2012 Higher Education Directory®

Published by
Higher Education Publications, Inc.

Edited by
Mary Pat Rodenhouse

Editor Emerita
Jeanne M. Burke

Reston, Virginia

2012

2012 Edition

Higher Education Publications, Inc.
1801 Robert Fulton Drive, Suite 340
Reston, VA 20191-4387
(888) 349-7715
(571) 313-0478
FAX (571) 313-0526
Email: info@hepinc.com
Internet address: www.hepinc.com

Carnegie classification codes with permission from The Carnegie Foundation for the Advancement of Teaching.

Internet addresses (URL's) were originally drawn from lists maintained by Washington and Lee University and the University of North Carolina-Chapel Hill and through the annual survey sent out by Higher Education Publications, Inc.

Printed in the United States of America

ISBN-10: 0-914927-67-1; ISBN-13: 978-0-914927-67-9
ISSN 0736-0797
Library of Congress Catalogue Card Number: 83-641119
Library of Congress Cataloging-in Publication Data

HEP. . . Higher Education Directory®
Reston, VA; Higher Education Publications.
V.: 28cm
Annual
Began with issue for 1983.

A directory of accredited postsecondary, degree-granting institutions in the U.S., its possessions and territories accredited by regional, national, professional and specialized agencies recognized as accrediting bodies by the U.S. Secretary of Education and the Council for Higher Education Accreditation (CHEA) which honors recognition provided by the former Council on Postsecondary Accreditation (COPA)/Commission on Recognition of Postsecondary Accreditation (CORPA)
Description based on 2012.
Cover title: 2012 Higher Education Directory®
Spine title: 2012 Higher Education Directory® Thirtieth Edition

ISSN 0736-0797 = The Higher Education Directory®.

1. Education, Higher—United States—Directories.
2. Recognized accrediting agencies and associations—United States—Directories.
3. Acronyms, explanatory notes and symbols—United States—Directories.
4. Institution changes (additions, deletions, mergers and name changes)—United States—Directories.
5. Administrative officers, titles and title codes—United States—Directories.
6. United States Department of Education offices, statewide agencies for higher education and educational associations (and consortia)—United States—Directories.
7. Religious affiliation by denomination.
8. Carnegie classification codes.
9. Statistics.
10. Universities and colleges—United States—Directories.
11. College administrators alphabetical listing, phone numbers—United States—Directories.
12. Regional, national, professional and specialized accreditation alphabetical listing—United States—Directories.
13. Institutional FICE & Unit ID Number listing—United States—Directories.
14. Institutional alphabetical listing—United States—Directories.

I. Higher Education Publications, Inc.
II. Title: Higher Education Directory®.

L901.E34 378.73-dc19 83-641119 AACR 2 MARC-S

Table of Contents

Acknowledgments

Twenty-nine years ago on September 26, 1982, Higher Education Publications, Inc. was formed to continue producing a directory to succeed the Department of Education's *Education Directory: Colleges and Universities*.

When we undertook this project, we worked toward three main goals: To publish accurate data, to make the directory more usable, and to have the directory ready for distribution much earlier in the academic year.

We continue to meet these objectives and more, while keeping the changing landscape of reference publishing in mind. We upgraded our HED-Connect online updating system again this year based on feedback from last year's users and we are very pleased with the results. A special thanks to everyone who helped to improve the online updating system by giving us their comments.

The response to the HED-Connect online update system was excellent. Nearly 60% of this year's survey updates were submitted online. You can expect more innovations and improvements to the HED-Connect system in the coming months.

We continue to work on a tight schedule starting in mid-June to distribution in November—especially when you consider the complexity and increase in the size of the database.

We thank the thousands of people who have supplied us the necessary data contained in the directory. We had a response/update rate of 99.5%—truly outstanding! We are most appreciative of the many subscribers who have supported us in our efforts to bring you the most accurate and current information available. And, a special thanks to Ted Manning and Judith Eaton.

The accuracy and completeness of the contents of the 2012 edition was assured by a group of editors, updating and proofing specialists including Jodi Mondragon, Jeanne Burke, Emmy Brown, Doris Jean Schreiber, Mary Pat Rodenhouse, Jackie Hafner and Pat Parks. Barbara Herrman handled our in-house typesetting. Mark Schreiber managed the HED-Connect update system and the database.

Throughout the remainder of this year and into next you will see new products and services from Higher Education Publications, Inc. Last year, we released HED-Connect, the *Higher Education Directory* online. This version of the directory is updated continually throughout the academic year. This year and next we will continue to add new, useful data to HED-Connect. Also, look for HED-Connect smart phone apps early next year. We feel that our move to the Internet will continue to provide you with the most complete and accurate information on the higher education community.

Frederick F. Hafner
Publisher

Reston, Virginia

Preface

Within the past several years, the traditional guidelines for recognition of accrediting agencies by the U.S. Secretary of Education have changed.

The *Higher Education Directory* (HED) makes use of accreditation at four points: (a) selection of institutions to be listed; (b) noting the institutional accreditation and accredited programs within each institution listing; (c) providing a listing of accrediting agencies with names, addresses, etc.; (d) index of accreditations.

Before 1998, the HED had relied on the recognition of accrediting agencies by the U.S. Secretary of Education to identify accrediting agencies whose actions are used in these four ways.

The Secretary (or the predecessor, the Commissioner of Education) has recognized accrediting agencies since 1952. From the beginning the recognition has been limited by statute to those agencies whose accreditation was used for Federal purposes. For the first forty years the interpretation of "Federal purposes" was expansive: the use of a list of institutions or programs to advise service members, or the possibility of future need for a list of accredited programs was sufficient to allow an agency access to the recognition process. In that period the recognition criteria were phrased in general terms of good practice. As a result the Federal list came to include almost all legitimate accrediting agencies, both agencies that accredited institutions and agencies that accredited programs.

With the passage of the 1992 amendments to the Higher Education Act the Congress introduced two significant changes of policy: (a) Federal recognition was restricted to those agencies whose accreditation was used to establish institutional eligibility for participation in federal programs; (b) the Secretary was obliged to place in the criteria for recognition a number of requirements of recognized accrediting agencies focused squarely on the administration of Federal student financial aid.

As a result a number of well-established, legitimate accrediting agencies were excluded from Federal recognition. In practice, the Secretary has dropped these from the list as their terms of recognition have expired. In each case the agency has received a letter from the Secretary emphasizing that this action does not reflect on the quality or integrity of the agency's activities, but is a result of the statutory changes in the understanding of "Federal purposes" for recognizing accrediting agencies. Since the "Federal purpose" is restricted to agencies accrediting institutions, the agencies dropped from the list are those accrediting programs exclusively. For example, among them are the agencies dealing with programs in architecture, in library and information studies, and in business (including graduate programs in business administration.)

From the start of the publication the HED relied on the federal list. This reliance and the changes in the federal recognition criteria led to the elimination from the HED listings of programs accredited by the accrediting agencies dropped from the Secretary's recognition. Thus, well known institutions were not shown as having an accredited program in architecture or business administration, while others were not shown as having accredited programs in library and information studies; yet in many cases the programs were among the premier programs in their disciplines.

The HED seeks to be both a comprehensive and an accurate guide to higher education and the HED has sought to identify reliable recognition of accrediting agencies other than that of the Secretary of Education. Beginning in 1975 the Council on Postsecondary Accreditation conducted a well-respected recognition process for accrediting agencies, and published a list of the agencies, both institutional and programmatic, that it recognized. From 1975 through the dissolution of COPA in 1993 there was substantial overlap of the COPA list and the Federal list. After 1993 the COPA recognition process was continued by the Commission on the Recognition of Postsecondary Accreditation (CORPA).

The Council on Higher Education Accreditation (CHEA), formed in 1996, now conducts recognition reviews based on its recognition policies and procedures. The recognition provisions deal with matters of good practice, and do not include the specific Federal student aid provisions now in the federal regulations. This is a two-tier process: an accreditor is first reviewed for its eligibility for CHEA recognition and, if the accreditor is deemed eligible for a recognition review, it then submits material for recognition consideration. Fifty-six (56) accreditors are recognized by CHEA as of 2011. CHEA eligibility and recognition standards are contained in the CHEA *Recognition of Accrediting Organizations: Policy and Procedures* (2010, revised), available on the CHEA web-site at www.chea.org.

In this edition, the HED has used the Secretary's list, supplemented by the most recent COPA/CORPA/CHEA list for agencies that accredit only programs within accredited institutions. Reference has been made to the Secretary's list of earlier years to identify agencies that were recognized and have been dropped because of the eligibility change noted above. No accreditation by an agency not recognized by either the Secretary or COPA/CORPA/CHEA has been included.

A footnote for clarity: some agencies, especially in the health sciences, accredit both programs within institutions and institutions whose sole program is the accredited program. Such agencies continue to meet the Secretary's eligibility requirements and many are on the Secretary's list although they are primarily program accrediting agencies. The agencies dropped from the Secretary's list are those that accredit programs only, and for the most part require a program to be within the offerings of an already-accredited institution.

Thurston E. Manning[1]

[1]Thurston Manning is a former president of North Central Association of Colleges and Schools and former president of the Council on Postsecondary Accreditation, COPA.

Foreword

The 2012 edition of the *Higher Education Directory®* contains listings of accredited, degree-granting institutions of postsecondary education in the United States and its territories.

Criteria for Listing in this Directory

To be listed in this Directory, an institution must meet the following guidelines:

(1) They are degree-granting (legally authorized to offer and are offering a program of college-level studies leading toward a degree[1]);
(2) They have submitted the information required for listing; and
(3) They meet one of the following criteria for listing:
  A. The institution is accredited at the college level by an accrediting agency that is recognized by the U.S. Secretary of Education;
  B. The institution holds pre-accredited status with an accrediting agency recognized by the U.S. Secretary of Education whose recognition includes the pre-accreditation status;
  C. The institution is accredited at the college level by an accrediting agency recognized by the Council for Higher Education Accreditation (CHEA).

"College level" means a postsecondary associate, baccalaureate, post-baccalaureate, or rabbinical education program.

Verification of Accreditations

Verification of each accreditation for all institutions was done by comparing the accreditation against the current Directory (and updated lists) for each respective regional, national, professional and specialized association or agency, along with telephone calls to numerous accrediting associations whenever there was a question of accuracy. Over 19,000 accreditations were verified through September 2011.

The reader is reminded that many institutions have programs which may not be recognized by a professional or specialized association, but are considered fine programs. The institutions may or may not have sought such recognition.

General Organization of the Directory

Our approach to the organization of the material is to make the desired information readable and easy to find. There are four indexes which are cross-referenced to the main institutional listing.

A. Prologue
  1. Accrediting agencies with addresses. Regional accrediting commissions are listed alphabetically while national, professional and specialized bodies are listed alphabetically under headings showing their specialties.
  2. Acronyms used in the Directory for accrediting bodies are listed alphabetically.
  3. Explanatory notes and symbols.
  4. U.S. postal abbreviations of states.
  5. Institution changes.
  6. Administrative officers' description and job codes.
  7. U.S. Department of Education offices.
  8. Statewide agencies of higher education.
  9. Higher education associations.
  10. Consortia of institutions of higher education.
  11. Association name index.
  12. Religious affiliation by denomination.
  13. Carnegie classification codes.
  14. Statistical data.

B. College and university listings by state with institutional characteristics and administrative officers.
  1. Institution Name. If an * appears before the institution's name, it is a part of a system. A line between institutions separates two systems.
  2. Alpha Code. The first institution listed on a page is coded (A), the second (B), etc. The Administrators' index is also coded to enable the reader to locate the desired institution quickly.
  3. Address.
  4. County.
  5. FICE Identification. This was the Federal Interagency Commission on Education number originally assigned by the Department of Education. We continue to use the term FICE. However, the Department of Education in their Office of Student Financial Assistance uses OPEID, Office of Postsecondary Education Identification. OPEID consists of the first six digits of the FICE plus two more digits indicating branch campuses. Numbers beginning with 66 are for accredited institutions for which we cannot locate a FICE or OPEID number. These are identification numbers only.
  6. Telephone Number.
  7. Unit ID Number. A unique number developed by the National Center for Education Statistics (NCES) for the Education Department's IPEDS Reports.
  8. Carnegie Classification Code. (see page **xlix**)
  9. Main FAX Number.
  10. School Calendar.
  11. URL (Universal Resource Locator).
  12. Date Established.
  13. Annual Tuition & Fees for 2011-12 school year.
  14. Fall 2010 Enrollment. Head count (not FTE) in degree programs as reported on the latest IPEDS survey.
  15. Type of Student Body.
  16. Affiliation or Control.
  17. IRS Status.
  18. Highest Degree Offered.
  19. Program. This is the general type of education offered.
  20. Accreditation (see page **viii**). **N.B. Institutional accreditation is in bold face.**
  21. Administrative and academic officers with job classification code (see page **xxvii** for descriptions).

C. Index of administrators is an alphabetical listing of all the administrators with their most direct phone number and E-mail address. The page and reference letter indicate the page on which the administrator's institution listing begins.

D. Index of regional, national, professional and specialized accreditation alphabetically by state. This index standardizes and simplifies reviewing of the 128 accrediting classifications.

E. FICE number index. Numeric listing of FICE number and school.

F. Alphabetic index of institutions.

---

[1]The *Higher Education Directory®* lists degree-granting institutions approved by regional, national, professional or specialized accrediting agencies.

Accrediting Agencies

The following regional, national, professional and specialized accrediting agencies are recognized by the U.S. Secretary of Education or the Council for Higher Education Accreditation (CHEA). The U.S. Department of Education (USDE) dates specified are the date of initial listing as a U.S. Department of Education recognized agency, the date of the U.S. Secretary's most recent grant of renewed recognition based on the last full review of the agency by the National Advisory Committee on Institutional Quality and Integrity, and the date of the agency's next scheduled review for renewal of recognition.[1] The Council for Higher Education (CHEA) date reflects initial or continued recognition by CHEA.

Regional Accrediting Bodies

Delaware, District of Columbia, Maryland, New Jersey, New York, Pennsylvania, Puerto Rico, Virgin Islands

Commission on Higher Education
Middle States Association of Colleges and Schools M
USDE: 1952/2007/2012 CHEA: 2002
3624 Market Street, Second Floor West
Philadelphia, PA 19104-2680
(267) 284-5000 Fax (215) 662-5950
Elizabeth H. Sibolski, President
E-mail: info@msche.org
URL: www.msche.org

Connecticut, Maine, Massachusetts, New Hampshire, Rhode Island, Vermont

Commission on Institutions of Higher Education
New England Association of Schools and Colleges EH
USDE: 1952/2008/2013 CHEA: 2002
209 Burlington Road
Bedford, MA 01730-1433
(781) 271-0022 Fax (781) 271-0950
Barbara E. Brittingham, Director
E-mail: bbrittingham@neasc.org
URL: www.neasc.org

Arizona, Arkansas, Colorado, Illinois, Indiana, Iowa, Kansas, Michigan, Minnesota, Missouri, Nebraska, New Mexico, North Dakota, Ohio, Oklahoma, South Dakota, West Virginia, Wisconsin, Wyoming

The Higher Learning Commission
North Central Association of Colleges and Schools NH
USDE: 1952/2008/2013 CHEA: 2003
230 South LaSalle Street, Suite 7-500
Chicago, IL 60604-1413
(800) 621-7440 Fax (312) 263-7462
Sylvia Manning, President
E-mail: info@hlcommission.org
URL: www.ncahigherlearningcommission.org

Alaska, Idaho, Montana, Nevada, Oregon, Utah, Washington

Northwest Commission on Colleges and Universities NW
USDE: 1952/2008/2012 CHEA: 2001
8060 165th Avenue, NE, Suite 100
Redmond, WA 98052
(425) 558-4224 Fax (425) 376-0596
Sandra E. Elman, President
E-mail: selman@nwccu.org
URL: www.nwccu.org

Alabama, Florida, Georgia, Kentucky, Louisiana, Mississippi, North Carolina, South Carolina, Tennessee, Texas, Virginia

Commission on Colleges
Southern Association of Colleges and Schools SC
USDE: 1952/2006/2012 CHEA: 2003
1866 Southern Lane
Decatur, GA 30033-4097
(800) 248-7701 Fax (404) 679-4528
Belle S. Wheelan, President
E-mail: bwheelan@sacscoc.org
URL: www.sacscoc.org

California, Hawaii, American Samoa, Guam, Commonwealth of the Northern Marianas, Federated States of Micronesia, Republic of the Marshall Islands, Republic of Palau

Accrediting Commission for Senior Colleges and Universities
Western Association of Schools and Colleges WC
USDE: 1952/2007/2012 CHEA: 2003
985 Atlantic Avenue, Suite 100
Alameda, CA 94501
(510) 748-9001 Fax (510) 748-9797
Ralph A. Wolff, Executive Director
E-mail: wascsr@wascsenior.org
URL: www.wascweb.org

Accrediting Commission for Community and Junior Colleges
Western Association of Schools and Colleges WJ
USDE: 1952/2008/2013 CHEA: 2003
10 Commercial Boulevard, Suite 204
Novato, CA 94949
(415) 506-0234 Fax (415) 506-0238
Barbara A. Beno, President
E-mail: accjc@accjc.org
URL: www.wascweb.org

[1]U.S. Department of Education, Nationally Recognized Accrediting Agencies, www2.ed.gov/admins/finaid/accred/accreditation.html.

National, Professional and Specialized Accrediting Bodies

Acupuncture

Accreditation Commission for Acupuncture and Oriental Medicine (ACAOM)
USDE: 1988/2006/2011
Maryland Trade Center 3
14502 Greenview Drive, Suite 300B
Laurel, MD 20708
(301) 313-0855 Fax (301) 313-0912
William W. Goding, Interim Executive Director
E-mail: william.goding@acaom.org
URL: www.acaom.org

First-professional master's degree, professional master's level certificate and diploma programs and professional post-graduate doctoral programs in acupuncture and Oriental medicine, and freestanding institutions that offer such programs **ACUP**

Allied Health

Accrediting Bureau of Health Education Schools (ABHES)
USDE: 1969/2005/2011
7777 Leesburg Pike, Suite 314N
Falls Church, VA 22043
(703) 917-9503 Fax (703) 917-4109
Carol Moneymaker, Executive Director
E-mail: cmoneymaker@abhes.org
URL: www.abhes.org

Institutions specializing in allied health education **ABHES**
Specialized programs for
- Medical laboratory technician **MLTAB**
- Medical assistant **MAAB**
- Surgical technologist **SURTEC**

Commission on Accreditation of Allied Health Education Programs (CAAHEP)
CHEA: 2001
1361 Park Street
Clearwater, FL 33756
(727) 210-2350 Fax (727) 210-2354
Kathleen Megivern, Executive Director
E-mail: mail@caahep.org
URL: www.caahep.org

The Commission on Accreditation of Allied Health Education Programs (CAAHEP) is recognized as an accrediting agency for accreditation of education for the allied health occupations. In carrying out its accreditation activities, CAAHEP cooperates with the Committees on Accreditation sponsored by various allied health and medical specialty organizations. CAAHEP is the coordinating agency for accreditation of education for the following allied health occupations:
- Anesthesiologist assistant **AA**
- Blood bank technology **BBT**
- Cardiovascular technologist **CVT**
- Cytotechnologist **CYTO**
- Diagnostic medical sonographer **DMS**
- Electroneurodiagnostic technologist **EEG**
- Emergency medical technician-paramedic **EMT**
- Exercise science **EXSC**
- Kinesiotherapy **KIN**
- Medical assistant **MAC**
- Medical illustrator **MIL**
- Orthotist/prosthetist **OPE**
- Perfusionist **PERF**
- Polysomnographic technologist **POLYT**
- Surgeon assistant **SURGA**
- Surgical technologist **SURGT**

Anesthesiologist Assistant

Commission on Accreditation of Allied Health Education Programs (see listing under Allied Health)
Accreditation Review Committee for the Anesthesiologist Assistant
2027 Burnside Drive
Allen, TX 75013
(469) 656-1103
Jennifer Anderson Warwick, Executive Director
E-mail: arcaamember@gmail.com

Post-baccalaureate programs for anesthesiologist assistant **AA**

Art

Commission on Accreditation
National Association of Schools of Art and Design (NASAD)
USDE: 1966/2008/2012
11250 Roger Bacon Drive, Suite 21
Reston, VA 20190
(703) 437-0700 Fax (703) 437-6312
Samuel Hope, Executive Director
E-mail: info@arts-accredit.org
URL: www.arts-accredit.org

Institutions and departments within institutions offering degree and non-degree granting programs in art/design and art/design-related programs **ART**

Aviation

Aviation Accreditation Board International
CHEA: 2002
3410 Skyway Drive
Auburn, AL 36830
(334) 844-2431 Fax (334) 844-2432
Gary W. Kiteley, Executive Director
E-mail: bavenva@auburn.edu
URL: www.aabi.aero

Non-engineering programs for aviation **AAB**

Bible College Education

Commission on Accreditation
Association for Biblical Higher Education (ABHE)
USDE: 1952/2007/2012 CHEA: 2001
5850 T. G. Lee Boulevard, Suite 130
Orlando, FL 32822
(407) 207-0808 Fax (407) 207-0840
Randall E. Bell, Director
E-mail: rebell@abhe.org
URL: www.abhe.org

Bible colleges and institutions offering undergraduate programs **BI**

Blood Bank Technology

Commission on Accreditation of Allied Health Education Programs (see listing under Allied Health)
American Association of Blood Banks (AABB)
8101 Glenbrook Road
Bethesda, MD 20814-2749
(301) 907-6977 Fax (301) 907-6895
Sharon Moffett, Director of Education
E-mail: aabb@aabb.org
URL: www.aabb.org

Programs for blood bank technologist **BBT**

Business

AACSB International-The Association to Advance Collegiate Schools of Business
CHEA: 2002
777 South Harbour Island Boulevard, Suite 750
Tampa, FL 33602
(813) 769-6500 Fax (813) 769-6559
Jerry Trapnell, Executive Vice President and Chief Accreditation Officer
E-mail: accreditation@aacsb.edu
URL: www.aacsb.edu

Programs for:
- Business and management education **BUS**
- Accounting **BUSA**

Accrediting Council for Independent Colleges and Schools (ACICS)
USDE: 1956/2006/2011 CHEA: 2001
750 First Street NE, Suite 980
Washington, DC 20002-4223
(202) 336-6780 Fax (202) 842-2593
Albert C. Gray, Executive Director
E-mail: agray@acics.org
URL: www.acics.org

Private, postsecondary institutions offering specialized associate, associate, baccalaureate and master's degree programs to educate students for professional, technical, or occupational careers **ACICS**

Accreditation Council for Business Schools and Programs (ACBSP)
CHEA: 2001
11520 West 119th Street
Overland Park, KS 66213
(913) 339-9356 Fax (913) 339-6226
Douglas Viehland, Executive Director
E-mail: info@acbsp.org
URL: www.acbsp.org

Business administration, management, accounting and related business fields **ACBSP**

International Assembly for Collegiate Business Education
CHEA: 2011
P.O. Box 3960
Olathe, KS 66063
(913) 631-3009 Fax (913) 631-9154
Dennis N. Gash, President
E-mail: iacbe@iacbe.org
URL: www.iacbe.org

Undergraduate and graduate level business programs in institutions that grant bachelor's and/or graduate degrees **IACBE**

Cardiovascular Technology

Commission on Accreditation of Allied Health Education Programs (see listing under Allied Health)
Joint Review Committee on Education in Cardiovascular Technology (JRC-CVT)
6 Pine Knoll Drive
Beverly, MA 01915-1425
(978) 456-5594
William W. Goding, Executive Director
E-mail: office@jrccvt.org
URL: www.jrccvt.org

Programs for cardiovascular technology **CVT**

Chiropractic

The Council on Chiropractic Education (CCE)
USDE: 1974/2006/2011 CHEA: 2005

8049 North 85th Way
Scottsdale, AZ 85258-4321
(480) 443-8877 Fax (480) 483-7333
Lee Van Dusen, Executive Director
E-mail: cce@cce-usa.org
URL: www.cce-usa.org

Programs leading to and institutions offering the Doctorate of Chiropractic (D.C.) degree **CHIRO**

Christian Studies Education

Accreditation Commission
Transnational Association of Christian Colleges and Schools (TRACS)
USDE: 1991/2005/2011 CHEA: 2001
15935 Forest Road
Forest, VA 24551
(434) 525-9539 Fax (434) 525-9538
T. Paul Boatner, President
E-mail: info@tracs.org
URL: www.tracs.org

Christian liberal arts institutions which offer a certificate/diploma, associate, baccalaureate and graduate degrees **TRACS**

Clinical Laboratory Sciences

National Accrediting Agency for Clinical Laboratory Sciences (NAACLS)
CHEA: 2002
5600 North River Road, Suite 720
Rosemont, IL 60018
(773) 714-8880 Fax (773) 714-8886
Dianne M. Cearlock, Chief Executive Officer
E-mail: naaclsinfo@naacls.org
URL: www.naacls.org

Programs for:
- diagnostic molecular scientist **DMOLS**
- histologic technician/technologist **HT**
- medical laboratory technician **MLTAD**
- medical technologist **MT**
- pathologists' assistant **PA**

Clinical Pastoral Education

Accreditation Commission
Association for Clinical Pastoral Education, Inc. (ACPEI)
USDE: 1969/2007/2012
1549 Clairmont Road, Suite 103
Decatur, GA 30033-4635
(404) 320-1472 Fax (404) 320-0849
Teresa E. Snorton, Executive Director
E-mail: acpe@acpe.edu
URL: www.acpe.edu

Basic, advanced and supervisory clinical pastoral education programs **PAST**

Construction Education

American Council for Construction Education (ACCE)
CHEA: 2011
1717 North Loop 1604 East, Suite 320
San Antonio, TX 78232-1570
(210) 495-6161 Fax (210) 495-6168
Michael Holland, Executive Vice President
E-mail: mholland@acce-hq.org
URL: www.acce-hq.org

Associate and baccalaureate degree programs **CONST**

Continuing Education

Accrediting Commission
Accrediting Council for Continuing Education and Training (ACCET)
USDE: 1978/2008/2013
1722 N Street NW
Washington, DC 20036
(202) 955-1113 Fax (202) 955-1118
Roger J. Williams, Executive Director
E-mail: rjwilliams@accet.org
URL: www.accet.org

Institutions offering noncollegiate continuing education and institutions offering occupational associate degree programs **CNCE**

Cosmetology

National Accrediting Commission of Career Arts and Sciences (NACCAS)
USDE: 1970/2006/2010
4401 Ford Avenue, Suite 1300
Alexandria, VA 22302-1432
(703) 600-7600 Fax (703) 379-2200
Anthony Mirando, Executive Director
E-mail: naccas@naccas.org
URL: www.naccas.org

Postsecondary schools and departments of cosmetology arts and sciences and massage therapy **COSME**

Counseling and Related Educational Programs

Council for Accreditation of Counseling and Related Educational Programs (CACREP)
CHEA: 2002
1001 North Fairfax Street, Suite 510
Alexandria, VA 22314
(703) 535-5990 Fax (703) 739-6209
Carol L. Bobby, Executive Director
E-mail: cacrep@cacrep.org
URL: www.cacrep.org

Master's degree programs in addiction counseling, career counseling, marriage, couple and family counseling, mental health counseling, school counseling, student affairs and college counseling and doctorate degree programs in counselor education and supervision **CACREP**

Culinary Arts

Accrediting Commission
American Culinary Federation
CHEA: 2004
180 Center Place Way
St. Augustine, FL 32095
(904) 824-4468 Fax (904) 825-4758
Candice Childers, Assistant Director of Accreditation
E-mail: acf@acfchefs.net
URL: www.acfchefs.org

Programs in culinary arts which award certificates, diplomas or associate degrees and bachelor degree programs in culinary management **ACFEI**

Cytotechnology

Commission on Accreditation of Allied Health Education Programs (see listing under Allied Health)
Cytotechnology Programs Review Committee
American Society of Cytopathology
100 West 10th Street, Suite 605
Wilmington, DE 19801
(302) 543-6583 Fax (302) 543-6597
Debby MacIntyre, CPRC Coordinator
E-mail: dmacintyre@cytopathology.org
URL: www.cytopathology.org

Programs for the cytotechnologist **CYTO**

Dance

Commission on Accreditation
National Association of Schools of Dance (NASD)
USDE: 1983/2008/2012
11250 Roger Bacon Drive, Suite 21
Reston, VA 20190
(703) 437-0700 Fax (703) 437-6312
Samuel Hope, Executive Director
E-mail: info@arts-accredit.org
URL: www.arts-accredit.org

Institutions and departments within institutions offering degree and non-degree-granting programs in dance and dance-related disciplines **DANCE**

Dental and Dental Auxiliary Programs

Commission on Dental Accreditation
American Dental Association (ADA)
USDE: 1952/2006/2012
211 East Chicago Avenue
Chicago, IL 60611
(800) 621-8099 Fax (312) 440-2915
Anthony Ziebert, Director
E-mail: zieberta@ada.org
URL: www.ada.org

Programs leading to:
- D.D.S. or D.M.D. degree, advanced general dentistry and specialty programs **DENT**
- Dental hygiene **DH**
- Dental assisting **DA**
- Dental laboratory technology **DT**

Diagnostic Medical Sonography

Commission on Accreditation of Allied Health Education Programs (see listing under Allied Health)
Joint Review Committee on Education in Diagnostic Medical Sonography
6021 University Boulevard, Suite 500
Ellicot City, MD 21043-6090
(443) 973-3251 Fax (866) 738-3444
Cindy Weiland, Executive Director
E-mail: mail@jrcdms.org
URL: www.jrcdms.org

Programs for the diagnostic medical sonographer **DMS**

Dietetics

Commission on Accreditation for Dietetics Education
American Dietetic Association
USDE: 1974/2007/2012
120 South Riverside Plaza, Suite 2000
Chicago, IL 60606-6995
(312) 899-4872 Fax (312) 899-4817
Ulric K. Chung, Executive Director
E-mail: uchung@eatright.org
URL: www.eatright.org/cade

Coordinated programs in dietetics **DIETC**
Didactic programs **DIETD**
Post-baccalaureate internships **DIETI**
Dietetic technician programs **DIETT**

Distance Education and Training

Accrediting Commission
Distance Education and Training Council (DETC)
USDE: 1959/2007/2012 CHEA: 2001
1601 18th Street NW, Suite 2
Washington, DC 20009
(202) 234-5100 Fax (202) 332-1386
Michael P. Lambert, Executive Director
E-mail: detc@detc.org
URL: www.detc.org

Distance education institutions including associate, baccalaureate, master's, and doctoral degree-granting programs primarily through the distance learning method **DETC**

Electroneurodiagnostic Technology

Commission on Accreditation of Allied Health Education Programs (see listing under Allied Health)
Committee on Accreditation for Education in Electroneurodiagnostic Technology
6654 South Sycamore Street
Littleton, CO 80120
(303) 738-0770 Fax (303) 738-3223
Theresa Sisneros, Executive Director
E-mail: office@coa-end.org
URL: http://coa-end.org

Programs for the electroneurodiagnostic technolocist **EEG**

Emergency Medical Services

Commission on Accreditation for Allied Health Programs (see listing under Allied Health)
Committee on Educational Programs for the Emergency Medical Services Professions
4101 West Green Oaks Boulevard, Suite 305-599
Arlington, TX 76016
(817) 330-0080 Fax (817) 330-0089
George Hatch, Executive Director
E-mail: george@coaemsp.org
URL: www.coaemsp.org

Programs for the emergency medical technician-paramedic **EMT**

Engineering

ABET, Inc.
CHEA: 2003
111 Market Place, Suite 1050
Baltimore, MD 21202
(410) 347-7700 Fax (410) 625-2238
Michael Milligan, Executive Director
E-mail: abet@abet.org
URL: www.abet.org

Baccalaureate programs in computer science **CS**
Basic (baccalaureate) and advanced (master's) level programs in engineering **ENG**
Applied science programs at the associate, baccalaureate and master's level **ENGR**
Associate and baccalaureate degree programs in engineering technology **ENGT**

English Language

Commission on English Language Program Accreditation (CEA)
USDE: 2003/2005/2011
801 North Fairfax Drive, Suite 402A
Alexandria, VA 22314
(703) 519-2070 Fax (703) 519-2071
Teresa D. O'Donnell, Executive Director
E-mail: todonnell@cea-accredit.org
URL: www.cea-accredit.org

Non-degree-granting English language programs and institutions **CEA**

Exercise Sciences

Commission on Accreditation of Allied Health Education Programs (see listing under Allied Health)
Committee on Accreditation for the Exercise Sciences
401 West Michigan Street
Indianapolis, IN 46202
(317) 637-9200 Fax (317) 634-7817
Traci Sue Rush, Executive Director
E-mail: trush@acsm.org
URL: www.coaes.org

Programs for exercise science of related departments **EXSC**

Family and Consumer Sciences

Council for Accreditation
American Association of Family and Consumer Sciences (AAFCS)
CHEA: 2001
400 North Columbus Street, Suite 202
Alexandria, VA 22314
(703) 706-4600 Fax (703) 706-4663
Carolyn W. Jackson, Executive Director
E-mail: accreditation@aafcs.org
URL: www.aafcs.org

Baccalaureate programs in family and consumer sciences **AAFCS**

Fire and Emergency

International Fire Service Accreditation Congress Degree Assembly
CHEA: 2011
1700 West Tyler
Stillwater, OK 74078
(405) 744-8303 Fax (405) 744-8802
Clayton Moorman, Manager
E-mail: cmoorman@ifsac.org
URL: www.ifsac.org

Undergraduate fire and emergency related programs **IFSAC**

Forestry

Society of American Foresters (SAF)
CHEA: 2001
5400 Grosvenor Lane
Bethesda, MD 20814-2198
(301) 897-8720 Fax (301) 897-3690
Carol Redelsheimer, Director of Science and Education
E-mail: redelsheimer@safnet.org
URL: www.safnet.org

Programs leading to a bachelor's or higher first-professional degree in forestry **FOR**

Funeral Service Education

Committee on Accreditation
American Board of Funeral Service Education (ABFSE)
USDE: 1972/2002/2010 CHEA: 2011
3414 Ashland Avenue, Suite G
St. Joseph, MO 64506
(816) 233-3747 Fax (816) 233-3793
Gretchen Warner, Executive Director
E-mail: exdir@abfse.org
URL: www.abfse.org

Institutions and programs awarding diplomas, associate and bachelor's degrees in funeral service or mortuary science **FUSER**

Healthcare Management

Commission on Accreditation of Healthcare Management Education (CAHME)
USDE: 1970/2007/2012 CHEA: 2003
2111 Wilson Boulevard, Suite 700
Arlington, VA 22201
(703) 351-5010 Fax (703) 991-5989
John S. Lloyd, President and CEO, Director of Accreditation Operations
E-mail: jlloyd@cahme.org
URL: www.cahme.org

Graduate programs in healthcare management **HSA**

Histologic Technology

See Clinical Laboratory Sciences

Home Study Education

See Distance Education and Training

Industrial Technology

The Association of Technology, Management, and Applied Engineering
CHEA: 2002
1390 Eisenhower Place
Ann Arbor, MI 48108
(734) 677-0720 Fax (734) 677-0046
Rick Coscarelli, Executive Director
E-mail: atmae@atmae.org
URL: http://atmae.org

Technology, applied technology, engineering technology and technology-related programs at the associate, baccalaureate and master's degree level **NAIT**

Interior Design

Council for Interior Design Accreditation (CIDA)
CHEA: 2002
206 Grandville Avenue, Suite 350
Grand Rapids, MI 49503
(616) 458-0400 Fax (616) 458-0460
Holly Mattson, Executive Director
E-mail: info@accredit-id.org
URL: www.accredit-id.org

First professional degree level programs (master's and baccalaureate degrees) **CIDA**

Journalism and Mass Communications

Accrediting Committee
Accrediting Council on Education in Journalism and Mass Communications (ACEJMC)
CHEA: 2002
University of Kansas School of Journalism
Stauffer-Flint Hall
1435 Jayhawk Boulevard
Lawrence, KS 66045-7575
(785) 864-3973 Fax (785) 864-5225
Susanne Shaw, Executive Director
E-mail: sshaw@ku.edu
URL: www2.ku.edu/~acejmc

Units within institutions offering professional baccalaureate and master's degree programs in journalism and mass communications **JOUR**

Kinesiotherapy

Commission on Accreditation of Allied Health Education Programs (see listing under Allied Health)
Committee on Accreditation of Education Programs for Kinesiotherapy
118 College Drive #5142
Hattiesburg, MS 39406-0002
(601) 266-5371 Fax (601) 266-4445
Jerry W. Purvis, Executive Director
E-mail: jerry.purvis@usm.edu
URL: http://akta.org

Kinesiotherapy programs **KIN**

Landscape Architecture

Landscape Architectural Accreditation Board
American Society of Landscape Architects (ASLA)
CHEA: 2003
636 Eye Street, NW
Washington, DC 20001-3736
(202) 898-2444 Fax (202) 898-1185
Ron Leighton, Executive Director
E-mail: rleighton@asla.org
URL: www.asla.org

Baccalaureate and master's programs leading to the first professional degree **LSAR**

Law

Council of the Section of Legal Education and Admissions to the Bar
American Bar Association (ABA)
USDE: 1952/2007/2011
321 North Clark Street, 21st Fl
Chicago, IL 60654
(312) 988-6738 Fax (312) 988-5681
Hulett H. Askew, Consultant on Legal Education
E-mail: legaled@americanbar.org
URL: www.americanbar.org/groups/legal_education.html

Programs in legal education; professional schools of law **LAW**

Librarianship

Committee on Accreditation
American Library Association (ALA)
CHEA: 2001
50 East Huron Street
Chicago, IL 60611-2729
(800) 545-2433 Fax (312) 280-2433
Karen O'Brien, Director of Accreditation
E-mail: accred@ala.org
URL: www.ala.org/accreditation

Master's programs leading to the first professional degree **LIB**

Marriage and Family Therapy

Commission on Accreditation for Marriage and Family Therapy Education
American Association for Marriage and Family Therapy (AAMFT)
USDE: 1978/2006/2011 CHEA: 2003
112 South Alfred Street
Alexandria, VA 22314-3061
(703) 838-9808 Fax (703) 838-9805
Tanya A. Tamarkin, Director of Education Affairs
E-mail: ttamarkin@aamft.org
URL: www.aamft.org

Clinical training programs at the master's, doctorate and post-graduate levels **MFCD**

Massage Therapy

Commission on Massage Therapy Accreditation
USDE: 2002/2004/2011
5335 Wisconsin Avenue NW, Suite 440
Washington, DC 20015
(202) 895-1518 Fax (202) 895-1519
Kate Ivane Henrioulle, Executive Director
E-mail: khenrioulle@comta.org
URL: www.comta.org

Institutions that award postsecondary certificates, diplomas, and associate degrees in the practice of massage therapy, bodywork, aesthetics/esthetics and skin care **COMTA**

Medical Assistant Education

(see listing under Allied Health)
Accrediting Bureau of Health Education Schools (ABHES)

Medical assistant programs **MAAB**

Commission on Accreditation of Allied Health Education Programs (see listing under Allied Health)
Medical Assisting Education Review Board
20 North Wacker Drive, Suite 1575
Chicago, IL 60606-2963
(312) 899-1500 Fax (312) 899-1259
Anna L. Johnson, Executive Director of Accreditation
E-mail: ajohnson@maerb.org
URL: www.maerb.org

One and two year medical assistant programs **MAC**

Medical Illustrator Education

Commission on Accreditation of Allied Health Education Programs (see listing under Allied Health)
Accreditation Review Committee for the Medical Illustrator
Saint Luke's Hospital Instructional Resources
32531 Meadowlark Way
Pepper Pike, OH 44124
(216) 595-9363 Fax (216) 595-9360
Kathy Jung, Chair, ARC-MI
E-mail: kijung@aol.com
URL: www.caahep.org/arc-mi

Programs for medical illustrator **MIL**

Medical Laboratory Technician Education

(see listing under Allied Health)
Accrediting Bureau of Health Education Schools (ABHES)

Schools and programs for the medical laboratory technician **MLTAB**

(see listing under Clinical Laboratory Sciences)
National Accrediting Agency for Clinical Laboratory Sciences (NAACLS)

Programs for medical laboratory technician
(certificate) **MLTC**
(associate degree) **MLTAD**

Medical Technology

(see listing under Clinical Laboratory Sciences)
National Accrediting Agency for Clinical Laboratory Sciences (NAACLS)

Programs for medical technologist **MT**

Medicine

Liaison Committee on Medical Education (LCME) of the Council on Medical Education of the American Medical Association and the Association of American Medical Colleges
USDE: 1952/2007/2012
The LCME is administered in odd-numbered years, beginning each July 1, by:
Council on Medical Education of the American Medical Association (AMA)
515 North State Street
Chicago, IL 60610
(312) 464-4933 Fax (312) 464-5830
Barbara Barzansky, Interim Secretary
E-mail: barbara.barzansky@ama-assn.org
URL: www.ama-assn.org

The LCME is administered in even-numbered years, beginning each July 1, by:
Association of American Medical Colleges (AAMC)
2450 N Street NW
Washington, DC 20037-1127
(202) 828-0596 Fax (202) 828-1125
Dan Hunt, LCME Secretary
E-mail: dhunt@aamc.org
URL: www.aamc.org

Programs leading to the M.D. degree **MED**

Midwifery Education

Midwifery Education Accreditation Council (MEAC)
USDE: 2001/2003/2010
PO Box 984
LaConner, WA 98257
(360) 466-2080 Fax (480) 907-2936
Jo Anne Myers-Ciecko, Executive Director
E-mail: executivedirector@meacschools.org
URL: www.meacschools.org

Accreditation of direct-entry midwifery educational institutions and programs conferring degrees and certificates **MEAC**

Montessori Teacher Education

Commission on Accreditation
Montessori Accreditation Council for Teacher Education (MACTE)
USDE: 1995/2003/2010
313 Second Street, SE, Suite 112
Charlottesville, VA 22902
(434) 202-7793 Fax (888) 525-8838
Rebecca Pelton, Executive Director
E-mail: rebecca@macte.org
URL: www.macte.org

Montessori teacher-education programs and institutions **MACTE**

Music

Commission on Accreditation
National Association of Schools of Music (NASM)
USDE: 1952/2008/2012
11250 Roger Bacon Drive, Suite 21
Reston, VA 20190
(703) 437-0700 Fax (703) 437-6312
Samuel Hope, Executive Director
E-mail: info@arts-accredit.org
URL: www.arts-accredit.org

Institutions and departments within institutions offering degree and non-degree-granting programs in music and music-related disciplines **MUS**

Naturopathic Medical Education

Council on Naturopathic Medical Education (CNME)
USDE: 2003/2010/2013
PO Box 178
Great Barrington, MA 01230
(413) 528-8877 Fax (413) 528-8880
Daniel Seitz, Executive Director
E-mail: council@cnme.org
URL: www.cnme.org

Graduate-level, four-year naturopathic medical education programs **NATUR**

Nuclear Medicine Technology

Joint Review Committee on Educational Programs in Nuclear Medicine Technology
CHEA: 2002
2000 West Danforth Road, Suite 130 #203
Edmund, OK 73003
(405) 285-0546 Fax (405) 285-0579
Jan M. Winn, Executive Director
E-mail: jrcnmt@coxinet.net
URL: www.jrcnmt.org

Programs for the nuclear medicine technologist **NMT**

Nurse Anesthetists

Council on Accreditation of Nurse Anesthesia Educational Programs
USDE: 1955/2007/2012 CHEA: 2011
222 South Prospect Avenue, Suite 304
Park Ridge, IL 60068-4001
(847) 692-7050 Fax (847) 692-6968
Francis Gerbasi, Director of Accreditation and Education
E-mail: fgerbasi@aana.com
URL: www.aana.com

Nurse anesthesia educational institutions and programs at the certificate, master's and doctoral degree levels **ANEST**

Nurse-Midwifery

Accreditation Commission for Midwifery Education
USDE: 1982/2006/2012
8403 Colesville Road, Suite 1550
Silver Spring, MD 20910
(240) 485-1802 Fax (240) 485-1818
Susan E. Stone, Chair, Accreditation Commission
E-mail: susan.stone@frontierschool.edu
URL: www.midwife.org/accreditation

Pre-certification, basic certificate and master's degree nurse-midwifery educational programs **MIDWF**

Nursing

Commission on Collegiate Nursing Education (CCNE)
USDE: 2000/2007/2012
One Dupont Circle NW, Suite 530
Washington, DC 20036-1120
(202) 887-6791 Fax (202) 887-8476
Jennifer Butlin, Director
E-mail: jbutlin@aacn.nche.edu
URL: www.aacn.nche.edu/accreditation

Baccalaureate and higher degree nursing education **NURSE**

Accrediting Commission
National League for Nursing (NLNAC)
USDE: 1952/2007/2012 CHEA: 2001
3343 Peachtree Road NE, Suite 850
Atlanta, GA 30326
(404) 975-5000 Fax (404) 975-5020
Sharon J. Tanner, Executive Director
E-mail: stanner@nlnac.org
URL: www.nlnac.org

Programs in:
- Practical nursing (certificate) **PNUR**
- Diploma nurse education **DNUR**
- Associate degree **ADNUR**
- Baccalaureate and higher degree nurse education **NUR**

Occupational Education

Council on Occupational Education (COE)
USDE: 1969/2007/2011
7840 Roswell Road, Bldg 300, Suite 325
Atlanta, GA 30350
(770) 396-3898 Fax (770) 396-3790
Gary Puckett, Executive Director
E-mail: info@council.org
URL: www.council.org

Occupational/vocational institutions that grant the applied associate degree in specific career and technical education **COE**

Occupational Therapy

Accreditation Council for Occupational Therapy Education
American Occupational Therapy Association
USDE: 1952/2007/2012 CHEA: 2002
4720 Montgomery Lane, PO Box 31220
Bethesda, MD 20824-1220
(301) 652-2682 Fax (301) 652-7711
Neil Harvison, Director of Accreditation
E-mail: nharvison@aota.org
URL: www.aota.org

Occupational therapy programs **OT**
Occupational therapy assistant programs **OTA**

Opticianry

Commission on Opticianry Accreditation
CHEA: 2010
PO Box 592
Canton, NY 13617
(703) 468-0566 Fax (888) 306-9036
Debra White, Director of Accreditation
E-mail: director@COAccreditation.com
URL: www.coaccreditation.com

Two-year opticianry degree programs **OPD**
One year programs for opthalmic laboratory technician **OPLT**

Optometry

Accreditation Council on Optometric Education
American Optometric Association (AOA)
USDE: 1952/2008/2013 CHEA: 2001
243 North Lindbergh Boulevard
St. Louis, MO 63141
(314) 991-4100 Fax (314) 991-4101
Joyce L. Urbeck, Administrative Director
E-mail: jlurbeck@aoa.org
URL: www.theacoe.org

Programs in:
- First professional **OPT**
- Optometric residency **OPTR**
- Optometric technology **OPTT**

Orthotic and Prosthetic Education

Commission on Accreditation of Allied Health Education Programs (see listing under Allied Health)
National Commission on Orthotic and Prosthetic Education (NCOPE)
330 John Carlyle Street, Suite 200
Alexandria, VA 22314
(703) 836-7114 Fax (703) 836-0838
Robin C. Seabrook, Executive Director
E-mail: rseabrook@ncope.org
URL: www.ncope.org

Programs for orthotic and prosthetic education **OPE**

Osteopathic Medicine

Commission on Osteopathic College Accreditation
American Osteopathic Association
USDE: 1952/2006/2016
Department of Education
142 East Ontario Street
Chicago, IL 60611-2864
(312) 202-8048 Fax (312) 202-8202
Konrad C. Miskowicz-Retz, Director
E-mail: kretz@osteopathic.org
URL: www.osteopathic.org

Programs leading to and institutions offering the D.O. (Doctor of Osteopathy/Osteopathic Medicine) degree **OSTEO**

Perfusion

Commission on Accreditation of Allied Health Education Programs (see listing under Allied Health)
Accreditation Committee for Perfusion Education
6654 South Sycamore Street
Littleton, CO 80120
(303) 738-0770 Fax (303) 738-3223
Theresa Sisneros, Executive Director
E-mail: ac-pe@msn.com
URL: www.ac-pe.org

Programs for the perfusionist **PERF**

Pharmacy

Accreditation Council for Pharmacy Education (ACPE)
USDE: 1952/2006/2012 CHEA: 2004
135 South LaSalle Street, Suite 4100
Chicago, IL 60603
(312) 664-3575 Fax (312) 664-4652
Peter H. Vlasses, Executive Director
E-mail: csinfo@acpe-accredit.org
URL: www.acpe-accredit.org

Professional degree programs in pharmacy **PHAR**

Physical Therapy

Commission on Accreditation in Physical Therapy Education
American Physical Therapy Association (APTA)
USDE: 1977/2007/2012 CHEA: 2002
Trans Potomac Plaza
1111 North Fairfax Street
Alexandria, VA 22314
(703) 706-3245 Fax (703) 684-7343

Mary Jane Harris, Director
E-mail: maryjaneharris@apta.org
URL: www.apta.org

Professional programs for the physical therapist **PTA**
Programs for the physical therapist assistant **PTAA**

Physician Assistant

Accreditation Review Commission on Education for the Physician Assistant (ARC-PA)
CHEA: 2004
12000 Findley Road, Suite 240
John's Creek, GA 30097
(770) 476-1224 Fax (770) 476-1738
John McCarty, Executive Director
E-mail: arc-pa@arc-pa.org
URL: www.arc-pa.org

Programs for the physician assistant **ARCPA**

Planning (City and Regional)

Planning Accreditation Board
CHEA: 2001
53 West Jackson Boulevard, Suite 1315
Chicago, IL 60604
(312) 662-1440 Fax (312) 662-1460
Shonagh Merits, Executive Director
E-mail: pab@planning.org
URL: www.planningaccreditationboard.org

Bachelor and master's level programs in planning **PLNG**

Podiatry

Council on Podiatric Medical Education
American Podiatric Medical Association (APMA)
USDE: 1952/2006/2011 CHEA: 2004
9312 Old Georgetown Road
Bethesda, MD 20814-1621
(301) 571-9200 Fax (301) 571-4903
Alan R. Tinkleman, Director
E-mail: artinkleman@apma.org
URL: www.cpme.org

Colleges and programs of podiatric medicine, including first professional and doctorate degree programs **POD**

Polysomnographic Technology

Commission on Accreditation of Allied Health Education Programs (see listing under Allied Health)
Committee on Accreditation for Polysomnographic Technologists Education
6 Pine Knoll Drive
Beverly, MA 01915-1425
(774) 855-4100
William W. Goding, Executive Director
E-mail: office@coapsg.org
URL: www.coapsg.org

Programs for polysomnographic technology **POLYT**

Psychology

Commission on Accreditation
American Psychological Association (APA)
USDE: 1970/2005/2011 CHEA: 2002
750 First Street NE
Washington, DC 20002-4242
(202) 336-5979 Fax (202) 336-5978
Susan F. Zlotlow, Director Program Consultation and Accreditation
E-mail: apaaccred@apa.org
URL: www.apa.org/ed/accred.html

Doctoral programs in:
- Clinical psychology **CLPSY**
- Counseling psychology **COPSY**
- Combined professional-scientific psychology **PSPSY**
- School psychology **SCPSY**
- Pre-doctoral internship program in professional psychology **IPSY**
- Post-doctoral residency in professional psychology **PDPSY**

Public Affairs and Administration

Commission on Peer Review and Accreditation
National Association of Schools of Public Affairs and Administration (NASPAA)
CHEA: 2004
1029 Vermont Avenue, NW, Suite 1100
Washington, DC 20005
(202) 628-8965 Fax (202) 626-4978
Crystal Calarusse, Academic Director
E-mail: copra@naspaa.org
URL: www.naspaa.org

Master's degree programs in public affairs, public policy and administration **SPAA**

Public Health

Council on Education for Public Health (CEPH)
USDE: 1974/2007/2013
800 Eye Street NW, Suite 202
Washington, DC 20001-3710
(202) 789-1050 Fax (202) 789-1895
Laura Rasar King, Executive Director
E-mail: lking@ceph.org
URL: www.ceph.org

Baccalaureate and graduate level programs in schools of public health and public health programs outside of schools of public health **PH**

Rabbinical and Talmudic Education

Accreditation Commission
Association of Advanced Rabbinical and Talmudic Schools (AARTS)
USDE: 1974/2007/2012 CHEA: 2011
11 Broadway, Suite 405
New York, NY 10004
(212) 363-1991 Fax (212) 533-5335
Bernard Fryshman, Executive Vice President
E-mail: BFryshma@nyit.edu

Advanced rabbinical and Talmudic schools **RABN**

Radiologic Technology

Joint Review Committee on Education in Radiologic Technology
USDE: 1957/2006/2011 CHEA: 2004
20 North Wacker Drive, Suite 2850
Chicago, IL 60606-3182
(312) 704-5300 Fax (312) 704-5304
Leslie F. Winter, Chief Executive Director
E-mail: mail@jrcert.org
URL: www.jrcert.org

Programs for:
- Magnetic resonance **RADMAG**
- Medical dosimetry **RADDOS**
- Radiographer **RAD**
- Radiation therapist technologist **RTT**

Recreation, Park and Leisure Studies

Council on Accreditation of Parks, Recreation, Tourism and Related Professions
National Recreation and Park Association
CHEA: 2003
22377 Belmont Ridge Road
Ashburn, VA 20148-4501
(703) 858-2195 Fax (703) 858-0794
Danielle Price, Accreditation Manager
E-mail: info@nrpa.org
URL: www.nrpa.org

Baccalaureate degree programs in recreation, park resources and leisure studies **NRPA**

Rehabilitation Education

Commission on Standards and Accreditation
Council on Rehabilitation Education (CORE)
CHEA: 2001
1699 Woodfield Road, Suite 300
Schaumburg, IL 60173
(847) 944-1345 Fax (847) 944-1346
Sue Ouellette, Executive Director
E-mail: souellet@niu.edu
URL: www.core-rehab.org

Rehabilitation counselor education programs at the master's level **CORE**

Social Work

Commission on Accreditation
Council on Social Work Education (CSWE)
1701 Duke Street, Suite 200
Alexandria, VA 22314-3457
(703) 683-8080 Fax (703) 683-8099
Stephen M. Holloway, Director, Office of Social Work Accreditation
E-mail: info@cswe.org
URL: www.cswe.org

Master's and baccalaureate degree programs **SW**

Speech-Language Pathology and Audiology

Council on Academic Accreditation
American Speech-Language-Hearing Association (ASHA)
USDE: 1967/2003/2010
2200 Research Boulevard
Rockville, MD 20850-3289
(301) 897-5700 Fax (301) 571-0457
Patrima L. Tice, Director Credentialing
E-mail: accreditation@asha.org
URL: www.asha.org

Master's and doctoral degree programs in:
- Audiology **AUD**
- Speech-language pathology **SP**

Surgical Assisting and Technology

(see listing under Allied Health)
Accrediting Bureau of Health Education Schools (ABHES)

Surgical technologist programs **SURTEC**

Commission on Accreditation of Allied Health Education Programs (see listing under Allied Health)
Accreditation Review Council On Education in Surgical Technology and Surgical Assisting
6 West Dry Creek Circle, Suite 110
Littleton, CO 80120

(303) 694-9262 Fax (303) 741-3655
Keith Orloff, Executive Director
E-mail: info@arcstsa.org
URL: www.arcst.org

Programs for the surgical technologist **SURGT**
Programs for the surgical assistant **SURGA**

Teacher Education

National Council for Accreditation of Teacher Education (NCATE)
USDE: 1952/2006/2011 CHEA: 2002
2010 Massachusetts Avenue NW, Suite 500
Washington, DC 20036-1023
(202) 466-7496 Fax (202) 296-6620
James G. Cibulka, President
E-mail: ncate@ncate.org
URL: www.ncate.org

Baccalaureate and graduate programs for the preparation of teachers and other professional personnel for elementary and secondary schools **TED**

Accreditation Committee
Teacher Education Accreditation Council (TEAC)
USDE: 2003/2005/2011 CHEA: 2001
One Dupont Circle NW, Suite 320
Washington, DC 20036-1110
(202) 466-7236 Fax (202) 466-7238
Mark LaCelle-Peterson, President
E-mail: teac@teac.org
URL: www.teac.org

Professional teacher education programs in institutions offering baccalaureate and graduate degrees for the preparation of K-12 teachers **TEAC**

Theatre

Commission on Accreditation
National Association of Schools of Theatre (NAST)
USDE: 1982/2008/2012
11250 Roger Bacon Drive, Suite 21
Reston, VA 20190
(703) 437-0700 Fax (703) 437-6312
Samuel Hope, Executive Director
E-mail: info@arts-accredit.org
URL: www.arts-accredit.org

Institutions and departments within institutions offering degree granting and non-degree-granting programs in theatre and theatre-related disciplines **THEA**

Theology

Commission on Accrediting
Association of Theological Schools (ATS)
USDE: 1952/2004/2011 CHEA: 2001
10 Summit Park Drive
Pittsburgh, PA 15275-1103
(412) 788-6505 Fax (412) 788-6510
Daniel O. Aleshire, Executive Director
E-mail: ats@ats.edu
URL: www.ats.edu

Freestanding schools, as well as schools or programs affiliated with larger institutions, offering graduate professional education for ministry and graduate study of theology **THEOL**

Trade and Technical Education

Accrediting Commission of Career Schools and Colleges (ACCSC)
USDE: 1967/2005/2016
2101 Wilson Boulevard, Suite 302
Arlington, VA 22201
(703) 247-4212 Fax (703) 247-4533
Michale McComis, Executive Director
E-mail: info@accsc.org
URL: www.accsc.org

Private, postsecondary degree-granting and non-degree-granting institutions that are predominantly organized to educate students for trade, occupational or technical careers **ACCSC**

Veterinary Medicine

Council on Education
American Veterinary Medical Association (AVMA)
USDE: 1952/2007/2012 CHEA: 2001
1931 North Meacham Road, Suite 100
Schaumburg, IL 60173
(800) 248-2862 Fax (847) 925-1329
David E. Granstrom, Director Education and Research
E-mail: avmainfo@avma.org
URL: www.avma.org

Colleges of veterinary medicine offering programs leading to a D.V.M./D.M.V. professional degree **VET**

Other

New York State Board of Regents
USDE: 1952/2007/2012
State Education Department
The University of the State of New York
89 Washington Avenue, Room 1106B
Albany, NY 12234
(518) 474-5889 Fax (518) 473-4000
John B. King, Jr., Commissioner of Education
E-mail: jking@mail.nysed.gov
URL: www.nysed.gov

Degree-granting institutions of higher education in New York that designate the agency as their sole or primary nationally recognized accrediting agency for purposes of establishing elibility to participate in Higher Education Act programs **NY**

Accrediting Agencies Recognized for their Pre-accreditation Categories[1]

Under the terms of the Higher Education Act and other Federal legislation providing funding assistance to postsecondary education, an institution or program is eligible to apply for participation in certain Federal programs if, in addition to meeting other statutory requirements, it is accredited by a nationally recognized accrediting agency—or if it is an institution with respect to which the U.S. Secretary of Education has determined that there is satisfactory assurance the institution or program will meet the accreditation standards of such agency or association within a reasonable time. An institution or program may establish satisfactory assurance of accreditation by acquiring pre-accreditation status with a nationally recognized accrediting agency which has been recognized by the U.S. Secretary of Education for the award of such status. According to the Criteria for Nationally Recognized Accrediting Agencies, if an accrediting agency has developed a pre-accreditation status, it must demonstrate that it applies criteria and follows procedures that are appropriately related to those used to award accreditation status. The criteria for recognition also requires an agency's standards for pre-accreditation to permit an institution or program to hold pre-accreditation no more than five years.

The following is a list of accrediting agencies recognized by the U.S. Secretary of Education for their pre-accreditation categories and the categories which are recognized.

Regional Institution Accrediting Bodies

Middle States Association of Colleges and Schools
Commission on Higher Education: *Candidate for Accreditation*

New England Association of Schools and Colleges:
Commission on Institutions of Higher Education: *Candidate for Accreditation*

North Central Association of Colleges and Schools
Commission on Institutions of Higher Education: *Candidate for Accreditation*

Northwest Commission on Colleges and Universities:
Candidate for Accreditation

Southern Association of Colleges and Schools
Commission on Colleges: *Candidate for Accreditation*

Western Association of Schools and Colleges
Accrediting Commission for Community and Junior Colleges: *Candidate for Accreditation*

Western Association of Schools and Colleges
Accrediting Commission for Senior Colleges and Universities: *Candidate for Accreditation*

National, Institutional and Specialized Accrediting Bodies

Accreditation Commission for Acupuncture and Oriental Medicine: *Candidate for Accreditation*

Accreditation Commission for Midwifery Education: *Pre-accreditation*

Accreditation Council for Pharmaceutical Education: *Candidate, Pre-candidate*

American Association for Marriage and Family Therapy,
Commission on Accreditation for Marriage and Family Therapy Education: *Candidate for Accreditation*

American Dietetic Association
Commission on Accreditation for Dietetics Education: *Pre-accreditation*

American Optometric Association
Accreditation Council on Optometric Education: *Preliminary Approval* (for professional degree programs); *Candidacy Pending* (for optometric residency programs in Veterans Administration facilities)

American Osteopathic Association
Commission on Osteopathic College Accreditation: *Provisional Accreditation*

American Physical Therapy Association
Commission on Accreditation in Physical Therapy Education: *Candidate for Accreditation*

American Podiatric Medical Association
Council on Podiatric Medical Education: *Candidate for Accreditation*

American Speech-Language-Hearing Association
Council on Academic Accreditation: *Candidate for Accreditation*

American Veterinary Medical Association
Council on Education: *Reasonable Assurance of Accreditation*

Association for Biblical Higher Education
Commission on Accreditation: *Candidate for Accreditation*

Association of Advanced Rabbinical and Talmudic Schools
Accreditation Commission: *Correspondent, Candidate for Accreditation*

Association of Theological Schools
Commission on Accrediting: *Candidate for Accredited Membership*

Council on Naturopathic Medical Education: *Pre-accreditation*

Council on Occupational Education: *Candidate for Accreditation*

Midwifery Education Accreditation Council: *Pre-accreditation*

Teacher Education Accreditation Council Accreditation Committee: *Pre-accreditation*

Transnational Association of Christian Colleges and Schools
Accreditation Commission: *Candidate for Accreditation*

[1]U.S. Department of Education, Nationally Recognized Accrediting Agencies and Associations, www2.ed.gov/admins/finaid/accred/accreditation_pg8.html.

Abbreviations, Explanatory Notes and Symbols

Abbreviations

Listed below are the abbreviations used in this Directory for the recognized regional accrediting commissions and the recognized national, professional and specialized accrediting bodies. Addresses for these associations can be found under our listing of Accrediting Agencies beginning on page viii.

The recognized regional accrediting commissions are indicated throughout this Directory by the following abbreviations:

EH New England Association of Schools and Colleges, Commission on Institutions of Higher Education (NEASC-CIHE)

M Middle States Association of Colleges and Schools, Commission on Higher Education (MSA/CHE)

NH North Central Association of Colleges and Schools, The Higher Learning Commission (NCA)

NW Northwest Commission on Colleges and Universities (NWCCU)

SC Southern Association of Colleges and Schools, Commission on Colleges (SACS)

WC Western Association of Schools and Colleges, Accrediting Commission for Senior Colleges and Universities (WASC-Sr)

WJ Western Association of Schools and Colleges, Accrediting Commission for Community and Junior Colleges (WASCACCJC)

National, professional and specialized accrediting agencies and associations are listed below. Wherever possible, degree levels are shown by the following symbols: (C) diploma/certificate; (A) associate; (B) baccalaureate; (M) master's; (S) beyond master's but less than doctorate; (FP) first professional; (D) doctorate.

AA Commission on Accreditation of Allied Health Education Programs: anesthesiologist assistant (M)

AAB Aviation Accreditation Board International: aviation (A,B)

AAFCS American Association of Family and Consumer Sciences: family and consumer sciences (B)

ABHES Accrediting Bureau of Health Education Schools: allied health (C,A,B)

ACBSP Accreditation Council for Business Schools and Programs: business administration, management, accounting and related business fields (A,B,M)

ACCSC Accrediting Commission of Career Schools and Colleges: occupational, trade and technical education (A,B,M)

ACFEI American Culinary Federation, Inc.: culinary arts and culinary management (C,A,B)

ACICS Accrediting Council for Independent Colleges and Schools: business and business-related programs (C,A,B,M)

ACUP Accreditation Commission for Acupuncture and Oriental Medicine: acupuncture (C,FP,M,D)

ADNUR National League for Nursing: nursing (A)

ANEST Council on Accreditation of Nurse Anesthesia Educational Programs: nurse anesthesia (C,M,D)

ARCPA Accreditation Review Commission on Education for the Physician Assistant: physician assisting programs (C,A,B,M)

ART National Association of Schools of Art and Design: art and design (C,A,B,M,D)

AUD American Speech-Language-Hearing Association: audiology (M,D)

BBT Commission on Accreditation of Allied Health Education Programs: blood bank technology (C,M)

BI Association for Biblical Higher Education: bible college education (C,A,B,M,D)

BUS AACSB-The Association to Advance Collegiate Schools of Business: business and management (B,M,D)

BUSA AACSB-The Association to Advance Collegiate Schools of Business: accounting (B,M,D)

CACREP Council for Accreditation of Counseling & Related Education programs: addiction counseling, career counseling, marriage, couple and family counseling, mental health counseling, school counseling, student affairs and college counseling and counselor education and supervision (M,D)

CEA Commission on English Language Program Accreditation: english language (C)

CHIRO Council on Chiropractic Education: chiropractic education (FP)

CIDA Council for Interior Design Accreditation: interior design (B,M)

CLPSY American Psychological Association: clinical psychology (D)

CNCE Accrediting Council for Continuing Education and Training: continuing education (C,A)

COE Council on Occupational Education: occupational, trade, and technical education (A)

COMTA Commission on Massage Therapy Accreditation: massage therapy, bodywork, aesthetics/esthetics and skin care (C,A)

CONST American Council for Construction Education: construction education (A,B)

COPSY American Psychological Association: counseling psychology (D)

CORE Council on Rehabilitation Education: rehabilitation counseling (M)

COSME National Accrediting Commission of Career Arts and Sciences: cosmetology and massage therapy (C)

CS ABET, Inc.: computer science (B)

CVT Commission on Accreditation of Allied Health Education Programs: cardiovascular technology (C,A,B)

CYTO Commission on Accreditation of Allied Health Education Programs: cytotechnology (C,A,B,M)

DA American Dental Association: dental assisting (C,A)

DANCE National Association of Schools of Dance: dance (C,B,M,D)

DENT American Dental Association: dentistry (FP)

DETC Distance Education and Training Council: home study schools (A,B,M,FP,D)

DH American Dental Association: dental hygiene (C,A)

DIETC American Dietetic Association: coordinated dietetics programs (B,M)

DIETD American Dietetic Association: didactic dietetics programs

DIETI American Dietetic Association: dietetic post-baccalaureate internships

DIETT American Dietetic Association: dietetic technician (A)

DMOLS National Accrediting Agency for Clinical Laboratory Sciences: diagnostic molecular scientist (C,B)

DMS Commission on Accreditation of Allied Health Education Programs: diagnostic medical sonography (C,A,B)

DNUR National League for Nursing: nursing (C)

DT American Dental Association: dental laboratory technology (C,A)

EEG Commission on Accreditation of Allied Health Education Programs: electroneurodiagnostic technology (C,A)

EMT Commission on Accreditation of Allied Health Education Programs: emergency medical technician-paramedic (C,A,B)

ENG ABET, Inc.: engineering (B,M)

ENGR ABET, Inc.: applied science (A,B,M)

ENGT ABET, Inc.: engineering technology (A,B)

EXSC Commission on Accreditation of Allied Health Education Programs: exercise science (B,M)

FOR Society of American Foresters: forestry (B,M,FP)

FUSER American Board of Funeral Service Education: funeral service education (C,A,B)

HSA Commission on Accreditation of Healthcare Management Education: healthcare management (M)

HT National Accrediting Agency for Clinical Laboratory Sciences: histologic technology (C,A,B)

IACBE International Assembly for Collegiate Business Education: business programs in institutions that grant bachelor/graduate degrees (A,B,M,D)

IFSAC International Fire Service Accreditation Congress Degree Assembly: fire and emergency related degree (A,B)

IPSY American Psychological Association: pre-doctoral internships in professional psychology

JOUR Accrediting Council on Education for Journalism and Mass Communications: journalism and mass communications (B,M)

KIN Commission on Accreditation of Allied Health Education Programs: kinesiotherapy (B)

LAW American Bar Association: law (FP)

LIB American Library Association: librarianship (FP)

LSAR American Society for Landscape Architects: landscape architecture (B,M)

MAAB Accrediting Bureau of Health Education Schools: medical assisting (C)

MAC Commission on Accreditation of Allied Health Education Programs: medical assisting (C,A)

MACTE Montessori Accreditation Council for Teacher Education: Montessori teacher education

MEAC Midwifery Education Accreditation Council: midwifery education (C,A)

MED Liaison Committee on Medical Education: medicine (FP)

MFCD American Association for Marriage and Family Therapy: marriage and family therapy (M,D)

MIDWF Accreditation Commission for Midwifery Education: nurse midwifery (C,M,D)

MIL Commission on Accreditation of Allied Health Education Programs: medical illustrator (M)

MLTAB Accrediting Bureau of Health Education Schools: medical laboratory technician (C)

MLTAD National Accrediting Agency for Clinical Laboratory Sciences: medical laboratory technician (A)

MT National Accrediting Agency for Clinical Laboratory Sciences: medical technology (C,B)

MUS National Association of Schools of Music: music (B,M,D)

NAIT The Association of Technology, Management, and Applied Engineering: technology, applied technology, engineering technology and technology-related programs (A,B,M)

NATUR Council on Naturopathic Medical Education: naturopathic medical education (FP)

NMT Joint Review Committee on Educational Programs in Nuclear Medicine Technology: nuclear medicine technology (C,A,B)

NRPA National Recreation and Park Association: recreation, park resources, and leisure studies (B)

NUR National League for Nursing: nursing (B,M)

NURSE Commission on Collegiate Nursing Education: nursing (B,M)

NY New York State Board of Regents:
Degree-granting institutions of higher education in New York that designate the agency as their sole or primary nationally recognized accrediting agency for purposes of establishing elibility to participate in Higher Education Act programs

OPD Commission on Opticianry Accreditation: opticianry (A)

OPE Commission on Accreditation of Allied Health Education Programs: orthotics and prosthetics (C,B,M)

OPLT Commission on Opticianry Accreditation: opthalmic laboratory technician (C)

OPT American Optometric Association: optometry (FP)

OPTR American Optometric Association: optometric residency programs

OPTT American Optometric Association: optometric technician (A)

OSTEO American Osteopathic Association, Office of Osteopathic Education: osteopathic medicine (FP)

OT American Occupational Therapy Association: occupational therapy (B,M,D)

OTA American Occupational Therapy Association: occupational therapy assistant (C,A)

PA National Accrediting Agency for Clinical Laboratory Sciences: pathologist's assistant (C,A,B,M)

PAST Association for Clinical Pastoral Education: clinical pastoral education

PDPSY American Psychological Association: post-doctorate residency in professional psychology

PERF Commission on Accreditation of Allied Health Education Programs: perfusionist (C,B,M)

PH Council on Education for Public Health: public health (B,M,D)

PHAR Accreditation Council for Pharmaceutical Education: pharmacy (FP)

PLNG Planning Accreditation Board: certified planning (B,M)

PNUR National League for Nursing: practical nursing (C)

POD American Podiatric Medical Association: podiatry (FP)

POLYT Commission on Accreditation of Allied Health Education Programs: polysomnographic technologist education (C,A)

PSPSY American Psychological Association: combined professional-scientific psychology (D)

PTA American Physical Therapy Association: physical therapy (M,D)

PTAA American Physical Therapy Association: physical therapy assistant (A)

RABN Association of Advanced Rabbinical and Talmudic Schools: rabbinical and Talmudic education (B,M,D)

RAD Joint Review Committee on Education in Radiologic Technology: radiography (C,A,B)

RADDOS Joint Review Committee on Education in Radiologic Technology: medical dosimetry (C,B)

RADMAG Joint Review Committee on Education in Radiologic Technology: magnetic resonance (C,B)

RTT Joint Review Committee on Education in Radiologic Technology: radiation therapist/technologist (C,A,B)

SCPSY American Psychological Association: school psychology (D)

SP American Speech-Language-Hearing Association: speech-language pathology (M,D)

SPAA National Association of Schools of Public Affairs and Administration: public affairs and administration (M)

SURGA Commission on Accreditation of Allied Health Education Programs: surgical assistant (C,A)

SURGT Commission on Accreditation of Allied Health Education Programs: surgical technology (C,A)

SURTEC Accrediting Bureau of Health Education Schools: surgical technologist (C,A)

SW Council on Social Work Education: social work (B,M)

TEAC Teacher Education Accreditation Council: teacher education (B, M,D)

TED National Council for Accreditation of Teacher Education: teacher education (B,M,S,D)

THEA National Association of Schools of Theatre: theatre (B,M,D)

THEOL Association of Theological Schools: theology (M,FP,D)

TRACS Transnational Association of Christian Colleges and Schools: christian studies education (C,A,B,M,D)

VET American Veterinary Medical Association: veterinary medicine (FP)

Explanatory Notes and Symbols

Associate degree: includes junior colleges, community colleges, technical institutes, and schools offering at least a two-year program of college-level studies, either leading to an associate degree wholly or principally creditable toward a baccalaureate degree.

Baccalaureate: includes those institutions offering programs of studies leading to the customary bachelor of arts or bachelor of science degrees.

First professional degree: includes those institutions that offer the academic requirements for selected professions based on programs that require at least two academic years of previous college work for entrance and a total of at least six years of college work for completion.

Master's: includes those institutions offering the customary first graduate degree, master of arts or master of science degree in the liberal arts and sciences, or the next degree in the same field after the first professional degree.

Beyond master's but less than doctorate: includes those institutions offering "postgraduate pre-doctoral degrees".

Graduate non-degree granting: includes institutions offering work beyond the bachelor's level but not conferring degrees. In some instances the degrees are conferred by cooperating institutions.

Doctorate: includes those institutions offering a Ph.D. or its equivalent in any field.

Postdoctoral research only: includes institutions operating solely for the purpose of research at the postdoctoral level.

First Talmudic degree: undergraduate degree granted by accredited Rabbinical schools. The schools in New York "using this designation do not imply that the 'First Talmudic Degree' is equivalent to any secular academic degree recognized by the Board of Regents".*

Second Talmudic degree: graduate degree granted by accredited Rabbinical schools. The schools in New York "using this designation do not imply that the 'Second Talmudic Degree' is equivalent to any secular academic degree recognized by the Board of Regents".*

---

*The University of the State of New York, The State Education Department, Albany, New York, letter August 17, 1983.

Type of Program

Occupational: refers to programs beyond high school designed to provide students with knowledge and skills necessary for immediate employment.

Two-year principally bachelor's creditable: refers to the first two years of college work.

Liberal arts and general: refers to four or five year baccalaureate or postbaccalaureate degree programs in the liberal arts and sciences.

Teacher preparatory programs: refers to programs of at least four years duration.

Professional programs: refers to separate programs of at least four years beyond high school and organized around a professionally oriented academic discipline.

Business, fine arts, music, nursing, religious, or technical emphasis: refers to programs that are organized around a specific discipline.

Symbols

* The institution is part of a system.

Used preceding any of the acronyms for the accrediting agencies the following symbols indicate that:

The accrediting agency has stated publicly that the institution or program is preliminary or provisionally accredited, accredited with some reservations, or approved on probation.

@ The institution or program has attained a pre-accredited status.

& The institution is covered under the regional accreditation of the parent institution.

U.S. Postal Abbreviation of States and Territories

Alabama .... AL
Alaska .... AK
American Samoa .... AS
Arizona .... AZ
Arkansas .... AR
California .... CA
Colorado .... CO
Connecticut .... CT
Delaware .... DE
District of Columbia .... DC
Florida .... FL
Georgia .... GA
Guam .... GU
Hawaii .... HI
Idaho .... ID
Illinois IL
Indiana .... IN
Iowa .... IA
Kansas .... KS
Kentucky .... KY
Louisiana .... LA
Maine .... ME
Maryland .... MD
Marshall Islands .... MH
Massachusetts .... MA
Michigan .... MI
Micronesia .... FM
Minnesota .... MN
Mississippi .... MS
Missouri .... MO
Montana .... MT
Nebraska .... NE
Nevada .... NV
New Hampshire .... NH
New Jersey .... NJ
New Mexico .... NM
New York .... NY
North Carolina .... NC
North Dakota .... ND
Northern Marianas .... MP
Ohio .... OH
Oklahoma .... OK
Oregon .... OR
Palau .... PW
Pennsylvania .... PA
Puerto Rico .... PR
Rhode Island .... RI
South Carolina .... SC
South Dakota .... SD
Tennessee .... TN
Texas .... TX
Utah .... UT
Vermont .... VT
Virgin Islands VI
Virginia .... VA
Washington .... WA
West Virginia .... WV
Wisconsin .... WI
Wyoming .... WY

Institution Changes

Institutions and Offices Added

	FICE/ID Number
Alaska	
Career Academy	025410
Arizona	
Sonoran Desert Institute	667057
Arkansas	
Shorter College	667054
California	
Abraham Lincoln University	667049
Alhambra Medical University	667052
American Career College-Ontario	039713
Carrington College California - Citrus Heights	667042
Cedars-Sinai Medical Center Graduate Program in Biomedical Sciences and Tra	667071
Eternity Bible College	667045
Everest College-Anaheim	011107
Everest College-Gardena	011123
Everest College-Hayward	011121
Everest College-LA Wilshire	007606
Everest College-Reseda	011109
Heald College, Modesto	667043
International Technological University	667070
John Paul the Great Catholic University	667072
Kensington College	033083
Los Angeles ORT College	025703
New York Film Academy, Los Angeles	041188
Riverside Community College District	667039
San Bernardino Community College District	667040
San Joaquin Valley College-Hesperia	667044
Sanford-Burnham Graduate School of Biomedical Sciences	667069
Shepherd University School of Theology	667056
Stanton University	667053
United Education Institute	025593
Unitek College	041697
West Coast Ultrasound Institute	036393
West Hills Community College District	667041
Colorado	
Colorado Academy of Veterinary Technology	667048
IntelliTec Medical Institute	008635
Florida	
Academy for Practical Nursing and Health Occupations	033463
FastTrain of Ft. Lauderdale	041320
FastTrain of Jacksonville	041322
FastTrain of Miami	041319
FastTrain of Tampa	041321
Fortis College	030542
Rasmussen College - Fort Myers	667062
Rasmussen College - Tampa/Brandon	667067
Stenotype Institute of Jacksonville	008417
Ultimate Medical Academy-Clearwater	035493
University of South Florida Manatee-Sarasota	667058
Illinois	
Rasmussen College - Aurora	667060
Rasmussen College - Mokena/Tinley Park	667064
Rasmussen College - Rockford	667065
Rasmussen College - Romeoville/Joliet	667066
Tribeca Flashpoint Media Arts Academy	667083
Kansas	
Pinnacle Career Institute	026130
Kentucky	
Daymar College-Louisville East	667081
Daymar College-Madisonville	667079
Daymar College-Scottsville	667080
Maine	
Institute for Doctoral Studies in the Visual Arts	667036
Maryland	
Bais HaMedrash & Mesivta of Baltimore	667075
Lincoln College of Technology	007936
Michigan	
Keweenaw Bay Ojibwa Community College	667037
Minnesota	
Rasmussen College - Blaine	667061
Nebraska	
Alegent Health School of Radiologic Technology	008492
New Jersey	
Yeshiva Gedolah Zichron Leyma	667078
New York	
Be'er Yaakov Talmudic Seminary	667076
Memorial Hospital School of Nursing	012203
Saint Paul's School of Nursing-Staten Island	009479
Samaritan Hospital School of Nursing	009248
SBI Campus-An Affiliate of Sanford-Brown	011647

	FICE/ID Number
St. Paul's School of Nursing	012364
Yeshiva Gedolah Ohr Yisrael	667077

Ohio

Bexley Hall Seminary	037473
Daymar College-New Boston	667082

Pennsylvania

Reformed Episcopal Seminary	667050
The Commonwealth Medical College	667004

Puerto Rico

Universal Career Community College	033263

Tennessee

Mid-South Christian College	667046

Texas

Anamarc College	037563
Kaplan College	031158
Kaplan College	025919
Lincoln College of Technology	008353
Redeemer Theological Seminary	667055
Texas School of Business	023122
Texas School of Business-Friendswood	667051
The Academy of Health Care Professions	034263

Virginia

Aviation Institute of Maintenance	038834
Bon Secours Memorial College of Nursing	010043
Medical Careers Institute	667038
Sentara College of Health Sciences	031065

Washington

Everest College	023001
Interface College	667047

Wisconsin

Rasmussen College - Appleton	667059
Rasmussen College - Green Bay	667063
Rasmussen College - Wausau	667068

Institutions and Offices Dropped

FICE/ID Number

Alabama

American Sentinel University 666067
(No longer accredited)

Alaska

Alaska Christian College 041386
(Not degree granting)

California

American InterContinental University 666646
(Closed)

Bethany University 001121
(Closed)

Crimson Technical College 025964
(Not degree granting)

Colorado

American Pathways University 666652
(AALE accreditation no longer recognized)

Remington College-Colorado Springs Campus 031105
(Not degree granting)

Connecticut

St. Basil College Seminary 001408
(Voluntarily withdrew from institutional accreditation)

Florida

IMPAC University 666334
(No longer accredited)

Jones College 001498
(Closed)

Universidad FLET/FLET University 666312
(No longer accredited)

Georgia

Holy Spirit College 666661
(AALE accreditation no longer recognized)

Indiana

Aviation Institute of Maintenance 031763
(Not degree granting)

Harrison College 666432
(Closed)

Massachusetts

University of Massachusetts School of Law-Dartmouth 031277
(Part of University of Massachusetts)

Missouri

Midwest University 035283
(Voluntarily withdrew from institutional accreditation)

New Hampshire

Magdalen College 022233
(No longer accredited)

Institution Changes

FICE/ID Number

New York

Kol Yaakov Torah Center 022567
(No longer accredited)

Yeshiva Nesivos Hatorah 666410
(No longer accredited)

Yeshiva Zichron Aryeh 039343
(No longer accredited)

Ohio

Academy of Court Reporting, Akron, OH 666464
(Closed)

Rhode Island

Sanford-Brown Institute-Cranston 007844
(Not degree granting)

Utah

Mountainland Applied Technology College 034133
(Not degree granting)

Virginia

Everest College 009267
(Not degree granting)

Skyline College 025354
(No longer accredited)

Skyline College 666149
(Closed)

Merged Institutions

California

Jesuit School of Theology at Berkeley *into* 010333
Santa Clara University 001326

Mennonite Brethren Biblical Seminary *into* 010368
Fresno Pacific University 001253

Illinois

Springfield College in Illinois *into* 001761
Benedictine University 001767

Louisiana

Northshore Technical College Ascension Campus *into* 015047
River Parishes Community College 037894

New York

New York Institute of Technology - Manhattan Campus *into* 002782
New York Institute of Technology 004804

Sage College of Albany *into* 002811
The Sage Colleges 002810

FICE/ID Number

Sage Graduate School *into* 666955
The Sage Colleges 002810

Tennessee

Lambuth University *into* 003498
The University of Memphis 003509

Name Changes

Arizona

from: Coconino County Community College 031004
to: Coconino Community College

from: Southwestern College 007113
to: Arizona Christian University (formerly Southwestern College)

from: The Art Center Design College 024915
to: Southwest University of Visual Arts

Arkansas

from: Ouachita Technical College 009976
to: College of the Ouachitas

California

from: American Career College-Anaheim 022418
to: American Career College-Los Angeles

from: California School of Culinary Arts 032103
to: Le Cordon Bleu College of Culinary Arts in Los Angeles

from: Carrington College California 666086
to: Carrington College California - Administrative Office

from: Coleman College 666259
to: Coleman University

from: Dell'Arte International School of Physical Theater 030256
to: Dell'Arte International School of Physical Theatre

from: Dongguk Royal University 031095
to: Dongguk University

from: Redwoods Community College District 001185
to: College of the Redwoods Community College District

from: Riverside Community College District 001270
to: Riverside City College

from: Saybrook Graduate School & Research Center 021206
to: Saybrook University

from: The American Musical and Dramatic Academy 666721
to: AMDA College and Conservatory of the Performing Arts

from: TUI University 041279
to: Trident University International

from: West Hills Community College District 001176
to: West Hills College Coalinga

Institution Changes

FICE/ID Number

Colorado

from: Denver Academy of Court Reporting 021887
to: Prince Institute-Rocky Mountains

from: Mesa State College 001358
to: Colorado Mesa University

from: University of Colorado Denver 004508
to: University of Colorado Denver|Anschutz Medical Campus

District of Columbia

from: National Defense Intelligence College 666393
to: National Intelligence University

from: Trinity College 001460
to: Trinity Washington University

from: University of the District of Columbia 001441
to: University System of the District of Columbia

Florida

from: Americare School of Nursing-Fern Park 033903
to: Lincoln Tech Fern Park Orlando Campus

from: Gulf Coast Community College 001490
to: Gulf Coast State College

from: Institute of Allied Medical Professions 040834
to: Cambridge Institute of Allied Health & Technology

from: Le Cordon Bleu Program College of the Culinary Arts 666064
to: Le Cordon Bleu College of Culinary Arts in Orlando

from: Polytechnic University of the Americas 666238
to: Polytechnic University Puerto Rico

from: Rasmussen College - Pasco 666425
to: Rasmussen College - New Port Richey

from: St. Johns River Community College 001523
to: St. Johns River State College

from: Valencia Community College 006750
to: Valencia College

Georgia

from: Atlanta Christian College 001547
to: Point University

from: Brown College of Court Reporting and Medical Transcription 020609
to: Brown College of Court Reporting

from: DeVry University - Stockbridge 666532
to: DeVry University - Henry County

from: Heart of Georgia Technical College 022795
to: Oconee Falls Line Technical College-South Campus

from: Medical College of Georgia 001579
to: Georgia Health Sciences University

from: Sandersville Technical College 031555
to: Oconee Fall Line Technical College-North Campus

FICE/ID Number

Hawaii

from: Pacific Rim Christian College 667010
to: New Hope Christian College-Hawaii

Illinois

from: DeVry University - Corporate Office 001672
to: DeVry University - Home Office

from: West Suburban College of Nursing 006250
to: Resurrection University

Iowa

from: Mount Mercy College 001880
to: Mount Mercy University

Kentucky

from: Asbury College 001952
to: Asbury University

from: Frontier School of Midwifery & Family Nursing 030070
to: Frontier Nursing University

from: Pikeville College 001980
to: University of Pikeville

from: Southwestern College 666447
to: Lincoln College of Technology

Louisiana

from: Northshore Technical College Sullivan Campus 006756
to: Northshore Technical Community College

Maryland

from: College of Notre Dame of Maryland 002065
to: Notre Dame of Maryland University

Massachusetts

from: Bridgewater State College 002183
to: Bridgewater State University

from: Fitchburg State College 002184
to: Fitchburg State University

from: Framingham State College 002185
to: Framingham State University

from: Longy School of Music 021430
to: Longy School of Music of Bard College

from: Salem State College 002188
to: Salem State University

from: Western New England College 002226
to: Western New England University

from: Westfield State College 002189
to: Westfield State University

from: Worcester State College 002190
to: Worcester State University

Michigan

from: Michigan Theological Seminary 031353
to: Moody Theological Seminary-Michigan

FICE/ID Number

Minnesota

from: Alexandria Technical College 005544
to: Alexandria Technical & Community College

from: Rasmussen College - Eden Prairie 011686
to: Rasmussen College - Bloomington

Missouri

from: DeVry University - St. Louis West Center 666214
to: DeVry University - St. Louis

from: Hannibal-La Grange College 009089
to: Hannibal-La Grange University

from: IHM Health Studies Center 667021
to: IHM Academy of EMS

from: Saint Luke's College 009782
to: Saint Luke's College of Health Sciences

Nebraska

from: Midland Lutheran College 002553
to: Midland University

Nevada

from: University of Southern Nevada 040653
to: Roseman University of Health Sciences

New Mexico

from: College of Santa Fe 002649
to: Santa Fe University of Art and Design

from: The Art Center Design College 666524
to: Southwest University of Visual Arts

New York

from: Albany Law School of Union University 002886
to: Albany Law School

from: Crouse Hospital School of Nursing 006445
to: Crouse Hospital College of Nursing

from: Long Island University Rockland Graduate Campus 666077
to: Long Island University Hudson Graduate Center at Rockland

from: Long Island University Westchester Graduate Campus 666078
to: Long Island University Hudson Graduate Center at Westchester

from: New York Institute of Technology Main Campus - Old Westbury 004804
to: New York Institute of Technology

from: Russell Sage College 002810
to: The Sage Colleges

from: The American Musical and Dramatic Academy 007572
to: AMDA College and Conservatory of the Performing Arts

North Carolina

from: Carolina Evangelical Divinity School 039395
to: Carolina Graduate School of Divinity

FICE/ID Number

from: DeVry University - Morrisville 666562
to: DeVry University - Raleigh/Durham

from: John Wesley College 002935
to: Laurel University

North Dakota

from: Rasmussen College - Fargo 004846
to: Rasmussen College - Fargo/Moorhead

Ohio

from: Heidelberg College 003048
to: Heidelberg University

from: Kent State University Stark Campus 003054
to: Kent State University at Stark

from: Lourdes College 003069
to: Lourdes University

from: Mercy College of Northwest Ohio 030970
to: Mercy College of Ohio

from: Southwestern College 666471
to: Lincoln College of Technology

from: Southwestern College 666472
to: Lincoln College

from: Southwestern College 012128
to: Lincoln College of Technology

from: Southwestern College 666473
to: Lincoln College of Technology

Oklahoma

from: Oklahoma State University - Okmulgee 003172
to: Oklahoma State University Institute of Technology-Okmulgee

Oregon

from: Western Culinary Institute 030226
to: Le Cordon Bleu College of Culinary Arts in Portland

from: Western States Chiropractic College 012309
to: University of Western States

Pennsylvania

from: Allied Medical and Technical Institute 030115
to: Fortis Institute

from: Pennsylvania Culinary Institute 030068
to: Le Cordon Bleu Institute of Culinary Arts in Pittsburgh

from: Sanford-Brown Institute-Monroeville 666526
to: Sanford-Brown Institute-Wilkins Township

from: Tri-State Business Institute 030108
to: Fortis Institute

from: Triangle Tech-Erie School 020902
to: Triangle Tech, Erie

Puerto Rico

from: Colegio Pentecostal Mizpa 031983
to: Universidad Pentecostal Mizpa

Institution Changes

	FICE/ID Number
Tennessee	
from: Emmanuel School of Religion *to:* Emmanuel Christian Seminary	012547
from: Harding University Graduate School of Religion *to:* Harding School of Theology	004081
from: Johnson Bible College *to:* Johnson University	003495
from: Medvance Institute *to:* Fortis Institute	023263
from: Visible School - Music and Worship Arts College *to:* Visible Music College	039823
Texas	
from: Academy of Oriental Medicine at Austin *to:* AOMA Graduate School of Integrative Medicine	031564
from: Austin Community College *to:* Austin Community College District	012015
from: Parker College of Chiropractic *to:* Parker University	023053
Utah	
from: College of Eastern Utah *to:* Utah State University-College of Eastern Utah	003676
from: Utah Career College *to:* Broadview University	011166
Virginia	
from: Union Theological Seminary and Presbyterian School of Christian Education *to:* Union Presbyterian Seminary	003743
Washington	
from: Mars Hill Graduate School *to:* The Seattle School of Theology and Psychology	034664
West Virginia	
from: Pierpont Community and Technical College *to:* Pierpont Community & Technical College	040385

Codes and Descriptions of Administrative Officers

(01) **Chief Executive Officer (President/Chancellor)** - Directs all affairs and operations of a higher education institution.

(02) **Chief Executive Officer Within a System (President/Chancellor)** - Directs all affairs and operations of a campus or an institution which is part of a university-wide system.

(03) **Executive Vice President** - Responsible for all or most functions and operations of an institution under the direction of the Chief Executive Officer.

(04) **Administrative Assistant to the President** - Senior administrative assistant to the Chief Executive Officer.

(05) **Chief Academic Officer** - Directs the academic program of the institution. Typically includes academic planning, teaching, research, extensions and coordination of interdepartmental affairs.

(06) **Registrar** - Responsible for student registration, scheduling of classes, examinations and classroom facilities, student records and related matters.

(07) **Director of Admissions** - Responsible for the recruitment, selection and admission of students.

(08) **Head Librarian** - Directs the activities of all institutional libraries.

(09) **Director of Institutional Research** - Conducts research and studies on the institution including design of studies, data collection, analysis and reporting.

(10) **Chief Financial/Business Officer** - Directs business and financial affairs including accounting, purchasing, investments, auxiliary enterprises and related business matters.

(11) **Chief of Operations/Administration** - Responsible for administrative functions that are generally non-academic and non-financial.

(12) **Director of Branch Campus** - Official who is in charge of a branch campus.

(13) **Director, Computing and Information Management** - Coordinates computing systems and the flow of information to and from computing operations.

(14) **Director, Computer Center** - Directs the institution's major data processing facilities and services.

(15) **Director, Personnel Services** - Administers the institution's personnel policies and programs for staff or faculty and staff.

(16) **Chief, Personnel** - Responsible for establishing and directing personnel policies including government related requirements.

(17) **Chief, Health Care Professions** - Senior administrator of academic health care programs, hospitals, clinic or affiliated healthcare programs.

(18) **Chief, Facilities/Physical Plant** - Responsible for the construction, rehabilitation and maintenance of buildings and grounds.

(19) **Director, Security/Safety** - Manages campus police. Responsible for security programs, training, traffic and parking regulations.

(20) **Associate Academic Officer** - Responsible for many of the functions and operations under the direction of the Chief Academic Officer.

(21) **Associate Business Officer** - Assists and reports to the Chief Business Officer.

(22) **Director, Affirmative Action/Equal Opportunity** - Responsible for the institution's program relating to affirmative action and equal opportunity.

(23) **Director, Health Services** - Directs the operation of clinics, medical staff and other programs which provide institutional health services.

(24) **Director, Educational Media** - Responsible for audio-visual services and multi-media learning devices.

(25) **Contract Administrator** - Conducts administrative activities in connection with contracts and grants.

(26) **Chief Public Relations Officer** - Directs public relations program. May include alumni relations, publication, marketing and development.

(27) **Chief Information Officer** - Provides information about the institution to students, faculty, staff and the public.

(28) **Director of Diversity** - Responsible for the institution's programs relating to diversity.

(29) **Director, Alumni Relations** - Coordinates alumni activities between the institution and the alumni.

(30) **Chief, Development** - Organizes and directs programs connected with the fund raising activities of the institution.

(31) **Chief Community Relations Officer** - Directs the educational (usually non-credit), cultural and recreational services to the community.

(32) **Chief Student Life Officer** - Responsible for the direction of student life programs including counseling and testing, housing, placement, student union, relationships with student organizations and related functions.

(33) **Dean of Men** - Directs student life activities solely concerned with male students.

(34) **Dean of Women** - Directs student life activities solely concerned with female students.

(35) **Director, Student Affairs** - Assists Chief Student Life Officer in the non-academic student life activities.

(36) **Director, Student Placement** - Directs the operation of the student placement office to provide career counseling and job placement services to undergraduates, graduates and alumni.

(37) **Director, Student Financial Aid** - Directs the administration of all forms of student aid.

(38) **Director, Student Counseling** - Directs non-academic counseling and testing for students including referral to outside agencies.

(39) **Director, Student Housing** - Manages student housing operations.

(40) **Director, Bookstore** - Responsible for the operation of the bookstore including purchasing, advertising, sales, employment, inventory and related functions.

(41) **Athletic Director** - Manages intramural and intercollegiate programs including employment, scheduling, promotion, maintenance and related functions.

(42) **Chaplain, Director Campus Ministry** - Plans, directs the pastoral ministry and religious activities.

(43) **Director, Legal Services (General Counsel)** - Salaried staff person responsible for advising on legal rights, obligations and related matters.

(44) **Director, Annual or Planned Giving** - Operates the annual giving from all supporters of the institutions.

(45) **Chief Planning Officer** - Directs the long-range planning and the allocation of the institution's resources.

(46) **Chief, Research and Development (not fundraising)** - Initiates and directs research in using the facilities and personnel in new areas of academic and scientific exploration.

Dean or Director. Serves as the principal administrator for the institutional program indicated:

(47) **Agriculture**
(48) **Architecture**
(49) **Art and Sciences**
(50) **Business**
(51) **Continuing Education**
(52) **Dentistry**
(53) **Education**
(54) **Engineering**
(55) **Evening Division**
(56) **Extension**
(57) **Fine Arts**
(58) **Graduate Programs**
(59) **Home Economics**
(60) **Journalism/Communications**
(61) **Law**
(62) **Library Services**
(63) **Medicine**
(64) **Music**
(65) **Natural Resources**
(66) **Nursing**
(67) **Pharmacy**
(68) **Physical Education**
(69) **Public Health**
(70) **Social Work**
(71) **Special Session**
(72) **Technology**
(73) **Theology**
(74) **Veterinary Medicine**
(75) **Vocational/Occupational Education**
(76) **Allied Health Sciences**
(77) **Computer Science**
(78) **Cooperative Education**
(79) **Humanities**
(80) **Government/Public Affairs**
(81) **Mathematics/Sciences**
(82) **Political Science/International Affairs**
(83) **Social and Behavioral Sciences**
(87) **Summer School/Session**
(89) **Freshmen Studies**
(92) **Honors Program**
(93) **Minority Students**
(94) **Women's Studies**
(97) **General Studies**
(106) **Online Education/E-learning**
(107) **Professional Studies**

(84) **Director, Enrollment Management** - Plans, develops, and implements strategies to sustain enrollment. Supervises administration of all admissions and financial aid operations.

(85) **Director, Foreign Students** - Directs student life activities solely concerned with foreign students.

(86) **Director, Government Relations** - Coordinates institution's relations with local, state, and federal government.

(90) **Director, Academic Computing** - Responsible for operation and coordination of the institution's various academic computer facilities and labs.

(91) **Director, Administrative Computing** - Responsible for operation of the institution's administrative computing facility.

(96) **Director of Purchasing** - Coordinates purchasing of goods and services.

(100) **Chief of Staff** - Senior non-secretarial staff assistant to the President/Chancellor. Manages administration and operations of The Office of the President.

(101) **Secretary of the Institution/Board of Governors** - Responsible for liaison between the Board and the institution. Maintains governance and official Board records.

(102) **Director, Foundation/Corporate Relations** - Directs institution's efforts in the area of soliciting grants and gifts from foundations and corporations.

(103) **Director, Workforce Development** - Directs the institution's efforts in course development and instruction for students and the community in skills necessary to gain employment.

(104) **Director, Study Abroad** - Coordinates and advises students and faculty on academic studies conducted internationally.

(105) **Director, Web Services** - Directs the development, operations and content of the institution's web sites.

(88) Use this code for those titles that do not fit the above positions.

(00) **President Emeritus**

United States Department of Education Offices

Arne Duncan (A)
Secretary of Education
United States Department of Education
400 Maryland Avenue, SW
Washington, DC 20202
(202) 401-3000
FAX: (202) 260-7867
URL: www.ed.gov

Tony Miller (B)
Deputy Secretary of Education
United States Department of Education
400 Maryland Avenue, SW
Room 7W310
Washington, DC 20202
(202) 401-3000
FAX: (202) 260-7867
E-MAIL: tony.miller@ed.gov
URL: www.ed.gov

Eduardo Ochoa (C)
Assistant Secretary
Office of Postsecondary Education
United States Department of Education
1990 K Street, NW
Washington, DC 20006
(202) 502-7750
FAX: (202) 502-7677
E-MAIL: eduardo.ochoa@ed.gov
URL: www2.ed.gov/about/offices/list/ope/index.html

Melissa Lewis (D)
Executive Director
National Advisory Committee on Institutional Quality & Integrity
Office of Postsecondary Education
United States Department of Education
1990 K Street, NW
Room 8060
Washington, DC 20006
(202) 219-7009
FAX: (202) 219-7005
E-MAIL: melissa.lewis@ed.gov
URL: www.ed.gov/about/bdscomm/list/naciqi.html

Ms. Kay Gilcher (E)
Director
Accreditation Division
Office of Postsecondary Education
U.S. Department of Education
1990 K Street, NW
Room 8027
Washington, DC 20006-8509
(202) 502-7693
FAX: (202) 219-7005
URL: www.ed.gov/admins/finaid/accred/index.html

Mr. Thomas Weko (F)
Associate Commissioner
Postsecondary, Adult and Career Education Division
National Center for Education Statistics
1990 K Street, NW
Room 8107
Washington, DC 20006
(202) 502-7643
E-MAIL: tom.weko@ed.gov
URL: www.nces.ed.gov

Ms. Melissa Lewis (G)
Executive Director
National Committee on Foreign Medical Education
and Accreditation (NCFMEA)
U.S. Department of Education
1990 K Street, NW
Room 8060
Washington, DC 20006
(202) 219-7009
FAX: (202) 219-7005
E-MAIL: melissa.lewis@ed.gov
URL: www2.ed.gov/about/bdscomm/list/ncfmea.html

Statewide Agencies of Higher Education

ALABAMA

Alabama Commission on Higher Education (H)
PO Box 302000
Montgomery, AL 36130-2000
(334) 242-1998
FAX: (334) 242-0268
Dr. Gregory G. Fitch
Executive Director
E-MAIL: gregory.fitch@ache.alabama.gov
URL: www.ache.alabama.gov

State of Alabama Department of Postsecondary Education (I)
135 South Union Street
PO Box 302130
Montgomery, AL 36130
(334) 293-4524
FAX: (334) 293-4526
Dr. Freida Hill
Chancellor
E-MAIL: freida.hill@dpe.edu
URL: www.accs.cc

ALASKA

Alaska Commission on Postsecondary Education (J)
PO Box 110505
Juneau, AK 99811-0505
(907) 465-6740
FAX: (907) 465-3293
Ms. Diane Barrans
Executive Director
E-MAIL: ACPE.execdirector@alaska.gov
URL: www.akadvantage.alaska.gov

ARIZONA

Arizona Board of Regents (K)
2020 North Central Avenue
Suite 230
Phoenix, AZ 85004-4593
(602) 229-2500
FAX: (602) 229-2555
Thomas K. Anderes Ph.D.
President
E-MAIL: tom.anderes@azregents.edu
URL: www.azregents.edu

Arizona Commission for Postsecondary Education (L)
2020 North Central Avenue
Suite 650
Phoenix, AZ 85004-4503
(602) 258-2435
FAX: (602) 258-2483
Dr. April L. Osborn
Executive Director
E-MAIL: acpe@azhighered.gov
URL: www.azhighered.gov

ARKANSAS

Arkansas Department of Higher Education (M)
114 East Capitol Avenue
Little Rock, AR 72201
(501) 371-2030
FAX: (501) 371-2003
Mr. Shane Broadway
Interim Director of Higher Education
E-MAIL: shane.broadway@adhe.edu
URL: www.adhe.edu

CALIFORNIA

California Postsecondary Education Commission (N)
770 L Street
Suite 1160
Sacramento, CA 95814-3366
(916) 445-1000
FAX: (916) 327-4417
Ms. Karen Humphrey
Executive Director
E-MAIL: khumphrey@cpec.ca.gov
URL: www.cpec.ca.gov

Board of Governors California Community Colleges (O)
1102 Q Street
4th Floor
Sacramento, CA 95811
(916) 322-4005
FAX: (916) 322-4783
Dr. Jack Scott
Chancellor
E-MAIL: jscott@cccco.edu
URL: www.cccco.edu

COLORADO

Colorado Department of Higher Education (P)
1560 Broadway
Suite 1600
Denver, CO 80202
(303) 866-2723
FAX: (303) 866-4266
Mr. Joseph Garcia
Executive Director
E-MAIL: josephgarcia.executivedirector@dhe.state.co.us
URL: highered.colorado.gov

Colorado Community College System (Q)
9101 East Lowry Boulevard
Denver, CO 80230-6011
(303) 595-1552
FAX: (303) 620-4043
Dr. Nancy J. McCallin
President
E-MAIL: president@cccs.edu
URL: www.cccs.edu

CONNECTICUT

Board of Governors for Higher Education (R)
Connecticut Department of Higher Education
61 Woodland Street
Hartford, CT 06105-2326
(860) 947-1800
FAX: (860) 947-1310
Mr. Michael P. Meotti
Commissioner Higher Education
E-MAIL: meotti@ctdhe.org
URL: www.ctdhe.org

Board of Trustees of Community-Technical Colleges (S)
61 Woodland Street
Hartford, CT 06105
(860) 244-7601
FAX: (860) 244-7886
Mr. Marc S. Herzog
Chancellor
E-MAIL: mherzog@commnet.edu
URL: www.commnet.edu

DELAWARE

Delaware Higher Education Office (T)
820 North French Street, 5F
Carvel State Office Building
Wilmington, DE 19801
(302) 577-5240
FAX: (302) 577-6765
Ms. Maureen Laffey
Director
E-MAIL: dheo@doe.k12.de.us
URL: www.doe.k12.de.us/dheo

Delaware Technical & Community College (U)
PO Box 897
Dover, DE 19903
(302) 739-4053
FAX: (302) 739-6225
Dr. Orlando J. George Jr.
President
E-MAIL: pres@dtcc.edu
URL: www.dtcc.edu

DISTRICT OF COLUMBIA

Office of the State Superintendent of Education Government of the District of Columbia (V)
810 First Street, NE
9th Floor
Washington, DC 20002
(202) 727-3471
FAX: (202) 727-2019
Hosanna Mahaley
State Superintendent of Education
E-MAIL: osse@dc.gov
URL: www.osse.dc.gov

District of Columbia Education Licensure Commission (W)
810 First Street, NE
2nd Floor
Washington, DC 20002
(202) 724-2095
FAX: (202) 724-0227
Ms. Robin Y. Jenkins
Executive Director
E-MAIL: robin.jenkins@dc.gov
URL: www.osse.dc.gov

FLORIDA

Board of Governors State University System of Florida (X)
325 West Gaines Street
Suite 1614
Tallahassee, FL 32399-0400
(850) 245-0466
FAX: (850) 245-9685
Frank T. Brogan
Chancellor
E-MAIL: chancellor@flbog.edu
URL: www.flbog.edu

State of Florida Department of Education Division of Florida Colleges (Y)
325 West Gaines Street
1544 Turlington Building
Tallahassee, FL 32399-0400
(850) 245-9449
FAX: (850) 245-9525
Dr. Willis N. Holcombe
Chancellor
E-MAIL: will.holcombe@fldoe.org
URL: www.fldoe.org/cc

GEORGIA

Board of Regents of the University System of Georgia (Z)
270 Washington Street, SW
Atlanta, GA 30334
(404) 656-2202
FAX: (404) 657-6979
Mr. Henry Huckaby
Chancellor
E-MAIL: chancellor@usg.edu
URL: www.usg.edu

University System of Georgia (a)
270 Washington Street, SW
Atlanta, GA 30334
(404) 656-2213
FAX: (404) 657-4130
Dr. Susan Campbell Lounsbury
Asst Vice Chanc for Research & Policy Analysis
E-MAIL: susan.campbell@usg.edu
URL: www.usg.edu

HAWAII

State Post-Secondary Education Commission (A)
University of Hawaii at Manoa
2444 Dole Street
Bachman Hall, Room 209
Honolulu, HI 96822
(808) 956-8213
FAX: (808) 956-5156
Compliance Officer/Director
E-MAIL: bor@hawaii.edu

IDAHO

Idaho State Board of Education (B)
PO Box 83720
Boise, ID 83720-0037
(208) 334-2270
FAX: (208) 334-2632
Dr. Mike Rush
Executive Director
E-MAIL: mike.rush@osbe.idaho.gov
URL: boardofed.idaho.gov

ILLINOIS

Illinois Board of Higher Education (C)
431 East Adams
2nd Floor
Springfield, IL 62701-1404
(217) 782-2551
FAX: (217) 782-8548
Mr. George W. Reid
Executive Director
E-MAIL: reid@ibhe.org
URL: www.ibhe.org

Illinois Community College Board (D)
401 East Capitol Avenue
Springfield, IL 62701-1874
(217) 785-0123
FAX: (217) 785-7495
Mr. Geoffrey S. Obrzut
President/CEO
E-MAIL: geoffrey.obrzut@illinois.gov
URL: www.iccb.org

INDIANA

Indiana Commission for Higher Education (E)
101 West Ohio Street
Suite 550
Indianapolis, IN 46204
(317) 464-4400
FAX: (317) 464-4410
Mrs. Teresa Lubbers
Commissioner for Higher Education
E-MAIL: Teresal@che.in.gov
URL: www.che.in.gov

IOWA

Board of Regents, State of Iowa (F)
11260 Aurora Avenue
Urbandale, IA 50322-7905
(515) 281-3934
FAX: (515) 281-6420
Mr. Robert Donley
Executive Director
E-MAIL: bdonley@iastate.edu

Iowa College Student Aid Commission (G)
603 East 12th Street
5th Floor
Des Moines, IA 50319
(515) 725-3410
FAX: (515) 725-3401
Ms. Karen Misjak
Executive Director
E-MAIL: karen.misjak@iowa.gov
URL: www.iowacollegeaid.org

Iowa Department of Education Division of Community Colleges and Workforce Preparation (H)
400 East 14th Street
Grimes State Office Building
Des Moines, IA 50319-0146
(515) 281-8260
FAX: (515) 281-6544
Roger Utman Ph. D.
Administrator
E-MAIL: roger.utman@iowa.gov
URL: www.iowa.gov/educate

Iowa Association of Community College Trustees (I)
855 East Court Avenue
Des Moines, IA 50309
(515) 282-4692
FAX: (515) 282-3743
M. J. Dolan J.D.
Executive Director
E-MAIL: mjdolan@iacct.com
URL: www.iacct.com

KANSAS

Kansas Board of Regents (J)
1000 SW Jackson
Suite 520
Topeka, KS 66612-1368
(785) 296-3421
FAX: (785) 296-0983
Dr. Andy Tompkins
President and CEO
E-MAIL: atompkins@ksbor.org
URL: www.kansasregents.org

Kansas Legislative Research Department (K)
Room 68 West, State Capitol Building
300 SW 10th Avenue
Topeka, KS 66612-1504
(785) 296-3181
FAX: (785) 296-3824
Mr. Alan Conroy
Director
E-MAIL: kslegres@klrd.ks.gov
URL: www.kslegislature.org/klrd

KENTUCKY

Kentucky Council on Postsecondary Education (L)
1024 Capital Center Drive
Suite 320
Frankfort, KY 40601-8204
(502) 573-1555
FAX: (502) 573-1535
Dr. Robert L. King
President
E-MAIL: mary.morse@ky.gov
URL: cpe.ky.gov

Kentucky Community & Technical College System (M)
300 North Main Street
Versailles, KY 40383
(859) 256-3132
FAX: (859) 256-3116
Dr. Michael B. McCall
President
E-MAIL: president@kctcs.edu
URL: www.kctcs.edu

LOUISIANA

Board of Regents (N)
PO Box 3677
Baton Rouge, LA 70821-3677
(225) 342-4253
FAX: (225) 342-9318
Mr. James E. Purcell
Commissioner of Higher Education
E-MAIL: jim.purcell@la.gov
URL: www.regents.state.la.us

Department of Education (O)
Box 94064
Baton Rouge, LA 70804-9064
(225) 342-3607
FAX: (225) 342-7316
Mr. Ollie S. Tyler
Acting Superintendent
URL: www.louisianaschools.net

MAINE

Department of Education Office of Higher Education (P)
23 State House Station
Augusta, ME 04333
(207) 624-6846
FAX: (207) 624-6841
Mr. Harry Osgood
Higher Education Specialist
E-MAIL: harry.osgood@maine.gov

MARYLAND

Maryland Higher Education Commission (Q)
839 Bestgate Road
Suite 400
Annapolis, MD 21401
(410) 260-4516
FAX: (410) 260-3204
Ms. Elisabeth A. Sachs
Interim Secretary of Higher Education
E-MAIL: esachs@mhec.state.md.us
URL: www.mhec.state.md.us

MASSACHUSETTS

Massachusetts Department of Higher Education (R)
1 Ashburton Place
Room 1401
McCormack Building
Boston, MA 02108
(617) 994-6901
FAX: (617) 727-6656
Richard M. Freeland Ph.D.
Commissioner
URL: www.mass.edu

MICHIGAN

Department of Licensing and Regulatory Affairs Bureau of Commercial Services, Licensing Division Private Postsecondary Schools (S)
PO Box 30714
Okemos, MI 48864
(517) 373-6551
FAX: (517) 335-3630
Mr. Michael Beamish
Manager
E-MAIL: beamishm@michigan.gov
URL: www.michigan.gov/lara

Workforce Development Agency, State of Michigan Division of Lifelong Learning (T)
201 North Washington Square
Victor Building, 2nd Floor
Lansing, MI 48913
(517) 373-3430
FAX: (517) 373-2759
Ms. Dianne Duthie
Director
E-MAIL: duthied@michigan.gov
URL: admin.michiganops.net

MINNESOTA

Minnesota Office of Higher Education (U)
1450 Energy Park Drive
Suite 350
St. Paul, MN 55108-5227
(651) 642-0567
FAX: (651) 642-0597
Dr. Sheila Wright
Director
E-MAIL: info.ohe@state.mn.us
URL: www.ohe.state.mn.us

Minnesota State Colleges and Universities (V)
30 7th Street East
Wells Fargo Place, Suite 350
St. Paul, MN 55101
(651) 201-1696
FAX: (651) 297-7465
Dr. Steven R. Rosenstone
Chancellor
E-MAIL: steven.rosenstone@so.mnscu.edu
URL: www.mnscu.edu

MISSISSIPPI

Board of Trustees of State Institutions of Higher Learning (W)
3825 Ridgewood Road
Jackson, MS 39211
(601) 432-6623
FAX: (601) 432-6972
Dr. Hank Bounds
Commissioner of Higher Education
URL: www.mississippi.edu

Mississippi Community College Board (X)
3825 Ridgewood Drive
Jackson, MS 39211
(601) 432-6684
FAX: (601) 432-6480
Dr. Eric Clark
Executive Director
E-MAIL: info@mscjc.edu
URL: www.mscjc.edu

MISSOURI

Coordinating Board for Higher Education Department of Higher Education (Y)
205 Jefferson Street, 11th Floor
PO Box 1469
Jefferson City, MO 65102-1469
(573) 751-2361
FAX: (573) 751-6635
Dr. David R. Russell
Commissioner of Higher Education
E-MAIL: david.russell@dhe.mo.gov
URL: www.dhe.mo.gov

MONTANA

Office of the Commissioner of Higher Education (Z)
PO Box 203201
Academic, Research & Student Affairs
Helena, MT 59620-3201
(406) 444-0312
FAX: (406) 444-1469
Dr. Sylvia Moore
Deputy Commissioner
E-MAIL: smoore@montana.edu
URL: www.mus.edu

NEBRASKA

Coordinating Commission for Postsecondary Education (a)
PO Box 95005
Lincoln, NE 68509-5005
(402) 471-2847
FAX: (402) 471-2886
Dr. Marshall A. Hill
Executive Director
E-MAIL: marshall.hill@nebraska..gov
URL: www.ccpe.state.ne.us

NEVADA

Nevada System of Higher Education (b)
2601 Enterprise Road
Reno, NV 89512
(775) 784-4901
FAX: (775) 784-1127
Mr. Daniel J. Klaich
Chancellor
E-MAIL: chancellor@nevada.edu
URL: www.nevada.edu

NEW HAMPSHIRE

New Hampshire Department of Education Division of Higher Education Higher Education Commission (c)
101 Pleasant Street
Concord, NH 03301
(603) 271-0256
FAX: (603) 271-1953
Director
URL: www.education.nh.gov

Community College System of New Hampshire (d)
26 College Drive
Concord, NH 03301-7407
(603) 271-2739
FAX: (603) 271-2725
Ms. J. Bonnie Newman
Chancellor
E-MAIL: jbnewman@ccsnh.edu
URL: www.ccsnh.edu

NEW JERSEY

New Jersey Higher Education (e)
20 West State Street
PO Box 542
Trenton, NJ 08625-0542
(609) 292-4310
FAX: (609) 292-7225
E-MAIL: nj_che@che.state.nj.us
URL: www.state.nj.us/highereducation

NEW MEXICO

New Mexico Higher Education Department (A)
2048 Galisteo Street
Santa Fe, NM 87505
(505) 476-8404
FAX: (505) 476-8454
Dr. Jose Garcia
Cabinet Secretary
E-MAIL: jose.garcia@state.nm.us
URL: www.hed.state.nm.us

NEW YORK

New York State Education Department (B)
89 Washington Avenue
Room 111
Albany, NY 12234
(518) 474-5844
FAX: (518) 473-4909
Mr. John B. King Jr.
Commissioner
E-MAIL: commissioner@mail.nysed.gov

State University of New York (C)
Room T7
SUNY Plaza
353 Broadway
Albany, NY 12246
(518) 320-1303 or (518) 320-1276
FAX: (518) 320-1543 or (518) 320-1570
Ms. Johanna Duncan-Poitier
Chanc Deputy for Educ Pipeline & VC for Cmty Coll
E-MAIL: johanna.duncan-poitier@suny.edu
URL: www.suny.edu

New York State Education Department (D)
Education Building Annex
Room 977
Albany, NY 12234
(518) 486-3633
FAX: (518) 486-2254
Mr. John D'Agati
Deputy Commissioner
E-MAIL: jdagati@mail.nysed.gov
URL: www.highered.nysed.gov

NORTH CAROLINA

Space Utilization and Analysis (E)
UNC General Administration
910 Raleigh Road
PO Box 2688
Chapel Hill, NC 27515
(919) 962-4569
FAX: (919) 962-0488
Mr. Jeffrey D. Hill
Director
E-MAIL: jdh@northcarolina.edu
URL: www.northcarolina.edu

North Carolina Community College System (F)
200 West Jones Street
Raleigh, NC 27603
(919) 807-6950
FAX: (919) 807-7166
Dr. Scott Ralls
President
E-MAIL: ralls@nccommunitycolleges.edu
URL: www.nccommunitycolleges.edu

NORTH DAKOTA

North Dakota University System (G)
600 East Boulevard Avenue
Department 215
State Capitol, 10th Floor
Bismarck, ND 58505-0230
(701) 328-2960
FAX: (701) 328-2961
Mr. William G. Goetz
Chancellor
URL: www.ndus.edu

OHIO

Ohio Board of Regents (H)
30 East Broad Street
36th Floor
Columbus, OH 43215
(614) 466-0887
FAX: (614) 466-5866
Mr. Jim M. Petro
Chancellor
E-MAIL: regents@regents.state.oh.us
URL: www.regents.ohio.gov

OKLAHOMA

Oklahoma State Regents for Higher Education (I)
655 Research Parkway
Suite 200
Oklahoma City, OK 73104
(405) 225-9100
FAX: (405) 225-9230
Dr. Glen D. Johnson
Chancellor
E-MAIL: gjohnson@osrhe.edu
URL: www.okhighered.org

OREGON

Oregon State Board of Higher Education (J)
PO Box 751
Portland, OR 97207-0751
(541) 346-5716
FAX: (503) 725-5709
Mr. Charles L. Triplett III
Board Secretary
E-MAIL: charles_triplett@ous.edu
URL: www.ous.edu/dept/board

Governor's Office of Education (K)
160 State Capitol
Salem, OR 97301
(503) 378-5690
FAX: (503) 378-3225
Education Policy Advisor
E-MAIL: marjorie.lowe@state.or.us
URL: www.state.or.us/agencies.ns/12100/12106/index.html

Department of Community Colleges and Workforce Development (L)
255 Capitol Street, NE
Salem, OR 97310
(503) 947-2433
FAX: (503) 378-8434
Dr. Camille Preus
Commissioner
E-MAIL: camille.preus@state.or.us
URL: www.odccwd.state.or.us

PENNSYLVANIA

Pennsylvania Department of Education Liaison to Postsecondary and Higher Education Institutions (M)
333 Market Street
12th Floor
Harrisburg, PA 17126-0333
(717) 772-3623
FAX: (717) 772-3622
Ms. Patricia Landis
Chief, Division of Higher Education
E-MAIL: plandis@pa.gov
URL: www.education.state.pa.us

Liaison to Postsecondary and Higher Education Institutions (N)
333 Market Street
12th Floor
Department of Education
Harrisburg, PA 17126-0333
(717) 783-8228
FAX: (717) 772-3622
Ms. Patricia Landis
Division Chief - Higher and Career Education
E-MAIL: plandis@state.pa.us
URL: www.education.state.pa.us

RHODE ISLAND

Rhode Island Board of Governors for Higher Education (O)
80 Washington Street
Suite 524
Providence, RI 02903
(401) 456-6000
FAX: (401) 456-6028
Mr. Ray M. DiPasquale
Acting Commissioner of Higher Education
E-MAIL: rmdipasquale@ribghe.org
URL: www.ribghe.org

Community College of Rhode Island (P)
400 East Avenue
Warwick, RI 02886
(401) 825-2188
FAX: (401) 825-2166
Mr. Ray M. Di Pasquale
President
E-MAIL: rmdipasquale@ccri.edu
URL: www.ccri.edu

SOUTH CAROLINA

South Carolina Commission on Higher Education (Q)
1333 Main Street
Suite 200
Columbia, SC 29201
(803) 737-2275
FAX: (803) 737-2297
Dr. Garrison Walters
Executive Director
E-MAIL: gwalters@che.sc.gov
URL: www.che.sc.gov

South Carolina State Board for Technical and Comprehensive Education (R)
111 Executive Center Drive
Columbia, SC 29210
(803) 896-5280
FAX: (803) 896-5281
Dr. Darrel Staat
System President
E-MAIL: staatd@sctechsystem.edu
URL: www.sctechsystem.edu

SOUTH DAKOTA

South Dakota Board of Regents (S)
306 East Capitol Avenue
Suite 200
Pierre, SD 57501-2545
(605) 773-3455
FAX: (605) 773-5320
Dr. Jack R. Warner
Executive Director and Chief Executive Officer
E-MAIL: jack.warner@sdbor.edu
URL: www.sdbor.edu

South Dakota Department of Education (T)
Office of the Secretary
800 Governors Drive
Pierre, SD 57501-2291
(605) 773-5669
FAX: (605) 773-6139
Dr. Melody Schopp
Secretary
E-MAIL: melody.schopp@state.sd.us
URL: www.doe.sd.gov

TENNESSEE

Tennessee Higher Education Commission (U)
404 James Robertson Parkway
Parkway Towers
Suite 1900
Nashville, TN 37243-0830
(615) 741-3605
FAX: (615) 741-6230
Dr. Richard G. Rhoda
Executive Director
E-MAIL: richard.rhoda@tn.gov

Tennessee Board of Regents (V)
1415 Murfreesboro Road
Suite 324
Nashville, TN 37217
(615) 366-4482
FAX: (615) 366-3903
Dr. Paula Myrick Short
Vice Chancellor for Academic Affairs
E-MAIL: paula.short@tbr.edu
URL: www.tbr.edu

University of Tennessee Board of Trustees (W)
719 Andy Holt Tower
Knoxville, TN 37996-0170
(865) 974-3245
FAX: (865) 974-3074
Ms. Catherine S. Mizell
General Counsel and Secretary
E-MAIL: cmizell@tennessee.edu
URL: www.tennessee.edu/system/

TEXAS

Texas Higher Education Coordinating Board (X)
PO Box 12788
Austin, TX 78711
(512) 427-6101
FAX: (512) 427-6127
Dr. Raymund A. Paredes
Commissioner of Higher Education
E-MAIL: raymund.paredes@thecb.state.tx.us
URL: www.thecb.state.tx.us

Texas Higher Education Coordinating Board P-16 Initiatives (Y)
PO Box 12788
Austin, TX 78711-2788
(512) 427-6545
FAX: (512) 427-6444
Dr. Judith Loredo
Assistant Commissioner
E-MAIL: judy.loredo@thecb.state.tx.us
URL: www.thecb.state.tx.us

UTAH

Utah State Board of Regents (Z)
60 South 400 West
Salt Lake City, UT 84101-1284
(801) 321-7103
FAX: (801) 321-7156
Dr. William A. Sederburg
Commissioner of Higher Education
E-MAIL: wsederburg@utahsbr.edu
URL: www.utahsbr.edu

VERMONT

Vermont Department of Education School Finance Team (a)
120 State Street
Montpelier, VT 05620-2501
(802) 828-5139
FAX: (802) 828-1631
URL: www.education.vermont.gov

VIRGINIA

State Council of Higher Education for Virginia (b)
101 North Fourteenth Street
James Monroe Building
9th Floor
Richmond, VA 23219
(804) 225-2600
FAX: (804) 371-7911
Mr. Peter Blake
Interim Director
E-MAIL: peterblake@schev.edu
URL: www.schev.edu

Virginia Community College System (c)
101 North Fourteenth Street
James Monroe Building
Richmond, VA 23219
(804) 819-4903
FAX: (804) 819-4760
Dr. Glenn DuBois
Chancellor
E-MAIL: gdubois@vccs.edu
URL: www.vccs.edu

WASHINGTON

Higher Education Coordinating Board (d)
917 Lakeridge Way, SW
PO Box 43430
Olympia, WA 98504-3430
(360) 753-7810
FAX: (360) 753-7808
Mr. Don Bennett
Executive Director
E-MAIL: info@hecb.wa.gov
URL: www.hecb.wa.gov

State Board for Community and Technical Colleges (e)
PO Box 42495
1300 Quince Street, SE
Olympia, WA 98504-2495
(360) 704-4355
FAX: (360) 704-4415
Mr. Charles N. Earl
Executive Director
E-MAIL: cearl@sbctc.edu
URL: www.sbctc.edu

WEST VIRGINIA

West Virginia Higher Education Policy Commission (f)
1018 Kanawha Boulevard, East
Suite 700
Charleston, WV 25301-2800
(304) 558-0699
FAX: (304) 558-1011
Dr. Brian Noland
Chancellor
E-MAIL: noland@hepc.wvnet.edu
URL: wvhepcnew.wvnet.edu

WISCONSIN

Higher Educational Aids Board **(A)**
PO Box 7885
Madison, WI 53707-7885
(608) 267-2206
FAX: (608) 267-2808
E-MAIL: heabmail@wisconsin.gov
URL: heab.wi.gov

Wisconsin Technical College System **(B)**
PO Box 7874
Madison, WI 53707-7874
(608) 266-7983
FAX: (608) 266-1285
Mr. Daniel Clancy
President
E-MAIL: dan.clancy@wtcsystem.edu
URL: www.wtcsystem.edu

WYOMING

Wyoming Community College Commission **(C)**
2020 Carey
8th Floor
Cheyenne, WY 82002
(307) 777-7763
FAX: (307) 777-6567
Dr. Jim Rose
Executive Director
E-MAIL: jrose@commission.wcc.edu
URL: www.communitycolleges.wy.edu

AMERICAN SAMOA

Board of Higher Education (American Samoa) American Samoa Community College **(D)**
PO Box 2609
Pago Pago, AS 96799
(684) 699-9155
FAX: (684) 699-6259
E-MAIL: info@amsamoa.edu
URL: www.amsamoa.edu

FEDERATED STATES OF MICRONESIA

Board of Regents College of Micronesia-FSM **(E)**
PO Box 159
Kolonia Pohnpei, FM 96941
(691) 320-2480
FAX: (691) 320-2479
E-MAIL: national@comfsm.fm
URL: www.comfsm.fm

PUERTO RICO

Council on Higher Education of Puerto Rico **(F)**
PO Box 19900
San Juan, PR 00910-1900
(787) 641-7100
FAX: (787) 641-2573
Ms. Carmen L. Berrios
President
E-MAIL: cberrios@cge.gobierno.pr
URL: www.gobierno.pr/cespr/inicio

Higher Education Associations

AACSB International-The Association to Advance Collegiate Schools of Business (A)
777 South Harbour Island Boulevard
Suite 750
Tampa, FL 33602-5730
(813) 769-6500
FAX: (813) 769-6559
Mr. John J. Fernandes
President and Chief Executive Officer
E-MAIL: mediarelations@aacsb.edu
URL: www.aacsb.edu

AAUW (B)
1111 Sixteenth Street, NW
Washington, DC 20036
(800) 326-2289
FAX: (202) 872-1425
E-MAIL: connect@aauw.org
URL: www.aauw.org

ABET, Inc. (C)
111 Market Place
Suite 1050
Baltimore, MD 21202
(410) 347-7700
FAX: (410) 625-2238
Michael K. J. Milligan Ph.D., PE
Executive Director
E-MAIL: info@abet.org
URL: www.abet.org

FHI360 (D)
1825 Connecticut Avenue, NW
Washington, DC 20009-5721
(202) 884-8000
FAX: (202) 884-8400
Dr. Albert J. Siemens
Chief Executive Officer
E-MAIL: contact@fhi.org
URL: www.fhi360.org

Academy of Legal Studies in Business (E)
Miami University
Department of Finance
3111 FSB
Oxford, OH 45056
(513) 529-1574
FAX: (513) 523-8180
Dr. Daniel J. Herron
Executive Secretary
E-MAIL: herrondj@muohio.edu
URL: www.alsb.org

Accreditation Commission for Acupuncture and Oriental Medicine (ACAOM) (F)
14502 Greenview Drive
Suite 300B
Laurel, MD 20708
(301) 313-0855
FAX: (301) 313-0912
Dr. Annette M. Donawa
Director of Accreditation Services
E-MAIL: annette.donawa@acaom.org
URL: www.acaom.org

Accreditation Committee for Perfusion Education (G)
6654 South Sycamore Street
Littleton, CO 80120
(303) 738-0770
FAX: (303) 738-3223
Ms. Theresa Sisneros
Executive Director
E-MAIL: ac-pe@msn.com
URL: www.ac-pe.org

Accreditation Council for Business Schools and Programs (H)
11520 West 119th Street
Overland Park, KS 66213
(913) 339-9356
FAX: (913) 339-6226
Mr. Douglas Viehland CAE
Executive Director
E-MAIL: info@acbsp.org
URL: www.acbsp.org

Accreditation Council for Pharmacy Education (I)
20 North Clark
Suite 2500
Chicago, IL 60602
(312) 664-3575
FAX: (312) 664-4652
Dr. Peter H. Vlasses, PharmD BCPS
Executive Director
E-MAIL: pvlasses@acpe-accredit.org
URL: www.acpe-accredit.org

Accreditation Review Commission on Education for the Physican Assistant (ARC-PA) (J)
12000 Findley Road
Suite 150
John's Creek, GA 30097
(770) 476-1224
FAX: (770) 476-1738
Mr. John McCarty
Executive Director
E-MAIL: arc-pa@arc-pa.org
URL: www.arc-pa.org

Accreditation Review Committee for the Anesthesiologist's Assistant (K)
2027 Burnside Drive
Allen, TX 75013
(469) 656-1103
Ms. Jennifer Anderson Warwick
Executive Director
E-MAIL: arcaamember@gmail.com
URL: www.caahep.org/arc-aa

Accreditation Review Committee for the Medical Illustrator (L)
32531 Meadowlark Way
Pepper Pike, OH 44124
(216) 595-9363
FAX: (216) 595-9360
E-MAIL: kijung@aol.com
URL: www.caahep.org/arc-mi

Accreditation Review Council on Education in Surgical Technology and Surgical Assisting (M)
6 West Dry Creek Circle
Suite 110
Littleton, CO 80120
(303) 694-9262
FAX: (303) 741-3655
Mr. Keith Orloff
Executive Director
E-MAIL: info@arcstsa.org
URL: www.arcstsa.org

Accrediting Bureau of Health Education Schools (N)
7777 Leesburg Pike
Suite 314 N
Falls Church, VA 22043
(703) 917-9503
FAX: (703) 917-4109
Ms. Carol Moneymaker
Executive Director
E-MAIL: info@abhes.org
URL: www.abhes.org

Accrediting Commission of Career Schools and Colleges (O)
2101 Wilson Boulevard
Suite 302
Arlington, VA 22201
(703) 247-4212
FAX: (703) 247-4533
Dr. Michale McComis
Executive Director
E-MAIL: info@accsc.org
URL: www.accsc.org

Accrediting Council for Continuing Education & Training (ACCET) (P)
1722 N Street, NW
Washington, DC 20036
(202) 955-1113
FAX: (202) 955-1118
Mr. Roger J. Williams
Executive Director
E-MAIL: rjwilliams@accet.org
URL: www.accet.org

Accrediting Council for Independent Colleges and Schools (Q)
750 First Street, NE
Suite 980
Washington, DC 20002-4241
(202) 336-6780
FAX: (202) 464-5621
Dr. Albert Gray
Executive Director & CEO
E-MAIL: agray@acics.org
URL: www.acics.org

Accrediting Council on Education in Journalism and Mass Communications (R)
University of Kansas, School of Journalism
1435 Jayhawk Boulevard
Stauffer-Flint Hall
Lawrence, KS 66045-7575
(785) 864-3973
FAX: (785) 864-5225
Prof. Susanne Shaw
Executive Director
E-MAIL: sshaw@ku.edu
URL: www.ku.edu/~acejmc

ACT, Inc. (S)
500 ACT Drive
Box 168
Iowa City, IA 52243
(319) 337-1079
FAX: (319) 337-1059
Dr. Jon S. Whitmore
CEO
URL: www.act.org

ACUTA: The Association for Information Communications Technology Professionals in Higher Education (T)
152 West Zandale Drive
Suite 200
Lexington, KY 40503-2486
(859) 278-3338
FAX: (859) 278-3268
Ms. Corinne Hoch
Interim Executive Director
E-MAIL: choch@acuta.org
URL: www.acuta.org

Alabama Association of Independent Colleges and Universities (U)
5950 Carmichael Place
Suite 213
Montgomery, AL 36117
(334) 356-2220
FAX: (334) 356-2202
Gen. Paul M. Hankins
President
E-MAIL: hankinsp@knology.net
URL: www.aaicu.net

American Academy for Liberal Education (AALE) (V)
526 King Street
Suite 203
Alexandria, VA 22314
(703) 299-9030
FAX: (703) 299-9031
Prof. Charles Butterworth
President
E-MAIL: aaleinfo@aale.org
URL: www.aale.org

National Academy of Kinesiology (W)
1607 North Market Street
Champaign, IL 61820
(217) 403-7545
FAX: (217) 351-2674
Ms. Kim Scott
Business Manager
E-MAIL: kims@hkusa.com
URL: www.nationalacademyofkinesiology.org

American Academy of Microbiology Committee on Postgraduate Educational Programs (X)
1752 N Street, NW
Washington, DC 20036-2804
(202) 942-9225
FAX: (202) 942-9353
Ms. Peggy McNult
Manager
E-MAIL: college@asmusa.org
URL: www.asm.org/cpep

American Anthropological Association (Y)
2200 Wilson Boulevard
Suite 600
Arlington, VA 22201
(703) 528-1902
FAX: (703) 528-3546
Mr. William E. Davis
Executive Director
E-MAIL: bdavis@aaanet.org
URL: www.aaanet.org

American Association for Adult and Continuing Education (AAACE) (Z)
10111 Martin Luther King, Jr. Highway
Suite 200C
Bowie, MD 20720
(301) 459-6261
FAX: (301) 459-6241
Dr. Clare Klunk
President
E-MAIL: aaace10@aol.com
URL: www.aaace.org

American Association for Employment in Education, Inc. (a)
3040 Riverside Drive
Suite 117
Columbus, OH 43221
(614) 485-1111
Mr. Doug Peden
Executive Director
E-MAIL: execdir@aaee.org
URL: www.aaee.org

American Association for Vocational Instructional Materials (b)
220 Smithonia Road
Winterville, GA 30683
(706) 742-5355
FAX: (706) 742-7005
Mr. Gary Farmer
Director
E-MAIL: gary@aavim.com
URL: www.aavim.com

American Association for Women in Community Colleges (c)
PO Box 30808
Salt Lake City, UT 84130-0808
(801) 957-4225
FAX: (801) 957-4440
Dr. Cynthia Bioteau
President
E-MAIL: aawccsupport@gmail.com
URL: www.aawccnatl.org

American Association of Blood Banks Committee on Accreditation of Specialist in Blood Banking Technology Schools (d)
8101 Glenbrook Road
Bethesda, MD 20814-2749
(301) 215-6482
FAX: (301) 907-6895
Ms. Sharon D. Moffett CAE
Director Education
E-MAIL: professionaldevelopment@aabb.org
URL: www.aabb.org

American Association of Colleges for Teacher Education (e)
1307 New York Avenue, NW
Suite 300
Washington, DC 20005-4701
(202) 293-2450
FAX: (202) 457-8095
Dr. Sharon P. Robinson
President & Chief Executive Officer
E-MAIL: aacte@aacte.org
URL: www.aacte.org

American Association of Colleges of Nursing (f)
1 Dupont Circle, NW
Suite 530
Washington, DC 20036-1120
(202) 463-6930
FAX: (202) 785-8320
Dr. Geraldine Bednash
CEO and Executive Director
E-MAIL: pbednash@aacn.nche.edu
URL: www.aacn.nche.edu

American Association of Colleges of Osteopathic Medicine (g)
5550 Friendship Boulevard
Suite 310
Chevy Chase, MD 20815-7231
(301) 968-4142
FAX: (301) 968-4101
Stephen C. Shannon DO, MPH
President and CEO
E-MAIL: president@aacom.org
URL: www.aacom.org

American Association of Collegiate Registrars and Admissions Officers (AACRAO) (A)
1 Dupont Circle, NW
Suite 520
Washington, DC 20036-1135
(202) 293-9161
FAX: (202) 872-8857
Mr. Jerome H. Sullivan
Executive Director
E-MAIL: sullivanj@aacrao.org
URL: www.aacrao.org

American Association of Community Colleges (B)
1 Dupont Circle, NW
Suite 410
Washington, DC 20036
(202) 728-0200, ext. 235
FAX: (202) 452-1461
Dr. Walter G. Bumphus
President/CEO
E-MAIL: wbumphus@aacc.nche.edu
URL: www.aacc.nche.edu

American Association of Family and Consumer Sciences (AAFCS) (C)
400 North Columbus Street
Suite 202
Alexandria, VA 22314
(703) 706-4600
FAX: (703) 706-4663
Ms. Carolyn W. Jackson
Executive Director
E-MAIL: accreditation@aafcs.org
URL: www.aafcs.org

American Association of Medical Assistants (D)
20 North Wacker Drive
Suite 1575
Chicago, IL 60606
(312) 899-1500
FAX: (312) 899-1259
Mr. Donald A. Balasa J.D., MBA
Executive Director
URL: www.aama-ntl.org

American Association of Physics Teachers (E)
One Physics Ellipse
College Park, MD 20740-3845
(301) 209-3311
FAX: (301) 209-0845
Dr. Beth A. Cunningham
Executive Officer
E-MAIL: eo@aapt.org
URL: www.aapt.org

American Association of Presidents of Independent Colleges and Universities (F)
Box 7070
Provo, UT 84602-7070
(801) 422-5625
FAX: (801) 422-0617
Mr. John B. Stohlton
Executive Director
E-MAIL: john_stohlton@byu.edu
URL: www.aapicu.org

American Association of School Administrators (G)
801 North Quincy Street
Suite 700
Arlington, VA 22203-1730
(703) 528-0700
FAX: (703) 841-1543
Dr. Daniel A. Domenech
Executive Director
E-MAIL: ddomenech@aasa.org
URL: www.aasa.org

American Association of State Colleges and Universities (H)
1307 New York Avenue, NW
5th Floor
Washington, DC 20005-4701
(202) 293-7070
FAX: (202) 296-5819
Dr. Muriel A. Howard
President
E-MAIL: howardm@aascu.org
URL: www.aascu.org

American Association of Teachers of Slavic and Eastern European Languages (I)
University of Southern California
3501 Trousdale Parkway
THH 255L
Los Angeles, CA 90089-4353
(213) 740-2734
FAX: (213) 740-8550
Dr. Elizabeth Durst
Executive Director
E-MAIL: aatseel@usc.edu
URL: www.aatseel.org

American Association of University Professors (J)
1133 19th Street, NW
Suite 200
Washington, DC 20036
(202) 737-5900
FAX: (202) 737-5526
Dr. Martin D. Snyder
Senior Associate General Secretary
E-MAIL: aaup@aaup.org
URL: www.aaup.org

American Bar Association Office of the Consultant on Legal Education and Admissions to the Bar (K)
321 North Clark Street
21st Floor
Chicago, IL 60654-7598
(312) 988-6746
FAX: (312) 988-5681
Mr. Hulett H. Askew
Consultant on Legal Education
E-MAIL: bucky.askew@americanbar.org
URL: www.americanbar.org/groups/legal_education

American Board of Funeral Service Education Committee on Accreditation (L)
3414 Ashland Avenue
Suite G
St. Joseph, MO 64506
(816) 233-3747
FAX: (816) 233-3793
Dr. Gretchen Warner
Executive Director
E-MAIL: exdir@abfse.org
URL: www.abfse.org

American Catholic Philosophical Association (M)
University of St. Thomas
3800 Montrose Boulevard
Houston, TX 77006
(713) 942-3483
FAX: (713) 525-6964
Dr. R. E. Houser
National Secretary
E-MAIL: acpa@stthom.edu
URL: www.acpaweb.org

American Chemical Society Committee on Professional Training (N)
1155 Sixteenth Street, NW
Washington, DC 20036
(202) 872-4589
FAX: (202) 872-6066
Ms. Cathy A. Nelson
Assistant Director
E-MAIL: cpt@acs.org
URL: www.acs.org/cpt

American College of Nurse-Midwives (O)
8403 Colesville Road
Suite 1550
Silver Spring, MD 20910
(240) 485-1800
FAX: (240) 485-1818
Ms. Lorrie Kaplan
Executive Director
E-MAIL: info@acnm.org
URL: www.midwife.org

American College Personnel Association (P)
1 Dupont Circle, NW
Suite 300
Washington, DC 20036-1188
(202) 835-2272
FAX: (202) 296-3286
Mr. Gregory Roberts
Executive Director
E-MAIL: info@acpa.nche.edu
URL: www.myacpa.org

American Collegiate Retailing Association (Q)
Sam Walton College of Business
University of Arkansas
WJWH 538
Fayetteville, AR 72701
(479) 575-2643
Ms. Claudia Mobley
President
E-MAIL: cmobley@walton.uark.edu
URL: www.acraretail.org

American Conference of Academic Deans (ACAD) (R)
1818 R Street, NW
Washington, DC 20009
(202) 884-7419
FAX: (202) 265-9532
Mrs. Laura A. Rzepka
Executive Director
E-MAIL: info@acad-edu.org
URL: www.acad-edu.org

American Council for Construction Education (S)
1717 North Loop 1604 East
Suite 320
San Antonio, TX 78232-1570
(210) 495-6161
FAX: (210) 495-6168
Mr. Michael Holland
Executive Vice President
E-MAIL: acce@acce-hq.org
URL: www.acce-hq.org

American Council of Trustees and Alumni (T)
1726 M Street, NW
Suite 802
Washington, DC 20036-4525
(202) 467-6787
FAX: (202) 467-6784
Ms. Anne D. Neal
President
E-MAIL: info@goacta.org
URL: www.goacta.org

American Council on Education (U)
1 Dupont Circle, NW
Washington, DC 20036
(202) 939-9300
FAX: (202) 464-4899
Molly Corbett Broad
President
E-MAIL: acepresident@acenet.edu
URL: www.acenet.edu

American Council on Education Center for Lifelong Learning (V)
1 Dupont Circle, NW
Suite 250
Washington, DC 20036
(202) 939-9470
FAX: (202) 833-5692
Assistant Vice President, Lifelong Learning
E-MAIL: credit@ace.nche.edu
URL: www.acenet.edu

American Council on Education Office of Institutional Initiatives (W)
1 Dupont Circle, NW
Suite 86
Washington, DC 20036
(202) 939-9389
FAX: (202)939-9302
Dr. Claire Van Ummersen
Senior Adviser
E-MAIL: cvanummersen@acenet.edu
URL: www.acenet.edu

American Counseling Association (X)
5999 Stevenson Avenue
Alexandria, VA 22304
(800) 347-6647
FAX: (800) 473-2329
Mr. Richard Yep
Executive Director
E-MAIL: ryep@counseling.org
URL: www.counseling.org

American Culinary Federation Education Foundation Accrediting Commission (Y)
180 Center Place Way
St. Augustine, FL 32095
(904) 824-4468
FAX: (904) 825-4758
E-MAIL: cchilders@acfchefs.net
URL: www.acfchefs.org

American Dental Association Commission on Dental Accreditation (Z)
211 East Chicago Avenue
19th Floor
Chicago, IL 60611
(312) 440-2940
FAX: (312) 440-2915
Dr. Anthony Ziebert
Director
E-MAIL: zieberta@ada.org
URL: www.ada.org/117.aspx

American Dietetic Association Commission on Accreditation for Dietetics Education (a)
120 South Riverside Plaza
Suite 2000
Chicago, IL 60606-6995
(312) 899-4872
FAX: (312) 899-4817
Mr. Ulric Chung
Executive Director
E-MAIL: uchung@eatright.org
URL: www.eatright.org/cade

American Educational Research Association (b)
1430 K Street, NW
Suite 1200
Washington, DC 20005
(202) 238-3200
FAX: (202) 238-3250
Dr. Felice J. Levine
Executive Director
E-MAIL: flevine@aera.net
URL: www.aera.net

American Forensic Association (c)
Box 256
River Falls, WI 54022-0256
(800) 228-5424
FAX: (715) 425-9533
Dr. James W. Pratt
Executive Secretary
E-MAIL: amforensicassoc@aol.com
URL: www.americanforensics.org

American Institute of Architecture Students (d)
1735 New York Avenue, NW
Washington, DC 20006-5209
(202) 626-7472
FAX: (202) 626-7414
Mr. Joshua Caulfield
Executive Director
E-MAIL: mailbox@aias.org
URL: www.aias.org

American Library Association Office for Accreditation (e)
50 East Huron Street
Chicago, IL 60611-2795
(312) 280-2432
FAX: (312) 280-2433
Karen O'Brien
Director, Office for Accreditation
E-MAIL: accred@ala.org
URL: www.ala.org/accreditation

American Mathematical Association of Two Year Colleges (f)
Southwest Tennessee Community College
5983 Macon Cove
Memphis, TN 38134
(901) 333-6243
FAX: (901) 333-6251
Dr. Cheryl Cleaves
Executive Director of Office Operations
E-MAIL: amatyc@amatyc.org
URL: www.amatyc.org

American Occupational Therapy Association (g)
4720 Montgomery Lane
PO Box 31220
Bethesda, MD 20824-1220
(301) 652-6611 Ext. 2202
FAX: (301) 652-1417
Dr. Neil Harvison
Dir Accreditation & Acad Affs
E-MAIL: accred@aota.org
URL: www.aota.org

Higher Education Associations

American Optometric Association Accreditation Council on Optometric Education (A)
243 North Lindbergh Boulevard
Floor 1
St. Louis, MO 63141-7881
(314) 991-4100
FAX: (314) 991-4101
Ms. Joyce L. Urbeck
Administrative Director
E-MAIL: jlurbeck@aoa.org
URL: www.theacoe.org

American Osteopathic Association (B)
142 East Ontario Street
Commission on Osteopathic College Accreditation
Chicago, IL 60611
(312) 202-8048
FAX: (312) 202-8202
Konrad C. Miskowicz-Retz Ph.D.
Secretary
E-MAIL: kretz@osteopathic.org
URL: www.aoacoca.org

American Physical Therapy Association (C)
1111 North Fairfax Street
Alexandria, VA 22314
(703) 684-2782
FAX: (703) 684-7343
Mr. John D. Barnes
Chief Executive Officer
E-MAIL: johnbarnes@apta.org
URL: www.apta.org

American Political Science Association (D)
1527 New Hampshire Avenue, NW
Washington, DC 20036
(202) 483-2512
FAX: (202) 483-2657
Dr. Michael Brintnall
Executive Director
E-MAIL: apsa@apsanet.org
URL: www.apsanet.org

American Psychological Association Commission on Accreditation (E)
750 First Street, NE
Washington, DC 20002-4242
(202) 336-5979
FAX: (202) 336-5978
Dr. Susan F. Zlotlow
Dir. Program Consultation & Accred
E-MAIL: apaaccred@apa.org
URL: www.apa.org/ed/accreditation

American Real Estate and Urban Economics Association (F)
PO Box 3061110
Tallahassee, FL 32306-1110
(850) 644-7898
FAX: (850) 644-4077
E-MAIL: elaffitte@areuea.org
URL: www.areuea.org

American Society for Engineering Education (G)
1818 N Street, NW
Suite 600
Washington, DC 20036
(202) 331-3545
FAX: (202) 265-8504
Mr. Norman L. Fortenberry
Executive Director
E-MAIL: n.fortenberry@asee.org
URL: www.asee.org

American Society for Microbiology (H)
1752 N Street, NW
Washington, DC 20036
(202) 942-9264
FAX: (202) 942-9329
Ms. Amy Chang
Director, Education Department
E-MAIL: education@asmusa.org
URL: www.asm.org

American Society of Cytopathology Cytotechnology Programs Review Committee (CPRC) (I)
100 West 10th Street
Suite 605
Wilmington, DE 19801
(302) 543-6583
FAX: (302) 543-6597
Ms. Deborah A. MacIntyre
Coordinator, CPRC
E-MAIL: asc@cytopathology.org
URL: www.cytopathology.org

American Society of Landscape Architects Landscape Architectural Accreditation Board (J)
636 Eye Street, NW
Washington, DC 20001-3736
(202) 898-2444
FAX: (202) 898-1185
Mr. Ron Leighton
Education/Academic Affairs Director
E-MAIL: rleighton@asla.org
URL: www.asla.org

American Speech-Language-Hearing Association Council on Academic Accreditation in Audiology and Speech-Language Pathology (K)
2200 Research Boulevard
Rockville, MD 20850
(800) 498-2071
FAX: (301) 571-0481
Dr. Arlene A. Pietranton
Executive Director
E-MAIL: accreditation@asha.org
URL: www.asha.org

American Student Government Association (L)
412 NW 16th Avenue
Gainesville, FL 32601-4203
(352) 373-6907
FAX: (352) 373-8120
Mr. W. H. Oxendine Jr.
Executive Director
E-MAIL: info@asgaonline.com
URL: www.asgaonline.com

American Veterinary Medical Association (M)
1931 North Meacham Road
Schaumburg, IL 60173
(847) 925-8070
FAX: (847) 285-5732
Dr. David E. Granstrom
Director Education and Research
E-MAIL: dgranstrom@avma.org
URL: www.avma.org

APPA (N)
1643 Prince Street
Alexandria, VA 22314-2818
(703) 684-1446, ext. 229
FAX: (703) 549-2772
E. Lander Medlin
Executive Vice President
E-MAIL: lander@appa.org
URL: www.appa.org

Association for Asian Studies (O)
825 Victors Way
Suite 310
Ann Arbor, MI 48108
(734) 665-2490
FAX: (734) 665-3801
Mr. Michael Paschal
Executive Director
E-MAIL: mpaschal@asian-studies.org
URL: www.asian-studies.org

Association for Biblical Higher Education Commission on Accreditation (P)
5850 T.G. Lee Boulevard
Suite 130
Orlando, FL 32822
(407) 207-0808
FAX: (407) 207-0840
Dr. Ralph E. Enlow Jr.
President
E-MAIL: info@abhe.org
URL: www.abhe.org

Association for Business Communication (Q)
PO Box 6143
Nacogdoches, TX 75962-6143
(936) 468-6280
FAX: (936) 468-6281
Dr. Betty S. Johnson
Executive Director
E-MAIL: abcjohnson@sfasu.edu
URL: www.businesscommunication.org

Association for Business Simulation and Experiential Learning (R)
c/o School of Business
Arcadia University
450 South Easton Road
Glenside, PA 19038
(215) 572-2849
FAX: (215) 572-4489
Dr. Annette Halpin
VP/Executive Director
E-MAIL: absel@email.com
URL: www.absel.org

The Association for Canadian Studies in the United States (ACSUS) (S)
2030 M Street, NW
Suite 350
Washington, DC 20036
(202) 775-9007
FAX: (202) 775-0061
Mr. David Archibald
Executive Director
E-MAIL: info@acsus.org
URL: www.acsus.org

Association for Clinical Pastoral Education, Inc. (T)
1549 Clairmont Road
Suite 103
Decatur, GA 30033
(404) 320-1472
FAX: (404) 320-0849
Executive Director
E-MAIL: acpe@acpe.edu
URL: www.acpe.edu

Association of College and University Religious Affairs (U)
Macalester College
1600 Grand Avenue
St. Paul, MN 55105
(651) 696-6293
RevDr. Lucy Forster-Smith
President
E-MAIL: forstersmith@macalester.edu
URL: www.site.acuraonline.net

Association for Consortium Leadership (V)
4900 Powhatan Avenue
Norfolk, VA 23529-0293
(757) 683-3183
FAX: (757) 683-4515
Dr. Lawrence G. Dotolo
Executive Director
E-MAIL: lgdotolo@aol.com
URL: www.national-acl.com

Association for Continuing Higher Education (W)
University of Oklahoma Outreach
OCCE Administration Building
1700 Asp Avenue
Norman, OK 73072-6400
(800) 807-2243
FAX: (405) 325-4888
Ynez Walske
Executive Secretary
E-MAIL: admin@acheinc.org
URL: www.acheinc.org

Association for Education in Journalism and Mass Communication (X)
234 Outlet Pointe Boulevard
Suite A
Columbia, SC 29210-5667
(803) 798-0271
FAX: (803) 772-3509
Ms. Jennifer H. McGill
Executive Director
E-MAIL: aejmchq@aol.com
URL: www.aejmc.org

Association for General and Liberal Studies (Y)
c/o Rebecca Amato, University College
Ball State University
Muncie, IN 47306
(765) 285-8406
FAX: (765) 285-2167
Mr. Paul W. Ranieri
Executive Director
E-MAIL: pranieri@bsu.edu
URL: www.agls.org

Association for Institutional Research (Z)
1435 East Piedmont Drive
Suite 211
Tallahassee, FL 32308
(850) 385-4155
FAX: (850) 385-5180
Dr. Randy L. Swing
Executive Director
E-MAIL: executivedirector@airweb.org
URL: www.airweb.org

Cultural Vistas (a)
10400 Little Patuxent Parkway
Suite 250
Columbia, MD 21044-3519
(410) 997-2200
FAX: (410) 992-3924
Ms. Elizabeth G. Chazottes
President & CEO
E-MAIL: aipt@aipt.org
URL: www.aipt.org

Association for Library and Information Science Education (ALISE) (b)
65 East Wacker Place
Suite 1900
Chicago, IL 60601
(312) 795-0996
FAX: (312) 419-8950
Ms. Kathleen Combs
Executive Director
E-MAIL: contact@alise.org
URL: www.alise.org

Association for Prevention Teaching and Research (c)
1001 Connecticut Avenue, NW
Suite 610
Washington, DC 20036
(202) 463-0550
FAX: (202) 463-0555
E-MAIL: info@aptrweb.org
URL: www.aptrweb.org

Association for the Study of Higher Education (ASHE) (d)
UNLV
4505 South Maryland Parkway
Box 3068
Las Vegas, NV 89154-3068
(702) 895-2737
FAX: (702) 895-4269
Dr. Kimberly Nehls
Executive Director
E-MAIL: ASHE@unlv.edu
URL: www.ashe.ws

Association for Theatre in Higher Education (ATHE) (e)
PO Box 1290
Boulder, CO 80306-1290
(888) 284-3737
FAX: (303) 530-2168
Ms. Nancy Erickson
Executive Director
E-MAIL: administrativedirector@athe.org
URL: www.athe.org

Association of Advanced Rabbinical and Talmudic Schools Accreditation Commission (f)
11 Broadway
Suite 405
New York, NY 10004
(212) 363-1991
FAX: (212) 533-5335
Dr. Bernard Fryshman
Executive Vice President

Association of American Colleges and Universities (g)
1818 R Street, NW
Washington, DC 20009
(202) 387-3760
FAX: (202) 265-9532
Dr. Carol G. Schneider
President
E-MAIL: info@aacu.org
URL: www.aacu.org

Association of American Law Schools (h)
1201 Connecticut Avenue, NW
Suite 800
Washington, DC 20036-2605
(202) 296-8851
FAX: (202) 296-8869
Ms. Susan Westerberg Prager
Executive Director
E-MAIL: aals@aals.org
URL: www.aals.org

Association of American Medical Colleges (i)
2450 N Street, NW
Washington, DC 20037-1127
(202) 828-0400
FAX: (202) 828-1125
Dr. Darrell G. Kirch
President/CEO
E-MAIL: aamcpresident@aamc.org
URL: www.aamc.org

Association of American Universities (A)
1200 New York Avenue, NW
Suite 550
Washington, DC 20005
(202) 408-7500
FAX: (202) 408-8184
Dr. Hunter R. Rawlings III
President
URL: www.aau.edu

Association of American University Presses (B)
28 West 36th Street
Suite 602
New York, NY 10018
(212) 989-1010
FAX: (212) 989-0275
Mr. Peter Givler
Executive Director
E-MAIL: info@aaupnet.org
URL: www.aaupnet.org

Association of Catholic Colleges and Universities (C)
1 Dupont Circle, NW
Suite 650
Washington, DC 20036
(202) 457-0650
FAX: (202) 728-0977
Michael Galligan-Stierle Ph.D.
President/CEO
E-MAIL: accu@accunet.org
URL: www.accunet.org

Association of College and University Housing Officers-International (D)
941 Chatham Lane
Suite 318
Columbus, OH 43221-2416
(614) 292-0099
FAX: (614) 292-3205
Ms. Sallie Traxler
Executive Director
E-MAIL: office@acuho-i.org
URL: www.acuho-i.org

Association of College Unions International (E)
One City Centre
Suite 200
120 West Seventh Street
Bloomington, IN 47404-3925
(812) 245-2284
FAX: (812) 245-6710
Ms. Marsha Herman-Betzen
Executive Director
E-MAIL: acui@acui.org
URL: www.acui.org

Association of Collegiate Conference and Events Directors-International (F)
419 Canyon Avenue
#311
Fort Collins, CO 80521
(970) 449-4960
FAX: (970) 449-4965
Ms. Deborah Blom
Executive Director
E-MAIL: deborah@acced-i.org
URL: www.acced-i.org

Association of Collegiate Schools of Architecture (G)
1735 New York Avenue, NW
Washington, DC 20006
(202) 785-2324
FAX: (202) 628-0448
Michael Monti Ph.D.
Executive Director
E-MAIL: info@acsa-arch.org
URL: www.acsa-arch.org

Association of Collegiate Schools of Planning (H)
c/o Donna Dodd, Association Manager
6311 Mallard Trace Drive
Tallahassee, FL 32312
(850) 385-2054
FAX: (850) 385-2084
Dr. Cheryl Contant
President
E-MAIL: president@acsp.org
URL: www.acsp.org

Association of Community College Trustees (I)
1233 20th Street, NW
Suite 301
Washington, DC 20036
(202) 775-4667
FAX: (202) 223-1297
Mr. J. Noah Brown
President and CEO
E-MAIL: nbrown@acct.org
URL: www.acct.org

Association of Departments of English (J)
26 Broadway
3rd Floor
New York, NY 10004-1789
(646) 576-5130
FAX: (646) 458-0033
Dr. David Laurence
Director
E-MAIL: ade@mla.org
URL: www.ade.org

Association of Departments of Foreign Languages (K)
26 Broadway
3rd Floor
New York, NY 10004-1789
(646) 576-5140
FAX: (646) 458-0033
Dr. Nelly Furman
Director
E-MAIL: adfl@mla.org
URL: www.adfl.org

The Association of Educational Publishers (L)
300 Martin Luther King Boulevard
Suite 200
Wilmington, DE 19801
(302) 295-8350
FAX: (302) 778-1110
Ms. Charlene F. Gaynor
Chief Executive Officer
E-MAIL: mail@aepweb.org
URL: www.aepweb.org

Association of Governing Boards of Universities and Colleges (M)
1133 20th Street, NW
Suite 300
Washington, DC 20036
(202) 296-8400
FAX: (202) 223-7053
Mr. Richard Legon
President
E-MAIL: rickl@agb.org
URL: www.agb.org

Association of Graduate Liberal Studies Programs (N)
c/o Duke University
Box 90095
Durham, NC 27708-0095
(919) 684-1987
FAX: (919) 681-8905
Mr. David L. Gitomer
President
E-MAIL: info@aglsp.org
URL: www.aglsp.org

Association of Jesuit Colleges and Universities (O)
1 Dupont Circle, NW
Suite 405
Washington, DC 20036
(202) 862-9893
FAX: (202) 862-8523
Rev. Gregory F. Lucey S.J.
President
E-MAIL: glucey@ajcunet.edu
URL: www.ajcunet.edu

Association of Military Colleges and Schools of the United States (P)
3604 Glenbrook Road
Fairfax, VA 22031-3211
(703) 272-8406
Dr. Rudy Ehrenberg
Executive Director
E-MAIL: amcsus@cox.net
URL: www.amcsus.org

Association of Performing Arts Presenters (Q)
1211 Connecticut Avenue, NW
Suite 200
Washington, DC 20036
(202) 833-2787
FAX: (202) 833-1543
E-MAIL: info@artspresenters.org
URL: www.apap365.org

Association of Practical Theology (R)
Princeton Theological Seminary
Tennent Hall
108 Stockton Street
Princeton, NJ 08540
(609) 497-7739
FAX: (609) 279-9014
Mr. Gordon Mikoski
President
E-MAIL: gordon.mikoski@ptsem.edu
URL: www.practicaltheology.org

Association of Presbyterian Colleges and Universities (S)
100 Witherspoon Street
Louisville, KY 40202-1396
(502) 569-5509
FAX: (502) 569-8077
Mr. Gary Luhr
Executive Director
E-MAIL: gary.luhr@pcusa.org
URL: www.presbyteriancolleges.org

Association of Private Sector Colleges and Universities (APSCU) (T)
1101 Connecticut Avenue, NW
Suite 900
Washington, DC 20036
(202) 336-6700
FAX: (202) 336-6828
Mr. Brian Moran
Interim CEO/President
E-MAIL: brian.moran@apscu.org
URL: www.apscu.org

Association of Public and Land-Grant Universities (U)
1307 New York Avenue, NW
Suite 400
Washington, DC 20005-4722
(202) 478-6040
FAX: (202) 478-6046
M. Peter McPherson
President
E-MAIL: pmcpherson@aplu.org
URL: www.aplu.org

Association of Research Libraries (V)
21 Dupont Circle, NW
Suite 800
Washington, DC 20036
(202) 296-2296
FAX: (202) 872-0884
Mr. Charles B. Lowry
Executive Director
E-MAIL: clowry@arl.org
URL: www.arl.org

Association of Schools of Allied Health Professions (W)
4400 Jenifer Street, NW
Suite 333
Washington, DC 20015
(202) 237-6481
FAX: (202) 237-6485
Dr. Thomas Elwood
Executive Director
E-MAIL: thomas@asahp.org
URL: www.asahp.org

Association of Specialized and Professional Accreditors (X)
3304 North Broadway Street, #214
Chicago, IL 60657
(773) 857-7900
FAX: (773) 857-7901
Mr. Joseph Vibert
Executive Director
E-MAIL: aspa@aspa-usa.org
URL: www.aspa-usa.org

Association of Teacher Educators (Y)
PO Box 793
Manassas, VA 20113
(703) 331-0911
FAX: (703) 331-3666
Mr. David Ritchey
Executive Director
E-MAIL: dritchey@ate1.org
URL: www.ate1.org

Association of Teachers of Technical Writing (Z)
University of North Texas
Dept. of Linguistics & Technical Communication
1155 Union Circle #305298
Denton, TX 76203-5017
(940) 565-4458
Dr. Brenda R. Sims
Executive Secretary
E-MAIL: sims@unt.edu
URL: www.attw.org

The Association of Technology, Management, and Applied Engineering (ATMAE) (a)
1390 Eisenhower Place
Ann Arbor, MI 48108
(734) 677-0720
FAX: (734) 677-0046
Mr. Rick Coscarelli
Executive Director
E-MAIL: rcoscarelli@atmae.org
URL: atmae.org

Association of Theological Schools in the United States and Canada The Commission on Accrediting (b)
10 Summit Park Drive
Pittsburgh, PA 15275-1103
(412) 788-6505
FAX: (412) 788-6510
Dr. Daniel O. Aleshire
Executive Director
E-MAIL: ats@ats.edu
URL: www.ats.edu

Association of University Programs in Health Administration (c)
2000 14th Street North
Suite 780
Arlington, VA 22201-2543
(703) 894-0940
FAX: (703) 894-0941
Ms. Lydia Middleton MBA, CAE
President & CEO
E-MAIL: lmiddleton@aupha.org
URL: www.aupha.org

Association of University Research Parks (d)
6262 North Swan Road
Suite 100
Tucson, AZ 85718
(520) 529-2521
FAX: (520) 529-2499
Ms. Eileen Walker
CEO
E-MAIL: info@aurp.net
URL: www.aurp.net

Association of University Summer Sessions (e)
PO Box 210066, Room 221
University of Arizona
Tucson, AZ 85721-0066
(520) 626-8488
FAX: (520) 621-2099
Ms. Debbie Milora
Recorder
E-MAIL: dmiller@u.arizona.edu

Broadcast Education Association (f)
1771 N Street, NW
Washington, DC 20036-2891
(202) 429-5355
FAX: (202) 775-2981
Ms. Heather Birks
Executive Director
E-MAIL: hbirks@nab.org
URL: www.beaweb.org

The Carnegie Foundation for the Advancement of Teaching (g)
51 Vista Lane
Stanford, CA 94305
(650) 566-5100
FAX: (650) 326-0278
Dr. Anthony S. Bryk
President
E-MAIL: bryk@carnegiefoundation.org
URL: www.carnegiefoundation.org

Center for Women Policy Studies (h)
1776 Massachusetts Avenue, NW
Suite 450
Washington, DC 20036
(202) 872-1770
FAX: (202) 296-8962
Leslie R. Wolfe
President
E-MAIL: cwps@centerwomenpolicy.org
URL: www.centerwomenpolicy.org

Center on Education and Training for Employment (i)
The Ohio State University
1900 Kenny Road
Columbus, OH 43210-1016
(614) 292-9072
FAX: (614) 292-1260
Mr. Robert A. Mahlman
Director
E-MAIL: mahlman.1@osu.edu
URL: www.cete.org

Higher Education Associations

College and University Professional Association for Human Resources (CUPA-HR) (A)
1811 Commons Point Drive
Knoxville, TN 37932
(865) 637-7673
Fax: (865) 637-7674
Mr. Andy Brantley
President and Chief Executive Officer
E-mail: abrantley@cupahr.org
URL: www.cupahr.org

College Art Association (B)
50 Broadway, Floor 21
New York, NY 10004
(212) 691-1051
Fax: (212) 627-2381
Ms. Linda Downs
Executive Director
E-mail: nyoffice@collegeart.org
URL: www.collegeart.org

The College Board (C)
45 Columbus Avenue
New York, NY 10023
(212) 713-8000
Fax: (212) 713-8282
Governor Gaston Caperton
President
E-mail: gcaperton@collegeboard.org
URL: www.collegeboard.org

College English Association (D)
James Madison University
English Department
MC 1801
Harrisonburg, VA 22807
Mr. Robert Hoskins
Executive Director
E-mail: hoskinrv@jmu.edu
URL: cea-web.org

College Media Advisers (E)
2301 Vanderbilt Place
VU Station B351669
Nashville, TN 37235-1669
(615) 322-6610
Fax: (615) 343-2756
Mr. Christopher Carroll
Executive Director
E-mail: chris.carroll@vanderbilt.edu
URL: www.collegemedia.org

Columbia Scholastic Press Association (F)
Columbia University
Mail Code 5711
New York, NY 10027-6902
(212) 854-9400
Fax: (212) 854-9401
Mr. Edmund J. Sullivan
Executive Director
E-mail: cspa@columbia.edu
URL: www.columbia.edu/cu/cspa

Commission on Accreditation for Health Informatics and Information Management Education (CAHIIM) (G)
233 North Michigan Avenue
21st Floor
Chicago, IL 60601-5800
(312) 233-1183
Fax: (312) 233-1483
Dr. Claire Dixon-Lee
Executive Director CAHIIM
E-mail: claire.dixon-lee@ahima.org
URL: www.cahiim.org

Commission on Accreditation for Marriage and Family Therapy Education (H)
112 South Alfred Street
Alexandria, VA 22314
(703) 253-0457
Fax: (703) 253-0508
Ms. Tatiana A. Tamarkin
Director of Educational Affairs
E-mail: ttamarkin@aamft.org
URL: www.aamft.org

Commission on Accreditation of Allied Health Education Programs (I)
1361 Park Street
Clearwater, FL 33756
(727) 210-2350
Fax: (727) 210-2354
Dr. Kathleen Megivern J.D., CAE
Executive Director
E-mail: megivern@caahep.org
URL: www.caahep.org

Commission on Accreditation of Healthcare Management Education (CAHME) (J)
2111 Wilson Boulevard
Suite 700
Arlington, VA 22201
(703) 351-5010
Fax: (703) 991-5989
Mr. John S. Lloyd MBA, MPH
President & CEO
E-mail: jlloyd@cahme.org
URL: www.cahme.org

Commission on Accreditation of Rehabilitation Facilities (CARF) (K)
6951 E. Southpoint Road
Tucson, AZ 85756
(520) 325-1044
Fax: (520) 318-1129
Dr. Brian J. Boon Ph.D.
President & CEO
E-mail: info@carf.org
URL: www.carf.org

Commission on Collegiate Nursing Education (CCNE) (L)
One Dupont Circle, NW
Suite 530
Washington, DC 20036-1120
(202) 887-6791
Fax: (202) 887-8476
Dr. Jennifer Butlin
Executive Director
E-mail: jbutlin@aacn.nche.edu
URL: www.aacn.nche.edu/accreditation

Commission on English Language Program Accreditation (CEA) (M)
801 North Fairfax Street
Suite 402A
Alexandria, VA 22314
(703) 519-2070
Fax: (703) 519-2071
Ms. Teresa D. O'Donnell
Executive Director
E-mail: todonnell@cea-accredit.org
URL: www.cea-accredit.org

Commission on Independent Colleges and Universities (CICU) (N)
17 Elk Street
PO Box 7289
Albany, NY 12224
(518) 436-4781
Fax: (518) 436-0417
Ms. Laura L. Anglin
President
E-mail: mail@cicu.org
URL: www.cicu.org, www.nycolleges.org

Commission on Massage Therapy Accreditation (O)
5335 Wisconsin Avenue, NW
Suite 440
Washington, DC 20015
(202) 895-1518
Fax: (202) 895-1519
Ms. Kate Ivane Henrioulle
Executive Director
E-mail: khenrioulle@comta.org
URL: www.comta.org

Commission on Opticianry Accreditation (P)
PO Box 592
Canton, NY 13617
(703) 468-0566
Mrs. Debra White
Director of Accreditation
E-mail: director@coaccreditation.com
URL: www.coaccreditation.com

Committee on Accreditation for Education in Electroneurodiagnostic Technology (Q)
6654 South Sycamore Street
Littleton, CO 80120
(303) 738-0770
Fax: (303) 738-3223
Ms. Theresa Sisneros
Executive Director
E-mail: office@coa-end.org
URL: www.coa-end.org

Committee on Accreditation for the Exercise Sciences (R)
401 West Michigan Street
Indianapolis, IN 46202
(317) 637-9200
Fax: (317) 634-7817
E-mail: trush@acsm.org
URL: www.coaes.org

Committee on Accreditation of Education Programs for Kinesiotherapy (S)
University of Southern Mississippi
118 College Drive, #5142
Hattiesburg, MS 39406-0001
(601) 266-5371
Fax: (601) 266-4445
Jerry W. Purvis
E-mail: copskt@akta.org
URL: www.akta.org

Committee on Educational Programs for the Emergency Medical Services Professions (T)
4101 West Green Oaks Boulevard
Suite 305-599
Arlington, TX 76016
(817) 330-0080
Fax: (817) 330-0089
Dr. George Hatch
Executive Director
E-mail: george@coaemsp.org
URL: www.coaemsp.org

Committee on Institutional Cooperation (U)
1819 South Neil Street
Suite D
Champaign, IL 61820
(217) 333-8475
Fax: (217) 244-7127
Ms. Barbara McFadden Allen
Director
E-mail: cic@staff.cic.net
URL: www.cic.net

Conference on College Composition and Communication (V)
1111 West Kenyon Road
Urbana, IL 61801-1096
(800) 369-6283
Fax: (217) 328-0977
Mr. Kent Williamson
Executive Secretary-Treasurer
E-mail: kwilliamson@ncte.org
URL: www.ncte.org/cccc

Council for Accreditation of Counseling and Related Educational Programs (CACREP) (W)
1001 North Fairfax Street, Suite 510
Alexandria, VA 22314
(703) 535-5990
Fax: (703) 739-6209
Dr. Carol L. Bobby
President and CEO
E-mail: cacrep@cacrep.org
URL: www.cacrep.org

Council for Adult and Experiential Learning (X)
55 East Monroe
Suite 1930
Chicago, IL 60603
(312) 499-2600
Fax: (312) 499-2601
Ms. Pamela Tate
President
E-mail: ptate@cael.org
URL: www.cael.org

The Council for Advancement and Support of Education (Y)
1307 New York Avenue, NW
Suite 1000
Washington, DC 20005-4701
(202) 478-5655
Fax: (202) 387-4973
Mr. John Lippincott
President
E-mail: lippincott@case.org
URL: www.case.org

Council for Agricultural Science and Technology (CAST) (Z)
4420 West Lincoln Way
Ames, IA 50014-3447
(515) 292-2125
Fax: (515) 292-4512
Dr. John M. Bonner
Executive Vice President
E-mail: cast@cast-science.org
URL: www.cast-science.org

Council for Aid to Education (a)
215 Lexington Avenue
21st Floor
New York, NY 10016-6023
(212) 661-5800
Fax: (212) 661-9766
Dr. Roger Benjamin
President & CEO
E-mail: rbenjamin@cae.org
URL: www.cae.org

Council for Christian Colleges & Universities (b)
321 8th Street, NE
Washington, DC 20002-6158
(202) 546-8713
Fax: (202) 548-5205
Dr. Paul R. Corts
President
E-mail: council@cccu.org
URL: www.cccu.org

Council for Economic Education (c)
122 East 42nd Street
Suite 2600
New York, NY 10168
(212) 730-7007 or (800) 338-1192
Fax: (212) 730-1793
Ms. Nan Morrison
President and CEO
E-mail: njmorrison@councilforeconed.org
URL: www.councilforeconed.org

Council for Higher Education Accreditation (d)
1 Dupont Circle, NW
Suite 510
Washington, DC 20036-1135
(202) 955-6126
Fax: (202) 955-6129
Dr. Judith Eaton
President
E-mail: chea@chea.org
URL: www.chea.org

Council for Interior Design Accreditation (formerly FIDER) (e)
206 Grandville Avenue, SW
Suite 350
Grand Rapids, MI 49503
(616) 458-0400
Fax: (616) 458-0460
Ms. Holly Mattson
Executive Director
E-mail: info@accredit-id.org
URL: www.accredit-id.org

Institute of International Education Council for International Exchange of Scholars (f)
1400 K Street, NW
Suite 700
Washington, DC 20005
(202) 686-4000
Fax: (202) 686-4029
Dr. Edward Roslof
Executive Director
E-mail: scholars@iie.org
URL: www.cies.org

Council for Research in Music Education (g)
University of Illinois at Urbana-Champaign
1114 West Nevada
Urbana, IL 61801
(217) 333-1027
Dr. Eve Harwood
Editor
E-mail: crme@illinois.edu
URL: bcrme.press.illinois.edu

Council for the Advancement of Standards in Higher Education (h)
One Dupont Circle, NW
Suite 300
Washington, DC 20036-1188
(202) 862-1400
Fax: (202) 296-3286
Ms. Phyllis L. Mable
Executive Director
E-mail: phyllismable@aol.com
URL: www.cas.edu

Council of Colleges of Acupuncture and Oriental Medicine (CCAOM) (A)
600 Wyndhurst Avenue
Suite 112
Baltimore, MD 21210
(410) 464-6041
Fax: (410) 464-6042
Mr. David M. Sale
Executive Director
E-mail: executivedirector@ccaom.comcastbiz.net
URL: www.ccaom.org

Council of Colleges of Arts and Sciences (B)
PO Box 8795
c/o The College of William and Mary
Williamsburg, VA 23187-8795
(757) 221-1784
Dr. Anne-Marie McCartan
Executive Director
E-mail: ccas@wm.edu
URL: www.ccas.net

Council of Graduate Schools (C)
1 Dupont Circle, NW
Suite 230
Washington, DC 20036
(202) 223-3791
Fax: (202) 331-7157
Dr. Debra W. Stewart
President
E-mail: dstewart@cgs.nche.edu
URL: www.cgsnet.org

Council of Independent Colleges (D)
1 Dupont Circle, NW
Suite 320
Washington, DC 20036-1142
(202) 466-7230
Fax: (202) 466-7238
Dr. Richard Ekman
President
E-mail: cic@cic.nche.edu
URL: www.cic.edu

The Council of Writing Program Administrators (E)
Grand Valley State University
Department of Writing
326 Lake Ontario Hall
Allendale, MI 49401
(616) 331-8147
Dr. Keith Rhodes
Secretary
E-mail: rhodekei@gvsu.edu
URL: www.wpacouncil.org

Council on Accreditation of Nurse Anesthesia Educational Programs (COA) (F)
222 Prospect Avenue
Park Ridge, IL 60068-4010
(847) 655-1154
Fax: (847) 692-7137
Francis Gerbasi CRNA,Ph.D.
Executive Director COA
E-mail: fgerbasi@aana.com
URL: www.aana.com

Council on Aviation Accreditation dba Aviation Accreditation Board International (G)
3410 Skyway Drive
Auburn, AL 36830
(334) 844-2431
Fax: (334) 844-2432
Mr. Gary W. Kiteley
Executive Director
E-mail: kitelgw@auburn.edu
URL: www.aabi.aero

Council on Chiropractic Education (H)
8049 North 85th Way
Scottsdale, AZ 85258-4321
(480) 443-8877
Fax: (480) 483-7333
Lee Van Dusen
President
E-mail: cce@cce-usa.org
URL: www.cce-usa.org

Council on Education for Public Health (I)
800 Eye Street, NW
Suite 202
Washington, DC 20001
(202) 789-1050
Fax: (202) 789-1895
Ms. Laura Rasar King
Executive Director
E-mail: lking@ceph.org
URL: www.ceph.org

Council on Governmental Relations (J)
1200 New York Avenue, NW
Suite 750
Washington, DC 20005
(202) 289-6655
Fax: (202) 289-6698
Mr. Anthony DeCrappeo
President
E-mail: tdecrappeo@cogr.edu
URL: www.cogr.edu

Council on Higher Education Solutions for Adults (K)
104 Johnson Street
Marshall, TX 75670
(903) 472-2762
Fax: (903) 935-3890
Dr. Tracy Andrus
President/CEO
E-mail: chesa1962@gmail.com
URL: www.chesa1.com

Council on Law in Higher Education (L)
9386 Via Classico West
Wellington, FL 33411
(561) 792-4440
Fax: (561) 792-4441
Mr. Daren Bakst
President
E-mail: moss@clhe.org
URL: www.clhe.org

Council on Naturopathic Medical Education (M)
PO Box 178
Great Barrington, MA 01238
(413) 528-8877
Fax: (413) 528-8880
Dr. Daniel Seitz J.D., Ed.D
Executive Director
E-mail: danseitz@cnme.org
URL: www.cnme.org

Council on Occupational Education (N)
7840 Roswell Road
Building 300, Suite 325
Atlanta, GA 30350
(800) 917-2081
Fax: (770) 396-3790
Dr. Gary Puckett
President
E-mail: puckettg@council.org
URL: www.council.org

Council on Podiatric Medical Education (O)
9312 Old Georgetown Road
Bethesda, MD 20814-1698
(301) 581-9290
Fax: (301) 571-4903
Mr. Alan Tinkleman
Director
E-mail: artinkleman@apma.org
URL: www.cpme.org

Council on Rehabilitation Education (CORE) (P)
1699 Woodfield Road
Suite 300
Schaumburg, IL 60173
(847) 944-1345
Fax: (847) 944-1346
Dr. Sue Ouellette
Executive Director
E-mail: souellet@niu.edu
URL: www.core-rehab.org

Council on Social Work Education (Q)
1701 Duke Street
Suite 200
Alexandria, VA 22314-3457
(703) 683-8080
Fax: (703) 683-8099
Dr. Stephen Holloway
Director Office of Social Work Accreditation
E-mail: accreditation@cswe.org
URL: www.cswe.org

Council on Undergraduate Research (R)
734 15th Street, NW
Suite 550
Washington, DC 20005
(202) 783-4810
Fax: (202) 783-4811
Dr. Nancy Hensel
Executive Officer
E-mail: cur@cur.org
URL: www.cur.org

CSAB, Inc. (S)
817 Loyola Drive
Towson, MD 21204
(410) 339-5456
Ms. Liz Glazer
Executive Director
E-mail: csab@csab.org
URL: www.csab.org

Decision Sciences Institute (T)
75 Piedmont Road
Suite 340
Atlanta, GA 30303
(404) 413-7711
Fax: (404) 413-7714
Ms. Carol J. Latta
Executive Director
E-mail: clatta@gsu.edu
URL: www.decisionsciences.org

Direct Marketing Association, Inc. (U)
1120 Avenue of the Americas
New York, NY 10036-6700
(212) 768-7277
Fax: (212) 768-7353
Mr. Lawrence M. Kimmel
CEO
E-mail: ceo@the-dma.org
URL: www.the-dma.org

Direct Marketing Education Foundation, Inc. (V)
1120 Avenue of the Americas
14th Floor
New York, NY 10036-6700
(212) 768-7277
Fax: (212) 790-1561
Terri L. Bartlett
President
E-mail: dmef@directworks.org
URL: www.directworks.org

Distance Education and Training Council (W)
1601 Eighteenth Street, NW
Suite 2
Washington, DC 20009
(202) 234-5100
Fax: (202) 332-1386
Mr. Michael P. Lambert
Executive Director
E-mail: info@detc.org
URL: www.detc.org

Education Commission of the States (X)
700 Broadway
Suite 810
Denver, CO 80203-3460
(303) 299-3600
Fax: (303) 296-8332
Mr. Roger Sampson
President
E-mail: ecs@ecs.org
URL: www.ecs.org

Education Development Center, Inc. (Y)
55 Chapel Street
Newton, MA 02458-1060
(617) 969-7100
Fax: (617) 969-5979
Mr. Luther S. Luedtke
President
E-mail: comment@edc.org
URL: www.edc.org

EDUCAUSE (Z)
1150 18th Street, NW
Suite 900
Washington, DC 20036-3816
(202) 872-4200
Fax: (202) 872-4318
Diana Oblinger Ph.D.
President
E-mail: doblinger@educause.edu
URL: www.educause.edu

Financial Management Association International (a)
University of South Florida
College of Business Administration
4202 East Fowler Avenue, BSN 3331
Tampa, FL 33620-5500
(813) 974-2084
Fax: (813) 974-3318
Mr. Jack S. Rader
Executive Director
E-mail: fma@coba.usf.edu
URL: www.fma.org

Friends Association for Higher Education (b)
1501 Cherry Street
Philadelphia, PA 19102
(215) 241-7116
Fax: (215) 241-7028
Ms. Kori Heavner
FAHE Coordinator
E-mail: fahe@quaker.org
URL: www.earlham.edu/~fahe

The George Washington University HEATH Resource Center Graduate School of Education and Human Development (c)
2134 G Street, NW
Washington, DC 20052-0001
E-mail: askheath@gwu.edu
URL: www.heath.gwu.edu

The Gerontological Society of America (d)
1220 L Street, NW
Suite 901
Washington, DC 20005-4018
(202) 842-1275
Fax: (202) 842-1150
Mr. James Appleby
Executive Director
E-mail: geron@geron.org
URL: www.geron.org

Graduate Record Examinations Board (e)
Educational Testing Service
Mail Stop 57L
Rosedale Road
Princeton, NJ 08541
(609) 683-2014
Fax: (609) 683-2040
Dr. David G. Payne
Vice President
E-mail: dpayne@ets.org
URL: www.ets.org

H. Wiley Hitchcock Institute for Studies in American Music (f)
Brooklyn College/CUNY
2900 Bedford Avenue
Brooklyn, NY 11210-2889
(718) 951-5655
Dr. Jeffrey Taylor
Director
E-mail: isam@brooklyn.cuny.edu
URL: www.hisam.org

Higher Education Resource Services (HERS) (g)
University of Denver
1901 East Asbury Avenue
Denver, CO 80208
(303) 871-6866
Fax: (303) 871-6766
Dr. Judith White
President/Executive Director
E-mail: jwhite28@du.edu
URL: www.hersnet.org

The Higher Learning Commission, a Commission of The North Central Association of Colleges and Schools (h)
230 South LaSalle Street
Suite 7-500
Chicago, IL 60604-1413
(312) 263-0456 / (800) 621-7440
Fax: (312) 263-7462
Ms. Sylvia Manning
President
E-mail: info@hlcommission.org
URL: www.ncahlc.org

Hispanic Association of Colleges and Universities (i)
8415 Datapoint Drive
Suite 400
San Antonio, TX 78229
(210) 692-3805
Fax: (210) 692-0823
Dr. Antonio R. Flores
President
E-mail: hacu@hacu.net
URL: www.hacu.net

IACLEA (International Association of Campus Law Enforcement Administrators) (A)
342 North Main Street
West Hartford, CT 06117-2507
(860) 586-7517
FAX: (860) 586-7550
Mr. Peter J. Berry CAE
Chief Staff Officer
E-MAIL: info@iaclea.org
URL: www.iaclea.org

The Institute for Higher Education Policy (B)
1320 19th Street, NW
Suite 400
Washington, DC 20036
(202) 861-8223
FAX: (202) 861-9307
Michelle A. Cooper Ph.D.
President
E-MAIL: institute@ihep.org
URL: www.ihep.org

Institute of International Education (C)
809 United Nations Plaza
New York, NY 10017-3580
(212) 883-8200
FAX: (212) 984-5496
E-MAIL: info@iie.org
URL: www.iie.org

Intercollegiate Broadcasting System, Inc. (D)
367 Windsor Highway
New Windsor, NY 12553-7900
(845) 565-0003
FAX: (845) 565-7446
Mr. Fritz Kass
Director-Operations
E-MAIL: ibshq@aol.com
URL: www.collegeradio.tv

International Assembly for Collegiate Business Education (E)
PO Box 3960
Olathe, KS 66063
(913) 631-3009
FAX: (913) 631-9154
Mr. Dennis N. Gash
President
E-MAIL: iacbe@iacbe.org
URL: www.iacbe.org

International Association of Baptist Colleges and Universities (F)
8120 Sawyer Brown Road
Suite 108
Nashville, TN 37221-1410
(615) 673-1896
Dr. Michael Arrington
Executive Director
E-MAIL: marrington@baptistschools.org
URL: www.baptistschools.org

International Communication Association (G)
1500 21st Street, NW
Washington, DC 20036
(202) 955-1444
FAX: (202) 955-1448
Dr. Michael Haley
Executive Director
E-MAIL: mhaley@icahdq.org
URL: www.icahdq.org

International Council on Education for Teaching (H)
National-Louis University
1000 Capitol Drive
Wheeling, IL 60090
(847) 947-5881
FAX: (847) 947-5881
Dr. Darrell A. Bloom
President
E-MAIL: contact@icet4u.org
URL: www.icet4u.org

Joint Review Committee on Education in Cardiovascular Technology (JRC-CVT) (I)
6 Pine Knoll Drive
Beverly, MA 01915-1425
(978) 456-5594
Mr. William W. Goding
Executive Director
E-MAIL: office@jrccvt.org
URL: www.jrccvt.org

Joint Review Committee on Education in Diagnostic Medical Sonography (J)
6021 University Boulevard
Suite 500
Ellicott City, MD 21043-6090
(443) 973-3251
Mr. Gerry Magat
Accreditation Coordinator
E-MAIL: mail@jrcdms.org
URL: www.jrcdms.org

Joint Review Committee on Education in Radiologic Technology (K)
20 North Wacker Drive
Suite 2850
Chicago, IL 60606-3182
(312) 704-5300
FAX: (312) 704-5304
Leslie F. Winter
Chief Executive Officer
E-MAIL: mail@jrcert.org
URL: www.jrcert.org

Joint Review Committee on Educational Programs in Nuclear Medicine Technology (L)
2000 West Danforth Road
Suite 130, #203
Edmond, OK 73003
(405) 285-0546
FAX: (405) 285-0579
Ms. Jan M. Winn
Executive Director
E-MAIL: jrcnmt@coxinet.net
URL: www.jrcnmt.org

Journalism Association of Community Colleges (M)
PO Box 163509
Sacramento, CA 95816
(562) 860-2451, ext 2619
FAX: (562) 467-5044
Mr. Rich Cameron
Communications Director
E-MAIL: rich@rcameron.com
URL: www.jacconline.org

LASPAU: Academic and Professional Programs for the Americas (N)
25 Mount Auburn Street
Suite 300
Cambridge, MA 02138-6095
(617) 495-5255
FAX: (617) 495-8990
Dr. Peter DeShazo
Executive Director
E-MAIL: laspau-info@calists.harvard.edu
URL: www.laspau.harvard.edu

Law School Admission Council (O)
PO Box 40
Newtown, PA 18940
(215) 968-1101
FAX: (215) 968-1169
Mr. Daniel Bernstine
President
URL: www.lsac.org

Liaison Committee on Medical Education (LCME) American Medical Association (P)
515 North State Street
Chicago, IL 60654
(312) 464-4933
FAX: (312) 464-5830
Barbara Barzansky Ph.D.,MHPE
LCME Secretary, 2011-2012
E-MAIL: barbara.barzansky@ama-assn.org
URL: www.lcme.org

Linguistic Society of America (Q)
1325 Eighteenth Street, NW
Archibald A. Hill, Suite #211
Washington, DC 20036-6501
(202) 835-1714
FAX: (202) 835-1717
Ms. Alyson Reed
Executive Director
E-MAIL: lsa@lsadc.org
URL: www.lsadc.org

Lutheran Educational Conference of North America (R)
PMB #377
2601 South Minnesota Avenue
Suite 105
Sioux Falls, SD 57105-4750
(605) 271-9894
FAX: (605) 271-9895
Mr. William E. Hamm
President
E-MAIL: hamm@lutherancolleges.org
URL: www.lutherancolleges.org

Middle States Commission on Higher Education (S)
3624 Market Street
2nd Floor West
Philadelphia, PA 19104
(267) 284-5025
FAX: (215) 662-5501
E-MAIL: info@msche.org
URL: www.msche.org

Midwest Association of Colleges and Employers (T)
100 East Grand Avenue
Suite 330
Des Moines, IA 50309
(515) 244-6515
FAX: (515) 243-2049
Ms. Laura Kestner
President
E-MAIL: e-mail@mwace.org
URL: www.mwace.org

Midwestern Higher Education Compact (U)
1300 South Second Street
Suite 130
Minneapolis, MN 55454-1079
(612) 626-8288
FAX: (612) 626-8290
Mr. Larry A. Isaak
President
E-MAIL: mhec@mhec.org
URL: www.mhec.org

Midwifery Education Accreditation Council (MEAC) (V)
PO Box 984
LaConner, WA 98257
(360) 466-2080
FAX: (480) 907-2936
Ms. Jo Anne Myers-Ciecko
Executive Director
E-MAIL: executivedirector@meacschools.org
URL: www.meacschools.org

Modern Language Association (W)
26 Broadway
3rd Floor
New York, NY 10004-1789
(646) 576-5000
FAX: (646) 458-0030
Dr. Rosemary G. Feal
Executive Director
E-MAIL: info@mla.org
URL: www.mla.org

Montessori Accreditation Council for Teacher Education (MACTE) (X)
313 Second Street S.E.
Suite 112
Charlottesville, VA 22902
(434) 202-7793
FAX: (888) 525-8838
Ms. Rebecca Pelton
Executive Director
E-MAIL: rebecca@macte.org
URL: www.macte.org

NACAS (Y)
3 Boar's Head Lane
Suite B
Charlottesville, VA 22903-4610
(434) 245-8425
FAX: (434) 245-8453
Dr. Bob Hassmiller CAE
Chief Executive Officer
E-MAIL: bob@nacas.org
URL: www.nacas.org

NASH (Z)
1250 H Street, NW
Suite 700
Washington, DC 20005
(202) 248-5149
FAX: (202) 293-2605
Dr. Kevin Reilly
President
E-MAIL: jane@nash-bc.org
URL: www.nashonline.org

NASPA-Student Affairs Administrators in Higher Education (a)
111 K Street, NE
10th Floor
Washington, DC 20002-4409
(202) 265-7500
FAX: (202) 898-5737
Dr. Gwendolyn J. Dungy
Executive Director
E-MAIL: office@naspa.org
URL: www.naspa.org

National Academic Advising Association (b)
2323 Anderson Avenue
Suite 225
Manhattan, KS 66502-2912
(785) 532-5717
FAX: (785) 532-7732
Dr. Charlie L. Nutt
Executive Director
E-MAIL: nacada@ksu.edu
URL: www.nacada.ksu.edu

The National Academy of Education (c)
500 5th Street, NW
Suite 307
Washington, DC 20001
(202) 334-2341
FAX: (202) 334-2350
E-MAIL: info@naeducation.org
URL: www.naeducation.org

National Accreditation Council for Blind and Low Vision Services (d)
7017 Pearl Road
Middleburg Heights, OH 44130
(440) 545-1601
Mr. Steven K. Hegedeos
Executive Director
E-MAIL: steve@nacasb.org
URL: www.nacasb.org

National Accrediting Agency for Clinical Laboratory Sciences (e)
5600 North River Road
Suite 720
Rosemont, IL 60018
(773) 714-8880
FAX: (773) 714-8886
Dr. Dianne M. Cearlock Ph.D
CEO
E-MAIL: dcearlock@naacls.org
URL: www.naacls.org

National Accrediting Commission of Cosmetology Arts and Sciences (f)
4401 Ford Avenue
Suite 1300
Alexandria, VA 22302-1432
(703) 600-7600
FAX: (703) 379-2200
Dr. Tony Mirando
Executive Director
E-MAIL: naccas@naccas.org
URL: www.naccas.org

National Association for College Admission Counseling (g)
1050 North Highland Street
Suite 400
Arlington, VA 22201
(703) 836-2222
FAX: (703) 836-8015
Ms. Joyce E. Smith
Chief Executive Officer
E-MAIL: jsmith@nacacnet.org
URL: www.nacacnet.org

National Association for Equal Opportunity in Higher Education (h)
209 Third Street, SE
Washington, DC 20003
(202) 552-3300
FAX: (202) 552-3330
Lezli Baskerville Esquire
President & CEO
E-MAIL: presidentsoffice@nafeo.org
URL: www.nafeo.org

National Association for Ethnic Studies, Inc. (i)
Colorado State University
Department of Ethnic Studies
1790 Campus Delivery
Fort Collins, CO 80523-1790
970-491-3927
FAX: 970-491-2717
E-MAIL: naes@ethnicstudies.org
URL: www.ethnicstudies.org

National Association for Legal Support of Alternative Schools (A)
PO Box 2823
Santa Fe, NM 87504-2823
(505) 474-0300
FAX: (505) 474-0300
Mr. Ed Nagel
Coordinator
E-MAIL: nalsas@msn.com

National Association for Practical Nurse Education and Service, Inc. (B)
1940 Duke Street
Suite 200
Alexandria, VA 22314
(703) 933-1003
FAX: (703) 940-4089
Helen Larsen J.D.
Executive Director
E-MAIL: educationdept@napnes.org
URL: www.napnes.org

National Association of Agricultural Educators (C)
300 Garrigus Building
University of Kentucky
Lexington, KY 40546-0215
(859) 257-2224
FAX: (859) 323-3919
Dr. Wm. Jay Jackman
Executive Director
E-MAIL: jjackman.naae@uky.edu
URL: www.naae.org

The National Association of College & University Food Services (D)
2525 Jolly Road
Suite 280
Okemos, MI 48864
(517) 332-2494
FAX: (517) 332-8144
Dr. Joseph H. Spina Ph.D., CAE
Executive Director
E-MAIL: jspina@nacufs.org
URL: www.nacufs.org

National Association of College and University Attorneys (E)
1 Dupont Circle, NW
Suite 620
Washington, DC 20036
(202) 833-8390
FAX: (202) 296-8379
Ms. Kathleen Curry Santora Esq.
CEO
E-MAIL: ksantora@nacua.org
URL: www.nacua.org

National Association of College and University Business Officers (F)
1110 Vermont Avenue, NW
Suite 800
Washington, DC 20005
(202) 861-2500
FAX: (202) 861-2583
Mr. John Walda
President
E-MAIL: john.walda@nacubo.org
URL: www.nacubo.org

National Association of College Stores (G)
500 East Lorain Street
Oberlin, OH 44074-1294
(440) 775-7777
FAX: (440) 775-4769
Mr. Brian E. Cartier
Chief Executive Officer
E-MAIL: info@nacs.org
URL: www.nacs.org

National Association of College Wind and Percussion Instructors (H)
308 Hillcrest Drive
Kirksville, MO 63501
(660) 665-2558
FAX: (660) 627-3233
Dr. Richard Weerts
Executive Secretary-Treasurer
URL: www.nacwpi.org

National Association of Colleges and Employers (I)
62 Highland Avenue
Bethlehem, PA 18017-9085
(610) 868-1421
FAX: (610) 868-0208
Dr. Marilyn Mackes
Executive Director
E-MAIL: cnader@naceweb.org
URL: www.naceweb.org

National Association of Educational Procurement (J)
5523 Research Park Drive
Suite 340
Baltimore, MD 21228
(443) 543-5540
FAX: (443) 543-5550
Ms. Doreen Murner
CEO
E-MAIL: dmurner@naepnet.org
URL: www.naepnet.org

National Association of Independent Colleges and Universities (K)
1025 Connecticut Avenue, NW
Suite 700
Washington, DC 20036-5405
(202) 785-8866
FAX: (202) 835-0003
Dr. David L. Warren
President
E-MAIL: geninfo@naicu.edu
URL: www.naicu.edu

National Association of Schools of Art and Design (L)
11250 Roger Bacon Drive
Suite 21
Reston, VA 20190
(703) 437-0700
FAX: (703) 437-6312
Samuel Hope
Executive Director
E-MAIL: info@arts-accredit.org
URL: www.arts-accredit.org

National Association of Schools of Dance (M)
11250 Roger Bacon Drive
Suite 21
Reston, VA 20190
(703) 437-0700
FAX: (703) 437-6312
Samuel Hope
Executive Director
E-MAIL: info@arts-accredit.org
URL: www.arts-accredit.org

National Association of Schools of Music (N)
11250 Roger Bacon Drive
Suite 21
Reston, VA 20190
(703) 437-0700
FAX: (703) 437-6312
Samuel Hope
Executive Director
E-MAIL: info@arts-accredit.org
URL: www.arts-accredit.org

National Association of Schools of Public Affairs and Administration (NASPAA) (O)
1029 Vermont Avenue, NW
Suite 1100
Washington, DC 20005
(202) 628-8965
Ms. Laurel McFarland
Executive Director
E-MAIL: naspaa@naspaa.org
URL: www.naspaa.org

National Association of Schools of Theatre (P)
11250 Roger Bacon Drive
Suite 21
Reston, VA 20190
(703) 437-0700
FAX: (703) 437-6312
Samuel Hope
Executive Director
E-MAIL: info@arts-accredit.org
URL: www.arts-accredit.org

National Association of State Directors of Teacher Education and Certification (Q)
1225 Providence Road
PMB #116
Whitinsville, MA 01588
(508) 380-1202
FAX: (508) 278-5342
Mr. Roy Einreinhofer
Executive Director
E-MAIL: rje@nasdtec.com
URL: www.nasdtec.org

National Association of Student Financial Aid Administrators (R)
1101 Connecticut Avenue, NW
Suite 1100
Washington, DC 20036-4303
(202) 785-0453
FAX: (202) 785-1487
Mr. Justin Draeger
President
E-MAIL: web@nasfaa.org
URL: www.nasfaa.org

National Catholic Educational Association (S)
1005 North Glebe Road
Sutie 525
Arlington, VA 22201
(571) 257-0010
FAX: (703) 243-0025
Ms. Karen M. Ristau Ed.D.
President
E-MAIL: kristau@ncea.org
URL: www.ncea.org

National Coalition for Campus Childrens Centers (T)
950 Glenn Drive
Suite 150
Folsom, CA 95630
(877) 736-6222
FAX: (916) 932-2209
Ms. Tonya Palla
Executive Director
E-MAIL: info@campuschildren.org
URL: www.campuschildren.org

National Collegiate Athletic Association (U)
PO Box 6222
Indianapolis, IN 46206
(317) 917-6222
FAX: (317) 917-6364
Mr. Todd Petr
Managing Director of Research
E-MAIL: tpetr@ncaa.org
URL: www.ncaa.org

National Commission on Orthotic and Prosthetic Education (NCOPE) (V)
330 John Carlyle Street
Suite 200
Alexandria, VA 22314
(703) 836-7114
FAX: (703) 836-0838
Ms. Robin C. Seabrook
Executive Director
E-MAIL: rseabrook@ncope.org
URL: www.ncope.org

National Communication Association (W)
1765 N Street, NW
Washington, DC 20036
(202) 464-4622
FAX: (202) 464-4600
Nancy Kidd Ph.D.
Executive Director
E-MAIL: inbox@natcom.org
URL: www.natcom.org

National Council for Accreditation of Teacher Education (X)
2010 Massachusetts Avenue, NW
Suite 500
Washington, DC 20036
(202) 466-7496
FAX: (202) 296-6620
Dr. James G. Cibulka
President
E-MAIL: ncate@ncate.org
URL: www.ncate.org

National Council for Continuing Education and Training (Y)
PO Box 162551
Austin, TX 78716-2551
(512) 306-8686
FAX: (512) 306-8753
Sunil Gupta
President
E-MAIL: nccet@sbcglobal.net
URL: www.nccet.org

National Council of Instructional Administrators (NCIA) Dept of Educational Administration (Z)
141 Teachers College Hall
PO Box 880360
University of Nebraska - Lincoln
Lincoln, NE 68588-0360
(402) 472-3727
FAX: (402) 472-4300
Dr. Linda Uzureau
Executive Director
E-MAIL: ncia@unl.edu
URL: ncia.unl.edu

National Council of University Research Administrators (a)
1015 18th Street, NW
Suite 901
Washington, DC 20036
(202) 466-3894
FAX: (202) 223-5573
Mrs. Kathleen M. Larmett
Executive Director
E-MAIL: info@ncura.edu
URL: www.ncura.edu

National Education Association (b)
1201 Sixteenth Street, NW
Washington, DC 20036
(202) 822-7110
FAX: (202) 822-7624
Ms. Valerie Wilk
Higher Education Coordinator
E-MAIL: vwilk@nea.org
URL: www.nea.org/he

National Forensic Association (c)
Bradley University
Department of Communication
Global Communications Center, #313
Peoria, IL 61625
(300) 077-2439
FAX: (309) 677-3446
Prof. Dan Smith
National Secretary
E-MAIL: dan@bradley.edu
URL: www.nationalforensics.org

National League for Nursing (d)
61 Broadway
33rd Floor
New York, NY 10006
(212) 363-5555 / (800) 669-1656
FAX: (212) 812-0392
Dr. Beverly L. Malone
Chief Executive Officer
E-MAIL: oceo@nln.org
URL: www.nln.org

National League for Nursing (NLNAC) (e)
3343 Peachtree Road NE
Suite 850
Atlanta, GA 30326
(404) 975-5000
FAX: (404) 296-5819
Ms. Sharon J. Tanner
CEO
E-MAIL: sjtanner@nlnac.org
URL: www.nlnac.org

Literacy Research Association, Inc. (f)
7044 South 13th Street
Oak Creek, WI 53154-1429
(414) 908-4924
FAX: (414) 768-8001
Mr. Christopher Roper
Executive Director
E-MAIL: c.roper@LiteracyResearchAssociation.org
URL: www.LiteracyResearchAssociation.org

National Recreation and Park Association Council on Accreditation for Parks, Recreation, Tourism and Related Professions (COAPRT) (g)
22377 Belmont Ridge Road
Ashburn, VA 20148-4501
(703) 858-2195
FAX: (703) 858-0794
Ms. Danielle Price
Accreditation Manager
E-MAIL: coaprt@nrpa.org
URL: www.nrpa.org

Higher Education Associations

National Rural Education Association (A)
Purdue University
Beering Hall of Liberal Arts & Education
100 North University Street
West Lafayette, IN 47907
(765) 494-0086
FAX: (765) 496-1228
Dr. John Hill
Executive Director
E-MAIL: jehill@purdue.edu
URL: www.nrea.net

National Safety Council College and University Initiative (B)
1121 Spring Lake Drive
Itasca, IL 60143
(630) 775-2227
FAX: (630) 775-2310
Ms. Sloane Grubb
Volunteer Manager, (College&University Oversight)
E-MAIL: sloane.grubb@nsc.org
URL: www.nsc.org

National Society for Experiential Education (C)
c/o Talley Management Group, Inc.
19 Mantua Road
Mt. Royal, NJ 08061
(856) 423-3427
FAX: (856) 423-3420
Haley Brust
Executive Director
E-MAIL: nsee@talley.com
URL: www.nsee.org

National Writing Project (D)
2105 Bancroft Way
#1042
University of California
Berkeley, CA 94720-1042
(510) 642-0963
FAX: (510) 643-1226
Dr. Sharon J. Washington
Executive Director
E-MAIL: nwp@nwp.org
URL: www.nwp.org

New England Association of Schools and Colleges, Inc. Commission on Institutions of Higher Education (E)
209 Burlington Road
Bedford, MA 01730-1433
(781) 541-5447
FAX: (781) 271-0950
Dr. Barbara Brittingham
Director of the Commission
E-MAIL: cihe@neasc.org
URL: cihe.neasc.org

New England Board of Higher Education (F)
45 Temple Place
Boston, MA 02111
(617) 357-9620, ext. 128
FAX: (617) 338-1577
Dr. Michael K. Thomas
President and CEO
E-MAIL: mthomas@nebhe.org
URL: www.nebhe.org

North American Association of Summer Sessions (G)
Continuing Education & Professional Development
Bradley University
1501 W. Bradley Avenue
Peoria, IL 61625
(866) 880-9607
FAX: (309) 677-3321
Ms. Janet Lange
Executive Director
E-MAIL: lange@bradley.edu
URL: www.naass.org

North Central Association Commission on Accreditation and School Improvement (H)
9115 Westside Parkway
Alpharetta, GA 30009
(678) 392-2285
FAX: (770) 346-9260
Mr. Mark A. Elgart
President/CEO
URL: www.advanc-ed.org

North Central Conference on Summer Sessions (I)
Bradley University
Peoria, IL 61625
(309) 677-2374
FAX: (309) 677-3321
Mr. Jon C. Neidy
Director of Summer and Interim Sessions
E-MAIL: neidy@bradley.edu

Northwest Commission on Colleges and Universities (J)
8060 165th Avenue, NE
Suite 100
Redmond, WA 98052
(425) 558-4224
FAX: (425) 376-0596
Dr. Sandra E. Elman
President
E-MAIL: ruthb@nwccu.org
URL: www.nwccu.org

Organizational Systems Research Association (K)
Morehead State University
Department of Information Systems
150 University Boulevard, Box 2478
Morehead, KY 40351-1689
(606) 783-2718
FAX: (606) 783-5025
Dr. Donna R. Everett
Executive Director
E-MAIL: d.everett@moreheadstate.edu
URL: www.osra.org

Pennsylvania Association of Colleges and Universities (L)
950 Walnut Bottom Road
Suite 15-214
Carlisle, PA 17015
(800) 687-9010
FAX: (717) 240-0673
URL: www.pacu.org

Quality Education for Minorities (QEM) Network (M)
1818 N Street, NW
Suite 350
Washington, DC 20036
(202) 659-1818
FAX: (202) 659-5408
Dr. Shirley M. McBay
President
E-MAIL: qemnetwork@qem.org
URL: qemnetwork.qem.org

Society for College and University Planning (N)
1330 Eisenhower Place
Ann Arbor, MI 48108
(734) 764-2000
FAX: (734) 661-0157
Ms. Jolene Knapp, CAE
Executive Director
E-MAIL: info@scup.org
URL: www.scup.org

Society for Slovene Studies (O)
Suzzallo Library
Box 352900
University of Washington
Seattle, WA 98195
(206) 543-5588
Mr. Michael Biggins
Secretary
E-MAIL: mbiggins@uw.edu
URL: www.slovenestudies.com

Society for the Advancement of Scandinavian Study (P)
Brigham Young University
3168 JFSB
Provo, UT 84602-6702
(801) 422-5598
Mr. Steven P. Sondrup
Managing Editor
E-MAIL: sass.subscriptions@gmail.com
URL: www.scandinavianstudy.org

Society for Values in Higher Education (Q)
Portland State University
PO Box 751-SVHE
Portland, OR 97207-0751
(503) 725-2575
FAX: (503) 725-2577
Ms. Pamela Montgomery
Director
E-MAIL: society@pdx.edu
URL: www.svhe.org

Society of American Foresters (R)
5400 Grosvenor Lane
Bethesda, MD 20814-2198
(866) 897-8720
FAX: (301) 897-3690
Mr. Michael T. Goergen Jr.
Executive Vice President & CEO
E-MAIL: goergenm@safnet.org
URL: www.safnet.org

Society of American Foresters (SAF) (S)
5400 Grosvenor Lane
Bethesda, MD 20814-2198
(301) 897-8720
FAX: (301) 897-3690
Director of Science and Education
E-MAIL: ScienceEd@safnet.org
URL: www.safnet.org

Society of Professors of Education (T)
University of West Georgia
Department of ELPS
1600 Maple Street
Carrollton, GA 30118-5160
(678) 839-6132
FAX: (678) 839-6097
Dr. Robert C. Morris
Secretary-Treasurer
E-MAIL: rmorris@westga.edu

Southeastern Universities Research Association (U)
1201 New York Avenue, NW
Suite 430
Washington, DC 20005
(202) 408-7872
FAX: (202) 408-8250
Dr. Jerry Draayer
President
E-MAIL: draayer@sura.org
URL: www.sura.org

Southern Association for College Student Affairs (V)
Armstrong Atlantic State University
11935 Abercorn Street
Savannah, GA 31419
(912) 344-2510
FAX: (912) 344-3468
Dr. Joe Buck
Executive Director
E-MAIL: joe.buck@armstrong.edu
URL: www.sacsa.org

Southern Association of Colleges and Schools Commission on Colleges (W)
1866 Southern Lane
Decatur, GA 30033-4097
(404) 679-4500
FAX: (404) 679-4528
Dr. Belle S. Wheelan
President
E-MAIL: bwheelan@sacscoc.org
URL: www.sacscoc.org

Southern Regional Education Board (X)
592 Tenth Street, NW
Atlanta, GA 30318-5790
(404) 875-9211
FAX: (404) 872-1477
Dr. David S. Spence
President
E-MAIL: dave.spence@sreb.org
URL: www.sreb.org

Southern States Communication Association (Y)
Valdosta State University
Communication Arts
1500 N. Patterson
Valdosta, GA 31698
(229) 333-5820
FAX: (229) 293-6182
Dr. Carl M. Cates
Executive Director
E-MAIL: director@ssca.net
URL: www.ssca.net

State Higher Education Executive Officers (Z)
3035 Center Green Drive
Suite 100
Boulder, CO 80301-2205
(303) 541-1600
FAX: (303) 541-1639
Dr. Paul E. Lingenfelter
President
E-MAIL: sheeo@sheeo.org
URL: www.sheeo.org

Teacher Education Accreditation Council (TEAC) (a)
One Dupont Circle, NW
Suite 320
Washington, DC 20036-1110
(202) 466-7236
FAX: (202) 466-7238
Mr. Mark LaCelle-Peterson
President
E-MAIL: teac@teac.org
URL: www.teac.org

Tennessee Independent Colleges and Universities Association (b)
1031 17th Avenue South
Nashville, TN 37212
(615) 242-6400
FAX: (615) 242-8033
Dr. Claude O. Pressnell Jr.
President
E-MAIL: pressnell@ticua.org
URL: www.ticua.org

Transnational Association of Christian Colleges and Schools (TRACS) (c)
PO Box 328
Forest, VA 24551
(434) 525-9539
FAX: (434) 525-9538
Dr. T. Paul Boatner
President
E-MAIL: info@tracs.org
URL: www.tracs.org

The Tuition Exchange, Inc. (d)
3 Bethesda Metro Center
Suite 700
Bethesda, MD 20814
(301) 941-1827
FAX: (301) 657-9776
Mr. Robert D. Shorb
Executive Director/CEO
E-MAIL: rshorb@tuitionexchange.org
URL: www.tuitionexchange.org

UNCF (e)
8260 Willow Oaks Corporate Drive
PO Box 10444
Fairfax, VA 22031-8044
(800) 331-2244
FAX: (703) 205-3575
Dr. Michael L. Lomax
President & CEO
URL: www.uncf.org

University Aviation Association (f)
3410 Skyway Drive
Auburn, AL 36830-6444
(334) 844-2434
FAX: (334) 844-2432
Ms. Carolyn Williamson
Executive Director
E-MAIL: uaamail@uaa.aero
URL: www.uaa.aero

Midtown Detroit, Inc. (g)
3939 Woodward Avenue
Suite 100
Detroit, MI 48201
(313) 420-6000
FAX: (313) 420-6200
Ms. Susan Mosey
President
E-MAIL: detroitmidtown@yahoo.com
URL: www.detroitmidtown.com

University Film and Video Association (h)
Emerson College - VMA
120 Boylston Street
Boston, MA 02116
(866) 647-8382
Mr. Rob Sabal
E-MAIL: ufvahome@gmail.com
URL: www.ufva.org

University Photographers' Association of America (i)
Moraine Valley Community College
9000 West College Park
Palos Hills, IL 60465
(708) 974-5495
FAX: (708) 974-0681
Mr. Glenn Carpenter
UPAA President
E-MAIL: carpenter@morainevalley.edu
URL: www.upaa.org

University Professional & Continuing Education Association (UPCEA) (A)
1 Dupont Circle, NW
Suite 615
Washington, DC 20036
(202) 659-3130
FAX: (202) 785-0374
Dr. Robert J. Hansen
Executive Director & CEO
E-MAIL: postmaster@upcea.edu
URL: www.upcea.edu

Urban Affairs Association (B)
University of Wisconsin-Milwaukee
PO Box 413
Milwaukee, WI 53201-0413
(414) 229-3025
E-MAIL: info@uaamail.com
URL: www.urbanaffairsassociation.org

Western Association of Schools and Colleges Accrediting Commission for Community and Junior Colleges (C)
10 Commercial Boulevard
Suite 204
Novato, CA 94949
(415) 506-0234
FAX: (415) 506-0238
Dr. Barbara A. Beno
President
E-MAIL: accjc@accjc.org
URL: www.accjc.org

Western Association of Schools and Colleges Accrediting Commission for Schools (D)
533 Airport Boulevard
Suite 200
Burlingame, CA 94010
(650) 696-1060
FAX: (650) 696-1867
Dr. David E. Brown
Executive Director
E-MAIL: mail@acswasc.org

Western Association of Schools and Colleges Accrediting Commission for Senior Colleges and Universities (E)
985 Atlantic Avenue
Suite 100
Alameda, CA 94501
(510) 748-9001
FAX: (510) 748-9797
Mr. Ralph A. Wolff
President & Executive Director
E-MAIL: wascsr@wascsenior.org
URL: www.wascsenior.org

Western Interstate Commission for Higher Education (F)
3035 Center Green Drive
Suite 200
Boulder, CO 80301-2204
(303) 541-0201
FAX: (303) 541-0245
Dr. David A. Longanecker
President
E-MAIL: dlonganecker@wiche.edu
URL: www.wiche.edu

Women in Higher Education (G)
5376 Farmco Drive
Madison, WI 53704
(608) 251-3232
FAX: (608) 284-0601
Ms. Mary Dee Wenniger
E-MAIL: women@wihe.com
URL: www.wihe.com

Consortia of Institutions of Higher Education

Alliance for Higher Education (A)
PO Box 836696
Richardson, TX 75083-6696
(972) 883-4920
FAX: (972) 883-4919
URL: www.ntxrcic.org

Arkansas' Independent Colleges and Universities (B)
One Riverfront Place
Suite 610
US Bank Building
North Little Rock, AR 72114
(501) 378-0843
FAX: (501) 374-1523
Mr. Rex Nelson
President
E-MAIL: rnelson@arkindcolleges.org
URL: www.arkindcolleges.org

Associated Colleges of Central Kansas (C)
210 South Main Street
McPherson, KS 67460
(620) 241-5150
FAX: (620) 241-5153
URL: www.acck.edu

Associated Colleges of the Midwest (D)
205 West Wacker Drive
Suite 220
Chicago, IL 60606
(312) 263-5000
FAX: (312) 263-5879
Dr. Christopher Welna
President
E-MAIL: acm@acm.edu
URL: www.acm.edu

Associated Colleges of the Twin Cities (ACTC) (E)
570 Asbury Street
Suite 109
St. Paul, MN 55104
(651) 556-1863
FAX: (651) 294-8959
Dr. Carole Chabries
Executive Director
E-MAIL: info@actc-mn.org
URL: www.actc-mn.org

Association of Independent California Colleges and Universities (F)
1100 Eleventh Street
Suite 10
Sacramento, CA 95814
(916) 446-7626
FAX: (916) 446-7948
Ms. Kristen Soares
President
E-MAIL: aiccu@aiccu.edu
URL: www.aiccu.edu

Association of Independent Colleges and Universities in Massachusetts (G)
11 Beacon Street
Suite 1224
Boston, MA 02108-3093
(617) 742-5147
FAX: (617) 742-3089
Mr. Richard Doherty
President
E-MAIL: richard.doherty@bc.edu
URL: www.masscolleges.org -or- www.aicum.org

Association of Independent Colleges and Universities in New Jersey (H)
797 Springfield Avenue
Summit, NJ 07901-1107
(908) 277-3738
FAX: (908) 277-0851
Mr. John B. Wilson
President and CEO
E-MAIL: jbwilson@njcolleges.org
URL: www.njcolleges.org

Association of Independent Colleges and Universities of Michigan (I)
124 West Allegan Street
Suite 650
Lansing, MI 48933-1707
(517) 372-9160
FAX: (517) 372-9165
Dr. Edward O. Blews Jr.
President

Association of Independent Colleges and Universities of Nebraska (J)
635 South 14th Street
Suite 310
Lincoln, NE 68508
(402) 434-2818
FAX: (402) 434-2825
Mr. Thomas O'Neill
President
E-MAIL: tiponeill2@aol.com

Association of Independent Colleges and Universities of Ohio (K)
41 South High Street
Suite 2424
Columbus, OH 43215
(614) 228-2196
FAX: (614) 228-8406
Mr. C. Todd Jones
President & General Counsel
E-MAIL: tjones@aicuo.edu
URL: www.aicuo.edu

Association of Independent Colleges and Universities of Pennsylvania (L)
101 North Front Street
Harrisburg, PA 17101-1405
(717) 232-8649
FAX: (717) 233-8574
Dr. Don L. Francis
President
E-MAIL: francis@aicup.org
URL: www.aicup.org

Association of Independent Colleges and Universities of Rhode Island (M)
30 Exchange Terrace
Providence, RI 02903
(401) 272-8270
FAX: (401) 272-9194
Mr. Daniel Egan
President
E-MAIL: pmulcahey@aicuri.org
URL: www.aicuri.org

Association of Independent Colleges of Art & Design (N)
3957 22nd Street
San Francisco, CA 94114-3205
(415) 642-8595
Mr. William O. Barrett
Executive Director
URL: www.aicad.org

Association of Independent Kentucky Colleges and Universities (O)
484 Chenault Road
Frankfort, KY 40601
(502) 695-5007
FAX: (502) 695-5057
Dr. Gary S. Cox
President
E-MAIL: gary.cox@aikcu.org
URL: www.aikcu.org

Association of Vermont Independent Colleges (P)
PO Box 254
Montpelier, VT 05601
(802) 828-8826
Susan Stitely
President
E-MAIL: sstitely@vermont-icolleges.org
URL: www.vermont-icolleges.org

Atlanta Regional Council for Higher Education (Q)
133 Peachtree Street NE
Suite 4925
Atlanta, GA 30303-2923
(404) 651-2668
FAX: (404) 880-9816
Mr. Michael A. Gerber
President
E-MAIL: arche@atlantahighered.org
URL: www.atlantahighered.org

Boston Theological Institute (R)
210 Herrick Road
Newton Centre, MA 02459
(617) 527-4880
FAX: (617) 527-1073
Dr. Rodney Petersen
Executive Director
E-MAIL: btioffice@bostontheological.org
URL: www.bostontheological.org

Central Pennsylvania Consortium (S)
c/o Franklin & Marshall College
PO Box 3003
Lancaster, PA 17604-3003
(717) 291-4282
FAX: (717) 358-4455
Ms. Kathryn Missildine
Executive Assistant
E-MAIL: kathy.missildine@fandm.edu
URL: www.fandm.edu/cpc

CHESLA (T)
21 Talcott Notch Rd
Suite 1
Farmington, CT 06032
(860) 678-7788
FAX: (860) 678-0006
Ms. Gloria F. Ragosta
Executive Director
E-MAIL: ragostag@theccic.org
URL: www.chesla.org

Christian College Consortium (U)
255 Grapevine Road
Wenham, MA 01984-1813
(978) 867-4755
FAX: (978) 867-4650
Dr. Stan Gaede
President
E-MAIL: stan.gaede@gordon.edu
URL: www.ccconsortium.org

Colleges of Worcester Consortium, Inc. (V)
484 Main Street
Suite 500
Worcester, MA 01608
(508) 754-6829
FAX: (508) 797-0069
Mr. Mark Bilotta
CEO
E-MAIL: mbilotta@cowc.org
URL: www.cowc.org

Community College Leadership Consortium & Futures Assembly (W)
University of Florida, College of Education
Box 117049
229 Norman Hall
Gainesville, FL 32611-7049
(352) 273-4300
FAX: (352) 846-2697
Dr. Dale F. Campbell
Director
E-MAIL: dfc@coe.ufl.edu
URL: futures.education.ufl.edu/index.html

The Consortium for Graduate Study in Management (X)
5585 Pershing Avenue
Suite 240
St. Louis, MO 63112-1795
(314) 877-5500
FAX: (314) 877-5505
Mr. Peter J. Aranda III
Executive Director and CEO
E-MAIL: recruiting@cgsm.org
URL: www.cgsm.org

Consortium for the Advancement of Adult Higher Education (Y)
4025 South Riverpoint Parkway
Mail Stop CF-K601
Phoenix, AZ 85040
(602) 557-1153
Dr. Sue Salter Dietrich
Executive Director
E-MAIL: sue.dietrich@ipd.org
URL: www.caahe.org

Consortium of College & University Media Centers (Z)
Indiana University
601 East Kirkwood Ave
Franklin Hall 0009
Bloomington, IN 47405-1223
(812) 855-6049
FAX: (812)855-2103
Aileen Scales
Executive Director
E-MAIL: ccumc@ccumc.org
URL: www.ccumc.org

Consortium of Universities of the Washington Metropolitan Area (a)
1025 Connecticut Avenue, NW
Suite 705
Washington, DC 20036
(202) 331-8080
FAX: (202) 331-7925
Mr. John B. Childers
President & CEO
E-MAIL: childers@consortium.org
URL: www.consortium.org

Consortium on Financing Higher Education (b)
238 Main Street
Suite 402
Cambridge, MA 02142-1046
(617) 253-5030
FAX: (617) 258-8280
Dr. Kristine E. Dillon
President
E-MAIL: kedillon@mit.edu
URL: www.cofhe.org

Cooperating Raleigh Colleges (c)
Meredith College
3800 Hillsborough Street
Raleigh, NC 27607-5298
(919) 760-8538
FAX: (919) 760-2194
Ms. Jenny Spiker
Director
E-MAIL: crc@meredith.edu
URL: www.crcraleighcolleges.org

Council of Independent Colleges in Virginia (d)
PO Box 1005
Bedford, VA 24523
(540) 586-0606
FAX: (540) 586-2630
Mr. Robert B. Lambeth Jr.
President
E-MAIL: lambeth@cicv.org
URL: www.cicv.org

Council of North Central Two Year Colleges (e)
513 Split Rock Drive
Jefferson City, MO 65109
(573) 634-4848
FAX: (573) 634-4811
Dr. James S. Kellerman
Executive Director
E-MAIL: cnctyc@embarqmail.com
URL: www.cnctyc.org

Council of Presidents (f)
410 Eleventh Avenue, SE
Suite 101
Olympia, WA 98501
(360) 292-4100
FAX: (360) 292-4110
Mr. Mike Rellly
Executive Director
E-MAIL: mreilly@cop.wsu.edu
URL: www.cop.wsu.edu

Federation of Independent Illinois Colleges and Universities (g)
1123 South Second Street
Springfield, IL 62704
(217) 789-1400
FAX: (217) 789-6259
Mr. David W. Tretter
President
E-MAIL: davetretter@federationedu.org
URL: www.federationedu.org

Five Colleges, Incorporated (h)
97 Spring Street
Amherst, MA 01002
(413) 256-8316
FAX: (413) 256-0249
Dr. Neal B. Abraham
Executive Director
E-MAIL: nabraham@fivecolleges.edu
URL: www.fivecolleges.edu

Georgia Independent College Association (i)
600 West Peachtree St. NW
Suite 1510
Atlanta, GA 30308
(404) 233-5433
FAX: (404) 233-6309
Dr. Susanna Baxter
President
E-MAIL: sbaxter@georgiacolleges.org
URL: www.georgiacolleges.org

Graduate Theological Foundation Oxford/Rome/Indiana Consortia (A)
Dodge House
415 Lincoln Way East
Mishawaka, IN 46544-2213
(800) 423-5983
Bethany Morgan MBA
Registrar
E-MAIL: information@gtfeducation.org
URL: www.gtfeducation.org

Great Lakes Colleges Association (B)
535 West William
Suite 301
Ann Arbor, MI 48103
(734) 661-2350
FAX: (734) 661-2349
Dr. Richard A. Detweiler
President
E-MAIL: detweiler@glca.org
URL: www.glca.org

Greater Cincinnati Consortium of Colleges and Universities (C)
Northern Kentucky University
241 Campbell Hall
Highland Heights, KY 41099
(859) 392-2424
Ms. Janet Piccirillo
Executive Director
E-MAIL: gcccu@nku.edu
URL: www.gcccu.org

Hartford Consortium for Higher Education (D)
31 Pratt Street
4th Floor
Hartford, CT 06103
(860) 702-3808
FAX: (860) 241-1130
Ms. Margaret W. Nareff
Executive Director
E-MAIL: mnareff@metrohartford.com
URL: www.hartfordconsortium.org

Higher Education Consortium for Urban Affairs, Inc. (HECUA) (E)
2233 University Avenue West
Suite 210
St. Paul, MN 55114
(651) 646-8831
FAX: (651) 659-9421
Dr. Jenny Keyser
Executive Director
E-MAIL: hecua@hecua.org
URL: www.hecua.org

Higher Education Consortium of Metropolitan St. Louis (F)
8420 Delmar Boulevard
Suite 504
St. Louis, MO 63124
(314) 991-2700
FAX: (314) 991-2874
URL: www.heccstl.com

Higher Education Data Sharing Consortium (G)
Franklin and Marshall College
PO Box 3003
Lancaster, PA 17604-3003
(717) 358-4448
FAX: (717) 358-4456
Sandra Atkins
Assistant Director
E-MAIL: satkins@e-heds.org
URL: www.e-heds.org

Independent Colleges and Universities of Missouri (H)
PO Box 1865
Jefferson City, MO 65102-1865
(573) 635-9160
FAX: (573) 635-6258
Dr. Marianne Inman
President
E-MAIL: bill@molobby.com
URL: www.icum.org

Independent Colleges and Universities of Texas, Inc. (I)
PO Box 13105
Austin, TX 78701-3105
(512) 472-9522
FAX: (512) 472-2371
Dr. Carol McDonald
President
E-MAIL: carol.mcdonald@icut.org
URL: www.icut.org

Independent Colleges of Indiana Inc. (J)
3135 North Meridian Street
Indianapolis, IN 46208
(317) 236-6090
FAX: (317) 236-6086
Dr. Richard Ludwick
President and CEO
E-MAIL: rludwick@icindiana.org
URL: www.icindiana.org

Independent Colleges of Washington (K)
600 Stewart Street
Suite 600
Seattle, WA 98101
(206) 623-4494
FAX: (206) 625-9621
Ms. Violet A. Boyer
President & CEO
E-MAIL: violet@icwashington.org
URL: www.icwashington.org

Inter-University Consortium for Political and Social Research (L)
The University of Michigan
Institute for Social Research
PO Box 1248
Ann Arbor, MI 48106-1248
(734) 615-8400
FAX: (734) 647-8200
Dr. George Alter
Acting Director
E-MAIL: netmail@icpsr.umich.edu
URL: www.icpsr.umich.edu

Iowa Association of Independent Colleges and Universities (M)
505 Fifth Avenue
Suite 1030
Des Moines, IA 50309
(515) 282-3175
FAX: (515) 282-8177
Mr. Gary W. Steinke
President
E-MAIL: president@iaicu.org
URL: www.iowaprivatecolleges.org

Kansas Independent College Association (N)
700 S. Kansas Avenue
Suite 622 A
Topeka, KS 66603
(785) 235-9877
FAX: (785) 235-1437
Dr. Douglas A. Penner
President
E-MAIL: dpenner@kscolleges.org
URL: www.kscolleges.org

Kentuckiana Metroversity (O)
200 West Broadway
Suite 800
Louisville, KY 40202
(502) 213-4562
Kathleen Mandlehr Ed.D.
Executive Director
E-MAIL: ktmand01@louisville.edu
URL: www.metroversity.org

Lehigh Valley Association of Independent Colleges (P)
130 West Greenwich Street
Bethlehem, PA 18018
(610) 625-7888
FAX: (610) 625-7891
Dr. Evelyn C. Lynch
Executive Director
E-MAIL: lynche@lvaic.org
URL: www.lvaic.org

Louisiana Association of Independent Colleges and Universities (Q)
320 Third Street
Suite 104
Baton Rouge, LA 70801
(225) 389-9885
FAX: (225) 389-0149
Ms. Mary Ann Coleman
President
E-MAIL: maryann@laicu.org
URL: www.laicu.org

Maine Independent Colleges Association (R)
University of New England
11 Hills Beach Road
Biddeford, ME 04005
(207) 602-2306
FAX: (207) 602-5925
Dr. Danielle N. Ripich
President
E-MAIL: dripich@une.edu
URL: www.une.edu

Maryland Independent College and University Association (S)
60 West Street
Suite 201
Annapolis, MD 21401
(410) 269-0306
FAX: (410) 269-5905
Ms. Tina M. Bjarekull
President
E-MAIL: lstrayer@micua.org
URL: www.micua.org

Midwest Universities Consortium for International Activities, Inc. (T)
4700 South Hagadorn Road
Suite 150
East Lansing, MI 48823-6808
(517) 432-0661
FAX: (517) 432-4457
Dr. Philip R. Smith
President & Executive Director
E-MAIL: mucia@msu.edu
URL: www.muciainc.org

Minnesota Private College Council (U)
445 Minnesota Street
Suite 500
St. Paul, MN 55101
(651) 228-9061
FAX: (651) 228-0379
E-MAIL: colleges@mnprivatecolleges.org
URL: www.mnprivatecolleges.org

Mississippi Association of Independent Colleges and Universities (V)
PO Box 2933
Ridgeland, MS 39158-2933
(601) 957-2052
FAX: (601) 977-0233
Dr. E. Harold Fisher
Executive Director
E-MAIL: ehfisher@bellsouth.net

National Student Exchange (W)
4656 West Jefferson
Suite 140
Fort Wayne, IN 46804
(260) 436-2634
FAX: (260) 436-5676
Ms. Bette Worley
President
E-MAIL: bworley@nse2.org
URL: www.nse.org

New England Faculty Development Consortium (X)
New England Institute of Technology
1408 Division Road
East Greenwich, RI 02818
(401) 739-5000
Mr. Thomas R. Thibodeau
President
E-MAIL: tthibodeau@neit.edu
URL: www.nefdc.org

New Hampshire College & University Council (Y)
3 Barrell Court
Suite 100
Concord, NH 03301-8543
(603) 225-4199
FAX: (603) 225-8108
E-MAIL: horgan@nhcuc.org
URL: www.nhcuc.org

New Jersey Association of State Colleges and Universities (Z)
150 West State Street
Trenton, NJ 08608
(609) 989-1100
FAX: (609) 989-7017
Dr. Darryl G. Greer
CEO
E-MAIL: njascu@njascu.org
URL: www.njascu.org

New Jersey Council of County Colleges (a)
330 West State Street
Trenton, NJ 08618
(609) 392-3434
FAX: (609) 392-8158
Dr. Lawrence A. Nespoli
President
E-MAIL: info@njccc.org
URL: www.njccc.org

New Mexico Independent College Fund (b)
c/o St. John's College
Office of the President
1160 Camino Cruz Blanca
Santa Fe, NM 87505
(505) 984-6098
FAX: (505) 984-6031
E-MAIL: president@sjcsf.edu
URL: www.sjcsf.edu

New Orleans Educational Telecommunications Consortium, Inc. (c)
5000 West Esplanade Avenue
#290
Metairie, LA 70006
(504) 524-0350
E-MAIL: noetc@noetc.org
URL: www.noetc.org

North Carolina Independent Colleges and Universities (d)
530 North Blount Street
Raleigh, NC 27604
(919) 832-5817
FAX: (919) 833-0794
Dr. A. Hope Williams
President
E-MAIL: williams@ncicu.org
URL: www.ncicu.org

North Carolina Piedmont Automated Library System (NC-PALS) (e)
Bennett College
900 E. Washington Street
Greensboro, NC 27401
(336) 517-2158
FAX: (336) 370-8653
Dr. Millicent Rainey
Chair of the Executive Board
E-MAIL: mrainey@bennett.edu
URL: www.nc-pals.org

North Dakota Independent College Fund (f)
University of Mary
7500 University Drive
Bismarck, ND 58504-9652
(701) 355-8222
FAX: (701) 255-7687
Mr. Neal Kalberer
Executive Director
E-MAIL: kalberer@umary.edu

Northeast Consortium of Colleges and Universities in Massachusetts (g)
Merrimack College
315 Turnpike Street
North Andover, MA 01845
(978) 837-5131
FAX: (978) 837-5403
Ms. Linda Murphy
Assistant Vice President of Personnel
E-MAIL: murphyl@merrimack.edu
URL: www.merrimack.edu

Northeast Ohio Council on Higher Education (h)
1422 Euclid Avenue
Suite 840
Cleveland, OH 44115
(216) 420-9200
FAX: (216) 420-9292
Ms. Ann Womer Benjamin
Executive Director
E-MAIL: awomerbenjamin@noche.org
URL: www.noche.org

Oak Ridge Associated Universities (i)
PRES-CAB-22
PO Box 117
Oak Ridge, TN 37831-0117
(865) 576-3300
FAX: (865) 576-3816
Mr. Harry A. Page
President and CEO
E-MAIL: andy.page@orau.org
URL: www.orau.org

The Ohio College Association, Inc. (j)
10 West Broad Street
Suite 450
Columbus, OH 43215
(614) 464-1266
FAX: (614) 464-9281
Ms. Cindy McQuade
URL: www.ohiocollege.org

Consortia of Institutions of Higher Education

Oklahoma Independent Colleges and Universities (A)
PO Box 57148
Oklahoma City, OK 73157-7148
(405) 371-1780
Lesa Smaligo
Executive Director
E-MAIL: lesa@oicu.org
URL: www.oicu.org

Oregon Independent Colleges Association (B)
7150 SW Hampton
Suite 101
Portland, OR 97223
(503) 639-4541
FAX: (503) 639-4851
Dr. Gary K. Andeen
President & CEO
E-MAIL: andeen@oicanet.org
URL: www.oicanet.org

Pennsylvania State System of Higher Education Foundation, Inc. (C)
2986 North Second Street
Harrisburg, PA 17110
(717) 720-4056
FAX: (717) 720-7082
Ms. Jennifer S. Scipioni
President/CEO
E-MAIL: jscipioni@thepafoundation.org
URL: www.thepafoundation.org

Pittsburgh Council on Higher Education (D)
201 Wood Street
Pittsburgh, PA 15222-1912
(412) 392-4217
FAX: (412) 392-4218
Mr. Kenneth P. Service
Executive Director
E-MAIL: kservice@pointpark.edu
URL: www.pchepa.org

Quad-Cities Graduate Study Center (E)
331 W. 3rd Street
Suite 100, Room 128
Davenport, IA 52801
(563) 322-0016
Marti Clyde
Director
E-MAIL: qc@gradcenter.org
URL: www.gradcenter.org

Quad-Cities Graduate Study Center (F)
WIU - QC Campus
3561 60th Street
Moline, IL 61265
(309) 762-9481
Shirley Moore
Administrative Assistant
E-MAIL: shirley@gradcenter.org
URL: www.gradcenter.org

South Carolina Independent Colleges & Universities, Inc. (G)
PO Box 12007
Columbia, SC 29211
(803) 799-7122
FAX: (803) 254-7504
Mr. Michael G. LeFever
President & CEO
E-MAIL: mike@scicu.org
URL: www.scicu.org

South Metropolitan Higher Education Consortium (H)
One University Parkway
University Park, IL 60484
(708) 534-4984
FAX: (708) 534-8458
Ms. Genevieve Boesen
Executive Director
E-MAIL: gboesen@govst.edu
URL: www.southmetroed.org

Southern Regional Education Board (I)
592 10th Street, NW
Atlanta, GA 30318-5776
(404) 875-9211, ext. 221
FAX: (404) 872-1477
Mr. Dave Spence
President
E-MAIL: dave.spence@sreb.org
URL: www.sreb.org

Southwestern Ohio Council for Higher Education (SOCHE) (J)
3155 Research Boulevard
Suite 204
Dayton, OH 45420-4015
(937) 258-8890
FAX: (937) 258-8899
Dr. Sean Creighton
Executive Director
E-MAIL: soche@soche.org
URL: www.soche.org

Texas International Education Consortium (K)
1103 West 24th Street
Austin, TX 78705
(512) 477-9283, ext. 114
FAX: (512) 322-9079
Dr. Ronald Aqua
President & CEO
E-MAIL: ron.aqua@tiec.org
URL: www.tiec.org

Tuition Plan Consortium (L)
700 Rosedale
Suite 1620
St. Louis, MO 63112
(314) 727-0900
FAX: (314) 727-0930
Ms. Barbara Floreth
Vice President
E-MAIL: barb@pc529.com
URL: www.privatecollege529plan.com

University City Science Center (M)
3711 Market Street
8th Floor
Philadelphia, PA 19104
(215) 966-6000
FAX: (215(966-6002
Dr. Stephen Tang
President & CEO
E-MAIL: info@sciencecenter.org
URL: www.sciencecenter.org

The Virginia College Fund (N)
4900 Augusta Avenue
Suite 101
Richmond, VA 23230
(804) 355-3271
FAX: (804) 359-5765
Mr. James K. Dill
President
E-MAIL: jkdill@thevcf.org
URL: www.thevcf.org

Virginia Tidewater Consortium for Higher Education (O)
4900 Powhatan Avenue
Norfolk, VA 23508-1836
(757) 683-3183
FAX: (757) 683-4515
Dr. Lawrence G. Dotolo
President
E-MAIL: lgdotolo@aol.com
URL: www.vtc.odu.edu

Washington Theological Consortium (P)
487 Michigan Avenue, NE
Washington, DC 20017
(202) 832-2675
FAX: (202) 526-0818
Rev. John Crossin OSFS
Executive Director
E-MAIL: wtc@washtheocon.org
URL: www.washtheocon.org

West Virginia Independent Colleges & Universities, Inc. (Q)
900 Lee Street
Suite 910
Charleston, WV 25301
(304) 345-5525
FAX: (304) 345-5526
Mr. Ben Exley IV
Executive Director
E-MAIL: benexley@wvicu.org
URL: www.wvicu.org

Wisconsin Association of Independent Colleges and Universities (R)
122 West Washington Avenue
Suite 700
Madison, WI 53703-2723
(608) 256-7761
FAX: (608) 256-7065
Dr. Rolf Wegenke
President
E-MAIL: mail@waicu.org
URL: www.waicu.org

NAME INDEX
US Department of Education Offices, Statewide Agencies of Higher Education, Higher Education Associations, Consortia of Institutions of Higher Education

Institutions By Religious Affiliation

African Methodist Episcopal
Allen University ... SC
Edward Waters College ... FL
Paul Quinn College ... TX
Payne Theological Seminary ... OH
Shorter College ... AR
Wilberforce University ... OH

African Methodist Episcopal Zion Church
Clinton Junior College ... SC
Hood Theological Seminary ... NC
Livingstone College ... NC

Alabama Baptist State Convention
Judson College ... AL

American Baptist
Alderson Broaddus College ... WV
American Baptist Seminary of the West .. CA
Bacone College ... OK
Eastern University ... PA
Franklin College of Indiana ... IN
Judson University ... IL
Linfield College ... OR
Northern Seminary ... IL
Ottawa University ... KS
Ottawa University Arizona ... AZ
Ottawa University Jeffersonville ... IN
Ottawa University Kansas City ... KS
Ottawa University Wisconsin ... WI
Palmer Theological Seminary of Eastern University ... PA
University of Sioux Falls ... SD

Assemblies Of God Church
American Indian College of the Assemblies of God ... AZ
Assemblies of God Theological Seminary MO
Bethel College ... VA
Central Bible College ... MO
Evangel University ... MO
Global University ... MO
North Central University ... MN
Northwest University ... WA
Southeastern University ... FL
Southwestern Assemblies of God University ... TX
Trinity Bible College ... ND
Valley Forge Christian College ... PA
Vanguard University of Southern California ... CA
Zion Bible College ... MA

Baptist
American Baptist College ... TN
Arkansas Baptist College ... AR
Arlington Baptist College ... TX
Baptist Bible College ... MO
Baptist Bible College and Seminary ... PA
Baptist Missionary Association Theological Seminary ... TX
Baptist University of the Americas ... TX
Baylor University ... TX
Bethel University ... MN
Bluefield College ... VA
Boston Baptist College ... MA
Brewton-Parker College ... GA
Campbell University ... NC
Campbellsville University ... KY
Cedarville University ... OH
Central Baptist College ... AR
Central Baptist Theological Seminary ... KS
Central Baptist Theological Seminary ... VA
Central Baptist Theological Seminary of Minneapolis ... MN
Chowan University ... NC
Dallas Baptist University ... TX
Gardner-Webb University ... NC
Georgetown College ... KY
Hardin-Simmons University ... TX
Howard Payne University ... TX
Huntsville Bible College ... AL
International Baptist College ... AZ
Jacksonville College ... TX
Liberty University ... VA
Maple Springs Baptist Bible College & Seminary ... MD
Missouri Baptist University ... MO
Morris College ... SC
Northland International University ... WI
Oakland City University ... IN
Selma University ... AL
Shaw University ... NC
Shorter University ... GA
Simmons College of Kentucky ... KY
Southeastern Baptist College ... MS
Temple Baptist College ... OH
Tennessee Temple University ... TN
The John Leland Center for Theological Studies ... VA
Trinity Baptist College ... FL
Truett McConnell College ... GA
University of the Cumberlands ... KY
Virginia Baptist College ... VA
Virginia Intermont College ... VA
Virginia Union University ... VA
Washington Baptist University ... VA

Brethren Church
Ashland University ... OH

Christian Church (Disciples Of Christ)
Barton College ... NC
Bethany College ... WV
Chapman University ... CA
Christian Theological Seminary ... IN
Columbia College ... MO
Culver-Stockton College ... MO
Eureka College ... IL
Jarvis Christian College ... TX
Lexington Theological Seminary ... KY
Lynchburg College ... VA
Midway College ... KY
Northwest Christian University ... OR
Phillips Theological Seminary ... OK
Texas Christian University ... TX
Transylvania University ... KY
William Woods University ... MO

Christian Churches And Churches of Christ
Boise Bible College ... ID
Central Christian College of the Bible ... MO
Cincinnati Christian University ... OH
Crossroads College ... MN
Dallas Christian College ... TX
Emmanuel Christian Seminary ... TN
Great Lakes Christian College ... MI
Johnson University ... TN
Kentucky Christian University ... KY
Lincoln Christian University ... IL
Manhattan Christian College ... KS
Nebraska Christian College ... NE
Piedmont College ... GA
Point University ... GA

Christian Methodist Episcopal
Lane College ... TN
Miles College ... AL
Texas College ... TX

Christian Reformed Church
Calvin College ... MI
Calvin Theological Seminary ... MI
Dordt College ... IA

Church Of Christ
Pepperdine University ... CA

Church Of God
Anderson University ... IN
Colegio Biblico Pentecostal De Puerto Rico ... PR
Lee University ... TN
Mid-America Christian University ... OK
Pentecostal Theological Seminary ... TN
The University of Findlay ... OH
Warner Pacific College ... OR
Warner University ... FL

Church of God in Christ
All Saints Bible College ... TN

Church of New Jerusalem
Bryn Athyn College of the New Church ... PA

Church Of The Brethren
Bethany Theological Seminary ... IN
Bridgewater College ... VA
Elizabethtown College ... PA
Manchester College ... IN
McPherson College ... KS

Church Of The Nazarene
Eastern Nazarene College ... MA
MidAmerica Nazarene University ... KS
Mount Vernon Nazarene University ... OH
Nazarene Bible College ... CO
Nazarene Theological Seminary ... MO
Northwest Nazarene University ... ID
Olivet Nazarene University ... IL
Point Loma Nazarene University ... CA
Southern Nazarene University ... OK
Trevecca Nazarene University ... TN

Churches Of Christ
Abilene Christian University ... TX
Amridge University ... AL
Crowley's Ridge College ... AR
Faulkner University ... AL
Freed-Hardeman University ... TN
Harding School of Theology ... TN
Harding University Main Campus ... AR
Heritage Christian University ... AL
Lipscomb University ... TN
Lubbock Christian University ... TX
Mid-Atlantic Christian University ... NC
Ohio Valley University ... WV
Southwestern Christian College ... TX
York College ... NE

Cumberland Presbyterian
Bethel University ... TN
Memphis Theological Seminary ... TN

Evangelical Congregational Church
Evangelical Theological Seminary ... PA

Evangelical Covenant Church Of America
North Park University ... IL

Evangelical Free Church Of America
Trinity International University ... IL
Trinity International University, Florida Regional Center ... FL

Evangelical Lutheran Church In America
Augsburg College ... MN
Augustana College ... IL
Augustana College ... SD
Bethany College ... KS
California Lutheran University ... CA
Capital University ... OH
Carthage College ... WI
Concordia College ... MN
Finlandia University ... MI
Gettysburg College ... PA
Grand View University ... IA
Gustavus Adolphus College ... MN
Lenoir-Rhyne University ... NC
Luther College ... IA
Luther Seminary ... MN
Lutheran School of Theology at Chicago IL
Lutheran Theological Seminary at Gettysburg ... PA
Lutheran Theological Seminary at Philadelphia ... PA
Lutheran Theological Southern Seminary SC
Midland University ... NE
Muhlenberg College ... PA
Newberry College ... SC
Pacific Lutheran Theological Seminary ... CA
Pacific Lutheran University ... WA
Roanoke College ... VA
St. Olaf College ... MN
Susquehanna University ... PA
Texas Lutheran University ... TX
Thiel College ... PA
Trinity Lutheran Seminary ... OH
Wartburg College ... IA
Wartburg Theological Seminary ... IA
Wittenberg University ... OH

Evangelical Lutheran Synod
Bethany Lutheran College ... MN

Fellowship Of Grace Brethren Churches
Grace College and Seminary ... IN

Free Methodist
Central Christian College of Kansas ... KS
Greenville College ... IL
Seattle Pacific University ... WA
Spring Arbor University ... MI

Free Will Baptist Church
California Christian College ... CA
Free Will Baptist Bible College ... TN
Hillsdale Free Will Baptist College ... OK

Friends
Earlham College and Earlham School of Religion ... IN
George Fox University ... OR
Guilford College ... NC
Malone University ... OH
William Penn University ... IA
Wilmington College ... OH

Greek Orthodox
Hellenic College-Holy Cross Greek Orthodox School of Theology ... MA

Interdenominational
Carolina Graduate School of Divinity ... NC
Denver Seminary ... CO
Evangelical Seminary of Puerto Rico ... PR
Faith Evangelical College & Seminary ... WA
God's Bible School and College ... OH
INSTE Bible College ... IA
Interdenominational Theological Center .. GA
Messiah College ... PA
Oak Hills Christian College ... MN
Palm Beach Atlantic University ... FL
Phoenix Seminary ... AZ
Rocky Mountain College ... MT
Shepherd University School of Theology . CA
South Florida Bible College ... FL
Wesley Biblical Seminary ... MS

Jewish
Academy for Jewish Religion ... CA
Hebrew Union College-Jewish Institute of Religion ... OH
Hebrew Union College-Jewish Institute of Religion (California Branch) ... CA
Hebrew Union College-Jewish Institute of Religion (New York Branch) ... NY
Rabbi Isaac Elchanan Theological Seminary ... NY
Reconstructionist Rabbinical College ... PA

Latter-day Saints
Brigham Young University ... UT
Brigham Young University Hawaii ... HI
Brigham Young University-Idaho ... ID
Latter-Day Saints Business College ... UT

Lutheran
Valparaiso University ... IN

Lutheran Church - Missouri Synod
Concordia College ... AL
Concordia College ... NY
Concordia Seminary ... MO
Concordia Theological Seminary ... IN
Concordia University ... CA
Concordia University ... MI
Concordia University ... NE
Concordia University ... OR
Concordia University Chicago ... IL
Concordia University Texas ... TX
Concordia University Wisconsin ... WI
Concordia University, St. Paul ... MN

Mennonite Brethren Church
Fresno Pacific University ... CA
Tabor College ... KS

Mennonite Church
Associated Mennonite Biblical Seminary . IN
Bethel College ... KS
Bluffton University ... OH
Eastern Mennonite University ... VA
Goshen College ... IN
Hesston College ... KS
Rosedale Bible College ... OH

Missionary Church
Bethel College ... IN

Moravian Church
Moravian College ... PA
Salem College ... NC

Multiple Protestant Denominations
Huston-Tillotson University ... TX
LeMoyne-Owen College ... TN
Paine College ... GA

Non-denominational
Belmont University ... TN
Carolina Bible College ... NC
Clearwater Christian College ... FL
Faith Theological Seminary ... MD
Montreat College ... NC
Providence Christian College ... CA

University of Fort Lauderdale ... FL
Williamson Christian College ... TN

North American Baptist
Sioux Falls Seminary ... SD

Original Free Will Baptist Church
Mount Olive College ... NC

Other Protestant
Beulah Heights University ... GA
Mars Hill College ... NC
Ohio Christian University ... OH
Saint Louis Christian College ... MO
Urshan Graduate School of Theology ... MO

Pentecostal Church of God
Messenger College ... MO
Universidad Pentecostal Mizpa ... PR

Pentecostal Holiness Church
Emmanuel College ... GA
Southwestern Christian University ... OK

Pentecostal/Charismatic Non-Denominational
Christian Life College ... IL

Presbyterian Church (U.S.A.)
Agnes Scott College ... GA
Austin College ... TX
Austin Presbyterian Theological Seminary ... TX
Belhaven University ... MS
Blackburn College ... IL
Bloomfield College ... NJ
Buena Vista University ... IA
Carroll University ... WI
Columbia Theological Seminary ... GA
Davidson College ... NC
Davis & Elkins College ... WV
Eckerd College ... FL
Grove City College ... PA
Hampden-Sydney College ... VA
Hanover College ... IN
Hastings College ... NE
Jamestown College ... ND
King College ... TN
Lees-McRae College ... NC
Louisville Presbyterian Theological Seminary ... KY
Lyon College ... AR
Macalester College ... MN
Mary Baldwin College ... VA
Maryville College ... TN
McCormick Theological Seminary ... IL
Millikin University ... IL
Missouri Valley College ... MO
Monmouth College ... IL
Muskingum University ... OH
Peace College ... NC
Pittsburgh Theological Seminary ... PA
Presbyterian College ... SC
Princeton Theological Seminary ... NJ
Queens University of Charlotte ... NC
Rhodes College ... TN
San Francisco Theological Seminary ... CA
Schreiner University ... TX
St. Andrews Presbyterian College ... NC
Sterling College ... KS
Stillman College ... AL
Tusculum College ... TN
Union Presbyterian Seminary ... VA
University of Dubuque ... IA
University of Pikeville ... KY
University of the Ozarks ... AR
Warren Wilson College ... NC
Waynesburg University ... PA
Westminster College ... PA
Whitworth University ... WA
Wilson College ... PA

Presbyterian Church In America
Covenant College ... GA
Covenant Theological Seminary ... MO
Grace Mission University ... CA
Knox Theological Seminary ... FL
Presbyterian Theological Seminary in America ... CA

Protestant Episcopal
Church Divinity School of the Pacific ... CA
Episcopal Divinity School ... MA
General Theological Seminary ... NY
Nashotah House ... WI
Protestant Episcopal Theological Seminary in Virginia ... VA
Saint Augustine's College ... NC
Saint Paul's College ... VA
Seabury-Western Theological Seminary ... IL
Seminary of the Southwest ... TX
Sewanee: The University of the South ... TN
Trinity Episcopal School for Ministry ... PA
Voorhees College ... SC

Reformed Church In America
Central College ... IA
Hope College ... MI
New Brunswick Theological Seminary ... NJ
Northwestern College ... IA
Western Theological Seminary ... MI

Reformed Episcopal Church
Reformed Episcopal Seminary ... PA

Reformed Presbyterian Church
Evangelia University ... CA
Geneva College ... PA
Reformed Presbyterian Theological Seminary ... PA

Roman Catholic
Alvernia University ... PA
Ancilla College ... IN
Anna Maria College ... MA
Aquinas College ... MI
Aquinas College ... TN
Aquinas Institute of Theology ... MO
Assumption College ... MA
Assumption College for Sisters ... NJ
Athenaeum of Ohio ... OH
Ave Maria School of Law ... FL
Avila University ... MO
Barry University ... FL
Bayamon Central University ... PR
Belmont Abbey College ... NC
Benedictine College ... KS
Benedictine University ... IL
Blessed John XXIII National Seminary ... MA
Boston College ... MA
Brescia University ... KY
Briar Cliff University ... IA
Cabrini College ... PA
Caldwell College ... NJ
Calumet College of Saint Joseph ... IN
Canisius College ... NY
Cardinal Stritch University ... WI
Carlow University ... PA
Carroll College ... MT
Catholic Theological Union ... IL
Chestnut Hill College ... PA
Christ the King Seminary ... NY
Christendom College ... VA
Christian Brothers University ... TN
Clarke University ... IA
College of Mount St. Joseph ... OH
College of Our Lady of the Elms ... MA
College of Saint Benedict ... MN
College of Saint Elizabeth ... NJ
College of Saint Mary ... NE
College of St. Joseph ... VT
College of the Holy Cross ... MA
Conception Seminary College ... MO
Creighton University ... NE
DePaul University ... IL
DeSales University ... PA
Divine Word College ... IA
Dominican School of Philosophy and Theology ... CA
Dominican University ... IL
Donnelly College ... KS
Duquesne University ... PA
Edgewood College ... WI
Emmanuel College ... MA
Fairfield University ... CT
Felician College ... NJ
Fontbonne University ... MO
Franciscan University of Steubenville ... OH
Gannon University ... PA
Georgetown University ... DC
Georgian Court University ... NJ
Gonzaga University ... WA
Gwynedd-Mercy College ... PA
Holy Apostles College and Seminary ... CT
Holy Cross College ... IN
Holy Family University ... PA
Immaculata University ... PA
Immaculate Conception Seminary of Seton Hall University ... NJ
John Carroll University ... OH
Kenrick-Glennon Seminary-Kenrick School of Theology ... MO
King's College ... PA
La Roche College ... PA
La Salle University ... PA
Laboure College ... MA
Lewis University ... IL
Loras College ... IA
Lourdes University ... OH
Loyola Marymount University ... CA
Loyola University Chicago ... IL
Loyola University Maryland ... MD
Loyola University New Orleans ... LA
Madonna University ... MI
Marian Court College ... MA
Marian University ... IN
Marian University ... WI
Marquette University ... WI
Marygrove College ... MI
Marymount College ... CA
Marymount University ... VA
Marywood University ... PA
Mercy College of Health Sciences ... IA
Mercy College of Ohio ... OH
Mercyhurst College ... PA
Merrimack College ... MA
Misericordia University ... PA
Mount Angel Seminary ... OR
Mount Carmel College of Nursing ... OH
Mount Marty College ... SD
Mount Mary College ... WI
Mount Mercy University ... IA
Mount St. Mary's College ... CA
Mount St. Mary's University ... MD
Neumann University ... PA
Newman University ... KS
Notre Dame College ... OH
Notre Dame of Maryland University ... MD
Notre Dame Seminary, Graduate School of Theology ... LA
Oblate School of Theology ... TX
Ohio Dominican University ... OH
Our Lady of Holy Cross College ... LA
Our Lady of the Lake College ... LA
Our Lady of the Lake University ... TX
Pontifical Catholic University of Puerto Rico-Arecibo Campus ... PR
Pontifical Catholic University of Puerto Rico-Mayaguez Campus ... PR
Pontifical College Josephinum ... OH
Pontifical Faculty of the Immaculate Conception at the Dominican House of Studies ... DC
Pontifical John Paul II Institute for Studies on Marriage and Family ... DC
Presentation College ... SD
Providence College ... RI
Quincy University ... IL
Regis University ... CO
Rivier College ... NH
Rockhurst University ... MO
Rosemont College ... PA
Sacred Heart Major Seminary/College and Theologate ... MI
Sacred Heart School of Theology ... WI
Saint Anselm College ... NH
Saint Bernard's School of Theology & Ministry ... NY
Saint Charles Borromeo Seminary ... PA
Saint Francis Medical Center College of Nursing ... IL
Saint Francis Seminary ... WI
Saint Francis University ... PA
Saint Gregory the Great Seminary ... NE
Saint John's Seminary ... CA
Saint John's Seminary ... MA
Saint John's University ... MN
Saint Joseph College ... CT
Saint Joseph Seminary College ... LA
Saint Joseph's College ... IN
Saint Joseph's College of Maine ... ME
Saint Joseph's Seminary ... NY
Saint Joseph's University ... PA
Saint Leo University ... FL
Saint Louis University ... MO
Saint Martin's University ... WA
Saint Mary Seminary and Graduate School of Theology ... OH
Saint Mary's College ... IN
Saint Mary's College of California ... CA
Saint Mary's Seminary and University ... MD
Saint Mary's University of Minnesota ... MN
Saint Mary-of-the-Woods College ... IN
Saint Meinrad Seminary and School of Theology ... IN
Saint Michael's College ... VT
Saint Norbert College ... WI
Saint Patrick's Seminary & University ... CA
Saint Peter's College ... NJ
Saint Vincent College ... PA
Saint Vincent Seminary ... PA
Saint Xavier University ... IL
Salve Regina University ... RI
Seattle University ... WA
Seminary of the Immaculate Conception ... NY
Seton Hall University ... NJ
Seton Hall University School of Law ... NJ
Seton Hill University ... PA
Siena Heights University ... MI
Silver Lake College ... WI
Spring Hill College ... AL
SS. Cyril and Methodius Seminary ... MI
St. Ambrose University ... IA
St. Anthony College of Nursing ... IL
St. Bonaventure University ... NY
St. Catharine College ... KY
St. Catherine University ... MN
St. Gregory's University ... OK
St. John Vianney College Seminary ... FL
St. John Vianney Theological Seminary ... CO
St. John's University ... NY
St. Mary's University ... TX
St. Thomas University ... FL
St. Vincent De Paul Regional Seminary ... FL
Stonehill College ... MA
The Catholic University of America ... DC
The College of Saint Scholastica ... MN
The College of Saint Thomas More ... TX
The Pontifical Catholic University of Puerto Rico ... PR
The University of Scranton ... PA
Thomas More College ... KY
Trinity Washington University ... DC
University of Dallas ... TX
University of Dayton ... OH
University of Detroit Mercy ... MI
University of Great Falls ... MT
University of Mary ... ND
University of Notre Dame ... IN
University of Saint Francis ... IN
University of Saint Mary ... KS
University of Saint Mary of the Lake-Mundelein Seminary ... IL
University of Saint Thomas ... MN
University of San Diego ... CA
University of San Francisco ... CA
University of St. Francis ... IL
University of St. Thomas ... TX
University of the Incarnate Word ... TX
University of the Sacred Heart ... PR
Ursuline College ... OH
Villanova University ... PA
Viterbo University ... WI
Walsh University ... OH
Wheeling Jesuit University ... WV
Xavier University ... OH
Xavier University of Louisiana ... LA

Russian Orthodox
Holy Trinity Orthodox Seminary ... NY

Seventh-day Adventist
Andrews University ... MI
Atlantic Union College ... MA
Florida Hospital College of Health Sciences ... FL
Griggs University ... MI
Kettering College of Medical Arts ... OH
La Sierra University ... CA
Loma Linda University ... CA
Oakwood University ... AL
Pacific Union College ... CA
Southern Adventist University ... TN
Southwestern Adventist University ... TX
Union College ... NE
Universidad Adventista de las Antillas ... PR
Walla Walla University ... WA
Washington Adventist University ... MD

Southern Baptist
Blue Mountain College ... MS
California Baptist University ... CA
Carson-Newman College ... TN
Charleston Southern University ... SC
Clear Creek Baptist Bible College ... KY
East Texas Baptist University ... TX
Golden Gate Baptist Theological Seminary ... CA
Hannibal-La Grange University ... MO
Houston Baptist University ... TX
Louisiana College ... LA
Mid-Continent University ... KY
Midwestern Baptist Theological Seminary ... MO
Mississippi College ... MS
New Orleans Baptist Theological Seminary ... LA
North Greenville University ... SC
Oklahoma Baptist University ... OK
Ouachita Baptist University ... AR
Samford University ... AL
Southeastern Baptist Theological Seminary ... NC
Southwest Baptist University ... MO
Southwestern Baptist Theological Seminary ... TX
The Baptist College of Florida ... FL
The Southern Baptist Theological Seminary ... KY
Union University ... TN
University of Mary Hardin-Baylor ... TX
University of Mobile ... AL
Wayland Baptist University ... TX
William Carey University ... MS

Williams Baptist College .... AR
Wingate University .... NC

The Christian And Missionary Alliance
Crown College .... MN
Nyack College .... NY
Simpson University .... CA

Unification Church
Unification Theological Seminary .... NY

Unitarian Universalist
Meadville/Lombard Theological School ... IL
Starr King School for the Ministry .... CA

United Brethren Church
Huntington University .... IN

United Church Of Christ
Bangor Theological Seminary .... ME
Catawba College .... NC
Cedar Crest College .... PA
Chicago Theological Seminary IL
Doane College .... NE
Eden Theological Seminary .... MO
Elmhurst College IL
Heidelberg University .... OH
Lakeland College .... WI
Lancaster Theological Seminary .... PA
Northland College .... WI
The Defiance College .... OH
Tougaloo College .... MS
United Theological Seminary of the Twin Cities .... MN

United Methodist
Adrian College .... MI
Albion College .... MI
Albright College .... PA
American University .... DC
Andrew College .... GA
Baker University .... KS
Baldwin-Wallace College .... OH
Bennett College for Women .... NC
Bethune Cookman University .... FL
Birmingham-Southern College .... AL
Brevard College .... NC
Centenary College of Louisiana .... LA
Central Methodist University .... MO
Claflin University .... SC
Claremont School of Theology .... CA
Clark Atlanta University .... GA
Columbia College .... SC
Cornell College .... IA
Dakota Wesleyan University .... SD
DePauw University .... IN
Dillard University .... LA
Emory & Henry College .... VA
Emory University .... GA
Ferrum College .... VA
Florida Southern College .... FL
Garrett-Evangelical Theological Seminary IL
Greensboro College .... NC
Hamline University .... MN
Hendrix College .... AR
High Point University .... NC
Hiwassee College .... TN
Huntingdon College .... AL
Iliff School of Theology .... CO
Iowa Wesleyan College .... IA
Kansas Wesleyan University .... KS
Kentucky Wesleyan College .... KY
LaGrange College .... GA
Lebanon Valley College .... PA
Lindsey Wilson College .... KY
Lon Morris College .... TX
Louisburg College .... NC
Lycoming College .... PA
MacMurray College IL
Martin Methodist College .... TN
McKendree University IL
McMurry University .... TX
Methodist Theological School in Ohio ..... OH
Methodist University .... NC
Millsaps College .... MS
Morningside College .... IA
Nebraska Wesleyan University .... NE
North Carolina Wesleyan College .... NC
North Central College IL
Ohio Northern University .... OH
Ohio Wesleyan University .... OH
Oklahoma City University .... OK
Otterbein University .... OH
Pfeiffer University .... NC
Philander Smith College .... AR
Randolph College .... VA
Randolph-Macon College .... VA
Reinhardt University .... GA
Rust College .... MS
Saint Paul School of Theology .... MO
Shenandoah University .... VA
Simpson College .... IA
Southern Methodist University .... TX
Southwestern College .... KS
Southwestern University .... TX
Spartanburg Methodist College .... SC
Tennessee Wesleyan College .... TN
Texas Wesleyan University .... TX
Union College .... KY
United Theological Seminary .... OH
University of Evansville .... IN
University of Indianapolis .... IN
University of Mount Union .... OH
Virginia Wesleyan College .... VA
Wesley College .... DE
Wesley Theological Seminary .... DC
Wesleyan College .... GA
West Virginia Wesleyan College .... WV
Wiley College .... TX
Wofford College .... SC
Young Harris College .... GA

Wesleyan Church
Allegheny Wesleyan College .... OH
Houghton College .... NY
Indiana Wesleyan University .... IN
Oklahoma Wesleyan University .... OK
Somerset Christian College .... NJ
Southern Wesleyan University .... SC

Wisconsin Evangelical Lutheran Synod
Martin Luther College .... MN

Carnegie Classification Code Definitions*

This year, the Higher Education Directory lists the updated 2010 Carnegie Classifications. The 2010 Classification update retains the same structure of classifications initially adopted in 2005. Due to space limitation, the *Higher Education Directory* ® only lists the original classification framework—now called the basic classification—which was substantially revised in 2005. These new codes are listed below:

Associate's Colleges: Includes institutions where all degrees are at the associate's level, or where bachelor's degrees account for less than 10 percent of all undergraduate degrees. Excludes institutions eligible for classification as Tribal Colleges or Special Focus Institutions.

Assoc/Pub-R-S: Associate's — Public Rural-serving Small
Assoc/Pub-R-M: Associate's — Public Rural-serving Medium
Assoc/Pub-R-L: Associate's — Public Rural-serving Large
Assoc/Pub-S-SC: Associate's — Public Suburban-serving Single Campus
Assoc/Pub-S-MC: Associate's — Public Suburban-serving Multicampus
Assoc/Pub-U-SC: Associate's — Public Urban-serving Single Campus
Assoc/Pub-U-MC: Associate's — Public Urban-serving Multicampus
Assoc/Pub-Spec: Associate's — Public Special Use
Assoc/PrivNFP: Associate's — Private Not-for-profit
Assoc/PrivFP: Associate's — Private For-profit
Assoc/Pub2in4: Associate's — Public 2-year Colleges under Universities
Assoc/Pub4: Associate's — Public 4-year, Primarily Associate's
Assoc/PrivNFP4: Associate's — Private Not-for-profit 4-year, Primarily Associate's
Assoc/PrivFP4: Associate's — Private For-profit 4-year, Primarily Associate's

Doctorate-granting Universities. Includes institutions that award at least 20 doctoral degrees per year (excluding doctoral-level degrees that qualify recipients for entry into professional practice, such as the JD, MD, PharmD, DPT, etc.). Excludes Special Focus Institutions and Tribal Colleges.

RU/VH: Research Universities (very high research activity)
RU/H: Research Universities (high research activity)
DRU: Doctoral/Research Universities

Master's Colleges and Universities. Includes institutions that award at least 50 master's degrees per year. Excludes Special Focus Institutions and Tribal Colleges.

Master's/L: Master's Colleges and Universities (larger programs)
Master's/M: Master's Colleges and Universities (medium programs)
Master's/S: Master's Colleges and Universities (smaller programs)

Baccalaureate Colleges. Includes institutions where baccalaureate degrees represent at least 10 percent of all undergraduate degrees and that award fewer than 50 master's degrees or fewer than 20 doctoral degrees per year. Excludes Special Focus Institutions and Tribal Colleges.

Bac/A&S: Baccalaureate Colleges — Arts & Sciences
Bac/Diverse: Baccalaureate Colleges — Diverse Fields
Bac/Assoc: Baccalaureate/Associate's Colleges

Special Focus Institutions. Institutions awarding baccalaureate or higher-level degrees where a high concentration of degrees is in a single field or set of related fields. Excludes Tribal Colleges.

Spec/Faith: Theological seminaries, Bible colleges, and other faith-related institutions
Spec/Medical: Medical schools and medical centers
Spec/Health: Other health profession schools
Spec/Engg: Schools of engineering
Spec/Tech: Other technology-related schools
Spec/Bus: Schools of business and management
Spec/Arts: Schools of art, music, and design
Spec/Law: Schools of law
Spec/Other: Other special-focus institutions

Tribal Colleges. Colleges and universities that are members of the American Indian Higher Education Consortium, as identified in IPEDS Institutional Characteristics.

Tribal: Tribal Colleges

*All data provided by The Carnegie Foundation for the Advancement of Teaching. For more detailed information on the revised Carnegie Codes, please visit www.carnegiefoundation.org/classifications/

Statistics

Institutions of Higher Education by Control, Level and State

STATE	TWO YEAR		FOUR YEAR		TOTAL		SYSTEM	GRAND
	PRIVATE	PUBLIC	PRIVATE	PUBLIC	PRIVATE	PUBLIC	OFFICE	TOTAL
AL	6	27	28	16	34	43	2	79
AK	2	1	3	3	5	4	1	10
AZ	22	19	45	4	67	23	1	91
AR	3	22	13	11	16	33	2	51
CA	94	115	263	35	357	150	29	536
CO	23	14	40	14	63	28	3	94
CT	1	12	23	8	24	20	2	46
DE	1	3	4	2	5	5	1	11
DC	2	0	15	3	17	3	0	20
FL	61	9	123	32	184	41	1	226
GA	10	34	55	27	65	61	1	127
HI	2	6	11	4	13	10	2	25
ID	1	3	8	4	9	7	0	16
IL	17	47	119	12	136	59	6	201
IN	14	14	61	15	75	29	2	106
IA	2	18	44	3	46	21	3	70
KS	8	24	24	11	32	35	0	67
KY	11	16	46	8	57	24	1	82
LA	17	37	15	17	32	54	4	90
ME	3	7	14	8	17	15	2	34
MD	4	16	29	15	33	31	1	65
MA	5	16	88	14	93	30	2	125
MI	2	29	58	15	60	44	1	105
MN	6	30	58	11	64	41	3	108
MS	5	15	11	9	16	24	0	40
MO	25	21	76	13	101	34	3	138
MT	6	8	5	6	11	14	1	26
NE	5	8	20	7	25	15	2	42
NV	5	1	6	6	11	7	1	19
NH	2	7	14	5	16	12	2	30
NJ	3	19	31	21	34	40	2	76
NM	2	18	11	8	13	26	0	39
NY	42	39	195	44	237	83	5	325
NC	2	59	62	16	64	75	2	141
ND	3	4	8	7	11	11	1	23
OH	55	28	89	33	144	61	2	207
OK	8	12	20	18	28	30	0	58
OR	6	16	28	8	34	24	1	59
PA	81	16	118	46	199	62	1	262
RI	0	1	9	3	9	4	0	13
SC	5	20	28	13	33	33	0	66
SD	1	5	10	6	11	11	1	23
TN	14	13	65	10	79	23	2	104
TX	36	64	87	48	123	112	8	243
UT	4	5	18	6	22	11	1	34
VT	1	1	16	5	17	6	1	24
VA	17	24	74	17	91	41	1	133
WA	7	28	34	11	41	39	2	82
WV	12	10	13	12	25	22	2	49
WI	4	17	42	13	46	30	2	78
WY	2	7	0	1	2	8	0	10
AS	0	1	0	0	0	1	0	1
GU	0	1	1	1	1	2	0	3
MH	0	1	0	0	0	1	0	1
MP	0	0	0	1	0	1	0	1
PR	8	0	43	14	51	14	3	68
FM	0	1	0	0	0	1	0	1
PW	0	1	0	0	0	1	0	1
VI	0	0	0	1	0	1	0	1
Total	**678**	**990**	**2321**	**701**	**2999**	**1691**	**116**	**4806**

50 Largest Universities by Fall 2010 Enrollment

Institution	Enrollment
1. Arizona State University	70440
2. University of Central Florida	56337
3. The Ohio State University Main Campus	56064
4. Liberty University	55223
5. University of Minnesota-Twin Cities	51721
6. University of Texas at Austin	51195
7. University of Florida	49827
8. Texas A & M University	49129
9. University of South Florida	47800
10. Walden University	47456
11. Air University	47222
12. Michigan State University	47137
13. Ashford University	46830
14. Ohio University (all campuses)	45343
15. Pacific Northwest University of Health Sciences	44650
16. Penn State University Park	43998
17. New York University	43797
18. University of Wisconsin-Madison	42595
19. Indiana University Bloomington	42464
20. University of Washington	42446
21. Florida International University	42197
22. University of Michigan-Ann Arbor	41480
23. University of Cincinnati Main Campus	41357
24. Kansas City University of Medicine & Biosciences	41013
25. Florida State University	40416
26. Purdue University Main Campus	39726
27. University of Maryland University College	39577
28. American Public University System	39296
29. University of Arizona	39086
30. University of Houston	39000
31. Rutgers the State University of New Jersey New Brunswick Campus	38912
32. University of California-Los Angeles	38157
33. Grand Canyon University	37441
34. Temple University	37367
35. University of Maryland College Park	37200
36. University of Southern California	36896
37. University of North Texas	36067
38. California State University-Fullerton	35590
39. California State University-Northridge	35272
40. University of Georgia	34677
41. North Carolina State University	34376
42. The University of Texas at Arlington	32975
43. Brigham Young University	32947
44. Boston University	32727
45. Utah Valley University	32670
46. Texas State University-San Marcos	32572
47. George Mason University	32562
48. University of Missouri - Columbia	32415
49. Virginia Commonwealth University	32303
50. University of California-Davis	32290

Institutions by Control and Tuition Range

Tuition	Public*	Private	Total
0 - 1,000	122	266	388
1,001 - 2,000	198	10	208
2,001 - 4,000	599	48	647
4,001 - 6,000	339	95	434
6,001 - 8,000	217	108	325
8,001 - 10,000	98	148	246
Over 10,000	118	2324	2442
Total	**1691**	**2999**	**4690**

* Figures for Public Institutions are In-State Tuitions

Universities, Colleges and Schools

by State*

*Includes the District of Columbia and, separately, U.S. Service Schools, American Samoa, Federated States of Micronesia, Guam, Marshall Islands, Northern Marianas, Palau, Puerto Rico, and Virgin Islands.

ALABAMA

Alabama Agricultural and Mechanical University (A)

4900 Meridian Street, Normal AL 35762-1357

County: Madison   FICE Identification: 001002
Unit ID: 100654
Telephone: (256) 372-5230   Carnegie Class: Master's L
FAX Number: (256) 372-5244   Calendar System: Semester
URL: www.aamu.edu
Established: 1875   Annual Undergrad Tuition & Fees (In-State): $6,090
Enrollment: 5,814   Coed
Affiliation or Control: State   IRS Status: 501(c)3
Highest Offering: Doctorate
Program: Liberal Arts And General; Teacher Preparatory; Professional
Accreditation: SC, AAFCS, CORE, CS, DIETD, ENG, ENGT, FOR, PLNG, SP, SW, TED

01 President ... Dr. Andrew HUGINE, JR.
05 Vice Pres Academic Affairs ... Dr. Daniel K. WIMS
10 VP of Business & Finance ... Mr. Ralph JOHNSON
46 Interim VP Inst Rsrch/Spons Pgms ... Dr. Lloyd WALKER
32 Interim VP Student Affairs ... Mr. Jeffery BURGIN
20 Associate Provost ... Dr. Lloyd WALKER
21 Comptroller ... Mr. Norman JONES
15 Director Human Resources ... Ms. Nancy VAUGHN
18 Director Physical Facilities ... Mr. Walter ALEXANDER
06 Registrar ... Mr. Cedric ARRINGTON
07 Director of Admissions ... Ms. Venita KING
37 Interim Director of Financial Aid ... Ms. Deborah GORDON
88 Director of Emergency Management ... Mr. Allen VITAL
23 Director Student Health Center ... Dr. Martin VAN SHERRILL
36 Dir Career Development Services ... Ms. Carolyn LEWIS
09 Interim Dir Institutional Research ... Dr. Frank ARCHER, III
26 Director Info & Public Relations ... Mr. Jerome SAINTJONES
31 Interim Dir of Auxiliary/Housing ... Mr. Walter ALEXANDER
14 Director Computer Services ... Mr. Raymond TURNER
19 Chief of Police ... Ms. Monica RAY
08 Interim Dean Learn Resources Center ... Dr. Gary BUSH
41 Director of Athletics ... Ms. Betty AUSTIN
39 Director of Residential Life ... Mr. Kenneth MADDOX
96 Interim Director of Purchasing ... Ms. Delores HUDSON
58 Dean Graduate School ... Dr. Vann NEWKIRK
49 Dean School Arts/Science ... Dr. Matthew EDWARDS
47 Dean Sch Agricul/Environ Sci ... Dr. Robert TAYLOR
53 Interim Dean School of Education ... Dr. Delores PRICE
54 Dean Sch Engineering Technology ... Dr. Trent MONTGOMERY
60 Dean School of Business ... Dr. Amin SARKAR
88 Interim Dean University College ... Dr. Juarine STEWART
100 Chief of Staff ... Dr. Kevin ROLLE

Alabama Southern Community College (B)

PO Box 2000, Monroeville AL 36460-2000

County: Monroe   FICE Identification: 001034
Unit ID: 101949
Telephone: (251) 575-3156   Carnegie Class: Assoc/Pub-R-S
FAX Number: (251) 575-5356   Calendar System: Semester
URL: www.ascc.edu
Established: 1965   Annual Undergrad Tuition & Fees (In-State): $3,210
Enrollment: 1,500   Coed
Affiliation or Control: State   IRS Status: 501(c)3
Highest Offering: Associate Degree
Program: Occupational; 2-Year Principally Bachelor's Creditable
Accreditation: SC, ADNUR

01 President ... Dr. Reginald SYKES
05 Vice Pres for Lrng/Academic Affairs ... Dr. Lee L. TAYLOR
10 VP Finance/Administrative Services ... Mr. Roger CHANDLER
32 Dean of Student Development ... Mrs. Ann CLANTON
08 Dean of Library Services ... Ms. LaShannon HOLLINGER
06 Registrar ... Ms. Jana HORTON
37 Director of Financial Aid ... Ms. Amy ROWELL
20 Assoc Dean Academic Affairs ... Dr. Melissa HAAB
26 Director of Public Information ... Ms. Stephanie PETTIS
18 Chief Facilities/Physical Plant ... Mr. Tom REED

Alabama State University (C)

915 S Jackson Street, Montgomery AL 36101-0271

County: Montgomery   FICE Identification: 001005
Unit ID: 100724
Telephone: (334) 229-4200   Carnegie Class: Master's L
FAX Number: (334) 834-6861   Calendar System: Semester
URL: www.alasu.edu
Established: 1867   Annual Undergrad Tuition & Fees (In-State): $7,164
Enrollment: 5,705   Coed
Affiliation or Control: State   IRS Status: 501(c)3
Highest Offering: Doctorate
Program: Liberal Arts And General; Teacher Preparatory
Accreditation: SC, ACBSP, @CORE, MUS, OT, PTA, SW, TED, THEA

01 President ... Dr. William H. HARRIS
03 Chief Oper Ofcr/Exec Vice Pres ... Dr. John F. KNIGHT, JR.
05 Int Provost/Vice Pres Academic Affs ... Dr. Alfred SMITH
10 Vice President Business & Finance .. Mr. Freddie C. GALLOT, JR.
26 Vice Pres Marketing/ Communications ... Ms. Danielle KENNEDY-LAMAR
18 Vice Pres Buildings & Grounds ... Mr. Kippy TATE
15 Vice Pres Human Resources ... Mrs. Carmen DOUGLAS
32 Int Assoc Vice Pres Student Affairs ... Mr. Ricky DRAKE
20 Assoc Vice Pres Academic Affairs ... Dr. Alfred S. SMITH
35 Asst Vice Pres to Student Affairs ... Mr. Ricky DRAKE
21 Asst VP Business & Finance/ Comptrol ... Mrs. Alondrea J. PRITCHETT
09 Director Institutional Research ... Vacant
08 Dean Libraries/Learning Resource ... Dr. Janice FRANKLIN
06 Director Records Registration ... Ms. Karen PRESTAGE
07 Int Director Admissions/Recruiting ... Vacant
14 Director of Academic Computing/MIS ... Mr. Larry COBB
37 Director Student Financial Aid ... Mrs. Dorenda ADAMS
36 Dir Placement Svcs/Cooperative Educ .... Mrs. Mary K. WILLIAMS
27 Director University Relations ... Mr. Kenneth MULLINAX
50 Int Dean College Business Admin ... Dr. LaQuita BOOTH
89 Dean University College ... Dr. Evelyn HODGE
53 Dean College of Education ... Dr. John GOODEN
64 Dean Visual & Performing Arts ... Dr. Tommie T. STEWART
58 Dean Graduate Studies ... Dr. William PERSONS
81 Dean College of Sci Math & Tech ... Dr. Cajetan AKAJUOBI
49 Int Dean Col of Lib Arts & Soc Sci ... Dr. Sharron HERRON-WILLIAMS
51 Director Cmty Svcs/Cont Education ... Mr. Olan L. WESLEY
30 Assoc Vice President of Development ... Ms. Zillah FLUKER
29 Director Alumni Relations ... Mr. Cromwell HANDY
23 Director Student Health Services ... Ms. Gwendolyn MANN
19 Exec Dir Police & Campus Security ... Mr. Henry C. DAVIS
38 Dir Counseling & Development Svcs ... Mrs. Jessyca M. DARRINGTON
39 Int Dir Housing/Residential Life ... Mrs. Queen GREEN
41 Director of Athletics ... Mr. Stacy DANLEY
25 Director Grants & Contracts .... Dr. Linda PHAIRE-WASHINGTON
88 Director Internal Audit ... Vacant
96 Director of Purchasing ... Ms. Ann SMITH

Amridge University (D)

1200 Taylor Road, Montgomery AL 36117-3553

County: Montgomery   FICE Identification: 025034
Unit ID: 100690
Telephone: (800) 351-4040   Carnegie Class: Bac/A&S
FAX Number: (334) 387-3878   Calendar System: Semester
URL: www.amridgeuniversity.edu
Established: 1967   Annual Undergrad Tuition & Fees: $8,420
Enrollment: 759   Coed
Affiliation or Control: Churches Of Christ   IRS Status: 501(c)3
Highest Offering: Doctorate
Program: Liberal Arts And General; Professional; Religious Emphasis
Accreditation: SC

01 President ... Dr. Michael C. TURNER
05 Academic Vice President/Dean ... Dr. Stanley PATTERSON
06 Registry Officer ... Mrs. Elaine P. TARENCE
07 Admissions ... Mrs. Ora DAVIS
08 Director of Library ... Ms. Kay S. NEWMAN
10 Chief Business Officer ... Mrs. B. P. TURNER
13 Director of Computing/Information ... Mr. Clayton F. SCHMIDT
37 Financial Aid Officer/Counselor ... Mrs. Lisa BYRD
42 Director of Church Relations ... Mr. Curtis SAMPLEY
88 Director of World Missions ... Mr. Demar ELAM
29 Director of Alumni Relations ... Mr. Ed SMITH
09 Director of Institutional Research ... Dr. J. H. WHITE
14 Director of Computer Center ... Mr. Jack TEMPLE
18 Chief Facilities/Physical Plant ... Mr. Robert SHIRLEY
24 Director of Educational Media ... Mr. Thomas PATTERSON
38 Director of Student Counseling ... Dr. Wayne PERRY
26 Chief Public Relations Officer ... Mrs. Laina COSTANZA
42 Chaplain/Director Campus Ministry ... Dr. Leon F. ESTEP
44 Director Annual/Planned Giving ... Mr. Ed SMITH
73 Dean of School of Religion ... Dr. Rodney CLOUD
88 Dean School of Human Services ... Dr. Dale BERTRAM
90 Director Academic Computing ... Mr. Donnie E. CROSBY
15 Director Personnel Services ... Vacant

Andrew Jackson University (E)

2919 John Hawkins Parkway, Birmingham AL 35244-1095

County: Jefferson   FICE Identification: 041292
Unit ID: 420361
Telephone: (205) 871-9288   Carnegie Class: Not Classified
FAX Number: (205) 871-9294   Calendar System: Trimester
URL: www.aju.edu
Established: 1994   Annual Undergrad Tuition & Fees: $1,592
Enrollment: 510   Coed
Affiliation or Control: Proprietary   IRS Status: Proprietary
Highest Offering: Master's
Program: Liberal Arts And General; Business Emphasis
Accreditation: DETC

00 CEO ... Mr. Eugene V. WADE
01 President ... Dr. Salvatore MONACO
05 Dean of Academic Programs ... Dr. Patricia NEELY
07 Director of Admissions ... Ms. Tammy J. KASSNER
20 Director of Academic Affairs ... Vacant
06 Registrar ... Ms. Bell N. WOODS

Athens State University (F)

300 N Beaty Street, Athens AL 35611-1902

County: Limestone   FICE Identification: 001008
Unit ID: 100812
Telephone: (256) 233-8100   Carnegie Class: Bac/Diverse
FAX Number: (256) 233-8164   Calendar System: Semester
URL: www.athens.edu
Established: 1822   Annual Undergrad Tuition & Fees (In-State): $5,340
Enrollment: 3,624   Coed
Affiliation or Control: State   IRS Status: 501(c)3
Highest Offering: Baccalaureate
Program: Liberal Arts And General; Teacher Preparatory
Accreditation: SC, ACBSP, TED

01 President ... Dr. Robert K. GLENN
05 Vice President for Academic Affairs ... Dr. Denver BETTS
20 Associate VP for Academic Affairs ... Vacant
32 Vice Pres for Enroll & Student Supp ... Mr. Jim HUTTO
10 Vice President for Financial Aff ... Mr. Mike MCCOY
21 Associate Business Officer ... Mr. Evan THORNTON
26 Vice Pres for University Advance ... Mr. Richard MOULD
08 Director of Libraries ... Dr. Robert BURKHARDT
50 Dean College of Business ... Dr. Linda SHONESY
53 Dean College of Education ... Dr. Debra BAIRD
49 Dean College of Arts & Sciences ... Dr. Ronald FRITZE
36 Dir of Career Services ... Mr. Larry KEENUM
37 Dir of Student Financial Services ... Ms. Sarah MCABEE
06 Registrar ... Ms. Teresa SUIT
07 Director of Admissions & Records ... Ms. Necedah HENDERSON
35 Director of Student Activities ... Ms. Tena BULLINGTON
29 Director of Alumni Affairs/Ann Giv ... Ms. Trish DI LULLO
30 Director of Development ... Mr. Dennis STORY
88 Director of Printing & Public Rels ... Mr. Guy MCCLURE
09 Director of Institutional Research ... Ms. Sylvia CORREA
18 Director of Physical Plant ... Mr. Jerry BRADFORD
15 Director of Human Resources ... Ms. Suzanne SIMS
102 Director of Gov Corp & Found Rel ... Ms. Lynne INGRAM
36 Director of Student Recruitment ... Ms. Deborah SCHAUS

Auburn University (G)

Auburn AL 36849

County: Lee   FICE Identification: 001009
Unit ID: 100858
Telephone: (334) 844-4000   Carnegie Class: RU/H
FAX Number: N/A   Calendar System: Semester
URL: www.auburn.edu
Established: 1856   Annual Undergrad Tuition & Fees (In-State): $8,698
Enrollment: 26,070   Coed
Affiliation or Control: State   IRS Status: 501(c)3
Highest Offering: Doctorate
Program: Liberal Arts And General; Teacher Preparatory; Professional
Accreditation: SC, AAB, ART, AUD, BUS, BUSA, CACREP, CIDA, CLPSY, CONST, COPSY, CORE, CS, DIETD, ENG, FOR, JOUR, LSAR, MFCD, MUS, NURSE, PHAR, PLNG, SP, SPAA, SW, TED, THEA, VET

01 President ... Dr. Jay GOGUE
03 Executive Vice President ... Dr. Donald L. LARGE
05 Interim Provost/VP Acad Affairs ... Dr. Timothy R. BOOSINGER
29 Vice President Alumni Affairs ... Dr. Deborah L. SHAW
30 Interim Vice President Development ... Mr. Robert W. WELLBAUM
32 Vice President Student Affaris ... Dr. Ainsley CARRY
46 Assoc Provost/VP Research ... Dr. John M. MASON
20 Associate Provost ... Dr. Emmett WINN
56 Assistant Vice President Outreach ... Dr. Royrickers COOK
58 Dean Graduate School ... Dr. George FLOWERS
84 Dean of Enrollment Services ... Dr. Charles W. ALDERMAN
11 Asst Vice Pres Auxiliary Services ... Mr. Robert C. RITENBAUGH
15 Asst Vice Pres Human Resources ... Ms. Lynne B. HAMMOND
65 Exec Dir Nat Resource Mgmt Dev Inst ... Dr. Larry FILLMER
26 Executive Director Comm/Marketing ... Ms. Deedie K. DOWDLE
28 Assoc Provost Multicultural Affs ... Dr. Overtoun JENDA
20 Assoc Provost Undergrad Studies ... Dr. Constance C. RELIHAN
21 Assoc Vice Pres Business & Finance ... Ms. Marcie SMITH
43 General Counsel ... Mr. Lee F. ARMSTRONG
101 Secretary to Board of Trustees ... Mr. C. Grant DAVIS
14 Exec Dir Information Technology ... Mr. Bliss BAILEY
37 Exec Dir Student Financial Services ... Mr. Michael C. REYNOLDS
11 Director Public Affairs ... Mr. Brian C. KEETER
22 Director Affirmative Action/EEO ... Ms. Kelley G. TAYLOR
86 Director Governmental Affairs ... Ms. Sherri FULFORD
09 Director Inst Research & Assessment ... Dr. James A. CLARK
41 Director of Athletics ... Mr. John O. JACOBS, JR.
06 Registrar ... Ms. Laura Ann FOREST
40 Director University Bookstore ... Ms. Catherine LEE
88 Director JCS Museum of Art ... Dr. Marilyn LAUFER
56 Director AL Cooperative Extension ... Dr. W. Gaines SMITH
39 Director Housing & Residential Life ... Ms. Kim L. TRUPP
92 Director Honors College ... Dr. James R. HANSEN
10 Chief Business Officer ... Dr. Donald L. LARGE
36 Director Career Center ... Mrs. Nancy M. BERNARD
13 Associate Executive Director IT ... Mr. William C. WADE
96 Asst Director Procurement Services ... Ms. Marilyn SANFORD
47 Dean of Agriculture ... Dr. William D. BATCHELOR
48 Dean Architect Design/Construction ... Dr. Vini NATHAN
49 Dean of Liberal Arts ... Dr. Anne-Katrin GRAMBERG
50 Dean of Business ... Dr. Bill HARDGRAVE
53 Dean of Education ... Dr. Betty Lou WHITFORD
54 Dean of Engineering ... Dr. Larry BENEFIELD
65 Dean of Forestry/Wildlife Sciences ... Dr. James P. SHEPARD
59 Dean of Human Sciences ... Dr. June M. HENTON
66 Dean of Nursing ... Dr. Gregg NEWSCHWANDER
67 Dean of Pharmacy ... Dr. R. Lee EVANS, JR.
81 Interim Dean Sciences & Mathematics ... Dr. Charles SAVRDA
74 Interim Dean Veterinary Medicine ... Dr. Calvin M. JOHNSON
08 Dean University Libraries ... Dr. Bonnie MACEWAN

Auburn University at Montgomery (A)

PO Box 244023, Montgomery AL 36124-4023
County: Montgomery FICE Identification: 008310
Unit ID: 100830
Telephone: (334) 244-3000 Carnegie Class: Master's L
FAX Number: (334) 244-3762 Calendar System: Semester
URL: www.aum.edu
Established: 1967 Annual Undergrad Tuition & Fees (In-State): $7,580
Enrollment: 5,811 Coed
Affiliation or Control: State IRS Status: 501(c)3
Highest Offering: Doctorate
Program: Teacher Preparatory; Professional
Accreditation: SC, BUS, CACREP, CYTO, MT, NURSE, SPAA, TED

01 Chancellor .... Dr. John G. VERES, III
05 Provost .... Dr. Jeffery S. ELWELL
30 Vice Chanc Advancement/Alumni Svcs .... Ms. Carolyn GOLDEN
10 Vice Chancellor Finance .... Ms. Wanda MEADOWS
20 Assoc Provost Acad/Grad Affs .... Dr. Jeffrey M. BARKSDALE
28 Asst Prov Diversity/MultiCultural .... Mr. Timothy SPRAGGINS
07 Director of Admissions .... Ms. Valerie S. CRAWFORD
15 Director of Human Resources .... Ms. Cassandra TARVER-ROSS
26 Communications Manager .... Mr. Frank MILES
37 Director of Financial Aid .... Mr. Anthony RICHEY
32 Interim Dean of Students .... Dr. Yulanda TYRE
08 Dean of Library .... Ms. Lucy L. FARROW
41 Athletic Director .... Mr. Steve CROTZ
39 Director of Residential Housing .... Mr. Daryl MORRIS
27 Chief Information Officer .... Dr. Jeffery ANDERSON
18 Sr Director of Facilities .... Mr. Dorsey SMITH
38 Director Student Counseling .... Dr. Yulanda TYRE
09 Director Inst Effectiveness .... Ms. Jennifer GOOD
19 Chief Campus Police .... Ms. Nell ROBINSON
13 Asst Chief Information Officer .... Ms. Carolyn D. RAWL
13 Asst Chief Information Officer .... Mr. Jon FISHER
96 Dir Procurement/Payment Services .... Ms. Lori LAMBERTH
36 Director Career Development .... Mr. Keith CULLEN
40 Director of Bookstore .... Mr. Jeffrey P. VINZANT
06 Registrar .... Ms. Elizabeth WARD
25 Director of Sponsored Programs .... Ms. Fariba S. DERAVI
29 Program Manager Alumni Services .... Ms. Carolyn GOLDEN
85 Coord Intl Student Admissions .... Mr. Ron BLAESING
35 Director Student Life .... Mrs. Lakecia HARRIS
49 Dean of Liberal Arts .... Dr. Michael BURGER
50 Dean of Business .... Dr. Jane R. GOODSON
51 Senior Dir of Continuing Education .... Ms. Kathy GUNTER
53 Dean of Education .... Dr. Jennifer A. BROWN
66 Dean of Nursing .... Dr. Gregg NEWSCHWANDER
81 Dean of Sciences .... Dr. Karen STINE
85 Asst Provost Intl Affairs .... Mr. Jacques L. FUQUA, JR.
84 Dean of Admissions/Recruiting .... Mr. Tyler PETERSON
19 Sr Director of Public Safety .... Mr. Ricky ADAMS
88 Vice Chanc University Outreach .... Dr. Katherine JACKSON

Bevill State Community College (B)

1411 Indiana Avenue, Jasper AL 35501
County: Walker FICE Identification: 005733
Unit ID: 102429
Telephone: (205) 387-0511 Carnegie Class: Assoc/Pub-R-M
FAX Number: (205) 387-5192 Calendar System: Semester
URL: www.bscc.edu
Established: 1965 Annual Undergrad Tuition & Fees (In-State): $4,110
Enrollment: 4,660 Coed
Affiliation or Control: State IRS Status: 501(c)3
Highest Offering: Associate Degree
Program: Occupational; 2-Year Principally Bachelor's Creditable
Accreditation: SC, ADNUR, EMT, PNUR, SURGT

01 President .... Dr. Anne MCNUTT
03 Executive Vice President .... Mr. Mark ELLARD
05 Dean of Instruction .... Dr. Charles MURRAY
32 Dean of Students .... Dr. Kim ENNIS

Birmingham-Southern College (C)

900 Arkadelphia Road, Birmingham AL 35254-0001
County: Jefferson FICE Identification: 001012
Unit ID: 100937
Telephone: (205) 226-4600 Carnegie Class: Bac/A&S
FAX Number: (205) 226-4627 Calendar System: 4/1/4
URL: www.bsc.edu
Established: 1856 Annual Undergrad Tuition & Fees: $28,250
Enrollment: 1,521 Coed
Affiliation or Control: United Methodist IRS Status: 501(c)3
Highest Offering: Master's
Program: Liberal Arts And General; Teacher Preparatory; Professional
Accreditation: SC, ARCPA, BUS, MUS, TED

01 President .... Gen. Charles C. KRULAK
05 Provost .... Dr. Mark SCHANTZ
11 Vice President Administration .... Mr. Lane ESTES
30 Int VP Institutional Advancement .... Ms. Karen CARROLL
27 Vice President Communications .... Mr. Bill WAGNON
13 Vice Pres Information Technology .... Mr. Anthony HAMBEY
84 Vice Pres of Enrollment Management .... Ms. Kathleen ROSSMANN
32 Assoc Vice Pres Student Development .... Dr. David EBERHARDT
07 Assoc Vice President of Admissions .... Ms. Sheri SALMON
04 Exec Assistant to the President .... Ms. Lauren MCCURDY
20 Associate Provost .... Dr. Susan HAGEN
20 Assistant Provost .... Ms. Martha A. STEVENSON
06 Dean of Records .... Mr. Danny K. BROOKS
42 Chaplain .... Rev. Jack HINNEN
29 Director of Alumni Affairs .... Ms. Lisa HARRISON
23 Director of Health Services .... Ms. Yvette SPENCER
39 Director of Residence Life .... Mr. Jonathan LUCIA
08 Director of the Library .... Ms. Charlotte FORD
18 Director of Facilities & Events .... Ms. Anne CURRY
07 Director of Admission-Operations .... Mr. Jon CROOK
07 Director of Admission-Recruitment .... Vacant
37 Director of Financial Aid .... Ms. Jo Ann BENNETT
15 Director of Human Resources .... Ms. Susan E. KINNEY
26 Director of Church Relations .... Ms. Laura SISSON
38 Director Personal Counseling .... Ms. Sara HOOVER
41 Athletic Director .... Mr. Joe DEAN, JR.
19 Chief of Campus Police .... Mr. Randy YOUNGBLOOD
36 Director of Career Counseling .... Mr. Michael LEBEAU
30 Director Advancement Services .... Mr. Jeff SHERRELL
88 Dir of Interim & Contract Learning .... Dr. Katy LEONARD
28 Director of Multi-Cultural Affairs .... Ms. Erica BROWN
68 Dir Physical Fitness & Recreation .... Mr. Mike ROBINSON
88 Director of Leadership Studies .... Vacant
88 Director of Service Learning .... Ms. Kristin HARPER
88 Sports Information Director .... Ms. Sarah ERRECA
27 Communications Specialist .... Ms. Patricia COLE
88 Communications Specialist .... Mr. Richard RUSH
27 Assoc Dir of Comm Publications .... Ms. Tracy THOMAS
88 Assc Dir Communications-New Media .... Mr. Mike HAMILTON
88 Assoc Dir of International Programs .... Ms. Anne LEDVINA
88 Manager of Printing Services .... Mr. Jerome DAVIS
40 Manager of the Bookstore .... Mr. William ALEXANDER
96 Coordinator of Purchasing .... Ms. Cassandra BROWN

Bishop State Community College (D)

351 N Broad Street, Mobile AL 36603-5898
County: Mobile FICE Identification: 001030
Unit ID: 102030
Telephone: (251) 405-7000 Carnegie Class: Assoc/Pub-U-MC
FAX Number: (251) 438-3249 Calendar System: Semester
URL: www.bishop.edu
Established: 1965 Annual Undergrad Tuition & Fees (In-State): $3,264
Enrollment: 2,616 Coed
Affiliation or Control: State IRS Status: 501(c)3
Highest Offering: Associate Degree
Program: Occupational; 2-Year Principally Bachelor's Creditable
Accreditation: SC, ACBSP, ACFEI, ADNUR, EMT, FUSER, PNUR, PTAA

01 President .... Dr. James LOWE, JR.
05 Dean of Instructional Services .... Dr. Latitia MCCANE
12 Director of Southwest Campus .... Mr. Roderick MCSWAIN
12 Director of Carver Campus .... Dr. Betty LESLIE
12 Director of Central Campus .... Mrs. Madeline STOKES
05 Dean of Technical School .... Vacant
32 Dean of Students .... Dr. Terry HAZZARD
10 Dean of Business/Finance .... Mrs. Brenda TAYLOR
35 Assistant to the Dean of Students .... Mrs. Wanda DANIELS
09 Coordinator Institutional Planning .... Ms. Aundrea WHEELER-DUNNER
15 Director of Human Resources .... Mrs. Marcella SIMS
18 Director of Physical Plant .... Mr. Lorenzo GRAYSON
26 Director of Public Relations .... Mr. Herb JORDAN
103 Coordinator Workforce Development .... Mr. Jim KELLEN
103 Dir Workforce Dev/Lifelong Learning .... Mr. Charles PORTER
37 Mgr Student Fin Aid/Veterans Svcs .... Dr. Samuel CHUKS

Calhoun Community College (E)

PO Box 2216, Decatur AL 35609-2216
County: Limestone FICE Identification: 001013
Unit ID: 101514
Telephone: (256) 306-2500 Carnegie Class: Assoc/Pub-R-L
FAX Number: (256) 306-2877 Calendar System: Semester
URL: www.calhoun.edu
Established: 1963 Annual Undergrad Tuition & Fees (In-State): $3,144
Enrollment: 12,139 Coed
Affiliation or Control: State IRS Status: 501(c)3
Highest Offering: Associate Degree
Program: Occupational; 2-Year Principally Bachelor's Creditable
Accreditation: SC, ACBSP, ADNUR, DA, EMT, MLTAD, PNUR, PTAA, SURGT

01 President .... Dr. Marilyn C. BECK
05 Vice Pres Instruction/Student Succ .... Ms. Alicia TAYLOR
32 Dean of Student Affairs .... Dr. Kermit CARTER
10 Dean for Business & Finance .... Mr. Jack BURROW
07 Dir Admissions & Records/Registrar .... Dr. Dan OPALEWSKI
08 Head Librarian .... Ms. Lucinda BEDDOW
37 Director Student Financial Aid .... Mrs. Deborah BYRD
14 Director Information Systems .... Mrs. Laquita NELSON
30 Director Development/Foundation .... Ms. Terri BRYSON
12 Dean Research Park Campus .... Ms. Terri BRYSON
55 Director Evening Program .... Dr. Vinetta WESLEY
29 Director of Alumni Relations .... Ms. Janet KINCHERLOW-MARTIN
18 Director of Physical Plant .... Mr. Bruce CAUSEY
09 Dean Planning/Research & Grants .... Dr. Debra HENDERSHOT
103 Director of Workforce Development .... Mr. Jim SWINDELL
84 Coord Enrollment Management .... Ms. Samantha NELSON
26 Chief Public Relations Officer .... Ms. Janet KINCHERLOW-MARTIN

Central Alabama Community College (F)

1675 Cherokee Road, Alexander City AL 35010
County: Tallapoosa FICE Identification: 001007
Unit ID: 100760
Telephone: (256) 234-6346 Carnegie Class: Assoc/Pub-R-M
FAX Number: (256) 234-0384 Calendar System: Semester
URL: www.cacc.edu
Established: 1963 Annual Undergrad Tuition & Fees (In-State): $3,270
Enrollment: 2,448 Coed
Affiliation or Control: State IRS Status: 501(c)3
Highest Offering: Associate Degree
Program: Occupational; 2-Year Principally Bachelor's Creditable
Accreditation: SC, ADNUR

01 President .... Dr. Stephen B. FRANKS
03 Vice President .... Vacant
05 Provost/CAO/Dean of Instruction .... Dr. Melenie BOLTON
32 Provost/Dean of Students .... Ms. Amanda HARKINS
10 Dean of Business Operations .... Mr. Lynn SPRAGGINS
35 Associate Dean of Student Services .... Ms. Glenda BLAND
09 Asc Dean Instruction/Instl Effectiv .... Ms. Sherie FLEMING
08 Librarian .... Ms. Denita OLIVER
06 Registrar .... Ms. Janice STEPHENS
26 Chief Public Relations Officer .... Mr. Brett PRITCHARD
37 Director Student Financial Aid .... Ms. Cindy ENTREKIN
38 Director Student Counseling .... Vacant
30 Advancement Officer .... Mr. Michael LOVETT

Chattahoochee Valley Community College (G)

2602 College Drive, Phenix City AL 36869-7960
County: Russell FICE Identification: 012182
Unit ID: 101028
Telephone: (334) 291-4900 Carnegie Class: Assoc/Pub-R-M
FAX Number: (334) 291-4944 Calendar System: Semester
URL: www.cv.edu
Established: 1973 Annual Undergrad Tuition & Fees (In-State): $3,312
Enrollment: 1,734 Coed
Affiliation or Control: State IRS Status: 501(c)3
Highest Offering: Associate Degree
Program: Occupational; 2-Year Principally Bachelor's Creditable
Accreditation: SC

01 President .... Dr. Donald G. CANNON
05 Dean of Instruction .... Vacant
32 Dean of Student & Admin Services .... Dr. David HODGE
103 Dean of Workforce Development .... Ms. Janet ORMOND
81 Chair of Mathematics & Science .... Mr. Earl COOK
57 Chair of Language & Fine Arts .... Ms. Susan LOCKWOOD
76 Chair of Health Sciences .... Ms. Resa LORD
88 Program Dir Public Safety Academy .... Ms. Mary SIMONTON
83 Chair of Social Sciences .... Dr. Ellen GUNTER
50 Chair Business & Information Tech .... Ms. Debra PLOTTS
08 Director Learning Resources Center .... Ms. Xueying CHEN
37 Director of Financial Aid .... Mrs. Joan WATERS
18 Director Facilities & Maintenance .... Mr. Johann WELLS
45 Dir of Institutional Effectiveness .... Vacant
26 Director of Marketing .... Vacant
41 Director of Athletics .... Mr. Adam THOMAS
38 Director of Counseling & Advising .... Ms. Cynthia FLOYD
27 Director of Information Systems .... Mr. Jody NOLES
88 Director of Student Development .... Ms. Vickie WILLIAMS
51 Director of Adult Education .... Ms. Darlene THOMPSON
15 Director of Human Resources .... Ms. Debbie BOONE
30 Director of Development .... Ms. Karen KELLY
10 Chief Financial Officer .... Ms. Brenda KELLEY
55 Evening Coordinator .... Mr. Reggie GORDY
88 Dir Trng for Existing Bus & Indus .... Vacant

Columbia Southern University (H)

21982 University Lane, Orange Beach AL 36561-3845
County: Baldwin FICE Identification: 041215
Unit ID: 450933
Telephone: (251) 981-3771 Carnegie Class: Master's L
FAX Number: (251) 981-3815 Calendar System: Other
URL: www.columbiasouthern.edu
Established: 1993 Annual Undergrad Tuition & Fees: $4,800
Enrollment: 17,594 Coed
Affiliation or Control: Proprietary IRS Status: Proprietary
Highest Offering: Doctorate
Program: Occupational; 2-Year Principally Bachelor's Creditable; Liberal Arts And General; Professional; Business Emphasis
Accreditation: DETC

01 President .... Mr. Robert G. MAYES, JR.
03 Provost .... Dr. Terry DIXON
11 Corporate Vice President .... Ms. Chantell COOLEY
05 VP Academics & Administration .... Dr. Karen J. SMITH
10 Vice President of Business Affairs .... Mr. Thomas COOLEY
27 VP of Marketing and Outreach .... Mr. Billy HAYES
13 Chief Information Officer .... Mr. Ken STYRON
88 VP of Business Development .... Mr. Rick COOPER
20 Assoc VP for Academic Services .... Mr. Elwin JONES
26 Associate VP of Marketing .... Ms. Jessica MCBRIDE
07 Assoc VP Admissions & Student Svcs .... Ms. Kathy COLE
06 Registrar .... Ms. Rachel FARRIS

09 Director of Institutional Research .... Dr. Katherine ODOM
32 Dean of Students .... Mr. F. Poche WAGUESPACK
97 Dean of Undergraduate Programs .... Ms. Nichole GOTSCHALL
58 Dean of Graduate Programs .... Dr. Mark PANTALEO
21 Director of Business Affairs .... Mr. Pat TROUP
37 Director of Financial Aid .... Mr. Aaron COLLINS
16 Director Employee Relations & Trng .... Ms. Sue BUTTS
45 Director of Quality Assurance .... Ms. Tina SHIPP
24 Director of Curriculum Development .... Mr. Brad MILLS
08 Director of Learning Resources .... Ms. Marsha HINNEN

Concordia College (A)

1804 Green Street, Selma AL 36703-3323
County: Dallas FICE Identification: 010554
Unit ID: 101073
Telephone: (334) 874-5700 Carnegie Class: Bac/Diverse
FAX Number: (334) 874-5755 Calendar System: Semester
URL: www.concordiaselma.edu
Established: 1922 Annual Undergrad Tuition & Fees: $8,090
Enrollment: 653 Coed
Affiliation or Control: Lutheran Church - Missouri Synod
IRS Status: 501(c)3
Highest Offering: Baccalaureate
Program: 2-Year Principally Bachelor's Creditable; Liberal Arts And General; Teacher Preparatory; Business Emphasis
Accreditation: SC

01 Chief Executive Officer .... Dr. Tilahun M. MENDEDO
05 Dean Academic Affs/Dir Special Pgms . Dr. Cheryl WASHINGTON
32 Acting Dean of Student Services .... Dr. Stanford ANGION
10 Business Manager/Dir of Purchasing .... Mr. Mike HARRIS
37 Director Financial Aid .... Mrs. Tharsteen BRIDGES
09 Research/Planning and Evaluation .... Mrs. Ruthie J. ORSBORN
64 Director of Music .... Mr. Bobby MCKENZIE
08 Librarian .... Mr. Scott WHITING
06 Registrar .... Mrs. Chinester GRAYSON
84 Director Enrollment Management .... Mrs. Gwendolyn MOORE
29 Director Alumni Affairs/Devel Ofc .... Mrs. Minnie MCMILLAN
30 Development Officer .... Dr. Kevin STEWART
18 Chief Facilities/Physical Plant .... Mr. Jeff HESTERMAN
27 Chief Information Officer .... Mrs. Christine WEERTS
36 Dir Student Placement/Counseling .... Ms. Sadie JARETT

*Education Corporation of America (B)

3660 Grandview Parkway Suite 300,
Birmingham AL 35243
County: Jefferson Identification: 666006
Telephone: (205) 329-7900 Carnegie Class: N/A
FAX Number: (205) 329-7906
URL: www.ecacolleges.com

01 President & Chief Executive Officer .... Mr. Tom A. MOORE, JR.
03 Exec VP/Chief Operations Officer .... Mr. Roger M. MILLER
05 Exec VP/Chf Compl Ofcr/Gen Counsel .... Mr. Roger L. SWARTZWELDER
26 Exec VP/Chief Marketing Officer .... Mr. Charles S. TRIERWEILER
10 Exec VP/Chief Financial Officer .... Mr. Christopher BOEHM
16 Exec VP/Human Resource & People Dev .... Mr. Michael C. WILLIAMS
13 Exec VP/Chief Info & Security Ofcr ..... Mr. Ronald G. MAILLETTE
84 Exec VP Campus Development .... Mr. William R. OWENS
05 Exec VP Academics .... Dr. Patricia KAPPER
20 SVP Compliance & Curriculum .... Ms. Judy E. LIMA
20 SVP Academic Operations & Training .... Ms. Shirley S. WILKINSON
36 SVP Career Services .... Mr. Scot STAPLETON
26 SVP Marketing Communications .... Mr. Donald W. KEITH
88 Regional VP & Operations Mgr .... Mr. Michael LARGENT
88 Regional VP & Operations Mgr .... Dr. Sara LAWHORNE
88 Regional VP Operations Gen Mgr .... Mr. David PODESTA
37 Vice President Student Finance .... Ms. Kathy CHEATHAM
21 Vice President Controller .... Mr. Ryan BREWER
15 VP Employee Services & Compliance .... Mr. J. Michael KELLY
07 Corporate VP Admissions .... Mr. Dean MAHAFFEY
88 VP Marketing .... Mr. Jason MANN
18 SVP Facilities & Interior Design .... Ms. Celeste PRESTENBACH
91 Vice Pres IT Operations & Support .... Mr. Lloyd J. WEAVER
15 VP Human Resources Regional .... Mr. Mitchell J. SRAIL

*Virginia College (C)

488 Palisades Boulevard, Birmingham AL 35209
County: Jefferson FICE Identification: 030106
Unit ID: 420307
Telephone: (205) 802-1200 Carnegie Class: Master's S
FAX Number: (205) 271-8225 Calendar System: Quarter
URL: www.vc.edu
Established: 1993 Annual Undergrad Tuition & Fees: $14,000
Enrollment: 1,900 Coed
Affiliation or Control: Proprietary IRS Status: Proprietary
Highest Offering: Master's
Program: Occupational; 2-Year Principally Bachelor's Creditable
Accreditation: ACICS, ACFEI, CIDA, SURGT

02 Campus President .... Ms. Lisa BACON
05 Academic Dean .... Dr. Jon CRISPIN
10 Controller .... Mr. Donny VINES

*Virginia College (D)

2021 Drake Avenue SW, Huntsville AL 35801
County: Madison Identification: 666400
Unit ID: 420316
Telephone: (256) 533-7387 Carnegie Class: Bac/Assoc
FAX Number: (256) 533-7785 Calendar System: Quarter
URL: www.vc.edu
Established: 1993 Annual Undergrad Tuition & Fees: $14,000
Enrollment: 731 Coed
Affiliation or Control: Proprietary IRS Status: Proprietary
Highest Offering: Baccalaureate
Program: 2-Year Principally Bachelor's Creditable
Accreditation: ACICS

02 Campus President .... Mr. James D. FOSTER
05 Vice President Academic Affairs .... Dr. James W. HICKS, JR.
07 Director of Admissions .... Ms. Angela BECK
37 Director of Student Finance .... Ms. Samantha L. WILLIAMS
36 Director of Career Services .... Mr. Greg COX
08 Librarian .... Ms. Dorothy J. BOWDEN
06 Registrar .... Ms. Bridget K. DAVIS

*Virginia College (E)

3725 Airport Boulevard, Suite 165, Mobile AL 36608
County: Mobile Identification: 666069
Unit ID: 445090
Telephone: (251) 343-7227 Carnegie Class: Assoc/PrivFP
FAX Number: (251) 343-7287 Calendar System: Quarter
URL: www.vc.edu
Established: 2001 Annual Undergrad Tuition & Fees: $18,320
Enrollment: 731 Coed
Affiliation or Control: Proprietary IRS Status: Proprietary
Highest Offering: Associate Degree
Program: Occupational
Accreditation: ACICS, SURGT

02 Campus President .... Mr. Eric BERRIOS
07 Director of Admissions .... Ms. April MARTIN
06 Registrar .... Ms. Sidna K. UTSEY
10 Campus Controller .... Ms. Donna CASSIDY

*Virginia College (F)

6200 Atlanta Highway, Montgomery AL 36117-2802
County: Montgomery Identification: 666408
Unit ID: 452115
Telephone: (334) 277-3390 Carnegie Class: Not Classified
FAX Number: (334) 277-0773 Calendar System: Quarter
URL: www.vc.edu
Established: 2008 Annual Undergrad Tuition & Fees: $21,900
Enrollment: 878 Coed
Affiliation or Control: Proprietary IRS Status: Proprietary
Highest Offering: Associate Degree
Program: 2-Year Principally Bachelor's Creditable
Accreditation: ACICS, SURGT

02 Campus President .... Christopher M. DUCOTE
05 Academic Dean .... Stevan MCCRORY
37 Director of Financial Planning .... Alexander LEWIS
07 Director of Admissions .... Bevin YESKEVICZ
36 Director of Career Services .... Arnesha HOGANS

Enterprise State Community College (G)

PO Box 1300, Enterprise AL 36331-1300
County: Coffee FICE Identification: 001015
Unit ID: 101143
Telephone: (334) 347-2623 Carnegie Class: Assoc/Pub-R-M
FAX Number: (334) 393-6223 Calendar System: Semester
URL: www.escc.edu
Established: 1963 Annual Undergrad Tuition & Fees (In-State): $3,930
Enrollment: 2,923 Coed
Affiliation or Control: State IRS Status: 501(c)3
Highest Offering: Associate Degree
Program: Occupational; 2-Year Principally Bachelor's Creditable
Accreditation: SC

01 President .... Dr. Nancy W. CHANDLER
05 Dean of Instruction .... Dr. Judith G. MILLER
84 Associate Dean Enrollment Mgmt .... Mr. M. Gary DEAS
32 Dean of Students .... Dr. Jeffrey COATS
10 Dean Administration & Finance ... Ms. Alonzetta LANDRUM-SIMS
12 Dean Alabama Aviation Center Ozark .... Mr. Tom KIRK
30 Assoc Dean Inst Advancement .... Ms. Susan STECK
26 Director of Public Relations .... Mrs. Montez M. VICKERS
37 Director Student Financial Aid .. Dr. Henry L. QUISENBERRY, JR.
14 Director Information Technology .... Dr. Sue BAUM
55 Director Evening Division .... Mr. Carl HOLBROOK
15 Director Personnel Services .... Ms. Angel LYNK

Faulkner University (H)

5345 Atlanta Highway, Montgomery AL 36109-3398
County: Montgomery FICE Identification: 001003
Unit ID: 101189
Telephone: (334) 272-5820 Carnegie Class: Bac/Diverse
FAX Number: (334) 386-7107 Calendar System: Semester
URL: www.faulkner.edu
Established: 1942 Annual Undergrad Tuition & Fees: $15,880
Enrollment: 3,302 Coed
Affiliation or Control: Churches Of Christ IRS Status: 501(c)3
Highest Offering: Doctorate
Program: Liberal Arts And General; Teacher Preparatory; Professional
Accreditation: SC, LAW, TED

01 President .... Dr. Billy D. HILYER
05 Vice President Academic Affairs .... Dr. Jack E. TUCCI
10 Vice President Financial Services .... Mrs. Wilma D. PHILLIPS
30 Vice President for Advancement .... Dr. Ben BRUCE
56 Vice Pres Extended Education Svcs .... Mr. Jim SPRATLIN
32 Vice President Student Services .... Mr. Joey WIGINTON
84 Vice President Enrollment .... Mr. Keith MOCK
61 Dean Jones School of Law .... Mr. Charles NELSON
49 Dean College Arts & Sciences .... Dr. Dave RAMPERSAD
50 Dean College Business/Exec Educ .... Dr. Dave KHADANGA
73 Dean College of Biblical Studies .... Dr. Cecil MAY
53 Interim Dean College of Education .... Dr. Jendia GRISSETT
88 Assoc Dean/Director of Law Library .... Mr. Tim CHINARIS
21 Assistant Vice President of Finance .... Mr. Jamie HORN
88 Asst Vice President Development .... Mr. Billy CAMP
88 Assoc Vice President Extended Svcs .... Mr. Mark HUNT
06 Registrar .... Mr. Don REYNOLDS
35 Dean of Students .... Mr. Faires AUSTIN
16 Director Human Resources/Diversity .... Mrs. Renee DAVIS
37 Director Student Financial Aid .... Mr. Buddy JACKSON
12 Director Mobile Center .... Mrs. Diane NEWELL
12 Director Birmingham Center .... Mr. Tim PARKER
12 Director Huntsville Center .... Ms. Barbara GAMBLE
41 Athletic Director .... Mr. Brent BARKER
08 Director of Libraries .... Mrs. Barbara KELLY
09 Director of Institutional Research .... Vacant
88 Director of International Studies .... Dr. Ed HICKS
26 Director of Public Relations .... Ms. Leigh BRANNAN
07 Director of Admissions .... Mr. Neil SCOTT
88 Director Student Success .... Vacant
29 Director of Alumni Relations .... Mr. Joel DILBECK
88 Director Quality Enhancement Plng .... Dr. Cindy WALKER
92 Director of Honors Program .... Dr. Robert WOODS
19 Security Coordinator .... Vacant
36 Director Career Services .... Mrs. Marie OTTINGER
38 Counselor .... Ms. Donna PUTNAM
04 Exec Assistant to the President .... Mrs. Lanette TAYLOR

Fortis College (I)

3590 Pleasant Valley Road, Mobile AL 36609
County: Mobile FICE Identification: 023410
Unit ID: 371052
Telephone: (251) 344-1203 Carnegie Class: Not Classified
FAX Number: (251) 344-1299 Calendar System: Other
URL: www.fortiscollege.edu
Established: 1978 Annual Undergrad Tuition & Fees: N/A
Enrollment: 212 Coed
Affiliation or Control: Proprietary IRS Status: Proprietary
Highest Offering: Associate Degree
Program: Occupational
Accreditation: ABHES, DA

01 Campus Director .... Mr. Walter BEQUETTE

Gadsden State Community College (J)

1001 Geo Wallace Drive, PO Box 227,
Gadsden AL 35902-0227
County: Etowah FICE Identification: 001017
Unit ID: 101240
Telephone: (256) 549-8200 Carnegie Class: Assoc/Pub-R-L
FAX Number: (256) 549-8444 Calendar System: Semester
URL: www.gadsdenstate.edu
Established: 1925 Annual Undergrad Tuition & Fees (In-State): $3,780
Enrollment: 7,031 Coed
Affiliation or Control: State IRS Status: 501(c)3
Highest Offering: Associate Degree
Program: Occupational; 2-Year Principally Bachelor's Creditable
Accreditation: SC, ACBSP, ADNUR, EMT, MLTAD, RAD

01 President .... Dr. Raymond W. STAATS
03 Vice President .... Dr. Valerie RICHARDSON
86 Vice President Government Relations .... Mr. John E. BLUE, II
05 Dean of Instructional Services .... Dr. Jim L. JOLLY
10 Dean Financial/Administrative Svcs .... Dr. James R. PRUCNAL
72 Dean Tech Educ/Workforce Develop .... Mr. Tim GREEN
04 Ast to Pres Chrk Cty Ops/Hlth Sci .... Dr. Martha LAVENDER
30 Assoc Dean Instnl Advance/Cmty Svc .... Ms. Pam JOHNSON
20 Assoc Dean Instructional Services .... Dr. Karen BLYTHE-SMITH
56 Assoc Dean for Distance Education .... Ms. Sara POOVEY
32 Asc Dean Stdnt Svcs/Instl Effective .... Dr. Teresa R. RHEA
26 Coordinator Public Relations .... Ms. Kay S. FOSTER
19 Director Safety & Security .... Mr. Sam LEDBETTER
21 Director of Financial Services .... Ms. Jacqueline HENDERSON
28 Director of Diversity & Compliance .... Ms. Michele BRADFORD
13 Director of Computer Services .... Mr. Jeff W. GREEN
16 Director Human Resources .... Ms. Kim S. COBB
41 Athletic Director .... Mr. Mike CANCILLA
38 Assoc Dean Stdnt Svcs & Counse Svcs ... Dr. Cheryl C. VICKERS
75 Director HBCU Initiatives .... Ms. Tarva VAUGHN
51 Director Adult Education .... Mr. Joe CAVENDAR
37 Director of Financial Aid .... Ms. Kelly D'EATH
06 Assistant to President/Registrar .... Mrs. Jennie P. DOBSON

George C. Wallace Community College - Dothan (A)

1141 Wallace Drive, Dothan AL 36303-9234
County: Dale FICE Identification: 001018
Unit ID: 101286
Telephone: (334) 983-3521 Carnegie Class: Assoc/Pub-R-M
FAX Number: (334) 983-6066 Calendar System: Semester
URL: www.wallace.edu
Established: 1947 Annual Undergrad Tuition & Fees (In-State): $3,330
Enrollment: 4,874 Coed
Affiliation or Control: State IRS Status: 501(c)3
Highest Offering: Associate Degree
Program: Occupational; 2-Year Principally Bachelor's Creditable; Business Emphasis
Accreditation: SC, ADNUR, EMT, MAC, PNUR, PTAA, RAD

01	President	Dr. Linda C. YOUNG
32	Dean of Student Affs/Sparks Campus	Ms. Jacqueline B. SCREWS
32	Dean of Student Dev/Wallace Campus	Mr. Mark SHOPE
05	Dean of Instructional Affairs	Dr. Mike BABB
10	Dean of Business Affairs	Mr. Lynn BELL
07	Director Enroll Svcs/Registrar	Mr. Keith SAULSBERRY
08	Dir Learning Resources Ctrs System	Mr. A. P. HOFFMAN
37	Director of Financial Aid	Ms. Erma PERRY
14	AS-400 Progm/Sys Admin	Mr. Gordon FREE
15	Director of Human Resources	Ms. Betty ROBERTS
09	Dir Institutional Effectiveness	Mr. Frank BAREFIELD
40	Bookstore Manager	Ms. Lori WATKINS
38	Director Student Counseling	Ms. Jean DAGOSTIN
21	Director of Accounting & Finance	Ms. Kay GAMBLE
26	Dir Public Relations & Marketing	Ms. Sally BUCHANAN
30	Dean Institutional Svcs/Com Dev	Dr. Ashli BOUTWELL

George Corley Wallace State Community College - Selma (B)

PO Box 2530, 3000 Earl Goodwin Pkwy, Selma AL 36702-2530
County: Dallas FICE Identification: 005699
Unit ID: 101301
Telephone: (334) 876-9227 Carnegie Class: Assoc/Pub-R-M
FAX Number: (334) 876-9250 Calendar System: Semester
URL: www.wccs.edu
Established: 1963 Annual Undergrad Tuition & Fees (In-State): $3,851
Enrollment: 2,116 Coed
Affiliation or Control: State IRS Status: 501(c)3
Highest Offering: Associate Degree
Program: Occupational; 2-Year Principally Bachelor's Creditable
Accreditation: SC, ADNUR, PNUR

01	President	Dr. James M. MITCHELL
05	Vice President for Instruction	Dr. Robert MCCONNELL
20	Instructional Administrator	Mr. Raji GOURDINE
10	Business Manager	Mrs. Bonita ALLEN
32	Dean of Students	Mrs. Donitha GRIFFIN
08	Librarian	Ms. Minnie CARSTARPHEN
66	Director Associate Degree Nursing	Ms. Becky CASEY
37	Director of Financial Aid/Cmty Educ	Mrs. Chenetta LEE
38	Counselor College Division	Ms. Anessa KIDD
09	Director of Institutional Research	Mr. Robby BENNETT
26	Director of Marketing/Col Relations	Mr. Johnny MOSS
19	Director Security/Safety	Mr. Ray MOORE
40	Director of Bookstore	Ms. Leigh Ann SMITH
41	Athletic Director	Mr. Marcus HANNAH
15	Personnel Specialist	Mrs. Helen COSBY
18	Act Chief Facilities/Physical Plant	Mr. Jimmie GOLDSBY
28	Director of Diversity	Vacant

Heritage Christian University (C)

PO Box HCU, Florence AL 35630-0050
County: Lauderdale FICE Identification: 021997
Unit ID: 101453
Telephone: (256) 766-6610 Carnegie Class: Spec/Faith
FAX Number: N/A Calendar System: Semester
URL: www.hcu.edu
Established: 1971 Annual Undergrad Tuition & Fees: $11,792
Enrollment: 208 Coed
Affiliation or Control: Churches Of Christ IRS Status: 501(c)3
Highest Offering: Master's
Program: Religious Emphasis
Accreditation: BI

01	President	Mr. Dennis H. JONES
05	Vice President of Academic Affairs	Dr. Bill BAGENTS
10	VP Business/Finance/Operations	Mr. Freddie P. MOON
32	Dean of Students	Mr. Cory COLLINS
58	Director of Graduate Studies	Dr. Jeremy BARRIER
30	Director Institutional Advancement	Mr. Philip GOAD
06	Registrar	Mrs. Charlotte ORR
08	Librarian	Miss Jamie S. COX
42	Director of Christian Service	Mr. Brad MCKINNON
84	Dir Enrollment Svcs/Stdnt Fin Aid	Mr. Larry DAVENPORT

Herzing University (D)

280 W Valley Avenue, Birmingham AL 35209-4816
County: Jefferson FICE Identification: 010193
Unit ID: 101365
Telephone: (205) 916-2800 Carnegie Class: Bac/Diverse
FAX Number: (205) 916-2807 Calendar System: Semester
URL: www.herzing.edu
Established: 1965 Annual Undergrad Tuition & Fees: $8,400
Enrollment: 938 Coed
Affiliation or Control: Proprietary IRS Status: Proprietary
Highest Offering: Baccalaureate
Program: Occupational; Technical Emphasis
Accreditation: &NH

01	President	Donald E. LEWIS

† Regional accreditation is carried under the parent institution in Madison, WI.

Huntingdon College (E)

1500 East Fairview Avenue, Montgomery AL 36106-2148
County: Montgomery FICE Identification: 001019
Unit ID: 101435
Telephone: (334) 833-4222 Carnegie Class: Bac/Diverse
FAX Number: (334) 833-4486 Calendar System: Semester
URL: www.huntingdon.edu
Established: 1854 Annual Undergrad Tuition & Fees: $20,990
Enrollment: 1,107 Coed
Affiliation or Control: United Methodist IRS Status: 501(c)3
Highest Offering: Baccalaureate
Program: Liberal Arts And General
Accreditation: SC, MUS

01	President	Rev. J. Cameron WEST
10	Treasurer & Sr VP for Plng & Admin	Mr. Jay A. DORMAN
30	VP for College & Alumni Relations	Mr. Anthony J. LEIGH
84	VP for Enrollment Management	Ms. Laura H. DUNCAN
05	Provost & Dean of the College	Dr. Sidney J. STUBBS
32	VP Student Life & Dean of Students	Dr. Frank R. PARSONS, JR.
20	Asst VP for Academic Enrichment	Dr. Erastus C. DUDLEY
27	Assoc VP for Comm and Marketing	Ms. Suellen S. OFE
35	Coordinator of Student Activities	Ms. Sara Beth TERRY
06	Registrar	Ms. Maryann M. BECK
13	Dir of Technology Support Services	Mr. Richard K. BRUNER
36	Dir of the Center for Career & Voc	Mr. Christopher CLARK
37	Dir Student Financial Services	Mr. Tommy G. DISMUKES
37	Dir of Student Financial Aid	Ms. Belinda G. DUETT
18	Director of Facilities and Grounds	Mr. T. Michael DUNN
40	Manager Follett Bookstore	Mr. Victor WYATT
23	Director of Student Health	Ms. Camilla IRVIN
04	Exec Asst to President/Corp Secy	Ms. Sandra B. KELSER
08	Director Houghton Memorial Library	Mr. Eric A. KIDWELL
07	Director of Admission	Mr. Joseph C. MILLER
21	Comptroller	Ms. Tina S. NIXON
39	Director of Residence Life	Ms. Sandra Betts HALL
41	Director of Athletics	Mr. Hugh H. PHILLIPS
42	Chaplain and Dir of Community Svcs	Rev. Brian L. SMITH
19	Chief of Security	Mr. Michael S. WARD
104	Dir College Travel & Event Planning	Ms. Jane T. WILLIAMS

Huntsville Bible College (F)

904 Oakwood Avenue NW, Huntsville AL 35811-1632
County: Madison FICE Identification: 038943
Unit ID: 449348
Telephone: (256) 539-0834 Carnegie Class: Assoc/PrivNFP4
FAX Number: (256) 539-0854 Calendar System: Semester
URL: www.hbc1.edu
Established: 1986 Annual Undergrad Tuition & Fees: $3,960
Enrollment: 121 Coed
Affiliation or Control: Baptist IRS Status: 501(c)3
Highest Offering: Baccalaureate
Program: Liberal Arts And General; Religious Emphasis
Accreditation: BI

01	President	Dr. John L. CLAY
05	Academic Dean	Dr. Willie T. BROWN
20	Dean of Instruction	Dr. Willie T. BROWN
06	Registrar	Mr. Jermaine TURNER

ITT Technical Institute (G)

6270 Park South Drive, Bessemer AL 35022-5655
County: Jefferson Identification: 666530
Unit ID: 414568
Telephone: (205) 497-5700 Carnegie Class: Spec/Tech
FAX Number: (205) 497-5799 Calendar System: Quarter
URL: www.itt-tech.edu
Established: 1994 Annual Undergrad Tuition & Fees: N/A
Enrollment: 1,020 Coed
Affiliation or Control: Proprietary IRS Status: Proprietary
Highest Offering: Baccalaureate
Program: Technical Emphasis
Accreditation: ACICS

† Branch campus of ITT Technical Institute, Knoxville, TN.

ITT Technical Institute (H)

9238 Madison Boulevard, Suite 500, Madison AL 35758
County: Madison Identification: 666695
Unit ID: 451945
Telephone: (256) 542-2900 Carnegie Class: Not Classified
FAX Number: (256) 542-2950 Calendar System: Quarter
URL: www.itt-tech.edu
Established: N/A Annual Undergrad Tuition & Fees: N/A
Enrollment: 454 Coed
Affiliation or Control: Proprietary IRS Status: Proprietary
Highest Offering: Baccalaureate
Program: Technical Emphasis
Accreditation: ACICS

† Branch campus of ITT Technical Institute, Orange, CA.

ITT Technical Institute (I)

3100 Cottage Hill Road, Bldg 3, Mobile AL 36606-2913
County: Mobile Identification: 666165
Unit ID: 450252
Telephone: (251) 472-4760 Carnegie Class: Assoc/PrivFP4
FAX Number: N/A Calendar System: Quarter
URL: www.itt-tech.edu
Established: 2006 Annual Undergrad Tuition & Fees: N/A
Enrollment: 475 Coed
Affiliation or Control: Proprietary IRS Status: Proprietary
Highest Offering: Baccalaureate
Program: Technical Emphasis
Accreditation: ACICS

† Branch campus of ITT Technical Institute, Orange, CA.

J.F. Drake State Technical College (J)

3421 Meridian Street N, Huntsville AL 35811-1584
County: Madison FICE Identification: 005260
Unit ID: 101462
Telephone: (256) 539-8161 Carnegie Class: Assoc/Pub-R-S
FAX Number: (256) 539-6439 Calendar System: Semester
URL: www.drakestate.edu
Established: 1961 Annual Undergrad Tuition & Fees (In-State): $3,144
Enrollment: 1,561 Coed
Affiliation or Control: State IRS Status: 501(c)3
Highest Offering: Associate Degree
Program: Occupational; 2-Year Principally Bachelor's Creditable; Technical Emphasis
Accreditation: @SC, COE

01	President	Dr. Helen T. MCALPINE
05	Dean of Instruction/Student Svcs	Dr. Patricia SIMS
10	Business Manager/Treasurer	Ms. Patricia HUGHES
103	Director of Workforce Development	Mr. Ricky WILLINGHAM
88	Dir of Accreditation & Program Dev	Dr. John REUTTER
20	Associate Dean of Instruction	Dr. Kemba CHAMBERS
15	Director of Human Resources	Vacant
14	Director Computer Services	Vacant
08	Director of Library Services	Mrs. Carla CLIFT
07	Director of Admissions	Ms. Monica SUDEALL
37	Director Student Financial Aid	Ms. Jennifer O'LINGER
26	Director of Public Relations	Mrs. Marty DUBEY
36	College Counselor	Mrs. April CLEMENT
86	Dir Title III Federal/State Rels	Ms. Ina WILSON
09	Director of Institutional Research	Mr. Harold BATTS
32	Student Services Management Dir	Vacant
51	Director of Adult Education	Mr. Ryan SMITH

J.F. Ingram State Technical College (K)

PO Box 220350, Deatsville AL 36022-0350
County: Elmore FICE Identification: 030025
Unit ID: 101471
Telephone: (334) 285-5177 Carnegie Class: Assoc/Pub-R-S
FAX Number: (334) 285-5328 Calendar System: Semester
URL: www.ingram.cc.al.us
Established: 1965 Annual Undergrad Tuition & Fees (In-State): $3,924
Enrollment: 1,166 Coed
Affiliation or Control: State IRS Status: 501(c)3
Highest Offering: Associate Degree
Program: Occupational; Technical Emphasis
Accreditation: COE

01	President	Mr. Douglas CHAMBERS
05	Dean of Instruction	Dr. James T. MERK
32	Dean of the College & Students	Mr. James E. WILSON
45	Dean of Strategic Planning and Eval	Mrs. Monica GREENE
15	Personnel/Inst Effectiveness	Dr. James T. MERK
07	Director of Admissions & Registrar	Mrs. Bonita OWENSBY
10	Director of Fiscal Affairs	Mrs. Dawnelle ROBINSON
36	Asst Transition Specialist	Mrs. Mary KING

Jacksonville State University (L)

700 Pelham Road N, Jacksonville AL 36265-1602
County: Calhoun FICE Identification: 001020
Unit ID: 101480
Telephone: (256) 782-5781 Carnegie Class: Master's L
FAX Number: (256) 782-5291 Calendar System: Semester
URL: www.jsu.edu
Established: 1883 Annual Undergrad Tuition & Fees (In-State): $6,112
Enrollment: 9,504 Coed
Affiliation or Control: State IRS Status: 501(c)3
Highest Offering: Doctorate
Program: Liberal Arts And General; Teacher Preparatory; Professional
Accreditation: SC, ART, BUS, CACREP, CS, DIETD, JOUR, MUS, NAIT, NURSE, SW, TED, THEA

01	President	Dr. William A. MEEHAN
05	Provost/VP Academic/Student Affairs	Dr. Rebecca O. TURNER

10 Vice Pres Admin/Business Affairs ... Mr. Clint CARLSON
30 Actg Vice Pres Inst Advancement ... Ms. Melanie DELAP
13 Actg Vice Pres Info Technology ... Mr. Vinson HOUSTON
20 Assoc Vice Pres Academic Affairs ... Dr. Joe DELAP
84 Assoc VP Enrol Mgmt/Student Affairs ... Dr. Tim KING
08 Dean of Library Services ... Mr. John-Bauer GRAHAM
58 Dean College Graduate Studies ... Dr. William D. CARR
49 Dean College Arts & Sciences ... Dr. James E. WADE
66 Dean College Nursing/Hlth Sciences ... Dr. Sarah V. LATHAM
53 Dean College Education/Prof Studies ... Dr. John HAMMETT
50 Dean Col Commerce/Business Admin ... Dr. William FIELDING
21 University Controller ... Ms. Allyson BARKER
07 Director of Admissions ... Mr. Andy GREEN
45 Dir Institutional Support Services ... Mr. Joe WHITMORE
44 Director Institutional Development ... Mr. Earl WARREN
39 Director Residence Life ... Mr. Kevin HOULT
88 Dir International House/Programs ... Dr. John J. KETTERER
29 Director of Alumni Relations ... Ms. Kaci OGLE
15 Director of Human Resources ... Ms. Rosalynn MARTIN
37 Director Financial Aid ... Ms. Vickie ADAMS
72 Director Department of Technology ... Mr. Terry MARBUT
41 Director Athletics ... Mr. Warren KOEGEL
09 Director Inst Research & Assessment ... Dr. Alicia SIMMONS
06 Registrar ... Ms. Kelly OSTERBIND
18 Director Physical Plant ... Mr. George F. LORD
36 Director Career Placement Services ... Ms. Rebecca E. TURNER
38 Dir Counseling/Disability Sppt Svcs ... Ms. Julie NIX
35 Director Student Life ... Mr. Terry CASEY
96 Director of Purchasing ... Ms. Pamela L. FINDLEY
26 Dir of Marketing/Communications ... Mr. Tim GARNER

James H. Faulkner State Community College (A)

1900 Highway 31 S, Bay Minette AL 36507-2698
County: Baldwin FICE Identification: 001060
Unit ID: 101161
Telephone: (251) 580-2100 Carnegie Class: Assoc/Pub-S-MC
FAX Number: (251) 580-2253 Calendar System: Semester
URL: www.faulknerstate.edu
Established: 1965 Annual Undergrad Tuition & Fees (In-State): $3,264
Enrollment: 4,620 Coed
Affiliation or Control: State IRS Status: 501(c)3
Highest Offering: Associate Degree
Program: Occupational; 2-Year Principally Bachelor's Creditable
Accreditation: SC, ACFEI, ADNUR, DA, EMT, PNUR, SURGT

01 President ... Dr. Gary L. BRANCH
05 Dean of Instruction ... Ms. Emily MARTIN
32 Dean of Student Development ... Dr. Brenda J. KENNEDY
35 Dean of Student Services ... Mr. Michael NIKOLAKIS
11 Dean Administrative Services ... Mr. Jim FITZ-GERALD
103 Dean of Workforce Development ... Ms. Patty HUGHSTON
26 Director College Relations ... Vacant
06 Registrar ... Ms. Betty SHEFFIELD
08 Dir Learning Resource ... Ms. Rheena ELMORE
37 Financial Aid Officer ... Ms. Chere VOGLER
88 Director High School Relations ... Ms. Carmelita MIKKELSEN
18 Director of Buildings & Ground ... Mr. Jim FITZ-GERALD
51 Director of Continuing Education ... Vacant
19 Director of Campus Police ... Mr. Larry JOHNSON
15 Director Human Resources ... Mrs. Laura BURKS
09 Dir Institutional Effectiveness/Dev ... Ms. Linda CALDWELL
66 Director Nursing & Allied Health ... Ms. Jean GROHAM
13 Coordinator Technology Services ... Mr. Brian STRICKLAND

Jefferson Davis Community College (B)

PO Box 958, Brewton AL 36427-0958
County: Escambia FICE Identification: 001021
Unit ID: 101499
Telephone: (251) 867-4832 Carnegie Class: Assoc/Pub-R-S
FAX Number: (251) 867-7399 Calendar System: Semester
URL: www.jdcc.edu
Established: 1965 Annual Undergrad Tuition & Fees (In-State): $3,788
Enrollment: 1,314 Coed
Affiliation or Control: State IRS Status: 501(c)3
Highest Offering: Associate Degree
Program: Occupational; 2-Year Principally Bachelor's Creditable
Accreditation: SC, ADNUR

01 Interim President ... Ms. Kathleen V. HALL
11 Director of Admin/Personnel ... Ms. Sherry J. MARTIN
05 Interim Dean of Instruction ... Dr. Carol BATES
10 Dean of Business Affairs ... Mr. Bernie WALL
32 Dean of Student Affairs ... Mr. David JONES
20 Associate Dean of Instruction ... Vacant
06 Registrar ... Ms. Robin SESSIONS
13 Director of MIS ... Mr. Anthony HARDY
26 Director Mktg & Community Relations ... Vacant
08 Librarian ... Mr. Jeffrey FAUST
37 Financial Aid Director ... Ms. Vanessa M. KYLES
09 Dir Institutional Research/Testing ... Ms. Carolyn WOODS
18 Chief Facilities/Physical Plant ... Mr. Richard LYNN
88 Dir Stdnt Support Svcs/Development ... Dr. Beth BILLY

Jefferson State Community College (C)

2601 Carson Road, Birmingham AL 35215-3098
County: Jefferson FICE Identification: 001022
Unit ID: 101505
Telephone: (205) 853-1200 Carnegie Class: Assoc/Pub-U-MC
FAX Number: (205) 983-5918 Calendar System: Semester
URL: www.jeffstateonline.com
Established: 1963 Annual Undergrad Tuition & Fees (In-State): $3,690
Enrollment: 9,700 Coed
Affiliation or Control: State IRS Status: 501(c)3
Highest Offering: Associate Degree
Program: Occupational; 2-Year Principally Bachelor's Creditable
Accreditation: SC, ACBSP, ACFEI, ADNUR, CONST, EMT, FUSER, MLTAD, PNUR, PTAA, RAD

01 President ... Dr. Judy M. MERRITT
03 Vice President ... Dr. Joe E. MORRIS
05 Dean of Instruction ... Dr. Joe E. MORRIS
75 Dean Career & Technical Education ... Ms. Norma G. BELL
30 Dean Campus Development/Campus Svcs ... Mr. Keith A. BROWN
10 Director Financial Services ... Ms. Mary WATSON
21 Business Manager ... Mr. J. Brian WILKINSON
32 Director of Student Services ... Dr. Linda J. HOOTON
97 Assoc Dean Transf Gen Stds Shelby ... Ms. Jeanette ROGERS
97 Assoc Dean Transf Gen Stds Jeffrsn ... Dr. Aliakbar R. YAZDI
106 Associate Dean Distance Education ... Mr. Alan B. DAVIS
51 Director College/Cmty/Corp Educ ... Ms. Kay C. POTTER
09 Info Svc/Institutional Research ... Ms. Peggy L. VANDERGRIFT
13 Director Information Technology ... Ms. Peggy L. VANDERGRIFT
37 Director Financial Aid ... Ms. Tracy R. ADAMS
84 Dean of Enrollment Services ... Dr. Phillip M. HOBBS
18 Director Maintenance ... Mr. Bill MIXON
08 Director of Learning Resources ... Ms. Barbara GOSS
36 Director Career/Job Resource Center ... Ms. Nancy F. BEAUCHAMP
07 Director Admissions and Retention ... Ms. Lillian OWENS
15 Director Human Resources ... Ms. Ruby RUSSELL
26 Director Media Relations ... Mr. David BOBO
96 Purchasing Coordinator ... Mr. Andy TERRY
19 Director Safety & Security ... Mr. Mark BAILEY

Judson College (D)

302 Bibb Street, Marion AL 36756-2504
County: Perry FICE Identification: 001023
Unit ID: 101541
Telephone: (334) 683-5100 Carnegie Class: Bac/A&S
FAX Number: (334) 683-5147 Calendar System: Semester
URL: www.judson.edu
Established: 1838 Annual Undergrad Tuition & Fees: $13,600
Enrollment: 312 Female
Affiliation or Control: Alabama Baptist State Convention
IRS Status: 501(c)3
Highest Offering: Baccalaureate
Program: Liberal Arts And General; Teacher Preparatory
Accreditation: SC, MUS, @SW

01 President ... Dr. David E. POTTS
05 Vice Pres & Academic Dean ... Dr. Sara B. KISER
32 Vice Pres & Dean of Students ... Mrs. Sandra S. FOWLER
07 Vice President Admissions ... Mrs. Charlotte S. CLEMENTS
10 Vice President Business Affairs ... Mr. Dennis W. FRODSHAM
30 VP Institutional Advancement ... Dr. Terry SMITH MORGAN
43 VP and General Counsel ... Mr. Bill MATHEWS

Lawson State Community College (E)

3060 Wilson Road, SW, Birmingham AL 35221-1798
County: Jefferson FICE Identification: 001059
Unit ID: 101569
Telephone: (205) 925-2515 Carnegie Class: Assoc/Pub-U-MC
FAX Number: (205) 925-8526 Calendar System: Semester
URL: www.lawsonstate.edu
Established: 1949 Annual Undergrad Tuition & Fees (In-State): $4,100
Enrollment: 3,570 Coed
Affiliation or Control: State IRS Status: 501(c)3
Highest Offering: Associate Degree
Program: Occupational; 2-Year Principally Bachelor's Creditable
Accreditation: SC, ACBSP, ADNUR, DA, PNUR

01 President ... Dr. Perry W. WARD
05 Vice Pres Instructional Services ... Dr. Bruce CRAWFORD
11 Vice President of Administration ... Mrs. Sharon CREWS
35 Dean of Students ... Dr. Cynthia ANTHONY
09 Director of Institutional Research ... Dr. Randy GLAZE
20 Academic Dean ... Dr. Sherri DAVIS
75 Asc Dean Business/Information Tech ... Dr. Alice MILTON
49 Asc Dn Liberal Arts/Coll Trans Pgms ... Dr. Karl PRUITT
76 Assoc Dean of Health Occupations ... Dr. Shelia MARABLE
75 Asst Dean Career Technical Programs ... Mr. Donald SLEDGE
84 Asst Dean of Admissions/Records ... Mr. Darren ALLEN
07 Director of Admissions ... Mr. Jeff SHELLEY
08 Librarian ... Ms. Sandra HENDERSON
37 Director Student Financial Aid ... Ms. Cassandra MATTHEWS
15 Director of Personnel Services ... Mrs. Vergie SPEARS
30 Chief Development ... Dr. Myrtes GREEN
26 Chief Public Relations Officer ... Mrs. Geri ALBRIGHT
18 Chief Facilities/Physical Plant ... Vacant
19 Director Safety/Security ... Mr. Walter WILLIAMS
13 Dir Computing and Information Mgmt ... Dr. Randy GLAZE
40 Director Bookstore ... Mr. Al YOUNG
31 Director Auxiliary Services ... Dr. Craig LAWRENCE
41 Athletic Director ... Mrs. Eleanor PITTS
06 Registrar ... Ms. Lori CHISEM
91 Director of Academic Computing ... Dr. Alice MILTON
24 Director Educational Media ... Ms. Sandra HENDERSON

39 Director Student Housing ... Mr. Robert SMITH
29 Coordinator Alumni Relations ... Mrs. Janice ORANGE
35 Coordinator Student Affairs ... Mrs. Sandra HOWARD
38 Coordinator Student Counseling ... Mrs. Janice WILLIAMS
84 Coordinator Enrollment Management ... Mrs. Phyllis YOUNGER

Lurleen B. Wallace Community College (F)

PO Drawer 1418, 1000 Dannelly Blvd, Andalusia AL 36420-1224
County: Covington FICE Identification: 008988
Unit ID: 101602
Telephone: (334) 222-6591 Carnegie Class: Assoc/Pub-R-S
FAX Number: (334) 881-2300 Calendar System: Semester
URL: www.lbwcc.edu
Established: 1969 Annual Undergrad Tuition & Fees (In-State): $3,270
Enrollment: 1,929 Coed
Affiliation or Control: State IRS Status: 501(c)3
Highest Offering: Associate Degree
Program: Occupational; 2-Year Principally Bachelor's Creditable; Technical Emphasis
Accreditation: SC, ADNUR, DMS, EMT, SURGT

01 President ... Dr. Herbert H. RIEDEL
05 Dean of Instruction ... Ms. Peggy LINTON
32 Dean of Student Affairs ... Ms. Judy H. HALL
10 Chief Financial Officer ... Mrs. Linda A. HARTIN
12 Vice Pres Greenville Campus Direct ... Dr. James D. KRUDOP
103 Assoc Dean Adult Educ/Workforce Dev ... Mr. Jimmy HUTTO
14 Assoc Dean Instr/Info Technology ... Mr. Greg APLIN
15 Director of Human Resources ... Ms. Peige JOSEY
09 Dir Inst Effectiveness & Quality ... Mr. Terry ZHU
18 Dir College Facilities/Maintenance ... Mr. Tim JONES
07 Director Admissions & Records ... Ms. Mackie STEPHENS
41 Athletic Director ... Mr. Steve HELMS
08 Director of Learning Resources ... Ms. Mary Beth GREEN
88 Director Student Support Services ... Mr. Jason CAIN
88 Dir Upward Bound/Andalusia Camp Dir ... Mr. Bridges ANDERSON
21 Assistant Chief Financial Officer ... Ms. Cynthia DONALDSON
37 Dir Financial Aid MacArthur/Luverne ... Ms. Wanda S. BASS
37 Dir Fin Aid Andalusia/Greenville ... Ms. Donna BASS
26 Public Info Officer/Dir Mktg & Dev ... Ms. Renée LEMAIRE

Marion Military Institute (G)

1101 Washington Street, Marion AL 36756-3213
County: Perry FICE Identification: 001026
Unit ID: 101648
Telephone: (800) 664-1842 Carnegie Class: Assoc/Pub-R-S
FAX Number: (334) 683-2380 Calendar System: Semester
URL: www.marionmilitary.edu
Established: 1842 Annual Undergrad Tuition & Fees (In-State): $6,700
Enrollment: 452 Coed
Affiliation or Control: State IRS Status: 501(c)3
Highest Offering: Associate Degree
Program: 2-Year Principally Bachelor's Creditable
Accreditation: SC

01 President ... Col. David J. MOLLAHAN
10 VP for Finance and Business Affairs ... Vacant
05 Vice President & Academic Dean ... Dr. Susan G. STEVENSON
41 Director of Athletics ... Dr. Michelle IVEY
32 VP for Student Affairs & Commandant ... Col. Thomas L. TATE
29 Director of Alumni Affairs ... Mrs. Carrie R. WILLIAMS
30 VP for Institutional Advancement ... Mrs. Suzanne MCKEE
88 ROTC Professor of Military Science ... LtCol. Sean RYAN
84 Interim VP for Enrollment Mgmt ... Mr. David IVEY
09 Director of Institutional Research ... Mrs. Donna LEEMON
06 Registrar ... Mrs. Wanda CALAME
38 Director of Guidance ... Ms. Brenda A. COOK
37 Director of Financial Aid ... Ms. Jacqueline WILSON
08 Library Director ... Mrs. Kelly A. GRIFFITHS
18 Supt of Buildings & Grounds ... Mr. Brian HALE
17 Director of Health Services ... Mr. Brandon TAYLOR

Miles College (H)

5500 Myron Massey Boulevard, Fairfield AL 35064-2621
County: Jefferson FICE Identification: 001028
Unit ID: 101675
Telephone: (205) 929-1000 Carnegie Class: Bac/Diverse
FAX Number: (205) 929-1453 Calendar System: Semester
URL: www.miles.edu
Established: 1905 Annual Undergrad Tuition & Fees: $8,200
Enrollment: 1,839 Coed
Affiliation or Control: Christian Methodist Episcopal IRS Status: 501(c)3
Highest Offering: Baccalaureate
Program: Liberal Arts And General; Teacher Preparatory
Accreditation: SC, SW, TED

01 President ... Dr. George T. FRENCH, JR.
05 Dean Academic Affairs ... Dr. Kenneth JONES
100 Special Asst/Chief of Staff ... Mr. Kenneth COACHMAN
10 Chief Financial Ofcr/Business Affs ... Mrs. Diana W. KNIGHTON
07 Director Admissions & Recruitment ... Mr. Christopher ROBERTSON
06 Registrar ... Vacant
08 Librarian ... Dr. Geraldine BELL
30 Director Institutional Development ... Mr. W. Frank TOPPING
32 Dean Student Affairs ... Ms. Griena KNIGHT

36 Director Career Planning/Placement ... Dr. Glenda BROWN-WADE
26 Director College Relations ... Dr. Rickey C. LEE
09 Dir Institutional Effective/Rsrch ... Dr. Bashen WELCH
37 Director Financial Aid ... Mr. Percy LANIER
18 Director Physical Plant ... Mr. Edward JENKINS
25 Director Sponsored Programs ... Vacant
35 Director Student Activities ... Mrs. Dorothy ROWE
38 Dir Counseling/Advising/Testing ... Dr. Joyce WOOD
84 Dir Enrollment Mgmt/Alumni Affs ... Mr. Charles CROCKROM, SR.
15 Director Personnel Services ... Mrs. Verlanda TATE
42 Chaplain ... Rev. Larry BATIE
14 Manager of Data Processing ... Ms. Jackie HUDSON

Northeast Alabama Community College (A)

PO Box 159, 138 Alabama Highway 35,
Rainsville AL 35986-0159
County: DeKalb/Jackson FICE Identification: 001031
Unit ID: 101897
Telephone: (256) 638-4418 Carnegie Class: Assoc/Pub-R-M
FAX Number: (256) 638-3052 Calendar System: Semester
URL: www.nacc.edu
Established: 1963 Annual Undergrad Tuition & Fees (In-State): $3,144
Enrollment: 3,435 Coed
Affiliation or Control: State IRS Status: 501(c)3
Highest Offering: Associate Degree
Program: Occupational; 2-Year Principally Bachelor's Creditable; Business Emphasis
Accreditation: SC, ADNUR, EMT, PNUR

01 President ... Dr. J. David CAMPBELL
05 Dean of Instruction ... Dr. Joseph D. BURKE
56 Dean of Extended Day Program ... Ms. Marilyn REECE
32 Dean of Student Services ... Ms. Tonie M. NIBLETT
11 Dean of Admin Services/Registrar ... Mr. Larry D. GUFFEY
37 Director of Financial Aid ... Mr. Nixon WILLMON
103 Dir Workforce Devel/Skills Training ... Mr. Mike KENNAMER
26 Chief Public Relations Officer ... Mrs. Debra A. BARRENTINE
07 Dir Admissions & Student Services ... Mrs. Tonie M. NIBLETT
09 Dir Instl Planning & Assessment ... Ms. Martha BANKS
18 Chief Facilities/Physical Plant ... Mr. Kent JONES
06 Registrar/Chief Bus Ofcr/Dir Purchg ... Mr. Larry D. GUFFEY
30 Development Director ... Ms. Heather RICE
19 Director of Security ... Mr. Norman SMITH

Northwest - Shoals Community College (B)

800 George Wallace Boulevard,
Muscle Shoals AL 35661-3205
County: Colbert FICE Identification: 005697
Unit ID: 101736
Telephone: (256) 331-5200 Carnegie Class: Assoc/Pub-R-M
FAX Number: (256) 331-5222 Calendar System: Semester
URL: www.nwscc.edu
Established: 1963 Annual Undergrad Tuition & Fees (In-State): $3,216
Enrollment: 4,489 Coed
Affiliation or Control: State IRS Status: 501(c)3
Highest Offering: Associate Degree
Program: Occupational; 2-Year Principally Bachelor's Creditable
Accreditation: SC, ADNUR, EMT

01 President ... Dr. Humphrey LEE
05 Vice President of Instruction ... Dr. Glenda COLAGROSS
10 Chief Fiscal Officer ... Dr. Paul MERRILL
32 Vice Pres of Student Development ... Dr. Karen BERRYHILL
35 Assoc Dean Students/Athletic Admin ... Mr. Charles TAYLOR
09 Assc Dean Instl Effect/Dist Ed/Dev ... Mr. John MCINTOSH
20 Assoc Dean Instructional Programs ... Mr. Timmy JAMES
26 Director Mktg/Public Rels/Promo Svc ... Mr. Tom CARTER
30 Acting Director of Development ... Ms. Dianne PACE
37 Director of Financial Aid ... Ms. Laurel TURBYFILL
08 Chair Learning Resource Center ... Mrs. Rachel TRAPP
07 Dir Recruitment/Admissions/Records ... Mr. Tom CARTER
15 Director of Human Resources ... Ms. Pam TOWNSEND
29 Director of Alumni Relations ... Vacant
36 Director of the Career Center ... Ms. Linda WAIDE
84 Director of Enrollment Management ... Mr. Tom CARTER
14 Director of Management Info Systems ... Mr. Alan MITCHELL
19 Chief Safety Officer ... Mr. Sammie WASHINGTON
07 Coordinator Admissions ... Ms. Sheila WILLIAMS

Oakwood University (C)

7000 Adventist Boulevard, NW, Huntsville AL 35896-0003
County: Madison FICE Identification: 001033
Unit ID: 101912
Telephone: (256) 726-7000 Carnegie Class: Bac/Diverse
FAX Number: (256) 726-8335 Calendar System: Semester
URL: www.oakwood.edu
Established: 1896 Annual Undergrad Tuition & Fees: $14,822
Enrollment: 1,915 Coed
Affiliation or Control: Seventh-day Adventist IRS Status: 501(c)3
Highest Offering: Master's
Program: Occupational; Liberal Arts And General; Teacher Preparatory
Accreditation: SC, ACBSP, DIETD, DIETI, NUR, SW, TED

01 President ... Dr. Leslie POLLARD
05 Vice President Academic Affairs ... Dr. Garland DULAN
10 Vice President Financial Affairs ... Ms. Sabrina COTTON
32 Vice President Student Services ... Vacant
30 Vice President Development ... Vacant
13 Vice Pres Information Technology ... Vacant
20 Asst Vice Pres Academic Affairs ... Dr. Roy MALCOLM
21 Asst VP Financial Affs/Controller ... Mrs. Gail CALDWELL
15 Asst Vice Pres Student Services ... Mr. Philip NIXON
16 Director Human Resources ... Mrs. Sylvia GERMANY
25 Director Sponsored Programs ... Mrs. Marcia BURNETTE
26 Director Public Relations ... Ms. Michelle SOLOMON
07 Director Enrollment Management ... Mrs. Joyce SMITH
37 Director Financial Aid ... Ms. Joylyn TROTMAN
06 Director Records ... Mrs. Shirley SCOTT
39 Residence Life Coordinator-Men ... Mr. Tracey HOLIDAY
08 Director Library Services ... Mrs. Paulette JOHNSON
09 Director Inst Effectiveness ... Mrs. Janis NEWBORN
18 Director Physical Plant ... Mr. Colins ALEXANDER
19 Director Security ... Mr. Lewis EAKINS
29 Director Alumni Relations ... Ms. Barbara STOVALL
36 Director Career Services & Testing ... Mrs. Sonia PAUL
38 Dir Counseling & Health Services ... Dr. Janice LEWIS-THOMAS
51 Dir Adult & Continuing Education ... Dr. Rachel WILLIAMS
42 Chaplain ... Mr. T. Marshall KELLY
46 Dir Research & Faculty Dev ... Vacant
89 Director Freshmen Studies ... Mr. James HUTCHINSON
50 Chair Business & Info Systems ... Vacant
53 Chair Education ... Dr. James MBYIRUKIRA
59 Chair Family & Consumer Sciences ... Dr. Marta SOVYANHADI
60 Chair English & Foreign Languages ... Dr. Derek BOWE
64 Chair Music ... Dr. Audley CHAMBERS
65 Chair Biological Sciences ... Dr. Safawo GULLO
65 Chair Chemistry ... Dr. Kenneth LAI HING
66 Chair Nursing ... Dr. Flora FLOOD
68 Chair Health & Physical Education ... Dr. Howard SHAW
70 Chair Social Work ... Dr. George ASHLEY
73 Chair Religion & Theology ... Dr. Agniel SAMSON
81 Chair Math & Computer Science ... Mrs. Kathleen DOBBINS
82 Chair History ... Dr. Ciro SEPULVEDA
83 Chair Psychology ... Dr. Howard WEEMS
60 Chair Communication ... Dr. Rennae ELLIOTT
96 Director Purchasing ... Mrs. Belita NEWBY

Prince Institute of Professional Studies (D)

7735 Atlanta Highway, Montgomery AL 36117-4231
County: Montgomery FICE Identification: 022960
Unit ID: 101958
Telephone: (334) 271-1670 Carnegie Class: Assoc/PrivFP
FAX Number: (334) 271-1671 Calendar System: Quarter
URL: www.princeinstitute.edu
Established: 1976 Annual Undergrad Tuition & Fees: $11,400
Enrollment: 114 Coed
Affiliation or Control: Proprietary IRS Status: Proprietary
Highest Offering: Associate Degree
Program: Occupational
Accreditation: ACICS

01 Director ... Mrs. Patricia L. HILL
05 Dean of Academic Affairs ... Ms. Ann C. SCHMIDT
07 Director of Admissions ... Ms. Sherry A. HILL
03 Assistant Director ... Mrs. Candace H. SHEPHERD
37 Financial Aid Administrator ... Mr. Reginald JAMES

Reid State Technical College (E)

PO Box 588, Evergreen AL 36401-0588
County: Conecuh FICE Identification: 005692
Unit ID: 101994
Telephone: (251) 578-1313 Carnegie Class: Assoc/Pub-R-S
FAX Number: (251) 578-5355 Calendar System: Semester
URL: www.rstc.edu
Established: 1966 Annual Undergrad Tuition & Fees (In-State): $3,360
Enrollment: 743 Coed
Affiliation or Control: State IRS Status: 501(c)3
Highest Offering: Associate Degree
Program: Occupational; Technical Emphasis
Accreditation: ACBSP, COE

01 President ... Dr. Douglas M. LITTLES
05 Dean of College ... Ms. F. Diannah ROWSER
32 Asst Dean Students/Enrollment Mgmt ... Dr. Tangela PURIFOY
103 Assoc Dean Workforce Development ... Dr. Alesia K. STUART
84 Asst Dean Enrollment Management ... Dr. Tangela PURIFOY
09 Assoc Dean for Institutional Effect ... Ms. Wilma Quarker SMITH
37 Director Financial Aid ... Ms. Christy GOODWIN
07 Dir of Recruiting/Retention/Plcmt ... Ms. Coretta BOYKIN
38 Director of Counseling ... Dr. Linda G. ALFORD
21 Business Manager ... Mr. David J. RHODES

Remington College, Mobile Campus (F)

828 Downtowner Loop W, Mobile AL 36609-5404
County: Mobile FICE Identification: 026055
Unit ID: 366535
Telephone: (251) 343-8200 Carnegie Class: Assoc/PrivFP4
FAX Number: (251) 343-0577 Calendar System: Quarter
URL: www.remingtoncollege.edu
Established: 1986 Annual Undergrad Tuition & Fees: $30,900
Enrollment: 512 Coed
Affiliation or Control: Proprietary IRS Status: Proprietary
Highest Offering: Associate Degree
Program: Occupational; 2-Year Principally Bachelor's Creditable; Technical Emphasis
Accreditation: ACCSC

01 President ... Mr. Stephen M. BACKMAN
05 Director of Education ... Ms. Cindy MCMILLAN
37 Financial Aid Director ... Ms. Linda K. CALVANESE
07 Director of Admissions ... Mr. Brent MALVEAUX
36 Dir of Career Services & Placement ... Ms. Ellen JONES

Samford University (G)

800 Lakeshore Drive, Birmingham AL 35229-0001
County: Jefferson FICE Identification: 001036
Unit ID: 102049
Telephone: (205) 726-2011 Carnegie Class: Master's M
FAX Number: (205) 726-2171 Calendar System: 4/1/4
URL: www.samford.edu
Established: 1841 Annual Undergrad Tuition & Fees: $23,963
Enrollment: 4,715 Coed
Affiliation or Control: Southern Baptist IRS Status: 501(c)3
Highest Offering: Doctorate
Program: Liberal Arts And General; Teacher Preparatory; Professional; Fine Arts Emphasis
Accreditation: SC, ANEST, BUS, CIDA, DIETD, LAW, MUS, NURSE, PHAR, TED, THEOL

01 President ... Dr. T. Andrew WESTMORELAND
03 Provost/Exec Vice President ... Dr. J. Bradley CREED
32 Vice President for Student Affairs ... Dr. Phil KIMREY
30 Vice President of Advancement ... Mr. W. Randall PITTMAN
10 Vice President of Business Affairs ... Mr. Harry B. BROCK, III
11 Vice Pres Operations/Planning ... Dr. Sarah C. LATHAM
21 Associate VP Decision Support ... Dr. Tatyana KARAMAN
05 Associate Provost ... Dr. Mary Sue BALDWIN
20 Assistant Provost ... Dr. Nancy BIGGIO
04 Assistant to the President ... Dr. Michael D. MORGAN
13 Chief Information Officer ... Mr. David HAKANSON
21 Controller ... Mr. Mike DARWIN
41 Athletic Director ... Mr. Martin NEWTON
88 Director of Academic Success Pgm ... Ms. Bridget ROSE
07 Director of Admissions ... Mr. Brian WILLETT
88 Interim Director Adult Degree Pgm ... Ms. Laura LEE
88 Director of Advancement Services ... Mrs. Judi F. AUCOIN
29 Director Alumni & Parent Programs ... Mr. David GOODWIN
44 Director of Annual Giving ... Ms. Sheri RANSOME
40 Director of the Bookstore ... Mr. Alan B. MORRIS
21 Director of Business Services ... Mr. Mike MCCORMACK
88 Director of Capital Planning & Imp ... Mr. David T. WHITT
36 Director Career Development Center ... Vacant
38 Director Counseling Services ... Vacant
88 Dir Event Management & Space Utiliz ... Mr. Ken ENGLAND
18 Director of Facilities Management ... Mr. Mark FULLER
37 Director of Financial Aid ... Mr. Lane M. SMITH
15 Director of Human Resources ... Mr. Fred R. ROGAN
09 Director Inst Effectiveness ... Mrs. Karen G. HAMBY
104 Director of International Education ... Dr. David SHIPLEY
43 Director Investments and Legal Svcs ... Ms. Lisa IMBRAGULIO
08 Director of Library ... Ms. Kimmetha D. HERNDON
26 Director of Media/Public Relations ... Mr. William A. NUNNELLEY
19 Director of Pub Safety & Emer Mgmt ... Mr. Mike COPPAGE
39 Director Residence Life & Univ Svcs ... Ms. Lauren M. TAYLOR
88 Director of Risk Mmgt & Insurance ... Mr. James A. CLEMENT
23 Director Student Health Services ... Mrs. Shauna N. YELTON
88 Director Venue Management ... Mr. Sean WRIGHT
105 Director of Web Services ... Mr. Josh THOMAS
07 Dean of Admissions ... Mr. Jason BLACK
06 Dean Academic Services/Registrar ... Mr. Paul G. AUCOIN
06 Associate Registrar ... Mrs. Nancy B. MILLER
42 Assistant Dean for Spritual Life ... Dr. Matthew S. KERLIN
35 Assistant Dean of Student Services ... Mr. Garry L. ATKINS
35 Assistant Dean for Campus Life ... Ms. Renie MOSS
50 Dean Brock School of Business ... Dr. J. Howard FINCH
49 Dean Howard College Arts/Sciences ... Dr. David W. CHAPMAN
64 Dean School of the Arts ... Dr. Joseph HOPKINS
53 Dean Education/Professional Studies ... Dr. Jean A. BOX
66 Dean Ida Moffett School of Nursing ... Dr. Nena F. SANDERS
67 Dean McWhorter School of Pharmacy ... Dr. Charlie SANDS
73 Dean Beeson School of Divinity ... Dr. Timothy F. GEORGE
61 Dean Cumberland School of Law ... Mr. John L. CARROLL

Selma University (H)

1501 Lapsley Street, Selma AL 36701-5232
County: Dallas FICE Identification: 001037
Unit ID: 102058
Telephone: (334) 872-2533 Carnegie Class: Spec/Faith
FAX Number: (334) 872-7746 Calendar System: Semester
URL: www.selmauniversity.org
Established: 1878 Annual Undergrad Tuition & Fees: $5,750
Enrollment: 300 Coed
Affiliation or Control: Baptist IRS Status: 501(c)3
Highest Offering: Master's
Program: Liberal Arts And General; Religious Emphasis
Accreditation: BI

01 President ... Dr. Alvin A. CLEVELAND, SR.
05 Dean ... Dr. Kayarda LOWE

Shelton State Community College (A)

9500 Old Greensboro Road, Tuscaloosa AL 35405-8522
County: Tuscaloosa FICE Identification: 005691
Unit ID: 102067
Telephone: (205) 391-2211 Carnegie Class: Assoc/Pub-R-L
FAX Number: (205) 391-2426 Calendar System: Semester
URL: www.sheltonstate.edu
Established: 1953 Annual Undergrad Tuition & Fees (In-State): $4,080
Enrollment: 5,759 Coed
Affiliation or Control: State IRS Status: 501(c)3
Highest Offering: Associate Degree
Program: Occupational; 2-Year Principally Bachelor's Creditable
Accreditation: #SC, ADNUR, PNUR

01 President ... Dr. Mark A. HEINRICH
100 Assistant to the President ... Dr. Graham HATCHER
26 Spec Asst to Pres for External Affs ... Ms. Camille P. COCHRANE
10 Dean of Business Services ... Vacant
32 Dean of Student Services ... Dr. Thomas HUEBNER
13 Dean Technology/Instl Rsrch ... Ms. Michelle JARRELL
12 Director Fredd Campus/Title III ... Mr. Ronald RANGE
20 Assoc Dean ... Ms. Linda GROTE
20 Assoc Dn Trng Existing Bus/Industry ... Mr. Jason MOORE
21 Associate Dean of Business Services ... Ms. DeLane BAILEY
06 Asst Dean Student Svcs/Registrar ... Mr. Byron ABSTON
76 Assistant Dean for Health Services ... Ms. Gladys HILL
35 Asst Dean for Student Services ... Ms. Jeanetta HARGROW
35 Assistant Dean Student Services ... Ms. Susan MOHUN
37 Asst Dean Financial Aid ... Ms. Amanda HARBISON
15 Director of Personnel Services ... Mr. Johnny F. PARKER
88 Director Special Projects ... Ms. Channing HOWINGTON
08 Director Library Services ... Dr. Debbie J. GRIMES
30 Director Institutional Advancement ... Vacant
103 Director Workforce Development ... Mr. Lew DRUMMOND
25 Director Grant/Resource Development ... Vacant
88 Director Adult Education ... Dr. Fran TURNER
38 Counseling Center Coordinator ... Ms. Holly ELLIOTT

Snead State Community College (B)

PO Box 734, Boaz AL 35957-0734
County: Marshall FICE Identification: 001038
Unit ID: 102076
Telephone: (256) 593-5120 Carnegie Class: Assoc/Pub-R-M
FAX Number: (256) 593-7180 Calendar System: Semester
URL: www.snead.edu
Established: 1898 Annual Undergrad Tuition & Fees (In-State): $4,416
Enrollment: 2,483 Coed
Affiliation or Control: State IRS Status: Exempt
Highest Offering: Associate Degree
Program: Occupational; 2-Year Principally Bachelor's Creditable
Accreditation: SC, ADNUR, PNUR

01 President ... Dr. Robert EXLEY
10 Chief Financial Officer ... Mr. Mark RICHARD
05 Chief Academic Officer/CSSO ... Dr. Larry MILLER
13 Chief IT Officer ... Mr. Randy MALTBIE
26 Director of PR/Marketing ... Ms. Shelley SMITH
38 Director of Testing ... Ms. Jessamine HUFFMAN
07 Dir Admissions & Records ... Mr. Jason CANNON
09 Assoc Dean Academic Planning/Rsrch ... Dr. Jason WATTS
81 Science Division Director ... Ms. Deborah RHODEN
79 Humanities Division Director ... Dr. Cynthia DENHAM
83 Social Science Division Director ... Mr. Alan BATES
81 Mathematics Division Director ... Mr. Blake LEETH
50 Business Division Director ... Mr. Vann SCOTT
75 Technology Division Director ... Mr. Greg RANDALL
103 Director Community Education ... Ms. Teresa WALKER
76 Director Health Sciences ... Ms. Amy LANGLEY
41 Athletic Director ... Mr. Sean ABERNATHY
08 Head Librarian ... Mr. John MILLER
15 Human Resources Specialist ... Ms. Barbara KILPATRICK
18 Director of Physical Plant ... Mr. Steve WILLIAMS
37 Director of Financial Aid ... Ms. Darylann THOMAS

South University (C)

5355 Vaughn Road, Montgomery AL 36116-1120
County: Montgomery FICE Identification: 004463
Unit ID: 101116
Telephone: (334) 395-8800 Carnegie Class: Bac/Assoc
FAX Number: (334) 395-8859 Calendar System: Quarter
URL: www.southuniversity.edu
Established: 1887 Annual Undergrad Tuition & Fees: $15,735
Enrollment: 732 Coed
Affiliation or Control: Proprietary IRS Status: Proprietary
Highest Offering: Master's
Program: Occupational; 2-Year Principally Bachelor's Creditable; Professional
Accreditation: &SC, MAC, NURSE, PTAA

01 President ... Mr. Victor K. BIEBIGHAUSER
05 Dean of Academic Affairs ... Mr. Donald A. EDWARDS, JR.
32 Dean of Student Affairs ... Ms. Patricia MCCORMICK
37 Director of Financial Aid ... Ms. Yvonne R. MILLER
07 Director of Admissions ... Ms. Anna M. PEARSON

† Regional accreditation is carried under the parent institution in Savannah, GA.

Southeastern Bible College (D)

2545 Valleydale Road, Birmingham AL 35244-2083
County: Shelby FICE Identification: 022704
Unit ID: 102261
Telephone: (205) 970-9200 Carnegie Class: Spec/Faith
FAX Number: (205) 970-9207 Calendar System: Semester
URL: www.sebc.edu
Established: 1935 Annual Undergrad Tuition & Fees: $11,600
Enrollment: 189 Coed
Affiliation or Control: Independent Non-Profit IRS Status: 501(c)3
Highest Offering: Baccalaureate
Program: Liberal Arts And General; Religious Emphasis
Accreditation: BI

01 President ... Dr. Don HAWKINS
05 Vice Pres for Education/Provost ... Dr. Vicki L. WOLFE
10 Vice Pres for Operations ... Mr. Paul WILLARD
30 Vice Pres for Advancement ... Mr. Cliff MCARDLE
32 Dean of Students ... Ms. Kristie HARRICK
42 Campus Pastor ... Mr. Micah SIMPSON
49 Int Chair of Dept Arts/Sciences ... Dr. Dwain WALDREP
53 Chair of Dept of Education ... Dr. Lynn GANNETT-MALICK
73 Chair of Dept of Biblical Studies ... Dr. Jason SNYDER
04 Admin Asst to the President ... Mrs. Anita SCROGGINS
06 Registrar ... Mr. Joel WOLFE
08 Librarian ... Mr. Paul ROBERTS
09 Coord Institutional Effectiveness ... Mrs. Michelle HOWER
18 Facilities Director ... Mr. David POWLESS
26 Director of Alumni/Public Relations ... Mrs. Jenny ELLISON
37 Director Student Financial Aid ... Mr. Jay POWELL
55 Director of ACHIEVE Adult Education ... Mr. Steven CLECKLER

Southern Union State Community College (E)

PO Box 1000, Wadley AL 36276-1000
County: Randolph FICE Identification: 001040
Unit ID: 251260
Telephone: (256) 395-2211 Carnegie Class: Assoc/Pub-R-M
FAX Number: (256) 395-2215 Calendar System: Semester
URL: www.suscc.edu
Established: 1922 Annual Undergrad Tuition & Fees (In-State): $3,840
Enrollment: 4,869 Coed
Affiliation or Control: State IRS Status: 501(c)3
Highest Offering: Associate Degree
Program: Occupational; 2-Year Principally Bachelor's Creditable
Accreditation: SC, ADNUR, EMT, RAD, SURGT

01 President ... Dr. Amelia PEARSON
05 Dean of Academics ... Dr. Mary Jean WHITE
32 Dean of Students ... Ms. Tiffany SANDERS
97 Assoc Dean of Instruction ... Mr. Steve SPRATLIN
72 Assoc Dean of Technology ... Mr. Bud EDWARDS
20 Assoc Dean Student Development ... Mr. Gary BRANCH
13 Director Management Info Systems ... Ms. Cherly JORDAN
41 Athletic Director ... Mr. Ron RADFORD
30 Director Institutional Advancement ... Vacant
06 Registrar ... Ms. Catherine STRINGFELLOW
26 Chief Public Relations Officer ... Ms. Shondae BROWN
10 Chief Business Officer ... Mr. Ben JORDAN
35 Coordinator of Student Life ... Ms. Lori DANIEL

Spring Hill College (F)

4000 Dauphin Street, Mobile AL 36608-1791
County: Mobile FICE Identification: 001041
Unit ID: 102234
Telephone: (251) 380-4000 Carnegie Class: Master's S
FAX Number: (251) 460-2182 Calendar System: Semester
URL: www.shc.edu
Established: 1830 Annual Undergrad Tuition & Fees: $26,730
Enrollment: 1,390 Coed
Affiliation or Control: Roman Catholic IRS Status: 501(c)3
Highest Offering: Master's
Program: Liberal Arts And General; Teacher Preparatory
Accreditation: SC, NURSE

01 President ... Rev. Richard P. SALMI, SJ
05 Provost/Vice Pres Academic Affairs ... Dr. George E. SIMS
10 Vice President Business & Finance ... Ms. Rhonda SHIRAZI
32 Vice Pres Student Affs/Dn Stdnts ... Mr. Joe DEIGHTON
84 Vice Pres Enrollment Mgmt ... Mrs. Laura ALLSUP
20 Assistant VP for Academic Affairs ... Ms. Theresa MCGONAGLE CRIDER
58 Assoc Provost Grad & Cont Studies ... Mrs. Ramona M. HILL
35 Associate Dean of Students ... Ms. Margarita PEREZ
07 Director of Admissions ... Mr. Brian STUDEBAKER
21 Controller ... Vacant
37 Director of Financial Aid ... Mrs. Ellen FOSTER
06 Registrar ... Mr. Stuart MOORE
88 Director Student Development Center ... Ms. Josetta MULLOY
29 Director of Alumni & Parents ... Mrs. Monde DONALDSON
91 Director Administrative Computing ... Mr. Mac HORTON
90 Dir Information Technology Services ... Mr. Glenn R. BELL
16 Director of Personnel ... Ms. Patricia A. DAVIS
19 Director of Public Safety/Security ... Mr. James CROSBY
23 Director of Health Services ... Mrs. Melissa MELTON
38 Counselor ... Ms. Lynda OLEN
42 Director of Campus Ministry ... Ms. Maureen BERGAN
40 Bookstore Manager ... Ms. Genevieve MORRIS
41 Director Athletics & Recreation ... Mr. James HALL
31 Dir Foley CommunityService Center ... Dr. Kathleen ORANGE
26 Dir Communications/Instl Mktng ... Mr. John KERR
96 Director of Purchasing ... Ms. Karen STANTON
36 Coordinator of Career Services ... Ms. Elizabeth DEXTER-WILSON

Stillman College (G)

3601 Stillman Boulevard, POB 1430, Tuscaloosa AL 35403-1430
County: Tuscaloosa FICE Identification: 001044
Unit ID: 102270
Telephone: (205) 349-4240 Carnegie Class: Bac/A&S
FAX Number: (205) 366-8996 Calendar System: Semester
URL: www.stillman.edu
Established: 1876 Annual Undergrad Tuition & Fees: $15,088
Enrollment: 1,078 Coed
Affiliation or Control: Presbyterian Church (U.S.A.) IRS Status: 501(c)3
Highest Offering: Baccalaureate
Program: Liberal Arts And General; Teacher Preparatory
Accreditation: SC, #IACBE, MUS, NURSE, TED

01 President ... Dr. Ernest MCNEALEY
05 Vice President Academic Affairs ... Vacant
10 Vice President Fiscal Affairs ... Mr. Sama MONDEH
32 Vice President for Students Affairs ... Dr. Sharon WHITTAKER-DAVIS
30 Associate VP for Development ... Mr. Gregory EUBANKS
84 Asst VP/Dean Enrollment Management ... Vacant
09 Director of Institutional Research ... Ms. Cynthia D. LEATHERWOOD
21 Asst Vice Pres External Affairs ... Mrs. Lois GWINN
26 Asst Vice President/Marketing & PR ... Miss Veronica CLARK
06 Registrar ... Mrs. Barbara SMITH
08 Dean of Library ... Mr. Robert HEATH
37 Director of Financial Aid ... Mrs. Jacqueline MORRIS
29 Director of Alumni Affairs ... Mrs. Aretha THOMAS
38 Director of Student Development Ctr ... Ms. Jacqueline CURRIE
13 Director of Info Tech ... Mr. Dominic MURUAKO
07 Director of Admissions ... Mrs. Victoria BOMAN
19 Chief of Campus Police ... Mr. James TAGGART
41 Athletic Director ... Mr. Curtis CAMPBELL
42 College Chaplain ... Dr. Mark MCCORMICK
49 Dean of Arts & Sciences ... Dr. Mary Jane KROTZER
53 Dean of Professional Education ... Dr. Linda BRADFORD
15 Human Resources Director ... Mrs. Patricia WILSON

Talladega College (H)

627 W Battle Street, Talladega AL 35160-2354
County: Talladega FICE Identification: 001046
Unit ID: 102298
Telephone: (256) 362-0206 Carnegie Class: Bac/A&S
FAX Number: (256) 761-9206 Calendar System: Semester
URL: www.talladega.edu
Established: 1867 Annual Undergrad Tuition & Fees: $17,996
Enrollment: 710 Coed
Affiliation or Control: Independent Non-Profit IRS Status: 501(c)3
Highest Offering: Baccalaureate
Program: Liberal Arts And General; Teacher Preparatory; Professional; Business Emphasis
Accreditation: SC, SW

01 President ... Dr. Billy C. HAWKINS
05 Provost/Vice Pres Academic Affairs ... Dr. Evelyn M. WHITE
10 Vice President of Finance and Admin ... Dr. Gerald WILLIAMS
32 Vice President Student Affairs ... Mrs. Jacqueline PADDIO
30 Vice Pres Institutional Advancement ... Ms. Casandra BLASSINGAME
18 Director Facilities Management ... Mr. Gary LAWSON
26 Director of Public Relations ... Vacant
37 Director Financial Aid ... Ms. Sheoneta ASHLEY
07 Director of Admissions ... Mr. Charles HANKS
09 Director of Institutional Research ... Vacant
32 Director of Student Activities ... Mr. Anthony JONES
41 Athletic Director ... Mr. Wilberto RAMOS
08 Librarian ... Vacant
14 Information Technology Director ... Mr. Quintin LATIN
36 Director of Career Placement ... Ms. Delores TRAYLOR
40 Materials Management/Bookstore ... Ms. Sharonda HUTCHINSON
15 Director of Human Resources ... Mrs. Brenda RHODEN
19 Chief Campus Police ... Vacant
50 Dean Div Administration & Business ... Vacant
79 Dean Div Humanities/Fine Arts ... Vacant
81 Dean Div of Natural Sci/Math ... Dr. Charlie STINSON
83 Dean Div EWJ Social Sciences/Educ ... Dr. Lisa LONG
23 Health Services on Campus ... Mrs. Valarie ALFRED
25 Title III Coor/Grants Administrator ... Mrs. Nicola LAWLER
29 Director Alumni Relations ... Mr. Seddrick HILL

Trenholm State Technical College (I)

PO Box 10048, Montgomery AL 36108
County: Montgomery FICE Identification: 005734
Unit ID: 102313
Telephone: (334) 420-4200 Carnegie Class: Assoc/Pub-R-S
FAX Number: (334) 420-4206 Calendar System: Semester
URL: www.trenholmstate.edu
Established: 1963 Annual Undergrad Tuition & Fees (In-State): $3,990
Enrollment: 1,789 Coed
Affiliation or Control: State IRS Status: 501(c)3
Highest Offering: Associate Degree
Program: Occupational; 2-Year Principally Bachelor's Creditable; Technical Emphasis

Accreditation: ACFEI, COE, DA, DMS, EMT, MAC, PNUR, RAD

01 President ... Mr. Samuel MUNNERLYN
10 Dean of Finance/Administrative Svcs ... Ms. Deborah GRIGGS
05 Dean of Instruction ... Ms. Barbara A. SPEARS
30 Dean of Development ... Dr. Suresh C. KAUSHIK
32 Interim Dean of Students ... Ms. Beverly ROSS
103 Dean of Workforce Development ... Mr. Wilford HOLT
13 Assoc Dean of IT ... Mr. Charles HARRIS
09 Director of Institutional Research ... Dr. Mimi JOHNSON
18 Director Physcial Facilities ... Mr. Dennis MONROE
37 Director Student Financial Aid ... Ms. Betty EDWARDS
07 Director of Admissions/Registrar ... Mrs. Tennie S. MCBRYDE
27 Public Information Officer ... Mr. Michael EVANS
15 Director of Human Resources ... Ms. Pam ROLLINS
51 Dir Title III/Marketing/Cont Educ ... Ms. Arlinda KNIGHT
36 Coordinator Job Placement ... Ms. Benee EDWARDS

Tri-State Institute (A)

100 London Parkway Suite 150, Birmingham AL 35211

County: Jefferson Identification: 666683
Unit ID: 455628
Telephone: (205) 940-7800 Carnegie Class: Not Classified
FAX Number: (205) 942-6708 Calendar System: Other
URL: www.tristateinstitute.com
Established: 2008 Annual Undergrad Tuition & Fees: N/A
Enrollment: 226 Coed
Affiliation or Control: Proprietary IRS Status: Proprietary
Highest Offering: Associate Degree
Program: Occupational
Accreditation: ACICS, DH

01 Campus President ... Ms. Carolyn H. GREENE
05 Academic Dean ... Mr. Bob PALMATIER

† Branch campus of Fortis Institute, Erie, PA.

Troy University (B)

University Avenue, Troy AL 36082-0001

County: Pike FICE Identification: 001047
Unit ID: 102368
Telephone: (334) 670-3100 Carnegie Class: Master's L
FAX Number: (334) 670-3774 Calendar System: Semester
URL: www.troy.edu
Established: 1887 Annual Undergrad Tuition & Fees (In-State): $6,412
Enrollment: 29,689 Coed
Affiliation or Control: State IRS Status: 501(c)3
Highest Offering: Doctorate
Program: Liberal Arts And General; Teacher Preparatory; Professional
Accreditation: SC, ACBSP, ADNUR, CACREP, CORE, MUS, NUR, SPAA, SW, TED

01 Chancellor ... Dr. Jack HAWKINS, JR.
05 Sr Vice Chanc for Academic Affairs ... Dr. Earl INGRAM
32 Sr Vice Chanc Student Svcs/Admin ... Dr. John R. DEW
30 Sr Vice Chanc Advance/External Affs ... Dr. John SCHMIDT
10 Sr VC for Finance & Business Affs ... Dr. James BOOKOUT
12 Vice Chancellor Troy Global Campus ... Vacant
12 Vice Chancellor Troy Dothan ... Dr. Don JEFFREY
12 Vice Chancellor Troy Phenix City ... Dr. David WHITE
35 Dean of Student Svcs Troy Dothan ... Mr. Bob WILLIS
49 Assoc Dean Col Arts/Sci Troy Dothan ... Dr. Robert SAUNDERS
50 Assoc Dean Col Bus Troy Dothan ... Dr. Orrin AMES
53 Assoc Dean Col of Educ Troy Dothan ... Dr. Robin BYNUM
12 Vice Chanc Troy Montgomery ... Mr. Ray WHITE
49 Assoc Dean Arts/Sci Troy Montgomery ... Dr. Fred BEATTY
53 Assoc Dean Col Educ Troy Montgomery ... Dr. Pamela ARRINGTON
30 Assoc Vice Chanc for Development ... Dr. Jean LALIBERTE
37 Assoc Vice Chanc for Financial Aid ... Ms. Carol BALLARD
20 Associate Provost for Academics ... Dr. Lee VARDAMAN
27 Assoc VC for Mktg/Communication ... Mrs. Donna SCHUBERT
06 Registrar ... Mrs. Vickie MILES
84 Dean Enrollment Services ... Mr. Buddy STARLING
08 Dean Library Services ... Dr. Henry STEWART
15 Senior Director Human Resources ... Dr. Toni TAYLOR
13 Chief Technology Officer ... Mr. Greg PRICE
26 Director University Relations ... Mr. Tom DAVIS
29 Director Alumni Affairs ... Ms. Faith W. WARD
36 Coordinator Career Services ... Mr. Josh WOODEN
18 Director Facilities/Physical Plant ... Mr. Mark SALMON
60 Director of Journalism ... Dr. Steven PADGETT
04 Exec Assistant to the Chancellor ... Mr. Dave BARRON
38 Director Student Counseling ... Mrs. Teresa P. RODGERS
07 Director of Graduate Admissions ... Mrs. Brenda CAMPBELL
88 Dir Not for Profit/Assoc Controller ... Mrs. Lauri DORRILL
106 eCampus Dir Educational Technology ... Mr. Ronnie CREEL
86 Director of Federal/State Govt Rels ... Mr. Marcus PARAMORE
86 Dir of Local Governmental Relations ... Mr. Alan BOOTHE
44 Director of Annual Giving ... Mrs. Bronda DENISON
25 Director Sponsored Programs ... Mrs. Judy FULMER
62 Dir of Library Svcs Troy Dothan ... Mr. Chris SHAFFER
62 Dir of Library Svcs Troy Montgomery ... Mr. Kent SNOWDEN
20 Dean Undergrad Pgms/Assoc Provost ... Dr. Hal FULMER
35 Dean of Student Svcs Troy Campus ... Mr. Herbert REEVES
49 Interim Dean Arts & Sciences ... Dr. Don JEFFREY
50 Dean Business ... Dr. Judson EDWARDS
53 Dean Education ... Dr. Lance TATUM
58 Dean Graduate Pgms/Assoc Provost ... Dr. Dianne BARRON
76 Dean Health/Human Services ... Dr. Damon ANDREW
57 Dean Communication/Fine Arts ... Dr. Maryjo COCHRAN
35 Dean Student Svcs Troy Montgomery ... Vacant
35 Dean Student Svcs Troy Phenix City ... Ms. Mary A. RAGLAND
50 Assoc Dean Col Bus Troy Montgomery ... Dr. Anthony RHEE

Tuskegee University (C)

Tuskegee AL 36088

County: Macon FICE Identification: 001050
Unit ID: 102377
Telephone: (334) 727-8011 Carnegie Class: Bac/Diverse
FAX Number: (334) 727-5276 Calendar System: Semester
URL: www.tuskegee.edu
Established: 1881 Annual Undergrad Tuition & Fees: $17,720
Enrollment: 2,946 Coed
Affiliation or Control: Independent Non-Profit IRS Status: 501(c)3
Highest Offering: Doctorate
Program: Liberal Arts And General; Teacher Preparatory; Professional
Accreditation: SC, BUS, DIETD, ENG, MT, NUR, #OT, SW, TED, VET

01 President ... Dr. Gilbert L. ROCHON
05 Provost ... Dr. Luther S. WILLIAMS
10 VP Finance/Chief Financial Officer ... Mr. Stephen A. MARTIN
46 Vice Pres Sponsored Pgms/Research ... Dr. Shaikr JEELANI
30 Vice Pres University Advancement ... Ms. Cheryl M. THOMAS
84 VP/Dir Admissions/Enrollment Mgmt ... Dr. Cynthia SELLERS
32 Vice Pres for Student Services ... Dr. Cynthia SELLERS
101 Exec Asst to Pres/Secy to the Board ... Vacant
13 Asst Vice Pres/Chief Info Tech Ofcr ... Vacant
45 Assistant VP for Budget & Planning ... Ms. Belinda HOGUE
20 Assoc Provost & Director Intl Pgms ... Dr. Eloise CARTER
49 Int Dean Liberal Arts/Education ... Dr. Carlton E. MORRIS
47 Dean Agric/Environment/Natural Sci ... Dr. Walter A. HILL
50 Int Dean Col Business/Orgnztn/Mgmt ... Dr. Tejnder SARA
54 Dean Col Engr/Architecture/Phys Sci ... Dr. Legand L. BURGE
74 Dean Col Vet Med/Nurs/Allied Health ... Dr. Tsegaye HABTEMARIAM
08 Director of Library Services ... Mrs. Juanita ROBERTS
29 Alumni Affairs Director ... Mr. Willie M. BURNETTE
86 Director Federal Relations ... Mrs. Willa HALL SMITH
42 Dean of the Chapel ... Dr. Gregory S. GRAY
26 VP Communications/Public Rels/Mktg ... Mr. Kevin J. MCLIN, SR.
51 Int Assoc Prov Cont Educ/Extension ... Dr. Ntam BAHARANYI
36 Assoc Dir Career Devel/Placement ... Ms. Sarah STRINGER
21 Bursar ... Ms. Barbara CHISHOLM
37 Director of Financial Aid ... Mr. A. D. JAMES
09 Assoc Dir Inst Analysis/Evaluation ... Mr. Willie J. JACKSON
15 Interim Director Personnel Services ... Ms. Patricia SCOTT
18 Project Mgr Sodexho/Physical Plant ... Mr. Tony WARD
91 Director of Applications Support ... Mr. James E. COOPER
06 Registrar ... Mrs. Edrice LEFTWICH
38 Director Student Counseling ... Dr. Joyce RHODEN
96 Director of Purchasing ... Vacant

United States Sports Academy (D)

One Academy Drive, Daphne AL 36526-7055

County: Baldwin FICE Identification: 021706
Unit ID: 102395
Telephone: (251) 626-3303 Carnegie Class: Spec/Other
FAX Number: (251) 626-3874 Calendar System: Semester
URL: www.ussa.edu
Established: 1972 Annual Undergrad Tuition & Fees: $8,520
Enrollment: 508 Coed
Affiliation or Control: Independent Non-Profit IRS Status: 501(c)3
Highest Offering: Doctorate
Program: Professional
Accreditation: SC

01 President ... Dr. Thomas P. ROSANDICH
05 Vice President & CAO ... Dr. Thomas J. ROSANDICH
20 Dean of Academic Affairs ... Vacant
10 Dean of Admin & Finance ... Ms. Holly H. MCLELLAN
32 Director of Student Services ... Dr. Timothy FOLEY
51 Assoc Dn Cont Ed/Distance Learning ... Ms. Betsy R. SMITH
27 Director of Communications ... Mr. Duwayne ESCOBEDO
06 Registrar ... Ms. Tiffany KERSTEN
08 Director of Library/Archivist ... Mr. Greg TYLER
37 Director of Financial Aid ... Mr. Timothy SHARIT
18 Building and Grounds ... Mr. Robert ZIMLICH

*University of Alabama System Office (E)

401 Queen City Avenue, Tuscaloosa AL 35401-1551

County: Tuscaloosa FICE Identification: 008004
Unit ID: 100733
Telephone: (205) 348-5861 Carnegie Class: N/A
FAX Number: (205) 348-9788
URL: www.uasystem.ua.edu

01 Chancellor ... Dr. Malcolm PORTERA
101 Sec Board & Exec Asst to Chanc ... Mr. Michael A. BOWNES
05 Vice Chancellor Academic Affairs ... Dr. Charles R. NASH
10 Vice Chancellor Financial Affairs ... Mr. Ray HAYES
26 Vice Chancellor System Relations ... Mrs. Kellee C. REINHART
88 Vice Chancellor Intl Pgm/Outreach ... Dr. Arthur N. DUNNING
43 General Counsel ... Mr. Ralph SMITH
21 General Auditor ... Ms. Sabrina B. HEARN

*The University of Alabama (F)

Tuscaloosa AL 35487-0100

County: Tuscaloosa FICE Identification: 001051
Unit ID: 100751
Telephone: (205) 348-6010 Carnegie Class: RU/H
FAX Number: (205) 348-9046 Calendar System: Semester
URL: www.ua.edu
Established: 1831 Annual Undergrad Tuition & Fees (In-State): $11,077
Enrollment: 30,323 Coed
Affiliation or Control: State IRS Status: 501(c)3
Highest Offering: Doctorate
Program: Liberal Arts And General; Teacher Preparatory; Professional
Accreditation: SC, AAFCS, ART, BUS, BUSA, CACREP, CEA, CIDA, CLPSY, CORE, CS, DANCE, DIETC, DIETD, ENG, JOUR, LAW, LIB, MUS, NURSE, SP, SW, TED, THEA

02 President ... Dr. Robert E. WITT
05 Provost/Executive Vice President ... Dr. Judy L. BONNER
10 Vice Pres for Financial Affairs ... Dr. Lynda GILBERT
30 Vice President for Advancement ... Dr. Pamela H. PARKER
46 Vice President for Research ... Dr. Joe BENSON
32 Vice Pres for Student Affairs ... Dr. Mark NELSON
31 Vice Pres for Community Affairs ... Dr. Samory T. PRUITT
14 Vice Provost/Chief Information Ofcr ... Dr. John MCGOWAN
18 Assistant VP University Facilities ... Mr. Duane LAMB
18 Ast VP Univ Facilities/Construction ... Mr. Tim LEOPARD
19 Asst Vice Pres Public Safety ... Mr. W. Steven TUCKER
20 Asst Provost Academic Affairs ... Dr. Mark NELSON
11 Asst Provost for Administration ... Ms. Dorothy J. MARTIN
15 Assoc Vice Pres Human Resources ... Ms. Charlotte M. HARRIS
21 Assoc Vice President for Finance ... Ms. Reba J. ESSARY
21 Assoc Vice Pres Financial Affairs ... Ms. Dana S. KEITH
26 Asst VP University Relations ... Ms. Deborah LANE
29 Asst VP for Alumni Affs/Annual Fund ... Mr. Calvin BROWN
85 Asst VP Internatl Ed/Global Affairs ... Dr. B. Jane STANFIELD
06 University Registrar ... Mr. W. Michael GEORGE
09 Director Inst Research/Assessment ... Dr. Lorne KUFFELL
36 Exec Director of Career Center ... Mr. Jerry L. PASCHAL
07 Dir of Undergraduate Admissions ... Ms. Mary K. SPIEGEL
22 Dir & University Compliance Officer ... Ms. Gwendolyn D. HOOD
11 Chief Admin Officer CCHS/RSHC ... Mr. John B. MAXWELL, JR.
37 Director of Student Financial Aid ... Ms. Jeanetta C. ALLEN
84 Director Enrollment Management ... Mrs. Terri TERRY
39 Director Dept of Housing/Res Cmty ... Dr. David P. JONES
40 Director of University Supply Store ... Ms. Teresa SHREVE
41 Athletic Director ... Mr. Mal M. MOORE
43 University Counsel ... Mr. George B. GORDON
08 Dean of University Libraries ... Dr. Louis A. PITSCHMANN
49 Dean of Arts & Sciences ... Dr. Robert F. OLIN
50 Dean Col Commerce & Business Admin ... Dr. J. Michael HARDIN
51 Dean College of Continuing Studies ... Dr. Carolyn C. DAHL
53 Dean College of Education ... Dr. James E. MCLEAN
54 Dean College of Engineering ... Dr. Charles L. KARR
58 Dean Graduate School/Asst Acad VP ... Dr. David A. FRANCKO
59 Dean Human Environmental Sciences ... Dr. Milla BOSCHUNG
60 Dean Col of Communication/Info Sci ... Dr. Loy SINGLETON
61 Dean School of Law ... Mr. Kenneth C. RANDALL
62 Dir Sch of Library/Info Studies ... Dr. Elizabeth S. AVERSA
38 Manager Stdnt Support Svcs-Trio Pgm ... Ms. Wendy L. COGBURN
96 Asc Purchasing Mgr Genl Procurement ... Ms. Pollye HARDY
96 Asc Purchas Mgr Facil Procurement ... Mr. Lane COX
76 Interim Dean Cmty Health Sciences ... Dr. Thad ULZEN
66 Dean Capstone College of Nursing ... Dr. Sara E. BARGER
70 Interim Dean School of Social Work ... Dr. Lucinda L. ROFF
92 Interim Dean of Honors College ... Dr. Shane SHARPE
94 Chair of Women's Studies ... Dr. DoVeanna F. MINOR

*University of Alabama at Birmingham (G)

1530 3rd Avenue S, Birmingham AL 35294-0001

County: Jefferson FICE Identification: 001052
Unit ID: 100663
Telephone: (205) 934-4011 Carnegie Class: RU/VH
FAX Number: N/A Calendar System: Semester
URL: www.uab.edu
Established: 1969 Annual Undergrad Tuition & Fees (In-State): $6,264
Enrollment: 17,543 Coed
Affiliation or Control: State IRS Status: 501(c)3
Highest Offering: Doctorate
Program: Liberal Arts And General; Teacher Preparatory; Professional
Accreditation: SC, ANEST, ARCPA, ART, BUS, BUSA, CACREP, CLPSY, CORE, CS, CYTO, DENT, DIETI, ENG, HSA, IPSY, MED, MT, MUS, NMT, NURSE, OPT, OPTR, OT, PH, PTA, RTT, SPAA, SW, TED, THEA

02 President ... Dr. Carol Z. GARRISON
05 Interim Provost ... Dr. Linda C. LUCAS
10 Vice Pres Financial Affairs/Admin ... Mr. Richard L. MARGISON
17 CEO UAB Health System ... Dr. Will FERNIANY
30 Vice Pres Dev/Alumni/External Rels ... Dr. Shirley S. KAHN
13 Int Vice Pres Info Technology ... Dr. Doug RIGNEY
28 Vice Pres for Equity and Diversity ... Dr. Louis DALE
46 Vice Pres for Research/Economic Dev ... Dr. Richard B. MARCHASE
63 Vice Pres/Dean School of Medicine ... Dr. Ray L. WATTS
11 Vice Prov Admin/Quality Improvement ... Mr. Harlan M. SANDS
20 Vice Prov Student/Faculty Success ... Dr. Suzanne E. AUSTIN
43 University Counsel ... Mr. W. John DANIEL
49 Dean College of Arts & Sciences ... Dr. Thomas DILORENZO
50 Dean School of Business ... Dr. David R. KLOCK
52 Interim Dean School of Dentistry ... Dr. Michael S. REDDY
53 Dean School of Education ... Dr. Deborah L. VOLTZ

54 Interim Dean School of Engineering .... Dr. Melinda M. LALOR
76 Dean School of Health Professions .... Dr. Harold P. JONES
66 Dean School of Nursing .... Dr. Doreen C. HARPER
88 Dean School of Optometry .... Dr. Rodney NOWAKOWSKI
69 Dean School of Public Health .... Dr. Max MICHAEL, III
58 Dean Graduate School .... Dr. Bryan D. NOE
18 Assoc Vice President Facilities .... Mr. Brooks H. BAKER, III
21 Assoc VP Business/Auxiliary Svcs ...... Mr. Christopher CLIFFORD
29 Assoc VP Alumni/Annual Giving .... Ms. Rebecca WATSON
44 Asst Vice Pres Development .... Mr. Alton WHITT
26 Assoc VP Public Relations & Mktg .... Ms. Dale TURNBOUGH
84 Assoc Provost Enrollment Management .... Dr. Brent GAGE
21 Assoc Vice Pres Finance .... Ms. Patricia A. RACYNSKI
35 Asst Vice Pres for Student Life .... Mr. Andrew J. MARSCH, III
45 Assoc Provost Planning/Analysis .... Dr. Glenna G. BROWN
08 Director Mervyn Sterne Library .... Dr. Jerry W. STEPHENS
08 Director Lister Hill Library .... Mr. Scott PLUTCHAK
41 Athletic Director .... Mr. Brian W. MACKIN
15 Chief Human Resources Officer .... Ms. Alesia M. JONES
09 Associate Director Inst Research .... Ms. Mary Beth ADAMS
19 Chief of Police .... Mr. Anthony B. PURCELL
07 Director Undergraduate Admissions .... Ms. Chenise RYAN
37 Director of Financial Aid .... Ms. Janet B. MAY
06 University Registrar .... Ms. Stella COCORIS
39 Director Student Housing/Resid Life .... Mr. Marc BOOKER
36 Director Career Services .... Ms. Suzanne SCOTT-TRAMMELL
38 Director Student Counseling .... Ms. Susan HART

*University of Alabama in Huntsville (A)

301 Sparkman Drive, Huntsville AL 35899-1911
County: Madison FICE Identification: 001055
Unit ID: 100706
Telephone: (256) 824-1000 Carnegie Class: RU/VH
FAX Number: (256) 824-6073 Calendar System: Semester
URL: www.uah.edu
Established: 1950 Annual Undergrad Tuition & Fees (In-State): $8,094
Enrollment: 7,614 Coed
Affiliation or Control: State IRS Status: 501(c)3
Highest Offering: Doctorate
Program: Liberal Arts And General; Teacher Preparatory; Professional
Accreditation: SC, ART, BUS, CS, ENG, MUS, NURSE, TED

02 President .... Dr. Robert A. ALTENKIRCH
05 Provost & Exec VP Academic Affairs .... Dr. Vistasp KARBHARI
10 VP Finance & Administration .... Mr. Ray PINNER
28 VP Diversity .... Ms. Delois SMITH
30 Interim VP University Advancement .... Mr. Ray PINNER
46 VP Research .... Dr. John M. HORACK
43 University Counsel .... Mr. Robert W. RIEDER, JR.
20 Associate Provost .... Mr. Brent M. WREN
08 Dean Library .... Vacant
58 Dean Graduate Studies .... Dr. Rhonda K. GAEDE
66 Dean College of Nursing .... Dr. C. Fay RAINES
81 Dean College of Science .... Dr. John FIX
79 Dean College of Liberal Arts .... Mr. Glenn DASHER
32 Dean of Students .... Ms. Regina G. HYATT
54 Dean College of Engineering .... Dr. Shankar MAHALINGAM
50 Dean College Business Admin .... Dr. Caron ST. JOHN
44 Assoc VP Gift Development .... Vacant
88 Assoc VP Research .... Dr. Thomas M. KOSHUT
29 Assoc VP for Advancement .... Mr. Joel C. LONERGAN
29 Assoc VP for Special Events .... Ms. April HARRIS
39 Assoc VP University Housing & CBO .... Mr. John MAXON
18 Asst VP Facilities & Operations .... Mr. Michael S. FINNEGAN
11 Asst VP Finance & Business Services .... Mr. Robert LEONARD
21 Asst VP Budgets & Fin Planning .... Mr. Chih LOO
84 Assoc Provost Enrollment Services .... Ms. Ingrid HAYES
102 Asst VP Corporate Relations .... Vacant
88 Asst VP Human Resources .... Ms. Laurel LONG
06 Registrar .... Ms. Janet WALLER
13 Interim CIO .... Dr. John P. MCGOWAN
09 Director Institutional Research .... Ms. Deborah STOWERS
88 Interim Director CAO .... Dr. Pat REARDON
88 Dir Center Space Plsm & Aeron Res .... Dr. Gary ZANK
88 Interim Director Propulsion Res .... Dr. Robert FREDERICK
88 Dir Ctr for Mgmt of Science & Tech .... Dr. P. J. BALLENGER
88 Director Research Institute .... Dr. Richard G. RHOADES
88 Director CMSA .... Dr. Mikel D. PETTY
88 Director SMAP Center .... Dr. Gary MADDUX
88 Acting Director Rotocraft Center .... Ms. Susan O'BRIEN
104 Director Global Studies Program .... Dr. David JOHNSON
88 Director Earth Systems Science Ctr .... Dr. John R. CHRISTY
88 Dir Ctr for Mgmt & Economic Res .... Mr. Jeff S. THOMPSON
88 Director Humanities Center .... Dr. Brian J. MARTINE
15 Dir Employee Rels & Compliance .... Ms. Cynthia R. BACKUS
85 Dir Office of International Pgms .... Dr. John R. POTTENGER
88 Principal Assoc Dir SMAP Center .... Dr. James R. CLARK
88 Interim Director CMR .... Mr. Fred C. SAUTTER
37 Director Financial Aid .... Mr. Andrew M. WEAVER
51 Director Div Continuing Education .... Ms. Karen CLANTON
41 Director Intercollegiate Athletics .... Dr. E. J. BROPHY
88 Exec Dir Student Success Center .... Dr. Diana BELL
38 Dir Student Counseling Svcs .... Dr. Larry CANTOR
86 Director Public Affairs .... Mr. Ray GARNER
21 Director Internal Audit .... Ms. Sabrina HEARN
88 Asst Director University Center .... Mr. Nate BAILIE
19 Director Public Safety .... Mr. Michael R. SNELLGROVE
25 Director Sponsored Programs .... Ms. Gloria GREENE
91 Director Administrative Computing .... Mr. Malcolm RICE
07 Director Admissions .... Ms. Sandra BARINOWSKI
93 Coord Undergrad Minority Studies .... Ms. Rosemary ROBINSON

04 Sr Exec Assistant to the President .... Ms. Mary Beth WALKER
23 Dir Family Staff Clinic .... Ms. Louise O'KEEFE
40 Bookstore General Manager .... Ms. Amber HILL

University of Mobile (B)

5735 College Parkway, Mobile AL 36613-2842
County: Mobile FICE Identification: 001029
Unit ID: 101693
Telephone: (251) 675-5990 Carnegie Class: Bac/Diverse
FAX Number: (251) 675-6293 Calendar System: Semester
URL: www.umobile.edu
Established: 1961 Annual Undergrad Tuition & Fees: $16,880
Enrollment: 1,673 Coed
Affiliation or Control: Southern Baptist IRS Status: 501(c)3
Highest Offering: Master's
Program: 2-Year Principally Bachelor's Creditable; Liberal Arts And General; Teacher Preparatory; Professional
Accreditation: SC, ACBSP, ADNUR, MUS, NURSE

01 President .... Dr. Mark R. FOLEY
05 Vice Pres for Academic Affairs .... Dr. Audrey C. EUBANKS
10 Vice President for Business Affairs .... Mr. J. Steve LEE
30 Vice President for Development .... Mr. Brian BOYLE
84 VP Enrollment Svcs/Campus Life .... Mrs. Kim LEOUSIS
44 Director Foundations/Stewardship .... Ms. Marty PITTMAN
20 Associate VP for Academic Affairs .... Dr. Anne B. LOWERY
21 Associate VP for Business Affairs .... Mrs. Carol CAMP
20 Assoc VP Academic Svcs/Registrar .... Dr. Donald K. BERRY
84 Assoc VP for Enrollment Services .... Ms. Marie BATSON
04 Assistant to the President .... Dr. Fred G. LACKEY
26 Director of Marketing .... Ms. Lesa MOORE
41 Athletic Director .... Mr. Joe NILAND
07 Director of Enrollment Services .... Mrs. Charity WITTNER
08 Director of Library Services .... Mr. Jeffrey D. CALAMETTI
26 Director of Public Relations .... Mrs. Kathy L. DEAN
09 Director of Inst Effectiveness .... Dr. Anne B. LOWERY
50 Dean School of Business .... Dr. Jane FINLEY
49 Dean College of Arts & Sciences .... Dr. Dwight STEEDLEY
53 Dean School of Education .... Dr. Peter KINGSFORD
66 Dean School of Nursing .... Dr. Richard MCELHANEY
51 Dean Center for Adult Programs .... Dr. Pam BUCHANAN
73 Dean School of Christian Studies .... Dr. Cecil R. TAYLOR
58 Dean School of Graduate Programs .... Dr. Anne B. LOWERY
39 Director of Residential Life .... Mr. Kris NELSON
29 Director Alumni/Parent Relations .... Mrs. Hali GIVENS
90 Director Academic Computing Lab .... Mr. Mitch DAVIS
42 Director of Campus Ministries .... Mr. Neal LEDBETTER
15 Director of Human Resources .... Mrs. Diane BLACK
13 Exec Dir Computer Info Tech Svcs .... Mr. Mitch E. DAVIS
18 Dir of Institutional Operations .... Mrs. Vicky BURGIN
38 Director Student Retention .... Mrs. Shirley SUTTERFIELD

University of Montevallo (C)

Station 6001, Montevallo AL 35115-6001
County: Shelby FICE Identification: 001004
Unit ID: 101709
Telephone: (205) 665-6000 Carnegie Class: Master's M
FAX Number: (205) 665-6003 Calendar System: Semester
URL: www.montevallo.edu
Established: 1896 Annual Undergrad Tuition & Fees (In-State): $8,502
Enrollment: 3,045 Coed
Affiliation or Control: State IRS Status: 501(c)3
Highest Offering: Beyond Master's But Less Than Doctorate
Program: Liberal Arts And General; Teacher Preparatory; Professional
Accreditation: SC, AAFCS, ART, BUS, CACREP, DIETD, MUS, SP, SW, TED

01 President .... Dr. John W. STEWART, III
05 VP Academic Affairs .... Dr. Terry G. ROBERSON
32 VP Student Affairs .... Dr. Kimberly A. BARRETT
30 Vice Pres Advancement .... Vacant
10 VP Business Affairs .... Ms. DeAnna M. SMITH
11 Sr VP for Administratiave Affairs .... Dr. Michelle JOHNSTON
18 Dir Physical Plant .... Mr. David R. PRITCHETT
35 Dir Student Life .... Ms. Robyn W. BOYD
06 Assoc Registrar .... Ms. Amanda T. FOX
08 Dir Libraries .... Ms. Rosemary H. ARNESON
07 Dir Admissions .... Mr. Lynn GURGANUS
29 Dir Development/Alumni Relations .... Ms. Racheal B. BANKS
14 Interim Dir Computer Center .... Mr. Frank WHIDDEN
26 Dir Public Relations .... Ms. Cynthia K. SHACKELFORD
37 Dir of Student Financial Services .... Ms. Maria D. PARKER
38 Dir Counseling Center .... Dr. Tammi S. DAHLE
19 Police Chief .... Ms. Shelley M. TYREE
39 Dir Housing & Residence Life .... Mr. John DENSON
41 Dir Athletics .... Mr. James E. HERLIHY
15 Dir Personnel Services .... Ms. Barbara FORREST
51 Dir Reg Insvc & Continuing Ed ..... Ms. Rebecca L. RICHARDSON
58 Dir Graduate Admissions & Records .... Ms. Rebecca HARTLEY
49 Dean College Arts & Sciences .... Dr. Mary Beth ARMSTRONG
50 Dean College of Business .... Vacant
53 Dean College of Education .... Dr. Anna E. MCEWAN
57 Dean College of Fine Arts .... Dr. William CLOW

University of North Alabama (D)

One Harrison Plaza, Florence AL 35632-0001
County: Lauderdale FICE Identification: 001016
Unit ID: 101879
Telephone: (256) 765-4100 Carnegie Class: Master's L
FAX Number: (256) 765-4329 Calendar System: Semester
URL: www.una.edu
Established: 1830 Annual Undergrad Tuition & Fees (In-State): $7,308
Enrollment: 7,279 Coed
Affiliation or Control: State IRS Status: 501(c)3
Highest Offering: Beyond Master's But Less Than Doctorate
Program: Liberal Arts And General; Teacher Preparatory; Professional
Accreditation: SC, ACBSP, ART, CACREP, CEA, CS, ENGR, MUS, NURSE, SW, TED

01 President .... Dr. William G. CALE, JR.
05 Vice Pres Acad Affairs & Provost .... Dr. John THORNELL
88 Vice Provost for Intl Affairs .... Dr. Chunsheng ZHANG
10 VP for Business/Financial Affairs .... Dr. Steve SMITH
32 Vice President Student Affairs .... Mr. David P. SHIELDS, JR.
30 Vice President for Advancement .... Dr. Alan G. MEDDERS
49 Dean College of Arts & Sciences .... Dr. Vagn K. HANSEN
50 Dean College of Business .... Dr. Kerry P. GATLIN
53 Dean College of Education .... Dr. Donna P. JACOBS
66 Dean College of Nursing .... Dr. Birdie I. BAILEY
20 Assoc VP Academic Support .... Dr. Thomas C. CALHOUN, JR.
13 Dean Information Technologies .... Vacant
31 Director University Events .... Mr. Bret JENNINGS
41 Director of Athletics .... Mr. Mark LINDER
21 Controller .... Ms. Donna F. TIPPS
86 Director Governmental Relations .... Vacant
44 Dir Annual Giving/Donor Research .... Dr. Judy T. JACKSON
39 Director of Housing .... Ms. Audrey MITCHELL
37 Director Student Financial Services .... Mr. Ben J. BAKER
15 Asst Dir Human Resources/Affirm Act .... Vacant
26 Director University Communications .... Mr. Joshua L. WOODS
24 Dir Educational Technology Services .... Ms. Debbie CHAFFIN
18 Director Facilities Admin/Planning .... Mr. Michael B. GAUTNEY
19 Director of University Police .... Mr. Robert G. PASTULA
51 Dir Continuing Studies and Outreach .... Ms. Lavonne GATLIN
23 Director University Health Services .... Ms. Cynthia L. WOOD
35 Dir Judicial Affairs/Stdnt Aff Plng .... Dr. Kimberly GREENWAY
40 Manager University Bookstore .... Vacant
91 Director Computer/Telecomm Services .... Vacant
07 Director of Admissions .... Ms. Kim MAULDIN
09 Dir Inst Rsrch/Plng & Assessment .... Dr. Andrew L. LUNA
29 Director Alumni Relations .... Ms. Carol S. LYLES
96 Director of Procurement .... Ms. Cindy H. CONLON
28 Dir Diversity/Institutional Equity .... Dr. Lelon O. DAVIDSON
36 Dir Career Planning & Development .... Ms. Melissa T. MEDLIN
06 Registrar .... Ms. Tina SHARP

University of South Alabama (E)

307 University Boulevard, N, Mobile AL 36688-0002
County: Mobile FICE Identification: 001057
Unit ID: 102094
Telephone: (251) 460-6101 Carnegie Class: RU/H
FAX Number: N/A Calendar System: Semester
URL: www.usouthal.edu
Established: 1963 Annual Undergrad Tuition & Fees (In-State): $7,380
Enrollment: 15,007 Coed
Affiliation or Control: State IRS Status: 501(c)3
Highest Offering: Doctorate
Program: Liberal Arts And General; Teacher Preparatory; Professional
Accreditation: SC, ARCPA, AUD, BUS, CS, EMT, ENG, MED, MUS, NURSE, OT, PTA, RAD, RTT, SP, SW, TED

01 President .... Mr. V. Gordon MOULTON
05 Sr Vice Pres Academic Affairs .... Dr. G. David JOHNSON
30 Vice Pres Developmental/Alumni Rels .... Dr. Joseph F. BUSTA
10 Vice President Financial Affairs .... Mr. M. Wayne DAVIS
23 Vice President Health Sciences .... Dr. Ronald FRANKS
32 VP Stdnt Affairs/Special Asst Pres .... Dr. John SMITH
46 Vice President for Research .... Dr. Russ LEA
84 Assoc Vice Pres Enrollment Services .... Dr. J. David STEARNS
58 Assoc VP Acad Affs/Dean Grad Sch .... Dr. B. Keith HARRISON
14 Assoc Vice Pres Computer Services .... Mr. David K. BLOUGH
46 Assoc VP IRPA & Regional Campuses .... Dr. Joan EXLINE
15 Asst Vice President Human Resources . Ms. Pamela HENDERSON
17 Dean College of Medicine .... Dr. Samuel J. STRADA
86 Exec Dir Government Relations .... Mr. William J. FULFORD
88 Dir Student Acad Success/Retention .... Dr. Nicole T. CARR
88 Director of Assessment .... Ms. Cecelia MARTIN
26 Director of Public Relations .... Mr. Keith AYERS
41 Director of Athletics .... Dr. Joel ERDMANN
07 Director of Admissions .... Ms. Norma J. TANNER
85 Director Intl Student Services .... Ms. Donna PIGG
07 Director New Student Recruitment .... Mr. Christopher LYNCH
09 Director of Institutional Research .... Dr. Gordon E. MILLS, JR.
06 Registrar .... Ms. Melissa WOLD
29 Director Alumni Relations .... Ms. Carol N. KITTRELL
19 Director Campus Security .... Mr. Zeke AULL, JR.
37 Director of Financial Aid .... Ms. Emily JOHNSTON
36 Director Career Services .... Ms. Bevley D. WHITE
12 Director USA Baldwin County .... Vacant
18 Director Facilities Management .... Mr. Chris WILLIS
38 Director Student Counseling/Test .... Dr. Al E. CLARK
88 Manager New Student Orientation .... Mr. Scott R. SMITH
28 Manager Multicultural Student Affs ..... Dr. Carl G. CUNNINGHAM
96 Purchasing Agent .... Mr. Robert M. BROWN
54 Dean College of Engineering .... Dr. John STEADMAN
51 Dean Continuing Educ/Spec Pgms .... Dr. Vaughn S. MILLNER
49 Dean of Arts and Sciences .... Dr. Andrzej WIERZBICKI
08 Dean of University Libraries .... Dr. Richard J. WOOD
50 Dean Mitchell College of Business .... Dr. Carl C. MOORE
53 Dean of Education .... Dr. Richard L. HAYES
66 Dean of College of Nursing .... Dr. Debra C. DAVIS
76 Dean of Allied Health Professions .... Dr. Richard TALBOTT
77 Dean Computer & Information Science .... Dr. Alec YASINSAC

The University of West Alabama (A)

205 N Washington Street, Livingston AL 35470-2099
County: Sumter FICE Identification: 001024
Unit ID: 101587
Telephone: (205) 652-3400 Carnegie Class: Master's L
FAX Number: (205) 652-3718 Calendar System: Semester
URL: www.uwa.edu
Established: 1835 Annual Undergrad Tuition & Fees (In-State): $6,524
Enrollment: 5,094 Coed
Affiliation or Control: State IRS Status: 501(c)3
Highest Offering: Beyond Master's But Less Than Doctorate
Program: Liberal Arts And General; Teacher Preparatory; Professional
Accreditation: #SC, ACBSP, ADNUR, TED

01 President ... Dr. Richard D. HOLLAND
05 Provost ... Dr. David M. TAYLOR
10 Vice President Financial Affairs ... Mr. T. Raiford NOLAND
30 Vice Pres Institutional Advancement ... Mr. Clemit W. SPRUIELL
32 Vice President for Student Affairs ... Mr. Thomas D. BUCKALEW
49 Dean of Liberal Arts ... Dr. Tim EDWARDS
50 Dean of Business ... Dr. Ken TUCKER
53 Dean of Teacher Education ... Dr. Kathy CHANDLER
81 Dean of Natural Science/Math ... Dr. Venkat SHARMA
58 Dean of Graduate Studies ... Dr. Kathy CHANDLER
51 Dean Continuing Education ... Dr. Tina N. JONES
106 Dean Online Programs ... Dr. Martha HOCUTT
66 Chairperson of Nursing ... Mrs. Marsha CANNON
08 Director of Library ... Dr. Neil SNIDER
09 Dir Institutional Effectiveness ... Mrs. Patricia PRATT
41 Athletic Director ... Vacant
35 Director of Student Life & Housing ... Mr. Luther GREMMELS
06 Registrar ... Mrs. Susan SPARKMAN
37 Director Student Financial Aid ... Mr. Don RAINER
13 Director Information Systems ... Mr. Michael PRATT
18 Director of Physical Plant ... Mr. Robert L. HOLYCROSS
40 Director of Auxiliary Services ... Ms. Mamie REED
36 Director Career Services/Placement ... Ms. Tammy S. WHITE
29 Director Alumni Relations ... Mrs. Tyanne S. STONE
38 Director Student Success Center ... Dr. Vicki P. SPRUIELL
86 Director Government Relations ... Mr. Clemit W. SPRUIELL
07 Director of Admissions ... Vacant
96 Director of Purchasing ... Mr. Lawson C. EDMONDS
89 Director Freshmen Studies ... Dr. James GENTSCH
92 Director Honors Program ... Dr. Lesa SHAUL
15 Director Personnel Services ... Mrs. Jessie W. EGBERT
20 Associate Academic Officer ... Mrs. Patricia PRATT
26 Chief Public Relations Officer ... Ms. Betsy COMPTON
19 Director of Security/Safety ... Mr. Jeff MANUEL
103 Director Workforce Development ... Mr. Kenneth WALKER
105 Director of Web Services ... Mrs. Christi GEORGE
101 Secretary Board of Trustees ... Mrs. Earlene LINDSEY
28 Director of Diversity ... Dr. David M. TAYLOR

Wallace State Community College - Hanceville (B)

PO Box 2000, 801 Main Street, NW,
Hanceville AL 35077-2000
County: Cullman FICE Identification: 007871
Unit ID: 101295
Telephone: (256) 352-8000 Carnegie Class: Assoc/Pub-R-M
FAX Number: (256) 352-8228 Calendar System: Semester
URL: www.wallacestate.edu
Established: 1966 Annual Undergrad Tuition & Fees (In-State): $3,230
Enrollment: 6,371 Coed
Affiliation or Control: State IRS Status: 501(c)3
Highest Offering: Associate Degree
Program: Occupational; 2-Year Principally Bachelor's Creditable
Accreditation: SC, ACBSP, ADNUR, DA, DH, DMS, EMT, MAC, MLTAD, OTA, POLYT, PTAA, RAD

01 President ... Dr. Vicki HAWSEY
10 Business Manager/Treasurer ... Janice MORGAN
20 Int Technical Dean ... Wayne MANORD
32 Vice President for Students ... Dr. Tomesa SMITH
26 Dean of Institutional Outreach ... Melinda EDWARDS
72 Dean of Technical Education ... Vacant
76 Dean of Health Sciences ... Lisa GERMAN
88 Auxiliary Director ... Sid BORDEN
08 Librarian ... Lisa HULLETT
07 Director Admissions & Registrar ... Linda SPERLING
09 Director of Planning & Assessment ... Vacant
37 Director of Financial Aid ... Becky GRAVES
56 Extended Day Program Director ... Wayne MANORD
15 Director of Human Resources ... Alyce FLANAGAN
30 Director Institutional Development ... Suzanne HARBIN
18 Director of Plant Operations ... Phil STUDDARD
26 Director of Communication/Marketing ... Kristen HOLMES
38 Director of Advising ... Donnie RICE
84 Director Enrollment Management ... Jennifer HILL

ALASKA

Alaska Bible College (C)

Box 289, 200 College Road, Glennallen AK 99588-0289
FICE Identification: 008843
Unit ID: 102580
Telephone: (907) 822-3201 Carnegie Class: Not Classified
FAX Number: (907) 822-5027 Calendar System: Semester
URL: www.akbible.edu
Established: 1966 Annual Undergrad Tuition & Fees: $7,030
Enrollment: 79 Coed
Affiliation or Control: Independent Non-Profit IRS Status: 501(c)3
Highest Offering: Baccalaureate
Program: Religious Emphasis
Accreditation: BI

01 President ... Mr. Nick RINGGER
05 Vice President Academic Affairs ... Mr. Kevin NEWMAN
32 VP Student Development/Dean of Men ... Mr. Bob WENDT
10 Vice Pres Business Administration ... Vacant
06 Registrar/Bookkeeper ... Miss Carol REIMER
08 Librarian ... Mrs. Pamela HORST
07 Director Admissions/Recruiting ... Mrs. Nikki PALMER
27 Director of Communications ... Ms. Michelle EASTTY

Alaska Pacific University (D)

4101 University Drive, Anchorage AK 99508-4672
County: Anchorage FICE Identification: 001061
Unit ID: 102669
Telephone: (907) 561-1266 Carnegie Class: Master's S
FAX Number: (907) 562-4276 Calendar System: Semester
URL: www.alaskapacific.edu
Established: 1957 Annual Undergrad Tuition & Fees: $27,000
Enrollment: 732 Coed
Affiliation or Control: Independent Non-Profit IRS Status: 501(c)3
Highest Offering: Master's
Program: Liberal Arts And General; Teacher Preparatory
Accreditation: NW, TED

01 President ... Dr. Don BANTZ
04 Assistant to the President ... Ms. Debbie ROLL
05 Academic Dean ... Ms. Tracy STEWART
10 Dean of Administration & Finance ... Ms. Deborah JOHNSTON
32 Dean of Students ... Mr. Kelly SMITH
06 Registrar ... Ms. Donna DOUGHERTY
07 Director of Admissions ... Ms. Jennifer JENSEN
37 Director of Financial Aid ... Ms. Jo HOLLAND
18 Director Facilities Management ... Ms. Kathy MINCKS
13 Director Information Technology ... Mr. Michael BAKER
30 Chief Development Officer ... Vacant
40 Assistant Campus Store Manager ... Ms. Lydia HARVEY
42 Chaplain ... Rev. Doug LINDSAY
29 Alumni Relations ... Ms. Jessica HARRIS
15 Director Personnel Services ... Ms. Kathleen MINER

† Granted candidacy at the Doctorate level.

Career Academy (E)

1415 E. Tudor Road, Anchorage AK 99507-1033
County: Anchorage FICE Identification: 025410
Unit ID: 103501
Telephone: (907) 563-7575 Carnegie Class: Not Classified
FAX Number: (907) 563-8330 Calendar System: Other
URL: www.careeracademy.edu
Established: N/A Annual Undergrad Tuition & Fees: $10,495
Enrollment: 410 Coed
Affiliation or Control: Proprietary IRS Status: Proprietary
Highest Offering: Associate Degree
Program: Occupational
Accreditation: ACCSC

01 Director ... Ms. Linda STURE

Charter College (F)

2221 E Northern Lights Blvd, #120,
Anchorage AK 99508-4157
County: Anchorage FICE Identification: 025769
Unit ID: 102845
Telephone: (907) 277-1000 Carnegie Class: Bac/Assoc
FAX Number: (907) 274-3342 Calendar System: Quarter
URL: www.chartercollege.edu
Established: 1985 Annual Undergrad Tuition & Fees: $11,530
Enrollment: 883 Coed
Affiliation or Control: Proprietary IRS Status: Proprietary
Highest Offering: Baccalaureate
Program: Occupational; 2-Year Principally Bachelor's Creditable
Accreditation: ACICS

01 President ... Dr. Richard MACLEAN
03 Vice President ... Vacant
32 Director of Financial Aid ... Ms. Amanda HOKE
36 Director of Career Services ... Ms. Wendy NOVAK
08 Librarian ... Ms. Lisa DEBUSK
07 Director of Admission ... Ms. Irene LEE
11 Administrative Coordinator ... Ms. Traci RICKETTS
32 Director of Student Success ... Ms. Catherine HEBDON

Ilisagvik College (G)

PO Box 749, Barrow AK 99723-0749
County: North Slope Borough FICE Identification: 034613
Unit ID: 434584
Telephone: (907) 852-3333 Carnegie Class: Tribal
FAX Number: (907) 862-2729 Calendar System: Semester
URL: www.ilisagvik.cc
Established: 1996 Annual Undergrad Tuition & Fees: $6,270
Enrollment: 591 Coed
Affiliation or Control: Independent Non-Profit IRS Status: 501(c)3
Highest Offering: Associate Degree
Program: Occupational; 2-Year Principally Bachelor's Creditable
Accreditation: NW

01 President ... Mrs. Brooke GONDARA
06 Registrar ... Ms. Ann CAHOON
09 Director of Institutional Research ... Ms. Sharyl MESINA
10 Chief Business Officer ... Mr. Andy STEMP
15 Director Human Resources ... Ms. Nancy MONNIN
18 Chief Facilities/Physical Plant ... Mr. Chris SMITH
26 Chief Public Relations Officer ... Ms. Pearl BROWER
30 Chief Development ... Mr. Robbie GONDARA
32 Chief Student Life Officer ... Ms. Sarah BERGMAN
35 Director Student Affairs ... Ms. Pearl BROWER
36 Director Student Placement ... Ms. Janelle EVERETT
37 Director Student Financial Aid ... Mr. Fred MILLER
38 Director Student Counseling ... Ms. Jennifer KISER

*University of Alaska System (H)

910 Yukon Drive, Fairbanks AK 99775-5000
County: Fairbanks FICE Identification: 008005
Unit ID: 103529
Telephone: (907) 450-8000 Carnegie Class: N/A
FAX Number: (907) 450-8012
URL: www.alaska.edu

01 President ... Mr. Patrick K. GAMBLE
26 Vice President for Univ Relations ... Ms. Wendy REDMAN
05 Vice President for Academic Affairs ... Mr. Dan JULIUS
10 Vice Pres for Finance & Admin ... Mr. Joe TRUBACZ
46 Associate Vice President Budget ... Ms. Michelle RIZK
09 Assoc Vice Pres Research & Planning ... Ms. Gwen WHITE
43 General Counsel ... Mr. Roger BRUNNER
15 Chief Human Resources Officer ... Ms. Beth BEHNER
17 Associate Vice President for Health ... Vacant
102 President of Foundation ... Ms. Mary RUTHERFORD
13 Chief Info Technology Officer ... Mr. Steve SMITH
86 Director Federal Relations ... Ms. Martha STEWART
26 Director of Public Affairs ... Ms. Kate RIPLEY

*University of Alaska Anchorage (I)

3211 Providence Drive, Anchorage AK 99508-8000
County: Anchorage FICE Identification: 011462
Unit ID: 102553
Telephone: (907) 786-1800 Carnegie Class: Master's L
FAX Number: (907) 786-4888 Calendar System: Semester
URL: www.uaa.alaska.edu
Established: 1954 Annual Undergrad Tuition & Fees (In-State): $5,294
Enrollment: 20,559 Coed
Affiliation or Control: State IRS Status: 501(c)3
Highest Offering: Master's
Program: Occupational; 2-Year Principally Bachelor's Creditable; Liberal Arts And General; Teacher Preparatory; Professional
Accreditation: NW, ADNUR, ART, BUS, DA, DH, @DIETD, DIETI, ENG, ENGR, JOUR, MAC, MLTAD, MT, MUS, NUR, PH, SW, TED

02 Chancellor ... Gen. Tom CASE
05 Provost ... Dr. Michael DRISCOLL
11 Vice Chancellor Administrative Svcs ... Dr. William SPINDLE
09 Sr Vice Provst Inst Effectiveness ... Ms. Renee M. CARTER-CHAPMAN
84 Assoc Vice Chanc Enrollment Mgmt ... Mr. Eric R. PEDERSEN
30 Vice Chancellor Univ Advancement ... Ms. Megan OLSON
32 Vice Chancellor Student Affairs ... Dr. Bruce SCHULTZ
26 Asst Vice Chanc University Rels ... Ms. Kristin DESMITH
91 Assoc Vice Chanc Information Tech ... Dr. Richard A. WHITNEY
09 Assoc VP of Institutional Research ... Dr. Gary RICE
18 Assoc Vice Chanc. Facilities ... Mr. Christopher TURLETES
96 Assoc VC Financial Services ... Ms. Sandi CULVER
44 AVC of Development ... Ms. Beth ROSE
20 Assc VC Acad/Multicul Stdnt Success ... Ms. Vara ALLEN-JONES
35 Dean of Students ... Dr. Dewain LEE
37 Director Student Financial Aid ... Mr. Ted MALONE
88 Director AHAINA Student Programs ... Vacant
35 Director Student Life & Leadership ... Ms. Annie ROUTE
07 Director of Admissions ... Ms. Cecile MITCHELL
28 Dir Campus Diversity & Compliance ... Ms. Marva WATSON
29 Director Alumni Relations ... Vacant
41 Director Athletics ... Dr. Steve COBB
06 Interim University Registrar ... Ms. Shirlee WILLIS-HASLIP
36 Director Career Services Ctr ... Ms. Diane KOZAK
15 Director Human Resources ... Mr. Ron KAMAHELE
08 Dean Consortium Library ... Mr. Stephen J. ROLLINS
63 Director Biomedical Program ... Dr. Dennis VALEZENO
88 Director Native Student Services ... Mr. William TEMPLETON
50 Dean Col Business & Public Policy ... Dr. Elisha BAKER
51 Dean Community/Tech College ... Dr. Karen R. SCHMITT
83 Dean Col Health/Social Welfare ... Dr. Cheryl EASLEY
54 Dean School of Engineering ... Dr. Robert LANG
49 Interim Dean Arts & Sciences Colleg ... Dr. Kim PETERSON
53 Interim Dean College of Education ... Dr. Patricia CHESBRO
92 Dean Honors College ... Mr. Ronald SPATZ

*University of Alaska Fairbanks (J)

215 Signers' Hall, Admissions, Fairbanks AK 99775-7480
County: Fairbanks North Star Borough FICE Identification: 001063
Unit ID: 102614
Telephone: (907) 474-7500 Carnegie Class: RU/H
FAX Number: (907) 474-5379 Calendar System: Semester
URL: www.uaf.edu
Established: 1917 Annual Undergrad Tuition & Fees (In-State): $5,570
Enrollment: 10,713 Coed

Affiliation or Control: State IRS Status: 501(c)3
Highest Offering: Doctorate
Program: Occupational; 2-Year Principally Bachelor's Creditable; Liberal Arts And General; Teacher Preparatory; Professional
Accreditation: NW, BUS, BUSA, CS, DH, EMT, ENG, FOR, #JOUR, MAC, MUS, SW, TED

02 Chancellor ... Mr. Brian D. ROGERS
05 Provost ... Dr. Susan M. HENRICHS
11 Vice Chancellor Administrative Svcs ... Ms. Pat PITNEY
18 Assoc VC Facilities ... Mr. Scott BELL
30 VC Advancement ... Mr. John (Jake) POOLE
32 Vice Chancellor for Students ... Dr. Mike SFRAGA
45 Vice Chancellor Research ... Dr. Mark MYERS
21 Assoc VC for Financial Services ... Mr. Raaj KURAPATI
44 Director of Development ... Ms. Emily DRYGAS
58 Interim Dean Graduate School ... Dr. Lawrence DUFFY
81 Dean Col of Natural Science/Math ... Dr. Paul LAYER
35 Assoc Vice Chanc for Student Life ... Mr. Don FOLEY
31 VC Rural/Cmty & Native Educ ... Ms. Bernice JOSEPH
12 Director UAF Comm/Tech College ... Ms. Susan WHITENER
47 Dean Sch of Natural Res/Ag Sciences ... Dr. Carol E. LEWIS
88 Dean Sch Fisheries & Ocean Sciences ... Dr. Mike CASTELLINI
50 Dean School of Management ... Dr. Mark HERRMANN
54 Dean Col of Engineering & Mines ... Dr. Doug GOERING
88 Dir Intl Arctic Research Center ... Dr. Larry HINZMAN
88 Dir Institute of Arctic Biology ... Dr. Brian M. BARNES
54 Director Inst Northern Engineering ... Dr. Daniel WHITE
15 Director UAF Human Resources ... Ms. Kris RACINA
19 Chief of Police ... Mr. Sean MCGEE
37 Director Financial Aid ... Ms. Deanna L. DIERINGER
26 Director of Community Advocacy ... Ms. Ann RINGSTAD
41 Director Athletics ... Mr. Forrest KARR
39 Director Residence Life ... Ms. Laura L. MCCOLLOUGH
56 Vice Provost for Extension/Outreach ... Mr. Fred SCHLUTT
40 Director of Aux/Recharge/Cntrct Ops ... Mr. Robert HOLDEN
85 Director International Programs ... Ms. Donna ANGER
88 Fire Chief ... Mr. Doug SCHRAGE
88 Dir Institute of Marine Science ... Dr. Terry WHITLEDGE
49 Interim Dean College of Lib/Arts ... Dr. Burns COOPER
53 Interim Dean School of Education ... Dr. Allan MOROTTI
12 Director Bristol Bay Campus ... Dr. Deborah MCLEAN-NELSON
12 Director Chukchi Campus ... Ms. Pauline HARVEY
12 Director Interior Aleutians Campus ... Ms. Clara ANDERSON
12 Director Kuskokwim Campus ... Ms. Mary C. PETE
12 Director Northwest Campus ... Dr. Linda HAUGEN
28 Director of Diversity ... Vacant
23 Director Health and Counseling ... Dr. B.J ALDRICH
29 Exec Director Alumni Association ... Mr. Joe HAYES
07 Registrar & Dir Office Admissions ... Mr. Mike EARNEST
88 Director Geophysical Institute ... Dr. Roger W. SMITH
21 Director Business Operations ... Ms. Amanda WALL
36 Director Career Services ... Ms. Patti PICHA
38 Director Academic Advising Center ... Ms. Linda M. HAPSMITH
92 Interim Director Honors Program ... Dr. Gary LAURSEN
94 Coordinator Women's Studies ... Dr. Sine ANAHITA
45 Dir Planning/Analysis/Inst Research ... Mr. Ian OLSON
49 Assoc Dean College of Liberal Arts ... Ms. Anita HARTMANN
26 Director Marketing/Communications ... Mr. Scott J. MCCREA
08 Dean of Libraries ... Dr. Bella GERLICH
88 Director UA Museum of the North ... Dr. Carol DIEBEL
14 Dir Arctic Reg Supercomputing Ctr ... Dr. Greg NEWBY
13 Chief Info Technology Officer ... Mr. Karl KOWALSKI
20 Vice Provost & Accreditation Ofcr ... Dr. Dana THOMAS
88 Director for Disability Services ... Ms. Mary MATTHEWS
96 Dir of Procurement & Contract Svcs ... Mr. John HEBARD
88 Director Wood Center Student Union ... Mrs. Lydia ANDERSON
46 AVC Research ... Dr. John BLAKE
46 AVC Research ... Dr. Nettie LABELLE-HAMER

*University of Alaska Southeast (A)

11120 Glacier Highway, Juneau AK 99801-8681
County: Juneau FICE Identification: 001065
Unit ID: 102632
Telephone: (907) 796-6000 Carnegie Class: Master's S
FAX Number: N/A Calendar System: Semester
URL: www.uas.alaska.edu
Established: 1956 Annual Undergrad Tuition & Fees (In-State): $4,961
Enrollment: 842 Coed
Affiliation or Control: State IRS Status: 501(c)3
Highest Offering: Master's
Program: Occupational; Liberal Arts And General; Teacher Preparatory; Professional
Accreditation: NW, TED

02 Chancellor ... Mr. John PUGH
05 Provost & Executive Dean SCE ... Dr. Richard CAULFIELD
75 Associate Dean Sch of Career Educ ... Ms. Robin GILCRIST
46 Vice Provost for Research ... Dr. Marsha SOUSA
20 Vice Provost for Academic Programs ... Ms. Carol HEDLIN
11 Vice Chanc & Director Admin Svcs ... Ms. Carol GRIFFIN
88 Assistant VC Admin Svcs ... Mr. James DANIELSON
12 Sitka Campus Director ... Dr. Jeffrey JOHNSTON
12 Ketchikan Campus Director ... Dr. Tony MANSUETO
49 Dean of Arts & Sciences ... Dr. Marsha SOUSA
88 Interim Dean School of Management ... Mr. John BLANCHARD
88 Director UAS Ctr for Mine Training ... Mr. Mike BELL
53 Dean Education & Graduate Studies ... Dr. Deborah LO
37 Financial Aid Officer ... Ms. Corinne SOLTIS
26 Dir of Marketing/Public Relations ... Ms. Katie BAUSLER
06 Registrar ... Ms. Barbara HEGEL
84 Dean Enrollment Management ... Mr. Joseph NELSON

09 Institutional Effectiveness Manager ... Ms. Diane MEADOR
10 Director Business Services ... Mr. Tom DIENST
15 Director Personnel Services ... Mr. Kirk MCALLISTER
18 Director Facilities Services ... Mr. Keith GERKEN
08 Interim Director Library Services ... Ms. Elise TOMLINSON
13 Director Information/Technology ... Mr. Michael CIRI
30 Dir Development/Alumni Relations ... Ms. Lynne JOHNSON
29 Annual Fund Alumni Rels Manager ... Ms. Keni CAMPBELL
32 Dean of Students ... Dr. Jessie GRANT
21 Chief Budget Officer ... Ms. Barbara HYDE
88 Director Learning Center ... Ms. Hildegard SELLNER

*Prince William Sound Community College (B)

PO Box 97, Valdez AK 99686-0097
County: Valdez-Cordova-Glennallen Identification: 666659
Unit ID: 103361
Telephone: (907) 834-1612 Carnegie Class: Assoc/Pub-R-M
FAX Number: (907) 834-1611 Calendar System: Semester
URL: www.pwscc.edu
Established: 1978 Annual Undergrad Tuition & Fees (In-State): $3,500
Enrollment: 2,000 Coed
Affiliation or Control: State IRS Status: 501(c)3
Highest Offering: Associate Degree
Program: Occupational; 2-Year Principally Bachelor's Creditable
Accreditation: NW

02 President ... Mr. Douglas DESORCIE
05 Dean of Instruction ... Mr. Wes LUNDBURG
10 Business Manager ... Mr. Steve SHIELL
06 Registrar ... Ms. Shannon FOSTER
07 Director Admiss/Fin Aid/ Stdnt Svc ... Mr. Chris WASHCO
15 Director Personnel Services ... Ms. Ana HINKLE
26 Chief Public Relations Officer ... Ms. Wendy GOLDSTEIN
38 Director Student Counseling ... Vacant
88 Director of Training ... Mr. Alan SORUM

ARIZONA

American Graduate School of Education (C)

7665 South Research Drive, Tempe AZ 85284-1812
County: Maricopa Identification: 667017
Telephone: (480) 428-6034 Carnegie Class: Not Classified
FAX Number: (480) 428-6033 Calendar System: Semester
URL: www.agse.edu
Established: 2006 Annual Graduate Tuition & Fees: $7,300
Enrollment: 200 Coed
Affiliation or Control: Other IRS Status: 501(c)3
Highest Offering: Master's; No Undergraduates
Program: Teacher Preparatory
Accreditation: DETC

01 President ... Mr. Michael TURICO
05 Exec VP Curriculum/Assessment Dev ... Dr. Sharon BOLSTER
106 Exec VP Trainining/Online Learning ... Dr. Marilynn D. HENLEY
32 Exec VP Student Affairs ... Mr. Tim MOMAN

American Indian College of the Assemblies of God (D)

10020 N 15th Avenue, Phoenix AZ 85021-2199
County: Maricopa FICE Identification: 021999
Unit ID: 103787
Telephone: (602) 944-3335 Carnegie Class: Bac/Diverse
FAX Number: (602) 943-8299 Calendar System: Semester
URL: www.aicag.edu
Established: 1957 Annual Undergrad Tuition & Fees: $9,990
Enrollment: 85 Coed
Affiliation or Control: Assemblies Of God Church IRS Status: 501(c)3
Highest Offering: Baccalaureate
Program: 2-Year Principally Bachelor's Creditable; Teacher Preparatory; Religious Emphasis
Accreditation: NH

01 President ... Dr. David L. DEGARMO
05 Vice President for Academic Affairs ... Dr. Boyd TOLBERT
10 Exec Director of Financial Services ... Rev. Paul HENNING
32 Executive Dir of Student Services ... Rev. Vincent ROUBIDEAUX
42 Campus Pastor ... Rev. Jimmy E. DEMPSEY
06 Registrar ... Ms. Jennifer ROUBIDEAUX
84 Director Enrollment Mgmt/ Admissions ... Ms. Sandra M. GONZALES
37 Student Financial Aid Director ... Ms. Candita WOODIS
08 Library Director ... Rev. John S. ROSE
30 Director of Advancement ... Ms. Kathryn MILLS-SMITH

Anthem College (E)

1515 East Indian School Road, Phoenix AZ 85014
County: Maricopa FICE Identification: 022631
Unit ID: 104805
Telephone: (602) 279-9700 Carnegie Class: Not Classified
FAX Number: N/A Calendar System: Other
URL: www.anthem.edu
Established: 1982 Annual Undergrad Tuition & Fees: $23,624
Enrollment: 1,748 Coed
Affiliation or Control: Proprietary IRS Status: Proprietary
Highest Offering: Baccalaureate
Program: Occupational
Accreditation: ACICS

01 Campus President ... Mr. James HADLEY

Argosy University, Phoenix (F)

2233 W Dunlap Avenue, Phoenix AZ 85021
County: Maricopa Identification: 666790
Unit ID: 436094
Telephone: (602) 216-2600 Carnegie Class: Spec/Health
FAX Number: (602) 216-3151 Calendar System: Semester
URL: www.argosy.edu/phoenix
Established: 1997 Annual Undergrad Tuition & Fees: $14,580
Enrollment: 896 Coed
Affiliation or Control: Proprietary IRS Status: Proprietary
Highest Offering: Doctorate
Program: Professional
Accreditation: &NH, CLPSY

01 Campus President ... Bart LERNER
05 Vice President of Academic Affairs ... Norma J. PATTERSON
32 Director of Student Services ... Jacqueline MARTINEZ
07 Director of Admissions ... Rachel RIUTTA
16 Regional Human Resources Director ... Tommy COMER
10 Business Manager ... Richard BINDER
37 Dir of Student Financial Services ... Cameraon ROBB
06 Registrar ... Vacant
04 Executive Assistant ... Elizabeth MIRABAL

† Regional accreditation is carried under the parent institution, Argosy University in Chicago, IL.

Arizona Automotive Institute (G)

6829 N 46th Avenue, Glendale AZ 85301-3597
County: Maricopa FICE Identification: 010847
Unit ID: 103963
Telephone: (623) 934-7273 Carnegie Class: Assoc/PrivFP
FAX Number: (623) 937-5000 Calendar System: Quarter
URL: www.aai.edu
Established: 1968 Annual Undergrad Tuition & Fees: $27,790
Enrollment: 1,734 Coed
Affiliation or Control: Proprietary IRS Status: Proprietary
Highest Offering: Associate Degree
Program: Occupational
Accreditation: ACCSC

01 Executive Director ... Dennis DEL VALLE
05 Director of Education ... Bret IDASPE

Arizona Christian University (formerly Southwestern College) (H)

2625 E Cactus Road, Phoenix AZ 85032-7042
County: Maricopa FICE Identification: 007113
Unit ID: 105899
Telephone: (602) 489-5300 Carnegie Class: Bac/Diverse
FAX Number: (602) 404-2159 Calendar System: Semester
URL: www.arizonachristian.edu
Established: 1960 Annual Undergrad Tuition & Fees: $18,968
Enrollment: 464 Coed
Affiliation or Control: Independent Non-Profit IRS Status: 501(c)3
Highest Offering: Baccalaureate
Program: Liberal Arts And General; Teacher Preparatory
Accreditation: NH

01 President ... Mr. Len MUNSIL
05 Provost ... Dr. Gary P. DAMORE
10 Chief Financial Officer ... Mr. Douglas REMY
11 Vice President for Operations ... Mr. Don MITCHELL
84 Vice Pres Enrollment & Marketing ... Ms. Heather KIM
18 Vice Pres for Facilities Expansion ... Mr. Paul HENDRICKS
100 Chief of Staff ... Mr. Brant NYHART
04 Executive Assistant to President ... Ms. Tiffani EDWARDS
44 Director of Advancement ... Mr. Daniel MILLS
20 Academic Dean ... Dr. William P. BAKER
32 Dean of Student Services ... Mr. Charles HUNTER
88 Dean of Accred/Plng & Program ... Vacant
51 Acting Dean Adult Degree Completion ... Vacant
41 Athletic Director ... Mr. Rick ROTH
21 Business Office Manager ... Ms. June TAYLOR
06 Registrar ... Mr. Lambert CRUZ
37 Director Financial Aid ... Ms. Jill GOLIKE
34 Dean of Women ... Ms. Peg FORREST
08 Head Librarian ... Mr. Sean J. MCNULTY
39 Director of Residence Life ... Mr. Anthony SUAREZ
13 Information Technology Director ... Mr. Joel HAYS
19 Dir Campus Min & Campus Safety ... Mr. James FARLEY

Arizona College of Allied Health (I)

4425 W Olive Avenue, Suite 300, Glendale AZ 85302-3851
County: Maricopa FICE Identification: 031150
Unit ID: 421708
Telephone: (602) 222-9300 Carnegie Class: Assoc/PrivFP
FAX Number: (602) 200-8726 Calendar System: Other
URL: www.arizonacollege.edu
Established: 1991 Annual Undergrad Tuition & Fees: $13,525
Enrollment: 832 Coed

Affiliation or Control: Proprietary IRS Status: Proprietary
Highest Offering: Associate Degree
Program: 2-Year Principally Bachelor's Creditable; Nursing Emphasis
Accreditation: **ABHES**

01 President .... Mr. Nick MANSOUR
11 Vice President for Operations .... Ms. Dawn SMITH
37 Financial Aid Director .... Mr. Matthew CALHOUN

Arizona School of Acupuncture and Oriental Medicine (A)

4646 E Fort Lowell Road, Suite 103,
Tucson AZ 85712-1100
County: Pima FICE Identification: 036955
Unit ID: 446039
Telephone: (520) 795-0787 Carnegie Class: Spec/Health
FAX Number: (520) 795-1481 Calendar System: Quarter
URL: www.asaom.edu
Established: 1996 Annual Graduate Tuition & Fees: $47,226
Enrollment: 48 Coed
Affiliation or Control: Proprietary IRS Status: Proprietary
Highest Offering: Master's; No Undergraduates
Program: Professional
Accreditation: **ACUP**

01 CEO/Founder .... Mr. David EPLEY
05 Education Director .... Ms. Laurel INMAN
37 Financial Aid Advisor .... Ms. Susan WAGNER
20 Academic/Clinic Dean .... Mr. Don LIGHTNER
07 Dean of Admissions .... Ms. Laurel INMAN

Arizona State University (B)

300 E. University Drive, Tempe AZ 85281
County: Maricopa FICE Identification: 001081
Unit ID: 104151
Telephone: (480) 965-9011 Carnegie Class: RU/VH
FAX Number: N/A Calendar System: Semester
URL: www.asu.edu
Established: 1885 Annual Undergrad Tuition & Fees (In-State): $9,720
Enrollment: 70,440 Coed
Affiliation or Control: State IRS Status: 501(c)3
Highest Offering: Doctorate
Program: Liberal Arts And General; Professional
Accreditation: **NH**, AAB, ART, AUD, BUS, BUSA, CACREP, CIDA, CLPSY, CONST, COPSY, CS, DIETD, DIETI, ENG, ENGT, HSA, IPSY, JOUR, LAW, LSAR, MUS, NAIT, NRPA, NURSE, PLNG, SCPSY, SP, SPAA, SW

01 President .... Dr. Michael M. CROW
05 Exec Vice President and Provost .... Dr. Elizabeth D. CAPALDI
10 Exec Vice President/Treasurer & CFO .... Dr. Morgan R. OLSEN
03 Sr Vice Pres/Sec of the University ... Dr. Christine K. WILKINSON
45 Sr Vice Pres & University Planner .... Mr. Richard H. STANLEY
46 Sr Vice Pres Knowledge Enterprise .... Dr. R. F. SHANGRAW
43 Sr Vice President & General Counsel .... Mr. Jose A. CARDENAS
32 Sr VP Educ Outreach & Student Svcs .... Dr. James A. RUND
41 Vice Pres of University Athletics .... Ms. Lisa L. LOVE
13 Chief Information Officer .... Mr. Gordon D. WISHON
26 Vice President for Public Affairs .... Mr. Virgil N. RENZULLI
88 Vice Pres Education Partnerships .... Dr. Eugene E. GARCIA
20 Sr Vice Pres Academic Affairs .... Dr. David A. YOUNG
20 Vice President Academic Personnel .... Dr. Mark S. SEARLE
106 Exec Vice Provost/Dean ASU Online .... Dr. Philip R. REGIER
102 President/CEO ASU Foundation .... Mr. Johnnie D. RAY
16 Asst VP & Chief Human Resources Ofc .... Mr. Kevin J. SALCIDO
46 Univ Chief Research Officer ..... Dr. Sethuraman PANCHANATHEN
100 VP/Chief of Staff .... Mr. Jim O'BRIEN
57 Dean Herberger Inst for Design/Arts .... Dr. Kwang-Wu KIM
50 Dean WP Carey School of Business .... Mr. Robert F. MITTELSTAEDT
54 Dean Ira A Fulton Schls of Engr .... Dr. Paul C. JOHNSON
58 Exec Vice Prov/Dean Graduate Col .... Dr. Maria T. ALLISON
92 Dean of Barrett Honors College .... Dr. Mark JACOBS
12 VP of West Campus /Dean New College .... Dr. Elizabeth LANGLAND
60 Dean Cronkite Sch Journal/Mass Comm .... Mr. Christopher CALLAHAN
61 Interim Dean College of Law .... Mr. Douglas SYLVESTER
49 Vice Pres/Dean Col Lib Arts & Sci .... Dr. Quentin D. WHEELER
66 Dean College of Nursing & Health In . Dr. Bernadette M. MELNYK
88 Dean School of Sustainability .... Dr. Sander VAN DER LEEUW
53 Dean Mary Lou Fulton Teachers Col .... Dr. Mari E. KOERNER
72 Vice Prov/Dean College Tech & Innov ..... Dr. Mitzi M. MONTOYA
20 Vice Prov/Dean University College .... Dr. Frederick C. COREY
79 Dean Humanities CLAS .... Dr. Neal A. LESTER
88 Dean Natural Sciences CLAS .... Dr. Sid P. BACON
88 Dean School of Life Sciences CLAS .... Dr. Robert E. PAGE
83 Dean Social Sciences CLAS .... Dr. Linda C. LEDERMAN

Arizona Western College (C)

2020 Avenue 8E, Yuma AZ 85365
County: Yuma FICE Identification: 001071
Unit ID: 104160
Telephone: (928) 317-6000 Carnegie Class: Assoc/Pub-R-L
FAX Number: (928) 344-7730 Calendar System: Semester
URL: www.azwestern.edu
Established: 1963 Annual Undergrad Tuition & Fees (In-District): $2,100
Enrollment: 8,545 Coed
Affiliation or Control: State/Local IRS Status: 501(c)3
Highest Offering: Associate Degree
Program: Occupational; 2-Year Principally Bachelor's Creditable
Accreditation: **NH**, ADNUR, RAD

01 President .... Dr. Glenn MAYLE
10 Vice President Admin Services .... Mr. Dan HANN
13 Vice President Info Tech Services .... Mr. Paul NEUMAN
05 Vice Pres Academic & Student Svcs .... Dr. Eric SOULSBY
102 Executive Director AWC Foundation .... Mrs. Denise SWEET-MCGREGOR
26 Dir Public Relations & Marketing .... Mrs. Lori STOFFT
09 Director Instnl Effect/Rsrch/Grants .... Dr. Mary SCHAAL
20 Dean of Instruction .... Mrs. Linda ELLIOTT-NELSON
84 Dean of Enrollment Services .... Dr. Llewellyn YOUNG
103 Dean of Business & Workforce Devel .... Mrs. Lynn LABRIE
38 Dean Student Retention/Support Svcs .... Mr. Bryan DOAK
75 Dean of Career & Technical Educ .... Mr. Daniel BARAJAS
21 Associate VP for Business Services .... Ms. Carole COLEMAN
15 Director of Human Resources .... Ms. Ruth WHISLER
96 Director of Purchasing & Aux Svcs .... Mr. Denis PONDER
18 Director Facilities Mgmt & Planning .... Mr. Bill SMITH
14 Director of Tech & Network Services .... Mr. Don RINEY
08 Director of Library Services .... Ms. Angie CREEL-ERB
41 Director of Athletics .... Mr. Jerry SMITH
19 Chief of Police .... Mr. John EDMUNDSON
35 Dean for Campus Life .... Ms. Mary Kay HARTON
12 Associate Dean La Paz County Svcs .... Mr. Jim BROUILLETTE
12 Assoc Dean for South Yuma County .... Mr. Everardo MARTINEZ
37 Director of Financial Aid .... Ms. Lisa SEALE
85 Coordinator of Intl Student Program .... Mr. Ken KUNTZELMAN
07 Director of Admissions/Registrar .... Ms. Amy PIGNATORE
106 Associate Dean for Distance Educ .... Mrs. Jana MOORE
88 Director of Testing Services .... Mrs. Leticia MARTINEZ
105 Webmaster II .... Mr. Damien BATES

The Art Institute of Phoenix (D)

2233 W Dunlap Avenue, Phoenix AZ 85021-2859
County: Maricopa FICE Identification: 040513
Unit ID: 428444
Telephone: (602) 331-7500 Carnegie Class: Spec/Arts
FAX Number: (602) 331-5301 Calendar System: Quarter
URL: www.artinstitutes.edu/phoenix
Established: 1995 Annual Undergrad Tuition & Fees: $28,860
Enrollment: 1,300 Coed
Affiliation or Control: Proprietary IRS Status: Proprietary
Highest Offering: Baccalaureate
Program: 2-Year Principally Bachelor's Creditable; Professional; Fine Arts Emphasis
Accreditation: **ACICS**, ACFEI, CIDA

01 President .... Mr. Kevin LAMOUNTAIN
05 Dean of Academic Affairs .... Dr. Meryl EPSTEIN
07 Senior Director of Admissions .... Ms. Stacey TILL
32 Dean of Student Affairs .... Vacant
36 Director of Career Services .... Ms. Kristin FRANK
10 Director of Admin & Fin Svcs .... Ms. Lori RYAN
15 Director of Human Resources .... Ms. Kristin ROBINSON
09 Dir of Institutional Effectiveness .... Ms. Jessica MARQUIS
13 Director of Technology .... Mr. Josh KOENIG
37 Director of Student Financial Svcs .... Ms. Abigail GARCIA
06 Registrar .... Ms. Barbara HICKS

The Art Institute of Tucson (E)

5099 East Grant Road, Suite 100, Tucson AZ 85712-2733
County: Pima FICE Identification: 037405
Unit ID: 444927
Telephone: (520) 318-2700 Carnegie Class: Spec/Arts
FAX Number: (520) 881-4794 Calendar System: Quarter
URL: www.artinstitutes.edu/tucson
Established: 1996 Annual Undergrad Tuition & Fees: $23,088
Enrollment: 496 Coed
Affiliation or Control: Proprietary IRS Status: Proprietary
Highest Offering: Baccalaureate
Program: 2-Year Principally Bachelor's Creditable; Professional
Accreditation: **ACICS**

01 Campus Director .... Mr. R. William VAN ZWOL
05 Dean .... Mr. Mark HINRICHS

Asian Institute of Medical Studies (F)

3131 N Country Club Road Ste 100,
Tucson AZ 85716-1650
County: Pima FICE Identification: 041193
Telephone: (520) 322-6330 Carnegie Class: Not Classified
FAX Number: (520) 322-5661 Calendar System: Quarter
URL: www.asianinstitute.edu
Established: 2000 Annual Undergrad Tuition & Fees: N/A
Enrollment: 25 Coed
Affiliation or Control: Independent Non-Profit IRS Status: 501(c)3
Highest Offering: Master's
Program: Professional
Accreditation: **ACUP**

01 President .... Mr. Alex HOLLAND
07 Admissions Director .... Ms. Margaret GRAGG

Brighton College (G)

7332 E Butherus Drive, Scottsdale AZ 85260
County: Maricopa Identification: 666710
Telephone: (800) 231-3803 Carnegie Class: Not Classified
FAX Number: (602) 212-0502 Calendar System: Other
URL: www.brightoncollege.edu
Established: 1961 Annual Undergrad Tuition & Fees: $7,800
Enrollment: 500 Coed
Affiliation or Control: Proprietary IRS Status: Proprietary
Highest Offering: Associate Degree
Program: Occupational; 2-Year Principally Bachelor's Creditable; Technical Emphasis
Accreditation: **DETC**

01 President .... Kathleen MIRABILE

Brookline College (H)

2445 West Dunlap Avenue, Phoenix AZ 85021
County: Maricopa FICE Identification: 022188
Unit ID: 104090
Telephone: (602) 242-6265 Carnegie Class: Bac/Assoc
FAX Number: (602) 973-2572 Calendar System: Other
URL: www.brooklinecollege.edu
Established: 1979 Annual Undergrad Tuition & Fees: $19,975
Enrollment: 1,636 Coed
Affiliation or Control: Proprietary IRS Status: Proprietary
Highest Offering: Baccalaureate
Program: Occupational
Accreditation: **ACICS**, @PTAA

01 Director .... Ms. Donna GREEN

Brookline College (I)

1140 South Priest Drive, Tempe AZ 85281
County: Maricopa Identification: 666403
Unit ID: 404055
Telephone: (480) 545-8755 Carnegie Class: Assoc/PrivFP
FAX Number: (480) 926-1371 Calendar System: Other
URL: www.brooklinecollege.edu
Established: 1979 Annual Undergrad Tuition & Fees: $13,750
Enrollment: 579 Coed
Affiliation or Control: Proprietary IRS Status: Proprietary
Highest Offering: Baccalaureate
Program: Occupational; Technical Emphasis
Accreditation: **ACICS**

01 Campus Director .... Mrs. Cheryl KINDRED

† Branch campus of Brookline College, Phoenix, AZ.

Brookline College (J)

5441 E 22nd Street, Suite 125, Tucson AZ 85711-5444
County: Pima Identification: 666402
Unit ID: 438179
Telephone: (520) 748-9799 Carnegie Class: Assoc/PrivFP
FAX Number: (520) 748-9355 Calendar System: Semester
URL: www.brooklinecollege.edu
Established: 1995 Annual Undergrad Tuition & Fees: $13,750
Enrollment: 984 Coed
Affiliation or Control: Proprietary IRS Status: Proprietary
Highest Offering: Baccalaureate
Program: Occupational; Liberal Arts And General
Accreditation: **ACICS**

01 Director .... Ms. Leigh Anne PECHOTA

† Branch campus of Brookline College, Phoeniz, AZ.

Brown Mackie College-Phoenix (K)

13430 North Black Canyon Highway, Phoenix AZ 85029
County: Maricopa Identification: 666782
Unit ID: 456612
Telephone: (602) 337-3044 Carnegie Class: Not Classified
FAX Number: (480) 375-2450 Calendar System: Other
URL: www.brownmackie.edu
Established: N/A Annual Undergrad Tuition & Fees: $11,124
Enrollment: 510 Coed
Affiliation or Control: Proprietary IRS Status: Proprietary
Highest Offering: Baccalaureate
Program: Occupational; 2-Year Principally Bachelor's Creditable; Business Emphasis
Accreditation: **ACICS**, OTA, SURTEC

01 President .... Connie SCOLLARD
07 Senior Director of Admissions .... Mike CRANCE
05 Dean of Academic Affairs .... Vacant

† Branch campus of Brown Mackie College, Tuscon, AZ.

Brown Mackie College-Tucson (L)

4585 E Speedway Boulevard, Tucson AZ 85712-5300
County: Pima FICE Identification: 009451
Unit ID: 104364
Telephone: (520) 319-3300 Carnegie Class: Bac/Diverse
FAX Number: (520) 325-0108 Calendar System: Other
URL: www.brownmackie.edu
Established: 1972 Annual Undergrad Tuition & Fees: $12,204
Enrollment: 728 Coed
Affiliation or Control: Proprietary IRS Status: Proprietary
Highest Offering: Baccalaureate
Program: Occupational; 2-Year Principally Bachelor's Creditable; Business Emphasis

Accreditation: ACICS, OTA, SURTEC

01 President .... Mr. Tim BUSH
05 Dean of Academic Affairs .... Mr. Michael O'DONNELL
07 Senior Director of Admissions .... Vacant
06 Registrar .... Vacant
32 Director of Student Services .... Mr. Kris JOHNSON
36 Director of Career Services .... Mr. Frank MAISH

The Bryman School (A)

2250 W Peoria Avenue, Suite A100, Phoenix AZ 85029-4923
County: Maricopa FICE Identification: 030764
Unit ID: 384209
Telephone: (602) 274-4300 Carnegie Class: Assoc/PrivFP
FAX Number: (602) 248-9087 Calendar System: Other
URL: www.brymanschool.edu
Established: N/A Annual Undergrad Tuition & Fees: $21,800
Enrollment: 1,450 Coed
Affiliation or Control: Proprietary IRS Status: Proprietary
Highest Offering: Associate Degree
Program: Occupational; 2-Year Principally Bachelor's Creditable; Technical Emphasis
Accreditation: ACICS, MAAB

01 Campus President .... Mr. Shawn ALEXANDER
05 Dean of Education .... Ms. Susan PINKERTON
37 Director of Financial Aid .... Mrs. Erin JOHNSON
07 Director of Admissions .... Mr. John PALUMBO
11 Office Manager .... Ms. Bonnie EASON
36 Career Service Director .... Mr. Rick RUSCH
32 Student Services Director .... Mr. James CANDELERIA

Carrington College - Mesa (B)

630 W Southern Avenue, Mesa AZ 85210-5005
County: Maricopa FICE Identification: 023352
Unit ID: 103909
Telephone: (480) 212-1600 Carnegie Class: Not Classified
FAX Number: (480) 827-0022 Calendar System: Other
URL: www.carrington.edu
Established: N/A Annual Undergrad Tuition & Fees: $13,295
Enrollment: 1,099 Coed
Affiliation or Control: Proprietary IRS Status: Proprietary
Highest Offering: Associate Degree
Program: Occupational; 2-Year Principally Bachelor's Creditable
Accreditation: ACICS, DH, PTAA

01 Executive Campus Director .... Ms. Val COLMONE

Carrington College - Phoenix (C)

8503 N 27th Avenue, Phoenix AZ 85051-4096
County: Maricopa FICE Identification: 021006
Unit ID: 103893
Telephone: (602) 393-5900 Carnegie Class: Assoc/PrivFP
FAX Number: N/A Calendar System: Other
URL: www.carrington.edu
Established: N/A Annual Undergrad Tuition & Fees: $13,295
Enrollment: 977 Coed
Affiliation or Control: Proprietary IRS Status: Proprietary
Highest Offering: Associate Degree
Program: Occupational; 2-Year Principally Bachelor's Creditable
Accreditation: ACICS

01 Interim Executive Campus Director .... Mr. Edward CONNOLLY
05 Dean Academic Affairs .... Ms. Susan OPALKA

Carrington College - Tucson (D)

3550 N Oracle Road, Tucson AZ 85705-3591
County: Pima FICE Identification: 030898
Unit ID: 103927
Telephone: (520) 888-5885 Carnegie Class: Not Classified
FAX Number: (520) 887-3005 Calendar System: Semester
URL: www.carrington.edu
Established: N/A Annual Undergrad Tuition & Fees: $13,295
Enrollment: 867 Coed
Affiliation or Control: Proprietary IRS Status: Proprietary
Highest Offering: Associate Degree
Program: Occupational; 2-Year Principally Bachelor's Creditable
Accreditation: ACICS

01 Executive Campus Director .... Mr. Luis ARMENDARIZ

Carrington College - Westside (E)

2701 W Bethany Home Road, Phoenix AZ 85017-1705
County: Maricopa Identification: 666248
Unit ID: 250601
Telephone: (602) 433-1333 Carnegie Class: Not Classified
FAX Number: (602) 433-1414 Calendar System: Semester
URL: www.carrington.edu
Established: 1976 Annual Undergrad Tuition & Fees: $13,295
Enrollment: 694 Coed
Affiliation or Control: Proprietary IRS Status: Proprietary
Highest Offering: Associate Degree
Program: 2-Year Principally Bachelor's Creditable
Accreditation: ACICS, RAD

01 Campus Director .... Rick CARSON

Central Arizona College (F)

8470 N Overfield Road, Coolidge AZ 85128-9779
County: Pinal FICE Identification: 007283
Unit ID: 104346
Telephone: (520) 494-5444 Carnegie Class: Assoc/Pub-S-MC
FAX Number: (520) 494-5008 Calendar System: Semester
URL: www.centralaz.edu
Established: 1962 Annual Undergrad Tuition & Fees (In-District): $2,100
Enrollment: 7,117 Coed
Affiliation or Control: Local IRS Status: 501(c)3
Highest Offering: Associate Degree
Program: Occupational; 2-Year Principally Bachelor's Creditable
Accreditation: NH, ADNUR, DIETT, MAC, RAD

01 President .... Mr. Dennis JENKINS
05 VP Instructional Pgms & Svcs/CAO .... Vacant
81 Dean of Comm/Math & Learning Supp .... Dr. Steven GONZALES
76 Dean of Health Careers & Sciences .... Mr. Julian EASTER
88 Dean of Professional & Technical Ed .... Dr. Georgia WHITE
49 Dean of Arts & Social Sciences .... Ms. Terri ACKLAND
10 Vice President Financial & Admn Svc .... Mr. Chris WODKA
13 Associate VP Technology Svcs .... Mr. Richard KING
09 Associate VP Inst Effectiveness .... Vacant
16 Vice President Human Resources .... Mr. James KIMSEY
32 Vice President Student Services .... Dr. Doris HELMICH
102 Exec Director for the Foundation .... Vacant
09 Exec Dir Institutional Research .... Mr. William BROWN
08 Director Library Services .... Mr. Jeffrey MIDDLETON
26 Dir Media & Community Events .... Mr. Thomas DICAMILLO
37 Director of Financial Aid .... Ms. Elisa JUAREZ
41 Athletic Director .... Mr. Chuck SCHNOOR
39 Director of Residence/ Life .... Mr. Nev KRAGULJEVIC
19 Chief Campus Police Officer .... Mr. Luis MARTINEZ
18 Exec Director of Facilities .... Mr. Ernesto VALENZUELA
96 Director of Purchasing .... Mr. Mark SALAZ
06 Registrar .... Ms. Veronica DURAN
07 Director of Recruitment .... Mr. Luis SANCHEZ
15 Director of HR Services .... Mr. T.J FERRER
21 Exec Dir Accounting Svc/Comptroller .... Ms. Luisa OTT
35 Dean Student Life .... Dr. Philip TOMPKINS
84 Dean Recruitment & Admissions .... Dr. James MOORE

Cochise College (G)

4190 W Highway 80, Douglas AZ 85607-6190
County: Cochise FICE Identification: 001072
Unit ID: 104425
Telephone: (800) 966-7943 Carnegie Class: Assoc/Pub-R-L
FAX Number: (520) 417-4006 Calendar System: Semester
URL: www.cochise.edu
Established: 1962 Annual Undergrad Tuition & Fees (In-District): $1,970
Enrollment: 5,252 Coed
Affiliation or Control: Local IRS Status: 170(c)1
Highest Offering: Associate Degree
Program: Occupational; 2-Year Principally Bachelor's Creditable
Accreditation: NH, ADNUR

01 President .... Dr. J. D. ROTTWEILER
05 VP for Instruction/Provost .... Dr. Verlyn FICK
10 Vice President Administration .... Mr. Kevin S. BUTLER
13 Vice Pres Information Technology .... Mr. Carlos CARTAGENA
15 Vice Pres Human Resources .... Ms. Wendy DAVIS
49 Dean of Liberal Arts .... Mr. Chuck HOYACK
56 Dean of Extended Learning .... Ms. Sheila DEVOE HEIDMAN
32 Dean of Student Services .... Dr. James (Bo) HALL
09 Director of Institutional Research .... Dr. Jerome V. WARD
20 Director Curr/Learning/Assessment .... Dr. Judith E. DOERR
06 Director Admissions & Rec/Registrar .... Ms. Debbie QUICK
08 Director of College Libraries .... Ms. Pat HOTCHKISS
21 Director of Budgeting Services .... Ms. Sandy BRYAN
18 Director of Facilities Maintenance .... Mr. Frank DYKSTRA
35 Asst Dean of Student Services .... Mr. Mark BOGGIE
27 Director Office of External Affairs .... Ms. Denise MERKEL
72 Dean of Business & Technology .... Mr. Bruce RICHARDSON
81 Dean of Math/Science & Health Sci .... Dr. Richard (Bubba) HALL
106 Director of Online Campus .... Mr. George SELF
37 Director of Financial Aid .... Ms. Karen BENNETT
39 Director of Housing & Student Life .... Mr. Agustin GALVAN
88 Director Ctr for Economic Research .... Dr. Robert CARREIRA
51 Director Ctr for Lifelong Learning .... Vacant
26 Director Marketing & Creative Svcs .... Mr. Ed ROSKOWSKI

Coconino Community College (H)

2800 S Lone Tree Road, Flagstaff AZ 86001-2701
County: Coconino FICE Identification: 031004
Unit ID: 404426
Telephone: (928) 527-1222 Carnegie Class: Assoc/Pub-R-M
FAX Number: (928) 226-4106 Calendar System: Semester
URL: www.coconino.edu
Established: 1991 Annual Undergrad Tuition & Fees (In-State): $2,640
Enrollment: 2,550 Coed
Affiliation or Control: State IRS Status: 501(c)3
Highest Offering: Associate Degree
Program: 2-Year Principally Bachelor's Creditable
Accreditation: NH

01 President .... Dr. Leah L. BORNSTEIN
05 Vice President for Academic Affairs .... Dr. Kathleen A. CORAK
10 VP for Business & Administration .... Ms. Jami VAN ESS
32 Director of Student Services .... Ms. Veronica HIPOLITO
12 Executive Dean for Page Campus .... Mr. Lloyd HAMMONDS
51 Exec Dir of Cmty & Corp Learning .... Mr. John CARDANI
49 Dean of Art & Sciences .... Dr. Ingrid LEE
15 Director for Human Resources .... Ms. Theresa ALVARADO
09 Dir Institutional Research/Assess .... Dr. Stephen CHAMBERS
37 Director for Financial Aid .... Mr. Robert VOYTEK
06 Registrar/Dir Enrollment Services .... Ms. Kimmi GRULKE
88 Dean of Occupational/Profess Tech .... Dr. Monica BAKER
18 Director Facilities .... Mr. Mark EASTON
13 Chief Technical Officer .... Mr. Joe TRAINO
96 Director Purchasing/Auxiliary Svcs .... Mr. Robert SEDILLO
21 Controller .... Ms. Cindy COOK
30 Director Institutional Advancement .... Mr. Scott TALBOOM
04 Exec Assistant to the President .... Ms. Joan WHITE

CollegeAmerica-Flagstaff (I)

3012 East Route 66, Flagstaff AZ 86004-6323
County: Coconino FICE Identification: 031203
Unit ID: 103945
Telephone: (928) 213-6060 Carnegie Class: Assoc/PrivFP
FAX Number: (928) 226-8593 Calendar System: Other
URL: www.collegeamerica.edu
Established: 1964 Annual Undergrad Tuition & Fees: N/A
Enrollment: 285 Coed
Affiliation or Control: Proprietary IRS Status: Proprietary
Highest Offering: Baccalaureate
Program: Occupational
Accreditation: ACCSC

01 Executive Director .... Ms. Suzanne SCALES

CollegeAmerica-Phoenix (J)

9801 N Metro Parkway East, Phoenix AZ 85051
County: Maricopa Identification: 666017
Telephone: (602) 257-7522 Carnegie Class: Not Classified
FAX Number: (602) 246-3063 Calendar System: Semester
URL: www.collegeamerica.edu
Established: 2004 Annual Undergrad Tuition & Fees: N/A
Enrollment: N/A Coed
Affiliation or Control: Proprietary IRS Status: Proprietary
Highest Offering: Associate Degree
Program: Occupational; 2-Year Principally Bachelor's Creditable
Accreditation: ACCSC

01 Assoc Director .... Mr. Marty JIUNTA

† Branch campus of CollegeAmerica-Flagstaff

DeVry University - Mesa Center (K)

1201 S Alma School Road, Suite 5450, Mesa AZ 85210-2011
County: Maricopa Identification: 666190
Unit ID: 405137
Telephone: (480) 827-1511 Carnegie Class: Not Classified
FAX Number: (480) 827-2552 Calendar System: Semester
URL: www.devry.edu
Established: 1931 Annual Undergrad Tuition & Fees: $15,294
Enrollment: 452 Coed
Affiliation or Control: Proprietary IRS Status: Proprietary
Highest Offering: Master's
Program: Occupational; Professional; Business Emphasis
Accreditation: &NH

01 Center Dean .... Wallis STEMM

† Regional accreditation is carried under the parent institution in Downers Grove, IL.

DeVry University - Northeast Phoenix Center (L)

18500 N Allied Way, Suite 150, Phoenix AZ 85054-3102
County: Maricopa Identification: 666191
Unit ID: 437307
Telephone: (480) 657-3223 Carnegie Class: Not Classified
FAX Number: (480) 657-3222 Calendar System: Semester
URL: www.devry.edu
Established: 1999 Annual Graduate Tuition & Fees: $18,040
Enrollment: 97 Coed
Affiliation or Control: Proprietary IRS Status: Proprietary
Highest Offering: Master's; No Undergraduates
Program: Occupational; Professional; Business Emphasis
Accreditation: &NH

01 Center Dean .... Mr. Gary STARK, JR.

† Regional accreditation is carried under the parent institution in Downers Grove, IL.

DeVry University - Phoenix Campus (M)

2149 W Dunlap Avenue, Phoenix AZ 85021-2995
County: Maricopa FICE Identification: 008322
Unit ID: 104531
Telephone: (602) 870-9222 Carnegie Class: Master's M
FAX Number: (602) 870-1209 Calendar System: Semester
URL: www.devry.edu
Established: 1967 Annual Undergrad Tuition & Fees: $15,294

Enrollment: 1,915 Coed
Affiliation or Control: Proprietary IRS Status: Proprietary
Highest Offering: Master's
Program: Occupational; Professional; Business Emphasis
Accreditation: &NH, ENGT, MT

01 Metro President .... Mr. Craig JACOB
03 Group Vice President .... Mr. James DUGAN
05 Dean of Academic Affairs .... Mr. Geoffrey GATES
07 Director of Admissions .... Ms. Cathy TELLES
08 Director of Library Services .... Ms. Margot CASSIDY
06 Registrar .... Ms. Jill JAMERSON
32 Dean of Student Central .... Mr. Michael CHASE
11 Sr Director Finance & Admin .... Ms. Vicki L. MAY
15 Human Resources Business Partner .... Mr. Adam WINTER
31 Director of Outreach Services .... Ms. Cheryl BUNTING
36 Director of Career Services .... Ms. Deena HANDLER

† Regional accreditation is carried under the parent institution in Downers Grove, IL.

Diné College (A)

One Circle Drive, Tsaile AZ 86556-9998
County: Apache FICE Identification: 008246
Unit ID: 105297
Telephone: (928) 724-6671 Carnegie Class: Tribal
FAX Number: (928) 724-3327 Calendar System: Semester
URL: www.dinecollege.edu
Established: 1968 Annual Undergrad Tuition & Fees (In-District): $850
Enrollment: 2,149 Coed
Affiliation or Control: Local IRS Status: 501(c)3
Highest Offering: Baccalaureate
Program: Occupational; 2-Year Principally Bachelor's Creditable
Accreditation: NH

01 Interim President .... Ms. Marie R. ETSITTY
05 Int VP of Academic & Student Pgms .... Ms. Priscilla WEAVER
11 Vice President for Admin & Finance .... Mr. Ronald BELLOLI
30 VP of Institutional Advancement .... Mr. Curtis R. BENALLY
06 Registrar .... Ms. Louise LITZIN
20 Interim Dean .... Mr. Edison CURTIS
37 Director Student Financial Aid .... Mr. Gary SEGAY
15 Dir Department of Human Resources .... Ms. Evelyn MEADOWS
18 Supt Maintenance Operations .... Mr. Delbert PAQUIN
21 Controller .... Ms. Jolene WHEELER
26 Public Relations Director .... Mr. Ed MCCOMBS
09 Director of Institutional Research .... Vacant

Dunlap-Stone University (B)

11225 N 28th Drive, Suite B201, Phoenix AZ 85029-5610
County: Maricopa Identification: 666315
Telephone: (602) 648-5750 Carnegie Class: Not Classified
FAX Number: (602) 648-5755 Calendar System: Other
URL: www.dunlap-stone.edu
Established: 1995 Annual Undergrad Tuition & Fees: $8,200
Enrollment: 492 Coed
Affiliation or Control: Proprietary IRS Status: Proprietary
Highest Offering: Baccalaureate
Program: Professional; Business Emphasis
Accreditation: DETC

01 President .... Dr. Donald N. BURTON
106 Vice President Online Programs .... Mrs. Caulyne BARRON
06 Registrar .... Ms. Lisa FRITSCH

Eastern Arizona College (C)

615 N Stadium Avenue, Thatcher AZ 85552-0769
County: Graham FICE Identification: 001073
Unit ID: 104577
Telephone: (928) 428-8233 Carnegie Class: Assoc/Pub-R-L
FAX Number: (928) 428-8462 Calendar System: Semester
URL: www.eac.edu
Established: 1888 Annual Undergrad Tuition & Fees (In-District): $1,600
Enrollment: 6,791 Coed
Affiliation or Control: State/Local IRS Status: 501(c)3
Highest Offering: Associate Degree
Program: Occupational; 2-Year Principally Bachelor's Creditable
Accreditation: NH

01 President .... Mr. Mark BRYCE
03 Executive Vice President .... Mr. Brent MCEUEN
10 Chief Business Officer .... Mr. Timothy CURTIS
05 Provost .... Mrs. Jeanne BRYCE
20 Dean of Instruction .... Mr. Michael CROCKETT
20 Dean of Instruction .... Dr. Phil MCBRIDE
20 Dean of Curriculum and Instruction .... Dr. Janice LAWHORN
32 Dean of Students .... Dr. Gary SORENSEN
06 Associate Dean/Registrar .... Dr. Randall SKINNER
38 Assistant Dean of Counseling .... Ms. Sharon ALLEN
12 Director of Discovery Park Campus .... Mr. Paul ANGER
21 Director Fiscal Control/Controller .... Mr. Darwin WEECH
37 Director of Financial Aid .... Mrs. Sharon MONTOYA
14 Director of Information Resources .... Mr. Thomas THOMPSON
09 Director of Institutional Research .... Mr. Glen SNIDER
08 Director of Library Services .... Mrs. Karen JAGGERS
26 Director of Marketing & Public Rels .... Mr. Todd HAYNIE
18 Director of Physical Resources .... Mr. Dan WELKER
30 Executive Director EAC Foundation .... Mr. David UDALL
35 Director of Student Life .... Mr. Danny BATTRAW
41 Athletic Director .... Mr. James BAGNALL
15 Assoc Director Admin Support EEO Co .... Ms. Lauri AVILA
04 Exec Asst to the President and DGB .... Mrs. Laurie PENNINGTON

Embry-Riddle Aeronautical University-Prescott Campus (D)

3200 Willow Creek Road, Prescott AZ 86301-3270
County: Yavapai FICE Identification: 021047
Unit ID: 104586
Telephone: (800) 888-3728 Carnegie Class: Bac/Diverse
FAX Number: (928) 777-3740 Calendar System: Semester
URL: www.erau.edu
Established: 1978 Annual Undergrad Tuition & Fees: $28,680
Enrollment: 1,705 Coed
Affiliation or Control: Independent Non-Profit IRS Status: 501(c)3
Highest Offering: Master's
Program: Occupational; Liberal Arts And General; Professional
Accreditation: &SC, AAB, ENG

01 President .... Dr. John P. JOHNSON
05 Exec Vice President and CAO .... Mr. Frank AYERS
20 Associate VP for Academics .... Dr. Richard BLOOM
32 Dean of Students .... Mr. Larry STEPHAN
50 Director of Business & Finance .... Mr. David HALL
84 Dean of Enrollment Management .... Mr. Thomas RAJALA
15 Manager HR & Student Employment .... Ms. Sara HEFFELFINGER
13 Director of Information Technology .... Ms. Nancy BARRETT
37 Director Financial Aid .... Mr. Daniel LUPIN
06 Director Records & Registration .... Ms. Mary LAHANN
26 Asst Director of Media Relations .... Mr. Bob ROSS
30 Senior Director of Development .... Mr. Steven BOBINSKY
09 Director of Institutional Research .... Ms. Maria FRANCO

† Regional accreditation is carried under the parent institution in Daytona Beach, FL.

Everest College Phoenix (E)

10400 N 25th Avenue, Suite 190, Phoenix AZ 85021-1610
County: Maricopa FICE Identification: 022950
Unit ID: 103644
Telephone: (602) 942-4141 Carnegie Class: Assoc/PrivFP4
FAX Number: (602) 943-0960 Calendar System: Other
URL: www.everest-college.com
Established: 1982 Annual Undergrad Tuition & Fees: $16,526
Enrollment: 527 Coed
Affiliation or Control: Proprietary IRS Status: Proprietary
Highest Offering: Baccalaureate
Program: Occupational; 2-Year Principally Bachelor's Creditable
Accreditation: NH

01 Campus President .... Mr. Todd M. MCDONALD
07 Director of Admissions .... Mr. Nick THORESON

Fortis College, Phoenix (F)

555 N 18th Street, Suite 110, Phoenix AZ 85006
County: Maricopa Identification: 666761
Unit ID: 456180
Telephone: (602) 254-3099 Carnegie Class: Not Classified
FAX Number: (602) 254-3183 Calendar System: Semester
URL: www.fortis.edu
Established: 2008 Annual Undergrad Tuition & Fees: $11,350
Enrollment: 267 Coed
Affiliation or Control: Proprietary IRS Status: Proprietary
Highest Offering: Associate Degree
Program: Occupational
Accreditation: ACCSC

01 Campus Director .... Glen THARP

† Branch campus of Fortis College, Centerville, OH. Tuition varies by degree program.

Frank Lloyd Wright School of Architecture (G)

Taliesin W, PO Box 4430, Scottsdale AZ 85261-4430
County: Maricopa FICE Identification: 025332
Unit ID: 104665
Telephone: (480) 860-2700 Carnegie Class: Spec/Arts
FAX Number: (480) 860-8472 Calendar System: Other
URL: www.taliesin.edu
Established: 1932 Annual Undergrad Tuition & Fees: $30,000
Enrollment: 32 Coed
Affiliation or Control: Independent Non-Profit IRS Status: 501(c)3
Highest Offering: Master's
Program: Professional
Accreditation: NH

01 Academic Dean & Dir of Curriculum .... Mr. Victor SIDY
08 Dean of Libraries .... Ms. Elizabeth AL-HAZZAM DAWASARI
07 Dir Admissions/Registrar/Fin Aid .... Ms. Pamela STEFANSSON
10 Vice President Finance .... Ms. Lisa MURPHY
30 Director of Development .... Mr. Ralph PHILLIPS
20 Education Coordinator .... Ms. Madalena MAESTRI

Golf Academy of America (H)

2031 N. Arizona Ave Suite 2, Chandler AZ 85225
County: Maricopa Identification: 666023
Unit ID: 430166
Telephone: (800) 342-7342 Carnegie Class: Assoc/PrivFP
FAX Number: (480) 857-1580 Calendar System: Semester
URL: www.golfacademy.edu
Established: 1996 Annual Undergrad Tuition & Fees: $33,824
Enrollment: 274 Coed
Affiliation or Control: Proprietary IRS Status: Proprietary
Highest Offering: Associate Degree
Program: Occupational; Business Emphasis
Accreditation: ACICS

01 President .... Mr. Chris HUNKLER
12 Campus Director .... Mr. Tim EBERLEIN

† Branch campus of Virginia College, Birmingham, AL.

Grand Canyon University (I)

3300 W Camelback Road, Phoenix AZ 85017-3030
County: Maricopa FICE Identification: 001074
Unit ID: 104717
Telephone: (602) 639-7500 Carnegie Class: Master's L
FAX Number: N/A Calendar System: Semester
URL: www.gcu.edu
Established: 1949 Annual Undergrad Tuition & Fees: $8,320
Enrollment: 37,441 Coed
Affiliation or Control: Proprietary IRS Status: Proprietary
Highest Offering: Doctorate
Program: Liberal Arts And General; Teacher Preparatory; Professional
Accreditation: NH, ACBSP, NURSE

01 President .... Dr. Kathy PLAYER
00 Chief Executive Officer .... Mr. Brian MUELLER
03 Executive Vice President .... Mr. Stan MEYER
11 Chief Administrative Officer .... Vacant
15 Vice President Human Resources .... Vacant
05 Chief Academic Officer .... Dr. Cheri ST. ARNAULD
26 Vice Pres of Marketing .... Ms. Christel MOSBY
50 Dean Ken Blanchard Col of Business .... Dr. Kevin BARKSDALE
53 Dean College of Education .... Dr. Kimberly LAPRADE
66 Dean College of Nursing .... Dr. Anne MCNAMARA
49 Dean of College of Arts and Science .... Dr. Mark WOODEN
58 Dean Graduate Studies .... Dr. Hank RAADA
57 Dean of Fine Arts and Production .... Mr. Claude PENSIS

Harrison Middleton University (J)

1105 East Broadway Road, Tempe AZ 85282-1505
County: Maricopa Identification: 666169
Telephone: (877) 248-6724 Carnegie Class: Not Classified
FAX Number: (800) 762-1622 Calendar System: Other
URL: www.hmu.edu
Established: 1998 Annual Undergrad Tuition & Fees: $30,350
Enrollment: 400 Coed
Affiliation or Control: Proprietary IRS Status: Proprietary
Highest Offering: Doctorate
Program: Liberal Arts And General
Accreditation: DETC

01 President .... Mr. David CURD
06 Director of Accreditation/Registrar .... Ms. Susan CHIARAMONTE
10 Director of Finance .... Mr. Walter MILLER

International Baptist College (K)

2211 W Germann Road, Chandler AZ 85286
County: Maricopa FICE Identification: 033473
Unit ID: 436614
Telephone: (480) 245-7903 Carnegie Class: Spec/Faith
FAX Number: (480) 245-7908 Calendar System: Semester
URL: www.ibconline.edu
Established: 1980 Annual Undergrad Tuition & Fees: $10,400
Enrollment: 84 Coed
Affiliation or Control: Baptist IRS Status: 501(c)3
Highest Offering: Doctorate
Program: Occupational; 2-Year Principally Bachelor's Creditable; Teacher Preparatory; Religious Emphasis
Accreditation: TRACS

01 President .... Mr. David W. BROCK
00 Chancellor .... Dr. Jerry C. TETREAU
32 Student Life Director .... Mr. Nathan MESTLER
05 Acting Academic Dean .... Mr. Jeffrey G. CAUPP
58 Acting Grad School Administrator .... Mr. Steve REYNOLDS
10 Chief Financial Officer .... Mr. Walt BAINES
08 Media Center Director .... Mrs. Kay SPROUL
33 Dean of Men .... Mr. Nathan MESTLER
34 Dean of Women .... Ms. Marcia GAMMON
06 Registrar .... Mrs. Bethany MESTLER
37 Financial Aid Administrator .... Mrs. Jane BUSHEY

ITT Technical Institute (L)

10220 North 25th Avenue, Suite 100, Phoenix AZ 85021
County: Maricopa Identification: 666696
Unit ID: 451972
Telephone: (602) 749-7900 Carnegie Class: Not Classified
FAX Number: (602) 749-7950 Calendar System: Quarter

URL: www.itt-tech.edu
Established: N/A Annual Undergrad Tuition & Fees: N/A
Enrollment: 568 Coed
Affiliation or Control: Proprietary IRS Status: Proprietary
Highest Offering: Baccalaureate
Program: Technical Emphasis
Accreditation: ACICS

† Branch campus of ITT Technical Institute, Tucson, AZ.

ITT Technical Institute (A)

5005 S Wendler Drive, Tempe AZ 85282-6321
County: Maricopa FICE Identification: 020652
Unit ID: 105172
Telephone: (602) 437-7500 Carnegie Class: Spec/Tech
FAX Number: (602) 437-7505 Calendar System: Quarter
URL: www.itt-tech.edu
Established: 1963 Annual Undergrad Tuition & Fees: N/A
Enrollment: 829 Coed
Affiliation or Control: Proprietary IRS Status: Proprietary
Highest Offering: Baccalaureate
Program: Technical Emphasis
Accreditation: ACICS

ITT Technical Institute (B)

1455 W River Road, Tucson AZ 85704-5829
County: Pima FICE Identification: 023611
Unit ID: 105163
Telephone: (520) 408-7488 Carnegie Class: Spec/Tech
FAX Number: (520) 292-9899 Calendar System: Quarter
URL: www.itt-tech.edu
Established: 1984 Annual Undergrad Tuition & Fees: N/A
Enrollment: 521 Coed
Affiliation or Control: Proprietary IRS Status: Proprietary
Highest Offering: Baccalaureate
Program: Technical Emphasis
Accreditation: ACICS

Kaplan College (C)

13610 N Black Canyon Highway, #104,
Phoenix AZ 85029-6323
County: Maricopa FICE Identification: 020712
Unit ID: 105118
Telephone: (602) 548-1955 Carnegie Class: Assoc/PrivFP
FAX Number: (602) 548-1956 Calendar System: Semester
URL: www.kaplancollege.com
Established: 1972 Annual Undergrad Tuition & Fees: $11,900
Enrollment: 543 Coed
Affiliation or Control: Proprietary IRS Status: Proprietary
Highest Offering: Associate Degree
Program: Occupational
Accreditation: ACCSC, MAC

01 Director .... Mr. Jake ELSEN

Lamson College (D)

875 West Elliot Road, Suite 206, Tempe AZ 85284-1141
County: Maricopa FICE Identification: 025215
Unit ID: 104984
Telephone: (480) 898-7000 Carnegie Class: Assoc/PrivFP
FAX Number: (480) 967-6645 Calendar System: Other
URL: www.lamsoncollege.edu
Established: 1889 Annual Undergrad Tuition & Fees: N/A
Enrollment: 258 Coed
Affiliation or Control: Proprietary IRS Status: Proprietary
Highest Offering: Associate Degree
Program: Occupational; 2-Year Principally Bachelor's Creditable
Accreditation: ACICS, SURGT

01 Campus Director .... Mr. Dino MEYER

Le Cordon Bleu College of Culinary Arts in Scottsdale (E)

8100 E Camelback Road, Ste 1001,
Scottsdale AZ 85251-3940
County: Maricopa FICE Identification: 026167
Unit ID: 262332
Telephone: (480) 990-3773 Carnegie Class: Spec/Other
FAX Number: (480) 990-0351 Calendar System: Other
URL: www.chefs.edu/scottsdale
Established: 1986 Annual Undergrad Tuition & Fees: $17,550
Enrollment: 1,362 Coed
Affiliation or Control: Proprietary IRS Status: Proprietary
Highest Offering: Baccalaureate
Program: Occupational
Accreditation: ACCSC, ACFEI

01 President .... Mr. Lloyd KIRSCH
11 Vice President Administration .... Ms. Jennifer JILOG
37 Vice Pres/Director of Financial Aid .... Ms. Maria IARKOVA
36 Director Career Services .... Ms. Kathleen DOELLER
06 Registrar .... Ms. Polly GIBSON
07 Director of Admission .... Mr. Martin HOWIE

*Maricopa County Community College District Office (F)

2411 W 14th Street, Tempe AZ 85281-6941
County: Maricopa FICE Identification: 001075
Unit ID: 105136
Telephone: (480) 731-8000 Carnegie Class: N/A
FAX Number: (480) 731-8850
URL: www.maricopa.edu

01 Chancellor .... Dr. Rufus GLASPER
05 Executive Vice Chancellor/ Provost .... Dr. Maria HARPER-MARINICK
26 VC Resource Devel/Community Rels .... Dr. Steven HELFGOT
10 Vice Chanc Business Services .... Ms. Debra THOMPSON
16 Vice Chancellor Human Resources .... Ms. Nikki R. JACKSON
13 Vice Chanc Information Technologies .... Mr. George KAHKEDJIAN
21 Assoc Vice Chanc Business Services .... Ms. Gaye MURPHY
22 Dir Center Workforce Development .... Mr. Randy KIMMENS
30 Exec Director Resource Development .... Ms. Mary O'CONNOR
09 Dir Inst Effectiveness & Outcomes .... Vacant
18 Assoc Vice Chanc Cap Plng/Spec Proj .... Mr. J. Lionel DIAZ

*Chandler-Gilbert Community College (G)

2626 E Pecos Road, Chandler AZ 85225-2499
County: Maricopa FICE Identification: 030722
Unit ID: 364025
Telephone: (480) 732-7000 Carnegie Class: Assoc/Pub-U-MC
FAX Number: (480) 732-7090 Calendar System: Semester
URL: www.cgc.maricopa.edu
Established: 1992 Annual Undergrad Tuition & Fees (In-District): $1,854
Enrollment: 12,296 Coed
Affiliation or Control: State/Local IRS Status: 501(c)3
Highest Offering: Associate Degree
Program: 2-Year Principally Bachelor's Creditable
Accreditation: NH, ADNUR, DIETT

02 President .... Dr. Linda LUJAN
05 Vice President Academic Affairs .... Dr. William GUERRIERO
32 Vice President Student Affairs .... Mr. William H. CRAWFORD, III
11 Vice Pres Administrative Services .... Dr. Jacalyn A. ASKIN
12 Provost Williams Campus .... Mr. John SCHROEDER
49 Dean of Arts and Sciences .... Vacant
31 Dean of Community Affairs .... Vacant
32 Dean of Student Affairs .... Mr. Daniel HERBST
10 Assoc Dean Finance/Business Svcs .... Vacant
07 Dir Admissions/Registr & Records .... Ms. Linda SHAW
13 Director Information Technology .... Mr. Victor NAVARRO
09 Dir Research/Planning/Development .... Ms. Mary DAY
24 Dir Instructional Tech & Media Svcs .... Mr. Tim KEEFE
36 Dir Career/Education Planning Svcs .... Mrs. Mary FREDERICK
85 Director International Education .... Ms. Annie JIMENEZ
32 Director College Student Services .... Ms. Dawn GRUICHICH
18 Dir Buildings and Grounds .... Mr. Bruce SCHARBACH
35 Director Student Life .... Mr. Mike GREENE
41 Director Athletics .... Mr. Jeff MASON
19 Director College Safety .... Mr. Robert EVERETT
37 Director Financial Aid .... Ms. Nanci REGEHR
21 Manager College Fiscal Services .... Mr. Tom NICOL
15 Manager College Employee Services .... Vacant
26 Coordinator Marketing/Public Rel .... Ms. Trish NIEMANN
27 Coordinator of Marketing .... Ms. Carol CRANE
28 Coordinator of Diversity .... Ms. Lori GIRSHICK
28 Coordinator of Diversity .... Ms. Caryl TERRELL-BAMIRO
25 Project Coordinator Admin Svcs .... Ms. Trina LARSON

*Estrella Mountain Community College (H)

3000 N Dysart Road, Avondale AZ 85392
County: Maricopa FICE Identification: 031563
Unit ID: 384333
Telephone: (623) 935-8000 Carnegie Class: Assoc/Pub-U-MC
FAX Number: (623) 935-8008 Calendar System: Semester
URL: www.estrellamountain.edu
Established: 1990 Annual Undergrad Tuition & Fees (In-District): $2,280
Enrollment: 8,122 Coed
Affiliation or Control: State/Local IRS Status: 501(c)3
Highest Offering: Associate Degree
Program: Occupational; 2-Year Principally Bachelor's Creditable
Accreditation: NH, ADNUR

02 President .... Dr. Ernest LARA
05 Vice President of Academic Affairs .... Dr. Bryan TIPPETT
32 Vice President Student Affairs .... Dr. Debbie KUSHIBAB
11 Vice President Admin Services .... Ms. Sue TAVAKOLI
75 Vice President Occupational Educ .... Dr. Clay GOODMAN
20 Dean of Academic Affairs .... Ms. Joyce M. JACKSON
20 Dean of Academic Affairs .... Dr. Sylvia ORR
13 Director Information Technology .... Mr. Richard MARMON
35 Dean of Student Services .... Dr. Lauren SHELLENBARGER
08 Division Chair Information Resource .... Ms. Nikol PRICE
09 Dean Planning/Rsrch/Effectiveness .... Dr. Rene G. WILLEKENS
18 Director Facilities Planning/Devel .... Mr. Randy MAULDIN
07 Director of Enrollment Services .... Mr. Frank AMPARO
10 Manager College Fiscal Services .... Ms. Leda JOHNSON
26 Chief Public Relations Officer .... Mr. Ralph CAMPBELL
37 Director Student Financial Aid .... Ms. Rosanna SHORT
21 Manager College Budget .... Ms. Maggie CASTILLO

*Gateway Community College (I)

108 N 40th Street, Phoenix AZ 85034-1795
County: Maricopa FICE Identification: 008303
Unit ID: 105145
Telephone: (602) 286-8000 Carnegie Class: Assoc/Pub-U-MC
FAX Number: (602) 286-8003 Calendar System: Semester
URL: www.gatewaycc.edu/
Established: 1968 Annual Undergrad Tuition & Fees (In-District): $1,854
Enrollment: 7,346 Coed
Affiliation or Control: State/Local IRS Status: 501(c)3
Highest Offering: Associate Degree
Program: Occupational; 2-Year Principally Bachelor's Creditable
Accreditation: NH, ADNUR, DMS, EEG, NMT, PTAA, RAD, RTT, SURGT

02 President .... Dr. Eugene GIOVANNINI
05 Vice President Academic Affairs .... Dr. Paula NORBY
05 Vice Pres of Academic Affairs .... Dr. Michael GLISSON
32 Vice President Student Affairs .... Dr. Diana MUNIZ
11 Vice President Administrative Svcs .... Ms. Janet LANGLEY
35 Dean Student Services .... Dr. Dan LUFKIN
20 Associate Dean Academic Affairs .... Ms. Gloria STAHMER
07 Supervisor Admissions/Reg & Rec .... Ms. Brenda STARCK
09 Dir Inst Plng/Rsrch/Effectiveness .... Dr. Sue KATER
10 Chief Business Officer .... Ms. Janet LANGLEY
18 Chief Facilities/Physical Plant .... Mr. Charles POURE
26 Director Marketing & Public Rels .... Ms. Christine LAMBRAKIS
30 Director Inst Advance & Entrep Pgm .... Ms. Susie PULIDO
37 Director Student Financial Aid .... Ms. Suzanne RINGLE

*Glendale Community College (J)

6000 W Olive Avenue, Glendale AZ 85302-3006
County: Maricopa FICE Identification: 001076
Unit ID: 104708
Telephone: (623) 845-3000 Carnegie Class: Assoc/Pub-U-MC
FAX Number: (623) 845-3329 Calendar System: Semester
URL: www.gc.maricopa.edu
Established: 1965 Annual Undergrad Tuition & Fees (In-District): $1,854
Enrollment: 21,373 Coed
Affiliation or Control: State/Local IRS Status: 170(c)1
Highest Offering: Associate Degree
Program: Occupational; 2-Year Principally Bachelor's Creditable
Accreditation: NH, ADNUR

02 President .... Dr. Irene KOVALA
05 VP Academic Affairs .... Dr. Ronald D. NATALE, II
32 VP Student Affairs .... Mr. Alberto SANCHEZ
11 VP Admin Services & Planning .... Mr. Greg ROGERS
20 Dean of Academic Affairs .... Dr. Fernando CAMOU
20 Acting Dean of Academic Affairs .... Mr. Gary MARRER
20 Acting Dean of Academic Affairs .... Ms. Rachelle HALL
84 Dean Enrollment Services .... Ms. Mary D. BLACKWELL
35 Dean Student Life .... Dr. Osaro IGHODARO
12 Dean GCC North Site .... Mr. Charles F. JEFFERY
37 Director Financial Aid .... Ms. Ellen NEEL
18 Director Facilities .... Mr. Al GONZALES
21 Director College Business Services .... Mr. Herman GONZALEZ
30 Director Institutional Advancement .... Ms. Patricia R. VOGEL
09 Director Research Planning & Devel .... Dr. Alka ARORA SINGH
15 Manager College Employee Svcs .... Ms. June S. FESSENDEN
44 Asst Director of Development .... Ms. Judy SANCHEZ
38 Dept Chair Counseling .... Mr. David GERKIN
08 Dept Chair Librarian .... Mr. Frank TORRES
19 Director College Safety .... Ms. Debra PALOK
04 Admin Assistant to College Pres .... Vacant

*Mesa Community College (K)

1833 W Southern Avenue, Mesa AZ 85202-4866
County: Maricopa FICE Identification: 001077
Unit ID: 105154
Telephone: (480) 461-7000 Carnegie Class: Assoc/Pub-U-MC
FAX Number: (480) 461-7805 Calendar System: Semester
URL: www.mesacc.edu/
Established: 1965 Annual Undergrad Tuition & Fees (In-District): $1,824
Enrollment: 26,609 Coed
Affiliation or Control: State/Local IRS Status: 501(c)3
Highest Offering: Associate Degree
Program: Occupational; 2-Year Principally Bachelor's Creditable
Accreditation: NH, ADNUR, DH, FUSER

02 President .... Dr. Shouan PAN
05 Vice Pres Academic Affairs .... Dr. James MABRY
32 Vice Pres Student Affairs .... Dr. Sonya PEARSON
11 Vice Pres Admin Services .... Mr. Jeff DARBUT
13 Vice Pres Information Technology .... Mr. Sasan POUREETEZADI
12 Provost Red Mountain/Downtown Ctr .... Ms. Jo WILSON
09 Dean of Inst Planning & Analysis .... Mr. Matthew ASHCRAFT
35 Dean of Student Affairs .... Ms. Joan GROVER
20 Dean Instruction .... Dr. Rodney HOLMES
81 Dean Instruction .... Ms. Carol ACHS
72 Dean Instruction .... Mr. Roger YOHE
06 Registrar .... Dr. Barbara BOROS
15 Associate Dean Human Resources .... Dr. Emily WEINACKER
18 Director Facilities .... Mr. Richard CLUFF
21 Dean Administrative Services .... Mr. Kurt CONOVER
26 Director of Institutional Advance .... Ms. Sonia FILAN
30 Director of Development .... Mr. Jared LANGKILDE
37 Dir Fin Aid/Scholarships .... Ms. Patricia PEPPIN
38 Dept Chair Counseling .... Dr. Karen HARDIN

*Paradise Valley Community College (A)

18401 N 32nd Street, Phoenix AZ 85032-1210
County: Maricopa FICE Identification: 026236
Unit ID: 364016
Telephone: (602) 787-6500 Carnegie Class: Assoc/Pub-U-MC
FAX Number: (602) 787-6625 Calendar System: Semester
URL: www.pvc.maricopa.edu
Established: 1985 Annual Undergrad Tuition & Fees (In-District): $2,280
Enrollment: 10,282 Coed
Affiliation or Control: State/Local IRS Status: 501(c)3
Highest Offering: Associate Degree
Program: Occupational; 2-Year Principally Bachelor's Creditable
Accreditation: NH, ADNUR, DIETT

02 President Dr. Paul DALE
05 Vice President of Academic Affairs Dr. Mary Lou MOSLEY
11 Interim VP Administrative Services Mr. Anthony ASTI
20 Dean of Academic Affairs Dr. Denise DIGIANFILIPPO
32 Vice President of Student Affairs Dr. Sandra MILLER HOLST
35 Dean of Student Affairs Dr. Shirley GREEN
13 Dean of Information Technology Mr. Paul GOLISCH
07 Supervisor of Admissions Ms. Stella NAPOLES
10 Chief Business Officer Ms. Sandy MCDILL
15 Director Personnel Services Ms. Laurel SMITH
18 Chief Facilities/Physical Plant Mr. David MATUS
37 Director Student Financial Aid Mr. Kenneth CLARKE
38 Director Student Counseling Dr. James RUBIN
06 Registrar Dr. Shirley GREEN
36 Director Student Placement Ms. Norma CHANDLER
26 Chief Public Relations Officer Ms. Nicole DELEON
09 Director of Institutional Research Mr. John SNELLING
19 Director Security/Safety Mr. Scott MEEK
41 Athletic Director Mr. Greg SILCOX

*Phoenix College (B)

1202 W Thomas Road, Phoenix AZ 85013-4234
County: Maricopa FICE Identification: 001078
Unit ID: 105428
Telephone: (602) 285-7800 Carnegie Class: Assoc/Pub-U-MC
FAX Number: (602) 285-7700 Calendar System: Semester
URL: www.pc.maricopa.edu
Established: 1920 Annual Undergrad Tuition & Fees (In-District): $2,160
Enrollment: 13,000 Coed
Affiliation or Control: State/Local IRS Status: 501(c)3
Highest Offering: Associate Degree
Program: Occupational; 2-Year Principally Bachelor's Creditable; Technical Emphasis
Accreditation: NH, ADNUR, DA, DH, HT, MAAB, MLTAD

02 President Dr. Anna SOLLEY
05 VP of Academic Affairs Ms. Casandra KAKAR
11 VP Administrative Services Mr. Paul DEROSE
32 Vice Pres Student Affairs Ms. Yira BRIMAGE
35 Dean of Student Affairs Vacant
20 Dean of Academic Affairs Mr. Wilbert NELSON
103 Dean of Workforce Development Dr. Sharon HALFORD
14 Associate Dean of Technology Vacant
08 Department Chair Library Ms. Elizabeth SALIBA
38 Department Chair Counseling Ms. Nancy NAVARRETE
06 Dir Admissions/Registration/Records Ms. Kathy FRENCH
41 Athletic Director Ms. Samantha EZELL
37 Director Financial Aid Ms. Genevieve WATSON
35 Director Student Leadership Ms. Genesis TOOLE
84 Director Advisement Enrollment Ms. Cheryl AXTELL
09 Dir Instl Plng/Rsrch/Effectiveness Ms. Jan BINDER
19 Director of College Safety Mr. Wil MCFADDEN
30 Dir Institutional Advancement Ms. Eileen ARCHIBALD
18 Director of Facilities Mr. Douglas MCCARTHY
10 Manager Business Services Ms. Angela GENNA
15 Supv College Employee Services Ms. Mary Helen ESCALANTE
29 Coord Alumni/Comm Relations Mr. Frank LUNA
04 Assistant to the President Ms. Renee PERRY

*Rio Salado College (C)

2323 W 14th Street, Tempe AZ 85281-6950
County: Maricopa FICE Identification: 021775
Unit ID: 105668
Telephone: (480) 517-8000 Carnegie Class: Assoc/Pub-U-MC
FAX Number: (480) 377-4719 Calendar System: Semester
URL: www.riosalado.edu
Established: 1978 Annual Undergrad Tuition & Fees (In-District): $2,310
Enrollment: 31,763 Coed
Affiliation or Control: State/Local IRS Status: 501(c)3
Highest Offering: Associate Degree
Program: Occupational; 2-Year Principally Bachelor's Creditable; Business Emphasis
Accreditation: NH, DA, DH

02 President Dr. Chris BUSTAMANTE
05 Vice President Teaching & Learning Dr. Vernon SMITH
10 Vice Pres Business & Employee Svcs Mr. Todd SIMMONS
32 Vice President Student Services Ms. Kishia BROCK
13 Vice President Information Services Mr. Edward KELTY
20 Dean of Instruction Mr. Rick KEMP
105 Dean of Instruction Ms. Dana REID
20 Dean of Instruction Dr. Jo JORGENSON
84 Dean Student Enrollment Services Vacant
26 Director Inst Advancement Mr. Kevin BILDER
07 Assoc Dean of Enrollment Services Ms. Ruby MILLER
37 Director of Financial Aid Mr. Ryan CHASE
09 Dir Research Planning & Development Ms. Genevieve WINTERS
18 Director of Facilities Mr. Ernest ADKINS
19 Director College Safety Ms. Margaret TURNER-SAMPLE
21 Director College Business Services Ms. Devi BALA
15 Manager College Employee Services Ms. Ginger MARTINDALE
28 Director of Diversity Dr. Sharon KOBERNA
08 Faculty Chair Library Ms. Hazel DAVIS
17 Faculty Chair Nursing Vacant
25 Assoc Dir Grants/Corp Development Ms. Barbara KHALSA
85 Director International Education Ms. Erma ABEYTA

*Scottsdale Community College (D)

9000 E Chaparral, Scottsdale AZ 85256-2626
County: Maricopa FICE Identification: 008304
Unit ID: 105747
Telephone: (480) 423-6000 Carnegie Class: Assoc/Pub-U-SC
FAX Number: (480) 423-6200 Calendar System: Semester
URL: www.scottsdalecc.edu
Established: 1969 Annual Undergrad Tuition & Fees (In-District): $1,950
Enrollment: 11,257 Coed
Affiliation or Control: State/Local IRS Status: 501(c)3
Highest Offering: Associate Degree
Program: Occupational; 2-Year Principally Bachelor's Creditable
Accreditation: NH, ACFEI, ADNUR

02 President Dr. Jan L. GEHLER
05 Vice Pres Academic/Student Affairs Dr. Daniel P. CORR
11 Vice Pres Administrative Services Mr. Carl COUCH
13 Vice Pres Information Technology Mr. Dustin FENNELL
20 Vice Pres Occupational Educ Dr. Dean E. HERMANSON
32 Dean of Student Affairs Dr. Donna YOUNG
84 Dean of Student Enrollment Ms. Gia TAYLOR
07 Director of Admissions Ms. Fran WATKINS
09 Director of Institutional Research Dr. Laurie COHEN
30 Director of Development Vacant
08 Director of Library Services Dr. Pat LOKEY
37 Director Financial Aid/Placement Ms. Stacie BECK
18 Director Buildings/Grounds Mr. Samuel J. VAN CLEAVE
19 Director of College Safety Mr. Les STRICKLAND
26 Dir of Marketing/Public Relations Ms. Denise KRONSTEINER
51 Director Continuing Education Vacant
41 Athletic Director Men Mr. Art C. BECKER
41 Athletic Director Women Ms. Darcel COCO
88 Dir of Southwest Studies Program Mr. Marshall TRIMBLE
38 Director Student Advisement Mr. Michael CORNELIUS

*South Mountain Community College (E)

7050 S 24th Street, Phoenix AZ 85042-5806
County: Maricopa FICE Identification: 021466
Unit ID: 105792
Telephone: (602) 243-8000 Carnegie Class: Assoc/Pub-U-MC
FAX Number: (602) 243-8329 Calendar System: Semester
URL: www.southmountaincc.edu
Established: 1979 Annual Undergrad Tuition & Fees (In-District): $2,310
Enrollment: 6,218 Coed
Affiliation or Control: State/Local IRS Status: 501(c)3
Highest Offering: Associate Degree
Program: Occupational; 2-Year Principally Bachelor's Creditable
Accreditation: NH, MACTE

02 President Dr. Shari L. OLSON
05 Interim Vice Pres Academic Affairs Ms. Helen SMITH
11 Int Vice Pres Administrative Svcs Ms. Janet ORTEGA
32 Interim Vice Pres Student Affairs Dr. Lauren SHELLENBARGER
20 Assoc Dean Career Tech Educ Ms. Cindy ODGERS
84 Int Assoc Dean Enrollment Services Ms. Chris HAINES
35 Assoc Dean Student Development Mr. Raul MONREAL
12 Assoc Dean Extended Campuses Dr. Cheryl CRUTCHER
37 Director Financial Aid Ms. Inez MORENO-WEINERT
06 Director of Registration & Records Ms. Della GARCIA
09 Dean Research/Plng & Development Ms. Damita KALOOSTIAN
10 Chief Business Officer Ms. Dzung TRAN
18 Director of Facilities Mr. Jim THARP
26 Director Marketing/Public Relations Mr. Robert PRICE
21 Manager Fiscal Services Mr. David MORRIS
15 Coordinator Human Resources Ms. Vanessa LOGAN
07 Coordinator Advisement/Recruitment Ms. Christine NEILL
36 Coordinator Job Placement Ms. Suzanne HIPPS

Midwestern University (F)

19555 N 59th Avenue, Glendale AZ 85308-6814
County: Maricopa Identification: 666001
Unit ID: 423643
Telephone: (623) 572-3400 Carnegie Class: Spec/Med
FAX Number: (623) 572-3410 Calendar System: Quarter
URL: www.midwestern.edu
Established: 1900 Annual Undergrad Tuition & Fees: N/A
Enrollment: 2,450 Coed
Affiliation or Control: Independent Non-Profit IRS Status: 501(c)3
Highest Offering: First Professional Degree
Program: Professional
Accreditation: &NH, ANEST, ARCPA, DENT, @OPT, OSTEO, OT, PERF, PHAR, POD, @PTA

01 President & CEO Dr. Kathleen H. GOEPPINGER
03 Exec Vice Pres/Chief Operating Ofcr Dr. Arthur G. DOBBELAERE
10 Sr Vice Pres/Chief Financial Ofcr Mr. Gregory J. GAUS
05 VP/CAO Pharmacy & Health Sci Educ Dr. Mary LEE
05 VP/CAO Medicine & Dentistry Educ Dr. Dennis PAULSON
21 Vice President Finance Mr. Dean MALONE
26 Vice President University Relations Dr. Karen JOHNSON
15 VP Human Resources/Administration Ms. Angela MARTY
32 Dean of Student Services Dr. Ross KOSINSKI
76 Dean College of Health Sciences Dr. Jackie SMITH
63 Dean Arizona Coll Osteopathic Med Dr. Lori KEMPER
67 Dean College of Pharmacy-Glendale Dr. Dennis MCCALLIAN
52 Dean College of Dental Medicine Dr. Russell GILPATRICK
06 Registrar Ms. Christy SCHENK
07 Director of Admissions Mr. James WALTER
18 Chief Facilities/Physical Plant Mr. Bill FRANTZ
30 Director Development Ms. Christine CLOUSE
37 Director Student Financial Aid Mr. Edmund Thomas BILLARD
09 Director of Institutional Research Dr. Kevin HYNES
96 Director of Purchasing Ms. Carol VANDIJK
13 Director Information Technology Mr. Erik CARROLL
19 Director Security/Safety Mr. Ronald ENOS

† Regional accreditation is carried under the parent institution in Downers Grove, IL.

Mohave Community College (G)

1971 E. Jagerson Avenue, Kingman AZ 86409-1238
County: Mohave FICE Identification: 011864
Unit ID: 105206
Telephone: (928) 757-0879 Carnegie Class: Assoc/Pub-S-MC
FAX Number: (928) 757-0836 Calendar System: Semester
URL: www.mohave.edu
Established: 1971 Annual Undergrad Tuition & Fees (In-District): $1,968
Enrollment: 8,995 Coed
Affiliation or Control: State/Local IRS Status: 501(c)3
Highest Offering: Associate Degree
Program: Occupational; 2-Year Principally Bachelor's Creditable; Technical Emphasis
Accreditation: NH, ADNUR, DH, PTAA, SURGT

01 President Dr. Michael KEARNS
03 Vice President for Administration Dr. H. Lynn CUNDIFF
05 Dean of Instruction Dr. Michael ROURKE
32 Dean of Student Services Ms. Jann WOODS
10 Dean of Business Services Mr. Dick MACDONALD
30 Assoc Vice Pres College Advancement Dr. Alan KLAAS
13 Associate VP for Information Tech Mr. Francisco PORRAS
106 Campus Dean Distance Education Ms. Diana STITHEM
12 Campus Dean Bullhead City Mr. Shawn BRISTLE
12 Campus Dean Lake Havasu Dr. Nicolas SANCHEZ
12 Campus Dean Neal Kingman Dr. Fred GILBERT
12 Campus Dean North Mohave Ms. Carolyn HAMBLIN
06 Registrar Mr. John WILSON
21 Bursar Ms. Camille HOLDEN
37 Director Student Financial Aid Mr. Bill OSBORN
09 Dir of Institutional Research Mr. Bob FAUBERT
08 Director of Library Services Ms. Claudia TIMMANN
26 Chief Public Relations Officer Ms. Charlotte KELLER
07 Director of Recruitment/Admissions Mr. David SHABAZZ
35 Dir Student Services Distance Educ Ms. Ana MASTERSON
35 Dir Stdnt Svcs Neal Campus Kingman Ms. Shirley JOHNSON-CRAFT
35 Dir Student Svcs Lake Havasu Campus Mr. Tim KEITH
35 Dir Stdnt Svcs Bullhead Cty Campus Mr. Todd MILLER
15 Director Personnel Services Ms. Jenny DIXON

National Paralegal College (H)

6516 N 7th Street, Suite 103, Phoenix AZ 85014-1262
County: Maricopa Identification: 666175
Telephone: (800) 371-6105 Carnegie Class: Not Classified
FAX Number: (866) 347-2744 Calendar System: Other
URL: nationalparalegal.edu
Established: 2003 Annual Undergrad Tuition & Fees: $13,944
Enrollment: N/A Coed
Affiliation or Control: Proprietary IRS Status: Proprietary
Highest Offering: Baccalaureate
Program: Occupational; 2-Year Principally Bachelor's Creditable; Business Emphasis
Accreditation: DETC

01 President Avi KATZ
05 Dean/Director Mark GELLER
32 Student Services Director David COHEN
20 Educational Director Stephen HAAS

Northcentral University (I)

10000 E University Drive, Prescott Valley AZ 86314-2336
County: Yavapai FICE Identification: 038133
Unit ID: 444130
Telephone: (928) 541-7777 Carnegie Class: DRU
FAX Number: (928) 541-7817 Calendar System: Other
URL: www.ncu.edu
Established: 1996 Annual Undergrad Tuition & Fees: $8,800
Enrollment: 10,179 Coed
Affiliation or Control: Proprietary IRS Status: Proprietary
Highest Offering: Doctorate
Program: Teacher Preparatory; Professional; Business Emphasis
Accreditation: NH, ACBSP, @TEAC

01 President ... Dr. Clinton D. GARDNER
05 Interim Provost ... Dr. Clinton D. GARDNER
10 Executive VP & Chief Financial Ofcr ... Mr. Christopher LYNNE
04 Director Office of the President ... Ms. Stephnie HOPPLE
50 Dean School of Business & Tech Mgmt ... Dr. Lee SMITH
53 Dean School of Education ... Dr. Dennis LESSARD
83 Dean School of Psychology ... Dr. Heather FREDERICK
97 Chair of General Education ... Ms. Melinda LYONS
21 Controller ... Ms. Shannyn STERN
11 Vice President Operations ... Mr. Eric STODDARD
06 Registrar ... Ms. Rebekah BLAKLEY
37 Dir of Learner Financial Services ... Ms. Valerie STEINBOCK
08 Director of Library Services ... Mr. Ed SALAZAR
15 Director of Human Resources ... Ms. Karry LAYETTE
26 Director of Marketing ... Mr. Kevin LUSTIG
88 Director of Writing Program ... Dr. Renee RAMSEY
45 Director of Planning & Quality Assu ... Ms. Linda R. BOITOS
50 Director of Strategic Business Know ... Vacant
83 Director of Marriage & Family Ther ... Dr. Branden H. HENLINE
84 Enrollment Manager ... Mr. Bob HANKS

Northern Arizona University (A)

South San Francisco Street, Flagstaff AZ 86011-0001
County: Coconino FICE Identification: 001082
Unit ID: 105330
Telephone: (928) 523-9011 Carnegie Class: RU/H
FAX Number: (928) 523-1848 Calendar System: Semester
URL: www.nau.edu
Established: 1899 Annual Undergrad Tuition & Fees (In-State): $8,826
Enrollment: 25,204 Coed
Affiliation or Control: State IRS Status: 501(c)3
Highest Offering: Doctorate
Program: Liberal Arts And General; Teacher Preparatory; Professional
Accreditation: NH, BUS, CACREP, CONST, CS, DH, ENG, FOR, MUS, NRPA, NURSE, PTA, SP, SW, TED

01 President ... Dr. John D. HAEGER
03 Executive Vice President ... Dr. M.J MCMAHON
05 Provost ... Dr. Elizabeth S. GROBSMITH
30 Vice President Univ Advancement ... Dr. Mason GERETY
32 Sr VP Enrollment Mgmt/Student Affs ... Mr. David BOUSQUET
09 Vice Pres Plng/Budget/Inst Research ... Dr. Patricia N. HAEUSER
10 Vice President Finance/Admin ... Dr. Jennus L. BURTON
46 Vice President Research ... Dr. Laura HUENNEKE
56 Sr VP Extended Campuses ... Mr. Fred HURST
14 Chief Information Tech Officer ... Mr. Fred ESTRELLA
35 Assoc Vice President Student Affs ... Dr. Sarah L. BICKEL
28 Assoc Vice President of Diversity ... Dr. David E. CAMACHO
84 Int Exec Dir Enrollment Services ... Mr. Paul ORSCHELN
88 Assoc VP Economic Develop & Sustain ... Mr. Richard M. BOWEN
12 Assoc VP/Campus Executive Officer ... Mr. Larry GOULD
86 VP Govt Affairs/Business Ptnr ... Ms. Christy FARLEY
20 Vice Provost Undergraduate Studies ... Dr. Karen L. PUGLIESI
85 Vice Provost Center Intl Education ... Mr. Harvey CHARLES
20 Associate Provost Academic Admin ... Dr. Debra LARSON
08 Dean/University Librarian ... Ms. Cynthia A. CHILDREY
53 Interim Dean College of Education ... Dr. Gypsy DENZINE
58 Dean of Graduate College ... Dr. Ramona N. MELLOTT
54 Dean Col Engr/Forestry/Natural Sci ... Dr. Paul JAGODZINSKI
50 Int Dean W.A. College of Business ... Dr. Mason GERETY
49 Dean College of Arts & Letters ... Dr. Michael VINCENT
83 Dean Col Social/Behavioral Sci ... Dr. Michael STEVENSON
17 Exec Dean Col of Health/Human Svcs ... Dr. Leslie SCHULZ
06 University Registrar ... Ms. Pamela L. ANASTASSIOU
43 Office of Legal Affairs ... Mr. Mark NEUMAYR
37 Director Financial Aid ... Ms. Michelle CASTILLO
15 Assoc VP Human Resources ... Ms. Diane VERKEST
19 Director NAU Police Dept ... Mr. Gregory T. FOWLER
22 Director Affirmative Action ... Ms. Priscilla L. MILLS
23 Director Health Services ... Ms. Elizabeth M. APPLEBEE
29 Director Alumni Relations ... Mr. Neil E. GOODELL
41 Athletic Director ... Mr. James E. FALLIS
36 Dir Gateway Student Success Center ... Dr. Eileen MAHONEY
07 Director of Admissions ... Mr. Paul ORSCHELN
26 Interim Director of Public Affairs ... Mr. Thomas BAUER
35 Dean of Students ... Dr. Rick L. BRANDEL
38 Dir Counseling & Testing Center ... Dr. Christopher S. GUNN
96 Director of Purchasing ... Ms. Becky E. MCGAUGH

Northland Pioneer College (B)

PO Box 610, Holbrook AZ 86025-0610
County: Navajo FICE Identification: 011862
Unit ID: 105349
Telephone: (928) 524-7311 Carnegie Class: Assoc/Pub-R-L
FAX Number: (928) 524-7312 Calendar System: Semester
URL: www.npc.edu
Established: 1973 Annual Undergrad Tuition & Fees (In-State): $1,475
Enrollment: 3,950 Coed
Affiliation or Control: State IRS Status: 501(c)3
Highest Offering: Associate Degree
Program: Occupational; 2-Year Principally Bachelor's Creditable
Accreditation: NH, ADNUR

01 President ... Dr. Jeanne SWARTHOUT
05 Vice Pres Learning/Student Services ... Mr. Mark H. VEST
11 Vice Pres Administrative Services ... Mr. Blaine HATCH
13 Director of Information Services ... Mr. Eric BISHOP
06 Registrar/Dir Enrollment Mgmt ... Mr. Jake HINTON-RIVERA
04 Assistant to the President ... Mr. Russell DICKERSON
10 Director of Financial Services ... Ms. Maderia ELLISON
21 Comptroller ... Mr. John H. BREMER
15 Director of Human Resources ... Mr. Daniel WATTRON
37 Financial Aid Coordinator ... Ms. Beaulah BOB-PENNYPACKER
88 Director of Developmental Services ... Mr. Rickey JACKSON
50 Dean of Career & Technical Educ ... Ms. Peggy BELKNAP
49 Dean of Arts & Sciences ... Dr. Eric HENDERSON
66 Dean of Nursing ... Vacant
18 Chief Facilities/Physical Plant ... Mr. David HUISH
26 Dir of Marketing/Public Relations ... Ms. Ann HESS
09 Director of Institutional Research ... Vacant
88 Network and Systems Administrator ... Mr. Robert GODFREY
88 Director Small Business Development ... Ms. Tracy MANCUSO
08 Head Librarian ... Ms. Trudy BENDER

Ottawa University Arizona (C)

10020 N 25th Avenue, Phoenix AZ 85021-1660
County: Maricopa Identification: 666066
Unit ID: 105367
Telephone: (602) 371-1188 Carnegie Class: Master's M
FAX Number: (602) 371-0035 Calendar System: Semester
URL: www.ottawa.edu
Established: 1977 Annual Undergrad Tuition & Fees: $10,560
Enrollment: 1,054 Coed
Affiliation or Control: American Baptist IRS Status: 501(c)3
Highest Offering: Master's
Program: Liberal Arts And General; Teacher Preparatory
Accreditation: &NH

01 President ... Mr. Kevin EICHNER
05 Univ Provost/Chief Academic Officer ... Dr. Terry HAINES
10 Vice Pres Administration/CFO ... Mr. J. Clark RIBORDY
26 Mgr Public Relations & Publications ... Ms. Paula PAINE
30 Vice Pres University Advancement ... Mr. Paul BEAN
86 VP Regulatory/Governmental Affairs ... Dr. Donna LEVENE
88 Vice President for APOS ... Dr. Brian SANDUSKY
07 Assistant VP Enrollment ... Mr. Bill HAMMOND
06 University Registrar ... Ms. Karen ADAMS
21 Director Business Operations ... Mr. Tom CORLEY
37 Director Student Financial Aid ... Mr. Howard FISCHER
11 Director of Administration ... Ms. Peggie LANZONE
21 Director Finance/Controller ... Ms. Brenda GUENTHER
15 Director Human Resources ... Ms. Joanna WALTERS
20 Dean of Instruction ... Dr. Karen MILLS
88 Vice President for APOS ... Mr. Brian MESSER
12 Campus Executive ... Dr. Mary VANIS

† Regional accreditation is carried under the parent institution in Ottawa, KS.

The Paralegal Institute (D)

7332 E Butherus Drive, Scottsdale AZ 85260
County: Maricopa FICE Identification: 030737
Unit ID: 105385
Telephone: (800) 354-1254 Carnegie Class: Not Classified
FAX Number: (602) 212-0502 Calendar System: Other
URL: www.theparalegalinstitute.edu
Established: 1974 Annual Undergrad Tuition & Fees: $9,000
Enrollment: 360 Coed
Affiliation or Control: Proprietary IRS Status: Proprietary
Highest Offering: Associate Degree
Program: Occupational; 2-Year Principally Bachelor's Creditable; Business Emphasis
Accreditation: DETC

01 President ... Kathleen MIRABILE
26 Vice President Marketing ... Chris CARAWAY
07 Dir Student Aquisitions/Admissions ... Keith SCHEIB

Penn Foster College (E)

14300 N Northsight Blvd, Suite 120,
Scottsdale AZ 85260-3673
County: Maricopa FICE Identification: 004049
Unit ID: 211486
Telephone: (480) 947-6644 Carnegie Class: Not Classified
FAX Number: (480) 951-6030 Calendar System: Semester
URL: www.pennfostercollege.edu
Established: 1974 Annual Undergrad Tuition & Fees: $2,640
Enrollment: 30,000 Coed
Affiliation or Control: Proprietary IRS Status: Proprietary
Highest Offering: Baccalaureate
Program: Occupational
Accreditation: DETC, MAAB

01 President ... Dr. Richard W. FERRIN
05 Chief Academic Officer ... Ms. Connie DEMPSEY

Phoenix Institute of Herbal Medicine and Acupuncture (F)

301 E Bethany Home Road, Ste A-100,
Phoenix AZ 85012-1275
County: Maricopa FICE Identification: 036175
Unit ID: 447698
Telephone: (602) 274-1885 Carnegie Class: Spec/Health
FAX Number: (602) 274-1895 Calendar System: Semester
URL: www.pihma.edu
Established: 1996 Annual Graduate Tuition & Fees: $12,473
Enrollment: 140 Coed
Affiliation or Control: Proprietary IRS Status: Proprietary
Highest Offering: Master's; No Undergraduates
Program: Professional
Accreditation: ACUP

01 President ... Ms. Catherine NIEMIEC

Phoenix School of Law (G)

4041 N Central Avenue, Suite 100, Phoenix AZ 85012
County: Maricopa FICE Identification: 041314
Unit ID: 450942
Telephone: (602) 682-6800 Carnegie Class: Not Classified
FAX Number: (602) 682-6999 Calendar System: Semester
URL: www.phoenixlaw.edu
Established: N/A Annual Graduate Tuition & Fees: $38,828
Enrollment: 380 Coed
Affiliation or Control: Proprietary IRS Status: Proprietary
Highest Offering: First Professional Degree; No Undergraduates
Program: Professional
Accreditation: LAW

01 Dean ... Ms. Shirley L. MAYS
05 Assoc Dean for Academic Affairs ... Ms. Penny L. WILLRICH
07 Dean of Admissions ... Ms. Barbara Kaye MILLER
20 Asst Dean for Academic Admin ... Ms. Ann E. WOODLEY

Phoenix Seminary (H)

4222 E Thomas Road, Suite 400, Phoenix AZ 85018-7607
County: Maricopa FICE Identification: 034784
Unit ID: 381459
Telephone: (602) 850-8000 Carnegie Class: Spec/Faith
FAX Number: (602) 850-8080 Calendar System: Semester
URL: www.phoenixseminary.edu
Established: 1988 Annual Graduate Tuition & Fees: $10,500
Enrollment: 191 Coed
Affiliation or Control: Interdenominational IRS Status: 501(c)3
Highest Offering: Doctorate; No Undergraduates
Program: Religious Emphasis
Accreditation: @NH, THEOL

01 President ... Dr. Darryl L. DELHOUSAYE
03 Executive Vice President/Provost ... Dr. W. B. HUNTER
11 Vice President of Administration ... Dr. Rae LARSON
05 Vice President of Acad Engagement ... Dr. Charles MOODY
20 Dir Acad Services/Admiss/Assess ... Ms. Roma ROYER
06 Registrar ... Mr. Lee P. RICHARDS
84 Director of Enrollment ... Mr. Eric CHANNING
08 Director of Library Services ... Mr. Doug OLBERT
10 Director of Finance ... Mr. Dave HESTON
37 Financial Aid Officer ... Mrs. Lynn GORDON
30 Director of Advancement ... Mrs. Rhonda MILLIGAN
44 Associate Director of Advancement ... Ms. Shannon COX

Pima County Community College District (I)

4905 C East Broadway Boulevard, Tucson AZ 85709-1005
County: Pima FICE Identification: 007266
Unit ID: 105525
Telephone: (520) 206-4500 Carnegie Class: Assoc/Pub-U-MC
FAX Number: (520) 206-4535 Calendar System: Semester
URL: www.pima.edu
Established: 1966 Annual Undergrad Tuition & Fees (In-District): $1,910
Enrollment: 35,365 Coed
Affiliation or Control: State/Local IRS Status: 501(c)3
Highest Offering: Associate Degree
Program: Occupational; 2-Year Principally Bachelor's Creditable
Accreditation: NH, ADNUR, DA, DH, DT, HT, MLTAD, RAD, SURGT

01 Chancellor ... Dr. Roy FLORES
05 Provost/Exec Vice Chancellor ... Dr. Suzanne MILES
10 Exec Vice Chanc for Administration ... Dr. David BEA
14 Acting Vice Chanc Information Tech ... Ms. Cindy DOOLING
16 Vice Chanc for Human Resources ... Ms. Janet MAY
12 President Downtown Campus ... Dr. Luba CHLIWNIAK
12 President Northwest Campus ... Dr. Alex KAJSTURA
12 President East Campus ... Ms. Charlotte A. FUGETT
12 President Community Campus ... Dr. Suzanne MILES
12 President West Campus ... Dr. Louis ALBERT
12 President Desert Vista Campus ... Dr. Johnson BIA
04 Assistant Vice Chancellor ... Ms. Deborah YOKLIC
21 Asst Vice Chanc for Finance ... Ms. Diane GROOVER
21 Asst VC for Business Services ... Mr. Bill HOWARD
91 Asst VC Information Technology ... Mr. Keith MCINTOSH
15 Asst VC for Personnel Services ... Ms. Doreen ARMSTRONG
20 Vice Provost Academic Svcs ... Dr. Mary Ann MARTINEZ-SANCHEZ
26 Asst Vice Chancellor for Marketing ... Vacant
32 Asst Vice Chanc for Student Dev ... Ms. Leticia MENCHACA
18 Asst Vice Chancellor Facilities ... Mr. Bill WARD
09 Exec Dir Institutional Research ... Ms. Nicola RICHMOND
37 Executive Director Financial Aid ... Ms. Anna REESE
102 Executive Director Foundation ... Ms. Cheryl HOUSE
41 Executive Director of Athletics ... Mr. Edgar SOTO
19 Exec Director Dept of Public Safety ... Ms. Stella BAY
66 Dean Nursing/Health Rel Prof ... Ms. Marty MAYHEW
06 Director Admissions/Registrar ... Mr. Michael TULINO
96 Director of Purchasing ... Mr. Thomas HARRINGTON

Pima Medical Institute-Mesa (A)

957 S Dobson Road, Mesa AZ 85202-2903
County: Maricopa FICE Identification: 011570
Unit ID: 260691
Telephone: (480) 644-0267 Carnegie Class: Assoc/PrivFP
FAX Number: (480) 649-5249 Calendar System: Other
URL: www.pmi.edu
Established: 1972 Annual Undergrad Tuition & Fees: N/A
Enrollment: 1,536 Coed
Affiliation or Control: Proprietary IRS Status: Proprietary
Highest Offering: Baccalaureate
Program: Occupational
Accreditation: ABHES, OTA, PTAA, RAD

01 Campus Director ..... Ms. Kristen TORRES

Pima Medical Institute-Tucson (B)

3350 E Grant Road, Suite 200, Tucson AZ 85716-2932
County: Pima FICE Identification: 022171
Unit ID: 105534
Telephone: (520) 326-1600 Carnegie Class: Assoc/PrivFP
FAX Number: (520) 326-4125 Calendar System: Other
URL: www.pmi.edu
Established: 1972 Annual Undergrad Tuition & Fees: N/A
Enrollment: 697 Coed
Affiliation or Control: Proprietary IRS Status: Proprietary
Highest Offering: Associate Degree
Program: Occupational
Accreditation: ABHES, OTA, PTAA, RAD

01 Director ..... Mr. Dale BERG

Prescott College (C)

220 Grove Avenue, Prescott AZ 86301-2912
County: Yavapai FICE Identification: 020653
Unit ID: 105589
Telephone: (928) 778-2090 Carnegie Class: Master's S
FAX Number: (928) 776-5137 Calendar System: Semester
URL: www.prescott.edu
Established: 1966 Annual Undergrad Tuition & Fees: $26,819
Enrollment: 1,156 Coed
Affiliation or Control: Independent Non-Profit IRS Status: 501(c)3
Highest Offering: Doctorate
Program: Liberal Arts And General; Teacher Preparatory
Accreditation: NH

01 President ..... Dr. Kristin R. WOOLEVER
05 Exec VP of Academic Affairs/Provost ..... Dr. Paul BURKHARDT
10 Vice President of Financial Affairs ..... Ms. Catherine BOLAND
30 VP for Insitutional Advancement ..... Ms. Marjory SENTE
84 VP of Enrollment Management ..... Mr. Timothy ROBISON
32 VP of Student Life ..... Ms. Laurie SILVER
06 Registrar ..... Ms. Mary TREVOR
37 Financial Aid Director ..... Ms. Mary Frances CAUSEY
04 Executive Assistant ..... Ms. Cathy CHURCH
88 Dean Resident Degree Program ..... Dr. Jack HERRING
20 Director of Academic Operations ..... Ms. Tricia GOFFENA-BEYER
18 Director of Facilities ..... Mr. Greg LAZZELL
08 Director of Library ..... Mr. Richard LEWIS
90 Co-Director of ITS ..... Ms. Kistie SIMMONS
91 Co-Director of ITS ..... Mr. Jordan AMERMAN
21 Director of Financial Services ..... Ms. Anne LABRUZZO
07 Director of ADGP Admissions ..... Mr. Ted BOURAS
07 Director of RDP Admissions ..... Ms. Michelle TISSOT

The Refrigeration School (D)

4210 E Washington Street, Phoenix AZ 85034-1816
County: Maricopa FICE Identification: 011689
Unit ID: 105659
Telephone: (602) 275-7133 Carnegie Class: Assoc/PrivFP
FAX Number: (602) 267-4805 Calendar System: Other
URL: www.refrigerationschool.com
Established: 1965 Annual Undergrad Tuition & Fees: $24,755
Enrollment: 500 Coed
Affiliation or Control: Proprietary IRS Status: Proprietary
Highest Offering: Associate Degree
Program: Occupational
Accreditation: ACCSC

01 Executive Director ..... Ms. Sherry JONES
37 Financial Aid Director ..... Ms. Jael MARTINEZ
07 Admissions Director ..... Ms. Melissa CAIRNS

Sanford-Brown College (E)

9630 North 25th Avenue, Phoenix AZ 85021
County: Maricopa Identification: 666739
Unit ID: 458654
Telephone: (480) 444-1112 Carnegie Class: Not Classified
FAX Number: (480) 444-1200 Calendar System: Semester
URL: www.sanfordbrown.edu/phoenix
Established: 2009 Annual Undergrad Tuition & Fees: N/A
Enrollment: 518 Coed
Affiliation or Control: Proprietary IRS Status: Proprietary
Highest Offering: Associate Degree
Program: 2-Year Principally Bachelor's Creditable
Accreditation: ACICS, MAAB

01 Campus President ..... Mr. George FITZPATRICK
05 Director of Education ..... Ms. Cheryl PIETKIEWICZ

Sessions College for Professional Design (F)

398 South Mill Avenue, Suite 300, Tempe AZ 85281
County: Maricopa Identification: 667018
Telephone: (480) 212-1704 Carnegie Class: Not Classified
FAX Number: (480) 212-1705 Calendar System: Semester
URL: www.sessions.edu
Established: 1997 Annual Undergrad Tuition & Fees: $9,100
Enrollment: 30 Coed
Affiliation or Control: Proprietary IRS Status: Proprietary
Highest Offering: Associate Degree
Program: Occupational; 2-Year Principally Bachelor's Creditable
Accreditation: DETC

00 CEO ..... Ms. Doris GRANATOWSKI
01 President ..... Mr. Gordon DRUMMOND
03 Executive Vice President ..... Mr. Louis J. SCHILT
05 Chief Academic Officer ..... Ms. Tara MACKAY
10 Chief Financial Officer/Bursar ..... Ms. Carole Anne BAILO
32 Director of Student Services ..... Ms. Nomi ALTABEF

Sonoran Desert Institute (G)

10245 East Via Linda, Ste 110, Scottsdale AZ 85258-5316
County: Maricopa Identification: 667057
Telephone: (480) 314-2102 Carnegie Class: Not Classified
FAX Number: (480) 314-2138 Calendar System: Semester
URL: www.sdi.edu
Established: 2000 Annual Undergrad Tuition & Fees: N/A
Enrollment: N/A Coed
Affiliation or Control: Proprietary IRS Status: Proprietary
Highest Offering: Associate Degree
Program: Occupational
Accreditation: DETC

01 President ..... Thomas A. KUBE

Southwest College of Naturopathic Medicine & Health Sciences (H)

2140 E Broadway Road, Tempe AZ 85282-1751
County: Maricopa FICE Identification: 031070
Unit ID: 420246
Telephone: (480) 858-9100 Carnegie Class: Spec/Health
FAX Number: (480) 858-9116 Calendar System: Quarter
URL: www.scnm.edu
Established: 1993 Annual Graduate Tuition & Fees: $24,656
Enrollment: 349 Coed
Affiliation or Control: Independent Non-Profit IRS Status: 501(c)3
Highest Offering: First Professional Degree; No Undergraduates
Program: Professional
Accreditation: NH, NATUR

01 President/Chief Executive Officer ..... Paul A. MITTMAN
17 Exec VP Academic & Clinical Affairs ..... Christine L. GIRARD
10 Vice Pres Finance & Administration ..... Marion DAVIS
32 Vice President Student Affairs ..... Melissa WINQUIST

Southwest Institute of Healing Arts (I)

1100 E Apache Boulevard, Tempe AZ 85281-5822
County: Maricopa FICE Identification: 035933
Unit ID: 442879
Telephone: (480) 994-9244 Carnegie Class: Assoc/PrivFP
FAX Number: (480) 994-3228 Calendar System: Other
URL: www.swiha.edu
Established: 1992 Annual Undergrad Tuition & Fees: $8,600
Enrollment: 498 Coed
Affiliation or Control: Proprietary IRS Status: Proprietary
Highest Offering: Associate Degree
Program: Occupational
Accreditation: CNCE

01 President/Owner ..... Mrs. K. C. MILLER
05 Director of Education ..... Mr. Brad BOUTE
07 Director of Admissions ..... Mr. Jason JAEGER
37 Director of Student Financial Aid ..... Mrs. Kerry WATERS
32 Director Student Services ..... Ms. Amanda SLATER

Southwest University of Visual Arts (J)

2525 N Country Club Road, Tucson AZ 85716-2505
County: Pima FICE Identification: 024915
Unit ID: 104188
Telephone: (520) 325-0123 Carnegie Class: Spec/Arts
FAX Number: (520) 325-5535 Calendar System: Semester
URL: www.theartcenter.edu
Established: 1983 Annual Undergrad Tuition & Fees: $27,540
Enrollment: 555 Coed
Affiliation or Control: Proprietary IRS Status: Proprietary
Highest Offering: Master's
Program: Fine Arts Emphasis
Accreditation: NH, CIDA

01 President ..... Mrs. Sharmon WOODS
07 Director of Admissions ..... Ms. Amy WOODS
32 Director of Student Services ..... Ms. Amy WOODS
12 Director of Albuquerque Campus ..... Ms. Cindy WHITAKER
06 Registrar ..... Ms. Stephanie GASSER

Thunderbird School of Global Management (K)

1 Global Place, Glendale AZ 85306-3236
County: Maricopa FICE Identification: 001070
Unit ID: 103778
Telephone: (602) 978-7011 Carnegie Class: Spec/Bus
FAX Number: (602) 978-8238 Calendar System: Trimester
URL: www.thunderbird.edu
Established: 1946 Annual Graduate Tuition & Fees: N/A
Enrollment: 1,309 Coed
Affiliation or Control: Independent Non-Profit IRS Status: 501(c)3
Highest Offering: Master's; No Undergraduates
Program: Professional; Business Emphasis
Accreditation: NH, BUS

01 President ..... Dr. Angel CABRERA
05 Provost ..... Dr. David BOWEN
46 Sr VP Thunderbird Corporate Lrng ..... Ms. Beth STOOPS
10 Chief Financial Officer ..... Mr. Timothy PROPP
58 Vice President Full-time Program ..... Dr. Kay KECK
30 Vice Pres & Chief Development Ofcr ..... Ms. Joan NEICE
26 Associate Vice President Marketing ..... Mr. Phil SCHLESINGER
27 Assoc VP Information Services ..... Ms. Carol HAMMOND
07 Asst VP Admissions & Recruiting ..... Mr. Jay BRYANT
21 Assoc VP Finance/Admin Services ..... Mr. Chris LEE
36 Assoc VP for Prof Career Devel ..... Mr. Kip HARRELL
20 Dean of Faculty ..... Dr. Dale DAVISON
13 Director IT Operations ..... Mr. Jim HERNDON
06 Registrar/Assoc VP Acad Operations ..... Mr. James SCOTT
37 Director Student Financial Aid ..... Mrs. Catherine KING-TODD
11 Senior Director Operations ..... Ms. Joyce ROGERS
20 Assoc Dir Acad/International Svcs ..... Ms. Felicia WELCH
04 Exec Assistant to the President ..... Ms. Mary Ellen PRUNENCA

Tohono O'odham Community College (L)

PO Box 3129, Sells AZ 85634-3129
County: Pima FICE Identification: 037844
Unit ID: 442781
Telephone: (520) 383-8401 Carnegie Class: Tribal
FAX Number: (520) 383-0029 Calendar System: Semester
URL: www.tocc.cc.az.us
Established: 1998 Annual Undergrad Tuition & Fees: $1,435
Enrollment: 240 Coed
Affiliation or Control: Tribal Control IRS Status: 501(c)3
Highest Offering: Associate Degree
Program: Occupational; 2-Year Principally Bachelor's Creditable
Accreditation: NH

01 Interim President ..... Ms. Jane LATANE
05 Vice President for Education ..... Ms. Juana JOSE
32 Vice Pres of Student Services ..... Ms. Sylvia HENDRICKS
11 Vice President of Admin Services ..... Dr. Robert LEDMAN
46 Vice President Inst Devel/Research ..... Vacant
75 Dept Chair Occupational Pgms ..... Mr. George MIGUEL
07 Director of Admissions/Records ..... Mr. Leslie LUNA
25 Sponsored Projects ..... Mr. Samuel OROZCO
97 Dept Chair for General Education ..... Vacant
08 Librarian ..... Ms. Elaine CUBBINS
37 Director of Financial Aid ..... Mr. Al RIVERA
88 Director Project NATIVE ..... Ms. Camille MARTINEZ-YADEN
88 Director Project NATIVE ..... Dr. Sandra LUCAS
30 Director of Fundraising ..... Ms. Andrea AHMED

Universal Technical Institute (M)

10695 W Pierce Street, Avondale AZ 85323-7946
County: Maricopa FICE Identification: 008221
Unit ID: 106041
Telephone: (623) 245-4600 Carnegie Class: Assoc/PrivFP
FAX Number: (623) 245-4601 Calendar System: Other
URL: www.uticorp.com
Established: 1965 Annual Undergrad Tuition & Fees: $25,200
Enrollment: 2,857 Coed
Affiliation or Control: Proprietary IRS Status: Proprietary
Highest Offering: Associate Degree
Program: Occupational
Accreditation: ACCSC

01 Campus President ..... Mr. Michael ROMANO
05 Director of Education ..... Ms. Maria WALTERS
32 Director of Student Services ..... Mr. Jamie BALES
10 Director of Campus Accounting ..... Mr. Dale KENNEDY
07 Admissions Director ..... Mr. Eric MURRY
36 Director of Graduate Employment ..... Ms. Cheryl RADKE
37 Director of Financial Aid ..... Ms. Terri MEIXSEL-CORDERO
38 Counselor ..... Ms. Heather GONZALES
18 Maintenance Director ..... Mr. George MICKENS

University of Advancing Technology (A)

2625 W Baseline Road, Tempe AZ 85283-1056
County: Maricopa — FICE Identification: 025590
Unit ID: 363934
Telephone: (602) 383-8228 — Carnegie Class: Bac/Diverse
FAX Number: (602) 383-8250 — Calendar System: Other
URL: www.uat.edu
Established: 1983 — Annual Undergrad Tuition & Fees: $19,500
Enrollment: 1,037 — Coed
Affiliation or Control: Proprietary — IRS Status: Proprietary
Highest Offering: Master's
Program: Technical Emphasis
Accreditation: NH

01 President ... Mr. Jason PISTILLO
03 Executive Vice President ... Vacant
10 Treasurer/General Counsel ... Mr. Robert WRIGHT
05 Provost ... Mr. Dave BOLMAN

University of Arizona (B)

1401 E University Blvd, Tucson AZ 85721-0001
County: Pima — FICE Identification: 001083
Unit ID: 104179
Telephone: (520) 621-2211 — Carnegie Class: RU/VH
FAX Number: (520) 621-9323 — Calendar System: Semester
URL: www.arizona.edu
Established: 1885 — Annual Undergrad Tuition & Fees (In-State): $9,286
Enrollment: 39,086 — Coed
Affiliation or Control: State — IRS Status: 501(c)3
Highest Offering: Doctorate
Program: Liberal Arts And General; Teacher Preparatory; Professional
Accreditation: NH, ART, AUD, BUS, BUSA, CEA, CLPSY, CORE, DANCE, DIETD, ENG, IPSY, JOUR, LAW, LIB, LSAR, MED, MUS, NURSE, PERF, PH, PHAR, PLNG, SCPSY, SP, SPAA, THEA

01 President ... Dr. Eugene SANDER
05 Exec VP Academic Affairs/Provost ... Dr. Meredith HAY
100 Senior VP/Chief of Staff ... Dr. Jacqueline MOK
10 Senior Vice Pres Business Affairs ... Mr. Milton M. CASTILLO
32 Vice President Student Affairs ... Ms. Melissa VITO
63 Dean College of Medicine ... Dr. Steven GOLDSCHMID
17 Vice President Health Affairs ... Dr. William M. CRIST
30 Vice President External Relations ... Mr. Stephen MACCARTHY
40 VP Research/Economic Development ... Dr. Leslie P. TOLBERT
86 Vice Provost Outreach ... Mr. Michael A. PROCTOR
84 Asst VP Enrollment Management ... Ms. Kasandra URQUIDEZ
43 VP Legal Affairs/General Counsel ... Dr. Betty GEORGE
20 Vice Provost Academic Affairs ... Dr. Gail BURD
13 Chief Information Officer ... Ms. Michelle NORIN
21 Sr Associate VP Business Affairs ... Mr. Robert R. SMITH
31 Assoc VP Community Relations ... Mr. Jaime P. GUTIERREZ
88 Associate VP Univ Research Parks ... Mr. Bruce A. WRIGHT
27 Asst Vice President Communications ... Mr. Johnny CRUZ
46 Assoc VP Research ... Dr. Andrew COMRIE
86 Assoc VP Government Relations ... Mr. J. Gregory FAHEY
45 Assoc VP Academic Res/Plng/Mgmt ... Mr. Ed FRISCH
15 Vice Pres Human Resources ... Ms. Allison VAILLANCOURT
06 Registrar/Enrollment Management ... Dr. Beth ACREE
21 Asst Vice President/Budget Director ... Mr. Jim FLORIAN
21 Assoc Vice President Financial Svcs ... Mr. Charles INGRAM
37 Director Student Financial Aid ... Mr. John NAMETZ
08 Dean of Libraries ... Ms. Carla STOFFLE
29 Exec Director Alumni Association ... Ms. Melinda BURKE
23 Director Campus Health ... Dr. Harry MCDERMOTT
36 Director Career Services ... Ms. Eileen MCGARRY
22 Dir Equal Oppty/Affirmative Action ... Ms. Mary Beth TUCKER
41 Athletic Director ... Mr. Greg BYRNE
18 Director Facilities Management ... Mr. Christopher M. KOPACH
47 Dean Col Agriculture/Life Sciences ... Mr. Shane BURGESS
48 Dean Col Arch & Landscape Arch ... Dr. Jan CERVELLI
50 Dean Eller College of Management ... Dr. Leonard JESSUP
53 Dean College of Education ... Dr. Ronald MARX
54 Dean College of Engineering ... Dr. Jeff GOLDBERG
61 Dean College of Law ... Mr. Lawrence PONOROFF
57 Dean College of Fine Arts ... Dr. Jory HANCOCK
79 Dean College of Humanities ... Dr. Mary WILDNER-BASSETT
81 Dean College of Science ... Dr. Joaquin RUIZ
83 Dean Coll of Social/Behav Science ... Dr. John P. JONES
66 Dean College of Nursing ... Dr. Joan SHAVER
67 Dean College of Pharmacy ... Dr. Lyle BOOTMAN
69 Dean Zuckerman AZ Col Public Hlth ... Dr. Iman A. HAKIM
12 Exec Officer UA South ... Dr. James W. SHOCKEY
92 Dean Honors College ... Dr. Patricia MACCORQUODALE
88 Dean College of Optical Sciences ... Dr. James C. WYANT
09 Assoc Vice Provost Inst Research ... Dr. Richard KROC
26 Chief Public Relations/News Svcs ... Ms. Jennifer FITZENBERGER

University of Phoenix (C)

4615 E Elwood Street, Phoenix AZ 85040-1958
County: Maricopa — FICE Identification: 020988
Unit ID: 105516
Telephone: (480) 557-2000 — Carnegie Class: Master's L
FAX Number: N/A — Calendar System: Other
URL: www.phoenix.edu
Established: 1976 — Annual Undergrad Tuition & Fees: N/A
Enrollment: 398,579 — Coed
Affiliation or Control: Proprietary — IRS Status: Proprietary
Highest Offering: Doctorate
Program: Liberal Arts And General; Teacher Preparatory; Professional
Accreditation: NH, CACREP, NURSE, TEAC

01 President University of Phoenix ... Dr. William PEPICELLO
00 President & COO Apollo Group ... Mr. Joseph L. D'AMICO
05 Provost/Sr VP Academic Affairs ... Dr. Alan DRIMMER
88 Sr VP & CFO Apollo Group ... Mr. Brian L. SWARTZ
03 Executive VP Campus Operations ... Mr. Jerrad TAUSZ
102 Exec VP Corp Rels & Educ Alliances ... Mr. Barry FEIERSTEIN
26 Exec VP Public Affairs ... Ms. Sara JONES
31 Exec Vice Pres External Affairs ... Ms. Terri BISHOP
13 Executive VP Technology Strategies ... Mr. Jay GOIN
88 EVP Integration/Design Improvement ... Mr. Vince GRELL
43 Exec VP/Gen Counsel & Secretary ... Mr. Robert MOYA
05 Senior VP Academic Research ... Dr. Adam HONEA
11 Chief Operating Officer UOPX ... Ms. Dianne PUSCH
20 Senior VP Academic Excellence ... Mr. Jorge KLOR DE ALVA
10 Sr VP of Financial Services ... Mr. Jeff SONNENBERG
84 Senior Vice President Enrollment ... Ms. Trish ELLIOTT
32 Sr Vice President Student Services ... Ms. Nancy CERVASIO
86 Sr VP National/Government Affairs ... Dr. Susan MITCHELL
106 Regional Vice President Online ... Ms. Cheri SORENSEN
88 Vice President of University Svcs ... Ms. Evelyn GASKIN
66 Exec Dir/Dean College Social Sci ... Dr. Lynn HALL
37 VP Student Financial Aid ... Ms. Shawn TEBBEN
100 VP Academic Administration ... Mr. Lee FINKEL
102 VP Cmty Investment & Foundation ... Ms. Pat GOTTFRIED
20 Vice President Academic Operations ... Dr. Russ PADEN
46 VP Academic Affair/Apollo Publishng ... Mr. David BICKFORD
43 VP University Legal/General Counsel ... Mr. Dan LITTERAL
09 Assoc Vice Pres Inst Research ... Mr. Jay KLAGGE
20 Assoc VP of Academic Affairs ... Dr. Dawn IWAMOTO
20 Assoc VP of Academic Affairs ... Dr. Marla KELSEY
29 Exec Director Alumni Relations ... Ms. Alanna VITUCCI
27 Chief Technology Officer ... Mr. Michael WHITE
26 Chief Mktg & Prod Development ... Mr. Rob WRUBEL
07 Sr Director of Admissions ... Mr. Marc BOOKER
06 Registrar ... Ms. Audra MCQUARIE
16 Chief Human Resources Officer ... Mr. Fred NEWTON
09 Sr Director Institutional Assess ... Mr. Wayne FORAKER
28 Org Diversity Officer ... Ms. Victoria JONES
04 Assistant to the President ... Ms. Sandy MEYER
12 Campus Director Harrisburg PA ... Ms. Beth SIGLER
12 Campus Director Boston ... Mr. Josh CHUMLEY
12 VP/Campus Director Cleveland ... Ms. Gina CUFFARI
12 VP/Campus Director San Diego ... Ms. Kim SAVICH
12 State VP Oklahoma/Director Tulsa ... Ms. Lori SANTIAGO
12 Campus Director Oregon ... Mr. Flint HOLLAND
12 Assoc Campus Director Memphis TN ... Mr. Mark AMREIN
12 Campus Director Oklahoma City OK ... Mr. Troy THOMAS
12 Vice President/Director Atlanta GA ... Mr. Michael HEARON
12 Campus Director South Florida ... Ms. Leslie KRISTOF
12 VP Dir Canada/Europe/Middle East ... Mr. Pete MARTINEZ
12 VP/Campus Director Vancouver Campus ... Mr. Daren HANCOTT
12 Vice President Director Far East ... Mr. Jason SCHROTT
12 Campus Director Western Washington ... Ms. Alexis LIM
12 Campus Director Puerto Rico Campus ... Mr. Jorge RIVERA
12 Campus Director North Florida ... Mr. Dan MACFERRAN
12 Campus Director Tucson ... Mr. Gregg JOHNSON
12 Campus Director Kansas City MO ... Ms. Jeannine LAKE
12 Vice Pres/Director Utah Campus ... Dr. Darris HOWE
12 State VP New Mexico/Dir Albuquerque ... Mr. Randy LICHTENFELD
12 VP/Director Detroit ... Ms. Janice CARDWELL
12 Director Reno Campus ... Ms. Kathy GAMBOA
12 VP/Director San Antonio Campus ... Mr. Wally HEDGECOCK
12 Campus Director Louisville Campus ... Mr. Scot MALL
12 Assoc Campus Dir Chattanooga TN ... Mr. Marc CROSBY
12 Campus Director Idaho Campus ... Mr. Bill BACH
12 VP/Director New Jersey Campus ... Mr. Todd CUNNINGHAM
12 Campus Dir West Michigan Campus ... Mr. Todd PEULER
12 Campus Director Online Netherlands ... Mr. Stephen ZEMBLE
12 Campus Director Wisconsin Campus ... Mr. Dave STEFFAN
12 Campus Director Central FL Campus ... Vacant
12 Campus Director Chicago IL ... Mr. Jeremiah HOOD
12 Campus Director Hawaii Campus ... Ms. Kristine AVERILL
12 Campus Director Phoenix Campus ... Mr. David FITZGERALD
12 Campus Director SoCal Campus ... Mr. Bryan NEWMAN
12 Campus Director Charlotte NC ... Ms. Shannon ECKARD
12 Campus Director Sacremento CA ... Mr. Scott LEWIS
12 Campus Director Jackson MS ... Ms. Tiffany DILLER
12 Campus Director Reston VA ... Mr. Erik GREENBURG
12 Campus Dir Las Vegas Campus ... Mr. Charlie NGUYEN
12 Campus Director Bay Area Campus ... Ms. Stacy MCAFEE
12 Campus Director Lafayette LA ... Ms. Corell HEBERT
12 VP/Director West Florida ... Ms. Lisa NUCCI
12 Assoc Campus/Div Director Austin ... Mr. Michael CULLUP
12 Campus Director Pittsburg PA ... Mr. Troy MALOVEY
12 Campus Director Columbus GA ... Ms. Shelby FRUTCHEY
12 Campus Director Omaha, NE ... Mr. Jason PFAFF
12 Campus Director Cincinnati Campus ... Ms. Chris MONTAGNINO
12 Assoc Campus Dir Springfield MO ... Ms. Yalonda PINNELL
12 Campus Dir Des Moines ... Mr. Christopher MASON
12 Campus Director Wichita Campus ... Ms. Carrie MORRIS-SMITH
12 Campus Director Eastern Washington ... Mr. Paul GREEN
12 Campus Director Central Valley ... Ms. Ann TYE
12 Assoc Campus Directr Madison WI ... Ms. Briana HOULIHAN
12 Campus Director Dallas Campus ... Ms. Jennifer RODRIGUEZ
12 Campus Director Columbus OH ... Ms. Heather LOUGHLEY
12 Campus Dir NW Arkansas (Rogers) ... Mr. Luke CAMPBELL
12 Acting Campus Director Connecticut ... Mr. Mike MORLEY
12 Campus Director Richmond VA ... Mr. Gregg CROWE
12 Campus Director Columbia SC ... Ms. Stephanie JACKSON
12 Assoc Campus Dir NW Indianapolis ... Ms. Jennifer KHADIVAR
12 Acting Director Calgary Canada ... Mr. Mike BROUSSEAU
12 Campus Director Washington DC ... Mr. Joe MARZANO
12 Campus Dir Colorado Springs ... Ms. Brittany NIELSON
12 Campus Director Nashville TN ... Mr. Mark MENDOZA
12 Campus Director Raleigh NC ... Ms. Candice MORGAN
12 Assoc Campus Director Savannah GA ... Ms. Melissa JACKSON
12 Camp Dir El Paso TX/Santa Teresa NM ... Ms. Barbara JANOWSKI
12 Campus Director Birmingham AL ... Mr. Roger ROCHA
12 Assoc Campus Dir Little Rock AR ... Mr. Randy MCCORMICK
12 Assoc Campus Director St Louis MO ... Mr. Adam WRIGHT
12 Assoc Campus Director Schaumburg IL ... Mr. Tony ALBRUSCATO
12 Director Cheyenne & Fort Collins ... Mr. Brent SEIFRIED
50 Exec Dir/Dean Sch of Advanced Studi ... Dr. Freda HARTMAN
65 Exec Dir/Dean College Natural Sci ... Dr. Hinrich EYLERS
53 Exec Dir/Dean of Education ... Dr. Meredith CURLEY
88 Exec Dir/Dean Sch Advanced Studies ... Dr. Jeremy MORELAND
66 Exec Dir/College of Nursing ... Dr. Pam FULLER
88 Exec Dir/Dean College of IS&T ... Dr. Blair SMITH
79 Exec Dir/Dean College of Humanities ... Dr. Barb BADERMAN
88 Exec Dir/Dean Criminal Justice/Sec ... Dr. James NESS
50 Assoc VP/Dean School of Business ... Dr. Brian LINDQUIST

† Tuition is a weighted average for all campuses using 24 credits.

Western International University (D)

9215 N Black Canyon Highway, Phoenix AZ 85021-2718
County: Maricopa — FICE Identification: 021715
Unit ID: 106102
Telephone: (602) 943-2311 — Carnegie Class: Master's M
FAX Number: (602) 371-8637 — Calendar System: Other
URL: www.west.edu
Established: 1978 — Annual Undergrad Tuition & Fees: $13,300
Enrollment: 2,975 — Coed
Affiliation or Control: Proprietary — IRS Status: Proprietary
Highest Offering: Master's
Program: Professional; Business Emphasis
Accreditation: NH

01 President ... Ms. Tracy LORENZ
03 Vice President ... Dr. Alan DRIMMER
45 VP Strategy & Development ... Ms. Allison POOLEY
90 VP Academic Technology ... Vacant
106 VP Online Services ... Vacant
88 VP of Administration ... Mr. Kris MCCALL
11 Interim COO ... Dr. Mark CAMERON
05 Assoc Director Academic Affairs ... Mr. Robert DORFMAN
09 Dir Assessment/Institutional Effect ... Ms. Kay LOOK
11 Exec Director University Services ... Ms. Jo ARNEY
07 Regional Director of Enrollment ... Ms. Karen JANITELL
06 Registrar/Dir Internatl Operations ... Ms. Hue HASLIM
10 Reg Dir of Finance/Administration ... Mr. Roger WALTON

Yavapai College (E)

1100 E Sheldon Street, Prescott AZ 86301-3297
County: Yavapai — FICE Identification: 001079
Unit ID: 106148
Telephone: (928) 445-7300 — Carnegie Class: Assoc/Pub-R-L
FAX Number: (928) 776-2119 — Calendar System: Semester
URL: www.yc.edu
Established: 1966 — Annual Undergrad Tuition & Fees (In-District): $1,608
Enrollment: 8,410 — Coed
Affiliation or Control: Local — IRS Status: 501(c)3
Highest Offering: Associate Degree
Program: Occupational; 2-Year Principally Bachelor's Creditable
Accreditation: NH, ADNUR, IFSAC, RAD

01 President ... Dr. Penelope WILLS
05 Vice Pres Academic/Student Affairs ... Dr. Gregory GILLESPIE
10 Exec VP Finance/Administrative Svcs ... Mr. Clint EWELL
30 VP College Development/Foundation ... Mr. Steve WALKER
20 Dean District Student/Academic Svcs ... Ms. Barbara R. WING
20 Dean Instruct/Stdnt Svcs Verde Camp ... Mr. Tom SCHUMACHER
88 Dean Career Technical Education ... Mr. John MORGAN
66 Dn Sci/Nursing/Allied Hlth/Dir Athl ... Mr. Scott FARNSWORTH
35 Assoc Dean Student Svcs Prescott ... Ms. Sandy GARBER
07 Assoc Dean Student Services Verde ... Ms. Barbie DUNCAN
26 Director of Marketing/Public Inform ... Ms. Katie HOESCHLER
37 Director of Financial Aid ... Ms. Terri ECKEL
09 Dir Inst Planning/Research/Assess ... Mr. Tom HUGHES
15 Human Resources Director ... Ms. Rose HURLEY
19 Director of Campus Safety ... Mr. Joe CAPELLI
21 Assoc Business Officer/Comptroller ... Mr. Frank D'ANGELO
07 Recruitment Officer ... Mr. Jeff RHOADS
18 Facilities Director ... Mr. David LAURENCE
13 Chief Information Officer ... Mr. Patrick BURNS
88 Paralegal Director ... Ms. Ruth HARRISON
06 Registrar ... Ms. Sheila JARRELL
29 Director Alumni Relations ... Ms. Barbara CLAY BAUGH
96 Director of Purchasing ... Ms. Phyllis LEWELLEN
88 Custom Training Coordinator ... Ms. Ginger JOHNSON
36 Coordinator Career Services ... Mr. Michael BROWN

ARKANSAS

Arkansas Baptist College (F)

1621 Martin Luther King Drive, Little Rock AR 72202-6099
County: Pulaski — FICE Identification: 001087
Unit ID: 106306
Telephone: (501) 370-4000 — Carnegie Class: Bac/Assoc
FAX Number: (501) 372-7992 — Calendar System: Semester
URL: www.arkansasbaptist.edu
Established: 1884 — Annual Undergrad Tuition & Fees: $7,800
Enrollment: 1,119 — Coed

Affiliation or Control: Baptist IRS Status: 501(c)3
Highest Offering: Baccalaureate
Program: 2-Year Principally Bachelor's Creditable; Liberal Arts And General
Accreditation: NH

01 President ..... Dr. Fitz HILL
04 President's Executive Assistant ..... Ms. Patsy BIGGS
10 Exec VP/Chief Financial Officer ..... Mr. Billy OWENS
100 Chief of Staff ..... Mrs. LaCresha NEWTON
05 Vice President of Academic Affairs ..... Dr. Barbara HOLMES
32 Vice President Student Affairs ..... Dr. V. C. HENDERSON
30 Director of Development ..... Mr. Larry BONE
09 Director of Institutional Research ..... Mrs. Jerelyn L. DUNCAN
103 Dir of Adult Ed & Workforce Dev ..... Ms. Arma HART
07 Director of Admissions/Recruitment ..... Mr. Alfred DORSEY
84 Dean of Enrollment Management ..... Ms. Rosie TONEY
06 Registar ..... Ms. Delores VOLIBER
37 Director of Financial Aid ..... Ms. Patricia PROCTOR
08 Director of Library/Media Services ..... Mrs. Joyce CAMPBELL
26 Assoc Dir Public Relations/Mktg ..... Mrs. Terri CLARK
21 Business Manager ..... Ms. Rita NEWBURN
34 Dean of Women ..... Vacant
35 Asst Dean of Student Affairs ..... Mr. Brian MILLER
33 Dean of Men ..... Mr. Donald NORTHCROSS
19 Chief of Campus Safety ..... Mr. Curtis JOHNSON
18 Facilities Director ..... Mr. Bryan RUSHER

Arkansas Northeastern College (A)

2501 S Division Street, Blytheville AR 72315-5111
County: Mississippi FICE Identification: 012860
Unit ID: 107327
Telephone: (870) 762-1020 Carnegie Class: Assoc/Pub-R-M
FAX Number: (870) 763-3704 Calendar System: Semester
URL: www.anc.edu
Established: 1974 Annual Undergrad Tuition & Fees (In-District): $1,875
Enrollment: 2,003 Coed
Affiliation or Control: State/Local IRS Status: 501(c)3
Highest Offering: Associate Degree
Program: Occupational; 2-Year Principally Bachelor's Creditable
Accreditation: NH, ADNUR, DA, EMT

01 President ..... Dr. Robert MYERS
03 Executive Vice President ..... Mrs. June WALTERS
05 Vice President of Instruction ..... Ms. Mary DEMENT
10 Vice President for Finance ..... Dr. James SHEMWELL
32 Vice Pres Student Svcs/Registrar ..... Mrs. Laura YARBROUGH
30 Vice President for Advancement ..... Mrs. Sherri BENNETT
09 Vice President MITS/Human Resources .. Mr. James W. MCCLAIN
26 Dean Development/College Relations ..... Ms. Rachel GIFFORD
72 Dean Tech Programs & Training ..... Mrs. Robin SINGLETON
49 Dean Arts & Sciences ..... Mrs. Deborah PARKER
12 Dean Occupatl Pgms/Ext Campus Ops ..... Mr. Gene BENNETT
66 Dean Nursing/Allied Hlth/PE/Rec ..... Mrs. Brenda HOLIFIELD
88 Coordinator University Center ..... Vacant
31 Coordinator Community Education ..... Mrs. Sharyn STEVENSON
08 Director of College Library ..... Mrs. Bronwyn MORGAN
07 Counselor Admissions & Careers ..... Mr. Johnny MOORE
36 Coordinator of Placement Services ..... Mrs. Pauline LINAM
37 Director Financial Aid ..... Vacant
72 Dean MITS ..... Mrs. Ruby MEADOR
21 Controller ..... Mr. Curt ELLINGTON
15 Human Resources & ADA Coordinator ..... Mrs. Carol WILF
90 Director Academic Tech Services ..... Mr. James ODOM
18 Director Physical Plant and Grounds ..... Mr. Ralph HILL
88 Director Talent Search/Educ Opp Ctr ..... Ms. Niki JOHNS
88 Director Student Support Services ..... Ms. Lisa MCGHEE

*Arkansas State University System (B)

2222 Cottondale Lane, Suite 230, Little Rock AR 72202
County: Pulaski Identification: 666187
Telephone: (501) 660-1000 Carnegie Class: N/A
FAX Number: (501) 660-1010
URL: www.asusystem.edu

01 President ..... Dr. Charles L. WELCH
04 Exec Assistant to the President ..... Ms. Pam KAIL
10 Vice President for Finance ..... Ms. Julie BATES
86 Vice Pres Governmental Relations ..... Mr. Robert EVANS
102 System VP/President ASU Foundation ..... Mr. Steve OWENS
43 Legal Counsel ..... Ms. Lucinda MCDANIEL
88 Internal Auditor ..... Ms. Jo LUNBECK

*Arkansas State University (C)

PO Box 600, State University AR 72467
County: Craighead FICE Identification: 001090
Unit ID: 106458
Telephone: (870) 972-2100 Carnegie Class: Master's L
FAX Number: (870) 972-3465 Calendar System: Semester
URL: www.astate.edu
Established: 1909 Annual Undergrad Tuition & Fees (In-State): $6,934
Enrollment: 13,415 Coed
Affiliation or Control: State IRS Status: 501(c)3
Highest Offering: Doctorate
Program: Liberal Arts And General; Teacher Preparatory; Professional
Accreditation: NH, ADNUR, ANEST, ART, BUS, CACREP, CORE, DMS, ENG, JOUR, MLTAD, MT, MUS, NUR, PTA, PTAA, RAD, RTT, SP, SPAA, SW, TED

02 Interim Chancellor ..... Dr. G. Daniel HOWARD
04 Exec Assistant to the Chancellor ..... Mr. Thomas MOORE
05 Int Exec Vice Chancellor & Provost ..... Dr. Glendell JONES
10 VC Finance & Administration ..... Mr. Ed KREMERS
32 Vice Chancellor Student Affairs ..... Dr. William R. STRIPLING
30 VC University Advancement ..... Mr. Cristian MURDOCK
86 Exec Dir Governmental Relations ..... Mr. Robert EVANS
41 Director of Athletics ..... Dr. Dean LEE
88 Assoc Vice Chanc Academic Affairs ..... Dr. Lynita M. COOKSEY
21 Assoc Vice Chancellor Finance ..... Mr. Russ HANNAH
11 Assoc Vice Chanc Administration ..... Dr. J. W MASON
35 Assoc Vice Chanc Student Affairs ..... Dr. Lonnie R. WILLIAMS
88 Asst Vice Chanc Student Affairs ..... Mr. Craig JOHNSON
14 Asst VC Information Technology/CIO ..... Mr. Mark HOETING
18 Asst Vice Chancellor Facilities ..... Mr. Al STOVERINK
51 Dean Continuing Educ/Cmty Outreach ..... Dr. Beverly BOALS-GILBERT
37 Dir of Financial Aid & Scholarship ..... Mr. Terry FINNEY
09 Dir Instnl Research/Plng/Assessment ..... Dr. Kathryn C. JONES
06 Registrar ..... Ms. Tracy FINCH
07 Director of Admissions ..... Ms. Tammy FOWLER
39 Director of Residence Life ..... Mr. Patrick DIXON
38 Dean of Student Development ..... Mr. Randall TATE
19 Interim Dir of University Police ..... Mr. Randy MARTIN
28 Director of Disability Services ..... Dr. Jenifer R. MASON
36 Director of Career Services ..... Ms. Sharon BECKER
38 Director Student Counseling ..... Dr. Phil HESTAND
23 Director Student Health Center ..... Ms. Renata VAUGHN
29 Director of Alumni Relations ..... Ms. Beth SMITH
26 Director of University Relations ..... Ms. Christy VALENTINE
27 Director of Media Relations ..... Ms. Gina BOWMAN
88 Director Pub & Creative Services ..... Mr. Mark REEVES
44 Executive Director of Development ..... Dr. Jim PROCK
96 Director of Purchasing ..... Ms. Carol BARNHILL
62 Int Dean of Library/Info Resources ..... Mr. Jeff BAILEY
47 Int Dean Col Agriculture/Technology ..... Dr. David BEASLEY
54 Dn Coll of Sci & Math/Agri/Engineer ..... Dr. Andy NOVOBILSKI
50 Dean College of Business ..... Dr. Len FREY
53 Interim Dean College of Education ..... Dr. Gregory MEEKS
58 Dean of Graduate School ..... Dr. Andrew SUSTICH
60 Interim Dean Col of Communications ..... Dr. Osa AMIENYI
66 Dean College of Nursing Health Prof ..... Dr. Susan N. HANRAHAN
88 Dean University College ..... Dr. Lynita M. COOKSEY
57 Interim Dean Fine Arts ..... Dr. Dale MILLER
79 Int Dean College Humanities/Soc Sci ..... Dr. Carol O'CONNOR
92 Dean Honors Program ..... Dr. Andrew SUSTICH
54 Dean College of Engineering ..... Dr. David BEASLEY

*Arkansas State University-Beebe (D)

PO Box 1000, Beebe AR 72012-1000
County: White FICE Identification: 001091
Unit ID: 106449
Telephone: (501) 882-3600 Carnegie Class: Assoc/Pub2in4
FAX Number: (501) 882-8970 Calendar System: Semester
URL: www.asub.edu
Established: 1927 Annual Undergrad Tuition & Fees (In-State): $2,850
Enrollment: 4,683 Coed
Affiliation or Control: State IRS Status: 501(c)3
Highest Offering: Associate Degree
Program: Occupational; 2-Year Principally Bachelor's Creditable
Accreditation: NH, EMT, MLTAD

02 Chancellor ..... Dr. Eugene MCKAY
100 Assistant to Chancellor ..... Dr. Stephanie N. NICHOLS
03 Vice Chancellor ASU-Heber Springs ..... Dr. James C. BOYETT
03 Vice Chancellor of ASU-Searcy ..... Mr. Don HARLAN
05 Vice Chanc External/Advanced Pgms ..... Mr. Barry N. FARRIS
05 Vice Chancellor Academic Affairs ..... Dr. Theodore J. KALTHOFF
32 Vice Chancellor Student Services ..... Dr. Deborah A. GARRETT
10 Vice Chanc Finance & Administration ..... Mr. Jerry H. CARLISLE
30 Vice Chanc Inst Advancement ..... Dr. Keith PINCHBACK
26 Director of Public Information ..... Dr. Colbie M. FALWELL
06 Registrar ..... Ms. Amy J. MAHAN
08 Head Librarian ..... Ms. Tracy D. SMITH
15 Director of Human Resources ..... Ms. Susan A. COLLIE
19 Chief of Police ..... Mr. James J. MARTIN
18 Director of Physical Plant ..... Mr. Jerry L. THOMPSON
37 Director Student Financial Aid ..... Ms. Louise DRIVER
09 Director of Institutional Research ... Ms. Bonnie SMYTH-MCGAHA
14 Director of Computer Service ..... Mr. Wade FINCHER
21 Business Manager ..... Mr. Robbins MILLER
21 Controller ..... Ms. Sharon A. BEEN
84 Director of Enrollment Management ..... Mr. David M. MAYES
38 Dir Student Success and Retention ..... Ms. Krystal N. MARTIN
36 Job Placement Coordinator ..... Vacant
39 Director of Student Life ..... Ms. Angie D. TOTTY
24 Director of Learning Center ..... Ms. Rebecca E. WOLF
72 Director Advanced Tech/Allied Hlth ..... Dr. Keith MCCLANAHAN
106 Director of Distance Learning ..... Ms. Rhonda DURHAM
96 Dir Administrative Support Services ..... Ms. Stephanie CREED
12 Dir ASU-Beebe Degree Ctr at LRAFB . Ms. Nancy A. SHEFFLETTE
07 Director of Admissions ..... Ms. Robin A. HAYES
35 Coordinator of Campus Life ..... Mr. Neil A. OUTAR
105 Website Coordinator ..... Mr. Rikky L. FREE
31 Coord Marketing/Community Relations ..... Mrs. Rose Mary JACKSON

*Arkansas State University-Mountain Home (E)

1600 S College Street, Mountain Home AR 72653-5326
County: Baxter Identification: 666311
Unit ID: 420538
Telephone: (870) 508-6100 Carnegie Class: Assoc/Pub2in4
FAX Number: (870) 508-6287 Calendar System: Semester
URL: www.asumh.edu
Established: 1995 Annual Undergrad Tuition & Fees (In-District): $3,030
Enrollment: 1,583 Coed
Affiliation or Control: State/Local IRS Status: 501(c)3
Highest Offering: Associate Degree
Program: Occupational; Business Emphasis
Accreditation: NH, FUSER

02 Chancellor ..... Dr. Ed COULTER
05 Provost/VC Academic/Student Affairs ..... Dr. Patricia A. BAILEY
11 Vice Chanc Administrative Affairs ..... Mr. John DAVIDSON
30 Vice Chancellor Development ..... Ms. Carol MILLER-GRESHAM
84 Assoc VC Enrollment Management ..... Mrs. Rosalyn R. BLAGG
46 Assoc VC Rsrch/Sp Prog/Dist Lrng ..... Mrs. Karen S. HOPPER
06 Registrar ..... Mrs. Rosalyn R. BLAGG
18 Chief Facilities/Physical Plant ..... Mr. Nickey L. ROBBINS
26 Chief Public Relations Officer ..... Mrs. Christy C. KEIRN
35 Director Student Affairs ..... Vacant
37 Director Student Financial Aid ..... Mr. Clay BERRY

*Arkansas State University-Newport (F)

7648 Victory Boulevard, Newport AR 72112-8912
County: Jackson Identification: 666153
Unit ID: 440402
Telephone: (870) 512-7800 Carnegie Class: Assoc/Pub2in4
FAX Number: (870) 512-7807 Calendar System: Semester
URL: www.asun.edu
Established: 1991 Annual Undergrad Tuition & Fees (In-State): $2,700
Enrollment: 2,102 Coed
Affiliation or Control: State IRS Status: 501(c)3
Highest Offering: Associate Degree
Program: Occupational; 2-Year Principally Bachelor's Creditable
Accreditation: NH

02 Chancellor ..... Dr. Larry N. WILLIAMS
04 Assistant to the Chancellor ..... Ms. Laura KING
05 Vice Chancellor Academic Affairs ..... Dr. Sandra MASSEY
10 Vice Chancellor Fiscal Affairs ..... Mr. Bob STIGER
32 Vice Chancellor Student Affairs ..... Dr. Mary ROBERTSON
12 Vice Chancellor Jonesboro Tech Ctr ..... Ms. Linda SHARP
12 Vice Chanc Marked Tree Tech Ctr ..... Mr. Jeff BOOKOUT
88 Division Chair University Studies ..... Mr. Ike WHEELER
75 Division Chair Occupational Studies ..... Mr. Duane DOYLE
88 Division Chair Crim Just/Univ Ctr ..... Dr. Allen MOONEYHAN
88 Director of Business/Transportation ..... Mr. Bentley WALLACE
06 Registrar/Director of Admissions ..... Mr. Robert SUMMERS
13 Director of Computer Services ..... Ms. Tamya STALLINGS
15 Director Human Resources ..... Ms. Bettye DAVIS
18 Director of Physical Plant ..... Mr. David WINSTON
21 Business Manager ..... Ms. Melissa WATSON
102 Director of Grants Management ..... Ms. Monika PHILLIPS
51 Director Cont Ed/Business Outreach ..... Ms. Patricia CALHOUN
37 Director Student Financial Aid ..... Ms. Deana TIMS
32 Director Student Services ..... Ms. Ashley BUCHMAN
38 Counselor ..... Ms. Amber GRADY
08 Librarian ..... Ms. Jennifer BALLARD
24 Director of Learning Resource Ctr ..... Ms. Christy MANN
19 Public Safety Officer ..... Mr. Jeff GRIZZLE
40 Bookstore Manager ..... Ms. Debara FISHER
96 Director of Procurement ..... Ms. Lee WEBB
17 Director of Nursing ..... Mr. Scott COWELL

Arkansas Tech University (G)

1509 North Boulder Avenue, Russellville AR 72801-2222
County: Pope FICE Identification: 001089
Unit ID: 106467
Telephone: (479) 968-0389 Carnegie Class: Master's L
FAX Number: (479) 964-0522 Calendar System: Semester
URL: www.atu.edu
Established: 1909 Annual Undergrad Tuition & Fees (In-State): $5,070
Enrollment: 9,815 Coed
Affiliation or Control: State IRS Status: 501(c)3
Highest Offering: Beyond Master's But Less Than Doctorate
Program: Liberal Arts And General; Teacher Preparatory; Professional
Accreditation: NH, BUS, CS, EMT, ENG, MAC, MUS, NRPA, NUR, PTAA, TED

01 President ..... Dr. Robert C. BROWN
32 VP Student Services/Univ Rels ..... Ms. Susie S. NICHOLSON
05 Vice President Academic Affairs ..... Dr. John WATSON
11 Vice President Administration ..... Mr. David MOSELEY
32 Vice President Student Services ..... Ms. Susie NICKOLSON
30 Vice President for Development ..... Ms. Jayne W. JONES
20 Assoc Vice Pres Academic Affairs ..... Dr. David UNDERWOOD
06 Registrar ..... Ms. Tammy RHODES
07 Director of Admissions ..... Ms. Shauna H. DONNELL
09 Director of Institutional Research ..... Mr. Wyatt WATSON
36 Director Student Placement ..... Vacant
08 Librarian ..... Mr. William PARTON
21 Controller ..... Mr. Gary HODGES
84 Director of Enrollment Management ..... Ms. Shauna DONNELL
38 Dir Learning Asst/Testing Center ..... Ms. Tockie HEMPHILL
14 Director Computer Services ..... Mr. Merrell E. SHOPTAW
27 Director News Bureau ..... Vacant
15 Director Human Resources ..... Ms. Angela REYNOLDS
37 Director Student Financial Aid ..... Ms. Shirley M. GOINES
29 Director Alumni Association ..... Mr. Kelly DAVIS
24 Director Virtual Learning Center ..... Mr. Ken WESTER
85 Director of International Students ..... Ms. Amy PENNINGTON
18 Director of Physical Plant Services ..... Mr. Brian LASEY
26 Chief Public Relations Officer ..... Ms. Susie S. NICHOLSON

96 Director of Purchasing .... Ms. Beth FOSTER
92 Director of Honors Program .... Dr. Jan JENKINS
22 Director of Affirmative Action .... Ms. Jennifer FLEMING
35 Director Student Affairs .... Vacant
58 Dean of Graduate College .... Dr. Mary GUNTER
53 Dean of College of Education .... Dr. Eldon CLARY
49 Dean College of Arts & Humanities .... Dr. Micheal TARVER
50 Dean of College of Business .... Dr. Edward BASHAW
77 Dean of College of Applied Science .... Dr. William HOEFLER
81 Dean College of Natural & Health Sc .... Dr. Richard R. COHOON
51 Dn Col Prof Studies Cmty Outreach .... Dr. Mary Ann ROLLANS
10 Chief Business Officer .... Vacant

Black River Technical College (A)

PO Box 468, Pocahantas AR 72455-0468
County: Randolph　FICE Identification: 020522
Unit ID: 106625
Telephone: (870) 248-4000　Carnegie Class: Assoc/Pub-R-M
FAX Number: (870) 248-4100　Calendar System: Semester
URL: www.blackrivertech.org
Established: 1991　Annual Undergrad Tuition & Fees (In-State): $2,190
Enrollment: 2,508　Coed
Affiliation or Control: State　IRS Status: 501(c)3
Highest Offering: Associate Degree
Program: Occupational; 2-Year Principally Bachelor's Creditable
Accreditation: NH, DIETT, EMT

01 President .... Dr. Wayne HATCHER
05 Vice President General Education .... Dr. Roger JOHNSON
72 Vice President Technical Education .... Mrs. Angela CALDWELL
10 Vice President of Finance .... Mrs. Loretta WILLIAMS
32 Vice President Student Affairs .... Dr. Michael A. SULLENS
30 Vice President of Development .... Dr. Jan ZIEGLER
37 Director Student Financial Aid .... Mrs. Brandi CHESTER
06 Registrar .... Mrs. Kimberly BIGGER

Bryan College (B)

3704 West Walnut, Rogers AR 72756-1825
County: Benton　Identification: 666252
Unit ID: 454458
Telephone: (479) 899-6644　Carnegie Class: Assoc/PrivFP
FAX Number: (417) 862-9554　Calendar System: Semester
URL: www.bryancolleges.edu
Established: 2007　Annual Undergrad Tuition & Fees: $17,500
Enrollment: 292　Coed
Affiliation or Control: Proprietary　IRS Status: Proprietary
Highest Offering: Associate Degree
Program: Occupational; 2-Year Principally Bachelor's Creditable
Accreditation: ACICS

01 President .... Mr. Brian STEWART
03 Executive Director .... Mr. Bob ROARK

† Branch campus of Bryan College, Springfield, MO.

Central Baptist College (C)

1501 College Avenue, Conway AR 72034-6470
County: Faulkner　FICE Identification: 001093
Unit ID: 106713
Telephone: (501) 329-6872　Carnegie Class: Bac/Diverse
FAX Number: (501) 329-2941　Calendar System: Semester
URL: www.cbc.edu
Established: 1952　Annual Undergrad Tuition & Fees: $11,600
Enrollment: 742　Coed
Affiliation or Control: Baptist　IRS Status: 501(c)3
Highest Offering: Baccalaureate
Program: Liberal Arts And General; Teacher Preparatory
Accreditation: NH

01 President .... Mr. Terry KIMBROW
05 Vice President Academic Affairs .... Dr. Gary MCALLISTER
10 Vice President Financial Affairs .... Mr. Don JONES
30 VP for Institutional Advancement .... Mrs. Sancy FAULK
06 Registrar .... Mrs. Phylis HOFFMANN
08 Librarian .... Mrs. Rachel WHITTINGHAM
26 Director of Public Relations .... Mrs. Deanna OTT
88 Dir of Project Development .... Mr. Curt CROOK
37 Financial Aid Director .... Mrs. Tonya HAMMONTREE
32 Dean Student Services .... Mr. B. J. SULLIVAN
88 Director of Special Events .... Ms. Jessica FAULKNER
91 Director of Technical Services .... Mr. Doug BIBLE
41 Athletic Director .... Mr. Lyle MIDDLETON
07 Director of Recruitment .... Mr. Ryan JOHNSON

College of the Ouachitas (D)

One College Circle, Malvern AR 72104-0816
County: Hot Spring　FICE Identification: 009976
Unit ID: 107521
Telephone: (501) 337-5000　Carnegie Class: Assoc/Pub-R-S
FAX Number: (501) 337-9382　Calendar System: Semester
URL: www.coto.edu
Established: 1991　Annual Undergrad Tuition & Fees (In-State): $2,550
Enrollment: 1,542　Coed
Affiliation or Control: State　IRS Status: 501(c)3
Highest Offering: Associate Degree
Program: Occupational; 2-Year Principally Bachelor's Creditable; Technical Emphasis
Accreditation: NH

01 President .... Dr. J. Barry BALLARD
10 Vice Pres Finance & Administration .... Dr. Roger COOMER
05 Vice President of Instruction .... Dr. Martin EGGENSPERGER
09 Vice Pres for Planning & Assessment .... Ms. June PRINCE
103 VP Workforce and Adult Education .... Dr. Blake ROBERTSON
32 Vice President Student Affairs .... Vacant
06 Registrar .... Ms. Linda JOHNSON
08 Library Director .... Ms. Mary Ann HARPER
37 Director of Financial Aid .... Ms. Teresa AVERY
13 Director of Computer Services .... Mr. David SEE
30 Dir Develop/Chief Public Rels Ofcr .... Ms. Amber CHILDERS
36 Director Career Center .... Mr. Ruben KEISLER
88 Dir TRIO Student Support Services .... Ms. Marshel JOHNSON
88 Director Career Pathways .... Mr. Billy FRANCIS

Crowley's Ridge College (E)

100 College Drive, Paragould AR 72450-9775
County: Greene　FICE Identification: 001095
Unit ID: 106810
Telephone: (870) 236-6901　Carnegie Class: Assoc/PrivNFP4
FAX Number: (870) 236-7748　Calendar System: Semester
URL: www.crc.edu
Established: 1964　Annual Undergrad Tuition & Fees: $9,800
Enrollment: 201　Coed
Affiliation or Control: Churches Of Christ　IRS Status: 501(c)3
Highest Offering: Baccalaureate
Program: Liberal Arts And General
Accreditation: NH

01 President .... Mr. Ken HOPPE
05 Vice President for Academic Affairs .... Mr. Phil WILKERSON
32 Vice President for Student Affairs .... Mr. Art SMITH
30 Vice President for Advancement .... Mr. Richard JOHNSON
06 Registrar .... Mr. Paul MCFADDEN
37 Director Student Financial Services .... Mr. David W. GOFF
26 Director Public Information .... Mrs. Andrea JOHNSON
07 Director Admissions/Student Life .... Mrs. Nancy JONESHILL
41 Athletic Director/Campus Minister .... Mr. Paul MCFADDEN
08 Director Learning Center .... Mr. Mark WARNICK
21 Business Office Manager .... Mrs. Sonia JOHNSON
18 Physical Plant Manager .... Mr. Larry KITCHENS
27 Director of Information Services .... Mr. Larry JOHNSON

East Arkansas Community College (F)

1700 Newcastle Road, Forrest City AR 72335-9598
County: Saint Francis　FICE Identification: 012260
Unit ID: 106883
Telephone: (870) 633-4480　Carnegie Class: Assoc/Pub-R-S
FAX Number: (870) 633-7222　Calendar System: Semester
URL: www.eacc.edu
Established: 1974　Annual Undergrad Tuition & Fees (In-District): $2,340
Enrollment: 1,505　Coed
Affiliation or Control: Local　IRS Status: 501(c)3
Highest Offering: Associate Degree
Program: Occupational; 2-Year Principally Bachelor's Creditable
Accreditation: NH, ADNUR, EMT

01 President .... Dr. Coy F. GRACE
05 Vice President Academic Affairs .... Dr. Jeff B. WATSON
10 Vice President Business Affairs .... Mr. Morris BOYDSTUN
32 Vice President Student Affairs .... Mrs. Catherine T. COLEMAN
37 Director Student Financial Aid .... Mr. Alvin COLEMAN
08 Director Library Services .... Mrs. Paige LAWS
84 Director Enrollment Mgmt/Registrar .... Mrs. Sharon COLLIER
26 Director of Public Relations/Mktg .... Mrs. Elizabeth C. LOEB
09 Director of Institutional Research .... Mrs. Alberta COLEMAN
15 Director Personnel Services .... Mrs. Yvonne RUCKER-FRANKLIN
18 Director Physical Plant .... Mr. Glenn FORD
38 Director Educational Guidance Svcs .... Mrs. Michelle WILSON
96 Director of Purchasing .... Mrs. Nancy HERBERT
04 Assistant to the President .... Mrs. Jan C. HAVEN
51 Director of Continuing Education .... Mrs. Lindsay MIDKIFF

Ecclesia College (G)

9653 Nations Drive, Springdale AR 72762-8159
County: Benton　FICE Identification: 038553
Unit ID: 446233
Telephone: (479) 248-7236　Carnegie Class: Spec/Faith
FAX Number: (479) 248-1455　Calendar System: Semester
URL: www.ecollege.edu
Established: 1975　Annual Undergrad Tuition & Fees: $15,050
Enrollment: 179　Coed
Affiliation or Control: Independent Non-Profit　IRS Status: 501(c)3
Highest Offering: Baccalaureate
Program: Liberal Arts And General; Religious Emphasis
Accreditation: BI

01 President .... Mr. Oren PARIS, III
05 Vice President of Academics .... Dr. Robert HEADRICK
10 Vice Pres of Business & Finance .... Mr. Shannon WORTHEN
32 Vice Pres of Student Development .... Mr. Jesse E. WADKINS
30 Vice President of Advancement .... Mr. Mike NOVAK
07 Director of Admissions .... Mr. Titus W. HOFER
26 Vice Pres of Communications .... Ms. Angie P. SNYDER
37 Director Student Financial Aid .... Mr. Jesse E. WADKINS
41 Athletic Director .... Mr. Oren PARIS, III
06 Registrar .... Mrs. Donna BROWN
08 Head Librarian .... Mrs. Joanne CAMPBELL
36 Director Career Development .... Vacant
39 Director Student Housing .... Vacant
88 Director Work Learning .... Mr. Nic STICE

Harding University Main Campus (H)

915 E Market, Searcy AR 72149-0001
County: White　FICE Identification: 001097
Unit ID: 107044
Telephone: (501) 279-4000　Carnegie Class: Master's L
FAX Number: (501) 279-4600　Calendar System: Semester
URL: www.harding.edu
Established: 1924　Annual Undergrad Tuition & Fees: $15,554
Enrollment: 6,810　Coed
Affiliation or Control: Churches Of Christ　IRS Status: 501(c)3
Highest Offering: Doctorate
Program: Occupational; Liberal Arts And General; Teacher Preparatory; Professional
Accreditation: NH, ACBSP, ARCPA, CIDA, DIETD, ENG, MUS, NUR, @PHAR, @PTA, @SP, SW, TED

01 President .... Dr. David B. BURKS
03 Executive Vice President .... Dr. James W. CARR
05 Provost .... Dr. Larry LONG
30 Sr Vice President for Development .... Mr. Floyd DANIEL
10 Vice President Finance .... Mr. Mel SANSOM
44 Vice President Advancement .... Dr. Mike WILLAMS
42 Vice President of Spiritual Life .... Mr. Bruce MCLARTY
07 Assistant Vice President Admissions .... Mr. Glenn DILLARD
06 Registrar .... Mrs. Janice HURD
38 Director of Counseling .... Dr. Lew MOORE
26 Director of Public Relations .... Mr. David CROUCH
37 Director Student Financial Aid .... Mr. Jon ROBERTS
58 Director of Graduate Studies .... Mr. Pat BASHAW
08 Librarian .... Mrs. Ann DIXON
09 Director of Institutional Research .... Dr. Marty SPEARS
18 Chief Facilities/Physical Plant .... Mr. Danny DERAMUS
29 Director Alumni Relations .... Mrs. Liz HOWELL
93 Director of Minority Students .... Dr. Butch GARDNER
15 Director Personnel Services .... Mr. David ROSS
36 Director Student Placement .... Mrs. Deb BASHAW
96 Director of Purchasing .... Vacant
32 Dean of Students/Vice Pres .... Dr. David COLLINS
35 Assistant Dean of Students .... Mr. Zoal NEAL
33 Assistant Dean of Students .... Mr. Stu VARNER
34 Assistant Dean of Students .... Mrs. Sheri SHEARIN
92 Dean of Honors College .... Dr. Warren CASEY
50 Dean School of Business .... Dr. Bryan BURKS
53 Dean School of Education .... Dr. Tony FINLEY
66 Dean School of Nursing .... Dr. Cathleen M. SHULTZ
79 Dean College of Arts & Humanities .... Dr. Warren CASEY
81 Dean College of Sciences .... Dr. Travis THOMPSON
04 Assistant to the President .... Mr. Nate COPELAND

† See Also Affiliate: Harding Graduate School of Religion, TN.

Henderson State University (I)

1100 Henderson Street, Arkadelphia AR 71999-0001
County: Clark　FICE Identification: 001098
Unit ID: 107071
Telephone: (870) 230-5000　Carnegie Class: Master's M
FAX Number: (870) 230-5144　Calendar System: Semester
URL: www.hsu.edu
Established: 1890　Annual Undergrad Tuition & Fees (In-State): $5,688
Enrollment: 3,877　Coed
Affiliation or Control: State　IRS Status: 501(c)3
Highest Offering: Beyond Master's But Less Than Doctorate
Program: Liberal Arts And General; Teacher Preparatory; Professional
Accreditation: NH, BUS, CACREP, DIETD, MUS, NURSE, TED

01 President .... Dr. Charles L. WELCH
05 Provost/Vice Pres Academic Affairs .... Dr. Vernon MILES
10 Vice Pres Finance & Administration .... Mr. Bobby G. JONES
32 Vice President Student Services .... Ms. Gail M. STEPHENS
04 VP Univ/Cmty Rels/Exec Ast to Pres .... Ms. Doris N. WRIGHT
43 General Counsel .... Ms. Elaine KNEEBONE
28 Int Assistant to Pres for Diversity .... Dr. Duane JACKSON
35 Dean of Student Services .... Mr. Chad FIELDING
36 Assoc Dean of Student Services .... Ms. Pam LIGON
13 Director Computer/Communication Svc .... Mr. David H. EPPERHART
30 Director Development .... Mr. Billy TARPLEY
41 Director Athletics .... Mr. T. Kale GOBER
26 Director of Public Relations .... Ms. Penny A. MURPHY
49 Dean Ellis College Arts/Sciences .... Dr. Maralyn T. SOMMER
50 Int Dean of School of Business .... Dr. Carl STARK
53 Dean Teachers College Henderson .... Dr. Judy HARRISON
58 Dean of Graduate School .... Dr. Marck BEGGS
06 Registrar .... Mr. Tom GATTIN
08 Director Huie Library .... Mr. Robert F. YEHL
18 Director Physical Plant .... Mr. John C. CORLEY
15 Director of Human Resources .... Ms. Kathy TAYLOR
19 Director of University Police .... Mr. Jonathan CAMPBELL
38 Director of Counseling .... Ms. Deborah COLLINS
07 Director Univ Relations/Admissions .... Ms. Vikita B. HARDWRICK
37 Director of Financial Aid .... Ms. Vicki TAYLOR
92 Director of Honors College .... Dr. David T. THOMSON
88 Director of Student Research .... Dr. Martin CAMPBELL
96 Director of Purchasing .... Mr. Tim JONES
24 Dir Multi Media Learning Center .... Ms. Jennifer HOLBROOK
39 Director Residence Life .... Mr. Cris MCGOUGH

85 Director International Students .... Dr. Drew SMITH
29 Coordinator of Alumni Services .... Ms. Sherry WRIGHT

Hendrix College (A)

1600 Washington Avenue, Conway AR 72032-3080
County: Faulkner FICE Identification: 001099
Unit ID: 107080
Telephone: (501) 329-6811 Carnegie Class: Bac/A&S
FAX Number: (501) 450-1200 Calendar System: Semester
URL: www.hendrix.edu
Established: 1876 Annual Undergrad Tuition & Fees: $43,944
Enrollment: 1,461 Coed
Affiliation or Control: United Methodist IRS Status: 501(c)3
Highest Offering: Master's
Program: Liberal Arts And General
Accreditation: NH, MUS, TED

01 President .... Dr. J. Timothy CLOYD
04 Executive Assistant to President .... Ms. Donna PLEMMONS
30 Exec Vice Pres/Dean Inst Advance .... Mr. W. Ellis ARNOLD, III
05 Provost .... Dr. Robert L. ENTZMINGER
27 Exec Vice Pres & Chief Communicat .... Mr. Frank COX
10 Executive Vice President and CFO .... Mr. Tom SIEBENMORGEN
45 Exec Vice Pres and Strategic Plng .... Ms. Karen R. FOUST
18 Assoc VP Operations & Facilities .... Mr. Loyd RYAN
32 Vice President Student Affairs .... Dr. Karla CARNEY-HALL
35 Dean of Students .... Dr. James N. WILTGEN, JR.
26 Exec Director of Communications .... Ms. Helen S. PLOTKIN
06 Registrar .... Ms. Xinying WANG
08 Director of Libraries .... Ms. Amanda MOORE
13 Exec Vice Pres & Chief Info Office .... Mr. David J. HINSON
29 Director Alumni Relations .... Ms. Pamela OWEN
37 Director of Financial Aid .... Ms. Kristina BURFORD
40 Bookstore Manager .... Ms. Dee Dee ALLEN
79 Area Head/Humanities .... Dr. Alex VERNONE
81 Area Head/Natural Sciences .... Dr. Carl BURCH
83 Area Head/Social Sciences .... Dr. Allison SHUTT
42 Chaplain .... Rev. Wayne CLARK
07 Director of Admission .... Mr. Fred BAKER
15 Director Personnel Services .... Ms. Vicki LYNN
20 Associate Academic Officer .... Dr. David SUTHERLAND
21 Associate Business Officer .... Mr. Shawn MATHIS
36 Director Career Services .... Ms. Christy COKER
38 Director Student Counseling .... Ms. Mary Anne SIEBERT

ITT Technical Institute (B)

4520 S University Avenue, Little Rock AR 72204-9925
County: Pulaski Identification: 666531
Unit ID: 413839
Telephone: (501) 565-5550 Carnegie Class: Spec/Tech
FAX Number: (501) 565-4747 Calendar System: Quarter
URL: www.itt-tech.edu
Established: 1993 Annual Undergrad Tuition & Fees: N/A
Enrollment: 638 Coed
Affiliation or Control: Proprietary IRS Status: Proprietary
Highest Offering: Baccalaureate
Program: Technical Emphasis
Accreditation: ACICS

† Branch campus of ITT Technical Institute, Thornton, CO.

John Brown University (C)

2000 W University Street, Siloam Springs AR 72761-2121
County: Benton FICE Identification: 001100
Unit ID: 107141
Telephone: (479) 524-9500 Carnegie Class: Bac/Diverse
FAX Number: (479) 524-9548 Calendar System: Semester
URL: www.jbu.edu
Established: 1919 Annual Undergrad Tuition & Fees: $20,766
Enrollment: 2,131 Coed
Affiliation or Control: Independent Non-Profit IRS Status: 501(c)3
Highest Offering: Master's
Program: Liberal Arts And General; Teacher Preparatory
Accreditation: NH, CONST, ENG, IACBE, TED

01 President .... Dr. Charles POLLARD
03 Executive Vice President .... Vacant
10 Vice Pres Finance & Administration .... Mrs. Kim HADLEY
84 Vice Pres Enrollment Management .... Mr. Donald W. CRANDALL
30 Vice Pres of University Advancement .... Dr. Jim KRALL
32 Vice Pres for Student Development .... Dr. Stephen T. BEERS
05 VP Academic Affairs/Dean of Faculty .... Dr. Ed ERICSON, III
88 Dean Degree Completion Program .... Mr. Dan LAMBERT
42 Campus Pastor/Assoc Dean of Stdnts .... Mr. Rod REED
06 Registrar .... Mrs. Rebecca LAMBERT
21 Controller .... Mr. Tom PERRY
13 Chief Information Systems Ofcr .... Mr. Paul NAST
18 Director of Facilities Services .... Mr. Steve BRANKLE
44 Director of Planned Giving .... Mr. Eric GREENHAW
08 Director of Library .... Mrs. Mary HABERMAS
85 Director International Programs .... Mr. Bill STEVENSON
29 Director of Alumni/Parent Relations .... Mr. Jerry ROLLENE
37 Director of Financial Aid .... Mr. Kim ELDRIDGE
41 Athletic Director .... Ms. Robyn DAUGHERTY
38 Director of Counseling .... Dr. Tim DINGER

Lyon College (D)

PO Box 2317, Batesville AR 72503-2317
County: Independence FICE Identification: 001088
Unit ID: 106342
Telephone: (870) 307-7000 Carnegie Class: Bac/A&S
FAX Number: (870) 307-7001 Calendar System: Semester
URL: www.lyon.edu
Established: 1872 Annual Undergrad Tuition & Fees: $22,906
Enrollment: 630 Coed
Affiliation or Control: Presbyterian Church (U.S.A.) IRS Status: 501(c)3
Highest Offering: Baccalaureate
Program: Liberal Arts And General; Teacher Preparatory
Accreditation: NH, TED

01 President .... Dr. Donald V. WEATHERMAN
05 Dean of the Faculty .... Dr. Virginia F. WRAY
10 Vice President Business & Finance .... Mr. Kenneth J. RUETER
11 Vice Pres for Administration .... Mr. David L. HERINGER
32 Vice President Student Life .... Dr. F. Bruce JOHNSTON
06 Registrar/Dir Inst Research/Comm .... Mr. Donald R. TAYLOR
08 Director Library .... Mr. Dean COVINGTON
26 Director Public Relations .... Mr. Bob R. QUALLS
29 Dir Alumni Services & Development .... Ms. Gina GARRETT
15 Director Personnel .... Mrs. Clarinda L. FOOTE
37 Director of Financial Assistance .... Mr. Tommy TUCKER
36 Director Career Development .... Ms. Vicki WEBB
13 Director Information Services .... Mr. Charles NEAL
41 Director of Athletics .... Mr. Kevin JENKINS
42 Chaplain .... Rev. Nancy MCSPADDEN
104 Director Nichols Intl Studies Pgm .... Dr. Virginia F. WRAY
53 Director of Teacher Education .... Dr. Kathy PILLOW-PRICE
07 Director of Admissions .... Mr. Josh MANNING

Mid-South Community College (E)

2000 W Broadway, West Memphis AR 72301-3829
County: Crittenden FICE Identification: 023482
Unit ID: 107318
Telephone: (870) 733-6722 Carnegie Class: Assoc/Pub-S-SC
FAX Number: (870) 733-6799 Calendar System: Semester
URL: www.midsouthcc.edu
Established: 1992 Annual Undergrad Tuition & Fees (In-District): $2,550
Enrollment: 2,340 Coed
Affiliation or Control: State/Local IRS Status: 501(c)3
Highest Offering: Associate Degree
Program: Occupational; 2-Year Principally Bachelor's Creditable
Accreditation: NH

01 President .... Dr. Glen F. FENTER
03 Executive Vice President .... Dr. Barbara C. BAXTER
05 Vice Pres Learning & Instruction .... Ms. Judith SCHERER
10 Vice Pres Finance & Administration .... Mrs. Susan MARSHALL
32 Vice President Student Affairs .... Mr. Dwayne SCOTT
26 Director Marketing/Public Rels .... Mr. Len GRICE
37 Director of Financial Aid .... Ms. LaChelle DAVENPORT
08 Director of Library Media Center .... Ms. Rene JONES
06 Registrar/Dir Institutional Rsrch .... Ms. Leslie ANDERSON
07 Director of Admissions .... Mr. Jeremy REECE
15 Director of Human Resources .... Ms. Jackie BRUBAKER
18 Director Facilities/Physical Plant .... Mr. Randy WEBB
30 Director of Advancement .... Vacant
38 Director of Student Counseling .... Vacant

National Park Community College (F)

101 College Drive,
Hot Springs National Park AR 71913-9174
County: Garland FICE Identification: 012105
Unit ID: 106980
Telephone: (501) 760-4222 Carnegie Class: Assoc/Pub-R-M
FAX Number: (501) 760-4100 Calendar System: Semester
URL: www.npcc.edu
Established: 1973 Annual Undergrad Tuition & Fees (In-District): $2,540
Enrollment: 3,853 Coed
Affiliation or Control: State/Local IRS Status: 501(c)3
Highest Offering: Associate Degree
Program: Occupational; 2-Year Principally Bachelor's Creditable; Technical Emphasis
Accreditation: NH, ADNUR, COE, EMT, MLTAD, RAD

01 President .... Dr. Sally CARDER
05 Exec Vice Pres for Instruction .... Dr. Gordon WATTS
10 Vice President for Business Affairs .... Ms. Janis SAWYER
32 Vice President Student Services .... Ms. Margaret PICKING
72 Assoc Vice Pres Technical Education .... Mr. David HUGHES
04 Assistant to the President .... Dr. Susan ALDRIDGE
20 Assoc Dean for Academic Affairs .... Dr. Brad MOODY
35 Director of Student Affairs .... Ms. Holly GARRETT-MILLER
15 Director of Human Resources .... Ms. Janet BREWER
08 Director of the Library .... Ms. Sara SEAMAN
37 Director of Financial Aid .... Ms. Lisa HOPPER
26 Chief Public Relations Officer .... Ms. Jill JOHNSON
30 Chief Development .... Ms. Lisa CAREY
38 Director Student Counseling .... Mr. Ron CHESSER

North Arkansas College (G)

1515 Pioneer Drive, Harrison AR 72601-5599
County: Boone FICE Identification: 012261
Unit ID: 107460
Telephone: (870) 743-3000 Carnegie Class: Assoc/Pub-R-M
FAX Number: (870) 391-3250 Calendar System: Semester
URL: www.northark.edu
Established: 1974 Annual Undergrad Tuition & Fees (In-District): $1,920
Enrollment: 2,421 Coed
Affiliation or Control: State/Local IRS Status: 501(c)3
Highest Offering: Associate Degree
Program: Occupational; 2-Year Principally Bachelor's Creditable; Nursing Emphasis
Accreditation: NH, @ACBSP, ADNUR, EMT, MLTAD, RAD, SURGT

01 President .... Dr. Jacquelyn ELLIOTT
05 Vice President of Learning .... Dr. Gwen GRESHAM
10 Vice Pres Finance & Administration .... Mr. Donald SUGG
30 Vice Pres Institutional Advancement .... Dr. Jim STOCKTON
31 Executive Director .... Vacant
101 Secretary of the Institution .... Mrs. B.J MARCIL
49 Dean Arts and Science .... Dr. Laura BERRY
50 Dean Business and Tech Programs .... Mr. Ed PROCTOR
66 Dean Allied Health/Nursing .... Mrs. Cindy MAYO
08 Director of Libraries .... Mr. Jim ROBB
44 Director Institutional Advancement .... Mrs. Katherine VAUGHN
88 Title III Director .... Mrs. Cindy MAYO
88 Title III Director .... Mrs. Nell BONDS
41 Athletic Director .... Mr. Jerry THOMASON
15 Director Human Resources .... Mrs. Kris GREENING
18 Chief Facilities/Physical Plant .... Mr. Kevin SOMERS
96 Director of Purchasing .... Mrs. Sandra JONES
37 Director Student Financial Aid .... Mrs. Jennifer HADDOCK
06 Registrar .... Mrs. Charla JENNINGS
07 Director of Admissions .... Vacant
26 Director of Public Relations .... Mrs. Micki SOMERS
90 Director Academic Computing .... Mr. Rick WILLIAMS
91 Director Administrative Computing .... Mr. Glenn COLMAN
103 Director Workforce Development .... Mrs. Amy BELL

NorthWest Arkansas Community College (H)

1 College Drive, Bentonville AR 72712-5091
County: Benton FICE Identification: 030633
Unit ID: 367459
Telephone: (479) 636-9222 Carnegie Class: Assoc/Pub-R-L
FAX Number: (479) 619-4335 Calendar System: Semester
URL: www.nwacc.edu
Established: 1989 Annual Undergrad Tuition & Fees (In-District): $2,748
Enrollment: 8,365 Coed
Affiliation or Control: State/Local IRS Status: 501(c)3
Highest Offering: Associate Degree
Program: Occupational; 2-Year Principally Bachelor's Creditable
Accreditation: NH, EMT, IFSAC, PTAA

01 President .... Dr. Becky PANEITZ
05 Sr Vice Pres Learning/Provost .... Dr. Steve GATES
10 Vice Pres for Finance .... Mr. Marty PARSONS
20 Interim Vice Pres for Learning .... Dr. Marvin GALLOWAY
26 VP for Public Relations/Foundation .... Mr. Wyley ELLIOTT
32 Vice Pres Learner Services .... Mr. Todd KITCHEN
103 Assoc VP Corporate Learning .... Ms. Susan PIKE
91 Assoc VP Information Technology Svc .... Ms. Paige FRANCIS
18 Assoc Vice Pres for Operations .... Mr. Jim HESSLER
25 Assoc Vice Pres Grants/Research .... Dr. Ricky TOMPKINS
20 AVP Global Bus/Computer Information .... Mr. Tim CORNELIUS
88 AVP Ofc Corporate/NonCredit Lrng .... Ms. Renee CAMPBELL
102 Executive Director of Foundation .... Ms. Meredith BRUNEN
88 Exec Director of Public Relations .... Mr. Mark SCOTT
86 Exec Dir Community/Government Rels .... Mr. Jim HALL
21 Director of Accounting .... Mr. John HIXSON
21 Dir of Budget/Analytical Services .... Ms. Gulizar BAGGSON
26 Director of Marketing .... Mr. Rob HANLON
15 Director of Human Resources .... Ms. Wendi CADLE
56 Director of Distance Learning .... Dr. Kate BURKES
50 Exec Dir of Business Development .... Ms. Teresa WHITMIRE
88 Director of Building Sciences .... Mr. Rick MAYES
88 Coordinator Culinary & Hospitality .... Mr. Michael KUEFNER
88 Exec Dir for High School Rels .... Dr. Diana JOHNSON
31 Dean of Community Education .... Mr. Ben ALDAMA
88 Director of Learning Resources .... Ms. Louise LAMB
09 Ex Dir Institutional Effectiveness .... Vacant
06 Registrar .... Ms. Taysha CARTER
07 Director of Admissions .... Vacant
35 Director Student Affairs .... Mr. Dale MONTGOMERY
37 Director Student Financial Aid .... Ms. Michelle CORDELL
38 Director Student Counseling .... Mr. Eric VEST
84 Director Enrollment Management .... Ms. Brooke HOLT
96 Dir Procurement/Disbursement Svcs .... Mr. Jack THOMPSON
51 Business Manager & Continuing Educ .... Vacant
88 Event Coordinator .... Ms. Diane BOSS

Ouachita Baptist University (I)

410 Ouachita Street, Arkadelphia AR 71998-0001
County: Clark FICE Identification: 001102
Unit ID: 107512
Telephone: (870) 245-5000 Carnegie Class: Bac/A&S
FAX Number: (870) 245-5500 Calendar System: Semester
URL: www.obu.edu
Established: 1886 Annual Undergrad Tuition & Fees: $20,630
Enrollment: 1,504 Coed
Affiliation or Control: Southern Baptist IRS Status: 501(c)3
Highest Offering: Baccalaureate
Program: Liberal Arts And General; Teacher Preparatory
Accreditation: NH, BUS, DIETD, MUS, TED

01 President ... Dr. Rex M. HORNE, JR.
44 Vice Pres Institutional Advancement ... Dr. Wesley KLUCK
05 Vice President Academic Affairs ... Dr. Stan POOLE
11 Vice President for Admin Services ... Dr. Brett POWELL
32 Vice President for Student Services ... Dr. Keldon HENLEY
30 Vice President for Development ... Mrs. Terry G. PEEPLES
27 Vice Pres for Communications ... Mr. Trennis HENDERSON
04 Asst to President/Administration ... Mr. Philip W. HARDIN
07 Director of Admissions Counseling ... Mrs. Lori MOTL
09 Director of Institutional Research ... Mr. Phil HARDIN
15 Director of Human Resources ... Mrs. Sherri PHELPS
18 Chief Facilities/Physical Plant ... Mr. John HARDMAN
29 Director of Alumni Relations ... Mrs. Lauren LAND
35 Director of Student Affairs ... Dr. Keldon HENLEY
20 Assoc Vice Pres Academic Affairs ... Dr. Doug REED
26 Vice Pres for Communications ... Mr. Trennis HENDERSON
36 Director of Student Placement ... Mrs. Mallory MODDELMOG
38 University Counselor ... Mr. Dan JARBOE
08 Librarian ... Dr. Ray GRANADE
06 Registrar/Director of Admissions ... Mrs. Judy JONES
37 Director Student Financial Svcs ... Mrs. Susan HURST
96 Director of Purchasing ... Ms. Kim HUNTER
92 Director Honors Program ... Dr. Barbara PEMBERTON
13 Dir Information Technology Services ... Mr. Bill PHELPS
39 Director of Housing ... Ms. Margaret FRAZIER
41 Athletic Director ... Mr. David SHARP
43 General Counsel ... Mr. Bryan MCKINNEY
21 Director of Financial Services ... Mrs. Kim HUNTER
40 Bookstore Manager ... Mrs. Yvonne CLOUD
57 Dean of School of Fine Arts ... Dr. Scott HOLSCLAW
50 Dean of the School of Business ... Mr. Bryan MCKINNEY
53 Dean Sch of Interdisciplinary Stds ... Dr. Stan POOLE
73 Dean School of Christian Studies ... Dr. Danny HAYS
53 Dean School of Education ... Dr. Merribeth BRUNING
79 Dean School of Humanities ... Dr. Jeff ROOT
81 Dean School of Natural Sciences ... Dr. Joe JEFFERS
83 Dean School of Social Sciences ... Dr. Randall WIGHT

Ozarka College (A)

PO Box 10, Melbourne AR 72556-0010
County: Izard — FICE Identification: 020870
Unit ID: 107549
Telephone: (870) 368-7371 — Carnegie Class: Assoc/Pub-R-S
FAX Number: (870) 368-2091 — Calendar System: Semester
URL: www.ozarka.edu
Established: 1991 — Annual Undergrad Tuition & Fees (In-State): $2,720
Enrollment: 1,563 — Coed
Affiliation or Control: State — IRS Status: 501(c)3
Highest Offering: Associate Degree
Program: Occupational; 2-Year Principally Bachelor's Creditable
Accreditation: NH

01 President ... Dr. Richard L. DAWE
05 Vice President Academic Affairs ... Dr. Michael L. DELONG
10 Vice President Finance ... Ms. Tina WHEELIS
32 Vice President of Student Services ... Mr. Ron C. HELM
45 Director Planning/IR ... Mrs. Joan R. STIRLING
13 Director of Information Systems ... Mr. Scott PINKSTON
04 Assistant to the President ... Mrs. Nancy DUST
30 Director of College Advancement ... Ms. Suellen DAVIDSON
29 Development Officer/Dir Alumni Rels ... Vacant
37 Director of Financial Aid ... Ms. Laura LAWRENCE
07 Director of Admissions ... Mrs. Brandy GORE
18 Chief Facilities/Physical Plant ... Mr. Ronny RUSH
06 Registrar ... Mrs. Zeda WILKERSON

Philander Smith College (B)

900 W. Daisy L. Gatson Bates Drive,
Little Rock AR 72202-3799
County: Pulaski — FICE Identification: 001103
Unit ID: 107600
Telephone: (501) 375-9845 — Carnegie Class: Bac/Diverse
FAX Number: (501) 370-5277 — Calendar System: Semester
URL: www.philander.edu
Established: 1877 — Annual Undergrad Tuition & Fees: $11,760
Enrollment: 696 — Coed
Affiliation or Control: United Methodist — IRS Status: 501(c)3
Highest Offering: Baccalaureate
Program: Liberal Arts And General; Teacher Preparatory; Business Emphasis
Accreditation: NH, ACBSP, SW, TED

01 President ... Dr. Walter M. KIMBROUGH
04 Assistant to the President ... Mr. Michael HUTCHINSON
05 Vice President of Academic Affairs ... Dr. Frank R. JAMES
10 Vice President for Fiscal Affairs ... Mr. Terry WALLACE
32 Vice President of Student Affairs ... Dr. Juliana MOSLEY
30 Vice Pres Inst Advancement ... Dr. Shannon FLEMING
43 General Counsel ... Mr. Eric WALKER
06 Registrar ... Ms. Bertha OWENS
42 Chaplain/Dir Ofc Religious Life ... Rev. Ronnie MILLER-YOW
20 Associate Dean of Instruction ... Dr. Jesse HARGROVE
35 Dean of Students/Residential Life ... Mr. Ronnie WILLIAMS
15 Director of Human Resources ... Mrs. Molly GOZA
37 Director of Financial Aid ... Mr. David PAGE
18 Director of Physical Plant ... Mr. Henry JEMISON
26 Director Marketing/Public Relations ... Ms. Sericia COLE
08 Director of the Library ... Ms. Theresa OJEZUA
07 Dir of Admissions/Recruitment ... Mr. George GRAY
29 Director of Alumni Relations ... Ms. Yvonne ALEXANDER

41 Athletic Director ... Mr. James JOHNSON
13 Director Computer Information Sys ... Mr. Ben JOHNSON
09 Director of Institutional Research ... Ms. Beverly RICHARDSON
19 Chief of Security ... Mr. Jack MATLOCK
51 Director of Continuing Education ... Mr. Bruce JAMES
88 Mission Center Director ... Mrs. Cynthia BURROUGHS
38 Director Student Counseling ... Vacant
40 Bookstore Manager ... Mrs. Veda MAXWELL
17 Nurse ... Ms. Christal WALLER
36 Career Counseling/Placement Coord ... Ms. Rhonda LOVELACE
49 Int Division Chair Natural Sciences ... Ms. Anjela DANIELS
50 Division Chair of Business ... Dr. Adrian PRICE
53 Division Chair of Education ... Dr. Jesse HARGROVE
70 Director of Social Work ... Ms. Angela SANDERS
79 Chair Division of Humanities ... Dr. James RUSH
83 Chair Div of Social Sciences ... Dr. Raphael LEWIS

Pulaski Technical College (C)

3000 W Scenic Drive, North Little Rock AR 72118-3399
County: Pulaski — FICE Identification: 020753
Unit ID: 107664
Telephone: (501) 812-2200 — Carnegie Class: Assoc/Pub-U-SC
FAX Number: (501) 771-2844 — Calendar System: Semester
URL: www.pulaskitech.edu
Established: 1991 — Annual Undergrad Tuition & Fees (In-State): $3,000
Enrollment: 11,206 — Coed
Affiliation or Control: State — IRS Status: 501(c)3
Highest Offering: Associate Degree
Program: Occupational; 2-Year Principally Bachelor's Creditable; Technical Emphasis
Accreditation: NH, ACFEI, DA, OTA

01 President ... Dr. Dan F. BAKKE
05 Vice President for Instruction ... Mr. Augusta FARVER
32 Vice President for Student Services ... Ms. Cindy HARKEY
10 Vice President for Finance ... Ms. Patricia PALMER
30 Vice President College Advancement ... Ms. Carol LANGSTON
88 VP for Economic Development ... Ms. Mary Ann SHOPE
44 Chief Development Officer ... Ms. Joyce TAYLOR
84 Dean Enrollment Svcs ... Ms. Beth TRAFFORD
07 Director of Admissions ... Mr. Clark ATKINS
38 Director of Counseling/Advising ... Ms. Lisa FISHER
08 Library Director ... Ms. Wendy DAVIS
18 Director of Physical Plant ... Mr. Stuart SMITH
09 Director of Institutional Research ... Ms. Tara SMITH
96 Director of Purchasing ... Mr. Tim WALBERT
13 Chief Information Officer ... Mr. David HARRIS
15 Director of Human Resources ... Mr. Essie CLEVELAND
04 Assistant to the President ... Ms. Tena CARRIGAN
37 Director of Financial Aid ... Ms. Lavonne JUHL
26 Dir of Public Relations/Marketing ... Mr. Tim JONES
72 Dean Technical Education Division ... Mr. Mike SNEED
81 Dean Mathematics/Nat Social Scis ... Mr. Ben RAINS
50 Dean Business Division ... Ms. Christy SHERRILL
88 Dean Information Technology Div ... Mr. David DURR
57 Dean Fine Arts & Humanities ... Mr. Joey COLE
06 Registrar ... Ms. Virginia PEYTON
76 Dean Allied Health/Human Services ... Ms. Pam CICIRELLO

Remington College-Little Rock (D)

19 Remington Drive, Little Rock AR 72204-8202
County: Pulaski — Identification: 666286
Unit ID: 438869
Telephone: (501) 312-0007 — Carnegie Class: Assoc/PrivFP
FAX Number: (501) 225-3819 — Calendar System: Quarter
URL: www.remingtoncollege.edu
Established: 1998 — Annual Undergrad Tuition & Fees: $14,745
Enrollment: 391 — Coed
Affiliation or Control: Proprietary — IRS Status: Proprietary
Highest Offering: Associate Degree
Program: Occupational
Accreditation: ACCSC

01 President ... Mr. Randall HAYES
05 Director of Education ... Mr. Jonathan PORTER

† Branch campus of Remington College, Mobile, AL.

Rich Mountain Community College (E)

1100 College Drive, Mena AR 71953-2500
County: Polk — FICE Identification: 021111
Unit ID: 107743
Telephone: (479) 394-7622 — Carnegie Class: Assoc/Pub-R-S
FAX Number: (479) 394-7295 — Calendar System: Semester
URL: www.rmcc.edu
Established: 1983 — Annual Undergrad Tuition & Fees (In-District): $2,040
Enrollment: 1,116 — Coed
Affiliation or Control: State/Local — IRS Status: 501(c)3
Highest Offering: Associate Degree
Program: Occupational; 2-Year Principally Bachelor's Creditable
Accreditation: NH

01 Interim President ... Dr. Steve ROOK
05 Vice Pres Academic Affairs ... Dr. Steve ROOK
32 Vice Pres Student Affairs/Registrar ... Mr. Phillip WILSON
10 VP Administration/CFO ... Ms. Brenda GILLOGLY
13 Dir of Information Technology ... Mr. J. Mark BARTON
08 Director Library Services ... Ms. Mary SHEAHAN
37 Financial Aid Director ... Ms. Mary STANDERFER
30 Director of Development ... Ms. Jaclyn KEETER
18 Director of Physical Plant ... Mr. Steve WILLSON
53 Director of Adult Basic Education ... Ms. Julie BLACK
09 Director of Institutional Research ... Vacant
15 Director of Human Resources ... Vacant
07 Director of Admissions ... Ms. Tammy YOUNG
21 Controller ... Ms. Patricia HALL
26 Chief Public Relations Officer ... Ms. Judi WHITE
40 Bookstore Manager ... Mr. Andrew MATTHEWS
21 Fiscal Project Coordinator ... Ms. Amy TILLEY

Shorter College (F)

604 Locus Street, North Little Rock AR 72114
County: Pulaski — Identification: 667054
Telephone: (501) 374-6305 — Carnegie Class: Not Classified
FAX Number: (501) 374-9333 — Calendar System: Semester
URL: www.shorterjrcollege.com
Established: 1886 — Annual Undergrad Tuition & Fees: N/A
Enrollment: N/A — Coed
Affiliation or Control: African Methodist Episcopal — IRS Status: 501(c)3
Highest Offering: Associate Degree
Program: Occupational; 2-Year Principally Bachelor's Creditable
Accreditation: @TRACS

01 President ... Dr. Katherine MITCHELL

South Arkansas Community College (G)

300 S West Avenue, PO Box 7010,
El Dorado AR 71731-7010
County: Union — FICE Identification: 020746
Unit ID: 107974
Telephone: (870) 862-8131 — Carnegie Class: Assoc/Pub-R-S
FAX Number: (870) 864-7190 — Calendar System: Semester
URL: www.southark.edu
Established: 1992 — Annual Undergrad Tuition & Fees (In-State): $3,460
Enrollment: 1,781 — Coed
Affiliation or Control: State — IRS Status: 501(c)3
Highest Offering: Associate Degree
Program: Occupational; 2-Year Principally Bachelor's Creditable
Accreditation: NH, EMT, OTA, PTAA, RAD, SURGT

01 President ... Dr. Barbara JONES
05 VP of Academic Learning ... Dr. Valeriano CANTU
10 Vice President for Fiscal Affairs ... Mr. Lathan HAIRSTON
32 Vice Pres of Student Services ... Dr. Curtis HILL
84 Dean of Enrollment Services ... Mr. Dean INMAN
08 Director Library Media Center ... Mrs. Francis KUYKENDALL
31 Dean & Dir Corporate/Community Educ ... Ms. Lynda RICHARDSON
37 Director of Financial Aid ... Ms. Veronda TATUM
04 Admin Assistant to the President ... Ms. Susan JORDAN
26 Chief Information Officer ... Dr. Tim KIRK
27 Public Information Officer ... Mr. Heath WALDROP
15 Director Personnel Services ... Mrs. Becky RIGGS
18 Chief Facilities/Physical Plant ... Vacant
30 Institutional Advance/Foundation ... Ms. Cynthia REYNA
09 Director of Institutional Research ... Dr. Stephanie TULLY-DARTEZ
96 Director of Purchasing ... Ms. Ann SOUTHALL
07 Publicity & Student Recruitment ... Mr. Randy JERRY
49 Dean of Liberal Arts ... Mr. Phillip BALLARD
76 Dean Health/Natural Sciences ... Dr. George ROBERTS
50 Dean Business/Technical Education ... Mr. Jim ROOMSBURG

Southeast Arkansas College (H)

1900 Hazel Street, Pine Bluff AR 71603-3900
County: Jefferson — FICE Identification: 005707
Unit ID: 107637
Telephone: (870) 543-5900 — Carnegie Class: Assoc/Pub-R-M
FAX Number: (870) 543-5927 — Calendar System: Semester
URL: www.seark.edu
Established: 1991 — Annual Undergrad Tuition & Fees (In-State): $2,700
Enrollment: 2,190 — Coed
Affiliation or Control: State — IRS Status: 501(c)3
Highest Offering: Associate Degree
Program: Occupational; 2-Year Principally Bachelor's Creditable; Technical Emphasis
Accreditation: NH, ADNUR, EMT, RAD, SURGT

01 President ... Dr. Stephen HILTERBRAN
05 Vice President Academic Affairs ... Ms. Linda E. LEWIS
32 Vice President Student Affairs ... Ms. Linda E. LEWIS
10 Vice President Financial Affairs ... Ms. Debbie WALLACE
76 VP Assessment/Nursing/Allied Health ... Ms. Diann W. WILLIAMS
30 VP College Affairs/Advancement ... Dr. Kaleybra M. MOREHEAD
21 Controller ... Ms. Stephanie SMITH-BROWN
13 Director of Technology Services ... Ms. JoAnn DUPRA
06 Registrar ... Ms. Laqueta HILL
07 Director of Admissions ... Ms. Barbara DUNN
15 Director of Personnel Services ... Ms. Dena CHILDS
18 Chief Facilities/Physical Plant ... Mr. David BRADFORD
28 Director of Diversity ... Dr. Kaleybra MOREHEAD
29 Dir Alumni Relations/Development ... Dr. Kaleybra MOREHEAD
37 Director Student Financial Aid ... Ms. Donna COX

Southern Arkansas University (I)

100 E University Street, Magnolia AR 71753-5000
County: Columbia — FICE Identification: 001107
Unit ID: 107983

Telephone: (870) 235-4000 Carnegie Class: Master's M
FAX Number: (870) 235-5005 Calendar System: Semester
URL: www.saumag.edu
Established: 1909 Annual Undergrad Tuition & Fees (In-State): $5,580
Enrollment: 3,379 Coed
Affiliation or Control: State IRS Status: 501(c)3
Highest Offering: Master's
Program: Liberal Arts And General; Teacher Preparatory; Professional
Accreditation: NH, ADNUR, BUS, MUS, NUR, SW, TED

01 President .... Dr. David F. RANKIN
05 Vice President Academic Affairs .... Dr. David L. CROUSE
11 VP Administration/General Counsel .... Mr. Roger W. GILES
32 Vice President Student Affairs .... Dr. Donna Y. ALLEN
18 Vice President of Facilities .... Mr. C. Jasper LEWIS
10 Vice President for Finance .... Mr. Darrell R. MORRISON
49 Dean Col Liberal/Perform Arts .... Dr. Trey BERRY
50 Dean College of Business .... Dr. Lisa C. TOMS
53 Dean College of Education .... Dr. Zaidy MOHDZAIN
72 Dean College of Sci & Technology .... Dr. Scott MCKAY
58 Dean School of Graduate Studies .... Dr. Kim K. BLOSS
06 Registrar .... Dr. G. Edward NIPPER
84 Dean Enrollment Services .... Ms. Sarah E. JENNINGS
08 Director of Library .... Mr. Daniel R. PAGE
14 Director Info Technology Services .... Mr. Mike A. ARGO
38 Director Counsel/Testing Center .... Ms. Paula WASHINGTON-WOODS
35 Interim Dean of Students .... Ms. Sandra E. SMITH
29 Director of Alumni Affairs .... Ms. Ceil L. BRIDGES
30 Director of Development .... Ms. Jeanie BISMARK
37 Director of Financial Aid .... Ms. Bronwyn C. SNEED
51 Director of Continuing Education .... Ms. Sandra L. WALKER
41 Director of Athletics .... Mr. Jay D. ADCOX
88 Director Student Support Services .... Ms. Eunice E. WALKER
36 Director of Placement Services .... Ms. Wilma L. WILLIAMS
27 Director of Communications Center .... Mr. Aaron J. STREET
28 Director of Diversity .... Mr. Cledis D. STUART
21 Coordinator of Fringe Benefits .... Mr. D. Alan DAVIS

Southern Arkansas University Tech (A)

6415 Spellman Road, Camden AR 71701
County: Calhoun FICE Identification: 007738
Unit ID: 107992
Telephone: (870) 574-4500 Carnegie Class: Assoc/Pub2in4
FAX Number: (870) 574-4520 Calendar System: Semester
URL: www.sautech.edu
Established: 1967 Annual Undergrad Tuition & Fees (In-State): $3,420
Enrollment: 1,996 Coed
Affiliation or Control: State IRS Status: 501(c)3
Highest Offering: Associate Degree
Program: Occupational; 2-Year Principally Bachelor's Creditable
Accreditation: NH

01 Chancellor .... Dr. Corbet J. LAMKIN
05 VC for Academic Affairs .... Mr. Gary ODEN
10 VC for Finance & Administration .... Mrs. Gaye MANNING
56 VC for Extended Education .... Mr. Robert GUNNELS
32 VC for Student Services .... Dr. Reginald COOPER
13 VC for Information Technology .... Mrs. Valerie WILSON
26 Director of Communications .... Mrs. Kim COKER
09 Director of Research .... Mr. Lee SANDERS
84 Director of Enrollment Services .... Mrs. Patricia SINDLE
103 Director of Career Pathways .... Vacant
31 Director of SCES .... Mr. Robert WHITE
75 Director of B & I Training .... Mr. Mike BASHFORD
88 Director of Career Academy .... Mr. Terry STARKEY
88 Director of AETA .... Mr. Randy HARPER
88 Director of AFTA .... Mrs. Rachel NIX
14 Director of IIS .... Mrs. Laura JOHNSON
37 Director of Financial Aid .... Mr. Jeff JEFFERSON
18 Director of Physical Plant .... Mr. Gerald MANNING
35 Director of Student Life .... Mr. David MCLEANE
06 Registrar .... Mr. Wayne BANKS
08 Director of LRC .... Ms. Allison MALONE
76 Dept Chair Allied Health .... Mrs. Julia SMITH
04 Assistant to the Chancellor .... Mrs. Paula BERGSTROM
15 Human Resources Director .... Mrs. Olivia CLACK
21 Controller .... Mr. Dale TOMMEY
45 Chief PAD Officer .... Dr. Diane ATCHISON
39 Residential Advisor .... Mrs. Angela AMIDAN
96 Buyer/Bookstore Manager .... Mrs. Sonya HOLLIS
43 Legal Counsel .... Ms. Mary THOMASON
51 Director of Adult Education .... Mrs. Barbara HAMILTON

*University of Arkansas System Office (B)

2404 N University Avenue, Little Rock AR 72207-3608
County: Pulaski FICE Identification: 008008
Unit ID: 108056
Telephone: (501) 686-2500 Carnegie Class: N/A
FAX Number: (501) 686-2507
URL: www.uasys.edu

01 President .... Dr. B. Alan SUGG
04 Assistant to the President .... Ms. Angela HUDSON
05 Vice President Academic Affairs .... Dr. Daniel E. FERRITOR
10 Vice President for Finance .... Ms. Barbara GOSWICK
11 Vice President for Administration .... Ms. Ann KEMP
26 Vice President University Relations .... Ms. Melissa RUST
47 Vice President Agriculture .... Dr. Mark J. COCHRAN
43 General Counsel .... Mr. Fred H. HARRISON
88 Director Internal Audit .... Mr. Jacob W. FLOURNOY
21 Assoc Vice President for Finance .... Ms. Rita FLEMING

*University of Arkansas Main Campus (C)

Fayetteville AR 72701-1201
County: Washington FICE Identification: 001108
Unit ID: 106397
Telephone: (479) 575-2000 Carnegie Class: RU/VH
FAX Number: (479) 575-2361 Calendar System: Semester
URL: www.uark.edu
Established: 1871 Annual Undergrad Tuition & Fees (In-State): $7,174
Enrollment: 21,405 Coed
Affiliation or Control: State IRS Status: 501(c)3
Highest Offering: Doctorate
Program: Liberal Arts And General; Teacher Preparatory; Professional
Accreditation: NH, AAFCS, BUS, BUSA, CACREP, CEA, CIDA, CLPSY, CORE, CS, DIETD, ENG, JOUR, LAW, LSAR, MUS, NURSE, SP, SW, TED

02 Chancellor .... Dr. G. David GEARHART
04 Executive Asst to the Chancellor .... Ms. Gloria SUTHERLAND
05 Provost & Vice Chanc Academic Affs .... Dr. Sharon GABER
10 Vice Chanc Finance & Administration .... Dr. Donald O. PEDERSON
30 Vice Chanc University Advancement .... Mr. Brad E. CHOATE
86 Vice Chanc Govt & Cmty Relations .... Mr. Richard B. HUDSON
09 Vice Provost Planning/Dir Inst Res .... Dr. Kathy M. VAN LANINGHAM
46 Vice Provost Research/Econ Dev .... Dr. James M. RANKIN
35 Vice Prov Stdnt Affs/Dean Students .... Dr. Daniel PUGH
28 Vice Provost for Diversity .... Mr. Charles ROBINSON
84 Vice Prov Enrol Mgt/Dean Admissions .... Dr. Suzanne MCCRAY
26 Assoc Vice Chanc Univ Relations .... Mr. John N. DIAMOND
15 Assoc Vice Chanc Human Resources .... Ms. Debbie MCLOUD
18 Assoc Vice Chanc Facilities Mgmt .... Mr. Mike JOHNSON
21 Assoc Vice Chanc Business Affairs .... Mr. David O. MARTINSON
08 Dean of Libraries .... Ms. Carolyn H. ALLEN
49 Dean of Arts & Sciences .... Dr. Robin ROBERTS
50 Dean Sam Walton College of Business .... Dr. Dan L. WORRELL
47 Dean of Agriculture .... Dr. Michael E. VAYDA
53 Dean Education/Health Professions .... Dr. Tom SMITH
48 Dean of Architecture .... Mr. Jeff SHANNON
51 Interim Dean of Graduate School .... Dr. Todd SHIELDS
54 Dean of Engineering .... Dr. Ashok SAXENA
92 Dean Honors College .... Dr. Robert MCMATH
61 Dean of the Law School .... Ms. Cynthia E. NANCE
29 Executive Director of Alumni Assoc .... Mr. Mike D. MACECHKO
22 Director of Affirmative Action .... Mr. Willyerd R. COLLIER
37 Director of Financial Aid .... Ms. Kattie WING
38 Dir of Counseling/Psych Services .... Dr. Jonathan C. PERRY
25 Director Research & Sponsored Pgms .... Ms. Rosemary H. RUFF
19 Director University Police .... Mr. Steve GAHAGANS
36 Dir of Career Development Center .... Ms. Barbara BATSON
14 Director of Computing Services .... Mr. Robert E. ZIMMERMAN
06 Registrar .... Mr. Dave DAWSON
96 Director of Purchasing .... Ms. Linda FAST
58 Director Graduate & Intl Admissions .... Ms. Lynn MOSESSO

*University of Arkansas at Fort Smith (D)

PO Box 3649, Fort Smith AR 72913-3649
County: Sebastian FICE Identification: 001110
Unit ID: 108092
Telephone: (479) 788-7000 Carnegie Class: Bac/Assoc
FAX Number: (479) 788-7003 Calendar System: Semester
URL: www.uafortsmith.edu
Established: 1928 Annual Undergrad Tuition & Fees (In-District): $5,267
Enrollment: 7,716 Coed
Affiliation or Control: State/Local IRS Status: 501(c)3
Highest Offering: Baccalaureate
Program: Occupational; Liberal Arts And General; Teacher Preparatory
Accreditation: NH, ADNUR, DH, DMS, MUS, NAIT, NUR, RAD, SURGT, TED

02 Chancellor .... Dr. Paul B. BERAN
05 Provost and Sr Vice Chancellor .... Dr. Ray WALLACE
04 Vice Chancellor Univ Relations .... Dr. Arleene BREAUX
30 Vice Chancellor Univ Advancement .... Dr. Marta LOYD
10 Vice Chanc Finance & Administration .... Mr. Mark HORN
32 Vice Chancellor Student Affairs .... Dr. Lee KREHBIEL
11 Vice Chanc for Operations .... Dr. Kyle PARKER
20 Assoc Provost Academic Affairs .... Dr. Brenda MITCHELL
31 Assoc Vice Chanc Campus/Cmty Events .... Mr. Stacey JONES
79 Dean Col Humanities/Social Sci .... Dr. Henry RINNE
76 Dean College of Health Sciences .... Dr. Carolyn MOSLEY
53 Dean College of Education .... Dr. John R. JONES
50 Dean College of Business .... Dr. Steve WILLIAMS
72 Dean Col Applied Science/Technology .... Dr. Georgia HALE
72 Dean Col Sci/Tech/Engineering/Math .... Dr. Mark ARANT
60 Dean Col of Languages/Communication .... Dr. Joe HARDIN
88 Dean Student Success .... Ms. Diana ROWDEN
84 Dean of Enrollment Management .... Ms. Penny PENDLETON
16 Dir Human Resources/EEO Officer .... Ms. Bev MCCLENDON
51 Director of Lifelong Learning .... Mr. Jeff ADAMS
12 Dir Western Arkansas Tech Ctr .... Dr. Darrel C. RINK
45 Ex Dir Institutional Effectiveness .... Mr. Darin DOUBRAVA
36 Exec Director Career Services .... Mr. Pat WIDDERS
88 Exec Dir of International Relations .... Mr. Takeo SUZUKI
88 Director of Instructional Devel .... Vacant
06 Registrar .... Mr. Wayne WOMACK
08 Director of Library Services .... Vacant
39 Interim Director of Student Housing .... Ms. Beth EPPINGER
37 Director Student Financial Aid .... Mr. Alan PIXLEY
38 Director of Advisement .... Ms. Julie MOSLEY
36 Director of Career Services .... Mr. Ron ORICK
29 Director of Alumni Affairs .... Ms. Elizabeth UNDERWOOD
07 Director of Admissions .... Mr. Mark LLOYD
26 Director Marketing & Communications .... Mr. Jeff HARMON
41 Director of Athletics .... Mr. Dustin SMITH
27 Director of Public Information .... Ms. Sondra LAMAR
18 Director of Plant Operations .... Mr. Danny COWART
21 Interim Controller .... Mr. Robert WILSON
96 Director of Business Services .... Ms. Debbie BREEDLOVE

*University of Arkansas at Little Rock (E)

2801 S University Avenue, Little Rock AR 72204-1099
County: Pulaski FICE Identification: 001101
Unit ID: 106245
Telephone: (501) 569-3000 Carnegie Class: DRU
FAX Number: (501) 569-8915 Calendar System: Semester
URL: www.ualr.edu
Established: 1927 Annual Undergrad Tuition & Fees (In-State): $6,642
Enrollment: 13,176 Coed
Affiliation or Control: State IRS Status: 501(c)3
Highest Offering: Doctorate
Program: Occupational; Liberal Arts And General; Teacher Preparatory; Professional
Accreditation: NH, ADNUR, ART, AUD, BUS, CONST, CORE, CS, ENG, ENGT, LAW, MUS, NUR, RADDOS, SP, SPAA, SW, TED, THEA

02 Chancellor .... Dr. Joel E. ANDERSON
05 Provost & VC Academic Affairs .... Dr. Sandra L. ROBERSTSON
32 Vice Chanc Education/Student Svcs .... Dr. Charles W. DONALDSON
10 Vice Chanc Finance & Administration .... Dr. Robert H. ADAMS
44 Vice Chanc University Advancement .... Mr. Bill M. WALKER
58 Vice Prov Rsrch/Dn Grad School .... Dr. Patrick J. PELLICANE
13 Vice Chanc Information Services .... Ms. Jeannie WINSTON
100 Chief of Staff/Director of Budget .... Dr. Sandra L. ROBERTSON
11 Assoc Vice Chanc Facilities Mgt .... Mr. David MILLAY
21 Associate Vice Chancellor Finance .... Mr. Steven J. MCCLELLAN
30 Executive Director Development .... Mr. Bob G. DENMAN
88 Assoc Vice Chanc for Advancement .... Ms. Joni C. LEE
35 Div Chief Student Dev/Dean Students .... Vacant
84 Div Chief Enrollment Plng/Registrar .... Mr. Charles DONALDSON
06 Registrar Records & Registration .... Ms. Joyce HALL
15 Director of Human Resource Devel .... Ms. Annette MURDOCK-TANGYE
21 Director of Financial Services .... Ms. Stacey L. HOGUE
18 Director of Physical Plant .... Mr. David L. MILLAY
80 Director Arkansas Institute of Govt .... Dr. Roby D. ROBERTSON
88 Director Ark Institute Econ Advance .... Mr. Jim L. YOUNGQUIST
27 Director of Communications .... Ms. Judy G. WILLIAMS
09 Director Institutional Research .... Ms. Rita M. STERLING
08 Director of the Library .... Ms. Wanda DOLE
19 Director of Public Safety .... Mr. Brad KING
40 Director of Bookstore .... Ms. Brenda R. THOMAS
46 Director of Research/Sponsored Pgms .... Mr. Allen D. STANLEY
37 Director Financial Aid .... Ms. Tammy HARRISON
41 Director of Athletics .... Mr. Chris PETERSON
29 Director of Alumni Relations .... Mr. Christopher O'NEAL
36 Director of Student Placement .... Vacant
07 Director of Admissions .... Ms. Tammy HARRISON
38 Director Student Counseling .... Vacant
96 Director of Purchasing .... Mr. J. D. LOCHALA
20 Associate Academic Officer .... Dr. Christina S. DRALE
20 Associate Academic Officer .... Dr. Karen J. WHEELER
50 Dean of Business Administration .... Dr. Anthony F. CHELTE
53 Dean of Education .... Dr. Angela M. SEWALL
79 Dean Arts/Human/Social Science .... Dr. Deborah J. BALDWIN
54 Dean of Eng & Information Technolog .... Dr. Eric SANDGREN
81 Dean of Science & Mathematics .... Dr. Michael GEALT
61 Dean of Bowen School of Law .... Mr. John M. DIPIPPA
107 Dean of Professional Studies .... Dr. Angela L. BRENTON
26 Chief Public Relations Officer .... Ms. Judy G. WILLIAMS
28 Director of Diversity .... Ms. Adjoa A. AIYETORO

*University of Arkansas for Medical Sciences (F)

4301 W Markham, Little Rock AR 72205-7199
County: Pulaski FICE Identification: 001109
Unit ID: 106263
Telephone: (501) 686-5000 Carnegie Class: Spec/Med
FAX Number: (501) 686-5905 Calendar System: Semester
URL: www.uams.edu
Established: 1879 Annual Undergrad Tuition & Fees (In-State): $6,826
Enrollment: 2,836 Coed
Affiliation or Control: State IRS Status: 501(c)3
Highest Offering: Doctorate
Program: Occupational; 2-Year Principally Bachelor's Creditable; Liberal Arts And General; Professional
Accreditation: NH, CYTO, DH, DIETI, DMS, EMT, HSA, IPSY, MED, MT, NMT, NURSE, PH, PHAR, RAD, SURGT

02 Chancellor .... Dr. Daniel RAHN
05 Vice Chancellor Academic Affairs .... Dr. Larry MILNE
10 Vice Chancellor Finance & CEO .... Mrs. Melony GOODHAND

26 Vice Chancellor Communications ... Ms. Pat TORVESTAD
30 Vice Chancellor Development ... Dr. Kent WESTBROOK
11 Vice Chancellor Campus Operations ... Mr. Mark KENNEDAY
08 Director of Library ... Ms. Mary RYAN
27 Chief Information Officer ... Mr. David MILLER
15 Director Human Resources ... Mr. Hosea LONG
37 Director Financial Services ... Ms. Gloria KEMP
63 Dean College of Medicine ... Dr. Debra H. FISER
76 Dean Col Health Related Professions ... Dr. Douglas MURPHY
66 Dean College of Nursing ... Dr. Lorraine FRAZIER
67 Dean College of Pharmacy ... Dr. Stephanie F. GARDNER
58 Dean of the Graduate School ... Dr. Robert E. MCGEHEE, JR.

*University of Arkansas at Monticello (A)

346 University Drive, Monticello AR 71656-3596
County: Drew   FICE Identification: 001085
Unit ID: 106485
Telephone: (870) 367-6811   Carnegie Class: Master's S
FAX Number: (870) 460-1321   Calendar System: Semester
URL: www.uamont.edu
Established: 1909   Annual Undergrad Tuition & Fees (In-State): $5,290
Enrollment: 3,638   Coed
Affiliation or Control: State   IRS Status: 501(c)3
Highest Offering: Master's
Program: Occupational; 2-Year Principally Bachelor's Creditable; Liberal Arts And General; Teacher Preparatory
Accreditation: NH, COE, EMT, FOR, MUS, NUR, SW, TED

02 Chancellor ... Dr. Jack LASSITER
05 Provost/Vice Chanc for Acad Affs ... Mr. David RAY
10 Vice Chanc Finance & Administration ... Mr. Jay JONES
30 Vice Chanc Advancement/Univ Rels ... Dr. Clay BROWN
32 Vice Chanc Student Affairs ... Mr. Jay HUGHES
12 Vice Chanc UAM Col of Tech Crossett ... Ms. Linda RUSHING
12 Vice Chanc UAM Col of Tech McGehee ... Mr. Bob WARE
20 Assoc Vice Chanc Academic Affs ... Dr. Ranelle EUBANKS
06 Assc Vice Chanc Acad Affs/Registrar ... Dr. Debbie BRYANT
09 Director of Institutional Research ... Dr. Debbie BRYANT
07 Director of Admissions ... Mrs. Mary WHITING
84 Director of Enrollment Mgmt ... Mrs. Mary WHITING
08 Director of Library ... Ms. Sandra CAMPBELL
13 Director Information Technology ... Mr. Bobby HOYLE
26 Director of Media Services ... Mr. James L. BREWER
37 Director of Financial Aid ... Mrs. Susan BREWER
21 Assoc VC for Finance ... Mrs. Debbie GASAWAY
18 Chief Facilities/Physical Plant ... Mr. Jim HUDGINS
38 Dir Counseling/Testing Services ... Ms. Laura HUGHES
96 Director of Purchasing ... Mrs. Gay PACE
29 Director of Alumni Affairs ... Mr. Colt ROAN
35 Dean of Students/Dir Govt Relations ... Mr. Scott KUTTENKULER

*University of Arkansas at Pine Bluff (B)

1200 N University Drive, Pine Bluff AR 71601-2799
County: Jefferson   FICE Identification: 001086
Unit ID: 106412
Telephone: (870) 575-8000   Carnegie Class: Bac/Diverse
FAX Number: (870) 543-8009   Calendar System: Semester
URL: www.uapb.edu
Established: 1873   Annual Undergrad Tuition & Fees (In-State): $4,990
Enrollment: 3,792   Coed
Affiliation or Control: State   IRS Status: 501(c)3
Highest Offering: Master's
Program: Liberal Arts And General; Teacher Preparatory; Professional
Accreditation: NH, AAFCS, ART, @DIETD, MUS, NAIT, NUR, SW, TED

02 Chancellor ... Dr. Lawrence A. DAVIS, JR.
04 Assistant to the Chancellor ... Mrs. Liz F. STRICKLAND
05 Vice Chancellor Academic Affairs ... Dr. Mary E. BENJAMIN
10 Vice Chanc Finance & Admin ... Ms. Pauline THOMAS
30 Director of Development ... Mrs. Margaret MARTIN-HALL
20 Associate Academic Officer ... Dr. Verma JONES
08 Librarian ... Mr. Edward J. FONTENETTE
91 Director of Technical Services ... Mrs. Willette TOTTEN
37 Director of Financial Aid ... Mrs. Janice KEARNEY
09 Director of Institutional Research ... Mrs. Margaret TAYLOR
15 Director Human Resources ... Ms. Gladys BENFORD
36 Director Career Services/Admissions ... Mrs. Mary JONES
26 Director Public Relations/Info ... Mrs. Tisha ARNOLD
35 Dir Student Life/Enrollment Mgmt ... Mr. Leon CRUMBLIN
38 Director Student Counseling ... Ms. Joyce VAUGHN
06 Registrar ... Mrs. Erica FULTON
19 Chief of Police ... Mr. Maxcie THOMAS
18 Chief Facilities/Physical Plant ... Mr. Russell WILLS
29 Director of Alumni Affairs ... Mr. John KUYKENDALL
96 Director of Purchasing ... Mrs. A. Kay TURNER
32 Admin Coordinator Student Affairs ... Mr. Elbert BENNETT
47 Int Dean Agricult/Fisheries/Hum Sci ... Dr. James GARNER
49 Interim Dean Arts & Sciences ... Dr. Yolanda PAGE
53 Dean School of Education ... Dr. Calvin JOHNSON
51 Dean Continuing Education ... Dr. Alfred ARRINGTON
50 Dean School of Business/Management ... Dr. Carla MARTIN
92 Dean Honors College ... Dr. Carolyn F. BLAKELY

*Cossatot Community College of the University of Arkansas (C)

183 College Drive, PO Box 960, De Queen AR 71832-0960
County: Sevier   FICE Identification: 022209
Unit ID: 106795
Telephone: (870) 584-4471   Carnegie Class: Assoc/Pub2in4
FAX Number: (870) 642-3320   Calendar System: Semester
URL: cccua.edu
Established: 1991   Annual Undergrad Tuition & Fees (In-District): $1,978
Enrollment: 1,465   Coed
Affiliation or Control: State/Local   IRS Status: 501(c)3
Highest Offering: Associate Degree
Program: Occupational; 2-Year Principally Bachelor's Creditable
Accreditation: NH, ACBSP

02 Chancellor ... Mr. Steve COLE
05 Vice Chancellor of Academics ... Mrs. Maria PARKER
45 VC of Planning and Facilities ... Mr. Mike KINKADE
10 Vice Chancellor Business/Finance ... Mrs. Charlotte JOHNSON
30 Exec Director Inst Advancement ... Vacant
32 Director of Student Services ... Mr. Shaun CLARK
37 Director Student Financial Aid ... Mrs. Denise HAMMOND
26 Director of Marketing ... Ms. Alisha LEWIS
09 Director of Inst Research/Registrar ... Mrs. Brenda MORRIS
103 Dir of Public Svc/Workforce Dev ... Mrs. Tammy COLEMAN
12 Dean of Ashdown Campus ... Mr. Milton HIGGINBOTHAM
15 Director of Human Resources ... Mrs. Lilly BELL-JOHNSON
25 Director of Grants ... Mr. Mark RILEY
13 Information Manager ... Mr. David BLACKWELL

*Phillips Community College of the University of Arkansas (D)

PO Box 785, Helena AR 72342-0785
County: Phillips   FICE Identification: 001104
Unit ID: 107619
Telephone: (870) 338-6474   Carnegie Class: Assoc/Pub2in4
FAX Number: (870) 338-7542   Calendar System: Semester
URL: www.pccua.edu
Established: 1965   Annual Undergrad Tuition & Fees (In-District): $2,300
Enrollment: 2,178   Coed
Affiliation or Control: State/Local   IRS Status: 501(c)3
Highest Offering: Associate Degree
Program: Occupational; 2-Year Principally Bachelor's Creditable
Accreditation: NH, ACBSP, ADNUR, MLTAD

02 Chancellor ... Dr. Steven MURRAY
05 Vice Chancellor for Instruction ... Dr. Deborah KING
10 Vice Chanc Finance & Administration ... Vacant
32 Vice Chanc Student Svcs/Registrar ... Mr. Lynn BOONE
30 Vice Chanc Col Advancement/Bus Dev ... Mrs. Rhonda ST. COLUMBIA
12 Vice Chancellor Stuttgart Campus ... Dr. Susan LUEBKE
12 Vice Chancellor DeWitt Campus ... Mrs. Carolyn TURNER

*University of Arkansas Community College at Batesville (E)

2005 White Drive, PO Box 3350, Batesville AR 72503-3350
County: Independence   FICE Identification: 020735
Unit ID: 106999
Telephone: (870) 612-2000   Carnegie Class: Assoc/Pub2in4
FAX Number: (870) 793-4988   Calendar System: Semester
URL: www.uaccb.edu
Established: 1975   Annual Undergrad Tuition & Fees (In-District): $2,440
Enrollment: 1,705   Coed
Affiliation or Control: State/Local   IRS Status: 501(c)3
Highest Offering: Associate Degree
Program: Occupational; 2-Year Principally Bachelor's Creditable
Accreditation: NH, ADNUR, EMT

02 Chancellor ... Ms. Deborah J. FRAZIER
04 Assistant to the Chancellor ... Ms. Tina PAUL
05 Vice Chancellor for Academics ... Dr. Cliff JONES
32 VC Enrollment Mgmt/Student Services ... Mr. Brian BERRY
10 Vice Chancellor Finance and Admin ... Mr. Gayle COOPER
09 VC Research/Planning/Assessment ... Dr. Anne AUSTIN
09 Dir of Institutional Research ... Mr. Blake CANNON
84 Director of Enrollment Management ... Mr. Scott POST
106 Director of Distance Learning ... Ms. Tammy JOLLEY
49 Chair Div of Arts & Humanities ... Ms. Susan BESHEARS
50 Chair Div Business/Tech/Public Svc ... Ms. Tamara GRIFFIN
76 Chair Div Nursing/Allied Health ... Ms. Rebecca KING
81 Chair Div of Math and Science ... Mr. Douglas MUSE
51 Chair Div Community and Tech Educ ... Ms. Kathleen MCNAMEE
13 Director Information Services ... Mr. Steve COLLINS
06 Dir Student Information/Registrar ... Ms. Shelly MOSER
37 Director of Financial Aid ... Ms. Kristen CROSS
30 Director of Development ... Ms. Tina PAUL
18 Director of Maintenance ... Mr. Heath WOOLDRIDGE
36 Director Student Development ... Ms. Louise HUGHES
38 Career & Counseling Services Coord ... Ms. Heather GARCIA
08 Director Library ... Ms. Linda BENNETT
21 Controller ... Mr. Adam ADAIR
15 Personnel Officer ... Ms. Alexa SMITH
96 Purchasing Agent ... Ms. Peggy JACKSON
40 Bookstore Manager ... Vacant

*University of Arkansas Community College at Hope (F)

PO Box 140, 2500 S Main Street, Hope AR 71802-0140
County: Hempstead   FICE Identification: 005732
Unit ID: 107725
Telephone: (870) 777-5722   Carnegie Class: Assoc/Pub2in4
FAX Number: (870) 777-5957   Calendar System: Semester
URL: www.uacch.edu
Established: 1991   Annual Undergrad Tuition & Fees (In-State): $2,258
Enrollment: 1,557   Coed
Affiliation or Control: State   IRS Status: 501(c)3
Highest Offering: Associate Degree
Program: Occupational; 2-Year Principally Bachelor's Creditable; Business Emphasis
Accreditation: NH, EMT, FUSER

02 Chancellor ... Mr. Chris THOMASON
05 Vice Chancellor for Academics ... Mrs. Jennifer METHVIN
32 Vice Chancellor Student Services ... Mr. Bobby JAMES
10 Vice Chancellor for Finance ... Mr. Jerald BARBER
08 Librarian ... Ms. Marielle MCFARLAND
51 Director of Cont Educ/Ind Relations ... Ms. Jolane COOK
26 Communications Coordinator ... Mr. Brent TALLEY
24 Director of Telecommunications ... Mr. Dave PHILLIPS
15 Human Resources Officer ... Ms. Kathryn HOPKINS

*University of Arkansas Community College at Morrilton (G)

1537 University Boulevard, Morrilton AR 72110-9601
County: Conway   FICE Identification: 005245
Unit ID: 107585
Telephone: (501) 354-2465   Carnegie Class: Assoc/Pub2in4
FAX Number: (501) 977-2134   Calendar System: Semester
URL: www.uaccm.edu
Established: 1961   Annual Undergrad Tuition & Fees (In-State): $3,300
Enrollment: 2,462   Coed
Affiliation or Control: State   IRS Status: 501(c)3
Highest Offering: Associate Degree
Program: Occupational; 2-Year Principally Bachelor's Creditable
Accreditation: NH

02 Chancellor ... Dr. Larry D. DAVIS
05 Vice Chancellor Academic Services ... Ms. Diana ARN
10 Vice Chancellor for Finance ... Ms. Lisa GUNDERMAN
11 Vice Chancellor for Administration ... Dr. Linda M. BIRKNER
32 Vice Chancellor Student Services ... Mr. Darren JONES
09 Director of Institutional Research ... Ms. Wanda F. HENSLEY
08 Librarian ... Mr. Leroy GATTIN
06 Registrar ... Ms. Linda HOLLAND
37 Financial Aid Director ... Mrs. Teresa Y. CASH
13 Director of Computer Services ... Mr. Richard O. GROWNS
18 Director of the Physical Plant ... Mr. C. Allen HOLLOWAY
27 Chief Information Officer ... Ms. Mary CLARK
07 Director of Admissions ... Ms. Susan DEWEY
31 Coordinator of Community Outreach ... Vacant

University of Central Arkansas (H)

201 Donaghey Avenue, Conway AR 72035-0001
County: Faulkner   FICE Identification: 001092
Unit ID: 106704
Telephone: (501) 450-5000   Carnegie Class: Master's L
FAX Number: (501) 450-5003   Calendar System: Semester
URL: www.uca.edu
Established: 1907   Annual Undergrad Tuition & Fees (In-State): $7,183
Enrollment: 11,444   Coed
Affiliation or Control: State   IRS Status: 501(c)3
Highest Offering: Doctorate
Program: Occupational; Liberal Arts And General; Teacher Preparatory; Professional
Accreditation: NH, ART, BUS, CIDA, CS, DIETD, DIETI, MUS, NURSE, OT, PTA, SCPSY, SP, TED, THEA

01 Interim President ... Mr. Tom COURTWAY
100 Chief of Staff ... Mr. Jack GILLEAN
05 Provost & VP Academic Affairs ... Dr. Lance R. GRAHN
10 VP Finance/Administration ... Ms. Diane D. NEWTON
32 Vice President Student Services ... Mr. Ronnie D. WILLIAMS
84 Vice President for Enrollment Mgmt ... Dr. Robert W. PARRENT
43 General Counsel ... Mr. Tom COURTWAY
26 VP for University & Govt Relations ... Mr. Jeffery L. PITCHFORD
30 VP for UCA Advancement ... Ms. Shelley MEHL
41 Athletics Director ... Dr. Brad TEAGUE
15 Assoc Vice Pres for Human Resources ... Dr. Graham GILLIS
85 Assoc VP for Intl Engagement ... Dr. Alex CHEN
20 Assoc VP Academic Dev/Dir Diversity ... Vacant
46 Asst Provost/Dir Sponsored Pgms ... Dr. Timothy N. ATKINSON
20 Associate Provost ... Vacant
21 Controller ... Ms. Mary Kay DUNAWAY
58 Assoc Provost/Dean of Graduate Sch ... Dr. Elaine M. MCNIECE
51 Dean Academic Outreach/Extended Pgm ... Vacant
50 Dean of Col Business Administration ... Dr. Patricia K. CANTRELL
53 Dean of College of Education ... Dr. Diana G. POUNDER
76 Dean of Col Health/Applied Science ... Dr. Neil W. HATTLESTAD
49 Dean of Liberal Arts ... Dr. Maurice A. LEE
81 Dean Col Natural Science/Math ... Dr. Steven W. RUNGE
57 Dean Fine Arts & Communication ... Dr. Rollin R. POTTER
35 Dean of Students ... Dr. Gary A. ROBERTS

92 Dean of Honors College .... Dr. Richard I. SCOTT
07 Interim Director Admissions .... Ms. Penny HATFIELD
08 Library Director .... Mr. Art LICHTENSTEIN
06 Registrar .... Mr. Anthony D. SITZ
09 Director Institutional Research .... Ms. Melissa L. GOFF
13 Chief Information Officer .... Dr. Jonathan A. GLENN
37 Director Student Financial Aid .... Ms. Cheryl C. LYONS
36 Dir Career Svcs/Cooperative Educ ..... Dr. Kathy RICE-CLAYBORN
19 Director University Police .... Mr. Larry K. JAMES
38 Director Counseling Center .... Dr. Maurice E. NESS
39 Asst VP for Housing & Contract Svcs .... Mr. Rick L. MCCOLLUM
29 Director of Alumni Services .... Mrs. Jan A. NEWCOMER
21 Director Internal Audits .... Ms. Pamela L. MASSEY
18 Director Physical Plant .... Mr. Larry D. LAWRENCE
27 Dir Publications/Creative Services .... Mr. Richard R. HANCOCK
96 Director of Purchasing .... Ms. Cassandra MCCUIEN-SMITH
21 Director Student Accounts .... Mr. Jason A. RANKIN

University of the Ozarks (A)

415 College Avenue, Clarksville AR 72830-2880
County: Johnson FICE Identification: 001094
Unit ID: 107558
Telephone: (479) 979-1000 Carnegie Class: Bac/Diverse
FAX Number: (479) 979-1355 Calendar System: Semester
URL: www.ozarks.edu
Established: 1834 Annual Undergrad Tuition & Fees: $22,050
Enrollment: 630 Coed
Affiliation or Control: Presbyterian Church (U.S.A.) IRS Status: 501(c)3
Highest Offering: Baccalaureate
Program: Liberal Arts And General; Teacher Preparatory
Accreditation: NH, IACBE, TED

01 President .... Dr. Rick D. NIECE
05 Sr VP Acad Affairs/Dean Faculty .... Dr. Daniel L. TADDIE
03 Exec Vice Pres/Chief Development .... Mr. Steve G. EDMISTEN
10 Chief Financial Officer .... Mr. Jeff SCACCIA
84 Vice Pres for Enrollment Management .... Ms. Kimberly MYRICK
07 Dean of Admissions & Financial Aid .... Ms. Jana D. HART
42 Chaplain .... Rev. Nancy BENSON-NICOL
35 Dean of Students .... Mr. Joe W. HOING
39 Dean of Residential & Campus Life .... Ms. Sherrie AREY
06 Registrar .... Ms. Wilma K. HARRIS
08 Librarian .... Mr. Stuart P. STELZER
27 Director of Public Information .... Mr. Larry A. ISCH
36 Director Student Placement .... Ms. Kim A. SPICER
29 Director Alumni Affairs .... Ms. Lori A. MCBEE
41 Athletic Director .... Mr. Jimmy CLARK
31 Director Campus/Community Relations .... Ms. Sheree A. NIECE
26 Chief Public Relations Officer .... Mr. Larry A. ISCH
30 Director of Development .... Ms. Brandy COX
18 Chief Facilities/Physical Plant .... Mr. Mike QUALLS
88 Director Jones Learning Center .... Ms. Julia H. FROST
90 Director Academic Computing .... Mr. Nathan SAIN
09 Director of Institutional Research .... Mr. Randolph L. PETERSON
96 Director of Purchasing .... Mr. Darrell W. WILLIAMS
89 Director of Freshmen Studies .... Mr. Stacy KEY
14 Director Computer Services .... Mr. Rick OTTO
32 Chief Student Life Officer .... Ms. Sherrie AREY
20 Associate Academic Dean .... Dr. Elissa HEIL
21 Business Manager .... Mr. Darrell W. WILLIAMS
81 Chair Division Sciences/Mathematics .... Dr. Frank KNIGHT
50 Chair Division of Business .... Dr. Robert C. HILTON
53 Chair Division of Education .... Dr. Glenda EZELL
79 Chair Division Humanities/Fine Arts .... Dr. David M. STRAIN
37 Student Financial Aid Counselor .... Ms. Melody JOHNSON

Williams Baptist College (B)

60 W Fulbright Avenue, Walnut Ridge AR 72476
County: Lawrence FICE Identification: 001106
Unit ID: 107877
Telephone: (870) 886-6741 Carnegie Class: Bac/Diverse
FAX Number: (870) 886-3924 Calendar System: Semester
URL: www.wbcoll.edu
Established: 1941 Annual Undergrad Tuition & Fees: $12,620
Enrollment: 636 Coed
Affiliation or Control: Southern Baptist IRS Status: 501(c)3
Highest Offering: Baccalaureate
Program: Liberal Arts And General
Accreditation: NH, TED

01 President .... Dr. Jerol B. SWAIM
05 Vice President Academic Affairs .... Dr. Kenneth M. STARTUP
30 Vice Pres Institutional Advancement .... Dr. Eric A. TURNER
84 VP for Enrollment Mgmt/Student Svcs ...... Mrs. Angela D. FLIPPO
26 Vice President of College Relations .... Dr. Brett COOPER
32 Dean of Students .... Mrs. Susan M. WATSON
44 Director of Development .... Vacant
06 Registrar .... Mrs. Tonya D. BOLTON
08 Librarian .... Mrs. Pamela MERIDITH
37 Director Student Financial Aid .... Mrs. Barbara J. TURNER
38 Director Student Counseling .... Dr. Gary V. GREGORY
42 Director Campus Ministry .... Mr. Josh MCCARTY
18 Chief Facilities/Physical Plant .... Vacant
36 Director Student Placement .... Mrs. Dolores B. MAGEE
29 Director of Alumni Relations .... Mr. Aaron ANDREWS

CALIFORNIA

Abraham Lincoln University (C)

3530 Wilshire Blvd, Ste 1430, Los Angeles CA 90010
County: Los Angeles Identification: 667049
Telephone: (213) 252-5100 Carnegie Class: Not Classified
FAX Number: (213) 252-5112 Calendar System: Trimester
URL: www.alu.edu
Established: 1996 Annual Undergrad Tuition & Fees: $7,500
Enrollment: N/A Coed
Affiliation or Control: Independent Non-Profit IRS Status: 501(c)3
Highest Offering: First Professional Degree
Program: Professional
Accreditation: DETC

01 President & CEO .... Mr. Roy WINTER
11 Director of Administration .... Ms. Jessica PARK
05 Dean & Academic Dean .... Ms. Carole BUCKNER
32 Dean of Student Affairs .... Dr. Daryl FISHER-OGDEN
61 Dean School of Law .... Ms. Carole BUCKNER
07 Manager of Admissions .... Mr. Jason PESIGAN
06 Registrar .... Ms. Elizabeth GOMEZ
35 Student Services Coordinator .... Ms. Jin CHUNG
13 Technology Manager .... Mr. Myeong KIM

Academy for Jewish Religion (D)

574 Hilgard Avenue, Los Angeles CA 90024-3234
County: Los Angeles Identification: 666636
Unit ID: 457271
Telephone: (310) 824-1586 Carnegie Class: Not Classified
FAX Number: (310) 824-1614 Calendar System: Trimester
URL: www.ajrca.org
Established: 2001 Annual Graduate Tuition & Fees: $19,965
Enrollment: 55 Coed
Affiliation or Control: Jewish IRS Status: 501(c)3
Highest Offering: Master's; No Undergraduates
Program: Professional; Religious Emphasis
Accreditation: @WC

01 President .... Rabbi Mel GOTTLIEB
05 Dean of Academic Affairs .... Dr. Tamar FRANKIEL
37 Director Student Financial Aid .... Ms. Lauren GOLDNER
06 Registrar .... Ms. Reesa ROTMAN
07 Director of Admissions .... Ms. Janet BARZILAY
26 Chief Public Relations Officer .... Ms. Cheryl AZAIR
88 Dean of Cantorial School .... Cantor Nathan LAM
73 Dean of Rabbinical School .... Rabbi Mel GOTTLIEB
88 Associate Dean of Cantorial School .... Cantor Perryne ANKER

Academy of Art University (E)

79 New Montgomery Street,
San Francisco CA 94105-3410
County: San Francisco FICE Identification: 007531
Unit ID: 108232
Telephone: (415) 274-2200 Carnegie Class: Spec/Arts
FAX Number: (415) 274-8665 Calendar System: Semester
URL: www.academyart.edu
Established: 1929 Annual Undergrad Tuition & Fees: $22,200
Enrollment: 17,697 Coed
Affiliation or Control: Proprietary IRS Status: Proprietary
Highest Offering: Master's
Program: Fine Arts Emphasis
Accreditation: WC, ART, CIDA

01 President .... Ms. Elisa STEPHENS

Academy of Chinese Culture and Health Sciences (F)

1601 Clay Street, Oakland CA 94612-1540
County: Alameda FICE Identification: 032883
Unit ID: 108269
Telephone: (510) 763-7787 Carnegie Class: Spec/Health
FAX Number: (510) 834-8646 Calendar System: Other
URL: www.acchs.edu
Established: 1982 Annual Undergrad Tuition & Fees: $16,250
Enrollment: 150 Coed
Affiliation or Control: Independent Non-Profit IRS Status: 501(c)3
Highest Offering: Master's; No Lower Division
Program: Professional
Accreditation: ACUP

01 Acting President .... Mr. Joseph KO
03 Vice President .... Mr. Phillip TOU
11 Dean of Administration .... Ms. Jane ZHANG

Acupuncture and Integrative Medicine College-Berkeley (G)

2550 Shattuck Avenue, Berkeley CA 94704-2724
County: Alameda FICE Identification: 033274
Unit ID: 384306
Telephone: (510) 666-8248 Carnegie Class: Spec/Health
FAX Number: (510) 666-0111 Calendar System: Quarter
URL: www.aimc.edu
Established: 1990 Annual Undergrad Tuition & Fees: $11,525
Enrollment: 128 Coed
Affiliation or Control: Independent Non-Profit IRS Status: 501(c)3
Highest Offering: Master's; No Lower Division
Program: Professional
Accreditation: ACUP

01 President .... Dr. Terri POWERS
05 Academic Dean .... Mr. Yeaji SUH
20 Clinic Dean .... Dr. Glen OBERMAN
06 Registrar .... Ms. Carol KNOX
51 Continuing Education/Events Dir .... Mr. Erin OLENICK
07 Director of Admissions .... Mr. Benjamin DERAUF

Advanced College (H)

13180 Paramount Boulevard, South Gate CA 90280-7956
County: Los Angeles FICE Identification: 037863
Unit ID: 444343
Telephone: (562) 408-6969 Carnegie Class: Not Classified
FAX Number: (562) 408-0471 Calendar System: Other
URL: www.advancedcollege.edu
Established: 1999 Annual Undergrad Tuition & Fees: $25,925
Enrollment: 225 Coed
Affiliation or Control: Proprietary IRS Status: Proprietary
Highest Offering: Associate Degree
Program: Occupational
Accreditation: COE

01 Chief Executive Officer .... Dr. Mehdi KARIMPOR
11 Director of Operations .... Dr. Mehdi KARIMPOUR
66 Director Vocational Nursing .... Dr. Minnie L. DOUGLAS

Advanced Training Associates (I)

1810 Gillespie Way, Suite 104, El Cajon CA 92020-1234
County: San Diego FICE Identification: 035324
Unit ID: 444361
Telephone: (619) 596-2766 Carnegie Class: Not Classified
FAX Number: (619) 596-4526 Calendar System: Other
URL: www.advancedtraining.edu
Established: 2000 Annual Undergrad Tuition & Fees: $11,650
Enrollment: 51 Coed
Affiliation or Control: Proprietary IRS Status: Proprietary
Highest Offering: Associate Degree
Program: Occupational; Technical Emphasis
Accreditation: COE

01 President .... Joann ZAKARIN
03 Operations Manager .... Valerie PHILLIPS

Alhambra Medical University (J)

25 S. Raymond Ave., Suite 201, Alhambra CA 91801
County: Los Angeles Identification: 667052
Telephone: (626) 289-7719 Carnegie Class: Not Classified
FAX Number: (626) 289-8641 Calendar System: Quarter
URL: www.amuedu.com/about-amu/about-amu.html
Established: 2005 Annual Graduate Tuition & Fees: $13,282
Enrollment: N/A Coed
Affiliation or Control: Proprietary IRS Status: Proprietary
Highest Offering: Master's; No Undergraduates
Program: Professional
Accreditation: @ACUP

01 President .... Dr. Jonathan WU
05 Academic Dean .... Jerome JIANG
23 Director of University Clinic .... Megan HAH
07 Director of Admissions .... Fanny HSU
06 Registrar .... Qing MA
08 Librarian .... Yue LU

Allan Hancock College (K)

800 S College Drive, Santa Maria CA 93454-6399
County: Santa Barbara FICE Identification: 001111
Unit ID: 108807
Telephone: (805) 922-6966 Carnegie Class: Assoc/Pub-R-L
FAX Number: (805) 928-7905 Calendar System: Semester
URL: www.hancockcollege.edu
Established: 1920 Annual Undergrad Tuition & Fees (In-District): $908
Enrollment: 11,297 Coed
Affiliation or Control: State/Local IRS Status: 501(c)3
Highest Offering: Associate Degree
Program: Occupational; 2-Year Principally Bachelor's Creditable
Accreditation: WJ

01 Superintendent/President .... Dr. Jose M. ORTIZ
10 Assoc Supt/VP Administrative Svcs .... Dr. Elizabeth MILLER
05 Assoc Supt/VP Academic Affairs .... Mr. Luiz P. SANCHEZ
32 Int VP Student Services .... Dr. Jose M. ORTIZ
18 Vice Pres Facilities & Operations .... Mr. Felix HERNANDEZ
35 Interim Dean Student Services .... Mr. Rob PARISI
20 Dean Academic Affairs .... Dr. Paul MURPHY
20 Dean Academic Affairs .... Ms. Roanna BENNIE
20 Dean Academic Affairs .... Dr. Anne CREMAROSA
20 Dean Academic Affairs .... Ms. Ardis NEILSEN
88 Dean Counseling & Matriculation .... Dr. Charles OSIRIS
12 Dean The Extended Campus .... Mr. Ricky RANTZ
41 Assoc Dean Athletics/Health .... Ms. Kim ENSING
08 Int Dean Lrng Resources/Cmty Educ .... Ms. Nancy MEDDINGS
102 Executive Director AHC Foundation .... Mr. Jeff COTTER
88 Artistic Director PCPA .... Mr. Mark BOOHER

13 Director Information Technology .... Ms. Carol VAN NAME
15 Director Human Resources .... Ms. Cyndi MESAROS
21 Director Business Services .... Mr. Richard CARMODY
07 Director Admissions & Records .... Ms. Adela ESQUIVEL-SWINSON
37 Director Student Financial Aid .... Mr. Robert PARISI
26 Dir Public Affairs & Publications .... Mrs. Rebecca ALARCIO
40 Director Bookstore Services .... Mr. William HOCKENSMITH
88 Director EOPS & Special Outreach .... Mr. Will BRUCE
88 Dir Learning Assistance Program .... Dr. Robert PARISI
18 Director Plant Services .... Mr. Rex VAN DEN BERG
09 Director Inst Research & Planning .... Dr. Laurie PEMBERTON
19 Dir Public Safety/Chief of Police .... Lt. Kim GRAHAM
88 Director College Achvmt Now (CAN) .... Mr. Francisco DORAME
88 Dir Title V Learning College Grant .... Ms. Carmela VIGNOCCHI
88 Director Cal-SOAP .... Ms. Diana PEREZ
25 Director of Institutional Grants .... Dr. Suzanne VALERY
81 Counselor/Coordinator MESA .... Ms. Christine REED
88 Managing Director PCPA .... Mr. Michael BLACK

*Alliant International University President's Office (A)

One Beach Street, Suite 200,
San Francisco CA 94133-1221

County: San Francisco — Identification: 666132
Unit ID: 110431
Telephone: (415) 955-2000 — Carnegie Class: N/A
FAX Number: (414) 955-2062
URL: www.alliant.edu

01 President .... Dr. Geoffrey COX
05 Provost/Vice Pres Academic Affairs .... Dr. Russ NEWMAN
10 Vice Pres Finance/Admin/CFO/CSO .... Mr. Tarun BHATIA
11 VP Administration/General Counsel .... Ms. Jennifer TREESE WILSON
09 Assoc Provost Inst Research .... Ms. Patty MULLEN
53 Dean Grad School of Education .... Dr. Karen Schuster WEBB
88 Systemwide Dean CSPP .... Dr. Morgan SAMMONS
15 Chief Human Resources Officer .... Ms. Kristine COMBS
88 University Ombudsperson .... Ms. Jacyn LEWIS
96 Director of Procurement .... Mr. Mehdi RAJABZADEH
21 Asst VP Budget/Fin Plng/Analysis .... Mr. Rohinton BHANDARI
88 Controller .... Ms. Sheryl KOGA

*Alliant International University-Fresno & Sacramento (B)

5130 E Clinton Way, Fresno CA 93727-2014

County: Fresno — FICE Identification: 011117
Unit ID: 110440
Telephone: (559) 456-2777 — Carnegie Class: Not Classified
FAX Number: (559) 253-2267 — Calendar System: Semester
URL: www.alliant.edu
Established: 1973 — Annual Graduate Tuition & Fees: $28,350
Enrollment: 311 — Coed
Affiliation or Control: Independent Non-Profit — IRS Status: 501(c)3
Highest Offering: Doctorate; No Undergraduates
Program: Liberal Arts And General; Teacher Preparatory; Professional
Accreditation: WC, CLPSY, MFCD

02 Director Campus/Student Services .... Ms. Penny SCHAFER
88 Dean of Forensic Studies .... Dr. Eric HICKEY
83 Dir Clinical PsyD & PhD Program .... Dr. Kevin J. O'CONNOR
88 Interim Director Forensic Program .... Dr. Jana PRICE-SHARPS
88 Director Organizational Psych Pgm .... Dr. Toni KNOTT
07 Director of Admissions .... Mr. Brian EVANS
08 Director of Library Service .... Ms. Louise COLBERT-MAR

*Alliant International University-Irvine (C)

2855 Michelle Drive, Suite 300, Irvine CA 92606

County: Orange — Identification: 666157
Unit ID: 11046804
Telephone: (949) 812-7440 — Carnegie Class: Not Classified
FAX Number: (714) 508-6926 — Calendar System: Semester
URL: www.alliant.edu
Established: 1991 — Annual Graduate Tuition & Fees: $22,000
Enrollment: 240 — Coed
Affiliation or Control: Independent Non-Profit — IRS Status: 501(c)3
Highest Offering: Doctorate; No Undergraduates
Program: Teacher Preparatory; Professional
Accreditation: WC, MFCD

02 Director Campus/Student Services .... Ms. Nicole CAMARAS
53 Director Educational Psych Program .... Dr. Donald WOFFORD
07 Director of Admissions CSFS .... Mr. Robert PETTAY
88 Assistant Dir Forensic Psychology .... Dr. Sean STERLING

*Alliant International University-Los Angeles (D)

1000 S Fremont Avenue, Unit 5,
Alhambra CA 91803-1360

County: Los Angeles — FICE Identification: 010013
Unit ID: 110459
Telephone: (626) 284-2777 — Carnegie Class: Not Classified
FAX Number: (626) 284-0550 — Calendar System: Semester
URL: www.allliant.edu
Established: 1970 — Annual Graduate Tuition & Fees: $29,700
Enrollment: 729 — Coed
Affiliation or Control: Independent Non-Profit — IRS Status: 501(c)3
Highest Offering: Doctorate; No Undergraduates
Program: Professional
Accreditation: WC, CLPSY, MFCD

02 Dir of Campus & Student Services .... Ms. Stephanie BYERS-BELL
83 Dir Clin PhD Pgm & Field Training .... Dr. Ellin BLOCH
88 Dean Cal Sch Organizationl Stds/Bus .... Dr. Jay FINKELMAN
53 Dir Clinical Psychology PsyD Pgm .... Dr. David KATZ
53 Director Educational Psy Pgm .... Dr. Carlton PARKS
88 Int Forensic Academic Pgm Director .... Dr. Tracy FASS
28 Director I-MERIT .... Dr. Kumea SHORTER-GOODEN
53 Teacher Education Program Director .... Dr. Barbara STEIN-STOVER
20 Associate Dean CSPP .... Dr. Tracy HELLER
07 Admissions Assistant .... Mr. Sam KIM

*Alliant International University-San Diego (E)

10455 Pomerado Road, San Diego CA 92131-1799

County: San Diego — FICE Identification: 001158
Unit ID: 110468
Telephone: (858) 635-4000 — Carnegie Class: DRU
FAX Number: (858) 693-8562 — Calendar System: Semester
URL: www.alliant.edu
Established: 1952 — Annual Undergrad Tuition & Fees: $16,680
Enrollment: 4,236 — Coed
Affiliation or Control: Independent Non-Profit — IRS Status: 501(c)3
Highest Offering: Doctorate
Program: Liberal Arts And General; Teacher Preparatory; Professional
Accreditation: WC, CLPSY, MFCD

32 Assoc Vice Pres for Student Life .... Dr. Mike PITTENGER
02 Provost/Vice Pres Academic Affairs .... Dr. Russ NEWMAN
03 Vice President and Univ Counsel .... Ms. Jennifer WILSON
09 Assoc Provost for Rsrch & Scholar .... Dr. Sharon FOSTER
11 Assoc Provost for Administration .... Dr. Tracy HELLER
50 Dean Marshall Goldsmith Sch of Mgmt .... Dr. Jim GOODRICH
26 Chief Marketing Officer .... Mrs. Madeleine WIENER
06 University Registrar .... Mr. Paul WELCH
37 Director of Financial Aid .... Ms. Deborah SPINDLER
08 University Librarian .... Mr. Scott ZIMMER
39 Director Housing & Residence Life .... Ms. Meghan MURRAY
83 Director Clinical PhD Program .... Dr. Adele RABIN
83 Dir Marriage & Family Therapy Pgm .... Dr. Scott WOOLLEY
53 Systemwide Director TESOL Pgms .... Dr. Mary Ellen BUTLER-PASCOE
53 Syst Dir Educational Leadership .... Dr. Suzanne POWER
25 Dir of Grants and Contracts .... Mrs. Jean FREISER

*Alliant International University-San Francisco (F)

One Beach Street, San Francisco CA 94133-1221

County: San Francisco — FICE Identification: 011881
Unit ID: 110477
Telephone: (415) 955-2100 — Carnegie Class: Not Classified
FAX Number: (415) 955-2179 — Calendar System: Semester
URL: www.alliant.edu
Established: 1970 — Annual Graduate Tuition & Fees: $21,190
Enrollment: 975 — Coed
Affiliation or Control: Independent Non-Profit — IRS Status: 501(c)3
Highest Offering: Doctorate; No Undergraduates
Program: Teacher Preparatory; Professional
Accreditation: WC, CLPSY

02 Director of Campus/Student Services .... Mr. Ned DOHERTY
06 Registrar .... Ms. Rachel MAYEDA
07 Director of Admissions .... Ms. Julie AQUINO
37 Director of Student Financial Aid .... Ms. Tracy BABBITT
08 Director Library Services .... Mr. Joseph TALLY
83 Associate Dean CSPP .... Dr. Diane ADAMS
83 Int Dir Clinical Psychology PhD Pgm .... Dr. Natalie PORTER
83 Dir Clinical Psychology PsyD Pgm .... Dr. Valata JENKINS-MONROE
83 Dir Japan Clinical Psychology Pgm .... Dr. Reiko TRUE
83 Dir HK Clinical Psychology PsyD Pgm .... Dr. Alex LEUNG
88 Dir Organizational Psych Programs .... Dr. Ira LEVIN
53 Asst Dean Graduate Sch of Education .... Dr. Trudy DAY
53 Dir Educational Psychology Program .... Dr. James HIRAMOTO
88 Director Disabilities Services .... Dr. Nina GHISELLI

Allied American University (G)

22952 Alcalde Drive, Laguna Hills CA 92653-1337

County: Orange — Identification: 666452
Telephone: (888) 384-0849 — Carnegie Class: Not Classified
FAX Number: (949) 707-2978 — Calendar System: Other
URL: www.allied.edu
Established: 2008 — Annual Undergrad Tuition & Fees: $7,500
Enrollment: 1,042 — Coed
Affiliation or Control: Proprietary — IRS Status: Proprietary
Highest Offering: Baccalaureate
Program: Liberal Arts And General
Accreditation: DETC

01 President & CEO .... Charli HISLOP
05 Academic Dean .... Dr. Alex LAZO
06 Registrar .... Christopher BISHOP
32 Director of Student Affairs .... Frank VAZQUEZ
07 Director of Admissions .... Lindsay OGLESBY

AMDA College and Conservatory of the Performing Arts (H)

6305 Yucca Street, Los Angeles CA 90028

Identification: 666721
Telephone: (323) 469-3300 — Carnegie Class: Not Classified
FAX Number: (323) 469-5246 — Calendar System: Semester
URL: www.amda.edu
Established: 1964 — Annual Undergrad Tuition & Fees: $29,960
Enrollment: 1,183 — Coed
Affiliation or Control: Independent Non-Profit — IRS Status: 501(c)3
Highest Offering: Baccalaureate
Program: Liberal Arts And General; Fine Arts Emphasis
Accreditation: THEA

01 Artistic Director/President .... David MARTIN
05 Executive Director/Vice President .... Jan MARTIN
07 Director of Admissions .... Karen JACKSON
07 Director of Admissions .... Charlotte FRANCOVALLE

American Academy of Dramatic Arts, Los Angeles Campus (I)

1336 N La Brea Avenue, Hollywood CA 90028-7504

County: Los Angeles — FICE Identification: 021069
Unit ID: 108852
Telephone: (323) 464-2777 — Carnegie Class: Assoc/PrivNFP
FAX Number: (323) 464-1250 — Calendar System: Other
URL: www.aada.org
Established: 1974 — Annual Undergrad Tuition & Fees: $30,500
Enrollment: 95 — Coed
Affiliation or Control: Independent Non-Profit — IRS Status: 501(c)3
Highest Offering: Associate Degree
Program: 2-Year Principally Bachelor's Creditable; Fine Arts Emphasis
Accreditation: &M, THEA

01 Acting President/COO .... Ms. Susan ZECH
12 Managing Director .... Ms. Barbara HODGEN
07 Director of Admissions .... Ms. Karen HIGGINBOTHAM
05 Director of Instruction .... Ms. Theresa HAYES
37 Director Student Financial Aid .... Mr. Jorge RAMIREZ
06 Registrar .... Ms. Irma ROA
08 Head Librarian .... Ms. Sally LAPORTE

† Regional accreditation is carried under the parent institution in New York, NY.

American Baptist Seminary of the West (J)

2606 Dwight Way, Berkeley CA 94704-3097

County: Alameda — FICE Identification: 001120
Unit ID: 108861
Telephone: (510) 841-1905 — Carnegie Class: Spec/Faith
FAX Number: (510) 841-2446 — Calendar System: Semester
URL: www.absw.edu
Established: 1871 — Annual Undergrad Tuition & Fees: $16,200
Enrollment: 95 — Coed
Affiliation or Control: American Baptist — IRS Status: 501(c)3
Highest Offering: Master's
Program: Professional; Religious Emphasis
Accreditation: THEOL

01 President .... Dr. Paul MARTIN
03 Vice President .... Rev. Michelle M. HOLMES
05 Academic Dean .... Dr. LeAnn SNOW
10 Chief Financial Officer .... Ms. Regina PRIDGEON
06 Registrar/Dir Academic Admin .... Mr. Blake HORRIDGE
07 Director of Recruitment .... Ms. Marie ONWUBUARIRI

American Career College-Los Angeles (K)

4021 Rosewood Avenue, Los Angeles CA 90004

County: Los Angeles — FICE Identification: 022418
Unit ID: 441052
Telephone: (323) 668-7555 — Carnegie Class: Not Classified
FAX Number: (322) 953-3654 — Calendar System: Other
URL: www.americancareer.com
Established: 1978 — Annual Undergrad Tuition & Fees: $15,788
Enrollment: 1,764 — Coed
Affiliation or Control: Proprietary — IRS Status: Proprietary
Highest Offering: Associate Degree
Program: Occupational
Accreditation: ABHES, SURTEC

American Career College-Ontario (L)

3130 East Sedona Court, Ontario CA 91764

County: San Bernardino — FICE Identification: 039713
Unit ID: 447768
Telephone: (951) 739-0788 — Carnegie Class: Not Classified
FAX Number: (951) 739-0798 — Calendar System: Other
URL: www.americancareer.com
Established: 2006 — Annual Undergrad Tuition & Fees: $15,288
Enrollment: 1,416 — Coed
Affiliation or Control: Proprietary — IRS Status: Proprietary
Highest Offering: Associate Degree
Program: Occupational

Accreditation: **ABHES**, SURTEC

01 Campus President .... Mr. Scott WARDALL

American Career College-Orange County (A)

1200 North Magnolia Avenue, Anaheim CA 92801-2607
County: Orange Identification: 667073
Unit ID: 441052
Telephone: (714) 952-9066 Carnegie Class: Not Classified
FAX Number: (714) 952-1819 Calendar System: Other
URL: www.americancareercollege.edu
Established: 2000 Annual Undergrad Tuition & Fees: $33,158
Enrollment: 1,652 Coed
Affiliation or Control: Proprietary IRS Status: Proprietary
Highest Offering: Associate Degree
Program: Occupational
Accreditation: **ABHES**, SURGT, SURTEC

01 Executive Director .... Ms. Rita TOTTEN

American College of Traditional Chinese Medicine (B)

455 Arkansas Street, San Francisco CA 94107-2813
County: San Francisco FICE Identification: 030782
Unit ID: 430591
Telephone: (415) 282-7600 Carnegie Class: Spec/Health
FAX Number: (415) 282-0856 Calendar System: Quarter
URL: www.actcm.edu
Established: 1980 Annual Undergrad Tuition & Fees: $12,900
Enrollment: 270 Coed
Affiliation or Control: Independent Non-Profit IRS Status: 501(c)3
Highest Offering: Master's; No Lower Division
Program: Professional
Accreditation: **ACUP**

01 President .... Lixin HUANG
05 Vice President Academic Affairs .... Elizabeth GOLDBLATT
58 Dean of Masters Program .... Megan HAUNGS
17 Dean of Clinical Education .... John KOLENDA
20 Chief Academic & Clinic Adviser .... Stanley LEUNG
06 Registrar .... Jim HABLE
32 Director of Student Services .... Lee SWAIN
84 Dir of Recruitment/Enrollment Mgmt .... Yuwen CHIU
10 Controller .... Reno GOLEZ
20 Asst Dean of Clinical Education .... Jung KIM
20 Asst to the Dean of Master's Pgm .... Richard ALBERTA
24 Director of Learning Resources .... Aileen HUANG
27 Director of Communications .... Alissa COHAN
37 Financial Aid Administrator .... Daryl CULLEN
14 Network Administrator .... Yan LI
08 Library Administrator .... Sara WANG
07 Admissions Counselor .... Yumiko TOMOBE
88 Academic Advisor .... Andrea NATTA
04 Admn Asst/Asst to President .... Lena LIU
30 Development Officer .... Bria LARSON
18 Facilities Manager .... Jorge MEJIA

American Conservatory Theater (C)

30 Grant Avenue, 6th floor, San Francisco CA 94108-5800
County: San Francisco FICE Identification: 020992
Unit ID: 109086
Telephone: (415) 439-2350 Carnegie Class: Spec/Arts
FAX Number: (415) 834-3210 Calendar System: Semester
URL: www.act-sf.org
Established: 1969 Annual Graduate Tuition & Fees: $19,346
Enrollment: 26 Coed
Affiliation or Control: Independent Non-Profit IRS Status: 501(c)3
Highest Offering: Master's; No Undergraduates
Program: Professional; Fine Arts Emphasis
Accreditation: **WC**

01 Executive Director .... Ellen RICHARD
88 Artistic Director .... Carey PERLOFF
05 Conservatory Director .... Melissa SMITH
20 Director of Academic Affairs .... Jack SHARRAR
37 Director of Financial Aid .... Jerry LOPEZ

American Film Institute Conservatory (D)

2021 N Western Avenue, Los Angeles CA 90027-1657
County: Los Angeles FICE Identification: 022220
Unit ID: 108870
Telephone: (323) 856-7600 Carnegie Class: Spec/Arts
FAX Number: (323) 467-4578 Calendar System: Semester
URL: www.afi.com
Established: 1969 Annual Graduate Tuition & Fees: $37,750
Enrollment: 338 Coed
Affiliation or Control: Independent Non-Profit IRS Status: 501(c)3
Highest Offering: Master's; No Undergraduates
Program: Professional; Fine Arts Emphasis
Accreditation: **WC**, ART

01 Director American Film Institute .... Mr. Bob GAZZALE
11 Chief Operating Officer .... Ms. Nancy HARRIS
05 Exec Vice Dean of Conservatory .... Mr. Joe PETRICCA
20 Vice Dean for Production/Post Prod .... Mr. Phil LINSON
20 Dean of Conservatory .... Mr. Robert MANDEL
32 Vice Dean Fellow Affairs .... Ms. Carolyn BROOKS
57 Artistic Director .... Mr. Frank PIERSON
57 Artistic Director .... Mr. Roger BIRNBAUM
06 Registrar .... Ms. Cheryl REINSCHMIDT
15 Manager Human Resources .... Ms. Roschoune FRANKLIN
37 Financial Aid Director .... Ms. Trina RODLER
07 Admissions Manager .... Ms. Karin T. TUCKER
30 Consultant for Development .... Ms. Molly MROESZYNSKI
08 Librarian .... Mr. Robert VAUGHN
13 Chief Information Officer .... Mr. Paul JACQUES

American Graduate University (E)

733 N Dodsworth Avenue, Covina CA 91724-2408
County: Los Angeles Identification: 666982
Unit ID: 109095
Telephone: (626) 966-4576 Carnegie Class: Not Classified
FAX Number: (626) 915-1709 Calendar System: Other
URL: www.agu.edu
Established: 1969 Annual Graduate Tuition & Fees: $1,180
Enrollment: 1,150 Coed
Affiliation or Control: Proprietary IRS Status: Proprietary
Highest Offering: Master's; No Undergraduates
Program: Professional; Business Emphasis
Accreditation: **DETC**

01 President/Dir Academic Affairs .... Mr. Paul R. MCDONALD
11 Vice President Administration .... Ms. Marie SIRNEY
32 Director of Student Services .... Ms. Sherrie ANGSTER
06 Registrar .... Ms. Debbie MCDONALD

American Jewish University (F)

15600 Mulholland Drive, Los Angeles CA 90077-1599
County: Los Angeles FICE Identification: 002741
Unit ID: 116846
Telephone: (310) 476-9777 Carnegie Class: Bac/A&S
FAX Number: (310) 471-1278 Calendar System: Semester
URL: www.ajula.edu
Established: 1947 Annual Undergrad Tuition & Fees: $24,744
Enrollment: 274 Coed
Affiliation or Control: Independent Non-Profit IRS Status: 501(c)3
Highest Offering: Master's
Program: Liberal Arts And General; Teacher Preparatory; Professional
Accreditation: **WC**

01 President .... Dr. Robert WEXLER
03 Sr VP & Provost .... Mr. Mark BOOKMAN
05 VP & Dean Ziegler School .... Rabbi Bradley ARTSON
51 VP Whizin Center for Cont Educ .... Dr. Gady LEVY
10 VP Finance/Admin & Technology .... Ms. Zofia YALOVSKY
30 Sr VP Development .... Rabbi Jay STREAR
42 Rector .... Dr. Elliot DORFF
08 Library Director .... Mr. Paul MILLER
06 Registrar .... Mr. Arnie WEISBERG
27 Sr Director of Comm & Recruitment .... Ms. Iris WASKOW
37 Director of Financial Aid .... Ms. Larisa ZADOYEN
53 Dean Fingerhut School of Education .... Ms. Miriam HELLER-STERN
49 Dean College of Arts & Sciences .... Vacant
88 Dean Nonprofit Management Program .... Ms. Nina LIEBERMAN GILADI
39 Director Residence Life .... Mr. Jacob GOWN
07 Director Undergraduate Admissions .... Mr. Matt SPOONER

American University of Armenia (G)

300 Lakeside Drive, 12th Floor, Oakland CA 94612
County: Alameda Identification: 666013
Telephone: (510) 987-9452 Carnegie Class: Not Classified
FAX Number: (510) 208-3576 Calendar System: Semester
URL: www.aua.am
Established: 1991 Annual Graduate Tuition & Fees: $6,400
Enrollment: 302 Coed
Affiliation or Control: Independent Non-Profit IRS Status: 501(c)3
Highest Offering: Master's; No Undergraduates
Program: Professional
Accreditation: **WC**

01 President .... Dr. Brue BOGHOSIAN

American University of Health Sciences (H)

1600 E Hill St Building #1, Signal Hill CA 90755
County: Los Angeles FICE Identification: 032253
Unit ID: 433004
Telephone: (562) 988-2278 Carnegie Class: Assoc/PrivFP4
FAX Number: (562) 988-1791 Calendar System: Quarter
URL: www.auhs.edu
Established: 1994 Annual Undergrad Tuition & Fees: $32,000
Enrollment: 115 Coed
Affiliation or Control: Proprietary IRS Status: Proprietary
Highest Offering: Master's
Program: Professional
Accreditation: **ACICS**

01 President .... Ms. Kim DANG
11 Chief Operating Officer .... Pastor Gregory A. JOHNSON

Anaheim University (I)

1240 S State College Blvd, Ste 110, Anaheim CA 92806-5152
County: Orange Identification: 666651
Telephone: (714) 772-3330 Carnegie Class: Not Classified
FAX Number: (714) 772-3331 Calendar System: Other
URL: www.anaheim.edu
Established: 1996 Annual Graduate Tuition & Fees: N/A
Enrollment: N/A Coed
Affiliation or Control: Proprietary IRS Status: Proprietary
Highest Offering: Master's; No Undergraduates
Program: Professional
Accreditation: **DETC**

01 President .... Dr. William B. HARTLEY
05 Vice President of Academic Affairs .... Dr. David NUNAN

Antelope Valley College (J)

3041 W Avenue K, Lancaster CA 93536-5426
County: Los Angeles FICE Identification: 001113
Unit ID: 109350
Telephone: (661) 722-6300 Carnegie Class: Assoc/Pub-S-SC
FAX Number: (661) 722-6333 Calendar System: Semester
URL: www.avc.edu
Established: 1929 Annual Undergrad Tuition & Fees (In-District): $864
Enrollment: 14,555 Coed
Affiliation or Control: State/Local IRS Status: 501(c)3
Highest Offering: Associate Degree
Program: Occupational; 2-Year Principally Bachelor's Creditable
Accreditation: **WJ**, RAD

01 President/Superintendent .... Dr. Jackie L. FISHER, SR.
05 VP Academic Affs/Student Services .... Ms. Sharon LOWRY
10 Vice Pres Administrative Services .... Mr. Thomas BRUNDAGE
15 Vice President Human Resources .... Mr. Michael TURNER
07 Dean Enrollment Services .... Ms. LaDonna TRIMBLE
88 Director Disabled Students .... Dr. Louis LUCERO
26 Director Public Relations .... Mr. Steve STANDERFER
18 Dir Facilities Plng/Campus Devel .... Mr. Doug JENSEN
13 Director Information Technology .... Mr. Calvin MADLOCK
30 Dir Inst Advancement & Foundation .... Ms. Bridget RAZO
46 Director Inst Research & Planning .... Mr. Ted YOUNGLOVE
96 Buyer .... Ms. Crystal MOHAIR
37 Director Financial Aid .... Ms. Sherrie PADILLA
68 Dean PE/Athlet/Visual and Perf Arts .... Mr. Newton CHELETTE
79 Dean of Inst Res/Language Arts ... Dr. Charlotte FORTE-PARNELL
83 Dean Soc & Beh Sci/Bus/Comp Stds .... Dr. Tom O'NEIL
38 Dean Counseling & Matriculation .... Vacant
76 Dean Health Sciences .... Dr. Karen COWELL
35 Dean of Student Develop & Services .... Dr. Jill ZIMMERMAN
75 Dean of Technical Education .... Ms. Margaret DRAKE
81 Dean of Math/Science & Engineering .... Dr. Les UHAZY

Antioch University Los Angeles (K)

400 Corporate Pointe, Culver City CA 90230
County: Los Angeles Identification: 666236
Unit ID: 245838
Telephone: (310) 578-1080 Carnegie Class: Master's L
FAX Number: (310) 822-4824 Calendar System: Quarter
URL: www.antiochla.edu
Established: 1972 Annual Undergrad Tuition & Fees: $24,900
Enrollment: 810 Coed
Affiliation or Control: Independent Non-Profit IRS Status: 501(c)3
Highest Offering: Master's
Program: Liberal Arts And General
Accreditation: **&NH**

01 Interim President .... Dr. Tex BOGGS
05 Provost/VP Academic Affairs .... Dr. Luis PEDRAJA
10 Chief Financial Officer .... Mr. David HOUSER
06 Registrar .... Ms. Emelita DACANAY
07 Director of Admissions .... Mr. Michael NEE
15 Director Human Resources .... Mr. Robert STAPP
18 Chief Operations Officer .... Ms. Sandy LEE
26 Dir Communications/Public Relations .... Ms. Joanna GERBER
37 Dir Student Financial Aid .... Mr. Chris FREEMAN
35 Dir Student Advocacy & Services .... Mr. Josh WILLIAMS

† Regional accreditation is carried under the parent institution in Yellow Springs, OH.

Antioch University Santa Barbara (L)

602 Anacapa Street, Santa Barbara CA 93101
County: Santa Barbara Identification: 666231
Unit ID: 245847
Telephone: (805) 962-8179 Carnegie Class: Master's S
FAX Number: (805) 962-4786 Calendar System: Quarter
URL: www.antiochsb.edu
Established: 1977 Annual Undergrad Tuition & Fees: $16,308
Enrollment: 369 Coed
Affiliation or Control: Independent Non-Profit IRS Status: 501(c)3
Highest Offering: Doctorate
Program: Liberal Arts And General; Professional
Accreditation: **&NH**

01 President ..... Dr. Nancy LEFFERT
05 Provost/VP Academic Affairs ..... Dr. Bill RICHARDSON
09 Executive Dean Institutional Rsrch ..... Mr. Richard WHITNEY
30 Associate Director of Development ..... Ms. Kristine SCHWARZ
06 Registrar ..... Ms. Julia DUBIEL
84 Director of Enrollment Management ..... Mr. Steve WEIR
37 Assistant Director of Financial Aid ..... Ms. Babette WILLENS
10 Chief Financial Officer ..... Ms. Deb CARAWAY
15 Director of Human Resources ..... Ms. Nanci BRAUNSCHWEIGER
58 Chair Graduate Psychology Programs ..... Dr. Elizabeth WOLFSON
53 Chair Education Program ..... Dr. Marianne D'EMIDIO CASTON
88 Chair Psychology Doctoral Program ..... Dr. Barbara LIPINSKI
97 Chair Undergraduate Studies ..... Dr. Britt ANDREATTA
57 Chair Master of Fine Arts ..... Vacant
50 Chair Global Business/Management ..... Vacant

† Regional accreditation is carried under the parent institution in Yellow Springs, OH.

Applied Professional Training, Inc. (A)

5751 Palmer Way, Suite D, Carlsbad CA 92010-7247
County: San Diego — Identification: 666245
Telephone: (800) 431-8488 — Carnegie Class: Not Classified
FAX Number: (888) 431-8588 — Calendar System: Semester
URL: www.aptc.edu
Established: 1993 — Annual Undergrad Tuition & Fees: $3,500
Enrollment: 800 — Coed
Affiliation or Control: Proprietary — IRS Status: Proprietary
Highest Offering: Associate Degree
Program: Occupational; 2-Year Principally Bachelor's Creditable
Accreditation: DETC

01 President/Chief Executive Officer ..... Mr. Steven W. BLUME

Argosy University, Inland Empire (B)

3401 Centre Lake Drive, Suite 200, Ontario CA 91761
County: San Bernardino — Identification: 666007
Unit ID: 450526
Telephone: (909) 472-0800 — Carnegie Class: Bac/A&S
FAX Number: N/A — Calendar System: Semester
URL: www.argosy.edu/inlandempire
Established: 2006 — Annual Undergrad Tuition & Fees: $14,580
Enrollment: 710 — Coed
Affiliation or Control: Proprietary — IRS Status: Proprietary
Highest Offering: Doctorate
Program: Professional
Accreditation: &NH

01 Campus President ..... Dr. James COX
05 Vice President Academic Affairs ..... Dr. Marilyn AL-HASSAN
07 Senior Director of Admissions ..... Wendy VASQUEZ-OSBORN
32 Director of Student Services ..... Michele CORTEZ
10 Area Business Manager ..... Michael ANDRUSKI

† Regional accreditation is carried under the parent institution in Chicago, IL.

Argosy University, Los Angeles (C)

5230 Pacific Concourse Drive, Los Angeles CA 90045
County: Los Angeles — Identification: 666011
Unit ID: 447272
Telephone: (310) 531-9700 — Carnegie Class: Bac/A&S
FAX Number: (310) 531-9801 — Calendar System: Semester
URL: www.argosy.edu/losangeles
Established: 2005 — Annual Undergrad Tuition & Fees: $14,580
Enrollment: 555 — Coed
Affiliation or Control: Proprietary — IRS Status: Proprietary
Highest Offering: Doctorate
Program: Professional
Accreditation: &NH

01 Campus President ..... Dr. James COX
05 Vice President of Academic Affairs ..... Dr. Marilyn AL-HASSAN
07 Senior Director of Admissions ..... Michele A. MONROE
32 Director of Student Services ..... Jacqueline GOMEZ-JURADO
10 Area Business Manager ..... Vacant

† Regional accreditation is carried under the parent institution in Chicago, IL.

Argosy University, Orange County (D)

601 South Lewis Street, Orange CA 92868
County: Orange — Identification: 666180
Unit ID: 436438
Telephone: (714) 620-3700 — Carnegie Class: DRU
FAX Number: (714) 620-3802 — Calendar System: Semester
URL: www.argosy.edu/orangecounty
Established: 1999 — Annual Undergrad Tuition & Fees: $14,580
Enrollment: 925 — Coed
Affiliation or Control: Proprietary — IRS Status: Proprietary
Highest Offering: Doctorate
Program: Professional
Accreditation: &NH, CLPSY

01 Campus President ..... Dr. James COX
05 Vice President Academic Affairs ..... Dr. Marilyn AL-HASSAN
07 Director of Admissions ..... Christina SHADE
32 Director of Student Services ..... Michael NOEL
10 Area Business Manager ..... Vacant
06 Registrar ..... Mark WILLS

† Regional accreditation is carried under the parent institution in Chicago, IL.

Argosy University, San Diego (E)

1615 Murray Canyon Rd, Suite 100,
San Diego CA 92108-4423
County: San Diego — Identification: 666034
Unit ID: 450544
Telephone: (619) 321-3000 — Carnegie Class: Bac/Assoc
FAX Number: (619) 321-3005 — Calendar System: Semester
URL: www.argosy.edu/sandiego
Established: 2005 — Annual Undergrad Tuition & Fees: $14,580
Enrollment: 353 — Coed
Affiliation or Control: Proprietary — IRS Status: Proprietary
Highest Offering: Doctorate
Program: Professional
Accreditation: &NH

01 Interim Campus President ..... Dr. James COX
05 Vice President of Academic Affairs ..... Dr. Marilyn AL-HASSAN
07 Director of Admissions ..... Pierre-Carly LAFAILLE
32 Director of Student Services ..... Steve BURNS
10 Area Business Manager ..... Mike ANDRUSKI

† Regional accreditation is carried under the parent institution, Argosy University in Chicago, IL.

Argosy University, San Francisco Bay Area (F)

1005 Atlantic Avenue, Alameda CA 94501-1148
County: Contra Costa — Identification: 666081
Unit ID: 121983
Telephone: (510) 217-4700 — Carnegie Class: Spec/Health
FAX Number: (510) 217-4800 — Calendar System: Semester
URL: www.argosy.edu/sanfrancisco
Established: 1998 — Annual Undergrad Tuition & Fees: $14,580
Enrollment: 867 — Coed
Affiliation or Control: Proprietary — IRS Status: Proprietary
Highest Offering: Doctorate
Program: Professional
Accreditation: &NH, #CLPSY

01 Campus President ..... Dr. Richard BOOROM
05 Vice President of Academic Affairs ..... Dr. Gladys ATO
32 Director of Student Services ..... Lewis BUNDY
07 Director of Admissions ..... John STOFAN
10 Business Manager ..... Michael TOLIVER
15 Human Resources Manager ..... Sophia WARITH

† Regional accreditation is carried under the parent institution in Chicago, IL.

Art Center College of Design (G)

1700 Lida Street, Pasadena CA 91103-1999
County: Los Angeles — FICE Identification: 001116
Unit ID: 109651
Telephone: (626) 396-2200 — Carnegie Class: Spec/Arts
FAX Number: N/A — Calendar System: Semester
URL: www.artcenter.edu
Established: 1930 — Annual Undergrad Tuition & Fees: $32,592
Enrollment: 1,586 — Coed
Affiliation or Control: Independent Non-Profit — IRS Status: 501(c)3
Highest Offering: Master's
Program: Professional
Accreditation: WC, ART

01 President ..... Dr. Lorne M. BUCHMAN
10 Sr VP/Chief Financial Officer ..... Mr. Rich HALUSCHAK
05 Provost ..... Mr. Fred FEHLAU
30 Sr VP Development &External Affairs ..... Ms. Arwen DUFFY
18 Senior Vice President Operations ..... Mr. George FALARDEAU
07 VP Admissions/Enrollment Mgmt ..... Ms. Kit BARON
32 Dean of Students ..... Mr. Jeffrey HOFFMAN
88 VP Exhibitions ..... Mr. Steve NOWLIN
08 VP Library Director ..... Mrs. Elizabeth GALLOWAY
13 VP Information Technology ..... Ms. Theresa ZIX
15 Executive Director Human Resources ..... Ms. Nancy TORRES DUGGAN
21 Controller ..... Ms. Diane WITTENBERG
37 Director Financial Aid ..... Ms. Clema MCKENZIE
29 Director of Alumni Affairs ..... Ms. Kristine BOWNE
26 Director Marketing & Communication ..... Mr. Jered GOLD
06 Director of Enrollment & Registrar ..... Mr. William GARTRELL
09 Director of Institutional Research ..... Ms. Esmeralda NAVA
19 Dir Environmental Health & Safety ..... Ms. Vicky MCCORMICK
102 Assoc Director Foundation Relations ..... Vacant
36 Director Career Development ..... Ms. Jean MITSUNAGA
18 Director of Facilities ..... Mr. Jess RIVAS
96 Director of Purchasing ..... Ms. Monica MATSUO

The Art Institute of California-Hollywood (H)

5250 Lankershim Boulevard, North Hollywood CA 91601
County: Los Angeles — FICE Identification: 031254
Unit ID: 410502
Telephone: (213) 251-3636 — Carnegie Class: Spec/Arts
FAX Number: (213) 385-3545 — Calendar System: Quarter
URL: www.artinstitutes.edu/hollywood
Established: 1991 — Annual Undergrad Tuition & Fees: $18,798
Enrollment: 1,775 — Coed
Affiliation or Control: Proprietary — IRS Status: Proprietary
Highest Offering: Baccalaureate
Program: Occupational
Accreditation: ACICS

01 President ..... Mr. Roger GOMEZ
05 Assoc Dean of Academic Affairs ..... Dr. Karen NOWAK
37 Director of Student Financial Svcs ..... Ms. Adis CEBALLOS
32 Dean of Student Affairs ..... Mr. Nate GAMB
06 Registrar ..... Ms. Lorena LOPEZ

The Art Institute of California-Inland Empire (I)

674 East Brier Drive, San Bernardino CA 92408-2800
County: San Bernardino — FICE Identification: 016471
Unit ID: 448576
Telephone: (909) 915-2100 — Carnegie Class: Not Classified
FAX Number: (909) 915-2130 — Calendar System: Semester
URL: www.artinstitutes.edu/inlandempire
Established: 2006 — Annual Undergrad Tuition & Fees: $18,748
Enrollment: 1,938 — Coed
Affiliation or Control: Proprietary — IRS Status: Proprietary
Highest Offering: Baccalaureate
Program: Liberal Arts And General
Accreditation: ACCSC

01 President ..... Mr. Eman EL-HOUT

The Art Institute of California-Los Angeles (J)

2900 31st Street, Santa Monica CA 90405-3035
County: Los Angeles — Identification: 666045
Unit ID: 432533
Telephone: (310) 752-4700 — Carnegie Class: Spec/Arts
FAX Number: (310) 752-4708 — Calendar System: Quarter
URL: www.aila.artinstitutes.edu
Established: 1997 — Annual Undergrad Tuition & Fees: $30,550
Enrollment: 2,275 — Coed
Affiliation or Control: Proprietary — IRS Status: Proprietary
Highest Offering: Baccalaureate
Program: Occupational; 2-Year Principally Bachelor's Creditable
Accreditation: ACICS, CIDA

01 President ..... Laura SOLOFF
05 Dean of Academic Affairs ..... Shelley GLICKSTEIN
36 Director of Career Services ..... Scott SAUNDERS
07 Director of Admissions ..... AJ ANTUN
10 Dir Administrative/Financial Svcs ..... Mohamed AMMAR
16 Director of Human Resources ..... Rebecca ELLIS
06 Registrar ..... Dave ANTER
08 Director Learning Resource Center ..... Mary EDWARDS
26 Director of Public Relations ..... Michelles ESTRELLADO
37 Director Student Financial Services ..... Cynthia GALARZA
88 Culinary Arts Program Director ..... Christophe BERNARD
20 Graphic Arts Program Director ..... Susanne MANHEIMER
20 Media Arts/Animation Prgm Director ..... Aaron LYLE
20 Video Production Program Director ..... David SCHREIBER
13 Director Technology ..... Glenn BELL
24 Interactive Media Design Prgm Dir ..... Jan MCWILLIAM
88 Interior Design Program Director ..... Joanne KRAVETZ
32 Director Student Development ..... Don KOHN
35 Dean of Student Affairs ..... Eric POMPEI
88 Game Art Design Program Director ..... Eric ELDER

The Art Institute of California-Orange County (K)

3601 W Sunflower Avenue, Santa Ana CA 92704-7931
County: Orange — Identification: 666182
Unit ID: 441973
Telephone: (714) 830-0200 — Carnegie Class: Spec/Arts
FAX Number: (714) 556-1923 — Calendar System: Quarter
URL: www.artinstitutes.edu/orangecounty
Established: 2000 — Annual Undergrad Tuition & Fees: $25,500
Enrollment: 2,135 — Coed
Affiliation or Control: Proprietary — IRS Status: Proprietary
Highest Offering: Baccalaureate
Program: Occupational; Liberal Arts And General; Fine Arts Emphasis
Accreditation: ACICS, CIDA

01 President ..... Mr. Gregory J. MARICK
07 Director of Admissions ..... Mr. Harry RAMOS
26 Director of PR & Marketing ..... Ms. Amy ROCHA
18 Facilities Director ..... Mrs. Margaret CARROLL

† Branch campus of The Art Institute of California-Los Angeles, Santa Monica, CA.

The Art Institute of California-Sacramento (L)

2850 Gateway Oaks Drive, Suite 100,
Sacramento CA 95833-4348
County: Sacramento — Identification: 666619
Unit ID: 450094

Telephone: (916) 830-6320 Carnegie Class: Not Classified
FAX Number: (916) 830-6344 Calendar System: Quarter
URL: www.artinstitutes.edu/sacramento
Established: 2007 Annual Undergrad Tuition & Fees: $22,950
Enrollment: 735 Coed
Affiliation or Control: Proprietary IRS Status: Proprietary
Highest Offering: Baccalaureate
Program: Liberal Arts And General; Professional; Technical Emphasis
Accreditation: ACICS

01 President ....Terry A. MARLINK

† Branch campus of The Art Institute of California-Los Angeles, Santa Monica, CA.

The Art Institute of California-San Diego (A)

7650 Mission Valley Road, San Diego CA 92108-4423
County: San Diego FICE Identification: 023276
Unit ID: 117113
Telephone: (858) 598-1200 Carnegie Class: Spec/Arts
FAX Number: (619) 291-3206 Calendar System: Quarter
URL: www.the-art-institutes.info
Established: 1981 Annual Undergrad Tuition & Fees: $24,144
Enrollment: 2,040 Coed
Affiliation or Control: Proprietary IRS Status: Proprietary
Highest Offering: Baccalaureate
Program: Occupational; Liberal Arts And General
Accreditation: ACCSC, ACFEI

01 President ....Elizabeth ERICKSON
05 Dean of Academic Affairs ....Rebecca BROWNING
10 Chief Financial Officer ....Beverly MILLER
32 Dean of Student Affairs ....Jennifer DONALDSON
07 Director of Admissions ....Melissa CARRILLO
15 Human Resources Director ....Carol CAMPO
36 Director of Career Services ....Jean BRANAN
37 Director Student Financial Services ....Laverne ARBERRY-LAMB
06 Registrar ....Jesse ROGERS

The Art Institute of California-San Francisco (B)

1170 Market Street, San Francisco CA 94102-4908
County: San Francisco FICE Identification: 007236
Unit ID: 117928
Telephone: (888) 493-3261 Carnegie Class: Spec/Arts
FAX Number: (415) 863-6344 Calendar System: Quarter
URL: www.aisf.artinstitutes.edu
Established: 1939 Annual Undergrad Tuition & Fees: $22,700
Enrollment: 1,462 Coed
Affiliation or Control: Proprietary IRS Status: Proprietary
Highest Offering: Master's
Program: Occupational; 2-Year Principally Bachelor's Creditable; Liberal Arts And General
Accreditation: ACICS

01 President ....Mr. Byron CHUNG
05 Dean of Academic Affairs ....Dr. Caren MEGHREBLIAN
32 Dean of Student Affairs ....Mr. Clark DAWOOD
07 Director of Admissions ....Mr. Louic GARCIA
36 Director of Career Services ....Ms. Donna DESSART
37 Director of Student Financial Svcs ....Ms. Erin MUSIL
26 Director of Public Relations ....Ms. Jennifer TOMARO
15 Director of Human Resources ....Mr. John MCCULLOUGH

† Branch campus of The Art Institute of California-Los Angeles, Santa Monica, CA.

The Art Institute of California-Sunnyvale (C)

1120 Kifer Road, Sunnyvale CA 94086-5303
County: Santa Clara Identification: 666620
Unit ID: 451848
Telephone: (408) 962-6400 Carnegie Class: Not Classified
FAX Number: N/A Calendar System: Other
URL: www.artinstitutes.edu/sunnyvale
Established: N/A Annual Undergrad Tuition & Fees: N/A
Enrollment: 564 Coed
Affiliation or Control: Proprietary IRS Status: Proprietary
Highest Offering: Baccalaureate
Program: Liberal Arts And General
Accreditation: ACICS

01 President ....Mr. Tim HANSEN

† Branch campus of The Art Institute of California-Hollywood, Los Angeles, CA.

Aviation & Electronic Schools of America (D)

PO Box 1810, 111 S Railroad Street,
Colfax CA 95713-1810
County: Placer FICE Identification: 041253
Telephone: (800) 345-2742 Carnegie Class: Not Classified
FAX Number: (530) 346-8466 Calendar System: Other
URL: www.aesa.com
Established: 1988 Annual Undergrad Tuition & Fees: N/A
Enrollment: 300 Coed
Affiliation or Control: Proprietary IRS Status: Proprietary
Highest Offering: Associate Degree
Program: Occupational; 2-Year Principally Bachelor's Creditable; Technical Emphasis
Accreditation: COE

01 President/Exec Vice President ....Mr. James P. DOYLE
05 Director Education ....Mr. James P. DOYLE
07 Acting Director of Admissions ....Mr. James P. DOYLE
10 Controller ....Ms. Lorie SUAREZ
32 Dir Student Services/Registrar ....Ms. Christina BUSH

Azusa Pacific University (E)

901 E Alosta Avenue, Azusa CA 91702-7000
County: Los Angeles FICE Identification: 001117
Unit ID: 109785
Telephone: (626) 969-3434 Carnegie Class: DRU
FAX Number: (626) 969-7180 Calendar System: Semester
URL: www.apu.edu
Established: 1899 Annual Undergrad Tuition & Fees: $37,164
Enrollment: 9,258 Coed
Affiliation or Control: Independent Non-Profit IRS Status: 501(c)3
Highest Offering: Doctorate
Program: Liberal Arts And General; Teacher Preparatory; Professional
Accreditation: WC, ART, CLPSY, IACBE, MUS, NURSE, PTA, SW, TED, THEOL

01 President ....Dr. Jon R. WALLACE
05 Provost ....Dr. Mark STANTON
26 Exec Vice Pres External Affairs ....Mr. David E. BIXBY
11 Exec Vice President Administration ....Mr. John C. REYNOLDS
32 Senior Vice Pres for Student Life ....Dr. Terry FRANSON
10 Vice President Business Affairs/CFO ....Mr. Bob L. JOHANSEN
43 VP Legal Affs/Cmty Rels/Gen Counsel ....Mr. Mark DICKERSON
84 VP for Enrollment Mangement ....Mr. David DUFAULT-HUNTER
88 Sr VP People/Organiz Development ....Mrs. Deana L. PORTERFIELD
20 Vice Provost Undergraduate Programs ....Dr. Diane GUIDO
58 Vice Provost Graduate Programs/Rsch ....Dr. Paul GRAY
35 AVP Student Life/Chief Judicial Ofc ....Mr. Willie HAMLETT
84 AVP Academic Enrollment/Student Svc ....Mrs. Heather PETRIDIS
26 Assoc VP University Relations ....Mr. David PECK
49 Dean College Liberal Arts/Sci ....Dr. David WEEKS
83 Int Dean School Behav/Appl Sciences ....Dr. Rose LIEGLER
50 Dean School of Business Mgmt ....Dr. Ilene BEZJIAN
53 Dean School of Education ....Dr. Helen WILLIAMS
73 Dean Haggard School of Theology ....Dr. Scott DANIELS
64 Acting Dean School of Music ....Mr. Don NEUFELD
66 Dean School of Nursing ....Dr. Aja LESH
51 Dean Ctr Adult/Professional Studies ....Dr. Fred GARLETT
35 Assoc Dean Students/Dir Student Act ....Mrs. Shino SIMONS
15 Exec Director Human Resources ....Ms. Brenda YOUNG
13 Associate Vice President/CIO ....Mr. Don DAVIS
30 Executive Director Development ....Mrs. Louise FURROW
21 Executive Director Finance ....Mr. Stephen GREY
88 Exec Director University Services ....Mr. Roger HODSDON
42 Campus Pastor ....Mr. Woody MOORWOOD
37 Dir Graduate Student Financial Svcs ....Ms. Michelle MORZOV
06 Registrar-Graduate ....Mrs. Norma MOCABEE
06 Registrar-Undergraduate & CAPS ....Mrs. Jennifer MOORE
29 Director Alumni Relations ....Mr. Craig WALLACE
09 Director Acad Info Mgmt Analysis ....Vacant
41 Director Athletics ....Mr. Gary PINE
38 Director Counseling Center ....Dr. Bill FIALA
37 Director UG/CAPS Student Finan Svcs ....Mr. Todd ROSS
18 Director Facilities Management ....Mr. Dennis ROBBINS
92 Director of Honors Program ....Dr. Vicky BOWDEN
07 Director Undergraduate Admissions ....Mr. David BURKE
36 Director Career Services ....Ms. Lynn PEARSON

Barstow Community College District (F)

2700 Barstow Road, Barstow CA 92311-6699
County: San Bernardino FICE Identification: 001119
Unit ID: 109907
Telephone: (760) 252-2411 Carnegie Class: Assoc/Pub-S-SC
FAX Number: (760) 252-1875 Calendar System: Semester
URL: www.barstow.edu
Established: 1959 Annual Undergrad Tuition & Fees (In-District): $936
Enrollment: 5,483 Coed
Affiliation or Control: State/Local IRS Status: 501(c)3
Highest Offering: Associate Degree
Program: Occupational; 2-Year Principally Bachelor's Creditable
Accreditation: WJ

01 President ....Dr. Thom M. ARMSTRONG
04 Exec Assistant to the President ....Mrs. Michelle HENDERSON
10 Vice President Administrative Svcs ....Mr. Virgil STANFORD
05 Acting VP Academic Affairs ....Dr. Bill ORR
32 Vice President Student Services ....Mr. Cal BRINKERHOFF
16 Interim VP Human Resources ....Ms. Trinda BEST
09 Dean Research Planning & Dev ....Dr. Robert PACHECO
103 Dean Workforce & Economic Dev ....Mr. Ken EAVES
49 Interim Dean of Instruction ....Mr. David GROSSMAN
27 Director Public Information ....Ms. Maureen O. STOKES
18 Director Maintenance & Operations ....Mr. Dwight CALLOWAY
21 Director Fiscal Services ....Ms. Shawna L. ROBBINS
84 Director Enrollment Services ....Ms. Heather CALDON
41 Athletic Director ....Mr. Gary SCHWARTZ
35 Director Student Dev & Outreach ....Mrs. Joann GARCIA
88 Director CTE Grants ....Ms. Sandra THOMAS
88 Director Military Programs ....Mr. Jerry PETERS
88 Director Special Program & Services ....Ms. Jessica BETTENCOURT
40 Bookstore Manager ....Mrs. Kimberly YOUNG
21 Budget Analyst ....Mrs. Debbie WYNNE

Bethesda Christian University (G)

730 N Euclid Street, Anaheim CA 92801-4115
County: Orange FICE Identification: 032663
Unit ID: 110060
Telephone: (714) 517-1945 Carnegie Class: Spec/Faith
FAX Number: (714) 517-1948 Calendar System: Semester
URL: www.bcu.edu
Established: 1976 Annual Undergrad Tuition & Fees: $7,005
Enrollment: 275 Coed
Affiliation or Control: Independent Non-Profit IRS Status: 501(c)3
Highest Offering: Doctorate
Program: Religious Emphasis
Accreditation: BI, TRACS

01 President ....Pastor Yoo Chul JIN
05 Chief Academic Officer ....Dr. Man Tae KIM
10 Chief Business Officer ....Dr. Chan HEO
08 Head Librarian ....Ms. Ho K. WOO
07 Director of Admissions ....Ms. Jee Won HA

Biola University (H)

13800 Biola Avenue, La Mirada CA 90639-0001
County: Los Angeles FICE Identification: 001122
Unit ID: 110097
Telephone: (562) 903-6000 Carnegie Class: DRU
FAX Number: (562) 903-4748 Calendar System: 4/1/4
URL: www.biola.edu
Established: 1908 Annual Undergrad Tuition & Fees: $29,908
Enrollment: 6,123 Coed
Affiliation or Control: Independent Non-Profit IRS Status: 501(c)3
Highest Offering: Doctorate
Program: Liberal Arts And General; Teacher Preparatory; Professional
Accreditation: WC, ACBSP, ART, CLPSY, MUS, NURSE, THEOL

01 President ....Dr. Barry H. COREY
05 Provost ....Dr. David NYSTROM
30 Vice President Advancement ....Dr. Adam MORRIS
11 Vice President University Services ....Mr. Gregory R. BALSANO
10 Vice President Finance ....Mr. Michael PIERCE
32 Vice Pres Student Devel & Univ Plng ....Dr. Chris GRACE
84 Vice Pres Enrollment Management ....Mr. Greg VAUGHAN
26 Vice Pres University Comm & Mktg ....Mrs. Irene NELLER
20 Vice Provost/Undergraduate Educ ....Dr. Patricia PIKE
20 Vice Provost/Fac Dev & Univ Assess ....Dr. Pete MENJARES
28 Vice Provost/Multi-Eth & Cross Cult ....Dr. Doretha O'QUINN
73 Dean Talbot School Theology ....Dr. Dennis DIRKS
83 Dean Rosemead School Psychology ....Dr. Clark CAMPBELL
88 Dean Cook Sch Intercultural Studies ....Dr. Douglas PENNOYER
08 Dean of the Library ....Dr. Rodney M. VLIET
87 Director Summer Session & Interterm ....Dr. Pete MENJARES
35 Dean of Students ....Mr. Danny PASCHALL
06 Dean Academic Records/Inst Research ....Mr. Ken GILSON
15 Director Human Resources ....Mr. Ronald G. MOORADIAN
37 Director Financial Aid ....Mr. Jonathan CHOY
46 Director Financial Planning/Opers ....Ms. Sandie WEAVER
21 Director Financial Mgmt/Reporting ....Mr. David KOONTZ
13 Director Information Systems ....Mr. Gary WYTCHERLEY
29 Director Alumni Relations ....Mr. Richard BEE
19 Director Campus Safety ....Mr. John O. OJEISEKHOBA
90 Director Technology Services ....Mr. Steven R. EARLE
36 Director Career Services ....Ms. Jeanie JANG
41 Athletic Director ....Dr. David HOLMQUIST
42 Dean of Spiritual Development ....Dr. Todd PICKETT
40 Manager Bookstore ....Mr. Harry EDWARDS
24 Supervisor Media Center ....Ms. Jill WATSON
18 Director Facilities Services ....Mr. Brian PHILLIPS
38 Director Student Counseling ....Dr. Melanie TAYLOR
96 Director of Purchasing ....Mr. Jim SAMPLES
09 Dean of University Assessment ....Dr. Deborah TAYLOR

Brandman University (I)

16355 Laguna Canyon Road, Irvine CA 92618
County: Orange Identification: 666638
Unit ID: 262086
Telephone: (949) 753-4774 Carnegie Class: Not Classified
FAX Number: (714) 753-7875 Calendar System: Other
URL: www.brandman.edu
Established: 1958 Annual Undergrad Tuition & Fees: $11,280
Enrollment: 6,849 Coed
Affiliation or Control: Independent Non-Profit IRS Status: 501(c)3
Highest Offering: Master's
Program: Liberal Arts And General
Accreditation: WC

01 Chancellor ....Dr. Gary BRAHM
12 Campus Director ....Ms. Jan HARTZ
05 Associate Dean of Education ....Ms. Patricia CLARK-WHITE
07 Director of Admissions ....Ms. Leticia ESPINOZA

† A member of the Chapman University System.

Brooks Institute (A)

1321 Alameda Padre Serra, Santa Barbara CA 93103
County: Santa Barbara　FICE Identification: 001123
Unit ID: 110185
Telephone: (805) 966-3888　Carnegie Class: Spec/Arts
FAX Number: (805) 564-1475　Calendar System: Semester
URL: www.brooks.edu
Established: 1945　Annual Undergrad Tuition & Fees: $26,820
Enrollment: 916　Coed
Affiliation or Control: Proprietary　IRS Status: Proprietary
Highest Offering: Master's
Program: Occupational; Liberal Arts And General; Professional; Fine Arts Emphasis
Accreditation: ACICS

01 President ..... Dr. Sue KIRKMAN
03 Provost ..... David LITSCHEL
10 Vice President of Finance ..... Timothy HALSEY
07 Vice President Marketing/Admissions ..... Elmo FRAZER
05 Director of Academic Affairs ..... Amanda BREY
26 Manager Media & Alumni Relations ..... Bethany INNOCENTI
28 Director of Regulatory Compliance ..... Denese PHILLIPS
36 Dir Career Services/Student Service ..... Maggie TOMAS
91 Director of Information Technology ..... Greg LAWLER
06 Registrar ..... Alice NGUYEN
08 Librarian ..... Susan SHIRAS
15 Director of Human Resources ..... Jamie PLATT

Brooks Institute (B)

5301 North Ventura Avenue, Ventura CA 93001-1023
County: Ventura　Identification: 666250
Telephone: (805) 585-8000　Carnegie Class: Not Classified
FAX Number: (805) 585-8001　Calendar System: Semester
URL: www.brooks.edu
Established: 1945　Annual Undergrad Tuition & Fees: $21,600
Enrollment: 1,855　Coed
Affiliation or Control: Proprietary　IRS Status: Proprietary
Highest Offering: Master's
Program: Occupational; Liberal Arts And General; Professional; Fine Arts Emphasis
Accreditation: ACICS

01 President ..... Dr. Sue KIRKMAN

Bryan College (C)

2317 Gold Meadow Way, Gold River CA 95670-4443
County: Sacramento　FICE Identification: 033993
Unit ID: 439826
Telephone: (916) 649-2400　Carnegie Class: Assoc/PrivFP
FAX Number: (916) 641-8649　Calendar System: Quarter
URL: www.bryancollege.edu
Established: 1996　Annual Undergrad Tuition & Fees: $17,550
Enrollment: 611　Coed
Affiliation or Control: Proprietary　IRS Status: Proprietary
Highest Offering: Associate Degree
Program: Occupational; 2-Year Principally Bachelor's Creditable; Technical Emphasis
Accreditation: ACCSC

01 President ..... Mr. John LEDESMA
53 Director of Education ..... Mr. Matthew BRANDSTETTER
88 Dir of Student & Alumni Outreach ..... Mr. Jeff HORTON
07 Director of Admissions ..... Ms. Orquedia CHAVEZ
37 Director Student Financial Aid ..... Mr. Ramiro ONTIVEROS
06 Registrar ..... Mr. Michael KRYSHAK

Bryan College (D)

3580 Wilshire Boulevard, Suite 400,
Los Angeles CA 90010
County: Los Angeles　FICE Identification: 007164
Unit ID: 110219
Telephone: (213) 484-8850　Carnegie Class: Not Classified
FAX Number: (213) 483-3936　Calendar System: Semester
URL: www.bryancollege.edu
Established: 1940　Annual Undergrad Tuition & Fees: $12,270
Enrollment: 946　Coed
Affiliation or Control: Proprietary　IRS Status: Proprietary
Highest Offering: Associate Degree
Program: Occupational; 2-Year Principally Bachelor's Creditable
Accreditation: ACICS

01 President ..... Mr. John KOLACINSKI

Butte College (E)

3536 Butte Campus Drive, Oroville CA 95965-8399
County: Butte　FICE Identification: 008073
Unit ID: 110246
Telephone: (530) 895-2511　Carnegie Class: Assoc/Pub-R-L
FAX Number: (530) 895-2345　Calendar System: Semester
URL: www.butte.edu
Established: 1966　Annual Undergrad Tuition & Fees (In-District): $1,084
Enrollment: 13,293　Coed
Affiliation or Control: State/Local　IRS Status: 501(c)3
Highest Offering: Associate Degree
Program: Occupational; 2-Year Principally Bachelor's Creditable
Accreditation: WJ, EMT

01 Superintendent/President ..... Dr. Kimberly PERRY
05 Vice President of Learning ..... Dr. Kenneth MEIER
11 CBO/VP Administrative Services ..... Mr. Andrew SULESKI
45 Vice President Planning & Info ..... Mr. Les JAURON
32 Vice President Student Services ..... Mr. Allen RENVILLE
75 Dean Career/Technical Education ..... Mr. Michael DUNBAUGH
97 Dean of Transfer & General Educ ..... Ms. Samia YAQUB
37 Dean Financial Aid/Special Programs ..... Ms. Karen MICALIZIO
15 Director Human Resources ..... Ms. Claudia TRUJILLO
18 Dir Facilities Planning/Management ..... Mr. Mike MILLER
09 Director of Institutional Research ..... Dr. Baba ADAM
07 Director Admissions/Records ..... Mr. Clinton SLAUGHTER
08 Director Library Services ..... Dr. Luozhu CEN
12 Director Chico/Glenn Centers ..... Mr. Rudy FLORES
103 Dir Contract Education & Training ..... Ms. Annie RAFFERTY
26 Director of Marketing/Public Rels ..... Ms. Lisa DELABY
41 Athletic Director ..... Mr. Craig RIGSBEE
13 Director Information Services ..... Mr. Doug CREMER
30 Director Institutional Advancement ..... Mr. John GLIHA
37 Director Student Financial Aid ..... Ms. Carolyn STEPHEN
76 Director of Allied Health Programs ..... Ms. Denise ADAMS
21 Associate Business Officer ..... Mr. Trevor STEWART
38 Coordinator of Counseling ..... Ms. Susan CAREY

Cabrillo College (F)

6500 Soquel Drive, Aptos CA 95003-3194
County: Santa Cruz　FICE Identification: 001124
Unit ID: 110334
Telephone: (831) 479-6100　Carnegie Class: Assoc/Pub-R-L
FAX Number: (831) 479-6425　Calendar System: Semester
URL: www.cabrillo.edu
Established: 1959　Annual Undergrad Tuition & Fees (In-District): $964
Enrollment: 15,387　Coed
Affiliation or Control: State/Local　IRS Status: 501(c)3
Highest Offering: Associate Degree
Program: Occupational; 2-Year Principally Bachelor's Creditable
Accreditation: WJ, DH, MAC, RAD

01 President ..... Dr. Brian KING
05 Vice President for Instruction ..... Dr. Renee KILMER
10 Asst Supt/Vice Pres Business Svcs ..... Ms. Victoria LEWIS
32 Asst Supt/Vice Pres Student Svcs ..... Dr. Dennis BAILEY-FOUGNIER
13 Int Dean of Information Technology ..... Dr. Craig HAYWARD
08 Librarian ..... Mr. Georg ROMERO
27 Director Marketing & Communications ..... Ms. Kristin FABOS
15 Director Personnel/Human Resources ..... Ms. Loree L. MCCAWLEY
21 Director Business Services ..... Mr. Graciano MENDOZA
07 Director Admissions & Records ..... Ms. Tama BOLTON
09 Dir Planning/Research/Knowledge Sys ..... Dr. Craig HAYWARD
18 Director Facilities Plng/Purchasing ..... Mr. Joe NUGENT
37 Dir Financial Aid/Scholarships ..... Ms. Deborah B. SORIA
40 Bookstore Manager ..... Ms. Robin ELLIS

California Baptist University (G)

8432 Magnolia Avenue, Riverside CA 92504-3297
County: Riverside　FICE Identification: 001125
Unit ID: 110361
Telephone: (951) 689-5771　Carnegie Class: Master's L
FAX Number: (951) 351-1808　Calendar System: Semester
URL: www.calbaptist.edu
Established: 1950　Annual Undergrad Tuition & Fees: $25,654
Enrollment: 4,715　Coed
Affiliation or Control: Southern Baptist　IRS Status: 501(c)3
Highest Offering: Master's
Program: Liberal Arts And General; Teacher Preparatory
Accreditation: WC, ACBSP, MUS, NURSE

01 President ..... Dr. Ronald L. ELLIS
04 Admin Asst to the Presidet ..... Ms. Ann CRAMER
10 Vice President for Finance & Admin ..... Mr. Mark HOWE
32 VP Enrollment & Student Services ..... Mr. Kent DACUS
27 Vice Pres Marketing & Communication ..... Dr. Mark A. WYATT
88 Director of Conferences & Events ..... Mr. Earl HARRIS
26 Director of Marketing ..... Mr. Jeremy ZIMMERMAN
26 Director of Communications ..... Ms. Yvonne HESTER
30 Interim VP Institution Advancement ..... Dr. Arthur CLEVELAND
106 VP for Online & Prof Studies ..... Mr. David POOLE
07 Director of Enrollment Services ..... Mr. Ted MEYER
05 Provost ..... Dr. Jonathan K. PARKER
45 Assoc Provost Institution Planning ..... Dr. Neal MCBRIDE
20 Associate Provost ..... Dr. Dawn Ellen JACOBS
20 Dean of Academic Services ..... Dr. Tracy WARD
102 Grants Administrator ..... Ms. Lauren SAVORD
29 Director Alumni Relations ..... Ms. Carrie SMITH
35 Dean of Students ..... Mr. Anthony LAMMONS
84 Assoc Dean Enrollment Services ..... Mr. Allen JOHNSON
84 Assoc Dean Graduate Enrollment ..... Ms. Gail RONVEAUX
06 Registrar ..... Ms. Shawnn KONING
08 Director of Library ..... Mr. Steve EMERSON
21 Director of Financial Services ..... Mr. Calvin SPARKMAN
18 Director Facilities/Physical Plant ..... Mr. Steve SMITH
37 Director Financial Aid ..... Ms. Rebecca SANCHEZ
14 Dir Information Technology Services ..... Mr. Scott TRACY
72 Dean of Technology ..... Mr. Tran HONG
15 Human Resources Manager ..... Ms. Julie FRESQUEZ
19 Director of Public Safety ..... Mr. Jim WALTERS
36 Director Career Services ..... Mrs. Kushi JONES
41 Athletic Director ..... Dr. Micah PARKER
38 Director of Enrollment Advising ..... Ms. Shelly RUPARD
85 Director of International Students ..... Mr. Jonathan BELLO
09 Director of Assessment ..... Mr. Phil MARTINEZ
39 Director of Residence Life ..... Mr. Daron HUBBERT
40 Director of University Bookstore ..... Ms. Carol BRACEY
105 Web Site Manager ..... Mr. John DICESARE
42 Dean Spiritual Life/Campus Minister ..... Mr. John MONTGOMERY
53 Dean School of Education ..... Dr. John SHOUP
54 Dean School of Engineering ..... Dr. Anthony DONALDSON
64 Dean School of Music ..... Dr. Gary BONNER
66 Dean School of Nursing ..... Dr. Constance L. MILTON
66 Director of RN-BSN Program ..... Dr. Geneva OAKS
73 Dean School of Christian Ministries ..... Dr. Chris MORGAN
82 Dean School of Behavioral Sciences ..... Dr. H. Bruce STOKES
49 Interim Dean College of Arts & Sci ..... Dr. James LU
50 Dean School of Business ..... Dr. Andrew K. HERRITY
106 Dean for Online and Prof Studies ..... Dr. Dirk DAVIS
76 Dean of College of Allied Health ..... Dr. Charles SANDS

California Christian College (H)

4881 E University Avenue, Fresno CA 93703-3599
County: Fresno　FICE Identification: 008844
Unit ID: 110918
Telephone: (559) 251-4215　Carnegie Class: Spec/Faith
FAX Number: (559) 251-4231　Calendar System: Semester
URL: www.calchristiancollege.org
Established: 1955　Annual Undergrad Tuition & Fees: $7,610
Enrollment: 20　Coed
Affiliation or Control: Free Will Baptist Church　IRS Status: 501(c)3
Highest Offering: Baccalaureate
Program: 2-Year Principally Bachelor's Creditable; Liberal Arts And General; Religious Emphasis
Accreditation: TRACS

01 President ..... Mr. Wendell L. WALLEY
05 Academic Dean ..... Dr. James H. COX
06 Registrar ..... Vacant
10 Chief Business Officer ..... Mrs. Anna-Jean WALLEY
09 Dir Institutional Effectiveness ..... Ms. Ingrid VOSS
08 Head Librarian ..... Mrs. Nancy SINGH
37 Coordinator Financial Aid ..... Ms. Melinda SCROGGINS
07 Admissions Representative ..... Vacant
39 Director Student Housing ..... Vacant

California Coast University (I)

925 N. Spurgeon Street, Santa Ana CA 92701-3515
County: Orange　FICE Identification: 041276
Unit ID: 110936
Telephone: (714) 547-9625　Carnegie Class: Not Classified
FAX Number: (714) 547-5777　Calendar System: Other
URL: www.calcoast.edu
Established: 1973　Annual Undergrad Tuition & Fees: $9,500
Enrollment: 6,500　Coed
Affiliation or Control: Proprietary　IRS Status: Proprietary
Highest Offering: Doctorate
Program: Professional; Business Emphasis
Accreditation: DETC

01 President ..... Dr. Thomas M. NEAL
05 Chief Academic Officer ..... Dr. Cynthia TEEPLE
20 Director of Academic Affairs ..... Mr. Douglas PETRIKAT

California College of the Arts (J)

1111 Eighth Street, San Francisco CA 94107-2247
County: San Francisco　FICE Identification: 001127
Unit ID: 110370
Telephone: (415) 703-9500　Carnegie Class: Spec/Arts
FAX Number: (510) 655-3541　Calendar System: Semester
URL: www.cca.edu
Established: 1907　Annual Undergrad Tuition & Fees: $36,969
Enrollment: 1,860　Coed
Affiliation or Control: Independent Non-Profit　IRS Status: 501(c)3
Highest Offering: Master's
Program: Professional
Accreditation: WC, ART, CIDA

01 President ..... Mr. Stephen BEAL
05 Provost ..... Mr. Mark BREITENBERG
10 Sr VP Finance & Administration ..... Mr. David KIRSHMAN
30 Sr Vice President of Advancement ..... Ms. Susan AVILA
11 Vice President of Operations ..... Ms. Jennifer STEIN
84 Vice Pres of Enrollment Management ..... Ms. Sheri MCKENZIE
26 Vice President for Communications ..... Ms. Chris BLISS
35 Vice President Student Affairs ..... Mr. George SEDANO
20 Assoc Provost ..... Ms. Melanie CORN
06 Registrar ..... Mr. Jerry ALLEN
37 Director Financial Aid ..... Ms. Silvia MARQUEZ
15 Director Human Resources ..... Ms. Sharyn SCHNEIDER
29 Director Alumni Relations ..... Ms. Jessica RUSSELL
36 Director of Career Services ..... Ms. Olivia MARTINEZ
21 Controller ..... Mr. Ken TANZER
27 Co-Chief Information Officer ..... Mr. Scott EMERY
27 Co-Chief Information Officer ..... Mrs. Mindy JASPERSON
07 Director Undergrad Admissions ..... Ms. Robynne ROYSTER
38 Director Student Counseling ..... Dr. Tara RECH
09 Director of Institutional Research ..... Mr. David MECKEL
18 Chief Facilities/Physical Plant ..... Ms. Deborah FELDMANN
96 Director of Purchasing ..... Ms. Jackie CRADDOCK
07 Director Graduate Admissions ..... Mr. Noel DAHL

California College San Diego (A)

2820 Camino Del Rio S, Ste 300,
San Diego CA 92108-3821

County: San Diego — FICE Identification: 021108
Unit ID: 110945
Telephone: (619) 680-4430 — Carnegie Class: Spec/Health
FAX Number: (619) 295-5985 — Calendar System: Other
URL: www.cc-sd.edu
Established: 1978 — Annual Undergrad Tuition & Fees: $15,800
Enrollment: 1,400 — Coed
Affiliation or Control: Proprietary — IRS Status: Proprietary
Highest Offering: Master's
Program: Occupational; 2-Year Principally Bachelor's Creditable
Accreditation: ACCSC

01 Chief Operating Officer ... Mrs. Barbara THOMAS
05 Executive Director ... Dr. Ken WEBB

California Culinary Academy (B)

350 Rhode Island Street, San Francisco CA 94103

County: San Francisco — FICE Identification: 022202
Unit ID: 111009
Telephone: (888) 897-3222 — Carnegie Class: Assoc/PrivFP
FAX Number: (415) 771-2194 — Calendar System: Other
URL: www.baychef.com
Established: 1977 — Annual Undergrad Tuition & Fees: N/A
Enrollment: 2,045 — Coed
Affiliation or Control: Proprietary — IRS Status: Proprietary
Highest Offering: Associate Degree
Program: Occupational
Accreditation: ACCSC, ACICS, ACFEI

01 President ... Peter LEE
10 Vice Pres of Finance & Accounting ... Jim MIRR
05 Dean of Student & Academic Affairs ... Rocco LAMANNA
11 Vice President of Operations ... Christina BRENNER
07 Director of Admissions ... Sanjay KETTY
37 Director of Student Finance ... Vacant
36 Director of Career Services ... Lisa WILSON

California Institute of the Arts (C)

24700 McBean Parkway, Valencia CA 91355-2397

County: Los Angeles — FICE Identification: 001132
Unit ID: 111081
Telephone: (661) 255-1050 — Carnegie Class: Spec/Arts
FAX Number: (661) 254-8352 — Calendar System: Semester
URL: www.calarts.edu
Established: 1961 — Annual Undergrad Tuition & Fees: $37,684
Enrollment: 1,467 — Coed
Affiliation or Control: Independent Non-Profit — IRS Status: 501(c)3
Highest Offering: Doctorate
Program: Professional; Fine Arts Emphasis
Accreditation: WC, ART, DANCE, MUS, THEA

01 President ... Dr. Steven D. LAVINE
05 Provost ... Vacant
10 Vice Pres/Chief Financial Officer ... Vacant
88 Vice Pres for Special Projects ... Lynn R. ROSENFELD
30 Vice Pres/Chief Advancement Officer ... Bianca ROBERTS
88 Vice Pres Internatioal Relations ... Carol KIM
20 Associate Provost ... Jacqueline ELAM
13 Assoc Vice President and CIO ... Michael CARTER
21 Assoc Vice President and Controller ... Karla TALAVERA
18 Asst Vice President Facilities ... Jesse SMITH
20 Asst Provost for Academic Affairs ... Justine GARRETT
28 Asst Provost Equity and Diversity ... Matthew SHENODA
84 Assoc Provost Enrollment Management ... Audrey TANNER
57 Dean School of Art ... Thomas LAWSON
64 Dean Herb Alpert School of Music ... David ROSENBOOM
88 Dean School of Critical Studies ... Vacant
88 Dean Sharon D. Lund School of Dance ... Stephan KOPLOWITZ
88 Dean School Film & Video ... Steve ANKER
88 Dean School of Theater ... Travis PRESTON
32 Dean of Students ... Yvonne GUY
08 Dean Div of Library & Info Resource ... Jeffrey GATTEN
26 Executive Director Public Affairs ... Wendy SHATTUCK
37 Director of Financial Aid ... Bobbi HEUER
88 Director Community Arts Partnership ... Glenna AVILA
29 Director Alumni Relations ... Nicole STARK
15 Director of Human Resources ... Annabelle BALTIERRA
06 Registrar ... Nancy WHITTEMORE
07 Director of Admissions ... Molly RYAN

California Institute of Integral Studies (D)

1453 Mission Street, 4th Floor,
San Francisco CA 94103-2557

County: San Francisco — FICE Identification: 012154
Unit ID: 110316
Telephone: (415) 575-6100 — Carnegie Class: DRU
FAX Number: (415) 575-1264 — Calendar System: Semester
URL: www.ciis.edu
Established: 1968 — Annual Undergrad Tuition & Fees: $22,140
Enrollment: 1,235 — Coed
Affiliation or Control: Independent Non-Profit — IRS Status: 501(c)3
Highest Offering: Doctorate
Program: Professional
Accreditation: WC, #CLPSY

01 President ... Mr. Joseph L. SUBBIONDO
05 Academic Vice President ... Dr. Judie WEXLER
32 Dean of Students/Director Diversity ... Ms. Shirley STRONG
29 Dean of Alumni/Dir of Travel Stds ... Dr. Richard BUGGS
20 Dean Academic Plng/Administration ... Mr. Chip B. GOLDSTEIN
10 Controller/Director Finance ... Mr. Ken ABIKO
30 Director of Development ... Ms. Dorotea REYNA
16 Director of Human Resources ... Ms. S. Michelle COLEMAN
07 Dean Admissions & Financial Aid ... Mr. Michael GRIFFIN
13 Director of Info Systems Technology ... Mr. Scott CILIBERTI
08 Library Director ... Ms. Lise DYCKMAN
06 Registrar ... Mr. Dan GURLER
26 Director of Communications ... Mr. Jim David MARTIN
37 Director of Financial Aid ... Ms. Marisol NEALON
51 Director of Public Programs ... Mr. Karim BAER
18 Director Facilities & Operations ... Mr. Jonathan MILLS
40 Bookstore Manager ... Mr. Steven SWANSON
85 International Student Advisor ... Ms. Jody O'CONNOR

California Institute of Technology (E)

1200 E California Boulevard, Pasadena CA 91125-0001

County: Los Angeles — FICE Identification: 001131
Unit ID: 110404
Telephone: (626) 395-6811 — Carnegie Class: RU/VH
FAX Number: (626) 795-1547 — Calendar System: Trimester
URL: www.caltech.edu
Established: 1891 — Annual Undergrad Tuition & Fees: $37,704
Enrollment: 2,175 — Coed
Affiliation or Control: Independent Non-Profit — IRS Status: 501(c)3
Highest Offering: Doctorate
Program: Liberal Arts And General; Professional
Accreditation: WC, ENG

01 President ... Dr. Jean-Lou A. CHAMEAU
04 Executive Assistant to President ... Mrs. Mary L. WEBSTER
05 Provost ... Dr. Edward M. STOLPER
88 Vice President/Director JPL ... Dr. Charles ELACHI
10 Vice President Business & Finance ... Mr. Dean W. CURRIE
30 Vice President Devel/Alumni Rels ... Mr. Peter B. DERVAN
32 Vice President Student Affairs ... Dr. Anneila I. SARGENT
43 General Counsel ... Ms. Victoria D. STRATMAN
20 Vice Provost ... Dr. Melany L. HUNT
20 Vice Provost ... Dr. Morteza GHARIB
15 Assoc Vice Pres HR/Campus Svcs ... Ms. Julia M. MCCALLIN
44 Asst Vice President Development ... Ms. Kristi L. NEWTON
31 Assoc VP Campus & Cmty Relations . Ms. Denise NELSON NASH
86 Director Govt Rels ... Mr. Hall P. DAILY
35 Senior Dir for Student Activities ... Mr. Tom N. MANNION
26 Asst VP Marketing & Communications ... Ms. Kristen BROWN
81 Chair Biology Division ... Dr. Stephen L. MAYO
81 Chair Chemistry & Chemical Engr Div . Dr. Jacqueline K. BARTON
54 Chair Engr & Applied Science Div ... Dr. Ares J. ROSAKIS
65 Chair Geology/Planet Science Div ... Dr. Kenneth FARLEY
79 Chair Humanities/Social Science Div ... Dr. Jonathan N. KATZ
81 Chair Physics/Math/Astro Division ... Dr. B. T. SOIFER
06 Registrar ... Mrs. Mary N. MORLEY
07 Director of Admissions ... Mr. Jarrid WHITNEY
08 University Librarian ... Ms. Kimberly DOUGLAS
14 Chief Information Officer ... Mr. Rich E. FAGEN
18 Assoc Vice Pres for Facilities ... Mr. James W. COWELL, JR.
18 Director Facilities Management ... Mr. William J. IRWIN
19 Manager Security Office ... Mr. Gregg HENDERSON
22 Director Employee Affirm Act/ Rels ... Ms. April WHITE CASTENADA
23 Director Health Services ... Dr. Stuart C. MILLER
25 Director Sponsored Research ... Dr. Richard P. SELIGMAN
29 Executive Director Alumni Assoc ... Ms. Alexandra C. TOBEK
37 Director Financial Aid ... Mr. Don CREWELL
36 Director Career Development ... Ms. Lauren B. STOLPER
40 Manager Bookstore ... Ms. Karyn SEIXAS
41 Director Athletics & Physical Ed ... Ms. Betsy MITCHELL
58 Dean of Graduate Studies ... Dr. Joseph E. SHEPHERD
28 Dean of Students ... Dr. D. R. KIEWIET
88 Associate Dean of Students ... Dr. Barbara C. GREEN
85 Director International Student Pgm ... Ms. Marjory GOODING
96 Dir of Purchasing & Payment Svcs ... Ms. Tina LOWENTHAL

California Intercontinental University (F)

1470 Valley Vista Drive, Suite 150,
Diamond Bar CA 91765-3954

County: Los Angeles — Identification: 666670
Telephone: (909) 396-6090 — Carnegie Class: Not Classified
FAX Number: (909) 804-5151 — Calendar System: Other
URL: www.caluniversity.edu
Established: 2003 — Annual Undergrad Tuition & Fees: $18,000
Enrollment: 215 — Coed
Affiliation or Control: Proprietary — IRS Status: Proprietary
Highest Offering: Doctorate
Program: Professional; Business Emphasis
Accreditation: DETC

01 Chief Executive Officer ... Mr. Senthil B. KUMAR
05 Chief Academic Officer ... Vacant

California International Business University (G)

520 West Ash Street 3rd Floor, San Diego CA 92101

County: San Diego — Identification: 666711
Telephone: (619) 702-9400 — Carnegie Class: Not Classified
FAX Number: (619) 702-9476 — Calendar System: Quarter
URL: www.cibu.edu
Established: 1994 — Annual Undergrad Tuition & Fees: $12,000
Enrollment: 220 — Coed
Affiliation or Control: Independent Non-Profit — IRS Status: 501(c)3
Highest Offering: Doctorate
Program: Professional; Business Emphasis
Accreditation: ACICS

01 President ... Dr. Michael L. MCMANUS

California Lutheran University (H)

60 W Olsen Road, Thousand Oaks CA 91360-2787

County: Ventura — FICE Identification: 001133
Unit ID: 110413
Telephone: (805) 492-2411 — Carnegie Class: Master's L
FAX Number: (805) 493-3513 — Calendar System: Semester
URL: www.clunet.edu
Established: 1959 — Annual Undergrad Tuition & Fees: $32,860
Enrollment: 3,931 — Coed
Affiliation or Control: Evangelical Lutheran Church In America
IRS Status: 501(c)3
Highest Offering: Doctorate
Program: Liberal Arts And General; Teacher Preparatory; Professional
Accreditation: WC, TED

01 President ... Dr. Christopher KIMBALL
05 Provost/Vice Pres Academic Affairs ... Ms. Leanne NEILSON
30 Vice Pres University Advancement ... Mr. Stephen WHEATLY
10 Vice Pres Admin/Finance/Treasurer ... Ms. Karen DAVIS
32 Vice Pres Stdnt Life/Dean of Stdnts ... Mr. William ROSSER
84 VP Enrollment Mgmt & Marketing ... Dr. Mathew WARD
08 Assoc Provost for Information Svcs ... Mr. Julius BIANCHI
18 Assoc Vice Pres Facilities ... Mr. Ryan VAN OMMEREN
26 Assc Vice Pres University Relations ... Ms. Lynda FULFORD
49 Dean College Arts & Sciences ... Dr. Joan GRIFFIN
53 Dean of School of Education ... Dr. George PETERSEN
50 Dean of School of Business ... Dr. Charles MAXEY
88 Director Church Relations ... Rev. Arne BERGLAND
15 Director of Human Resources ... Ms. Susan TOLLE
06 Director Academic Svcs/Registrar ... Ms. Maria KOHNKE
42 University Pastor ... Rev. Scott MAXWELL-DOHERTY
42 University Pastor ... Rev. Melissa MAXWELL-DOHERTY
44 Director Estate & Gift ... Ms. Shannon YASMAN
41 Director Athletics ... Mr. Daniel KUNTZ
55 Director of Adult Degree Program ... Ms. Gina LAMONICA
36 Director of Career Services ... Ms. Cindy LEWIS
35 Director Multicultural/Intl Pgm ... Dr. Juanita HALL
21 Dir of Budget/Management Analysis ... Ms. Barbara REX
29 Director Alumni Relations ... Ms. Rachel RONNING LINDGREN
38 Director Counseling Services ... Dr. Alan GOODWIN
19 Director Security/Safety ... Mr. Frederick MILLER

California Maritime Academy (I)

200 Maritime Academy Drive, Vallejo CA 94590-0644

County: Solano — FICE Identification: 001134
Unit ID: 111188
Telephone: (707) 654-1000 — Carnegie Class: Bac/Diverse
FAX Number: (707) 654-1001 — Calendar System: Semester
URL: www.csum.edu
Established: 1929 — Annual Undergrad Tuition & Fees (In-State): $7,574
Enrollment: 857 — Coed
Affiliation or Control: State — IRS Status: 501(c)3
Highest Offering: Baccalaureate
Program: Occupational; Liberal Arts And General; Technical Emphasis
Accreditation: WC, ENG, ENGT, IACBE

01 President ... Dr. William B. EISENHARDT
05 Provost/VP Academic Affairs ... Dr. Gerald JAKUBOWSKI
10 Vice Pres Administration/Finance ... Vacant
30 VP University Advancement ... Mr. Thomas DUNWORTH
20 Academic Dean ... Mr. Stephen PRONCHICK
20 Assoc VP Academic Affairs ... Mr. Steve KRETA
88 Master of Training Ship ... Capt. Harry BOLTON
21 Budget Officer ... Mr. Steve MASTRO
06 Director of Student Records ... Ms. Deborah L. FISCHER
08 Director of Library ... Mr. Richard ROBISON
07 Dir Admissions/Enrollment Services ... Mr. Marc MCGEE
37 Director of Financial Aid ... Vacant
88 Executive Director CMA Services ... Ms. Diane RAWICZ
88 Director Ctr Excellence & Learning ... Mr. Howard JACKSON
36 Director Career Development ... Mr. James DALSKE
18 Director Facilities Planning ... Mr. Roger JAECKEL
19 Chief Security Officer ... Chief Roseann RICHARD
22 Director of Human Resources ... Ms. Kay MILLER
41 Director of Athletics ... Mr. Marv CHRISTOPHER
26 Director Public Relations ... Ms. Jennifer WHITTY
32 Dean of Students ... Dr. Debborah HEBERT
40 Bookstore Manager ... Ms. Beth AYERS
96 Purchasing Manager ... Ms. Vineeta DHILLON
29 Alumni Coordinator ... Ms. Sylvia REGALADO

California Miramar University (A)

9750 Miramar Road Suite 180, San Diego CA 92126-7501

County: San Diego — Identification: 666713
Telephone: (858) 653-3000 — Carnegie Class: Not Classified
FAX Number: (858) 653-6786 — Calendar System: Other
URL: www.calmu.edu
Established: 2005 — Annual Undergrad Tuition & Fees: $7,050
Enrollment: N/A — Coed
Affiliation or Control: Proprietary — IRS Status: Proprietary
Highest Offering: Doctorate
Program: Professional
Accreditation: DETC, ACICS

01 President ... Dr. Dominic MWENJA

California National University for Advanced Studies (B)

8550 Balboa Boulevard, Suite 210,
Northridge CA 91325-3576

County: Los Angeles — Identification: 666786
Telephone: (800) 782-2422 — Carnegie Class: Not Classified
FAX Number: (818) 830-2418 — Calendar System: Trimester
URL: www.cnuas.edu
Established: 1993 — Annual Undergrad Tuition & Fees: $5,932
Enrollment: 703 — Coed
Affiliation or Control: Proprietary — IRS Status: Proprietary
Highest Offering: Master's
Program: Professional
Accreditation: DETC

01 President ... Dr. Carlton BRYANT
32 Vice Pres Student Affs/Registrar ... Ms. Stephanie SMITH
05 Director of Instruction ... Dr. Carol BACKER
50 Dean Business Administration ... Dr. Philip CHONG
54 Associate CNU Col of Engineering ... Dr. Robert RYAN
06 Consult to CNU VP Stdt Affs/Registr ... Mr. Philip CHONG
14 MIS Director ... Mr. Charles NG

California Northstate College of Pharmacy (C)

10811 International Drive, Rancho Cordova CA 95670

County: Sacramento — Identification: 667020
Telephone: (916) 631-8108 — Carnegie Class: Not Classified
FAX Number: (916) 631-8127 — Calendar System: Semester
URL: www.californiacollegeofpharmacy.org
Established: 2008 — Annual Graduate Tuition & Fees: $39,624
Enrollment: N/A — Coed
Affiliation or Control: Independent Non-Profit — IRS Status: 501(c)3
Highest Offering: Doctorate; No Undergraduates
Program: Professional
Accreditation: @WC, @PHAR

01 President ... Dr. Alvin CHEUNG
05 Dean ... Dr. David HAWKINS
11 Vice President of Operations ... Mr. Norman FONG
20 Assoc Dean Academic Affs/Research ... Dr. John MARTIN
32 Asst Dean Student Affs/Admissions ... Ms. Cyndi PORTER
08 Director of Library Resources ... Mr. Scott MINOR
06 Registrar ... Ms. Lisa ERCK

California Southern University (D)

930 Roosevelt, Irvine CA 92620

County: Orange — Identification: 666770
Telephone: (714) 882-7800 — Carnegie Class: Not Classified
FAX Number: (714) 480-0834 — Calendar System: Semester
URL: www.calsouthern.edu
Established: 1978 — Annual Undergrad Tuition & Fees: $5,280
Enrollment: N/A — Coed
Affiliation or Control: Independent Non-Profit — IRS Status: 501(c)3
Highest Offering: Doctorate
Program: Liberal Arts And General; Professional
Accreditation: DETC

01 President ... Dr. Carroll RYAN

*The California State University System Office (E)

401 Golden Shore, Long Beach CA 90802-4210

County: Los Angeles — FICE Identification: 001136
Unit ID: 110501
Telephone: (562) 951-4000 — Carnegie Class: N/A
FAX Number: (562) 951-4986
URL: www.calstate.edu

01 Chancellor ... Dr. Charles B. REED
03 Executive Vice Chancellor & CAO ... Dr. Ephraim P. SMITH
30 Vice Chanc Univ Rels/Advancement ... Mr. Garrett ASHLEY
15 Vice Chancellor Human Resources ... Ms. Gail BROOKS
100 Chief of Staff ... Ms. Sandra B. GEORGE
10 Executive Vice Chancellor & CFO ... Dr. Benjamin F. QUILLIAN
43 General Counsel ... Ms. Christine HELWICK
96 Dir Contract Services/Procurement ... Mr. Tom ROBERTS

*California Polytechnic State University-San Luis Obispo (F)

1 Grand Avenue, San Luis Obispo CA 93407-9000

County: San Luis Obispo — FICE Identification: 001143
Unit ID: 110422
Telephone: (805) 756-1111 — Carnegie Class: Master's L
FAX Number: (805) 756-5400 — Calendar System: Quarter
URL: www.calpoly.edu
Established: 1901 — Annual Undergrad Tuition & Fees (In-State): $7,333
Enrollment: 18,360 — Coed
Affiliation or Control: State — IRS Status: 501(c)3
Highest Offering: Master's
Program: Liberal Arts And General; Teacher Preparatory; Professional; Technical Emphasis
Accreditation: WC, ART, BUS, CONST, CS, DIETD, DIETI, ENG, FOR, LSAR, MUS, NAIT, NRPA, PLNG

02 President ... Dr. Jeffrey D. ARMSTRONG
100 Interim Chief of Staff ... Mr. Matthew J. ROBERTS
05 Provost/Vice Pres Academic Affs ... Dr. Robert D. KOOB
10 Vice Pres Administration & Finance ... Mr. Lawrence R. KELLEY
32 Vice President Student Affairs ... Dr. Cornel N. MORTON
30 Vice Pres University Advancement ... Vacant
88 Exec Dir CP Corp/Assoc VP Comm Svcs ... Ms. Bonnie D. MURPHY
28 Associate VP Inclusive Exc/Ombuds ... Dr. W. David CONN
35 Assoc Vice Pres Student Affairs ... Dr. Denise M. CAMPBELL
21 Associate Vice Pres Finance ... Mr. Richard M. RAMIREZ
44 Assoc VP Univ Adv/Chief Dev Officer ... Mr. Michael D. MCCALL
26 Assoc VP Strategic Communications ... Mr. Chip VISCI
15 Assoc Vice Pres Academic Personnel ... Dr. Al LIDDICOAT
39 Dir Univ Housing & Assoc VP/SA ... Mr. Preston C. ALLEN
20 Vice Provost Programs & Planning ... Dr. Erling A. SMITH
46 Assoc Vive Provost Systems/Res Mgmt ... Ms. Kimi M. IKEDA
07 Asst VP Admiss/Recruitment/Fin Aid ... Mr. James L. MARAVIGLIA
21 Asst Vice President Admin & Finance ... Ms. Karen WEBB
06 Registrar/Dir of Academic Records ... Mr. Cem SUNATA
22 Dir Employment Eq & Fac Recruit ... Ms. Martha CODY
41 Athletic Director ... Mr. Don OBERHELMAN
18 Director Facility Services ... Mr. Mark A. HUNTER
18 Dir Facil Planning/Capital Projects ... Mr. Robert KITAMURA
23 Director Health/Counseling Services ... Dr. Martin E. BRAGG
38 Interim Head of Counseling Services ... Dr. Elie N. AXELROTH
32 ASI Executive Director ... Mr. Richard G. JOHNSON
32 Director Student Life & Leadership ... Mr. Ken BARCLAY
40 Director El Corral Bookstore ... Mr. Frank CAWLEY
19 University Police Department ... Chief William WATTON
35 Dean of Students ... Dr. Jean DECOSTA
51 Dean Continuing Education ... Dr. Brian TIETJE
46 Dean Research & Graduate Pgm ... Dr. Susan C. OPAVA
27 Dean of Information Services/CIO ... Dr. Michael D. MILLER
47 Dean Agriculture/Food & Env Sci ... Dr. David J. WEHNER
48 Dean Architect/Environmental Design ... Mr. R. Thomas JONES
50 Dean Orfalea College of Business ... Dr. David P. CHRISTY
54 Dean Engineering ... Vacant
49 Dean Liberal Arts ... Dr. Linda H. HALISKY
81 Dean Science & Mathematics ... Dr. Philip S. BAILEY, JR.
53 Director CSM School of Education ... Dr. Bob DETWEILER
29 Interim Director Alumni Relations ... Ms. Tracee DEHAHN
36 Dir Career Services & Testing Svcs ... Mr. Martin C. SHIBATA
09 Director Inst Planning/Analysis ... Mr. Brent S. GOODMAN
37 Director Financial Aid ... Ms. Lois M. KELLY
15 Director Human Resources ... Ms. Beth E. GALLAGHER
96 Dir Contract Procrurement Risk Mgmt ... Mr. Dru ZACHMEYER
104 Director of International Education ... Dr. Raymond ZEUSCHNER
94 Int Chair Women's & Gender Studies ... Dr. Jean M. WILLIAMS
92 Director University Honors Program ... Dr. Sema E. ALPTEKIN

*California State Polytechnic University-Pomona (G)

3801 W Temple Avenue, Pomona CA 91768-2557

County: Los Angeles — FICE Identification: 001144
Unit ID: 110529
Telephone: (909) 869-7659 — Carnegie Class: Master's L
FAX Number: (909) 869-4535 — Calendar System: Quarter
URL: www.csupomona.edu
Established: 1938 — Annual Undergrad Tuition & Fees (In-State): $4,830
Enrollment: 20,747 — Coed
Affiliation or Control: State — IRS Status: 501(c)3
Highest Offering: Master's
Program: Liberal Arts And General; Teacher Preparatory; Professional
Accreditation: WC, ART, BUS, CIDA, CS, DIETD, DIETI, ENG, ENGT, LSAR, PLNG, SPAA

02 President ... Dr. J. Michael ORTIZ
05 Provost/VP Academic Affairs ... Dr. Marten DENBOER
32 Vice President Student Affairs ... Dr. Douglas R. FREER
11 Vice Pres Administrative Affairs ... Dr. Edwin A. BARNES
30 Vice Pres University Advancement ... Mr. Scott C. WARRINGTON
20 Assoc VP Academic Programs ... Dr. Claudia L. PINTER-LUCKE
18 Assoc VP Facilities Planning & Mgmt ... Vacant
35 Assoc VP & Dean of Students ... Dr. Rebecca L. GUTIERREZ-KEETON
84 Assoc VP Enroll Management & Svcs ... Ms. Kathleen A. STREET
20 Int Assoc Vice Pres Faculty Affairs ... Mr. Gary HAMILTON
46 Assoc VP Research Research ... Vacant
26 Assoc Vice Pres for Univ Relations ... Dr. Ron H. FREMONT, II
10 Assoc VP Finance/Admin Svcs ... Mr. Darwin LABORDO
35 Assoc VP Student Services ... Dr. Kevin T. COLANER
35 Assoc VP Student Affairs ... Ms. Christi R. CHISLER
13 Chief Information Officer ... Mr. John W. MCGUTHRY
28 Admin in Charge D/HR/Employee Svcs ... Ms. Sharon L. REITER
04 Exec Assistant to the President ... Ms. Sandra L. DAVIS
47 Dean College of Agriculture ... Dr. Lester C. YOUNG
49 Dean Col Letters/Arts/Soc Sci ... Dr. Carol RICHARDSON
50 Dean Col of Business Admin ... Dr. Richard S. LAPIDUS
54 Dean College of Engineering ... Dr. Mahyar AMOUZEGAR
48 Dean Col Environmental Design ... Mr. Michael WOO
88 Dean Collins Sch of Hosp Mgmt ... Mr. Andrew H. FEINSTEIN
81 Interim Dean College of Science ... Mr. Donald P. CODUTO
53 Dean College Educ/Integrat Stds ... Dr. Peggy KELLY
56 Dean Extended University ... Vacant
44 Interim Assoc VP for Development ... Ms. Michelle L. MOYER
08 Dean University Library ... Mr. Ray WANG
41 Director of Athletics ... Mr. Brian R. SWANSON
86 Dir of Government/External Affairs ... Mr. Doug P. GLAESER
19 Chief of Police ... Mr. Michael W. GUERIN
102 Exec Dir Cal Poly Pomona Found Inc ... Mr. G. Paul STOREY
37 Director Student Financial Aid ... Ms. Diana Y. MINOR
06 Registrar/Academic Records Svcs ... Ms. Maria L. MARTINEZ
96 Director of Procurement ... Ms. Kathleen A. PRUNTY
84 Exec Dir Admissions and Outreach ... Ms. Deborah L. BRANDON
30 Exec Director Capital Campaign ... Mr. Robert G. BALZER

*California State University-Bakersfield (H)

9001 Stockdale Highway, Bakersfield CA 93311-1022

County: Kern — FICE Identification: 007993
Unit ID: 110486
Telephone: (661) 654-2011 — Carnegie Class: Master's L
FAX Number: (661) 654-3194 — Calendar System: Quarter
URL: www.csub.edu
Established: 1965 — Annual Undergrad Tuition & Fees (In-State): $6,682
Enrollment: 7,906 — Coed
Affiliation or Control: State — IRS Status: 501(c)3
Highest Offering: Master's
Program: Occupational; Liberal Arts And General; Teacher Preparatory; Professional; Nursing Emphasis
Accreditation: WC, BUS, NURSE, SPAA, SW, TED

02 President ... Dr. Horace MITCHELL
100 Executive Asst to the President ... Ms. Evelyn YOUNG
04 Presidential Aide ... Ms. Stella M. CHAVEZ
05 Provost/Vice Pres Academic Affairs ... Dr. Soraya COLEY
11 Vice Pres Business/Admin Services ... Mr. Michael A. NEAL
32 Int Vice President Student Affairs ... Dr. John HULTSMAN
86 Exec Dir Government/Foundation Rels ... Ms. Beverly BYL
84 Assoc VP for Enrollment Management ... Dr. Jacqueline MIMMS
12 Int Assoc VP Antelope Valley Center ... Dr. Jess DEEGAN
20 Assoc VP for Academic Programs ... Dr. Carl KEMNITZ
20 Assoc VP for Faculty Affairs ... Dr. Beth RIENZI
15 AVP Human Res/Administrative Svcs ... Ms. Kellie GARCIA
88 Spec Asst to Provost Academic Aff ... Dr. Edwin SASAKI
21 Asst Vice Pres Fiscal Services ... Mr. Douglas WADE
14 Asst Vice Pres Info Technology Svcs ... Mr. Clarke SANFORD
18 Asst VP Facilities Management/Dev ... Mr. Pat JACOBS
09 Asst VP Inst Rsrch/Planning/Assess ... Dr. Laura HECHT
25 Assoc Provost for Grants & Resource ... Dr. Julio BLANCO
50 Dean Business/Public Administration ... Dr. John EMERY
53 Dean Social Sciences and Education ... Dr. Kathleen KNUTZEN
79 Dean Arts & Humanities ... Dr. Richard COLLINS
81 Dean Natural Sciences & Mathematics ... Dr. Julio BLANCO
56 Dean Extended University Division ... Dr. Craig KELSEY
58 Dir of Academic Operation & Support ... Dr. John DIRKSE
08 Dean University Library ... Dr. Rodney M. HERSBERGER
35 Dean Student Life ... Vacant
06 Registrar ... Ms. Rita GUSTAFSON
88 Director Academic Advising ... Dr. Isabel SUMAYA
91 Dir Admn Computing Svcs/CMS Pgm Dir ... Mr. Kallya SHENOY
07 Director Admissions & Records ... Vacant
29 Director Alumni Relations ... Ms. Shannon HILL
41 Director Athletics ... Mr. Jeffrey KONYA
36 Dir for Cmty Engagement/Career Dev ... Ms. Jane EVARIAN
88 Interim Director Children's Center ... Dr. Christie HOWELL
96 Dir Contract Services/Procurement ... Mr. Michael CHAVEZ
38 Admin Supervisor Counseling Center ... Dr. Beth RIENZI
106 Director E-Learning Services ... Vacant
18 Director Facilities Operations ... Dr. Felix GARCERA
37 Director Financial Aid/Scholarships ... Dr. Ron RADNEY
92 Director Hawk Honors Program ... Dr. Michael FLACHMANN
39 Director Housing & Residential Life ... Ms. Crystal BECKS
88 Director Information Tech Support ... Vacant
26 Dir Public Affairs & Communications ... Mr. Robert MESZAROS
88 Director Safety & Risk Management ... Ms. Juli SMITH
88 Dir Svcs Students w/Disabilities ... Ms. Janice CLAUSEN
17 Director Student Health Services ... Dr. Oscar RICO
88 Director Student Recreation Center ... Mr. Mark HARRIMAN
88 Director Student Union ... Ms. Laura CATHERMAN
88 Director Telecommunications ... Mr. David WATTS
88 Director Outreach Services ... Mr. Steve WATKIN
19 Director University Police ... Chief Marty WILLIAMSON
40 Bookstore Manager ... Ms. Kelly SWANSON
88 Director of Food Services ... Mr. David CORRAL

*California State University-Channel Islands (I)

One University Drive, Camarillo CA 93012-8599

County: Ventura — FICE Identification: 039803
Unit ID: 441937
Telephone: (805) 437-8400 — Carnegie Class: Master's S
FAX Number: (805) 437-8414 — Calendar System: Semester

URL: www.csuci.edu
Established: 2002 Annual Undergrad Tuition & Fees (In-District): $2,864
Enrollment: 3,828 Coed
Affiliation or Control: State/Local IRS Status: 501(c)3
Highest Offering: Master's
Program: Liberal Arts And General
Accreditation: WC, NURSE

02 President .... Dr. Richard R. RUSH
05 Provost/Vice Pres Academic Affairs .... Dr. Dawn NEUMAN
10 Vice Pres Finance/Administration .... Ms. Joanne COVILLE
32 Vice President for Student Affairs .... Dr. Wm. Gregory SAWYER
26 Vice President for Advancement .... Vacant
100 Chief of Staff .... Dr. Therese EYERMANN
20 AVP Academic Programs & Planning .... Dr. Steve LEFEVRE
88 AVP for Faculty Affairs .... Dr. Renny CHRISTOPHER
25 AVP Research/Sponsored Programs .... Mr. Sadiq SHAH
18 AVP Ops/Planning/Construction .... Mr. Dave CHAKRABORTY
15 AVP for Human Resources .... Ms. Anna PAVIN
35 AVP for Student Affairs .... Mr. Ed LEBIODA
88 AVP Co-Curricular Programs .... Dr. George MORTEN
88 Dean of Faculty .... Vacant
84 AVP & Dean of Enrollment Management ... Dr. Jane SWEETLAND
56 AVP & Dean Extended Education .... Dr. Gary BERG
08 Dean University Library .... Ms. Amy WALLACE
19 Dir Public Safety/Chief of Police .... Mr. John REID
06 Registrar .... Vacant
13 Chief Information Officer .... Dr. Michael BERMAN
07 Director Admissions & Recruitment .... Ms. Ginger REYES
27 Dir of Communication/Marketing .... Ms. Nancy GILL
30 AVP for Univ Development .... Ms. Nichole IPACH
37 Int Dir Fin Aid/Admiss/Records .... Mr. Richard MONTIEL
09 Director of Institutional Research .... Dr. Nelle MOFFETT
29 Assoc Dir Development/Alumni Rels .... Ms. Tania GARCIA
21 Director Special Projects for F&A .... Ms. Caroline DOLL
39 Dir Housing & Residential Education .... Ms. Cindy DERRICO
104 Assoc Dir Ctr International Affairs .... Ms. Mayomi KOWTA
96 Manager of Procurement .... Ms. Valerie PATSCHECK

*California State University-Chico (A)

400 W First Street, Chico CA 95929-0001
County: Butte FICE Identification: 001146
Unit ID: 110538
Telephone: (530) 898-6116 Carnegie Class: Master's L
FAX Number: (530) 898-6824 Calendar System: Semester
URL: www.csuchico.edu
Established: 1887 Annual Undergrad Tuition & Fees (In-State): $6,294
Enrollment: 15,989 Coed
Affiliation or Control: State IRS Status: 501(c)3
Highest Offering: Master's
Program: Liberal Arts And General; Teacher Preparatory; Professional
Accreditation: WC, ART, BUS, CONST, CS, DIETD, DIETI, ENG, JOUR, MUS, NAIT, NRPA, NURSE, SP, SPAA, SW, TED, THEA

02 President .... Dr. Paul J. ZINGG
100 Chief of Staff/Dir of Govt Rels .... Ms. Karla J. ZIMMERLEE
05 Provost/Vice Pres Academic Affairs .... Dr. Sandra M. FLAKE
10 Vice President Business/Finance .... Ms. Lorraine B. HOFFMAN
32 Vice President Student Affairs .... Mr. Drew CALANDRELLA
30 Vice Pres University Advancement .... Mr. Richard ELLISON
45 Vice Prov Planning/Res Allocation .... Dr. Arno RETHANS
84 Vice Provost Enrollment Management .... Ms. Meredith KELLEY
13 Vice Prov Information Resource .... Mr. William POST
15 Asst Vice Pres Faculty Affairs .... Ms. Rhonda ALLEN
21 Asst Vice Pres Financial Svcs .... Mr. David FOREMAN
46 Vice Provost for Reseach .... Dr. E.K. (Eun) PARK
47 Dean College of Agriculture .... Dr. Jennifer RYDER-FOX
51 Dean Continuing Education .... Ms. Debra E. BARGER
72 Dean Col Engr/Comp Sci/Const Mgmt .... Dr. Michael G. WARD
83 Dean Col Behavior & Social Sci .... Dr. Gayle E. HUTCHINSON
50 Dean College of Business .... Vacant
79 Dean College Humanities/Fine Arts .... Dr. Joel ZIMBELMAN
81 Int Dean College Natural Sciences .... Dr. Frederika (Fraka) HARMSEN
60 Dean College Communication & Educ .... Ms. Maggie PAYNE
26 Director Public Affairs .... Mr. Joe WILLS
29 Director Alumni Relations .... Ms. Susan M. ANDERSON
09 Director Institutional Research .... Mr. William R. ALLEN
06 Registrar .... Ms. Jean H. IRVING
07 Director of Admissions .... Mr. Allan C. BEE
36 Director Student Placement .... Mr. Jamie STARMER
37 Director Financial Aid/Scholarships .... Mr. Dan REED
38 Int Dir Psyc Counslng/Wellness/ Tstg .... Dr. Mimi L. BOMMERSBACH
18 Int Dir Facilities Management Svcs .... Mr. Dennis FRAZIER
96 Director of Procurement .... Ms. Sara RUMIANO
92 Director Univ Honors Program .... Dr. Frank LI
20 Associate Academic Officer .... Mr. Arno RETHANS
35 Interim Director Student Affairs .... Ms. Connie HUYCK
28 Coordinator of Diversity .... Mr. Tray ROBINSON

*California State University-Dominguez Hills (B)

1000 E Victoria Street, Carson CA 90747-0005
County: Los Angeles FICE Identification: 001141
Unit ID: 110547
Telephone: (310) 243-3300 Carnegie Class: Master's L
FAX Number: N/A Calendar System: Semester
URL: www.csudh.edu
Established: 1960 Annual Undergrad Tuition & Fees (In-State): $4,650
Enrollment: 14,477 Coed
Affiliation or Control: State IRS Status: 501(c)3
Highest Offering: Master's
Program: Liberal Arts And General; Teacher Preparatory; Professional
Accreditation: WC, ACBSP, CS, MT, MUS, NURSE, OPE, OT, SPAA, SW, TED, THEA

02 President .... Dr. Mildred GARCIA
05 Provost/VP Academic Affairs .... Vacant
10 Vice Pres Administration/Finance .... Ms. Mary Ann RODRIGUEZ
84 Vice Pres Enroll Mgmt/Stdnt Affairs .... Dr. Susan E. BORREGO
30 Vice President Univ Advancement .... Mr. Greg SAKS
20 Assoc VP Faculty Affairs .... Dr. Clarence "Gus" MARTIN
11 Assoc VP Administration/Finance .... Ms. Karen J. WALL
86 Dir University & Govt Relations .... Mr. David GAMBOA
44 Assoc Vice President Development .... Ms. Andrea SALA
13 Assoc VP Information Tech .... Mr. Ronald F. BERGMANN
35 Assoc Vice President Student Life .... Dr. Daniels SONJA
21 Assoc VP Resource Management .... Dr. Janna BERSI
88 Assoc VP Student Success Services .... Dr. William FRANKLIN
04 Exec Assistant to the Pres .... Ms. Ann CAMP
41 Director of Athletics .... Mr. Patrick GUILLEN
26 Senior Media Relations Officer .... Ms. Brenda KNEPPER
37 Director of Financial Aid .... Ms. Delores LEE
06 Int Dir Student Records/Info Svcs .... Ms. Brandy MCLELLAND
38 Dir Student Health & Psych Services .... Dr. Janie MACHARG
15 Asst Vice Pres Human Resources/Mgmt .... Mr. Mark SEIGLE
09 Assoc Director Institutional Rsrch ... Mr. Pete VAN HAMERSVELD
19 Chief of Police .... Ms. Susan SLOAN
25 Director of Research/Funded Project .... Vacant
49 Acting Dean College of Liberal Arts .... Dr. Carol TUBBS
107 Int Dean Col Professional Studies .... Dr. Larry ORTIZ
50 Int Dean Col of Bus Admin/Pub Plcy .... Dr. Kaye BRAGG
56 Dean College of Ext & Intl Educ .... Dr. Margaret GORDON
83 Dean Col of Natural & Behav Sci .... Dr. Laura ROBLES
08 Dean of the Library .... Ms. Sandra PARHAM
18 Director of Physical Plant .... Vacant
21 Accounting Director .... Ms. Cecilia PATZ
96 Director of Procurement & Contracts .... Mr. Emmit WILLIAMS
88 Director Outreach and Info Services .... Dr. Gayle BALL-PARKER

*California State University-East Bay (C)

25800 Carlos Bee Boulevard, Hayward CA 94542-3001
County: Alameda FICE Identification: 001138
Unit ID: 110574
Telephone: (510) 885-3000 Carnegie Class: Master's L
FAX Number: (510) 885-3808 Calendar System: Quarter
URL: www.csueastbay.edu
Established: 1957 Annual Undergrad Tuition & Fees (In-State): $5,745
Enrollment: 12,897 Coed
Affiliation or Control: State IRS Status: 501(c)3
Highest Offering: Doctorate
Program: Liberal Arts And General; Teacher Preparatory; Professional
Accreditation: WC, BUS, ENG, MUS, NUR, SP, SW, TED

02 President .... Dr. Leroy M. MORISHITA
100 Chief of Staff .... Dr. Donald T. SAWYER
05 Provost/VP Academic Affairs .... Dr. James HOUPIS
10 Vice President Admin & Finance/CFO .... Vacant
30 Vice President Univ Advancement .... Mr. Robert BURT
84 VP Plng/Enroll Mgmt/Student Affs .... Dr. Linda DALTON
20 Interim Assoc Provost Acad Affairs .... Ms. Linda S. DOBB
58 AVP Academic Pgms/Graduate Studies .... Dr. Susan OPP
45 Sr Dir Budget & Res for Acad Affs .... Ms. Carol REESE
21 Assoc VP Risk Mgmt/Internal Control .... Ms. Nyassa LOVE
18 Director Facilities Planning & Ops .... Mr. James ZAVAGNO
15 Asst Vice Pres Human Resources .... Mr. James CIMINO
07 Assoc VP Enrollment Dev and Mgmt .... Dr. Gregory SMITH
09 Assoc VP Planning & Inst Research ... Dr. A. Amber MACHAMER
36 Associate Vice Pres Student Affairs .... Mr. Stanley HEBERT, III
27 Assoc VP University Communications .... Mr. Jay COLOMBATTO
21 Assoc VP Finance .... Ms. Debbie BROTHWELL
46 Assoc VP Research/Sponsored Pgms .... Vacant
49 Int Dean Col of Ltrs/Arts/Soc Sci .... Dr. Kathleen ROUNTREE
50 Dean College of Business/Economics .... Dr. Terri SWARTZ
53 Dean Col of Educ/Allied Studies .... Dr. Carolyn NELSON
81 Dean College of Science .... Dr. Michael LEUNG
12 Exec Director Concord Campus .... Dr. Emily BRIZENDINE
08 University Librarian .... Ms. Linda S. DOBB
29 Director of Alumni Relations .... Ms. Kate SHAHEED
13 Chief Information Officer .... Vacant
21 University Controller .... Mr. Darrell HAYDON
88 Exec Director of Student Retention .... Ms. Diana BALGAS
18 Director Facilities Operations .... Mr. Robert ANDREWS
23 Exec Director Student Health Svcs .... Ms. Andrea WILSON
24 Director Media & Technology Svcs .... Mr. Roger C. PARKER
41 Director of Athletics .... Ms. Debby DEANGELIS
19 Director University Police Dept .... Mr. James HODGES
39 Dir Housing & Residential Life .... Mr. Martin CASTILLO
38 Dir Stdnt Ctr for Acad Achieve .... Mr. John WHITMAN
51 Exec Dir Continuing/Intl Educ .... Mr. Brian COOK
38 Dir Counseling/Psychological Svcs .... Dr. Brian REINHARDT
22 Dir of Equity & Diversity .... Ms. Linda NOLAN
37 Director Student Financial Aid .... Ms. Rhonda JOHNSON
35 Dir Ofc Stdnt Dev/Judicial Affs .... Ms. Carol NOWICKI
96 Dir Procurement & Support Svcs .... Ms. Rita PETH
36 Dir Acad Adv and Career Educ .... Mr. Lawrence BLISS

*California State University-Fresno (D)

5200 N. Barton Avenue, Fresno CA 93740-8027
County: Fresno FICE Identification: 001147
Unit ID: 110556
Telephone: (559) 278-4240 Carnegie Class: Master's L
FAX Number: (559) 278-4715 Calendar System: Semester
URL: www.csufresno.edu
Established: 1911 Annual Undergrad Tuition & Fees (In-State): $5,675
Enrollment: 20,932 Coed
Affiliation or Control: State IRS Status: 501(c)3
Highest Offering: Doctorate
Program: Liberal Arts And General; Teacher Preparatory; Professional
Accreditation: WC, BUS, CACREP, CIDA, CONST, CORE, DIETD, DIETI, ENG, MUS, NRPA, NURSE, PH, PTA, SP, SPAA, SW, TED, THEA

02 President .... Dr. John D. WELTY
05 Provost/Vice Pres Academic Affairs .... Dr. William A. COVINO
10 VP Administration/Chief Fin Ofcr .... Ms. Cynthia TENIENTE-MATSON
30 Vice Pres University Advancement .... Dr. Peter N. SMITS
32 Vice Pres Student Affairs .... Dr. Paul M. OLIARO
15 Int Assoc VP Academic Personnel .... Dr. Ted WENDT
26 Assoc VP University Communications .... Ms. Shirley ARMBRUSTER
20 Associate Provost .... Dr. Ellen JUNN
20 Assoc VP/Dean Undergrad Students .... Dr. Dennis L. NEF
45 Assoc Vice President Research .... Dr. Thomas H. MCCLANAHAN
44 Assoc Vice Pres Univ Development .... Mr. R. Kent CLARK
21 Assoc VP for Financial Services .... Mr. Clinton MOFFITT
18 Associate Vice President Facilities .... Mr. Robert BOYD
84 Assoc Vice Pres Enrollment Services .... Mr. Bernie VINOVRSKI
51 Dean/Assoc VP Continuing/Global Ed .... Dr. Lynnette ZELEZNY
47 Dean Agricultural Science/Tech .... Dr. Charles D. BOYER
79 Dean of Arts & Humanities .... Dr. Vida SAMIIAN
50 Dean Craig School of Business .... Dr. Robert HARPER
53 Dean of Kremen School of Education .... Dr. Paul BEARE
54 Dean of Engineering .... Dr. Ramakrishna NUNNA
76 Dean of Health/Human Services .... Dr. Andrew HOFF
83 Dean of Social Sciences .... Dr. Luz GONZALEZ
81 Interim Dean of Sciences & Math .... Dr. Andrew HOFF
08 Dean of Library Services .... Mr. Peter MCDONALD
58 Dean of Graduate Studies .... Dr. Sharon BROWN-WELTY
23 Int Dir Univ Health/Psyc Svcs Oper .... Mr. Dirk RUTHRAUFF
19 Director of Public Safety .... Mr. David HUERTA
41 Director of Athletics .... Mr. Thomas BOEH
16 Director of Human Resources .... Ms. Janice PARTEN
13 Technology Services .... Vacant
09 Dir of Research Plng/Assessment .... Ms. Christina LEIMER
37 Director of Financial Aid .... Ms. Maria HERNANDEZ
06 Registrar .... Ms. Tina BEDDALL
27 Director of Publications .... Mr. Bruce WHITWORTH
29 Executive Director Alumni Relations .... Ms. Jacquelyn GLASENER
36 Director of Career Services .... Ms. Rita BOCCHINFUSO-COHEN
39 Director Univ Courtyard (Housing) .... Ms. Erin BOELE
96 Dir Procurement & Support Services .... Mr. Brian COTHAM
07 Director of Admissions .... Ms. Vivian FRANCO
35 Director of Student Involvement .... Ms. Sally RAMAGE
40 Bookstore Manager .... Mr. Ron DURHAM

*California State University-Fullerton (E)

PO Box 34080, 800 N State Col Blvd, Fullerton CA 92831-3547
County: Orange FICE Identification: 001137
Unit ID: 110565
Telephone: (657) 278-2011 Carnegie Class: Master's L
FAX Number: (657) 278-2649 Calendar System: Semester
URL: www.fullerton.edu
Established: 1957 Annual Undergrad Tuition & Fees (In-State): $5,540
Enrollment: 35,590 Coed
Affiliation or Control: State IRS Status: 501(c)3
Highest Offering: Doctorate
Program: Liberal Arts And General; Teacher Preparatory; Professional
Accreditation: WC, ANEST, ART, BUS, BUSA, CACREP, CS, DANCE, ENG, JOUR, MIDWF, MUS, NURSE, PH, SP, SPAA, SW, TED, THEA

02 President .... Dr. Milton A. GORDON
04 Executive Assistant to President .... Mr. Patrick CARROLL
05 Actg Vice President Academic Affs .... Dr. Steven MURRAY
10 VP Administration & Finance/CFO .... Dr. Willie HAGAN
30 Vice Pres University Advancement .... Ms. Pamela HILLMAN
13 VP Info Tech/Chief Info Tech Ofcr .... Mr. Amir DABIRIAN
102 AVP Development/CFO Foundation .... Mr. Ira UNTERMAN
44 Assoc VP University Advancement .... Mrs. Carrie STEWART
58 AVP Graduate Studies/Research .... Dr. Dorota HUIZINGA
26 Assoc VP Strategic Communications .... Mr. Jeffrey COOK
20 Assoc Vice Pres Academic Affairs .... Dr. James DIETZ
86 Asc VP Public Affs/Government Rels .... Mr. Owen HOLMES
84 Asst Vice Pres Enrollment Services .... Ms. Nancy DORITY
29 Exec Director Alumni Relations .... Ms. Dianna L. FISHER
06 Registrar .... Ms. Melissa WHATLEY
08 University Librarian .... Mr. Richard POLLARD
36 Director Career Development Center .... Mr. Jim CASE
45 Chief Budget Planning & Strategy .... Vacant
15 Actg Exec Director Human Resources .... Mr. Bill BARRETT
23 Acting Director Health Center .... Dr. Howard WANG
18 Director Physical Plant .... Mr. Willem VAN DER POL
19 Director University Police .... Ms. Judith KING
28 Director Diversity/Equity Programs .... Ms. Rosamaria GOMEZ-AMARO
37 Acting Director Financial Aid .... Ms. Jessica SCHUTTE
41 Director of Athletics .... Mr. Brian QUINN
84 Dir Enrollment Svcs Center-El Toro .... Dr. Charles MOORE
85 Dir International Educ/Exchange .... Ms. Lay Tuan TAN
35 Assoc VP of Student Affairs .... Ms. Kandy MINK-SALAS
09 Asst VP Inst Res/Analytical Stds .... Dr. Edward SULLIVAN

96 Director of Contracts & Procurement ... Mr. Don GREEN
21 Associate Vice President of Finance ... Mr. Brian JENKINS
38 Act Exec Dir Stdnt Hlth/Counseling ... Mr. Howard WANG
51 Dean University Extended Educ Svcs ... Dr. Harry NORMAN
79 Dean Humanities/Social Science ... Dr. Angela DELLA VOLPE
81 Actg Dean Natural Sciences & Math ... Dr. Robert KOCH
50 Dean Business & Economics ... Dr. Anil PURI
83 Dean Health & Human Development ... Dr. Shari MCMAHAN
57 Dean of the Arts ... Dr. Joseph ARNOLD
53 Dean of Education ... Dr. Claire CAVALLARO
54 Dean Engineering & Computer Science ... Dr. Raman UNNIKRISHNAN
60 Dean Communications ... Dr. William BRIGGS
35 Dean of Students ... Dr. Lea JARNAGIN

California State University-Long Beach (A)

1250 Bellflower Boulevard, Long Beach CA 90840-0119
County: Los Angeles FICE Identification: 001139
Unit ID: 110583
Telephone: (562) 985-4111 Carnegie Class: Master's L
FAX Number: (562) 985-5419 Calendar System: Semester
URL: www.csulb.edu
Established: 1949 Annual Undergrad Tuition & Fees (In-State): $5,652
Enrollment: 27,252 Coed
Affiliation or Control: State IRS Status: 501(c)3
Highest Offering: Doctorate
Program: Liberal Arts And General; Teacher Preparatory; Professional
Accreditation: WC, AAFCS, ART, BUS, CEA, CS, DANCE, DIETD, DIETI, ENG, HSA, IPSY, KIN, MUS, NRPA, NURSE, PH, PTA, RTT, SP, SPAA, SW, TED, THEA

02 President ... Dr. F. K. ALEXANDER
05 Provost/Sr Vice Pres Academic Affs ... Dr. Donald PARA
11 Vice Pres Administration/Finance ... Ms. Mary E. STEPHENS
32 Vice President Student Services ... Dr. Douglas W. ROBINSON
30 Vice Pres University Rels/Devel ... Ms. Andrea TAYLOR
04 Exec Assistant to the President ... Dr. Karen NAKAI
10 Assoc VP Financial Management ... Ms. Sharon TAYLOR
20 Assoc Academic Officer/Vice Provost ... Dr. David DOWELL
35 Assoc Vice Pres Student Services ... Dr. Mary Ann TAKEMOTO
27 Asst Vice Pres Public Affairs ... Ms. Toni A. BERON-HUDSON
29 Asst Vice Pres Alumni Rel/Spec Proj ... Ms. Janice HATANAKA
88 Asst VP Ctr for International Educ ... Dr. Jeet JOSHEE
09 Asst VP Institutional Research ... Dr. Van NOVACK
18 Assoc Vice Pres Phys Plng/Facil Mgt ... Mr. David SALAZAR
58 Assoc VP/Grad & Undergrad Programs ... Dr. Cecile LINDSAY
46 Assoc Vice Pres University Research ... Dr. T. C. YIH
84 Asst Vice Pres Enrollment Services ... Mr. Thomas ENDERS
13 Asst VP Information Technology ... Ms. Janet FOSTER
16 Assoc VP Budget/Human Resource Mgmt ... Mr. Scott APEL
91 Int Assoc VP Academic Technology ... Mr. Roman KOCHAN
76 Dean College Health/Human Svcs ... Dr. Kenneth MILLAR
50 Dean College of Business Admin ... Dr. Michael SOLT
53 Dean College of Education ... Dr. Marquita GRENOT-SCHEYER
54 Int Dean College of Engineering ... Dr. Forouzan GOLSHANI
57 Dean College of the Arts ... Dr. Raymond TORRES-SANTOS
81 Dean Col Natural Science/Math ... Dr. Laura KINGSFORD
49 Dean College of Liberal Arts ... Dr. Gerry RIPOSA
56 Dean University Extension Services ... Dr. Jeet JOSHEE
08 Dean Library/Learning Resources ... Mr. Roman KOCHAN
39 Director Housing Administration ... Ms. Carol ROBERTS-CORB
15 Director Staff Personnel Services ... Vacant
41 Director Athletics ... Mr. Victor CEGLES
88 Dir Student Rels/Academic Support ... Ms. Donna GREEN
07 Director of Admissions ... Ms. Marie ALFORD
36 Director Career Plng & Placement ... Mr. Manuel PEREZ
23 Director Health Services ... Dr. Michael CARBUTO
19 Director Public Safety ... Mr. Fernando SOLORZANO
38 Director Counseling/Psych Services . Dr. Paul RATANASIRIPONG
37 Director Financial Aid/Admissions ... Mr. Nicolas VALDIVIA
25 Director Found Grants/Contracts ... Ms. Sandra SHEREMAN
102 Executive Director Foundation ... Dr. Brian NOWLIN
28 Director of Equity & Diversity ... Vacant
26 Chief Public Relations Officer ... Ms. Toni A. BERON-HUDSON
96 Director of Purchasing ... Ms. Laurinda FULLER
40 General Manager/49'er Shops ... Mr. Donald PENROD

California State University-Los Angeles (B)

5151 State University Drive, Los Angeles CA 90032-8530
County: Los Angeles FICE Identification: 001140
Unit ID: 110592
Telephone: (323) 343-3000 Carnegie Class: Master's L
FAX Number: (323) 343-2670 Calendar System: Quarter
URL: www.calstatela.edu
Established: 1947 Annual Undergrad Tuition & Fees (In-State): $5,506
Enrollment: 20,142 Coed
Affiliation or Control: State IRS Status: 501(c)3
Highest Offering: Doctorate
Program: Liberal Arts And General; Teacher Preparatory; Professional
Accreditation: WC, ART, BUS, CACREP, CORE, CS, DIETC, DIETD, ENG, MUS, NURSE, SP, SPAA, SW, TED

02 President ... Dr. James M. ROSSER
05 Provost/Vice Pres Academic Affairs ... Dr. Ashish VAIDYA
32 Vice President Student Affairs ... Dr. Anthony R. ROSS
13 Vice Pres/Chief Technology Officer ... Mr. Peter QUAN
10 VP Administration & CFO ... Ms. Lisa M. CHAVEZ
44 Vice Pres Institutional Advancement ... Mr. Kyle C. BUTTON
20 Assoc VP Academic Affairs ... Dr. Cheryl L. NEY
11 Assoc VP Admin & Finance ... Mr. Jose GOMEZ
21 Asst VP Admin & Finance/Budget ... Ms. Mae SANTOS
35 Asst VP Student Affs/Student Svcs ... Ms. Nancy WADA-MCKEE
30 Asst VP University Development ... Ms. Collette G. ROCHA
29 Executive Director Alumni Relations ... Vacant
26 Exec Director Public Affairs ... Ms. Nancy MIRON
41 Director Intercollegiate Athletics ... Dr. Daniel BRIDGES
83 Dean Natural & Social Sciences ... Dr. James P. HENDERSON
08 University Librarian ... Ms. Alice K. KAWAKAMI
06 Univ Registrar & Dir of Enrollment ... Ms. Joan V. WOOSLEY
58 Interim Dean Grad Studies/Research ... Dr. Alan MUCHLINSKI
88 Acting Assoc Dean Graduate Studies ... Dr. Philip LAPOLT
09 Director Institutional Research ... Dr. Mark PAVELCHAK
36 Director Career Placement & Plng ... Mr. Christopher LENZ
37 Director Student Financial Services ... Ms. Tamie NGUYEN
23 Director Health Center ... Dr. Monica JAZZABI
39 Director Housing Svc/Residence Life ... Mr. Stephen FLEISCHER
22 Director Equal Opportunity Pgm ... Ms. Becky HOPKINS
18 Director Facilities/Physical Plant ... Mr. Randy SHARP
19 Director Public Safety ... Mr. Gregory D. KING
15 Asst VP Human Resources Management ... Ms. Lisa SANCHEZ
85 Director Intl Programs & Services ... Ms. Amy WANG
43 University Counsel ... Mr. Victor I. KING
07 Director of Outreach & Admissions ... Mr. Vince LOPEZ
96 Director Procurement & Contracts ... Mr. Thomas JOHNSON
09 Assoc Dir Institutional Research ... Mr. Mark ROBINSON
28 Equity & Diversity Specialist ... Vacant
40 Manager Bookstore ... Mr. Todd MURPHY
88 Dean Undergraduate Studies ... Dr. Alfredo G. GONZALEZ
49 Dean Arts & Letters ... Dr. Peter MCALLISTER
54 Dean Engr/Computer Science/Tech ... Dr. Keith MOO-YOUNG
51 Dean Extended Studies & Intl Pgms ... Dr. Jose GALVAN
76 Dean Health & Human Services ... Dr. Beatrice YORKER
53 Dean Charter College of Education ... Dr. Mary FALVEY
50 Dean Business & Economics ... Dr. James A. GOODRICH

† Grants Joint Doctoral degree in cooperation with the University of California-Los Angeles.

*California State University-Monterey Bay (C)

100 Campus Center, Seaside CA 93955-8000
County: Monterey FICE Identification: 032603
Unit ID: 409698
Telephone: (831) 582-3000 Carnegie Class: Master's S
FAX Number: (831) 582-3783 Calendar System: Semester
URL: www.csumb.edu
Established: 1994 Annual Undergrad Tuition & Fees (In-State): $4,884
Enrollment: 4,790 Coed
Affiliation or Control: State IRS Status: 501(c)3
Highest Offering: Master's
Program: Liberal Arts And General
Accreditation: WC, @SW, TED

02 President ... Dr. Dianne F. HARRISON
05 Provost ... Dr. Kathryn CRUZ-URIBE
11 Vice Pres Admin & Finance/CFO ... Mr. Kevin SAUNDERS
30 Vice Pres University Advancement ... Vacant
32 Vice Pres Student Affairs ... Dr. Ronnie HIGGS
26 Dir of Govt & External Relations ... Mr. Justin WELLNER
35 Dean of Student Life ... Dr. Christine ERICKSON
10 Assoc Vice President for Finance ... Mr. John FITZGIBBON
100 Chief of Staff to President ... Dr. Patti HIRAMOTO
06 Registrar ... Ms. Sheila HERNANDEZ
22 Interim Director EEO ... Ms. Tamberly PETROVICH
37 Director Financial Aid ... Ms. Angeles FUENTES
15 Assoc Vice Pres Human Resources ... Ms. Linda WIGHT
19 Chief of Police ... Chief Earl LAWSON
18 Chief Facilities/Physical Plant ... Mr. John MARKER
21 Associate Business Officer ... Mr. John FITZGIBBON
07 Dir for Admissions & Recruitment ... Mr. David LINNEVERS
29 Director Alumni Relations ... Ms. Pilar GOSE
41 Athletic Director ... Mr. Vince OTOUPAL
20 Associate Academic Officer ... Dr. Mary BOYCE
84 Assoc VP Enrollment Management ... Dr. Ronnie HIGGS
96 Director of Purchasing ... Mr. Art EVJEN

*California State University-Northridge (D)

18111 Nordhoff Street, Northridge CA 91330-0001
County: Los Angeles FICE Identification: 001153
Unit ID: 110608
Telephone: (818) 677-1200 Carnegie Class: Master's L
FAX Number: N/A Calendar System: Semester
URL: www.csun.edu
Established: 1958 Annual Undergrad Tuition & Fees (In-State): $5,900
Enrollment: 35,272 Coed
Affiliation or Control: State IRS Status: 501(c)3
Highest Offering: Doctorate
Program: Liberal Arts And General; Teacher Preparatory; Professional
Accreditation: WC, AAFCS, ART, BUS, CACREP, CIDA, CONST, CS, DIETD, DIETI, ENG, JOUR, MUS, NURSE, PH, PTA, RAD, SP, SW, TED, THEA

02 President ... Dr. Jolene M. KOESTER
05 Provost/Vice Pres Academic Affairs ... Dr. Harry HELLENBRAND
10 Vice President Admin/Finance ... Mr. Thomas MCCARRON
32 VP Student Affairs/Dean of Students ... Dr. William WATKINS
44 Vice Pres University Advancement ... Dr. Vance T. PETERSON
13 Vice President IT/CIO ... Ms. Hilary BAKER
88 Exec Director University Corp ... Mr. Rick EVANS
20 Vice Provost Academic Affairs ... Dr. Cynthia Z. RAWITCH
100 Chief of Staff ... Dr. Barbara L. GROSS
18 Assoc VP Facilities Dev/Operations ... Mr. Colin J. DONAHUE
58 Assoc VP Grad Studies/Intl Pgms ... Dr. Mack I. JOHNSON
30 Assoc Vice Pres Development ... Ms. Maureen F. FITZGERALD
21 Associate VP Financial Services ... Ms. Deborah WALLACE
15 Interim Assoc VP of Human Resources ... Ms. Jill A. SMITH
29 Asst Vice Pres Alumni Relations ... Mr. D. G. (Gray) MOUNGER
26 Assoc VP Marketing/Communications ... Ms. Stacy LIEBERMAN
20 Senior Dir Undergraduate Studies ... Dr. Elizabeth T. ADAMS
91 Director of Academic Resources ... Ms. Diane S. STEPHENS
07 Director of Admissions and Records ... Ms. Patty R. LORD
08 Dean University Library ... Dr. Mark STOVER
51 Dean College of Extended Learning ... Dr. Joyce A. FEUCHT-HAVIAR
79 Dean College of Humanities ... Dr. Elizabeth A. SAY
50 Dean College Business/Economics ... Dr. William P. JENNINGS
53 Dean College of Education ... Dr. Michael E. SPAGNA
57 Dean College Arts/Media/Commun ... Dr. Robert BUCKER
83 Dean Col Social/Behavioral Sci ... Dr. Stella Z. THEODOULOU
76 Dean Col Health/Human Development ... Dr. Sylvia A. ALVA
81 Dean College Science & Math ... Dr. Jerry STINNER
54 Dean College Engr/Computer Science ... Dr. S. K. RAMESH
09 Director Institutional Research ... Dr. Bettina HUBER
37 Director Financial Aid/Scholarships ... Mrs. Lili C. VIDAL
38 Director Univ Counseling Services ... Dr. Mark STEVENS
36 Director Career Center ... Ms. Ann N. MOREY
25 Dir Research/Sponsored Projects ... Mr. Scott L. PEREZ
18 Int Exec Dir Physical Plant Mgmt ... Mr. Lynn WIEGERS
19 Director of Police Services ... Ms. Anne P. GLAVIN
28 Director of Equity and Diversity ... Ms. Lauren N. NILE
86 Dir Government/Community Relations ... Ms. Brittny MCCARTHY
23 Director Student Health Center ... Dr. Linda REID-CHASSIAKOS
39 Dir Student Housing/Conf Services ... Mr. Timothy J. TREVAN
40 Director Matador Bookstore ... Ms. Amy C. BERGER
41 Director of Athletics ... Mr. Rick MAZZUTO
85 Dir Student Devel/Intl Programs ... Mr. Thomas E. PIERNIK
92 Dir General Education Honors Pgm ... Dr. Beth A. WIGHTMAN
96 Manager Purchasing ... Ms. Deborah FLUGUM
84 Director Enrollment Management ... Dr. William WATKINS

*California State University-Sacramento (E)

6000 J Street, Sacramento CA 95819-2694
County: Sacramento FICE Identification: 001150
Unit ID: 110617
Telephone: (916) 278-6011 Carnegie Class: Master's L
FAX Number: (916) 278-6664 Calendar System: Semester
URL: www.csus.edu
Established: 1947 Annual Undergrad Tuition & Fees (In-State): $6,572
Enrollment: 27,033 Coed
Affiliation or Control: State IRS Status: 501(c)3
Highest Offering: Doctorate
Program: Liberal Arts And General; Teacher Preparatory; Professional
Accreditation: WC, ART, BUS, CACREP, CIDA, CONST, CORE, CS, DIETD, DIETI, EMT, ENG, HT, MUS, NRPA, NURSE, PTA, SP, SW

02 President ... Dr. Alexander GONZALEZ
05 Provost/Vice Pres Academic Affairs ... Dr. Joseph F. SHELEY
11 Vice President Administration & CFO ... Dr. Ming-Tung "Mike" LEE
26 Vice Pres University Advancement ... Dr. Carole HAYASHINO
32 Vice President Student Affairs ... Dr. Lori VARLOTTA
15 Vice President for Human Resources ... Dr. David L. WAGNER
25 Asst VP Research/Contract Admin ... Mr. David EARWICKER
20 Vice Provost ... Vacant
45 Assoc VP Academic Affs/Planning ... Vacant
18 Assoc Vice Pres Facilities Mgmt ... Dr. Ali IZADIAN
27 Assoc Vice President Public Affairs ... Ms. Gloria MORAGA
30 Assoc Vice President Development ... Ms. Rebecca THOMPSON
84 AVP Enrollment Mgmt/Student Support ... Mr. Edward MILLS
35 AVP Student Affairs/Campus Life ... Mr. Michael SPEROS
21 Interim Assoc VP Financial Svcs ... Ms. Justine HEARTT
13 VP & Chief Information Officer ... Dr. Larry GILBERT
43 University Counsel ... Dr. Christine LOVELY
09 Director Institutional Research ... Dr. Jing WANG
07 Director Outreach & Admissions ... Mr. Emiliano DIAZ
08 Dean University Library ... Ms. Tabzeera DOSU
29 Director Alumni Relations ... Ms. Jennifer BARBER
19 Director Public Safety ... Mr. Daniel J. DAVIS
39 Director Residential Life ... Mr. Michael SPEROS
41 Director Intercollegiate Athletics ... Dr. Terry WANLESS
36 Director Academic Adv/Career Ctrs ... Dr. Beth MERRITT MILLER
37 Director Financial Aid ... Mr. Craig YAMAMOTO
22 Director of Employment Equity ... Dr. Susan HOUGH
40 Bookstore Director ... Ms. Julia MILARDOVICH
04 Executive Assistant to President ... Ms. Carol ENSLEY
06 University Registrar ... Mr. Dennis GEYER
85 Director Global Education ... Dr. Jack GODWIN
23 Dir Student Health Ctr & Psych Svcs . Dr. Joy STEWART-JAMES
96 Mgr Procurement/Contract Services ... Mr. John GUION
49 Dean College of Arts & Letters ... Dr. Edward INCH
50 Dean College of Business Admin ... Dr. Sanjay VARSHNEY
53 Dean College of Education ... Dr. Vanessa SHEARED
54 Dean College of Engr/Computer Sci ... Dr. Emir J. MACARI
76 Dean College of Health/Human Svcs ... Dr. Fred BALDINI
81 Dean College of Natural Sci/Math ... Dr. Jill TRAINER
51 Dean College Continuing Education ... Ms. Alice K. TOM
83 Dean College Soc Sci/Interdisc Stds ... Dr. Charles W. GOSSETT
58 Acting Dean Graduate Studies ... Dr. Chevelle NEWSOME

*California State University-San Bernardino (A)

5500 University Parkway, San Bernardino CA 92407-2393
County: San Bernardino FICE Identification: 001142
Unit ID: 110510
Telephone: (909) 537-5000 Carnegie Class: Master's L
FAX Number: N/A Calendar System: Quarter
URL: www.csusb.edu
Established: 1960 Annual Undergrad Tuition & Fees (In-State): $5,865
Enrollment: 16,400 Coed
Affiliation or Control: State IRS Status: 501(c)3
Highest Offering: Doctorate
Program: Liberal Arts And General; Teacher Preparatory; Professional
Accreditation: WC, ART, BUS, CORE, CS, DIETD, MUS, NURSE, SPAA, SW, TED, THEA

02 President Dr. Albert K. KARNIG
05 Provost/Vice Pres Academic Affairs Dr. Andrew R. BODMAN
10 Vice Pres Administration/Finance Mr. Robert GARDNER
32 Vice President Student Affairs Dr. Frank L. RINCON
30 Vice Pres University Advancement Mr. Larry SHARP
13 Interim Vice Pres Info Tech/CIO Ms. Lorraine FROST
04 Spec Asst to Pres Ext Govt Rel Ms. Pamela LANGFORD
86 Spec Asst to Pres Federal Relations Dr. Clifford YOUNG
20 Assoc Provost Academic Programs Dr. Jenny ZORN
88 Assoc Provost Research Dr. Jeffrey M. THOMPSON
16 Assoc Provost Academic Personnel Dr. Risa DICKSON
21 Assoc VP Budget & Financial Opers Mr. Bob WILSON
84 Assoc VP Enrollment Mgmt Ms. Olivia ROSAS
35 Assoc VP Student Development Ms. Helga KRAY
88 Assoc VP IRT Ms. Lorraine FROST
88 Associate VP Development Ms. Cindi PRINGLE
26 Asst VP Public Affairs Mr. Sid ROBINSON
15 Asst VP Human Resources Mr. Dale T. WEST
09 Director Institutional Research Ms. Muriel LOPEZ-WAGNER
36 Int Placement Services Coordinator Ms. Carol DIXON
06 Acting Dir Student Recs/Regis/Eval Ms. Mary CHOUINARD
07 Director Admissions/Recruitment Ms. Olivia ROSAS
38 Director Counseling Center Dr. Patricia SMITH
08 University Librarian Mr. Cesar CABALLERO
37 Director Financial Aid Ms. Roseanna RUIZ
45 Director Plng Design/Construction Mr. Hamid U. AZHAND
18 Sr Director Facilities Services Mr. Tony SIMPSON
41 Director Athletics Dr. Kevin L. HATCHER
29 Director Alumni Affairs Ms. Pam LANGFORD
96 Director Purchasing Ms. Kathy HANSEN
28 Director Diversity (faculty) Dr. Risa DICKSON
28 Director Diversity (staff) Mr. Dale T. WEST
40 Director Bookstore Ms. Lyly BIRD
94 Dir Gender & Sexuality Studies Dr. Todd JENNINGS
92 Director University Honors Program Dr. Allen BUTT
56 Dean of Extended Learning Dr. Tatiana KARMANOVA
49 Dean College of Arts & Letters Dr. Eri F. YASUHARA
81 Interim Dean Col Natural Sciences Dr. David MAYNARD
83 Dean Col Social/Behavioral Sciences Dr. Jamal R. NASSAR
53 Dean College of Education Dr. Jay FIENE
50 Dean College of Business Dr. Lawrence D. ROSE
58 Dean Graduate Studies Dr. Sandra KAMUSIKIRI
12 Dean CSUSB Palm Desert Dr. Fred E. JANDT
89 Dean Freshman Studies Dr. J. Milton CLARK

*California State University-San Marcos (B)

333 S Twin Oaks Valley Road,
San Marcos CA 92096-0001
County: San Diego FICE Identification: 030113
Unit ID: 366711
Telephone: (760) 750-4000 Carnegie Class: Master's M
FAX Number: (760) 750-4030 Calendar System: Semester
URL: www.csusm.edu
Established: 1989 Annual Undergrad Tuition & Fees (In-State): $4,884
Enrollment: 9,641 Coed
Affiliation or Control: State IRS Status: 501(c)3
Highest Offering: Doctorate
Program: Liberal Arts And General; Teacher Preparatory
Accreditation: WC, NURSE, @SP, TED

02 President Dr. Karen S. HAYNES
04 Executive Assistant Ms. Joyce BRUGGEMAN
10 Vice President Finance/Admin Svcs Ms. Linda HAWK
05 Vice President Academic Affairs Dr. Emily CUTRER
32 Vice President of Student Affairs Dr. Eloise STIGLITZ
30 Vice Pres University Advancement Mr. Neal HOSS
20 Assoc Vice Pres Academic Affairs Dr. David BARSKY
20 Assoc VP Planning/Acad Resources Vacant
84 Assoc Vice Pres Enrollment Mgmt Mr. Darren BUSH
15 Assoc VP Human Resource/Equal Oppty Ms. Joanne SHYDIAN
44 Assoc VP Development/Campaign Dir Mr. Bruce GENUNG
22 Assoc VP Diversity & Educ Equity Mr. Derrick CRAWFORD
49 Dean Col Hum Arts/Behav & Soc Sci Dr. Adam SHAPIRO
50 Dean Col Business Administration Dr. Dennis GUSEMAN
53 Dean Col Educ/Health & Human Svcs Dr. Don CHU
08 Dean of Library Services Ms. Barbara PREECE
81 Dean Col of Science & Mathematics Dr. Katherine KANTARDJIEFF
56 Dean of Extended Studies Mr. Michael SCHRODER
88 Dean Instructional/Info Technology Mr. Wayne VERES
37 Director Financial Aid Ms. Vonda GARCIA
06 Registrar Mr. Thomas SWANGER
07 Dir of Admissions & Recruitment Vacant
09 Chief of Staff/Dir Inst Plng & Anal Mr. Matthew CEPPI
18 Director Facility Services Mr. Gary CINNAMON
21 Associate Business Officer Vacant
29 Director Alumni/Parent Relations Ms. Lori BROCKETT
96 Director Procurment/Support Svcs Ms. Bella NEWBERG
38 Director Undergraduate Advising Mr. Andres FAVELA

† Grants Joint Doctoral degree in cooperation with the University of California-San Diego.

*California State University-Stanislaus (C)

1 University Circle, Turlock CA 95382-0299
County: Stanislaus FICE Identification: 001157
Unit ID: 110495
Telephone: (209) 667-3012 Carnegie Class: Master's L
FAX Number: (209) 667-3206 Calendar System: Semester
URL: www.csustan.edu
Established: 1957 Annual Undergrad Tuition & Fees (In-State): $5,805
Enrollment: 8,305 Coed
Affiliation or Control: State IRS Status: 501(c)3
Highest Offering: Doctorate
Program: Liberal Arts And General; Teacher Preparatory; Professional
Accreditation: WC, ART, BUS, MUS, NURSE, SPAA, SW, TED, THEA

02 President Dr. Hamid SHIRVANI
05 Provost/VP Academic Affairs Dr. James T. STRONG
10 Vice President Business/Finance Mr. Russell GIAMBELLUCA
30 Vice President Univ Advancement Ms. Susana GAJIC-BRUYEA
50 Dean College of Business Admin Dr. Linda I. NOWAK
53 Dean College of Education Dr. Kathy NORMAN
76 Dean College Human & Health Sci Vacant
49 Dean College of the Arts Mr. Daryl J. MOORE
79 Int Dean Col Humanities/Social Sci Dr. James A. TUEDIO
65 Int Dean College Natural Sciences Dr. Robert MARINO
20 Associate Vice President/ALO Dr. Halyna M. KORNUTA
13 Assoc Vice Pres for Info Technology Mr. Carl E. WHITMAN
32 VP Enrollment/Student Affairs Dr. Suzanne M. ESPINOZA
35 AVP Student Affair/Dean of Students Mr. Ronald J. NOBLE
21 Assoc Vice Pres Financial Svcs Ms. Claire TYSON
18 Int Assoc VP Facilities Services Ms. Melody MAFFEI
20 Int Vice Pres Faculty Affairs/HR Mr. Dennis W. SHIMEK
08 Interim Dean Library Services Ms. Annie Y. HOR
27 Assoc Vice Pres Communications/PA Mr. David L. TONELLI
88 Assoc Vice Pres Auxiliary Services Mr. John W. REHO
06 Registrar Ms. Lisa M. BERNARDO
88 Exec Director Retention Svcs Vacant
88 Int Director EOP/Advising Mr. Fernando BELTRAN
29 Dir Alumni Relations/Annual Giving Mr. Jacob N. MCDOUGAL
51 Int Exec-in-Chg Univ Extended Educ Dr. Majorie A. JAASMA
37 Director Financial Aid Ms. Noelia GONZALEZ
41 Director Athletics Dr. Milton E. RICHARDS
09 Director of Institutional Research Dr. Angel A. SANCHEZ
15 Senior Manager HR & Compliance Ms. Gina B. LEGURIA
22 Campus Compliance Officer Ms. Wendy D. SMITH
96 Director University Business Svcs Ms. Clyta L. POLHEMUS
38 Director Psychological Counseling Dr. Daniel BERKOW

*Humboldt State University (D)

1 Harpst Street, Arcata CA 95521-8222
County: Humboldt FICE Identification: 001149
Unit ID: 115755
Telephone: (707) 826-3011 Carnegie Class: Master's M
FAX Number: (707) 826-5555 Calendar System: Semester
URL: www.humboldt.edu
Established: 1913 Annual Undergrad Tuition & Fees (In-State): $7,084
Enrollment: 7,902 Coed
Affiliation or Control: State IRS Status: 501(c)3
Highest Offering: Master's
Program: Liberal Arts And General; Teacher Preparatory; Professional
Accreditation: WC, ART, ENG, FOR, MUS, NURSE, SW

02 President Dr. Rollin C. RICHMOND
04 Special Assistant to the President Ms. Denice HELWIG
05 Provost/Vice Pres Academic Affairs Dr. Robert A. SNYDER
20 Vice Prov Acad Pgms/Undergrad Stds Dr. Jena BURGES
32 VP Student Affairs & Enroll Mgmt Dr. Peg BLAKE
11 Vice Pres Administrative Affairs Mr. Burt NORDSTROM
30 Vice President of Advancement Mr. Frank WHITLATCH
88 Assoc Vice President Faculty Affs Dr. Colleen MULLERY
10 Assoc Vice Pres Business Services Ms. Carol TERRY
88 Assoc VP Development & Alumni Rels Ms. Laura JACKSON
26 Assoc VP for Mktg & Communications Vacant
18 Director Facilities Management Mr. Gary KRIETSCH
88 Director University Budget Office Mr. David ROWE
20 Director of Academic Resources Mr. Volga KOVAL
06 Registrar Ms. Grace DEMPSEY
07 Director of Admissions Mr. Scott HAGG
15 Director Human Resources Ms. Tammy CURTIS
08 Dean of Library Ms. Teresa GRENOT
29 Director Alumni Relations Mr. Dean HART
44 Director Planned Giving Ms. Kimberley PITTMAN-SCHULZ
19 Chief of University Police Chief Thomas DEWEY
41 Athletic Director Mr. Dan COLLEN
39 Director of Housing Mr. John CAPACCIO
40 Asst Director Bookstore Ms. Roberta DUGGAN
13 Chief Information Officer Ms. Anna KIRCHER
36 Director Career Devel Center Ms. Annie BOLICK-FLOSS
28 Director Diversity & Inclusion Ms. Radha WEBLEY
46 Dean of Research & Sponsored Prgms Dr. Rhea WILLIAMSON
85 Director International Programs Vacant
104 Study Abroad Advisor Ms. Penelope SHAW
35 Dean Student Affairs Ms. Randi DARNALL BURKE
37 Director Student Financial Aid Ms. Kim COUGHLIN-LAMPHEAR
09 Dir Institutional Research & Plng Dr. Jacqueline NAGATSUKA
96 Director of Contracts & Procurement Mr. Dave BUGBEE
90 Manager Desktop IT Mr. Steve DARNALL
14 Director Central IT Mr. Josh CALLAHAN
23 Dir Health/Counseling/Psych Svcs Dr. Rebecca STAUFFER
56 Director Extended Education Mr. Carl F. HANSEN
79 Dean Col Arts/Humanities/Soc Sci Dr. Kenneth AYOOB
107 Dean College Professional Studies Dr. John LEE
81 Dean Col Natural Resources/Science Dr. Steven SMITH
21 Director Financial Services Ms. Lynne SANDSTROM

*San Diego State University (E)

5500 Campanile Drive, San Diego CA 92182-8000
County: San Diego FICE Identification: 001151
Unit ID: 122409
Telephone: (619) 594-5200 Carnegie Class: RU/H
FAX Number: (619) 594-8894 Calendar System: Semester
URL: www.sdsu.edu
Established: 1897 Annual Undergrad Tuition & Fees (In-State): $6,578
Enrollment: 30,016 Coed
Affiliation or Control: State IRS Status: 501(c)3
Highest Offering: Doctorate
Program: Teacher Preparatory; Professional
Accreditation: WC, ART, AUD, BUS, BUSA, CIDA, CLPSY, CORE, CS, DIETD, ENG, HSA, JOUR, KIN, MFCD, MIDWF, NURSE, PH, SP, SPAA, SW, TED, THEA

02 President Dr. Elliot HIRSHMAN
05 Provost Dr. Nancy A. MARLIN
10 Vice President Business Affairs Ms. Sally F. ROUSH
32 Vice President Student Affairs Dr. James R. KITCHEN
30 VP University Relations/Development Ms. Mary Ruth CARLETON
46 Vice President for Research Dr. Stephen WELTER
20 Assoc Vice Pres Academic Affairs Dr. Ethan A. SINGER
11 Assoc Vice President Operations Mr. Robert SCHULZ
88 Assoc Vice Pres Faculty Affairs Dr. Edith BENKOV
21 Assoc VP for Financial Operations Mr. Scott BURNS
15 Interim Assoc VP Administration Ms. Jessica RENTTO
85 Asst Vice President Intl Programs Dr. Alan R. SWEEDLER
27 Assoc VP Marketing & Communications Mr. Jack F. BERESFORD
35 Associate Vice Pres Student Affairs Mr. Eric RIVERA
88 Exec Dir St Affs Ldrshp/Cmpus Life Ms. Martha RUEL
29 Exec Director Alumni Association Mr. James S. HERRICK
23 Int Director Student Health Svcs Ms. Martha RUEL
100 Chief of Staff President's Office Ms. Andrea ROLLINS
23 Student Health Svcs Medical Dir Dr. Gregg LICHTENSTEIN
88 Asst Vice Pres Academic Affairs Dr. Sandra COOK
38 Director Counseling/Psych Services Dr. Sandy JORGENSEN-FUNK
08 Int Dean Library/Information Access Ms. Gale ETSCHMAIER
37 Dir Financial Aid & Scholarships Ms. Chrys M. DUTTON
45 Exec Dir Research Foundation Mr. Bob E. WOLFSON
51 Dean of Extended Studies Dr. Joe SHAPIRO
58 Assoc Dean of Graduate Affairs Dr. Radmila PRISLIN
49 Dean of Undergraduate Studies Dr. Geoffrey W. CHASE
79 Dean of College Arts & Letters Dr. Paul WONG
81 Dean of College of Sciences Dr. Stanley MALOY
54 Dean of College of Engineering Dr. David T. HAYHURST
50 Dean of College of Business Admin Dr. Michael CUNNINGHAM
76 Dean of Col Health/Human Services Dr. Marilyn NEWHOFF
53 Dean of College of Education Dr. Ric A. HOVDA
12 Dean Imperial Valley Campus Mr. David PEARSON
57 Dean of Profess Studies/Fine Arts Dr. Joyce M. GATTAS
84 Assoc Exec Dir Enrollment Services Ms. Rita GAJOLI
19 Director Public Safety Mr. John BROWNING
28 Chief Diversity Officer Dr. Aaron I. BRUCE
06 Registrar Ms. Rayanne WILLIAMS
07 Director of Admissions Ms. Beverly ARATA
36 Director Career Services Mr. James TARBOX
39 Director Housing Administration Ms. Patricia FRANCISCO
40 CEO Aztec Shops Mrs. Donna TUSACK
41 Director Intercollegiate Athletics Mr. Jim STERK
85 Asc Dir Intl Stdt Ctr/Int Std Advis Ms. Jane KALIONZES
88 Director Environ Health & Safety Mr. Terry GEE
13 Sr Director Information & Tech/CIO Mr. Rich PICKETT
09 Dir Univ Analytic Stds/Instnl Rsrch Ms. Sally FARRIS
31 Dir Community Rels/Special Projects Mr. Tyler SHERER
96 Mgr Contract/Procurement Mgmt Ms. Cathy GARCIA
21 Controller Ms. Loretta LEAVITT

*San Francisco State University (F)

1600 Holloway Avenue, San Francisco CA 94132-1740
County: San Francisco FICE Identification: 001154
Unit ID: 122597
Telephone: (415) 338-1111 Carnegie Class: Master's L
FAX Number: (415) 338-2514 Calendar System: Semester
URL: www.sfsu.edu
Established: 1899 Annual Undergrad Tuition & Fees (In-State): $5,688
Enrollment: 29,718 Coed
Affiliation or Control: State IRS Status: 501(c)3
Highest Offering: Doctorate
Program: Liberal Arts And General
Accreditation: WC, AAFCS, ART, BUS, CACREP, CORE, CS, DIETD, DIETI, ENG, JOUR, MT, MUS, NRPA, NURSE, PH, PTA, SP, SPAA, SW, TED, THEA

02 President ... Dr. Robert A. CORRIGAN
05 University Provost ... Dr. Sue V. ROSSER
44 Vice Pres University Advancement ... Mr. Robert NAVA
10 Interim Exec VP/CFO ... Ms. Nancy K. HAYES
32 VP Student Affairs/Dean of Students ... Dr. J.E.(Penny) SAFFOLD
100 Interim Chief of Staff ... Ms. Patricia B. BARTSCHER
45 AVP Academic Planning/Development ... Dr. Linda BUCKLEY
20 Assoc VP Academic Resources ... Dr. John J. KIM
46 Assoc VP Research Sponsored Pgm ... Dr. Jaylan TURKKAN
20 Associate VP Academic Affairs .. Dr. Enrique RIVEROS-SCHAFER
85 Assoc VP International Education ... Dr. Yenbo WU
18 Assoc VP Capital Plan Design Const ... Mr. Simon Y. LAM
13 Interim AVP Division Info Tech ... Ms. Phoebe KWAN
84 Senior AVP Enrollment Management ... Dr. Jo VOLKERT
18 Sr Assoc VP Physical Plng & Develop ... Ms. Marilyn LANIER
21 Acting Assoc VP Fiscal Affairs/ Cont ... Ms. Agnes WONG-NICKERSON
16 Assoc VP HR/Safety & Risk Mgt ... Ms. Lori GENTLES
45 AVP Planning & Strategic Initiativ ... Mr. Gene CHELBERG
50 Interim Dean College Business ... Ms. Caran COLVIN
53 Dean College Education ... Dr. Jake E. PEREA
88 Dean College Ethnic Studies ... Dr. Kenneth P. MONTEIRO
51 Director College Extended Learning ... Vacant
69 Dean College Health Human Svcs ... Dr. Don TAYLOR
79 Dean College of Arts and Humanities ... Dr. Paul SHERWIN
81 Dean College Science & Engineering ... Dr. Sheldon AXLER
15 Dean Faculty Affairs & Prof Dev ... Dr. Sacha BUNGE
58 Dean Graduate Studies ... Dr. Ann HALLUM
88 Dean Undergraduate Studies ... Dr. Gail EVANS
43 University Counsel ... Ms. Patricia B. BARTSCHER
102 Exec Director SFState Foundation ... Mr. Robert NAVA
31 Director Inst Civic/Cmty Engagement ... Dr. Gerald EISMAN
08 University Librarian ... Ms. Deborah C. MASTERS
24 Director Academic Technology ... Dr. Maggie BEERS
85 Director International Programs ... Ms. Hildy HEATH
88 Director Testing Center ... Mr. Gerald F. CARRIG
30 Associate Vice Pres Development ... Ms. Donna BLAKEMORE
86 Director Government & Community Rel ... Ms. Lisbet SUNSHINE
27 Director University Communications ... Ms. Ellen GRIFFIN
88 Exec Dir Univ Property Management ... Mr. Mark GOODRICH
88 Director EHOS ... Vacant
39 Director Residential Life ... Dr. Mary Ann BEGLEY
37 Director Student Financial Aid ... Ms. Barbara HUBLER
88 Director Student Outreach Services ... Dr. Frieda LEE
07 Director Undergraduate Admissions ... Mr. John PLISKA
21 Director Univ Budget Planning ... Mr. Andrew SOM
06 Registrar ... Ms. Suzanne DMYTRENKO
41 Director Athletics ... Dr. Michael J. SIMPSON
36 Acting Director Career Center ... Mr. Alan FISK
38 Director Counseling & Psych Svcs ... Dr. Derethia DUVAL
88 Director Disability Pgms/Res Ctr ... Mr. Gene CHELBERG
88 Dir Education Opportunity Program ... Mr. Oscar M. GARDEA
19 Chf of Police/Dir of Public Safety ... Chief Patrick WASLEY
23 Medical Dir Student Health Svcs ... Dr. Alastair SMITH
35 Dir LEAD/Assoc Dn Stdnts/Stdnt Life ... Mr. Joseph D. GREENWELL
96 Director Procurement Department ... Mr. Stephen C. SMITH
29 Director Alumni Relations ... Mr. Doug HUPKE

† Grants additional Doctoral degrees in cooperation with the UC-Berkeley and UC-San Francisco.

*San Jose State University (A)

One Washington Square, San Jose CA 95192-0001

County: Santa Clara — FICE Identification: 001155
Unit ID: 122755
Telephone: (408) 924-1000 — Carnegie Class: Master's L
FAX Number: (408) 924-1018 — Calendar System: Semester
URL: www.sjsu.edu
Established: 1857 — Annual Undergrad Tuition & Fees (In-State): $6,240
Enrollment: 29,076 — Coed
Affiliation or Control: State — IRS Status: 501(c)3
Highest Offering: Master's
Program: Liberal Arts And General; Teacher Preparatory; Professional; Business Emphasis
Accreditation: WC, ART, BUS, CEA, CS, DANCE, DIETD, DIETI, ENG, JOUR, LIB, MT, MUS, NAIT, NRPA, NURSE, OT, PH, PLNG, SP, SPAA, SW, TED, THEA

02 President ... Dr. Mohammed QAYOUMI
11 Vice Pres Administration & Finance ... Mr. Shawn BIBB
32 Vice President Student Affairs ... Mr. Jason LAKER
30 Int VP University Advancement ... Ms. Nancy BUSSANI
13 VP Info Technology & CIO ... Mr. William NANCE
45 Vice Provost Academic Budgets/Plng ... Vacant
14 Int Assoc VP Univ Computing/Telecom ... Mr. Don BAKER
09 Assoc VP Institutional Research ... Dr. Sutee SUJITPARAPITAYA
05 Provost/Vice Pres Acad Affairs ... Dr. Gerry SELTER
04 Exec Assistant to the President ... Mr. William NANCE
20 Associate Vice Pres Faculty Affairs ... Dr. Joan MERDINGER
58 Assoc VP Graduate Studies/Research ... Dr. Pamela STACKS
20 Assoc VP Undergrad Studies ... Dr. Dennis JAEHNE
21 VP Admin Systems/Finance ... Ms. Josee LAROCHELLE
18 Assoc VP for Facilities/Operations ... Mr. Anton KASHIRI
15 Associate VP Human Resources ... Ms. Maria DEGUEVARA
26 Assoc VP Public Affairs ... Mr. Lawrence CARR
44 Director Devel/Alumni Rels ... Mr. Paul RICHARDSON
51 Assoc VP/Dean Intl/Extended Stds ... Dr. Mark NOVAK
84 Int Assoc VP Enroll/Academic Svcs ... Ms. Colleen BROWN
08 Dean of the University Library ... Dr. Ruth KIFER
28 Equity & Diversity Manager ... Mr. Barrett MORRIS
27 Director Communications/Public Affs ... Mr. Cyril MANNING
29 Director Alumni Relations ... Mr. Paul RICHARDSON
06 Registrar ... Ms. Marion SOFISH
41 Director Intercollegiate Athletics ... Mr. Thomas BOWEN
96 Director Procurement Services ... Vacant
40 Director Spartan Bookstore ... Vacant
19 Chief of Police ... Mr. Peter DECENA
36 Director Career Center ... Ms. Cheryl ALLMEN-VINNEDGE
38 Int Director Counseling Services ... Mr. Kell FUJIMOTO
37 Director Fin Aid/Schlarship Ofc ... Ms. Coleetta MCELROY
39 Dir University Housing Svcs ... Mr. Victor CULATTA
23 Dir Student Health Center ... Dr. Roger ELROD
49 Dean College of Applied Sci & Art ... Dr. Charles BULLOCK
50 Dean College of Business ... Dr. David STEELE
53 Dean College of Education ... Dr. Elaine CHIN
54 Dean College of Engineering ... Dr. Belle WEI
79 Dean College of Humanities/Arts ... Dr. Karl TOEPFER
81 Dean College of Science ... Dr. J. Michael PARRISH
83 Dean College Social Sciences ... Dr. Sheila BIENENFELD

*Sonoma State University (B)

1801 E Cotati Avenue, Rohnert Park CA 94928-3609

County: Sonoma — FICE Identification: 001156
Unit ID: 123572
Telephone: (707) 664-2880 — Carnegie Class: Master's L
FAX Number: (707) 664-2505 — Calendar System: Semester
URL: www.sonoma.edu
Established: 1960 — Annual Undergrad Tuition & Fees (In-State): $5,508
Enrollment: 8,395 — Coed
Affiliation or Control: State — IRS Status: 501(c)3
Highest Offering: Master's
Program: Liberal Arts And General; Teacher Preparatory; Professional
Accreditation: WC, ART, BUS, CACREP, MUS, NUR, TED

02 President ... Dr. Ruben ARMINANA
05 Provost & Vice Pres Academic Affs ... Dr. Andrew ROGERSON
10 Vice Pres Administration & Finance ... Mr. Laurence FURUKAWA-SCHLERETH
26 Vice President University Affairs ... Mr. Dan CONDRON
30 Vice President Development ... Ms. Patricia MCNEILL
32 Interim Vice Pres Stdnt Affs/ Enroll ... Mr. Matthew LOPEZ-PHILLIPS
20 Assoc VP for Faculty Affairs ... Dr. Melinda BARNARD
21 Assoc VP for Admin & Finance ... Ms. Letitia COATE
35 Asst VP Stdnt Affs/Enrollment Mgmt ... Mr. Chuck RHODES
09 Director Institutional Research ... Dr. Marilyn SARGENT
14 Acting CIO/Sr Dir Common Mgmt Sys ... Mr. Jason WENRICK
08 Library Dean ... Ms. Barbara BUTLER
70 Dean School of Arts & Humanities ... Dr. William BABULA
50 Dean Sch of Business/Economic ... Dr. William SILVER
53 Interim Dean School of Education ... Dr. Carlos AYALA
81 Interim Dean School Science & Tech ... Dr. Lynn STAUFFER
83 Dean School of Social Sciences ... Dr. Elaine A. LEEDER
56 Dean School of Extended Education ... Dr. Mark MERICKEL
38 Dir of Counseling/Psych Services ... Dr. Lisa WYATT
37 Director of Financial Aid ... Mrs. Susan GUTIERREZ
18 Sr Dir Facilities Services/CPDC ... Mr. Christopher DINNO
27 Assoc VP for Communications & Mktg ... Ms. Susan KASHACK
41 Director Athletics ... Mr. William J. FUSCO
19 Interim Chief Police Services ... Ms. Sally MILLER
21 Sr Director Univ Business Services ... Ms. Gloria OGG
88 Sr Director Entrepreneurial Srvcs ... Mr. Neil MARKLEY
06 Registrar ... Ms. Lisa NOTO
07 Director of Admissions ... Mr. Gustavo FLORES
29 Dir Alumni Relations/Annual Giving ... Ms. Laurie OGG
36 Mg Dir Advising/Career/EOP Ctr ... Ms. Joyce CHONG
28 Mg Dir Employee Rel/Comp Svcs ... Ms. Joyce SUZUKI

California University of Management and Sciences (C)

721 North Euclid Street, Anaheim CA 92801

County: Orange — FICE Identification: 041331
Telephone: (714) 533-3946 — Carnegie Class: Not Classified
FAX Number: (714) 533-7778 — Calendar System: Quarter
URL: www.calums.edu
Established: 1998 — Annual Undergrad Tuition & Fees: $7,365
Enrollment: 178 — Coed
Affiliation or Control: Independent Non-Profit — IRS Status: 501(c)3
Highest Offering: Master's
Program: 2-Year Principally Bachelor's Creditable; Professional; Business Emphasis
Accreditation: ACICS

01 President ... David PARK
03 Vice President ... Jason SHIN
05 Academic Dean ... Mohammad SAFARZADEH
20 Program Director ... Il Soo LEE
11 Registrar/Director Administration ... Jeffrey BEASCA
07 Admissions Officer ... Lisa LEE
32 Director of Student Services ... Janet LAURIN
08 Library Director ... Edwin FOLLICK
90 Academic Computing/Network Support ... James KIM

California Western School of Law (D)

225 Cedar Street, San Diego CA 92101-3090

County: San Diego — FICE Identification: 013103
Unit ID: 111391
Telephone: (619) 239-0391 — Carnegie Class: Spec/Law
FAX Number: (619) 525-7092 — Calendar System: Trimester
URL: www.cwsl.edu
Established: 1928 — Annual Graduate Tuition & Fees: $42,600
Enrollment: 983 — Coed
Affiliation or Control: Independent Non-Profit — IRS Status: 501(c)3
Highest Offering: First Professional Degree; No Undergraduates
Program: Professional
Accreditation: LAW

01 President & Dean ... Dean Steven R. SMITH
05 Associate Dean Academic Affairs ... Prof. William C. ACEVES
11 Associate Dean Administration ... Prof. Laura M. PADILLA
30 Assistant Dean External Affairs ... Mr. David D. BOWERS
32 Asst Dean Students/Diversity Svcs ... Ms. Kathleen SEIBEL
36 Assistant Dean Career Services ... Ms. Courtney MIKLUSAK
88 Asst Dean Mission Development ... Mr. James M. COOPER
37 Exec Director Financial Aid ... Mr. William KAHLER
40 Exec Dir Sworwood Bookstore ... Ms. Crystal L. HENGEL
13 Exec Director Computer Services ... Ms. Mary Lou MITCHELL
18 Exec Dir Facilities Management ... Ms. Jolie L. CARTIER
88 Ex Dir Inst for Criminal Def Advoc ... Prof. Justin P. BROOKS
88 Exec Dir Inst of Health Law Studies ... Prof. Bryan A. LIANG
08 Director Law Library ... Prof. Phyllis C. MARION
10 Chief Financial Officer ... Ms. Pamela A. DUFFY
07 Director of Admissions ... Ms. Traci D. HOWARD
06 Registrar ... Ms. Diane SHRAGG
88 Director MCL/LLM Program ... Prof. Jacquelyn H. SLOTKIN
26 Chief Public Relations Officer ... Ms. Pamela HARDY
29 Director Alumni Relations ... Ms. Lori BOYLE
15 Director Personnel Services ... Ms. Rikklyn S. UEDA
28 Director of Diversity ... Ms. Marion E. CLOETE
21 Associate Business Officer ... Ms. Ruth GOULDING
35 Director Student Affairs ... Ms. Kathleen SEIBEL

Cambridge Junior College (E)

990-A Klamath Lane, Yuba City CA 95993-8978

County: Sutter — FICE Identification: 038743
Unit ID: 446093
Telephone: (530) 674-9199 — Carnegie Class: Not Classified
FAX Number: (530) 671-7319 — Calendar System: Other
URL: www.cambridge.edu
Established: N/A — Annual Undergrad Tuition & Fees: N/A
Enrollment: 195 — Coed
Affiliation or Control: Proprietary — IRS Status: Proprietary
Highest Offering: Associate Degree
Program: Occupational
Accreditation: ACICS

01 Director ... Ms. Sandy FOWLER

*Carrington College California - Administrative Office (F)

7801 Folsom Boulevard, Suite 210, Sacramento CA 95826-2620

County: Sacramento — Identification: 666086
Unit ID: 125532
Telephone: (916) 388-2800 — Carnegie Class: N/A
FAX Number: (916) 381-1609
URL: www.carrington.edu

01 President ... Dr. Jeff AKENS

*Carrington College California - Antioch (G)

2157 Country Hills Drive, Antioch CA 94509-7435

County: Contra Costa — Identification: 666041
Unit ID: 437927
Telephone: (925) 522-7777 — Carnegie Class: Assoc/PrivFP
FAX Number: (925) 755-0079 — Calendar System: Other
URL: www.carrington.edu
Established: 1997 — Annual Undergrad Tuition & Fees: $40,956
Enrollment: 520 — Coed
Affiliation or Control: Proprietary — IRS Status: Proprietary
Highest Offering: Associate Degree
Program: Occupational; 2-Year Principally Bachelor's Creditable
Accreditation: &WJ, MAC

02 Executive Campus Director ... Mr. Mitch CHARLES

† Regional accreditation is carried under the parent institution in Sacramento, CA.

*Carrington College California - Citrus Heights (H)

7301 Greenback Lane, Suite A, Citrus Heights CA 95621

County: Sacramento — Identification: 667042
Unit ID: 450702
Telephone: (916) 722-8200 — Carnegie Class: Not Classified
FAX Number: (916) 772-6883 — Calendar System: Other
URL: www.carrington.edu
Established: N/A — Annual Undergrad Tuition & Fees: $17,056
Enrollment: 806 — Coed
Affiliation or Control: Proprietary — IRS Status: Proprietary
Highest Offering: Associate Degree
Program: Occupational; 2-Year Principally Bachelor's Creditable
Accreditation: &WJ, SURGT

02 Executive Campus Director ... Mr. Jeff ORTEGA

† Regional accreditation is carried under the parent institution in Sacramento, CA.

*Carrington College California - Emeryville (A)

6001 Shellmound Street, Suite 145,
Emeryville CA 94608-1020
County: Alameda Identification: 666372
Unit ID: 445355
Telephone: (510) 420-5400 Carnegie Class: Assoc/PrivFP
FAX Number: (510) 601-0793 Calendar System: Other
URL: www.carrington.edu
Established: 2000 Annual Undergrad Tuition & Fees: $17,056
Enrollment: 306 Coed
Affiliation or Control: Proprietary IRS Status: Proprietary
Highest Offering: Associate Degree
Program: 2-Year Principally Bachelor's Creditable; Professional
Accreditation: &WJ, MAC

02 Executive Campus Director .... Mr. Frederick HOLLAND
05 Dean Academic Affairs .... Ms. Jennifer EVANS

† Regional accreditation is carried under the parent institution in Sacramento, CA.

*Carrington College California - Pleasant Hill (B)

380 Civic Drive, Suite 300, Pleasant Hill CA 94523-1984
County: Contra Costa Identification: 666043
Unit ID: 438258
Telephone: (925) 609-6650 Carnegie Class: Assoc/PrivFP
FAX Number: (925) 609-6666 Calendar System: Other
URL: www.carrington.edu
Established: 1997 Annual Undergrad Tuition & Fees: $17,056
Enrollment: 568 Coed
Affiliation or Control: Proprietary IRS Status: Proprietary
Highest Offering: Associate Degree
Program: Occupational; 2-Year Principally Bachelor's Creditable
Accreditation: &WJ, MAC, @PTAA

02 Executive Campus Director ....Ms. La Shawn WELLS
05 Dean of Academic Affairs ....Ms. Karen LEWIS
08 Librarian ....Ms. Sarah Jo NEUBAUER

† Regional accreditation is carried under the parent institution in Sacramento, CA.

*Carrington College California - Sacramento (C)

8909 Folsom Boulevard, Sacramento CA 95826-9823
County: Sacramento FICE Identification: 009748
Unit ID: 125532
Telephone: (916) 361-1660 Carnegie Class: Assoc/PrivFP
FAX Number: (916) 361-6666 Calendar System: Other
URL: www.carrington.edu
Established: 1967 Annual Undergrad Tuition & Fees: $17,056
Enrollment: 1,416 Coed
Affiliation or Control: Proprietary IRS Status: Proprietary
Highest Offering: Associate Degree
Program: Occupational; 2-Year Principally Bachelor's Creditable
Accreditation: WJ, DH, MAC

02 Executive Director .... Ms. Sue SMITH
06 Registrar ....Ms. Ryanne GREEN-QUARLES
07 Director of Admissions ....Vance KLINKE
08 Librarian ....Ms. Kirsten KLINGHAMMER
05 Dean of Academic Affairs .... Ms. Helen FAIRCHILD

*Carrington College California - San Jose (D)

6201 San Ignacio Avenue, San Jose CA 95119-1325
County: Santa Clara Identification: 666042
Unit ID: 437936
Telephone: (408) 360-0840 Carnegie Class: Assoc/PrivFP
FAX Number: (408) 360-0848 Calendar System: Other
URL: www.carrington.edu
Established: 1989 Annual Undergrad Tuition & Fees: $17,056
Enrollment: 1,006 Coed
Affiliation or Control: Proprietary IRS Status: Proprietary
Highest Offering: Baccalaureate
Program: Occupational; 2-Year Principally Bachelor's Creditable
Accreditation: &WJ, DH, MAC, SURGT

02 Executive Campus Director .... Mr. Tim GIENAPP

† Regional accreditation is carried under the parent institution in Sacramento, CA.

*Carrington College California - San Leandro (E)

15555 E 14th Street, Suite 500,
San Leandro CA 94578-9930
County: Alameda Identification: 666751
Unit ID: 246974
Telephone: (510) 276-3888 Carnegie Class: Assoc/PrivFP
FAX Number: (510) 276-3653 Calendar System: Other
URL: www.carrington.edu
Established: 1967 Annual Undergrad Tuition & Fees: $17,056
Enrollment: 908 Coed
Affiliation or Control: Proprietary IRS Status: Proprietary
Highest Offering: Associate Degree
Program: Occupational; 2-Year Principally Bachelor's Creditable
Accreditation: &WJ, MAC

02 Executive Campus Director ....Ms. Michelle A. KREUZER
05 Dean of Academic Affairs .... Ms. Pat CHANNELL
06 Registrar ....Mr. Michael BORGES
07 Director of Admissions .... Ms. Tiffany RHODES
08 Librarian ....Mr. Chris BROWN
37 Director Student Finance .... Ms. Kimberly RORABAUGH
36 Director of Career Services ....Vacant

† Regional accreditation is carried under the parent institution in Sacramento, CA.

*Carrington College California - Stockton (F)

1313 W Robinhood Drive, Suite B,
Stockton CA 95207-5509
County: San Joaquin Identification: 666140
Unit ID: 450696
Telephone: (209) 956-1240 Carnegie Class: Assoc/PrivFP
FAX Number: (209) 956-1244 Calendar System: Semester
URL: www.carrington.edu
Established: 1967 Annual Undergrad Tuition & Fees: $25,472
Enrollment: 665 Coed
Affiliation or Control: Proprietary IRS Status: Proprietary
Highest Offering: Associate Degree
Program: Occupational; 2-Year Principally Bachelor's Creditable
Accreditation: &WJ, MAC

02 Executive Campus Director .... Mr. David KAYE
07 Director of Admissions ....Mrs. Anna MELI

† Regional accreditation is carried under the parent institution in Sacramento, CA.

Casa Loma College-Van Nuys (G)

6725 Kester Avenue, Van Nuys CA 91405
County: Los Angeles FICE Identification: 006731
Unit ID: 111638
Telephone: (818) 785-2726 Carnegie Class: Not Classified
FAX Number: (818) 785-2191 Calendar System: Other
URL: www.casalomacollege.edu
Established: N/A Annual Undergrad Tuition & Fees: N/A
Enrollment: 587 Coed
Affiliation or Control: Independent Non-Profit IRS Status: 501(c)3
Highest Offering: Associate Degree
Program: Occupational
Accreditation: ABHES

01 Campus Director/Controller .... Ms. Veronica PANTOJA
66 Director of Nursing ....Ms. Barbara BRIDGES
06 Registrar .... Ms. Christina CARRILLO
07 Director of Admissions ....Ms. Deanna BERNAL
26 Director Public Relations ....Ms. Claire BUHN
36 Director Career Services ....Mr. Paul BOYCHUK
37 Director Studend Financial Aid ....Ms. Rosleen AURORA

CBD College (H)

5724 West Third Street, Los Angeles CA 90036
County: Los Angeles FICE Identification: 032503
Unit ID: 439367
Telephone: (323) 937-7772 Carnegie Class: Not Classified
FAX Number: (323) 937-4472 Calendar System: Other
URL: www.cbd.edu
Established: 1982 Annual Undergrad Tuition & Fees: $28,744
Enrollment: 335 Coed
Affiliation or Control: Independent Non-Profit IRS Status: 501(c)3
Highest Offering: Associate Degree
Program: Occupational
Accreditation: CNCE, SURTEC

01 President .... Mr. Alan HESHEL

Cedars-Sinai Medical Center Graduate Program in Biomedical Sciences and Translational Medicine (I)

8700 Beverly Blvd Atrium Bld 2nd Fl,
Los Angeles CA 90048
County: Los Angeles Identification: 667071
Telephone: (310) 423-6252 Carnegie Class: Not Classified
FAX Number: N/A Calendar System: Trimester
URL: www.cedars-sinai.edu
Established: N/A Annual Graduate Tuition & Fees: N/A
Enrollment: N/A Coed
Affiliation or Control: Independent Non-Profit IRS Status: 501(c)3
Highest Offering: Doctorate; No Undergraduates
Program: Professional
Accreditation: @WC

01 President ....Thomas PRISELAC
05 Graduate Educ Program Coordinator .... Emma YATES

Cerritos College (J)

11110 Alondra Boulevard, Norwalk CA 90650-6298
County: Los Angeles FICE Identification: 001161
Unit ID: 111887
Telephone: (562) 860-2451 Carnegie Class: Assoc/Pub-S-SC
FAX Number: (562) 467-5005 Calendar System: Semester
URL: www.cerritos.edu
Established: 1955 Annual Undergrad Tuition & Fees (In-District): $676
Enrollment: 22,735 Coed
Affiliation or Control: State/Local IRS Status: 501(c)3
Highest Offering: Associate Degree
Program: Occupational; 2-Year Principally Bachelor's Creditable
Accreditation: WJ, ADNUR, DA, DH, PTAA

01 President ....Dr. Linda L. LACY
05 VP of Academic Affairs .... Mr. William C. FARMER
10 VP of Business Services ....Mr. David EL FATTAL
32 Vice President Student Services ....Dr. Stephen JOHNSON
20 Dean of Academic Affairs ....Vacant
88 Exec Dean Cmty/Industr/Tech Educ ....Vacant
07 Dean of Admissions/Records & Svcs .....Ms. Stephanie MURGUIA
38 Dean of Counseling Services ....Dr. Renee DeLong CHOMIAK
08 Dean of the Library & LRC ....Mr. Carl BENGSTON
88 Dean Disabled Student Pgms & Svcs ....Dr. Lucinda ABORN
88 Dean of Student Support Services ....Ms. Kim WESTBY
50 Instr Dean Business/Humanities/SS ....Ms. Rachel MASON
57 Instr Dean Fine Arts/Communications .... Dr. Connie MAYFIELD
76 Instr Dean Health Occupations ....Vacant
83 Dean Academic Success ....Dr. Bryan REECE
49 Instr Dean Liberal Arts ....Dr. Linda ROSE
68 Instr Dean Physical Educ/Athletics .... Dr. Daniel SMITH
54 Instr Dean Science/Engineering/Math ...... Dr. Carolyn CHAMBERS
73 Instruction Dean of Technology ....Vacant
14 Director of Information Technology .... Ms. Lee KRICHMAR
21 Director of Fiscal Services ....Vacant
35 Director of Student Activities .... Ms. Holly BOGDANOVICH
16 Interim VP of Human Resources .... Mr. Victor COLLINS
36 Dir of Career/Assessment Services .... Ms. Theresa LOPEZ
18 Director Physical Plant ....Mr. Robert RIFFLE
44 Executive Director Foundation .... Mr. Steven RICHARDSON
88 Director Community Advancement .... Ms. Bellegran GOMEZ
26 Director Public & Governmental Rels ....Mr. Mark WALLACE
96 Director of Purchasing ....Ms. Jenney HO
15 Asst Director Human Resources .. Ms. Adriana FLORES-CHURCH
104 Web Administrator ....Mr. Ty BOWMAN
19 Chief of Campus Police ....Mr. Richard BUKOWIECKI
28 Dir Adult Edu/Diversity Programs .... Ms. Graciela VASQUEZ
31 Director Community Education .... Dr. Patricia ROBBINS SMITH
88 Director Child Development Center ....Ms. Debra WARD
88 Director Foster/Kinship Care Ed Pgm .... Ms. Lori SWITANOWSKI
88 Operations Manager ....Mr. Arcadio AVILA
18 Facilities Manager .... Mr. Thomas RICHEY
88 Payroll Manager ....Ms. Deanna HART
21 Accounting Manager ....Mr. Shawn JONES
21 Budget Manager ....Ms. Suzie PAYNE
13 Manager Information Technology ....Mr. Patrick O'DONNELL
23 Director Student Health Services ....Ms. Nancy MONTGOMERY
85 Director International Student Svcs ....Ms. Danita KURTZ
88 Director of CalWORKs Services ....Ms. Norma RODRIGUEZ
09 Dir of Research & Planning ....Ms. Kay NGUYEN
88 Director Adv Trans Tech Proj ....Ms. Jannet MALIG
88 PeopleSoft Database Administrator ....Ms. Maria MENDEZ
88 PeopleSoft Database Administrator ....Mr. Michael SALAZAR
88 Director of Pathway Programs ....Ms. Maggie CORDERO
22 Mgr Emp Svcs/Fac & Staff Div Ofcr ....Ms. Cynthia CONVEY

*Chabot-Las Positas Community College District (K)

5020 Franklin Drive, Pleasanton CA 94588-3354
County: Alameda Identification: 666925
Telephone: (925) 485-5208 Carnegie Class: N/A
FAX Number: (925) 485-5256
URL: www.clpccd.org

01 Chancellor ....Dr. Joel L. KINNAMON
10 Vice Chanc Business Services .... Mr. Lorenzo LEGASPI
05 Vice Chanc Educational Svcs/Plng ....Vacant
18 Vice Chanc Facilities/Bond .... Mr. Jeffrey KINGSTON
16 Vice Chanc HR Svcs/Org Dev ....Dr. Mary Anne GULARTE
26 Exec Dist Dir Pub Rels/Govt Affairs ....Ms. Laura WEAVER

*Chabot College (L)

25555 Hesperian Boulevard, Hayward CA 94545-2400
County: Alameda FICE Identification: 001162
Unit ID: 111920
Telephone: (510) 723-6600 Carnegie Class: Assoc/Pub-S-MC
FAX Number: (510) 782-9315 Calendar System: Semester
URL: www.chabotcollege.edu
Established: 1961 Annual Undergrad Tuition & Fees (In-District): $622
Enrollment: 15,148 Coed
Affiliation or Control: State/Local IRS Status: 501(c)3
Highest Offering: Associate Degree
Program: Occupational; 2-Year Principally Bachelor's Creditable
Accreditation: WJ, DH, MAC

02 President ....Dr. Celia BARBERENA
05 Vice President Academic Services ....Dr. George A. RAILEY, JR.
32 Vice President Student Services ....Dr. Howard J. IRVIN
10 Vice President Business Services ....Ms. Rita BROWN

04 Exec Asst to the College President ... Ms. Karen L. SILVA
08 Dean Instr-Learning Resource ... Vacant
38 Div Dean Counseling/Guidance ... Dr. Matt KRITSCHER
41 Dean Health/PE/Athletics ... Mr. Dale WAGONER
07 Director of Admissions & Records ... Mrs. Paulette LINO
37 Director of Financial Aid ... Ms. Kathryn LINZMEYER
19 Director Safety & Security ... Sgt. Keith STIVER
09 Director of Institutional Research ... Dr. Carolyn ARNOLD
15 Director Human Resources ... Dr. Mary Anne GULARTE
18 Chief Facilities/Physical Plant ... Mr. Tim NELSON
26 Int Chief Public Relations Officer ... Ms. Laura WEAVER
35 Director Student Life ... Ms. Danielle PRECIADO
96 Manager Purchasing/Warehouse Svcs ... Mr. Andrew D. HOWE

Las Positas College (A)

3000 Campus Hill Drive, Livermore CA 94551-7623
County: Alameda　FICE Identification: 030357
Unit ID: 366401
Telephone: (925) 424-1000　Carnegie Class: Assoc/Pub-S-MC
FAX Number: (925) 443-0742　Calendar System: Semester
URL: www.laspositascollege.edu
Established: 1975　Annual Undergrad Tuition & Fees (In-District): $1,341
Enrollment: 9,220　Coed
Affiliation or Control: State/Local　IRS Status: 501(c)3
Highest Offering: Associate Degree
Program: Occupational; 2-Year Principally Bachelor's Creditable
Accreditation: WJ

02 President ... Dr. Kevin G. WALTHERS
05 Int Vice President Academic Svcs ... Ms. Marge MALONEY
32 Int Vice President Student Svcs ... Mr. Jeff BAKER
10 Vice Pres Business Services ... Mr. Bob KRATOCHVIL
04 Exec Assistant to the President ... Ms. Jennifer ADAMS
35 Interim Dean of Student Services ... Ms. Kimberly TOMLINSON
79 Int Dean Arts and Communication ... Dr. John RUYS
75 Dean Bus/Comp/Applied Technologies ... Dr. Janice NOBLE
81 Dean Math/Sci/Engr/Public Safety ... Dr. Neal ELY
76 Dean PE/Health and Wellness ... Ms. Dyan MILLER
07 Dean of Admissions/Records ... Ms. Sylvia RODRIQUEZ
45 Director of Research & Planning ... Mr. Rajinder SAMRA
37 Financial Aid/Veterans Assistance ... Ms. Andi SCHREIBMAN
19 Director of Safety/Security ... Vacant
26 Exec Dir Public Info & Marketing ... Ms. Laura WEAVER
08 Head Librarian ... Ms. Cheryl WARREN
102 LPC Foundation Executive Director ... Dr. Ted KAYE
41 Health/Athletic Director ... Ms. Dyan MILLER
18 Project Planner/Manager Facilities ... Mr. Jeffrey KINGSTON

Chaffey College (B)

5885 Haven Avenue, Rancho Cucamonga CA 91737-3002
County: San Bernardino　FICE Identification: 001163
Unit ID: 111939
Telephone: (909) 652-6000　Carnegie Class: Assoc/Pub-S-MC
FAX Number: (909) 652-6006　Calendar System: Semester
URL: www.chaffey.edu
Established: 1883　Annual Undergrad Tuition & Fees (In-District): $864
Enrollment: 19,773　Coed
Affiliation or Control: State/Local　IRS Status: 501(c)3
Highest Offering: Associate Degree
Program: Occupational; 2-Year Principally Bachelor's Creditable
Accreditation: WJ, ADNUR, DA, RAD

01 Superintendent/President ... Dr. Henry D. SHANNON
11 VP/Chief Admin Officer Chino Campus ... Vacant
05 VP Instruction & Student Services ... Dr. Sherrie L. GUERRERO
11 Int VP Admin Svcs & External Rels ... Dr. Ciriaco PINEDO
10 Int Vice Pres Business Operations .. Mr. Stephen W. MENZEL, JR.
15 Exec Director Human Resources ... Ms. Lisa BAILEY
44 Int Exec Dir Found & Alum Rel ... Mr. Nick NAZARIAN
85 Director Transfer Center/Intl Pgms ... Ms. Jenny DANNELLEY
32 Director Student Activities ... Ms. Susan STEWART
07 Administrator Admissions/Records ... Ms. Kathy LUCERO
19 Dir Public Safety/Chief of Police ... Mr. David RAMIREZ
21 Director Accounting Services ... Ms. Kim ERICKSON
06 Registrar ... Vacant
29 Director Alumni Relations ... Vacant
21 Director Administrative Systems ... Ms. Melanie SIDDIQI
88 Director Technical Services ... Mr. Michael FINK
88 Director Childrens Center ... Ms. Birgit MONKS
23 Director Health Services ... Ms. Katherine PEEK
75 Dean DD/PD/Vocation ... Vacant
18 Dir Maintenance and Central Plant ... Mr. Bruce COOK
37 Director Financial Aid ... Ms. Patricia BOPKO
96 Manager Purchasing Services ... Mr. Mark LOGAN
31 Director Auxiliary Services ... Mr. Jared CEJA
26 Director Marketing ... Ms. Peggy CARTWRIGHT
09 Director Institutional Research ... Mr. Jim FILLPOT
21 Director Budgeting Services ... Ms. Anita UNDERCOFFER
88 Director Museum Gallery ... Ms. Rebecca TRAWICK
88 Manager Facilities Development ... Ms. Sarah RILEY
12 Dean Chino Campus ... Dr. Teresa HULL
88 Dean Language Arts ... Mr. Michael DINIELLI
50 Dean Business & Applied Technology ... Mr. Sid BURKS
81 Interim Dean Mathematics & Science ... Ms. Merrill DEMING
83 Int Dean Social & Behavioral Sci ... Ms. Merrill DEMING
38 Dean Counseling & Matriculation ... Dr. Lori WAITE
76 Dean Health Sciences ... Dr. Teresa HULL
88 Int Dean Visual Performing Arts ... Mr. Michael DINIELLI
68 Int Dean Physical Education ... Mr. Frank PINKERTON
08 Dean Instructional Support ... Ms. Laura HOPE
04 Exec Assistant Supt/Pres Office ... Ms. Kathy NAPOLI

Chapman University (C)

One University Drive, Orange CA 92866-1099
County: Orange　FICE Identification: 001164
Unit ID: 111948
Telephone: (714) 997-6815　Carnegie Class: Master's L
FAX Number: (714) 997-6713　Calendar System: 4/1/4
URL: www.chapman.edu
Established: 1861　Annual Undergrad Tuition & Fees: $40,234
Enrollment: 6,881　Coed
Affiliation or Control: Christian Church (Disciples Of Christ)
IRS Status: 501(c)3
Highest Offering: Doctorate
Program: Liberal Arts And General; Teacher Preparatory; Professional
Accreditation: WC, BUS, DANCE, LAW, MFCD, MUS, PTA, @SP, TEAC, THEA

01 President ... Dr. James L. DOTI
05 Chancellor ... Dr. Daniele C. STRUPPA
03 Executive Vice President & COO ... Mr. Harold W. HEWITT, JR.
30 Exec VP University Advancement ... Ms. Sheryl BOURGEOIS
32 Vice Chancellor & Dean of Students ... Dr. Jerry PRICE
84 Vice Chancellor/Dean Enrollment Mgt ... Mr. Micheal PELLY
20 Vice Chancellor for Academic Admin ... Dr. Raymond SFEIR
15 Vice Chan for Faculty Affairs & ALO ... Dr. Karen GRAHAM
49 Dean Wilkinson Col Hum/Soc Sci ... Dr. Patrick QUINN
61 Dean School of Law ... Dr. Tom CAMPBELL
50 Dean School Business/Economics ... Vacant
53 Dean College of Educational Studies ... Dr. Donald CARDINAL
88 Dean College of Film & Media Arts ... Mr. Robert BASSETT
88 Dean College of Performing Arts ... Mr. Dale MERRILL
81 Dean Col of Science & Technology ... Dr. Menas KAFATOS
88 Dean/Artistic Dir Center for Arts ... Dr. William HALL
88 Director Ctr for Global Education ... Dr. James COYLE
97 Vice Chancellor Undergrad Education ... Dr. Jeanne GUNNER
45 Vice President Campus Planning ... Mr. Kris OLSEN
16 Vice President of Human Resources ... Ms. Becky CAMPOS
43 Assoc Vice Pres of Legal Affairs ... Ms. Janine DUMONTELLE
21 Assoc Vice President & Controller ... Mr. Behzad BINESH
07 Asst VC/Chief Admissions Officer ... Mr. Michael DRUMMY
88 Assistant Chancellor ... Ms. Iris GERBASI
88 Dir Assesmnt/Strat Curr Initiatives ... Mr. Joseph SLOWENSKY
18 Director of Facilities ... Mr. Alan SMITH
26 Director Public Relations ... Ms. Mary PLATT
08 Dean of Library ... Ms. Charlene BALDWIN
29 Director Alumni Relations ... Ms. Dea MARCANO
13 Chief Information Officer ... Ms. Shari WATERS
09 Director of Institutional Research ... Dr. Marisol ARREDONDO
06 Registrar ... Dr. Jack FARRELL
46 Director Sponsored Research ... Vacant
37 Director Financial Aid ... Mr. Jack MILLIS
85 Director Intl Student Services ... Ms. Susan SAMS
19 Chief of Public Safety ... Mr. Randy BURBA
39 Assoc Dean/Director Residence Life ... Ms. Deborah MILLER
41 Athletic Director ... Mr. David CURREY
42 Dean of the Chapel ... Dr. Gail STEARNS
04 Associate to the President ... Ms. Ann CAMERON
88 Assistant to the Chancellor ... Ms. Christina D. MARSHALL
22 Equal Opportunity Officer ... Mr. Eduardo MONGE
23 Director Student Health Services ... Ms. Jacqueline DEATS
35 Director Student LEAD ... Ms. Tami OTSUKA
36 Director Career Development ... Ms. Barbara HUBERT
38 Assoc Dean/Dir Student Psych Couns ... Ms. Jeannie WALKER
96 Director of Purchasing ... Ms. Pam AMES
04 Assistant to the President ... Ms. Dorothy FAROL

Charles Drew University of Medicine & Science (D)

1730 E 118th Street, Los Angeles CA 90059-3025
County: Los Angeles　FICE Identification: 010365
Unit ID: 111966
Telephone: (323) 563-4800　Carnegie Class: Spec/Health
FAX Number: (323) 563-5987　Calendar System: Semester
URL: www.cdrewu.edu
Established: 1966　Annual Undergrad Tuition & Fees: $14,500
Enrollment: 324　Coed
Affiliation or Control: Independent Non-Profit　IRS Status: 501(c)3
Highest Offering: Master's
Program: Occupational; 2-Year Principally Bachelor's Creditable; Liberal Arts And General; Professional
Accreditation: WC, DMS, RAD

01 President & CEO ... Dr. David M. CARLISLE
45 EVP Research & Health Affairs ... Dr. Keith NORRIS
11 Senior Administrator ... Mr. Nathaniel CLARK
10 Vice Pres Finance/Chief Fin Ofcr ... Mr. Ron LAU
05 Dean of Academic Affairs ... Dr. Ronald A. EDELSTEIN
63 Provost/Dean College of Medicine ... Dr. Richard S. BAKER
76 Dean College of Science & Health .. Dr. Gail ORUM-ALEXANDER
32 Assoc Dean Med Student Affairs ... Dr. Daphne CALMES
88 Assoc Dean Col of Science & Health ... Dr. Rosslynn BYOUS
35 Assoc Dean of Medical Students ... Dr. Nancy HANNA
27 IT Manager ... Mr. Matt CULLEN
84 Director Enrollment Svcs/Registrar ... Dr. Joseph MARRON
08 Director of Library ... Ms. Darlene PARKER-KELLY
09 Director of Institutional Research ... Mr. Alvin HEARD
35 Director Medical Student Affairs ... Vacant
15 Director of Human Resources ... Dr. Toni C. ELBOUSHI

Charter College-Oxnard (E)

2000 Outlet Center Drive, Suite 150, Oxnard CA 93036
County: Ventura　Identification: 666675
Telephone: (805) 973-1240　Carnegie Class: Not Classified
FAX Number: (775) 284-9900　Calendar System: Other
URL: www.chartercollege.edu
Established: 2009　Annual Undergrad Tuition & Fees: N/A
Enrollment: N/A　Coed
Affiliation or Control: Proprietary　IRS Status: Proprietary
Highest Offering: Baccalaureate
Program: Occupational; 2-Year Principally Bachelor's Creditable
Accreditation: ACICS

01 Campus President ... Ms. Cecelia BURRILL

† Branch campus of Charter College, Anchorage, AK.

Church Divinity School of the Pacific (F)

2451 Ridge Road, Berkeley CA 94709-1217
County: Alameda　FICE Identification: 001165
Unit ID: 112127
Telephone: (510) 204-0700　Carnegie Class: Spec/Faith
FAX Number: (510) 644-0712　Calendar System: Semester
URL: www.cdsp.edu
Established: 1893　Annual Graduate Tuition & Fees: $16,320
Enrollment: 74　Coed
Affiliation or Control: Protestant Episcopal　IRS Status: 501(c)3
Highest Offering: Doctorate; No Undergraduates
Program: Professional
Accreditation: THEOL

01 President & Dean ... Dr. W. Mark RICHARDSON
05 Dean Academic Affairs ... Dr. Linda L. CLADER
10 Chief Financial Officer ... Mr. Steve ARGYRIS
30 Vice President for Advancement ... Mr. Jerry CAMPBELL
32 Dean of Students ... Rev. Jan WOOD
06 Registrar ... Ms. Margo WEBSTER
07 Director of Recruitment ... Ms. Dianne SMITH
27 Director of Communications ... Mr. Barry HOLTZCLAW
37 Director of Financial Aid ... Ms. Kathleen ANTOKHIN

Citrus College (G)

1000 W Foothill Boulevard, Glendora CA 91741-1899
County: Los Angeles　FICE Identification: 001166
Unit ID: 112172
Telephone: (626) 963-0323　Carnegie Class: Assoc/Pub-S-SC
FAX Number: (626) 914-8618　Calendar System: Semester
URL: www.citruscollege.edu
Established: 1915　Annual Undergrad Tuition & Fees (In-District): $864
Enrollment: 12,388　Coed
Affiliation or Control: State/Local　IRS Status: 501(c)3
Highest Offering: Associate Degree
Program: Occupational; 2-Year Principally Bachelor's Creditable; Business Emphasis
Accreditation: WJ, DA

01 Superintendent/President ... Dr. Geraldine M. PERRI
05 Vice President Academic Affairs ... Dr. Irene MALMGREN
32 Vice President Student Services ... Vacant
10 Vice Pres Finance/Admin Services ... Mrs. Carol R. HORTON
07 Dean Admissions & Records ... Ms. Lois PAPNER
51 Dean Career/Technical/Continuing Ed ... Mr. James LANCASTER
38 Dean of Counseling ... Dr. Lucinda OVER
16 Director Human Resources ... Dr. Robert SAMMIS
102 Director Foundation/Grants ... Ms. June STEPHENS
88 Director Performing Arts ... Mr. Greg HINRICHSEN
35 Dean of Students ... Ms. Martha MCDONALD
18 Director Facilities & Construction ... Mr. Fred DIAMOND
103 Director Workforce Development ... Vacant
09 Director of Institutional Research ... Dr. Lan HAO
06 Registrar ... Vacant
37 Director Financial Aid ... Ms. Lilia MEDINA
96 Director of Purchasing ... Mr. Robert IVERSON
21 Director of Fiscal Services ... Ms. Rosalinda BUCHWALD
26 Director of Communication ... Ms. Paula GREEN
23 Director of Health Sciences ... Dr. Maureen RENAGHAN
28 Staff Diversity Officer ... Mrs. Brenda FINK
13 Chief Information Services Officer ... Ms. Linda WELZ
19 Campus Security Supervisor ... Mr. Tony GIANNONE
83 Dean Social & Behavioral Sciences ... Dr. Mike HURTADO
41 Dean of Physical Educ & Athletics ... Ms. Jody WISE
79 Dean of Lang Arts & Enrollment Mgt ... Dr. Samuel LEE
50 Dean Business CSIS/Dist Ed/Library ... Dr. Stephen LINDSEY
65 Dean Physical & Natural Science ... Mr. Eric RABITOY
57 Dean of Fine & Performing Arts ... Mr. Robert SLACK
81 Dean Mathematics/Health Sciences ... Mr. James MCCLAIN
15 Director of Human Resources ... Dr. Robert SAMMIS

City College of San Francisco (H)

33 Gough Street, San Francisco CA 94103-1292
County: San Francisco　FICE Identification: 001167
Unit ID: 112190
Telephone: (415) 239-3000　Carnegie Class: Assoc/Pub-U-MC
FAX Number: (415) 239-3919　Calendar System: Semester
URL: www.ccsf.edu
Established: 1935　Annual Undergrad Tuition & Fees (In-District): $720
Enrollment: 35,760　Coed
Affiliation or Control: State/Local　IRS Status: 501(c)3
Highest Offering: Associate Degree
Program: Occupational; 2-Year Principally Bachelor's Creditable
Accreditation: WJ, ACFEI, DA, EMT, MAC, RAD, RTT

01 Chancellor ... Dr. Don Q. GRIFFIN
10 Vice Chanc Finance/Administration ... Mr. Peter A. GOLDSTEIN
05 Vice Chancellor Academic Affairs ... Dr. Alice MURILLO
32 Vice Chanc Student Development ... Ms. Lindy MCKNIGHT
46 Vice Chanc Research & Policy ... Ms. Phyllis MCGUIRE
11 Vice Chanc Campuses & Enroll Svcs ... Mr. Jorge BELL
43 Vice Chanc Legal Services ... Vacant
12 Dean Civic Center Campus ... Mr. Carl JEW
12 Dean Southeast Campus ... Mr. Jorge BELL
12 Dean Mission Campus ... Mr. Jorge BELL
12 Dean Downtown/Business School ... Dr. David DORE
26 Dean of Marketing/Public Relations ... Vacant
35 Dean Student Affairs ... Dr. Veronica HUNNICUTT
37 Dean Financial Aid & EOPS ... Mr. Roland MONTEMAYOR
07 Dean Admissions & Records ... Ms. Marylou LEYBA
20 Int Dean Instruction/Curriculum ... Mr. Tom BOEGEL
16 Dean Human Resourc/Library/Lrng Res ... Ms. Clara H. STARR
38 Dean/Dir Counseling/Student Support ... Vacant
06 Dean Matriculation ... Vacant
51 Dean Contract Educ/Voc Educ ... Vacant
85 Dean Chinatown/Intl Educ/ESL ... Ms. Joanne LOW
49 Dean Liberal Arts ... Ms. Bob DAVIS
83 Dean Behavioral/Social Sciences ... Dr. Fred CHAVARIA
81 Dean Science & Math ... Mr. David YEE
68 Dean J Adams Campus/Sch Hlth Educ ... Mr. Terry HALL
30 Dean College Development ... Dr. Kathleen SULLIVAN ALIOTO
88 Assoc Dean (Non-Credit) Admiss/Recs ... Ms. Lidia JENKINS
13 Director Information Services ... Mr. Doug RE
15 Director Employee Relations ... Mr. Steve HALE
18 Superintendent Buildings/Grounds ... Vacant
103 Dir Cal Works Education & Training . Mr. Roland MONTEMAYOR
09 Asst Dir of Institutional Research ... Mr. Steven SPURLING
27 Chief Information Technology Office ... Dr. David HOTCHKISS
96 Director of Purchasing ... Ms. Kathy HENNIG
19 Chief of Police ... Mr. Andre BARNES
88 ADA Compliance Officer ... Dr. Leilani BATTISTE
21 Assoc Vice Chanc/CFO ... Mr. John BILMONT
25 Dean Grants & Resource Dev ... Ms. Kristin CHARLES
86 Assoc Vice Chanc Governmtl Rel ... Ms. Leslie SMITH
06 Assoc Dean Registration/Records ... Ms. Monika LIU
37 Director Financial Aid ... Dr. Rose ROBERSON
88 Director Small Bus Dev Ctr ... Mr. Albert DIXON
88 Dean Faculty Support Svcs ... Dr. Minh-Hoa TA
23 Assoc Dean Student Health Svcs ... Ms. Sunny CLARK

City of Hope (A)

1500 East Duarte Road, Duarte CA 91010-3000
County: Los Angeles FICE Identification: 035924
Unit ID: 441238
Telephone: (626) 256-4673 Carnegie Class: Spec/Med
FAX Number: (626) 301-8105 Calendar System: Semester
URL: cityofhope.org
Established: 1994 Annual Graduate Tuition & Fees: N/A
Enrollment: 80 Coed
Affiliation or Control: Independent Non-Profit IRS Status: 501(c)3
Highest Offering: Doctorate; No Undergraduates
Program: Professional
Accreditation: WC

01 Dean ... John J. ROSSI
05 Associate Dean ... Steven NORVAC

*Claremont University Consortium (B)

150 E Eighth Street, Claremont CA 91711-3910
County: Los Angeles Identification: 666003
Telephone: (909) 621-8026 Carnegie Class: N/A
FAX Number: (909) 621-8517
URL: www.cuc.claremont.edu

01 Chief Executive Officer ... Mr. Robert WALTON
10 Vice President/CFO ... Mr. Ken PIFER
32 Vice President of Student Affairs ... Dr. Denise HAYES
18 VP Facilities Management/Planning ... Mr. Tim MORRISON
101 Sec to Brd of Overseers/Ast to CEO ... Ms. Bonnie CLEMENS

*Claremont Graduate University (C)

150 E 10th Street, Claremont CA 91711-5909
County: Los Angeles FICE Identification: 001169
Unit ID: 112251
Telephone: (909) 621-8000 Carnegie Class: RU/H
FAX Number: (909) 621-8390 Calendar System: Semester
URL: www.cgu.edu
Established: 1925 Annual Graduate Tuition & Fees: $36,804
Enrollment: 2,265 Coed
Affiliation or Control: Independent Non-Profit IRS Status: 501(c)3
Highest Offering: Doctorate; No Undergraduates
Program: Liberal Arts And General; Teacher Preparatory; Professional
Accreditation: WC, BUS

02 President ... Dr. Deborah A. FREUND
04 Exec Asst to the President ... Ms. Donna STANDLEA
05 Exec Vice President and Provost ... Dr. Jacob ADAMS
10 Senior VP for Finance and Admin ... Dr. Steven N. GARCIA
30 Vice President for Advancement ... Vacant
84 Vice Provost for Enrollment Mgmt ... Vacant
46 Vice Provost/Research ... Dr. Dean GERSTEIN
88 Vice Provost/Transdisciplin Studies ... Dr. Wendy MARTIN
20 Assistant Provost ... Dr. Scott SIMPSON
16 Assoc VP for Human Resources ... Ms. Brenda LESWICK
47 Chair Botany Department ... Dr. Lucinda MCDADE
79 Dean School of Arts & Humanities ... Dr. Janet BRODIE
50 Dean Drucker-Ito Grad School of Mgt ... Dr. Hideki YAMAWAKI
83 Dean School of Behavioral & Org Sci ... Dr. Stewart DONALDSON
69 Dean School of Cmty & Global Health ... Dr. Anderson JOHNSON
53 Dean School of Educational Studies ... Dr. Margaret GROGAN
77 Dean Sch Information Systems & Tech ... Dr. Thomas HORAN
81 Dean Sch of Mathematical Sciences ... Dr. Ellis CUMBERBATCH
82 Dean Sch of Politics & Economics ... Dr. Jean SCHROEDEL
73 Dean School of Religion ... Dr. Tammi SCHNEIDER
09 Institutional Research Officer ... Ms. Jeannette GURROLA
30 Senior Director of Development ... Mr. Mike AVILA
21 Asst VP/Asst Treasurer ... Mr. Dean CALVO
29 Director Alumnae /Alumni Relations ... Ms. Monika MOORE
26 Director University Communications ... Ms. Esther WILEY
06 Registrar ... Mr. Cliff RAMIREZ
37 Director Student Financial Aid ... Ms. Susie GUILBAULT
85 International Student Coordinator ... Vacant
07 Director of Admissions ... Ms. Julia EVANS
36 Director Career Management ... Ms. Fatma KASSAMALI
18 Director of Facilities ... Mr. DeWayne HURST
39 Director Real Estate & Housing Svcs ... Ms. Katherine RUBEL
13 Exec Dir Office Information Tech ... Mr. Travis WYNBERRY
27 Chief Information Officer ... Mr. Daris BOUTHILLIER
91 Application Services Director ... Mr. Manoj CHITRE
101 Secretary to the Board ... Ms. Louise WEBBER

*Claremont McKenna College (D)

500 E 9th Street, Claremont CA 91711-6400
County: Los Angeles FICE Identification: 001170
Unit ID: 112260
Telephone: (909) 621-8000 Carnegie Class: Bac/A&S
FAX Number: (909) 621-8790 Calendar System: Semester
URL: www.claremontmckenna.edu
Established: 1946 Annual Undergrad Tuition & Fees: $41,995
Enrollment: 1,278 Coed
Affiliation or Control: Independent Non-Profit IRS Status: 501(c)3
Highest Offering: Master's
Program: Liberal Arts And General
Accreditation: WC

02 President and CEO ... Pamela B. GANN
05 Vice President & Dean of Faculty ... Gregory HESS
30 Vice President for Development ... Ernie ISEMINGER
10 Vice Pres Business Admin/Treasurer ... Robin J. ASPINALL
11 VP for Planning and Administration ... Matthew G. BIBBENS
32 Vice President for Student Affairs ... Jefferson HUANG
07 VP & Dean Admission/Financial Aid ... Richard C. VOS
21 VP and Chief Investment Officer ... James J. FLOYD
37 Assoc Vice Pres Admis/Financial Aid ... Georgette DEVERES
26 Assoc VP Public Affs/Communications ... Richard RODNER
13 Assoc VP/Chief Technology Officer ... Cynthia HUMES
29 Vice President for Alumni Relations ... John P. FARANDA
06 Registrar/Director of IR ... Elizabeth MORGAN
36 Assoc Dean/Dir Career Services ... Diana SEDER
18 Dir Facilities and Campus Services ... Brian WORLEY
15 Director of Human Resources ... Andrea GALE
32 Dean of Students ... Mary SPELLMAN
104 Director of Off-Campus Study ... Kristen MALLORY
41 Athletic Director ... Michael SUTTON
04 Special Assistant to the President ... Cheryl M. AGUILAR

*Claremont School of Theology (E)

1325 N College Avenue, Claremont CA 91711-3199
County: Los Angeles FICE Identification: 001288
Unit ID: 124283
Telephone: (909) 447-2500 Carnegie Class: Spec/Faith
FAX Number: (909) 626-7062 Calendar System: Semester
URL: www.cst.edu
Established: 1885 Annual Graduate Tuition & Fees: $16,070
Enrollment: 213 Coed
Affiliation or Control: United Methodist IRS Status: 501(c)3
Highest Offering: Doctorate; No Undergraduates
Program: Professional
Accreditation: WC, THEOL

02 President ... Dr. Jerry D. CAMPBELL
05 Vice President Academic Affs & Dean ... Dr. Philip CLAYTON
10 VP for Administration & Finance/ CFO ... Dr. Lynn O'LEARY-ARCHER
30 Vice President of Development ... Mr. Duane DYER
21 Assoc VP for Finance & Planning ... Mr. Gamward QUAN
27 Director of Communications ... Mr. Jon HOOTEN
06 Registrar ... Ms. Jennie ALLEN
07 Director of Admission ... Ms. Jennifer MCGOWAN
08 Dir of Library/Technological Svcs ... Mr. John DICKASON
42 Dir Church Rels & Ministry Resource ... Dr. Karen DALTON
37 Director of Financial Aid ... Ms. LaNae HERRERA
22 Affirmative Action Officer ... Ms. Elaine WALKER

*Keck Graduate Institute (F)

535 Watson Drive, Claremont CA 91711-4817
County: Los Angeles FICE Identification: 038533
Unit ID: 440031
Telephone: (909) 607-7855 Carnegie Class: Assoc/PrivNFP4
FAX Number: (909) 607-8086 Calendar System: Semester
URL: www.kgi.edu
Established: 1997 Annual Graduate Tuition & Fees: $38,470
Enrollment: 151 Coed
Affiliation or Control: Independent Non-Profit IRS Status: 501(c)3
Highest Offering: Doctorate; No Undergraduates
Program: Professional
Accreditation: WC

02 President ... Dr. Sheldon M. SCHUSTER
06 Registrar ... Adam PAVE

Cleveland Chiropractic College (G)

590 N Vermont Avenue, Los Angeles CA 90004-2196
County: Los Angeles FICE Identification: 021474
Unit ID: 112312
Telephone: (323) 660-6166 Carnegie Class: Spec/Health
FAX Number: (323) 660-5387 Calendar System: Trimester
URL: www.clevelandchiropractic.edu
Established: 1908 Annual Undergrad Tuition & Fees: $6,532
Enrollment: 301 Coed
Affiliation or Control: Independent Non-Profit IRS Status: 501(c)3
Highest Offering: First Professional Degree
Program: Professional
Accreditation: &NH, CHIRO

01 President ... Dr. Carl S. CLEVELAND, III
30 VP Inst Advancement/Alumni Svcs ... Dr. John NAB
05 Provost ... Ms. Ashley CLEVELAND
10 Controller ... Mrs. Yvonne MOORE
11 Chief Operating Officer ... Mr. Jeff KARP
08 College Librarian ... Ms. Marian HICKS
37 Director Financial Aid/Admissions ... Ms. Sunshine GARCIA
20 Associate Dean ... Dr. Stephan MAYER
17 Chair Clinical Sciences ... Dr. Keith HENRY
32 Dir Student Services & Alumni Rels ... Mr. Michael BROWN
20 Director Undergraduate Studies ... Mr. Christopher PEDITTO
06 Registrar ... Mr. Bryan REEDER
13 Info Systems Technology Director ... Mr. Kurt BARNETT
09 Research Director ... Dr. James BRANTINGHAM
15 Director Human Resources ... Mr. J. Dale MARRANT
18 Physical Plant Manager ... Mr. Daniel GRANADOS
76 Coord Prerequisite Health Science ... Ms. Ivette TAPIA

† Regional accreditation is carried under parent institution in Overland Park, KS.

CNI College (H)

702 West Town and Country Road, Orange CA 92868
County: Orange FICE Identification: 032423
Telephone: (714) 437-9697 Carnegie Class: Not Classified
FAX Number: (714) 437-9356 Calendar System: Other
URL: www.cnicollege.edu
Established: N/A Annual Undergrad Tuition & Fees: N/A
Enrollment: 718 Coed
Affiliation or Control: Proprietary IRS Status: Proprietary
Highest Offering: Associate Degree
Program: Occupational
Accreditation: ABHES, SURTEC

01 President ... Mr. James BUFFINGTON

*Coast Community College District Administration Offices (I)

1370 Adams Avenue, Costa Mesa CA 92626-5429
County: Orange FICE Identification: 008711
Unit ID: 112376
Telephone: (714) 438-4600 Carnegie Class: N/A
FAX Number: (714) 438-4882
URL: www.cccd.edu

01 Chancellor ... Dr. Andrew C. JONES
10 Vice Chancellor Finance & Adm Svcs ... Mr. Andrew DUNN
16 Vice Chancellor Human Resources ... Dr. Deborah D. HIRSH
05 Vice Chanc Educ Svcs & Technology ... Mr. Nabil ABU-GHAZALEH
26 Dir Public Affairs/Mktg & Govt Rels ... Dr. Martha PARHAM
96 Director of Purchasing ... Mr. John ERIKSEN

*Coastline Community College (J)

11460 Warner Avenue, Fountain Valley CA 92708-2597
County: Orange FICE Identification: 020635
Unit ID: 112385
Telephone: (714) 546-7600 Carnegie Class: Assoc/Pub-S-MC
FAX Number: (714) 241-6277 Calendar System: Semester
URL: www.coastline.edu
Established: 1976 Annual Undergrad Tuition & Fees (In-District): $896
Enrollment: 10,251 Coed
Affiliation or Control: State/Local IRS Status: 501(c)3
Highest Offering: Associate Degree
Program: Occupational; 2-Year Principally Bachelor's Creditable
Accreditation: WJ

02 President ... Dr. Loretta P. ADRIAN
05 Acting Vice President Instruction ... Dr. Dan JONES
11 Interim VP of Admin Services ... Ms. Christine NGUYEN
32 Interim VP Student Svcs & Econ Dev ... Ms. Lois WILKERSON
46 Admin Dean Instr Systems Devel ... Mr. Dan JONES
38 Interim Dean of Counseling ... Mr. Bill KERWIN
56 Dean of Instruction Distance Lrng ... Mr. Vince RODRIGUEZ
12 Actg Dean of Instruction Costa Mesa ... Dr. Ted BOEHLER
12 Actg Dean Instruction Garden Grove ... Dr. Ted BOEHLER

12 Dean Instruction Westminster ... Mr. Vinicio LOPEZ
26 Director of Mktg/PR & Govt Affairs ... Mrs. Michelle MA
06 Registrar/Director of Admissions ... Ms. Jennifer MCDONALD
37 Dir Student Financial Aid & EOPS ... Ms. Cynthia PIENKOWSKI
18 Director Maintenance & Operations ... Mr. David CANT
21 Interim Director Fiscal Services ... Mr. Richard KUDLIK
102 Executive Director Foundation ... Ms. Mariam KHOSRAVANI
40 Director Bookstore ... Mr. Michael BARE
14 Interim Director Computer Services ... Mr. Anthony MACIEL
09 Director Research/Planning/Develop ... Dr. Jorge R. SANCHEZ
56 Dean of Military Programs ... Ms. Joycelyn GROOT
88 Manager Contract Education Programs ... Mr. Peter MAHARAJ
72 Dean of Lrng Tech Innovation & Supp ... Mr. Ted BOEHLER
24 Director of Electronic Media ... Ms. Judy GARVEY
15 Director of Personnel Services ... Vacant
88 Director of Telecourse Production ... Ms. Laurie MELBY
88 Director of Instructional Design ... Mr. Robert NASH
106 Director of eLearning Rsrch and Dev ... Mr. Dave THOMPSON
103 Interim Dir Workforce & Econ Dev ... Ms. Sallie SALINAS

Golden West College (A)

15744 Golden West Street,
Huntington Beach CA 92647-2748
County: Orange FICE Identification: 001206
Unit ID: 115126
Telephone: (714) 892-7711 Carnegie Class: Assoc/Pub-S-MC
FAX Number: (714) 895-8243 Calendar System: Semester
URL: www.gwc.info
Established: 1966 Annual Undergrad Tuition & Fees (In-District): $926
Enrollment: 13,684 Coed
Affiliation or Control: State/Local IRS Status: Exempt
Highest Offering: Associate Degree
Program: Occupational; 2-Year Principally Bachelor's Creditable
Accreditation: WJ, ADNUR

02 President ... Mr. Wes BRYAN
05 Vice President Student Success . Dr. Fabienne MCPHAIL NAPLES
11 Vice Pres Student & Admin Support ... Ms. Janet M. HOULIHAN
38 Dean Counseling ... Dr. David L. BAIRD
08 Dean Lrng Res/Online Inst/New Media ... Vacant
72 Dean Career & Tech Ed and Business .. Mr. Omid POURZANJANI
81 Dean Soc Science/Math & Sciences ... Mr. Jeff COURCHAINE
49 Dean Arts & Letters ... Dr. David D. HUDSON
23 Assoc Dean/Dir Student Health Svcs ... Mr. Robin BACHMANN
09 Assoc Dean Inst Research/Planning .. Mr. Dwayne E. THOMPSON
88 Dean Criminal Justice & Health Prof ... Mr. Ron LOWENBERG
35 Administrative Director Stdnt Svcs ... Ms. Shirley A. DONNELLY
15 Director Personnel Services ... Mrs. Crystal D. CRANE
21 Director Fiscal Services ... Ms. Louise COMER
102 Director Foundation/Community Rels ... Ms. Margie J. BUNTEN
35 Director Student Activities ... Ms. Valerie A. VENEGAS
07 Director of Admissions ... Ms. Jennifer L. ORTBERG
37 Director of Financial Aid ... Vacant
18 Chief Facilities/Physical Plant ... Mr. Joseph B. DOWLING
68 Dean Health PE & Athletics ... Mr. Albert GASPARIAN

Orange Coast College (B)

2701 Fairview Road, POB 5005,
Costa Mesa CA 92628-5005
County: Orange FICE Identification: 001250
Unit ID: 120342
Telephone: (714) 432-0202 Carnegie Class: Assoc/Pub-S-MC
FAX Number: (714) 432-5609 Calendar System: Semester
URL: www.orangecoastcollege.edu
Established: 1947 Annual Undergrad Tuition & Fees (In-District): $624
Enrollment: 23,331 Coed
Affiliation or Control: State/Local IRS Status: 501(c)3
Highest Offering: Associate Degree
Program: Occupational; 2-Year Principally Bachelor's Creditable
Accreditation: WJ, ACFEI, CVT, DA, DIETT, DMS, EEG, MAC, POLYT, RAD

02 President ... Dr. Dennis HARKINS
05 Vice President Instruction ... Dr. Melinda NISH
32 Vice President Student Services ... Ms. Kristin CLARK
11 Vice Pres Administrative Services ... Dr. Richard PAGEL
84 Dean Enrollment Services ... Vacant
38 Dean of Counseling ... Dr. Hue PHAM
35 Dean of Student Services ... Dr. Kathyrn MUELLER
26 Director Community Relations ... Mr. Jeffrey HOBBS
102 Director Foundation ... Mr. Douglas BENNETT
09 Director of IR/Planning and IE ... Ms. Sheri STERNER
07 Director Admiss/Records/Enroll Tech ... Mr. Efren GALVAN
15 Director Personnel Services ... Ms. Laurel FRANCIS
18 Assistant Director M & O ... Mr. Mark GOODE
37 Director Student Financial Aid ... Ms. Melissa MOSER
13 Director Infomration Technology ... Mr. Craig OBERLIN
23 Associate Dean Health Services ... Ms. Sylvia WORDEN
88 Manager Child Care Center ... Ms. Sue BIERLICH
35 Associate Dean Student Services ... Mr. Madjid NIROUMAND
40 Director Bookstore ... Mr. William KIRCHINGER
41 Athletic Director ... Mr. Steve TAMANAHA
88 Dean of Consumer & Health Sciences ... Mr. Kevin BALLINGER
68 Dean of Physical Education & Athl ... Mr. Kevin BALLINGER
72 Dean of Technology ... Dr. Doug BENOIT
50 Dean of Business & Computer Science ... Dr. Doug BENOIT
83 Dean of Social & Behavioral Science ... Mr. Paul ASIM
88 Dean of Literature & Languages ... Dr. Michael MANDELKERN
81 Dean of Math & Sciences ... Dr. Robert MENDOZA
57 Dean of Visual & Performing Arts ... Mr. Joe POSHEK
62 Dean of Library and Media Services ... Mr. Joe POSHEK

103 Director Career & Cmty Education ... Ms. Corine DOUGHTY
105 Director Web Services ... Mr. Glen PROFETA

Cogswell Polytechnical College (C)

1175 Bordeaux Drive, Sunnyvale CA 94089-1299
County: Santa Clara FICE Identification: 001177
Unit ID: 112394
Telephone: (408) 541-0100 Carnegie Class: Bac/Diverse
FAX Number: (408) 747-0764 Calendar System: Semester
URL: www.cogswell.edu
Established: 1887 Annual Undergrad Tuition & Fees: $19,668
Enrollment: 238 Coed
Affiliation or Control: Independent Non-Profit IRS Status: 501(c)3
Highest Offering: Baccalaureate
Program: Liberal Arts And General; Professional; Technical Emphasis
Accreditation: WC

01 President ... Dr. Chester D. HASKELL
05 Dean of the College ... Mr. Michael MARTIN
10 Vice President Finance ... Mr. Rejino CASTANEDA
07 VP for Admissions & Recruiting ... Ms. Jackie DONOHOE
06 Registrar ... Ms. Milla ZLATANOV
08 Librarian ... Ms. Vivian KOBAYASHI
04 Executive Assistant ... Ms. Lucy MCDONALD

The Colburn School (D)

200 S Grand Avenue, Los Angeles CA 90012-3007
County: Los Angeles Identification: 666233
Telephone: (213) 621-2200 Carnegie Class: Not Classified
FAX Number: (213) 621-2110 Calendar System: Semester
URL: www.colburnschool.edu
Established: 2003 Annual Undergrad Tuition & Fees: N/A
Enrollment: 130 Coed
Affiliation or Control: Independent Non-Profit IRS Status: 501(c)3
Highest Offering: Baccalaureate
Program: Music Emphasis
Accreditation: MUS

01 President & CEO ... Mr. Sal KARDAN
10 Chief Financial Officer ... Mr. Seth WEINTRAUB

† Full room, board, and tuition are provided to accepted students through the school's endowment.

Coleman University (E)

8888 Balboa Avenue, San Diego CA 92123-1506
County: San Diego FICE Identification: 007296
Unit ID: 112446
Telephone: (858) 499-0202 Carnegie Class: Bac/Assoc
FAX Number: (858) 499-0233 Calendar System: Quarter
URL: www.coleman.edu
Established: 1963 Annual Undergrad Tuition & Fees: $35,200
Enrollment: 503 Coed
Affiliation or Control: Independent Non-Profit IRS Status: 501(c)3
Highest Offering: Master's
Program: Occupational; Professional; Technical Emphasis
Accreditation: ACICS

01 President ... Mr. Paul S. PANESAR
12 Vice Pres/Branch Mgr San Marcos ... Ms. Darlene S. ANKTON
05 Vice President/Dean of Academics ... Ms. Sheryl L. RIDENS
10 Chief Financial Officer ... Mr. Mohsen GHARAHBAGHIAN
06 Registrar ... Ms. Karen S. HYNES
21 Business Manager ... Ms. Elizabeth A. GALINDO
36 Director Career Services ... Mr. John D. BULLOCK
18 Site Manager ... Mr. Keith R. WISSWELL
08 Head Librarian ... Mr. Manuel A. BERNAD
105 Web Master ... Mr. Chris J. CAREY
37 Director Student Financial Aid ... Mr. Axel N. HERNANDEZ
15 Human Resource Generalist ... Ms. Maria HAMZAVI
26 Chief Public Relations Officer ... Ms. Bobbie A. STROHM

Coleman University (F)

1284 West San Marcos Boulevard,
San Marcos CA 92078-4073
County: San Diego Identification: 666259
Telephone: (760) 747-3990 Carnegie Class: Not Classified
FAX Number: (760) 752-9808 Calendar System: Quarter
URL: www.coleman.edu
Established: 1963 Annual Undergrad Tuition & Fees: $23,990
Enrollment: 155 Coed
Affiliation or Control: Independent Non-Profit IRS Status: 501(c)3
Highest Offering: Associate Degree
Program: Occupational; 2-Year Principally Bachelor's Creditable; Technical Emphasis
Accreditation: ACICS

01 President ... Mr. Paul PANESAR

College of the Canyons (G)

26455 Rockwell Canyon Road,
Santa Clarita CA 91355-1899
County: Los Angeles FICE Identification: 008903
Unit ID: 111461
Telephone: (661) 259-7800 Carnegie Class: Assoc/Pub-S-SC
FAX Number: (661) 259-8302 Calendar System: Semester
URL: www.canyons.edu
Established: 1967 Annual Undergrad Tuition & Fees (In-District): $1,050
Enrollment: 22,968 Coed
Affiliation or Control: State/Local IRS Status: 501(c)3
Highest Offering: Associate Degree
Program: Occupational; 2-Year Principally Bachelor's Creditable
Accreditation: WJ, ADNUR

01 Chancellor ... Dr. Dianne G. VAN HOOK
10 Asst Supt/VP Business Services ... Ms. Sharlene COLEAL
15 Asst Supt/Vice Pres Human Resources ... Ms. Diane FIERO
46 Asst Supt/VP Inst Dev/Tech/Online ... Dr. Barry GRIBBONS
11 Asst Supt/VP CCC & Econ Development ... Dr. Dena MALONEY
18 Asst Supt/VP Facil Plan Op/Const ... Mr. Jim SCHRAGE
32 Asst Superintendent/VP Student Svcs ... Dr. Michael WILDING
05 Int Asst Supt/Vice Pres Instruction ... Dr. Floyd MOOS
20 Assoc Vice Pres Academic Affairs ... Ms. Audrey GREEN
13 Assoc VP Information Technology ... Mr. Jim TEMPLE
57 Div Dean Fine & Performing Arts ... Dr. Carmen DOMINGUEZ
76 Div Dean Allied Health & Pub Safety ... Ms. Cynthia DORROH
79 Division Dean Humanities ... Dr. Michael MCMAHAN
41 Division Dean PE/Athletic Director ... Mr. Len MOHNEY
83 Div Dean Social Sci & Business ... Dr. Patty ROBINSON
81 Div Dean Math/Science & Engineering ... Mr. Omar TORRES
106 Dean Educ Tech/Lrng Resrc/Dist Educ ... Mr. James GLAPA-GROSSKLAG
75 Dean Career Technical Education ... Ms. Kristin HOUSER
35 Dean Student Services ... Mr. Mike JOSLIN
88 Dean Instructional Support ... Dr. Kevin KISTLER
06 Dean Enrollment Services ... Ms. Deborah RIO
88 Dean ECE/AOC & Teacher Training ... Ms. Diane STEWART
103 Interim Dean Economic Development ... Mr. Peter BELLAS
66 Asst Dean Allied Health/Dir Nursing ... Dr. Diane MOREY
88 Assistant Dean of Students CCC ... Mr. Ryan THEULE
21 Controller Fiscal Services ... Ms. Cindy GRANDGEORGE
102 COO COC Foundation/Int Dir UC ... Ms. Cathy RITZ
30 Chief Devel Officer COC Foundation ... Mr. Murray WOOD
86 Managing Director Govt Rels/Advoc ... Mr. Eric HARNISH
26 Managing Director PR & Marketing ... Mr. Bruce BATTLE
96 Director Contracts Proc & Risk Mgmt ... Mr. Jon AASTED
88 Director Student Business Office ... Ms. Kathleen BENZ
37 Director Financial Aid ... Mr. Tom BILBRUCK
88 Director Professional Development ... Ms. Leslie CARR
19 Director Campus Safety ... Ms. Tammy CASTOR
88 Director MESA ... Ms. Susan CROWTHER
88 Director Student Development ... Ms. Allison KORSE-DEVLIN
30 Director Development ... Ms. Michele EDMONSON
88 Director Budget Development ... Ms. Donna HAYWOOD
100 Dir Distance & Accelerated Learning ... Mr. John MAKEVICH
09 Director of Institutional Research ... Dr. Daylene MEUSCHKE
36 Director Career Services ... Mr. Anthony MICHAELIDES
06 Dir Admissions/Records/Online Svcs ... Ms. Jasmine RUYS
88 Dir Outreach & School Relations ... Ms. Kari SOFFA
88 Director Small Business Dev Ctr ... Mr. Steven TANNEHILL
88 Dir Reentry Pgm & Veterans Affair ... Mr. Renard THOMAS
16 Director Human Resources ... Ms. Donna VOOGT
25 Director Grants Development ... Ms. Theresa ZUZEVICH
23 Director Student Health & Wellness ... Vacant
88 Int Director Pub Safety Instr Pgms ... Mr. Steven MCLEAN
91 Asst Director Mgmt Info Systems ... Mr. Mike BREZINA
14 Asst Dir Information Technology ... Mr. Michael GUNTHER

College of the Desert (H)

43-500 Monterey Avenue, Palm Desert CA 92260-9399
County: Riverside FICE Identification: 001182
Unit ID: 113573
Telephone: (760) 346-8041 Carnegie Class: Assoc/Pub-S-MC
FAX Number: (760) 341-8678 Calendar System: Semester
URL: www.collegeofthedesert.edu
Established: 1958 Annual Undergrad Tuition & Fees (In-District): $1,008
Enrollment: 12,143 Coed
Affiliation or Control: State/Local IRS Status: 501(c)3
Highest Offering: Associate Degree
Program: Occupational; 2-Year Principally Bachelor's Creditable
Accreditation: WJ, ADNUR

01 President ... Mr. Jerry R. PATTON
05 Vice Pres Academic Affairs ... Mr. Farley HERZEK
11 Vice President Business Affairs ... Dr. Edwin DEAS
32 Interim Vice Pres Student Affairs ... Mr. Adrian GONZALES
15 Exec Dir Human Res/Employee Rels ... Mr. Robert BLIZINSKI
30 Instnl Advance & Title V Dir ... Ms. Pam LICALSI
84 Dean of Enrollment Services ... Dr. Annebelle NERY
38 Dean Student Support Programs ... Mr. Adrian GONZALES
102 Exec Dir of Foundation ... Mr. Jim HUMMER
09 Dean Info Tech & Inst Research ... Ms. Bina ISAAC
18 Director of Maintenance/Operations ... Mr. Steve RENEW
26 Director Public Relations ... Ms. Pam LICALSI
29 Director Alumni Relations ... Mr. Gene MARCHU
37 Director Financial Aid ... Mr. Ken LIRA
96 Director of Fiscal Services ... Mr. Wade ELLIS
06 Registrar/Director of Admissions ... Ms. Sally TIAGA

College of Marin (I)

835 College Avenue, Kentfield CA 94904-2590
County: Marin FICE Identification: 001178
Unit ID: 118347
Telephone: (415) 457-8811 Carnegie Class: Assoc/Pub-S-MC
FAX Number: (415) 485-0135 Calendar System: Semester
URL: www.marin.edu
Established: 1926 Annual Undergrad Tuition & Fees (In-District): $1,080
Enrollment: 7,463 Coed
Affiliation or Control: State/Local IRS Status: 501(c)3

Highest Offering: Associate Degree
Program: Occupational; 2-Year Principally Bachelor's Creditable
Accreditation: WJ, ADNUR, DA

01 Superintendent/President ... Dr. David W. COON
05 Int Vice Pres Student Learning ... Ms. Angelina DUARTE
10 Vice President Operations ... Mr. A.J HARRISON, II
16 Exec Dean Human Res/Labor Relations ... Ms. Linda BEAM
84 Dean Enrollment Services ... Mr. Bob BALESTRERI
49 Dean Arts & Humanities ... Dr. David SNYDER
103 Dean Wkfce Dev/Col & Cmty Prntrshps ... Ms. Nanda SCHORSKE
81 Dean Math/Sciences ... Mr. Jim ARNOLD
21 Director Fiscal Services ... Ms. Peggy ISOZAKI
09 Dir Plng/Rsch/ Inst Effectiveness ... Dr. Chialin HSIEH
37 Director Financial Aid/Career Pgms ... Mr. David COOK
18 Director Maintenance & Operations ... Mr. Robert H. THOMPSON
13 Director Information Technology ... Mr. Marshall NORTHCOTT
35 Dir Student Affairs/Health Center ... Dr. Arnulfo CEDILLO
19 Chief of Police/Director of Safety ... Mr. Mitch LEMAY
68 Dir Physical Educ/Athletics ... Mr. Matt MARKOVICH
76 Interim Director Health Sciences ... Ms. Debra LEWIS
31 Int Dir Cmty Svc/Lifelong Lrng ... Ms. Janice AUSTIN
26 Dir Communications/Community Rels ... Ms. Cathy SUMMA-WOLFE

College of the Redwoods Community College District (A)

7351 Tompkins Hill Road, Eureka CA 95501-9300
County: Humboldt | FICE Identification: 001185
Unit ID: 121707
Telephone: (707) 476-4100 | Carnegie Class: Assoc/Pub-R-L
FAX Number: (707) 476-4400 | Calendar System: Semester
URL: www.redwoods.edu
Established: 1964 | Annual Undergrad Tuition & Fees (In-District): $864
Enrollment: 17,660 | Coed
Affiliation or Control: State/Local | IRS Status: 501(c)3
Highest Offering: Associate Degree
Program: Occupational; 2-Year Principally Bachelor's Creditable
Accreditation: WJ, DA, NAIT

01 Interim President ... Dr. Utpal GOSWAMI
04 Assistant to the President ... Ms. Michelle ANDERSON
11 VP Administrative Services ... Mr. Lee LINDSEY
32 VP Student Services ... Dr. Keith SNOW-FLAMER
05 VP of Instruction ... Dr. Utpal GOSWAMI
15 Director Human Resources ... Ms. Ahn FIELDING
12 Vice President of Del Norte Campus ... Ms. Anita JANIS
12 Vice Pres of Mendocino Coast Campus ... Dr. Geisce LY
41 Athletic Director ... Mr. Joseph HASH
37 Director Financial Aid ... Ms. Lynn THIESEN
22 Director EOPS ... Ms. Cheryl TUCKER
88 Director Disabled Student Pgm Svcs ... Vacant
18 Director Facilities & Planning ... Mr. Tim FLANAGAN
19 Director Maintenance & Operations ... Mr. Gary PATRICK
26 Public Information Officer ... Mr. Paul DEMARK
35 Dean Student Development ... Ms. Melissa GREEN
20 Dean Academic Affairs ... Dr. Rachel ANDERSON
17 Dean Health Occupations/Public Svcs ... Dr. Pat GIRCZYC
72 Int Dean Career & Technical Educ ... Mr. Mike PETERSON
13 Dean Info Technology/Distance Educ ... Dr. Maggie LYNCH
08 Director Learning Resource Center ... Ms. Mary Grace BARRICK
09 Director of Institutional Research ... Ms. Angeline HILL
07 Manager Admissions & Records ... Ms. Kathy GOODLIVE
88 Coord Basic Law Enforcement Academy ... Mr. Ron WATERS
24 Coord Technology Infrastructure ... Mr. Paul AGPAWA

College of the Sequoias (B)

915 S Mooney Boulevard, Visalia CA 93277-2234
County: Tulare | FICE Identification: 001186
Unit ID: 123217
Telephone: (559) 730-3700 | Carnegie Class: Assoc/Pub-R-L
FAX Number: (559) 730-3894 | Calendar System: Semester
URL: www.cos.edu
Established: 1925 | Annual Undergrad Tuition & Fees (In-District): $799
Enrollment: 13,470 | Coed
Affiliation or Control: State/Local | IRS Status: 501(c)3
Highest Offering: Associate Degree
Program: Occupational; 2-Year Principally Bachelor's Creditable
Accreditation: WJ, @PTAA

01 Superintendent/President ... Dr. William T. SCROGGINS
05 Vice President Academic Services ... Dr. Duncan GRAHAM
10 Dean Fiscal Services ... Ms. Leangela MILLER
32 Vice President Student Services ... Ms. Frances GUZMAN
37 Dean Student Svcs/Financial Aid ... Ms. Tamara RAVALIN
38 Dean Counseling/Matriculation ... Ms. Chris KNOX
75 Dean Academic Svcs/Voc Educ ... Mr. Larry DUTTO
81 Dean Science/Math/Eng ... Dr. Robert URTECHO
76 Dean Allied Health/Phys Education ... Mrs. Cindy DELAIN
49 Dean Arts & Letters ... Ms. Jennifer VEGA-LA SERNA
15 Dean Human Resources/Legal Affairs ... Mr. John BRATSCH
18 Dean Facilities/Facilities Plng ... Mr. Eric MITTLESTEAD
30 Exec Dir Found/Inst Advancement ... Mr. Steve RENTON
66 Director Nursing & Allied Health ... Mrs. Karen ROBERTS
08 Dir Library/Instructional Tech ... Mrs. Kathie LEWIS
09 Director of Research ... Mr. Tim GARNER
06 Registrar/Record Technician ... Ms. Irene GARCIA
27 Public Information Officer ... Mr. Steve RENTON
41 Athletic Director ... Mr. Lamel HARRIS
19 Chief Campus Police ... Mr. Robert MASTERSON
38 Div Chr Stdt Counsel/Hlth Std/Wk Ex ... Ms. Hunter CHURCH-GONZALES
40 Bookstore Manager ... Ms. Dorianna MENDIETTA
23 Head Nurse/Health Center ... Ms. Stephanie YOCUM
32 Student Activities Coordinator ... Mrs. Debbie DOUGLASS
103 Program Coord Workforce Development ... Ms. Louann WALDNER
36 Coord Career/Placement Center ... Ms. Bethany AZEVEDO

College of the Siskiyous (C)

800 College Avenue, Weed CA 96094-2899
County: Siskiyou | FICE Identification: 001187
Unit ID: 123484
Telephone: (530) 938-5200 | Carnegie Class: Assoc/Pub-R-M
FAX Number: (530) 938-5506 | Calendar System: Semester
URL: www.siskiyous.edu
Established: 1957 | Annual Undergrad Tuition & Fees (In-District): $1,104
Enrollment: 2,732 | Coed
Affiliation or Control: State/Local | IRS Status: 501(c)3
Highest Offering: Associate Degree
Program: Occupational; 2-Year Principally Bachelor's Creditable
Accreditation: WJ

01 Superintendent/President ... Mr. Randall C. LAWRENCE
04 Exec Assistant to the President ... Ms. Kathy GASSAWAY
05 Vice President Student Learning ... Dr. Robert FROST
11 VP Administrative &Technology Svcs ... Mr. Steve CROW
08 Assistant Dean Learning Resources ... Ms. Nancy SHEPARD
32 Director Student Life ... Mr. Doug HAUGEN
09 Director Planning Assess & Research ... Ms. Kristy ANDERSON
41 Director Athletics ... Mr. Dennis ROBERTS
20 Interim Dean Student Learning ... Mr. Joe ZAGORSKI
12 Director Yreka Campus ... Ms. Sarah WHITIS
07 Director of Enrollment Services ... Ms. Meghan WITHERELL
15 Director Personnel ... Ms. Nancy MILLER
37 Interim Asst Dir Financial Aid ... Mrs. Andrea CASTRO
18 Chief Facilities/Physical Plant ... Mr. Mark HEALY
26 Int Chief Public Relations Officer ... Ms. Dawn SLABAUGH
28 Director of Diversity ... Ms. Nancy MILLER
96 Director of Purchasing ... Ms. Lori LUDDON

Columbia College Hollywood (D)

18618 Oxnard Street, Tarzana CA 91356-1411
County: Los Angeles | FICE Identification: 021102
Unit ID: 112570
Telephone: (800) 785-0585 | Carnegie Class: Spec/Arts
FAX Number: (818) 345-9053 | Calendar System: Quarter
URL: www.columbiacollege.edu
Established: 1952 | Annual Undergrad Tuition & Fees: $17,685
Enrollment: 330 | Coed
Affiliation or Control: Independent Non-Profit | IRS Status: 501(c)3
Highest Offering: Baccalaureate
Program: Liberal Arts And General; Fine Arts Emphasis
Accreditation: ART

01 President/CEO ... Mr. Richard KOBRITZ
05 Dean of the College ... Mr. Alan L. GANSBERG
10 Treasurer ... Mr. Theodore O'KARMA
22 Compliance & Accreditation Manager ... Mr. Brian SYMONDS
21 Director of Finance ... Mr. Richard CROWE
32 Dean of Students ... Mr. Andrew KESLER
35 Dean of Student Services ... Dr. Steve MARTINEZ
13 Director of IT and Production Svcs ... Mr. Ronald REEVES
07 Director of Admissions ... Ms. Carmen MUNOZ
37 Financial Aid Manager ... Mr. Jan HASTINGS
36 Student Placement ... Ms. Marie ROSE

Community Christian College (E)

251 Tennessee Street, Redlands CA 92373-4438
County: San Bernardino | FICE Identification: 038744
Unit ID: 446163
Telephone: (909) 335-8863 | Carnegie Class: Assoc/PrivNFP
FAX Number: (909) 335-9101 | Calendar System: Quarter
URL: www.cccollege.edu
Established: 1995 | Annual Undergrad Tuition & Fees: $10,875
Enrollment: 74 | Coed
Affiliation or Control: Independent Non-Profit | IRS Status: 501(c)3
Highest Offering: Associate Degree
Program: 2-Year Principally Bachelor's Creditable; Liberal Arts And General
Accreditation: TRACS

01 President ... Rev. Robert JOHNSON
05 Vice President for Academic Affairs ... Dr. John HARBISON
10 Vice Pres for Finance ... Mr. Jason SCHROCK

Concord Law School of Kaplan University (F)

10866 Wilshire Blvd, Suite 1200,
Los Angeles CA 90024-4356
County: Los Angeles | FICE Identification: 041259
Telephone: (310) 689-3200 | Carnegie Class: Not Classified
FAX Number: (310) 470-3547 | Calendar System: Other
URL: info.concordlawschool.edu
Established: 1998 | Annual Undergrad Tuition & Fees: $9,984
Enrollment: 1,300 | Coed
Affiliation or Control: Proprietary | IRS Status: Proprietary
Highest Offering: First Professional Degree
Program: Professional
Accreditation: &NH, DETC

01 Interim Dean and VP Business Dev ... Stephen BURNETT
03 Associate Dean ... Cassandra C. COLCHAGOFF
05 Dean of Faculty ... Gregory BRANDES
30 Director of External Affairs ... Donna SKIBBE
32 Dean of Students ... Dr. Martha SIEGEL
88 Associate Dean of EJD Program ... Kiyoko TATSUI
13 Associate Dean of Technology ... Vacant
13 Director of Technology Operations ... Christopher RUBIO
13 Director of Technology ... Erin FROYD
88 Director of Legal Writing Programs ... Linda HIEMER
35 Director of Student Services ... Rick STEADMAN
07 Regional Director of Admissions ... Vacant
26 Publicist ... Holly BARNHILL
89 Assoc Dean of First-Year Programs ... Steven BRACCI

† Regional accreditation is carried under the parent institution in Cedar Rapids, IA.

Concorde Career College (G)

12951 Euclid Street, Suite 101,
Garden Grove CA 92840-1451
County: Orange | FICE Identification: 008071
Unit ID: 123679
Telephone: (714) 703-1900 | Carnegie Class: Assoc/PrivFP
FAX Number: (714) 530-8421 | Calendar System: Semester
URL: www.concorde.edu
Established: 1960 | Annual Undergrad Tuition & Fees: N/A
Enrollment: 850 | Coed
Affiliation or Control: Proprietary | IRS Status: Proprietary
Highest Offering: Associate Degree
Program: Occupational; Nursing Emphasis
Accreditation: ACCSC, DH, @PTAA

12 Campus Director ... Christopher F. BECKER

Concorde Career College (H)

12412 Victory Boulevard, North Hollywood CA 91606-3134
County: Los Angeles | FICE Identification: 007607
Unit ID: 124937
Telephone: (818) 766-8151 | Carnegie Class: Assoc/PrivFP
FAX Number: (818) 766-1587 | Calendar System: Quarter
URL: www.concordecareercolleges.com
Established: 1955 | Annual Undergrad Tuition & Fees: $13,100
Enrollment: 590 | Coed
Affiliation or Control: Proprietary | IRS Status: Proprietary
Highest Offering: Associate Degree
Program: Occupational
Accreditation: ACCSC, PTAA, SURGT

01 Director ... Dr. Madeline VOLKER

Concorde Career College (I)

201 E Airport Drive, Suite A, San Bernadino CA 92408
FICE Identification: 008537
Unit ID: 124706
Telephone: (909) 884-8891 | Carnegie Class: Assoc/PrivFP
FAX Number: (909) 884-1831 | Calendar System: Semester
URL: www.concorde.edu
Established: 1970 | Annual Undergrad Tuition & Fees: $14,251
Enrollment: 720 | Coed
Affiliation or Control: Proprietary | IRS Status: Proprietary
Highest Offering: Associate Degree
Program: Occupational
Accreditation: ACCSC, DH, SURGT

01 Campus President ... Fred FARIDIAN

Concorde Career College (J)

4393 Imperial Avenue, Suite 100,
San Diego CA 92113-1962
County: San Diego | FICE Identification: 007930
Unit ID: 120661
Telephone: (619) 688-0800 | Carnegie Class: Assoc/PrivFP
FAX Number: (619) 220-4177 | Calendar System: Semester
URL: www.concorde.edu
Established: N/A | Annual Undergrad Tuition & Fees: N/A
Enrollment: 621 | Coed
Affiliation or Control: Proprietary | IRS Status: Proprietary
Highest Offering: Associate Degree
Program: Occupational
Accreditation: ACCSC, @PTAA, SURGT

01 Campus President ... Mr. Harry STRONG

Concordia University (K)

1530 Concordia W, Irvine CA 92612-3299
County: Orange | FICE Identification: 020705
Unit ID: 112075
Telephone: (949) 854-8002 | Carnegie Class: Master's L
FAX Number: (949) 854-6854 | Calendar System: Semester
URL: www.cui.edu
Established: 1972 | Annual Undergrad Tuition & Fees: $26,700
Enrollment: 2,927 | Coed
Affiliation or Control: Lutheran Church - Missouri Synod
IRS Status: 501(c)3

Highest Offering: Master's
Program: Liberal Arts And General; Teacher Preparatory
Accreditation: WC, NURSE

01 President .... Dr. Kurt J. KRUEGER
05 Exec Vice Pres/Provost .... Dr. Mary K. SCOTT
32 Exec Vice Pres Student & Enroll Svc .... Dr. Gary R. MCDANIEL
30 Exec Vice Pres Advancement .... Mr. Timothy J. JAEGER
10 Exec Vice Pres/Finance .... Mr. Kevin TILDEN
20 Vice Pres/Associate Provost .... Dr. Peter SENKBEIL
85 Vice Pres Interntl/Cultural Rels .... Dr. Cheryl WILLIAMS
49 Dean School of Arts and Sciences .... Dr. Timothy L. PREUSS
50 Dean School Business/Profess Stds .... Dr. Timothy C. PETERS
53 Dean School of Education .... Dr. Janice NELSON
73 Dean Christ College .... Dr. Steven P. MUELLER
06 Registrar .... Prof. Kenneth R. CLAVIR
08 Director of Library Services .... Prof. Carolina BARTON
24 Director Educational Media .... Prof. John RANDALL
35 Dean of Students .... Mr. Derek VERGARA
38 Assoc Dean Student Affairs/Advising .... Mrs. Dian VIESELMEYER
43 General Counsel .... Mr. Ronald VAN BLARCOM
07 Exec Dir Admissions .... Mr. Rick HARDY
15 Director of Human Resources .... Mrs. Pamela CLAVIR
41 Athletic Director .... Prof. David BIRELINE
39 Director Residence Life .... Ms. Kimberly CHAMBERLAIN
19 Director Security/Safety .... Mr. Steven RODRIGUEZ
29 Director of Alumni Relations .... Mr. Michael BERGLER
84 Exec Dir Financial Services .... Ms. Lori MCDONALD
36 Director of Career Services .... Mrs. Victoria JAFFEE
88 Director Major Gift Planning .... Mr. Dennis COX
13 IT Services Manager .... Mr. Chris HARRIS
21 Bursar .... Mr. Edgar LOPEZ
85 Exec Director Global Programs .... Dr. Dan WAITE

*Contra Costa Community College District Office (A)

500 Court Street, Martinez CA 94553-1278
County: Contra Costa FICE Identification: 001189
Unit ID: 112817
Telephone: (925) 229-1000 Carnegie Class: N/A
FAX Number: (925) 370-2019
URL: www.4cd.edu

01 Chancellor .... Dr. Helen BENJAMIN
05 VC Education and Technology .... Mr. Mojden MEHDIZADEH
11 Vice Chanc Admin Services .... Vacant
15 VC Human Resources/Chief Negotiator .... Mr. Eugene C. HUFF

*Contra Costa College (B)

2600 Mission Bell Drive, San Pablo CA 94806-3195
County: Contra Costa FICE Identification: 001190
Unit ID: 112826
Telephone: (510) 235-7800 Carnegie Class: Assoc/Pub-S-MC
FAX Number: (510) 236-6768 Calendar System: Semester
URL: www.contracosta.edu
Established: 1948 Annual Undergrad Tuition & Fees (In-District): $864
Enrollment: 7,946 Coed
Affiliation or Control: State/Local IRS Status: 501(c)3
Highest Offering: Associate Degree
Program: Occupational; 2-Year Principally Bachelor's Creditable
Accreditation: WJ, DA

02 President .... Mr. McKinley WILLIAMS
03 Acting Vice President .... Ms. Donna FLOYD
32 Acting Sr Dean of Student Services .... Ms. Vicki FERGUSON
05 Senior Dean of Instruction .... Vacant
75 Dean Economic Development .... Ms. Priscilla LEADON
07 Director of Admissions & Records .... Mr. Michael ALDACO
10 Director Business Services .... Ms. Mariles MAGALONG
09 Director of Institutional Research .... Vacant
37 Director Student Financial Aid .... Ms. Viviane LAMOTHE
18 Chief Facilities/Physical Plant .... Mr. Bruce KING

*Diablo Valley College (C)

321 Golf Club Road, Pleasant Hill CA 94523-1544
County: Contra Costa FICE Identification: 001191
Unit ID: 113634
Telephone: (925) 685-1230 Carnegie Class: Assoc/Pub-S-MC
FAX Number: (925) 685-1551 Calendar System: Semester
URL: www.dvc.edu
Established: 1949 Annual Undergrad Tuition & Fees (In-District): $780
Enrollment: 20,910 Coed
Affiliation or Control: State/Local IRS Status: 501(c)3
Highest Offering: Associate Degree
Program: Occupational; 2-Year Principally Bachelor's Creditable
Accreditation: WJ, ACFEI, DA, DH

02 President .... Mr. Peter GARCIA
05 Vice President Instruction .... Ms. Susan E. LAMB
32 Interim VP Student Services .... Ms. Donna FLOYD
10 Vice President Finance and Admin .... Mr. Chris LEIVAS
12 Exec Dean San Ramon Campus .... Dr. Kevin HORAN
20 Interim Senior Dean of Instruction .... Mr. Ted WIEDEN
84 Dean Outreach/Enroll Mgt/ Matric .... Ms. Elizabeth HAUSCARRIAGUE
12 Dean San Ramon Campus .... Ms. Kathleen COSTA
35 Dean Student Life .... Mr. William OYE
41 Dean of PE/Athl/Dance/Athletic Dir .... Ms. Christina WORSLEY
62 Director of the Library Services .... Mr. Andy KIVEL
38 Dean Counseling & Support Services .... Mr. Terry ARMSTRONG
26 Director of Media & Communications .... Ms. Chrisanne KNOX
57 Dean Applied & Fine Arts .... Mr. Michael ALMAGUER
54 Int Dean Phys Sci/Engr/Bio Sci .... Mr. Ray GORALKA
50 Interim Dean English & Social Sci .... Ms. Ellen KRUSE
81 Dean Math/Computer Science & Bus .... Ms. Rachel WESTLAKE
37 Dean EOPS/Fin Aid/CalWORKS .... Ms. Emily STONE
75 Dean Career Tech Ed & Econ Develop .... Ms. Kim SCHENK

*Los Medanos College (D)

2700 E Leland Road, Pittsburg CA 94565-5197
County: Contra Costa FICE Identification: 010340
Unit ID: 117894
Telephone: (925) 439-2181 Carnegie Class: Assoc/Pub-S-MC
FAX Number: (925) 427-1599 Calendar System: Semester
URL: www.losmedanos.edu
Established: 1973 Annual Undergrad Tuition & Fees (In-District): $874
Enrollment: 9,966 Coed
Affiliation or Control: State/Local IRS Status: 501(c)3
Highest Offering: Associate Degree
Program: Occupational; 2-Year Principally Bachelor's Creditable
Accreditation: WJ

02 Interim President .... Mr. Richard LIVINGSTON
03 Vice President .... Mr. Bruce CUTLER
10 Director of Business Services .... Ms. Sandy SMITH
04 Int Senior Executive Assistant .... Ms. Eileen VALENZUELA
26 Dir of Marketing & Media Design .... Ms. Barbara CELLA
102 Senior Foundation Director .... Ms. Ruth GOODIN
05 Senior Dean Instruction .... Vacant
32 Senior Dean of Student Svcs .... Ms. Gail NEWMAN
88 Dean Career Technical Education .... Ms. Kiran KAMATH
32 Dean Student Development .... Dr. Blas GUERRERO
49 Dean Liberal Arts and Sciences .... Mr. Gil RODRIGUEZ
07 Director of Admissions .... Ms. Robin ARMOUR
37 Director of Financial Aid .... Ms. Loretta CANTO-WILLIAMS
14 Computer & Network Svcs Supervisor .... Mr. Mike BECKER

Copper Mountain College (E)

6162 Rotary Way, Box 1398, Joshua Tree CA 92252-6102
County: San Bernardino FICE Identification: 035424
Unit ID: 395362
Telephone: (760) 366-3791 Carnegie Class: Assoc/Pub-S-SC
FAX Number: (760) 366-5255 Calendar System: Semester
URL: www.cmccd.edu
Established: 1999 Annual Undergrad Tuition & Fees (In-District): $1,080
Enrollment: 2,728 Coed
Affiliation or Control: State/Local IRS Status: 501(c)3
Highest Offering: Associate Degree
Program: Occupational; 2-Year Principally Bachelor's Creditable
Accreditation: WJ

01 Superintendent/President .... Dr. Roger WAGNER
05 Vice Pres for Academic Affairs .... Dr. Wei ZHOU
32 Vice President for Student Services .... Mr. Greg BROWN
15 Director of Human Resources .... Ms. Andrea RIESGO
18 Chief of Facilities .... Mr. Dan CAIN
12 Director of Base Programs .... Mr. Gregg CHESTERMAN
102 Executive Director of Foundation .... Ms. Sandy SMITH
10 Chief Business Officer .... Ms. Meredith PLUMMER
37 Director of Financial Aid .... Mr. Brian HEINEMANN
76 Dir Hlth Science-Registered Nursing .... Ms. Ellie SMITH
91 Director of Information Systems .... Mr. Steve KEMP
26 Dir Marketing & Community Relations .... Vacant

Cuesta College (F)

PO Box 8106, San Luis Obispo CA 93403-8106
County: San Luis Obispo FICE Identification: 001192
Unit ID: 113193
Telephone: (805) 546-3100 Carnegie Class: Assoc/Pub-R-L
FAX Number: (805) 546-3904 Calendar System: Semester
URL: www.cuesta.edu
Established: 1963 Annual Undergrad Tuition & Fees (In-District): $898
Enrollment: 11,588 Coed
Affiliation or Control: State/Local IRS Status: 501(c)3
Highest Offering: Associate Degree
Program: Occupational; 2-Year Principally Bachelor's Creditable
Accreditation: #WJ, EMT

01 Superintendent/President .... Dr. Gilbert H. STORK
05 VP/Asst Supt Academic Affairs .... Dr. A. Cathleen GREINER
10 VP/Asst Supt Administrative Svcs .... Ms. Toni SOMMER
32 VP/Asst Supt Student Services .... Dr. Linda FONTANILLA
12 Exec Dean North Co Campus/S Co Ctrs .... Ms. Sandee MCLAUGHLIN
35 Dean of Students .... Vacant
30 Int Exec Dir Foundation/Inst Adv .... Dr. Barbara GEORGE
08 Director Library/Lrng Resources/DE .... Mr. Mark STENGEL
35 Coordinator Student Life/Leadership .... Mr. Anthony GUTIERREZ
13 Director of Computer Services .... Ms. Janice M. HOUSE
26 Director Marketing & Communication .... Mr. Stephan GUNSAULUS
37 Director of Financial Aid .... Ms. Noherny ORNELAS
66 Director of Nursing .... Ms. Marcia SCOTT
15 Exec Dir Human Res Labor Relations .... Mr. William BENJAMIN
19 Director of Public Safety .... Mr. Joseph ARTEAGA
40 Director of Bookstore .... Ms. Trudy BELL
41 Director of Athletics .... Mr. Robert MARIUCCI
18 Dir Maintenance/Operations/Grounds .... Mr. Terry REECE
38 Director Counseling Services .... Mr. Candelario MUNOZ
103 Dir Workforce Econ Devel Cmty Pgm .... Dr. Matthew GREEN
23 Coordinator of Health Services .... Ms. Vicki SAWZAK
81 Dean Ac Aff Sci/Math/Nursing/PE .... Ms. Deborah WULFF
79 Dean Ac Aff Arts/Humanities/Soc Sci .... Dr. Pamela RALSTON
103 Dean Ac Aff Workforce Econ Dev .... Mr. John CASCAMO
76 Associate Director of Allied Health .... Ms. Lisa WEARDA
07 Director of Admissions & Records .... Vacant
09 Director of Institutional Research .... Dr. Ryan CARTNAL
96 Director of General Services .... Ms. Maryanne ZARYCKA
21 Director Fiscal Services .... Mr. Christopher GREEN
102 Director Foundation Programs .... Ms. Karen TACKET

The Culinary Institute of America at Greystone (G)

2555 Main Street, Saint Helena CA 94574-9504
County: Napa Identification: 666260
Unit ID: 19050301
Telephone: (707) 967-1100 Carnegie Class: Not Classified
FAX Number: (707) 967-1113 Calendar System: Semester
URL: www.ciachef.edu/california/
Established: 1997 Annual Undergrad Tuition & Fees: $28,770
Enrollment: 247 Coed
Affiliation or Control: Independent Non-Profit IRS Status: 501(c)3
Highest Offering: Associate Degree
Program: Occupational; Technical Emphasis
Accreditation: &M

01 President .... Dr. Tim RYAN
03 VP/Dean of Culinary Education .... Mr. Mark ERICKSON
05 Director of Education .... Mr. Adam BUSBY

† Regional accreditation is carried under the parent institution in Hyde Park, NY.

Deep Springs College (H)

HC 72 Box 45001, Via Dyer, NV 89010-9803
County: Inyo FICE Identification: 001194
Unit ID: 113528
Telephone: (760) 872-2000 Carnegie Class: Not Classified
FAX Number: (760) 874-7077 Calendar System: Other
URL: www.deepsprings.edu
Established: 1917 Annual Undergrad Tuition & Fees: $0
Enrollment: 26 Male
Affiliation or Control: Independent Non-Profit IRS Status: 501(c)3
Highest Offering: Associate Degree
Program: 2-Year Principally Bachelor's Creditable
Accreditation: WJ

01 President .... Mr. David NEIDORF
05 Dean of College .... Mr. Kenneth CARDWELL
88 Ranch Manager .... Mr. Ken MITCHELL
11 VP Operations .... Mr. David WELLE
21 Office Manager .... Ms. Iris POPE
18 Mechanic & Plant Manager .... Mr. Padraic MACLEISH
88 Chef .... Mr. Jonathan DEWEESE
88 Farm Manager .... Mr. Mark DUNN

Dell'Arte International School of Physical Theatre (I)

P.O. Box 816, 131 H Street, Blue Lake CA 95525
County: Humboldt FICE Identification: 030256
Unit ID: 113537
Telephone: (707) 668-5663 Carnegie Class: Not Classified
FAX Number: (707) 668-5665 Calendar System: Other
URL: www.dellarte.com
Established: N/A Annual Graduate Tuition & Fees: $11,850
Enrollment: 42 Coed
Affiliation or Control: Independent Non-Profit IRS Status: 501(c)3
Highest Offering: Master's; No Undergraduates
Program: Professional; Fine Arts Emphasis
Accreditation: THEA

01 Producing Artistic Director .... Mr. Michael FIELDS
11 Administrative Director .... Ms. Stephanie WETZEL
26 Marketing Director/IT Development .... Mr. Gannon ROGERS

Design Institute of San Diego (J)

8555 Commerce Avenue, San Diego CA 92121-2685
County: San Diego FICE Identification: 022980
Unit ID: 113582
Telephone: (858) 566-1200 Carnegie Class: Spec/Arts
FAX Number: (858) 566-2711 Calendar System: Semester
URL: www.disd.edu
Established: 1977 Annual Undergrad Tuition & Fees: $14,400
Enrollment: 306 Coed
Affiliation or Control: Proprietary IRS Status: Proprietary
Highest Offering: Baccalaureate
Program: Professional
Accreditation: ACICS, CIDA

01 President .... Mr. Arthur ROSENSTEIN
05 Vice President .... Ms. Gloria ROSENSTEIN
07 Director of Admissions .... Ms. Paula PARRISH
11 Campus Director .... Ms. Margot BLANK DOUCETTE
37 Director Financial Aid .... Ms. Jackie GLORIA

32 Director of Student Services .... Ms. Tena MOIOLA
08 Librarian .... Ms. Lisa SCHATTMAN
06 Registrar .... Ms. Tracy GULINO
07 Outreach & Admissions .... Ms. Liz BARRY

DeVry University - Bakersfield (A)

3000 Ming Avenue, Bakersfield CA 93304-4136

County: Kern Identification: 666486
Telephone: (661) 833-7120 Carnegie Class: Not Classified
FAX Number: N/A Calendar System: Semester
URL: www.devry.edu
Established: 1931 Annual Undergrad Tuition & Fees: $15,294
Enrollment: 386 Coed
Affiliation or Control: Proprietary IRS Status: Proprietary
Highest Offering: Baccalaureate
Program: Occupational; Professional; Business Emphasis
Accreditation: &NH

01 Center Dean .... George SHEARER

† Regional accreditation is carried under the parent institution in Downers Grove, IL.

DeVry University - Colton (B)

1090 E. Washington Street, Suite H,
Colton CA 92324-8180

County: San Bernadino Identification: 666487
Telephone: (909) 514-1808 Carnegie Class: Not Classified
FAX Number: (909) 514-1836 Calendar System: Semester
URL: www.devry.edu
Established: 1931 Annual Undergrad Tuition & Fees: $15,294
Enrollment: 424 Coed
Affiliation or Control: Proprietary IRS Status: Proprietary
Highest Offering: Master's
Program: Professional; Business Emphasis
Accreditation: &NH

01 Center Dean .... Michael MILFORD

† Regional accreditation is carried under the parent institution in Downers Grove, IL.

DeVry University - Daly City (C)

2001 Junipero Serra Blvd, Ste 161,
Daly City CA 94014-3899

County: San Mateo Identification: 666493
Telephone: (650) 991-3520 Carnegie Class: Not Classified
FAX Number: (650) 992-3840 Calendar System: Semester
URL: www.devry.edu
Established: 1931 Annual Undergrad Tuition & Fees: $15,294
Enrollment: 276 Coed
Affiliation or Control: Proprietary IRS Status: Proprietary
Highest Offering: Master's
Program: Professional; Business Emphasis
Accreditation: &NH

01 Center Dean .... William MINNICH

† Regional accreditation is carried under the parent institution in Downers Grove, IL.

DeVry University - Fremont Campus (D)

6600 Dumbarton Circle, Fremont CA 94555-3615

County: Alameda Identification: 666829
Unit ID: 432171
Telephone: (510) 574-1200 Carnegie Class: Not Classified
FAX Number: (510) 742-0868 Calendar System: Semester
URL: www.devry.com
Established: 1931 Annual Undergrad Tuition & Fees: $15,294
Enrollment: 2,022 Coed
Affiliation or Control: Proprietary IRS Status: Proprietary
Highest Offering: Master's
Program: Occupational; Professional; Business Emphasis
Accreditation: &NH, ENGT

01 Metro President .... Michael CUBBIN
07 Sr Director of Admissions .... Tianna COHEN-PAUL
37 Student Finance Manager .... Carolyn TORRES
13 Information Technology Director .... Muhammad KHAN
77 Program Dean GSP .... Dave WALKER
06 Registrar .... Evelyn ANDREWS
15 Human Resources Business Partner .... Monica STINSON
05 Dean of International Admissions .... Chow LEE
32 Manager of Student Services .... Stefanie CORNELL
36 Director of Career Services .... Sandra DIXON
39 Director of Residence Life .... Timothy BLOOD
54 Dean of Engineering Tech Programs .... Dennis MUELLER

† Regional accreditation is carried under the parent institution in Downers Grove, IL.

DeVry University - Fresno (E)

7575 North Fresno Street, Fresno CA 93720-2458

County: Fresno Identification: 666494
Telephone: (559) 439-8595 Carnegie Class: Not Classified
FAX Number: (559) 439-8598 Calendar System: Semester
URL: www.devry.edu
Established: 1931 Annual Undergrad Tuition & Fees: $15,294
Enrollment: 600 Coed
Affiliation or Control: Proprietary IRS Status: Proprietary
Highest Offering: Master's
Program: Professional; Business Emphasis
Accreditation: &NH

02 Campus President .... Joseph COPPOLA

† Regional accreditation is carried under the parent institution in Downers Grove, IL.

DeVry University - Irvine Center (F)

430 Exchange, Suite 250, Irvine CA 92602-1303

County: Orange Identification: 666192
Unit ID: 434788
Telephone: (714) 734-5560 Carnegie Class: Not Classified
FAX Number: (714) 730-8451 Calendar System: Semester
URL: www.devry.edu
Established: 1997 Annual Undergrad Tuition & Fees: $15,294
Enrollment: 255 Coed
Affiliation or Control: Proprietary IRS Status: Proprietary
Highest Offering: Master's
Program: Occupational; Professional; Business Emphasis
Accreditation: &NH

01 Center Dean .... Ms. Michelle ARENCIVIA

† Regional accreditation is carried under the parent institution in Downers Grove, IL.Terrace, IL.

DeVry University - Long Beach Campus (G)

3880 Kilroy Airport Way, Long Beach CA 90806-2452

County: Los Angeles Identification: 666988
Unit ID: 420282
Telephone: (562) 427-0861 Carnegie Class: Not Classified
FAX Number: (562) 997-5368 Calendar System: Semester
URL: www.devry.edu
Established: 1931 Annual Undergrad Tuition & Fees: $15,294
Enrollment: 1,400 Coed
Affiliation or Control: Proprietary IRS Status: Proprietary
Highest Offering: Master's
Program: Occupational; Professional; Business Emphasis
Accreditation: &NH, ENGT

01 Campus President .... Ivonna EDKINS
07 Director of Admissions .... Frederick THOMAS
36 Dean of Career & Student Services .... Carmen ORTIZ
15 Human Resources Manager .... Beatrice MICALIZIO
05 Manager of Academic Support Center .... John ROLLINS
08 Librarian .... Colleen BRISKI

† Regional accreditation is carried under the parent institution in Downers Grove, IL.

DeVry University - Oakland Center (H)

505 14th St., Ste. 100, Oakland CA 94612

County: San Francisco Identification: 666194
Telephone: (510) 267-1340 Carnegie Class: Not Classified
FAX Number: N/A Calendar System: Semester
URL: www.devry.edu
Established: 1931 Annual Undergrad Tuition & Fees: $15,294
Enrollment: 170 Coed
Affiliation or Control: Proprietary IRS Status: Proprietary
Highest Offering: Master's
Program: Occupational; Professional; Business Emphasis
Accreditation: &NH

01 Center Dean .... Kurt SCHAKE

† Regional accreditation is carried under the parent institution in Downers Grove, IL.

DeVry University - Palmdale (I)

39115 Trade Center Dr. Ste. 100,
Palmdale CA 93551-3649

County: Los Angeles Identification: 666495
Telephone: (661) 224-2920 Carnegie Class: Not Classified
FAX Number: (661) 266-4986 Calendar System: Semester
URL: www.devry.edu
Established: 1931 Annual Undergrad Tuition & Fees: $15,294
Enrollment: 536 Coed
Affiliation or Control: Proprietary IRS Status: Proprietary
Highest Offering: Master's
Program: Professional; Business Emphasis
Accreditation: &NH

01 Center Dean .... Ms. Susan ISHII

† Regional accreditation is carried under the parent institution in Downers Grove, IL.

DeVry University - Pomona Campus (J)

901 Corporate Center Drive, Pomona CA 91768-2642

County: Los Angeles FICE Identification: 023329
Unit ID: 113607
Telephone: (909) 622-8866 Carnegie Class: Master's L
FAX Number: (909) 623-5666 Calendar System: Semester
URL: www.devry.edu
Established: 1931 Annual Undergrad Tuition & Fees: $15,294
Enrollment: 3,339 Coed
Affiliation or Control: Proprietary IRS Status: Proprietary
Highest Offering: Master's
Program: Occupational; Professional; Business Emphasis
Accreditation: &NH, ENGT

01 Metro President .... Scott SAND
05 Dean Academic Affairs .... Walter BROWN
37 Director of Student Finance .... Catherine THOMAS
32 Dean Student Central .... Stacey WEINSTEIN
07 Senior Director of Admissions .... Devin DODSON
36 Director of Career Services .... Larry BURNS
08 Director of Library Services .... Nicole BIRD
15 Human Resources Business Partner .... Makisha ALEXANDER
10 Director of Finance/Administration .... Raymond WONG
72 Dean of Electronics .... Alan PRICE
50 Dean of Business Program .... Walter BROWN
31 Director of Community Outreach .... Kenneth CHAN

† Regional accreditation is carried under the parent institution in Downers Grove, IL.

DeVry University - Sacramento (K)

2216 Kausen Drive, Ste. 1, Sacramento CA 95758-7115

Identification: 666497
Telephone: (916) 478-2847 Carnegie Class: Not Classified
FAX Number: (916) 478-2849 Calendar System: Semester
URL: www.devry.edu
Established: 1931 Annual Undergrad Tuition & Fees: $15,294
Enrollment: 919 Coed
Affiliation or Control: Proprietary IRS Status: Proprietary
Highest Offering: Master's
Program: Professional; Business Emphasis
Accreditation: &NH, ENGT

01 Campus Director .... Marcela IGLESIAS

† Regional accreditation is carried under the parent institution in Downers Grove, IL.

DeVry University - San Diego Center (L)

2655 Camino Del Rio North, Ste 201,
San Diego CA 92108-1633

County: San Diego Identification: 666193
Unit ID: 437264
Telephone: (619) 683-2446 Carnegie Class: Not Classified
FAX Number: (619) 683-2448 Calendar System: Semester
URL: www.devry.edu
Established: 2002 Annual Undergrad Tuition & Fees: $15,294
Enrollment: 786 Coed
Affiliation or Control: Proprietary IRS Status: Proprietary
Highest Offering: Master's
Program: Occupational; Professional; Business Emphasis
Accreditation: &NH

01 Center Dean .... Pamela DALY

† Regional accreditation is carried under the parent institution in Downers Grove, IL.

DeVry University - San Jose (M)

2160 Lundy Avenue, Suite 250, San Jose CA 95131-1862

County: Santa Clara Identification: 666523
Telephone: (408) 571-3760 Carnegie Class: Not Classified
FAX Number: (408) 577-1246 Calendar System: Semester
URL: www.devry.edu
Established: 1931 Annual Undergrad Tuition & Fees: $15,294
Enrollment: 446 Coed
Affiliation or Control: Proprietary IRS Status: Proprietary
Highest Offering: Master's
Program: Professional; Business Emphasis
Accreditation: &NH

01 Center Dean .... Nils SEDWICK

† Regional accreditation is carried under the parent institution in Downers Grove, IL.

DeVry University - Sherman Oaks Campus (N)

15301 Ventura Blvd, #100, Bldg D,
Sherman Oaks CA 91403-6654

County: Los Angeles Identification: 666065
Unit ID: 439181
Telephone: (818) 713-8111 Carnegie Class: Not Classified
FAX Number: N/A Calendar System: Semester
URL: www.devry.edu
Established: 1931 Annual Undergrad Tuition & Fees: $15,294
Enrollment: 1,291 Coed
Affiliation or Control: Proprietary IRS Status: Proprietary
Highest Offering: Master's
Program: Occupational; Professional; Business Emphasis

Accreditation: &NH, ENGT

01 Campus President .... Brian PORTER
05 Dean of Academic Affairs .... Sue MCDONALD
07 Director of Admissions .... Stan GERSH
12 Graduate Center Dean .... Nadeem KHATTAK
36 Director of Career Services .... Hassan AKMAL

† Regional accreditation is carried under the parent institution in Downers Grove, IL.

Dominican School of Philosophy and Theology (A)

2301 Vine Street, Berkeley CA 94708-1816
County: Alameda FICE Identification: 001296
Unit ID: 113704
Telephone: (510) 849-2030 Carnegie Class: Spec/Faith
FAX Number: (510) 849-1372 Calendar System: Semester
URL: www.dspt.edu
Established: 1932 Annual Undergrad Tuition & Fees: $13,800
Enrollment: 79 Coed
Affiliation or Control: Roman Catholic IRS Status: 501(c)3
Highest Offering: Master's
Program: Professional
Accreditation: WC, THEOL

01 President .... Rev. Michael SWEENEY
11 Vice President Administration .... Mr. Peter MACLEOD
30 Vice Pres Institutional Advancement .... Mrs. Mariciel MAHONEY
05 Academic Dean .... Rev. Christopher M. RENZ
07 Director of Admissions .... Mr. John D. KNUTSEN
06 Registrar .... Ms. Teresa OLSON
21 Office Manager/Dir Student Services .... Ms. Colleen POWER
26 Director of Communications .... Ms. Heidi MCKENNA
36 Career Development Director .... Mr. Paul KIRCHER

Dominican University of California (B)

50 Acacia Avenue, San Rafael CA 94901-2298
County: Marin FICE Identification: 001196
Unit ID: 113698
Telephone: (415) 457-4440 Carnegie Class: Master's M
FAX Number: (415) 485-3205 Calendar System: Semester
URL: www.dominican.edu
Established: 1890 Annual Undergrad Tuition & Fees: $36,900
Enrollment: 2,267 Coed
Affiliation or Control: Independent Non-Profit IRS Status: 501(c)3
Highest Offering: Master's
Program: Liberal Arts And General; Teacher Preparatory; Professional
Accreditation: WC, NURSE, OT

01 President .... Dr. Mary B. MARCY
05 Exec VP and Chief Academic Officer .... Dr. Luis CALINGO
10 Chief Financial Officer .... Ms. Cecilia MINALGA
26 Vice Pres External Relations .... Ms. Maureen KEEFE
32 VP Student Life/Dean of Students .... Dr. John F. KENNEDY
84 Vice Pres of Enrollment Management .... Vacant
20 Associate VP Academic Affairs .... Dr. Sherry VOLK
27 Director of Marketing .... Ms. Nancy BULETTE
04 Assistant to the President .... Ms. Mary Jane BAIRD
100 Asst Spec Projects/Trustee Liaison .... Dr. Francoise LEPAGE
79 Dean Sch Arts/Humanities/Social Sci .... Dr. Nicola PITCHFORD
76 Dean of School Health/Natural Sci .... Dr. Martha NELSON
53 Dean School of Educ/Counsel Psych .... Dr. Edward KUJAWA
50 Dean School of Business/Leadership .... Dr. Dan MOSHAVI
88 Asc Dean Sch of Health/Natural Sci .... Dr. Sibdas GHOSH
35 Associate Dean of Students .... Mr. Paul RACCANELLO
18 Exec Dir Facilities/Physical Plant .... Mr. Jacques CHARTON
08 Executive Director Library Services .... Mr. Gary GORKA
09 Exec Dir of Institutional Research .... Ms. Jenny LI
37 Director of Financial Aid .... Ms. Shanon LITTLE
07 Asst VP of Undergrad Admissions .... Ms. Rebecca FINN KENNEY
13 Chief Technology Officer .... Mr. Jackson RATCLIFFE
06 Registrar .... Ms. Marianne STICKEL
29 Director of Alumni Relations .... Ms. Tracy HOGAN
88 President Alumni Association .... Mr. Pepe GONZALEZ
15 Director of Human Resources .... Ms. Christine GODFREY
36 Director Student Placement .... Ms. Susan FYLES
28 Director Diversity .... Dr. Suresh APPAVOO
92 Director Honors Program .... Dr. Diara SPAIN
38 Director Student Counseling .... Dr. Chuck BILLINGS
26 Public Relations Officer .... Mr. David ALBEE
85 Exec Director Intl & Global Educ .... Dr. Jayati GHOSH
30 Director of Advancement .... Ms. Sarah ANDREWS

Dongguk University (C)

440 Shatto Place, Los Angeles CA 90020-1704
County: Los Angeles FICE Identification: 031095
Unit ID: 122117
Telephone: (213) 487-0110 Carnegie Class: Spec/Health
FAX Number: (213) 487-0527 Calendar System: Quarter
URL: www.dula.edu
Established: 1979 Annual Undergrad Tuition & Fees: $11,600
Enrollment: 171 Coed
Affiliation or Control: Independent Non-Profit IRS Status: 501(c)3
Highest Offering: Master's; No Lower Division
Program: Professional
Accreditation: ACUP

01 President .... Dr. Un Kyo SEO
05 Office of the Provost/Admissions .... Mr. Seok Joo AUM
10 Director of Finance .... Mr. Albert KIM
37 Financial Aid Officer .... Ms. Julia PARK
06 Registrar .... Mr. Hoon SEO
63 Director of Oriental Medical Center .... Mr. Chul WON
18 Director of Facilities .... Mr. Arturo AGUIRRE
21 Office Manager .... Ms. Bo Yoon CHOI
85 International Student Advisor .... Mr. Phillip YEW

El Camino College (D)

16007 Crenshaw Boulevard, Torrance CA 90506-0002
County: Los Angeles FICE Identification: 001197
Unit ID: 113980
Telephone: (310) 660-3670 Carnegie Class: Assoc/Pub-S-SC
FAX Number: (310) 660-7798 Calendar System: Semester
URL: www.elcamino.edu
Established: 1947 Annual Undergrad Tuition & Fees (In-District): $899
Enrollment: 25,739 Coed
Affiliation or Control: State/Local IRS Status: 501(c)3
Highest Offering: Associate Degree
Program: Occupational; 2-Year Principally Bachelor's Creditable
Accreditation: WJ, ADNUR, RAD

01 President .... Dr. Thomas M. FALLO
05 Vice President Academic Affairs .... Dr. Francisco M. ARCE
11 Vice Pres Administrative Services .... Ms. Jo Ann HIGDON
32 Vice Pres Student/Community Advance .... Dr. Jeanie NISHIME
15 Int Vice Pres of Human Resources .... Ms. Lynn SOLOMITA
30 Dean Community Advancement .... Mr. Jose ANAYA
45 Dean Planning/Research/Development .... Vacant
72 Dean Industry & Technology .... Dr. Stephanie RODRIGUEZ
81 Dean Math/Physical Sciences .... Dr. Donald GOLDBERG
50 Dean of Business .... Dr. Virginia RAPP
83 Dean Behavioral & Social Science .... Dr. Gloria MIRANDA
68 Dean Health/Exer/Science/Sport .... Mr. Rory NATIVIDAD
57 Dean Fine Arts .... Dr. Connie FITZSIMONS
76 Dean Natural Sciences .... Dr. Jean SHANKWEILER
79 Dean Humanities .... Mr. Tom LEW
38 Dean Counseling Matriculation Svcs .... Dr. Regina SMITH
84 Dean of Enrollment Services .... Mr. Arvid SPOR
27 Director of Information Systems .... Mr. John WAGSTAFF
31 Director of Community Relations .... Ms. Ann GARTEN
66 Interim Director of Nursing .... Ms. Kim BAILY
07 Dir Admissions/Records/Registrar .... Mr. Bill MULROONEY
10 Chief Business Officer .... Dr. Jo Ann HIGDON
20 Associate Academic Officer .... Vacant
26 Chief Public Relations Officer .... Ms. Ann M. GARTEN
102 Executive Director Foundation .... Ms. Katie GLEASON
36 Director Student Placement .... Dr. Regina SMITH
96 Acting Director of Purchasing .... Mr. Rocky BONURA
40 Director of Bookstore .... Ms. Julie BOURLIER
19 Chief of Campus Police .... Mr. Michael TREVIS
18 Director of Facilities Plng/Svcs .... Mr. Robert GANN
35 Director of Student Affairs .... Mr. Harold TYLER
37 Director Student Financial Aid .... Ms. Hortense COOPER
09 Director Institutional Research .... Ms. Irene GRAFF
28 Director of Diversity .... Ms. Leisa BIGGERS
21 Business Manager .... Ms. Janice ELY
25 Resource Devel/Grants Coordinator .... Vacant

El Camino College Compton Center (E)

1111 E Artesia Boulevard, Compton CA 90221-5393
County: Los Angeles FICE Identification: 001188
Unit ID: 112686
Telephone: (310) 900-1600 Carnegie Class: Assoc/Pub-S-SC
FAX Number: (310) 605-1458 Calendar System: Semester
URL: www.compton.edu
Established: 1927 Annual Undergrad Tuition & Fees (In-State): $864
Enrollment: 8,729 Coed
Affiliation or Control: State IRS Status: 501(c)3
Highest Offering: Associate Degree
Program: Occupational; 2-Year Principally Bachelor's Creditable
Accreditation: &WJ

01 Interim Chief Executive Officer .... Dr. Keith CURRY
11 Vice President Admin Services .... Ms. JoAnn HIGDON
05 Vice President Academic Affairs .... Ms. Barbara PEREZ
32 Interim Dean Student Services .... Ms. Valerie O'GUYNN
15 Dean Human Resources/Risk Mgmt .... Mrs. Rachelle SASSER
20 Dean Academic Affairs .... Dr. Susan DEVER
76 Dean Health/Human Services .... Ms. Wanda MORRIS
55 Director Evening Division .... Vacant
88 Dir Special Programs & Services .... Mr. Robert BUTLER
08 Librarian .... Ms. Eleanor SONIDO
88 Director CalWORKs & DSPS .... Ms. Patricia BONACIC
22 Interim Director EOP & S .... Ms. Elizabeth MARTINEZ
41 Director of Athletics .... Mr. Albert OLGUIN
09 Director Institutional Research .... Ms. Irene GRAFF
37 Director Financial Aid .... Dr. Mytha PASCUAL
31 Director Outreach & Relations .... Mr. Ricky SHABAZZ
10 Chief Business Officer .... Mr. Daniel VILLANUEVA
35 Director Student Support Services .... Mr. Macheo SHABAKA
88 Director Title V .... Vacant
18 Director Facilities .... Mr. Fred STURNER
13 Supervisor MIS .... Mr. Rudy RAMOS

† Regional accreditation is carried under the parent institution in Torrance, CA.

Emperor's College of Traditional Oriental Medicine (F)

1807-B Wilshire Boulevard, Santa Monica CA 90403-5678
County: Los Angeles FICE Identification: 026090
Unit ID: 114114
Telephone: (310) 453-8300 Carnegie Class: Spec/Health
FAX Number: (310) 829-3838 Calendar System: Quarter
URL: www.emperors.edu
Established: 1983 Annual Undergrad Tuition & Fees: $14,000
Enrollment: 216 Coed
Affiliation or Control: Proprietary IRS Status: Proprietary
Highest Offering: Doctorate
Program: Professional
Accreditation: ACUP

01 Chief Executive Officer .... Yun KIM
05 Academic Dean .... Jacques MORAMARCO
07 Director of Admissions .... Lisa ROCCHETTI
37 Financial Aid Officer .... Farida LUGEMBE
11 Administrator .... George PARK

Empire College School of Business (G)

3035 Cleveland Avenue, Santa Rosa CA 95403-2100
County: Sonoma FICE Identification: 009032
Unit ID: 114123
Telephone: (707) 546-4000 Carnegie Class: Assoc/PrivFP
FAX Number: (707) 546-4058 Calendar System: Other
URL: www.empcol.edu
Established: 1961 Annual Undergrad Tuition & Fees: $11,500
Enrollment: 557 Coed
Affiliation or Control: Proprietary IRS Status: Proprietary
Highest Offering: Associate Degree
Program: Occupational; Technical Emphasis
Accreditation: ACICS

01 President .... Mr. Roy HURD
26 Vice Pres Marketing/Administration .... Mrs. Sherie HURD
05 Director of Education .... Mrs. Vickie SAVINO
07 Director of Admissions .... Ms. Dahnja STRAUB
37 Director Student Financial Aid .... Mrs. Mary O'BRIEN
11 Director of Administrative Svcs .... Mr. David YARBROUGH
10 Director of Accounting .... Ms. Susanne RICHARDS
36 Director Student Placement .... Ms. Lucille INMAN
40 Bookstore Manager .... Ms. Kass VON DER MEHDEN
06 Registrar .... Ms. Margareta CAMPBELL
38 Student Success Advisor .... Ms. Mae Rose BELLAGIO
38 Student Success Advisor .... Ms. Nora SONGSTER

Epic Bible College (H)

4330 Auburn Blvd., Sacramento CA 95841
County: Sacramento FICE Identification: 034033
Unit ID: 124487
Telephone: (916) 348-4689 Carnegie Class: Spec/Faith
FAX Number: (916) 334-2315 Calendar System: Trimester
URL: www.EPIC.edu
Established: 1974 Annual Undergrad Tuition & Fees: $8,784
Enrollment: 306 Coed
Affiliation or Control: Independent Non-Profit IRS Status: 501(c)3
Highest Offering: Baccalaureate
Program: Liberal Arts And General; Religious Emphasis
Accreditation: TRACS

01 President .... Dr. Ronald W. HARDEN
05 Vice President of Academics .... Dr. Greg L. HARTLEY
09 Director of Assessment .... Dr. Ronald W. HARDEN
08 Director Learning Resource .... Carol SIMON
10 Chief Financial Officer .... C. Steven CHANEY
37 Director of Financial Aid .... David PINESCHI
06 Director of Records .... Kathy CLARKE

Eternity Bible College (I)

2136 Winifred Street, Simi Valley CA 93063
County: Ventura Identification: 667045
Telephone: (805) 581-1233 Carnegie Class: Not Classified
FAX Number: (805) 581-1245 Calendar System: Semester
URL: www.eternitybiblecollege.com
Established: 2004 Annual Undergrad Tuition & Fees: N/A
Enrollment: 117 Coed
Affiliation or Control: Independent Non-Profit IRS Status: 501(c)3
Highest Offering: Baccalaureate
Program: Religious Emphasis
Accreditation: @BI

01 President .... Joshua WALKER
05 Academic Dean .... Spencer MACCUISH
07 Director of Admissions .... Nicole CARTENSEN

Evangelia University (J)

2660 West Woodland Drive, Suite 200,
Anaheim CA 92801-2650
County: Orange Identification: 666640
Telephone: (714) 527-0691 Carnegie Class: Not Classified
FAX Number: (714) 527-0693 Calendar System: Other
URL: www.evangelia.edu
Established: 1999 Annual Undergrad Tuition & Fees: $2,880

Enrollment: 50 Coed
Affiliation or Control: Reformed Presbyterian Church IRS Status: 501(c)3
Highest Offering: Master's
Program: Liberal Arts And General; Religious Emphasis
Accreditation: @TRACS

01 President .... Dr. David H. SHIN
05 Academic Dean .... Bo Min LEE
11 Dean Admin/Chief Operating Officer .... Benjamin JEONG
06 Registrar/Foreign Student Advisor .... Charley LEE
57 Chair Masters of Arts Program .... Cha Hi WON
32 Dean of Students .... Ki Won HAN
20 Associate Academic Dean .... David KIM

Everest College-Anaheim (A)

511 N. Brookhurst, Ste 300, Anaheim CA 92801
County: Orange FICE Identification: 011107
Unit ID: 371982
Telephone: (714) 953-6500 Carnegie Class: Not Classified
FAX Number: (714) 953-4163 Calendar System: Quarter
URL: www.everest.edu/campus/anaheim
Established: 1969 Annual Undergrad Tuition & Fees: $16,305
Enrollment: 772 Coed
Affiliation or Control: Proprietary IRS Status: Proprietary
Highest Offering: Associate Degree
Program: Occupational
Accreditation: ACCSC

01 President .... Mr. Greg WAITE

Everest College-City of Industry (B)

12801 Crossroads Parkway S,
City of Industry CA 91746-3412
County: Los Angeles FICE Identification: 030426
Unit ID: 372037
Telephone: (562) 908-2500 Carnegie Class: Assoc/PrivFP
FAX Number: (562) 908-7656 Calendar System: Quarter
URL: www.everest-college.com
Established: 1989 Annual Undergrad Tuition & Fees: $13,518
Enrollment: 1,148 Coed
Affiliation or Control: Proprietary IRS Status: Proprietary
Highest Offering: Associate Degree
Program: Occupational
Accreditation: ACCSC, MAAB

01 President .... Ms. Sherry TOMAN

Everest College-Gardena (C)

1045 W. Redondo Beach Blvd, Ste 275,
Gardena CA 90247
County: Los Angeles FICE Identification: 011123
Unit ID: 119456
Telephone: (310) 527-7105 Carnegie Class: Not Classified
FAX Number: (310) 527-7985 Calendar System: Quarter
URL: www.everest.edu/campus/gardena
Established: N/A Annual Undergrad Tuition & Fees: $17,292
Enrollment: 758 Coed
Affiliation or Control: Proprietary IRS Status: Proprietary
Highest Offering: Associate Degree
Program: Occupational
Accreditation: ACCSC

01 Director/Admissions .... Mr. Victor ARIOLA

Everest College-Hayward (D)

22336 Main Street, 1st Floor, Hayward CA 94541
County: Alameda FICE Identification: 011121
Unit ID: 109332
Telephone: (510) 582-9500 Carnegie Class: Not Classified
FAX Number: (510) 537-9645 Calendar System: Quarter
URL: www.everest.edu/campus/hayward
Established: 2001 Annual Undergrad Tuition & Fees: $17,292
Enrollment: 420 Coed
Affiliation or Control: Proprietary IRS Status: Proprietary
Highest Offering: Associate Degree
Program: Occupational
Accreditation: ACCSC

01 Campus President .... Mr. Zae PERRIN

Everest College-LA Wilshire (E)

3460 Wilshire Blvd, Ste 500, Los Angeles CA 90010
County: Los Angeles FICE Identification: 007606
Unit ID: 119368
Telephone: (213) 388-9950 Carnegie Class: Not Classified
FAX Number: (213) 388-9907 Calendar System: Quarter
URL: www.everest.edu/campus/la_wilshire
Established: 1960 Annual Undergrad Tuition & Fees: $17,300
Enrollment: 341 Coed
Affiliation or Control: Proprietary IRS Status: Proprietary
Highest Offering: Associate Degree
Program: Occupational
Accreditation: ACCSC

01 President .... Mr. Rob LADENDECKER

Everest College-Ontario Metro (F)

1819 South Excise Avenue, Ontario CA 91761-8525
County: San Bernadino Identification: 666621
Unit ID: 440299
Telephone: (909) 484-4311 Carnegie Class: Not Classified
FAX Number: (909) 484-1162 Calendar System: Other
URL: www.everestcollege.edu
Established: 2002 Annual Undergrad Tuition & Fees: $13,572
Enrollment: 1,162 Coed
Affiliation or Control: Proprietary IRS Status: Proprietary
Highest Offering: Baccalaureate
Program: Occupational
Accreditation: ACICS

01 College President .... Mr. Richard MALLOW

† Branch campus of Everest College, Springfield, MO.

Everest College-Reseda (G)

18040 Sherman Way, Ste 400, Reseda CA 91335-4631
County: Los Angeles FICE Identification: 011109
Unit ID: 119359
Telephone: (818) 774-0550 Carnegie Class: Not Classified
FAX Number: (818) 774-1577 Calendar System: Quarter
URL: www.everest.edu/campus/reseda
Established: 1969 Annual Undergrad Tuition & Fees: $18,538
Enrollment: 864 Coed
Affiliation or Control: Proprietary IRS Status: Proprietary
Highest Offering: Associate Degree
Program: Occupational
Accreditation: ACCSC, MAAB

01 President .... Ms. Lani TOWNSEND

Everest College-San Bernardino (H)

217 Club Center Drive, Suite A, San Bernardino CA 92408
County: San Bernardino FICE Identification: 004494
Unit ID: 119508
Telephone: (909) 777-3300 Carnegie Class: Not Classified
FAX Number: (909) 777-3550 Calendar System: Other
URL: www.everest.edu/campus/san_bernardino
Established: 1969 Annual Undergrad Tuition & Fees: N/A
Enrollment: 847 Coed
Affiliation or Control: Proprietary IRS Status: Proprietary
Highest Offering: Associate Degree
Program: Occupational
Accreditation: ACICS, MAC

01 President .... Ms. Jennifer WHITE

† Tuition varies by degree program.

Everest College-West LA (I)

3000 S Robertson Boulevard, Ste 300,
Los Angeles CA 90034-3158
County: Los Angeles Identification: 666749
Unit ID: 368805
Telephone: (310) 840-5777 Carnegie Class: Assoc/PrivFP
FAX Number: (310) 287-2344 Calendar System: Quarter
URL: www.everest.edu/campus/west_los_angeles
Established: 1987 Annual Undergrad Tuition & Fees: $16,937
Enrollment: 340 Coed
Affiliation or Control: Proprietary IRS Status: Proprietary
Highest Offering: Associate Degree
Program: Occupational; 2-Year Principally Bachelor's Creditable
Accreditation: ACCSC, MAC

01 College President .... Mr. Michael NIELSEN

Expression College for Digital Arts (J)

6601 Shellmound Street, Emeryville CA 94608-1021
County: Alameda FICE Identification: 039733
Unit ID: 447458
Telephone: (510) 654-2934 Carnegie Class: Spec/Arts
FAX Number: (510) 658-3414 Calendar System: Quarter
URL: www.expression.edu
Established: 1999 Annual Undergrad Tuition & Fees: $18,750
Enrollment: 1,149 Coed
Affiliation or Control: Proprietary IRS Status: Proprietary
Highest Offering: Baccalaureate
Program: Professional
Accreditation: ACCSC

01 Executive Director .... Mr. Kirk ENGEL
88 Chief Creative Officer .... Mr. Spencer NILSEN

Fashion Careers College (K)

1923 Morena Boulevard, San Diego CA 92110-3555
County: San Diego FICE Identification: 022343
Unit ID: 114372
Telephone: (619) 275-4700 Carnegie Class: Assoc/PrivFP
FAX Number: (619) 275-0635 Calendar System: Quarter
URL: www.fashioncareerscollege.com
Established: 1979 Annual Undergrad Tuition & Fees: $23,150
Enrollment: 98 Coed
Affiliation or Control: Proprietary IRS Status: Proprietary
Highest Offering: Associate Degree
Program: Occupational
Accreditation: ACICS

00 Founder .... Ms. Patricia G. O'CONNOR
01 President .... Ms. Judy THACKER
10 Vice President/CFO .... Mr. Andrew BISAHA
36 Placement Director .... Ms. Fran LAMBERT
32 Director of Student Services .... Ms. Tanya MCANEAR
37 Financial Aid Director .... Ms. Alexis LYTLE
07 Admissions Advisor .... Ms. Saundra FLORES
06 Business Office Director/Registrar .... Mr. Peter MAMONIS, JR.
11 Office Manager .... Mr. Sean FOUST
88 Student Director/General Manager .... Ms. Karen ROQUE-SHAVER
05 Director of Education .... Ms. Susan SUAREZ
20 Assistant to Director of Education .... Ms. Sharlene BORROMEO

Fashion Institute of Design and Merchandising-Los Angeles (L)

919 S Grand Avenue, Los Angeles CA 90015-1421
County: Los Angeles FICE Identification: 011112
Unit ID: 114354
Telephone: (213) 624-1200 Carnegie Class: Spec/Arts
FAX Number: (213) 624-9354 Calendar System: Quarter
URL: www.fidm.edu
Established: 1969 Annual Undergrad Tuition & Fees: $25,586
Enrollment: 4,424 Coed
Affiliation or Control: Proprietary IRS Status: Proprietary
Highest Offering: Baccalaureate
Program: Occupational; 2-Year Principally Bachelor's Creditable; Business Emphasis
Accreditation: WC, WJ, ART

01 President .... Mrs. Tonian HOHBERG
10 Vice President Finance .... Ms. Annie JOHNSON
45 Vice President Planning .... Mrs. Vivien LOWY
05 Vice President Education .... Mrs. Barbara BUNDY
20 Dean of Academic Development .... Dr. Carol ROOKSTOOL
12 Director Orange County Campus .... Ms. Dorothy METCALFE
12 Director San Francisco Campus .... Ms. Barbara CUPPER
27 Exec Director Industry Relations .... Ms. Sharon RYAN
08 Director Library .... Ms. Kathy BAILON
06 Registrar .... Mr. Michael GILBERT
37 Director Financial Aid .... Ms. Norine FULLER
26 Director Public Relations .... Ms. Shirley WILSON
88 Director Adv Fashion Design .... Ms. Mary STEPHENS
09 Director Institutional Research .... Mrs. Andrea HELEKAR
38 Articulation Officer .... Mr. Ben WEINBERG
21 Director Student Financial Services .... Mr. Chris JENNINGS
96 Director of Purchasing .... Mrs. Darlene LATINVILLE
97 Chair General Educ/Dean Education .... Ms. Sheryl RABINOVICH
72 Chair Apparel Manufacturing Mgmt .... Ms. Roni MILLER START

Fashion Institute of Design and Merchandising-Orange County (M)

17590 Gillette Avenue, Irvine CA 92614-5610
County: Orange Identification: 666004
Unit ID: 114415
Telephone: (949) 851-6200 Carnegie Class: Assoc/PrivFP
FAX Number: (949) 851-6808 Calendar System: Quarter
URL: www.fidm.edu
Established: 1981 Annual Undergrad Tuition & Fees: $26,010
Enrollment: 395 Coed
Affiliation or Control: Proprietary IRS Status: Proprietary
Highest Offering: Baccalaureate
Program: Occupational; 2-Year Principally Bachelor's Creditable; Business Emphasis
Accreditation: &WJ, ART

01 Regional Campus Director .... Dorothy METCALFE
05 Regional Education Director .... Jim NEMMERT
07 Admission Director .... Mike MIRABELLA
36 Career Center Director .... Michelle PALTY
08 Branch Librarian .... Rebecca MARKMAN

† Regional accreditation is carried under the parent institution in Los Angeles, CA.

Fashion Institute of Design and Merchandising-San Diego (N)

350 10th Avenue, 3rd Floor, San Diego CA 92101
County: San Diego Identification: 666005
Unit ID: 248846
Telephone: (619) 235-2049 Carnegie Class: Assoc/PrivFP
FAX Number: (619) 232-4322 Calendar System: Quarter
URL: www.fidm.edu
Established: 1985 Annual Undergrad Tuition & Fees: $26,685
Enrollment: 287 Coed
Affiliation or Control: Proprietary IRS Status: Proprietary
Highest Offering: Associate Degree
Program: Occupational; 2-Year Principally Bachelor's Creditable; Business Emphasis
Accreditation: &WJ, ART

01 Campus Director .... Ms. Denise BACA
05 Education Director .... Ms. Katherine SLAUTA

07 Admissions Director .... Ms. Denise BACA

† Regional accreditation is carried under the parent institution in Los Angeles, CA.

Fashion Institute of Design and Merchandising-San Francisco (A)

55 Stockton Street, San Francisco CA 94108-5829
County: San Francisco FICE Identification: 013041
Unit ID: 114390
Telephone: (415) 675-5200 Carnegie Class: Assoc/PrivFP
FAX Number: (415) 296-7299 Calendar System: Quarter
URL: www.fidm.edu
Established: 1973 Annual Undergrad Tuition & Fees: $26,010
Enrollment: 933 Coed
Affiliation or Control: Proprietary IRS Status: Proprietary
Highest Offering: Associate Degree
Program: Occupational; 2-Year Principally Bachelor's Creditable; Business Emphasis
Accreditation: &WJ, ART

01 Campus Director .... Ms. Barbara CUPPER
05 Education Director .... Ms. Kim WETZEL

† Regional accreditation is carried under the parent institution in Los Angeles, CA.

Feather River College (B)

570 Golden Eagle Avenue, Quincy CA 95971-9124
County: Plumas FICE Identification: 008597
Unit ID: 114433
Telephone: (530) 283-0202 Carnegie Class: Assoc/Pub-R-M
FAX Number: (530) 283-3757 Calendar System: Semester
URL: www.frc.edu
Established: 1968 Annual Undergrad Tuition & Fees (In-District): $1,159
Enrollment: 3,360 Coed
Affiliation or Control: State/Local IRS Status: 501(c)3
Highest Offering: Associate Degree
Program: 2-Year Principally Bachelor's Creditable
Accreditation: WJ

01 Superintendent/President .... Dr. Ron TAYLOR
10 Chief Financial Officer .... Mr. Jim SCOUBES
05 Chief Instructional Officer .... Dr. Derek LERCH
32 Chief Student Services Officer .... Dr. Lisa KAUFMAN KELLY
15 Director Human Resources/EEO .... Ms. Jamie CANNON
18 Director of Facilities .... Mr. Nick BOYD
06 Registrar/Dir of Admissions .... Ms. Leslie MIKESELL
37 Director Student Financial Aid .... Ms. Barbara CORMACK
96 Purchasing Agent .... Ms. Tamara CLINE

Fielding Graduate University (C)

2112 Santa Barbara Street,
Santa Barbara CA 93105-3538
County: Santa Barbara FICE Identification: 020961
Unit ID: 114549
Telephone: (805) 687-1099 Carnegie Class: DRU
FAX Number: (805) 687-4590 Calendar System: Trimester
URL: www.fielding.edu
Established: 1974 Annual Graduate Tuition & Fees: $23,160
Enrollment: 1,565 Coed
Affiliation or Control: Independent Non-Profit IRS Status: 501(c)3
Highest Offering: Doctorate; No Undergraduates
Program: Professional
Accreditation: WC, #CLPSY

01 President .... Dr. Richard S. MEYERS
04 Assistant to the President .... Ms. Nancy OSBORNE
05 Provost .... Dr. Gloria WILLINGHAM
10 VP and Chief Financial Officer .... Ms. Lisa LEWIS
15 VP HR & Administration .... Dr. Anna MCDONALD
30 VP Advancement & Development .... Mr. David EDELMAN
46 Assoc Provost Research & Learning .... Dr. Daniel R. SEWELL
84 Assoc Provost Enrollment Mgmt .... Dr. Monique L. SNOWDEN
53 Dean School of Educ Ldrshp & Change .... Dr. Judy V. WITT
88 Dean School of Human & Org Dev .... Dr. Charles MCCLINTOCK
83 Interim Dean School of Psychology .... Dr. Gerardo RODRIGUEZ-MENENDEZ

Five Branches University: Graduate School of Traditional Chinese Medicine (D)

3031 Tisch Way, Ste 507, San Jose CA 95128
County: Santa Clara Identification: 667008
Telephone: (408) 260-0208 Carnegie Class: Not Classified
FAX Number: (408) 261-3166 Calendar System: Semester
URL: www.fivebranches.edu
Established: 2005 Annual Undergrad Tuition & Fees: $14,000
Enrollment: 275 Coed
Affiliation or Control: Independent Non-Profit IRS Status: 501(c)3
Highest Offering: Master's; No Lower Division
Program: Professional
Accreditation: ACUP

01 President/CEO .... Ron ZAIDMAN
05 VP Academic Affairs .... Joanna ZHAO
06 Registrar .... Gina HUANG
07 Associate Director of Admissions .... Nancy BURNS
10 Chief Financial Officer .... Liana CHEN
58 Associate Director Doctoral .... Candace LUO
58 Associate Director Doctoral .... E-Sing HONG
58 Director Chinese Masters of TCM .... Ching CHI
58 Director Korean Masters of TCM .... Heerei PARK

Five Branches University: Graduate School of Traditional Chinese Medicine (E)

200 7th Avenue, Santa Cruz CA 95062-4669
County: Santa Cruz FICE Identification: 031313
Unit ID: 114585
Telephone: (831) 476-9424 Carnegie Class: Spec/Health
FAX Number: (831) 476-8928 Calendar System: Semester
URL: www.fivebranches.edu
Established: 1984 Annual Undergrad Tuition & Fees: $14,000
Enrollment: 230 Coed
Affiliation or Control: Independent Non-Profit IRS Status: 501(c)3
Highest Offering: Master's; No Lower Division
Program: Professional
Accreditation: ACUP

01 President .... Ron ZAIDMAN
05 Academic Dean .... Joanna ZHAO
07 Admissions Director .... Eleonor MENDELSON
32 Director of Student Services .... Ana LOBATO
37 Director Student Financial Aid .... Mecca MATILDA
08 Librarian .... Jim EMDY
17 Clinic Director .... Joanna ZHAO
84 Director of Enrollment Management .... Ali POLK

*Foothill-De Anza Community College District System Office (F)

12345 El Monte Road, Los Altos Hills CA 94022-4597
County: Santa Clara FICE Identification: 009020
Unit ID: 114831
Telephone: (650) 949-6100 Carnegie Class: N/A
FAX Number: (650) 941-1638
URL: www.fhda.edu

01 Chancellor .... Dr. Linda THOR
10 Vice Chancellor Business Services .... Mr. Kevin MCELROY
16 Vice Chancellor Human Resources .... Ms. Dorene NOVOTNY
13 Vice Chancellor Technology .... Dr. Fred SHERMAN
18 Exec Dir Facility Oper/Constr Mgmt .... Mr. Charles ALLEN

*De Anza College (G)

21250 Stevens Creek Boulevard,
Cupertino CA 95014-5793
County: Santa Clara FICE Identification: 004480
Unit ID: 113333
Telephone: (408) 864-5678 Carnegie Class: Assoc/Pub-S-MC
FAX Number: (408) 864-5698 Calendar System: Quarter
URL: www.deanza.edu
Established: 1967 Annual Undergrad Tuition & Fees (In-District): $816
Enrollment: 23,280 Coed
Affiliation or Control: State/Local IRS Status: 501(c)3
Highest Offering: Associate Degree
Program: Occupational; 2-Year Principally Bachelor's Creditable
Accreditation: WJ, MLTAD

02 President .... Dr. Brian MURPHY
05 Vice Pres of Instruction .... Dr. Christina ESPINOSA-PIEB
32 Vice Pres of Student Services .... Ms. Stacy A. COOK
10 Vice Pres Finance/Educ Resources .... Ms. Letha JEANPIERRE
20 Dean of Academic Services .... Ms. Christina ESPINOSA PIEB
35 Dean Student Development/EOPS .... Ms. Michele LEBLEU BURNS
38 Int Dean Counseling & Matriculation .... Mr. Gordon POON
07 Dean Admissions & Records .... Ms. Kathleen MOBERG
37 Director Student Financial Aid .... Ms. Cindy CASTILLO
09 Director of Institutional Research .... Dr. Andrew LAMANQUE
15 Director Personnel Services .... Ms. Margaret MICHAELIS
18 Exec Dir Facilities/Physical Plant .... Mr. Charles ALLEN
21 Director Budget & Personnel .... Ms. Margaret MICHAELIS
26 Director Marketing/Communications .... Ms. Marisa SPATAFORE
30 Chief Development .... Ms. Marie FOX
84 Director Enrollment Management .. Ms. Christina ESPINOSA PIEB
28 Director of Diversity .... Vacant
96 Director of Purchasing .... Ms. Carmen REDMOND

*Foothill College (H)

12345 El Monte Road, Los Altos Hills CA 94022-4599
County: Santa Clara FICE Identification: 001199
Unit ID: 114716
Telephone: (650) 949-7777 Carnegie Class: Assoc/Pub-S-MC
FAX Number: (650) 949-7375 Calendar System: Quarter
URL: www.foothill.edu
Established: 1958 Annual Undergrad Tuition & Fees (In-District): $1,114
Enrollment: 16,896 Coed
Affiliation or Control: State/Local IRS Status: 501(c)3
Highest Offering: Associate Degree
Program: Occupational; 2-Year Principally Bachelor's Creditable
Accreditation: WJ, DA, DH, DMS, EMT, RAD

02 President .... Dr. Judy C. MINER
45 VP Instr/Educational Resources .... Dr. Shirley TREANOR
09 VP Instr/Institutional Research .... Ms. Kimberlee MESSINA
05 Int VP Instr/Student Development .... Dr. Denise SWETT
32 Dean Instruction/Student Affairs .... Ms. Patricia HYLAND
31 Dean Community Services .... Vacant
56 Dean Intl & Distance Education .... Mr. George S. BEERS
103 Interim VP of Workforce Education .... Mr. John MUMMERT
32 Dean Counseling/Student Services .... Ms. Laureen BALDUCCI
55 Dean Middlefield College .... Dr. Denise SWETT
15 Vice Chancellor Personnel Services .... Dr. Doreen NOVOTNY
102 Executive Director Foundation .... Ms. Sheryl ALEXANDER
26 Assoc VP of External Relations .... Mr. Kurt HUEG
19 Director & Chief of Police .... Mr. Ronald LEVINE
35 Dir Student Services & Activities .... Ms. Daphne SMALL
10 Chief Business Officer .... Mr. Kevin MCELROY
96 Director of Purchasing .... Ms. Carmen REDMOND
18 Manager Buildings & Grounds .... Ms. Marilyn WILLIAMS
40 Bookstore Manager .... Mr. Romeo PAULE
37 Manager Financial Aid .... Mr. Kevin HARRAL
88 Pgm Admin NASA Ames Internship .... Vacant
23 Coordinator Student Health Services .... Ms. Lorraine N. KITAJIMA
76 Div Dean Biology/Health Science .... Ms. Phyllis SPRAGGE
50 Interim Div Dean Bus/Social Science .... Mr. Glenn VIOLETTE
77 Div Dean Computer/Tech/Info Systems .... Ms. Judy BAKER
57 Div Dn Fine Arts/Communications .... Mr. Mark ANDERSON
88 Division Dean Language Arts .... Mr. Paul STARER
68 Int Div Dean PE/Human Performance .... Ms. Laurie BERTANI
81 Div Dean Physical Science/Math/Engr .... Dr. Peter MURRAY

Franciscan School of Theology (I)

1712 Euclid Avenue, Berkeley CA 94709-1294
County: Alameda FICE Identification: 011792
Unit ID: 114734
Telephone: (510) 848-5232 Carnegie Class: Spec/Faith
FAX Number: (510) 549-9466 Calendar System: Semester
URL: www.fst.edu
Established: 1968 Annual Graduate Tuition & Fees: $13,080
Enrollment: 64 Coed
Affiliation or Control: Independent Non-Profit IRS Status: 501(c)3
Highest Offering: Master's; No Undergraduates
Program: Professional
Accreditation: WC, THEOL

01 President .... Fr. Joseph CHINNICI, OFM
05 Dean .... Fr. William SHORT, SM
06 Registrar .... Ms. Jenna NIELSEN
07 Director of Admissions .... Mr. Vince NIMS
30 Associate Development Director .... Mr. Franklin FONG
10 Chief Financial Officer .... Ms. Carolyn RODKIN

Fremont College (J)

18000 Studebaker Road, 9th Floor, Cerritos CA 90703
County: Los Angeles FICE Identification: 030399
Unit ID: 372073
Telephone: (562) 809-5100 Carnegie Class: Assoc/PrivFP
FAX Number: (562) 809-7100 Calendar System: Other
URL: www.fremont.edu
Established: 1985 Annual Undergrad Tuition & Fees: N/A
Enrollment: 350 Coed
Affiliation or Control: Proprietary IRS Status: Proprietary
Highest Offering: Baccalaureate
Program: Occupational; 2-Year Principally Bachelor's Creditable
Accreditation: ACCSC

01 Chairman/CEO .... Dr. Sabrina KAY
11 Director of Operations .... Mr. Tony WONG
37 Asst Director of Financial Aid .... Ms. Jacqueline BUCKREIS

Fresno Pacific University (K)

1717 S Chestnut Avenue, Fresno CA 93702-4798
County: Fresno FICE Identification: 001253
Unit ID: 114813
Telephone: (559) 453-2000 Carnegie Class: Master's M
FAX Number: (559) 453-2007 Calendar System: Semester
URL: www.fresno.edu
Established: 1944 Annual Undergrad Tuition & Fees: $24,790
Enrollment: 3,314 Coed
Affiliation or Control: Mennonite Brethren Church IRS Status: 501(c)3
Highest Offering: Master's
Program: Liberal Arts And General; Teacher Preparatory
Accreditation: WC, NURSE

01 President .... Dr. D. Merrill EWERT
05 Interim Provost .... Dr. Stephen VARVIS
10 Vice President Business Affairs .... Ms. Diane CATLIN
30 Vice President for Advancement .... Mr. Mark DEFFENBACHER
13 Vice Pres of Information Services .... Mr. Alan OURS
50 Interim Dean School of Business .... Dr. Richard KREIGBAUM
79 Dean Sch of Humanities/Rel/Soc Sci .... Dr. Kevin REIMER
53 Dean School of Education .... Dr. Gary GRAMENZ
78 Dean School of Natural Sciences .... Dr. Karen CIANCI
42 Dean of Spiritual Formation .... Rev. Angulus WILSON
32 Dean of Student Life .... Dr. Randy WORDEN
06 Registrar .... Ms. Linda PRYCE-SHEEHAN
08 Interim Director of Library .... Mr. Kevin ENNS-REMPEL
36 Director of Career Resource Center .... Ms. Alicia ANDRADE
18 Facilities Manager .... Mr. Barry LOCKTON

15 Human Resources Director ... Mrs. Carol DEBELLIS
25 Director of Grants & Research ... Vacant
27 Publications Director ... Mr. Wayne STEFFEN
29 Alumni Director ... Mrs. Charity BROWN
37 Director of Financial Aid ... Ms. April POWELL
38 Counseling Coordinator ... Vacant
40 Bookstore Manager ... Ms. Erin NOEL
41 Athletic Director ... Mr. Dennis JANZEN
19 Director of Security ... Mr. Gary MEJIA
26 Chief Public Relations Officer ... Ms. Diana MOCK
28 Director of Diversity ... Vacant
07 Director of Admissions ... Ms. Rina CAMPBELL

Fuller Theological Seminary (A)

135 N Oakland, Pasadena CA 91182-1780
County: Los Angeles FICE Identification: 001200
Unit ID: 114840
Telephone: (626) 584-5200 Carnegie Class: Spec/Faith
FAX Number: (626) 584-5672 Calendar System: Quarter
URL: www.fuller.edu
Established: 1947 Annual Graduate Tuition & Fees: $16,908
Enrollment: 2,981 Coed
Affiliation or Control: Independent Non-Profit IRS Status: 501(c)3
Highest Offering: Doctorate; No Undergraduates
Program: Professional
Accreditation: WC, CLPSY, THEOL

01 President ... Dr. Richard J. MOUW
05 Provost & Sr Vice President ... Dr. C. Douglas MCCONNELL
10 Vice President for Finance ... Mr. John WARD
30 Vice President Seminary Advancement ... Mr. Joe B. WEBB
11 Executive VP for Administration ... Vacant
84 VP for Enrollment & Student Affairs ... Dr. Wendy WAKEMAN
73 Dean School of Theology ... Dr. Howard J. LOEWEN
88 Dean School of Psychology ... Dr. Winston E. GOODEN
88 Asst Dean Sch Intercultural Studies ... Ms. Toni WALKER
56 Assoc Provost Cont/Extended Educ ... Vacant
26 Assoc Vice Pres for Public Affairs ... Mr. Fred MESSICK
21 Asst Vice Pres for Finance ... Dr. David R. ADAMS
08 Assoc Provost Library Services & IT ... Dr. David BUNDY
73 Assoc Dean/Advanced Theol Studies ... Dr. Eugen MATEI
88 Assoc Dean School of Psychology ... Vacant
27 Asst Provost Library/IT & CIO ... Mr. Michael MURRAY
06 Registrar ... Mr. David E. KIEFER
14 Director Management Info Svcs ... Vacant
88 Assoc Dean Doctor of Ministry Pgm ... Mr. Kurt FREDRICKSON
15 Director of Human Resources ... Ms. Teresa LEWIS
32 Dean of Students ... Vacant
39 Director of Student Housing ... Mr. David SMITH
04 Exec Asst to President & Trustees ... Ms. Wendy WALKER
18 Director of Campus Facilities ... Mr. Randall R. SMITH
31 Director of Auxiliary Services ... Mrs. Jeanne HANDOJO
24 Director of Academic Tech Center ... Vacant
43 General Counsel ... Ms. Rita K. ROWLAND
29 Assoc VP Alumni & Church Rels ... Ms. Mary HUBBARD GIVEN
96 Director of Purchasing ... Ms. Silvia GUTIERREZ
36 Asst to Dean of Stdnts/Career Svcs ... Vacant
85 Dir Student Affs/International Svcs ... Mr. Sam BANG
37 Director Student Financial Services ... Mr. David RICHARDS
07 Assoc Director of Admissions ... Mr. Chad CAIN

Gavilan College (B)

5055 Santa Teresa Boulevard, Gilroy CA 95020-9599
County: Santa Clara FICE Identification: 001202
Unit ID: 114938
Telephone: (408) 848-4800 Carnegie Class: Assoc/Pub-S-SC
FAX Number: (408) 848-4801 Calendar System: Semester
URL: www.gavilan.edu
Established: 1919 Annual Undergrad Tuition & Fees (In-District): $918
Enrollment: 5,733 Coed
Affiliation or Control: State/Local IRS Status: 501(c)3
Highest Offering: Associate Degree
Program: Occupational; 2-Year Principally Bachelor's Creditable
Accreditation: WJ

01 Superintendent/President ... Dr. Steven M. KINSELLA
05 Exec Vice Pres Instructional Svcs ... Dr. Kathleen A. ROSE
11 Vice Pres Administrative Services ... Mr. Joseph KEELER
32 Vice President Student Services ... Mr. John PRUITT
06 Registrar ... Ms. Candice WHITNEY
08 Head Librarian ... Vacant
37 Director Student Financial Aid ... Ms. Veronica MARTINEZ
09 Director of Institutional Research ... Dr. Randy BROWN
15 Director Personnel Services ... Vacant
18 Chief Facilities/Physical Plant ... Mr. Jeff GOPP
13 Dir Computing & Information Mgmt ... Ms. Mimi ARVIZU
19 Director Security/Safety ... Ms. Ana HIPOL
26 Director Public Information ... Ms. Jan CHARGIN
23 Director Health Services ... Ms. Alice DUFRESNE-REYES
41 Athletic Director ... Mr. Ron HANNON
40 Director Bookstore ... Ms. Alexis BOLIN
49 Dean Liberal Arts/Sci/Dir Cont Educ ... Ms. Fran LOZANO
72 Dean Career Technical Education ... Ms. Sherrean CARR
07 Director of Admissions ... Ms. Candice WHITNEY

Glendale Community College (C)

1500 N Verdugo Road, Glendale CA 91208-2894
County: Los Angeles FICE Identification: 001203
Unit ID: 115001
Telephone: (818) 240-1000 Carnegie Class: Assoc/Pub-S-SC
FAX Number: (818) 549-9436 Calendar System: Semester
URL: www.glendale.edu
Established: 1927 Annual Undergrad Tuition & Fees (In-District): $878
Enrollment: 18,182 Coed
Affiliation or Control: State/Local IRS Status: 501(c)3
Highest Offering: Associate Degree
Program: Occupational; 2-Year Principally Bachelor's Creditable
Accreditation: WJ

01 Superintendent/President ... Dr. Dawn LINDSAY
11 Vice Pres Administrative Services ... Mr. Ron NAKASONE
05 Vice Pres Instructional Services ... Dr. Mary MIRCH
32 Vice President Student Services ... Dr. Ricardo PEREZ
31 Assoc VP Instruct Svcs Cont/Cmty Ed ... Dr. Karen HOLDEN-FERKICH
15 Associate Vice Pres Human Resources ... Ms. Vicki NICHOLSON
07 Dean Admissions/Records ... Ms. Sharon COMBS
45 Dean Research/Planning/Grants ... Dr. Edward KARPP
06 Registrar ... Ms. Michelle MORA
20 Dean of Instructional Services ... Dr. Kristin BRUNO
20 Dean of Instructional Services ... Mr. Ronald HARLAN
32 Dean Student Affairs ... Dr. Paul SCHLOSSMAN
35 Dean of Student Services ... Dr. Jewel A. PRICE
13 Dean Information & Technology ... Mr. Arnel PASCUA
08 Assoc Dean Library/Lrng Resource ... Ms. Brenda JONES
37 Associate Dean Financial Aid ... Dr. Patricia HURLEY
10 Int Director Business Services ... Ms. Susan COURTEY

Golden Gate Baptist Theological Seminary (D)

201 Seminary Drive, Mill Valley CA 94941-3197
County: Marin FICE Identification: 001204
Unit ID: 115047
Telephone: (415) 380-1300 Carnegie Class: Not Classified
FAX Number: (415) 383-1302 Calendar System: Semester
URL: www.ggbts.edu
Established: 1944 Annual Graduate Tuition & Fees: $5,040
Enrollment: 2,057 Coed
Affiliation or Control: Southern Baptist IRS Status: 501(c)3
Highest Offering: Doctorate; No Undergraduates
Program: Professional
Accreditation: WC, THEOL

00 President Emeritus ... Dr. William O. CREWS
01 President/Chairman of the Faculty ... Dr. Jeff IORG
30 Vice Pres Institutional Advancement ... Dr. Thomas O. JONES
10 Vice President Business & Finance ... Mr. Gary GROAT
05 Vice President Academic Affairs ... Dr. D. Michael MARTIN
84 VP Enrollment/Student Svcs/Dn Stdts ... Dr. Adam GROZA
21 Controller ... Mr. Harrison WEAVER
06 Registrar ... Ms. Jennifer PEACH
08 Director of Library Services ... Ms. Kelly CAMPBELL
12 Director SC Campus ... Dr. Reggie THOMAS
12 Director PNW Campus ... Dr. Mark BRADLEY
12 Director Arizona Campus ... Dr. David JOHNSON
12 Director Rocky Mountain Campus ... Dr. Steve VETETO
13 Director Information Technology ... Mr. Jeff COLBERT
15 Director Personnel Services ... Vacant
18 Chief Facilities/Physical Plant ... Mr. Robert DVORAK
40 Director Bookstore ... Mr. Darren DRAEGER
07 Director Admissions ... Ms. Karen ROBINSON
44 Director of Development ... Mr. Jeff JONES
84 Director Enrollment Management ... Ms. Karen ROBINSON
39 Resident Life Manager ... Mr. Shane TANIGAWA

Golden Gate University (E)

536 Mission Street, San Francisco CA 94105-2968
County: San Francisco FICE Identification: 001205
Unit ID: 115083
Telephone: (415) 442-7000 Carnegie Class: Master's L
FAX Number: (415) 495-2671 Calendar System: Trimester
URL: www.ggu.edu
Established: 1901 Annual Undergrad Tuition & Fees: $17,400
Enrollment: 3,778 Coed
Affiliation or Control: Independent Non-Profit IRS Status: 501(c)3
Highest Offering: Doctorate
Program: Professional; Business Emphasis
Accreditation: WC, LAW

01 President ... Dr. Daniel D. ANGEL
05 VP of Academic Affairs ... Ms. Barbara H. KARLIN
10 VP of Business Affairs & CFO ... Mr. Robert D. HITE
30 VP of University Advancement ... Ms. Elizabeth A. BRADY
13 Assoc VP Technology & Telecom ... Vacant
61 Dean School of Law ... Ms. Drucilla S. RAMEY
50 Dean Ageno School of Business ... Mr. Terry R. CONNELLY
88 Dean School of Taxation ... Ms. Mary CANNING
88 Dean School of Accounting ... Ms. Mary CANNING
49 Dean Undergraduate Programs ... Dr. Cherron HOPPES
100 Assistant to the President ... Dr. John FYFE
12 Dean Cyber Campus ... Mr. Marvin WEINBAUM
32 Dean of Students & Student Affairs ... Ms. Janine MIXON
08 Director University Library ... Ms. Janice CARTER
08 Associate Dean Law Library ... Mr. Michael DAW
15 Director Human Resources/EEO ... Ms. Terri SHULTIS
84 Director Enrollment Services ... Mr. Louis D. RICCARDI, JR.
06 University Registrar ... Mr. Steven LIND
27 Chief Information Officer ... Mr. Scott CILIBERTI
26 Director Marketing & Communications ... Ms. Tasia S. NEEVE
88 Director PLUS Program ... Dr. Karen MCROBIE
09 Dir Planning/Resources/Analysis ... Dr. Mercy LIM
18 Director Business Svcs/Facilities ... Mr. Mike KOPERSKI
21 Controller ... Ms. Sheryl KOGA
37 Director Student Financial Aid ... Mr. Steven LIND
38 Clinical Director/Counseling Svcs ... Ms. Michael Anne CONLEY

Golf Academy of America (F)

1950 Camino Vida Roble, Suite 125, Carlsbad CA 92008
County: San Diego FICE Identification: 015609
Unit ID: 122366
Telephone: (800) 342-7342 Carnegie Class: Assoc/PrivFP
FAX Number: (760) 734-1642 Calendar System: Semester
URL: www.golfacademy.edu
Established: 1974 Annual Undergrad Tuition & Fees: $33,824
Enrollment: 329 Coed
Affiliation or Control: Proprietary IRS Status: Proprietary
Highest Offering: Associate Degree
Program: Occupational; Business Emphasis
Accreditation: ACICS

01 President ... Mr. Chris HUNKLER
12 Campus Director ... Mr. Richard IORIO

† Branch campus of Virginia College, Birmingham, AL.

Grace Mission University (G)

1645 West Valencia Drive, Fullerton CA 92833-3860
County: Orange Identification: 666642
Telephone: (714) 525-0088 Carnegie Class: Not Classified
FAX Number: (714) 525-0089 Calendar System: Semester
URL: www.gmuedu.org
Established: 1995 Annual Undergrad Tuition & Fees: $5,420
Enrollment: 145 Coed
Affiliation or Control: Presbyterian Church In America IRS Status: 501(c)3
Highest Offering: Master's
Program: Professional; Religious Emphasis
Accreditation: @BI, @TRACS

01 President ... Kwangsin KIM
03 Executive Vice President ... Dr. Kyunam CHOI
05 Academic Dean ... Dr. Hyunwan KIM

Graduate Theological Union (H)

2400 Ridge Road, Berkeley CA 94709-1212
County: Alameda FICE Identification: 001207
Unit ID: 115214
Telephone: (510) 649-2400 Carnegie Class: Spec/Faith
FAX Number: (510) 649-1417 Calendar System: Semester
URL: www.gtu.edu
Established: 1962 Annual Graduate Tuition & Fees: $26,500
Enrollment: 256 Coed
Affiliation or Control: Independent Non-Profit IRS Status: 501(c)3
Highest Offering: Doctorate; No Undergraduates
Program: Professional; Religious Emphasis
Accreditation: WC, THEOL

01 President ... Dr. James A. DONAHUE
05 Dean/Vice Pres Academic Affairs ... Dr. Arthur HOLDER
10 Vice Pres Administration/Finance ... Mr. Steven G. ARGYRIS
30 Vice President for Advancement ... Vacant
32 VP Student Affairs/Dean Students ... Dr. Maureen A. MALONEY
07 Assistant Dean for Admissions ... Dr. Kathleen KOOK
08 Library Director ... Mr. Robert BENEDETTO
37 Dir Consortial Registration/Fin Aid ... Mr. Carlos PEREZ
13 Chief Information Officer ... Mr. Jeffrey DIGREORIO
26 Director of Communications ... Ms. Joanne BROWN
18 Building & Grounds Engineer ... Mr. Curtis OSBORNE
15 Personnel Officer ... Ms. Debi WALKER
44 Assoc Director of Major Gifts ... Vacant
04 Executive Assistant to President ... Ms. Teresa JOYE

*Grossmont-Cuyamaca Community College District (I)

8800 Grossmont College Drive, El Cajon CA 92020-1799
County: San Diego FICE Identification: 007006
Unit ID: 115287
Telephone: (619) 644-7010 Carnegie Class: N/A
FAX Number: (619) 644-7936
URL: www.gcccd.edu

01 Chancellor ... Dr. Cindy MILES
10 Vice Chanc Business Services ... Ms. Sue REARIC
16 Int Assoc Vice Chanc Human Res ... Mr. Don AVERILLL

*Cuyamaca College (J)

900 Rancho San Diego Parkway, El Cajon CA 92019-4304
County: San Diego FICE Identification: 021113
Unit ID: 113218
Telephone: (619) 660-4000 Carnegie Class: Assoc/Pub-S-MC
FAX Number: (619) 660-4399 Calendar System: Quarter
URL: www.cuyamaca.edu
Established: 1978 Annual Undergrad Tuition & Fees (In-District): $1,048
Enrollment: 10,239 Coed
Affiliation or Control: State/Local IRS Status: 501(c)3
Highest Offering: Associate Degree
Program: Occupational; 2-Year Principally Bachelor's Creditable
Accreditation: WJ

02 President .... Dr. Mark J. ZACOVIC
05 Vice President Instruction .... Dr. Robin STEINBACK
32 Vice Pres Student Svcs .... Dr. Julianna BARNES
11 Vice Pres Administrative Services .... Ms. Arleen SATELE
20 Dean of Instruction Div I .... Dr. Madelaine WOLFE
20 Dean of Instruction Div II .... Ms. Danene SOARES
51 Dean of Cont Edu/Workforce Training .... Dr. Darlene SPOOR
08 Dean Learning & TechnologyResources .... Ms. Connie ELDER
88 Acting Assistant Dean EOPS .... Ms. Nanyamka HILL
41 Assoc Dean Athletics/Athletic Dir .... Mr. Scott HERRIN
35 Assoc Dean Student Affairs .... Dr. Lauren WEINER
07 Dean Counseling & Enrollment Svc .... Ms. Susan TOPHAM
37 Director of Financial Aid .... Mr. Ray REYES
06 Acting Supv Admissions & Records .... Mr. Victor DEVORE
18 Facilities/Physical Plant .... Mr. Bruce FARNHAM

*Grossmont College (A)

8800 Grossmont College Drive, El Cajon CA 92020-1799
County: San Diego FICE Identification: 001208
Unit ID: 115296
Telephone: (619) 644-7000 Carnegie Class: Assoc/Pub-S-MC
FAX Number: (619) 644-7922 Calendar System: Semester
URL: www.grossmont.edu
Established: 1961 Annual Undergrad Tuition & Fees (In-District): $1,080
Enrollment: 19,783 Coed
Affiliation or Control: State/Local IRS Status: 501(c)3
Highest Offering: Associate Degree
Program: Occupational; 2-Year Principally Bachelor's Creditable
Accreditation: WJ, ADNUR, CVT, OTA

02 President .... Dr. Sunita COOKE
05 Vice Pres of Academic Affairs .... Dr. Barbara BLANCHARD
32 Vice President of Student Services .... Dr. John COLSON
38 Dean Counseling & Enrollment Svcs .... Dr. Wendy STEWART
72 Dean Career & Technical Workforce .... Mr. Fred ALLEN
81 Int Dean Math/Natural Sci/Phys Educ .... Dr. Chris HILL
60 Dean Arts/Languages/Communication .... Mr. Steve BAKER
79 Dean English/Social & Behav Sci .... Dr. Janet CASTANOS
08 Dean of Learning Resources .... Ms. Kerry KILBER
35 Associate Dean Student Affairs .... Mr. Agustin ALBARRAN
09 Director of Institutional Research .... Dr. Jerry BUCKLEY
10 Chief Business Officer .... Mr. Tim FLOOD
15 Director Personnel Services .... Ms. Amber GREEN
18 Chief Facilities/Physical Plant .... Mr. Tim FLOOD
26 Int Chief Public Relations Officer .... Mr. Rick GRIFFIN
36 Director Student Placement .... Ms. Nancy DAVIS
37 Director Student Financial Aid .... Mr. Michael COPENHAVER
96 Director of Purchasing .... Ms. Linda BERTOLUCCI

Hands-on Medical Massage School (B)

2015 Park Avenue, Redlands CA 92373
County: San Bernardino Identification: 667024
Telephone: (909) 793-4263 Carnegie Class: Not Classified
FAX Number: (909) 793-5763 Calendar System: Semester
URL: www.handsonmedicalmassage.com
Established: 2003 Annual Undergrad Tuition & Fees: N/A
Enrollment: N/A Coed
Affiliation or Control: Proprietary IRS Status: Proprietary
Highest Offering: Associate Degree
Program: Occupational
Accreditation: @COE

01 Director .... Ms. Carola JANIAK

Hartnell College (C)

411 Central Avenue, Salinas CA 93901-1697
County: Monterey FICE Identification: 001209
Unit ID: 115393
Telephone: (831) 755-6700 Carnegie Class: Assoc/Pub-R-L
FAX Number: (831) 755-6751 Calendar System: Semester
URL: www.hartnell.edu
Established: 1920 Annual Undergrad Tuition & Fees (In-District): $872
Enrollment: 9,812 Coed
Affiliation or Control: State/Local IRS Status: 501(c)3
Highest Offering: Associate Degree
Program: Occupational; 2-Year Principally Bachelor's Creditable
Accreditation: WJ

01 Superintendent/President .... Dr. Phoebe K. HELM
30 Vice President Advancement .... Ms. Beverly GROVA
32 VP Student Affairs/Athletics .... Dr. Esteban SORIANO
11 VP Support Operations .... Vacant
13 VP Information Systems .... Vacant
20 VP Academic Affairs .... Dr. Suzanne FLANNIGAN
68 Interim Dean Athletics .... Mr. Daniel TERESA
15 Assoc VP Human Resources/EEO .... Dr. Terri PYER
21 Controller .... Mr. Al MUNOZ
06 Dean Student Affairs .... Ms. Mary DOMINGUEZ

Harvey Mudd College (D)

301 Platt Boulevard, Claremont CA 91711-5990
County: Los Angeles FICE Identification: 001171
Unit ID: 115409
Telephone: (909) 621-8000 Carnegie Class: Bac/A&S
FAX Number: (909) 621-8360 Calendar System: Semester
URL: www.hmc.edu
Established: 1955 Annual Undergrad Tuition & Fees: $773
Enrollment: 42,410 Coed
Affiliation or Control: Independent Non-Profit IRS Status: 501(c)3
Highest Offering: Baccalaureate
Program: Liberal Arts And General; Professional; Technical Emphasis
Accreditation: WC, ENG

01 President .... Dr. Maria M. KLAWE
30 Vice President Advancement .... Mr. Marc ARCHAMBAULT
10 Vice President/Treasurer .... Mr. Andrew R. DORANTES
05 Dean of the Faculty .... Dr. Robert CAVE
07 Vice Pres/Dean of Admissions .... Ms. Thyra BRIGGS
32 Vice Pres/Dean of Students .... Dr. Marguerite BROWNING
13 VP/CIO .... Mr. Joseph VAUGHAN
09 Asst VP Institutional Research .... Dr. Janel H. HASTINGS
06 Registrar .... Ms. Noel KELLER
26 Director of College Relations .... Ms. Stephanie GRAHAM
28 Director Institutional Diversity .... Mr. Gary KELLY
15 Director of Human Resources .... Ms. Cynthia A. BECKWITH
18 Chief Facilities/Physical Plant .... Ms. Theresa POTTER
29 Director of Alumni Relations .... Vacant
37 Director of Student Financial Aid .... Ms. Gilma LOPEZ
20 Associate Academic Officer .... Vacant
101 Exec Asst to the Pres/Secy to Board .... Ms. Karen ANGEMI

*Heald College, Central Office (E)

601 Montgomery Street, 14th Floor,
San Francisco CA 94111-2618
County: San Francisco Identification: 666712
Telephone: (415) 808-1400 Carnegie Class: N/A
FAX Number: (415) 808-1598
URL: www.heald.edu

01 President/CEO .... Ms. Eeva DESHON
05 Sr VP/Chief Academic Ofcr .... Mr. Terry RAWLS

*Heald College, Concord (F)

5130 Commercial Circle, Concord CA 94520-5617
County: Contra Costa FICE Identification: 020798
Unit ID: 115533
Telephone: (925) 288-5800 Carnegie Class: Assoc/PrivFP
FAX Number: (925) 288-5896 Calendar System: Quarter
URL: www.heald.edu
Established: 1863 Annual Undergrad Tuition & Fees: $17,300
Enrollment: 1,015 Coed
Affiliation or Control: Proprietary IRS Status: Proprietary
Highest Offering: Associate Degree
Program: Occupational
Accreditation: &WJ, DA, MAC

02 Campus President .... Ms. Shirley LLAFET
03 Campus Vice President .... Mr. Keith WOODMAN
05 Dean of Educational Programs .... Mr. Kevin KENNY
07 Director of Admissions .... Mr. Dan CHEW
36 Director of Career Services .... Ms. Kimberly BOUTTE
10 Business Office Manager .... Ms. Amalia COTA

† Regional accreditation is carried under the parent institution Heald College, Central Office in San Francisco, CA

*Heald College, Fresno (G)

255 W Bullard Avenue, Fresno CA 93704-1706
County: Fresno FICE Identification: 008093
Unit ID: 115472
Telephone: (559) 438-4222 Carnegie Class: Assoc/PrivFP
FAX Number: (559) 438-6368 Calendar System: Quarter
URL: www.heald.edu
Established: 1863 Annual Undergrad Tuition & Fees: $14,790
Enrollment: 2,030 Coed
Affiliation or Control: Proprietary IRS Status: Proprietary
Highest Offering: Associate Degree
Program: Occupational
Accreditation: &WJ, MAC

02 Campus President .... Ms. Carolyn PIERCE
07 Senior Director of Admissions .... Ms. Tina MATHIS
05 Director of Academic Affairs .... Ms. Jenny SAECHAO
36 Director of Career Services .... Ms. Stephanie HAUSLADEN
10 Director of Financial Services .... Ms. Hortencia HODGE
37 Director of Financial Aid .... Mr. Kevin HOOVER
38 Director of Student Services .... Mr. Michael NEWTON
20 Assoc Director of Academic Affairs .... Ms. Pha MOUAVANGSOU
50 Business Program Director .... Mr. Randey PORTER
97 General Education Program Director .... Ms. Krista HALL
61 Criminal Justice Program Director .... Mr. Mike ROBISON
88 Paralegal Program Director .... Ms. Joanne ALLEN
72 Technology Program Director .... Mr. Michael BLACKSTON
76 Healthcare Program Director .... Ms. Darlene LISTOPAD
88 Med Insurance Billing/Codng Pgm Dir .... Ms. Pamela LOCKE
67 Pharmacy Technology Program Dir .... Ms. Denise WALSH

† Regional accreditation is carried under the parent institution Heald College, Central Office in San Francisco, CA

*Heald College, Hayward (H)

25500 Industrial Boulevard, Hayward CA 94545-2349
County: Alameda FICE Identification: 025929
Unit ID: 371779
Telephone: (510) 783-2100 Carnegie Class: Assoc/PrivFP
FAX Number: (510) 783-3287 Calendar System: Quarter
URL: www.heald.edu
Established: 1863 Annual Undergrad Tuition & Fees: $17,300
Enrollment: 1,105 Coed
Affiliation or Control: Proprietary IRS Status: Proprietary
Highest Offering: Associate Degree
Program: Occupational
Accreditation: &WJ, DA, MAC

02 Campus President .... Dr. Nick DAVIS
11 Regional VP/Campus Operations .... Ms. Barbara GORDON
05 Dean of Educational Programs .... Ms. Lisa RATTO
36 Director of Career Services .... Ms. Caren FLORES
07 Director of Admissions .... Mr. Jose SAES

† Regional accreditation is carried under the parent institution Heald College, Central Office in San Francisco, CA

*Heald College, Milpitas (I)

341 Great Mall Parkway, Milpitas CA 95035-8008
County: Santa Clara FICE Identification: 025932
Unit ID: 115490
Telephone: (408) 934-4900 Carnegie Class: Assoc/PrivFP
FAX Number: (408) 934-7777 Calendar System: Quarter
URL: www.heald.edu
Established: 1863 Annual Undergrad Tuition & Fees: $17,300
Enrollment: 890 Coed
Affiliation or Control: Proprietary IRS Status: Proprietary
Highest Offering: Associate Degree
Program: Occupational
Accreditation: &WJ, MAC

02 Campus President .... Mr. Elmo FRAZER
05 Dean of Educational Programs .... Dr. Nelly MANGRO
07 Director of Admissions .... Mr. Clarence HARDIMAN
36 Director of Career Services .... Ms. Joellen SUTTERFIELD
10 Business Office Manager .... Ms. Merrynoll BARRERA

† Regional accreditation is carried under the parent institution Heald College, Central Office in San Francisco, CA

*Heald College, Modesto (J)

5260 Pirrone Court, Salida CA 95368
County: Stanislaus Identification: 667043
Unit ID: 459930
Telephone: (209) 416-3700 Carnegie Class: Not Classified
FAX Number: (209) 416-3690 Calendar System: Quarter
URL: www.heald.edu
Established: N/A Annual Undergrad Tuition & Fees: $17,300
Enrollment: 287 Coed
Affiliation or Control: Proprietary IRS Status: Proprietary
Highest Offering: Associate Degree
Program: Occupational
Accreditation: &WJ

02 Campus President .... Mr. Ezra SALAS

† Regional accreditation is carried under the parent institution Heald College, Central Office in San Francisco, CA

*Heald College, Rancho Cordova (K)

2910 Prospect Park Drive,
Rancho Cordova CA 95670-6005
County: Sacramento FICE Identification: 007477
Unit ID: 115454
Telephone: (916) 638-1616 Carnegie Class: Assoc/PrivFP
FAX Number: (916) 638-1580 Calendar System: Quarter
URL: www.heald.edu
Established: 1863 Annual Undergrad Tuition & Fees: $14,650
Enrollment: 1,058 Coed
Affiliation or Control: Proprietary IRS Status: Proprietary
Highest Offering: Associate Degree
Program: Occupational; 2-Year Principally Bachelor's Creditable
Accreditation: &WJ, MAC

02 Campus President .... Ms. Ada GERARD
07 Director of Admissions .... Ms. Christi ARMES
05 Director of Academic Affairs .... Ms. Nancy PLUNKETT
36 Director of Career Services .... Ms. Lorraine BEAMAN
10 Director of Financial Services .... Mr. William (Bill) CAMPBELL

† Regional accreditation is carried under the parent institution Heald College, Central Office in San Francisco, CA

*Heald College, Roseville (L)

7 Sierra Gate Plaza, Roseville CA 95678-6602
County: Sacramento FICE Identification: 025931
Unit ID: 363387
Telephone: (916) 789-8600 Carnegie Class: Assoc/PrivFP
FAX Number: (916) 896-8616 Calendar System: Quarter
URL: www.heald.edu
Established: 1863 Annual Undergrad Tuition & Fees: $14,650
Enrollment: 1,039 Coed
Affiliation or Control: Proprietary IRS Status: Proprietary
Highest Offering: Associate Degree
Program: Occupational
Accreditation: &WJ, MAC

02 Campus President .... Mr. Guy ADAMS
05 Director Academic Affairs .... Mr. John ROTH

10 Business Manager .... Ms. Kaia RHODES
36 Director Career Services .... Ms. Tina RIVERA

† Regional accreditation is carried under the parent institution Heald College, Central Office in San Francisco, CA

*Heald College, Salinas (A)

1450 N Main Street, Salinas CA 93906-5100

County: Salinas FICE Identification: 030340
Unit ID: 409874
Telephone: (831) 443-1700 Carnegie Class: Assoc/PrivFP
FAX Number: (831) 443-1050 Calendar System: Quarter
URL: www.heald.edu
Established: 1863 Annual Undergrad Tuition & Fees: $13,095
Enrollment: 1,479 Coed
Affiliation or Control: Proprietary IRS Status: Proprietary
Highest Offering: Associate Degree
Program: Occupational
Accreditation: &WJ, MAC

02 Campus President .... Ms. Maria EMBRY
07 Director of Admissions .... Mr. Christian MORENO
10 Director of Financial Services .... Ms. Lolita PARIAN
05 Director of Academic Affairs .... Mr. Jorge GARCIA
36 Director of Career Services .... Ms. Belyn WILSON

† Regional accreditation is carried under the parent institution Heald College, Central Office in San Francisco, CA

*Heald College, San Francisco (B)

875 Howard Street, Suite 100,
San Francisco CA 94105-2206

County: San Francisco FICE Identification: 007234
Unit ID: 115515
Telephone: (415) 808-3000 Carnegie Class: Assoc/PrivFP
FAX Number: (415) 808-3005 Calendar System: Quarter
URL: www.heald.edu
Established: 1863 Annual Undergrad Tuition & Fees: $17,300
Enrollment: 482 Coed
Affiliation or Control: Proprietary IRS Status: Proprietary
Highest Offering: Associate Degree
Program: Occupational
Accreditation: &WJ, MAC

02 Campus President .... Ms. Debbie JONES
05 Director of Academic Affairs .... Mr. Robb ERSKINE
36 Director of Career Services .... Ms. Carolyn BURNS
07 Director of Admissions .... Mr. Cary KEPLAN
10 Business Manager .... Ms. Toi KAWAII

† Regional accreditation is carried under the parent institution Heald College, Central Office in San Francisco, CA

*Heald College, Stockton (C)

1605 E March Lane, Stockton CA 95210-6632

County: San Joaquin FICE Identification: 025933
Unit ID: 371760
Telephone: (209) 473-5200 Carnegie Class: Assoc/PrivFP
FAX Number: (209) 477-2739 Calendar System: Quarter
URL: www.heald.edu
Established: 1863 Annual Undergrad Tuition & Fees: $14,650
Enrollment: 1,545 Coed
Affiliation or Control: Proprietary IRS Status: Proprietary
Highest Offering: Associate Degree
Program: Occupational
Accreditation: &WJ, DA, MAC

02 Campus President .... Mr. Sandy LAMBA
05 Director of Academic Affairs .... Mrs. Lisa DIANDA
06 Registrar .... Mr. John WHEETLEY
07 Director of Admission .... Mrs. Hola MOTOUAPUAKA
10 Director of Financial Services .... Ms. Karen BOWERS
36 Director of Career Services .... Ms. Shalana PENNYWEIT

† Regional accreditation is carried under the parent institution Heald College, Central Office in San Francisco, CA

Hebrew Union College-Jewish Institute of Religion (California Branch) (D)

3077 University Avenue, Los Angeles CA 90007-3796

County: Los Angeles FICE Identification: 004055
Unit ID: 203049
Telephone: (213) 749-3424 Carnegie Class: Spec/Faith
FAX Number: (213) 747-6128 Calendar System: Other
URL: www.huc.edu
Established: 1875 Annual Undergrad Tuition & Fees: $21,000
Enrollment: 88 Coed
Affiliation or Control: Jewish IRS Status: 501(c)3
Highest Offering: Doctorate
Program: Teacher Preparatory; Professional; Religious Emphasis
Accreditation: &M

05 Dean .... Dr. Joshua HOLO
53 Director of School of Education .... Mr. Michael ZELDIN
58 Director of Graduate School .... Dr. Sharon GILLERMAN
73 Director of Judaic Studies .... Dr. Leah HOCHMAN
30 Director of Development West .... Ms. Fredi REMBAUGH
08 Librarian .... Dr. Yaffa WEISMAN
42 Director of Spiritual Growth .... Rabbi Richard LEVY
70 School Jewish Nonprofit Management .... Mr. Richard SIEGEL
32 Director of Student Life .... Ms. Madelyn KATZ
11 Director of Operations .... Ms. Joan SPEARMAN

† Regional accreditation is carried under the parent institution in New York, NY.

Henley-Putnam University (E)

25 Metro Drive, Suite 500, San Jose CA 95110-1339

County: Santa Clara Identification: 666120
Telephone: (408) 453-9900 Carnegie Class: Not Classified
FAX Number: (408) 453-9700 Calendar System: Quarter
URL: www.henley-putnam.edu
Established: 2001 Annual Undergrad Tuition & Fees: $23,760
Enrollment: N/A Coed
Affiliation or Control: Proprietary IRS Status: Proprietary
Highest Offering: Doctorate
Program: Professional
Accreditation: DETC

00 Chief Executive Officer .... Jim P. KILLIN
01 President .... Dr. Michael H. CORCORAN
05 Chief Academic Officer .... Dr. Tina PITT
07 Director of Admissions .... Nancy REGGIO
32 Dean of Student Services .... Patrick CLARK

Holy Names University (F)

3500 Mountain Boulevard, Oakland CA 94619-1699

County: Alameda FICE Identification: 001183
Unit ID: 115728
Telephone: (510) 436-1000 Carnegie Class: Master's M
FAX Number: (510) 436-1199 Calendar System: Semester
URL: www.hnu.edu
Established: 1868 Annual Undergrad Tuition & Fees: $30,050
Enrollment: 1,216 Coed
Affiliation or Control: Independent Non-Profit IRS Status: 501(c)3
Highest Offering: Master's
Program: Liberal Arts And General; Teacher Preparatory; Professional
Accreditation: WC, NURSE

01 President .... Dr. William J. HYNES
05 Vice President for Academic Affairs .... Dr. Lizbeth J. MARTIN
10 Vice President for Finance/Admin .... Mr. Stuart KOOP
32 Vice President for Student Affairs .... Mr. Michael S. MILLER
30 Vice President for Inst Advancement .... Ms. Davorka CVITKOVIC
37 Dean of Student Financial Services .... Mr. Murad DIBBINI
07 Dean of Admission & Recruiting .... Mr. Brian O'ROURKE
58 Director of ABD Program .... Ms. Nancy FLINN
06 Associate Registrar .... Ms. Jeanette CALIXTO
08 Director of Library Services .... Ms. Karen SCHNEIDER
37 Dir Student Financial Assistance .... Mr. Richard COLLINGS
31 Director Campus Services .... Mr. Luis GUERRA
42 Director of Campus Ministry .... Ms. Carrie REHAK
41 Director of Athletics .... Mr. Dennis JONES
26 Director Marketing/Communications .... Ms. Lesley SIMS
29 Director of Alumni Relations .... Mr. John MCCOY
13 Director Information Technology .... Ms. Elena OLKHOVSKAYA
19 Director Campus Safety .... Ms. Dana KIRKPATRICK
15 Director Human Resources .... Ms. Patricia BARTON

Hope International University (G)

2500 E Nutwood Avenue, Fullerton CA 92831-3104

County: Orange FICE Identification: 001252
Unit ID: 120537
Telephone: (714) 879-3901 Carnegie Class: Bac/Diverse
FAX Number: (714) 681-7451 Calendar System: 4/1/4
URL: www.hiu.edu
Established: 1928 Annual Undergrad Tuition & Fees: $23,600
Enrollment: 1,257 Coed
Affiliation or Control: Independent Non-Profit IRS Status: 501(c)3
Highest Offering: Master's
Program: 2-Year Principally Bachelor's Creditable; Liberal Arts And General; Teacher Preparatory; Professional; Religious Emphasis
Accreditation: WC, BI, MFCD

01 President .... Dr. John L. DERRY
05 Vice President for Academic Affairs .... Dr. Paul ALEXANDER
10 Vice President for Business/Finance .... Mr. Frank SCOTTI
30 Vice Pres Institutional Advancement .... Mr. Michael MULRYAN
32 Vice President for Student Affairs .... Mr. Mark COMEAUX
84 Vice Pres for Enrollment Management .... Mrs. Teresea I. SMITH
08 Librarian .... Mrs. Robin HARTMAN
06 Registrar .... Mr. Ron ARCHER
07 Director Undergraduate Admissions .... Mr. Butch ELLIS
37 Director of Financial Aid .... Mrs. Shannon O'SHIELDS
41 Athletic Director .... Mr. John TUREK
18 Director of Campus Facilities .... Mr. Steve MULLINS
09 Assc VP for Education Effectiveness .... Dr. Tamsen MURRAY
26 Chief Public Relations Officer .... Mr. Michael MULRYAN
36 Dir Student Career Svcs & Retention .... Ms. Beth I. LEE
38 Director Student Counseling .... Dr. Laura L. STEELE
42 Chaplain/Director Campus Ministry .... Vacant
85 Director of International Studies .... Ms. Weili C. LIN
49 Dean College of Arts and Sciences .... Dr. Steve EDGINGTON
53 Dean College of Education .... Dr. George E. WEST
50 Dean College of Business & Mgmt .... Dr. James WOEST
88 Dean College of Ministry & Bib Stds .... Dr. Joe GRANA
83 Dean College of Psych & Counseling .... Dr. Laura L. STEELE

Horizon College of San Diego (H)

5331 Mt Alifan Dr, San Diego CA 92111

County: San Diego FICE Identification: 041405
Unit ID: 457226
Telephone: (858) 695-8587 Carnegie Class: Not Classified
FAX Number: (858) 695-9527 Calendar System: Semester
URL: www.horizoncollege.org
Established: 1993 Annual Undergrad Tuition & Fees: $17,040
Enrollment: 107 Coed
Affiliation or Control: Independent Non-Profit IRS Status: 501(c)3
Highest Offering: Baccalaureate
Program: Liberal Arts And General; Religious Emphasis
Accreditation: @BI

01 President .... Mr. F. Chapin MARSH, III
32 Dean of Students .... Mr. Wayne KINDE

Humphreys College (I)

6650 Inglewood Street, Stockton CA 95207-3896

County: San Joaquin FICE Identification: 001212
Unit ID: 115773
Telephone: (209) 478-0800 Carnegie Class: Bac/Diverse
FAX Number: (209) 478-8721 Calendar System: Quarter
URL: www.humphreys.edu
Established: 1896 Annual Undergrad Tuition & Fees: $12,250
Enrollment: 1,175 Coed
Affiliation or Control: Independent Non-Profit IRS Status: 501(c)3
Highest Offering: First Professional Degree
Program: Liberal Arts And General; Professional
Accreditation: WC

01 President .... Dr. Robert G. HUMPHREYS
05 Dn Instruction/Dir Arts & Sciences .... Dr. Robert G. HUMPHREYS, JR.
11 Dean Administration/Ofc Admin Pgm .... Ms. Wilma OKAMOTO-VAUGHN
09 Dean of Institutional Research .... Mr. Jess BONDS
61 Dean Law School .... Mr. Patrick L. PIGGOTT
06 Registrar .... Ms. Maria GARCIA-MILLER
07 Dir Admission/Placement/Public Rels .... Ms. Santa LOPEZ
26 Chief Public Relations Officer .... Vacant
08 Head Librarian .... Dr. Stanislav PERKNER
88 Director Paralegal Studies .... Ms. Rowena WALKER
88 Director Court Reporting Program .... Mrs. Kay REINDL
10 Chief Business Officer .... Ms. Carol KRAMLICH
37 Director Student Financial Aid .... Ms. Rita FRANCO
20 Associate Dean of Instruction .... Ms. Cynthia BECERRA
13 Director of Information Services .... Mr. Fabian ECHEVARRIA

ICDC College (J)

5422 West Sunset Boulevard, Los Angeles CA 90027

County: Los Angeles FICE Identification: 033953
Unit ID: 437662
Telephone: (323) 468-0404 Carnegie Class: Not Classified
FAX Number: (323) 468-0417 Calendar System: Other
URL: www.learncareer.com
Established: N/A Annual Undergrad Tuition & Fees: $15,157
Enrollment: 3,194 Coed
Affiliation or Control: Proprietary IRS Status: Proprietary
Highest Offering: Associate Degree
Program: Occupational; 2-Year Principally Bachelor's Creditable
Accreditation: ACCSC

Imperial Valley College (K)

380 E Aten Road, Imperial CA 92251-0158

County: Imperial FICE Identification: 001214
Unit ID: 115861
Telephone: (760) 352-8320 Carnegie Class: Assoc/Pub-R-L
FAX Number: (760) 355-2663 Calendar System: Semester
URL: www.imperial.edu
Established: 1922 Annual Undergrad Tuition & Fees (In-District): $1,080
Enrollment: 8,991 Coed
Affiliation or Control: Local IRS Status: 501(c)3
Highest Offering: Associate Degree
Program: Occupational; 2-Year Principally Bachelor's Creditable
Accreditation: WJ, EMT

01 Int Superintendent/President .... Dr. Victor JAIME
05 Vice President Academic Services .... Mrs. Kathy BERRY
32 Int Vice President Student Services .... Ms. Janis MAGNO
10 Vice President Business Services .... Mr. John LAU
15 Assoc Vice President Human Services .... Mr. Travis GREGORY
13 Vice Pres Info Technology .... Mr. Todd FINNELL
103 Dean Economic & Worforce Develop .... Mr. Efrain SILVA
76 Dean of Health and Public Safety .... Mrs. Tina AGUIRRE
62 Dean Lrng Svcs/Instructional Tech .... Dr. Taylor RUHL
84 Dean of Enrollment Services .... Mrs. Jan MAGNO
38 Dean of Counseling .... Mr. Ted CEASAR
35 Dean Student Develop/Campus Events .... Mr. Sergio LOPEZ
07 Director of Admissions and Records .... Ms. Gloria CARMONA
37 Director of Financial Aid .... Ms. Lisa SEALS
09 Dir Research/Planning/Grant Admin .... Ms. Dawn CHUN
26 Dir of Media & Community Relations .... Mr. Bill GAY
59 Dir Child/Family/Consumer Sciences .... Ms. Rebecca GREEN

Infotech Career College (A)

16900 Lakewood Boulevard, Suite 209,
Bellflower CA 90706
County: Los Angeles FICE Identification: 041327
Unit ID: 450960
Telephone: (562) 804-1239 Carnegie Class: Not Classified
FAX Number: (562) 866-7739 Calendar System: Other
URL: www.infotech.edu
Established: 1998 Annual Undergrad Tuition & Fees: N/A
Enrollment: 276 Coed
Affiliation or Control: Proprietary IRS Status: Proprietary
Highest Offering: Associate Degree
Program: Occupational
Accreditation: #COE

01 School Director ....Ms. Amita GARG

Institute of Technology (B)

564 West Herndon Avenue, Clovis CA 93612
County: Fresno FICE Identification: 030675
Unit ID: 431141
Telephone: (559) 297-4500 Carnegie Class: Not Classified
FAX Number: (559) 297-5822 Calendar System: Semester
URL: www.it-colleges.edu
Established: N/A Annual Undergrad Tuition & Fees: N/A
Enrollment: 1,314 Coed
Affiliation or Control: Proprietary IRS Status: Proprietary
Highest Offering: Associate Degree
Program: Occupational; Technical Emphasis
Accreditation: ACCSC, ACFEI

01 President ....Joseph HAYDOCK

Institute of Transpersonal Psychology (C)

1069 E Meadow Circle, Palo Alto CA 94303-4231
County: Santa Clara FICE Identification: 022676
Unit ID: 110778
Telephone: (650) 493-4430 Carnegie Class: Spec/Health
FAX Number: (650) 493-6835 Calendar System: Quarter
URL: www.itp.edu
Established: 1975 Annual Graduate Tuition & Fees: $28,140
Enrollment: 446 Coed
Affiliation or Control: Independent Non-Profit IRS Status: 501(c)3
Highest Offering: Doctorate; No Undergraduates
Program: Professional
Accreditation: WC

01 President & CEO ....Dr. Neal KING
05 Provost/VP for Academic Affairs ....Dr. Paul ROY
10 CFO/VP for Finance/Compliance Ofcr ....Mr. Charles RANDALL

Interior Designers Institute (D)

1061 Camelback Road, Newport Beach CA 92660-3228
County: Orange FICE Identification: 025203
Unit ID: 116226
Telephone: (949) 675-4451 Carnegie Class: Spec/Arts
FAX Number: (949) 759-0667 Calendar System: Quarter
URL: www.idi.edu
Established: 1984 Annual Undergrad Tuition & Fees: $17,950
Enrollment: 317 Coed
Affiliation or Control: Proprietary IRS Status: Proprietary
Highest Offering: Master's
Program: Professional
Accreditation: ACCSC, CIDA

01 Executive Director ....Ms. Judy DEATON
37 Financial Aid Director ....Ms. Sharon DEATON

International Academy of Design and Technology (E)

2450 Del Paso Road, Sacramento CA 95834
Identification: 666740
Unit ID: 450447
Telephone: (916) 285-9468 Carnegie Class: Not Classified
FAX Number: (916) 285-6986 Calendar System: Other
URL: www.iadtsacramento.com
Established: 1977 Annual Undergrad Tuition & Fees: $17,000
Enrollment: 599 Coed
Affiliation or Control: Proprietary IRS Status: Proprietary
Highest Offering: Baccalaureate
Program: Fine Arts Emphasis
Accreditation: ACICS

01 President ....Ms. Patricia A. HOFFMAN

† Branch campus of International Academy of Design & Technology, Tampa, FL.

International Reformed University and Seminary (F)

125 S. Vermont Avenue, Los Angeles CA 90004
County: Los Angeles FICE Identification: 041357
Telephone: (213) 381-0081 Carnegie Class: Not Classified
FAX Number: (213) 381-0010 Calendar System: Semester
URL: www.iruniv.org
Established: 1979 Annual Undergrad Tuition & Fees: $4,500
Enrollment: 160 Coed
Affiliation or Control: Proprietary IRS Status: Proprietary
Highest Offering: First Professional Degree
Program: Religious Emphasis
Accreditation: @BI

01 Acting President ....Mr. John E. WHANG

International Technological University (G)

355 W. San Fernando Street, San Jose CA 95113
County: Santa Clara Identification: 667070
Telephone: (888) 488-4968 Carnegie Class: Not Classified
FAX Number: (408) 331-1026 Calendar System: Semester
URL: www.itu.edu
Established: 1994 Annual Graduate Tuition & Fees: N/A
Enrollment: 1,173 Coed
Affiliation or Control: Independent Non-Profit IRS Status: 501(c)3
Highest Offering: Doctorate; No Undergraduates
Program: Professional
Accreditation: @WC

01 Acting President ....Yau-Gene CHAN
05 Academic & Exec VP/CFO ....Dr. Gerald A. CORY

International Theological Seminary (H)

3225 Tyler Avenue, El Monte CA 91731-3355
County: Los Angeles Identification: 666360
Unit ID: 396985
Telephone: (626) 448-0023 Carnegie Class: Not Classified
FAX Number: (626) 350-6343 Calendar System: Quarter
URL: www.itsla.edu
Established: 1982 Annual Undergrad Tuition & Fees: $9,720
Enrollment: 85 Coed
Affiliation or Control: Independent Non-Profit IRS Status: 501(c)3
Highest Offering: Doctorate
Program: Religious Emphasis
Accreditation: THEOL

01 President ....Dr. C. Melvin LOUCKS
05 Academic Dean ....Dr. Jaretha J. JIMENA-PALMER
10 Vice President for Finance ....Mr. James LIM
06 Registrar ....Mr. Zhahui YANG
30 Vice Pres Seminary Advancement ....Dr. Peter CHOU

ITT Technical Institute (I)

362 N Clovis Avenue, Clovis CA 93612-0300
County: Fresno Identification: 666144
Unit ID: 448451
Telephone: (559) 325-5400 Carnegie Class: Assoc/PrivFP4
FAX Number: N/A Calendar System: Quarter
URL: www.itt-tech.edu
Established: 2006 Annual Undergrad Tuition & Fees: N/A
Enrollment: 598 Coed
Affiliation or Control: Proprietary IRS Status: Proprietary
Highest Offering: Baccalaureate
Program: Technical Emphasis
Accreditation: ACICS

† Branch campus of ITT Technical Institute, Rancho Cordova, CA.

ITT Technical Institute (J)

1140 Galaxy Way, Suite 400, Concord CA 94520
County: Contra Costa Identification: 666697
Unit ID: 456427
Telephone: (925) 674-8200 Carnegie Class: Not Classified
FAX Number: N/A Calendar System: Quarter
URL: www.itt-tech.edu
Established: N/A Annual Undergrad Tuition & Fees: N/A
Enrollment: 445 Coed
Affiliation or Control: Proprietary IRS Status: Proprietary
Highest Offering: Baccalaureate
Program: Technical Emphasis
Accreditation: ACICS

† Branch campus of ITT Technical Institute, San Bernardino, CA.

ITT Technical Institute (K)

16916 S Harlan Road, Lathrop CA 95330-8737
County: San Joaquin Identification: 666533
Unit ID: 437219
Telephone: (209) 858-0077 Carnegie Class: Spec/Tech
FAX Number: (209) 858-0277 Calendar System: Quarter
URL: www.itt-tech.edu
Established: 1997 Annual Undergrad Tuition & Fees: N/A
Enrollment: 723 Coed
Affiliation or Control: Proprietary IRS Status: Proprietary
Highest Offering: Baccalaureate
Program: Technical Emphasis
Accreditation: ACICS

† Branch campus of ITT Technical Institute, San Dimas, CA.

ITT Technical Institute (L)

4000 West Metropolitan Dr, Ste. 100, Orange CA 92868
County: Orange FICE Identification: 023219
Unit ID: 116484
Telephone: (714) 941-2400 Carnegie Class: Spec/Tech
FAX Number: (714) 535-1802 Calendar System: Quarter
URL: www.itt-tech.edu
Established: 1983 Annual Undergrad Tuition & Fees: N/A
Enrollment: 994 Coed
Affiliation or Control: Proprietary IRS Status: Proprietary
Highest Offering: Baccalaureate
Program: Technical Emphasis
Accreditation: ACICS

ITT Technical Institute (M)

2051 Solar Drive, Suite 150, Oxnard CA 93036-0641
County: Ventura Identification: 666534
Unit ID: 413848
Telephone: (805) 988-0143 Carnegie Class: Bac/Assoc
FAX Number: (805) 988-1813 Calendar System: Quarter
URL: www.itt-tech.edu
Established: 1993 Annual Undergrad Tuition & Fees: N/A
Enrollment: 474 Coed
Affiliation or Control: Proprietary IRS Status: Proprietary
Highest Offering: Baccalaureate
Program: Technical Emphasis
Accreditation: ACICS

† Branch campus of ITT Technical Institute, Sylmar, CA.

ITT Technical Institute (N)

10863 Gold Center Drive,
Rancho Cordova CA 95670-6034
County: Sacramento FICE Identification: 021209
Unit ID: 108250
Telephone: (916) 851-3900 Carnegie Class: Spec/Tech
FAX Number: (916) 851-9225 Calendar System: Quarter
URL: www.itt-tech.edu
Established: 1954 Annual Undergrad Tuition & Fees: N/A
Enrollment: 755 Coed
Affiliation or Control: Proprietary IRS Status: Proprietary
Highest Offering: Baccalaureate
Program: Technical Emphasis
Accreditation: ACICS

ITT Technical Institute (O)

670 E Carnegie Drive, San Bernardino CA 92408-3519
County: San Bernardino FICE Identification: 030704
Unit ID: 381909
Telephone: (909) 806-4600 Carnegie Class: Bac/Assoc
FAX Number: (909) 806-4699 Calendar System: Quarter
URL: www.itt-tech.edu
Established: 1986 Annual Undergrad Tuition & Fees: N/A
Enrollment: 1,513 Coed
Affiliation or Control: Proprietary IRS Status: Proprietary
Highest Offering: Baccalaureate
Program: Technical Emphasis
Accreditation: ACICS

ITT Technical Institute (P)

9680 Granite Ridge Drive, San Diego CA 92123-2662
County: San Diego FICE Identification: 022916
Unit ID: 116466
Telephone: (858) 571-8500 Carnegie Class: Spec/Tech
FAX Number: (858) 571-1277 Calendar System: Quarter
URL: www.itt-tech.edu
Established: 1981 Annual Undergrad Tuition & Fees: N/A
Enrollment: 1,654 Coed
Affiliation or Control: Proprietary IRS Status: Proprietary
Highest Offering: Baccalaureate
Program: Technical Emphasis
Accreditation: ACICS

ITT Technical Institute (Q)

650 W Cienega Avenue, San Dimas CA 91773-2933
County: Los Angeles FICE Identification: 022915
Unit ID: 116475
Telephone: (909) 971-2300 Carnegie Class: Spec/Tech
FAX Number: (626) 337-5271 Calendar System: Quarter
URL: www.itt-tech.edu
Established: 1982 Annual Undergrad Tuition & Fees: N/A
Enrollment: 907 Coed
Affiliation or Control: Proprietary IRS Status: Proprietary
Highest Offering: Baccalaureate
Program: Technical Emphasis
Accreditation: ACICS

ITT Technical Institute (R)

12669 Encinitas Avenue, Sylmar CA 91342-3664
County: Los Angeles FICE Identification: 023218
Unit ID: 244011
Telephone: (818) 364-5151 Carnegie Class: Bac/Assoc

FAX Number: (818) 364-5150 Calendar System: Quarter
URL: www.itt-tech.edu
Established: 1982 Annual Undergrad Tuition & Fees: N/A
Enrollment: 1,046 Coed
Affiliation or Control: Proprietary IRS Status: Proprietary
Highest Offering: Baccalaureate
Program: Technical Emphasis
Accreditation: ACICS

ITT Technical Institute (A)

2555 West 190th Street, Suite 125, Torrance CA 90504
County: Los Angeles FICE Identification: 030874
Unit ID: 378406
Telephone: (310) 965-5900 Carnegie Class: Spec/Tech
FAX Number: (310) 380-1557 Calendar System: Quarter
URL: www.itt-tech.edu
Established: 1986 Annual Undergrad Tuition & Fees: N/A
Enrollment: 905 Coed
Affiliation or Control: Proprietary IRS Status: Proprietary
Highest Offering: Baccalaureate
Program: Technical Emphasis
Accreditation: ACICS

John F. Kennedy University (B)

100 Ellinwood Way, Pleasant Hill CA 94523-4817
County: Contra Costa FICE Identification: 004484
Unit ID: 116712
Telephone: (925) 969-3300 Carnegie Class: Master's M
FAX Number: (925) 969-3399 Calendar System: Quarter
URL: www.jfku.edu
Established: 1964 Annual Undergrad Tuition & Fees: $19,275
Enrollment: 1,626 Coed
Affiliation or Control: Independent Non-Profit IRS Status: 501(c)3
Highest Offering: Doctorate
Program: Liberal Arts And General; Professional
Accreditation: WC, #CLPSY

01 President .... Dr. Steven A. STARGARDTER
10 CFO/Chief Operations Officer .... Ms. Ladene DIAMOND
05 Vice President of Academic Affairs .... Dr. Donald CAMPBELL
30 Vice President of Advancement .... Mrs. Anne Marie TAYLOR
09 Vice Pres of Institutional Research .... Dr. Sandi TATMAN
13 Director of Information Technology .... Ms. Mary HUNTER
15 Director of Human Resources .... Ms. Theresa ROGERS
61 College of Law Dean .... Mr. Dean BARBIERI
97 College of Undergraduate Studies .... Dr. Michael GRANEY-MULHOLLAND
58 College of Professional Studies .... Dr. Ruth FASSINGER
07 Interim Director Admissions .... Ms. Cathy SANTINI
37 Director Financial Aid .... Ms. Mindy BERGERON
06 Registrar .... Mr. Micheal RAINE
08 Acting University Librarian .... Mrs. Claudia CHESTER
18 Director of Facilities .... Mr. David L. SADLER

John Paul the Great Catholic University (C)

10174 Old Grove Road, Ste 200, San Diego CA 92131
County: San Diego Identification: 667072
Telephone: (858) 653-6740 Carnegie Class: Not Classified
FAX Number: (858) 653-3791 Calendar System: Quarter
URL: www.jpcatholic.com
Established: 2006 Annual Undergrad Tuition & Fees: N/A
Enrollment: N/A Coed
Affiliation or Control: Independent Non-Profit IRS Status: 501(c)3
Highest Offering: Master's
Program: Professional; Religious Emphasis
Accreditation: @WC

01 President .... Derry CONNOLLY
05 Provost .... Domini IUCCO
10 CFO .... Greg BREEN
11 VP for Administration .... Lidy CONNOLLY
88 VP for Strategic Partnerships .... Joe SZALKIEWICZ
32 Dean of Students .... Fr. Dan BARRON, OMV
88 Director of Film Production .... Tom DUNN
07 Dir of Admissions & Recruitment .... Martin HAROLD
13 Director of IT .... Kevin MEZIERE
37 Director of Financial Aid .... Lisa WILLIAMS
06 Registrar .... Liz MAMARIL
42 Chaplain .... Fr. Richard HUSTON

Kaplan College (D)

1914 Wible Road, Bakersfield CA 93304
County: Kerns Identification: 666291
Unit ID: 447102
Telephone: (661) 836-6300 Carnegie Class: Assoc/PrivFP
FAX Number: (661) 394-6056 Calendar System: Semester
URL: www.kaplancollege.edu
Established: 2005 Annual Undergrad Tuition & Fees: $14,401
Enrollment: 846 Coed
Affiliation or Control: Proprietary IRS Status: Proprietary
Highest Offering: Associate Degree
Program: Occupational
Accreditation: ACICS

01 President .... Ms. Mary WHITLOCK

† Branch campus of Kaplan College, Sacramento, CA.

Kaplan College (E)

14355 Roscoe Boulevard, Panorama City CA 91402-4222
County: Los Angeles FICE Identification: 030445
Unit ID: 424424
Telephone: (818) 672-3000 Carnegie Class: Assoc/PrivFP
FAX Number: (818) 672-8919 Calendar System: Other
URL: www.kaplancollege.edu
Established: 1996 Annual Undergrad Tuition & Fees: $14,648
Enrollment: 237 Coed
Affiliation or Control: Proprietary IRS Status: Proprietary
Highest Offering: Associate Degree
Program: 2-Year Principally Bachelor's Creditable
Accreditation: ACICS

01 Executive Director .... Mr. Bruno SABLAN

Kaplan College (F)

4330 Watt Avenue, Suite 400, Sacramento CA 95821-7000
County: Sacramento FICE Identification: 023519
Unit ID: 118259
Telephone: (916) 649-8168 Carnegie Class: Assoc/PrivFP
FAX Number: (916) 649-8344 Calendar System: Quarter
URL: www.kaplancollege.edu
Established: 1982 Annual Undergrad Tuition & Fees: N/A
Enrollment: 492 Coed
Affiliation or Control: Proprietary IRS Status: Proprietary
Highest Offering: Associate Degree
Program: Occupational
Accreditation: ACICS

01 Executive Director .... Lisia MOORE
05 Director of Education .... Kanita LIPJANKIC
37 Director of Student Financial Aid .... Vacant
07 Director of Admissions .... Keever JANKOVICH
36 Director of Career .... Julie MUIR

Kaplan College (G)

5172 Kiernan Court, Salida CA 95368
County: Stanislaus FICE Identification: 023063
Unit ID: 366960
Telephone: (209) 543-7000 Carnegie Class: Assoc/PrivFP
FAX Number: (209) 543-1755 Calendar System: Other
URL: www.kaplancollege.edu
Established: 2005 Annual Undergrad Tuition & Fees: $28,990
Enrollment: 610 Coed
Affiliation or Control: Proprietary IRS Status: Proprietary
Highest Offering: Associate Degree
Program: Occupational
Accreditation: ACCSC, MAAB

01 Executive Director .... Mr. Bill JONES

Kaplan College (H)

9055 Balboa Avenue, San Diego CA 92123-1509
County: San Diego FICE Identification: 020917
Unit ID: 118277
Telephone: (858) 279-4500 Carnegie Class: Assoc/PrivFP
FAX Number: (858) 279-4885 Calendar System: Other
URL: www.kaplancollege.com
Established: 1976 Annual Undergrad Tuition & Fees: $31,552
Enrollment: 1,521 Coed
Affiliation or Control: Proprietary IRS Status: Proprietary
Highest Offering: Associate Degree
Program: Occupational
Accreditation: ACCSC, MAAB

01 President .... Mr. Kevin PREHN
05 Director of Education .... Mr. Michael TURNER
11 Director of Operations .... Mr. David MOVSESIAN

Kaplan College (I)

722 West March Lane, Stockton CA 95207
County: San Joaquin FICE Identification: 025654
Unit ID: 384193
Telephone: (209) 462-8777 Carnegie Class: Not Classified
FAX Number: (209) 462-3219 Calendar System: Other
URL: stockton.kaplancollege.com
Established: 2005 Annual Undergrad Tuition & Fees: $12,807
Enrollment: 521 Coed
Affiliation or Control: Proprietary IRS Status: Proprietary
Highest Offering: Associate Degree
Program: Occupational
Accreditation: ACCSC, MAAB

01 Executive Director .... Mr. Robert BAYLES

Kaplan College (J)

2022 University Drive, Vista CA 92083-7736
County: San Diego FICE Identification: 025490
Unit ID: 118286
Telephone: (760) 630-1555 Carnegie Class: Assoc/PrivFP
FAX Number: (760) 630-1656 Calendar System: Quarter
URL: www.kaplancollege.com
Established: 1976 Annual Undergrad Tuition & Fees: $32,093
Enrollment: 1,210 Coed
Affiliation or Control: Proprietary IRS Status: Proprietary
Highest Offering: Associate Degree
Program: Occupational; Technical Emphasis
Accreditation: ACCSC, MAAB

01 Campus President .... Mr. Graham NOTT
05 Director of Education .... Mr. Mike WITTEMAN
07 Director of Admissions .... Ms. Renee CODNER
36 Director of Career Services .... Ms. Jaye BEATTY
37 Director of Financial Aid .... Ms. Kathy SMITH
66 Director of Nursing .... Ms. Beth BUNYI

Kensington College (K)

2428 N. Grand Avenue, Suite D, Santa Ana CA 92705-8708
County: Orange FICE Identification: 033083
Unit ID: 397270
Telephone: (714) 542-8086 Carnegie Class: Not Classified
FAX Number: (714) 245-2425 Calendar System: Semester
URL: www.kensingtoncollege.edu
Established: 1991 Annual Undergrad Tuition & Fees: $11,250
Enrollment: 40 Coed
Affiliation or Control: Proprietary IRS Status: Proprietary
Highest Offering: Master's
Program: Business Emphasis
Accreditation: ACICS

01 President .... Mr. Larry D. MADOSKI
58 Dean of Graduate Studies .... Dr. Guy LANGVARDT
37 Financial Aid Director .... Mr. Bobby PEPITO

*Kern Community College District (L)

2100 Chester Avenue, Bakersfield CA 93301-4099
County: Kern FICE Identification: 006994
Unit ID: 436313
Telephone: (661) 336-5100 Carnegie Class: N/A
FAX Number: (661) 336-5134
URL: www.kccd.edu

01 Chancellor .... Ms. Sandra V. SERRANO
05 Vice Chanc Educational Services .... Vacant
11 Vice Chanc Operations Management .... Mr. Sean P. JAMES
16 Vice Chanc Human Resources .... Mr. Abe ALI
10 Chief Financial Officer .... Mr. Tom J. BURKE
13 Asst Dir Information Technology .... Mr. David W. PALINSKY
91 Assistant Director Information Tech .... Mr. Eddie D. ALVARADO
43 General Counsel .... Mr. Frank W. RONICH

*Bakersfield College (M)

1801 Panorama Drive, Bakersfield CA 93305-1299
County: Kern FICE Identification: 001118
Unit ID: 109819
Telephone: (661) 395-4011 Carnegie Class: Assoc/Pub-U-MC
FAX Number: (661) 395-4241 Calendar System: Semester
URL: www.bakersfieldcollege.edu
Established: 1913 Annual Undergrad Tuition & Fees (In-District): $902
Enrollment: 19,512 Coed
Affiliation or Control: State/Local IRS Status: 501(c)3
Highest Offering: Associate Degree
Program: Occupational; 2-Year Principally Bachelor's Creditable
Accreditation: WJ, EMT, RAD

02 President .... Dr. Greg CHAMBERLAIN
05 Int Vice President Academic Affairs .... Ms. Nan GOMEZ-HEITZEBERG
32 Vice President Student Services .... Dr. Joyce ESTER
09 Dir Institutional Research/Planning .... Dr. Ann MORGAN
20 Dean of Student Learning .... Mr. Stephen EATON
90 Dean Learning Resources/Info Tech .... Dr. Bonnie SUDERMAN
88 Dean Learning Support Services .... Ms. Joyce COLEMAN
30 Director Foundation & Development .. Mr. Michael STEPANOVICH
11 Exec Dir Administrative Services .... Mr. LaMont SCHIERS
12 Director Delano Center .... Mr. Rich MCCROW
37 Director Financial Aid .... Mrs. Joan H. WEGNER
07 Director Enrollment Services .... Mrs. Suzanne A. VAUGHN
26 Director Marketing & Public Info .... Mrs. Amber CHIANG
04 Admin Assistant to the President .... Ms. Debborah SPOHN
13 Director Information Services .... Vacant
20 Dean of Student Learning .... Dr. Rebecca FLORES
66 Director of Nursing .... Ms. Cindy COLLIER
41 Director of Athletics .... Vacant
75 Dean Career & Tech Education .... Dr. Hamid EYDGAHI
20 Dean Instruction .... Dr. Daniel O'CONNOR

*Cerro Coso Community College (N)

College Heights Boulevard, Ridgecrest CA 93555-7777
County: Kern FICE Identification: 010111
Unit ID: 111896
Telephone: (760) 384-6100 Carnegie Class: Assoc/Pub-U-MC
FAX Number: (760) 375-4776 Calendar System: Semester
URL: www.cerrocoso.edu
Established: 1973 Annual Undergrad Tuition & Fees (In-District): $1,008
Enrollment: 6,482 Coed
Affiliation or Control: State/Local IRS Status: 501(c)3
Highest Offering: Associate Degree

Program: Occupational; 2-Year Principally Bachelor's Creditable
Accreditation: WJ

02 President ..... Ms. A. Jill BOARD
05 Vice President Academic Affairs ..... Dr. Corey MARVIN
32 Vice President of Student Services ..... Ms. Heather OSTASH
12 Dir Eastern Sierra College Center ..... Ms. Deanna CAMPBELL
12 Dir South Kern & Kern River Valley ..... Dr. Erie JOHNSON
75 Dean Career Technical Education ..... Ms. Valerie KARNES
21 Director of Admin Services ..... Ms. Gale LEBSOCK
38 Dir of Students & Counseling Svcs ..... Ms. Paula SUOREZ
37 Dir Financial Aid & Scholarships ..... Ms. JoAnn SPILLER
07 Dir Admiss/Records/Veteran Affs ..... Dr. David CORNELL
10 Accounting Manager ..... Ms. Lisa COUCH
15 Human Resources Manager ..... Mr. Clint DOUGHERTY
09 Institutional Researcher ..... Ms. Tina TUTTLE
88 Child Development Coordinator ..... Ms. Jennifer SAN NICOLAS
26 Public Rel/Marketing & Dev Mgr ..... Ms. Natalie DORRELL
13 Information Technology Manager ..... Mr. Michael CAMPBELL
41 Dir Student Programs & Athletics ..... Ms. Kimberlee KELLY

*Porterville College (A)

100 E College Avenue, Porterville CA 93257-6058
County: Tulare FICE Identification: 001268
Unit ID: 121363
Telephone: (559) 791-2200 Carnegie Class: Assoc/Pub-U-MC
FAX Number: (559) 784-4779 Calendar System: Semester
URL: www.portervillecollege.edu
Established: 1927 Annual Undergrad Tuition & Fees (In-District): $938
Enrollment: 4,110 Coed
Affiliation or Control: State/Local IRS Status: 501(c)3
Highest Offering: Associate Degree
Program: Occupational; 2-Year Principally Bachelor's Creditable
Accreditation: WJ

02 President ..... Dr. Rosa F. CARLSON
05 Vice President Academic Affairs ..... Dr. Ann BEHELER
32 Vice President Student Services ..... Mr. Steven SCHULTZ
04 Administrative Asst to President ..... Ms. Carol BROWN
20 Dean Academic Affairs ..... Dr. Antonia ECUNG
75 Dean Career & Technical Education ..... Mr. Bill HENRY
10 Director Administrative Services ..... Ms. Donna BERRY
18 Maintenance & Operations Manager ..... Mr. John WORD
06 Director Admissions/Records ..... Ms. Virginia GURROLA
26 Director Public Information ..... Mr. Will LLOYD
15 Human Resources Manager ..... Ms. Resa HESS
35 Student Programs/Athletics ..... Mr. Eric MENDOZA
09 Institutional Researcher ..... Mr. Michael CARLEY
08 Interim Director Library ..... Ms. Lorie BARKER
88 Director CalWorks/EOPS ..... Ms. Maria ROMAN
21 Accounting Manager ..... Ms. Sonia HUCKABAY
88 Program Manager Child Dev Center ..... Ms. Karen BALL
105 Graphic Designer/Website Coord ..... Ms. Randy MORGAN
13 Information Technology Manager ..... Mr. Chris CRAIG
37 Interim Director Financial Aid ..... Ms. Erin CRUZ

The King's University (B)

14800 Sherman Way, Los Angeles CA 91405-2233
County: Los Angeles FICE Identification: 035163
Unit ID: 439701
Telephone: (818) 779-8040 Carnegie Class: Spec/Faith
FAX Number: (818) 779-8241 Calendar System: Quarter
URL: www.kingsuniversity.edu
Established: 1997 Annual Undergrad Tuition & Fees: $9,675
Enrollment: 536 Coed
Affiliation or Control: Independent Non-Profit IRS Status: 501(c)3
Highest Offering: Doctorate
Program: Professional; Religious Emphasis
Accreditation: BI, TRACS

01 President ..... Dr. Jack W. HAYFORD
05 Exec VP & Chief Academic Officer ..... Dr. Paul G. CHAPPELL
10 Chief Business Officer ..... Mr. Dan J. DEHART
106 Dean Online Education ..... Prof. Donald C. BRUBAKER
58 Dean of Doctoral Programs ..... Dr. Wesley M. PINKHAM
09 Director of Institutional Research ..... Dr. Wesley M. PINKHAM
32 Chief Student Life Officer ..... Dr. Michael J. GREGG
07 Director of Admissions ..... Mrs. Marilyn J. CHAPPELL
06 Registrar ..... Mrs. Martha S. BRANTLEY
37 Director Student Financial Aid ... Mr. Norman V. STOPPENBRINK
08 Head Librarian ..... Prof. Barbara L. TARR
30 Chief Development ..... Mr. Lee S. MIMMS
18 Chief Facilities Physical Plant ..... Dr. Michael J. GREGG
13 Director Computing & Info Mgmt ... Mr. Edmond M. MUGWANYA
15 Director Personnel Services ..... Mrs. JoAnne L. HILL
38 Director Stdnt Counseling/Chaplain ..... Dr. Dale A. BUFFINGTON
36 Director Student Placement ..... Dr. Jody D. SMITH
106 Administrator Online Education ... Mr. Michael E. MCKENDRICKS
40 Director Bookstore ..... Mr. Michael B. CLEMENS
21 Student Accounts Officer ..... Ms. June M. HADLEY
90 Dir Acad Computing/Dir Student Affs ..... Prof. Donald C. BRUBAKER
29 Director Alumni Relations ..... Dr. Jody D. SMITH
96 Director of Purchasing ..... Mr. Michael B. CLEMENS
24 Director Educational Media ..... Mr. Irwin K. LOUIE
85 Director Foreign Students ..... Mrs. Marilyn J. CHAPPELL
28 Director of Diversity ..... Dr. Michael J. GREGG
102 Dir Foundation/Corporate Relations ..... Mr. Lee S. MIMMS
26 Chief Public Relations Officer ..... Mrs. Janis A. GORAIEB

LA College International (C)

3200 Wilshire Boulevard, #400,
Los Angeles CA 90010-1308
County: Los Angeles FICE Identification: 023124
Unit ID: 116040
Telephone: (213) 381-3333 Carnegie Class: Bac/Assoc
FAX Number: (213) 383-9369 Calendar System: Other
URL: www.lac.edu
Established: 1982 Annual Undergrad Tuition & Fees: $16,900
Enrollment: 156 Coed
Affiliation or Control: Proprietary IRS Status: Proprietary
Highest Offering: Baccalaureate
Program: Occupational; 2-Year Principally Bachelor's Creditable; Technical Emphasis
Accreditation: ACICS

01 Campus Director ..... Mr. Dean DUNBAR
05 Dir Academic Development/Education ..... Ms. Jodie RICE
07 Director of Admissions ..... Mr. Brian JENETTE
37 Financial Aid Director ..... Ms. Anastasia KLINE
36 Director of Student & Career Svcs ..... Vacant
13 IT Director ..... Mr. David KOPACK

La Sierra University (D)

4500 Riverwalk Parkway, Riverside CA 92515-8247
County: Riverside FICE Identification: 001215
Unit ID: 117627
Telephone: (951) 785-2000 Carnegie Class: Master's M
FAX Number: (951) 785-2901 Calendar System: Quarter
URL: www.lasierra.edu
Established: 1922 Annual Undergrad Tuition & Fees: $25,881
Enrollment: 2,096 Coed
Affiliation or Control: Seventh-day Adventist IRS Status: 501(c)3
Highest Offering: Doctorate
Program: Liberal Arts And General; Teacher Preparatory; Professional; Business Emphasis
Accreditation: WC, MUS, SW, @THEOL

01 President ..... Dr. Randal R. WISBEY
05 Provost ..... Dr. Steve PAWLUK
10 Vice President for Finance ..... Mr. David GERIGUIS
32 Vice President for Student Life ..... Ms. Yamilet BAZAN
30 Vice President Development ..... Dr. Jeffry M. KAATZ
84 Vice Pres Enrollment Services ..... Mr. David R. LOFTHOUSE
26 VP Communication/Integrated Mktg ..... Dr. Marilyn THOMSEN
21 Associate Vice President Finance ..... Ms. Pamela CHRISPENS
20 Associate Provost ..... Dr. Barbara FAVORITO
49 Dean College Arts/Sciences ..... Dr. James W. BEACH
50 Dean School of Business ..... Dr. John THOMAS
53 Dean School of Education ..... Dr. Clinton VALLEY
73 Dean School of Religion ..... Dr. John W. WEBSTER
35 Dean of Students ..... Ms. Sue CURTIS
26 Exec Dir University Relations ..... Mr. Larry BECKER
55 Director Adult Evening Program ..... Ms. Nancy DITTEMORE
29 Director Alumni Relations ..... Ms. Julie NARDUCCI
15 Director Human Resources ..... Ms. Dell Jean VAN FOSSEN
08 Director Library ..... Ms. Kitty SIMMONS
37 Director Student Financial Services ..... Ms. Esther KINZER
42 Director Campus Ministries ..... Mr. Samuel E. LEONOR, JR.
13 Director Information Technology ..... Mr. Geoff INGRAM
09 Director of Institutional Research ..... Mr. Guru UPPALA
18 Director Physical Plant ..... Mr. Al VALDEZ
38 Director Counseling Center ..... Ms. Minerva SAJJADI
92 Director Honors Program ..... Dr. Douglas R. CLARK
07 Director of Admissions/Registrar ..... Ms. Faye SWAYZE
36 Director Career Services ..... Mr. Natan VIGNA
96 Coordinator of Purchasing ..... Vacant

Laguna College of Art & Design (E)

2222 Laguna Canyon Road,
Laguna Beach CA 92651-1136
County: Orange FICE Identification: 023305
Unit ID: 117168
Telephone: (949) 376-6000 Carnegie Class: Spec/Arts
FAX Number: (949) 376-6009 Calendar System: Semester
URL: www.lcad.edu
Established: 1961 Annual Undergrad Tuition & Fees: $23,730
Enrollment: 448 Coed
Affiliation or Control: Independent Non-Profit IRS Status: 501(c)3
Highest Offering: Master's
Program: Professional
Accreditation: WC, ART

01 President ..... Dr. Jonathan BURKE
05 Vice President Academic Affairs ..... Dr. Helene GARRISON
30 Vice Pres of Development ..... Mr. Domenick IETO
07 Dean of Admissions ..... Mr. Mike RIVAS
10 Chief Financial Officer ..... Mr. Jim GODEK
06 Registrar ..... Ms. Laura PATRICK
08 Library Director ..... Ms. Jennifer WORMSER
04 Assistant to the President ..... Ms. Jennifer DANIELS
37 Dir Financial Aid/Student Services ..... Mr. Andy WU

Lake Tahoe Community College (F)

1 College Drive, South Lake Tahoe CA 96150-4524
County: El Dorado FICE Identification: 012907
Unit ID: 117195
Telephone: (530) 541-4660 Carnegie Class: Assoc/Pub-S-SC
FAX Number: (530) 541-7852 Calendar System: Quarter
URL: www.ltcc.edu
Established: 1975 Annual Undergrad Tuition & Fees (In-District): $876
Enrollment: 2,937 Coed
Affiliation or Control: State/Local IRS Status: 501(c)3
Highest Offering: Associate Degree
Program: Occupational; 2-Year Principally Bachelor's Creditable; Business Emphasis
Accreditation: WJ

01 Superintentent/President ..... Dr. Kindred MURILLO
04 Admin Assistant to President ..... Ms. Julie BOOTH
05 VP Academic Affs/Stdnt Svcs ..... Dr. Thomas GREENE
10 Vice President Business Services ..... Vacant
20 Dean of Instruction ..... Ms. Cynthea PRESTON
20 Interim Dean of Instruction ..... Mr. Kurt GREEN
08 Director of Library ..... Ms. Lisa FOLEY
07 Director of Admissions/Records ..... Ms. Cheri JONES
21 Director of Fiscal Services ..... Mr. Marc SABELLA
15 Director of Human Resources ..... Ms. Susan WALTER
18 Interim Director of Maintenance ..... Mr. Craig GRASTEIT
14 Director of Computer Services ..... Mr. Bill KING
88 Director Child Development Center ..... Ms. Michelle SOWER
37 Director Financial Aid ..... Ms. Julie CATHIE
75 Director of Vocational Education ..... Dr. Virginia BOYAR
09 Director of Institutional Research ..... Mr. Aaron MCVEAN
26 Public Information Officer ..... Ms. Christina PROCTOR
102 Foundation Director ..... Ms. Melonie GUTTRY
40 Bookstore Manager ..... Mr. Lor COLLIN
96 Purchasing Agent ..... Mr. Bob ROSEBLADE

Lassen Community College (G)

PO Box 3000, 478-200 Highway 139,
Susanville CA 96130-3000
County: Lassen FICE Identification: 001217
Unit ID: 117274
Telephone: (530) 257-6181 Carnegie Class: Assoc/Pub-R-M
FAX Number: (530) 251-8872 Calendar System: Semester
URL: www.lassencollege.edu
Established: 1925 Annual Undergrad Tuition & Fees (In-District): $647
Enrollment: 3,030 Coed
Affiliation or Control: State/Local IRS Status: 501(c)3
Highest Offering: Associate Degree
Program: Occupational; 2-Year Principally Bachelor's Creditable
Accreditation: WJ

01 District Superintendent/President ..... Mr. Bill STUDT
04 Assistant to President ..... Ms. Julie L. JOHNSTON
05 Vice Pres of Academic Affairs ..... Vacant
11 Dean of Administrative Services ..... Mr. Dave CLAUSEN
09 Dir Research/Assoc Dean Academics ..... Dr. Kayleigh CARABAJAL
08 Librarian ..... Vacant
37 Director Financial Aid ..... Mr. Matt LEVINE
35 Director Student Life ..... Mr. Francis BEAUJON
41 Athletic Director ..... Mr. John JONES
18 Chief Facilities/Physical Plant ..... Mr. Eric RULOFSON
15 Human Resources Manager ..... Ms. Vickie RAMSEY
14 Data Processing Manager ..... Vacant
40 Bookstore Manager ..... Ms. Heather PARKER

Le Cordon Bleu College of Culinary Arts in Los Angeles (H)

530 East Colorado Boulevard, Pasadena CA 91101
County: Los Angeles FICE Identification: 032103
Unit ID: 423980
Telephone: (626) 229-1300 Carnegie Class: Assoc/PrivFP
FAX Number: (626) 204-3907 Calendar System: Quarter
URL: www.chefs.edu/los-angeles
Established: 1994 Annual Undergrad Tuition & Fees: $47,910
Enrollment: 2,756 Coed
Affiliation or Control: Proprietary IRS Status: Proprietary
Highest Offering: Associate Degree
Program: Occupational
Accreditation: ACICS, ACFEI

01 President ..... Mr. Tony BONDI

Life Chiropractic College West (I)

25001 Industrial Boulevard, Hayward CA 94545-2801
County: Alameda FICE Identification: 022285
Unit ID: 117520
Telephone: (510) 780-4500 Carnegie Class: Spec/Health
FAX Number: (510) 780-4525 Calendar System: Quarter
URL: www.lifewest.edu
Established: 1976 Annual Undergrad Tuition & Fees: $20,400
Enrollment: 334 Coed
Affiliation or Control: Independent Non-Profit IRS Status: 501(c)3
Highest Offering: First Professional Degree; No Lower Division
Program: Professional
Accreditation: CHIRO

01 President ..... Dr. Brian KELLY
05 Dean ..... Dr. Joseph E. FERGUSON
10 Chief Financial Officer ..... Mr. Reza BADIEE
17 Dean of Clinic ..... Dr. Scott DONALDSON
51 Dean Postgraduate & Cont Education ..... Dr. Kendra HOLLOWAY
32 Dean of Students ..... Mrs. Jackie BIRON
30 Director Institutional Advancement ..... Ms. Cheryl NICKERSON

09 Director of Planning .... Dr. George C. CASEY
46 Research Director .... Dr. Dale JOHNSON
08 Director Library .... Ms. Annette OSENGA
07 Director of Admissions & Recruiting .... Mr. Carlos ALICEA
16 Human Resources Director .... Ms. Nilofer RAHIMI
40 Bookstore Director .... Ms. Toni MORLAN
37 Director Financial Aid .... Ms. Brenda R. JOHNSON
18 Chief Facilities/Physical Plant .... Mr. Ralph ROGERS
06 Manager Student Records .... Mrs. Robbie SHERWOOD
38 Academic Counselor .... Ms. Lori PINO

Life Pacific College (A)

1100 Covina Boulevard, San Dimas CA 91773-3298
County: Los Angeles FICE Identification: 022706
Unit ID: 117104
Telephone: (909) 599-5433 Carnegie Class: Spec/Faith
FAX Number: (909) 599-6690 Calendar System: Semester
URL: www.lifepacific.edu
Established: 1923 Annual Undergrad Tuition & Fees: $12,560
Enrollment: 509 Coed
Affiliation or Control: Other IRS Status: 501(c)3
Highest Offering: Baccalaureate
Program: Teacher Preparatory; Religious Emphasis
Accreditation: WC, BI

01 President .... Dr. Robert FLORES
04 Exec Assistant to the President .... Rev. Pasha JOHNSON
05 Vice President Academic Affairs .... Mr. Michael SALMEIER
32 Director Student Life .... Mr. Scott MARTZ
10 Chief Financial Officer .... Rev. Jarrod KULA
08 Librarian .... Mr. Keith DAWSON
06 Registrar .... Ms. Amber COFFEY
18 Director of Campus Operations .... Mr. Scott MARTZ
37 Director of Financial Aid .... Mrs. Becky HUYCK
20 Assoc Acad Dean NonTrad Pgms .... Rev. Brian TOMHAVE
30 Advancement Director .... Ms. Lynnette LOZOYA
40 Bookstore Director .... Mrs. Marilyn CLARK
09 Director of Institutional Research .... Rev. Bruce PRIMROSE
13 Director Information Technology .... Mr. Kenneth MILLER

Lincoln University (B)

401 15th Street, Oakland CA 94612-2801
County: Alameda FICE Identification: 006975
Unit ID: 117557
Telephone: (510) 628-8010 Carnegie Class: Master's S
FAX Number: (510) 628-8012 Calendar System: Semester
URL: www.lincolnuca.edu
Established: 1919 Annual Undergrad Tuition & Fees: $11,170
Enrollment: 542 Coed
Affiliation or Control: Independent Non-Profit IRS Status: 501(c)3
Highest Offering: Master's
Program: Liberal Arts And General; Professional; Business Emphasis
Accreditation: ACICS

01 President/Rector .... Dr. Mikhail BRODSKY
05 Dean .... Mr. William HESS
07 Director of Admissions & Records .... Ms. Peggy AU
08 Chief Librarian .... Ms. Nicole Y. MARSH
32 Director of Student Services .... Ms. Annique DALLEY
37 Chief Financial Aid Director .... Mr. James PETERSON
10 Controller .... Ms. Sherry LIANG
20 Asst Dean Academic Affairs .... Ms. Mariya ORSHANSKY

Logos Evangelical Seminary (C)

9358 Telstar Avenue, El Monte CA 91731-2816
County: Los Angeles FICE Identification: 039454
Unit ID: 397553
Telephone: (626) 571-5110 Carnegie Class: Not Classified
FAX Number: (626) 571-5119 Calendar System: Semester
URL: www.logos-seminary.edu
Established: 1989 Annual Graduate Tuition & Fees: $8,420
Enrollment: 153 Coed
Affiliation or Control: Other IRS Status: 501(c)3
Highest Offering: Doctorate; No Undergraduates
Program: Religious Emphasis
Accreditation: @WC, THEOL

01 President .... Dr. Felix LIU
05 Academic Dean .... Dr. Ekron CHEN
10 Director of Business Affairs .... Mr. Sonny GAN
32 Associate Dean of Students .... Mr. Godwin NGAI
30 Director of Advancement .... Mr. James YU

Loma Linda University (D)

Loma Linda CA 92350-0001
County: San Bernardino FICE Identification: 001218
Unit ID: 117636
Telephone: (909) 558-1000 Carnegie Class: Spec/Med
FAX Number: (909) 558-0242 Calendar System: Quarter
URL: www.llu.edu
Established: 1905 Annual Undergrad Tuition & Fees: $28,422
Enrollment: 4,359 Coed
Affiliation or Control: Seventh-day Adventist IRS Status: 501(c)3
Highest Offering: Doctorate
Program: Occupational; Liberal Arts And General; Professional
Accreditation: WC, ANEST, ARCPA, CLPSY, CYTO, DENT, DH, DIETC, DMS, MED, MFCD, MT, NURSE, OT, PH, PHAR, PTA, PTAA, RAD, RTT, SP, SW

01 President .... Dr. Richard H. HART
05 Provost .... Dr. Ronald L. CARTER
10 Sr Vice President Financial Affairs .... Mr. Rodney NEAL
30 Sr Vice President Advancement .... Mrs. Rachelle BUSSELL
27 Vice President Information Systems .... Dr. David P. HARRIS
84 VP Enrollment Mgmt/Student Services .... Dr. Rick E. WILLIAMS
63 Dean of Medicine .... Dr. H. Roger HADLEY
52 Dean of Dentistry .... Dr. Charles J. GOODACRE
69 Dean of Public Health .... Dr. Tricia Y. PENNIECOOK
66 Dean of Nursing .... Dr. Marilyn M. HERRMANN
76 Dean of Allied Health Professions .... Dr. Craig R. JACKSON
67 Dean School of Pharmacy .... Dr. W. William HUGHES
83 Dean Sch Science/Technology .... Dr. Beverly J. BUCKLES
73 Dean of School of Religion .... Dr. Jon PAULIEN
06 Director of Records .... Ms. Erin SEHEULT
58 Dean Faculty of Graduate Studies .... Dr. Anthony J. ZUCCARELLI
08 Director of University Libraries .... Ms. Carlene DRAKE
38 Director of Counseling .... Dr. William G. MURDOCH
43 General Legal Counsel .... Mr. Kent A. HANSEN
33 Dean of Men .... Mr. John NAFIE
34 Dean of Women .... Ms. Lynette BATES
37 Director Student Financial Aid .... Ms. Verdell SCHAEFER
09 Dir Educational Effectiveness .... Dr. Kirk CAMPBELL
15 Director Personnel Services .... Vacant
18 Director Campus Engineering .... Mr. Randy STEVENS
96 Director of Purchasing .... Mr. Tim HICKMAN
40 Campus Bookstore Manager .... Ms. Melodi HAMILTON
42 Campus Chaplain .... Pastor Terry SWENSON

Long Beach City College (E)

4901 E Carson Street, Long Beach CA 90808-1780
County: Los Angeles FICE Identification: 001219
Unit ID: 117645
Telephone: (562) 938-4111 Carnegie Class: Assoc/Pub-U-MC
FAX Number: (562) 938-4118 Calendar System: Semester
URL: www.lbcc.edu
Established: 1927 Annual Undergrad Tuition & Fees (In-District): $802
Enrollment: 26,517 Coed
Affiliation or Control: State/Local IRS Status: 501(c)3
Highest Offering: Associate Degree
Program: Occupational; 2-Year Principally Bachelor's Creditable
Accreditation: WJ, ADNUR

01 Superintendent-President .... Mr. Eloy OAKLEY
03 Executive VP Academic Affairs .... Mr. Donald BERZ
10 Vice Pres Administrative Services .... Ms. Ann-Marie GABEL
25 Vice Pres Econ & Resourc Devel .... Ms. Lou Anne BYNUM
16 Vice President Human Resources .... Ms. Rose DELGAUDIO
32 Vice Pres Student Support Services .... Dr. Greg PETERSON
12 Assoc Vice President PCC Campus .... Dr. Byron BRELAND
15 Assoc VP Human Resources .... Ms. Cindy VYSKOCIL
13 Assoc VP Instruct & Info Tech .... Mr. Jay FIELD
07 Dean Admissions/Records .... Mr. Ross MIYASHIRO
09 Dean Academic Services .... Dr. Meena SINGHAL
38 Dean Counseling/Stdt Support Svcs .... Dr. Kaneesha TARRANT
57 Dean Creative Arts/Applied Sciences .... Mr. Gary SCOTT
37 Dean Financial Aid Programs .... Mr. Michael MACCALLUM
88 Dean of Language Arts .... Dr. Jose Ramon NUNEZ
41 Director of Athletics .... Ms. Connie SEARS
32 Dean Student Affairs .... Ms. Sabrina SANDERS
76 Dean School Health & Science .... Mr. Paul CREASON
75 Dean Trades/Career Technolgy .... Dr. Gregory SCHULZ
102 Exec Director Foundation .... Dr. Ginny BAXTER
26 Exec Dir Public Affairs & Marketing .... Mr. Chi-Chung KEUNG
96 Director Business Support Services .... Mr. Mike COLLINS
45 Assoc Dean Inst Effectiveness .... Dr. Eva BAGG
18 Director of Facilities .... Mr. Tim WOOTTON
21 Director Fiscal Services & Payroll .... Mr. John THOMPSON
50 Dean Business and Social Science .... Ms. Laura WAN
88 Dean Student Success .... Dr. Bobbi VILLALOBOS

*Los Angeles Community College District Office (F)

770 Wilshire Boulevard, Los Angeles CA 90017
County: Los Angeles FICE Identification: 001221
Unit ID: 117681
Telephone: (213) 891-2000 Carnegie Class: N/A
FAX Number: N/A
URL: www.laccd.edu

01 Chancellor .... Dr. Daniel J. LAVISTA
43 General Counsel .... Ms. Camille A. GOULET
03 Deputy Chancellor .... Dr. Adriana D. BARRERA
05 VC Educ Support Svcs/Inst Effective .... Dr. Yasmin DELAHOUSSAYE
103 Vice Chanc Econ Workforce Devel .... Mr. Felicito CAJAYON

*East Los Angeles College (G)

1301 Avenida Cesar Chavez,
Monterey Park CA 91754-6001
County: Los Angeles FICE Identification: 022260
Unit ID: 113856
Telephone: (323) 265-8650 Carnegie Class: Assoc/Pub-U-MC
FAX Number: (323) 265-8763 Calendar System: Semester
URL: www.elac.edu
Established: 1945 Annual Undergrad Tuition & Fees (In-District): $958
Enrollment: 34,681 Coed
Affiliation or Control: State/Local IRS Status: 501(c)3
Highest Offering: Associate Degree
Program: Occupational; 2-Year Principally Bachelor's Creditable
Accreditation: WJ

02 President .... Mr. Ernest H. MORENO
05 VP Academic Affairs .... Dr. Richard MOYER
103 VP Workforce & Econ Devel .... Ms. Renee D. MARTINEZ
32 VP Student Services/Special Pgms .... Mr. Oscar VALERIANO
11 VP Administrative Services .... Mr. Tom FURUKAWA
88 Assoc VP Administrative Services .... Ms. Erlinda DE OCAMPO
20 Dean Academic Affairs Sciences .... Ms. Karen DAAR
88 Dean Academic Affairs Economic Dev .... Ms. Gayle BROSSEAU
36 Dean Academic Affs/Career Tech Educ .... Ms. Laura M. RAMIREZ
49 Dean Academic Affairs Liberal Arts .... Ms. Kerrin MCMAHAN
49 Dean Academic Affairs Liberal Arts .... Ms. Vi LY
07 Dean Admissions .... Mr. Jeremy P. ALLRED
12 Dean Academic Affairs Southgate Ctr .... Mr. Alfonso RIOS
30 Dean Resource & Institutional Dev .... Ms. Selina CHI
09 Dean Institutional Effectiveness .... Dr. Ryan CORNNER
51 Dean Continuing Education .... Ms. Adrienne A. MULLEN
35 Dean Student Activities .... Ms. Sonia LOPEZ
88 Dean EOP&S .... Ms. Danelle FALLERT
88 Dean CalWORKS .... Ms. Angelica TOLEDO
25 Assoc Dean Resource Development .... Dr. John RUDE
25 Assistant Dean Grants Management .... Ms. Martha ERMIAS
26 Chief Public Relations Officer .... Mr. Richard ANDERSON
22 Affirmative Action Officer .... Ms. Maria E. YEPES
37 Financial Aid Manager .... Ms. Lindy FONG
40 Director Student Store .... Ms. Joyce GARCIA
41 Athletic Director (Men/Women) .... Mr. Allen J. CONE
28 Director of Diversity .... Ms. Maria Elena YEPES
88 Child Development Director .... Mr. Michael SIMONE
38 Department Chair Counseling .... Mr. Daniel ORNELAS
21 College Fiscal Administrator .... Ms. Erlinda N. DEOCAMPO
08 Library Coordinator .... Ms. Choonhee L. RHIM
85 Foreign Student Advisement .... Ms. Nancy C. WONG
88 Director Vincent Price Art Museum .... Ms. Karen RAPP

*Los Angeles City College (H)

855 N Vermont Avenue, Los Angeles CA 90029-9990
County: Los Angeles FICE Identification: 001223
Unit ID: 117788
Telephone: (323) 953-4000 Carnegie Class: Assoc/Pub-U-MC
FAX Number: (323) 953-4013 Calendar System: Semester
URL: www.lacitycollege.edu
Established: 1929 Annual Undergrad Tuition & Fees (In-District): $1,080
Enrollment: 20,430 Coed
Affiliation or Control: Local IRS Status: 501(c)3
Highest Offering: Associate Degree
Program: Occupational; 2-Year Principally Bachelor's Creditable
Accreditation: WJ, DIETT, DT, RAD

02 President .... Dr. Jamillah K. MOORE
05 Int Vice President Academic Affairs .... Dr. Mary CALLAHAN
11 Vice President of Administration .... Mr. Paul CARLSON
32 Vice President of Student Services .... Dr. Lawrence BRADFORD
20 Acting Dean of Academic Affairs .... Dr. Thelma DAY
20 Dean of Academic Affairs .... Ms. Allison JONES
45 Dean Planning/Instl Effectiveness .... Dr. Edward PAI
84 Dean of Enrollment Services .... Mr. William MARMOLEJO
103 Dean Workforce Development .... Ms. A. Alex DAVIS
35 Assoc Dean Student Svcs Access .... Mr. Jeremy VILLAR
37 Assoc Dean Financial Aid .... Mr. Jeremy VILLAR
35 Assoc Dean Office of Student Life .... Mr. Earic PETERS
40 Bookstore Director .... Ms. Christi O'CONNOR
85 Director International Students .... Dr. Reginald BRADY
15 Human Resources Manager .... Ms. Lenore SAUNDERS
66 Nursing Department Chair .... Ms. Betsy MANCHESTER
38 Counseling Chairperson .... Ms. Reri PUMPHREY

*Los Angeles Harbor College (I)

1111 Figueroa Place, Wilmington CA 90744-2397
County: Los Angeles FICE Identification: 001224
Unit ID: 117690
Telephone: (310) 233-4000 Carnegie Class: Assoc/Pub-U-MC
FAX Number: (310) 233-4223 Calendar System: Semester
URL: www.lahc.edu
Established: 1949 Annual Undergrad Tuition & Fees (In-District): $938
Enrollment: 10,511 Coed
Affiliation or Control: State/Local IRS Status: 501(c)3
Highest Offering: Associate Degree
Program: Occupational; 2-Year Principally Bachelor's Creditable
Accreditation: WJ, ADNUR

02 President .... Mr. Marvin MARTINEZ
04 Executive Assistant to President .... Ms. Danielle JACK
05 Vice President Academic Affairs .... Mr. Luis M. ROSAS
11 Vice Pres Administrative Services .... Dr. Ann W. TOMLINSON
32 Vice President Student Services .... Mrs. Abbie L. PATTERSON
21 Assoc Vice Pres Administrative Svcs .... Mr. Nestor TAN
20 Dean of Academic Affairs .... Mrs. Kristi V. BLACKBURN
20 Dean of Academic Affairs .... Dr. David HUMPHREYS
07 Dean Admissions/Records/Eve Ops .... Mr. David M. CHING
35 Dean Student Life .... Ms. Nina R. MALONE
35 Dean Student Services .... Vacant
83 Div Chair Behavioral/Social Sci .... Mr. Bradley J. YOUNG
50 Division Chairperson Business .... Mr. Stanley C. SANDELL
60 Div Chairperson Communications .... Ms. Carmen CARRILLO
57 Div Chair Humanities/Fine Arts .... Mr. Mark D. WOOD
81 Div Chairperson Math/Phys Science .... Mr. Lauren J. MCKENZIE
76 Act Div Chairperson Health Sciences .... Ms. Lynn YAMAKAWA
68 Div Chairperson Physical Education .... Mr. Nabeel M. BARAKAT
88 Div Chrp Sci & Fam/Consum Stds .... Mrs. Joyce E. PARKER

08 Division Chairperson Library ... Mr. Jonathan LEE
38 Division Chairperson Counseling ... Mrs. Joy P. FISHER
09 Director of Institutional Research ... Dr. Robert RICHARDS
41 Athletic Director ... Mr. George SWADE
29 Dir Alumni Rels/Chief Development ... Vacant
37 Director Student Financial Aid ... Mrs. Sheila U. MILLMAN
18 Facilities Manager ... Mr. William C. ENGLERT
31 Community Services Manager .. Ms. Carla R. MUSSA-MULDOON
40 College Enterprise Manager ... Mr. Mark A. ZANKICH
85 Foreign Student Advisor ... Mr. Paul GRADY

*Los Angeles Mission College (A)

13356 Eldridge Avenue, Sylmar CA 91342-3244
County: Los Angeles FICE Identification: 012550
Unit ID: 117867
Telephone: (818) 364-7600 Carnegie Class: Assoc/Pub-U-MC
FAX Number: (818) 364-7826 Calendar System: Semester
URL: www.lamission.edu
Established: 1975 Annual Undergrad Tuition & Fees (In-District): $936
Enrollment: 11,357 Coed
Affiliation or Control: State/Local IRS Status: 501(c)3
Highest Offering: Associate Degree
Program: Occupational; 2-Year Principally Bachelor's Creditable
Accreditation: WJ

02 President ... Dr. Monte E. PEREZ
05 Vice President Academic Affairs . Ms. Alma JOHNSON-HAWKINS
11 Vice President Administrative Svcs ... Vacant
32 Vice President of Student Services ... Mr. Joe RAMIREZ
20 Dean of Academic Affairs ... Dr. Nadia SWERDLOW
88 Associate Dean of Academic Affairs ... Ms. Cathy BRINKMAN
88 Assistant Dean of Title V HSI ... Mrs. Susan RHI-KLEINERT
09 Act Dean Inst Rsrch/Plng/Info Tech ... Ms. Hanh TRAN
26 Chief Public Relations Officer ... Ms. Darlene MONTES
88 Director Child Development Center ... Ms. Monica MORENO
41 Athletic Director ... Mr. John KLITSNER
08 Head Librarian ... Ms. Sandy THOMSEN
38 Head Student Counseling ... Ms. Suzanne RITCHESON
37 Student Financial Aid Manager ... Mr. Dennis J. SCHROEDER
31 Community Services Manager ... Vacant
18 Chief Facilities/Physical Plant ... Mr. Walter J. BORTMAN
88 EOP & S/Care Director ... Ms. Ludi VILLEGAS-VIDAL

*Los Angeles Pierce College (B)

6201 Winnetka Avenue, Woodland Hills CA 91371-0001
County: Los Angeles FICE Identification: 001226
Unit ID: 117706
Telephone: (818) 347-0551 Carnegie Class: Assoc/Pub-U-MC
FAX Number: (818) 710-9844 Calendar System: Semester
URL: www.piercecollege.edu
Established: 1947 Annual Undergrad Tuition & Fees (In-District): $958
Enrollment: 21,230 Coed
Affiliation or Control: State/Local IRS Status: 501(c)3
Highest Offering: Associate Degree
Program: Occupational; 2-Year Principally Bachelor's Creditable
Accreditation: WJ, ADNUR

02 President ... Dr. Kathleen BURKE-KELLY
05 Vice President Academic Affairs ... Ms. Anna DAVIES
11 Vice President Administration ... Mr. Kenneth B. TAKEDA
32 Vice President Student Services ... Dr. Joy MCCASLIN
10 Assoc Vice President Admin Services ... Mr. Bruce ROSKY
10 Assoc Vice President Admin Services ... Mr. Larry KRAUS
08 Chairman Library Services ... Ms. Florence K. ROBIN
38 Chair Student Counseling ... Mr. Rudy DOMPE
20 Dean of Academic Affairs ... Mr. Paul WHALEN
20 Dean of Academic Affairs ... Dr. Donna Mae VILLANUEVA
07 Dean Admissions/Records ... Mr. Marco DE LA GARZA
35 Dean Student Services ... Ms. Phyllis BRAXTON
35 Dean Student Services ... Mr. David FOLLOSCO
37 Dean Financial Aid ... Mr. Marco DE LA GARZA
09 Director Institutional Research ... Ms. Carol KOZERACKI
26 Public Information Officer ... Ms. Doreen CLAY
31 Director Community Services ... Ms. Cindy CHANG
102 Director of Foundation ... Vacant
36 Director Student Placement ... Mr. Richard SKIDMORE
22 Compliance Officer ... Ms. Sylvia SILVA
18 Director of College Facilities ... Mr. Paul NIEMAN

*Los Angeles Southwest College (C)

1600 W Imperial Highway, Los Angeles CA 90047-4899
County: Los Angeles FICE Identification: 007047
Unit ID: 117715
Telephone: (323) 241-5225 Carnegie Class: Assoc/Pub-U-MC
FAX Number: (323) 241-5220 Calendar System: Semester
URL: www.lasc.edu
Established: 1967 Annual Undergrad Tuition & Fees (In-District): $1,102
Enrollment: 8,427 Coed
Affiliation or Control: State/Local IRS Status: 501(c)3
Highest Offering: Associate Degree
Program: Occupational; 2-Year Principally Bachelor's Creditable
Accreditation: WJ

02 President ... Dr. Jack E. DANIELS, III
03 Executive Vice President ... Ms. Trudy J. WALTON
10 Vice President Admin Services ... Mr. Ferris E. TRIMBLE
46 Dean Resource Development ... Ms. Felicia DUENAS
09 Dean Institutional Effectiveness ... Dr. Daniel WALDEN
103 Dean Workforce Development ... Dr. Elmer BUGG
05 Dean Academic Affairs ... Dr. Michael A. SUTLIFF
05 Dean Academic Affairs ... Ms. Stephanie L. BRASLEY
32 Dean Student Services ... Dr. Patrick JEFFERSON
38 Chairperson Counseling ... Mr. Reggie MORRIS
08 Chairperson Library ... Ms. Shelley WERTS
07 Sr Admissions & Records Supervisor . Ms. Kimberly CARPENTER
26 Public Relations Manager ... Dr. Louella BENSON
18 Director of College Facilities ... Mr. Randy CRAIG
37 Manager Student Financial Aid ... Ms. Kathleen STIGER
88 Dean TRIO ... Dr. Oscar COBIAN
04 Exec Asst to President ... Ms. Jessica MARTIN

*Los Angeles Trade-Technical College (D)

400 W Washington Boulevard,
Los Angeles CA 90015-4108
County: Los Angeles FICE Identification: 001227
Unit ID: 117724
Telephone: (213) 763-7000 Carnegie Class: Assoc/Pub-U-MC
FAX Number: (213) 763-5393 Calendar System: Semester
URL: www.lattc.edu
Established: 1925 Annual Undergrad Tuition & Fees (In-District): $1,080
Enrollment: 16,066 Coed
Affiliation or Control: State/Local IRS Status: 501(c)3
Highest Offering: Associate Degree
Program: Occupational; 2-Year Principally Bachelor's Creditable
Accreditation: WJ, ACFEI

02 President ... Dr. Roland CHAPDELAINE
05 Vice President of Academic Affairs ... Vacant
11 Vice President Administration ... Dr. Mary GALLAGHER
103 Vice President Workforce Devel ... Ms. Marcy J. DRUMMOND
32 Vice President Student Services ... Mr. Ramon S. CASTILLO
21 Assoc Vice Pres Administrative Svcs ... Mr. William GASPER
35 Dean Student Services ... Vacant
20 Dean of Academic Affairs ... Mr. Vincent JACKSON
20 Dean Academic Affairs ... Ms. Cynthia MORLEY-MOWER
20 Dean Academic Affairs ... Ms. Leticia BARAJAS
84 Dean Enrollment Management ... Dr. Raul CARDOZA
37 Manager Financial Aid/EOP&S ... Ms. Cecilia KWAN
09 Dean Research & Planning ... Ms. Anna BADALYAN
88 Dean Matriculation/Student Success ... Ms. Dorothy SMITH
35 Associate Dean Student Services ... Mr. Luis DORADO
18 Chief Facilities/Physical Plant ... Mr. Bill SMITH
06 Registrar ... Ms. Carolyn CLARK
10 Chief Business Officer ... Mr. Marcus ANGLIN
38 Chair Student Counseling ... Mr. Maurice BURNETT
96 Director of Purchasing ... Mr. Galen BULLOCK
102 Director Foundation/Corporate Rels ... Dr. Rhea CHUNG
26 Public Relations Manager ... Mr. David YSAIS

*Los Angeles Valley College (E)

5800 Fulton Avenue, Valley Glen CA 91401-4096
County: Los Angeles FICE Identification: 001228
Unit ID: 117733
Telephone: (818) 947-2600 Carnegie Class: Assoc/Pub-U-MC
FAX Number: (818) 947-2602 Calendar System: Semester
URL: www.lavc.edu
Established: 1949 Annual Undergrad Tuition & Fees (In-District): $444
Enrollment: 19,888 Coed
Affiliation or Control: State/Local IRS Status: 501(c)3
Highest Offering: Associate Degree
Program: Occupational; 2-Year Principally Bachelor's Creditable
Accreditation: WJ, ADNUR

02 President ... Dr. A. Susan CARLEO
05 Vice President Academic Affairs ... Dr. Sandra L. MAYO
10 Vice Pres Administrative Services ... Mr. Tom V. JACOBSMEYER
32 Acting Vice Pres Student Services ... Mr. Florentino MANZANO
11 Assoc Vice Pres Administrative Svcs ... Mr. Raul D. GONZALEZ
21 Financial Analyst ... Ms. Violet AMRIKHAS
45 Chief Financial Anaylist ... Mr. Tom HILTABIDDLE
20 Dean Academic Affairs ... Dr. Laurie NALEPA
20 Dean Academic Affairs ... Dr. Carole YEE
20 Dean Academic Affairs ... Mr. Dennis J. REED
88 Dean Economic Development ... Dr. Deborah A. DICESARE
84 Dean of Enrollment Services ... Vacant
08 Chairperson of Library Service ... Ms. Georgianna W. SAMPLER
37 Financial Aid Manager ... Vacant
09 Dean Research & Planning ... Ms. Michelle R. FOWLES
35 Associate Dean Student Services ... Ms. Elizabeth ORTIZ
88 Associate Dean of EOPS ... Dr. Sherri RODRIGUEZ
88 Associate Dean DSPS ... Mr. David M. GREEN
35 Assoc Dean of Student Services ... Ms. Annie G. REED
102 Director Foundation/Alumni Rels ... Mr. Raul V. CASTILLO
26 Public Relations Manager ... Ms. Jennifer C. FONG
18 Director of College Facilities ... Mr. Tom LOPEZ
40 Bookstore Manager ... Vacant
13 Manager College Info Svcs ... Mr. Aaron WEATHERSBY
31 Community Services Manager ... Mr. Michael B. ATKIN
38 Director Student Counseling ... Ms. Barbara GOLDBERG
22 Compliance Officer ... Ms. Charmagne SHEARRILL
41 Athletic Director ... Ms. Deidra STARK

*West Los Angeles College (F)

9000 Overland Avenue, Culver City CA 90230-5002
County: Los Angeles FICE Identification: 008596
Unit ID: 125471
Telephone: (310) 287-4200 Carnegie Class: Assoc/Pub-U-MC
FAX Number: (310) 841-0396 Calendar System: Semester
URL: www.wlac.edu
Established: 1969 Annual Undergrad Tuition & Fees (In-District): $1,118
Enrollment: 11,140 Coed
Affiliation or Control: State/Local IRS Status: 501(c)3
Highest Offering: Associate Degree
Program: Occupational; 2-Year Principally Bachelor's Creditable
Accreditation: WJ, DH

02 President ... Mr. Nabil S. ABU-GHAZALEH
11 Vice President Administrative Svcs ... Mr. John R. OESTER
05 Vice President Academic Affairs ... Mr. Robert L. SPRAGUE
32 Vice President Student Services ... Ms. Betsy A. REGALADO
45 Dean Institutional Effectivness ... Vacant
84 Dean Student Svcs Enrollment ... Mr. John M. GOLTERMANN
97 Dean General Education/Transfer ... Dr. Judith Ann FRIEDMAN
20 Dean Advance Program Development ... Mr. Mark PRACHER
75 Dean Career/Technology Education ... Ms. Ara AGUIAR
35 Dean of Student Support Services ... Dr. Shalamon DUKE
09 Dean of Research and Planning ... Ms. Rebecca TILLBERG
56 Dean Distance Learning/Inst Tech ... Mr. Eric ICHON
35 Assoc Dean Student Svcs Activities ... Ms. Celena ALCALA
11 Associate Dean Contract Ed ... Mr. Barry SLOAN
20 Associate Dean Trio ... Ms. Kathy S. WALTON
88 Associate Dean Hospitality ... Ms. Tara MARRAY
88 Academic Senate President ... Dr. Adrienne FOSTER
21 Chief Financial Administrator ... Ms. Maureen O'BRIEN
102 Actg Exec Director WLAC Foundation ... Mr. John R. OESTER
26 Dir Advtg/Marketing/Public Rels ... Ms. Michelle LONG-COFFEE
41 Athletic Director ... Mr. Steve AGGERS
18 Facilities Manager ... Mr. Allan HANSEN
19 Sheriff/Deputy ... Mr. Alfred A. GUERRERO
37 Financial Aid Manager ... Mr. Glenn SCHENK
40 College Enterprise Manager ... Mr. Larry PACKHAM
88 Operations Manager ... Mr. Bruce HICKS
22 Compliance Officer ... Vacant

Los Angeles County College of Nursing and Allied Health (G)

1237 N Mission Road, Los Angeles CA 90033-1083
County: Los Angeles FICE Identification: 006165
Unit ID: 117803
Telephone: (323) 226-4911 Carnegie Class: Assoc/Pub-Spec
FAX Number: (323) 226-6343 Calendar System: Semester
URL: www.ladhs.org/wps/portal/CollegeOfNursing/
Established: 1895 Annual Undergrad Tuition & Fees (In-District): $4,925
Enrollment: 274 Coed
Affiliation or Control: Local IRS Status: 501(c)3
Highest Offering: Associate Degree
Program: Occupational; 2-Year Principally Bachelor's Creditable
Accreditation: WJ

01 Provost ... Ms. Nancy W. MILLER
05 Dean of Nursing Programs ... Ms. Barbara COLLIER
06 Reg/Admiss Ofcr/Dn Admn/Stdnt Svcs ... Ms. Maria C. CABALLERO
51 Dir Continuing Education Programs ... Ms. Tammy BLASS

Los Angeles Film School (H)

6353 Sunset Boulevard, Hollywood CA 90028
County: Los Angeles FICE Identification: 040373
Unit ID: 436429
Telephone: (323) 464-5200 Carnegie Class: Not Classified
FAX Number: (323) 646-0770 Calendar System: Other
URL: www.lafilm.edu
Established: 1999 Annual Undergrad Tuition & Fees: $43,300
Enrollment: 2,083 Coed
Affiliation or Control: Proprietary IRS Status: Proprietary
Highest Offering: Associate Degree
Program: 2-Year Principally Bachelor's Creditable; Fine Arts Emphasis
Accreditation: ACCSC

01 President/CEO ... Ms. Diana DERYCZ-KESSLER

Los Angeles ORT College (I)

6435 Wilshire Blvd, Los Angeles CA 90048
County: Los Angeles FICE Identification: 025703
Unit ID: 368780
Telephone: (323) 966-5444 Carnegie Class: Not Classified
FAX Number: (323) 966-5455 Calendar System: Other
URL: www.laort.edu
Established: 1985 Annual Undergrad Tuition & Fees: $11,450
Enrollment: 303 Coed
Affiliation or Control: Independent Non-Profit IRS Status: 501(c)3
Highest Offering: Associate Degree
Program: Occupational; Technical Emphasis
Accreditation: CNCE

*Los Rios Community College District Office (J)

1919 Spanos Court, Sacramento CA 95825-3981
County: Sacramento FICE Identification: 001231
Unit ID: 117900
Telephone: (916) 568-3021 Carnegie Class: N/A
FAX Number: (916) 568-3023
URL: www.losrios.edu

01 Chancellor ... Dr. Brice W. HARRIS
30 Vice Chanc Resource Devel/ Planning ... Dr. Sandra G. KIRSCHENMANN
05 Vice Chancellor Education/Tech ... Dr. Susan L. LORIMER
10 Deputy Chanc Finance/Admin/Hum Res ... Mr. Jon SHARPE
13 Assoc Vice Chanc Information Tech ... Mr. Mick HOLSCLAW
15 Assoc Vice Chanc Personnel Svcs ... Mr. Ryan COX
21 Assoc Vice Chancellor Finance ... Ms. Theresa MATISTA
26 Assoc Vice Chanc Communications/Res ... Ms. Susie S. WILLIAMS
103 Assoc Vice Chanc Corp & Econ Devel ... Dr. Daniel THROGMORTON
32 Assoc Vice Chanc Student Services ... Ms. Victoria ROSARIO
43 General Counsel ... Mr. Jan P. SHERRY
18 Director Facilities Maintenance ... Mr. Pablo MANZO
09 Director Institutional Research ... Ms. Flora B. YEN
103 Director Workforce/Economic Devel ... Mr. Walter DIMANTOVA
04 Chancellor's Executive Assistant ... Ms. Jeannie FREEMAN
96 Director General Services ... Mr. O.D BURR

*American River College (A)

4700 College Oak Drive, Sacramento CA 95841-4286
County: Sacramento | FICE Identification: 001232
Unit ID: 109208
Telephone: (916) 484-8011 | Carnegie Class: Assoc/Pub-U-MC
FAX Number: (916) 484-8674 | Calendar System: Semester
URL: www.arc.losrios.edu
Established: 1955 | Annual Undergrad Tuition & Fees (In-District): $894
Enrollment: 35,264 | Coed
Affiliation or Control: State/Local | IRS Status: 501(c)3
Highest Offering: Associate Degree
Program: Occupational; 2-Year Principally Bachelor's Creditable
Accreditation: WJ, EMT, FUSER

02 President ... Dr. David VIAR
05 Vice President of Instruction ... Ms. Colleen H. OWINGS
32 Vice President of Student Services ... Dr. Pamela D. WALKER
10 Vice President of Admin Services ... Mr. Raymond DI GUILIO
20 Assoc Vice President of Instruction ... Dr. Lisa LAWRENSON
62 Assoc VP of Instruction/Lrng Res ... Dr. David REDFIELD
103 Assoc VP Workforce Development ... Dr. Cris MCCULLOUGH
09 Dean Planning/Rsch/Tech/Prof Dev ... Dr. Jane DE LEON
27 Public Information Officer ... Dr. Stephen PEITHMAN
30 Director of College Advancement ... Ms. Kirsten DUBRAY
37 Financial Aid Supervisor ... Ms. Maritza LAVU
07 Dean of Enrollment Services ... Dr. Robin NEAL
57 Dean Fine & Applied Arts ... Dr. David NEWNHAM
83 Dean Behavioral Sci/Social Science ... Ms. Carol POTTORFF
79 Dean Humanities ... Vacant
38 Dean Counseling & Student Services ... Ms. Brenda THAMES
88 Dean of English ... Ms. Tammy MONTGOMERY
81 Dean of Mathematics ... Ms. Nancy REITZ
68 Dean of Physical Educ/Athletics ... Ms. Jean SNUGGS
81 Dean Science/Engineering ... Dr. Rina ROY
75 Dean of Technical/Vocational Educ ... Ms. Gabriel M. MEEHAN
56 Dean Off-Campus Education ... Mr. James V. THOMPSON
38 Dean Student Support Services ... Ms. Eddie WEBB
66 Dean Health & Education ... Dr. Steven BOYD
56 Dean Natomas Education Center ... Ms. Sheryl GESSFORD
35 Dean Student Development ... Mr. Manuel PEREZ
50 Dean Computer Science/Info Tech/Bus ... Dr. Derrick BOOTH

*Cosumnes River College (B)

8401 Center Parkway, Sacramento CA 95823-5799
County: Sacramento | FICE Identification: 007536
Unit ID: 113096
Telephone: (916) 691-7344 | Carnegie Class: Assoc/Pub-U-MC
FAX Number: (916) 691-7375 | Calendar System: Semester
URL: www.crc.losrios.edu
Established: 1970 | Annual Undergrad Tuition & Fees (In-District): $780
Enrollment: 15,946 | Coed
Affiliation or Control: State/Local | IRS Status: 501(c)3
Highest Offering: Associate Degree
Program: Occupational; 2-Year Principally Bachelor's Creditable
Accreditation: WJ, DIETT, MAC

02 President ... Dr. Deborah J. TRAVIS
05 VP Instruction & Student Learning ... Mr. Whitney YAMAMURA
11 VP Admin Svcs & Student Support ... Dr. Donald WALLACE
32 VP Student Svcs/Enrollment Mgmt ... Ms. Celia ESPOSITO-NOY
84 Dean Student Svcs/Enrollment Mgmt ... Ms. Christine THOMAS
20 Dean Instruction/Student Learning ... Dr. Judith BEACHLER
08 Dean Learning Res/College Tech ... Mr. Stephen MCGLOUGHLIN
38 Dean Counseling & Student Services ... Mr. Michael MARION
50 Dean Business & Family Science ... Mr. Jamey NYE
79 Dean Humanities & Social Science ... Ms. Virginia REYNOLDS
41 Dean PE & Athletics ... Ms. Elizabeth BELYEA
81 Dean Science/Math/Engineering ... Dr. Robert MONTANEZ
72 Dean Careers & Technology ... Mr. Robert JOHNSON
45 Dean of College Planning & Research ... Ms. Katherine MCLAIN
06 Registrar/Admissions & Records ... Mr. Richard ANDREWS
18 Chief Facilities/Physical Plant ... Mr. Cory WATHEN
26 Public Information Officer ... Ms. Kristie WEST

*Folsom Lake College (C)

10 College Parkway, Folsom CA 95630-6798
County: Sacramento | FICE Identification: 038713
Unit ID: 444219
Telephone: (916) 608-6500 | Carnegie Class: Assoc/Pub-U-MC
FAX Number: (916) 608-6584 | Calendar System: Semester
URL: www.flc.losrios.edu
Established: 2004 | Annual Undergrad Tuition & Fees (In-District): $1,038
Enrollment: 9,027 | Coed
Affiliation or Control: State/Local | IRS Status: 501(c)3
Highest Offering: Associate Degree
Program: 2-Year Principally Bachelor's Creditable
Accreditation: WJ

02 President ... Dr. Thelma SCOTT-SKILLMAN
11 Vice President Administration ... Kathleen KIRKLIN
05 Vice President Instruction ... Vacant
32 VP Student Devel/Enrollment Mgmt ... Dr. Denise NOLDON
88 Executive Director VAPAC ... David PIER
30 Chief Development ... Vacant
20 Dean of Instruction ... Dr. Monica PACTOL
20 Dean of Instruction & Technology ... Gary HARTLEY
20 Dean of Career & Tech Educ ... Dr. Stu VAN HORN
20 Dean of Instruction/EDC ... Dale VAN DAM
20 Dean of Instruction/VAPA ... David WILLIAMS
35 Director Student Affairs ... Aiden ELY
07 Admissions & Records Supervisor ... Christine WURZER
40 Bookstore Manager ... Rob MULLIGAN
10 Business Services Supervisor ... Joany HARMAN
18 Campus Operations Supervisor ... Colleen JOHNSON
12 Educational Center Supervisor ... Adrienne ANDREWS
37 Financial Aid Supervisor ... Carol THOMAS
26 Public Information Officer ... Scott CROW
04 Assistant to the President ... Beth SPRINKEL
09 Research Analyst ... Chris OLSON

*Sacramento City College (D)

3835 Freeport Boulevard, Sacramento CA 95822-1386
County: Sacramento | FICE Identification: 001233
Unit ID: 122180
Telephone: (916) 558-2111 | Carnegie Class: Assoc/Pub-U-MC
FAX Number: (916) 558-2449 | Calendar System: Semester
URL: www.scc.losrios.edu
Established: 1916 | Annual Undergrad Tuition & Fees (In-District): $972
Enrollment: 24,781 | Coed
Affiliation or Control: State/Local | IRS Status: 501(c)3
Highest Offering: Associate Degree
Program: Occupational; 2-Year Principally Bachelor's Creditable
Accreditation: WJ, DA, DH, OTA, PTAA

02 President ... Dr. Kathryn JEFFERY
05 Vice Pres Instructional Services ... Dr. Mary TURNER
10 Vice Pres Administrative Services ... Mr. Robert J. MARTINELLI
32 Vice President Student Services ... Mr. Michael C. POINTDEXTER
20 Associate Vice Pres Instruction ... Mr. Rick IDA
20 Associate Vice Pres Instruction ... Mrs. Julia A. JOLLY
35 Associate Vice Pres Student Svcs ... Ms. Juanita CHRYSANTHOU
13 Dean Information Technology ... Dr. Elaine ADER
07 Dean Enrollment/Student Services ... Ms. Christine HERNANDEZ
46 Dean Planning/Research/Development ... Dr. Marybeth BUECHNER
08 Dean Learning Resources ... Ms. Rhonda RIOS-KRAVITZ
36 Dean Counseling/Student Success ... Mr. David RASUL
40 Director VII College Store ... Mr. Randy CLEM
66 Director IV Nursing ... Ms. Dale S. COHEN
18 Director III College Operations ... Mr. Gregory HAYMAN
26 Director College Advancement ... Mrs. Mary LELAND
27 Public Information Officer ... Ms. Amanda DAVIS
35 Student Leadership & Development ... Ms. Kim BEYRER
76 Dean Science & Allied Health ... Mr. James COLLINS
50 Dean Business ... Vacant
38 Dean Matriculation/Student Develop ... Vacant
79 Dean Humanities/Fine Arts ... Mr. Chris IWATA
88 Dean Languages/Literature ... Mr. Albert GARCIA
72 Dean Advanced Technology ... Mrs. Donnetta WEBB
41 Dean PE/Health/Athletics ... Mr. Mitchell L. CAMPBELL
81 Dean Statistics/Math/Engineering ... Mrs. Anne LICCIARDI
83 Dean Behavorial & Social Science ... Dr. Frank MALARET
56 Dean Davis Center ... Mr. Don PALM
56 Dean West Sacramento Ctr ... Dr. Debra LUFF

Loyola Marymount University (E)

1 LMU Drive, Los Angeles CA 90045-2659
County: Los Angeles | FICE Identification: 011649
Unit ID: 117946
Telephone: (310) 338-2700 | Carnegie Class: Master's L
FAX Number: N/A | Calendar System: Semester
URL: www.lmu.edu
Established: 1911 | Annual Undergrad Tuition & Fees: $37,605
Enrollment: 9,069 | Coed
Affiliation or Control: Roman Catholic | IRS Status: 501(c)3
Highest Offering: Doctorate
Program: Liberal Arts And General; Teacher Preparatory; Professional
Accreditation: WC, ART, BUS, DANCE, ENG, LAW, MUS, TED, THEA, THEOL

01 President ... Mr. David W. BURCHAM
00 Chancellor ... Rev. Patrick J. CAHALAN, SJ
03 Exec Vice President & Provost ... Vacant
04 Special Assistant to the President ... Rev. Joseph LABRIE, SJ
05 Interim Sr VP/Chief Academic Ofcr ... Dr. Joseph HELLIGE
10 Sr Vice Pres/Chief Financial Ofcr ... Mr. Tom O. FLEMING
26 Sr Vice Pres University Relations ... Mr. Dennis SLON
32 Sr Vice Pres for Student Affairs ... Dr. Elena M. BOVE
11 Sr Vice Pres for Administration ... Ms. Lynne B. SCARBORO
85 Vice President Intercultural Affs ... Dr. Abbie ROBINSON-ARMSTRONG
15 Vice President for Human Resources ... Ms. Rebecca CHANDLER
86 VP for Comm/Government Relations ... Ms. Kathleen FLANAGAN
84 Vice Pres Enrollment Management ... Dr. Anne PRISCO
18 Vice Pres Facilities Management ... Mr. Rick GARCIA
20 Vice Pres Undergraduate Studies ... Dr. Rae Linda BROWN
21 Vice Pres for Finance/Controller ... Ms. Lori A. HUSEIN
28 Assoc VP Intercultural Affairs ... Mr. Marshall SAUCEDA
21 AVP Auxiliary Mgmt & Business Affs ... Mr. Raymond A. DENNIS
39 Assoc Vice Pres of Student Life ... Mr. Richard ROCHELEAU
09 Assoc Vice Pres Inst Effectiveness ... Ms. Margaret KASIMATIS
35 Dean of Students ... Dr. Linda MCMURDOCK
08 Dean of University Libraries ... Ms. Kristine BRANCOLINI
06 University Registrar ... Ms. Rosenia ST. ONGE
61 Dean Loyola Law School/Sr VP ... Mr. Victor J. GOLD
50 Dean Business Administration ... Dr. Dennis DRAPER
57 Dean Communication/Fine Arts ... Prof. Barbara BUSSE
88 Dean School of Film & TV ... Prof. Stephen G. UJLAKI
49 Dean Liberal Arts ... Dr. Paul T. ZELEZA, SJ
54 Dean Science & Engineering ... Dr. Richard PLUMB
53 Dean School of Education ... Dr. Shane MARTIN
30 Ex Dir Dev Plnd Gvng/Princpal Gifts ... Ms. Joanie POHAS
29 Exec Dir Alumni Rels/Annual Giving ... Ms. Lisa PIUMETTI FARLAND
102 Exec Dir Corporate/Foundation Rels ... Ms. Noelle GERVAIS
42 Director of Campus Ministry ... Rev. James D. ERPS
07 Director of Admissions ... Mr. Matthew X. FISSINGER
37 Director of Financial Aid ... Ms. Catherine GRAHAM
36 Dir Career Devel/Placement Svcs ... Ms. Laura WESLEY
23 Medical Director ... Daniel HYSLOP, M.D.
41 Athletic Director ... Dr. William HUSAK
19 Chief of Public Safety ... Mr. Hampton CANTRELL
44 Director of Annual Giving ... Mr. Kevin J. DELANEY
92 Director of Honors Program ... Dr. Brad STONE
94 Director of Women's Studies ... Dr. Nancy JABBRA
88 Dir Real Estate/Faculty Housing ... Ms. Kirsten ANDRESEN

Marymount College (F)

30800 Palos Verdes Drive E,
Rancho Palos Verdes CA 90275-6299
County: Los Angeles | FICE Identification: 010474
Unit ID: 118541
Telephone: (310) 377-5501 | Carnegie Class: Assoc/PrivNFP
FAX Number: (310) 377-6223 | Calendar System: Semester
URL: www.marymountpv.edu
Established: 1932 | Annual Undergrad Tuition & Fees: $28,121
Enrollment: 793 | Coed
Affiliation or Control: Roman Catholic | IRS Status: 501(c)3
Highest Offering: Baccalaureate
Program: 2-Year Principally Bachelor's Creditable; Business Emphasis
Accreditation: WC

01 President ... Dr. Michael S. BROPHY
10 Vice President of Finance ... Mr. James REEVES
05 Dean of Academic Affairs ... Dr. Ariane SCHAUER
30 Dean Institutional Advancement ... Mr. Bret PRICHARD
07 Dean of Admission & Enrollment Mgmt ... Dr. Len HIGHTOWER
32 Dean of Students ... Ms. Shane ARMSTRONG
20 Associate Academic Officer ... Ms. Susie MARTIN
08 Librarian ... Ms. Mary MCMILLAN
37 Director Student Financial Aid ... Ms. Tracie HUNTER
15 Director Personnel Services ... Ms. Karen THORDARSON
18 Chief Facilities/Physical Plant ... Mr. Michael CLIFFORD
26 Chief Public Relations Officer ... Ms. Kelly CURTIS
29 Director Alumni Relations ... Ms. Megan MCCORMICK
36 Director Student Placement ... Ms. Virginia WADE
38 Director Student Counseling ... Dr. David DRAPER
96 Director of Purchasing ... Ms. Denise QUINONES
06 Registrar ... Ms. Lynn ELLIOTT
35 Dir Student Life & Engagement ... Ms. Kelly KRUSEE
84 Director of Enrollment Management ... Ms. Paula AVERY
09 Director of Institutional Research ... Mr. Michael SEMENOFF
21 Associate Business Officer ... Ms. Kathleen RUIZ

The Master's College and Seminary (G)

21726 Placerita Canyon Road,
Santa Clarita CA 91321-1200
County: Los Angeles | FICE Identification: 001220
Unit ID: 117751
Telephone: (661) 259-3540 | Carnegie Class: Bac/Diverse
FAX Number: N/A | Calendar System: Semester
URL: www.masters.edu
Established: 1927 | Annual Undergrad Tuition & Fees: $26,260
Enrollment: 1,070 | Coed
Affiliation or Control: Independent Non-Profit | IRS Status: 501(c)3
Highest Offering: Doctorate
Program: Liberal Arts And General; Teacher Preparatory
Accreditation: WC, MUS

01 President ... Dr. John MACARTHUR
03 Exec Vice President and Provost ... Dr. Mark TATLOCK
05 Vice President Academic Affairs ... Dr. John A. HUGHES
32 Dean of Student Life ... Mr. Joe KELLER
58 Vice President Graduate School ... Dr. Richard L. MAYHUE
15 Vice President of Operations ... Mr. Bob HOTTON
30 Int Vice President for Development ... Mr. Mark AYDELOTTE
88 Director of Educational Partnership ... Vacant
10 Chief Financial Officer ... Mr. Jason HARTUNG
11 Chief of Operations ... Mr. Jason HARTUNG
06 Registrar ... Mr. Don GILMORE
08 Director Library Services ... Mr. John STONE
20 Associate Dean of Students ... Vacant
07 Director Enrollment ... Miss Hollie GORSH

41 Athletic Director .... Mr. Steve WALDECK
37 Director Financial Aid .... Mr. Gary EDWARDS
35 Director Campus Activities .... Mr. Peter BARGAS
29 Director Alumni Affairs .... Miss Polly MEREDITH
09 Director of Institutional Research .... Mr. John M. WALTER
36 Director Student Placement .... Mr. Rick WAHLER
85 International Students Advisor .... Miss Lisa LAGEORGE

† The Master's Seminary is located at 13248 Roscoe Boulevard, Sun Valley, CA 91352.

Mendocino College (A)

1000 Hensley Creek Road, Ukiah CA 95482-7821

County: Mendocino FICE Identification: 011672
Unit ID: 118684
Telephone: (707) 468-3000 Carnegie Class: Assoc/Pub-R-L
FAX Number: (707) 468-3120 Calendar System: Semester
URL: www.mendocino.edu
Established: 1973 Annual Undergrad Tuition & Fees (In-District): $850
Enrollment: 3,987 Coed
Affiliation or Control: State/Local IRS Status: 501(c)3
Highest Offering: Associate Degree
Program: Occupational; 2-Year Principally Bachelor's Creditable
Accreditation: WJ, EMT

01 Superintendent/President .... Ms. Kathryn G. LEHNER
05 VP of Education & Student Services .... Ms. Meridith RANDALL
11 Vice Pres Administrative Services .... Dr. Larry PERRYMAN
08 Head Librarian .... Mr. John KOETZNER
32 Dean Student Services .... Vacant
20 Dean of Instruction .... Ms. Virginia GULEFF
12 Dean Lake & Willits Centers .... Mr. Mark RAWITSCH
75 Dean Career and Technical Education .... Ms. Susan GOFF
15 Director Human Resources .... Ms. Karen CHATY
18 Maintenance and Operations Supvsr .... Mr. Steve OLIVERIA
26 Director Public Info & Marketing .... Vacant
41 Director Athletics .... Mr. Tom GANG
21 Director Fiscal Services .... Ms. Eileen CICHOCKI
14 Director Information Technology .. Ms. Karen CHRISTOPHERSON
09 Director of Institutional Research .... Mr. Charles DUFFY
07 Director Admissions/Registrar .... Ms. Kristie A. ANDERSON
37 Asst Dean Stdnt Financial Aid/EOPS .... Ms. Jacquline BRADLEY

Menlo College (B)

1000 El Camino Real, Atherton CA 94027-4301

County: San Mateo FICE Identification: 001236
Unit ID: 118693
Telephone: (800) 556-3656 Carnegie Class: Bac/Diverse
FAX Number: (650) 543-4496 Calendar System: Semester
URL: www.menlo.edu
Established: 1927 Annual Undergrad Tuition & Fees: $34,476
Enrollment: 589 Coed
Affiliation or Control: Independent Non-Profit IRS Status: 501(c)3
Highest Offering: Baccalaureate
Program: Liberal Arts And General; Business Emphasis
Accreditation: WC

01 President .... Dr. James KELLY
05 Provost .... Dr. James WOOLEVER
84 Vice President Enrollment Mgmt .... Mr. David PLACEY
30 VP for Institutional Advancement .... Ms. Catherine REEVES
10 Chief Financial Officer .... Mr. Nilo VENTURA
20 Dean for Academic Affairs .... Dr. Dale HOCKSTRA
107 Dean of Professional Studies Pgm .... Dr. James WOOLEVER
18 Director Facilities & Operations .... Mr. Robert TALBOTT
08 Dean Library Services .... Dr. William WALTERS
41 Director of Athletics .... Mr. Keith SPATARO
35 Associate Dean of Student Affairs .... Ms. Sharyn MOORE
37 Director Office of Financial Aid .... Ms. Anne HEATON-DUNLAP
36 Director of Career Services .... Ms. Mary ROBINS
09 Assessment Coordinator .... Ms. Ivana IZVONAR
21 Controller .... Ms. Raagini ALI
26 Director of Commun/PR & Marketing .... Ms. Darcy BLAKE
32 Dean of Student Affairs .... Ms. Yasmin LAMBIE-SIMPSON
39 Director of Housing .... Mr. Jessie GUILLIOT
07 Director Office of Admissions .... Ms. Priscila DE SOUZA
06 Registrar .... Ms. Mary RANDERS
29 Director of Alumni Relations .... Vacant

Merced College (C)

3600 M Street, Merced CA 95348-2898

County: Merced FICE Identification: 001237
Unit ID: 118718
Telephone: (209) 384-6000 Carnegie Class: Assoc/Pub-R-L
FAX Number: (209) 384-6043 Calendar System: Semester
URL: www.mccd.edu
Established: 1962 Annual Undergrad Tuition & Fees (In-District): $1,116
Enrollment: 11,000 Coed
Affiliation or Control: State/Local IRS Status: 501(c)3
Highest Offering: Associate Degree
Program: Occupational; 2-Year Principally Bachelor's Creditable; Business Emphasis
Accreditation: WJ, DMS, RAD

01 President .... Dr. Benjamin T. DURAN
04 Executive Assistant to President .... Mrs. Stacey HICKS
05 Vice President Instruction .... Dr. Marianne TORTORICI
32 Vice Pres Student Personnel Svcs .... Dr. Anne NEWINS
11 Vice Pres District Admin Services .... Ms. Mazie BREWINGTON
12 Dean Los Banos Campus .... Dr. Brenda LATHAM
81 Dean Instructional Services .... Dr. Douglas KAIN
71 Dean Instructional Services .... Mrs. Delores CABEZUT-ORTIZ
47 Dean Instructional Services .... Mr. Jim ANDERSEN
50 Dean Instructional Services .... Dr. Bobby ANDERSON
83 Dean Instructional Services .... Dr. Myshel PIMMENTEL
103 Dean Instructional Services .... Mrs. Karyn DOWER
35 Dean of Student Services .... Mr. Mario CORDOVA
35 Dean of Student Services .... Dr. Everett LOVELACE
26 Chief Public Relations Officer .... Mr. Robin SHEPARD
14 Director Info Technology Services .... Mr. Don PETERSON
18 Director Maint./Transp./Facilities .... Mr. Rick SOUHRADA
06 Registrar & Dir Financial Aid .... Mrs. Sharon REINHARDT
08 Director Learning Resources Center .... Dr. Susan WALSH

Mills College (D)

5000 MacArthur Boulevard, Oakland CA 94613-1301

County: Alameda FICE Identification: 001238
Unit ID: 118888
Telephone: (510) 430-2255 Carnegie Class: Master's M
FAX Number: (510) 430-3314 Calendar System: Semester
URL: www.mills.edu
Established: 1852 Annual Undergrad Tuition & Fees: $38,066
Enrollment: 1,596 Female
Affiliation or Control: Independent Non-Profit IRS Status: 501(c)3
Highest Offering: Doctorate
Program: Liberal Arts And General; Teacher Preparatory
Accreditation: WC

01 President .... Ms. Alecia A. DECOUDREAUX
05 Provost & Dean of the Faculty .... Dr. Sandra C. GREER
10 Interim VP Finance & Treasurer .... Ms. Jamie NICKEL
26 VP for Opers/Chief Public Rels Ofcr ... Ms. Renee JADUSHLEVER
30 VP for Institutional Advancement .. Ms. Cynthia BRANDT STOVER
43 Vice President & General Counsel .... Ms. Therese M. LEONE
20 Vice Provost .... Dr. Andrew WORKMAN
21 Assoc VP for Student Fin/Admin Svcs .... Mr. David GIN
07 Dean of Undergraduate Admission .... Ms. Giulietta AQUINO
32 Dean Student Life/Vice Provost .... Ms. Joi LEWIS
101 Asst Secretary of Board of Trustees .... Dr. Marianne SHELDON
38 Assoc Dean/Dir Counsel/Psych Svcs .... Ms. Dorian NEWTON
06 Registrar .... Ms. Kristen SMITH
18 Director of Campus Facilities .... Ms. Linda ZITZNER
41 Director of Athletics .... Ms. Themy ADACHI
29 Exec Dir of Alumnae Relations .... Ms. Laura GOBBI
09 Dir Acad Assess/Inst Research/Plng .... Ms. Alice KNUDSEN

MiraCosta Community College District (E)

One Barnard Drive, Oceanside CA 92056-3899

County: San Diego FICE Identification: 001239
Unit ID: 118912
Telephone: (760) 757-2121 Carnegie Class: Assoc/Pub-S-MC
FAX Number: (760) 795-6609 Calendar System: Semester
URL: www.miracosta.edu
Established: 1934 Annual Undergrad Tuition & Fees (In-District): $924
Enrollment: 14,571 Coed
Affiliation or Control: State/Local IRS Status: 501(c)3
Highest Offering: Associate Degree
Program: Occupational; 2-Year Principally Bachelor's Creditable
Accreditation: #WJ, SURGT

01 Superintendent/President .... Dr. Francisco RODRIGUEZ
04 Exec Assistant to Supt/President .... Ms. Evelyn DALBY
04 Exec Assistant to Supt/President .... Ms. Jeanne SWANSON
05 Vice President Instructional Svcs .... Ms. Pam DEEGAN
32 Vice President Student Services .... Dr. Richard J. ROBERTSON
10 Vice President Business/Admin Svcs .... Mr. James AUSTIN
12 Dean San Elijo Campus .... Ms. Sally FOSTER
20 Dean Academic Information Svcs .... Mr. Mario VALENTE
38 Dean Counseling/Student Develop .... Vacant
07 Dean Admissions/Student Support .... Mr. Gilbert HERMOSILLO
88 Associate Dean San Elijo Campus .... Ms. Nikki SCHAPER
51 Interim Dean Community Education .... Dr. Alketa WOJCIK
49 Dean Arts/Letters .... Ms. Dana SMITH
81 Dean Math/Sciences .... Mr. Carlos LOPEZ
75 Dean Career/Technical Education .... Dr. Al TACCONE
88 Director Small Business Dev Ctr .... Mr. Sudershan SHAUNAK
31 Director Community Services .... Ms. Linda KUROKAWA
06 Registrar .... Ms. Alicia TERRY
09 Director Institutional Research .... Ms. Kimberly COUTTS
26 Interim Director Marketing/Commun .... Ms. Cheryl BROOM
102 Director Foundation/Fund Devel .... Ms. Linda FOGERSON
18 Director Facilities .... Mr. Tom MACIAS
37 Director Financial Aid .... Ms. JoAnn BERNARD
88 Director Risk Management .... Mr. Joseph MAZZA
88 Director Cashiering Services .... Ms. Jo FERRIS
15 Director Human Resources .... Ms. Sheri WRIGHT
36 Director Career Center .... Ms. Donna DAVIS
88 Director Transfer Center .... Ms. Lise FLOCKEN
96 Director Purchasing/Material Mgmt .... Ms. Susan ASATO
88 Director Retention Services .... Dr. Edward POEHLERT
21 Director Fiscal Services .... Ms. Myeisha ARMSTRONG
19 Director Campus Police .... Chief Robert NORCROSS
106 Director Online Education .... Dr. James JULIUS

Monterey Institute of International Studies (F)

460 Pierce Street, Monterey CA 93940-2691

County: Monterey FICE Identification: 001241
Unit ID: 119058
Telephone: (831) 647-4100 Carnegie Class: Master's L
FAX Number: (831) 647-4199 Calendar System: Semester
URL: www.miis.edu
Established: 1955 Annual Undergrad Tuition & Fees: $32,800
Enrollment: 757 Coed
Affiliation or Control: Other IRS Status: 501(c)3
Highest Offering: Master's
Program: Professional
Accreditation: &EH, BUS

01 President .... Dr. Sunder RAMASWAMY
10 Exec Dir Finance/Business Ops/Admin .... Mr. Jai SHANKAR
05 Provost & Chief Academic Officer .... Dr. Amy SANDS
30 Exec Director of Inst Advancement .... Mr. Kevin WASBAUER
04 Exec Asst to the President .... Ms. Barbara BURKE
06 Registrar .... Mr. Seamus DORRIAN
84 Exec Director of Enrollment Mgmt .... Ms. Jill STOFFERS
07 Admissions Officer .... Ms. Sherre KRUFT
36 Dean of Advising & Career Services .... Mr. Tate MILLER
37 Director Financial Aid .... Ms. Regina GARNER
08 Librarian .... Mr. Peter LIU
88 Program Mgr/Custom Language Svcs .... Ms. Alicia BRENT
15 Manager Human Resources .... Mr. Michael ULIBARRI
13 Dir Information Technology Services .... Mr. John GRUNDER
35 Director Student Services .... Ms. Ashley ARROCHA
29 Director Alumni Relations .... Ms. Leah GOWRON
21 Controller .... Mr. Steve MARINO
19 Director of Security .... Mr. Jeremy VONDENBENKEN
24 Media Services Supervisor .... Mr. Vince MASCAL
18 Campus Services Manager .... Vacant
79 Dean School Trans Inter & Lang Ed .... Dr. Renee JOURDENAIS
82 Dean School Intl Policy & Mgmt .... Dr. Yuwei SHI
26 Exec Director of Communications .... Mr. Jason WARBURG

† Regional accrediation is carried under parent institution Middlebury College, VT.

Monterey Peninsula College (G)

980 Fremont Street, Monterey CA 93940-4799

County: Monterey FICE Identification: 001242
Unit ID: 119067
Telephone: (831) 646-4010 Carnegie Class: Assoc/Pub-R-L
FAX Number: (831) 655-2627 Calendar System: Semester
URL: www.mpc.edu
Established: 1947 Annual Undergrad Tuition & Fees (In-District): $928
Enrollment: 10,182 Coed
Affiliation or Control: State/Local IRS Status: 501(c)3
Highest Offering: Associate Degree
Program: Occupational; 2-Year Principally Bachelor's Creditable
Accreditation: WJ, ADNUR

01 Superintendent/President .... Dr. Douglas GARRISON
05 Vice President Academic Affairs .... Vacant
11 Vice Pres Administrative Services .... Mr. Stephen MA
32 Vice President Student Services .... Mr. Carsbia ANDERSON
20 Dean Instruction .... Ms. Laura FRANKLIN
45 Dean Instructional Planning .... Mr. Michael GILMARTIN
15 Associate Dean of Human Resources .... Ms. Barbara LEE
35 Dean of Student Services .... Mr. Larry WALKER
09 Director of Institutional Research .... Dr. Rosaleen RYAN
06 Registrar .... Ms. Vera COLEMAN
08 Librarian .... Ms. Stephanie TETTER
37 Financial Aid Officer .... Ms. Claudia MARTIN
41 Athletic Director .... Mr. Lyndon SCHUTZLER
18 Director Facilities/Physical Plant .... Mr. Steve MORGAN
26 Public Relations Officer .... Vacant
96 Purchasing Agent .... Mr. Pete BUECHEL

Mount St. Mary's College (H)

12001 Chalon Road, Los Angeles CA 90049-1599

County: Los Angeles FICE Identification: 001243
Unit ID: 119173
Telephone: (310) 954-4000 Carnegie Class: Master's S
FAX Number: (310) 954-4379 Calendar System: Semester
URL: www.msmc.la.edu
Established: 1925 Annual Undergrad Tuition & Fees: $30,696
Enrollment: 2,864 Female
Affiliation or Control: Roman Catholic IRS Status: 501(c)3
Highest Offering: Doctorate
Program: Occupational; 2-Year Principally Bachelor's Creditable; Liberal Arts And General; Teacher Preparatory; Professional
Accreditation: WC, NURSE, PTA

01 President .... Dr. Ann MCELANEY-JOHNSON
05 Provost .... Dr. Eleanor SIEBERT
30 Vice Pres Institutional Advancement .... Dr. Stephanie CUBBA
10 Vice Pres Administration & Finance .... Mr. Chris MCALARY
13 VP Info Support Svcs/Enroll Mgmt .... Mr. Larry SMITH
32 Vice President Student Affairs .... Dr. Jane LINGUA
20 Assistant Provost .... Dr. Karol DEAN
09 Asst VP Inst Planning & Research .... Dr. Heather BROWN
35 Asst VP Student Affairs .... Ms. Bernadette ROBERT
58 Graduate Dean .... Dr. Linda MOODY

55 Dean of Weekend College ... Mr. Merrill RODIN
84 Director Enrollment Management ... Mr. Dean KILGOUR
06 Registrar ... Ms. Rocio DELEON
26 Director of Public Relations ... Ms. Debbie REAM
15 Director of Human Resources ... Ms. Susan LUSK
18 Director of Facilities Mgmt ... Ms. Barbara TELL
37 Director of Student Financing ... Ms. La Royce DODD
08 Director of MSMC Libraries ... Ms. Claudia REED
28 Director of Diversity ... Dr. Pam HALDEMAN
29 Director Alumni Relations ... Ms. Elizabeth ROBLES
38 Director Student Counseling ... Dr. Susan SALEM
07 Director of Admissions ... Ms. Yvonne BERUMEN
36 Director Career Services ... Ms. Marlene SIMON

Mt. San Antonio College (A)

1100 N Grand, Walnut CA 91789-1399
County: Los Angeles — FICE Identification: 001245
Unit ID: 119164
Telephone: (909) 594-5611 — Carnegie Class: Assoc/Pub-S-SC
FAX Number: (909) 598-2303 — Calendar System: Semester
URL: www.mtsac.edu
Established: 1946 — Annual Undergrad Tuition & Fees (In-District): $836
Enrollment: 38,741 — Coed
Affiliation or Control: State/Local — IRS Status: 501(c)3
Highest Offering: Associate Degree
Program: Occupational; 2-Year Principally Bachelor's Creditable
Accreditation: WJ, EMT, HT, RAD

01 President/CEO ... Dr. William T. SCROGGINS
05 Vice President Instruction ... Dr. Virginia BURLEY
11 Vice President Administrative Svcs ... Mr. Michael D. GREGORYK
32 Vice President Student Services ... Dr. Audrey YAMAGATA-NOJI
15 Vice President Human Resources ... Ms. Annette LORIA
20 Dean Instructional Services ... Ms. Terri LONG
35 Dean Student Services ... Ms. Carolyn KEYS
14 Chief Technology Officer ... Mr. Victor BELINSKI
84 Dean Enrollment Management ... Dr. George BRADSHAW
21 Director Fiscal Services ... Ms. Linda BALDWIN
37 Director Financial Aid ... Ms. Susan Y. JONES
46 Director Grants ... Ms. Adrienne PRICE
26 Director Marketing & Public Affairs ... Mr. Clarence BROWN
09 Dir Research & Inst Effectiveness ... Ms. Barbara MCNEICE-STALLARD
18 Director Facilities Planning & Mgmt ... Mr. Gary NELLESEN
35 Director Student Life ... Dr. Maryann TOLANO-LEVEQUE
36 Director Career & Transfer Services ... Ms. Heidi LOCKHART
50 Dean Business Division ... Dr. Joumana MCGOWAN
96 Purchasing Manager ... Mr. Tom MIEKLE
68 Dean Physical Education ... Mr. Joe JENNUM
38 Dean Counseling & Matriculation ... Mr. Tom MAUCH
79 Dean Humanities & Social Science ... Mr. Jim JENKINS
72 Dean Tech/Health Science ... Dr. Sarah DAUM
65 Dean Natural Sciences ... Mr. Larry L. REDINGER
88 Dean Arts ... Dr. Susan LONG
51 Dean Continuing Education ... Ms. Donna BURNS

Mt. San Jacinto College (B)

1499 N State Street, San Jacinto CA 92583-2399
County: Riverside — FICE Identification: 001246
Unit ID: 119216
Telephone: (951) 487-6752 — Carnegie Class: Assoc/Pub-S-MC
FAX Number: (951) 654-9712 — Calendar System: Semester
URL: www.msjc.edu
Established: 1962 — Annual Undergrad Tuition & Fees (In-District): $870
Enrollment: 18,697 — Coed
Affiliation or Control: State/Local — IRS Status: 501(c)3
Highest Offering: Associate Degree
Program: Occupational; 2-Year Principally Bachelor's Creditable
Accreditation: WJ

01 Superintendent/President ... Dr. Roger W. SCHULTZ
04 Executive Assistant to the S/P ... Ms. Kathy S. DONNELL
05 Vice Pres Instructional Svcs ... Dr. Dennis ANDERSON
32 Vice President Student Services ... Dr. William K. VINCENT
35 Dean Student Services ... Ms. JoAnna QUEJADA
10 Vice President Business Svcs ... Ms. Becky ELAM
18 Director Facilities Planning ... Vacant
16 Vice President of Human Resources ... Ms. Irma RAMOS
19 Chief of Police ... Mr. John ORTEGA
20 Dean of Instruction/Gen Educ ... Mr. Carlos LOPEZ
20 Dean of Academic Programs ... Dr. Richard ROWLEY
21 Dean of Business Services ... Ms. Beth GOMEZ
72 Dean Instruct Acad Success/Tech ... Ms. Patricia JAMES
13 Assoc Dean of Information Tech ... Mr. Brian ORLAUSKI
41 Dean of Athletics ... Mr. Patrick SPRINGER
38 Dean Counseling/Stdnt Sppt Svcs ... Mr. Tom SPILLMAN
56 Dean of Off-Site Programs ... Mrs. Laurie MCLAUGHLIN
103 Dean Career Education - MVC ... Ms. Joyce JOHNSON
103 Dean Career Education - SJC ... Dr. Michael CONNER
27 Public Information Officer ... Ms. Karin MARRIOTT
09 Associate Dean of Research ... Mr. Charles HAWKINS
37 Supervisor Financial Aid ... Ms. Lesia NAVARRO
07 Director Enrollment Management-SJC ... Ms. Cheri NAISH
84 Assoc Dean Enrollment Mgmt ... Ms. Susan LOOMIS
45 Assoc Dean Institutional Planning ... Ms. Rebecca TEAGUE
102 Foundation Director ... Vacant
66 Dean of Nursing and Allied Health ... Dr. Kathleen WINSTON
96 Assoc Dean Purchasing ... Ms. Teri SISCO

Mount Sierra College (C)

101 E Huntington Drive, Monrovia CA 91016-3414
County: Los Angeles — FICE Identification: 031287
Unit ID: 398130
Telephone: (626) 873-2144 — Carnegie Class: Bac/Diverse
FAX Number: (626) 359-5961 — Calendar System: Quarter
URL: www.mtsierra.edu
Established: 1991 — Annual Undergrad Tuition & Fees: $20,350
Enrollment: 465 — Coed
Affiliation or Control: Proprietary — IRS Status: Proprietary
Highest Offering: Baccalaureate
Program: Occupational; Professional
Accreditation: ACCSC

01 President ... Mr. Vaughn HARTUNIAN
11 Chief Operating Officer ... Mr. Z. Greg KAHWAJIAN
07 Director of Admissions ... Mr. Patrick AZADIAN
37 Director of Student Accounts ... Ms. Joyce BOYLAN
06 Registrar ... Ms. Jeanette ANDERSON

MTI College (D)

5221 Madison Avenue, Sacramento CA 95841-3037
County: Sacramento — FICE Identification: 012912
Unit ID: 118198
Telephone: (916) 339-1500 — Carnegie Class: Assoc/PrivFP
FAX Number: (916) 339-0305 — Calendar System: Quarter
URL: www.mticollege.edu
Established: 1965 — Annual Undergrad Tuition & Fees: $25,550
Enrollment: 877 — Coed
Affiliation or Control: Proprietary — IRS Status: Proprietary
Highest Offering: Associate Degree
Program: Occupational
Accreditation: WJ

01 President ... Mr. John A. ZIMMERMAN
10 Vice Pres/Chief Financial Officer ... Mr. David W. ALLEN

Musicians Institute (E)

6752 Hollywood Boulevard, Hollywood CA 90028
County: Los Angeles — FICE Identification: 021618
Unit ID: 119270
Telephone: (323) 462-1384 — Carnegie Class: Spec/Arts
FAX Number: (323) 462-6978 — Calendar System: Quarter
URL: www.mi.edu
Established: 1977 — Annual Undergrad Tuition & Fees: $22,500
Enrollment: 1,234 — Coed
Affiliation or Control: Proprietary — IRS Status: Proprietary
Highest Offering: Baccalaureate
Program: Music Emphasis
Accreditation: MUS

01 President ... Mr. Hisatake SHIBUYA
11 Vice Pres Operations/General Mgr ... Mr. Tak SAKIMOTO
05 Vice President of Education ... Ms. Beth MARLIS
10 Vice Pres Business Development ... Vacant

Napa Valley College (F)

2277 Napa-Vallejo Highway, Napa CA 94558-6236
County: Napa — FICE Identification: 001247
Unit ID: 119331
Telephone: (707) 253-3000 — Carnegie Class: Assoc/Pub-U-MC
FAX Number: (707) 253-3015 — Calendar System: Semester
URL: www.napavalley.edu
Established: 1942 — Annual Undergrad Tuition & Fees (In-District): $966
Enrollment: 7,533 — Coed
Affiliation or Control: State/Local — IRS Status: 501(c)3
Highest Offering: Associate Degree
Program: Occupational; 2-Year Principally Bachelor's Creditable
Accreditation: WJ, EMT

01 Superintendent/President ... Dr. Edna V. BAEHRE-KOLOVANI
10 Vice President Business & Finance ... Mr. John NAHLEN
05 Vice President Instruction ... Ms. Sue NELSON
32 Vice President Student Service/NMA ... Mr. Oscar DE HARO
15 Dean Human Resources ... Ms. Laura ECKLIN
20 Dean of Instruction ... Ms. Faye SMYLE
45 Dean Research/Planning/ Development ... Ms. Judith P. WALTER-BURKE
37 Int Dean Fin Aid/EOPS/DSPS/WIII ... Ms. Windy MARTINEZ
51 Int Dir Adult/Cont Ed Up Val Campus ... Ms. Christina RIVERS
07 Int Assoc Dean Admissions/Records ... Ms. Jessica MILLIKAN
18 Dir Camp Plng/Constr/Risk Mgmt Svcs ... Mr. Daniel J. TERAVEST
102 Executive Director Foundation ... Ms. Sonia WRIGHT
38 Division Chair Counseling ... Ms. Lauralyn BAUER
13 Int Dir Info Technology/Netwk Admin ... Mr. Robert BUTLER
26 Director Community Relations ... Ms. Betty M. MALMGREN
19 Police Chief ... Mr. Kenneth L. ARNOLD
18 Director Facilities Services ... Mr. Matt CHRISTENSEN
40 Bookstore Manager ... Ms. Sherry MELTON
88 Counselor/Coord Trans Center ... Ms. Gwen KELL
09 Research Analyst ... Ms. Robyn WORNALL
96 Business Services Assistant ... Ms. Solange KADA
84 Enrollment Management ... Ms. Sue NELSON

The National Hispanic University (G)

14271 Story Road, San Jose CA 95127-3823
County: Santa Clara — FICE Identification: 025184
Unit ID: 119544
Telephone: (408) 254-6900 — Carnegie Class: Bac/A&S
FAX Number: (408) 254-1369 — Calendar System: Semester
URL: www.nhu.edu
Established: 1981 — Annual Undergrad Tuition & Fees: $9,810
Enrollment: 609 — Coed
Affiliation or Control: Proprietary — IRS Status: Proprietary
Highest Offering: Baccalaureate
Program: Liberal Arts And General; Teacher Preparatory
Accreditation: WC

01 President ... Dr. David P. LOPEZ
05 Provost ... Dr. Juan NECOCHEA
20 Vice Provost ... Ms. Adriana AYALA
06 Director Admiss & Records/Registrar ... Ms. Pamela BUSTILLO
84 Director of Outreach & Recruitment ... Mr. Augustin CERVANTES
77 Director Computer Science ... Dr. Julio GARCIA
09 Director Institutional Research ... Dr. Isabel VALLEJO
37 Director Student Financial Aid ... Mr. Diondrae COLLIER
81 Coordinator Mathematics & Science ... Dr. Yazmin ROSA-BAUZA
88 Dir Childhood Development ... Dr. Edirle MENEZES
97 Chair Liberal Studies ... Dr. Carlos NAVARRO
53 Chair of Teacher Education ... Ms. Neva HOFEMANN
50 Chair of Business Administration ... Dr. George GUIM

National Test Pilot Institute (H)

PO Box 658, Mojave CA 93502-0658
County: Kern — Identification: 667009
Telephone: (616) 824-2977 — Carnegie Class: Not Classified
FAX Number: (661) 824-2943 — Calendar System: Other
URL: www.ntps.edu
Established: 1981 — Annual Graduate Tuition & Fees: N/A
Enrollment: N/A — Coed
Affiliation or Control: Independent Non-Profit — IRS Status: 501(c)3
Highest Offering: Master's; No Undergraduates
Program: Professional
Accreditation: ENG

01 Director ... Sean ROBERTS
03 Deputy Director ... Gregory V. LEWIS
10 Business Manager ... Lynda MATOS

National University (I)

11255 N Torrey Pines Road, La Jolla CA 92037-1011
County: San Diego — FICE Identification: 011460
Unit ID: 119605
Telephone: (858) 642-8000 — Carnegie Class: Master's L
FAX Number: (858) 642-8714 — Calendar System: Other
URL: www.nu.edu
Established: 1971 — Annual Undergrad Tuition & Fees: $17,400
Enrollment: 16,249 — Coed
Affiliation or Control: Independent Non-Profit — IRS Status: 501(c)3
Highest Offering: Master's
Program: 2-Year Principally Bachelor's Creditable; Liberal Arts And General; Teacher Preparatory; Professional
Accreditation: WC, #IACBE, NURSE

01 Interim University President ... Ms. Patricia E. POTTER
05 Provost ... Dr. Eileen HEVERON
11 Exec Vice Pres Admin & Business ... Mr. Richard E. CARTER
13 Vice President of Info Technology ... Mr. Christopher KRUG
32 Vice President for Student Services ... Dr. Joseph ZAVALA
20 Associate Provost ... Ms. Debra BEAN
09 AVP Inst Rsrch/Planning & Analysis ... Vacant
12 AVP Regional Oper San Diego Region ... Mr. Mark MOSES
12 AVP Regional Oper Southern Region ... Dr. Daren UPHAM
12 AVP Regional Oper Northern Region ... Dr. Mahvash YADEGAR
15 AVP Human Resources ... Mr. Alan HONEYCUTT
30 Exec Dir of Dev & Alumni Relations ... Mr. Robert FREELEN
53 Dean School of Education ... Dr. Kenneth FAWSON
50 Dean School Business & Management ... Dr. Ronald UHLIG
49 Dean College of Letters & Sciences ... Dr. Michael MCANEAR
54 Dean Engineering & Technology ... Dr. George BECKWITH
60 Dean School of Media/Communication ... Ms. Karla BERRY
76 Dean Health and Human Services ... Dr. Michael LACOURSE
06 Registrar ... Ms. Jo Ellen SHENDY
27 Director Communications ... Mr. Michael BURGOS
08 Director Library Services ... Ms. Anne-Marie SECORD
37 Director Financial Aid ... Ms. Valerie RYAN
26 Dir Information/Community Relations ... Mr. David NEVILLE
18 Director of Facilities ... Mr. Craig CROSBY
07 Director of Marketing ... Ms. Kendra LOSEE
88 Director of Credentials ... Mr. Brad DAMON

New York Film Academy, Los Angeles (J)

3801 Barham Boulevard, Los Angeles CA 90068
County: Los Angeles — FICE Identification: 041188
Telephone: (818) 733-2600 — Carnegie Class: Not Classified
FAX Number: (818) 733-4074 — Calendar System: Semester
URL: www.nyfa.edu
Established: 2006 — Annual Undergrad Tuition & Fees: $34,800
Enrollment: 635 — Coed
Affiliation or Control: Proprietary — IRS Status: Proprietary
Highest Offering: Master's

Program: Fine Arts Emphasis
Accreditation: ART

05 Provost .... Mr. Michael YOUNG
20 Academic Dean .... Ms. Patricia BECKMAN-WELLS
11 Senior Director .... Ms. Jean SHERLOCK

NewSchool of Architecture and Design (A)

1249 F Street, San Diego CA 92101-6634
County: San Diego FICE Identification: 030439
Unit ID: 119775
Telephone: (619) 684-8800 Carnegie Class: Spec/Arts
FAX Number: (619) 684-8880 Calendar System: Quarter
URL: www.newschoolarch.edu
Established: 1980 Annual Undergrad Tuition & Fees: $22,995
Enrollment: 640 Coed
Affiliation or Control: Proprietary IRS Status: Proprietary
Highest Offering: Master's
Program: Professional
Accreditation: ACICS

01 President .... Dr. Steven ALTMAN
05 Dean .... Mr. Christopher GENIK
10 Director Finance & Administration .... Mr. Robert GIROLAMO
32 Director Student Affairs .... Ms. Charlene ALSBAUGH
48 Graduate Chair Arch .... Mr. Kurt HUNKER
48 Undergraduate Chair Architecture .... Mr. Len ZEGARSKI
88 Chair Construction Mgmt .... Dr. Linda THOMAS-MOBLEY
88 Chair Landscape Architecture .... Ms. Leslie RYAN
88 Chair Digital Media Arts .... Mr. Avery CALDWELL
09 Director of Institutional Research .... Ms. Nga PHAN
06 Registrar .... Mr. Victor PARGA
07 Director Admissions .... Mr. John KIM
37 Director of Financial Aid .... Mr. Mike NELSON
38 Director of Advising and Retention .... Vacant
21 Business Services .... Ms. Terre CORTEZ-FARAH
36 Director Career Services .... Ms. Ellyn LESTER
29 Director Alumni Relations .... Vacant
08 Library .... Ms. Karen KINNEY
20 Faculty Coordinator .... Mr. Michael STEPNER
26 Marketing Manager .... Ms. Lisa APOLINSKI

*North Orange County Community College District (B)

1830 W Romneya Drive, Anaheim CA 92801-1819
County: Orange FICE Identification: 009742
Unit ID: 120023
Telephone: (714) 808-4500 Carnegie Class: N/A
FAX Number: (714) 808-4791
URL: www.nocccd.edu

01 Chancellor .... Dr. Ned DOFFONEY
10 Vice Chancellor Finance/Facilities .... Mr. Fred WILLIAMS
15 Vice Chancellor Human Resources .... Mr. Jeff O. HORSLEY
05 Vice Chancellor of Instruction .... Vacant
13 District Director Information Svcs .... Ms. Deborah LUDFORD
04 Exec Admin Aide to Chancellor .... Ms. Violet R. AYON
26 District Dir Public & Govt Affairs .... Ms. Kai STEARNS MOORE
22 Dist Director Equity & Diversity .... Mr. Kenneth I. ROBINSON

*Cypress College (C)

9200 Valley View, Cypress CA 90630-5897
County: Orange FICE Identification: 001193
Unit ID: 113236
Telephone: (714) 484-7000 Carnegie Class: Assoc/Pub-S-MC
FAX Number: (714) 527-8238 Calendar System: Semester
URL: www.cypresscollege.edu
Established: 1966 Annual Undergrad Tuition & Fees (In-District): $896
Enrollment: 15,963 Coed
Affiliation or Control: State/Local IRS Status: 501(c)3
Highest Offering: Associate Degree
Program: Occupational; 2-Year Principally Bachelor's Creditable
Accreditation: WJ, ADNUR, DA, DH, DMS, FUSER, RAD

02 President .... Dr. Michael J. KASLER
03 Executive Vice President .... Dr. Robert SIMPSON
11 Vice Pres of Administrative Svcs .... Ms. Karen CANT
07 Dean Admissions & Records/Business .... Mr. Dave WASSENAAR
08 Int Dean Library/Lrng Resource Ctr .... Mr. Eldon YOUNG
38 Dean Counseling/Student Devel .... Mr. Paul DEDIOS
06 Registrar .... Ms. Regina FORD
102 Exec Dir Foundation Cypress College .... Mr. Raul ALVAREZ
32 Dean Student Support Services .... Dr. Richard RAMS
88 Director Disabled Student Services .... Dr. Kimberly BARTLETT
90 Manager Systems Technology Svcs .... Mr. Michael KAVANAUGH
37 Manager Financial Aid .... Mr. Keith COBB
84 Matriculation Manager .... Ms. Kristine NELSON
09 Dir Institutional Research/ Planning .... Dr. Santanu BANDYOPADHYAY
18 Director Physical Plant/Facilities .... Mr. Albert MIRANDA
19 Director Campus Security .... Ms. Shirley SMITH

*Fullerton College (D)

321 E Chapman Avenue, Fullerton CA 92832-2095
County: Orange FICE Identification: 001201
Unit ID: 114859
Telephone: (714) 992-7000 Carnegie Class: Assoc/Pub-S-MC
FAX Number: (714) 992-9930 Calendar System: Semester
URL: www.fullcoll.edu
Established: 1913 Annual Undergrad Tuition & Fees (In-District): $1,112
Enrollment: 22,354 Coed
Affiliation or Control: State/Local IRS Status: 501(c)3
Highest Offering: Associate Degree
Program: Occupational; 2-Year Principally Bachelor's Creditable; Liberal Arts And General
Accreditation: WJ

02 President .... Dr. Rajen VURDIEN
05 Vice President Instruction .... Vacant
32 Vice President Student Services .... Dr. Toni DUBOIS
11 Vice President Administrative Svcs .... Vacant
50 Dean Business & CIS .... Ms. Ann HOVEY
57 Dean Fine Arts .... Mr. Robert JENSEN
79 Dean Humanities .... Mr. Dan WILLOUGHBY
81 Dean Math/Computer Science .... Mr. Mark GREENHALGH
49 Interim Dean Natural Sciences .... Dr. Carol MATTSON
68 Interim Dean Physical Education .... Dr. Susan BEERS
83 Dean Social Sciences .... Mr. Dan TESAR
54 Dean Technology & Engr .... Mr. Scott MCKENZIE
37 Director of Financial Aid .... Mr. Greg RYAN
23 Director Health Center .... Ms. Christine KIGER
18 Director Physical Plant .... Ms. Christine FIGHERA
40 Manager Bookstore .... Mr. Nick KARVIA
88 Dean Student Support Services .... Mr. Robert MIRANDA
35 Director Student Affairs .... Ms. Darlene JENSEN
06 Registrar .... Ms. Rena NEGRETE
19 Director Campus Safety .... Mr. Steve SELBY
38 Dean Counseling/Student Development .... Ms. Lisa CAMPBELL
62 Dean Library Services .... Ms. Jackie BOLL
07 Dean Admissions & Records .... Mr. Albert ABUTIN
13 Academic Computing .... Mr. Co HO
09 Director of Institutional Research .... Dr. Kenneth MEEHAN
88 Director Transfer Center .... Ms. Lily ESPINOZA
26 Public Information Officer .... Ms. Andrea HANSTEIN
04 Exec Assistant to the President .... Vacant

North-West College (E)

2121 W Garvey Avenue N, West Covina CA 91790-2051
County: Los Angeles FICE Identification: 011707
Unit ID: 120078
Telephone: (626) 960-5046 Carnegie Class: Not Classified
FAX Number: (626) 960-9190 Calendar System: Semester
URL: www.northwestcollege.com
Established: N/A Annual Undergrad Tuition & Fees: N/A
Enrollment: 288 Coed
Affiliation or Control: Proprietary IRS Status: Proprietary
Highest Offering: Associate Degree
Program: Occupational; 2-Year Principally Bachelor's Creditable
Accreditation: ACCSC

01 Vice President .... Mr. Mitchell FUERST

Northwestern Polytechnic University (F)

47671 Westinghouse Drive, Fremont CA 94539-7474
County: Alameda Identification: 666759
Unit ID: 120166
Telephone: (510) 592-9688 Carnegie Class: Spec/Engg
FAX Number: (510) 657-8975 Calendar System: Trimester
URL: www.npu.edu
Established: 1984 Annual Undergrad Tuition & Fees: $9,000
Enrollment: 869 Coed
Affiliation or Control: Independent Non-Profit IRS Status: 501(c)3
Highest Offering: Doctorate
Program: Technical Emphasis
Accreditation: ACICS

01 President .... Dr. George HSIEH
05 Dean of Academic Affairs .... Dr. Pochang HSU
07 Director of Admissions .... Ms. Judy WENG
06 Registrar .... Ms. Lily HSIAO
10 Director of Operations .... Dr. Bill WU
46 Director of Institutional Research .... Dr. Tai HSU
15 Director Personnel Services .... Ms. Linda REN
18 Chief Facilities/Physical Plant .... Mr. Dennis YU
32 Director Student Affairs .... Dr. Mariam GHAZVINI
36 Director Student Placement .... Mr. Michael TANG
38 Director Student Counseling .... Ms. Monica SINHA
35 Chief Student Life Officer .... Dr. John KU

Notre Dame de Namur University (G)

1500 Ralston Avenue, Belmont CA 94002-1908
County: San Mateo FICE Identification: 001179
Unit ID: 120184
Telephone: (650) 508-3500 Carnegie Class: Master's M
FAX Number: (650) 508-3660 Calendar System: Semester
URL: www.ndnu.edu
Established: 1851 Annual Undergrad Tuition & Fees: $26,610
Enrollment: 1,790 Coed
Affiliation or Control: Independent Non-Profit IRS Status: 501(c)3
Highest Offering: Master's
Program: Liberal Arts And General; Teacher Preparatory; Professional
Accreditation: WC

01 President .... Dr. Judith M. GREIG
05 Provost .... Dr. Diana DEMETRULIAS
10 Vice Pres Finance & Administration .... Mr. Henry ROTH
20 Dean of Students .... Ms. Jean CONDE
84 Vice President of Enrollment .... Mr. Hernan BUCHELI
30 Vice Pres Institutional Advancement .... Mr. Michael ROMO
04 Exec Assistant to the President .... Ms. Gina DORST
49 Dean Arts & Sciences .... Vacant
50 Dean Business & Management .... Ms. Barbara CAULLEY
53 Dean Education & Leadership .... Dr. Joanne ROSSI
06 Registrar .... Ms. Sandra LEE
36 Director Career Development .... Ms. Carrie MCKNIGHT
37 Director Financial Aid .... Ms. Susan PACE
38 Director Student Counseling .... Dr. Dennis C. DOW
41 Athletic Director .... Mr. Josh DOODY
42 Director Spirituality .... Vacant
19 Chief Public Safety .... Mr. David MEFFORD
23 Director Health Services .... Ms. Karen HACKETT
29 Director Events/Alumni Relations .... Vacant
26 Director Communication .... Mr. Richard ROSSI
15 Director Human Resources .... Ms. Mary HAESLOOP
28 Director for Mission and Diversity .... Dr. Bobby VAUGHN

Occidental College (H)

1600 Campus Road, Los Angeles CA 90041-3314
County: Los Angeles FICE Identification: 001249
Unit ID: 120254
Telephone: (323) 259-2500 Carnegie Class: Bac/A&S
FAX Number: (323) 259-2958 Calendar System: Semester
URL: www.oxy.edu
Established: 1887 Annual Undergrad Tuition & Fees: $40,939
Enrollment: 2,102 Coed
Affiliation or Control: Independent Non-Profit IRS Status: 501(c)3
Highest Offering: Master's
Program: Liberal Arts And General
Accreditation: WC

01 President .... Dr. Jonathan VEITCH
05 Dean of the College .... Dr. Jorge GONZALEZ
11 Vice President Admin/Finance .... Mr. Michael GROENER
30 Vice Pres Institutional Advancement .... Mr. Dennis COLLINS
07 Vice Pres Admission & Financial Aid .... Mr. Vincent CUSEO
43 VP Legal Affairs & General Counsel .... Mr. Carl BOTTERUDE
13 VP for Information Technology Svcs .... Dr. Pamela MCQUESTEN
10 Assoc Vice President & Controller .... Ms. Barbara VALIENTE
18 Assoc VP for Facilities Management .... Mr. Michael STEPHENS
04 Exec Assistant to the President .... Ms. Rebecca STOLZ
32 Dean of Students .... Dr. Barbara AVERY
06 Registrar .... Mr. Victor T. EGITTO
08 Librarian .... Dr. Robert KIEFT
37 Director of Financial Aid .... Ms. Maureen MCRAE
29 Actg Director of Alumni Relations .... Ms. Dana VALK
36 Director Career Development Center .... Ms. Valerie SAVIOR
15 Director of Human Resources .... Mr. Richard LEDWIN
26 Director of Communications .... Mr. Jim TRANQUADA
09 Director Institutional Research .... Mr. Michael D. TAMADA
44 Int Dir Advance Svc Operations .... Ms. Regan REMULLA
39 Ast Dn Stdnts Resid Life/Hsng Svc .... Mr. Tim CHANG
19 Director of Campus Safety .... Ms. Hollis B. NIETO

Ohlone College (I)

43600 Mission Boulevard, Fremont CA 94539-0390
County: Alameda FICE Identification: 004481
Unit ID: 120290
Telephone: (510) 659-6000 Carnegie Class: Assoc/Pub-S-SC
FAX Number: N/A Calendar System: Semester
URL: www.ohlone.edu
Established: 1966 Annual Undergrad Tuition & Fees (In-District): $1,134
Enrollment: 11,801 Coed
Affiliation or Control: State/Local IRS Status: 501(c)3
Highest Offering: Associate Degree
Program: Occupational; 2-Year Principally Bachelor's Creditable
Accreditation: WJ, ADNUR, PTAA

01 President/Superintendent .... Dr. Gari BROWNING
10 Vice Pres Administrative Services .... Vacant
05 Vice President Academic Affairs .... Dr. James WRIGHT
32 Vice President Student Services .... Dr. Ron TRAVENICK
13 Assoc Vice Pres Information Tech .... Mr. Bruce GRIFFIN
20 Assoc Vice Pres Academic Affairs .... Dr. Leta STAGNARO
15 Assoc Vice Pres Human Resources .... Ms. Shairon ZINGSHEIM
08 Dean Learning Resource/Instruc Tech .... Ms. Lesley BUEHLER
39 Dean of Counseling .... Vacant
09 Dean Institutional Research .... Mr. Michael BOWMAN
57 Dean Fine Arts/Business .... Mr. Walter BIRKEDAHL
76 Dean Health Sciences & Env Studies .... Ms. Gale CARLI
83 Dean Humanities/Social Sci & Math .... Ms. Mikelyn STACEY
81 Dean Science & Technology .... Dr. Ron QUINTA
88 Dean Deaf Studies .... Dr. Genie GERTZ
102 Executive Director Foundation .... Mr. Dave SMITH
35 Director EOPS/Student Services .... Ms. Debra TRIGG
21 Dean Business Services .... Ms. Joanne SCHULTZ
30 Director College Advancement .... Ms. Patrice BIRKEDAHL
40 Bookstore Manager .... Vacant
19 Chief Safety & Security .... Mr. Steve OSAWA
18 Director Facilities/Physical Plant .... Mr. Lucky LOFTON
37 Director Financial Aid .... Ms. Deborah GRIFFIN
96 Director of Purchasing .... Vacant
07 Director Admissions & Records .... Vacant
92 Director International Programs .... Mr. Eddie WEST
84 Director Enrollment Mgmt .... Ms. Kimberly ROBBIE

Olivet University (A)

250 Fourth Street, San Francisco CA 94103-3117
County: San Francisco Identification: 666176
Telephone: (415) 371-0002 Carnegie Class: Not Classified
FAX Number: (415) 371-0003 Calendar System: Semester
URL: www.olivetu.us
Established: 1992 Annual Undergrad Tuition & Fees: $12,888
Enrollment: 570 Coed
Affiliation or Control: Independent Non-Profit IRS Status: 501(c)3
Highest Offering: Master's
Program: Liberal Arts And General; Professional; Religious Emphasis
Accreditation: BI

01 University President ....Dr. William WAGNER
03 Vice President ....Dr. Joseph Ray TALLMAN
05 Academic Dean ....Dr. Tracy DAVIS
32 Dean of Students ....Mrs. Julia TZENG
10 Chief Financial Officer ....Mr. Barnabas JUNG
11 Chief Operating Officer ....Mr. Walker TZENG
08 Librarian ....Mrs. Biehwa CHEN MA

Otis College of Art and Design (B)

9045 Lincoln Boulevard, Westchester CA 90045-3550
County: Los Angeles FICE Identification: 001251
Unit ID: 120403
Telephone: (310) 665-6800 Carnegie Class: Spec/Arts
FAX Number: (310) 665-6805 Calendar System: Semester
URL: www.otis.edu
Established: 1918 Annual Undergrad Tuition & Fees: $35,404
Enrollment: 1,226 Coed
Affiliation or Control: Independent Non-Profit IRS Status: 501(c)3
Highest Offering: Master's
Program: Professional
Accreditation: WC, ART

01 President ....Mr. Samuel HOI
05 Chief Acad Officer/Provost ....Dr. Kerry WALK
10 VP of Administration & Finance Svcs ....Mr. William SCHAEFFER
84 VP Enrollment Management ....Mr. Marc MEREDITH
30 VP Institutional Advancement ....Ms. Carrie STEWART
32 Dean of Students ....Dr. Laura KIRALLA
51 Dean of Continuing Education ....Ms. Amy GANTMAN
07 Dean of Admissions ....Ms. Yvette SOBKY-SHAFFER
06 Registrar ....Ms. Anna MANZANO
08 Director of Library ....Ms. Sue MABERRY
37 Director of Financial Aid ....Ms. Jessika VASQUEZ-HUERTA
88 Director of Galleries & Exhibitions ....Ms. Meg LINTON
15 Director of Human Resources ....Ms. Dana LOPEZ
36 Career Services Specialist ....Ms. Denise GIANOUSSOPOULOS
13 Director of Information Systems ....Mr. Robert WALTERS
18 Director of Facilities ....Mr. Claude NICA
26 Chief Public Relations Officer ....Ms. Margi REEVE
29 Director Alumni Relations ....Ms. Ceres MADOO
96 Director of Purchasing ....Ms. Barbara TECLE
38 Director Student Counseling ....Dr. Fred BARNES

Oxman College (C)

375 Third Avenue, San Francisco CA 94118
County: San Francisco Identification: 667025
Telephone: (415) 751-6461 Carnegie Class: Not Classified
FAX Number: (415) 751-6458 Calendar System: Other
URL: www.oxmancollege.com
Established: 1991 Annual Undergrad Tuition & Fees: N/A
Enrollment: N/A Coed
Affiliation or Control: Proprietary IRS Status: Proprietary
Highest Offering: Associate Degree
Program: Occupational; Nursing Emphasis
Accreditation: COE

Pacific College (D)

3160 Redhill Avenue, Costa Mesa CA 92626-3402
County: Orange FICE Identification: 032993
Unit ID: 422695
Telephone: (800) 867-2243 Carnegie Class: Not Classified
FAX Number: (714) 662-1702 Calendar System: Semester
URL: www.pacific-college.edu
Established: 1993 Annual Undergrad Tuition & Fees: $29,500
Enrollment: 400 Coed
Affiliation or Control: Proprietary IRS Status: Proprietary
Highest Offering: Baccalaureate
Program: Occupational; 2-Year Principally Bachelor's Creditable; Nursing Emphasis
Accreditation: ACCSC

01 President ....Mr. William L. NELSON

Pacific College of Oriental Medicine (E)

7445 Mission Valley Road, #105,
San Diego CA 92108-4408
County: San Diego FICE Identification: 030277
Unit ID: 378576
Telephone: (619) 574-6909 Carnegie Class: Spec/Health
FAX Number: (619) 574-6641 Calendar System: Trimester
URL: www.pacificcollege.edu
Established: 1986 Annual Undergrad Tuition & Fees: $17,725
Enrollment: 588 Coed
Affiliation or Control: Proprietary IRS Status: Proprietary
Highest Offering: Doctorate
Program: Professional
Accreditation: ACCSC, ACUP

01 President ....Mr. Jack MILLER
11 Chief Operating Officer ....Ms. Elaine GATES-MILINER
07 Vice Pres of Admissions/Marketing ....Ms. Suzanne KARSTEN
12 Campus Director NY Campus ....Ms. Gina LEPORE
12 Campus Director CH Campus ....Mr. Edward LAMADRID
05 Director of Academic Affairs ....Ms. Stacy GOMES
06 Registrar ....Mr. Troy HALL
20 Academic Dean ....Mr. Bob DAMONE
37 Financial Aid Director ....Ms. Kyle POSTON
26 Director of Adv and Marketing ....Ms. Gail VOGT
23 Director of Clinical Services ....Mr. Greg SPERBER
08 Head Librarian ....Ms. Naomi BROERING
13 Director of Information Technology ....Mr. Roland ZAKARIA
15 Office Manager ....Ms. Cindy FLOYD
40 Bookstore Manager ....Ms. Nayeli CORONA
21 Bursar/Property Manager ....Ms. Patti HINES
27 Pacific Symposium & Events Coord ....Ms. Tiffany HANSEN

Pacific Lutheran Theological Seminary (F)

2770 Marin Avenue, Berkeley CA 94708-1597
County: Alameda FICE Identification: 001254
Unit ID: 120740
Telephone: (510) 524-5264 Carnegie Class: Spec/Faith
FAX Number: (510) 524-2408 Calendar System: Semester
URL: www.plts.edu
Established: 1950 Annual Graduate Tuition & Fees: $12,180
Enrollment: 100 Coed
Affiliation or Control: Evangelical Lutheran Church In America
IRS Status: 501(c)3
Highest Offering: Master's; No Undergraduates
Program: Professional; Religious Emphasis
Accreditation: THEOL

01 President ....Dr. Phyllis ANDERSON
05 Dean of the Faculty ....Dr. Michael AUNE
10 VP for Finance and Operations ....Ms. Debora OW
30 Director of Development ....Mr. Joel WUDEL
07 Director of Admissions ....Dr. Steve CHURCHILL
08 Library Director ....Mr. Robert BENEDETTO

Pacific Oaks College (G)

5 Westmoreland Place, Pasadena CA 91103-3592
County: Los Angeles FICE Identification: 001255
Unit ID: 120768
Telephone: (800) 388-1330 Carnegie Class: Spec/Other
FAX Number: N/A Calendar System: Semester
URL: www.pacificoaks.edu
Established: 1945 Annual Undergrad Tuition & Fees: $27,252
Enrollment: 560 Coed
Affiliation or Control: Independent Non-Profit IRS Status: 501(c)3
Highest Offering: Master's
Program: Teacher Preparatory; Professional
Accreditation: WC

01 President ....Dr. Michael HOROWITZ
10 Associate Vice President of Finance ....Mr. Kevin WILSON
32 Assoc Vice Pres Student Services ....Mr. Frank FRIAS
04 Executive Assistant to President ....Ms. Amy DILGREN
05 Chief Academic Officer ....Vacant
37 Director of Financial Aid ....Mr. Seph RODRIGUEZ
13 IT Director ....Ms. Terry UTTER
06 Registrar/Director Enrollment Svcs ....Mr. Jeff ROAMES
08 Dir Instruct Sites/Library Svcs ....Ms. Erin BARTA
09 Dir Ctr Stdnt Achievmt/Res/Enrich ....Ms. Pat MEDA
20 Academic Dir/Instructional Sites ....Dr. Laila AAEN
88 Academic Director MFT ....Ms. Connie DESTITO
15 Human Resources Manager ....Ms. Carolyn MATHIS
22 Program Director Human Development ....Dr. Joseph T. SUNDEEN
88 Pgm Dir Early Childhood Education ....Ms. Aki OHSEKI
18 Manager of Facilities ....Vacant

Pacific School of Religion (H)

1798 Scenic Avenue, Berkeley CA 94709-1323
County: Alameda FICE Identification: 001256
Unit ID: 120795
Telephone: (510) 849-8200 Carnegie Class: Spec/Faith
FAX Number: (510) 845-8948 Calendar System: Semester
URL: www.psr.edu
Established: 1866 Annual Graduate Tuition & Fees: $14,910
Enrollment: 639 Coed
Affiliation or Control: Independent Non-Profit IRS Status: 501(c)3
Highest Offering: Doctorate; No Undergraduates
Program: Professional; Religious Emphasis
Accreditation: WC, THEOL

01 President ....Dr. Riess POTTERVELD
05 Vice President & Academic Dean ....Dr. Tat-Siong Benny LIEW
10 Chief Financial Officer ....Mr. Steve ARGYRIS
30 VP for Institutional Advancement ....Ms. Kathi MCSHANE
20 Asst Dean Academic Pgms/Registrar ....Ms. Delphine HWANG
32 Minister & Coordinator of Cmty Life ....Vacant
08 Library Director GTU ....Mr. Robert BENEDETTO
07 Dir of Recruitment & Admissions ....Ms. Nicole NAFFAA
15 Personnel Director ....Ms. Deborah WALKER
04 Executive Asst to President ....Ms. Marjorie WILKES

Pacific States University (I)

1516 S Western Avenue, Los Angeles CA 90006-4298
County: Los Angeles FICE Identification: 031633
Unit ID: 120838
Telephone: (323) 731-2383 Carnegie Class: Spec/Bus
FAX Number: (323) 731-7276 Calendar System: Quarter
URL: www.psuca.edu
Established: 1928 Annual Undergrad Tuition & Fees: $18,900
Enrollment: 196 Coed
Affiliation or Control: Independent Non-Profit IRS Status: 501(c)3
Highest Offering: Doctorate
Program: Liberal Arts And General; Professional; Business Emphasis
Accreditation: ACICS

01 President ....Dr. Jin Q. KIM
04 Special Assistant to the President ....Dr. Joan B. WILSON
11 Vice President ....Mr. Jin KIM
05 University Dean Emeritus ....Mr. Meyer POLLACK
50 Director College of Business ....Dr. Kamol SOMVICHIAN
77 Dir Col Computer Sci/Info Systems ....Dr. John MA
88 Director ESL Program ....Ms. Karen CHEN
08 University Librarian ....Ms. Deborah HULL
06 Registrar/Student Financial Aid ....Ms. Namyoung CHAH
10 Financial Affairs Officer ....Mr. Keith K. KIM
20 Associate Dean ....Dr. Min Sang KIM

Pacific Union College (J)

One Angwin Avenue, Angwin CA 94508-9797
County: Napa FICE Identification: 001258
Unit ID: 120865
Telephone: (707) 965-6311 Carnegie Class: Bac/A&S
FAX Number: (707) 965-6390 Calendar System: Quarter
URL: www.puc.edu
Established: 1882 Annual Undergrad Tuition & Fees: $25,965
Enrollment: 1,436 Coed
Affiliation or Control: Seventh-day Adventist IRS Status: 501(c)3
Highest Offering: Master's
Program: Liberal Arts And General; Teacher Preparatory; Professional
Accreditation: WC, ADNUR, IACBE, MUS, NUR, SW

01 President ....Dr. Heather J. KNIGHT
05 Vice Pres Admin & Academic Dean ....Dr. Nancy LECOURT
10 Vice Pres Financial Administration ....Dr. Dave LAWRENCE
32 Vice President Student Life ....Dr. Lisa BISSELL PAULSON
30 Vice President Advancement ....Ms. Pam SADLER
84 Vice Pres Marketing and Enrollment ....Ms. Julie LEE
33 Dean of Men ....Mr. James I. BOYD, JR.
34 Dean of Women ....Miss Janice R. WOOD
08 Director Library Services ....Mr. Adu WORKU
37 Director Student Financial Services ....Ms. Laurie WHEELER
13 Director Information Technology ....Ms. Maria LOPEZ
06 Director Registration & Records ....Mrs. Marlo WATERS
15 Director Human Resources ....Mr. Gayln K. BOWERS
21 Director Budgets & Fiscal Services ....Mr. William L. COCHRAN
38 Director Counseling Center ....Mrs. Laurie HALVERSEN
18 Chief Facilities/Physical Plant ....Mr. Dan BROWN
20 Associate Academic Officer ....Mr. Edwin MOORE

Pacifica Graduate Institute (K)

249 Lambert Road, Carpinteria CA 93013-3019
County: Carpinteria FICE Identification: 031268
Unit ID: 115746
Telephone: (805) 969-3626 Carnegie Class: DRU
FAX Number: (805) 565-1932 Calendar System: Quarter
URL: www.pacifica.edu
Established: 1974 Annual Graduate Tuition & Fees: $25,965
Enrollment: 670 Coed
Affiliation or Control: Proprietary IRS Status: Proprietary
Highest Offering: Doctorate; No Undergraduates
Program: Professional
Accreditation: WC

01 President ....Dr. Stephen AIZENSTAT
03 Executive Vice President & Provost ....Dr. Carol S. PEARSON
11 Chief Administrative Officer ....Dr. Alex MIRANDA
10 Chief Financial Officer ....Mr. David HENKEL
07 Director of Admissions ....Ms. Wendy OVEREND

Palmer College of Chiropractic, West Campus (L)

90 E Tasman Drive, San Jose CA 95134-1617
County: Santa Clara FICE Identification: 021849
Unit ID: 120944
Telephone: (408) 944-6000 Carnegie Class: Spec/Health
FAX Number: (408) 944-6111 Calendar System: Quarter
URL: www.palmer.edu
Established: 1978 Annual Graduate Tuition & Fees: $29,800
Enrollment: 311 Coed
Affiliation or Control: Independent Non-Profit IRS Status: 501(c)3
Highest Offering: First Professional Degree; No Undergraduates
Program: Professional
Accreditation: &NH, CHIRO

00 Chancellor ... Dr. Dennis M. MARCHIORI
01 President ... Dr. William C. MEEKER
05 Vice Chancellor for Academics ... Dr. Robert E. PERCUOCO
32 Vice Chancellor Student Success ... Dr. Kevin A. CUNNINGHAM
11 Vice Chancellor Support Services ... Mr. Robert E. LEE
84 Vice Chancellor for Enrollment ... Mr. J. Michael NOVAK
10 Vice Chancellor for Administration ... Mr. Thomas L. TIEMEIER
30 VC for Institutional Advancement ... Vacant
17 Vice Chancellor for Clinic Affairs ... Dr. Kurt W. WOOD
46 Vice Chancellor for Research ... Dr. Christine G. GOERTZ
26 Exec Dir for Marketing & PR ... Mr. Darren R. GARRETT
29 Executive Director for Alumni ... Dr. Mickey G. BURT
88 Exec Dir Office of Strategic Dev ... Dr. Judy M. SILVESTRONE
20 Dean of Academic Affairs ... Dr. Thomas A. SOUZA
23 Dean of Clinics ... Dr. Gregory J. SNOW
35 Dean of Student Services ... Dr. William N. DUMONTHIER
09 Sr Dir Institutional Plng/Research ... Dr. Dustin C. DERBY
21 Senior Dir for Financial Affairs ... Ms. Alexis A. VANDER HORN
13 Senior Director of IT ... Mr. Mike A. BENEDICT
15 Senior Human Resources Director ... Ms. Michelle K. WALKER
40 Senior Director of Bookstores ... Ms. Carol A. HOYT
88 Senior Director for Assessment ... Dr. Robert E. PERCUOCO
24 Sr Dir Center for Teaching/Lrng ... Vacant
09 Director of Research ... Dr. Robert COOPERSTEIN
06 Registrar ... Ms. Eliana NATHAN
07 Campus Enrollment Director ... Ms. Julie J. BEHN

† Regional accreditation is carried under the parent institution in Davenport, IA.

Palo Alto University (A)

1791 Arastradero Road, Palo Alto CA 94304
County: San Mateo FICE Identification: 021383
Unit ID: 120698
Telephone: (800) 818-6136 Carnegie Class: Spec/Health
FAX Number: (650) 433-3888 Calendar System: Quarter
URL: www.paloaltou.edu
Established: 1975 Annual Undergrad Tuition & Fees: $17,901
Enrollment: 575 Coed
Affiliation or Control: Independent Non-Profit IRS Status: 501(c)3
Highest Offering: Doctorate
Program: Professional
Accreditation: WC, CLPSY

01 President ... Dr. Allen CALVIN
05 Academic Vice President ... Dr. William FROMING
32 Vice President Student Services ... Ms. Elizabeth HILT
08 VP Information Resource/Library Dir ... Ms. Christine KIDD
10 Vice Pres Business Affairs/CFO ... Ms. June KLEIN
17 Dir of Clinical Training-Ph.D. Pgm ... Dr. Robert RUSSELL
17 Dir of Clinical Training-Psy.D. Pgm ... Dr. Jim BRECKENRIDGE
23 Director of Clinic ... Dr. Robert REISER
06 Registrar ... Ms. Nora MARQUEZ
37 Director of Financial Aid ... Ms. America BRYANT

Palo Verde College (B)

One College Drive, Blythe CA 92225-9561
County: Riverside FICE Identification: 001259
Unit ID: 120953
Telephone: (760) 921-5500 Carnegie Class: Assoc/Pub-S-MC
FAX Number: (760) 921-5590 Calendar System: Semester
URL: www.paloverde.edu
Established: 1947 Annual Undergrad Tuition & Fees (In-District): $780
Enrollment: 3,898 Coed
Affiliation or Control: State/Local IRS Status: 501(c)3
Highest Offering: Associate Degree
Program: Occupational; 2-Year Principally Bachelor's Creditable
Accreditation: WJ

01 Superintendent/President ... Dr. James HOTTOIS
05 Vice Pres Instructional Services ... Mr. William SMITH
32 Vice President of Student Services ... Ms. Diana RODRIGUEZ
04 Admin Asst to Supt/Pres/Foundation ... Ms. Denise HUNT
66 Nursing & Allied Health Coord ... Ms. Sharron BURGESON
106 Dean of Distance Learning ... Ms. Vicki ATTAWAY
12 Director Needles Center ... Ms. Cristen MANN
51 Dean of Career/Tech/Cont Educ ... Mr. George WALTERS
08 Librarian ... Ms. June TURNER
06 Registrar ... Ms. Melinda WALNOHA
88 Site Supervsr Child Dev/Teacher Ctr ... Ms. Maria KEHL
09 Institutional Research/Professor ... Mr. Brian THIEBAUX
18 Facilities & Operations Manager ... Mr. Albert BRAMBILA
13 Director of Information Technology ... Mr. Adam HOUSTON
26 Outreach & Events Coordinator ... Ms. Sarah FRID
36 Transfer & Career Ctr Dir/Counselor ... Ms. Hortensia RIVERA
45 Dir Econ Dev Center/Inst Research ... Vacant
37 Financial Aid Officer ... Ms. Linda PRATT
40 Bookstore Assistant ... Ms. Denise TAYLOR
15 Human Resource Manager ... Ms. Debbie MITCHELL
21 Fiscal Services Manager ... Ms. Russi EGAN
20 Instructional Service Manager ... Ms. Lisa HOLMES

Palomar College (C)

1140 W Mission Road, San Marcos CA 92069-1487
County: San Diego FICE Identification: 001260
Unit ID: 120971
Telephone: (760) 744-1150 Carnegie Class: Assoc/Pub-S-MC
FAX Number: (760) 744-8123 Calendar System: Semester
URL: www.palomar.edu
Established: 1946 Annual Undergrad Tuition & Fees (In-District): $780
Enrollment: 28,700 Coed
Affiliation or Control: State/Local IRS Status: 501(c)3
Highest Offering: Associate Degree
Program: Occupational; 2-Year Principally Bachelor's Creditable
Accreditation: WJ, ADNUR, DA, EMT

01 Superintendent/President ... Mr. Robert P. DEEGAN
05 Asst Supt/Vice Pres Instruction ... Ms. Berta CUARON
32 Asst Supt/VP Student Services ... Mr. Mark VERNOY
10 Asst Supt/VP Finance/Admin Svcs ... Vacant
16 Asst Supt/VP Human Resources ... Mr. John TORTAROLO
04 Assistant to the President ... Ms. Cheryl ASHOUR
79 Dean Languages & Literature ... Mr. Steve MCDONALD
81 Dean Math/Natural & Health Sciences ... Mr. Dan SOURBEER
38 Dean Counseling Services ... Ms. Lynda HALTTUNEN
75 Dean Career/Tech/Extended Educ Div ... Ms. Wilma G. OWENS
50 Dean Arts/Media/Bus & Computer Sci ... Ms. Norma MIYAMOTO
83 Int Dean Social/Behavioral Sciences ... Ms. Judy CATER
14 Director Info Systems & Services ... Mr. Jose VARGAS
84 Director Enrollment Svcs/Admissions ... Mr. Herman C. LEE
09 Director Institutional Research ... Ms. Michelle BARTON
18 Int Director of Facilities ... Ms. Kelley HUDSON-MACISAAC
35 Director Student Affairs ... Ms. Sherry TITUS
37 Director Student Financial Aid ... Ms. Mary SANAGUSTIN
21 Associate Business Officer ... Vacant
26 Int Chief Public Relations Officer ... Ms. Laura GROPEN
30 Chief of Development ... Mr. Richard TALMO
51 Director Extended Education ... Vacant
19 Interim Chief of Police ... Mr. Tony CRUZ
23 Director Health Services ... Ms. Jayne CONWAY
41 Director Athletics ... Mr. Scott CATHCART
24 Supervisor Media Equipment ... Mr. Lee HOFFMANN

Pardee RAND Graduate School of Policy Studies (D)

1776 Main Street, Santa Monica CA 90407-2138
County: Los Angeles FICE Identification: 010441
Unit ID: 121628
Telephone: (310) 393-0411 Carnegie Class: Spec/Other
FAX Number: (310) 451-6978 Calendar System: Quarter
URL: www.prgs.edu
Established: 1970 Annual Graduate Tuition & Fees: $25,000
Enrollment: 102 Coed
Affiliation or Control: Independent Non-Profit IRS Status: 501(c)3
Highest Offering: Doctorate; No Undergraduates
Program: Professional
Accreditation: WC

01 Dean ... Dr. Susan MARQUIS
05 Associate Dean ... Ms. Rachel SWANGER
06 Registrar ... Ms. Mary PARKER

Pasadena City College (E)

1570 E Colorado Boulevard, Pasadena CA 91106-2041
County: Los Angeles FICE Identification: 001261
Unit ID: 121044
Telephone: (626) 585-7123 Carnegie Class: Assoc/Pub-S-SC
FAX Number: (626) 585-7910 Calendar System: Semester
URL: www.pasadena.edu
Established: 1924 Annual Undergrad Tuition & Fees (In-District): $912
Enrollment: 27,027 Coed
Affiliation or Control: State/Local IRS Status: 501(c)3
Highest Offering: Associate Degree
Program: Occupational; 2-Year Principally Bachelor's Creditable
Accreditation: WJ, DA, DH, DT, MAC, RAD

01 Superintendent/President ... Dr. Mark W. ROCHA
05 Vice President for Instruction ... Dr. Jacqueline W. JACOBS
11 Vice Pres Admin Services ... Mr. Richard VAN PELT
32 Vice Pres Student/Learning Svcs ... Dr. Robert H. BELL
88 Vice Pres Educational Svcs ... Mr. Robert B. MILLER
15 Vice President of Human Resources ... Dr. Benedict LASTIMADO
13 Vice Pres Info Technology ... Mr. Dwayne P. CABLE
43 General Counsel ... Ms. Gail F. COOPER
30 Interim Dean External Relations ... Mrs. Elaine F. CHAPMAN
09 Dean Planning & Research ... Dr. Crystal KOLLROSS
75 Assoc Dean Voc Educ/Economic Devel ... Ms. Ellen L. LIGONS
35 Asst Dean Student Activities ... Mr. Scott W. THAYER
31 Assoc Dean Extended Learning Center ... Ms. Elaine CHAPMAN
38 Assoc Dean Counseling/Curr Liaison ... Dr. Cynthia D. OLIVO
88 Assistant Dean Special Services ... Dr. Kent YAMAUCHI
07 Assoc Dean Admissions/Records ... Dr. Margaret RAMEY
75 Assoc Dean Community Skills Center ... Mr. Rick L. HODGE
84 Assoc Dean Enroll/Instruc Data Mgmt ... Dr. Sabah ALQUADDOOMI
20 Assoc Dean of Academic Support ... Mr. Robert B. MILLER
37 Assistant Dean Financial Aid ... Ms. Kim MILES
56 Asst Dean Ext Opportunity Program ... Ms. Kathleen RODARTE
08 Assistant Dean Library Services ... Ms. Mary Ann LAUN
91 Director Admin Computing Services ... Mr. Dale PITTMAN
26 Director of Public Relations ... Mr. Juan F. GUTIERREZ
24 Director Media Services ... Ms. Johari DEWITT-ROGERS
18 Chief Facilities/Physical Plant ... Dr. Richard VAN PELT
96 Dir Business & Purchasing Services ... Ms. Sherry P. HASSAN

Patten University (F)

2433 Coolidge Avenue, Oakland CA 94601-2699
County: Alameda FICE Identification: 004490
Unit ID: 121071
Telephone: (510) 261-8500 Carnegie Class: Bac/Diverse
FAX Number: (510) 534-4344 Calendar System: Semester
URL: www.patten.edu
Established: 1944 Annual Undergrad Tuition & Fees: $13,440
Enrollment: 1,138 Coed
Affiliation or Control: Independent Non-Profit IRS Status: 501(c)3
Highest Offering: Master's
Program: 2-Year Principally Bachelor's Creditable; Liberal Arts And General; Teacher Preparatory; Religious Emphasis
Accreditation: #WC

01 President ... Dr. Gary R. MONCHER
05 Chief Academic Officer ... Dr. Kenneth ROMINES
11 Vice Pres of University Services ... Ms. Darla CUADRA
10 Chief Business Officer ... Mr. Andy GANES
06 Registrar ... Ms. Cindi HOGEBOOM
07 Director of Admissions ... Ms. Kimberly GUERRA
08 Library Director ... Mr. Joshua ADARKWA
84 Dean Enrollment Services ... Mr. Robert OLIVERA
19 Director Security/Safety ... Mr. Richard SWANSON
32 Dean Student Services ... Ms. Tatiana GUADAMUZ
37 Director Student Financial Aid ... Mr. Dennis CLARK
39 Director Student Housing ... Ms. Marche SIMON
41 Athletic Director ... Mr. Robert OLIVERA
20 Associate Academic Officer ... Ms. Darlene WILLIAMS
26 Chief Public Relations Officer ... Dr. Glenn KUNKEL
21 Associate Business Officer ... Ms. Robin SPENCER

Pepperdine University (G)

24255 Pacific Coast Highway, Malibu CA 90263-0001
County: Los Angeles FICE Identification: 010149
Unit ID: 121150
Telephone: (310) 506-4000 Carnegie Class: DRU
FAX Number: (310) 506-4861 Calendar System: Semester
URL: www.pepperdine.edu
Established: 1937 Annual Undergrad Tuition & Fees: $40,752
Enrollment: 7,604 Coed
Affiliation or Control: Church Of Christ IRS Status: 501(c)3
Highest Offering: Doctorate
Program: Liberal Arts And General; Teacher Preparatory; Professional
Accreditation: WC, BUS, CLPSY, DIETD, LAW, MUS

01 President ... Dr. Andrew K. BENTON
100 Chief of Staff ... Ms. Marne D. MITZE
03 Executive Vice President ... Mr. Gary A. HANSON
04 Execute Assistant ... Ms. Beverly GANDY
05 Provost ... Dr. Darryl TIPPENS
00 Chancellor Emeritus ... Dr. Charles B. RUNNELS
30 Sr VP Advancement & Public Affairs ... Mr. Keith HINKLE
10 Senior Vice President Investments ... Mr. Jeff PIPPIN
43 General Counsel ... Mr. Marc P. GOODMAN
11 Chief Administrative Officer ... Mr. Phil E. PHILLIPS
10 Chief Business Officer ... Mrs. Edna POWELL
10 Chief Financial Officer ... Mr. Paul B. LASITER
13 Vice Provost & Chief Info Officer ... Dr. Timothy M. CHESTER
26 Assoc Vice Pres for Public Affairs ... Mr. Rick GIBSON
21 Assoc VP Campus Ops/Business Svcs ... Mr. Alex PANG
06 Assoc VP & University Registrar ... Mr. Hung V. LE
104 Dean of International Programs ... Dr. Charles F. HALL
84 Dean of Admission/Enrollment Mgmt ... Mr. Michael E. TRUSCHKE
32 Dean of Student Affairs ... Dr. Mark DAVIS
08 Dean of Libraries ... Mr. Mark S. ROOSA
61 Dean of the School of Law ... Dr. Deanell TACHA
50 Dean of School of Business/Mgmt ... Dr. Linda LIVINGSTON
53 Dean of Graduate School Educ/Psych ... Dr. Margaret J. WEBER
49 Dean of Seaver College ... Dr. Rick R. MARRS
80 Dean School of Public Policy ... Dr. James R. WILBURN
42 University Chaplain ... Mr. David LEMLEY
29 Exec Director for Alumni Affairs ... Mr. Bob CLARD
16 Assoc VP Center for Human Resources ... Mrs. Lauren COSENTINO
88 Director for Church Relations ... Dr. Jerry RUSHFORD
88 Managing Dir Center for the Arts ... Ms. Rebecca CARSON
88 Director of Special Programs ... Ms. Kanet THOMAS
39 Director Housing and Residence Life ... Ms. Kerri HEATH
85 Director Intl Student Services ... Mr. Rich DAWSON
26 Dir Public Relations and News ... Mr. Jerry DERLOSHON
23 Director of Student Health Services ... Ms. Nancy SAFINICK
36 Director Career Center ... Mr. Brad D. DUDLEY
41 Director of Athletics ... Dr. Steven POTTS
19 Director of Public Safety ... Mr. Earl CARPENTER
18 Managing Dir Fac/Physical Plant ... Mr. Robert E. BULLARD
37 Director Student Financial Aid ... Mrs. Janet LOCKHART
38 Director Student Counseling ... Ms. Connie HORTON
96 Director of Payroll & Purchasing ... Mr. David BRANT
09 Director of Institutional Research ... Ms. Lily PANG
44 Director Estate & Gift Planning ... Ms. Stephanie BUCKLEY

*Peralta Community Colleges District Office (H)

333 E Eighth Street, Oakland CA 94606-2889
County: Alameda FICE Identification: 001265
Unit ID: 121178
Telephone: (510) 466-7200 Carnegie Class: N/A
FAX Number: (510) 835-4078
URL: www.peralta.edu

01 Interim Chancellor ... Dr. Wise E. ALLEN
27 Assoc VC Information Technology ... Mr. Minh LAM
26 Exec Dir Public Info/Commun & Media ... Mr. Jeffrey HEYMAN

*Berkeley City College (A)

2050 Center Street, Berkeley CA 94704-1183
County: Alameda FICE Identification: 022427
Unit ID: 125170
Telephone: (510) 981-2800 Carnegie Class: Assoc/Pub-U-MC
FAX Number: (510) 841-7333 Calendar System: Semester
URL: www.berkeleycitycollege.edu
Established: 1974 Annual Undergrad Tuition & Fees (In-District): $964
Enrollment: 7,461 Coed
Affiliation or Control: State/Local IRS Status: 501(c)3
Highest Offering: Associate Degree
Program: 2-Year Principally Bachelor's Creditable
Accreditation: WJ

02 President .... Dr. Betty INCLAN
05 Vice President of Instruction .... Ms. Krista JOHNS
32 Vice President of Student Services .... Dr. May K. CHEN
88 Division Dean II .... Vacant
35 Dean of Student Support Services .... Ms. Brenda JOHNSON
10 Business Services Manager .... Ms. Shirley SLAUGHTER
51 Dir Program Adult College Education . Dr. Nola HADLEY TORRES
88 Dir of Special Projects .... Ms. Terri TRICOMI
27 Public Information Officer .... Ms. Shirley FOGARINO

*College of Alameda (B)

555 Ralph Appezzato Memorial Pkwy,
Alameda CA 94501-2109
County: Alameda FICE Identification: 006720
Unit ID: 108667
Telephone: (510) 522-7221 Carnegie Class: Assoc/Pub-U-MC
FAX Number: (510) 337-0619 Calendar System: Semester
URL: www.peralta.edu
Established: 1968 Annual Undergrad Tuition & Fees (In-District): $1,080
Enrollment: 6,516 Coed
Affiliation or Control: State/Local IRS Status: 501(c)3
Highest Offering: Associate Degree
Program: Occupational; 2-Year Principally Bachelor's Creditable
Accreditation: WJ, DA

02 President .... Dr. Jannett N. JACKSON
05 Vice President of Instruction .... Dr. Rebecca J. KENNEY
32 Vice President of Student Services .... Dr. Kerry COMPTON
56 Dir Extended Opportunity Pgm & Svcs .... Ms. Toni COOK
26 Chief Public Relations Officer ..... Ms. Shirleen SCHERMERHORN
35 Dean Student Services .... Mr. Alexis S. MONTEVIRGEN
10 Business & Administrative Svcs Mgr .... Ms. Connie WILLIS
50 Division Dean-Division I .... Mr. Gary PERKINS
88 Dean Acad Pathways/Student Success .... Mr. Maurice JONES
84 Dean Enrollment Services .... Dr. Alexis S. MONTEVIRGEN

*Laney College (C)

900 Fallon Street, Oakland CA 94607-4893
County: Alameda FICE Identification: 001266
Unit ID: 117247
Telephone: (510) 834-5740 Carnegie Class: Assoc/Pub-U-MC
FAX Number: (510) 464-3528 Calendar System: Semester
URL: www.laney.edu
Established: 1953 Annual Undergrad Tuition & Fees (In-District): $1,118
Enrollment: 13,793 Coed
Affiliation or Control: State/Local IRS Status: 501(c)3
Highest Offering: Associate Degree
Program: Occupational; 2-Year Principally Bachelor's Creditable
Accreditation: WJ

02 President .... Dr. Elnora T. WEBB
05 Vice President .... Dr. Eileen WHITE
10 Business/Admin Services Manager .... Ms. MaryBeth BENVENUTTI
49 Div Dean Liberal Arts .... Mr. Marco MENENDEZ
81 Div Dean Mathematics and Science .... Dr. Inger STARK
75 Div Dean Career & Technical Educ .... Mr. Peter CRABTREE
20 Dean Student Wellness & Development .... Dr. Tina VASCONCELLOS
31 Dean Cmty Leadership & Civic Engag .... Mr. Newin P. ORANTE
04 Executive Assistant to President .... Ms. Maisha JAMESON
37 Int Director Student Financial Aid .... Mr. Gary NICHOLES
41 Director Athletics .... Mr. John BEAM
88 Director APASS Program .... Ms. Lilia CELHAY
88 Director Gateway to College Pgm .... Mr. Anthony FLORES
88 Director TRIO Supp Services Pgm .... Vacant
88 Director Green Jobs Program .... Vacant

*Merritt College (D)

12500 Campus Drive, Oakland CA 94619-3196
County: Alameda FICE Identification: 001267
Unit ID: 118772
Telephone: (510) 531-4911 Carnegie Class: Assoc/Pub-U-MC
FAX Number: (510) 436-2405 Calendar System: Semester
URL: www.merritt.edu
Established: 1953 Annual Undergrad Tuition & Fees (In-District): $882
Enrollment: 7,105 Coed
Affiliation or Control: State/Local IRS Status: 501(c)3
Highest Offering: Associate Degree
Program: Occupational; 2-Year Principally Bachelor's Creditable
Accreditation: WJ, DIETT, RAD

02 President .... Dr. Robert A. ADAMS
05 Vice President of Instruction .... Dr. Linda BERRY
32 Vice President of Student Services .... Dr. Eric GRAVENBERG
96 Vice Chancellor of General Services .... Dr. Sadiq IKHARO
35 Vice Chancellor Student Services .... Dr. Jacob NG
15 Vice Chancellor for Human Resources .... Ms. Trudy LARGENT
20 Assoc Vice Chanc Academic Affairs .... Dr. Michael ORKIN
26 Exec Dir Marketing/Public Rels/Comm .... Mr. Jeffrey HEYMAN
08 Head Librarian .... Mr. Timothy HACKETT
06 Registrar .... Ms. Susana DE LA TORRE
18 Director of Facilities & Operations .... Mr. Robert BECKWITH
37 Director of Financial Aid .... Ms. Judy COHEN
10 Business/Admin Service Manager .... Ms. Alice MAREZ

Perelandra College (E)

8697-C LaMesa Boulevard, PMB 21, La Mesa CA 91942
County: San Diego Identification: 666475
Telephone: (619) 335-0441 Carnegie Class: Not Classified
FAX Number: (619) 512-4291 Calendar System: Other
URL: www.perelandra.edu
Established: 2002 Annual Undergrad Tuition & Fees: $6,000
Enrollment: 22 Coed
Affiliation or Control: Independent Non-Profit IRS Status: 501(c)3
Highest Offering: Master's
Program: Liberal Arts And General
Accreditation: DETC

01 President .... Mr. Ken KUHLKEN
06 Registrar .... Mr. James GARFIELD
32 Director of Student Resources .... Ms. Pam FOX KUHLKEN

Phillips Graduate Institute (F)

5445 Balboa Boulevard, Encino CA 91316-1509
County: Los Angeles FICE Identification: 022372
Unit ID: 110307
Telephone: (818) 386-5600 Carnegie Class: Spec/Health
FAX Number: (818) 386-5636 Calendar System: Semester
URL: www.pgi.edu
Established: 1971 Annual Graduate Tuition & Fees: $24,600
Enrollment: 245 Coed
Affiliation or Control: Independent Non-Profit IRS Status: 501(c)3
Highest Offering: Doctorate; No Undergraduates
Program: Professional
Accreditation: WC

01 President .... Dr. Yolanda J. NUNN GORMAN
05 Vice President Academic Affairs .... Dr. Deborah BUTTITTA
10 Vice President Finance - CFO .... Ms. Tanya PONTEP
11 Vice Pres Administrative Affairs .... Ms. Karen L. JACKSON
30 Int VP Development/External Affairs .... Ms. Ellen FAULK
07 Director of Admissions .... Ms. Kimberly BELL
08 Director Library .... Ms. Caroline SISNEROS
37 Financial Aid Director .... Vacant
13 IT/Operations Director .... Mr. Ed NILA
06 Registrar .... Ms. Jeanne GENTILLON
09 Dir Institutional Rsrch/Assess/Plng .... Ms. Elizabeth TREBOW
15 Director Human Resources .... Ms. Theresa WRAY
51 Coordinator Continuing Education .... Ms. Jocceline HERNANDEZ

Pima Medical Institute-Chula Vista (G)

780 Bay Boulevard, Suite 101,
Chula Vista CA 91910-5261
County: San Diego Identification: 666272
Unit ID: 434140
Telephone: (619) 425-3200 Carnegie Class: Assoc/PrivFP
FAX Number: (619) 425-3450 Calendar System: Semester
URL: www.pmi.edu
Established: 1972 Annual Undergrad Tuition & Fees: $10,408
Enrollment: 1,000 Coed
Affiliation or Control: Proprietary IRS Status: Proprietary
Highest Offering: Associate Degree
Program: Occupational
Accreditation: ABHES, RAD

01 Campus Director .... Ms. Kathy HOERSCH

† Branch campus of Pima Medical Institute, Tucson, AZ.

Pitzer College (H)

1050 N Mills Avenue, Claremont CA 91711-6110
County: Los Angeles FICE Identification: 001172
Unit ID: 121257
Telephone: (909) 621-8129 Carnegie Class: Bac/A&S
FAX Number: (909) 621-8770 Calendar System: Semester
URL: www.pitzer.edu
Established: 1963 Annual Undergrad Tuition & Fees: $40,130
Enrollment: 1,070 Coed
Affiliation or Control: Independent Non-Profit IRS Status: 501(c)3
Highest Offering: Baccalaureate
Program: Liberal Arts And General
Accreditation: WC

01 President .... Dr. Laura SKANDERA TROMBLEY
05 Vice Pres Acad Affs/Dean of Faculty .... Dr. Alan JONES
10 Treasurer/Vice Pres Administration .... Mr. Yuet LEE
30 Int Vice Pres College Advancement .... Mr. Adrian STEVENS
07 Vice Pres Admissions/Financial Aid .... Dr. Arnaldo RODRIGUEZ
32 Vice Pres Student Affairs .... Mr. Jim MARCHANT
26 VP Marketing/Public Relations .... Ms. Kira POPLOWSKI
44 Associate Vice Pres of Development .... Ms. Joy KLIEWER
20 Associate Dean of Faculty .... Vacant
88 Assistant Dean of Faculty .... Vacant
06 Registrar .... Ms. Cheryl MORALES
37 Director Financial Aid .... Ms. Margaret CAROTHERS
07 Director Admission .... Mr. Angel PEREZ
09 Director of Institutional Research .... Dr. Jeff LEWIS
15 Director Human Resources .... Ms. Marni BOBICH
18 Director Facilities .... Mr. Larry BURIK
21 Associate Treasurer .... Ms. Lori YOSHINO
36 Director Career Services .... Ms. Karen SUAREZ
29 Director Alumni Relations .... Ms. Jean GRANT
38 Director Student Counseling .... Dr. Rebecca KORNBLUH

Platt College (I)

1000 S Fremont Avenue, Building A9W,
Alhambra CA 91803-8845
County: Los Angeles FICE Identification: 030627
Unit ID: 260789
Telephone: (626) 300-5444 Carnegie Class: Bac/Assoc
FAX Number: (626) 457-8295 Calendar System: Other
URL: www.plattcollege.edu
Established: 1987 Annual Undergrad Tuition & Fees: $17,991
Enrollment: 358 Coed
Affiliation or Control: Proprietary IRS Status: Proprietary
Highest Offering: Baccalaureate
Program: Occupational
Accreditation: ACCSC

01 Executive Director .... Mr. Nicholas EWELL

Platt College (J)

3700 Inland Empire Blvd, Ste 400, Ontario CA 91764-4906
County: San Bernardino Identification: 666056
Unit ID: 432384
Telephone: (909) 941-9410 Carnegie Class: Bac/Assoc
FAX Number: (909) 941-9660 Calendar System: Other
URL: www.plattcollege.edu
Established: 1997 Annual Undergrad Tuition & Fees: $57,750
Enrollment: 672 Coed
Affiliation or Control: Proprietary IRS Status: Proprietary
Highest Offering: Baccalaureate
Program: Occupational
Accreditation: ACCSC

01 Campus President .... Mr. Daryl GOLDBERG
05 Regional Dean of Academics .... Ms. Crystal NASIO
60 Visual Communication Dept Chair .... Ms. Patricia DENYS
75 Paralegal Studies Dept Chair .... Mr. Ugo NWAOHA
75 Info Tech Networking Dept Chair .... Mr. Jeffrey JACKSON
36 Career Services Director .... Ms. Megan FEYER
37 Financial Aid Director .... Mr. Daniel RAMOS
07 Admissions Director .... Mr. Steven WILLIAMS

† Branch campus of Platt College, Ahambra, CA.

Platt College (K)

6250 El Cajon Boulevard, San Diego CA 92115-3919
County: San Diego FICE Identification: 023043
Unit ID: 121275
Telephone: (619) 265-0107 Carnegie Class: Spec/Arts
FAX Number: (619) 265-8655 Calendar System: Semester
URL: www.platt.edu
Established: 1980 Annual Undergrad Tuition & Fees: $27,957
Enrollment: 340 Coed
Affiliation or Control: Proprietary IRS Status: Proprietary
Highest Offering: Baccalaureate
Program: Occupational; Professional
Accreditation: ACCSC

00 Chairman .... Mr. Robert D. LEIKER
01 President .... Mrs. Meg LEIKER
03 Vice President .... Mr. Alfred MEDRO
05 Dean of Education .... Ms. Marketa HANCOVA

Point Loma Nazarene University (L)

3900 Lomaland Drive, San Diego CA 92106-2899
County: San Diego FICE Identification: 001262
Unit ID: 121309
Telephone: (619) 849-2200 Carnegie Class: Master's L
FAX Number: (619) 849-2579 Calendar System: Semester
URL: www.pointloma.edu
Established: 1902 Annual Undergrad Tuition & Fees: $28,300
Enrollment: 3,560 Coed
Affiliation or Control: Church Of The Nazarene IRS Status: 501(c)3
Highest Offering: Beyond Master's But Less Than Doctorate
Program: Liberal Arts And General; Teacher Preparatory; Professional
Accreditation: WC, ACBSP, DIETD, MUS, NURSE, @SW

01 President .... Dr. Bob BROWER
05 Provost/Chief Academic Officer .... Dr. Kerry FULCHER
10 VP Finance/Administrative Svcs .... Mr. George LATTER
26 Vice President External Relations .... Dr. Joe WATKINS
32 Vice Pres for Student Development .... Dr. Caye SMITH
88 Vice Pres Spiritual Development .... Dr. Mary PAUL
15 Assoc VP for Human Resources .... Mrs. Joyce FALK

37 Assoc Vice President for Finance .... Mrs. Cindy CHAPPELL
35 Assc VP Stdnt Dev/Chf Diversity Ofc .... Dr. Jeffrey CARR
30 Assoc VP University Advancement .... Vacant
21 Assoc VP for Budget/Accounting .... Ms. Sonia CHIN
84 Assoc VP Enrollment .... Mr. Scott SHOEMAKER
20 Vice Prov Academic Administration .... Dr. Mark PITTS
88 Vice Prov Program Dev and Accred .... Dr. Maggie BAILEY
35 Dean of Students .... Mr. Jeff BOLSTER
13 Chief Information Officer .... Mr. Sam YOUNG
09 Dir Institutional Effectiveness .... Dr. Ruth HEINRICHS
12 Director of Wesleyan Center .... Dr. Mark MANN
18 Director of Physical Plant .... Mr. Richard SCHULT
86 Dir Cmty Outreach/Government Rels .... Ms. Megan EKARD
88 Director Center Pastoral Leadship .... Dr. Norm SHOEMAKER
42 Director of Church Relations .... Rev. Ron FAY
88 Director of Outreach Ministries .... Ms. Becky MODESTO
88 Director of Discipleship Ministries .... Ms. Sylvia CORTEZ
88 Director of Worship Ministries .... Mr. George WILLIAMSON
49 Dean College of Arts & Sciences .... Dr. Kathy MCCONNELL
83 Dean College of Social Sciences .... Dr. Holly IRWIN-CHASE
07 Director Graduate Admissions .... Mr. Dejon DAVIS
07 Director Undergraduate Admissions .... Mr. Eric GROVES
08 Director of Ryan Library .... Dr. Frank QUINN
31 Director Community Life .... Ms. Melissa BURT-GRACIK
06 Dir Records/Institutional Research .... Ms. Cheryl GAUGHAN
26 Director Marketing/Creative Svcs .... Ms. Michele CORBETT
36 Director of Career Services .... Mr. Charles HOWARD
24 Director of Academic Support Center .... Dr. Kim BOGAN
23 Director of Wellness Center .... Mr. Jim COIL
19 Director of Public Safety .... Mr. Mark GALBRAITH
29 Director of Alumni Relations .... Ms. Sheryl SMEE
40 Bookstore Manager .... Mrs. Janet RAMPENTHAL
28 Dir Multicultural/Intnl Stdnt Svcs .... Ms. Lily DAVIS
41 Athletic Director .... Mr. Ethan HAMILTON
42 University Chaplain .... Rev. Mark CARTER
88 Director of Nicholson Commons .... Mr. Milton KARAHADIAN
94 Dir Stevenson Ctr for Women's Stds .... Dr. Linda BEAIL
104 Director Study Abroad .... Mr. Frank SERNA

Pomona College (A)

550 N College Avenue, #206, Claremont CA 91711-6301
County: Los Angeles FICE Identification: 001173
Unit ID: 121345
Telephone: (909) 621-8000 Carnegie Class: Bac/A&S
FAX Number: (909) 621-8403 Calendar System: Semester
URL: www.pomona.edu
Established: 1887 Annual Undergrad Tuition & Fees: $39,572
Enrollment: 1,546 Coed
Affiliation or Control: Independent Non-Profit IRS Status: 501(c)3
Highest Offering: Baccalaureate
Program: Liberal Arts And General
Accreditation: WC

01 President .... Dr. David W. OXTOBY
05 Vice President/Dean of College .... Dr. Cecilia CONRAD
45 Vice President Planning .... Dr. Richard A. FASS
10 Vice President/Treasurer .... Dr. Karen SISSON
30 VP for Institutional Advancement .... Mr. Chris B. PONCE
32 Vice President/Dean of Students .... Mrs. Miriam FELDBLUM
07 VP of Admissions & Financial Aid .... Mr. Seth ALLEN
04 Special Assistant to President .... Dr. Teresa SHAW
06 Registrar .... Ms. Margaret ADORNO
26 Director Public Relations .... Mr. Mark WOOD
29 Director Alumni Relations .... Ms. Nancy J. TRESER-OSGOOD
37 Director Financial Aid .... Ms. Mary BOOKER
36 Director Career Development .... Vacant
15 Director Human Resources .... Ms. Brenda RUSHFORTH
41 Director Physical Education .... Mr. Charles KATSIAFICAS
44 Director Annual Giving .... Mr. Craig ARTEAGA-JOHNSON
21 Assoc Treasurer/Controller .... Ms. Mary Lou WOODS
09 Director of Institutional Research .... Dr. Jennifer RACHFORD
18 Chief Facilities/Physical Plant .... Mr. Robert ROBINSON

Presbyterian Theological Seminary in America (B)

15605 Carmenita Rd., Santa Fe Springs CA 90670
County: Los Angeles FICE Identification: 041228
Telephone: (562) 926-1023 Carnegie Class: Not Classified
FAX Number: (562) 926-1025 Calendar System: Semester
URL: www.ptsa.edu
Established: 1977 Annual Undergrad Tuition & Fees: $5,760
Enrollment: 213 Coed
Affiliation or Control: Presbyterian Church In America IRS Status: 501(c)3
Highest Offering: First Professional Degree
Program: Professional; Religious Emphasis
Accreditation: BI

01 President .... Dr. In Soo KIM
05 Academic Dean .... Dr. Sang Meyng LEE
10 Dean of Administration .... Rev. Hee Duk HYUN
32 Dean of Students/Student Ministry .... Rev. Byung Ik OH
85 Dean/Director of Intl Students .... Rev. Jeffrey FRICK
08 Head Librarian .... Mrs. Haesan CHOI
06 Registrar .... Mrs. Mi PARK
88 Administrator .... Mrs. Michelle YOON

Professional Golfers Career College (C)

26109 Ynez Road, Temecula CA 92591-6013
County: Riverside FICE Identification: 033673
Unit ID: 437750
Telephone: (951) 719-2994 Carnegie Class: Assoc/PrivFP
FAX Number: (951) 719-1643 Calendar System: Semester
URL: www.golfcollege.edu
Established: 1990 Annual Undergrad Tuition & Fees: $26,000
Enrollment: 659 Coed
Affiliation or Control: Proprietary IRS Status: Proprietary
Highest Offering: Associate Degree
Program: Occupational; 2-Year Principally Bachelor's Creditable; Business Emphasis
Accreditation: ACICS

01 President .... Dr. Tim SOMERVILLE

Providence Christian College (D)

1539 E. Howard Street, Pasadena CA 91104
County: Los Angeles FICE Identification: 041539
Unit ID: 455770
Telephone: (866) 323-0233 Carnegie Class: Not Classified
FAX Number: N/A Calendar System: Semester
URL: www.providencecc.net
Established: 2002 Annual Undergrad Tuition & Fees: $21,789
Enrollment: 60 Coed
Affiliation or Control: Non-denominational IRS Status: 501(c)3
Highest Offering: Baccalaureate
Program: Liberal Arts And General
Accreditation: @WC

01 President .... Dr. J. Derek HALVORSON
05 Academic Dean .... Dr. Russ REEVES
06 Registrar .... Patty TSAI
11 Director of Operations .... Dawn DIRKSEN
84 Director of Enrollment Management .... Larissa KAMPS
30 Director of Development .... Jack HOEKSTRA
32 Dean of Student Life .... Steve KORTENHOEVEN

*Rancho Santiago Community College District (E)

2323 N Broadway, Santa Ana CA 92706-1606
County: Orange FICE Identification: 006991
Unit ID: 438665
Telephone: (714) 480-7450 Carnegie Class: N/A
FAX Number: (714) 796-3915
URL: www.rsccd.edu

01 Chancellor .... Dr. Raul RODRIGUEZ
16 Exec Vice Chanc Human Resources .... Mr. John DIDION
10 Vice Chanc Business & Fiscal Svcs .... Mr. Peter HARDASH
05 Asst Vice Chanc Education Svcs .... Mr. Enrique PEREZ
45 Ast VC Facility Plng/Dist Spprt Svc .... Vacant
86 Exec Dir of Public Aff & Govt Rels .... Vacant

*Santa Ana College (F)

1530 W 17th Street, Santa Ana CA 92706-3398
County: Orange FICE Identification: 001284
Unit ID: 121619
Telephone: (714) 564-6000 Carnegie Class: Assoc/Pub-S-MC
FAX Number: (714) 564-6379 Calendar System: Semester
URL: www.sac.edu
Established: 1915 Annual Undergrad Tuition & Fees (In-District): $1,388
Enrollment: 27,007 Coed
Affiliation or Control: State/Local IRS Status: 501(c)3
Highest Offering: Associate Degree
Program: Occupational; 2-Year Principally Bachelor's Creditable
Accreditation: WJ, ADNUR, OTA

02 President .... Dr. Erlinda MARTINEZ
05 Vice President Academic Affairs .... Dr. Linda ROSE
32 Vice President Student Services .... Dr. Sara LUNDQUIST
51 Vice President Continuing Education .... Vacant
35 Dean Student Affairs .... Dr. Lilia TANAKEYOWMA
11 Vice Pres Administrative Svcs .... Paul FOSTER
07 Director Admissions & Records .... Mark LIANG
06 Registrar .... Chris TRUONG
50 Dean Business Division .... Dr. Allen DOOLEY
35 Assoc Dean Student Development .... Dr. Loy NASHUA
38 Dean Counseling .... Dr. Micki BRYANT
37 Director of Financial Aid .... Robert MANSON
41 Dean Exercise Sci/Health/Athletics .... Avie BRIDGES
57 Dean Fine & Performing Arts .... Sylvia C. TURNER
30 Director College Advancement .... Christina ROMERO
18 Interim Plant Manager .... Ron JONES
79 Dean Humanities & Social Sciences .... Vacant
81 Dean Science/Math/Health Sciences .... Carol COMEAU
72 Dean Career Educ/Workforce Develop .... Bart HOFFMAN
56 Associate Dean EOPS .... Marsha GABLE
88 Associate Dean DSPS .... Elyse CHAPLIN

*Santiago Canyon College (G)

8045 E Chapman Avenue, Orange CA 92869-4512
County: Orange FICE Identification: 036957
Unit ID: 399212
Telephone: (714) 628-4900 Carnegie Class: Assoc/Pub-S-MC
FAX Number: (714) 628-4723 Calendar System: Semester
URL: www.sccollege.edu
Established: 1997 Annual Undergrad Tuition & Fees (In-District): $760
Enrollment: 12,698 Coed
Affiliation or Control: State/Local IRS Status: 501(c)3
Highest Offering: Associate Degree
Program: Occupational; 2-Year Principally Bachelor's Creditable
Accreditation: WJ

02 President .... Mr. Juan A. VAZQUEZ
04 Assistant to the President .... Ms. Lynn MANZANO
32 Vice President Student Services .... Dr. John HERNANDEZ
05 Int Vice President Academic Affairs .... Mr. Aracely MORA
51 Vice President Continuing Educ .... Mr. Jose VARGAS
11 Vice Pres Administrative Services .... Mr. Steve KAWA
38 Dean Counseling .... Ms. Ruth BABESHOFF
41 Assoc Dean Athletics .... Mr. Martin STRINGER
79 Dean Arts/Hum/Soc Sci/Library .... Mr. John WEISPFENNING
36 Dean Career Tech Education .... Ms. Tricia EVANS
20 Dean Instruction/Student Services .... Ms. Lori FASBINDER
20 Dean Instruction/Student Services .... Mr. Jim KENNEDY
35 Assoc Dean Student Development .... Ms. Lorrie JORDAN
07 Assoc Dean of Admissions & Records .... Ms. Linda MISKOVIC
37 Associate Dean Financial Aid .... Mr. Syed RIZVI
06 Registrar .... Ms. Denise PENNOCK
18 Physical Plant Manager .... Mr. Rich CURIA

Rio Hondo College (H)

3600 Workman Mill Road, Whittier CA 90601-1699
County: Los Angeles FICE Identification: 001269
Unit ID: 121886
Telephone: (562) 692-0921 Carnegie Class: Assoc/Pub-S-SC
FAX Number: (562) 699-7386 Calendar System: Semester
URL: www.riohondo.edu
Established: 1960 Annual Undergrad Tuition & Fees (In-District): $864
Enrollment: 21,764 Coed
Affiliation or Control: State/Local IRS Status: 501(c)3
Highest Offering: Associate Degree
Program: Occupational; 2-Year Principally Bachelor's Creditable
Accreditation: WJ

01 Superintendent/President .... Dr. Ted MARTINEZ, JR.
05 Vice President Academic Svcs .... Dr. Paul PARNELL
10 Vice President Finance/Business .... Ms. Teresa DREYFUSS
32 Vice President Student Services .... Mr. Henry GEE
86 Dir Govt & Community Relations .... Mr. Russell CASTANEDA-CALLEROS
16 Director Human Resources .... Ms. Yolanda EMERSON
26 Director Mktg & Communications .... Ms. Susan HERNEY
35 Director Student Activities .... Ms. Cathy BUTLER
07 Dir Admissions & Records/Registrar .... Ms. Judy G. PEARSON
38 Dean Counseling & Student Dev .... Dr. Walter JONES
30 Executive Director RHC Foundation .... Ms. Kerry FRANCO
37 Director Financial Aid & Veteran's .... Ms. Elizabeth CORIA
18 Interim Dir Facilities Services .... Mr. John S. RAMIREZ
96 Director of Purchasing .... Mr. Timothy CONNELL

*Riverside Community College District (I)

3845 Market Street, Riverside CA 92501
County: Riverside Identification: 667039
Telephone: (951) 222-8000 Carnegie Class: N/A
FAX Number: (951) 222-8036
URL: www.rccd.edu

01 Chancellor .... Dr. Gregory W. GRAY
05 Vice Chancellor Academic Affairs .... Dr. Ray MAGHROORI
10 Vice Chancellor Admin & Finance .... Dr. Jim BUYSSE
28 Vice Chanc Diversity/Human Resource .... Ms. Melissa KANE
100 Chief of Staff/Exec Asst to Chanc .... Ms. Chris CARLSON
12 Act President Moreno Valley College .... Dr. Tom HARRIS
12 Act President Norco College .... Dr. Debbie DI THOMAS
12 President Riverside City College .... Dr. Cynthia AZARI
09 Dean Institutional Research .... Mr. David TORRES
66 Dean School of Nursing .... Dr. Sandy BAKER
84 Dean Enrollment Services .... Ms. Joy CHAMBERS

*Moreno Valley College (J)

16130 Lasselle Street, Moreno Valley CA 92551
County: Riverside Identification: 666771
Unit ID: 460394
Telephone: (951) 571-6100 Carnegie Class: Not Classified
FAX Number: N/A Calendar System: Semester
URL: www.rcc.edu
Established: 2010 Annual Undergrad Tuition & Fees (In-District): $1,114
Enrollment: 10,684 Coed
Affiliation or Control: State/Local IRS Status: 501(c)3
Highest Offering: Associate Degree
Program: 2-Year Principally Bachelor's Creditable
Accreditation: WJ, DA, DH

02 Acting President .... Dr. Tom HARRIS
05 Vice President Academic Affairs .... Dr. Lisa CONYERS
10 Interim Vice Pres Business Services .... Mr. David BOBBITT
32 Vice President Student Services .... Dr. Greg SANDOVAL
20 Interim Dean of Instruction .... Dr. Carlos TOVARES
35 Dean of Student Support Services .... Vacant

*Norco College (A)

2001 Third Street, Norco CA 92860
County: Riverside Identification: 666772
Unit ID: 460464
Telephone: (951) 372-7000 Carnegie Class: Not Classified
FAX Number: N/A Calendar System: Semester
URL: www.rcc.edu
Established: N/A Annual Undergrad Tuition & Fees (In-District): $1,080
Enrollment: 10,540 Coed
Affiliation or Control: State/Local IRS Status: 501(c)3
Highest Offering: Associate Degree
Program: 2-Year Principally Bachelor's Creditable
Accreditation: WJ

02 Interim President .... Dr. Debbie DITHOMAS
10 Int Vice Pres Business Services .... Mr. Laurence THURMAN
05 Interim Vice Pres Academic Affairs .... Dr. Diane DIECKMEYER
32 Interim Vice Pres Student Services .... Dr. Monica GREEN
75 Assoc Dean Career & Technical Educ .... Mr. Kevin FLEMING
08 Dean Library/Learning Resources .... Mr. Damon NANCE

*Riverside City College (B)

4800 Magnolia Avenue, Riverside CA 92506
County: Riverside FICE Identification: 001270
Unit ID: 121901
Telephone: (951) 222-8000 Carnegie Class: Assoc/Pub-U-MC
FAX Number: (951) 222-8036 Calendar System: Semester
URL: www.rcc.edu
Established: 1916 Annual Undergrad Tuition & Fees (In-District): $832
Enrollment: 35,000 Coed
Affiliation or Control: State/Local IRS Status: 501(c)3
Highest Offering: Associate Degree
Program: Occupational; 2-Year Principally Bachelor's Creditable
Accreditation: WJ, ADNUR, ARCPA, EMT

02 President .... Dr. Cynthia AZARI
10 Vice President Business Services .... Mr. Norm GODIN
32 Vice President Student Services .... Dr. Edward BUSH
28 VC Diversity/Human Resources .... Ms. Melissa KANE
20 Dean of Instruction .... Mrs. Virginia MCKEE-LEONE
75 Vice Pres Career/Technical Programs .... Mr. Ron VITO
18 Assoc Vice Chancellor Facilities .... Mr. Orin WILLIAMS
21 Assoc Vice Chanc Finance .... Mr. Aaron BROWN
30 AVC Strategic Comm and Relations .... Mr. James PARSONS
20 Associate Vice Chanc Instruction .... Ms. Sylvia THOMAS
88 District Dean Open Campus .... Vacant
66 Dean School of Nursing .... Dr. Sandy BAKER
08 Exec Dean Technology/Lrng Resource .... Dr. Bernard FRADKIN
103 Exec Dean Workforce Development .... Dr. Shelagh CAMAK
70 Dean Public Safety Educ/Trng .... Dr. Cordell BRIGGS
88 Assoc Dean Early Childhood Educ .... Ms. Debbie WHITAKER
24 Prod/Artistic Dir Perform Riverside .... Ms. Rey O'DAY
25 Director Grant & Contract Services .... Mr. Richard KEELER
07 Dean Enrollment Services .... Ms. Joy CHAMBERS
37 Dean Financial Aid .... Mrs. Eugenia VINCENT
28 Director Diversity/HR .... Mr. Arturo ALCARAZ
41 Dean PE/Athletics .... Mr. Barry MEIER
09 District Dir Institutional Research .... Mr. David TORRES
21 Director Accounting Services .... Ms. Doretta SOWELL
23 District Director Health Services .... Ms. Renee KIMBERLING
19 Chief of Police .... Mr. James MIYASHIRO
72 Dean Technology/Economic Dev .... Dr. John TILLQUIST
14 Director Software Development .... Mr. Rick HERMAN
102 Director Foundation/Alumni Affairs .... Mrs. Amy CARDULLO

Sage College (C)

12125 Day Street, Building L,
Moreno Valley CA 92557-6720
FICE Identification: 030695
Unit ID: 410520
Telephone: (951) 781-2727 Carnegie Class: Assoc/PrivFP
FAX Number: (951) 781-0570 Calendar System: Semester
URL: www.sagecollege.edu
Established: 1973 Annual Undergrad Tuition & Fees: $11,825
Enrollment: 587 Coed
Affiliation or Control: Proprietary IRS Status: Proprietary
Highest Offering: Associate Degree
Program: Occupational; 2-Year Principally Bachelor's Creditable
Accreditation: ACICS

01 Executive Director .... Ms. Lauren SOMMA
11 Assistant Director .... Ms. Sharon GOUPEL

Sage College (D)

2820 Camino Del Rio South Ste 100,
San Diego CA 92108-3821
County: San Diego Identification: 666304
Telephone: (619) 683-2727 Carnegie Class: Not Classified
FAX Number: (619) 683-2777 Calendar System: Other
URL: www.sagecollege.edu
Established: 1973 Annual Undergrad Tuition & Fees: N/A
Enrollment: N/A Coed
Affiliation or Control: Proprietary IRS Status: Proprietary
Highest Offering: Associate Degree
Program: Occupational; 2-Year Principally Bachelor's Creditable
Accreditation: ACICS

01 Administrator .... Ms. Tiffany EWING

Saint John's Seminary (E)

5012 Seminary Road, Camarillo CA 93012-2598
County: Ventura FICE Identification: 001299
Unit ID: 123855
Telephone: (805) 482-2755 Carnegie Class: Spec/Faith
FAX Number: (805) 482-3470 Calendar System: Semester
URL: www.stjohnsem.edu
Established: 1939 Annual Graduate Tuition & Fees: $13,500
Enrollment: 91 Male
Affiliation or Control: Roman Catholic IRS Status: 501(c)3
Highest Offering: Master's; No Undergraduates
Program: Professional
Accreditation: WC, THEOL

01 Rector .... RevMgr. Craig A. COX
05 Interim Academic Dean .... Rev. Kevin MCCRACKEN, CM
07 Director of Admissions .... Dr. Mark FISCHER
06 Registrar .... Ms. Esme TAKAHASHI

Saint Mary's College of California (F)

1928 Saint Mary's Road, Moraga CA 94556-2744
County: Contra Costa FICE Identification: 001302
Unit ID: 123554
Telephone: (925) 631-4000 Carnegie Class: Master's L
FAX Number: (925) 376-8497 Calendar System: 4/1/4
URL: www.stmarys-ca.edu
Established: 1863 Annual Undergrad Tuition & Fees: $37,000
Enrollment: 3,917 Coed
Affiliation or Control: Roman Catholic IRS Status: 501(c)3
Highest Offering: Doctorate
Program: Liberal Arts And General; Teacher Preparatory; Professional
Accreditation: WC, MACTE

01 President .... Bro. Ronald J. GALLAGHER
05 Provost/Vice President Acad Affairs .... Dr. Bethami DOBKIN
32 Vice Provost Student Affairs .... Dr. Jane CAMARILLO
20 Vice Provost Undergrad Academics .... Dr. Richard M. CARP
10 Vice President for Finance/CFO .... Mr. Peter MICHELL
30 Vice President Development .... Dr. Keith E. BRANT
26 Vice Pres College Communications .... Mr. Michael G. BESEDA
88 Vice President for Mission .... Dr. Carole SWAIN
84 Vice Provost Enrollment Services .... Mr. Michael BESEDA
107 Vice Prov Graduate/Professnl Stds .... Dr. Christopher SINDT
27 Asst Vice Pres of Communications .... Ms. Elizabeth SMITH
30 Asst Vice President of Development .... Ms. Lisa MOORE
43 College Counsel .... Mr. Larry NUTI
53 Dean School of Education .... Dr. Phyllis METCALF-TURNER
50 Dean School Econ & Business Admin .... Dr. Zhan LI
81 Dean School of Science .... Dr. Roy WENSLEY
49 Dean School Liberal Arts .... Dr. Steve WOOLPERT
35 Dean of Students .... Mr. Scott KIER
08 Dean Academic Resources .... Ms. Patricia KREITZ
42 Director Mission & Ministry .... Ms. Marie LAWLER
07 Dean of Admissions .... Mr. Michael MCKEON
15 Director Human Resources .... Mr. Eduardo SALAZ
58 Asc Dean/Dir Graduate Business Pgms .... Mr. Guido KRICKX
06 Registrar .... Ms. Julia ODOM
20 Assistant Dean of Students .... Mr. Jim SCIUTO
37 Director of Financial Aid .... Ms. Priscilla MUHA
58 Director of HPE&R .... Dr. Stephen MILLER
57 Director MFA in Creative Writing .... Ms. Marilyn ABILDSKOV
29 Director Alumni/Volunteer Engagemnt .... Mr. Chris CARTER
14 Director of Information Technology .... Mr. Dennis RICE
13 Chief Technology Officer .... Dr. Edward BIGLIN
19 Director of Public Safety .... Mr. Bill FOLEY
38 Director of Counseling Center .... Vacant
41 Dir of Athletic & Recreation Sports .... Mr. Mark C. ORR
88 Director of Hearst Art Gallery .... Ms. Carrie BREWSTER
71 Director of January Term Program .... Dr. Sue FALLIS
18 Exec Director of Physical Plant .... Mr. Joseph KEHOE
102 Director of Foundation & Corp Rels .... Ms. Elizabeth GALLAGHER
44 Director of the Annual Fund .... Mr. Daniel G. LEWIS
36 Director of Career Devel Center .... Ms. Patty BISHOP
23 Director Health & Wellness Center .... Ms. Sue PETERS
26 Media Relations Officer .... Mr. Michael MCALPIN
86 Director Community & Govt Relations .... Mr. Tim FARLEY
94 Director Women's Resource Ctr .... Ms. Sharon SOBOTTA
88 Associate Director of CILSA .... Ms. Jennifer PIGZA
21 Director of Finance/Controller .... Ms. Jeanne DEMATTEO
88 Director Ctr International Programs .... Ms. M. Susan MILLER-REID
88 Director of Food Services .... Mr. Matt CARROLL
39 Director Conferences & Housing .... Ms. Marie LUCERO
92 Director High Potential Program .... Ms. Angelica GARCIA
28 Dir of Delphine Intercultural Ctr .... Ms. Joan CUBE
09 Director of Institutional Research .... Mr. Sam AGRONOW
96 Purchasing/Buyer .... Ms. Janie MINGUILLON
88 Dir New Student/Family Programs .... Ms. Maisha BEASLEY

Saint Patrick's Seminary & University (G)

320 Middlefield Road, Menlo Park CA 94025-3596
County: San Mateo FICE Identification: 010074
Unit ID: 122250
Telephone: (650) 325-5621 Carnegie Class: Not Classified
FAX Number: (650) 322-0997 Calendar System: Semester
URL: www.stpatricksseminary.org
Established: 1894 Annual Undergrad Tuition & Fees: $15,382
Enrollment: 93 Male
Affiliation or Control: Roman Catholic IRS Status: 501(c)3
Highest Offering: Master's
Program: Professional; Religious Emphasis
Accreditation: WC, THEOL

01 President/Rector & Vice Chancellor .... Rev. James L. MCKEARNEY
03 Vice Rector/Academic Dean .... Rev. Gladstone H. STEVENS
10 Vice Pres of Business & Finance .... Ms. Jennifer M. MORRIS
26 Vice President for External Affairs .... Rev. James MYERS
32 Dean of Students .... Rev. Vincent BUI
08 Librarian .... Ms. Gretchen LEWIS
06 Registrar .... Ms. Nuria ORTIZ

The Salvation Army College for Officer Training at Crestmont (H)

30840 Hawthorne Boulevard,
Rancho Palos Verdes CA 90275-5300
County: Los Angeles FICE Identification: 036954
Unit ID: 122269
Telephone: (310) 377-0481 Carnegie Class: Not Classified
FAX Number: (310) 541-6126 Calendar System: Quarter
URL: www.crestmont.edu
Established: 1878 Annual Undergrad Tuition & Fees: $7,191
Enrollment: 91 Coed
Affiliation or Control: Other IRS Status: 501(c)3
Highest Offering: Associate Degree
Program: 2-Year Principally Bachelor's Creditable; Religious Emphasis
Accreditation: WJ

01 CEO/Principal Col for Officer Trng .... Major Tim FOLEY
03 Assistant Principal .... Major Brian SAUNDERS
05 Director of Curriculum .... Major Brian JONES
10 Director of Business Administration .... Capt. Kelly NOLAN
32 Director of Campus Services .... Major Cindy FOLEY

Samra University of Oriental Medicine (I)

3545 Wilshire Boulevard, Suite 350,
Los Angeles CA 90010
County: Los Angeles FICE Identification: 026193
Unit ID: 122287
Telephone: (213) 381-2221 Carnegie Class: Spec/Health
FAX Number: (213) 381-1701 Calendar System: Quarter
URL: www.samra.edu
Established: 1969 Annual Undergrad Tuition & Fees: $7,200
Enrollment: 177 Coed
Affiliation or Control: Independent Non-Profit IRS Status: 501(c)3
Highest Offering: Master's; No Lower Division
Program: Professional
Accreditation: ACUP

01 President .... Dr. Taecheong CHOO
05 Academic Dean .... Vacant
88 Assoc Dean Chinese/English Section .... Ms. Deannie JANOWITZ
88 Associate Dean Korean Section .... Dr. Youngjune YOON
37 Financial Aid Administrator .... Vacant
10 Senior Fiscal Officer .... Mr. David HAN
23 Clinic Manager .... Ms. Munghwa CHUNG
08 Librarian .... Vacant

Samuel Merritt University (J)

370 Hawthorne Avenue, Oakland CA 94609-3108
County: Alameda FICE Identification: 007012
Unit ID: 122296
Telephone: (510) 869-6511 Carnegie Class: Spec/Health
FAX Number: (510) 869-6525 Calendar System: Semester
URL: www.samuelmerritt.edu
Established: 1909 Annual Undergrad Tuition & Fees: $35,686
Enrollment: 1,365 Coed
Affiliation or Control: Independent Non-Profit IRS Status: 501(c)3
Highest Offering: Doctorate
Program: Professional
Accreditation: WC, ANEST, ARCPA, NURSE, OT, POD, PTA

01 President .... Dr. Sharon C. DIAZ
05 Academic Vice President/Provost .... Dr. Scot FOSTER
10 Vice President Business Affairs/CFO .... Mr. Gregory GINGRAS
84 Vice President Enrollment Services .... Mr. John GARTEN-SHUMAN
20 Assistant Academic Vice President .... Dr. Penny BAMFORD
35 Asst Vice President Student Affairs .... Mr. Craig ELLIOTT
21 Asst VP Finance & Admin/Controller .... Mr. Kenneth BOXTON
04 Assistant to the President .... Ms. Margrette PETERSON
09 Director Institutional Research .... Ms. Nandini DASGUPTA
66 Dean & Professor of Nursing .... Dr. Audrey BERMAN
63 Dean Podiatric Medicine .... Dr. John VENSON
88 Chair Dept Physical Therapy .... Dr. Terry NORDSTROM
88 Chair Dept Occupational Therapy .... Dr. Kate HAYNER
66 Chair ABSN .... Dr. Nancy HAUGEN
66 Chairperson Undergraduate Nursing .... Dr. Margaret EARLY
06 Registrar .... Ms. Anne SCHER
08 Library Director .... Ms. Barbara RYKEN
37 Director Financial Aid .... Ms. Mary ROBINSON
07 Director Admission .... Ms. Anne SEED
88 Dir Family Nurse Practitioner Pgm .... Ms. Suzanne AUGUST-SCHWARTZ
29 Director of Alumni Relations .... Ms. Carla ROSS
18 Director Facilities Management .... Ms. Lillian HARVIN
88 Director Physician Assistant Pgm .... Dr. Michael DEROSA
15 Exec Director Human Resources .... Ms. Elaine LEMAY

100 Exec Director Ofc of the President .... Ms. Stephanie BANGERT
30 Chief Development Officer .... Ms. Sue SYLVESTER
12 Site Manager Sacramento .... Ms. Rene ENGELHART
12 Site Manager San Mateo .... Dr. Mileva LEWIS SAULO
12 Site Manager San Francisco ... Ms. Zenobia COLLINS JOHNSON
13 Dir of Information Tech Svcs .... Mr. Blair SIMMONS
26 Assoc Dir Media Rels/Publication .... Ms. Elizabeth VALENTE

*San Bernardino Community College District (A)

114 S. Del Rosa Drive, San Bernardino CA 92401
County: San Bernardino　Identification: 667040
Telephone: (909) 382-4091　Carnegie Class: N/A
FAX Number: (909) 382-0153
URL: www.sbccd.edu

01 Chancellor .... Bruce BARRON
10 Int Vice Chancellor Fiscal Services .... Charlie NG
15 Vice Chancellor Human Resources .... Jack MIYAMOTO

*Crafton Hills College (B)

11711 Sand Canyon Road, Yucaipa CA 92399-1799
County: San Bernardino　FICE Identification: 009272
Unit ID: 113111
Telephone: (909) 794-2161　Carnegie Class: Assoc/Pub-U-MC
FAX Number: (909) 794-0423　Calendar System: Semester
URL: www.craftonhills.edu
Established: 1972　Annual Undergrad Tuition & Fees (In-District): $909
Enrollment: 6,108　Coed
Affiliation or Control: State/Local　IRS Status: 501(c)3
Highest Offering: Associate Degree
Program: Occupational; 2-Year Principally Bachelor's Creditable
Accreditation: WJ, EMT

02 President .... Ms. Gloria M. HARRISON
05 Vice President of Instruction .... Dr. Cheryl A. MARSHALL
32 Vice President Student Services .... Ms. Rebeccah WARREN-MARLATT
11 Vice President Administrative Svcs .... Mr. Mike STRONG
20 Dean Stdnt Svcs/Stdnt Development .... Mr. Joe CABRALES
35 Dean Student Services .... Ms. Kirsten S. COLVEY
49 Dean of Arts & Sciences .... Mr. Richard HOGREFE
81 Dean Math/English/Reading/Inst Supp .... Mr. Raju HEGDE
88 Dean Career Educ & Human Devel .... Ms. June Y. YAMAMOTO
30 Director Resource Development .... Ms. Cheryl BARDOWELL
09 Director Research & Planning .... Mr. Keith WURTZ
40 Director Bookstore .... Ms. Gloriann CHAVEZ
88 Director EOPS/CARE .... Ms. Rejoice CHAVIRA
25 Director Grant Mgt & Development .... Ms. Karen CHILDERS
37 Director Financial Aid .... Mr. John W. MUSKAVITCH
32 Director Student Life .... Ms. Ericka PADDOCK
18 Director Facilities/Opers/Maint .... Vacant
13 Director Technology Services .... Mr. Wayne BOGH
26 Director Marketing/Public Relations .Ms. Alisa SPARKIA MOORE
08 Librarian .... Ms. Laura WINNINGHAM

*San Bernardino Valley College (C)

701 S Mt. Vernon Avenue,
San Bernardino CA 92410-2798
County: San Bernardino　FICE Identification: 001272
Unit ID: 123527
Telephone: (909) 384-4400　Carnegie Class: Assoc/Pub-U-MC
FAX Number: N/A　Calendar System: Semester
URL: www.valleycollege.edu
Established: 1926　Annual Undergrad Tuition & Fees (In-District): $1,114
Enrollment: 13,857　Coed
Affiliation or Control: State/Local　IRS Status: 501(c)3
Highest Offering: Associate Degree
Program: Occupational; 2-Year Principally Bachelor's Creditable
Accreditation: WJ, ADNUR

02 President .... Dr. Debra S. DANIELS
05 Vice President Instruction .... Dr. Larry BUCKLEY
11 Vice President Administrative Svcs .... Mr. Jim HANSEN
07 Assoc Dean Admissions/Records .... Mr. Dan ANGELO
32 Vice President Student Services .... Mr. Damon BELL
08 Dean Library/Learning Support Serv .... Ms. Marie MESTAS
38 Dean Counseling/Matriculation .... Mr. Marco COTA
26 Director Marketing/Public Relations .... Mr. Craig PETINAK
88 Director Child Development Ctr .... Mr. Mark MERJIL
23 Director Health Services .... Ms. Elaine AKERS
31 Director Resource Development .... Mrs. Donna HOFFMAN
40 Director Bookstores .... Ms. Gloriann CHAVEZ
09 Director Institutional Research .... Dr. James SMITH
37 Director Student Financial Aid .... Mr. Joseph NGUYEN
41 Div Dean SS/Human Development & PE ..... Dr. Cory SCHWARTZ
50 Div Dean Math/Bus & Computer Tech .... Ms. Haragewen KINDE
76 Division Dean Sciences .... Dr. Susan BANGASSER
79 Division Dean Arts & Humanities .... Dr. Kay WEISS
72 Int Dean AT/TRANS/CULA .... Dr. Kay RAGAN
75 Dean Stdnt Success/Special Services .... Dr. Zelma RUSS

San Diego Christian College (D)

2100 Greenfield Drive, El Cajon CA 92019-1157
County: San Diego　FICE Identification: 012031
Unit ID: 112084
Telephone: (619) 201-8700　Carnegie Class: Bac/A&S
FAX Number: (619) 201-8749　Calendar System: Semester
URL: www.sdcc.edu
Established: 1970　Annual Undergrad Tuition & Fees: $23,924
Enrollment: 372　Coed
Affiliation or Control: Independent Non-Profit　IRS Status: 501(c)3
Highest Offering: Baccalaureate
Program: Liberal Arts And General; Teacher Preparatory
Accreditation: WC

01 President .... Dr. Paul E. AGUE
04 Exec Assistant to the President .... Mrs. Sarah CLARK
10 VP for Finance & Administration .... Mr. Ken YODER
05 VP for Academic Affairs .... Dr. Jon DEPRIEST
32 VP for Student Life .... Vacant
84 VP for Enrollment & Marketing .... Mr. Mitch FISK
07 Director of Enrollment Services .... Mrs. Susie M. PARKS
07 Director of Admissions .... Ms. Candice DELGIUDICE
42 Director of Spiritual Life .... Mr. Steve JENKINS
35 Director of Student Life .... Mrs. April FISK
30 Director of Advancement .... Mr. Victor CONNER
15 Director of Human Resources .... Mr. Robert JENSEN
08 Director of Library Services .... Ms. Ruth MARTIN
29 Alumni Services .... Mrs. Susie PARKS
09 Director of Assessment .... Mrs. Lundie CARSTENSEN
41 Athletic Director .... Mr. Chris BANDO
23 Director of Health Services .... Mr. Malia JENKINS
28 Director of Diversity .... Mr. Carl CALDERSON

*San Diego Community College District Administrative Offices (E)

3375 Camino Del Rio South, San Diego CA 92108-3883
County: San Diego　FICE Identification: 008895
Unit ID: 122339
Telephone: (619) 388-6500　Carnegie Class: N/A
FAX Number: (619) 388-6913
URL: www.sdccd.edu

01 Chancellor .... Dr. Constance M. CARROLL
05 Vice Chanc Instructional Svcs .... Dr. Otto LEE
10 Exec Vice Chanc Business Services .... Vacant
15 Vice Chancellor Human Resources .... Vacant
18 Vice Chanc Facilities Management .... Mr. David UMSTOT
32 Vice Chancellor Student Services .... Ms. Lynn C. NEAULT
26 Director Pub Info & Govt Relations ...... Mr. Richard DITTBENNER
43 Director Legal Services & EEO .... Ms. Mary ROGERS

*San Diego City College (F)

1313 Park Boulevard, San Diego CA 92101-4787
County: San Diego　FICE Identification: 001273
Unit ID: 122320
Telephone: (619) 388-3400　Carnegie Class: Not Classified
FAX Number: (619) 388-3063　Calendar System: Semester
URL: www.sdcity.edu
Established: 1914　Annual Undergrad Tuition & Fees (In-District): $1,114
Enrollment: 15,157　Coed
Affiliation or Control: State/Local　IRS Status: 501(c)3
Highest Offering: Associate Degree
Program: Occupational; 2-Year Principally Bachelor's Creditable
Accreditation: WJ, ADNUR

02 President .... Dr. Terrence BURGESS
05 Vice President Instruction .... Mrs. Mary BENARD
32 Vice President Student Services .... Mr. Peter WHITE
11 Vice Pres Administrative Services .... Dr. Jerry DAVIS
35 Dean of Student Affairs .... Ms. Denise WHISENHUNT
08 Int Dean Information/Learning Tech .... Mr. Robbi EWELL
79 Int Dean School of Arts/Humanities .... Ms. Trudy GERALD
50 Dean Sch Business/Info Tech .... Dr. Randall BARNES
88 Dean Student Develop/Matriculation .... Ms. Helen ELIAS
88 Acting Dn Engr & Tech/Math/Sci/Nurs ...... Dr. Minou SPRADLEY
56 Director Off-Campus Programs .... Ms. Jeanie TYLER
18 Chief Facilities/Physical Plant .... Mr. Derrall CHANDLER
92 Director Honors Program .... Dr. Kelly MAYHEW
07 Admissions & Records Supervisor .... Ms. Lou HUMPHRIES
22 Affirmative Action Officer .... Mr. Edwin HIEL
40 Bookstore Supervisor .... Ms. DeeDee PORTER
26 Public Information Officer .... Ms. Heidi BUNKOWSKE
88 PgmMgr Disabled Student Services .... Ms. Debra WRIGHT-HOWARD
37 Financial Aid Supervisor .... Mr. Gregory SANCHEZ
88 Director EOPS .... Mr. Gerald RAMSEY
83 Dean Behav & Soc Sci/Consumer Stds .... Ms. Lori ERRECA
68 Dean Health/Exercise Sci/Athletics .... Ms. Kathy MCGINNIS

*San Diego Mesa College (G)

7250 Mesa College Drive, San Diego CA 92111-4998
County: San Diego　FICE Identification: 001275
Unit ID: 122375
Telephone: (619) 388-2600　Carnegie Class: Assoc/Pub-U-MC
FAX Number: (619) 388-2929　Calendar System: Semester
URL: www.sdmesa.edu
Established: 1962　Annual Undergrad Tuition & Fees (In-District): $814
Enrollment: 25,972　Coed
Affiliation or Control: State/Local　IRS Status: 501(c)3
Highest Offering: Associate Degree
Program: Occupational; 2-Year Principally Bachelor's Creditable
Accreditation: WJ, DA, #PTAA, RAD

02 Interim President .... Ms. Elizabeth ARMSTRONG
05 Vice President Instruction .... Dr. Tim MCGRATH
32 Act Vice President Student Services .... Mr. Brian STOCKERT
11 Vice Pres Administrative Services .... Mr. Ron PEREZ
84 Dean Student Devel/Matriculation .... Ms. Joi Lin BLAKE
79 Dean Arts & Languages .... Mr. Jonathan FOHRMAN
76 Dean Health Sciences/Public Svc .... Ms. Margie FRITCH
81 Dean School Math/Natural Sciences .... Dr. Mary I. TOSTE
77 Dean Sch Bus/Comp Stds/Econ Dev .... Dr. Jill BAKER
62 Dean Lrng Resource/Educational Tech .... Mr. William P. CRAFT
68 Dean PE/Health Educ & Athletics .... Mr. Dave EVANS
79 Interim Dean Humanities .... Dr. Chris SULLIVAN
83 Int Dean Social/Behav Sci/Mult Stds ... Dr. Charlotta ROBERTSON
35 Dean Student Affairs .... Ms. Ashanti HANDS
46 Dn Instruct Svcs/Resource Dev/Rsrch ..Dr. Yvonne P. BERGLAND
27 Public Information Officer .... Ms. Lina HEIL
37 Financial Aid Officer .... Ms. Gilda MALDONADO
07 Student Svcs Supervisor Admission .... Ms. Ivonne ALVAREZ

*San Diego Miramar College (H)

10440 Black Mountain Road, San Diego CA 92126-2999
County: San Diego　FICE Identification: 011820
Unit ID: 122384
Telephone: (619) 388-7800　Carnegie Class: Assoc/Pub-U-MC
FAX Number: (619) 388-7901　Calendar System: Semester
URL: www.sdmiramar.edu
Established: 1969　Annual Undergrad Tuition & Fees (In-District): $1,114
Enrollment: 12,490　Coed
Affiliation or Control: State/Local　IRS Status: 501(c)3
Highest Offering: Associate Degree
Program: 2-Year Principally Bachelor's Creditable
Accreditation: WJ

02 President .... Dr. Patricia HSIEH
05 Interim Vice President Instruction .... Dr. Randy BARNES
32 Vice President Student Services .... Vacant
10 Vice President Admin Services .... Mr. Brett BELL
49 Dean of Liberal Arts .... Dr. Louis ASCIONE
36 Dean Career Tech/Wrkfce Initiatives .... Mr. Greg NEWHOUSE
50 Dean Business/Mathematics/Science .... Dr. Paulette HOPKINS
61 Dean of Public Safety .... Mr. George BEITEY
20 Physical Sciences Co-Chair .... Dr. Linda WOODS
26 Public Info Ofcr/Dir Alumni Rels .... Ms. Sandi TREVISAN
37 Financial Aid Officer .... Ms. Teresa VILABOY
06 Registrar .... Ms. Lynn NEAULT
15 Director Personnel Services .... Mr. Will SURBROOK
18 Chief Facilities/Physical Plant .... Mr. Dane LINDSAY
88 Child Development .... Ms. Dawn BURGESS
35 Dean of Student Affairs .... Ms. Adela JACOBSON
08 Library Chair .... Ms. Mary HART
07 Admissions Supervisor .... Ms. Dana STACK
88 Chair Admin Justice/Police Acad .... Mr. Steve LICKISS
50 Chair Business .... Mr. Alan VIERSEN
72 Chair Fire Science .... Ms. Mary KJARTANSON
79 Chair Arts & Humanities .... Mr. Robert FRITSCH
81 Chair Math .... Mr. Harvey WILENSKY
83 Chair Social Sciences .... Mr. Thomas SCHILZ
88 Chair Trade/Ind/Aviation Mtn Tech .... Mr. David BUSER
88 Spec Proj Mgr/Advanc Transp Tech .... Mr. Greg NEWHOUSE
88 Chair Diesel Technology .... Mr. Dan WILLKIE
38 Chair Counseling .... Mr. David NAVARRO
76 Chair Dept of Natural Sciences .... Dr. Marie MCMAHON
68 Chair Exercise Science .... Mr. Rod PORTER
60 Chair Comm/English & World Language .... Ms. Sheryl GOBBLE
88 Co-Chair Automotive .... Mr. Joseph YOUNG

San Francisco Art Institute (I)

800 Chestnut Street, San Francisco CA 94133-2206
County: San Francisco　FICE Identification: 003948
Unit ID: 122454
Telephone: (415) 771-7020　Carnegie Class: Spec/Arts
FAX Number: (415) 749-4590　Calendar System: Semester
URL: www.sfai.edu
Established: 1871　Annual Undergrad Tuition & Fees: $34,046
Enrollment: 562　Coed
Affiliation or Control: Independent Non-Profit　IRS Status: 501(c)3
Highest Offering: Master's
Program: Professional; Fine Arts Emphasis
Accreditation: WC, ART

01 President .... Charles DESMARAIS
05 Vice Pres/Dean Academic Affairs .... Jeannene PRZYBLYSKI
58 Dean of Graduate Programs .... Vacant
10 Chief Operating Officer .... Espi SANJANA
84 VP for Enrollment and Stdnt Affs .... Vacant
15 HR Administrator .... Joannie PACHECO
32 Dean of Student/VP Student Affairs .... Yunny YIP
06 Dir Registration & Student Records .... Martha SCHLITT
91 Director of Information Tech .... Andrew SIMAS
08 Director of Library Services .... Jeff GUNDERSON
26 Dir of Marketing & Communications .... Robert VALENTINE
20 Assoc Dean of Academic Admin .... Jennifer RISSLER
90 Dir Digital Stds/Trans Dscplny Tech .... Paul KLEIN
18 Facilities Manager .... Dave VARDANEGA
04 Exec Asst to the President .... Lydian REED
88 Director of Special Events .... Vacant
32 Dir Student Affairs for Campus Life .... Vacant
37 Dir of Student Financial Aid .... Larry BLAIR
38 Director of Counseling Services .... Marina TALLEY
07 Director of Admissions .... Elizabeth O'BRIEN
102 Dir Foundations/Corporate Relations .... Karen WEBER
21 Controller .... Susan WAYLAND

36 Assoc Dean of Stdnts/Dir Career Res .... Megann SEPT
96 Admin Services Director .... Heather HICKMAN
29 Dir of Advance & Alumni Relations .... Lael KOPKE
30 VP of Development & Alumni Rel .... Dr. Lee S. THEISEN

San Francisco Conservatory of Music (A)

50 Oak Street, San Francisco CA 94102-6011
County: San Francisco FICE Identification: 001278
Unit ID: 122506
Telephone: (415) 864-7326 Carnegie Class: Spec/Arts
FAX Number: (415) 503-6299 Calendar System: Semester
URL: www.sfcm.edu
Established: 1917 Annual Undergrad Tuition & Fees: $36,500
Enrollment: 398 Coed
Affiliation or Control: Independent Non-Profit IRS Status: 501(c)3
Highest Offering: Beyond Master's But Less Than Doctorate
Program: Professional; Music Emphasis
Accreditation: WC, MUS

01 President .... Colin MURDOCH
05 Dean .... Mary Ellen POOLE
32 Associate Dean of Student Life .... Jason SMITH
10 Vice Pres Finance & Administration .... Kathryn WITTENMYER
30 Vice President of Advancement .... Elizabeth TOUMA
07 Director of Admission .... Melissa COCCO-MITTEN
56 Director Preparatory/Extension .... Joan GORDON
26 Communications Manager .... Joseph SARGENT
30 Director of Development .... Murrey NELSON
04 Executive Assistant to President .... Jennifer GAMBARO
31 Performance Outreach Manager .... Elisabeth LOWRY
20 Assistant to the Dean .... Alice BECKETT
15 Human Resources Manager .... Michael PATTERSON
37 Director of Financial Aid .... Doris HOWARD
18 Chief Facilities Engineer .... David MITCHELL
06 Registrar .... Erika JOHNSON
08 Head Librarian .... Kevin MCLAUGHLIN

San Francisco Theological Seminary (B)

105 Seminary Road, San Anselmo CA 94960-2997
County: Marin FICE Identification: 001279
Unit ID: 122603
Telephone: (415) 451-2800 Carnegie Class: Spec/Faith
FAX Number: (415) 451-2852 Calendar System: Semester
URL: www.sfts.edu
Established: 1871 Annual Graduate Tuition & Fees: $10,600
Enrollment: 373 Coed
Affiliation or Control: Presbyterian Church (U.S.A.) IRS Status: 501(c)3
Highest Offering: Doctorate; No Undergraduates
Program: Professional; Religious Emphasis
Accreditation: WC, THEOL

01 President .... Dr. James L. MCDONALD
05 Dean of the Seminary .... Dr. Elizabeth LIEBERT
30 Interim VP Inst Advancement .... Rev. Scott SHELDON
10 Vice Pres Administration/ Finance .... Ms. Barbara BRENNER-BUDER
84 Director of Enrollment .... Ms. Elizabeth MCCORD
04 Exec Administrator to President .... Ms. Bonnie JOHNSTON
42 Chaplain & Assoc Dean Student Srvce .... Mr. Scott CLARK
36 Dir Vocational Formation Placement .... Rev. Leslie VEEN
06 Registrar .... Dr. Polly COOTE
21 Controller .... Ms. Susan BURNNETT
18 Chief of Physical Plant .... Mr. Gary MILLER
91 Director of IT .... Mr. Larry PICKARD
39 Director Student Housing .... Ms. Gail LU
15 Dir Human Resources .... Ms. Bonnie BLANK
44 Director of Annual Gifts .... Ms. Sarah CAMPBELL
26 Director of Communications .... Ms. Holly WOOLARD

San Joaquin College of Law (C)

901 Fifth Street, Clovis CA 93612-1312
County: Fresno FICE Identification: 025000
Unit ID: 122649
Telephone: (559) 323-2100 Carnegie Class: Spec/Law
FAX Number: (559) 323-5566 Calendar System: Semester
URL: www.sjcl.edu
Established: 1969 Annual Graduate Tuition & Fees: $17,000
Enrollment: 213 Coed
Affiliation or Control: Independent Non-Profit IRS Status: 501(c)3
Highest Offering: Doctorate; No Undergraduates
Program: Professional
Accreditation: WC

01 Dean .... Janice L. PEARSON
05 Dean Academic Affairs .... Sally A. PERRING
11 Director of Operations .... Joan K. LASSLEY
10 Chief Financial Officer .... Jill A. RANDLES
32 Director of Student Services .... Joyce K. MORODOMI
37 Financial Aid Administrator .... Jeannie M. LEWIS
08 Library Director .... Peter K. ROONEY
26 Public Relations Director .... Missy M. CARTIER
16 Chief of Personnel .... Gwen A. WATT
30 Chief Development .... Robin L. LEPPO
84 Director Enrollment Management .... Diane M. STEEL
61 Law Program Coordinator .... Pat A. SMITH

San Joaquin Delta College (D)

5151 Pacific Avenue, Stockton CA 95207-6370
County: San Joaquin FICE Identification: 001280
Unit ID: 122658
Telephone: (209) 954-5151 Carnegie Class: Assoc/Pub-U-MC
FAX Number: (209) 954-5644 Calendar System: Semester
URL: www.deltacollege.edu
Established: 1935 Annual Undergrad Tuition & Fees (In-District): $864
Enrollment: 18,610 Coed
Affiliation or Control: State/Local IRS Status: 501(c)3
Highest Offering: Associate Degree
Program: Occupational; 2-Year Principally Bachelor's Creditable
Accreditation: WJ, ACFEI, ADNUR

01 Superintendent/President .... Dr. Jeff MARSEE
05 Asst Supt/VP of Instruction .... Dr. Kathleen HART
32 Vice President of Student Services .... Ms. Trudy WALTON
10 Vice President of Business Services .... Vacant
15 VP Human Res/Employee Relations .... Mr. Vince BROWN
13 Vice Pres Information Technology .... Mr. Lee BELARMINO
09 Dean Plng Research/Regional Educ .... Dr. Matthew WETSTEIN
103 Dean Workforce/Economic Development .... Dr. Hazel M. HILL
97 Dean General Education & Transfer .... Dr. Charles JENNINGS
08 Div Dean Library/Learning Res/Lang .... Mr. Joe GONZALES
12 Associate Dean of Tracy Center .... Dr. Jessie GARZA-RODERICK
27 Dir Public Information/Marketing .... Vacant
21 Interim Director of Finance .... Mr. Jerry MCCLEAN
18 Director Facilities Management .... Ms. Maria BAKER
07 Director of Admissions .... Ms. Catherine MOONEY
37 Director of Financial Aid/Vet Svcs .... Ms. Denise C. DONN
96 Director of Purchasing .... Ms. Maria BERNARDINO

San Joaquin Valley College, Inc. (E)

8400 W Mineral King Avenue, Visalia CA 93291-9283
County: Tulare FICE Identification: 021207
Unit ID: 122685
Telephone: (559) 651-2500 Carnegie Class: Assoc/PrivFP
FAX Number: (559) 651-0574 Calendar System: Quarter
URL: www.sjvc.edu/campus/Visalia/
Established: 1977 Annual Undergrad Tuition & Fees: $12,550
Enrollment: 1,252 Coed
Affiliation or Control: Proprietary IRS Status: Proprietary
Highest Offering: Associate Degree
Program: Occupational; 2-Year Principally Bachelor's Creditable
Accreditation: WJ, ARCPA, DH

01 President .... Mr. Mark PERRY
00 Chief Executive Officer .... Mr. Michael PERRY
05 College Director .... Mr. Don WRIGHT
11 Vice President of Administration .... Ms. Wendy MENDES
84 Vice Pres of Enrollment Services .... Mr. Joseph HOLT
10 Chief Financial Officer .... Mr. Russ LEBO
37 Director of Student Financial Aid .... Mr. Kevin ROBINSON
96 Director of Purchasing .... Mr. Ralph ORTIZ

San Joaquin Valley College-Bakersfield (F)

201 New Stine Road, Suite 200,
Bakersfield CA 93309-2668
County: Kern FICE Identification: 023135
Unit ID: 122694
Telephone: (661) 834-0126 Carnegie Class: Assoc/PrivFP
FAX Number: (661) 834-1021 Calendar System: Quarter
URL: www.sjvc.edu/campus/Bakersfield/
Established: 1981 Annual Undergrad Tuition & Fees: $12,550
Enrollment: 877 Coed
Affiliation or Control: Proprietary IRS Status: Proprietary
Highest Offering: Associate Degree
Program: Occupational; 2-Year Principally Bachelor's Creditable
Accreditation: &WJ, SURGT

12 Campus Director .... Kelly WALTERS

† Regional accreditation is carried under the parent institution in Visalia, CA.

San Joaquin Valley College-Fresno (G)

295 E Sierra Avenue, Fresno CA 93710-3616
County: Fresno Identification: 666008
Unit ID: 262457
Telephone: (559) 448-8282 Carnegie Class: Assoc/PrivFP
FAX Number: (559) 448-8250 Calendar System: Quarter
URL: www.sjvc.edu/campus/Fresno/
Established: 1981 Annual Undergrad Tuition & Fees: $12,550
Enrollment: 870 Coed
Affiliation or Control: Proprietary IRS Status: Proprietary
Highest Offering: Associate Degree
Program: Occupational; 2-Year Principally Bachelor's Creditable
Accreditation: &WJ, SURGT

01 President .... Mr. Mark A. PERRY
12 Campus Director .... Dr. John SWIGER

† Regional accreditation is carried under the parent institution in Visalia, CA.

San Joaquin Valley College-Fresno Aviation Campus (H)

4985 E Andersen Avenue, Fresno CA 93721-1501
County: Fresno Identification: 666009
Unit ID: 422020
Telephone: (559) 453-0123 Carnegie Class: Assoc/PrivFP
FAX Number: (559) 453-0133 Calendar System: Quarter
URL: www.sjvc.edu
Established: 1991 Annual Undergrad Tuition & Fees: $11,230
Enrollment: 75 Coed
Affiliation or Control: Proprietary IRS Status: Proprietary
Highest Offering: Associate Degree
Program: Occupational; 2-Year Principally Bachelor's Creditable; Technical Emphasis
Accreditation: &WJ

01 President .... Mr. Mark PERRY
12 Campus Director .... Mr. Jack P. MACFARLANE

† Regional accreditation is carried under the parent institution in Visalia, CA.

San Joaquin Valley College-Hesperia (I)

9329 Mariposa Road, Hesperia CA 92344-8000
County: San Barnardino Identification: 667044
Unit ID: 456852
Telephone: (760) 948-1947 Carnegie Class: Not Classified
FAX Number: (760) 948-1704 Calendar System: Quarter
URL: www.sjvc.edu/campus/Hesperia/
Established: N/A Annual Undergrad Tuition & Fees: $12,925
Enrollment: 233 Coed
Affiliation or Control: Proprietary IRS Status: Proprietary
Highest Offering: Associate Degree
Program: Occupational; 2-Year Principally Bachelor's Creditable
Accreditation: &WJ, SURGT

12 Campus Director .... Ms. Melanie BLACKWELL

† Regional accreditation is carried under the parent institution in Visalia, CA.

San Joaquin Valley College-Modesto (J)

5380 Pirrone Road, Salida CA 95368-9090
County: Stanislaus Identification: 666128
Unit ID: 447351
Telephone: (209) 543-8800 Carnegie Class: Assoc/PrivFP
FAX Number: (209) 543-8320 Calendar System: Other
URL: www.sjvc.edu/campus/Modesto/
Established: 1977 Annual Undergrad Tuition & Fees: $17,310
Enrollment: 500 Coed
Affiliation or Control: Proprietary IRS Status: Proprietary
Highest Offering: Associate Degree
Program: Occupational; 2-Year Principally Bachelor's Creditable
Accreditation: &WJ

12 Director .... Mr. Sean C. HANCOCK

† Regional accreditation is carried under the parent institution in Visalia, CA.

San Joaquin Valley College-Rancho Cordova (K)

11050 Olson Drive, Suite 210,
Rancho Cordova CA 95670-5600
County: Sacramento Identification: 666133
Unit ID: 448372
Telephone: (916) 638-7582 Carnegie Class: Assoc/PrivFP
FAX Number: (916) 638-7553 Calendar System: Quarter
URL: www.sjvc.edu/campus/Rancho_Cordova/
Established: N/A Annual Undergrad Tuition & Fees: $17,517
Enrollment: 356 Coed
Affiliation or Control: Proprietary IRS Status: Proprietary
Highest Offering: Associate Degree
Program: Occupational; 2-Year Principally Bachelor's Creditable
Accreditation: &WJ

01 President .... Mr. Mark PERRY
12 Campus Director .... Mr. Jeff RUTHERFORD

† Regional accreditation is carried under the parent institution in Visalia, CA.

San Joaquin Valley College-Rancho Cucamonga (L)

10641 Church Street, Rancho Cucamonga CA 91730-6862
County: San Bernardino Identification: 666096
Unit ID: 442444
Telephone: (909) 948-7582 Carnegie Class: Assoc/PrivFP
FAX Number: (909) 948-3860 Calendar System: Quarter
URL: www.sjvc.edu/campus/Rancho_Cucamonga/
Established: N/A Annual Undergrad Tuition & Fees: $17,310
Enrollment: 1,003 Coed
Affiliation or Control: Proprietary IRS Status: Proprietary

Highest Offering: Associate Degree
Program: Occupational; 2-Year Principally Bachelor's Creditable
Accreditation: &WJ

01 President .... Mr. Mark PERRY
12 Campus Director .... Ms. Sherril HEIN

† Regional accreditation is carried under the parent institution in Visalia, CA.

*San Jose/Evergreen Community College District (A)

4750 San Felipe Road, San Jose CA 95135-1599
County: Santa Clara FICE Identification: 029042
Unit ID: 122737
Telephone: (408) 274-6700 Carnegie Class: N/A
FAX Number: (408) 531-8722
URL: www.sjeccd.org

01 Chancellor .... Dr. Rita CEPEDA
11 Vice Chanc Administrative Services .... Ms. Jeanine HAWK
05 Vice Chanc Educational Services .... Vacant
15 Vice Chanc Human Resources .... Ms. Kim L. GARCIA
84 Dean Enrollment Services .... Mr. Octavio CRUZ
09 Int Ex Dir Rsrch & Instnl Effect .... Ms. Oleg BESPALOV
18 Dir Facilities/Const Mgmt/Operation .... Mr. Robert DIAS
07 Director Admiss/Records San Jose .... Mr. Carlo SANTOS
10 Director of Fiscal Services .... Mr. Peter FITZSIMMONS
13 Dir Information Technology Sys Svc .... Mr. Thomas ONWILER
28 Dir of Employment Svcs/Diversity .... Mr. Sam HO

*Evergreen Valley College (B)

3095 Yerba Buena Road, San Jose CA 95135-1598
County: Santa Clara FICE Identification: 012452
Unit ID: 114266
Telephone: (408) 274-7900 Carnegie Class: Assoc/Pub-U-MC
FAX Number: (408) 238-3179 Calendar System: Semester
URL: www.evc.edu
Established: 1975 Annual Undergrad Tuition & Fees (In-District): $908
Enrollment: 9,922 Coed
Affiliation or Control: State/Local IRS Status: 501(c)3
Highest Offering: Associate Degree
Program: 2-Year Principally Bachelor's Creditable
Accreditation: WJ, ADNUR

02 President .... Mr. Henry C. YONG
05 Acting VP Academic Affairs .... Mr. Keith AYTCH
32 Vice Pres Student Services .... Ms. Irma ARCHULETA
10 VP Administrarive Services .... Mr. Henry GEE
50 Dean Business & Workforce Devel .... Dr. Jonathan KING
66 Acting Dean Nursing & Allied Health .... Ms. Sandra DEWOLFE
62 Dean Language Arts/Library/Lrng Res .... Dr. Keith AYTCH
81 Dean Math/Science/Engineering .... Dr. Wei ZHOU
83 Dean Soc Sci/PE/Arts/Humanities .... Mr. Mark GONZALES
84 Dean Enrollment Services .... Mr. Octavio CRUZ
38 Dean Student Counseling .... Ms. Tammeil GILKERSON
35 Director Student Life .... Mr. Victor GARZA, JR.
37 Director Financial Aid .... Ms. Alma TANON
88 Director Student Services Pgm .... Mr. Savander PARKER
88 Director CalWorks/WIN .... Ms. Elizabeth TYRRELL
11 Supervisor Administrative Services .... Ms. Lauren MCKEE
19 District Police Chief .... Mr. Ray AGUIRRE

*San Jose City College (C)

2100 Moorpark Avenue, San Jose CA 95128-2799
County: Santa Clara FICE Identification: 001282
Unit ID: 122746
Telephone: (408) 298-2181 Carnegie Class: Assoc/Pub-U-MC
FAX Number: (408) 298-1935 Calendar System: Semester
URL: www.sjcc.edu
Established: 1921 Annual Undergrad Tuition & Fees (In-District): $780
Enrollment: 12,364 Coed
Affiliation or Control: State/Local IRS Status: 501(c)3
Highest Offering: Associate Degree
Program: Occupational; 2-Year Principally Bachelor's Creditable
Accreditation: #WJ, DA

02 President .... Dr. Barbara KAVALIER
11 Vice President Administrative Svcs .... Mr. James WILLIAMS
32 Vice President Student Services .... Ms. Marie-Elaine BURNS
07 Director Admissions & Records .... Vacant
88 Executive Director WIN Program .... Ms. Marilyn BRODIE
37 Director Student Financial Aid .... Mr. Takeo KUBO
92 Director Honors Program .... Vacant
41 Athletic Director .... Mr. Donald STAGNARO
04 Assistant to the President .... Ms. Isabel MACIAS
88 Dean Applied Science/Bus/Careers .... Mr. Kishan VUJJENI
79 Dean Humanities/Social Science .... Dr. Patrick GERSTER
71 Dean Special Programs .... Dr. Romero JALOMO
88 Int Dean Language Arts .... Ms. Virginia SCALES
81 Dean Mathematics/Sciences Division .... Ms. Leandra MARTIN
38 Dean Counseling & Matriculation .... Mr. Romero JALOMO

*San Mateo County Community College District Office (D)

3401 CSM Drive, San Mateo CA 94402-3699
County: San Mateo FICE Identification: 004697
Unit ID: 122782
Telephone: (650) 574-6500 Carnegie Class: N/A
FAX Number: (650) 574-6566
URL: www.smccd.edu

01 Chancellor .... Mr. Ron D. GALATOLO
03 Interim Executive Vice Chancellor .... Ms. Kathy BLACKWOOD
16 Vice Chanc Employee Rels/Human Res .... Mr. Harry JOEL
05 Vice Chanc Educational Svcs/Plng .... Dr. Jing LUAN
18 Vice Chanc Facil Plng/Maint/Oper .... Mr. Jose NUNEZ
88 Vice Chanc Auxilliary Services .... Mr. Tom BAUER
31 Director of Community/Govt Rels .... Ms. Barbara W. CHRISTENSEN
10 Interim Chief Financial Officer .... Mr. Raymond CHOW
14 Chief Technology Officer .... Mr. Frank M. VASKELIS

*Cañada College (E)

4200 Farm Hill Boulevard, Redwood City CA 94061-1099
County: San Mateo FICE Identification: 006973
Unit ID: 111434
Telephone: (650) 306-3100 Carnegie Class: Assoc/Pub-S-MC
FAX Number: (650) 306-3457 Calendar System: Semester
URL: www.canadacollege.net
Established: 1968 Annual Undergrad Tuition & Fees (In-District): $624
Enrollment: 7,222 Coed
Affiliation or Control: State/Local IRS Status: 501(c)3
Highest Offering: Associate Degree
Program: Occupational; 2-Year Principally Bachelor's Creditable
Accreditation: WJ, RAD

02 Interim President .... Mr. James KELLER
32 Vice President of Student Services .... Ms. Robin RICHARDS
05 Vice President of Instruction .... Dr. Sarah PERKINS
84 Dean Enrollment Services .... Ms. Kim LOPEZ
06 Assistant Registrar .... Ms. Ruth MILLER
10 Chief Business Officer .... Ms. Victoria NUNES
26 Director of Marketing .... Mr. Robert HOOD
44 Dir Plng/Research/Student Success .... Mr. Gregory STOUP
18 Facilities Manager .... Mr. Danny GLASS
37 Director Financial Aid .... Ms. Margie CARRINGTON
103 Dean Business/Worforce & Athletics .... Ms. Linda HAYES
79 Dean of Humanities & Social Science .... Mr. David JOHNSON
81 Dean Science & Technology .... Dr. Janet STRINGER

*College of San Mateo (F)

1700 W Hillsdale Boulevard, San Mateo CA 94402-3795
County: San Mateo FICE Identification: 001181
Unit ID: 122791
Telephone: (650) 574-6161 Carnegie Class: Assoc/Pub-S-MC
FAX Number: (650) 574-6680 Calendar System: Semester
URL: www.collegeofsanmateo.edu
Established: 1922 Annual Undergrad Tuition & Fees (In-District): $1,080
Enrollment: 9,500 Coed
Affiliation or Control: State/Local IRS Status: 501(c)3
Highest Offering: Associate Degree
Program: Occupational; 2-Year Principally Bachelor's Creditable
Accreditation: WJ, DA

02 President .... Mr. Michael CLAIRE
05 Vice President Instruction .... Dr. Susan ESTES
32 Vice President Student Services .... Ms. Jennifer HUGHES
07 Dean Admissions & Records .... Dr. Henry VILLAREAL
38 Dean Counsel/Advis/Matriculation .... Ms. Marsha RAMEZANE
30 Dir College Development & Marketing .... Ms. Beverly MADDEN
18 Chief Facilities/Physical Plant .... Ms. Karen POWELL
46 Dean Articulation & Research .... Dr. John J. SEWART
79 Dean Language Arts Division .... Dr. Sandra STEFANI COMERFORD
68 Dean Phys Educ/Athletics Division .... Mr. Andreas WOLF
81 Dean Math/Science Division .... Dr. Charlene FRONTIERA
83 Dean Creative Arts/Social Sci Div .... Dr. Kevin HENSON
72 Dean Business & Technology Division .... Ms. Kathleen ROSS

*Skyline College (G)

3300 College Drive, San Bruno CA 94066-1698
County: San Mateo FICE Identification: 007713
Unit ID: 123509
Telephone: (650) 738-4100 Carnegie Class: Assoc/Pub-S-MC
FAX Number: (650) 738-4338 Calendar System: Semester
URL: www.skylinecollege.edu
Established: 1969 Annual Undergrad Tuition & Fees (In-District): $780
Enrollment: 10,561 Coed
Affiliation or Control: State/Local IRS Status: 501(c)3
Highest Offering: Associate Degree
Program: Occupational; 2-Year Principally Bachelor's Creditable
Accreditation: WJ, SURGT

02 President .... Ms. Regina STANBACK STROUD
05 Int Vice President Instruction .... Mr. Michael WILLIAMSON
32 Int Vice President Student Services .... Mr. Joseph MADRIGAL
84 Dean Enrollment Svcs/Financial Aid .... Dr. John MOSBY
09 Dean Plng/Rsrch/Instl Effective .... Dr. Robert JOHNSTONE
10 Director Business Service .... Ms. Eloisa BRIONES
83 Dean Social Science/Creative Arts .... Ms. Donna J. BESTOCK
50 Dean Business Division .... Ms. Margery MEADOWS
60 Dean Language Arts .... Ms. Connie BERINGER
68 Dean Physical Education .... Mr. Joseph MORELLO
81 Dean Science/Math/Technology .... Mr. Michael WILLIAMSON
38 Dean Counsel/Advising/Matriculation .... Mr. Richard WALLACE
18 Chief Facilities/Physical Plant .... Mr. Richard INOKUCHI
103 Dir Workforce Development Center .... Mr. William WATSON
37 Director Financial Aid/CalWk .... Ms. Maria ESCOBAR
26 Communications Manager .... Ms. Christianne MARRA

Sanford-Burnham Graduate School of Biomedical Sciences (H)

10901 North Torrey Pines Road, La Jolla CA 92037
County: San Diego Identification: 667069
Telephone: (858) 646-3100 Carnegie Class: Not Classified
FAX Number: (858) 646-3199 Calendar System: Quarter
URL: sanfordburnham.org
Established: 2005 Annual Graduate Tuition & Fees: N/A
Enrollment: N/A Coed
Affiliation or Control: Independent Non-Profit IRS Status: 501(c)3
Highest Offering: Master's; No Undergraduates
Program: Professional
Accreditation: @WC

01 President .... Dr. Kristiina VUORI
10 Exec VP/Chief Financial Officer .... Dr. Gary RAISL
05 Dean .... Dr. Guy SALVESEN
15 Vice Pres Human Res/Org Effect .... Ms. Beth ALTON
30 Vice President Inst Advancement .... Mr. Philip GRAHAM
27 Vice President Communications .... Ms. Andrea MOSER

Santa Barbara Business College (I)

5300 California Ave, Bakersfield CA 93309-2139
County: Kern FICE Identification: 025779
Unit ID: 122834
Telephone: (661) 835-1100 Carnegie Class: Assoc/PrivFP
FAX Number: (661) 835-0242 Calendar System: Semester
URL: www.sbbcollege.edu
Established: 1982 Annual Undergrad Tuition & Fees: $28,910
Enrollment: 972 Coed
Affiliation or Control: Proprietary IRS Status: Proprietary
Highest Offering: Associate Degree
Program: Occupational; 2-Year Principally Bachelor's Creditable
Accreditation: ACICS

01 President .... Matthew JOHNSTON
07 Director of Admissions .... Holly ORTIZ
26 Marketing Coordinator .... Monica RAYMOND

Santa Barbara Business College (J)

34275 Monterey Ave, Rancho Mirage CA 92270
Identification: 666582
Telephone: (760) 341-2602 Carnegie Class: Not Classified
FAX Number: (760) 341-2607 Calendar System: Semester
URL: www.sbbcollege.com
Established: 2008 Annual Undergrad Tuition & Fees: N/A
Enrollment: N/A Coed
Affiliation or Control: Proprietary IRS Status: Proprietary
Highest Offering: Associate Degree
Program: Occupational; 2-Year Principally Bachelor's Creditable
Accreditation: ACICS

01 President .... Matthew JOHNSON
07 Director of Admissions .... Holly ORTIZ
26 Marketing Coordinator .... Monica RAYMOND

Santa Barbara Business College (K)

506 Chapala Street, Santa Barbara CA 93101-3412
County: Santa Barbara FICE Identification: 009989
Telephone: (805) 967-9677 Carnegie Class: Not Classified
FAX Number: (805) 967-4248 Calendar System: Semester
URL: www.sbbcollege.edu
Established: 1888 Annual Undergrad Tuition & Fees: $7,100
Enrollment: 100 Coed
Affiliation or Control: Proprietary IRS Status: Proprietary
Highest Offering: Associate Degree
Program: Occupational; 2-Year Principally Bachelor's Creditable
Accreditation: ACICS

01 President .... Matthew JOHNSTON
07 Director of Admissions .... Holly ORTIZ

Santa Barbara Business College (L)

303 E Plaza Drive, Santa Maria CA 93454
County: Santa Barbara FICE Identification: 025780
Unit ID: 122852
Telephone: (805) 922-8256 Carnegie Class: Assoc/PrivFP
FAX Number: (805) 346-1857 Calendar System: Semester
URL: www.sbbcollege.edu
Established: 1980 Annual Undergrad Tuition & Fees: $18,090
Enrollment: 328 Coed
Affiliation or Control: Proprietary IRS Status: Proprietary
Highest Offering: Associate Degree
Program: Occupational; 2-Year Principally Bachelor's Creditable
Accreditation: ACICS

01 President .... Matthew JOHNSTON
07 Director of Admissions .... Holly ORTIZ
26 Marketing Coordinator .... Monica RAYMOND

Santa Barbara Business College (A)

4839 Market Street, Ventura CA 93003
County: Ventura Identification: 666099
Unit ID: 433420
Telephone: (805) 339-2999 Carnegie Class: Assoc/PrivFP
FAX Number: (805) 339-2994 Calendar System: Other
URL: www.sbbcollege.edu
Established: 2003 Annual Undergrad Tuition & Fees: $29,190
Enrollment: 492 Coed
Affiliation or Control: Proprietary IRS Status: Proprietary
Highest Offering: Associate Degree
Program: Occupational; 2-Year Principally Bachelor's Creditable
Accreditation: ACICS

01 President .... Matthew JOHNSTON
07 Director of Admissions .... Holly ORTIZ
26 Marketing Coordinator .... Monica RAYMOND

† Branch campus of Santa Barbara Business College, Santa Barbara, CA.

Santa Barbara City College (B)

721 Cliff Drive, Santa Barbara CA 93109-2394
County: Santa Barbara FICE Identification: 001285
Unit ID: 122889
Telephone: (805) 965-0581 Carnegie Class: Assoc/Pub-R-L
FAX Number: (805) 963-7222 Calendar System: Semester
URL: www.sbcc.edu
Established: 1909 Annual Undergrad Tuition & Fees (In-District): $1,096
Enrollment: 17,849 Coed
Affiliation or Control: State/Local IRS Status: 501(c)3
Highest Offering: Associate Degree
Program: Occupational; 2-Year Principally Bachelor's Creditable
Accreditation: WJ, ACFEI, ADNUR, DMS, RAD

01 Superintendent/President .... Dr. Andreea M. SERBAN
05 Exec Vice Pres Educational Programs .... Dr. Jack FRIEDLANDER
51 Vice President Continuing Education .... Dr. Ofelia ARELLANO
10 Vice President Business Services .... Mr. Joseph SULLIVAN
15 Vice Pres Human Resources/Legal Aff .... Ms. Susan EHRLICH
14 Vice President Info Technology .... Dr. Paul BISHOP
72 Dean Educational Programs .... Mr. Ben PARTEE
38 Dean Educational Programs .... Mr. Keith C. MCLELLAN
81 Dean Educational Programs .... Ms. Marilynn SPAVENTA
57 Dean Educational Programs .... Dr. Alice SCHARPER
53 Dean Educational Programs .... Dr. Diane HOLLEMS
72 Dean Educational Programs .... Dr. Doug HERSH
08 Librarian .... Mr. Kenley NEUFELD
102 Exec Dir Foundation for SBCC .... Ms. Vanessa PATTERSON
09 Sr Director Institutional Research .... Mr. Robert ELSE
27 College Information Officer .... Ms. Joan GALVAN
37 Director of Student Financial Aid .... Mr. Brad HARDISON
30 Director Campus Development .... Mr. Alex PITTMON
18 Director of Facilities & Operations .... Ms. Julie HENDRICKS
07 Director of Admissions .... Ms. Allison CURTIS
85 Director International Students .... Ms. Carola SMITH
96 Manager of Purchasing .... Mr. Robert MORALES

Santa Clara University (C)

500 El Camino Real, Santa Clara CA 95053-0001
County: Santa Clara FICE Identification: 001326
Unit ID: 122931
Telephone: (408) 554-4000 Carnegie Class: Master's L
FAX Number: (408) 554-2700 Calendar System: Quarter
URL: www.scu.edu
Established: 1851 Annual Undergrad Tuition & Fees: $41,790
Enrollment: 8,831 Coed
Affiliation or Control: Independent Non-Profit IRS Status: 501(c)3
Highest Offering: Doctorate
Program: Liberal Arts And General; Teacher Preparatory; Professional
Accreditation: WC, BUS, BUSA, ENG, LAW, THEOL

01 President .... Rev. Michael E. ENGH, SJ
05 Provost .... Mr. Dennis JACOBS
10 Vice President Admin & Finance .... Mr. Robert D. WARREN
43 General Counsel .... Mr. John OTTOBONI
26 Vice President University Relations .... Mr. Robert GUNSALUS
04 Exec Assistant to the President .... Dr. Molly MC DONALD
04 Assistant to the President .... Vacant
49 Dean of Arts & Sciences .... Dr. Atom YEE
50 Dean of Business .... Dr. S. Andrew STARBIRD
53 Dean Educ & Counseling Psychology .... Vacant
54 Dean of Engineering .... Dr. Godfrey MUNGAL
61 Dean of Law .... Dr. Donald J. POLDEN
73 Dean Jesuit School of Theology .... Rev. Kevin F. BURKE, SJ
88 Dean Academic Support Services .... Ms. Elaine BORELLI
20 Senior Vice Provost .... Dr. Don C. DODSON
20 Vice Provost Undergraduate Studies .... Dr. Diane E. JONTE-PACE
32 Vice Provost for Student Life .... Ms. Jeanne ROSENBERGER
84 Vice Provost for Enrollment Mgmt .... Mr. Mike SEXTON
20 Vice Provost Planning/Admin .... Dr. Charles F. EREKSON
27 Vice Provost Info Services/CIO .... Dr. Ronald L. DANIELSON
88 Assoc Provost Undergraduate Studies .... Dr. Philip R. KESTEN
88 Assoc Provost Research Initiatives .... Dr. Amy M. SHACHTER
88 Assoc Provost Faculty Development .... Dr. William SUNDSTROM
07 Dean Admission .... Ms. Sandra L. HAYES
84 Assoc Vice Provost Enrollment Mgt .... Dr. Richard TOOMEY
27 Assoc Vice President Mktg/Comm .... Mr. Richard GIACCHETTI
21 Assoc Vice President Finance .... Mr. Harry M. FONG
15 Asst Vice President Human Resources .... Vacant
88 Asst Vice President University Oper .... Mr. Joe SUGG
30 Asst Vice President Development .... Ms. Nancy CALDERON
31 Asst Vice Pres Auxiliary Services .... Ms. Jane BARRANTES
35 Assoc Dean for Student Life .... Mr. Matthew DUNCAN
06 Registrar .... Ms. Monica L. AUGUSTIN
29 Executive Dir of Alumini Relations .... Ms. Kathy KALE
41 Director Athletics and Recreation .... Dr. Daniel COONAN
08 University Librarian .... Vacant
08 Law Librarian .... Dr. Mary D. HOOD
14 Director of Information Technology .... Mr. Carl FUSSELL
24 Director Media Services .... Ms. Nancy CUTLER
36 Director Career Center .... Ms. Elspeth ROSSETTI
09 Director Institutional Research .... Ms. Barbara A. STEWART
25 Director Sponsored Projects .... Ms. Linda J. CAMPBELL
38 Director Health & Counseling Svcs .... Vacant
85 Int Exec Dir International Programs .... Dr. Terry SHOUP
21 Director Budget .... Mr. Dennis ROBERTS
88 Chief Investment Officer .... Mr. John E. KERRIGAN
21 Controller .... Ms. Sarah J. GATENBY
18 Director of Facilities .... Mr. Jeffrey R. CHARLES
96 Director University Support Service .... Mr. Ed MERRYMAN
19 Director Campus Safety Services .... Mr. Philip BELTRAN
40 General Manager Bookstore .... Mrs. Deborah KENDALL
42 Director of Campus Ministry .... Rev. Jack R. TREACY, SJ
22 Director of Affirmative Action .... Vacant
88 Director de Saisset Museum .... Ms. Rebecca M. SCHAPP
88 Exec Dir Ignatian Ctr Jesuit Educ .... Rev. Michael MCCARTHY, SJ
88 Managing Dir Ctr Sci/Tech/Society .... Mr. Thane KREINER
88 Managing Dir Ctr Sci/Tech/Society .... Ms. Radha BASU
88 Exec Dir Markkula Ctr Applied Ethic .... Mr. Kirk O. HANSON

Santa Monica College (D)

1900 Pico Boulevard, Santa Monica CA 90405-1628
County: Los Angeles FICE Identification: 001286
Unit ID: 122977
Telephone: (310) 434-4000 Carnegie Class: Assoc/Pub-S-MC
FAX Number: (310) 434-4386 Calendar System: Semester
URL: www.smc.edu
Established: 1929 Annual Undergrad Tuition & Fees (In-District): $961
Enrollment: 35,232 Coed
Affiliation or Control: State/Local IRS Status: 501(c)3
Highest Offering: Associate Degree
Program: Occupational; 2-Year Principally Bachelor's Creditable
Accreditation: WJ, ADNUR

01 Superintendent/President .... Dr. Chui L. TSANG
03 Executive Vice President .... Mr. Randal R. LAWSON
10 Vice President Business/Admin .... Mr. Robert G. ISOMOTO
16 Vice President Human Resources .... Ms. Marcia WADE
05 Vice President Academic Affairs .... Mr. Jeffery SHIMIZU
45 Vice Pres Planning & Development .... Vacant
84 Vice Pres Enrollment Development .... Ms. Teresita RODRIGUEZ
32 Vice President Student Affairs .... Mr. Michael TUITASI
20 Dean Academic Affairs .... Ms. Erica LEBLANC
46 Dean Institutional Effectiveness .... Vacant
15 Dean Human Resources .... Mrs. Sherri LEE-LEWIS
08 Dean Learning Resources .... Ms. Mona MARTIN
85 Dean International Education .... Ms. Kelley BRAYTON
56 Dean External Programs .... Ms. Katharine MULLER
38 Dean Counseling/Retention .... Ms. Brenda BENSON
14 Dean Information Technology .... Ms. Jocelyn CHONG
43 Campus Counsel .... Mr. Robert MYERS
106 Director Online Services & Support .... Ms. Julie YARRISH
51 Associate Dean Emeritus College .... Mr. Ron FURUYAMA
35 Dean Student Life .... Ms. Deyna HEARN
20 Dean Instructional Services .... Dr. Georgia LORENZ
17 Associate Dean of Health Sciences .... Dr. Ida DANZEY
07 Dean Enrollment Services .... Ms. Kiersten ELLIOTT
86 Sr Director Government Relations .... Mr. Don GIRARD
37 Assoc Dean Financial Aid/Scholarshp .... Mr. Steve MYROW
18 Chief Dir Facilities Management .... Ms. J.C SAUNDERS-KEURJIAN
21 Director Fiscal Services .... Mr. Chris BONVENUTO
09 Director Institutional Research .... Ms. Hannah ALFORD
104 Assoc Dean International Education .... Ms. Denise KINSELLA
41 Project Manager Athletics .... Mr. Joe CASCIO
88 Dean of Special Programs .... Dr. Leonard CRAWFORD
102 Director of Grants .... Ms. Laurel MCQUAY-PENINGER
88 Director Performing Arts Center .... Ms. Dale FRANZEN
30 Actg Dir Institutional Advancement .... Mr. Charles POTTS
31 Director Community Relations .... Ms. Judy NEVEAU
88 Director of Classified Personnel .... Ms. Dori MACDONALD
88 Director Network Services .... Mr. Bob DAMMER
25 Director of Contracts .... Mr. Charlie YEN
96 Director of Purchasing .... Ms. Cynthia MOORE
19 Dean Camp Security Stdnt Hlth/Safe .... Dr. Albert VASQUEZ
27 Public Information Officer .... Mr. Bruce SMITH
04 Admin Asst to the President .... Ms. Lin D. CALDWELL
13 Director Management Info Systems .... Mr. Dexter L. JOHNSTON
24 Mgr Media & Reprographic Services .... Mr. Albert DESALLES
40 Bookstore Manager .... Mr. David DEVER
103 Dean Workforce Development .... Dr. Patricia RAMOS
101 Coordinator Board of Trustees .... Ms. Lisa ROSE
88 Assoc Dean Outreach & Recruitment .... Ms. Sonali PERERA-BRIDGES
88 Director Radio Station (KCRW) .... Ms. Jennifer FERRO
88 Director Facilities Programming .... Ms. Linda SULLIVAN
30 Actg Dean Institutional Development .... Ms. Carol HAMILTON
88 Assoc Dean Stdnt Success Initiative .... Mr. Roberto GONZALEZ
88 Dir Sustainability Coordination .... Ms. Genevieve BERTONE
75 Dir Small Business Devlopment Ctr .... Ms. Michelle KING
88 Assoc Dir Dual Enroll/Instr Svcs .... Ms. Maral HYELER

Santa Rosa Junior College (E)

1501 Mendocino Avenue, Santa Rosa CA 95401-4395
County: Sonoma FICE Identification: 001287
Unit ID: 123013
Telephone: (707) 527-4011 Carnegie Class: Assoc/Pub-R-L
FAX Number: (707) 527-4816 Calendar System: Semester
URL: www.santarosa.edu
Established: 1918 Annual Undergrad Tuition & Fees (In-District): $742
Enrollment: 31,467 Coed
Affiliation or Control: State/Local IRS Status: 501(c)3
Highest Offering: Associate Degree
Program: Occupational; 2-Year Principally Bachelor's Creditable
Accreditation: WJ, DA, DH, @DIETT, EMT, RAD

01 Superintendent/President .... Dr. Robert F. AGRELLA
12 Vice President Petaluma Campus .... Dr. Jane SALDANA-TALLEY
05 VP Acad Affs/Asst Superintendent .... Dr. Mary Kay RUDOLPH
10 Vice President Business Services .... Mr. Doug ROBERTS
32 VP Student Svcs/Asst Superindendent .... Mr. Ricardo D. NAVARRETTE
16 VP Human Resources .... Ms. Karen FURUKAWA
11 Dean Facilities Planning/Operations .... Mr. Tony ICHSAN
14 Director Information Technology .... Mr. Scott CONRAD
04 Executive Assistant to CEO/BOT .... Ms. Maria GAITAN
75 Dean Career/Tech Ed/Economic Dev .... Ms. Lorraine WILSON
88 Dean Curriculum/Education Support .... Dr. Abraham FARKAS
49 Dean Liberal Arts & Sciences .... Dr. Kris ABRAHAMSON
08 Dean Learning Res/Educ Tech .... Ms. Cherry LI-BUGG
88 Dean Counseling/Support Services .... Mr. Marty LEE
88 Dean Public Safety .... Ms. April CHAPMAN
81 Dean Sci/Tech/Engr/Math .... Ms. Kerry CAMPBELL-PRICE
17 Dean Health Sciences .... Dr. Ezbon JEN
50 Dean Business/Professional Studies .... Mr. Steve COHEN
83 Dean Arts/Comm/Behav & Soc Sci .... Dr. Tyra BENOIT
79 Dean Language Arts/Acad Foundation .... Mr. Victor CUMMINGS
41 Dean KiniseologylDance/Athletic Dir .... Mr. James FORKUM
88 Dean Disabled Students Pgm & Svcs .... Ms. Patie WEGMAN
72 Dean Instruction & Technical Svcs .... Mr. Robert CHUDNOFSKY
35 Dean Student Services .... Vacant
84 Dean Instruction & Enrollment Mgmt .... Vacant
88 Dean Early Childhood Education .... Mr. Joel GORDON
88 Dean Matriculation & Student Dev .... Ms. Ruth MCMULLEN
47 Dean Career/Tech Svcs & Agriculture .... Vacant
19 Interim Chief of Police .... Mr. Joe PALLA
103 Director Economic/Workforce Dev .... Mr. Charles ROBBINS
21 Director of Fiscal Services .... Ms. Kate JOLLEY
37 Director Student Financial Services .... Ms. Kris SHEAR
18 Director Facility Operations .... Mr. Paul BIELEN
23 Director Student Health Services .... Ms. Susan QUINN
09 Director Institutional Research .... Dr. KC GREANEY
35 Dir Student Affs/New Student Pgm .... Mr. Robert ETHINGTON
96 Director Purchasing & Graphics .... Mr. Tim BOSMA
40 Director Bookstore .... Ms. Lorraine FAZZOLARE
44 Director Alumni Rels & Foundation .... Ms. Kate MCCLINTOCK
66 Director Nursing Program .... Ms. Susan CRAWFORD
06 Dir Acad Records/Intl Admissions .... Ms. Freyja PEREIRA
07 Director Admissions/Enrollment Svcs .... Ms. Diane TRAVERSI
51 Director Continuing Education .... Ms. Betsy ROBERTS
15 Assistant Director Human Resources .... Ms. Sabrina MEYER
26 Public Relations Manager .... Ms. Susan BAGBY MATTHEWS
90 Manager Instructional Computing .... Mr. Josh ADAMS
36 Manager Career Development Svcs .... Ms. Catherine WILSON
24 Manager Media Services .... Mr. Russ BOWDEN
24 Manager Media Services Petaluma .... Mr. Matt PEARSON

Saybrook University (F)

747 Front Street, 3rd Floor, San Francisco CA 94111-1920
County: San Francisco FICE Identification: 021206
Unit ID: 123095
Telephone: (800) 825-4480 Carnegie Class: Spec/Health
FAX Number: (415) 433-9271 Calendar System: Semester
URL: www.saybrook.edu
Established: 1971 Annual Graduate Tuition & Fees: $21,400
Enrollment: 605 Coed
Affiliation or Control: Independent Non-Profit IRS Status: 501(c)3
Highest Offering: Doctorate; No Undergraduates
Program: Professional
Accreditation: WC

01 President .... Dr. Mark SCHULMAN
05 Vice President of Academic Affairs .... Dr. Daniel R. SEWELL
11 Int Vice President for Operations .... Mr. Michael CAIRNS
26 VP Communications/External Affairs .... Ms. Sigrid BADINELLI
06 Registrar .... Mr. Aaron HIATT
08 Director of Library Services .... Vacant
37 Director Student Financial Aid .... Ms. Shandel ROBERTS
04 Exec Assistant to the President .... Ms. Ann LUCKIESH
07 Director of Admissions .... Ms. Cathy FUSCO
16 Director of Human Resources .... Ms. Kim SRODA
13 Director IT and Network Resource .... Mr. Laurens DEHAAN
29 Director Alumni Relations .... Dr. George AIKEN
09 Director of Institutional Research .... Mr. Scott KERLIN

School of Urban Missions (G)

735 105th Avenue, Oakland CA 94603-3603
County: Alameda Identification: 666021
Unit ID: 447953
Telephone: (510) 567-6174 Carnegie Class: Spec/Faith
FAX Number: (510) 568-1024 Calendar System: Trimester
URL: www.sum.edu
Established: 1999 Annual Undergrad Tuition & Fees: $7,820

Enrollment: 234 Coed
Affiliation or Control: Independent Non-Profit IRS Status: 501(c)3
Highest Offering: Baccalaureate
Program: Occupational; Religious Emphasis
Accreditation: BI

01 President/Chancellor .... Rev. George NEAU
05 Chief Academic Officer .... Dr. Richard MILLER
10 Vice President Finance .... Mrs. Judy LITTLETON
30 Chief Development/Dir of Admissions .... Ms. Diana SEARLE
42 Dean of Student Ministry .... Dr. Kenneth SEARLE
08 Director of the Library .... Ms. Kristin ABRAMS
32 Dean of Student Life .... Ms. Sharon JIMENEZ
06 Institutional Research/Registrar .. Ms. D'Lonkia JENKINS-CARTER
37 Director of Financial Aid .... Ms. Kathryn MANGAN
07 Director Recruitment .... Mr. Mike SAVAGE

† Affiliated with School of Urban Missions-New Orleans, Gretna, LA.

Scripps College (A)

1030 Columbia, Claremont CA 91711-3948
County: Los Angeles FICE Identification: 001174
Unit ID: 123165
Telephone: (909) 621-8000 Carnegie Class: Bac/A&S
FAX Number: (909) 621-8323 Calendar System: Semester
URL: www.scrippscollege.edu
Established: 1926 Annual Undergrad Tuition & Fees: $41,950
Enrollment: 946 Female
Affiliation or Control: Independent Non-Profit IRS Status: 501(c)3
Highest Offering: Baccalaureate
Program: Liberal Arts And General
Accreditation: WC

01 President .... Dr. Lori BETTISON-VARGA
05 Vice Pres/Dean of the Faculty .... Dr. Amy MARCUS-NEWHALL
30 VP for Institutional Advancement .... Ms. Patricia F. GOLDSMITH
10 Vice President for Business Affairs .... Ms. Joanne COVILLE
32 Interim Dean of Students .... Ms. Rebecca LEE
07 Vice President for Enrollment .... Ms. Victoria ROMERO
29 Director of Alumnae Relations .... Ms. Emily RANKIN
09 Director of Research & Planning .... Mr. Marc FIGUEROA
04 Executive Asst to the President .... Ms. Linda R. SCOTT
37 Director of Financial Aid .... Mr. David LEVY
15 Director of Human Resources .... Ms. Peggy BOOK
20 Associate Dean of Faculty .... Dr. Thierry BOUCQUEY
08 Librarian .... Ms. Judy B. HARVEY-SAHAK
06 Registrar .... Ms. Lauren KIM
26 VP for Communications & Marketing .... Vacant
36 Director of Career Planning .... Ms. Vicki P. KLOPSCH
13 Director of Information Technology .... Mr. Jeff SESSLER
18 Director of Facilities .... Mr. Niel ERRICKSON
104 Director of Off-Campus Study .... Ms. Neva BARKER

The Scripps Research Institute (B)

10550 N Torrey Pines Road, TPC19,
La Jolla CA 92037-1000
County: San Diego FICE Identification: 033213
Unit ID: 435338
Telephone: (858) 784-8469 Carnegie Class: Not Classified
FAX Number: (858) 784-2802 Calendar System: Quarter
URL: www.scripps.edu
Established: 1989 Annual Graduate Tuition & Fees: $29,000
Enrollment: 249 Coed
Affiliation or Control: Independent Non-Profit IRS Status: 501(c)3
Highest Offering: Doctorate; No Undergraduates
Program: Professional
Accreditation: WC

01 Dean Graduate Studies .... Dr. James R. WILLIAMSON

Shasta Bible College and Graduate School (C)

2951 Goodwater Avenue, Redding CA 96002-1544
County: Shasta FICE Identification: 023593
Unit ID: 123280
Telephone: (530) 221-4275 Carnegie Class: Spec/Faith
FAX Number: (530) 221-6929 Calendar System: Semester
URL: www.shasta.edu
Established: 1972 Annual Undergrad Tuition & Fees: $7,000
Enrollment: 64 Coed
Affiliation or Control: Independent Non-Profit IRS Status: 501(c)3
Highest Offering: Master's
Program: Religious Emphasis
Accreditation: TRACS

01 President .... Dr. David R. NICHOLAS
04 Assistant to the President .... Ms. Lanell E. WREN
05 Academic Dean .... Dr. Stephen G. BROWN
32 Vice President for Student Life .... Dr. Keith STONE
07 Director of Admissions .... Mr. George A. GUNN
18 Chief Facility/Physical Plant .... Ms. Lanell E. WREN
06 Registrar .... Mrs. Faith MCCARTHY
10 Business Affairs .... Mrs. Mary MCENTIRE
37 Financial Aid Officer .... Ms. Linda ILES
106 Coordinator External Education .... Mrs. Faith MCCARTHY

Shasta College (D)

PO Box 496006, 11555 Old Oregon Tr,
Redding CA 96049-6006
County: Shasta FICE Identification: 001289
Unit ID: 123299
Telephone: (530) 242-7500 Carnegie Class: Assoc/Pub-R-L
FAX Number: (530) 225-4990 Calendar System: Semester
URL: www.shastacollege.edu
Established: 1950 Annual Undergrad Tuition & Fees (In-District): $485
Enrollment: 10,025 Coed
Affiliation or Control: State/Local IRS Status: Exempt
Highest Offering: Associate Degree
Program: Occupational; 2-Year Principally Bachelor's Creditable
Accreditation: WJ, DH

01 Superintendent/President .... Mr. Joe WYSE
05 VP Academic and Student Affairs .... Vacant
11 VP Administrative Services .... Vacant
15 Assoc VP of Human Resources .... Ms. Patricia DEMO
14 Assoc VP Info Services/Technology .... Mr. Doug MELINE
13 Supv Info Services Technology .... Mr. James CRANDALL
45 Director of Research & Planning .... Mr. Marc BEAM
21 Comptroller .... Ms. Nancy FUNK
84 Dean of Student Services .... Mr. Kevin O'RORKE
57 Dean Arts/Communications/Soc Sci .... Dr. Ralph PERRIN
65 Dean Bus/Ag/Industry/Technology .... Ms. Eva JIMENEZ
66 Dean Health Sciences & Univ Prog .... Ms. Wanda SPRATT
41 Athletic Dir/Dean PE/Safety/Con Sci .... Mr. Gary HOUSER
79 Dean Science/Language Arts/Math .... Mr. Morris RODRIGUE
56 Dean Extended Education .... Mr. Thomas ORR, II
103 Dean Economic & Workforce Devel .... Mr. Brad BANGHART
08 Associate Dean Library Services .... Ms. Janet ALBRIGHT
37 Financial Aid Director .... Ms. Connie BARTON
88 Director EOPS/DSPS/SSS .... Ms. Sandra HAMILTON-SLANE
35 Director Student Development .... Ms. Kate MAHAR
06 Chief Records Technician .... Ms. Sheree WHALEY
18 Director Physical Plant .... Mr. George ESTRADA
88 Director Food Services .... Ms. Denise AXTELL
19 Interim Director of Campus Safety .... Mr. James BARTON
88 Supervisor HazMat Compliance Pgm .... Mr. Dave FREEMAN
102 Executive Director SC Foundation .... Mr. Scott THOMPSON
40 Bookstore Manager .... Ms. Josee GENDRON

Shepherd University School of Theology (E)

1111 W. Sunset Boulevard, Los Angeles CA 90012
County: Los Angeles Identification: 667056
Telephone: (213) 481-1313 Carnegie Class: Not Classified
FAX Number: N/A Calendar System: Semester
URL: shepherduniversity.edu
Established: N/A Annual Undergrad Tuition & Fees: N/A
Enrollment: 65 Coed
Affiliation or Control: Interdenominational IRS Status: 501(c)3
Highest Offering: Doctorate
Program: Religious Emphasis
Accreditation: @THEOL

01 President .... Juan Carlos ORTIZ
05 Vice Pres & Academic Dean .... Shalom Y. KIM

Sierra College (F)

5000 Rocklin Road, Rocklin CA 95677-3397
County: Placer FICE Identification: 001290
Unit ID: 123341
Telephone: (916) 624-3333 Carnegie Class: Assoc/Pub-S-MC
FAX Number: (916) 630-4530 Calendar System: Semester
URL: www.sierracollege.edu
Established: 1914 Annual Undergrad Tuition & Fees (In-District): $1,080
Enrollment: 20,715 Coed
Affiliation or Control: State/Local IRS Status: 501(c)3
Highest Offering: Associate Degree
Program: Occupational; 2-Year Principally Bachelor's Creditable
Accreditation: WJ

01 Superintendent/President .... Mr. William H. DUNCAN
05 Vice President Instruction .... Dr. Rachel ROSENTHAL
10 Vice Pres Finance & Administration .... Vacant
32 Vice Pres Student Services .... Ms. Mandy DAVIES
15 Vice Pres Human Resources .... Dr. Kim MYERS
04 Exec Assistant Presidents Office .... Ms. Jeannette BISCHOFF
08 Dean Library/Learning Resource Ctr .... Mr. Brian HALEY
50 Dean Business & Technology .... Vacant
81 Dean Science & Mathematics .... Ms. Heather ROBERTS
49 Dean Liberal Arts .... Ms. Debra SUTPHEN
68 Dean PE & Athletics .... Mr. John VOLEK
66 Associate Dean Nursing .... Vacant
21 Director of Finance .... Ms. Kerri HESTER
18 Dir of Facilities & Construction .... Ms. Laura DOTY
88 Director Economic Development .... Vacant
37 Financial Svcs Program Manager .... Ms. Linda WILLIAMS
31 Community Education Pgm Manager .... Ms. Adele HAMLETT
22 EEO Program Manager .... Mr. Cameron ABBOTT
26 Marketing/PR Supervisor .... Ms. Sue MICHAELS
39 Residence Life Supervisor .... Mr. Jon HAMBLEN

Silicon Valley University (G)

2160 Lundy Avenue, Suite 110, San Jose CA 95131
FICE Identification: 038103
Unit ID: 444848
Telephone: (408) 435-8989 Carnegie Class: Master's S
FAX Number: (408) 955-0887 Calendar System: Semester
URL: www.svuca.edu
Established: 1997 Annual Undergrad Tuition & Fees: $10,000
Enrollment: 612 Coed
Affiliation or Control: Proprietary IRS Status: Proprietary
Highest Offering: Master's
Program: Professional
Accreditation: ACICS

01 President .... Mr. Jerry SHIAO

Simpson University (H)

2211 College View Drive, Redding CA 96003-8606
County: Shasta FICE Identification: 001291
Unit ID: 123457
Telephone: (530) 224-5600 Carnegie Class: Bac/A&S
FAX Number: (530) 226-4860 Calendar System: Other
URL: www.simpsonu.edu
Established: 1921 Annual Undergrad Tuition & Fees: $21,600
Enrollment: 1,225 Coed
Affiliation or Control: The Christian And Missionary Alliance
IRS Status: 501(c)3
Highest Offering: Master's
Program: Liberal Arts And General; Teacher Preparatory
Accreditation: WC

01 President .... Dr. Larry J. MCKINNEY
03 Executive Vice President .... Mr. Bradley E. WILLIAMS
05 Provost .... Dr. Stanley A. CLARK
32 Vice President Student Development .... Dr. Richard W. BROWN
102 VP Marketing & Dev/Foundation .... Mr. Gordon B. FLINN
84 VP Enrollment Management .... Dr. Herb TOLBERT
10 Controller .... Mrs. Jill K. AULT
20 Associate Provost & UG Dean .... Mr. Robin K. DUMMER
18 Director of Facilities .... Mr. Merlin D. WEBER
04 Exec Assistant to the President .... Mrs. Regina ERICKSON
08 Dir Lib Svcs/Ast Prof Librarianship .... Mr. Larry L. HAIGHT
06 Registrar .... Miss Wendy A. RIDDLE
84 Director of Undergraduate Admission .... Mrs. Kendell M. KLUTTZ
07 Dir of Grad and Cont Admissions .... Mrs. Marie E. MOE
13 Director of IS .... Mr. S. Curtis DODDS
41 Director of Athletics .... Mr. Joseph E. GRIFFIN
35 Director of Student Life .... Mr. Joseph C. SLAVENS
44 Director of Advancement Services .... Mrs. Elizabeth A. SPENCER
38 Director of Wellness Center .... Dr. Michael C. SCHILL
09 Director Institutional Rsrch/Assess .... Mrs. Brooks CLARK
39 Bookstore Manager .... Miss Karen LUND
15 Human Resources Manager .... Mrs. Kori D. OECHSLI
19 Director of Auxiliary Services .... Mr. Edward D. SCHNEIDER
39 Residence Life Supervisor .... Mr. Mark L. RIPPETOE
26 Director of Marketing .... Mr. Mark U. WOOD
29 Director of University Relations .... Mr. Matthew B. KLUTTZ
42 Director of Spiritual Formation .... Mr. Travis G. OSBORNE
13 Database Administrator .... Mr. Richard L. ARCHIBALD
23 Health Center Coordinator .... Mrs. Connie C. ECHOLS
36 Career Services Counselor .... Mrs. Pamela A. SCHALO
51 Dean of Continuing Studies .... Mrs. Patty A. TAYLOR
73 Dean, AW Tozer Seminary .... Dr. Sarah C. SUMNER
54 Dean Educ/Assoc Prof Education .... Dr. Glee R. BROOKS
37 Director Student Financial Services .... Mrs. Melissa A. HUDSON

Soka University of America (I)

1 University Drive, Aliso Viejo CA 92656-8081
County: Orange FICE Identification: 038144
Unit ID: 399911
Telephone: (949) 480-4000 Carnegie Class: Bac/A&S
FAX Number: (949) 480-4001 Calendar System: Semester
URL: www.soka.edu
Established: 2001 Annual Undergrad Tuition & Fees: $26,294
Enrollment: 441 Coed
Affiliation or Control: Independent Non-Profit IRS Status: 501(c)3
Highest Offering: Master's
Program: Liberal Arts And General
Accreditation: WC

01 President/Professor of Economics .... Dr. Daniel Y. HABUKI
04 Exec Asst to the President .... Mr. Hiro SAKAI
10 Vice President Finance & Admin/CFO .... Mr. Archibald E. ASAWA
05 Provost/Vice Pres Academic Affairs .... Dr. Tomoko TAKAHASHI
04 Assistant to the President .... Mr. Arnold KAWASAKI
20 Dean of Faculty/Prof of Economics .... Dr. Edward M. FEASEL
58 Dean of Graduate School .... Dr. Tomoko TAKAHASHI
07 Dean of Enrollment Svcs/Records .... Ms. Nirmala SHARMA
32 Dean of Students .... Dr. Jay HEFFRON
88 Dir Envir Hlth/Sfty/Security/Event .... Mr. George WESSON
31 Director of Community Relations .... Ms. Wendy WETZEL HARDER
41 Director of Athletics & Recreation .... Mr. Mike MOORE
35 Director of Student Services .... Dr. Hyon MOON
39 Dir Stdt Activities/Resident Life .... Ms. Michelle HOBBY-MEARS
30 Director of Philanthropy .... Ms. Linda KENEDY
13 Director Info Tech/Int Dir Library .... Mr. Saeed FAKHRI RAVARI
84 Dir Student Recruitment Programs .... Ms. Marilyn GOVE
44 Dir of International Development .... Mr. Hideki ABERA
15 Director of Human Resources .... Ms. Katherine KING
104 Dir Study Abroad & Intl Internships .... Mr. Alex H. OKUDA
06 Registrar .... Ms. Nancy YOSHIMURA
18 Chief of Operations .... Mr. Tom HARKENRIDER

Solano Community College (A)

4000 Suisun Valley Road, Fairfield CA 94534-3197
County: Solano FICE Identification: 001292
Unit ID: 123563
Telephone: (707) 864-7000 Carnegie Class: Assoc/Pub-S-SC
FAX Number: (707) 864-0361 Calendar System: Semester
URL: www.solano.edu
Established: 1945 Annual Undergrad Tuition & Fees (In-District): $1,080
Enrollment: 11,836 Coed
Affiliation or Control: State/Local IRS Status: 501(c)3
Highest Offering: Associate Degree
Program: Occupational; 2-Year Principally Bachelor's Creditable
Accreditation: WJ

01 Superintendent/President ....Dr. Jowel C. LAGUERRE
05 Exec VP Academic & Student Affairs ....Mr. Arturo REYES
10 Vice President Finance & Admin ....Mr. Yulian LIGIOSO
13 Interim Chief Info Systems Officer ....Mr. James ENNIS
07 Director of Admissions/Records ....Ms. Barbara FOUNTAIN
38 Dean Counseling/Special Services ....Mr. Erin VINES
37 Dean Financial Aid and EOPS ....Vacant
21 Director of Fiscal Services ....Ms. Susan FOFT
84 Director Enrollment Management ....Vacant
16 Director Human Resources ....Ms. Karen ULRICH
18 Director Facilities ....Mr. David FROEHLICH
35 Dir Student Development/Mesa ....Mr. Mostafa GHOUS
06 Registrar ....Ms. Barbara FOUNTAIN
09 Int Director Research and Planning ....Dr. Chris MYERS
36 Employment Development Ofcr ....Mr. Zafer SUN
30 Exec Dir of Institutional Advancmnt ....Mr. Peter BOSTIC
14 Director Computer Services ....Mr. James ENNIS
49 Interim Dean School of Liberal Arts ....Dr. Jeffrey LAMB
88 Dean School Human Performance/Devel ....Vacant
79 Dean School of Sciences ....Dr. Betsy JULIAN
76 Dn Sch Career Technical Ed/Business ....Mrs. Maire MORINEC
12 Center Dean Vallejo ....Dr. Jerry KEA
12 Center Dean Vacaville/TAFB/Nut Tree ....Dr. Shirley LEWIS
88 Director Children's Programs ....Ms. Christie SPECK
88 Director Small Bus Development Ctr ....Mr. Charles EASON
88 Director Theater Operations ....Mr. Chris GUPTIL
96 Purchasing Tech/Buyer ....Ms. Laura SCOTT

South Baylo University (B)

1126 N Brookhurst Street, Anaheim CA 92801-1702
County: Orange FICE Identification: 025973
Unit ID: 123633
Telephone: (714) 533-1495 Carnegie Class: Spec/Health
FAX Number: (714) 533-6040 Calendar System: Quarter
URL: www.southbaylo.edu
Established: 1977 Annual Undergrad Tuition & Fees: $12,000
Enrollment: 544 Coed
Affiliation or Control: Independent Non-Profit IRS Status: 501(c)3
Highest Offering: Master's
Program: Professional
Accreditation: ACUP

01 President ....Dr. Jason SHIN
05 Academic Dean ....Dr. Pia MELEN
11 Vice President Administration ....Dr. David KWON
07 Director of Admission ....Dr. Young Jin AHN
06 Registrar ....Ms. Michelle PARK
10 Director of Finance ....Ms. Michelle JANG
15 Operations/Personnel Director ....Dr. Sohila MOHIYEDDINI
36 Program Student Advisor ....Dr. Henry CHOI
08 Director of Libraries ....Dr. Edwin FOLLICK
13 Dir Computer Information System ....Mr. James KIM
88 Director of Clinics ....Dr. Sang Jo KIM
37 Financial Aid Officer ....Ms. Mimi PARK
35 Stdnt/Alumni/English LG Coordinator ....Ms. Rocio SALAS-BELTRAN
85 International Student Advisor ....Ms. Michelle PARK
88 Doctoral Clerkship Coordinator ....Dr. Sheng LI
88 Doctoral Program Director ....Dr. John FANG
88 Master Program Director ....Dr. Hanjik KIM

South Coast College (C)

2011 W Chapman Avenue, Orange CA 92868-2609
County: Orange FICE Identification: 022774
Unit ID: 123642
Telephone: (714) 867-5009 Carnegie Class: Assoc/PrivFP
FAX Number: (714) 867-5026 Calendar System: Quarter
URL: www.southcoastcollege.com
Established: 1961 Annual Undergrad Tuition & Fees: $10,400
Enrollment: 445 Coed
Affiliation or Control: Proprietary IRS Status: Proprietary
Highest Offering: Associate Degree
Program: Occupational
Accreditation: ACICS

01 President ....Ms. Jean GONZALEZ
03 Vice President ....Ms. Lonnie SKELTON
11 Director of Operations ....Mr. Kevin MAGNER
37 Director of Financial Aid ....Ms. Melanie SARACCO

*South Orange County Community College District (D)

28000 Marguerite Parkway, Mission Viejo CA 92692-3697
County: Orange FICE Identification: 033433
Unit ID: 432144
Telephone: (949) 582-4500 Carnegie Class: N/A
FAX Number: (949) 364-2726
URL: www.socccd.org

01 Chancellor ....Mr. Gary POERTNER
05 Vice Chanc Technology/Learning Svcs ....Dr. Robert S. BRAMUCCI
16 Vice Chancellor Human Resources ....Dr. David P. BUGAY
26 Dir Public Affairs/Intergovtl Rels ....Ms. Tere FLUEGEMAN
10 Vice Chancellor Business Services ....Ms. Debra FITZSIMONS

*Irvine Valley College (E)

5500 Irvine Center Drive, Irvine CA 92618-4399
County: Orange FICE Identification: 025395
Unit ID: 116439
Telephone: (949) 451-5100 Carnegie Class: Assoc/Pub-S-MC
FAX Number: (949) 451-5270 Calendar System: Semester
URL: www.ivc.edu
Established: 1979 Annual Undergrad Tuition & Fees (In-District): $1,080
Enrollment: 14,037 Coed
Affiliation or Control: State/Local IRS Status: 501(c)3
Highest Offering: Associate Degree
Program: Occupational; 2-Year Principally Bachelor's Creditable
Accreditation: WJ

02 President ....Dr. Glenn R. ROQUEMORE
05 Vice President Instruction ....Dr. Stephen C. JUSTICE
10 Director Fiscal Services ....Mr. Davit KHACHATRYAN
32 Vice President Student Services ....Dr. Gwendolyn PLANO
39 Dean Counseling Services ....Dr. Elizabeth CIPRES
62 Dean School of Library Services ....Dr. Karima FELDHUS
57 Dean Fine Arts/Bus Scis/Online Educ ....Dr. Roger OWENS
76 Dean Health Sci/Phys Educ/Athletic ....Mr. Keith SHACKLEFORD
81 Dean Math/Sciences/Engineering ....Dr. Kathleen SCHRADER
75 Dean Career Tech Ed & Workforce Dev ....Dr. David GATEWOOD
102 Director Foundation ....Mr. Al TELLO
07 Director Admiss/Records/Enroll Svcs ....Ms. Arleen ELSEROAD
18 Dir Facilities & Maintenance ....Mr. John EDWARDS
19 Chief of Police ....Mr. Will GLEN
88 Child Development Center Manager ....Ms. Becky THOMAS
37 Director Financial Aid ....Mr. Darryl COX
35 Director Student Affairs ....Ms. Helen LOCKE
31 Director of Outreach/Community Rels ....Vacant
14 Director Technology Services ....Mr. Tran HONG
51 Director Extended Education ....Mr. David ANDERSON, JR.
88 Director CACT Project ....Dr. Larry DE SHAZER
06 Registrar/Admissions/Records ....Mr. Ben GUZMAN
09 Research & Planning Analyst ....Mr. Christopher TARMAN
26 Director of Public Info & Marketing ....Ms. Diane G. OAKS

*Saddleback College (F)

28000 Marguerite Parkway, Mission Viejo CA 92692-3635
County: Orange FICE Identification: 008918
Unit ID: 122205
Telephone: (949) 582-4500 Carnegie Class: Assoc/Pub-S-MC
FAX Number: (949) 347-0438 Calendar System: Semester
URL: www.saddleback.edu
Established: 1968 Annual Undergrad Tuition & Fees (In-District): $1,184
Enrollment: 27,057 Coed
Affiliation or Control: State/Local IRS Status: 501(c)3
Highest Offering: Associate Degree
Program: Occupational; 2-Year Principally Bachelor's Creditable
Accreditation: WJ, ADNUR, EMT

02 President ....Dr. Tod A. BURNETT
05 Actg Vice President of Instruction ....Dr. Donald BUSCHE
32 Vice President of Student Services ....Dr. Juan AVALOS
07 Director Admissions & Records ....Ms. Jane ROSENKRANS
45 Director Planning/Research/Grants ....Ms. Gretchen BENDER
06 Registrar ....Ms. Joyce SEMANIK
19 Director Security/Safety ....Mr. Harry PARMER
26 Director Public Information ....Ms. Jennie MCCUE
102 Director College Foundation ....Mr. Dave JENKIN
35 Director Student Development ....Ms. Audra DIPADOVA
31 Director of Community Education ....Ms. Estella GARRISON
88 Director Emeritus Institute ....Ms. Sandy MARZILLI
66 Director of Nursing ....Ms. Tammy RICE
10 Director of Fiscal Services ....Ms. Carol HILTON
15 Director Human Resources ....Ms. Teddi LORCH
18 Dir Facilities/Maint/Operation ....Mr. John OZUROVICH
37 Director Financial Assistance ....Mr. Christian ALVARADO
96 Director of Purchasing ....Ms. Brandye D'LENA
85 Intl Student Program Specialist ....Ms. Monika CONNOLLY
92 Honors Program ....Ms. Alannah ROSENBERG
38 Dean Counseling Svcs/Special Pgms ....Ms. Jerilyn CHUMAN
57 Dean Fine Arts ....Mr. Bart MCHENRY
75 Dean Bus Sci/Voc Educ/Econ Devel ....Mr. Rocky CIFONE
76 Dean Hlth Sci/Human Svcs & Emeritus ....Dr. Donna RANE-SZOSTAK
81 Dean Math/Science & Engineering ....Dr. James WRIGHT
79 Dean Liberal Arts/Learning Res ....Dr. Kevin O'CONNOR
83 Dean Social & Behavioral Sciences ....Dr. Patricia FLANIGAN
72 Dean Advance Tech Appl Science ....Mr. Don TAYLOR
68 Dean Physical Educ/Athltc Dir ....Mr. Tony LIPOLD
84 Chair Enrollment Management ....Vacant
35 Asst Dean Couns Svcs/Spec Pgms ....Mr. Terence NELSON

Southern California College of Optometry (G)

2575 Yorba Linda Boulevard, Fullerton CA 92831-1699
County: Orange FICE Identification: 001230
Unit ID: 123943
Telephone: (714) 870-7226 Carnegie Class: Spec/Health
FAX Number: (714) 879-9834 Calendar System: Quarter
URL: www.scco.edu
Established: 1904 Annual Undergrad Tuition & Fees: $29,100
Enrollment: 394 Coed
Affiliation or Control: Independent Non-Profit IRS Status: 501(c)3
Highest Offering: Doctorate
Program: Professional
Accreditation: WC, OPT, OPTR

01 President ....Dr. Kevin L. ALEXANDER
05 Vice Pres/Dean Academic Affairs ....Dr. Morris S. BERMAN
10 Vice Pres of Financial Affairs/CFO ....Ms. Lisa ALBERS
30 Vice Pres Advancement/Marketing ....Mr. Paul A. STOVER
88 Vice Pres Interprofessional Affairs ....Dr. John H. NISHIMOTO
17 Vice Pres & Dean Clinical Affairs ....Dr. Julie A. SCHORNACK
32 Vice President of Student Affairs ....Dr. Lorraine I. VOORHEES
04 Special Assistant to President ....Mr. William HEATON, JR.
46 Associate Dean for Research ....Dr. Jerry PAUGH
18 Director Campus Operations ....Mr. Gregory SMITH
51 Director Continuing Education ....Ms. Susan ATKINSON
25 Director Invest & Restricted Funds ....Mr. Cameron R. BENSON
15 Director Human Resources ....Mr. Dennis GABY
27 Director of Communications ....Ms. Debra J. MARKS
13 Director of Information Technology ....Mr. Gary W. GRAY
37 Director Financial Aid ....Ms. Tami A. SATO
07 Director of Admissions ....Dr. Jane Ann MUNROE
08 Director of Library Services ....Ms. Donnajean MATTHEWS
24 Director Multi-Media Services ....Mr. L. Ernie CARRILLO
40 Manager Campus Store ....Ms. Debra WOODS

Southern California Institute of Architecture (H)

960 E 3rd Street, Los Angeles CA 90013-1822
County: Los Angeles FICE Identification: 020758
Unit ID: 123952
Telephone: (213) 613-2200 Carnegie Class: Spec/Arts
FAX Number: (213) 613-2260 Calendar System: Semester
URL: www.sciarc.edu
Established: 1972 Annual Undergrad Tuition & Fees: $30,250
Enrollment: 503 Coed
Affiliation or Control: Independent Non-Profit IRS Status: 501(c)3
Highest Offering: Master's
Program: Professional
Accreditation: WC

01 Director ....Mr. Eric O. MOSS
04 Director's Assistant ....Ms. Sarah POLLE
05 Director Academic Affairs ....Ms. Hsin-Ming FUNG
11 Chief Operating Officer ....Mr. Jamie BENNETT
30 Chief Development Officer ....Mr. Bill KRAMER
58 Graduate Program Director ....Ms. Hsin-Ming FUNG
88 Undergraduate Program Director ....Mr. Chris GENIK
05 Academic Affairs Manager ....Mr. Paul HOLLIDAY
20 Academic Programs Assistant ....Ms. Emily REITER
10 Finance Director ....Mr. Christopher BANKS
15 Human Resources Director ....Ms. Melissa BURGESS
07 Admissions Director ....Mr. J. J. JACKMAN
37 Financial Aid Director ....Ms. Helen LARA
08 Library Manager ....Mr. Kevin MCMAHON
90 Director of IT ....Mr. Vic JABRASSIAN
88 Wood & Metal Shopmaster ....Mr. Rodney ROJAS
88 Wood & Metal Shopmaster ....Mr. Katsumi MUROI
20 Academic Counselor ....Mr. Peter DUNG
06 Registrar/Chf of Staff/Intl Advisor ....Ms. Lisa RUSSO

Southern California Institute of Technology (I)

222 S Harbor Boulevard, Suite 200,
Anaheim CA 92805-3758
County: Orange FICE Identification: 031136
Unit ID: 399869
Telephone: (714) 300-0300 Carnegie Class: Bac/Diverse
FAX Number: (714) 300-0311 Calendar System: Quarter
URL: www.scitech.edu
Established: 1987 Annual Undergrad Tuition & Fees: $15,000
Enrollment: 755 Coed
Affiliation or Control: Proprietary IRS Status: Proprietary
Highest Offering: Baccalaureate
Program: Technical Emphasis
Accreditation: ACCSC

01 President ....Dr. Parviz SHAMS
03 Vice President ....Mrs. Nazila SHAMS
32 Student Services ....Ms. Anel NEVAREZ
05 Dean of Education ....Mr. Saravana RAMAN
07 Dean of Admissions ....Ms. JoDell PINESETT
13 MIS ....Mr. Arian SHAMS

Southern California Seminary (J)

2075 E Madison Avenue, El Cajon CA 92019-1108
County: San Diego FICE Identification: 033323
Unit ID: 117575
Telephone: (619) 201-8999 Carnegie Class: Spec/Faith
FAX Number: (619) 201-8975 Calendar System: Trimester
URL: www.socalsem.edu
Established: 1946 Annual Undergrad Tuition & Fees: $205
Enrollment: 13,068 Coed
Affiliation or Control: Independent Non-Profit IRS Status: 501(c)3

Highest Offering: Doctorate
Program: Religious Emphasis
Accreditation: TRACS

00 Chancellor ... Dr. George W. HARE
01 President ... Dr. Gary F. COOMBS
03 Executive Vice President ... Mr. Randolph E. GILL
05 Vice President for Academics ... Dr. Chuck EMERT
32 Vice President of Student Services ... Vacant
58 Dean of Graduate Biblical Studies ... Dr. Peter OH
83 Dean of Behavioral Science ... Dr. Barry LORD
73 Dean of Undergrad Biblical Studies ... Mr. Ezequiel SERRATO
06 Registrar ... Mrs. Cheryl OBST
37 Director of Financial Aid ... Mrs. Yuli MARTINEZ
08 Seminary Librarian ... Miss Jennifer EWING

Southern California University of Health Sciences (A)

16200 E Amber Valley Drive, Whittier CA 90604-4051
County: Los Angeles FICE Identification: 001229
Unit ID: 117672
Telephone: (562) 947-8755 Carnegie Class: Spec/Health
FAX Number: (562) 947-5724 Calendar System: Trimester
URL: www.scuhs.edu
Established: 1911 Annual Undergrad Tuition & Fees: $28,158
Enrollment: 559 Coed
Affiliation or Control: Independent Non-Profit IRS Status: 501(c)3
Highest Offering: First Professional Degree
Program: Professional
Accreditation: WC, ACUP, CHIRO

01 President ... Dr. John SCARINGE
05 Vice President of Academic Affs ... Dr. J. Todd KNUDSEN
10 VP Admin & Finance/CFO ... Mr. Thomas K. ARENDT
84 Assoc VP Enroll Mgmt/Stdnt Affs ... Ms. Debra MITCHELL
88 Interim Dean of Chiropractic ... Dr. Mike SACKETT
11 Director Administrative Svcs ... Ms. Theresa EGGLESTON
88 Dean Acupuncture/Oriental Medicine ... Dr. Wen-Shuo WU
10 Controller ... Mrs. Kelly GALLO
09 Dean Supportive/Inst Research ... Dr. Melea FIELDS
07 Exec Director of Enrollment Svcs ... Dr. Peter HANNA
06 Registrar ... Mr. Choury DEVELLE
13 Senior Programmer/Operations Mgr ... Mr. Mike ROCKE
32 Director of Student Affairs ... Dr. Steven JAFFE
23 Director Health Svs/Chief of Staff ... Dr. Stanley EWALD
30 Exec Director of Inst Mktg/Advance ... Dr. Hubert CHANG
18 Chief Facilities/Physical Plant ... Mr. Jerry BAUER
37 Finacial Aid Counselor ... Ms. Juana LOPEZ
08 Exec Dir of Seabury Learning Center ... Ms. Kathleen E. SMITH
29 Director of Alumni ... Ms. Sheila HANES
96 Accounts Payable/Purchasing Coord ... Mrs. Catherine MCBRIDE

Southern California University School of Oriental Medicine and Acupuncture (B)

1541 Wilshire Boulevard, 3rd Floor,
Los Angeles CA 90017-2211
County: Los Angeles Identification: 666665
Telephone: (213) 413-9500 Carnegie Class: Not Classified
FAX Number: (213) 413-5400 Calendar System: Quarter
URL: www.scusoma.edu
Established: N/A Annual Undergrad Tuition & Fees: $12,000
Enrollment: 135 Coed
Affiliation or Control: Proprietary IRS Status: Proprietary
Highest Offering: Master's
Program: Professional
Accreditation: ACUP

01 President ... Brian H. KIM
05 Academic Dean ... Dr. Katherine H S. CHO

Southwestern College (C)

900 Otay Lakes Road, Chula Vista CA 91910-7299
County: San Diego FICE Identification: 001294
Unit ID: 123800
Telephone: (619) 421-6700 Carnegie Class: Assoc/Pub-S-SC
FAX Number: (619) 482-6413 Calendar System: Semester
URL: www.swccd.edu
Established: 1961 Annual Undergrad Tuition & Fees (In-District): $1,080
Enrollment: 19,476 Coed
Affiliation or Control: State/Local IRS Status: 501(c)3
Highest Offering: Associate Degree
Program: Occupational; 2-Year Principally Bachelor's Creditable
Accreditation: WJ, ADNUR, DH, EMT, MLTAD, SURGT

01 Interim Superintendent/President ... Dr. Denise WHITTAKER
05 Act Vice President Academic Affairs ... Ms. Angelica SUAREZ
10 Int VP Business & Financial Affairs ... Mr. Robert TEMPLE
32 Vice President Student Affairs ... Dr. Angelica SUAREZ
16 Actg Vice Pres Human Resources ... Mr. Jospeh QUARELS
12 Act Dean Ed Ctr Otay Mesa/San Ysidr ... Ms. Silvia CORNEJO-DARCY
12 Dean HEC Natl City/Crown Cove ... Ms. Christine PERRI
79 Dean Language & Literature ... Dr. Joel LEVINE
81 Dean Math/Science Engineering ... Ms. Kathy TYNER
35 Dean Student Services ... Ms. Mia C. MCCLELLAN
51 Dean Cont Ed/Econ & Wrkfrc Dev ... Dr. Mark MEADOWS
38 Dean Counseling & Matriculation ... Ms. Beatrice ZAMORA-AGUILAR
88 Dean Career/Tech Ed & Learning Asst ... Ms. Trish U. AXSOM
68 Dean Health/Exercise Sci/Athletics ... Mr. Terry DAVIS
83 Dean Social Sciences & Humanities ... Dr. Viara GIRAFFE
60 Dean Arts & Communication ... Ms. Donna C. ARNOLD
88 Dean Instructional Support Services ... Dr. Mink STAVENGA
26 Chief Comm Cmty & Gov Rels Officer ... Mr. Chris BENDER
15 Director Human Resources ... Ms. Jackie OSBORNE
09 Dir Inst Rsrch Grants & Planning ... Vacant
18 Dir Facilities Ops & Planning ... Mr. John BROWN
13 Director Computer Systems & Svcs ... Mr. Steve BOSSI
40 Director Bookstore ... Ms. Patti LARKIN
88 Dir Center Ops San Ysidro ... Ms. Silvia CORNEJO-DARCY
21 Director Payroll & Risk Mgmt ... Mr. Thomas BEASLEY
37 Director Financial Aid ... Ms. Linda THROWER
96 Dir Contract Purchasing & Cntrl Svc ... Ms. Priya JEROME

Southwestern Law School (D)

3050 Wilshire Boulevard, Los Angeles CA 90010-1106
County: Los Angeles FICE Identification: 001295
Unit ID: 123970
Telephone: (213) 738-6700 Carnegie Class: Spec/Law
FAX Number: (213) 383-1688 Calendar System: Semester
URL: www.swlaw.edu
Established: 1911 Annual Graduate Tuition & Fees: $41,300
Enrollment: 1,095 Coed
Affiliation or Control: Independent Non-Profit IRS Status: 501(c)3
Highest Offering: Master's; No Undergraduates
Program: Professional
Accreditation: LAW

01 Dean/Chief Executive Officer ... Mr. Bryant G. GARTH
03 Chief Operating Officer ... Ms. Janice A. MANIS
10 Chief Financial Officer ... Mr. Paul KALUSH
04 Corporate Secretary ... Ms. Janis K. YOKOYAMA
05 Vice Dean for Academic Affairs ... Mr. Austen PARRISH
46 Associate Dean of Research ... Mr. Michael DORFF
08 Associate Dean of Library Services ... Ms. Linda A. WHISMAN
32 Assoc Dean/Dean of Stdnts & Div Aff ... Ms. Nyree GRAY
20 Associate Dean for Academic Admin ... Ms. Doreen E. HEYER
36 Associate Dean Career Services ... Mr. Gary J. GREENER
43 Associate Dean/General Counsel ... Mr. Patrick PYLE
30 Assoc Dean for Institutional Advanc ... Ms. Debra L. LEATHERS
27 Associate Dean for Public Affairs ... Ms. Leslie R. STEINBERG
07 Asst Dean of Admissions ... Ms. Lisa L. GEAR
06 Asst Dean Regist/Academic Records ... Ms. Carolyn HAITH
35 Asst Dean of Student Affairs ... Dr. Robert MENA
04 Special Assistant to the Dean ... Ms. Anne WILSON
37 Director of Financial Aid ... Ms. Peggy LOEWY-WELLISCH
13 Chief Information Systems Officer ... Ms. Bo SUZOW
88 Associate Dean of Special Projects ... Dr. Jane POWELL

Stanbridge College (E)

2041 Business Center Drive, Irvine CA 92612
County: Orange FICE Identification: 038893
Unit ID: 446561
Telephone: (949) 794-9090 Carnegie Class: Not Classified
FAX Number: (949) 794-9098 Calendar System: Other
URL: www.stanbridge.edu
Established: N/A Annual Undergrad Tuition & Fees: $29,968
Enrollment: 336 Coed
Affiliation or Control: Proprietary IRS Status: Proprietary
Highest Offering: Baccalaureate
Program: Occupational; 2-Year Principally Bachelor's Creditable; Business Emphasis
Accreditation: ACCSC

01 Chief Executive Officer ... Yasith WEERASURIYA
10 Chief Financial Officer ... Nazi MASOUM
37 Director of Financial Aid ... Brian SILVANO
07 Director of Admissions ... Edward RIEPMA
32 Director of Student Services ... Danielle STEVENS
66 Director of Nursing ... Debbie LIEU
75 Director of Occupational Therapy ... Satch PURCELL
88 Director of Physical Therapy ... Dr. Scott BENNIE
106 Director of Online Programs ... Dr. Robert WOLF
05 Dean of Instruction ... Tim POWERS
20 Director of Education ... John WALKER
105 VP of Internet and Media Technology ... Monir BOKTOR

Stanford University (F)

Stanford CA 94305-1684
County: Santa Clara FICE Identification: 001305
Unit ID: 243744
Telephone: (650) 723-2300 Carnegie Class: RU/VH
FAX Number: (650) 725-6847 Calendar System: Quarter
URL: www.stanford.edu
Established: 1885 Annual Undergrad Tuition & Fees: $40,050
Enrollment: 15,666 Coed
Affiliation or Control: Independent Non-Profit IRS Status: 501(c)3
Highest Offering: Doctorate
Program: Liberal Arts And General; Professional
Accreditation: WC, ARCPA, BUS, CLPSY, ENG, IPSY, LAW, MED, TED

01 President ... Mr. John L. HENNESSY
43 Vice President & General Counsel ... Ms. Debra L. ZUMWALT
05 Provost ... Mr. John W. ETCHEMENDY
30 Vice President for Development ... Mr. Martin SHELL
10 Vice President Business Affairs/CFO ... Mr. Randy LIVINGSTON
26 Vice President for Public Affairs ... Mr. David F. DEMAREST
15 Vice President of Human Resources ... Mr. David JONES
29 President of Alumni Associaton ... Mr. Howard E. WOLF
46 Vice Provost/Dean of Research ... Dr. Ann ARVIN
20 Vice Provost for Academic Affairs ... Dr. Stephanie KALFAYAN
88 Vice Provost Faculty Development ... Ms. Karen COOK
20 Vice Provost Undergrad Education ... Mr. Harry J. ELAM
18 Vice Provost for Land & Buildings ... Mr. Robert C. REIDY
21 Vice Provost Budget & Auxiliaries ... Mr. Timothy R. WARNER
32 Vice Provost Student Affairs ... Mr. Gregory E. BOARDMAN
04 Sr Assistant to the President ... Mr. Jeffrey H. WACHTEL
63 Dean School of Medicine ... Dr. Philip A. PIZZO
50 Dean Graduate School Business ... Dr. Garth SALONER
65 Dean School of Earth Sciences ... Dr. Pamela A. MATSON
53 Dean School of Education ... Dr. Claude STEELE
54 Dean School of Engineering ... Dr. James D. PLUMMER
49 Dean School Humanities & Sciences ... Mr. Richard P. SALLER
61 Dean School of Law ... Dr. Larry D. KRAMER
87 Dean Summer Session/Cont Stds ... Dr. Charles L. JUNKERMAN
42 Dean for Religious Life ... Rev. William L. MCLENNAN
88 Director Hoover Institution ... Dr. John RAISIAN
88 Director Stanford Lin Accelerator ... Dr. Persis DRELL
13 Executive Director IT Services ... Mr. Bill CLEBSCH
86 Director Government Relations ... Mr. Larry N. HORTON
08 University Librarian ... Mr. Michael A. KELLER
41 Athletic Director ... Mr. Bob BOWLSBY
07 Director of Admission ... Mr. Robert K. PATTERSON
88 CEO Stanford Management Company ... Mr. John POWERS
16 Director of Compensation ... Ms. Linda S. LEE
21 Director of Business Development ... Ms. Susan L. WEINSTEIN
06 Registrar ... Mr. Thomas BLACK
36 Director Career Development Center ... Mr. Lance M. CHOY
09 Director of Institutional Research ... Ms. Rana GLASGAL
37 Director of Student Financial Aid ... Ms. Karen S. COOPER
27 Director Stanford News Service ... Mr. Dan STOBER
19 Director Public Safety ... Ms. Laura L. WILSON
96 Chief Procurement Officer ... Mr. Stuart DAVIS
35 Director of Student Activities ... Ms. Nanci HOWE
28 Director of Diversity ... Mr. Tommy Lee WOO
38 Director Student Counseling ... Dr. Ronald ALBURCHER

Stanton University (G)

12666 Brookhurst Street, Garden Grove CA 92840
County: Orange Identification: 667053
Telephone: (714) 539-6561 Carnegie Class: Not Classified
FAX Number: (714) 539-6542 Calendar System: Quarter
URL: www.stantonuniversity.com
Established: N/A Annual Undergrad Tuition & Fees: N/A
Enrollment: N/A Coed
Affiliation or Control: Proprietary IRS Status: Proprietary
Highest Offering: Master's
Program: Professional
Accreditation: @ACUP

01 President ... Dr. Franklin R. TURNER

Starr King School for the Ministry (H)

2441 Le Conte Avenue, Berkeley CA 94709-1299
County: Alameda FICE Identification: 004080
Unit ID: 123916
Telephone: (510) 845-6232 Carnegie Class: Spec/Faith
FAX Number: (510) 845-6273 Calendar System: Semester
URL: www.sksm.edu
Established: 1904 Annual Graduate Tuition & Fees: $18,236
Enrollment: 90 Coed
Affiliation or Control: Unitarian Universalist IRS Status: 501(c)3
Highest Offering: Master's; No Undergraduates
Program: Professional
Accreditation: THEOL

01 President ... Dr. Rebecca PARKER
05 Dean of the Faculty ... Dr. Dorsey BLAKE
32 Dean of Students ... Ms. Becky LEYSER
06 Registrar ... Ms. Kat CROSWELL
07 Director of Admissions ... Ms. Crystal WESTON

*State Center Community College District (I)

1525 E Weldon Avenue, Fresno CA 93704-6398
County: Fresno FICE Identification: 001306
Unit ID: 123925
Telephone: (559) 226-0720 Carnegie Class: N/A
FAX Number: (559) 229-7039
URL: www.scccd.edu

01 Chancellor ... Dr. Deborah G. BLUE
10 Vice Chancellor Finance & Admin ... Mr. Edwin ENG
16 Assoc Vice Chanc Human Resources ... Mr. Randy ROWE
11 Assoc Vice Chanc District Ops ... Mr. Brian SPEECE
20 Assoc Vice Ch Workforce Dev/Ed Svcs ... Vacant
09 Vice President Adm Recs & Inst Res ... Dr. John CUMMINGS
15 District Dean of Human Resources ... Ms. Diane CLEROU
26 Exec Dir Public/Legislative Rels ... Dr. Teresa PATTERSON
102 Executive Director of Foundation ... Ms. Gurdeep SIHOTA HE'BERT
25 Director Grants/External Funding ... Ms. Shelly CONNER
96 Director of Purchasing ... Mr. Randy VOGT
21 Director of Finance ... Vacant

13 Director of Information Systems ....Mr. John BENGTSON
88 Director of Classified Personnel ....Ms. Nancy KAST
18 Director Maintenance/Operations ....Mr. Carl SIMMS
43 General Counsel ....Mr. Gregory TAYLOR
19 Chief of Police ....Chief Joseph CALLAHAN

*Fresno City College (A)

1101 E University Avenue, Fresno CA 93741-0002
County: Fresno FICE Identification: 001307
Unit ID: 114789
Telephone: (559) 442-4600 Carnegie Class: Assoc/Pub-U-MC
FAX Number: (559) 237-4232 Calendar System: Semester
URL: www.fresnocitycollege.edu
Established: 1910 Annual Undergrad Tuition & Fees (In-District): $864
Enrollment: 29,774 Coed
Affiliation or Control: State/Local IRS Status: 501(c)3
Highest Offering: Associate Degree
Program: Occupational; 2-Year Principally Bachelor's Creditable
Accreditation: WJ, DH, EMT, RAD, SURGT

02 President ....Mr. Tony CANTU
05 Vice President of Instruction ....Ms. Kelly FOWLER
32 Vice President of Student Services ....Dr. Christopher M. VILLA
10 Vice Pres Administrative Services ....Mr. Michael GUERRA
07 Vice Pres Admissions/Records ....Mr. John H. CUMMINGS
08 Dean Library/Stdnt Lrng Support Svc ....Mr. James M. TUCKER
50 Dean Business Division ....Dr. Timothy WOODS
57 Dean Fine Perform Commun Arts .....Dr. Jothany L. BLACKWOOD
79 Dean Humanities Division ....Ms. Jennifer JOHNSON
54 Dean Math/Science/Engineering Div .....Dr. Ashok V. NAIMPALLY
83 Dean Social Sciences Division ....Dr. Margaret E. MERICLE
76 Dean Health Sciences Division ....Dr. Carolyn C. DRAKE
72 Dean Applied Technology Div ....Mr. Richard I. CHRISTL
38 Dean Counseling-Guidance ....Dr. Mark SANCHEZ
88 Dean of Students/EOPS ....Dr. Lee FARLEY
103 Dean Workforce Dev & Welfare Reform ..Ms. Natalie C. DOCKINS
75 Director FCC Training Institute ....Mr. Charles FRANCIS
88 Director Disabled Stdnt Pgms & Svcs ....Dr. Janice EMERZIAN
09 Director Institutional Research ....Dr. Lijuan ZHAI
88 Director Police Academy ....Mr. Richard LINDSTROM
35 Director of Student Activities ....Mr. Sean HENDERSON
26 Director Marketing/Communications ....Ms. Cris M. BREMER
37 Director Financial Aid ....Mr. Sonny SILVA
27 Public Information Officer ....Ms. Kathleen BONILLA
41 Athletic Director ....Ms. Susan YATES
38 Director Student Support Svcs & ETS ....Ms. Ginna BEARDEN
72 Director of Technology ....Mr. Don LOPEZ
36 Director Career Advancement ....Vacant
66 Director of Nursing ....Ms. Stephanie R. ROBINSON
88 Director CalWORKs Program ....Ms. Anne WATTS

*Reedley College (B)

995 N Reed Avenue, Reedley CA 93654-2099
County: Fresno FICE Identification: 001308
Unit ID: 117052
Telephone: (559) 638-3641 Carnegie Class: Assoc/Pub-U-MC
FAX Number: (559) 638-5040 Calendar System: Semester
URL: www.reedleycollege.edu
Established: 1926 Annual Undergrad Tuition & Fees (In-District): $780
Enrollment: 15,384 Coed
Affiliation or Control: State/Local IRS Status: 501(c)3
Highest Offering: Associate Degree
Program: Occupational; 2-Year Principally Bachelor's Creditable
Accreditation: WJ

02 President ....Dr. Barbara A. HIOCO
05 Vice President of Instruction ....Dr. Marilyn BEHRINGER
11 Int Vice Pres Administrative Svcs ....Ms. Cheryl SULLIVAN
32 Vice President of Student Services ....Mr. Michael WHITE
75 Dean of Instruction/Vocational Educ ....Mr. David CLARK
79 Dean of Instruction/Humanities ....Mr. Thomas WEST
81 Dean Instruct/Math/Sci/Tech/PE/Hlth ....Mr. Jan DEKKER
27 Public Information Officer ....Ms. Lucy RUIZ
88 Director Disabled Stdnt Prgms/Svcs ....Dr. Janice EMERZIAN
22 Director EOPS ....Mr. Eluterio ESCAMILLA
13 Director of Technology ....Mr. Gary SAKAGUCHI
37 Financial Aid Manager ....Ms. Chris CORTES
07 Admissions & Records Mgr/Registrar ....Ms. Leticia ALVAREZ

Taft College (C)

29 Emmons Park Drive, Taft CA 93268-1437
County: Kern FICE Identification: 001309
Unit ID: 124113
Telephone: (661) 763-7700 Carnegie Class: Assoc/Pub-S-SC
FAX Number: (661) 763-7705 Calendar System: Semester
URL: www.taftcollege.edu
Established: 1922 Annual Undergrad Tuition & Fees (In-District): $1,095
Enrollment: 7,820 Coed
Affiliation or Control: State/Local IRS Status: 501(c)3
Highest Offering: Associate Degree
Program: Occupational; 2-Year Principally Bachelor's Creditable
Accreditation: WJ, DH

01 Interim Superintendent/President ....Dr. Richard GIESE
05 Vice President of Instruction ....Ms. Patricia BENCH
32 Vice Pres of Student Services ....Mr. Brock MCMURRAY
04 Assistant to the President ....Ms. Shelley KLEIN
13 Director Information Services ....Mr. Adrian AGUNDEZ
20 Associate Dean of Instruction ....Mr. Val GARCIA
38 Lead Counselor ....Ms. Darcy BOGLE
08 Director of Library & LRC ....Vacant
46 Coord Inst Research/Assessment/Plng ....Dr. Eric BERUBE
41 Director Athletics ....Ms. Kanoe BANDY
15 Director Human Resources ....Ms. Jana PETERS
21 Director of Business Services ....Mr. Jim NICHOLAS
07 Dir of Enrollment Services ....Mr. Brian MCKEE
18 Supervisor Maintenance/Operations ....Mr. Michael CAPELA
10 Chief Business Officer ....Mr. Ronald ERREA
37 Director Student Financial Aid ....Ms. Barbara WINGLER

Taft Law School (D)

3700 South Susan Street, Office 200,
Santa Ana CA 92704-6954
County: Orange Identification: 666398
Unit ID: 454689
Telephone: (714) 850-4800 Carnegie Class: Spec/Law
FAX Number: (714) 708-2082 Calendar System: Other
URL: www.taftu.edu
Established: 1976 Annual Undergrad Tuition & Fees: $6,845
Enrollment: 217 Coed
Affiliation or Control: Proprietary IRS Status: Proprietary
Highest Offering: Doctorate
Program: Professional
Accreditation: DETC

01 President ....Mr. David L. BOYD
05 Dean ....Mr. Robert K. STROUSE
32 Director Student Services ....Ms. Joan L. SLAVIN
20 Associate Dean ....Ms. Melody JOLLY

Thomas Aquinas College (E)

10,000 N Ojai Road, Santa Paula CA 93060-9621
County: Ventura FICE Identification: 023580
Unit ID: 124292
Telephone: (805) 525-4417 Carnegie Class: Bac/A&S
FAX Number: (805) 525-9342 Calendar System: Semester
URL: www.thomasaquinas.edu
Established: 1971 Annual Undergrad Tuition & Fees: $22,850
Enrollment: 355 Coed
Affiliation or Control: Independent Non-Profit IRS Status: 501(c)3
Highest Offering: Baccalaureate
Program: Liberal Arts And General
Accreditation: WC

01 President ....Dr. Michael F. MCLEAN
04 Secretary to the President ....Miss Kelly BAILEY
26 Asst to Pres/Dir College Relations ....Mrs. Anne S. FORSYTH
30 Vice Pres for Devel & Gen Counsel .....Mr. John Q. MASTELLER
11 Vice President for Admn & Finance ....Mr. Peter L. DELUCA
05 Academic Dean ....Dr. Brian KELLY
46 Director of Development ....Mr. Robert A. BAGDAZIAN
44 Director of Gift Planning ....Mr. Thomas J. SUSANKA
07 Director of Admissions ....Mr. Jonathan P. DALY
21 Supervisor Business/Finance ....Mr. Michael COLLINS
37 Director of Financial Aid ....Mr. Gregory J. BECHER
32 Asst Dean for Student Affairs ....Dr. John J. GOYETTE
06 Registrar ....Dr. Sean D. COLLINS
36 Director of Student Placement ....Mr. Mark R. KRETSCHMER
08 Librarian ....Mrs. Viltis A. JATULIS
42 Chaplain ....Fr. Cornelius M. BUCKLEY
27 Communications Manager ....Mr. Christopher WEINKOPF
13 Development Database Manager ....Mr. James HARRISON

Thomas Jefferson School of Law (F)

1155 Island Avenue, San Diego CA 92101
County: San Diego FICE Identification: 010854
Unit ID: 126049
Telephone: (619) 297-9700 Carnegie Class: Spec/Law
FAX Number: (619) 294-4713 Calendar System: Semester
URL: www.tjsl.edu
Established: 1969 Annual Graduate Tuition & Fees: $41,000
Enrollment: 1,120 Coed
Affiliation or Control: Independent Non-Profit IRS Status: 501(c)3
Highest Offering: Doctorate; No Undergraduates
Program: Professional
Accreditation: LAW

01 Dean and President ....Rudolph C. HASL
20 Assoc Dean Acad Affs/Prof of Law ....Eric MITNICK
32 Assoc Dean for Student Affairs ....M. Elizabeth (Beth) KRANSBERGER
26 Asst Dean Communications/Admin ....Lori WULFEMEYER
30 Asst Dean Development/Alumni Rels ....Karen GOYETTE
18 Asst Dean Facilities Services ....Lisa BRUCE
36 Director for Career Services ....Beverly BRACKER
08 Interim Library Director ....Patrick MEYER
10 Chief Financial Officer ....Nancy VU
37 Director Financial Assistance ....Marc BERMAN
06 Registrar ....Kim GRENNAN
35 Student Services Director ....Lisa FERREIRA
21 Director of Business Office ....Christine MOORE
88 Dir Clin/Judicial Educ & Acad Cnslr ....Judybeth TROPP
07 Director of Admissions ....Timothy "Tim" SPEARMAN
15 Director of Personnel Services ....Lisa CHIGOS

Touro College Los Angeles (G)

1317 N Crescent Heights Boulevard,
West Hollywood CA 90046-4506
County: Los Angeles FICE Identification: 041425
Unit ID: 459727
Telephone: (323) 822-9700 Carnegie Class: Not Classified
FAX Number: (310) 654-2086 Calendar System: Semester
URL: www.touro.edu/losangeles/
Established: 2005 Annual Undergrad Tuition & Fees: $16,100
Enrollment: 110 Coed
Affiliation or Control: Independent Non-Profit IRS Status: 501(c)3
Highest Offering: Master's
Program: Liberal Arts And General
Accreditation: WC

01 President ....Dr. Alan KADISH
05 Founding Dean/Chief Academic Ofcr ....Dr. Esther LOWY
07 Director of Admissions ....Mrs. Samira MILLER
09 Dir Inst Research/Assessment ....Dr. Michael HAMLIN
10 Chief Business Officer/Bursar ....Mr. Kamran MANUEL
37 Dir Student Fin Aid/Registrar ....Ms. Rivka WEINBERG

Touro University-California (H)

1310 Club Drive, Vallejo CA 94592
County: Solano FICE Identification: 041426
Unit ID: 459736
Telephone: (707) 638-5200 Carnegie Class: Not Classified
FAX Number: (707) 638-5255 Calendar System: Semester
URL: www.tu.edu
Established: 1997 Annual Undergrad Tuition & Fees: $40,800
Enrollment: 1,403 Coed
Affiliation or Control: Independent Non-Profit IRS Status: 501(c)3
Highest Offering: Doctorate
Program: Teacher Preparatory; Professional
Accreditation: WC, ARCPA, OSTEO, PH, PHAR

01 President & CEO ....Dr. Alan KADISH
05 Provost & COO ....Dr. Marilyn HOPKINS
32 Dean of Students ....Dr. Donald HAIGHT
35 Associate Dean of Students ....Dr. James BINKERD
06 Registrar ....Dr. Harold BORRERO
07 Director of Admissions ....Dr. Donald HAIGHT
09 Director of Institutional Research ....Dr. Meiling TANG
10 Chief Business Officer/CFO ....Mr. Reed GOERTLER
15 Director Human Resources ....Ms. Kathy LOWE
11 Associate VP of Administration ....Mr. Jay RITCHIE
08 Director University Library ....Ms. Tamara TRUJILLO
63 Dean College of Osteopathic Med ....Dr. Michael CLEARFIELD
67 Dean College of Pharmacy ....Dr. Katherine KNAPP
53 Dean Col of Education & Health Sci ....Dr. Jim O'CONNOR
13 Director of Information Technology ....Ms. Julia PERHAC
26 Director of External Relations ....Mr. Jesus MENA
29 Director Alumni Relations ....Dr. Irene FAVREAU
37 Director of Student Financial Aid ....Ms. Lynne MOSELEY
30 Chief Officer of Advancement ....Mr. James SOTIROS
35 Director of Student Activities ....Rabbi Elchonon TENENBAUM
23 Director of Student Health Center ....Ms. Lorraine NALLEY

Trident University International (I)

5665 Plaza Drive, Third Floor, Cypress CA 90630-5023
County: Orange FICE Identification: 041279
Unit ID: 450979
Telephone: (714) 816-0366 Carnegie Class: DRU
FAX Number: (714) 816-0367 Calendar System: Semester
URL: www.tuiu.edu
Established: 1998 Annual Undergrad Tuition & Fees: $9,440
Enrollment: 7,307 Coed
Affiliation or Control: Proprietary IRS Status: Proprietary
Highest Offering: Doctorate
Program: Liberal Arts And General; Professional; Business Emphasis
Accreditation: WC

01 President/CEO ....Mr. Kenneth J. SOBASKI
10 Vice President Finance ....Ms. Caroline ROOK
26 Vice President Marketing ....Mr. Jose MARRERO
05 Vice Pres Academic Affairs/CAO ....Dr. Paul WATKINS
13 VP Computing/Info Management ....Mr. Vahid SHARIAT
15 Vice Pres Human Resources ....Ms. Lynne BERNSTEIN
20 Assoc Vice Pres Academic Affairs ....Dr. Afshin AFROOKHTEH
04 Senior Assistant to President ....Ms. Nancy YOU
30 Director Business Development ....Mr. Rafael ITZHAKI
06 Registrar/Dir of Admissions ....Ms. Wei REN
37 Director Student Financial Aid ....Ms. Renita VERNER
09 Director of Institutional Research ....Dr. Shelia LEWIS
08 Head Librarian ....Ms. AnnMarie ZIADIE
21 Chief Financial/Business Officer ....Mr. Robert TORMEY
50 Dean Business/Info Tech Management .. Dr. Anthony CULPEPPER
76 Dean Educ/Health Sciences ....Dr. Mihaela TANASESCU
25 Assoc Dean Special Projects ....Dr. Steven GOLD

United Education Institute (J)

6055 Pacific Blvd, Huntington Park CA 90255
County: Los Angeles FICE Identification: 025593
Telephone: (323) 319-9500 Carnegie Class: Not Classified
FAX Number: N/A Calendar System: Other
URL: www.uei.edu
Established: 1986 Annual Undergrad Tuition & Fees: $16,040
Enrollment: 4,370 Coed
Affiliation or Control: Proprietary IRS Status: Proprietary

Highest Offering: Associate Degree
Program: Occupational
Accreditation: CNCE

01 Area President ... Mr. Al NEDERHOOD

United States University (A)

830 Bay Boulevard, Chula Vista CA 91911
County: San Diego
FICE Identification: 040053
Unit ID: 447050
Telephone: (619) 477-6310
Carnegie Class: Bac/A&S
FAX Number: (619) 477-7340
Calendar System: Semester
URL: www.usuniversity.edu
Established: 1997
Annual Undergrad Tuition & Fees: $6,500
Enrollment: 317
Coed
Affiliation or Control: Proprietary
IRS Status: Proprietary
Highest Offering: Master's
Program: Liberal Arts And General; Teacher Preparatory; Professional; Nursing Emphasis
Accreditation: WC

01 President and CEO ... Dr. Yoram NEUMANN
05 Provost and CAO ... Dr. Edith F. NEUMANN
11 COO ... Tom FINALY
10 CFO ... Joshua KIM
27 CIO ... Roy FINALY
20 Associate Provost ... Dr. Shelia LEWIS
06 Registrar and Campus Director ... Veronica GARCIA
76 Director School of Health Science ... Dr. Rosalinda MILLA
97 Director School of Liberal Studies ... Dr. Elizabeth ARCHER
53 Director School of Education ... Vacant
66 Director School of Nursing ... Vacant

† Additional campus located in Cypress, CA.

Unitek College (B)

4670 Auto Mall Parkway, Fremont CA 94538
County: Alameda
FICE Identification: 041697
Telephone: (888) 735-4355
Carnegie Class: Not Classified
FAX Number: (510) 249-9125
Calendar System: Other
URL: www.unitekcollege.edu
Established: 1992
Annual Undergrad Tuition & Fees: $21,630
Enrollment: 613
Coed
Affiliation or Control: Proprietary
IRS Status: Proprietary
Highest Offering: Baccalaureate
Program: Occupational; 2-Year Principally Bachelor's Creditable; Nursing Emphasis
Accreditation: ACCSC

University of Antelope Valley (C)

44055 Sierra Hwy, Lancaster CA 93534
County: Los Angeles
FICE Identification: 034275
Unit ID: 442930
Telephone: (661) 726-1911
Carnegie Class: Not Classified
FAX Number: (661) 726-5158
Calendar System: Other
URL: www.uav.edu
Established: N/A
Annual Undergrad Tuition & Fees: N/A
Enrollment: 967
Coed
Affiliation or Control: Proprietary
IRS Status: Proprietary
Highest Offering: Master's
Program: Occupational; 2-Year Principally Bachelor's Creditable
Accreditation: ACICS, EMT

01 President ... Mr. Marco JOHNSON
03 Vice President/CEO ... Ms. Sandra JOHNSON
05 Dean of Academic Affairs ... Mr. Ronald FELTS
06 Dean of Records ... Mrs. Jaime PRYOR
37 Financial Aid Officer ... Mr. Araceli JIMENEZ
20 Chief Academic Officer ... Ms. Spring ZUTES
10 Director of Operations ... Ms. Crystal STEPHENS

*University of California Office of the President (D)

1111 Franklin Street, Oakland CA 94607-5200
County: Alameda
FICE Identification: 001311
Unit ID: 124557
Telephone: (510) 987-0700
Carnegie Class: N/A
FAX Number: (510) 987-0328
URL: www.ucop.edu

01 President ... Mark G. YUDOF
05 Provost/Exec Vice Pres Acad Affairs ... Lawrence H. PITTS
10 Exec Vice President/CFO ... Peter J. TAYLOR
11 Exec Vice Pres Business Operations ... Nathan E. BROSTROM
26 Sr Vice Pres External Relations ... Daniel M. DOOLEY
47 Vice Pres Agriculture/Nat Resources ... Daniel M. DOOLEY
17 Sr Vice Pres Health Sciences & Svcs ... John D. STOBO
43 General Counsel/VP Legal Affairs ... Charles F. ROBINSON
32 Vice President Student Affairs ... Judy K. SAKAKI
88 Exec Vice Pres Laboratory Mgmt ... Bruce B. DARLING
25 Sr Vice Pres Compliance/Audit ... Sheryl S. VACCA
27 CIO/Vice Pres for Investments ... Marie N. BERGGREN
15 Vice Pres Human Resources/Benefits ... Dwaine B. DUCKETT
46 Vice Pres Research/Graduate Studies ... Steven V W. BECKWITH
21 Vice President Budget ... Patrick J. LENZ

*University of California-Berkeley (E)

Berkeley CA 94720-0001
County: Alameda
FICE Identification: 001312
Unit ID: 110635
Telephone: (510) 642-6000
Carnegie Class: RU/VH
FAX Number: (510) 643-5499
Calendar System: Semester
URL: www.berkeley.edu
Established: 1868
Annual Undergrad Tuition & Fees (In-State): $13,393
Enrollment: 25,540
Coed
Affiliation or Control: State
IRS Status: 501(c)3
Highest Offering: Doctorate
Program: Liberal Arts And General; Teacher Preparatory; Professional
Accreditation: WC, BUS, CLPSY, CS, DIETD, ENG, FOR, IPSY, JOUR, LAW, LSAR, OPT, OPTR, PH, PLNG, SCPSY, SW

02 Chancellor ... Robert J. BIRGENEAU
05 Exec Vice Chancellor & Provost ... George W. BRESLAUER
11 Vice Chanc Administration/Finance ... John WILTON
32 Vice Chancellor Student Affairs ... Harry LE GRANDE
26 Vice Chanc University Relations ... Scott BIDDY
46 Vice Chancellor Research ... Graham FLEMING
18 Vice Chancellor Facilities Services ... Edward DENTON
100 Assoc Chancellor/Chief of Staff ... Beata FITZPATRICK
31 Assc Chanc Govt/Cmty Campus Liaison ... Linda M. WILLIAMS
25 Asst VC Research Admin & Compliance ... Patrick SCHLESINGER
13 Assoc Vice Chanc Info Technology ... Shelton WAGGENER
10 Assoc Vice Chanc Finance/Controller ... Delphine REGALIA
84 Assoc Vice Chanc Admiss/Enrollment ... Vacant
43 Chief Campus Counsel ... Christopher M. PATTI
26 Assoc Vice Chanc Public Affairs ... Claire HOLMES
21 Asst VC Business & Admin Svcs ... Ron T. COLEY
88 Asc Vice Chanc Budget/Resource Plng ... Erin S. GORE
07 Assoc Vice Chanc Undergrad Admiss ... Walter A. ROBINSON
35 Dean of Students ... Jonathan POULLARD
37 Director Financial Aid ... Vacant
08 University Librarian ... Thomas C. LEONARD
06 Assoc Registrar ... Walter WONG
38 Director Counsel Psychological Svcs ... Jeff PRINCE
36 Director Career Center ... Thomas C. DEVLIN
87 Director Summer Sessions ... Richard RUSSO
41 Dir Intercol Athletics & Rec Sports ... Sandy BARBOUR
58 Dean of the Graduate Division ... Andrew J. SZERI
56 Dean of University Extension ... Diana WU
61 Dean of Law ... Christopher EDLEY, JR.
88 Dean of Optometry ... Dennis M. LEVI
54 Dean School of Engineering ... Shankar SASTRY
88 Dean of Environmental Design ... Jennifer WOLCH
65 Dean of Natural Resources ... J. Keith GILLESS
50 Dean of Haas School of Business ... Richard K. LYONS
70 Dean of Social Welfare ... Lorraine T. MIDANIK
88 Dean School of Information ... AnnaLee SAXENIAN
69 Dean of Public Health ... Stephen M. SHORTELL
53 Dean of Education ... Judith W. LITTLE
60 Dean of Journalism ... Neil HENRY
88 Dean of Chemistry ... Richard MATHIES
80 Dean Goldman School/Public Pol ... Henry BRADY
79 Dean of Arts and Humanities ... Anthony CASCARDI
88 Interim Dean of Biological Sciences ... G. Steven MARTIN
81 Dean Mathematical/Physical Sciences ... Mark RICHARDS
83 Dean of Social Sciences ... Carla HESSE
97 Dean of the Undergraduate Division ... Tyler STOVALL

*University of California-Davis (F)

One Shields Avenue, Davis CA 95616-5270
County: Yolo
FICE Identification: 001313
Unit ID: 110644
Telephone: (530) 752-1011
Carnegie Class: RU/VH
FAX Number: N/A
Calendar System: Quarter
URL: www.ucdavis.edu
Established: 1905
Annual Undergrad Tuition & Fees (In-State): $14,055
Enrollment: 32,290
Coed
Affiliation or Control: State
IRS Status: 501(c)3
Highest Offering: Doctorate
Program: Liberal Arts And General; Teacher Preparatory; Professional
Accreditation: WC, ARCPA, BUS, CS, DIETD, DIETI, ENG, IPSY, LAW, LSAR, MED, MT, PH, VET

02 Chancellor ... Dr. Linda P. KATEHI
05 Provost & Exec Vice Chancellor ... Dr. Ralph J. HEXTER
03 Associate Chancellor ... Mr. Karl M. ENGELBACH
46 Vice Chancellor Research ... Dr. Harris A. LEWIN
04 Assistant Executive Vice Chancellor ... Ms. Marie H. CARTER-DUBOIS
32 Vice Chancellor Student Affairs ... Dr. Fred E. WOOD
26 Vice Chancellor External Relations ... Dr. Beverly A. SANDEEN
45 VC Administration & Resource Mgmt ... Mr. John A. MEYER
76 Vice Chanc Human Health Sciences ... Dr. Claire POMEROY
17 CEO Hospital/Clinics ... Ms. Ann M. RICE
31 Assoc Exec VC Campus Cmty Relations ... Mr. Rahim REED
15 Assoc VC Human Resources ... Ms. Karen S. HULL
10 Assoc VC Accounting/Financial Svcs ... Mr. J. Michael ALLRED
30 Vice Chancellor Development ... Vacant
35 Assoc Vice Chanc Student Affairs ... Ms. Emily GALINDO
35 Assoc Vice Chanc Student Affairs ... Ms. Lora J. BOSSIO
21 Assoc Vice Chancellor Budget ... Ms. Kelly M. RATLIFF
18 Assoc Vice Chancellor/Safety Svcs ... Ms. Jill PARKER
88 Asst VC Capital Resource Mgmt ... Mr. Karl F. MOHR
45 Asst Vice Chanc Campus Planning ... Mr. Robert B. SEGAR
88 Asst VC Env.Plng & Sustainability ... Dr. Sid ENGLAND
27 Assoc VC University Communications ... Mr. Mitchel BENSON
86 Asst VC Govt & Community Relations ... Ms. Marjorie M. DICKINSON
35 Asst Vice Chanc Student Affairs ... Ms. Griselda CASTRO
12 Exec Director Mondavi Center ... Dr. Don ROTH
13 Vice Provost Info/Educ Tech ... Mr. Peter M. SIEGEL
53 Vice Provost Undergraduate Studies ... Dr. Pat A. TURNER
85 Vice Prov Univ Outreach/Intl Pgms ... Dr. William B. LACY
20 Vice Provost Academic Affairs ... Dr. Maureen L. STANTON
88 Assoc Vice Provost Internatl Pgms ... Dr. Adrienne MARTIN
43 Campus Counsel ... Mr. Steven A. DROWN
06 Registrar ... Dr. Frank Y. WADA
08 University Librarian ... Vacant
58 Dean of Graduate Studies ... Dr. Jeffery C. GIBELING
47 Dean of Agricultural/Envir Sciences ... Dr. Neal K. VAN ALFEN
81 Dean of Biological Sciences ... Dr. James E. HILDRETH
54 Dean of Engineering ... Dr. Enrique J. LAVERNIA
83 Dean Social Sciences ... Dr. George R. MANGUN
81 Dean Math & Physical Science ... Dr. Winston T. KO
79 Dean Humanities/Arts & Culture ... Dr. Jessie A. OWENS
61 Dean School of Law ... Dr. Kevin R. JOHNSON
50 Dean Graduate School of Management ... Dr. Steven C. CURRALL
63 Dean School of Medicine ... Dr. Claire POMEROY
74 Dean Veterinary Medicine ... Dr. Bennie I. OSBORN
53 Dean School of Education ... Dr. Harold LEVINE
56 Dean of University Extension ... Mr. Dennis F. PENDLETON
37 Interim Director Financial Aid ... Ms. Kathryn A. MALONEY
09 Dir Student Affairs Research/Info ... Ms. Gillian BUTLER
29 AVC/Exec Director Alumni Relations ... Mr. Richard R. ENGEL
23 Director Student Health Services ... Dr. Michelle S. FAMULA
38 Director Counseling Center ... Dr. Emil R. RODOLFA
36 Director Internship & Career Center ... Dr. Subhash H. RISBUD
39 Director Student Housing ... Ms. Emily GALINDO
40 Director Bookstore ... Mr. Charles P. KRATOCHVIL
41 Int Dir Intercollegiate Athletics ... Ms. Nona E. RICHARDSON
27 Director News Service ... Ms. Claudia MORAIN
96 Director Material Management ... Ms. Janice KING
07 Director Admissions ... Ms. Lora J. BOSSIO

*University of California-Hastings College of the Law (G)

200 McAllister Street, San Francisco CA 94102-4978
County: San Francisco
FICE Identification: 003947
Unit ID: 110398
Telephone: (415) 565-4600
Carnegie Class: Spec/Law
FAX Number: (415) 565-4005
Calendar System: Semester
URL: www.uchastings.edu
Established: 1878
Annual Graduate Tuition & Fees: $41,200
Enrollment: 1,337
Coed
Affiliation or Control: State
IRS Status: 501(c)3
Highest Offering: First Professional Degree; No Undergraduates
Program: Professional
Accreditation: LAW

02 Chancellor and Dean ... Mr. Frank H. WU
05 Academic Dean ... Ms. Shauna MARSHALL
43 General Counsel ... Ms. Elise TRAYNUM
10 Chief Financial Officer ... Mr. David SEWARD
20 Associate Academic Dean ... Mr. C. Keith WINGATE
08 Director Law Library ... Ms. Jenni PARRISH
15 Executive Director Human Resources ... Ms. Marie HAIRSTON
19 Chief Public Safety ... Mr. Bill PALMINI
06 Registrar ... Ms. Gina BARNETT
07 Assistant Dean Admissions ... Mr. Greg CANADA
32 Director Student Services ... Ms. Rupa BHANDARI
72 Director Information Technology ... Mr. Eric NOBLE
36 Asst Dean Career & Profess Devel ... Ms. Sari ZIMMERMAN
26 Assistant Dean Communications ... Mr. Michael TREVINO
22 Director LEOP ... Ms. Jan JEMISON
23 Student Health Manager/Admin Nurse ... Ms. Laurie BROOKNER
21 Controller ... Ms. Deborah TRAN
37 Assistant Dean Financial Aid ... Ms. Linda BISESI
40 Bookstore Manager ... Vacant
18 Property Manager ... Ms. Pansy MAR
96 Director of Purchasing ... Mr. Darryl SWEET
44 Sr Asst Dean Institutional Advance ... Ms. Amy SOLLINS

*University of California-Irvine (H)

Campus Drive, Irvine CA 92697-0001
County: Orange
FICE Identification: 001314
Unit ID: 110653
Telephone: (949) 824-5011
Carnegie Class: RU/VH
FAX Number: (949) 824-5451
Calendar System: Quarter
URL: www.uci.edu
Established: 1965
Annual Undergrad Tuition & Fees (In-State): $12,749
Enrollment: 27,676
Coed
Affiliation or Control: State
IRS Status: 501(c)3
Highest Offering: Doctorate
Program: Liberal Arts And General; Teacher Preparatory; Professional
Accreditation: WC, BUS, CEA, ENG, IPSY, #LAW, MED, MT, NURSE, PLNG

02 Chancellor ... Michael V. DRAKE
05 Executive Vice Chancellor & Provost ... Michael R. GOTTFREDSON
10 Vice Chanc Admin/Business Services ... Wendell C. BRASE
46 Vice Chancellor for Research ... John C. HEMMINGER
32 Interim Vice Chanc Student Affairs ... Thomas A. PARHAM
30 Interim Vice Chanc Univ Advancement ... Dan ALDRICH
45 Vice Chanc Planning & Budget ... Meredith MICHAELS
20 Vice Provost for Academic Planning ... Michael P. CLARK
16 Vice Provost for Academic Personnel ... Herbert KILLACKEY
21 Assoc Vice Chanc Admin/Business Svc ... Paige L. MACIAS

29 Asst Vice Chanc Alumni Relations ... Jorge ANCONA
35 Assoc Vice Chancellor Stdnt Affairs ... Daniel J. DOOROS
22 Asst Executive Vice Chancellor OEOD ... Kirsten K. QUANBECK
100 Associate Chancellor ... Ramona AGRELA
20 Associate Exec Vice Chancellor ... Michael R. ARIAS
35 Asst Vice Chanc/Dean of Students ... Rameen A. TALESH
84 Asst Vice Chanc Enrollment Services ... Brent W. YUNEK
06 University Registrar ... Elizabeth C. BENNETT
43 Chief Campus Counsel ... Diane F. GEOCARIS
51 Dean Continuing Education ... Gary W. MATKIN
08 Interim University Librarian ... Lorelei A. TANJI
37 Director Financial Aid ... Christopher SHULTZ
36 Interim Director Career Center ... Linda R. DRAKE
41 Director Athletics ... Michael A. IZZI
09 Dir Office Institutional Research ... Michael POSTON
58 Dean Graduate Division ... Frances M. LESLIE
20 Dean Undergraduate Education ... Sharon V. SALINGER
63 Dean School of Medicine ... Ralph V. CLAYMAN
61 Dean of Law School ... Erwin CHEMERINSKY
81 Dean Biological Sciences ... Albert F. BENNETT
81 Dean Physical Sciences ... Kenneth C. JANDA
83 Dean School of Social Sciences ... Barbara DOSHER
50 Dean Paul Merage School of Business ... Andrew J. POLICANO
79 Dean Humanities ... Vicki L. RUIZ
49 Dean Arts ... Joseph S. LEWIS
83 Dean Social Ecology ... Valerie JENNESS
54 Interim Dean School of Engineering ... Dimitri PAPAMOSCHOU
77 Dean Bren Sch of Info & Comp Sci ... Hal S. STERN
88 Chair Academic Senate ... Craig MARTENS
53 Chair Department of Education ... Deborah L. VANDELL
13 CIO and Asst Vice Chancellor IT ... Dana F. ROODE
96 Director Materiel & Risk Management ... Harry B. GUNTHER
26 Director Media Relations ... Cathy LAWHON
28 Director ADVANCE Program ... Douglas M. HAYNES

*University of California-Los Angeles (A)

405 Hilgard Avenue, Los Angeles CA 90095-1405
County: Los Angeles — FICE Identification: 001315
Unit ID: 110662
Telephone: (310) 825-4321 — Carnegie Class: RU/VH
FAX Number: N/A — Calendar System: Quarter
URL: www.ucla.edu
Established: 1919 — Annual Undergrad Tuition & Fees (In-State): $11,618
Enrollment: 38,157 — Coed
Affiliation or Control: State — IRS Status: 501(c)3
Highest Offering: Doctorate
Program: Liberal Arts And General; Professional
Accreditation: WC, BUS, CLPSY, CS, CYTO, DENT, DIETI, EMT, ENG, ENGR, ENGT, HSA, IPSY, LAW, LIB, MED, NMT, NURSE, PDPSY, PH, PLNG, RAD, SW, THEA

02 Chancellor ... Gene D. BLOCK
03 Exec Vice Chancellor/Provost ... Scott WAUGH
10 Administrative Vice Chancellor ... Jack J. POWAZEK
32 Vice Chancellor Student Affairs ... Janina MONTERO
26 Vice Chancellor External Affairs ... Rhea TURTELTAUB
45 VC Finance/Budget/Capital Pgms ... Steven A. OLSEN
17 VC Med Sciences/Dean Med School ... A. Eugene WASHINGTON
46 Vice Chancellor Research ... James S. ECONOMOU
58 VC Grad Studies/Dean Grad Div ... Claudia MITCHELL-KERNAN
16 Vice Chanc Academic Personnel ... Thomas RICE
43 Vice Chancellor Legal Affairs ... Kevin REED
82 Vice Provost International Studies ... Nicholas J. ENTRIKIN
88 Vice Provost/Dean Undergrad Educ ... Judith L. SMITH
88 Assoc VC and CEO Hospital Systems ... David T. FEINBERG
24 Assoc V Provost Instr Development ... Larry L. LOEHER
35 Vice Prov Faculty Diversity/Develop ... Rosina BECERRA
88 Asst Provost ... Margaret LEAL-SOTELO
13 Vice Provost Information Technology ... James DAVIS
88 Assoc Vice Chanc Acad Plng/Budget ... Glyn DAVIES
27 Assoc Vice Chanc Univ Communication ... Lawrence H. LOKMAN
86 Asst Vice Chanc Govt/Cmty Rels ... Keith S. PARKER
18 Assoc Vice Chanc General Services ... Jack POWAZEK
30 Assoc Vice Chancellor Development ... Tracie CHRISTENSEN
21 Assoc Vice Chancellor/Controller ... Susan K. ABELES
15 Assoc Vice Chanc Campus Human Res ... Lubbe LEVIN
32 Assoc VC Dean Student & Campus Life ... Robert J. NAPLES
29 Asst Vice Chanc/Exec Dir Alumni Rel ... Ralph AMOS
88 Executive Director Volunteer Center ... Antoinette MONGELLI
84 Assoc VC Student Academic Svcs ... Thomas E. LIFKA
25 Asst VC Res Policy & Compliance ... Ann M. POLLACK
23 Asst VC Student Development/Health ... Vacant
06 Registrar ... Anita COTTER
88 Vice Prov Intel Prop/Indust Rels ... Kathryn ATCHISON
20 Assistant Provost ... Maryann J. GRAY
87 Asst Prov Academic Program Dev ... David UNRUH
09 Dir Analysis/Information Management ... Caroline S. WEST
08 University Librarian ... Gary E. STRONG
19 Chief of Police ... James HERREN
07 Dir Undergrad Admiss/Rels w/Schools ... Vu TRAN
36 Director Career Center ... Kathy L. SIMS
37 Director Financial Aid Office ... Ronald W. JOHNSON
38 Dir Student Psychological Services ... Elizabeth GONG-GUY
85 Dir Ctr for Intl Students/Scholars ... Robert B. ERICKSEN
91 Asst Vice Chanc Adm Info Systems ... Andrew WISSMILLER
41 Director Intercollegiate Athletics ... Daniel G. GUERRERO
39 Asst VC Housing & Hospitality Svcs ... Peter ANGELIS
22 Director Staff Affirmative Action ... Linda C. AVILA
96 Director of Purchasing ... William S. PROPST
88 Executive Director ASUCLA ... Robert WILLIAMS
51 Dean of Extension ... Cathy SANDEEN
53 Dean Grad Sch Educ/Info Studies ... Aimee DORR
54 Dean Sch of Engr & Applied Sci ... Vijay K. DHIR
61 Interim Dean School of Law ... Stephen C. YEAZELL
50 Dean Anderson Grad Sch Management ... Judy D. OLIAN
52 Dean School of Dentistry ... No Hee PARK
66 Dean School of Nursing ... Courtney LYDER
88 Dean Sch of the Arts/Architecture ... Christopher WATERMAN
88 Dean School of Theater/Film/TV ... Teri SCHWARTZ
69 Dean School of Public Health ... Linda ROSENSTOCK
80 Dean School of Public Affairs ... Franklin D. GILLIAM, JR.
79 Dean of Humanities ... Timothy STOWELL
88 Dean of Life Sciences ... Victoria SORK
88 Dean of Physical Sciences ... Joseph RUDNICK
83 Dean of Social Sciences ... Alessandro DURANTI
90 Director Academic Tech Svcs ... William LABATE
40 Divisional Manager Textbooks ... Anne COLLUM

*University of California-Merced (B)

5200 North Lake Road, Merced CA 95343
County: Merced — Identification: 666371
Unit ID: 445188
Telephone: (209) 228-4400 — Carnegie Class: Not Classified
FAX Number: (209) 228-4424 — Calendar System: Semester
URL: www.ucmerced.edu
Established: 1868 — Annual Undergrad Tuition & Fees (In-District): $14,370
Enrollment: 3,802 — Coed
Affiliation or Control: State/Local — IRS Status: 501(c)3
Highest Offering: Master's
Program: Liberal Arts And General; Teacher Preparatory; Professional
Accreditation: WC

02 Chancellor ... Dr. Dorothy LELAND
03 Executive Vice Chancellor & Provost ... Dr. Keith ALLEY
11 Vice Chancellor Administration ... Mary E. MILLER
32 Vice Chancellor Student Affairs ... Dr. Jane F. LAWRENCE
46 Vice Chancellor Research ... Dr. Samuel TRAINA
04 Associate Chancellor ... Janet YOUNG
35 Associate Vice Chancellor Students ... Dr. Charles NIES
84 Assoc Vice Chanc Enrollment Mgmt ... Kevin M. BROWNE
23 Assoc Vice Chanc Health & Wellness ... Dr. Fuji COLLINS
06 University Registrar ... Dr. Laurie HERBRAND
07 Director of Admissions ... Encarnacion RUIZ
08 Int University Librarian ... Donald A. BARCLAY
37 Director of Financial Aid ... Diana RALLS
85 Director of International Programs ... Rebecca SWEELEY
56 Director of Extension & Summer Pgms ... Kevin M. BROWNE
19 Chief of Police ... Rita SPAUR
27 Exec Director of Communications ... Patti W. WAID
41 Director of Campus Athletics & Rec ... David DUNHAM
39 Director of Student Housing ... Leslie SANTOS
58 Dean Graduate Studies ... Dr. Samuel TRAINA
65 Dean Natural Sciences ... Dr. Juan MEZA
54 Dean Engineering ... Dr. E. Daniel HIRLENAN
79 Dean School of SSHA ... Dr. Mark S. ALDENDERFER

*University of California-Riverside (C)

900 University Avenue, Riverside CA 92521
County: Riverside — FICE Identification: 001316
Unit ID: 110671
Telephone: (951) 827-1012 — Carnegie Class: RU/VH
FAX Number: (951) 827-3800 — Calendar System: Quarter
URL: www.ucr.edu
Established: 1954 — Annual Undergrad Tuition & Fees (In-State): $12,923
Enrollment: 20,746 — Coed
Affiliation or Control: State — IRS Status: 501(c)3
Highest Offering: Doctorate
Program: Liberal Arts And General; Teacher Preparatory; Professional
Accreditation: WC, BUS, CS, ENG, SCPSY

02 Chancellor ... Dr. Timothy P. WHITE
04 Associate Chancellor ... Ms. Cynthia R. GIORGIO
05 Exec Vice Chancellor/Provost ... Dr. Dallas RABENSTEIN
11 Vice Chanc Finance/Business Opers ... Ms. Gretchen S. BOLAR
32 Vice Chancellor Student Affairs ... Mr. James W. SANDOVAL
26 Vice Chanc University Advancement ... Mr. Peter A. HAYASHIDA
46 Vice Chancellor Research ... Dr. Charles LOUIS
17 VC Hlth Affs/Dean School of Med ... Dr. G. Richard OLDS
20 Vice Provost Academic Personnel ... Dr. David F. BOCAIN

*University of California-San Diego (D)

9500 Gilman Drive, La Jolla CA 92093-0014
County: San Diego — FICE Identification: 001317
Unit ID: 110680
Telephone: (858) 534-2230 — Carnegie Class: RU/VH
FAX Number: (858) 534-6523 — Calendar System: Quarter
URL: www.ucsd.edu
Established: 1960 — Annual Undergrad Tuition & Fees (In-State): $12,157
Enrollment: 29,899 — Coed
Affiliation or Control: State — IRS Status: 501(c)3
Highest Offering: Doctorate
Program: Liberal Arts And General; Professional
Accreditation: WC, AUD, BUS, CEA, CLPSY, @DIETI, DMS, ENG, IPSY, MED, PHAR

02 Chancellor ... Dr. Marye Anne FOX
05 Executive VC Academic Affairs ... Dr. Suresh SUBRAMANI
30 VC External and Business Affairs ... Mr. Steven W. RELYEA
32 Vice Chancellor Student Affairs ... Ms. Penny E. RUE
11 Vice Chanc Resource Mgmt/Planning ... Mr. Gary C. MATTHEWS
65 Vice Chancellor Marine Sciences ... Dr. Anthony D. HAYMET
63 VC Health Science/Dean Sch Med ... Dr. David A. BRENNER
46 Vice Chancellor Research ... Dr. Sandra BROWN
18 Vice Chanc Resource Mgmt/Planning ... Mr. Gary C. MATTHEWS
100 Associate Chancellor/Chief of Staff ... Ms. Clare M. KRISTOFCO
56 Assoc VC Public Pgms/Dean Univ Ext ... Dr. Mary L. WALSHOK
43 Chief Campus Counsel ... Mr. Daniel W. PARK
21 AVC Business Fin Svcs/Controller ... Mr. Don A. LARSON
23 AVC Student Health/Wellness ... Ms. Karen J. CALFAS
26 University Communications ... Ms. Clare M. KRISTOFCO
20 Asst Vice Chanc Academic Affairs ... Ms. Kristina L. LARSEN
35 Assoc Vice Chanc Student Affairs ... Mr. Edward J. SPRIGGS
16 Asst Vice Chanc Human Resources ... Mr. Thomas R. LEET
88 Associate Vice Chancellor Research ... Mr. George TYNAN
84 Asst Vice Chanc Admiss/Enroll Svcs ... Ms. Mae W. BROWN
14 Asst VC Admin Computing/Teleco ... Mr. Min YAO
45 Assoc Vice Chanc Campus Planning ... Dr. Jeffrey A. STEINDORF
09 Associate Dean of Research ... Dr. David D. SWORDER
08 University Librarian ... Mr. Brian E C. SCHOTTLAENDER
06 University Registrar ... Mr. William R. HAID
23 CEO UCSD Medical Center ... Mr. Thomas E. JACKIEWICZ
28 Assoc Chancellor/Chief Diversity ... Dr. Sandra DALEY
29 Assistant Vice Chancellor ... Mr. Armin AFSAHI
96 Senior Director Purchasing ... Mr. Ted JOHNSON
54 Dean Jacobs Sch of Engineering ... Dr. Frieder SEIBLE
49 Dean Arts & Humanities ... Dr. Seth LERER
81 Dean Div of Biological Sciences ... Dr. Steve A. KAY
83 Dean of Social Sciences ... Dr. Jeffrey ELMAN
82 Dean Rady School of Management ... Mr. Robert S. SULLIVAN
81 Dean Physical Science ... Dr. Mark H. THIEMENS
82 Dean Sch Intl Rels/Pacific Stds ... Dr. Peter F. COWHEY
58 Dean Graduate Studies ... Dr. Kim E. BARRETT
12 Provost John Muir College ... Dr. Susan SMITH
12 Prov Thurgood Marshall Coll ... Mr. Allan HAVIS
12 Provost Earl Warren College ... Mr. Steven ADLER
12 Provost Revelle College ... Dr. Don WAYNE
12 Provost Eleanor Roosevelt College ... Dr. Alan C. HOUSTON
12 Provost Sixth College ... Dr. Naomi ORESKES
38 Director Stdt Psych/Counseling Svcs ... Dr. Reina JUAREZ

*University of California-San Francisco (E)

513 Parnassus Avenue, Room S-126,
San Francisco CA 94143-0402
County: San Francisco — FICE Identification: 001319
Unit ID: 110699
Telephone: (415) 476-9000 — Carnegie Class: Spec/Med
FAX Number: (415) 476-9634 — Calendar System: Quarter
URL: www.ucsf.edu
Established: 1864 — Annual Undergrad Tuition & Fees (In-State): N/A
Enrollment: 2,735 — Coed
Affiliation or Control: State — IRS Status: 501(c)3
Highest Offering: Doctorate
Program: Professional
Accreditation: WC, DENT, DIETI, IPSY, MED, MIDWF, NURSE, PHAR, PTA

02 Chancellor ... Dr. Susan DESMOND-HELLMANN
03 Executive Vice Chancellor & Provost ... Dr. Jeffrey A. BLUESTONE
100 Assistant Chancellor ... Ms. Angelique LOSCAR
10 Sr Vice Chanc Finance & Admin ... Mr. John E. PLOTTS
05 Vice Provost Academic Affairs ... Dr. Sally MARSHALL
17 Dean of Medicine ... Dr. Samuel HAWGOOD
20 Vice Chanc Student Academic Affairs ... Dr. Joseph I. CASTRO
18 Asst VC Cap Pgms/Camp Architect ... Mr. Michael BADE
32 Assoc VC Camp Life Svcs & FM ... Ms. Angela HAWKINS
21 Vice Chancellor Finance ... Mr. Eric VERMILLION
30 Int VC Univ Develop & Alumni Rels ... Ms. Janice EISELE
26 VC Strat Communications & Univ Rels ... Ms. Barbara FRENCH
91 VC & Chief Info Officer - ITS ... Mr. Elazar HAREL
22 VC Diversity & Outreach ... Dr. Renee NAVARRO
06 Associate Registrar ... Ms. Jina SHAMIM
37 Director Student Financial Services ... Ms. Carrie STEERE-SALAZAR
43 Chief Campus Counsel ... Ms. Marcia CANNING
08 University Librarian/AVC ... Ms. Karen BUTTER
19 Chief of Police ... Ms. Pamela ROSKOWSKI
22 Dir Affirm Action/Equal Oppty/Diver ... Mr. Michael B. ADAMS
66 Dean of Nursing ... Dr. David VLAHOV
52 Dean of Dentistry ... Dr. John FEATHERSTONE
67 Dean of Pharmacy ... Dr. Mary Anne KODA-KIMBLE
35 Director Student Life ... Mr. Eric KOENIG
39 Assoc Director of Housing Services ... Mr. Jim JACOBS
96 Exec Dir Camp Procurmt/Bus Contract ... Mr. James HINE
07 Registrar ... Mr. Douglas CARLSON
15 Director Human Resources ... Mr. Mike TYBURSKI
36 Dir Career/Professional Development ... Mr. William LINDSTAEDT
23 Director Student Health Services ... Mr. Henry KAHN
40 Bookstore Manager ... Mr. Jim SOBCZYK

*University of California-Santa Barbara (F)

552 University Road, Santa Barbara CA 93106-0001
County: Santa Barbara — FICE Identification: 001320
Unit ID: 110705
Telephone: (805) 893-8000 — Carnegie Class: RU/VH
FAX Number: N/A — Calendar System: Quarter
URL: www.ucsb.edu
Established: 1909 — Annual Undergrad Tuition & Fees (In-State): $12,527
Enrollment: 22,218 — Coed
Affiliation or Control: State — IRS Status: 501(c)3

Highest Offering: Doctorate
Program: Liberal Arts And General; Teacher Preparatory
Accreditation: WC, CS, DANCE, ENG, IPSY, PSPSY

02 Chancellor ... Dr. Henry T. YANG
04 Exec Assistant to the Chancellor ... Mr. Kevin R. MCCAULEY
05 Exec Vice Chanc/Chief Academic Ofcr ... Dr. Glenn E. LUCAS
46 Vice Chancellor Research ... Dr. Michael S. WITHERELL
11 Sr Assoc Vice Chancellor Admin Svcs ... Mr. Marc FISHER
88 Assoc Vice Chancellor Admin Svcs ... Mr. Ronald CORTEZ
26 Vice Chanc Inst Advancement ... Vacant
32 Vice Chancellor Student Affairs ... Dr. Michael D. YOUNG
45 Assistant Chanc Budget & Planning ... Mr. Todd G. LEE
16 Assoc Vice Chanc Acad Personnel ... Dr. John E. TALBOTT
28 Asc VC Diversity/Equity/Acad Policy ... Dr. Maria HERRERA-SOBEK
20 Acting AVC Academic Programs ... Dr. Ronald W. TOBIN
30 Assoc Vice Chancellor Development ... Mr. Gary A. GREINKE
27 Assoc Vice Chanc Public Affairs ... Vacant
84 Asst Vice Chanc Enrollment Svcs/Mgt ... Ms. Christine N. VAN GIESON
88 Exec Dir Student Acad Support Svc ... Ms. Mary JACOB
29 Asst Vice Chanc Alumni Affairs ... Mr. George THURLOW, III
88 Dean College Creative Studies ... Dr. Bruce H. TIFFNEY
54 Acting Dean College of Engineering ... Dr. Larry COLDREN
58 Dean Graduate Division ... Ms. Gale M. MORRISON
53 Dean Gevirtz Graduate Sch Educ ... Ms. Jane CONOLEY
65 Dean Bren School of Env Sci & Mgmt ... Dr. Steven D. GAINES
56 Dean UC Santa Barbara Extension ... Dr. Michael T. BROWN
35 Dean of Students ... Dr. Yonie HARRIS
79 Dean Humanities/Fine Arts ... Dr. David B. MARSHALL
81 Dean Math/Life & Physical Sciences ... Dr. Pierre WILTZIUS
87 Dean Summer Sessions ... Dr. Carol BRAUN PASTERNACK
83 Dean Social Sciences ... Dr. Melvin L. OLIVER
85 Director Intl Students/Scholars ... Ms. Mary J. JACOB
06 Acting Registrar ... Ms. Marsha BANKSTON
15 Interim Director Human Resources ... Ms. Tricia HIEMSTRA
21 Director Accounting Svcs & Controls ... Mr. Jim R. CORKILL
37 Acting Director Financial Aid ... Mr. Michael MILLER
88 Acting Dir Audit & Advisory Service ... Mr. Robert TARSIA
07 Director Admissions & Outreach ... Ms. Christine N. VAN GIESON
09 Director Institutional Research ... Dr. Steven C. VELASCO
23 Director Student Health Svcs ... Dr. Mary FERRIS
39 Exec Dir Housing Residential Svcs ... Mr. Wilfred E. BROWN
40 Director of UCSB Bookstore ... Mr. Alan KIRBY
19 Chief of Police ... Mr. Dustin OLSON
41 Director Intercollegiate Athletics ... Mr. Mark MASSARI
86 Dir Governmental Relations ... Ms. Kirsten DECHLER
88 Director Finance/Administration ... Mr. Eric J. SONQUIST
08 Co-Acting University Librarian ... Ms. Sherry DEDECKER
08 Co-Acting University Librarian ... Ms. Lucia SNOWHILL
88 Director Orientation Programs ... Ms. Kim R. PARENT
44 Interim Dir Capital Development ... Mr. Chuck HAINES
46 Acting Dir Campus Planning & Design ... Ms. Alissa HUMMER
44 Assoc Vice Chancellor Development ... Mr. Gary A. GREINKE
31 Director Arts & Lectures ... Ms. Celesta BILLECI
88 Director Disabled Students Pgm ... Mr. Gary R. WHITE
104 Campus Dir Education Abroad Program ... Dr. Juan E. CAMPO
88 Director Env Health & Safety ... Ms. Pam LOMBARDO
88 Director MultiCultural Center ... Ms. Zaveeni KHAN-MARCUS
38 Director Counseling Services ... Dr. Jeanne STANFORD
94 Director Women's Center ... Ms. Alka ARORA
88 Ombudsperson ... Ms. Priscilla MORI
88 Exec Dir Instructional Devel ... Mr. George H. MICHAELS
36 Director Career Services ... Mr. Micael S. KEMP
13 Assoc VC for IT and CIO ... Mr. Tom PUTNAM
43 UCSB Legal Counsel ... Mr. David BIRNBAUM
88 Equal Opport Sexual Harras/Title IX ... Mr. Ricardo ALCAINO
18 Director Design & Construction ... Mr. Jack WOLEVER
88 Director Univ Center/Events Center ... Mr. Alan KIRBY
68 Director of Recreation ... Mr. Jon SPAVENTA
24 Director Instructional Computing ... Mr. William KOSELUK
92 Honors Coord/Academic Advisor ... Ms. Rocio ANGELES
92 Honors Coord/Academic Advisor ... Mr. Scott KASSNER
96 Strategic Sourcing Specialist ... Mr. Chris CURLESS

*University of California-Santa Cruz (A)

1156 High Street, Santa Cruz CA 95064-1077
County: Santa Cruz FICE Identification: 001321
Unit ID: 110714
Telephone: (831) 459-0111 Carnegie Class: RU/VH
FAX Number: (831) 459-0146 Calendar System: Quarter
URL: www.ucsc.edu
Established: 1962 Annual Undergrad Tuition & Fees (In-State): $13,417
Enrollment: 17,175 Coed
Affiliation or Control: State IRS Status: 501(c)3
Highest Offering: Doctorate
Program: Liberal Arts And General; Professional
Accreditation: WC, ENG, IPSY

02 Chancellor ... Dr. George R. BLUMENTHAL
05 Campus Provost/Exec Vice Chancellor ... Dr. Alison GALLOWAY
10 Vice Chanc Business/Admin Services ... Christina L. VALENTINO
32 Vice Chancellor Student Affairs ... Dr. Felicia E. MCGINTY
45 Vice Chancellor Planning/Budget ... Ms. Peggy DELANEY
46 Vice Chancellor Research ... Dr. Bruce MARGON
30 Vice Chanc of University Relations ... Ms. Donna M. MURPHY
13 Vice Provost Information Technology ... Dr. Mary DOYLE
20 Interim V Prov/Dean Undergrad Educ ... Dr. Mark CIOC
20 Vice Provost Academic Affairs ... Dr. Herbert LEE
88 Sr Dir Silicon Valley Initiative ... Mr. Gordon RINGOLD
16 Asst VC Academic Personnel ... Dr. Pamela PETERSON
08 University Librarian ... Ms. Virginia STEEL
07 Assoc VC Enrollment Mgmt ... Ms. Michelle WHITTINGHAM
49 Dean of Humanities ... Dr. William LADUSAW
81 Dean Physical & Biological Sci ... Dr. Paul KOCH
49 Dean of the Arts ... Dr. David YAGER
83 Dean of Social Sciences ... Dr. Sheldon KAMIENIECKI
54 Dean of Engineering ... Dr. Arthur RAMIREZ
58 Vice Prov/Dean of Graduate Studies ... Dr. Tyrus MILLER
65 Director Institute Marine Sciences ... Dr. Gary B. GRIGGS
81 Director Institute Particle Physics ... Dr. Steven RITZ
88 Director UCO/Lick Observatory ... Dr. Michael BOLTE
12 Provost Stevenson College ... Dr. Alice YANG
12 Provost Cowell College ... Dr. Faye CROSBY
12 Provost Crown College ... Dr. F. Joel FERGUSON
12 Provost Merrill College ... Dr. Lourdes MARTINEZ-ESCHAZABAL
12 Provost Porter College ... Dr. David Evan JONES
12 Provost Kresge College ... Dr. Juan POBLETE
12 Provost Oakes College ... Dr. Pedro CASTILLO
12 Provost College Eight ... Dr. Kimberly LAU
12 Provost College Nine & Ten ... Dr. Helen SHAPIRO
06 Registrar ... Ms. Pamela HUNT-CARTER
09 Director Institutional Research ... Dr. Julian L. FERNALD
15 Director Staff Human Resources ... Ms. Charlotte MORENO
18 Int Assoc VC & Campus Arthitect ... Mr. John BARNES
29 Exec Director of Alumni Relations ... Ms. Carolyn CHRISTOPHERSON
37 Staff Director Financial Aid ... Ms. Ann DRAPER
22 Staff Dir EEO/Affirmative Action ... Mr. Ashish SAHNI
86 Director Government Relations ... Ms. Donna M. BLITZER
38 Interim Director Student Counseling ... Dr. Maryjan MURPHY
96 Director of Purchasing ... Mr. John BONO
35 Asst Vice Chanc Student Affairs ... Ms. Alma SIFUENTES

University of East-West Medicine (B)

595 Lawrence Expressway, Sunnyvale CA 94085
County: Santa Clara FICE Identification: 039953
Unit ID: 447801
Telephone: (408) 636-7705 Carnegie Class: Spec/Health
FAX Number: (408) 992-0448 Calendar System: Trimester
URL: www.uewm.edu
Established: 1997 Annual Undergrad Tuition & Fees: $30,855
Enrollment: 500 Coed
Affiliation or Control: Proprietary IRS Status: Proprietary
Highest Offering: Master's
Program: Professional
Accreditation: ACUP

00 CEO ... Mr. Jerry WANG
01 President ... Dr. Ying Qiu WANG

University of LaVerne (C)

1950 Third Street, La Verne CA 91750-4443
County: Los Angeles FICE Identification: 001216
Unit ID: 117140
Telephone: (909) 593-3511 Carnegie Class: DRU
FAX Number: (909) 593-0965 Calendar System: Semester
URL: www.laverne.edu
Established: 1891 Annual Undergrad Tuition & Fees: $31,300
Enrollment: 9,562 Coed
Affiliation or Control: Independent Non-Profit IRS Status: 501(c)3
Highest Offering: Doctorate
Program: Liberal Arts And General; Teacher Preparatory; Professional
Accreditation: WC, CLPSY

01 President ... Dr. Devorah A. LIEBERMANPH.
05 Provost ... Dr. Gregory DEWEY
03 Executive Vice President ... Mr. Philip A. HAWKEY
30 Vice President Univ Advancement ... Dr. Jean BJERKE
20 Vice Provost ... Dr. Homa SHABAHANG
49 Dean College Arts & Sciences ... Dr. Jonathan REED
50 Dean College Business/Public Mgmt ... Dr. Ibrahim (Abe) HELOU
53 Dean College of Educ/Org Leadership ... Dr. Mark GOOR
61 Dean College of Law ... Dr. Allen K. EASLEY
32 Dean Student Affairs ... Dr. Loretta RAHMANI
84 Assoc VP Academic Sppt/Retent Svcs ... Ms. Adeline CARDENAS-CLAGUE
12 Dean Regional Campus Admin ... Dr. Stephen L. LESNIAK
10 Associate Vice President of Finance ... Ms. Lori K. GORDIEN CASE
21 Associate Vice Pres & Treasurer ... Mr. Avedis (Avo) KECHICHIAN
20 Assoc VP Academic/Faculty Affairs ... Dr. Alfred P. CLARK
09 Assoc VP University-Wide Assessment ... Dr. Aghop DER-KARABETIAN
07 Dean of Admissions ... Mr. Chris KRZAK
27 Chief Marketing Officer ... Mr. Fred A. CHYR
16 Chief Human Resources Officer ... Ms. Jody L. BOMBA
13 Chief Information Officer ... Dr. Clive K. HOUSTON-BROWN
35 Associate Dean Student Affairs ... Ms. Ruby S. MONTANO-CORDOVA
88 Asst Dean Grad Acad Supp/Ret Svcs ... Ms. Jo Nell BAKER
88 Director Intl Recruitment/Admission ... Dr. Jeffrey NONEMAKER
18 Dir Physical Plant Operations/Svs ... Mr. Robert D. BEEBE
37 Director of Financial Aid ... Ms. Leatha E. WEBSTER
26 Director of Public Relations ... Mr. Charles BENTLEY
29 Director Alumni Relations ... Ms. Beth ELMORE
38 Director Student Counseling ... Dr. Richard R. ROGERS
88 Director Student Accounts ... Ms. Xochitl E. MARTINEZ
104 Director Intl/Study Abroad Ctr ... Mr. Philip HOFER
96 Director of Purchasing ... Mrs. Deborah S. DEACY
28 Director Multicultural Affairs ... Mr. Daniel L. LOERA
23 Dir Health Svcs/Svcs for Stds-Disab ... Ms. Cynthia K. DENNE
39 Asst Dean/Dir Housing/Res Life Ed ... Mr. Juan REGALADO
36 Director Career Services ... Mrs. Paula E. VERDUGO
88 Int Dir Center Teaching/Learning ... Dr. Lisa R. RODRIGUEZ
19 Director Campus Safety ... Mr. Michael W. NUNEZ
41 Athletic Director ... Ms. Julie KLINE
06 Registrar ... Mrs. Marilyn S. DAVIES
08 University Librarian ... Ms. Vinaya L. TRIPURANENI

University of the Pacific (D)

3601 Pacific Avenue, Stockton CA 95211-0197
County: San Joaquin FICE Identification: 001329
Unit ID: 120883
Telephone: (209) 946-2011 Carnegie Class: DRU
FAX Number: (209) 946-2845 Calendar System: Semester
URL: www.pacific.edu
Established: 1851 Annual Undergrad Tuition & Fees: $16,290
Enrollment: 6,717 Coed
Affiliation or Control: Independent Non-Profit IRS Status: 501(c)3
Highest Offering: Doctorate
Program: Liberal Arts And General; Teacher Preparatory; Professional
Accreditation: WC, ART, BUS, CS, DENT, DH, ENG, LAW, MUS, PHAR, PTA, SP, TED

01 President ... Pamela A. EIBECK
05 Provost ... Maria G. PALLAVICINI
10 Vice President Business & Finance ... Patrick D. CAVANAUGH
32 Vice President Student Life ... Elizabeth B. GRIEGO
30 Vice President Development ... Chris JOHNSTON
26 Vice Pres External Relations ... Ted LELAND
101 VP & Secretary to Board of Regents ... Mary Lou LACKEY
21 Associate VP Business/Finance ... Larry BREHM
84 Assoc Provost for Enrollment Svcs ... Robert ALEXANDER
26 Assoc VP Marketing/Univ Relations ... Richard ROJO
51 Asst Provost Ctr Prof & Cont Educ ... Barbara L. SHAW
08 Dean of the Library ... C. Brigid WELCH
58 Dean Research/Graduate Studies ... Jin GONG
25 Sponsored Pgms Administrator ... Carol BRODIE
29 Exec Dir of Alumni Relations ... William COEN
37 Director of Financial Aid ... Lynn FOX
07 Director of Admissions ... Rich TOLEDO
06 Registrar ... Ann GILLEN
09 Director Institutional Research ... Mike ROGERS
35 Director Student Activities ... Jason VELO
96 Director of Purchasing ... Ronda MARR
92 Director Honors Program ... George RANDELS
93 Director Multicultural Affairs ... Ines RUIZ-HUSTON
94 Director Gender Studies ... Becky BEAL
38 Director of Counseling Services ... Stacie TURKS
39 Director of Housing ... Steven JACOBSON
36 Director of Career Resource Center ... Diane FARRELL
41 Director of Athletics ... Lynn KING
42 University Chaplain ... Donna MCNIEL
13 Chief Information Officer ... Malik RAHMAN
15 Director of Human Resources ... Jane L. LEWIS
40 Director of Bookstore ... Nicole CASTILLO
19 Director of Public Safety ... Michael BELCHER
18 Director of Physical Plant ... Scott HEATON
28 Dir of Div/Asst to Prov for Acad ... Arturo OCAMPO
61 Dean McGeorge School of Law .. Elizabeth RINDSKOPF PARKER
54 Dean Sch of Eng/Comp Science ... Ravi JAIN
67 Dean Sch of Pharm/Hlth Sciences ... Phillip R. OPPENHEIMER
64 Dean Conservatory of Music ... Giulio ONGARO
52 Dean School of Dentistry ... Patrick FERRILLO
53 Dean School of Education ... Lynn BECK
49 Dean College of the Pacific ... Tom KRISE
50 Dean School Business/Public Admin ... Lewis GALE
82 Int Dean Sch International Studies ... Cynthia WAGNER WEICK

University of Philosophical Research (E)

3910 Los Feliz Boulevard, Los Angeles CA 90027
County: Los Angeles Identification: 666373
Telephone: (323) 663-2167 Carnegie Class: Not Classified
FAX Number: (323) 663-9443 Calendar System: Quarter
URL: www.uprs.edu
Established: 1998 Annual Graduate Tuition & Fees: $5,500
Enrollment: 205 Coed
Affiliation or Control: Independent Non-Profit IRS Status: 501(c)3
Highest Offering: Master's; No Undergraduates
Program: Liberal Arts And General
Accreditation: DETC

01 President/Chief Executive Officer ... Dr. Obadiah HARRIS
05 Dean of Academic Affairs ... Dr. Debashish BANERJI
06 Registrar ... Ms. Maja D'AOUST

University of Redlands (F)

PO Box 3080, Redlands CA 92373-0999
County: San Bernardino FICE Identification: 001322
Unit ID: 121691
Telephone: (909) 793-2121 Carnegie Class: Master's L
FAX Number: (909) 793-2029 Calendar System: Semester
URL: www.redlands.edu
Established: 1907 Annual Undergrad Tuition & Fees: $37,302
Enrollment: 4,431 Coed
Affiliation or Control: Independent Non-Profit IRS Status: 501(c)3
Highest Offering: Doctorate
Program: Liberal Arts And General; Teacher Preparatory; Professional
Accreditation: WC, MUS, SP

01 President ... Dr. James R. APPLETON
03 Executive Vice President/COO ... Mr. Phillip L. DOOLITTLE
05 Vice President Academic Affairs ... Dr. David FITE
26 Vice President University Relations ... Mr. Neil A. MACREADY
32 Vice President/Dean Student Life ... Ms. Charlotte G. BURGESS
27 Vice Pres Mktg/Strategic Commun ... Ms. Gail GUGE
30 Assoc Vice Pres Development ... Mr. Ray WATTS
84 Assoc Vice Pres of Enrollment Mgmt ... Ms. Nancy SVENSON
91 Assoc VP Integrated Tech Sys/CIO ... Mr. Hamid ETESAMNIA
10 Treasurer/Chief Financial Officer ... Mr. Cory NOMURA
21 Director Financial Ops & Controller ... Ms. Patricia M. CAUDLE
58 Dean School of Business ... Dr. Stuart NOBLE-GOODMAN
53 Dean School of Education ... Dr. James VALADEZ
49 Interim Dean Arts & Sciences ... Dr. Kathy OGREN
07 Dean of Admiss/Col Arts & Science ... Mr. Paul M. DRISCOLL
28 Asc Dean Campus Diversity/Inclusion .. Ms. Leela MADHAVARAU
42 Chaplain ... Rev. John T. WALSH
06 Registrar ... Ms. Patricia G. HALL
104 Director Study Abroad ... Ms. Sarah N. FALKENSTIEN
37 Interim Director of Financial Aid ... Ms. Lisa VAN MEETEREN
90 Dir Academic Computing/Instruct ... Vacant
64 Dean School of Music ... Dr. Andrew GLENDENING
81 Director Center of Sciences & Math ... Dr. Barbara M. MURRAY
88 Director of Environmental Programs ... Dr. Lamont C. HEMPEL
08 Director of Library Services ... Ms. Gabriela SONNTAG
15 Director of Human Resources ... Ms. Roberta G. DELLHIME
22 EEO & Employee Relations Manager ... Vacant
09 Director of Institutional Research ... Ms. Wendy MCEWEN
19 Director of Public Safety ... Mr. Jeffrey TALBOTT
18 Interim Director of Physical Plant ... Mr. Roger CELLINI
29 Director of Alumni Relations ... Mr. John SERBEIN
20 Director of Acad Support Services ... Vacant
38 Director Student Counseling ... Mr. Ruben ROBLES
41 Director of Athletics ... Mr. Jeffrey MARTINEZ
96 Director of Purchasing ... Ms. Sandi TAYLOR
36 Director Student Placement ... Ms. Kathryn WOOD

University of San Diego (A)

5998 Alcala Park, San Diego CA 92110-2492
County: San Diego — FICE Identification: 010395
Unit ID: 122436
Telephone: (619) 260-4600 — Carnegie Class: DRU
FAX Number: (619) 260-6833 — Calendar System: 4/1/4
URL: www.sandiego.edu
Established: 1949 — Annual Undergrad Tuition & Fees: $38,582
Enrollment: 8,201 — Coed
Affiliation or Control: Roman Catholic — IRS Status: 501(c)3
Highest Offering: Doctorate
Program: Liberal Arts And General; Teacher Preparatory; Professional
Accreditation: WC, BUS, BUSA, CACREP, ENG, IPSY, LAW, MFCD, NURSE, TED

01 President ... Dr. Mary E. LYONS
04 Special Assistant to the President ... Ms. Elaine ATENCIO
05 Executive Vice President & Provost ... Dr. Julie H. SULLIVAN
10 Vice Pres Business Services & Admin ... Mr. Leendert R. HERING
42 Vice President Mission & Ministry ... Msgr. Daniel J. DILLABOUGH
32 Vice President Student Affairs ... Ms. Carmen M. VAZQUEZ
30 Vice President Univ Relations ... Dr. Timothy L. O'MALLEY
49 Dean College of Arts & Sciences ... Dr. Mary K. BOYD
50 Dean School of Business Admin ... Dr. David F. PYKE
61 Dean School of Law ... Mr. Stephen FERRUOLO
53 Dean Sch Leadership/Educ Sciences ... Dr. Paula A. CORDEIRO
66 Dean School Nursing/Health Science ... Dr. Sally B. HARDIN
88 Dean School of Peace Studies ... Fr. William R. HEADLEY
51 Dean Prof & Continuing Education ... Dr. Jason LEMON
35 Dean of Student Affairs ... Dr. Donald GODWIN
20 Associate Provost ... Dr. Thomas R. HERRINTON
20 Associate Provost ... Dr. Andrew T. ALLEN
20 Assoc Provost International Affairs ... Dr. Kimberly EHERENMAN
28 Assoc Provost for Incl & Diversity ... Dr. Carlton FLOYD
13 Vice Provost & Chief Info Officer ... Mr. Christopher W. WESSELLS
41 Executive Director Athletics ... Mr. Ky L. SNYDER
21 Assoc Vice Pres Business Svcs/ Admin ... Ms. Patricia T. OLIVER PUTNAM
16 Chief Human Resources Officer ... Dr. David M. BLAKE
18 Asst VP Facilities Management ... Mr. Roger G. MANION
26 Asst Vice Pres Public Affairs ... Ms. Pamela GRAY PAYTON
19 Asst Vice President Public Safety ... Mr. Larry E. BARNETT
43 General Counsel ... Ms. Kelly C. DOUGLAS
06 University Registrar ... Ms. Susan H. BUGBEE
07 Director of Admissions & Enrollment ... Mr. Stephen F. PULTZ
08 University Librarian ... Dr. Theresa BYRD
09 Exec Dir Inst Research & Planning ... Dr. Cel JOHNSON
54 Director Engineering ... Dr. Kathleen A. KRAMER
90 Senior Director Academic Tech Svcs ... Ms. Shahra MESHKATY
91 Dir Administrative Info Services ... Ms. Indra BISHOP
102 Sr Director Foundation Relations ... Ms. Annette KETNER
86 Sr Dir Community/Govt Relations ... Mr. Thomas R. CLEARY
44 Senior Director Planned Giving ... Mr. John A. PHILLIPS
29 Director Alumni Relations ... Mr. Charles BASS
44 Director Annual Giving ... Mr. Philip GARLAND
40 Director Bookstore ... Ms. Katherine MISSELL
36 Director Career Services ... Ms. Linda M. SCALES
38 Director Counseling Center ... Dr. Stephen D. SPRINKLE
37 Director Financial Aid Services ... Ms. Judith LEWIS LOGUE
92 Director of Honors Program ... Dr. James P. BOLENDER
39 Director Housing ... Mr. Rick HAGAN
85 Dir International Students/Scholars ... Ms. Yvette M. FONTAINE
104 Dir International Studies Abroad ... Ms. Kira A. ESPIRITU

93 Director Multicultural Center ... Dr. Mayte PEREZ-FRANCO
27 Senior Director Media Relations ... Ms. Elizabeth HARMAN
96 Director Procurement Services ... Ms. Dawn L. ANDERSON
25 Director Sponsored Programs ... Ms. Kim EUDY
23 Director Student Health Center ... Ms. Pamela J. SIKES

University of San Francisco (B)

2130 Fulton Street, San Francisco CA 94117-1080
County: San Francisco — FICE Identification: 001325
Unit ID: 122612
Telephone: (415) 422-5555 — Carnegie Class: DRU
FAX Number: (415) 422-2303 — Calendar System: 4/1/4
URL: www.usfca.edu
Established: 1855 — Annual Undergrad Tuition & Fees: $37,424
Enrollment: 9,557 — Coed
Affiliation or Control: Roman Catholic — IRS Status: 501(c)3
Highest Offering: Doctorate
Program: Liberal Arts And General; Teacher Preparatory; Professional
Accreditation: WC, BUS, LAW, NURSE

01 President ... Rev. Stephen A. PRIVETT, SJ
05 Provost/Vice Pres Academic Affairs ... Dr. Jennifer E. TURPIN
00 Chancellor ... Rev. John J. LO SCHIAVO, SJ
10 Vice President Business & Finance ... Mr. Charles E. CROSS
26 Vice Pres for Communications ... Mr. David F. MACMILLAN
30 Vice President Development ... Mr. George B. ATTERBURY
32 Vice Provost University Life ... Dr. Peter J. NOVAK
43 University Counsel ... Ms. Donna J. DAVIS
20 Vice Provost ... Dr. Gerardo MARIN
20 Vice Provost ... Dr. Salvador D. ACEVES
20 Vice Provost/Dean Academic Svcs ... Dr. Elizabeth J. JOHNSON
15 Asst Vice Pres Human Resource ... Ms. Martha A. PEUGH-WADE
21 Asst Vice Pres Financial Reporting ... Ms. Kimberly L. KVAAL
18 Asst Vice Pres Facilities Mgmt ... Mr. Michael LONDON
28 Assoc Vice Provost Diversity ... Dr. Mary J. WARDELL
42 Director University Ministry ... Ms. Julia A. DOWD
04 Exec Assistant to the President ... Ms. Jaci E. NEESAM
08 Dean of Libraries ... Mr. Tyrone H. CANNON
37 Assoc Dean Acad Svcs/Dir Fin Aid ... Ms. Susan L. MURPHY
06 Assoc Dean University Registrar ... Mr. Robert L. BROMFIELD
85 Dir International Student Services ... Ms. Lisa KOSIEWICZ
41 Executive Director of Athletics ... Mr. Scott A. SIDWELL
07 Director of Admissions ... Mr. Michael HUGHES
09 Director of Institutional Research ... Dr. Alan L. ZIAJKA
36 Director of Career Services ... Mr. James CATIGGAY
29 Director of Alumni Relations ... Ms. Annette M. ANTON
13 Chief Info Officer/Info Tech Svcs ... Mr. Stephen GALLAGHER
26 Director of Media Relations ... Mr. Gary MCDONALD
38 Director Counseling Center ... Dr. Barbara J. THOMAS
19 Director of Public Safety ... Mr. Daniel LAWSON
39 Director of Residence Life ... Mr. Steve NYGAARD
24 Dir Ctr for Instruction/Technology ... Dr. John BANSAVICH
96 Director of Purchasing ... Ms. Janet L. TEYMOURTASH
35 Chief Student Life Officer ... Dr. Peter J. NOVAK
88 Asst Human Resources Director ... Ms. Diane L. NELSON
50 Actg Dean School of Management ... Dr. Mike WEBBER
49 Act Dean College Arts & Sciences ... Dr. Marcelo F. CAMPERI
53 Dean School of Education ... Dr. Walter H. GMELCH
66 Dean School of Nursing ... Dr. Judith KARSHMER
61 Dean of the School of Law ... Mr. Jeffrey S. BRAND

University of Southern California (C)

University Park, Los Angeles CA 90089-0012
County: Los Angeles — FICE Identification: 001328
Unit ID: 123961
Telephone: (213) 740-2311 — Carnegie Class: RU/VH
FAX Number: (213) 740-8502 — Calendar System: Semester
URL: www.usc.edu
Established: 1880 — Annual Undergrad Tuition & Fees: $42,162
Enrollment: 36,896 — Coed
Affiliation or Control: Independent Non-Profit — IRS Status: 501(c)3
Highest Offering: Doctorate
Program: Occupational; Liberal Arts And General; Teacher Preparatory; Professional
Accreditation: WC, ANEST, ARCPA, BUS, BUSA, CEA, CLPSY, CS, DENT, DH, DIETI, ENG, HSA, IPSY, JOUR, LAW, LSAR, MED, MUS, OT, PDPSY, PH, PHAR, PLNG, PTA, SPAA, SW

01 President ... Dr. C.L M. NIKIAS
05 Provost and Sr VP Academic Affairs ... Prof. Elizabeth GARRETT
03 Sr Vice Pres Administration ... Mr. Todd R. DICKEY
10 Sr Vice President & CFO ... Mr. Robert ABELES
26 Sr Vice Pres University Relations ... Mr. Thomas SAYLES
30 SR VP University Advancement ... Mr. Albert R. CHECCIO
30 VP for Development ... Ms. Courtney SURLS
43 General Counsel/Secretary of Univ ... Ms. Carol MAUCH AMIR
32 Vice President Student Affairs ... Dr. Michael L. JACKSON
07 VP Admissions and Planning ... Dr. L. Katharine HARRINGTON
46 VP for Research ... Dr. Randolph W. HALL
21 Chief Investment Officer ... Ms. Lisa MAZZOCCO
45 Vice Pres Academic Planning/Budget ... Vacant
41 Athletic Director ... Mr. Patrick C. HADEN
100 Chief of Staff/Chief of Protocol ... Mr. Dennis CORNELL
88 Dean Leventhal School of Accounting ... Dr. William W. HOLDER
60 Dean Annenberg Sch Communications . Dr. Ernest J. WILSON, III
48 Dean School of Architecture ... Mr. Qingyun MA
50 Dean Marshall School of Business ... Mr. James G. ELLIS
88 Dean School of Cinematic Arts ... Dr. Elizabeth M. DALEY
52 Dean School of Dentistry ... Dr. Avishai SADAN
53 Dean Rossier School of Education ... Dr. Karen S. GALLAGHER
54 Dean Viterbi School of Engineering ... Dr. Yannis C. YORTSOS
57 Dean Roski School of Fine Arts ... Dr. Rochelle STEINER
88 Dean Davis School of Gerontology ... Dr. Gerald C. DAVISON
61 Dean Gould School of Law ... Mr. Robert K. RASMUSSEN
63 Dean Keck School of Medicine ... Dr. Carmen A. PULIAFITO
64 Dean Thornton School of Music ... Dr. Robert A. CUTIETTA
67 Dean School of Pharmacy ... Dr. R. Pete L. VANDERVEEN
70 Dean School of Social Work ... Dr. Marilyn L. FLYNN
88 Dean School of Theatre ... Ms. Madeline PUZO
88 Dean School of Policy/Plng/Devel ... Dr. Jack H. KNOTT
49 Dean Dornsife Col Ltrs Arts & Sci ... Dr. Howard GILLMAN
42 Dean Religious Life ... Mr. Varun SONI
06 Dean Academic Records & Registrar ... Vacant
08 Dean University Libraries ... Ms. Catherine QUINLAN
07 Dean of Admission ... Mr. Timothy BRUNOLD
21 Asc Sr VP Financial & Business Svcs ... Mr. Robert V. JOHNSON
36 Assoc Sr VP Career/Protective Svcs ... Dr. Charles E. LANE
21 Assoc Sr VP/University Comptroller ... Mr. Erik D. BRINK
27 Assoc Sr Vice Pres Public Relations ... Ms. Nicole MALEC
29 Assoc Sr VP and CEO Alumni Assn ... Mr. Scott M. MORY
18 Assoc VP Facilities Management Svcs ... Vacant
18 Assoc VP Facilities Mgmt Svcs ... Mr. John WELSH
36 Asst VP Career Services ... Dr. Mary K. CAMPBELL
36 Exec Dir Career Plng/Placement ... Ms. Eileen B. KOHAN
28 Exec Dir Office of Equity/Diversity ... Vacant
38 Director Student Counseling Service ... Dr. Ilene ROSENSTEIN
96 Director of Purchasing Services ... Ms. Juliana H. HUEHN-JOHNSON
15 Director Personnel Services ... Ms. Maria E. CHACON
07 Vice Provost/Enrollment Policy/Mgmt ... Vacant
20 Executive Vice Provost ... Dr. Michael W. QUICK
20 Vice Provost Faculty Affairs ... Dr. Martin L. LEVINE
20 Vice Prov for Graduate Programs ... Dr. Sarah PRATT
20 Vice Prov for Undergraduate Program ... Dr. Eugene N. BICKERS
27 Vice Prov for Info Tech Svcs/CIO ... Mr. Ilee RHIMES
20 Vice Prov for Planning and Budget ... Mr. Robert A. COOPER
20 Vice Prov for Innovation ... Ms. Krisztina HOLLY
20 Vice Prov for Global Initiatives ... Dr. Kenneth J. MCGILLIVRAY
20 Vice Prov for Faculty & Pgm Devel ... Dr. Beth MEYEROWITZ

University of the West (D)

1409 Walnut Grove Avenue, Rosemead CA 91770-3709
County: Los Angeles — FICE Identification: 036963
Unit ID: 449870
Telephone: (626) 571-8811 — Carnegie Class: Bac/Diverse
FAX Number: (626) 571-1413 — Calendar System: Semester
URL: www.uwest.edu
Established: 1991 — Annual Undergrad Tuition & Fees: $12,990
Enrollment: 216 — Coed
Affiliation or Control: Independent Non-Profit — IRS Status: 501(c)3
Highest Offering: Doctorate
Program: Liberal Arts And General
Accreditation: WC

01 President ... Dr. Chin Shun WU
04 Special Advisor to President ... Dr. Arthur PETERSON
05 Dean of Academic Affairs ... Dr. William HOWE
84 Dean of Enrollment and Students ... Mr. Heemanshu BHAGAT
10 Exec Dir Finance/Administration ... Mr. Jeffrey LIN
08 Director of Library ... Ms. Ling Ling KUO
06 Registrar ... Mrs. Carmela CHANEY
07 Admissions Officer ... Ms. Grace HSIAO
39 Residential Student Life Coord ... Ven. De HONG
73 Chair Dept of Religious Studies ... Dr. Kenneth LOCKE
50 Chair Dept of Business Admin ... Dr. Bill CHEN

Vanguard University of Southern California (E)

55 Fair Drive, Costa Mesa CA 92626-6597
County: Orange — FICE Identification: 001293
Unit ID: 123651
Telephone: (714) 556-3610 — Carnegie Class: Bac/Diverse
FAX Number: (714) 957-9317 — Calendar System: Semester
URL: www.vanguard.edu
Established: 1920 — Annual Undergrad Tuition & Fees: $27,675
Enrollment: 1,961 — Coed
Affiliation or Control: Assemblies Of God Church — IRS Status: 501(c)3
Highest Offering: Master's
Program: Liberal Arts And General; Teacher Preparatory; Professional
Accreditation: WC, NURSE, THEA

01 President ... Dr. Carol A. TAYLOR
04 Exec Assistant to the President ... Ms. Shree CARTER
05 Provost/Vice President Acad Affairs ... Dr. Jeff HITTENBERGER
20 Assoc Provost/Dean Col Arts & Sci ... Dr. Michael D. WILSON
107 Director Sch Professional Studies ... Ms. Jamie BROWNLEE
73 Director for Graduate Religion ... Dr. Richard ISRAEL
53 Director for Graduate Education ... Dr. Doug GROVE
83 Director for Graduate Psychology ... Dr. Jerre WHITE
06 Registrar ... Ms. Judy HAMILTON
09 Director of Institutional Research ... Dr. Ludmilla PRASLOVA
08 Head Librarian ... Ms. Alison ENGLISH
41 Athletic Director ... Mr. Bob WILSON
10 Vice President Business/Finance ... Ms. Lettie COWIE
21 Director of Business Services ... Vacant
19 Director of Campus Safety Services ... Mr. Paul TURGEON
27 Chief Information Officer ... Mr. Derek DENSBERGER
15 Director of Human Resources ... Mr. Joe BAFFA
18 Director of Facility Services ... Mr. Bruce CROUCH
40 Bookstore Manager ... Ms. Carol KING

32 Vice President Student Affairs ... Dr. Ann HAMILTON
42 Campus Pastor ... Dr. Vince BERESFORD
39 Director of Residence Life ... Mr. Tim YOUNG
39 Student Housing Coordinator ... Ms. Allison HESSE
24 Director of Learning Skills ... Ms. Barbi ROUSE
38 Director of Counseling Services ... Dr. Beth LORANCE
36 Dir of Career Planning/Placement ... Mr. Hassan ARCHER
84 VP for Enrollment Management ... Ms. Kim JOHNSON
07 Director of Undergrad Admissions ... Vacant
07 Director of Graduate Admissions ... Mr. Drake LEVASHEFF
37 Director of Student Financial Svcs ... Ms. Robyn FOURNIER
30 VP University Advancement ... Ms. Kelly KANNWISCHER
29 Director of Alumni Relations ... Mr. Joel GACKLE
26 Chief Communications Officer ... Ms. Kelly KANNWISCHER
86 Director of Veteran/Government Rels ... Mr. Brent THEOBALD

*Ventura County Community College District (A)

255 W Stanley Avenue, Suite 150,
Ventura CA 93001-1348
County: Ventura — FICE Identification: 006863
Unit ID: 125019
Telephone: (805) 652-5500 — Carnegie Class: N/A
FAX Number: (805) 652-7700
URL: www.vcccd.edu

01 Chancellor ... Dr. James MEZNEK
10 Vice Chanc Business Svcs/Fin Mgmt ... Ms. Susan JOHNSON
15 Vice Chanc of Human Resources ... Ms. Patricia PARHAM

*Moorpark College (B)

7075 Campus Road, Moorpark CA 93021-1695
County: Ventura — FICE Identification: 007115
Unit ID: 119137
Telephone: (805) 378-1400 — Carnegie Class: Assoc/Pub-U-MC
FAX Number: (805) 378-1499 — Calendar System: Semester
URL: www.moorparkcollege.edu
Established: 1967 — Annual Undergrad Tuition & Fees (In-State): $898
Enrollment: 15,379 — Coed
Affiliation or Control: State — IRS Status: 501(c)3
Highest Offering: Associate Degree
Program: Occupational; 2-Year Principally Bachelor's Creditable
Accreditation: WJ, ADNUR, RAD

02 President ... Dr. Pam EDDINGER
03 Executive Vice President ... Mr. Edward KNUDSON
10 Vice President Business Services ... Ms. Iris INGRAM
04 Executive Assistant to President ... Ms. Louise CHRISTENER
66 Dean Student Learning ... Ms. Lori BENNETT
57 Dean Student Learning ... Ms. Patricia EWINS
50 Dean Student Learning ... Dr. Kim HOFFMANS
88 Dean of Student Learning ... Dr. Lisa MILLER
79 Dean Student Learning ... Ms. Inajane NICKLAS
49 Dean Student Learning ... Dr. Julius SOKENU
18 Director Maintainence/Operations ... Mr. John SINUTKO
88 College Business Services Manager ... Ms. Darlene MELBY
41 Athletic Director ... Mr. Howard DAVIS
06 Registrar ... Ms. Kathy COLBORN
37 Student Financial Aid Officer ... Vacant

*Oxnard College (C)

4000 S Rose Avenue, Oxnard CA 93033-6699
County: Ventura — FICE Identification: 012842
Unit ID: 120421
Telephone: (805) 986-5800 — Carnegie Class: Assoc/Pub-U-MC
FAX Number: (805) 986-5908 — Calendar System: Semester
URL: www.oxnardcollege.edu
Established: 1975 — Annual Undergrad Tuition & Fees (In-District): $1,054
Enrollment: 7,918 — Coed
Affiliation or Control: State/Local — IRS Status: 501(c)3
Highest Offering: Associate Degree
Program: Occupational; 2-Year Principally Bachelor's Creditable
Accreditation: WJ, DH

02 President ... Dr. Richard DURAN
05 Exec Vice Pres of Student Learning ... Dr. Erika ENDRIJONAS
11 Vice President of Business Services ... Dr. John AL-AMIN
32 Dean of Student Services ... Dr. Karen ENGELSEN
79 Dean Liberal Studies ... Ms. Marjorie PRICE
41 Director of Athletics ... Mr. Jonas CRAWFORD
88 Dean Career &Technical Education ... Ms. Carmen GUERRERO
81 Dean Math Science/Health ... Dr. Carolyn INOUYE
18 Director Maintenance/Operations ... Mr. Will DEITS
40 Bookstore Manager ... Ms. Diane RAUSCH
06 Registrar ... Ms. Susan CABRAL
88 Director STEM ... Dr. Cynthia HERRERA

*Ventura College (D)

4667 Telegraph Road, Ventura CA 93003-3899
County: Ventura — FICE Identification: 001334
Unit ID: 125028
Telephone: (805) 654-6400 — Carnegie Class: Assoc/Pub-U-MC
FAX Number: (805) 654-6466 — Calendar System: Semester
URL: www.venturacollege.edu
Established: 1925 — Annual Undergrad Tuition & Fees (In-District): $818
Enrollment: 13,711 — Coed
Affiliation or Control: State/Local — IRS Status: 501(c)3
Highest Offering: Associate Degree
Program: Occupational; 2-Year Principally Bachelor's Creditable
Accreditation: WJ, EMT

02 President ... Dr. Robin CALOTE
05 Exec Vice Pres Student Learning ... Dr. Ramiro SANCHEZ
10 Vice President Business Services ... Mr. David KEEBLER
04 Exec Assistant to the President ... Ms. Laura BROWER
75 Dean Career & Tech Education ... Vacant
50 Dean Economic Dev/Off-Campus Pgm ... Vacant
60 Dean Communication/Learning Res Ctr ... Ms. Kathleen SCOTT
81 Dean Mathematics & Sciences ... Mr. David OLIVER
68 Dean Physical Education/Athletics ... Mr. Tim HARRISON
83 Dean Social Sciences/Humanities ... Ms. Gwen HUDDLESTON
38 Dean Student Services ... Ms. Victoria LUGO
88 Asst Dean Career Tech Education ... Ms. Karen GORBACK
106 Asst Dean Distance Education ... Vacant
31 Asst Dean Economic Development ... Dr. Karen GORBACK
32 Asst Dean Student Services ... Mr. David BRANSKY
30 Executive Director Foundation ... Mr. Norbert N. TAN
102 Director Development Foundation ... Ms. Diana DUNBAR
06 Registrar ... Ms. Susan BRICKER
18 Director Maintenance/Operations ... Mr. Robert FOREST
35 Coordinator Student Activities ... Mr. Rick TREVINO
37 Financial Aid Officer ... Ms. Audren MORRIS
13 Director Institutional Technology ... Mr. Rick SHAW
09 Institutional Research ... Mr. Michael CALLAHAN
85 International Students ... Ms. Rosie STUTTS
12 Coordinator Off Campus Programs ... Dr. Art SANDFORD
25 Coordinator Resource Development ... Mr. Gary VAN METER
103 Dir Center of Excellence ... Ms. Sharon DWYER
84 Enrollment Management ... Ms. Connie BAKER
23 Director Student Health Center ... Ms. Elaine TENNEN
19 Campus Police ... Lt. Robert ESCOBEDO

Victor Valley College (E)

18422 Bear Valley Road, Victorville CA 92395-5850
County: San Bernardino — FICE Identification: 001335
Unit ID: 125091
Telephone: (760) 245-4271 — Carnegie Class: Assoc/Pub-S-SC
FAX Number: (760) 245-9744 — Calendar System: Semester
URL: www.vvc.edu
Established: 1961 — Annual Undergrad Tuition & Fees (In-District): $36
Enrollment: 13,198 — Coed
Affiliation or Control: State/Local — IRS Status: 501(c)3
Highest Offering: Associate Degree
Program: Occupational; 2-Year Principally Bachelor's Creditable
Accreditation: #WJ, EMT

01 Superintendent/President ... Dr. Christopher O'HEARN
05 Int Exec VP/Instruction/Stdnt Svcs ... Mr. Peter ALLAN
11 Vice President Admin Services ... Dr. G. H. JAVAHERIPOUR
15 Vice President Human Resources ... Ms. Fusako YOKOTOBI
76 Dean Health Science & Public Safety ... Dr. Patricia LUTHER
81 Dean STEM ... Dr. Lori KILDAL
79 Dean Acad Pgms Humanities/Soc Sci ... Dr. Paul WILLIAMS
75 Dean Vocational Education ... Vacant
21 Director Fiscal Services ... Mrs. Mary PRINGLE
07 Director of Admissions ... Mrs. Greta MOON
26 Director Public Info & Marketing ... Mr. William GREULICH
41 Director Athletics/Athletic Trainer ... Mrs. Jaye TASHIMA
18 Director Maintenance/Operations ... Mr. Christopher HYLTON
37 Director Financial Aid ... Vacant
13 Director MIS ... Ms. Deanna TURNBEAU
40 Director Auxiliary Services/ASB Adv ... Mr. Robert SEWELL
35 Dean Student Services ... Dr. Tim JOHNSTON
18 Director Facilities Construction ... Mr. Steve GARCIA
19 Chief Campus Police ... Mr. Leonard KNIGHT
72 Exec Dean Technology/Info Resource ... Mr. Frank SMITH
22 Dir Disabled Student/ADA Compl Ofcr ... Vacant
88 Director Child Development Center ... Ms. Kelley JOHNSON
88 Dir Extended Optnty Pgms/Svcs/CARE ... Mr. Carl SMITH
09 Exec Dean Inst Effectiveness ... Mrs. Virginia MORAN
55 Dir Evening Opers/Inst Support Pgm ... Mr. Rolando REGINO

West Coast Ultrasound Institute (F)

291 S. La Cienega Blvd, Ste 500, Beverly Hills CA 90211
County: Los Angeles — FICE Identification: 036393
Unit ID: 441229
Telephone: (310) 289-5123 — Carnegie Class: Not Classified
FAX Number: (310) 289-5136 — Calendar System: Quarter
URL: www.wcui.edu
Established: 1998 — Annual Undergrad Tuition & Fees: $22,339
Enrollment: 834 — Coed
Affiliation or Control: Proprietary — IRS Status: Proprietary
Highest Offering: Associate Degree
Program: Occupational
Accreditation: ACCSC

01 Campus Director ... Ms. Mele KRAMER

West Coast University (G)

12215 Victory Boulevard, North Hollywood CA 91606-3206
County: Los Angeles — FICE Identification: 036983
Unit ID: 443331
Telephone: (818) 299-5500 — Carnegie Class: Spec/Health
FAX Number: (818) 299-5545 — Calendar System: Semester
URL: www.westcoastuniversity.edu
Established: 1909 — Annual Undergrad Tuition & Fees: $33,544
Enrollment: 830 — Coed
Affiliation or Control: Proprietary — IRS Status: Proprietary
Highest Offering: Master's
Program: Professional
Accreditation: ACICS, DH, NURSE

01 President ... Dr. Barry T. RYAN
03 Executive Director ... Mr. Ladd GRAHAM
05 Provost ... Dr. Jeb EGBERT
11 Associate Provost/Administration ... Mr. Wayne FLETCHER
66 Dean of Nursing-Los Angeles Campus ... Dr. Rosanne CURTIS
20 Academic Dean ... Dr. Miriam KAHAN
66 Dean of Nursing-Ontario Campus ... Dr. Cathy EARL

*West Hills Community College District (H)

9900 Cody Street, Coalinga CA 93210
County: Fresno — Identification: 667041
Telephone: (559) 934-2100 — Carnegie Class: N/A
FAX Number: (559) 934-2810
URL: www.westhillscollege.com

01 Chancellor ... Dr. Frank P. GORNICK
09 VC Inst Effect/Enrollment Mgmt ... Mr. Pedro AVILA
05 VC Educ Svcs/Workforce Development ... Dr. Carole GOLDSMITH
10 Vice Chancellor Business Services ... Mr. Ken STOPPENBRINK
102 Exec Director WHCC Foundation ... Ms. Frances SQUIRE
90 Assoc VC Academic & Info Systems ... Mr. Keith STEARNS
15 Director of Human Resources ... Vacant
37 Director of Financial Aid ... Vacant
21 Director of Fiscal Services ... Ms. Tammy WEATHERMAN
26 Director of Marketing ... Vacant
25 Director of Grants ... Ms. Cathy BARABE
25 Director of Special Grant Programs ... Mr. David CASTILLO
103 Director of Special Grant Programs ... Mr. Robert PIMENTEL
25 Director of Special Grant Programs ... Mr. Riley TALFORD
25 Director of Special Grant Programs ... Ms. Anita WRIGHT
13 Director of Info Tech Services ... Ms. Michelle KOZLOWSKI
88 Director of Child Dev Centers ... Ms. Kathy WATTS

*West Hills College Coalinga (I)

300 Cherry Lane, Coalinga CA 93210-1399
County: Fresno — FICE Identification: 001176
Unit ID: 125462
Telephone: (559) 934-2000 — Carnegie Class: Assoc/Pub-S-MC
FAX Number: N/A — Calendar System: Semester
URL: www.westhillscollege.com/coalinga
Established: 1932 — Annual Undergrad Tuition & Fees (In-District): $624
Enrollment: 2,493 — Coed
Affiliation or Control: State/Local — IRS Status: 501(c)3
Highest Offering: Associate Degree
Program: Occupational; 2-Year Principally Bachelor's Creditable; Business Emphasis
Accreditation: WJ

02 President ... Dr. Willard LEWALLEN
05 Vice President of Educational Svcs ... Ms. Jill STEARNS
32 Vice President of Student Services ... Mr. Marlon HALL
35 Assoc Dean of Student Services ... Mr. Mark GRITTON
20 Assoc Dean of Student Learning ... Ms. Raquel RODRIGUEZ
88 Director of CAMP Grant ... Mr. Eliseo GAMINO
47 Director of Farm of the Future ... Mr. Richard LARSON
85 Dir of International Student Srvcs ... Mr. Daniel TAMAYO
88 Director of Title IV Projects ... Ms. Bertha FELIX-MATA
12 Director of North District Center ... Dr. Marcel HETU
17 District Director of Health Careers ... Mr. Charles FREEMAN

*West Hills College Lemoore (J)

555 College Avenue, Lemoore CA 93245-9248
County: Kings — FICE Identification: 041113
Unit ID: 448594
Telephone: (559) 925-3000 — Carnegie Class: Assoc/Pub-R-M
FAX Number: (559) 924-1243 — Calendar System: Semester
URL: www.westhillscollege.com/lemoore
Established: 2002 — Annual Undergrad Tuition & Fees (In-District): $864
Enrollment: 3,229 — Coed
Affiliation or Control: State/Local — IRS Status: 501(c)3
Highest Offering: Associate Degree
Program: Occupational; 2-Year Principally Bachelor's Creditable; Business Emphasis
Accreditation: WJ

02 President ... Mr. Don WARKENTIN
05 Vice President of Educational Svcs ... Mr. Dave BOLT
32 Vice President of Student Services ... Ms. Sylvia DORSEY-ROBINSON
35 Dean of Student Services ... Mr. Jose LOPEZ
20 Interim Dean of Educational Svcs ... Mr. James PRESTON
88 Dean of Categorical Programs ... Mr. Joel RUBLE
17 District Director of Health Careers ... Mr. Charles FREEMAN
41 Dir of Athletics/Health/Physical Ed ... Mr. Bob CLEMENT

*West Valley-Mission Community College District (K)

14000 Fruitvale Avenue, Saratoga CA 95070-5698
County: Santa Clara — FICE Identification: 029139
Unit ID: 125222
Telephone: (408) 741-2011 — Carnegie Class: N/A
FAX Number: (408) 867-8273
URL: www.wvm.edu

01 Chancellor .... Mr. John E. HENDRICKSON
11 Vice Chancellor Admin Services .... Mr. Ed MADULI
15 Assoc Vice Chanc Human Resources .... Mr. Brad DAVIS
14 Director Information Systems .... Mr. Ron SMITH
18 Director of Facilities .... Mr. Javier CASTRUITA
30 Dean Advancement .... Ms. Cynthia SCHELCHER
19 Interim Director Public Safety .... Mr. Chris ROLEN
26 Director Public Affs/Community Rels .... Vacant
04 Special Assistant to the Chancellor .... Mr. Albert MOORE

*Mission College (A)

3000 Mission College Boulevard,
Santa Clara CA 95054-1897

County: Santa Clara — FICE Identification: 021191 — Unit ID: 118930
Telephone: (408) 988-2200 — Carnegie Class: Assoc/Pub-S-MC
FAX Number: (408) 496-0462 — Calendar System: Semester
URL: www.missioncollege.org
Established: 1976 — Annual Undergrad Tuition & Fees (In-District): $1,074
Enrollment: 10,538 — Coed
Affiliation or Control: State/Local — IRS Status: 501(c)3
Highest Offering: Associate Degree
Program: Occupational; 2-Year Principally Bachelor's Creditable
Accreditation: WJ

02 President .... Dr. Laurel JONES
05 Vice Pres of Instruction .... Dr. Norma AMBRIZ-GALAVIZ
32 Vice President Student Services .... Dr. Penny JOHNSON
11 Vice Pres Administrative Services .... Dr. Worku NEGASH
35 Dean of Student Support Services .... Mr. Daniel SANIDAD
103 Dean of Educational Instruction .... Mr. Danny NGUYEN
20 Educational Dean of Instruction .... Ms. Stephanie KASHIMA
31 Director Community Services .... Vacant
27 Marketing & Communications Director .... Mr. Peter ANNING
08 Instructional Dean and Library Dean .... Mr. Tim KARAS
24 Dean Instructional Technology .... Ms. Mina JAHAN
19 Interim Chief of Police .... Lt. Chris ROLAN
18 Manager of Facilities .... Mr. Don HOUSTON
07 Assistant Director of Admissions .... Mr. Ed GREEN
37 Director of Financial Aid .... Ms. Rita GROGAN
04 Exec Assistant to the President .... Ms. Linda ANGELOTTI
81 Applied Science Division .... Ms. Janice MORGAN
88 Language Arts Division .... Mr. Myo MYINT
60 Communications Division .... Mr. Rob DEWIS
81 Mathematics and Science Division .... Ms. Thais WINSOME
83 Liberal Studies Division .... Mr. Keith JOHNSON
35 Student Services Division .... Ms. Char PERLAS

*West Valley College (B)

14000 Fruitvale Avenue, Saratoga CA 95070-5698

County: Santa Clara — FICE Identification: 001338 — Unit ID: 125499
Telephone: (408) 867-2200 — Carnegie Class: Assoc/Pub-S-MC
FAX Number: (408) 867-5033 — Calendar System: Semester
URL: www.westvalley.edu
Established: 1963 — Annual Undergrad Tuition & Fees (In-District): $936
Enrollment: 11,752 — Coed
Affiliation or Control: State/Local — IRS Status: 501(c)3
Highest Offering: Associate Degree
Program: Occupational; 2-Year Principally Bachelor's Creditable
Accreditation: WJ

02 President .... Dr. Lori GASKIN
05 Vice President Instruction .... Ms. Kuni HAY
32 Vice President Student Services .... Dr. Victoria HINDES
11 Vice Pres Administrative Services .... Mr. Michael John RENZI
20 Dean Instruction .... Dr. Celine PINET
30 Dean Advancement .... Ms. Cindy SCHELCHER
36 Dean Career Programs/Workforce Dev .... Mr. Frank KOBAYASHI
72 Dean Info Technology & Services .... Mr. Fred CHOW
32 Dean of Student Services .... Ms. Ginny ARAGON
15 Assoc Vice Chanc Human Resources .... Mr. Bradley DAVIS
07 Director of Admissions .... Ms. Herlisa HAMP
18 Chief Facilities/Physical Plant .... Mr. Bill TAYLOR
26 Chief Public Relations Officer .... Mr. Bradley DAVIS
37 Director Student Financial Aid .... Ms. Maritza CANTARERO
09 Director of Institutional Research .... Ms. Inge BOND
35 Director Student Affairs .... Dr. Michelle DONOHUE-MENDOZA
29 Director Alumni Relations .... Ms. Cindy SCHELCHER
56 Coord Instruct Tech/Distance Lrng .... Ms. Lisa KAAZ

Western State University College of Law (C)

1111 N State College Boulevard, Fullerton CA 92831-3014

County: Orange — FICE Identification: 010832 — Unit ID: 126030
Telephone: (714) 459-1000 — Carnegie Class: Spec/Law
FAX Number: (714) 526-1062 — Calendar System: Semester
URL: www.wsulaw.edu
Established: 1966 — Annual Graduate Tuition & Fees: $38,885
Enrollment: 468 — Coed
Affiliation or Control: Proprietary — IRS Status: Proprietary
Highest Offering: Doctorate; No Undergraduates
Program: Professional
Accreditation: WC, LAW

01 Dean .... Mr. William E. ADAMS
05 Associate Dean for Academic Affairs .... Ms. Susan KELLER
07 Director of Admissions .... Ms. Gloria SWITZER
32 Assistant Dean of Students .... Mr. Charles SHEPPARD
15 Director Human Resources .... Ms. Peggy SAVALA
06 Asst Dir Student Services/Registrar .... Ms. Shari HARTMANN
37 Director Financial Assistance .... Ms. Donna ESPINOZA
36 Director of Career Services .... Ms. Ana BIDOGLIO
08 University Librarian .... Prof. Patricia O'CONNOR
18 Director Facilities .... Mr. Jon EVANS
10 Business Office Manager .... Ms. Theresa CARROLL
30 Director of Development .... Mr. James CHEYDLEUR
29 Asst Dir of Alumni Relations .... Mr. Tim MALLORY

Western University of Health Sciences (D)

309 E 2nd Street, Pomona CA 91766-1854

County: Los Angeles — FICE Identification: 024827 — Unit ID: 112525
Telephone: (909) 623-6116 — Carnegie Class: Spec/Med
FAX Number: N/A — Calendar System: Semester
URL: www.westernu.edu
Established: 1977 — Annual Graduate Tuition & Fees: N/A
Enrollment: 2,917 — Coed
Affiliation or Control: Independent Non-Profit — IRS Status: 501(c)3
Highest Offering: Doctorate; No Undergraduates
Program: Professional
Accreditation: WC, ARCPA, DENT, NURSE, @OPT, OSTEO, PHAR, @POD, PTA, VET

01 President .... Dr. Philip PUMERANTZ
05 Provost/COO .... Dr. Benjamin COHEN
46 Exec Vice Provost for Academic Dev .... Dr. Gary GUGELCHUK
44 Senior Vice Pres of Advancement .... Dr. Thomas FOX
20 Vice Provost .... Dr. Sheree ASTON
32 Vice President of Student Affairs .... Dr. Beverly SANKS GUIDRY
15 Executive Director Human Resources .... Ms. Linda EMILIO
25 Asst VP Spnsrd Pgms/Contract Mgt .... Mr. Matthew KATZ
67 Dean College of Pharmacy .... Dr. Daniel ROBINSON
10 Chief Financial Officer/Treasurer .... Mr. Kevin SHAW
07 Director Admiss COP/CGN .... Ms. Kathy FORD
07 Director Admissions COMP/MSHS .... Ms. Susan HANSON
07 Director Admissions CO/CPM/CDM .... Ms. Marie ANDERSON
07 Director Admissions CVM/PT/PA .... Ms. Karen HUTTON-LOPEZ
37 Director Financial Aid .... Mr. Otto REYER
52 Dean College of Dentistry .... Dr. Steven W. FRIEDRICHSEN
88 Founding Dean College of Optometry .... Dr. Elizabeth HOPPE
88 Founding Dean College of Podiatry .... Dr. Lawrence HARKLESS
63 Dn Col Osteopath Med/VP Clinic Affs .... Dr. Clinton ADAMS
76 Dean College Allied Health Profess .... Dr. Stephanie BOWLIN
66 Dean College of Graduate Nursing .... Dr. Karen HANFORD
88 Chair Dept of Physical Therapy .... Dr. Denise SCHILLING
76 Chair Dept of Health Sciences .... Dr. Tina MEYER
88 Chair Physician Assistant Program .... Mr. Roy GUIZADO
63 Chair Department Family Medicine .... Dr. Alan CUNDARI
74 Dean College of Veterinary Medicine .... Dr. Phil NELSON
40 Bookstore Director .... Ms. Elizabeth GUERRA
88 Dir Ctr Disability Issues/Hlth Prof .... Ms. Brenda PREMO
23 Medical Director .... Dr. David CONNETT
06 Asst Vice Pres Univ Enroll/Registr .... Ms. Kimberly DEKRUIF
08 Director of University Library .... Ms. Patricia VADER
91 Exec Director Information Tech .... Ms. Denise WILCOX
96 Director of Procurement Services .... Mr. Michael BUTLER
26 Exec Director of Public Affairs .... Mr. Jeff KEATING
88 Dir Learning Enhancement/Acad Devel .... Mr. David HACKER
09 Director of Institutional Research .... Dr. Juan RAMIREZ
18 Exec Dir Facilities/Physical Plant .... Mr. Todd CLARK
35 Director of Univ Student Affairs .... Ms. Michelle EMMERT
88 Dir of Outcomes Assmnt & IPE Educ .... Dr. Jordan ORZOFF

Westminster Theological Seminary in California (E)

1725 Bear Valley Parkway, Escondido CA 92027-4128

County: San Diego — FICE Identification: 022768 — Unit ID: 125718
Telephone: (760) 480-8474 — Carnegie Class: Spec/Faith
FAX Number: (760) 480-0252 — Calendar System: Semester
URL: www.wscal.edu
Established: 1979 — Annual Graduate Tuition & Fees: $10,715
Enrollment: 137 — Coed
Affiliation or Control: Independent Non-Profit — IRS Status: 501(c)3
Highest Offering: Master's; No Undergraduates
Program: Professional
Accreditation: WC, THEOL

01 President .... Dr. W. Robert GODFREY
03 Executive Vice President .... Mr. Steven OEVERMAN
05 Academic Dean .... Dr. Dennis JOHNSON
10 Business Manager .... Mr. Dan TERHORST
08 Library Director .... Mr. John G. BALES
32 Dean of Students .... Dr. Julius KIM
06 Registrar .... Ms. Heather GIDEON

Westmont College (F)

955 La Paz Road, Santa Barbara CA 93108-1089

County: Santa Barbara — FICE Identification: 001341 — Unit ID: 125727
Telephone: (805) 565-6000 — Carnegie Class: Bac/A&S
FAX Number: (805) 565-7006 — Calendar System: Semester
URL: www.westmont.edu
Established: 1937 — Annual Undergrad Tuition & Fees: $46,990
Enrollment: 1,354 — Coed
Affiliation or Control: Independent Non-Profit — IRS Status: 501(c)3
Highest Offering: Baccalaureate
Program: Liberal Arts And General; Teacher Preparatory
Accreditation: WC, MUS

01 President .... Dr. Gayle D. BEEBE
03 Executive Vice President .... Mr. Cliff LUNDBERG
05 Provost and Dean of Faculty .... Vacant
10 Vice President Finance .... Mr. Douglas W. JONES
11 Vice President for Administration .... Mr. Christopher D. CALL
32 Vice President & Dean of Students .... Mrs. Jane H. HIGA
30 Vice President for Advancement .... Dr. Reed SHEARD
06 Registrar .... Mr. Robert KUNTZ
07 Dean of Admissions .... Mr. Silvio VAZQUEZ
08 Director Library/Information Svcs .... Mrs. Debra QUAST
09 Assoc Provost/Dir of Inst Research .... Dr. William A. WRIGHT
13 VP Information Technology & CIO .... Dr. Reed SHEARD
15 Director of Human Resources .... Ms. Beth CAUWELS
18 Director of Physical Plant .... Mr. Thomas BEVERIDGE
19 Manager Security & Public Safety .... Mr. Thomas G. BAUER
21 Controller .... Mr. Paul V. LARSON
23 Director of Student Health Services .... Dr. David HERNANDEZ
24 Coord Media Services/Asst Librarian .... Ms. Mary LOGUE
26 Director of Public Affairs .... Mrs. Nancy L. PHINNEY
29 Exec Director Alumni & Parent Rels .... Mrs. Teri BRADFORD ROUSE
35 Associate Dean of Students .... Mr. Timothy B. WILSON
88 Assoc Dean of Students for Res Life .... Mr. Stu CLEEK
36 Director of Career/Life Planning .... Mr. Dana C. ALEXANDER
88 Director of Campus Life .... Ms. Angela L. D'AMOUR
88 Director of Internships/Practica .... Mrs. Jennifer TAYLOR
37 Director of Financial Aid .... Mr. Sean SMITH
38 Director Counseling Services .... Mrs. Marcy O'HARA
39 Director of Housing .... Mr. David W. KING
40 Bookstore Manager .... Mrs. Marilyn LOPPNOW
41 Athletic Director .... Mr. David ODELL
42 Campus Pastor .... Rev. Ben PATTERSON
44 Director of Planned Giving .... Mr. Bob FREELOVE
45 Director of Campus Planning .... Mr. Randy JONES
96 Director Procurement/Auxiliary Svcs .... Mr. Troy HARRIS
28 Director of Intercultural Programs .... Ms. Elena YEE
43 College Counsel .... Ms. Toya COOPER
20 Associate Academic Officer .... Dr. Tatiana NAZARENKO

Westwood College-Anaheim (G)

1551 S Douglass Road, Anaheim CA 92806-5949

County: Orange — Identification: 666047 — Unit ID: 437848
Telephone: (714) 704-2727 — Carnegie Class: Bac/Diverse
FAX Number: (714) 939-2011 — Calendar System: Quarter
URL: www.westwood.edu
Established: 1953 — Annual Undergrad Tuition & Fees: $14,317
Enrollment: 1,159 — Coed
Affiliation or Control: Proprietary — IRS Status: Proprietary
Highest Offering: Baccalaureate
Program: 2-Year Principally Bachelor's Creditable; Liberal Arts And General
Accreditation: ACCSC, ACICS

01 Executive Director .... Mr. Lou OSBORN

† Branch campus of Westwood College-Denver North. Denver, CO.

Westwood College-Inland Empire (H)

20 W Seventh Street, Upland CA 91786-7148

County: San Bernardino — Identification: 666104 — Unit ID: 440484
Telephone: (909) 931-7550 — Carnegie Class: Bac/Diverse
FAX Number: (909) 931-9195 — Calendar System: Other
URL: www.westwood.edu
Established: 2001 — Annual Undergrad Tuition & Fees: $14,317
Enrollment: 1,337 — Coed
Affiliation or Control: Proprietary — IRS Status: Proprietary
Highest Offering: Baccalaureate
Program: Occupational; Technical Emphasis
Accreditation: ACCSC, ACICS

01 Campus President .... Mrs. Tina MILLER
05 Campus Academic Dean .... Dr. Luka MBEWE
07 Director of Admissions .... Ms. Alma SALAZAR
32 Director of Student Services .... Ms. Megan FEYER
37 Director of Financial Aid .... Ms. Erin VARGAS
06 Registrar .... Ms. Connie KUANG

† Branch campus of Westwood College-Denver North, Denver, CO.

Westwood College-Los Angeles Campus (I)

3250 Wilshire Boulevard, Suite 400,
Los Angeles CA 90010-1437

County: Los Angeles — FICE Identification: 030727 — Unit ID: 122843
Telephone: (213) 739-9999 — Carnegie Class: Bac/Diverse
FAX Number: (213) 382-2468 — Calendar System: Quarter
URL: www.westwood.edu
Established: 1997 — Annual Undergrad Tuition & Fees: N/A
Enrollment: 5,257 — Coed
Affiliation or Control: Proprietary — IRS Status: Proprietary
Highest Offering: Master's
Program: Occupational

Accreditation: ACICS

01 Campus President .... Mr. DeWayne JOHNSON
07 Director of Admissions .... Mr. Brian WILLINGHAM

Westwood College-South Bay (A)

19700 S Vermont Avenue, #100, Torrance CA 90502-1148
County: Los Angeles FICE Identification: 011626
Unit ID: 121381
Telephone: (310) 965-0888 Carnegie Class: Bac/Diverse
FAX Number: (310) 516-8232 Calendar System: Other
URL: www.westwood.edu
Established: 2002 Annual Undergrad Tuition & Fees: $24,900
Enrollment: 742 Coed
Affiliation or Control: Proprietary IRS Status: Proprietary
Highest Offering: Baccalaureate
Program: Occupational; Technical Emphasis
Accreditation: ACICS

01 Campus President .... Mr. Christopher TUREN

Whittier College (B)

13406 E Philadelphia St, PO Box 634,
Whittier CA 90608-4413
County: Los Angeles FICE Identification: 001342
Unit ID: 125763
Telephone: (562) 907-4200 Carnegie Class: Bac/A&S
FAX Number: (562) 907-4242 Calendar System: 4/1/4
URL: www.whittier.edu
Established: 1887 Annual Undergrad Tuition & Fees: $38,874
Enrollment: 1,664 Coed
Affiliation or Control: Independent Non-Profit IRS Status: 501(c)3
Highest Offering: Master's
Program: Liberal Arts And General; Teacher Preparatory; Professional
Accreditation: WC, LAW, SW

01 President .... Dr. Sharon D. HERZBERGER
10 Vice Pres Finance & Administration .... Mr. James DUNKELMAN
05 VP Academic Affs/Dean of Faculty .... Dr. Charlotte BORST
61 VP Legal Education/Dean Sch of Law .... Ms. Penelope BRYAN
30 Vice President College Advancement .... Ms. Elizabeth POWER ROBISON
84 Vice President Dean of Enrollment .... Mr. Fred PFURSICH
32 Dean of Students .... Dr. Jeanne ORTIZ
37 Director of Student Financial Aid .... Mr. David CARNEVALE
06 Registrar .... Mr. Wayne VAN ELLIS
08 Librarian .... Vacant
20 Dir Whtr Scholar Pgm/Assc Acad Dean .... Ms. Doreen O'CONNOR-GOMEZ
29 Director of Alumni Relations .... Vacant
27 Director of Communications .... Ms. Dana RAKOCZY
14 Director of Computing Services .... Mr. Troy GREENUP
09 Director of Institutional Research .... Mr. Fritz SMITH
39 Director for Resident Life .... Mrs. Delaphine HUDSON
41 Director of Athletics .... Mr. Rob COLEMAN
53 Dir Lib Educ Pgm/Assoc Acad Dean .... Dr. Fritz SMITH
07 Director of Admissions .... Mr. Kieron MILLER
15 Director of Human Resources .... Vacant
21 Exec Director Finance/Business Svcs .... Ms. Hoang HAU
35 Director Student Activies .... Mr. Rick CLARK
18 Director Facilities/Physical Plant .... Mr. Ken BOHAN
26 Director Public Relations .... Mrs. Dana RAKOCZY
19 Director of Campus Safety .... Mr. Timm BROWNE

William Jessup University (C)

333 Sunset Boulevard, Rocklin CA 95765-3707
County: Placer FICE Identification: 001281
Unit ID: 122728
Telephone: (916) 577-2200 Carnegie Class: Spec/Faith
FAX Number: (916) 577-2203 Calendar System: Semester
URL: www.jessup.edu
Established: 1939 Annual Undergrad Tuition & Fees: $21,800
Enrollment: 721 Coed
Affiliation or Control: Independent Non-Profit IRS Status: 501(c)3
Highest Offering: Baccalaureate
Program: 2-Year Principally Bachelor's Creditable; Liberal Arts And General; Teacher Preparatory; Religious Emphasis
Accreditation: WC, BI

01 President .... Dr. John JACKSON
05 Vice President for Academic Affairs .... Ms. Rhonda CAPRON
32 Vice Pres for Student Development .... Dr. Paul BLEZIEN
11 Vice Pres Finance/Administration .... Mr. Gene DEYOUNG
30 Vice President for Advancement .... Mr. Eric HOGUE
20 Interim Academic Dean .... Dr. Portia HOPKINS
88 Accreditation Liason Officer .... Dr. Kay LLOVIO
107 School of Professional Studies Dir .... Mr. Sam HEINRICH
15 Director of Human Resources .... Ms. DeDe HUDAK
10 Controller .... Ms. Diane KIM
08 Library Director .... Mr. Kevin PISCHKE
29 Director of Alumni/Church Relations .... Mr. Jim JESSUP
44 Director University Fund .... Ms. Kathleen TUCKER
35 Associate Dean of Students .... Mr. Tom STEPHENS
06 Registrar .... Mrs. Tina PETERSEN
07 Director of Admission .... Mr. Vance PASCUA
37 Financial Aid Director .... Mr. Korey COMPAAN
09 Institutional Research Director .... Mrs. Karen LAMBRECHTSEN
42 Director of Campus Ministries .... Mr. Daniel GLUCK
41 Athletic Director .... Mr. Farnum SMITH
18 Facilities Director .... Mr. Brian SULLIVAN

Woodbury University (D)

7500 Glenoaks Boulevard, Burbank CA 91510-7520
County: Los Angeles FICE Identification: 001343
Unit ID: 125897
Telephone: (818) 767-0888 Carnegie Class: Master's M
FAX Number: (818) 767-7520 Calendar System: Semester
URL: www.woodbury.edu
Established: 1884 Annual Undergrad Tuition & Fees: $29,994
Enrollment: 1,628 Coed
Affiliation or Control: Independent Non-Profit IRS Status: 501(c)3
Highest Offering: Master's
Program: Professional; Business Emphasis
Accreditation: WC, ACBSP, ART, CIDA

01 President .... Kenneth R. NIELSEN
05 Vice Pres Academic Affairs .... David M. ROSEN
10 Vice Pres Finance & Administration .... Ken JONES
84 VP Enrollment Mgmt/Univ Marketing .... Don E. ST. CLAIR
30 Vice Pres University Advancement .... Richard M. NORDIN
13 VP Information Technology/Planning .... Steve DYER
32 VP Student Development .... Phyllis A. CREMER
04 Exec Assistant to the President .... Seta JAVOR
35 Dean of Students .... Anne R. EHRLICH
50 Dean School of Business .... Andre VAN NIEKERK
48 Dean School of Architecture .... Norman MILLAR
88 Dean School of Media/Culture/Design .... Edward CLIFT
44 Sr Director of Development .... Rose NIELSEN
88 Ex Dir Inst for Exclnce Teach/Lrng .... Paul W. DECKER
06 Assistant Registrar .... Tamara L. BLOK
84 Director of Enrollment Services .... Celeastia WILLIAMS
08 University Librarian .... Nedra PETERSON
15 Director of Human Resources .... Rachelle H. PRINCE
36 Director of Career Services .... Liana JINDARYAN
18 Director of Physical Plant .... Jerry W. TRACY
38 Director of Student Counseling .... Monica VALDIVIA
07 Director of Admissions .... Ruth G. LORENZANA
88 Director Transdisciplinary Studies .... Douglas CREMER
35 Coord Student Involvement/Leadershp .... Janice L. BLAIR

World Mission University (E)

500 Shatto Place, Suite 600, Los Angeles CA 90020-1789
County: Los Angeles FICE Identification: 038683
Unit ID: 401223
Telephone: (213) 385-2322 Carnegie Class: Spec/Faith
FAX Number: (213) 385-2332 Calendar System: Semester
URL: www.wmu.edu
Established: 1989 Annual Undergrad Tuition & Fees: $5,100
Enrollment: 288 Coed
Affiliation or Control: Independent Non-Profit IRS Status: 501(c)3
Highest Offering: First Professional Degree
Program: Religious Emphasis
Accreditation: BI, @THEOL, TRACS

01 President .... Dr. Dong Sun LIM
05 Exec Vice Pres/Chief Acad Officer .... Dr. Sung Jin LIM
26 Vice Pres of Collegiate Relations .... Dr. John E. MCKENNA
42 Vice President of Church Relations .... Rev. Choon Min KANG
32 Dean of Student Svcs/Financial Aid .... Mr. John B. PARK
30 Director of Development .... Ms. Keum Hee LEE
10 Director of Business .... Mr. Sun Young CHOI
06 Registrar .... Mr. Solomon BAHK

The Wright Institute (F)

2728 Durant Avenue, Berkeley CA 94704-1796
County: Alameda FICE Identification: 008846
Unit ID: 126012
Telephone: (510) 841-9230 Carnegie Class: Spec/Health
FAX Number: (510) 841-0167 Calendar System: Trimester
URL: www.wrightinst.edu
Established: 1969 Annual Graduate Tuition & Fees: $26,600
Enrollment: 390 Coed
Affiliation or Control: Independent Non-Profit IRS Status: 501(c)3
Highest Offering: Doctorate; No Undergraduates
Program: Professional
Accreditation: WC, CLPSY

01 President .... Mr. Peter DYBWAD
05 Dean .... Dr. Charles ALEXANDER
11 Administrator .... Ms. Tricia O'REILLY
07 Director of Admissions .... Ms. Melissa DELANEY
08 Librarian .... Mr. Jason STRAUSS
06 Registrar .... Ms. Virginia MORGAN

WyoTech-Fremont (G)

420 Whitney Place, Fremont CA 94539-7663
County: Alameda FICE Identification: 007190
Unit ID: 123208
Telephone: (510) 490-6900 Carnegie Class: Assoc/PrivFP
FAX Number: (510) 490-8599 Calendar System: Quarter
URL: www.wyotech.com
Established: 1965 Annual Undergrad Tuition & Fees: $28,768
Enrollment: 1,926 Coed
Affiliation or Control: Proprietary IRS Status: Proprietary
Highest Offering: Associate Degree
Program: Occupational
Accreditation: ACCSC

01 President .... Mr. Joe PAPPALY
07 Vice President of Admissions .... Mr. Jae LEE
05 Director of Education .... Mr. Michael LEE
36 Director of Career Services .... Mr. Michael QUINNINE
37 Director of Financial Aid .... Mrs. Kathleen CLOUGH
06 Registrar .... Ms. Liz GUSTAFSON
11 Dir Compliance/Administrative Svcs .... Ms. Cheryl L. PAGUIA

WyoTech-Long Beach (H)

2161 Technology Place, Long Beach CA 90810-3800
County: Los Angeles FICE Identification: 012873
Unit ID: 398574
Telephone: (562) 624-9530 Carnegie Class: Assoc/PrivFP
FAX Number: (562) 437-8111 Calendar System: Quarter
URL: www.wyotech.edu
Established: 1969 Annual Undergrad Tuition & Fees: $25,133
Enrollment: 1,050 Coed
Affiliation or Control: Proprietary IRS Status: Proprietary
Highest Offering: Associate Degree
Program: Occupational; Technical Emphasis
Accreditation: ACCSC, MAAB

01 Interim President .... Mr. John L. ANDREWS

WyoTech-Sacramento (I)

980 Riverside Parkway, West Sacramento CA 95605-1507
County: Yolo Identification: 666292
Unit ID: 445452
Telephone: (916) 376-8888 Carnegie Class: Assoc/PrivFP
FAX Number: (916) 617-2069 Calendar System: Quarter
URL: www.wyotech.com
Established: 2004 Annual Undergrad Tuition & Fees: $27,500
Enrollment: 1,594 Coed
Affiliation or Control: Proprietary IRS Status: Proprietary
Highest Offering: Associate Degree
Program: Occupational; Technical Emphasis
Accreditation: ACCSC

01 Campus President .... Mr. John HURD

† Branch campus of Wyoming Technical Institute, Laramie, WY.

Yeshiva Ohr Elchonon Chabad/ West Coast Talmudical Seminary (J)

7215 Waring Avenue, Los Angeles CA 90046-7660
County: Los Angeles FICE Identification: 022624
Unit ID: 126076
Telephone: (323) 937-3763 Carnegie Class: Spec/Faith
FAX Number: (323) 937-9456 Calendar System: Semester
Established: 1953 Annual Undergrad Tuition & Fees: $11,500
Enrollment: 130 Male
Affiliation or Control: Independent Non-Profit IRS Status: 501(c)3
Highest Offering: Baccalaureate
Program: Professional
Accreditation: RABN

01 Chief Executive Officer .... Rabbi Ezra B. SCHOCHET
03 Executive Vice President .... Rabbi Mendel SPALTER
05 Curriculum Suprv/Education Counsel .... Rabbi Shimon RAICHIK
37 Director Student Financial Aid .... Mrs. Hendy TAUBER
06 Registrar .... Rabbi Chaim CITRON
38 Director Student Counseling .... Rabbi Mendel SCHAPIRO
08 Head Librarian .... Rabbi Ben Zion OSTER

Yo San University of Traditional Chinese Medicine (K)

13315 W Washington Boulevard, Los Angeles CA 90066
County: Los Angeles FICE Identification: 030982
Unit ID: 401250
Telephone: (310) 577-3000 Carnegie Class: Spec/Health
FAX Number: (310) 577-3033 Calendar System: Trimester
URL: www.yosan.edu
Established: 1989 Annual Undergrad Tuition & Fees: $12,200
Enrollment: 185 Coed
Affiliation or Control: Independent Non-Profit IRS Status: 501(c)3
Highest Offering: Master's; No Lower Division
Program: Professional
Accreditation: ACUP

01 President .... Lawrence RYAN
05 Dean of Academic & Clinical Educ .... Lawrence LAU
11 Dean of Admin & Student Affairs .... Steven CARTER
10 Chief Financial Officer .... Tracy WANG
20 Assistant Academic Dean .... Andrea MURCHISON
07 Admissions Director .... Daouia AMRIR
37 Financial Aid Coordinator .... Ed MERVINE
21 Controller .... Mariani MAY

*Yosemite Community College District (L)

PO Box 4065, Modesto CA 95352-4065
County: Stanislaus FICE Identification: 009146
Unit ID: 126100
Telephone: (209) 575-6509 Carnegie Class: N/A
FAX Number: (209) 575-6565
URL: www.yosemite.edu

01 Chancellor ....Dr. Joan E. SMITH
03 Executive Vice Chancellor ....Ms. Teresa M. SCOTT
13 Asst Chancellor Information Tech ....Ms. Gina ROSE
16 Vice Chancellor Human Resources ....Ms. Diane WIRTH

*Columbia College (A)

11600 Columbia College Drive, Sonora CA 95370-8580
County: Tuolumne FICE Identification: 007707
Unit ID: 112561
Telephone: (209) 588-5100 Carnegie Class: Assoc/Pub-R-M
FAX Number: (209) 588-5104 Calendar System: Semester
URL: www.columbia.yosemite.cc.ca.us
Established: 1968 Annual Undergrad Tuition & Fees (In-District): $936
Enrollment: 3,764 Coed
Affiliation or Control: State/Local IRS Status: 501(c)3
Highest Offering: Associate Degree
Program: Occupational; 2-Year Principally Bachelor's Creditable
Accreditation: WJ, ACFEI

02 President ....Dr. Dennis GERVIN
05 Acting Vice Pres Student Learning ....Dr. Dennis GERVIN
11 VP College & Administrative Svcs ....Mr. Gary WHITFIELD
20 Dean Instructional Svcs/Voc Educ ....Mr. Chris VITELLI
49 Dean of Instruction/Arts & Sciences ....Mr. Michael TOROK
24 Director of Info Tech & Media Svcs ....Mr. Brian DEMOSS
07 Dir of Student Success & Matric ....Vacant
41 Athletic Director ....Mr. Michael TOROK
37 Financial Aid Manager ....Ms. Marnie SHIVELY
27 Public Information Officer ....Vacant
31 Director Community Services ....Vacant
30 Chief Development ....Vacant
40 Bookstore Manager ....Mr. Jeff WHALEN
18 Manager Facilities/Operations ....Ms. Judy LANCHESTER

*Modesto Junior College (B)

435 College Avenue, Modesto CA 95350-9977
County: Stanislaus FICE Identification: 001240
Unit ID: 118976
Telephone: (209) 575-6498 Carnegie Class: Assoc/Pub-R-L
FAX Number: (209) 575-6630 Calendar System: Semester
URL: www.mjc.edu
Established: 1921 Annual Undergrad Tuition & Fees (In-District): $624
Enrollment: 19,431 Coed
Affiliation or Control: State/Local IRS Status: 501(c)3
Highest Offering: Associate Degree
Program: Occupational; 2-Year Principally Bachelor's Creditable
Accreditation: WJ, DA, MAC

02 Acting President ....Dr. Karen WALTERS DUNLAP
05 Vice President for Instruction ....Dr. Karen WALTERS DUNLAP
32 Actg Vice Pres for Student Services ....Dr. Don LOW
11 Int VP College/Administrative Svcs ....Dr. Carmen FERNANDEZ
57 Div Dean Arts/Humanit & Communicat ....Mr. Mike SUNDQUIST
83 Div Dean Busi/Behav/Social Sci ....Dr. Dina HUMBLE
76 Div Dean Inst/All Hlth/Fam/Con Sci ....Dr. Maurice MCKINNON
79 Div Dean Literature/Language Arts ....Mr. Patrick BETTENCOURT
54 Div Dean Science/Math/Engineering ....Mr. Brian SANDERS
47 Dean Agri/Envir Science/Tech Ed ....Mr. Mark ANGLIN
31 Dean of Community & Economic Devel ....Mr. George J. BOODROOKAS
68 Dean Phys/Rec/Health Educ/Athl Dir ....Dr. William KAISER
84 Director Matriculation/Enroll Svcs ....Vacant
09 Director of Institutional Research ....Vacant
37 Director Student Financial Aid ....Ms. Myra E. RUSH
35 Director Student Dev/Campus Life ....Vacant
26 Director Marketing/Public Relations ....Vacant
40 Manager College Bookstore ....Ms. Rhonda T. GREEN

*Yuba Community College District (C)

2088 North Beale Road, Marysville CA 95901
County: Yuba Identification: 666478
Telephone: (530) 741-6700 Carnegie Class: N/A
FAX Number: (530) 634-7704
URL: www.yccd.edu

01 Chancellor ....Dr. Douglas B. HOUSTON
05 VC Educ Planning & Services ....Dr. Beatriz ESPINOZA
11 VC Administrative Services ....Al ALT
13 Director Information Technologies ....Karen TRIMBLE
86 Director Public & Governmental Rels ....Dr. Adrian LOPEZ
30 Director Institutional Development ....Dr. Phil KREBS
15 Director HR & Personnel ....Vacant
10 Director Fiscal Services ....Kuldeep KAUR
18 Director Facilities Planning ....George PARKER
96 Director Purchasing ....Malinda BOGDONOFF

*Woodland Community College (D)

2300 East Gibson Road, Woodland CA 95776-5156
County: Yolo FICE Identification: 041438
Unit ID: 455512
Telephone: (530) 661-5711 Carnegie Class: Assoc/Pub-R-M
FAX Number: (530) 666-9028 Calendar System: Semester
URL: www.yccd.edu/woodland/
Established: 2008 Annual Undergrad Tuition & Fees (In-District): $884
Enrollment: 4,000 Coed
Affiliation or Control: State/Local IRS Status: 501(c)3
Highest Offering: Associate Degree
Program: Occupational; 2-Year Principally Bachelor's Creditable
Accreditation: WJ

02 President ....Dr. Angela R. FAIRCHILDS

*Yuba College (E)

2088 N Beale Road, Marysville CA 95901-7699
County: Yuba FICE Identification: 001344
Unit ID: 126119
Telephone: (530) 741-6700 Carnegie Class: Assoc/Pub-R-L
FAX Number: (530) 741-3541 Calendar System: Semester
URL: www.yccd.edu
Established: 1927 Annual Undergrad Tuition & Fees (In-District): $956
Enrollment: 8,490 Coed
Affiliation or Control: State/Local IRS Status: 501(c)3
Highest Offering: Associate Degree
Program: Occupational; 2-Year Principally Bachelor's Creditable
Accreditation: WJ, RAD

02 President ....Dr. Kay ADKINS
05 Vice Pres Academic/Student Services ....Dr. Kevin TRUTNA
07 Dir Admissions & Enrollment Svcs ....Dr. Kendyl MAGNUSON
88 Director Disabled Students/Pgm/Svcs ....Ms. Jan PONTICELLI
37 Dean Financial Aid/EOPS/TRIO ....Dr. Marisela ARCE
50 Dean Bus/Soc Sci/Cosmetology ....Dr. Ed DAVIS
88 Dir Child Dev Ctr/AmeriCorps ....Ms. Laurie SCHEUERMANN
106 Dean Distributive Ed & Media Svcs ....Ms. Martha MILLS
88 Dir Upward Bound/SSS ....Ms. Yvette SANTANA-SOTO
57 Dean Fine Arts/Language Arts ....Mr. Walter MASUDA
68 Dn Hlth/PE/Rec/Ath/Pub Safety ....Mr. Rod BEILBY
20 Dean Instruction/Learning Res ....Mr. Ken NATHER
32 Dean Student Services ....Dr. Stacey COOK
19 Director Public Safety ....Mr. Rolfe APPEL
81 Dn Math/Engr/Sci/Hlth/Applied Tech ....Vacant
09 Dir Plng/Rsrch & Student Success ....Mr. Erik COOPER
38 Dn Stdnt Dev/DSPS/Vets/Stdnt Succ ....Vacant
26 Pub Info Ofcr/Dir Cmty Ed/Camp Life ....Ms. Miriam ROOT
66 Dir Nursing/Allied Health ....Ms. Sheila SCROGGINS

COLORADO

Adams State College (F)

208 Edgemont Boulevard, Alamosa CO 81102-0001
County: Alamosa FICE Identification: 001345
Unit ID: 126182
Telephone: (719) 587-7011 Carnegie Class: Master's M
FAX Number: (719) 587-7522 Calendar System: Semester
URL: www.adams.edu
Established: 1921 Annual Undergrad Tuition & Fees (In-State): $5,627
Enrollment: 3,237 Coed
Affiliation or Control: State IRS Status: 501(c)3
Highest Offering: Master's
Program: 2-Year Principally Bachelor's Creditable; Liberal Arts And General; Teacher Preparatory
Accreditation: NH, CACREP, MUS, NURSE, TEAC

01 President ....Dr. David P. SVALDI
05 Vice President for Academic Affairs ....Dr. Frank J. NOVOTNY
10 VP Finance/Governmental Relations ....Mr. Bill MANSHEIM
84 Sr VP Enrollment Mgmt/Program Devel ....Dr. Michael MUMPER
30 Vice President Inst Advancement ....Vacant
18 AVP Facil Plng/Design/ Construction ....Mr. Eric VAN DE BOOGAARD
56 Asst VP Extended Campus - Academics ....Mr. Walter ROYBAL
21 Asst Vice Pres Budget & Technology ....Ms. Heather HEERSINK
20 Assoc Provost Academic Affairs ....Vacant
32 Dean Student Affairs ....Mr. Kenneth L. MARQUEZ
09 Senior Analyst Inst Research ....Mrs. Andrea BENTON-MESTAS
08 Director Library ....Mr. David GOETZMAN
37 Director Student Financial Aid ....Mr. Philip SCHROEDER
07 Director of Admissions ....Mr. Eric CARPIO
06 Registrar ....Ms. Belen MAESTAS
31 Exec Dir Community Partnerships ....Ms. Mary HOFFMAN
13 Chief Information Officer ....Mr. Mike E. NICHOLSON
41 Athletic Director ....Mr. Larry MORTENSEN
27 Asst to President Communications ....Ms. Julie WAECHTER
31 Director of Auxiliary Services ....Mr. Bruce DEL TONDO
38 Director Counseling/Career Services ....Mr. Gregg ELLIOTT
15 Director Human Resources ....Ms. Tracy ROGERS
102 Executive Director ASC Foundation ....Ms. Tammy L. LOPEZ
29 Director Alumni Relations ....Ms. Lori L. LASKE
96 Director of Purchasing ....Ms. Renee VIGIL
19 Dir Adams State College Police Dept ....Mr. Joel SHULTS
40 Director Bookstore ....Mr. Darrell MEIS
27 Interim Director Communications ....Mr. Mark SCHOENECKER
88 Chair English/Theatre/Communication ....Dr. David MAZEL
50 Chair Business & Economics ....Dr. Kurt KEISER
53 Chair Education ....Dr. Donna STOUT
81 Chair Chemistry/Computer Sci/Math ....Dr. Matthew S. NEHRING
81 Chair Biology/Earth Science ....Dr. Brent YBARRONDO
28 Director of Diversity ....Ms. Isabel MEDINA KEISER

Aims Community College (G)

Box 69, Greeley CO 80632-0069
County: Weld FICE Identification: 007582
Unit ID: 126207
Telephone: (970) 330-8008 Carnegie Class: Assoc/Pub-R-M
FAX Number: (970) 330-5705 Calendar System: Semester
URL: www.aims.edu
Established: 1967 Annual Undergrad Tuition & Fees (In-District): $2,621
Enrollment: 5,340 Coed
Affiliation or Control: Local IRS Status: 501(c)3
Highest Offering: Associate Degree
Program: Occupational; 2-Year Principally Bachelor's Creditable
Accreditation: NH, ADNUR, EMT, IFSAC, SURGT

01 President ....Dr. Marilynn LIDDELL
10 Chief Administrative Officer ....Mr. Mike KELLY
27 Chief Information Officer ....Vacant
05 Chief Academic Officer ....Ms. Donna SOUTHER
20 Academic Dean ....Mr. Jeff REYNOLDS
20 Academic Dean ....Dr. Dan DOHERTY
32 Dean for Student Services ....Dr. Patricia MATIJEVIC
51 Dean Continuing Education ....Mr. Steven KAHLA
43 Special Assistant Legal Affairs ....Ms. Sandra OWENS
30 Dir Inst Advancement/Foundation ....Ms. Julie BUDERUS
15 Director Human Resources ....Vacant
21 Budget Director ....Mr. Daniel ERBERT
21 Controller ....Vacant
18 Chief Facilities Management Officer ....Mr. Michael MILLSAPPS
37 Director Student Financial Assist ....Ms. Teri DORCHUCK
06 Registrar/Director Admissions ....Mr. Stuart THOMAS
38 Director Student Success Center ....Ms. Paula YANISH
09 Dir Inst Effectiveness & Assessment ....Ms. Lee Ann SAPPINGTON
13 Director Technology ....Mr. Bill WAGGONER
35 Director Student Life ....Mr. Ron FAY
12 Assoc Dean Loveland Campus ....Ms. Heather LELCHOOK
12 Assoc Dean Ft Lupton Campus ....Ms. Brenda RASK
12 Director Windsor Auto/Tech Ctr ....Mr. Fred BROWN
75 Associate Dean Career & Tech Ed ....Ms. Brenda RASK
08 Assoc Dean Learning/Org Dev ....Mr. Rob UMBAUGH
66 Associate Dean Nursing ....Ms. Nina KIRK

American Sentinel University (H)

2260 South Xanadu Way, Ste 310, Aurora CO 80014
County: Arapahoe FICE Identification: 041277
Telephone: (303) 991-1575 Carnegie Class: Not Classified
FAX Number: (303) 991-1577 Calendar System: Other
URL: www.americansentinel.edu
Established: 2000 Annual Undergrad Tuition & Fees: $10,500
Enrollment: 1,302 Coed
Affiliation or Control: Proprietary IRS Status: Proprietary
Highest Offering: Master's
Program: Occupational; 2-Year Principally Bachelor's Creditable; Professional; Nursing Emphasis
Accreditation: DETC, NURSE

01 President ....Ms. Mary A. ADAMS
05 Interim Provost/CEO ....Dr. Rick OLIVER
50 Dean Business & Technology ....Dr. Danettee LANCE

Anthem College (I)

350 Blackhawk Street, Aurora CO 80011-8754
County: Arapahoe Identification: 666510
Unit ID: 410539
Telephone: (720) 859-7900 Carnegie Class: Assoc/PrivFP
FAX Number: (303) 344-1376 Calendar System: Other
URL: www.cambridgecollege.com
Established: 1993 Annual Undergrad Tuition & Fees: $20,700
Enrollment: 321 Coed
Affiliation or Control: Proprietary IRS Status: Proprietary
Highest Offering: Associate Degree
Program: Occupational
Accreditation: ACICS, MAAB, SURTEC

01 Campus President ....Ms. Janet MACK
05 Dean of Education ....Vacant
07 Director of Admissions ....Ms. Amy MARSHALL

† Branch campus of The Bryman School, AZ.

Arapahoe Community College (J)

5900 S Santa Fe Drive, PO Box 9002,
Littleton CO 80160-9002
County: Arapahoe FICE Identification: 001346
Unit ID: 126289
Telephone: (303) 797-4222 Carnegie Class: Assoc/Pub-S-MC
FAX Number: (303) 797-5935 Calendar System: Semester
URL: www.arapahoe.edu
Established: 1965 Annual Undergrad Tuition & Fees (In-State): $4,142
Enrollment: 9,218 Coed
Affiliation or Control: State IRS Status: 501(c)3
Highest Offering: Associate Degree
Program: Occupational; 2-Year Principally Bachelor's Creditable
Accreditation: NH, ADNUR, CEA, EMT, FUSER, MAC, MLTAD, PTAA

01 President ....Dr. Diana DOYLE
03 Executive Vice President ....Mr. David SHELLBERG
05 Vice President Instruction ....Dr. Diane HEGEMAN
10 Chief Financial Officer ....Mr. Joseph LORENZO, JR.
11 Chief Operating Officer ....Mr. David J. CASTRO
103 Dean Community/Workforce Partnershp ....Mr. Matt MCKEEVER
32 Dean of Student Services ....Ms. Connie SIMPSON
38 Director of Advising and Retention ....Mr. Michael MCMANUS
07 Director Admissions & Records ....Ms. Darcy BRIGGS
37 Dir of Student Financial Services ....Ms. Dorothy SHALLCROSS
31 Exec Dir of Community/Workforce Pgm ....Ms. Kim K. LARSON-COONEY
79 Dean Liberal Arts & Prof Programs ....Dr. Janna OAKES
76 Dean Health/Sciences & Engineering ....Ms. Linda COMEAUX

50 Dean Math/Business & Technology .... Dr. Cindy SOMERS
49 Dean Arts/Design/Social/Behav Sci .... Ms. Kathy HOLT
102 Executive Director Foundation .... Ms. Courtney LOEHFELM
21 Controller .... Ms. Pat BOULEY
19 Chief of Police .... Mr. Dennis GOODWIN
09 Manager Institutional Research .... Ms. Mary SHERMAN
08 Director Learning Resource Center .... Mr. Malcolm BRANTZ
26 Dir of Marketing/Public Relations .... Mr. Murry UNELL
35 Director Student Affairs .... Ms. Heather WILCOX
96 Director of Purchasing .... Mr. Jay WEST
18 Facilities Manager .... Mr. Larry OTTO

Argosy University, Denver (A)

7600 East Eastman Avenue, Denver CO 80231
County: Denver Identification: 666654
Unit ID: 448734
Telephone: (303) 923-4110 Carnegie Class: Not Classified
FAX Number: (303) 923-4112 Calendar System: Semester
URL: www.argosy.edu
Established: 2006 Annual Undergrad Tuition & Fees: $14,580
Enrollment: 540 Coed
Affiliation or Control: Proprietary IRS Status: Proprietary
Highest Offering: Doctorate
Program: Professional
Accreditation: &NH

01 Campus President .... Dr. Marcia BANKIRER
07 Director of Admissions .... Mr. Randal CARSON
32 Director of Student Services .... Mr. Thomas HARTMAN
10 Business Manager .... Mr. Richard BINDER
15 Director of Human Resources .... Ms. Nancy CRISTADORO
37 Director of Student Financial Svcs .... Ms. Jamie ESQUIBEL

† Regional accreditation is carried under the parent institution in Chicago, IL.

The Art Institute of Colorado (B)

1200 Lincoln Street, Denver CO 80203-2172
County: Denver FICE Identification: 020789
Unit ID: 126702
Telephone: (303) 837-0825 Carnegie Class: Spec/Arts
FAX Number: (303) 860-8520 Calendar System: Quarter
URL: www.artinstitutes.edu/denver
Established: 1952 Annual Undergrad Tuition & Fees: $31,168
Enrollment: 2,235 Coed
Affiliation or Control: Proprietary IRS Status: Proprietary
Highest Offering: Baccalaureate
Program: Occupational
Accreditation: NH, ACFEI, CIDA

01 President .... Mr. David C. ZORN
05 Dean of Education .... Mr. Jon KERBAUGH
07 Senior Director of Admissions .... Ms. Sarah JOHNSON
32 Director of Student Services .... Ms. Debi PITTS
10 Director Admin & Financial Services .... Ms. Wendy BUTLER
37 Director of Financial Aid .... Ms. Sophia LEUTH
06 Registrar .... Ms. Angel BLACK
38 Counselor .... Ms. Kristen ELDREDGE

Aspen University (C)

720 S Colorado Blvd, Suite 1150N, Denver CO 80246
County: Denver FICE Identification: 040803
Unit ID: 454829
Telephone: (800) 441-4746 Carnegie Class: Master's M
FAX Number: (303) 336-1144 Calendar System: Other
URL: www.aspen.edu
Established: 1987 Annual Undergrad Tuition & Fees: $6,100
Enrollment: 768 Coed
Affiliation or Control: Proprietary IRS Status: Proprietary
Highest Offering: Doctorate
Program: Business Emphasis
Accreditation: DETC, NURSE

01 President .... Dr. Gerry WILLIAMS
06 Registrar .... Ms. Suzanne PARTAIN
07 Director of Admissions .... Ms. Barbara MAX

Bel-Rea Institute of Animal Technology (D)

1681 S Dayton Street, Denver CO 80247-3048
County: Arapahoe FICE Identification: 012670
Unit ID: 126359
Telephone: (800) 950-8001 Carnegie Class: Assoc/PrivFP
FAX Number: (303) 751-9969 Calendar System: Quarter
URL: www.bel-rea.com
Established: 1971 Annual Undergrad Tuition & Fees: $9,656
Enrollment: 857 Coed
Affiliation or Control: Proprietary IRS Status: Proprietary
Highest Offering: Associate Degree
Program: Occupational
Accreditation: ACCSC

01 Director .... Paulette KAUFMAN
37 Director Student Financial Aid .... Stasi BONTINELLI
32 Director Student Services .... Cynthia MEDINA

Boulder College of Massage Therapy (E)

6255 Longbow Drive, Boulder CO 80301-3295
County: Boulder FICE Identification: 030131
Unit ID: 126410
Telephone: (800) 442-5131 Carnegie Class: Assoc/PrivNFP
FAX Number: (303) 530-2204 Calendar System: Quarter
URL: www.bcmt.org
Established: 1975 Annual Undergrad Tuition & Fees: $12,100
Enrollment: 11,252 Coed
Affiliation or Control: Independent Non-Profit IRS Status: 501(c)3
Highest Offering: Associate Degree
Program: Occupational
Accreditation: ACCSC

01 President .... Mr. Brent NILSON
05 Director of Education .... Ms. Joni MASSE
37 Financial Aid Advisor .... Ms. Kira CLARK

College for Financial Planning (F)

8000 E Maplewood Avenue, Suite 200,
Greenwood Village CO 80111-4727
County: Denver Identification: 666809
Unit ID: 126526
Telephone: (303) 220-1200 Carnegie Class: Not Classified
FAX Number: (303) 220-4940 Calendar System: Other
URL: www.cffp.edu
Established: 1972 Annual Undergrad Tuition & Fees: $3,900
Enrollment: 11,000 Coed
Affiliation or Control: Proprietary IRS Status: Proprietary
Highest Offering: Master's
Program: Professional
Accreditation: NH

01 President .... Mr. John SEARS
05 Vice President Academic Affairs .... Dr. Jesse ARMAN
10 Vice President Business Development .... Mr. Dirk PANTONE
07 Sr Dir Enrollment & Student Svcs .... Mr. Brett SANBORN
06 Registrar .... Ms. Viviane PRICE
38 Director Student Service Center .... Mr. Brett SANBORN

CollegeAmerica Colorado Springs (G)

3645 Citadel Drive S, Colorado Springs CO 80909-5320
County: El Paso Identification: 666293
Unit ID: 448752
Telephone: (719) 637-0600 Carnegie Class: Bac/Assoc
FAX Number: (719) 637-0806 Calendar System: Other
URL: www.collegeamerica.edu
Established: 1964 Annual Undergrad Tuition & Fees: $15,957
Enrollment: 564 Coed
Affiliation or Control: Proprietary IRS Status: Proprietary
Highest Offering: Baccalaureate
Program: Occupational
Accreditation: ACCSC

01 Executive Director .... Mrs. Rozann R. KUNSTLE

† Branch campus of CollegeAmerica Denver, Denver, CO.

CollegeAmerica Denver (H)

1385 S Colorado Blvd, 5th Floor, Denver CO 80222
County: Denver FICE Identification: 025943
Unit ID: 126872
Telephone: (303) 300-8740 Carnegie Class: Bac/Assoc
FAX Number: (303) 692-9156 Calendar System: Other
URL: www.collegeamerica.edu
Established: 1964 Annual Undergrad Tuition & Fees: $23,700
Enrollment: 800 Coed
Affiliation or Control: Proprietary IRS Status: Proprietary
Highest Offering: Baccalaureate
Program: Occupational
Accreditation: ACCSC

01 Executive Director .... Mr. Nathan LARSON
05 Academic Director .... Mr. Greg LAMPARD
37 Director of Financial Aid .... Ms. Ruby ROWE
07 Director of Admissions .... Ms. Jaclyn HAACK
06 Registrar .... Ms. Gwen ESTRIDGE

CollegeAmerica Fort Collins (I)

4601 S Mason, Fort Collins CO 80525-3740
County: Larimer Identification: 666362
Unit ID: 448761
Telephone: (970) 225-4860 Carnegie Class: Spec/Health
FAX Number: (970) 225-6059 Calendar System: Other
URL: www.collegeamerica.edu
Established: 2001 Annual Undergrad Tuition & Fees: $19,750
Enrollment: 477 Coed
Affiliation or Control: Proprietary IRS Status: Proprietary
Highest Offering: Baccalaureate
Program: 2-Year Principally Bachelor's Creditable; Professional; Business Emphasis
Accreditation: ACCSC

01 Campus Director .... Mr. Joel SCIMECA
07 Assistant Director of Admission .... Ms. Kristy MCNEAR
37 Financial Aid Director .... Ms. Laura MITCHELL
14 Network Administrator .... Mr. Craig R. SANDERS
32 Director Student Services/Placement .... Mr. Michael REY
06 Registrar .... Ms. Linda KLINE
08 Librarian .... Ms. Risa LUMLEY
35 Student Services Coordinator .... Ms. Oonah MANKIN
50 Dept Chair of Business & Computers .... Ms. Story STRINGER
76 Dept Chair of Healthcare .... Ms. Kai SCOTT

† Branch campus of CollegeAmerica Denver, Denver, CO.

Colorado Academy of Veterinary Technology (J)

1017 Cheyenne Meadows Road,
Colorado Springs CO 80906
County: El Paso Identification: 667048
Telephone: (719) 219-9636 Carnegie Class: Not Classified
FAX Number: (719) 302-5577 Calendar System: Quarter
URL: www.coloradovettech.com
Established: 2007 Annual Undergrad Tuition & Fees: $15,595
Enrollment: 2 Coed
Affiliation or Control: Proprietary IRS Status: Proprietary
Highest Offering: Associate Degree
Program: Occupational
Accreditation: COE

01 Site Director .... Dr. Steve RUBIN
05 Chief Academic Officer .... Mrs. Ramona CRANE
38 Director Student Counseling .... Mrs. Lisa BRUBAKER

Colorado Christian University (K)

8787 W Alameda Avenue, Lakewood CO 80226-7499
County: Jefferson FICE Identification: 009401
Unit ID: 126669
Telephone: (303) 963-3000 Carnegie Class: Master's M
FAX Number: (303) 963-3001 Calendar System: Semester
URL: www.ccu.edu
Established: 1914 Annual Undergrad Tuition & Fees: $22,610
Enrollment: 2,733 Coed
Affiliation or Control: Independent Non-Profit IRS Status: 501(c)3
Highest Offering: Master's
Program: 2-Year Principally Bachelor's Creditable; Liberal Arts And General; Teacher Preparatory; Professional
Accreditation: NH, MUS, NURSE

01 President .... Mr. William L. ARMSTRONG
10 Senior Vice President & CFO .... Mr. Daniel COHRS
05 VP College Adult & Graduate Studies .... Vacant
05 VP Acad Affairs College UG Studies .... Dr. Cherri S. PARKS
30 VP of Development .... Mr. Paul ELDRIDGE
32 VP for Student Development .... Mr. Jim S. MCCORMICK
20 Asst VP of Acad Affairs/Dean CAGS .... Mrs. Sarah SCHERLING
11 Asst VP for Administrative Services .... Mr. Ronald W. BENTON
35 Asst VP Stdnt Pgm/Dean of Students ..... Mrs. Sharon M. FELKER
42 Asst VP of Student Life/Ministry .... Mr. Joe WALTERS
50 Dean School of Business .... Dr. Gary EWEN
50 Dean of Business and Technology .... Dr. Mellani J. DAY
53 Dean School of Education .... Dr. Sara E. DALLMAN
53 Dean of Ed/Curriculum & Instruction .... Dr. Wendy WENDOVER
79 Dean Sch Humanities & Sciences .... Dr. William R. SAXBY
64 Dean School of Music .... Mr. Steven T. TAYLOR
73 Dean School of Theology .... Dr. Sidney S. BUZZELL
41 Athletic Director .... Mr. Darren A. RICHIE
21 Controller .... Mrs. Teresa HAGAR
38 Director of Counseling Services .... Dr. Joannie L. DEBRITO
44 Director of Development .... Mr. David J. NYE
18 Director of Facilities .... Mr. Mathew J. GOTHARD
37 Director of Financial Aid .... Mr. Steve M. WOODBURN
23 Director of Health Services .... Mrs. Donna HORWATH
15 Director of Human Resources .... Mr. Rick GARRIS
13 Sr Dir of Information Systems/Tech .... Mr. Bryan SHOLTEN
08 Library Director .... Mrs. Gayle C. GUNDERSON
36 Director of Life Directions Center .... Mrs. Joy STRICKLAND
06 Registrar .... Mrs. Linda K. PERCIANTE
39 Director of Residence Life .... Mr. Josh KUSCH
19 Director of Security .... Mr. Harry G. CAROTHERS
26 Dir of University Communications .... Mrs. Lisa L. ZELLER
07 Dean of Admissions .... Mr. Derry EBERT
29 Director Alumni Relations .... Mr. Daniel WESTERMANN

Colorado College (L)

14 E La Cache Poudre St.,
Colorado Springs CO 80903-3294
County: El Paso FICE Identification: 001347
Unit ID: 126678
Telephone: (719) 389-6000 Carnegie Class: Bac/A&S
FAX Number: (719) 634-4180 Calendar System: Other
URL: www.coloradocollege.edu
Established: 1874 Annual Undergrad Tuition & Fees: $39,900
Enrollment: 2,066 Coed
Affiliation or Control: Independent Non-Profit IRS Status: 501(c)3
Highest Offering: Master's
Program: Liberal Arts And General; Teacher Preparatory
Accreditation: NH

01 President .... Dr. Jill TIEFENTHALER

04 Director Office of the President .... Vacant
05 Dean of College & Faculty .... Dr. Susan ASHLEY
10 Vice Pres Business/Finance & Treas .... Mr. Robert G. MOORE
13 VP for Information Management .... Vacant
30 Vice Pres for College Advancement .... Mr. Stephen ELDER
32 VP Student Life/Dean of Students .... Mr. Mike EDMONDS
43 Dir Bus Contract Svcs/Legal Council .... Mr. Chris MELCHER
41 Director of Athletics .... Mr. Ken RALPH
84 Vice Pres Enrollment Management .... Mr. Mark HATCH
27 Director of Communications .... Ms. Jane TURNIS
18 Director of Facilities .... Vacant
96 Director of Purchasing .... Ms. Gina ARMS
42 Chaplain .... Dr. Bruce CORIELL
35 Associate Dean of Students .... Ms. Ginger MORGAN
37 Director of Financial Aid .... Mr. James M. SWANSON
88 Asst Vice Pres for Development .... Mr. Jay MALONEY
91 Director of Information Technology .... Mr. Dave ARMSTRONG
88 Director Advancement Services .... Ms. Cathey BARBEE
88 Assistant VP for Advancement .... Ms. Diane BENNINGHOFF
88 Dir Investment/Endowment Admin .... Ms. Stacy LUTZ-DAVIDSON
88 Director of Budget .... Ms. Lyrae WILLIAMS
88 Director Internal Audit .... Ms. Yolanda LYONS
09 Director of Institutional Research .... Ms. Amanda UDIS-KESSLER
39 Director Residential Life .... Mr. John LAUER
29 Director Alumni & Parent Relations .... Mr. Jay ENGLN
15 Director Human Resources .... Ms. Barbara WILSON
87 Dean of Summer Programs .... Mr. Eric POPKIN
36 Director Career Center .... Mr. Geoff FALEN
28 Director Minority & Intl Students .... Ms. Rochelle MASON
23 Medical Director .... Ms. Judith REYNOLDS
19 Director Campus Safety .... Mr. Ron SMITH
104 Director International Programs .... Dr. Inger BULL
91 Director Enterprise Info Svcs .... Mr. Vishvas PARADKAR
105 Director Web Communications .... Ms. Karen TO
20 Associate Dean of the College .... Mr. Victor NELSON-CISNEROS
21 Controller .... Mr. John CALDERHEAD
06 Registrar .... Mr. Phillip C. APODACA
20 Associate Dean of the Faculty .... Dr. Jeffrey NOBLETT
07 Director of Admissions .... Mr. Roberto GARCIA
08 Library Director .... Ms. Carol DICKERSON
40 Bookstore Manager .... Ms. Stephanie DAIGLE

Colorado Heights University (A)

3001 S Federal Boulevard, Denver CO 80236-2711
County: Denver FICE Identification: 032893
Unit ID: 367839
Telephone: (303) 936-8441 Carnegie Class: Spec/Bus
FAX Number: (303) 937-4224 Calendar System: Semester
URL: www.chu.edu
Established: 1990 Annual Undergrad Tuition & Fees: $15,355
Enrollment: 530 Coed
Affiliation or Control: Independent Non-Profit IRS Status: 501(c)3
Highest Offering: Master's
Program: Liberal Arts And General; Professional; Business Emphasis
Accreditation: ACICS

01 Interim President .... Dr. Brad YEAGER
05 Dean of Academic Affairs .... Dr. Brad YEAGER
10 Director of Finance/Accountant .... Ms. Erin ONSAGER
50 Dir of MBA and BA Intl Business .... Dr. Brad YEAGER
06 Registrar .... Mr. Million KAHSAY
88 Dir of Theater & Event Center .... Ms. Felica GOETT
08 Librarian .... Ms. Schanie CAIRNS
15 Director of Human Resources .... Ms. Debra POWELL
37 Financial Aid Counselor .... Ms. Beba PREDIC
84 Director Enrollment Services .... Vacant
39 Dir Residence Life/Security .... Mr. Daniil YUSUFOV
07 Director of Recruiting .... Mr. Jason JOHNSON
13 Director Information Technology .... Mr. John ADAMS
18 Director of Facilities .... Mr. Jose GALLEGOS
88 Food Services .... Ms. Cindy ROATH

Colorado Mesa University (B)

1100 North Avenue, Grand Junction CO 81501-3122
County: Mesa FICE Identification: 001358
Unit ID: 127556
Telephone: (970) 248-1020 Carnegie Class: Bac/A&S
FAX Number: (970) 248-1076 Calendar System: Semester
URL: www.mesastate.edu
Established: 1925 Annual Undergrad Tuition & Fees (In-State): $5,238
Enrollment: 8,130 Coed
Affiliation or Control: State IRS Status: 501(c)3
Highest Offering: Doctorate
Program: Occupational; Liberal Arts And General; Professional
Accreditation: NH, EMT, MUS, NURSE, RAD, TED

01 President .... Mr. Tim FOSTER
05 Vice Pres Academic/Student Affairs .... Dr. Carol FUTHEY
10 Vice President Financial/Admin Svcs .... Mr. Patrick DOYLE
31 Vice Pres Community College Affairs .... Mrs. Brigitte SUNDERMANN
96 Asst Vice Pres Auxiliary Services .... Mr. Andy RODRIGUEZ
32 Dean of Students .... Mr. John MARSHALL
13 Director Information Technology .... Mr. Jeremy BROWN
09 Director Institutional Research .... Ms. Sonia BRANDON
08 Library Director .... Ms. Elizabeth BRODAK
25 Director Sponsored Programs .... Ms. Cindy LUEB
20 Assistant Academic Officer .... Mr. Steve WERMAN
21 Controller .... Mr. Joe TAYLOR
21 Director Budget .... Ms. Whitney SUTTON
30 Director of Development .... Ms. Kristi POLLARD
37 Director Financial Aid .... Mr. Curt MARTIN
18 Director of Facilities Services .... Mr. Kent MARSH
29 Director of Alumni Association .... Mr. Rick ADLEMAN
41 Athletic Director .... Mr. Butch MILLER
26 Act Director Marketing/Publications .... Ms. Dana NUNN
39 Director Housing & Residence Life .... Mr. Troy SEPPELT
06 Registrar .... Ms. Holly TEAL
07 Director of Admissions .... Mr. Jared MEIER
15 Director of Human Resources .... Ms. Barbara CASE-KING
20 Interim Director Academic Services .... Ms. Millie MOLAND
40 Bookstore Manager .... Ms. Tracy BRODRICK

Colorado Mountain College (C)

831 Grand Avenue, Glenwood Springs CO 81602-3961
County: Garfield FICE Identification: 004506
Unit ID: 126711
Telephone: (970) 945-8691 Carnegie Class: Assoc/Pub-R-L
FAX Number: (970) 947-8385 Calendar System: Semester
URL: www.coloradomtn.edu
Established: 1965 Annual Undergrad Tuition & Fees (In-District): $1,590
Enrollment: 6,088 Coed
Affiliation or Control: Local IRS Status: 501(c)3
Highest Offering: Baccalaureate
Program: Occupational; 2-Year Principally Bachelor's Creditable
Accreditation: NH, ADNUR, EMT

01 President .... Dr. Stanley JENSEN
03 Senior Vice President .... Dr. Jill BOYLE
05 Sr Vice President Academic Affairs .... Dr. Brad TYNDALL
12 VP CMC/Aspen Campus CEO .... Mr. Joseph MAESTAS
10 CFO .... Ms. Linda ENGLISH
09 VP Institutional Effectiveness .... Dr. Meeta GOEL
32 VP Student Affairs .... Mr. Brad BANKHEAD
15 Vice President of Human Resources .... Ms. Jan ASPELUND
26 Public Relations Officer .... Ms. Debbie CRAWFORD
13 Chief Information Officer .... Ms. Debbie CRAWFORD
07 Dir Pre-Enrollment Svcs/Registrar .... Mr. Bill SOMMERS
37 Director of Financial Aid .... Mr. Gary LEWIS
18 Director of College Facilities .... Mr. Sam SKRAMSTAD
27 Director of Marketing/Publications .... Mr. Doug STEWART
96 Director of Purchasing .... Mr. Steve BOYD
20 Developmental Education Coordinator .... Ms. Krisan CROW

Colorado Northwestern Community College (D)

500 Kennedy Drive, Rangely CO 81648-3598
County: Rio Blanco FICE Identification: 001359
Unit ID: 126748
Telephone: (970) 675-2261 Carnegie Class: Assoc/Pub-R-M
FAX Number: (970) 675-5046 Calendar System: Semester
URL: www.cncc.edu
Established: 1962 Annual Undergrad Tuition & Fees (In-District): $2,888
Enrollment: 1,383 Coed
Affiliation or Control: State/Local IRS Status: 170(c)1
Highest Offering: Associate Degree
Program: Occupational; 2-Year Principally Bachelor's Creditable
Accreditation: NH, DH

01 President .... Mr. Russell GEORGE
11 Vice Pres Administration .... Mr. Gene BILODEAU
05 Vice Pres Instruction/Student Svcs .... Mr. David SMITH
10 Vice Pres Business/Administration .... Mr. Don BRANTLEY
84 Dean of Enrollment Services .... Ms. Tresa ENGLAND
21 Chief Finance Officer .... Mr. Christopher BISHOP
08 Library Director .... Ms. Leana COX
15 Human Resource Specialist .... Ms. Penny HANCOCK
26 Marketing Dir/Exec Asst to Pres .... Ms. Becky DUBBERT
18 Facilities Director .... Mr. Bobby BURNS
102 Foundation Director .... Ms. Becky NIEMI
09 Director of Institutional Research .... Ms. Lisa LASEVERE
38 Director Student Counseling .... Ms. Charity STOLWORTHY
96 Director of Purchasing .... Mr. Roger HANNA
56 Director of Distance Learning .... Vacant
37 Financial Aid Technician .... Ms. Merrie BYERS
12 Dean of Instruction in Rangely .... Ms. Judy ALLRED
12 Dean of Instruction in Craig .... Mr. Dan MINOR

Colorado School of Healing Arts (E)

7655 W Mississippi, Suite 100, Lakewood CO 80226-4332
County: Jefferson FICE Identification: 035844
Unit ID: 381732
Telephone: (303) 986-2320 Carnegie Class: Assoc/PrivFP
FAX Number: (303) 980-6594 Calendar System: Quarter
URL: www.csha.net
Established: 1986 Annual Undergrad Tuition & Fees: $11,620
Enrollment: 204 Coed
Affiliation or Control: Proprietary IRS Status: Proprietary
Highest Offering: Associate Degree
Program: Occupational; 2-Year Principally Bachelor's Creditable; Technical Emphasis
Accreditation: ACCSC

01 Executive Director & Owner .... Mr. Dennis SIMPSON
03 Director .... Ms. Gina SIMPSON
05 Director of Education Deg Pgm .... Mr. Mark BRAUKMAN
06 Registrar .... Ms. Melinda PHINPRAPHAT
07 Admissions Representatives .... Ms. Tiffany LAYNE
08 Head Librarian .... Ms. Kris WILL
36 Career Advisor/Placement .... Mr. Mark SOBOLESKE
37 Financial Aid Administrator .... Ms. Andrea NIECE
40 Bookstore Manager .... Mr. Greg SENICH
53 Director of Education Cert Pgm .... Ms. Chris SMITH

Colorado School of Mines (F)

1500 Illinois Street, Golden CO 80401-1843
County: Jefferson FICE Identification: 001348
Unit ID: 126775
Telephone: (303) 273-3000 Carnegie Class: RU/H
FAX Number: (303) 273-3278 Calendar System: Semester
URL: www.mines.edu
Established: 1874 Annual Undergrad Tuition & Fees (In-State): $14,454
Enrollment: 5,093 Coed
Affiliation or Control: State IRS Status: 501(c)3
Highest Offering: Doctorate
Program: Professional; Technical Emphasis
Accreditation: NH, ENG

01 President .... Dr. M. W. SCOGGINS
05 Provost .... Dr. Terry PARKER
10 Sr Vice Pres Finance & Admin .... Ms. Kirsten VOLPI
88 Sr Vice Pres Strat Enterprises .... Dr. Nigel T. MIDDLETON
32 Vice Pres Student Life .... Dr. Don FOX
30 VP for Institutional Advancement .... Mr. Brian WINKELBAUER
20 Assoc Vice Pres Academic Affairs .... Dr. Wendy HARRISON
100 Chief of Staff .... Mr. Peter HAN
06 Registrar .... Ms. Lara MEDLEY
07 Director of Admissions .... Mr. Bruce P. GOETZ
08 Librarian .... Ms. Joanne V. LERUD-HECK
14 Director of Computer Center .... Mr. Derek J. WILSON
26 Director Integrated Marketing Comm .... Ms. Karen GILBERT
37 Director of Financial Aid .... Ms. Jill ROBERTSON
51 Director of Special Programs .... Dr. Gary L. BAUGHMAN
58 Dean Graduate Studies/Research .... Dr. Thomas BOYD
18 Director of Plant Facilities .... Mr. Gary BOWERSOCK
22 Affirmative Action Officer .... Mr. Michael DOUGHERTY
39 Director of Student Housing .... Ms. Rebecca FLINTOFT
38 Director Student Development .... Mr. Ronald L. BRUMMETT
41 Athletic Director .... Mr. Thomas SPICER
04 Spec Assistant to the President .... Ms. Carol R. CHAPMAN
09 Director of Institutional Research .... Ms. Tricia DOUTHIT
15 Director Personnel Services .... Mr. Michael DOUGHERTY
84 Director Enrollment Management .... Ms. Heather BOYD
35 Director Student Affairs .... Mr. Derek MORGAN
36 Director Student Placement .... Mr. Ronald L. BRUMMETT
19 Director Public Safety .... Mr. Keith TURNEY
94 Exec Dir Women in Sci Eng & Math .... Ms. Deb LASICH
92 Director Honors Program .... Dr. Ken OSGOOD
96 Director Purchasing .... Mr. John C. KANE
93 Director Minority Engineering Pro .... Mr. Khahn VU
91 Director Information Services .... Mr. George E. FUNKEY
29 Director Alumni Relations .... Ms. Anita PARISEAU

Colorado School of Trades (G)

1575 Hoyt Street, Lakewood CO 80215-2996
County: Jefferson FICE Identification: 011572
Unit ID: 126784
Telephone: (800) 234-4594 Carnegie Class: Assoc/PrivFP
FAX Number: (303) 233-4723 Calendar System: Other
URL: www.schooloftrades.edu
Established: 1947 Annual Undergrad Tuition & Fees: $18,900
Enrollment: 145 Coed
Affiliation or Control: Proprietary IRS Status: Proprietary
Highest Offering: Associate Degree
Program: Occupational
Accreditation: ACCSC

01 President .... Mr. Robert E. MARTIN

Colorado School of Traditional Chinese Medicine (H)

1441 York Street, Suite 202, Denver CO 80206-2127
County: Denver FICE Identification: 036863
Unit ID: 381352
Telephone: (303) 329-6355 Carnegie Class: Spec/Health
FAX Number: (303) 388-8165 Calendar System: Trimester
URL: www.cstcm.edu
Established: 1989 Annual Undergrad Tuition & Fees: $14,950
Enrollment: 112 Coed
Affiliation or Control: Proprietary IRS Status: Proprietary
Highest Offering: Master's
Program: Occupational; Professional
Accreditation: ACUP

01 Administrative Director .... Vladimir DIBRIGIDA

*Colorado State University System Office (I)

410 17th Street, Suite 2440, Denver CO 80202-4426
County: Denver FICE Identification: 033437
Telephone: (303) 534-6290 Carnegie Class: N/A
FAX Number: (303) 534-6298
URL: www.csusystem.edu

01 Chancellor ... Mr. Joseph BLAKE
05 Chief Academic Officer ... Dr. George DENNISON
43 General Counsel ... Mr. Michael NOLSER
10 Chief Financial Officer ... Mr. Rich SCHWEIGERT
26 Director of Public Relations ... Mr. Brad BOHLANDER
86 Government Relations Coordinator ... Vacant
04 Executive Asst to President ... Ms. Melanie GEARY

*Colorado State University (A)

Fort Collins CO 80523-0015
County: Larimer FICE Identification: 001350
Unit ID: 126818
Telephone: (970) 491-1101 Carnegie Class: RU/VH
FAX Number: (970) 491-0501 Calendar System: Semester
URL: www.colostate.edu
Established: 1870 Annual Undergrad Tuition & Fees (In-State): $8,042
Enrollment: 26,356 Coed
Affiliation or Control: State IRS Status: 501(c)3
Highest Offering: Doctorate
Program: Liberal Arts And General; Teacher Preparatory; Professional
Accreditation: NH, BUS, CACREP, CEA, CIDA, CONST, COPSY, DIETC, DIETD, ENG, ENGR, FOR, IPSY, JOUR, LSAR, MFCD, MUS, OT, SW, TEAC, VET

02 President ... Dr. Anthony A. FRANK
05 Senior Executive VP/Provost ... Dr. Rick MIRANDA
46 Vice President for Research ... Dr. William H. FARLAND
10 Assoc VP for Finance and Budgets ... Ms. Lynn JOHNSON
11 VP for University Operations ... Ms. Amy PARSONS
30 VP Advancement/Strategic Initiative ... Mr. Brett B. ANDERSON
84 Vice Pres for Enrollment/Access ... Dr. Robin C. BROWN
20 Vice Prov for Undergraduate Affairs ... Dr. Alan LAMBORN
58 Vice Prov Graduate Ed/Asst VP Rsch ... Dr. Peter DORHOUT
27 VP for External Relations ... Mr. Tom MILLIGAN
90 VP for IT/Dean of Libraries ... Dr. Patrick BURNS
91 Director of Acad Comp/Network Svc ... Mr. Scott BAILY
15 Interim Dir Human Resource Svcs ... Mr. Tony DECROSTA
36 Director Career Services ... Ms. Ann MALEN
08 Exec Assoc Dean of Libraries ... Vacant
07 Assoc VP Enroll/VP for Diversity ... Ms. Mary R. ONTIVEROS
29 Exec Director Alumni Relations ... Ms. Colleen D. MEYER
41 Athletic Director ... Mr. Paul KOWALCZYK
43 Deputy General Counsel ... Mr. Jason L. JOHNSON
47 Dean Agriculture Sciences ... Dr. Craig BEYROUTY
88 Int Dean Applied Human Sciences ... Dr. Nancy K. HARTLEY
50 Dean of Business ... Dr. Ajay MENON
54 Dean of Engineering ... Dr. Sandra L. WOODS
49 Dean of Liberal Arts ... Dr. Ann M. GILL
62 VP for IT/Dean of Libraries ... Dr. Patrick BURNS
65 Dean of Natural Resources ... Dr. Joyce BERRY
81 Dean of Natural Sciences ... Dr. Janice L. NERGER
74 Dean of Veterinary Med & Biomed Sci ... Dr. Lance PERRYMAN
56 Director Cooperative Extension Svcs ... Dr. Lou SWANSON
06 Registrar ... Ms. Sandra CALHOUN
18 Chief Facilities/Physical Plant ... Mr. Brian J. CHASE
22 Dir of Equal Opportunity ... Ms. Diana PRIETO
37 Director of Student Financial Aid ... Ms. Sandy CALHOUN
39 Exec Dir Housing & Dining Services ... Dr. James DOLAK
40 Director of Bookstore ... Mr. John PARRY
96 Director of Purchasing ... Mr. Frank KRAPPES
92 Director University Honors Program ... Dr. Robert KELLER
94 Director Women's Programs & Studies ... Ms. Kathy SISNEROS
09 Director of Institutional Research ... Dr. Laura JENSEN

*Colorado State University-Pueblo (B)

2200 Bonforte Boulevard, Pueblo CO 81001-4901
County: Pueblo FICE Identification: 001365
Unit ID: 128106
Telephone: (719) 549-2100 Carnegie Class: Master's S
FAX Number: (719) 549-2650 Calendar System: Semester
URL: www.colostate-pueblo.edu
Established: 1933 Annual Undergrad Tuition & Fees (In-State): $6,269
Enrollment: 7,379 Coed
Affiliation or Control: State IRS Status: 501(c)3
Highest Offering: Master's
Program: Liberal Arts And General; Teacher Preparatory; Professional
Accreditation: NH, BUS, ENG, ENGT, MUS, NUR, SW, TEAC

02 Interim President ... Dr. Julio S. LEON
05 Provost/VP for Academic Affairs ... Dr. Peter DORHOUT
10 Interim VP Finance & Administration ... Mr. Mike FARLEY
84 Asst Vice Pres Enrollment Mgmt ... Mr. Joe MARSHALL
88 Asst Provost Assess/Student Lrng ... Dr. Erin FREW
32 Dean Student Life/Development ... Dr. Zav DADABHOY
08 Dean Library ... Ms. Rhonda GONZALES
51 Dean Continuing Education ... Dr. James MALM
50 Dean Hasan School of Business ... Dr. Sue HANKS
79 Dean Col of Humanities/Soc Sci ... Dr. Roy SONNEMA
54 Dean Engr/Educ/Profess Studies ... Dr. Hector CARRASCO
81 Dean Science/Math ... Dr. Richard KREMINSKI
102 Executive Director Foundation ... Ms. Dena Sue POTESTIO
26 Exec Director External Affairs ... Ms. Cora ZALETEL
09 Dir Institutional Research/Analysis ... Dr. Lin CHANG
21 Controller ... Mr. Harvey WILDS
37 Director Student Financial Services ... Mr. Sean MCGIVNEY
06 Registrar ... Ms. Katie VELARDE
36 Director Career Center ... Mrs. Michelle B. GJERDE
14 Dir Info Tech Svcs/Chief Tech Ofcr ... Vacant
41 Director Athletics ... Mr. Joe FOLDA
18 Dir Facilities/Construction/Plng ... Mr. Craig CASON
15 Director Human Resources ... Mr. Ken NUFER
39 Director Residence Life & Housing ... Ms. Rhonda UBER
31 Director Auxiliary Services ... Mr. A. Ramon GARCIA
23 Student Health Services Nurse ... Ms. Carlotta FENDRICH
29 Director Alumni Relations ... Ms. Tracy SAMORA
38 Director Student Counseling ... Vacant
89 Director First Year Programs ... Dr. Derek LOPEZ
22 Director Affirmative Action ... Ms. LaNeeca WILLIAMS
85 Assoc Dir International Programs ... Ms. Annie WILLIAMS
04 Executive Asst to the President ... Ms. Trisha MACIAS

Colorado Technical University (C)

3151 South Vaughn Way, Aurora CO 80014
County: Arapahoe Identification: 666732
Unit ID: 430087
Telephone: (303) 632-2300 Carnegie Class: Master's M
FAX Number: (303) 694-6673 Calendar System: Quarter
URL: www.coloradotech.edu
Established: 1996 Annual Undergrad Tuition & Fees: $11,370
Enrollment: 1,300 Coed
Affiliation or Control: Proprietary IRS Status: Proprietary
Highest Offering: Doctorate
Program: Technical Emphasis
Accreditation: &NH

01 President ... Dr. Mark PIEFFER
11 Director of Operations ... Mr. Jeremy L. WALKER
37 Director of Financial Aid ... Ms. Terry BARGAS
10 Controller ... Ms. Rebecca ZARNES
07 Director of Admissions ... Mr. Shebon KELIN
13 Manager of IT ... Mr. Tom FELDZYNSKI
08 Librarian ... Ms. Tracy TREASE
15 Human Resources ... Ms. Renae STOKKE

† Regional accreditation is carried under the parent institution in Colorado Springs, CO.

Colorado Technical University (D)

4435 N Chestnut Street, Colorado Springs CO 80907-3896
County: El Paso FICE Identification: 010148
Unit ID: 126827
Telephone: (719) 598-0200 Carnegie Class: DRU
FAX Number: (719) 598-3740 Calendar System: Quarter
URL: www.coloradotech.edu
Established: 1965 Annual Undergrad Tuition & Fees: $10,665
Enrollment: 2,947 Coed
Affiliation or Control: Proprietary IRS Status: Proprietary
Highest Offering: Doctorate
Program: Occupational; 2-Year Principally Bachelor's Creditable; Professional; Technical Emphasis
Accreditation: NH, ENG

00 CEO ... Mr. Jeremy WHEATON
01 Campus President ... Mr. Bentley RAYBURN
05 Vice President of Education ... Dr. Luis VELEZ
07 Vice President of Admissions ... Ms. Beth BRAATEN
10 Vice President of Operations ... Mr. Scott MCGUIRE
16 Dir of Human Resources ... Ms. Jan SUHR
08 Dir of University Libraries ... Ms. Amy PHILLIPS
37 Dir of Student Financial Services ... Ms. Cindy RUBEK
36 Director of Career Services ... Mr. Jason RAMSEY
36 Career Services Manager ... Mr. Mike BOYD
13 Manager of Information Systems ... Mr. Thomas LEIGH
54 Dean Engineering/Computer Science ... Dr. Bruce HARMON
88 Dean of Management ... Dr. Les KEFFEL
76 Dean of Health Sciences ... Dr. Diana KOSTRZEWSKI

Community College of Aurora (E)

16000 E Centre Tech Parkway, Aurora CO 80011-9036
County: Arapahoe FICE Identification: 022769
Unit ID: 126863
Telephone: (303) 360-4700 Carnegie Class: Assoc/Pub-S-MC
FAX Number: (303) 360-4761 Calendar System: Semester
URL: www.ccaurora.edu
Established: 1983 Annual Undergrad Tuition & Fees (In-State): $3,400
Enrollment: 7,610 Coed
Affiliation or Control: State IRS Status: 501(c)3
Highest Offering: Associate Degree
Program: Occupational; 2-Year Principally Bachelor's Creditable
Accreditation: NH, EMT

01 President ... Dr. Linda S. BOWMAN
05 Interim Vice President Instruction ... Vacant
11 Vice Pres Administrative Services ... Mr. Richard MAESTAS
84 VP Enrollment Mgmt/Student Services ... Vacant
07 Director Admissions & Registrar ... Ms. Kristen CUSACK
21 Controller ... Ms. Mercy ABRAHAM
15 Director of Human Resources ... Ms. Cindy HESSE
08 Director Learning Resource Center ... Vacant
37 Director Financial Aid and Advising ... Mr. John YOUNG
32 Director Student Life ... Ms. Angie TIEDEMAN
27 Director College Communications ... Ms. Liz VANLANDINGHAM
09 Director of Institutional Research ... Dr. David BAILEY
18 Facilities Manager ... Mr. Jim MARSHALL
25 Coordinator of Grants & Funding ... Dr. Chris WARD

Community College of Denver (F)

P.O. Box 173363, Denver CO 80217-3363
County: Denver FICE Identification: 009542
Unit ID: 126942
Telephone: (303) 556-2600 Carnegie Class: Assoc/Pub-U-MC
FAX Number: (303) 556-8555 Calendar System: Semester
URL: www.ccd.edu
Established: 1967 Annual Undergrad Tuition & Fees (In-State): $3,956
Enrollment: 9,005 Coed
Affiliation or Control: State IRS Status: 501(c)3
Highest Offering: Associate Degree
Program: Occupational; 2-Year Principally Bachelor's Creditable
Accreditation: NH, DH, MAC, RAD

01 Interim President ... Mr. Cliff RICHARDSON
05 Provost/Vice Pres Learning ... Dr. Bernice HARRIS
10 Vice Pres Finance & Admin/CFO ... Mr. Duane RISSE
32 Vice Pres Student Development ... Ms. Leslie MCCLELLON
102 Vice Pres Economic/Resource Devel ... Vacant
75 Dean Career/Technical Education ... Dr. Chris BUDDEN
49 Dean Language/Arts/Behavioral Sci ... Dr. Amy RELL
88 Dean Educational Advancement ... Ms. Nancy STORY
35 Dean of Students/Ed Plng/Advising ... Mr. Ryan ROSS
84 Dean of Enrollment Svcs/Registrar ... Mr. Dan OPALEWSKI
12 Dean Lowry Campus ... Ms. Jan JOOST
35 Director Office of Student Life ... Vacant
37 Director Financial Aid ... Ms. Karla NASH
07 Director Recruit/Student Outreach ... Mr. Ari Senghor ROSNER-SALAZAR
15 Director Human Resources ... Ms. Rhonda PYLICAN
13 Executive Director IT Services ... Mr. Andy CORBETT
09 Exec Dir Inst Research & Planning ... Ms. Margaret PURYEAR

Concorde Career College (G)

111 N Havana Street, Aurora CO 80010-4314
County: Arapahoe FICE Identification: 008871
Unit ID: 126687
Telephone: (303) 861-1151 Carnegie Class: Assoc/PrivFP
FAX Number: (303) 839-5478 Calendar System: Other
URL: www.concorde.edu
Established: 1969 Annual Undergrad Tuition & Fees: $14,786
Enrollment: 651 Coed
Affiliation or Control: Proprietary IRS Status: Proprietary
Highest Offering: Associate Degree
Program: Occupational
Accreditation: ACCSC, @PTAA, RAD, SURGT

01 Campus President ... Mr. Al SHORT
05 Academic Dean ... Ms. Cindy ODDD
37 Director of Financial Aid ... Ms. Nancy DISATE
07 Director of Admissions ... Mr. Michael COMO

Denver School of Nursing (H)

1401 19th Street, Denver CO 80202
County: Adams FICE Identification: 041483
Unit ID: 454856
Telephone: (303) 292-0015 Carnegie Class: Not Classified
FAX Number: (720) 974-0290 Calendar System: Quarter
URL: www.denverschoolofnursing.edu
Established: N/A Annual Undergrad Tuition & Fees: $15,379
Enrollment: 430 Coed
Affiliation or Control: Proprietary IRS Status: Proprietary
Highest Offering: Baccalaureate
Program: Nursing Emphasis
Accreditation: @NH, ACCSC

01 President ... Mr. David O'DONNELL
05 Dir of General Education/ Operations ... Dr. Vanessa DAVIS WARNER
32 Director of Student Services ... Ms. Jenny BURTON
66 Dean/Dir of Nursing Education Prgms ... Dr. Deb BANIK

Denver Seminary (I)

6399 S Santa Fe Drive, Littleton CO 80120-2912
County: Arapahoe FICE Identification: 001352
Unit ID: 126979
Telephone: (303) 761-2482 Carnegie Class: Spec/Faith
FAX Number: (303) 761-8060 Calendar System: Semester
URL: www.denverseminary.edu
Established: 1950 Annual Graduate Tuition & Fees: $13,950
Enrollment: 993 Coed
Affiliation or Control: Interdenominational IRS Status: 501(c)3
Highest Offering: Doctorate; No Undergraduates
Program: Professional
Accreditation: NH, CACREP, THEOL

01 President ... Dr. Mark S. YOUNG
00 Chancellor ... Dr. Gordon MACDONALD
05 Provost/Dean ... Dr. Randolph M. MACFARLAND
10 Vice President of Finance ... Ms. Deborah KELLAR
30 Vice President of Advancement ... Dr. Jim HOWARD
32 Vice President of Student Services ... Mr. Robert JONES
35 Dean of Student Services ... Mr. Tony LEMUS
20 Associate Academic Dean ... Dr. W. David BUSCHART
20 Associate Academic Dean ... Dr. Don PAYNE
06 Registrar/Dir Educ Services ... Ms. Pam BETKER
88 Dir Educational Projects ... Mrs. Lisa LINHART
88 Director of Accounting ... Mrs. Kristy EDLUND
07 Director of Admissions ... Vacant
44 Director of Development ... Mr. Chris JOHNSON
40 Director of Auxiliary Services ... Mr. Kent B. QUACKENBUSH
13 Director of Information Systems ... Mr. Jason ADAMS

27 Director of Communications .... Ms. Pam BURTON
88 Dir Educational Technology .... Dr. Venita DOUGHTY
18 Director of Physical Plant .... Mr. Tom PECORA
37 Director of Financial Aid .... Mr. Joel LAOS
08 Director of Library .... Dr. Keith P. WELLS
73 Director of DMin Program .... Dr. David R. OSBORN
15 Director of Human Resources .... Ms. Zandy WENNERSTROM

DeVry University - Colorado Springs Center (A)

1175 Kelly Johnson Boulevard,
Colorado Springs CO 80920-3928
County: El Paso Identification: 666511
Unit ID: 363378
Telephone: (719) 632-3000 Carnegie Class: Not Classified
FAX Number: (719) 866-6770 Calendar System: Semester
URL: www.devry.edu
Established: 2001 Annual Undergrad Tuition & Fees: $15,294
Enrollment: 490 Coed
Affiliation or Control: Proprietary IRS Status: Proprietary
Highest Offering: Master's
Program: Occupational; Professional; Business Emphasis
Accreditation: &NH

01 Center Dean .... Judy LESSER

† Regional accreditation is carried under the parent institution in Downers Grove, IL.

DeVry University - Denver South Center (B)

6312 S Fiddlers Green Circle #150E,
Greenwood Village CO 80111-4943
County: Denver FICE Identification: 007648
Unit ID: 127042
Telephone: (303) 329-3000 Carnegie Class: Not Classified
FAX Number: (303) 329-4486 Calendar System: Semester
URL: www.devry.edu
Established: 2001 Annual Undergrad Tuition & Fees: $15,294
Enrollment: 387 Coed
Affiliation or Control: Proprietary IRS Status: Proprietary
Highest Offering: Master's
Program: Occupational; Professional; Business Emphasis
Accreditation: &NH

01 Center Dean .... Mr. Peter DINNEEN

† Regional accreditation is carried under the parent institution in Downers Grove, IL.

DeVry University - Westminster Campus (C)

1870 W 122nd Avenue, Westminster CO 80234-2010
County: Denver Identification: 666227
Unit ID: 440590
Telephone: (303) 280-7400 Carnegie Class: Master's S
FAX Number: (303) 452-3606 Calendar System: Semester
URL: www.devry.edu
Established: 2003 Annual Undergrad Tuition & Fees: $15,294
Enrollment: 1,129 Coed
Affiliation or Control: Proprietary IRS Status: Proprietary
Highest Offering: Master's
Program: Occupational; Professional; Business Emphasis
Accreditation: &NH, ENGT

01 Metro President .... Mr. James CALDWELL
06 Registrar .... Ms. Lisa BARRY
10 Director of Student Finance .... Mr. Cliff DEFFKE
07 Senior Director of Admissions .... Mr. Matthew HANUSA
05 Dean of Academic Affairs .... Mr. Michael WASSON
15 Human Resources Business Partner .... Mr. Daryl SMITH
32 Dean of Student Affairs .... Ms. Sheila SCOTT
54 Dean of Engineering Technology .... Ms. Martha KEUL
36 Director of Career Services .... Ms. Laurie SEIN
97 Dean of General Education & Busines .... Mr. Martin GLOEGE

† Regional accreditation is carried under the parent institution in Downers Grove, IL.

Everest College (D)

14280 E Jewell Avenue, Suite 100, Aurora CO 80012
County: Arapahoe Identification: 666412
Unit ID: 366544
Telephone: (303) 745-6244 Carnegie Class: Assoc/PrivFP
FAX Number: (303) 745-6245 Calendar System: Other
URL: www.everest.edu
Established: 1895 Annual Undergrad Tuition & Fees: $14,759
Enrollment: 636 Coed
Affiliation or Control: Proprietary IRS Status: Proprietary
Highest Offering: Associate Degree
Program: Occupational
Accreditation: ACICS, MAC

01 President .... Ms. Carissa BARTON

† Branch campus of Everest College, Denver, CO.

Everest College (E)

1815 Jet Wing Drive, Colorado Springs CO 80916
County: El Paso FICE Identification: 004503
Unit ID: 126401
Telephone: (719) 638-6580 Carnegie Class: Assoc/PrivFP
FAX Number: (719) 638-6818 Calendar System: Quarter
URL: www.everest-college.com
Established: 1897 Annual Undergrad Tuition & Fees: $14,271
Enrollment: 719 Coed
Affiliation or Control: Proprietary IRS Status: Proprietary
Highest Offering: Associate Degree
Program: Occupational; 2-Year Principally Bachelor's Creditable
Accreditation: ACICS, MAC

01 President .... Mr. Randy ATWATER
05 Dean of Education .... Ms. Heidi GODBOLD
07 Director Admissions .... Ms. Dawn COLLINS
37 Director Student Finance .... Mrs. Meng JOHNSON
36 Director Career Services .... Mr. James PROBY

Everest College (F)

9065 Grant Street, Denver CO 80229-4339
County: Adams FICE Identification: 004507
Unit ID: 127787
Telephone: (303) 457-2757 Carnegie Class: Assoc/PrivFP
FAX Number: (303) 457-4030 Calendar System: Quarter
URL: www.cci.edu
Established: 1895 Annual Undergrad Tuition & Fees: $35,136
Enrollment: 752 Coed
Affiliation or Control: Proprietary IRS Status: Proprietary
Highest Offering: Associate Degree
Program: Occupational
Accreditation: ACICS, MAC, #SURGT

01 President .... Mr. Bruce PILEGGI
05 Academic Dean .... Mr. Raines GUINN
07 Director of Admissions .... Ms. Jennifer HEDRICK
37 Director of Student Finance .... Ms. Kim MARTINEZ
36 Director of Career Services .... Ms. Diane BOOREN
06 Registrar .... Mr. Bruce DOUGHTY

Fort Lewis College (G)

1000 Rim Drive, Durango CO 81301-3999
County: La Plata FICE Identification: 001353
Unit ID: 127185
Telephone: (970) 247-7010 Carnegie Class: Bac/A&S
FAX Number: (970) 247-7175 Calendar System: Semester
URL: www.fortlewis.edu
Established: 1911 Annual Undergrad Tuition & Fees (In-State): $4,924
Enrollment: 3,864 Coed
Affiliation or Control: State IRS Status: 170(c)1
Highest Offering: Baccalaureate
Program: Liberal Arts And General; Teacher Preparatory
Accreditation: NH, BUS, ENG, MUS, TEAC

01 President .... Dr. Dene Kay THOMAS
05 Provost/Vice Pres Academic Affairs .... Dr. Barbara MORRIS
10 Vice Pres Finance & Administration .... Mr. Steven J. SCHWARTZ
84 Assoc Vice Pres Enrollment Mgmt .... Dr. Carol SMITH
32 Vice President Student Affairs .... Dr. Glenna W. SEXTON
20 Assoc Vice Pres Academic Affairs .... Dr. Kenneth PEPION
09 Exec Dir of Institutional Research .... Mr. Richard A. MILLER
21 Director Budget .... Ms. Michele PETERSON
06 Registrar .... Ms. Kathy KENDALL
21 Controller .... Ms. Valerie L. BORGE
25 Director of Grants Management .... Ms. Angela ROCHAT
37 Director Financial Aid .... Ms. Elaine S. REDWINE
07 Director of Admission .... Mr. Andrew BURNS
38 Director Counseling/Student Dev Ctr ... Dr. Susan K. MCGINNESS
08 Director of the Library .... Vacant
18 Dir Physical Plant/College Engr .... Mr. Wayne KJONAAS
15 Dir Human Resources/Equal Opptnty .... Mr. Darren MATHEWS
39 Dir Stdnt Housing/Conferences Svcs .... Ms. Julie N. LOVE
41 Athletic Director .... Vacant
13 Director Computing & Telecomm .... Mr. Matt MCGLAMERY
83 Dean Sch Natural & Behavioral Sci .... Dr. Maureen BRANDON
50 Dean School of Business Admin .... Dr. Gary LINN
49 Dean School Arts/Hum/Social Sci .... Dr. Linda SCHOTT
28 Coord Equal Opport/Judicial Affs .... Dr. Haeryon KIM
29 Director Alumni Relations .... Mr. Ross NELSON
96 Director of Purchasing .... Mr. Wayne J. HERMES
40 Bookstore Manager .... Ms. Brooke INGLE

Front Range Community College (H)

3645 W 112th Avenue, Westminster CO 80031-2105
County: Adams FICE Identification: 007933
Unit ID: 127200
Telephone: (303) 404-5000 Carnegie Class: Assoc/Pub-S-MC
FAX Number: (303) 466-1623 Calendar System: Semester
URL: www.frontrange.edu
Established: 1968 Annual Undergrad Tuition & Fees (In-State): $2,600
Enrollment: 20,092 Coed
Affiliation or Control: State IRS Status: 501(c)3
Highest Offering: Associate Degree
Program: Occupational; 2-Year Principally Bachelor's Creditable
Accreditation: NH, ADNUR, DA, MAC, PNUR

01 President .... Mr. Andrew R. DORSEY
04 Asst to the President .... Ms. Kimberly STEFANSKI
10 Vice Pres Finance & Administration .... Ms. Jennifer SOBANET
05 Chief Academic Officer .... Dr. James BUTZEK
21 Controller .... Ms. Acqunetta LIKKEL
21 Director of Budget & Contracts .... Ms. Stephanie MORAN
12 Vice Pres Westminster Camp .... Ms. Therese BROWN
12 Vice Pres Larimer Campus .... Dr. James BUTZEK
12 Vice Pres Boulder County Campus .... Dr. Linda CURRAN
06 Registrar .... Ms. Yolanda ESPINOZA
72 Dean of Career Technical Ed .... Mr. Keith BOGGS
106 Dean of OnLine Learning .... Ms. Tammy VERCAUTEREN
20 Dean of Instruction Larimer .... Ms. Sharon ROBINSON
20 Dean of Instruction Larimer .... Vacant
20 Dean of Instruction Boulder County .... Vacant
20 Dean of Instruction Westminster .... Ms. Catherine PELLISH
32 Dean of Student Svcs Larimer .... Dr. Kris BINARD
32 Dean of Student Svcs Boulder County .... Dr. Stacey L. HOGAN
32 Dean of Student Svcs Westminster .... Ms. Renee TASTAD
88 Dean/Exec Dir of Secondary Programs .... Dr. Phyllis ABT
16 Director of Human Resources .... Ms. Myra PASCO
09 Director of Institutional Research .... Ms. Kim WALLACE
37 Dir of Financial Aid Campus Wide .... Ms. Carolee GOLDSMITH
08 Director of Library Services .... Vacant
18 Director of Facilities Westminster .... Mr. Patrick O'NEILL
18 Director of Facilities Larimer .... Mr. Scott MCKELVEY
35 Director Student Life Westminister .... Ms. Amy ROSDIL
35 Director Student Life Larimer .... Ms. Erin SMITH
35 Dir Student Life Boulder County .... Ms. Amanda CLANCY
102 Director of Foundation .... Mr. Chuck CROWE
26 Dir of Marketing & Communications .... Ms. Marian MAHARAS
27 Public Information Officer .... Mr. John FEELEY
13 Director of Information Technology .... Ms. Janet WAGGONER
40 Director of Auxiliary Services .... Mr. Wes GEARY

Heritage College (I)

12 Lakeside Lane, Denver CO 80212-7413
County: Jefferson FICE Identification: 026110
Unit ID: 262509
Telephone: (303) 477-7240 Carnegie Class: Assoc/PrivFP
FAX Number: (303) 477-7276 Calendar System: Other
URL: www.heritage-education.com
Established: 1986 Annual Undergrad Tuition & Fees: $23,900
Enrollment: 703 Coed
Affiliation or Control: Proprietary IRS Status: Proprietary
Highest Offering: Associate Degree
Program: Occupational
Accreditation: ABHES

01 College Director Denver .... Jennifer SPRAGUE
03 President of Residential Schools .... Richard K. SHEPARD
05 Director of Education .... Kai STONE
20 Education Specialist .... Nancy BOUCNEAU
07 Director of Admissions .... Elyse SCHMINKE
06 Registrar .... Julia WILLIAMS
36 Director of Career Services .... Michelle TYMOCZKO
37 Director of Financial Aid .... Anne RUSK
11 Director of Campus Management .... Shannon BEELER
04 Assistant to the Vice President .... Tari VONDRASEK
37 National Director of Financial Aid .... Callie PARRECO
22 Director of Compliance .... Bill PASCHALL
12 Director Jacksonville .... Sonnie WILLINGHAM
12 Director Fort Myers .... Eva HUTSON
12 Director Oklahoma City .... Cheryl MORRIS
12 Director Kansas City .... Larry CARTMILL
84 National Director of Admissions .... Joe SALLUSTIO
36 National Director of Career Svcs .... Betty BALL
20 National Director of Education .... Brian DYK

Holmes Institute of Consciousness Studies (J)

573 Park Point Drive, Golden CO 80401
County: Jefferson Identification: 666255
Telephone: (720) 496-1370 Carnegie Class: Not Classified
FAX Number: (303) 526-0913 Calendar System: Quarter
URL: www.holmesinstitute.org
Established: 1972 Annual Graduate Tuition & Fees: $18,900
Enrollment: 140 Coed
Affiliation or Control: Independent Non-Profit IRS Status: 501(c)3
Highest Offering: Master's; No Undergraduates
Program: Liberal Arts And General
Accreditation: DETC

01 Dir of HICS/Dir of Education .... RevDr. Lynn CONNOLLY
06 Registrar .... Ms. Maureen THURSTON

Iliff School of Theology (K)

2201 S University Boulevard, Denver CO 80210-4798
County: Denver FICE Identification: 001354
Unit ID: 127273
Telephone: (303) 744-1287 Carnegie Class: Spec/Faith
FAX Number: (303) 777-3387 Calendar System: Quarter
URL: www.iliff.edu
Established: 1892 Annual Graduate Tuition & Fees: $16,920
Enrollment: 330 Coed
Affiliation or Control: United Methodist IRS Status: 501(c)3
Highest Offering: Doctorate; No Undergraduates
Program: Professional; Religious Emphasis
Accreditation: NH, THEOL

01 President ... Dr. David G H. TRICKETT
05 Vice Pres/Dean Academic Affairs ... Dr. Albert HERNANDEZ
10 Vice President for Business Affairs ... Ms. Kelly L. MCCORMICK
30 VP of Institutional Advancement ... Ms. Peggy SANDGREN
26 VP of Marketing Communications ... Ms. Greta GLOVEN
32 Dean Enrollment & Student Services ... Mr. David WORLEY
06 Registrar ... Ms. Carmen E. DOSTER
08 Director Library & Information Svcs ... Dr. Deborah CREAMER
07 Director Admission/Financial Aid ... Ms. Peggy J. BLOCKER
28 Associate Dean of Diversities ... Dr. Edward ANTONIO

Institute of Business and Medical Careers (A)

3842 South Mason Street, Fort Collins CO 80526
County: Larimer FICE Identification: 030063
Unit ID: 372329
Telephone: (970) 223-2669 Carnegie Class: Assoc/PrivFP
FAX Number: (970) 223-2796 Calendar System: Quarter
URL: www.ibmc.edu
Established: 1987 Annual Undergrad Tuition & Fees: $28,500
Enrollment: 820 Coed
Affiliation or Control: Proprietary IRS Status: Proprietary
Highest Offering: Associate Degree
Program: Occupational
Accreditation: ACICS

00 CEO ... Mr. Richard LAUB
01 President ... Mr. Steven STEELE

Institute of Taoist Education and Acupuncture (B)

325 West South Boulder Road, Ste 2, Louisville CO 80027
County: Boulder FICE Identification: 041212
Unit ID: 454838
Telephone: (720) 890-8922 Carnegie Class: Not Classified
FAX Number: (720) 890-7719 Calendar System: Other
URL: www.itea.edu
Established: 1996 Annual Graduate Tuition & Fees: N/A
Enrollment: 32 Coed
Affiliation or Control: Independent Non-Profit IRS Status: 501(c)3
Highest Offering: Master's; No Undergraduates
Program: Professional
Accreditation: ACUP

01 President ... Sandra LILLIE
05 Director ... Hilary SKELLON
06 Registrar ... Claudia O'NIELL
10 Financial Administrator ... Angela SMITH

IntelliTec College (C)

2315 E Pikes Peak Avenue,
Colorado Springs CO 80909-6096
County: El Paso FICE Identification: 022537
Unit ID: 128179
Telephone: (719) 632-7626 Carnegie Class: Assoc/PrivFP
FAX Number: (719) 632-7451 Calendar System: Quarter
URL: www.intelliteccollege.edu
Established: 1965 Annual Undergrad Tuition & Fees: $19,700
Enrollment: 560 Coed
Affiliation or Control: Proprietary IRS Status: Proprietary
Highest Offering: Associate Degree
Program: Occupational
Accreditation: ACCSC

01 COO/Executive Director ... Mr. Edwin KRAUS
06 Registrar ... Ms. Tammy ALESH

IntelliTec College (D)

772 Horizon Drive, Grand Junction CO 81506-3994
County: Mesa FICE Identification: 030669
Unit ID: 128188
Telephone: (970) 245-8101 Carnegie Class: Assoc/PrivFP
FAX Number: (970) 243-8074 Calendar System: Quarter
URL: www.intelliteccollege.edu
Established: 1984 Annual Undergrad Tuition & Fees: $21,840
Enrollment: 834 Coed
Affiliation or Control: Proprietary IRS Status: Proprietary
Highest Offering: Associate Degree
Program: Occupational
Accreditation: ACCSC

01 President ... Mr. Michael SCHRANZ
05 Director ... Mr. Mike GROVES

IntelliTec College (E)

3673 Parker Boulevard, Suite 250, Pueblo CO 81008-2211
County: Pueblo Identification: 666366
Telephone: (719) 542-3181 Carnegie Class: Not Classified
FAX Number: (719) 242-6686 Calendar System: Other
URL: www.intelliteccollege.com
Established: 2004 Annual Undergrad Tuition & Fees: $11,343
Enrollment: 310 Coed
Affiliation or Control: Proprietary IRS Status: Proprietary
Highest Offering: Associate Degree
Program: Occupational; Technical Emphasis
Accreditation: ACCSC

01 President ... Mr. Michael V. SCHRANZ
12 Director ... Dr. Miguel ELIAS

IntelliTec Medical Institute (F)

2345 North Academy Boulevard,
Colorado Springs CO 80909
County: El Paso FICE Identification: 008635
Unit ID: 127839
Telephone: (719) 596-7400 Carnegie Class: Not Classified
FAX Number: (719) 596-2464 Calendar System: Other
URL: www.intellitecmedical.edu
Established: 1966 Annual Undergrad Tuition & Fees: $19,155
Enrollment: 487 Coed
Affiliation or Control: Proprietary IRS Status: Proprietary
Highest Offering: Associate Degree
Program: Occupational
Accreditation: ABHES, DA

01 Campus Director ... Mr. Todd MATTHEWS

ITT Technical Institute (G)

500 E 84th Avenue, Suite B12, Thornton CO 80229-5338
County: Arapahoe FICE Identification: 023217
Unit ID: 244154
Telephone: (303) 288-4488 Carnegie Class: Spec/Tech
FAX Number: (303) 288-8166 Calendar System: Quarter
URL: www.itt-tech.edu
Established: 1984 Annual Undergrad Tuition & Fees: N/A
Enrollment: 568 Coed
Affiliation or Control: Proprietary IRS Status: Proprietary
Highest Offering: Baccalaureate
Program: Technical Emphasis
Accreditation: ACICS

Johnson & Wales University - Denver Campus (H)

7150 Montview Boulevard, Denver CO 80220-1866
County: Denver Identification: 666411
Unit ID: 439288
Telephone: (303) 256-9300 Carnegie Class: Bac/Assoc
FAX Number: (303) 256-9333 Calendar System: Quarter
URL: www.jwu.edu/denver
Established: 2000 Annual Undergrad Tuition & Fees: $25,107
Enrollment: 1,532 Coed
Affiliation or Control: Independent Non-Profit IRS Status: 501(c)3
Highest Offering: Baccalaureate
Program: Occupational; 2-Year Principally Bachelor's Creditable
Accreditation: &EH, DIETD

01 President ... Ms. Bette MATKOWSKI
05 VP and Dean of Academic Affairs ... Dr. Richard WISCOTT
32 Dean of Students ... Mr. Jeff EDERER
20 Associate Dean of Academic Affairs ... Mr. Antonio BARREIRO
30 Exec Dir of Institutional Advance ... Ms. Ginny A. DAVIS
11 Director of Operations ... Mr. JD SAWYER
07 Director of Admissions ... Ms. Kim MEDINA
06 Dir of Student Acad & Financial Ser ... Ms. Kimberly BUXTON-HAMEL
35 Director Student Affairs ... Ms. Denise KUPETZ
36 Dir Experiential Educ/Career Svcs ... Ms. Laura DEAN
26 Dir Public Relations/Cmty Affairs ... Ms. Lindsay TRACY
15 Human Resources Representative ... Ms. Rodena BARR
41 Athletic Director ... Mr. Jeff CULVER
88 Dean of Culinary Education ... Mr. Jorge DE LA TORRE
88 Dean of Experiential Education ... Dr. Gregory F. LORENZE

† Regional accreditation is carried under the parent institution in Providence, RI.

Jones International University (I)

9697 E Mineral Avenue, Centennial CO 80112-3408
County: Arapahoe FICE Identification: 035343
Unit ID: 444723
Telephone: (800) 811-5663 Carnegie Class: Master's L
FAX Number: (303) 799-0966 Calendar System: Other
URL: www.jiu.edu
Established: 1993 Annual Undergrad Tuition & Fees: $13,840
Enrollment: 7,674 Coed
Affiliation or Control: Proprietary IRS Status: Proprietary
Highest Offering: Doctorate
Program: Teacher Preparatory; Professional; Business Emphasis
Accreditation: NH

01 Chief Operating Officer ... Mr. Richard COX, JR.
05 Sr Vice Chancellor Academics ... Dr. Lynn PAYNE
10 Chief Financial Officer ... Vacant
84 Vice Chancellor Admissions & Enroll ... Vacant
50 Dean School of Business ... Dr. Richard THOMPSON
53 Dean School of Education ... Dr. Debora SCHEFFEL

Kaplan College (J)

500 E 84th Avenue, Suite W200,
Thornton CO 80229-5316
County: Adams FICE Identification: 021676
Unit ID: 381796
Telephone: (303) 295-0550 Carnegie Class: Assoc/PrivFP
FAX Number: (303) 295-0102 Calendar System: Quarter
URL: www.kaplancollege.com
Established: 1977 Annual Undergrad Tuition & Fees: $14,961
Enrollment: 260 Coed
Affiliation or Control: Proprietary IRS Status: Proprietary
Highest Offering: Associate Degree
Program: Occupational
Accreditation: ACCSC

01 Executive Director ... Mr. Evan MELLMAN

Lamar Community College (K)

2401 S Main, Lamar CO 81052-3999
County: Prowers FICE Identification: 001355
Unit ID: 127389
Telephone: (719) 336-2248 Carnegie Class: Assoc/Pub-R-S
FAX Number: (719) 336-2448 Calendar System: Semester
URL: www.lamarcc.edu
Established: 1937 Annual Undergrad Tuition & Fees (In-State): $4,376
Enrollment: 1,051 Coed
Affiliation or Control: State IRS Status: 501(c)3
Highest Offering: Associate Degree
Program: Occupational; 2-Year Principally Bachelor's Creditable
Accreditation: NH

01 President ... Mr. John MARRIN
05 Vice Pres of Academic Services ... Dr. Deborah LOPER
11 VP Administrative & Student Svcs ... Mrs. Cheryl SANCHEZ
84 Vice Pres Enrollment Services ... Mr. Chad DE BONO
20 Dean of Academic Services ... Mr. Curtis TURNER
26 Director of Communication ... Mrs. Anne-Marie CRAMPTON
06 Registrar/Dean Student Services ... Mrs. Kimberly BRIGHT
08 Library Tech ... Ms. Ellen LOVELL
18 Director of Facilities ... Mr. Sean LIRLEY
15 Director Personnel Services ... Ms. Gwen GRUENLOH
39 Director Student Housing ... Mr. Zack DRUCE
38 Director Student Counseling ... Mr. Don BRIGHT
96 Director of Purchasing ... Mrs. Ava BAIR
40 Director Bookstore ... Mrs. Sheila DIETERLE
41 Athletic Director ... Mr. Craig BROOKS
37 Director Financial Aid ... Mrs. Teale HEMPHILL
07 Director of Admissions ... Mrs. Amber THOMPSON
09 Director of Institutional Research ... Mrs. Lisa LAFEVRE

Lincoln College of Technology (L)

11194 East 45th Avenue, Denver CO 80239
County: Denver FICE Identification: 007547
Unit ID: 126951
Telephone: (303) 722-5724 Carnegie Class: Assoc/PrivFP
FAX Number: (303) 778-8264 Calendar System: Other
URL: www.lincolnedu.com
Established: 1963 Annual Undergrad Tuition & Fees: N/A
Enrollment: 1,233 Coed
Affiliation or Control: Proprietary IRS Status: Proprietary
Highest Offering: Associate Degree
Program: Occupational
Accreditation: ACCSC

01 Executive Director ... Mr. Robert LANTZY
07 Director Admissions ... Ms. Jennifer HASH
05 Director of Education ... Mr. Ted HRDLICKA

McKinley College (M)

2001 Lowe Street, Fort Collins CO 80525-3474
County: Larimer Identification: 666237
Telephone: (970) 207-4550 Carnegie Class: Not Classified
FAX Number: (877) 599-5863 Calendar System: Other
URL: www.mckinleycollege.edu
Established: 2004 Annual Undergrad Tuition & Fees: $3,100
Enrollment: N/A Coed
Affiliation or Control: Proprietary IRS Status: Proprietary
Highest Offering: Associate Degree
Program: Occupational; 2-Year Principally Bachelor's Creditable
Accreditation: DETC

01 President ... Ann ROHR

Metropolitan State College of Denver (N)

PO Box 173362, Denver CO 80217-3362
County: Denver FICE Identification: 001360
Unit ID: 127565
Telephone: (303) 556-3022 Carnegie Class: Bac/Diverse
FAX Number: (303) 556-3912 Calendar System: Semester
URL: www.mscd.edu
Established: 1963 Annual Undergrad Tuition & Fees (In-State): $4,834
Enrollment: 23,948 Coed
Affiliation or Control: State IRS Status: 501(c)3
Highest Offering: Master's
Program: Liberal Arts And General; Teacher Preparatory; Professional
Accreditation: NH, ART, CS, DIETD, ENGT, IPSY, MUS, NRPA, NUR, SW, TED

01 President ... Dr. Stephen M. JORDAN
04 Exec Asst to President ... Ms. Mary Lou LAWRENCE
05 Vice President Academic Affairs ... Dr. Vicki GOLICH

10 Vice Pres Finance & Administration .... Ms. Natalie LUTES
44 Vice Pres Institutional Advancement .... Dr. Carrie BESNETTE HAUSER
32 Vice President Student Services .... Vacant
13 Interim VP for IT .... Vacant
20 Assoc VP for Academic Affairs .... Dr. Sheila THOMPSON
84 Assoc VP for Enrollment Services .... Mrs. Judi DIAZ-BONACQUISTI
29 Assoc VP for Development/Alumni Rel .... Ms. Cherrelyn NAPUE
50 Dean School Business .... Dr. John COCHRAN
107 Dean School Professional Studies .... Dr. Sandra HAYNES
49 Dean School Letters/Arts/Science .... Dr. Joan L. FOSTER
35 Dean Student Life .... Ms. Emilia PAUL
22 Exec Director EEO/Asst to President .... Dr. Percy A. MOREHOUSE, JR.
56 Director of Extended Education .... Ms. Carol SVENDSEN
06 Registrar .... Ms. Paula MARTINEZ
15 Exec Director Human Resources .... Ms. Judith L. ZEWE
37 Director Financial Aid .... Ms. Cindy HEJL
38 Director Counseling Center .... Dr. Gail BRUCE-SANFORD
41 Athletic Director .... Ms. Joan MCDERMOTT
35 Director Student Activities .... Ms. Brooke DILLING
36 Director Career Services .... Ms. Bridgette COBLE
28 Int Assoc to Pres Inst Diversity .... Dr. Myron ANDERSON

Morgan Community College (A)

920 Barlow Road, Fort Morgan CO 80701-4399

County: Morgan | FICE Identification: 009981 | Unit ID: 127617
Telephone: (970) 542-3100 | Carnegie Class: Assoc/Pub-R-M
FAX Number: (970) 542-3114 | Calendar System: Semester
URL: www.morgancc.edu
Established: 1967 | Annual Undergrad Tuition & Fees (In-State): $2,836
Enrollment: 1,965 | Coed
Affiliation or Control: State | IRS Status: Exempt
Highest Offering: Associate Degree
Program: Occupational; 2-Year Principally Bachelor's Creditable
Accreditation: NH, ADNUR, PTAA

01 President .... Dr. Kerry HART
10 Vice Pres Finance/Admin Services .... Ms. Susan CLOUGH
05 Vice President of Instruction .... Ms. Betty MCKIE
84 Vice President of Student Success .... Mr. Kent BAUER
04 Assistant to the President .... Ms. Jane FRIES
12 Center Director .... Ms. Mary ANDERSEN
12 Center Director .... Ms. Nancy BARDEN
12 Center Director .... Ms. Kellie OVERTURF
12 Center Director .... Ms. Valerie RHOADES
09 Dir of Institutional Effectiveness .... Mr. Charles DUELL
27 Dir of Communications & Marketing .... Ms. Katie BARRON
30 Director of Development .... Vacant
37 Director of Financial Aid .... Ms. Sally NESTOR
07 Director of Admissions .... Ms. Kim MAXWELL
15 Director of Personnel Services .... Vacant
08 Dir of Learning Resource Center .... Ms. April AMACK
96 Director of Purchasing .... Ms. Julie BEYDLER
40 Director of Bookstore .... Ms. Anita ERTLE
18 Coordinator of M & O .... Mr. Seth NOBLE
36 Voc Guidance/Placement Counselor .... Mr. Dan MARLER
66 Director of Nursing .... Ms. Kathy FRISBIE
14 Director Information Technology .... Mr. Michael SHRIVER

Naropa University (B)

2130 Arapahoe Avenue, Boulder CO 80302-6697

County: Boulder | FICE Identification: 021175 | Unit ID: 127653
Telephone: (303) 444-0202 | Carnegie Class: Master's L
FAX Number: (303) 444-0410 | Calendar System: Semester
URL: www.naropa.edu
Established: 1974 | Annual Undergrad Tuition & Fees: $25,000
Enrollment: 1,063 | Coed
Affiliation or Control: Independent Non-Profit | IRS Status: 501(c)3
Highest Offering: Master's
Program: Liberal Arts And General
Accreditation: NH

01 President .... Dr. Stuart C. LORD
04 Assistant to the President .... Ms. Cathy CHEN-ORTEGA
10 Vice President Business & Finance .... Vacant
05 Vice Pres Acad Affs/Dean Faculty .... Mr. Stuart J. SIGMAN
11 Chief Administrative Officer .... Mr. Todd KILBURN
30 Vice Pres Development/Ext Relations .... Ms. Jill GRAMMER
32 VP Student Affairs/Enrollment Mgmt .... Ms. Cheryl BARBOUR
13 Assistant Vice President for IT .... Mr. Harvey NICHOLS
07 Dean of Admissions .... Ms. Susan BOYLE
97 Associate Dean Undergrad Educ .... Mr. Mark A. MILLER
35 Dean of Students .... Mr. Robert CILLO
39 Director of Student Housing .... Ms. Lisa CONSTANTINO
06 Registrar .... Ms. Jamie PETA
08 Librarian .... Mr. Mark KILLE
18 Director of Facilities .... Mr. Don RASMUSSEN
37 Dir Student Financial Services .... Ms. Nancy MORRELL
15 Director of Human Resources .... Mr. James ROBINSON-LONG
106 Director of Online Curriculum Devel .... Mr. Jirka HLADIS
29 Alumni Relations Officer .... Ms. Melissa HOLLAND
14 Assistant Director Technical .... Mr. Mike PAXTON
28 Chief Diversity Officer .... Ms. Suzanne BENALLY
19 Safety & Security Manager .... Mr. Steve JEWELL

National Theatre Conservatory (C)

1101 13th Street, Denver CO 80204-2157

County: Denver | FICE Identification: 025179 | Unit ID: 260196
Telephone: (303) 446-4855 | Carnegie Class: Not Classified
FAX Number: (303) 623-0693 | Calendar System: Semester
URL: www.denvercenter.org
Established: 1983 | Annual Graduate Tuition & Fees: N/A
Enrollment: 28 | Coed
Affiliation or Control: Independent Non-Profit | IRS Status: 501(c)3
Highest Offering: Master's; No Undergraduates
Program: Professional
Accreditation: NH

01 President .... Mr. Randy WEEKS
05 Director of Education .... Mr. Daniel RENNER
06 Registrar .... Vacant

Nazarene Bible College (D)

1111 Academy Park Loop, Colorado Springs CO 80910-3704

County: El Paso | FICE Identification: 013007 | Unit ID: 127714
Telephone: (719) 884-5000 | Carnegie Class: Spec/Faith
FAX Number: (719) 884-5199 | Calendar System: Trimester
URL: www.nbc.edu
Established: 1964 | Annual Undergrad Tuition & Fees: $10,800
Enrollment: 949 | Coed
Affiliation or Control: Church Of The Nazarene | IRS Status: 501(c)3
Highest Offering: Baccalaureate
Program: Professional; Religious Emphasis
Accreditation: NH, BI

01 President .... Dr. Harold B. GRAVES
05 Vice President for Academic Affairs .... Dr. Gary W. STREIT
32 Vice Pres for Student Development .... Prof. Laurel L. MATSON
10 Vice President for Finance .... Mr. J. Mike ARRAMBIDE
106 Dean of Online Education .... Dr. Alan D. LYKE
84 Vice President Marketing/Recruiting .... Dr. Jay W. OTT
08 Library Director .... Prof. Ann M. ATTIG
37 Financial Aid Officer .... Mr. Malcolm E. BRITTON
09 Director of Institutional Research .... Vacant
06 Registrar .... Prof. Laurel L. MATSON

Northeastern Junior College (E)

100 College Drive, Sterling CO 80751-2399

County: Logan | FICE Identification: 001361 | Unit ID: 127732
Telephone: (970) 521-6600 | Carnegie Class: Assoc/Pub-R-M
FAX Number: (970) 521-6636 | Calendar System: Semester
URL: www.njc.edu
Established: 1941 | Annual Undergrad Tuition & Fees (In-State): $2,667
Enrollment: 2,497 | Coed
Affiliation or Control: State | IRS Status: 501(c)3
Highest Offering: Associate Degree
Program: Occupational; 2-Year Principally Bachelor's Creditable
Accreditation: NH

01 President .... Dr. Lance BOLTON
05 Vice President Academic Services .... Mr. Stanton GARTIN
10 Vice Pres Finance & Administration .... Ms. Brenda LAUER
32 Dean of Student Success .... Ms. Steve SMITH
84 Dean New Student Enroll/Admissions .... Mr. Andrew LONG
29 Alumni Director .... Mr. Jack ANNAN
45 Executive Director NJC Foundation .... Ms. Cinthia JOHNSON
06 Director Records/Admission Process .... Ms. Angela ANDERSON
37 Director of Financial Aid .... Ms. Alice WEINGARDT
35 Dir Resident Life & Student Activit .... Mr. David MCNABB
18 Physical Plant Director .... Mr. David CRAWFORD
15 Human Resources Director .... Ms. Tammy KALLSEN
41 Athletic Director .... Ms. Marci HENRY
96 Director of Purchasing/AR .... Ms. Annie SHALLA
09 Dir of Inst Research/Plng/Devel .... Mr. Derek HERBERT
26 Director of Marketing .... Ms. Barbara BAKER
21 Assistant Controller .... Ms. Deb COUNTY
13 Director Information Technology .... Ms. Cherie BRUNGARDT
40 Bookstore Director .... Mr. Brock BASEGGIO

Otero Junior College (F)

1802 Colorado Avenue, La Junta CO 81050-3346

County: Otero | FICE Identification: 001362 | Unit ID: 127778
Telephone: (719) 384-6831 | Carnegie Class: Assoc/Pub-R-S
FAX Number: (719) 384-6933 | Calendar System: Semester
URL: www.ojc.edu
Established: 1941 | Annual Undergrad Tuition & Fees (In-State): $4,700
Enrollment: 1,823 | Coed
Affiliation or Control: State | IRS Status: 501(c)3
Highest Offering: Associate Degree
Program: Occupational; 2-Year Principally Bachelor's Creditable
Accreditation: NH, ADNUR

01 President .... Mr. James T. RIZZUTO
11 Vice Pres Administrative Services .... Mr. Gary A. ASHIDA
05 Int Vice Pres Instructional Svcs .... Dr. James HERRELL
32 Vice President Student Services .... Mr. Jeff PAOLUCCI
20 Assoc Dean Instructional Services .... Mr. Jim HERRELL
08 Director Learning Resources .... Ms. Sue KEEFER
38 Director Advising/Guidance/Recruit .... Mr. Brad SMITH
41 Athletic Director .... Mr. Gary ADDINGTON
15 Director of Human Resources .... Mrs. Marlene F. BOETTCHER
18 Director of Physical Plant .... Mr. Wayne W. STUCHLIK
40 Bookstore Manager .... Mrs. Debra NICHOLSON
37 Director of Financial Aid .... Mrs. Janet CARRILLO
88 Director of Auxilliary Services .... Mr. Carl S. OTTEMAN
26 Director Marketing/Public Relations .... Mrs. Almabeth KAESS
14 Director of Computer Services .... Mr. Mark ALLEN

Pikes Peak Community College (G)

5675 S Academy Boulevard, Colorado Springs CO 80906-5498

County: El Paso | FICE Identification: 008896 | Unit ID: 127820
Telephone: (719) 502-2000 | Carnegie Class: Assoc/Pub-U-MC
FAX Number: (719) 502-2201 | Calendar System: Semester
URL: www.ppcc.edu
Established: 1968 | Annual Undergrad Tuition & Fees (In-State): $6,268
Enrollment: 15,299 | Coed
Affiliation or Control: State | IRS Status: 501(c)3
Highest Offering: Associate Degree
Program: Occupational; 2-Year Principally Bachelor's Creditable
Accreditation: NH, ACFEI, DA, EMT

01 President .... Dr. Lance BOLTON
04 Exec Assistant to the President .... Ms. Kimberly BARNETT
05 Vice President Educational Services .... Ms. Cindy BUCKLEY
11 Vice Pres Administrative Services .... Mr. Mike YOUNG
32 Interim VP Student Services .... Mr. Jeffrey HORNER
20 Asst to VP Educational Services .... Ms. Julie HAZEL
84 Director Enrollment Services .... Mr. Jeff HORNER
37 Director of Financial Aid .... Ms. Sherri MCCULLOUGH
08 Director of Libraries .... Ms. Carole OLDS
16 Exec Dir of Human Resource Services .... Mr. Carlton BROOKS
27 Exec Dir Marketing/Communications .... Ms. Allison SWICKARD
21 Director of Business Svcs .... Ms. Eileen HOGUE
06 Registrar .... Ms. Twila HUMPHREY
102 Exec Dir Found/Res/Cmty Development .... Mr. Jon STEPLETON
18 Dir Facilities/Maintenance/Opers .... Vacant
13 Director Information Technology .... Mr. Cyrillc PARENT
19 Director Public Safety .... Mr. Ken HILTE
88 Director Student Support Services .... Mr. Edmond QUESADA
88 Dir Military & Veteran Programs .... Ms. Cheri ARFSTEN
76 Dean Hlth Environ/Natural/Phys/Scis ... Ms. Mary-Ann WERMERS
81 Dean Mathematics & Language .... Ms. Carol JONAS-MORRISON
50 Dean Business/Social/Behav Scis .... Vacant
60 Dean Comm/Humanities/Tech Studies .... Ms. Taffy MULLIKEN
36 Dir of Career Planning & Advising .... Mr. Lincoln WULF
35 Dean of Students .... Ms. Jennifer SENGENBERGER
96 Director of Purchasing .... Ms. Rockie HURRELL
38 Director Student Counseling ...... Ms. Melanie LINDSAY-BRISBIN
88 Dean of High School Programs .... Ms. Chelsy HARRIS
09 Director of Institutional Research .... Dr. Tim GRIFFIN

Pima Medical Institute-Denver (H)

7475 Dakin Street, Westminster CO 80221

County: Denver | Identification: 666171 | Unit ID: 404912
Telephone: (303) 426-1800 | Carnegie Class: Assoc/PrivFP
FAX Number: (303) 430-4048 | Calendar System: Other
URL: www.pmi.edu
Established: 1988 | Annual Undergrad Tuition & Fees: $10,150
Enrollment: 1,144 | Coed
Affiliation or Control: Proprietary | IRS Status: Proprietary
Highest Offering: Associate Degree
Program: Occupational
Accreditation: ABHES, OTA, PTAA, RAD

01 Campus Director .... Ms. Sue ANDERSON

† Branch campus of Pima Medical Institute, Tucson, AZ.

Platt College (I)

3100 S Parker Road, Suite 200, Aurora CO 80014-3141

County: Arapahoe | FICE Identification: 030149 | Unit ID: 260813
Telephone: (303) 369-5151 | Carnegie Class: Bac/Diverse
FAX Number: (303) 745-1433 | Calendar System: Quarter
URL: www.plattcolorado.edu
Established: 1986 | Annual Undergrad Tuition & Fees: $19,320
Enrollment: 179 | Coed
Affiliation or Control: Proprietary | IRS Status: Proprietary
Highest Offering: Baccalaureate
Program: Nursing Emphasis
Accreditation: ACCSC, NUR

01 President/CEO .... Mr. Jerald B. SIRBU
05 Vice President of Academic Affairs .... Dr. Julie BASLER
10 Director of Financial Services .... Ms. Kimberly E. ADAMACHE
37 Director of Financial Aid/Registrar .... Ms. Margie ROSE
08 Head Librarian .... Ms. Laura CULLERTON
66 Dean of Nursing Program .... Ms. Hollie CAMPANELLA

Prince Institute-Rocky Mountains (A)

9051 Harlan Street, Suite 20, Westminster CO 80030-2901
County: Jefferson FICE Identification: 021887
Unit ID: 126924
Telephone: (303) 427-5292 Carnegie Class: Assoc/PrivFP
FAX Number: (303) 427-5383 Calendar System: Quarter
URL: www.princeinstitute.edu
Established: 1976 Annual Undergrad Tuition & Fees: $11,700
Enrollment: 150 Coed
Affiliation or Control: Proprietary IRS Status: Proprietary
Highest Offering: Associate Degree
Program: Occupational; Technical Emphasis
Accreditation: ACICS

01 Campus Director .... Ms. Sue KUHL

Pueblo Community College (B)

900 W Orman Avenue, Pueblo CO 81004-1499
County: Pueblo FICE Identification: 021163
Unit ID: 127884
Telephone: (719) 549-3200 Carnegie Class: Assoc/Pub-R-L
FAX Number: (719) 544-1179 Calendar System: Semester
URL: www.pueblocc.edu
Established: 1933 Annual Undergrad Tuition & Fees (In-State): $3,175
Enrollment: 7,943 Coed
Affiliation or Control: State IRS Status: 501(c)3
Highest Offering: Associate Degree
Program: Occupational; 2-Year Principally Bachelor's Creditable
Accreditation: NH, ACFEI, ADNUR, DA, DH, EMT, OTA, PNUR, PTAA

01 President .... Ms. Patricia ERJAVEC
10 Vice Pres Administration & Finance .... Ms. Colleen ARMSTRONG
05 Vice Pres of Learning .... Ms. Laura SOLANO
32 Vice President of Student Services .... Ms. Lucinda MIHELICH
12 Dean Fremont Campus .... Ms. Jennifer HERMAN
12 Dean of SCCC East Campus .... Dr. Lynn URBAN
12 Dean of SCCC West Campus .... Ms. Shannon SOUTH
76 Dean Health Professions .... Ms. Sue KOCHEVAR
49 Dean of Arts & Science .... Dr. Lana CARTER
72 Dean of Business & Technology .... Dr. David COCKRELL
102 Exec Dir Foundation/Alumni Rels .... Ms. Diane PORTER
07 Director Admissions & Records .... Ms. Maija KURTZ
21 Controller .... Ms. Gayle PETTINARI
37 Director Financial Aid .... Mr. Ron SWARTWOOD
15 Director Human Resources .... Ms. JanDee HAAG
14 Director of Computer Services .... Mr. Bryan CRAWFORD
18 Director Facility Svcs/Capital Plng .... Mr. Clifford KITCHEN
35 Director Student Activities/Col Ctr .... Mr. Joel ZARR
38 Director Learning Center .... Mr. Ross BARNHART
08 Director Library Services .... Ms. Jeanne W. GARDNER
27 Dir Communications/Community Rels .... Ms. Erin HERGERT
36 Director of Career & Counseling .... Mr. Dennis JOHNSON
84 Director of Recruitment .... Ms. Carriann MARTINEZ
06 Registrar .... Ms. Maija KURTZ
09 Dir Plng/Accreditation/Effective .... Dr. Patricia DIAWARA
96 Purchasing Agent .... Ms. Leanne CORSENTINO
26 Chief Public Relations Officer .... Mr. Gary FRANCHI
31 Dean of Community Educ & Training .... Ms. Juanita FUENTES
103 Dean of Economic & Workforce Devel .... Mr. Vukich JOHN
88 Director of Academic Advising .... Mr. Gage MICHAEL

Red Rocks Community College (C)

13300 W Sixth Avenue, Lakewood CO 80228-1255
County: Jefferson FICE Identification: 009543
Unit ID: 127909
Telephone: (303) 914-6600 Carnegie Class: Assoc/Pub-S-MC
FAX Number: (303) 914-6666 Calendar System: Semester
URL: www.rrcc.edu
Established: 1969 Annual Undergrad Tuition & Fees (In-State): $3,492
Enrollment: 9,803 Coed
Affiliation or Control: State IRS Status: 501(c)3
Highest Offering: Associate Degree
Program: Occupational; 2-Year Principally Bachelor's Creditable
Accreditation: NH, ARCPA, MAC, RAD

01 President .... Dr. Michele HANEY
04 Assistant to the President .... Ms. Kathy SCHISSLER
11 Vice Pres Administrative Services .... Ms. Peggy MORGAN
05 Vice President Instruction .... Ms. Colleen JORGENSEN
32 Vice Pres Stdnt Svcs/Enrollment Mgt .... Mr. Bruce WALTHERS
20 Dean .... Ms. Marilyn SMITH
20 Dean .... Mr. Rick REEVES
13 Dean Technology .... Mr. Wayne CARUOLO
25 Dean Instruction Strategic Planning .... Ms. Joan SMITH
88 Dean of Instruct/Exec Dir RMEC-OSHA .... Ms. Joan SMITH
85 Director International Education .... Ms. Linda YAZDANI
07 Dir Student Recruitment/Advising .... Ms. Linda CROOK
21 Controller .... Ms. Kathy KAOUDIS
84 Director Enrollment Services .... Vacant
30 Exec Dir Advancement & Foundation .... Vacant
37 Director Financial Aid .... Ms. Linda CROOK
06 Director Enrollment Services .... Dr. Dean RATHE
36 Director Student Employment .... Ms. Nancy CARLSON
18 Director Facilities .... Mr. Mark BANA
16 Director Human Resources .... Mr. Bill DIAL
102 Exec Director RRCC Foundation .... Vacant
27 Director Marketing/Communications .... Ms. Kim REIN
35 Director Student Activities .... Ms. Carolyn MATTERN
88 Dir Childhood Ed & Support Svcs .... Ms. Kathleen DEVRIES

09 Director Institutional Research .... Mr. Andrew STEVENS
96 Coordinator Purchasing .... Ms. Renee ARCHULETA

Redstone College (D)

10851 W 120th Avenue, Broomfield CO 80021-3401
County: Broomfield FICE Identification: 007297
Unit ID: 126605
Telephone: (303) 466-1714 Carnegie Class: Assoc/PrivFP
FAX Number: (303) 469-3797 Calendar System: Other
URL: www.redstone.edu
Established: 1965 Annual Undergrad Tuition & Fees: $13,274
Enrollment: 738 Coed
Affiliation or Control: Proprietary IRS Status: Proprietary
Highest Offering: Associate Degree
Program: Occupational
Accreditation: ACICS

01 Executive Director .... Mr. Mike COULING
05 Pgm Dir Advanced Electronics Tech .... Mr. Tim BRAA
07 Director of Admissions .... Ms. Cate CLARK
11 Director of Campus Operations .... Ms. Alicia HARBIN
06 Registrar .... Ms. Vicki MIDDEKER

Regis University (E)

3333 Regis Boulevard, Denver CO 80221-1099
County: Denver FICE Identification: 001363
Unit ID: 127918
Telephone: (303) 458-4100 Carnegie Class: Master's L
FAX Number: (303) 458-4921 Calendar System: Semester
URL: www.regis.edu
Established: 1877 Annual Undergrad Tuition & Fees: $24,902
Enrollment: 11,069 Coed
Affiliation or Control: Roman Catholic IRS Status: 501(c)3
Highest Offering: Doctorate
Program: Liberal Arts And General; Teacher Preparatory; Professional
Accreditation: NH, CACREP, NURSE, @PHAR, PTA, TEAC

01 President .... Rev. Michael J. SHEERAN
00 Chancellor .... Rev. David M. CLARKE
05 Provost Emeritus .... Dr. Allan L. SERVICE
43 Legal Counsel .... Mr. Stanley ERECKSON
05 VP for Academic Affairs .... Dr. Patricia A. LADEWIG
30 Vice President University Relations .... Ms. Julie A. CROCKETT
11 Vice President Administration .... Ms. Karen B. WEBBER
32 Vice President Mission .... Dr. Thomas E. REYNOLDS
10 Vice President/CFO .... Mr. Chuck DAHLMAN
88 VP New Ventures/Strategic Alliances .... Dr. William J. HUSSON
84 Assoc VP Enrollment Services .... Mr. Bill HATHAWAY-CLARK
88 Assoc VP University Services .... Ms. Susan LAYTON
15 Assoc VP Human Resources .... Mr. Tony L. CROW
18 Assoc VP Physical Plant .... Mr. Michael J. REDMOND
20 Asst VP Academic Affairs .... Mr. Steve JACOBS
28 Asst VP for Diversity .... Ms. Sandra L. MITCHELL
26 Asst VP University Relations .... Ms. Marycate LUMPP
27 Chief Information Officer .... Mr. Peter L. GRECO
107 Dean Professional Studies .... Dr. Roxanne GONZALES
76 Dean Health Professions .... Dr. Janet HOUSER
49 Dean of Regis College .... Dr. Paul D. EWALD
08 Dean of Libraries .... Dr. Ivan K. GAETZ
35 Dean of Students .... Ms. Diane M. MCSHEEHY
07 Director of Admissions .... Mr. Victor L. DAVOLT
88 Exec Dir/CPS Mktg and Enrollment .... Mr. Jerry MOSIER
88 Dir/RHCHP Admissions and Student Op .... Ms. Kim FRISCH
37 Director Financial Aid .... Ms. Elinor MILLER
06 Director Registration .... Ms. Cathy GORRELL
06 Director Academic Records .... Ms. Terry GAURMER
38 Director Personal Counseling .... Dr. Chaney GIVENS
29 Exec Dir Alumni/Parent Programs .... Ms. Penny DEMPSEY ST. JOHN
19 Director of Campus Safety .... Mr. William T. WILLIAMS
09 Director of Institutional Research .... Ms. Paula HARMER
25 Director Academic Grants .... Mr. Donald BRIDGER
42 Director of University Ministry .... Mr. Pete ROGERS
36 Director of Career Services .... Mr. Richard DELLIVENERI
41 Director Athletics .... Ms. Ann MARTIN

Rocky Mountain College of Art & Design (F)

1600 Pierce Street, Lakewood CO 80214-1433
County: Denver FICE Identification: 007649
Unit ID: 127945
Telephone: (303) 753-6046 Carnegie Class: Spec/Arts
FAX Number: (303) 759-4970 Calendar System: Semester
URL: www.rmcad.edu
Established: 1963 Annual Undergrad Tuition & Fees: $27,648
Enrollment: 684 Coed
Affiliation or Control: Proprietary IRS Status: Proprietary
Highest Offering: Master's
Program: Fine Arts Emphasis
Accreditation: NH, ART, CIDA

01 President .... Dr. Maria PUZZIFERRO
45 Chief Financial Officer .... Mr. Mark FULLER
26 VP Marketing .... Ms. Rebecca NEWMAN
32 Dean of Students .... Vacant
07 VP Admissions .... Mr. Joe LEONHARDT
13 VP of Information Technology .... Mr. Chris MINCHEFF
37 Financial Aid Director .... Ms. Tammy DYBDAHL

05 Dean of Academic Affairs .... Dr. Kiki GILDERHUS
106 Dean of Academic Affairs - Online .... Ms. Lauren PILLOTE
06 Registrar .... Mr. Chuck KING
09 Director Institutional Research .... Dr. Ally OSTROWSKI
15 Human Resources Director .... Ms. Carrie BRANCHEAU
10 Controller .... Ms. Becky SKOUGSTAD
08 Head Librarian .... Mr. Hugh THURLOW
35 Director Student Activities .... Mr. David BOURASSA

Rocky Vista University (G)

8401 South Chambers Road, Parker CO 80134
County: Douglas Identification: 667002
Telephone: (303) 373-2008 Carnegie Class: Not Classified
FAX Number: N/A Calendar System: Other
URL: www.rockyvistauniversity.org
Established: 1983 Annual Graduate Tuition & Fees: $43,384
Enrollment: 321 Coed
Affiliation or Control: Independent Non-Profit IRS Status: 501(c)3
Highest Offering: Doctorate; No Undergraduates
Program: Professional
Accreditation: @OSTEO

01 President .... Dr. Robert ROEHRICH
05 Dean/CAO .... Dr. Bruce DUBIN
20 Vice Dean .... Dr. Thomas MOHR
10 Vice Pres Admin & Finance/CAO .... Dr. Thomas SABAN
43 Vice Pres & General Counsel .... Mr. J. Andrew USERA

St. John Vianney Theological Seminary (H)

1300 S Steele Street, Denver CO 80210-2526
County: Denver Identification: 666127
Telephone: (303) 282-3427 Carnegie Class: Not Classified
FAX Number: (303) 282-3453 Calendar System: Semester
URL: www.sjvdenver.org
Established: 1999 Annual Graduate Tuition & Fees: $25,910
Enrollment: 127 Male
Affiliation or Control: Roman Catholic IRS Status: 501(c)3
Highest Offering: Master's; No Undergraduates
Program: Professional; Religious Emphasis
Accreditation: THEOL

01 Rector .... Msgr. Michael GLENN
03 Vice Rector .... Rev. Jorge RODRIGUEZ
05 Academic Dean .... Rev. Andreas HOECK
06 Registrar .... Dr. Richard NEYENS

Southwest Acupuncture College (I)

6620 Gunpark Drive, Boulder CO 80301-3339
County: Boulder Identification: 666618
Unit ID: 436261
Telephone: (303) 581-9955 Carnegie Class: Not Classified
FAX Number: (303) 581-9933 Calendar System: Semester
URL: www.acupuncturecollege.edu
Established: 1997 Annual Graduate Tuition & Fees: N/A
Enrollment: 120 Coed
Affiliation or Control: Proprietary IRS Status: Proprietary
Highest Offering: Master's; No Undergraduates
Program: Professional
Accreditation: ACUP

01 Campus Director .... Valerie HOBBS

† Branch campus of Southwest Acupuncture College, Santa Fe, NM.

Trinidad State Junior College (J)

600 Prospect, Trinidad CO 81082-2396
County: Las Animas FICE Identification: 001368
Unit ID: 128258
Telephone: (719) 846-5621 Carnegie Class: Assoc/Pub-R-M
FAX Number: (719) 846-5667 Calendar System: Semester
URL: www.trinidadstate.edu
Established: 1925 Annual Undergrad Tuition & Fees (In-State): $3,378
Enrollment: 1,916 Coed
Affiliation or Control: State IRS Status: 501(c)3
Highest Offering: Associate Degree
Program: Occupational; 2-Year Principally Bachelor's Creditable
Accreditation: NH, ENGR

01 President .... Mr. Felix LOPEZ
05 Vice President of Academic Affairs .... Dr. Sandra VELTRI
11 Vice President Administrative Svcs .... Mr. Michael HICKMAN
12 Assoc Vice President/Alamosa Campus .... Ms. Marta SHOMAN
32 VP Stdnt Svcs/Inst Advancement .... Mr. Kerry GABRIELSON
49 Dean Arts & Sciences .... Ms. Debbie ULIBARRI
35 Dean Student Svcs/Alamosa Campus .... Mr. David PEARSE
20 Dean of Instruction/Alamosa Campus .... Mr. Rolando RAEL
30 Director of Devel/College Relations .... Ms. Toni DEANGELIS
15 Human Resources Director .... Ms. Lorrie VELASQUEZ
37 Director Financial Aid .... Ms. Wilma ATENCIO
06 Registrar/Institutional Research .... Ms. Annette LUJAN
07 Admission/Recruitment Specialist .... Ms. Erin COMDEN
18 Director Facilities/Physical Plant .... Mr. Louis MANTELLI
10 Controller .... Ms. Juanita PENA
32 Dir Stdnt Sprt Svcs/Advisory Coord .... Vacant
14 Distance Lrng/Audio Visual Coord .... Mr. Doug BAK
08 Library Resource Manager .... Mr. Wayne RIVERA
35 Coordinator of Student Life .... Ms. Charlene DURAN

*University of Colorado System Office (A)

1800 Grant Street, Suite 800, Denver CO 80203
County: Denver FICE Identification: 007996
Unit ID: 128300
Telephone: (303) 860-5600 Carnegie Class: N/A
FAX Number: (303) 860-5610
URL: www.cu.edu

01 President Mr. Bruce D. BENSON
05 Assoc VP & Academic Affairs Officer Dr. Kathleen BOLLARD
100 Senior VP & Chief of Staff Mr. Leonard DINEGAR
10 VP & Chief Financial Officer Ms. Kelly FOX
43 VP University Counsel/Secy Board Mr. Dan WILKERSON
16 Sr AVP/Chief Human Resource Ofcr Ms. Jill POLLOCK
86 VP Government Relations Ms. Tanya KELLY-BOWRY
26 Assoc VP University Relations Mr. Ken MCCONNELLOGUE
21 Asst VP & University Controller Mr. Robert KUEHLER
11 Assistant VP Administration Vacant
31 Dir Business & Community Relations Ms. Elizabeth COLLINS

*University of Colorado Boulder (B)

Boulder CO 80309-0001
County: Boulder FICE Identification: 001370
Unit ID: 126614
Telephone: (303) 492-1411 Carnegie Class: RU/VH
FAX Number: N/A Calendar System: Semester
URL: www.colorado.edu
Established: 1876 Annual Undergrad Tuition & Fees (In-State): $9,152
Enrollment: 29,952 Coed
Affiliation or Control: State IRS Status: 501(c)3
Highest Offering: Doctorate
Program: Liberal Arts And General; Teacher Preparatory; Professional
Accreditation: NH, AUD, BUS, CEA, CLPSY, CS, ENG, IPSY, #JOUR, LAW, MUS, SP, TED

02 Chancellor Dr. Phillip P. DISTEFANO
05 Provost & Exec Vice Chancellor Dr. Russell MOORE
10 Sr Vice Chanc Budget & Finance Mr. Richard F. PORRECA
46 Vice Chancellor for Research Dr. Stein STURE
11 Vice Chancellor Administration Mr. Frank W. BRUNO
32 Int Vice Chanc Student Affairs Ms. Deborah J. COFFIN
28 Int Vice Chanc for Diversity/Equity Dr. Robert BOSWELL
21 Assc VC Budget & Finance/Controller Mr. Steven L. MCNALLY
13 Assoc VC & Chief Information Offcr Dr. Lawrence M. LEVINE
100 Senior Advisor to the Chancellor Ms. Mary Jo WHITE
30 Vice President for Development Ms. Carolyn WHITEHEAD
29 Exec Director of Alumni Relations Ms. Deborah W. FOWLKES
58 Dean of the Graduate School Dr. John A. STEVENSON
61 Dean of Law Dr. Philip J. WEISER
49 Dean of Arts & Science Dr. Todd GLEESON
54 Dean of Engineering Dr. Robert H. DAVIS
50 Dean of Business Dr. David L. IKENBERRY
53 Dean of Education Dr. Loretta SHEPARD
64 Dean of Music Dr. Daniel P. SHER
60 Dean Journalism/Mass Communication Vacant
51 Dean Continuing Ed & Prof Studies Ms. Anne K. HEINZ
62 Dean of Libraries Mr. James F. WILLIAMS
37 Director of Financial Aid Ms. Gwen E. POMPER
07 Director of Admissions Mr. Kevin L. MACLENNAN
06 Registrar Ms. Barbara J. TODD
09 Director of Institutional Research Dr. Lou MCCLELLAND
25 Director of Contracts Grants Mr. Randall W. DRAPER
15 Exec Director of Human Resources Ms. Candice BOWEN
41 Athletic Director Mr. Michael R. BOHN
19 Director of Public Safety Mr. Joe E. ROY, II
23 Director of Student Health Center Dr. Donald MISCH
36 Director of Career Services Dr. Lisa E. SEVERY
88 Director of Museum Dr. Patrick KOCIOLEK

*University of Colorado at Colorado Springs (C)

1420 Austin Bluffs Parkway, Colorado Springs CO 80918
County: El Paso FICE Identification: 004509
Unit ID: 126580
Telephone: (719) 255-8227 Carnegie Class: Master's L
FAX Number: (719) 255-3362 Calendar System: Semester
URL: www.uccs.edu
Established: 1965 Annual Undergrad Tuition & Fees (In-State): $8,042
Enrollment: 8,900 Coed
Affiliation or Control: State IRS Status: 501(c)3
Highest Offering: Doctorate
Program: Liberal Arts And General
Accreditation: NH, BUS, CACREP, CLPSY, CS, DIETD, ENG, NURSE, TED

02 Chancellor Dr. Pam SHOCKLEY-ZALABAK
05 Provost Dr. Margaret (Peg) BACON
10 Vice Chanc Administration & Finance Dr. Brian BURNETT
11 Assoc Vice Chanc Admin & Finance Susan SZPYRKA
32 Vice Chanc Student Success Dr. Homer A. WESLEY, III
30 Vice Chanc Univ Advancement Martin WOOD
20 Sr Vice Chanc Academic Affairs Dr. David MOON
43 Legal Counsel Jenny WATSON-WILLITS
25 Director of Sponsored Programs Gwen GENNARO
08 Dean of Library Teri SWITZER
07 Director of Admissions & Records John SALNAITIS
09 Director of Institutional Research Dr. Robyn MARSCHKE
15 Human Resources Cynthia CORWIN
19 Director of Public Safety Jim SPICE
29 Director Alumni & Community Rels Jennifer HANE
37 Director Finan Aid/Stdnt Employment Vacant
40 Manager of Bookstore Tamara MOORE
18 Chief Facilities/Physical Plant Gary REYNOLDS
26 Director Media Relations Tom HUTTON
38 Director Student Counseling Dr. Z. Benek ALTAYLI
41 Director of Athletics Stephen W. KIRKHAM
13 Director of Information Technology Jerry WILSON
21 Director Resource Management Gayanne SCOTT
49 Dean of Letters/Arts/Science Dr. Thomas CHRISTENSEN
50 Dean of Business Dr. Venkateshwar REDDY
53 Dean of Education Dr. Mary SNYDER
54 Dean of Engineering/Applied Science Dr. Ramaswami DANDAPANI
80 Assoc Dean of Public Affairs Dr. Terry SCHWARTZ
66 Dean Nursing/Health Sciences Dr. Nancy SMITH
58 Dean of Graduate School Dr. Janenne NELSON
28 Director of Diversity Dr. Kee WARNER
39 Director Campus Housing Ralph GIESE
88 Director of Sustainability Linda KOGAN

*University of Colorado Denver|Anschutz Medical Campus (D)

1380 Lawrence Street, Denver CO 80204
County: Denver FICE Identification: 004508
Unit ID: 126562
Telephone: (303) 315-2500 Carnegie Class: RU/H
FAX Number: N/A Calendar System: Semester
URL: www.ucdenver.edu
Established: 1912 Annual Undergrad Tuition & Fees (In-State): $7,214
Enrollment: 18,142 Coed
Affiliation or Control: State IRS Status: 501(c)3
Highest Offering: Doctorate
Program: Professional
Accreditation: NH, ARCPA, BUS, BUSA, CACREP, CS, DENT, DMS, ENG, HSA, IPSY, LSAR, MED, MIDWF, MUS, NURSE, PH, PHAR, PLNG, PTA, SPAA, TED

02 Chancellor Dr. Jerry WARTGROW
03 VP Health Affairs/Exec VC AMC Ms. Lily MARKS
10 Vice Chancellor Admin/Finance Mr. Jeffrey PARKER
30 VC Advancement & Chief of Staff Vacant
46 Vice Chancellor for Research Dr. Richard TRAYSTMAN
17 VC Health Affairs/Dean of Medicine Dr. Richard D. KRUGMAN
05 Provost & VC Academic/Student Affs Dr. Roderick NAIRN
52 Dean School of Dental Medicine Dr. Denise KASSEBAUM
66 Dean College of Nursing Dr. Patricia MORITZ
67 Dean School of Pharmacy Dr. Ralph ALTIERE
69 Dean CO School of Public Health Vacant
58 Dean Graduate School Dr. Barry SHUR
64 Dean College of Arts and Media Dr. David DYNAK
80 Dean School of Public Affairs Dr. Paul TESKE
49 Dean College of Liberal Arts & Sci Dr. Dan J. HOWARD
48 Dean College of Arch/Planning Mr. Mark GELERNTER
50 Dean Business School Ms. Sueann AMBRON
53 Dean School of Education Dr. Rebecca KANTOR
54 Dean College of Engineering Dr. Marc INGBER
46 Assoc VC for Research Vacant
20 Assoc VC Academic Affairs Vacant
20 Assoc VC Faculty Affairs Dr. Laura GOODWIN
32 Assoc VC Student Affairs Dr. Raul CARDENAS
28 Assoc VC Diversity/Inclusion Vacant
21 Assoc VC Budget/Finance Ms. Lisa ESGAR
18 Assoc VC Facilities Management Mr. David C. TURNQUIST
15 Asst VC Human Resources Mr. Kevin JACOBS
13 Asst VC Information Technology Svcs Mr. Russell POOLE
88 Asst VC Academic Tech/Extd Learning Mr. Robert TOLSMA
84 Asst VC Enrollment Management Ms. Barbara EDWARDS
88 Asst VC Student Success Ms. Peggy LORE
35 Asst VC Univ Life/Dean of Students Dr. Samantha ORTIZ
06 Interim Registrar Ms. Ingrid ESCHHOLZ
09 Director Institutional Research Dr. Christine STROUP-BENHAM
08 Director Auraria Library Dr. Mary SOMERVILLE
08 Director Denison Library Hlth Sci Mr. Jerry PERRY
26 Director PR/Media Relations Ms. Jacque MONTGOMERY
37 Interim Director Financial Aid Svcs Mr. Evan ICOLARI
19 Chief of Police Mr. Doug ABRAHAM
29 Director Alumni Relations Ms. Joy FRENCH
43 Assistant University Counsel Mr. Christopher PUCKETT

University of Denver (E)

2199 S. University Blvd., Denver CO 80208-0001
County: Denver FICE Identification: 001371
Unit ID: 127060
Telephone: (303) 871-2000 Carnegie Class: RU/H
FAX Number: (303) 871-3301 Calendar System: Quarter
URL: www.du.edu
Established: 1864 Annual Undergrad Tuition & Fees: $37,833
Enrollment: 11,842 Coed
Affiliation or Control: Independent Non-Profit IRS Status: 501(c)3
Highest Offering: Doctorate
Program: Liberal Arts And General; Teacher Preparatory; Professional
Accreditation: NH, ART, BUS, BUSA, CEA, CLPSY, COPSY, ENG, IPSY, LAW, LIB, MUS, SW

01 Chancellor Dr. Robert D. COOMBE
05 Provost Dr. Gregg O. KVISTAD
43 University Counsel Mr. Paul H. CHAN
10 Vice Chanc Business/Financial Affs Mr. Craig WOODY
41 Vice Chanc Athletics and Recreation Ms. Peg BRADLEY-DOPPES
30 Vice Chanc University Advance Mr. Ed HARRIS
26 Vice Chancellor Communications Vacant
14 Vice Chanc University Tech Services Ms. Cindy CROUCH
84 Vice Chancellor for Enrollment Mr. Thomas WILLOUGHBY
37 Director of Financial Aid Mr. Chris GEORGE
04 Assistant to the Chancellor Ms. Claire BROWNELL
20 Associate Provost Academic Program Dr. Jennifer KARAS
32 Assoc Provost Student Life Dr. Patti HELTON
28 Assoc Provost Multicult Excellence Dr. James MORAN
58 Vice Provost Graduate Studies Dr. Barbara WILCOTS
08 Dean Libraries Ms. Nancy T. ALLEN
34 Dean The Women's College Dr. Lynn GANGONE
45 Associate Provost Planning/Budget Ms. Julia MCGAHEY
06 Registrar Mr. Dennis M. BECKER
21 Controller/Assistant Treasurer Ms. Margaret HENRY
36 Director Career Center Ms. Mary M. HAWKINS
22 EO/ADA Compliance Director Ms. Kathryne GROVE
18 Director Facilities Management Mr. Jeff BEMELEN
09 Director Institutional Research Dr. Ali WALTON
15 Director Human Resources Ms. Amy KING
19 Director Campus Safety Mr. Donald ENLOE
96 Director University Business Svcs Mr. Joe BENSON
91 Director Admin Information Systems Ms. Susan LUTZ
23 Exec Dir of Univ Health Services Dr. Sam ALEXANDER
79 Dean Arts/Humanities/Social Science Dr. Anne MCCALL
81 Dean Natural Science/Math Dr. Alayne PARSON
50 Dean College of Business Dr. Christine RIORDAN
61 Dean College of Law Mr. Martin J. KATZ
82 Dean Graduate Sch Intl Studies Mr. Christopher R. HILL
70 Dean Graduate Sch Social Work Dr. James WILLIAMS
55 Dean University College Dr. James DAVIS
53 Dean College of Education Dr. Greg M. ANDERSON
64 Director Lamont School of Music Mr. F. Joseph DOCKSEY
88 Dir Special Community Programs Dr. Cathy GRIEVE
57 Director School of Art/Art History Dr. Gwen CHANZIT
07 Director of Enrollment Services Ms. Anne GROSS
35 Student Programs & Greek Life Mr. Carl JOHNSON

University of Northern Colorado (F)

501 20th Street, Greeley CO 80639-6900
County: Weld FICE Identification: 001349
Unit ID: 127741
Telephone: (970) 351-1890 Carnegie Class: DRU
FAX Number: (970) 351-1880 Calendar System: Semester
URL: www.unco.edu
Established: 1889 Annual Undergrad Tuition & Fees (In-State): $6,576
Enrollment: 12,348 Coed
Affiliation or Control: State IRS Status: 501(c)3
Highest Offering: Doctorate
Program: Liberal Arts And General; Teacher Preparatory; Professional
Accreditation: NH, AUD, BUS, BUSA, CACREP, COPSY, CORE, DIETD, DIETI, MUS, NURSE, PH, SCPSY, SP, TED

01 President Ms. Kay NORTON
05 Provost/Vice Pres Academic Affairs Vacant
11 Vice President Administration Ms. Michelle QUINN
43 Vice President & University Counsel Mr. Dan SATRIANA
26 VP Univ Advancement/Univ Relations Mr. Chuck LEONHARDT
30 Vice Pres Development/Alumni Rels Ms. Victoria GORRELL
58 Asst VP Res/Extend Stds/DnGrad Sch Dr. Robbyn WACKER
20 Ast VP Undergrad Stds/Dean Univ Col Dr. Thomas SMITH
10 Asst Vice President Budgets/Analysl Ms. Susan SIMMERS
13 Asst VP Information Technology Ms. Jeanette VANGALDER
84 Asst Vice Pres for Enrollment Mgmt Mr. Tobias GUZMAN
49 Dean Humanities & Social Sciences Dr. David CALDWELL
50 Dean Business Administration Dr. Donald GUDMUNDSON
53 Dean Education/Behavorial Sciences Dr. Eugene SHEEHAN
76 Dean Natural & Health Sciences Dr. Denise BATTLES
57 Dean Performing Visual Arts Dr. Andrew SVEDLOW
08 Interim Dean University Libraries Ms. Helen REED
35 Dean of Students Dr. Raul CARDENAS
102 Exec Director University Foundation Ms. Polly KURTZ
06 Registrar Mr. Charlie COUCH
07 Director of Admissions Mr. Randall LANGSTON
25 Dir Sponsored Pgms/Academic Res Ms. Michele SCHWIETZ
37 Dir Student Financial Resources Mr. Marty SOMERO
36 Director of Career Services Ms. Renee WELCH
15 Director of Human Resources Mr. Marshall PARKS
29 Asst VP Alumni/Donor Relations Mr. Michael JOHNSON
18 Director Facilities Management Mr. Kirk LEICHLITER
41 Director Intercollegiate Athletics Mr. Jay HINRICHS
39 Director of Residence Life Ms. Jenna FINLEY
38 Director Student Counseling Ms. Kim WILCOX
19 Chief of University Police Mr. Mikel LONGMAN
44 Director of Annual Giving Mr. Michael MUSKIN
27 Dir Communications/Media Relations Mr. Nate HAAS
96 Director of Purchasing Ms. Cristal SWAIN

University of the Rockies (G)

555 E Pikes Peak Ave, Suite 108,
Colorado Springs CO 80903-3612
County: El Paso FICE Identification: 035453
Unit ID: 441308
Telephone: (719) 442-0505 Carnegie Class: Spec/Health
FAX Number: (719) 389-0359 Calendar System: Other
URL: www.rockies.edu
Established: 1998 Annual Graduate Tuition & Fees: $17,170
Enrollment: 1,489 Coed
Affiliation or Control: Proprietary IRS Status: Proprietary
Highest Offering: Doctorate; No Undergraduates

Program: Professional
Accreditation: NH

01 President .... Dr. Charlita SHELTON
03 Vice President/Campus Director .... Dr. Robert EDELBROCK
05 Provost .... Dr. Tina PARSCAL
20 Vice President of Academic Services .... Dr. Barbara DIERKS
20 Vice Pres of Academic Affs Online .... Ms. Linda HIEMER
32 Director of Student Affairs .... Ms. Janet BRUGGER
58 Dean School of Prof Psychology .... Dr. David STEPHENS
106 Dean Sch Organizational Leadership .... Dr. J. Stephen KIRKPATRICK
26 Campus PR/Marketing Specialist .... Ms. Melissa BLEVINS
37 Director of Financial Aid .... Ms. Jami FLEMING
15 Director of Human Resources .... Ms. Barbara HENRY-QUINN
06 Associate Campus Registrar .... Ms. Katina JORDAN
07 Campus Enrollment Services Manager .. Ms. Carolyn SCHNEIDER
28 Director of Diversity .... Dr. Amy KAHN

U.S. Career Institute (A)

2001 Lowe Street, Fort Collins CO 80525
County: Laramer — Identification: 666776
Telephone: (970) 207-4500 — Carnegie Class: Not Classified
FAX Number: (970) 223-1678 — Calendar System: Other
URL: www.uscareerinstitute.edu
Established: N/A — Annual Undergrad Tuition & Fees: N/A
Enrollment: N/A — Coed
Affiliation or Control: Proprietary — IRS Status: Proprietary
Highest Offering: Associate Degree
Program: Occupational
Accreditation: DETC

01 President .... Ann ROHR
03 Chief Executive Officer .... Cole P. THOMPSON

Western State College (B)

Gunnison CO 81231-0001
County: Gunnison — FICE Identification: 001372
Unit ID: 128391
Telephone: (970) 943-0120 — Carnegie Class: Bac/A&S
FAX Number: (970) 943-7069 — Calendar System: Semester
URL: www.western.edu
Established: 1911 — Annual Undergrad Tuition & Fees (In-State): $3,922
Enrollment: 2,233 — Coed
Affiliation or Control: State — IRS Status: 501(c)3
Highest Offering: Baccalaureate
Program: Liberal Arts And General; Teacher Preparatory; Professional
Accreditation: NH, MUS

01 President .... Dr. Jay W. HELMAN
05 Vice President Academic Affairs .... Dr. Jessica YOUNG
10 Vice Pres Finance & Administration .... Mr. W. Bradley BACA
32 Vice President of Student Affairs .... Mr. Gary PIERSON
30 Vice Pres Institutional Advancement .... Mr. Thomas F. BURGGRAF, JR.
20 Assoc Vice Pres Academic Affairs .... Dr. Kevin NELSON
21 Assoc Vice Pres Finance & Admin .... Ms. Julie FEIER
07 Director of Admissions .... Mr. Tim ALBERS
35 Assoc Vice Pres Student Affairs .... Ms. Shelley JANSEN
06 Registrar .... Ms. Debra CLARK
37 Director Student Financial Aid .... Mr. Eric CRONKRIGHT
104 Dir Intl Student Pgms/Study Abroad .... Ms. Jerri PURALEWSKI
41 Athletic Director .... Dr. R. Greg WAGGONER
15 Director of Human Resources .... Ms. Kim GAILEY
40 Director Retail Operations .... Ms. Teri HAUS
91 Director Administrative Computing .... Mr. Chad ROBINSON
08 Director Library Services .... Ms. Nancy GAUSS
51 Director Extended Studies .... Ms. Layne Meredith NELSON
39 Director Residence Life .... Ms. Carrie BUCHANAN
36 Director Career Svcs/Internships .... Ms. Svea WHITING
26 Director of Public Relations .... Ms. Tracey KOEHLER
29 Director of Alumni Relations .... Ms. Tonya VANHEE
44 Director Annual & Special Gifts .... Ms. Deb HOSKINS
09 Director Institutional Research .... Mr. Doug DRIVER
18 Chief Facilities/Physical Plant .... Mr. Paul MORGAN
35 Director of Student Affairs .... Vacant
84 Director of Enrollment Management .... Mr. Tim ALBERS
28 Director of Multicultural Center .... Ms. Sally ROMERO
96 Director of Purchasing .... Mr. Thornton REESE

*Westwood College (C)

7604 Technology Way Suite 400, Denver CO 80237
County: Denver — Identification: 667029
Telephone: (303) 846-1700 — Carnegie Class: N/A
FAX Number: N/A
URL: www.westwood.edu

01 System President & CEO .... Mr. George BURNETT

*Westwood College-Denver North (D)

7350 N Broadway, Denver CO 80221-3653
County: Adams — FICE Identification: 007548
Unit ID: 127024
Telephone: (303) 426-7000 — Carnegie Class: Bac/Diverse
FAX Number: (303) 426-4647 — Calendar System: Other
URL: www.westwood.edu
Established: 1953 — Annual Undergrad Tuition & Fees: $14,227
Enrollment: 797 — Coed
Affiliation or Control: Proprietary — IRS Status: Proprietary
Highest Offering: Baccalaureate
Program: Occupational; Technical Emphasis
Accreditation: ACCSC, ACICS, MAC

00 Alta Colleges Chairman .... Mr. Kirk RIEDINGER
02 Alta Colleges President .... Mr. James TURNER
12 Campus President .... Ms. Natalie WILLIAMS

*Westwood College-Denver South (E)

3150 S Sheridan Boulevard, Denver CO 80227-5507
County: Denver — Identification: 666512
Unit ID: 381787
Telephone: (303) 934-1122 — Carnegie Class: Bac/Diverse
FAX Number: (303) 934-2583 — Calendar System: Quarter
URL: www.westwood.edu
Established: 1953 — Annual Undergrad Tuition & Fees: $14,050
Enrollment: 350 — Coed
Affiliation or Control: Proprietary — IRS Status: Proprietary
Highest Offering: Baccalaureate
Program: Occupational
Accreditation: ACCSC, ACICS

02 Executive Director .... Daniel C. SNYDER
04 Executive Assistant .... Donna REICHERT
05 Campus Academic Dean .... Bob STUDINGER
07 Director of Admissions .... Daniel VOPAT
06 Registrar .... Kristin HUSBY
08 Librarian .... Jessica KING
10 Director of Finance .... Vacant
36 Director of Career Services .... Randall SCHALHAMER
32 Director Student Affairs .... Maureen WALLACE

† Branch campus of Westwood College-Denver North, Denver, CO.

William Howard Taft University (F)

600 South Cherry Street, Suite 525, Denver CO 80246
County: Denver — FICE Identification: 041004
Telephone: (303) 867-1155 — Carnegie Class: Not Classified
FAX Number: (303) 867-1156 — Calendar System: Trimester
URL: www.taft.edu
Established: 1976 — Annual Undergrad Tuition & Fees: N/A
Enrollment: N/A — Coed
Affiliation or Control: Proprietary — IRS Status: Proprietary
Highest Offering: Doctorate
Program: 2-Year Principally Bachelor's Creditable; Liberal Arts And General; Professional
Accreditation: DETC

01 President .... Mr. Jerome ALLEY
03 Chief Operating Officer .... Mr. Robert K. STROUSE
11 Director of Administration .... Ms. Christine A. BALDWIN

† Tuition varies by degree program.

Yorktown University (G)

4340 East Kentucky Avenue, Ste 457,
Denver CO 80246-2079
County: Denver — Identification: 666409
Telephone: (303) 757-0059 — Carnegie Class: Not Classified
FAX Number: (720) 528-7761 — Calendar System: Other
URL: www.yorktownuniversity.edu
Established: 1999 — Annual Graduate Tuition & Fees: N/A
Enrollment: 5 — Coed
Affiliation or Control: Proprietary — IRS Status: Proprietary
Highest Offering: Master's; No Undergraduates
Program: Professional
Accreditation: DETC

01 President .... Dr. Richard J. BISHIRJIAN
05 Chief Academic Officer .... Dr. Lewis PRINGLE
07 Director of Admissions .... Christopher G. EVANS

CONNECTICUT

Albertus Magnus College (H)

700 Prospect Street, New Haven CT 06511-1189
County: New Haven — FICE Identification: 001374
Unit ID: 128498
Telephone: (203) 773-8550 — Carnegie Class: Master's L
FAX Number: (203) 773-9539 — Calendar System: Semester
URL: www.albertus.edu
Established: 1925 — Annual Undergrad Tuition & Fees: $37,374
Enrollment: 1,961 — Coed
Affiliation or Control: Independent Non-Profit — IRS Status: 501(c)3
Highest Offering: Master's
Program: Liberal Arts And General
Accreditation: EH, IACBE

01 President .... Dr. Julia M. MCNAMARA
05 Provost/Vice Pres Academic Affairs .... Dr. John J. DONOHUE
10 Vice President Finance/Treasurer .... Mrs. Jeanne E. MANN
13 VP Information Technology Services .... Mr. Steven GSTALDER
29 Asc VP Development/Alumni Relations .... Ms. Carolyn A. BEHAN KRAUS
32 Dean for Student Services .... Ms. Maureen V. MORRISON
07 Dean for Admission/Financial Aid .... Mr. Richard J. LOLATTE
20 Academic Dean Day Program .... Dr. Sean P. O'CONNELL
35 Assistant Dean for Student Life .... Ms. Jennifer DUROCHER
06 Registrar .... Ms. Claudia SCHIAVONE
08 Director Library/Information Svcs .... Ms. Anne LEENEY-PANAGROSSI
55 Dean for School of New Dimensions .... Dr. Irene RIOS
09 Dir Assessment/Institutional Rsrch .... Vacant
37 Director Financial Aid .... Mr. Andrew FOSTER
58 Dean of Evening/Graduate Program .... Vacant
90 Director Academic Computing .... Mr. Robert HUBBARD
41 Director of Athletics .... Mr. Michael S. SPINNER
58 Director MALS Program .... Ms. Julia COASH
89 Director of Freshmen Advising .... Vacant
92 Director of Honors Program .... Dr. Christine ATKINS
96 Dir Purchas/Pub Sfty/Spec Projects .... Mr. James A. SCHAFRICK
15 Director Human Resources .... Mrs. Diane L. NUNN
18 Director of Facilities Services .... Mr. Edward J. THOMASI, SR.
26 Dir Communications/Community Rels .... Ms. Rosanne ZUDEKOFF
36 Director Career Services .... Ms. Suzanne YURKO WALL
42 Director of Campus Ministry .... Sr. Helen KIERAN, OP

Beth Benjamin Academy of Connecticut (I)

132 Prospect Street, Stamford CT 06901-1202
County: Fairfield — FICE Identification: 029120
Unit ID: 414975
Telephone: (203) 325-4351 — Carnegie Class: Not Classified
FAX Number: (203) 323-6073 — Calendar System: Trimester
Established: 1976 — Annual Undergrad Tuition & Fees: $5,300
Enrollment: 60 — Male
Affiliation or Control: Independent Non-Profit — IRS Status: 501(c)3
Highest Offering: First Talmudic Degree
Program: Teacher Preparatory; Professional
Accreditation: RABN

01 Rosh Hayeshiva .... Rabbi S. SCHUSTAL
04 Associate Rosh Hayeshiva .... Rabbi M. HERSHKOWITZ
05 Dean .... Rabbi Michael BENDER

*Board of Trustees of Community-Technical Colleges (J)

61 Woodland Street, Hartford CT 06105-2391
County: Hartford — Identification: 666784
Telephone: (860) 566-8760 — Carnegie Class: N/A
FAX Number: (860) 244-7886
URL: www.commnet.edu

01 Chancellor .... Mr. Marc S. HERZOG
04 Assistant to the Chancellor .... Ms. Pamela COLEMAN
03 Deputy Chancellor .... Vacant
05 Chief Academic Officer .... Dr. Paul SUSEN
16 Dir of Employee/Labor Relations .... Vacant
09 Director of Institutional Research .... Dr. Corby COPERTHWAITE
26 Dir Comm/Syst Advance/Asst Chanc .... Ms. Mary Anne COX
86 Director of Governmental Affairs .... Ms. Meghan COLLINS-FANNING
15 Director of Personnel Services .... Ms. Coreen SUMPLE
28 Dir Sys Ofcr Equity/Diversity Aware .... Mr. Kenneth ARMSTRONG
13 Chief Information Officer .... Mr. Kenneth SPELKE
10 Chief Financial/Administrative Ofcr .... Ms. Vicky GREENE
18 Chief Facilities .... Ms. Lenell KITTLITZ
20 Associate Academic Officer .... Mr. Phil COCCHIOLA
43 Mgr of Labor Relations/Asst Counsel .... Ms. Marjorie LONDON

*Asnuntuck Community College (K)

170 Elm Street, Enfield CT 06082-3800
County: Hartford — FICE Identification: 011150
Unit ID: 128577
Telephone: (860) 253-3000 — Carnegie Class: Assoc/Pub-S-SC
FAX Number: (860) 253-3007 — Calendar System: Semester
URL: www.acc.commnet.edu
Established: 1972 — Annual Undergrad Tuition & Fees (In-State): $3,490
Enrollment: 1,836 — Coed
Affiliation or Control: State — IRS Status: 501(c)3
Highest Offering: Associate Degree
Program: Occupational; 2-Year Principally Bachelor's Creditable
Accreditation: EH

02 President .... Dr. Martha MCLEOD
05 Dean of Academic Affairs .... Ms. Barbara MCCARTHY
10 Dean of Administration .... Mr. Timothy J. HURLOCK
32 Dean Student Services .... Ms. Kathleen KELLEY
15 Director Personnel .... Mr. Joe BLEICHER
51 Director of Continuing Education .... Mr. Jim LOMBELLA
07 Director Admissions .... Mr. Tim ST. JAMES
06 Registrar .... Ms. Gail LABBADIA
37 Director Financial Aid .... Ms. Donna JONES-SEARLE
09 Director Institutional Research .... Ms. Qing L. MACK
30 Director Institutional Advancement .... Vacant
18 Chief Facilities/Physical Plant .... Mr. Joseph MULLER
96 Fiscal Administrative Officer .... Mr. Duncan D. MORRIS

*Capital Community College (L)

950 Main Street, Hartford CT 06103-1207
County: Hartford — FICE Identification: 007635
Unit ID: 129367
Telephone: (860) 906-5000 — Carnegie Class: Assoc/Pub-U-SC
FAX Number: (860) 520-7906 — Calendar System: Semester
URL: www.ccc.commnet.edu
Established: 1967 — Annual Undergrad Tuition & Fees (In-State): $3,490

Enrollment: 4,518 Coed
Affiliation or Control: State IRS Status: 501(c)3
Highest Offering: Associate Degree
Program: Occupational; 2-Year Principally Bachelor's Creditable
Accreditation: EH, ADNUR, EMT, MAC, PTAA, RAD

02 President ....Dr. Wilfredo NIEVES
05 Academic Dean ....Dr. Mary Ann AFFLECK
32 Dean of Student Services ....Ms. Doris B. ARRINGTON
11 Dean of Administration ....Mr. Lester PRIMUS
51 Dean Continuing Educ/Community Svcs ....Ms. Linda GUZZO
09 Director of Institutional Research ....Ms. Jenny WANG
10 Director Finance/Administration ....Mr. Ted HALE
06 Registrar ....Mr. Patrick TUCKER
08 Director of Library Services ....Ms. Jessica VANDERHOFF
88 Disabilities Coordinator ....Ms. Glaisma PEREZ-SILVA
07 Director of Admissions ....Ms. Marsha BALL-DAVIS
37 Director of Financial Aid ....Ms. Margaret MALASPINA
14 Director of Computer Services ....Mr. Roger FERRARO
66 Dir Cont Educ Nurse/Allied Health ....Ms. Ruth KREMS
36 Dir of Career Planning/Development ....Ms. Linda DOMENITZ
26 Director of Information/Marketing ....Ms. Jane BRONFMAN
15 Director of Human Resources ....Mr. Henry BURGOS
20 Associate Academic Officer ....Mr. C. Raymond HUGHES
30 Director Institutional Advancement ....Mr. John MCNAMARA

*Gateway Community College (A)

60 Sargent Drive, New Haven CT 06511-5970
County: New Haven FICE Identification: 008037
Unit ID: 130396
Telephone: (203) 285-2000 Carnegie Class: Assoc/Pub-U-MC
FAX Number: (203) 285-2018 Calendar System: Semester
URL: www.gwcc.commnet.edu
Established: 1968 Annual Undergrad Tuition & Fees (In-State): $3,490
Enrollment: 7,328 Coed
Affiliation or Control: State IRS Status: 501(c)3
Highest Offering: Associate Degree
Program: Occupational; 2-Year Principally Bachelor's Creditable
Accreditation: EH, ADNUR, DIETT, NMT, RAD, RTT

02 President ....Dr. Dorsey L. KENDRICK
11 Dean of Administrative Services ....Mr. Louis S. D'ANTONIO
46 Dean of Research & Development ....Ms. Mary Ellen CODY
05 Dean of Learning ....Dr. Mark KOSINSKI
31 Dean Community Services ....Ms. Victoria BOZZUTO
15 Director Personnel/Contract Admin ....Ms. Lucille BROWN
04 Executive Assistant to President ....Ms. Carol G. MCHUGH
09 Director Institutional Research ....Dr. Vincent P. TONG
27 Director Public Info & Marketing ....Ms. Evelyn GARD
10 Director Finance & Admin Svcs ....Ms. Jill RAIOLA
30 Director Institutional Advancement ....Vacant
08 Director Learning Resources Center ....Ms. Clara OGBAA
07 Director of Admissions ....Ms. Kim SHEA
36 Director Career Development Center ....Mr. Michael BUCCILLI
06 Registrar ....Mr. David M. SWIRSKY
37 Director Financial Aid ....Mr. Raymond ZEEK
38 Director Student Counseling ....Ms. Tina MCHUGH
35 Director of College Life ....Ms. Roberta PRIOR
24 Director Educational Technologies ....Ms. Wendy SAMBERG
25 Grants Facilitator ....Vacant
13 Director Computer Services ....Mr. Lawrence SALAY
24 Director Early Learning Center ....Ms. Marjorie WEINER
51 Coord Center for Education Svcs ....Mr. Luis F. MELENDEZ
50 Chair Business Department ....Mr. Richard REES
79 Chair Humanities Department ....Mr. Chester H. SCHNEPF
83 Chair Social Sciences Department ....Mr. Daniel P. COURCEY
88 Coord Early Childhood Education ....Ms. Susan E. LOGSTON
88 Coord Drug/Alcohol Rehab Couns ....Ms. Cheryl SHANNON
16 Coordinator Human Services Programs ....Mr. Jonah COHEN
67 Coordinator Pharmacy Tech Program ....Ms. Louise A. PETROKA
81 Chair Math/Natural Sci Department ....Mr. Miguel GARCIA
50 Director Business & Industry Svcs ....Mr. John VINCZE
88 Director Dietetic Technician Pgm ....Mrs. Marcia S. DORAN
76 Director Allied Health ....Ms. Marcia DORAN
20 Associate Dean of Learning ....Vacant
88 Director Credit Free Programming ....Vacant
54 Dir Engineering/Applied Technology ....Mr. Paul SILBERQUIT
18 Chief Facilities/Physical Plant ....Mr. Lucian SIMONE

*Housatonic Community College (B)

900 Lafayette Boulevard, Bridgeport CT 06604-4704
County: Fairfield FICE Identification: 004513
Unit ID: 129543
Telephone: (203) 332-5000 Carnegie Class: Assoc/Pub-R-M
FAX Number: (203) 332-5123 Calendar System: Semester
URL: www.hcc.commnet.edu
Established: 1966 Annual Undergrad Tuition & Fees (In-State): $3,490
Enrollment: 6,197 Coed
Affiliation or Control: State IRS Status: 501(c)3
Highest Offering: Associate Degree
Program: Occupational; 2-Year Principally Bachelor's Creditable
Accreditation: EH, OTA, PTAA

02 President ....Ms. Anita GLINIECKI
05 Academic Dean ....Ms. Elizabeth ROOP
11 Dean of Administration ....Mr. Ralph TYLER
31 Dean of Outreach ....Mr. Gary KECSKES
32 Dean of Students ....Dr. Avis D. HENDRICKSON
20 Associate Dean Academics ....Mr. Alan BARKLEY
06 Registrar ....Mr. Jim CONNOLLY
07 Director of Admissions ....Ms. Deloris Y. CURTIS
08 Librarian ....Ms. Shelly STROHM
37 Director of Financial Aid ....Ms. Barbara SUROWIEC
26 Public Relations Associate ....Mr. Anson SMITH
19 Director of Security ....Mr. Christopher GOUGH
09 Director of Institutional Research ....Ms. Jan SCHAEFFLER
14 Director of Computer Services ....Mr. Anthony VITOLA
16 Director Personnel/Labor Relations ....Ms. Brenda ALEXANDER
30 Director Resource Development ....Mrs. Maureen DOWDLE
29 Director Alumni Relations ....Mrs. Maureen DOWDLE
35 Director of Student Life ....Ms. Linda BAYUSIK
15 Personnel Officer ....Ms. Theresa EISENBACH
10 Business Manager ....Vacant
51 Coordinator Continuing Education ....Ms. Deborah KUCHMAS
18 Coordinator of Facilities ....Mr. Richard HENNESSEY

*Manchester Community College (C)

PO Box 1046, Great Path, Manchester CT 06045-1046
County: Hartford FICE Identification: 001392
Unit ID: 129695
Telephone: (860) 512-3000 Carnegie Class: Assoc/Pub-S-SC
FAX Number: (860) 512-3631 Calendar System: Semester
URL: www.mcc.commnet.edu
Established: 1963 Annual Undergrad Tuition & Fees (In-State): $3,490
Enrollment: 7,540 Coed
Affiliation or Control: State IRS Status: 501(c)3
Highest Offering: Associate Degree
Program: Occupational; 2-Year Principally Bachelor's Creditable
Accreditation: EH, ACFEI, OTA, PTAA, SURGT

02 President ....Dr. Gena GLICKMAN
05 Dean of Academic Affairs ....Dr. Joanne RUSSELL
32 Dean of Student Affairs ....Dr. G. Duncan HARRIS
11 Dean of Administrative Affairs ....Mr. James MCDOWELL
30 Acting Dean of Advancement ....Mr. Martin HART
51 Dean of Continuing Education ....Ms. Melanie HABER
20 Associate Dean of Academic Affairs ....Dr. Pamela MITCHELL-CRUMP
10 Director Finance & Admin Services ....Ms. Regina FERRANTE
07 Director of Admissions ....Mr. Peter HARRIS
06 Registrar ....Ms. Natalie DURANT
08 Director of Library Services ....Dr. Randolph FOURNIER
13 Director of Information Technology ....Mr. Barry GRANT
09 Director Plng/Research & Assessment ....Mr. David NIELSEN
15 Director of Human Resources ....Ms. Deborah WILSON
18 Dir Facilities Management/ Planning ....Ms. Darlene MANCINI-BROWN
26 Dir Marketing and Public Relations ....Ms. Charlene TAPPAN
37 Financial Aid Officer ....Ms. Ivette RIVERA-DREYER
72 Director Ctr Business/Technologies ....Ms. Catherine SEAVER
83 Director Social Science/Hospitality ....Dr. Christopher PAULIN
81 Dir Math/Science/Health Careers ....Ms. Marcia JEHNINGS
79 Director of Liberal Arts ....Mr. Michael STEFANOWICZ
41 Director of Athletics and Fitness ....Ms. Cynthia WASHBURNE
19 Director of Public Safety ....Ms. Susan GIBBENS
44 Coordinator Annual Giving ....Ms. Sara VINCENT
38 Dir Counseling and Career Svcs ....Mr. Carl OCHNIO
84 Director of Enrollment Management ....Mr. Peter HARRIS

*Middlesex Community College (D)

100 Training Hill Road, Middletown CT 06457-4889
County: Middlesex FICE Identification: 008038
Unit ID: 129756
Telephone: (860) 343-5800 Carnegie Class: Assoc/Pub-S-SC
FAX Number: (860) 344-7488 Calendar System: Semester
URL: www.mxcc.commnet.edu
Established: 1966 Annual Undergrad Tuition & Fees (In-State): $3,490
Enrollment: 2,952 Coed
Affiliation or Control: State IRS Status: 501(c)3
Highest Offering: Associate Degree
Program: Occupational; 2-Year Principally Bachelor's Creditable
Accreditation: EH, OPD, RAD

02 President ....Dr. Anna WASESCHA
05 Dean of Academics ....Vacant
10 Dean Finance & Administration ....Mr. David SYKES
32 Dean of Students ....Dr. Adrienne MASLIN
51 Dean Continuing Education ....Mr. Reid SMALLEY
06 Registrar ....Ms. Susan SALOWITZ
08 Director Library Services ....Ms. Lan LIU
37 Director Financial Aid ....Ms. Irene MARTIN
30 Director Institutional Advancement ....Mr. Greg KLINE
07 Director of Admissions ....Ms. Mensimah SHABAZZ
09 Director of Institutional Research ....Mr. Paul CARMICHAEL
13 Director Information Technology ....Ms. Annie SCOTT
35 Coordinator Student Activities ....Ms. Judy MAZGULSKI
88 Director Child Care Services ....Ms. Hilary PHELPS
18 Chief Facilities/Physical Plant ....Mr. Steven CHESTER
103 Director of Business & Industry ....Mr. Ian CANNING
15 Director Personnel Services ....Ms. Josephine AGNELLO-VELEY
26 Chief Public Relations Officer ....Ms. Marlene OLSON
50 Chair Business ....Ms. Donna LEONOWICH
83 Chair Social & Behavioral ....Ms. Judith FELTON
81 Interim Chair Mathematics ....Ms. Pamela FROST
49 Chair Arts & Humanities ....Dr. Donna BONTATIBUS
81 Chair Science & Health ....Dr. Marci SWEDE

*Naugatuck Valley Community College (E)

750 Chase Parkway, Waterbury CT 06708-3089
County: New Haven FICE Identification: 006982
Unit ID: 129729
Telephone: (203) 575-8044 Carnegie Class: Assoc/Pub-R-L
FAX Number: (203) 575-8096 Calendar System: Semester
URL: www.nvcc.commnet.edu
Established: 1964 Annual Undergrad Tuition & Fees (In-State): $3,510
Enrollment: 7,195 Coed
Affiliation or Control: State IRS Status: 501(c)3
Highest Offering: Associate Degree
Program: Occupational; 2-Year Principally Bachelor's Creditable
Accreditation: EH, ADNUR, ENGT, PTAA, RAD

02 President ....Dr. Daisy Cocco DE FILIPPIS
11 Dean of Administration ....Mr. James TROUP
05 Dean Learning/Student Development ....Dr. Sandra PALMER
31 Dean Community/Economic Development ....Vacant
35 Acting Dean of Student Services ....Ms. Lillian ORTIZ
30 Actg Assoc Dean of Resource Devel ....Mr. Waldemar KOSTRZEWA
13 Assoc Dean Information Technology ....Mr. Conal LARKIN
20 Actg Assoc Dean of Academic Affairs ....Ms. Estela LOPEZ
06 Registrar ....Ms. Joan ARBUSTO
37 Director of Financial Aid ....Ms. Catherine HARDY
07 Director of Admissions ....Ms. Linda STANGO
22 Affirmative Action Officer ....Mr. Ron CLYMER
08 Director of Learning Resource Ctr ....Dr. Samuel BROWN
10 Director of Finance/Admin Services ....Ms. Lisa PALEN
26 Dir of Marketing/Public Relations ....Mr. Thomas VIOLANTE
32 Director of Student Activities ....Ms. Karen BLAKE
18 Chief Facilities/Physical Plant ....Mr. Robert DIVJAK
09 Director of Institutional Research ....Ms. Lauren FRIEDMAN
38 Actg Dir Student Development Svcs ....Mr. Bernd MATTHEIS
15 Director of Human Resources ....Mr. Arthur DUBOIS

*Northwestern Connecticut Community-Technical College (F)

Park Place E, Winsted CT 06098-1798
County: Litchfield FICE Identification: 001398
Unit ID: 130040
Telephone: (860) 738-6300 Carnegie Class: Assoc/Pub-S-SC
FAX Number: (860) 738-6488 Calendar System: Semester
URL: www.nwctc.commnet.edu
Established: 1965 Annual Undergrad Tuition & Fees (In-State): $3,490
Enrollment: 1,800 Coed
Affiliation or Control: State IRS Status: 501(c)3
Highest Offering: Associate Degree
Program: Occupational; 2-Year Principally Bachelor's Creditable
Accreditation: EH, MAC, PTAA

02 President ....Dr. Barbara DOUGLASS
11 Dean of Administration ....Dr. Steven R. FRAZIER
05 Acting Dean of Academic Affairs ....Dr. Patricia A. BOUFFARD
51 Dean of Continuing Education ....Dr. John C. NORMAN
07 Director of Admissions ....Ms. Joanne NARDI
08 Director of Library Services ....Mr. James PATTERSON
06 Registrar ....Ms. Debra REYNOLDS
15 Director of Human Resources ....Ms. Fran PISTILLI
37 Financial Aid Officer ....Mr. Louis BRISTOL
14 Director of Computer Services ....Mr. Joseph DANAJOVITS
88 Dir CEDHH ....Mr. Gary GRECO
38 Dir of Student Development ....Ms. Ruth GONZALEZ
09 Director of Institutional Research ....Ms. Caitlin BOGER-HAWKINS
26 Director Marketing/Public Relations ....Mr. Grantley ADAMS
10 Director Financial/Admin Services ....Ms. Kimberly DRAGAN

*Norwalk Community College (G)

188 Richards Avenue, Norwalk CT 06854-1655
County: Fairfield FICE Identification: 001399
Unit ID: 130004
Telephone: (203) 857-7000 Carnegie Class: Assoc/Pub-R-L
FAX Number: (203) 857-7287 Calendar System: Semester
URL: www.ncc.commnet.edu
Established: 1961 Annual Undergrad Tuition & Fees (In-State): $3,406
Enrollment: 6,740 Coed
Affiliation or Control: State IRS Status: 501(c)3
Highest Offering: Associate Degree
Program: Occupational; 2-Year Principally Bachelor's Creditable
Accreditation: EH, ADNUR, MAC, PTAA

02 President ....Dr. David L. LEVINSON
05 Dean of Academic Affairs ....Dr. Pamela EDINGTON
11 Dean of Administration ....Ms. Rose R. ELLIS
32 Dean of Students ....Dr. Robert BAER
44 Dean of Advancement ....Ms. Barbara DROTMAN
09 Dean of Institutional Effectiveness ....Dr. Vanessa MOREST
30 Executive Director of Development ....Ms. Jane KIEFER
51 Director of Continuing Education ....Mr. David CHASE
08 Director of Library Services ....Ms. Linda LERMAN
46 Director of Inst Research/Info Svcs ....Mr. Robert J. JALBERT, JR.
37 Financial Aid Officer ....Ms. Norma L. MCNERNEY
66 Director of Nursing Education ....Dr. Mary E. SCHULER
06 Registrar ....Ms. Danita BROWN
15 Director Human Resources ....Ms. Virginia C. DELLAMURA
26 Director of Public Relations ....Ms. Madeline K. BARILLO
36 Director Career Development ....Mr. Patrick O. BOLAND
38 Director Student Counseling ....Ms. Catherine MILLER

35 Acting Director Student Activities .... Mr. Andres GOMEZ
96 Director of Purchasing .... Ms. Gwen BROWN
10 Director Finance/Administration .... Ms. Carrie MCGEE-YUROF
18 Chief Facilities/Physical Plant .. Mr. Anthony (Tony) CENTOPANTI

*Quinebaug Valley Community College (A)

742 Upper Maple Street, Danielson CT 06239-1440
County: Windham FICE Identification: 010530
Unit ID: 130217
Telephone: (860) 412-7200 Carnegie Class: Assoc/Pub-R-M
FAX Number: (860) 412-7222 Calendar System: Semester
URL: www.qvcc.commnet.edu
Established: 1971 Annual Undergrad Tuition & Fees (In-State): $3,490
Enrollment: 2,288 Coed
Affiliation or Control: State IRS Status: 501(c)3
Highest Offering: Associate Degree
Program: Occupational; 2-Year Principally Bachelor's Creditable
Accreditation: EH, MAC

02 President .... Dr. Ross TOMLIN
32 Dean of Student Services .... Mr. David BATY
11 Dean of Administrative Services .... Mr. David BULL
08 Director of Library Services .... Ms. Sharon MOORE
37 Director of Student Financial Aid .... Mr. Alfred WILLIAMS
84 Director Enrollment & Research .... Vacant
51 Director Ctr for Cmty/Profess Lrng .... Ms. Jill O'HAGAN
14 Director Computer/Telecomm Svcs .... Mr. Kevin ANDERSON
07 Director of Admissions .... Vacant
09 Director of Institutional Research .... Dr. Donna SOHAN
10 Chief Business Officer .... Ms. Michelle WEISS
15 Dir Personnel Svcs/Aff Action Ofcr .... Mr. Dennis SIDOTI
18 Chief Facilities/Physical Plant .... Mr. David STIFEL
26 Chief Public Relations Officer .... Ms. Susan BREAULT
30 Director of College Development .... Ms. Monique WOLANIN
05 Chief Academic Office .... Dr. Amy DESONIA
06 Registrar .... Mr. Antonio VELOSO

*Three Rivers Community College (B)

574 New London Turnpike, Norwich CT 06360
County: New London FICE Identification: 009765
Unit ID: 129808
Telephone: (860) 886-0177 Carnegie Class: Assoc/Pub-R-M
FAX Number: (860) 886-0691 Calendar System: Semester
URL: www.trcc.commnet.edu
Established: 1963 Annual Undergrad Tuition & Fees (In-State): $3,490
Enrollment: 5,161 Coed
Affiliation or Control: State IRS Status: 501(c)3
Highest Offering: Associate Degree
Program: Occupational; 2-Year Principally Bachelor's Creditable
Accreditation: EH, ACBSP, ADNUR, ENGT

02 President .... Dr. Grace S. JONES
05 Academic Dean .... Ms. Ann Z. BRANCHINI
11 Dean of Administrative Services .... Mr. Michael LOPEZ
32 Dean of Student Services .... Dr. Karin EDWARDS
06 Registrar .... Ms. Christine LANGUTH
38 Director of Counseling .... Mr. John RICH
08 Director Learning Resources .... Ms. Mildred HODGE
15 Director Human Resources .... Ms. Louise J. SUMMA
37 Director Student Financial Aid .... Ms. Hong Yu KOVIC
18 Director of Facilities .... Mr. Arnie DE LA ROSSA
10 Director of Finance & Admin Svcs .... Ms. Gayle O'NEILL
30 Director Institutional Advancement .... Ms. Sandra ALLYN-GAUTHIER
26 Public Relations Associate .... Ms. Christina LEVERE

*Tunxis Community College (C)

271 Scott Swamp Road, Farmington CT 06032-3187
County: Hartford FICE Identification: 009764
Unit ID: 130606
Telephone: (860) 255-3500 Carnegie Class: Assoc/Pub-S-SC
FAX Number: (860) 255-3417 Calendar System: Semester
URL: www.tunxis.commnet.edu
Established: 1969 Annual Undergrad Tuition & Fees (In-State): $3,491
Enrollment: 4,200 Coed
Affiliation or Control: State IRS Status: 501(c)3
Highest Offering: Associate Degree
Program: Occupational; 2-Year Principally Bachelor's Creditable
Accreditation: EH, @ACBSP, DA, DH, PTAA

02 President .... Dr. Cathryn L. ADDY
05 Dean of Academic Affairs .... Dr. Michael ROOKE
32 Dean of Student Services .... Dr. Kirk PETERS
11 Dean of Administration .... Mr. Charles CLEARY
45 Dean of Institutional Effectiveness .... Dr. David C. ENGLAND
10 Dir Finance/Administrative Services .... Ms. Nancy ESCHENBRENNER
30 Dir of Institutional Advancement .... Vacant
15 Director Human Resources .... Ms. Pamela KOWAR
08 Director Library Services .... Dr. Lisa LAVOIE
13 Director Information Technology .... Mr. Robert WAHL
07 Director of Admissions .... Mr. Peter MCCLUSKEY
35 Director Academic Support Center .... Ms. Kathleen SCHWAGER
09 Director of Institutional Research .... Vacant
37 Director Financial Aid Services .... Mr. David WELSH
26 Dir of Marketing/Public Relations .... Vacant
18 Director of Facilities .... Mr. John LODOVICO

90 Coord Academic Info Technology .... Mr. Steven MEAD
91 Coord Admin Information Technology .... Mrs. Mary Ann DIORIO

Charter Oak State College (D)

55 Paul Manafort Drive, New Britain CT 06053-2142
County: Hartford FICE Identification: 032343
Unit ID: 128780
Telephone: (860) 832-3800 Carnegie Class: Bac/A&S
FAX Number: (860) 832-3999 Calendar System: Other
URL: www.charteroak.edu
Established: 1973 Annual Undergrad Tuition & Fees (In-State): $6,144
Enrollment: 2,278 Coed
Affiliation or Control: State IRS Status: 501(c)3
Highest Offering: Baccalaureate
Program: Liberal Arts And General
Accreditation: EH

01 President .... Mr. Edward KLONOSKI
05 Provost .... Dr. Shirley M. ADAMS
20 Dean Undergraduate Programs .... Dr. Dana WILKIE
10 Chief Financial/Administrative Ofcr .... Mr. Clifford S. WILLIAMS
13 Chief Information Officer .... Mr. George F. CLAFFEY, JR.
09 Dir Institutional Effectiveness .... Mr. David A. HEMENWAY
06 Registrar .... Ms. Jennifer WASHINGTON
37 Dir Financial Aid/Veterans Benefits .... Ms. Deborah FLINN
20 Director Academic Services .... Ms. Linda LARKIN
07 Director Admissions .... Ms. Lori GAGNE PENDLETON
45 Coordinator Special Assessments .... Dr. Maryanne LEGROW
106 Director Distance Learning .... Ms. Susan H. ISRAEL
26 Director Marketing/Public Relations .... Ms. Carolyn HEBERT

Connecticut College (E)

270 Mohegan Avenue, New London CT 06320-4125
County: New London FICE Identification: 001379
Unit ID: 128902
Telephone: (860) 447-1911 Carnegie Class: Bac/A&S
FAX Number: (860) 439-2700 Calendar System: Semester
URL: www.conncoll.edu
Established: 1911 Annual Undergrad Tuition & Fees: $54,970
Enrollment: 1,887 Coed
Affiliation or Control: Independent Non-Profit IRS Status: 501(c)3
Highest Offering: Master's
Program: Liberal Arts And General; Teacher Preparatory
Accreditation: EH

01 President .... Mr. Leo I. HIGDON, JR.
05 Dean of the Faculty .... Dr. Roger L. BROOKS
10 Vice President for Finance .... Mr. Paul L. MARONI
30 Vice President College Advancement .... Mr. Gregory T. WALDRON
08 Vice Pres of Info Svcs/Librarian .... Dr. W. Lee HISLE
11 Vice President for Administration ...... Mr. Ulyssess B. HAMMOND
26 Vice President College Relations .... Ms. Patricia M. CAREY
07 VP of Admission & Financial Aid .... Ms. Martha C. MERRILL
15 Asst VP HR/Professional Development .... Ms. Cheryl L. MILLER
20 Dean of the College .... Dr. Armando BENGOCHEA
35 Dean of Student Life .... Dr. Jocelyn BRIDDELL
28 Dean of Multicultural Affairs .... Dr. Elizabeth GARCIA
20 Dean of Studies .... Dr. Theresa P. AMMIRATI
20 Associate Dean of Faculty .... Prof. Abigail A. VAN SLYCK
06 Registrar .... Ms. Elisabeth S. LABRIOLA
09 Director of Institutional Research .... Dr. John D. NUGENT
21 Controller .... Ms. Amanda B. MAYFIELD
36 Director of Placement .... Vacant
37 Director of Financial Aid .... Ms. Elaine F. SOLINGA
41 Director of Athletics .... Mr. Francis SHIELDS
29 Director of Alumni Relations .... Ms. Bridget MCSHANE
38 Director Student Counseling .... Dr. Janet D. SPOLTORE
84 Director Enrollment Management .... Vacant
18 Chief Facilities/Physical Plant .... Mr. James NORTON
96 Director of Purchasing .... Mr. Marco J. MICHAUD
88 Secretary of the College .... Ms. Bonnie WELLS

*Connecticut State University System Office (F)

39 Woodland Street, Hartford CT 06105-2337
County: Hartford Identification: 666656
Unit ID: 129011
Telephone: (860) 493-0000 Carnegie Class: N/A
FAX Number: (860) 493-0009
URL: www.ctstateu.edu

01 Acting Chancellor .... Dr. Louise FEROE
05 Sr Vice Chancellor Academic Affairs .... Dr. Louise FEROE
09 Assoc Vice Chanc Strat Plng/IR .... Dr. William J. GAMMELL
15 Assoc Vice Chanc Human Resources .... Mr. David TRAINOR
86 Assoc Vice Chanc Govt Relations .... Ms. Jill FERRAIOLO
26 Asst Vice Chanc Public Affairs .... Mr. Bernard KAVALER
04 Administrative Assistant .... Ms. Carmen L. DIAZ
101 Assoc Board Affairs/Secy to BOT .... Ms. Erin FITZGERALD
10 Chief Financial Officer .... Ms. Pamela KEDDERIS
13 Chief Information Officer .... Dr. Wendy CHANG
21 Exec Dir Finance & Administration .. Mr. Thomas MASCIADRELLI

*Central Connecticut State University (G)

1615 Stanley Street, New Britain CT 06050-4010
County: Hartford FICE Identification: 001378
Unit ID: 128771
Telephone: (860) 832-3200 Carnegie Class: Master's L
FAX Number: (860) 832-2522 Calendar System: Semester
URL: www.ccsu.edu
Established: 1849 Annual Undergrad Tuition & Fees (In-State): $8,055
Enrollment: 12,477 Coed
Affiliation or Control: State IRS Status: 501(c)3
Highest Offering: Doctorate
Program: Liberal Arts And General; Teacher Preparatory; Professional
Accreditation: EH, ANEST, CACREP, CONST, CORE, CS, ENG, ENGT, EXSC, MFCD, MUS, NAIT, NURSE, SW, TED

02 President .... Dr. John W. MILLER
04 Assistant to the President .... Ms. Courtney MCDAVID
05 Provost/Vice Pres Academic Affs .... Dr. Carl R. LOVITT
30 Vice Pres Institutional Advancement .... Mr. Chris GALLIGAN
32 Vice President Student Affairs .... Dr. Laura TORDENTI
35 Asst Vice Pres/Dean of Students .... Vacant
20 Associate VP Academic Affairs .... Dr. Joseph P. PAIGE
44 Assoc VP Institutional Advancement .... Mr. Nicholas PETTINICO, JR.
58 Associate VP Graduate Studies .... Dr. Paulette LEMMA
26 Assoc VP Marketing/Communications .... Dr. Mark W. MCLAUGHLIN
88 Special Assistant to the President .... Ms. Carolyn MAGNAN
11 Chief Administrative Officer .... Dr. Richard R. BACHOO
10 Interim Chief Financial Officer .... Ms. Kim CHAGNON
15 Chief Human Resources Officer .... Ms. Anne B. ALLING
13 Chief Information Officer .... Mr. James ESTRADA
28 Interim Chief Diversity Officer .... Ms. Rosa RODRIGUEZ
49 Dean School Arts & Sciences .... Dr. Susan PEASE
50 Dean School of Business .... Dr. Siamack SHOJAI
53 Dean School Educ & Prof Studies .... Dr. Mitch SAKOFS
72 Dean School Engineering/Technology .... Dr. Zdzislaw KREMENS
82 Dir Center International Education .... Dr. Nancy B. WAGNER
51 Dir Continuing Educ/Cmty Engagement .... Vacant
07 Director Admissions & Recruitment .... Mr. Lawrence HALL
41 Director Athletics .... Mr. Paul SCHLICKMANN
39 Director Residence Life .... Ms. Jean ALICANDRO
19 Director Public Safety .... Mr. Jason B. POWELL
37 Director Student Financial Aid .... Mr. Richard BISHOP
44 Director Institutional Advancement .... Ms. Cynthia B. CAYER
27 Media Relations Officer .... Ms. Janice PALMER
08 Interim Director Library Services .... Mr. Carl ANTONUCCI
36 Dir Ctr Advising/Career Exploration .... Mr. Kenneth POPPE
23 Director Health Services .... Dr. Christopher R. DIAMOND
24 Director Academic Technology .... Mr. Scott M. ERARDI
06 Registrar .... Ms. Susan PETROSINO
38 Director Counseling & Wellness .... Mr. Timothy CORBITT
10 Asst Chief Admin Ofcr/Dir Facil Mgt .... Mr. Salvatore CINTORINO
21 Director of Business Services .... Ms. Lori JAMES
96 Purchasing Manager .... Mr. Thomas BRODEUR
09 Director of Institutional Research .... Ms. Yvonne KIRBY

*Eastern Connecticut State University (H)

83 Windham Street, Willimantic CT 06226-2295
County: Windham FICE Identification: 001425
Unit ID: 129215
Telephone: (860) 465-5000 Carnegie Class: Master's S
FAX Number: (860) 465-4485 Calendar System: Semester
URL: www.easternct.edu
Established: 1889 Annual Undergrad Tuition & Fees (In-State): $8,555
Enrollment: 5,606 Coed
Affiliation or Control: State IRS Status: 501(c)3
Highest Offering: Master's
Program: 2-Year Principally Bachelor's Creditable; Liberal Arts And General; Teacher Preparatory; Professional
Accreditation: EH, SW, TED

02 President .... Dr. Elsa M. NUNEZ
03 Executive Vice President .... Dr. Michael E. PERNAL
05 Vice President for Academic Affairs .... Dr. Rhona C. FREE
10 Vice Pres Finance/Administration .... Mr. Dennis A. HANNON
32 Vice Pres Student Affairs .... Mr. Ken BEDINI
30 Vice Pres Institutional Advance .... Mr. Kenneth J. DELISA
21 Assoc Vice Pres Finance & Admin .... Mr. James HOWARTH
09 Asst Dir of Institutional Research .... Dr. Brian R. LASHLEY
41 Interim Director of Athletics .... Mr. Michael STENKO
08 Director of Library Services .... Ms. Patricia S. BANACH
37 Actg Director of Financial Aid .... Mr. Patrick KELLY
07 Interim Director of Admissions .... Mr. Christopher DORSEY
36 Acting Director of Career Services .... Mr. Clifford MARRETT
29 Director of Alumni Affairs .... Mr. Michael STENKO
06 Interim Registrar .... Ms. Jennifer HUOPPI
19 Director of Public Safety .... Mr. Jeffrey A. GAREWSKI
39 Acting Director Housing/Res Life .... Ms. Angela BAZIN
40 Director of Bookstore .... Mr. Ben BLAKE
42 Director of Campus Ministry .... Rev. Laurence LAPOINTE
18 Dir of Facilities Mgmt/Planning .... Ms. Nancy TINKER
26 Director University Relations .... Mr. Edward H. OSBORN
49 Dean of Arts & Sciences .... Dr. Carmen R. CID
51 Dean of Continuing Education .... Dr. Rochelle P. GIMENEZ
58 Int Dean Educ/Prof Studies/Grad Pgm .... Dr. Jaime GOMEZ
96 Assoc Dir Fiscal Affs/Acquisition .... Mr. David ROBERTS
38 Director of Counseling & Psych Svcs .... Dr. Mercy ARAIS

*Southern Connecticut State University (I)

501 Crescent Street, New Haven CT 06515-0901
County: New Haven FICE Identification: 001406
Unit ID: 130493
Telephone: (203) 392-5200 Carnegie Class: Master's L

FAX Number: (203) 392-7149 Calendar System: Semester
URL: www.southernct.edu
Established: 1893 Annual Undergrad Tuition & Fees (In-State): $8,248
Enrollment: 11,964 Coed
Affiliation or Control: State IRS Status: 501(c)3
Highest Offering: Doctorate
Program: Liberal Arts And General; Teacher Preparatory; Professional
Accreditation: EH, CACREP, CS, EXSC, #LIB, MFCD, NURSE, PH, SP, SW, TED

02 Interim President ....Dr. Stanley F. BATTLE
04 Admin Assistant to the President ....Ms. Beth Ann H. JOHNSON
05 Provost/Vice Pres Academic Affairs ....Vacant
03 Executive Vice President ....Mr. James E. BLAKE
32 Vice Pres Student/University Affs ....Vacant
30 Vice President Inst Advancement ....Vacant
16 Assoc VP for Human Resources ....Ms. Jaye BAILEY
20 Assoc VP Academic Student Services ....Ms. Kimberly M. CRONE
43 Employment and Labor ....Ms. Diane MAZZA
18 Assoc VP Capitol Budgeting/Fac Ops ....Mr. Robert G. SHEELEY
13 Chief Information Technology Ofcr ....Dr. Wendy CHANG
49 Dean School Arts & Sciences ....Dr. Donna Jean A. FREDEEN
50 Dean School of Business ....Dr. Ellen DURNIN
53 Dean School Education ....Dr. Michael SAMPSON
58 Dean School Graduate Studies ....Dr. Holly CRAWFORD
70 Dean School Health/Human Svcs ....Dr. Gregory PAVEZA
44 Assoc to VP Dir Major/Planned Gifts ....Vacant
41 Director Intercollegiate Athletics ....Ms. Patricia NICOL
26 Director of Public Affairs ....Mr. Patrick DILGER
29 Director Alumni Affairs ....Ms. Michelle JOHNSTON
88 Dir Resource Dev Programs/Athletics ....Mr. Gregg R. CRERAR
07 Dir Admissions/Enrollment Mgmt ....Vacant
06 Registrar ....Vacant
08 Director of Library Services ....Dr. Christina BAUM
09 Director of Institutional Research ....Vacant
91 Director Computer Svcs/Admin ....Mr. John O. YOUNG
90 Director Computer Svcs/Academic ....Vacant
15 Director of Human Resources ....Vacant
19 Director of Public Safety ....Mr. Joseph M. DOOLEY
25 Director of Sponsored Research ....Ms. Patricia M. ZIBLUK
37 Director of Financial Aid ....Vacant
36 Director of Career Services ....Ms. Marguerite S. FADDEN
23 Director of Health Services ....Dr. Diane S. MORGENTHALER
35 Director of Student Affairs ....Dr. Peter F. TROIANO
46 Director Ofc of Mgmt/Info/Research ....Mr. Richard RICCARDI
28 Exec Asst to Pres Divers/Equity Pgm ....Dr. Marcia SMITH-GLASPER
38 Director of Counseling Services ....Dr. Julie LIEFELD
96 Purchasing Manager ....Ms. Jane MAILHIOT
21 University Controller ....Ms. Lise M. BRULE
92 Director of Honors Program ....Dr. Terese GEMME
94 Director of Women's Studies ....Dr. Yi-Chun Tricia LIN

*Western Connecticut State University (A)

181 White Street, Danbury CT 06810-6885
County: Fairfield FICE Identification: 001380
Unit ID: 130776
Telephone: (203) 837-8200 Carnegie Class: Master's M
FAX Number: (203) 837-8276 Calendar System: Semester
URL: www.wcsu.edu
Established: 1903 Annual Undergrad Tuition & Fees (In-State): $8,104
Enrollment: 6,582 Coed
Affiliation or Control: State IRS Status: 501(c)3
Highest Offering: Doctorate
Program: Liberal Arts And General; Teacher Preparatory; Professional
Accreditation: EH, CACREP, MUS, NURSE, SW, TED

02 President ....Dr. James W. SCHMOTTER
05 Provost/Vice Pres Academic Affairs ....Dr. Jane MCBRIDE GATES
10 Vice Pres Finance & Administration ....Mr. Paul REIS
30 Int Assoc VP Inst Advancement ....Mr. Paul M. STEINMETZ
32 Vice Pres Student Affs/Ext Affs ....Dr. Walter B. BERNSTEIN
88 Dean of Visual/Performing Arts ....Dr. Daniel GOBLE
35 Dean of Student Affairs ....Dr. Walter CRAMER
49 Int Dean of Arts & Sciences ....Dr. Abbey ZINK
50 Dean of Ancell Business ....Dr. Allen MORTON
107 Int Dean of Professional Studies ....Dr. Maryann ROSSI
58 Int Dean of Graduate/External Pgms ....Dr. Burton PERETTI
16 Assoc Vice Pres Human Resources ....Mr. Charles P. SPIRIDON
18 Assoc Vice Pres for Facilities ....Vacant
14 Chief Information Officer ....Ms. Lorraine CAPOBIANCO
21 Director Fiscal Affairs/Controller ....Mr. Sean LOUGHRAN
44 Director of Development ....Ms. Jane VON TRAPP
22 Ex Asst to Pres/Chief Diversity Ofc ....Ms. Carolyn LANIER
06 Registrar ....Ms. Lourdes CRUZ
84 Enrollment Management Officer ....Vacant
08 Director of Library Services ....Dr. Edward O'HARA
09 Director of Inst Research/Assess ....Dr. Jerry WILCOX
25 Director of Grant/Programs ....Vacant
38 Director of Counseling Svcs ....Dr. Michael SCHWARZCHILD
37 Dir Financial Aid/Veterans Affairs ....Ms. Nancy BARTON
36 Director of Career Devel Center ....Ms. Maureen C. GERNERT
26 Director University Relations ....Mr. Paul STEINMETZ
39 Dir of Housing & Residence Life ....Mr. Ron MASON
35 Director Student Life ....Dr. Paul M. SIMON
41 Director of Athletics ....Mr. Edward FARRINGTON
29 Director of Alumni Affairs ....Ms. Tammy MCINERNEY
07 Director of Admissions ....Mr. Steven GOETSCH
15 Director of Employee Relations ....Mr. Frederic CRATTY
45 Dir of Facilities Plng & Engr ....Mr. Peter VISENTIN
11 Director of Administrative Services ....Mr. Mark R. CASE

88 Dir Environmental & Facilities Svcs ....Mr. Luigi MARCONE
88 Dir Facil Utilization & Promotion ....Mr. John MURPHY
21 Director of Fin Planning & Budgets ....Ms. Mary Ann DEASE
19 Director of University Police ....Mr. Neil MCLAUGHLIN

Fairfield University (B)

1073 N Benson Road, Fairfield CT 06824-5195
County: Fairfield FICE Identification: 001385
Unit ID: 129242
Telephone: (203) 254-4000 Carnegie Class: Master's L
FAX Number: (203) 254-4101 Calendar System: Semester
URL: www.fairfield.edu
Established: 1942 Annual Undergrad Tuition & Fees: $39,990
Enrollment: 5,232 Coed
Affiliation or Control: Roman Catholic IRS Status: 501(c)3
Highest Offering: Doctorate
Program: Liberal Arts And General; Teacher Preparatory; Professional
Accreditation: EH, ANEST, BUS, CACREP, ENG, MFCD, NURSE, TED

01 President ....Rev. Jeffrey P. VON ARX, SJ
04 Executive Asst to the President ....Rev. Charles H. ALLEN, SJ
03 Executive Vice President ....Mr. William WEITZER
04 Assistant to the President ....Mrs. Elizabeth BAGLEY
05 Sr Vice President Academic Affairs ....Rev. Paul J. FITZGERALD, SJ
30 Vice President Univ Advancement ....Ms. Stephanie FROST
10 Vice President Finance/Treasurer ....Ms. Julie L. DOLAN
11 VP Administration/Student Affairs ....Dr. Mark C. REED
26 Vice Pres Mktg & Communications ....Ms. Rama SUDHAKAR
42 VP Mission Identity/Univ Chaplain ....Rev. Gerald R. BLASZCZAK, SJ
20 Assoc Vice Pres Academic Affairs ....Dr. Mary Frances MALONE
21 Associate Vice Pres for Finance ....Mr. Michael S. MACCARONE
84 Assoc Academic VP for Enroll Mgmt ....Ms. Judith M. DOBAI
32 Assoc Vice Pres/Dean of Students ....Dr. Thomas C. PELLEGRINO
18 Assoc Vice Pres Facilities Mgmt ....Mr. David W. FRASSINELLI
38 Asst Vice Pres/Dir Counseling Svcs ....Dr. Susan N. BIRGE
88 Asst VP Admin/Stdnt Affs ....Mr. James D. FITZPATRICK
09 AVP Institutional Research/Planning ....Dr. Ann K. STEHNEY
44 Asst Vice President for Development ....Ms. Julianna DAVIS
07 Director of Undergraduate Admission ....Ms. Karen A. PELLEGRINO
07 Director of Graduate Admission ....Ms. Marianne L. GUMPPER
06 University Registrar ....Mr. Robert C. RUSSO
14 Dir Computing/Network Services ....Mr. Michael GRAHAM-CORNELL
37 Director of Financial Aid ....Vacant
36 Director of Career Planning ....Ms. Cathleen M. BORGMAN
29 Director of Alumni Relations ....Ms. Janet A. CANEPA
42 Director of Campus Ministry ....Rev. Michael J. DOODY, SJ
19 Director of Public Safety ....Mr. Todd A. PELAZZA
41 Director of Athletics ....Mr. Eugene P. DORIS
49 Dean College Arts & Science ....Dr. Robbin D. CRABTREE
50 Dean Charles F Dolan Sch of Bus ....Dr. Donald E. GIBSON
54 Dean School of Engineering ....Dr. Jack BEAL
53 Dean Grad Sch of Educ/Allied Prof ....Dr. Susan D. FRANZOSA
66 Dean School of Nursing ....Dr. Suzanne H. CAMPBELL
51 Dean University College ....Dr. Robbin D. CRABTREE
20 Dean of Academic Engagement ....Dr. Elizabeth BOQUET
88 Dean of Exploratory Acad Advising ....Dr. Debnam CHAPPELL
88 Sr Assoc Dean Stdnts/Dir Univ Act ....Mr. Matthew A. DINNAN
35 Assoc Dean Stdnts/Dir Stdnt Devel ....Dr. Joseph DEFEO
28 Assoc Dn Stdnts/Dir Stdnt Div Pgm ....Mr. William H. JOHNSON
85 Dir of International Programs ....Mr. Christopher JOHNSON
92 Director of Honors Program ....Dr. John E. THIEL
08 Univ Librarian/Dir of Library Svcs ....Ms. Joan T. OVERFIELD
39 Dir Residence Life/Asst Dean Stdnts ....Ms. Karen A. DONOGHUE
23 Director of Student Health Center ....Ms. Judith WEINDLING
15 Director Human Resources ....Mr. Mark J. GUGLIELMONI
96 Director of Purchasing ....Mr. Nicholas J. PAPILLO

Goodwin College (C)

One Riverside Drive, East Hartford CT 06118-2777
County: Hartford FICE Identification: 022449
Unit ID: 129154
Telephone: (860) 528-4111 Carnegie Class: Assoc/PrivNFP
FAX Number: (860) 291-9550 Calendar System: Semester
URL: www.goodwin.edu
Established: 1999 Annual Undergrad Tuition & Fees: $18,800
Enrollment: 2,700 Coed
Affiliation or Control: Independent Non-Profit IRS Status: 501(c)3
Highest Offering: Baccalaureate
Program: 2-Year Principally Bachelor's Creditable
Accreditation: EH, ADNUR, HT, MAAB, MAC

01 President ....Mr. Mark E. SCHEINBERG
03 Executive Vice President/Provost ....Ms. Ann B. CLARK
10 Vice President for Finance/CFO ....Mr. Jerry D. EMLET
05 Vice President for Academic Affairs ....Ms. Judith D. ZIMMERMAN
45 Vice Pres for Inst Effectiveness ....Ms. Janet L. JEFFORD
30 Vice Pres Col Rels & Advancement ....Mr. Todd J. ANDREWS
18 Vice Pres for Phys Facilities & IT ....Mr. Bryant L. HARRELL
84 Vice President for Enrollment ....Mr. Daniel NOONAN
88 Dean of Magnet Schools ....Mr. Alan KRAMER
35 Dean of Students ....Dr. Sandy WIRTH
07 Director of Admissions ....Mr. Nicholas LENTINO
36 Director of Career Services ....Mr. David ZOPPOLI
26 Director of Communications ....Mr. Lee SAWYER
44 Assoc Dir of Developmnt/Annual Fund ....Ms. Leia BELL
21 Director of Finance & Business Svcs ....Ms. Sharon N. DADDONA
37 Director of Financial Aid ....Mr. William MANGINI

09 Dir Inst Research/Educ Assessment ....Dr. Alan J. STURTZ
08 Director of Library Services ....Ms. Marilyn L. NOWLAN
106 Director of Online Learning ....Dr. Kavita LEONE
06 Assistant Dean/Registrar ....Ms. Denise SCHWABE
32 Assistant Dean for Student Life ....Ms. Joy CASTELLO-BUTLER
13 Director of Information Technology ....Mr. Dan REGO
29 Alumni Relations Coordinator ....Ms. Vanessa PERGOLIZZI
04 Executive Assistant to President ....Ms. Ann ZAJCHOWSKI
97 Dept Chair General Educ & Business ....Dr. Henriette M. PRANGER
76 Dept Chair Health/Natural Sciences ....Ms. Danielle S. WILKEN
66 Dept Chair/Director Nursing ....Ms. Janice COSTELLO
83 Dept Chair Social Sci & Education ....Dr. Clifford THERMER

Hartford Seminary (D)

77 Sherman Street, Hartford CT 06105-2260
County: Hartford FICE Identification: 001387
Unit ID: 129491
Telephone: (860) 509-9500 Carnegie Class: Spec/Faith
FAX Number: (860) 509-9509 Calendar System: Semester
URL: www.hartsem.edu
Established: 1834 Annual Graduate Tuition & Fees: $10,800
Enrollment: 155 Coed
Affiliation or Control: Independent Non-Profit IRS Status: 501(c)3
Highest Offering: Doctorate; No Undergraduates
Program: Professional; Religious Emphasis
Accreditation: EH, THEOL

01 President ....Dr. Heidi HADSELL
05 Academic Dean ....Dr. James NIEMAN
11 Director of Admin and Facilities ....Ms. Roseann LEZAK JANOW
30 Chief Development Officer ....Rev. Jonathan LEE
07 Admissions Manager ....Ms. Vanessa AVERY
88 Director Religion Research Inst ....Dr. David A. ROOZEN
88 Director Doctor of Ministry Program ....Dr. James NIEMAN
88 Director of Islamic Center ....Dr. Ingrid MATTSON
08 Library Director ....Dr. Steven BLACKBURN
44 Dir of Annual Fund & Database Admin ....Ms. Janine HEWITT
10 Comptroller ....Ms. Lilyne HOLLINGWORTH
84 Dir Enrollment Management/Registrar ....Ms. Karen ROLLINS
04 Exec Assistant to the President ....Ms. Mary ZEMAN
27 Director of Communications ....Mr. David BARRETT

Holy Apostles College and Seminary (E)

33 Prospect Hill Road, Cromwell CT 06416-2005
County: Middlesex FICE Identification: 001389
Unit ID: 129534
Telephone: (860) 632-3010 Carnegie Class: Spec/Faith
FAX Number: (860) 632-3030 Calendar System: Semester
URL: www.holyapostles.edu
Established: 1956 Annual Undergrad Tuition & Fees: $9,890
Enrollment: 312 Coed
Affiliation or Control: Roman Catholic IRS Status: 501(c)3
Highest Offering: Beyond Master's But Less Than Doctorate
Program: Liberal Arts And General; Professional
Accreditation: EH

01 President & Rector ....V.Rev. Douglas L. MOSEY
03 Vice Rector ....Rev. John HILLIER
03 Vice President ....Rev. Gregoire J. FLUET
11 Vice Pres Admin Affairs ....Deacon James F. PAPILLO
05 Academic Dean ....Vacant
42 Spiritual Director ....Rev. Addison HALLOCK
07 Director of Admissions ....Rev. Bradley W. PIERCE
10 Finance Officer ....Mr. William RUSSELL
08 Director of Library Services ....Ms. Clare ADAMO
06 Registrar ....Dr. Cynthia TOOLIN

Lincoln College of New England (F)

2279 Mount Vernon Road, Southington CT 06489-1057
County: Hartford FICE Identification: 009407
Unit ID: 128683
Telephone: (860) 628-4751 Carnegie Class: Bac/Assoc
FAX Number: (860) 628-6444 Calendar System: Semester
URL: www.lincolncollegene.edu
Established: 1966 Annual Undergrad Tuition & Fees: $18,500
Enrollment: 950 Coed
Affiliation or Control: Proprietary IRS Status: Proprietary
Highest Offering: Baccalaureate
Program: Occupational; 2-Year Principally Bachelor's Creditable
Accreditation: EH, DA, DH, DIETT, FUSER, MAC, NMT, OTA

01 President ....Mrs. Kathryn REGJO
04 Executive Assistant to President ....Mrs. Rita W. SCHOOLNIK
05 Vice Pres Academic Affairs ....Dr. Gil LINNE
11 Vice Pres Operations & Stdnt Affs ....Mr. John F. LE CONCHE
10 Chief Financial Officier ....Mr. Kevin MILLER
07 Vice Pres Admissions ....Mr. Anthony REICH
07 Vice Pres Admissions On-Line ....Mr. Matthew HAWES
10 Director of Administrative Services ....Mrs. Denise LEWICKI
32 Dean of Student Life ....Miss Kimberly MARTINEZ
35 Assoc Dean of Student Services ....Mrs. Cynthia A. CLARK
35 Exec Dir Student Services On-Line ....Mr. Spencer MCNIVEN
20 Associate Dean of Academic Affairs ....Mrs. Angela P. KIERNAN
20 Dean of Academic Affairs On-Line ....Mrs. Denise ALBERLE-CANNATA
20 Dean of Academic Affairs-Suffield ....Mr. Ken ZANE
06 Registrar-Ground Campuses ....Mrs. Stephanie L. CROMBIE

06 Registrar On-Line ... Mr. Fletcher BROWN
08 Director of Library Services ... Mrs. Valeri E. WALLACE
37 Regional Director of Financial Aid ... Mrs. Gina D. SWENTON
09 Dir Instl Effectiveness/Integrity ... Dr. Hans J. KUSS
19 Director Campus Safety & Security ... Mr. David C. ALLING
36 Director of Career Services- Ground ... Mr. Christopher FRYER
36 Director of Career Services On-Line ... Mr. Bob MCNAMARA
18 Supt of Buildings & Grounds ... Mr. Leonard ROY
13 IT Administrator-Southington ... Mr. Edward D. CONNELLY
13 IT Administrator- Suffield ... Mr. Dominic RIONI
13 IT Administrator - Hartford ... Mr. David HEINTZ
13 IT Administrator On-Line ... Mr. Steve MEANS

Lyme Academy College of Fine Arts (A)

84 Lyme Street, Old Lyme CT 06371-2333
County: New London FICE Identification: 030794
Unit ID: 129686
Telephone: (860) 434-5232 Carnegie Class: Spec/Arts
FAX Number: (860) 434-8725 Calendar System: Semester
URL: www.lymeacademy.edu
Established: 1976 Annual Undergrad Tuition & Fees: $24,860
Enrollment: 97 Coed
Affiliation or Control: Independent Non-Profit IRS Status: 501(c)3
Highest Offering: Baccalaureate
Program: Fine Arts Emphasis
Accreditation: EH, ART

01 President ... Ms. Debra PETKE
30 Vice President External Affairs ... Ms. Joanne DONAGHUE
10 Controller ... Ms. Wendy MASSE
05 Actg Dean/Vice Pres Academic Affs ... Ms. Sally SEAMAN
07 Director Admissions/Cont Educ ... Ms. Sarah CHURCHILL
06 Registrar & Financial Aid ... Mr. James FALCONER
51 Int Director Continuing Education ... Ms. Renee BEYAR

Mitchell College (B)

437 Pequot Avenue, New London CT 06320-4498
County: New London FICE Identification: 001393
Unit ID: 129774
Telephone: (860) 701-5000 Carnegie Class: Bac/Diverse
FAX Number: (860) 701-5090 Calendar System: Semester
URL: www.mitchell.edu
Established: 1938 Annual Undergrad Tuition & Fees: $27,714
Enrollment: 992 Coed
Affiliation or Control: Independent Non-Profit IRS Status: 501(c)3
Highest Offering: Baccalaureate
Program: Liberal Arts And General; Teacher Preparatory; Business Emphasis
Accreditation: EH

01 President ... Dr. Mary Ellen JUKOSKI
03 Senior Vice President ... Mr. Kevin MAYNE
05 VP Acad Affs/Dean of the College ... Dr. Laurence CONNER
10 Vice Pres Administration & Finance ... Ms. Dyann J. BAKER
32 Vice President for Student Affairs ... Mr. Jason EBBELING
41 Director Of Athletics ... Ms. Maureen WHITE
06 Registrar ... Mr. Kevin P. KELLY
88 Director of Thames Academy ... Ms. Tammy VUKSINIC
08 Director of Library Services ... Ms. Suzanne M. BARTELS
15 Director of Human Resources ... Ms. Susan L. DEVLIN
09 Dir Institutional Rsrch & Assesment ... Ms. Melanie R. SULLIVAN
37 Director of Financial Aid ... Ms. Jacqueline C. STOLTZ
38 Director FYC and Ctr for Teaching ... Dr. David J. BRAILEY
84 Assoc VP Enrollment Mgmt ... Ms. Susan BIBEAU
35 Director of Student Activities ... Ms. Cheri HENAULT
27 Director of Communications ... Ms. Renee K. FOURNIER
29 Director of Alumni Relations ... Ms. Carol BROWN
102 Director of Parent Programs ... Ms. Kimberly S. HODGES
36 Director of Career Center ... Dr. Catherine ERIK-SOUSSI
88 Director of Learning Resource Ctr ... Dr. Peter LOVE
31 Title III Activity Director & PM ... Ms. Kathleen E. NEAL
96 Purchasing Manager ... Ms. Jill RAKOFF
26 Dir Public Relations & Marketing ... Ms. Renee K. FOURNIER
39 Director of Residence Life ... Ms. Christine GALLAGHER
18 Director of Facilities ... Ms. Rebecca HELLER
21 Accounting Manager ... Ms. Wendy HODGE
88 Bursar ... Ms. Leah BRENNAN
13 Chief Technology Officer ... Mr. Chuck KEELER

Paier College of Art (C)

20 Gorham Avenue, Hamden CT 06514-3902
County: New Haven FICE Identification: 007459
Unit ID: 130110
Telephone: (203) 287-3031 Carnegie Class: Spec/Arts
FAX Number: (203) 287-3021 Calendar System: Semester
URL: www.paiercollegeofart.edu
Established: 1946 Annual Undergrad Tuition & Fees: $12,960
Enrollment: 218 Coed
Affiliation or Control: Proprietary IRS Status: Proprietary
Highest Offering: Baccalaureate
Program: Liberal Arts And General
Accreditation: ACCSC

01 President ... Mr. Jonathan E. PAIER
03 Vice President ... Mr. Daniel L. PAIER
05 Dean of the College ... Mr. Francis COOLEY
10 Director Finance ... Mrs. Maureen E. PAIER
57 Director Design/Graphics ... Mr. Peter MISERENDINO
102 Director Foundation/Arts ... Mr. Robert E. ZAPPALORTI
08 Librarian ... Ms. Beth HARRIS
37 Director Student Financial Aid ... Mr. John DE ROSE
32 Director of Student Services ... Mrs. Maureen DEROSE
20 Assistant to the Dean ... Ms. Angela DEROSE
88 Director Interior Design ... Mr. Pierre STRAUCH
88 Director Photography ... Mr. Peter BENSON
07 Admissions Secretary ... Ms. Lynn PASCALE

Post University (D)

800 Country Club Road, Waterbury CT 06723-2540
County: New Haven FICE Identification: 001401
Unit ID: 130183
Telephone: (203) 596-4500 Carnegie Class: Bac/Diverse
FAX Number: (203) 756-5810 Calendar System: Semester
URL: www.post.edu
Established: 1890 Annual Undergrad Tuition & Fees: $26,000
Enrollment: 782 Coed
Affiliation or Control: Proprietary IRS Status: Proprietary
Highest Offering: Master's
Program: Occupational; 2-Year Principally Bachelor's Creditable; Liberal Arts And General; Professional
Accreditation: EH

00 Chancellor ... Dr. Thomas SAMPH
01 President ... Dr. Ronald W. OGRODNIK
05 VP for Academic Affairs ... Dr. William H. MCDONALD
10 Vice President Finance & Admin ... Mr. Scott T. ALLEN
84 Director of Admissions ... Mr. Jay E. MURRAY
32 VP for Student Svcs & Intl Rels ... Mr. John WALLACE
06 Registrar ... Mr. Keith GAUVIN
41 Director of Athletics ... Mr. Anthony FALLACARO
15 Human Resources Director ... Ms. Madelaine KELSEY
08 Library Director ... Ms. Tracy RALSTON
13 Chief Information Officer ... Mr. Michael STATMORE
26 Director of Communications ... Ms. Kelly STATMORE
36 Director Career Services ... Mr. Chris SZPRYNGEL
35 Dean of Students ... Ms. Erica KLUGE
40 Campus Store Manager ... Mrs. Frances R. KAMINSKY
19 Director of Campus Safety ... Mr. Robert TANSLEY
38 Director Student Counseling ... Ms. Lisa ANTEL
07 Vice President of ADP Enrollment ... Ms. Veronica MARRERO
37 Director Financial Aid ... Ms. Regina FAULDS
37 Director Office of Student Finance ... Ms. Michelle GAMBACINI
100 President Online Education Institut ... Mr. Frank MULGREW
26 Chief Marketing Officer ... Mr. Marcelo S. PARRAVICINI
37 Director of Student Assistance ... Vacant
88 Director of Military Programs ... Mr. Edmund LIZOTTE
50 Dean of School of Business ... Dr. Donald MROZ
53 Dean of School of Education ... Ms. Jane BAILEY

Quinnipiac University (E)

275 Mount Carmel Avenue, Hamden CT 06518-1908
County: New Haven FICE Identification: 001402
Unit ID: 130226
Telephone: (203) 582-8200 Carnegie Class: Master's L
FAX Number: (203) 582-4703 Calendar System: Semester
URL: www.quinnipiac.edu
Established: 1929 Annual Undergrad Tuition & Fees: $36,130
Enrollment: 8,166 Coed
Affiliation or Control: Independent Non-Profit IRS Status: 501(c)3
Highest Offering: First Professional Degree
Program: Liberal Arts And General; Professional
Accreditation: EH, ARCPA, BUS, CS, LAW, NUR, OT, PA, PERF, PTA, RAD, TED

01 President ... Dr. John L. LAHEY
03 Sr Vice President/Exec Assoc to Pres ... Ms. Jean L. HUSTED
05 Sr Vice Pres Academic/Student Affs ... Dr. Mark A. THOMPSON
10 Sr Vice Pres Financial Affairs ... Dr. Patrick J. HEALY
11 Sr Vice Pres Administration ... Dr. Richard C. FERGUSON
30 Vice President Devel/Alumni Affairs ... Mr. Donald J. WEINBACH
07 Vice Pres/Dean of Admissions ... Ms. Joan I. MOHR
32 Vice President & Dean of Students ... Dr. Manuel C. CARREIRO
26 Vice President for Public Affairs ... Ms. Lynn M. BUSHNELL
15 Vice President for Human Resources ... Mr. Ronald MASON
20 Assoc Vice Pres Academic Affairs ... Dr. Edward KAVANAGH
44 Associate Vice Pres for Development ... Ms. Dianna PATEGAS
18 Assoc Vice Pres Facilities Mgmt ... Mr. Joseph D. RUBERTONE
27 Assoc VP for Information Services ... Ms. Janice WACHTARZ
88 Assoc VP for Human Resources ... Ms. Anna SPRAGG
88 Assoc VP for Faculty Relations ... Ms. Sarah STEELE
28 AVP Acad Affs/Chief Diversity Ofcr ... Dr. Diana M. ARIZA
35 Assoc Dean of Student Affairs ... Ms. Carol T. BOUCHER
38 Asst Dean Career Svcs Sch Comm ... Ms. Jennifer BURNS
38 Asst Dean Career Svcs Sch Hlth Sci ... Ms. Cynthia L. CHRISTIE
19 Chief of Security ... Mr. David BARGER
08 Director of Arnold Bernhard Library ... Mr. Charles GETCHELL
32 Dir Stdnt Ctr/Stdnt Leadership Dev ... Mr. Daniel W. BROWN
41 Director of Athletics & Recreation ... Mr. Jack J. MCDONALD
40 Campus Store Manager ... Mr. Andrew A. TRANQUILLI
85 Director International Education ... Vacant
21 Controller ... Mr. Daniel R. JOHNSON
96 Assoc Dir of Administrative Svcs ... Ms. Maria BIMONTE-YERGANIAN
29 Director of Alumni & Parent Affairs ... Mr. Nicholas George WORMLEY
06 Registrar ... Ms. Dorothy M. LAURIA
37 Sr Director of Financial Aid ... Mr. Dominic YOIA
84 Director Enrollment Management ... Ms. Joan I. MOHR
09 Director of Institutional Research ... Mr. Edward GILLEN
50 Dean School of Business ... Dr. Matthew L. O'CONNOR
49 Dean College of Arts & Sciences ... Dr. Hans BERGMANN
76 Dean School of Health Sciences ... Dr. Edward R. O'CONNOR
61 Dean School of Law ... Mr. Brad SAXTON
60 Dean School of Communications ... Mr. Lee KAMLET
53 Int Dean School of Education ... Dr. Gary ALGER
63 Dean of the School of Medicine ... Dr. Bruce KOEPPEN
72 Dean Academic Technology ... Dr. John PATON
94 Dean/Director of Women's Studies ... Ms. Michele HOFFNUNG
36 Asst Dean Career Devel Sch Bus ... Ms. Jill Anne FERRALL
88 Asst Dean Career Svcs Col Arts/Sci ... Dr. Annalisa J. ZINN
61 Associate Dean School of Law ... Mr. David S. KING

Rensselaer at Hartford (F)

275 Windsor Street, Hartford CT 06120-2991
County: Hartford FICE Identification: 002804
Unit ID: 129428
Telephone: (860) 548-2400 Carnegie Class: Master's L
FAX Number: (860) 548-7887 Calendar System: Semester
URL: www.ewp.rpi.edu/hartford
Established: 1955 Annual Graduate Tuition & Fees: $33,840
Enrollment: 430 Coed
Affiliation or Control: Independent Non-Profit IRS Status: 501(c)3
Highest Offering: Master's; No Undergraduates
Program: Professional
Accreditation: &M

01 Vice President and Dean ... Dr. John A. MINASIAN
06 Registrar ... Ms. Doris M. MATSIKAS
32 Student Services Administrator ... Ms. Natalie SUTERA
08 Library Director ... Ms. Mary DIXEY
14 Director Technical & Info Services ... Mr. Brian CLEMENT
18 Director Operations & Facilities ... Mr. Paul J. MURPHY
37 Financial Aid Officer ... Mr. John GONYEA
20 Asst Dean for Academic Programs ... Dr. Houman YOUNESSI
84 Director Enrollment & Marketing ... Mrs. Kristin GALLIGAN

† Regional accreditation is carried under the parent institution, Rensselaer Polytechnic Institute, NY.

Sacred Heart University (G)

5151 Park Avenue, Fairfield CT 06825-1000
County: Fairfield FICE Identification: 001403
Unit ID: 130253
Telephone: (203) 371-7999 Carnegie Class: Master's L
FAX Number: (203) 365-7652 Calendar System: Semester
URL: www.sacredheart.edu
Established: 1963 Annual Undergrad Tuition & Fees: $32,724
Enrollment: 6,283 Coed
Affiliation or Control: Independent Non-Profit IRS Status: 501(c)3
Highest Offering: Doctorate
Program: Liberal Arts And General; Teacher Preparatory; Professional; Business Emphasis
Accreditation: EH, BUS, NURSE, OT, PTA, SW, TED

01 President ... Dr. John J. PETILLO
11 Sr VP for Finance & Administration ... Mr. Michael J. KINNEY
05 Vice President for Academic Affairs ... Dr. Thomas V. FORGET
32 Vice President Plng/Student Affairs ... Mr. James M. BARQUINERO
15 Vice President for Human Resources ... Mr. Robert M. HARDY
30 VP Marketing & Communication ... Mr. Michael L. IANNAZZI
88 VP for Mission & Catholic Identity ... Dr. Michael J. HIGGINS
10 Vice President for Finance ... Mr. Philip J. MCCABE
13 Vice Pres for Technology & Security ... Mr. Michael D. TRIMBLE
45 VP for Strategic Planning & Admin ... Dr. David L. COPPOLA
20 Vice Provost for Academic Programs ... Ms. Mary Lou DEROSA
49 Dean College of Arts & Sciences ... Dr. Seamus CAREY
50 Interim Dean College of Business ... Dr. Rupendra PALIWAL
53 Dean College of Educ & Health Prof ... Dr. Patricia W. WALKER
35 Dean of Students ... Mr. Lawrence J. WIELK
21 Controller ... Mr. Peter J. WARD
06 Registrar ... Mrs. Dona J. PERRONE
88 Bursar ... Ms. Alice M. AVERY
08 University Librarian ... Dr. Peter FERRIBY
16 Exec Dir for Human Resources ... Mrs. Julia E. NOFRI
27 Director of Communications ... Mrs. Funda F. ALP
105 Director Web Content ... Mrs. Nancy D. BOUDREAU
44 Director of Annual Giving ... Ms. Judite VAMVAKIDES
41 Director of Athletics ... Mr. Donald COOK
84 Dir of Enrollment Research ... Ms. Deanna FIORENTINO
09 Director of Institutional Research ... Dr. Xiaomei FENG
19 Director of Security ... Mr. Jack FERNANDEZ
25 Director of Grants ... Dr. Virginia M. HARRIS
36 Director of Career Development ... Mrs. Patricia A. KLAUSER
88 Director of Divisional Budget ... Mrs. JudyAnn RICCIO
38 Director Counseling Center ... Dr. Mary Jo MASON
92 Director Honors Program ... Dr. Jason J. MOLITIERNO
39 Director of Student Housing ... Mr. Joel R. QUINTONG
42 Director of Campus Ministry ... Fr. Jerry RYLE
88 Dir GE Foundations Scholar Pgm ... Ms. Virginia L. STEPHENS
88 General Manager WSHU ... Mr. George J. LOMBARDI
96 Director of Purchasing ... Mrs. Donna STERN

Saint Joseph College (H)

1678 Asylum Avenue, West Hartford CT 06117-2791
County: Hartford FICE Identification: 001409
Unit ID: 130314
Telephone: (860) 232-4571 Carnegie Class: Master's L
FAX Number: (860) 233-5695 Calendar System: Semester
URL: www.sjc.edu

Established: 1932 Annual Undergrad Tuition & Fees: $28,960
Enrollment: 2,326 Female
Affiliation or Control: Roman Catholic IRS Status: 501(c)3
Highest Offering: Doctorate
Program: Liberal Arts And General; Teacher Preparatory; Professional
Accreditation: **EH**, DIETD, DIETI, MFCD, NURSE, @PHAR, SW

01 President ... Dr. Pamela T. REID
05 Provost ... Dr. Michelle KALIS
10 Vice President Finance & Admin ... Mr. Shawn M. HARRINGTON
30 VP Institutional Advancement ... Mr. Douglas NELSON
84 VP Enrollment Management ... Dr. Gary SHERMAN
32 VP Student Affairs ... Dr. Cheryl A. BARNARD
21 Assoc VP of Finance/Controller ... Mr. William HAWKINS
15 Director of Human Resources ... Ms. Deborah SPENCER
58 Dean Sch of Grad & Prof Studies ... Dr. Daniel NUSSBAUM
67 Dean School of Pharmacy ... Dr. Joseph OFOSU
53 Dean School of Education ... Dr. Kathleen BUTLER
76 Dean School of Health Natl Sci ... Dr. Sandra AFFENITO
79 Dean School of Humanities Soc Sci ... Dr. Wayne STEELY
08 Librarian ... Ms. Linda O. GEFFNER
06 Registrar ... Ms. Allison MISKY
26 Dir of Marketing & Communications ... Ms. Cynthia MARIANI
18 Int Director of Facilities ... Mr. Kevin COCHRAN
29 Dir of Alumni Rels/Annual Giving ... Mr. Steve KUMNICK
07 Director of Admissions ... Ms. Nancy WUNDERLY
37 Director of Financial Aid ... Ms. Elizabeth BAKER
36 Director of Career Services ... Mr. Stephen SEWARD
92 Director of Honors Program ... Dr. Agnes B. CURRY
35 Director Student Activities ... Ms. Tracy LAKE
09 Director of Institutional Research ... Mr. Michael BRODERICK
101 Exec Asst to Pres/Secy to Board ... Ms. Ruth FOXMAN
04 Exec Asst to Pres/Dir Spec Event ... Ms. Kelley STREETER

St. Vincent's College (A)

2800 Main Street, Bridgeport CT 06606-4292
County: Fairfield FICE Identification: 006191
Unit ID: 130448
Telephone: (203) 576-5235 Carnegie Class: Assoc/PrivNFP
FAX Number: (203) 576-5893 Calendar System: Semester
URL: www.stvincentscollege.edu
Established: 1991 Annual Undergrad Tuition & Fees: $14,531
Enrollment: 585 Coed
Affiliation or Control: Independent Non-Profit IRS Status: 501(c)3
Highest Offering: Baccalaureate
Program: Occupational; 2-Year Principally Bachelor's Creditable
Accreditation: **EH**, ADNUR, MAC, RAD

01 President ... Dr. Martha K. SHOULDIS
10 Interim Chief Financial Officer ... Mr. John GLECKLER
05 Vice President/Dean ... Dr. Joanne R. WOLFERTZ
20 Dean of Academic Services ... Dr. Susan CAPASSO
11 Director of Administrative Services ... Mrs. Janice N. FAYE
16 Human Resources Officer ... Dr. Joanne R. WOLFERTZ
37 Director of Financial Aid ... Mrs. Mary L. RICH
06 Registrar ... Mr. Joseph MACIONUS
07 Director of Admissions & Marketing ... Mr. Joseph MARRONE
51 Director Education ... Ms. Tatiana RAMPINO
08 Librarian ... Mrs. Vicky JACOBSON
66 Chair of Nursing-ADN ... Mrs. Margo M. MCCARTHY
66 Chair of Nursing-BSN ... Dr. Sharon MAKOWSKI
88 Chair of Radiography ... Ms. Terry HINE
97 Chair of General Education ... Dr. Susan CAPASSO
88 Chair of Medical Assisting ... Ms. Holly MULRENAN

Sanford-Brown College-Farmington (B)

270 Farminton Avenue, Suite 245,
Farmington CT 06032-1909
County: Hartford FICE Identification: 012877
Unit ID: 129613
Telephone: (860) 882-1690 Carnegie Class: Not Classified
FAX Number: (860) 882-1691 Calendar System: Quarter
URL: www.sanfordbrown.edu
Established: N/A Annual Undergrad Tuition & Fees: N/A
Enrollment: 148 Coed
Affiliation or Control: Proprietary IRS Status: Proprietary
Highest Offering: Associate Degree
Program: Occupational
Accreditation: **ACICS**, MAAB

01 President ... Mr. Kurtis M. PETERSON

Trinity College (C)

300 Summit Street, Hartford CT 06106-3100
County: Hartford FICE Identification: 001414
Unit ID: 130590
Telephone: (860) 297-2000 Carnegie Class: Bac/A&S
FAX Number: (860) 297-2257 Calendar System: Semester
URL: www.trincoll.edu
Established: 1823 Annual Undergrad Tuition & Fees: $44,070
Enrollment: 2,179 Coed
Affiliation or Control: Independent Non-Profit IRS Status: 501(c)3
Highest Offering: Master's
Program: Liberal Arts And General
Accreditation: **EH**, ENG

01 President ... Dr. James F. JONES, JR.
05 Dean of the Faculty ... Dr. Rena FRADEN
10 Vice Pres Finance & Ops/Treasurer ... Mr. Paul MUTONE
30 Vice Pres College Advancement ... Mr. Ronald A. JOYCE
32 Dean of Students ... Mr. Frederick ALFORD
101 Secretary of the College ... Mr. William H. REYNOLDS, JR.
07 Dean Admissions/Financial Aid ... Mr. Larry DOW
20 Associate Academic Dean ... Dr. Sheila FISHER
20 Associate Academic Dean ... Dr. Melanie STEIN
27 Director of Media Relations ... Ms. Michele J. JACKLIN
31 Director of Community Relations ... Mr. Jason ROJAS
37 Director of Financial Aid ... Ms. Kelly O'BRIEN
06 Registrar ... Ms. Patricia MCGREGOR
18 Dir of Facilities Mgmt/Plng & Svcs ... Ms. Sally KATZ
15 Director of Human Resources ... Ms. Beth IACAMPO
21 Director of Business Operations ... Mr. Alan R. SAUER
21 Budget Director ... Ms. Marcia PHELAN JOHNSON
19 Director of Campus Safety ... Mr. Charles MORRIS
44 Director of Development ... Ms. Gretchen ORSCHIEDT
44 Director of Institutional Support ... Ms. Amy F. BROUGH
36 Director of Career Services ... Mr. Peter BENNETT
21 Comptroller ... Mr. Guy DRAPEAU
13 Director of Computer/Commun Systems ... Ms. Suzanne ABER
41 Director of Athletics ... Mr. Michael D. RENWICK
09 Director of Institutional Research ... Dr. James J. HUGHES
32 Director of Campus Life ... Ms. Amy DEBAUN
42 College Chaplain ... Rev. Allison READ
28 Dean of Multicultural Affairs ... Ms. Karla SPURLOCK-EVANS
38 Director Student Counseling ... Dr. Randolph LEE
96 Director of Purchasing ... Mr. Michael S. ELLIOTT
88 Dean of Urban and Global Studies ... Dr. Xiangming CHEN
29 Director of Alumni Relations ... Ms. Katherine DECONTI
08 Head Librarian ... Dr. Richard S. ROSS
26 Director of Communications ... Ms. Jenny HOLLAND

University of Bridgeport (D)

126 Park Avenue, Bridgeport CT 06604-5620
County: Fairfield FICE Identification: 001416
Unit ID: 128744
Telephone: (203) 576-4000 Carnegie Class: Master's L
FAX Number: (203) 576-4653 Calendar System: Semester
URL: www.bridgeport.edu
Established: 1927 Annual Undergrad Tuition & Fees: $27,330
Enrollment: 5,155 Coed
Affiliation or Control: Independent Non-Profit IRS Status: 501(c)3
Highest Offering: Doctorate
Program: Occupational; Liberal Arts And General; Teacher Preparatory; Professional
Accreditation: **EH**, ACBSP, ACUP, ART, CHIRO, DH, ENG, NATUR

01 President ... Mr. Neil Albert SALONEN
04 Executive Assistant to President ... Ms. Joan E. FLORCZAK
05 Provost & VP for Academic Affairs ... Dr. Hans VAN DER GIESSEN
10 VP Administration & Finance ... Dr. Susan D. WILLIAMS
88 Vice Pres International Programs ... Dr. Thomas J. WARD
30 Vice Pres for University Relations ... Ms. Mary Jane FOSTER
18 VP of Facilities ... Mr. George ESTRADA
09 Exec Asst Pres Plng/Inst Research ... Ms. Barbara A. GABIANELLI
07 Associate VP of Admissions ... Mr. Bryan J. GROSS
32 Dean of Students ... Mr. Kenneth M. HOLMES
15 Dir Human Resources/Affirm Act Ofcr ... Dr. Melitha R. PRZYGODA
21 Controller ... Mr. Thomas A. DEBRIZZI, JR.
27 Assoc VP Information Tech & CIO ... Ms. Diane C. MIRVIS
37 Director of Financial Aid ... Vacant
13 Director Information Technology ... Ms. Susan ASKEW
90 Director of Academic Computing ... Mr. Abdelshakour A. ABUZNEID
19 Exec Director of Campus Security ... Ms. April J. VOURNELIS
38 Director of Counseling Services ... Vacant
06 University Registrar ... Mr. Christian HANSEN
85 Director of Intl Student Affairs ... Ms. Yumin WANG
39 Dir Residential Life/Stdnt Conduct ... Mr. Robert VASS
96 Director of Purchasing ... Ms. Jacqueline A. REEVES
35 Dir Campus Activit & Cmty Service ... Ms. Colleen POWERS
12 Director of Waterbury Center ... Ms. Karen RINGWOOD
12 Director of Stamford Center ... Ms. Maureen MALONEY
29 Director Alumni Relations ... Ms. Susan BUTLER
44 Director of Annual Giving ... Ms. Meems ELLENBERG
26 Dir Public Info & Media Affairs ... Ms. Leslie H. GEARY
43 University Counsel ... Mr. Michael D. BROMLEY
41 Athletic Director ... Mr. James M. MORAN
51 Dean Continuing/Profess Studies ... Mr. Michael J. GIAMPAOLI
23 Director of Health Center ... Ms. Melissa H. LOPEZ
88 Director of Acupuncture Institute ... Dr. Jennifer BRETT
40 Manager of the Bookstore ... Mr. Gary M. REEVES
42 Director of Interfaith Center ... Vacant
36 Director of Career Services ... Ms. Antonia M. COLOGNESI
54 VP Grad Stds/Research & Dean Engr ... Dr. Tarek M. SOBH
49 Dean Arts & Sciences ... Dr. Stephen E. HEALEY
53 Dean School of Education ... Dr. Allen P. COOK
88 Dean College of Chiropractic ... Dr. Frank A. ZOLLI
88 Dean College Naturopathic Medicine ... Dr. Guru Sandesh Singh KHALSA
50 Dean School of Business ... Vacant
17 Vice Provost Div of Health Science ... Dr. David M. BRADY
97 Director Div of General Studies ... Dr. Edward V. GEIST
89 Director First Year Studies ... Ms. Roxie L. RAY
52 Dir Fones Sch of Dental Hygiene ... Dr. Margaret H. ZAYAN
56 Director for Distance Learning ... Mr. Kris BICKELL
24 Media Services Coordinator ... Ms. Lynn DORSEY
57 Dir Shintaro Akatsu Sch of Design ... Mr. Richard W. YELLE
88 Dir Physician Assistant Institute ... Dr. Daniel CERVONKA
102 Director of Institutional Grants ... Ms. Gabrielle E. JAZWIECKI

University of Connecticut (E)

Storrs CT 06269-0001
County: Tolland FICE Identification: 001417
Unit ID: 129020
Telephone: (860) 486-2000 Carnegie Class: RU/VH
FAX Number: N/A Calendar System: Semester
URL: www.uconn.edu
Established: 1881 Annual Undergrad Tuition & Fees (In-State): $10,670
Enrollment: 30,034 Coed
Affiliation or Control: State IRS Status: 501(c)3
Highest Offering: Doctorate
Program: Liberal Arts And General; Teacher Preparatory; Professional
Accreditation: **EH**, ART, AUD, BUS, BUSA, CACREP, CEA, CLPSY, CS, DIETC, DIETD, DIETI, DMOLS, ENG, JOUR, LAW, LSAR, MFCD, MUS, NURSE, PHAR, PTA, SCPSY, SP, SPAA, SW, TED

01 President ... Susan HERBST
100 Chief of Staff ... Rachel RUBIN
05 Provost/Exec VP Academic Affairs ... Peter NICHOLLS
17 Interim VP Health Affairs ... Philip AUSTIN
10 Vice Pres/Chief Financial Officer ... Richard D. GRAY
11 Vice Pres/Chief Operating Officer ... Barry FELDMAN
32 Vice President for Student Affairs ... John SADDLEMIRE
15 VP Human Res/Payroll Services ... Donna B. MUNROE
46 Vice President for Research ... Suman SINGHA
101 Executive Secretary to the Board ... Rachel RUBIN
26 Assoc Vice Pres/Communications ... James WALTER
41 Director Division of Athletics ... Jeffrey HATHAWAY
43 Asst Attorney General/Gen Counsel ... Ralph URBAN
13 Assoc VP/Chief Info Officer ... David GILBERTSON
21 Assoc Vice President Budget Office ... Paul MCDOWELL
19 Assoc VP Public & Environ Safety ... Robert S. HUDD
28 Assoc Vice Pres/Diversity & Equity ... Dana MCGEE
35 Asst Vice Pres for Student Affairs ... Cynthia F. JONES
102 Pres Univ Connecticut Foundation ... John MARTIN
20 Vice Prov Undergrd Ed/Reg Camp Admn ... Douglas COOPER
20 Vice Provost Academic Admin ... Nancy BULL
84 VP Enrollment Planning & Mgmt ... Lee MELVIN
08 Vice Provost Library Admin Svcs ... Brinley FRANKLIN
12 Director Stamford Campus ... Sharon WHITE
12 Director Avery Point Campus ... Michael ALFULTIS
12 Director Waterbury Campus ... William J. PIZZUTO
12 Interim Director Hartford Campus ... Michael MENARD
12 Director Torrington Campus ... Michael MENARD
20 Assoc Vice Prov Teaching & Learning ... Keith BARKER
92 Assoc Vice Prov/Director Honors Pgm ... Lynne GOODSTEIN
25 AVP Rsrch/Exec Dir Sponsrd Pgms ... Michael CROUCH
86 Director Government Relations ... Gail GARBER
86 Dir Govt Relations/Health Affairs ... Joann LOMBARDO
06 Registrar ... Jeffrey C. VON MUNKWITZ-SMITH
27 Manager Media Communications ... Michael KIRK
09 Director Institutional Research ... Pamela J. ROELFS
07 Int Director Undergrad Admissions ... Brian USHER
37 Director Student Financial Aid ... Jean MAIN
29 Director Alumni Relations ... Lisa LEWIS
23 Director Student Health Services ... Michael KURLAND
18 Director Facilities Management ... Eugene ROBERTS
15 Director of Human Resources ... Aliza WILDER
94 Director of Women's Studies ... Manish DESAI
96 Dir Procurement/Logistical Svcs ... Matthew LARSON
47 Dean Col of Agric/Natural Resources ... Gregory WEIDEMANN
50 Dean of Business ... P. Christopher EARLEY
53 Dean of Education ... Thomas DEFRANCO
54 Dean of Engineering ... Mun YOUNG CHOI
51 Int Dir Center Continuing Studies ... Peter DIPLOCK
57 Dean of Fine Arts ... David G. WOODS
58 Int Vice Prov Grad Ed/Dean Grad Sch ... Charles LOWE
82 Exec Director Office Intl Affairs ... Elizabeth MAHAN
61 Dean of Law ... Jeremy PAUL
49 Dean of Liberal Arts/Sciences ... Jeremy TEITELBAUM
66 Dean of Nursing ... Anne R. BAVIER
67 Dean of Pharmacy ... Robert L. MCCARTHY
70 Dean of Social Work ... Salome RAHEIM
52 Dean of Dental Medicine ... Roderick L. MACNEIL
63 Interim Dean of Medicine ... Bruce T. LIANG
35 Asst Dean of Students ... Gay DOUGLAS
38 Dir Student Couns/Mental Health Svc ... Barry SCHREIER
39 Exec Director Residential Life ... Steve KREMER
45 Exec Dir Ofc of Inst Effectiveness ... Karla FOX

University of Connecticut Health Center (F)

263 Farmington Avenue, Farmington CT 06030-1827
County: Hartford FICE Identification: 009867
Unit ID: 243762
Telephone: (860) 679-2000 Carnegie Class: Not Classified
FAX Number: (860) 679-1255 Calendar System: Other
URL: www.uchc.edu
Established: 1961 Annual Undergrad Tuition & Fees (In-State): $32,533
Enrollment: 866 Coed
Affiliation or Control: State IRS Status: 501(c)3
Highest Offering: First Professional Degree
Program: Professional
Accreditation: **&EH**, DENT, MED, PH

01 President ... Dr. Susan HERBST
10 Assoc VP/Chief Financial Ofcr ... Mr. John BIANCAMANO
45 Assoc Vice President of Budget ... Ms. M. Lisa DANVILLE
30 Assoc VP Development ... Ms. Dina PLAPLER
16 Assoc Vice Pres Human Resources ... Vacant

46 Assoc VP Research Admin (Emeritus) .... Mr. Leonard P. PAPLAUSKAS
21 Assistant Vice President Finance .... Mr. Jeffrey P. GEOGHEGAN
08 Associate Director Library .... Ms. Evelyn B. MORGEN
52 Dean School of Dental Medicine .... Dr. Monty R. MACNEIL
63 Dean School of Medicine .... Dr. Philip E. AUSTIN
53 Assoc Dean Education/Patient Care .... Dr. Steven LEPOWSKY
35 Assoc Dean Medical Student Affairs .... Dr. Anthony J. ARDOLINO
93 Asc Dn/Dir Dept Hlth Career Op Pgms .... Dr. Marja M. HURLEY
17 Hospital Director .... Dr. Mike SUMMERER

† Regional accreditation is carried under the parent institution in Storrs, CT.

University of Hartford (A)

200 Bloomfield Avenue, West Hartford CT 06117-1599
County: Hartford　FICE Identification: 001422
Unit ID: 129525
Telephone: (860) 768-4100　Carnegie Class: Master's L
FAX Number: (860) 768-4070　Calendar System: Semester
URL: www.hartford.edu
Established: 1877　Annual Undergrad Tuition & Fees: $30,754
Enrollment: 7,180　Coed
Affiliation or Control: Independent Non-Profit　IRS Status: 501(c)3
Highest Offering: Doctorate
Program: Liberal Arts And General; Teacher Preparatory; Professional
Accreditation: EH, ART, BUS, CLPSY, DANCE, ENG, ENGT, MT, MUS, NURSE, PTA, RAD, TED, THEA

01 President .... Dr. Walter HARRISON
05 Provost .... Ms. Sharon VASQUEZ
10 Vice Pres Finance & Administration .... Mr. Arosha JAYAWICKREMA
30 Vice Pres Institutional Advancement .... Mrs. Cathy VOELKER
32 Vice Pres Student Affs/Dean Stdnts .... Mr. J. Lee PETERS
21 Asst Vice Pres Finance/Controller .... Ms. Kimberly KENNISON
35 Asst Vice Pres Student Development .... Ms. DeLois LINDSEY
04 Senior Advisor to the President .... Ms. Susan FITZGERALD
35 Assoc Vice Pres for Student Life .... Mr. Irwin NUSSBAUM
21 Assoc Vice Pres/Treasurer .... Mr. Thomas J. PERRA
43 General Counsel & Univ Secretary .... Mr. Thomas DORER
20 Assoc Provost/Dean UG Studies .... Dr. Guy C. COLARULLI
20 Asst Provost/Dean of Faculty Devel .... Dr. Frederick SWEITZER
07 Dean of Admission .... Mr. Richard A. ZEISER
04 Exec Assistant to the President .... Ms. Ilena ROSENSTEIN
15 Exec Dir Human Resources & Devel .... Ms. Lisa BELANGER
08 Director University Libraries . Ms. RandiLynn ASHTON-PRITTING
37 Director Student Financial Aid .... Ms. Jennifer FUHRMANN
06 Director Registration & Records .... Ms. Doreen LAY
38 Dir Counsel & Personal Development .... Dr. David ALBERT
36 Director Career Center .... Mr. John KNIERING
14 Chief Info Ofcr/Ex Dir Info Tech .... Mr. George BROPHY
19 Director Public Safety .... Mr. John SCHMALTZ
23 Director Health Services .... Ms. Mary NORRIS
24 Director Media Technology Services .... Mr. Sebastian SORRENTINO
25 Dir Inst Prtnrshp/Sponsored Rsrch .... Dr. Peter LISI
29 Director Alumni & Parent Relations .... Ms. Kandyce AUST
18 Senior Director of Facilities .... Mr. Norman YOUNG
41 Director Athletics .... Ms. Patricia MEISER-MCKNETT
104 Director International Studies .... Ms. Sarah REUTER
09 Director Institutional Research .... Ms. Sarah NOELL
94 Director of Women's Center .... Ms. Patricia MCKENNA-GRANT
88 Director of Judicial Process .... Ms. Helena SAJKO
96 Director of Purchasing .... Mr. Dennis M. GACIOCH
92 Director of University Honors .... Dr. Donald JONES
88 Dean University Programs .... Mr. R. J. MCGIVNEY
57 Acting Dean Hartford Art School .... Ms. Mary FREY
72 Dean College Engineer/Tech/Arch .... Dr. Louis MANZIONE
58 Dean Graduate Studies .... Dr. Peter DIFFLEY
49 Dean College Arts & Science .... Dr. Joseph VOELKER
50 Dean Barney School of Business .... Dr. James W. FAIRFIELD-SONN
12 Dean Hillyer College .... Dr. David H. GOLDENBERG
53 Dean College of Education .... Dr. Ralph MUELLER
88 Dean Hartt School .... Dr. Aaron FLAGG

University of New Haven (B)

300 Boston Post Road, West Haven CT 06516-1999
County: New Haven　FICE Identification: 001397
Unit ID: 129941
Telephone: (203) 932-7000　Carnegie Class: Master's L
FAX Number: (203) 931-6060　Calendar System: Other
URL: www.newhaven.edu
Established: 1920　Annual Undergrad Tuition & Fees: $31,500
Enrollment: 5,949　Coed
Affiliation or Control: Independent Non-Profit　IRS Status: 501(c)3
Highest Offering: Doctorate
Program: Liberal Arts And General; Professional
Accreditation: EH, CS, DH, DIETD, ENG

01 President .... Dr. Steven H. KAPLAN
10 Vice Pres Finance/Treasurer of Univ .... Mr. George S. SYNODI
30 Vice President Univ Advancement .... Mr. Richard TUCHMAN
32 Vice President for Student Affairs .... Dr. Margaret JABLONSKI
04 Sp Ast to Pres/Athletic Adv/Outrch .... Mr. William M. LEETE
05 Provost/Vice Pres Academic Affs .... Dr. David P. DAUWALDER
84 Vice Pres Enrollment Management .... Mr. Jim MCCOY
18 Vice President for Facilities .... Mr. Thomas E. BEEBE
15 Vice President Human Resources .... Ms. Caroline KOZIATEK
20 Asc Prov Grad Stds/Rsrch/Fac Devel .... Dr. Ira H. KLEINFELD
21 Assoc Vice Pres for Finance .... Mr. Patrick TORRE
13 Assoc VP Institutional Technology .... Mr. Vincent P. MANGIACAPRA
26 Associate VP for Advancement .... Ms. Juli ROEBUCK
35 Assoc VP Stdnt Affs/Dean of Students .. Ms. Rebecca D. JOHNSON
88 Asst Provost Experiential Learning .... Dr. Christie MONTGOMERY-BORONICO
08 University Librarian .... Ms. Hanko H. DOBI
44 Director of Development .... Ms. Jacqueline K. KORAL
06 Registrar for Undergraduate Records .... Ms. Nancy BAKER
06 Registrar for Graduate Records .... Ms. Virginia KLUMP
07 Director of Admissions .... Mr. Kevin J. PHILLIPS
07 Director of Graduate Admissions .... Ms. Eloise GORMLEY
28 Director of Intercultural Relations .... Ms. Wanda TYLER
29 Director of Alumni Relations .... Ms. Jennifer PJATAK
38 Director of Counseling .... Dr. Deborah EVERHART
09 Director Institutional Research .... Dr. Elizabeth JOHNSTON-O'CONNOR
19 Chief of University Police .... Chief Henry A. STARKEL
41 Director of Athletics .... Ms. Deborah CHIN
85 Director of Intl Student Services .... Ms. Andrea HOGAN
37 Director of Financial Aid .... Ms. Karen FLYNN
35 Director Student Activities .... Mr. Gregory OVEREND
96 Director of Procurement Services .... Mr. David ROBERTS
85 Director International Admissions .... Mr. Joseph SPELLMAN
88 Dir Student Accounts/Risk Manager .... Mr. Marc MANIATIS
26 Director of Marketing Services .... Ms. Sandy ABBAGNARO
88 Dean of University College .... Mr. Arthur GOON
49 Dean College Arts & Sciences .... Dr. Ronald NOWACZYK
50 Dean College Business .... Dr. Richard HIGHFIELD
54 Int Dean Tagliatela Col Engineering .... Dr. Ali J. MONTAZAR
51 Dn HCL Col Crimnl Just/Forensic Sci .... Dr. Richard H. WARD

Wesleyan University (C)

Middletown CT 06459-0001
County: Middlesex　FICE Identification: 001424
Unit ID: 130697
Telephone: (860) 685-2000　Carnegie Class: Bac/A&S
FAX Number: (860) 685-2001　Calendar System: Semester
URL: www.wesleyan.edu
Established: 1831　Annual Undergrad Tuition & Fees: $43,404
Enrollment: 3,215　Coed
Affiliation or Control: Independent Non-Profit　IRS Status: 501(c)3
Highest Offering: Doctorate
Program: Liberal Arts And General
Accreditation: EH

01 President .... Dr. Michael S. ROTH
05 Vice Pres Academic Affairs/Provost .... Dr. Robert ROSENTHAL
10 Vice President/Treasurer .... Dr. John MEERTS
26 Vice President University Relations .... Ms. Barbara-Jan WILSON
101 Secretary of University .... Ms. Marianne CALNEN
28 Vice President for Diversity .... Dr. Sonia B. MAÑJON
32 Vice Pres of Student Affairs .... Mr. Michael J. WHALEY
07 Dean of Admissions & Financial Aid .... Ms. Nancy H. MEISLAHN
35 Asst Vice Pres/Dean of Students .... Mr. Richard CULLITON
09 Director of Institutional Research .... Mr. Michael E. WHITCOMB
37 Director Financial Aid .... Vacant
29 Asst VP Alumni/Parent Relations .... Ms. Gemma F. EBSTEIN
27 Asst Vice Pres University Relations .... Ms. Ann GOODWIN
20 Associate Provost .... Dr. Karen L. ANDERSON
18 Asst Vice President for Facilities .... Ms. Joyce TOPSHE
58 Director of Graduate Liberal Stds .... Ms. Sheryl CULOTTA
06 Registrar .... Ms. Anna VAN DER BURG
08 Librarian .... Ms. Patricia TULLY
36 Director Career Development .... Mr. Michael A. SCIOLA
15 Director Human Resources .... Ms. Julia HICKS
19 Director Public Safety .... Mr. David A. MEYER
31 Dir Community Svcs/Volunteerism .... Ms. Catherine CRIMMINS LECHOWICZ
41 Director of Athletics .... Mr. John S. BIDDISCOMBE
88 Director of Strategic Initiatives .... Dr. Charles G. SALAS

Yale University (D)

New Haven CT 06520
County: New Haven　FICE Identification: 001426
Unit ID: 130794
Telephone: (203) 432-4771　Carnegie Class: RU/VH
FAX Number: N/A　Calendar System: Semester
URL: www.yale.edu
Established: 1701　Annual Undergrad Tuition & Fees: $40,500
Enrollment: 11,701　Coed
Affiliation or Control: Independent Non-Profit　IRS Status: 501(c)3
Highest Offering: Doctorate
Program: Liberal Arts And General; Teacher Preparatory; Professional
Accreditation: EH, ARCPA, BUS, CLPSY, ENG, FOR, HSA, IPSY, LAW, MED, MIDWF, MUS, NURSE, PH, THEOL

01 President .... Richard C. LEVIN
05 Provost .... Peter SALOVEY
86 Vice Pres & Dir New Haven/State Aff .... Bruce D. ALEXANDER
101 Vice President & Secretary .... Linda K. LORIMER
10 Vice Pres Finance & Business Ops .... Shauna KING
30 Vice President Development .... Inge T. REICHENBACH
43 Vice President & General Counsel .... Dorothy K. ROBINSON
16 Vice Pres/Chief HR Officer .... Michael A. PEEL
20 Deputy Provost Science & Tech .... Steven M. GIRVIN
20 Deputy Provost of the Arts .... Barbara SHAILOR
20 Deputy Provost Arts and Humanities .... Emily P. BAKEMEIR
20 Deputy Prov Health Affairs .... Stephanie SPANGLER
20 Deputy Provost Academic Resources .... J. Lloyd SUTTLE
11 Assoc VP of Administration .... Janet E. LINDNER
18 Assoc VP Facilities .... John H. BOLLIER
21 Assoc VP Financial Plng & Analysis .... Stephen C. MURPHY
27 Chief Commun Ofcr/Spec Asst to Pres .... Thomas G. MATTIA
96 Assoc VP & Chief Procurement Ofcr .... John A. MAYES
102 Assoc VP/Dir Corp & Found Rels .... Patricia E. PEDERSEN
08 University Librarian .... Susan GIBBONS
09 Director Institutional Research .... John R. GOLDIN
13 Assoc VP & Univ CIO .... Leonard PETERS
19 Chief University Police .... Ronnell A. HIGGINS
06 University Registrar .... Gabriel G. OLSZEWSKI
07 Dean Undergraduate Admissions .... Jeffrey BRENZEL
20 Dean Undergraduate Education .... Joseph W. GORDON
35 Dean Student Affairs .... Mr. W. Marichal GENTRY
29 Exec Director Assoc of Yale Alumni .... Mark R. DOLLHOPF
37 Director University Financial Aid .... Caesar T. STORLAZZI
27 Assoc CIO .... Charles POWELL
22 Dir Ofc Equal Opportunities .... Valarie J. STANLEY
23 Director University Health Services .... Dr. Paul GENECIN
90 Sr Dir Academic Technology .... Peggy A. MCCREADY
25 Exec Dir Univ Grant & Contract Admn .... Michael GLASGOW
36 Director Career Services .... Allyson L. MOORE
91 Director ITS Finance & Admin .... Frank M. MURO, JR.
44 Univ Director Planned Giving .... Eileen B. DONAHUE
39 Dir Grad & Prof Student Housing .... George E. LONGYEAR, JR.
41 Director Athletics .... Thomas A. BECKETT
42 University Chaplain .... Sharon KUGLER
85 Director Intl Students & Scholars .... Ann KUHLMAN
48 Dean of the School of Architecture .... Robert A M. STERN
49 Dean of Yale College .... Mary MILLER
50 Dean School of Management .... Sharon M. OSTER
54 Dean Faculty of Engineering .... Ms. T. Kyle VANDERLICK
57 Dean of the School of Art .... Robert STORR
58 Dean of Grad Sch Arts & Science .... Thomas D. POLLARD
57 Dean of the School of Drama .... James A. BUNDY
61 Dean of the Law School .... Robert C. POST
64 Dean of the School of Music .... Robert L. BLOCKER
65 Dean Sch of Forestry & Environ Stds .... Sir Peter CRANE
73 Dean of the Divinity School .... Harold W. ATTRIDGE
88 Director Inst of Sacred Music .... Martin D. JEAN
63 Dean of School of Medicine .... Dr. Robert J. ALPERN
66 Dean of the School of Nursing .... Margaret GREY
69 Dean of Public Health .... Paul C. CLEARY
28 Chief Diversity Officer .... Deborah STANLEY-MCAULAY
104 Dean Intl & Professional Experience .... Jane EDWARDS

DELAWARE

Delaware College of Art and Design (E)

600 N Market Street, Wilmington DE 19801-3007
County: New Castle　FICE Identification: 041398
Unit ID: 432524
Telephone: (302) 622-8000　Carnegie Class: Assoc/PrivNFP
FAX Number: (302) 622-8870　Calendar System: Semester
URL: www.dcad.edu
Established: 1997　Annual Undergrad Tuition & Fees: $20,023
Enrollment: 235　Coed
Affiliation or Control: Independent Non-Profit　IRS Status: 501(c)3
Highest Offering: Associate Degree
Program: 2-Year Principally Bachelor's Creditable; Fine Arts Emphasis
Accreditation: M, ART

01 President .... Mr. Stuart BARON

Delaware State University (F)

1200 N DuPont Highway, Dover DE 19901-2275
County: Kent　FICE Identification: 001428
Unit ID: 130934
Telephone: (302) 857-6060　Carnegie Class: Master's M
FAX Number: (302) 857-6069　Calendar System: Semester
URL: www.desu.edu
Established: 1891　Annual Undergrad Tuition & Fees (In-State): $7,056
Enrollment: 3,975　Coed
Affiliation or Control: State　IRS Status: 501(c)3
Highest Offering: Doctorate
Program: Liberal Arts And General; Teacher Preparatory; Professional
Accreditation: M, BUS, DIETD, NUR, NURSE, SW, TED

01 President .... Dr. Harry L. WILLIAMS
04 Assistant to the President .... Ms. Natasha A. ADAMS
05 Int Provost & V Chair Academic Affs .... Dr. Alton THOMPSON
10 Vice Pres Finance & Administration .... Mr. Amir MOHAMMADI
30 Vice Pres Institutional Advancement .... Mrs. Carolyn CURRY
88 General Counsel .... Mr. Thomas PRESTON
32 Vice Pres Student Affairs .... Mr. Kemal ATKINS
18 Director of Facilities .... Mr. Randy JONES
06 Registrar .... Mr. Terrell HOLMES
07 Director of Admissions .... Ms. Erin HILL
62 Dean of Library Services .... Ms. Rebecca BATSON
37 Director of Financial Aid .... Ms. Lynn IOCANO
09 Director of Institutional Research .... Dr. Phyllis Y. EDAMATSU
29 Director of Alumni Relations .... Ms. Lorene K. ROBINSON
36 Director Career Planning/Placement .... Mrs. Robin ROBERTS
38 Director of Student Counseling .... Mr. Ralph ROBINSON
27 News Director .... Mr. Carlos HOLMES
41 Director of Athletics .... Mr. Derek CARTER
15 Director of Human Resources .... Ms. Irene HAWKINS
46 Vice President for Research .... Dr. Noureddine MELIKECHI

*Delaware Technical and Community College Central Office (A)

Box 897, Dover DE 19903-0897

County: Kent FICE Identification: 008074
Unit ID: 130882
Telephone: (302) 739-3737 Carnegie Class: N/A
FAX Number: (302) 739-6225
URL: www.dtcc.edu

01 President .... Dr. Orlando J. GEORGE, JR.
05 Vice President for Academic Affairs .... Ms. Stephanie S. SMITH
10 Vice President for Finance .... Mr. Gerard M. MCNESBY
15 Vice Pres Human Res/College Rels .... Dr. Hope W. MURRAY
43 Vice Pres/Chief Legal Counsel .... Mr. Brian D. SHIREY
102 Assoc VP Institutional Advancement .... Dr. Barbara S. RIDGELY
20 Asst Vice Pres Educational Support .... Dr. Kimberly L. JOYCE
21 Asst Vice President for Finance .... Ms. Carol C. RHODES
15 Asst Vice Pres Human Resources .... Ms. Patricia A. DEPLASCO
26 Acting Asst VP for Marketing & PR .... Ms. Lisa C. HASTINGS-SHEPPARD
20 Asst VP Curriculum & Instruction .... Dr. June S. TURANSKY
09 Director of Institutional Research .... Ms. Tracy L. BAKOWSKI
13 Chief Technology Officer .... Mr. Robert H. MESSNER
106 Director of E-Learning .... Dr. Richard C. KRALEVICH
104 International Education Director .... Ms. Taryn E. GASSNER

*Delaware Technical and Community College Owens Campus (B)

Box 610, Georgetown DE 19947-0610

County: Sussex FICE Identification: 007053
Unit ID: 130891
Telephone: (302) 856-5400 Carnegie Class: Assoc/Pub-R-M
FAX Number: (302) 858-5455 Calendar System: Semester
URL: www.dtcc.edu/owens
Established: 1967 Annual Undergrad Tuition & Fees (In-State): $2,980
Enrollment: 4,882 Coed
Affiliation or Control: State IRS Status: 501(c)3
Highest Offering: Associate Degree
Program: Occupational; 2-Year Principally Bachelor's Creditable
Accreditation: M, ACBSP, ADNUR, DMS, ENGT, MLTAD, OTA, PTAA, RAD

02 Vice President & Campus Director .... Dr. Ileana M. SMITH
05 Dean of Instruction .... Dr. June S. TURANSKY
32 Dean of Student Services .... Dr. Ann L. DELNEGRO
30 Asst Dean of Inst Advancement .... Vacant
20 Assistant Dean of Instruction .... Mr. Christopher M. MOODY
04 Assistant to the Campus Director .... Ms. Bobbi J. BARENDS
31 Director Corporate/Community Pgms .... Dr. Michael R. OWENS
15 Human Resources Director .... Ms. Maribeth B. DOCKETY
11 Director of Administrative Services .... Mr. Linford P. FAUCETT
06 Registrar & Director of Admissions .... Mr. Willie G. THOMAS
08 Head Librarian .... Dr. Shirin JAMASB
26 Chief Public Relations Officer .... Mrs. Leanne PHILLIPS-LOWE
37 Director of Student Financial Aid .... Ms. Veronica E. ONEY
84 Director of Enrollment Management .... Vacant
18 Asst Dir of Administrative Services .... Mr. George E. BOOTH
10 Business Manager .... Mr. Robert W. HEARN, JR.
21 Assistant Business Manager .... Vacant
29 Alumni Coordinator .... Ms. Alison BUCKLEY

*Delaware Technical and Community College Stanton-Wilmington Campus (C)

400 Stanton-Christiana Road, Newark DE 19713-2197

County: New Castle FICE Identification: 021449
Unit ID: 130916
Telephone: (302) 454-3900 Carnegie Class: Assoc/Pub-U-MC
FAX Number: (302) 368-6620 Calendar System: Semester
URL: www.dtcc.edu/stanton
Established: 1968 Annual Undergrad Tuition & Fees (In-State): $2,980
Enrollment: 7,241 Coed
Affiliation or Control: State IRS Status: 501(c)3
Highest Offering: Associate Degree
Program: Occupational; 2-Year Principally Bachelor's Creditable
Accreditation: M, ACBSP, ACFEI, ADNUR, DH, DMS, ENGT, HT, MAC, NMT, OTA, PTAA, RAD

02 Vice President & Campus Director .... Mr. Lawrence H. MILLER
03 Assistant Campus Director .... Mr. Mark T. BRAINARD
05 Dean Instruction Stanton/Wilmington .... Dr. Frances H. LEACH
32 Dean Stdnt Svcs Stanton/Wilmington .... Dr. Regan HICKS-GOLDSTEIN
35 Asst Dean Student Services Stanton .... Mrs. Cornelia JOHNSON
35 Asst Dean Student Svcs Wilmington .... Mrs. Margaret Rose HENRY
20 Asst Dean of Instruction Stanton .... Mr. Robert J. BRADLEY
20 Asst Dean of Instruction Wilmington .... Dr. Kathern R. FRIEL
04 Assistant to the Campus Director .... Dr. Jacquita L. WRIGHT-HENDERSON
91 Systems Admin Director DIET .... Mr. Kenneth J. WEAVERLING
31 Dir of Corporate/Community Pgms .... Dr. Susan E. ZAWISLAK
15 Director of Human Resources .... Dr. Jacqueline D. JENKINS
11 Director Administrative Services .... Mr. John A. FOGELGREN
37 Financial Aid Officer .... Dr. Debra J. TROXLER
06 Registrar Stanton/Wilmington .... Mrs. Collette M. HAYES
08 Head Librarian Stanton .... Mrs. Regina A. WELLS
08 Head Librarian Wilmington .... Mrs. Donna M. ABED
10 Business Manager .... Mr. Daniel R. EHMANN
21 Assistant Business Manager .... Dr. Mary M Y. CHEN
88 Asst Director Admin Services .... Mr. Eddie CUNNINGHAM

*Delaware Technical and Community College Terry Campus (D)

100 Campus Drive, Dover DE 19904-1383

County: Kent FICE Identification: 011727
Unit ID: 130907
Telephone: (302) 857-1000 Carnegie Class: Assoc/Pub-R-M
FAX Number: (302) 857-1296 Calendar System: Semester
URL: www.dtcc.edu/terry
Established: 1972 Annual Undergrad Tuition & Fees (In-State): $2,980
Enrollment: 3,351 Coed
Affiliation or Control: State IRS Status: 501(c)3
Highest Offering: Associate Degree
Program: Occupational; 2-Year Principally Bachelor's Creditable
Accreditation: M, ACBSP, ADNUR, EMT, PNUR

02 Vice President & Campus Director .... Mr. Daniel L. SIMPSON
05 Dean Instruction .... Mr. John M. BUCKLEY
32 Dean Student Services .... Ms. Jennifer P. MOSLEY
04 Assistant to the Campus Director .... Dr. Susan D. LOONEY
31 Director Corporate & Community Pgms .... Vacant
15 Director of Human Resources .... Ms. Charlotte T. LISTER
11 Director of Administrative Services .... Mr. William J. AYERS
37 Director Student Financial Aid .... Ms. Jennifer J. GRUNDEN
08 Head Librarian .... Dr. Margaret R. PROUSE
10 Business Manager .... Mr. James A. GREENWELL
06 Registrar/Admissions Coordinator .... Ms. Nauleen A. PERRY

Goldey-Beacom College (E)

4701 Limestone Road, Wilmington DE 19808-0551

County: New Castle FICE Identification: 001429
Unit ID: 130989
Telephone: (302) 998-8814 Carnegie Class: Spec/Bus
FAX Number: (302) 998-8631 Calendar System: Semester
URL: www.gbc.edu
Established: 1886 Annual Undergrad Tuition & Fees: $19,860
Enrollment: 1,013 Coed
Affiliation or Control: Independent Non-Profit IRS Status: 501(c)3
Highest Offering: Master's
Program: Liberal Arts And General; Professional; Business Emphasis
Accreditation: M, ACBSP, IACBE

01 President .... Dr. Mohammad ILYAS
26 Vice President External Affairs .... Dr. Gary L. WIRT
10 Vice Pres Finance/Administration .... Mrs. Kristine M. SANTOMAURO
05 Dean of Academic Affairs .... Mrs. Alison Boord WHITE
32 Dean of Students .... Mrs. Bernadette H. WIMBERLEY
07 Director of Admissions .... Mr. Larry EBY
84 Dean Enrollment Mgmt/Registrar .... Mrs. Jane H. LYSLE
91 Dean of Information Technology/ACC .... Mrs. Emily S. JACKSON
21 Controller .... Mrs. Susan M. MANNERING
08 Director of Library .... Vacant
40 Director of Auxiliary Services .... Mrs. Valerie J. HASTINGS-CANDELORO
30 Dir of Development/Alumni Relations .... Mrs. Marsha A. CORCORAN
39 Director of Housing/Residence Life .... Mr. Kevin MARTIN
36 Career Service Specialist .... Mrs. Rebecca LEYSON
36 Career Service Specialist .... Mrs. Lynne LEPORE
18 Director of Facilities .... Mr. Meezie FOSTER
41 Athletic Director .... Mr. Chris E. MORGAN

University of Delaware (F)

104 Hullihen Hall, Newark DE 19716

County: New Castle FICE Identification: 001431
Unit ID: 130943
Telephone: (302) 831-2000 Carnegie Class: RU/VH
FAX Number: N/A Calendar System: 4/1/4
URL: www.udel.edu
Established: 1743 Annual Undergrad Tuition & Fees (In-State): $11,192
Enrollment: 21,177 Coed
Affiliation or Control: State Related IRS Status: 501(c)3
Highest Offering: Doctorate
Program: Liberal Arts And General; Teacher Preparatory; Professional
Accreditation: M, BUS, BUSA, CEA, CLPSY, DIETD, DIETI, ENG, ENGT, IPSY, MT, MUS, NURSE, PTA, SPAA, TED

01 President .... Dr. Patrick T. HARKER
05 Provost .... Dr. Thomas APPLE
03 Exec Vice President/Univ Treasurer .... Mr. Scott R. DOUGLASS
11 Vice President for Finance & Admin .... Ms. Jennifer DAVIS
101 Vice Pres & University Secretary .... Mr. Pierre D. HAYWARD
30 VP Development & Alumni Relations .... Ms. Monica M. TAYLOR
26 Vice Pres Communications/Marketing .... Mr. David L. BROND
13 Vice Pres Information Technologies .... Mr. Carl JACOBSON
43 Vice Pres and General Counsel .... Mr. Lawrence WHITE
100 VP/Chief of Staff .... Ms. Patricia WILSON
18 VP Facilities & Auxillary Services .... Mr. David SINGLETON
46 Senior Vice Provost for Research .... Dr. Mark A. BARTEAU
58 Vice Provost Graduate and Prof Educ .... Dr. Charles RIORDAN
20 Deputy Provost .... Dr. Nancy BRICKHOUSE
20 Assoc Provost Academic Affairs .... Dr. Margaret ANDERSEN
51 Asst Provost Prof Cont Studies .... Dr. James K. BROOMALL
84 Assoc Provost Admin/Enrollment Svcs .... Ms. Margaret B. BOTTORFF
32 Vice Pres for Student Life .... Dr. Michael A. GILBERT
09 Director Institutional Research .... Dr. Heather A. KELLY
29 Director Alumni Relations .... Ms. Cynthia B. CAMPANELLA
08 Vice Provost/Director Libraries .... Ms. Susan BRYNTESON
37 Director Student Financial Services .... Ms. Melissa STONE
36 Director Career Services Center .... Mr. Matthew BRINK
19 Exec Director Public Safety .... Mr. Albert J. HOMIAK, JR.
47 Dean Agriculture/Natural Resources .... Dr. Robin W. MORGAN
49 Dean Arts & Sciences .... Dr. George H. WATSON
50 Dean Business & Economics .... Dr. Bruce W. WEBER
54 Interim Dean College of Engineering .... Dr. Babatunde A. OGUNNAIKE
65 Dean of Earth/Ocean/Environment .... Dr. Nancy M. TARGETT
76 Dean of Health Sciences .... Dr. Kathleen S. MATT
53 Dean Education/Human Development .... Dr. Lynn OKAGAKI
92 Director University Honors Program .... Dr. Michael A. ARNOLD
107 Assoc Prov Grad/Professional Edu .... Dr. John E. SAWYER
07 Director Admissions .... Mr. Louis L. HIRSH
15 Director Human Resources .... Mr. Jerry CUTLER
96 Director of Procurement Services .... Ms. Debra C. REESE
06 University Registrar .... Mr. Jeffrey L. PALMER
21 Director Budget .... Mr. Michael S. JACKSON
28 Director Equity and Inclusion .... Ms. Rebecca R. FOGERTY
35 Dean of Students/AVP Student Life .... Ms. Dawn M. THOMPSON
38 Director Ctr for Couns/Student Dev .... Dr. Charles L. BEALE
39 Director Housing Assignment Service .... Ms. Linda CAREY
41 Director Athletics & Recreation .... Mr. Bernard MUIR

Wesley College (G)

120 N State Street, Dover DE 19901-3876

County: Kent FICE Identification: 001433
Unit ID: 131098
Telephone: (302) 736-2300 Carnegie Class: Bac/Diverse
FAX Number: (302) 736-2301 Calendar System: Semester
URL: www.wesley.edu
Established: 1873 Annual Undergrad Tuition & Fees: $21,565
Enrollment: 2,109 Coed
Affiliation or Control: United Methodist IRS Status: 501(c)3
Highest Offering: Master's
Program: Liberal Arts And General; Teacher Preparatory; Professional
Accreditation: M, NUR, #TED

01 President .... Dr. William N. JOHNSTON
05 Vice President for Academic Affairs .... Dr. Patricia DWYER
10 VP Finance/Dir Human Resource .... Mr. Eric NELSON
30 Vice Pres Institutional Advancement .... Mr. Chris WOOD
20 Assoc VP for Academic Affairs .... Dr. Colleen DI RADDO
32 Dean of Students .... Ms. Mary-Alice OZECHOSKI
51 Exec Dir Wesley College New Castle .... Dr. Zoann PARKER
84 Dean of Enrollment Management .... Dr. Howard BALLENTINE
42 Dir Spiritual Life and Comm Involv .... Ms. Erica BROWN
21 Dir Acctg and Business Systems .... Mr. Scott SLACUM
43 General Counsel .... Mr. David WILKS
06 Registrar .... Ms. Rayann FRYATT
88 Head of School Campus/Community Sch .... Ms. Patricia HERMANCE
12 Part-time Admin Coord DAFB .... Ms. Tracey LUNDBLAD
08 Director of the Parker Library .... Mr. Roger GETZ
20 Director of Academic Support Svcs .... Ms. Charlene STEPHENS
36 Asst Dir Academic Support Services .... Ms. Christine MCDERMOTT
26 Dir Publications & Campus Photograp .... Ms. Leigh Ann LITTLE
09 Director of Institutional Research .... Mr. Richard FRANCE
46 Dir Data Analy & Inst Assessment .... Dr. Chul LEE
07 Director of Undergrad Admissions .... Mr. Arthur JACOBS
41 Exec Dir of Sports & Recreation .... Mr. Mike DRASS
18 Director of the Physical Plant .... Mr. Chuck ARTHUR
40 Director of the Bookstore .... Mr. Kris MCGLOTHIN
19 Director of Safety/Security .... Mr. Walter BEAUPRE
23 Director Student Health Services .... Ms. Jill MASER
44 Dir of the Annual Wesley Fund .... Ms. Cathy NOSEL
88 Dir of The Wesley Fund .... Ms. Cathy ANDERSON
39 Director of Residence Life .... Mr. Kevin HANSBURY
35 Director of Student Activities .... Ms. Sarah SMITH
37 Dir of Student Financial Planning .... Mr. Michael HALL
38 Director of Counseling .... Ms. Ann ROGGE
85 Director of Global Initiatives .... Mr. Kevin CULLEN
29 Director Alumni Affairs .... Ms. Amanda DOWNES
88 Dir Campus Community High School .... Ms. Heidi GREENE
41 Assoc Dir of Sports & Rec .... Mr. Tripp KEISTER
04 Assistant to the President .... Ms. Ellen COLEMAN
88 Supervisor Finance Office .... Ms. Zoe BELL

Widener University School of Law (H)

PO Box 7474, Wilmington DE 19803-0474

County: New Castle FICE Identification: 012962
Unit ID: 211945
Telephone: (302) 477-2100 Carnegie Class: Not Classified
FAX Number: (302) 477-2282 Calendar System: Semester
URL: www.law.widener.edu
Established: 1971 Annual Undergrad Tuition & Fees: $36,350
Enrollment: 1,681 Coed
Affiliation or Control: Independent Non-Profit IRS Status: 501(c)3
Highest Offering: First Professional Degree
Program: Professional
Accreditation: LAW

01 President .... Dr. James T. HARRIS, III
05 Interim Sr Vice President & Provost .... Dr. Stephn C. WILHITE

20 Dean ... Ms. Linda L. AMMONS
11 Sr Vice Pres Administration/Finance ... Mr. Joseph J. BAKER
30 Vice Pres University Advancement ... Ms. Linda S. DURANT
12 Vice Dean Delaware Campus ... Mr. Patrick KELLY
12 Vice Dean Harrisburg Campus ... Ms. Robyn L. MEADOWS
32 Dean of Students Harrisburg Campus ... Mr. Keith E. SEALING
35 Assoc Dean Student Academic Svcs ... Ms. Susan GOLDBERG
07 Assistant Dean Admission ... Ms. Barbara L. AYARS
29 Asst Dean Development/Alumni Rels ... Ms. Deborah M. MCCREERY
06 Assistant Dean Registrar ... Ms. Dorothy D. HEMPHILL
37 Director of Financial Aid ... Ms. Eleanor A. KELLY
61 Assistant Dean Legal Education Inst ... Ms. Eileen A. GRENA
36 Asst Dean Career Development ... Ms. Lea Nora RUFFIN
21 Assistant Dean Business & Admin ... Mr. Verne R. SMITH
13 Chief Information Officer ... Mr. Peter D. SHOUDY
18 Director of Operations ... Mr. Carl G. PIERCE
08 Director Legal Information Center ... Mr. Michael J. SLINGER
09 Director of Institutional Research ... Dr. Stephen W. THORPE
26 Chief Public Relations Officer ... Ms. Mary E. ALLEN
35 Assistant Dean for Student Affairs ... Mr. Edmund LUCE

† Branch campus of Widener University in Pennsylvania. This listing reflects the administrators for the school of law for the Harrisburg (PA) and Delaware campuses.

Wilmington University (A)

320 N Dupont Highway, New Castle DE 19720-6491
County: New Castle — FICE Identification: 007948
Unit ID: 131113
Telephone: (302) 356-4636 — Carnegie Class: DRU
FAX Number: (302) 328-5902 — Calendar System: Trimester
URL: www.wilmu.edu
Established: 1967 — Annual Undergrad Tuition & Fees: $9,290
Enrollment: 10,101 — Coed
Affiliation or Control: Independent Non-Profit — IRS Status: 501(c)3
Highest Offering: Doctorate
Program: Liberal Arts And General; Professional
Accreditation: M, CACREP, IACBE, NURSE, TED

01 President ... Dr. Jack P. VARSALONA
05 Provost/Vice Pres Academic Affairs ... Dr. Betty J. CAFFO
11 University Vice Pres Admin Affs ... Ms. Carole D. PITCHER
10 Vice President/CFO Financial Affs ... Ms. Heather A. O'CONNELL
32 University Vice Pres Student Affs ... Dr. LaVerne T. HARMON
84 Asst Vice Pres Enrollment Mgmt ... Ms. Eileen G. DONNELLY
88 Asst Vice Pres Administrative Affs ... Dr. Peter A. BAILEY
20 Asst Vice Pres Academic Affairs ... Dr. James D. WILSON, JR.
20 Asst Vice Pres Academic Affairs ... Dr. Richard D. GOCHNAUER
21 Asst Vice President/Controller ... Mr. David R. LEWIS
15 Asst Vice Pres/Chief Human Res Ofcr ... Mr. P. Donald HAGERMANN
26 Asst Vice Pres Public Relations ... Dr. Christopher G. PITCHER
04 Asst Vice Pres/President's Office ... Dr. Thomas B. CUPPLES
04 Asst Vice Pres/President's Office ... Dr. Angela C. SUCHANIC
88 Asst Vice Pres Student Admin Svcs ... Ms. Erin DIMARCO
13 Asst VP Cust Svc & Information Tech ... Ms. Eileen G. DONNELLY
35 Asst VP Student Affairs ... Ms. Tina M. SCOTT
08 Director Library ... Mr. James M. MCCLOSKEY
24 Director of Educational Technology ... Mr. Kevin G. BARRY
13 Dir Information Technology ... Mr. Bryan E. STEINBERG
41 Director Athletics ... Mr. Frank C. AIELLO
07 Director of Admissions ... Vacant
18 Chief Facilities/Physical Plant ... Mr. William P. QUINN
29 Director Alumni Relations ... Ms. Patricia L. JENNINGS
36 Director Student Placement ... Dr. Regina C. ALLEN-SHARPE
96 Director of Purchasing ... Mr. Mark S. PARIS
26 Director University Relations ... Dr. Jacque R. VARSALONA
37 Director Student Financial Services ... Ms. Trudy E. HITE
50 Dean College of Business ... Dr. Robert E. EDELSON
53 Dean College of Education ... Dr. John C. GRAY
76 Dean College of Health Professions ... Ms. Sheila M. SHARBAUGH
83 Dean College Social/Behavioral Sci ... Dr. Christian A. TROWBRIDGE
49 Dean College of Arts and Sciences ... Ms. Johanna L. ADAMS
72 Dean College of Technology ... Dr. Edward L. GUTHRIE

DISTRICT OF COLUMBIA

American University (B)

4400 Massachusetts Avenue, NW, Washington DC 20016-8002
FICE Identification: 001434
Unit ID: 131159
Telephone: (202) 885-1000 — Carnegie Class: DRU
FAX Number: N/A — Calendar System: Semester
URL: www.american.edu
Established: 1893 — Annual Undergrad Tuition & Fees: $38,071
Enrollment: 13,047 — Coed
Affiliation or Control: United Methodist — IRS Status: 501(c)3
Highest Offering: Doctorate
Program: Liberal Arts And General; Teacher Preparatory; Professional
Accreditation: M, BUS, CLPSY, IPSY, JOUR, LAW, MUS, SPAA, TED

01 President ... Dr. Cornelius M. KERWIN
05 Provost ... Dr. Scott A. BASS
30 Vice President Development ... Dr. Thomas MINAR
10 Vice President Finance & Treasurer ... Mr. Donald MYERS
32 Vice President Campus Life ... Dr. Gail S. HANSON
43 Vice President General Counsel ... Ms. Mary E. KENNARD
11 Vice Provost for Administration ... Ms. Violeta ETTLE
18 Asst Vice Pres Facilities/Admn Svcs ... Mr. Jorge J. ABUD
21 Assistant Vice President Finance ... Mr. Douglas KUDRAVETZ
35 Asst Vice Pres and Dean of Students ... Dr. Robert HRADSKY
35 Asst Vice President Campus Life ... Dr. Fanta AW
29 Asst Vice President of Alumni Rels ... Ms. Raina LENNEY
84 Exec Director for Enrollment ... Dr. Sharon ALSTON
13 Asst VP & Chief Information Officer ... Mr. David L. SWARTZ
100 Chief of Staff ... Mr. David E. TAYLOR
20 Sr Vice Provost & Dean Acad Affairs ... Dr. Phyllis PERES
58 Vice Provost Grad Studies & Rsrch ... Dr. Jonathan G. TUBMAN
20 Int Vice Provost Undergrad Studies ... Dr. Virginia (Lyn) STALLINGS
49 Dean College Arts & Sciences ... Dr. Peter STARR
60 Dean Sch of Communication ... Mr. Larry KIRKMAN
50 Dean Kogod School of Business ... Dr. Michael J. GINZBERG
61 Dean Washington College of Law ... Dr. Claudio GROSSMAN
82 Dean School of Intl Service ... Dr. James GOLDGEIER
80 Dean School of Public Affairs ... Dr. William M. LEOGRANDE
15 Exec Director Human Resources ... Ms. Beth MUHA
36 Exec Director Career Center ... Ms. Katherine STAHL
09 Dir Institutional Rsrch/Assessment ... Ms. Karen L. FROSLID JONES
26 Exec Dir University Comm/Marketing ... Dr. Teresa (Terry) FLANNERY
06 University Registrar ... Vacant
08 University Librarian ... Mr. William A. MAYER
21 Controller ... Mr. John R. SMIELL
88 Bursar ... Mr. Mark WELCH
21 Exec Director Budget and Payroll ... Ms. Nana AN
88 Exec Dir Risk Mgmt/Safety Svcs ... Ms. Patricia L. KELSHIAN
88 Assoc Director Student Accounts ... Ms. Minh N. PHUNG
88 Assoc Director Student Accounts ... Mr. Darrell COOK
42 University Chaplain ... Mr. Joseph T. ELDRIDGE
30 Asst Vice President Development ... Ms. Abbey SILBERMAN
19 Director Public Safety ... Mr. Michael MCNAIR
37 Director Financial Aid ... Mr. Brian LEE SANG
38 Director of Counseling Center ... Dr. Wanda COLLINS
25 Director Contracting & Procurement ... Mr. Brian BLAIR
07 Director of Admissions ... Mr. Gregory GRAUMAN
85 Director Intl Student/Scholar Svcs ... Dr. Fanta AW
92 Int Dir University Honors Program ... Dr. Michael L. MANSON
41 Director Athletics & Recreation ... Mr. Keith GILL
28 Director of Multicultural Affairs ... Ms. Tiffany SPEAKS
96 Director of Purchasing ... Ms. Hallie PORTER
104 Director Study Abroad ... Ms. Sara E. DUMONT

The Catholic University of America (C)

620 Michigan Avenue, NE, Washington DC 20064-0002
FICE Identification: 001437
Unit ID: 131283
Telephone: (202) 319-5000 — Carnegie Class: RU/H
FAX Number: (202) 319-4441 — Calendar System: Semester
URL: www.cua.edu
Established: 1887 — Annual Undergrad Tuition & Fees: $33,780
Enrollment: 6,967 — Coed
Affiliation or Control: Roman Catholic — IRS Status: 501(c)3
Highest Offering: Doctorate
Program: Liberal Arts And General; Teacher Preparatory; Professional
Accreditation: M, CLPSY, ENG, IPSY, LAW, LIB, MUS, NURSE, SW, TED, THEOL

01 President ... Mr. John H. GARVEY
100 VP University Rels/Chief of Staff ... Mr. Frank G. PERSICO
05 Provost ... Dr. James F. BRENNAN
10 Vice Pres Finance & Treasurer ... Ms. Cathy R. WOOD
30 Vice Pres University Development ... Vacant
32 Vice President Student Life ... Mrs. Susan D. PERVI
21 Vice President Business Services ... Vacant
84 Vice Pres Enrollment Management ... Mr. Michael HENDRICKS
35 Assoc VP Student Life/Dean Students ... Mr. Jonathan C. SAWYER
26 Assoc Vice Pres for Public Affairs ... Mr. Victor B. NAKAS
43 University Counsel ... Ms. Sarah M. PHELPS
15 Assoc VP/Chief Human Resources ... Ms. Christine PETERSON
18 Assoc VP Facilities Operations ... Mr. Carl A. PETCHIK
41 Assoc VP & Director Athletics ... Dr. Michael S. ALLEN
88 Assoc VP for Campus Services ... Mr. Timothy CARNEY
44 Asst Vice Pres Development ... Ms. Amy WILSON
25 Assoc Prov Sponsored Research ... Mr. Ralph ALBANO
58 Dean Graduate Studies ... Dr. James GREENE
48 Dean of Architecture ... Mr. Randall OTT
49 Dean of Arts & Sciences ... Dr. Lawrence R. POOS
54 Dean of Engineering ... Dr. Charles C. NGUYEN
61 Dean of Law ... Ms. Veryl V. MILES
64 Dean of Music ... Dr. Grayson WAGSTAFF
70 Dean Natl Catholic Sch Social Svcs ... Dr. James R. ZABORA
66 Dean of Nursing ... Dr. Patricia MCMULLEN
73 Dean Theology/Religious Studies ... R.Msgr. Kevin W. IRWIN
55 Dean Metropolitan Sch Profess Stds ... Dr. Sara M. THOMPSON
62 Int DeanLibrary/Information Sci ... Dr. Ingrid HSIEH-YEE
79 Dean of Philosophy ... Rev. Kurt J. PRITZL
88 Dean of Canon Law ... Rev. Robert J. KASLYN, SJ
07 Dean of Admissions ... Ms. Christine MICA
13 Chief Information Officer ... Mr. Ziaeddin MAFAHER
08 Director of Libraries ... Mr. Stephen CONNAGHAN
06 Registrar ... Ms. Adriana FARELLA
36 Director of Career Services ... Vacant
29 Exec Director Alumni Relations ... Ms. Kyra A. LYONS
19 Director of Public Safety ... Ms. Thomasine JOHNSON
38 Director of Counseling Center ... Dr. T. Monroe RAYBURN
23 Medical Director of Health Center ... Dr. Loretta STAUDT
37 Director of Financial Aid ... Mr. Donald BOSSE
39 Director of Housing Services ... Ms. Heidi E. ZEICH
44 Director Annual Giving ... Vacant
42 Dir Univ Campus Ministry ... Rev. Jude DEANGELO, OFM CONV
09 Dir Inst Research/Assessment ... Mr. Brian A. JOHNSTON
92 Director Univ Honors Program ... Dr. Peter SHOEMAKER
96 Director of Procurement Services ... Mr. Norman BROWN
22 Equal Opportunity Officer ... Ms. Christine PETERSON
40 Manager Bookstore ... Ms. Tammy ROGERS

Corcoran College of Art and Design (D)

500 17th Street, NW, Washington DC 20006-4804
FICE Identification: 011950
Unit ID: 131308
Telephone: (202) 639-1801 — Carnegie Class: Spec/Arts
FAX Number: (202) 639-1802 — Calendar System: Semester
URL: www.corcoran.edu
Established: 1890 — Annual Undergrad Tuition & Fees: $28,980
Enrollment: 1,110 — Coed
Affiliation or Control: Independent Non-Profit — IRS Status: 501(c)3
Highest Offering: Master's
Program: Liberal Arts And General
Accreditation: M, ART

01 Director & CEO of Gallery & College ... Mr. Fred BOLLERER
05 Provost ... Ms. Catherine ARMOUR
10 Vice President of Finance ... Mr. Stephen GOLDSMITH
15 Vice President of Human Resources ... Ms. Nancy RIEGLE
26 Vice President of Communications ... Ms. Kristin GUITER
20 Assoc Provost/Dean Undergrad Stds ... Mr. Andy GRUNDBERG
32 Dean of Students ... Mr. John DICKSON
84 Associate Dean of Enrollment ... Vacant
11 Senior Director of Operations ... Mr. Steve BROWN
06 Registrar ... Ms. Curren MCCLANE
08 Library Director ... Ms. Margo ASCENCIO
37 Director of Financial Aid ... Ms. Diane MORRIS
51 Director of Continuing Education ... Ms. Doris OSTRANDER

Gallaudet University (E)

800 Florida Avenue, NE, Washington DC 20002-3695
FICE Identification: 001443
Unit ID: 131450
Telephone: (202) 651-5000 — Carnegie Class: Master's S
FAX Number: (202) 651-5508 — Calendar System: Semester
URL: www.gallaudet.edu
Established: 1864 — Annual Undergrad Tuition & Fees: $11,986
Enrollment: 1,477 — Coed
Affiliation or Control: Independent Non-Profit — IRS Status: 501(c)3
Highest Offering: Doctorate
Program: Liberal Arts And General; Teacher Preparatory; Professional
Accreditation: M, ACBSP, AUD, CACREP, CLPSY, SP, SW, TED

01 President ... Dr. T. Alan HURWITZ
05 Provost ... Dr. Stephen F. WEINER
10 Vice Pres Admin & Finance/Treasurer ... Mr. Paul KELLY
30 Vice Pres Dev & Alumni Relations ... Dr. Lynne MURRAY
100 Chief of Staff ... Mr. Don BEIL
101 Spec Asst to Pres/Board Liaison ... Ms. Deborah DESTEFANO
84 Chief Enrollment Mgmt Officer ... Dr. Catherine ANDERSEN
28 Assoc Provost Diversity/Inclusion ... Dr. Angela MCCASKILL
27 Chief Information Officer ... Dr. Cynthia KING
88 Dean Laurent Clerc Nat Deaf Ed Ctr ... Mr. Edward H. BOSSO
49 Dean Arts/Sciences/Technologies ... Dr. Isaac AGBOOLA
58 Dean Graduate Sch & Prof Pgms ... Dr. Carol ERTING
32 Dean Student Affairs ... Mr. Dwight BENEDICT
88 Actg Dean Prof Services & Outreach ... Dr. Stephen WEINER
88 Exec Dir Academic Quality ... Dr. Patricia HULSEBOSCH
21 Executive Director Finance ... Ms. Jean CIBUZAR
45 Director University Budget ... Ms. Debra LIPKEY
96 Exec Dir Business Support Services ... Mr. Gary ALLER
18 Executive Director Facilities ... Dr. Meloyde BATTEN-MICKENS
86 Exec Dir Pgm Dev & Govt Rels ... Mr. Fred WEINER
102 Dir Corp and Foundations Relations ... Vacant
26 Exec Dir Public & Media Relations ... Ms. Catherine MURPHY
09 Dir Research & Info Services ... Ms. Sarah DUCRAY
29 Director Alumni Relations ... Mr. Samuel SONNENSTRAHL
16 Director Human Resources Svcs ... Ms. Elaine VANCE
90 Director Technology Services Oper ... Mr. Earl PARKS
88 Dir Technology Servcies Enterprise ... Mr. Harvey GROSSINGER
14 Info Security Officer/Network Dir ... Mr. Jon MITCHINER
88 Director Library Public Services ... Ms. Sarah HAMRICK
88 University Ombuds ... Ms. Suzanne ROSEN SINGLETON
88 Dir Library Deaf Collection/Archive ... Mr. Ulf HEDBERG
22 Director Equal Opportunity Programs ... Ms. Sharrell MCCASKILL

George Washington University (F)

2121 I Street, NW, Washington DC 20052-0002
FICE Identification: 001444
Unit ID: 131469
Telephone: (202) 994-1000 — Carnegie Class: RU/VH
FAX Number: (202) 994-0458 — Calendar System: Semester
URL: www.gwu.edu
Established: 1821 — Annual Undergrad Tuition & Fees: $44,148
Enrollment: 25,135 — Coed
Affiliation or Control: Independent Non-Profit — IRS Status: 501(c)3
Highest Offering: Doctorate
Program: 2-Year Principally Bachelor's Creditable; Liberal Arts And General; Teacher Preparatory; Professional

Accreditation: M, ARCPA, BUS, BUSA, CACREP, CIDA, CLPSY, CORE, CS, DMS, EMT, ENG, HSA, LAW, MED, MT, MUS, NURSE, PH, PTA, SP, SPAA, TED

01 President ... Dr. Steven KNAPP
100 Chief of Staff President's Office ... Ms. Barbara A. PORTER
05 Provost & Exec VP Academic Affairs ... Dr. Steven LERMAN
30 Vice Pres for Dev/Alumni Relations ... Mr. Michael J. MORSBERGER
10 Exec Vice President & Treasurer ... Mr. Louis H. KATZ
43 Senior Vice Pres & General Counsel ... Ms. Beth NOLAN
32 Sr VP Student/Acad Support Svcs ... Dr. Robert A. CHERNAK
26 Vice President External Relations ... Ms. Lorraine A. VOLES
28 Vice Provost Diversity & Inclusion ... Dr. Terri Harris REED
15 Chief Human Resources Officer ... Mr. Louis N. LEMIEUX
13 Chief Information Officer ... Mr. David STEINOUR
20 Assoc VP Grad Studies/Acad Affairs ... Dr. Diane C. MARTIN
45 Assoc VP for Academic Planning ... Dr. Craig W. LINEBAUGH
20 Assoc VP for Academic Operations ... Dr. Jeffrey LENN
21 Senior Associate VP for Finance ... Mr. David D. LAWLOR
11 Senior Assoc VP of Operations ... Ms. Alicia M. O'NEIL
35 Senior Assoc VP & Dean of Students ... Dr. Peter A. KONWERSKI
88 Associate VP & Chief Admin Officer ... Mr. Frederic A. SIEGEL
89 Assoc VP & Dean of Freshmen . Ms. Helen CANNADAY SAULNY
90 Asst VP for Acad Technologies ... Ms. P. B. GARRETT
88 Asst VP of IR/Acad Plng/Assessment ... Dr. Cheryl BEIL
107 Dean Col of Professional Studies ... Dr. Kathleen M. BURKE
46 Vice President for Research ... Dr. Leo M. CHALUPA
21 Chief Budget Officer ... Ms. Vanessa R. ROSE
21 University Comptroller ... Ms. Debra L. DICKENSON
09 Director Inst Research & Planning ... Mr. Joachim W. KNOP
86 Assistant Vice President DC Affairs ... Mr. Bernard DEMCZUK
87 Associate VP for International Pgms ... Dr. Donna SCARBORO
08 University Librarian ... Mr. Jack A. SIGGINS
26 Asst VP for Communications ... Ms. Sarah GEGENHEIMER BALDASSARO
27 Exec Director of Media Relations ... Ms. Candace E. SMITH
29 Associate VP Alumni Relations ... Ms. Adrienne A. RULNICK
06 Registrar ... Ms. Elizabeth A. AMUNDSON
07 Assoc VP & Dean Undergrad Admiss ... Dr. Kathryn M. NAPPER
38 Director Counseling Center ... Dr. John R. DAGES
37 Assoc VP & Director Financial Aid ... Mr. Daniel E. SMALL
36 Exec Director Career Center ... Ms. Marva GUMBS
18 Associate VP Facilities ... Vacant
85 Director International Services ... Mr. Joseph G. LEONARD
19 Sr Assoc VP Safety & Security ... Mr. Darrell L. DARNELL
22 Exec Dir Equal Employ Opportunity ... Ms. Lydia M. MARTINEZ
23 Director Student Health Services ... Dr. Isabel GOLDENBERG
40 Director GW Bookstore ... Mr. Robert C. BLAKE
49 Dean Columbian Col Arts/Sciences ... Dr. Marguerite BARRATT
63 Interim Dean Medicine & Health Sci ... Dr. Jeffrey S. AKMAN
69 Dean School of Public Health ... Dr. Lynn R. GOLDMAN
61 Interim Dean Law School ... Mr. Gregory E. MAGGS
54 Dean Engineer/Applied Science ... Dr. David DOLLING
53 Dean Education/Human Development ... Dr. Michael J. FEUER
50 Dean School of Business ... Dr. Doug GUTHRIE
82 Dean Elliott School Intl Affairs ... Dr. Michael E. BROWN
66 Dean School of Nursing ... Dr. Jean JOHNSON
82 Dean Graduate Sch Political Mgmt ... Dr. Christopher ARTERTON
41 Director Athletics/Recreation ... Mr. Jack KVANCZ
84 Asst VP Grad Student Enroll Mgmt ... Dr. Kristin WILLIAMS
92 Director University Honors Program ... Dr. Maria H. FRAWLEY
93 Director Multicultural Student Svc ... Mr. Michael R. TAPSCOTT

Georgetown University (A)

37th & O Streets, NW, Washington DC 20057-1947

FICE Identification: 001445
Unit ID: 131496
Telephone: (202) 687-0100 Carnegie Class: RU/VH
FAX Number: N/A Calendar System: Semester
URL: www.georgetown.edu
Established: 1789 Annual Undergrad Tuition & Fees: $40,920
Enrollment: 16,871 Coed
Affiliation or Control: Roman Catholic IRS Status: 501(c)3
Highest Offering: Doctorate
Program: Liberal Arts And General; Professional
Accreditation: M, ANEST, BUS, CEA, HSA, LAW, MED, MIDWF, NURSE

01 President ... Dr. John (Jack) J. DEGIOIA
03 Senior Vice President ... Dr. Spiros DIMOLITSAS
101 Secretary of the University ... Mr. Edward M. QUINN
100 Chief of Staff ... Mr. Joseph FERRARA
05 Provost ... Dr. James J. O'DONNELL
17 Exec Vice Pres Health Sciences ... Dr. Howard J. FEDEROFF
61 Exec Vice Pres/Dean of Law School ... Dr. William M. TREANOR
26 Vice Pres for Advancement ... Mr. R. Bartley MOORE
42 Vice Pres for Mission and Ministry ... Rev. Philip L. BOROUGHS, SJ
10 Senior Vice Pres & Treasurer ... Mr. Christopher L. AUGOSTINI
13 Interim Vice Pres Info Svcs/CIO ... Mr. Kevin MURPHY
15 VP/Chief Human Resources Ofcr ... Ms. Mary Anne MAHIN
27 VP Public Affairs & Strategic Dev ... Mr. Erik SMULSON
18 VP Univ Facilities/Student Housing ... Ms. Karen S. FRANK
32 Vice President for Student Affairs ... Dr. Todd OLSON
28 VP for Inst Diversity & Equity ... Ms. Rosemary KILKENNY
19 Vice President University Safety ... Mr. Rocco DELMONACO, JR.
29 Associate VP Alumni Relations ... Mr. William G. REYNOLDS
88 Assoc VP for Auxiliary Services ... Ms. Margie BRYANT
30 Assoc VP University Development ... Mr. Matthew T. LAMBERT
90 Assoc VP Univ Information Svcs ... Dr. Ardoth HASSLER
43 Vice President & General Counsel ... Ms. Stephanie TSACOUMIS
06 Registrar ... Mr. John Q. PIERCE, IV
07 Dean Undergraduate Admissions ... Mr. Charles A. DEACON
08 University Librarian ... Ms. Artemis G. KIRK
09 Exec Director Inst Research ... Dr. Michael D. MCGUIRE
37 Dean Student Financial Svcs ... Ms. Patricia A. MCWADE
25 Associate Dean for Research Admin ... Ms. Mary E. SCHMIEDEL
49 Dean Georgetown College ... Dr. Chester GILLIS
82 Dean School Foreign Service ... Dr. Carol LANCASTER
50 Dean School of Business ... Dr. David A. THOMAS
63 Dean Medical School ... Dr. Stephen R. MITCHELL
66 Dean Sch of Nursing/Health Stds ... Dr. Martin Y. IGUCHI
51 Dean School Summer/Cont Educ ... Dr. Robert L. MANUEL
58 Interim Dean of Graduate School ... Dr. Gerald MARA
86 Asst to President Federal Relations ... Mr. Scott S. FLEMING
31 Asst Vice Pres for External Rels ... Ms. Linda GREENAN
85 Exec Dir International Programs ... Ms. Kathryn S. BELLOWS
36 Exec Director Career Center ... Dr. J. Michael SCHAUB
22 Int Dir Diversity Equity & Aff Act ... Mr. Michael W. SMITH
24 Exec Dir Classroom Educ/Tech Svcs ... Mr. Mark J. COHEN
38 Director Counseling & Psych Svcs ... Dr. Philip W. MEILMAN
41 Director Athletics ... Mr. Lee REED
20 Associate Provost ... Ms. Marcia B. MINTZ
20 Associate Provost Academics ... Ms. Marjory S. BLUMENTHAL
96 Director Purchasing & Contracts ... Ms. Geneva THORNE

Howard University (B)

2400 Sixth Street, NW, Washington DC 20059-0001

FICE Identification: 001448
Unit ID: 131520
Telephone: (202) 806-6100 Carnegie Class: RU/H
FAX Number: (202) 806-5934 Calendar System: Semester
URL: www.howard.edu
Established: 1867 Annual Undergrad Tuition & Fees: $20,171
Enrollment: 10,594 Coed
Affiliation or Control: Independent Non-Profit IRS Status: 501(c)3
Highest Offering: Doctorate
Program: Occupational; Liberal Arts And General; Teacher Preparatory; Professional
Accreditation: M, ARCPA, ART, BUS, BUSA, CLPSY, COPSY, CS, DENT, DH, DIETC, ENG, IPSY, JOUR, LAW, MED, MT, MUS, NURSE, OT, PHAR, PTA, RTT, SP, SPAA, SW, TED, THEA, THEOL

01 President ... Dr. Sidney RIBEAU
05 Provost/Chief Academic Officer ... Dr. James H. WYCHE
17 SVP & Exec Dean for Health Sciences ... Dr. Eve J. HIGGINBOTHAM
10 Senior Vice President & CFO ... Mr. Robert TAROLA
45 Sr VP Strategic Planning ... Dr. Hassan MINOR, JR.
03 Executive VP & COO ... Mr. Troy A. STOVALL
101 Senior Vice Pres/Secretary of Univ ... Ms. Artis G. HAMPSHIRE-COWAN
43 General Counsel ... Ms. Norma B. LEFTWICH
30 Vice President Development ... Ms. Nesta BERNARD
11 Senior Executive for Operations ... Dr. Marian WILSON
100 Chief of Staff ... Mr. Andrew RIVERS
17 CEO University Hospital ... Mr. Larry WARREN
20 Associate Provost ... Dr. Joseph P. REIDY
46 AVP for Research Health Sciences ... Dr. Kristy F. WOODS
46 Associate Provost Academic Research ... Dr. Fitzgerald B. BRAMWELL
32 Vice President Student Affairs ... Dr. Barbara GRIFFIN
13 Chief Information Officer ... Mr. Quentin CANTLO
10 Deputy Chief Financial Officer ... Ms. Bridget SARIKAS
58 Interim Dean Graduate School ... Dr. Charles BETSEY
49 Dean College of Arts & Sciences ... Dr. James A. DONALDSON
50 Dean School of Business ... Dr. Barron H. HARVEY
61 Dean School of Law ... Mr. Kurt L. SCHMOKE
63 Dean College of Medicine ... Dr. Robert E. TAYLOR
52 Dean College of Dentistry ... Dr. Leo E. ROUSE
54 Dean Col Engr/Arch/Computr Sciences .. Dr. James W. MITCHELL
53 Dean School of Education ... Dr. Leslie T. FENWICK
60 Dean School of Communications ... Vacant
88 Dean Col Phar/Nur/Allied Hlth Sci ... Dr. Beatrice ADDERLEY-KELLY
70 Dean School of Social Work ... Dr. Cudore L. SNELL
73 Dean School of Divinity ... Dr. Alton B. POLLARD, III
48 Director School of Architecture ... Prof. Bradford C. GRANT
66 Assoc Dean Division of Nursing ... Dr. Mary H. HILL
67 Associate Dean School of Pharmacy ... Dr. Anthony K. WUTOH
76 Assoc Dean/Div Allied Health Sci ... Dr. Allan JOHNSON
57 Assoc Dean/Division of Fine Arts ... Dr. Tritobia H. BENJAMIN
84 Director of Enrollment Management ... Mr. Steven L. JOHNSON
07 Director of Admissions ... Ms. Linda SANDERS-HAWKINS
37 Director Financial Aid ... Mr. Derek KINDLE
42 Dean Andrew Rankin Chapel ... Dr. Bernard L. RICHARDSON
35 Dean Student Life & Activities ... Ms. Tonya L. GUILLORY
39 Dean of Residence Life ... Mr. Marc D. LEE
36 Director Career Services Office ... Dr. Joan M. BROWNE
23 Director Student Health Center ... Dr. Evelyn TREAKLE-MOORE
09 Dir University Research & Plng ... Vacant
08 Interim Dir University Libraries ... Dr. Arthuree R. WRIGHT
88 Director Health Sciences Library ... Ms. Cynthia L. HENDERSON
88 Director Law Library ... Ms. Rhea BALLARD-THROWER
24 Dir Teaching Learning & Assmnt Ctr ... Dr. Theresa M. REDD
92 Director of Honors Program ... Dr. Daniel A. WILLIAMS, III
94 Director of Women's Studies ... Dr. Rebecca L. REVIÈRE
30 Sr Dir for Advancement Services ... Mr. Brent E. SWINTON
29 Acting Director Alumni Relations ... Mr. Spencer CHENIER
44 Director of Annual Giving ... Ms. Christie ASKEW
26 Exec Dir Comm & Marketing ... Dr. Judi M. LATTA
16 Chief of Talent Management ... Mr. Jimmy JONES
16 Director of Employment ... Ms. Kym WILSON
22 Dir Equal Employment Opportunity ... Mr. Antwan LOFTON
18 Assoc VP Administrative Services ... Mr. Michael HARRIS
96 Associate VP Materials Management ... Mr. Paul ASHLEY
40 Director University Bookstore ... Mr. Antwan D. CLINTON
19 Chief of Campus Police ... Mr. Leroy K. JAMES
41 Athletics Director ... Mr. Louis PERKINS, JR.
31 Director HU Community Association ... Ms. Maybelle T. BENNETT

The Institute of World Politics (C)

1521 16th Street, NW, Washington DC 20036-1464

FICE Identification: 041144
Unit ID: 455804
Telephone: (202) 462-2101 Carnegie Class: Spec/Other
FAX Number: (202) 464-0335 Calendar System: Semester
URL: www.iwp.edu
Established: 1990 Annual Graduate Tuition & Fees: $26,950
Enrollment: 140 Coed
Affiliation or Control: Independent Non-Profit IRS Status: 501(c)3
Highest Offering: Master's; No Undergraduates
Program: Professional
Accreditation: M

01 President ... Dr. John LENCZOWSKI
10 Vice President for Finance/Admin ... Mr. Jim HOLMES
30 Vice Pres Institutional Advancement ... Ms. Tricia LLOYD
05 Dean/Chief Academic Officer ... Dr. Charles Roger SMITH
20 Vice Dean Academic Affairs ... Dr. David J. KLOCEK
11 Director of Operations ... Mr. Brooks SOMMER
06 Registrar ... Mrs. Hasanna BENSON-TYUS
44 Development Officer ... Mr. Justin STEBBINS
84 Director Student Recruitment ... Mr. Colin PARKS
08 Director Libraries/Info Svcs ... Mr. Jim STAMBAUGH
32 Dir Student Affs/Admissions Coord ... Mr. Jason C. JOHNSRUD
04 Asst to President/Development Ofcr ... Ms. Kathy CARROLL
27 Communications Officer ... Mr. Charles VAN SOMEREN
37 Director of Financial Aid ... Ms. Ingrid ABERNATHY
21 Busines Manager & Bursar ... Mr. Donald BROWN

Pontifical Faculty of the Immaculate Conception at the Dominican House of Studies (D)

487 Michigan Avenue, NE, Washington DC 20017-1585

FICE Identification: 012803
Unit ID: 131405
Telephone: (202) 495-3820 Carnegie Class: Spec/Faith
FAX Number: (202) 495-3873 Calendar System: Semester
URL: www.dhs.edu
Established: 1902 Annual Graduate Tuition & Fees: $15,370
Enrollment: 83 Coed
Affiliation or Control: Roman Catholic IRS Status: 501(c)3
Highest Offering: Master's; No Undergraduates
Program: Professional; Religious Emphasis
Accreditation: M, THEOL

01 President ... Fr. Steven BOGUSLAWSKI, OP
05 Vice President/Academic Dean ... Fr. Gabriel O'DONNELL, OP
30 Vice President for Advancement ... Fr. Joseph FOX, OP
20 Secretary of Studies ... Fr. Brian CHRZASTEK, OP
08 Librarian ... Fr. Bernard MULCAHY, OP
18 Director of Facilities ... Br. Gerard THAYER, OP
42 Chaplain to Commuter Students ... Fr. Andrew HOFER, OP
06 Registrar ... Mr. Tobias NATHE
10 Treasurer/Director of Financial Aid ... Ms. Shauna ROYE
29 Director Alumni and Friends ... Ms. Margaret PERRY
14 IT Director ... Mr. Carlos MOLINA
88 Writing Tutor ... Fr. Raymond VANDEGRIFT, OP
36 Director of Career Placement ... Dr. Jem SULLIVAN
04 Admin Assistant to President ... Mrs. Honya WEEKS

Pontifical John Paul II Institute for Studies on Marriage and Family (E)

620 Michigan Ave, NE, McGivney Hall,
Washington DC 20064

FICE Identification: 041427
Unit ID: 455813
Telephone: (202) 526-3799 Carnegie Class: Not Classified
FAX Number: (202) 269-6090 Calendar System: Other
URL: www.johnpaulii.edu
Established: 1988 Annual Graduate Tuition & Fees: $15,800
Enrollment: 88 Coed
Affiliation or Control: Roman Catholic IRS Status: 501(c)3
Highest Offering: Doctorate; No Undergraduates
Program: Professional
Accreditation: M

01 President ... Rev. Livio MELINA
03 Vice President ... Carl A. ANDERSON
05 Provost ... Dr. David L. SCHINDLER
06 Registrar ... Joseph C. ATKINSON
07 Director of Admissions ... Sara L. TRUDEAU
20 Dean ... Rev. Antonio LOPEZ
20 Associate Dean for Academic Affairs ... David S. CRAWFORD
11 Assoc Dean Progams & Administration ... Nick J. BAGILEO

† Affiliated with The Catholic University of America, DC.

Potomac College (A)

4000 Chesapeake Street, NW,
Washington DC 20016-1860

FICE Identification: 032183
Unit ID: 384412
Telephone: (202) 686-0876 Carnegie Class: Spec/Bus
FAX Number: (202) 686-0818 Calendar System: Semester
URL: www.potomac.edu
Established: 1991 Annual Undergrad Tuition & Fees: $13,350
Enrollment: 335 Coed
Affiliation or Control: Proprietary IRS Status: Proprietary
Highest Offering: Baccalaureate
Program: Business Emphasis
Accreditation: M

01 President ... Cathleen RAFFAELI
05 Vice President Academic Affairs ... Dr. Cathy EBERHART
07 Vice President Admissions ... Wendy DAVIDSON
11 Vice President Operations ... Chet WHITE
10 Vice President Finance ... Brian CARTER
09 Director Inst Assessment & Effectiv ... Walter PERSON
37 Director Financial Aid ... Melva CARTY
15 Outsourced, DHR ... Kara GIBBS
06 Registrar ... Tim FINKLEA
08 Director of Learning Resource Ctr ... Edward ROBINSON

Radians College (B)

1025 Vermont Avenue, Ste 200, Washington DC 20005

Identification: 667005
Telephone: (202) 291-9020 Carnegie Class: Not Classified
FAX Number: (202) 291-8013 Calendar System: Other
URL: www.radianscollege.com
Established: 2005 Annual Undergrad Tuition & Fees: N/A
Enrollment: N/A Coed
Affiliation or Control: Proprietary IRS Status: Proprietary
Highest Offering: Associate Degree
Program: Occupational; 2-Year Principally Bachelor's Creditable
Accreditation: @M

01 President ... Mr. Seelan ABRAHAM
05 Vice Pres Academic Administration ... Dr. Stephanie JACKSON

Sanz College (C)

529 14th Street, NW, Washington DC 20045

Identification: 666591
Telephone: (202) 872-4700 Carnegie Class: Not Classified
FAX Number: (202) 872-9009 Calendar System: Semester
URL: www.sanz.edu
Established: 1939 Annual Undergrad Tuition & Fees: $32,100
Enrollment: 13 Coed
Affiliation or Control: Proprietary IRS Status: Proprietary
Highest Offering: Associate Degree
Program: Occupational; 2-Year Principally Bachelor's Creditable
Accreditation: COE

01 Campus Director ... Dr. Aamir QURESHI
05 Director of Education ... Ms. Rene DAVIS

† National accreditation is carried under parent institution in Falls Church, VA.

Strayer University (D)

1133 15th Street, NW, Washington DC 20005-2710

FICE Identification: 001459
Unit ID: 131803
Telephone: (202) 408-2400 Carnegie Class: Master's L
FAX Number: (202) 419-1423 Calendar System: Quarter
URL: www.strayer.edu
Established: 1892 Annual Undergrad Tuition & Fees: $19,080
Enrollment: 2,384 Coed
Affiliation or Control: Proprietary IRS Status: Proprietary
Highest Offering: Master's
Program: Occupational; Liberal Arts And General; Professional
Accreditation: M

01 President ... Dr. Sondra F. STALLARD
05 Provost & Chief Academic Officer ... Dr. Michael PLATTER
20 Senior Vice Pres of Academic Admin ... Ms. Randi S. REICH
10 Senior VP/Chief Financial Officer ... Mr. Mark C. BROWN
43 Senior VP/General Counsel ... Mr. Gregory FERENBACH
32 Senior Vice Provost Student Affairs .. Ms. Mariana VALDEZ-FAULI
88 Senior Vice Pres Operations-Area 2 ... Mr. Randall T. JONES
88 Region IV Vice President ... Mr. Lamar FARR
12 Region III Vice President ... Mr. Carter J. SMITH
13 VP/Chief Technology Officer ... Mr. Kevin P. O'REAGAN
11 Senior Vice Pres Administration ... Ms. Lysa A. HLAVINKA
07 Vice Pres University Admissions ... Mr. Reginald RAINEY
26 Vice President Corp Communications ... Ms. Sonya G. UDLER
12 Regional Vice President ... Mr. James F. MCCOY
35 Dean of Online Students ... Ms. Tammy BIRD
06 University Registrar ... Mr. Robert BERWICK
20 Dean of Online Academics ... Ms. Sheena R. BHASIN
20 Director of Academic Programs/Admin ... Ms. Cyndi L. WASTLER
20 Dean of Academic Training & Devel ... Dr. Eric F. GROSSE
58 Dean of Graduate Studies ... Dr. Joel O. NWAGBARAOCHA
35 Dean of Students ... Ms. Jacqueline PALMER
37 Director of Financial Aid ... Mr. Alan J. SMITH
08 University Librarian ... Mr. David A. MOULTON
30 Director of Business Development ... Ms. Ann P. BERGER
18 Director of Real Estate ... Mr. Geoffrey ROTH
106 Academic Dean Global Region ... Dr. L. Ward ULMER
20 Region I Academic Dean ... Dr. William CARMICHAEL
20 Region IV Academic Dean ... Dr. Lucy RABENDA-BAJKOWSKA
20 Region III Academic Dean ... Ms. Joyce MAYFIELD
20 Strayer Online Dean of Faculty ... Ms. Catherine DATTE
88 Director Training/Quality Assurance ... Ms. Deepali KALA
14 Dir Tech Applications/Info Literacy ... Dr. Bryant PAYDEN
16 Director Human Resources ... Mr. Edward YOST
20 Arlington Campus Dean ... Ms. E. Maggie SIZER
12 Arlington Campus Director ... Ms. Corey ROSSO
20 Alexandria Campus Dean ... Dr. Abed H. ALMALA
12 Alexandria Campus Director ... Ms. Amy PROPER
20 Center City Campus Dean ... Mr. Izzeldin BAKHIT
12 Center City Campus Director ... Mr. Isaac WALTERS
20 Anne Arundel Campus Dean ... Dr. Twila LINDSAY
12 Anne Arundel Campus Director ... Mr. Valtroud HARVEY
20 Birmingham Campus Dean ... Dr. Vidal ADADEVOH
12 Birmingham Campus Director ... Ms. Stephanie GOWER
20 Chesapeake Campus Dean ... Dr. Muleka KIKWEBATI
12 Chesapeake Campus Director ... Ms. Jeanne POINDEXTER
20 Research Triangle Park Campus Dean ... Mr. Donald WEST
12 Research Triangle Park Campus Dir ... Ms. Cherry CLARK
20 Chamblee Campus Dean ... Dr. Charles M. SMITH
12 Chamblee Campus Director ... Mr. Paul LAWSON
20 Delaware County Campus Dean ... Dr. Joseph GRECO
12 Delaware County Campus Director ... Ms. Lauren ZUCKER
20 Cobb County Campus Dean ... Ms. LaRoyce MORGAN
12 Cobb County Campus Director ... Mr. Bruce REESE
20 Charleston Campus Dean ... Mr. Rufus ROBINSON
12 Charleston Campus Director ... Ms. Keona TIMMONS
20 Chesterfield Campus Dean ... Ms. Carol WILLIAMS
12 Chesterfield Campus Director ... Ms. Cheryl VAUGHAN
20 Christiana Campus Dean ... Dr. Antony JACOB
12 Christiana Campus Director ... Ms. Hannah RICHARDSON
20 Columbia Campus Dean ... Dr. Pender GBENEDIO
12 Columbia Campus Director ... Ms. Florence SPENCER
20 Henrico Campus Dean ... Mr. Bob NOLLEY
12 Henrico Campus Director ... Ms. Carla GREEN
20 Fredericksburg Campus Dean ... Mr. James BLACKER
12 Fredericksburg Campus Director ... Ms. Amy RIDPATH
20 Greensboro Campus Dean ... Dr. Johnny ELUKA
12 Greensboro Campus Director ... Ms. Nashanta WHITAKER
20 Lower Bucks Campus Dean ... Mr. Gary WHITE
12 Lower Bucks Campus Director ... Mr. Lamar FARR
20 Greenville Campus Dean ... Mr. Peter MCDANIEL
12 Greenville Campus Director ... Ms. Kelly HUMPHRIES
20 King of Prussia Campus Dean ... Dr. Eugene GARONE
12 King of Prussia Campus Director ... Ms. Monique STERLING
20 Loudoun Campus Dean ... Ms. Myra ROBINSON
12 Loudoun Campus Director ... Mr. Tyrone TINDELL
20 Manassas Campus Dean ... Ms. Melba WILLIAMS
12 Manassas Campus Director ... Ms. Shirin SAGHAFI
20 North Raleigh Campus Dean ... Dr. Pang-Jen CRAIG KUNG
12 North Raleigh Campus Director ... Ms. Kenya DUKES
20 Morrow Campus Dean ... Dr. Virgil MENSAH-DARTEY
12 Morrow Campus Director ... Ms. Toni STURDIVANT
20 Nashville Campus Dean ... Dr. Udoh UDOM
12 Nashville Campus Director ... Ms. Denise SILVA
20 Newport News Campus Dean ... Dr. Gianpaolo CAPPUZZO
12 Newport News Campus Director ... Ms. Charlotte IZZARD
20 North Charlotte Campus Dean ... Dr. Kazem KAN-SHAGHAGHI
12 North Charlotte Campus Director ... Ms. Dianna ANDERSON
20 Owings Mills Campus Dean ... Mr. Barry THOMAS
12 Owings Mills Campus Director ... Dr. Doreen LUCAS
20 Shelby Oaks Campus Dean ... Dr. Ron DAVIS
12 Shelby Oaks Campus Director ... Ms. Jenna BAILEY
20 Penn Center West Campus Dean ... Dr. George MARUSCHOCK
12 Penn Center West Campus Director ... Ms. Carly BROWN
20 Prince Georges Campus Dean ... Mr. Willie STRAIT
12 Prince Georges Campus Director ... Ms. Chinneta COLLINS
20 Rockville Campus Dean ... Dr. Jerald L. FEINSTEIN
12 Rockville Campus Director ... Mr. Huot HE
20 Tampa East Campus Dean ... Dr. Yamil GUEVARA
12 Tampa East Campus Director ... Mr. Jeffrey KEITH
20 Roswell Campus Dean ... Dr. Keva YARBROUGH
12 Roswell Campus Director ... Ms. Diana BONSIGNORE
20 South Charlotte Campus Dean ... Dr. Johnnie D. WOODARD
12 South Charlotte Campus Director ... Mr. Mark LOMAS
20 Virginia Beach Campus Dean ... Dr. Hermann BAYER
12 Virginia Beach Campus Director ... Mr. Tom LOTITO
20 Takoma Park Campus Dean ... Mr. Doug EARHART
12 Takoma Park Campus Director ... Mr. Melvin MENNS
20 Tampa Westshore Campus Dean ... Dr. Mohammad SUMADI
12 Tampa Westshore Campus Director ... Ms. Jennifer PORTER
20 Woodbridge Campus Dean ... Dr. Michael I. OTAIGBE
12 Woodbridge Campus Director ... Ms. Niaomi CARTER
20 Thousand Oaks Campus Dean ... Dr. Jeannie OLIVER
12 Thousand Oakes Campus Director ... Ms. Lottie MINOR
20 Washington Campus Dean ... Dr. Chandra QUAYE
12 Washington Campus Director ... Mr. Haroon MOKEL
20 White Marsh Campus Dean ... Ms. A. Kobina ARMOO
12 White Marsh Campus Director ... Ms. Yanka CAMPBELL

Trinity Washington University (E)

125 Michigan Avenue, NE, Washington DC 20017-1090

FICE Identification: 001460
Unit ID: 131876
Telephone: (202) 884-9000 Carnegie Class: Master's L
FAX Number: (202) 884-9229 Calendar System: Semester
URL: www.trinitydc.edu
Established: 1897 Annual Undergrad Tuition & Fees: $20,575
Enrollment: 2,305 Female
Affiliation or Control: Roman Catholic IRS Status: 501(c)3
Highest Offering: Master's
Program: Liberal Arts And General; Teacher Preparatory; Professional
Accreditation: M, NURSE, TED

01 President ... Ms. Patricia A. MCGUIRE
04 Assistant to the President ... Ms. Cassandra BOSTON
05 Vice President Academic Affairs ... Ms. Virginia BROADDUS
84 Vice Pres Enrollment Services ... Ms. Cathy GEIER
30 Vice Pres Institutional Advancement ... Ms. Ann PAULEY
49 Dean College of Arts & Science ... Dr. Elizabeth CHILD
53 Int Dean School of Education ... Dr. Antoinette MITCHELL
107 Dean School of Professional Studies ... Dr. Telaekah BROOKS
66 Dean Sch Nursing/Health Professions ... Dr. Mary ROMANELLO
07 Vice President of CAS Admissions ... Ms. Kelly GOSNELL
84 Executive Director Enrollment Devel ... Ms. Kavita FREEMAN
44 Director of Development ... Ms. Judy TART
32 Dean of Student Services ... Ms. Michelle BOWIE
15 Director of Human Resources ... Ms. Carole KING
41 Athletic Director ... Ms. Tracy RENKEN
18 Exec Dir Facilities Services ... Mr. Gary BRICHER
29 Director Alumnae Affairs ... Ms. Margy REAGAN

University System of the District of Columbia (F)

4200 Connecticut Avenue, NW,
Washington DC 20008-1174

FICE Identification: 001441
Unit ID: 131399
Telephone: (202) 274-5000 Carnegie Class: Master's S
FAX Number: (202) 274-5304 Calendar System: Semester
URL: www.udc.edu
Established: 1976 Annual Undergrad Tuition & Fees (In-District): $7,000
Enrollment: 5,855 Coed
Affiliation or Control: Local IRS Status: 501(c)3
Highest Offering: Doctorate
Program: Occupational; 2-Year Principally Bachelor's Creditable; Liberal Arts And General; Teacher Preparatory; Professional
Accreditation: M, ACBSP, ADNUR, CACREP, CS, DIETD, ENG, FUSER, LAW, NUR, SP, SW, TED

01 President ... Dr. Allen SESSOMS
05 Int Provost/VP Academic Affairs ... Ms. Graeme BAXTER
32 Vice President for Student Affairs ... Dr. Valerie EPPS
16 Vice President Human Resources ... Mr. Mark FARLEY
18 VP Facilities & Real Estate ... Ms. Barbara JUMPER
07 Assoc VP Admission/Recruit ... Ms. Ann-Marie WATERMAN
09 Assoc Provost Inst Rsrch & Acc ... Dr. Ansar AHMED
12 CEO UDC Community College ... Dr. Jonathan GUEVERRA
20 Executive Asst to the Provost ... Mr. Herman PRESCOTT
10 Chief Financial Officer ... Mr. Ibrahim H. KOROMA
49 Senior Dean Arts & Sciences ... Dr. Rachel PETTY
50 Dean Sch Business & Public Mgmt ... Dr. Charlie MAHONE
61 Dean School of Law ... Ms. Katherine S. BRODERICK
54 Actg Dean Engineering/Applied Scis ... Dr. Beverly HARTLINE
56 Dean Agriculture Urban Stablity ... Dr. Gloria WYCHE-MOORE
06 University Registrar ... Ms. LaVerne M. HILL-FLANAGAN
21 Director of Finance ... Mr. Steven GRAUBART
37 Director Student Financial Aid ... Mr. Willis PARKER
26 Dir Marketing & Communications ... Ms. Susan BODIKER
08 Dean Learning Resources ... Mr. Albert J. CASCIERO
88 Director Institute Gerontology ... Ms. Jessyna MCDONALD
88 Director Ctr for Res & Urban Policy ... Dr. Chinue AKUKWE
86 Director of Government Affairs ... Ms. Aimee OCCHETTI
25 Director Grants Administration ... Ms. Cassandra PARKER
15 Director Human Resources ... Vacant
41 Athletic Director ... Ms. Patricia A. THOMAS
43 Deputy University Counsel ... Ms. Andrea BAGWELL
88 General Manager UDC Cable TV ... Mr. Edward JONES, JR.
18 Chief Facilities/Physical Plant ... Mr. Armando PRIETO
29 Exec Director of Alumni Affairs ... Ms. Jacquelyn MALCOLM
30 Exec Director of Development ... Ms. Felicia BRANT
09 Director of Institutional Research ... Dr. David CARUTH
38 Director Student Counseling ... Dr. Jane D. OFFEL
96 Director of Procurement ... Ms. Mary A. HARRIS
27 Media Liaison and Univ Spokesperson ... Mr. Alan ETTER
88 Dean Student Achievement ... Ms. Hermina P. PETERS
103 Dean Workforce Dept ... Ms. Cornelia V. SPINNER
19 Dir Public Safety/Chief of Police ... Mr. Larry E. VOLTZ
92 Director TRIO Program ... Ms. Saundra M. CARTER
36 Director Career Services ... Mr. Clifton L. COATES
86 Director State & Local Affairs ... Mr. Thomas E. REDMOND
85 Director International Affairs ... Mr. Paul N. TENNASSEE
11 Director Financial Operations ... Mr. William C. NELSON
88 Director STEM ... Ms. Barbara J. HOLMES
29 Director Alumni Affairs ... Mr. Joseph LIBERTELLI
89 Dir 1st Yr Experience Programs ... Mr. Esteban OLIVERAS
102 Diretor Sponsored Programs ... Ms. Jovita WELLS
13 Dir Information Technology ... Mr. Hakeem P. FAHM
88 Dir Small Business Develop Ctr ... Ms. Candice MILES
49 Acting Assistant Dean ... Dr. April MASSEY

Washington Theological Union (G)

6896 Laurel Street, NW, Washington DC 20012-2016

FICE Identification: 010065
Unit ID: 164243
Telephone: (202) 726-8800 Carnegie Class: Spec/Faith
FAX Number: (202) 726-1716 Calendar System: Semester
URL: www.wtu.edu
Established: 1969 Annual Graduate Tuition & Fees: $17,160
Enrollment: 230 Coed

Affiliation or Control: Independent Non-Profit IRS Status: 501(c)3
Highest Offering: Doctorate; No Undergraduates
Program: Professional; Religious Emphasis
Accreditation: **M**, THEOL

01 President .... Rev. Frederick J. TILLOTSON, O.CARM.
05 Academic Dean .... Dr. C. Colt ANDERSON
10 Chief Financial Officer .... Mr. Wayne WISSMAN
06 Registrar/Dir Student Financial Aid .... Deacon Bartholomew J. MERELLA
08 Director of the Library .... Mr. Alexander M. MOYER
73 Chair Department Pastoral Studies .... Dr. Lawrence LENOIR
32 Dean of Students .... Dr. Kathleen BROWN
26 Director of Communications/PR .... Ms. Kerry TURNER
07 Dir of Enrollment/Admiss Services .... Ms. Cynthia CAMERON
15 Director of Human Resources .... Sr. Lisa M. DROVER
30 Director of Development .... Ms. Joan KNETEMANN
13 Director of Technology .... Ms. Neha PAUL

Wesley Theological Seminary (A)

4500 Massachusetts Avenue, NW,
Washington DC 20016-5690
FICE Identification: 001464
Unit ID: 131973
Telephone: (202) 885-8600 Carnegie Class: Spec/Faith
FAX Number: (202) 885-8605 Calendar System: Semester
URL: www.wesleyseminary.edu
Established: 1882 Annual Graduate Tuition & Fees: $15,850
Enrollment: 670 Coed
Affiliation or Control: United Methodist IRS Status: 501(c)3
Highest Offering: Doctorate; No Undergraduates
Program: Professional; Religious Emphasis
Accreditation: **M**, THEOL

01 President .... Dr. David MCALLISTER-WILSON
10 Vice Pres Finance/Administration .... Ms. June STOWE
30 Vice President for Development .... Rev. Terry BRADFIELD
04 Special Assistant to the President .... Ms. Jane S. DELAND
05 Dean .... Dr. Amy G. ODEN
32 Assoc Dean Acad Admin/Cmty Life .... Rev. Shelby M. HAGGRAY
07 Director of Admissions .... Rev. William D. ALDRIDGE
06 Registrar .... Mr. Drew THIEMANN
08 Director of Library .... Dr. William FAUPEL
15 Director Human Resources .... Ms. Barbara W. DONELSON
18 Chief Facilities/Physical Plant .... Mr. Donald RICE
37 Director Student Financial Aid .... Ms. Mary VIBERT
29 Director Alumni Relations .... Ms. Mauri BISHOP
26 Director of Marketing .... Ms. Alison BURTT

FLORIDA

Academy for Five Element Acupuncture (B)

305 SE Second Avenue, Gainesville FL 32601-6811
County: Alachua FICE Identification: 035243
Unit ID: 451079
Telephone: (352) 335-2332 Carnegie Class: Spec/Health
FAX Number: (352) 337-2535 Calendar System: Trimester
URL: www.acupuncturist.edu
Established: 1998 Annual Graduate Tuition & Fees: $41,200
Enrollment: 78 Coed
Affiliation or Control: Independent Non-Profit IRS Status: 501(c)3
Highest Offering: Master's; No Undergraduates
Program: Professional
Accreditation: **ACUP**

01 President .... Ms. Misti OXFORD-PICKERAL
11 Vice President Administration .... Ms. Joanne EPSTEIN
05 Academic Dean .... Mr. Chuck GRAHAM
37 Financial Aid Administrator .... Mr. Glenn MORRIS
06 Registrar .... Ms. Angela XISTRIS

Academy for Practical Nursing and Health Occupations (C)

5154 Okeechobee Blvd #201, West Palm Beach FL 33417
County: Palm Beach FICE Identification: 033463
Unit ID: 412173
Telephone: (561) 683-1400 Carnegie Class: Not Classified
FAX Number: (561) 683-6773 Calendar System: Other
URL: www.apnho.com
Established: 1978 Annual Undergrad Tuition & Fees: $18,571
Enrollment: 384 Coed
Affiliation or Control: Independent Non-Profit IRS Status: 501(c)3
Highest Offering: Associate Degree
Program: Occupational; 2-Year Principally Bachelor's Creditable; Nursing Emphasis
Accreditation: **COE**

01 President .... Lois M. GACKENHEIMER

Acupuncture & Massage College (D)

10506 N Kendall Drive, Miami FL 33176-1509
County: Miami-Dade FICE Identification: 034145
Unit ID: 439969
Telephone: (305) 595-9500 Carnegie Class: Spec/Health
FAX Number: (305) 595-2622 Calendar System: Semester
URL: www.amcollege.edu
Established: 1983 Annual Undergrad Tuition & Fees: $45,000
Enrollment: 210 Coed
Affiliation or Control: Proprietary IRS Status: Proprietary
Highest Offering: Master's
Program: Professional; Technical Emphasis
Accreditation: **ACCSC**, ACUP

00 Chief Executive Officer .... Ms. Nancy E. BROWNE
01 President .... Dr. Richard M. BROWNE
05 Academic Dean .... Dr. Lana MONCHEK
17 Clinic Director .... Dr. Wei LU
37 Financial Aid Director .... Ms. Judith GALVIS
07 Admissions Director .... Mr. Joe CALARESO
06 Registrar/Student Services .... Ms. Maria GARCIA

American InterContinental University (E)

2250 N Commerce Parkway, Weston FL 33326-3233
County: Broward Identification: 666336
Unit ID: 438601
Telephone: (954) 446-6100 Carnegie Class: Bac/Diverse
FAX Number: (954) 446-6301 Calendar System: Quarter
URL: www.aiuniv.edu
Established: 1998 Annual Undergrad Tuition & Fees: $19,366
Enrollment: 849 Coed
Affiliation or Control: Proprietary IRS Status: Proprietary
Highest Offering: Master's
Program: Professional; Business Emphasis
Accreditation: **&NH**, ACBSP

01 President .... Dr. Hisham SHABAN
10 Controller .... Mr. Don BLACKMAN
32 Interim Director of Student Affairs .... Mrs. Alice OLIVER
05 Interim VP of Academic Affairs .... Dr. John CAMPBELL
06 Coordinator Registrar Office & Rec .... Ms. Dawn LEAMING
09 Int Dir Institutional Effectiveness .... Dr. Fabian CONE
08 Head Librarian .... Ms. Sharon ARGOV
37 Director Financial Aid .... Mr. Travis BROWN
22 Director Regulatory Operations .... Mrs. Helen GALLAGHER
16 Director of Human Resource .... Ms. Sharmane BUCHANAN
36 Director of Career Service .... Mrs. Elizabeth BALACHANDRAN
13 Director Information Technology .... Mr. Juan RODRIGUEZ
04 Admin Assistant to the President .... Ms. Lisabelle TORRES

† Regional accreditation is carried under the parent institution in Hoffman Estates, IL.

Angley College (F)

1700 South Woodland Boulevard, Deland FL 32720-4257
County: Volusia FICE Identification: 035954
Unit ID: 441399
Telephone: (386) 740-1215 Carnegie Class: Assoc/PrivFP4
FAX Number: (386) 740-2077 Calendar System: Semester
URL: www.angley.edu
Established: 1999 Annual Undergrad Tuition & Fees: $14,301
Enrollment: 401 Coed
Affiliation or Control: Proprietary IRS Status: Proprietary
Highest Offering: Baccalaureate
Program: Occupational; 2-Year Principally Bachelor's Creditable
Accreditation: **ACICS**

01 President .... Mr. Raymond NUNZIATA
05 Director of Education .... Ms. Nancy CLARK
06 Registrar .... Ms. Betty HOLLENBECK

Argosy University, Sarasota (G)

5250 17th Street, Sarasota FL 34235-8246
County: Sarasota FICE Identification: 025906
Unit ID: 137148
Telephone: (941) 379-0404 Carnegie Class: DRU
FAX Number: (941) 379-9464 Calendar System: Semester
URL: www.argosy.edu/sarasota
Established: 1976 Annual Undergrad Tuition & Fees: $14,580
Enrollment: 1,701 Coed
Affiliation or Control: Proprietary IRS Status: Proprietary
Highest Offering: Doctorate
Program: Professional
Accreditation: **&NH**, CACREP

01 Interim Campus President .... Dr. Sandra WISE
05 Vice President of Academic Affairs .... Dr. Earl WILLIAMS
10 Business Manager .... Mike MAGOWAN
07 Director of Admissions .... Melissa HICKSON
06 Registrar .... Diana GIFFORD
37 Director of Student Finance .... Deborah KERRIS
32 Director of Student Services .... Vacant

† Regional accreditation is carried under the parent institution in Chicago, IL.

Argosy University, Tampa (H)

1403 N. Howard Avenue, Tampa FL 33607
County: Hillsborough Identification: 666082
Unit ID: 428268
Telephone: (813) 393-5290 Carnegie Class: Master's S
FAX Number: (813) 874-1989 Calendar System: Semester
URL: www.argosy.edu/tampa
Established: 1997 Annual Undergrad Tuition & Fees: $14,580
Enrollment: 684 Coed
Affiliation or Control: Proprietary IRS Status: Proprietary
Highest Offering: Doctorate
Program: Professional
Accreditation: **&NH**, CLPSY

01 Campus President .... Patricia MEREDITH
05 Vice President of Academic Affairs .... Tomi WAHLSTROM
07 Director of Admissions .... Josh STAGNER
32 Director of Student Services .... Iris CRAWFORD
10 Business & Finance Manager .... Sarah WELLS
15 Human Resources Manager .... Jillian CONRAD

† Regional accreditation is carried under the parent institution in Chicago, IL.

The Art Institute of Fort Lauderdale (I)

1799 SE 17th Street, Fort Lauderdale FL 33316-3000
County: Broward FICE Identification: 010195
Unit ID: 132338
Telephone: (954) 463-3000 Carnegie Class: Spec/Arts
FAX Number: (954) 523-7676 Calendar System: Quarter
URL: www.aifl.edu
Established: 1968 Annual Undergrad Tuition & Fees: $22,595
Enrollment: 2,785 Coed
Affiliation or Control: Proprietary IRS Status: Proprietary
Highest Offering: Baccalaureate
Program: Occupational; Liberal Arts And General
Accreditation: **ACICS**, ACFEI, CIDA

01 President .... Charles J. NAGELE
10 Vice Pres Admin/Financial Services .... Maria V. BARRON
32 Dean of Student Services .... Kathy F. DEANER
05 Dean of Academic Affairs .... Peter C. WEST
20 Associate Dean of Academic Affairs .... David WALCZAK
06 Registrar .... Laura N. TENGERES
07 Senior Director of Admissions .... Mike MORLEY
37 Director Student Financial Services .... Joyce CUMMINGS
36 Director of Career Services .... Wendy WAGNER-LIND
15 Director of Human Resources .... Ilana CORUM
09 Dir Institutional Effectiveness .... Michael P. KAIN

ATI Career Training Center (J)

2890 NW 62nd Street, Fort Lauderdale FL 33309-1737
County: Broward FICE Identification: 022159
Unit ID: 137892
Telephone: (954) 973-4760 Carnegie Class: Assoc/PrivFP
FAX Number: (954) 973-6422 Calendar System: Quarter
URL: www.aticareertraining.edu
Established: 1979 Annual Undergrad Tuition & Fees: $29,500
Enrollment: 379 Coed
Affiliation or Control: Proprietary IRS Status: Proprietary
Highest Offering: Associate Degree
Program: Occupational
Accreditation: **ACCSC**

00 CEO & Vice Chairman .... Mr. Arthur BENJAMIN
01 President & COO .... Mr. Carli STRENGTH
05 Executive Director .... Mr. Errol STEPHENSON

ATI Career Training Center (K)

7265 NW 25th Street, Miami FL 33122-1707
County: Miami-Dade FICE Identification: 030355
Unit ID: 136738
Telephone: (305) 573-1600 Carnegie Class: Not Classified
FAX Number: (305) 599-9721 Calendar System: Other
URL: www.aticareertraining.edu
Established: 1945 Annual Undergrad Tuition & Fees: $24,973
Enrollment: 710 Coed
Affiliation or Control: Proprietary IRS Status: Proprietary
Highest Offering: Associate Degree
Program: Occupational; Technical Emphasis
Accreditation: **ACCSC**

01 Director .... Ms. Maribel CINTRON
05 Director of Education .... Ms. Sandra AQUINO
20 Assistant Director of Education .... Mr. Victor CALDERON
36 Director of Career Services .... Mr. Scott DUDEK

ATI Career Training Center (L)

3501 Northwest 9th Avenue, Oakland Park FL 33309-5900
County: Broward FICE Identification: 022932
Unit ID: 136747
Telephone: (954) 563-5899 Carnegie Class: Not Classified
FAX Number: (954) 568-0874 Calendar System: Other
URL: www.aticareertraining.edu
Established: 1988 Annual Undergrad Tuition & Fees: $22,500
Enrollment: 569 Coed
Affiliation or Control: Proprietary IRS Status: Proprietary
Highest Offering: Associate Degree
Program: Occupational
Accreditation: **ACCSC**

01 Executive Director .... Mr. Dwight BERRY
04 Assistant to Executive Director .... Ms. Lukita ALTERMA

Atlantic Institute of Oriental Medicine (A)

100 E Broward Boulevard, Suite 100,
Fort Lauderdale FL 33301-3510
County: Broward FICE Identification: 034296
Unit ID: 439446
Telephone: (954) 763-9840 Carnegie Class: Spec/Health
FAX Number: (954) 763-9844 Calendar System: Trimester
URL: www.atom.edu
Established: 1994 Annual Graduate Tuition & Fees: $13,000
Enrollment: 129 Coed
Affiliation or Control: Independent Non-Profit IRS Status: 501(c)3
Highest Offering: Master's; No Undergraduates
Program: Professional
Accreditation: ACUP

01 President .... Johanna C. YEN
05 Academic Dean .... Yan CHENG

Ave Maria School of Law (B)

1025 Commons Circle, Naples FL 34119
County: Collier FICE Identification: 036914
Unit ID: 442295
Telephone: (239) 687-5300 Carnegie Class: Spec/Law
FAX Number: N/A Calendar System: Semester
URL: www.avemarialaw.edu
Established: 2000 Annual Graduate Tuition & Fees: $35,947
Enrollment: 475 Coed
Affiliation or Control: Roman Catholic IRS Status: 501(c)3
Highest Offering: First Professional Degree; No Undergraduates
Program: Professional
Accreditation: LAW

01 President and Dean .... Mr. Eugene R. MILHIZER
04 Executive Assistant to the Dean .... Ms. Pamela KRAMER
05 Assoc Dean Academic Affairs .... Mr. Patrick QUIRK
32 Assoc Dean for Student Affairs .... Ms. Kaye A. CASTRO
42 Chaplain .... Fr. Michael ORSI
06 Registrar .... Ms. Angela KOJIRO
37 Director of Financial Aid .... Mr. Kevin MCGOWAN
30 Director of Develop & External Affs .... Mr. John KNOWLES
07 Assistant Dean of Admissions .... Ms. Monique MCCARTHY
36 Director of Career Services .... Ms. Victoria RYAN
08 Director of Library/InfoTech .... Ms. Roberta STUDWELL
13 Network Operations Manager .... Mr. John DEPRISCO
91 Database Administrator .... Mr. Ken THIONGO
24 Audio-Visual Coordinator .... Mr. Tony PETRO
11 Director of Administrative Services .... Ms. Virginia TRAVER
40 Bookstore Manager .... Vacant

Ave Maria University (C)

5050 Ave Maria Boulevard, Ave Maria FL 34142-9505
County: Collier FICE Identification: 039413
Unit ID: 446048
Telephone: (877) 283-8648 Carnegie Class: Bac/A&S
FAX Number: (239) 352-2392 Calendar System: Semester
URL: www.avemaria.edu
Established: 2002 Annual Undergrad Tuition & Fees: $17,945
Enrollment: 825 Coed
Affiliation or Control: Independent Non-Profit IRS Status: 501(c)3
Highest Offering: Doctorate
Program: Liberal Arts And General; Religious Emphasis
Accreditation: SC

01 Chancellor/CEO .... Mr. Thomas S. MONAGHAN
03 President/COO .... Mr. Nicholas J. HEALY, JR.
05 Sr Vic Pres Admin/VP Academic Affs .... Dr. John E. SITES
13 VP Technology Systems & Engineering .... Mr. Bryan MEHAFFEY
26 Vice Pres of University Relations .... Dr. Carole V. CARPENTER
32 Vice President for Student Affairs .... Mr. Dan A. DENTINO
10 Chief Financial Officer .... Mr. Paul RONEY
84 Vice Pres Enrollment Mgmt/Finan Aid .... Dr. Dennis GRACE
08 Director of Library Services .... Mr. J. Robert VERBESEY
15 Human Resources & Privacy Ofcr .... Ms. Rebecca ZMUDA
18 Director Physical Plant & Security .... Mr. Thomas R. MINICK
21 Controller .... Mr. Anthony BEATA
44 Director Planned Giving .... Mr. Jeffrey MCMANUS
88 Director of Mission/Outreach .... Mr. William MAGUIRE
35 Director of Student Life .... Ms. Julie COSDEN
42 Director of Campus Ministry .... Fr. Robert M. GARRITY
07 Interim Director of Admissions .... Mr. Jason FABAZ
37 Managing Financial Aid Director .... Mrs. Anne HART
39 Director Resident Life .... Mr. Lucas CONDIT
29 Alumni Liaison/Phoneathon Manager .... Mr. Gary HUBER
38 Mental Health Counselor .... Ms. Sharon O'REILLY
41 Athletic Director .... Mr. Brian SCANLAN

Aviator College of Aeronautical Science & Technology (D)

3800 St. Lucie Blvd, Fort Pierce FL 34946
County: Saint Lucie FICE Identification: 039863
Unit ID: 447847
Telephone: (772) 672-8222 Carnegie Class: Not Classified
FAX Number: (772) 489-8383 Calendar System: Semester
URL: www.aviator.edu
Established: 1984 Annual Undergrad Tuition & Fees: N/A
Enrollment: 42 Coed
Affiliation or Control: Proprietary IRS Status: Proprietary
Highest Offering: Associate Degree
Program: Occupational
Accreditation: ACCSC

01 President .... Mr. Michael E. COHEN
10 Vice Pres & Chief Financial Officer .... Ms. T. J. METE
05 Director of Education .... Mr. Pierre LAVIAL
06 Registrar .... Ms. Roxanne PALMER

The Baptist College of Florida (E)

5400 College Drive, Graceville FL 32440-3306
County: Jackson FICE Identification: 021596
Unit ID: 132408
Telephone: (850) 263-3261 Carnegie Class: Spec/Faith
FAX Number: (850) 263-7506 Calendar System: Semester
URL: www.baptistcollege.edu
Established: 1943 Annual Undergrad Tuition & Fees: $9,100
Enrollment: 625 Coed
Affiliation or Control: Southern Baptist IRS Status: 501(c)3
Highest Offering: Master's
Program: 2-Year Principally Bachelor's Creditable; Teacher Preparatory; Religious Emphasis
Accreditation: SC, MUS

01 President .... Dr. Thomas A. KINCHEN
03 Senior Vice President/CFO .... Dr. R. C. HAMMACK
30 Vice President for Development .... Mr. Charles R. PARKER
05 Dean of Faculty .... Dr. G. Robin JUMPER
06 Registrar .... Ms. Stephanie W. ORR
26 Director of Marketing .... Mrs. Sandra K. RICHARDS
09 Director of Institutional Research .... Vacant
37 Director of Financial Aid & VA .... Mrs. Angela W. RATHEL
32 Dean of Students .... Dr. Roger C. RICHARDS
07 Director of Admissions .... Mrs. Sandra K. RICHARDS
18 Maintenance Director .... Mr. Huie G. WILSON
21 Associate Business Officer .... Ms. Polly K. FLOYD
30 Director of Development .... Vacant

Barry University (F)

11300 NE Second Avenue, Miami Shores FL 33161-6695
County: Dade FICE Identification: 001466
Unit ID: 132471
Telephone: (305) 899-3000 Carnegie Class: DRU
FAX Number: (305) 899-3054 Calendar System: Semester
URL: www.barry.edu
Established: 1940 Annual Undergrad Tuition & Fees: $28,160
Enrollment: 8,995 Coed
Affiliation or Control: Roman Catholic IRS Status: 501(c)3
Highest Offering: Doctorate
Program: Liberal Arts And General; Teacher Preparatory; Professional
Accreditation: SC, ANEST, ARCPA, BUS, CACREP, HT, LAW, MACTE, NURSE, OT, PERF, POD, SW, THEOL

01 President .... Sr. Linda BEVILACQUA
00 President Emerita .... Sr. Jeanne O'LAUGHLIN
05 Provost .... Dr. Linda PETERSON
10 Vice President Business & Finance .... Mr. Bruce EDWARDS
32 Vice President Student Affairs .... Dr. Michael J. GRIFFIN
30 Vice Pres Institutional Advancement .... Vacant
43 General Counsel .... Mr. David DUDGEON
49 Dean College of Arts/Sciences .... Dr. Karen A. CALLAGHAN
66 Dean College of Health Sciences .... Dr. Pegge L. BELL
51 Dean School of Adult/Continuing Ed .... Dr. Carol Rae SODANO
50 Dean School of Business .... Dr. Tomislav MANDAKOVIC
53 Dean School of Education .... Dr. Terry PIPER
88 Int Dean Human Perf/Leisure Sci .... Dr. Darlene KLUKA
61 Dean School of Law .... Dr. Leticia M. DIAZ
63 Dean School of Podiatric Medicine .... Dr. Jeffrey JENSEN
70 Interim Dean School of Social Work .... Dr. Phyllis SCOTT
09 Vice Provost Plng/Assess/Inst Rsrch .. Dr. Christopher STARRATT
90 Chief Technology Officer .... Ms. Yvette BROWN
84 Asst Vice Provost Enrollment Svcs .... Ms. Angela SCOTT
35 Assoc VP Student Affs/Dean Students .... Dr. Maria L. ALVAREZ
35 Assoc Vice Pres Student Affairs .... Dr. Eileen MCDONOUGH
18 Assoc VP Business Svcs & Fac Mgmt .... Ms. Monica SOTO
30 Assoc Vice Pres Inst Advancement .... Mr. Tom SEVERINO
21 Assoc VP Finance & Chief Acc Office .... Ms. Susan KIRKLAND
26 Asst VP Communication/Marketing .... Mr. Michael S. LADERMAN
15 Associate VP Human Resources .... Ms. Jennifer N. BOYD-PUGH
29 Asst VP Alumni Relations .... Mrs. Elizabeth REED
91 Assoc VP Admin Information Systems .... Ms. Traci SIMPSON
42 Director Campus Ministry/Chaplain .... Vacant
105 Assistant VP Enroll Mktg/Internet .... Mr. Michel SILY
19 Executive Director of Public Safety .... Mr. George E. WILHELM
08 Dir Library Svcs/Libr Dir .... Mr. Thomas MESSNER
44 Director for Major Gifts .... Ms. Victoria CHAMPION
44 Director Annual Fund .... Vacant
06 University Registrar .... Ms. Cynthia A. CHRUSZCZYK
36 Director Career Services .... Mr. John MORIARTY
39 Director Housing and Residence Life .. Mr. Matthew R. CAMERON
92 Director Honors Program .... Dr. Pawena SIRIMANGKALA
96 Director of Purchasing .... Ms. Sandra MADISON
37 Director Financial Aid .... Mr. Howard D. HUMESTON
38 Director Student Counseling Center .... Dr. James SCOTT
40 Manager Bookstore .... Ms. Claudia HADJEZ

Bay Medical Center (G)

615 N Bonita Avenue, Panama City FL 32401-3600
County: Bay FICE Identification: 011127
Unit ID: 439464
Telephone: (800) 422-2418 Carnegie Class: Not Classified
FAX Number: (850) 747-6115 Calendar System: Semester
URL: www.baymedical.org/Career-Center.aspx
Established: 1969 Annual Graduate Tuition & Fees: $21,825
Enrollment: 51 Coed
Affiliation or Control: Independent Non-Profit IRS Status: 501(c)3
Highest Offering: Master's; No Undergraduates
Program: Occupational; Professional
Accreditation: ANEST

01 President/CEO .... Mr. Steve JOHNSON
05 Pgm Dir Gooding Inst of Nurse Anest .... Ms. Amanda BROWN
20 Anesthesia Program Coordinator .... Ms. Geniece MCPEAK

Beacon College (H)

105 E Main Street, Leesburg FL 34748-5162
County: Lake FICE Identification: 033733
Unit ID: 384254
Telephone: (352) 787-7660 Carnegie Class: Bac/A&S
FAX Number: (352) 787-0721 Calendar System: Semester
URL: www.beaconcollege.edu
Established: 1989 Annual Undergrad Tuition & Fees: $28,650
Enrollment: 141 Coed
Affiliation or Control: Independent Non-Profit IRS Status: 501(c)3
Highest Offering: Baccalaureate
Program: Liberal Arts And General
Accreditation: SC

01 Interim President .... Dr. John HUTCHINSON
05 Vice President of Academic Affairs .... Dr. Shelly CHANDLER
32 Vice President of Student Services .... Dr. Robert BRIDGEMAN
30 Vice Pres Institutional Advancement .... Dr. Walter ZIELINSKI
10 Vice Pres Finance & Administartion .... Mr. Calvin SANSON
06 Registrar .... Ms. Kim BAGGETT
18 Director of Facilities .... Mr. Chris HALL
35 Director of Student Life .... Ms. Maria GEORGO
37 Director of Financial Aid .... Ms. Shawna WELLS-BOOTH
08 Coordinator of Library Resources .... Ms. Dianna WADE
13 Director Information Technology .... Mr. Scott HUGHES
04 Exec Assistant to the President .... Ms. Tamara FULTON

Bethune Cookman University (I)

640 Dr. Mary McLeod Bethune Blvd,
Daytona Beach FL 32114-3099
County: Volusia FICE Identification: 001467
Unit ID: 132602
Telephone: (386) 481-2000 Carnegie Class: Bac/Diverse
FAX Number: (386) 481-2010 Calendar System: Semester
URL: www.cookman.edu
Established: 1904 Annual Undergrad Tuition & Fees: $13,990
Enrollment: 3,577 Coed
Affiliation or Control: United Methodist IRS Status: 501(c)3
Highest Offering: Master's
Program: Liberal Arts And General; Teacher Preparatory; Nursing Emphasis
Accreditation: SC, NUR, TED

01 President .... Dr. Trudie K. REED
10 Exec VP Finance/Administration .... Mr. E. Dean MONTGOMERY
05 Vice Pres Academic Affairs .... Dr. Sarah WILLLIAMS
30 Vice Pres Institutional Advancement .... Dr. Hiram POWELL
32 Vice Pres Student Affairs .... Dr. Dwaun J. WARMACK
09 Vice Pres Inst Research/Plng & Accr .... Dr. Willis WALTER
21 Assoc Vice Pres Finance/Budget .... Mrs. Melissa PETERS
33 ASC VP Student Affs/Dir of Housing .... Mr. Fulton POSTON
29 Asst VP/Director Alumni Affairs .... Ms. Sharon BOSTICK-ISSAC
44 Asst VP/Dir of Planned/Major Gifts .... Vacant
26 Assoc Dir/Communications/Mktg .... Mrs. Meredith RODRIGUEZ
20 Assoc Vice President Acad Affs .... Vacant
36 Dir Career Place/Outreach Services .... Ms. Davita BONNER
08 Director Library/LRC .... Dr. Tasha LUCAS-YOUMANS
06 Registrar .... Mrs. Annie REDD
07 Director Admissions .... Mrs. Aixa MELENDEZ
37 Director Financial Aid .... Mr. Joseph L. COLEMAN
23 Director Health Services .... Ms. Colleen O'BRIEN
41 Athletics Director .... Mr. Lynn THOMPSON
42 Chaplain/Dir of Religious Life .... Rev. Walter MONROE
19 Director of Security .... Capt. Melvin WILLIAMS
15 Director Human Resources .... Mrs. Cynthia HAWKINS
18 Chief Facilities/Physical Plant .... Mr. Ervin ROSS, JR.
92 Director of Honors Program .... Dr. Masood POORANDI
27 Chief Information Officer .... Mr. Franklin PATTERSON
66 Dean School of Nursing .... Dr. Willie M. SESSION
50 Dean School of Business .... Dr. Aubrey E. LONG
53 Dean School of Education .... Dr. Carol B. JOHNSON
79 Dean Sch of Arts & Humanities .... Dr. James BROOKS
81 Dean Sch Science/Engineering/Math .... Dr. Herbert THOMPSON
83 Dean School of Social Sciences .... Dr. Dorcas MCCOY
58 Dean of Graduate Studies .... Dr. Sharon NOWELL

Brevard Community College (J)

1519 Clearlake Road, Cocoa FL 32922-6597
County: Brevard FICE Identification: 001470
Unit ID: 132693
Telephone: (321) 632-1111 Carnegie Class: Assoc/Pub-R-L
FAX Number: (321) 633-4565 Calendar System: Semester
URL: www.brevardcc.edu
Established: 1960 Annual Undergrad Tuition & Fees (In-District): $2,820
Enrollment: 18,096 Coed
Affiliation or Control: Local IRS Status: 501(c)3
Highest Offering: Associate Degree
Program: Occupational; 2-Year Principally Bachelor's Creditable

Accreditation: SC, DA, DH, EMT, MLTAD, RAD, SURGT

01 President .... Dr. James A. DRAKE
03 Exec Vice Pres/General Counsel .... Mr. James H. RICHEY
05 Provost & Dean of Faculty .... Dr. Philip SIMPSON
30 VP Advancement & Public Affairs .... Mr. James ROSS
84 VP Enrollment Mgmt/Student Success .... Dr. John F. DIETRICH
45 Vice Pres for Planning/Assessment .... Mr. Robert A. SHEARER
10 AVP Financial Services .... Mr. Mark CHERRY
15 AVP/Exec Dir Human Resources .... Ms. Darla FERGUSON
12 Provost Cocoa Campus .... Dr. Ethel NEWMAN
12 Provost Melbourne Campus .... Dr. Joe Lee SMITH
12 Provost Palm Bay Campus .... Dr. Beverly J. SLAUGHTER
12 Int Provost Titusville Campus .... Dr. Linda MIEDEMA
12 Provost Virtual Campus .... Dr. Kathy COBB
76 Provost Health Sciences .... Dr. Barbara AKE
103 Provost Workforce Trng & Devel .... Ms. Mildred COYNE
37 Dean Student Financial Aid .... Ms. Joan BUCHANAN
84 Dean Enrollment Management .... Ms. Kathleen PETERS
102 Executive Director Foundation .... Mr. Richard BEAGLEY
04 Executive Asst to the President .... Ms. Terry MARTIN
31 Exec Dir Business Trng/Cmty Ed .Ms. Kieta OSTEEN-COCHRANE
88 Exec Director Aerospace Program .... Dr. Al KOLLER
18 Director Maint/Plant Operations .... Mr. Richard MOON
96 Director Budgets & Purchasing .... Ms. Ann KNOTTS
06 Registrar .... Ms. Stephanie BURNETTE
28 Dir Office for Student Diversity .... Ms. Teri JONES
13 Chief Information Officer .... Mr. Tim MARSHALL
41 Athletic Director .... Mr. Ernie ROSSEAU

Broward College (A)

111 E Las Olas Boulevard,
Fort Lauderdale FL 33301-2298

County: Broward FICE Identification: 001500
Unit ID: 132709
Telephone: (954) 201-6500 Carnegie Class: Assoc/Pub-U-MC
FAX Number: (954) 201-7576 Calendar System: Trimester
URL: www.broward.edu
Established: 1959 Annual Undergrad Tuition & Fees (In-State): $2,838
Enrollment: 40,392 Coed
Affiliation or Control: State IRS Status: 501(c)3
Highest Offering: Baccalaureate
Program: Occupational; 2-Year Principally Bachelor's Creditable; Teacher Preparatory
Accreditation: SC, ADNUR, DA, DH, DMS, EMT, MAC, MUS, PTAA

01 President .... Mr. J. David ARMSTRONG
32 Vice Pres Student Affairs .... Mrs. Angelia MILLENDER
05 Vice Pres Academic Affairs .... Dr. Linda HOWDYSHELL
26 VP Public Affairs and Marketing .... Ms. Aileen IZQUIERDO
11 Vice President of Operations .... Mr. Alex DENIS
102 Executive Director BC Foundation .... Ms. Nancy BOTERO
10 Interim Chief Financial Officer .... Mr. Jayson IROFF
15 Assoc Vice President HR & Equity .... Ms. Denese EDSALL
13 Vice President Info Technology .... Ms. Patti BARNEY
12 Interim Provost Central Campus .... Mr. David ASENCIO
12 Provost North Campus .... Dr. Barbara J. BRYAN
12 Interim Provost South Campus .... Mr. Jorge GUERRA
86 Int Asst to Pres Govt Relations .... Mr. Jayson IROFF
88 Assoc Vice President Economic Dev .... Mr. Norm SEAVERS
21 Interim Comptroller .... Ms. Karen ROBERTS
37 Director of Student Financial Svcs .... Mr. Robert ROBBINS
06 Registrar .... Mr. Willie ALEXANDER
08 Dean of Libraries/Learning Res .... Mr. Miguel MENENDEZ
09 Director Enterprise Business Intel .... Ms. Wendy CLINK
84 Director Enrollment Management .... Ms. Laura ANTCZAK
29 Director Alumni Relations .... Ms. Simone CHAMPAGNIE

Brown Mackie College-Miami (B)

One Herald Plaza, Miami FL 33132-1418

County: Miami-Dade Identification: 666110
Unit ID: 447290
Telephone: (305) 341-6600 Carnegie Class: Assoc/PrivFP4
FAX Number: (305) 373-8814 Calendar System: Other
URL: www.brownmackie.edu
Established: 2004 Annual Undergrad Tuition & Fees: $13,896
Enrollment: 972 Coed
Affiliation or Control: Proprietary IRS Status: Proprietary
Highest Offering: Baccalaureate
Program: Occupational; 2-Year Principally Bachelor's Creditable; Business Emphasis
Accreditation: ACICS

01 President .... Ms. Julia M. DENNISTON
05 Dean of Academic Affairs .... Mr. Thomas CHAMBERLAIN
07 Senior Director of Admissions .... Mr. Greg KING
06 Registrar .... Ms. Lourdes PAONESSA

† Branch campus of Brown Mackie College, Cincinnati, OH.

Cambridge Institute of Allied Health & Technology (C)

5150 Linton Boulevard, Suite 340, Delray Beach FL 33484

County: Palm Beach FICE Identification: 040834
Unit ID: 454865
Telephone: (561) 381-4990 Carnegie Class: Not Classified
FAX Number: (561) 381-4992 Calendar System: Other
URL: www.cambridgehealth.edu
Established: N/A Annual Undergrad Tuition & Fees: $17,500
Enrollment: 397 Coed
Affiliation or Control: Proprietary IRS Status: Proprietary
Highest Offering: Associate Degree
Program: Occupational
Accreditation: ABHES, DMS, NMT, RAD, RTT

01 President .... Mr. Terry LAPIER

Carlos Albizu University Miami Campus (D)

2173 NW 99th Avenue, Miami FL 33172-2209

County: Miami-Dade Identification: 666814
Unit ID: 132842
Telephone: (305) 593-1223 Carnegie Class: Master's M
FAX Number: (305) 592-7930 Calendar System: Semester
URL: www.albizu.edu
Established: 1980 Annual Undergrad Tuition & Fees: $11,910
Enrollment: 1,078 Coed
Affiliation or Control: Independent Non-Profit IRS Status: 501(c)3
Highest Offering: Doctorate
Program: Professional
Accreditation: &M, CLPSY

01 President .... Dr. Ileana RODRIGUEZ-GARCIA
05 Chanc/Chf Acad Ofcr/Coord Cont Educ .... Dr. Carmen ROCA
32 Director Student Service/Counseling .... Mr. Peter RUBIO
83 Director of Undergrad Psychology .... Dr. Francisco MARTINEZ-MESA
53 Dir Education/Undergrad Programs .... Mr. Rafael MARTINEZ
88 Director of Clinical Training .... Dr. Gerald SPECTER
88 Director of Psychological Services .... Vacant
58 Director of Masters Programs .... Ms. Diana BARROSO
30 Director of Development .... Vacant
10 Director of Finance .... Ms. Eunice PIERRE-LOUIS
11 Director of Administration .... Mr. Magdiel BELETTE
37 Financial Aid Officer .... Dr. Ramona MORALES
06 Registrar .... Mrs. Fina CAMPA
08 Library Director .... Ms. Mary BISHOP
13 Director of ITS .... Ms. Gabriel NUNEZ
15 Director of Human Resources .... Vacant
09 Director of Institutional Research .... Mrs. Mirta MIRANDA
50 Int Director Business Program .... Mr. Orlando RIVERO
18 Administration Facilities Manager .... Mr. Magdiel BELETTE
20 Associate Academic Officer .... Vacant
29 Alumni Relations Officer .... Mr. Marco BOWER
36 Director Career & Retention .... Dr. Claudia DOLINSKY
84 Director Enrollment Management .... Mr. Rafeal VASQUEZ
96 Director of Purchasing .... Ms. Elsa VEGA
07 Asst Director of Admissions .... Ms. Carmen VAZQUEZ

† Regional accreditation is carried under the parent institution in San Juan, PR.

Central Florida Institute (E)

6000 Cinderland Pkwy, Orlando FL 32810

County: Orange Identification: 667022
Unit ID: 439525
Telephone: (407) 253-5354 Carnegie Class: Not Classified
FAX Number: (407) 294-3453 Calendar System: Other
URL: www.cfi.edu
Established: 1997 Annual Undergrad Tuition & Fees: N/A
Enrollment: 793 Coed
Affiliation or Control: Proprietary IRS Status: Proprietary
Highest Offering: Associate Degree
Program: Occupational
Accreditation: ABHES, DMS

01 School Director .... Mr. Richard COVINGTON

Central Florida Institute (F)

30522 US Highway 19 N, Ste 300,
Palm Harbor FL 34684-4436

County: Pinellas FICE Identification: 034254
Unit ID: 439525
Telephone: (727) 786-4707 Carnegie Class: Assoc/PrivFP
FAX Number: (727) 781-9421 Calendar System: Other
URL: www.cfinstitute.com
Established: 1998 Annual Undergrad Tuition & Fees: N/A
Enrollment: 512 Coed
Affiliation or Control: Proprietary IRS Status: Proprietary
Highest Offering: Associate Degree
Program: Occupational; Technical Emphasis
Accreditation: ABHES, CVT, DMS, POLYT, SURGT, SURTEC

01 School Director .... Mr. Ross BATTIATA
05 Director of Education .... Mr. Jason FREE
06 Registrar .... Ms. Ivonne DURANT
07 Director of Admissions .... Ms. Kathy MCCABE
23 Director of Health Education .... Ms. Sondra CRANFORD
37 Director of Financial Aid .... Mr. David ROCK
32 Dir Career/Student Support Svcs .... Ms. Lolita JOHNS
36 Career Services Advisor .... Ms. Betty GRESS
04 Executive Assistant .... Ms. Caitlin BEAVER-JONES

† Tuition is variable based on program.

Centura Institute (G)

6359 Edgewater Drive, Orlando FL 32810

County: Orange FICE Identification: 039394
Unit ID: 446446
Telephone: (407) 275-9696 Carnegie Class: Assoc/PrivFP
FAX Number: (407) 275-4499 Calendar System: Semester
URL: www.centura.edu
Established: 2002 Annual Undergrad Tuition & Fees: N/A
Enrollment: 189 Coed
Affiliation or Control: Proprietary IRS Status: Proprietary
Highest Offering: Associate Degree
Program: Occupational
Accreditation: ACCSC

01 Director .... Mrs. Danielle BROWN

Chipola College (H)

3094 Indian Circle, Marianna FL 32446-3065

County: Jackson FICE Identification: 001472
Unit ID: 133021
Telephone: (850) 526-2761 Carnegie Class: Assoc/Pub4
FAX Number: (850) 718-2388 Calendar System: Semester
URL: www.chipola.edu
Established: 1947 Annual Undergrad Tuition & Fees (In-District): $3,000
Enrollment: 2,294 Coed
Affiliation or Control: State/Local IRS Status: 501(c)3
Highest Offering: Baccalaureate
Program: Occupational; 2-Year Principally Bachelor's Creditable
Accreditation: SC

01 President .... Dr. Gene PROUGH
05 Sr VP Instructional/Student Svcs .... Dr. Sarah CLEMMONS
10 Vice President of Finance .... Mr. Steve YOUNG
32 Vice Pres of Student Affairs .... Dr. Jayne ROBERTS
13 Associate VP Information Systems .... Mr. Dennis F. EVERETT
16 Assoc VP of Human Resources .... Mrs. Karan P. DAVIS
45 Assoc Dean Institutional Dev/Plng .... Mrs. Gail C. HARTZOG
26 Director Public Relations .... Mr. Bryan C. CRAVEN
18 Physical Plant Manager .... Mr. Harry FLEENER
37 Director of Financial Aid .... Mrs. Sybil CLOUD
40 Bookstore Manager .... Mrs. Jennifer MEREDITH
41 Director of Athletics .... Dr. Dale O'DANIEL

City College (I)

853 State Road 436, Suite 200,
Casselberry FL 32707-5365

County: Seminole FICE Identification: 030799
Unit ID: 417327
Telephone: (407) 831-9816 Carnegie Class: Assoc/PrivNFP
FAX Number: (407) 831-1147 Calendar System: Quarter
URL: www.citycollegeorlando.edu
Established: 1997 Annual Undergrad Tuition & Fees: $13,570
Enrollment: 182 Coed
Affiliation or Control: Independent Non-Profit IRS Status: 501(c)3
Highest Offering: Associate Degree
Program: Occupational
Accreditation: ACICS

01 President .... Mrs. Esther FIKE
05 Executive Director .... Mr. Cliff PHILLIPS

City College (J)

2000 W Commercial Boulevard,
Fort Lauderdale FL 33309-1916

County: Broward FICE Identification: 025154
Unit ID: 244233
Telephone: (954) 492-5353 Carnegie Class: Bac/Assoc
FAX Number: (954) 491-1965 Calendar System: Quarter
URL: www.citycollege.edu
Established: 1983 Annual Undergrad Tuition & Fees: $9,850
Enrollment: 2,005 Coed
Affiliation or Control: Independent Non-Profit IRS Status: 501(c)3
Highest Offering: Baccalaureate
Program: Occupational
Accreditation: ACICS

01 President .... Esther FIKE
03 Executive Director .... David (Skip) HIGLEY
36 Director of Career Development .... Sodia ROSE-STEPHENS
05 Director of Education .... Thomas CARPENTER
07 Director of Admissions .... Audrey MANGUM
10 Director of Financial Affairs .... Ginger RUBACK
13 Director of Technologies .... Jeffrey A. CLAYTON
08 Director of Library .... Julia FULLER
06 Registrar .... James THRONE
15 Human Resources Generalist .... Patricia BURKHART
37 Director Student Financial Aid .... Ginger UNGER-RUBACK

City College (K)

7001 NW Fourth Boulevard, Gainesville FL 32607

County: Alachua Identification: 666413
Unit ID: 406547
Telephone: (352) 335-4000 Carnegie Class: Bac/Assoc
FAX Number: (352) 335-4303 Calendar System: Quarter
URL: www.citycollege.edu
Established: 1986 Annual Undergrad Tuition & Fees: $8,735
Enrollment: 280 Coed
Affiliation or Control: Independent Non-Profit IRS Status: 501(c)3
Highest Offering: Baccalaureate
Program: Occupational; 2-Year Principally Bachelor's Creditable

Accreditation: ACICS

01 Executive Director .... Mr. Steve SCHWAB

† Branch campus of City College, Fort Lauderdale, FL.

City College (A)

9300 S Dadeland Blvd, Suite PH, Miami FL 33156
County: Miami-Dade Identification: 666414
Unit ID: 434539
Telephone: (305) 666-9242 Carnegie Class: Bac/Assoc
FAX Number: (305) 666-9243 Calendar System: Quarter
URL: www.citycollege.edu
Established: 1997 Annual Undergrad Tuition & Fees: $14,320
Enrollment: 354 Coed
Affiliation or Control: Independent Non-Profit IRS Status: 501(c)3
Highest Offering: Baccalaureate
Program: Occupational; 2-Year Principally Bachelor's Creditable
Accreditation: ACICS

01 Executive Director .... Ms. Marciela HOWARD
05 Director of Education .... Dr. Mathew ABRAHAM
06 Registrar .... Ms. Donysha GIVENS
07 Director of Admissions .... Ms. Ana HERNANDEZ

† Branch campus of City College, Fort Lauderdale, FL.

Clearwater Christian College (B)

3400 Gulf-to-Bay Boulevard, Clearwater FL 33759-4595
County: Pinellas FICE Identification: 001473
Unit ID: 133085
Telephone: (727) 726-1153 Carnegie Class: Bac/A&S
FAX Number: (727) 723-8566 Calendar System: Semester
URL: www.clearwater.edu
Established: 1966 Annual Undergrad Tuition & Fees: $16,250
Enrollment: 568 Coed
Affiliation or Control: Non-denominational IRS Status: 501(c)3
Highest Offering: Master's
Program: Liberal Arts And General; Teacher Preparatory
Accreditation: SC

01 President .... Dr. Richard A. STRATTON
05 Vice President for Academic Affairs .... Dr. Mary C. DRAPER
10 Vice Pres for Financial Affairs .... Mr. Randy T. LIVINGSTON
30 Vice Pres Institutional Advancement .... Mr. Terry D. WILD
32 Vice President for Student Life .... Mr. Ryan DUPEE
06 Registrar .... Mr. Thomas CANNON
26 Dean of Institutional Advancement .... Mr. Benjamin PUCKETT
35 Dean of Students .... Mr. Todd BARTON
09 Director Institutional Research .... Dr. Mary DRAPER
37 Director of Financial Aid .... Mr. Ryan MCNAMARA
38 Director of Guidance & Career Svcs ... Mrs. Lisa DOLLENMAYER
41 Athletic Director .... Mr. James WHITAKER
29 Alumni Director .... Mr. Benjamin PUCKETT
08 Director of the Library .... Mrs. Elizabether WERNER
50 Chair of Business Studies Division .... Dr. Ian DUNCAN
49 Chair of Humanities Division .... Dr. Dan HURST
73 Chair of Biblical Studies Division .... Dr. Philip BURGGRAFF
53 Chair of Education Division .... Dr. Philip LARSEN
81 Chair of Science Division .... Dr. Jonathan HENRY
57 Chair of Fine Arts Division .... Dr. Craig RALSTON
07 Director of Admissions .... Mr. Brian JOHNSON
15 Director of Human Resources .... Mrs. Vicki LIVINGSTON
21 Accounting Manager .... Mr. Ryan MCCLURE
18 Director of Campus Plant .... Mr. Roy SQUIRES
13 Director of Information Technology .... Mr. Kevin GAULT
19 Chief of Campus Security .... Mr. Richard SCHLOSSER
88 Director of Custodial Services .... Mrs. Kelly MACLEOD
88 Director of Food Service .... Mr. Dennis BURGGRAFF
96 Director of Auxiliary Services .... Mr. Joe VALENTIN

College of Business and Technology (C)

8991 SW 107th Avenue, Suite 200, Miami FL 33176-1412
County: Miami-Dade FICE Identification: 030716
Unit ID: 417318
Telephone: (305) 273-4499 Carnegie Class: Assoc/PrivFP
FAX Number: (305) 270-0779 Calendar System: Semester
URL: www.cbt.edu
Established: 1988 Annual Undergrad Tuition & Fees: $11,500
Enrollment: 436 Coed
Affiliation or Control: Proprietary IRS Status: Proprietary
Highest Offering: Associate Degree
Program: Occupational; 2-Year Principally Bachelor's Creditable; Technical Emphasis
Accreditation: ACICS

01 President .... Mr. Fernando N. LLERENA
03 Executive Director .... Mr. Luis E. LLERENA
05 Regional Director of Education .... Mrs. Gladys P. LLERENA
37 Financial Aid Director .... Mrs. Yazmin PALMA
36 Career Services Director .... Ms. Jakelin MIRANDA
06 Registrar .... Ms. Maria GONZALEZ
07 Director of Admissions .... Mrs. Ivet RIOS
50 Program Director .... Dr. Stephanie ETTER
10 Finance Director .... Ms. Maricel SPEZZACATENA
31 Corporate Director of Public Affair .... Ms. Monica LLERENA
84 Managing Director of Strategy .... Mrs. Ines CANO
85 International Relations Director .... Ms. Veronica VILLEGAS

12 Campus Director .... Mr. Kennedy FERNANDEZ
12 Campus Director .... Mr. Hector DUENAS
12 Campus Director .... Mr. Julian VALDEZ

College of Central Florida (D)

3001 S.W. College Road, Ocala FL 34474
County: Marion FICE Identification: 001471
Unit ID: 132851
Telephone: (352) 237-2111 Carnegie Class: Assoc/Pub-R-L
FAX Number: (352) 873-5847 Calendar System: Semester
URL: www.cf.edu
Established: 1957 Annual Undergrad Tuition & Fees (In-District): $2,956
Enrollment: 8,710 Coed
Affiliation or Control: Local IRS Status: 501(c)3
Highest Offering: Baccalaureate
Program: Occupational; 2-Year Principally Bachelor's Creditable
Accreditation: SC, ADNUR, DA, EMT, PNUR, PTAA

01 Interim President .... Dr. James D. HARVEY
03 Senior Vice President .... Dr. James D. HARVEY
05 Interim VP Instruction .... Dr. Mark PAUGH
30 Vice Pres Institutional Advancement .... Mrs. Joan STEARNS
32 Vice President Student Affairs .... Dr. Timothy WISE
12 Provost/VP Citrus County Campus .... Dr. Vernon LAWTER, JR.
12 Provost Levy Center/Exec Dir Plng .... Mrs. Marilyn LADNER
31 Exec Dir College/Comm Relations .... Dr. Jillian RAMSAMMY
50 Assoc VP for Careers & Tech Educ .... Dr. Cheryl FANTE
49 AVP for Liberal Arts & Sciences .... Dr. Mark PAUGH
08 Dean Learning Resources .... Mr. Richard BAZILE
51 Dir Corp Training/Continuing Educ .... Ms. Donnah ROSS
15 Human Resources Director .... Ms. Gilda CROCKER
37 Director Financial Aid .... Ms. Judy MENADIER
84 Dean Enrollment Management .... Ms. Lyn POWELL
26 Director Marketing/Public Rels .... Dr. Joe WALLACE
09 Director Inst Effectiveness .... Dr. Lawrence KUSZYNSKI
13 Chief Information Officer .... Ms. Kathy ANDERSON
06 Registrar .... Ms. Devona SEWELL
18 Director Facilities .... Mr. Tommy MORELOCK
96 Director of Purchasing .... Mr. Stewart TRAUTMAN
29 Annual Fund/Alumni Devel Coord .... Ms. Pamela CALERO
07 Director of Admissions/Records .... Mrs. Teri LITTLE-BERRY

Concorde Career Institute (E)

7960 Arlington Expressway, Ste 120,
Jacksonville FL 32211-7429
County: Duval FICE Identification: 020896
Unit ID: 133845
Telephone: (904) 725-0525 Carnegie Class: Assoc/PrivFP
FAX Number: (904) 721-9944 Calendar System: Semester
URL: www.concorde.edu
Established: 1988 Annual Undergrad Tuition & Fees: $14,050
Enrollment: 500 Coed
Affiliation or Control: Proprietary IRS Status: Proprietary
Highest Offering: Associate Degree
Program: Occupational
Accreditation: ACCSC, @PTAA, SURGT

01 Campus Director .... Melissa RYAN

Concorde Career Institute (F)

10933 Marks Way, Miramar FL 33025
County: Broward FICE Identification: 022751
Unit ID: 133854
Telephone: (954) 731-8880 Carnegie Class: Not Classified
FAX Number: (954) 484-2961 Calendar System: Other
URL: www.concorde.edu
Established: N/A Annual Undergrad Tuition & Fees: N/A
Enrollment: 380 Coed
Affiliation or Control: Proprietary IRS Status: Proprietary
Highest Offering: Associate Degree
Program: Occupational
Accreditation: ACCSC

01 Campus President .... Dan GRIMM

Concorde Career Institute (G)

4202 West Spruce, Tampa FL 33607-4127
County: Hillsborough FICE Identification: 021727
Unit ID: 133863
Telephone: (813) 874-0094 Carnegie Class: Not Classified
FAX Number: (813) 872-6884 Calendar System: Other
URL: www.concorde.edu
Established: N/A Annual Undergrad Tuition & Fees: N/A
Enrollment: 575 Coed
Affiliation or Control: Proprietary IRS Status: Proprietary
Highest Offering: Associate Degree
Program: Occupational
Accreditation: ACCSC

01 Campus President .... Donna HALLAM

Dade Medical College (H)

3401 NW 7th Street, Miami FL 33125-4013
County: Miami-Dade FICE Identification: 038323
Unit ID: 444574
Telephone: (305) 644-1171 Carnegie Class: Not Classified
FAX Number: (305) 644-1129 Calendar System: Other
URL: www.dademedical.edu
Established: 1999 Annual Undergrad Tuition & Fees: N/A
Enrollment: 1,600 Coed
Affiliation or Control: Proprietary IRS Status: Proprietary
Highest Offering: Associate Degree
Program: 2-Year Principally Bachelor's Creditable; Nursing Emphasis
Accreditation: ABHES, RAD

01 Chief Executive Officer .... Mr. Ernesto PEREZ
10 Chief Financial Officer .... Mr. Chris GRESSETT

Daytona College (I)

425 South Nova Road, Ormond Beach FL 32174-8449
County: Volusia FICE Identification: 039396
Unit ID: 447014
Telephone: (386) 267-0565 Carnegie Class: Assoc/PrivFP
FAX Number: (386) 267-0567 Calendar System: Semester
URL: www.daytonacollege.edu
Established: 1996 Annual Undergrad Tuition & Fees: $9,800
Enrollment: 198 Coed
Affiliation or Control: Proprietary IRS Status: Proprietary
Highest Offering: Associate Degree
Program: Occupational
Accreditation: ACCSC

01 President .... Mr. Roger BRADLEY
05 Director .... Ms. Jo Ann MOORMAN

Daytona State College (J)

PO Box 2811, Daytona Beach FL 32120-2811
County: Volusia FICE Identification: 001475
Unit ID: 133386
Telephone: (386) 506-3000 Carnegie Class: Assoc/Pub4
FAX Number: (386) 506-4489 Calendar System: Semester
URL: www.DaytonaState.edu
Established: 1958 Annual Undergrad Tuition & Fees (In-District): $3,074
Enrollment: 18,820 Coed
Affiliation or Control: Local IRS Status: 501(c)3
Highest Offering: Baccalaureate
Program: Occupational; 2-Year Principally Bachelor's Creditable
Accreditation: SC, ADNUR, DA, DH, EMT, MAC, OTA, PTAA, SURGT

01 Interim President .... Mr. Frank LOMBARDO
03 Executive Vice President .... Mr. Brian T. BABB
05 VP Academic Affairs .... Dr. Michael VITALE
45 VP Planning/Development/Inst Effect .. Dr. Angela M. FALCONETTI
11 VP Administrative Services .... Mr. Peter X. MCCARTHY
13 VP Information Services .... Mr. Roberto LOMBARDO
102 VP Foundation .... Ms. Donna Sue SANDERS
86 VP Governmental Relations .... Ms. Sharon CROW
84 VP Enrollment .... Dr. Thomas LOBASSO
50 VP College of Business Admin .... Dr. Eileen HAMBY
88 VP WDSC-TV and Economic Development ..... Dr. Bob WILLIAMS
15 Assoc VP Human Resources .... Ms. Robin BARR
103 Dean Workforce Development .... Mrs. Mary BRUNO
84 Dean Enrollment Management .... Dr. Richard PASTOR
10 VP Accounting .... Mr. Dennis MICARE
88 Assoc VP Accreditatio/ Compliance .... Dr. Nancy MORGAN
08 Head Librarian .... Ms. Mercedes CLEMENT
88 Director Assessment .... Ms. Janet SLEDGE
17 Assoc VP Col Health Human Pub Svc .... Dr. James GREENE
72 Assoc VP School of Technology .... Dr. Ron EAGLIN
08 Assoc VP/Dir Library & Acad Support ... Dr. Michelle MCCRANEY
53 Assoc VP College of Education .... Ms. Kristy PRESSWOOD
106 Dean Col of Online Studies .... Dr. Rob SAUM
88 Assoc VP Alternative Services .... Ms. Judy CAMPBELL
64 Interim AVP Mike Curb Col Arts/Sci .... Ms. Susan PATE
32 Dean of Students .... Mr. Keith KENNEDY
18 Director Facilities Planning .... Mr. Steven ECKMAN
09 Assoc VP Institutional Research .... Ms. Susan ANTILLON
37 Director Financial Aid .... Ms. Aileen MORRISSEY
41 Dean Athletics .... Mr. Will DUNNE
19 Director Campus Safety .... Mr. Bill TILLARD
12 Provost New Smyrna Beach Campus .... Mr. Glynn JOHNSTON
12 Provost DeLand & Deltona Campuses .... Mr. Bill WETHERELL
12 Provost Flagler/Palm Coast Campus .... Mr. Kent RYAN
43 College Counsel .... Mr. Brian BABB
88 Director Ctr for Business/Industry .... Mr. Frank MERCER
35 Asst Dean Student Activities .... Mr. Bruce COOK
96 Assoc VP Purch & Business Svcs .... Ms. Janet PARISH
38 Director Academic Advising .... Ms. LeeAnn DAVIS
07 Director Admissions/Recruitment .... Ms. Karen SANDERS
21 Assoc VP Accounting .... Ms. Cass FOWLER
06 Director Student Accounts .... Ms. Amy IVERSON

DeVry University - Fort Lauderdale (K)

600 Corporate Drive, Suite 200,
Ft. Lauderdale FL 33334-3603
County: Broward Identification: 666525
Telephone: (954) 938-3083 Carnegie Class: Not Classified
FAX Number: (954) 938-7446 Calendar System: Semester
URL: www.devry.edu
Established: 1931 Annual Undergrad Tuition & Fees: $15,294
Enrollment: 322 Coed
Affiliation or Control: Proprietary IRS Status: Proprietary
Highest Offering: Master's
Program: Professional; Business Emphasis
Accreditation: &NH

01 Center Dean .... Antoinette CUPPARI

† Regional accreditation is carried under the parent institution in Downers Grove, IL.

DeVry University - Jacksonville (A)

5200 Belfort Road, Suite 175, Jacksonville FL 32256-6040
County: Duval Identification: 666527
Telephone: (904) 367-4942 Carnegie Class: Not Classified
FAX Number: (904) 731-4121 Calendar System: Semester
URL: www.devry.edu
Established: 1931 Annual Undergrad Tuition & Fees: $15,294
Enrollment: 247 Coed
Affiliation or Control: Proprietary IRS Status: Proprietary
Highest Offering: Master's
Program: Professional; Business Emphasis
Accreditation: &NH

01 Campus Director .... Abel OKAGBARE

† Regional accreditation is carried under the parent institution in Downers Grove, IL.

DeVry University - Miami Center (B)

8700 W Flagler St., Suite 100, Miami FL 33174-2535
County: Miami-Dade Identification: 666197
Unit ID: 438762
Telephone: (305) 229-4833 Carnegie Class: Not Classified
FAX Number: (305) 221-8887 Calendar System: Semester
URL: www.devry.edu
Established: 1931 Annual Undergrad Tuition & Fees: $15,294
Enrollment: 241 Coed
Affiliation or Control: Proprietary IRS Status: Proprietary
Highest Offering: Master's
Program: Occupational; Professional; Business Emphasis
Accreditation: &NH

01 Center Dean .... David COLE

† Regional accreditation is carried under the parent institution in Downers Grove, IL.

DeVry University - Miramar Campus (C)

2300 SW 145th Avenue, Miramar FL 33027-4150
County: Broward Identification: 666196
Unit ID: 439163
Telephone: (954) 499-9700 Carnegie Class: Master's L
FAX Number: N/A Calendar System: Semester
URL: www.devry.edu
Established: 1931 Annual Undergrad Tuition & Fees: $15,294
Enrollment: 1,577 Coed
Affiliation or Control: Proprietary IRS Status: Proprietary
Highest Offering: Master's
Program: Occupational; Professional; Business Emphasis
Accreditation: &NH, ENGT

01 Metro President .... Mr. Joshua PADRON
37 Director of Student Finance .... Ms. Maria MAURO
05 Associate Provost Curriculum .... Mr. Jesus FERNANDEZ
15 HR Business Partner .... Ms. Maria VALDESPINO
07 Director of Admissions .... Mr. Todd OXENDINE
06 Registrar .... Ms. Susan JENKINS
72 Dean of Technology Programs .... Mr. Raef YASSIN
97 Dean of College of Liberal Arts .... Ms. Tracey ROBINSON
50 Dean of Business & CIS .... Mr. Willie WILBORN
08 Director of Library Services .... Dr. Mary HOWREY
36 Director of Career Services .... Ms. Elizabeth LUGO-MARTINEZ
31 Director of Community Outreach .... Ms. Keisha SMITH

† Regional accreditation is carried under the parent institution in Downers Grove, IL.

DeVry University - Orlando Campus (D)

4000 Millenia Boulevard, Orlando FL 32839-2426
County: Orange Identification: 666112
Unit ID: 439163
Telephone: (407) 345-2800 Carnegie Class: Master's L
FAX Number: (407) 345-2829 Calendar System: Semester
URL: www.devry.com
Established: 1931 Annual Undergrad Tuition & Fees: $15,294
Enrollment: 2,367 Coed
Affiliation or Control: Proprietary IRS Status: Proprietary
Highest Offering: Master's
Program: Occupational; Professional; Business Emphasis
Accreditation: &NH, ENGT

01 Metro President .... Mr. Steve BROWN
08 Director of Library Services .... Ms. Candace KELLER-RABER
10 Dean of Finance/Administration .... Mr. Wes CAMPBELL
32 Manager Student Services .... Mr. Jameer ABASS
07 Director of Admissions .... Ms. Sheryl NICHOLS
05 Dean of Academic Affairs .... Dr. Eddie WACHTER
97 Dean General Education .... Mr. Dusty MADDOX
37 Manager Student Finance .... Mr. Dale THOMAS
15 HR Business Partner .... Ms. Robin HUDSON
36 Director of Career Services .... Ms. Kathleen EMERY
06 Registrar .... Ms. Sheila DIAL
58 Dean of Graduate Studies .... Ms. Carol BULL

† Regional accreditation is carried under the parent institution in Downers Grove, IL.

DeVry University - Orlando North Center (E)

1800 Pembrook Drive, Suite 160, Orlando FL 32810-6372
County: Orange Identification: 666198
Unit ID: 437334
Telephone: (407) 659-0900 Carnegie Class: Not Classified
FAX Number: (407) 659-0901 Calendar System: Semester
URL: www.devry.edu
Established: 1998 Annual Undergrad Tuition & Fees: $15,294
Enrollment: 314 Coed
Affiliation or Control: Proprietary IRS Status: Proprietary
Highest Offering: Master's
Program: Occupational; Professional; Business Emphasis
Accreditation: &NH

01 Center Dean .... Elisabeth SAUTNER

† Regional accreditation is carried under the parent institution in Downers Grove, IL.

DeVry University - Tampa Center (F)

5540 W Executive Dr., Ste. 100, Tampa FL 33609-1002
County: Hillsborough Identification: 666199
Unit ID: 434885
Telephone: (813) 288-8994 Carnegie Class: Not Classified
FAX Number: (813) 288-8980 Calendar System: Semester
URL: www.devry.edu
Established: 1931 Annual Undergrad Tuition & Fees: $15,294
Enrollment: 351 Coed
Affiliation or Control: Proprietary IRS Status: Proprietary
Highest Offering: Master's
Program: Occupational; Professional; Business Emphasis
Accreditation: &NH

01 Campus Dean .... Lynn KOHLER

† Regional accreditation is carried under the parent institution in Downers Grove, IL.

DeVry University - Tampa East (G)

6700 Lakeview Center Drive, Ste 150, Tampa FL 33619-1121
County: Hillsborough Identification: 666528
Telephone: (813) 664-4260 Carnegie Class: Not Classified
FAX Number: (813) 740-2790 Calendar System: Semester
URL: www.devry.edu
Established: 1931 Annual Undergrad Tuition & Fees: $15,294
Enrollment: 402 Coed
Affiliation or Control: Proprietary IRS Status: Proprietary
Highest Offering: Master's
Program: Professional; Business Emphasis
Accreditation: &NH

01 Center Dean .... Nicole BETHUNE-WALKER

† Regional accreditation is carried under the parent institution in Downers Grove, IL.

Digital Media Arts College (H)

5400 Broken Sound Blvd, Suite 100, Boca Raton FL 33487
County: Palm Beach FICE Identification: 041274
Unit ID: 451060
Telephone: (561) 391-1148 Carnegie Class: Bac/Diverse
FAX Number: (561) 998-3430 Calendar System: Semester
URL: www.dmac.edu
Established: 2002 Annual Undergrad Tuition & Fees: $17,460
Enrollment: 393 Coed
Affiliation or Control: Proprietary IRS Status: Proprietary
Highest Offering: Master's
Program: Professional; Fine Arts Emphasis
Accreditation: @SC, ACICS

01 President .... Dr. Alan STUTTS
03 Exec Vice President/Dir of Finance .... Mr. David MURVIN

Dragon Rises College of Oriental Medicine (I)

1000 NE 16th Ave., Building F, Gainesville FL 32601-4557
County: Alachua FICE Identification: 038883
Unit ID: 449481
Telephone: (352) 371-2833 Carnegie Class: Spec/Health
FAX Number: (352) 371-2867 Calendar System: Semester
URL: www.dragonrises.edu
Established: 2001 Annual Undergrad Tuition & Fees: $15,220
Enrollment: 57 Coed
Affiliation or Control: Proprietary IRS Status: Proprietary
Highest Offering: Master's
Program: Professional
Accreditation: ACUP

01 Director .... Mr. Bruce PAGEL
05 Academic Dean .... Mr. Kenney EBERSOLE
23 Clinic Director .... Mr. Jamin NICHOLS
32 Dean of Student Services .... Ms. Ruth HAYES-MORRISON
37 Financial Aid Administrator .... Ms. Kate ELLISON

East West College of Natural Medicine (J)

3808 N Tamiami Trail, Sarasota FL 34234-5362
County: Sarasota FICE Identification: 034297
Unit ID: 439394
Telephone: (941) 355-9080 Carnegie Class: Spec/Health
FAX Number: (941) 355-3243 Calendar System: Quarter
URL: www.ewcollege.org
Established: 1994 Annual Undergrad Tuition & Fees: $14,700
Enrollment: 99 Coed
Affiliation or Control: Proprietary IRS Status: Proprietary
Highest Offering: Master's
Program: Professional
Accreditation: ACUP

01 President/CEO .... Ms. Cynthia O'DONNELL
05 Academic Dean .... Dr. Ellen Catherine COVER
20 Assistant Dean .... Mr. Jonathan D. WALD

Eckerd College (K)

4200 54th Avenue S, Saint Petersburg FL 33711-4700
County: Pinellas FICE Identification: 001487
Unit ID: 133492
Telephone: (727) 867-1166 Carnegie Class: Bac/A&S
FAX Number: (727) 864-1877 Calendar System: 4/1/4
URL: www.eckerd.edu
Established: 1958 Annual Undergrad Tuition & Fees: $34,546
Enrollment: 2,346 Coed
Affiliation or Control: Presbyterian Church (U.S.A.) IRS Status: 501(c)3
Highest Offering: Baccalaureate
Program: Liberal Arts And General
Accreditation: SC

01 President .... Dr. Donald R. EASTMAN, III
05 Exec Vice Pres/Provost/Dean Faculty .... Dr. Betty H. STEWART
10 CFO .... Mr. Christopher P. BRENNAN
03 Vice President .... Dr. Lisa A. METS
30 Vice President Advancement .... Mr. Matthew S. BISSET
51 Vice Pres/Dean of Special Programs .... Dr. James E. DEEGAN
32 Vice Pres/Dean for Student Life .... Dr. James J. ANNARELLI
07 Dean of Admissions & Financial Aid .... Mr. John SULLIVAN
20 Assistant to the Pres Academic Affs .... Dr. Kathryn J. WATSON
26 Exec Dir Marketing/Communication .... Ms. Valerie GLIEM
21 Associate Chief Financial Officer .... Ms. Luz ARCILA
20 Assoc Dean Institutional Effective .... Dr. Suzan HARRISON
30 Assoc VP Advancement .... Mr. Tom SCHNEIDER
88 Academic Director of PEL .... Dr. Margret SKAFTADOTTIR
105 Dir Web/Marketing/Communication .... Mr. Casey PAQUET
27 Director Media Relations .... Ms. Alizza PUNZALAN HALL
88 Director of ASPEC .... Mr. Raymond KULLA
88 Director of CALA .... Dr. Norman SMITH
88 Director of International Education .... Ms. Diane L. FERRIS
85 Dir International Student Programs .... Mr. Olivier DEBURE
13 Dir of Information Tech .... Dr. John A. DUFF
09 Director Institutional Research .... Ms. Sharon GRUBIS
06 Registrar .... Ms. Linda SWINDALL
06 Student Enrollment Manager PEL .... Ms. Lin JORGENSEN
08 Director of Library .... Ms. Jamie W. GILL
38 Director Counseling Center .... Dr. Scott C. STRADER
29 Director Alumni Relations .... Ms. Tanner KENNEDY
19 Director Campus Safety .... Mr. Adam COLBY
36 Director Career Resources .... Ms. Caroline MURPHY
37 Director Financial Aid .... Dr. Pat E. WATKINS
41 Athletic Director .... Dr. Robert FORTOSIS
07 Director of Admission .... Ms. Maria FURTADO
42 Chaplain .... Rev. Doug MCMAHON
88 Director of Sponsored Research .... Vacant
21 Controller .... Ms. Robin SMALLEY
35 Assistant Dean of Student Affairs .... Ms. Lorisa LORENZO
88 Asst Dean Students for Campus Act .... Mr. Fred SABOTA
28 Assoc Dn Stdnt Affs/Dir Mltcltl-Div .... Ms. Lena L. WILFALK
87 Dir Conferences and Summer School .... Ms. Cheryl GOLD

Edison State College (L)

8099 College Parkway, SW, Fort Myers FL 33919-5566
County: Lee FICE Identification: 001477
Unit ID: 133508
Telephone: (239) 489-9300 Carnegie Class: Assoc/Pub4
FAX Number: (239) 489-9103 Calendar System: Semester
URL: www.edison.edu
Established: 1961 Annual Undergrad Tuition & Fees (In-District): $3,469
Enrollment: 17,537 Coed
Affiliation or Control: Local IRS Status: 501(c)3
Highest Offering: Baccalaureate
Program: Occupational; 2-Year Principally Bachelor's Creditable; Liberal Arts And General; Teacher Preparatory; Professional
Accreditation: SC, ADNUR, CVT, DH, EMT, RAD

01 District President .... Dr. Kenneth P. WALKER
10 VP Financial Services .... Ms. Gina DOEBLE

30 Vice President of Development ... Ms. Tracey GALLOWAY
38 Vice President Inst Research ... Dr. Edith PENDLETON
05 Chief Academic Officer ... Dr. Steve ATKINS
12 Pres Charlotte County Campus ... Dr. Patricia LAND
12 Pres Collier County Campus ... Vacant
06 Registrar ... Mrs. Billee SILVA
28 Vice President Human Resources ... Ms. Pamela FAIRFAX
96 Director of Purchasing ... Mrs. Lisa TUDOR
49 Dean Arts & Sciences ... Dr. Robert BEESON
09 Dean Inst Research ... Mr. Kevin COUGHLIN
107 Dean Professional/Tech Studies ... Mr. William ROSHON
66 Dean School of Nursing ... Vacant
32 Dean Student Services ... Ms. Patricia NEWELL
20 Associate Academic Officer ... Dr. Robert BEESON
49 Assoc Dn Arts & Sci/Assoc Acad Ofcr ... Dr. Rodney DENNISON
88 Associate Dean College Prep ... Dr. Eileen DELUCA
29 Director Alumni Relations ... Ms. Barbara WELLS
18 Director Facilities Plant/Mgmt ... Mr. Steve NICE
26 Director of Marketing ... Ms. Catherine BERGERSON
96 Director Student Support Services ... Ms. Paula DAILY
35 Director of Student Life ... Ms. Amy TEPROVICH
88 Director of Student Counseling ... Ms. Jeanette FRITZ
13 Director Technology Services ... Mr. Mark TRASK
62 Campus Dir Lrng Resources Collier ... Mr. Antony VALENTI
62 Campus Dir Lrng Resources Charlotte ... Ms. Mary Ann WALTON
62 Dir Learning Resources Lee ... Mr. William SHULUK

Edward Waters College (A)

1658 Kings Road, Jacksonville FL 32209-6199
County: Duval FICE Identification: 001478
Unit ID: 133526
Telephone: (904) 470-8000 Carnegie Class: Bac/Diverse
FAX Number: (904) 470-8039 Calendar System: Semester
URL: www.ewc.edu
Established: 1866 Annual Undergrad Tuition & Fees: $10,470
Enrollment: 769 Coed
Affiliation or Control: African Methodist Episcopal IRS Status: 501(c)3
Highest Offering: Baccalaureate
Program: Liberal Arts And General
Accreditation: **SC**, IACBE

01 President ... Mr. Nathaniel GLOVER
04 Spec Advisor to the President . Ms. Brenda PRIESTLY-JACKSON
03 Executive Vice President/VPIA ... Dr. Eurmon HERVEY
25 Dir of Title III/Sponsored Programs ... Mrs. Lois M. WASHBURN
88 Executive Business Auditor ... Mr. George DANDELAKE
10 Acting Vice Pres Business & Finance ... Mr. Randolph MITCHELL
32 Vice President Student Affairs ... Dr. James EWERS
05 Vice Pres of Academic Affairs ... Dr. Bertha MINUS
101 Secy of the College/Clerk BOT ... Mrs. Linda FOSTER
06 Registrar ... Mr. Lindsey BARNETTE
08 Director Library Services ... Ms. Vivian BROWN-CARMEN
15 Director Human Resources ... Mr. Michael Q. ROGERS
37 Director Financial Aid ... Ms. Janice NOWAK
88 Dir of Teacher Education ... Dr. Marie SNOW
20 Dean of the Faculty ... Dr. Reuben PERECHI
88 Chair Business Administration ... Dr. Francis IKEOKWU
43 General Counsel ... Mr. Michael FREED
09 Dir Inst Plng/Research & Effectiv ... Mr. Robert PULTZ
88 Director Upward Bound ... Dr. Delacy SANFORD
36 Director Career Planning ... Ms. Helen BRITT
18 Director Physical Plants ... Mr. Larry WILLIAMS
29 Assistant VP Inst Advancement ... Ms. Wanda J. WILLIS
96 Director of Auxiliary Services ... Mr. Anthony RODGERS
07 Director of Admissions ... Mr. Edward ALEXANDER
26 Director Comm & Marketing ... Vacant
88 Director of TRIO ... Dr. Sabrina EDWARDS
31 Director Community Resource Center ... Mrs. Marie HEATH
88 Director of Advising ... Dr. Thelecia WILSON
89 Director of First-Year Experience ... Dr. Mel C. NORWOOD, II
88 Director of FAME ... Mrs. Gladys CLAY
41 Director of Athletics ... Mr. Johnny REMBERT
13 Director of IT and Safety ... Mr. Bernard CHAPPLE

Embry-Riddle Aeronautical University (B)

600 S Clyde Morris Boulevard,
Daytona Beach FL 32114-3900
County: Volusia FICE Identification: 001479
Unit ID: 133553
Telephone: (386) 226-6000 Carnegie Class: Master's M
FAX Number: (386) 226-6459 Calendar System: Semester
URL: www.erau.edu
Established: 1926 Annual Undergrad Tuition & Fees: $28,680
Enrollment: 5,089 Coed
Affiliation or Control: Independent Non-Profit IRS Status: 501(c)3
Highest Offering: Doctorate
Program: Occupational; Liberal Arts And General; Professional
Accreditation: **SC**, AAB, ACBSP, ENG

01 President ... Dr. John P. JOHNSON
05 Exec Vice President and CAO ... Mr. Richard HEIST
10 Vice Pres/Chief Financial Officer ... Mr. Eric B. WEEKES
30 VP of Instititutional Advancement ... Mr. Daniel MONTPLAISIR
15 Vice President Human Resources ... Ms. Irene MCREYNOLDS
32 Dean of Students ... Ms. Sonja TAYLOR
84 Assoc VP Enrollment Management ... Vacant
26 Assistant Director Communications ... Ms. Mary VAN BUREN
37 Director Financial Aid ... Ms. Barbara DRYDEN
09 Director Institutional Research ... Ms. Maria FRANCO
36 Executive Director Career Services ... Ms. Lisa KOLLAR
07 Director UG Admissions ... Mr. Robert J. ADAMS
13 Chief Information Officer ... Ms. Cindy BIXLER
29 Exec Director Alumni Relations ... Ms. Michele BERG
06 Director Records & Registration ... Mrs. Valerie KRUSE
88 Director Univ Veterans Affairs ... Ms. Faith DESLAURIERS
41 Director of Athletics ... Mr. Steven G. RIDDER
28 Director of Diversity Initiatives ... Ms. Cindy OAKLEY-PAULIK
35 Director Student Activities ... Mr. Aaron CLEVENGER
38 Director Student Academic Support ... Mr. Richard NICOLS

Embry-Riddle Aeronautical University-Worldwide (C)

600 S Clyde Morris Boulevard,
Daytona Beach FL 32114-3900
County: Volusia Identification: 666089
Unit ID: 426314
Telephone: (800) 522-6787 Carnegie Class: Spec/Tech
FAX Number: (386) 226-6984 Calendar System: Other
URL: www.erau.edu
Established: 1970 Annual Undergrad Tuition & Fees: $11,160
Enrollment: 16,423 Coed
Affiliation or Control: Independent Non-Profit IRS Status: 501(c)3
Highest Offering: Master's
Program: Occupational; Liberal Arts And General; Professional
Accreditation: **&SC**

01 President ... Dr. John P. JOHNSON
05 Exec Vice President & CAO Worldwide ... Dr. John WATRET
20 Assoc VP Academic Affairs ... Dr. Barry FARBROTHER
84 Assoc VP Mktg & Enrollment Mgmt ... Mr. Bill HAMPTON
45 Assoc VP Institutional Effectivenes ... Ms. Joan MILLER
10 Assoc VP & Chief Business Officer ... Mr. Robert JOST
26 Executive Director of Marketing ... Mr. Mark DIFABIO
09 Director of Institutional Research ... Ms. Maria FRANCO
29 Exec Director Alumni Relations ... Ms. Michele BERG
07 Director of Admissions ... Ms. Linda DAMMER

† Regional accreditation is carried under the parent institution in Daytona Beach, FL.

Everest Institute (D)

530 West 49th Street, Hialeah FL 33012-3605
County: Dade Identification: 666271
Unit ID: 136011
Telephone: (305) 558-9500 Carnegie Class: Assoc/PrivFP
FAX Number: (305) 558-4419 Calendar System: Other
URL: www.everest.edu/hialeah
Established: 1977 Annual Undergrad Tuition & Fees: $22,100
Enrollment: 710 Coed
Affiliation or Control: Proprietary IRS Status: Proprietary
Highest Offering: Associate Degree
Program: Occupational
Accreditation: **ACICS**, MAAB, SURGT

01 President ... Mr. Michael ESCALANTE

† Branch campus of Everest Institute, Miami, FL.

Everest Institute (E)

9020 SW 137th Avenue, Miami FL 33186-1410
County: Miami-Dade FICE Identification: 030032
Unit ID: 409670
Telephone: (305) 386-9900 Carnegie Class: Assoc/PrivFP
FAX Number: (305) 388-1740 Calendar System: Other
URL: www.everest.edu
Established: 1977 Annual Undergrad Tuition & Fees: $15,600
Enrollment: 819 Coed
Affiliation or Control: Proprietary IRS Status: Proprietary
Highest Offering: Associate Degree
Program: 2-Year Principally Bachelor's Creditable
Accreditation: **ACICS**, MAAB, SURGT

01 President ... Darrell RHOTEN
04 Assistant to the President ... Carolina MARTE
05 Academic Dean ... Claudette THOMPSON

Everest Institute (F)

111 NW 183rd Street, Suite 200, Miami FL 33169-4538
County: Miami-Dade FICE Identification: 021218
Unit ID: 135957
Telephone: (305) 949-9500 Carnegie Class: Assoc/PrivFP
FAX Number: (305) 949-7303 Calendar System: Other
URL: www.everest.edu
Established: 1977 Annual Undergrad Tuition & Fees: $15,100
Enrollment: 968 Coed
Affiliation or Control: Proprietary IRS Status: Proprietary
Highest Offering: Associate Degree
Program: Occupational; 2-Year Principally Bachelor's Creditable; Technical Emphasis
Accreditation: **ACICS**, MAAB

01 Campus President ... Peter BASTIONY
05 Academic Dean ... Mike GIACCHINO
07 Director of Admissions ... Kevin WILKINSON
37 Director of Finance ... Angela MACKEY
36 Director of Career Services ... Paul CASTELLANOS
20 Associate Dean ... Rose-Marie MURRAY
06 Registrar ... Tonia SMITH
10 Business Office Manager ... Mauricio ROSAS

Everest University-Brandon Campus (G)

3924 Coconut Palm Drive, Tampa FL 33619-1354
County: Hillsborough Identification: 666416
Unit ID: 260293
Telephone: (813) 621-0041 Carnegie Class: Master's M
FAX Number: (813) 623-5769 Calendar System: Quarter
URL: www.everest.edu
Established: 1890 Annual Undergrad Tuition & Fees: $14,650
Enrollment: 9,932 Coed
Affiliation or Control: Proprietary IRS Status: Proprietary
Highest Offering: Master's
Program: Occupational; 2-Year Principally Bachelor's Creditable; Business Emphasis
Accreditation: **ACICS**, MAC, RAD, SURGT

01 President ... Mr. Todd PEARSON
03 Vice President ... Mr. Rod KIRKWOOD
05 Associate Academic Dean ... Mr. Thomas MOORE-PIZON
04 Assistant to the President ... Ms. Stephanie CORSON
06 Registrar ... Ms. Ingrid ZEKAN
07 Director of Admissions ... Ms. Shandretta POINTER
08 Head Librarian ... Ms. Madeline LOCK
10 Director Student Accounts ... Ms. Courtenay LOPEZ
36 Director Student Placement ... Ms. Millie REED
37 Director Student Financial Aid ... Mr. Michael WERNON
32 Director Student Services ... Ms. Dolly BROWN

† Branch campus of Everest University, Tampa, FL.

Everest University-Jacksonville Campus (H)

8226 Phillips Highway, Jacksonville FL 32256-1240
County: Duval Identification: 666994
Unit ID: 438902
Telephone: (904) 731-4949 Carnegie Class: Assoc/PrivFP4
FAX Number: (904) 731-0599 Calendar System: Quarter
URL: www.everest.edu
Established: 2000 Annual Undergrad Tuition & Fees: $13,200
Enrollment: 1,195 Coed
Affiliation or Control: Proprietary IRS Status: Proprietary
Highest Offering: Master's
Program: Liberal Arts And General; Professional
Accreditation: **ACICS**, MAAB

01 President ... Dr. Peter NEIGLER
04 Assistant to the President ... Ms. Chantel HASSEON
05 Academic Dean for Lanier Programs ... Dr. James ARTLEY
05 Actg Academic Dean Modular Programs ... Dr. James ARTLEY
20 Associate Academic Dean ... Dr. Tameiko ALLEN GRANT
07 Director of Admissions ... Mr. Robin MANNING
36 Director of Career Service ... Ms. Marta ROTH
37 Director Student Financial Aid ... Ms. Cathy KIMBALL
10 Director Student Accounts ... Ms. Donna WILHELM

† Branch campus of Everest University-Pinnellas Campus, Largo, FL.

Everest University-Lakeland Campus (I)

995 E Memorial Boulevard, Suite 110,
Lakeland FL 33801-1919
County: Polk Identification: 666415
Unit ID: 367909
Telephone: (863) 686-1444 Carnegie Class: Bac/Assoc
FAX Number: (863) 688-9881 Calendar System: Quarter
URL: www.everest.edu
Established: 1890 Annual Undergrad Tuition & Fees: $15,600
Enrollment: 750 Coed
Affiliation or Control: Proprietary IRS Status: Proprietary
Highest Offering: Master's
Program: Occupational; Business Emphasis
Accreditation: **ACICS**, MAC

01 President ... Mr. Rod KIRKWOOD
05 Academic Dean ... Mr. Charlie ZARUBA
07 Admissions Director ... Mr. Allen GOFF
36 Career Services Director ... Ms. Carly THOMPSON
37 Student Finance Director ... Ms. Linda WAGNER
10 Business Director ... Ms. Ariel MILLIGAN
08 Librarian ... Ms. Betty MARTINEZ

† Branch campus of Everest University-Pinnellas Campus, Largo, FL.

Everest University-Largo (J)

1199 East Bay Drive, Largo FL 33770-2556
County: Pinellas FICE Identification: 025998
Unit ID: 137810
Telephone: (727) 725-2688 Carnegie Class: Bac/Assoc
FAX Number: (727) 373-4412 Calendar System: Quarter
URL: www.everest.edu
Established: 1890 Annual Undergrad Tuition & Fees: $23,636
Enrollment: 691 Coed
Affiliation or Control: Proprietary IRS Status: Proprietary
Highest Offering: Master's

Program: Occupational; Business Emphasis
Accreditation: ACICS

01 President .... Vacant
05 Chief Academic Officer .... Ms. Mamie ANDREWS
07 Director of Admissions .... Ms. Jill MALONE
07 Director of High School Admissions .... Ms. Theresa AMICO
37 Director of Student Finance .... Mr. Will SCOTT
36 Director of Career Services .... Ms. Carmela NASTASI
10 Business Manager .... Mr. Will SCOTT
08 Librarian .... Ms. Candice PASCUAL
32 Director of Student Services .... Vacant
20 Associate Dean of Academics-Modular .... Vacant
20 Associate Dean of Academic-Linear .... Ms. Heidi DINDIAL-THOMPSON

Everest University-Melbourne Campus (A)

2401 N Harbor City Boulevard, Melbourne FL 32935-6609
County: Brevard — Identification: 666417
Unit ID: 420006
Telephone: (321) 253-2929 — Carnegie Class: Bac/Assoc
FAX Number: (321) 255-2017 — Calendar System: Quarter
URL: www.everest.edu
Established: 1996 — Annual Undergrad Tuition & Fees: $14,328
Enrollment: 896 — Coed
Affiliation or Control: Proprietary — IRS Status: Proprietary
Highest Offering: Master's
Program: Occupational; Business Emphasis
Accreditation: ACICS, MAC

01 President .... Mr. Mark W. JUDGE
05 Academic Dean .... Ms. Jennie LESSER
07 Admissions Director .... Mr. Timothy ALEXANDER
37 Director of Student Finance .... Ms. Ida LISKA
36 Career Plan Placement Director .... Mrs. Catherine MALLOZZI
10 Director of Student Accounts .... Mr. Bryan CAPPS

† Branch campus of Everest University-North Orlando Campus, Orlando, FL.

Everest University-North Orlando Campus (B)

5421 Diplomat Circle, Orlando FL 32810-5674
County: Orange — FICE Identification: 001499
Unit ID: 136288
Telephone: (407) 628-5870 — Carnegie Class: Bac/Assoc
FAX Number: (407) 628-1344 — Calendar System: Quarter
URL: www.everest.edu
Established: 1918 — Annual Undergrad Tuition & Fees: $12,780
Enrollment: 1,609 — Coed
Affiliation or Control: Proprietary — IRS Status: Proprietary
Highest Offering: Master's
Program: Business Emphasis
Accreditation: ACICS, MAC

01 President .... Charlie HARDIMAN
03 Vice President .... Vacant
12 President of Branch Campus .... Louise A. STEINKEOWAY
12 President of Melbourne Branch .... Mark JUDGE
05 Academic Dean .... William FORD
07 Director of Admissions .... Kenny ANDERSON
08 Librarian .... Tamara DUJARDIAN
37 Financial Aid Supervisor .... Linda KAISRLIK
06 Registrar .... Katonia WARREN
36 Director Student Placement .... Danielle THORNTON
10 Chief Business Officer .... Sharon MENDOZA
35 Director Student Service .... Liane PARDO

Everest University-Orange Park (C)

805 Wells Road, Orange Park FL 32073-2301
County: Clay — Identification: 666590
Unit ID: 445434
Telephone: (904) 264-9122 — Carnegie Class: Bac/Assoc
FAX Number: (904) 264-9952 — Calendar System: Quarter
URL: www.everest.edu
Established: 2003 — Annual Undergrad Tuition & Fees: $15,030
Enrollment: 339 — Coed
Affiliation or Control: Proprietary — IRS Status: Proprietary
Highest Offering: Baccalaureate
Program: Business Emphasis
Accreditation: ACICS, MAAB

01 President .... Mr. Bruce JONES
05 Academic Dean .... Mr. Mark CORNETT
37 Director Financial Aid .... Ms. Kristine HIBBARD
32 Director Student Services .... Ms. Dawn SCHAUB

† Branch campus of Everest University, Tampa, FL.

Everest University-Pompano Beach Campus (D)

225 N Federal Highway, Pompano Beach FL 33062
County: Broward — FICE Identification: 008146
Unit ID: 134149
Telephone: (954) 783-7339 — Carnegie Class: Master's S
FAX Number: (954) 943-2547 — Calendar System: Quarter
URL: www.everest.edu
Established: 1940 — Annual Undergrad Tuition & Fees: $19,900
Enrollment: 1,752 — Coed
Affiliation or Control: Proprietary — IRS Status: Proprietary
Highest Offering: Master's
Program: 2-Year Principally Bachelor's Creditable; Professional; Business Emphasis
Accreditation: ACICS, MAAB

01 President .... Mr. Stephen GUIDRY
05 Academic Dean .... Dr. Jeannette SHELDON
07 Director Admissions .... Mr. Martin LEVERT
07 Director Admissions .... Ms. Amanda MCLURE
37 Director Student Finance .... Mr. Todd FOX
06 Registrar .... Ms. Stacey MILLER
20 Associate Academic Dean .... Ms. Latrenda SMALL
36 Director Career Planning/Placement .... Ms. Andrea MITCHELL
08 Librarian .... Ms. Keri ENTERLINE
10 Director Student Accounts .... Mr. Trevor BLOW
04 Admin Assistant to the President .... Ms. Fumiko NYE
32 Director of Student Services .... Mr. Darnell DOVERVAN

Everest University-South Orlando Campus (E)

9200 Southpark Center Loop, Orlando FL 32819-8606
County: Orange — Identification: 666418
Unit ID: 390701
Telephone: (407) 851-2525 — Carnegie Class: Bac/Assoc
FAX Number: (407) 345-8671 — Calendar System: Quarter
URL: www.everest.edu
Established: 1953 — Annual Undergrad Tuition & Fees: $20,000
Enrollment: 1,100 — Coed
Affiliation or Control: Proprietary — IRS Status: Proprietary
Highest Offering: Master's
Program: 2-Year Principally Bachelor's Creditable; Professional; Business Emphasis
Accreditation: ACICS, MAC

01 President .... Mr. John BUCK
10 Vice President of Finance .... Mr. Sami FANEK
05 Dean of Academics .... Dr. M. Brad MILLER
07 Director of Admissions .... Vacant
37 Director of Student Finance .... Ms. Sherri WILLIAMS
88 Director of Student Accounts .... Mr. Jerry THOMPSON
36 Director of Career Services .... Ms. Veena GARIB
32 Director of Student Services .... Mr. Tony GAFFNEY

† Branch campus of Everest University-North Orlando Campus, Orlando, FL.

Everest University-Tampa Campus (F)

3319 W Hillsborough Avenue, Tampa FL 33614-5801
County: Hillsborough — FICE Identification: 001534
Unit ID: 137801
Telephone: (813) 879-6000 — Carnegie Class: Bac/Assoc
FAX Number: (813) 871-2483 — Calendar System: Quarter
URL: www.everest.edu
Established: 1890 — Annual Undergrad Tuition & Fees: $18,720
Enrollment: 1,587 — Coed
Affiliation or Control: Proprietary — IRS Status: Proprietary
Highest Offering: Master's
Program: Occupational; 2-Year Principally Bachelor's Creditable; Professional; Business Emphasis
Accreditation: ACICS, MAC

01 President .... Mr. Thomas M. BARLOW
04 Assistant to the President .... Ms. Maida AVELLANET
05 Academic Dean .... Ms. Theo EGGLESTON
07 Director of Admissions .... Mr. Donnie BROUGHTON
37 Director of Financial Aid .... Mr. Brian JONES
32 Director of Student Services .... Ms. Yolanda WILLIAMS
10 Director of Student Accounts .... Ms. Janet GENAO
20 Associate Academic Dean .... Ms. Dena SEIDEN
06 Lead Registrar .... Ms. Kim LARKIN
08 University Librarian .... Ms. Judith COLE

Everglades University (G)

5002 T-Rex Avenue, Suite 100, Boca Raton FL 33431-4493
County: Palm Beach — FICE Identification: 031085
Unit ID: 385619
Telephone: (888) 772-6077 — Carnegie Class: Bac/Diverse
FAX Number: (561) 912-1191 — Calendar System: Semester
URL: www.evergladesuniversity.edu
Established: 1990 — Annual Undergrad Tuition & Fees: $22,989
Enrollment: 1,161 — Coed
Affiliation or Control: Independent Non-Profit — IRS Status: 501(c)3
Highest Offering: Master's
Program: Professional
Accreditation: SC

01 President/CEO .... Ms. Kristi L. MOLLIS
05 Vice President of Academic Affairs .... Dr. Jayne MOSCHELLA
37 Regional Director of Financial Aid .... Mrs. Seeta SINGH MOONILALL
84 Regional Dir Enrollment Management .... Mrs. Marci TULLY
88 Director of Fundraising .... Vacant
09 Director Inst Effectiveness .... Mr. Chee PIONG
08 Director of Library Services .... Ms. Amanda SARRA
12 Vice President Boca Raton Campus .... Ms. Carla SANOIR
12 Vice President Online Division .... Ms. Sheila KELL
12 Interim Vice President Sarasota .... Ms. Caroline KING
12 Vice President of Orlando Campus .... Ms. Sherry PARKER
20 Dean of Academics Online .... Vacant
20 Dean of Academics Sarasota .... Dr. Christine GRAHAM
20 Dean of Academics Orlando .... Dr. Usha PALANISWAMY
20 Assistant Dean Boca Raton .... Mr. Jared BEZET
07 Director of Admissions Boca .... Mr. Mark SCHILLACI
07 Director of Admissions Online Boca .... Mr. Ron BARONA
07 Director of Admissions Orlando .... Mr. Michael CIMMINO
07 Director of Admission Sarasota .... Mr. John THORPE
04 Assistant to the President .... Ms. Christina OAKLEY
37 Online Financial Aid Director Boca .... Ms. Roxana SPIREA
37 Asst Financial Aid Director Online .... Ms. Fatima FLORES
37 Financial Aid Director Sarasota .... Mrs. Courtney ROBERTSON
37 Financial Aid Director Orlando .... Vacant
37 Asst Financial Aid Director Boca .... Ms. Anne RODNE
06 Head Registrar .... Mr. Adrian KACZOR
06 Registrar Online Division .... Ms. Tanecia NATTO
06 Registrar Boca .... Ms. Shelly PAUL
06 Registrar Orlando .... Ms. Jennifer WILLIAMS
06 Registrar Sarasota .... Ms. Fay HUANG
50 Department Chair of Business .... Vacant
50 Dept Chair of Construction Mgmt .... Mr. William FLUELLEN
88 Department Chair of Aviation .... Mr. Michael FLYNN
76 Department Chair Allied Health .... Ms. Tammy FOGARTY
97 Department Chair General Education .... Vacant
88 Librarian Boca Raton .... Mr. Joseph GREMILLION
88 Librarian Sarasota .... Ms. Ellen TURNER
08 Librarian Orlando .... Mr. Zachary ENGLISH
21 Business Manager .... Vacant
32 Dir of Student Services Online .... Ms. Daneweise JEAN-JOSPEH
32 Dir of Student Services Boca Raton .... Ms. LaTrista FUNCHES
32 Dir of Student Services Sarasota .... Ms. Caroline KING
32 Dir of Student Services Orlando .... Ms. Kayli LEWIS
88 Bursar Online Division .... Ms. Angela SMITH
88 Bursar Online Division .... Ms. Samantha ISAAC
40 Bursar/Bookstore Manager Boca .... Ms. Megan TALBOTT
40 Bookstore Manager Online Division .... Ms. Pamela PETERSON
40 Bursar/Bookstore Manager Sarasota .... Ms. Anita WENDZEL
40 Bursar/Bookstore Manager Orlando .... Ms. Mabel RASMUSSEN
88 Online Trainer .... Mr. Ronnie ABUKHALAF

FastTrain of Ft. Lauderdale (H)

51 North State Road 7, Plantation FL 33317
County: Broward — FICE Identification: 041320
Telephone: (954) 730-8711 — Carnegie Class: Not Classified
FAX Number: (954) 730-8067 — Calendar System: Quarter
URL: www.fasttrain.edu
Established: 1990 — Annual Undergrad Tuition & Fees: $17,150
Enrollment: 88 — Coed
Affiliation or Control: Proprietary — IRS Status: Proprietary
Highest Offering: Associate Degree
Program: Occupational
Accreditation: ACICS

01 Director .... Mr. Elliot LOPEZ

FastTrain of Jacksonville (I)

10752 Deerwood Park Blvd S, Ste 201, Jacksonville FL 32256
County: Duval — FICE Identification: 041322
Telephone: (904) 265-3278 — Carnegie Class: Not Classified
FAX Number: (904) 265-3283 — Calendar System: Quarter
URL: www.fasttrain.edu
Established: 1990 — Annual Undergrad Tuition & Fees: $17,150
Enrollment: 130 — Coed
Affiliation or Control: Proprietary — IRS Status: Proprietary
Highest Offering: Associate Degree
Program: Occupational
Accreditation: ACICS

FastTrain of Miami (J)

5555 West Flagler Street, Miami FL 33134
County: Miami-Dade — FICE Identification: 041319
Telephone: (305) 262-4748 — Carnegie Class: Not Classified
FAX Number: (305) 261-2544 — Calendar System: Quarter
URL: www.fasttrain.edu
Established: 1990 — Annual Undergrad Tuition & Fees: $17,150
Enrollment: 48 — Coed
Affiliation or Control: Proprietary — IRS Status: Proprietary
Highest Offering: Associate Degree
Program: Occupational
Accreditation: ACICS

01 Director .... Ms. Ana COLLADO

FastTrain of Tampa (K)

2156 University Square Mall, Tampa FL 33612
County: Hillsborough — FICE Identification: 041321
Telephone: (813) 874-0660 — Carnegie Class: Not Classified
FAX Number: (813) 874-0662 — Calendar System: Quarter
URL: www.fasttrain.edu
Established: 1990 — Annual Undergrad Tuition & Fees: $17,150
Enrollment: 37 — Coed
Affiliation or Control: Proprietary — IRS Status: Proprietary
Highest Offering: Associate Degree

Program: Occupational
Accreditation: ACICS

01 Campus Director .... Mr. Jose GONZALES

Flagler College (A)

74 King Street, Saint Augustine FL 32084-4342
County: Saint Johns FICE Identification: 007893
Unit ID: 133711
Telephone: (904) 829-6481 Carnegie Class: Bac/Diverse
FAX Number: (904) 824-6017 Calendar System: Semester
URL: www.flagler.edu
Established: 1968 Annual Undergrad Tuition & Fees: $14,510
Enrollment: 13,860 Coed
Affiliation or Control: Independent Non-Profit IRS Status: 501(c)3
Highest Offering: Baccalaureate
Program: Liberal Arts And General; Teacher Preparatory; Business Emphasis
Accreditation: SC, @TEAC

01 President .... Dr. William T. ABARE, JR.
00 Chancellor .... Dr. William L. PROCTOR
10 Vice President Business Services .... Mr. Kenneth S. RUSSOM
30 Vice President Inst Advancement .... Mr. Mark WHITTAKER
05 Dean Academic Affairs .... Dr. Alan WOOLFOLK
26 Exec Director College Relations .... Ms. Donna DELORENZO
21 Executive Director of Finance .... Ms. Pamela F. LEYDON
09 Director Inst Research & Planning .... Dr. Randi HAGEN
27 Director of Public Information .... Mr. Brian L. THOMPSON
84 Vice President for Enrollment Mgmt .... Mr. Marc G. WILLIAR
32 Dean of Student Services .... Mr. Daniel P. STEWART
20 Associate Dean of Academic Affairs .... Mr. Yvan J. KELLY
35 Assistant Dean of Student Services .... Dr. Dirk HIBLER
38 Associate Dean of Counseling .... Dr. Glenn GOLDBERG
06 Registrar .... Mrs. Miriam C. ROBERSON
37 Director of Financial Aid .... Mr. Christopher D. HAFFNER
36 Director of Career Services .... Vacant
08 Director of Library Services .... Mr. Michael A. GALLEN
41 Director Intercollegiate Athletics .... Mr. Jud DAMON
19 Director of Safety & Security .... Mr. Kerry DAVIS
40 Bookstore Manager .... Mr. Bob SMITH
24 Director Educational Media Services .... Mr. Steven I. SKIPP
13 Director Technology Services .... Mr. Joseph S. PROVENZA
39 Director of Residence Life .... Ms. Rachel T. GREEN
35 Director of Student Activities .... Ms. Carley JAMES
12 Dean Flagler College - Tallahassee .... Vacant
88 Dir of Disability Services .... Ms. Eva Lynn FRANCISCO
18 Superintendent of Plant & Grounds .... Mr. Victor CHENEY
04 Assistant to the President .... Ms. Mary Jane DILLON
21 Director of Business Services .... Mr. Larry D. WEEKS
29 Director Alumni Relations .... Ms. Margo BROWN
44 Director Annual Fund .... Mr. Jeffrey DAVITT
15 Human Resource Analysis .... Ms. Tricia KRISTOFF
31 Director of College Relations .... Ms. Laura STEVENSON
88 Senior Woman Admin Athletic Dept .... Ms. Taylor MOTT

Florida Career College (B)

410 Park Place Boulevard, Clearwater FL 33759-3924
County: Pinellas FICE Identification: 025862
Unit ID: 364885
Telephone: (727) 724-1037 Carnegie Class: Not Classified
FAX Number: (727) 723-7630 Calendar System: Other
URL: www.careercollege.edu
Established: 2006 Annual Undergrad Tuition & Fees: $16,744
Enrollment: 265 Coed
Affiliation or Control: Proprietary IRS Status: Proprietary
Highest Offering: Associate Degree
Program: Occupational
Accreditation: COE

01 Chief Executive Officer .... Mr. Julio SOCORRO
03 Executive Director .... Mr. Samuel HUTKIN

Florida Career College (C)

3750 West 18th Avenue, Hialeah FL 33012-7028
County: Miami-Dade Identification: 666624
Telephone: (305) 825-3231 Carnegie Class: Not Classified
FAX Number: (305) 825-3436 Calendar System: Other
URL: www.careercollege.edu
Established: 2006 Annual Undergrad Tuition & Fees: N/A
Enrollment: N/A Coed
Affiliation or Control: Proprietary IRS Status: Proprietary
Highest Offering: Baccalaureate
Program: Occupational; 2-Year Principally Bachelor's Creditable
Accreditation: ACICS

01 Executive Director .... Mr. Silvio D. FRYDMAN

Florida Career College (D)

3383 North State Road 7,
Lauderdale Lakes FL 33319-5617
County: Broward Identification: 666622
Telephone: (954) 733-7551 Carnegie Class: Not Classified
FAX Number: (954) 733-7558 Calendar System: Other
URL: www.careercollege.edu
Established: 1982 Annual Undergrad Tuition & Fees: N/A
Enrollment: N/A Coed
Affiliation or Control: Proprietary IRS Status: Proprietary
Highest Offering: Baccalaureate
Program: Occupational; 2-Year Principally Bachelor's Creditable
Accreditation: ACICS

01 Executive Director .... Mr. Gilbert DELGADO

Florida Career College (E)

1321 SW 107th Avenue, Suite 201B,
Miami FL 33174-2521
County: Miami-Dade FICE Identification: 023058
Unit ID: 133997
Telephone: (305) 553-6065 Carnegie Class: Assoc/PrivFP4
FAX Number: (305) 225-0128 Calendar System: Quarter
URL: www.careercollege.edu
Established: 1982 Annual Undergrad Tuition & Fees: $17,100
Enrollment: 3,958 Coed
Affiliation or Control: Proprietary IRS Status: Proprietary
Highest Offering: Baccalaureate
Program: Occupational; 2-Year Principally Bachelor's Creditable; Technical Emphasis
Accreditation: ACICS

01 President/CEO .... Mr. David KNOBEL
03 Executive Director .... Ms. Erica MATTHEW
88 Associate Executive Director .... Mr. Eduardo SAMA
88 Associate Executive Director .... Ms. Muriel GUTIERREZ
88 Area Executive Director .... Mr. Gilbert DELGADO
88 Area Executive Director .... Mr. Michael SCHWAM
05 Director of Education .... Mr. Anthony RICHIEZ
37 Financial Aid Director .... Ms. Vanessa ALFARO
06 Registrar .... Ms. Jessica RIVERA
07 Director of Admission .... Ms. Heidi CRUZ

Florida Career College (F)

7891 Pines Boulevard, Pembroke Pines FL 33024-6916
County: Broward Identification: 666025
Telephone: (954) 965-7272 Carnegie Class: Not Classified
FAX Number: (954) 983-2707 Calendar System: Quarter
URL: www.careercollege.edu
Established: 1982 Annual Undergrad Tuition & Fees: $15,250
Enrollment: 895 Coed
Affiliation or Control: Proprietary IRS Status: Proprietary
Highest Offering: Baccalaureate
Program: Occupational; 2-Year Principally Bachelor's Creditable
Accreditation: ACICS

01 Executive Director .... Dr. Gilbert DELGADO
05 Director of Education .... Mr. Max ANER
26 Vice Pres Communication .... Mr. Peter LUNDBERG

Florida Christian College (G)

1011 Bill Beck Boulevard, Kissimmee FL 34744-5301
County: Osceola FICE Identification: 021567
Unit ID: 132879
Telephone: (407) 847-8966 Carnegie Class: Spec/Faith
FAX Number: (321) 206-2007 Calendar System: Semester
URL: www.fcc.edu
Established: 1976 Annual Undergrad Tuition & Fees: $13,272
Enrollment: 325 Coed
Affiliation or Control: Independent Non-Profit IRS Status: 501(c)3
Highest Offering: Baccalaureate
Program: 2-Year Principally Bachelor's Creditable; Teacher Preparatory; Professional; Religious Emphasis
Accreditation: SC, BI

01 President .... Mr. William BEHRMAN
03 Exec Vice President .... Dr. Terry ALLCORN
10 Chief Financial Officer .... Mrs. Ann BEEKMAN
43 General Counsel .... Dr. David PETERS
05 Vice President Academics .... Dr. Brian SMITH
06 Registrar .... Mrs. Diane ADAMS
08 Librarian .... Mrs. Linda STARK
07 Director of Admissions .... Mrs. Kellie SPENCER
18 Executive Director of Operations .... Mr. Paul PEPPARD
35 Executive Director of Student Life .... Mrs. Sandra PEPPARD
37 Director of Financial Aid .... Mr. Bryce FOULKE
21 Director of Financial Reporting .... Vacant
15 Director of Human Resources .... Mrs. Eileen ADAMS
13 Director of Information Technology .... Mr. Glenn FEASTER
09 Director of Institutional Research .... Mr. Bruce DUSTERHOFT
105 Director of Online Development .... Mr. James BYRD
88 Director of Special Events .... Mrs. Glinda CAMERON
41 Athletic Director .... Mr. Bryce BOW
39 Residence Director .... Mr. Robert MEHLENBACHER
29 Alumni Director .... Mr. Alan TISON
04 Exec Assistant to the President .... Mrs. Nancy BRADDS
04 Assistant to the President .... Mr. Mark DURBIN

Florida Coastal School of Law (H)

8787 Baypine, Jacksonville FL 32256-8528
County: Duval FICE Identification: 033743
Unit ID: 434715
Telephone: (904) 680-7700 Carnegie Class: Spec/Law
FAX Number: (904) 680-7777 Calendar System: Semester
URL: www.fcsl.edu
Established: 1995 Annual Graduate Tuition & Fees: $36,889
Enrollment: 1,748 Coed
Affiliation or Control: Proprietary IRS Status: Proprietary
Highest Offering: First Professional Degree; No Undergraduates
Program: Professional
Accreditation: LAW

01 Dean & Professor of Law .... Mr. C. Peter GOPLERUD
05 Vice Dean .... Mrs. Teresa H. DAVLANTES
10 Vice Pres Finance & Administration .... Mr. Bruce WILSON
30 Dir of Institutional Advancement .... Mrs. Margaret DEES
20 Associate Dean Academic Affairs .... Mrs. Rosa L. DUBOSE
32 Assistant Dean of Students .... Mr. Thomas TAGGART
08 Professor/Director of Law Library .... Mrs. Alma (Nickie) SINGLETON
04 Assistant to the Dean .... Ms. Denise SACCO
36 Director of Career Services .... Mrs. Ellen SEFTON
06 Registrar .... Ms. Bridgette WAINES
37 Director Financial Aid .... Mr. Roger COLLINS
14 Director Information Technology .... Mr. Mark SABATTINI
26 Asst Dir Marketing/Communications .... Mr. Brooks TERRY
15 Director of Human Resources .... Mrs. Stacie SMITH
18 Facilities Manager .... Mr. Jay LEHMANN
20 Assistant Dean of Academic Affairs .... Ms. Bethany REICH

Florida College (I)

119 N Glen Arven Avenue,
Temple Terrace FL 33617-5578
County: Hillsborough FICE Identification: 001482
Unit ID: 133809
Telephone: (813) 988-5131 Carnegie Class: Bac/Assoc
FAX Number: (813) 899-6772 Calendar System: Semester
URL: www.floridacollege.edu
Established: 1944 Annual Undergrad Tuition & Fees: $13,180
Enrollment: 478 Coed
Affiliation or Control: Independent Non-Profit IRS Status: 501(c)3
Highest Offering: Baccalaureate
Program: Liberal Arts And General; Religious Emphasis
Accreditation: SC, MUS

01 President .... Dr. Harry E. PAYNE, JR.
05 Vice Pres of Acad & Student Affairs .... Dr. Douglas H. NORTHCUTT
20 Dean of Academics .... Dr. Daniel W. PETTY
32 Dean of Student Services .... Dr. Brian CRISPELL
10 Chief Business Officer .... Mr. Ronnie STACKPOLE
37 Director Student Financial Aid .... Mrs. Lisa MCCLISTER
84 Director of Enrollment Management .... Mr. Paul CASEBOLT
09 Director of Institutional Research .... Dr. M. Thaxter DICKEY
06 Registrar .... Ms. Beth A. GRANT
44 Director of Planned Giving .... Mr. Douglas R. NERLAND
08 Director of Library .... Mrs. Wanda DICKEY
90 Director of Academic Computing .... Mr. M. Ray HINDS
91 Director of Information Technology .... Mr. William J. MCKINNEY
30 Director Institutional Development .... Mr. Douglas R. NERLAND
26 Director of Alumni/Public Relations .... Mr. Ralph R. WALKER, JR.
27 Director of Marketing .... Mr. Jared BARR
40 Manager of Bookstore .... Mr. Jeff NUNLEY

Florida College of Integrative Medicine (J)

7100 Lake Ellenor Drive, Orlando FL 32809-5721
County: Orange FICE Identification: 032383
Unit ID: 434441
Telephone: (407) 888-8689 Carnegie Class: Spec/Health
FAX Number: (407) 888-8211 Calendar System: Semester
URL: www.fcim.edu
Established: 1990 Annual Undergrad Tuition & Fees: $15,125
Enrollment: 135 Coed
Affiliation or Control: Proprietary IRS Status: Proprietary
Highest Offering: Master's; No Lower Division
Program: Professional
Accreditation: ACUP

01 President .... Mr. Larry LAN
03 Vice President .... Ms. Jenjen HAN
11 Chief Administrative Officer .... Mr. Robert P. LYNCH
05 Academic Dean .... Dr. Lin CHAI

Florida College of Natural Health (K)

616 67th Street Circle East, Bradenton FL 34208-6087
County: Sarasota Identification: 666830
Unit ID: 438294
Telephone: (941) 744-1244 Carnegie Class: Assoc/PrivFP
FAX Number: (941) 744-1242 Calendar System: Other
URL: www.fcnh.com
Established: 1998 Annual Undergrad Tuition & Fees: N/A
Enrollment: 205 Coed
Affiliation or Control: Proprietary IRS Status: Proprietary
Highest Offering: Associate Degree
Program: Occupational
Accreditation: ACCSC, COMTA

01 Director .... Mrs. Ronnie FULTON

† Branch campus of Florida College of Natural Health, Pompano Beach, FL.

Florida College of Natural Health (L)

2600 Lake Lucien Drive, Suite 240,
Maitland FL 32751-7253
County: Seminole Identification: 666513
Unit ID: 438285

Telephone: (407) 261-0319 Carnegie Class: Assoc/PrivFP
FAX Number: (407) 261-0342 Calendar System: Other
URL: www.fcnh.com
Established: 1995 Annual Undergrad Tuition & Fees: $21,990
Enrollment: 437 Coed
Affiliation or Control: Proprietary IRS Status: Proprietary
Highest Offering: Associate Degree
Program: Occupational
Accreditation: ACCSC, COMTA

01 Director .... Ms. Stephanie DUCKSWORTH

† Branch campus of Florida College of Natural Health, Pompano Beach, FL.

Florida College of Natural Health (A)

7925 NW 12th Street, #201, Miami FL 33126-1821
County: Miami-Dade Identification: 666514
Unit ID: 420103
Telephone: (305) 597-9599 Carnegie Class: Assoc/PrivFP
FAX Number: (305) 597-9110 Calendar System: Other
URL: www.fcnh.com
Established: 1993 Annual Undergrad Tuition & Fees: N/A
Enrollment: 228 Coed
Affiliation or Control: Proprietary IRS Status: Proprietary
Highest Offering: Associate Degree
Program: Occupational
Accreditation: ACCSC, COMTA

01 Campus Director .... Ms. Debra STARR-COHEN

† Branch campus of Florida College of Natural Health, Pompano Beach, FL.

Florida College of Natural Health (B)

2001 W Sample Road, #100,
Pompano Beach FL 33064-1342
County: Broward FICE Identification: 030086
Unit ID: 387925
Telephone: (954) 975-6400 Carnegie Class: Assoc/PrivFP
FAX Number: (954) 975-9633 Calendar System: Other
URL: www.fcnh.com
Established: 1986 Annual Undergrad Tuition & Fees: $11,720
Enrollment: 433 Coed
Affiliation or Control: Proprietary IRS Status: Proprietary
Highest Offering: Baccalaureate
Program: Occupational
Accreditation: ACCSC, COMTA

01 President .... Mr. Stephen LAZARUS
10 Controller .... Ms. Barbara KRANE
03 Vice President of Compliance .... Ms. Melissa WADE
05 Vice President of Education .... Ms. Dawnette CABALUNA

Florida Gateway College (C)

149 SE College Place, Lake City FL 32025-2007
County: Columbia FICE Identification: 001501
Unit ID: 135160
Telephone: (386) 752-1822 Carnegie Class: Assoc/Pub-R-M
FAX Number: (386) 755-1521 Calendar System: Semester
URL: www.fgc.edu
Established: 1947 Annual Undergrad Tuition & Fees (In-State): $2,924
Enrollment: 3,032 Coed
Affiliation or Control: State IRS Status: 501(c)3
Highest Offering: Associate Degree
Program: Occupational; 2-Year Principally Bachelor's Creditable; Liberal Arts And General; Teacher Preparatory; Nursing Emphasis
Accreditation: SC, ADNUR, EMT, PTAA

01 President .... Dr. Charles W. HALL
05 Vice Pres Instruction/Student Svcs .... Mr. Charles CARROLL
10 Vice President Business Services .... Ms. Marilyn HAMM
04 Assistant to the President .... Ms. Karyn CONGRESSI
49 Dean of Arts & Sciences .... Dr. Brian DOPSON
75 Dean of Occupational Programs .... Ms. Tracy HICKMAN
32 Dean Student Services .... Dr. Linda CROLEY
14 Exec Dir Info Technology/CIO .... Mr. Mike DAVIS
47 Exec Dir of Industrial & Agricult .... Mr. John PIERSOL
13 Exec Dir Library & Community Svcs .... Mr. Jim MORRIS
53 Exec Dir Teacher Prep Academy .... Ms. Pamela CARSWELL
102 Executive Director Foundation .... Mr. Mike LEE
26 Exec Dir Media & Community Info .... Mr. Mike MCKEE
37 Director Financial Aid .... Mrs. Debberin TUNSIL
84 Director Enrollment Management .... Ms. Sandra JOHNSTON
15 Director Human Resources .... Ms. Sharon BEST
06 Registrar .... Ms. Gayle HUNTER
21 Director Business Services .... Mr. Van SMITHEY
66 Director Nursing Programs .... Ms. Mattie JONES
25 Director of Grants .... Dr. Laurel SEMMES
09 Director of Research/Institutional .... Ms. Patty ANDERSON
18 Chief Facilities/Physical Plant .... Mr. George SCOTT
96 Director of Purchasing .... Mr. Bill BROWN
36 Director Advising/Student Dev .... Dr. Margaret MCLAUGHLIN
88 Dir Banner Center for Water Resourc .... Mr. Tim ATKINSON

Florida Hospital College of Health Sciences (D)

671 Winyah Drive, Orlando FL 32803-1204
County: Orange FICE Identification: 031155
Unit ID: 133872
Telephone: (407) 303-9798 Carnegie Class: Spec/Health
FAX Number: (407) 303-9408 Calendar System: Trimester
URL: www.fhchs.edu
Established: 1992 Annual Undergrad Tuition & Fees: $10,030
Enrollment: 2,741 Coed
Affiliation or Control: Seventh-day Adventist IRS Status: 501(c)3
Highest Offering: Master's
Program: Occupational; 2-Year Principally Bachelor's Creditable; Professional
Accreditation: SC, ADNUR, ANEST, DMS, MT, NMT, NUR, OTA, RAD

01 President .... Dr. David E. GREENLAW
05 Sr VP for Academic Administration .... Dr. Donald E. WILLIAMS
10 Sr VP for Finance/CFO .... Mr. Robert A. CURREN
11 VP for Operations .... Mr. Ruben O. MARTINEZ
32 VP for Student Services .... Mr. Stephen H. ROCHE
26 VP Marketing & Public Relations .... Mr. Lewis HENDERSHOT
106 VP for Educational Tech/Distance Ed .... Dr. Dan LIM
20 Associate VP for Academic Admin .... Dr. Len ARCHER
09 Dir of Accreditation & Inst Effect .... Dr. Roy LUKMAN
37 Director of Financial Aid .... Mrs. Starr S. BENDER
06 Registrar .... Dr. Janet CALDERON
45 Dir of Grant Management .... Ms. Stefanie JOHNSON
88 Director Ctr for Acad Achievement .... Ms. Yvette C. SALIBA
08 Library Director .... Ms. Deanna L. FLORES
42 Campus Chaplain .... Mr. Reynold ACOSTA
07 Director of Enrollment Services .... Mrs. Katie R. SHAW
21 Chief Accountant .... Mr. Grayson GOODMAN
39 Director of Residence Hall .... Mr. David A. BRYANT
30 Development Officer .... Mr. Eddie D. BRAGA
16 Director of Human Resources .... Mr. Fred W. STEPHENS
13 Director of Information Technology .... Mrs. Fely A. RUGLESS
04 Executive Asst to the President .... Mrs. Dawn H. CREFT

Florida Institute of Technology (E)

150 W University Boulevard, Melbourne FL 32901-6975
County: Brevard FICE Identification: 001469
Unit ID: 133881
Telephone: (321) 674-8000 Carnegie Class: DRU
FAX Number: (321) 984-8461 Calendar System: Semester
URL: www.fit.edu
Established: 1958 Annual Undergrad Tuition & Fees: $34,990
Enrollment: 8,985 Coed
Affiliation or Control: Independent Non-Profit IRS Status: 501(c)3
Highest Offering: Doctorate
Program: Liberal Arts And General; Teacher Preparatory; Professional; Technical Emphasis
Accreditation: SC, AAB, CLPSY, CS, ENG

01 President .... Dr. Anthony J. CATANESE
04 Exec Asst to Pres & Ombudsman .... Mrs. Suzee S. LOUCHE
05 Executive Vice Pres & COO .... Dr. T. Dwayne MCCAY
30 Sr Vice Pres/Chief Development Ofcr .... Dr. Kenneth STACKPOOLE
10 Sr Vice Pres Financial Affairs/CFO .... Dr. Robert E. NIEBUHR
10 Sr Vice Pres Management Services .... Mr. Jack ARMUL
88 Dean College of Aeronautics .... Capt. Winston SCOTT
50 Dean College of Business .... Dr. S. Ann BECKER
54 Dean College of Engineering .... Dr. Frederic HAME
83 Dean Col of Psychology/Liberal Arts .... Dr. Mary Beth KENKEL
49 Dean College Science .... Dr. Hamid RASSOUL
08 Dean of Libraries .... Dr. Celine LANG
20 Sr Vice Pres Academic Affairs .... Dr. Gordon NELSON
88 Vice Pres Strategic Initiatives .... Dr. Clifford R. BRAGDON
46 Vice President Research .... Mr. Frank KINNEY
21 Vice Pres/Fin Planning & Control .... Mr. Richard RUMMEL
32 Vice President Student Affairs .... Dr. Randall L. ALFORD
27 Vice Pres Marketing & Communication .... Mr. Wesley SUMNER
88 Vice Pres Support Services .... Dr. Joni OGLESBY
106 Dean Online/Assoc Vice Pres .... Dr. Mary BONHOMME
84 Assoc Vice Pres Enrollment Mgmt .... Mr. Gary HAMME
13 Interim Assoc Vice Pres/CIO .... Dr. Richard NEWMAN
86 Asst Vice Pres Inst Compliance .... Dr. Monica BALOGA
35 Asst VP Student Affs/Dean of Stdnt .... Mr. Rodney BOWERS
29 Asst VP Alum Rel/Exec Dir Alum Assn .... Mr. Bino CAMPANINI
06 Registrar .... Ms. Charlotte YOUNG
88 Director Academic Support Services .... Mr. Rodd NEWCOMBE
41 Director Athletics .... Mr. William K. JURGENS
19 Director Campus Security .... Mr. Kevin GRAHAM
36 Director Career Services .... Ms. Dona E. GAYNOR
38 Dir Counseling/Psychological Svcs .... Dr. Robyn TAPLEY
88 Director Creative Services .... Ms. Judi E. TINTERA
88 Dir Environ & Regulatory Compliance .... Mr. Greg PEEBLES
18 Director Facilities Operations .... Mr. John M. MILBOURNE
37 Director Financial Aid .... Mr. Jay LALLY
88 Director Funk Ctr for Textile Arts .... Ms. Carla FUNK
07 Assoc Director Graduate Admissions .... Ms. Cheryl-Ann BROWN
07 Director Grad Adm Online Learning .... Ms. Carolyn P. FARRIOR
58 Director Graduate Programs .... Ms. Rosemary LAYNE
85 Director Intl Students/Scholar Svcs .... Ms. Judith BROOKE
09 Director Institutional Research .... Ms. Leslie L. SAVOIE
07 Director Undergraduate Admission .... Mr. Michael PERRY

Florida Keys Community College (F)

5901 College Road, Key West FL 33040-4397
County: Monroe FICE Identification: 001485
Unit ID: 133960
Telephone: (305) 296-9081 Carnegie Class: Assoc/Pub-R-S
FAX Number: (305) 292-5155 Calendar System: Trimester
URL: www.fkcc.edu
Established: 1963 Annual Undergrad Tuition & Fees (In-District): $3,574
Enrollment: 1,937 Coed
Affiliation or Control: State/Local IRS Status: 501(c)3
Highest Offering: Associate Degree
Program: Occupational; 2-Year Principally Bachelor's Creditable; Fine Arts Emphasis
Accreditation: SC

01 President .... Dr. Lawrence TYREE
05 Provost .... Mrs. Brittany SYNDER
10 Vice Pres Financial & Admin Svcs .... Mrs. Jean MAUK
32 Director Student Services .... Mrs. Michelle CHERRY
51 Dir Lifelong Learning and Cont Educ .... Mrs. Cathy TORRES
04 Exec Director Pres Office .... Mrs. Debbie LEONARD
26 Director College and Public Rels .... Mrs. Amber ERNST-LEONARD
84 Director Enrollment Services .... Mrs. Cheryl MALSHEIMER
08 Dir Learning Resources .... Mrs. Juana CAREAGA
37 Director Student Financial Aid .... Mrs. Susan URBAN
46 Dean Student Affs & Accreditation .... Mrs. Erika MACWILLIAMS
18 Dir Purchasing and Plant Opers .... Mr. Douglas PRYOR
13 Director of IT .... Mr. Bryan GILCHRIST
15 Director Human Resources .... Mr. Charles MCGINNIS
46 Grant Administrator .... Ms. Joanne PRESTON
76 Dean of Allied Health & Nursing .... Ms. Debra ALLISH
88 Dean of Marine Sciences and Tech .... Dr. Patrick RICE
102 Dir Of FKCC Foundation .... Mrs. Patti CAREY
20 Director Academic Affairs .... Mr. Michael MCPHERSON
21 Manager Business Services .... Mrs. Paula JIMENEZ
88 Centers Director .... Mr. Christopher FLETCHER

Florida Medical Training Institute-Coconut Creek (G)

7451 Wiles Road, Suite 105, Coral Springs FL 33067
County: Broward Identification: 666612
Telephone: (954) 752-1414 Carnegie Class: Not Classified
FAX Number: (954) 752-2721 Calendar System: Other
URL: www.fmti.edu
Established: 1999 Annual Undergrad Tuition & Fees: N/A
Enrollment: N/A Coed
Affiliation or Control: Proprietary IRS Status: Proprietary
Highest Offering: Associate Degree
Program: Occupational
Accreditation: ABHES

01 Campus Director .... Mr. Stewart JUSIM

Florida Memorial University (H)

15800 NW 42nd Avenue, Miami Gardens FL 33054-6199
County: Miami-Dade FICE Identification: 001486
Unit ID: 133979
Telephone: (305) 626-3600 Carnegie Class: Master's S
FAX Number: (305) 626-3769 Calendar System: Semester
URL: www.fmuniv.edu
Established: 1879 Annual Undergrad Tuition & Fees: $14,024
Enrollment: 1,892 Coed
Affiliation or Control: Independent Non-Profit IRS Status: 501(c)3
Highest Offering: Master's
Program: Liberal Arts And General; Teacher Preparatory
Accreditation: SC, ACBSP, CS, MUS, SW

01 President .... Dr. Henry LEWIS, III
05 Provost and VP Academic Affairs .... Dr. Makola ABDULLAH
20 Associate Provost .... Dr. Denise CALLWOOD-BRATHWAITE
04 Assistant to President .... Ms. Rachel TURNER
49 Dean of Arts and Sciences .... Dr. William HOPPER
88 Associate VP for Auxiliary Services .... Mr. Archie BOUIE
100 Chief of Staff .... Dr. Mary O'BANNER
10 Vice Pres Business/Fiscal Affairs .... Mr. Tony VALENTINE
11 Vice President for Administration .... Dr. Harold CLARKE, JR.
32 Interim VP for Student Affairs .... Ms. Danneal JONES
30 Vice Pres Institutional Advancement .... Dr. Adriene WRIGHT
88 Director of Aviation .... Dr. Arnold TOLBERT
50 Dean Business Administration .... Dr. Abbass ENTESSARI
53 Dean Division Education .... Dr. Mildred BERRY
81 Chair Natural Science .... Dr. Rose Mary STIFFIN
83 Chair Social Sciences .... Dr. Priye TORULAGHA
88 Chair Visual and Performing Arts .... Dr. Dawn BATSON-BOREL
89 Director Freshman Studies Dept .... Dr. Jeffrey SWAIN
77 Chair Comp Science/Math & Tech .... Dr. Ben WONGSAROJ
79 Chair Division Humanities .... Dr. William JONG-EBOT
08 Director University Library .... Mrs. Gloria OSWALD
84 Director of Enrollment Mgmt .... Mr. Roscoe WARREN
06 Registrar .... Mrs. Lelia A. EFFORD
09 Director of Institutional Research .... Dr. Carlos CANAS
45 Assoc VP Intitutional Effectiveness .... Dr. Sandra THOMPSON
42 Director of Church Relations .... Mrs. Patricia CARTER
15 Director Human Resources Management .... Mrs. Valerie A. WILLIAMS
88 Dir Property and Risk Management .... Mr. Alphonso BURNSIDE
41 Director of Athletics .... Mr. Robert SMITH
36 Director Career Development .... Ms. Athena JACKSON
37 Interim Director Financial Aid .... Mr. Kozman STROMAN
39 Director Residential Life .... Mrs. Jacklan ALEXANDER
07 Director of Admissions .... Mrs. Peggy Murray MARTIN
19 Chief of Security .... Chief Terrance WILSON
18 Dir Facility Mgmt/Plant Operations .... Mr. David JACCARINO

42 Campus Minister ... Rev. Wendell PARIS
29 Director Alumni Affairs ... Mrs. Sheila POWELL-COHEN
38 Lead Counselor ... Mr. Michael MOSS
35 Director Student Affairs ... Mr. C. Vernon MARTIN, JR.
85 Actg International Student Advisor ... Mr. Trevor LEWIS
13 Asst Chief Information Officer ... Mr. Orlando HUERTAS
55 Dir of Evening and Weekend Program ... Mrs. Gladys GONZALEZ
88 Director of Assessment ... Dr. Richard YAKLICH

Florida National College Hialeah Campus (A)

4425 W 20th Avenue, Hialeah FL 33012-4108

County: Dade
FICE Identification: 025476
Unit ID: 408844
Telephone: (305) 821-3333
Carnegie Class: Assoc/PrivFP4
FAX Number: (305) 362-0595
Calendar System: Semester
URL: www.fnc.edu
Established: 1982
Annual Undergrad Tuition & Fees: $13,170
Enrollment: 1,842
Coed
Affiliation or Control: Proprietary
IRS Status: Proprietary
Highest Offering: Baccalaureate
Program: 2-Year Principally Bachelor's Creditable
Accreditation: SC

01 President/CEO ... Mrs. Maria REGUEIRO
09 VP of Assessment & Research/FA Dir ... Mr. Omar SANCHEZ
11 Vice President of Operations ... Mr. Frank ANDREU
05 Vice President of Academic Affairs ... Mrs. Caridad SANCHEZ
10 Controller ... Mrs. Lourdes NIEVES
88 Accreditation Liaison ... Mrs. Barbara RODRIGUEZ
07 Director of Admissions ... Mr. Guillermo ARAYA
06 College Registrar ... Mr. Jose L. VALDES
08 Library Director ... Mr. Patrick BYRNES
32 Director of Student Services ... Mrs. Tricia FOSTER
105 Distance Learning Director ... Mrs. Sandra LOMENA
12 Campus Dean ... Mr. Jorge ALFONSO
88 Military Academic Advisor ... Mr. Manuel MARES
88 Education Specialist ... Mrs. Jelenny HERNANDEZ
36 Job Placement Officer ... Mr. Candido AVEILLE
84 Enrollment Manager ... Mr. Robert SMATT
50 Business & Economics Division Head ... Dr. James BULLEN
76 Allied Health Division Head ... Dr. Loreto ALMONTE
66 RN Program Director ... Mrs. Oneida SEGURA
66 PN Nursing Division Director ... Mrs. Maida BURGOS
79 Humanities and Fine Arts Division ... Mrs. Barbara RODRIGUEZ
88 ESL Division Head ... Mrs. Lidia MORALES

Florida National College South Campus (B)

11865 SW 26th Street Unit H-3, Miami FL 33175

Identification: 666691
Unit ID: 40884401
Telephone: (305) 226-9999
Carnegie Class: Not Classified
FAX Number: (305) 226-4439
Calendar System: Semester
URL: www.fnc.edu
Established: 2002
Annual Undergrad Tuition & Fees: $13,170
Enrollment: 837
Coed
Affiliation or Control: Proprietary
IRS Status: Proprietary
Highest Offering: Baccalaureate
Program: 2-Year Principally Bachelor's Creditable
Accreditation: &SC

01 President/CEO ... Mrs. Maria C. REGUEIRO
09 VP of Assessment & Research/FA ... Mr. Omar SANCHEZ
11 Vice President of Operations ... Mr. Frank ANDREU
05 Vice President of Academic Affairs ... Mrs. Caridad SANCHEZ
10 Controller ... Mrs. Lourdes NIEVES
88 Accreditation Liaison ... Mrs. Barbara RODRIGUEZ
07 Director of Admissions ... Mr. Guillermo ARAYA
06 College Registrar ... Mr. Jose L. VALDES
08 Library Director ... Mr. Patrick BYRNES
32 Director of Student Services ... Mrs. Tricia FOSTER
12 Interim Campus Dean ... Mr. Guillermo ARAYA
36 Job Placement Officer ... Mrs. Heydee CUERVO
88 Academic Advisor ... Mrs. Melissa LOPEZ
50 Business & Economics Division Head ... Dr. James BULLEN
76 Allied Health Division Head ... Dr. Loreto ALMONTE
66 PN Nursing Division Director ... Mrs. Maida BURGOS
66 RN Program Director ... Mrs. Oneida SEGURA
79 Humanities and Fine Arts Division ... Mrs. Barbara RODRIGUEZ
88 ESL Division Head ... Mrs. Lidia MORALES

† Regional accreditation is carried under the parent institution Florida National College, Hialeah, FL.

Florida National College Training Center (C)

4206 West 12th Avenue, Hialeah FL 33012

Identification: 666690
Unit ID: 40884402
Telephone: (305) 231-3326
Carnegie Class: Not Classified
FAX Number: (305) 819-9616
Calendar System: Semester
URL: www.fnc.edu
Established: 2004
Annual Undergrad Tuition & Fees: $13,170
Enrollment: 140
Coed
Affiliation or Control: Proprietary
IRS Status: Proprietary
Highest Offering: Baccalaureate
Program: 2-Year Principally Bachelor's Creditable
Accreditation: &SC

01 President/CEO ... Mrs. Maria REGUEIRO
09 VP of Assessment & Research/FA ... Mr. Omar SANCHEZ
11 Vice President of Operations ... Mr. Frank ANDREU
05 Vice President of Academic Affairs ... Mrs. Caridad SANCHEZ
10 Controller ... Mrs. Lourdes NIEVES
88 Accreditation Liaison ... Mrs. Barbara RODRIGUEZ
07 Director of Admissions ... Mr. Guillermo ARAYA
06 College Registrar ... Mr. Jose L. VALDES
08 Library Director ... Mr. Patrick BYRNES
32 Director of Student Services ... Mrs. Tricia FOSTER
12 Interim Campus Dean ... Mr. Jose L. VALDEZ
36 Job Placement Officer ... Mrs. Genobeba DELGADO
88 Academic Advisor ... Mr. Manuel MARES
76 Allied Health Division Head ... Dr. Loreto ALMONTE
88 ESL Division Head ... Mrs. Lidia MORALES

† Regional accreditation is carried under the parent institution Florida National College, Hialeah, FL.

Florida Southern College (D)

111 Lake Hollingsworth Drive, Lakeland FL 33801-5698

County: Polk
FICE Identification: 001488
Unit ID: 134079
Telephone: (863) 680-4111
Carnegie Class: Bac/Diverse
FAX Number: (863) 680-4112
Calendar System: Semester
URL: www.flsouthern.edu
Established: 1885
Annual Undergrad Tuition & Fees: $26,112
Enrollment: 2,291
Coed
Affiliation or Control: United Methodist
IRS Status: 501(c)3
Highest Offering: Master's
Program: Liberal Arts And General
Accreditation: SC, NURSE

01 President ... Dr. Anne B. KERR
05 Provost ... Dr. Kyle FEDLER
10 Vice President Finance & Admin ... Mr. Terry DENNIS
26 Vice President External Relations ... Dr. Robert H. TATE
32 Dean of Student Development ... Vacant
84 Vice Pres/Dean Enrollment Mgmt ... Mr. John GRUNDIG
30 Vice President Advancement ... Dr. Matthew R. THOMPSON
26 Vice President of Marketing & Comm ... Mr. David A. WEAGLE
08 Director of the Library ... Mr. Randall M. MACDONALD
07 Director of Admissions ... Mr. Bill C. LANGSTON, II
06 Registrar ... Ms. Sally L. THISSEN
09 Dir Inst Research/Effectiveness ... Dr. Kenneth M. REAVES
36 Director of Career Development ... Ms. Xuchitl COSO
37 Director of Student Financial Aid ... Mr. William L. HEALY
29 Director of Alumni Relations ... Vacant
41 Athletic Director ... Mr. Peter E. MEYER
42 Chaplain Director Campus Ministry ... Rev. Timothy S. WRIGHT
19 Director Security/Safety ... Mr. William CAREW
15 Director Personnel Services ... Ms. Katherine PAWLAK
18 Construction Manager ... Mr. Hank HILLHOUSE
20 Associate Provost ... Dr. Daniel SILBER
31 Director of Community Living ... Ms. Mindy BAINE
38 Director Student Counseling ... Dr. Carol BALLARD

Florida State College at Jacksonville (E)

501 W State Street, Jacksonville FL 32202-4097

County: Duval
FICE Identification: 001484
Unit ID: 133702
Telephone: (904) 646-2300
Carnegie Class: Assoc/Pub4
FAX Number: N/A
Calendar System: Semester
URL: www.fscj.edu
Established: 1963
Annual Undergrad Tuition & Fees (In-District): $2,984
Enrollment: 46,354
Coed
Affiliation or Control: Local
IRS Status: 501(c)3
Highest Offering: Baccalaureate
Program: Occupational; 2-Year Principally Bachelor's Creditable
Accreditation: SC, ACBSP, ACFEI, ADNUR, DH, DIETT, EMT, FUSER, HT, MLTAD, OTA, PTAA, SURGT

01 College President ... Dr. Steven R. WALLACE
05 Exec VP for Inst/Student Svcs ... Dr. Donald W. GREEN, JR.
12 Interim Campus President Downtown .. Dr. Christal M. ALBRECHT
12 Campus President Urban Resource Ctr ... Ms. Jana KOOI
12 Campus President-Kent/Int Provost ... Dr. Margarita A. CABRAL-MALY
12 Campus President-North ... Dr. Barbara A. DARBY
12 Campus President-South ... Dr. Denis G. WRIGHT
13 Vice President of Technology ... Dr. Robert J. RENNIE
11 Vice Pres of Administrative Svcs ... Mr. Steven P. BOWERS
15 Vice President of Human Resources ... Dr. Christine C. ARAB
30 VP Student Devel/Cmty Education ... Dr. Tracy A. PIERCE
43 Gen Counsel/VP Strategic Intiative ... Ms. Jeanne M. MILLER
20 Assoc VP of Educational Tech ... Mr. Dennis M. REIMAN
103 Assoc VP Workforce Devel/Adult Ed . Mr. James D. SIMPSON, III
18 Assoc VP Facilities Mgmt and Const ... Mr. Charles M. STRATMANN
10 Assoc Vice Pres of Financial Svcs ... Ms. Peggy L. BOORD
96 Assoc VP of Purchasing/Bus Svcs ... Mr. Laurence I. SNELL
15 Employee Svcs Dir/Col Equity Ofcr ... Ms. Elaine TISDALE
31 Exec Director of Cultural Programs ... Dr. Milton A. RUSSOS
88 Exec Dir Military Educ Institute ... Adm. James E. STEVENSON
102 Exec Director of the Foundation ... Mr. Robert L. STAMP
88 Dir Svcs for Stdnts w/Disabilities ... Ms. Denise J. GIARRUSSO
41 Dir Athletics and Physical Educ ... Mr. George E. SANDERS
84 Dist Dir Enroll Svcs/Coll Registrar ... Mr. Peter J. BIEGEL
37 Director Student Financial Aid ... Ms. Michele BOWLES
45 Director of Resource Development ... Dr. Phyllis R. RENNIGER
88 Director Aviation Ctr of Excellence ... Mr. Gene V. MILOWICKI
06 Registrar ... Ms. Lori G. COLLINS
07 Director of Admissions ... Ms. Roz DEXTER-HARRIS
09 Director of Institutional Research ... Mr. Greg MICHALSKI
26 Chief Public Relations Officer ... Ms. Celine MACARTHUR

Florida Technical College (F)

1199 S Woodland Boulevard, Deland FL 32720-7415

County: Volusia
Identification: 666419
Unit ID: 432393
Telephone: (386) 734-3303
Carnegie Class: Not Classified
FAX Number: (386) 734-5150
Calendar System: Quarter
URL: www.ftccollege.edu
Established: 1997
Annual Undergrad Tuition & Fees: $26,500
Enrollment: 346
Coed
Affiliation or Control: Proprietary
IRS Status: Proprietary
Highest Offering: Associate Degree
Program: 2-Year Principally Bachelor's Creditable
Accreditation: ACICS

01 Executive Director ... Mr. Alex RODRIGUEZ
06 Registrar ... Ms. Soraya CARDANES
07 Director of Admissions ... Mr. Christopher MERCADO

Florida Technical College (G)

4715 South Florida Avenue, Suite 4, Lakeland FL 33813-2101

County: Polk
FICE Identification: 025981
Unit ID: 432409
Telephone: (866) 967-8822
Carnegie Class: Not Classified
FAX Number: (866) 619-7600
Calendar System: Quarter
URL: www.flatech.edu
Established: 1990
Annual Undergrad Tuition & Fees: $29,970
Enrollment: 300
Coed
Affiliation or Control: Proprietary
IRS Status: Proprietary
Highest Offering: Associate Degree
Program: Occupational
Accreditation: ACICS

01 Executive Director ... Lisa Marie VELARDI

Florida Technical College (H)

12689 Challenger Parkway, Suite 130, Orlando FL 32826

County: Orange
FICE Identification: 022187
Unit ID: 134112
Telephone: (407) 447-7300
Carnegie Class: Assoc/PrivFP
FAX Number: (407) 447-7301
Calendar System: Quarter
URL: www.flatech.edu
Established: 1982
Annual Undergrad Tuition & Fees: $15,895
Enrollment: 475
Coed
Affiliation or Control: Proprietary
IRS Status: Proprietary
Highest Offering: Associate Degree
Program: Occupational; 2-Year Principally Bachelor's Creditable; Technical Emphasis
Accreditation: ACICS

00 President/CEO ... Mr. David RUGGIERI
01 Executive Director ... Mr. Gabriel GARCES
05 Director of Education ... Mr. Angel MEDINA
07 Director of Admissions ... Ms. Audrey HARDEN
37 Director of Financial Aid ... Ms. Deborah DIAZ

Fortis College (I)

7757 West Flagler Street, Ste 230, Miami FL 33144

County: Miami-Dade
FICE Identification: 030542
Telephone: (305) 717-7000
Carnegie Class: Not Classified
FAX Number: (786) 388-5464
Calendar System: Quarter
URL: www.fortis.edu
Established: 1978
Annual Undergrad Tuition & Fees: $12,000
Enrollment: 894
Coed
Affiliation or Control: Proprietary
IRS Status: Proprietary
Highest Offering: Associate Degree
Program: Occupational
Accreditation: COE

01 President ... Ms. Denyse ANTUNES

Fortis College (J)

560 Wells Road, Orange Park FL 32073-2999

County: Clay
FICE Identification: 034343
Unit ID: 439792
Telephone: (904) 269-7086
Carnegie Class: Assoc/PrivFP
FAX Number: (904) 269-6664
Calendar System: Semester
URL: www.fortis.edu
Established: 1985
Annual Undergrad Tuition & Fees: $13,125
Enrollment: 535
Coed
Affiliation or Control: Proprietary
IRS Status: Proprietary
Highest Offering: Associate Degree
Program: Occupational; 2-Year Principally Bachelor's Creditable
Accreditation: ACICS, SURGT

01 Campus President ... Mr. Wyman DICKEY

Fortis College (A)

3910 US Highway 301N, Suite 200,
Tampa FL 33619-1283

County: Hillsborough FICE Identification: 023057
Unit ID: 136075
Telephone: (813) 620-1446 Carnegie Class: Assoc/PrivFP
FAX Number: (813) 620-1641 Calendar System: Quarter
URL: www.fortis.edu
Established: 1978 Annual Undergrad Tuition & Fees: $19,300
Enrollment: 159 Coed
Affiliation or Control: Proprietary IRS Status: Proprietary
Highest Offering: Associate Degree
Program: 2-Year Principally Bachelor's Creditable; Nursing Emphasis
Accreditation: ACICS

01 Director ... Mr. Ray NUNZIATA
05 Director of Education ... Ms. Tonja HELTON
66 Director of Nursing ... Dr. Joanna HILL

Fortis College (B)

1573 W Fairbanks Avenue, Suite 100,
Winter Park FL 32789-4679

County: Orange FICE Identification: 022455
Unit ID: 132806
Telephone: (407) 843-3984 Carnegie Class: Assoc/PrivFP
FAX Number: (407) 843-9828 Calendar System: Quarter
URL: www.fortiscollege.edu
Established: 1985 Annual Undergrad Tuition & Fees: $18,350
Enrollment: 488 Coed
Affiliation or Control: Proprietary IRS Status: Proprietary
Highest Offering: Associate Degree
Program: Occupational
Accreditation: ACCSC, MAC

01 School Director ... Mr. Mark GUTMANN
06 Registrar/Business Manager ... Ms. Lisa BEARD
36 Career Services Director ... Ms. Catherine READY
37 Financial Aid Director ... Ms. Julie HALL
07 Admissions Director ... Mr. Antivan HARRINGTON

Full Sail Real World Education (C)

3300 University Boulevard, Suite160,
Winter Park FL 32792-7429

County: Orange FICE Identification: 023621
Unit ID: 134237
Telephone: (407) 679-0100 Carnegie Class: Master's L
FAX Number: (407) 679-9685 Calendar System: Other
URL: www.fullsail.edu
Established: 1979 Annual Undergrad Tuition & Fees: $36,905
Enrollment: 15,695 Coed
Affiliation or Control: Proprietary IRS Status: Proprietary
Highest Offering: Master's
Program: Occupational; 2-Year Principally Bachelor's Creditable
Accreditation: ACCSC

00 Co-Chairman ... Mr. Jon PHELPS
00 Co-Chairman ... Mr. Ed HADDOCK
00 Co-Chairman ... Mr. Bill HEAVENER
01 President ... Mr. Garry JONES
07 Vice President of Admissions ... Ms. Mary Beth PLANK

Golf Academy of America (D)

510 South Hunt Club Blvd., Apopka FL 32703

County: Seminole Identification: 666186
Unit ID: 430157
Telephone: (800) 342-7342 Carnegie Class: Assoc/PrivFP
FAX Number: (407) 699-6653 Calendar System: Semester
URL: www.golfacademy.edu
Established: 1986 Annual Undergrad Tuition & Fees: $33,824
Enrollment: 289 Coed
Affiliation or Control: Proprietary IRS Status: Proprietary
Highest Offering: Associate Degree
Program: Occupational; Business Emphasis
Accreditation: ACICS

01 President ... Mr. Chris HUNKLER
12 Campus Director ... Mr. Bradley G. TURNER

† Branch campus of Virginia College, Birmingham, AL.

Gulf Coast State College (E)

5230 W Highway 98, Panama City FL 32401-1058

County: Bay FICE Identification: 001490
Unit ID: 134343
Telephone: (850) 769-1551 Carnegie Class: Assoc/Pub-R-L
FAX Number: (850) 913-3319 Calendar System: Semester
URL: www.gulfcoast.edu
Established: 1957 Annual Undergrad Tuition & Fees (In-State): $2,370
Enrollment: 7,632 Coed
Affiliation or Control: State Related IRS Status: 501(c)3
Highest Offering: Baccalaureate
Program: Occupational; 2-Year Principally Bachelor's Creditable; Teacher Preparatory
Accreditation: SC, ACFEI, ADNUR, DA, DH, EMT, PTAA, RAD, SURGT

01 President ... Dr. Jim KERLEY
11 Vice Pres Administration & Finance ... Mr. John D. MERCER
05 VP Academic Affairs & Learn Support ... Dr. George BISHOP
75 Chief Economic Dev Officer ... Dr. Jeffry J. STEVENSON
32 VP Student Affairs ... Dr. Melissa LAVENDER
20 Assoc VP Academic Affairs ... Dr. Cheryl L. FLAX-HYMAN
27 Chief Information Officer ... Mr. Herman G. DANIELS
08 Director of Library ... Ms. Lori DRISCOLL
07 Director of Enrollment Services ... Ms. Sharon O. TODD
15 Exec Director of Human Resources ... Ms. Roberta MACKEY
18 Superintendent Grounds & Bldg Svcs ... Mr. Dennis STORCK
28 Assoc Dir Retention/Stdnt Diversity ... Dr. Carrie B. BAKER
26 Exec Director Media & Community Rel ... Mr. Christopher P. THOMES
96 Coordinator of Purchasing ... Ms. Tonia E. LAWSON
37 Director of Financial Aid ... Mr. Christopher J. WESTLAKE
09 Coordinator Institutional Research ... Ms. Dee NIELSEN
30 Chief Development Officer ... Vacant

Heritage Institute-Fort Myers (F)

6630 Orion Drive, Suite 202, Fort Meyers FL 33912-7130

County: Lee FICE Identification: 025971
Unit ID: 135124
Telephone: (239) 936-5822 Carnegie Class: Not Classified
FAX Number: (239) 225-9117 Calendar System: Other
URL: www.heritage-education.com
Established: 2001 Annual Undergrad Tuition & Fees: $24,950
Enrollment: 723 Coed
Affiliation or Control: Proprietary IRS Status: Proprietary
Highest Offering: Associate Degree
Program: Occupational
Accreditation: ABHES

01 Director ... Ms. Eva HUTSON

Heritage Institute-Jacksonville (G)

4130 Salisbury Road, Suite 1100, Jacksonville FL 32216

County: Duval FICE Identification: 030358
Unit ID: 372772
Telephone: (904) 332-0910 Carnegie Class: Not Classified
FAX Number: (904) 332-0920 Calendar System: Other
URL: www.heritage-education.com/campus_jacksonville.htm
Established: 2001 Annual Undergrad Tuition & Fees: N/A
Enrollment: 469 Coed
Affiliation or Control: Proprietary IRS Status: Proprietary
Highest Offering: Associate Degree
Program: Occupational
Accreditation: ABHES

01 Director ... Ms. Sonnie WILLINGHAM

Herzing University (H)

1865 SR 436, Winter Park FL 32792

County: Orange Identification: 666422
Unit ID: 386472
Telephone: (407) 478-0500 Carnegie Class: Bac/Assoc
FAX Number: (407) 478-0501 Calendar System: Trimester
URL: www.herzing.edu
Established: 1965 Annual Undergrad Tuition & Fees: $17,200
Enrollment: 410 Coed
Affiliation or Control: Proprietary IRS Status: Proprietary
Highest Offering: Master's
Program: 2-Year Principally Bachelor's Creditable; Nursing Emphasis
Accreditation: &NH, MLTAB, PTAA

01 President ... Mrs. Heather ANTONACCI
37 Director Financial Aid ... Ms. Krista KUHR
07 Director of Admissions ... Ms. Lauren RUSTON
05 Academic Dean ... Vacant
06 Registrar ... Ms. Lori GUISEPPI
29 Director Alumni Relations ... Ms. Sharon ROSEN

† Regional accreditation is carried under the parent institution in Madison, WI.

Hillsborough Community College (I)

PO Box 31127, 39 Columbia Drive, Tampa FL 33631-3127

County: Hillsborough FICE Identification: 007870
Unit ID: 134495
Telephone: (813) 253-7000 Carnegie Class: Assoc/Pub-U-MC
FAX Number: (813) 253-7183 Calendar System: Semester
URL: www.hccfl.edu
Established: 1968 Annual Undergrad Tuition & Fees (In-State): $2,422
Enrollment: 30,936 Coed
Affiliation or Control: State IRS Status: 501(c)3
Highest Offering: Associate Degree
Program: Occupational; 2-Year Principally Bachelor's Creditable
Accreditation: SC, ACFEI, ADNUR, DA, DH, @DIETT, DMS, EMT, MUS, NMT, OPD, RAD, RTT

01 President ... Dr. Ken ATWATER
10 Vice President Administration/CFO ... Ms. Barbara LARSON
03 Senior Vice President ... Mr. Robert WOLF
05 Vice President for Academic Affairs ... Mr. Craig JOHNSON
14 Int Vice Pres Info Technology ... Mr. Stephen GORHAM
32 VP Student Services/Enrollment Mgt ... Dr. Ken RAY
12 Campus President Dale Mabry ... Dr. Robert P. CHUNN
12 Campus President Ybor City Campus ... Dr. Shawn ROBINSON
12 Campus President Plant City Campus ... Dr. Felix HAYNES
12 Campus President Brandon Campus ... Dr. Carlos SOTO
12 Campus President South Shore Campus ... Dr. Allen WITT
22 Asst to Pres Equity/Special Pgms ... Dr. Joan HOLMES
26 Exec Dir Marketing/Public Relations ... Ms. Ashley CARL
09 Spc Asst to Pres Strat Plng & Analy ... Dr. Paul NAGY
102 Director HCC Foundation ... Dr. Adrienne GARCIA
43 College Attorney ... Ms. Martha K. KOEHLER
15 Director Human Resources ... Ms. Sue FLAIG
21 Controller ... Ms. Bonnie J. CARR
75 Director Technical Programs ... Dr. Ginger CLARK
20 Director Assoc in Arts Programs ... Dr. Karen GRIFFIN
90 Director of Academic Technology ... Mr. Richard SENKER
75 Dean Public Services Programs ... Mr. Jack EVANS
88 Dean Environmental Programs ... Vacant
88 Dean Assoc in Science Pgrams ... Dr. Ellen CANGI
88 Dean Assoc in Arts/Hum/Comm Pgms ... Dr. Mary BENDICKSON
81 Dean Assoc in Math/Science ... Mr. Robert WYNEGAR
76 Dean Health/Wellness & Sports Tech ... Dr. Amy ANDERSON
37 Financial Aid Director ... Ms. Linda CLEMONS
35 Student Services Systems Officer ... Ms. Kathy CECIL
18 Director Facilities/Physical Plant ... Mr. David CABECEIRAS
96 Director of Purchasing ... Ms. Vonda MELCHIOR
31 Dir of Community & Govt Relations ... Ms. Sarah (Sally) EVERETT

Hobe Sound Bible College (J)

PO Box 1065, Hobe Sound FL 33475-1065

County: Martin FICE Identification: 021889
Unit ID: 134510
Telephone: (772) 546-5534 Carnegie Class: Spec/Faith
FAX Number: (772) 545-1422 Calendar System: Semester
URL: www.hsbc.edu
Established: 1960 Annual Undergrad Tuition & Fees: $5,360
Enrollment: 128 Coed
Affiliation or Control: Independent Non-Profit IRS Status: 501(c)3
Highest Offering: Baccalaureate
Program: Liberal Arts And General; Religious Emphasis
Accreditation: BI

01 President ... Mr. P. Daniel STETLER
05 Academic Dean ... Dr. Clifford W. CHURCHILL
10 Director of Finances ... Mr. Kendall STRAIGHT
11 Director of Administration ... Mr. Wesley HOLDEN
32 Dean of Students ... Mr. John S. JONES
33 Dean of Men ... Mr. Jonathan STRATTON
08 Librarian ... Mr. Phil JONES
26 Public Relations Director ... Mr. Jonathan HEATH
06 Registrar ... Ms. Kristel GLICK
07 Director of Admissions ... Mrs. Judy FAY
30 Director of Development ... Mr. Patrick DAVIS
51 Dean of External Studies ... Mr. Dalbert N. WALKER

Hodges University (K)

2655 Northbrooke Drive, Naples FL 34119-7932

County: Collier FICE Identification: 030375
Unit ID: 367884
Telephone: (239) 513-1122 Carnegie Class: Master's S
FAX Number: (239) 598-6253 Calendar System: Trimester
URL: www.hodges.edu
Established: 1990 Annual Undergrad Tuition & Fees: $11,530
Enrollment: 2,580 Coed
Affiliation or Control: Independent Non-Profit IRS Status: 501(c)3
Highest Offering: Master's
Program: Liberal Arts And General
Accreditation: SC, IACBE, MAC

01 President ... Dr. Terry MCMAHAN
05 Exec Vice Pres Academic Affairs ... Dr. Jeanette BROCK
32 Exec Vice Pres Student Services ... Mr. John WHITE
10 Vice President of Finance ... Mr. Randy ELDRIDGE
06 Vice Pres of Student Records Mgt ... Ms. Carol MORRISON
84 Vice President of Enrollment Mgt ... Ms. Rita LAMPUS
35 Vice Pres of Student Development ... Mr. Ron BOWMAN
37 VP of Student Financial Assistance ... Mr. Joseph GILCHRIST
38 Director Student Counseling ... Mr. Micki ERICKSON
26 Chief Public Relations Officer ... Mr. Joe TURNER
09 Dir Institutional Effective/Rsrch ... Dr. Diane BALL
30 Chief Development ... Mr. Louis TRAINA

Indian River State College (L)

3209 Virginia Avenue, Fort Pierce FL 34981-5596

County: Saint Lucie FICE Identification: 001493
Unit ID: 134608
Telephone: (772) 462-4722 Carnegie Class: Assoc/Pub4
FAX Number: (772) 462-4796 Calendar System: Semester
URL: www.irsc.edu
Established: 1960 Annual Undergrad Tuition & Fees (In-District): $2,976
Enrollment: 17,511 Coed
Affiliation or Control: Local IRS Status: 501(c)3
Highest Offering: Baccalaureate
Program: Occupational; 2-Year Principally Bachelor's Creditable; Liberal Arts And General; Teacher Preparatory
Accreditation: SC, ADNUR, DA, DH, DT, EMT, MAC, MLTAD, NUR, PTAA, RAD, SURGT

01 President ... Dr. Edwin R. MASSEY
32 Vice President Student Affairs ... Mr. Frank WATKINS

05 Vice President Academic Affairs ... Dr. Henri Sue BYNUM
10 Vice Pres Administration/Finance ... Mr. Barry A. KEIM
38 Vice Pres Applied Science & Tech ... Dr. Alan L. ROBERTS
45 Associate VP Institutional Effectiv ... Dr. Christina HART
04 Exec Assistant to the President ... Mr. Andrew TREADWELL
12 Vice Pres/Provost-Fort Pierce ... Dr. Mary G. LOCKE
12 Provost Pt St Lucie/St Lucie W ... Dr. Harvey E. ARNOLD
12 Provost Okeechobee ... Mr. Sam SMITH
12 Provost Stuart ... Ms. Patricia ALAN
12 Provost Vero Beach ... Dr. David SULLIVAN
12 Dean Northwest Center ... Mr. Andre HAWKINS
18 Dean Auxiliary Services/Facility ... Mr. Allen BOTTORFF
72 Dean Institutional Tech ... Mr. Paul R. O'BRIEN
30 Dean of Public Services ... Dr. Stephen HUNTSBERGER
72 Dean Advanced Technology ... Mr. Jose L. FARINOS
93 Associate Dean Minority Affairs ... Ms. Adriene JEFFERSON
51 Associate Dean Developmental Ed ... Dr. Anthony IACONO
20 Asst Dean Educational Services ... Mr. Steven W. PAYNE
50 Assistant Dean Business Technology ... Mr. Cedric GIBSON
15 Associate Dean Human Resources ... Ms. Shelia DANIELS
14 Associate Dean Data Processing ... Ms. Patricia D. PFEIFFER
21 Assistant Dean Finance ... Mr. Joe MAZUR
08 Associate Dean Learning Resources ... Ms. Patricia C. PROFETA
49 Associate Dean of Arts & Sciences ... Mr. Casey LUNCEFORD
103 Associate Dean of CCTI ... Ms. Jan PAGANO
75 Associate Dean Industrial Education ... Ms. Donna RIVETT
76 Associate Dean of Health Science ... Ms. Jane P. CEBELAK
09 Associate Dean Research/Reports ... Mr. Gerald L. MOCK
66 Administrative Director of Nursing ... Ms. Ann HUBBARD
102 Executive Director Foundation ... Ms. Ann DECKER
30 Director Institutional Advancement ... Ms. Michelle ABALDO
41 Director Athletics ... Mr. Scott KIMMELMAN
36 Director Student Success Services ... Ms. Flossie JACKSON
84 Director Enrollment Management ... Ms. Eileen STORCK
37 Director Student Financial Aid ... Ms. Mary LEWIS
06 Registrar/Dir Student Affs/Admiss ... Ms. Karen CHAPDELAINE
96 Purchasing Agent ... Mr. Don WINDHAM
38 Director Student Counseling ... Ms. Dale HAYES
51 Admin Dir Baccalaureate Programs ... Mr. Ian NEUHARD
35 Director Student Affairs ... Ms. Sharon LOWE

International Academy of Design and Technology (A)

5104 Eisenhower Boulevard, Tampa FL 33634-6313
County: Hillsborough | FICE Identification: 030314
Unit ID: 134080
Telephone: (813) 881-0007 | Carnegie Class: Spec/Arts
FAX Number: (813) 884-9327 | Calendar System: Quarter
URL: www.academy.edu
Established: 1984 | Annual Undergrad Tuition & Fees: $15,775
Enrollment: 1,475 | Coed
Affiliation or Control: Proprietary | IRS Status: Proprietary
Highest Offering: First Professional Degree
Program: Fine Arts Emphasis
Accreditation: **ACICS**, CIDA

01 President ... Dr. Karen O'DONNELL
10 Vice President of Finance ... Tim COPPOLA
05 Dean/Chief Academic Officer ... Phil BULONE
07 Director of Admissions ... Dewey MCGUIRK
32 Director of Student Services ... Amanda WILLIAMS
36 Director of Career Services ... Carl STORCK
08 Learning Resource Center Coord ... Elaine NERI
37 Director Student Financial Aid ... Jameson STEVENS
35 Manager of Student Services ... Kimberly FORTENBERRY

International Academy of Design and Technology-Online (B)

5104 Eisenhower Boulevard, Tampa FL 33634-6313
County: Hillsborough | Identification: 666631
Unit ID: 456296
Telephone: (813) 881-0007 | Carnegie Class: Not Classified
FAX Number: (813) 357-2505 | Calendar System: Quarter
URL: www.iadt.edu
Established: 1977 | Annual Undergrad Tuition & Fees: $13,887
Enrollment: 2,117 | Coed
Affiliation or Control: Proprietary | IRS Status: Proprietary
Highest Offering: Baccalaureate
Program: Professional; Fine Arts Emphasis
Accreditation: **ACICS**

01 President ... Mr. Mark PAGE
05 Director of Education ... Ms. Dawn CARLSON
06 Registrar ... Ms. Nicole BELLFIELD
07 VP of Admissions ... Mr. Michael WASHINGTON

ITT Technical Institute (C)

13500 Powers Court, Suite 100, Fort Myers FL 33912
County: Lee | Identification: 666669
Unit ID: 456436
Telephone: (239) 603-8700 | Carnegie Class: Not Classified
FAX Number: N/A | Calendar System: Quarter
URL: www.itt-tech.edu
Established: N/A | Annual Undergrad Tuition & Fees: N/A
Enrollment: 288 | Coed
Affiliation or Control: Proprietary | IRS Status: Proprietary
Highest Offering: Baccalaureate
Program: Technical Emphasis
Accreditation: **ACICS**

† Branch campus of ITT Technical Institute, San Diego, CA.

ITT Technical Institute (D)

3401 S University Drive, Fort Lauderdale FL 33328-2021
County: Broward | Identification: 666536
Unit ID: 409069
Telephone: (954) 476-9300 | Carnegie Class: Spec/Tech
FAX Number: (954) 476-6889 | Calendar System: Quarter
URL: www.itt-tech.edu
Established: 1991 | Annual Undergrad Tuition & Fees: N/A
Enrollment: 830 | Coed
Affiliation or Control: Proprietary | IRS Status: Proprietary
Highest Offering: Baccalaureate
Program: Technical Emphasis
Accreditation: **ACICS**

† Branch campus of ITT Technical Institute, Fort Wayne, IN.

ITT Technical Institute (E)

7011 A.C. Skinner Parkway, Ste. 140,
Jacksonville FL 32244-6630
County: Duval | Identification: 666537
Unit ID: 407063
Telephone: (904) 573-9100 | Carnegie Class: Spec/Tech
FAX Number: (904) 573-0512 | Calendar System: Quarter
URL: www.itt-tech.edu
Established: 1990 | Annual Undergrad Tuition & Fees: N/A
Enrollment: 700 | Coed
Affiliation or Control: Proprietary | IRS Status: Proprietary
Highest Offering: Baccalaureate
Program: Technical Emphasis
Accreditation: **ACICS**

† Branch campus of ITT Technical Institute, Tampa, FL.

ITT Technical Institute (F)

1400 International Parkway South,
Lake Mary FL 32746-1607
County: Orange | FICE Identification: 030876
Unit ID: 372578
Telephone: (407) 660-2900 | Carnegie Class: Spec/Tech
FAX Number: (407) 660-2566 | Calendar System: Quarter
URL: www.itt-tech.edu
Established: 1989 | Annual Undergrad Tuition & Fees: N/A
Enrollment: 670 | Coed
Affiliation or Control: Proprietary | IRS Status: Proprietary
Highest Offering: Baccalaureate
Program: Technical Emphasis
Accreditation: **ACICS**

ITT Technical Institute (G)

7955 NW 12th Street, Suite 119, Miami FL 33126-1823
County: Miami-Dade | Identification: 666026
Unit ID: 430263
Telephone: (305) 477-3080 | Carnegie Class: Spec/Tech
FAX Number: (305) 477-7561 | Calendar System: Quarter
URL: www.itt-tech.edu
Established: 1996 | Annual Undergrad Tuition & Fees: N/A
Enrollment: 853 | Coed
Affiliation or Control: Proprietary | IRS Status: Proprietary
Highest Offering: Baccalaureate
Program: Technical Emphasis
Accreditation: **ACICS**

† Branch campus of ITT Technical Institute, Lake Mary, FL.

ITT Technical Institute (H)

877 Executive Ctr. Dr. W, Ste. 100,
St. Petersburg FL 33702
County: Pinellas | Identification: 666163
Unit ID: 450207
Telephone: (727) 209-4700 | Carnegie Class: Assoc/PrivFP4
FAX Number: N/A | Calendar System: Quarter
URL: www.itt-tech.edu
Established: 2006 | Annual Undergrad Tuition & Fees: N/A
Enrollment: 335 | Coed
Affiliation or Control: Proprietary | IRS Status: Proprietary
Highest Offering: Baccalaureate
Program: Technical Emphasis
Accreditation: **ACICS**

† Branch campus of ITT Technical Institute, Lake Mary, FL.

ITT Technical Institute (I)

4809 Memorial Highway, Tampa FL 33634-7350
County: Hillsborough | FICE Identification: 022865
Unit ID: 134909
Telephone: (813) 885-2244 | Carnegie Class: Spec/Tech
FAX Number: (813) 888-8451 | Calendar System: Quarter
URL: www.itt-tech.edu
Established: 1981 | Annual Undergrad Tuition & Fees: N/A
Enrollment: 918 | Coed
Affiliation or Control: Proprietary | IRS Status: Proprietary
Highest Offering: Baccalaureate
Program: Technical Emphasis
Accreditation: **ACICS**

Jacksonville University (J)

2800 University Boulevard N, Jacksonville FL 32211-3394
County: Duval | FICE Identification: 001495
Unit ID: 134945
Telephone: (904) 256-8000 | Carnegie Class: Master's M
FAX Number: N/A | Calendar System: Semester
URL: www.ju.edu
Established: 1934 | Annual Undergrad Tuition & Fees: $27,900
Enrollment: 3,688 | Coed
Affiliation or Control: Independent Non-Profit | IRS Status: 501(c)3
Highest Offering: Doctorate
Program: Liberal Arts And General; Teacher Preparatory; Professional; Business Emphasis
Accreditation: **SC, AAB, BUS, DANCE, DENT, MUS, NURSE**

01 President ... Dr. Kerry D. ROMESBURG
05 Senior VP for Academic Affairs ... Dr. Lois S. BECKER
10 VP for Finance & Administration ... Mr. George C. SCADUTO
84 Vice Pres Enrollment Management ... Mr. Terry E. WHITTUM
32 Vice President for Student Life ... Dr. John A. BALOG
30 Vice Pres University Advancement ... Mr. Michael HOWLAND
26 VP Univ Rel & External Affairs ... Dr. Derek J. HALL
13 VP Info Tech & Chief Info Officer ... Mr. Tom HALL
04 Exec Assistant to the President ... Ms. Dolores STARR
41 Athletic Director ... Mr. C. Alan VERLANDER
06 Registrar ... Ms. Carolyn BARRETT
09 Director of Institutional Research ... Ms. Carolyn M. BARNETT
07 Director of Admissions ... Vacant
08 Director of the Library ... Mr. David JONES
35 Dean of Students ... Dr. Bryan F. COKER
36 Career Development Coordinator ... Ms. Devan COUGHLIN
37 Dir Student Financial Assistance ... Ms. Breanne SIMKIN
29 Asst VP for Institutional Advance ... Vacant
21 Controller ... Ms. Liza MULLINS
11 Exec Dir Budgets/Business Opers ... Ms. Ellen M. PAIGE
96 Director of Purchasing ... Mr. Michael J. BOBBIN
40 Director of the Bookstore ... Ms. Kimberly BANKS
42 Campus Minister ... Mr. Lance BEAUCHAMP
15 Director of Human Resources ... Mr. James V. WILLIAMS
57 Dean College of Fine Arts ... Mr. William E. HILL
49 Dean Col of Arts & Sciences ... Dr. Douglas HAZZARD
50 Interim Dean College of Business ... Dr. William CROSBY
51 Assoc Dean of Continuing Studies ... Vacant
53 Interim Dean School of Education ... Dr. Douglas HAZZARD
64 Chairman Division of Music ... Mr. Robert TUDOR
66 Dean School of Nursing ... Dr. Judith ERICKSON
79 Chair Div of Humanities ... Dr. Scott KIMBROUGH
81 Chair Division of Science & Math ... Dr. Lee Ann J. CLEMENTS
38 Director Student Counseling ... Ms. Kristin R. ALBERTS
83 Chair Division of Social Science ... Dr. Sherry JACKSON
88 Chair Division of Naval Science ... Capt. Charles BERDAR
88 Chair Div of Theatre Arts & Dance ... Mr. Brian PALMER
57 Chair Division Art/Art History ... Ms. Dana L. CHAPMAN
18 Chief Facilities/Physical Plant ... Mr. Joe COLEMAN

Johnson & Wales University (K)

1701 NE 127th Street, North Miami FL 33181-2518
County: Miami-Dade | Identification: 666423
Unit ID: 414823
Telephone: (305) 892-7000 | Carnegie Class: Bac/Assoc
FAX Number: (305) 892-7030 | Calendar System: Quarter
URL: www.jwu.edu
Established: 1992 | Annual Undergrad Tuition & Fees: $25,107
Enrollment: 2,098 | Coed
Affiliation or Control: Independent Non-Profit | IRS Status: 501(c)3
Highest Offering: Baccalaureate
Program: Occupational; 2-Year Principally Bachelor's Creditable
Accreditation: **&EH**

01 President North Miami Campus ... Mrs. Loreen M. CHANT
03 Vice Pres/Dean of Academic Affairs ... Mr. Larry RICE
05 Dean of Culinary Education ... Mr. Bruce M. OZGA
100 Executive Administrator ... Mr. Jordan FICKESS
32 Director of Student Acad Services ... Ms. Maheen CARROLL
07 Director of Admissions ... Mr. Jeffrey GREENIP
11 Director of Administration ... Mr. Barry VOGEL
18 Director of Facilities Management ... Mr. Paul ZAHN
26 Dir of Comm & Media Relations ... Mrs. Tonya EVANS
30 Director of Development & Alumni ... Mr. Peter ROOD
35 Dean of Students ... Ms. Ismare MONREAL
37 Director of Student Financial Svcs ... Mr. Chris MAGNAN
38 Director of Student Success ... Ms. Martha SACKS
13 Director of Campus IT Services ... Mr. Michael GRAZIOTTI
19 Director Campus Safety & Security ... Mr. Yakir FERNANDEZ
23 Director of Student Health Services ... Ms. Roberta ADAMONIS
36 Director Exp Education & Career Svc ... Ms. Darlene CANTOR
39 Director of Residential Life ... Mr. Dan OFSTEIN
41 Director of Athletics & Campus Rec ... Mr. David GRAHAM
96 Director of Purchasing ... Mr. Shawn RAY
29 Manager of Alumni Relations ... Ms. Karen MCGIBBON
44 Development Relations Officer ... Ms. Yudit ARTEAGA
15 Campus Human Resources Manager ... Ms. Dolly DURAN
40 Bookstore Manager ... Mr. Darryl LERNER
08 Director of Library Services ... Ms. Nicole COVONE
85 International Student Advisor ... Ms. Nicole GRAHAM

92 Honors Program Coordinator .... Ms. Carol KORIS

† Regional accreditation is carried under the parent institution in Providence, RI.

Jones College (A)

5353 Arlington Expressway, Jacksonville FL 32211-5588
County: Duval FICE Identification: 001497
Unit ID: 135063
Telephone: (904) 743-1122 Carnegie Class: Bac/Diverse
FAX Number: (904) 743-4446 Calendar System: Trimester
URL: www.jones.edu
Established: 1918 Annual Undergrad Tuition & Fees: $7,410
Enrollment: 667 Coed
Affiliation or Control: Independent Non-Profit IRS Status: 501(c)3
Highest Offering: Baccalaureate
Program: Business Emphasis
Accreditation: ACICS

00 Corporate President & CEO .... Dorothy D. JONES
01 President of the College .... Frank M. MCCAFFERTY
05 Dean of the College .... Dee THORNTON
10 Business Officer .... Kathy DANE
37 Director of Financial Assistance .... Becky DAVIS
07 Diretor of Admissions .... Linda VAUGHN
36 Director of Career Development .... Richard SMITH
13 Director IT .... Holly KELLEY
08 Librarian .... Kevin DOBYNS

Jose Maria Vargas University (B)

8300 S Palm Drive, Pembroke Pines FL 33025
FICE Identification: 041620
Telephone: (954) 322-4460 Carnegie Class: Not Classified
FAX Number: (954) 322-4131 Calendar System: Semester
URL: www.jmvu.edu
Established: N/A Annual Undergrad Tuition & Fees: $5,088
Enrollment: N/A Coed
Affiliation or Control: Proprietary IRS Status: Proprietary
Highest Offering: Master's
Program: Occupational; 2-Year Principally Bachelor's Creditable; Teacher Preparatory
Accreditation: ACICS, @TEAC

01 President .... Dr. Alicia F. PARRA DE ORTIZ
05 Vice President of Academic Affairs .... Clara GONZALEZ
10 Vice President of Finance .... Lelis Antonio ORTIZ ALVAREZ
08 Library Director .... Desiree ROLAND
18 Facilities/Purchasing Director .... Erika Jose ORTIZ PARRA
21 Director of Budgeting .... Edith PAREDES
06 Registrar .... Lelis ORTIZ PARRA
32 Director of Student Development .... Ezer TOSSAS
58 Coord of Research/Grad Studies .... Lori N. KIJANCA

Kaplan College (C)

10131 Pines Boulevard, Pembroke Pines FL 33026
Identification: 666752
Unit ID: 458238
Telephone: (888) 972-4141 Carnegie Class: Not Classified
FAX Number: N/A Calendar System: Semester
URL: www.kaplancollege.com
Established: N/A Annual Undergrad Tuition & Fees: N/A
Enrollment: 118 Coordinate
Affiliation or Control: Proprietary IRS Status: Proprietary
Highest Offering: Associate Degree
Program: 2-Year Principally Bachelor's Creditable
Accreditation: ACICS

01 Executive Director .... Mr. Steve NELSON

† Branch campus of Kaplan Career Institute, Harrisburg, PA.

Keiser Career College (D)

6812 Forest Hills Blvd, Suite D-1, Greenacres FL 33413
County: Palm Beach FICE Identification: 031239
Telephone: (561) 433-2330 Carnegie Class: Not Classified
FAX Number: (561) 433-9025 Calendar System: Other
URL: www.keisercareer.edu
Established: 1988 Annual Undergrad Tuition & Fees: $14,885
Enrollment: 1,780 Coed
Affiliation or Control: Proprietary IRS Status: Proprietary
Highest Offering: Associate Degree
Program: Occupational
Accreditation: ACCSC, MAAB, SURGT, SURTEC

01 Vice President .... Ms. Elizabeth HOULIHAN

Keiser Career College (E)

6700 South Point Pkwy, Ste 400, Jacksonville FL 32216
County: Duval FICE Identification: 035533
Unit ID: 443270
Telephone: (904) 448-9499 Carnegie Class: Not Classified
FAX Number: (904) 448-9270 Calendar System: Other
URL: www.keisercareer.edu
Established: 1988 Annual Undergrad Tuition & Fees: $14,885
Enrollment: 155 Coed
Affiliation or Control: Proprietary IRS Status: Proprietary
Highest Offering: Associate Degree
Program: Occupational
Accreditation: ACCSC

01 Campus Vice President .... Shawn HUMPHREY

Keiser Career College (F)

17395 NW 59th Avenue, Miami Lakes FL 33015-5111
County: Miami-Dade Identification: 666290
Unit ID: 42817001
Telephone: (305) 820-5003 Carnegie Class: Not Classified
FAX Number: (305) 820-5455 Calendar System: Quarter
URL: www.keisercareer.edu
Established: 2002 Annual Undergrad Tuition & Fees: N/A
Enrollment: N/A Coed
Affiliation or Control: Proprietary IRS Status: Proprietary
Highest Offering: Associate Degree
Program: Occupational
Accreditation: ACCSC, MAAB, SURGT, SURTEC

01 Vice President .... Marion DAMOUR
05 Dean Academics .... Craig MUNNS

† Branch campus of Keiser Career College, Greenacres, FL.

Keiser Career College (G)

11208 Blue Heron Boulevard, Suite A,
St. Petersburg FL 33716
County: Pinellas Identification: 666758
Unit ID: 42817002
Telephone: (727) 576-6500 Carnegie Class: Not Classified
FAX Number: (727) 576-6589 Calendar System: Semester
URL: www.keisercareer.edu
Established: 1988 Annual Undergrad Tuition & Fees: N/A
Enrollment: N/A Coed
Affiliation or Control: Proprietary IRS Status: Proprietary
Highest Offering: Associate Degree
Program: Occupational
Accreditation: ACCSC, MAAB, SURTEC

01 President .... Mr. Jeff SLAGLE

† Branch campus of Keiser Career College, Greenacres, FL.

Keiser University (H)

1500 NW 49th Street, Fort Lauderdale FL 33309-3700
County: Broward FICE Identification: 021519
Unit ID: 135081
Telephone: (954) 776-4456 Carnegie Class: Bac/Assoc
FAX Number: (954) 771-4894 Calendar System: Semester
URL: www.keiseruniversity.edu
Established: 1977 Annual Undergrad Tuition & Fees: $14,176
Enrollment: 16,968 Coed
Affiliation or Control: Proprietary IRS Status: Proprietary
Highest Offering: Doctorate
Program: Occupational
Accreditation: SC, ACFEI, #ARCPA, DMS, MAAB, MAC, MLTAD, NURSE, OTA, PTAA, RAD

01 Chancellor .... Dr. Arthur KEISER
12 Campus President .... Mr. Steven BROOKS
26 Reg Dir Media & Public Relations .... Ms. Kimberly DALE

Keiser University (I)

10330 S Federal Highway,
Port Saint Lucie FL 34952-5605
County: Saint Lucie Identification: 666289
Unit ID: 437990
Telephone: (772) 398-9990 Carnegie Class: Not Classified
FAX Number: (772) 335-9619 Calendar System: Semester
URL: www.keiseruniversity.edu
Established: 1977 Annual Undergrad Tuition & Fees: $8,250
Enrollment: 488 Coed
Affiliation or Control: Proprietary IRS Status: Proprietary
Highest Offering: Associate Degree
Program: Occupational
Accreditation: &SC, SURGT

01 Campus President .... Dr. Thomas CREOLA

† Regional accreditation is carried under the parent institution Keiser University, Fort Lauderdale, FL.

Keiser University (J)

2085 Vista Parkway, West Palm Beach FL 33411-2719
County: Palm Beach Identification: 667032
Unit ID: 428170
Telephone: (561) 471-6000 Carnegie Class: Assoc/PrivFP
FAX Number: (561) 471-7849 Calendar System: Quarter
URL: www.keiseruniversity.edu
Established: N/A Annual Undergrad Tuition & Fees: $14,176
Enrollment: 1,790 Coed
Affiliation or Control: Proprietary IRS Status: Proprietary
Highest Offering: Doctorate
Program: Occupational
Accreditation: &SC

01 Campus President .... Mr. Gary VONK
03 Executive Vice Chancellor/COO .... Mr. Peter CROCITTO

† Regional accreditation is carried under the parent institution Keiser University, Fort Lauderdale, FL.

Key College (K)

225 E Dania Beach Blvd, Suite 130,
Dania Beach FL 33004-3042
County: Broward FICE Identification: 023251
Unit ID: 134422
Telephone: (954) 923-4440 Carnegie Class: Assoc/PrivFP
FAX Number: (954) 923-9226 Calendar System: Quarter
URL: www.keycollege.edu
Established: 1982 Annual Undergrad Tuition & Fees: $10,815
Enrollment: 107 Coed
Affiliation or Control: Proprietary IRS Status: Proprietary
Highest Offering: Associate Degree
Program: 2-Year Principally Bachelor's Creditable; Business Emphasis
Accreditation: ACICS

01 President .... Mr. Ronald DOOLEY
05 Director of Academic Affairs .... Vacant
07 Director of Admissions .... Vacant
37 Director of Financial Aid .... Ms. Amber YOUNG
06 Registrar .... Mr. Jose MIRANDA

Knox Theological Seminary (L)

5554 N Federal Highway, Fort Lauderdale FL 33308-3209
County: Broward FICE Identification: 039923
Telephone: (954) 771-0376 Carnegie Class: Not Classified
FAX Number: (954) 351-3343 Calendar System: Semester
URL: www.knoxseminary.edu
Established: 1989 Annual Undergrad Tuition & Fees: $7,080
Enrollment: 112 Coed
Affiliation or Control: Presbyterian Church In America IRS Status: 501(c)3
Highest Offering: Doctorate
Program: Religious Emphasis
Accreditation: THEOL

01 President & CEO .... Dr. Ronald J. KOVACK
05 Dean of Faculty .... Dr. Warren GAGE
32 Dir Student Svcs/Dean of Students .... Mr. Al JIRON

Lake-Sumter Community College (M)

9501 US Highway 441, Leesburg FL 34788-8751
County: Lake FICE Identification: 001502
Unit ID: 135188
Telephone: (352) 787-3747 Carnegie Class: Assoc/Pub-S-MC
FAX Number: (352) 365-3548 Calendar System: Semester
URL: www.lscc.edu
Established: 1962 Annual Undergrad Tuition & Fees (In-District): $2,997
Enrollment: 4,886 Coed
Affiliation or Control: State/Local IRS Status: 501(c)3
Highest Offering: Associate Degree
Program: Occupational; 2-Year Principally Bachelor's Creditable
Accreditation: SC, ADNUR

01 President .... Dr. Charles R. MOJOCK
10 VP Business Affairs .... Mr. Richard M. SCOTT
05 VP Academic-Student Affairs .... Dr. Barbara C. HOWARD
21 Controller .... Mr. John FROMAN
75 Dean Career & Technical Programs .... Dr. Mary Jo RAGER
53 Dean General Ed & Transfer Programs .... Mr. Gary SLIGH
15 Exec Director Human Resources .... Mr. Tim KANE
13 Chief Information Officer .... Mr. Douglas GUILER
09 Exec Dir Planning & IE .... Dr. Kristy LISLE
32 Assistant VP Student Affairs .... Vacant
30 Exec Dir Inst Advance & Foundation .... Ms. Rosanne BRANDEBURG
18 Director College Facilities .... Mr. Donald BALL
08 Director Libraries .... Ms. Denise K. ENGLISH
35 Director Student Development .... Ms. Claire BRADY
21 Director Budget & Accounting .... Ms. Sue FAGAN
66 Director Nursing .... Dr. Margaret WACKER
08 Director Learning Center .... Ms. Marion J. KANE
26 Director College Relations .... Ms. Pat LANDSMAN
37 Director Financial Aid .... Ms. Audrey WILLIAMS
06 Director Enrollment Services .... Ms. Kelli COLOBORNE
41 Athletic Director .... Mr. Michael K. MATULIA
88 Director Youth Outreach Programs .... Mr. Reinaldo CORTES
106 Director Distance Learning .... Ms. Jacquie BUSBOOM

Le Cordon Bleu College of Culinary Arts in Miami (N)

3221 Enterprise Way, Miramar FL 33025-3929
County: Broward Identification: 666369
Unit ID: 446835
Telephone: (954) 438-8882 Carnegie Class: Assoc/PrivFP
FAX Number: (954) 438-9519 Calendar System: Other
URL: www.chefs.edu/miami
Established: 2002 Annual Undergrad Tuition & Fees: $39,500
Enrollment: 762 Coed
Affiliation or Control: Proprietary IRS Status: Proprietary
Highest Offering: Associate Degree
Program: Occupational
Accreditation: ACCSC, ACFEI

01 President ....Mr. Bob KANE

† Branch campus of Le Cordon Bleu Institute of Culinary Arts, Pittsburgh, PA.

Le Cordon Bleu College of Culinary Arts in Orlando (A)

8511 Commodity Circle, Orlando FL 32819-9002
County: Orange Identification: 666064
Unit ID: 442231
Telephone: (407) 888-4000 Carnegie Class: Assoc/PrivFP
FAX Number: (407) 888-4019 Calendar System: Quarter
URL: www.chefs.edu/orlando
Established: 2002 Annual Undergrad Tuition & Fees: $17,500
Enrollment: 1,000 Coed
Affiliation or Control: Proprietary IRS Status: Proprietary
Highest Offering: Associate Degree
Program: 2-Year Principally Bachelor's Creditable; Professional; Technical Emphasis
Accreditation: ACICS, ACFEI

01 President ....Joe HARDIMAN
07 Vice President of Admissions ....Ken FIIGUEROA
22 Director of Regulatory Operations ....Sean MURPHY
05 Director of Education ....Chef William MATHER
06 Registrar ....Laura HARRELSON

† Branch campus of International Academy of Design & Technology, Tampa, FL.

Lincoln Tech Fern Park Orlando Campus (B)

7275 Estapona Circle, Fern Park FL 32730-2351
County: Seminole FICE Identification: 033903
Unit ID: 439437
Telephone: (407) 673-7406 Carnegie Class: Assoc/PrivFP
FAX Number: (407) 339-0295 Calendar System: Quarter
URL: www.americareschools.com
Established: 1991 Annual Undergrad Tuition & Fees: N/A
Enrollment: 525 Coed
Affiliation or Control: Proprietary IRS Status: Proprietary
Highest Offering: Associate Degree
Program: Occupational
Accreditation: ABHES, DA, SURTEC

01 Executive Director ....Mr. Justin BERKOWITZ
05 Director of Education ....Ms. Gabriel HAWKINS

Lincoln College of Technology (C)

2410 Metrocentre Boulevard,
West Palm Beach FL 33407-3155
County: Palm Beach FICE Identification: 022808
Unit ID: 136066
Telephone: (561) 842-8324 Carnegie Class: Assoc/PrivFP4
FAX Number: (561) 842-9503 Calendar System: Other
URL: www.lincolncollegeoftechnology.com
Established: 1982 Annual Undergrad Tuition & Fees: $17,536
Enrollment: 2,690 Coed
Affiliation or Control: Proprietary IRS Status: Proprietary
Highest Offering: Baccalaureate
Program: Occupational; Technical Emphasis
Accreditation: ACICS, ACFEI

01 President ....Mr. Charles HALLADAY

Lynn University (D)

3601 N Military Trail, Boca Raton FL 33431-5598
County: Palm Beach FICE Identification: 001505
Unit ID: 132657
Telephone: (561) 237-7000 Carnegie Class: DRU
FAX Number: (561) 237-7100 Calendar System: Semester
URL: www.lynn.edu
Established: 1962 Annual Undergrad Tuition & Fees: $31,700
Enrollment: 2,109 Coed
Affiliation or Control: Independent Non-Profit IRS Status: 501(c)3
Highest Offering: Doctorate
Program: Liberal Arts And General; Business Emphasis
Accreditation: SC, IACBE, MUS

01 President ....Dr. Kevin M. ROSS
100 Chief of Staff ....Dr. Jason L. WALTON
00 President Emeritus ....Dr. Donald E. ROSS
11 Sr Vice Pres Administration ....Mr. Gregory J. MALFITANO
05 Vice President Academic Affairs ....Dr. Cynthia M. PATTERSON
84 Vice Pres Enrollment Management ....Dr. Gareth FOWLES
10 Vice President Business & Finance ....Ms. Laurie LEVINE
32 Vice President for Student Life ....Dr. Phil RIORDAN
26 Vice Pres Marketing & Communication ....Ms. Michele M. MORRIS
30 Vice Pres Development/Alumni Affs ....Ms. Judith L. NELSON
13 Chief Information Officer ....Mr. Chris G. BONIFORTI
88 Dean of Administration ....Mr. Thomas J. HEFFERNAN
35 Dean of Students ....Mr. Paul S. TURNER
20 Academic Dean ....Dr. Gregg C. COX
43 General Counsel ....Ms. Margaret E. RUDDY
88 Exec Dir Stdnt Administrative Svcs ....Ms. Evelyn C. NELSON
08 Library Director ....Vacant
39 Director Housing & Residence Life ....Ms. Joy DOLIBER
36 Director Career Development ....Vacant
41 Director of Athletics ....Dr. Kristen L. MORAZ
18 Director Auxiliary Services ....Mr. Matthew P. CHALOUX
23 Director Health Center ....Ms. Rita ALBERT
27 Director of Marketing ....Mrs. Carol A. HERZ
31 Director of Public Relations ....Mr. Joshua GLANZER
44 Director of Regional Development ....Mr. Jay J. BRANDT
29 Director Alumni Affairs ....Mr. Matthew R. ROOS
42 Chaplain ....Fr. Martin C. DEVEREAUX
07 Dir Undergraduate Day Admissions ....Mr. Juan C. TAMAYO
37 Dir Student Financial Assistance ....Mrs. Chan J. PARK
38 Director of the Counseling Center ....Ms. Nicole R. OVEDIA
96 Director of Purchasing ....Mr. Alfredo H. BONIFORTI
06 Registrar ....Ms. Angela K. ROGERS
21 Director of Accounting ....Mr. Michael C. BOLDUC
07 Dir Intnl/Graduate Admissions ....Mr. Stefano PAPALEO
51 Director Distance Learning ....Dr. Mary L. TEBES
09 Director of Institutional Research ....Dr. Leslie A. WASSON
15 Director of Employee Services ....Mrs. Carole E. DODGE
40 Bookstore Manager ....Ms. Rita D. LOUREIRO
50 Dean College Business & Management ....Vacant
49 Dean College of Liberal Educ ....Dr. Katrina CARTER-TELLISON
88 Dean School of Aeronautics ....Dr. Jeffrey C. JOHNSON
53 Dean Ross College of Education ....Vacant
60 Dean College Intl Communications ....Dr. David L. JAFFE
88 Dean College Hospitality Mgmt ....Vacant
64 Dean Conservatory of Music ....Dr. Jon H. ROBERTSON
88 Dean Inst Achievement Learning ....Dr. Marsha A. GLINES

MedVance Institute of Fort Lauderdale (E)

4850 W Oakland Park Blvd, Suite 200,
Lauderdale Lakes FL 33313-7261
County: Broward Identification: 666269
Unit ID: 443438
Telephone: (954) 587-7100 Carnegie Class: Assoc/PrivFP
FAX Number: (954) 587-7704 Calendar System: Other
URL: www.medvance.edu
Established: 2003 Annual Undergrad Tuition & Fees: $13,600
Enrollment: 560 Coed
Affiliation or Control: Proprietary IRS Status: Proprietary
Highest Offering: Associate Degree
Program: Occupational
Accreditation: ABHES, RAD, SURGT, SURTEC

01 Director ....Mr. Mike BEAUREGARD

† Branch campus of MedVance Institute, Baton Rouge, LA.

Meridian Career Institute (F)

7020 Professioinal Pkwy E, Sarasota FL 34240
County: Sarasota FICE Identification: 023268
Unit ID: 244279
Telephone: (941) 377-4880 Carnegie Class: Not Classified
FAX Number: (941) 378-2842 Calendar System: Other
URL: www.meridian.edu
Established: 1982 Annual Undergrad Tuition & Fees: $11,500
Enrollment: 392 Coed
Affiliation or Control: Proprietary IRS Status: Proprietary
Highest Offering: Associate Degree
Program: Occupational
Accreditation: ACCSC

01 President ....Mr. Wayne A. SLATER

Miami Ad School (G)

955 Alton Road, Miami Beach FL 33139-5203
County: Miami-Dade FICE Identification: 031256
Unit ID: 428000
Telephone: (305) 538-3193 Carnegie Class: Assoc/PrivFP
FAX Number: (305) 538-3724 Calendar System: Quarter
URL: www.miamiadschool.com
Established: 1993 Annual Undergrad Tuition & Fees: $17,200
Enrollment: 172 Coed
Affiliation or Control: Proprietary IRS Status: Proprietary
Highest Offering: Associate Degree
Program: Occupational
Accreditation: COE

01 President ....Ms. Pipa SEICHRIST

Miami Dade College (H)

300 NE Second Avenue, Miami FL 33132-2296
County: Miami-Dade County FICE Identification: 001506
Unit ID: 135717
Telephone: (305) 237-8888 Carnegie Class: Assoc/Pub4
FAX Number: (305) 237-7913 Calendar System: Semester
URL: www.mdc.edu/main/
Established: 1960 Annual Undergrad Tuition & Fees (In-State): $3,165
Enrollment: 57,294 Coed
Affiliation or Control: State IRS Status: 501(c)3
Highest Offering: Baccalaureate
Program: Occupational; 2-Year Principally Bachelor's Creditable; Liberal Arts And General; Teacher Preparatory
Accreditation: SC, ADNUR, ARCPA, ART, DANCE, DH, DMS, EMT, FUSER, HT, MLTAD, MUS, NUR, OPD, PTAA, RAD, THEA

01 College President ....Dr. Eduardo J. PADRON
05 College Provost ....Dr. Rolando MONTOYA
10 Vice Provost Business Affairs ....Mr. E. H. LEVERING
13 Vice Provost Information Technology ....Mr. Karl HERLEMAN
18 Int Vice Provost Facilities Opers ....Mr. Patrick REBULL
15 Vice Provost Human Resources ....Ms. Iliana CASTILLO-FRICK
09 Assoc Provost Inst Effectiveness ....Dr. Joanne BASHFORD
20 Vice Provost for Education ....Dr. Pamela MENKE
12 Campus President Hialeah Campus ....Vacant
12 Campus President Kendall ....Dr. Lourdes OROZA
12 Campus Pres Medical Ctr Campus ....Dr. Armando FERRER
12 Campus President North Campus ....Dr. Jose VICENTE
12 Campus President Wolfson Campus ....Vacant
12 Campus President Homestead Campus ....Dr. Jeanne JACOBS
12 Campus Pres InterAmerican Cmps ....Dr. Gina CORTES-SUAREZ
21 Assoc Vice Prov Business Affs ....Mr. Gregory KNOTT
32 Director Student Services ....Dr. Rene GARCIA
102 Exec Director MDC Foundation ....Mr. L. J RODRIGUEZ
37 Collegewide Financial Aid Director ....Ms. Mercedes AMAYA
93 Director Employee Relations/EOP/ADA ....Dr. Joy C. RUFF
07 Collegewide Director Admissions ....Ms. Dulce BELTRAN
26 Chief Public Rels Officer/Dir Comm ....Mr. Juan MENDIETA
29 Director Annual Giving/Alumni Rels ....Ms. Nairobi ABRAMS
35 Chief Student Life Officer ....Ms. Teresa REIGOSA
36 Dir Testing Admin/Pgm Evaluation ....Mr. Silvio RODRIGUEZ
28 Director of Diversity ....Dr. Joy C. RUFF
38 Director Student Advisement ....Ms. Paola DOCUMET
84 Director Enrollment Management ....Dr. Rene GARCIA
96 Director of Purchasing ....Mr. Roman MARTINEZ
41 Director Athletics & Student Life ....Mr. Anthony FIORENZA
06 Collegewide Registrar ....Ms. Dulce BELTRAN
09 Director of Institutional Research ....Dr. David M. KAISER
43 Legal Counsel ....Ms. Carmen DOMINGUEZ
86 Director Governmental Affairs ....Ms. Victoria HERNANDEZ
100 Chief of Staff ....Mr. George ANDREWS
103 Dean Workforce Education & Develop ....Dr. Donna JENNINGS
104 Int Program Manager Study Abroad ....Ms. Eva FERNANDEZ
105 College Webmaster ....Mr. Andrew SEAGA
08 Head Librarian ....Ms. Glendora PHIPPS
85 Director Foreign Students ....Ms. Tere COLLADA

Miami International University of Art & Design (I)

1501 Biscayne Boulevard, Suite 100,
Miami FL 33132-1418
County: Miami-Dade FICE Identification: 008878
Unit ID: 134811
Telephone: (305) 428-5700 Carnegie Class: Spec/Arts
FAX Number: (305) 374-7946 Calendar System: Quarter
URL: www.aimiu.aii.edu
Established: 1965 Annual Undergrad Tuition & Fees: $22,700
Enrollment: 1,628 Coed
Affiliation or Control: Proprietary IRS Status: Proprietary
Highest Offering: Master's
Program: Fine Arts Emphasis
Accreditation: SC, CIDA

01 President ....Ms. Erika FLEMING
05 Chief Academic Officer ....Mr. Paul COX
10 Dir Admin & Financial Services ....Mr. Joseph GIANNATTASIO
32 Dean of Student Affairs ....Mr. John OSBORNE
07 Director of Admissions ....Mr. Kevin RYAN
08 Librarian ....Mr. Daniel CROMER

North Florida Community College (J)

325 NW Turner Davis Drive, Madison FL 32340-1610
County: Madison FICE Identification: 001508
Unit ID: 136145
Telephone: (850) 973-2288 Carnegie Class: Assoc/Pub-R-S
FAX Number: (850) 973-1696 Calendar System: Semester
URL: www.nfcc.edu
Established: 1958 Annual Undergrad Tuition & Fees (In-State): $2,745
Enrollment: 1,727 Coed
Affiliation or Control: State IRS Status: 501(c)3
Highest Offering: Associate Degree
Program: Occupational; 2-Year Principally Bachelor's Creditable
Accreditation: SC

01 President ....Mr. John GROSSKOPF
05 Dean of Academic Affairs/CAO ....Dr. Sharon ERLE
11 Dean Administrative Svcs & CBO ....Ms. Amelia MULKEY
07 Dean of Enrollment/Student Services ....Ms. Mary Anne WHEELER
09 Manager of Networking Systems ....Mr. John SIRMON
15 Director of Personnel Services ....Mr. Bill HUNTER
08 Head Librarian ....Ms. Kay HOGAN
88 SSS and Disability Coordinator ....Ms. Nancy LILLIS
88 Director of Public Safety Academy ....Mr. Rick DAVIS
06 Registrar ....Ms. Mary Anne WHEELER
18 Chief Facilities/Physical Plant ....Mr. Dale HACKLE
21 Controller ....Ms. Edna EALY
26 Public Information Officer ....Ms. Kim SCARBORO
29 Dir Foundation Alumni Relations ....Ms. Gina RUTHERFORD
37 Director Student Financial Aid ....Ms. Peggy HARRIS
28 Director of Diversity ....Ms. Denise BELL
32 Director Student Services ....Ms. Kim HALFHILL
96 Director of Purchasing ....Ms. Sarah NEWSOME

Northwest Florida State College (A)

100 College Boulevard, Niceville FL 32578-1295
County: Okaloosa FICE Identification: 001510
Unit ID: 136233
Telephone: (850) 678-5111 Carnegie Class: Assoc/Pub4
FAX Number: (850) 729-5215 Calendar System: Semester
URL: www.nwfsc.edu
Established: 1963 Annual Undergrad Tuition & Fees (In-District): $3,000
Enrollment: 10,445 Coed
Affiliation or Control: Local IRS Status: 501(c)3
Highest Offering: Baccalaureate
Program: Occupational; 2-Year Principally Bachelor's Creditable; Liberal Arts And General; Teacher Preparatory; Professional
Accreditation: SC, DA, NURSE

01 President ... Dr. Ty HANDY
05 Vice Pres for Instruction ... Dr. Sasha JARRELL
11 Vice Pres Administrative Services ... Dr. Gary YANCEY
12 Vice President NWFSC/UWF FWB Campus ... Dr. David L. GOETSCH
10 Assoc Vice Pres Business Services ... Ms. Donna K. UTLEY
32 Dist Dean of Students/Athletic Dir ... Mr. Mickey ENGLETT
30 Director Inst Resource Development ... Vacant
07 Dean Enrollment Services/Registrar ... Ms. Christine C. BISHOP
09 Director of Institutional Research ... Ms. Janice W. HENDERSON
15 Director Human Resources/Diversity ... Ms. Nancy MURPHY
37 Director Financial Aid/Veteran Affs ... Ms. Patricia BENNETT
18 Facilities Director ... Mr. Sam JONES
44 Dir Resource Dev/College Foundation ... Mrs. Cristie KEDROSKI
36 Director Student Counseling ... Ms. Dianne AVILLION
08 Director Learning Resources Center ... Ms. Janice HENDERSON
26 Director Marketing/Public Relations ... Ms. Sylvia BRYAN
96 Coordinator of Purchasing ... Ms. Dedria LUNDERMAN
06 Registrar ... Ms. Christine C. BISHOP

Nova Southeastern University (B)

3301 College Avenue, Fort Lauderdale FL 33314-7796
County: Broward FICE Identification: 001509
Unit ID: 136215
Telephone: (954) 262-7300 Carnegie Class: RU/H
FAX Number: (954) 262-3800 Calendar System: Other
URL: www.nova.edu
Established: 1964 Annual Undergrad Tuition & Fees: $23,200
Enrollment: 28,741 Coed
Affiliation or Control: Independent Non-Profit IRS Status: 501(c)3
Highest Offering: Doctorate
Program: Liberal Arts And General; Teacher Preparatory; Professional
Accreditation: SC, AA, ARCPA, AUD, CLPSY, DENT, DMS, IACBE, IPSY, LAW, MFCD, NURSE, OPT, OPTR, OSTEO, OT, PH, PHAR, PTA, SP

01 President ... Dr. George L. HANBURY, II
05 Exec VP & Provost for Acad Affs ... Dr. Frank DE PIANO
11 Exec Vice Pres for Administration ... Vacant
10 Vice President Finance ... Mr. David HERON
00 Chancellor Nova Southeastern Univ ... Mr. Ray FERRERO, JR.
17 Chancellor Health Professions (HPD) ... Dr. Fred LIPPMAN
20 Vice Chancellor/Provost (HPD) ... Dr. Irving ROSENBAUM
09 VP Institutional Effectiveness ... Dr. Ronald CHENAIL
86 Vice Pres Community/Govt Affairs ... Dr. Larry A. CALDERON
08 Vice Pres Info Svcs/Univ Librarian ... Ms. Lydia M. ACOSTA
43 Vice President Legal Affairs ... Mr. Joel BERMAN
46 Vice Pres Research Tech Transfer ... Dr. Gary S. MARGULES
30 Vice President Inst Advancement ... Ms. Joanne FERCHLAND-PARELLA
18 Vice President Facilities Mgmt ... Mr. John J. SANTULLI, II
13 Vice Pres Info Tech/Chief Info Ofcr ... Mr. Tom WEST
37 Asc VP Stdnt Enrollment/Stdnt Svcs ... Dr. Stephanie BROWN
21 Assoc Vice Pres Business Services ... Mr. Marc CROCQUET
15 Associate Vice Pres Human Resources ... Mr. Mark A. JONES
20 Asc Prov Div Appld Intdscplnry Stds ... Dr. Margaret A. MALMBERG
26 Exec Director University Relations ... Mr. David DAWSON
19 Director Public Safety ... Mr. James EWING
09 Exec Dir of Institutional Research ... Dr. Blair T. ATHERTON
45 Exec Dir Accreditation Planning ... Dr. Dian MOORHOUSE
24 Exec Dir Ed Tech/Digital Media Prod ... Ms. Toni MCLEOD
25 Exec Director Grants & Contracts ... Ms. Barbara STERRY
86 Director Licensure/State Relations ... Dr. Greg F. STIBER
84 Director Enrollment Management ... Ms. Maria P. DILLARD
12 Headmaster University School ... Dr. Jerry CHERMAK
27 Director University Publications ... Mr. Ron RYAN
29 Director Alumni Relations ... Ms. Sara DUCUENNOIS
36 Director of Career Development ... Ms. Shari SAPERSTEIN
06 University Registrar ... Ms. Elaine G. POFF
41 Director of Athletics ... Mr. Michael MOMINEY
39 Dir Residential Life & Housing ... Ms. Aarika CAMP
96 Director of Purchasing ... Mr. Mike COROMINAS
23 Asst Dir of Campus Recreation ... Mr. Tom VIRTUCCI
26 Director of Public Affairs ... Ms. Julie SPECHLER
63 Dean College Osteopathic Medicine ... Dr. Anthony SILVAGNI
67 Dean College Pharmacy ... Dr. Andres MALAVE
88 Dean College Optometry ... Dr. David LOSHIN
76 Dean College Allied Health ... Dr. Richard E. DAVIS
77 Int Dean Grad Sch Computer/Info Sci ... Dr. Amon SEAGULL
61 Dean Shepard Broad Law Center ... Mr. Athornia STEELE
65 Dean Oceanographic Center ... Dr. Richard DODGE
50 Dn W Huizenga Grad Sch Bus/Entrepr ... Dr. Michael FIELDS
49 Dean Farquhar Col Arts & Sciences ... Dr. Donald ROSENBLUM
88 Dean Center Psychological Stds ... Ms. Karen GROSBY
83 Dean Grad Sch Humanities/Social Sci ... Dr. Honggang YANG
53 Dean Sch Education & Human Services ... Dr. H. Wells SINGLETON
88 Dean Mailman Segal Institute ... Dr. Roni LEIDERMAN
63 Dean College of Medical Sciences ... Dr. Harold LAUBAUCH
52 Dean College of Dental Medicine ... Dr. Robert A. UCHIN
35 Dean of Student Affairs ... Dr. Brad WILLIAMS

Palm Beach Atlantic University (C)

901 S Flagler Drive, West Palm Beach FL 33401
County: Palm Beach FICE Identification: 008849
Unit ID: 136330
Telephone: (561) 803-2000 Carnegie Class: Master's M
FAX Number: (561) 803-2186 Calendar System: Semester
URL: www.pba.edu
Established: 1968 Annual Undergrad Tuition & Fees: $23,800
Enrollment: 3,659 Coed
Affiliation or Control: Interdenominational IRS Status: 501(c)3
Highest Offering: Doctorate
Program: Occupational; Liberal Arts And General; Teacher Preparatory; Professional
Accreditation: SC, IACBE, MUS, NURSE, PHAR

01 President ... Mr. William B. FLEMING
05 Provost ... Dr. Joseph A. KLOBA
10 Interim VP Business Affs/CFO ... Mrs. Renae MURRAY
04 Assoc VP Pres & Trustee Relations ... Vacant
30 Vice President Development ... Mr. William M B. FLEMING, JR.
32 Vice President Student Development ... Vacant
09 Asst Vice Pres Rsrch/Effectiveness ... Mrs. Carolanne BROWN
14 Asst Vice Pres Technology Services ... Mr. Phillip MAJOR
26 Assoc VP Univ Relations & Marketing ... Mrs. Rebecca PEELING
51 Dean MacArthur School of Leadership ... Dr. James A. LAUB
49 Dean School of Arts & Sciences ... Dr. J. Barton STARR
50 Interim Dean School of Business ... Dr. Leslie TURNER
53 Dean School of Education ... Dr. Gene SALE
57 Dean School of Music/Fine Arts ... Dr. Lloyd MIMS
66 Dean School of Nursing ... Dr. Joanne MASELLA
67 Dean Gregory School of Pharmacy ... Dr. Mary FERRILL
60 Dean School Communication/Media ... Dr. J. Duane MEEKS
73 Dean School of Ministry ... Dr. Randy E. RICHARDS
06 Dean Academic Records/Advising ... Ms. Audrey SCHOFIELD
08 Dean of the Library ... Mr. Steven BAKER
20 Dean of Faculty ... Vacant
15 Director of Human Resources ... Ms. Mona L. HICKS
18 Director of Physical Plant ... Mr. Michael STEGER
21 Controller ... Mrs. Renae MURRAY
29 AVP Alumni Relations/Annual Fund ... Ms. Delesa MORRIS
31 Coordinator Community Services ... Mrs. Cindy LAMERSON
38 Director of Student Success Center ... Mrs. Andrea DYBEN
37 Director of Financial Aid ... Mr. Todd MARTIN
35 Dean of Students ... Mr. Kevin ABEL
40 Director of Campus Store ... Mrs. Abbie ROSEMEYER
41 Director of Athletics ... Mr. Robert WHITE
42 Director of Campus Ministries ... Mr. Mark KAPRIVE
19 Director of Safety & Security ... Mr. Terry WHEELER
92 Director of Supper Honors Program ... Dr. Tom ST. ANTOINE
07 Dean of Admissions ... Mr. Joe SHARP

Palm Beach State College (D)

4200 Congress Avenue, Lake Worth FL 33461-4796
County: Palm Beach FICE Identification: 001512
Unit ID: 136358
Telephone: (561) 967-7222 Carnegie Class: Assoc/Pub-S-MC
FAX Number: (561) 868-3504 Calendar System: Semester
URL: www.palmbeachstate.edu
Established: 1933 Annual Undergrad Tuition & Fees (In-District): $2,880
Enrollment: 29,534 Coed
Affiliation or Control: Local IRS Status: 501(c)3
Highest Offering: Baccalaureate
Program: Occupational; 2-Year Principally Bachelor's Creditable
Accreditation: SC, ADNUR, DA, DH, DMS, EMT, MAC, MACTE, RAD, SURGT

01 President ... Dr. Dennis P. GALLON
05 Vice President for Academic Affairs ... Dr. Sharon A. SASS
10 Vice President Admin/Business Svcs ... Mr. Richard A. BECKER
32 Vice President for Student Services ... Dr. Patricia J. ANDERSON
102 CEO Foundation ... Ms. Suellen MANN
12 Provost Glades Center ... Dr. Marcia HARDNEY
12 Provost South Campus ... Dr. Bernadette MENDONEZ RUSSELL
12 Provost Eissey Campus ... Dr. Jean WIHBEY
12 Provost Central Campus ... Dr. Maria M. VALLEJO
35 Dean Student Services/Central ... Ms. Penny J. MCISAAC
35 Dean Student Services/Boca Raton ... Ms. Nicole P. BANKS
35 Dean Student Services/Eissey ... Mr. Scott MACLACHLAN
35 Dean Educational Services/Glades ... Dr. Barry L. MOORE
84 Dean Enrollment Management ... Vacant
103 Dean Workforce ... Ms. Patricia V. RICHIE
37 Director Financial Aid ... Ms. Susan KADIR
41 Dir Student Activities/Athletics ... Mr. David HOLSTEIN
09 Dir Institutional Effectiveness ... Dr. Jennifer D. CAMPBELL
86 Director Government Relations ... Ms. Erin S. MCCOLSKEY
18 Director Facilities ... Mr. John T. WASUKANIS
15 Director Human Resources ... Dr. Ellen GRACE
26 Dir College Relations & Marketing ... Dr. Grace H. TRUMAN
21 Controller ... Mr. James E. DUFFIE
06 Registrar/Director Admissions ... Mr. Edward MUELLER
96 Director of Purchasing ... Ms. Jodi HART
27 Chief Information Officer ... Mr. Anthony PARZIALE
13 Director Information Technology ... Mr. Chuck H. ZETTLER
29 Director Alumni Relations ... Ms. Suellen MANN
25 Manager Grant Development ... Ms. Maureen CAPP
88 Project Reports Coordinator ... Ms. Karen M. LIPPE

Palmer College of Chiropractic, Florida Campus (E)

4777 City Center Parkway, Port Orange FL 32129-4153
County: Volusia Identification: 666330
Telephone: (386) 763-2709 Carnegie Class: Not Classified
FAX Number: (386) 763-2635 Calendar System: Quarter
URL: www.palmer.edu
Established: 2002 Annual Undergrad Tuition & Fees: $30,220
Enrollment: 740 Coed
Affiliation or Control: Independent Non-Profit IRS Status: 501(c)3
Highest Offering: First Professional Degree
Program: Professional
Accreditation: &NH, CHIRO

00 Chancellor ... Dr. Dennis M. MARCHIORI
01 President ... Dr. Peter A. MARTIN
05 Vice Chancellor for Academics ... Dr. Robert E. PERCUOCO
32 Vice Chancellor Student Success ... Dr. Kevin A. CUNNINGHAM
11 Vice Chancellor Support Services ... Mr. Robert E. LEE
84 Vice Chancellor for Enrollment ... Mr. J. Michael NOVAK
10 Vice Chancellor for Administration ... Mr. Thomas L. TIEMEIER
17 Vice Chancellor for Clinic Affairs ... Dr. Kurt W. WOOD
46 Vice Chancellor for Research ... Dr. Christine G. GOERTZ
26 Exec Dir for Marketing & PR ... Mr. Darren R. GARRETT
29 Executive Director for Alumni ... Dr. Mickey G. BURT
88 Exec Dir Office of Strategic Dev ... Dr. Judy M. SILVESTRONE
20 Dean of Academic Affairs ... Dr. Donald F. GRAN
21 Senior Dir for Financial Affairs ... Ms. Alexis A. VANDERHORN
13 Senior Director IT ... Mr. Mike A. BENEDICT
09 Sr Dir Institutional Plng/Research ... Dr. Dustin C. DERBY
40 Senior Director of Bookstores ... Ms. Carol A. HOYT
15 Sr Director of Human Resources ... Ms. Michelle K. WALKER
24 Sr Dir/Center for Teaching/Lrng ... Dr. Dana J. LAWRENCE
88 Senior Director for Assessment ... Vacant
07 Campus Enrollment Director ... Ms. Jessica BLUMENFELD
46 Director of Research ... Dr. Liang ZHANG
37 Manager of Financial Planning ... Ms. Carmen AFGHANI
35 Director of Student Services ... Ms. Melissa L. LINGO
23 Dean of Clinics ... Dr. Albert J. LUCE
06 Registrar ... Mr. Jason BREWER
08 Librarian ... Mr. Daniel W. WRIGHT

† Regional accreditation is carried under the parent institution in Davenport, IA.

Pasco-Hernando Community College (F)

10230 Ridge Road, New Port Richey FL 34654-5199
County: Pasco FICE Identification: 010652
Unit ID: 136400
Telephone: (727) 847-2727 Carnegie Class: Assoc/Pub-S-MC
FAX Number: (727) 816-1815 Calendar System: Semester
URL: www.phcc.edu
Established: 1972 Annual Undergrad Tuition & Fees (In-District): $2,844
Enrollment: 10,762 Coed
Affiliation or Control: State/Local IRS Status: 501(c)3
Highest Offering: Associate Degree
Program: Occupational; 2-Year Principally Bachelor's Creditable
Accreditation: SC, ADNUR, DH, EMT

01 President ... Dr. Katherine M. JOHNSON
05 VP Instruction/Prov West Campus ... Dr. Burt H. HARRES, JR.
32 VP Stdnt Devel/Enrollment Mgmt ... Dr. Timothy L. BEARD
10 Vice Pres Administration & Finance ... Mr. Kenneth R. BURDZINSKI
12 Provost of the East Campus ... Dr. Randall H. STOVALL
12 Provost of the North Campus ... Dr. Stanley M. GIANNET
12 Assoc Provost Spring Hill Campus ... Ms. Bonnie M. CLARK
103 Dean of Workforce Development ... Mr. Edwin G. GOOLSBY
24 Dean of Institutional Technology ... Mr. Paul G. WRIGHT
20 Asst Dean Instructional Services ... Dr. Michelle J. BALON
17 Dean Health Occupations ... Ms. Jayme S. ROTHBERG
49 Interim Dean Arts and Sciences ... Vacant
35 Assoc Dean Student Act/Engagement ... Mr. Robert E. BADE
21 Dean Admin/Finance/Comptroller ... Mr. Brian S. HORN
84 Dean Student Enroll/Retention ... Ms. Donna R. BURDZINSKI
09 Assoc Dean Inst Research/Assessment ... Mr. Michael MALIZIA
13 Director of Management Info Svcs ... Ms. Janice L. SCOTT
30 Dir Inst Advancement/Exec Dir Found ... Ms. Arla S. ALTMAN
66 Associate Dean of Nursing ... Ms. Billie J. GABBARD
07 Dir Admissions & Student Records ... Ms. Debra K. MARVEL
37 Asst Dean Financial Aid/Vet Svcs ... Ms. Rebecca S. SHANAFELT
43 Gen Counsel/Exec Dir Govt Relations ... Mr. Stephen C. SCHROEDER
08 Director of Libraries ... Mr. Raymond J. CALVERT
41 Athletics Director/Instructor ... Mr. James E. JOHNSON
26 Exec Dir Marketing/Public Relation ... Ms. Lucy T. MILLER
18 Director of Facilities ... Mr. Keith V. BRAUN
15 Exec Director of Human Resources ... Ms. Vivian M. FRIEND
40 Auxiliary Services Manager ... Mr. John D. COLLINS
28 Coord of Disabilities Services ... Mr. Ron THIESSEN
22 Dist Coord Multicul Std Affs/Eq Svc ... Mr. Imani D. ASUKILE
96 Purchasing Agent ... Ms. Debra B. WHITTAKER

Pensacola State College (G)

1000 College Boulevard, Pensacola FL 32504-8998
County: Escambia FICE Identification: 001513
Unit ID: 136473

Telephone: (850) 484-1000 Carnegie Class: Assoc/Pub-R-L
FAX Number: (850) 484-1826 Calendar System: Semester
URL: www.pensacolastate.edu
Established: 1948 Annual Undergrad Tuition & Fees (In-District): $2,727
Enrollment: 11,676 Coed
Affiliation or Control: Local IRS Status: 501(c)3
Highest Offering: Baccalaureate
Program: 2-Year Principally Bachelor's Creditable
Accreditation: SC, ACFEI, ADNUR, DH, EMT, MAC, PTAA, RAD, SURGT

01 President ....Dr. Ed MEADOWS
05 Vice Pres for Instructional Affairs ....Dr. Erin SPICER
32 Vice President Student Affairs ....Mr. Tom GILLIAM
10 Vice President for Business ....Mrs. Gean Ann EMOND
103 VP Workforce Educ/Academic Support ....Dr. Jason HURST
12 Dean Milton Campus ....Ms. Anthea AMOS
12 Dean Warrington Campus ....Ms. Frances DUNCAN
28 Assoc Vice Pres Inst Diversity ....Dr. Gael FRAZER
30 Exec Dir Col Devel/Alumni Affairs ....Ms. Patrice WHITTEN
13 Exec Director MIS/Telecom Systems ....Mrs. Carolyn PHILLIPS
86 Exec Director of Govt Relations ....Mr. Larry BRACKEN
26 Director Marketing & College Info ....Ms. MaryEllen ROY
06 Registrar ....Ms. Martha CAUGHEY
09 Dean Instnl Effectiveness & Grants ....Ms. Debbie DOUMA
18 Director Physical Plant ....Mr. Walt WINTER
14 Director Computer Svcs/Telecommun ....Mr. William MELOY
15 Director Human Resources/EA/EO ....Ms. Tammy HENDERSON
37 Dir Fin Aid/Veteran Affairs/Scholar ....Ms. Karen KESSLER
36 Director Student Job Services ....Mr. Gil BIXEL
31 Dean Community Education ....Dr. Rebecca CAUSEY
19 Public Safety Director ....Mr. Hank SHIRAH
43 General Counsel ....Mr. Thomas J. GILLIAM
35 Director Student Life ....Mr. Peter WILKIN
08 Int District Dept Head Libraries ....Ms. Winifred BRADLEY
96 Director of Purchasing ....Ms. Angie C. JONES
21 Associate Business Officer ....Ms. Jackie PADILLA
29 Director Alumni Relations ....Ms. Breena BRUI
07 Director of Admissions ....Ms. Martha CAUGHEY
38 Director Student Counseling ....Ms. Kathy DUTREMBLE
41 Director Athletics ....Mr. Bill HAMILTON
84 Coordinator Enrollment Management ....Ms. Kathy DUTREMBLE

Polk State College (A)

999 Avenue H, NE, Winter Haven FL 33881-4299
County: Polk FICE Identification: 001514
Unit ID: 136516
Telephone: (863) 297-1000 Carnegie Class: Assoc/Pub-R-L
FAX Number: (863) 297-1065 Calendar System: Trimester
URL: www.polk.edu
Established: 1964 Annual Undergrad Tuition & Fees (In-District): $3,725
Enrollment: 11,925 Coed
Affiliation or Control: Local IRS Status: 501(c)3
Highest Offering: Baccalaureate
Program: Occupational; 2-Year Principally Bachelor's Creditable; Technical Emphasis
Accreditation: SC, ADNUR, CVT, EMT, OTA, PTAA, RAD

01 President ....Dr. Eileen HOLDEN
05 Vice Pres Academic/Student Svcs ....Dr. Ken ROSS
30 Assoc Vice Pres Development ....Ms. Tracy PORTER
10 Vice President Administration/CFO ....Mr. Peter A. ELLIOTT
26 Assoc VP Communications/Public Affs ....Mr. David STEELE
32 Dean Student Services-Lakeland ....Mr. Reggie WEBB
32 Dean Student Services-Winter Haven ....Mr. Charles LYLE
20 District Dn Academic/Student Svcs ....Dr. Patricia JONES
12 Provost Lakeland Campus ....Mr. Stephen E. HULL
12 Provost Winter Haven Campus ....Dr. Sharon MILLER
66 Director of Nursing ....Dr. Annette HUTCHERSON
06 Registrar ....Ms. Kathy BUCKLEW
21 Comptroller ....Ms. Teresa VOROUS
18 District Director Facilities ....Mr. George URBANO
37 Director Financial Aid ....Ms. Olivia MAULTSBY
22 Director of Equity & Diversity ....Ms. Val BAKER
41 Athletic Diredtor ....Mr. Bing TYUS
09 Dir Inst Research/Effective/Plng ....Mr. Peter USINGER
15 Director Personnel Services ....Ms. Jill HALL
84 Director Enrollment Management ....Mr. Reginald WEBB
96 Director of Purchasing ....Ms. Wendy GELTCH
27 Coordinator College Information ....Mr. Thomas E. DOWLING

Polytechnic University Puerto Rico (B)

8180 NW 36th Street, Suite 401, Miami FL 33166-6674
County: Miami-Dade Identification: 666238
Unit ID: 456481
Telephone: (305) 418-4220 Carnegie Class: Spec/Bus
FAX Number: (305) 418-4325 Calendar System: Trimester
URL: www.pupr.edu
Established: 2001 Annual Undergrad Tuition & Fees: $12,900
Enrollment: 178 Coed
Affiliation or Control: Independent Non-Profit IRS Status: 501(c)3
Highest Offering: Master's
Program: Professional; Technical Emphasis
Accreditation: &M

01 President ....Mr. Ernesto VAZQUEZ-BARQUET
03 VP & Campus Director ....Mr. Jose ORLANDO RIVERA
05 Vice Pres Academic Affairs ....Dr. Miguel RIESTRA
20 Academic Director ....Mr. Ernesto CASTRO
11 Vice Pres Administration/ Finance ....Mr. Ernesto VASQUEZ-MARTINEZ
07 Director of Admissions ....Ms. Teresa CARDONA
26 Marketing Director ....Mr. Luis MERCADO
37 Dir of Financial Aid/HR Coordinator ....Mr. Sergio VILLOLDO
06 Registrar & Finance Officer ....Ms. Taima GONZALEZ-LOPEZ
04 Administrative Assistant ....Ms. Diane PEREZ

† Regional accreditation is carried under the parent institution, Universidad Politecnica de Puerto Rico, San Juan, PR.

Professional Golfers Career College (C)

16349 Phil Ritson Way, Winter Garden FL 34787
County: Orange Identification: 666300
Telephone: (407) 905-2200 Carnegie Class: Not Classified
FAX Number: (407) 905-2241 Calendar System: Semester
URL: www.golfcollege.edu
Established: 2005 Annual Undergrad Tuition & Fees: $13,000
Enrollment: 185 Coed
Affiliation or Control: Proprietary IRS Status: Proprietary
Highest Offering: Associate Degree
Program: Occupational
Accreditation: ACICS

01 President ....Mr. Tim SOMMERVILLE
10 Chief Financial Officer ....Ms. Sandi SOMMERVILLE

Professional Training Center (D)

13926 SW 47th Street, Miami FL 33175-4404
County: Miami-Dade FICE Identification: 033484
Unit ID: 436702
Telephone: (305) 220-4120 Carnegie Class: Assoc/PrivFP
FAX Number: (305) 220-2889 Calendar System: Other
URL: www.ptcmatt.com
Established: 1994 Annual Undergrad Tuition & Fees: $38,595
Enrollment: 712 Coed
Affiliation or Control: Proprietary IRS Status: Proprietary
Highest Offering: Associate Degree
Program: Occupational; 2-Year Principally Bachelor's Creditable
Accreditation: ACICS, RAD

01 Chief Executive Officer ....Mr. Marc A. MATTIA
03 Campus Director ....Mr. Mike BEAUREGARD
06 Academic Registrar ....Mr. John KRAMER
07 Director of Admissions ....Vacant
15 Human Resources Director ....Ms. Jeannie HIDALGO
37 Student Finance Director ....Vacant
32 Student Services Director ....Vacant
36 Placement Director ....Mrs. Maria RODRIGUEZ
08 Librarian ....Ms. Ophelia WIETZ
51 Continuing Education Dept Director ....Ms. Lillian RUIZ
97 Dir of Assoc & General Education ....Dr. Victor FERNANDEZ
67 Pharmacy Director ....Mrs. Alicia TUMA
76 Diagnostic Med Sonography Pgm Dir ..Dr. Victor M. FERNANDEZ
88 Imaging Director ....Ms. Deborah HUGHES

Rasmussen College - Fort Myers (E)

9160 Forum Corporate Parkway, Fort Myers FL 33905
County: Lee Identification: 667062
Unit ID: 13830902
Telephone: (239) 477-2100 Carnegie Class: Not Classified
FAX Number: (239) 477-2101 Calendar System: Quarter
URL: www.rasmussen.edu
Established: 1900 Annual Undergrad Tuition & Fees: $16,340
Enrollment: 676 Coed
Affiliation or Control: Proprietary IRS Status: Proprietary
Highest Offering: Baccalaureate
Program: Occupational; 2-Year Principally Bachelor's Creditable
Accreditation: &NH, MAAB

02 Campus Director ....Eric WHITEHOUSE

† Regional accreditation is carried under the parent institution in Lake Elmo, MN.

Rasmussen College - New Port Richey (F)

7660 Little Road, New Port Richey FL 34654
Identification: 666425
Unit ID: 138336
Telephone: (727) 942-0069 Carnegie Class: Bac/Assoc
FAX Number: (727) 938-5709 Calendar System: Quarter
URL: www.rasmussen.edu
Established: 1968 Annual Undergrad Tuition & Fees: $16,340
Enrollment: 946 Coed
Affiliation or Control: Proprietary IRS Status: Proprietary
Highest Offering: Baccalaureate
Program: Occupational; 2-Year Principally Bachelor's Creditable
Accreditation: &NH, MAAB

01 Campus Director ....Mrs. Claire WALKER

† Regional accreditation is carried under parent institution in Lake Elmo, MN.

Rasmussen College - Ocala (G)

4755 SW 46th Court, Ocala FL 34474
County: Marion FICE Identification: 008501
Unit ID: 138309
Telephone: (352) 629-1941 Carnegie Class: Bac/Assoc
FAX Number: (352) 629-0926 Calendar System: Quarter
URL: www.rasmussen.edu
Established: 1968 Annual Undergrad Tuition & Fees: $16,340
Enrollment: 1,318 Coed
Affiliation or Control: Proprietary IRS Status: Proprietary
Highest Offering: Baccalaureate
Program: Occupational; 2-Year Principally Bachelor's Creditable
Accreditation: &NH, MAAB

01 Campus Director ....Mr. Pete BEASLEY

† Regional accreditation carried under the parent institution in Lake Elmo, MN.

Rasmussen College - Tampa/ Brandon (H)

4042 Park Oaks Boulevard, Tampa FL 33610
County: Hillsborough Identification: 667067
Unit ID: 13830903
Telephone: (813) 246-7600 Carnegie Class: Not Classified
FAX Number: (813) 621-4835 Calendar System: Quarter
URL: www.rasmussen.edu
Established: 1900 Annual Undergrad Tuition & Fees: $16,340
Enrollment: 18 Coed
Affiliation or Control: Proprietary IRS Status: Proprietary
Highest Offering: Baccalaureate
Program: Occupational; 2-Year Principally Bachelor's Creditable
Accreditation: &NH

01 Campus Director ....Margaret COOK

† Regional accreditation is carried under the parent institution in Lake Elmo, MN.

Reformed Theological Seminary (I)

1231 Reformation Drive, Oviedo FL 32765-7197
County: Seminole Identification: 666628
Unit ID: 372763
Telephone: (407) 366-9493 Carnegie Class: Not Classified
FAX Number: (407) 366-9425 Calendar System: Semester
URL: www.rts.edu
Established: 1989 Annual Graduate Tuition & Fees: $14,315
Enrollment: 470 Coed
Affiliation or Control: Independent Non-Profit IRS Status: 501(c)3
Highest Offering: Doctorate; No Undergraduates
Program: Professional; Religious Emphasis
Accreditation: &SC, &THEOL

00 Chancellor & CEO ....Dr. Robert C. CANNADA
00 Chancellor & CEO Elect ....Dr. Michael A. MILTON
01 President ....Dr. Donald W. SWEETING
11 Vice President of Administration ....Mr. Robert E. EMEOTT
30 Chief Development Officer ....Rev. Lynwood C. PEREZ
05 Academic Dean ....Dr. Mark D. FUTATO
32 Dean of Students ....Mr. Scott REDD
07 Director of Admissions ....Mr. Tom NELSON
06 Registrar ....Mr. Lanny CONLEY
58 Director of Doctor of Ministry ....Dr. Steven L. CHILDERS
08 Library Director ....Mr. John R. MUETHER
40 Bookstore Manager ....Mr. Greg THOMPSON
18 Superv Facilities/Physical Plant ....Mr. Gary MILLER
04 Assistant to the President ....Ms. Cristi MANSFIELD
36 Director of Placement ....Rev. Michael J. GLODO

† Regional accreditation is carried under the parent institution in Jackson, MS.

Remington College-Tampa Campus (J)

6302 E Martin Luther King Dr, #400, Tampa FL 33619
County: Hillsborough FICE Identification: 007586
Unit ID: 135939
Telephone: (813) 935-5700 Carnegie Class: Bac/Assoc
FAX Number: (813) 935-7415 Calendar System: Quarter
URL: www.remingtoncollege.edu
Established: 1948 Annual Undergrad Tuition & Fees: $30,900
Enrollment: 260 Coed
Affiliation or Control: Proprietary IRS Status: Proprietary
Highest Offering: Baccalaureate
Program: Occupational; Technical Emphasis
Accreditation: ACCSC, NURSE

01 President ....Dr. Rosalie LAMPONE
06 Registrar ....Ms. Mary BALTES
36 Director Student Placement ....Ms. Deborah HOFFMAN
37 Director Student Financial Aid ....Ms. Connie ROBINSON

Ringling College of Art and Design (K)

2700 N Tamiami Trail, Sarasota FL 34234-5895
County: Sarasota FICE Identification: 012574
Unit ID: 136774
Telephone: (941) 351-5100 Carnegie Class: Spec/Arts
FAX Number: (941) 359-7517 Calendar System: Semester
URL: www.ringling.edu
Established: 1931 Annual Undergrad Tuition & Fees: $34,840
Enrollment: 1,368 Coed
Affiliation or Control: Independent Non-Profit IRS Status: 501(c)3

Highest Offering: Baccalaureate
Program: Professional; Fine Arts Emphasis
Accreditation: SC, ART, CIDA

01 President ... Dr. Larry R. THOMPSON
04 Spec Asst to Pres Media & Cmty Rels ... Ms. Christine M. LANGE
05 Vice President for Academic Affairs ... Ms. Melody WEILER
30 VP Development/Alumni Relations ... Mr. Lance BURCHETT
10 Vice President for Finance & Admin ... Ms. Tracy A. WAGNER
15 VP Human/Organizational Development ... Ms. Christine C. DEGEORGE
21 Asst VP for Fin & Admn/Controller ... Ms. Monica K. WAID
18 Asst VP/Dir Facilities Operations ... Mr. Jeffrey A. POLESHEK
29 Asst VP of Dev/Alumni Relations ... Ms. Terri J. ARNELL
32 Vice President for Student Life ... Dr. Tammy WALSH
07 Dean of Admissions ... Mr. James H. DEAN
20 Assoc Vice Pres Faculty Affairs ... Mr. David JACKSON
51 Director of Continuing Studies ... Ms. Diane ZORN
06 Dir Advising/Records & Registration ... Ms. Donna M. ANDERSON
44 Director of Development ... Ms. Christine P. JOHNSON
90 Director Institutional Technology ... Dr. Mahmoud PEGAH
36 Director Career Services ... Mr. Charles KOVACS
26 Dir of Marketing & Communications ... Mr. James H. DEAN
37 Director of Financial Aid ... Mr. Kurt WOLF
19 Director of Public Safety ... Mr. Richard E. TUBBS
08 Director of Library Services ... Ms. Kathleen L. LIST
09 Dir of Student Outcomes Assessment ... Dr. Alison L. WATKINS

The Robert E. Webber Institute for Worship Studies (A)

151 Kingsley Avenue, Orange Park FL 32073-5640
County: Clay — Identification: 666616
Telephone: (904) 264-2172 — Carnegie Class: Not Classified
FAX Number: (904) 278-2878 — Calendar System: Semester
URL: www.iws.edu
Established: 1998 — Annual Graduate Tuition & Fees: $4,686
Enrollment: 134 — Coed
Affiliation or Control: Independent Non-Profit — IRS Status: 501(c)3
Highest Offering: Doctorate; No Undergraduates
Program: Professional; Religious Emphasis
Accreditation: BI

01 Chief Executive Officer ... Dr. James R. HART
05 Chief Academic Officer ... Dr. Andrew E. HILL
10 Chief Financial Officer ... Ms. Lea A. MONTGOMERY
06 Registrar ... Ms. Laura B. RITTER
07 Director of Admissions ... Mr. Mark MURRAY
08 Head Librarian ... Ms. Monica I. LOPEZ
29 Director Alumni Relations ... Dr. Kent L. WALTERS
42 Dean of the Chapel ... Dr. Darrell A. HARRIS
106 Dir of Distance Learning Technology ... Dr. Sam L. HOROWITZ
88 Administrative Support Specialist ... Ms. Sydney K. ASHMEAD
30 Administrative Asst for Advancement ... Ms. Sandy DINKINS
45 Dir Strategic Plng/Accreditation ... Dr. Steve HUNTLEY
13 Director of Information Technology . Dr. James Kenneth RUSHING

Rollins College (B)

1000 Holt Avenue, Winter Park FL 32789-4499
County: Orange — FICE Identification: 001515
Unit ID: 136950
Telephone: (407) 646-2000 — Carnegie Class: Master's L
FAX Number: (407) 646-2600 — Calendar System: Semester
URL: www.rollins.edu
Established: 1885 — Annual Undergrad Tuition & Fees: $38,400
Enrollment: 3,226 — Coed
Affiliation or Control: Independent Non-Profit — IRS Status: 501(c)3
Highest Offering: Master's
Program: Liberal Arts And General; Teacher Preparatory; Professional
Accreditation: SC, BUS, CACREP, MUS

01 President ... Dr. Lewis DUNCAN
05 Vice President Acad Affairs/Provost ... Dr. Carol BRESNAHAN
45 VP for Planning/Dean of the College ... Dr. Laurie JOYNER
10 Vice President Business/Finance ... Mr. Jeffrey EISENBARTH
30 VP for Institutional Advancement ... Dr. Ronald KORVAS
27 Chief Information Officer ... Dr. Pat SCHOKNECHT
20 Dean of the Faculty ... Vacant
32 Dean of Student Affairs ... Dr. Karen HATER
84 Dean of Enrollment Management ... Mr. David ERDMANN
51 Dean Hamilton Holt School ... Vacant
50 Dean of Graduate Business School ... Dr. Craig MCALLASTER
08 Director of Olin Library ... Dr. Jonathan MILLER
41 Athletic Director ... Ms. Pennie PARKER
21 Assoc VP Finance/Asst Treasurer ... Mr. William SHORT
30 Assoc Vice Pres Development ... Ms. Lisa THOMSON
29 Assoc VP Alumni Relations ... Dr. Sharon CARRIER
26 Assistant VP of Public Relations ... Ms. Ann Marie VARGA
88 Assistant VP Strategic Marketing ... Ms. Lisa JUNKERMAN
15 Asst VP Human Res/Risk Management ... Ms. Maria MARTINEZ
42 Dean of the Chapel ... Dr. Patrick POWERS
88 Exec Director Student Services ... Ms. Meghan HARTE
37 Director of Financial Aid ... Mr. Steve BOOKER
20 Assoc Dean Academic Administration ... Ms. Toni STROLLO HOLBROOK
09 Director of Institutional Research ... Mr. Udeth LUGO
104 Director of International Programs ... Ms. Giselda BEAUDIN
07 Director of Admission ... Ms. Holly POHLIG
39 Director of Residential Life ... Mr. Leon HAYNER
36 Director of Career Services ... Mr. Ray ROGERS
38 Director of Personal Counseling ... Dr. Joanne VOGEL
35 Dir Student Involvement Leadership ... Mr. Brent TURNER
18 Director of Facilities Management ... Mr. Scott BITIKOFER
96 Director of Business Services ... Ms. Kathy WELCH
19 Campus Security Director ... Mr. Ken MILLER
44 Director of Annual Giving ... Ms. Leslie CARNEY
44 Director of Planned Giving ... Ms. Amanda HOPKINS
102 Director of Foundation Relations ... Mr. Joseph MONTI
40 Manager of Bookstore ... Ms. Mary VITELLI
04 Exec Assistant to the President ... Dr. Lorrie KYLE

St. John Vianney College Seminary (C)

2900 SW 87th Avenue, Miami FL 33165-3244
County: Miami-Dade — FICE Identification: 008075
Unit ID: 137272
Telephone: (305) 223-4561 — Carnegie Class: Spec/Faith
FAX Number: (305) 223-0650 — Calendar System: Semester
URL: www.sjvcs.edu
Established: 1959 — Annual Undergrad Tuition & Fees: $17,900
Enrollment: 75 — Male
Affiliation or Control: Roman Catholic — IRS Status: 501(c)3
Highest Offering: Baccalaureate
Program: Liberal Arts And General
Accreditation: SC

01 Rector & President ... V.Rev. Roberto GAZA
05 Academic Dean ... Dr. Ramon SANTOS
06 Registrar ... Mrs. Bonnie DE ANGULO
08 Librarian ... Mrs. Maria RODRIGUEZ
32 Dean of Students ... Rev. Lucian PIERRE
38 Director of Counseling ... Vacant
09 Institutional Research Director ... Dr. Jose ORTA
42 Spiritual Director ... Rev. Juan Carlos RIOS

St. Johns River State College (D)

5001 St. Johns Avenue, Palatka FL 32177-3897
County: Putnam — FICE Identification: 001523
Unit ID: 137281
Telephone: (386) 312-4200 — Carnegie Class: Assoc/Pub-R-L
FAX Number: (386) 312-4229 — Calendar System: Semester
URL: www.sjrstate.edu
Established: 1958 — Annual Undergrad Tuition & Fees (In-District): $3,060
Enrollment: 7,468 — Coed
Affiliation or Control: State/Local — IRS Status: 501(c)3
Highest Offering: Baccalaureate
Program: Occupational; 2-Year Principally Bachelor's Creditable
Accreditation: SC

01 President ... Mr. Joe PICKENS
03 Exec Vice President/General Counsel ... Dr. Melissa C. MILLER
32 Vice President Student Affairs ... Dr. Gilbert L. EVANS, JR.
05 Vice President Academic Affairs ... Dr. Melanie A. BROWN
10 Vice President Business Affairs ... Mr. Albert P. LITTLE
11 Vice Pres Administrative Affairs ... Mrs. Annette W. BARRINEAU
30 Vice Pres Develop/External Affairs ... Mrs. Caroline D. TINGLE
09 VP for Research & Inst Effective ... Dr. Rosalind M. HUMERICK
103 Vice Pres Workforce Development ... Dr. Anna M. LEBESCH
13 Chief Information Officer ... Mr. Paul M. HAWKINS
12 Provost St Augustine Campus ... Dr. Gregory K. MCLEOD
12 Provost Orange Park/Dir Govt Rels ... Mr. James C. ROY
49 Dean of Arts & Sciences ... Dr. Laura L. BOILINI
57 Dean of Florida School of the Arts ... Mr. Alain R. HENTSCHEL
88 Director of Testing & Acad Success ... Mrs. Jane T. CRAWFORD
38 Director of Counsel/Acad Advise ... Ms. Sara J. MYERS
08 Dean of Library Services ... Mrs. Carmen M. CUMMINGS
66 Dean Nursing ... Dr. Mary A. LANEY
76 Dean of Allied Health Programs ... Dr. Thomas D. BAXTER
88 Assoc Dean Arts & Sci/Assoc Provost ... Mr. Michael J. KELLER
53 Associate Dean of Teacher Education ... Mrs. Carey A. BASS
88 Exec Director TH Center for the Art ... Mr. James A. WALSH
37 Dir Financial Aid/Veteran Affairs ... Mr. John W. BODIFORD
88 Director of Dual Enrollment ... Mrs. Melissa PERRY
51 Dir of Cont/Community Education ... Mrs. Meghan DEPUTY
26 Director of Public Relations ... Mrs. Susan B. KESSLER
88 Director Criminal Justice ... Mr. Gary A. KILLAM
07 Director of Admissions and Records ... Mrs. Susanne B. LINEBERGER
41 Director of Athletics ... Mr. Ross JONES, JR.
18 Facilities Director ... Mr. Michael CANADAY
96 Dir of Purchasing & Cont Admin ... Mrs. Beverly BARKER

Saint Leo University (E)

33701 State Road 52 W, Saint Leo FL 33574-6665
County: Pasco — FICE Identification: 001526
Unit ID: 137032
Telephone: (352) 588-8200 — Carnegie Class: Master's L
FAX Number: (352) 588-8654 — Calendar System: Semester
URL: www.saintleo.edu
Established: 1889 — Annual Undergrad Tuition & Fees: $18,870
Enrollment: 15,565 — Coed
Affiliation or Control: Roman Catholic — IRS Status: 501(c)3
Highest Offering: Beyond Master's But Less Than Doctorate
Program: Liberal Arts And General; Teacher Preparatory; Professional
Accreditation: SC, IACBE, SW

01 President ... Dr. Arthur F. KIRK, JR.
05 VP Academic Affairs ... Dr. Maribeth DURST
51 VP Continuing Ed/Student Services ... Dr. Edward DADEZ
84 VP Enrollment & Online Programs ... Ms. Kathryn MCFARLAND
10 VP Business Affairs ... Mr. Frank MEZZANINI
30 VP University Advancement ... Mr. David OSTRANDER
04 Assistant to the President ... Dr. David PERSKY
20 Associate VP Academic Affairs ... Dr. Jeffrey ANDERSON
09 Evaluation & Research Specialist ... Dr. Laura BLASI
51 Associate VP Continuing Education ... Dr. Beth CARTER
43 Associate VP/General Counsel ... Mr. Michael GRADISHER
84 Associate VP Enrollment ... Mr. Scott RHODES
45 Assoc VP Assessment/Inst Research ... Dr. Jeffrey ANDERSON
90 Associate VP/CIO ... Mr. Les LLOYD
42 Asst to the Pres for Univ Ministry ... Fr. Stephan BROWN
32 Assistant VP Student Services ... Mr. Kenneth POSNER
38 Dir Counseling & Career Services ... Mr. Lawson JOLLY
49 Dean School of Arts & Sciences ... Dr. Mary SPOTO
75 Dean School of Educ/Social Svcs ... Dr. Carol WALKER
50 Dean School of Business ... Dr. Michael NASTANSKI
58 Dir Graduate Studies in Business ... Dr. Lorrie MCGOVERN
58 Dir Grad Studies in Crim Justice ... Dr. Robert DIEMER
58 Dir Grad Studies in Education ... Dr. Karen HAHN
58 Dir Grad Studies in Social Work ... Dr. Cindy LEE
58 Dir Graduate Studies in Theology ... Fr. Anthony KISSEL
06 Registrar ... Mrs. Karen HATFIELD
08 Director Library Services ... Mr. Brent SHORT
07 Assoc VP of UG Admission/Advising ... Mr. Jeff WALSH
88 Director Instructional Technology ... Dr. Susan COLARIC
88 Dir Academic Student Support Svcs ... Dr. Joanne MACEACHRAN
11 Director Academic Administration ... Mr. Joseph TADEO
41 Director Athletics ... Mr. Fran REIDY
26 Director University Communications ... Ms. Maureen MOORE
18 Director Physical Plant ... Mr. Jose CABAN
19 Exec Dir Campus Security & Safety ... Mr. Robert SULLIVAN
23 Director Health Center ... Ms. Teresa DADEZ
88 Asst Director Disability Services ... Ms. Amanda BECKER
35 Director Campus Life ... Ms. Ana DI DONATO
29 Director Alumni Relations ... Mr. Eddie KENNY
88 Director Parent Relations ... Mr. Stephen KUABASEK
44 Exec Director Development ... Ms. Dawn PARISI
85 Assoc Director International Svcs ... Ms. Paige RAMSEY-HAMACHER
15 Human Resources Manager ... Ms. Theresa KLUENDER

St. Petersburg College (F)

PO Box 13489, Saint Petersburg FL 33733-3489
County: Pinellas — FICE Identification: 001528
Unit ID: 137078
Telephone: (727) 341-4772 — Carnegie Class: Bac/Assoc
FAX Number: (727) 341-3318 — Calendar System: Semester
URL: www.spcollege.edu
Established: 1927 — Annual Undergrad Tuition & Fees (In-District): $2,955
Enrollment: 32,454 — Coed
Affiliation or Control: Local — IRS Status: 501(c)3
Highest Offering: Baccalaureate
Program: Occupational; 2-Year Principally Bachelor's Creditable; Teacher Preparatory; Professional
Accreditation: SC, ADNUR, DH, EMT, FUSER, IFSAC, MLTAD, NURSE, OPE, PTAA, RAD

01 President ... Dr. William D. LAW
05 Sr Vice Pres Academic/Student Affs ... Dr. Anne M. COOPER
88 VP Bacc Pgms & University Ptnrshps ... Kay M. BURNISTON
32 VP Academic/Student Affairs ... Dr. Tonjua L. WILLIAMS
11 VP Admin/Bus Svcs & Info Technology .. Dr. Douglas S. DUNCAN
46 VP Economic Dev & Innov Projects ... Dennis L. JONES
18 VP Facilities Plng/Inst Svcs ... Susan M. REITER
15 Vice Pres Human Resources ... Patty JONES
30 VP Inst Advance/Exec Dir Foundation ... Frances NEU
45 Assoc VP Business Svcs ... Jamelle CONNER
84 Assoc VP Enrollment Mgmt ... Dr. Pat RINARD
37 Assoc VP Financial Asst Svcs ... Michael J. BENNETT
104 Assoc VP Univ Partnership Center ... Catherine C. KENNEDY
84 Dir Enrollment Management/Athletics ... Mark STRICKLAND
26 Dir Marketing/Public Information ... Michael O'KEEFFE
88 Dir Baccalaureate Student Success ... Jason KRUPP
43 Acting General Counsel ... Suzanne GARDNER
12 Campus Exec Offcr Allstate Center ... J. C. BROCK
12 Provost Clearwater Campus ... Dr. Stanley VITTETOE
12 Provost/Health Education Center ... Dr. Phil NICOTERA
12 Provost St Petersburg Campus ... Dr. Karen K. WHITE
12 Provost Seminole Campus ... Dr. James OLLIVER
12 Provost Tarpon Springs Campus ... Dr. Conferlete CARNEY
12 Campus Exec Officer Downtown Center ... Yvonne ULMER
22 Dir Equal Access/Equal Opportunity ... Pam SMITH
96 Dir Procurement & Asset Mgmt ... Paul SPINELLI
38 Dir Student Success ... Jo DVORACSEK
88 Dean College of Public Safety Admin ... Brian FRANK
88 Dean Col of Policy/Legal Studies ... Susan S. DEMERS
83 Dean Social & Behavioral Sciences ... Dr. Joseph SMILEY
88 Principal St. Pete Collegiate High ... Starla METZ
88 President Faculty Senate ... Maureen MAHONEY

St. Thomas University (G)

16401 NW 37th Avenue, Miami Gardens FL 33054-6498
County: Miami-Dade — FICE Identification: 001468
Unit ID: 137476
Telephone: (305) 625-6000 — Carnegie Class: Master's L
FAX Number: (305) 628-6510 — Calendar System: Semester
URL: www.stu.edu
Established: 1962 — Annual Undergrad Tuition & Fees: $23,910
Enrollment: 2,501 — Coed
Affiliation or Control: Roman Catholic — IRS Status: 501(c)3
Highest Offering: Doctorate

Program: Liberal Arts And General; Teacher Preparatory; Professional
Accreditation: SC, LAW, THEOL

01 President .... Msgr. Franklyn M. CASALE
05 Provost & Chief Academic Officer .... Dr. Gregory S. CHAN
10 Vice Pres Finance/Administration .... Mr. Terrence O'CONNER
61 Dean of Law School .... Mr. Douglas RAY
30 Vice Pres University Advancement .... Dr. Beverly BACHRACH
45 Vice Pres for Planning & Enrollment .... Dr. Beatriz G. ROBINSON
20 Assoc Provost Academic Support Svcs .... Dr. Susan B. ANGULO
84 Dean Enrollment Management .... Mr. Andre LIGHTBOURN
26 Director Marketing/Communications .... Ms. Marivi PRADO
06 Assoc Prov Records/Acad Computing .... Ms. Maria ABDEL
37 Director Financial Aid .... Ms. Anh T. DO
08 University Librarian .... Mr. Larry TREADWELL
21 Controller .... Ms. Maribel RAMIREZ
18 Director Facilities/Physical Plant .... Mr. Juan ZAMORA
09 Director Institutional Research .... Dr. Jerry A. WEINBERG
36 Director Career Services .... Mr. Timothy DEPALMA
41 Athletic Director .... Ms. Laura COURTLEY-TODD
32 Dean of Students .... Mr. Isaac CARTER
15 Assoc Director Human Resources .... Ms. Lenore PRADO
25 Assoc Dir Grant Writing/Publication .... Ms. Susan L. SMITH
38 Assoc Director Health & Wellness .... Vacant
73 Interim Dean School of Theology .... Dr. Mary CARTER-WAREN
12 Dean Biscayne College .... Dr. Scott ZERMAN
27 Chief Information Officer .... Mr. Rudy IBARRA
29 Director Alumni Relations .... Mr. Jerry BERNFELD
44 Director Annual Giving .... Ms. Janine LAUDISIO
11 Director for Administration .... Ms. Sylvia RODRIGUEZ

St. Vincent De Paul Regional Seminary (A)

10701 S Military Trail, Boynton Beach FL 33436-4899
County: Palm Beach FICE Identification: 008223
Unit ID: 136701
Telephone: (561) 732-4424 Carnegie Class: Spec/Faith
FAX Number: (561) 737-2205 Calendar System: Semester
URL: www.svdp.edu
Established: 1963 Annual Graduate Tuition & Fees: $32,740
Enrollment: 97 Coed
Affiliation or Control: Roman Catholic IRS Status: 501(c)3
Highest Offering: Master's; No Undergraduates
Program: Religious Emphasis
Accreditation: SC, THEOL

01 Rector/President .... Rev. Keith BRENNAN
03 Vice Rector .... Rev. Jose ALFARO
05 Academic Dean/Registrar .... Dcn. Dennis DEMES
10 Treasurer .... Mr. Keith PARKER
08 Director of the Library .... Mr. Arthur QUINN

Sanford-Brown Institute (B)

1201 W Cypress Creek Road, Ste 101,
Fort Lauderdale FL 33309
County: Broward Identification: 667031
Unit ID: 385008
Telephone: (954) 308-7400 Carnegie Class: Assoc/PrivFP
FAX Number: (954) 375-6900 Calendar System: Other
URL: www.sanfordbrown.edu/Fort-Lauderdale
Established: 1989 Annual Undergrad Tuition & Fees: $13,900
Enrollment: 835 Coed
Affiliation or Control: Proprietary IRS Status: Proprietary
Highest Offering: Associate Degree
Program: Occupational; Technical Emphasis
Accreditation: ACICS, DA, DH, DMS, MAAB, SURTEC

01 President .... Mr. Michael LABELLE

† Branch campus of Sanford-Brown College, Atlanta, GA.

Sanford-Brown Institute (C)

10255 Fortune Parkway, Suite #501,
Jacksonville FL 32256-0757
County: Duval FICE Identification: 026164
Unit ID: 404505
Telephone: (904) 363-6221 Carnegie Class: Assoc/PrivFP
FAX Number: (904) 363-6824 Calendar System: Other
URL: www.sanfordbrown.edu/Jacksonville
Established: 1977 Annual Undergrad Tuition & Fees: $13,875
Enrollment: 1,002 Coed
Affiliation or Control: Proprietary IRS Status: Proprietary
Highest Offering: Associate Degree
Program: Occupational
Accreditation: ACICS, DH, MAAB, SURGT, SURTEC

01 Executive Director .... Ms. Aida SHEHU

Sanford-Brown Institute (D)

5701 E Hillsborough Ave, Suite 1417,
Tampa FL 33610-5428
County: Hillsborough Identification: 666027
Unit ID: 379029
Telephone: (813) 621-0072 Carnegie Class: Assoc/PrivFP
FAX Number: (813) 626-0392 Calendar System: Other
URL: www.sanfordbrown.edu/Tampa
Established: 1984 Annual Undergrad Tuition & Fees: N/A
Enrollment: 678 Coed
Affiliation or Control: Proprietary IRS Status: Proprietary
Highest Offering: Associate Degree
Program: Occupational
Accreditation: ACICS, MAAB

01 President .... Mr. Steeve DUMERVE

† Branch campus of Sanford-Brown Institute, Jacksonville, FL.

Santa Fe College (E)

3000 NW 83rd Street, Gainesville FL 32606-6200
County: Alachua FICE Identification: 001519
Unit ID: 137096
Telephone: (352) 395-5000 Carnegie Class: Assoc/Pub-R-L
FAX Number: (352) 395-5581 Calendar System: Semester
URL: www.sfcollege.edu
Established: 1965 Annual Undergrad Tuition & Fees (In-District): $3,071
Enrollment: 17,630 Coed
Affiliation or Control: Local IRS Status: 501(c)3
Highest Offering: Baccalaureate
Program: Occupational; 2-Year Principally Bachelor's Creditable
Accreditation: SC, ADNUR, CONST, CVT, DA, DH, EMT, NMT, PNUR, RAD, SURGT

01 President .... Dr. Jackson N. SASSER
05 Vice Pres Academic Affairs .... Dr. Edward BONAHUE
10 Chief Financial Ofcr/VP Admin Affs .... Ms. Ginger GIBSON
11 Vice Pres College Services .... Mr. Guy L. YORK
32 Vice President Student Affairs .... Dr. Portia L. TAYLOR
30 Vice President Development .... Mr. Chuck CLEMONS
04 Assistant to the President .... Mr. Lawrence D. KEEN
20 Associate VP Academic Affairs .... Dr. Curtis JEFFERSON
13 Assoc VP Information Tech Services .... Mr. Timothy C. NESLER
18 Assoc VP Facilities Services .... Mr. William REESE
25 Asst VP/Development/Grants/Projects .. Ms. Joan M. SUCHORSKI
20 Asst Vice Pres Academic Affairs .... Dr. Dave YONUTAS
90 Asst VP/Academic Affs .... Mr. Kim KENDALL
35 Assoc VP Student Affs/Financial Aid .... Mr. Steven H. FISHER
26 Assoc VP College/Community Rels .... Ms. Bennye J. ALLIGOOD
35 Asst Vice Pres Student Affairs .... Mr. John COWART
09 Assoc VP Inst Effect/Rsrch/Plng .... Vacant
43 Legal Counsel .... Ms. Patti P. LOCASCIO
06 College Registrar .... Ms. Lynn SULLIVAN
88 Dir High Sch Dual Enrollment Pgm ... Ms. Linda LANZA-KADUCE
88 Director Advisement Center .... Ms. Emilia HODGE
41 Athletic Director .... Mr. Jim KEITES
08 Director Library Service .... Ms. Myra STERRETT
19 Chief of Police/Dir Inst Pub Safety .... Capt. Daryl JOHNSTON
35 Director Student Life .... Mr. Dan RODKIN
96 Director of Purchasing .... Mr. David SHLAFER
28 Director of Diversity .... Ms. Elizabeth O'REGGIO
37 Director Student Financial Aid .... Ms. Maureen MCFARLANE
15 Director Human Resources .... Ms. Lela ELMORE
38 Coordinator Student Counseling .... Mr. Mardell COLEMAN

Schiller International University (F)

8560 Ulmerton Road, Largo FL 33771
County: Pinellas FICE Identification: 023141
Unit ID: 404338
Telephone: (727) 736-5082 Carnegie Class: Spec/Bus
FAX Number: (727) 734-0359 Calendar System: Semester
URL: www.schiller.edu
Established: 1964 Annual Undergrad Tuition & Fees: $18,660
Enrollment: 212 Coed
Affiliation or Control: Proprietary IRS Status: Proprietary
Highest Offering: Master's
Program: Occupational; Liberal Arts And General; Business Emphasis
Accreditation: ACICS

01 President .... Dr. Michele Z. GEIGLE
05 Provost .... Dr. Angela P. CARNEY
07 Director of Admissions .... Ms. Betty RUSZKOWSKI

Seminole State College of Florida (G)

100 Weldon Boulevard, Sanford FL 32773-6199
County: Seminole FICE Identification: 001520
Unit ID: 137209
Telephone: (407) 708-4722 Carnegie Class: Assoc/Pub-S-SC
FAX Number: (407) 708-2139 Calendar System: Semester
URL: www.seminolestate.edu
Established: 1965 Annual Undergrad Tuition & Fees (In-District): $3,131
Enrollment: 18,028 Coed
Affiliation or Control: Local IRS Status: 501(c)3
Highest Offering: Baccalaureate
Program: Occupational; 2-Year Principally Bachelor's Creditable
Accreditation: SC, ADNUR, EMT, PTAA

01 President .... Dr. E. Ann MCGEE
09 Vp Institutional Effect/Innovation .... Dr. Carol HAWKINS
10 VP Admin & Financial Svcs/CFO .... Mr. Joseph SARNOVSKY
05 Int VP Educ Pgms/Chief Acad Ofcr .... Dr. James HENNINGSEN
32 Int VP Stdnt Success/Chf Stdnt Affs .... Ms. Marcia ROMAN
13 VP Information Tech/Resources/CIO .... Mr. Dick T. HAMANN
102 Executive Director Foundation .... Mr. John GYLLIN
21 Associate VP Finance & Budget .... Ms. Lynn POWERS
26 Assoc VP College Relations & Mktg .... Mr. Michael GARLICH
12 Provost Altamonte Springs .... Ms. Lynn COLON
12 Provost of Oviedo Campus .... Mrs. Lisa VALENTINO
28 Asst to Pres Diversity & Equity .... Ms. Yolanda WILLIAMS
45 Dean of Planning & Assessment .... Dr. Christine ROBINSON
08 Dean of Learning Resources .... Ms. Patricia D. DESALVO
49 Dean of Art & Sciences .... Dr. Laura ROSS
36 Dean of Career Programs .... Ms. Angela M. KERSENBROCK
88 Provost Economic Dev/Employer Svcs .... Mr. Michael STALEY
51 Dean of Adult Education .... Mr. Robert LEDFORD
86 Director of Government Relations .... Mr. Donald PAYTON
91 Dir Network/Telecomm Infrastructure .... Mr. Julio VALENTIN
38 Director Counseling/Educ Planning .... Ms. Patry ENGLISH
53 Director of Education Curriculum .... Vacant
15 Director of Human Resources .... Dr. Claudia SALVANO
06 Int Dir Enrollment Svcs/Registrar .... Mr. John SCARPINO
88 Dir Student Success Initiatives .... Dr. Marcia ROMAN
90 Director Academic Computing .... Mr. Michael HOLMES
37 Director Student Financial Aid .... Mr. Robert LYNN
09 Director Institutional Research .... Dr. Mark MORGAN
18 Dir Facilities Planning/Constr/Mgmt .... Mrs. Adie PRICE
35 Director Student Life .... Mr. Randy PAWLOWSKI
96 Director of Purchasing & Auxiliary .... Mr. Scott ROCHE
41 Director Intercollegiate Athletics .... Mr. John SCARPINO
07 Dir Student Recruitment & Admission .... Mrs. Pamela PELAEZ
36 Dir Career Development Services .... Mrs. Christy KING
25 Director Grants Development .... Dr. Angela ALBERT
88 Director Enterprise System .... Ms. Pilar ACOSTA

South Florida Bible College (H)

1100 South Federal Highway, Deerfield Beach FL 33441
County: Broward FICE Identification: 032643
Unit ID: 366003
Telephone: (954) 545-4500 Carnegie Class: Spec/Faith
FAX Number: (954) 480-9755 Calendar System: Semester
URL: www.sfbc.edu
Established: 1985 Annual Undergrad Tuition & Fees: $5,075
Enrollment: 125 Coed
Affiliation or Control: Interdenominational IRS Status: 501(c)3
Highest Offering: Doctorate
Program: Professional; Religious Emphasis
Accreditation: @BI

01 President .... Dr. Joseph GUADAGNINO
03 Provost .... Mary A. DRABIK
10 Chief Financial Officer .... Beatrice GUADAGNINO
06 Registrar .... Katie SLAUGHTER
08 Librarian .... Timothy SKINNER
05 Dean of Faculty .... Esa AUTERO
32 Dean of Students .... Dr. Thomas DRABIK

South Florida Community College (I)

600 W College Drive, Avon Park FL 33825-9399
County: Highlands FICE Identification: 001522
Unit ID: 137315
Telephone: (863) 453-6661 Carnegie Class: Assoc/Pub-R-M
FAX Number: (863) 453-0165 Calendar System: Trimester
URL: www.southflorida.edu
Established: 1965 Annual Undergrad Tuition & Fees (In-District): $2,986
Enrollment: 6,064 Coed
Affiliation or Control: Local IRS Status: 501(c)3
Highest Offering: Associate Degree
Program: Occupational; 2-Year Principally Bachelor's Creditable
Accreditation: SC, DA, DH, RAD

01 President .... Dr. Norman L. STEPHENS, JR.
05 Vice Pres Educational/Stdnt Svcs .... Dr. Leana REVELL
11 Vice Pres Administrative Services .... Mr. Glenn W. LITTLE
51 Dean Adult & Continuing Education .... Dr. Michael MCLEOD
75 Dean Applied Science & Tech .... Mr. J. Kevin BROWN
49 Dean Arts & Sciences .... Dr. Kimberly BATTY-HERBERT
88 Dean Cultural Programming .... Mr. Douglas M. ANDREWS
45 Dean Resource Development .... Mr. Donald L. APPELQUIST
32 Dean Student Services .... Mrs. Annie ALEXANDER-HARVEY
84 Assoc Dean Enrollment Svcs/Univ Rel .... Mrs. Laura M. WHITE
12 Director DeSoto Campus .... Mrs. Suzanne DEMERS
12 Director Hardee Campus .... Ms. Teresa CRAWFORD
12 Director Lake Placid Center .... Mr. Randall K. PAEPLOW
21 Controller .... Mrs. Anita A. KOVACS
26 Director Community Relations .... Ms. Deborah BELL
72 Director Educational Tech Center .... Mrs. Melanie M. JACKSON
15 Director Human Res/EA-EO & ADA Ofcr .... Mrs. Susie HALE
18 Dir Phys Plant/Opers/Maintenance .... Mr. Roberto FLORES
06 Registrar .... Dr. Deborah M. FUSCHETTI
41 Athletic Director .... Mr. Richard J. HITT
36 Director Career Development Center .... Mrs. Colleen RAFATTI
37 Director Financial Aid .... Ms. Susie JOHNSON
13 Director Information Technology .... Dr. Linda WARD
09 Director Instl Res/Curriculum Devel .... Mr. Daniel D. MCAULIFF
38 Director Student Counseling .... Ms. Judy ZEMKO
08 Library Services .... Ms. Lena PHELPS-ELLERKER
40 Manager College Bookstore .... Mr. Gene HALEY
96 Coordinator Purchasing .... Mr. Richard PEAVY
10 Chief Business Officer .... Mrs. Anita A. KOVACS

South University (J)

9801 Belevedere Road, Royal Palm Beach FL 33411
County: Palm Beach Identification: 666117
Unit ID: 133465
Telephone: (561) 273-6500 Carnegie Class: Bac/Diverse
FAX Number: (561) 273-6420 Calendar System: Quarter
URL: www.southuniversity.edu
Established: 1899 Annual Undergrad Tuition & Fees: $15,735
Enrollment: 946 Coed
Affiliation or Control: Proprietary IRS Status: Proprietary

Highest Offering: Master's
Program: Occupational; 2-Year Principally Bachelor's Creditable; Liberal Arts And General
Accreditation: &SC, NURSE, PTAA

01 President .... Mr. David MCGUIRE
05 Dean of Academic Affairs .... Vacant
32 Dean of Student Affairs .... Ms. Maria SANTOS
07 Director of Admissions .... Mr. Gary MALISOS
37 Director of Financial Aid .... Ms. Kacey ATKINSON
10 Director of Finance .... Ms. Luz ARROYO
13 Director Computing/Info Management .... Ms. Sharon JACKSON
21 Business Officer .... Ms. Rowena GEISLER
06 Registrar .... Ms. Michelle BELKIN
08 Head Librarian .... Mr. David BOSCA
36 Career Services Coordinator .... Ms. Jessica RENARD

† Regional accreditation is carried under the parent institution in Savannah, GA.

Southeastern University (A)

1000 Longfellow Boulevard, Lakeland FL 33801-6099
County: Polk FICE Identification: 001521
Unit ID: 137564
Telephone: (863) 667-5000 Carnegie Class: Bac/Diverse
FAX Number: (863) 667-5200 Calendar System: Semester
URL: www.seuniversity.edu
Established: 1935 Annual Undergrad Tuition & Fees: $17,718
Enrollment: 2,779 Coed
Affiliation or Control: Assemblies Of God Church IRS Status: 501(c)3
Highest Offering: Master's
Program: Liberal Arts And General; Teacher Preparatory; Religious Emphasis
Accreditation: SC, IACBE, SW

01 President .... Dr. Kent INGLE
03 Executive Vice President .... Mr. Del CHITTIM
05 Vice President for Academic Affairs ... Dr. William C. HACKET, JR.
10 Vice Pres Finance/Administration .... Vacant
30 VP for University Advancement .... Mr. Brian C. CARROLL
06 Dir Student Records/Registrar .... Mr. Anthony G. DE SOUZA
09 Assoc VPAA/Dean Inst Research .... Dr. Andrew H. PERMENTER
08 Dean of Library Services .... Mrs. Grace VEACH
37 Director Student Financial Services .... Mrs. Carol B. BRADLEY
07 Director of Admission .... Ms. Betania TORRES
15 Director Human Resources .... Mrs. Clara S. ENGLISH
29 Director Alumni Relations .... Ms. Jebapriya ARUL
18 Chief Facilities/Physical Plant .... Mr. Norman M. ALDERMAN
88 Director of Academic Success .... Mrs. Pamela CROSBY
36 Director of Career Services .... Mrs. Jacquelyn SMALL
21 Controller .... Mr. Randy PATRICK
26 Public Relations Officer .... Mr. Edward MANER
38 Director Student Counseling .... Dr. James (Emory) WELCH
35 VP for Student Development .... Mr. James (Chris) OWEN
84 VP for Enrollment Management .... Mr. Roy ROWLAND, IV
96 Director of Purchasing .... Mr. David W. DUPAUL
88 Dir of Institutional Effectiveness .... Mr. Andrew MILLER

Southern Career College (B)

950 Regency Square Blvd, Suite 1100,
Jacksonville FL 32225
County: Duval FICE Identification: 025982
Unit ID: 134121
Telephone: (904) 724-2229 Carnegie Class: Assoc/PrivFP
FAX Number: (904) 720-0920 Calendar System: Quarter
URL: www.flatech.edu
Established: 1960 Annual Undergrad Tuition & Fees: $14,100
Enrollment: 185 Coed
Affiliation or Control: Proprietary IRS Status: Proprietary
Highest Offering: Associate Degree
Program: Occupational
Accreditation: ACICS

01 Executive Director/Academic Dean .... Mr. Don SLAYTER

Southern Technical College (C)

1485 Florida Mall Ave, Orlando FL 32809-7733
County: Orange FICE Identification: 039035
Unit ID: 446552
Telephone: (407) 438-6000 Carnegie Class: Not Classified
FAX Number: (407) 438-6005 Calendar System: Semester
URL: www.southerntech.edu
Established: 1956 Annual Undergrad Tuition & Fees: $30,900
Enrollment: 1,357 Coed
Affiliation or Control: Proprietary IRS Status: Proprietary
Highest Offering: Associate Degree
Program: Occupational
Accreditation: ACICS

01 Dean .... Mr. Dwayne ORE

Southwest Florida College (D)

1685 Medical Lane, Fort Myers FL 33907-1158
County: Lee FICE Identification: 022788
Unit ID: 366553
Telephone: (239) 939-4766 Carnegie Class: Bac/Assoc
FAX Number: (239) 790-2118 Calendar System: Quarter
URL: www.swfc.edu
Established: 1974 Annual Undergrad Tuition & Fees: $11,880
Enrollment: 2,316 Coed
Affiliation or Control: Proprietary IRS Status: Proprietary
Highest Offering: Baccalaureate
Program: Occupational; 2-Year Principally Bachelor's Creditable; Teacher Preparatory; Professional; Business Emphasis
Accreditation: ACICS, MAAB

01 President .... Dr. Stephen CALABRO
05 Chief Academic Officer .... Dr. Barbara CALABRO
20 VP of Academic Affairs .... Dr. Melanie YERK

State College of Florida, Manatee-Sarasota (E)

PO Box 1849, Bradenton FL 34206-7046
County: Manatee FICE Identification: 001504
Unit ID: 135391
Telephone: (941) 752-5000 Carnegie Class: Assoc/Pub-U-MC
FAX Number: (941) 758-6830 Calendar System: Semester
URL: www.scf.edu
Established: 1957 Annual Undergrad Tuition & Fees (In-District): $3,074
Enrollment: 11,371 Coed
Affiliation or Control: Local IRS Status: 501(c)3
Highest Offering: Baccalaureate
Program: Occupational; 2-Year Principally Bachelor's Creditable
Accreditation: SC, ADNUR, DH, NUR, OTA, PTAA, RAD

01 President .... Dr. Lars A. HAFNER
04 Exec Assistant to President/Board .... Ms. Pamela MORRIS
10 Vice President Business/Admin Svcs .. Dr. Carol F. PROBSTFELD
05 VP Academic Quality & Success .... Dr. W. Jack CROCKER
20 Assoc VP Acad Quality & Success .... Mr. Gary RUSSELL
32 VP Educational & Student Services .... Dr. Donald R. BOWMAN
12 Provost Bradenton/VP Baccalaureate .... Dr. Michael J. MEARS
12 Provost Lakewood Ranch/Dean BSN .... Dr. Bonnie HESSELBERG
12 Provost Venice Campus .... Ms. Darlene WEDLER-JOHNSON
102 Exec Dir SCF Foundation Inc .... Ms. Peg LOWERY
15 Executive Director Human Resources .... Ms. Margaret Z. BECK
21 Assoc VP Finance .... Ms. Karen A. KESTER
38 Assoc VP Student Development .... Dr. Helen T. MEYER
06 Assoc VP Student Services .... Ms. MariLynn J. LEWY
31 Assoc VP Corporate & Community Dev .... Ms. Daisy VULOVICH
25 Assoc VP Eval & Compl & Inst Effect .... Mr. Bradley W. DAVIS
45 Assoc VP Facilities & Planning .... Ms. Traci STEEN
51 Director Inst of Continuing/Cmty Ed .... Ms. Cynthia HUNTER
19 Director Business Svc/Public Safety ... Mr. Timothy LANGENBACK
22 Equity Officer .... Ms. Gloria TRACY
72 Director Career & Technical Ed .... Dr. Idelia P. PHILLIPS
08 Director Library Services .... Ms. Tracy ELLIOTT
09 Director Institutional Research .... Ms. Su-hua MEN
14 Chief Information Officer .... Mr. Feng HOU
26 Director Public Affairs & Marketing .... Ms. Katherine WALKER
37 Director Financial Aid .... Mr. Jack TONEY
40 Manager Bookstore .... Mrs. Betty J. GIBSON
36 Director Career Resource Centers .... Ms. Denise D. GATCH
41 Director Athletics .... Mr. Matt ENNIS
103 Director Inst Workforce Development .... Mr. David AUXIER
88 Director Academic Resource Centers .... Ms. Jacquelyn MCNEIL
43 General Counsel .... Mr. Steve PROUTY
88 Head of SCF Collegiate School .... Ms. Kelly MONOD

*State University System of Florida, Board of Governors (F)

325 W Gaines Street, Suite 1614,
Tallahassee FL 32399-0400
County: Leon FICE Identification: 008068
Unit ID: 137449
Telephone: (850) 245-0466 Carnegie Class: N/A
FAX Number: (850) 245-9685
URL: www.flbog.edu

01 Chancellor .... Mr. Frank T. BROGAN
05 Vice Chanc Academic/Student Affairs .... Dr. Dorothy J. MINEAR
10 Vice Chanc Budget & Finance .... Mr. Tim JONES
43 General Counsel .... Ms. Vikki SHIRLEY
22 Inspector General & Compliance .... Mr. Derry HARPER
101 Corporate Secretary .... Ms. Mikey BESTEBREURTJE
100 Chief of Staff .... Mr. Randy A. GOIN, JR.

*Florida Agricultural and Mechanical University (G)

Tallahassee FL 32307
County: Leon FICE Identification: 001480
Unit ID: 133650
Telephone: (850) 599-3000 Carnegie Class: DRU
FAX Number: (850) 599-3952 Calendar System: Semester
URL: www.famu.edu
Established: 1887 Annual Undergrad Tuition & Fees (In-State): $5,571
Enrollment: 13,284 Coed
Affiliation or Control: State IRS Status: 501(c)3
Highest Offering: Doctorate
Program: Occupational; Liberal Arts And General; Teacher Preparatory; Professional
Accreditation: SC, CS, ENG, ENGT, JOUR, LAW, LSAR, NUR, #OT, PH, PHAR, PTA, SW, TED

02 President .... Dr. James H. AMMONS
05 Provost/Vice Pres Academic Affs ... Dr. Cynthia HUGHES-HARRIS
10 Vice Pres Admin & Financial Svcs .... Ms. Teresa HARDEE
32 Interim Vice Pres Student Affairs .... Mr. William HUDSON, JR.
30 Interim VP University Relations .... Mrs. Sharon SAUNDERS
25 Interim VP for Sponsored Research .... Dr. Kinfe K. REDDA
88 VP Audit and Compliance .... Dr. Charles O'DUOR
13 Interim CIO Enterprise Technology .... Mr. Michael JAMES
35 Assoc Vice Pres Student Affairs .... Mr. Henry KIRBY
44 Asst VP University Development .... Vacant
20 Associate VP for Academic Affairs .... Vacant
21 Asst Vice Pres Planning & Budgeting .... Vacant
06 University Registrar .... Dr. Agatha ONWUNLI
43 University Attorney .... Atty. Avery MCKNIGHT
07 Director of Admissions .... Ms. Barbara COX
08 Director of University Libraries .... Dr. Lauren SAPP
37 Director of Financial Aid .... Ms. Marcia CONLIFFE
36 Director of The Career Center .... Dr. Delores DEAN
09 Director of Institutional Research .... Dr. Kwadwo OWUSU-ADUEMIRI
28 Director of EEO .... Ms. Carrie GAVIN
26 Chief Public Relations Officer .... Mrs. Sharon SAUNDERS
21 University Controller .... Mr. Vinod SHARMA
15 Assistant VP for Human Resources .... Ms. Nellie WOODRUFF
29 Director of Alumni Affairs .... Mrs. Carmen CUMMINGS
51 Director of Continuing Education .... Mrs. Phyllis WATSON
49 Dean of Arts & Sciences .... Dr. Ralph TURNER
50 Dean of Business and Industry ..... Dr. Shawnta FRIDAY-STROUD
66 Interim Dean of Nursing .... Dr. Ruena NORMAN
67 Interim Dean of Pharmacy .... Dr. Seth ABLOREDEPPEY
53 Dean of Education .... Dr. Genniver BELL
54 Interim Dean Engr Sci/Tech/Agricult .... Dr. Samuel DONALD
48 Dean of Architecture .... Mr. Rodner B. WRIGHT
97 Dean of General Studies .... Dr. Dorothy HENDERSON
60 Dean of Journalism .... Dr. James M. HAWKINS
58 Interim Dean of Graduate Studies .... Dr. Verian THOMAS
76 Dean of Allied Health Sciences .... Dr. Barbara MOSLEY
54 Interim Dean FAMU/FSU Engineering .... Dr. John COLLIER
61 Dean College of Law .... Mr. Leroy PERNELL
19 Director of Security .... Mr. Calvin ROSS
23 Director of Student Health Services .... Ms. Tanya TATUM
41 Director of Athletics .... Mr. Derek HORNE
18 Assoc VP Facilities/Plng/Phys Plnt .... Mr. Joseph BAKKER
38 Director Counseling Services .... Dr. Yolanda BOGAN
96 Director of Purchasing .... Ms. Stephany FALL
101 Chief of Staff/BOT Liaison .... Mrs. Rosalind FUSE-HALL
04 Assistant to the President .... Mrs. Patricia WOODARD
88 Int Director Environmental Sciences .... Dr. Michael ABAZINGE
86 Director of Governmental Relations .... Mr. Tola THOMPSON

*Florida Atlantic University (H)

PO Box 3091, 777 Glades Road,
Boca Raton FL 33431-0991
County: Palm Beach FICE Identification: 001481
Unit ID: 133669
Telephone: (561) 297-3000 Carnegie Class: RU/H
FAX Number: (561) 297-3942 Calendar System: Semester
URL: www.fau.edu
Established: 1961 Annual Undergrad Tuition & Fees (In-State): $5,372
Enrollment: 28,394 Coed
Affiliation or Control: State IRS Status: 501(c)3
Highest Offering: Doctorate
Program: Liberal Arts And General; Teacher Preparatory; Professional
Accreditation: SC, BUS, CACREP, CORE, CS, ENG, #MED, MUS, NURSE, PLNG, SP, SPAA, SW, TED

02 President .... Dr. Mary Jane SAUNDERS
03 Vice President & Associate Provost .... Dr. Joyanne G. STEPHENS
30 Sr Vice Pres Univ Advancement .... Mr. Randy TALBOT
45 Vice President Strategic Planning .... Dr. Gitanjali KAUL
63 Vice President College of Medicine .... Dr. Michael FRIEDLAND
05 Univ Prov/Chief Academic Officer .... Dr. Brenda CLAIBORNE
10 VP Finance/Chief Fiscal Officer .... Mr. Dennis CRUDELE
32 Vice President Student Affairs .... Dr. Charles L. BROWN
46 Vice President Research .... Dr. Barry ROSSON
88 Assoc Vice Pres Univ Architect Ofc .... Mr. Tom DONAUDY
46 Associate Vice President Research .... Vacant
20 Assoc Provost Acad Budget/Planning .... Dr. Norman KAUFMAN
13 Assoc Provost Info Resource Mgmt .... Mr. Jason BALL
29 Vice President Alumni Relations .... Mr. Bradford W. CREWS
27 Asst Vice Pres Creative Services .... Ms. Jan BOND
21 Assoc Bus Ofcr/Assoc VP For Admin .... Ms. Dorothy RUSSELL
35 Interim Assoc Dean Student Affairs .... Mr. Terry MENA
43 General Counsel .... Mr. David KIAN
27 University Ombudsman .... Ms. Patricia SINGER
22 Director EEO Programs .... Ms. Paula BEHUL
84 Assoc Provost Enrollment Management .... Vacant
20 Assoc Provost Personnel & Programs .... Dr. Diane ALPERIN
80 Dean of Design and Social Inquiry .... Dr. Rosalyn Y. CARTER
49 Interim Dean of Arts & Letters .... Dr. Heather COLTMAN
50 Dean of Business .... Dr. Dennis COATES
53 Dean of Education .... Dr. Valerie BRISTOR
54 Int Dean of Engineering/Comp Sci .... Dr. Mohammad ILYAS
66 Dean of Nursing .... Dr. Marlaine SMITH
81 Dean of Science .... Dr. Gary PERRY
92 Dean of Honors College .... Dr. Jeff BULLER
58 Dean Graduate College .... Dr. Barry T. ROSSON
20 Dean Undergraduate Studies .... Dr. Edward E. PRATT
53 Asst Dean/PK-12 Sch/Educational Pgm .... Dr. Glenn THOMAS
07 Director Undergraduate Admissions .... Ms. Barbara PLETCHER
90 Director Enterprise Computing Svcs . Mr. Mehran BASIRATMAND
91 Dir Univ Administrative Systems .... Ms. Kay RECKTENWALD
25 Dir Sponsored Programs .... Ms. JoAnn MORETTI
09 Director Inst Effective/Analysis .... Vacant

24 Dir University Learning Resources ... Mrs. Molly MUNRO
06 Registrar ... Mr. Harry DEMIK
08 Dean University Library ... Dr. William MILLER
15 Interim Director Personnel Services ... Ms. Marie MASCARO
41 Athletics Director ... Mr. Craig ANGELOS
39 Director Student Housing ... Ms. Jill ECKARDT
36 Dir Career Devel Ctr/Student Place ... Ms. Sandra JAKUBOW
21 Director Business Services ... Ms. Stacy VOLNICK
85 Director Intl Students/Scholar Svcs ... Dr. Mihaela METIANU
37 Director Student Financial Aid ... Ms. Carole PFEILSTICKER
23 Director Student Health Services ... Ms. Cathie L. WALLACE
19 Dir Safety & Security/Chief Police ... Chief Charles LOWE
86 Director Government Relations ... Mr. David MANN
45 Director Facilities Planning ... Mr. Robert RICHMAN
18 Director Physical Plant ... Mr. John SINGER
42 Director Campus Ministries ... Vacant
38 Director Student Counseling ... Dr. Kirk DOUGHER
96 Director of Purchasing ... Mr. Ed SCHIFF
28 Assoc Dir Multicultural Affairs ... Dr. Indgrid JONES
88 Director Student Union ... Dr. Larry FAERMAN
88 Dir Office Students w/Disabilities ... Ms. Nicole ROKOS
88 Assoc Director Student Orientation ... Ms. Christine LYNCH
88 Assoc Dir Student Dev/Activities ... Ms. Michele PERKINS
21 University Controller ... Mrs. Stacey SEMMEL
57 Director School of the Arts ... Vacant
60 Dir Sch of Comm/Multimedia Studies ... Dr. Susan REILLY
88 Director School of Accounting ... Dr. Somnath BHATTACHARYA
88 Dir Complex Systems/Brain Sciences ... Dr. Janet BLANKS
70 Director School of Social Work ... Dr. Michele HAWKINS
80 Dir School of Public Administration ... Dr. Khi THAI
48 Director School of Architecture ... Dr. Deirdre HARDY
88 Dir Center for Env/Urban Solutions ... Dr. James MURLEY
104 Director of International Programs ... Dr. Catherine MESCHIEVITZ
88 Assoc Provost Lifelong Learning ... Dr. Herbert SHAPIRO
94 Director Women's Studies ... Dr. Josephine A. BEOKU-BETTS
65 Dir Pine Jog Environ Education Ctr ... Vacant
53 Dir K Slattery Educ Research Ctr ... Ms. Lydia BARTRAM
54 Dir SeaTech Inst for Ocean Engr ... Dr. Manhar DHANAK
54 Dir Intermodal Trans Safety/Sec Ctr ... Dr. Pete SCARLATOS
88 Dir Harbor Brnch Oceanographic Inst ... Dr. Margaret LEINEN

*Florida Gulf Coast University (A)

10501 FGCU Boulevard S, Fort Myers FL 33965-6565
County: Lee
FICE Identification: 032553
Unit ID: 433660
Telephone: (239) 590-1000
Carnegie Class: Master's L
FAX Number: (239) 590-1166
Calendar System: Semester
URL: www.fgcu.edu
Established: 1991
Annual Undergrad Tuition & Fees (In-State): $5,533
Enrollment: 12,038
Coed
Affiliation or Control: State
IRS Status: 501(c)3
Highest Offering: Doctorate
Program: Liberal Arts And General; Teacher Preparatory; Professional
Accreditation: SC, ANEST, BUS, CACREP, ENG, MT, NURSE, OT, PTA, SPAA, SW

02 President ... Dr. Wilson G. BRADSHAW
05 Provost & VP Academic Affairs ... Dr. Ronald B. TOLL
10 Vice Pres Admin Services/Finance ... Mr. Steve L. MAGIERA
30 Vice Pres University Advancement ... Mr. Steve L. MAGIERA
32 Vice President Student Affairs ... Dr. J. Michael ROLLO
20 Assoc Prov/Assoc VP Academic Affs ... Vacant
13 Assoc Vice Pres Admin Services ... Mr. Duncan MCBRIDE
45 Asc Prov/Asc VP Plng & Inst Perfrmc ... Dr. Paul SNYDER
25 Assoc VP Research/Sponsored Pgms ... Dr. Thomas J. ROBERTS
26 Asst VP Community Rels/Marketing ... Mr. Ken SCHEXNAYDER
04 Asst to Pres/University Ombudsman ... Ms. Helen MAMARCHEV
21 Controller/Asst VP Admin Services ... Ms. Linda BACHELER
35 Dean Student Affairs ... Ms. Michele YOVANOVICH
49 Dean College Arts & Sciences ... Dr. Donna Price HENRY
20 Dean of Undergraduate Studies ... Vacant
50 Dean Lutgert College of Business ... Dr. Hudson ROGERS
53 Dean College of Education ... Dr. Marcia GREENE
76 Dean College Health Professions ... Dr. Mitchell CORDOVA
54 Dean Whitaker College Engineering ... Dr. Susan BLANCHARD
72 Dean Academic & Media Tech Svcs ... Vacant
107 Int Dean Col Professional Studies ... Dr. Tony BARRINGER
62 Dean Library Services ... Dr. Kathleen MILLER
45 Assoc Dean Plng/Inst Performance ... Dr. George ALEXANDER
38 Asst Dean Counselng/Stdnt Hlth Svcs ... Dr. Jon L. BRUNNER
43 Asst Dean Judicial Affairs ... Ms. Cindy LYONS
58 Dir Grad Studies/Spec Asst to Pres ... Dr. Greg TOLLEY
07 Director of Admissions ... Mr. Marc LAVIOLETTE
15 Director Human Resources ... Mr. Steven BELCHER
96 Director of Procurement Svcs ... Ms. Maryan EGAN
19 Director Campus Police & Safety ... Chief Steven C. MOORE
100 Chief of Staff/Univ Spokesperson ... Ms. Susan EVANS
18 Director Facilities Planning ... Mr. Barrett GENSON
91 Director Computing Services ... Ms. Mary BANKS
37 Director Student Financial Aid ... Mr. Jorge LOPEZ-ROSADO
06 University Registrar ... Ms. Susan BYARS
23 Director Student Health Services ... Ms. Eileen DONDERO
41 Director Intercollegiate Athletics ... Mr. Kenneth KAVANAGH
28 Director Equity & Diversity ... Mr. Jimmy MYERS
85 Director International Services ... Ms. Elaine HOZDIK
106 Dir Web/E-learning/Publication Svcs ... Mr. David JAEGER
72 Director Academic & Event Tech ... Ms. Pat O'CONNOR-BENSON
36 Director Career Development Svcs ... Mr. Reid LENNERTZ
31 Dir Center for Civic Engagement ... Ms. Jessica RHEA
29 Director Alumni Relations ... Ms. Lindsey TOUCHETTE
43 General Counsel ... Ms. Vee LEONARD
92 Director Honors Program ... Dr. Sean KELLY

09 Director Inst Research/Analysis ... Dr. Robert VINES
21 Director University Budgets ... Mr. David VAZQUEZ
39 Director University Housing ... Dr. Brian FISHER
86 Director Government Relations ... Ms. Jennifer GOEN
51 Int Ex Dir Cont Ed/Off-Campus Pgms ... Mr. John GUERRA
84 Director Enrollment Management ... Vacant
88 General Manager/WGCU ... Mr. Rick JOHNSON
40 Manager The University Store ... Ms. Laura JENSEN

*Florida International University (B)

University Park, 11200 SW 8 Street, Miami FL 33199-0001
County: Miami-Dade
FICE Identification: 009635
Unit ID: 133951
Telephone: (305) 348-2000
Carnegie Class: RU/H
FAX Number: N/A
Calendar System: Semester
URL: www.fiu.edu
Established: 1965
Annual Undergrad Tuition & Fees (In-State): $5,102
Enrollment: 42,197
Coed
Affiliation or Control: State
IRS Status: 501(c)3
Highest Offering: Doctorate
Program: Liberal Arts And General; Teacher Preparatory; Professional
Accreditation: SC, ANEST, ART, BUS, BUSA, CACREP, CIDA, CONST, CS, DIETC, DIETD, ENG, IPSY, JOUR, LAW, LSAR, #MED, MUS, NURSE, OT, PH, PTA, SP, SPAA, SW, TED, THEA

02 President ... Dr. Mark ROSENBERG
100 Chief of Staff ... Mr. Javier MARQUES
05 Exec VP Academic Affs/Provost ... Dr. Douglas WARTZOK
20 Vice Provost Academic Affairs ... Dr. Irma BECERRA-FERNANDEZ
20 Vice Prov Acad Plng/Accountability ... Dr. Elizabeth BEJAR
10 CFO & Sr VP for Administration ... Dr. Kenneth JESSELL
30 Vice President for Advancement ... Mr. Robert CONRAD
32 VP Student Affairs ... Dr. Rosa JONES
09 Assoc VP Planning & Inst Research ... Mr. Jeffery GONZALEZ
46 VP for Research ... Dr. Andres GIL
13 Vice President/CIO ... Mr. Robert GRILLO
88 Vice Pres for Engagement ... Dr. Divina GROSSMAN
12 Int Vice Prov Biscayne Bay Campus ... Mr. Stephen MOLL
84 Int Assoc VP Enrollment Management ... Mr. Steve KELLY
35 Assoc VP Stdnt Affs Biscayne Bay ... Ms. Cathy AKENS
45 Assoc VP Strategic Development ... Ms. Liane MARTINEZ
15 Assoc Vice Pres Human Resources ... Dr. Jaffus HARDRICK
18 Assoc VP Facilities Operations ... Mr. John CAL
07 Director/Undergraduate Admissions ... Mr. Barry TAYLOR
20 Assoc VP Academic Administration ... Ms. Tonja MOORE
49 Dean College Arts & Sciences ... Dr. Kenneth FURTON
50 Exec Dean College Business Admin ... Dr. Joyce ELAM
54 Dean Col Engineering/Computing ... Dr. Amir MIRMIRAN
53 Dean College of Education ... Dr. Delia GARCIA
88 Int Dean Sch Hospitality Management ... Dr. Joan REMINGTON
60 Dean School Journ/Mass Communic ... Dr. Lillian KOPENHAVER
66 Int Dean Col Nursing/Health Science ... Dr. Sharon PONTIOUS
69 Int Dean College of Public Health ... Dr. Michele CICCAZZO
61 Dean College of Law ... Mr. R. Alexander ACOSTA
63 Dean College of Medicine ... Dr. John ROCK
88 Dean Undergraduate Studies ... Dr. Douglas ROBERTSON
58 Int Dean University Graduate School ... Dr. Kevin O'SHEA
92 Interim Dean Honors College ... Dr. Lesley NORTHUP
48 Int Dean Col Architectur & the Arts ... Mr. Brian SCHRINER
77 Int Dir Sch Computing/Info Sciences ... Dr. Jainendra NAVLAKHA
64 Director School of Music ... Mr. Orlando GARCIA
38 Director Counseling/Psych Svcs ... Dr. Cheryl NOWELL
22 Director Equal Opportunity Program ... Ms. Shirlyon J. MCWHORTER
88 Director School Accounting ... Dr. Ruth MCEWEN
88 Director Multicultural Pgms & Svcs ... Mr. Robert M. COATIE
62 Dean of Libraries ... Dr. Laura PROBST
25 Assoc VP Sponsored Research ... Dr. Joseph BARABINO
41 Athletics Director ... Mr. Pete GARCIA
86 Asst VP for Government Affairs ... Ms. Michelle PALACIO
06 Int University Registrar ... Ms. Andrea JAY
86 VP for Government Relations ... Mr. Steve SAULS
88 Director Protocol & Special Events ... Ms. Josefina CAGIGAL
37 Director Student Financial Aid ... Mr. Francisco VALINES
36 Director Career Services ... Dr. Imani FREDRICKS-LOWMAN
23 Int Director Univ Health Services ... Dr. Oscar LOYNAZ
39 Executive Director Student Housing ... Mr. James R. WASSENAAR, JR.
85 Director Intl Student/Scholar Svcs ... Ms. Ana M. SIPPIN
88 Director Disability Student Svcs ... Ms. Amanda NIGUIDULA
88 Director Internal Audit ... Mr. Allen VANN
24 Director Media & Technology Support ... Ms. Debra SHERIDAN
21 Associate VP and Univ Controller ... Ms. Cecilia HAMILTON
14 Assistant VP Univ Technology Svcs ... Vacant
88 Int Dir Environmentl Health/Safety ... Mr. William YOUNGBLUT
19 Director Public Safety ... Chief Bill KING
29 Assoc Vice Pres Alumni Affairs ... Mr. Bill DRAUGHON
27 Director Media Relations ... Ms. Maydel SANTANA-BRAVO
43 Interim General Counsel ... Ms. Isis CARBAJAL DE GARCIA

*Florida State University (C)

Tallahassee FL 32306-9936
County: Leon
FICE Identification: 001489
Unit ID: 134097
Telephone: (850) 644-2525
Carnegie Class: RU/VH
FAX Number: (850) 644-9936
Calendar System: Semester
URL: www.fsu.edu
Established: 1851
Annual Undergrad Tuition & Fees (In-State): $5,825
Enrollment: 40,416
Coed
Affiliation or Control: State
IRS Status: 501(c)3
Highest Offering: Doctorate
Program: Liberal Arts And General; Teacher Preparatory; Professional
Accreditation: SC, AAFCS, ART, BUS, BUSA, CACREP, CIDA, CLPSY, CORE, CS, DANCE, DIETD, DIETI, ENG, IPSY, LAW, LIB, MED, MFCD, MUS, NURSE, PLNG, PSPSY, SP, SPAA, SW, TED, THEA

02 President ... Dr. Eric J. BARRON
05 Prov/Ex Vice Pres Academic Affs ... Dr. Garnett S. STOKES
10 Sr Vice Pres Finance & Admin ... Mr. John R. CARNAGHI
32 Vice President Student Affairs ... Dr. Mary B. COBURN
46 Vice President Research ... Dr. Kirby KEMPER
26 Vice President University Relations ... Ms. Elizabeth MARYANSKI
88 VP Academic Quality/External Pgms ... Dr. Robert E. BRADLEY
30 VP University Advancement ... Mr. Thomas W. JENNINGS
04 Executive Assistant to President ... Ms. Cheryl BAKKER
45 Assoc Vice President for Research ... Dr. Ross ELLINGTON
18 Associate VP for Facilities ... Mr. Dennis A. BAILEY
21 Assoc VP Finance/Administration ... Mr. Paul A. STROUTS
21 Assoc VP Budget/Planing/Fin Svcs ... Mr. Rafael G. ALVAREZ
16 Asst Vice Pres for Human Resources ... Ms. Joyce A. INGRAM
88 Dir Academic Pgm Professional Svcs ... Mr. Bill LINDNER
20 Interim Dean Faculties/Dep Provost ... Dr. Jennifer N. BUCHANAN
49 Dean Arts & Sciences ... Dr. Joseph A. TRAVIS
50 Dean Business ... Dr. Caryn BECK-DUDLEY
53 Dean Education ... Dr. Marcy P. DRISCOLL
59 Dean Human Sciences ... Dr. Billie COLLIER
88 Dean Communication & Information ... Dr. Larry DENNIS
66 Interim Dean Nursing ... Dr. Dianne SPEAKE
88 Dean Criminology ... Dr. Thomas BLOMBERG
61 Dean Law ... Mr. Donald WEIDNER
83 Dean Social Sciences ... Dr. David W. RASMUSSEN
70 Dean Social Work ... Dr. Nicholas MAZZA
88 Dean Motion Picture Arts ... Mr. Frank PATTERSON
64 Dean Music ... Dr. Don GIBSON
57 Dean Visual Arts/Theatre/Dance ... Dr. Sally E. MCRORIE
88 Director of Theatre ... Mr. Charles C. JACKSON
54 Interim Dean Engineering ... Dr. John COLLIER
63 Dean Medicine ... Dr. John FOGARTY
58 Dean Graduate Studies ... Dr. Nancy MARCUS
88 Dean Undergraduate Studies ... Dr. Karen L. LAUGHLIN
35 Dean of Students ... Dr. Jeanine WARD-ROOF
12 Dean Panama City Branch Campus ... Dr. George DEPUY
07 Asst VP Admissions and Records ... Mr. John BARNHILL
06 University Registrar ... Ms. Kimberly BARBER
07 Director Admissions ... Ms. Janice FINNEY
92 Director University Honors Program ... Dr. James MATHES
37 Director Student Financial Aid ... Mr. Darryl MARSHALL
08 Director Libraries ... Ms. Julia ZIMMERMAN
27 Chief Information Officer ... Mr. Michael BARRETT
90 Dir University Computing Services ... Mr. Randy MCCAUSLAND
43 University Attorney ... Ms. Betty J. STEFFENS
88 Asst VP of University Relations ... Dr. Jeanette DEDIEMAR
104 Director International Programs ... Dr. James E. PITTS
45 Chief Budget Officer ... Mr. Michael P. LAKE
09 Director Institutional Research ... Dr. Richard BURNETTE
86 Director Governmental Relations ... Ms. Kathleen M. DALY
41 Director Intercollegiate Athletics ... Mr. Randy SPETMAN
38 Director Student Counseling ... Dr. Nikki PRITCHETT
19 Director Public Safety ... Mr. David L. PERRY
23 Director Student Health Services ... Dr. Lesley SACHER
36 Director Career Center ... Dr. Jeff GARIS
29 Director Alumni Affairs ... Mr. Scott ATWELL
88 Inspector General ... Mr. David COURY
28 Dir Office of Diversity/Equal Oppty ... Ms. Renisha L. GIBBS
96 Director of Purchasing ... Ms. Martha DOOLITTLE
20 Associate VP for Academic Affairs ... Dr. Joe NOSARI
20 Assistant VP for Academic Affairs ... Ms. Anne BLANKENSHIP
39 Director Student Housing ... Ms. Adrienne FRAME
88 Director Environmental Health ... Mr. Thomas JACOBSON
88 Director Technology Service/Support ... Mr. Harvey BUCHANAN
88 Director Conferences ... Ms. Susann RUDASILL
46 Director Sponsored Research ... Mr. Gregory THOMPSON
88 Director IT Security ... Mr. Joseph LAZOR
88 Asst VP for Administrative Services ... Dr. Perry CROWELL
18 Director Facilities Planning ... Mr. Mark BERTOLAMI
88 Director Union/Student Activities ... Mr. William CLUTTER
88 Director Campus Recreation ... Ms. Alicia CREW

*New College of Florida (D)

5800 Bay Shore Road, Sarasota FL 34243-2109
County: Sarasota
FICE Identification: 001507
Unit ID: 262129
Telephone: (941) 487-4100
Carnegie Class: Bac/A&S
FAX Number: (941) 487-4101
Calendar System: 4/1/4
URL: www.ncf.edu
Established: 1960
Annual Undergrad Tuition & Fees (In-State): $6,059
Enrollment: 801
Coed
Affiliation or Control: State
IRS Status: 501(c)3
Highest Offering: Baccalaureate
Program: Liberal Arts And General
Accreditation: SC

02 President ... Dr. Gordon E. MICHALSON, JR.
05 Provost ... Dr. Stephen MILES
10 Vice Pres Finance & Administration ... Mr. John U. MARTIN
79 Chair of Humanities ... Dr. Aron EDIDIN
81 Chair of Natural Sciences ... Dr. Paul SCUDDER
83 Chair of Social Sciences ... Dr. David HARVEY
08 Dean Cook Library ... Dr. Brian DOHERTY
84 Dean of Enrollment & Info Tech ... Ms. Kathleen KILLION
32 Dean of Students ... Dr. Wendy BASHANT
07 Associate Dean of Admissions ... Ms. Sonia WU
20 Associate Academic Officer ... Dr. Raymonda BURGMAN
21 Associate Business Officer ... Mr. William LAWHON

13 Director of Information Support ... Ms. Jennifer CROFFY
29 Director Alumnae/i Association ... Ms. Jessica ROGERS
06 Registrar ... Ms. Kathy ALLEN
26 Director Public Affairs ... Mr. Jake HARTVIGSEN
38 Director Counseling ... Dr. Anne E. FISHER
39 Director Residence Life ... Ms. Donita PACE
09 Director of Institutional Research ... Ms. Hui-Men WEN
15 Director Personnel Services ... Mr. Mark LEVENSON
18 Chief Facilities/Physical Plant ... Mr. Richard OLNEY
28 Director of Diversity ... Vacant
96 Director of Purchasing ... Mr. Jim BRETHERICK
37 Actg Director Student Financial Aid ... Ms. Tara KARAS
43 Director Legal Svcs/General Counsel ... Mr. David SMOLKER
25 Contract Administrator ... Ms. Jeanne WARE
72 Director of Technology Support ... Mr. Jeff SMITH
04 Assistant to the President ... Ms. Suzanne L. JANNEY
30 Chief Development ... Mr. Andrew WALKER
35 Director Student Affairs ... Mr. Tracy MURRY

*University of Central Florida (A)

PO Box 160000, Orlando FL 32816-0001

County: Orange
FICE Identification: 003954
Unit ID: 132903
Telephone: (407) 823-2000
Carnegie Class: RU/VH
FAX Number: N/A
Calendar System: Semester
URL: www.ucf.edu
Established: 1963
Annual Undergrad Tuition & Fees (In-State): $5,020
Enrollment: 56,337
Coed
Affiliation or Control: State
IRS Status: 501(c)3
Highest Offering: Doctorate
Program: Liberal Arts And General; Teacher Preparatory; Professional
Accreditation: SC, BUS, BUSA, CACREP, CEA, CLPSY, CS, ENG, ENGT, HSA, #MED, MT, MUS, NURSE, PTA, RAD, SP, SPAA, SW, TED

02 President ... Dr. John C. HITT
05 Provost & VP for Academic Affairs ... Dr. Tony G. WALDROP
100 Vice President and Chief of Staff ... Dr. John SCHELL
10 Vice Pres Administration & Finance ... Mr. William F. MERCK, II
26 Vice President University Relations ... Dr. Daniel HOLSENBECK
43 Vice President/General Counsel ... Mr. W. Scott COLE
46 VP Research and Commercialization ... Dr. M. J. SOILEAU
26 VP Strategy/Mktg/Comm/Admissions .. VAdm. Alfred HARMS, JR.
32 VP Student Dev/Enrollment Svcs ... Dr. Maribeth EHASZ
30 Vice Pres Development/Alumni Rels ... Mr. Robert HOLMES, JR.
31 Vice President for Community Rels ... Ms. Helen DONEGAN
63 VP Medical Affairs/Dean Med College ... Dr. Deborah GERMAN
49 Dean College of Arts & Humanities ... Dr. Jose B. FERNANDEZ
50 Dean College of Business Admin ... Dr. Thomas L. KEON
53 Dean College of Education ... Dr. Sandra L. ROBINSON
54 Dean College of Engr/Comp Sci ... Dr. Marwan SIMAAN
76 Dean College of Hlth/Pub Affs ... Dr. Michael FRUMKIN
88 Dean Rosen College Hospitality Mgt ... Dr. Abraham PIZAM
66 Dean College of Nursing ... Dr. Jean LEUNER
88 Dean College of Optics & Photonics ... Dr. Bahaa SALEH
81 Dean College of Sciences ... Dr. Peter T. PANOUSIS
92 Dean Burnett Honors College ... Dr. Alvin WANG
20 Vice Provost Academic Affairs ... Dr. Diane CHASE
13 Vice Provost Info Tech/Resources ... Dr. Joel L. HARTMAN
20 Vice Provost Academic Admin ... Dr. Edward NEIGHBOR
12 Int Vice Provost Regional Campuses ... Dr. Joyce DORNER
58 Vice Provost/Dean Graduate Studies ... Dr. Patricia J. BISHOP
88 Interim Vice Provost/Dean Undergrad ... Dr. Elliot VITTES
18 Assoc VP Facilities and Safety ... Ms. Lee KERNEK
29 Assoc Vice Pres Alumni Relations ... Mr. Tom MESSINA
86 Assoc VP for University Relations ... Mr. Fred KITTINGER
88 Assoc VP Rsrch & Commercialization ... Mr. Tom O'NEAL
07 Assoc VP Undergrad Admissions ... Dr. Gordon CHAVIS
21 Asst Vice Pres Admin/Finance ... Ms. Judith MONROE
27 Asst VP Director News & Information ... Mr. Grant HESTON
88 Assoc Vice Provost Faculty Relation ... Dr. Lin HUFF-CORZINE
09 Asst VP Institutional Research ... Dr. M. Paige BORDEN
37 Exec Dir Student Financial Asst ... Ms. Mary MCKINNEY
06 University Registrar ... Mr. Brian BOYD
08 Director Libraries ... Mr. Barry BAKER
15 Director Human Resources ... Mr. Mark A. ROBERTS
19 Director Public Safety/Police ... Mr. Richard BEARY
93 Director Multicul Acad Suppt Svcs ... Mr. Wayne JACKSON
14 Dir Comp Svcs/Telecommunications ... Mr. Robert YANCKELLO
38 Director Counseling Center ... Dr. Stacey PEARSON
41 Director of Athletics ... Mr. Keith TRIBBLE
22 Director EEO Affirmative Action ... Ms. Janet BALANOFF
23 Director Health Center ... Dr. J. Robert WIRAG
39 Director Housing and Residence Life ... Mrs. Christi HARTZLER
28 Director of Diversity Initiatives ... Dr. Valarie G. KING
96 Director of Purchasing ... Mr. Ray PUSKAS
36 Director Career Services ... Ms. Lynn HANSEN

*University of Florida (B)

Gainesville FL 32611-9500

County: Alachua
FICE Identification: 001535
Unit ID: 134130
Telephone: (352) 392-3261
Carnegie Class: RU/VH
FAX Number: N/A
Calendar System: Semester
URL: www.ufl.edu
Established: 1853
Annual Undergrad Tuition & Fees (In-State): $5,657
Enrollment: 49,827
Coed
Affiliation or Control: State
IRS Status: 501(c)3
Highest Offering: Doctorate
Program: Liberal Arts And General; Teacher Preparatory; Professional
Accreditation: SC, ARCPA, ART, AUD, BUS, BUSA, CACREP, CEA, CIDA, CLPSY, CONST, COPSY, DANCE, DENT, DIETD, DIETI, ENG, ENGR, FOR, HSA, IPSY, JOUR, LAW, LSAR, MED, MIDWF, MUS, NURSE, OT, PH, PHAR, PLNG, PTA, SCPSY, SP, TED, THEA, VET

02 President ... Dr. James B. MACHEN
05 Provost & Senior Vice President ... Dr. Joseph GLOVER
47 Sr Vice Pres Agric/Natural Res ... Dr. Jack M. PAYNE
17 Sr Vice Pres Health Affairs ... Dr. David S. GUZICK
30 Vice President Dev/Alumni Affairs ... Mr. Thomas J. MITCHELL
10 Vice President Business Affairs ... Mr. John E. POPPELL
32 Int Vice President Student Affairs ... Mr. David KRATZER
26 Vice President Univ Relations ... Ms. Jane A. ADAMS
15 Vice Pres Human Resources ... Ms. Paula V. FUSSELL
46 Vice President Research ... Dr. Winfred M. PHILLIPS
43 Vice President/General Counsel ... Ms. Jamie L. KEITH
13 Vice President & CIO ... Mr. Elias G. ELDAYRIE
86 Assoc VP Government Relations ... Ms. Marion S. HOFFMAN
26 Asc Vice Pres/Public Rel/Marketing ... Mr. William A. FLETCHER
21 Finance/Admin Assoc Vice President ... Mr. Fred CANTRELL
21 Finance/Admin Assoc Vice President ... Mr. Robert MILLER
18 Asst Vice Pres of Physical Plant ... Mr. Curtis A. REYNOLDS
20 Associate Provost ... Dr. Kathleen A. LONG
20 Associate Provost ... Dr. Angel KWOLEK-FOLLAND
92 Assoc Provost Undergrad Affairs ... Dr. Bernard A. MAIR
09 Asst Provost/Dir Inst Research/Plng ... Dr. Marie ZEGLEN
84 Vice Pres Enroll Mgmt/Assoc Provost ... Dr. Zina EVANS
35 Int Dean Stdnts/Asst VP Stdnt Affs ... Dr. Jen D. SHAW
08 Dean University Libraries ... Ms. Judith RUSSELL
50 Dean of Business Administration ... Dr. John KRAFT
49 Dean of Liberal Arts & Science ... Dr. Paul J. D'ANIERI
68 Dean Health/Human Performance ... Dr. Steve M. DORMAN
61 Dean of Law ... Mr. Robert H. JERRY
66 Dean of Nursing ... Dr. Kathleen A. LONG
67 Dean of Pharmacy ... Dr. William H. RIFFEE
54 Dean of Engineering ... Dr. Cammy ABERNATHY
47 Dean Agricultural/Life Sciences ... Dr. Teresa C. BALSER
60 Dean of Journalism/Communications ... Dr. John W. WRIGHT
76 Dean Pub Health/Health Professions ... Dr. Michael PERRI
53 Dean of Education ... Dr. Catherine H. EMIHOVICH
47 Int Dean IFAS Extension ... Dr. Millie FERRER
74 Dean of Veterinary Medicine ... Dr. Glen F. HOFFSIS
57 Dean of Fine Arts ... Ms. Lucinda LAVELLI
48 Dean Design Construction Planning ... Dr. Christopher SILVER
63 Dean of Medicine ... Dr. Michael L. GOOD
46 Dean of IFAS Research ... Dr. Mark R. MCLELLAN
52 Dean of Dentistry ... Dr. Teresa A. DOLAN
65 Sr Asc Dn/Dir Sch Natural Res/Envir ... Dr. James C. CATO
58 Dean Graduate School ... Dr. Henry T. FRIERSON
06 University Registrar ... Mr. Stephen J. PRITZ
23 Director of Student Health ... Dr. Phillip L. BARKLEY
38 Director of Counseling Center ... Dr. Sherry BENTON
37 Int Director Student Financial Aid ... Mr. Richard D. WILDER
36 Director of Placement Services ... Dr. Wayne E. WALLACE
14 Director of Computer Center ... Mr. Timothy J. FITZPATRICK
19 Director of University Police ... Ms. Linda J. STUMP
27 Assoc Director News & Public Affs ... Mr. Frank AHERN
27 Assoc Director News & Public Affs ... Mr. Stephen F. ORLANDO
24 Director of Academic Technology ... Dr. Fedro S. ZAZUETA
65 Director of Forestry ... Dr. Timothy L. WHITE
39 Director of Housing ... Mr. Norbert W. DUNKEL
41 Athletic Director ... Mr. Jeremy N. FOLEY
29 Int Exec Director Alumni Affairs ... Ms. Katie MARQUIS
15 Director Human Resources ... Ms. Jodi D. GENTRY
28 Director of Diversity ... Ms. Tamara COHEN
96 Director of Purchasing ... Ms. Lisa DEAL

*University of North Florida (C)

1 UNF Drive, Jacksonville FL 32224-7699

County: Duval
FICE Identification: 009841
Unit ID: 136172
Telephone: (904) 620-1000
Carnegie Class: Master's L
FAX Number: (904) 620-2414
Calendar System: Semester
URL: www.unf.edu
Established: 1965
Annual Undergrad Tuition & Fees (In-State): $5,449
Enrollment: 16,153
Coed
Affiliation or Control: State
IRS Status: 501(c)3
Highest Offering: Doctorate
Program: Liberal Arts And General; Teacher Preparatory; Professional
Accreditation: SC, ANEST, BUS, BUSA, CACREP, CONST, CS, DIETD, DIETI, ENG, HSA, MUS, NURSE, PH, PTA, SPAA, TED

02 President ... Mr. John A. DELANEY
05 Provost ... Dr. Mark E. WORKMAN
20 Associate Provost ... Dr. Bobby E. WALDRUP
20 Associate Provost ... Dr. Newton N. JACKSON
100 VP/Chief of Staff ... Dr. Thomas S. SERWATKA
86 VP Governmental Affairs ... Ms. Janet D. OWEN
43 VP/General Counsel ... Ms. Karen J. STONE
15 VP Human Resources ... Ms. Rachelle GOTTLIEB
10 VP Administration/Finance ... Ms. Shari A. SHUMAN
30 VP Institutional Advancement ... Dr. Pierre N. ALLAIRE
32 VP Student & International Affairs ... Dr. Mauricio GONZALEZ
84 Assoc VP for Enrollment Services ... Ms. Deborah M. KAYE
88 Assoc VP/Compliance Officer ... Dr. Joann N. CAMPBELL
21 Assoc VP Admin & Finance ... Mr. Scott BENNETT
13 Assoc VP Chief Info Officer ... Mr. Lance TAYLOR
44 Assoc VP Major Gifts ... Ms. Elizabeth M. HEAD
35 Assoc VP Student Affairs ... Mr. Everett J. MALCOLM, III
45 Asst VP Research ... Dr. Imeh D. EBONG
88 Asst VP Development ... Ms. Ann S. MCCULLEN
88 Asst VP Development ... Mr. Brandon T. MCCRAY
26 Asst VP Public Relations ... Ms. Sharon ASHTON
88 Asst VP Student Affairs ... Dr. Lucy S. CROFT
89 Dean of Undergraduate Studies ... Dr. Jeffrey W. COKER
58 Dean of the Graduate School ... Dr. James L. ROBERSON
08 Dean of the Library ... Dr. Shirley HALLBLADE
49 Dean College of Arts & Sciences ... Dr. Barbara HETRICK
50 Dean Coggin College of Business ... Dr. Ajay SAMANT
53 Dean College of Education ... Dr. Larry DANIEL
76 Dean Brooks College of Health ... Dr. Pam CHALLY
77 Dean Computing Engineering & Constr ... Dr. Peter A. BRAZA
51 Dean Continuing Education ... Mr. Robert WOOD
04 Executive Director Pres Office ... Mr. Donald A. SHEA
16 Dir Human Resources ... Ms. Sandra A. CUMMINGS
88 Dir Internal Auditing ... Mr. Robert L. BERRY
22 Dir Equal Oppty Programs ... Ms. Cheryl N. GONZALEZ
88 Dir Professional Dev Training ... Ms. Idania R. GROPPER
21 Chief Budget Officer ... Mr. Ricky B. ARJUNE
21 Controller ... Mr. Floyd HURST
88 Dir Environment Health/Safety ... Mr. Daniel D. ENDICOTT
88 Dir ADA Compliance ... Ms. Rocelia T. GONZALEZ
88 Treasurer ... Mr. Michael S. NEGLIA
18 Dir Univ Facilities Planning ... Mr. Zak OVADIA
88 Dir University Center ... Mr. George ANDROUIN
31 Dir Auxiliary Services ... Mr. Vince SMYTH
29 Dir Alumni Services ... Ms. Faith M. HALL
19 Dir Safety Security ... Mr. John E. DEAN
36 Dir Career Development Services ... Mr. Rick ROBERTS
85 Dir Intercultural Ctr for Peace ... Dr. Oupa SEANE
88 Dir Child Development Research Ctr ... Ms. Pam BELL
23 Chief Medical Officer ... Dr. Fred BECK
38 Dir Univ Counseling Center ... Dr. Theresa M. DINUZZO
88 Dir Women's Center ... Ms. Sheila D. SPIVEY
85 Dir The International Center ... Dr. Timothy ROBINSON
39 Dir Housing Residence Life ... Mr. Paul RIEL
41 Athletic Director ... Mr. Lee L. MOON
88 Dir Office of Faculty ... Dr. Francis D. RICHARD
88 Exec Dir of Assessment ... Dr. Judith E. MILLER
92 Dir Honors Program ... Dr. Mary O. BORG
37 Dir Student Financial Aid ... Mrs. Anissa AGNE
44 Assoc VP Institutional Advancement ... Mr. Rodney GRABOWSKI
06 Registrar ... Mrs. Megan R. KUEHNER
44 Associate Director Annual Giving ... Ms. Lynn M. BROWN
88 Associate Vice Pres for Major Gifts ... Ms. Elizabeth HEAD
07 Dir Admissions ... Mr. John YANCEY
25 Dir Contracts and Grants Acct ... Ms. Cheresa Y. HAMILTON
09 Dir Institutional Research ... Dr. Richard S. POWELL
88 Exec Dir FL Inst of Education ... Dr. Cheryl A. FOUNTAIN
104 Dir Study Abroad ... Ms. Anne S. FUGARD
88 Dir Small Business Dev Ctr ... Ms. Janice W. DONALDSON
88 Dir Disability Resource Center ... Dr. Kristine W. WEBB
96 Dir Purchasing ... Ms. Kathy RITTER
103 Dir Continuing Education ... Mr. Timothy W. GILES
40 Dir Bookstore ... Mr. Steve MOREAU

*University of South Florida (D)

4202 E Fowler Avenue, Tampa FL 33620-6100

County: Hillsborough
FICE Identification: 001537
Unit ID: 137351
Telephone: (813) 974-2011
Carnegie Class: RU/VH
FAX Number: (813) 974-5530
Calendar System: Semester
URL: www.usf.edu
Established: 1956
Annual Undergrad Tuition & Fees (In-State): $5,806
Enrollment: 47,800
Coed
Affiliation or Control: State
IRS Status: 501(c)3
Highest Offering: Doctorate
Program: Liberal Arts And General; Teacher Preparatory; Professional
Accreditation: SC, ANEST, ART, AUD, BUS, BUSA, CACREP, CEA, CLPSY, CORE, CS, ENG, ENGR, IPSY, JOUR, LIB, MED, MUS, NURSE, PH, @PHAR, PTA, SCPSY, SP, SPAA, SW, TED, THEA

02 President ... Dr. Judy L. GENSHAFT
100 Chief of Staff/President's Office ... Dr. Cynthia S. VISOT
05 Prov/Exec Vice Pres Academic Affs ... Dr. Ralph WILCOX
46 Sr VP Rsrch/Innovation/Global Affs ... Dr. Karen A. HOLBROOK
17 Sr Vice Pres USF Health ... Dr. Stephen K. KLASKO
20 Sr Vice Prov Faculty & Development ... Dr. Dwayne SMITH
10 Vice Pres Business & Finance ... Mr. Nick TRIVUNOVICH
11 Vice Pres Administrative Services ... Ms. Sandy LOVINS
30 Sr Vice Pres University Advancement ... Mr. Joel MOMBERG
32 Vice President Student Affairs ... Dr. Jennifer D. MENINGALL
13 Vice Pres Information Technology ... Mr. Michael PEARCE
26 VP Univ Communication/Marketing ... Mr. Michael HOAD
35 Assoc Vice Pres Student Affairs ... Dr. Denita SISCOE
35 Asst Vice Pres Student Affairs ... Dr. Kevin M. BANKS
35 Asst Vice Pres Student Affairs ... Mr. Guy CONWAY
11 Asst VP Administrative Services ... Vacant
40 Asst VP Auxiliary Services ... Mr. Jeffrey A. MACK
29 Assoc Vice Pres Alumni Affairs ... Mr. John HARPER
44 Assoc Vice Pres Development ... Mr. Rod GRABOWSKI
86 Asst Vice Pres Government Rels ... Mr. Mark WALSH
14 Assoc Vice Pres Info Technologies ... Mr. George W. ELLIS
22 Assoc VP for Diversity/Equal Oppty ... Dr. Ted WILLIAMS
84 Assoc VP Enrollment Planning & Mgmt ... Dr. Paul J. DOSAL
43 General Counsel ... Mr. Steven D. PREVAUX
39 Dean Housing/Residential Educ ... Ms. Ana HERNANDEZ
83 Int Dean Behavioral/Community Sci ... Dr. Catherine J. BATSCHE
50 Dean Business Administration ... Dr. Robert E. FORSYTHE
53 Dean Education ... Dr. Colleen S. KENNEDY
54 Dean Engineering ... Dr. John M. WIENCEK
57 Int Dean College of the Arts ... Dr. Barton LEE
49 Dean Arts & Sciences ... Dr. Eric EISENBERG
66 Dean Nursing ... Dr. Dianne MORRISON-BEEDY

69 Dean Public Health ... Dr. Donna PETERSEN
58 Dean Graduate School ... Dr. Karen D. LILLER
85 USF World ... Vacant
89 Dean of Undergraduate Studies ... Dr. W. Robert SULLINS
48 Dir Sch of Architecture/Cmty Design ... Mr. Robert MACLEOD
12 Regional Chanc Sarasota-Manatee ... Dr. Arthur M. GUILFORD
12 Regional Chanc USF St Petersburg ... Dr. Margaret SULLIVAN
12 Campus Exec Ofcr USF Polytechnic ... Dr. Marshall GOODMAN
21 Interim Comptroller ... Ms. Linda PETERSON
27 Director of News ... Ms. Lara WADE
06 University Registrar ... Ms. Angela W. DEBOSE
07 Director Admissions ... Mr. J. Robert SPATIG
18 Director Physical Plant ... Mr. Adrian CUARTA
31 Int Director Educational Outreach ... Dr. Sandra M. COOPER
21 University Budget Officer ... Ms. Bertha P. ALEXANDER
37 Director Financial Aid ... Ms. Billy Jo HAMILTON
38 Interim Director Counseling Ctr ... Dr. Dale A. HICKS
36 Director of the Career Center ... Dr. Drema K. HOWARD
19 Director University Police ... Mr. Thomas F. LONGO
08 USF Libraries Dean ... Dr. William GARRISON
40 Director University Bookstore ... Vacant
41 Director of Athletics ... Mr. Doug WOOLARD
28 Director of Diversity & Inclusion ... Ms. Patsy FELICIANO
96 Director Purchasing & Property Svcs ... Mr. Tom DIBELLA

*University of South Florida Manatee-Sarasota (A)

8350 Tamiami Trail, Sarasota FL 34243-2049
County: Manatee — Identification: 667058
Unit ID: 451671
Telephone: (941) 359-4200 — Carnegie Class: Not Classified
FAX Number: N/A — Calendar System: Semester
URL: www.sarasota.usf.edu
Established: 1956 — Annual Undergrad Tuition & Fees (In-State): $4,547
Enrollment: 1,803 — Coed
Affiliation or Control: State — IRS Status: 501(c)3
Highest Offering: Master's; No Lower Division
Program: Liberal Arts And General; Teacher Preparatory; Professional
Accreditation: **SC**

02 Regional Chancellor ... Dr. Arthur M. GUILFORD
32 Vice Chancellor Student Services ... Ms. Pamela DOERR
10 Vice Chancellor Business & Finance ... Mr. Ben ELLINOR
05 Vice Chancellor Academic Affairs ... Dr. Bonnie JONES
30 Senior Director of Development ... Ms. Alexis J. UPHAM

*University of South Florida St. Petersburg (B)

140 7th Avenue S, Saint Petersburg FL 33701-5016
County: Pinellas — FICE Identification: 009016
Unit ID: 448840
Telephone: (727) 873-4873 — Carnegie Class: Master's M
FAX Number: (727) 553-4131 — Calendar System: Semester
URL: www.stpete.usf.edu
Established: 1966 — Annual Undergrad Tuition & Fees (In-District): $4,610
Enrollment: 6,030 — Coed
Affiliation or Control: State/Local — IRS Status: 501(c)3
Highest Offering: Master's
Program: Liberal Arts And General; Teacher Preparatory; Professional
Accreditation: **SC**, BUS, BUSA, JOUR, TED

02 Regional Chancellor ... Dr. Margaret SULLIVAN
04 Special Asst to Regional Chancellor ... Ms. DeeLynn RIVINIUS
05 Reg Vice Chanc Academic Affairs ... Dr. Norine NOONAN
11 Reg Vice Chanc Admin/Financial Svcs ... Dr. Ashok DHINGRA
26 Reg Vice Chanc External Affairs ... Dr. Helen LEVINE
32 Reg Assoc Vice Chanc Student Affs ... Dr. Julie WONG
49 Dean College of Arts & Sciences ... Dr. Frank BIAFORA
50 Dean College of Business ... Dr. Maling EBRAHIMPOUR
53 Dean College of Education ... Dr. Vivian FUEYO
08 Dean of the Library ... Ms. Carol HIXSON
09 Dir Inst Res/Effectiveness ... Dr. J. E. GONZALEZ
19 Chief of Police ... Ms. Renee CHENEVERT
13 Director of Campus Computing ... Mr. Jeff REISBERG
16 Associate Director Human Resources ... Ms. Sandra CONWAY
37 Director of Financial Aid ... Ms. Erin DUNN
06 Director Records and Registration ... Ms. Linda CROSSMAN
07 Director Admissions & Marketing ... Ms. Holly KICKLITER
30 Executive Director of Development ... Ms. Kim HALL
18 Dir Facil Plng/Construction Svcs ... Mr. John DICKSON
96 Purchasing Manager ... Mr. Bill BENJAMIN

*University of West Florida (C)

11000 University Parkway, Pensacola FL 32514-5750
County: Escambia — FICE Identification: 003955
Unit ID: 138354
Telephone: (850) 474-2000 — Carnegie Class: RU/H
FAX Number: (850) 474-3131 — Calendar System: Semester
URL: uwf.edu
Established: 1963 — Annual Undergrad Tuition & Fees (In-State): $5,425
Enrollment: 11,599 — Coed
Affiliation or Control: State — IRS Status: 501(c)3
Highest Offering: Doctorate
Program: Liberal Arts And General; Teacher Preparatory; Professional
Accreditation: **SC**, BUS, ENG, MT, MUS, NURSE, PH, SW, TED

02 President ... Dr. Judy A. BENSE
05 Provost ... Dr. Chula G. KING
32 Vice President Student Affairs ... Dr. Kevin BAILEY
11 VP for Administrative Services ... Mr. Matthew ALTIER
20 Vice Provost ... Dr. George B. ELLENBERG
27 Sr Assoc VP University Affairs/CIO ... Mr. Mike F. DIECKMANN
30 Vice Pres for Development ... Dr. Kyle MARRERO
84 Assoc Vice Pres Enrollment Mgt ... Mrs. Susan J. MCKINNON
18 Assoc VP Facilities Develop & Opers ... Dr. James R. BARNETT
35 Associate Vice Pres Student Affairs ... Dr. James R. HURD
58 AVP Res & Dean of Grad Students ... Dr. Richard S. PODEMSKI
21 Asc VP Internal Audit/Mgmt Consultg ... Ms. J. Betsy BOWERS
15 Associate Vice Pres Human Resources ... Mrs. Sherell D. HENDRICKSON
96 Assoc VP Public Safety & Mgmt Svcs ... Mr. David J. O'BRIEN
28 Assoc VP Diversity/Intl Educ/Pgms ... Dr. Angela E. MCCORVEY
88 Executive Director ... Mr. J. Patrick CRAWFORD
43 Associate General Counsel ... Ms. Patricia D. LOTT
50 Dean of Business ... Dr. F. Edward RANELLI
49 Dean of Arts & Sciences ... Dr. Jane S. HALONEN
107 Dean of Professional Studies ... Dr. Pamela NORTHRUP
100 Chief of Staff ... Dr. Kimberly S. BROWN
08 Dean University Libraries ... Mr. Robert DUGAN
35 Associate Dean of Students ... Dr. LuSharon WILEY
10 Chief Budget Officer ... Dr. Susan E. STEPHENSON
21 Asst VP Financial Services ... Ms. Colleen M. ASMUS
06 Registrar ... Mrs. Ann H. DZIADON
13 Chief Technology Officer ... Mrs. Melanie J. HAVEARD
07 Director of Admissions ... Mr. Stephen MCKELLIPS
92 Director of Honors Program ... Dr. Gregory W. LANIER
37 Director of Financial Aid ... Ms. Cathy R. BROWN
19 Director of University Police ... Mr. John S. WARREN
39 Director of Housing/Residence Life ... Dr. Ruth L. DAVISON
38 Director Health & Counseling ... Dr. Rebecca E. KENNEDY
35 Assistant VP/Dean of Students ... Dr. Tammy L. MCGUCKIN
88 Director Facilities Planning ... Mr. Kenneth C. KLINDT
29 Director of Alumni Relations ... Ms. Katherine C. EHEREDGE
41 Athletic Director ... Mr. David L. SCOTT
26 Director Mktg & Creative Services ... Ms. Sabrina MCLAUGHLIN
09 Director Institutional Research ... Vacant
44 Director of Development ... Ms. Martha Lee BLODGETT
21 Director University Budgets ... Ms. Valerie Z. MONEYHAM
21 Director Business/Auxiliary Svcs ... Ms. Ellen P. TILL

Stenotype Institute of Jacksonville (D)

3563 Phillips Hwy, Bldg E Suite 501,
Jacksonville FL 32207
County: Duval — FICE Identification: 008417
Unit ID: 137537
Telephone: (904) 398-4141 — Carnegie Class: Not Classified
FAX Number: (904) 398-7878 — Calendar System: Trimester
URL: www.stenotype.edu
Established: N/A — Annual Undergrad Tuition & Fees: $14,900
Enrollment: 227 — Coed
Affiliation or Control: Proprietary — IRS Status: Proprietary
Highest Offering: Associate Degree
Program: Occupational
Accreditation: **ACICS**

01 Executive Director ... Carl MCGOWAN
05 Director of Education ... Carol CLARK
07 Director of Admissions ... LaNell DERBY

Stetson University (E)

421 N Woodland Boulevard, DeLand FL 32723-0001
County: Volusia — FICE Identification: 001531
Unit ID: 137546
Telephone: (386) 822-7000 — Carnegie Class: Master's L
FAX Number: (386) 822-8832 — Calendar System: 4/1/4
URL: www.stetson.edu
Established: 1883 — Annual Undergrad Tuition & Fees: $35,078
Enrollment: 3,756 — Coed
Affiliation or Control: Independent Non-Profit — IRS Status: 501(c)3
Highest Offering: Doctorate
Program: Liberal Arts And General; Teacher Preparatory; Professional
Accreditation: **SC**, BUS, BUSA, CACREP, LAW, MUS, TED

01 President ... Dr. Wendy B. LIBBY
05 Provost & Vice Pres Acad Affairs ... Dr. Beth PAUL
10 VP for Business Affairs & CFO ... Mr. F. Robert HUTH
26 Vice Pres for University Relations ... Ms. Linda P. DAVIS
84 VP Enrollmnt Mgmt ... Mr. Joel BAUMAN
26 VP for University Marketing ... Mr. Gregory CARROLL
32 Vice President for Campus Life ... Ms. Rina TOVAR
61 Interim Dean College of Law ... Mr. Royal C. GARDNER
49 Dean of College of Arts & Sciences ... Dr. Grady W. BALLENGER
50 Dean of School of Business Admin ... Dr. Stuart MICHELSON
64 Dean of School of Music ... Dr. Jean O. WEST
88 Assoc Provost for Faculty Devlpmnt ... Dr. Karen KAIVOLA
20 Asst Provost for Student Success ... Dr. Lua HANCOCK
06 Registrar ... Ms. Terri RICHARDS
08 Director DuPont-Ball Library ... Ms. Betty D. JOHNSON
12 Interim Director Celebration Campus ... Dr. Jay BRADEN
72 Assoc Vice Pres Technology ... Mr. R. William PENNEY
18 Assoc Vice Pres Facilities Mgmt ... Mr. Al ALLEN
21 Assoc Vice Pres for Finance ... Mr. Jeffrey MARGHEIM
30 Assoc Vice Pres for Univ Relations ... Vacant
07 Dean of Admissions ... Vacant
09 Dir Institutional Research & Plng ... Dr. Ray BARCLAY
42 University Chaplain ... Rev. Michael R. FRONK
44 Dir of Annual and Planned Giving ... Ms. Katheryn P. PEARCE
29 Director Alumni Relations ... Ms. Colleen M. COOPER
51 Director Continuing Education ... Mr. William R. O'CONNOR
36 Director Univ Career Services ... Ms. Robin KAZMAREK
85 Director of International Education ... Vacant
38 Director Counseling Center ... Ms. Cheryl HAMMOCK
41 Director of Athletics ... Mr. Jeffrey P. ALTIER
15 Director Human Resources ... Ms. Betty WHITEMAN
23 Director Health Services ... Ms. Deborah K. CASSIDY
96 Director of Purchasing ... Ms. Valinda WIMER
19 Chief Pubic Safety ... Mr. Robert MATUSICK

Tallahassee Community College (F)

444 Appleyard Drive, Tallahassee FL 32304-2895
County: Leon — FICE Identification: 001533
Unit ID: 137759
Telephone: (850) 201-6200 — Carnegie Class: Assoc/Pub-R-L
FAX Number: (850) 201-8682 — Calendar System: Semester
URL: www.tcc.fl.edu
Established: 1966 — Annual Undergrad Tuition & Fees (In-District): $2,518
Enrollment: 14,770 — Coed
Affiliation or Control: Local — IRS Status: 501(c)3
Highest Offering: Associate Degree
Program: Occupational; 2-Year Principally Bachelor's Creditable
Accreditation: **SC**, DA, DH, EMT

01 President ... Dr. Jim MURDAUGH
10 Vice Pres Administrative Svcs/CFO ... Dr. Teresa SMITH
13 Vice Pres Information Technology ... Vacant
05 Vice President for Academic Affairs ... Dr. Barbara SLOAN
32 Vice President for Student Affs ... Ms. Sharon JEFFERSON
103 Vice Pres Workforce/Economic Devel ... Dr. John CHAPIN
11 Asst VP Administrative Services ... Mr. Jerry SCHILLING
100 Chief of Staff ... Mr. Scott BALOG
12 Asst VP Florida Public Safety Inst ... Vacant
57 Dean Communications & Humanities ... Dr. Marge BANOCY-PAYNE
83 Dean History & Social Sciences ... Dr. Monte FINKELSTEIN
81 Dean Science & Math ... Dr. Frank BROWN
72 Dean Technology & Professional Pgms ... Ms. Kate STEWART
20 Dean Academic Support ... Dr. Sally SEARCH
08 Director of Library Services ... Ms. Deborah P. ROBINSON
76 Dean Health Care Professions ... Ms. Alice NIED
37 Director of Financial Aid ... Mr. William SPIERS
84 Dean Enrollment Management ... Dr. Sheri ROWLAND
15 Director of Human Resources ... Ms. Renae TOLSON
102 Director of TCC Foundation ... Mr. Robin JOHNSTON
41 Athletics Director ... Mr. Rob CHANEY
35 Director of Campus Life ... Mr. Douglas K. WADDELL
27 Director of Communications ... Ms. Alice MAXWELL
27 Director of Communications ... Ms. Susie HALL
19 Chief of Campus Police ... Mr. E. E. EUNICE
18 Dir Facilities/Construction/Plng ... Mr. David WILDES
21 Controller ... Ms. Patricia MANNING
45 Director of Educational Research ... Dr. Barbara J. GILL
09 Director of Institutional Research ... Ms. Margaret WINGATE
72 Dir Ctr for Instruct Tech/Dist Educ ... Mr. Chad CALL
106 Dir Center for Distance Learning ... Dr. Marilyn DICKEY
88 Dir Ctr for Teach/Learn/Ldrshp ... Dr. Karinda BARRETT
13 Manager Technical Support ... Mr. Chip SINGLETARY
18 Construction Coordinator ... Mr. Bill HUNTER
88 Dir Budget and General Services ... Mr. Curtis E. WATKINS, II
85 International Students Coordinator ... Ms. Betty JENSEN
14 Dir Management Information Systems ... Mr. John BURCH
25 Contracts and Grants Manager ... Ms. Vanessa LAWRENCE
88 Director Grants & Special Projects ... Mr. Charles WOOD
51 Director of Adult & Continuing Educ ... Ms. Carol EASLEY
29 Coord & Development Alumni Relation ... Ms. Lisa MASSING
96 Purchasing Manager ... Mr. Bobby HINSON

Talmudic College of Florida (G)

4000 Alton Road, Miami Beach FL 33140
County: Dade — FICE Identification: 025089
Unit ID: 137777
Telephone: (305) 534-7050 — Carnegie Class: Spec/Faith
FAX Number: (305) 534-8444 — Calendar System: Semester
URL: www.talmudicu.edu
Established: 1974 — Annual Undergrad Tuition & Fees: $10,500
Enrollment: 48 — Male
Affiliation or Control: Independent Non-Profit — IRS Status: 501(c)3
Highest Offering: Doctorate
Program: Teacher Preparatory; Professional
Accreditation: **RABN**

01 President ... Rabbi Yitzchak ZWEIG
05 Dean/Vice President ... Rabbi Yochanan ZWEIG
06 Registrar ... Rabbi Ira HILL
37 Director Student Financial Aid ... Ms. Stacy BROWN
20 Director Educational Programs ... Rabbi Yeshaya GREENBERG
07 Director of Admissions ... Rabbi Ariel EDRY

Teacher Education University (H)

1079 West Morse Boulevard, Suite B,
Winter Park FL 32789-3751
County: Orange — Identification: 666342
Telephone: (800) 523-1578 — Carnegie Class: Not Classified
FAX Number: (407) 740-8177 — Calendar System: Semester
URL: www.TEU.edu
Established: 2005 — Annual Undergrad Tuition & Fees: $3,960
Enrollment: N/A — Coed
Affiliation or Control: Proprietary — IRS Status: Proprietary
Highest Offering: Master's

Program: Teacher Preparatory
Accreditation: DETC

01 Chief Education/Academic Ofcr .... Ms. Kristi BORDELON
11 Chief Designated Administrator .... Ms. Amanda BOWERS
05 Academic Coordinator ....Ms. Charlotte LUGERING
07 Admissions Coordinator .... Ms. Anne MARION
06 Registrar ....Ms. Jennifer MORRISON

Trinity Baptist College (A)

800 Hammond Boulevard, Jacksonville FL 32221-1398
County: Duval FICE Identification: 031019
Unit ID: 137953
Telephone: (904) 596-2400 Carnegie Class: Spec/Faith
FAX Number: (904) 596-2531 Calendar System: Semester
URL: www.tbc.edu
Established: 1974 Annual Undergrad Tuition & Fees: $13,930
Enrollment: 230 Coed
Affiliation or Control: Baptist IRS Status: 501(c)3
Highest Offering: Master's
Program: 2-Year Principally Bachelor's Creditable; Teacher Preparatory; Religious Emphasis
Accreditation: TRACS

00 Chancellor ....Dr. Thomas C. MESSER
01 President/CEO .... Mr. Mac HEAVENER
03 Senior Vice President ....Dr. Matthew BEEMER
32 Dean of Students ....Mr. Jeremiah STANLEY
84 Director of Enrollment Management ....Mr. Brandon WILLIS
37 Director of Financial Aid .... Mr. Mark ELKINS

Trinity College of Florida (B)

2430 Welbilt Boulevard, Trinity FL 34655-4401
County: Pasco FICE Identification: 030282
Unit ID: 137962
Telephone: (727) 376-6911 Carnegie Class: Spec/Faith
FAX Number: (727) 376-0781 Calendar System: Semester
URL: www.trinitycollege.edu
Established: 1932 Annual Undergrad Tuition & Fees: $12,154
Enrollment: 201 Coed
Affiliation or Control: Independent Non-Profit IRS Status: 501(c)3
Highest Offering: Baccalaureate
Program: Religious Emphasis
Accreditation: BI

01 President ....Dr. Mark T. O'FARRELL
32 Vice President Student Affairs .... Rev. Al DEPOUTOT
05 Vice President Academic Affairs .... Dr. David BENEDICT
30 Vice President for Advancement .... Dr. Charlie MARTIN
10 Vice Pres for Business & Finance ...Mr. Richard C. HENRICKSEN
07 Vice Pres for Enrollment/Adult Ed ....Vacant
06 Registrar ....Mr. Zachary T. RANES
26 Asst VP Marketing/Communications ......Mr. Kevin D. O'FARRELL

Trinity International University, Florida Regional Center (C)

8190 W State Road 84, Davie FL 33324-4611
County: Broward FICE Identification: 012314
Unit ID: 135610
Telephone: (954) 382-6400 Carnegie Class: Bac/Diverse
FAX Number: (954) 382-6470 Calendar System: Semester
URL: www.tiu.edu/florida
Established: 1949 Annual Undergrad Tuition & Fees: $9,900
Enrollment: 247 Coed
Affiliation or Control: Evangelical Free Church Of America
IRS Status: 501(c)3
Highest Offering: Master's
Program: Liberal Arts And General; Teacher Preparatory
Accreditation: &NH

01 President .... Dr. G. Craig WILLIFORD
05 Exec Vice President/Provost .... Dr. Jeanette L. HSIEH
20 Chief Academic Officer ....Vacant
11 Exec Director & Assoc Dean .... Mr. Scott MCCLELLAND
20 Director of Academic Operations .... Ms. Deborah WILES
32 Director Student Services ....Mrs. Sarudzayi WILSON
10 Chief Operations Ofcr/Human Res ....Mrs. Ileana GIL
06 Director of Records .... Mr. Steve DAVIS
37 Financial Aid Director .... Ms. Karen GUAL

† Regional accreditation is carried under the parent institution in Deerfield, IL.

Ultimate Medical Academy-Clearwater (D)

1255 Cleveland Street, Clearwater FL 33756
County: Pinellas FICE Identification: 035493
Unit ID: 441371
Telephone: (727) 298-8685 Carnegie Class: Not Classified
FAX Number: (727) 446-2489 Calendar System: Semester
URL: www.ultimatemedical.edu
Established: N/A Annual Undergrad Tuition & Fees: $13,000
Enrollment: 812 Coed
Affiliation or Control: Proprietary IRS Status: Proprietary
Highest Offering: Associate Degree
Program: Occupational
Accreditation: ABHES

01 Campus Director .... Ms. Lori LEGROW

University of Fort Lauderdale (E)

4093 NW 16th Street, Lauderhille FL 33313-5809
County: Broward Identification: 666648
Unit ID: 457402
Telephone: (954) 486-7728 Carnegie Class: Not Classified
FAX Number: (954) 486-7667 Calendar System: Other
URL: www.uftl.edu
Established: N/A Annual Undergrad Tuition & Fees: N/A
Enrollment: 46 Coed
Affiliation or Control: Non-denominational IRS Status: 501(c)3
Highest Offering: Doctorate
Program: Professional; Religious Emphasis
Accreditation: @TRACS

01 Chancellor and CEO ....Dr. Henry B. FERNANDEZ
05 Chief Academic Officer .... Dr. Winnifred MCPHERSON
10 Chief Financial Officer .... Mr. Brian HANKERSON
09 VP Inst Effective/Compliance ....Ms. Laura TUCKER
07 Dir of Admission/Financial Aid Ofcr ....Ms. Chloris UNDERWOOD
06 Registrar .... Mr. Stephen ALLISON

University of Miami (F)

1252 Memorial Drive, Coral Gables FL 33146-2509
County: Miami-Dade FICE Identification: 001536
Unit ID: 135726
Telephone: (305) 284-2211 Carnegie Class: RU/VH
FAX Number: N/A Calendar System: Semester
URL: www.miami.edu
Established: 1925 Annual Undergrad Tuition & Fees: $39,654
Enrollment: 15,025 Coed
Affiliation or Control: Independent Non-Profit IRS Status: 501(c)3
Highest Offering: Doctorate
Program: Liberal Arts And General; Teacher Preparatory; Professional
Accreditation: SC, ANEST, BUS, BUSA, CEA, CLPSY, COPSY, DENT, ENG, HSA, IPSY, JOUR, LAW, MED, MIDWF, MUS, NURSE, PH, PTA, @TEAC

01 President .... Dr. Donna E. SHALALA
05 Exec Vice President & Provost .... Dr. Thomas J. LEBLANC
10 Sr Vice Pres for Business & Finance ....Mr. Joseph T. NATOLI
63 Sr VP & Dean School of Medicine ....Dr. Pascal J. GOLDSCHMIDT
21 Vice President Finance & Treasurer ....Mr. John R. SHIPLEY
43 Vice President and General Counsel ....Ms. Aileen M. UGALDE
32 Vice President Student Affairs .... Dr. Patricia A. WHITELY
30 Sr VP University Advancement .... Mr. Sergio M. GONZALEZ
17 Vice Pres Medical Administration .... Mr. William DONELAN
15 Vice President Human Resources ....Ms. Nerissa E. MORRIS
13 Vice Pres Information Technology ....Mr. Steve CAWLEY
26 Vice President for Communications ....Ms. Jacqueline R. MENENDEZ
21 Asst VP Business Services .... Mr. Humberto M. SPEZIANI
86 Vice President Government Relations .... Mr. Rodolfo J. FERNANDEZ
84 Vice President for Enrollment Mgmt ....Vacant
100 President's Chief of Staff ....Dr. Rebecca M. FOX
20 Sr Vice Prov/Dean Undergrad Educ .... Dr. William S. GREEN
46 Vice Provost for Research ....Vacant
20 Exec VP/Vice Prov Faculty Affairs ....Dr. David J. BIRNBACH
18 Vice Pres Real Estate & Facilities ....Mr. Larry D. MARBERT
41 Director of Athletics .... Mr. Shawn EICHORST
21 Assoc Vice Pres Budget & Planning .... Mr. Mark DIAZ
29 Associate VP Alumni Relations ....Ms. Donna A. ARBIDE
06 Assoc Vice President & Registrar ....Dr. Scott INGOLD
21 Asst Vice Pres Business & Finance ...... Ms. Sarah N. ARTECONA
26 Asst VP University Communications .... Mr. Todd M. ELLENBERG
86 Director of Government Affairs .... Ms. Shira KASTAN
09 Asst VP Planning & Inst Research .... Dr. Mary M. SAPP
19 Chief of Police ....Major David A. RIVERO
49 Dean College of Arts & Sciences .... Dr. Leonidas G. BACHAS
48 Dean School of Architecture .. Ms. Elizabeth M. PLATER-ZYBERK
50 Dean Business Administration .... Dr. Eugene ANDERSON
60 Dean School Communication .... Dr. Gregory J. SHEPHERD
53 Dean of Education .... Dr. Isaac PRILLELTENSKY
61 Dean of Law ....Ms. Patricia WHITE
64 Dean of Music ....Dr. Shelton G. BERG
65 Dean Marine & Atmospheric Science .... Dr. Roni AVISSAR
66 Dean of Nursing & Health Studies .... Dr. Nilda P. PERAGALLO
54 Dean College of Engineering .... Dr. James M. TIEN
58 Dean of the Graduate School ....Dr. Teresa A. SCANDURA
08 Dean and University Librarian .... Mr. William D. WALKER
35 Dean of Students ....Dr. Ricardo D. HALL
88 Asst VP of Enrollment Management ....Mr. James M. BAUER
12 Director Center Hemisphere Policy .... Dr. Susan K. PURCELL
38 Director Student Counseling ....Vacant
36 Director Career Services .... Mr. Christian GARCIA
85 Director Intl Student & Scholar Svc ....Ms. Teresa S. DE LA GUARDIA
39 Director Student Housing ....Mr. James G. SMART
96 Chief Purchasing Officer ....Ms. Susan R. MONTES
28 Exec Dir Equality Administration ....Ms. Wilhemena BLACK

University of St. Augustine for Health Sciences (G)

1 University Boulevard, Saint Augustine FL 32086-5799
County: Saint Johns FICE Identification: 031713
Unit ID: 367954
Telephone: (904) 826-0084 Carnegie Class: Spec/Health
FAX Number: (904) 826-0085 Calendar System: Trimester
URL: www.usa.edu
Established: 1979 Annual Undergrad Tuition & Fees: $32,085
Enrollment: 1,007 Coed
Affiliation or Control: Proprietary IRS Status: Proprietary
Highest Offering: Doctorate
Program: Professional
Accreditation: DETC, OT, PTA

01 President .... Dr. Wanda NITSCH
03 Vice President .... Dr. Cindy MATHENA
88 Dir Inst of Occupational Therapy ....Dr. Karen HOWELL
88 Program Dir Physical Therapy - SA .... Dr. Margaret NONNEMACHER
88 Program Dir Physical Therapy - SD .... Dr. Ellen LOWE
88 Program Dir Occupational Therapy SD ....Dr. Judith OLSON
88 Dir Trans Doctor Physical Therapy ....Dr. Jodi LIPHART
06 Registrar .... Ms. Diane RONDINELLI
07 Director of Admissions .... Mr. Steve JONES
51 Director of Continuing Education .... Ms. Lori HANKINS

University of Tampa (H)

401 W Kennedy Boulevard, Tampa FL 33606-1490
County: Hillsborough FICE Identification: 001538
Unit ID: 137847
Telephone: (813) 253-3333 Carnegie Class: Master's L
FAX Number: (813) 258-7207 Calendar System: Other
URL: www.ut.edu
Established: 1931 Annual Undergrad Tuition & Fees: $23,976
Enrollment: 6,600 Coed
Affiliation or Control: Independent Non-Profit IRS Status: 501(c)3
Highest Offering: Master's
Program: Liberal Arts And General; Teacher Preparatory; Professional
Accreditation: SC, BUS, MUS, NUR

01 President .... Dr. Ronald L. VAUGHN
05 Provost/Vice Pres Academic Affairs .... Dr. Janet M. MCNEW
10 Vice Pres Administration/Finance ....Mr. Richard W. OGOREK
84 Vice President Enrollment ....Mr. Dennis L. NOSTRAND
30 Vice Pres Development/Univ Rels ....Mr. Daniel T. GURA
45 Vice Pres Operations & Planning ....Dr. Linda W. DEVINE
13 Vice President Info Technology .... Ms. Donna R. ALEXANDER
21 Associate VP Admin/Finance ....Vacant
06 Registrar ....Ms. Michelle PELAEZ
08 Director of the Library .... Ms. Marlyn PETHE-COOK
29 Director of Alumni Relations .... Mr. James HARDWICK
44 Director of Annual Giving ....Mrs. Taylor A. PINKE
37 Director of Financial Aid .... Ms. Jacqueline LATORELLA
27 Director of Public Information .... Mr. Eric CARDENAS
32 Dean of Students ....Mr. Robert M. RUDAY
35 Asst Dn Stdnts/Dir Ofc Stdnt Ldrshp ....Ms. Stephanie A. RUSSELL HOLZ
36 Director of Career Services ....Mr. Tim HARDING
18 Director of Facilities Management ....Mr. David RAMSEY
91 Director Information Systems .... Mr. Jon ALBRECHT
15 Exec Director of Human Resources .... Ms. Donna B. POPOVICH
07 Sr Associate Director of Admissions ....Mr. Brent BENNER
41 Athletic Director ....Mr. Larry J. MARFISE
40 Manager Campus Store .... Mr. John MEYER
39 Director of Residence Life ....Ms. Krystal SCHOFIELD
50 Dean College of Business ....Dr. Frank GHANNADIAN
83 Dean Social Science/Math Education .... Dr. Ann V. GORMLY
81 Int Dean College Natural/Health Sci .... Dr. James GORE
57 Int Dean College of Arts/Letters .... Dr. Haig MARDIROSIAN
20 Assoc Provost & Dean of Acad Svcs .... Dr. Joseph SCLAFANI
51 Dir Graduate and Continuing Studies ....Dr. Don MORRILL
22 Affirmative Action Officer .... Ms. Donna B. POPOVICH
19 Director Safety & Security .... Mr. Kevin HOWELL
23 Dir Health Center/Stdnt Counseling ...... Ms. Sharon P. SCHAEFER
44 Director of Planned Giving .... Mr. William F. ROTH
90 Director of Instruction Services ....Mr. Steve MAGRIBY
38 Director Student Counseling .... Ms. Sharon P. SCHAEFER
96 Director of Procurement .... Ms. Cyn D. EZELL
09 Dir Institutional Effectiveness ....Dr. Jeanne ROBERTS
92 Director of Honors Program ....Dr. Gary S. LUTER

Valencia College (I)

PO Box 3028, Orlando FL 32802-3028
County: Orange FICE Identification: 006750
Unit ID: 138187
Telephone: (407) 299-5000 Carnegie Class: Assoc/Pub-U-MC
FAX Number: (407) 426-8970 Calendar System: Semester
URL: www.valenciacollege.edu
Established: 1967 Annual Undergrad Tuition & Fees (In-State): $2,972
Enrollment: 41,583 Coed
Affiliation or Control: State IRS Status: 501(c)3
Highest Offering: Baccalaureate
Program: Occupational; 2-Year Principally Bachelor's Creditable
Accreditation: SC, ADNUR, CEA, CVT, DH, DMS, EMT, RAD

01 President .... Dr. Sanford C. SHUGART
05 Exec VP/Chief Learning Officer ....Vacant
32 Vice President Student Affairs ....Dr. Joyce C. ROMANO
10 Vice Pres Administrative Svcs .... Mr. Keith W. HOUCK
30 Vice Pres Institutional Advancement .... Ms. Susan E. KELLEY
43 Vice Pres Policy & General Counsel ....Dr. William J. MULLOWNEY
16 Vice Pres Human Resources/Diversity ....Dr. Stanley H. STONE
12 Provost East Campus ....Dr. Ruth L. PRATHER
12 Provost Osceola Campus ....Dr. Kathleen A. PLINSKE
12 Campus President West Campus .... Dr. Falecia D. WILLIAMS
18 Asst Vice Pres Facilities Services ....Ms. Helene LOISELLE
103 Asst VP Workforce Development ....Vacant

21 Asst Vice Pres Financial Svcs .... Ms. Jacqueline D. LASCH
35 Asst Vice Pres Student Affairs .... Dr. Sonya F. JOSEPH
37 Asst VP Fin Aid/College Trans .... Ms. Linda DOWNING
07 Asst VP Admissions & Records .... Dr. Renee K. SIMPSON
31 Asst VP College/Community Rels .... Vacant
28 Asst VP Compliance/Diversity/Equ .... Dr. Martha W. WILLIAMS
09 Managing Director Research .... Dr. Jeffrey L. CORNETT
20 Asst Vice Pres Academic Affairs .... Vacant
35 Dean of Students East .... Ms. Linda B. VANCE
35 Dean of Students West .... Mr. Tyron S. JOHNSON
35 Dean of Students Osceola .... Ms. Jillian M. SZENTMIKLOSI
35 Dean of Students Winter Park .... Dr. Cheryl ROBINSON
102 Pres & CEO Valencia Foundation .... Ms. Geraldine M P. GALLAGHER
40 Director College Bookstore .... Mr. Todd A. HUNT
92 Director Honors Program .... Dr. Valerie C. BURKS
96 Director Procurement/Aux Svcs .... Mr. W. Edward AMES

Virginia College (A)

19 W Garden Street, Pensacola FL 32502-5678
County: Escambia FICE Identification: 031005
Unit ID: 389727
Telephone: (850) 436-8838 Carnegie Class: Assoc/PrivFP
FAX Number: (850) 436-2663 Calendar System: Quarter
URL: www.vc.edu
Established: 2001 Annual Undergrad Tuition & Fees: $17,423
Enrollment: 577 Coed
Affiliation or Control: Proprietary IRS Status: Proprietary
Highest Offering: Associate Degree
Program: Occupational
Accreditation: ACICS, SURGT

01 Campus President .... Dr. Kimberly COOLIDGE
05 Academic Dean .... Ms. Katheryn FOX
10 Controller .... Mr. Tim MOYE
37 Director of Financial Planning .... Ms. Pamela RODRIQUEZ
36 Director of Career Services .... Ms. Michelle SIMS
06 Registrar .... Ms. Susan M. PHILLIPS

† Branch campus of Virginia College, Birmingham, AL.

Warner University (B)

13895 Highway 27, Lake Wales FL 33859-2549
County: Polk FICE Identification: 008848
Unit ID: 138275
Telephone: (863) 638-1426 Carnegie Class: Master's S
FAX Number: (863) 638-1472 Calendar System: Semester
URL: www.warner.edu
Established: 1968 Annual Undergrad Tuition & Fees: $23,764
Enrollment: 1,082 Coed
Affiliation or Control: Church Of God IRS Status: 501(c)3
Highest Offering: Master's
Program: Liberal Arts And General; Teacher Preparatory
Accreditation: SC, @SW

01 President .... Dr. Gregory V. HALL
05 Vice Pres/Chief Academic Ofcr .... Dr. James G. MOYER
10 Vice Pres for Finance & Business .... Mr. Greg A. RODDEN
30 Vice President Advancement .... Mrs. Doris B. GUKICH
84 VP for Enrollment Mgmt & Marketing .... Mrs. Dawn M. RAFOOL
50 Dean of School of Business .... Dr. Cathy LEWIS-BRIM
49 Dean of Ministry/Arts & Sciences .... Dr. Steven DARR
53 Dean School of Education .... Dr. Bill RIGEL
32 Dean Student Affairs .... Dr. Wendi SANTEE
43 General Counsel .... Dr. Norman WHITE
06 Registrar .... Mrs. Sara F. KANE
07 Dean of Admissions .... Mr. Kevin JONES
37 Director Student Financial Aid .... Mrs. Lorrie STEEDLEY
21 Controller .... Mr. Dean MEADOWS
08 Librarian .... Mrs. Sherill HARRIGER
29 Director Alumni Relations .... Miss Kareen PICKETT
42 Campus Pastor .... Rev. Bob BECKLER
83 Chair Social & Natural Science .... Mrs. Erica SIRRINE
68 Chair Physical Educ/Rec/Health .... Mr. Trevor HALL
106 Online Church Ministries Coord .... Dr. Jeff HAYES
09 Director of Institutional Research .... Mrs. Lisa B. MURPHY
18 Chief Facilities/Physical Plant .... Mr. Bill BROWN
97 Director of General Studies .... Mrs. Kelly MILLS
79 Chair Ministry & Humanities .... Dr. Michael SANDERS
88 Chair of Traditional BA .... Dr. Melodi GUILBAULT
40 Director Bookstore .... Ms. Monica HAMILTON
13 Director of Institutional Tech .... Mr. Mark THOMAS
19 Director Campus Security .... Mr. Brian ROWLES

Webber International University (C)

PO Box 96, 1201 Scenic Highway N,
Babson Park FL 33827-0096
County: Polk FICE Identification: 001540
Unit ID: 138293
Telephone: (863) 638-1431 Carnegie Class: Bac/Diverse
FAX Number: (863) 638-2823 Calendar System: Semester
URL: www.webber.edu
Established: 1927 Annual Undergrad Tuition & Fees: $19,670
Enrollment: 758 Coed
Affiliation or Control: Independent Non-Profit IRS Status: 501(c)3
Highest Offering: Master's
Program: Business Emphasis
Accreditation: SC, IACBE

01 President .... Dr. H. Keith WADE
05 Academic Dean .... Dr. Charles SHIEH
10 Vice President Finance .... Ms. Christina JORDON
30 VP Institutional Advancement .... Mr. Steve WARNER
35 Dean of Student Life .... Ms. Johanna DEVERTEUIL
06 Registrar/Dir of Financial Aid .... Mrs. Kathy A. WILSON
36 Director Career Services .... Ms. Tonya WHITE
08 Head Librarian .... Ms. Sue DUNNING
26 Dir Public Relations/Athletic Dir .... Mr. Bill HEATH
30 Dir Institutional Development .... Mr. Rick WRIGHT
13 Director Information Technology .... Mr. Bob M. WEIS
55 Director for Adult Education .... Ms. Joann MCKENNA
18 Director of Campus Svcs/Maintenance .... Mr. Matt YENTES
40 Director of Bookstore .... Mr. Jay CULVER
07 Director of Admissions .... Mr. Michael MATTISON
09 Director of Institutional Effectiv .... Mrs. Treasa MCLEAN
50 Chair of Business Education .... Dr. Jeanette EBERLE
53 Chair of General Education Division .... Dr. Charles WUNKER

Wolford College (D)

1336 Creekside Boulevard, Suite 2,
Naples FL 34108-1931
County: Collier FICE Identification: 039393
Unit ID: 451130
Telephone: (239) 513-1135 Carnegie Class: Spec/Health
FAX Number: (239) 513-1368 Calendar System: Semester
URL: www.wolford.edu
Established: 2004 Annual Graduate Tuition & Fees: $43,270
Enrollment: 155 Coed
Affiliation or Control: Independent Non-Profit IRS Status: 501(c)3
Highest Offering: Master's; No Undergraduates
Program: Professional
Accreditation: ANEST

01 President .... Dr. Norman R. WOLFORD
05 Dean .... Dr. John NOLAN
10 Chief Financial Officer .... Ms. Lynda WATERHOUSE
37 Director of Financial Aid Services .... Mr. Gilberto CHANG
32 Dir Enrollment & Student Services .... Ms. Lori ELLISON

Yeshiva Gedolah Rabbinical College (E)

1140 Alton Road, Miami Beach FL 33139-4708
County: Dade FICE Identification: 032563
Unit ID: 363712
Telephone: (305) 653-8770 Carnegie Class: Spec/Faith
FAX Number: (305) 653-6790 Calendar System: Semester
Established: 1973 Annual Undergrad Tuition & Fees: $8,000
Enrollment: 47 Male
Affiliation or Control: Independent Non-Profit IRS Status: 501(c)3
Highest Offering: Master's
Program: Teacher Preparatory; Professional
Accreditation: @RABN

01 Executive Vice President .... Rabbi Benzion KORF
05 Dean .... Rabbi Abraham KORF
06 Registrar .... Ayelet BORTUNK

GEORGIA

Abraham Baldwin Agricultural College (F)

ABAC 1 - 2802 Moore Highway, Tifton GA 31793-2601
County: Tift FICE Identification: 001541
Unit ID: 138558
Telephone: (229) 391-5001 Carnegie Class: Assoc/Pub4
FAX Number: (229) 391-5051 Calendar System: Semester
URL: www.abac.edu
Established: 1908 Annual Undergrad Tuition & Fees (In-State): $3,778
Enrollment: 3,284 Coed
Affiliation or Control: State IRS Status: 501(c)3
Highest Offering: Baccalaureate
Program: Occupational; 2-Year Principally Bachelor's Creditable
Accreditation: SC, ADNUR

01 President .... Dr. David BRIDGES
05 Vice President of Academic Affairs .... Dr. Niles REDDICK
32 Vice President Student Affairs .... Dr. Gail DILLARD
10 Vice President for Fiscal Affairs .... Mr. John CLEMENS
30 VP External Affairs & Advancement .... Mr. Keith BARBER
08 Librarian .... Ms. Mildred GALENTINE-STEIS
35 Assistant Dean of Student Affairs .... Ms. Bernice HUGHES
13 Director Institutional Technology .... Dr. Chrystle M. ROSS
38 Dir Guidance/Testing/Student Place .... Dr. Maggie MARTIN
37 Director of Financial Aid .... Ms. Shawn THOMAS
44 Director of Development .... Mr. Melvin MERRILL
15 Director of Human Resources .... Mr. Richard SPANCAKE
26 Director of Public Relations .... Mr. Michael D. CHASON
09 Director Inst Research/Planning .... Ms. Amy HOWELL
84 Director Enrollment Management .... Ms. Donna WEBB
96 Director of Procurement .... Ms. Teri MATHIS
88 Director of College Enrichment .... Mr. Paul WILLIS
19 Chief of Police .... Mr. Bryan A. GOLDEN

† Part of the University System of Georgia.

Agnes Scott College (G)

141 E College Avenue, Decatur GA 30030-3797
County: DeKalb FICE Identification: 001542
Unit ID: 138600
Telephone: (404) 471-6000 Carnegie Class: Bac/A&S
FAX Number: (404) 471-6067 Calendar System: Semester
URL: www.agnesscott.edu
Established: 1889 Annual Undergrad Tuition & Fees: $32,195
Enrollment: 917 Female
Affiliation or Control: Presbyterian Church (U.S.A.) IRS Status: 501(c)3
Highest Offering: Master's
Program: Liberal Arts And General
Accreditation: SC

01 President .... Dr. Elizabeth KISS
05 VP Acad Affs/Dean of the College .... Dr. Carolyn J. STEFANCO
32 VP Student Life/Dean of Students .... Ms. Donna A. LEE
10 Vice President Business/Finance .... Mr. John P. HEGMAN
30 Vice Pres College Advancement .... Mr. Robert PARKER
84 Vice Pres Enrollment & Admission .... Ms. Laura MARTIN
13 Assoc VP Technology .... Ms. LaNeta COUNTS
20 Associate Dean of the College .... Dr. James K. DIEDRICK
35 Associate Dean of Students .... Ms. Suzanne ONORATO
42 Chaplain .... Rev. Kate COLUSSY-ESTES
04 Director Office of the President .... Ms. Lea Ann HUDSON
27 Senior Director of Communications .... Mr. J. D. FITE
44 Senior Director of Development .... Ms. Elizabeth K. WILSON
06 Registrar .... Ms. Angela DEWBERRY
35 Associate Dean of Students ..... Dr. Kijua SANDERS-MCMURTRY
08 Director of Library Services .... Ms. Elizabeth BAGLEY
29 Director of Alumnae Relations .... Ms. Kimberly VICKERS
36 Director Career Planning .... Ms. Catherine NEINER
18 Director of Facilities .... Mr. Tim BLANKENSHIP
15 Director of Human Resources .... Ms. Karen GILBERT
41 Director of Athletics .... Ms. Joeleen AKIN
28 Director of Multicultural Affairs .... Vacant
37 Director of Student Financial Aid .... Mr. Patrick BONONES
38 Director Personal Counseling .... Dr. Holly BYRD
09 Director of Institutional Research .... Ms. Katherine MCGUIRE
07 Director of Admissions .... Ms. Alexa GAETA
23 Director of Student Health .... Ms. Carole HOLCOMB

Albany State University (H)

504 College Drive, Albany GA 31705-2796
County: Dougherty FICE Identification: 001544
Unit ID: 138716
Telephone: (229) 430-4600 Carnegie Class: Master's M
FAX Number: (229) 430-4830 Calendar System: Semester
URL: www.asurams.edu
Established: 1903 Annual Undergrad Tuition & Fees (In-State): $5,214
Enrollment: 4,653 Coed
Affiliation or Control: State IRS Status: 501(c)3
Highest Offering: Beyond Master's But Less Than Doctorate
Program: Liberal Arts And General; Teacher Preparatory; Professional
Accreditation: SC, ACBSP, NUR, SPAA, SW, TED

01 President .... Dr. Everette J. FREEMAN
05 Vice President Academic Affairs .... Dr. Abiodun OJEMANKINDE
32 Vice Pres Student Affs .... Dr. Edgar L. BERRY
10 Vice President Fiscal Affairs .... Mr. Larry WAKEFIELD
30 Vice Pres Institutional Advance .... Mr. Clifford PORTER
13 Vice Pres Tech & Enrollment Svcs .... Ms. Virginia STEWART
20 Asst Vice Pres Academic Affairs .... Dr. Linda GRIMSLEY
21 Assoc Vice Pres Fiscal Affairs .... Vacant
06 Registrar .... Mrs. Arna T. ALBRITTEN
08 Librarian .... Dr. LaVerne MCLAUGHLIN
09 Asst VP of Institutional Research .... Dr. Ruth SALTER
27 Int Director Public Information .... Vacant
38 Dir Counsel/Test/Disability Svcs ... Dr. Stephanie HARRIS-JOLLY
14 Director of Information Technology .... Ms. Virginia STEWART
37 Director Financial Aid .... Mr. Thomas HARRIS, JR.
43 Chief of Staff & University Counsel .. Ms. Sharon "Nyota" TUCKER
15 Director of Human Resources Mgmt .... Mr. Steve GRANT
19 Director Police Department .... Mr. John FIELDS
41 Interim Director of Athletics .... Dr. Richard WILLIAMS
07 Director Admissions/Recruitment .... Mr. James BURRELL
18 Director of Facilities Management .... Mr. James OLIVER
35 Director Student Activities .... Ms. Gwinetta L. TRICE
38 Director Career Counseling Services ...... Ms. Glorya E. WILLIAMS
29 Director Alumni Affairs .... Ms. Wendy WILSON
96 Director of Business Services .... Ms. Lori W. BURNETT

† Part of the University System of Georgia.

Albany Technical College (I)

1704 S Slappey Boulevard, Albany GA 31701-3587
County: Dougherty FICE Identification: 005601
Unit ID: 138682
Telephone: (229) 430-3500 Carnegie Class: Assoc/Pub-R-M
FAX Number: (229) 430-3594 Calendar System: Quarter
URL: www.albanytech.edu
Established: 1961 Annual Undergrad Tuition & Fees (In-State): $3,024
Enrollment: 4,497 Coed
Affiliation or Control: State IRS Status: 501(c)3
Highest Offering: Associate Degree
Program: Occupational; 2-Year Principally Bachelor's Creditable; Technical Emphasis
Accreditation: SC, DA, MAC, RAD, SURGT

01 President ....Dr. Anthony O. PARKER
05 Vice President for Academic Affairs ......Ms. Shirley ARMSTRONG
32 VP Student Affairs/Enrollment Mgmt ....Ms. Pamela HEGLAR
46 Vice President Economic Development ....Mr. Matt TRICE
11 Vice Pres Administrative Services ....Mrs. Kathy SKATES
45 Vice Pres of Inst Effectiveness ....Ms. Vicki TUCKER
88 Associate Vice Pres of Adult Educ ....Mrs. Linda COSTON
04 Special Assistant to the President ....Mr. Joe NAJJAR
07 Dean of Admissions ....Ms. Lisa DE JESUS
06 Registrar ....Ms. Suzann CULPEPPER
37 Director of Financial Aid ....Ms. Helen CATT
36 Dir of Job Placement/Career Svcs ....Ms. Judy JIMMERSON
21 Director of Accounting Services ....Mrs. Karen THOMAS
20 Dean of Academic Affairs ....Dr. Dorothy GARNER
20 Dean of Academic Affairs ....Ms. Corine HUGHLEY
20 Dean of Academic Affairs ....Mr. Emmett GRISWOLD
55 Dean of Evening Administration ....Dr. Ed COOPER
88 Director of Business & Industry Svc ....Mr. Gary FRAGE
51 Dir Manufacturing Tech Ctr/Contg Ed ....Vacant
09 Director of Institutional Research ....Mr. Joe NAJJAR
26 Director of Public Rels/Information ....Ms. Wendy HOWELL
14 Director of Computer/Info Systems ....Mr. Bobby WIDNER
88 Director of Special Programs ....Vacant
18 Campus Operations Manager ....Mr. Lavon ACKLEY
56 Dir Spec Proj/Tech in Curriculum ....Ms. Elizabeth DEMING
35 Coordinator Student Activities ....Dr. Mary RICHARDSON

Altamaha Technical College (A)

1777 W Cherry Street, Jesup GA 31545-0612

County: Wayne FICE Identification: 030321
Unit ID: 366447
Telephone: (912) 427-5800 Carnegie Class: Assoc/Pub-R-S
FAX Number: (912) 427-5823 Calendar System: Semester
URL: www.altamahatech.edu
Established: 1989 Annual Undergrad Tuition & Fees (In-State): $2,550
Enrollment: 1,761 Coed
Affiliation or Control: State IRS Status: 501(c)3
Highest Offering: Associate Degree
Program: Occupational; 2-Year Principally Bachelor's Creditable
Accreditation: @SC, COE

01 President ....Ms. Lorette M. HOOVER
05 Vice President for Academic Affairs ....Dr. June MCCLAIN
11 Vice Pres Administrative Services ....Ms. Monica S. O'QUINN
32 Vice President for Student Affairs ....Ms. Karla C. EUBANKS
09 Dir of Institutional Effectiveness ....Mr. Lonnie V. ROBERTS
06 Registrar ....Mr. Chris MISSEL
07 Director of Admissions ....Mr. Chris JEANCAKE
15 Director Personnel Services ....Mrs. Janet CARTER
18 Chief Facilities/Physical Plant ....Dr. June MCCLAIN
20 Dean of Academic Affairs ....Dr. Ron SHAFER
20 Dean of Academic Affairs ....Mr. Walt PINDER
20 Dean of Academic Affairs ....Ms. Patsy WILKERSON
21 Director of Accounting ....Mrs. Melissa LAMB
30 Dir of Institutional Advancement ....Ms. Melinda LAAGER
36 Career Placement & Dev Coord ......Ms. Markisha MCCULLOUGH
37 Financial Aid Coordinator ....Mrs. Tina MANNING
28 Special Services Coordinator ....Ms. Tracy BRUMMETT
96 Purchasing Technician ....Ms. Kathy KOVACH
08 Director of Library Services ....Ms. Jessica EVERINGHAM
14 Director of Information Tech ....Mr. Richard COTHERN
40 Bookstore Manager ....Ms. Bertie SHIPES
18 Maintenance Manager ....Mr. Randy SMITH
38 Counseling & Special Svcs Director ...Ms. Cathy MONTGOMERY
29 Director Alumni Relations ....Vacant
20 Dean of Academic Support ....Ms. Sandra WILLIAMS

American InterContinental University (B)

6600 Pchtree-Dunwdy Rd, 500 Embassy,
Atlanta GA 30328

County: Fulton FICE Identification: 021136
Unit ID: 438586
Telephone: (404) 965-6500 Carnegie Class: Master's M
FAX Number: (404) 965-6501 Calendar System: Quarter
URL: atlanta.aiuniv.edu
Established: 1977 Annual Undergrad Tuition & Fees: $15,465
Enrollment: 2,116 Coed
Affiliation or Control: Proprietary IRS Status: Proprietary
Highest Offering: Master's
Program: Liberal Arts And General
Accreditation: &NH, ACBSP, CIDA

01 President ....Mr. Peter CORREA
10 Vice President of Finance ....Mr. Richard HAWKSHEAD
32 Vice President Student Affairs ....Ms. Janis HENRY
09 Dir Inst Rsrch/Assess & Effective ....Mrs. Patricia HAWKINS
22 Director of Compliance ....Ms. Helen GALLAGHER

† Regional accreditation is carried under the parent institution in Hoffman Estates, IL.

Andrew College (C)

501 College Street, Cuthbert GA 39840-5550

County: Randolph FICE Identification: 001545
Unit ID: 138761
Telephone: (229) 732-2171 Carnegie Class: Assoc/PrivNFP
FAX Number: (229) 732-2176 Calendar System: Semester
URL: www.andrewcollege.edu
Established: 1854 Annual Undergrad Tuition & Fees: $2,098
Enrollment: 273 Coed
Affiliation or Control: United Methodist IRS Status: 501(c)3
Highest Offering: Associate Degree
Program: 2-Year Principally Bachelor's Creditable; Fine Arts Emphasis
Accreditation: SC

01 President ....Dr. David C. SEYLE
04 Assistant to the President ....Mrs. Pennie R. SCROGGINS
10 Chief Financial Officer ....Mr. Bryan HELMS
07 Director Admissions & Financial Aid ....Mr. Blake COTY
21 Controller ....Mrs. Julie CADLE
30 Director of Development ....Mr. Wayne ANTHONY
32 Director of Student Life ....Dr. Sherri TAYLOR
41 Athletic Director ....Mr. Mike RIFFE
42 Chaplain ....Rev. Chris SHOEMAKER
08 Librarian ....Mrs. Karan PITTMAN
37 Coordinator Student Financial Aid ....Mrs. Amy THOMPSON
40 Director of Bookstore ....Mrs. Pat SWICK
88 Student Support Services Director ....Ms. Santee ARCHER
05 Dean of Academic Affairs ....Mr. Jason GOODNER
06 Registrar ....Ms. Rachel BUSH
13 Director Computer Services ....Mr. Paul MOORE
18 Director of Maintenance ....Mr. David HARPER
19 Chief of Police ....Mr. Bill BROWN
39 Director of Resident Housing ....Ms. Desi FRAZIER
105 Web Services ....Mr. Brice HERRIN
88 Director of AndrewServes ....Mrs. Rebecca WHITE
88 FOCUS Director ....Mrs. Bennie MATTOX
88 Director of Student Success Center ....Mrs. Christie COTY

Argosy University, Atlanta (D)

980 Hammond Drive, Suite 100, Atlanta GA 30328-6162

County: Fulton Identification: 666735
Unit ID: 367936
Telephone: (770) 671-1200 Carnegie Class: DRU
FAX Number: (770) 407-1110 Calendar System: Semester
URL: www.argosy.edu/atlanta
Established: 1990 Annual Undergrad Tuition & Fees: $14,580
Enrollment: 2,793 Coed
Affiliation or Control: Proprietary IRS Status: Proprietary
Highest Offering: Doctorate
Program: Professional
Accreditation: &NH, CACREP, CLPSY

01 Campus President ....Dr. Ronald SWANSON
05 Vice President Academic Affairs ....Dr. Murray BRADFIELD
32 Director Student Services ....Kim P. OUSLEY
07 Senior Director of Admissions ....Johanna COLLINS
08 Director Library Services ....Clara WILLIAMS
10 Dir of Admin & Financial Services ....Daniel FRAZIER

† Regional accreditation is carried under the parent institution, Argosy University in Chicago, IL.

Armstrong Atlantic State University (E)

11935 Abercorn Street, Savannah GA 31419-1997

County: Chatham FICE Identification: 001546
Unit ID: 139789
Telephone: (912) 344-2503 Carnegie Class: Master's L
FAX Number: N/A Calendar System: Semester
URL: www.armstrong.edu
Established: 1935 Annual Undergrad Tuition & Fees (In-State): $4,860
Enrollment: 7,682 Coed
Affiliation or Control: State IRS Status: 501(c)3
Highest Offering: Doctorate
Program: Occupational; Liberal Arts And General; Teacher Preparatory
Accreditation: SC, CS, HSA, MT, MUS, NMT, NURSE, PH, PTA, RAD, RTT, SP, TED

01 President ....Dr. Linda M. BLEICKEN
05 Int Vice President/Dean of Faculty ....Dr. Anne THOMPSON
10 Vice President Business & Finance ....Mr. David CARSON
32 Vice President Student Affairs ....Dr. Keith BETTS
30 Vice President for Advancement ....Mr. Scott JOYNER
20 Int Assistant VP Academic Affairs ....Dr. John KRAFT
21 Associate VP Business & Finance ....Mr. Marc MASCOLO
84 Assoc VP Enrollment Mgmt ....Vacant
08 University Librarian ....Mr. Doug FRAZIER
37 Director Financial Aid ....Ms. Lee Ann KIRKLAND
13 Chief Information Officer ....Vacant
49 Dean College of Liberal Arts ....Dr. Laura BARRETT
53 Dean College of Education ....Dr. Patricia WACHHOLZ
76 Dean Health Professions ....Dr. Shelley CONROY
72 Int Dean Science and Technology ....Dr. Robert GREGERSON
15 Director of Human Resources ....Ms. Rebecca CARROLL
35 Director Student Activities ....Mr. P. Al HARRIS
38 Director Counseling Services ....Mr. John MITCHELL
41 Athletic Director ....Ms. Lisa SWEANY
09 Director Institutional Research ....Vacant
18 Director Plant Operations ....Mr. David FAIRCLOTH
19 Chief Campus Police ....Mr. Wayne WILLCOX
26 Director Marketing & Communications ....Ms. Brenda FORBIS
29 Director Alumni Affairs ....Vacant
88 Director Faculty Development ....Dr. Teresa WINTERHALTER
28 Director Multicultural Affairs ....Mr. Michael SNOWDEN
06 Registrar ....Ms. Judy GINTER
07 Director of Admissions ....Ms. Stephanie WHALEY

† Part of the University System of Georgia.

The Art Institute of Atlanta (F)

6600 Peachtree Dunwoody Road, Atlanta GA 30328-1635

County: Fulton FICE Identification: 009270
Unit ID: 138813
Telephone: (770) 394-8300 Carnegie Class: Spec/Arts
FAX Number: (770) 394-0008 Calendar System: Quarter
URL: www.artinstitutes.edu/atlanta/
Established: 1949 Annual Undergrad Tuition & Fees: $23,535
Enrollment: 4,013 Coed
Affiliation or Control: Proprietary IRS Status: Proprietary
Highest Offering: Baccalaureate
Program: Fine Arts Emphasis
Accreditation: SC, ACFEI, ART, CIDA

01 President ....Mrs. Jo Ann KOCH
10 Dir of Admin and Financial Svcs ....Mr. Chris SCHWARZER
15 Director of Human Resources ....Ms. Joselyn CASSIDY
07 Senior Director of Admissions ....Ms. Joy MCCLURE
05 Dean of Academic Affairs ....Dr. Dan GARLAND
32 Dean of Student Affairs ....Ms. April SHAVKIN
37 Director of Student Financial Svcs ....Vacant
09 Dir of Inst Effectiveness/Research ....Dr. Michael T. HOEFER
08 Director of Library ....Ms. Gayle MEIER
13 Director of Technology ....Ms. TJ BONDS
06 Registrar ....Ms. Diana HILL
20 Associate Dean of Academic Affairs ....Vacant
36 Director of Career Services ....Mrs. Sharon BOLLING-CLAY
26 Director of Communications ....Ms. Kim RESNIK
40 Retail and Administrative Services ....Mr. Lewis HAWKINS
18 Director of Facilities ....Mr. Brandon GHOLSTON
38 Student Support Svcs Coordinator ....Ms. Elizabeth BUSH
39 Director of Residence Life/Housing ....Mr. Stephan MOORE
04 Exec Assistant to the President ....Ms. Rebecca CROWFOOT

Ashworth University (G)

6625 The Corners Parkway, Norcross GA 30092-3406

County: Gwinnett Identification: 666106
Telephone: (770) 729-8400 Carnegie Class: Not Classified
FAX Number: (770) 729-9296 Calendar System: Semester
URL: www.ashworthcollege.edu
Established: 2000 Annual Undergrad Tuition & Fees: $3,692
Enrollment: 12,000 Coed
Affiliation or Control: Proprietary IRS Status: Proprietary
Highest Offering: Master's
Program: 2-Year Principally Bachelor's Creditable; Professional
Accreditation: DETC

01 President ....Mr. Robert KLAPPER
05 Vice President Education ....Dr. Leslie GARGIULO

Athens Technical College (H)

800 US Highway 29 N, Athens GA 30601-1500

County: Clarke FICE Identification: 005600
Unit ID: 246813
Telephone: (706) 355-5000 Carnegie Class: Assoc/Pub-R-M
FAX Number: (706) 369-5753 Calendar System: Semester
URL: www.athenstech.edu
Established: 1958 Annual Undergrad Tuition & Fees (In-State): $3,090
Enrollment: 5,741 Coed
Affiliation or Control: State IRS Status: 501(c)3
Highest Offering: Associate Degree
Program: Occupational; 2-Year Principally Bachelor's Creditable; Technical Emphasis
Accreditation: SC, ACBSP, ADNUR, DA, DH, DMS, PTAA, RAD, SURGT

01 President ....Dr. Flora W. TYDINGS
05 Vice President Academic Affairs ....Dr. Joyce SANSING
32 Vice President Student Affairs ....Ms. Andrea DANIEL
11 Vice Pres Administrative Services ....Ms. Kathryn S. THOMAS
45 Vice Pres Economic Devel Services ....Mr. Jerry BARROW
12 Vice President of Off Campus Sites ....Dr. Larry D. SIEFFERMAN
09 Vice President Inst Effectiveness ....Dr. Daniel J. SMITH
13 Vice Pres Information Technology ....Mr. Dennis ASHWORTH
72 Dean Technical Education ....Ms. Susan LARSON
76 Dean Life Sciences ....Dr. Scott MARTIN
06 Registrar ....Ms. Caroline ANGELO
07 Director Admissions ....Mr. Lenzy REID
08 Director Library Services ....Ms. Carol STANLEY
08 Librarian Elbert County Campus ....Ms. Marci MANGLITZ
36 Director Student Support/Career Dev ....Ms. Celeste TAYLOR
37 Director Financial Aid ....Mr. Patrick HARRIS
88 Director Adult Education Programs ....Dr. Janie RODGERS
51 Director Community Education ....Vacant
12 Director Walton County Campus ....Mr. James E. HOGG
12 Director Greene County Campus ....Mr. Sibley BRYAN
50 Dean Business/Personal Services Div ....Ms. Diane CAMPBELL
35 Student Activities Director ....Mr. Yancey GULLEY
15 Director Human Resources ....Dr. Leslie CRICKENBERGER
18 Facilities Director ....Mr. Jim WALTER
30 Director Institutional Advancement ....Ms. Liz DALTON
21 Director of Accounting ....Ms. Sonya MCDANIEL
19 Director of College Relations ....Ms. Pamela R. GARDNER

Atlanta Metropolitan College (I)

1630 Metropolitan Parkway, SW, Atlanta GA 30310-4498

County: Fulton FICE Identification: 012165
Unit ID: 138901
Telephone: (404) 756-4000 Carnegie Class: Assoc/Pub-U-SC
FAX Number: (404) 756-4460 Calendar System: Semester

URL: www.atlm.edu
Established: 1974 Annual Undergrad Tuition & Fees (In-State): $3,400
Enrollment: 3,183 Coed
Affiliation or Control: State IRS Status: 501(c)3
Highest Offering: Associate Degree
Program: Occupational; 2-Year Principally Bachelor's Creditable
Accreditation: SC, ACBSP

01 President .... Dr. Gary A. MCGAHA, SR.
05 Vice Pres Academic Affairs .... Dr. Jerome DRAIN
10 Vice President Fiscal Affairs .... Mr. Freddie L. JOHNSON
32 Vice President Student Affairs .... Mrs. Cynthia EVERS
30 Vice Pres Institutional Advancement .... Mr. Larion WILLIAMS
20 Assoc Vice Pres Academic Affairs .... Vacant
21 Assoc VP Fiscal Affs/ Comptroller .... Mrs. Michelle ALSTON-BROWN
50 Dean Div Business/Computer Sci .... Ms. Cheryl BARNES
79 Dean Div Humanities/Fine Arts .... Dr. Frank JOHNSON
81 Dean Div of Sci/Math/Health Profess .... Dr. Bonita FLOURNOY
83 Dean Div of Social Science .... Dr. Grady CULPEPPER
06 Dir Enrollment Services/Registrar .... Mrs. Candace PERRY
15 Director of Human Resources .... Ms. Regina Ray SIMMONS
08 Director of the Library .... Mr. Robert QUARLES
35 Director of Student Activities .... Ms. Iris SHANKLIN
37 Director of Financial Aid .... Mrs. Alicia SCOTT
38 Director Counseling/Disability Svcs .... Ms. Tammy YOUNG
14 Data Processing Manager .... Mr. Walter CUMMINGS
13 Chief Information Officer .... Mr. Antonio W. TRAVIS
09 Director Inst Effectiveness .... Dr. Mark CUNNINGHAM
19 Director of Campus Safety .... Mr. Antonio LONG
35 Dir of Student Outreach & Access .... Mr. Stephen WOODALL
18 Dir Plant Operations/Facilities .... Mr. E. Keith WILLIAMS
40 Bookstore Manager .... Ms. Barbara SMITH

† Part of the University System of Georgia.

Atlanta Technical College (A)

1560 Metropolitan Parkway, SW, Atlanta GA 30310-4446
County: Fulton FICE Identification: 008543
Unit ID: 138840
Telephone: (404) 225-4000 Carnegie Class: Assoc/Pub-U-SC
FAX Number: (404) 225-4639 Calendar System: Semester
URL: www.atlantatech.edu
Established: 1967 Annual Undergrad Tuition & Fees (In-State): $4,453
Enrollment: 5,053 Coed
Affiliation or Control: State IRS Status: 501(c)3
Highest Offering: Associate Degree
Program: Occupational; Technical Emphasis
Accreditation: SC, COE, DA, DT, MAC

01 President .... Dr. Alvetta P. THOMAS
05 Vice President Academic Affairs .... Dr. Gladys CAMP
11 Vice Pres Administrative Services .... Mrs. Teresa BROWN
32 Student Services .... Mr. Vory BILLUPS
30 Vice President Economic Development .... Mr. Harold CRAIG
04 Assistant to the President .... Mrs. Joni WILLIAMS
45 Executive Vice President .... Dr. Rodney ELLIS
26 Director Communications & Marketing .... Mrs. Terreta RODGERS
37 Director of Financial Aid .... Mrs. Deborah CLARK
07 Director of Admissions .... Mr. Vory BILLUPS
88 Dean Industrial and Transportation .... Mr. Arthur GRIER
51 Director of Continuing Education .. Dr. Deborah JOHNSON-BLAKE
36 Director Career Placement .... Mr. Michael BURNSIDE
50 Dean Business and Public Services .... Mrs. Arriana DANIEL
88 Dean Health and Public Safety .... Dr. Constance ROWAN
06 Registrar .... Mrs. Niya EADY
15 Director Human Resources .... Ms. Marilyn SMITH-ROBINSON
18 Director of Facilities .... Mr. Isaac VINING
09 Director of Curriculum and Planning .... Dr. Murray J. WILLIAMS

Atlanta's John Marshall Law School (B)

1422 West Peachtree Street NW, Atlanta GA 30309
County: Fulton FICE Identification: 031733
Unit ID: 138929
Telephone: (404) 872-3593 Carnegie Class: Not Classified
FAX Number: (404) 872-3802 Calendar System: Semester
URL: www.johnmarshall.edu
Established: 1933 Annual Graduate Tuition & Fees: $33,860
Enrollment: 552 Coed
Affiliation or Control: Proprietary IRS Status: Proprietary
Highest Offering: First Professional Degree; No Undergraduates
Program: Professional
Accreditation: LAW

01 Dean .... Mr. Richardson R. LYNN
05 Assoc Dean Academics .... Vacant
32 Assoc Dean of Students .... Ms. Sheryl E. HARRISON
07 Assoc Dean Marketing/Recruiting .... Mr. Alan BOYER
10 Chief Financial Officer .... Mr. Allen BREZEL

Augusta State University (C)

2500 Walton Way, Augusta GA 30904-2200
County: Richmond FICE Identification: 001552
Unit ID: 138983
Telephone: (706) 737-1400 Carnegie Class: Master's L
FAX Number: (706) 737-1773 Calendar System: Semester
URL: www.aug.edu
Established: 1925 Annual Undergrad Tuition & Fees (In-State): $5,742
Enrollment: 6,750 Coed
Affiliation or Control: State IRS Status: 501(c)3
Highest Offering: Beyond Master's But Less Than Doctorate
Program: Occupational; 2-Year Principally Bachelor's Creditable; Liberal Arts And General; Teacher Preparatory
Accreditation: SC, ART, BUS, CACREP, MUS, NUR, SPAA, SW, TED

01 President .... Dr. William A. BLOODWORTH, JR.
05 Vice President Academic Affairs .... Dr. Samuel SULLIVAN
10 Vice President Business Operations .... Ms. Therese ROSIER
32 Vice President Student Services .... Dr. Joyce JONES
30 Vice Pres Development/Alumni Rels .... Ms. Helen HENDEE
20 Assoc VP for Academic Affairs .... Dr. Carol J. RYCHLY
20 Assoc VP for Academic Affairs .... Dr. Raymond A. WHITING
104 Asst VP for International Affairs .... Dr. Holly CARTER
45 Asst VP for Campus Development .... Mr. Jeffrey W. FOLEY
49 Dean College Arts/Sciences .... Dr. Robert R. PARHAM
50 Dean College of Business .... Dr. Marc D. MILLER
53 Dean College of Education .... Dr. Gordon EISENMAN
21 Director Financial Services .... Ms. Angela PRETTELT
51 Director Continuing Education .... Ms. Carolyn K. INGRAHAM
09 Director Institutional Research .... Ms. Mary FILPUS-LUYCKX
08 Librarian .... Ms. Camilla REID
07 Director Admissions/Registrar .... Ms. Katherine SWEENEY
29 Dir Alumni Relations/Annual Giving .... Mr. Wes ZAMZOW
36 Director Placement .... Ms. Julie GOLEY
37 Director Financial Aid .... Ms. Cynthia PARKS
15 Director Human Resources .... Mr. Walt ALEXANDERSON
38 Director Counseling Center .... Dr. Robert MAYS
35 Director Student Activities .... Mr. Eddie J. HOWARD
26 Dir Public Relations/Publications .... Ms. Kathy D. SCHOFE
41 Director Athletics .... Mr. Clint BRYANT
19 Director Public Safety .... Mr. Jasper COOKE
40 Director Business Services .... Mr. Karl MUNCHY
18 Director Plant Operations .... Mr. Dave W. FREEMAN
13 Director Information Technology .... Mr. Chip MATSON
88 Director Academic Advisement .... Ms. Kathryn T. THOMPSON
25 Director Grants Administration .... Ms. Kimberly F. GRAY
28 Director of Student Development ..... Ms. Karen A. MOBLEY-BELK
24 Director Media Services .... Ms. Rosemarie AXTON
21 Budget Director .... Ms. Aisha LAVIN
21 Controller Accounting Services .... Ms. Corina WARNER
88 Director Testing & Disability Svcs .... Ms. Angie KITCHENS

† Part of the University System of Georgia.

Augusta Technical College (D)

3200 Augusta Tech Drive, Augusta GA 30906-3399
County: Richmond FICE Identification: 005599
Unit ID: 138956
Telephone: (706) 771-4000 Carnegie Class: Assoc/Pub-R-M
FAX Number: (706) 771-4016 Calendar System: Quarter
URL: www.augustatech.edu
Established: 1961 Annual Undergrad Tuition & Fees (In-District): $3,780
Enrollment: 4,864 Coed
Affiliation or Control: State/Local IRS Status: 501(c)3
Highest Offering: Associate Degree
Program: Occupational
Accreditation: SC, CVT, DA, ENGT, MAC, OTA, PNUR, SURGT

01 President .... Mr. Terry D. ELAM
05 Vice President Academic Affairs .... Mr. C. Rick HALL
11 Vice Pres Administrative Services .... Ms. Janice G. RICHARDSON
32 Vice Pres Student Affairs .... Dr. Melissa M. FRANK-ALSTON
88 Vice President Economic Development .... Dr. Lisa PALMER
12 VP Ops Thomson/McDuffie Campus .... Mr. Ted DUZENSKI
12 VP Ops Waynesboro/Burke Campus .... Ms. Ella S. JONES
35 Dean Student Services .... Vacant
37 Director Financial Aid .... Ms. Beverly SMYRE HINES
07 Director Admissions .... Ms. Donna WENDT
30 Director Institutional Advancement .... Ms. Beverly PELTIER
06 Registrar .... Ms. Sabrina WHITE
45 Dir Inst Planning/Effectiveness .... Dr. Annabelle LEWIS
21 Director Accounting .... Ms. Sheila HILL
26 Dir Marketing/Public Relations .... Ms. Bonita JENKINS
15 Payroll/Benefits Manager .... Ms. Lori USRY
84 Enrollment Manager Thomson Campus .... Ms. Julie LANGHAM
36 Career Services Assistant .... Ms. Sharon GLENN
88 High School Coordinator .... Ms. Deborah HEREDIA
76 Dean Allied Health Science .... Dr. Gwen TAYLOR
72 Dean Industrial Technology .... Mr. James PRICE
50 Dean Business/Personal Svcs .... Ms. Debbie CLARK
97 Dean Gen Ed & Learning Support .... Mr. John RICHARDSON
54 Dean Information & Engineering Tech ...... Ms. JoAnne ROBINSON

Bainbridge College (E)

2500 E Shotwell Street, PO Box 990,
Bainbridge GA 39818-0990
County: Decatur FICE Identification: 011074
Unit ID: 139010
Telephone: (229) 248-2500 Carnegie Class: Assoc/Pub-R-M
FAX Number: (229) 248-2547 Calendar System: Semester
URL: www.bainbridge.edu
Established: 1970 Annual Undergrad Tuition & Fees (In-State): $3,142
Enrollment: 3,736 Coed
Affiliation or Control: State IRS Status: 501(c)3
Highest Offering: Associate Degree
Program: Occupational; 2-Year Principally Bachelor's Creditable
Accreditation: SC, ADNUR

01 President .... Dr. Richard CARVAJAL
05 Vice Pres Academic Affairs .... Dr. Mariam DITTMAN
10 Int Vice Pres of Business Affairs .... Mr. Shawn MCGEE
32 Int Dean of Student Services .... Ms. Connie SNYDER
49 Int Chair Arts & Sciences Div .... Dr. Tonya STRICKLAND
75 Int Chair Technical Studies Div .... Ms. Barbara STEPHENS
88 Int Chair Dept of Learning Support .... Dr. Michael KIRKLAND
08 Director Library .... Ms. Susan RALPH
51 Director of Continuing Education .... Ms. Ann WELLS
26 Chief Public Relations Officer .... Ms. Marcia A. MCRAE
37 Int Director of Financial Aid .... Mr. Richard MESSERSMITH
21 Controller .... Ms. Kay LIVINGSTON
18 Director of Plant Operations .... Mr. Leonard DEAN
91 Director of Technology Services .... Mr. Scott DUNN
35 Director Student Affairs .... Mr. David PRICE
30 Director of Development .... Mr. Emory SMITH
07 Director of Admissions .... Ms. Connie SNYDER
09 Research Analyst .... Dr. David BYRD
38 Counselor .... Ms. Arlene COOK

† Part of the University System of Georgia.

Bauder College (F)

384 Northyards Blvd, Ste 190 & 400,
Atlanta GA 30313-2439
County: Fulton FICE Identification: 011574
Unit ID: 139074
Telephone: (404) 237-7573 Carnegie Class: Bac/Assoc
FAX Number: (404) 237-1642 Calendar System: Quarter
URL: www.bauder.edu
Established: 1964 Annual Undergrad Tuition & Fees: $33,850
Enrollment: 1,499 Coed
Affiliation or Control: Proprietary IRS Status: Proprietary
Highest Offering: Baccalaureate
Program: Occupational; 2-Year Principally Bachelor's Creditable
Accreditation: SC

01 President/CEO .... Dr. Charles TAYLOR
05 Int Vice Pres for Academic Affairs .... Dr. Debbie GLINES
11 Vice President of Operations .... Chris CATHCART
09 Director Inst Effectiveness .... Dr. Robert PULTZ
10 Director of Finance .... Tanya JACKSON
07 Director of Admissions .... William KILGORE
07 Director of Admission - High School .... Dee BANKS
37 Director Financial Aid .... Mona Leiann MAY
36 Director of Career Services .... Andrea ROTH
20 Dean .... Melissa WILLIAMS
66 Director of Nursing .... Dr. Diana MEEKS-SJOSTROM
06 Head Registrar .... Absolom MEDLEY
08 Head Librarian .... Mary Kaye HOOKER
04 Executive Assistant .... Shannon KYRISCH
21 Director of Student Accounts .... LaTanya HARTSFIELD
32 Director Student Services .... Carolyn JENKINS

Berry College (G)

2277 Martha Berry Highway, NW,
Mount Berry GA 30149-0001
County: Floyd FICE Identification: 001554
Unit ID: 139144
Telephone: (706) 232-5374 Carnegie Class: Bac/A&S
FAX Number: (706) 236-2238 Calendar System: Semester
URL: www.berry.edu
Established: 1902 Annual Undergrad Tuition & Fees: $26,090
Enrollment: 2,087 Coed
Affiliation or Control: Independent Non-Profit IRS Status: 501(c)3
Highest Offering: Beyond Master's But Less Than Doctorate
Program: Liberal Arts And General; Teacher Preparatory; Professional
Accreditation: SC, BUS, MUS, TED

01 President .... Dr. Stephen R. BRIGGS
05 Vice President & Provost .... Dr. Katherine M. WHATLEY
10 Vice President Finance .... Mr. Brian I. ERB
32 VP Student Affairs and Enrollment .... Ms. Debbie HEIDA
30 Vice Pres Institutional Advancement .... Ms. Bettyann O'NEILL
84 VP of Enrollment Management .... Dr. Gary WATERS
35 Assoc Vice Pres Student Affairs .... Ms. Julie A. BUMPUS
50 Dean Campbell School of Business .... Dr. John GROUT
53 Dean Charter School of Education .... Dr. Jackie MCDOWELL
79 Dean School Humanities/Arts/Soc Sci .... Dr. Thomas D. KENNEDY
81 Dean School of Math/Natural Science .... Dr. Bruce CONN
78 Dean Stdnt Work/Experiential Lrng .... Mr. Rufus MASSEY
07 Director of Admissions .... Mr. Brett E. KENNEDY
08 Director of the Library .... Ms. Sherre Lee HARRINGTON
42 Interim Chaplain .... Mr. Jonathan HUGGINS
29 Director of Alumni Affairs .... Ms. Christina WATTERS
100 Chief of Staff .... Mr. Whit WHITAKER
27 Chief Information Officer .... Ms. Penny EVANS-PLANTS
38 Director of Counseling Center .... Dr. J. Marshall JENKINS
37 Director of Financial Aid .... Ms. Marcia MCCONNELL
36 Director of Career Center .... Mrs. Sue TARPLEY
06 Registrar .... Ms. Linda A. TENNANT
09 Director of Institutional Research .... Dr. Bryce DURBIN
18 Director Physical Plant .... Mr. Mark HOPKINS
20 Associate Provost .... Dr. Andy BRESSETTE
26 Asst VP Public Rels and Marketing .... Ms. Jeanne MATHEWS
89 Director First Year Experience .... Mrs. Katherine POWELL
92 Director Honors Program .... Dr. Brian CARROLL
94 Director Women's Studies .... Dr. Susan LOGSDON-CONRADSEN
96 Director Purchasing .... Mr. Brad BARRRIS
85 Director International Programs .... Ms. Sarah EGERER
15 Director Human Resources .... Mr. Harold NALLY

43 Director of Legal Services ... Mr. Danny PRICE
78 Dir Stdnt Work/Experiential Lrng ... Mr. Michael BURNES
88 Director of Employee Development ... Mr. Wes MORAN

Beulah Heights University (A)

892 Berne Street, SE, PO Box 18145,
Atlanta GA 30316-1873
County: Fulton FICE Identification: 030763
Unit ID: 139153
Telephone: (404) 627-2681 Carnegie Class: Spec/Faith
FAX Number: (404) 627-0702 Calendar System: Semester
URL: www.beulah.org
Established: 1918 Annual Undergrad Tuition & Fees: $5,590
Enrollment: 845 Coed
Affiliation or Control: Other Protestant IRS Status: 501(c)3
Highest Offering: Doctorate
Program: Religious Emphasis
Accreditation: BI, TRACS

01 President ... Dr. Benson M. KARANJA
05 Vice Pres/Dean Academic Affairs ... Dr. James B. KEILLER
88 VP for Academic Program Development ... Dr. Angelita HOWARD
09 Director for Assessment/Planning ... Ms. Hiuko ADAMS
32 VP Student Life/Enrollment Mgmt ... Pastor Shawn ADAMS
37 Director of Financial Aid ... Ms. Pat A. BANKS
08 Director of Library Services ... Mr. Pradeep K. DAS
06 Registrar ... Mrs. Jacquelyn B. ARMSTRONG
15 Human Resources Coordinator ... Vacant
07 Director of Admissions ... Mr. John DREHER
18 Facilities Director ... Mr. Harvey BRUMELOW
97 Chair Dept of General Studies ... Dr. Angelita HOWARD
73 Chair Dept of Religious Studies ... Mr. Walter TURNER
88 Chair Dept of Leadership Studies ... Ms. Betty G. PALMER
42 Dean of Chapel ... Bishop Johnathan E. ALVARADO
10 Chief Business Officer ... Miss Tammy GUELFO
20 Associate Academic Officer ... Dr. Mark HARDGROVE
21 Associate Business Officer ... Mr. Randy BREWER
26 Chief Public Relations/Dev Officer ... Mr. Peter KARANJA
29 Dir of Marketing/Enrollment/Almuni ... Miss Debbie CHAND

Brenau University (B)

500 Washington Street, SE, Gainesville GA 30501-3668
County: Hall FICE Identification: 001556
Unit ID: 139199
Telephone: (770) 534-6299 Carnegie Class: Master's L
FAX Number: (770) 534-6114 Calendar System: Semester
URL: www.brenau.edu
Established: 1878 Annual Undergrad Tuition & Fees: $21,124
Enrollment: 2,768 Coed
Affiliation or Control: Independent Non-Profit IRS Status: 501(c)3
Highest Offering: Doctorate
Program: Liberal Arts And General; Teacher Preparatory; Professional
Accreditation: SC, CIDA, DANCE, NURSE, OT, TED

01 President ... Dr. Ed L. SCHRADER
03 Exec VP/Chief Financial Ofcr ... Dr. Wayne W. DEMPSEY
05 Provost & VP For Academic Affairs ... Dr. Nancy F. KRIPPEL
100 Chief of Staff ... Ms. Jody Y. WALL
10 Vice President Financial Services ... Ms. Sandra D. THORNTON
32 Sr VP Enrollment Mgt/Student Svcs ... Mr. Scott A. BRIELL
30 Vice Pres External Relations ... Mr. J. Matthew THOMAS
13 Chief Information Tech Officer ... Mr. Chip L. ANDREWS
44 Sr VP Institutional Advancement ... Mr. James M. BARCO
09 Director of Research & Planning ... Dr. Robert E. CUTTINO
37 Assoc VP of EM & Dir Financial Aid ... Ms. Pam J. BARRETT
88 Assoc VP Info Tech & SACS Liaison ... Dr. Heather S. HARTMAN
07 Dean Graduate Admissions ... Ms. Christina C. WHITE
21 Controller ... Ms. Holly REYNOLDS
15 Director of Human Resources ... Ms. Kelley L. MADDOX
18 Director Facilities & Logistics ... Mr. Mike HOLLIMON
26 VP Communications/Publications ... Mr. David MORRISON
35 Dean of Student Success & Retention ... Ms. Valerie SIMMONS-WALSTON
36 Director of Career Services ... Mr. George BAGEL
24 Director of Learning Center ... Dr. Vince J. YAMILKOSKI
41 Athletic Director ... Mr. Mike LOCHSTAMPFOR
23 Chaplain ... Dr. Don HARRISON
53 Interim Dean College of Education ... Dr. David L. BARNETT
76 Dean College of Health & Sciences ... Dr. Gale H. STARICH
66 Chair Department of Nursing ... Dr. Keeta P. WILBORN
50 Dean College Business/Mass Commun ... Dr. Bill LIGHTFOOT
79 Dean College of Fine Arts & Human ... Dr. Andrea C. BIRCH
81 Chair Math & Science Department ... Dr. Latricia SCRIVEN
08 Dean of Library Services ... Ms. Marlene GIGUERE
88 Executive Director for Recruitment ... Mr. Nathan R. GOSS
06 Registrar & Dir of Student Records ... Ms. Barbara WILSON
29 Director Alumni Relations ... Ms. Natalie L. WALKER
19 Director Campus Safety & Security ... Ms. Paula LAND

Brewton-Parker College (C)

201 David-Eliza Fountain Circle,
Mount Vernon GA 30445-0197
County: Montgomery FICE Identification: 001557
Unit ID: 139205
Telephone: (912) 583-2241 Carnegie Class: Bac/Diverse
FAX Number: (912) 583-4498 Calendar System: Semester
URL: www.bpc.edu
Established: 1904 Annual Undergrad Tuition & Fees: $19,388
Enrollment: 778 Coed
Affiliation or Control: Baptist IRS Status: 501(c)3
Highest Offering: Baccalaureate
Program: 2-Year Principally Bachelor's Creditable; Liberal Arts And General; Teacher Preparatory; Business Emphasis
Accreditation: SC, MUS, TED

01 Acting President ... Dr. Mike SIMONEAUX
11 Interim Chief Operating Officer ... Mr. Randy F. MINTON
05 Interim Provost ... Dr. Christopher T. JONES
30 Interim VP Col Advancement ... Ms. Jessica L. JAMES
84 Vice Pres of Enrollment Services ... Mr. Jim BEALL
10 Chief Financial Officer ... Mrs. Natasha MASON
09 Dir of Assessment & Inst Research ... Dr. Carol S. O'DELL
32 Dean of Students ... Mrs. Sherrie HELMS
06 Registrar ... Mrs. Sara CROWE
07 Dir of Admiss & Intl Student Svcs ... Ms. Sandra CLAY
08 Librarian ... Mrs. Ann TURNER
26 Interim Director of Marketing ... Ms. Kelley M. ARNOLD
27 Director of News & Public Relations ... Ms. Kelley M. ARNOLD
35 Director of Student Activities ... Vacant
37 Director of Financial Aid ... Mr. Rick WOOLVERTON
42 Director of Campus Ministry ... Ms. Lauren PARNELL
18 Director of Plant Operations ... Mr. Ben HAMILTON
38 Dir Counseling & Career Services ... Mrs. Tonia SPAULDING
39 Director of Housing ... Mr. Greg COURSEY
15 Director Human Resources ... Mrs. Shirley ELLIS
40 Bookstore Manager ... Mrs. Lynn ADDISON
13 Interim Chief Information Officer ... Mr. David KIGHT
91 Computer Program/Analyst ... Vacant
29 Director Alumni Relations ... Ms. Jessica L. JAMES
25 Director Grants/Projects ... Ms. Jessica L. JAMES
41 Athletic Director ... Ms. Sheila SIMMONS
20 Academic Assistant to the Provost ... Mrs. Sadia AJOHDA
43 General Counsel ... Mr. John MANNING
50 Chair Business Division ... Mr. Randy F. MINTON
53 Chair Education Division ... Dr. Susan E. WHITE
49 Chair Arts & Sciences Division ... Dr. Ruth Ellen PORTER
73 Chair Christian Studies ... Dr. Jerry RAY

Brown College of Court Reporting (D)

1900 Emery St. NW, Atlanta GA 30318
County: Fulton FICE Identification: 020609
Unit ID: 139214
Telephone: (404) 876-1227 Carnegie Class: Assoc/PrivFP
FAX Number: (404) 876-4415 Calendar System: Quarter
URL: www.bccr.edu
Established: 1972 Annual Undergrad Tuition & Fees: $15,348
Enrollment: 242 Coed
Affiliation or Control: Proprietary IRS Status: Proprietary
Highest Offering: Associate Degree
Program: Occupational; 2-Year Principally Bachelor's Creditable
Accreditation: COE

01 Executive Director ... Sue C. SCHMITH
07 Director of Admissions ... Marita CAREY
05 Director of Education ... Shirley SOTONA

Brown Mackie College-Atlanta (E)

4370 Peachtree Road NE, Atlanta GA 30319
County: Gwinnett FICE Identification: 026214
Unit ID: 410283
Telephone: (404) 799-4500 Carnegie Class: Assoc/PrivFP
FAX Number: (404) 799-4522 Calendar System: Other
URL: www.brownmackie.edu
Established: 1987 Annual Undergrad Tuition & Fees: $11,124
Enrollment: 929 Coed
Affiliation or Control: Proprietary IRS Status: Proprietary
Highest Offering: Baccalaureate
Program: Occupational; 2-Year Principally Bachelor's Creditable; Business Emphasis
Accreditation: ACICS, OTA, SURTEC

01 President ... Mrs. Crystal CELESTINE
05 Dean of Academic Affairs ... Ms. Dominica AUSTIN
07 Senior Director of Admissions ... Mr. Trey MCCRAY
06 Registrar ... Ms. Pat HILDERBRANT

Carver College (F)

3870 Cascade Road SW, Atlanta GA 30331-2184
County: Fulton FICE Identification: 036353
Unit ID: 139287
Telephone: (404) 527-4520 Carnegie Class: Not Classified
FAX Number: (404) 527-4526 Calendar System: Semester
URL: www.carver.edu
Established: 1943 Annual Undergrad Tuition & Fees: $5,920
Enrollment: 108 Coed
Affiliation or Control: Independent Non-Profit IRS Status: 501(c)3
Highest Offering: Baccalaureate
Program: Religious Emphasis
Accreditation: #BI

01 President and COO ... Mr. Robert W. CRUMMIE
05 Vice Pres Academic Affs/Acad Dean ... Dr. Sujaya JAMES
32 Vice President of Student Affairs ... Mr. Jeffrey A. EASLEY
10 Vice President of Business Affairs ... Mr. Terry ALEXANDER
30 Vice President of Advancement ... Mrs. Carla M. CRUMMIE
07 Director of Admissions ... Ms. Bertha MACK
06 Registrar ... Ms. Olive JACKS
09 Dir Institutional Effectiveness ... Ms. Cynthia BIRKS
29 Director Alumni Affairs ... Mr. James FILE
42 Stdnt Director of Chapel Services ... Ms. Kola AMIGUN
73 Director of Bible/Theology Division ... Dr. Sujaya JAMES
97 Director of General Studies ... Mr. Benjamin JACKS
107 Director of Professional Studies ... Mr. Lester SMITH
08 Director of Library Services ... Ms. Lauren DENNY
18 Chief of Facilities/Physical Plant ... Mr. John MILLER
40 Director of Bookstore ... Mr. Thomas CAIN

Central Georgia Technical College (G)

3300 Macon Tech Drive, Macon GA 31206-3699
County: Bibb FICE Identification: 005763
Unit ID: 140304
Telephone: (478) 757-3400 Carnegie Class: Assoc/Pub-R-L
FAX Number: (478) 757-3454 Calendar System: Quarter
URL: www.centralgatech.edu
Established: 1966 Annual Undergrad Tuition & Fees (In-State): $3,515
Enrollment: 7,903 Coed
Affiliation or Control: State IRS Status: 501(c)3
Highest Offering: Associate Degree
Program: Occupational; Technical Emphasis
Accreditation: SC, DH, MLTAD, SURGT

01 President ... Dr. Michael D. MOYE
05 Vice President Academic Affairs ... Mr. Hank GRIFFETH
10 Vice President Administrative Svcs ... Ms. Elaine M. TRUELOVE
32 Vice President Student Affairs ... Dr. Eddy DIXON
31 Vice President Econ Dev & Comm Rel ... Ms. Rebecca R. LEE
12 Vice President Satellite Operations ... Mr. Hank GRIFFETH
18 Vice Pres Facilities/Ancillary Svcs ... Ms. Dana DAVIS
13 Vice Pres Information Technology ... Mr. Gardner J. LONG, II
20 Assoc Vice Pres Academic Affairs ... Ms. Joan THOMPSON
35 Dean of Student Affairs ... Ms. Pennie STRONG
06 Registrar ... Ms. Rosemary CULVERHOUSE
07 Director of Admissions ... Ms. Tammy CARTER
21 Director of Accounting Services ... Vacant
26 Director of Public Relations & Info ... Mr. James HARVEY, JR.
36 Director Career Services ... Mr. Tony TURNER
08 Director Library & Media Services ... Mr. Neil W. MCARTHUR
37 Director of Financial Aid ... Ms. Jackie WHITE
15 Director Human Resources ... Ms. Linda HAMPTON
105 Webmaster ... Ms. Margo S. KENIREY
18 Facilities Director ... Mr. Robert DOMINY
13 Director of Information Technology ... Mr. Ben HALL
51 Director of Continuing Education ... Mr. Clay TEAGUE

Chattahoochee Technical College (H)

980 South Cobb Drive, Marietta GA 30060
County: Barton FICE Identification: 030290
Unit ID: 366456
Telephone: (770) 528-4545 Carnegie Class: Not Classified
FAX Number: (770) 975-4126 Calendar System: Quarter
URL: www.chattahoocheetech.edu
Established: 1981 Annual Undergrad Tuition & Fees (In-State): $2,250
Enrollment: 6,642 Coed
Affiliation or Control: State IRS Status: 501(c)3
Highest Offering: Associate Degree
Program: Occupational
Accreditation: SC, ACFEI, COE, ENGT, MAC, PTAA, RAD

01 President ... Dr. Stanford CHANDLER
04 Administrative Asst to President ... Ms. Tammy COLLUM
05 Provost & Executive Vice President ... Mr. Ron NEWCOMB
20 Vice President Academic Affairs ... Dr. Trina BOTELER
10 Vice President for Finance ... Ms. Catrice HUFSTETLER
32 VP Student Affairs/Enrollment Mgmt ... Dr. Scott RULE
31 Vice Pres Community/Econ Develop ... Mr. Glenn RASCO
26 Exec Dir External Affs/Brd Liaison ... Ms. Jennifer NELSON
30 Exec Dir Advancement/Resource Devel ... Vacant
06 Registrar ... Ms. Shannon POLLOCK

Clark Atlanta University (I)

223 James P. Brawley Drive, SW, Atlanta GA 30314-4391
County: Fulton FICE Identification: 001559
Unit ID: 138947
Telephone: (404) 880-8000 Carnegie Class: DRU
FAX Number: N/A Calendar System: Semester
URL: www.cau.edu
Established: 1988 Annual Undergrad Tuition & Fees: $18,106
Enrollment: 3,941 Coed
Affiliation or Control: United Methodist IRS Status: 501(c)3
Highest Offering: Doctorate
Program: Liberal Arts And General; Teacher Preparatory; Professional
Accreditation: SC, BUS, CACREP, SPAA, SW, TED

01 President ... Dr. Carlton E. BROWN
05 Provost/VP for Academic Affairs ... Dr. Joseph H. SILVER, SR.
30 VP for Inst Advancement/Univ Rels ... Vacant
10 VP for Finance/Business Svcs ... Ms. Lucille MAUGE
84 Int VP for Enroll Svcs/Student Affs ... Dr. Randy GUNTER
88 VP for Research & Sponsored Pgms ... Dr. Marcus W. SHUTE
20 Assoc VP for Academic Affairs ... Dr. Jeffrey J. PHILLIPS
13 Assoc VP/Chief Info Ofcr ... Mr. Reginald BRINSON
21 Assoc VP/Controller ... Mr. Edward PATRICK
35 Assoc VP Student Affairs/Dean ... Ms. Ernita HEMMITT
09 Director Planning/Assessment/Rsrch ... Mr. Narendra H. PATEL
43 General Counsel ... Mr. Lance DUNNINGS
06 Registrar ... Ms. Angela FREEMAN

26 Director Strategic Communications .... Ms. Donna BROCK
29 Director Alumni Relations .... Ms. Gay-linn GATEWOOD-JASHO
15 Director Human Resources .... Ms. Valerie VINSON
07 Interim Director of Admissions .... Ms. Michelle DAVIS
38 Director University Counseling Ctr .... Dr. Marilyn LINEBERGER
36 Director Career Planning/Placement .... Ms. Ernita HEMMITT
37 Director Student Financial Aid .... Mr. Nigel EDWARDS
96 Director of Purchasing .... Ms. Donna BYRD
41 Acting Director of Athletics .... Mr. D'Wayne ROBINSON
42 University Chaplain .... Dr. Valerie EVERETT
49 Dean Arts & Sciences .... Dr. Shirley WILLIAMS-KIRKSEY
50 Dean Business Admin .... Dr. Lydia FLOYD
53 Dean Education .... Dr. Sean WARNER
70 Dean Social Work .... Dr. Vimala PILLARI
20 Dean Undergraduate Studies .... Dr. Alexa B. HENDERSON
58 Interim Dean Graduate Studies .... Dr. Bettye CLARK
19 Chief of Public Safety .... Chief Thomas TRAWICK
23 Director Health Services .... Ms. Janet SINGLETON
25 Manager Grants & Contracts Accting .... Mr. G. Keith WILLIAMS
39 Director of Residence Life .... Mr. Ernest MOORE
88 Director Instructional Media .... Mr. Frank EDWARDS
101 Coordinator for Board Relations .... Ms. Natalie BAKER
104 Dir International Educ/Study Abroad .... Dr. Paul M. BROWN
22 University Compliance Officer .... Mr. Robert CLARK
100 Chief of Staff/Spec Asst to Pres .... Ms. Cynthia BUSKEY
44 Director of Annual/Special Giving .... Ms. Nicole BLOUNT
88 Sr Director of Advancement .... Ms. Sylvia A. JACOBS
18 Director of Facilities .... Mr. Victor PANCHUK

Clayton State University (A)

2000 Clayton State Boulevard, Morrow GA 30260-0285
County: Clayton FICE Identification: 008976
Unit ID: 139311
Telephone: (678) 466-4000 Carnegie Class: Bac/Diverse
FAX Number: (770) 961-3700 Calendar System: Semester
URL: www.clayton.edu
Established: 1969 Annual Undergrad Tuition & Fees (In-State): $4,926
Enrollment: 6,604 Coed
Affiliation or Control: State IRS Status: 501(c)3
Highest Offering: Master's
Program: Occupational; Liberal Arts And General; Teacher Preparatory
Accreditation: SC, BUS, DH, MUS, NURSE, TED

01 President .... Dr. Thomas HYNES
05 Int Provost/Vice Pres Academic Affs .... Dr. Michael CRAFTON
10 VP for Operations/Planning/Budget .... Ms. Corlis CUMMINGS
32 Vice President for Student Affairs .... Dr. Brian HAYNES
26 Vice President External Affairs .... Mr. Steve STEPHENS
13 Vice President of Infor Tech & Svcs .... Dr. John S. BRYAN
20 Assoc Vice President Academic Affs .... Dr. Robert A. VAUGHAN, JR.
35 Asst Vice Pres Student Affairs .... Dr. Elaine MANGLITZ
41 Executive Director of Athletics .... Mr. Mason BARFIELD
88 Executive Director of Spivey Hall .... Mr. Samuel DIXON
15 Exec Dir Human Resources & Services .... Mr. John BROOKS
49 Dean of Arts & Sciences .... Dr. Nasser MOMAYEZI
36 Dean of Retention & Stdnt Placement .... Vacant
50 Dean of Business .... Dr. Alphonso OGBUEHI
76 Dean of Health Sciences .... Dr. Lisa EICHELBERGER
81 Dean Information/Mathematical Sci .... Dr. Lila ROBERTS
08 Dean of Library Services .... Dr. Gordon BAKER
46 Dean Assessmnt/Instructnl Developmt .... Dr. Jill LANE
51 Director of Continuing Education .... Ms. Janet WINKLER
06 University Registrar .... Ms. Rebecca GMEINER
07 Director of Admissions .... Ms. Betty MOMAYEZI
31 Director of Auxiliary Services .... Ms. Carolina AMERO
26 Director of University Relations .... Mr. John SHIFFERT
18 Director of Plant Operations .... Mr. Harun BISWAS
19 Director of Public Safety .... Mr. Bobby HAMIL
30 Actg Dir of Development/Alumni Rels .... Ms. Reda ROWELL
09 Director of Institutional Research .... Dr. Narem REDDY
24 Director Media Services .... Mr. Paul BAILEY
38 Director of Counseling Services .... Dr. Christine SMITH
37 Director Student Financial Aid .... Ms. Pat BARTON
88 Director Center Academic Assistance .... Dr. Mark DADDONA
96 Director of Purchasing .... Ms. Cindy KNIGHT
29 Director Alumni Relations .... Mr. Gid ROWELL

† Part of the University System of Georgia.

College of Coastal Georgia (B)

3700 Altama Avenue, Brunswick GA 31520-3632
County: Glynn FICE Identification: 001558
Unit ID: 139250
Telephone: (912) 279-5700 Carnegie Class: Assoc/Pub-R-M
FAX Number: (912) 262-3072 Calendar System: Semester
URL: www.ccga.edu
Established: 1961 Annual Undergrad Tuition & Fees (In-State): $4,426
Enrollment: 3,429 Coed
Affiliation or Control: State IRS Status: 501(c)3
Highest Offering: Baccalaureate
Program: Occupational; 2-Year Principally Bachelor's Creditable; Liberal Arts And General; Teacher Preparatory; Professional
Accreditation: SC, ACFEI, ADNUR, MLTAD, NUR, RAD

01 President .... Dr. Valerie HEPBURN
05 Vice President Academic Affairs .... Dr. Phil MASON
10 Vice President Business Affairs .... Mr. Jeffrey H. PRESTON
32 Vice President Student Affairs .... Dr. Gerald KIEL
20 Associate VP Academic Affairs .... Ms. Kay HAMPTON
20 Asst VP Academic Services .... Dr. Ann CROWTHER
29 Asst VP Alumni & Annual Giving .... Ms. Elizabeth WEATHERLY
21 Asst VP Business Affairs .... Mr. C. Tom SAUNDERS
37 Director Student Financial Aid .... Ms. Marsha MILLER
06 Registrar .... Ms. Lisa LESSEIG
08 Director Information Commons .... Ms. Debra HOLMES
09 Director Institutional Effectivenes .... Dr. Jim Hughes LYNCH
12 Director Camden Center .... Ms. Holly CHRISTENSEN
15 Director Human Resources .... Ms. Kathleen MORRIS
18 Chief Facilities/Physical Plant .... Mr. Gary STRICKLAND
50 Dean Sch of Business & Public Affs .... Dr. Craig FLEISHER
49 Dean Sch Art/Humanities & Soc Sci ... Dr. M. Karen HAMBRIGHT
81 Dean School of Math and Natural Sci .... Dr. Keith E. BELCHER
53 Dean School of Education & Teacher .... Dr. Kent LAYTON
66 Dean School of Nursing & Health Sci .... Dr. Patricia KRAFT
19 Chief of Police .... Mr. Brian SIPE
39 Director of Residence Life .... Dr. Michael BUTCHER
41 Director of Athletics .... Dr. William "Bee" CARLTON
27 Chief Information Officer .... Ms. Geri CULBREATH
07 Director of Admissions .... Mr. Eric L. FELVER
26 Director of Marketing & Public Rels .... Mr. John CORNELL
88 Coordinator Faculty & Admin Svcs .... Ms. Sandra J. BUNN
96 Director of Purchasing .... Ms. Karen O. MARTIN

† Part of the University System of Georgia.

Columbia Theological Seminary (C)

P.O. Box 520, 701 Columbia Drive,
Decatur GA 30031-0520
County: DeKalb FICE Identification: 001560
Unit ID: 139348
Telephone: (404) 378-8821 Carnegie Class: Spec/Faith
FAX Number: (404) 377-9696 Calendar System: 4/1/4
URL: www.ctsnet.edu
Established: 1828 Annual Graduate Tuition & Fees: N/A
Enrollment: 425 Coed
Affiliation or Control: Presbyterian Church (U.S.A.) IRS Status: 501(c)3
Highest Offering: Doctorate; No Undergraduates
Program: Professional; Religious Emphasis
Accreditation: SC, THEOL

01 President .... Dr. Stephen A. HAYNER
05 Exec VP Acad Affs/Dean of Faculty .... Dr. Deborah F. MULLEN
10 Vice Pres Business and Finance .... Mr. Martin SADLER
32 Vice President Student Services .... Rev. John WHITE
30 Vice Pres Institutional Advancement .... Mr. Doug TAYLOR
20 Assoc Dean Academic Administration .... Dr. Ann Clay ADAMS
08 Director of Library .... Dr. Sara MYERS
58 Interim Director Advanced Studies .... Dr. Marvin L. SIMMERS
06 Registrar .... Mr. Mike MEDFORD
07 Director of Admissions & Recruiting .... Rev. Monica WEDLOCK
26 Director of Communications .... Ms. Genie HAMBRICK

Columbus State University (D)

4225 University Avenue, Columbus GA 31907-5645
County: Muscogee FICE Identification: 001561
Unit ID: 139366
Telephone: (706) 507-8800 Carnegie Class: Master's L
FAX Number: (706) 568-2123 Calendar System: Semester
URL: www.columbusstate.edu
Established: 1958 Annual Undergrad Tuition & Fees (In-State): $6,404
Enrollment: 8,298 Coed
Affiliation or Control: State IRS Status: 501(c)3
Highest Offering: Doctorate
Program: 2-Year Principally Bachelor's Creditable; Liberal Arts And General; Teacher Preparatory; Professional
Accreditation: SC, ART, BUS, CACREP, MUS, NURSE, TED, THEA

01 President .... Dr. Timothy S. MESCON
05 Interim Provost/VP Academic Affairs .... Dr. Tom HACKETT
10 Vice President Business & Finance .... Mr. Tom HELTON
32 VP Student Affairs & Enrollment Mgt .... Dr. Gina SHEEKS
30 Vice Pres University Advancement .... Dr. Kayron M. LASKA
14 Chief Information Officer .... Mr. Abraham GEORGE
20 Assoc Provost Undergraduate Educ .... Dr. Tina BUTCHER
20 Interim Associate Provost .... Dr. Greg DOMIN
30 Assoc VP for Development .... Mr. Spence SEALY
21 Asst Vice Pres Business & Finance .... Mrs. Lougene BROWN
35 Assistant VP Student Affairs .... Dr. Darryl B. HOLLOMAN
18 Asst Vice President of Facilities .... Mr. Eddie WOODHOUSE
26 Asst VP for University Relations .... Mr. John LESTER
50 Dean College of Business & Comp Sci .... Dr. Linda HADLEY
81 Dean College of Letters & Sciences .... Dr. David LANOUE
53 Interim Dean College of Education .... Dr. Ellen ROBERTS
49 Interim Dean College of the Arts .... Dr. Gary WORTLEY
08 Interim Director Library .... Ms. Roberta FORD
84 Dean Students/Enrollment Management .... Mr. Aaron J. REESE
35 Sr Dir Student Life & Development .... Dr. Kimberly MULLEN
44 Dir Annual Giving/Alumni Relations .... Ms. Meri ROBINSON
29 Director Alumni Relations .... Mrs. Jennifer JOYNER
15 Human Resources Director .... Ms. Laurie S. JONES
09 Director Institutional Research .... Dr. Sri SITHARAMAN
41 Athletic Director .... Mr. Jay SPARKS
19 Chief Campus Police .... Mr. Rus DREW
51 Director Continuing Education .... Ms. Susan WIRT
39 Director Housing .... Mr. Todd MYRICK
37 Director Financial Aid .... Ms. Janis BOWLES
38 Director Counseling Center .... Dr. Dan ROSE
85 Director Center International Educ .... Dr. Neal R. MCCRILLIS
07 Director of Admissions .... Ms. Susan LOVELL
06 Registrar .... Mr. John H. BROWN
92 Director Honors Program .... Dr. Cindy HENNING
23 Director Student Health Services .... Ms. Rebecca TEW

† Part of the University System of Georgia.

Columbus Technical College (E)

928 Manchester Expressway, Columbus GA 31904-6572
County: Muscogee FICE Identification: 005624
Unit ID: 139357
Telephone: (706) 649-1800 Carnegie Class: Assoc/Pub-R-M
FAX Number: (706) 649-1885 Calendar System: Semester
URL: www.columbustech.edu
Established: 1961 Annual Undergrad Tuition & Fees (In-State): $2,575
Enrollment: 4,355 Coed
Affiliation or Control: State IRS Status: 501(c)3
Highest Offering: Associate Degree
Program: Occupational; 2-Year Principally Bachelor's Creditable; Technical Emphasis
Accreditation: SC, ADNUR, DA, DH, MAC, PNUR, RAD, SURGT

01 President .... Mr. J. Robert JONES
11 Vice President Administrative Svcs .... Ms. Betty JACKSON
05 Vice President Academic Affairs .... Dr. Linn STOREY
32 Vice President Student Affairs .... Interim Ms. Eleanor BERRY
18 Interim Vice President Operations .... Mr. Tommy WILSON
46 VP Institutional Effectiveness .... Dr. Michael LAMB
88 Vice President Economic Development .... Mr. James LOYD
06 Registrar .... Dr. Sarah BEECHAM
07 Director of Admissions .... Ms. Tara ASKEW
15 Director of Human Resources .... Ms. Patricia HOOD
26 Director of Communications .... Ms. Cheryl MYERS
37 Director Student Financial Aid .... Ms. Debbie HENSHAW
38 Director Student Counseling .... Ms. Olive VIDAL-KENDALL
30 Director Institutional Advancement .... Ms. Gloria DODDS

Covenant College (F)

14049 Scenic Highway, Lookout Mountain TN 30750-4164
County: Dade FICE Identification: 003484
Unit ID: 139393
Telephone: (706) 820-1560 Carnegie Class: Bac/Diverse
FAX Number: (706) 820-2165 Calendar System: Semester
URL: www.covenant.edu
Established: 1955 Annual Undergrad Tuition & Fees: $27,220
Enrollment: 1,049 Coed
Affiliation or Control: Presbyterian Church In America IRS Status: 501(c)3
Highest Offering: Master's
Program: Liberal Arts And General; Teacher Preparatory
Accreditation: SC

01 President .... Dr. Niel B. NIELSON
05 Vice Pres Academic Affairs & CFO .... Dr. Jeffrey B. HALL
30 Vice President Advancement .... Mr. Troy DUBLE
32 Vice Pres Student Development .... Mr. Brad VOYLES
08 Librarian .... Mr. Tad MINDEMAN
06 Dean of Records .... Mr. Rodney E. MILLER
42 Chaplain .... Mr. Aaron MESSNER
58 Director of Master of Education Pgm .... Dr. Jim DREXLER
21 Controller .... Mr. Robert E. HARBERT
18 Director of Physical Plant .... Mr. David NORTHCUTT
37 Director of Student Financial Plng .... Mrs. Brenda RAPIER
15 Director of Human Resources .... Vacant
41 Athletic Director .... Ms. Tami SMIALEK
13 Chief Information Officer .... Ms. Marjorie CROCKER
29 Director of Alumni Relations .... Mr. Marshall K. ROWE
24 Director of AV Services .... Mr. Matt WRIGHT
56 Director of Experiential Education .... Vacant
23 Director of Health Services .... Mrs. Barbara M. MICHAL
07 Dir Admissions & Church Relations .... Mr. Matthew BRYANT
09 Director of Institutional Research .... Dr. Kevin EAMES
26 Chief Public Relations Officer .... Ms. Jen ALLEN
20 Director of Academic Support .... Mrs. Janet HULSEY

Dalton State College (G)

650 College Drive, Dalton GA 30720-3797
County: Whitfield FICE Identification: 003956
Unit ID: 139463
Telephone: (706) 272-4436 Carnegie Class: Bac/Assoc
FAX Number: (706) 272-4588 Calendar System: Semester
URL: www.daltonstate.edu
Established: 1963 Annual Undergrad Tuition & Fees (In-State): $3,400
Enrollment: 5,600 Coed
Affiliation or Control: State IRS Status: 501(c)3
Highest Offering: Baccalaureate
Program: Occupational; 2-Year Principally Bachelor's Creditable; Liberal Arts And General; Teacher Preparatory; Professional
Accreditation: SC, ADNUR, BUS, MAC, MLTAD, RAD, SW, TED

01 President .... Dr. John O. SCHWENN
05 Vice President for Academic Affairs .... Dr. Sandra STONE
10 Vice Pres Fiscal Affairs .... Mr. Scott BAILEY
84 Vice Pres Enrollment & Student Svcs .... Dr. Jodi S. JOHNSON
20 Asst Vice President Academic Affs .... Dr. Andy MEYER
37 Director of Financial Aid/Vet Svcs .... Ms. Carol JONES
08 Librarian .... Ms. Lydia KNIGHT
09 Director Inst Research & Planning .... Dr. Henry M. CODJOE
21 Associate Business Officer .... Mr. Nick HENRY
07 Asst VP for Enrollment Services .... Dr. Angela HARRIS
18 Chief Facilities/Physical Plant .... Mr. Jack REYNOLDS
26 Director Marketing & Communication .... Ms. Pam PARTAIN

102 Director Foundation .... Mr. David ELROD
32 Director Student Activities .... Ms. Jami HALL
38 Director Student Counseling .... Ms. Linda WHEELER
15 Director Human Resources .... Ms. Faith MILLER
96 Interim Director of Purchasing .... Ms. Penny CORDELL
13 Director Information Technology .... Mr. Terry BAILEY
19 Director Public Safety .... Mr. Billy GEE
29 Director Alumni Relations .... Mr. Josh WILSON
39 Interim Director Student Housing .... Dr. Jodi JOHNSON
50 Dean School of Business .... Ms. Donna MAYO
53 Dean School of Education .... Dr. Calvin MEYER
49 Dean School of Liberal Arts .... Ms. Mary NIELSEN
81 Dean School of Nat Sci & Math .... Mr. Randall GRIFFUS
66 Dean School of Nursing .... Ms. Cordia STARLING
70 Dean School of Social Work .... Mr. Spencer ZEIGER
72 Dean School of Technology .... Mr. Charles JOHNSON

† Part of the University System of Georgia.

Darton College (A)

2400 Gillionville Road, Albany GA 31707-3098
County: Dougherty FICE Identification: 001543
Unit ID: 138691
Telephone: (229) 317-6000 Carnegie Class: Assoc/Pub-R-M
FAX Number: (229) 317-6651 Calendar System: Semester
URL: www.darton.edu
Established: 1963 Annual Undergrad Tuition & Fees (In-State): $3,042
Enrollment: 5,879 Coed
Affiliation or Control: State IRS Status: 501(c)3
Highest Offering: Associate Degree
Program: Occupational; 2-Year Principally Bachelor's Creditable
Accreditation: SC, ADNUR, CVT, DH, HT, MLTAD, OTA, PTAA

01 President .... Dr. Peter J. SIRENO
10 Vice Pres Business/Financial Svcs .... Mr. Ronnie A. HENRY
05 VP Academic Affairs .... Dr. F. Gary BARNETTE
32 VP Student Affs/Dean of Students .... Dr. F. Gary BARNETTE
21 Asst VP Business/Financial Svcs .... Mr. Stan BROWN
51 Interim Dir Cont Ed/Economic Dev .... Mr. Michael WHITE
08 Director Learning Resources Ctr .... Mrs. Mary WASHINGTON
07 Director Admissions .... Ms. Susan BOWEN
13 Director Office of Information Tech .... Mr. Tracy COSPER
18 Director Physical Plant .... Mr. D. Steve HARRIS
26 Director College Relations .... Ms. Krista ROBITZ
41 Athletic Director .... Mr. Michael KIEFER
06 Registrar .... Mrs. Frances CARR
37 Director Student Financial Aid .... Ms. Haley HOOKS
15 Director Personnel Services .... Mr. Ronnie HENRY
85 International Student Coordinator .... Ms. Diana GARNER
29 Director Alumni Relations .... Ms. Michelle SIMS
36 Director Student Placement .... Mr. Jason SWORDS
38 Director Student Counseling .... Ms. Carol Ann HAM
96 Director of Purchasing .... Mrs. Joy CAUSEY
89 Director Freshmen Studies .... Ms. Carol Ann HAM
92 Director Honors Program .... Ms. Shani CLARK
93 Director Minority Students .... Ms. Simonee PATTON
09 Director of Institutional Research .... Dr. Richard BALSLEY

† Part of the University System of Georgia.

DeKalb Technical College (B)

495 N Indian Creek Drive, Clarkston GA 30021-2397
County: DeKalb FICE Identification: 005622
Unit ID: 244446
Telephone: (404) 297-9522 Carnegie Class: Assoc/Pub-S-MC
FAX Number: (404) 297-4234 Calendar System: Quarter
URL: www.dekalbtech.edu
Established: 1961 Annual Undergrad Tuition & Fees (In-State): $4,044
Enrollment: 4,858 Coed
Affiliation or Control: State IRS Status: 501(c)3
Highest Offering: Associate Degree
Program: Occupational; 2-Year Principally Bachelor's Creditable; Technical Emphasis
Accreditation: SC, ENGT, MAC, MLTAD, OPD

01 Acting President .... Mr. Larry TEEMS
11 Vice Pres of Business & Financial .... Ms. Heather PENCE
03 Executive Vice President .... Vacant
05 Vice President Academic Affairs .... Dr. Tanya GORMAN
46 Vice Pres of Economic Development .... Mr. Richard SMITH
30 Vice President Inst Advancement .... Ms. Cynthia EDWARDS
20 Dean Academic Operations .... Mr. Julian P. WADE
20 Dean Academic Operations .... Mr. Marcus HICKS
20 Dean Academic Delivery .... Dr. Daisy DAVIS
20 Dean Academic Support .... Dr. Debra GORDON
32 Dean Student Services .... Ms. Amanda TAYLOR
15 Director of Human Resources .... Ms. Gale BELTON
26 Public Relations & Info Director .... Mr. Cory THOMPSON
06 Registrar .... Ms. Karen SILLS
07 Director of Admissions .... Mr. Terry RICHARDSON
09 Dir Inst Plng/Evaluat/Effectiveness .... Dr. Sue CHANDLER
50 Director Business & Comm Services .... Ms. Loretta HICKS
37 Director of Financial Aid .... Ms. Jerri HUEWITT
18 Director of Facilities & Auxil Svcs .... Mr. John GADSON
88 Director of Adult Literacy .... Dr. Martha COURSEY
29 Director Alumni Relations .... Vacant
36 Director Assessment & Career Svcs .... Mr. Keith SAGERS

DeVry University - Alpharetta Campus (C)

2555 Northwinds Parkway, Alpharetta GA 30009-2232
County: DeKalb Identification: 666989
Unit ID: 432162
Telephone: (770) 619-3600 Carnegie Class: Not Classified
FAX Number: (770) 664-8824 Calendar System: Semester
URL: www.devry.edu
Established: 1997 Annual Undergrad Tuition & Fees: $15,294
Enrollment: 1,078 Coed
Affiliation or Control: Proprietary IRS Status: Proprietary
Highest Offering: Master's
Program: Occupational; Professional; Business Emphasis
Accreditation: &NH, ENGT

01 Campus Dean .... Tonya GIBSON
07 Director of Admissions .... Karina KOPLOCK
08 Librarian .... Vacant

† Regional accreditation is carried under the parent institution in Downers Grove, IL.

DeVry University - Atlanta Buckhead Center (D)

3575 Piedmont Road NE, Atlanta GA 30305-1543
County: Fulton Identification: 666200
Unit ID: 437291
Telephone: (404) 760-1400 Carnegie Class: Not Classified
FAX Number: N/A Calendar System: Semester
URL: www.keller.edu
Established: 1998 Annual Graduate Tuition & Fees: $18,040
Enrollment: 205 Coed
Affiliation or Control: Proprietary IRS Status: Proprietary
Highest Offering: Master's; No Undergraduates
Program: Occupational; Professional; Business Emphasis
Accreditation: &NH

01 Center Dean .... Stephanie O'NEAL

† Regional accreditation is carried under the parent institution in Downers Grove, IL.

DeVry University - Atlanta Cobb/ Galleria Center (E)

100 Galleria Parkway, SE, Suite 100,
Atlanta GA 30339-3122
County: DeKalb Identification: 666257
Telephone: (770) 916-3704 Carnegie Class: Not Classified
FAX Number: N/A Calendar System: Semester
URL: www.devry.edu
Established: 1931 Annual Undergrad Tuition & Fees: $15,294
Enrollment: 609 Coed
Affiliation or Control: Proprietary IRS Status: Proprietary
Highest Offering: Master's
Program: Occupational; Professional; Business Emphasis
Accreditation: &NH

01 Center Dean .... Norma MARQUEZ

† Regional accreditation is carried under the parent institution in Downers Grove, IL.

DeVry University - Atlanta/ Perimeter Center (F)

2 Ravinia Drive, Suite 250, Atlanta GA 30346-2104
County: Fulton Identification: 666201
Unit ID: 437282
Telephone: (770) 391-6200 Carnegie Class: Not Classified
FAX Number: N/A Calendar System: Semester
URL: www.keller.edu
Established: 1993 Annual Graduate Tuition & Fees: $18,040
Enrollment: 194 Coed
Affiliation or Control: Proprietary IRS Status: Proprietary
Highest Offering: Master's; No Undergraduates
Program: Occupational; Professional; Business Emphasis
Accreditation: &NH

01 Center Dean .... Angelo BROWN

† Regional accreditation is carried under the parent institution in Downers Grove, IL.

DeVry University - Decatur Campus (G)

One West Court Square, Ste. 100,
Decatur GA 30030-2556
County: DeKalb FICE Identification: 009224
Unit ID: 139533
Telephone: (404) 270-2700 Carnegie Class: Master's L
FAX Number: (404) 292-8117 Calendar System: Semester
URL: www.devry.edu
Established: 1931 Annual Undergrad Tuition & Fees: $15,294
Enrollment: 3,912 Coed
Affiliation or Control: Proprietary IRS Status: Proprietary
Highest Offering: Master's
Program: Occupational; Professional; Business Emphasis
Accreditation: &NH, ENGT

01 Metro President .... Mr. Chris CHAVEZ
05 Dean of Academic Affairs .... Mr. John DUNBAR
08 Director of Library Services .... Ms. Mary Elizabeth ANTOINE
32 Student Services Manager .... Ms. Penny SAWYER
50 Dean of Business & Technology .... Mr. Charles THOMPSON
37 Dean of Student Finance .... Ms. Bianca SMITH
36 Director of Career Services .... Mr. Brian SHADIX
06 Registrar .... Ms. Marie BROWN
84 Director of Admissions .... Mr. Jimmy COPLES
31 Director of Community Outreach .... Mrs. Jeanne JOHNSON-WHATLEY
72 Dean of Technology Programs .... Mr. Keith WRIGHT
49 Dean of Arts & Sciences .... Mr. Dale BURGESS
15 HR Business Partner .... Mr. Felix ALEJANDRO

† Regional accreditation is carried under the parent institution in Downers Grove, IL.

DeVry University - Gwinnett Center (H)

3505 Koger Boulevard, Suite 170, Duluth GA 30096-7671
County: Gwinnett Identification: 666202
Unit ID: 440554
Telephone: (770) 381-4400 Carnegie Class: Not Classified
FAX Number: (770) 381-4411 Calendar System: Semester
URL: www.devry.edu
Established: 2001 Annual Undergrad Tuition & Fees: $15,294
Enrollment: 646 Coed
Affiliation or Control: Proprietary IRS Status: Proprietary
Highest Offering: Master's
Program: Occupational; Professional; Business Emphasis
Accreditation: &NH

01 Center Dean .... Anna MAKI

† Regional accreditation is carried under the parent institution in Downers Grove, IL.

DeVry University - Henry County (I)

675 Southcrest Parkway, Suite 100,
Stockbridge GA 30281-7973
County: Henry Identification: 666532
Telephone: (678) 284-4700 Carnegie Class: Not Classified
FAX Number: (770) 474-5011 Calendar System: Semester
URL: www.devry.edu
Established: 1931 Annual Undergrad Tuition & Fees: $15,294
Enrollment: 678 Coed
Affiliation or Control: Proprietary IRS Status: Proprietary
Highest Offering: Master's
Program: Professional; Business Emphasis
Accreditation: &NH

01 Center Dean .... Mr. Gregory PACE

† Regional accreditation is carried under the parent institution in Downers Grove, IL.

East Georgia College (J)

131 College Circle, Swainsboro GA 30401-3643
County: Emanuel FICE Identification: 010997
Unit ID: 139621
Telephone: (478) 289-2000 Carnegie Class: Assoc/Pub-R-S
FAX Number: (478) 289-2038 Calendar System: Semester
URL: www.ega.edu
Established: 1973 Annual Undergrad Tuition & Fees (In-State): $3,306
Enrollment: 3,063 Coed
Affiliation or Control: State IRS Status: 501(c)3
Highest Offering: Associate Degree
Program: Occupational; 2-Year Principally Bachelor's Creditable
Accreditation: SC

01 President .... Dr. John B. BLACK
05 Vice President for Academic Affairs .... Dr. Timothy D. GOODMAN
10 Vice President for Fiscal Affairs .... Mr. Cliff GAY
84 VP for Student/Enrollment Services .... Mr. Donald AVERY
43 VP for Legal & External Affairs .... Mrs. Mary C. SMITH
08 Librarian .... Mrs. Carol BRAY
06 Registrar .... Mrs. Janet STRACHER
27 Director of Public Information .... Mr. Gerald D. HOOKS
09 Director Institutional Research .... Mr. David GRIBBIN
37 Director of Financial Aid .... Mrs. Karen S. JONES
15 Director Human Resources .... Mrs. Tracy WOODS
30 Director of Development and Alumni .... Ms. Elizabeth GILMER
18 Director Facilities .... Mrs. Michelle GOFF
26 Director of Marketing .... Ms. Norma WOODS
13 Director of Computer Services .... Mr. Mike ROUNTREE
12 Director of the Statesboro Center .... Ms. Caroline MCMILLAN
19 Director of Security .... Mr. Drew DURDEN
35 Director Student Life .... Ms. Vicki SHERROD
04 Secretary to the President .... Mrs. Susan GRAY

† Part of the University System of Georgia.

Emmanuel College (K)

PO Box 129, Franklin Springs GA 30639-0129
County: Franklin FICE Identification: 001563
Unit ID: 139630

Telephone: (706) 245-7226 Carnegie Class: Bac/Diverse
FAX Number: (706) 245-4424 Calendar System: Semester
URL: www.ec.edu
Established: 1919 Annual Undergrad Tuition & Fees: $14,575
Enrollment: 795 Coed
Affiliation or Control: Pentecostal Holiness Church IRS Status: 501(c)3
Highest Offering: Baccalaureate
Program: Liberal Arts And General; Teacher Preparatory; Professional; Business Emphasis
Accreditation: **SC**

01 President ... Dr. Michael S. STEWART
32 Vice President for Student Life ... Mr. Jason CROY
05 Vice President for Academic Affairs ... Dr. John R. HENZEL, JR.
10 Vice President for Finance ... Dr. Kevin CRAWFORD
30 Vice President for Development ... Mr. Brian JAMES
84 Vice Pres Enrollment Mgmt/Marketing ... Ms. Wendy VINSON
08 Director of Library Services ... Mrs. Joye SLIFE
06 Registrar ... Mrs. Debra F. GRIZZLE
37 Director of Financial Aid ... Mr. Vince WELCH
13 Director of Information Technology ... Mr. Glenn TONEY
11 Director of Campus Operations ... Mr. Ron MCCULLAR
41 Director of Athletics ... Mr. Mike BONA
42 Director of Spiritual Life ... Mr. Chris MAXWELL
15 Director of Human Resources ... Mrs. Joann HARPER
26 Chief Public Relations Officer ... Mrs. Paula DIXON
38 Director of Student Counseling ... Mr. Sean WILLIAMSON
96 Director of Accounting Services ... Mrs. Anita RAY
18 Physical Plant Director ... Mr. Wayne CRIDER
09 Diredtor of Institutional Research ... Dr. Brian PEEK
29 Director Alumni Relations ... Mr. Harrell W. QUEEN

Emory University (A)

201 Dowman Drive, Atlanta GA 30322-0001
County: DeKalb FICE Identification: 001564
Unit ID: 139658
Telephone: (404) 727-6123 Carnegie Class: RU/VH
FAX Number: (404) 727-5997 Calendar System: Semester
URL: www.emory.edu
Established: 1836 Annual Undergrad Tuition & Fees: $41,164
Enrollment: 13,381 Coed
Affiliation or Control: United Methodist IRS Status: 501(c)3
Highest Offering: Doctorate
Program: Occupational; 2-Year Principally Bachelor's Creditable; Liberal Arts And General; Teacher Preparatory; Professional
Accreditation: **SC**, AA, ARCPA, BUS, CLPSY, DENT, DIETI, IPSY, LAW, MED, MIDWF, NURSE, PH, PTA, RAD, TED, THEOL

01 President ... Dr. James W. WAGNER
05 Provost/Exec VP Acad Affs ... Dr. Earl LEWIS
03 Exec Vice Pres for Finance/Admin ... Mr. Michael J. MANDL
17 Exec Vice Pres Health Affairs ... Dr. S. Wright CAUGHMAN
101 VP/Secretary of the University ... Dr. Rosemary MAGEE
04 VP/Deputy to the President ... Dr. Gary S. HAUK
43 Sr Vice Pres & General Counsel ... Mr. Stephen D. SENCER
30 Sr Vice Pres Devel/Alumni Rels ... Ms. Susan CRUSE
32 Sr Vice President/Dean Campus Life ... Dr. John L. FORD
46 Vice President for Research Admin ... Dr. David L. WYNES
29 Vice President Alumni Relations ... Ms. Allison DYKES
10 Vice President for Finance ... Ms. Edith C. MURPHREE
58 Vice Provost/Dean Graduate Sch ... Dr. Lisa A. TEDESCO
15 Vice President Human Resources ... Mr. Peter BARNES
26 Vice Pres Communications/Marketing ... Mr. Ron SAUDER
22 Vice President Equal Opportunity ... Vacant
86 Vice President Governmental Affairs ... Mr. John T. ENGELEN
18 Vice President Campus Services ... Mr. Matthew EARLY
25 Assoc Vice Pres for Research Admin ... Ms. Kerry PELUSO
10 Assoc Vice President & Controller ... Ms. Belva WHITE
35 Special Asst to Sr VP Campus Life ... Dr. Carolyn LIVINGSTON
28 Sr Vice Provost Community/Diversity ... Mr. Ozzie HARRIS
20 Sr Vice Prov for Academic Affairs ... Dr. Claire E. STERK
44 Sr Assoc Vice Pres Annual Giving ... Ms. Francine CRONIN
20 Sr Vice Prov for Undergrad Acad Aff ... Dr. Lynn ZIMMERMAN
88 Assoc Vice Prov Oper Student Svcs ... Ms. Heather MUGG
08 Vice Provost/Dir University Library ... Mr. Richard E. LUCE
14 CIO/Vice Provost Information Tech ... Dr. Richard A. MENDOLA
49 Dean of Emory College ... Dr. Robin FORMAN
12 Dean & CEO Oxford College ... Dr. Stephen H. BOWEN
63 Dean of Medicine ... Dr. Thomas J. LAWLEY
66 Dean of Nursing ... Dr. Linda MCCAULEY
73 Dean of Theology ... Dr. Jan LOVE
61 Dean of Law ... Mr. David PARTLETT
50 Dean of the Business School ... Dr. Lawrence M. BENVENISTE
69 Dean of Public Health ... Dr. James W. CURRAN
85 Dir Intl Student Scholar Program ... Ms. Lelia CRAWFORD
80 Pres & CEO of the Carter Center ... Dr. John HARDMAN
42 Dean of the Chapel & Religious Life ... Rev. Susan HENRY-CROWE
06 University Registrar ... Mr. Tom MILLEN
07 Dean of Admissions ... Ms. Jean JORDAN
27 Executive Director Marketing ... Ms. Jan GLEASON
37 Director Financial Aid ... Mr. Dean BENTLEY
36 Director Placement Service ... Mr. Paul FOWLER
19 Chief of Police ... Mr. Craig T. WATSON
23 Pres & CEO Emory Healthcare ... Mr. John T. FOX
41 Director Athletics/Recreation ... Mr. Timothy DOWNES
88 Director Yerkes Research Ctrs ... Dr. Stuart M. ZOLA
49 Director Institute Liberal Arts ... Dr. Walter L. REED
88 Director M C Carlos Museum ... Ms. Bonnie SPEED
40 University Bookstore Liaison ... Mr. Bruce COVEY
39 Exec Dir Res Life & Housing ... Dr. Andrea TRINKLEIN
38 Director Univ Counseling Center ... Dr. Mark MCLEOD
09 Director Institutional Research ... Dr. Daniel TEODORESCU
96 Director Contract Admin/Compliance ... Mr. Rex HARDAWAY

Everest Institute (B)

2460 Wesley Chapel Road, Suite 100, Decatur GA 30035-3420
County: DeKalb Identification: 666285
Unit ID: 438638
Telephone: (404) 327-8787 Carnegie Class: Assoc/PrivFP
FAX Number: (404) 327-8980 Calendar System: Quarter
URL: www.everest.edu
Established: N/A Annual Undergrad Tuition & Fees: N/A
Enrollment: 192 Coed
Affiliation or Control: Proprietary IRS Status: Proprietary
Highest Offering: Associate Degree
Program: Occupational
Accreditation: **ACCSC**, SURGT

01 President ... Mrs. Barbara HOLLIMAN

† Branch campus of Everest Institute, Cross Lanes, WV.

Fort Valley State University (C)

1005 State University Drive, Fort Valley GA 31030-4313
County: Peach FICE Identification: 001566
Unit ID: 139719
Telephone: (478) 825-6211 Carnegie Class: Bac/Diverse
FAX Number: (478) 825-6394 Calendar System: Semester
URL: www.fvsu.edu
Established: 1895 Annual Undergrad Tuition & Fees (In-State): $5,149
Enrollment: 3,566 Coed
Affiliation or Control: State IRS Status: 501(c)3
Highest Offering: Beyond Master's But Less Than Doctorate
Program: Occupational; Liberal Arts And General; Teacher Preparatory
Accreditation: **SC**, AAFCS, CORE, DIETD, ENGT, TED

01 President ... Dr. Larry E. RIVERS
03 Inerim Exeutive Vice President ... Dr. Canter BROWN, JR.
32 Vice Pres Student Affairs ... Dr. Terrance SMITH
10 Vice President Business & Finance ... Mr. Arthur HENDERSON
31 Vice President External Affairs ... Dr. Melody CARTER
05 Int Vice Pres for Academic Affairs ... Dr. Julius SCIPIO
09 VP Inst Research/Plng & Effec ... Dr. Vann NEWKIRK
88 Assoc VP for Land Grant Affair ... Dr. Mark LATTIMORE
04 Spec Asst to the Pres/Legal Counsel ... Dr. Canter BROWN
49 Int Dean of Arts/Sciences ... Dr. Keith MURPHY
21 Comptroller ... Mr. Kevin HOWARD
06 Registrar ... Mrs. Sharee LAWRENCE
13 Director for Information Technology ... Mr. Del KIMBROUGH
08 Dir University Libraries ... Dr. Annie PAYTON
07 Director Admissions ... Mr. Donavon O. COLEY
37 Int Director Financial Aid ... Ms. Freida JONES
88 Director Title III ... Dr. Melody CARTER
29 Director Alumni Affairs ... Ms. Clara BRASWELL
15 Director of Human Resources ... Dr. Dwayne CREW
19 Director Campus Safety ... Mr. Ken MORGAN
47 Int Dean Agriculture ... Dr. Gavindarajan KANNON
23 Director Health Services ... Mrs. Joann NOBLES
18 Int Director Plant & Maintenance ... Mr. Johann WELLS
36 Director Counsel/Career Development ... Ms. Simmons ROMELDA
26 Director Marketing/Communications ... Ms. Vickie OLDHAM
41 Director of Athletics ... Dr. Chico CALDWELL
88 Exec Dir Academic Success Ctr ... Dr. Said SEWELL
58 Dean Grad Studies/Extended Educ ... Dr. Anna HOLLOWAY
53 Dean Education ... Dr. Judy CARTER

† Part of the University System of Georgia.

Gainesville State College (D)

3820 Mundy Mill Rd, Oakwood GA 30566-3414
County: Hall FICE Identification: 001567
Unit ID: 139773
Telephone: (678) 717-3639 Carnegie Class: Assoc/Pub4
FAX Number: (678) 717-3859 Calendar System: Semester
URL: www.gsc.edu
Established: 1964 Annual Undergrad Tuition & Fees (In-State): $2,986
Enrollment: 8,874 Coed
Affiliation or Control: State IRS Status: 501(c)3
Highest Offering: Baccalaureate
Program: Occupational; 2-Year Principally Bachelor's Creditable
Accreditation: **SC**, ACBSP

01 President ... Dr. Martha T. NESBITT
05 Vice President Academic Affairs ... Dr. Al PANU
10 Vice President Business/Finance ... Mr. Paul GLASER
32 Vice Pres Student Devel/Enroll Mgmt ... Dr. Tom G. WALTER
30 Vice President Advancement ... Ms. Mary TRANSUE
12 Vice Pres/CEO Oconee Campus ... Dr. Margaret VENABLE
35 Assoc Vice Pres Student Development ... Dr. Alicia CAUDILL
21 Assoc Vice Pres Business & Finance ... Ms. Wanda ALDRIDGE
20 Associate VP Academic Affairs ... Dr. Chaudron GILLE
84 Assoc VP Enrollment Management ... Mr. Mack PALMOUR
88 Int Asst VP Academic Enrichment ... Dr. Kristen RONEY
06 Registrar ... Ms. Janice HARTSOE
07 Director of Admissions ... Mr. Mack PALMOUR
13 Director Information Technology ... Mr. Brandon A. HAAG
51 Director Cont Educ/Public Service ... Ms. Wendy THELLMAN
09 Director Institutional Research ... Ms. Betsy CANTRELL
35 Director Student Activities ... Dr. Cara RAY
37 Director Financial Aid ... Ms. Susan A. SMITH
28 Director Diversity Initiatives ... Dr. Christie CRUISE-HARPER
22 Affirmative Action/EEO Officer ... Dr. Joan H. MARLER
29 Director Alumni Affairs ... Ms. Jennifer HENDRICKSON
26 Director Public Rels/Marketing ... Ms. Sloan W. JONES
08 Director ACTT & Library ... Dr. Deborah PROSSER
15 Personnel Services Director ... Ms. Amy COLLINS
18 Director Plant Operations ... Mr. Bill MOODY
19 Director Public Safety ... Mr. Richard GOODSON
96 Director of Purchasing ... Ms. Bonnie JONES
38 Director Student Counseling ... Dr. Joy EVANS
40 Bookstore Manager ... Ms. Jackie MAULDIN
25 Grant Administrator ... Ms. Debbra PILGRIM
20 Director Student Academic Success ... Vacant
88 Director of Academic Advising ... Ms. Terri CARROLL
50 Dean Sch Bus Educ/Health/Wellness ... Dr. Maryellen COSGROVE
83 Dean School of Social Sciences ... Dr. Lee CHEEK, JR.
79 Int Dean Sch Humanities & Fine Arts ... Dr. Eric SKIPPER
81 Interim Dean STEM ... Dr. Danny LAU
36 Director Student Placement ... Vacant

† Part of the University System of Georgia.

Georgia Christian University (E)

6789 Peachtree Industrial Boulevard, Atlanta GA 30360
County: DeKalb Identification: 666641
Telephone: (770) 279-0507 Carnegie Class: Not Classified
FAX Number: (770) 279-0308 Calendar System: Other
URL: www.gcuniv.edu
Established: 1986 Annual Undergrad Tuition & Fees: $21,500
Enrollment: 320 Coed
Affiliation or Control: Independent Non-Profit IRS Status: 501(c)3
Highest Offering: Doctorate
Program: Professional; Religious Emphasis
Accreditation: **@TRACS**

01 President ... Dr. Paul C. KIM
03 Executive Vice President ... Dr. Victor YOON
05 Chief Academic Officer ... Dr. Hee Sook SONG
07 Director of Admissions ... Dr. Mi A KANG
08 Head Librarian ... Ms. Myo Ryoung KIM
10 Chief Financial Officer ... Ms. Eunice KIM
12 Director of Branch Campus ... Ms. Sun Hee CHOI
13 Director Information Technology ... Mr. Deok Joo MOON
18 Chief Facilities/Physical Plant ... Rev. Min Soo KIM
19 Director Security/Safety ... Mr. Samuel KIM
21 Associate Business Officer ... Mr. James D. CHONG
29 Director Alumni Relations ... Mr. Kyu Jong LEE
26 Chief Public Relations Officer ... Dr. Hyun Sung CHO
45 Chief Planning Officer ... Mr. Jo Kam CHUNG
96 Director of Purchasing ... Mr. Daniel KIM
06 Registrar ... Dr. Byong Kie CHOI
37 Director Student Financial Aid ... Dr. Hee Sook SONG
50 Dean Business ... Dr. Moon Ho SONG
53 Dean Education ... Dr. Young Jun KIM
58 Dean Graduate Programs ... Dr. Hee Kun KIM
64 Dean Music ... Dr. Soo Jin KIM
88 Dn Mission Stds/World Christianity ... Dr. Young Hwan KIM
73 Dean Theology ... Dr. Byong Kie CHOI
88 International Student Advisor ... Mr. Carlos CADLAON
46 Dir of Institutional Effectiveness ... Dr. Jong Sik CHANG
42 Associate Chaplain ... Rev. Chang Sun PYO

Georgia College & State University (F)

231 West Hancock Street, Milledgeville GA 31061-0490
County: Baldwin FICE Identification: 001602
Unit ID: 139861
Telephone: (478) 445-5004 Carnegie Class: Master's L
FAX Number: (478) 445-1191 Calendar System: Semester
URL: www.gcsu.edu
Established: 1889 Annual Undergrad Tuition & Fees (In-State): $8,344
Enrollment: 6,715 Coed
Affiliation or Control: State IRS Status: 501(c)3
Highest Offering: Beyond Master's But Less Than Doctorate
Program: Liberal Arts And General; Teacher Preparatory; Professional
Accreditation: **SC**, BUS, MUS, NUR, SPAA, TED

01 Interim President ... Dr. Stanley PRECZEWSKI
04 Exec Assistant to the President ... Ms. Monica STARLEY
05 Provost/VP Academic Affairs ... Dr. Sandra J. JORDAN
11 VP Administration & Operations ... Dr. Paul A. JONES
32 VP Student Affairs/Dean of Students ... Dr. Bruce HARSHBARGER
30 VP External Rel/University Advance ... Ms. Amy AMASON
20 Assoc Provost for Academic Affs ... Dr. Tom ORMOND
51 Assoc VP Extended University ... Dr. Mark PELTON
10 Chief Financial Officer ... Mr. Pete SHIELDS
88 Univ Architect/Dir Facilities Plng ... Mr. Michael RICKENBAKER
18 Director of Facilities Operations ... Mr. David SMITH
84 Asst VP Enrollment Management ... Ms. Suzanne PITTMAN
19 Director of Public Safety ... Vacant
35 Associate Vice Pres Student Affairs ... Dr. Paul K. JAHR
26 Assoc VP Strategic Communications ... Mr. Harry BATTSON
49 Dean College of Arts & Sciences ... Mr. Ken PROCTER
50 Dean College of Business ... Dr. Matthew A. LIAO-TROTH
53 Dean College of Education ... Dr. Jane HINSON
76 Dean College of Health Sciences ... Dr. Sandra GANGSTEAD
39 Exec Director University Housing ... Mr. Larry CHRISTENSON
09 Director of Institutional Research ... Dr. Ed HALE
12 Chf Admn Grad Prof Lrng Macon Ctr ... Dr. Doris CHRISTOPHER
12 Director Robins Center ... Dr. Howard WOODARD

13 Int Chief Information Officer ... Mr. Ed BOYD
08 Int Director of Libraries ... Ms. Nancy DAVIS BRAY
36 Director Career Center ... Ms. Mary ROBERTS
40 Director of University Bookstores ... Ms. Lynda GRABLE
16 Director Human Resources ... Ms. Diane KIRKWOOD
22 Dir Employment/Training/Diversity ... Ms. Yves-Rose SAINTDIC
91 Director Data Management Resources . Ms. Michelle HIGHTOWER
07 Director of Admissions ... Vacant
06 Registrar ... Ms. Kay ANDERSON
41 Director of Athetics ... Mr. Wendell STATON
29 Director Alumni Relations ... Mr. Herbert (Herby) AGNEW
31 Asst VP for Auxiliary Services ... Mr. Kyle CULLARS
43 General Counsel ... Mr. Marc CARDINALLI
38 Director of Counseling Services ... Dr. Anne REYNOLDS
37 Director Financial Aid ... Ms. Cathy CRAWLEY
88 Director Administrative Services ... Mr. Mark MEEKS
21 Chief Budget Officer ... Ms. Susan ALLEN
88 Director of Audit/Advisory Services ... Ms. Julia HANN
35 Director of Campus Life ... Mr. Tom MILES
88 Manager of Television Services ... Mr. Bill WENDT

Georgia Gwinnett College (A)

1000 University Center Lane, Lawrenceville GA 30043
County: Gwinnett — FICE Identification: 041429
Unit ID: 447689
Telephone: (678) 407-5000 — Carnegie Class: Not Classified
FAX Number: N/A — Calendar System: Semester
URL: www.ggc.usg.edu
Established: 2005 — Annual Undergrad Tuition & Fees (In-District): $4,846
Enrollment: 5,380 — Coed
Affiliation or Control: State/Local — IRS Status: 501(c)3
Highest Offering: Baccalaureate
Program: Liberal Arts And General
Accreditation: SC

01 President ... Dr. Daniel J. KAUFMAN
05 Vice Pres Academic/Student Affairs ... Dr. Stanley PRECZEWSKI
11 Vice Pres Facilities/Operations ... Mr. Eddie BEAUCHAMP
30 Vice President Advancement ... Dr. Gordon HARRISON

Georgia Health Sciences University (B)

1120 Fifteenth Street, Augusta GA 30912-0004
County: Richmond — FICE Identification: 001579
Unit ID: 140401
Telephone: (706) 721-0211 — Carnegie Class: Spec/Med
FAX Number: N/A — Calendar System: Semester
URL: www.georgiahealth.edu
Established: 1828 — Annual Undergrad Tuition & Fees (In-State): $8,908
Enrollment: 2,438 — Coed
Affiliation or Control: State — IRS Status: 501(c)3
Highest Offering: Doctorate
Program: Occupational; Professional
Accreditation: SC, ANEST, ARCPA, DENT, DH, DMS, IPSY, MED, MIL, MT, NMT, NURSE, OT, PH, PTA, RADDOS, RTT

01 President ... Dr. Ricardo AZZIZ
05 Exec VP for Acad Affairs/Provost ... Dr. Gretchen CAUGHMAN
11 Interim Sr VP for Admin/CAO ... Mr. William BOWES
10 Interim Sr VP Finance & Admin/CFO ... Mr. Dennis ROEMER
17 Exec Vice Pres Clinical Affairs ... Mr. David S. HEFNER
86 Asst to Pres External Affairs ... Mr. R. Bryan GINN, JR.
32 Vice Pres for Student Svcs & Dev ... Dr. Kevin B. FRAZIER
46 Interim Vice President for Research ... Dr. Mark W. HAMRICK
26 Assoc VP Exec Communications ... Ms. Deborah L. BARSHAFSKY
20 VP Instruction & Enrollment Mgmt ... Dr. Roman M. CIBIRKA
21 Chief Audit Officer ... Mr. Michael W. HILL
44 Assoc VP Advancement Programs ... Ms. Betty H. MEEHAN
43 General Counsel ... Mr. Andrew NEWTON
63 Dean of Medical College ... Dr. Peter F. BUCKLEY
52 Dean College of Dental Med ... Dr. Connie L. DRISKO
58 Interim Dean College of Grad Stds ... Dr. Edward INSCHO
66 Dean College of Nursing ... Dr. Lucy N. MARION
76 Dean Col of Allied Health Sciences ... Dr. E. Andrew BALAS
88 Dept Chair Biostatistics ... Dr. Varghese T. GEORGE
88 VP Institutional Effectiveness ... Mrs. Beth P. BRIGDON
46 Sr Assoc VP Research Administration ... Ms. Betty J. ALDRIDGE
21 Assoc VP for Finance/Controller ... Mr. Jim JONES
18 VP Facilities Service ... Mr. Philip HOWARD
51 Director Continuing Education ... Ms. Caro CASSELS
22 Dir Affirm Action/Equal Employ Opty ... Mr. Glenn POWELL
08 Interim Director of Libraries ... Dr. David KING
88 Assoc VP Materials Management ... Mr. James T. HARRIS
15 Assoc VP for Human Resources ... Ms. Susan A. NORTON
88 Assoc VP Enviro Health/Safety ... Dr. James S. DAVIS
19 Director Public Safety Division ... Mr. William E. MCBRIDE, JR.
07 Interim Director of Admissions ... Ms. Heather METRESS
28 Director Student Diversity Intl ... Ms. Beverly TARVER
35 Director of Campus Life Services ... Mr. Dale HARTENBURG
39 Director of Residence Life ... Mr. Thomas J. FITTS, JR.
29 Alumni Affairs Director ... Mr. Scott HENSON
88 Director Human Research Protection ... Ms. Ivy TILLMAN
102 Corp Foundation Develop Officer ... Ms. Eileen BRANDON
27 Director of University Comm ... Mr. Jack EVANS
40 Manager Bookstore ... Vacant

† Part of the University System of Georgia.

Georgia Highlands College (C)

3175 Cedartown Highway SE, Rome GA 30161-3897
County: Floyd — FICE Identification: 009507
Unit ID: 139700
Telephone: (706) 802-5000 — Carnegie Class: Assoc/Pub-R-M
FAX Number: (706) 295-6610 — Calendar System: Semester
URL: www.highlands.edu
Established: 1970 — Annual Undergrad Tuition & Fees (In-State): $1,236
Enrollment: 5,224 — Coed
Affiliation or Control: State — IRS Status: 501(c)3
Highest Offering: Associate Degree
Program: Occupational; 2-Year Principally Bachelor's Creditable
Accreditation: SC, ADNUR, DH

01 President ... Dr. John Randolph PIERCE
05 Vice President ... Dr. Renva WATTERSON
10 Vice Pres Finance/Administration ... Mr. Rob WHITAKER
15 Director Human Resources ... Ms. Ginni SILER
32 Director Student Support Services ... Ms. Sheryl BALLENGER
37 Director Financial Aid ... Vacant
06 Registrar ... Ms. Sandie DAVIS
09 Director of Institutional Research ... Dr. Laura MUSSELWHITE
21 Director of Accounting ... Mr. Jamie PETTY
29 Director Alumni Relations ... Ms. Alison LAMPKIN
35 Director Student Life ... Mr. John SPRANZA
14 Director Institutional Computer Ctr ... Mr. Jeff PATTY
08 Librarian ... Mr. Elijah SCOTT
19 Director Security ... Mr. John UPTON
26 Chief Public Relations Officer ... Ms. Dana DAVIS
40 Manager Bookstore ... Vacant
30 Development Officer ... Mr. John SOUTHWOOD
18 Chief Facilities/Physical Plant ... Mr. Phillip KIMSEY
96 Director of Purchasing ... Ms. Cynthia PARKER
12 Director Floyd Campus ... Mr. Todd JONES
83 Chairman Division Social Sciences ... Dr. Robert PAGE
76 Director Nursing ... Ms. Rebecca MADDOX
62 Chrm Div Learning Resources ... Dr. Diane LANGSTON
81 Chairman Division Science/PE ... Ms. Donna DAUGHERTY
81 Chairman Division of Mathematics ... Dr. Carla MOLDAVAN
79 Chairman Division of Humanities ... Dr. Jonathan HERSHEY
72 Director of Information Technology ... Mr. Jeff PATTY
12 Director Cartersville Campus ... Ms. Carolyn HAMRICK

† Part of the University System of Georgia.

Georgia Institute of Technology (D)

225 North Avenue, NW, Atlanta GA 30332-0002
County: Fulton — FICE Identification: 001569
Unit ID: 139755
Telephone: (404) 894-2000 — Carnegie Class: RU/VH
FAX Number: (404) 894-1277 — Calendar System: Semester
URL: www.gatech.edu
Established: 1885 — Annual Undergrad Tuition & Fees (In-State): $9,652
Enrollment: 20,720 — Coed
Affiliation or Control: State — IRS Status: 501(c)3
Highest Offering: Doctorate
Program: Professional
Accreditation: SC, ART, BUS, CONST, CS, ENG, IPSY, OPE, PLNG

01 President ... Dr. G. P. (Bud) PETERSON
05 Provost/Exec VP Academic Affairs ... Dr. Rafael BRAS
10 Executive Vice Pres Admin/Finance ... Mr. Steven SWANT
46 Executive Vice President Research ... Dr. Stephen CROSS
100 Assistant Vice Pres/Chief of Staff ... Ms. Lynn DURHAM
30 Vice President Development ... Mr. Barrett H. CARSON
26 Vice Pres Communications/Marketing ... Mr. Michael L. WARDEN
32 Vice President Student Affairs ... Dr. William SCHAFER
88 VP/ Director Ga Tech Res Inst ... Dr. Robert MCGRATH
25 Associate Vice Provost Research ... Ms. Jilda GARTON
86 Exec Dir Government/Cmty Relations ... Mr. Dene SHEHEANE
88 Vice Prov Entrprse Innovation Inst ... Mr. Stephen FLEMING
29 President Georgia Tech Alumni Assoc ... Mr. Joseph IRWIN
20 Sr Vice Provost Academic Affairs ... Dr. Anderson SMITH
84 Vice Prov Enrollment Services ... Dr. Paul KOHN
88 Vice Prov Grad & Undergrad Studies ... Dr. Raymond VITO
28 Vice President Institute Diversity ... Dr. Archie ERVIN
88 Vice Prov Acad Review & Faculty Dev ... Dr. Jack LOHMANN
88 Vice Provost GT Lorraine ... Dr. Yves BERTHELOT
88 Vice Provost GT Savannah ... Dr. David FROST
43 Assoc VP for Legal Affairs/Risk Mgt ... Mr. Patrick MCKENNA
21 Senior Vice Pres Admin & Finance .. Dr. Amir RAHNAMAY-AZAR
16 Assoc VP Human Resources ... Mr. M. Scott MORRIS
18 Assoc Vice President Facilities ... Mr. Charles G. RHODE
31 Vice President Campus Services ... Ms. Rosalind R. MEYERS
13 Interim Assoc VP Info Tech ... Mr. James O'CONNOR
41 Director of Athletics ... Mr. Dan RADAKOVICH
22 Senior Director Diversity Mgmt ... Ms. Pearl ALEXANDER
12 Dean Ivan Allen College ... Dr. Jacqueline J. ROYSTER
35 Dean of Students/Asst Vice Pres ... Mr. John STEIN
48 Dean College of Architecture ... Mr. Alan BALFOUR
77 Dean College of Computing ... Dr. Zvi GALIL
54 Dean College of Engineering ... Dr. Gary S. MAY
08 Dean & Director Libraries ... Ms. Catherine MURRAY-RUST
82 Dean College of Management ... Dr. Steven C. SALBU
81 Dean College of Sciences ... Dr. Paul HOUSTON
06 Registrar ... Ms. Reta PIKOWSKY
40 Director Bookstore ... Mr. Gerald J. MALONEY
19 Director of Security & Police ... Ms. Teresa CROCKER
51 V Prov/Dist Lrng/Professional Educ ... Dr. Nelson BAKER
78 Exec Dir Prof Practice Div ... Dr. Patrick ANTHONY
37 Director Student Financial Aid ... Ms. Marie MONS
23 Med Director Student Health Svcs ... Dr. Maureen OLSON
39 Actg Exec Director Housing/Transp ... Mr. Michael BLACK
09 Exec Dir Inst Research & Planning ... Ms. Sandra J. BRAMBLETT
85 Vice Provost Intl Initiatives ... Dr. Steven MCLAUGHLIN
104 Exec Dir International Education ... Ms. Amy HENRY
93 Dir Minority Education Development ... Mr. Gordon MOORE
36 Director Career Services ... Mr. Ralph MOBLEY
38 Director Counseling Center ... Dr. Ruperto PEREZ
53 Director Ctr Enhance Teach/Learning .. Dr. Donna C. LLEWELLYN
88 Acting Exec Dir Auxiliary Svcs ... Mr. Richard STEELE
07 Director Undergraduate Admission ... Mr. Richard CLARK
96 Director of Procurement Services ... Mr. Frans BARENDS
88 Director Budget Planning/Admin ... Mr. James KIRK
88 Director Capital Planning/Spce Mgt ... Mr. Howard WERTHEIMER
88 Exec Director Organizational Devel ... Mr. Chet WARZYNSKI
88 Bursar ... Ms. Carol PAYNE
25 Director Grants & Contracts Acctg ... Mr. James FORTNER

† Part of the University System of Georgia.

Georgia Military College (E)

201 E Greene Street, Milledgeville GA 31061-3398
County: Baldwin — FICE Identification: 001571
Unit ID: 139904
Telephone: (478) 445-2700 — Carnegie Class: Assoc/Pub-Spec
FAX Number: (478) 445-2688 — Calendar System: Quarter
URL: www.gmc.cc.ga.us
Established: 1879 — Annual Undergrad Tuition & Fees: $4,880
Enrollment: 1,549 — Coed
Affiliation or Control: Independent Non-Profit — IRS Status: 501(c)3
Highest Offering: Associate Degree
Program: 2-Year Principally Bachelor's Creditable
Accreditation: SC

01 President ... MajGen. Peter J. BOYLAN
03 Executive Vice President ... Col. Fred VAN HORN
05 Vice Pres Academic Affs/Dn Faculty ... Dr. Phillip M. HOLMES
10 Vice President Business Affairs ... Mr. Charles E. MADDEN
84 Vice Pres for Enrollment/Retention ... Ms. Donna FINDLEY
32 Vice Pres Student Svcs/Commandant ... Col. Patrick BEER
30 Vice Pres Institutional Advancement ... Mrs. Elizabeth SHEPPARD
13 Vice Pres Information Technology ... Mr. David HOHNADEL
21 Assoc Vice Pres Business Affairs ... Ms. Susan MEEKS
09 Director Institutional Research ... Dr. Paula PAYNE
41 Athletic Director ... Mr. Bert WILLIAMS
18 Director Facilities/Engineer ... Mr. Jeff GRAY
06 Registrar ... Mrs. Robin KNIGHT
08 Librarian ... Mr. Glen PHILLIPS
19 Chief of Security/Safety ... Mr. James HODNETT

Georgia Northwestern Technical College (F)

One Maurice Culberson Drive, Rome GA 30161
County: Floyd — FICE Identification: 005257
Unit ID: 141273
Telephone: (706) 295-6963 — Carnegie Class: Not Classified
FAX Number: (706) 295-6944 — Calendar System: Quarter
URL: www.gntc.edu
Established: 1966 — Annual Undergrad Tuition & Fees (In-State): $2,498
Enrollment: 8,200 — Coed
Affiliation or Control: State — IRS Status: 501(c)3
Highest Offering: Associate Degree
Program: Occupational
Accreditation: SC, ADNUR, COE, DA, DMS, MAC, OTA, RAD, RTT, SURGT

01 President ... Dr. Craig MCDANIEL
05 Provost ... Mr. Jeff KING
30 Vice Pres Econ Development ... Mr. Pete MCDONALD
20 Vice President Academic Affairs ... Ms. Mindy MCCANNON
09 Vice Pres Inst Effectiveness ... Ms. Heidi POPHAM
51 Vice President Adult Education ... Ms. Susan HACKNEY
11 Vice Pres Administrative Services ... Ms. Kelly BARNES
32 Assoc Vice Pres Student Services ... Dr. Steve BRADSHAW
06 Registrar ... Ms. Selena MAGNUSSON
08 Director of Library Services ... Ms. Linda FLOYD
35 Director of Student Affairs ... Mr. David MCBURNETT
37 Director of Financial Aid ... Ms. Sarah TWIGGS
18 Director Facilities Management ... Mr. Johnny TROTTER
26 Dir Marketing/Public Relations ... Ms. Amber JORDAN
15 Director of Human Resources ... Ms. Peggy CORDELL

Georgia Perimeter College (G)

3251 Panthersville Road, Decatur GA 30034-3897
County: DeKalb — FICE Identification: 001562
Unit ID: 244437
Telephone: (678) 891-2300 — Carnegie Class: Assoc/Pub-S-MC
FAX Number: N/A — Calendar System: Semester
URL: www.gpc.edu
Established: 1963 — Annual Undergrad Tuition & Fees (In-State): $3,550
Enrollment: 25,113 — Coed
Affiliation or Control: State — IRS Status: 501(c)3
Highest Offering: Associate Degree
Program: Occupational; 2-Year Principally Bachelor's Creditable
Accreditation: SC, ADNUR, DH

01 President ... Dr. Anthony S. TRICOLI
05 Vice President Academic Affairs ... Dr. Alan JACKSON
10 Exec Vice Pres Financial/Admin Affs ... Mr. Ron CARRUTH

30 Vice Pres Institutional Advancement ....Mr. Jeffrey TARNOWSKI
32 Vice Pres Student Affairs ....Dr. Vincent JUNE
38 Dir of Organizational Development ....Mr. Wallace WIEHE
32 Asst Vice Pres for Student Affs ....Ms. Coletta HASSELL
20 Asst VP for Academic Affairs ....Dr. Elizabeth MOLLOY
84 Assistant VP Enrollment Management ....Ms. Lisa FOWLER
88 Dir Center for Teaching & Learning ....Dr. Pamela MOOLENAR-WIRSY
13 Assoc VP/Chief Information Officer ....Mr. Reid J. CHRISTENBERRRY
12 Academic Dean Decatur Campus ....Dr. Barbara BROWN
12 Academic Dean Clarkston Campus ....Mr. Phil SMITH
12 Academic Dean Dunwoody Campus ....Dr. Margaret EHRLICH
12 Academic Dean Newton Campus ....Dr. Allan JACKSON
15 Dir HR Employment/Acad Svcs ....Mr. Thomas GEORGE
26 Director Public Relations ....Ms. Barbara OBRENTZ
88 Dir Human Res Conflict Management ....Ms. Karen TRUESDALE
45 Director Institutional Rsrch/Plng ....Dr. Godfrey F. NOE
41 Director Athletics ....Mr. Alfred BARNEY
21 Asst Vice Pres Finance ....Ms. Sheletha CHAMPION
29 Director Alumni Relations ....Mr. Collins FOSTER
37 Dir Student Financial Services ....Ms. Bridgett WILLIAMS
25 Director Grants/Sponsored Programs ....Ms. Ethel BROWN
28 Director of Disability Services ....Ms. Bonnie MARTIN
88 Dir Hum Res Cmp/Aff Act/Opn Rec Ofr ....Ms. Amanda REDDICK
96 Director of Logistical Services ....Mr. Brian Keith CHAPMAN
07 Assoc Dir Admissions & Records ....Mr. Doug RUCH

† Part of the University System of Georgia.

Georgia Southern University (A)

PO Box 8033, Statesboro GA 30460-8033
County: Bulloch FICE Identification: 001572
Unit ID: 139931
Telephone: (912) 478-4636 Carnegie Class: DRU
FAX Number: N/A Calendar System: Semester
URL: www.georgiasouthern.edu
Established: 1906 Annual Undergrad Tuition & Fees (In-State): $6,606
Enrollment: 19,691 Coed
Affiliation or Control: State IRS Status: 501(c)3
Highest Offering: Doctorate
Program: Liberal Arts And General; Teacher Preparatory; Professional
Accreditation: SC, ART, BUS, BUSA, CACREP, CIDA, CONST, CS, DIETD, ENGT, MUS, NRPA, NURSE, PH, SPAA, TED, THEA

01 President ....Dr. Brooks A. KEEL
05 Provost/Vice Pres Academic Affairs ....Dr. William T. MOORE
10 Vice Pres Business & Finance ....Dr. Ron CORE
32 VP Student Affairs & Enroll Mgmt ....Dr. Teresa THOMPSON
30 VP Univ Advance/GSU Foundation Pres ....Mr. William I. GRIFFIS
27 VP Information Technology/CIO ....Mr. Steve BURRELL
09 Assoc VP Strategic Rsrch & Analysis ....Dr. Jayne PERKINS BROWN
46 VP for Research ....Dr. Charles PATTERSON
35 Assoc VP & Dean of Students ....Dr. Georj L. LEWIS
04 Exec Associate to the President ....Ms. Marilyn BRUCE
43 Assoc Vice Pres for Legal Affairs ....Ms. Maura COPELAND
07 Director of Admissions ....Ms. Sarah SMITH
58 Dean College of Graduate Studies ....Dr. Charles PATTERSON
50 Dean College Business Admin ....Dr. Ronald SHIFFLER
53 Dean College Education ....Dr. Thomas KOBALLA
76 Dean College Health/Human Sci ....Dr. Jean BARTELS
49 Dean Col Liberal Arts/Social Sci ....Dr. Michael SMITH
81 Dean College Science & Tech ....Dr. Bret S. DANILOWICZ
72 Int Dean Col Information Technology ....Dr. Ronald SHIFFLER
51 Assoc Provost Continuing Education ....Dr. Anthony BRETTI
69 Int Dean College of Public Health ....Dr. Carolyn D. WOODHOUSE
62 Dean University Library ....Dr. Bede MITCHELL
88 Dir NCAA Compliance/Stdnt-Athl Svcs ....Mr. Keith ROUGHTON
88 Director Audit & Advisory Services ....Ms. Jana BRILEY
43 Associate University Attorney ....Vacant
26 Director Marketing & Communications ....Mr. Christian FLATHMAN
20 Associate Provost ....Dr. Kathy S. ALBERTSON
88 Director Academic Success Center ....Ms. Janet L. O'BRIEN
37 Director Financial Aid ....Ms. Connie MURPHEY
06 Registrar ....Mr. Michael DEAL
88 Director Auxiliary Services ....Mr. Edward D. MILLS
21 Controller ....Ms. Kim THOMPSON BROWN
15 Director Human Resources ....Mr. Paul MICHAUD
41 Athletic Director ....Mr. Sam BAKER
18 Director Physical Plant ....Mr. Ron DENNIS
19 Director Public Safety ....Mr. Michael RUSSELL
36 Director Career Services ....Col. Warren RILES
38 Director Counseling Services ....Dr. David P. MATTHEWS
88 Director Educ Opportunity Programs ....Ms. Joyya SMITH
23 Administrator Health Services ....Mr. Paul FERGUSON
39 Director University Housing ....Mr. Christopher MACDONALD
28 Dir Multicultural Student Center ....Dr. Consuela PENDER
88 Director Leadership/Outreach Pgms ....Dr. Todd DEAL
88 Director Advancement IT ....Ms. Janice WEST
29 Sr Dir Alumni Rels/Annual Giving ....Mr. Wendell TOMPKINS, JR.
86 Assoc VP Governmental Relations ....Mr. Russell KEEN
88 Director Botanical Garden ....Ms. Carolyn ALTMAN
13 Director Computing & Info Mgmt ....Mr. David EWING
90 Director Info Tech for Acad Affairs ....Ms. Pamela DEAL
31 Director Museum ....Dr. Brent THARP
40 Director Stores & Shops ....Mr. Richie AKINS
88 Director Wildlife Educ/Raptor Ctr ....Mr. Steven M. HEIN
96 Director of Materials Management ....Mr. George HORN
44 Director of Development ....Ms. Michelle PITTMAN
28 Director of Diversity Services ....Mr. Gary P. GAWEL

† Part of the University System of Georgia.

Georgia Southwestern State University (B)

800 GA Southwestern State Univ Dr,
Americus GA 31709-4693
County: Sumter FICE Identification: 001573
Unit ID: 139764
Telephone: (800) 338-0082 Carnegie Class: Master's S
FAX Number: N/A Calendar System: Semester
URL: www.gsw.edu
Established: 1906 Annual Undergrad Tuition & Fees (In-State): $11,824
Enrollment: 3,037 Coed
Affiliation or Control: State IRS Status: 501(c)3
Highest Offering: Beyond Master's But Less Than Doctorate
Program: Occupational; Liberal Arts And General; Teacher Preparatory; Professional
Accreditation: SC, BUS, NUR, TED

01 President ....Dr. Kendall A. BLANCHARD
05 Vice President Academic Affairs ....Dr. Brian U. ADLER
10 Vice Pres Business & Finance ....Mr. W. Cody KING
32 Vice President for Student Affairs ....Dr. Samuel T. MILLER
26 Vice Pres for University Relations ....Vacant
32 Dean of Students ....Dr. Gaye HAYES
09 Director Institutional Research ....Dr. Lisa A. COOPER
08 Director Library Services ....Ms. Vera WEISSKOPF
91 Dir Information/Instructional Tech ....Mr. Royce HACKETT
06 Registrar ....Ms. Krista SMITH
07 Director of Admissions ....Dr. Gaye HAYES
36 Director Career Services Center ....Ms. Etrat FATHI
37 Director Student Financial Aid ....Ms. Angela V. BRYANT
85 Director Foreign Students ....Mr. John FOX
27 Director Public Relations ....Mr. Stephen E. SNYDER
30 Director of Development ....Mr. Stephen E. SNYDER
53 Dean of Education ....Dr. Lettie WATFORD
50 Interim Dean of Business ....Dr. Elizabeth WILSON
66 Dean of Nursing ....Dr. Sandra D. DANIEL
49 Dean of Arts & Sciences ....Dr. J. Kelly MCCOY
77 Dean Computing & Mathematics ....Dr. Boris PELTSVERGER
15 Director of Human Resources ....Ms. Janet SIDERS
41 Athletic Director ....Ms. Jaclyn DONOVAN
51 Director of Continuing Education ....Ms. Karen HOLLOWAY
18 Director of Physical Plant ....Mr. George L. SMITH
38 Director Student Counseling ....Ms. Alma G. KEITA
96 Director of Purchasing ....Ms. Nancy ROOKS
29 Coord Alumni Relations/Annual Fund ....Ms. Kimberly COMER

† Part of the University System of Georgia.

Georgia State University (C)

PO Box 3999, Atlanta GA 30302-3999
County: Fulton FICE Identification: 001574
Unit ID: 139940
Telephone: (404) 413-2000 Carnegie Class: RU/VH
FAX Number: (404) 413-1380 Calendar System: Semester
URL: www.gsu.edu
Established: 1913 Annual Undergrad Tuition & Fees (In-State): $9,410
Enrollment: 31,538 Coed
Affiliation or Control: State IRS Status: 501(c)3
Highest Offering: Doctorate
Program: Liberal Arts And General; Teacher Preparatory; Professional
Accreditation: SC, ART, BUS, BUSA, CACREP, CEA, CLPSY, COPSY, CORE, DIETC, DIETD, EXSC, HSA, IPSY, LAW, MUS, NURSE, PH, PTA, SCPSY, SP, SPAA, SW, TED

01 President ....Dr. Mark P. BECKER
05 Sr VP Academic Affairs & Provost ....Dr. Risa I. PALM
10 Sr VP Finance & Administration ....Dr. Jerry J. RACKLIFFE
46 Vice President Research & Econ Dev ....Dr. James A. WEYHENMEYER
32 Vice President Student Affairs ....Dr. Douglass F. COVEY
30 Vice President Development ....Mr. Walter T. MASSEY
26 Vice Pres University Relations ....Ms. DeAnna J. HINES
43 University Attorney ....Dr. Kerry L. HEYWARD
49 Dean Arts & Sciences ....Dr. William J. LONG
50 Dean Business ....Dr. H. Fenwick HUSS
53 Dean Education ....Dr. Randy W. KAMPHAUS
76 Acting Dean Nursing & Health Prof ....Dr. Cecelia M. GRINDEL
69 Director Institute Public Health ....Dr. Michael P. ERIKSEN
61 Dean Law ....Dr. Steven J. KAMINSHINE
80 Dean Policy Studies ....Dr. Mary Beth WALKER
92 Dean Honors College ....Vacant
08 Dean University Library ....Dr. Nancy H. SEAMANS
20 Assoc Provost Academic Programs ....Dr. Timothy M. RENICK
88 Assoc Provost Strategic Initiatives ....Dr. Robert D. MORRIS
09 Assoc Provost Inst Effectiveness ....Dr. Peter LYONS
13 Assoc Provost Info Sys & Technology ....Mr. J. L. ALBERT
82 Assc Prov International Initiatives ....Dr. Jun LIU
45 Assoc VP Research Integrity ....Vacant
45 Associate Vice President Research ....Dr. Amy R. LEDERBERG
18 Assoc VP Facilities ....Vacant
21 Associate Vice President Finance ....Ms. Elizabeth R. JONES
30 Assoc VP Central Development ....Vacant
30 Assoc VP Constituent Programs Dev ....Mr. David J. FRABONI
35 Assoc VP Stdnt Affs/Dean Students ....Dr. Rebecca Y. STOUT
07 Asst VP Undergraduate Admissions ....Mr. Scott M. BURKE
84 Asst VP Student Retention ....Dr. Allison CALHOUN-BROWN
88 Asst VP Student Affairs Admin ....Ms. Carol M. CLARK
29 Asst VP Alumni Relations ....Ms. Christina C. MILLION
40 Asst VP Auxiliary Enterprises ....Mr. Wayne E. REED
21 Asst VP Finance & Comptroller ....Mr. Bruce R. SPRATT
15 Asst VP Human Resources ....Ms. Linda J. NELSON
22 Asst VP Opp Dev/Diversity Educ ....Ms. Linda J. NELSON
88 Asst VP Facilities Acquisition/Op ....Mr. Ramesh VAKAMUDI
19 Asst VP/Chief University Police ....Ms. Connie B. SAMPSON
25 Asst VP Research/Awards Admin ....Ms. Albertha W. BARRETT
06 Registrar ....Vacant
85 Dir Intl Students/Scholars Svcs ....Ms. Heather L. HOUSLEY
39 Director University Housing ....Ms. Marilyn A. DE LAROCHE
38 Director Psychological & Health Svc ....Dr. Jill LEE-BARBER
28 Director Diversity Programs ....Mr. John R. DAY
14 Director Business Support Services ....Mr. William F. PARASKA
13 Director Professional Services ....Mr. Julian O. ALLEN
88 Director Application Engineering ....Mr. John M. BANDY, JR.
13 Director Technology Engineering ....Mr. Keith E. CAMPBELL
88 Director Production Services ....Mr. William GRUSZKA
13 Director Technical Support Services ....Ms. June M. MOSS
36 Director University Career Svcs ....Mr. Kevin E. GAW
37 Director Financial Aid ....Mr. Louis B. SCOTT
96 Director of Business Services ....Mr. Larry J. MCCALOP
88 Dir Univ Auditing & Advisory Svcs ....Mr. Sterling ROTH
88 Director Design/Construction Svcs ....Ms. Kimberly P. BAUER
88 Director Facilities Planning ....Mr. Ramesh VAKAMUDI
88 Director Emergency Management ....Mr. D. Michael RADERSTORF
26 Director Govt & Community Affairs ....Vacant
41 Athletic Director ....Ms. Cheryl L. LEVICK
88 Special Advisor to President ....Mr. Thomas C. LEWIS
04 Assistant to the President ....Ms. Ethel M. BROWN
88 Assistant to the Provost ....Dr. Edgar C. TORBERT

† Part of the University System of Georgia.

Gordon College (D)

419 College Dr., Barnesville GA 30204-1746
County: Lamar FICE Identification: 001575
Unit ID: 139968
Telephone: (678) 359-5021 Carnegie Class: Assoc/Pub4
FAX Number: (678) 359-5080 Calendar System: Semester
URL: www.gdn.edu
Established: 1972 Annual Undergrad Tuition & Fees (In-State): $3,572
Enrollment: 5,009 Coed
Affiliation or Control: State IRS Status: 501(c)3
Highest Offering: Baccalaureate
Program: Occupational; 2-Year Principally Bachelor's Creditable; Teacher Preparatory
Accreditation: SC, ADNUR, NUR

01 Interim President ....Mrs. Shelley NICKEL
05 VP Academic Affairs ....Dr. Ed R. WHEELER
20 Associate VP Academic Affairs ....Dr. Richard BASKIN
10 VP Business Affairs ....Mr. Lee FRUITTICHER
32 VP Student Affairs ....Dr. Dennis R. CHAMBERLAIN
30 VP Institutional Advancement ....Mrs. Rhonda TOON
08 Librarian ....Ms. Nancy D. ANDERSON
37 Director of Financial Aid ....Mr. Larry G. MITCHAM
06 Registrar ....Ms. Janet F. BARRAS
15 Director of Human Resources ....Ms. Tonya L. JOHNSON
18 Director of Facilities ....Mr. Richard VEREEN
38 Director of Counseling Services ....Ms. Kristina L. HENDERSON
07 Director of Admissions ....Mr. Bennett FERGUSON
26 Chief Public Relations Officer ....Mrs. Tamara BOATWRIGHT
09 Director of Institutional Research ....Dr. Kelly MCMURRAY
19 Director of Public Safety ....Chief Jeff MASON
40 Bookstore Manager ....Mrs. Connie H. WADE
41 Athletic Director ....Mr. Todd DAVIS
39 Director of Resident Life ....Ms. Tonya R. COLEMAN
35 Director of Student Activities ....Mrs. Sharon LLOYD
13 Director of Computer Services ....Mr. Jeff HAYES
20 Director of Student Success ....Mr. Peter J. HIGGINS
21 Director of Business Services ....Ms. Sharon ELLIS
88 Comptroller ....Vacant

† Part of the University System of Georgia.

Gupton Jones College of Funeral Service (E)

5141 Snapfinger Woods Drive, Decatur GA 30035-4022
County: DeKalb FICE Identification: 010771
Unit ID: 139995
Telephone: (770) 593-2257 Carnegie Class: Assoc/PrivNFP
FAX Number: (770) 593-1891 Calendar System: Quarter
URL: www.gupton-jones.edu
Established: 1920 Annual Undergrad Tuition & Fees: $9,000
Enrollment: 118 Coed
Affiliation or Control: Independent Non-Profit IRS Status: 501(c)3
Highest Offering: Associate Degree
Program: Occupational; 2-Year Principally Bachelor's Creditable; Technical Emphasis
Accreditation: FUSER

01 President ....Ms. Patty S. HUTCHESON
05 Dean ....Mr. James HINZ
06 Registrar ....Ms. Felicia SMITH

Gwinnett College (F)

4230 Highway 29, Suite 11, Lilburn GA 30047-3447
County: Gwinnett FICE Identification: 025830
Unit ID: 140003
Telephone: (770) 381-7200 Carnegie Class: Not Classified
FAX Number: (770) 381-0454 Calendar System: Other
URL: www.gwinnettcollege.com
Established: 1976 Annual Undergrad Tuition & Fees: $9,250

Enrollment: 435 Coed
Affiliation or Control: Proprietary IRS Status: Proprietary
Highest Offering: Associate Degree
Program: Occupational; 2-Year Principally Bachelor's Creditable
Accreditation: ACICS

01 President Mr. Michael DAVIS

Gwinnett Technical College (A)

5150 Sugarloaf Parkway, Lawrenceville GA 30043-5702
County: Gwinnett FICE Identification: 022884
Unit ID: 140012
Telephone: (770) 962-7580 Carnegie Class: Assoc/Pub-S-SC
FAX Number: (770) 962-7985 Calendar System: Quarter
URL: www.gwinnetttech.edu
Established: 1984 Annual Undergrad Tuition & Fees (In-State): $2,524
Enrollment: 7,100 Coed
Affiliation or Control: State IRS Status: 501(c)3
Highest Offering: Associate Degree
Program: Occupational; 2-Year Principally Bachelor's Creditable; Technical Emphasis
Accreditation: SC, ACFEI, ADNUR, DA, EMT, MAC, RAD, SURGT

01 President Mrs. Sharon J. BARTELS
05 Vice President of Academic Affairs Dr. Cathy MAXWELL
26 Vice Pres Recruitment/Marketing Mr. Dave MCCULLOCH
32 Vice President of Student Affairs Dr. Tom TRAVIS
11 Vice President Administration Mr. David WELDEN
30 Vice Pres Institutional Advancement Mrs. Mary Beth BYERLY
88 Director of Economic Development Ms. Ann SECHRIST
16 Director Human Resources Mr. John SCHMEELK
09 Exec Dir Inst Effectiveness Mrs. Julie POST
21 Director of Accounting Mrs. Valerie STRICKLAND
06 Registrar Ms. Arlene CLARKE
08 Manager of Library Services Ms. Elissa CHECOV
46 Dir Assessment/Advisement/Ed Plng Ms. Brenda PYLE
36 Director of Career Services Ms. Ave MILLER
37 Director of Financial Aid Ms. Kristen GAST
53 Director of Adult Education Mr. Alberto LEYVA
07 Director of Admissions Dr. Florence HALLORAN
18 Dir Facilities/Campus Architect Mr. Eric LAWRENCE
19 Chief of Campus Police & Security Mr. Joseph MARKHAM
04 Assistant to the President Mrs. Debra SMITH

Herzing University (B)

3393 Peachtree Road NE, Suite 1003,
Atlanta GA 30326-1332
County: Fulton FICE Identification: 020897
Unit ID: 140340
Telephone: (404) 816-4533 Carnegie Class: Bac/Diverse
FAX Number: (404) 816-5576 Calendar System: Semester
URL: www.herzing.edu/atlanta/
Established: 1949 Annual Undergrad Tuition & Fees: $17,640
Enrollment: 627 Coed
Affiliation or Control: Proprietary IRS Status: Proprietary
Highest Offering: Baccalaureate
Program: Occupational; 2-Year Principally Bachelor's Creditable; Technical Emphasis
Accreditation: &NH

01 President Mr. Frank R. WEBSTER
05 Academic Dean Mrs. Marsha JOHNSON
36 Director of Career Services Mr. William SLATON
08 College Librarian Mr. Eric H. MURRAY
07 Director of Admissions Ms. Anissa ELDER
06 Registrar Ms. Fiona JIMILL
37 Director of Student Financial Aid Mrs. Stephanie GUNBY

† Regional accreditation is carried under the parent institution in Madison, WI.

Interactive College of Technology (C)

5303 New Peachtree Road, Chamblee GA 30341-2818
County: DeKalb FICE Identification: 022843
Unit ID: 138655
Telephone: (770) 216-2960 Carnegie Class: Assoc/PrivFP
FAX Number: (770) 216-2989 Calendar System: Semester
URL: www.ict-ils.edu
Established: 1986 Annual Undergrad Tuition & Fees: $7,800
Enrollment: 2,350 Coed
Affiliation or Control: Proprietary IRS Status: Proprietary
Highest Offering: Associate Degree
Program: Occupational
Accreditation: COE

01 President Mr. Elmer R. SMITH
05 Dean of the College Mr. Thomas BLAIR
12 Campus Director Pasadena Texas Mr. Rodrigo DORANTES
12 Campus Dir SW Houston Texas Ms. Cynthia BRYSON
12 Campus Dir North Houston Texas Ms. Samis NAGEL
12 Campus Director - New Port KY Ms. Tracy WILSON
12 Campus Directory - Morrow GA Ms. Amanda BLACKSHEAR

Interdenominational Theological Center (D)

700 Martin L. King, Jr. Drive, SW, Atlanta GA 30314-4143
County: Fulton FICE Identification: 001568
Unit ID: 140146
Telephone: (404) 527-7700 Carnegie Class: Spec/Faith
FAX Number: (404) 527-0901 Calendar System: Semester
URL: www.itc.edu
Established: 1958 Annual Graduate Tuition & Fees: $11,212
Enrollment: 413 Coed
Affiliation or Control: Interdenominational IRS Status: 501(c)3
Highest Offering: Doctorate; No Undergraduates
Program: Professional; Religious Emphasis
Accreditation: SC, THEOL

01 President Dr. Ronald E. PETERS
05 Interim VP for Acad Svcs/Provost Dr. Temba L. MAFICO
10 Vice Pres Admin Services Dr. Kevin STEWART
30 Vice Pres for Institutional Advance Ms. Fran L. DAY
06 Registrar Ms. Bobbie HALL
37 Financial Aid Director Ms. Tina GARNIGAN
15 Director Human Resources Ms. Michelle D. COOK
42 Chaplain/Counselor Dr. Willie GOODMAN
32 Coordinator Student/Community Life Dr. Francis T. BRYANT-LOWERY

ITT Technical Institute (E)

485 Oak Place, Suite 800, Atlanta GA 30349
County: Fulton Identification: 666595
Unit ID: 450243
Telephone: (404) 765-4600 Carnegie Class: Assoc/PrivFP4
FAX Number: (770) 904-4650 Calendar System: Quarter
URL: www.itt-tech.edu
Established: N/A Annual Undergrad Tuition & Fees: N/A
Enrollment: 706 Coed
Affiliation or Control: Proprietary IRS Status: Proprietary
Highest Offering: Baccalaureate
Program: Technical Emphasis
Accreditation: ACICS

† Branch campus of ITT Technical Institute, Greenfield, WI.

ITT Technical Institute (F)

10700 Abbotts Bridge Road, Duluth GA 30097-8460
County: Fulton Identification: 666325
Unit ID: 443526
Telephone: (678) 957-8510 Carnegie Class: Spec/Tech
FAX Number: (678) 417-2070 Calendar System: Quarter
URL: www.itt-tech.edu
Established: 2003 Annual Undergrad Tuition & Fees: N/A
Enrollment: 675 Coed
Affiliation or Control: Proprietary IRS Status: Proprietary
Highest Offering: Baccalaureate
Program: Technical Emphasis
Accreditation: ACICS

† Branch campus of ITT Technical Institute, Lake Mary, FL.

ITT Technical Institute (G)

2065 ITT Tech Way N.W., Kennesaw GA 30144
County: Cobb Identification: 666378
Unit ID: 446905
Telephone: (770) 426-2300 Carnegie Class: Assoc/PrivFP4
FAX Number: N/A Calendar System: Quarter
URL: www.itt-tech.edu
Established: N/A Annual Undergrad Tuition & Fees: N/A
Enrollment: 570 Coed
Affiliation or Control: Proprietary IRS Status: Proprietary
Highest Offering: Baccalaureate
Program: Technical Emphasis
Accreditation: ACICS

† Branch campus of ITT Technical Institute, Torrance, CA.

Kennesaw State University (H)

1000 Chastain Road #0101, Kennesaw GA 30144-5591
County: Cobb FICE Identification: 001577
Unit ID: 140164
Telephone: (770) 423-6000 Carnegie Class: Master's L
FAX Number: (770) 423-6543 Calendar System: Semester
URL: www.kennesaw.edu
Established: 1963 Annual Undergrad Tuition & Fees (In-State): $6,285
Enrollment: 23,452 Coed
Affiliation or Control: State IRS Status: 501(c)3
Highest Offering: Doctorate
Program: Liberal Arts And General; Teacher Preparatory; Professional
Accreditation: SC, ART, BUS, BUSA, CS, MACTE, MUS, NURSE, SPAA, SW, TED, THEA

01 President Dr. Daniel S. PAPP
05 Int Provost/Vice Pres Academic Affs Dr. W. Ken HARMON
30 Vice Pres University Advancement Dr. Wesley K. WICKER
32 Vice Pres Student Success Dr. Jerome RATCHFORD
11 Vice President for Operations Dr. Randy C. HINDS
58 VP Research/Dean Graduate College Dr. Charles J. AMLANER
31 Vice President External Affairs Ms. Arlethia PERRY-JOHNSON
28 Interim Chief Diversity Officer Ms. Linda M. LYONS
43 Univ Aty/Spec Asst Pres Leg Affairs Dr. Flora B. DEVINE
04 Faculty Exec Assistant to President Dr. Jorge PEREZ
20 Asst Vice Pres Academic Affairs Dr. Valerie D. WHITTLESEY
15 Asst Vice Pres Human Resources Svcs Mr. Rodney BOSSERT
84 Asst Vice Pres Enrollment Services Mr. Kim WEST
08 Actg Asst VP for Library Operations Mr. J. David EVANS
18 Asst Vice Pres Facilities Services Mr. John A. ANDERSON
21 Asst Vice Pres Financial Services Dr. Ashok K. ROY
20 AVP Academic Affairs/Dean Univ Col Dr. Ralph J. RASCATI
04 Exec Assistant to President Ms. Lynda K. JOHNSON
79 Dean Humanities/Social Science Dr. Richard VENGROFF
81 Interim Dean Mathematics/Science Dr. Ronald H. MATSON
53 Dean Bagwell College of Education Dr. Arlinda EATON
50 Int Dean Coles College of Business Dr. Kathy S. SCHWAIG
76 Dean WellStar Col Health/Human Svcs Dr. Richard L. SOWELL
49 Dean College of the Arts Mr. Joseph D. MEEKS
58 Assoc Provost Dr. Teresa M. JOYCE
35 Dean of Student Success Dr. Michael L. SANSEVIRO
51 Dean Continuing/Professional Educ Ms. Barbara S. CALHOUN
07 Asc Dn Enrol Svs/Ex Dir Univ Admiss Ms. Susan N. BLAKE
38 Asst Dean/Dir Student Success Svs Dr. Robert J. MATTOX
06 Registrar Mr. Kim WEST
90 Chief Tech Ofcr/Info Sys Architect Dr. John L. ISENHOUR
91 Dir Enterprise Systems & Services Mr. T. Wayne DENNISON
37 Director Student Financial Aid Mr. Rondall H. DAY
07 Dir Student Recruitment/Admissions Dr. Angela J. EVANS
40 Exec Dir Bookstore/Aux Svcs/Pgms Ms. Faye J. SILVERMAN
36 Director of Career Services Center Ms. Karen B. ANDREWS
41 Athletics Director Mr. Vaughn A. WILLIAMS
26 Director University Relations Ms. Frances L. HARRISON
29 Director Alumni Affairs Ms. Lisa A. DUKE
44 Director Annual Giving Vacant
46 Ex Dir Entrpr Info Mgt/Chf Data Ofr Mr. Erik R. BOWE
19 Director Public Safety Mr. Theodore J. COCHRAN
35 Director Student Life Ms. Katherine E. ALDAY
88 Dir Enterprise Info Reporting Ms. Donna R. HUTCHESON
09 Director of Institutional Research Dr. Charles J. AMLANER
10 Chief Business Officer Dr. Randy C. HINDS
96 Director of Purchasing Ms. Donna G. BERTRAND

† Part of the University System of Georgia.

LaGrange College (I)

601 Broad Street, La Grange GA 30240-2999
County: Troup FICE Identification: 001578
Unit ID: 140234
Telephone: (706) 880-8000 Carnegie Class: Bac/Diverse
FAX Number: (706) 880-8358 Calendar System: 4/1/4
URL: www.lagrange.edu
Established: 1831 Annual Undergrad Tuition & Fees: $23,212
Enrollment: 979 Coed
Affiliation or Control: United Methodist IRS Status: 501(c)3
Highest Offering: Master's
Program: Liberal Arts And General; Teacher Preparatory
Accreditation: SC, ACBSP, NUR

01 President Dr. Dan MCALEXANDER
05 Provost and Chief Academic Officer Dr. David GARRISON
10 Exec Vice President Administration Vacant
30 Vice President Advancement Mr. William JONES
84 Vice Pres Enrollment Management Mr. Dana PAUL
21 Vice Pres Finance & Operations Mr. Martin E. PIRRMAN
42 VP Spiritual Life & Church Relation Dr. Quincy D. BROWN
32 Dean of Student Affairs Dr. Jack C. SLAY
14 Director Infomation Technology Mr. James BLACKWOOD
06 Registrar Mr. Jimmy G. HERRING
08 Director Library Mr. Loren L. PINKERMAN
26 Director Communications/Marketing Mr. Dean A. HARTMAN
88 Director LaGrange Fund Mr. Andy BRUBAKER
37 Director Student Financial Aid Ms. Sylvia A. SMITH
41 Athletic Director Mrs. Jennifer D. CLAYBROOK
36 Director Student Placement Mrs. Diana GOLDWIRE
55 Director Evening College Mrs. Linda H. MCMULLEN
38 Director Student Counseling Mrs. Pamela TREMBLAY
44 Director Major Gifts Ms. Rebecca ROTH
40 Director Bookstore Mrs. Anita LANEY
09 Director Inst Research Dr. Doug FLOR
12 Director LaGrange College Albany Ms. Beth BROWN
35 Director Student Activities Vacant
18 Manager Facilities/Physical Plant Mr. Michael CONIGLIO
31 Events Coordinator Ms. Tammy ROGERS
04 Executive Assistant to President Mrs. Carla RHODES
29 Director Alumni & Cmty Relations Mrs. Martha PIRKLE
13 Director Admin Computing Mr. Brandon FETNER
15 Director Human Resources Mrs. Dawn COKER

Lanier Technical College (J)

2990 Landrum Education Drive, Oakwood GA 30566-3405
County: Hall FICE Identification: 005254
Unit ID: 140243
Telephone: (770) 531-6300 Carnegie Class: Assoc/Pub-R-M
FAX Number: (770) 531-6328 Calendar System: Semester
URL: www.laniertech.edu
Established: 1964 Annual Undergrad Tuition & Fees (In-State): $3,645
Enrollment: 4,432 Coed
Affiliation or Control: State IRS Status: 501(c)3
Highest Offering: Associate Degree
Program: Occupational; 2-Year Principally Bachelor's Creditable; Technical Emphasis
Accreditation: @SC, COE, DA, DH, MAC, MLTAD, RAD, SURGT

01 President Mr. Russell VANDIVER
103 Vice President Economic Development Vacant
05 Vice President Academic Affairs Dr. Linda M. BARROW
12 Vice President Operations Forsyth Dr. Joanne P. TOLLESON
32 Vice President Student Affairs Ms. Lisa WILSON

10 Vice Pres Administrative Services ....Ms. Laura ELDER
13 Vice President Technology ....Mr. Robbie VICKERS
04 Executive Assistant to President ....Ms. Becky SMITH
09 Dir of Institutional Effectiveness ....Mr. Brad GADBERRY
30 Director of Development ....Ms. Carol SPIRES
26 Director Public Relations Officer ....Mr. Dave PARRISH
20 Dean Academic Affairs ....Ms. Dianne BOWERS
20 Dean Academic Affairs ....Ms. Donna BRINSON
12 Director Satellite Campus ....Ms. Lisa MALOOF
12 Director Satellite Campus ....Mr. Tim MCDONALD
12 Director Satellite Campus ....Dr. Howard LEDFORD
07 Director of Admissions ....Mr. Mike MARLOWE
06 Registrar ....Ms. Sandi J. BAKER
37 Director Student Financial Aid ....Ms. Patsy GRIFFIN
84 Director Enrollment Management ....Ms. Deanna ORZA
36 Student Placement Specialist ....Ms. Melissa LAWRENCE
28 Coord Special Svcs/Minority Affairs ....Ms. Mallory SAFLEY
21 Director Administrative Services ....Ms. Janet BOHANON
15 Director of Human Resources ....Ms. Jill CANTRELL
18 Director of Facilities ....Mr. Carl PITTS

Le Cordon Bleu College of Culinary Arts in Atlanta (A)

1927 Lakeside Parkway, Tucker GA 30084-5865
County: DeKalb Identification: 666298
Unit ID: 443623
Telephone: (770) 938-4711 Carnegie Class: Assoc/PrivFP
FAX Number: (770) 938-4571 Calendar System: Quarter
URL: www.chefs.edu/atlanta
Established: 2003 Annual Undergrad Tuition & Fees: $16,142
Enrollment: 1,331 Coed
Affiliation or Control: Proprietary IRS Status: Proprietary
Highest Offering: Associate Degree
Program: Occupational; 2-Year Principally Bachelor's Creditable; Technical Emphasis
Accreditation: ACICS, ACFEI

01 President ....Mr. Glenn MACK
10 Controller ....Ms. Michelle BOWLING
07 Vice Pres of Marketing/Admissions ....Ms. Terri HOLTE
37 Director of Financial Aid ....Ms. Angelique STRICKLAND
05 Director of Education ....Mr. Jerald CASSIDY
11 Director of Campus Administration ....Ms. Pat NERI
88 Executive Chef ....Chef Todd KAZENSKE
06 Registrar ....Ms. Jessica BOLD
15 Human Resources Manager ....Ms. Staci BULLARD

† Branch campus of Le Cordon Bleu College of Culinary Arts, Portland, OR.

Life University (B)

1269 Barclay Circle, Marietta GA 30060-2996
County: Cobb FICE Identification: 020748
Unit ID: 140252
Telephone: (770) 426-2600 Carnegie Class: Bac/A&S
FAX Number: (770) 429-4819 Calendar System: Quarter
URL: www.life.edu
Established: 1974 Annual Undergrad Tuition & Fees: $8,415
Enrollment: 2,437 Coed
Affiliation or Control: Independent Non-Profit IRS Status: 501(c)3
Highest Offering: Doctorate
Program: 2-Year Principally Bachelor's Creditable; Liberal Arts And General; Professional
Accreditation: SC, CHIRO, DIETD, DIETI

01 President ....Dr. Guy F. RIEKEMAN
03 Executive Vice President/Provost ....Dr. Brian MCAULAY
10 Vice President Operations & Finance ....Mr. William JARR
30 Vice Pres of University Advancement ....Mr. Greg HARRIS
84 Executive Dir of Enrollment Mgmt ....Dr. Cynthia BOYD
41 Director of Athletics ....Mr. John BARRETT
15 Director of Human Resources ....Ms. Stella PETERSON
27 Chief Information Officer ....Mr. John ALTIKULAC
13 Director Information Technology ....Mr. Thorton MUIR
32 Executive Director Student Services ....Dr. Marc SCHNEIDER
104 Director of Global Initiatives ....Dr. John DOWNES
11 Asst Provost Administrative Service ....Dr. Tim GROSS
76 Dean College of Chiropractic ....Dr. Leslie KING
49 Dean College Undergraduate Studies ....Dr. Michael SMITH
23 Dean of Clinics ....Dr. Ralph DAVIS
06 Registrar ....Ms. Tiffany SMITH
08 Director of Learning Resources ....Ms. Susan STEWART
46 Director of Research ....Dr. Stephanie SULLIVAN
29 Alumni Relations Manager ....Ms. Leila TATUM
45 Director of Inst Effectiveness ....Dr. Vince ERARIO
09 Director of Institutional Research ....Mr. Tiannan ZHOU
18 Director Facilities/Physical Plant ....Mr. Richard SHAW
38 Director Student Success ....Dr. Lisa RUBIN
37 Director Student Financial Aid ....Ms. Melissa WATERS
35 Dir of Student Development ....Ms. Jennifer VALTOS
36 Director of Career Planning ....Ms. Susan DUDT
88 Dir of Student Administrative Svcs ....Ms. Kay FREELAND
26 Director of Communications ....Mr. Craig DEKSHENIEKS
28 Director of Diversity ....Dr. Jerry HARDEE
21 Budget Director ....Ms. Amy MCILVANE
44 Manager of Constituent Relations ....Mr. Tom MCCLESKEY

Lincoln College of Technology (C)

2359 Windy Hill Road, Marietta GA 30067
County: Cobb Identification: 666282
Unit ID: 434159
Telephone: (770) 226-0056 Carnegie Class: Assoc/PrivFP
FAX Number: (770) 226-0084 Calendar System: Semester
URL: www.lincolnedu.com
Established: 2001 Annual Undergrad Tuition & Fees: $19,577
Enrollment: 580 Coed
Affiliation or Control: Proprietary IRS Status: Proprietary
Highest Offering: Associate Degree
Program: Occupational; 2-Year Principally Bachelor's Creditable
Accreditation: ACICS

01 Executive Director ....Mr. Brian CAPOZZI

Luther Rice University (D)

3038 Evans Mill Road, Lithonia GA 30038-2454
County: DeKalb FICE Identification: 031009
Unit ID: 135364
Telephone: (770) 484-1204 Carnegie Class: Spec/Faith
FAX Number: (770) 484-1155 Calendar System: Semester
URL: www.lru.edu
Established: 1962 Annual Undergrad Tuition & Fees: $6,900
Enrollment: 1,159 Coed
Affiliation or Control: Independent Non-Profit IRS Status: 501(c)3
Highest Offering: Doctorate
Program: Liberal Arts And General; Professional
Accreditation: TRACS

01 President ....Dr. James L. FLANAGAN
10 Vice President Financial Affairs ....Mr. Louis B. HARDCASTLE
32 Vice President for Student Affairs ....Dr. Dennis D. DIERINGER
05 Chief Acad Officer/Dean Grad Pgm ....Dr. Brad K. ARNETT
08 Director of Library Services ....Mr. Hal HALLER
37 Director Student Financial Aid ....Mr. Gary W. COOK
30 Director Development/External Affs ....Mr. Russ L. SORROW
88 Asst to the Pres for Asian Affairs ....Dr. Kyung C. LIM
85 Asst to the Pres Global Strategy ....Dr. Ronald B. LONG
09 Director of Inst Effectiveness ....Dr. Ralph J. MCCANN
35 Coordinator of Academic Advising ....Dr. Dennis R. VINES
56 Coordinator of Distance Education ....Dr. Dennis R. VINES

Macon State College (E)

100 College Station Drive, Macon GA 31206-5145
County: Bibb FICE Identification: 007728
Unit ID: 140322
Telephone: (478) 471-2700 Carnegie Class: Bac/Diverse
FAX Number: (478) 471-2846 Calendar System: Semester
URL: www.maconstate.edu
Established: 1968 Annual Undergrad Tuition & Fees (In-State): $2,304
Enrollment: 6,041 Coed
Affiliation or Control: State IRS Status: 501(c)3
Highest Offering: Baccalaureate
Program: Liberal Arts And General
Accreditation: SC, ADNUR, CS, NUR, TED

01 President ....Dr. Jeff ALLBRITTEN
05 Vice President Academic Affairs ....Dr. Martha L. VENN
10 Vice President Fiscal Affairs ....Ms. Nancy STROUD
26 Vice President External Affairs ....Mr. Albert J. ABRAMS
30 Vice Pres Institutional Advancement ....Mr. John P. COLE
20 Assoc VP for Academic Affairs ....Vacant
84 Assoc Vice Pres Enrollment Services ....Ms. Dee MINTER
21 Asst Vice Pres Fiscal Affairs ....Vacant
30 Assoc Vice Pres Development/Alumni ....Ms. Sue CHIPMAN
09 Assoc VP Institutional Research ....Dr. Jeffrey V. STEWART, III
07 Director of Admissions ....Mr. Bruce APPLEWHITE
51 Director Continuing Education ....Mr. Albert J. ABRAMS
12 Assoc Dir of Warner Robins Campuses ....Mrs. Pella MURPHY
12 Exec Dir Warner Robins Campuses ....Vacant
13 Chief Information Officer ....Mr. Roger DIXON
06 Registrar ....Mr. Tom WAUGH
08 Director Library Services ....Ms. Pat BORCK
37 Director Financial Aid ....Ms. Pat SIMMONS
15 Dir Human Resources/EEO Officer ....Ms. Holly MORRISON
18 Director of Plant Operations ....Mr. David SIMS
44 Associate Director Development ....Ms. Beth BYERS
36 Director Counseling ....Ms. Ann LOYD
32 Dean of Students ....Ms. Lynn W. MCCRANEY
35 Asst Dean of Students ....Mr. Michael STEWART
88 Director Student Support Services ....Ms. Yolanda PETTY
27 Director Communications ....Mr. William H. WEAVER
21 Dir Business Services/Comptroller ....Mr. Brian STANLEY
96 Purchasing Manager ....Ms. Barbara BURNS
50 Dean of Business ....Dr. Varkey K. TITUS
66 Dean School of Nursing/Health ....Dr. Rebecca J. CORVEY
49 Dean Arts & Sciences ....Dr. Ron WILLIAMS
50 Dean Education ....Dr. Pamela BEDWELL
72 Dean Information Technology ....Dr. Alex KOOHANG
36 Director Career Services ....Vacant
90 Director Academic Resource Center ....Mr. Paul JOHNSON
91 Director Administrative Systems ....Ms. Beverly BERGMAN
88 Director Wellness Program ....Mr. James HAGLER
39 Director of Residence Life ....Dr. Chris SUMMERLIN
19 Director of Public Safety ....Mr. Shawn DOUGLAS
40 Director Auxiliary Services ....Mr. Kevin REID

† Part of the University System of Georgia.

Mercer University (F)

1400 Coleman Avenue, Macon GA 31207-0003
County: Bibb FICE Identification: 001580
Unit ID: 140447
Telephone: (478) 301-2700 Carnegie Class: Master's L
FAX Number: (478) 301-2108 Calendar System: Semester
URL: www.mercer.edu
Established: 1833 Annual Undergrad Tuition & Fees: $31,248
Enrollment: 8,236 Coed
Affiliation or Control: Independent Non-Profit IRS Status: 501(c)3
Highest Offering: Doctorate
Program: Liberal Arts And General; Teacher Preparatory; Professional
Accreditation: SC, ANEST, ARCPA, BUS, CACREP, CS, ENG, LAW, MED, MFCD, MUS, NURSE, PH, PHAR, @PTA, TED, THEOL

01 President and CEO ....Mr. William D. UNDERWOOD
00 Chancellor ....Dr. R. Kirby GODSEY
100 Senior VP and Chief of Staff ....Mr. Larry D. BRUMLEY
05 Provost ....Dr. Wallace L. DANIEL
10 Executive VP for Admin & Finance .....Dr. James S. NETHERTON
12 Sr VP Atlanta Campus ....Dr. Richard V. SWINDLE
30 Sr VP for University Advancement ....Mr. John A. PATTERSON
84 Sr Vice Pres Enrollment Mgmt ....Dr. Penny L. ELKINS
43 Vice President and General Counsel ....Mr. William G. SOLOMON
13 Chief Technology Officer ....Mr. Michael R. BELOTE
17 VP Health Sci/Dean Col Pharm & HS ....Dr. H. W. MATTHEWS
32 Vice President & Dean of Students ....Dr. Doug R. PEARSON
20 Sr V Prov Research/Dean Grad Stdnts ....Dr. D. Scott DAVIS
21 Treasurer & Assoc VP Finance ....Ms. Julia T. DAVIS
18 Assoc Vice President for Facilities ....Mr. Russell VULLO
15 Associate Vice Pres Personnel Admin ....Ms. Diane H. BACA
26 Assoc VP University Rels/Marketing ......Mr. Richard L. CAMERON
37 Assoc VP Student Financial Planning .....Ms. Carol K. WILLIAMS
49 Dean College of Liberal Arts ....Dr. Lake LAMBERT
61 Dean School of Law ....Mr. Gary J. SIMSON
63 Dean School of Medicine ....Dr. William F. BINA, III
54 Dean School of Engineering ....Dr. Wade H. SHAW
50 Dean Sch Business/Econ ....Dr. Scott DAVIS
73 Dean School of Theology ....Dr. R. Alan CULPEPPER
53 Dean College of Education ....Dr. Carl R. MARTRAY
66 Dean College of Nursing ....Dr. Linda A. STREIT
51 Dean College Cont/Prof Stds ....Dr. Priscilla R. DANHEISER
64 Dean School of Music ....Dr. John H. DICKSON
08 Dean of University Libraries ....Ms. Elizabeth D. HAMMOND
06 Registrar ....Dr. Marilyn P. MINDINGALL
50 Assoc Dn Sch Business/Econ-Atlanta ....Dr. Gina L. MILLER
41 Athletic Director ....Mr. Jim COLE
19 Chief Police Department ....Mr. Gary COLLINS
09 Director of Institutional Research ....Ms. Sarah E. MAY
96 Director of Purchasing ....Mr. Charles MIZE

Middle Georgia College (G)

1100 Second Street, SE, Cochran GA 31014-1599
County: Bleckley FICE Identification: 001581
Unit ID: 140483
Telephone: (478) 934-6221 Carnegie Class: Assoc/Pub4
FAX Number: (478) 934-3199 Calendar System: Semester
URL: www.mgc.edu
Established: 1884 Annual Undergrad Tuition & Fees (In-State): $3,622
Enrollment: 3,496 Coed
Affiliation or Control: State IRS Status: 501(c)3
Highest Offering: Baccalaureate
Program: Occupational; 2-Year Principally Bachelor's Creditable
Accreditation: SC, ADNUR, OTA

01 President ....Dr. Michael STOY
05 Vice President for Academic Affairs ....Dr. Mary Ellen WILSON
10 Vice President for Fiscal Affairs ....Ms. Lynn E. HOBBS
32 Vice Pres Student & Public Affairs ....Mr. John MCELVEEN
08 Director of Library Resources ....Mr. Paul ROBARDS
38 Director of Testing ....Mrs. Predita HOWARD
15 Director of Personnel ....Ms. Lisa CHASTAIN
37 Director of Financial Aid ....Mr. Jon FINKELSTEIN
40 Director of Bookstore ....Mr. Josh FOSKEY
07 Director of Admissions/Registrar ....Mrs. Jennifer BRANNON
26 Chief Public Relations Officer ....Ms. Alison MANNING
12 Director of Dublin Center ....Mr. Rodney CARR
12 Dir Eastman Campus/Chief Plng Ofcr ....Mr. Johnny MCMOY
12 Dir of Georgia Aviation Campus ....Mrs. Jennifer BRANNON

† Part of the University System of Georgia.

Middle Georgia Technical College (H)

80 Cohen Walker Drive, Warner Robins GA 31088-2729
County: Houston FICE Identification: 025086
Unit ID: 140085
Telephone: (478) 988-6800 Carnegie Class: Assoc/Pub-R-M
FAX Number: (478) 988-6813 Calendar System: Quarter
URL: www.middlegatech.edu
Established: 1973 Annual Undergrad Tuition & Fees (In-State): $2,268
Enrollment: 4,205 Coed
Affiliation or Control: State IRS Status: 501(c)3
Highest Offering: Associate Degree
Program: Occupational; 2-Year Principally Bachelor's Creditable; Technical Emphasis
Accreditation: SC, DA, DH, RAD, SURGT

01 President ....Dr. Ivan H. ALLEN
05 Vice President for Academic Affairs ....Dr. Amy L. HOLLOWAY
32 Vice President for Student Affairs ....Mr. Craig JACKSON
09 VP Economic Develop/Inst Support ....Mr. Jeffrey SCRUGGS
11 VP for Administrative Services ....Mrs. Michelle SINIARD
88 Vice President for Adult Education ....Ms. Brenda L. BROWN
07 Director of Admissions ....Mr. Dann WEBB
37 Director of Financial Aid ....Mr. Steve GREEN

06 Registrar .... Ms. Sonja JENKINS
08 Director of Library Services .... Dr. Dumont C. BUNN
15 Director of Human Resources .... Ms. Carol F. JONES
30 Director of Advancement .... Ms. Cheryl STELK
26 Marketing & PR Director .... Mrs. Janet H. KELLY
18 Maintenance Superintendent .... Mr. Joe PETERSDORFF

Morehouse College (A)

830 Westview Drive SW, Atlanta GA 30314-3773
County: Fulton FICE Identification: 001582
Unit ID: 140553
Telephone: (404) 681-2800 Carnegie Class: Bac/A&S
FAX Number: (404) 681-2650 Calendar System: Semester
URL: www.morehouse.edu
Established: 1867 Annual Undergrad Tuition & Fees: $23,792
Enrollment: 2,579 Male
Affiliation or Control: Independent Non-Profit IRS Status: 501(c)3
Highest Offering: Baccalaureate
Program: Liberal Arts And General; Teacher Preparatory
Accreditation: SC, BUS, MUS

01 President .... Dr. Robert M. FRANKLIN
05 Provost & Senior Vice President .... Dr. Weldon JACKSON
11 Vice President Campus Operations .... Mr. Andre E. BERTRAND
96 Purchasing Manager .... Mr. Kevin BRANCH
30 Vice Pres Institutional Advancement .... Mr. Phillip D. HOWARD
100 Chief of Staff .... Ms. Fran PHILLIPS-CALHOUN
32 VP Student Svcs and Enrollment Mgmt .... Dr. William BYNUM
10 Vice President Business Affairs/CFO .... Ms. Gwendolyn SYKES
20 Assoc Vice Pres Special Acad Pgms .... Dr. Anne W. WATTS
15 Assoc Vice Pres Human Resource .... Ms. Pamela WESTON
44 Exec Asst to Pres-Capital Campaign .... Ms. Kathleen JOHNSON
42 Dean Martin Luther King Jr Chapel .... Dr. Lawrence E. CARTER
06 Int Assoc Dean Records/Registration .... Ms. Kasi ROBINSON
07 Int Assoc Dean Admiss/Recruitment .... Mr. Danny BELLINGER
37 Director of Financial Aid .... Mr. James STOTTS
29 Director Alumni Rels/Annual Gvg Pgm .... Mr. Henry GOODGAME
26 Director Public Relations .... Ms. Toni O'NEAL MOSLEY
27 Publications Manager .... Ms. Vickie HAMPTON
36 Director of Placement .... Mr. Doug COOPER
36 Director of Placement .... Ms. Kellye BLACKBURN
41 Athletic Director .... Mr. Andre PATTILLO
39 Director Student Housing .... Mr. Maurice WASHINGTON
19 Chief of Campus Police .... Chief Vernon WORTHY
18 Int Superintendent Physical Plant .... Mr. Curtis DAVIS
85 Director Andrew Young Ctr Intl Pgms .... Mr. Julius COLES
86 Director Government Relations .... Ms. Denise MOORE
50 Dean Div of Business & Economics .... Dr. John E. WILLIAMS
81 Dean Div of Science & Mathematics .... Dr. John K. HAYNES
09 Director of Institutional Research .... Dr. Michael FLEMING
79 Dean Div of Humanities & Soc Sci .... Dr. Terry MILLS
35 Director Student Services .... Mr. Kevin BOOKER
38 Director of Student Counseling .... Dr. Gary WRIGHT

Morehouse School of Medicine (B)

720 Westview Drive, SW, Atlanta GA 30310-1495
County: Fulton FICE Identification: 024821
Unit ID: 140562
Telephone: (404) 752-1500 Carnegie Class: Spec/Med
FAX Number: (404) 752-1027 Calendar System: Semester
URL: www.msm.edu
Established: 1975 Annual Graduate Tuition & Fees: $30,000
Enrollment: 330 Coed
Affiliation or Control: Independent Non-Profit IRS Status: 501(c)3
Highest Offering: Doctorate; No Undergraduates
Program: Professional
Accreditation: SC, MED, PH

01 President .... Dr. John E. MAUPIN, JR.
05 Interim Dean/Sr VP Academic Affairs .... Dr. Sandra HARRIS-HOOKER
88 Sr Adv/Asst Dean Health Quality .... Vacant
86 Sr Adv for Strategic Mgmt/Gov Rels .... Dr. Virgina FLOYD
43 General Counsel .... Mr. Harold JORDAN
30 VP Institutional Advancement .... Mrs. Sally DAVIS
20 Sr Assoc Dean for Educ/Faculty Affs .... Dr. Martha ELKS
11 Assoc Dean Admin/Asst VP Finance .... Ms. Sandra E. WATSON
38 Director of Counseling .... Dr. Shawn GARRISON
37 Director of Financial Aid .... Ms. Cynthia H. HANDY
08 Interim Director of Library .... Mr. Joe SWANSON, JR.
09 Chief of Planning & Inst Research .... Ms. Andrea D. FOX
26 Exec Director of Marketing & Comm .... Ms. Cherie A. RICHARDSON
25 Director of Grants & Contracts .... Ms. Brenda G. WILLIS
29 Director of Alum Rel & Giving .... Ms. Carrie M. DUMAS
84 Director of Admissions .... Dr. Sterling A. ROAF
96 Director of Purchasing .... Mr. Linwood HILTON
15 Associate VP of Human Resources .... Ms. Denise BRITT
22 Chief Compliance Officer .... Ms. Lori J. COLLINS
100 Chief of Staff .... Mrs. Kimberly JACKSON
06 Interim Registrar .... Mrs. Adrienne L. WYATT
88 Assoc Dean for Clinical Affairs .... Dr. Lawrence L. SANDERS, JR.
27 Chief Information Officer .... Ms. Cigdem E. DELANO
19 Director of Public Safety .... Mr. Joseph CHEVALIER, JR.

Moultrie Technical College (C)

800 Veterans Parkway North, Moultrie GA 31788-1919
County: Colquitt FICE Identification: 005255
Unit ID: 140599
Telephone: (912) 891-7000 Carnegie Class: Assoc/Pub-R-M
FAX Number: (912) 891-7010 Calendar System: Quarter
URL: www.moultrietech.edu
Established: 1964 Annual Undergrad Tuition & Fees (In-State): $3,375
Enrollment: 2,616 Coed
Affiliation or Control: State IRS Status: 501(c)3
Highest Offering: Associate Degree
Program: Occupational; Technical Emphasis
Accreditation: COE, MAC, RAD, SURGT

01 President .... Dr. Tina K. ANDERSON
05 Vice President for Academic Affairs .... Jim GLASS
11 VP of Administrative Services .... Ken STRICKLAND
32 Vice President of Student Services .... Leigh WALLACE
21 Vice President Operations .... David EVANS
12 Dean of Instruction Moultrie Campus .... Tina STRICKLAND
12 Dean of Instruction Moultrie (IDC) .... Jerry SMITH
12 Dean of Instruction Ashburn .... Brandi GIDDENS
12 Dean of Instruction Tifton Campus .... Becky RICHARDSON
06 Registrar .... Wendi TOSTENSON
32 Director Student Affairs .... Lisa GRIFFIN
15 Director Human Resources .... Michael HEARD
18 Chief Facilities/Physical Plant .... Steve PEACOCK
26 Director of Marketing .... Jana WIGGINS
37 Director Student Financial Aid .... Judi LOVVORN
09 Dir of Institutional Effectiveness .... Tavarez HOLSTON
36 Career Services Specialist .... Bridgett ADAMS

North Georgia College & State University (D)

82 College Circle, Dahlonega GA 30597-1001
County: Lumpkin FICE Identification: 001585
Unit ID: 140669
Telephone: (706) 864-1400 Carnegie Class: Master's L
FAX Number: (706) 864-1478 Calendar System: Semester
URL: www.northgeorgia.edu
Established: 1873 Annual Undergrad Tuition & Fees (In-State): $6,452
Enrollment: 5,912 Coed
Affiliation or Control: State IRS Status: 501(c)3
Highest Offering: Doctorate
Program: 2-Year Principally Bachelor's Creditable; Liberal Arts And General; Teacher Preparatory; Professional
Accreditation: SC, ADNUR, BUS, CACREP, NUR, PTA, TED

01 President .... Dr. Bonita JACOBS
11 Vice Pres of Exec Affairs .... Mr. Billy WELLS
05 Interim Vice Pres for Acad Affairs .... Dr. Patricia DONAT
10 Vice President Business and Finance .... Mr. Frank J. MCCONNELL
30 Vice Pres Institutional Advancement .... Dr. Andrew LEAVITT
32 Vice Pres Student Affs/Dean Stdnts .... Dr. John CLOWER
41 Athletic Director .... Ms. Lindsay REEVES
13 Chief Information Officer .... Dr. Bryson PAYNE
20 Interim Asst VP for Acad Affairs .... Dr. Richard OATES
20 Interim Assoc VP for Acad Affairs .... Dr. Terry MCLEOD
20 Interim Assoc VP for Acad Affairs .... Dr. Kathy SISK
07 Director of Undergrad Admissions .... Ms. Jennifer CHADWICK
07 Director Cadet Admissions .... Mr. Keith ANTONIA
92 Honors Program Director .... Dr. Stephen SMITH
06 Registrar .... Ms. Jill BRADY
25 Director of Grants & Contracts .... Ms. Kelley ROBERTS
37 Director of Student Financial Aid .... Ms. Jill RAYNER
58 Exec Director Regional Engagement .... Dr. Donna GESSELL
88 Exec Director Inst Effectiveness .... Dr. Denise YOUNG
09 Director Institutional Research .... Ms. Linda ROWLAND
08 Director of Library Services .... Ms. Shawn TONNER
51 Dir of Public Services/Cont Educ .... Ms. Jane O'GORMAN
49 Dean of Arts & Letters .... Dr. Christopher JESPERSEN
50 Dean Mike Cottrell Sch of Business .... Dr. Max BURNS
53 Dean of School of Education .... Dr. Bob MICHAEL
65 Dean Sch of Science & Health Prof .... Dr. Michael BODRI
18 Assoc Vice Pres for Facilities .... Mr. Jeffrey DAVIS
104 Director Center Global Engagement .... Dr. Dlynn ARMSTRONG-WILLIAMS
40 Manager of Bookstore .... Ms. Laurie DAVIS
15 Director Human Resources .... Ms. Beth ARBUTHNOT
96 Director of Materials Mangement .... Mr. Alan SIBERT
16 Associate VP for Administration .... Dr. Brenda FINDLEY
18 Director of Plant Operations .... Mr. Todd BERMANN
19 Director/Chief of Public Safety .... Mr. Michael F. STAPLETON
29 Director of Alumni Affairs .... Mr. Gerald LORD
30 Director of Development .... Mr. Jeffrey S. BOGAN
26 Director of University Relations .... Ms. Kate MAINE
35 Dean of Students .... Ms. Laura WHITAKER-LEA
20 Commandant of Cadets .... Col. Tom PALMER
36 Director of Career Services .... Ms. Dora DITCHFIELD
38 Director Student Counseling/Dev .... Dr. Simon CORDERY
39 Director of Residence Life .... Ms. Alyson PAUL
23 Director of Student Health Services .... Ms. Karen TOMLINSON

† Part of the University System of Georgia.

North Georgia Technical College (E)

PO Box 65, Clarkesville GA 30523-0065
County: Habersham FICE Identification: 005619
Unit ID: 140678
Telephone: (706) 754-7700 Carnegie Class: Assoc/Pub-R-M
FAX Number: (706) 754-7777 Calendar System: Semester
URL: www.northgatech.edu
Established: 1943 Annual Undergrad Tuition & Fees (In-State): $3,849
Enrollment: 2,642 Coed
Affiliation or Control: State IRS Status: 501(c)3
Highest Offering: Associate Degree
Program: Occupational; 2-Year Principally Bachelor's Creditable; Technical Emphasis
Accreditation: SC, ACFEI, MAC, MLTAD

01 President .... Steve DOUGHERTY
05 Vice President of Academic Affairs .... Rex BISHOP
35 Vice President for Student Affairs .... Dr. Michael KING
06 Registrar .... Caroline FRICK
07 Director of Admissions .... Amanda MITCHELL
10 Chief Business Officer .... Mark IVESTER
15 Director Personnel Services .... Marcia PEYTON
18 Chief Facilities/Physical Plant .... Michael BOYD
26 Chief Public Relations Officer .... Sandra MAUGHON
29 Director Alumni Relations .... Cynthia BROWN
32 Chief Student Life Officer .... Sherry SEAL
36 Director Job Placement .... Daniel GREGG
37 Director Student Financial Aid .... Kim KELLEY
38 Director Student Counseling .... Vacant
84 Director Enrollment Management .... Amanda MITCHELL
96 Director of Purchasing .... Darline CHURCH
09 Director of Institutional Research .... Vacant
46 Dir Institutional Effectiveness .... Janet HENDERSON
20 Dean of Academics .... Kathie IVESTER
20 Dean of Academics .... Dan PRESSLEY
20 Dean of Academics .... Mindy GLANDER

Oconee Fall Line Technical College-North Campus (F)

1189 Deepstep Road, Sandersville GA 31082-9337
County: Washington FICE Identification: 031555
Unit ID: 420431
Telephone: (478) 553-2050 Carnegie Class: Assoc/Pub-R-S
FAX Number: (478) 553-2118 Calendar System: Semester
URL: www.oftc.edu
Established: 1996 Annual Undergrad Tuition & Fees (In-State): $1,662
Enrollment: 1,028 Coed
Affiliation or Control: State IRS Status: 501(c)3
Highest Offering: Associate Degree
Program: Occupational
Accreditation: COE

01 President .... Dr. Lloyd HORADAN
05 Vice Pres Academic/Student Affs .... Ms. Erica HARDEN
11 Vice Pres Administrative Services .... Ms. Rosemary SELBY
30 Vice Pres Economic Development .... Ms. Leigh EVANS
32 Dean Student Affairs .... Ms. Johnnie EDGE
06 Registrar .... Ms. Geri CLEMENTS
07 Director of Admissions .... Mr. Raydor CONEWAY
49 Dean Arts & Sciences/Business Svcs .... Ms. Michele STRICKLAND
15 Director Human Resources .... Ms. Sharon VEAL
18 Director Facilities/Physical Plant .... Mr. Jim HARRISON
26 Exec Director Marketing .... Ms. Jennifer AHRENS
37 Financial Aid Director .... Ms. Betty YOUNG
28 Dir of Spec Populations/Stdnt Life .... Ms. Dessie HALL
96 Director of Purchasing .... Ms. Penny KITCHENS

Oconee Falls Line Technical College-South Campus (G)

560 Pinehill Road, Dublin GA 31021-1599
County: Laurens FICE Identification: 022795
Unit ID: 140076
Telephone: (478) 275-6589 Carnegie Class: Assoc/Pub-R-M
FAX Number: (478) 275-6642 Calendar System: Semester
URL: www.oftc.edu
Established: 1984 Annual Undergrad Tuition & Fees (In-State): $1,662
Enrollment: 1,817 Coed
Affiliation or Control: State IRS Status: 501(c)3
Highest Offering: Associate Degree
Program: Occupational; Technical Emphasis
Accreditation: COE, MAC, RAD

01 President .... Dr. Lloyd HORADAN
05 Provost South Campus .... Mrs. Beth CRUMPTON
09 Vice Pres Inst Effectiveness .... Dr. Katie DAVIS
32 Dean Student Affairs .... Ms. Wanda COTICCHIO
06 Assistant Registrar .... Ms. Amber COCHRAN
18 Director Facilities .... Mr. Ragan GREEN
12 Dean Little Ocmulgee Instr Ctr .... Vacant
30 Exec Dir Inst Advancement .... Mrs. Jenny SHUMAN
19 Director Safety & Security .... Mr. Rick SWANSON
36 Director of Career Development .... Mrs. Cecile MILLER
76 Dean Allied Health/Prof Svcs .... Ms. Tammy BAYTO
37 Asst Director Financial Aid .... Ms. Teresa CRAFTON
08 Director Library Services .... Ms. Wendi MORRIS

Ogeechee Technical College (H)

One Joe Kennedy Boulevard, Statesboro GA 30458-8049
County: Bulloch FICE Identification: 030300
Unit ID: 366465
Telephone: (912) 681-5500 Carnegie Class: Assoc/Pub-R-M
FAX Number: (912) 486-7704 Calendar System: Semester
URL: www.ogeecheetech.edu
Established: 1987 Annual Undergrad Tuition & Fees (In-State): $3,240
Enrollment: 2,821 Coed
Affiliation or Control: State IRS Status: 501(c)3
Highest Offering: Associate Degree
Program: Occupational; 2-Year Principally Bachelor's Creditable
Accreditation: COE, DA, DMS, FUSER, MAC, OPD, RAD, SURGT

01 President .... Dr. Dawn H. CARTEE

04 Exec Assistant to the President ..... Ms. Charlene PEED
05 Vice President for Academic Affairs ..... Dr. Charlene LAMAR
88 Vice President Economic Development ..... Ms. Lori DURDEN
88 VP Institutional Effectiveness ..... Ms. Dianne STEWART
32 Vice President Student Affairs ..... Mr. Ryan FOLEY
10 Vice President for Administration ..... Ms. Eyvonne HART
13 VP Technology & Institutional Supp ..... Mr. Jeff DAVIS
30 VP College Advancement ..... Ms. Beth MATHEWS
26 VP Community & College Relations ..... Mr. Barry TURNER
09 Director Inst Research & Planning ..... Ms. Brandy TAYLOR
88 Dean for Adult Education ..... Mr. Michael K. BURRELL
20 Dean for Academic Affairs ..... Mr. John GROOVER
20 Dean for Academic Affairs ..... Ms. Teresa ALLEN
20 Dean for Academic Affairs ..... Mr. Bill BARTON
88 Dir Community & Resource Dev ..... Ms. Kathleen KOSMOSKI
84 Director for Admissions ..... Ms. Laura SAUNDERS
06 Registrar ..... Ms. Michelle MEYER
37 Director for Financial Aid ..... Ms. Letrell THOMAS
21 Director for Accounting ..... Ms. Patsy POWELL
15 Director for Human Resources ..... Mr. Steve MILLER
40 Director for Auxiliary Services ..... Mr. J.J ALTMAN
18 Director for Plant Operations ..... Mr. Buddy SAPP
19 Director Campus Safety & Security ..... Mr. Jeff SMITH
08 Director for Library Services ..... Dr. Lynn FUTCH

Oglethorpe University (A)

4484 Peachtree Road, NE, Atlanta GA 30319-2797
County: DeKalb FICE Identification: 001586
Unit ID: 140696
Telephone: (404) 261-1441 Carnegie Class: Bac/A&S
FAX Number: (404) 364-8500 Calendar System: Semester
URL: www.oglethorpe.edu
Established: 1835 Annual Undergrad Tuition & Fees: $28,900
Enrollment: 1,158 Coed
Affiliation or Control: Independent Non-Profit IRS Status: 501(c)3
Highest Offering: Master's
Program: Liberal Arts And General; Teacher Preparatory; Business Emphasis
Accreditation: SC

01 President ..... Dr. Lawrence M. SCHALL
05 Provost ..... Dr. Denise VON HERRMANN
10 Vice Pres for Business & Finance ..... Mr. Michael D. HORAN
30 Vice Pres Devel & Alumni Relations ..... Mr. Peter A. ROONEY
84 Vice Pres for Enrollment Management ..... Ms. Lucy LEUSCH
32 VP Stdnt Affairs/Dean of Students ..... Ms. Michelle HALL
04 Exec Assistant to the President ..... Ms. Terri WILLIAMS
08 Librarian ..... Ms. Anne SALTER
06 Registrar ..... Ms. Gail MEIS
09 Director of Institutional Research ..... Ms. Janet H. MADDOX
26 Exec Dir Marketing/Public Relations ..... Vacant
41 Interim Athletic Director ..... Mr. Jay GARDINER
37 Director of Financial Aid ..... Ms. Meg MCGINNISS
39 Director of Residence Life ..... Mr. Danny GLASSMAN
21 Director of Finance/Controller ..... Ms. Amy RENTENBACH
91 Director Administrative Computing ..... Ms. Joanne BOSSERT
27 Chief Information Officer ..... Mr. Cole MADDOX
29 Director of Alumni Relations ..... Ms. Barbara HENRY
36 Director of Career Counseling ..... Ms. Caroline WEIMAR
44 Director of Development Operations ..... Mr. John CARR
15 Director Human Resources ..... Mr. Wayne PHIPPS
55 Director Evening Degree Program ..... Ms. Lisa LITTLEFIELD
31 Dir Center for Civic Engagement ..... Ms. Tamara NASH
18 Director Facilities/Physical Plant ..... Mr. Walter HALL
40 Bookstore Manager ..... Mr. Charles M. WINGO

Okefenokee Technical College (B)

1701 Carswell Avenue, Waycross GA 31503-4016
County: Ware FICE Identification: 005511
Unit ID: 248776
Telephone: (912) 287-6584 Carnegie Class: Assoc/Pub-R-M
FAX Number: (912) 287-4865 Calendar System: Quarter
URL: www.okefenokeetech.edu
Established: 1965 Annual Undergrad Tuition & Fees (In-State): $2,105
Enrollment: 1,680 Coed
Affiliation or Control: State IRS Status: 501(c)3
Highest Offering: Associate Degree
Program: Occupational; Technical Emphasis
Accreditation: SC, COE, MAC, MLTAD, RAD, SURGT

01 President ..... Dr. Gail THAXTON
05 Int Vice Pres for Academic Affairs ..... Ms. Danita CANNON
11 VP of Administrative Services ..... Ms. Pamela FARR
46 Vice Pres for Economic Development ..... Mr. Andy BRANNEN
32 Vice President for Student Affairs ..... Ms. Danita CANNON
06 Registrar ..... Ms. Tara EICHFIELD
26 Public Relations/Information Dir ..... Ms. Cindy TANNER
18 Facilities Director ..... Mr. Chad BOYETT
36 Career Services Director ..... Mr. Charlie GIBSON
37 Director Student Financial Aid ..... Ms. Angie WILSON
09 Institutional Effectiveness Dir ..... Ms. Carol SHUGART
07 Director of Admissions ..... Mr. Neal MURPHY
15 Human Resources Coordinator ..... Ms. Cynthia LINDER
30 Coord of Resource Development ..... Ms. Cindy TANNER

Paine College (C)

1235 15th Street, Augusta GA 30901-3182
County: Richmond FICE Identification: 001587
Unit ID: 140720
Telephone: (706) 821-8200 Carnegie Class: Bac/Diverse
FAX Number: (706) 821-8373 Calendar System: Semester
URL: www.paine.edu
Established: 1882 Annual Undergrad Tuition & Fees: $12,502
Enrollment: 925 Coed
Affiliation or Control: Multiple Protestant Denominations IRS Status: 501(c)3
Highest Offering: Baccalaureate
Program: Liberal Arts And General; Teacher Preparatory; Professional
Accreditation: SC, ACBSP, TED

01 President ..... Dr. George C. BRADLEY
05 Provost and VP of Academic Affairs ..... Dr. Marcus D. TILLERY
49 Dean School of Arts and Sciences ..... Vacant
107 Dean School of Professional Studies ..... Vacant
10 VP of Admin & Fiscal Affairs ..... Mr. LeRoy SUMMERS
30 VP of Institutional Advancement ..... Mr. Brandon BROWN
32 VP/Dean of Student Affairs ..... Dr. Tina CARDENAS
04 Executive Asst to the President ..... Dr. Cheryl EVANS JONES
45 Dir Planning/Eval & Title III Coord ..... Dr. Cheryl EVANS JONES
88 Special Assistant to the President ..... Dr. Walter C. HOWARD
42 Campus Pastor ..... Dr. Luther FELDER
44 Asst VP Institutional Advancement ..... Ms. Frances WIMBERLY
20 Interim Assoc VP of Acad Affairs ..... Dr. Tina MARSHALL-BRADLEY
39 Director of Residence Life ..... Mr. LeMarcus J. HALL
21 Controller ..... Mrs. Burshunda HARDEN
88 Assistant Controller ..... Mrs. Melissa EVANS HALL
18 Maintenance Supervisor ..... Mr. Jason DENNIS
14 Dir of Information Technology Svcs ..... Mr. Michael HICKS
09 Director of Institutional Research ..... Mrs. Alice M. SIMPKINS
29 Director of Alumni Relations ..... Mrs. Mildred KENDRICK
26 Dir of Communications & Marketing ..... Ms. Natasha CARTER
08 Dir of Library/Learning Res Ctr ..... Mrs. Lyn DENNISON
06 Registrar ..... Ms. Castine RHOADES WILLIAMS
25 Director of Sponsored Programs ..... Mr. Geno CLARK
41 Athletics Director ..... Mr. Timothy DUNCAN
38 Director Counseling Center ..... Ms. Tiffaney WILLIAMS
36 Director of Career Services ..... Mrs. Deloris CROOM
23 College Nurse ..... Ms. Harriett S. JONES
07 Director of Admissions ..... Mr. Joseph TINSLEY
19 Chief of Campus Safety ..... Mr. James L. REID
40 Manager of The Lion's Shop ..... Ms. Antoinette DAWKINS
37 Sr Dir Financial Aid/Enroll Mgmt ..... Ms. Gerri BOGAN
15 Human Resource/Payroll Manager ..... Mrs. Rosalyn TUCKER
35 Director of Student Activities ..... Ms. Victoria SNYDER
106 Dean Online and Blended Programs ..... Mr. Andre FARLEY
96 Junior Buyer ..... Mr. Curtis WHITE
105 Website Designer ..... Mr. Kevin O. WILSON

Piedmont College (D)

PO Box 10, Demorest GA 30535-0010
County: Habersham FICE Identification: 001588
Unit ID: 140818
Telephone: (706) 778-3000 Carnegie Class: Master's L
FAX Number: (706) 776-0701 Calendar System: Semester
URL: www.piedmont.edu
Established: 1897 Annual Undergrad Tuition & Fees: $19,000
Enrollment: 2,676 Coed
Affiliation or Control: Christian Churches And Churches of Christ IRS Status: 501(c)3
Highest Offering: Doctorate
Program: Liberal Arts And General; Teacher Preparatory
Accreditation: SC, ACBSP, NUR

01 President ..... Dr. Danny P. HOLLINGSWORTH
05 Provost & VP Academic Affairs ..... Dr. James MELLICHAMP
11 Asst VP for Administrative Services ..... Mr. Parks MILLER
10 Asst VP Finance/Human Resources ..... Ms. Margie MEANS
12 Vice President Athens Campus ..... Dr. Mel PALMER
09 Asc VP Acad Affs/Plng/Dir Inst Rsch ..... Dr. Kenneth E. MELICHAR
30 Co-Dir Institutional Advancement ..... Ms. Brandy AYCOCK
30 Co-Dir Institutional Advancement ..... Mr. Justin SCALI
04 Assistant to the President ..... Ms. Debbie ZIMMERMAN
04 Assistant to the President ..... Ms. Kristen GRAY
32 Dean Student Affairs ..... Mr. Andrew B. DAVIS
42 Chaplain/Church Relations ..... Rev Dr. Ashley CLEERE
07 Director Graduate Admissions ..... Mr. Anthony COX
06 Registrar ..... Ms. Linda WOFFORD
08 College Librarian ..... Mr. Robert GLASS, JR.
37 Director of Financial Aid ..... Mr. David MCMILLION
07 Director of Admissions ..... Ms. Cindy PETERSON
13 Director Information Technology ..... Dr. Shahryar HEYDARI
15 Human Resources Specialist ..... Mr. Mark HARMON
26 Director of Public Relations ..... Mr. David E. PRICE
41 Dir of Intercollegiate Athletics ..... Mr. John L. DZIK
21 Compliance & Treasurery Officer ..... Ms. Leesa P. ANDERSON
36 Director Counseling/Career Services ..... Dr. Kel Lee CUTRELL
19 Director Security/Campus Police ..... Mr. Richard D. MARTIN
66 Dean School of Nursing/Health Sci ..... Dr. Linda SCOTT
50 Dean School of Business Admin ..... Dr. John MISNER
49 Dean School of Arts & Sciences ..... Dr. Steven NIMMO
53 Int Dean School of Education ..... Dr. J. Robert CUMMINGS
58 Dean of Graduate Studies ..... Dr. Marilyn BERRONG

Point University (E)

2605 Ben Hill Road, East Point GA 30344-9989
County: Fulton FICE Identification: 001547
Unit ID: 138868
Telephone: (404) 761-8861 Carnegie Class: Bac/Diverse
FAX Number: (404) 669-2024 Calendar System: Semester
URL: www.point.edu
Established: 1937 Annual Undergrad Tuition & Fees: $16,336
Enrollment: 1,046 Coed
Affiliation or Control: Christian Churches And Churches of Christ IRS Status: 501(c)3
Highest Offering: Baccalaureate
Program: 2-Year Principally Bachelor's Creditable; Liberal Arts And General; Teacher Preparatory; Religious Emphasis
Accreditation: SC, TED

01 President ..... Mr. Dean C. COLLINS
05 Chief Academic Officer ..... Dr. W. Darryl HARRISON
49 Vice Pres for Academic Affairs ..... Dr. Kimberly C. MACENCZAK
107 Vice Pres for Adult & Prof Studies ..... Dr. W. Darryl HARRISON
09 Vice Pres for Inst Effectiveness ..... Dr. Dennis E. GLENN
84 Vice Pres for Enrollment Management ..... Ms. Stacy BARTLETT
10 Vice Pres for Admin and CFO ..... Dr. Jeffrey A. HAVERLY
32 Vice Pres for Student Development ..... Mr. Samuel (Wye) W. HUXFORD
30 Vice President for Advancement ..... Ms. Emma W. MORRIS
41 Athletic Director ..... Mr. Kevin PORTER
08 Library Director ..... Mr. Michael L. BAIN
84 Asst VP for A&P Studies - Access ..... Ms. Carolyn COOK
07 Director of Admission ..... Ms. Tiffany SCHOENHOFF
06 Registrar ..... Mrs. Lisa SELLERS
37 Director of Financial Aid ..... Ms. Anna ENGLISH
21 Controller ..... Ms. Donna W. LANKFORD
18 Dir of Facilities and Maintenance ..... Mr. Jim ALDRIDGE
13 Director of Information Technology ..... Vacant
88 Chancellor ..... Dr. R. Edwin GROOVER
44 Director of Development ..... Vacant
26 Director of Communications ..... Ms. Sarah G. HUXFORD
29 Director of Alumni Relations ..... Ms. Pam ROSS

† Formerly Atlanta Christian College

Reinhardt University (F)

7300 Reinhardt Circle, Waleska GA 30183-2981
County: Cherokee FICE Identification: 001589
Unit ID: 140872
Telephone: (770) 720-5600 Carnegie Class: Bac/Diverse
FAX Number: (770) 720-5602 Calendar System: Semester
URL: www.reinhardt.edu
Established: 1883 Annual Undergrad Tuition & Fees: $17,670
Enrollment: 1,219 Coed
Affiliation or Control: United Methodist IRS Status: 501(c)3
Highest Offering: Master's
Program: Liberal Arts And General
Accreditation: SC, MUS

01 President ..... Dr. J. Thomas ISHERWOOD
04 Executive Assistant to President ..... Mrs. Bonnie H. DEBORD
05 VP & Dean for Academic Affairs ..... Dr. Robert L. DRISCOLL
10 Vice Pres Finance & Administration ..... Mr. Robert G. MCKINNON
30 VP Inst Advance/External Affairs ..... Mrs. JoEllen B. WILSON
32 VP Student Affairs/Dean of Students ..... Dr. Roger R. LEE
20 Assoc VP for Academic Affairs ..... Mrs. Margaret J. O'CONNOR
58 Assoc Vice Pres Graduate Studies ..... Dr. Margaret M. MORLIER
101 Asst Secretary Board of Trustees ..... Mrs. Bonnie H. DEBORD
18 Exec Director of Physical Plant ..... Mr. John W. YOUNG
26 Exec Dir Marketing/Communications ..... Mrs. Marsha S. WHITE
13 Exec Dir & CIO for Information Tech ..... Mrs. Virginia R. TOMLINSON
88 Exec Director of Funk Heritage Ctr ..... Dr. Joseph H. KITCHENS
07 Director of Admissions ..... Ms. Julie C. FLEMING
06 Registrar ..... Ms. Janet M. RODNING
09 Dir Instnl Research/Effectiveness ..... Ms. Cheryl A. NORRIS
08 Director of Library ..... Mr. Michael MARTINEZ
19 Director of Public Safety ..... Ms. Sherry N. CORNETT
29 Director of Alumni ..... Mrs. Jennifer W. MATTHEWS
42 University Chaplain ..... Rev. Leigh S. MARTIN
21 Controller ..... Mr. Peter J. BROMSTAD
37 Director Student Financial Aid ..... Mrs. Angie D. HARLOWE
41 Director of Athletics ..... Mr. William C. POPP
16 Director Human Resources ..... Mrs. Sandy B. MILTON
39 Director Residence Life ..... Ms. Nicole T. WESTON
23 Campus Nurse ..... Mrs. Allison STARTUP
35 Asst Dean of Students/Dir Stdnt Act ..... Dr. Walter P. MAY
38 Director of Counseling Svcs ..... Mr. Derek L. STRUCHTEMEYER
88 Dir Center for Student Success ..... Dr. Catherine B. EMANUEL
36 Director of Career Services ..... Mrs. Peggy C. FEEHERY
40 Bookstore Manager ..... Ms. Teresa GREGORY
105 Web Communication Manager ..... Mr. John C. PETTIBONE
106 Coordinator Online Education ..... Dr. Thomas M. REED
49 Dean School of Arts & Humanities ..... Dr. Arthur W. GLOWKA
81 Dean School of Maths & Sciences ..... Dr. Bill J. DEANGELIS
50 Int Dean McCamish School Business ..... Dr. Donald D. WILSON, JR.
53 Dean Price School of Education ..... Dr. James L. CURRY, JR.
64 Int Dean School of Music ..... Dr. Dennis K. MCINTIRE

Richmont Graduate University (G)

2055 Mt. Paran Road, NW, Atlanta GA 30327-2921
County: Fulton FICE Identification: 033554
Unit ID: 441104
Telephone: (404) 233-3949 Carnegie Class: Spec/Health
FAX Number: (404) 239-9460 Calendar System: Semester
URL: www.richmont.edu
Established: 1973 Annual Graduate Tuition & Fees: $13,200
Enrollment: 258 Coed
Affiliation or Control: Independent Non-Profit IRS Status: 501(c)3
Highest Offering: Master's; No Undergraduates
Program: Professional
Accreditation: SC

01 President ... Dr. C. Jeffrey TERRELL
03 Vice Pres/Chair of Integration ... Dr. Gary W. MOON
30 Vice President for Advancement ... Mr. Bob RODGERS, JR.
04 Assistant to the President ... Ms. Jennifer COOPER
05 Academic Dean ... Dr. Philip A. COYLE
10 Chief Financial Officer ... Mr. William J. MUELLER

Sanford-Brown College (A)

1140 Hammond Drive NE, Suite A 1150,
Atlanta GA 30328
County: Fulton FICE Identification: 021160
Unit ID: 420495
Telephone: (770) 576-4543 Carnegie Class: Not Classified
FAX Number: (773) 601-3881 Calendar System: Other
URL: www.sanfordbrown.edu/Atlanta
Established: N/A Annual Undergrad Tuition & Fees: $11,300
Enrollment: 1,605 Coed
Affiliation or Control: Proprietary IRS Status: Proprietary
Highest Offering: Associate Degree
Program: Occupational
Accreditation: ACICS, DMS, MAC

01 Campus President ... Mr. Chris KEY

Savannah College of Art and Design (B)

342 Bull Street, PO Box 3146, Savannah GA 31402-6263
County: Chatham FICE Identification: 021415
Unit ID: 140951
Telephone: (912) 525-5000 Carnegie Class: Spec/Arts
FAX Number: (912) 525-6263 Calendar System: Quarter
URL: www.scad.edu
Established: 1978 Annual Undergrad Tuition & Fees: $30,510
Enrollment: 10,461 Coed
Affiliation or Control: Independent Non-Profit IRS Status: 501(c)3
Highest Offering: Master's
Program: Fine Arts Emphasis
Accreditation: SC, CIDA

01 President ... Mrs. Paula S. WALLACE
03 COO - SCAD Group Inc. ... Mr. Brian F. MURPHY
84 Sr VP Marketing & Enrollment Mgmt ... Ms. Pamela RHAME
46 Sr Vice Pres College Resources ... Mr. Glenn E. WALLACE, JR.
05 Chief Academic Officer ... Mr. Tom FISCHER
10 Vice President for Business/Finance ... Mr. David LEOPARD
20 VP for Academic Services ... Dr. Gokhan OZAYSIN
12 Vice President for SCAD Atlanta ... Mr. Pharris D. (PJ) JOHNSON
12 Assoc VP for SCAD Hong Kong ... Mr. Grant PREISSER
13 VP for Educational Technology ... Mr. Andrew FULP
32 Vice President for Student Success ... Dr. Philip ALLETTO
15 Vice President for Human Resources ... Ms. Lesley HANAK
13 Asst VP for IM&T ... Mr. Harley LINGERFELT
106 Assistant VP for eLearning ... Mr. Darrell NAYLOR-JOHNSON
35 Dean of Students ... Mr. David PUGH
26 Director of Media Relations ... Ms. Sunny NELSON
29 Assoc VP Alumni & Career Success ... Ms. Alison H. DAVIS
08 Dean of Library/Academic Services ... Vacant
18 Exec Dir for Physical Resources ... Mr. John HOUSLEY
37 Director of Financial Aid ... Ms. Brenda CLARK
06 Registrar ... Ms. Margo MCLEOD
96 Director Procurement/Payment Svcs ... Ms. Mary GRANT
07 Executive Director of Admission ... Ms. Sara MALBROUGH
30 Exec Dir of Inst Advancement ... Ms. McLean HOOFF
19 Director of College Security ... Mr. Jeff SMITH
41 Athletics Director ... Mr. Steve LARSON
38 Dir Counseling/Student Support Svc ... Dr. Tamara KNAPP-GROSZ
20 Dean of Undergraduate Studies ... Ms. Beth GASKIN
58 Dean of Graduate Studies ... Dr. Edward DUPUY
88 Dean of School of Building Arts ... Mr. Herbert BRITO
88 Dean of School Communication Arts ... Mr. John LOWE
88 Dean of School of Design ... Mr. Victor ERMOLI
88 Dn Sch Film/Dig Media/PerformingArt ... Mr. Peter WEISHAR
57 Dean of School of Fine Arts ... Mr. Steve BLISS
49 Dean of School of Liberal Arts ... Mr. Robert EISINGER
88 Dean School of Fashion ... Mr. Michael FINK
88 Dean School of Foundation Studies ... Ms. Maureen GARVIN

Savannah State University (C)

3219 College Street, Savannah GA 31404-5308
County: Chatham FICE Identification: 001590
Unit ID: 140960
Telephone: (912) 358-4778 Carnegie Class: Bac/A&S
FAX Number: (912) 356-2256 Calendar System: Semester
URL: www.savannahstate.edu
Established: 1890 Annual Undergrad Tuition & Fees (In-State): $6,032
Enrollment: 4,080 Coed
Affiliation or Control: State IRS Status: 501(c)3
Highest Offering: Master's
Program: Liberal Arts And General
Accreditation: SC, BUS, ENGT, JOUR, SPAA, SW

01 Interim President ... Dr. Cheryl DOZIER
05 Interim Vice Pres Academic Affairs ... Dr. Mostafa SARHAN
10 Vice Pres Business & Finance ... Mr. Edward B. JOLLEY, JR.
32 Vice President Student Affairs ... Dr. Irvin CLARK
30 Vice President Advancement ... Vacant
20 Asst Vice Pres Academic Affairs ... Dr. Larry STOKES
84 Dir Enrollment Services/Registrar ... Mr. Timothy CRANFORD
07 Asst Director of Admissions ... Ms. Carol DOLAN
15 Director Human Resources ... Dr. Sandra M. BEST
08 Librarian ... Mrs. MaryJo FAYOYIN
26 Director Communications ... Ms. Loretta HEYWARD
27 Chief Information Officer ... Mr. Jeff DELANEY
18 Director Facilities/Physical Plant ... Mr. Ervin OGDEN
09 Dir Inst Resrch/Planning/Assessment ... Dr. Michael G. CROW
29 Director Alumni Relations ... Ms. Barbara MYERS
37 Director Financial Aid ... Mrs. Adrienne BROWN
19 Chief of Police ... Mr. Creighton ROBERTS
35 Director of Student Development ... Ms. Jacqueline AWE
50 Asst Dean College of Business ... Dr. Reginald LESEANE
83 Interim Dean Col Lib Arts/Soc Sci ... Dr. Michael SCHROEDER
72 Dean Col Science & Technology ... Dr. Derrek B. DUNN

† Part of the University System of Georgia.

Savannah Technical College (D)

5717 White Bluff Road, Savannah GA 31405-5521
County: Chatham FICE Identification: 005618
Unit ID: 140942
Telephone: (912) 443-5700 Carnegie Class: Assoc/Pub-R-M
FAX Number: (912) 443-5705 Calendar System: Quarter
URL: www.savannahtech.edu
Established: 1967 Annual Undergrad Tuition & Fees (In-State): $3,333
Enrollment: 5,777 Coed
Affiliation or Control: State IRS Status: 501(c)3
Highest Offering: Associate Degree
Program: Occupational; 2-Year Principally Bachelor's Creditable; Technical Emphasis
Accreditation: SC, ACFEI, DA, DH, ENGT, MAC, PNUR, SURGT

01 President ... Dr. Kathy S. LOVE
05 Vice President Academic Affairs ... Mr. Jim WHEELESS
11 Vice Pres Administrative Services ... Ms. Sue Z. TURNER
32 Vice President Student Affairs ... Mr. Jim NORDONE
45 Vice President Economic Development ... Dr. Ken BOYD
84 Exec Director Enroll Mgmt/Marketing ... Ms. Gail EUBANKS
07 Director of Admissions ... Ms. Gwendolyn MOORE
06 Registrar ... Ms. Regina THOMAS-WILLIAMS
18 Director Facilities ... Mr. Ken COOK
37 Director of Financial Aid ... Ms. Faith ANDERSON
38 Director Student Support Services ... Ms. Laurie HERRINGTON
15 Director Human Resources ... Ms. Melissa BANKS
12 Campus Dean Liberty Campus ... Ms. Terric O. SELLERS
12 Campus Dean Effingham Campus ... Mr. Robert SOLOMON
96 Purchasing Manager ... Mr. Kevin CHIEVES
88 Dean Public Services ... Dr. Gayle TREMBLE
76 Dean Allied Health ... Mr. Larry ROBERSON
75 Dean Industrial Technology ... Mr. Tal LOOS
50 Dean Business Technology ... Ms. Carol PAULK
97 Dean General Studies ... Mr. Al CUNNINGHAM

Shorter University (E)

315 Shorter Avenue, Rome GA 30165-4298
County: Floyd FICE Identification: 001591
Unit ID: 140988
Telephone: (706) 291-2121 Carnegie Class: Bac/A&S
FAX Number: (706) 236-1515 Calendar System: Semester
URL: www.shorter.edu
Established: 1873 Annual Undergrad Tuition & Fees: $17,870
Enrollment: 3,775 Coed
Affiliation or Control: Baptist IRS Status: 501(c)3
Highest Offering: Master's
Program: Liberal Arts And General; Teacher Preparatory; Professional
Accreditation: SC, MUS

01 President ... Dr. Donald V. DOWLESS
05 Provost ... Dr. Craig L. SHULL
11 VP for Administrative Affairs ... Vacant
10 Vice President for Finance & CFO ... Mrs. Stephanie R. OWENS
84 Vice Pres Enrollment Management ... Dr. John D. HEAD
30 Actg Vice Pres Development/Alumni ... Mrs. Suzanne SCOTT
32 VP Student Affairs/Dean of Students ... Dr. Debra FAUST
26 Vice President for Public Relations ... Mrs. Dawn C. TOLBERT
06 Registrar ... Mrs. Melissa TARRANT
29 Director of Alumni Relations ... Mr. Mark TUNNELL
35 Director of Student Activities ... Ms. Emily W. MESSER
08 Director of Libraries ... Vacant
09 Director of Inst Planning/Research ... Dr. Patricia A. DEWITT
90 Director of Academic Computing ... Mr. Anthony J. NICHOLS
56 Director Special Programs ... Vacant
13 Director of Information Technology ... Mr. Ryan HAYLOCK
18 Director of Facilities Management ... Mr. Dickerson E. TAYLOR
40 Bookstore Manager ... Ms. Jasmine RAGLAND
38 Director of Student Support Svcs ... Dr. Emily DERRICK
23 Director of Health Services ... Mrs. Mary SHOTWELL SMITH
41 Athletic Director ... Mr. Bill PETERSON
57 Dean School of the Arts ... Dr. Alan B. WINGARD
50 Dean College of Business ... Dr. Robert H. DARVILLE
49 Dean School of Liberal Arts ... Dr. Sabrena PARTON
73 Chair Dept of Christian Studies ... Dr. John CONNELL
53 Chair Department of Education ... Dr. Gary ROSS
79 Chair Department of Humanities ... Dr. Benjamin MCFRY
77 Chair Dept of Math/Computer Science ... Dr. Richard E. COWAN
60 Chair Dept of Communication Arts ... Dr. Dana HALL
81 Dean of Sciences & Mathematics ... Dr. Craig ALLEE
53 Dean School of Education ... Dr. Sandra LESLIE
56 Dean Coll Adult/Professional Pgms ... Dr. Barbara FINN
66 Dean School of Nursing ... Dr. Vanice W. ROBERTS
37 Director of Financial Aid ... Ms. Tara JONES
15 Director Human Resources ... Vacant
42 Campus Minister ... Rev. David E. ROLAND
44 Director of Annual Giving ... Mrs. Suzanne W. SCOTT
07 Director of Admissions ... Mr. Patrick MCELHANEY
102 Director of Foundation Relations ... Ms. Stephanie GRAVES
88 Chair Dept Natural Sciences ... Ms. Lisa M. KEITH
83 Chr Dpt Hist/Poli Sci/Psych/Soclgy ... Dr. Jill BORCHERT
39 Dir Residence Life/Student Conduct ... Mr. Joshua ARNOLD
104 Director of International Programs ... Ms. Laura MCRANEY
106 Director of Online Programs ... Mr. Sean BUTCHER

South Georgia College (F)

100 W College Park Drive, Douglas GA 31533-5098
County: Coffee FICE Identification: 001592
Unit ID: 140997
Telephone: (912) 260-4394 Carnegie Class: Assoc/Pub-R-S
FAX Number: (912) 260-4454 Calendar System: Semester
URL: www.sgc.edu
Established: 1906 Annual Undergrad Tuition & Fees (In-State): $3,500
Enrollment: 2,212 Coed
Affiliation or Control: State IRS Status: 501(c)3
Highest Offering: Associate Degree
Program: 2-Year Principally Bachelor's Creditable
Accreditation: SC, ADNUR

01 President ... Dr. Virginia M. CARSON
05 Vice Pres Academic Affairs ... Dr. Carl MCDONALD
32 Vice President for Student Success ... Mr. Wes S. BROWN
10 Vice President Business Affairs ... Ms. Wanda E. LLOYD
30 Dir Community/Foundation Relations ... Ms. Walda KIGHT
08 Librarian ... Ms. Jacqueline VICKERS
06 Registrar ... Dr. Randy BRASWELL
84 Exec Dir Enrollment/Information ... Mr. Wes S. BROWN
37 Director Financial Aid ... Ms. Becky RUMKER
15 Director Human Resources ... Mr. Keith NEWELL
18 Chief Facilities/Phys Plant ... Mr. Jim FOLDS
07 Director of Admissions ... Dr. Randy BRASWELL
12 Dir of Entry Programs and Planning ... Ms. Valerie WEBSTER
72 Director of Technology ... Ms. Lena HELMBRECHT
40 Director of Bookstore ... Ms. Daphne FRENCH
21 Associate Business Officer ... Ms. Peggy DOBBS
04 Assistant to the President ... Vacant
41 Athletic Director ... Mr. Robert BRUNEL
09 Dir of Institutional Effectiveness ... Ms. Danielle BUEHRER
39 Director of Residence Life ... Mr. Andy JOHNSON
35 Director of Student Life ... Ms. Sue MILLER

† Part of the University System of Georgia.

South Georgia Technical College (G)

900 South Georgia Tech Parkway,
Americus GA 31709-8167
County: Sumter FICE Identification: 005617
Unit ID: 141006
Telephone: (229) 931-2394 Carnegie Class: Assoc/Pub-R-M
FAX Number: (229) 931-2924 Calendar System: Quarter
URL: www.southgatech.edu
Established: 1948 Annual Undergrad Tuition & Fees (In-State): $3,873
Enrollment: 4,400 Coed
Affiliation or Control: State IRS Status: 501(c)3
Highest Offering: Associate Degree
Program: Occupational; Technical Emphasis
Accreditation: @SC, COE

01 President ... Sparky REEVES
11 Vice Pres Administrative Services ... Janice DAVIS
10 Vice Pres Business & Industry Svcs ... Wally SUMMERS
05 Vice President for Academic Affairs ... Robbie LATIMORE
12 Vice President Crisp County Center ... John WATFORD
09 Vice Pres of Institutional Support ... Karen J. WERLING
04 Special Assistant to the President ... Don SMITH
20 Dean of Instruction ... David KUIPERS
20 Dean of Instruction ... Raymond HOLT
26 Dir of Resource Devel & Marketing ... Su Ann BIRD
13 Technology Director ... Wray SKIPPER
37 Director of Financial Aid ... Michael WRIGHT
15 Director Personnel Services ... Sandy LARSON
36 Director of Career Services ... Cynthia CARTER
32 Director of Campus Life ... Brandan HARRELL
21 Director of Accounting ... Lea COE
88 Director of Administrative Services ... Mark BROOKS
55 Director of Instruction-Evening ... Lemond HALL
06 Registrar ... Julie PARTAIN
08 Librarian ... Jerry STOVALL
07 Director of Admissions ... Whitney CRISP
28 Director of Diversity ... Sandy LARSON
29 Director Alumni Relations ... SuAnn BIRD
35 Director Student Affairs ... Don SMITH
38 Director Student Counseling ... Cynthia CARTER
84 Director Enrollment Management ... Whitney CRISP
18 Chief Facilities/Physical Plant ... Jeff WISEMAN
30 Chief Development ... Wally SUMMERS
96 Purchasing Agent ... Gail CLARY

South University (H)

709 Mall Boulevard, Savannah GA 31406-4881
County: Chatham FICE Identification: 013039
Unit ID: 139579
Telephone: (912) 201-8000 Carnegie Class: Master's L
FAX Number: (912) 201-8070 Calendar System: Quarter
URL: www.southuniversity.edu

Established: 1899 Annual Undergrad Tuition & Fees: $15,285
Enrollment: 17,881 Coed
Affiliation or Control: Proprietary IRS Status: Proprietary
Highest Offering: Doctorate
Program: 2-Year Principally Bachelor's Creditable; Liberal Arts And General; Professional; Business Emphasis
Accreditation: **SC**, AA, ARCPA, MAC, NURSE, PHAR, PTAA

0 Chancellor .... Mr. John T. SOUTH, III
01 Campus President Savannah .... Mr. Todd CELLINI
12 President West Palm Beach .... Mr. David MCGUIRE
12 President Montgomery .... Mr. Victor K. BIEBIGHAUSER
12 President Columbia .... Mr. Brad KAUFFMAN
05 Vice Chanc Academic Affairs .... Dr. Steven K. YOHO
15 Assoc Chanc of Human Resources .... Ms. Trisha EARLS
13 Assoc Chanc Information Technology .... Mr. James FREYBURGER
10 Assoc Chancellor of Finance .... Ms. Katrina WIGREN
26 Assoc Chancellor Marketing .... Mr. Bruce CHONG
07 Assoc Chancellor Admissions .... Mr. Matthew MILLS
06 Registrar .... Mr. Bryan LOGIE
20 Dean of Academic Affairs .... Ms. Becky HAYES
17 Dean College of Health Professions .... Dr. A. William PAULSEN
37 Director of Student Financial Aid .... Ms. Tressa BRUSH
67 Dean School of Pharmacy .... Dr. James E. WYNN
32 Asst Dean Student Affairs/Pharmacy .... Ms. Gabriella FISCHER
08 Head Librarian .... Ms. Valerie E. YAUGHN
27 Asst Chancellor Communications .... Ms. Heather R. ASKEW
36 Director of Career Services .... Mr. Don HOLLAND
19 Director of Security .... Mr. Bill LYGHT

Southeastern Technical College (A)

3001 E First Street, Vidalia GA 30474-8817
County: Toombs FICE Identification: 030665
Unit ID: 368911
Telephone: (912) 538-3100 Carnegie Class: Assoc/Pub-R-S
FAX Number: (912) 538-3156 Calendar System: Semester
URL: www.southeasterntech.edu
Established: 1989 Annual Undergrad Tuition & Fees (In-State): $2,172
Enrollment: 1,982 Coed
Affiliation or Control: State IRS Status: 501(c)3
Highest Offering: Associate Degree
Program: Occupational; Technical Emphasis
Accreditation: **SC**, DH, MAC, MLTAD, RAD, SURGT

01 President .... Dr. Cathryn MITCHELL
03 Provost .... Mr. Larry CALHOUN
05 Vice Pres Academic Affairs .... Ms. Teresa COLEMAN
11 Vice Pres Administrative Services .... Ms. Denise POWELL
10 Vice President Fiscal Affairs .... Vacant
32 Vice President Student Affairs .... Dr. Barry DOTSON
84 Director Enrollment Services .... Mr. Brad HART
06 Registrar .... Ms. Karen VEREEN
37 Director Financial Aid .... Mr. Mitchell FAGLER
36 Director Job Placement .... Mr. Lance HELMS
103 Special Populations Coordinator .... Ms. Helen THOMAS
88 Fatherhood Initiative Coordinator .... Vacant
40 Bookstore Manager .... Ms. Brooke SALTER

Southern Crescent Technical College (B)

501 Varsity Road, Griffin GA 30223-2042
County: Spalding FICE Identification: 005621
Unit ID: 139986
Telephone: (770) 228-7348 Carnegie Class: Assoc/Pub-S-MC
FAX Number: (770) 229-3227 Calendar System: Quarter
URL: www.sctech.edu
Established: 1963 Annual Undergrad Tuition & Fees (In-State): $3,792
Enrollment: 6,227 Coed
Affiliation or Control: State IRS Status: 501(c)3
Highest Offering: Associate Degree
Program: Occupational; 2-Year Principally Bachelor's Creditable; Technical Emphasis
Accreditation: **SC**, DA, MAC, RAD, SURGT

01 Interim President .... Dr. Randall PETERS
05 Vice Pres for Academic Affairs .... Ms. Dawn HODGES
32 Vice Pres for Student Affairs .... Ms. Xenia JOHNS
31 Vice Pres for Economic Development .... Mr. Mark ANDREWS
11 Vice Pres Administrative Services .... Ms. Miriam JAMES
18 Vice Pres Facilities/Operations .... Mr. Jim BROWN
30 Vice President Advancement .... Ms. Barbara Jo COOK
09 Exec Dir Institutional Effective .... Ms. Christi ELLINGTON
08 Director of Library Services .... Ms. Kate WILLIAMS
06 Registrar .... Ms. Kathlyn BURDEN
26 Dir Marketing & Public Relations .... Ms. Anna TAYLOR
88 Dir of Administrative Services .... Ms. Gina BYRD
20 Dean of Academic Affairs .... Ms. Rebecca JOHNSON
20 Dean of Academic Affairs .... Dr. John POPE
20 Dean of Academic Affairs .... Ms. Karen WILLIAMS
20 Dean of Academic Affairs .... Mr. Steve CROMER
20 Dean of Academic Affairs .... Mr. Brad JESTER
106 Dean of Online Learning .... Ms. Tempie KITCHENS

Southern Polytechnic State University (C)

1100 South Marietta Parkway, Marietta GA 30060-2896
County: Cobb FICE Identification: 001570
Unit ID: 141097
Telephone: (678) 915-7778 Carnegie Class: Master's M
FAX Number: (678) 915-7483 Calendar System: Semester
URL: www.spsu.edu
Established: 1948 Annual Undergrad Tuition & Fees (In-State): $5,498
Enrollment: 5,514 Coed
Affiliation or Control: State IRS Status: 501(c)3
Highest Offering: Master's
Program: Liberal Arts And General; Professional; Technical Emphasis
Accreditation: **SC**, ACBSP, CONST, CS, ENGR, ENGT

01 President .... Dr. Lisa A. ROSSBACHER
05 Vice President for Academic Affairs .... Dr. Zvi SZAFRAN
32 Vice Pres Student/Enrollment Svcs .... Dr. Ron R. KOGER
30 VP for University Advancement .... Dr. Ron D. DEMPSEY
10 Vice President for Business/Finance .... Dr. Bill PRIGGE
13 Interim Chief Information Officer .... Dr. Ron KOGER
04 Exec Assistant to President .... Ms. Mary T. PHILLIPS
29 Exec Dir Strategic Mktg/Sustainblty .... Mr. James W. COOPER
22 Affirmative Action Officer .... Ms. Mary E. MCGEE
20 Assoc VP for Academic Affairs .... Mr. Dave CAUDILL
54 Assoc Dean Div of Engineering .... Dr. Tom CURRIN
48 Dean of Arch/Civil Engr Tech/Const .... Dr. Wilson C. BARNES
49 Dean of Arts & Sciences .... Dr. Thomas NELSON
77 Dean of Computing/Software Eng .... Dr. Han REICHGELT
72 Dean of Engr Technology/Mgmt .... Dr. Jeff RAY
56 Dean of Extended University .... Dr. Ruston HUNT
93 Dir of Adv/Tutoring/Tst/Intl Center .... Dr. Jeff ORR
58 Director of Graduate Studies .... Ms. Nikki PALAMIOTIS
104 Director of International Programs .... Dr. Richard BENNETT
08 Director of Library .... Dr. Joyce W. MILLS
78 Dir Center for Teaching Excellence .... Ms. Dawn RAMSEY
92 Director of Honors Program .... Dr. Nancy L. REICHERT
35 Dean of Students .... Mr. Barry D. BIRCKHEAD
36 Director of Career/Counseling Svcs .... Ms. Phyllis N. WEATHERLY
41 Dir Recreational Sports/Athletics .... Mr. Karl D. STABER
07 Dir Admissions/Student Recruitment .... Mr. Gary W. BUSH
09 Director of Institutional Research .... Mr. Dave CLINE
37 Dir of Scholarships/Financial Aid .... Mr. Gary MANN
06 Registrar .... Mr. Stephen A. HAMRICK
44 Director of Development .... Ms. Kit TRENSCH
26 Director of Public Relations .... Ms. Sylvia CARSON
21 Controller .... Mr. Arthur VAUGHN
21 Director of Budget and Grants .... Ms. Bonnie CHAMBERLIN
15 Director of Human Resources .... Dr. I. Charles AZEBEOKHAI
19 Int Chief of University Police .... Chief John BAUER
18 Dir of Facilities Management .... Mr. Steve KITCHEN
96 Dir Procurement/Mail Services .... Mr. Robert P. FORBES
31 Director Auxiliary Enterprises .... Ms. Kasey HELTON
90 Director Desktop Support .... Mr. Dave PARHAM
13 Dir of IT Enterprise Applications .... Mr. Kenneth HILL
91 Director of Info Tech Operations .... Mr. Ronald J. SKOPITZ
14 Dir IT Systems/Networks/Security .... Mr. Jim HERBERT

† Part of the University System of Georgia.

Southwest Georgia Technical College (D)

15689 US Highway 19 N, Thomasville GA 31792-2622
County: Thomas FICE Identification: 005615
Unit ID: 141158
Telephone: (229) 225-4096 Carnegie Class: Assoc/Pub-R-S
FAX Number: (229) 225-4330 Calendar System: Quarter
URL: www.southwestgatech.edu
Established: 1947 Annual Undergrad Tuition & Fees (In-State): $3,747
Enrollment: 1,683 Coed
Affiliation or Control: State IRS Status: 501(c)3
Highest Offering: Associate Degree
Program: Occupational
Accreditation: **SC**, ADNUR, MAC, MLTAD, SURGT

01 President .... Dr. Craig R. WENTWORTH
11 Vice Pres Administrative Services .... Mr. Paul ROBERTS
05 Vice Pres Academic Affairs .... Dr. Annie MCELROY
32 Vice President Student Affairs .... Ms. Joyce HALSTEAD
30 Vice President Economic Development .... Mr. Gary PITTS
09 VP Institutional Effectiveness .... Dr. Debbie GOODMAN
76 Dean Allied Health/Gen Education .... Ms. Carla BARROW
50 Dean Bus/Computer/Prof Svcs/T&I .... Mr. Dennis LEE
37 Director Financial Aid .... Ms. Amy SCOGGINS
26 Dir Marketing/Inst Devel/Pub Rels .... Ms. Amy MAISON
88 Executive Director Adult Education .... Mr. Dale ALDRIDGE
07 Director Admissions .... Ms. Wanda HANCOCK
06 Registrar .... Ms. Deborah GRAY
08 Director Library & Media Services .... Ms. Gail ROBERTS
36 Dir Career Placement & Development .... Dr. Jeanine LONG

Spelman College (E)

350 Spelman Lane, SW, Atlanta GA 30314-4399
County: Fulton FICE Identification: 001594
Unit ID: 141060
Telephone: (404) 681-3643 Carnegie Class: Bac/A&S
FAX Number: N/A Calendar System: Semester
URL: www.spelman.edu
Established: 1881 Annual Undergrad Tuition & Fees: $23,254
Enrollment: 2,171 Female
Affiliation or Control: Independent Non-Profit IRS Status: 501(c)3
Highest Offering: Baccalaureate
Program: Liberal Arts And General; Teacher Preparatory
Accreditation: **SC**, MUS, TED

01 President .... Dr. Beverly Daniel TATUM
05 Provost & VP of Academic Affairs .... Dr. Johnnella E. BUTLER
20 Vice Provost .... Dr. Myra BURNETT
10 VP Business/Financial Affairs/Treas .... Mr. Robert D. FLANIGAN, JR.
32 Vice President for Student Affairs .... Dr. Darnita KILLIAN
30 Vice Pres for College Relations .... Ms. Eloise ALEXIS
84 Vice Pres Enrollment Management .... Ms. Arlene CASH
30 Vice President for Development .... Ms. Kassandra JOLLEY
21 Assoc VP Business/Financial Affairs .... Mr. John CUNNINGHAM
88 Dir Investments & Financial Plng .... Ms. Rhonda HONEGAN
21 Controller .... Ms. April AUSTIN
100 Secretary of College/Chief of Staff .... Ms. Cathy DANIELS
26 Exec Dir of Communications .... Ms. Tomika DEPRIEST
04 Assistant to President .... Ms. Yvonne SKILLINGS
13 VP & CIO Media & Information Tech .... Ms. Delores BARTON
105 Dir Bonner Comm Svcs/Student Dev .... Vacant
20 Dean of Undergraduate Studies .... Dr. Desiree PEDESCLEAUX
42 Director Sisters Center for WISDOM .... Rev. Lisa D. RHODES
06 Registrar .... Dr. Frederick FRESH
07 Interim Director of Admissions .... Ms. Erica JOHNSON
27 Director Publications .... Ms. Jo Moore STEWART
29 Director of Alumnae Affairs .... Ms. Sharon OWENS
37 Director of Student Financial Svcs .... Ms. Lenora JACKSON
36 Director Career Planning/Devel .... Mr. Harold BELL
78 Director of Cooperative Education .... Mr. Keith WEBB
15 Director Human Resources .... Ms. Bernadette COHEN
38 Director Counseling Services .... Dr. Ave MARSHALL
09 Dir Inst Rsrch/Assessment/Planning .... Ms. Jill TRIPLETT
88 Director Women's Resource Center .... Dr. Beverly GUY-SHEFTALL
18 Director Facilities/Mgmt & Svcs .... Mr. Arthur E. FRAZIER, III
19 Director of Public Safety .... Mr. Steve BOWSER
24 Dir Educational Technology Svcs .... Ms. Jenell SARGENT
46 Associate Provost of Research .... Dr. Carmen SIDBURY
44 Director of Annual Giving .... Ms. DeShanna BROWN
102 Dir of Corp & Foundation Relations .... Ms. Shelese LANE
88 Director of Special Events .... Ms. Heather HAWES
39 Director Housing & Residential Life .... Ms. Alison CUMMINGS
86 Director Title III/Government Rels .... Ms. Helga GREENFIELD
88 Coordinator Intl/Commuter Students .... Ms. Letitia DENARD
08 Director of Woodruff Library .... Ms. Loretta PARHAM
23 Director Health Services .... Ms. Brenda DALTON
25 Director Sponsored Programs .... Mr. T.N. Nokware ADESEGUN
102 Assoc VP Advancement Operations .... Ms. Helga GREENFIELD
35 Dean Students .... Ms. Kimberly FERGUSON
40 Director Bookstore .... Ms. Deri CLELAND
41 Dir Phys Ed & Athletics/Sr Instr .... Ms. Germaine MCAULEY
96 Dir Adminstrative Support Svcs .... Ms. Jacqueline JAMES

Thomas University (F)

1501 Millpond Road, Thomasville GA 31792-7499
County: Thomas FICE Identification: 001555
Unit ID: 141167
Telephone: (229) 226-1621 Carnegie Class: Bac/Diverse
FAX Number: (229) 226-1653 Calendar System: Semester
URL: www.thomasu.edu
Established: 1950 Annual Undergrad Tuition & Fees: $12,600
Enrollment: 1,043 Coed
Affiliation or Control: Independent Non-Profit IRS Status: 501(c)3
Highest Offering: Master's
Program: Liberal Arts And General; Professional
Accreditation: **SC**, CORE, MT, NUR, SW

01 President .... Dr. Gary BONVILLIAN
05 Vice Pres of Academic Affairs .... Dr. Ann LANDIS
30 Vice Pres for Instnl Advancement .... Mr. Richard MUNROE
08 Univ Librarian/Dir Info Services .... Ms. Amber BROCK
06 Registrar .... Mrs. Lacey HARRISON
84 Exec Dir Enroll Mgmt/Student Svcs .... Mr. Micky WEST
07 Director of Admissions .... Ms. Kerri KNIGHT
38 Director of Student Support Svcs .... Ms. Faye R. JOHNSON
37 Director of Financial Aid .... Ms. Angela KEYS
41 Director of Athletics .... Mr. Michael D. LEE
10 Controller .... Ms. Sue STONE
18 Director of Physical Plant .... Mr. Randy WILCOX
32 Director of Student Life .... Mr. John RAINEY
44 Director of Annual Fund .... Ms. Melinda FRIDDELL
26 Director of Communications .... Mr. Brewer TURLEY
04 Assistant to the President .... Ms. Linda M. HERNDON

Toccoa Falls College (G)

107 North Chapel Drive, Toccoa Falls GA 30598-0068
County: Stephens FICE Identification: 001596
Unit ID: 141185
Telephone: (706) 886-6831 Carnegie Class: Bac/Diverse
FAX Number: (706) 282-6005 Calendar System: Semester
URL: www.tfc.edu
Established: 1907 Annual Undergrad Tuition & Fees: $16,710
Enrollment: 767 Coed
Affiliation or Control: Independent Non-Profit IRS Status: 501(c)3
Highest Offering: Baccalaureate
Program: Liberal Arts And General; Teacher Preparatory
Accreditation: **SC**, BI, IACBE, MUS

01 President .... Vacant
03 Provost .... Dr. Barbara K. BELLEFEUILLE
04 Sr Exec Administrative Assistant .... Mrs. Paula S. ELKINS
32 VP Student Development .... Mr. Lee P. YOWELL
30 Director for Advancement .... Vacant
10 Vice President for Finance .... Mr. R. Gregg SCHULTE
05 VP for Academic Affairs .... Dr. W. Brian SHELTON
42 Director Spiritual Form .... Rev. Jeffrey S. GANGEL

09 Director Institutional Research ... Dr. David W. MCCARTHY
08 Director Info Svcs/IT Dept/Library ... Miss Patricia J. FISHER
39 Director Residence/Community Life ... Mrs. Debbie MOORE
29 Director Alumni Assoc/Col Relations ... Miss Sharon SANDERSON
38 Dir Stdnt Health/Career Servs ... Mr. Johnathan C. KERR
37 Director Student Financial Aid ... Mr. Truitt FRANKLIN
07 Director of Admissions ... Ms. Joanna E. BRUCE
06 Registrar ... Mr. Kelly G. VICKERS
41 Athletic Director ... Mr. Lance E. MARTIN
18 Chief Facilities/Physical Plant ... Mr. Gerald WILLIAMSON
26 Chief Public Relations Officer ... Ms. Angela R. RAMAGE
15 Director Human Resources ... Ms. Mary K. RITCHEY
88 Director Retention Services ... Vacant
40 Director of Bookstore and Gift Shop ... Ms. Patricia MCGARVEY

Truett McConnell College (A)

100 Alumni Drive, Cleveland GA 30528-1264
County: White FICE Identification: 001597
Unit ID: 141237
Telephone: (706) 865-2134 Carnegie Class: Bac/Assoc
FAX Number: (706) 219-3339 Calendar System: Semester
URL: www.truett.edu
Established: 1946 Annual Undergrad Tuition & Fees: $15,010
Enrollment: 755 Coed
Affiliation or Control: Baptist IRS Status: 501(c)3
Highest Offering: Baccalaureate
Program: Liberal Arts And General
Accreditation: SC, MUS

01 President ... Dr. Emir CANER
05 Vice Pres Academic Services ... Dr. Brad REYNOLDS
11 Vice Pres Administrative Svcs ... Mr. David ARMSTRONG
30 Vice Pres Institutional Advancement ... Dr. Daniel P. MOOSBRUGGER
32 Vice President of Student Services ... Mr. Chris EPPLING
09 VP/Institutional Effectiveness ... Dr. Michel SIMONEAUX
04 Executive Assistant to President ... Mrs. Jeanavon BURROW
41 Athletic Director ... Mr. Chris EPPLING
06 Registrar/Dir Inst Research ... Mrs. Melissa FORTNER
37 Director of Financial Aid ... Mrs. Becky MOORE
08 Librarian ... Ms. Janice E. WILSON
29 Director of Alumni Relations ... Mr. Scott BAILEY
07 Director of Admissions ... Mr. Nathan RAYNOR
42 Director of Collegiate Ministries ... Mr. Keith WADE
40 Bookstore Manager ... Mr. Eddie O'BRIEN

University of Atlanta (B)

6685 Peachtree Industrial Boulevard,
Atlanta GA 30360-2116
County: DeKalb Identification: 666399
Telephone: (877) 503-4588 Carnegie Class: Not Classified
FAX Number: (678) 669-2439 Calendar System: Semester
URL: www.uofa.edu
Established: 2006 Annual Undergrad Tuition & Fees: $4,075
Enrollment: 610 Coed
Affiliation or Control: Proprietary IRS Status: Proprietary
Highest Offering: Doctorate
Program: Liberal Arts And General; Professional; Business Emphasis
Accreditation: DETC

01 President ... Mr. Nick MITHANI
03 Chief Executive Officer ... Mr. Alex MITHANI
05 Dean of Faculty ... Dr. James L. WILLIAMS
32 VP Student Affairs ... Ms. Nechelle ROBINSON
84 VP Enrollment Management ... Mr. Bill KAY

University of Georgia (C)

Athens GA 30602-0001
County: Clarke FICE Identification: 001598
Unit ID: 139959
Telephone: (706) 542-3000 Carnegie Class: RU/VH
FAX Number: N/A Calendar System: Semester
URL: www.uga.edu
Established: 1785 Annual Undergrad Tuition & Fees (In-State): $9,472
Enrollment: 34,677 Coed
Affiliation or Control: State IRS Status: 501(c)3
Highest Offering: Doctorate
Program: Liberal Arts And General; Teacher Preparatory; Professional
Accreditation: SC, AAFCS, ART, BUS, BUSA, CACREP, CIDA, CLPSY, COPSY, DANCE, DIETD, DIETI, ENG, FOR, JOUR, LAW, LSAR, MFCD, MUS, NRPA, PH, PHAR, SCPSY, SP, SPAA, SW, TED, THEA, VET

01 President ... Dr. Michael F. ADAMS
100 Chief of Staff ... Dr. Margaret A. AMSTUTZ
04 Assistant to the President ... Mr. Charles G. TONEY
04 Assistant to the President ... Mr. Matthew M. WINSTON, JR.
04 Assistant to the President ... Ms. Mary E. MCDONALD
05 Sr VP Academic Affs/Provost ... Mr. Jere W. MOREHEAD
10 Sr Vice Pres Finance/Administration ... Mr. Timothy P. BURGESS
26 Sr Vice Pres for External Affairs ... Mr. Thomas S. LANDRUM
20 Int Vice President for Instruction ... Dr. Laura D. JOLLY
46 Vice President for Research ... Dr. David C. LEE
11 Int Vice Pres Public Svc/Outreach ... Dr. Steve W. WRIGLEY
32 Vice President Student Affairs ... Dr. Rodney D. BENNETT
86 Vice President for Govt Relations ... Dr. Steve W. WRIGLEY
26 Vice President Public Affairs ... Dr. Thomas H. JACKSON, JR.
104 Assoc Prov for International Educ ... Dr. Kavita PANDIT
28 Int Assoc Prov for Inst Diversity ... Dr. Michelle G. COOK
45 Assoc Provost Academic Planning ... Mr. Robert G. BOEHMER
88 Assoc Provost/Economic Development ... Dr. Margaret W. DAHL
13 CIO & Associate Provost ... Dr. Barbara A. WHITE
08 University Librarian/Assoc Provost ... Dr. William G. POTTER
07 Assoc VP Admissions/Enroll Mgmt ... Ms. Nancy G. MCDUFF
21 Sr Assoc VP Finance/Administration ... Mr. Ryan A. NESBIT
18 Assoc Vice President Physical Plant ... Mr. Ralph F. JOHNSON
15 Associate VP Human Resources ... Mr. Tom GAUSVIK
43 Executive Director of Legal Affairs ... Mr. Stephen M. SHEWMAKER
49 Dean of Arts & Sciences ... Dr. Garnett S. STOKES
47 Dean of Agricultural & Environ Sci ... Dr. J. Scott ANGLE
61 Dean of Law ... Ms. Rebecca H. WHITE
67 Dean of Pharmacy ... Dr. Svein OIE
65 Dean Forestry & Natural Resources ... Dr. Michael L. CLUTTER
53 Dean of Education ... Dr. Arthur M. HORNE
58 Dean of the Graduate School ... Dr. Maureen GRASSO
50 Dean of Business ... Dr. Robert T. SUMICHRAST
60 Dean Journalism & Mass Comm ... Dr. E. Culpepper CLARK
59 Int Dean of Family/Consumer Science ... Dr. Anne L. SWEANEY
74 Dean of Veterinary Medicine ... Dr. Sheila W. ALLEN
70 Dean of Social Work ... Dr. Maurice C. DANIELS
48 Dean of Environment & Design ... Mr. Daniel J. NADENICEK
80 Dean of Public/International Affs ... Dr. Thomas P. LAUTH
69 Dean of Public Health ... Dr. Phillip L. WILLIAMS
88 Dean School of Ecology ... Dr. John L. GITTLEMAN
92 Director of Honors Program ... Dr. David S. WILLIAMS
41 Athletic Director ... Mr. William G. MCGARITY
22 Director of Equal Opportunity Ofc ... Mr. J. Steve SHI
06 Registrar ... Ms. Rebecca D. MACON
19 Chief of Police ... Chief James E. WILLIAMSON
37 Director of Student Financial Aid ... Ms. Bonnie JOERSCHKE
36 Director of Career Services Center ... Mr. Scott T. WILLIAMS
39 Executive Director of Housing ... Dr. Gerard J. KOWALSKI
23 Director of Health Services ... Dr. Jean E. CHIN
35 Dean of Students ... Dr. William M. MCDONALD
38 Dir Counseling/Psychological Svcs ... Dr. Gayle M. ROBBINS
51 Dir of Georgia Ctr Continuing Educ ... Dr. William CROWE
29 Exec Director of Alumni Relations ... Ms. Deborah H. DIETZLER
30 Assoc Vice Pres Development ... Mr. Robert S. HAWKINS
09 Director of Institutional Research ... Dr. Denise GARDNER
88 Director of Academic Enhancement ... Dr. Earl GINTER
84 Assoc VP Admissions/Enrollment Mgmt ... Ms. Nancy G. MCDUFF
93 Int Asc Dean Student Intercult Affs ... Dr. Willie BANKS, JR.
94 Interim Director of Women's Studies ... Dr. Juanita JOHNSON-BAILEY
96 Director of Purchasing ... Ms. Annette EVANS

† Part of the University System of Georgia.

University of West Georgia (D)

1601 Maple Street, Carrollton GA 30118-0001
County: Carroll FICE Identification: 001601
Unit ID: 141334
Telephone: (678) 839-5000 Carnegie Class: Master's L
FAX Number: (678) 839-4766 Calendar System: Semester
URL: www.westga.edu
Established: 1906 Annual Undergrad Tuition & Fees (In-State): $6,182
Enrollment: 11,283 Coed
Affiliation or Control: State IRS Status: 501(c)3
Highest Offering: Doctorate
Program: Occupational; Liberal Arts And General; Teacher Preparatory; Professional
Accreditation: SC, ART, BUS, BUSA, CACREP, CS, MUS, NURSE, SP, SPAA, TED, THEA

01 President ... Dr. Beheruz N. SETHNA
05 Vice Pres Academic Affairs ... Dr. Michael HORVATH
10 Vice President Business & Finance ... Mr. Jim SUTHERLAND
32 Vice President for Student Services ... Dr. Melanie MCCLELLAN
26 Vice President of Univ Advancement ... Mr. Michael RUFFNER
30 Director of Development ... Ms. Diane HOMESLEY
20 Associate VP for Academic Affairs ... Dr. Jon ANDERSON
84 Assoc VP for Enrollment Mgt ... Dr. Scott LINGRELL
20 Associate VP for Academic Affairs ... Dr. Myrna GANTNER
21 University Controller ... Mr. Richard SEARS
83 Dean of Social Sciences ... Dr. N. Jane MCCANDLESS
50 Dean of Business ... Dr. Faye S. MCINTYRE
53 Dean of Education ... Dr. Kim METCALF
79 Dean College of Arts and Humanities ... Dr. Randy HENDRICKS
81 Dean Science and Mathematics ... Dr. Bruce LANDMAN
92 Dean & Director of Honors College ... Dr. Donald R. WAGNER
06 Registrar ... Ms. Donna HALEY
07 Director of Admissions ... Vacant
08 Director of Libraries ... Ms. Lorene FLANDERS
37 Director of Financial Aid ... Ms. Kimberly L. JORDAN
36 Director of Career Services ... Ms. Wanda R. MCGUKIN
27 Chief Information Officer ... Mrs. Kathy KRAL
51 Director of Continuing Education ... Mr. James L. AGAN
15 Dir of Human Res/Affirm Action Ofcr ... Ms. Stephanie ROOKS
18 Director Facilities/Administration ... Mr. Robert S. WATKINS
19 Director of University Police ... Mr. Thomas J. MACKEL
23 Director of Health Services ... Dr. Leslie COTTRELL
35 Director of the Campus Center ... Mr. Matthew MILLER
39 Director of Residence Life ... Mr. Stephen WHITLOCK
41 Director of Athletics ... Mr. Daryl DICKEY
38 Assistant Dean of Student Services ... Dr. Gerald W. HALL
88 Dir Business Svcs/Auxiliary Enterpr ... Mr. Mark REEVES
09 Director Inst Research/Planning ... Dr. Ebenezer KOLAJO
29 Director of Alumni Relations ... Mr. H. Franklin PRITCHETT
93 Assoc Dir for Multicultural Svcs ... Mr. DeLandra HUNTER
89 Director of EXEL Center ... Mrs. Cheryl A. RICE
26 Asst Vice President of UA ... Ms. Jami BOWER
40 Bookstore Manager ... Vacant
25 Assoc VP Researc & Sponsored Ops ... Dr. Arlene HOME
55 Associate Dean Extended Degree Pgm ... Dr. Melanie N. CLAY
12 Administrative Coord Dalton Center ... Ms. Christy TALLEY
12 Director-Newnan Campus ... Ms. Cathy WRIGHT
44 Director of Planned Giving ... Mr. Ernie HENDERSON
28 Director of Diversity ... Dr. Jack JENKINS
24 Dept Manager of Learning Resources ... Mr. Brian MCCRARY
43 University Legal Counsel ... Ms. Jane SIMPSON
104 Dir of International Svcs & Pgms ... Dr. William SCHANIEL
102 Assoc Exec Dir of WG Foundation ... Mr. Bart GILLESPIE
66 Dean School of Nursing ... Dr. Kathyrn GRAMS

† Part of the University System of Georgia.

*University System of Georgia Office (E)

270 Washington Street, SW, Atlanta GA 30334-9007
County: Fulton FICE Identification: 008290
Telephone: (404) 656-2202 Carnegie Class: N/A
FAX Number: (404) 657-6979
URL: www.usg.edu

01 Chancellor ... Mr. Hank M. HUCKABY
04 Executive Assistant to Chancellor ... Ms. Sabrina THOMPSON
03 Chief Operating Officer ... Mr. Rob WATTS
05 Exec Vice Chanc/Chief Acad Officer ... Dr. Susan HERBST
10 Vice Chancellor Fiscal Affairs ... Ms. Usha RAMACHANDRAN
21 Chief Audit Officer ... Mr. John M. FUCHKO, III
26 Sr Vice Chanc External Affairs ... Mr. Thomas E. DANIEL
18 Vice Chancellor Facilities ... Ms. Linda DANIELS
13 Vice Chanc/Chief Info Officer ... Dr. Curt CARVER
100 Chief of Staff Academic Affairs ... Dr. Melinda SPENCER
09 Asst VC Rsrch & Policy Analysis I ... Dr. Susan CAMPBELL LOUNSBURY
27 Assoc Vice Chanc Media/Publications ... Mr. John MILLSAPS

Valdosta State University (F)

1500 N Patterson Street, Valdosta GA 31698-0010
County: Lowndes FICE Identification: 001599
Unit ID: 141264
Telephone: (229) 333-5800 Carnegie Class: Master's L
FAX Number: (229) 333-7400 Calendar System: Semester
URL: www.valdosta.edu
Established: 1906 Annual Undergrad Tuition & Fees (In-State): $5,696
Enrollment: 12,898 Coed
Affiliation or Control: State IRS Status: 501(c)3
Highest Offering: Doctorate
Program: 2-Year Principally Bachelor's Creditable; Liberal Arts And General; Teacher Preparatory
Accreditation: SC, ART, BUS, CACREP, #LIB, MFCD, MUS, NURSE, SP, SPAA, SW, TED, THEA

01 Interim President ... Dr. Louis H. LEVY
05 Provost & VP Academic Affairs ... Dr. Philip L. GUNTER
10 Vice President for Finance & Admin ... Ms. Sue E. MITCHELL
30 Vice President for Advancement ... Mr. John D. CRAWFORD
32 Vice Pres for Student Affairs ... Mr. Russell F. MAST
45 Asst to President Strategic Rsrch ... Vacant
49 Dean College of Arts & Sciences ... Dr. Connie L. RICHARDS
50 Dean College of Business Admin ... Dr. Wayne L. PLUMLY
57 Dean College of the Arts ... Dr. John C. GASTON
53 Interim Dean College of Education ... Dr. Julie LEE
58 Assoc VP for Rsrch & Dean of Grad ... Dr. Alfred FUCIARELLI
66 Dean College of Nursing ... Dr. Anita G. HUFFT
06 Registrar ... Mr. Stanley JONES
13 Chief Information Officer ... Mr. Joseph A. NEWTON
07 Director Admissions/Enrollment Mgmt ... Mr. Walter H. PEACOCK
08 Interim University Librarian ... Dr. Alan BERNSTEIN
37 Director of Financial Aid ... Mr. Douglas R. TANNER
31 Director of Public Services ... Mr. Bill MUNTZ
88 Dir of Publication & Design Service ... Mr. Jeff GRANT
36 Dir Career Services/Cooperative Ed ... Ms. Winifred V. COLLINS
15 Director of Human Resources ... Dr. Denise BOGART
72 Director Division Aerospace Studies ... LtCol. Marsha ALEEM
22 Director of Equal Oppty Pgms ... Dr. Maggie J. VIVERETTE
43 University Attorney ... Ms. Laverne L. GASKINS
18 Dir Phys Plant & Facilities Plng ... Mr. Ray SABLE
26 Dir Marketing & Cmty Relations ... Ms. Mary B. GOODING
38 Director of Counseling Center ... Dr. John GROTGEN
21 Director of Business Services ... Mr. William J. FILTZ

† Part of the University System of Georgia.

Waycross College (G)

2001 S Georgia Parkway, Waycross GA 31503-0110
County: Ware FICE Identification: 020550
Unit ID: 141307
Telephone: (912) 449-7500 Carnegie Class: Assoc/Pub-R-S
FAX Number: (912) 449-7614 Calendar System: Semester
URL: www.waycross.edu
Established: 1976 Annual Undergrad Tuition & Fees (In-State): $2,892
Enrollment: 1,109 Coed
Affiliation or Control: State IRS Status: 501(c)3
Highest Offering: Associate Degree
Program: Occupational; 2-Year Principally Bachelor's Creditable
Accreditation: SC

01 Interim President ... Dr. Mary Ellen WILSON

05 Int Vice Pres/Dean Academic Affairs .... Dr. Sara E. SELBY
10 Vice President Business Affairs .... Mr. Marcus LATHAM
84 Vice Pres Enrollment/Student Svcs .... Dr. Neil ASPINWALL
20 Assoc Dean for Academic Affairs .... Ms. Sara E. SELBY
08 Director of Library Services .... Ms. Sharon L. KELLY
32 Director for Student Life ....Ms. Sharon K. KOMANECKY
31 Director Development/Community Svcs .....Mr. Taylor HEREFORD
18 Director Physical Plant ....Mr. Harbin FARR
09 Director of Institutional Research ....Vacant
15 Director Personnel Services ....Vacant
30 Chief Devel/Public & Alumni Rels ....Mr. Taylor HEREFORD
13 Director of Computer Services .... Mr. Corry JOHNSON
37 Director Student Financial Aid ....Ms. Debbie M. HOWARD
06 Registrar/Director of Admissions ....Mr. Rob WINGFIELD
26 Chief Public Relations Officer ....Mr. Taylor HEREFORD
28 Director of Diversity .... Ms. Sara SELBY
29 Director Alumni Relations ....Mr. Taylor HEREFORD
38 Director Student Counseling .... Ms. Sharon KOMANECKY
96 Director of Purchasing .... Ms. Debbie MEEKS
35 Asst Director Student Support ....Ms. Angela HOLLAND-WASDIN
40 Bookstore Manager ....Mr. Harbin FARR

† Part of the University System of Georgia.

Wesleyan College (A)

4760 Forsyth Road, Macon GA 31210-4462
County: Bibb FICE Identification: 001600
Unit ID: 141325
Telephone: (478) 477-1110 Carnegie Class: Bac/A&S
FAX Number: (478) 757-4030 Calendar System: Semester
URL: www.wesleyancollege.edu
Established: 1836 Annual Undergrad Tuition & Fees: $18,500
Enrollment: 690 Female
Affiliation or Control: United Methodist IRS Status: 501(c)3
Highest Offering: Master's
Program: Liberal Arts And General; Teacher Preparatory
Accreditation: SC, MUS

01 President ....Ms. Ruth A. KNOX
05 Dean of the College ....Dr. Vivia L. FOWLER
30 VP Institutional Advancement ....Ms. Susan T. WELSH
10 Vice Pres Finance/Treasurer ....Mr. Richard P. MAIER
32 Vice Pres for Student Affairs ....Ms. Patricia M. GIBBS
84 Vice Pres for Enrollment Services .... Mr. C. Stephen FARR
06 Assistant Dean/Registrar ....Ms. Patricia R. HARDEMAN
04 Assistant to the President ....Ms. Denise W. HOLLOWAY
04 Assistant to the President ....Mrs. Sally A. HEMINGWAY
08 Library Director ....Ms. Sybil MCNEIL
13 Director of Information Services .... Mr. Kevin L. ULSHAFER
29 Director of Alumnae Affairs ....Ms. Cathy C. SNOW
26 Director of Communications ....Ms. Susan WELSH
44 Director of Annual Fund ....Ms. Dawn FREELIN
37 Director of Financial Aid ....Ms. Kizzy HOLMES
39 Director of Residence Life ....Ms. Stefanie SWANGER
18 Director of Physical Plant .... Ms. Kelly BLEDSOE
41 Athletic Director .... Ms. Patty GIBBS
42 Chaplain .... Rev. Bill HURDLE
19 Director Security/Safety ....Mr. Clinton BRANTLEY
15 Director Human Resources .... Ms. Meagon DAVIS
07 Director of Admissions .... Ms. Danielle LODGE
09 Director of Institutional Research .... Ms. Angie WRIGHT
32 Chief Student Life Officer ....Ms. Stefanie SWANGER
36 Director Career Development ....Ms. Monica MOODY
38 Director Student Counseling .... Ms. Jamie THAMES
96 Director of Purchasing .... Ms. Lindsay TIMMS
20 Associate Academic Officer .... Ms. Patricia R. HARDEMAN
21 Associate Business Officer ....Ms. Dawn P. NASH
40 Bookstore Manager .... Ms. Lindsay TIMMS

West Georgia Technical College (B)

176 Murphy Campus Boulevard, Waco GA 30182-2407
County: Haralson FICE Identification: 010487
Unit ID: 139278
Telephone: (770) 537-6000 Carnegie Class: Assoc/Pub-S-SC
FAX Number: (770) 537-7976 Calendar System: Quarter
URL: www.westgatech.edu
Established: 1968 Annual Undergrad Tuition & Fees (In-State): $2,625
Enrollment: 8,092 Coed
Affiliation or Control: State IRS Status: 501(c)3
Highest Offering: Associate Degree
Program: Occupational
Accreditation: SC, ADNUR, DH, MAC, MLTAD, RAD, SURGT

01 President .... Dr. Skip SULLIVAN
05 Vice President Academic Affairs .... Mr. Patrick K. HANNON
32 Vice President Student Affairs ....Mr. Eddie GORE
88 Vice Pres Adult Education ....Dr. Richard ROBINSON
30 Vice Pres Institutional Advancement ....Mrs. Dawn COOK
09 VP Institutional Effectiveness ....Dr. Kristen DOUGLAS
20 Asst Vice Pres For Curriculum .... Mrs. Sindi MCGOWAN
08 Director Library Services .... Mrs. Mary MCCLUNG
06 Registrar .... Mrs. Laura JAKUBIAK
27 Asst Dir Information Technology .... Mr. Brian HENDERSON
37 Financial Aid Director .... Ms. Nelda BURGESS
30 Director Economic Development .... Mr. Scotty PARKER
36 Director Career Services ....Mrs. Elise JOHNSON
12 Campus Director Carroll Campus ....Mr. Phil CARTER
12 Campus Director Coweta Campus ....Mrs. Tonya WHITLOCK
12 Campus Director Douglas Campus ....Mrs. Lisa DONEY
07 Director of Admissions .... Mrs. Mary ADERHOLD
15 Human Resources Coordinator ....Mrs. Sherri WALKER

18 Director Facilities & Security .... Mr. Michael JILES
51 Manager Continuing Education .... Mrs. Anita JONES

Westwood College-Atlanta Midtown (C)

1100 Spring Street, Suite 102, Atlanta GA 30309-2824
County: Fulton Identification: 666421
Unit ID: 445072
Telephone: (404) 745-9862 Carnegie Class: Bac/Assoc
FAX Number: (404) 892-7253 Calendar System: Semester
URL: www.westwood.edu
Established: 2004 Annual Undergrad Tuition & Fees: $14,227
Enrollment: 805 Coed
Affiliation or Control: Proprietary IRS Status: Proprietary
Highest Offering: Baccalaureate
Program: Occupational
Accreditation: ACICS, MAC

01 President of Campus .... Bryan GULEBIAN

† Branch campus of Westwood College-DuPage, Woodbridge, IL.

Westwood College-Atlanta Northlake (D)

2309 Parklake Drive NE Bldg 10, Atlanta GA 30345-2906
County: Dekalb Identification: 666597
Unit ID: 445276
Telephone: (866) 821-6146 Carnegie Class: Bac/Assoc
FAX Number: (770) 934-9539 Calendar System: Quarter
URL: www.westwood.edu
Established: N/A Annual Undergrad Tuition & Fees: $13,958
Enrollment: 586 Coed
Affiliation or Control: Proprietary IRS Status: Proprietary
Highest Offering: Baccalaureate
Program: Occupational; Liberal Arts And General
Accreditation: ACICS, MAC

01 Campus President .... Ms. Tina CLAY

† Branch campus of Westwood College-O'Hare Airport, Chicago, IL.

Wiregrass Georgia Technical College (E)

4089 Val Tech Road, Valdosta GA 31602
County: Lowndes FICE Identification: 005256
Unit ID: 141255
Telephone: (229) 333-2100 Carnegie Class: Assoc/Pub-R-M
FAX Number: (229) 333-2129 Calendar System: Quarter
URL: www.wiregrass.edu
Established: 1963 Annual Undergrad Tuition & Fees (In-State): $2,552
Enrollment: 5,408 Coed
Affiliation or Control: State IRS Status: 501(c)3
Highest Offering: Associate Degree
Program: Occupational; 2-Year Principally Bachelor's Creditable; Technical Emphasis
Accreditation: SC, DA, DH, MLTAD, SURGT

01 President .... Dr. Ray PERREN
03 Provost .... Ms. Lisa TOMBERLIN
50 VP for Academic Affairs .... Dr. Ron O'MEARA
11 VP for Administrative Services .... Ms. Keren WYNN
32 VP for Student Affairs .... Ms. Connie COFFEY
09 VP for Institutional Effectiveness .... Dr. Helen PENNY
88 VP for Adult Education ....Mr. Alvin PAYTON
46 VP for Economic Development .... Ms. Lidell GREENWAY
26 Executive Dir for Public Relations ....Ms. Angela HOBBY
30 Executive Director for Advancement ....Ms. Mona PAULK
27 Dir of Public Relations & Marketing .... Ms. Christina MOORE

Young Harris College (F)

PO Box 694, Young Harris GA 30582-0098
County: Towns FICE Identification: 001604
Unit ID: 141361
Telephone: (706) 379-3111 Carnegie Class: Assoc/PrivNFP
FAX Number: (706) 379-4319 Calendar System: Semester
URL: www.yhc.edu
Established: 1886 Annual Undergrad Tuition & Fees: $22,155
Enrollment: 820 Coed
Affiliation or Control: United Methodist IRS Status: 501(c)3
Highest Offering: Baccalaureate
Program: Liberal Arts And General
Accreditation: SC, MUS

01 President .... Dr. Cathy COX
05 Vice Pres for Academic Affairs .... Dr. Ron ROACH
10 Senior VP for Finance & Admin .... Mr. David LEOPARD
21 Vice President for Finance .... Mr. Wade M. BENSON
32 Vice President for Student Affairs .... Ms. Susan ROGERS
84 Vice Pres for Enrollment Management ....Mr. Clinton G. HOBBS
30 Vice President of Advancement .... Mr. Jay STROMAN
45 VP of Planning/Chief of Staff .... Ms. Rosemary R. ROYSTON
14 Vice President of Campus Technology ....Mr. Ken FANEUFF
29 Director of Alumni Relations ....Ms. Dana ENSLEY
20 Associate Academic Officer ....Dr. Keith DEFOOR
08 Librarian ....Ms. Dawn LAMADE
38 Counselor ....Ms. Lynne GRADY

06 Registrar ....Vacant
37 Director Student Financial Aid ....Ms. Linda ADAMS
07 Director of Admissions ....Vacant
15 Director Personnel Services ....Mr. Vince ROBELOTTO
26 Chief Public Relations Officer .... Ms. Denise COOK
18 Chief Facilities/Physical Plant .... Mr. Keith RAKER
19 Director of Safety & Compliance ....Ms. Krista MASSELL
41 Athletic Director .... Mr. Randy DUNN
42 Campus Minister .... Rev. Tim MOORE

HAWAII

Argosy University, Hawaii (G)

400 ABS Tower, 1001 Bishop Street, Honolulu HI 96813
County: Honolulu Identification: 666787
Unit ID: 366748
Telephone: (808) 536-5555 Carnegie Class: Master's S
FAX Number: (808) 536-5505 Calendar System: Semester
URL: www.argosy.edu/hawaii
Established: 1994 Annual Undergrad Tuition & Fees: $14,580
Enrollment: 510 Coed
Affiliation or Control: Proprietary IRS Status: Proprietary
Highest Offering: Doctorate
Program: Professional
Accreditation: &NH, CLPSY

01 Campus President .... Dr. Warren EVANS
32 Director of Student Services .... Cherie ANDRADE
07 Director of Admissions ....Vacant
10 Business Manager .... Alex SOUZA

† Regional accreditation is carried under the parent institution, Argosy University in Chicago, IL.

Babel University Professional School of Translation (H)

1110 University Avenue, Suite 510, Honolulu HI 96826
County: Honolulu Identification: 666350
Telephone: (808) 946-3773 Carnegie Class: Not Classified
FAX Number: (808) 946-3993 Calendar System: Other
URL: www.babel.edu
Established: 2000 Annual Graduate Tuition & Fees: $19,450
Enrollment: 69 Coed
Affiliation or Control: Proprietary IRS Status: Proprietary
Highest Offering: Master's; No Undergraduates
Program: Professional
Accreditation: DETC

01 Chancellor .... Dr. Miyoko YUASA

Brigham Young University Hawaii (I)

55-220 Kulanui Street, Laie Oahu HI 96762-1294
County: Honolulu FICE Identification: 001606
Unit ID: 230047
Telephone: (808) 675-3211 Carnegie Class: Bac/Diverse
FAX Number: (808) 675-3329 Calendar System: Semester
URL: www.byuh.edu
Established: 1955 Annual Undergrad Tuition & Fees: $4,450
Enrollment: 2,811 Coed
Affiliation or Control: Latter-day Saints IRS Status: 501(c)3
Highest Offering: Baccalaureate
Program: Liberal Arts And General; Teacher Preparatory; Professional
Accreditation: WC, SW

01 President .... Dr. Steven C. WHEELWRIGHT
05 Vice President for Academics ....Dr. Max L. CHECKETTS
11 VP for Administrative Services ....Mr. Michael B. BLISS
32 VP for Student Development & Svcs ....Dr. Debbie HIPPOLITE WRIGHT
100 Assistant to the President ....Dr. William G. NEAL
04 Administrative Asst to the Pres ....Ms. Lisa FEHOKO
20 Assoc Academic VP for Instruction ....Dr. D. Chad COMPTON
20 Assoc Academic VP for Curriculum ....Dr. Jennifer LANE
81 Dean College of Math and Sciences .... Dr. W. Jeffrey BURROUGHS
88 Dean College of Bus/Computing/Govt ....Dr. Glade TEW
88 Dean College of Human Development ....Dr. John BAILEY
88 Dean College of Lang/Culture & Arts ....Dr. Phillip MCARTHUR
13 University Technology Officer ....Mr. Kevin SCHLAG
07 Director Enrollment Services .... Mr. Arapata MEHA
41 Director of Athletics .... Mr. Ken WAGNER
08 Director University Library ....Michael ALDRICH
51 Director of Educational Outreach ....Mrs. Edna OWAN
88 Director Budget Services ....Mr. Steven TUELLER
96 Director of Purchasing & Travel .... Mr. Robert OWAN
19 Director Safety/Security & Risk Mgt ....Mr. Roy YAMAMOTO
15 Director of Human Resources .... Mrs. Tessie FAUSTINO
18 Director Facilities Management ....Mr. Judd WHETTEN
10 Director Financial Services ....Mr. Brian BLUM
40 Director Bookstore ....Mr. Kenway L. KUA
23 Director Health Center ....Dr. P. Douglas NIELSON
88 Dir Compliance & Internal Audit .... Mr. Adam R. JACOBSMEYER
36 Director Career Services ....Mrs. Jodi CHOWEN
39 Director Housing & Residential Life .... Mr. John A. ELKINGTON
38 Director of Counseling Services ....Dr. Paul BUCKINGHAM
35 Director Student Leadership & Honor ....Mr. David LUCERO
88 Director Food Services ....Mr. David KEALA

26 Director Communications .... Mr. Michael JOHANSON
88 Director Testing and Assessment .... Dr. Paul H. FREEBAIRN

† Affiliated with Brigham Young University, Provo, UT.

Chaminade University of Honolulu (A)

3140 Waialae Avenue, Honolulu HI 96816-1578
County: Honolulu FICE Identification: 001605
Unit ID: 141486
Telephone: (808) 735-4711 Carnegie Class: Master's L
FAX Number: (808) 735-4870 Calendar System: Semester
URL: www.chaminade.edu
Established: 1955 Annual Undergrad Tuition & Fees: $18,440
Enrollment: 2,806 Coed
Affiliation or Control: Independent Non-Profit IRS Status: 501(c)3
Highest Offering: Master's
Program: Liberal Arts And General; Teacher Preparatory; Professional
Accreditation: WC, MACTE

01 President .... Bro. Bernard PLOEGER, SM
04 Exec Assistant to the President .... Bro. Frank DAMM, SM
05 Provost .... Dr. Larry OSBORNE
30 VP for Institutional Advancement ..... Ms. Diane PETERS-NGUYEN
10 Vice President Finance/Facilities .... Dr. Daniel GILMORE
13 Dean of Info Services & Library .... Dr. Larry OSBORNE
84 Dean of Enrollment Management .... Ms. Joy BOUEY
32 Dean of Students .... Ms. Grissel BENITZ-HODGE
35 Associate Dean of Students .... Ms. Allison JEROME
88 Assoc Dean of Enrollment Mgmt .... Ms. Amy TAKIGUCHI
88 Dir Academic Advising/Retention .... Mr. Curtis WASHBURN
90 Director Network/Desktop Services .... Mr. Eddie PANG
55 Dir Adult Evening & Online Programs .... Mr. Skip LEE
91 Director of Management Info Svcs .... Mr. Jorge HERNANDEZ
29 Director of Alumni Relations .... Ms. Be-Jay KODAMA
41 Director of Athletics .... Mr. William VILLA
42 Director of Campus Ministry .... Ms. Kristina STONE
36 Dir Career Develop/Job Placement .... Ms. Kimberley GRAVES
18 Director of Facilities Operations .... Mr. Michael HAISEN
11 Director of Administrative Services .... Ms. Elaine OISHI
21 Director of Finance .... Ms. Aulani KAANOI
07 Director of Admissions .... Ms. Joy BOUEY
08 Director of Library .... Ms. Sharon LEPAGE
15 Director Personnel Services .... Mrs. Lucy STREETER
19 Supervisor of Security .... Mr. Melvin DECOSTA
38 Director of Student Counseling .... Dr. June YASUHARA
06 Registrar .... Mr. John MORRIS
09 Institutional Research Specialist .... Mr. Hieu NGUYEN
37 Director Student Financial Aid .... Ms. Amy TAKIGUCHI

Hawaii Pacific University (B)

1164 Bishop Street, Suite 800, Honolulu HI 96813-2882
County: Honolulu FICE Identification: 007279
Unit ID: 141644
Telephone: (808) 544-0200 Carnegie Class: Master's L
FAX Number: (808) 544-1136 Calendar System: Semester
URL: www.hpu.edu
Established: 1965 Annual Undergrad Tuition & Fees: $16,510
Enrollment: 8,339 Coed
Affiliation or Control: Independent Non-Profit IRS Status: 501(c)3
Highest Offering: Master's
Program: Liberal Arts And General; Teacher Preparatory; Professional
Accreditation: WC, NUR, SW

01 President .... Dr. Geoff BANNISTER
00 President Emeritus .... Mr. Chatt G. WRIGHT
05 Vice President of Academic Affairs .... Dr. John KEARNS
20 Assistant VP Academic Affairs .... Mr. Joe SCHMIEDL
56 Assoc VP Off-Campus/Military Pgm .... Mr. Robert CYBORON
88 Director Instructional Innovation .... Dr. Stephanie SCHULL
11 Vice President Administration .... Mr. E. Rick STEPIEN
35 Exec Dir Student Academic Services ... Ms. Deborah NAKASHIMA
84 Vice Pres Enrollment Management .... Mr. Scott STENSRUD
10 VP/Chief Financial Officer .... Mr. Kenneth T. UEMURA
09 Vice Pres Institutional Research .... Dr. Leslie CORREA
15 Vice President Human Resources .... Ms. Claire COOPER
30 Vice Pres Alumni & Univ Relations ..... Ms. Mary Ellen MCGILLAN
21 Associate VP/Controller .... Ms. Kathleen CLARK
50 Dean Business Administration .... Dr. Deborah CROWNE
66 Dean Nursing/Health Sciences .... Dr. Randy CAINE
81 Dean Natural/Computational Sciences .... Dr. Andrew BRITTAIN
60 Dean Humanities & Social Sciences .... Dr. Steven COMBS
89 Dean of Students .... Ms. Marites MCKEY
13 Chief Application Officer .... Mr. Robert SLIKE
106 Director Distance Education .... Dr. Langley FRISSELL
85 Dir Intl Admissions/Recruitment .... Ms. Lilian HALLSTROM
97 Assistant Dean General Education .... Dr. Malia SMITH
07 Director of Admissions .... Ms. Sara SATO
09 Academic Information Analyst .... Mr. John IGE
104 Director Intl Exchange/Study Abroad .... Dr. Jon DAVIDANN
36 Director Career Svcs Ctr/Co-op Educ ... Mr. Joseph BARRIENTOS
06 Registrar .... Mr. Richard L. YOUNT
37 Director Financial Aid .... Mr. Adam HATCH
41 Athletic Director .... Mr. Darren VORDERBRUEGGE
51 Assoc Dir Adult Learning Program .... Ms. Jill MERL
85 Dir International Student Services .... Ms. Ann NEWTON
105 Director Web Services .... Mr. Abe TOMA
08 University Librarian .... Ms. Kathleen CHEE
42 University Chaplain .... Rev. Dale BURKE
14 Director Computing Services .... Ms. Lisa CARPENTER
88 Dir Admin Support Operations .... Ms. Jamie KEMP
26 University Relations Asst Director .... Vacant

19 Assoc Director Security and Safety .... Mr. Wayne FERNANDEZ
18 Manager Facilities/Physical Plant .... Mr. Steve HENDRICKS
40 Bookstore Manager .... Ms. Shellee HEEN
29 Alumni/Parent Relations Coordinator .... Ms. Kris SMITH
38 Director Counseling/Behavioral Hlth .... Dr. Kevin BOWMAN
96 Procurement Director .... Mr. Kevin WETTER

Hawaii Tokai International College (C)

2241 Kapiolani Boulevard, Honolulu HI 96826-4310
County: Honolulu FICE Identification: 037603
Telephone: (808) 983-4100 Carnegie Class: Not Classified
FAX Number: (808) 983-4107 Calendar System: Quarter
URL: www.hawaiitokai.edu
Established: 1992 Annual Undergrad Tuition & Fees: $10,470
Enrollment: 117 Coed
Affiliation or Control: Independent Non-Profit IRS Status: 501(c)3
Highest Offering: Associate Degree
Program: 2-Year Principally Bachelor's Creditable; Liberal Arts And General
Accreditation: WJ

01 Chancellor .... Dr. Naoto YOSHIKAWA
05 Vice Chancellor .... Dr. Douglas FUQUA
11 Exec Director of Administration .... Mr. Yuzo OIDA
20 Dean of Instruction .... Dr. Deanna MADDEN
46 Director Program Development .... Ms. Wanda SAKO
08 Librarian .... Ms. Loraine ORIBIO
32 Director Student Services .... Ms. Laura SPROWLS
15 Human Resources Officer .... Ms. Janice DAWSON
21 Finance Department .... Mr. Mark GREENE
29 Alum Rel Coord/Std Sup Specialist .... Mr. Andrew FUJIMOTO

Heald College, Honolulu (D)

1500 Kapiolani Boulevard, Honolulu HI 96814-3797
County: Honolulu FICE Identification: 004546
Unit ID: 141468
Telephone: (808) 955-1500 Carnegie Class: Assoc/PrivFP
FAX Number: (808) 955-6964 Calendar System: Quarter
URL: www.heald.edu
Established: 1863 Annual Undergrad Tuition & Fees: $13,074
Enrollment: 1,985 Coed
Affiliation or Control: Proprietary IRS Status: Proprietary
Highest Offering: Associate Degree
Program: Occupational
Accreditation: &WJ, DA, MAC

01 Regional VP/Campus Operation .... Mrs. Evelyn A. SCHEMMEL
03 Campus Vice President .... Mr. Michael C. VAN LEAR
10 Director of Financial Services .... Mr. Arthur VALENCUELE
05 Director of Academic Affairs .... Mrs. Merrill W. CUTTING

† Regional accreditation is carried under the parent institution Heald College, Central Office in San Francisco, CA.

Institute of Clinical Acupuncture and Oriental Medicine (E)

100 N Beretania Street, Suite 203 B,
Honolulu HI 96817-4709
County: Honolulu FICE Identification: 037353
Unit ID: 444699
Telephone: (808) 521-2288 Carnegie Class: Spec/Health
FAX Number: (808) 521-2271 Calendar System: Semester
URL: www.orientalmedicine.edu
Established: 1996 Annual Graduate Tuition & Fees: $12,810
Enrollment: 40 Coed
Affiliation or Control: Proprietary IRS Status: Proprietary
Highest Offering: Master's; No Undergraduates
Program: Professional
Accreditation: ACUP

01 President .... Dr. Wai Hoa LOW
05 Chancellor Academic Affairs .... Dr. Edmund BERNAUER
63 Clinic Director .... Dr. Catherine Yu-Ling LOW

Kona University (F)

75-6099 Kuakini Hwy, Kailua-Kona HI 96740
County: Honolulu Identification: 666650
Telephone: (808) 791-5050 Carnegie Class: Not Classified
FAX Number: (808) 791-5051 Calendar System: Other
URL: www.kona.edu
Established: 1994 Annual Graduate Tuition & Fees: $4,600
Enrollment: 30 Coed
Affiliation or Control: Independent Non-Profit IRS Status: 501(c)3
Highest Offering: Master's; No Undergraduates
Program: Professional
Accreditation: DETC

01 President .... Dr. Matthew B. JAMES
03 Vice President .... Nancy MORENO-DERKS
13 Dir Info & Educational Technology .... Dr. Farhad SABA
05 Chief Academic Officer .... Dr. Matthew B. JAMES
26 Marketing Manager .... Daejin JEON
10 Director of Finance .... Vicky BONILLA
84 Director of Enrollment .... Virginia OMINE

New Hope Christian College-Hawaii (G)

290 Sand Island Access Road, Honolulu HI 96819
County: Honolulu Identification: 667010
Unit ID: 457484
Telephone: (808) 853-1040 Carnegie Class: Not Classified
FAX Number: (808) 853-1042 Calendar System: Semester
URL: www.pacrim.edu
Established: 1998 Annual Undergrad Tuition & Fees: $7,592
Enrollment: 108 Coed
Affiliation or Control: Independent Non-Profit IRS Status: 501(c)3
Highest Offering: Baccalaureate
Program: Religious Emphasis
Accreditation: @BI

00 Chancellor .... Dr. Wayne CORDEIRO
01 President .... Guy HIGASHI
05 Academic Vice President .... Dr. Randall FURUSHIMA
06 Registrar .... Martha STINTON
07 Admissions Director .... Lori HIGASHI
32 Director of Student Life .... Mia BURKE
10 Business Administrator .... James W. KAHLER

Remington College-Honolulu Campus (H)

1111 Bishop Street, Suite 400, Honolulu HI 96813-2811
County: Honolulu Identification: 666028
Unit ID: 372958
Telephone: (808) 942-1000 Carnegie Class: Bac/Assoc
FAX Number: (808) 533-3064 Calendar System: Quarter
URL: www.remingtoncollege.edu
Established: 1999 Annual Undergrad Tuition & Fees: $15,850
Enrollment: 628 Coed
Affiliation or Control: Proprietary IRS Status: Proprietary
Highest Offering: Baccalaureate
Program: 2-Year Principally Bachelor's Creditable; Liberal Arts And General
Accreditation: ACCSC

01 President .... Mr. Kenneth G. HEINEMANN
05 Director of Education .... Mr. Malcolm ROBERTS
37 Director of Financial Services .... Ms. Debbie USO
07 Director of Admissions .... Mr. Louis LAMAIR
36 Director of Career Services .... Ms. Zenaida CARAANG
06 Registrar .... Mrs. Diane SADLER
08 Director of Information Resources .... Mr. Glen ARAKAKI
04 Executive Assistant .... Ms. Lee SWEARINGER
76 Dept Chr Clinical Med Assisting .... Dr. Salvacion CHONG
77 Dept Chr Computer Networking Tech .... Mr. John SCOTT
83 Department Chair Criminal Justice .... Mr. Hector WEST
88 Dept Chair International Business ...... Mr. Mark LANGENBACHER

† Branch campus of Remington College, San Diego, CA.

Traditional Chinese Medical College of Hawaii (I)

65-1206 Mamalohoa Highway, Bldg 3,
Kamuela HI 96743-2288
County: Hawaii FICE Identification: 039994
Unit ID: 449579
Telephone: (808) 885-9226 Carnegie Class: Spec/Health
FAX Number: (808) 885-9227 Calendar System: Trimester
URL: www.tcmch.edu
Established: 1986 Annual Graduate Tuition & Fees: $15,950
Enrollment: 10 Coed
Affiliation or Control: Independent Non-Profit IRS Status: 501(c)3
Highest Offering: Master's; No Undergraduates
Program: Professional
Accreditation: ACUP

01 President .... Dr. Jacqueline HAHN
05 Academic Dean .... Ms. Megan J. YARBERRY
11 Director of Operations .... Ms. Cathleen KEENE

*University of Hawaii System Office (J)

2444 Dole Street, Honolulu HI 96822
County: Honolulu FICE Identification: 007885
Unit ID: 141963
Telephone: (808) 956-8207 Carnegie Class: N/A
FAX Number: (808) 956-5286
URL: www.hawaii.edu

01 President .... Dr. M. R. C GREENWOOD
05 Exec VP for Academic Affs/Provost .... Dr. Linda K. JOHNSRUD
46 Vice President for Research .... Dr. James R. GAINES
43 VP Legal Affs/Univ Gen Counsel .... Ms. Darolyn LENDIO
10 VP Budget and Finance/CFO .... Mr. Howard TODO
88 Vice President Community Colleges .... Dr. John MORTON
32 VP Student Affs and Univ/Comm Rels .... Mr. Rockne FREITAS
27 Vice President Info Tech/CIO .... Dr. David K. LASSNER
35 Assoc Vice Pres Student Affairs .... Mr. Lui HOKOANO
26 Assoc VP External Affs & Univ Rels .... Ms. Lynne T. WATERS
18 Assoc VP Capital Improvements .... Mr. Brian MINAAI
102 President UH Foundation .... Ms. Donna VUCHINICH
21 Director of Budget .... Vacant
16 System Director Human Resources .... Ms. Brenna HASHIMOTO
13 Director Management Info Systems .... Ms. Susan K. INOUYE

45 Director Off Research Services ..... Ms. Yaa-Yin FONG
21 Director Financial Management ..... Mr. Paul Y. KOBAYASHI, JR.
09 Dir Admin Operations/EVAAP ..... Ms. Sandra FURUTO
22 Director EEO/AA ..... Ms. Mie WATANABE
88 Director Creative Services ..... Ms. Cheryl S. ERNST
31 Dir Public Relations/Special Events ..... Vacant

University of Hawaii at Hilo (A)

200 W Kawili Street, Hilo HI 96720-4091
County: Hawaii FICE Identification: 001611
Unit ID: 141565
Telephone: (808) 974-7444 Carnegie Class: Bac/A&S
FAX Number: (808) 974-7622 Calendar System: Semester
URL: www.uhh.hawaii.edu
Established: 1947 Annual Undergrad Tuition & Fees (In-State): $5,640
Enrollment: 4,085 Coed
Affiliation or Control: State IRS Status: 501(c)3
Highest Offering: Doctorate
Program: Liberal Arts And General; Teacher Preparatory; Professional
Accreditation: WC, BUS, CEA, NUR, PHAR

02 Chancellor ..... Dr. Donald O. STRANEY
05 Vice Chancellor Academic Affair ..... Dr. Kenith SIMMONS
10 Vice Chanc Administrative Affs ..... Dr. Marcia SAKAI
46 Int Vice Chancellor for Research ..... Dr. Daniel E. BROWN
32 Vice Chancellor Student Affairs ..... Dr. Luoluo HONG
20 Asst VC for Academic Affairs ..... Vacant
21 Budget Director ..... Ms. Lois M. FUJIYOSHI
88 Director University Disability Svcs ..... Ms. Susan SHIRACHI
15 Director Human Resources ..... Mr. Kerwin S. IWAMOTO
18 Director Facilities Planner ..... Mr. Lo-Li CHIH
26 Director University Relations ..... Mr. Gerald L. DE MELLO
08 University Librarian ..... Dr. Linda Marie GOLIAN-LUI
24 Director Media Relations ..... Ms. Alyson Y. KAKUGAWA-LEONG
07 Director Admissions ..... Mr. James CROMWELL
38 Acting Director Counseling ..... Ms. Barbara B. HEINTZ
39 Director Housing ..... Mr. Miles K. NAGATA
35 Director Campus Center ..... Ms. Ellen I. KUSANO
37 Director Financial Aid ..... Mr. Jeff SCOFIELD
06 University Registrar ..... Ms. Cathy ZENZ
49 Dean College of Arts & Sciences ..... Dr. Randy HIROKAWA
50 Dean College of Business & Econ ..... Dr. Marcia SAKAI
67 Dean College of Pharmacy ..... Dr. John PEZZUTO
47 Dean Col Agri/Forestry/Nat Res Mgmt ..... Dr. William W. STEINER
51 Int Dean Cont Educ/Community Svcs ..... Dr. April K. SCAZZOLA
41 Director of Athletics ..... Mr. Dexter IRVIN
40 Bookstore Manager ..... Ms. Margot MASSA
85 Dir International Student Services ..... Dr. Ruth E. ROBISON
36 Director Career Services ..... Dr. Norman S. STAHL
22 Director EEO/AA ..... Ms. Kelly OAKS
09 Institutional Research Analyst ..... Mr. Brendan HENNESSEY
29 Director Marketing & Alumni ..... Ms. Yu Yok PEARRING
30 Senior Director of Development ..... Ms. Margaret SHIBA
94 Facilitator Women's Studies ..... Ms. Amy GREGG
23 Acting Director Medical Services ..... Ms. Lisa LYON
92 Honors Director ..... Vacant
88 Dir College of Hawaiian Language ..... Dr. Kalena SILVA

*University of Hawaii at Manoa (B)

2500 Campus Road, Honolulu HI 96822-2217
County: Honolulu FICE Identification: 001610
Unit ID: 141574
Telephone: (808) 956-8111 Carnegie Class: RU/VH
FAX Number: N/A Calendar System: Semester
URL: www.manoa.hawaii.edu
Established: 1907 Annual Undergrad Tuition & Fees (In-State): $9,100
Enrollment: 20,337 Coed
Affiliation or Control: State IRS Status: 501(c)3
Highest Offering: Doctorate
Program: Liberal Arts And General; Teacher Preparatory; Professional
Accreditation: WC, BUS, CEA, CLPSY, CORE, DH, DIETD, ENG, IPSY, LAW, LIB, MED, MT, MUS, NURSE, PH, PLNG, SP, SW, TED

02 Chancellor ..... Dr. Virginia S. HINSHAW
11 Vice Chanc Admin/Finance/ Operations ..... Ms. Kathleen D. CUTSHAW
05 Vice Chanc Academic Affs ..... Dr. Reed W. DASENBROCK
45 Vice Chanc Research/Grad Education ..... Dr. Gary K. OSTRANDER
32 Vice Chancellor for Students ..... Dr. Francisco J. HERNANDEZ
06 University Registrar ..... Mr. Stuart LAU
07 Director of Admissions ..... Dr. Alan I. YANG
08 Interim University Librarian ..... Ms. Paula T. MOCHIDA
37 Director Financial Aid Services ..... Ms. Jodie M. KUBA
38 Director Counsel/Student Devel Ctr ..... Dr. Allyson M. TANOUYE
18 Asst Vice Chanc for Campus Svcs ..... Mr. David T. HAFNER, JR.
23 Director University Health Center ..... Dr. Andrew W. NICHOLS
39 Director Student Housing ..... Mr. Michael W. KAPTIK
40 Director Bookstore/Auxiliary Svcs ..... Vacant
41 Athletic Director ..... Mr. James J. DONOVAN
56 Interim Dean Outreach College ..... Dr. William G. CHISMAR
50 Dean Shidler College of Business ..... Dr. V. Vance ROLEY
58 Int Dean Graduate Division ..... Dr. Patricia A. COOPER
88 Int Dean Sch of Travel Industry Mgt ..... Dr. Juanita C. LIU
53 Dean College of Education ..... Dr. Christine K. SORENSEN
54 Dean College of Engineering ..... Dr. Peter E. CROUCH
47 Int Dean Col Trop Agric & Human Res ..... Dr. Sylvia YUEN
63 Dean John A Burns Sch of Med ..... Dr. Jerris R. HEDGES
66 Dean Sch Nursing & Dental Hygiene ..... Dr. Mary G. BOLAND
70 Int Dn M P Thompson Sch of Soc Work ..... Dr. Noreen K. MOKUAU
61 Dean Wm S Richardson Sch of Law ..... Mr. Aviam SOIFER
48 Dean School of Architecture ..... Mr. Clark E. LLEWELLYN
49 Int Dean College Arts & Humanities ..... Mr. Thomas R. BINGHAM
65 Dean College Natural Sciences ..... Dr. William L. DITTO
83 Dean College Social Sciences ..... Dr. Richard A. DUBANOSKI
79 Dean College Lang Ling & Lit ..... Dr. Robert BLEY-VROMAN
88 Dean Sch Ocean & Earth Sci & Tech ..... Dr. Brian TAYLOR
88 Int Dean Pac and Asian Stds ..... Dr. Edward SHULTZ
88 Dn Hawaiinuiakea Sch Hawn Knowledge ..... Dr. Maenette BENHAM
27 Director of Cmty/Govt Affairs ..... Mr. Gregg T. TAKAYAMA
28 Dir Stdnt Equity/Exclnce/Diversity ..... Dr. Amefil AGBAYANI
36 Dir Career Devel/Student Employment ..... Ms. Myrtle CHING-RAPPA
15 Director Human Resources ..... Ms. Tammy KUNIYOSHI
88 Director Cancer Center ..... Dr. Michele CARBONE
88 Director Institute for Astronomy ..... Dr. Guenther HASINGER
88 Director Waikiki Aquarium ..... Dr. Andrew ROSSITER
88 Int Assc Dr Pac Biosci Research Ctr ..... Dr. Marilyn DUNLAP

*University of Hawaii - West Oahu (C)

96-129 Ala Ike, Pearl City HI 96782-3699
County: Honolulu FICE Identification: 021078
Unit ID: 141981
Telephone: (808) 454-4700 Carnegie Class: Bac/Diverse
FAX Number: (808) 453-6076 Calendar System: Semester
URL: www.uhwo.hawaii.edu
Established: 1976 Annual Undergrad Tuition & Fees (In-State): $5,246
Enrollment: 1,471 Coed
Affiliation or Control: State IRS Status: 501(c)3
Highest Offering: Baccalaureate
Program: Liberal Arts And General; Teacher Preparatory
Accreditation: WC

02 Chancellor ..... Dr. Gene I. AWAKUNI
05 Int Vice Chanc Academic Affairs ..... Dr. Joseph VLEY
32 Int Vice Chanc for Student Affairs ..... Dr. Susan NISHIDA
11 Vice Chanc Administrative Services ..... Ms. Ann NISHIMOTO
84 Director for Enrollment Management ..... Ms. Susan S. NISHIDA
09 Director of Institutional Research ..... Dr. Elaine LEE
26 Dir Public Relations & Marketing ..... Vacant
08 Head Librarian ..... Ms. Sarah S. GILMAN
06 Registrar ..... Ms. Robyn OSHIRO
37 Financial Aid Officer ..... Mr. Lester ISHIMOTO
15 Human Resources Specialist ..... Ms. Nancy K. NAKASONE
18 Facilities/Auxiliary Services Mgr ..... Mr. James (Kimo) YAMAGUCHI
10 Fiscal Officer ..... Ms. Lori FOO

*University of Hawaii Community Colleges (D)

2444 Dole Street, Honolulu HI 96822-2411
County: Honolulu FICE Identification: 006751
Unit ID: 420592
Telephone: (808) 956-7038 Carnegie Class: N/A
FAX Number: (808) 956-9219
URL: www.hawaii.edu

01 Vice Pres for Community Colleges ..... Dr. John F. MORTON
05 Assoc Vice Pres Academic Affairs ..... Dr. Peter QUIGLEY
11 Assoc Vice Pres Admin/Cmty Col Oper ..... Mr. Michael T. UNEBASAMI
04 Executive Assistant to the VP ..... Ms. Deborah NAKAGAWA

*Kapiolani Community College (E)

4303 Diamond Head Road, Honolulu HI 96816-4496
County: Honolulu FICE Identification: 001613
Unit ID: 141796
Telephone: (808) 734-9000 Carnegie Class: Assoc/Pub2in4
FAX Number: (808) 734-9162 Calendar System: Semester
URL: www.kcc.hawaii.edu
Established: 1957 Annual Undergrad Tuition & Fees (In-State): $2,388
Enrollment: 9,301 Coed
Affiliation or Control: State IRS Status: 501(c)3
Highest Offering: Associate Degree
Program: Occupational; 2-Year Principally Bachelor's Creditable
Accreditation: WJ, ACFEI, ADNUR, MAC, MLTAD, OTA, PTAA, RAD, SURGT

02 Chancellor ..... Dr. Leon RICHARDS
05 Vice Chancellor for Acad Affs ..... Dr. Louise PAGOTTO
10 Vice Chancellor for Admin Services ..... Mr. Milton HIGA
32 Vice Chanellor for Student Services ..... Ms. Mona LEE
49 Dean Arts and Sciences ..... Dr. Charles SASAKI
50 Dean Hospitality/Business/Legal ..... Dr. Frank HAAS
66 Dean Health Programs ..... Dr. Patricia O'HAGAN
51 Dean Community & Continuing Educ ..... Ms. Carol HOSHIKO
04 Special Asst to the Chancellor ..... Dr. Salvatore LANZILOTTI
88 Dir Culinary Inst of the Pacific ..... Mr. Conrad NONAKA
09 Dir Institutional Effectiveness ..... Dr. Robert FRANCO
08 Librarian ..... Ms. Susan MURATA
06 Registrar ..... Ms. Jerilyn LORENZO
37 Financial Aid Officer ..... Ms. Jennifer BRADLEY
18 Auxiliary Services Officer ..... Mr. Gordon MAN
29 Alumni Relations Coordinator ..... Ms. Louise YAMAMOTO
30 Development Officer ..... Ms. Linh HOANG
15 Director Personnel Office ..... Ms. Eileen TORIGOE
21 Fiscal Officer ..... Ms. Carol MASUTANI
35 Student Activities Coordinator ..... Mr. Keith KASHIWADA

*University of Hawaii Hawaii Community College (F)

200 W Kawili Street, Hilo HI 96720-4091
County: Hawaii FICE Identification: 005258
Unit ID: 383190
Telephone: (808) 974-7611 Carnegie Class: Assoc/Pub2in4
FAX Number: (808) 974-7692 Calendar System: Semester
URL: www.hawaii.hawaii.edu
Established: 1941 Annual Undergrad Tuition & Fees (In-State): $2,366
Enrollment: 3,815 Coed
Affiliation or Control: State IRS Status: 501(c)3
Highest Offering: Associate Degree
Program: Occupational; 2-Year Principally Bachelor's Creditable
Accreditation: WJ, ACFEI, ADNUR, CEA

02 Interim Chancellor ..... Ms. Noreen YAMANE
05 Int Vice Chanc Academic Affairs ..... Ms. Joni ONISHI
11 Vice Chanc Administrative Affairs ..... Mr. Michael LEIALOHA
32 Int Vice Chanc Student Affairs ..... Mr. James YOSHIDA
51 Int Dir Continuing Educ/Training ..... Ms. Deborah SHIGEHARA
21 Fiscal Officer ..... Ms. Jodi MINE
37 Student Financial Aid Officer ..... Ms. Sheryl LUNDBERG-SPRAGUE
12 Int Dir UH Center at West Hawaii ..... Ms. Beth SANDERS
06 Registrar ..... Mr. David LOEDING
15 Personnel Services Officer ..... Ms. Mari CHANG
07 Admissions Specialist ..... Ms. Dorinna MANUEL-CORTEZ

*University of Hawaii Honolulu Community College (G)

874 Dillingham Boulevard, Honolulu HI 96817-4598
County: Honolulu FICE Identification: 001612
Unit ID: 141680
Telephone: (808) 845-9211 Carnegie Class: Assoc/Pub2in4
FAX Number: (808) 845-9173 Calendar System: Semester
URL: www2.honolulu.hawaii.edu
Established: 1920 Annual Undergrad Tuition & Fees (In-State): $2,328
Enrollment: 4,725 Coed
Affiliation or Control: State IRS Status: 501(c)3
Highest Offering: Associate Degree
Program: Occupational; 2-Year Principally Bachelor's Creditable; Technical Emphasis
Accreditation: WJ

02 Chancellor ..... Mr. Michael T. ROTA
05 Vice Chancellor of Academic Affairs ..... Ms. Erika LACRO
11 Vice Chancellor of Admin Svcs ..... Mr. Ken KATO
32 Interim Dean of Student Services ..... Mr. Brian FURUTO
88 Int Dir PCATT ..... Ms. Rosemary SUMAJIT
88 Interim Dean Transport & Trades ..... Mr. Michael BARROS
27 Dean Communications & Services ..... Mr. Russell UYENO
20 Dean University College ..... Mr. Ralph KAM
24 Director Educational Media ..... Dr. Jon BLUMHARDT
21 Fiscal Officer ..... Mr. Derek INAFUKU
08 Librarian in Charge ..... Ms. Irene MESINA
37 Financial Aid Officer ..... Ms. Jannine OYAMA
15 Director Personnel Services ..... Ms. Sharene MORIWAKI
18 Chief Facilities/Physical Plant ..... Mr. Ken KATO
35 Director Student Affairs ..... Ms. Emily Ann KUKULIES
04 Int Exec Asst to the Chancellor ..... Ms. Billie LUEDER
06 Registrar ..... Ms. Farah DOIGUCHI
09 Director Management Info & Research ..... Ms. Lynn INOSHITA
36 Dir Student Placement/Counselor ..... Ms. Silvan CHUNG

*University of Hawaii Kauai Community College (H)

3-1901 Kaumualii Highway, Lihue HI 96766-9500
County: Kauai FICE Identification: 001614
Unit ID: 141802
Telephone: (808) 245-8311 Carnegie Class: Assoc/Pub2in4
FAX Number: (808) 245-8220 Calendar System: Semester
URL: kauai.hawaii.edu/
Established: 1964 Annual Undergrad Tuition & Fees (In-State): $2,970
Enrollment: 1,428 Coed
Affiliation or Control: State IRS Status: 501(c)3
Highest Offering: Associate Degree
Program: Occupational; 2-Year Principally Bachelor's Creditable
Accreditation: WJ, ACFEI, ADNUR

02 Chancellor ..... Dr. Helen COX
05 Vice Chanc Academic Affairs ..... Dr. James DIRE
32 Vice Chanc Student Affairs ..... Mr. Earl K. NISHIGUCHI
20 Actg Ast Dn Acad Suprt/Univ Ctr Dir ..... Ms. Ramona KINCAID
11 Director of Administrative Services ..... Mr. Gary NITTA
51 Director Continuing Educ/Training ..... Mr. Bruce GETZEN
08 Librarian ..... Mr. Robert KAJIWARA
06 Registrar ..... Mr. Leighton ORIDE
18 Chief Facilities/Physical Plant ..... Mr. Calvin SHIRAI
21 Associate Business Officer ..... Ms. Phyllis VIDINHA
37 Financial Aid Officer ..... Ms. Rebecca THOMPSON
22 AA/EEO Coordinator ..... Ms. Jo Rae BAPTISTE
35 Counselor ..... Mr. John CONSTANTINO
09 Institutional Researcher ..... Mr. Jonathan KALK

*University of Hawaii Leeward Community College (A)

96-045 Ala Ike, Pearl City HI 96782-3393
County: Honolulu FICE Identification: 004549
Unit ID: 141811
Telephone: (808) 455-0011 Carnegie Class: Assoc/Pub2in4
FAX Number: (808) 455-0471 Calendar System: Semester
URL: www.lcc.hawaii.edu
Established: 1968 Annual Undergrad Tuition & Fees (In-State): $2,910
Enrollment: 7,991 Coed
Affiliation or Control: State IRS Status: 501(c)3
Highest Offering: Associate Degree
Program: Occupational; 2-Year Principally Bachelor's Creditable
Accreditation: WJ, ACFEI

02 Chancellor ... Mr. Manuel J. CABRAL
03 Vice Chancellor/CAO ... Mr. Michael PECSOK
11 Vice Chancellor Admin Services ... Mr. Mark LANE
32 Dean Student Services ... Mr. Christopher MANASERI
72 Asst Dean Career & Tech Education ... Mr. Ron UMEHIRA
49 Asst Dean Arts & Sciences ... Mr. James GOODMAN
08 Librarian ... Mr. Christopher MATZ
06 Registrar ... Mr. Warren MAU
37 Financial Aid Officer ... Ms. Aileen LUM-AKANA
12 Coord Waianae Education Center ... Ms. Laurie LAWRENCE
91 Computer Center Manager ... Ms. Penny UYEHARA
15 Human Resources/EEO/AA Officer ... Mr. Michael WONG
19 Security Supervisor ... Mr. Talbort HOOK
24 Media Coordinator ... Ms. Leanne CHUN
35 Student Activities Coordinator ... Ms. Lexer CHOU
36 Placement Officer ... Vacant
18 Chief Facilities/Physical Plant ... Vacant

*University of Hawaii Maui College (B)

310 Kaahumanu Avenue, Kahului HI 96732-1644
County: Maui FICE Identification: 001615
Unit ID: 141839
Telephone: (808) 984-3500 Carnegie Class: Assoc/Pub4
FAX Number: (808) 984-3546 Calendar System: Semester
URL: maui.hawaii.edu
Established: 1931 Annual Undergrad Tuition & Fees (In-State): $1,227
Enrollment: 4,367 Coed
Affiliation or Control: State IRS Status: 501(c)3
Highest Offering: Baccalaureate
Program: Occupational; 2-Year Principally Bachelor's Creditable; Nursing Emphasis
Accreditation: WC, ACFEI, ADNUR, DA, DH

02 Chancellor ... Dr. Clyde SAKAMOTO
05 Vice Chanc Academic Affairs ... Dr. Jonathon MCKEE
32 Vice Chancellor of Student Affairs ... Mr. Alvin TAGOMORI
11 Vice Chanc of Administrative Affs ... Mr. David TAMANAHA
13 Vice Chanc Information Technology ... Dr. Jose BERNIER
20 Int Assistant Dean of Instruction ... Mr. David GROOMS
51 Director Continuing Educ/Training ... Ms. Lori TERAOAWACHI
08 Librarian ... Ms. Lisa SEPA
06 Registrar ... Mr. Stephen KAMEDA
12 Director University Center Maui ... Ms. Karen MURAOKA
07 Director of Admissions ... Mr. Stephen KAMEDA
09 Director of Institutional Research ... Dr. Jean PEZZOLI
15 Director Personnel Services ... Ms. Debbi BROWN
18 Chief Facilities/Physical Plant ... Mr. Robert BURTON
21 Associate Fiscal Officer ... Ms. Cindy YAMAMOTO
30 Chief Development ... Ms. Cordy MACLAUGHLIN
36 Director Student Placement ... Mr. Stephen KAMEDA
37 Director Student Financial Aid ... Ms. Cathy BIO
38 Director Student Counseling ... Mr. Shane PAYBA

*University of Hawaii Windward Community College (C)

45-720 Keaahala Road, Kaneohe HI 96744-3598
County: Honolulu FICE Identification: 011220
Unit ID: 141990
Telephone: (808) 235-7400 Carnegie Class: Assoc/Pub2in4
FAX Number: (808) 247-5362 Calendar System: Semester
URL: www.wcc.hawaii.edu
Established: 1972 Annual Undergrad Tuition & Fees (In-State): $2,970
Enrollment: 2,625 Coed
Affiliation or Control: State IRS Status: 501(c)3
Highest Offering: Associate Degree
Program: Occupational; 2-Year Principally Bachelor's Creditable
Accreditation: WJ

02 Chancellor ... Mr. Doug DYKSTRA
05 Vice Chancellor Academic Affairs ... Dr. Richard FULTON
32 Vice Chancellor Student Services ... Mr. Lui HOKOANA
11 Vice Chanc Administrative Services ... Mr. Clifford TOGO
75 Director Vocational/Cmty Education ... Dr. Bernadette HOWARD
08 Head Librarian ... Ms. Nancy HEU
06 Registrar ... Ms. Geri IMAI
09 Director of Institutional Research ... Mr. Jeffrey HUNT
37 Director Student Financial Aid ... Mr. Steven CHIGAWA
15 Personnel Officer ... Ms. Karen CHO
26 Marketing/Public Relations Dir ... Ms. Bonnie BEATSON
30 Chief Development ... Vacant

World Medicine Institute (D)

931 University Avenue, Suite 104,
Honolulu HI 96826-3266
County: Honolulu FICE Identification: 030725
Unit ID: 141936
Telephone: (808) 947-4788 Carnegie Class: Spec/Health
FAX Number: (808) 373-2899 Calendar System: Semester
URL: www.worldmedicineinstitute.com
Established: 1970 Annual Graduate Tuition & Fees: $9,786
Enrollment: 48 Coed
Affiliation or Control: Independent Non-Profit IRS Status: 501(c)3
Highest Offering: Master's; No Undergraduates
Program: Professional
Accreditation: ACUP

01 President ... Dr. Lillian CHANG
05 Academic Dean ... Ms. Gayle TODOKI

IDAHO

Boise Bible College (E)

8695 W Marigold Street, Boise ID 83714-1220
County: Ada FICE Identification: 022345
Unit ID: 142090
Telephone: (208) 376-7731 Carnegie Class: Spec/Faith
FAX Number: (208) 376-7743 Calendar System: Semester
URL: www.boisebible.edu
Established: 1945 Annual Undergrad Tuition & Fees: $9,720
Enrollment: 181 Coed
Affiliation or Control: Christian Churches And Churches of Christ
IRS Status: 501(c)3
Highest Offering: Baccalaureate
Program: Religious Emphasis
Accreditation: BI

01 President ... Mr. Terry E. STINE
05 Academic Dean ... Mr. Charles FABER
32 Dean of Students ... Mr. Travis JACOB
10 Chief Business Officer ... Mr. Jim VAUGHAN
30 Director of Development ... Mr. David DAVOLT
84 Director of Enrollment Services ... Mr. Ross KNUDSEN
07 Director of Admissions ... Mr. Russell GROVE
08 Head Librarian ... Mrs. Glennis THOMAS
37 Financial Aid Director ... Mrs. Joyce ANDERSON
04 Assistant to the President ... Mrs. Ricki CARR
40 Director of Bookstore ... Mrs. Debby GRAF

Boise State University (F)

1910 University Drive, Boise ID 83725-1000
County: Ada FICE Identification: 001616
Unit ID: 142115
Telephone: (208) 426-1000 Carnegie Class: Master's L
FAX Number: (208) 426-3765 Calendar System: Semester
URL: www.boisestate.edu
Established: 1932 Annual Undergrad Tuition & Fees (In-State): $7,188
Enrollment: 19,993 Coed
Affiliation or Control: State IRS Status: 501(c)3
Highest Offering: Doctorate
Program: Liberal Arts And General; Teacher Preparatory; Professional; Business Emphasis
Accreditation: NW, ACFEI, ART, BUS, BUSA, CACREP, CONST, CS, DMS, ENG, MUS, NUR, RAD, SPAA, SW, TED, THEA

01 President ... Dr. Robert W. KUSTRA
05 Provost/Vice Pres Academic Affairs ... Dr. Martin SCHIMPF
10 Vice President Finan/Administration ... Ms. Stacy PEARSON
32 Vice President Student Affairs ... Dr. Lisa HARRIS
30 Int Vice Pres Univ Advancement ... Ms. Rosemary REINHARDT
20 Associate VP for Academic Planning ... Dr. James MUNGER
21 Associate Vice Pres for Finance ... Ms. Jo Ellen DI NUCCI
46 AVP Strategic Research Initiatives ... Dr. Cheryl SCHRADER
08 Dean of University Libraries ... Dr. Marilyn MOODY
84 Exec Director Enrollment Services ... Ms. Mara AFFRE
29 Executive Director Alumni Affairs ... Mr. Mark ARSTEIN
17 Medical Services Director ... Dr. Vincent SERIO
06 Registrar ... Ms. Kristine COLLINS
43 Vice President/University Counsel ... Mr. Kevin SATTERLEE
18 Exec Director Campus Security ... Mr. Jon UDA
40 Director Bookstore ... Mr. Mike REED
24 Director Academic Technologies ... Mr. Dale PIKE
09 Dir Inst Analysis Assessment ... Mr. Steven P. SCHMIDT
26 Dir of Communications & Marketing ... Mr. Frank ZANG
41 Director Athletics ... Mr. Gene BLEYMAIER
13 Assoc VP Information Technologies ... Mr. Max DAVIS-JOHNSON
22 Director Affirmative Action/EEO ... Ms. Marla HENKEN
15 Exec Director Human Resources ... Mr. Pablo COBLENTZ
38 Director Counseling Center ... Dr. Dan TIMBERLAKE
37 Director Student Financial Aid ... Mr. David TOLMAN
96 Director of Purchasing ... Ms. Terri SPINAZZA
51 Dean Extended Studies ... Mr. Mark WHEELER
49 Int Dean of Arts & Sciences ... Dr. Tony ROARK
83 Dean of Social Science/Public Affs ... Dr. Melissa LAVITT
50 Dean of Business & Economics ... Dr. Pat SHANNON
53 Dean of Education ... Dr. Diane BOOTHE
58 Dean of the Graduate College ... Dr. Jack PELTON
76 Dean of Health Sciences ... Dr. Tim DUNNAGAN
54 Interim Dean College of Engineering ... Dr. Amy MOLL
07 Director of Admissions ... Ms. Jenny CERDA
35 Director Student Affairs ... Ms. Lynn HUMPHREY

Brigham Young University-Idaho (G)

Rexburg ID 83460-1650
County: Madison FICE Identification: 001625
Unit ID: 142522
Telephone: (208) 496-1411 Carnegie Class: Bac/Diverse
FAX Number: (208) 496-1103 Calendar System: Semester
URL: www.byui.edu
Established: 1888 Annual Undergrad Tuition & Fees: $3,470
Enrollment: 14,150 Coed
Affiliation or Control: Latter-day Saints IRS Status: 501(c)3
Highest Offering: Baccalaureate
Program: Occupational; Liberal Arts And General
Accreditation: NW, ADNUR, CIDA, EMT, ENG, ENGT, MAC, MUS, NUR, SW

01 President ... Dr. Kim B. CLARK
05 Academic Vice President ... Dr. Fenton L. BROADHEAD
46 University Resources Vice President ... Mr. Charles N. ANDERSEN
35 Stdnt Svcs/Activities Vice Pres ... Mr. Kevin T. MIYASAKI
30 Advancement Vice President ... Dr. Henry J. EYRING
20 Assoc Academic VP Instruction ... Mr. Kelly T. BURGENER
20 Assoc Academic Vice Pres Curriculum ... Dr. Bruce C. KUSCH
45 Assoc Acad VP Education/Acad Devel ... Dr. Rob EATON
20 Assoc Acad VP Support Services ... Dr. Richard K. PAGE
20 Assoc Acad VP Student Connections ... Dr. Guy M. HOLLINGSWORTH
32 Dean of Students ... Mr. Kip B. HARRIS
32 Student Well Being Mng Director ... Mr. Wynn N. HILL
51 Continuing Education Director ... Mr. Chad P. PRICE
13 Chief Technology Officer ... Mr. M. Spalding JUGGANAIKLOO
09 Inst Research & Assessment Director ... Dr. Scott J. BERGSTROM
06 Student Records & Registration ... Mr. Kyle R. MARTIN
37 Student Fin Aid/Scholarship Dir ... Mr. Aaron D. SANNS
08 University Librarian ... Dr. Martin H. RAISH
72 Academic Technology Svcs Director ... Mr. Kent L. BARRUS
21 Univ Operations Managing Director ... Mr. Wayne N. CLARK
15 Human Resources Director ... Ms. Carla J. RICKS
23 Student Health Svcs Administrator ... Mr. Shaun ORR
38 Student Counseling Center Director ... Mr. Reed J. STODDARD
19 University Security & Safety ... Mr. Garth M. GUNDERSON
07 Admissions Director ... Mr. Tyler R. WILLIAMS
29 Alumni/Cmty Connections Director ... Mr. Steven J. DAVIS
35 Student Activities Mng Director ... Mr. Derek R. FAY
26 University Rels & Services Mng Dir ... Mr. Bruce R. HOBBS
30 Philanthropies Director ... Mr. David G. RICHARDS
44 Annual Giving Director ... Mr. D. A. HANSEN
39 Housing & Student Living Director ... Dr. Troy J. DOUGHERTY
43 Legal Counsel ... Mr. Michael R. ORME
21 Financial Services Mng Director ... Mr. Russel K. BENEDICT
88 Academic Discovery Center Director ... Mrs. Amy R. LABAUGH
96 Purchasing & Travel Director ... Mr. Darin N. LEE
84 Enrollment Svcs Managing Director ... Mr. Rob J. GARRETT
27 University Communications Director ... Mr. Merv R. BROWN
40 University Store Manager ... Mr. Doug R. MASON
104 International Services Manager ... Mr. Mike R. OSWALD
04 Asst to Pres Strategy & Planning ... Mrs. Betty A. OLDHAM

Brown Mackie College-Boise (H)

9050 West Overland Road, Ste. 101, Boise ID 83709
County: Ada Identification: 666780
Unit ID: 455600
Telephone: (208) 321-8800 Carnegie Class: Not Classified
FAX Number: (208) 375-3249 Calendar System: Other
URL: www.brownmackie.edu
Established: 2008 Annual Undergrad Tuition & Fees: $11,520
Enrollment: 718 Coed
Affiliation or Control: Proprietary IRS Status: Proprietary
Highest Offering: Baccalaureate
Program: Occupational; 2-Year Principally Bachelor's Creditable; Business Emphasis
Accreditation: ACICS, OTA

01 President ... Steve KAINA
07 Senior Director of Admissions ... Vacant
05 Dean of Academic Affairs ... Rob ROBICHAUD

† Branch campus of Brown Mackie College, South Bend, IN.

Carrington College - Boise (I)

1122 N Liberty Street, Boise ID 83704-8742
County: Ada FICE Identification: 022180
Unit ID: 142054
Telephone: (208) 377-8080 Carnegie Class: Assoc/PrivFP
FAX Number: (208) 322-7658 Calendar System: Semester
URL: www.carrington.edu
Established: 1980 Annual Undergrad Tuition & Fees: $13,312
Enrollment: 777 Coed
Affiliation or Control: Proprietary IRS Status: Proprietary
Highest Offering: Associate Degree
Program: Occupational; 2-Year Principally Bachelor's Creditable
Accreditation: ACICS, DA, DH, MAAB, PNUR, @PTAA

01 Executive Director ... Vacant
05 Dean of Academic Affairs ... Mr. Bradley JAHN
36 Director Career Services ... Ms. Brenda SLUSSER

The College of Idaho (A)

2112 Cleveland Boulevard, Caldwell ID 83605-9990
County: Canyon FICE Identification: 001617
Unit ID: 142294
Telephone: (208) 459-5011 Carnegie Class: Bac/A&S
FAX Number: (208) 454-2077 Calendar System: Other
URL: www.collegeofidaho.edu
Established: 1891 Annual Undergrad Tuition & Fees: $21,940
Enrollment: 1,055 Coed
Affiliation or Control: Independent Non-Profit IRS Status: 501(c)3
Highest Offering: Master's
Program: Liberal Arts And General; Teacher Preparatory
Accreditation: NW

01 President .... Dr. Marvin HENBERG
05 Vice President Academic Affairs .... Dr. Mark SMITH
10 Chief Finance Officer .... Ms. Petra CARVER
32 Vice President Student Affairs .... Mr. Paul BENNION
30 Vice Pres College Relations .... Mr. Michael VANDERVELDEN
06 Registrar .... Ms. Ann KUCK
84 Dean Enrollment Management .... Mr. Brian BAVA
41 Director of Athletics .... Mr. Marty HOLLY
26 Dir of Marketing & Communications .... Mr. Dustin WUNDERLICH
29 Director of Alumni Relations .... Ms. Lisa DEDAPPER
44 Boone Fund Coordinator .... Ms. Tara WENSEL
20 Associate Dean .... Dr. Kathy SEIBOLD
08 Librarian .... Ms. Christine SCHUTZ
18 Director Maintenance & Operations .... Mr. Kyle ABRAHAMSON
21 Controller .... Ms. Deanna ROSS
37 Director of Financial Aid .... Mrs. Juanitta PEARSON
15 Human Resources Director .... Ms. Bev ROBINSON
36 Director Student Placement .... Ms. Dora GALLEGOS
85 Director of International Education .... Dr. Ellen BATT
92 Director of Honors Program .... Dr. Sue SCHAPER
89 Director of Freshman Studies .... Dr. Lynn WEBSTER
39 Director of Residential Life .... Ms. Jen NELSON
93 Director of Minority Affairs .... Mr. Arnold HERNANDEZ
42 Campus Minister .... Dr. Phil ROGERS
19 Director of Campus Safety .... Mr. Allan LAIRD
96 Director of Purchasing .... Ms. Peta CARVER
90 Director of Network Services .... Mr. Zane HOWE
09 Director Institutional Research .... Dr. Kristina MAZURAK
40 Bookstore Manager .... Ms. Susan HUNSBERGER
38 Counselor .... Ms. Marilyn SIMMONDS

College of Southern Idaho (B)

PO Box 1238, 315 Falls Avenue,
Twin Falls ID 83303-1238
County: Twin Falls FICE Identification: 001619
Unit ID: 142559
Telephone: (208) 733-9554 Carnegie Class: Assoc/Pub-R-L
FAX Number: (208) 736-3015 Calendar System: Other
URL: www.csi.edu
Established: 1964 Annual Undergrad Tuition & Fees (In-District): $2,640
Enrollment: 7,699 Coed
Affiliation or Control: Local IRS Status: 501(c)3
Highest Offering: Associate Degree
Program: Occupational; 2-Year Principally Bachelor's Creditable
Accreditation: NW, ADNUR, DH, EMT, MAC, RAD, SURGA, SURGT

01 President .... Dr. Gerald L. BECK
05 Exec VP/Chief Academic Officer .... Dr. D. Jeff FOX
11 Vice President of Administration .... Mr. J. Mike MASON
32 VP of Student Svc/Plng & Grant Dev .... Dr. Edit SZANTO
102 Executive Director Foundation .... Dr. Curtis H. EATON
20 Instructional Dean .... Dr. John S. MILLER
20 Instructional Dean .... Dr. Cindy R. BOND
20 Instructional Dean .... Dr. Todd K. SCHWARZ
76 Dean Health Sci/Human Svcs/Biology .... Dr. Mark A. SUGDEN
21 Dean of Finance .... Mr. Jeff M. HARMON
09 Dean of Information Technology .... Dr. Ken B. CAMPBELL
35 Dean of Students .... Mr. Graydon A. STANLEY
88 Dean of Student Services .... Mr. J. Scott SCHOLES
06 Director of Admissions & Records .... Ms. Gail SCHULL
38 Director of Advising .... Mr. Cesar PEREZ GARCIA
37 Director of Student Financial Aid .... Ms. Jennifer J. ZIMMERS
15 Director Human Resources .... Mr. Monty J. ARROSSA
18 Director Physical Plant .... Mr. Randy G. DILL
08 Director Library .... Ms. Teri L. FATTIG
26 Public Information Director .... Mr. Doug L. MAUGHAN
14 Director Data Services .... Mr. Jay N. SNEDDON
19 Director Security & Safety .... Mr. S. Boyd NELSON
41 Athletic Director .... Mr. Joel C. BATE
27 Sports Information Director .... Ms. Karen D. BAUMERT
85 Director of Foreign Students .... Ms. Samra CULUM
92 Coordinator Honors Program .... Ms. Kimberly PRESTWICH
04 Admin Assistant to the President .... Ms. Kathy S. DEAHL

Eastern Idaho Technical College (C)

1600 S 25th E, Idaho Falls ID 83404-5788
County: Bonneville FICE Identification: 011133
Unit ID: 142179
Telephone: (208) 524-3000 Carnegie Class: Assoc/Pub-R-S
FAX Number: (208) 524-3007 Calendar System: Semester
URL: www.eitc.edu
Established: 1969 Annual Undergrad Tuition & Fees (In-State): $1,350
Enrollment: 861 Coed
Affiliation or Control: State IRS Status: 501(c)3
Highest Offering: Associate Degree
Program: Occupational; 2-Year Principally Bachelor's Creditable; Technical Emphasis
Accreditation: NW, MAC, SURGT

01 President .... Mr. Burton L. WAITE
10 Vice President of Finance and Admin .... Mr. James STRATTON
05 VP of Instruction & Student Affairs .... Dr. Steven K. ALBISTON
06 Registrar .... Mrs. Suzanne FELT
10 Controller .... Mr. Don E. BOURNE
103 Mgr Workforce Trng/Cmty Education .... Mr. Kenneth W. ERICKSON
08 Librarian .... Mrs. Suzy RICKS
37 Financial Aid Director .... Mrs. Shayna SHARP
04 Administrative Assistant .... Mrs. Jacque LARSEN
26 Director of College Relations .... Mr. Todd WIGHTMAN
102 Foundation Director .... Mrs. Michelle P. ZIEL
07 Director of Admissions/Placement .... Mrs. Annalea AVERY
40 Bookstore Operator .... Mr. Devon H. GLOVER
50 Business/Office/Technology Div Mgr .... Mr. Christian J. GODFREY
97 General Education Division Manager .... Mrs. Peggy L. NELSON
76 Health Care Technology Div Manager .... Dr. Sharee ANDERSON
88 Trades/Industry Division Manager .... Mr. Kent E. BERGGREN
88 Adult Basic Education Div Manager .... Mrs. Melody CLEGG
09 Director of Institutional Research .... Mr. Douglas D. DEPRIEST
15 Director Human Resources .... Mrs. Isela GUTIERREZ
18 Chief Facilities/Physical Plant .... Mr. William C. BRYANT
29 Director Alumni Relations .... Mrs. Melissa M. BEAN

Idaho State University (D)

921 S 8th, Pocatello ID 83209-0009
County: Bannock FICE Identification: 001620
Unit ID: 142276
Telephone: (208) 282-0211 Carnegie Class: RU/H
FAX Number: (208) 282-4000 Calendar System: Semester
URL: www.isu.edu
Established: 1901 Annual Undergrad Tuition & Fees (In-State): $5,796
Enrollment: 14,489 Coed
Affiliation or Control: State IRS Status: 501(c)3
Highest Offering: Doctorate
Program: Occupational; Liberal Arts And General; Teacher Preparatory; Professional
Accreditation: NW, ACFEI, ADNUR, ARCPA, AUD, BUS, BUSA, CACREP, CLPSY, CS, DENT, DH, DIETD, DIETI, DT, EMT, ENG, ENGR, ENGT, MAC, MT, MUS, NAIT, NURSE, OT, PH, PHAR, PTA, PTAA, SP, SW, TED, THEA

01 President .... Dr. Arthur C. VAILAS
05 Int ProvostVP for Acad Affairs .... Dr. Barbara ADAMCIK
10 Vice President for Finance & Admin .... Mr. James A. FLETCHER
30 Vice Pres University Advancement .... Dr. Kent M. TINGFY
32 Vice Pres of Student Affairs .... Dr. Patricia TERRELL
46 Exec Dir of Research & Tech Trans .... Dr. Richard T. JACOBSEN
43 University Legal Counsel .... Mr. Bradley H. HALL
41 Athletic Director .... Mr. Jeff TINGEY
20 AVP/Exec Dean Div Health Sciences .... Dr. Linda HATZENBUEHLER
20 AVP for Academic Affairs .... Dr. Laura WOODWORTH-NEY
20 AVP for Academic Affairs .... Ms. Kay CHRISTENSEN
30 AVP for Development .... Vacant
18 AVP for Facilities Services .... Mr. Joseph HAN
58 Dean of Graduate School .... Dr. Thomas JACKSON
54 Dean College of Science & Engr .... Dr. George IMEL
67 Dean College of Pharmacy .... Dr. Paul S. CADY
50 Interim Dean College of Business .... Dr. Kregg AYTES
49 Dean College of Arts & Letters .... Dr. Kandi TURLEY-AMES
53 Dean College of Education .... Dr. Deborah L. HEDEEN
75 Dean College of Technology .... Dr. Marilyn DAVIS
12 Dean of Academic Pgm ISU-Meridian .... Dr. Bessie KATSILOMETES
12 Dean of Academic Pgm ISU-Id Falls .... Dr. Lyle W. CASTLE
08 University Librarian & Dean .... Ms. Sandra SHOPSHIRE
06 Registrar & Dir of Undergrad Admiss .... Ms. Laura MCKENZIE
14 Chief Information Officer .... Mr. Randy GAINES
29 Director Alumni Relations .... Ms. K.C FELT
09 Director Institutional Research .... Mr. Vince MILLER
37 Director Student Financial Aid .... Mr. Kent D. LARSON
15 Director Human Resources .... Mr. David J. MILLER
25 Director Sponsored Programs .... Ms. Dianne K. HORROCKS
23 Director Student Health Center .... Dr. Ronald SOLBRIG
22 Dir EEO/Affirm Action & Diversity .... Ms. Joyce HAMMOND-PERRY
19 Director Public Safety .... Mr. Stephen A. CHATTERTON
26 Director Marketing & Communication .... Mr. Mark LEVINE
86 Director Government Relations .... Mr. Kent KUNZ
88 Director Events Management .... Mr. George CASPER

ITT Technical Institute (E)

12302 W Explorer Drive, Boise ID 83713-1529
County: Ada FICE Identification: 004553
Unit ID: 142337
Telephone: (208) 322-8844 Carnegie Class: Spec/Tech
FAX Number: (208) 322-0173 Calendar System: Quarter
URL: www.itt-tech.edu
Established: 1969 Annual Undergrad Tuition & Fees: N/A
Enrollment: 555 Coed
Affiliation or Control: Proprietary IRS Status: Proprietary
Highest Offering: Baccalaureate
Program: Technical Emphasis
Accreditation: ACICS

Lewis-Clark State College (F)

500 8th Avenue, Lewiston ID 83501-2698
County: Nez Perce FICE Identification: 001621
Unit ID: 142328
Telephone: (208) 792-5272 Carnegie Class: Bac/Diverse
FAX Number: (208) 792-2831 Calendar System: Semester
URL: www.lcsc.edu
Established: 1893 Annual Undergrad Tuition & Fees (In-State): $5,348
Enrollment: 4,542 Coed
Affiliation or Control: State IRS Status: 501(c)3
Highest Offering: Baccalaureate
Program: Occupational; 2-Year Principally Bachelor's Creditable; Liberal Arts And General; Teacher Preparatory; Professional; Nursing Emphasis
Accreditation: NW, IACBE, MAC, NURSE, SW, TED

01 President .... Dr. J. Anthony FERNANDEZ
05 Provost/Academic Vice President .... Vacant
10 VP Finance and Administration .... Mr. Chet HERBST
75 Dean Professional/Technical Pgms .... Dr. Robert LOHRMEYER
51 Dean Community Programs .... Ms. Kathy MARTIN
20 Dean Academic Programs .... Vacant
35 Dean Student Services .... Dr. Andrew HANSON
08 Director of Library Services .... Ms. Susan NIEWENHOUS
103 Director of Workforce Training .... Dr. Linda STRICKLIN
07 Director of Admissions/Registrar .... Ms. Nikol LUTHER
09 Dir Planning/Research/Assessment .... Mr. Howard ERDMAN
13 Chief Technology Officer .... Mr. Allen SCHMOOCK
41 Athletic Director .... Mr. Gary PICONE
15 Director of Human Resources .... Ms. Vikki SWIFT
27 Director of College Communications .... Mr. Bert SAHLBERG
29 Director of Alumni Relations .... Ms. Renee OLSEN
37 Director of Student Financial Aid .... Ms. Laura HUGHES
30 Director of College Advancement .... Ms. Mary HASENOEHRL
18 Director of Physical Plant .... Mr. Matt GRAVES
36 Director Career & Advising Services .... Ms. Debra LYBYER
96 Director of Purchasing .... Ms. Sheila KOM

New Saint Andrews College (G)

PO Box 9025, Moscow ID 83843-1525
County: Latah Identification: 666166
Unit ID: 440396
Telephone: (208) 882-1566 Carnegie Class: Bac/A&S
FAX Number: (208) 882-4293 Calendar System: Other
URL: www.nsa.edu
Established: 1994 Annual Undergrad Tuition & Fees: $10,400
Enrollment: 150 Coed
Affiliation or Control: Independent Non-Profit IRS Status: 170(c)1
Highest Offering: Master's
Program: Liberal Arts And General; Religious Emphasis
Accreditation: TRACS

01 President .... Dr. Roy A. ATWOOD
03 Executive Vice President .... Mr. Bob HIERONYMUS
05 Interim Provost .... Mr. Ed IVERSON
20 Vice Provost .... Dr. Jonathan MCINTOSH
10 Dir Financial & Facility Services .... Mr. Eric BURNETT
08 Head Librarian .... Mr. Ed IVERSON
06 Registrar .... Mrs. Beverlee ATWOOD
32 Director Student Affairs .... Mr. Ben MERKLE
07 Director Admissions .... Mrs. Brenda SCHLECT
40 Bookstore Manager .... Mr. Eric BURNETT
09 Dir Institutional Effectiveness .... Mr. Bob HIERONYMUS
84 Director Student Recruitment .... Mr. John SAWYER

North Idaho College (H)

1000 W Garden Avenue, Coeur d'Alene ID 83814-2199
County: Kootenai FICE Identification: 001623
Unit ID: 142443
Telephone: (208) 769-3300 Carnegie Class: Assoc/Pub-R-M
FAX Number: (208) 765-2761 Calendar System: Semester
URL: www.nic.edu
Established: 1933 Annual Undergrad Tuition & Fees (In-District): $2,764
Enrollment: 6,347 Coed
Affiliation or Control: Local IRS Status: 501(c)3
Highest Offering: Associate Degree
Program: Occupational; 2-Year Principally Bachelor's Creditable
Accreditation: NW, ADNUR, RAD

01 President .... Dr. Priscilla J. BELL
05 Vice President for Instruction .... Mr. Jay LEE
10 Vice President for Resource Mgmt .... Mr. Ronald DORN
32 Vice President for Student Services .... Dr. Sheldon NORD
26 VP for Community Relations & Mktg .... Mr. John MARTIN
103 Dean of Prof/Tech/Workforce Educ .... Mr. Mike MIRES
97 Dean of General Studies .... Mr. Robert MURRAY
17 Dean of Nursing & Health Care Pgms .... Dr. Lita BURNS
06 Registrar .... Ms. Tami HAFT
09 Director of Inst Effectiveness .... Ms. Ann LEWIS
08 Librarian .... Vacant
13 Director of Information Technology .... Mr. Stephen A. RUPPEL
37 Director of Financial Aid .... Mr. Joseph BEKKEN
07 Director of Admissions .... Ms. Tami HAFT
15 Director of Human Resources .... Dr. Wade LARSON
18 Director of Facilities .... Mr. Mike HALPERN
26 Director of Public Relations .... Ms. Erna RHINEHART
30 Development Director .... Ms. Rayelle ANDERSON
35 Director Student Activities .... Mr. Dean BENNETT
36 Dir of Academic & Support Services .... Ms. Sally HINDERS
21 Controller .... Ms. Sarah GARCIA
72 Technology Coordinator .... Mr. Andy FINNEY
29 Alumni Relations Coordinator .... Ms. Katie LIEN

Northwest Nazarene University (I)

623 S. University Blvd., Nampa ID 83686-5897
County: Canyon FICE Identification: 001624
Unit ID: 142461

Telephone: (208) 467-8011 Carnegie Class: Master's L
FAX Number: (208) 467-8099 Calendar System: Semester
URL: www.nnu.edu
Established: 1913 Annual Undergrad Tuition & Fees: $24,030
Enrollment: 2,016 Coed
Affiliation or Control: Church Of The Nazarene IRS Status: 501(c)3
Highest Offering: Master's
Program: Liberal Arts And General; Teacher Preparatory; Professional
Accreditation: NW, ACBSP, CACREP, MUS, NURSE, SW, TED

01 President .... Dr. David C. ALEXANDER
05 Vice Pres Academic Affairs/Dean .... Dr. Burton J. WEBB
30 Vice Pres University Advancement .... Dr. Joel K. PEARSALL
10 Vice President Financial Affairs .... Mr. David C. PETERSON
84 Vice Pres Enrollment & Marketing .... Mrs. Stacey L. BERGGREN
32 Vice President Student Development .... Dr. Carey W. COOK
88 Vice Pres Spiritual & Ldrshp Dev .... Dr. Fred C. FULLERTON
06 Registrar .... Mrs. Nancy A. AYERS
08 Director of the Library .... Dr. Sharon I. BULL
29 Director of Alumni Relations .... Mr. Darl L. BRUNER
51 Dir Center for Professional Devel .... Dr. Larry M. MCMILLIN
42 Dean of the Chapel .... Rev. M. Gene SCHANDORFF
42 Director of Campus Ministry .... Ms. Julene M. TEGERSTRAND
40 Bookstore Manager .... Ms. Gail D. WALKER
39 Director of Residential Life .... Mrs. Karen L. PEARSON
38 Director Counseling Services .... Mrs. Stacy J. FREIBURGHAUS
07 Director of Admissions .... Mr. Mike B. MARSTON
21 Controller .... Mrs. Shirley J. HAIDLE
26 Director of Marketing & Media .... Mrs. Hollie M. LINDNER
35 Director of Campus Life .... Mr. Tim R. MILBURN
36 Director of Career Center .... Ms. Amanda F. MARBLE
13 Director Computing & Info Systems .... Dr. Eric J. KELLERER
24 Director of Media Technology .... Dr. Duane L. SLEMMER
37 Director of Financial Aid .... Mr. David KLAFFKE
93 Director of Multicultural Affairs .... Rev. Jamie COLEMAN
16 Director of Human Resources .... Ms. Sherry L. HARTMAN
41 Athletic Director .... Mr. Rich F. SANDERS
91 Senior Systems Analyst .... Vacant
18 Chief Facilities/Physical Plant .... Mr. C. Richard VAN SCHYNDEL

† Granted candidacy at the Doctorate level.

Stevens-Henager College-Boise (A)

1444 S. Entertainment Avenue, Boise ID 83709
County: Ada Identification: 666329
Telephone: (208) 383-4540 Carnegie Class: Not Classified
FAX Number: (208) 345-6999 Calendar System: Other
URL: www.stevenshenager.edu
Established: 2004 Annual Undergrad Tuition & Fees: $37,500
Enrollment: 854 Coed
Affiliation or Control: Proprietary IRS Status: Proprietary
Highest Offering: Baccalaureate
Program: Occupational; Professional
Accreditation: ACCSC

01 Campus Director .... Dr. Shane REEDER

University of Idaho (B)

Campus Drive, PO Box 443151, Moscow ID 83844-3151
County: Latah FICE Identification: 001626
Unit ID: 142285
Telephone: (208) 885-6111 Carnegie Class: RU/H
FAX Number: (208) 885-5540 Calendar System: Semester
URL: www.uidaho.edu
Established: 1889 Annual Undergrad Tuition & Fees (In-State): $5,856
Enrollment: 12,302 Coed
Affiliation or Control: State IRS Status: 501(c)3
Highest Offering: Doctorate
Program: Liberal Arts And General; Teacher Preparatory; Professional
Accreditation: NW, ART, BUS, BUSA, CIDA, CORE, CS, DIETC, ENG, FOR, IPSY, LAW, LSAR, MUS, NRPA, TED

01 President .... Dr. M. Duane NELLIS
05 Provost & Executive Vice President .... Dr. Douglas D. BAKER
10 Vice Pres Finance & Administration .... Mr. Ron SMITH
30 Vice Pres University Advancement .... Mr. Christopher D. MURRAY
46 Vice President Research .... Dr. John MCIVER
12 Assoc Vice Pres for Northern Idaho .... Dr. Richard REARDON
12 Assoc VP and CEO Boise Center .... Dr. Trudy J. ANDERSON
12 Assoc Vice Pres Idaho Falls Center .... Dr. Robert W. SMITH
27 Assoc Vice Pres Mktg/Strat Comm .... Vacant
18 Assistant Vice President Facilities .... Mr. Brian D. JOHNSON
21 Asst VP Aux Svcs/Ad Ops/Cap Plng .... Mr. Tyrone W. BROOKS
84 Asst Vice Pres Enrollmnt Managemnt .... Mr. Steve NEIHEISEL
28 Asst to Pres Diversity/Equity/Cmty .... Mr. Mark A. EDWARDS
19 Manager Parking & Trans Services .... Mr. Carl ROOT
20 Vice Provost Academic Affairs .... Dr. Jeanne M. CHRISTIANSEN
35 Vice Provost Student Affairs .... Dr. Bruce M. PITMAN
08 Dean Library Services .... Ms. Lynn N. BAIRD
15 Associate VP Human Resources .... Mr. Mychal COLEMAN
32 Dean of Students .... Dr. Bruce M. PITMAN
22 Dir Human Rights/Access/Inclusion .... Ms. Carmen A. SUAREZ
06 Registrar .... Ms. Nancy A. KROGH
07 Director of Admissions .... Mr. Michael LOEHRING
09 Director Inst Research & Assessment .... Dr. Archie A. GEORGE
24 Director Information Tech Services .... Mr. Antony OPHEIM
29 Director Alumni Relations .... Mr. Steven C. JOHNSON
36 Dir Career & Professional Planning .... Ms. Suzanne K L. BILLINGTON
37 Director Student Financial Aid .... Dr. Daniel D. DAVENPORT
38 Director Counseling & Testing Ctr .... Dr. Joan PULAKOS
39 Director University Residences .... Mr. Ray GASSER
41 Athletic Director .... Dr. Robert SPEAR
42 Director Campus Christian Center .... Ms. Sharon A. KEHOE
43 General University Counsel .... Mr. Kent E. NELSON
44 Director Annual Giving .... Ms. Mandy HANOUSEK
87 Director Summer & Dual Enrol Prog .... Ms. Nancy KROGH
92 Director Honors Program .... Dr. Alton CAMPBELL
93 Int Director Multicultural Affairs .... Dr. Mark A. EDWARDS
94 Director Women's Center .... Ms. Heather GASSER
40 Director Bookstore .... Mr. John Anthony BALES
96 Manager Purchasing .... Mr. Christopher P. JOHNSON
47 Dean College of Agri/Life Sciences .... Dr. John E. HAMMEL
48 Dean College of Art & Architecture .... Mr. Mark E. HOVERSTEN
49 Dean Col of Letters/Arts Soc Sci .... Dr. Katherine G. AIKEN
50 Dean College of Business & Econ .... Dr. John S. MORRIS
53 Dean College of Education .... Dr. Connie MANTLE-BROMLEY
54 Dean College of Engineering .... Dr. Donald M. BLACKKETTER
58 Dean Graduate Studies .... Dr. Nilsa BOSQUE-PEREZ
61 Dean College of Law .... Mr. Donald L. BURNETT, JR.
65 Dean College of Natural Resources .... Dr. Kurt PREGITZER
81 Dean College of Science .... Dr. Scott A. WOOD

ILLINOIS

Adler School of Professional Psychology (C)

17 North Dearborn, Chicago IL 60602
County: Cook FICE Identification: 020681
Unit ID: 142832
Telephone: (312) 662-4000 Carnegie Class: Spec/Health
FAX Number: (312) 662-4099 Calendar System: Semester
URL: www.adler.edu
Established: 1952 Annual Graduate Tuition & Fees: $31,000
Enrollment: 1,030 Coed
Affiliation or Control: Independent Non-Profit IRS Status: 501(c)3
Highest Offering: Doctorate; No Undergraduates
Program: Professional
Accreditation: NH, CLPSY, @CORE, IPSY

01 President .... Dr. Raymond E. CROSSMAN
04 Director Office of the President .... Ms. Mitzi NORTON
101 Board Secretary .... Ms. Mitzi NORTON
11 Vice President Administration .... Mrs. Jo Beth CUP
07 Associate Vice President Admissions .... Mr. Craig HINES
07 Director of Admissions .... Ms. Michelle BRICE
26 Assoce Vice President Marketing .... Mr. Mark BRANSON
06 Registrar .... Ms. Sheba JONES
29 Director Alumni Rels/Student Affs .... Vacant
35 Asst Director Student Affairs .... Ms. Tami RENNER
37 Director Student Financial Aid .... Ms. Terri ESCH
05 Vice President Academic Affairs .... Dr. Martha CASAZZA
20 Associate VP Academic Affairs .... Dr. Wendy PASZKIEWICZ
31 Director Community Engagement .... Ms. Nancy BOTHNE
88 Director MA Counseling Training .... Dr. Paul FITZGERALD
88 Director of Doctoral Training .... Dr. Eunice KIM
24 Director Learning & Educ Technology .... Mr. Zoaib MIRZA
10 Vice President Finance & IT .... Mr. Jeffrey GREEN
18 Director of Facilities .... Ms. Hope POPA
21 Controller .... Mr. Todd KRAUSE
13 Associate VP Technology .... Mr. Paul COLLINS
16 Assoc VP Human Resources .... Ms. Elinor HITE
23 Director Adler Community Health Svc .... Dr. Dan BARNES
08 Director Library .... Ms. Kerry COCHRANE
09 Director of Institutional Research .... Mr. Don HUFFMAN
12 Dean Vancouver Campus .... Dr. Larry AXELROD
30 Vice President of Development .... Mr. Anthony CHIMERA
44 Director of Annual Giving .... Mr. De-Anthony KING
102 Director Corp & Foundation Rels .... Ms. Kate LUX
103 Director Career Services .... Vacant
28 Dir Institute on Social Exclusion .... Dr. Lynn TODMAN
28 Director IPSSJ .... Dr. Elena QUINTANA

American Academy of Art (D)

332 S Michigan Avenue, Chicago IL 60604-4302
County: Cook FICE Identification: 001628
Unit ID: 142887
Telephone: (312) 461-0600 Carnegie Class: Spec/Arts
FAX Number: (312) 294-9570 Calendar System: Semester
URL: www.aaart.edu
Established: 1923 Annual Undergrad Tuition & Fees: $26,350
Enrollment: 471 Coed
Affiliation or Control: Proprietary IRS Status: Proprietary
Highest Offering: Baccalaureate
Program: Professional; Fine Arts Emphasis
Accreditation: NH, ACCSC

01 Director .... Mr. Richard H. OTTO
05 Academic Dean .... Mr. Duncan WEBB
06 Registrar .... Ms. Marcia R. THOMAS
36 Career Services Coordinator .... Ms. Alexis KOWALSKI
37 Financial Aid Director .... Ms. Ione FITZGERALD
08 Faculty Librarian .... Ms. Lindsay HARMON
88 Cultural Coordinator .... Ms. Lou Ann BURKHARDT
07 Director of Admissions .... Mr. Stuart ROSENBLOOM

American College of Education (E)

20 North Wacker Drive, Suite 1776, Chicago IL 60606
County: Cook Identification: 666242
Unit ID: 449889
Telephone: (312) 821-6300 Carnegie Class: Spec/Other
FAX Number: (312) 332-0860 Calendar System: Semester
URL: www.ace.edu
Established: 2006 Annual Graduate Tuition & Fees: $6,950
Enrollment: 3,183 Coed
Affiliation or Control: Proprietary IRS Status: Proprietary
Highest Offering: Master's; No Undergraduates
Program: Teacher Preparatory
Accreditation: NH

01 President .... Ms. Sandra DORAN
05 Provost .... Dr. Shawntel D. LANDRY
10 Sr Vice Pres Regulatory Compliance .... Mr. Robert V. MYERS
26 Exec Vice Pres Marketing/Develop .... Dr. Vernon JOHNSON

American InterContinental University (F)

5550 Prairie Stone Parkway Ste 400, Hoffman Estates IL 60192-3713
County: Cook Identification: 666723
Unit ID: 445027
Telephone: (877) 701-3800 Carnegie Class: Not Classified
FAX Number: N/A Calendar System: Quarter
URL: www.aiuonline.edu
Established: 1970 Annual Undergrad Tuition & Fees: N/A
Enrollment: 19,803 Coed
Affiliation or Control: Proprietary IRS Status: Proprietary
Highest Offering: Master's
Program: 2-Year Principally Bachelor's Creditable; Professional
Accreditation: NH, ACBSP, @TEAC

01 Chief Executive Officer .... Mr. Stephen TOBER
05 Provost/Chief Academic Officer .... Dr. Gregory WASHINGTON

*Argosy University (G)

205 North Michigan Ave 13th Floor, Chicago IL 60601
County: Cook FICE Identification: 021799
Unit ID: 145770
Telephone: (312) 899-9900 Carnegie Class: N/A
FAX Number: (312) 424-7282
URL: www.argosy.edu

01 University President .... Dr. Craig D. SWENSON
05 Vice President of Academic Affairs .... Dr. Kathryn TOOREDMAN
32 GVP West .... Mr. Michael FALOTICO
03 Executive Vice President .... Mr. Eric EVENSON
07 VP Admissions .... Mr. Jeff CROSS
26 VP of Marketing .... Mr. Daron RODRIGUEZ
15 Vice President Human Resources .... Mr. Gregory BERNIARD
32 VP Academic Ops & Student Services .... Ms. Julie JOHNSON
106 VP for Online & Distance Learning .... Ms. Kate NOONE
10 Vice President of Finance .... Mr. Ken STEVENS
50 Dean College of Business .... Cynthia LARSON
83 Dean Psychology and Behav Sciences .... Dr. Susan SANCES
76 Dean College of Health Sciences .... Ms. Kristin BENSON
53 Dean College of Education .... Ms. Cynthia KUCK
97 Dean Undergraduate Studies .... Ms. Ruki JAYARAMAN
12 Campus President Twin Cities .... Mr. Scott TJADEN
12 Campus President Atlanta .... Dr. Ronald SWANSON
12 Campus President Dallas .... Mr. Ronald HYSON
12 Campus President Hawaii .... Dr. Warren EVANS
12 Campus President Washington D.C. .... Mr. David EREKSON
12 Campus President Seattle .... Mr. Tom DYER
12 Campus President Sarasota .... Vacant
12 Campus President Orange County .... Dr. James COX
12 Campus President Schaumburg .... Mr. James CHITWOOD
12 Campus President Tampa .... Dr. Patricia MEREDITH
12 Campus President Phoenix .... Mr. Bart LERNER
12 Campus Pres San Francisco Bay Area .... Dr. Lucille SANSING
12 Campus President Inland Empire .... Dr. James COX
12 Campus President Nashville .... Dr. Sandra WISE
12 Int Campus President San Diego .... Dr. James COX
12 Campus President Los Angeles .... Dr. James COX
12 Campus President Salt Lake City .... Vacant
12 Campus President Denver .... Dr. Marcia BANKIRER

*Argosy University, Chicago (H)

225 North Michigan Ave., Suite 1300, Chicago IL 60601
County: Cook Identification: 666736
Unit ID: 145770
Telephone: (312) 777-7600 Carnegie Class: DRU
FAX Number: (312) 777-7748 Calendar System: Semester
URL: www.argosy.edu/chicago
Established: 1976 Annual Undergrad Tuition & Fees: $14,580
Enrollment: 1,464 Coed
Affiliation or Control: Proprietary IRS Status: Proprietary
Highest Offering: Doctorate
Program: Professional
Accreditation: &NH, CACREP, CLPSY

02 Campus President .... Dr. Michael FALOTICO
05 Vice President of Academic Affairs .... Vacant
07 Senior Director of Admissions .... Christa HOLTON
32 Director of Student Services .... Eric ZIEHLKE
08 Director of Library Services .... Qi CHEN
10 Dir of Admin & Financial Services .... Irene AYERS
16 Human Resources Generalist .... Kristina HOUSTON
06 Registrar .... Tyler SHIPPEN

37 Dir of Student Financial Services ... Lyudmila BERKOFF

† Regional accreditation is carried under the parent institution, Argosy University in Chicago, IL.

*Argosy University, Schaumburg (A)

999 N. Plaza Drive, Suite 111, Schaumburg IL 60173-5403
County: Cook
Identification: 666789
Unit ID: 420866
Telephone: (847) 969-4900
Carnegie Class: Spec/Health
FAX Number: (847) 969-4999
Calendar System: Semester
URL: www.argosy.edu/schaumburg
Established: 1994
Annual Undergrad Tuition & Fees: $14,580
Enrollment: 796
Coed
Affiliation or Control: Proprietary
IRS Status: Proprietary
Highest Offering: Doctorate
Program: Professional
Accreditation: &NH, CACREP, CLPSY

02 Campus President ... Dr. James CHITWOOD
05 Vice President of Academic Affairs ... Dr. David B. VANWINKLE
32 Director of Student Services ... Evelyn HUMPHRIES
07 Director of Admissions ... Catherine CURRAN
37 Director of Student Finance ... Gwen DODT
08 Director of Library Services ... Janan REYNA
10 Dir of Admin and Financial Services ... Lei XIE
06 Registrar ... Humera FATIMA

† Regional accreditation is carried under the parent institution, Argosy University in Chicago, IL.

Augustana College (B)

639-38th Street, Rock Island IL 61201-2296
County: Rock Island
FICE Identification: 001633
Unit ID: 143084
Telephone: (309) 794-7000
Carnegie Class: Bac/A&S
FAX Number: (309) 794-7422
Calendar System: Trimester
URL: www.augustana.edu
Established: 1860
Annual Undergrad Tuition & Fees: $32,235
Enrollment: 2,500
Coed
Affiliation or Control: Evangelical Lutheran Church In America
IRS Status: 501(c)3
Highest Offering: Baccalaureate
Program: Liberal Arts And General; Teacher Preparatory
Accreditation: NH, MUS, TED

01 President ... Mr. Steven C. BAHLS
05 Int VP Academic Affs/Dn of College ... Dr. Ellen HAY
10 Vice Pres Business & Finance ... Mr. Paul D. PEARSON
30 Vice President Advancement ... Ms. Lynn E. JACKSON
32 Vice Pres/Dean of Student Services ... Dr. Evelyn S. CAMPBELL
84 VP Enrollment/Communication/Plng ... Mr. W. Kent BARNDS
20 Associate Dean of the College ... Dr. Margaret E. FARRAR
25 Director Assessments/Grants Officer ... Vacant
42 Chaplain ... Rev. Richard W. PRIGGIE
06 College Registrar ... Ms. Liesl A. FOWLER
14 Director of ITS ... Mr. Chris VAUGHAN
08 Director of the Library ... Ms. Carla B. TRACY
26 Director of Public Relations ... Mrs. Kamara BEATTIE
36 Director of Career Development ... Mr. Eric ROWELL
29 Director Alumni/Parent Relations ... Ms. Kelly NOACK
37 Director of Student Financial Aid ... Ms. Susan STANDLEY
38 Director Student Counseling ... Mr. Michael W. TENDALL
09 Director of Institutional Research ... Vacant
41 Director of Athletics ... Mr. Mike ZAPOLSKI
15 Director Human Resources ... Mrs. Laura C. FORD
18 Director Facilities Services ... Mr. Dennis M. HITTLE
07 Director of Admissions/Recruitment ... Ms. Meghan M. COOLEY
28 Director of Diversity ... Mr. Mark A. ANDERSON

Aurora University (C)

347 S Gladstone Avenue, Aurora IL 60506-4892
County: Kane
FICE Identification: 001634
Unit ID: 143118
Telephone: (630) 892-6431
Carnegie Class: Master's L
FAX Number: (630) 844-5463
Calendar System: Semester
URL: www.aurora.edu
Established: 1893
Annual Undergrad Tuition & Fees: $19,250
Enrollment: 4,437
Coed
Affiliation or Control: Independent Non-Profit
IRS Status: 501(c)3
Highest Offering: Doctorate
Program: Liberal Arts And General; Teacher Preparatory; Professional
Accreditation: NH, NURSE, SW, TED

01 President ... Dr. Rebecca L. SHERRICK
05 Provost ... Dr. Andrew P. MANION
30 Exec Vice Pres Univ Advancement ... Mr. Theodore C. PARGE
10 Vice President for Finance ... Mrs. Beth W. REISSENWEBER
11 Vice President for Administration ... Mr. Thomas HAMMOND
84 Vice President Enrollment ... Dr. Donna DE SPAIN
32 Vice President for Student Life ... Dr. Lora DE LACEY
26 Vice President Public Relations ... Mr. Steven MCFARLAND
31 Vice President Community Relations ... Ms. Sarah R. RUSSE
30 VP for Development/Alumni Relations ... Ms. Teri TOMASZKIEWICZ
35 Dean of Student Life ... Ms. Amy LAMPHERE
37 Dean of Student Financial Services ... Mrs. Heather L. MCKANE
13 Chief Information Officer ... Ms. Celeste E. BRANDING
14 Dir of Administrative Computing ... Mr. Robt S. LOWE
20 Assistant Provost ... Ms. Ellen J. GOLDBERG
21 Controller ... Mr. Joseph ONZICK
06 Registrar ... Ms. Kate MALE
08 Director of the Library ... Mr. John W. LAW
15 Director of Human Resources ... Ms. Therese A. HOEHNE
19 Director of Campus Safety ... Mr. Michael GOHLKE
09 Director of Institutional Research ... Mr. Kenneth LEASK
44 Director Special Gifts ... Mr. Roger K. PAROLINI
41 Athletic Director ... Mr. Mark C. WALSH
28 Director of Diversity Affairs ... Dr. Gerald R. BUTTERS
38 Director of Counseling Center ... Ms. Marcia C. HANLON
107 Dean College of Professional Stds ... Dr. Fred L. MCKENZIE
66 Director of School of Nursing ... Dr. Carmella MORAN
70 Director of School of Social Work ... Dr. Fred R. MCKENZIE
49 Dean Arts/Sciences/Business ... Dr. Saib OTHMAN
68 Dir of Sch Health/Physical Educ ... Dr. Alicia C. COSKY
50 Director Dunham School of Business ... Dr. Charles EDWARDS
53 Dean Education ... Dr. Donald C. WOLD

Benedictine University (D)

5700 College Road, Lisle IL 60532-0900
County: DuPage
FICE Identification: 001767
Unit ID: 145619
Telephone: (630) 829-6000
Carnegie Class: DRU
FAX Number: (630) 960-1126
Calendar System: Semester
URL: www.ben.edu
Established: 1887
Annual Undergrad Tuition & Fees: $24,650
Enrollment: 6,892
Coed
Affiliation or Control: Roman Catholic
IRS Status: 501(c)3
Highest Offering: Doctorate
Program: Liberal Arts And General; Teacher Preparatory; Professional
Accreditation: NH, DIETD, DIETI, NURSE

00 Chancellor ... RtRev. Austin G. MURPHY, OSB
01 President ... Dr. William J. CARROLL
03 Executive Vice President ... Mr. Charles GREGORY
30 Chief Officer Advancement ... Vacant
05 Provost/Vice Pres Academic Affs ... Dr. Donald TAYLOR
32 Associate Vice Pres Student Life ... Mr. Marco MASINI
10 VP Business & Finance ... Mr. Allan GOZUM
09 Assoc Prov/Dir Inst Effectiveness ... Dr. David SONNENBERGER
42 Director University Ministry ... Mr. Mark KUROWSKI
84 Assoc Vice President of Enrollment ... Mrs. Kari GIBBONS
06 Registrar ... Mr. Bob BOSANAC
11 Executive Director Operations ... Vacant
08 Director Library Services ... Mr. Jack FRITTS
37 Associate Dean Financial Aid ... Ms. Diane BATTISTELLA
36 Director Career Development ... Ms. Julie COSIMO
23 Director Health Services ... Ms. Barbara ALLANACH
26 Exec Dir Marketing/Communications ... Ms. Mercy ROBB
105 Assoc Dir Online/Electronic Comm ... Ms. Nadia DARWISH
50 Dean College of Business ... Dr. Sandra GILL
81 Dean College of Science ... Dr. Ralph MEEKER
49 Dean College of Liberal Arts ... Dr. Maria DE LA CAMARA
51 Dean Col of Adult Profess Studies ... Vacant
53 Dean Col Education/Health Services ... Dr. Alan GORR
19 Chief of Police ... Mr. Michael SALATINO
18 Director Campus Services ... Mr. Jay L. STUART
39 Director of Residence Life ... Ms. Zeina ABUSOUD
29 Director of Alumni Relations ... Ms. Julie NELLIGAN
31 Director Community Development ... Ms. Denise WEST
15 Director of Personnel Resources ... Ms. Susan STROUGAL
35 Asst to Director Student Activities ... Ms. Katie BUELL
07 Acting Director of Enrollment ... Ms. Dayna CRABB
27 Chief Information Officer ... Mr. Charles WILLIAMS

Black Hawk College (E)

6600 34th Avenue, Moline IL 61265-5899
County: Rock Island
FICE Identification: 001638
Unit ID: 143279
Telephone: (309) 796-5000
Carnegie Class: Assoc/Pub-R-L
FAX Number: (309) 792-5976
Calendar System: Semester
URL: www.bhc.edu
Established: 1946
Annual Undergrad Tuition & Fees (In-District): $3,152
Enrollment: 6,677
Coed
Affiliation or Control: Local
IRS Status: 501(c)3
Highest Offering: Associate Degree
Program: Occupational; 2-Year Principally Bachelor's Creditable
Accreditation: NH, ADNUR, PTAA

01 President ... Dr. R. Gene GARDNER
05 Exec VP/VP Instruction/ITS ... Dr. Rose M. CAMPBELL
10 Chief Financial Officer ... Ms. Leslie ANDERSON
11 VP Administration ... Mr. Mike PHILLIPS
32 VP Student Services ... Dr. Richard VALLANDINGHAM
12 Vice President for East Campus ... Ms. Chanda DOWELL
15 Director of Human Resources ... Ms. Karen BOYD
13 Chief Information Officer ... Mr. Sam SCOMA
09 Director Plng & Inst Effectiveness ... Ms. Kathy MALCOLM
20 Dean Instruction/Academic Support ... Dr. Bettie TRUITT
20 Interim Dean Inst/Student Learning ... Dr. Michael RIVERA
32 Asst Dean of Student Support Svcs ... Dr. Kim ARMSTRONG
51 Assoc Dean Adult/Continuing Educ ... Ms. Glenda NICKE
44 Executive Director BHC Foundation ... Ms. Shelly CAIN
88 Director Small Business Devel Ctr ... Mr. Joel YOUNGS
26 Director Marketing/Public Relations ... Mr. John MEINEKE
37 Director of Financial Aid ... Ms. Joanna DYE
36 Director Career Services Center ... Dr. Bruce STOREY
40 Bookstore Manager ... Ms. Nyla WOOLARD
41 Division Director Athletics/Coach ... Mr. Gary HUBER
08 Librarian ... Ms. Charlet KEY
19 Chief of Police ... Mr. Richard FIEMS
22 EEO/Affirmative Action Officer ... Ms. Jo JOHNSON
24 Dir Teaching Lrng Ctr/Online Lrng ... Dr. Molly BAKER
81 Dept Chair Math/Comp Science ... Mr. Peter NODZENSKI
31 Director Bus & Community Educ Ctr ... Ms. Brenda BROWN
51 Director Adult Education ... Ms. Diane FALL
35 Asst Dean of Student Support Svc/EC ... Mr. B. J MCCULLUM
06 Registrar ... Ms. Linda TURNER
96 Purchasing Manager ... Mr. Mike MELEG
51 Department Chair Adult Education ... Ms. Julie STEIN
72 Dept Chair Bus & Office Tech ... Ms. Gwen JOHNSON
57 Dept Chair Comm & Fine Arts ... Ms. Michelle JOHNSON
79 Dept Chair Human/Languages/Journal ... Mr. Bill DESMOND
54 Dept Chair Natural Science/Engrng ... Mr. Brian GLASER
83 Dept Chair Social/Behav/Educ Stds ... Dr. Bruce LEBLANC
47 Department Chair Applied Science ... Mr. William GOOD
49 Dept Chair Liberal Arts/Sciences ... Ms. Deana BOBZIEN
66 Dept Chair Assoc Degree/Prac Nurs ... Ms. Karen BABER
76 Dept Chair Allied Health/HPE ... Ms. Betsey MORTHLAND
88 Dept Chair Counseling ... Mr. Joseph OBLETON
62 Dept Chair Lrg Resource Center ... Ms. Charlet KEY

Blackburn College (F)

700 College Avenue, Carlinville IL 62626-1498
County: Macoupin
FICE Identification: 001639
Unit ID: 143288
Telephone: (217) 854-3231
Carnegie Class: Bac/Diverse
FAX Number: (217) 854-5700
Calendar System: Semester
URL: www.blackburn.edu
Established: 1837
Annual Undergrad Tuition & Fees: $13,436
Enrollment: 595
Coed
Affiliation or Control: Presbyterian Church (U.S.A.)
IRS Status: 501(c)3
Highest Offering: Baccalaureate
Program: Liberal Arts And General; Teacher Preparatory
Accreditation: NH

01 President ... Dr. Miriam R. PRIDE
05 Provost ... Dr. Jeffery P. APER
10 Vice Pres Administration & Finance ... Ms. Heather BIGARD
04 Exec Asst to Pres/Asst Sec Bd Trust ... Ms. Ann M. ALLEN
32 Dean of Students ... Ms. Heidi HEINZ
07 Director of Admissions ... Ms. Alisha KAPP
88 Director of Transfer Admissions ... Mr. John MALIN
29 Sr Develop Ofcr/Alumni/Staff Rels ... Mr. Nate RUSH
37 Director of Financial Aid ... Ms. Jane KELSEY
08 Head Librarian ... Ms. Carol SCHAEFER
38 College Counselor ... Mr. Robert M. WEIS
06 College Registrar ... Ms. Dianna RUYLE
15 Director Personnel Services ... Ms. Ann ALLEN
36 Director Student Placement ... Ms. Suzanne KRUPICA
18 Director Physical Plant ... Mr. Richard BOWMAN
41 Director of Athletic Programs ... Ms. Sue HANSEN
42 Chaplain ... Vacant
26 Director of Public Relations ... Mr. Pete OSWALD
09 Director Institutional Research ... Dr. Kristi NELMS
21 Business Office Manager ... Ms. Mary WERRIES
44 Director of Annual Giving ... Ms. Jodi ROWE
30 Manager of Development Operations ... Mr. Glen KRUPICA

Blessing-Rieman College of Nursing (G)

Broadway at 11th, PO Box 7005, Quincy IL 62305-7005
County: Adams
FICE Identification: 006214
Unit ID: 143297
Telephone: (217) 228-5520
Carnegie Class: Spec/Health
FAX Number: (217) 223-4661
Calendar System: Semester
URL: www.brcn.edu
Established: 1891
Annual Undergrad Tuition & Fees: $17,089
Enrollment: 315
Coed
Affiliation or Control: Independent Non-Profit
IRS Status: 501(c)3
Highest Offering: Master's
Program: Professional; Nursing Emphasis
Accreditation: NH, NURSE

01 President College of Nursing ... Dr. Pamela S. BROWN

Bradley University (H)

1501 W Bradley Avenue, Peoria IL 61625-0001
County: Peoria
FICE Identification: 001641
Unit ID: 143358
Telephone: (309) 676-7611
Carnegie Class: Master's L
FAX Number: N/A
Calendar System: Semester
URL: www.bradley.edu
Established: 1897
Annual Undergrad Tuition & Fees: $26,704
Enrollment: 5,813
Coed
Affiliation or Control: Independent Non-Profit
IRS Status: 501(c)3
Highest Offering: Doctorate
Program: Liberal Arts And General; Teacher Preparatory; Professional
Accreditation: NH, ART, BUS, BUSA, CACREP, CONST, DIETD, @DIETI, ENG, ENGT, MUS, NUR, PTA, SW, TED, THEA

01 President ... Ms. Joanne K. GLASSER
05 Provost/Vice Pres Academic Affairs ... Dr. David GLASSMAN
20 Assistant Provost Academic Affairs ... Mrs. Linda J. PIZZUTI
10 Vice President Business Affairs ... Mr. Gary M. ANNA
30 Vice President Advancement ... Mr. Pat VICKERMAN
32 Vice Pres Student Affairs ... Dr. Alan G. GALSKY

27 Assoc VP University Communications ....Mr. Shelley EPSTEIN
26 Assoc VP University Marketing ....Ms. Susan ANDREWS
58 Dean Graduate School ....Dr. Charles MARIS
50 Dean Foster Col Business Admin ....Dr. Robert BAER
57 Dean Slane Col Communic/Fine Arts ...Dr. Jeffrey H. HUBERMAN
53 Dean Education & Health Sciences ....Dr. Joan L. SATTLER
54 Dean Engineering & Technology ....Dr. Richard T. JOHNSON
49 Dean Liberal Arts & Sciences ....Dr. Claire ETAUGH
84 Assoc Provost Enrollment Mgmt ....Ms. Angela M. ROBERSON
13 Assoc Provost Info Resources & Tech ....Mr. J. Chuck RUCH
08 Exec Director of the Library ....Ms. Barbara GALIK
38 Ex Dir Ctr For Stdnt Dev/Hlth Svcs ....Dr. Joyce SHOTICK
39 Ex Dir Ctr Residential Lvgn/Ldrshp ....Mr. Nathan THOMAS
88 Exec Dir Campus Rec & Athl Fac ....Mr. Mike KEUP
36 Exec Director Smith Career Center ....Ms. Jane C. LINNENBURGER
14 Exec Dir Computing Services ....Ms. Sandra HELMS
24 Ex Dir Instruct Tech/Media Svcs ....Mr. Nial L. JOHNSON
29 Exec Director of Alumni Relations ....Ms. Lori FAN
51 Executive Director Continuing Educ ....Ms. Janet LANGE
06 Registrar ....Mrs. Katherine M. BEATY
37 Exec Dir Enroll Mgmt/Dir Fin Asst ....Mr. David L. PARDIECK
07 Exec Director of Admissions ....Mr. Rodney SAN JOSE
19 Chief of Campus Police ....Mr. Brian JOSCHKO
15 Director of Human Resources ....Ms. Nena PEPLOW
18 Director Facilities Management ....Mr. Ron DOERZAPH
23 Medical Director ....Dr. Jessica HIGGS
27 Director Public Information ....Ms. M. Kathleen CONVER
41 Director Athletics ....Dr. Michael CROSS
78 Director Experiential Education ....Ms. Sharon ST. GERMAIN
87 Assoc Dir Summer/Interim Sessions ....Mr. Jon NEIDY
25 Int Dir Off/Teaching Excel/Fac Dev ....Mrs. Kim WILLIS
22 Director Affirmative Action/EEO ....Ms. Nena PEPLOW
28 Dir Multicultural Student Services ....Ms. Frances JONES
92 Director of Honors Program ....Dr. Robert FULLER
94 Director of Women's Studies ....Dr. Stacey M. ROBERTSON
09 Dir of Institutional Improvement ....Ms. Jennifer GRUENING
40 Manager Bookstore ....Mr. Paul KROENKE
21 Business Manager ....Mr. Kenneth GOLDIN
96 Accounts Payable Manager ....Mrs. Diane SMITH

Carl Sandburg College (A)

2400 Tom L. Wilson Boulevard, Galesburg IL 61401-9576
County: Knox FICE Identification: 007265
Unit ID: 143613
Telephone: (309) 344-2518 Carnegie Class: Assoc/Pub-R-M
FAX Number: (309) 344-1395 Calendar System: Semester
URL: www.sandburg.edu
Established: 1966 Annual Undergrad Tuition & Fees: $3,780
Enrollment: 3,483 Coed
Affiliation or Control: Independent Non-Profit IRS Status: 501(c)3
Highest Offering: Associate Degree
Program: Occupational; 2-Year Principally Bachelor's Creditable
Accreditation: NH, ADNUR, DH, FUSER, PNUR

01 President ....Dr. Lori L. SUNDBERG
32 Vice President of Student Services ....Mr. Steve NORTON
05 Vice President of Academic Services ....Ms. Julie GIBB
11 Vice President Administrative Svcs ....Mr. Samuel SUDHAKAR
08 Dean of Library ....Mr. Michael WALTERS
31 Dean Corporate & Community Svcs ....Ms. Sherry FOSTER
51 Dean Adult & Developmental Educ ....Mr. Jim RICH
75 Dean of Occupational Programs ....Vacant
76 Dean of Career Technical and Health ......Ms. Lauri WIECHMANN
12 Dean of Extension Services ....Ms. Debra MILLER
56 Director of Extension Services ....Ms. Linda THOMAS
36 Director of Business Svcs ....Mr. Larry BYRNE
37 Director Financial Aid ....Ms. Lisa HANSON
26 Director Marketing/Public Relations ....Ms. Robin DEMOTT
10 Chief Financial Officer/Treasurer ....Ms. Lisa BLAKE
102 Director Foundation ....Ms. Gena ALCORN
88 Director TRIO Upward Bound ....Mr. Tony BENTLEY
88 Director TRIO Student Support Svcs ....Ms. Misty LYON
07 Director of Recruitment ....Mrs. Marnie DUGAN
66 Associate Dean of Nursing ....Ms. Rosemary O'DANIEL
06 Dean of Student Support Services ....Ms. Carol KREIDER
46 Dean Hum Res/Organizational Devel .....Dr. Constance THURMAN

Catholic Theological Union (B)

5401 S Cornell Avenue, Chicago IL 60615-5698
County: Cook FICE Identification: 009232
Unit ID: 143659
Telephone: (773) 371-5400 Carnegie Class: Spec/Faith
FAX Number: (773) 324-8490 Calendar System: Semester
URL: www.ctu.edu
Established: 1967 Annual Graduate Tuition & Fees: $18,279
Enrollment: 470 Coed
Affiliation or Control: Roman Catholic IRS Status: 501(c)3
Highest Offering: Doctorate; No Undergraduates
Program: Professional; Religious Emphasis
Accreditation: THEOL

01 President ....Rev. Donald P. SENIOR, CP
05 Vice President/Academic Dean ....Sr. Barbara REID, OP
10 Vice Pres Finance & Administration ....Mr. Michael W. CONNORS
30 Director of Development ....Ms. Anne M. TIRPAK
26 Dir of Marketing & Communications ....Ms. Elizabeth J. WHITE
08 Director of the Library ....Ms. Melody L. MCMAHON
06 Registrar ....Mrs. Maria De Jesus LEMUS
07 Director of Admissions ....Ms. Kathy VAN DUSER
21 Comptroller ....Mrs. Joyce E. O'CONNOR
51 Director of Continuing Education ....Ms. Keiren O'KELLY
04 Assistant to the President ....Sr. Pam PAULOSKI, SP
35 Director of Student Services ....Ms. Christine HENDERSON
37 Director Student Financial Aid ....Ms. Kathy VAN DUSER

† The Graduate School of Theology and Ministry, accredited by the Association of Theological Schools and North Central Association (NCA), grants a Doctoral degree.

Chicago School of Professional Psychology (C)

325 N Wells Street, Chicago IL 60654-8158
County: Cook FICE Identification: 021553
Unit ID: 143978
Telephone: (312) 329-6600 Carnegie Class: Spec/Health
FAX Number: (312) 644-3333 Calendar System: Semester
URL: www.thechicagoschool.edu
Established: 1979 Annual Graduate Tuition & Fees: $31,911
Enrollment: 3,563 Coed
Affiliation or Control: Independent Non-Profit IRS Status: 501(c)3
Highest Offering: Doctorate; No Undergraduates
Program: Professional
Accreditation: NH, CLPSY

01 President ....Dr. Michele NEALON-WOODS
12 Interim Campus President Chicago ....Dr. Patricia BREEN
12 Campus President Washington DC ....Dr. Orlando TAYLOR
10 Vice Pres of Finance/Administration ....Ms. Carole ROBERTSON
11 Senior Vice President of Operations ....Vacant
102 President TCS Foundation ....Dr. Tim SHANNON
13 Vice Pres of Information Technology ....Vacant
26 Vice Pres of Marketing & Comm ....Ms. Dina SCHENK
32 Assoc VP Engagement/Student Affairs ....Vacant
05 Dean of Academic Affairs Chicago ....Dr. Ellis COPELAND
106 Dean of Academic Affairs Online Pgm ....Dr. Margie MARTYN
32 Director of Student Services ......Ms. Jennifer STRIPE-PORTILLO
07 Director of Admissions Chicago ....Ms. Andrea SCHMOYER
15 Assoc Vice Pres Human Resources ....Ms. Susan CRAIG
37 Assistant Director of Financial Aid ....Ms. Tamatha CONAWAY
36 Director of Career Services ....Ms. Aisha GHORI
08 Campus Librarian ....Vacant
09 Dir Institutional/Market Research ....Dr. George HAY
26 Dir Communications/Public Relations ....Ms. Lynne BAKER
36 Dir Office of Placement/Training ....Ms. Heather SHEETS
88 Assoc Director of Clincal Services ....Ms. Marilisa MOREA
88 Director of Community Partnerships ....Ms. Jill GLENN
07 Director of Admissions LA Campus ....Ms. Heather LA BELLE
88 Dir Center for Academic Excellence ....Dr. Katia MITOVA
28 Dir Multicultural/Diversity Studies ....Vacant
27 Dir of Institutional Publications ....Ms. Judy BEAUPRE
06 Registrar ....Ms. Lisa HINKLE
88 Dept Chair Clinical Psych PsyD ....Dr. Thomas BARRETT
88 Dept Chair Business Psych PsyD ....Dr. Keith CARROLL
88 Dept Chair School Psych Master's ....Dr. James WALSH
88 Dept Ch Forensic Psych PsyD/ Masters ....Dr. Michele HOY-WATKINS
88 Dept Chr Clinical-ABA PsyD/Masters ....Dr. Diana WALKER
88 Dept Chair Clincal-Counsel Master's ....Dr. Virginia QUINONEZ
35 Director of Student Affairs ....Ms. Shea WOLFE

Chicago State University (D)

9501 S King Drive, Chicago IL 60628-1598
County: Cook FICE Identification: 001694
Unit ID: 144005
Telephone: (773) 995-2000 Carnegie Class: Master's L
FAX Number: (773) 995-2563 Calendar System: Semester
URL: www.csu.edu
Established: 1867 Annual Undergrad Tuition & Fees (In-State): $10,653
Enrollment: 7,362 Coed
Affiliation or Control: State IRS Status: 501(c)3
Highest Offering: Doctorate
Program: Liberal Arts And General; Teacher Preparatory; Professional
Accreditation: NH, ACBSP, CACREP, MUS, NRPA, NUR, OT, @PHAR, SW, TED

01 President ....Dr. Wayne D. WATSON
04 Executive Assistant to President ....Vacant
05 Provost/Sr VP for Academic Affairs .....Dr. Sandra WESTBROOKS
43 Gen Counsel for Labor/Legal Affs ....Mr. Patrick CAGE
21 VP of Administration and Finance ....Mr. Glenn MEEKS
10 Acting Director Budget & Risk Mgmt .Mrs. Arrileen PATAWARAN
13 Chief Information Officer ....Mrs. Ce S. COLE DILLON
84 Vice Pres of Enrollment Management ...Mrs. Angela HENDERSON
09 Director Inst Research/Evaluations ....Vacant
49 Interim Dean Arts & Sciences ....Dr. David R. KANIS
53 Dean Education ....Dr. Sylvia GIST
67 Dean College of Pharmacy ....Dr. Miriam MOBLEY-SMITH
76 Dean College of Health Sciences ....Dr. Joseph A. BALOGUN
50 Dean College of Business ....Mr. Derrick K. COLLINS
08 Acting Dean of Library/Instruct Svc ....Dr. Richard DARGA
51 Interim Dean Cont Educ Nontrad Pgms ....Ms. Nelly MAYNARD
58 Dean School Grad/Prof Studies ....Dr. Justin AKUJIEZE
06 Interim Registrar ....Ms. Carnice HILL
21 Interim Bursar ....Ms. Mary C. LONG
84 Director of Enrollment Svcs ....Ms. Cheri SIDNEY
37 Director of Financial Aid ....Mrs. Brenda HOOKER
07 Director of Admissions ....Mr. Matthew HARRISON
29 Director Alumni Affairs ....Vacant
26 Director of Marketing & Public Rel ....Vacant
15 Director Human Resources ....Dr. Renee D. MITCHELL
36 Director of Career Development ....Mr. Lee JUNKANS
88 Interim Dir Latino Resource Center ....Mr. Fernando DIAZ
96 Director of Purchasing ....Ms. Janielle GRAHAM
18 Int Dir Facilities/Physical Plant ....Mr. Alan O'NEAL
20 Associate VP Academic Officer ....Dr. Debrah JEFFERSON
35 Dir of Student Act & Leadership Dev ....Mr. Jason FERGUSON
38 Director Counseling Center ....Dr. Michael C. EDWARDS

Chicago Theological Seminary (E)

5757 University Avenue, Chicago IL 60637-1579
County: Cook FICE Identification: 001661
Unit ID: 144014
Telephone: (773) 752-5757 Carnegie Class: Spec/Faith
FAX Number: (773) 752-0905 Calendar System: Semester
URL: www.ctschicago.edu
Established: 1855 Annual Graduate Tuition & Fees: $12,840
Enrollment: 228 Coed
Affiliation or Control: United Church Of Christ IRS Status: 501(c)3
Highest Offering: Doctorate; No Undergraduates
Program: Professional
Accreditation: NH, THEOL

01 President ....Dr. Alice HUNT
05 Academic Dean ....Dr. Ken STONE
10 Vice President for Finance & Admin ....Mr. Stephen MANNING
30 Vice President Development ....Vacant
06 Registrar ....Ms. Cheryl W. MILLER
08 Head Librarian ....Rev. Neil W. GERDES
84 Director of Enrollment ....Mr. Kim KING

Christian Life College (F)

400 E Gregory Street, Mount Prospect IL 60056-2522
County: Cook FICE Identification: 031993
Unit ID: 260947
Telephone: (847) 259-1840 Carnegie Class: Spec/Faith
FAX Number: (847) 259-3888 Calendar System: Semester
URL: www.christianlifecollege.edu
Established: 1950 Annual Undergrad Tuition & Fees: $10,590
Enrollment: 42 Coed
Affiliation or Control: Pentecostal/Charismatic Non-Denominational
IRS Status: 501(c)3
Highest Offering: Baccalaureate
Program: Religious Emphasis
Accreditation: TRACS

01 President ....Mr. Harry R. SCHMIDT
05 Academic Dean ....Mr. Wayne R. WACHSMUTH
08 Director of Library Services ....Mr. Christopher C. ULLMAN
10 Director of Finance ....Mr. Roger K. STEVENS
32 Dean of Students ....Vacant
06 Registrar ....Mr. Michael BELL

*City Colleges of Chicago (G)

226 W Jackson Boulevard, Chicago IL 60606-6998
County: Cook FICE Identification: 001647
Unit ID: 144500
Telephone: (312) 553-2500 Carnegie Class: N/A
FAX Number: (312) 553-2699
URL: www.ccc.edu

01 Chancellor ....Dr. Cheryl HYMAN
05 Int VC Academic Affs/Plan/Research ....Mr. Michael DAVIS
10 Vice Chancellor Finance ....Mr. Ken GOTSCH
15 Vice Chanc Human Resource/Staff Dev ....Ms. Patricia RIOS
13 Vice Chanc/Chief Information Ofcr ....Mr. Craig LYNCH
30 Vice Chanc Development ....Dr. Michael DAIGLER
09 Vice Chanc Strategy & Instnl Intel ....Dr. Alvin BISARYA
11 Vice Chanc Administrative Services ....Ms. Diane MINOR
04 Executive Board Administrator ....Ms. Regina HAWKINS
43 General Counsel ....Mr. James REILLY
27 Executive Director Communications ....Mr. Ronald SCHOFIELD

*City Colleges of Chicago Harold Washington College (H)

30 E Lake Street, Chicago IL 60601-2449
County: Cook FICE Identification: 001652
Unit ID: 144209
Telephone: (312) 553-5600 Carnegie Class: Assoc/Pub-U-MC
FAX Number: (312) 553-5964 Calendar System: Semester
URL: www.ccc.edu
Established: 1962 Annual Undergrad Tuition & Fees (In-District): $3,010
Enrollment: 8,721 Coed
Affiliation or Control: State/Local IRS Status: 501(c)3
Highest Offering: Associate Degree
Program: Occupational; 2-Year Principally Bachelor's Creditable
Accreditation: NH, ACBSP

02 President ....Mr. Donald LAACKMAN
05 Int Vice Pres Academic/Student Affs ....Mr. John H. METOYER
85 Vice Pres Intl & Non-Tradition Pgms ....Vacant
11 Director of Operational Services ....Mr. Andy HUH
37 Director of Financial Aid ....Mr. Francois HAJDUK
18 Chief Facilities/Physical Plant ....Mr. Richard WREN
21 Director Bus Admin & Aux Services ....Ms. Martha JAQUEZ
08 Librarian ....Ms. Sherry LEDBETTER
15 Human Resources Admin ....Mr. Brandon PENDLETON
20 Interim Dean of Instruction ....Ms. Donyel WILLIAMS

32 Dean of Student Services ... Mr. Wendell BLAIR
04 Assistant to the President ... Mr. Gabriel RAZO
88 Int Dean Public Agency/Special Pgms ... Mr. John HADER
20 Assistant Dean of Instruction ... Mr. George BICKFORD
13 Asst Dean of Information Technology ... Ms. Ewa BEJNAROWICZ
35 Assoc Dean of Student Services ... Mr. Robert BROWN
46 Asst Dean Research/Planning ... Ms. Keenan L. ANDREWS

City Colleges of Chicago Harry S Truman College (A)

1145 W Wilson Avenue, Chicago IL 60640-5691
County: Cook FICE Identification: 001648
Unit ID: 144184
Telephone: (773) 907-4700 Carnegie Class: Assoc/Pub-U-MC
FAX Number: (773) 907-4464 Calendar System: Semester
URL: www.trumancollege.edu
Established: 1956 Annual Undergrad Tuition & Fees (In-District): $3,070
Enrollment: 7,783 Coed
Affiliation or Control: State/Local IRS Status: 501(c)3
Highest Offering: Associate Degree
Program: Occupational; 2-Year Principally Bachelor's Creditable
Accreditation: NH, ADNUR

02 President ... Dr. Reagan F. ROMALI
05 Vice Pres Student/Academic Affs ... Dr. Pervez RAHMAN
06 Registrar ... Ms. My Linh TRAN
32 Dean of Student Services ... Ms. Brenda WEDDINGTON
35 Associate Dean of Student Services ... Mr. Corey WILLIAMS
35 Associate Dean of Student Services ... Mr. Mark LATUSZEK
56 Dean of Adult Education ... Mr. Armando MATA
51 Dean of Continuing Education ... Ms. Nancy KRAMER
20 Dean of Instruction ... Ms. Elizabeth ROEGER
20 Associate Dean of Instruction ... Vacant
10 Exec Dir Business/Operational Svcs ... Mr. Thomas DUNHAM
19 Director of Security ... Mr. Ira HUNTER
37 Director of Financial Aid ... Ms. Cynthia GRUNDEN
15 Int Human Resource Administrator ... Ms. Donika HODGES
27 Director of Public Relations ... Mr. Clifton DANIEL
18 Chief Engineer ... Mr. Brian MCCUE
72 Asst Dean Information Technology ... Mr. Mike KRITIKOS
24 Director Lakeview Learning Center ... Ms. Ellen SELLERGREN
09 Asst Dir of Research & Evaluation ... Ms. Ericka KILBURN
88 Director of Auxiliary Services ... Ms. Nina CAO

City Colleges of Chicago Kennedy-King College (B)

6301 South Halsted Street, Chicago IL 60621-3798
County: Cook FICE Identification: 001654
Unit ID: 144157
Telephone: (773) 602-5000 Carnegie Class: Assoc/Pub-U-MC
FAX Number: N/A Calendar System: Semester
URL: www.kennedyking.ccc.edu
Established: 1934 Annual Undergrad Tuition & Fees (In-District): $3,070
Enrollment: 4,108 Coed
Affiliation or Control: State/Local IRS Status: 501(c)3
Highest Offering: Associate Degree
Program: Occupational; 2-Year Principally Bachelor's Creditable
Accreditation: NH, DH

02 President ... Mr. Derrick HARDEN
05 Vice President for Academic Affairs .. Ms. Jacquie HOOD-MARTIN
32 Dean Student Services ... Ms. De Reese REID-HART
12 Dean-Dawson Tech Institute ... Mr. Selemon ASSIGNON
36 Dean Career Programs ... Ms. Kimberly CHAVIS
51 Dean Adult/Continuing Education ... Ms. Katonja WEBB
35 Assistant Dean Student Services ... Vacant
37 Director Financial Aid ... Ms. Tabitha O'NEIL
20 Director Academic Support Services ... Dr. Prentiss JACKSON
10 Director Business/Operation Svcs ... Mr. Christopher STENSON
06 Registrar ... Ms. Marlene SPARROW-OLOKO
09 Director of Institutional Research ... Mr. Andricus HUTCHERSON
18 Chief Facilities/Physical Plant ... Mr. Jerome DABNEY
26 Marketing Director ... Ms. Deborah CRABLE
15 Director Human Resources ... Mr. Rene ALVARADO
04 Assistant to the President ... Ms. Ukeyco RHYNS

*City Colleges of Chicago Malcolm X College (C)

1900 W Van Buren Street, Chicago IL 60612-3197
County: Cook FICE Identification: 001650
Unit ID: 144166
Telephone: (312) 850-7000 Carnegie Class: Assoc/Pub-U-MC
FAX Number: (312) 850-7039 Calendar System: Semester
URL: www.ccc.edu/malcolmx
Established: 1911 Annual Undergrad Tuition & Fees (In-District): $3,719
Enrollment: 4,802 Coed
Affiliation or Control: State/Local IRS Status: 501(c)3
Highest Offering: Associate Degree
Program: Occupational; 2-Year Principally Bachelor's Creditable
Accreditation: NH, #ARCPA, FUSER, RAD, SURGT

02 President ... Dr. Anthony E. MUNROE
05 Vice Pres Academic Affairs ... Dr. Darrylinn D. TODD
32 Dean Student Services/Enroll Mgmt ... Ms. Kimberly HOLLINGSWORTH
10 Exec Dir Business/Admin Svcs ... Mr. Christopher STINSON
04 Executive Assistant to President ... Ms. Mary H. JOHNSON
15 Human Resources Administrator ... Mr. Stanley BEAMON
20 Interim Dean Instructional Services ... Dr. Lynette STOKES-WILSON
09 Asst Dean Research & Planning ... Mr. Byron A. JAVIER
13 Asst Dean Information Technology ... Mr. Charles MCCLEANON
06 Registrar ... Mr. Eddie PHILLIPS
35 Assoc Dean Student Services ... Dr. Tasha WILLIAMS
07 Director Admissions/Financial Aid ... Mr. Marco SEPULVEDA
88 Director Child Care Center ... Ms. Erine WEEKES
19 Director Security/Public Safety ... Mr. Lorenzo CLEMONS
18 Chief Facilites/Physical Plant ... Mr. Eduardo JONES
18 Chief Facilites/Physical Plant ... Mr. John MORLEY
55 Assistant Dean Adult Education ... Mr. Victor CASTILLO
08 Librarian ... Ms. C.M WINTERS-PALACIO
21 Business Manager ... Ms. Angela LILY
40 Director Bookstore ... Ms. Kristen ROMAN
26 Coordinator Marketing ... Ms. Twania BREWSTER
75 Interim Dean Career Programs ... Mr. Ronald D. GRIMMETTE
56 Interim Dean Adult Education Pgms ... Mr. Emmanuel SARRIS
51 Interim Dean Continuing Education ... Mr. Aawon WISSMANN
88 Assoc Dean Student Development ... Ms. Lisa WILLIS
20 Associate Dean Instruction ... Ms. Stephanie OWEN

*City Colleges of Chicago Olive-Harvey College (D)

10001 S Woodlawn Avenue, Chicago IL 60628-1645
County: Cook FICE Identification: 009767
Unit ID: 144175
Telephone: (773) 291-6100 Carnegie Class: Assoc/Pub-U-MC
FAX Number: (773) 291-6304 Calendar System: Semester
URL: www.oliveharvey.ccc.edu
Established: 1970 Annual Undergrad Tuition & Fees (In-District): $3,070
Enrollment: 3,295 Coed
Affiliation or Control: State/Local IRS Status: 501(c)3
Highest Offering: Associate Degree
Program: Occupational; 2-Year Principally Bachelor's Creditable
Accreditation: NH

02 President ... Dr. Craig FOLLINS
04 Assistant to President ... Ms. Marcia JACKSON
05 VP Academic & Student Affairs ... Vacant
32 Dean Student Services ... Mr. Gregory ROBINSON
51 Dean Adult & Continuing Education ... Mr. Ileo LOTT
09 Asst Dean of Research/Planning ... Mrs. Christian COLLINS
13 Asst Dean Information Technology ... Mr. Savio PINTO
20 Dean of Instruction ... Dr. Vera AVERYHART-FULLARD
36 Dean of Career Programs ... Mr. Kevin SMITH
35 Assoc Dean of Student Services ... Dr. Ria PINKSTON-MCKEE
35 Assoc Dean of Student Services ... Ms. Michelle ADAMS
10 Exec Dir Business/Admin/Aux Svc ... Dr. Nikita JOHNSON
12 Director of South Chicago Lrng Ctr ... Ms. Irma SALDANA
37 Director Financial Aid ... Mr. Stacey ROBBINS
06 Registrar ... Mr. Eric HAYES
19 Director Security ... Mr. Michael ROSS
88 Director Child Development Center ... Ms. Tiffany CARTER
41 Director of Athletics ... Mr. Norman FUTRELL
15 Human Resource Administrator ... Ms. Sharon PRAYOR
88 Director of Auxiliary Services .... Ms. Angela ARRINGTON-JONES
26 Director Public Relations ... Mr. Ray NICHOLS
88 Exec Director of Transportation Pgm ... Ms. Joanne IVORY

*City Colleges of Chicago Richard J. Daley College (E)

7500 S Pulaski Road, Chicago IL 60652-1299
County: Cook FICE Identification: 001649
Unit ID: 144193
Telephone: (773) 838-7500 Carnegie Class: Assoc/Pub-U-MC
FAX Number: (773) 838-7524 Calendar System: Semester
URL: daley.ccc.edu
Established: 1960 Annual Undergrad Tuition & Fees (In-District): $3,070
Enrollment: 4,589 Coed
Affiliation or Control: State/Local IRS Status: 501(c)3
Highest Offering: Associate Degree
Program: Occupational; 2-Year Principally Bachelor's Creditable
Accreditation: NH, ADNUR

02 President ... Dr. Jose M. AYBAR
03 Vice President ... Dr. Keith MCCOY
05 Dean of Instruction ... Dr. Jacqueline WITHERSPOON
36 Dean Career & Economic Programs ... Ms. Benita HUNTER
88 Dean Adult Education ... Vacant
32 Dean of Student Services ... Dr. Gayle WARD
51 Dean Continuing Education ... Mrs. Jean JOHNSON
10 Exec Director Business Operations ... Ms. Emma L. ORTIZ
37 Director Financial Aid ... Mr. James LOAGUE
18 Chief Engineer/Physical Plant ... Mr. Tim SMITH
19 Director Security ... Mr. Robert HOGAN
21 Asst Director Business/Oper Svcs ... Ms. Crystal WASHINGTON
35 Assoc Dean Student Services ... Dr. Yesenia AVALOS
06 Registrar ... Mr. Milton WRIGHT
09 Director of Institutional Research ... Vacant
15 Administrator Human Resources ... Ms. Elinore MOORE

*City Colleges of Chicago Wilbur Wright College (F)

4300 N Narragansett Avenue, Chicago IL 60634-1591
County: Cook FICE Identification: 001655
Unit ID: 144218
Telephone: (773) 777-7900 Carnegie Class: Assoc/Pub-U-MC
FAX Number: (773) 481-8185 Calendar System: Semester
URL: www.ccc.edu/wright
Established: 1934 Annual Undergrad Tuition & Fees (In-District): $3,070
Enrollment: 9,050 Coed
Affiliation or Control: State/Local IRS Status: 501(c)3
Highest Offering: Associate Degree
Program: Occupational; 2-Year Principally Bachelor's Creditable
Accreditation: NH, ACBSP, OTA, RAD

02 President ... Mr. Jim PALOS
05 Vice President Academic Affairs ... Ms. Cynthia CORDES
10 Director Business ... Mrs. Nancy BECKMAN
32 Director Student Activities ... Ms. Kathleen ORDINARIO
08 Librarian ... Ms. Linda NEIL
37 Director Financial Aid ... Ms. Ronda ROCQUEMORE
09 Director of Institutional Research ... Mr. Brian TRZEBIATOWSKI
14 Director Computer Support ... Ms. Lula WALLACE
07 Assistant Dean Admissions ... Vacant
18 Director of Facilities ... Ms. Jackie LONQUIST
15 Director Personnel Services ... Ms. Kimberly WILLIAMSON
38 Director Student Counseling ... Ms. Maria LLOPIZ
19 Director of Security ... Mr. Jack MURPHY
06 Registrar ... Vacant
41 Athletic Director ... Mr. John MCDONNELL
36 Dean of Careers ... Vacant
20 Dean of Instruction ... Mr. Kevin LI
35 Dean Student Services ... Ms. Romell MURDEN
51 Dean of Continuing Education ... Dr. Alba PEZZAROSSI
76 Dean Allied Health ... Ms. Julie WHITE
53 Dean Adult Education ... Ms. Daisy MITCHELL
12 Dean Humboldt Park Center ... Ms. Madeline ROMAN-VARGAS
12 Assoc Dean Humboldt Park Center ... Mr. Marc SMIERCIAK
20 Associate Dean of Instruction ... Mr. Jeffrey JANULIS

College of DuPage (G)

425 Fawell Boulevard, Glen Ellyn IL 60137-6599
County: DuPage Identification: 006656
Unit ID: 144865
Telephone: (630) 942-2800 Carnegie Class: Assoc/Pub-S-SC
FAX Number: (630) 858-9399 Calendar System: Semester
URL: www.cod.edu
Established: 1966 Annual Undergrad Tuition & Fees (In-District): $3,960
Enrollment: 26,722 Coed
Affiliation or Control: State/Local IRS Status: 501(c)3
Highest Offering: Associate Degree
Program: Occupational; 2-Year Principally Bachelor's Creditable
Accreditation: NH, ACFEI, ADNUR, ART, DH, DMS, MAC, NMT, PNUR, PTAA, RAD, SURGT

01 President ... Dr. Robert L. BREUDER
05 Executive Vice President ... Dr. Joseph COLLINS
11 Senior Vice Pres Administration ... Mr. Thomas J. GLASER
13 Vice Pres Information Technology ... Mr. Chuck CURRIER
45 VP Planning & Inst Effectiveness ... Mr. James BENTE
15 Vice President Human Resources ... Ms. Linda SANDS-VANKERK
24 Asst VP Info Sys/Multimedia Svcs ... Ms. Donna BERLINER
20 Assoc VP Academic Affairs ... Dr. Glenda GALLISATH
27 Assoc VP Marketing & External Rels ... Mr. Joseph MOORE
84 Assoc VP Enrollment Management ... Mr. Earl DOWLING
102 Assoc VP Dev & Dir of Foundation ... Dr. Sharon MELLOR
49 Dean Liberal Arts ... Dr. Daniel LLOYD
50 Dean Business & Technology ... Ms. Karen M. RANDALL
75 Dean Health & Sciences ... Mr. Thomas CAMERON
51 Dean Cont Ed/Extended Learning ... Dr. Joseph CASSIDY
08 Dean Library ... Dr. Lisa A. STOCK
32 Dean Student Affairs ... Ms. Susan M. MARTIN
21 Asst VP Financial Affs/Controller ... Ms. Lynn SAPYTA
18 Dir Facilities Planning and Dev ... Mr. John WANDOLOWSKI
06 Dean Admiss/Registration/Records ... Ms. Jane L. SMITH
09 Director Research ... Dr. Harlan M. SCHWEER
30 Asst VP Resource Development ... Dr. Laura MANNION
88 Internal Auditor ... Mr. James E. MARTNER
88 Director Business Affairs ... Mr. Scott A. ENGEL
57 Director Performing Arts ... Mr. Stephen CUMMINS
41 Director Athletics ... Mr. Paul ZAKOWSKI
25 Director of Grants ... Ms. Carol ANGLET
86 Director Legislative Relations ... Ms. Mary Ann MILLUSH
19 Director & Chief COD Police Dept ... Mr. Mark FAZZINI
18 Director Facilities Operations ... Mr. Jim MA
79 Associate Dean Humanities ... Ms. Laura ORTIZ
60 Associate Dean Communications ... Ms. Beverly REED
26 Dir Marketing & Creative Svcs ... Ms. Laurie JORGENSEN
88 Dir Academic Partnerships ... Ms. Mary KLINEFELTER
57 Assoc Dean Fine & Applied Arts ... Ms. Cathryn WILKINSON
66 Director Nursing Programs ... Ms. Vickie GUKENBERGER
16 Director Labor & Emp Relations ... Ms. Mia IGYARTO
77 Assoc Dean Computer & App Tech ... Mr. John KRONENBURGER
83 Assoc Dean Social & Behav Sciences ... Ms. Jaime LEWANDOWSKI
81 Assoc Dean Math & Physical Sciences ... Mr. Thomas SCHRADER
88 Assoc Dean Health & Bio Sciences ... Ms. Karen SOLT
88 Associate Dean Learning Resources ... Ms. Ellen SUTTON

College of Lake County (H)

19351 W Washington Street, Grayslake IL 60030-1198
County: Lake FICE Identification: 007694
Unit ID: 146472
Telephone: (847) 543-2000 Carnegie Class: Assoc/Pub-S-MC
FAX Number: (847) 223-1017 Calendar System: Semester
URL: www.clcillinois.edu
Established: 1967 Annual Undergrad Tuition & Fees (In-District): $3,052
Enrollment: 18,091 Coed

Affiliation or Control: Local IRS Status: 501(c)3
Highest Offering: Associate Degree
Program: Occupational; 2-Year Principally Bachelor's Creditable
Accreditation: NH, ADNUR, DH, MAC, RAD, SURGT

01 President ... Dr. Girard W. WEBER
05 Vice President Educ Affairs ... Dr. Richard J. HANEY
11 Vice Pres Administrative Affs ... Mr. David AGAZZI
32 Vice Pres Student Development ... Ms. Darl E. DRUMMOND
88 Asst Vice Pres of Student Devel ... Ms. Karen HLAVIN
26 Executive Director/Public Relations ... Ms. Evelyn R. SCHIELE
12 Dean Southlake Campus ... Ms. Vicky CVITKOVIC
12 Dean Lakeshore Campus ... Dr. Alphonso BALDWIN
08 Dean Libraries/Instruction Svcs ... Ms. Cornelia E. BAKKER
10 Dean Business Services/Finance ... Mr. Ted P. POULOS
50 Dean of Business/Workforce Bus Div ... Ms. Lourdene HUHRA
76 Dean Biological/Health Sciences ... Dr. Denise ANASTASIO
83 Dean Social Sciences ... Dr. Jeffrey A. STOMPER
79 Dean Comm Arts/Humanities/Fine Arts ... Mr. Roland G. MILLER
81 Dean Engr/Math/Physical Science ... Mr. Gary MORGAN
51 Dean Adult Basic Education/GED/ESL ... Ms. Mary S. CHARUHAS
38 Dean Counsel/Advising/Transfer Ctr ... Ms. Julie E. DEGRAW
55 Assoc Dean Adult Education ... Vacant
54 Asc Dean Engr/Math/Physical Science ... Mr. Jose VELARDE
31 Assoc Dean Community Education ... Ms. Michele VAUGHN
103 Exec Dir Workforce/Prof Dev Inst ... Mr. Julian VAN WINKLE
41 Dir Athletics/Physical Activities ... Mr. Chad GOOD
21 Director Accounting Services ... Ms. Peggy PUGESEK
86 Dir Resource Dev/Legislative Affrs ... Mr. Nick C. KALLIERIS
14 Chief Info Ofcr/Info Tech Svcs ... Mr. Kamlesh SANGHVI
35 Executive Director of Student Life ... Ms. Felicia GANTHER
102 Executive Director CLC Foundation ... Mr. William DEVORE
16 Exec Director Human Resources ... Ms. Susan YASECKO
88 Director Student Services Lakeshore ... Mr. David WEATHERSPOON
18 Director Facilities ... Mr. Ted JOHNSON
88 Dir Children's Learning Center ... Ms. Sandra GROENINGER
88 Dir Ofc Students w/ Disabilities ... Mr. Thomas CROWE
19 Chief of Police/CLC Police Dept ... Mr. Kevin LOWRY
36 Exec Dir Career/Placement Services ... Ms. Sylvia M. JOHNSON
88 Dir Illinois Small Business Dev Ctr ... Ms. Jan L. BAUER
20 Asst Vice Pres Educational Affairs ... Ms. Alyssa O'BRIEN
20 Director Academic Support Services ... Ms. Adriane W. HUTCHINSON
66 Director Nursing Education ... Dr. Deborah JEZUIT
51 Dir Center for Personal Enrichment ... Vacant
88 Exec Dir James Lumber Ctr Perf Arts ... Ms. Gwethalyn BRONNER
88 Director Procurement Tech Asst Ctr ... Mr. Marc N. VIOLANTE
88 Director Judicial Services ... Ms. Margaret C. MILLER
29 Dir Alumni Relations/Special Events ... Ms. Julie SHROKA
23 Director Health Services ... Ms. Michelle M. GRACE
37 Director Financial Aid ... Ms. Kathleen JOHNSON
88 Dir Active Lrng Technologies ... Mr. Scott RIAL
88 Director Continuing Prof Devel ... Ms. Carol EWING
88 Director of Business Services ... Ms. Melanie SCHERER
84 Asst Director Enrollment Services ... Ms. Debra MICHELINI
15 Assistant Director Human Resources ... Ms. Kathleen SCATLIFFE-WALLACE
88 Director Green Jobs Initiative ... Mr. Stephen BELL
35 Director Student Support Services ... Ms. Zandra GENOUS
88 Director Technical Services ... Mr. James SENFT

The College of Office Technology (A)

1520 W Division Street, Chicago IL 60642-3312
County: Cook FICE Identification: 023378
Unit ID: 143075
Telephone: (773) 278-0042 Carnegie Class: Assoc/PrivFP
FAX Number: (773) 278-0143 Calendar System: Semester
URL: www.cotedu.com
Established: 1982 Annual Undergrad Tuition & Fees: $10,026
Enrollment: 378 Coed
Affiliation or Control: Proprietary IRS Status: Proprietary
Highest Offering: Associate Degree
Program: Occupational
Accreditation: ACICS

01 President ... Ms. Karla GALVA

Columbia College Chicago (B)

600 S Michigan Avenue, Chicago IL 60605-1996
County: Cook FICE Identification: 001665
Unit ID: 144281
Telephone: (312) 369-1000 Carnegie Class: Master's M
FAX Number: (312) 369-8069 Calendar System: Semester
URL: www.colum.edu
Established: 1890 Annual Undergrad Tuition & Fees: $20,094
Enrollment: 11,922 Coed
Affiliation or Control: Independent Non-Profit IRS Status: 501(c)3
Highest Offering: Master's
Program: Liberal Arts And General
Accreditation: NH, CIDA

01 President ... Dr. Warrick L. CARTER
10 Int VP Finance/Chief Financial Ofcr ... Ms. Debbie ROSSENBLUME
43 Vice President/General Counsel ... Ms. Annice KELLY
30 Vice Pres Institutional Advancement ... Dr. Eric WINSTON
88 Vice President Campus Environment ... Ms. Alicia M. BERG
45 Vice Pres Planning & Compliance ... Ms. Anne FOLEY
20 Vice President of Academic Affairs ... Dr. Louise LOVE
35 Vice President Student Affairs ... Mr. Mark KELLY
16 Vice Pres of Human Resources ... Ms. Ellen KRUTZ
21 Associate VP of Business Affairs ... Mr. Timothy BAUHS
100 Assoc Vice Pres/Chief of Staff ... Mr. Paul CHIARAVALLE
84 Assoc Vice Pres for Enrollment Mgmt ... Ms. Debra MCGRATH
18 Assoc VP Facilities/Operations ... Mr. John KAVOURIS
32 Assoc Vice Pres/Dean of Students ... Ms. Sharon WILSON-TAYLOR
08 Asc VP Research/Dean of the Library ... Ms. Jo CATES
26 Assoc VP & Chief Marketing Officer ... Ms. Diane DOYNE
13 Assoc VP PR/Marketing/Advertising ... Ms. Bernadette B. MCMAHON
21 Assoc Vice President & Controller ... Mr. Kevin DOHERTY
19 Assoc Vice Pres Safety & Security ... Mr. Robert KOVERMAN
07 Executive Director of Admissions ... Mr. Murphy MONROE
44 Asst Vice Pres Campaign Initiatives ... Ms. Kim CLEMENT
44 Assoc VP Institutional Advancement ... Mr. Michael ANDERSON
37 Exec Dir of Student Financial Svcs ... Ms. Jennifer WATERS
35 Asst Dean of Student Development ... Mr. William FRIEDMAN
88 Director of Degree Evaluation ... Ms. Susan SINDLINGER
26 Director of Public Relations ... Mr. Steve KAUFFMAN
15 Director Human Resources ... Ms. Patricia OLALDE
29 National Director Alumni Relations ... Mr. Charles BONILLA
96 Director of Purchasing ... Mr. Thomas RUSSELL
88 Exec Director Multi-Cultural Affs ... Ms. Shelia CARTER
85 Dir International Student Affairs ... Ms. Gigi POSEJPAL
06 Director of Records/Registrar ... Mr. Marvin COHEN
36 Director of Portfolio Center ... Mr. Tim LONG
39 Director of Residence Life ... Ms. Mary OAKES
09 AVP Planning/Exec Dir Inst Research ... Mr. Royal DAWSON
38 Director of Counseling Services ... Ms. Jackie SOWINSUI
88 Director of Latino Cultural Affairs ... Mr. Daniel ARANDA
88 Dir of New Stdnt Pgms & Orientation ... Ms. Emily EASTON
85 Exec Dir Academic Init & Intl Pgms ... Ms. Gillian MOORE
57 Dean School of Fine/Performing Arts ... Dr. Eliza NICHOLS
88 Dean School of Media Arts ... Dr. Robin BARGAR
49 Dean School Liberal Arts/Sciences ... Dr. Deborah HOLDSTEIN

Concordia University Chicago (C)

7400 Augusta Street, River Forest IL 60305-1499
County: Cook FICE Identification: 001666
Unit ID: 144351
Telephone: (708) 771-8300 Carnegie Class: Master's L
FAX Number: (708) 209-3176 Calendar System: Semester
URL: www.cuchicago.edu
Established: 1864 Annual Undergrad Tuition & Fees: $24,944
Enrollment: 5,223 Coed
Affiliation or Control: Lutheran Church - Missouri Synod
IRS Status: 501(c)3
Highest Offering: Doctorate
Program: Liberal Arts And General; Teacher Preparatory; Professional
Accreditation: NH, CACREP, MUS, TED

01 President ... Dr. John F. JOHNSON
05 Sr Vice President for Academics ... Dr. Manfred B. BOOS
30 Sr Vice Pres Development/Alumni ... Ms. Cindy SIMPSON
45 Sr VP for Planning & Research ... Mr. Alan E. MEYER
10 Vice President for Finance ... Mr. Tom HALLETT
11 Vice President for Administration ... Dr. Dennis E. WITTE
84 Vice Pres Enrollment & Marketing ... Ms. Evelyn P. BURDICK
32 Vice President Student Services ... Mr. Jeff HYNES
44 Asst Vice President of Major Gifts ... Mr. Tom J. FOOTE
84 Asst Vice President for Enrollment ... Ms. Gwen E. KANELOS
49 Dean College Arts & Sciences ... Dr. Gary WENZEL
53 Dean College Education ... Dr. Kevin BRANDON
50 Dean College of Business ... Vacant
58 Dean Col Graduate Innovative Pgms ... Dr. Thomas JANDRIS
88 Associate Director of CURES ... Ms. Elizabeth M. BECKER
37 Director Student Financial Planning ... Ms. Aida ASENCIO-PINTO
06 Registrar ... Ms. Connie PETTINGER
08 Director of Library Services ... Ms. Yana V. SERDYUK
88 Director of Degree Completion ... Dr. Carol J. REISECK
36 Director Career Plng/Placement Svcs ... Mr. Gerald PINOTTI
27 Director Marketing Communications ... Vacant
15 Director of Human Resources ... Ms. Elizabeth WOTEN
18 Director of Physical Plant ... Ms. Linda HOLOWICKI
11 Dean of Administration ... Mr. Glen D. STEINER
29 Director of Alumni Relations ... Ms. Paige CRAIG
38 Director Schmieding Counseling Ctr ... Dr. Carol A. JABS
31 Director of Auxiliary Services ... Mr. Pete D. BECKER
41 Director of Athletics ... Mr. Peter D. GNAN
21 Director of Business Services ... Ms. Anne FARMER
88 Director of Budget Services ... Ms. Tina NEPOMUCENO
39 Director Resident Life ... Mr. Andrew POLLOM
22 Affirmative Action Officer ... Vacant
42 Campus Pastor ... Rev. Jeffrey LEININGER
24 Dir of Media Production Services ... Mr. James A. KOSINSKY
19 Director of Public Safety ... Ms. Amberleigh BIRKHOLZ
88 Director of Academic Advising ... Ms. Rosemarie GARCIA-HILLS
26 Chief Public Relations Officer ... Vacant
96 Director of Purchasing ... Ms. Kathryn KLEMENT
91 Manager of Admin Information System ... Ms. Linda C. BERRY
40 Manager of Bookstore ... Vacant
85 International Student Advisor ... Vacant

Coyne College (D)

330 North Green Street, Chicago IL 60607-1300
County: Cook FICE Identification: 007549
Unit ID: 144485
Telephone: (773) 577-8100 Carnegie Class: Assoc/PrivFP
FAX Number: (312) 226-3818 Calendar System: Semester
URL: www.coynecollege.edu
Established: 1899 Annual Undergrad Tuition & Fees: N/A
Enrollment: 929 Coed
Affiliation or Control: Proprietary IRS Status: Proprietary
Highest Offering: Associate Degree
Program: Occupational; 2-Year Principally Bachelor's Creditable
Accreditation: ACCSC, MAAB

01 President ... Mr. Russell FREEMAN

Danville Area Community College (E)

2000 E Main Street, Danville IL 61832-5199
County: Vermilion FICE Identification: 001669
Unit ID: 144564
Telephone: (217) 443-3222 Carnegie Class: Assoc/Pub-R-L
FAX Number: (217) 443-8560 Calendar System: Semester
URL: www.dacc.edu
Established: 1946 Annual Undergrad Tuition & Fees (In-District): $3,210
Enrollment: 5,287 Coed
Affiliation or Control: State/Local IRS Status: 501(c)3
Highest Offering: Associate Degree
Program: Occupational; 2-Year Principally Bachelor's Creditable
Accreditation: NH, RAD

01 President ... Dr. Alice M. JACOBS
04 Admin Asst to the Pres/Board Sec ... Ms. Kerri L. THURMAN
05 VP Instruction & Student Svcs ... Mr. David L. KIETZMANN
15 Director Human Resources/AA Ofcr ... Ms. Jill A. CRANMORE
10 Chief Financial Officer ... Ms. Gail A. MORRISON
11 Director Administrative Services ... Mr. R. Michael CUNNINGHAM
07 Director Admissions & Registrar ... Ms. Stacy L. EHMEN
45 Director Grants and Planning ... Ms. Laura M. WILLIAMS
44 Foundation Executive Director ... Ms. Tracy D. WAHLFELDT
26 Director Marketing/Col Relations ... Ms. Lara L. CONKLIN
09 Dir Institutional Effectiveness ... Ms. Nancy A. BOESDORFER
88 Executive Director of JTP ... Mr. Brian C. HENSGEN
21 Controller ... Ms. Debra L. KNIGHT
37 Director of Financial Aid ... Ms. Janet M. INGARGIOLA
51 Dir Corporate/Community Education ... Ms. Sara L. VANDEWALKER
91 Director of Admin Data Systems ... Mr. Kim H. COLWELL
90 Director Computer & Network Svcs ... Mr. Jefferson D. WILLIAMS
88 Director of Adult Education ... Mr. Thomas G. SZOTT
50 Dean Business & Technology ... Mr. Bruce M. RAPE
49 Dean Liberal Arts and Library Servi ... Dr. Penny J. MCCONNELL
81 Dean Math & Sciences ... Ms. Kathy R. STURGEON
41 Athletic Director ... Mr. Tim M. BUNTON
88 Director Small Business Development ... Mr. Michael J. O'BRIEN
35 Director Student Support Services ... Ms. Vicky L. WELGE
36 Coordinator Career Services ... Ms. Carla M. BOYD
24 Director Instructional Media ... Mr. Jonathon L. SPORS
40 Coordinator Bookstore ... Ms. Cindy A. PARR-BARRETT
88 Coordinator Retention ... Ms. Cindy J. NICHOLS
88 Coordinator Recruitment ... Ms. Dawn S. NASSER

DePaul University (F)

25 E Jackson Boulevard, Chicago IL 60604-2287
County: Cook FICE Identification: 001671
Unit ID: 144740
Telephone: (312) 362-8000 Carnegie Class: DRU
FAX Number: (312) 362-5322 Calendar System: Quarter
URL: www.depaul.edu
Established: 1898 Annual Undergrad Tuition & Fees: $30,000
Enrollment: 25,145 Coed
Affiliation or Control: Roman Catholic IRS Status: 501(c)3
Highest Offering: Doctorate
Program: Liberal Arts And General; Teacher Preparatory; Professional
Accreditation: NH, ANEST, BUS, BUSA, CLPSY, LAW, MUS, NURSE, SPAA, SW

01 President ... Rev. Dennis H. HOLTSCHNEIDER
00 Chancellor ... Rev. John T. RICHARDSON, CM
05 Provost ... Dr. Helmut P. EPP
03 Executive Vice President ... Mr. Robert KOZOMAN
11 Vice President Admin/Sec of Univ ... Rev. Edward R. UDOVIC
32 Vice President Student Affairs ... Mr. James R. DOYLE
84 Sr Vice Pres Enrollment Management ... Dr. David H. KALSBEEK
10 Vice President for Finance ... Ms. Bonnie FRANKEL
15 Vice President Human Resources ... Mr. William W. SEITHEL
18 Vice President Facilities Operation ... Mr. Robert J. JANIS
43 Vice President & General Counsel ... Dr. Jose D. PADILLA
08 VP Teaching/Learning Resources ... Rev. Edward R. UDOVIC
29 Vice Pres Alumni Engagement/Outreac ... Dr. Patricia O'DONOGHUE
28 Vice Pres for Inst Diversity ... Ms. Elizabeth F. ORTIZ
27 VP Public Relations & Communication ... Ms. Cheryl PROCTOR-ROGERS
30 Senior Vice Pres for Development ... Ms. Mary FINGER
20 Assoc VP Academic Affairs ... Ms. Caryn CHADEN
20 Assoc VP Academic Affairs Online ... Mr. GianMario BESANA
45 Sr Exec Strategic Planning ... Dr. Jay BRAATZ
21 Sr Assoc VP Fiscal Admin ... Ms. Alyssa KUPKA
35 Assoc Vice Pres Student Affairs ... Ms. Cynthia SUMMERS
46 Assoc VP Faculty Devel/Research ... Dr. Rafaela WEFFER
35 Assoc Vice Pres Student Development ... Dr. Peggy BURKE
22 Assoc VP for Div Ed & Leadership ... Mr. Rico TYLER
20 Assoc Vice Pres Academic Affairs ... Ms. Kelly JOHNSON
09 Asst VP Inst Rsrch & Mkt Analytic ... Dr. Liz SANDERS
36 Assoc Vice President Career Svcs ... Ms. Carol MONTGOMERY
42 Assoc VP University Ministry ... Mr. Mark LABOE
21 Assoc VP Operations ... Mr. Mark TITZER
88 Asst Vice Pres Univ Marketing Comm ... Ms. Gwyn FRIEND
26 Asst Vice President Public Rels ... Ms. Denise MATTSON

88 Senior Executive University Mission .... Rev. Edward R. UDOVIC, CM
88 Treasurer .... Mr. Jeffrey BETHKE
88 Controller .... Mr. Mark HAWKINS
90 Director Academic Technology Devel .... Dr. Sharon GUAN
27 Director of Information Services .... Mr. Robert MCCORMICK
37 Director Financial Aid .... Ms. Paula LUFF
25 Director Sponsored Programs Rsrch .... Dr. Douglas PETCHER
26 Director Media Relations .... Mr. John HOLDEN
41 Athletic Director .... Ms. Jean PONSETTO
19 Director Public Safety .... Mr. Robert WACHOWSKI
38 Director Student Counseling .... Dr. Jeffery LANFEAR
51 Dean School for New Learning .... Ms. Marisa ALICEA
50 Dean College of Commerce .... Dr. Ray WHITTINGTON
64 Dean School of Music .... Dr. Donald E. CASEY
61 Dean College of Law .... Judge Warren WOLFSON
49 Dean Liberal Arts & Sciences .... Dr. Charles S. SUCHAR
57 Dean Theatre School .... Mr. John CULBERT
53 Dean School of Education .... Dr. Paul ZIONTS
88 Dean Computing & Digital Media .... Dr. David MILLER
06 Registrar .... Ms. Patricia HUERTA
07 Director of Admissions .... Ms. Carlene KLAAS
89 Dean College of Communication .... Dr. Jacqueline TAYLOR

*DeVry University - Home Office (A)

3005 Highland Parkway, Downers Grove IL 60515-5799

County: DuPage | FICE Identification: 001672 | Unit ID: 144777
Telephone: (800) 733-3879 | Carnegie Class: N/A
FAX Number: (630) 571-0317
URL: www.devry.edu

00 President & Chief Executive Officer .... Mr. Daniel HAMBURGER
01 Exec VP/President of DeVry Univ .... Mr. David J. PAULDINE
86 Sr VP Govt & Reg Affairs/CCO .... Ms. Sharon THOMAS-PARROTT
26 VP/Chief Marketing Officer .... Mr. John BIRMINGHAM
32 VP of Student & Career Services .... Mr. Claude TOLAND
10 Senior VP/CFO/Treasurer .... Mr. Richard GUNST
27 VP/Chief Information Officer .... Mr. Eric DIRST
43 VP/General Counsel/Corp Secretary .... Mr. Gregory DAVIS
84 VP Enrollment Management .... Ms. Erika ORRIS
88 VP Enrollment Management - Online .... Mr. Ted KULAWIAK
05 Provost/VP Academic Affairs .... Ms. Donna LORAINE
16 VP Human Resources .... Ms. Donna JENNINGS
88 VP Regulatory Affairs .... Mr. Thomas BABEL
88 Pres K-12/Prof & Intl Education .... Mr. Steven RIEHS
12 VP Metro Operations .... Mr. Rob PAUL
07 VP of Admissions - California .... Mr. Mark BUCK
07 VP of Admissions - Mountain .... Mr. Russell GILL
07 VP of Admissions - Northeast .... Ms. Marcy PRATT
07 VP of Admissions - Southeast .... Ms. Monal SHAH
07 VP of Admissions - North Central .... Ms. Virginia MECHNIG
07 VP of Admissions - South Central .... Mr. David WOOD
12 Group VP - North Central .... Ms. Terri JOHNSON
12 Group VP - South Central .... Ms. Stacy MUNOZ
12 Group VP - California .... Ms. Shelly DUBOIS
12 Group VP - Mountain .... Mr. Jim DUGAN
12 Group VP - Northeast .... Mr. Hal MCCULLOCH
12 Group VP - Southeast .... Mr. Julio TORRES

*DeVry University - Addison Campus (B)

1221 N Swift Road, Addison IL 60101-6106

County: DuPage | FICE Identification: 022966 | Unit ID: 144768
Telephone: (630) 953-1300 | Carnegie Class: Not Classified
FAX Number: (630) 953-1236 | Calendar System: Semester
URL: www.devry.edu
Established: 1931 | Annual Undergrad Tuition & Fees: $15,294
Enrollment: 1,794 | Coed
Affiliation or Control: Proprietary | IRS Status: Proprietary
Highest Offering: Baccalaureate
Program: Occupational; Professional; Business Emphasis
Accreditation: &NH, ENGT

02 Metro President .... Dr. Susan L. FRIEDBERG
08 Director of Library Sciences .... Mrs. Susan CHANG
07 Senior Director of Admissions .... Ms. Michelle ALFORD
05 Dean of Academic Affairs .... Ms. Janet ABRI
97 Dean of General Education .... Dr. Julie HAGEMANN
37 Director of Student Finance .... Ms. Sejal AMIN
32 Manager Student Services .... Mr. Michael KULCZYCKI
06 Assistant Registrar .... Ms. Heather WEBB
15 HR Business Partner .... Mr. Douglas OFFUTT
77 Program Dean .... Ms. Lyn WUNSCHL
36 Director of Career Services .... Ms. Kathleen MCCUEN

† Regional accreditation is carried under the parent institution in Downers Grove, IL.

*DeVry University - Chicago Campus (C)

3300 N Campbell Avenue, Chicago IL 60618-5994

County: Cook | FICE Identification: 010727 | Unit ID: 144759
Telephone: (773) 929-8500 | Carnegie Class: Master's L
FAX Number: (773) 348-1780 | Calendar System: Semester
URL: www.devry.edu
Established: 1931 | Annual Undergrad Tuition & Fees: $15,294
Enrollment: 2,446 | Coed
Affiliation or Control: Proprietary | IRS Status: Proprietary
Highest Offering: Baccalaureate
Program: Occupational; Professional; Business Emphasis
Accreditation: &NH, ENGT

02 Campus President .... Ms. Candace GOODWIN
06 Registrar .... Ms. Jacqueline LLOYD
07 Senior Director of Admissions .... Mr. Kelvin EASTER
05 Dean Academic Affairs .... Ms. Susan BRAUER
36 Director of Career Services .... Ms. Kelly JENKINS
37 Director of Student Finance .... Ms. Milena DOBRINA
08 Director of Library Services .... Dr. Cathy CARTER
15 HR Business Partner .... Ms. Nancy BOURQUE
26 Director of Community Outreach .... Ms. Karen KUSHINO
32 Manager Student Services .... Ms. Sara SPIEGEL
97 Dean of General Studies .... Ms. Carolyn BAIR

† Regional accreditation is carried under the parent institution in Downers Grove, IL.

*DeVry University - Chicago Loop Center (D)

225 W Washington Street, Ste 100, Chicago IL 60606-2418

County: Cook | Identification: 666203 | Unit ID: 439206
Telephone: (312) 372-4900 | Carnegie Class: Not Classified
FAX Number: (312) 372-4870 | Calendar System: Semester
URL: www.devry.edu
Established: 1973 | Annual Undergrad Tuition & Fees: $15,294
Enrollment: 1,550 | Coed
Affiliation or Control: Proprietary | IRS Status: Proprietary
Highest Offering: Master's
Program: Occupational; Professional; Business Emphasis
Accreditation: &NH

02 Campus Dean .... Mr. Piotr LECHOWSKI
07 Director of Admissions .... Ms. Ana THARAKAN

† Regional accreditation is carried under the parent institution in Downers Grove, IL.

*DeVry University - Chicago O'Hare Center (E)

8550 W Bryn Mawr Ave, Suite 450, Chicago IL 60631-3224

County: Cook | Identification: 666204 | Unit ID: 437352
Telephone: (773) 695-1000 | Carnegie Class: Not Classified
FAX Number: (773) 695-9118 | Calendar System: Semester
URL: www.devry.edu
Established: 1999 | Annual Undergrad Tuition & Fees: $15,294
Enrollment: 320 | Coed
Affiliation or Control: Proprietary | IRS Status: Proprietary
Highest Offering: Master's
Program: Occupational; Professional; Business Emphasis
Accreditation: &NH

02 Center Dean .... Oolka DIXIT

† Regional accreditation is carried under the parent institution in Downers Grove, IL.

*DeVry University - Downers Grove (F)

3005 Highland Parkway, Downers Grove IL 60515-5799

County: DuPage | Identification: 666791
Telephone: (630) 515-3000 | Carnegie Class: Not Classified
FAX Number: N/A | Calendar System: Semester
URL: www.devry.edu
Established: 1931 | Annual Undergrad Tuition & Fees: $15,294
Enrollment: 6,828 | Coed
Affiliation or Control: Proprietary | IRS Status: Proprietary
Highest Offering: Master's
Program: Professional; Business Emphasis
Accreditation: &NH

02 Center Dean .... Rowena KLEIN-ROBARTS

† Regional accreditation is carried under the parent institution in Downers Grove, IL.

*DeVry University - Elgin Center (G)

2250 Point Boulevard, Suite 250, Elgin IL 60123-7873

County: Kane | Identification: 666205 | Unit ID: 439215
Telephone: (847) 649-3980 | Carnegie Class: Not Classified
FAX Number: (847) 622-1246 | Calendar System: Semester
URL: www.devry.edu
Established: 1993 | Annual Undergrad Tuition & Fees: $15,294
Enrollment: 300 | Coed
Affiliation or Control: Proprietary | IRS Status: Proprietary
Highest Offering: Master's
Program: Occupational; Professional; Business Emphasis
Accreditation: &NH

02 Center Dean .... Mr. Timothy M. FLORER

† Regional accreditation is carried under the parent institution in Downers Grove, IL.

*DeVry University - Gurnee (H)

1075 Tri-State Parkway, Suite 800, Gurnee IL 60031-9126

County: Lake | Identification: 666535
Telephone: (847) 855-2649 | Carnegie Class: Not Classified
FAX Number: (847) 855-5932 | Calendar System: Semester
URL: www.devry.edu
Established: 1931 | Annual Undergrad Tuition & Fees: $15,294
Enrollment: 584 | Coed
Affiliation or Control: Proprietary | IRS Status: Proprietary
Highest Offering: Master's
Program: Professional; Business Emphasis
Accreditation: &NH

02 Center Dean .... Lewis ZANON

† Regional accreditation is carried under the parent institution in Downers Grove, IL.

*DeVry University - Lincolnshire Center (I)

25 Tri-State Int'l Center, Ste 130, Lincolnshire IL 60069-4460

County: Lake | Identification: 666206 | Unit ID: 439224
Telephone: (847) 940-7768 | Carnegie Class: Not Classified
FAX Number: (847) 940-7772 | Calendar System: Semester
URL: www.keller.edu
Established: 1984 | Annual Graduate Tuition & Fees: $18,040
Enrollment: 175 | Coed
Affiliation or Control: Proprietary | IRS Status: Proprietary
Highest Offering: Master's; No Undergraduates
Program: Occupational; Professional; Business Emphasis
Accreditation: &NH

02 Center Dean .... Roberta JANNSEN

† Regional accreditation is carried under the parent institution in Downers Grove, IL.

*DeVry University - Naperville Center (J)

2056 Westings Avenue, Suite 40, Naperville IL 60563-2361

County: DuPage | Identification: 666207
Telephone: (630) 428-9086 | Carnegie Class: Not Classified
FAX Number: (630) 428-4721 | Calendar System: Semester
URL: www.devry.edu
Established: 2002 | Annual Undergrad Tuition & Fees: $15,294
Enrollment: 536 | Coed
Affiliation or Control: Proprietary | IRS Status: Proprietary
Highest Offering: Master's
Program: Occupational; Professional; Business Emphasis
Accreditation: &NH

02 Center Dean .... Mary WAHLBECK

† Regional accreditation is carried under the parent institution in Downers Grove, IL.

*DeVry University - Schaumburg Center (K)

1051 Perimeter Drive, 9th Floor, Schaumburg IL 60173-5009

County: Cook | Identification: 666208 | Unit ID: 439251
Telephone: (847) 330-0040 | Carnegie Class: Not Classified
FAX Number: (847) 330-0046 | Calendar System: Semester
URL: www.keller.edu
Established: 1931 | Annual Graduate Tuition & Fees: $18,040
Enrollment: 312 | Coed
Affiliation or Control: Proprietary | IRS Status: Proprietary
Highest Offering: Master's; No Undergraduates
Program: Occupational; Professional; Business Emphasis
Accreditation: &NH

02 Center Dean .... Megan BAKER

† Regional accreditation is carried under the parent institution in Downers Grove, IL.

*DeVry University - Tinley Park Campus (L)

18624 W Creek Drive, Tinley Park IL 60477-6243

County: Cook | Identification: 666113 | Unit ID: 439242
Telephone: (708) 342-3300 | Carnegie Class: Not Classified
FAX Number: (708) 342-3712 | Calendar System: Semester
URL: www.devry.edu
Established: 2000 | Annual Undergrad Tuition & Fees: $15,294
Enrollment: 1,723 | Coed
Affiliation or Control: Proprietary | IRS Status: Proprietary
Highest Offering: Master's
Program: Occupational; Professional; Business Emphasis
Accreditation: &NH

02	Campus President	Mr. Jamal SCOTT
10	Director of Facilities	Mr. James MADORMA
07	Director of Admissions	Ms. Angela HOWARD
06	Registrar	Ms. Eva LUDWICZUK
15	HR Business Partner	Mr. Tremayne MCPHERSON
05	Dean of Academic Affairs	Mr. Stan LAN
72	Dean of Technology Programs	Mr. Craig WALDVOGEL
37	Director of Student Finance	Ms. Margaret CARMODY
08	Director of Library Services	Mr. Paul BURDEN

† Regional accreditation is carried under the parent institution in Downers Grove, IL.

Dominican University (A)

7900 W Division Street, River Forest IL 60305-1099

County: Cook FICE Identification: 001750
Unit ID: 148496

Telephone: (708) 366-2490 Carnegie Class: Master's L
FAX Number: (708) 524-5990 Calendar System: Semester
URL: www.dom.edu
Established: 1901 Annual Undergrad Tuition & Fees: $26,460
Enrollment: 3,748 Coed
Affiliation or Control: Roman Catholic IRS Status: 501(c)3
Highest Offering: Doctorate
Program: Liberal Arts And General; Teacher Preparatory; Professional
Accreditation: NH, ACBSP, DIETC, DIETD, LIB, SW

01	President	Dr. Donna M. CARROLL
05	Provost	Dr. Cheryl JOHNSON-ODIM
20	Associate Provost	Dr. David H. KRAUSE
11	Sr VP for Finance & Administration	Ms. Amy MCCORMACK
42	Vice Pres for Mission & Ministry	Sr. Diane KENNEDY, OP
30	Vice Pres University Advancement	Mrs. Grace J. CICHOMSKA
84	Vice Pres Enrollment Management	Dr. Mary Ann ROWAN
07	AVP Enroll Mgt/Dir Undergrad Admiss	Mr. Glenn HAMILTON
32	Dean of Students	Ms. Trudi GOGGIN
50	Dean School of Business	Dr. Arvid JOHNSON
62	Dean Grad School Library Science	Dr. Susan ROMAN
53	Dean School of Education	Dr. Colleen REARDON
70	Dean Graduate School Social Work	Dr. Mark RODGERS
49	Dean College of Arts & Science	Dr. Jeffrey CARLSON
88	Assistant Provost	Mr. Matthew J. HLINAK
08	Interim University Librarian	Ms. Inez RINGLAND
26	Chief Marketing/Communications Ofcr	Mr. Jeffrey KRAFT
27	Chief Information Officer	Mrs. Jill ALBIN HILL
06	Registrar	Mr. Michael Patrick MILLER
36	Director Career Development	Ms. Keli WOJCIECHOWSKI
29	Dir Alumnae/i Relations	Ms. Alysha COMSTOCK
88	Promoter of Mission Integration	Sr. Mary Ann MEUNINGHOFF, OP
09	Dir Institutional Rsch & Assessment	Ms. Elizabeth SILK
15	Director Human Resources	Ms. Roberta MCMAHON
18	Director/Physical Plant	Mr. Daniel BULOW
07	Director Transfer/Adult Admission	Mr. Michael MORSOVILLO
37	Director Financial Aid	Ms. Marie VON EBERS
23	Director Wellness Center	Ms. Elizabeth RITZMAN
41	Director Athletics	Mr. Erick BAUMANN
104	Director International Studies	Dr. Sue PONREMY

East-West University (B)

816 S Michigan Avenue, Chicago IL 60605-2185

County: Cook FICE Identification: 021686
Unit ID: 144883

Telephone: (312) 939-0111 Carnegie Class: Bac/A&S
FAX Number: (312) 939-0083 Calendar System: Quarter
URL: www.eastwest.edu
Established: 1980 Annual Undergrad Tuition & Fees: $16,695
Enrollment: 1,083 Coed
Affiliation or Control: Independent Non-Profit IRS Status: 501(c)3
Highest Offering: Baccalaureate
Program: Liberal Arts And General
Accreditation: NH

01	Chancellor	Dr. M. Wasiullah KHAN
05	Provost	Dr. Madhu JAIN
20	Associate Provost	Dr. Ekkehard T. WILKE
88	Assistant Provost for Acad Quality	Dr. Lawrence J. GORMAN
07	Associate Dean of Admissions	Mrs. Mettha M. ROSS
30	Assoc Dean Development/Univ Rels	Mr. Zafar A. MALIK
32	Director of Counseling/Student Affs	Ms. Melissa A. STEC
37	Director of Financial Aid	Ms. Elizabeth GUZMAN
06	Registrar	Mr. Matt S. MCCAW
04	Assistant to the Chancellor	Ms. Carolyn J. FOWLKES
19	Director of Security	Mr. Tasleem RAJA
26	Chief Public Relations Officer	Mr. John THOMAS
18	Chief Facilities/Physical Plant	Mr. Tasleem RAJA
10	Chief Business Officer	Dr. Madhu JAIN
44	Chief Development Officer	Ms. Judith BACON
38	Academic Counselor	Ms. Meco HARRIS
85	International Student Advisor	Mr. Rashed JAHANGIR

Eastern Illinois University (C)

600 Lincoln Avenue, Charleston IL 61920-3099

County: Coles FICE Identification: 001674
Unit ID: 144892

Telephone: (217) 581-5000 Carnegie Class: Master's L
FAX Number: (217) 581-2722 Calendar System: Semester
URL: www.eiu.edu
Established: 1895 Annual Undergrad Tuition & Fees (In-State): $10,534
Enrollment: 11,630 Coed
Affiliation or Control: State IRS Status: 501(c)3
Highest Offering: Beyond Master's But Less Than Doctorate
Program: Liberal Arts And General; Teacher Preparatory; Professional
Accreditation: NH, AAFCS, ART, BUS, BUSA, CACREP, DIETD, DIETI, JOUR, MUS, NAIT, NRPA, NURSE, SP, TED, THEA

01	President	Dr. William L. PERRY
05	Provost/Vice Pres Academic Affairs	Dr. Blair M. LORD
10	Vice President Business Affairs	Dr. William V. WEBER
32	Vice President Student Affairs	Dr. Daniel P. NADLER
30	Vice Pres University Advancement	Mr. Robert K. MARTIN
20	Associate VP Academic Affairs	Mr. Jeffrey F. CROSS
35	Associate Vice Pres Student Affairs	Vacant
13	Asst VP for Information Tech Svcs	Ms. Kathy S. REED
08	Dean of Library Services	Dr. Allen K. LANHAM
84	Dean Enrollment Management	Vacant
92	Dean Honors College	Dr. John STIMAC
15	Int Director Human Resources	Ms. Linda C. HOLLOWAY
43	General Counsel	Mr. Robert L. MILLER
22	Director Civil Rights	Ms. Cynthia D. NICHOLS
45	Dir Planning/Budgeting/Rsrch	Mr. Michael S. MAURER
07	Director of Admissions	Ms. Brenda L. MAJOR
37	Director of Financial Aid	Mr. Jerry A. DONNA
06	Registrar	Ms. Gayle S. HARVEY
29	Director Alumni Svc/Community Rels	Mr. Steven W. RICH
09	Director of Institutional Research	Vacant
18	Dir Facilities/Planning Management	Mr. Gary D. REED
96	Dir Procurmt/Disbursmt/Contract Svc	Mr. Monty R. BENNETT
38	Director of Counseling Center	Ms. Sandra K. COX
25	Director of Research & Grants	Dr. Robert W. CHESNUT
41	Director of Athletics	Ms. Barbara A. BURKE
93	Director of Minority Affairs	Ms. Mona DAVENPORT
39	Director of Housing/Dining Service	Mr. Mark A. HUDSON
51	Dean Continuing Education	Dr. William C. HINE
58	Dean Graduate School	Dr. Robert M. AUGUSTINE
81	Int Dean College Sciences	Dr. Godson C. OBIA
50	Dean Lumpkin Col Bus/Appl Sci	Dr. Mahyar IZADI
79	Dean College Arts/Humanities	Dr. Bonnie IRWIN
53	Dean College Education	Dr. Diane H. JACKMAN

Elgin Community College (D)

1700 Spartan Drive, Elgin IL 60123-7193

County: Kane FICE Identification: 001675
Unit ID: 144944

Telephone: (847) 697-1000 Carnegie Class: Assoc/Pub-S-MC
FAX Number: (847) 214-7995 Calendar System: Semester
URL: www.elgin.edu
Established: 1949 Annual Undergrad Tuition & Fees (In-District): $2,980
Enrollment: 12,214 Coed
Affiliation or Control: Local IRS Status: 501(c)3
Highest Offering: Associate Degree
Program: Occupational; 2-Year Principally Bachelor's Creditable
Accreditation: NH, ADNUR, COMTA, DA, HT, MLTAD, PTAA, RAD, SURGT

01	President	Dr. David SAM
10	VP Business/Fin/College Treasurer	Ms. Sharon KONNY
05	VP Teaching/Learning/Stdnt Dev	Ms. Rose DIGERLANDO
20	Asst VP Teach/Lrng/Stdnt Dev	Ms. Marcy THOMPSON
20	Dean Academic Dev/Learning Resource	Dr. Mi HU
50	Dean Business	Dr. Vincent PELLETIER
75	Dean Sustain/Safety & Career Tech	Dr. Jeff BOYD
83	Dean Comm/Behavioral Sciences	Dr. Ruixuan MAO
57	Dean Liberal/Visual/Performing Arts	Ms. Mary HATCH
81	Dean Math/Science & Engineer	Dr. James MCGEE
32	Dean of Student Development	Dr. Carol COWLES
88	Dean Adult Basic Education	Ms. Peggy HEINRICH
38	Assoc Dean Counsel/Career Svcs	Mr. John COFFIN
84	Assoc Dean Enrollment Management	Dr. Mary PERKINS
76	Int Dean Health Professions	Ms. Wendy MILLER
106	Assoc Dean Inst Improve/Dist Lrng	Mr. Timothy MOORE
08	Associate Dean Library	Mr. Brian BEECHER
71	Asc Dean TRIO/Reten/Stdnt Outreach	Dr. L. Bruce AUSTIN
18	Managing Director Facilities	Mr. Cal BYRD
16	Chief Human Resources Officer	Vacant
13	Chief Information Officer	Mr. Ned COONEN
26	Chief Marketing/Comm Officer	Ms. Paula AMENTA
30	Exec Dir Institutional Advancement	Vacant
20	Int Managing Dir Inst Comp/Curr	Ms. Sharon WILSON
45	Executive Dir Planning/Inst Effect	Dr. Philip GARBER
09	Director Institutional Research	Mr. David RUDDEN
37	Director Financial Aid/Scholarships	Ms. Amy PERRIN
19	Chief of Police	Mr. Emad EASSA
21	Controller	Ms. Heather SCHOLL
06	Assoc Dean Registration/Records	Dr. Jennifer MCCLURE
90	Director Academic Computing	Ms. Karin STACY
22	Paralegal/EEO/AA and FOIA Officer	Ms. Marilyn PRENTICE
07	Director of Admissions/Recruitment	Mr. Trevell EDDINS
41	Director Athletics & Wellness	Mr. Kent PAYNE
40	Exec Dir Aux Enterprises & Cont Ed	Mr. Frank HERNANDEZ
96	Director Business Services	Ms. Melissa TAIT
36	Director Career Services	Ms. Peggy GUNDRUM
27	Senior Director of Marketing	Mr. Jeffrey ARENA
35	Director Orientation/Student Life	Ms. Amybeth MAURER
88	Dir Small Business Devel Center	Mr. Kriss KNOWLES
14	Director Technology Services	Mr. Jeffery METZGER
101	Secretary to Board of Trustees	Ms. Eleanor MACKINNEY
04	Assistant to the President	Ms. Kathleen J. STOVER

Ellis University (E)

111 N Canal Street, Suite 380, Chicago IL 60606-7202

County: Cook FICE Identification: 041433
Unit ID: 452133

Telephone: (877) 355-4762 Carnegie Class: Bac/A&S
FAX Number: (312) 669-5005 Calendar System: Semester
URL: www.ellis.edu
Established: 2008 Annual Undergrad Tuition & Fees: $13,410
Enrollment: 1,338 Coed
Affiliation or Control: Independent Non-Profit IRS Status: 501(c)3
Highest Offering: Master's
Program: Professional; Business Emphasis
Accreditation: DETC

01	President	Dr. Roger H. WIDMER
10	Interim CFO	Randy WILLY
05	Chief Operating Officer	Dr. Virginia CARLIN
11	VP of Operations	Raymond RODRIGUEZ
20	Chief Academic Officer	Dr. Andrew CARPENTER
06	Registrar	Yahana TEGEGNE
07	Director of Admissions	LePra GEORGE

Elmhurst College (F)

190 Prospect, Elmhurst IL 60126-3296

County: DuPage FICE Identification: 001676
Unit ID: 144962

Telephone: (630) 279-4100 Carnegie Class: Master's M
FAX Number: (630) 617-3282 Calendar System: 4/1/4
URL: www.elmhurst.edu
Established: 1871 Annual Undergrad Tuition & Fees: $29,994
Enrollment: 3,430 Coed
Affiliation or Control: United Church Of Christ IRS Status: 501(c)3
Highest Offering: Master's
Program: Liberal Arts And General; Teacher Preparatory; Professional
Accreditation: NH, NURSE

01	President	Dr. S. Alan RAY
10	Sr VP of Finance & Administration	Ms. Denise P. JONES
05	Vice Pres Acad Affs/Dean of Faculty	Dr. Alzada TIPTON
27	VP and Chief Information Officer	Dr. James KULICH
26	VP for Communications & Public Affs	Mr. James W. WINTERS
29	Interim VP for Dev and Alumni Rels	Ms. Meg HOWES
30	Exec Director of Development	Ms. Ellen-Marie BONNER
32	Dean of Students	Dr. Eileen G. SULLIVAN
07	Dean of Admission	Mr. Gary F. ROLD
58	Dean of Adult and Grad Studies	Vacant
20	Associate Dean of Faculty	Dr. Heather HALL
20	Associate Dean of Faculty	Dr. Theodore LERUD
88	Exec Dir Center for Pro Excellence	Dr. Lawrence B. CARROLL
18	Exec Director Facilities Management	Mr. Bruce J. MATHER
42	Chaplain	Rev. H. Scott MATHENEY
06	Registrar	Mr. S. Dean ELLENS
08	Director of the Library	Ms. Susan S. STEFFEN
36	Director of Career Education	Ms. Peggy KILLIAN
21	Controller	Mr. Richard A. SCHEPLER
38	Director of Counseling Services	Dr. Amy SWARR
28	Director of Intercultural Education	Dr. Kathleen RUST
14	Director of Computer Services	Mr. James M. FRANCIS
88	Director Development Operations	Ms. Lisa BROSCH
29	Director of Alumni Relations	Ms. Samantha KILEY
44	Dir of Leadership Annual Giving	Ms. Filomena SPERO
88	Managing Dir of Public Affairs	Ms. Desiree CHEN
86	Exec Director Govt & Community Rels	Mr. Bob ROWLEY
16	Director of Human Resources	Mr. John NEWTON
19	Exec Director of Campus Security	Mr. Jeff KEDROWSKI
37	Director of Financial Aid	Ms. Ruth PUSICH
07	Director of Admission	Ms. Stephanie LEVENSON
07	Director Adult/Graduate Admission	Ms. Elizabeth D. KUEBLER
39	Director of Residence Life	Ms. Christine J. SMITH
41	Director Intercollegiate Athletics	Mr. Paul KROHN

Erikson Institute (G)

451 N. Lasalle, Chicago IL 60654

County: Cook FICE Identification: 035103
Unit ID: 409254

Telephone: (312) 755-2250 Carnegie Class: Spec/Other
FAX Number: (312) 755-0928 Calendar System: Semester
URL: www.erikson.edu
Established: 1966 Annual Graduate Tuition & Fees: $14,680
Enrollment: 284 Coed
Affiliation or Control: Independent Non-Profit IRS Status: 501(c)3
Highest Offering: Master's; No Undergraduates
Program: Professional
Accreditation: NH

01	President	Samuel J. MEISELS
05	Sr VP Academic Affs/Dean of Faculty	Aisha RAY
10	Vice President Finance/Operations	Susan WALLACE
88	Vice President Planning/Enrollment	Jeanne LOCKRIDGE
30	Vice Pres Institutional Advancement	Randy L. HOLGATE
44	Asst Dir Development Data Systems	Deborah HARP
13	Chief Information Officer	Jonathan FRANK
27	Chief Marketing/Communications Ofcr	Patricia NEDEAU
84	Dean of Enrollment Management	Michel FRENDIAN
51	Dir of Prof Devel & Continuing Educ	Deborah MANTIA

Eureka College (H)

300 E College Avenue, Eureka IL 61530-1500

County: Woodford FICE Identification: 001678
Unit ID: 144971

Telephone: (309) 467-3721 Carnegie Class: Bac/Diverse
FAX Number: (309) 467-6386 Calendar System: Semester
URL: www.eureka.edu
Established: 1855 Annual Undergrad Tuition & Fees: $17,940
Enrollment: 782 Coed
Affiliation or Control: Christian Church (Disciples Of Christ)
IRS Status: 501(c)3

Highest Offering: Baccalaureate
Program: Liberal Arts And General; Teacher Preparatory
Accreditation: NH

01 President ... Dr. J. David ARNOLD
04 Administrative Asst to President ... Ms. Jyl KRAUSE
05 Provost & Dean of the College ... Dr. Philip Acree CAVALIER
10 Chief Financial Officer ... Mr. Marc PASTERIS
32 Dean of Student Services ... Mr. Ken A. BAXTER
07 Dean of Admissions/Financial Aid ... Dr. Brian SAJKO
26 Director of College Relations ... Vacant
30 Chief Development Officer ... Mr. Michael MURTAGH
06 Registrar ... Mr. Scott WIGNALL
08 Library Director ... Mr. Tony GLASS
18 Director of Physical Plant ... Mr. Rod WESTFALL
42 Chaplain ... Rev. Bruce M. FOWLKES
14 Director of Computer Services ... Dr. Kanaka VIJITHA-KUMARA
37 Director of Financial Aid ... Mrs. Ellen M. RIGSBY
41 Athletic Director ... Mr. Paul BRYANT
29 Int Director Alumni Relations ... Mrs. Shellie SCHWANKE

Fox College (A)

6640 South Cicero Avenue, Bedford Park IL 60638
County: Cook FICE Identification: 025228
Unit ID: 145239
Telephone: (708) 636-7700 Carnegie Class: Assoc/PrivFP
FAX Number: (708) 636-8078 Calendar System: Semester
URL: www.foxcollege.edu
Established: 1932 Annual Undergrad Tuition & Fees: $14,680
Enrollment: 417 Coed
Affiliation or Control: Proprietary IRS Status: Proprietary
Highest Offering: Associate Degree
Program: 2-Year Principally Bachelor's Creditable
Accreditation: NH, MAAB, PTAA

01 President ... Mr. Carey CRANSTON

Garrett-Evangelical Theological Seminary (B)

2121 Sheridan Road, Evanston IL 60201-3298
County: Cook FICE Identification: 001682
Unit ID: 145275
Telephone: (847) 866-3900 Carnegie Class: Spec/Faith
FAX Number: (847) 866-3957 Calendar System: Semester
URL: www.garrett.edu
Established: 1853 Annual Graduate Tuition & Fees: $17,110
Enrollment: 349 Coed
Affiliation or Control: United Methodist IRS Status: 501(c)3
Highest Offering: Doctorate; No Undergraduates
Program: Professional; Religious Emphasis
Accreditation: NH, THEOL

01 President ... Dr. Philip A. AMERSON
11 VP for Admin/External Programming ... Dr. James A. NOSEWORTHY
05 Acad Dean/Vice Pres Acad Affairs ... Dr. Lallene J. RECTOR
30 Vice President for Development ... Dr. David L. HEETLAND
10 Vice President Business Affairs/CFO ... Mr. Arnold HENNING
21 Controller ... Ms. Ruth ELBAUM
32 Interim Dean of Students ... Rev. Cynthia A. WILSON
84 Assistant VP for Enrollment Mgmt ... Rev. Becky J. EBERHART
04 Assistant to the President ... Ms. Marjorie N. ECKHARDT
06 Registrar/Dir of Academic Studies ... Rev. Vince MCGLOTHIN-ELLER
08 Director of United Library ... Dr. Beth M. SHEPPARD
13 Director of Information Technology ... Mr. James D. CASH
18 Director of Buildings & Grounds ... Mr. John CARTER
39 Director of Housing & Food Service ... Ms. Barbara B. ADAMS
29 Dir Annual Gvg/Alum Rel/Hospitality ... Ms. Kay A. BURLINGHAM
26 Director of Communications & Events ... Mr. Shane NICHOLS
88 Director of Stewardship ... Ms. Elizabeth P. CAMPBELL
37 Director of Financial Aid ... Ms. Margaret C. HALLEN

Governors State University (C)

1 University Parkway, University Park IL 60484-0975
County: Will FICE Identification: 009145
Unit ID: 145336
Telephone: (708) 534-5000 Carnegie Class: Master's L
FAX Number: (708) 534-8399 Calendar System: Semester
URL: www.govst.edu
Established: 1969 Annual Undergrad Tuition & Fees (In-State): $8,936
Enrollment: 5,660 Coed
Affiliation or Control: State IRS Status: 501(c)3
Highest Offering: Doctorate
Program: Liberal Arts And General; Teacher Preparatory; Professional
Accreditation: NH, ACBSP, CACREP, HSA, NUR, OT, PTA, SP, SPAA, SW, TED

01 President ... Dr. Elaine P. MAIMON
03 Executive VP & Chief of Staff/Treas ... Dr. Gebeyehu EJIGU
05 Provost/VP Academic Affairs ... Dr. Terry C. ALLISON
11 Interim Vice Pres Admin & Planning ... Dr. Gebeyehu EJIGU
30 VP Advancement/CEO Foundation ... Ms. Joan T. VAUGHAN
43 Legal Counsel ... Ms. Alexis KENNEDY
22 Affirmative Action/EO ... Mr. Tony A. TYMKOW
45 Director Budget Planning/Inst Rsrch ... Dr. Jeffrey SLOVAK
09 Assoc Dir of Institutional Research ... Vacant
29 AVP Inst Advancement/Alumni Rels ... Ms. Rosemary D. HULETT
26 Director Public Affairs ... Mr. Eric J. MATANYI
50 Dean Col Business/Public Admin ... Dr. Ellen FOSTER CURTIS
49 Dean College Arts Sciences ... Dr. Reinhold HILL
76 Dean Col Health Professions ... Dr. Linda SAMSON
53 Dean College Education ... Dr. Deborah BORDELON
32 Dean Student Affairs & Services ... Dr. Sherilyn POOLE
84 Exec Director Enrollment Services ... Ms. Sharon EVANS
08 Dean Library Svc/Academic Computing ... Vacant
56 Dean Extend Lrng/Community Svcs ... Vacant
06 Registrar ... Ms. Michelle SMITH-WILLIAMS
37 Director Financial Aid ... Ms. Freda WHISETON-COMER
35 Acting Executive Dir Student Life ... Ms. Vanessa NEWBY
20 Associate Provost/AVP Academic Affs ... Dr. Peggy WOODARD
21 Director Business Operations ... Ms. Karen KISSEL
13 Exec Director Information Tech Svcs ... Mr. Peter J. MIZERA
15 Director Human Resources ... Ms. Gail BRADSHAW
18 Director Physical Plant ... Ms. Susan RAKSTANG
19 Int Director Dept Public Safety ... Mr. James MCGEE
38 Dir Stdnt Develop/Counseling Center ... Ms. Kelly MCCARTHY
36 Director of Career Services ... Ms. Darcie R. CAMPOS
96 Dir of Procurement/Auxillary Svcs ... Ms. Tracy SULLIVAN

Greenville College (D)

315 E College, Greenville IL 62246
County: Bond FICE Identification: 001684
Unit ID: 145372
Telephone: (618) 664-2800 Carnegie Class: Bac/Diverse
FAX Number: (618) 664-9775 Calendar System: 4/1/4
URL: www.greenville.edu
Established: 1892 Annual Undergrad Tuition & Fees: $22,198
Enrollment: 1,605 Coed
Affiliation or Control: Free Methodist IRS Status: 501(c)3
Highest Offering: Master's
Program: Liberal Arts And General; Teacher Preparatory; Professional
Accreditation: NH

01 President ... Dr. Larry LINAMEN
04 Assistant to the President ... Ms. Tamie HEICHELBECK
05 Provost ... Dr. Randy S. BERGEN
30 Vice Pres for Advancement ... Mr. Walter FENTON
10 Vice President for Finance ... Mrs. Dana FUNDERBURK
32 Vice Pres for Student Development ... Dr. Norman D. HALL
84 Vice Pres for Enrollment ... Mr. Michael RITTER
51 Assoc VP Strat Innov/Dn Prof Stds ... Dr. Dave HOLDEN
08 Director of Library ... Ms. Jane L. HOPKINS
06 Registrar ... Mrs. Michelle SUSSENBACH
29 Director Alumni Relations ... Ms. Pam TAYLOR
37 Director of Financial Aid ... Mrs. Marilae LATHAM
30 Director of Advancement ... Mr. Tim WAYMAN
42 Chaplain ... Mrs. Lori GAFFNER
18 Director of Facilities ... Mr. Chris KESTER
26 Director of Marketing ... Mr. Nathan BREWER
09 Dean of College Planning/Assessment ... Vacant
49 Dean School of Arts & Sciences ... Dr. Brad SHAW
53 Dean School of Educ/Dir Online ... Dr. Vickie COOK
41 Athletic Director ... Dr. Doug FAULKNER

Harper College (E)

1200 W Algonquin Road, Palatine IL 60067-7398
County: Cook FICE Identification: 003961
Unit ID: 149842
Telephone: (847) 925-6000 Carnegie Class: Assoc/Pub-S-SC
FAX Number: (847) 925-6034 Calendar System: Semester
URL: www.harpercollege.edu
Established: 1965 Annual Undergrad Tuition & Fees (In-District): $2,958
Enrollment: 17,678 Coed
Affiliation or Control: State/Local IRS Status: 501(c)3
Highest Offering: Associate Degree
Program: Occupational; 2-Year Principally Bachelor's Creditable
Accreditation: NH, ACBSP, ADNUR, CEA, DH, DIETT, DMS, MAC, MUS, RAD

01 President ... Dr. Kenneth L. ENDER
100 Chief of Staff ... Ms. Sheila QUIRK-BAILEY
101 Senior Executive to the President ... Mrs. Maria COONS
10 Exec VP Finance & Admin Services ... Dr. Ron ALLY
05 Provost ... Dr. Judith MARWICK
30 Chief Advancement Officer ... Ms. Catherine BROD
26 Chief Communications Officer ... Mr. Phil BURDICK
20 Associate Provost/Interdis St Succ ... Ms. Joan KINDLE
20 Assistant Provost/Support Services ... Ms. Diana SHARP
16 Chief Human Resources Officer ... Mr. Roger SPAYER
27 Chief Information Officer ... Mr. Patrick BAUER
21 Controller ... Mr. Bret BONNSTETTER
18 Executive Director of Facilities ... Mr. Thomas CRYLEN
88 Dean Career Programs ... Ms. Sally GRIFFITH
08 Dean Resources for Learning ... Ms. Njambi KAMOCHE
32 Dean Stdnt Affs/Welln & Campus Act ... Ms. Ashley KNIGHT
84 Dean Enrollment Services ... Ms. Maria MOTEN
51 Dean Continuing Education ... Dr. Mark MROZINSKI
35 Dean Student Development ... Ms. Sheryl OTTO
50 Dean Business & Social Science ... Ms. Michele' ROBINSON
81 Dean Mathematics & Sciences ... Mr. James ROZNOWSKI
88 Interim Dean Acad Enrch/Lang Stds ... Ms. Darice TROUT
49 Dean Liberal Arts ... Dr. Dennis WEEKS
88 Associate Dean Ctr Adjct Fac Engag ... Mr. Brian KNETL
93 Assoc Dean Ctr Multicultural Lrng ... Ms. Laura LABAUVE-MAHER
23 Asst Dean Well/Dir Hlth & Psy Svcs ... Ms. Shannon LENGERICH
76 Assistant Dean/Allied Health Dir ... Ms. Barbara SMALL
72 Assistant Dean ... Mr. John SMITH
88 Assistant Dean/Adult Education Dir ... Ms. Darice TROUT
88 Dir New Student Programs/Retention ... Ms. Vicki ATKINSON
13 Director IT Enterprise Systems ... Mr. Mike BABB
26 Director Marketing Services ... Mr. Mike BARZACCHINI
36 Director Career Svcs/Women's Pgm ... Ms. Kathleen CANFIELD
88 Acting Director Client Services ... Ms. Sue CONTARINO
09 Director Institutional Research ... Mr. Doug EASTERLING
106 Director Ctr for Innov Instruction ... Mr. Matthew ENSENBERGER
88 Dir Disability Svcs/ADA Compliance ... Mr. Scott FRIEDMAN
37 Dir Student Financial Assistance ... Ms. Laura MCGEE
14 Director Technical Services ... Dr. Regan MYERS
35 Director Student Activities ... Mr. Michael NEJMAN
07 Dir Student Recruitment & Outreach ... Mr. Robert PARZY
88 Campus Architect ... Mr. Stephen PETERSEN
38 Dir Academic Advising & Counseling ... Mr. Eric ROSENTHAL
44 Asc Exec Dir Found/Dir Major Gifts ... Ms. Katherine SAWYER
88 Dir Inst Effect/Outcomes Assess ... Ms. Darlene SCHLENBECKER
41 Director of Athletics & Fitness ... Mr. Doug SPIWAK
103 Director Adult Learning ... Ms. Nancy WAJLER

Harrington College of Design (F)

200 W Madison, 2nd Floor, Chicago IL 60606-3433
County: Cook FICE Identification: 020552
Unit ID: 145460
Telephone: (312) 939-4975 Carnegie Class: Spec/Arts
FAX Number: (312) 939-8005 Calendar System: Semester
URL: www.harringtoncollege.com
Established: 1931 Annual Undergrad Tuition & Fees: $19,300
Enrollment: 1,001 Coed
Affiliation or Control: Proprietary IRS Status: Proprietary
Highest Offering: Master's
Program: Professional; Fine Arts Emphasis
Accreditation: NH, ACICS, CIDA

01 President ... Mr. Erik I. PARKS
05 Academic Dean ... Vacant
07 Director of Admissions ... Ms. Jessie MCEWEN
10 Controller ... Mr. Mike THAYER
13 Director of IT & Facilities ... Mr. Bryan J. STYER
36 Director Career Services ... Ms. Camille HARRIS
08 Head Librarian ... Ms. Leigh GATES
37 Director of Financial Aid ... Mrs. Renee DAROSKY
06 Registrar ... Mr. Sam DELAROSA
35 Director Student Services ... Mr. Sam DELAROSA
09 Director of Institutional Research ... Mrs. Gretchen FRICKX

Heartland Community College (G)

1500 W Raab Road, Normal IL 61761-9446
County: McLean FICE Identification: 030838
Unit ID: 384342
Telephone: (309) 268-8000 Carnegie Class: Assoc/Pub-R-L
FAX Number: (309) 268-7999 Calendar System: Semester
URL: www.heartland.edu
Established: 1990 Annual Undergrad Tuition & Fees (In-District): $3,930
Enrollment: 5,886 Coed
Affiliation or Control: State/Local IRS Status: 501(c)3
Highest Offering: Associate Degree
Program: Occupational; 2-Year Principally Bachelor's Creditable
Accreditation: NH, ADNUR, RAD

01 President ... Dr. Allen GOBEN
05 Vice President Instruction ... Dr. Allan SAAF
10 Vice President Business Services ... Mr. Robert D. WIDMER
30 Vice Pres Institutional Advancement ... Dr. Helen KATZ
51 Vice President Continuing Education ... Ms. Mary Beth TRAKINAT
13 Chief Information Officer ... Mr. Doug MINTER
32 Dean Stdnt Engagement/Life/Wellness ... Dr. Kathleen COLLINS
84 Dean Enrollment Services ... Mr. Padriac SHINVILLE
18 Executive Director of Facilities ... Mr. James HUBBARD
11 Director of Administrative Services ... Ms. Valerie CRAWFORD
21 Controller ... Ms. Sue GILPIN
37 Director of Financial Aid ... Ms. Cheryl SCHAFFER
15 Exec Director Human Resources ... Mrs. Barb LEATHERS
26 Exec Director Marketing/Public Rels ... Ms. Janet HILL GETZ
09 Exec Director Inst Effectiveness ... Mr. David COOK
41 Director of Athletics ... Mr. Nate METZGER
29 Director Alumni Relations/Outreach ... Ms. Colleen REYNOLDS
36 Director Student Testing ... Ms. Kimberly KELLEY
38 Director of Advisement ... Ms. Cecilia OLIVARES

Hebrew Theological College (H)

7135 N Carpenter Road, Skokie IL 60077-3263
County: Cook FICE Identification: 001685
Unit ID: 145497
Telephone: (847) 982-2500 Carnegie Class: Spec/Faith
FAX Number: (847) 674-6381 Calendar System: Semester
URL: www.htc.edu
Established: 1922 Annual Undergrad Tuition & Fees: $18,740
Enrollment: 485 Coordinate
Affiliation or Control: Independent Non-Profit IRS Status: 501(c)3
Highest Offering: Baccalaureate
Program: Liberal Arts And General; Teacher Preparatory; Professional; Religious Emphasis
Accreditation: NH

01 Chancellor ... Rabbi Jerold ISENBERG
05 Rosh Hayeshiva-Chief Academic ... Rabbi Avraham FRIEDMAN
11 Vice President for Administration ... Rabbi Sender KUTNER
20 Dean Blitstein Institute ... Dr. Esther SHKOP
20 Dean AHS & LAS Men's Division ... Rabbi Michael MYERS

33 Mashgiach Ruchani-Dean ... Rabbi Zvi ZIMMERMAN
34 Menahel Ruchani-Dean ... Rabbi Binyamin OLSTEIN
34 Assistant Dean Blitstein Institute ... Ms. Rita LIPSHITZ
06 Registrar ... Rabbi Shmuel SCHUMAN
07 Director of Admissions ... Rabbi Joshua ZISOOK
30 Director of Development ... Rabbi Gershon SEIF
44 Development Coordinator ... Rabbi Yaakov FRIEDMAN
08 Librarian ... Rabbi Elie GINSPARG
88 Israel Program Liaison - Blitstein ... Mrs. Naomi POLLACK
88 Israel Program Liaison - Beis Midra ... Rabbi Joshua KANTER

† Separate campuses for male and female students.

Highland Community College (A)

2998 W Pearl City Road, Freeport IL 61032-9341
County: Stephenson FICE Identification: 001681
Unit ID: 145521
Telephone: (815) 235-6121 Carnegie Class: Assoc/Pub-R-M
FAX Number: (815) 235-6130 Calendar System: Semester
URL: www.highland.edu
Established: 1961 Annual Undergrad Tuition & Fees (In-District): $3,240
Enrollment: 2,226 Coed
Affiliation or Control: State/Local IRS Status: 501(c)3
Highest Offering: Associate Degree
Program: Occupational; 2-Year Principally Bachelor's Creditable
Accreditation: NH

01 President ... Dr. Joe M. KANOSKY
05 Vice Pres Academic Services ... Mr. Tim HOOD
11 Vice Pres Administrative Services ... Ms. Jill M. JANSSEN
15 Associate VP Human Resources ... Mrs. Rose A. FERGUSON
32 Assoc VP Student Services ... Mrs. Elizabeth L. GERBER
50 Dean Business & Technology ... Mr. Scott R. ANDERSON
79 Dean Humanities/Soc Science ... Dr. Thompson A. BRANDT
66 Assoc Dean Nursing & Allied Health ... Ms. Donna KAUKE
81 Assoc Dean Natural Science & Math ... Mr. George GOLDSWORTHY
84 Director Enrollment/Records ... Mr. Jeremy BRADT
51 Director Adult Education ... Mr. Mark JANSEN
41 Director Athletics ... Mr. Peter E. NORMAN
37 Director Financial Aid ... Ms. Kathy BANGASSER
91 Director ITS Admin Apps ... Vacant
90 Director ITS Network/Desktop & AV ... Mr. Nathan HENSAL
09 Director Institutional Research ... Dr. Michelle THRUMAN
08 Director Library Services ... Mrs. Judy MOORE
31 Director Marketing & Cmty Relations ... Mr. Pete WILLGING
88 Director Partners for Employment ... Ms. Kathy K. DAY
18 Director Physical Plant/Maint ... Mr. Kurt SIMPSON
88 Director Retired & Senior Vol Pgm ... Mr. Michael J. SHORE
88 Director Title IV Student Support ... Ms. Virginia A. WARE
88 Director Title IV Upward Bound ... Ms. Janet KAISER
40 Manager Bookstore ... Ms. Madonna KEENEY
21 Manager Accounting ... Ms. Mary J. LLOYD
04 Exec Asst to President/Board Sec ... Ms. Terri A. GRIMES
96 Purchasing & Insurance Specialist ... Ms. Teresa WILLIAMS
102 Foundation Executive Director ... Vacant

Illinois Central College (B)

1 College Drive, East Peoria IL 61635-0001
County: Tazewell FICE Identification: 006753
Unit ID: 145682
Telephone: (309) 694-5422 Carnegie Class: Assoc/Pub-R-L
FAX Number: (309) 694-5450 Calendar System: Semester
URL: www.icc.edu
Established: 1966 Annual Undergrad Tuition & Fees (In-District): $102
Enrollment: 7,705 Coed
Affiliation or Control: State/Local IRS Status: 501(c)3
Highest Offering: Associate Degree
Program: Occupational; 2-Year Principally Bachelor's Creditable
Accreditation: NH, ADNUR, DH, MAC, MLTAD, MUS, OTA, PTAA, RAD, SURGT

01 President ... Dr. John S. ERWIN
05 VP Academic Affairs ... Dr. William TAMMONE
10 Vice Pres Administration & Finance ... Mr. Bruce BUDDE
45 Vice Pres Plng/Org Effectiveness ... Dr. Vicky STEWART
26 Assoc Vice President of Marketing ... Dr. Cheryl FLIEGE
20 Assoc Vice Pres Academic Affairs ... Dr. Margaret A. SWANSON
30 Exec Dir/Chief Development Officer ... Ms. Robin BALLARD
15 Exec Director of Human Resources ... Mr. Patrick PARSONS
14 Director Technology Services ... Dr. Susan WHEELER
38 Director Advisement/Assess/Counsel ... Ms. Pam WILFINGER
37 Director Student Financial Services ... Ms. Beth MCCLAIN
07 Director Enrollment Services ... Ms. Emily POINTS
28 Executive Director of Diversity ... Dr. Rita ALI
18 Dir of Facilities Planning & Design ... Mr. Troy HATTERMANN
51 Assoc Dean Corporate/Community Ed ... Ms. Ellen GEORGE
88 Assoc Dean Inst Innovations & Learn ... Ms. Janice KINSINGER
83 Assoc Dean Social Sciences ... Vacant
81 Int Dean Math/Science/Engineering ... Mr. Tom PILAT
50 Interim Dean Business/Info Services .. Ms. Gina MCCONOUGHEY
32 Dean of Student Services ... Mr. Guy GOODMAN
57 Dean Arts & Communications ... Mr. Christopher GRAY
47 Assoc Dean Agricult/Industrial Tech ... Mr. Michael SLOAN
31 Dean Cmty Outreach/ICC N Coord ... Ms. Kay SUTTON
17 Dean Hlth/Pub Svcs/Peoria Campus ... Dr. Margaret SWANSON
60 Dean English/Social Sciences ... Dr. Jill WRIGHT

Illinois College (C)

1101 W College Avenue, Jacksonville IL 62650-2299
County: Morgan FICE Identification: 001688
Unit ID: 145691
Telephone: (217) 245-3000 Carnegie Class: Bac/A&S
FAX Number: (217) 245-3034 Calendar System: Semester
URL: www.ic.edu
Established: 1829 Annual Undergrad Tuition & Fees: $24,530
Enrollment: 880 Coed
Affiliation or Control: Independent Non-Profit IRS Status: 501(c)3
Highest Offering: Baccalaureate
Program: Liberal Arts And General; Teacher Preparatory
Accreditation: NH

01 President ... Dr. Axel D. STEUER
05 Vice President Academic Affairs ... Dr. Elizabeth H. TOBIN
10 Vice President Business Affairs ... Mr. Frank G. WILLIAMS
30 Vice President Advancement ... Vacant
84 Vice President for Enrollment ... Ms. Stephanie ELPERS
32 VP Student Affairs/Dean of Students ... Dr. Malinda L. CARLSON
18 Asst Vice Pres Campus Facilities ... Mr. Allen R. MAYS, JR.
20 Associate Dean of the College ... Mr. Nicholas P. CAPO
07 Associate Director Admissions ... Mr. Richard L. BYSTRY
29 Director Alumni Relations ... Mrs. Pamela S. MARTIN
26 Chief Public Relations Officer ... Ms. Kristin E. JAMISON
08 Librarian ... Vacant
37 Director Student Financial Aid ... Ms. Katherine A. TAYLOR
36 Director of Career Center ... Ms. Susan K. DRAKE
06 Registrar ... Dr. Glen W. CLATTERBUCK
21 Controller ... Ms. Melissa J. DYSSON
35 Director Student Activities ... Ms. Karen K. HOMOLKA
42 Chaplain ... Rev. Katrina E. JENKINS
88 Assoc Dir of Admissions/Recruitment ... Vacant
09 Advisor to Pres for Inst Research ... Dr. Robert A. SWEATMAN
15 Director Personnel Services ... Ms. Teresa C. SMITH
38 Director Student Counseling ... Vacant
28 Director of Diversity ... Mr. Herbert CALDWELL

Illinois College of Optometry (D)

3241 S Michigan Avenue, Chicago IL 60616-3878
County: Cook FICE Identification: 001689
Unit ID: 145628
Telephone: (312) 225-1700 Carnegie Class: Spec/Health
FAX Number: (312) 225-1724 Calendar System: Quarter
URL: www.ico.edu
Established: 1872 Annual Graduate Tuition & Fees: $31,660
Enrollment: 640 Coed
Affiliation or Control: Independent Non-Profit IRS Status: 501(c)3
Highest Offering: First Professional Degree; No Undergraduates
Program: Professional
Accreditation: NH, OPT, OPTR

01 President ... Dr. Arol R. AUGSBURGER
05 Vice Pres for Academic Affairs/Dean ... Dr. Kent DAUM
16 Vice President Human Res/Operations ... Mrs. Laura L. ROUNCE
17 Vice Pres for Patient Care Services ... Dr. Leonard V. MESSNER
10 VP for Finance & Business/CFO ... Mr. John BUDZYNSKI
30 VP Student/Alumni/College Devel ... Dr. Mark COLIP
22 Vice Pres Compliance/Risk Mgmt ... Dr. Valarie CONRAD
20 Associate Dean Academic Affairs ... Dr. Barclay BAKKUM
06 Asst Dean Academic Admin/Registrar ... Mrs. Lavern YOUNG
07 Director of Admissions ... Ms. Teisha JOHNSON
35 Sr Director Student Development ... Ms. Beth KARMIS
37 Director Student Financial Aid ... Ms. Melissa BARTOLD
29 Director Alumni Relations ... Ms. Connie M. SCAVUZZO
18 Chief Facilities/Physical Plant ... Mr. Opie NIMON
36 Director Student Placement ... Ms. Tracy FAULKNER

*Illinois Eastern Community Colleges System Office (E)

233 E Chestnut Street, Olney IL 62450-2298
County: Richland FICE Identification: 009135
Unit ID: 443368
Telephone: (618) 393-2982 Carnegie Class: N/A
FAX Number: (618) 392-4816
URL: www.iecc.edu

01 Chief Executive Officer ... Mr. Terry BRUCE
10 Chief Finance Officer/Treasurer ... Mr. Roger BROWNING
103 Dean Workforce Education ... Mr. Michael THOMAS
30 Assoc Dean Inst Development ... Mrs. Pam SCHWARTZ
36 Assoc Dean Career Ed & Econ Dev ... Mrs. Kathleen PAMPE
20 Assoc Dean Acad/Student Support Svc ... Mrs. Chris CANTWELL
05 Pgm Director College Support Svcs ... Ms. Rita S. ADAMS
88 Program Director SBDC ... Mr. Byron BRUMFIEL
85 Pgm Dir Intl Std/Dir Dist Std Rctmt ... Mrs. Pamela SWANSON-MADDEN
15 Director of Human Resources ... Mrs. Tara BUERSTER
88 Director Upward Bound ... Mrs. LeAnn HARTLEROAD
88 Director Student Advantage Network ... Mrs. Cora WEGER
22 Dir Economic/Educational Devel ... Ms. Kathy SWINSON
88 Director Talent Search ... Mrs. Carol REDMAN

*Illinois Eastern Community Colleges Frontier Community College (F)

Frontier Drive, Fairfield IL 62837-9801
County: Wayne FICE Identification: 020744
Unit ID: 403469
Telephone: (618) 842-3711 Carnegie Class: Assoc/Pub-R-L
FAX Number: (618) 842-4425 Calendar System: Semester
URL: www.iecc.edu/fcc
Established: 1976 Annual Undergrad Tuition & Fees (In-District): $2,762
Enrollment: 2,171 Coed
Affiliation or Control: State/Local IRS Status: 501(c)3
Highest Offering: Associate Degree
Program: Occupational; 2-Year Principally Bachelor's Creditable
Accreditation: &NH, ADNUR

02 President ... Dr. Tim TAYLOR
05 Dean of Instruction ... Mr. Bob BOYLES
32 Asst Dean of Student Services ... Mr. Jeff CUTCHIN
51 Assoc Dean Adult & Cont Education ... Mrs. Jervaise MCDANIEL
10 Director of Business ... Mrs. Lavonna MILLER
08 Director of Learning Resource Ctr ... Ms. Merna YOUNGBLOOD
88 Pgm Dir Emerg Prep/Indu Qual Mgmt ... Ms. Carrie DAGG
18 Supervisor of Building & Grounds ... Mr. Galen DUNN
37 Coordinator of Financial Aid ... Mr. Adam BOWLES
26 Coord of Public Info & Marketing ... Mrs. Karen BRYANT
88 Coord Literary Development Program ... Ms. Janet HERMAN
06 Coordinator of Registration/Records ... Ms. Mary ATKINS

*Illinois Eastern Community Colleges Lincoln Trail College (G)

11220 State Highway 1, Robinson IL 62454-5707
County: Crawford FICE Identification: 009786
Unit ID: 403478
Telephone: (618) 544-8657 Carnegie Class: Assoc/Pub-R-M
FAX Number: (618) 544-7423 Calendar System: Semester
URL: www.iecc.edu/ltc
Established: 1969 Annual Undergrad Tuition & Fees (In-District): $2,762
Enrollment: 1,062 Coed
Affiliation or Control: State/Local IRS Status: 501(c)3
Highest Offering: Associate Degree
Program: Occupational; 2-Year Principally Bachelor's Creditable
Accreditation: &NH, ADNUR

02 President ... Mr. Mitch HANNAHS
05 Dean of the College ... Ms. Kathy HARRIS
37 Director of Financial Aid ... Ms. Jennifer BARTHELEMY
07 Director of Admissions ... Ms. Becky L. MIKEWORTH
08 Director of Learning Resource Ctr ... Ms. Vicky BONELLI
10 Director of Business ... Ms. Jamie HENRY
36 Career Advisor ... Ms. Gayle ZARING
41 Interim Sports Center Manager/Coach ... Mr. Kevin BOWERS
18 Groundskeeper ... Mr. Dan LEGGITT
26 Coord Public Information/Marketing ... Ms. Danelle HEVRON

*Illinois Eastern Community Colleges Olney Central College (H)

305 North West Street, Olney IL 62450-1099
County: Richland FICE Identification: 001742
Unit ID: 145707
Telephone: (618) 395-7777 Carnegie Class: Assoc/Pub-R-M
FAX Number: (618) 392-3293 Calendar System: Semester
URL: www.iecc.edu/occ
Established: 1962 Annual Undergrad Tuition & Fees (In-District): $2,762
Enrollment: 1,603 Coed
Affiliation or Control: State/Local IRS Status: 501(c)3
Highest Offering: Associate Degree
Program: Occupational; 2-Year Principally Bachelor's Creditable
Accreditation: &NH, ADNUR, RAD

02 President ... Mr. Rodney RANES
05 Dean of Instruction ... Vacant
32 Assistant Dean Student Services ... Mrs. Chris WEBBER
76 Assoc Dean Nursing Allied Health ... Ms. Tamara FRALICKER
08 Director Learning Resource Center ... Mrs. Charlotte BRUCE
88 Director Cosmetology ... Ms. Linda MILLER
10 Director Business ... Mr. Doug SHIPMAN
41 Athletic Director/Coach ... Mr. Dennis CONLEY
37 Financial Aid Coordinator ... Mrs. Vicki STUCKEY
18 Operations/Maintenance Team Leader ... Mr. Larry GANGLOFF

*Illinois Eastern Community Colleges Wabash Valley College (I)

2200 College Drive, Mount Carmel IL 62863-2657
County: Wabash FICE Identification: 001779
Unit ID: 403487
Telephone: (618) 262-8641 Carnegie Class: Assoc/Pub-R-L
FAX Number: (618) 262-5347 Calendar System: Semester
URL: www.iecc.edu/wvc
Established: 1960 Annual Undergrad Tuition & Fees (In-District): $2,762
Enrollment: 5,584 Coed
Affiliation or Control: State/Local IRS Status: 501(c)3
Highest Offering: Associate Degree
Program: Occupational; 2-Year Principally Bachelor's Creditable
Accreditation: &NH, ADNUR

02 President ... Mr. Matt FOWLER
05 Interim Dean of Instruction ... Mr. Wayne MORRIS
32 Assistant Dean Student Services ... Mrs. Diana SPEAR
20 Director of Academic Advising ... Mr. Tim ZIMMER
08 Director of LRC ... Ms. Sandy CRAIG
60 Director of Broadcasting ... Mr. Kyle PEACH
41 Athletic Director ... Mr. Daniel SPARKS
26 Director of Public Info & Marketing ... Vacant
10 Director of Business ... Mrs. Cindy WALLS
37 Financial Aid Coordinator ... Ms. Melinda SILVERNALE
18 Groundskeeper ... Mr. Ron MARTIN

The Illinois Institute of Art (A)

350 N Orleans, Suite 136, Chicago IL 60654-1514
County: Cook　FICE Identification: 012584
Unit ID: 148177
Telephone: (312) 280-3500　Carnegie Class: Spec/Arts
FAX Number: (312) 777-8780　Calendar System: Quarter
URL: www.artinstitutes.edu/chicago
Established: 1916　Annual Undergrad Tuition & Fees: $21,996
Enrollment: 3,024　Coed
Affiliation or Control: Proprietary　IRS Status: Proprietary
Highest Offering: Baccalaureate
Program: Professional; Technical Emphasis
Accreditation: NH, ACFEI, CIDA

01 President/Chicago ... John B. JENKINS
04 Exec Assistant to the President ... Allison SANTOS
05 Vice President of Academic Affairs ... Vesna GRBOVIC
07 VP/Senior Director of Admissions ... Janis K. ANTON
20 Associate Dean of Academic Affairs ... Karen JANKO
20 Associate Dean of Academic Affairs ... Marlene ATKINS
06 Registrar ... LaVondra LACEY
09 Director of Assessment ... Dr. James BORLAND
08 Library Director ... Julie TEIPEL
88 Director of Transitional Studies ... Karine BRAVAIS-SLYMAN
88 Dir Media/Game Arts/Animation ... Jason HOPKINS
88 Director Digital Film/Vis Effects ... Scott PERRY
97 Director General Education ... Deann GROSSI
88 Dir Culinary Arts & Hospitality ... Mark FACKLAM
88 Dir Fashion Merch/Mktg Mgmt ... Dan ROBISON
88 Dir Fashion Design/Prod/Accessories ... Victoria SINON
88 Director Interior/Product Design ... Melissa MCATEE
88 Dir Visual Comm/Graphic Dsgn/Adv ... Perrin STAMATIS
88 Dir Foundations/Illustration/Design ... Jodie LAWRENCE
10 Dir Administration/Financial Svcs ... Robert SMETAK
21 Director of Accounting ... Diosa COLLADO
37 Director Student Financial Aid ... Paula PRICE
32 Dean of Student Affairs ... Betty KOURASIS
35 Asst Dean of Student Affairs ... Valarie RAND
38 Student Support/Disabilities Coord ... Dr. Suzana FLORES
40 Supply Store Manager ... Ricardo OLAVE
36 Director of Career Services ... Patricia GILLER
15 Director of Human Resources ... Ken HOGUE
13 Director of Technology ... Robert FREEMAN

Illinois Institute of Technology (B)

3300 S Federal Street, Chicago IL 60616-3793
County: Cook　FICE Identification: 001691
Unit ID: 145725
Telephone: (312) 567-3000　Carnegie Class: RU/H
FAX Number: (312) 567-3004　Calendar System: Semester
URL: www.iit.edu
Established: 1890　Annual Undergrad Tuition & Fees: $33,800
Enrollment: 7,774　Coed
Affiliation or Control: Independent Non-Profit　IRS Status: 501(c)3
Highest Offering: Doctorate
Program: Liberal Arts And General; Teacher Preparatory; Professional; Technical Emphasis
Accreditation: NH, BUS, CLPSY, CORE, CS, ENG, LAW, LSAR

01 President ... Dr. John L. ANDERSON
05 Provost ... Dr. Alan W. CRAMB
10 VP Finance & Administration ... Dr. Patricia LAUGHLIN
21 AVP & Controller ... Mr. Brian LAFFEY
21 AVP Finance ... Mr. David ULASZEK
11 Vice Pres Business & Operations ... Dr. John P. COLLINS
30 Vice Pres Institutional Advancement ... Ms. Elizabeth HUGHES
88 Vice Pres International Affairs ... Dr. Darsh T. WASAN
86 Vice President External Affairs ... Mr. David E. BAKER
43 Vice President General Counsel ... Ms. Mary Anne SMITH
31 VP Community Affairs & Outreach ... Mr. Leroy E. KENNEDY
27 Vice Pres Marketing/Communications ... Ms. Jeanne HARTIG
13 Chief Information Officer ... Mr. Ophir TRIGALO
04 Director President's Office ... Ms. Sandra LAPORTE
18 AVP Facilities/Real Estate & Const ... Mr. Terence FRIGO
11 Assoc Vice Pres Auxiliary Services ... Ms. Jean M. BINGHAM
07 Vice Prov UG Admissions & Fin Aid ... Mr. Gerald DOYLE
16 Associate VP Human Resources ... Ms. Antoinette MURRIL
20 Assoc Provost Undergrad Education ... Dr. Michael GOSZ
26 Assoc Dir Media Relations ... Mr. Evan VENIE
32 Dean of Students ... Ms. Katherine MURPHY-STETZ
61 Dean Chicago-Kent College of Law ... Mr. Harold J. KRENT
49 Dean College of Science & Letters ... Dr. Russell BETTS
54 Dean Armour Col of Engineering ... Dr. Natacha DEPAOLA
50 Dean Stuart School of Business ... Dr. Harvey KAHALAS
48 Dean College of Architecture ... Ms. Donna V. ROBERTSON
83 Dean College of Psychology ... Dr. M. Ellen MITCHELL
88 Dean Institute of Design ... Mr. Patrick F. WHITNEY
58 Dean Graduate College ... Dr. Ali CINAR
72 Dean School of Applied Technology ... Dr. C. Robert CARLSON
38 Director Counseling Center ... Dr. Daniel KAPLAN
06 Registrar ... Mr. Peter ZACHOCKI
36 Exec Director Career Management Ctr ... Mr. Bruce MUELLER
25 Director Sponsored Research ... Ms. Domenica G. PAPPAS
09 Director Institutional Information ... Dr. Carol-Ann EMMONS
44 Director Annual Giving ... Mr. Jason SMITH
29 Director Alumni & Donor Relations ... Mr. James ACTON
85 Director International Student Ctr ... Ms. Elizabeth MATTHEWS
37 Assoc Director Financial Aid ... Ms. Abigail MCGRATH
41 Athletic Director ... Mr. Enzley MITCHELL, IV
19 Director Public Safety ... Mr. Raymond MARTINEZ
08 Interim Dean of Galvin Library ... Ms. Kristin STANDAERT
22 Dir Equal Opp/Affirmative Action ... Ms. Candida MIRANDA
96 Director of Purchasing ... Mr. Frank FIORITO
28 Director Student Ctr for Diversity ... Ms. Lisa MONTGOMERY
35 Director Student Life ... Ms. Erin GRAY

Illinois State University (C)

School and North Streets, Normal IL 61790-0001
County: McLean　FICE Identification: 001692
Unit ID: 145813
Telephone: (309) 438-2111　Carnegie Class: DRU
FAX Number: (309) 438-2768　Calendar System: Semester
URL: www.ilstu.edu
Established: 1857　Annual Undergrad Tuition & Fees (In-State): $11,417
Enrollment: 21,134　Coed
Affiliation or Control: State　IRS Status: 501(c)3
Highest Offering: Doctorate
Program: Liberal Arts And General; Teacher Preparatory; Professional
Accreditation: NH, AAFCS, ART, AUD, BUS, BUSA, CIDA, CONST, CS, DIETD, DIETI, IPSY, MT, MUS, NAIT, NRPA, NURSE, SCPSY, SP, SW, TED, THEA

01 President ... Dr. C. Alvin BOWMAN, JR.
05 Vice Pres Academic Affs & Provost ... Dr. Sheri N. EVERTS
10 Vice President Finance & Planning ... Dr. Daniel LAYZEL
32 Vice President Student Affairs ... Mr. Steven L. ADAMS
26 Vice President Univ Advancement ... Ms. Erin MINNE
20 Associate Provost ... Dr. Jan MURPHY
35 Assoc Vice Pres Student Affairs ... Dr. Brent PATERSON
21 Assoc VP Finance & Planning ... Ms. Debra K. SMITLEY
91 Assoc Vice President Technology ... Dr. Mark WALBERT
58 Assoc VP Grad Std/Res/Intern Educ ... Dr. Rodney L. CUSTER
84 Assoc VP Enrollment Management . Dr. Jonathan M. ROSENTHAL
15 Assoc VP Human Resources ... Dr. Ira S. SCHOENWALD
86 Asst to Pres/Government Relations ... Mr. Philip ADAMS
08 Dean University Libraries ... Ms. Cheryl A. ELZY
06 University Registrar ... Mr. Jess D. RAY
07 Director Admissions ... Ms. Molly K. ARNOLD
20 Director University College ... Ms. Amelia NOEL-ELKINS
30 Exec Director of Development ... Ms. Joy D. HUTCHCRAFT
21 Exec Dir Financial Svcs/Comptroller ... Mr. Greg L. ALT
37 Director Financial Aid ... Ms. Jana ALBRECHT
29 Director Alumni Services ... Dr. Stephanie Ann EPP
36 Director Career Center ... Dr. Michael SCHERMER
18 Director Facilities Planning ... Dr. Richard C. RUNNER
19 Chief University Police ... Mr. Ronald D. SWAN
28 Director Diversity & Affirm Action ... Mr. Shane MCCREERY
23 Director Student Health Services ... Dr. Dwayne SACKMAN
39 Director University Housing ... Ms. Maureen BLAIR
41 Director of Athletics ... Dr. Sheahon ZENGER
85 Director International Studies ... Dr. Momar NDIAYE
92 Director Honors Program ... Dr. Kim PEREIRA
94 Director Women's Studies ... Dr. Alison BAILEY
96 Director of Purchasing ... Ms. Judy JOHNSON
49 Actg Dean College Arts & Sciences ... Dr. James PAYNE
50 Interim Dean College Business ... Dr. Scott JOHNSON
53 Dean College Education ... Dr. Deborah J. CURTIS
72 Dean College Applied Science/Tech ... Dr. Jeffrey A. WOOD
57 Dean College Fine Arts ... Dr. James MAJOR
66 Dean Mennonite College of Nursing ... Dr. Janet KREJCI
04 Assistant to the President ... Mr. Jay GROVES

Illinois Valley Community College (D)

815 N Orlando Smith Avenue, Oglesby IL 61348-9692
County: La Salle　FICE Identification: 001705
Unit ID: 145831
Telephone: (815) 224-2720　Carnegie Class: Assoc/Pub-R-L
FAX Number: (815) 224-3033　Calendar System: Semester
URL: www.ivcc.edu
Established: 1966　Annual Undergrad Tuition & Fees (In-District): $2,516
Enrollment: 4,507　Coed
Affiliation or Control: Local　IRS Status: 501(c)3
Highest Offering: Associate Degree
Program: Occupational; 2-Year Principally Bachelor's Creditable
Accreditation: NH, ADNUR, DA

01 President ... Dr. Jerry M. CORCORAN
45 VP Planning/Institutional Effective ... Dr. Lori E. SCROGGS
05 VP Learning & Student Development ... Dr. Rick R. PEARCE
10 Vice Pres Business Svcs/Finance ... Ms. Cheryl E. ROELFSEMA
20 Assoc Vice Pres Academic Affairs ... Ms. Sue L. ISERMANN
32 Assoc Vice Pres Student Services ... Ms. Tracy L. MORRIS
24 Director of Learning Technologies ... Ms. Emily B. VESCOGNI
31 Director Cmty Relations & Marketing ... Mr. Francis R. BROLLEY
13 Dir of Information Technology Svcs ... Mr. Harold B. BARNES
51 Dir Cont Educ/Business Services ... Ms. Jamie L. GAHM
15 Director Human Resources ... Ms. Glenna S. JONES
37 Director of Financial Aid ... Ms. Patricia A. WILLIAMSON
07 Director of Admissions/Records ... Mr. Mark J. GRZYBOWSKI
08 Head Librarian ... Ms. Jane H. NOREM
30 Director of Development ... Mr. Francis R. BROLLEY
96 Interim Director of Purchasing ... Ms. Laurie S. PITTMAN
18 Director of Facilities ... Mr. Gary K. JOHNSON
09 Director of Institutional Research ... Mr. Robert C. MATTSON
81 Dean Natural Science/Business ... Mr. Ron W. GROLEAU
66 Dean Health Professions/Nursing ... Mr. Michael E. GORMAN
75 Dean Career/Technical Programs ... Ms. Elaine NOVAK
79 Int Dn Humanities/Fine Arts/Soc Sci ... Dr. Jeffrey M. ANDERSON
88 Dean English/Mathematics/Education ... Ms. Marianne DZIK

Illinois Wesleyan University (E)

PO Box 2900, 1312 Park Street,
Bloomington IL 61702-2900
County: McLean　FICE Identification: 001696
Unit ID: 145646
Telephone: (309) 556-1000　Carnegie Class: Bac/A&S
FAX Number: (309) 556-3411　Calendar System: Other
URL: www.iwu.edu
Established: 1850　Annual Undergrad Tuition & Fees: $36,392
Enrollment: 2,094　Coed
Affiliation or Control: Independent Non-Profit　IRS Status: 501(c)3
Highest Offering: Baccalaureate
Program: Liberal Arts And General; Teacher Preparatory; Professional
Accreditation: NH, MUS, NURSE

01 President ... Dr. Richard F. WILSON
05 Provost & Dean of Faculty ... Dr. Jonathan D. GREEN
10 Vice President Business & Finance ... Mr. Daniel P. KLOTZBACH
30 Vice President for Advancement ... Mr. Martin W. SMITH
26 Vice President for Public Relations ... Mr. Matt KURZ
32 Int VP Student Affs/Dean Students ... Dr. Roger SCHNAITTER
07 Dean of Admissions ... Mr. Tony BANKSTON
84 Dean of Enrollment Management ... Mr. Robert MURRAY
09 AVP Instl Research/Plng/Evaluation ... Dr. Michael THOMPSON
86 Dir Government/Community Relations ... Mr. Carl F. TEICHMAN
04 Exec Assistant to the President ... Ms. Susan E. BASSI
20 Assoc Provost Acad Plng/Standards ... Dr. Frank A. BOYD
20 Associate Dean of the Faculty ... Dr. Irving EPSTEIN
20 Associate Dean of Curriculum ... Dr. Zahia DRICI
16 Assoc VP for Human Resources ... Ms. Catherine SPITZ
13 Asst Provost/Chief Technology Ofcr ... Mr. Trey SHORT
44 Associate Vice Pres for Advancement ... Mr. Benjamin J. RHODES
88 Associate Vice Pres for Advancement ... Mr. Steve D. SEIBRING
35 Asc Dean Stdnts/Co-Curricular/Pgmng ... Ms. Darcy L. GREDER
38 Director Student Counseling ... Dr. Annorrah MOORMAN
39 Director of Residential Life ... Mr. Matthew DAMSCHRODER
08 University Librarian ... Dr. Karen SCHMIDT
06 Registrar ... Dr. Leslie BETZ
42 University Chaplain ... Rev. Elyse NELSON WINGER
21 Controller ... Mr. John BRYANT
37 Director of Financial Aid ... Mr. Scott SEIBRING
64 Director of School of Music ... Dr. Mario J. PELUSI
57 Director of School of Art ... Prof. Miles C. BAIR
57 Director of School of Theatre Arts ... Dr. Curtis C. TROUT
66 Director of School of Nursing ... Dr. Victoria FOLSE
41 Director of Athletics ... Prof. Dennis BRIDGES
29 Director of Alumni Relations ... Ms. Ann HARDING
102 Dir Sponsored Pgms/Foundation Rels ... Vacant
44 Director of Annual Fund ... Mr. Jeffrey MAVROS
36 Director of Career Center ... Mr. Warren KISTNER
18 Director of Physical Plant ... Mr. Millard C. JORGENSON
27 Director of News Services ... Mr. Stewart I. SALOWITZ
93 Director Multicultural Student Affs ... Ms. Roshaunda ROSS
35 Director of Student Activities ... Mr. Colin STEWART
94 Director of Women's Studies Program ... Dr. Carole MYSCOFSKI
104 Director of International Office ... Ms. Stacey SHIMIZU
40 Bookstore Manager ... Mr. Thaddeus SUTTER

Institute for Clinical Social Work (F)

401 South State Street, Suite 822, Chicago IL 60605
County: Cook　FICE Identification: 025737
Unit ID: 145886
Telephone: (312) 935-4232　Carnegie Class: Spec/Health
FAX Number: (312) 935-4255　Calendar System: Semester
URL: www.icsw.edu
Established: 1981　Annual Graduate Tuition & Fees: $22,896
Enrollment: 105　Coed
Affiliation or Control: Independent Non-Profit　IRS Status: 501(c)3
Highest Offering: Doctorate; No Undergraduates
Program: Professional
Accreditation: NH

01 Director of Operations ... Maureen A. HEWITT
05 Dean/Chief Administrative Officer ... Amy ELDRIDGE
32 Student Services Coordinator ... Elizabeth OLER
37 Mgr Strategic Operations & Fin Aid ... Pierre SMITH
08 Head Librarian ... Scot AUSBORN
58 Director of Doctoral Studies ... R. Dennis SHELBY
88 Asst Director of Doctoral Studies ... Denise DUVAL

International Academy of Design and Technology (G)

1 N State Street, Suite 500, Chicago IL 60602-9736
County: Cook　FICE Identification: 021603
Unit ID: 146010
Telephone: (312) 980-9200　Carnegie Class: Spec/Arts
FAX Number: (312) 541-3929　Calendar System: Other
URL: www.iadtchicago.edu
Established: 1977　Annual Undergrad Tuition & Fees: $15,030
Enrollment: 1,411　Coed
Affiliation or Control: Proprietary　IRS Status: Proprietary
Highest Offering: Baccalaureate
Program: Occupational
Accreditation: ACICS, CIDA

01 President ... Mr. Robert NACHTSHEIM
05 Vice President of Academics ... Ms. Kathleen EMBRY
88 Reg Dir of Regulatory Operations ... Dr. Darlene ULMER

07 Senior Director of Admissions .... Ms. Catherine BROKENSHIRE
06 Associate Registrar .... Ms. Paris BALKCOM
08 Regional Librarian .... Ms. Kayte KORWITTS
36 Director of Career Services .... Ms. Cheryl PERILLO
37 Director of Financial Aid .... Mr. Ryan FROEHLE

International Academy of Design and Technology-Schaumberg (A)

935 National Parkway, Schaumberg IL 60173-5160
County: Cook Identification: 666141
Telephone: (847) 969-2800 Carnegie Class: Not Classified
FAX Number: (847) 969-2449 Calendar System: Quarter
URL: www.iadtschaumburg.com
Established: 2001 Annual Undergrad Tuition & Fees: $4,800
Enrollment: 288 Coed
Affiliation or Control: Proprietary IRS Status: Proprietary
Highest Offering: Baccalaureate
Program: Liberal Arts And General
Accreditation: ACICS

01 Campus Director .... Mr. Tom TIMMONS

† Branch campus of International Academy of Design and Technology, Chicago.

ITT Technical Institute (B)

1401 Feehanville Drive, Mount Prospect IL 60056-6005
County: Cook Identification: 666538
Unit ID: 260974
Telephone: (847) 375-8800 Carnegie Class: Spec/Tech
FAX Number: (847) 375-9022 Calendar System: Quarter
URL: www.itt-tech.edu
Established: 1986 Annual Undergrad Tuition & Fees: N/A
Enrollment: 513 Coed
Affiliation or Control: Proprietary IRS Status: Proprietary
Highest Offering: Baccalaureate
Program: Technical Emphasis
Accreditation: ACICS

† Branch campus of ITT Technical Institute, Indianapolis, IN.

ITT Technical Institute (C)

800 Jorie Blvd., Suite 100, Oak Brook IL 60523
County: DuPage Identification: 666118
Unit ID: 434557
Telephone: (630) 472-7000 Carnegie Class: Spec/Tech
FAX Number: (630) 455-6476 Calendar System: Quarter
URL: www.itt-tech.edu
Established: 1997 Annual Undergrad Tuition & Fees: N/A
Enrollment: 470 Coed
Affiliation or Control: Proprietary IRS Status: Proprietary
Highest Offering: Baccalaureate
Program: Technical Emphasis
Accreditation: ACICS

† Branch campus of ITT Technical Institute, Fort Wayne, IN.

ITT Technical Institute (D)

11551 184th Place, Orland Park IL 60467-4900
County: Cook Identification: 666539
Unit ID: 414586
Telephone: (708) 326-3200 Carnegie Class: Spec/Tech
FAX Number: N/A Calendar System: Quarter
URL: www.itt-tech.edu
Established: 1993 Annual Undergrad Tuition & Fees: N/A
Enrollment: 558 Coed
Affiliation or Control: Proprietary IRS Status: Proprietary
Highest Offering: Baccalaureate
Program: Technical Emphasis
Accreditation: ACICS

† Branch campus of ITT Technical Institute, Grand Rapids, MI.

John A. Logan College (E)

700 Logan College Road, Carterville IL 62918-2500
County: Williamson FICE Identification: 008076
Unit ID: 146205
Telephone: (618) 985-3741 Carnegie Class: Assoc/Pub-R-L
FAX Number: (618) 985-2248 Calendar System: Semester
URL: www.jalc.edu
Established: 1967 Annual Undergrad Tuition & Fees (In-District): $2,800
Enrollment: 6,787 Coed
Affiliation or Control: State/Local IRS Status: 501(c)3
Highest Offering: Associate Degree
Program: Occupational; 2-Year Principally Bachelor's Creditable
Accreditation: NH, CONST, DA, DH, DMS, MLTAD, OTA

01 President .... Dr. Robert L. MEES
05 Vice President Instruction Services .... Dr. Julia SCHROEDER
10 VP Business Svcs/College Facilities .... Mr. Brad MCCORMICK
11 Vice President Administration .... Dr. Tim DAUGHERTY
06 Dean Student Services .... Mr. Terry CRAIN
21 Dean Financial Operations .... Ms. Kim DIXON
20 Dean Instruction .... Dr. Deborah PAYNE
103 Dean Workforce Dev/Comm Educ .... Mr. Phil MINNIS
88 Assoc Dean Baccalaureate Transfer .... Mr. Mark HENSON
76 Assoc Dean Health/Public Svcs .... Dr. Valerie BARKO
51 Assoc Dean Continuing Education .... Mr. Barry HANCOCK
88 Assoc Dean Adult Basic/Secondary Ed .... Ms. Kay FLEMING
13 Assoc Dean Information Technology .... Mr. Robin H. PAULS
07 Associate Dean Admissions .... Vacant
37 Director of Student Financial Asst .... Ms. Sherry SUMMARY
08 Assoc Dean for Library Services .... Ms. Judy VINEYARD
30 Director of Development .... Vacant
26 Dir Community Relations/Marketing .... Mr. Steve O'KEEFE
35 Director of Student Activities .... Ms. Adrienne BARKLEY-GIFFIN
36 Director of Placement .... Ms. Lisa HUDGENS
102 Executive Director of Foundation .... Ms. Staci BYNUM
66 Director of Nursing .... Ms. Marilyn FALASTER
88 Director of Career Dev/Acad Support .... Ms. Christy MCBRIDE
15 Director of Human Resources/AAO .... Mr. Clay BREWER
18 Dir Building/Grounds/Campus Safety .... Mr. Dwight HOFFARD
09 Director Institutional Research .... Mr. Eric PULLEY
29 Dir of Scholarships/Alumni Svcs .... Ms. Stacy HOLLOWAY

John Marshall Law School (F)

315 S Plymouth Court, Chicago IL 60604-3968
County: Cook FICE Identification: 001698
Unit ID: 146241
Telephone: (312) 427-2737 Carnegie Class: Spec/Law
FAX Number: (312) 427-8307 Calendar System: Semester
URL: www.jmls.edu
Established: 1899 Annual Graduate Tuition & Fees: $32,880
Enrollment: 1,609 Coed
Affiliation or Control: Independent Non-Profit IRS Status: 501(c)3
Highest Offering: First Professional Degree; No Undergraduates
Program: Professional
Accreditation: NH, LAW

01 Dean .... Mr. John E. CORKERY
05 Assoc Dean Academic Affairs .... Dean Ralph RUEBNER
07 Assoc Dean Admissions/Stdnt Affairs ...... Mr. William B. POWERS
10 Chief Financial Officer .... Ms. Cynthia SAH
13 Chief Technology Officer .... Mr. Jim VELCO
45 Dean Outreach and Planning .... Mr. Rory Dean SMITH
26 Asst Dean Institutional Affairs .... Mr. John M. MCNAMARA
36 Asst Dean for Career Services .... Ms. Laurel A. HAJEK
20 Asst Dean for Academic Services .... Ms. Jodie NEEDHAM
06 Registrar .... Ms. Anna JOHNSON
15 Director Human Resources .... Mr. Martin D'AMBROSE
29 Director Alumni Relations/Aux Svcs .... Ms. Sherri BERENDT
44 Individual Gifts Officer .... Mr. Kevin HULL
37 Director Student Financial Aid .... Ms. Yara SANTANA

John Wood Community College (G)

1301 S 48th Street, Quincy IL 62305-8736
County: Adams FICE Identification: 012813
Unit ID: 146278
Telephone: (217) 224-6500 Carnegie Class: Assoc/Pub-R-M
FAX Number: (217) 224-4208 Calendar System: Semester
URL: www.jwcc.edu
Established: 1974 Annual Undergrad Tuition & Fees (In-District): $3,900
Enrollment: 2,501 Coed
Affiliation or Control: State/Local IRS Status: 501(c)3
Highest Offering: Associate Degree
Program: Occupational; 2-Year Principally Bachelor's Creditable
Accreditation: NH, MLTAD, SURGT

01 President .... Dr. Thomas KLINCAR
05 Vice President for Instruction .... Vacant
10 Vice Pres for Finance/Business Svcs .... Mr. Alan STEIGELMAN
32 Vice President for Student Services .... Dr. John LETTS
09 Dir Institutional Effectiveness .... Mr. Josh WELKER
88 Dean Transfer Education .... Dr. David SHINN
75 Dean Career/Technical/Workforce Ed .... Ms. Pam FOUST
84 Dean Enrollment Services .... Ms. Bonnie SCRANTON
07 Director Admissions .... Mr. Lee WIBBELL
21 Dean Fiscal Services .... Ms. Mary ARP
35 Director Support Services .... Dr. Sandra THOMAS
37 Director Financial Aid .... Ms. Melanie LECHTENBERG
13 Director Information Services .... Mr. Joshua BRUECK
47 Dept Chair Ag Sciences .... Mr. Gary SHUPE
76 Director Health Sciences .... Ms. Betty MCDONNELL
88 Associate Dean Transfer Education .... Mr. Kent HAWLEY
103 Assoc Dn Career Technical Workfc Ed .... Mr. Terry JENKINS
08 Dir Library Svcs/Acad Spprt Center .... Ms. Barbara LIEBER
26 Director Public Relations/Marketing .... Ms. Tracy ORNE
41 Director of Student Life/Athletics .... Mr. Mike ELBE
30 Director Advancement .... Ms. Barbara HOLTHAUS
36 Dir Career Services .... Mr. Cody BAGGETT
15 Director Human Resources .... Ms. Stacey O'BRIEN
18 Director Physical Plant .... Mr. Lou BARTA
19 Chief of Campus Police .... Mr. Bill LATOUR
40 Manager of Auxiliary Services .... Ms. Denise WILLIAMS
77 Dept Chair Ofc Technology/Comp Sci .... Ms. Carol SHARPE
50 Dept Chair Business .... Mr. Greg LEE
57 Dept Chair Fine Arts .... Mr. Gary DECLUE
81 Department Chair Mathematics .... Mr. David RIGSBEE
65 Dept Chair Natural Sciences .... Dr. Ivan PAUL
79 Dept Chair Language/Literature/Hum .... Ms. Valerie VLAHAKIS
88 Dept Chair Developmental Education .. Ms. Joyce MILLER-BOREN
83 Dept Chair Social/Behavior Science .... Mr. Randall EGDORF
88 Dept Chair Landscape/Loc Foods/Cons .... Mr. Gary WYCISLO

Joliet Junior College (H)

1215 Houbolt Road, Joliet IL 60431-8938
County: Will FICE Identification: 001699
Unit ID: 146296
Telephone: (815) 729-9020 Carnegie Class: Assoc/Pub-S-SC
FAX Number: (815) 729-4256 Calendar System: Semester
URL: www.jjc.edu
Established: 1901 Annual Undergrad Tuition & Fees (In-District): $3,090
Enrollment: 15,676 Coed
Affiliation or Control: State/Local IRS Status: 501(c)3
Highest Offering: Associate Degree
Program: Occupational; 2-Year Principally Bachelor's Creditable
Accreditation: NH, ACBSP, ACFEI, ADNUR, MUS

01 President .... Dr. Gena PROULX
05 Vice President Academic Affairs .... Dr. Valerie ROBERSON
11 Vice Pres Administrative Services .... Ms. Tammy RUST
09 VP Institutional Advancement/Rsrch .... Vacant
13 VP Information Technology .... Mr. Dwayne CABLE
35 Vice President Student Development ...... Dr. Betsy OUDENHOVEN
31 Dean Community/Economic Development ... Mr. Daniel KREIDLER
07 Director Admissions & Recruitment .... Ms. Jennifer KLOBERDANZ
88 Interim Dir Adult & Family Services .... Ms. Emilie MCCALLISTER
37 Director Financial Aid .... Mr. David SEWARD
15 Director Human Resources .... Ms. Joyce COLEMAN
06 Director Recruitment Svcs/Registrar .... Mr. Keith TILLMAN
18 Director Facility Services .... Mr. Patrick VAN DUYNE
21 Director Business/Auxiliary Svcs .... Ms. Judy MITCHELL
26 Dir Commun/External Relations .... Vacant
36 Director Career Services .... Ms. Mary J. WOLFERSBERGER
41 Director Athletics .... Mr. Wayne KING
21 Director Financial Svcs/Controller .... Mr. Jeffrey HEAP
19 Dir Campus Safety & Police Chief .... Mr. Peter COMANDA
30 Dir Inst Adv Exec Dir JJC Found .... Ms. Kristin MULVEY
08 Director Learning Resources .... Mr. TJ URBANSKI
40 Manager Bookstore .... Mr. Michael M. MAIER
88 Coord Transfer Articulation .... Ms. Angie KAYSEN-LUZBETAK
74 Coord Veterinary Medicine Tech .... Dr. Scott KELLER
38 Lead Counselor .... Ms. Mildred HOLMES

Judson University (I)

1151 N State Street, Elgin IL 60123-1498
County: Kane FICE Identification: 001700
Unit ID: 146339
Telephone: (847) 628-2500 Carnegie Class: Bac/Diverse
FAX Number: (847) 628-1027 Calendar System: 4/1/4
URL: www.judsonu.edu
Established: 1963 Annual Undergrad Tuition & Fees: $25,400
Enrollment: 1,178 Coed
Affiliation or Control: American Baptist IRS Status: 501(c)3
Highest Offering: Master's
Program: Liberal Arts And General; Teacher Preparatory
Accreditation: NH

01 President .... Dr. Jerry B. CAIN
10 Vice President Business Affairs .... Mr. Laine MALMQUIST
30 Vice President External Relations .... Mr. Tory GUM
05 Provost/Vice Pres Academic Affairs .... Dr. Dale SIMMONS
32 VP/Dean of Student Development .... Mrs. LeAnn PAULEY-HEARD
32 Dean of Stdnts/Dir Career Center .... Ms. Rolanda BURRIS
39 Director of Housing .... Mrs. Karen ALDRIDGE
06 College Registrar .... Ms. Ginny GUTH
07 Director of Admissions .... Ms. Nancy BINGER
15 Director Personnel Services .... Mr. Tom RUEGER
29 Director Alumni Relations .... Mrs. Bonnie BIENERT
08 Library Director .... Mr. Larry WILD
37 Director of Financial Aid .... Mr. Roberto SANTIZO
41 Athletic Director .... Ms. Nancy SMITH
18 Chief Facilities/Physical Plant .... Mr. Leonard J. NICOSIA
27 Director of Communications .... Ms. Mary DULABAUM

Kankakee Community College (J)

100 College Drive, Kankakee IL 60901-6505
County: Kankakee FICE Identification: 007690
Unit ID: 146348
Telephone: (815) 802-8100 Carnegie Class: Assoc/Pub-R-L
FAX Number: (815) 802-8101 Calendar System: Semester
URL: www.kcc.edu
Established: 1966 Annual Undergrad Tuition & Fees (In-District): $3,210
Enrollment: 4,219 Coed
Affiliation or Control: State/Local IRS Status: 501(c)3
Highest Offering: Associate Degree
Program: Occupational; 2-Year Principally Bachelor's Creditable
Accreditation: NH, MLTAD, PTAA

01 President .... Dr. John AVENDANO
04 Executive Secretary to President .... Ms. Rose MITCHELL
05 VP of Instructional & Stdnt Success .... Mr. Dennis SORENSEN
10 VP of Administration & Finance .... Ms. Vicki GARDNER
06 Registrar .... Ms. Michelle DRISCOLL
32 Dean of Student Development .... Ms. Julia WASKOSKY
35 Associate Dean of Student Develop .... Ms. Michelle DRISCOLL
09 Dir Institutional Research .... Dr. Vicki MAGEE
88 Dir Adult & Community Education .... Ms. Margaret COOPER
103 Director of Workforce Development .... Ms. Dana WASHINGTON
37 Director Financial Aid .... Mr. John PERRY
35 Coord Student Life .... Ms. Lindsey FRITZ
88 Director Fitness Center .... Mr. Dennis CLARK
41 Director Athletics .... Mr. Ted PETERSEN

15 Director Human Resources ... Mr. David CAGLE
21 Director Financial Affairs ... Ms. Beth NUNLEY
50 Asst Dean Business & Technology ... Mr. Paul CARLSON
51 Asst Dean Cont Educ & Career Svcs ... Ms. Mary POSING
18 Dir Campus Facilities & Security ... Mr. Rich SODERQUIST
88 Coordinator Small Business Devel ... Mr. Ken CRITE
81 Asst Dean Math/Science Division ... Ms. Virginia MAKEPEACE
76 Asst Dean Health Careers Div ... Ms. Kim MAU
88 Director Student Advisement ... Ms. Meredith PURCELL
76 Director Respiratory Therapist Pgm ... Ms. Nancy OZEE
76 Director Medical Lab Technology ... Ms. Glenda FORNERIS
83 Asst Dean Humanities/Social Science ... Mr. Mark LANTING
76 Director Radiology Technology Pgm ... Ms. Darla JEPSON
13 Director Information Tech Svcs ... Mr. Michael O'CONNOR
102 Exec Director of KCC Foundation ... Ms. Kelly MYERS
07 Coord Admissions & Recruitment ... Mrs. Oshunda CARPENTER-WILLIAMS
88 Director Institutional Tech/Fac Dev ... Ms. Donna SMITH
62 Director Learning Resource Center ... Ms. Karen BECKER
26 Director Marketing ... Ms. Kari SARGEANT
88 Dean of Sustainability ... Dr. Bert JACOBSON

Kaskaskia College (A)

27210 College Road, Centralia IL 62801-7878
County: Clinton FICE Identification: 001701
Unit ID: 146366
Telephone: (618) 545-3000 Carnegie Class: Assoc/Pub-R-L
FAX Number: (618) 532-1990 Calendar System: Semester
URL: www.kaskaskia.edu
Established: 1940 Annual Undergrad Tuition & Fees (In-District): $2,880
Enrollment: 5,391 Coed
Affiliation or Control: State/Local IRS Status: 501(c)3
Highest Offering: Associate Degree
Program: Occupational; 2-Year Principally Bachelor's Creditable
Accreditation: NH, ADNUR, DA, MLTAD, OTA, PTAA, RAD

01 President ... Dr. James C. UNDERWOOD
11 Vice Pres Administrative Services ... Mrs. Nancy KINSEY
05 Vice Pres Instructional Services ... Dr. Gregory LABYAK
32 Vice President of Student Services ... Mr. Sedgwick HARRIS
75 Dean Career & Technical Education ... Ms. Ava RAWLINGS
49 Dean of Arts & Sciences ... Ms. Kellie HENEGAR
66 Dean of Nursing ... Mrs. Susan BATCHELOR
09 Dean Inst Effectiveness ... Vacant
08 Director of LRC ... Ms. Arlene DUCKER
15 Dir Human Resources/Legal Counsel ... Ms. Rhonda BOEHNE
18 Director Facilities/Physical Plant ... Mr. Phillip ELLRICH
96 Director Purchasing/Auxiliary Svcs ... Mr. Craig ROPER
21 Dir of Internal Aud & Fin Reporting ... Mrs. Debra FUNDERBURK
06 Manager of Records & Registration ... Ms. Jan RIPPERDA
37 Director of Financial Aid ... Ms. Lisa COLLIER
88 Director of Radiologic Technology ... Mrs. Mimi POLCZYNSKI
88 Dir Physical Therapist Asst Pgm ... Ms. Jane HERRMANN
91 Director of Information Technology ... Ms. Gina SCHUETZ
27 Director of Public Information ... Ms. Cathy KARRICK
26 Director of Marketing ... Mr. Travis HENSON
40 Bookstore Manager ... Ms. Cheryl JOHNSON
88 Director Adult Education ... Ms. Lisa ATKINS
88 Project Director Business Svc Ctr ... Mr. Steve GRONER
50 Business Services Field Rep ... Mr. Art BORUM
41 Athletic Director ... Mr. Mitch KOESTER
10 Controller ... Vacant
88 Recruit Svcs/Multicultural Stdnts ... Ms. Amy TROUTT
38 Director of Advising & Reten Svcs ... Ms. Christin DALAVARIS
84 Dean of Enrollment Management ... Ms. Denise DERRICK
07 Dir Admissions/Records & Dual Cred ... Mrs. Cheryl BOEHNE
88 Director of Title III Program ... Mr. Robert BLINN
88 Dir Centralia Correctional Ctr Pgm ... Mr. George EVANS
30 Coord Inst Advancement Programs ... Mrs. Suzanne CHRIST

Kendall College (B)

900 N North Branch Street, Chicago IL 60642
County: Cook FICE Identification: 001703
Unit ID: 146393
Telephone: (312) 752-2000 Carnegie Class: Bac/Diverse
FAX Number: (312) 752-2021 Calendar System: Quarter
URL: www.kendall.edu
Established: 1934 Annual Undergrad Tuition & Fees: $22,095
Enrollment: 2,545 Coed
Affiliation or Control: Proprietary IRS Status: Proprietary
Highest Offering: Baccalaureate
Program: Occupational; 2-Year Principally Bachelor's Creditable; Liberal Arts And General; Teacher Preparatory; Professional; Business Emphasis
Accreditation: NH, ACFEI

01 President ... Dr. Karen GERSTEN
05 Provost ... Dr. Gwen HILLESHEIM
32 Dean of Student Affairs ... Ms. Kimberly SKARR
26 Vice President of Marketing ... Mr. Tom EHRHARDT
04 Assistant to the President ... Mrs. Helena VASILOPOULOS
10 Director of Finance ... Mr. Roald HENDERSON
06 Registrar ... Mr. Alex UNDERWOOD
15 Director of Human Resources ... Ms. Stephanie TOMINO
29 Director of Alumni Affairs ... Vacant
38 Director of Advising ... Ms. Amy HERRICK
08 Director Library Services ... Mrs. Iva M. FREEMAN
84 Director of Enrollment Management ... Mr. Tom MARIGLIANO
13 Director of Information Technology ... Vacant
26 Director of Marketing ... Vacant
37 Director of Financial Aid ... Mr. Chris MILLER

39 Director of Residence Life ... Ms. Jena HENSON
106 Academic Director ... Ms. Cheryl BONCUORE
97 Director of General Education ... Mr. Ryan BARTELMAY
18 Chief Facilities/Physical Plant ... Mr. Philip LITTLE
35 Director Student Life ... Vacant
09 Director of Institutional Research ... Mrs. Stacy VLAHAKIS
96 Procurement Manager ... Ms. Leigh BARBEAU

Kishwaukee College (C)

21193 Malta Road, Malta IL 60150-9600
County: De Kalb FICE Identification: 007684
Unit ID: 146418
Telephone: (815) 825-2086 Carnegie Class: Assoc/Pub-S-SC
FAX Number: (815) 825-2072 Calendar System: Semester
URL: www.kishwaukeecollege.edu
Established: 1967 Annual Undergrad Tuition & Fees (In-District): $3,000
Enrollment: 4,988 Coed
Affiliation or Control: State/Local IRS Status: 501(c)3
Highest Offering: Associate Degree
Program: Occupational; 2-Year Principally Bachelor's Creditable
Accreditation: NH, COMTA, RAD

01 President ... Dr. Thomas L. CHOICE
05 Vice President Instruction ... Dr. Jean V. KARTJE
10 Vice Pres of Finance/Administration ... Mr. Robert GALICK
32 Vice President Student Services ... Mr. Steve ULLNICK
81 Dean Math/Science/Business ... Vacant
83 Dean Arts/Communic/Social Science ... Dr. Tara CARTER
72 Dean Career Technologies ... Mrs. Sara POHL
76 Dean Health & Education ... Vacant
35 Dean of Student Services ... Ms. Nancy PARTCH
51 Dean Adult Educ/Transition Pgms ... Mrs. Evelina CICHY
102 Dir Kishwaukee Col Foundation Devel ... Mr. Marshall HAYES
14 Director Information Technology ... Mr. Scott ARMSTRONG
07 Dir Admissions/Registration/Records ... Ms. Jill BIER
37 Director Student Financial Aid ... Mrs. Pam WAGENER
66 Director Nursing ... Ms. Heather PETERS
41 Athletic Director ... Ms. Karen WILEY
40 Director Bookstore ... Mrs. Lynne DURIN
09 Dir Plng/Institutional Effective ... Mr. Kevin J. FUSS
27 Director of Marketing ... Ms. Kayte HAMEL
08 Library Director ... Ms. Anne-Marie EGGLESTON
15 Director Human Resources ... Mrs. Kate NOREIKO
21 Director of Business Affairs ... Ms. Beth YOUNG
18 Chief Facilities/Physical Plant ... Mr. Gary STROTHMAN

Knowledge Systems Institute (D)

3420 Main Street, Skokie IL 60076-2453
County: Cook FICE Identification: 026227
Unit ID: 260956
Telephone: (847) 679-3135 Carnegie Class: Spec/Tech
FAX Number: (847) 679-3166 Calendar System: Semester
URL: www.ksi.edu
Established: 1978 Annual Graduate Tuition & Fees: $7,690
Enrollment: 69 Coed
Affiliation or Control: Independent Non-Profit IRS Status: 501(c)3
Highest Offering: Master's; No Undergraduates
Program: Professional; Technical Emphasis
Accreditation: NH

01 Chancellor ... Dr. Shi-Kuo CHANG
03 Executive Director ... Ms. Judy PAN
05 Academic Dean ... Dr. Frederick THULIN
07 Chr Computer Sci/Admiss Committee ... Dr. Cheng-Yuan HSIEH

Knox College (E)

2 E South Street, Galesburg IL 61401-4999
County: Knox FICE Identification: 001704
Unit ID: 146427
Telephone: (309) 341-7000 Carnegie Class: Bac/A&S
FAX Number: (309) 341-7090 Calendar System: Trimester
URL: www.knox.edu
Established: 1837 Annual Undergrad Tuition & Fees: $34,464
Enrollment: 1,379 Coed
Affiliation or Control: Independent Non-Profit IRS Status: 501(c)3
Highest Offering: Baccalaureate
Program: Liberal Arts And General; Teacher Preparatory
Accreditation: NH, @TEAC

01 President ... Dr. Teresa L. AMOTT
05 VP Acad Affairs/Dean of College ... Dr. Lawrence B. BREITBORDE
10 Vice Pres for Finance & Admin Svcs ... Mr. Thomas B. AXTELL
30 Vice President for Advancement ... Ms. Beverly HOLMES
07 Vice Pres Enrollment/Dean of Admn ... Mr. Paul R. STEENIS
06 Registrar ... Mr. Kevin J. HASTINGS
32 Dean of Students ... Ms. Debbie SOUTHERN
20 Associate Dean of College ... Dr. Lori HASLEM
37 Director Financial Aid ... Ms. Ann BRILL
08 Librarian ... Mr. Jeffrey A. DOUGLAS
36 Interim Dir Ctr Career Pre-Prof Dev ... Ms. Terrie SALINE
14 Director Computer Center & Telecomm ... Mr. Steven JONES
15 Director Human Resources ... Ms. Gina ZINDT
18 Director Facilities Services ... Mr. Scott MAUST
21 Controller ... Ms. Bobby Jo MAURER
26 Director Public Relations ... Ms. Karrie HEARTLEIN
29 Dir Alumni & Constituent Programs ... Ms. Carol J. BROWN
38 Director of Counseling Services ... Dr. Daniel L. LARSON
41 Director of Athletics ... Mr. Chad EISELE

96 Director of Purchasing ... Mr. Ray BENSON
19 Director Campus Safety ... Mr. John SCHLAF
09 Dir Institutional Research/Assess ... Mr. Charles L. CLARK
102 Dir Corporate/Foundation Relations ... Ms. Sandra MEHL

Lake Forest College (F)

555 N Sheridan Road, Lake Forest IL 60045-2338
County: Lake FICE Identification: 001706
Unit ID: 146481
Telephone: (847) 234-3100 Carnegie Class: Bac/A&S
FAX Number: (847) 735-6291 Calendar System: Semester
URL: www.lakeforest.edu
Established: 1857 Annual Undergrad Tuition & Fees: $36,920
Enrollment: 1,387 Coed
Affiliation or Control: Independent Non-Profit IRS Status: 501(c)3
Highest Offering: Master's
Program: Liberal Arts And General
Accreditation: NH

01 President ... Mr. Stephen D. SCHUTT
05 Provost/Dean of Faculty ... Dr. Janet MCCRACKEN
10 Vice Pres of Business/Treasurer ... Mrs. Leslie T. CHAPMAN
30 VP of Development & Alumni Pgms ... Mr. Richard BARTOLOZZI
07 Vice Pres Admissions/Career Svcs ... Mr. William G. MOTZER, JR.
45 VP Budget/Planning/Controller ... Ms. Lori H. SUNDBERG
04 Executive Assistant to President ... Ms. Elizabeth A. PALM
32 Dean of Students ... Mr. Rob FLOT
35 Director of Residence Life ... Vacant
28 Interim Dir Intercult Rels ... Ms. Erin HOFFMAN
20 Asc Dean Facul/Dir Ctr Chicago Pgms ... Dr. Rand SMITH
20 Assoc Dean Facul/Dir Lrng/Tchng Ctr ... Dr. Richard MALLETTE
31 Director of Community Education ... Mr. Dan LEMAHIEU
37 Director of Financial Aid ... Mr. Gerard J. CEBRZYNSKI
41 Athletic Director ... Ms. Jacqueline SLAATS
08 Librarian & Director Info Svcs/Tech ... Mr. James R. CUBIT
06 Registrar ... Ms. Ruthane I. BOPP
38 Director of Counseling Services ... Mr. William T. DIVANE
29 Assoc Vice Pres for Alumni Relation ... Mr. Timothy STATE
09 Director of Institutional Research ... Ms. Lori H. SUNDBERG
15 Director of Human Resources ... Ms. Cynthia B. CARLSON
36 Director of Career Services ... Ms. Lisa HINKLEY
18 Director of Facilities Management ... Mr. David J. SIEBERT
26 Assoc VP for Comm//Mktg ... Ms. Elizabeth LIBBY
19 Director of Public Safety ... Mr. Richard L. COHEN

Lake Forest Graduate School of Management (G)

1905 W Field Court, Lake Forest IL 60045-4824
County: Lake FICE Identification: 023192
Unit ID: 146490
Telephone: (847) 234-5005 Carnegie Class: Spec/Bus
FAX Number: (847) 295-3656 Calendar System: Quarter
URL: www.lakeforestmba.edu
Established: 1946 Annual Graduate Tuition & Fees: $2,982
Enrollment: 734 Coed
Affiliation or Control: Independent Non-Profit IRS Status: 501(c)3
Highest Offering: Master's; No Undergraduates
Program: Professional; Business Emphasis
Accreditation: NH

01 President ... Mr. John N. POPOLI
05 Exec VP Educ Pgms & Solutions ... Mr. Christopher MULTHAUF
10 Vice Pres Finance/Administration ... Mr. Malcolm C. DOUGLAS
26 Exec VP Marketing & Admissions ... Mr. Curtis P. WANG
88 Vice Pres R&D and Innovation ... Ms. Kathleen M. LECK
16 VP Human Resources & Fundraising ... Ms. Stasia ZWISLER
13 VP Information Technology Services ... Mr. Gregory KOZAK
12 Associate Dean Schaumburg ... Ms. Gail KRACHTUS
12 Associate Dean Chicago ... Ms. Erica A. WILKE
12 Associate Dean Lake Forest ... Ms. Carol MODLIN
06 Registrar ... Ms. Christine L. PERLSTROM
29 Manager Alumni Relations & Events ... Ms. Jessica GARDNER
37 Associate Director of Financial Aid ... Ms. Rebecca KIM
07 Director of Admissions ... Ms. Carolyn BRUNE

Lake Land College (H)

5001 Lake Land Boulevard, Mattoon IL 61938-9366
County: Coles FICE Identification: 007644
Unit ID: 146506
Telephone: (217) 234-5253 Carnegie Class: Assoc/Pub-R-L
FAX Number: (217) 234-5400 Calendar System: Semester
URL: www.lakeland.cc.il.us
Established: 1966 Annual Undergrad Tuition & Fees (In-District): $2,904
Enrollment: 8,233 Coed
Affiliation or Control: State/Local IRS Status: 501(c)3
Highest Offering: Associate Degree
Program: Occupational; 2-Year Principally Bachelor's Creditable
Accreditation: NH, ADNUR, DH, PNUR, PTAA

01 President ... Mr. Scott LENSINK
04 Admin Assistant to President ... Ms. Lana FULLER
10 Vice President Business Services ... Mr. Ray RIECK
05 VP Academic Services ... Dr. Jim HULL
32 Vice President Student Services ... Dr. Tina STOVALL
30 Vice President Development ... Ms. Pam CRISMAN
103 Assoc Vice Pres Workforce Devel ... Ms. Linda VON BEHREN
20 Assoc Vice Pres Educational Svcs ... Dr. Deb HUTTI
88 Exec Dean Correctional Pgms ... Mr. Tom KERKHOFF

07 Dean of Admissions Services ... Mr. Jon VAN DYKE
50 Dean Center for Business & Industry ... Mr. Robert WESTCOTT
88 Assoc Dean Corrections-Taylorville ... Mr. John ALLEN
88 Assoc Dean Corrections-Graham ... Mr. Dennis MIHLBACHLER
88 Assoc Dean Corrections-Dwight ... Mr. Alan MORTENSEN
88 Assoc Dean Corrections-Dixon ... Mr. Brandon YOUNG
88 Assoc Dean Corrections-Western ... Mr. Tom THEISS
88 Assoc Dean Correction-IL River ... Mr. Tom ZABORAC
88 Assoc Dean Corrections-Jacksonville ... Mr. Steve BAHNEY
88 Assoc Dean Corrections-Lawrence ... Mr. Tim WATSON
88 Assoc Dean Corrections-Robinson ... Mr. Glen DONALDSON
88 Assc Dean Corrections-SW & Vandalia ... Mr. Steve DRAKE
88 Site Director Corrections-Hill ... Ms. Christine LEHR
88 Site Director Corr-Vienna & Shawnee ... Mr. Blake MCCONNELL
21 Comptroller ... Ms. Madge SHOOT
08 Director of the LRC ... Mr. Scott DRONE-SILVERS
26 Dir Communications/Creative Svcs ... Mrs. Kelly ALLEE
14 Director of Information Systems/Svc ... Mr. Lee SPANIOL
37 Director of Financial Aid ... Ms. Paula CARPENTER
19 Director Facilities Planning ... Mr. Michael KASDORF
15 Director of Human Resources ... Ms. Dawn SCHLECHTE
88 Director Learning Technologies ... Mr. Steve GARREN
25 Director Grant Development ... Ms. Emily RAMAGE
40 Director Auxiliary Services ... Ms. Chris KRAMER
29 Director Foundation & Alumni Svcs ... Mr. Dave COX
36 Director of Career Services ... Ms. Tina MOORE
38 Director of Student Counseling ... Ms. Emily HARTKE
18 Director of Physical Plant ... Mr. Durb ASKEW
41 Director of Athletics ... Mr. Dennis THRONEBURG
09 Director of Institutional Research ... Dr. Lynn BREER

Lakeview College of Nursing (A)

903 N Logan Avenue, Danville IL 61832-3788
County: Vermilion — FICE Identification: 010501
Unit ID: 146533
Telephone: (217) 443-5238 — Carnegie Class: Spec/Health
FAX Number: (217) 442-2279 — Calendar System: Semester
URL: www.lakeviewcol.edu
Established: 1987 — Annual Undergrad Tuition & Fees: $13,640
Enrollment: 289 — Coed
Affiliation or Control: Independent Non-Profit — IRS Status: 501(c)3
Highest Offering: Baccalaureate
Program: Professional; Nursing Emphasis
Accreditation: NH, NUR, NURSE

01 Interim Dean of Nursing ... Irene STEWARD
11 Associate CEO ... Ms. Sheila MINGEE
06 Registrar/Dir Enrollment ... Ms. Connie YOUNG
08 Library Dir/IT Coordinator ... Ms. Miranda SHAKE

Le Cordon Bleu College of Culinary Arts in Chicago (B)

361 W Chestnut Street, Chicago IL 60610
County: Cook — FICE Identification: 023522
Unit ID: 144467
Telephone: (312) 944-0882 — Carnegie Class: Assoc/PrivFP
FAX Number: (312) 944-8557 — Calendar System: Semester
URL: www.chefs.edu/chicago
Established: 1983 — Annual Undergrad Tuition & Fees: $17,525
Enrollment: 1,293 — Coed
Affiliation or Control: Proprietary — IRS Status: Proprietary
Highest Offering: Associate Degree
Program: Occupational
Accreditation: NH, ACFEI

01 President ... Mr. Kirk T. BACHMANN
05 VP Academic Affs/Dean Student Svcs ... Mr. Marshall J. SHAFKOWITZ

Lewis and Clark Community College (C)

5800 Godfrey Road, Godfrey IL 62035-2466
County: Madison — FICE Identification: 010020
Unit ID: 146603
Telephone: (618) 466-7000 — Carnegie Class: Assoc/Pub-S-SC
FAX Number: (618) 466-2798 — Calendar System: Semester
URL: www.lc.edu
Established: 1970 — Annual Undergrad Tuition & Fees (In-District): $3,300
Enrollment: 8,406 — Coed
Affiliation or Control: State/Local — IRS Status: 501(c)3
Highest Offering: Associate Degree
Program: Occupational; 2-Year Principally Bachelor's Creditable
Accreditation: NH, ADNUR, DA, DH, OTA

01 President ... Dr. Dale T. CHAPMAN
05 Vice President Academic Affairs ... Dr. Linda CHAPMAN
84 Vice President Enrollment Services ... Mr. Kent SCHEFFEL
32 Vice President Student Life ... Mr. George TERRY
11 Vice President Administration ... Mr. Gary AYRES
10 Assoc Vice Pres Finance ... Mrs. Mary SCHULTE
10 Assoc Vice President Accounting ... Mrs. Nancy KAISER
76 Dean Science/Math/Technology ... Dr. Sue CZERWINSKI-ALJETS
72 Dean Business & Liberal Arts ... Mrs. Jill LANE
88 Dean Corp & Comm Learning ... Mr. Thomas MONROE
27 Assoc Vice Pres Telecommunications ... Mrs. Julie MCPIKE
18 Assoc Vice Pres Cap Proj/Campus ... Mr. Christopher BACHMANN
102 Assoc Vice Pres Media & Found Rel ... Mrs. Lori ARTIS
20 Dir Academic Operations & Planning ... Mr. Nick MOEHN
09 Director Institutional Research ... Ms. Anne RAPPAPORT
51 Director Adult Education Program ... Mrs. Valorie HARRIS
07 Director Enrollment Ctr/Admissions ... Ms. Peggy HUDSON
88 Director Enrollment Center/Advising ... Mrs. Delfina DORNES
37 Dir Financial Aid/Stdnt Employment ... Mrs. Angela WEAVER
38 Dir Student Dev & Counseling ... Mrs. Kathy HABERER
35 Director Student Support Services ... Ms. Dolores PATRICK
15 Director Human Resources ... Mr. Bob BECHERER
06 Registrar ... Ms. Heidi SCOTT

Lewis University (D)

One University Parkway, Romeoville IL 60446-2200
County: Will — FICE Identification: 001707
Unit ID: 146612
Telephone: (815) 838-0500 — Carnegie Class: Master's L
FAX Number: (815) 838-9456 — Calendar System: Semester
URL: www.lewisu.edu
Established: 1932 — Annual Undergrad Tuition & Fees: $24,770
Enrollment: 6,139 — Coed
Affiliation or Control: Roman Catholic — IRS Status: 501(c)3
Highest Offering: Doctorate
Program: Occupational; Liberal Arts And General; Teacher Preparatory; Professional
Accreditation: NH, ACBSP, NURSE, @SW, TED

01 President ... Bro. James GAFFNEY, FSC
03 Executive Vice President ... Mr. Wayne J. DRAUDT
05 Provost ... Dr. Stephany S. SCHLACHTER
32 Vice President Student Services ... Mr. Joseph T. FALESE
10 Vice Pres for Business & Facilities ... Mr. Robert C. DE ROSE
84 Vice President Enrollment Mgmt ... Mr. Raymond KENNELLY
30 Vice Pres University Advancement ... Mr. Daniel J. ALLEN
07 Dean of Admission ... Mr. Andrew SISON
35 Dean of Student Services ... Ms. Kathryn SLATTERY
28 Assoc Vice Pres Mission ... Mr. Kurt SCHACKMUTH
49 Dean College Arts & Sciences ... Dr. Bonnie BONDAVALLI
50 Dean College Business ... Dr. Rami KHASAWNEH
66 Dean Col Nursing/Health Professions ... Dr. Peggy RICE
15 Assoc Vice Pres Human Resources ... Ms. Graciela DUFOUR
09 Dir Instl Data Analysis/Assessment ... Mrs. Vicky TUCKER
08 Director of Library ... Ms. Laura PATTERSON
06 Registrar ... Mr. Robert KEMPIAK
37 Director of Financial Aid ... Ms. Janeen DECHARINTE
26 Director Marketing/Communications ... Ms. Ramona LAMONTAGNE
41 Director of Athletics ... Mr. Daniel SCHUMACHER
23 Dir of Health & Counseling Services ... Dr. Shulmith MELLMAN
19 Director of Campus Security ... Mr. Gary BENDA
42 Director of University Ministry ... Bro. Philip JOHNSON, FSC
31 Dir of Meetings/Events/Conferences ... Mr. Robert ARNOLD
13 Chief Info Technology Officer ... Mr. John DALBY
85 Director International Student Svcs ... Mr. Michael FEKETE
14 Director Instl Data Administration ... Ms. Tammy KUSE
29 Exec Dir Alumni/Development Svcs ... Ms. Julie ZIENTEK
96 Director of Purchasing ... Mr. Jim KOENIG
36 Director of Career Services ... Mrs. Smret SMITH
38 Director Student Counseling ... Dr. Mellman SHULAMITH

Lexington College (E)

310 S Peoria, Suite 512, Chicago IL 60607-3534
County: Cook — FICE Identification: 025276
Unit ID: 146621
Telephone: (312) 226-6294 — Carnegie Class: Spec/Bus
FAX Number: (312) 226-6405 — Calendar System: Semester
URL: www.lexingtoncollege.edu
Established: 1977 — Annual Undergrad Tuition & Fees: $23,500
Enrollment: 57 — Female
Affiliation or Control: Independent Non-Profit — IRS Status: 501(c)3
Highest Offering: Baccalaureate
Program: Professional
Accreditation: NH

01 President ... Ms. Mary HUNT
05 Academic Dean ... Mrs. Jolene BIRMINGHAM
10 Manager of Business Office ... Ms. Estela GODINA
32 Director of Advising ... Vacant
26 Mgr Communications & Marketing ... Ms. Megan GOGGIN
37 Director of Financial Aid ... Ms. Maria LEBRON
06 Registrar ... Vacant
21 Associate Business Officer ... Ms. Diane MCDERMOTT
30 Director of Development ... Ms. Katherine CASKEY
35 Director Student Affairs ... Vacant

Lincoln Christian University (F)

100 Campus View Drive, Lincoln IL 62656-2167
County: Logan — FICE Identification: 001708
Unit ID: 146667
Telephone: (217) 732-3168 — Carnegie Class: Spec/Faith
FAX Number: (217) 732-5718 — Calendar System: Semester
URL: www.lincolnchristian.edu
Established: 1944 — Annual Undergrad Tuition & Fees: $14,340
Enrollment: 1,072 — Coed
Affiliation or Control: Christian Churches And Churches of Christ — IRS Status: 501(c)3
Highest Offering: Doctorate
Program: Liberal Arts And General; Religious Emphasis
Accreditation: NH, BI, THEOL

01 President ... Dr. Keith H. RAY
05 Provost ... Dr. Clay HAM
10 Vice President of Finance ... Miss Andrea SHORT
32 Vice Pres of Student Development ... Mr. Brian MILLS
30 VP of University Advancement ... Mr. Gordon D. VENTURELLA
84 VP of Enrollment Management ... Ms. Krista WONG
29 Assoc VP of Alumni Services ... Mr. Lynn LAUGHLIN
06 Registrar ... Mr. Shawn SMITH
08 Librarian ... Miss Nancy OLSON
37 Director of Financial Aid ... Miss Nancy SIDDENS
101 Admin Asst to Pres/Secy Bd of Gov ... Mrs. Linda SEGGELKE
13 Director of Campus Technology ... Mr. Mark HOUPT

Lincoln College (G)

300 Keokuk Street, Lincoln IL 62656-1699
County: Logan — FICE Identification: 001709
Unit ID: 146676
Telephone: (217) 732-3155 — Carnegie Class: Bac/Assoc
FAX Number: (217) 732-8859 — Calendar System: Semester
URL: www.lincolncollege.edu
Established: 1865 — Annual Undergrad Tuition & Fees: $23,000
Enrollment: 1,311 — Coed
Affiliation or Control: Independent Non-Profit — IRS Status: 501(c)3
Highest Offering: Baccalaureate
Program: 2-Year Principally Bachelor's Creditable
Accreditation: NH, IACBE

01 President ... Dr. Jonathan M. ASTROTH
05 Vice Pres Academic Affairs ... Dr. A. Gigi FANSLER
30 Vice President for Advancement ... Ms. Debbie ACKERMAN
10 Vice Pres Finance & Administration ... Mr. Greg A. EIMER
84 VP for Enroll Mgmt & Student Svcs ... Mr. Anthony CARDENAS
37 Director of Financial Aid ... Mr. Chris STECKMANN
06 Registrar ... Mrs. Debra J. HARMON
29 Coordinator Alumni Relations ... Ms. Kerri TAYLOR
38 Director of Counseling ... Ms. Michelle BAUER
08 Head Librarian ... Mr. Mike STARASTA
18 Director of Building & Grounds ... Ms. Ronda PIATT
23 Director of Health Services ... Ms. Diane STEPHENSON
21 Controller ... Mrs. Katherine PAPESCH
15 Director of Human Resources ... Mrs. Kathy STEFFENS
40 Bookstore Manager ... Mrs. Donna HUTCHISON
39 Director of Housing ... Mrs. Bridgett THOMAS
13 Director of Information Technology ... Mr. Randall SCHRADER
27 Director of Communications ... Vacant
35 Director of Student Development ... Mr. Steven SNODGRASS
07 Director of Admissions ... Mrs. Gretchen BREE
09 Director of Institutional Research ... Mr. David SMALLEY

Lincoln College of Technology (H)

8317 West North Avenue, Melrose Park IL 60160-1605
FICE Identification: 010316
Unit ID: 146700
Telephone: (708) 344-4700 — Carnegie Class: Not Classified
FAX Number: (708) 345-4380 — Calendar System: Semester
URL: www.lincolnedu.com
Established: 1950 — Annual Undergrad Tuition & Fees: $19,238
Enrollment: 1,705 — Coed
Affiliation or Control: Proprietary — IRS Status: Proprietary
Highest Offering: Associate Degree
Program: Occupational
Accreditation: ACCSC

01 President ... Ms. Helen CARVER

Lincoln Land Community College (I)

5250 Shepherd Road, PO Box 19256, Springfield IL 62794-9256
County: Sangamon — FICE Identification: 007170
Unit ID: 146685
Telephone: (217) 786-2200 — Carnegie Class: Assoc/Pub-R-L
FAX Number: (217) 786-2468 — Calendar System: Semester
URL: www.llcc.edu
Established: 1967 — Annual Undergrad Tuition & Fees (In-District): $3,015
Enrollment: 7,602 — Coed
Affiliation or Control: Local — IRS Status: 501(c)3
Highest Offering: Associate Degree
Program: Occupational; 2-Year Principally Bachelor's Creditable
Accreditation: NH, ADNUR, EEG, OTA, RAD

01 President ... Dr. Charlotte J. WARREN
11 Vice President Administrative Svcs ... Mr. Richard W. VERTREES
05 Vice President Academic Svcs ... Dr. Eileen G. TEPATTI
32 Vice President Student Services ... Ms. Lesley J. FREDERICK
103 Vice President Workforce Systems ... Dr. Judy JOZAITIS
13 Chief Information Officer ... Mr. Esteban CRUZ
04 Asst to Pres Planning & Inst Impr ... Ms. Iva G. BERGERON
15 Assoc Vice Pres Human Resources ... Ms. Junell A. RANSDELL
84 Assoc VP Enrollment Svcs/Registrar ... Ms. Tyra TAYLOR
45 Asc VP Budget/Finan Plng/Analysis ... Ms. Mary A. MCGEE
10 Asst VP Business & Fiscal Opers ... Dr. Maureen HARROP
37 Asst Vice President Financial Aid ... Mr. Lee BURSI
86 Asst VP Corp/Gov Trng & Econ Devel ... Ms. Paula J. LUEBBERT
18 Asst VP Facilities & Construction ... Mr. Hugh GARVEY
12 Exec Director Educ Service Area ... Mr. Scott R. STALLMAN
12 Exec Director Educ Service Area ... Ms. Jan M. TERRY
102 Exec Director LLCC Foundation ... Ms. Karen A. SANDERS
26 Exec Dir Public Relations/Marketing ... Ms. Lynn WHALEN
24 Exec Director Learning Lab ... Mrs. Julie CLEVENGER

88 Director Small Business Devel Ctr .... Mr. Kevin LUST
07 Director Admissions & Records .... Mr. Ronald J. GREGOIRE
96 Director Purchasing .... Ms. Sylvia M. STEMMONS
22 Dir Employ Bnft Svc/Eq Opty Cmpl Of .... Ms. Nicole M. RALPH
09 Director Institutional Research .... Ms. Susan SRBLJAN
30 Director Development .... Ms. Janet SEMANIK
38 Director Placement/Testing .... Ms. Tricia A. KUJAWA
32 Director Student Life .... Ms. Marci ROCKEY
19 Police Chief .... Mr. Bradley D. GENTRY
28 Dir Multicultural Awareness Center .... Ms. Blanca BERNASEK
21 Controller .... Ms. Karie L. LONGHTA
50 Dean Business & Technologies .... Mr. David A. GREEN
83 Dean Social Sciences .... Dr. Victor K. BRODERICK
72 Dean District Learning Resources .... Ms. Wendy L. HOWERTER
57 Dean Arts & Humanities .... Mr. David E. LAUBERSHEIMER
81 Dean Mathematics and Sciences .... Mr. William D. BADE
76 Dean Health Professions .... Dr. Cynthia L. MASKEY
08 Assoc Dean Library .... Vacant
72 Asc Dean Instruct Tech/Distance Ed .... Mrs. Becky PARTON

Loyola University Chicago (A)

1032 W. Sheridan Road, Chicago IL 60660
County: Cook FICE Identification: 001710
Unit ID: 146719
Telephone: (773) 274-3000 Carnegie Class: RU/H
FAX Number: (312) 915-7003 Calendar System: Semester
URL: www.luc.edu
Established: 1870 Annual Undergrad Tuition & Fees: $33,294
Enrollment: 15,951 Coed
Affiliation or Control: Roman Catholic IRS Status: 501(c)3
Highest Offering: Doctorate
Program: Liberal Arts And General; Teacher Preparatory; Professional; Business Emphasis
Accreditation: NH, BUS, BUSA, CLPSY, COPSY, DENT, DIETI, EMT, LAW, MED, MT, NURSE, SW, TED, THEA

01 President .... Rev. Michael J. GARANZINI, SJ
17 Sr VP & Provost Health Sciences .... Dr. Richard GAMELLI
05 Provost .... Dr. John P. PELISSERO
10 Sr Vice President Finance & CFO .... Mr. William G. LAIRD
45 Sr VP Cap Planning & Campus Mgmt ... Mr. Wayne MAGDZIARZ
32 Vice President Student Development .... Dr. Robert KELLY
43 Sr Vice President & General Counsel .... Ms. Ellen KANE-MUNRO
15 Sr VP Admin Svcs & Chief HR Officer ...... Mr. Thomas M. KELLY
30 Sr Vice President Advancement .. Mr. Jonathan R. HEINTZELMAN
86 Vice President Government Affairs .... Mr. Philip D. HALE
27 Vice President Information Services .... Ms. Susan M. MALISCH
04 Special Assistant to the President .... Ms. Lorraine G. SNYDER
84 Assoc Provost Enrollment Management ..... Mr. Paul G. ROBERTS
88 Assistant Provost Faculty Admin .... Dr. Anne H. REILLY
20 Vice Provost .... Dr. Nancy TUCHMAN
49 Dean of Arts & Sciences .... Dr. Francis L. FENNELL
50 Dean School of Business Admin .... Dr. Kathleen A. GETZ
60 Dean School of Communication .... Dr. Donald B. HEIDER
53 Dean School of Education .... Dr. David P. PRASSE
58 Dean of Graduate School .... Dr. Samuel A. ATTOH
61 Dean School of Law .... Dr. David N. YELLEN
63 Acting Dean Medical School .... Dr. Linda BRUBAKER
66 Dean School of Nursing .... Dr. Vicki A. KEOUGH
70 Dean School of Social Work .... Dr. Darrell P. WHEELER
51 Acting Dean Continuing & Prof Educ ...... Dr. Janet DEATHERAGE
35 Assoc VP & Dean of Students .... Ms. Jane F. NEUFELD
08 Dean University Libraries .... Mr. Robert A. SEAL
06 Director of Registration & Records .... Ms. Clare M. KORINEK
23 Director Student Wellness Center .... Ms. Diane C. ASARO
07 Director Undergraduate Admissions .... Ms. Lori A. GREENE
36 Director Career Development Center .... Dr. Darby SCISM
39 Director Residence Life .... Mr. Romando A. NASH
41 Director Athletics .... Dr. M.Grace CALHOUN
09 Director Institutional Research .... Dr. Richard S. HURST
85 Assoc Provost Global Affairs .... Dr. Patrick M. BOYLE
19 Director Campus Safety .... Mr. Robert FINE
29 Director Alumni Relations .... Ms. Nicole MEEHAN
37 Director Student Financial Aid .... Mr. Eric D. WEEMS
96 Manager of Purchasing .... Mr. Sam J. PERRY
12 Vice President & Director Rome Ctr .... Mr. Emilio IODICE
88 Assoc VP Development Operations .... Mr. Jamie S. ORSINI
28 Assoc Dean Student Diversity .... Mr. Javier CERVANTES
90 Director Academic Tech Services .... Mr. Bruce A. MONTES
88 Assoc VP Community Affairs/Outreach .... Ms. Jennifer R. CLARK
46 Assoc Provost Research Services .... Dr. Samuel A. ATTOH
88 Assistant Provost Administration .... Dr. Marian A. CLAFFEY
04 Asst to the President for Mission .... Dr. John J. HARDT
88 Special Assistant to the President .... Rev. John COSTELLO, SJ
26 VP Marketing & Communications .... Ms. Kelly SHANNON
20 Assoc Provost Academic Services .... Rev. Justin DAFFRON, SJ
88 Director Special Events .... Mr. Richard WILLIAMS
07 Dir Graduate & Professional Admiss .... Ms. Ann E. BEZBATCHENKO
18 Associate VP of Facilities .... Ms. Kana WIBBENMEYER
21 Assoc VP for Finance & Controller .... Mr. Thomas F. HICKEY
88 Assoc Provost Centers of Excellence .... Rev. Kevin GILLESPIE, SJ
88 Vice Provost Med Research/Grad Pgms ...... Dr. Richard KENNEDY
88 Assoc Provost Resource Management .... Dr. Paul E. GABRIEL
88 Dir Academic Business Operations .... Ms. Joanna PAPPAS
88 Dir Budgeting & Financial Planning .... Mr. Joseph M. FILIPIAK
107 Dean School of Professional Studies .... Mr. Jeffrey H. ROSEN
88 Dir Enrollment Systems Research .... Mr. Timothy HEUER
35 Assistant VP Student Development .... Mr. Jack MCLEAN
35 Assistant VP Student Development .... Dr. Dawn OVERSTREET
28 Dir Student Diversity & Multicultur .... Ms. Sadika SULAIMAN-HARA
88 Dir LUMA & Cultural Affairs .... Ms. Pam AMBROSE
88 Associate VP Major Giving .... Mr. Steve BERGFELD
88 Assoc VP Health Sciences Dev .... Mr. Shawn VOGEN
44 Director Annual Giving .... Ms. Shena KEITH
106 Dir Learning Technology & Assesment .... Ms. Carol SCHEIDENHELM
88 Dir Advancement Info Services .... Ms. Stacy HUGHES
21 Assoc VP Finance & Contoller .... Ms. Andrea SABITSANA
21 Assoc VP Sponsored Pgm Accounting .... Ms. Donna QUIRK
88 Treasurer .... Mr. Eric JONES
88 Associate VP Campus Services .... Mr. Timothy MCGURIMAN

Lutheran School of Theology at Chicago (B)

1100 E 55th Street, Chicago IL 60615-9985
County: Cook FICE Identification: 001712
Unit ID: 146728
Telephone: (773) 256-0700 Carnegie Class: Spec/Faith
FAX Number: (773) 256-0782 Calendar System: Semester
URL: www.lstc.edu
Established: 1860 Annual Graduate Tuition & Fees: $12,906
Enrollment: 282 Coed
Affiliation or Control: Evangelical Lutheran Church In America
IRS Status: 501(c)3
Highest Offering: Doctorate; No Undergraduates
Program: Professional; Religious Emphasis
Accreditation: NH, THEOL

01 Acting President .... Dr. Philip L. HOUGEN
05 Dean/Vice Pres for Academic Affairs .... Dr. Michael SHELLEY
04 Assistant to the President .... Ms. Patti DEBIAS
32 Dean Students/Dir of MA/MDiv Pgms .... Dr. Terrence BAEDER
11 Vice President for Operations .... Mr. Bob BERRIDGE
30 Vice President for Advancement ..... Mr. Mark H. VAN SCHARREL
10 Vice Pres Finance/Special Projects .... Mr. Richard HENSEY
07 Director of Admissions .... Dr. Scott CHALMERS
37 Dir Financial Aid/Admissions .... Ms. Dorothy DOMINIAK
06 Registrar .... Ms. Patricia A. BARTLEY
58 Director of Advanced Studies .... Dr. Esther MENN
26 Director of Communications/Mktg .... Ms. Janet BODEN
09 Exec for Administration/Assess/Plng .... Ms. Laura WILHELM
08 Director of Library .... Dr. Christine WENDEROTH
13 Dir of Information Technology Svcs .... Mr. Kenesa DEBELA

MacCormac College (C)

29 E Madison Street 2nd Floor, Chicago IL 60602-4405
County: Cook FICE Identification: 001716
Unit ID: 146816
Telephone: (312) 922-1884 Carnegie Class: Assoc/PrivNFP
FAX Number: (312) 922-4286 Calendar System: Semester
URL: www.maccormac.edu
Established: 1904 Annual Undergrad Tuition & Fees: $12,000
Enrollment: 208 Coed
Affiliation or Control: Independent Non-Profit IRS Status: 501(c)3
Highest Offering: Associate Degree
Program: 2-Year Principally Bachelor's Creditable
Accreditation: NH

01 President .... Dr. Marnelle ALEXIS
05 Academic Dean .... Dr. Gregory REID
10 Director of Finance/Human Resources ...... Mr. Mateusz GAWENDA
06 Registrar .... Ms. Mariza SILVA
37 Director of Financial Aid .... Mr. Robert GOMEZ
08 Librarian .... Mr. Greg PEKALA
07 Admissions Coord/Placement Director .... Ms. Ashlee FARNEY

MacMurray College (D)

447 E College Avenue, Jacksonville IL 62650-2590
County: Morgan FICE Identification: 001717
Unit ID: 146825
Telephone: (217) 479-7041 Carnegie Class: Bac/Diverse
FAX Number: (217) 245-0405 Calendar System: 4/1/4
URL: www.mac.edu
Established: 1846 Annual Undergrad Tuition & Fees: $19,900
Enrollment: 528 Coed
Affiliation or Control: United Methodist IRS Status: 501(c)3
Highest Offering: Baccalaureate
Program: Liberal Arts And General; Teacher Preparatory; Professional
Accreditation: NH, NURSE, SW

01 President .... Dr. Colleen HESTER
03 CFO & Vice President of Finance .... Ms. Jackie LOOSER
05 Vice Pres Academic Affairs .... Vacant
32 Vice President for Student Life .... Dr. Sally CAYAN
30 Exec Dir Institutional Advancement .... Ms. Bridget PHILLIPS
84 Chief Admissions Officer .... Ms. Alicia ZEONE
10 Controller .... Mr. Andrew SIDOCK
13 Director of IT/System Administrator .... Mr. Bob LOOSER
06 Registrar .... Dr. Allan METCALF
08 Librarian .... Ms. Susan EILERING
37 Director of Financial Aid .... Ms. Laci ENGELBRECHT
36 Coordinator Career Services .... Ms. Cori WAGNER
29 Director Alumni Relations .... Ms. Christina WELLS
09 Director of Institutional Research .... Vacant
18 Director of Facilities .... Mr. Larry TROWBRIDGE
26 Director of Public Relations .... Mr. Ted ROTH

McCormick Theological Seminary (E)

5460 S University Avenue, Chicago IL 60615-5108
County: Cook FICE Identification: 001721
Unit ID: 146977
Telephone: (773) 947-6300 Carnegie Class: Spec/Faith
FAX Number: (773) 288-2612 Calendar System: Semester
URL: www.mccormick.edu
Established: 1829 Annual Graduate Tuition & Fees: $17,200
Enrollment: 352 Coed
Affiliation or Control: Presbyterian Church (U.S.A.) IRS Status: 501(c)3
Highest Offering: Doctorate; No Undergraduates
Program: Professional
Accreditation: NH, THEOL

01 President .... Rev. Frank M. YAMADA
10 Vice President Finance/Operations .... Mr. David CRAWFORD
05 Vice Pres Acad Affs/Dean Faculty .... Dr. Luis R. RIVERA
32 Vice President for Student Affairs .... Rev Dr. Christine VOGEL
30 Co-VP Seminary Rels & Development .... Ms. Stephanie MOORE
30 Co-VP Seminary Rels & Development .... Mr. Sam EVANS
06 Registrar/Dir Stdnt Financial Plng .... Mr. Jim COURTNEY
29 Director of Alumni/ae & Church Rels .... Ms. Grayson VANCAMP
08 Director of JKM Library .... Dr. Christine WENDEROTH
15 Director Human Resources .... Ms. Karen PURNELL

McHenry County College (F)

8900 US Highway 14, Crystal Lake IL 60012-2796
County: McHenry FICE Identification: 007691
Unit ID: 147004
Telephone: (815) 455-3700 Carnegie Class: Assoc/Pub-S-SC
FAX Number: (815) 455-3999 Calendar System: Semester
URL: www.mchenry.edu
Established: 1967 Annual Undergrad Tuition & Fees (In-District): $3,180
Enrollment: 7,392 Coed
Affiliation or Control: State/Local IRS Status: 501(c)3
Highest Offering: Associate Degree
Program: Occupational; 2-Year Principally Bachelor's Creditable
Accreditation: NH

01 President .... Dr. Vicky SMITH
05 VP Academic & Student Affairs .... Dr. Anthony MIKSA
11 Interim VP Administrative Services .... Mr. Vern MANKE
10 CFO/Treasurer .... Mr. Larry WEST
13 Chief Information Officer .... Dr. Allen P. BUTLER
15 AVP of Human Resources .... Ms. Angelina CASTILLO
32 AVP Academic & Student Affairs .... Ms. Julietta PATRICK
09 Actg Exec Dir Institutional Effect .... Ms. Pat STEJSKAL
35 Dean of Students .... Vacant
18 Director of Physical Facilities .... Mr. Gregory EVANS
09 Director Institutional Research .... Mr. Joseph BAUMAN
19 Director Campus Public Safety .... Mr. Michael CLESCERI
26 Dir Marketing & Public Relations .... Mrs. Christina HAGGERTY
84 Director Enrollment Services .... Ms. Marianne DEVENNY
88 Dean of Student Success .... Dr. Flecia THOMAS
101 Asst to the President/Board Liaison ...... Mrs. Pat KRIEGERMEIER
72 Director Communication Technologies .... Mr. Dale NALEWAY
14 Director Computing Services .... Ms. Marilyn SCHICK
88 Director End User Services .... Mr. Geary SMITH
88 Director of Network Services .... Mr. Rob RASMUSSEN
88 Exec Dir of Shah Center Programs .... Ms. Catherine JONES
103 Dean of Adult Education .... Mr. Richard CLUTE
41 Director Athletics-Intramural & Rec .... Mr. Wally REYNOLDS
40 Director Bookstore .... Ms. Cathie SCHERMAN
55 Director Professional Development .... Ms. Patricia STEJSKAL
15 Director Employment Svcs/Diversity ...... Ms. Sandra HESS MOLL
102 Executive Director MCC Foundation .... Mr. Bill BRENNAN
88 Director of Children's Learning Ctr .... Ms. Taliashia BORDERS
83 Actg Exec Dean Educ/Social Science .... Mr. Jim FALCO
79 Executive Dean Humanities .... Dr. Thomas TAKAYAMA
81 Executive Dean Math & Science .... Ms. Amy MAXEINER
23 Dean Health Science .... Ms. Joan FLANAGAN
51 Exec Dean Cont & Professional Ed ...... Ms. Gwendolyn KOEHLER
75 Exec Dean Career & Technical Educ .... Mr. James FALCO
96 Director of Business Services .... Ms. Jennifer JONES
88 Director Food Services .... Ms. Sandra JOHNSTON
29 Director Alumni Relations .... Ms. Kathrine PFISTER
37 Director of Financial Aid .... Ms. Lynn MCCABE
53 Dean of Education .... Vacant
88 Director of High School Plus .... Mr. Tony CAPALBO
106 Director of Online Learning .... Dr. Raymond LAWSON

McKendree University (G)

701 College Road, Lebanon IL 62254-9990
County: Saint Clair FICE Identification: 001722
Unit ID: 147013
Telephone: (618) 537-4481 Carnegie Class: Master's L
FAX Number: (618) 537-6259 Calendar System: Semester
URL: www.mckendree.edu
Established: 1828 Annual Undergrad Tuition & Fees: $23,290
Enrollment: 3,299 Coed
Affiliation or Control: United Methodist IRS Status: 501(c)3
Highest Offering: Master's
Program: Liberal Arts And General; Teacher Preparatory; Professional
Accreditation: NH, IACBE, NURSE, TED

01 President .... Dr. James M. DENNIS
03 Senior Vice President .... Ms. Victoria A. DOWLING
04 Assistant to the President .... Ms. Patti J. DANIELS
05 Provost/Dean of the University .... Dr. Christine M. BAHR

10	Vice Pres Finance/Administration	Mrs. Sally A. MAYHEW
07	Vice Pres Admission & Financial Aid	Mr. Chris HALL
32	Vice President Student Affairs	Dr. Joni BASTIAN
09	Vice Pres Research Plng & Tech	Dr. Mary E. BORNHEIMER
30	Asst VP Dev/Alumni/Parent Relations	Ms. Kimberly A. MAYDEN
20	Associate Dean of the University	Dr. Tami EGGLESTON
12	Assoc Dean McKendree-at-Scott	Mr. Thomas A. PAWLOW
56	External Programs	Dr. Joseph J. CIPFL
13	Director Technology Information	Mr. George KRISS
06	Registrar/Asst Dean	Ms. Debra LARSON
08	Librarian	Ms. Rebecca SCHREINER
21	Comptroller/Budget Manager	Mr. Paul ZINK
26	Exec Dir Marketing/Communications	Mrs. Krysti H. CONNELLY
29	Director Alumni Relations	Vacant
44	Director of Annual Giving	Ms. Lauren FRIZZO
37	Director Financial Aid	Mr. James MYERS
36	Director Career Services	Ms. Jennifer K. PICKERELL
18	Director of Operations	Mr. Edward M. WILLETT
15	Director Human Resources	Ms. Shirley A. RENTZ
27	Director Media Relations	Ms. Lisa K. BRANDON
39	Director of Residence Life	Mr. Mitch NASSER
35	Director of Campus Activities	Mr. Craig L. ROBERTSON
41	Athletic Director	Dr. Todd A. REYNOLDS
42	Chaplain/Director Church Relations	Rev Dr. B. Timothy HARRISON
40	Bookstore Director	Ms. Rebecca B. MATHEWS
30	Director of Advancement Services	Mr. Scott L. BILLHARTZ
19	Superintendent Safety & Security	Mr. Monte C. LOWREY
44	Director of Major Gifts	Vacant
88	Director of Student Accounts	Vacant
28	Director of Diversity	Mr. Brent W. REEVES

Meadville/Lombard Theological School (A)

5701 S Woodlawn Avenue, Chicago IL 60637-1602

County: Cook — FICE Identification: 001723 — Unit ID: 147031

Telephone: (773) 256-3000 — Carnegie Class: Spec/Faith

FAX Number: (773) 753-1323 — Calendar System: Semester

URL: www.meadville.edu

Established: 1844 — Annual Graduate Tuition & Fees: $17,460

Enrollment: 99 — Coed

Affiliation or Control: Unitarian Universalist — IRS Status: 501(c)3

Highest Offering: Doctorate; No Undergraduates

Program: Professional; Religious Emphasis

Accreditation: THEOL

01	President	Dr. Lee BARKER
05	Provost	Dr. Sharon WELCH
10	Vice Pres Finance & Administration	Ms. Deborah BIEBER
30	Vice President of Development	Vacant
08	Dean of Library	Rev. Neil W. GERDES
32	Senior Director Student Services	Ms. Tina PORTER

Methodist College of Nursing (B)

415 St. Mark Court, Peoria IL 61603

County: Peoria — FICE Identification: 006228 — Unit ID: 147129

Telephone: (309) 672-5530 — Carnegie Class: Spec/Health

FAX Number: (309) 671-8303 — Calendar System: Semester

URL: www.mcon.edu

Established: 2000 — Annual Undergrad Tuition & Fees: $15,725

Enrollment: 472 — Coed

Affiliation or Control: Independent Non-Profit — IRS Status: 501(c)3

Highest Offering: Baccalaureate

Program: Nursing Emphasis

Accreditation: NH, NUR, NURSE

01	President	Dr. Kimberly JOHNSTON
05	Dean of Academic Affairs	Dr. Linda PENDERGAST
84	Dean Enrollment Management	Mr. David PETERSON
20	Dean Educational Tech & Faculty Dev	Dr. Eli COLLINS-BROWN
30	Director Business Svcs & Marketing	Ms. Kirstin MARSHALL
15	Director Human Resources	Ms. Linda MOORE
45	Director Inst Effectiveness	Dr. Marcus BABAOYE
13	Director Information Management	Mr. Bud SANDY

Midstate College (C)

411 W Northmoor Road, Peoria IL 61614-3558

County: Peoria — FICE Identification: 004568 — Unit ID: 147165

Telephone: (309) 692-4092 — Carnegie Class: Bac/Assoc

FAX Number: (309) 692-4873 — Calendar System: Quarter

URL: www.midstate.edu

Established: 1888 — Annual Undergrad Tuition & Fees: $13,875

Enrollment: 730 — Coed

Affiliation or Control: Proprietary — IRS Status: Proprietary

Highest Offering: Baccalaureate

Program: Occupational; 2-Year Principally Bachelor's Creditable; Business Emphasis

Accreditation: NH, MAC

01	President	Meredith N. BUNCH
03	Chief Executive Officer	Meredith N. BUNCH
05	Chief Academic Dean	Margaret J. STARR
88	Director of Assessment	Sheryl KRISTENSEN
10	Controller	Angie HATTEN
37	Director of Financial Assistance	Irene BIMROSE
26	Director of Marketing	Ashley SPAIN
32	Director of Student Affairs	Rhonda P. URBAN
36	Director of Career Services	Jennie GREENAN
08	Director of Library Resources	Zachary M. BROWN

Midwest College of Oriental Medicine (D)

4334 N Hazel, Suite 206, Chicago IL 60613-1429

County: Cook — Identification: 666090 — Unit ID: 439020

Telephone: (773) 975-1295 — Carnegie Class: Spec/Health

FAX Number: (773) 975-6511 — Calendar System: Quarter

URL: www.acupuncture.edu

Established: 1979 — Annual Undergrad Tuition & Fees: $11,759

Enrollment: 132 — Coed

Affiliation or Control: Proprietary — IRS Status: Proprietary

Highest Offering: Master's

Program: Professional

Accreditation: ACUP

01	President	Dr. William DUNBAR
05	Academic Dean/Research Director	Dr. Hui-Yan CAI
11	Administrative Director	Dr. Robert CHELNICK
88	Special Projects Director	Dr. Kristine L. LA POINT
37	Financial Aid Director	Ms. Jennifer RHYNER
07	Admissions Coord/Transfer Credit	Ms. Kelly A. WESTERLUND
06	Records Officer/Registrar	Ms. Amy L. BENISH
08	Librarian	Ms. Michelle C. KOPTEROS
32	Dean of Students	Ms. Olga GAJDOSIK
09	Research Director	Mr. Jin Hua XIE
63	Dean of Biomedicine Science	Dr. Donald L. MARTIN
85	Dean of Foreign Students	Dr. Duckin SUH
17	Internship Director	Dr. Alan D. URETZ
45	Clinic Tracking/Inst Evaluation	Ms. Deirdre M. DUNBAR
86	Compliance Officer	Mr. Harry S. HEIFETZ
91	Information Systems	Mr. Iosif G. LIFSHITS
26	Marketing/Student Affairs	Mr. Chris A. KRAJNIAK

Midwestern University (E)

555 31st Street, Downers Grove IL 60515-1200

County: DuPage — FICE Identification: 001657 — Unit ID: 143853

Telephone: (630) 969-4400 — Carnegie Class: Spec/Med

FAX Number: N/A — Calendar System: Quarter

URL: www.midwestern.edu

Established: 1900 — Annual Undergrad Tuition & Fees: $28,226

Enrollment: 2,131 — Coed

Affiliation or Control: Independent Non-Profit — IRS Status: 501(c)3

Highest Offering: Doctorate

Program: Professional

Accreditation: NH, ARCPA, DENT, OSTEO, OT, PHAR, PTA

01	President/CEO	Dr. Kathleen H. GOEPPINGER
03	Exec VP/Chief Operating Officer	Dr. Arthur G. DOBBELAERE
10	Sr VP/Chief Financial Officer	Mr. Gregory J. GAUS
21	Vice President Business Services	Mr. Dean P. MALONE
26	Vice President University Relations	Dr. Karen D. JOHNSON
05	VP/CAO Dental & Medical Education	Dr. Dennis J. PAULSON
05	VP/CAO Pharmacy & Health Sci Educ	Dr. Mary W L. LEE
11	VP Human Resources & Administration	Ms. Angela L. MARTY
63	Dean Chicago Col of Osteo Medicine	Dr. Karen J. NICHOLS
67	Dean Chicago College of Pharmacy	Dr. Nancy F. FJORTOFT
76	Dean College Health Sciences	Dr. Jacquelyn M. SMITH
52	Dean College of Dental Medicine IL	Dr. M. A. J. Lex MACNEIL
32	Dean for Student Services	Dr. Teresa A. DOMBROWSKI
88	Director Finance	Dr. Kimberly A. BROWN
08	University Librarian	Ms. Natalie K. REED
06	Registrar	Ms. Sue C. HARDWIDGE
46	Director Research & Sponsored Pgms	Dr. James M. WOODS
07	Director of Admissions	Mr. Michael J. LAKEN
30	Dir Development/Alumni Relations	Ms. Karen L. WYSOCKI
09	Director of Institutional Research	Dr. Kevin P. HYNES
14	Director Information Technology Svc	Mr. Erik P. CARROLL
15	Director Human Resources	Ms. Amy B. GIBSON
24	Director Media Resources	Ms. Kathleen A M. DOOLEY
18	Director Campus Facilities	Mr. Kevin M. MCCORMICK
37	Director Student Financial Services	Mr. Nathan ERNST

† Tuition rates vary by program

Millikin University (F)

1184 W Main Street, Decatur IL 62522-2084

County: Macon — FICE Identification: 001724 — Unit ID: 147244

Telephone: (217) 424-6211 — Carnegie Class: Bac/Diverse

FAX Number: (217) 424-3993 — Calendar System: Semester

URL: www.millikin.edu

Established: 1901 — Annual Undergrad Tuition & Fees: $27,852

Enrollment: 2,314 — Coed

Affiliation or Control: Presbyterian Church (U.S.A.) — IRS Status: 501(c)3

Highest Offering: Master's

Program: Liberal Arts And General; Teacher Preparatory; Professional; Nursing Emphasis

Accreditation: NH, ACBSP, ANEST, MUS, NURSE, TED

01	President	Dr. Harold G. JEFFCOAT
05	Vice President Academic Affairs	Mr. Barry N. PEARSON
10	Vice Pres Finance/Business Affs	Mr. Richard RIEDER
30	Vice Pres University Development	Mrs. Peggy S. LUY
84	Vice President of Enrollment	Mr. Rich L. DUNSWORTH
32	Dean of Students	Mr. Renardo A. HALL
100	Chief of Staff/Board Secretary	Ms. Marilyn S. DAVIS
49	Dean of Arts & Sciences	Dr. Randy M. BROOKS
57	Interim Dean of Fine Arts	Ms. Laura LEDFORD
107	Int Dean Col of Professional Stds	Dr. Deborah L. SLAYTON
50	Dean of Tabor School of Business	Dr. James G. DAHL
07	Dean of Admission & Financial Aid	Mrs. Stacey L. HUBBARD
06	Registrar	Mr. Walter G. WESSEL
29	Director of Alumni Relations	Dr. Janice G. DEVORE
44	Director of Major Gifts/Grant Devel	Mrs. Anne-Marie P. BERK
36	Director of Career Center	Ms. Pamela M. FOLGER
13	Director of Technology	Mrs. Patricia A. PETTIT
08	Director of the Library	Ms. Cindy FULLER
44	Director of Development	Mr. Dave E. BRANDON
41	Director of Athletics	Mr. Joe L. HAKES
53	Director of School of Education	Dr. Nancy I. GAYLEN
88	Director Kirkland Fine Arts Ctr	Mrs. Janiece L. SADDORIS-TRAUGHBER
28	Dir Ctr for Multicultural Stdnt Aff	Ms. Latrina L. DENSON
104	Interim Dir Center for Intl Educ	Mrs. Carmen ARAVENA
15	Director Human Resources	Ms. Diane L. LANE
21	Director of Fiscal Operations	Mrs. Ruby F. BRASE
21	Controller	Mrs. Vicki A. WRIGLEY
38	Director of Counseling Services	Mr. Kevin C. GRAHAM
92	Director of Honors Program	Dr. Cheryl L. CHAMBLIN
39	Asst Dean of Student Development	Mrs. Raphaella M. PALMER PRANGE
35	Director Student Programs	Ms. Elizabeth J. EVANS
37	Director of Financial Aid	Ms. Cheryl L. HOWERTON
51	Director of Extended Programs	Vacant
58	Director of MBA Program	Dr. Anthony F. LIBERATORE
64	Director School of Music	Dr. Stephen B. WIDENHOFER
87	Director of Summer School	Dr. James G. DAHL
09	Coord of Institutional Research	Mrs. Laura A. BIRCH
19	Director of Safety and Security	Mr. Dan DRAGO
105	Webmaster	Mr. Curtis D. SHIRLEY
66	Director School of Nursing	Dr. Deborah L. SLAYTON

Monmouth College (G)

700 E Broadway, Monmouth IL 61462-1963

County: Warren — FICE Identification: 001725 — Unit ID: 147341

Telephone: (309) 457-2311 — Carnegie Class: Bac/A&S

FAX Number: (309) 457-2141 — Calendar System: Semester

URL: www.monm.edu

Established: 1853 — Annual Undergrad Tuition & Fees: $35,950

Enrollment: 1,347 — Coed

Affiliation or Control: Presbyterian Church (U.S.A.) — IRS Status: 501(c)3

Highest Offering: Baccalaureate

Program: Liberal Arts And General; Teacher Preparatory

Accreditation: NH

01	President	Dr. Mauri A. DITZLER
05	Dean of Faculty	Dr. David M. TIMMERMAN
10	Vice President Finance & Business	Mr. Donald L. GLADFELTER
30	Vice Pres Devel/College Relations	Ms. Molly A. BALL
32	Vice Pres Student Life/Dn Students	Ms. Jacquelyn S. CONDON
84	Vice President Enrollment Mgmt	Mr. Omar G. CORREA
06	Registrar	Ms. Christine D. JOHNSTON
08	Director Hewes Library	Mr. Richard SAYRE
37	Director of Financial Aid	Ms. Jayne A. SCHRECK
29	Director of Alumni Programs	Ms. Lucy THOMPSON
26	Director College Communications	Mr. Jeffrey D. RANKIN
44	Director of Annual Giving	Ms. Susan SAVAGE
15	Director of Personnel Services	Mr. Mike MCNALL
18	Director Facilities Management	Mr. Earl WILFONG
20	Associate Dean of the Faculty	Dr. Frank GERSICH
21	Controller	Mrs. Debbie CLARK

Moody Bible Institute (H)

820 N Lasalle Boulevard, Chicago IL 60610-3263

County: Cook — FICE Identification: 001727 — Unit ID: 147369

Telephone: (312) 329-4000 — Carnegie Class: Spec/Faith

FAX Number: (312) 329-4109 — Calendar System: Semester

URL: www.moody.edu

Established: 1886 — Annual Undergrad Tuition & Fees: $9,906

Enrollment: 3,493 — Coed

Affiliation or Control: Independent Non-Profit — IRS Status: 501(c)3

Highest Offering: First Professional Degree

Program: Liberal Arts And General; Professional; Religious Emphasis

Accreditation: NH, BI, MUS, @THEOL

01	President	Dr. J. Paul NYQUIST
05	Provost & Dean of Education	Dr. Junias V. VENUGOPAL
11	Exec VP & Chief Operating Officer	Vacant
43	Vice President & General Counsel	Mr. Stephen A. OAKLEY
20	VP/Dean of Undergraduate School	Dr. Larry J. DAVIDHIZAR
58	VP/Dean of Graduate School	Dr. John A. JELINEK
16	Vice President Human Resources	Mr. Lloyd R. DODSON
88	Vice President Broadcasting	Mr. Collin LAMBERT
30	Vice President Stewardship	Mr. Tom MACADAM
13	Vice President Information Systems	Mr. Frank W. LEBER
26	Vice Pres Corporate Communications	Mrs. Christine GORZ
45	Vice Pres/Dean of Educ Services	Mr. William W. BLOCKER
84	Vice President of Student Services	Dr. Tom A. SHAW
18	Division Manager Facilities	Mr. Konrad FINCK
56	Dir Customer Rels/Distance Lrng Ctr	Mr. John KNIGHT

32 Dean of Students ... Dr. Timothy E. ARENS
07 Dean of Admissions ... Mr. Charles E. DRESSER
38 Associate Dean Counseling Services ... Mr. Steve BRASEL
35 Associate Dean for Student Programs ... Mr. Joseph M. GONZALES, JR.
36 Assoc Dean of Career Development ... Mr. Patrick FRIEDLINE
39 Associate Dean Residence Life ... Mr. Bruce R. NORQUIST
37 Director of Financial Aid ... Mr. Daniel GRIFFIN
06 Registrar/Director of Acad Records ... Mr. George MOSHER
08 Department Manager Library ... Mr. James PRESTON
29 Exec Director Alumni Association ... Mrs. Nancy HASTINGS
41 Athletic Director ... Mr. Donald K. MARTINDELL
10 Chief Fin Ofcr/Treasurer/Asst Secy ... Mr. Ken HEULITT
21 Controller ... Miss Linda WAHR
23 Admin of Health Service ... Miss Ann MEYER
96 Manager of Procurement Services ... Mr. Paul BRACKLEY
09 Institutional Researcher ... Mr. Gregory GAERTNER

† Tuition is paid through donor contributions. Fees are $1,739 per year.

Moraine Valley Community College (A)

9000 W College Parkway, Palos Hills IL 60465-0937
County: Cook FICE Identification: 007692
Unit ID: 147378
Telephone: (708) 974-4300 Carnegie Class: Assoc/Pub-S-SC
FAX Number: (708) 974-1184 Calendar System: Semester
URL: www.morainevalley.edu
Established: 1967 Annual Undergrad Tuition & Fees (In-District): $3,000
Enrollment: 18,628 Coed
Affiliation or Control: State/Local IRS Status: 501(c)3
Highest Offering: Associate Degree
Program: Occupational; 2-Year Principally Bachelor's Creditable
Accreditation: NH, ADNUR, COMTA, MAC, POLYT, RAD

01 President ... Dr. Vernon O. CRAWLEY
05 Vice President Academic Affairs ... Dr. Sylvia JENKINS
32 Vice President Student Devel ... Dr. Normah SALLEH-BARONE
11 Exec Vice Pres Administrative Svcs ... Mr. Andrew M. DUREN
10 Chief Financial Officer ... Mr. Robert STERKOWITZ
13 Chief Information Officer ... Mr. Jack LEIFEL
50 Dean Science/Business/Comp Tech ... Dr. Pamela HANEY
49 Dean Liberal Arts ... Mr. Walter FRONCZEK
38 Dean Counseling & Advising ... Ms. Joann WRIGHT
84 Dean Enrollment Services ... Mr. Sovoro BALASON
103 Dean Workforce Dev & Comm Svcs ... Vacant
36 Dean Career Programs ... Ms. Margaret MACHON
35 Dean Student Support Services ... Dr. Yolanda ISAACS
20 Dean Enrichment Services ... Dr. Nancy CURE
56 Asst Dean/Dir Academic Outreach ... Ms. Maureen FARRELL
32 Asst Dean Stdnt Life/Judicial Affs ... Mr. Chet SHAW
37 Director Financial Aid ... Ms. Laurie ANEMA
09 Dir Institutional Research/Planning ... Ms. Elizabeth REIS
19 Chief of Police ... Mr. Patrick O'CONNOR
15 Director Human Resources ... Ms. Lynn HARRINGTON
07 Director of Admissions/Recruitment ... Ms. Claudia ROSELLI
26 Director College & Cmty Relations ... Mr. Mark HORSTMEYER
18 Director Campus Operations ... Mr. Rick BRENNAN
40 Director Auxiliary Svcs ... Mr. Kashif SHAH
41 Director Athletics ... Mr. William FINN
85 Asst Dean Intl Student Admissions ... Ms. Diane VIVERITO
27 Director Mktg & Creative Services ... Ms. Delores J. BROOKS
44 Dir Res Devel/Extended Programs ... Dr. Sharon KATTERMAN
21 Controller ... Ms. Theresa O'CARROLL
42 Campus Minister ... Mr. Bill DROEL
88 Director Center Disability Services ... Ms. Debbie SIEVERS
96 Director of Purchasing ... Ms. Jane BENTLEY

Morrison Institute of Technology (B)

701 Portland Avenue, Morrison IL 61270-2959
County: Whiteside FICE Identification: 008880
Unit ID: 147396
Telephone: (815) 772-7218 Carnegie Class: Assoc/PrivNFP
FAX Number: (815) 772-7584 Calendar System: Semester
URL: www.morrison.tec.il.us
Established: 1973 Annual Undergrad Tuition & Fees: $15,100
Enrollment: 102 Coed
Affiliation or Control: Independent Non-Profit IRS Status: 501(c)3
Highest Offering: Associate Degree
Program: 2-Year Principally Bachelor's Creditable; Technical Emphasis
Accreditation: COE, ENGT

01 Chief Executive Officer ... Mr. Christopher D. SCOTT
05 Vice President of Academic Affairs ... Mr. James R. PROMBO

Morton College (C)

3801 S Central Avenue, Cicero IL 60804-4398
County: Cook FICE Identification: 001728
Unit ID: 147411
Telephone: (708) 656-8000 Carnegie Class: Assoc/Pub-S-SC
FAX Number: (708) 656-3297 Calendar System: Semester
URL: www.morton.edu
Established: 1924 Annual Undergrad Tuition & Fees (In-District): $2,396
Enrollment: 5,712 Coed
Affiliation or Control: State/Local IRS Status: 501(c)3
Highest Offering: Associate Degree
Program: Occupational; 2-Year Principally Bachelor's Creditable
Accreditation: NH, PTAA

01 President ... Dr. Leslie A. NAVARRO
05 Int VP Academic/Student Development ... Mr. Muhammad SIDDIQI
11 Vice Pres Administration ... Mr. Philip PENA
32 Director of Student Development ... Mr. Victor SANCHEZ
51 Dean Adult Educ/Cmty Prgms/Outreach ... Mr. James YOUNG
08 Director of Library ... Ms. Jennifer BUTLER
15 Director of Human Resources ... Mr. Kenneth STOCK
31 Director Community & Business Svcs ... Ms. Susan FELICE
09 Director Institutional Research ... Ms. Magda BANDA
18 Director of Facilities & Operations ... Mr. John S. POTEMPA
37 Director of Financial Aid ... Mr. Robert TEBBE

National-Louis University (D)

122 S Michigan Avenue, Chicago IL 60603
County: Cook FICE Identification: 001733
Unit ID: 147536
Telephone: (312) 261-3200 Carnegie Class: DRU
FAX Number: (312) 261-3200 Calendar System: Quarter
URL: www.nl.edu
Established: 1886 Annual Undergrad Tuition & Fees: $18,435
Enrollment: 6,616 Coed
Affiliation or Control: Independent Non-Profit IRS Status: 501(c)3
Highest Offering: Doctorate
Program: Liberal Arts And General; Teacher Preparatory; Professional
Accreditation: NH, IACBE, TED

01 President ... Dr. Nivine MEGAHED
05 Provost ... Dr. Christine J. QUINN
30 Vice Pres Institutional Advancement ... Vacant
15 Vice President Human Resources ... Mr. Tom BERGMANN
10 Vice Pres Finance & Administration ... Mr. Kent KAY
84 Assoc Vice Pres Enrollment Mgmt ... Vacant
14 Vice President Operational Services ... Mr. William P. ROBERTS
26 Vice Pres Marketing/Communications ... Dr. Joselyn ZIVIN
09 Vice Provost Institutional Effect ... Mr. Christopher DAVIS
50 Int Dean College of Mgmt/Business ... Dr. Walter ROETTGER
53 Dean Natl College of Education ... Dr. Alison HILSABECK
49 Int Dean College of Arts & Science ... Dr. Richard GREEN
08 Dean University Library ... Ms. Kathleen WALSH
32 Exec Dir Stdnt Affs/Ombudsperson ... Mr. Brisbane ROUZAN
12 Exec Director Milwaukee/Beloit ... Mr. Robert VANCE
12 Exec Director Florida Regional ... Dr. George VALCOURT
43 Exec Director of Legal Services ... Mrs. McCeil J. JOHNSON
28 Director of Employment/Diversity ... Ms. Erin HAULOTTE
37 Director of Student Finance ... Mr. Steve DIBENEDETTO
07 Director of Admissions/Registrar ... Vacant
36 Director of Career Services ... Mr. James OPON
29 President Alumni Advisory Board ... Dr. Russ RIENDEAU
51 Director Outreach Academic Pgm ... Ms. Karen HAWORTH
35 Director of Student Life ... Ms. Maria MEINTANIS
23 Student Health Services Coordinator ... Ms. Maria AGUILAR

National University of Health Sciences (E)

200 E Roosevelt Road, Lombard IL 60148-4583
County: DuPage FICE Identification: 001732
Unit ID: 147590
Telephone: (630) 629-2000 Carnegie Class: Spec/Health
FAX Number: (630) 889-6600 Calendar System: Trimester
URL: www.nuhs.edu
Established: 1906 Annual Undergrad Tuition & Fees: $8,558
Enrollment: 910 Coed
Affiliation or Control: Independent Non-Profit IRS Status: 501(c)3
Highest Offering: First Professional Degree
Program: Liberal Arts And General; Professional
Accreditation: NH, ACUP, CHIRO, COMTA, @NATUR

01 President ... Dr. James F. WINTERSTEIN
05 Vice President Academic Services ... Dr. Vincent F. DE BONO
10 Vice President Business Services ... Mr. Ron MENSCHING
11 Vice Pres Administrative Services ... Ms. Tracy MCHUGH
76 Dean College Allied Health Sciences ... Dr. Randy L. SWENSON
51 Dean Col Postprofessional Educ ... Dr. Jonathan SOLTYS
23 Dean of Clinics ... Dr. David PARISH
107 Dean Coll Professional Studies - FL ... Dr. Joseph STIEFEL
107 Dean Coll Professional Studies - IL ... Dr. Nicholas TRONGALE
46 Dean of Research ... Dr. Gregory D. CRAMER
09 Dean Institutional Analysis ... Dr. Shellee HANDLEY
32 Dean of Students ... Dr. Daniel R. DRISCOLL
88 Dean Academic Assessment ... Dr. Chad MAOLA
88 Dean Accreditation ... Mr. Keith WEROSH
08 Learning Resources Chair ... Ms. Joyce E. WHITEHEAD
06 Registrar ... Ms. Yesinia MALDONADO
84 Dir Communication/Enrollment Svcs ... Ms. Victoria SWEENEY
21 Director of Financial Services ... Ms. Sue UNGER
37 Director of Financial Aid ... Mr. Robert DAME
18 Director Maintenance & Facilities ... Mr. Tom ROHNER
15 Director of Human Resources ... Mr. Andrew WOZNIAK
30 Chief Development Officer ... Ms. Shawna MCDONOUGH
26 Chief Public Relations Officer ... Ms. Victoria SWEENEY
29 Director Alumni Development ... Ms. Shawna MCDONOUGH
13 Dir Management Information Services ... Mr. Kurt FALER
39 Coordinator of Housing ... Ms. Pam THOMAS

North Central College (F)

30 N Brainard Street, Naperville IL 60540-4607
County: DuPage FICE Identification: 001734
Unit ID: 147660
Telephone: (630) 637-5100 Carnegie Class: Master's M
FAX Number: (630) 637-5121 Calendar System: Trimester
URL: www.northcentralcollege.edu
Established: 1861 Annual Undergrad Tuition & Fees: $29,493
Enrollment: 2,902 Coed
Affiliation or Control: United Methodist IRS Status: 501(c)3
Highest Offering: Master's
Program: Liberal Arts And General
Accreditation: NH

01 President ... Dr. Harold R. WILDE
04 Exec Secy/Assistant to President ... Ms. Margaret A. WIORA
05 Vice President Academic Affairs ... Dr. R. Devadoss PANDIAN
10 Vice President Business Affairs ... Mr. Paul H. LOSCHEIDER
30 Vice Pres Institutional Advancement ... Mr. Rick E. SPENCER
84 VP Enrollment Management/Stdnt Svcs ... Ms. Laurie M. HAMEN
16 Asst Vice Pres Human Resources ... Ms. Michelle M. SKINDER
26 Asst Vice President Mktg/Communic ... Mr. James GODO
21 Asst VP for Business Operations ... Mr. Michael J. HUDSON
20 Associate Academic Dean ... Dr. Marti S. BOGART
07 Dean of Admissions ... Mr. Marty R. SAUER
32 Dean of Students ... Ms. Kimberly SLUIS
58 Dean of Graduate Pgms/Continuing Ed ... Dr. Peter S. BARGER
06 Registrar ... Mr. Jonathan M. PICKERING
08 Director of the Library ... Mr. John J. SMALL
36 Director of Career Development ... Mr. Jeffrey D. DENARD
37 Director of Financial Aid ... Mr. Marty ROSSMAN
23 Director of the Wellness Center ... Ms. Sally CARPENTER
31 Director of Cmty Educ/Conf/Camps ... Mr. Michael E. SQUIRE
41 Athletic Director ... Mr. James MILLER
21 AVP Finance/Controller ... Ms. Elizabeth A. LAKEN
39 Director of Residence Life ... Mr. Kevin E. MCCARTHY
42 Campus Chaplain ... Rev. Lynn L. PRIES
90 Director of Technology Services ... Dr. Kathy A. WILDERS
44 Director of Planned Giving ... Mr. Bruce NORTELL
09 Director of Institutional Research ... Mr. Jonathan M. PICKERING
29 Director Alumni Relations ... Mr. Adrian M. ALDRICH
28 Director of Multicultural Affairs ... Ms. Dorothy J. PLEAS

North Park University (G)

3225 W Foster Avenue, Chicago IL 60625-4895
County: Cook FICE Identification: 001735
Unit ID: 147679
Telephone: (773) 244-6200 Carnegie Class: Master's L
FAX Number: (773) 244-4953 Calendar System: Semester
URL: www.northpark.edu
Established: 1891 Annual Undergrad Tuition & Fees: $20,990
Enrollment: 3,254 Coed
Affiliation or Control: Evangelical Covenant Church Of America
IRS Status: 501(c)3
Highest Offering: Doctorate
Program: Liberal Arts And General; Teacher Preparatory; Professional
Accreditation: NH, IACBE, MUS, NURSE, THEOL

01 President ... Dr. David L. PARKYN
10 Executive Vice President/CFO ... Mr. Carl E. BALSAM
05 Provost ... Dr. Joseph JONES
84 Vice Pres for Enrollment/Marketing ... Mr. Nathan MOUTTET
30 Vice President for Development ... Ms. Mary M. SURRIDGE
73 Seminary President & Dean ... Vacant
49 Dean of Arts & Sciences ... Dr. Charles I. PETERSON
51 Dean School of Adult Learning ... Dr. Bryan WATKINS
50 Dean School of Business & NFP Mgmt ... Dr. Wesley LINDAHL
53 Dean School of Education ... Dr. Rebecca NELSON
64 Dean School of Music ... Dr. Craig JOHNSON
66 Dean School of Nursing ... Dr. Linda DUNCAN
09 Director of Institutional Research ... Dr. Robert STANLEY
28 Dean of Diversity & Intercult Pgm ... Dr. Terry LINDSAY
32 Dean of Student Development ... Ms. Andrea NEVELS
08 Director of Library ... Ms. Sally A. ANDERSON
07 Director of Admissions ... Mr. Mark OLSON
38 Director Counseling/Health Services ... Ms. Juanita BARRETT
37 Director Financial Aid Services ... Dr. Lucy G. SHAKER
14 Director of Computer Center ... Mr. Steven P. CLARK
15 Director of Human Resources ... Ms. Ingrid K. TENGLIN
18 Director of Environmental Services ... Mr. Carl H. WISTROM
19 Director of Security ... Mr. Daniel GOORIS
21 Director of Finance ... Mr. Lester H. CARLSTROM
26 Director of External Relations ... Vacant
41 Athletic Director ... Mr. Jack F. SURRIDGE
42 Director University Ministries ... Mr. Anthony ZAMBLE
36 Director of Career Planning ... Ms. Colette HANDS
06 Registrar ... Mr. Aaron D. SCHOOF
29 Alumni Relations Manager ... Ms. Melissa VELEZ LUCE

Northeastern Illinois University (H)

5500 N Saint Louis Avenue, Chicago IL 60625-4699
County: Cook FICE Identification: 001693
Unit ID: 147776
Telephone: (773) 583-4050 Carnegie Class: Master's L
FAX Number: (773) 442-4900 Calendar System: Semester
URL: www.neiu.edu
Established: 1867 Annual Undergrad Tuition & Fees (In-State): $788,5.2
Enrollment: 11,746 Coed
Affiliation or Control: State IRS Status: 501(c)3
Highest Offering: Master's
Program: Liberal Arts And General; Teacher Preparatory; Professional; Fine Arts Emphasis
Accreditation: NH, ART, CACREP, CORE, MUS, SW, TED

01 President ... Dr. Sharon K. HAHS
05 Provost ... Dr. Lawrence P. FRANK

10 Vice Pres Finance & Administration .... Mr. Mark WILCOCKSON
32 Vice President for Student Life .... Dr. Frank E. ROSS
30 Vice President Instnl Advancement .... Vacant
28 Assoc VP/Dean Diversity Intercultur ....Ms. Murrell J. DUSTER
20 Dean Academic Development .... Dr. Daniel LOPEZ, JR.
36 Director Office of Career Services ....Mr. Lorn B. COLEMAN
07 Associate VP Enrollment Services ....Dr. Janice HARRING-HENDON
21 Executive Director of Univ Budgets ....Dr. Helen C. ANG
08 Dean of Libraries & Learning Rscs .... Mr. Bradley F. BAKER
09 Director Institutional Research .... Mr. Blase E. MASINI
15 Human Resources Director ....Ms. Marta E. MASO
25 Director Sponsored Programs .... Ms. Louise M. ILLIAN
26 Asst VP Public Relations ....Ms. Erika M. KREHBIEL
37 Director Financial Aid ....Ms. Maureen T. AMOS
50 Dean College Business/Management ...... Dr. Amy B. HIETAPELTO
58 Dean of Graduate College .... Dr. Janet P. FREDERICKS
53 Dean College of Education ....Dr. Maureen D. GILLETTE
49 Dean College of Arts & Sciences ....Dr. Wamucii E. NJOGU
35 Dean of Students ....Dr. Michael T. KELLY
13 Exec Dir Univ Technology Services .... Mr. Kim TRACY
18 Asst Vice Pres Facilities Mgmt ....Ms. Nancy MEDINA
19 Director University Police Dept .... Mr. James C. LYON, JR.
21 Director Financial Affs/Controller .... Ms. Peggy HO
22 Dir Univ Outreach/Equal Employment ... Dr. Roberto A. SANABRIA
86 Director of Government Relations ....Ms. Suleyma PEREZ
06 Registrar .... Vacant
29 Director of Alumni Relations .... Ms. Damaris TAPIA
38 Director Counseling Office ....Dr. John HOEPPEL
96 Director of Purchasing/Auxil Svcs ....Mr. Robert FILIPP

Northern Illinois University (A)

De Kalb IL 60115-2825

County: De Kalb FICE Identification: 001737
Unit ID: 147703
Telephone: (815) 753-1000 Carnegie Class: RU/H
FAX Number: (815) 753-0198 Calendar System: Semester
URL: www.niu.edu
Established: 1895 Annual Undergrad Tuition & Fees (In-State): $10,513
Enrollment: 23,850 Coed
Affiliation or Control: State IRS Status: 501(c)3
Highest Offering: Doctorate
Program: Liberal Arts And General; Teacher Preparatory; Professional
Accreditation: NH, ART, AUD, BUS, BUSA, CACREP, CLPSY, CORE, DIETD, DIETI, ENG, ENGT, IPSY, LAW, MFCD, MT, MUS, NAIT, NURSE, PH, PTA, SCPSY, SP, SPAA, TED, THEA

01 President ....John G. PETERS
05 Executive Vice Pres & Provost ....Raymond W. ALDEN, III
20 Vice Provost Academic Planning/Dev .... Virginia CASSIDY
10 Exec Vice Pres/Chief of Operations .... Eddie R. WILLIAMS
30 Vice Pres Univ Advance/Development ....Michael P. MALONE
45 Vice Prov Resource Planning ....Joseph GRUSH
11 VP Admin/University Outreach ....Anne C. KAPLAN
32 Vice Pres Student Affs/Enroll Mgmt .... Brian O. HEMPHILL
46 Vice Pres for Research/Grad Studies ....Lisa C. FREEMAN
26 Vice Pres External Affairs .... Kathryn A. BUETTNER
43 VP/General Counsel/Legal Svcs ....Jerry D. BLAKEMORE
102 President NIU Foundation/Devel .... Mallory M. SIMPSON
13 Assoc Vice Pres Info Tech Services ....Walter L. CZERNIAK
18 Assoc Vice Pres Finance Facility Op .... Robert C. ALBANESE
15 Assoc VP Admin/Human Resources ...... Steven D. CUNNINGHAM
27 Asst Vice Pres for Public Affairs .... Melanie S. MAGARA
35 Assoc VP for Student Affairs ....John Raymond JONES
51 Assoc Vice President NIU Outreach ....John L. LEWIS
23 AVP Student Wellness/Health Service .... Linda HERRMANN
07 Assoc Vice Pres Admissions ....Katherine MCCARTHY
28 Asst Vice Pres Diversity/Equity ....James BRUNSEN
20 Vice Provost ....Earl J. SEAVER
50 Dean of Business .... Denise SCHOENBACHLER
53 Dean of Education .... Lemuel WATSON
54 Dean of Engineering/Engr Tech .... Promod VOHRA
61 Interim Dean of Law .... Leroy PERNELL
49 Dean Liberal Arts & Sciences ....Christopher MCCORD
76 Dean Health & Human Sciences ....Shirley A. RICHMOND
57 Dean Visual & Performing Arts .... Richard HOLLY
58 Dean Grad Sch/AVP Grad Studies .... Bradley BOND
85 Assoc Prov International Programs ....Deborah L. PIERCE
84 Asst Vice Prov Enrollment Services ....Brent A. GAGE
31 Exec Dir Community Relations .... Rena COTSONES
12 Director Lorado Taft Field Campus ....Dale W. HOPPE
12 Director Outreach Centers ....Brian VOLLMERT
12 Director NIU Naperville ....Brian BECKER
06 Director Registration & Records .... Adam STONE
09 Director of Institutional Research ....J. Daniel HOUSE
24 Director of Media Services ....Jay ORBIK
25 Director of Sponsored Projects .... David STONE
36 Exec Director of Career Services .... Cindy HENDERSON
37 Director of Student Financial Aid ....Kathleen D. BRUNSON
38 Director of Counseling/Student Dev .... Micky M. SHARMA
40 Director of University Bookstore ....Mitch KIELB
19 Police Chief/Public Safety .... Donald GRADY
41 Athletic Director .... Jeff COMPHER
91 Director Enterprise Info Systems ....Kimberly S. HENSLEY
39 Executive Director Housing & Dining ....Kelly WESENER
88 Director Access-Ability Resources .... Nancy KASINSKI
29 Director Alumni Relations ....Patricia ANDERSON
96 Director of Purchasing ....Al MUELLER

Northern Seminary (B)

660 E Butterfield Road, Lombard IL 60148-5698

County: DuPage FICE Identification: 001736
Unit ID: 147697
Telephone: (630) 620-2180 Carnegie Class: Spec/Faith
FAX Number: (630) 620-2190 Calendar System: Quarter
URL: www.seminary.edu
Established: 1913 Annual Graduate Tuition & Fees: $12,630
Enrollment: 157 Coed
Affiliation or Control: American Baptist IRS Status: 501(c)3
Highest Offering: Doctorate; No Undergraduates
Program: Professional; Religious Emphasis
Accreditation: NH, THEOL

01 President/Chief Academic Officer .... Dr. Alistair BROWN
05 Dean of Academic Programs .... Dr. Karen WALKER-FREEBURG
20 Dean of Academic Administration ....Mr. Blake WALTER
30 Exec Dir Advancement/Enroll Mgmt ....Mr. Greg HENSON
06 Registrar .... Ms. Marilyn R. MAST HEWITT
88 Director Doctoral Studies .... Dr. Karen WALKER-FREEBURG
32 Director Student Services ....Ms. Marilyn MAST HEWITT
15 Director Human Resources .... Vacant
13 Director of Information Technology ....Mr. Dwight HAWLEY

Northwestern College (C)

9700 W Higgins, Suite 750, Rosemont IL 60018-4742

County: Cook FICE Identification: 012362
Unit ID: 147749
Telephone: (847) 318-8550 Carnegie Class: Assoc/PrivFP
FAX Number: (847) 318-8558 Calendar System: Quarter
URL: www.northwesterncollege.edu
Established: 1902 Annual Undergrad Tuition & Fees: $16,520
Enrollment: 1,844 Coed
Affiliation or Control: Proprietary IRS Status: Proprietary
Highest Offering: Associate Degree
Program: Occupational; 2-Year Principally Bachelor's Creditable
Accreditation: NH, ACBSP, MAC, RAD

01 President .... Mr. Lawrence SCHUMACHER
03 Executive VP of Operations .... Mrs. Gail SCHUMACHER
11 Vice President of Campus Operations ....Mrs. Cynthia REYNOLDS
07 Senior Director of Admissions ....Mr. Mark SLIZ
10 Controller ....Ms. Leslie RODRIGUEZ
05 VP of Academic Affairs ....Mrs. Diane MAREK
13 VP of Technology ....Mr. David HOMAN
32 VP of Student Affairs ....Mrs. Barbara ANDERSON-SAPATA
08 Director of Library Services ....Ms. Sarah DULAY
12 Director of Bridgeview Campus .... Mr. Tony SAPATA
12 Director of Naperville Campus ....Ms. Mary REYNOLDS
12 Director of Chicago Campus ....Mr. Dimitrios KRIARAS
16 Chief Human Resources Officer ....Ms. Cheri CANFIELD
37 Director of Financial Assistance ....Mrs. Ethel ARROYO
38 Director of Counseling .... Ms. Alexandra DELLUTRI
106 Distance Education Director ....Ms. Jenifer VIENCEK
07 Director of Admissions ....Mr. Shahed KASEM
11 Dir of Administration Bridgeview .... Mrs. Margie BENNECKE
11 Director of Administration Chicago ....Mrs. Laura SORIA
66 Director of Nursing ....Ms. Lisa EVOY
06 Registrar ....Ms. Sharon FORBES
36 Career Development Coordinator .... Ms. Amy BUOSCIO
76 Program Director - AH ....Ms. Joyce MCNAMARA
97 Program Director - GE ....Mr. David COOPER
50 Program Director - SC ....Mr. Willie MORRIS
61 Program Director - LS ....Mr. John LOMBARDI

Northwestern University (D)

633 Clark Street, Evanston IL 60208-3854

County: Cook FICE Identification: 001739
Unit ID: 147767
Telephone: (847) 491-3741 Carnegie Class: RU/VH
FAX Number: (847) 491-7364 Calendar System: Quarter
URL: www.northwestern.edu
Established: 1851 Annual Undergrad Tuition & Fees: $41,592
Enrollment: 20,481 Coed
Affiliation or Control: Independent Non-Profit IRS Status: 501(c)3
Highest Offering: Doctorate
Program: Liberal Arts And General; Teacher Preparatory; Professional
Accreditation: NH, #ARCPA, AUD, BUS, CLPSY, ENG, HSA, IPSY, JOUR, LAW, MED, MFCD, MUS, OPE, PH, PTA, SP

01 President ....Dr. Morton O. SCHAPIRO
05 Provost ....Dr. Daniel I. LINZER
10 Sr Vice Pres Business/Finance .... Mr. Eugene S. SUNSHINE
32 Vice President Student Affairs ....Dr. William J. BANIS
26 Vice President University Relations ....Mr. Alan K. CUBBAGE
45 Vice Pres Administration & Planning ....Ms. Marilyn MCCOY
13 Vice Pres Information Technology .... Mr. Sean B. REYNOLDS
30 Vice Pres for Alumni Rel & Devel .... Mr. Robert MCQUINN
46 Vice President Research ....Mr. Joseph T. WALSH
88 Vice Pres/Chief Investment Officer .... Mr. William H. MCLEAN
43 Vice President/General Counsel ....Mr. Thomas G. CLINE
84 Associate Provost Univ Enrollment .... Mr. Michael E. MILLS
53 Associate Provost Undergrad Educ ... Dr. Ronald R. BRAEUTIGAM
20 Associate Provost Faculty Affairs ....Dr. James B. YOUNG
20 Assoc Provost Academic Initiatives .... Mr. Jake JULIA
21 Assoc Prov Budget/Facil/Analysis ....Ms. Jean E. SHEDD
86 Spec Asst to Pres for Govt Rels .... Mr. Bruce LAYTON
04 Assistant to the President .... Mr. Eugene Y. LOWE, JR.
100 Director Office of the President .... Ms. Judith V. REMINGTON
41 Athletic Director .... Mr. James J. PHILLIPS
72 Dean Sch Engr/Applied Science .... Dr. Julio M. OTTINO
50 Dean Graduate School of Management .... Dr. Sally E. BLOUNT
60 Dean School of Journalism ....Dr. John LAVINE
64 Dean School of Music .... Dr. Toni-Marie MONTGOMERY
63 Interim Dean Medical School ....Dr. Jeffrey L. GLASSROTH
51 Dean/Assoc Prov Conting Educ ....Dr. Thomas F. GIBBONS
58 Dean Graduate School ....Mr. Dwight A. MCBRIDE
60 Dean School of Communication .... Dr. Barbara J. O'KEEFE
53 Dean School of Education ....Dr. Penelope L. PETERSON
49 Dean College Arts & Science ....Dr. Sarah C. MANGELSDORF
61 Interim Dean School of Law .... Ms. Kimberly A. YURACKO
08 University Librarian ....Ms. Sarah M. PRITCHARD
36 Director of Univ Career Services .... Dr. Lonnie J. DUNLAP
35 Dean of Students ....Mr. Burgwell HOWARD
29 Asc VP Alum Rel/Ex Dir NW Alum Assn .... Ms. Catherine L. STEMBRIDGE
88 Assoc Vice President for Research ....Mr. Lewis SMITH
88 Assoc Vice President for Research ....Ms. Linda HICKE
88 Assoc VP for Rsrch Innov & New Vent ....Ms. Alicia LOFFLER
88 Assoc Vice President for Research ....Ms. Ann ADAMS
21 Assoc Vice Pres Budget Planning .... Mr. James M. HURLEY
18 Assoc Vice Pres Facilities Mgmt .... Mr. Ronald NAYLER
16 Assoc Vice Pres for Human Resources .... Ms. Pamela BEEMER
21 Assoc Vice Pres Finance/Controller ....Ms. Ingrid S. STAFFORD
07 Dean of Undergraduate Admissions ....Mr. Christopher WATSON
88 Ex Dir Technology Transfer Pgm .... Ms. Indrani MUKHARJI
23 Medical Director of Health Services .... Dr. John ALEXANDER
39 Director of Residential Life ....Ms. Mary GOLDENBERG
38 Director of Counseling/Psych Svcs ....Dr. John H. DUNKLE
42 University Chaplain ....Dr. Timothy S. STEVENS
09 Director Analytical Studies .... Vacant
88 Director University Housing .... Ms. Theresa M. DELIN
88 Dir Program Review/Spec Project .... Vacant
71 Planning/Special Projects Director .... Ms. Evelyn CALIENDO
88 Director Univ Center/Student Svcs ....Mr. Richard R. THOMAS
88 Director University Services ....Mr. Brian S. PETERS
06 Registrar ....Ms. Michele A. NEARY
37 Director Financial Aid ....Ms. Carolyn V. LINDLEY
15 Dir HR Consulting Svcs/Staffing ....Mr. Paul CORONA
19 Chief of University Police ....Mr. Bruce LEWIS
21 Director Auditing .... Ms. Betty L. MCPHILIMY
22 Dir Equal Emply Opppty/Affirm Act ....Ms. Pamela PIRTLE
96 Director University Svcs Purchasing ....Mr. Jim KONRAD

Oakton Community College (E)

1600 E Golf Road, Des Plaines IL 60016-1256

County: Cook FICE Identification: 009896
Unit ID: 147800
Telephone: (847) 635-1600 Carnegie Class: Assoc/Pub-S-MC
FAX Number: (847) 635-1992 Calendar System: Semester
URL: www.oakton.edu
Established: 1969 Annual Undergrad Tuition & Fees (In-District): $2,650
Enrollment: 6,064 Coed
Affiliation or Control: Local IRS Status: 501(c)3
Highest Offering: Associate Degree
Program: Occupational; 2-Year Principally Bachelor's Creditable; Business Emphasis
Accreditation: NH, ADNUR, MLTAD, PTAA

01 President .... Dr. Margaret B. LEE
05 Vice President Academic Affairs ....Dr. Thomas HAMEL
20 Assistant VP Academic Affairs ....Dr. Nancy PRENDERGAST
32 Vice President Student Affairs ....Dr. Joianne SMITH
10 Vice President Business & Finance ....Mr. Carl F. COSTANZA
51 VP Cont Educ & Trng/Workforce Dev .... Ms. Barbara RIZZO
13 Vice Pres Information Technology ....Ms. Bonnie LUCAS
76 Dean Science & Health Careers ....Dr. Adam HAYASHI
81 Dean Math & Technology ....Dr. Robert SOMPOLSKI
60 Dean Language/Humanities & the Arts ....Ms. Linda KORBEL
83 Dean Social Science/Business ....Mr. Bradley WOOTEN
26 Exec Director College Advancement .... Dr. Carlee DRUMMER
09 Director Research ....Dr. Trudy H. BERS
08 Director Library & Media Svcs ....Mr. Gary NEWHOUSE
32 Dean of Students/Office of Access .... Dr. Gregory JAMES
84 Dir of Student Recruitment/Outreach ....Ms. Michele BROWN
06 Director of Registrar Services ....Mr. Bruce OATES
35 Director of Student Life ....Ms. Ann Marie BARRY
88 Director of Student Success .... Mr. Sebastian CONTRERAS, JR.
41 Director of Athletics ....Mr. Bruce OATES
13 Director Systems & Network Svcs ....Mr. John WADE
50 Dir Business Institute/Prof Educ ....Ms. Lynn SEINFELD
21 Director of Accounting Services ....Mr. Raul GARCIA
21 Director of Business Services ....Ms. Doreen SCHWARTZ
15 Associate VP Human Resources ....Mr. D. Arnie OUDENHOVEN
18 Director of Facilities ....Ms. Leah SWANQUIST
14 Dir of Educ Computing/End User Svcs .... Ms. Renee KOZIMOR
07 Director of Enrollment Services ....Ms. Cheryl WARMANN
25 Dir of Grants & Alternative Funding .... Ms. Roxann MARSHBURN
88 Director of Learning Center ....Dr. Donna YOUNGER
51 Dir of Community & Adult Education .... Ms. Robyn BAILEY
28 Ethics Officer ....Mr. D. Arnie OUDENHOVEN

Olivet Nazarene University (F)

One University Avenue, Bourbonnais IL 60914-2345

County: Kankakee FICE Identification: 001741
Unit ID: 147828
Telephone: (815) 939-5011 Carnegie Class: Master's L
FAX Number: (815) 935-4998 Calendar System: Semester
URL: www.olivet.edu
Established: 1907 Annual Undergrad Tuition & Fees: $25,550
Enrollment: 4,550 Coed
Affiliation or Control: Church Of The Nazarene IRS Status: 501(c)3
Highest Offering: Doctorate
Program: Liberal Arts And General; Teacher Preparatory; Professional
Accreditation: NH, DIETD, ENG, MUS, NURSE, SW, TED

01 President .... Dr. John C. BOWLING
05 Vice President Academic Affairs .... Dr. Gregg CHENOWETH
10 Vice President for Finance .... Dr. Douglas E. PERRY
32 Vice President Student Development .... Dr. Walter W. WEBB
26 Vice Pres Institutional Advancement .... Dr. Brian ALLEN
58 Vice Pres for Grad & Adult Studies .... Mr. Ryan SPITTAL
49 Dean College of Arts & Sciences .... Dr. Janna MCLEAN
73 Dn Sch Theology/Christian Ministry .... Dr. Carl LETH
53 Dean School of Education .... Dr. Jim UPCHURCH
107 Dean School of Professional Studies .... Dr. Dennis CROCKER
29 Director of Alumni Relations .... Mr. Gary GRIFFIN
07 Director of Admissions .... Mrs. Susan WOLFF
06 Registrar .... Dr. Jim D. KNIGHT
08 Director of the Library .... Mrs. Kathy R. BOYENS
37 Director of Financial Aid .... Mr. Greg BRUNER
14 Director of Computer Center .... Mr. Dennis SEYMOUR
41 Athletic Director .... Mr. Gary NEWSOME
42 Chaplain .... Rev. Mark HOLCOMB
30 Exec Director of Development .... Mr. Dan J. FERRIS
35 Director Student Activities .... Mrs. Kathy STEINACKER
15 Director of Human Resources .... Mr. David PICKERING
18 Chief Facilities/Physical Plant .... Mr. Matt WHITIS
40 Bookstore Manager .... Mrs. Rachel PIAZZA
36 Career Specialist .... Mrs. Mary ANDERSON
85 International Student Advisor .... Mr. Tony GRIMM
27 Coord of Strategic Comm & Web .... Mrs. Heather DAY

Pacific College of Oriental Medicine (A)

65 East Wacker Place 21st Floor, Chicago IL 60601
County: Cook Identification: 666615
Unit ID: 442842
Telephone: (888) 729-4811 Carnegie Class: Not Classified
FAX Number: (773) 477-4109 Calendar System: Other
URL: www.pacificcollege.edu
Established: 1999 Annual Graduate Tuition & Fees: $11,129
Enrollment: 271 Coed
Affiliation or Control: Proprietary IRS Status: Proprietary
Highest Offering: Master's; No Undergraduates
Program: Professional
Accreditation: **ACUP**, ACCSC

01 Director/Chief Operating Officer .... Dr. Edward LAMADRID

† Branch campus of Pacific College of Oriental Medicine, San Diego CA.

Parkland College (B)

2400 W Bradley Avenue, Champaign IL 61821-1899
County: Champaign FICE Identification: 007118
Unit ID: 147916
Telephone: (217) 351-2200 Carnegie Class: Assoc/Pub-R-L
FAX Number: (217) 351-2581 Calendar System: Semester
URL: www.parkland.edu
Established: 1966 Annual Undergrad Tuition & Fees (In-District): $3,210
Enrollment: 9,715 Coed
Affiliation or Control: State/Local IRS Status: 501(c)3
Highest Offering: Associate Degree
Program: Occupational; 2-Year Principally Bachelor's Creditable
Accreditation: **NH**, ADNUR, DH, @DIETT, OTA, RAD, SURGT

01 President .... Dr. Thomas R. RAMAGE
04 Asst to President/Board of Trustees .... Ms. Nancy R. WILLAMON
05 Vice President Academic Services .... Dr. Kristine M. YOUNG
32 Vice President Student Services .... Dr. Linda H. MOORE
11 Vice Pres Administrative Svcs/ CFO .... Mr. Christopher M. RANDLES
30 Vice Pres Institutional Advancement .... Dr. Seamus REILLY
35 Dean of Students .... Ms. Marietta TURNER
75 Dean of Career & Transfer Prgms .... Mr. Randy FLETCHER
50 Dept Chair Bus & Agri Industries .... Mr. Bruce HENRIKSON
77 Department Chair Comp Science & IT .... Ms. Maria MOBASSERI
54 Dept Chair Engineering Science/Tech .... Ms. Catherine STALTER
79 Dept Chair Humanities .... Mr. Tom BARNARD
57 Dept Chair Fine & Applied Arts .... Ms. Nancy SUTTON
76 Dept Chair Health Professions .... Ms. Roberta SCHOLZE
81 Department Chair Mathematics .... Mr. Phil BLAZIER
65 Dept Chair Natural Sciences .... Ms. Kathy BRUCE
83 Dept Chair Social Sci & Human Svcs .... Mr. Paul SARANTAKOS
88 Dir Center for Academic Success .... Ms. Becky OSBORNE
09 Director Accountability & Research .... Mr. Kevin KNOTT
88 Director of Adult Basic Education .... Ms. Tawanna NICKENS
26 Dir Marketing & Public Relations .... Ms. Patty LEHN
103 Exec Director Workforce Development .... Mr. Minor JACKSON
102 Exec Director Parkland Foundation .... Mr. Carl R. MEYER
08 Director Library .... Ms. Anna Maria S. WATKIN
31 Director Community Education .... Ms. Jan SIMON
25 Director Grants and Contracts .... Mr. Ray SPENCER
07 Director Admissions/Enrollment Mgmt .... Mr. Reo WILHOUR
35 Director Student Life .... Dr. Thomas M. CAULFIELD
41 Director Athletics .... Mr. Rod M. LOVETT
36 Director Career Center .... Ms. Sandra L. SPENCER
38 Dir Counseling & Advising Center .... Ms. Donna TANNER-HAROLD
37 Director Financial Aid .... Mr. Tim WENDT
19 Director Public Safety .... Mr. Von YOUNG
18 Director Physical Plant .... Mr. James BUSTARD
15 Director Human Resources .... Ms. Kathleen CHARLESTON
21 Controller .... Mr. Dave DONSBACH
40 Manager of Bookstore .... Ms. Diane M. KIEST
44 Dir Planned and Major Gifts .... Mr. Michael HAGAN

Prairie State College (C)

202 S Halsted Street, Chicago Heights IL 60411-8226
County: Cook FICE Identification: 001640
Unit ID: 148007
Telephone: (708) 709-3500 Carnegie Class: Assoc/Pub-S-SC
FAX Number: (708) 755-2587 Calendar System: Semester
URL: www.prairiestate.edu
Established: 1957 Annual Undergrad Tuition & Fees (In-District): $3,120
Enrollment: 5,791 Coed
Affiliation or Control: State/Local IRS Status: 501(c)3
Highest Offering: Associate Degree
Program: Occupational; 2-Year Principally Bachelor's Creditable
Accreditation: **NH**, ADNUR, DH, SURGT

01 President .... Dr. Eric C. RADTKE
10 Vice Pres Finance & Administration .... Dr. Alan D. ROBERTSON
05 Vice Pres Academic Affs/Dean Facul .... Dr. Adenuga ATEWOLOGUN
31 Vice President Community/Econ Devel .... Ms. Terri L. WINFREE
32 VP Student Affairs/Dean of Students .... Ms. Mary B. REAVES
49 Dean Liberal Arts .... Dr. Susan R. SOLBERG
50 Dean Business/Mathematics & Science .... Dr. Debra L. PRENDERGAST
17 Dean Health & Industrial Technology .... Ms. Marie C. HANSEL
15 Exec Dir Human Resources/Empl Rels .... Ms. Lynita J. GEBHARDT
14 Exec Dir Info Technology Resources .... Vacant
56 Dean Adult Education .... Ms. Kim M. KUNCE
21 Controller/Dir of Business Svcs .... Mr. James M. EATON
08 Dean Acad Svcs & Dir of Library .... Vacant
51 Dean Corporate/Cont Professional Ed .... Mr. Edward JODELKA
35 Dean Student Services .... Ms. Shawn L. GOVAN
20 Associate Dean Faculty Affairs .... Ms. Patricia VALENZIANO
18 Director Physical Plant/Facilities .... Mr. Ronald P. LEET
26 Exec Dir Communications & Marketing .... Ms. Jennifer E. STONER
102 Executive Director Foundation .... Ms. Cathy K. KLOSS
35 Director Stdnt Life/Multicult Affs .... Dr. Consuelo BALLOM
91 Assoc Dir Admin Computer Services .... Mr. Roy E. MAURER
07 Director Enrollment Services .... Ms. Jaime M. MILLER
19 Dir Camp/Pub Safety/Chief of Police .... Mr. Norman D. MARTIN
88 Director Children's Learning Center .... Ms. Kellie E. CLARK
88 Director Disability Svcs/Testing .... Ms. Diane J. JANOWIAK
37 Director Financial Aid/Vet Affairs .... Ms. Alice GARCIA
09 Director Institutional Research .... Dr. Joseph H. WYCOFF
88 Director Institutional Support Svcs .... Ms. Paulette A. MAURER
41 Director Physical Ed/Athletics .... Mr. Edward J. SCHAFFER
88 Director Student Success Center .... Ms. Lee A. HELBERT
04 Exec Assistant to the President .... Ms. Patricia G. TROST

Principia College (D)

1 Maybeck Place, Elsah IL 62028-9799
County: Jersey FICE Identification: 001744
Unit ID: 148016
Telephone: (618) 374-2131 Carnegie Class: Bac/A&S
FAX Number: (618) 374-5500 Calendar System: Semester
URL: www.principiacollege.edu
Established: 1898 Annual Undergrad Tuition & Fees: $25,640
Enrollment: 529 Coed
Affiliation or Control: Independent Non-Profit IRS Status: 501(c)3
Highest Offering: Baccalaureate
Program: Liberal Arts And General; Teacher Preparatory
Accreditation: **NH**

01 President and Chief Executive .... Dr. Jonathan PALMER
05 Dean of Academics .... Dr. Scott SCHNEBERGER
88 Chief Investment Officer .... Mr. Howard E. BERNER, JR.
10 Chief Financial Officer .... Mr. Doug GIBBS
20 Associate Dean of Academics .... Dr. Joe RITTER
27 Director of Marketing .... Ms. Gretchen NEWBY
06 Registrar .... Mrs. Patricia LANGTON
07 Dean of Enrollment Mgt/Admissions .... Mr. Brian MCCAULEY
08 Director of Libraries .... Mrs. Lisa ROBERTS
13 Chief Technology Officer .... Mr. Richard BOOTH
104 Director of Principia Abroads .... Ms. Linda A. BOHAKER
30 Chief Advancement Officer .... Mr. Glenn WILLILAMS
41 Director of Athletics .... Mr. Lee ELLIS
15 Human Resources Manager .... Ms. Sharon Ann SMITH
18 Director of Facilities .... Mr. Ed GOEWERT
11 Director of Administration/Budget .... Mrs. Karen D. GRIMMER
21 Controller .... Mrs. Sara THORNDIKE
29 Director of Alumni Relations .... Mrs. Donna GIBBS
32 Dean of Students .... Ms. Dorsie GLEN
37 Director of College Financial Aid .... Mrs. Tami GAVALETZ
96 Purchasing Manager .... Vacant
38 Director Academic Career Advising .... Mrs. Midge BROWNING
09 Director of IEP .... Vacant

Quincy University (E)

1800 College Avenue, Quincy IL 62301-2699
County: Adams FICE Identification: 001745
Unit ID: 148131
Telephone: (217) 222-8020 Carnegie Class: Master's S
FAX Number: (217) 228-5257 Calendar System: Semester
URL: www.quincy.edu
Established: 1860 Annual Undergrad Tuition & Fees: $24,140
Enrollment: 1,907 Coed
Affiliation or Control: Roman Catholic IRS Status: 501(c)3
Highest Offering: Master's
Program: Liberal Arts And General; Teacher Preparatory
Accreditation: **NH**

01 President .... Dr. Robert GERVASI
05 Vice Pres for Academic Affairs .... Dr. Teresa REED
03 Vice Pres for Mission & Ministry .... Fr. John DOCTOR, OFM
10 Vice President for Business/Finance .... Mr. Tim WEIS
13 Chief Information Officer .... Mr. Daniel MICHAELS
84 Vice Pres for Enrollment Management .... Mrs. Syndi PECK
32 Vice Pres for Student Affairs .... Dr. Tiffany QUINZE
39 Director of Residence Life .... Mr. Jeff SPAIN
28 Dir Multicultural/Leadership Pgms .... Ms. Natasha RAMSEY
101 Corporate Secretary .... Dr. Teresa REED
21 Assoc VP for Finance/Controller .... Mrs. Jean M. GREEN
30 Assoc Vice President Advancement .... Mrs. Julie BELL
25 Grant Writer .... Ms. Julie BOLL
50 Dean School of Business .... Dr. Cynthia HALIEMUN
53 Dean School of Education .... Dr. Ann BEHRENS
51 Dean School Professional Studies .... Vacant
79 Chair Division of Humanities .... Dr. Terrence RIDDELL
81 Chair Division Science & Technology .... Dr. Lee ENGER
83 Chair Div Behavioral/Social Sci .... Dr. Wendy BELLER
57 Chr Div Communication & Fine Arts .... Dr. Barbara SCHLEPPENBACH
20 Dean Academic Support Services .... Dr. Chelona EDGERLY
08 Dean of Library/Info Resources .... Ms. Patricia TOMCZAK
92 Director of Honors Program .... Dr. Daniel STRUDWICK
06 Registrar .... Mrs. Barbara WELLMAN
09 Institution Research Specialist .... Mrs. Roberta PAUL
42 Director of Campus Ministry .... Br. Ed ARAMBASICH
37 Director of Financial Aid .... Ms. Lisa FLACK
27 Director of Communications .... Mr. Roman SALAMON
29 Director of Alumni Services .... Mr. Bill O'DONNELL
36 Director Career Planning/Placement .... Ms. Kristen LIESEN
41 Director of Athletics .... Mr. Marty BELL
18 Director of Facilities Management .... Mr. Shawn ELKINS
19 Director of Security .... Mr. Steve PATTERSON
15 Director of Human Resources .... Ms. Dana KEPPNER
38 Director of the Counseling Center .... Mrs. Molly DUNN-STEINKE
96 Director of Purchasing .... Mrs. Jennifer TRUITT
40 Manager of the Bookstore .... Mr. Chris HAGAN
88 Studio Manager WQUB .... Ms. Marifaith MUELLER
30 Coordinator of Development .... Mr. Matthew BERGMAN

Rasmussen College - Aurora (F)

2363 Sequoia Drive, Suite 131, Aurora IL 60506
Identification: 667060
Unit ID: 44867301
Telephone: (630) 888-3500 Carnegie Class: Not Classified
FAX Number: (630) 888-3501 Calendar System: Quarter
URL: www.rasmussen.edu
Established: 1900 Annual Undergrad Tuition & Fees: $16,340
Enrollment: 553 Coed
Affiliation or Control: Proprietary IRS Status: Proprietary
Highest Offering: Baccalaureate
Program: Occupational; 2-Year Principally Bachelor's Creditable
Accreditation: **&NH**, MAAB

01 Campus Director .... Susan CHENEY

† Regional accreditation is carried under the parent institution in Lake Elmo, MN.

Rasmussen College - Mokena/ Tinley Park (G)

8650 W. Spring Lake Drive, Mokena IL 60448
County: Will Identification: 667064
Unit ID: 44867303
Telephone: (815) 534-3300 Carnegie Class: Not Classified
FAX Number: (815) 534-3301 Calendar System: Quarter
URL: www.rasmussen.edu
Established: 1900 Annual Undergrad Tuition & Fees: $16,340
Enrollment: 42 Coed
Affiliation or Control: Proprietary IRS Status: Proprietary
Highest Offering: Baccalaureate
Program: Occupational; 2-Year Principally Bachelor's Creditable
Accreditation: **&NH**

01 Campus Director .... Staci HEGARTY

† Regional accreditation is carried under the parent institution in Lake Elmo, MN.

Rasmussen College - Rockford (H)

6000 E. State Street, 4th Floor, Rockford IL 61108
Identification: 667065
Unit ID: 448673
Telephone: (815) 316-4800 Carnegie Class: Not Classified
FAX Number: (815) 315-4801 Calendar System: Quarter
URL: www.rasmussen.edu
Established: 1900 Annual Undergrad Tuition & Fees: $16,340
Enrollment: 1,201 Coed
Affiliation or Control: Proprietary IRS Status: Proprietary
Highest Offering: Baccalaureate
Program: Occupational; 2-Year Principally Bachelor's Creditable
Accreditation: **&NH**, MAAB

02 Campus Director .... Craig STEEGE

† Regional accreditation is carried under the parent institution in Lake Elmo, MN.

Rasmussen College - Romeoville/ Joliet (A)

1400 West Normantown Road, Romeoville IL 60446

County: Will | Identification: 667066
Unit ID: 44867302
Telephone: (815) 306-2600 | Carnegie Class: Not Classified
FAX Number: (815) 306-2601 | Calendar System: Quarter
URL: www.rasmussen.edu
Established: 1900 | Annual Undergrad Tuition & Fees: $16,340
Enrollment: 382 | Coed
Affiliation or Control: Proprietary | IRS Status: Proprietary
Highest Offering: Baccalaureate
Program: Occupational; 2-Year Principally Bachelor's Creditable
Accreditation: &NH, MAAB

01 Campus Director .... Amy KING

† Regional accreditation is carried under the parent institution in Lake Elmo, MN.

Rend Lake College (B)

468 N Ken Gray Parkway, Ina IL 62846-9801

County: Jefferson | FICE Identification: 007119
Unit ID: 148256
Telephone: (618) 437-5321 | Carnegie Class: Assoc/Pub-R-L
FAX Number: (618) 437-5677 | Calendar System: Semester
URL: www.rlc.edu
Established: 1967 | Annual Undergrad Tuition & Fees (In-District): $2,790
Enrollment: 5,379 | Coed
Affiliation or Control: State/Local | IRS Status: 501(c)3
Highest Offering: Associate Degree
Program: Occupational; 2-Year Principally Bachelor's Creditable
Accreditation: NH, MLTAD, OTA, RAD

01 President .... Mr. Charley HOLSTEIN
05 VP of Academic Instruction .... Ms. Chris KUBERSKI
10 VP of Finance & Administration .... Mr. Robert CARLOCK
20 VP of Career Technical Instruction .... Ms. Lisa PAYNE
88 Dean of Special Programs .... Ms. Andrea WITTHOFT
26 Director Marketing & Information .... Mr. Chad COPPLE
37 Director Student Financial Aid .... Mr. Douglas CARLSON
38 Dean of Student Services .... Ms. Lisa PRICE
41 Athletic Director .... Vacant
18 Director Physical Plant .... Mr. C. Randall SHIVELY
102 CEO of RLC Foundation .... Ms. Patricia KERN
06 Director of Student Records .... Ms. Vickie SCHULTE

Resurrection University (C)

3 Erie Court, Oak Park IL 60302-2519

County: Cook | FICE Identification: 006250
Unit ID: 149763
Telephone: (708) 763-6530 | Carnegie Class: Spec/Health
FAX Number: (708) 763-1531 | Calendar System: Semester
URL: www.resu.edu
Established: 1982 | Annual Undergrad Tuition & Fees: $22,616
Enrollment: 220 | Coed
Affiliation or Control: Independent Non-Profit | IRS Status: 501(c)3
Highest Offering: Master's
Program: Liberal Arts And General; Nursing Emphasis
Accreditation: NH, NURSE

01 Interim President .... Dr. Beth A. BROOKS
66 Dean of Nursing .... Dr. Sandie SOLDWISCH
84 Director of Enrollment Management .... Dr. Cindy CRUZ
10 Director Business/Financial Affairs .... Ms. Therese A. SCANLAN
90 Program Analyst .... Mr. Zbigniew KUSNIERZ
37 Student Financial Aid .... Ms. Shirley HOWELL
06 Registrar .... Ms. Edy COOPER
32 Director of Student Services .... Ms. Carmelita GEE

Richland Community College (D)

One College Park, Decatur IL 62521-8513

County: Macon | FICE Identification: 010879
Unit ID: 148292
Telephone: (217) 875-7200 | Carnegie Class: Assoc/Pub-R-M
FAX Number: (217) 875-6961 | Calendar System: Semester
URL: www.richland.edu
Established: 1971 | Annual Undergrad Tuition & Fees (In-District): $2,880
Enrollment: 3,807 | Coed
Affiliation or Control: State/Local | IRS Status: 501(c)3
Highest Offering: Associate Degree
Program: Occupational; 2-Year Principally Bachelor's Creditable
Accreditation: NH, ADNUR, SURGT

01 President .... Dr. Gayle M. SAUNDERS
10 Vice President of Finance & Admin .... Mr. Greg E. FLORIAN
05 Vice Pres Student/Academic Affairs .... Dr. Tod TREAT
103 VP Econ Dev/Innov Wkfce Solutions .... Dr. Douglas BRAUER
106 Director Online Learning .... Mrs. Kona JONES
30 Exec Director Foundation & Develop .... Vacant
29 Dir Scholarships/Alumni Development .... Mrs. Kathy CARTER
51 Dean Continuing Education .... Mr. Terry ROBINSON
27 Exec Director of Public Information .... Ms. Lisa GREGORY
07 Dean Enrollment Services .... Mr. Marcus BROWN
06 Registrar .... Ms. Stephanie ZIMMERMAN
32 Director Student Engagement .... Mrs. Heather KIND-KEPPEL
38 Director Counseling and Advising .... Mrs. Deborah MCGEE
53 Dean Teaching/Learning Support Svcs .... Mrs. Sheryl BLAHNIK
81 Dean of Math & Sciences .... Dr. John CORDULACK
72 Dean of Business & Technology .... Mr. James HESS
37 Dir Financial Aid/Veteran Affairs .... Ms. Carmin E. ROSS
36 Director Career Services .... Mr. Michael DIGGS
16 Director Human Resources .... Mr. Richard GSCHWEND
57 Dean of Communications/Fine Arts .... Dr. Lily SIU
76 Dean of Health Professions .... Ms. Ellen COLBECK
18 Dir Tech Services & Operations .... Mr. David HOLTFRETER
19 Dir Campus Safety .... Mr. Greg FIRKUS

Robert Morris University (E)

401 South State Street, Chicago IL 60605-1225

County: Cook | FICE Identification: 001746
Unit ID: 148335
Telephone: (312) 935-6800 | Carnegie Class: Master's M
FAX Number: (312) 935-6660 | Calendar System: Other
URL: www.robertmorris.edu
Established: 1913 | Annual Undergrad Tuition & Fees: $21,600
Enrollment: 4,486 | Coed
Affiliation or Control: Independent Non-Profit | IRS Status: 501(c)3
Highest Offering: Master's
Program: Occupational; 2-Year Principally Bachelor's Creditable; Liberal Arts And General; Business Emphasis
Accreditation: NH, ADNUR, IACBE, MAC, SURGT

01 President .... Michael P. VIOLLT
05 Provost .... Mablene KRUEGER
88 Sr VP for Resource Administration .... Deborah BRODZINSKI
84 Sr VP for Enrollment Management .... Catherine LOCKWOOD
20 VP of Academic Administration .... Katie SUHAJDA
88 VP of Brand & Image .... Christine FISHER
10 VP for Business Affairs .... Ronald M. ARNOLD
09 VP for External Affairs .... Marie A. GIACOMELLI
37 VP of Financial Aid .... Leigh BRINSON
15 VP of Human Resources .... Nicole SKALUBA
88 VP for Information Systems .... Lisa CONTRERAS
88 VP for Marketing .... Connie ESPARZA
32 VP of Student Affairs .... Angela JORDAN
88 Dean of CCHES and Assessment .... Amy TWOREK
97 Dean of College of Liberal Arts .... Paula DIAZ
49 Dean of Institute of Art & Design .... Janice KAUSHAL
88 Dean/Exec Dir Inst of Culinary Arts .... Nancy ROTUNNO
58 Dean of Morris Grad School of Mgmt .... Kayed AKKAWI
50 Dean of Business Administration .... Larry NIEMAN
72 Dean of Inst of Technology & Media .... Basim KHARTABIL
76 Dean of Nursing & Health Studies .... Janet DAVIS
88 Dean of Integrated Learning .... Jennifer BUCKO
07 Dean of Admissions .... Ana MENDEZ
88 Sr Dir of Academic Administration .... Kathleen VIOLLT
96 Dir of Business Affairs .... Daniel BEDOLLA
13 Dir of Networking Services .... Gloria PLAZA
26 Dir of Public Relations .... Nancy DONOHOE
06 Dir of Student Information .... Stella MACH
39 Student Life Manager .... Janely RIVERA
35 Dir Student Services/Special Pgms .... Monique JONES
90 Dir of User Services .... Dipak PATEL
41 Athletic Dir .... Megan SMITH
21 Controller .... Melanie CARLIN
08 Institutional Library Dir .... Sue DUTLER
18 Institutional Dir of Operations .... Nino RANDAZZO
40 Dir of Bookstore Operations .... Julie MELLER
88 Assoc Dir of Career Development .... Stefanie CALDWELL
88 Dir of Admissions Info Systems .... Damaris RIVERA
88 Dir of High School Relations .... Knyja REED
88 Dir of Purchasing and Facilities .... Amy KECK
88 Dir of Data Administration .... Deana MIRANDA
88 Dir of Electronic Recruitment .... Sue POLZ
88 Dir of Human Resources .... Gregory TALL
88 Dir of System Integration & Audits .... Arlene REGNERUS

Rock Valley College (F)

3301 N Mulford Road, Rockford IL 61114-5699

County: Winnebago | FICE Identification: 001747
Unit ID: 148380
Telephone: (815) 921-7821 | Carnegie Class: Assoc/Pub-R-L
FAX Number: N/A | Calendar System: Semester
URL: www.rockvalleycollege.edu
Established: 1964 | Annual Undergrad Tuition & Fees (In-District): $2,804
Enrollment: 8,849 | Coed
Affiliation or Control: Local | IRS Status: 501(c)3
Highest Offering: Associate Degree
Program: Occupational; 2-Year Principally Bachelor's Creditable
Accreditation: NH, DH, SURGT

01 President .... Dr. Jack J. BECHERER
05 Provost/CAO .... Dr. Diane L. NYHAMMER
102 Executive Director Foundation .... Ms. Pamela OWENS
10 Vice Pres Administrative Services .... Mr. Sam OVERTON, JR.
32 Assoc VP Student Development .... Ms. Amy DIAZ
51 Assoc VP Outreach & Planning .... Mr. Michael MASTROIANNI
20 Assoc VP Academic Affairs .... Mr. Greg WEAR
13 Managing Dir Information Technology .... Vacant
15 Managing Dir Human Resource Svc .... Ms. Jessica JONES
96 Director Business Services .... Ms. Jacki MINNIHAN
84 Dir Enroll Mgmt & Judicial Affairs .... Ms. Lynn PERKINS
18 Director Facilities Planning & POM .... Mr. Thomas VIEL
26 Director Public Relations .... Ms. Nancy CHAMBERLAIN
88 Director Theatre & Arts Park .... Mr. Michael WEBB
19 Director Public Safety .... Mr. Joe DROUGHT
21 Director Financial Services .... Ms. Cynthia HAGGARD
37 Director Financial Aid .... Ms. Cyndi STONESIFER
09 Executive Director Inst Research .... Ms. Lisa MEHLIG
06 Registrar .... Ms. Michelle ROTHMEYER
35 Manager Student Life .... Ms. Quiana PRESTON
36 Coordinator Career Svcs/Placement .... Mr. Art DELGADO
07 Manager of Recruitment & Admissions .... Ms. Jennifer THOMPSON

Rockford Career College (G)

1130 S. Alpine Road, Rockford IL 61108

County: Winnebago | FICE Identification: 008545
Unit ID: 148399
Telephone: (815) 965-8616 | Carnegie Class: Assoc/PrivFP
FAX Number: (815) 965-0360 | Calendar System: Quarter
URL: www.rockfordcareercollege.edu
Established: 1862 | Annual Undergrad Tuition & Fees: $9,000
Enrollment: 740 | Coed
Affiliation or Control: Proprietary | IRS Status: Proprietary
Highest Offering: Associate Degree
Program: Occupational; 2-Year Principally Bachelor's Creditable
Accreditation: ACICS, MAC

01 President/CEO .... Mr. Steven GIBSON
10 Vice President/Dir of Finance .... Mr. Guary BERNADELLE
05 Dean of Academics .... Ms. Amy SEMENCHUCK
32 Dean of Students .... Ms. Karen GILBERT
22 Dir of Institutional Compliance .... Mr. Jack MARTIN
84 Director of Enrollment .... Mr. David JULIUS
15 Director of Human Resources .... Mr. Jim LAIBLE
36 Director Student Placement .... Ms. Monica WILLIAMS
37 Director of Financial Aid .... Ms. Lisa RUCH
26 Director of College Relations .... Mr. Jeff SWANBERG

Rockford College (H)

5050 E State Street, Rockford IL 61108-2393

County: Winnebago | FICE Identification: 001748
Unit ID: 148405
Telephone: (815) 226-4000 | Carnegie Class: Master's L
FAX Number: (815) 226-4119 | Calendar System: Semester
URL: www.rockford.edu
Established: 1847 | Annual Undergrad Tuition & Fees: $25,470
Enrollment: 1,330 | Coed
Affiliation or Control: Independent Non-Profit | IRS Status: 501(c)3
Highest Offering: Master's
Program: Liberal Arts And General; Teacher Preparatory; Professional
Accreditation: NH, IACBE, NUR

01 President .... Dr. Robert L. HEAD
05 Exec VP & Dean of the College .... Dr. Stephanie QUINN
30 Vice Pres Institutional Advancement .... Mr. Bernard SUNDSTEDT
10 Vice Pres Business/Operations/CFO .... Ms. Christina ANDERSON
84 Vice Pres Enrollment Management .... Mr. Barrett BELL
32 Dean of Student Life .... Mr. Bradley KNOTTS
11 Associate Vice President Operations .... Mr. Matthew PHILLIPS
13 Director of Information Technology .... Ms. Bonnie JOHNSON
58 Assoc VP Community/Graduate Educ .... Mr. Jeffrey FAHRENWALD
08 Librarian .... Mr. Jan FIGA
07 Director of Undergraduate Admission .... Ms. Jennifer NORDSTROM
88 Senior Development Officer .... Mr. John MCNAMARA
06 Registrar .... Ms. Anna J. JATTKOWSKI-HUDSON
36 Director Career Services .... Ms. Kelly COOPER
26 Interim Director of Communications .... Ms. Rita ELLIOTT
37 Director Financial Aid .... Mr. Todd FREE
12 Director of Kobe-Regents Center .... Ms. Michelle GRIGGS
38 Director Counseling .... Mrs. Sallyann ROBERTS
23 Director Health Services .... Mrs. Cecelia M. BRISTOL
18 Director Physical Plant .... Mr. Jerry BERG
19 Security Officer .... Mr. Roy RONCAL
40 Manager Bookstore .... Ms. Dawn MCCRAY
41 Athletic Director .... Mrs. Kristyn KING
15 Human Resource Manager .... Ms. Jennifer O'BRIEN

Roosevelt University (I)

430 S Michigan Avenue, Chicago IL 60605-1394

County: Cook | FICE Identification: 001749
Unit ID: 148487
Telephone: (312) 341-3500 | Carnegie Class: Master's L
FAX Number: (312) 341-3655 | Calendar System: Semester
URL: www.roosevelt.edu
Established: 1945 | Annual Undergrad Tuition & Fees: $25,000
Enrollment: 6,766 | Coed
Affiliation or Control: Independent Non-Profit | IRS Status: 501(c)3
Highest Offering: Doctorate
Program: Liberal Arts And General; Teacher Preparatory; Professional
Accreditation: NH, ACBSP, CACREP, CLPSY, MUS, @PHAR, TED

01 President .... Dr. Charles R. MIDDLETON
03 Provost & Exec Vice President .... Dr. James GANDRE
45 Vice Provost for Planning & Budgets .... Mr. Michael FORD
05 Asst V Provost Faculty/Acad Admin .... Dr. Samuel ROSENBERG
10 Sr VP of Finance/Admin and CFO .... Ms. Miroslava MEJIA KRUG
86 VP Govt Relations/Univ Outreach .... Ms. Lesley SLAVITT
84 VP Enrollment Mgmt & Student Svcs .... Dr. Sallye MCKEE
15 Vice President Human Resources .... Ms. Gretchen VAN NATTA
100 Chief of Staff & Asst Secy to BOT .... Mr. Brigham J. TIMPSON
12 Schaumburg Campus Provost .... Dr. Douglas KNERR
30 VP Inst Advancement and CAO .... Mr. Patrick WOODS
30 Asst Vice President for Development .... Ms. Mirna GARCIA

29 Asst VP Alumni Rels/Annual Giving .... Ms. June STINE
44 Asst Vice President Planned Giving .. Ms. Denise A. BRANSFORD
07 Asst Vice Pres Admissions .... Ms. Beth GIERACH
35 Asst VP Stdnt Svcs & Career Dev .... Mr. Eric TAMMES
09 Asst VP Institutional Research .... Mr. Joseph P. REGAN
88 Associate VP for Enrollment Service .... Vacant
21 Associate VP Finance .... Ms. Tangella MADDOX
32 Associate VP Student Services .... Ms. Tanya L. WOLTMANN
18 Assoc VP Physical Resources .... Mr. Steven A. HOSELTON
96 Assoc Vice President for Admin Svcs .... Ms. Laurie CASHMAN
85 Director of International Programs .... Ms. Rubee Li FULLER
13 Chief Information Officer .... Mr. Neeraj KUMAR
58 Int V Prov Research/Dean Grad Stds .... Ms. Linda JONES
49 Dean College Arts & Sciences .... Dr. Lynn Y. WEINER
50 Dean College Business Admin .... Dr. Terri L. FRIEL
64 Dean College of Performing Arts .... Mr. Henry FOGEL
107 Dean Col of Professional Studies .... Dr. John CICERO
53 Dean College of Education .... Dr. Holly STADLER
67 Dean College of Pharmacy .... Dr. George MACKINNON
39 Director of Residence Life .... Ms. Angela RYAN
26 Sr Director Public Relations .... Mr. Thomas R. KAROW
88 Exec Dir of Auditorium Theatre/RU .... Mr. Brett BATTERSON
08 University Librarian .... Mr. Richard UTTICH
06 Registrar .... Vacant
37 Director Financial Aid .... Mr. Walter J H. O'NEILL
38 Director Counseling Center .... Dr. Susan STOCK
36 Asst Vice Pres Career Development .... Mr. Eric TAMMES

Rosalind Franklin University of Medicine & Science (A)

3333 Green Bay Road, North Chicago IL 60064-3095

County: Lake FICE Identification: 001659
Unit ID: 145558

Telephone: (847) 578-3000 Carnegie Class: Spec/Med
FAX Number: (847) 578-3401 Calendar System: Quarter
URL: www.rosalindfranklin.edu
Established: 1912 Annual Undergrad Tuition & Fees: N/A
Enrollment: 1,937 Coed
Affiliation or Control: Independent Non-Profit IRS Status: 501(c)3
Highest Offering: Doctorate; No Lower Division
Program: Professional; Technical Emphasis
Accreditation: NH, ANEST, ARCPA, CLPSY, MED, PA, @PHAR, POD, PTA

01 President/Chief Executive Officer .... Dr. Michael WELCH
03 Exec Vice Pres/Chief Operating Ofcr .... Ms. Margot SURRIDGE
17 VP Medical Affs/Dean Medical School ... Dr. Russell ROBERTSON
05 VP Acad Affs/ Dean Col Hlth Prof .... Dr. Wendy RHEAULT
46 VP Research .... Dr. Ronald S. KAPLAN
67 Dean Col of Pharmacy .... Dr. Gloria MEREDITH
58 Dean Sch Grad PostDoc Stds .... Dr. Joseph X. DIMARIO
63 Dean Scholl Col Podiatric Med .... Dr. Nancy L. PARSLEY
10 Chief Financial Officer .... Ms. Roberta LANE
88 VP Faculty Affairs .... Dr. Timothy R. HANSEN
30 VP Institutional Advancement .... Ms. Tina M. ERICKSON
100 Director Office of the President .... Ms. Donna AGNEW
88 Chief Compliance Officer .... Mr. Bret MOBERG
45 Assoc VP Financial Plng/Analysis .... Mr. Eugene DAUN
88 Assoc VP Learning Resources .... Dr. Melanie SHURAN
09 Assoc VP Institutional Research .... Ms. Maryann DECAIRE
11 Assoc VP Operations .... Mr. Daniel ESTA
84 Assoc VP Stdnt Aff/Enrollment Mgmt .... Ms. Rebecca DURKIN
27 Chief Information Officer .... Mr. Richard LOESCH
29 Exec Dir Alumni/Community Affairs .... Ms. Martha KELLY BATES
15 Exec Dir of Human Resources .... Ms. Sherry BAGNO
26 Exec Dir Marketing/Communications .... Ms. Lee CONCHA
19 Director Campus Security .... Mr. Gordon BLANCHARD
18 Dir Facilities Management .... Mr. Robert D. JACKSON
25 Dir Sponsored Research .... Ms. Dora ESPINOZA
06 Registrar .... Mr. Timothy CARROLL
37 Dir Student Financial Services .... Ms. Maryann DECAIRE
88 Dir Academic/Retention Svcs .... Mr. Steven WEINAND
07 Dir Admissions/Recruitment .... Mr. La'Mont VAUGHN
32 Director Student Life .... Ms. Shelly BLOHOWIAK

Rush University (B)

600 S Paulina, Chicago IL 60612-3832

County: Cook FICE Identification: 009800
Unit ID: 148511

Telephone: (312) 942-7100 Carnegie Class: Spec/Med
FAX Number: (312) 942-2219 Calendar System: Quarter
URL: www.rushu.rush.edu
Established: 1971 Annual Undergrad Tuition & Fees: $32,000
Enrollment: 1,917 Coed
Affiliation or Control: Independent Non-Profit IRS Status: 501(c)3
Highest Offering: Doctorate
Program: Professional
Accreditation: NH, ANEST, #ARCPA, AUD, BBT, DIETI, DMS, HSA, IPSY, MED, MT, NURSE, OT, PERF, SP

01 President .... Dr. Larry J. GOODMAN
03 Executive Vice President/COO .... Mr. Peter W. BUTLER
17 Sr Vice Pres Medical Affs/Provost .... Dr. Thomas A. DEUTSCH
26 Sr Vice Pres Corp/External Affairs .... Mr. Avery MILLER
10 Senior Vice President Finance .... Mr. John MORDACH
30 Senior Vice President Philanthropy ...... Ms. Diane M. MCKEEVER
13 Sr Vice Pres/Chief Information Ofcr .... Mr. Lac VAN TRAN
43 Vice President Legal Affairs .... Mr. Max D. BROWN
15 Vice President Human Resource .... Ms. Mary E. SCHOPP
46 Vice President Research .... Dr. James L. MULSHINE
22 Assoc VP Equal Oppty Academic Affs .. Ms. Beverly B. HUCKMAN
25 Assoc Vice Pres Chief Compliance Of .... Dr. Cynthia E. BOYD
18 Vice Pres Campus Transformation .... Mr. Mick ZDEBLICK
20 Vice Provost .... Dr. Lois A. HALSTEAD
32 Assoc Prov Student Svcs/Registrar .... Dr. Gayle WARD
76 Dean College of Health Sciences .... Dr. David SHELLEDY
58 Dean The Graduate College .... Dr. Paul M. CARVEY
66 Dean College of Nursing .... Dr. Melanie DREHER
63 Dean Rush Medical College .... Dr. Thomas A. DEUTSCH
20 Assoc Dean Med/Student Pgm .... Dr. Keith BOYD
27 Asst Vice President Marketing .... Ms. Lori ALLEN
07 Dir Admiss Nursing/Allied Health .... Ms. Angela MASON-JOHNSON
08 Director Library .... Ms. Christine D. FRANK
35 Director Student Affairs .... Ms. Jill GABBERT
37 Director Student Financial Aid .... Mr. David J. NELSON
09 Director of Institutional Research .... Dr. James L. MULSHINE
38 Director Student Counsel Center .... Dr. Hilarie TEREBESSY
29 Director Alumni Relations .... Ms. Karyn REIF
85 Director International Services .... Ms. Helen LAVELLE
96 Director of Purchasing .... Mr. Michael MULROE
90 Asst Dir McCormick Educ Tech Ctr .... Mr. William FLEMING
21 Senior Manager Business Affairs .... Mr. William TICE

St. Anthony College of Nursing (C)

5658 E State Street, Rockford IL 61108-2468

County: Winnebago FICE Identification: 009987
Unit ID: 149028

Telephone: (815) 395-5091 Carnegie Class: Spec/Health
FAX Number: (815) 395-2275 Calendar System: Semester
URL: www.sacn.edu
Established: 1915 Annual Undergrad Tuition & Fees: $19,710
Enrollment: 188 Coed
Affiliation or Control: Roman Catholic IRS Status: 501(c)3
Highest Offering: Master's
Program: Professional; Nursing Emphasis
Accreditation: NH, NURSE

01 President .... Dr. Terese A. BURCH
05 Dean for Undergraduate Affairs .... Dr. Elizabeth M. CARSON
58 Dean for Graduate Affairs & Rsrch .... Dr. Shannon K. LIZER
32 Assoc Dean for Support Services .... Ms. Nancy A. SANDERS
08 College LRC/Med Library Director .... Ms. Heather KLEPITSCH

St. Augustine College (D)

1333-45 W Argyle Street, Chicago IL 60640-3501

County: Cook FICE Identification: 021854
Unit ID: 148876

Telephone: (773) 878-8756 Carnegie Class: Assoc/PrivNFP4
FAX Number: (773) 878-0937 Calendar System: Semester
URL: www.staugustine.edu
Established: 1980 Annual Undergrad Tuition & Fees: $8,760
Enrollment: 1,581 Coed
Affiliation or Control: Independent Non-Profit IRS Status: 501(c)3
Highest Offering: Baccalaureate
Program: 2-Year Principally Bachelor's Creditable; Liberal Arts And General
Accreditation: NH, SW

01 President .... Mr. Andrew C. SUND
05 Dean of Academic & Student Affairs .... Dr. Bruno BONDAVALLI
20 Dean of Instruction .... Mr. Lee MALTBY
10 VP for Finance .... Ms. Saundra FLEMING
30 VP for Institutional Advancement .... Mr. Alfredo CALIXTO
103 VP for Workforce Development .... Mr. Norman RUANO
09 VP Technology/Research & Systems .... Mr. Paul HECK
37 Director of Financial Aid .... Ms. Maria ZAMBONINO
15 Director Human Resources .... Mr. Teofilo CALERO
18 Director of Physical Facilities .... Mr. Pablo RODRIGUEZ
07 Director of Recruitment .... Ms. Gloria QUIROZ
12 Director Satellites .... Ms. Carmen RIVERA
24 Dir of Learning Resources Center .... Ms. Elizabeth GRUBY

Saint Francis Medical Center College of Nursing (E)

511 NE Greenleaf Street, Peoria IL 61603-3783

County: Peoria FICE Identification: 006240
Unit ID: 148575

Telephone: (309) 655-2201 Carnegie Class: Spec/Health
FAX Number: (309) 624-8973 Calendar System: Semester
URL: www.sfmccon.edu
Established: 1985 Annual Undergrad Tuition & Fees: $15,932
Enrollment: 525 Coed
Affiliation or Control: Roman Catholic IRS Status: 501(c)3
Highest Offering: Doctorate
Program: Nursing Emphasis
Accreditation: NH, NUR

01 President of the College .... Dr. Patricia A. STOCKERT
05 Dean Undergraduate Program .... Dr. Sue C. BROWN
58 Dean Graduate Program .... Dr. Janice F. BOUNDY
32 Asst Dean of Support Services .... Mr. Kevin N. STEPHENS
07 Director of Admissions/Registrar . Mrs. Janice E. FARQUHARSON
08 Librarian .... Ms. Leslie E. MENZ
38 College Counselor .... Mrs. Sally J. MCLAUGHLIN
37 Coord Student Fin/Financial Assist .... Mrs. Nancy S. PERRYMAN
21 Coord Student Finance/Accts Rec .... Mrs. Laura L. SIMMONS
04 Administrative Assistant .... Ms. Luann MORELOCK

St. John's College (F)

729 E. Carpenter St., Springfield IL 62702-5317

County: Sangamon FICE Identification: 030980
Unit ID: 148593

Telephone: (217) 525-5628 Carnegie Class: Spec/Health
FAX Number: (217) 757-6870 Calendar System: Semester
URL: www.stjohnscollegespringfield.edu
Established: 1991 Annual Undergrad Tuition & Fees: $14,776
Enrollment: 87 Coed
Affiliation or Control: Independent Non-Profit IRS Status: 501(c)3
Highest Offering: Baccalaureate
Program: Professional; Nursing Emphasis
Accreditation: NH, NUR

01 Chancellor .... Dr. Brenda R. JEFFERS
05 Academic Lead .... Ms. Casey SCHUMACHER
07 Admissions Officer/Registrar .... Ms. Linda S. QUIGLEY
32 Student Development Officer .... Ms. Beth M. BEASLEY
30 Development Officer .... Ms. Kristine MYSZKA
51 Director of Continuing Education .... Dr. Judy SHACKELFORD
37 Financial Aid Officer .... Ms. Mary BROWN

Saint Xavier University (G)

3700 W 103rd Street, Chicago IL 60655-3105

County: Cook FICE Identification: 001768
Unit ID: 148627

Telephone: (773) 298-3000 Carnegie Class: Master's L
FAX Number: (773) 779-9061 Calendar System: Semester
URL: www.sxu.edu
Established: 1846 Annual Undergrad Tuition & Fees: $26,280
Enrollment: 5,057 Coed
Affiliation or Control: Roman Catholic IRS Status: 501(c)3
Highest Offering: Master's
Program: Liberal Arts And General; Professional
Accreditation: NH, ACBSP, MUS, NURSE, SP, TED

01 President .... Ms. Christine M. WISEMAN
05 Provost .... Dr. Angela DURANTE
10 Vice President Business & Finance ...... Mr. Raymond P. CATANIA
30 Vice Pres University Advancement .... Dr. Steven J. MURPHY
26 Vice President University Relations . Mr. Robert C. TENCZAR, JR.
32 Vice President Student Affairs .... Mr. John P. PELRINE, JR.
45 Vice Pres Univ Mission & Heritage .... Sr. Susan M. SANDERS, RSM
09 VP Student Recruitment/Enroll Plng .... Dr. Kathleen CARLSON
13 Asst VP Instr Res & Tech .... Vacant
37 Asst VP Student Financial Services .... Ms. Susan SWISHER
35 Asst Vice Pres Student Affairs .... Ms. Carrie SCHADE
18 Asst Vice Pres Facilities Mgmt .... Mr. Peter SKACH
18 Asst VP Auxiliary Services .... Vacant
88 Director of Employee Services .... Vacant
21 Controller .... Ms. Tina FRODYMA
07 Asst VP Student Recruitment .... Vacant
20 Associate Provost .... Dr. Richard VENNERI
20 Associate Provost .... Dr. Dale FAST
20 Assistant Provost .... Ms. Maureen WOGAN
26 Executive Director Media Relation .... Ms. Karla THOMAS
56 Chief Campus Officer OPC .... Dr. Leslie PETTY
49 Dean College Arts/Sciences .... Dr. Kathleen ALAIMO
53 Dean School of Education .... Dr. S. Beverly GULLEY
50 Dean School of Management .... Dr. James BRODZINSKI
66 Dean School of Nursing .... Dr. Gloria JACOBSON
35 Dean of Students .... Ms. Eileen DOHERTY
24 Director Media Services .... Mr. Lee VAN SICKLE
08 Director Library .... Mr. Mark A. VARGAS
06 Director Records/Registration Svcs .... Ms. Barbara SUTTON
19 Dir Public Safety/Chief of Police .... Mr. Charles FRAZZINI
29 Director Alumni/Parent Relations .... Ms. Jamie MANAHAN
41 Director Athletics .... Mr. Robert HALLBERG
42 Director Campus Ministry .... Ms. Esther SANBORN
85 Director Center for Intl Education .... Ms. Colleen O'HARA
40 Director Bookstore Operations .... Ms. Donna GASIOR
96 Purchasing Coordinator .... Ms. Donna PAVLIK

Sanford-Brown College (H)

1101 Eastport Plaza Drive, Collinsville IL 62234

Identification: 666753
Unit ID: 391582

Telephone: (618) 344-5600 Carnegie Class: Not Classified
FAX Number: (314) 421-5256 Calendar System: Semester
URL: www.sanfordbrown.edu/Collinsville
Established: N/A Annual Undergrad Tuition & Fees: $16,321
Enrollment: 675 Coed
Affiliation or Control: Proprietary IRS Status: Proprietary
Highest Offering: Associate Degree
Program: Occupational
Accreditation: ACICS, MAAB

01 Campus Director .... Mr. Douglas GOODWIN

Sauk Valley Community College (I)

173 Illinois Route 2, Dixon IL 61021-9188

County: Lee FICE Identification: 001752
Unit ID: 148672

Telephone: (815) 288-5511 Carnegie Class: Assoc/Pub-R-M
FAX Number: (815) 288-1880 Calendar System: Semester
URL: www.svcc.edu
Established: 1965 Annual Undergrad Tuition & Fees (In-State): $3,168
Enrollment: 1,668 Coed

Affiliation or Control: State IRS Status: 501(c)3
Highest Offering: Associate Degree
Program: Occupational; 2-Year Principally Bachelor's Creditable
Accreditation: NH, RAD

01 President ..... Dr. George J. MIHEL
13 Dean Information Svcs/Int Acad VP ..... Mr. Alan D. PFEIFER
32 Dean of Student Services ..... Mr. Luis S. MORENO
10 Dean of Business Services ..... Ms. Paula MEYER
20 Dean of Instructional Services ..... Dr. Mary Lou KIDDER
09 Dean Institutional Research/ Plng ..... Mr. Thomas J. GOSPODARCZYK
76 Dean Health & Sciences ..... Ms. Janet D. LYNCH
18 Director Buildings & Grounds ..... Mr. John DITTO
15 Director of Human Resources ..... Ms. Kathryn SNOW
06 Registrar ..... Ms. Pam MEDEMA
14 Dir of Instructional Technology ..... Ms. Chris SHELLEY
41 Director of Athletics ..... Mr. Russ DAMHOFF
26 Coordinator College Relations ..... Vacant
37 Coord Student Financial Assistance ..... Ms. Debra STIEFEL

School of the Art Institute of Chicago (A)

37 S Wabash, Chicago IL 60603-3103
County: Cook FICE Identification: 001753
Unit ID: 143048
Telephone: (312) 899-5100 Carnegie Class: Spec/Arts
FAX Number: (312) 263-0141 Calendar System: Semester
URL: www.saic.edu
Established: 1866 Annual Undergrad Tuition & Fees: $36,930
Enrollment: 3,231 Coed
Affiliation or Control: Independent Non-Profit IRS Status: 501(c)3
Highest Offering: Master's
Program: Teacher Preparatory; Fine Arts Emphasis
Accreditation: NH, ART

01 President ..... Mr. Walter MASSEY
00 Chancellor ..... Mr. Tony JONES
05 Interim Dean of Faculty ..... Ms. Lisa WAINWRIGHT
11 Senior VP Planning & COO ..... Mr. Edward J. MCNULTY
84 Vice Pres Enrollment Management ..... Ms. Rose MILKOWSKI
30 VP for Institutional Advancement ..... Ms. Cheryl JESSOGNE
10 Vice President of Finance ..... Mr. Brian ESKER
15 Vice President for Human Resources ..... Mr. Michael NICOLAI
32 Vice Pres/Dean of Student Affairs ..... Dr. Felice DUBLON
20 Vice Provost ..... Mr. Paul COFFEY
35 Dean of Student Life ..... Ms. Deborah MARTIN
21 Exec Dir Academic Accounting ..... Ms. Sherry MISGEN
26 Exec Dir Enroll Mktg & Operations ..... Ms. Maryann SCHAEFER
27 Exec Director Mktg & Graphics ..... Ms. Ann WIENS
29 Assoc Director Alumni Relations ..... Ms. Emily CHAPMAN
38 Exec Director Student Counseling ..... Dr. Joseph BEHEN
84 Exec Director Enrollment Services ..... Ms. Jane BRUMITT
06 Director Registration & Records ..... Mr. Brad ERZ
08 Director of School Library ..... Ms. Claire EIKE
18 Assoc VP Facilities/Operations ..... Mr. Thomas BUECHELE
36 Asst Dean/Dir Career Development ..... Ms. Katharine SCHUTTA
07 Director of Undergrad Admissions ..... Mr. Scott RAMON
07 Director of Graduate Admissions ..... Mr. Andre VAN DE PUTTE
88 Exec Director Web E-Communication ..... Ms. Rae ULRICH
37 Director of Student Financial Svcs ..... Mr. Patrick JAMES
28 Director of Multicultural Affairs ..... Mr. James BRITT
23 Director of Health Services ..... Vacant
09 Enrollment Analyst ..... Mr. Bruce FELKNOR
49 Chair of Undergraduate Division ..... Ms. Tiffany HOLMES
58 Chair of Graduate Division ..... Ms. Candida ALVAREZ

Seabury-Western Theological Seminary (B)

2122 Sheridan Road, Evanston IL 60201-2976
County: Cook FICE Identification: 001754
Unit ID: 148724
Telephone: (847) 328-9300 Carnegie Class: Spec/Faith
FAX Number: (847) 328-9624 Calendar System: Semester
URL: www.seabury.edu
Established: 1858 Annual Graduate Tuition & Fees: N/A
Enrollment: 38 Coed
Affiliation or Control: Protestant Episcopal IRS Status: 501(c)3
Highest Offering: Doctorate; No Undergraduates
Program: Professional; Religious Emphasis
Accreditation: THEOL

01 Interim Dean & President ..... Mr. Robert G. BOTTOMS
03 Vice President & COO ..... Ms. Elizabeth BUTLER JAMESON
05 Academic Dean ..... Rev. Ellen WONDRA
30 VP for Advancement/Administration ..... Rev. Elizabeth S. BUTLER
10 Director of Finance ..... Mr. Mark MILIOTTO
04 Exec Assistant to the Dean ..... Br. Ronald A. FOX, BSG
51 Dir of Continuing Ed & Development ..... Ms. Ruth FREY
08 Director United Library ..... Ms. Beth SHEPPARD
06 Registrar & Admissions ..... Ms. Peggy PEARSON
18 Maintenance Superintendent ..... Mr. Wolfgang WALDERT
44 Annual Campaign Coordinator ..... Ms. Susan QUIGLEY

Shawnee Community College (C)

8364 Shawnee College Road, Ullin IL 62992-2206
County: Pulaski FICE Identification: 007693
Unit ID: 148821
Telephone: (618) 634-3200 Carnegie Class: Assoc/Pub-R-L
FAX Number: (618) 634-3300 Calendar System: Semester
URL: www.shawneecc.edu
Established: 1967 Annual Undergrad Tuition & Fees (In-District): $2,760
Enrollment: 3,915 Coed
Affiliation or Control: Local IRS Status: 501(c)3
Highest Offering: Associate Degree
Program: Occupational; 2-Year Principally Bachelor's Creditable
Accreditation: NH, MLTAD, OTA

01 President ..... Dr. Larry E. PETERSON
05 Vice Pres Instructional Services ..... Dr. Tim H. BELLAMEY
32 Int Vice President Student Svcs ..... Ms. Carolyn KINDLE
04 Asst to President/Human Res Ofcr ..... Ms. Beth DARDEN
20 Dean Instructional Services ..... Ms. Jean Ellen BOYD
51 Dean Adult Educ/Alternative Instruc ..... Mr. James DARDEN
10 Chief Financial Officer ..... Ms. Tiffiney RYAN
38 Student Support Services Director ..... Mr. Jeff MCGOY
35 Dean of Student Services ..... Ms. Dee BLAKELY
37 Dir Fin Aid/Coord Vet & Mil Personl ..... Ms. Tammy CAPPS
41 Athletic Director ..... Mr. Mike FITZGERALD
13 Director MIS ..... Mr. Chris CLARK
12 Director Metro Center ..... Dr. Sally WEST
66 Director of Nursing ..... Ms. Carol BELT
08 Head Librarian ..... Ms. Tracey JOHNSON
06 Registrar ..... Vacant
102 Dir Resource Development/Foundation ..... Mr. Greg LEGAN
21 Director of Business Services ..... Ms. Brandy WOODS
18 Facilities Director ..... Mr. Don KOCH
40 Bookstore Manager ..... Ms. Madonna SLIFE
88 Special Needs Counselor ..... Ms. Annie HUBBARD
88 Coord Ctr for Cmty/Economic Devel ..... Ms. Candy EASTWOOD
26 Public Relations Coordinator ..... Ms. Sharon FELKER
36 Career Services Coordinator ..... Ms. Leslie WELDON
50 Div Chair Business/Occup/Tech Dp ..... Ms. Phyllis SANDER
81 Division Chair Math/Science ..... Ms. Rhonda DILLOW
79 Div Chr Social Stds/Humanities/Comm ..... Ms. Susan WOOLRIDGE

Shimer College (D)

3424 S State Street, Second Floor, Chicago IL 60616-3893
County: Cook FICE Identification: 001756
Unit ID: 148849
Telephone: (312) 235-3500 Carnegie Class: Bac/A&S
FAX Number: (312) 235-3502 Calendar System: Semester
URL: www.shimer.edu
Established: 1853 Annual Undergrad Tuition & Fees: $24,600
Enrollment: 111 Coed
Affiliation or Control: Independent Non-Profit IRS Status: 501(c)3
Highest Offering: Baccalaureate
Program: Liberal Arts And General
Accreditation: NH

01 President ..... Mr. Edward NOONAN
10 Chief Financial Officer/Dir Ops ..... Mr. Marc L. HOFFMAN
05 Dean of the College ..... Dr. Barbara STONE
32 Dean of Students ..... Dr. B David GALT
30 Director of Development ..... Ms. Mary Pat BARBARI
37 Director of Financial Aid ..... Ms. Janet HENTHORN
07 Interim Director of Admissions ..... Ms. Cassie SHERMAN
08 Library Director ..... Ms. Colleen MCCARROLL
06 Registrar ..... Mr. James ULRICH
29 Director Alumni Relations ..... Mr. Aaron GARLAND

SOLEX College (E)

350 E. Dundee Road, Suite 200, Wheeling IL 60090
County: Cook FICE Identification: 041175
Unit ID: 459356
Telephone: (847) 229-9595 Carnegie Class: Not Classified
FAX Number: (847) 229-1919 Calendar System: Other
Established: 1995 Annual Undergrad Tuition & Fees: $17,200
Enrollment: 28 Coed
Affiliation or Control: Proprietary IRS Status: Proprietary
Highest Offering: Associate Degree
Program: Occupational; Business Emphasis
Accreditation: ACICS, COMTA

01 Executive Director ..... Mr. Leon E. LINTON

South Suburban College of Cook County (F)

15800 S State Street, South Holland IL 60473-1270
County: Cook FICE Identification: 001769
Unit ID: 149365
Telephone: (708) 596-2000 Carnegie Class: Assoc/Pub-S-SC
FAX Number: (708) 210-5710 Calendar System: Semester
URL: www.ssc.edu
Established: 1927 Annual Undergrad Tuition & Fees (In-District): $3,113
Enrollment: 7,161 Coed
Affiliation or Control: State/Local IRS Status: 501(c)3
Highest Offering: Associate Degree
Program: Occupational; 2-Year Principally Bachelor's Creditable
Accreditation: NH, ADNUR, MAC, MUS, OTA, PNUR

01 President ..... Mr. George DAMMER
05 Vice President Academic Services ..... Dr. Diane OSTOJIC
11 Vice Pres Administrative Services ..... Mr. Don MANNING
32 Vice President Student Development ..... Ms. Songie MILHOUSE
84 VP Enrollment/Community Education ..... Mrs. Jane Ellen STOCKER
35 Dean Student Development ..... Mr. Greg LAWRENCE
83 Dean Legal Studies/Soc & Behav Sci ..... Mr. Ronald KAWANNA, JR.
50 Dean Business & Technology ..... Mr. James COATES
51 Director Continuing Education ..... Ms. Shirley DREWENSKI
76 Dean Health Professions & Sciences ..... Mr. Jeff WADDY
57 Dean Fine Arts/Soc & Behav Sci/Bus ..... Mr. Tom GOVAN, JR.
66 Dean Nursing/Fine Arts/English/Hum ..... Ms. Marjorie ROACHE
10 Controller/Treasurer ..... Mr. Tim POLLERT
26 Director Public Rels/Pub & Found ..... Mr. Patrick RUSH
14 Director Network Systems/Info Tech ..... Mr. John MCCORMACK
35 Assoc Dean Student Services ..... Mrs. Patrice BURTON
88 Dir New Student Ctr & Retenion Svcs ..... Mrs. Jazaer FARRAR
84 Director Enrollment Services ..... Mrs. Robin RIHACEK
37 Director of Financial Aid ..... Mr. John SEMPLE
18 Director Physical Plant ..... Mr. Martin LAREAU
24 Dir Communication Svcs/Media Design ..... Mrs. Lisa MILLER
41 Athletic Director ..... Mr. Steve RUZICH
09 Director of Institutional Research ..... Mr. Kevin RIORDAN
15 Director Human Resources ..... Ms. Kim PIGATTI

Southeastern Illinois College (G)

3575 College Road, Harrisburg IL 62946-4925
County: Saline FICE Identification: 001757
Unit ID: 148937
Telephone: (618) 252-5400 Carnegie Class: Assoc/Pub-R-L
FAX Number: (618) 252-3156 Calendar System: Semester
URL: www.sic.edu
Established: 1960 Annual Undergrad Tuition & Fees (In-District): $5,500
Enrollment: 2,356 Coed
Affiliation or Control: State/Local IRS Status: 501(c)3
Highest Offering: Associate Degree
Program: Occupational; 2-Year Principally Bachelor's Creditable
Accreditation: NH, MLTAD, OTA

01 President ..... Dr. Jonah RICE
05 Vice President Instruction ..... Dr. Dana KEATING
10 VP Administration/Business Affairs ..... Mr. Tim WALKER
32 Dean of Enrollment Mgt & Stdnt Dev ..... Mr. Chad FLANNERY
20 Dean of Career & Technical Educ ..... Mrs. Karen WEISS
103 Assoc Dean of Workforce & Cmty Ed ..... Mrs. Lori COX
08 Head Librarian ..... Mr. Gary JONES
84 Director Enrollment Services ..... Ms. Sarah ADAMS
26 Marketing Coordinator ..... Ms. Angela WILSON
37 Financial Aid Director ..... Ms. Emily HENSON
13 Chief Information Officer ..... Mr. Greg MCCULLOCH
76 Director Allied Health & Nursing ..... Ms. Gina SIRACH
15 Human Resources Administrator ..... Mrs. Barbara POTTER
06 Registrar ..... Ms. Sarah ADAMS
18 Director of Environmental Services ..... Mr. Ed FITZGERALD

*Southern Illinois University (H)

Stone Center, Carbondale IL 62901-6801
County: Jackson FICE Identification: 008237
Unit ID: 149240
Telephone: (618) 536-3331 Carnegie Class: N/A
FAX Number: (618) 536-3404
URL: www.siu.edu

01 President ..... Dr. Glenn POSHARD
05 Vice President Academic Affairs ..... Dr. Paul SARVELA
10 Sr VP Financial/Admin Affs/Bd Treas ..... Dr. Duane STUCKY
88 Director Risk Management ..... Ms. Chris GLIDEWELL
86 Exec Dir of Governmental Public Aff ..... Mr. David GROSS
21 Exec Dir of Internal Audits ..... Ms. Kim LABONTE
43 Int General Couns & Legal Svcs ..... Mr. Jeffrey C. MCCLELLAN
04 Assistant to the President ..... Ms. Paula S. KEITH

*Southern Illinois University Carbondale (I)

425 Clocktower Drive, Carbondale IL 62901-4701
County: Jackson FICE Identification: 001758
Unit ID: 149222
Telephone: (618) 453-2121 Carnegie Class: RU/H
FAX Number: (618) 453-3250 Calendar System: Semester
URL: siuc.edu/
Established: 1869 Annual Undergrad Tuition & Fees (In-State): $11,038
Enrollment: 20,037 Coed
Affiliation or Control: State IRS Status: 501(c)3
Highest Offering: Doctorate
Program: Occupational; 2-Year Principally Bachelor's Creditable; Liberal Arts And General; Teacher Preparatory; Professional
Accreditation: NH, AAB, ARCPA, ART, BUS, BUSA, CACREP, CEA, CIDA, CLPSY, COPSY, CORE, CS, DH, DIETD, DIETI, DMS, ENG, ENGT, FOR, FUSER, IFSAC, IPSY, JOUR, LAW, MED, MLTAD, MUS, NAIT, NRPA, PH, PTAA, RADDOS, RTT, SP, SPAA, SW, TED, THEA

02 Chancellor ..... Dr. Rita CHENG
05 Provost & Vice Chancellor ..... Dr. John NICKLOW
32 Assoc VC Stdnt Life & Intercul Rels ..... Dr. Peter GITAU
30 Vice Chanc Inst Advancement ..... Dr. Rickey N. MCCURRY
10 VC for Administration and Finance ..... Mr. Kevin BAME
11 Exec Dir of Administration ..... Ms. Cathy HAGLER
46 Assoc VC Rsrch & Dir Rsrch Dev/Adv ..... Dr. Prudence M. RICE
28 Interim Assoc Chancellor Diversity ..... Dr. Linda MCCABE-SMITH
102 Asst Vice Chanc SIU Foundation ..... Mr. Bryan VAGNER
84 Int Asst Provost Enrollment Mgmt ..... Vacant
04 Assistant to the Chancellor ..... Mr. Jake BAGGOTT
49 Dean Liberal Arts ..... Dr. Alan C. VAUX

50 Dean Business/Administration ... Dr. J. D. CRADIT
53 Dean Education & Human Services ... Dr. Kenneth TEITELBAUM
54 Acting Dean Engineering ... Dr. Gary KOLB
58 Dean Graduate School ... Dr. John A. KOROPCHAK
61 Dean School of Law ... Dr. Cynthia FOUNTAINE
81 Dean Science ... Dr. Jay C. MEANS
63 Dean School of Medicine ... Dr. John K. DORSEY
47 Dean Agricultural Sciences ... Dr. Todd WINTERS
72 Dean Col Applied Sciences & Arts ... Mr. Terry OWENS
57 Dean Mass Comm/Media Arts ... Mr. Gary P. KOLB
08 Dean Library Affairs ... Mr. David H. CARLSON
07 Director Undergrad Admissions ... Ms. Patsy REYNOLDS
37 Director Student Financial Aid ... Ms. Terry HARFST
29 Associate VC Alumni Services ... Ms. Michelle SUAREZ
21 Director Budget ... Ms. Carol A. HENRY
09 Director Institutional Research ... Mr. Lawrence SCHILLING
88 University Ombudsman ... Mr. Donald BIXLER
13 Co-Interim Dir Information Tech ... Mr. Kevin BAME
13 Co-Interim Dir Information Tech ... Ms. Judith MARSHALL
27 Director University Communications ... Dr. Mike RUIZ
15 Director Human Resources ... Ms. Jennifer WATSON
39 Director University Housing ... Ms. Julie P. KIRCHMEIER
36 Int Director Univ Career Services ... Ms. Cynthia JENKINS
85 Int Director Intl Pgms & Svcs ... Ms. Carla E. COPPI
18 Director Plant/Service Operations ... Mr. Philip S. GATTON
19 Director of Public Safety ... Mr. Todd D. SIGLER
23 Director Student Health Center ... Dr. Ted W. GRACE
41 Director Intercollegiate Athletics ... Mr. Mario L. MOCCIA
51 Assoc Director Continuing Education ... Ms. Sandy RHOADS
06 Int Director Records & Registration ... Ms. Tiffany SPENCER
20 Assoc Provost for Academic Admin ... Ms. Susan LOGUE
38 Director Student Counseling Center ... Dr. Rosemary E. SIMMONS
96 Director of Purchasing ... Mr. Wallace S. BURMAN
35 Director Student Development ... Dr. Katherine L. SERMERSHEIM

*Southern Illinois University Edwardsville (A)

Edwardsville IL 62026-0001
County: Madison FICE Identification: 001759
Unit ID: 149231
Telephone: (618) 650-2000 Carnegie Class: Master's L
FAX Number: (618) 650-2270 Calendar System: Semester
URL: www.siue.edu
Established: 1957 Annual Undergrad Tuition & Fees (In-State): $8,865
Enrollment: 14,133 Coed
Affiliation or Control: State IRS Status: 501(c)3
Highest Offering: Beyond Master's But Less Than Doctorate
Program: Liberal Arts And General; Teacher Preparatory; Professional
Accreditation: NH, THEA, ANEST, BUS, BUSA, CONST, CS, DENT, ENG, JOUR, MLTAD, MUS, NURSE, PHAR, SP, SPAA, SW, TED

02 Chancellor ... Dr. Vaughn VANDEGRIFT
05 Interim Prov & VC for Academic Affs ... Dr. Ann M. BOYLE
11 Vice Chancellor for Administration ... Mr. Kenneth R. NEHER
26 VC Univ Rel & CEO SIUE Foundation ... Mr. Patrick HUNDLEY
32 Vice Chanc for Student Affairs ... Dr. Narbeth R. EMMANUEL
100 Executive Asst to the Chancellor ... Ms. Kimberly H. DURR
22 Asst Chanc for Institutional Compli ... Mr. Paul PITTS
20 Assoc Prov for Acad Plng & Pgm Dev ... Dr. Susan L. THOMAS
20 Acting Assc Prov Rsch/Dean Grad Sch ... Dr. Jerry B. WEINBERG
35 Assoc VC Stdnt Affs/Dean of Stdnts ... Dr. James W. KLENKE
35 Assoc VC for Student Affairs ... Ms. Lora MILES
13 Assoc VC for IT & CIO ... Ms. Jennifer VANDEVER
28 Assoc Prov Inst Diversity/Inclusion ... Dr. Venessa BROWN
88 Asst Prov for Acad Innov & Eff ... Ms. Victoria SCOTT
41 Asst VC Athletic Dev/Dir Athletics ... Dr. Bradley L. HEWITT
84 Asst VC for Enrollment Mgmt ... Mr. Scott BELOBRAJDIC
45 Asst VC for Planning & Budgeting ... Mr. Richard WALKER
49 Dean College of Arts & Sciences ... Dr. Aldemaro ROMERO
50 Dean School of Business ... Dr. Gary A. GIAMARTINO
52 Interim Dean Sch of Dental Medicine ... Dr. Bruce E. ROTTER
53 Dean School of Education ... Dr. Bette BERGERON
54 Dean School of Engineering ... Dr. Hasan SEVIM
66 Dean School of Nursing ... Dr. Marcia C. MAURER
67 Dean School of Pharmacy ... Dr. Gireesh V. GUPCHUP
62 Dean Library & Information Services ... Dr. Regina MCBRIDE
21 Budget Director ... Mr. William F. WINTER, JR.
27 Asst VC Univ Rel/Exec Dir Univ M&C ... Ms. Elizabeth M. KESERAUSKIS
51 Exec Director Educational Outreach ... Vacant
12 Exec Dir of East St Louis Center ... Dr. Venessa BROWN
88 Director Academic Advising ... Ms. Cheryle L. TUCKER-LOEWE
07 Director Admissions ... Mr. Todd C. BURRELL
29 Director Alumni Affairs ... Mr. Stephen E. JANKOWSKI
36 Director Career Dev Center ... Ms. Susan SEIBERT
38 Director Counseling Services ... Dr. Andrew B. KING
18 Director Facilities Management ... Mr. Robert B. WASHBURN
23 Director Health Services ... Ms. Riane B. GREENWALT
15 Director Human Resources ... Ms. Sherrie SENKFOR
09 Dir Institutional Rsrch & Studies ... Mr. Phillip M. BROWN
85 Director Ctr for International Pgms ... Dr. Ronald P. SCHAEFER
96 Director of Purchasing ... Ms. Nancy J. UFERT FAIRLESS
37 Director Student Financial Aid ... Ms. Sharon L. BERRY
102 Dir Univ Advancement/Foundation Ops ... Mr. Kevin MARTIN
39 Director University Housing ... Mr. Michael J. SCHULTZ
19 Director University Police ... Ms. Regina M. HAYS
06 Registrar ... Ms. Laura A. STROM

Southwestern Illinois College (B)

2500 Carlyle Avenue, Belleville IL 62221-5899
County: Saint Clair FICE Identification: 001636
Unit ID: 143215
Telephone: (618) 235-2700 Carnegie Class: Assoc/Pub-S-MC
FAX Number: (618) 277-0631 Calendar System: Semester
URL: www.swic.edu
Established: 1946 Annual Undergrad Tuition & Fees (In-District): $3,040
Enrollment: 82,154 Coed
Affiliation or Control: State/Local IRS Status: 501(c)3
Highest Offering: Associate Degree
Program: Occupational; 2-Year Principally Bachelor's Creditable
Accreditation: NH, ACFEI, ADNUR, MAC, MLTAD, PTAA, RAD

01 President - District ... Dr. Georgia COSTELLO
10 Board Treasurer/Controller ... Ms. Tammy L. CLARK
11 Vice Pres Administrative Svcs ... Mr. Bernie J. YSURSA
05 Vice Pres Instruction ... Mr. Clay L. BAITMAN
31 Vice Pres Community Svcs ... Dr. Valerie L. THAXTON
26 Vice Pres Mktg/Institutional Adv ... Mr. Mike R. FLEMING
09 Vice Pres Planning/Evaluation/Dev ... Mr. H. O. BROWNBACK
15 Vice Pres Human Resources/Org Devel ... Mr. Larry V. FRIEDERICH
32 Vice Pres Student Development ... Ms. Staci G. CLAYBORNE
20 Assoc Dean Instructional Services ... Ms. Patricia POU
12 Executive Director SWGCC ... Mr. Charles L. WHITEHEAD
12 Executive Director Red Bud Campus ... Mr. Mike REED
30 Interim Exec Director Foundation ... Mr. Gary E. GRAY
25 Grants Administrator ... Dr. Mark P. EICHENLAUB
08 Dean Learning Resources ... Ms. Laurie A. BINGEL
37 Director of Financial Aid/Placement ... Ms. Marsha K. GARNER
13 Chief Information Officer ... Mrs. Christine LEJA
18 Director of Physical Plant ... Mr. Ron R. HENDERSON
19 Director of Public Safety ... Mr. Mark A. GREEN
38 Interim Dean of Counseling ... Ms. Martha H. NELSON
96 Director of Purchasing ... Mr. Mike R. THOMAS
76 Dean Hlth Sci and Homeland Security ... Ms. Julie A. MUERTZ
50 Dean of Business Division ... Ms. Janet S. FONTENOT
72 Dean of Technical Education ... Mr. Brad SPARKS
81 Dean of Math & Science ... Ms. Amanda M. STARKEY
49 Dean of Liberal Arts ... Dr. Paul W. WREFORD
51 Director Adult Education/Cont Educ ... Dr. Suzanne C. DAILEY
07 Dean of Enrollment Services ... Ms. Michelle L. BIRK
28 Director of Diversity ... Ms. Donna MOODY
88 Director Green Jobs/Green Economy ... Ms. Karen STALLMAN
88 Dean of Success Programs ... Ms. Deborah ALFORD
88 Treasurer IL Green Economy Network ... Mr. Robert J. HILGENBRINK

Spertus College (C)

610 S Michigan Avenue, Chicago IL 60605-1994
County: Cook FICE Identification: 001663
Unit ID: 148982
Telephone: (312) 322-1700 Carnegie Class: Spec/Other
FAX Number: (312) 922-6406 Calendar System: Quarter
URL: www.spertus.edu
Established: 1924 Annual Graduate Tuition & Fees: $18,750
Enrollment: 343 Coed
Affiliation or Control: Independent Non-Profit IRS Status: 501(c)3
Highest Offering: Doctorate; No Undergraduates
Program: Liberal Arts And General; Teacher Preparatory; Professional
Accreditation: NH

01 President ... Dr. Hal M. LEWIS
05 Dean ... Dr. Dean BELL
51 Director for Public Programing ... Ms. Beth SCHENKER
10 Director Finance & Administration ... Mr. Charles DRAPER
88 Director Nonprofit Admin Program ... Dr. Karen BAIRD
37 Student Records/Financial Aid Mgr ... Ms. Lisa DEL SESTO

Spoon River College (D)

23235 N County Road 22, Canton IL 61520-9801
County: Fulton FICE Identification: 001643
Unit ID: 148991
Telephone: (309) 647-4645 Carnegie Class: Assoc/Pub-R-M
FAX Number: (309) 649-6235 Calendar System: Semester
URL: www.src.edu
Established: 1959 Annual Undergrad Tuition & Fees (In-District): $3,090
Enrollment: 2,373 Coed
Affiliation or Control: Local IRS Status: 501(c)3
Highest Offering: Associate Degree
Program: Occupational; 2-Year Principally Bachelor's Creditable
Accreditation: NH

01 President ... Dr. Robert E. RITSCHEL
05 Vice President Inst/Student Svcs ... Dr. Randall GREENWELL
11 Vice President Admin Services ... Mr. Brett STOLLER
31 Vice President Community Outreach ... Ms. Carol DAVIS
04 Executive Asst to the President ... Ms. Julie HAMPTON
36 Dean Career & Technical Education ... Mr. Robert OGLE
32 Dean Student Services ... Mr. Gary SCHINDLER
66 Dean Nursing ... Ms. Cheryl A. HOFFMAN
88 Dean Transfer Education ... Ms. Renee HIGGINS
18 Director Facilities ... Mr. Bob A. HAILE
53 Dir Secondary Education Programs ... Mr. Chad MURPHY
08 Director Library Services ... Ms. Kathleen A. MENANTEAUX
13 Chief Information Officer ... Mr. Raj SIDDARAJU
41 Director Athletics/Student Life ... Mr. Ron CLARK
21 Director Business Services ... Ms. Sarah GRAY
37 Director Financial Aid ... Ms. Salinda Jo BRANSON
40 Dir Purchasing & Auxiliary Services ... Mr. Brad T. O'BRIEN
15 Director Human Resources ... Ms. Michelle L. BUGOS
14 Director Technology Services ... Mr. Dean CLARY
84 Director Enrollment Services ... Ms. Missy A. WILKINSON
13 Director Information Services ... Ms. Patty SCHMIDT

09 Coord Institutional Reporting ... Ms. Neelima SINGH
26 Coordinator Marketing ... Ms. Anna R. BUEHRER
27 Coordinator College Information ... Ms. Sally SHIELDS

Taylor Business Institute (E)

318 W Adams Street, Suite 500, Chicago IL 60606
County: Cook FICE Identification: 011810
Unit ID: 149310
Telephone: (312) 658-5100 Carnegie Class: Assoc/PrivFP
FAX Number: (312) 658-0867 Calendar System: Quarter
URL: www.tbiil.edu
Established: 1962 Annual Undergrad Tuition & Fees: $13,500
Enrollment: 431 Coed
Affiliation or Control: Proprietary IRS Status: Proprietary
Highest Offering: Associate Degree
Program: Occupational
Accreditation: ACICS

01 President ... Mrs. Janice C. PARKER

Telshe Yeshiva-Chicago (F)

3535 W Foster Avenue, Chicago IL 60625-5598
County: Cook FICE Identification: 020732
Unit ID: 149329
Telephone: (773) 463-7738 Carnegie Class: Spec/Faith
FAX Number: (773) 463-2849 Calendar System: Semester
Established: 1960 Annual Undergrad Tuition & Fees: $14,200
Enrollment: 87 Male
Affiliation or Control: Independent Non-Profit IRS Status: 501(c)3
Highest Offering: Second Talmudic Degree
Program: Professional
Accreditation: RABN

01 President ... Rabbi Avrohom C. LEVIN
03 Executive Vice President ... Rabbi Yitzchok LEVIN
05 Vice President ... Rabbi Chaim D. KELLER
05 Vice President ... Rabbi Moshe SCHMELCZER
11 Administrative Director/Secretary ... Rabbi Shmuel ADLER

Toyota Technological Institute at Chicago (G)

1427 E. 60th Street, Chicago IL 60637-2902
County: Cook Identification: 666367
Unit ID: 445054
Telephone: (773) 834-2500 Carnegie Class: Assoc/PrivNFP4
FAX Number: (773) 834-9881 Calendar System: Quarter
URL: www.ttic.edu
Established: 2003 Annual Graduate Tuition & Fees: $30,000
Enrollment: 12 Coed
Affiliation or Control: Independent Non-Profit IRS Status: 501(c)3
Highest Offering: Doctorate; No Undergraduates
Program: Professional; Technical Emphasis
Accreditation: NH

01 Interim President ... Dr. Stuart A. RICE
05 Chief Academic Officer ... Dr. David MCALLESTER
10 Treasurer/Secretary of the Board ... Mr. Motohisa NOGUCHI
11 Chief Administrator ... Mr. Gary HAMBURG
58 Director of Graduate Studies ... Dr. Nathan SREBRO
21 Controller ... Ms. Anna RUFFULO
15 Human Resources Coordinator ... Ms. Carole FLEMMING

Tribeca Flashpoint Media Arts Academy (H)

28 North Clark Street, Suite 500, Chicago IL 60602
County: Cook Identification: 667083
Telephone: (312) 332-0707 Carnegie Class: Not Classified
FAX Number: (312) 506-0708 Calendar System: Semester
URL: www.tfa.edu
Established: 2007 Annual Undergrad Tuition & Fees: $25,500
Enrollment: 485 Coed
Affiliation or Control: Proprietary IRS Status: Proprietary
Highest Offering: Associate Degree
Program: Occupational; 2-Year Principally Bachelor's Creditable
Accreditation: ACICS

01 President ... Howard A. TULLMAN
05 Exec VP/Dean Academic Affairs ... Paula M. FROEHLE
10 Exec VP/Chief Financial Officer ... Mario CHRISTOPHER
15 Sr VP/Human Resources/Career Svcs ... Jill GEIMER
07 Sr VP/Director Admissions ... Heather SWANSON
11 Sr VP Operations ... Ernesto PARAS
26 VP Marketing/Business Development ... Edward GLASSMAN
13 VP Technology ... John SCHLAUCH
32 VP/Assoc Dean of Students ... Benjamin J. SPANNER
06 Registrar ... Brad BERGERON
21 Controller ... Laura PETRY

Trinity Christian College (I)

6601 W College Drive, Palos Heights IL 60463-0929
County: Cook FICE Identification: 001771
Unit ID: 149505
Telephone: (708) 597-3000 Carnegie Class: Bac/Diverse
FAX Number: (708) 385-5665 Calendar System: 4/1/4
URL: www.trnty.edu
Established: 1959 Annual Undergrad Tuition & Fees: $22,232

Enrollment: 1,491 Coed
Affiliation or Control: Independent Non-Profit IRS Status: 501(c)3
Highest Offering: Baccalaureate
Program: Liberal Arts And General; Teacher Preparatory; Professional
Accreditation: NH, ACBSP, NURSE, SW

01 President ... Dr. Steven TIMMERMANS
05 Provost ... Dr. Elizabeth RUDENGA
10 Vice Pres for Business & Finance ... Mr. James E. BELSTRA
26 Vice Pres for Admissions/Marketing ... Mr. Pete HAMSTRA
32 Vice President Student Development ... Mrs. Ginny CARPENTER
30 Vice Pres for Development ... Mr. Larryl HUMME
11 Vice Pres for Campus Development ... Dr. George VANDER VELDE
08 Director of Library Services ... Ms. Marcille FREDERICK
06 Registrar ... Mr. Chris HUANG
07 Director of Admissions ... Mr. Jeremy KLYN
36 Director Career Planning/Placement ... Mrs. Jackie MEDENBLIK
55 Director of Adult Studies Programs ... Dr. Lori SCREMENTI
29 Director of Alumni Relations ... Mr. Travis BANDSTRA
27 Dir of Marketing and Communications ... Ms. Kim FABIAN
88 Asst Dir Marketing/Graphic Designer ... Mr. Peter CLEVERING
44 Campaign Gifts Manager ... Vacant
14 Director of Computer Services ... Mr. Joe VELDERMAN
41 Director of Athletics ... Mr. Josh LENARZ
31 Director of Community Partnerships ... Ms. Anna ROSAS
42 Chaplain ... Dr. Willis VAN GRONINGEN
85 Director of Off-Campus Programs ... Dr. Burton J. ROZEMA
37 Director Financial Aid ... Ms. Denise COLEMAN
18 Director of Building/Grounds ... Mr. Tim TIMMONS
44 Director of Planned Giving ... Mr. Ken BOSS
21 Controller ... Mr. Mike TROCHUCK
28 Dir of Diversity/Acad Dean/Ed Prof ... Mr. Don WOO
92 Dean of Honors Program ... Dr. Aron REPPMANN
35 Director Student Affairs/Counseling ... Mrs. Ginny CARPENTER
84 Director Enrollment Management ... Mr. Pete HAMSTRA
09 Asst Registar for Inst Research ... Ms. Kimberly WILLIAMS
15 Human Resources Manager ... Mr. Larry BOER
20 Acad Dean/Mathematics Prof ... Dr. Sharon ROBBERT
20 Acad Dean/Social Work Prof ... Dr. Mackenzi HUYSER

Trinity College of Nursing & Health Sciences (A)

2122 25th Avenue, Rock Island IL 61201-5317
County: Rock Island FICE Identification: 006225
Unit ID: 146755
Telephone: (309) 779-7700 Carnegie Class: Spec/Health
FAX Number: (309) 779-7748 Calendar System: Semester
URL: www.trinitycollegeqc.edu
Established: 1994 Annual Undergrad Tuition & Fees: $13,272
Enrollment: 248 Coed
Affiliation or Control: Independent Non-Profit IRS Status: 501(c)3
Highest Offering: Baccalaureate
Program: Professional; Nursing Emphasis
Accreditation: NH, ADNUR, NURSE, RAD

01 Chancellor ... Dr. Susan C. WAJERT
05 Dean of Nursing & Health Sciences ... Ms. Tracy L. POELVOORDE
32 Dir of Student Svcs/External Rels ... Ms. Joann M. LAY

Trinity International University (B)

2065 Half Day Road, Deerfield IL 60015-1284
County: Lake FICE Identification: 001772
Unit ID: 149514
Telephone: (847) 945-8800 Carnegie Class: DRU
FAX Number: (847) 317-8090 Calendar System: Semester
URL: www.tiu.edu
Established: 1897 Annual Undergrad Tuition & Fees: $23,370
Enrollment: 2,730 Coed
Affiliation or Control: Evangelical Free Church Of America
IRS Status: 501(c)3
Highest Offering: Doctorate
Program: Liberal Arts And General; Teacher Preparatory; Professional
Accreditation: NH, THEOL

01 President ... Dr. Craig WILLIFORD
04 Assistant to President's Office ... Dr. Milo F. LUNDELL
03 Exec Vice President & Provost ... Dr. Jeanette HSIEH
05 Sr VP Education/Dean Divinity Sch ... Dr. Tite TIENOU
20 Sr Vice President Academic Affairs ... Dr. Robert HERRON
84 Sr VP for Enrollment Management ... Mr. Roger L. KIEFFER
32 Sr VP Stdnt Affs/Dn Stdnts/Athl Dir ... Dr. William O. WASHINGTON
13 Sr VP Information Technology/Plng ... Mr. Steven GEGGIE
30 Sr Vice Pres University Advancement ... Dr. David HOAG
10 Sr VP of Business & Finance/CFO ... Mr. Mike PICHA
44 Vice President of Development ... Mr. Carl JOHNSON
26 Vice Pres Communication/Marketing ... Mr. Gary CANTWELL
21 University Controller ... Mr. Paul EISENMENGER
73 Assoc Academic Dean Divinity School ... Dr. James R. MOORE
88 Assoc Dean of Nontraditional Educ ... Ms. Margaret R. CONNER
35 Assoc Dean of Undergraduate Stdnts ... Mr. Greg LEEPER
90 Director of Acad/Desktop Computing ... Mr. Chris MILLER
91 Director Administrative Computing ... Ms. Katie KEMP
23 Director of Health Services ... Ms. Barbara VIETMEIER
58 Assoc Dean of Graduate School ... Dr. Joyce A. SHELTON
61 Dean of Law School ... Mr. Donald R. MCCONNELL
42 Chaplain ... Rev. David WHITED
07 Director Undergraduate Admissions ... Mr. Aaron MAHL
07 Director TEDS & TGS Admissions ... Dr. Ron CAMPBELL
19 Director of Security Services ... Mr. Brian OLSON
96 Director Purchasing & Retail Svcs ... Mr. Patrick SMITH
15 Director of Human Resources ... Ms. Janet CRAIGMILES
06 Assoc University Registrar ... Mr. David SKINNER
37 Director of Financial Aid ... Ms. Patricia COLES
36 Director of Career Services ... Ms. Kelly MULLEN
36 Director of Placement ... Dr. Eugene SWANSTROM
08 University Librarian ... Dr. Robert H. KRAPOHL
29 Director of Alumni ... Mr. Ryan L. FINNELLY
27 Director of Publications ... Mr. Jeff CALHOUN
38 Director of Counseling Center ... Ms. Cathy CONWAY
28 Director of Ethnic Diversity ... Mr. Orlando FELICIANO
92 Director of Honors Program ... Dr. Steven POINTER
35 Director of Student Activities ... Mr. Adam GUSTINE
85 International Student Coordinator ... Mr. Felix THEONUGRAHA
39 Housing Coordinator ... Mrs. Amy HORTON

Triton College (C)

2000 Fifth Avenue, River Grove IL 60171-1995
County: Cook FICE Identification: 001773
Unit ID: 149532
Telephone: (708) 456-0300 Carnegie Class: Assoc/Pub-S-SC
FAX Number: (708) 583-3112 Calendar System: Semester
URL: www.triton.edu
Established: 1964 Annual Undergrad Tuition & Fees (In-District): $2,790
Enrollment: 16,432 Coed
Affiliation or Control: Local IRS Status: 501(c)3
Highest Offering: Associate Degree
Program: Occupational; 2-Year Principally Bachelor's Creditable; Business Emphasis
Accreditation: NH, ADNUR, CACREP, DMS, NMT, RAD, SURGT

01 President ... Dr. Patricia GRANADOS
10 Vice President Business Services ... Mr. Sean SULLIVAN
05 Vice President Academic Affairs ... Dr. Angela LATHAM
32 Vice Pres Student Affairs ... Mr. Douglas OLSON
101 Coord for Brd of Trustees/Exec Asst ... Ms. Susan PAGE
13 Assoc Vice Pres Information Systems ... Mr. Terence FELTON
21 Assoc VP Business Operations ... Mr. Kevin KENNEDY
18 Assoc VP Facilities ... Mr. John LAMBRECHT
20 Assoc Vice Pres Academic Affairs ... Ms. Cheryl ANTONICH
35 Dean of Student Services ... Mr. Quincy MARTIN
84 Dean of Enrollment Services ... Ms. Mary Rita MOORE
21 Director Finance ... Mr. James REYNOLDS
45 Director Planning & Accreditation ... Ms. Margaret STABILE
25 Director of Grants Development ... Dr. Sherry BURLINGAME
88 Director Teaching & Learning ... Dr. Mary Ann TOBIN
26 Executive Director Marketing ... Mr. Thomas OLSON
07 Director Admissions Services ... Mr. Sujith ZACHARIAH
37 Director Financial Aid ... Ms. Patricia ZINGA
19 Chief of Police ... Mr. Jeffrey SARGENT
102 Director Triton Foundation ... Ms. Susan KERR
31 Dir Spec Initiatives/Community Rels ... Ms. Lindsey WESTLEY
09 Dir Institutional Effectiveness ... Dr. William EDWARDS
14 Sr Tech Architect/Database Admin ... Mr. Humberto ESPINO
91 Director Programming Services ... Mr. Michael GARRITY
102 Asst Director Corporate Outreach ... Ms. Susan SMEDINGHOFF
90 Manager Online Technology ... Mr. Darren ROBARDS
86 Outreach/Communications Assistant ... Ms. Brenda JONES WATKINS
72 Instructional Technologist ... Ms. Marie-Ange ZICHER
49 Dean Arts & Sciences ... Mr. Jonathan PAVER
51 Dean of Continuing Education ... Mr. Paul JENSEN
76 Dean Health Careers & Pub Svc Pro ... Dr. Sue COLLINS
55 Interim Dean of Adult Education ... Ms. Elsa FIGUEROA
09 Dean of Academic Success ... Ms. Deborah BANESS KING
49 Asst Dean of Arts & Sciences ... Mr. Ric SEGOVIA
51 Asst Dean Continuing Education ... Mr. Jon GRIGALUNAS
29 Director Alumni Relations ... Ms. Lisa SCALESSI
50 Dean Business & Technology ... Ms. Antoinette BALDIN

University of Chicago (D)

5801 S Ellis Avenue, Chicago IL 60637-1496
County: Cook FICE Identification: 001774
Unit ID: 144050
Telephone: (773) 702-1234 Carnegie Class: RU/VH
FAX Number: N/A Calendar System: Quarter
URL: www.uchicago.edu
Established: 1891 Annual Undergrad Tuition & Fees: $41,853
Enrollment: 15,644 Coed
Affiliation or Control: Independent Non-Profit IRS Status: 501(c)3
Highest Offering: Doctorate
Program: Liberal Arts And General; Teacher Preparatory; Professional
Accreditation: NH, BUS, IPSY, LAW, MED, SW, THEOL

01 President ... Mr. Robert J. ZIMMER
05 Provost ... Mr. Thomas F. ROSENBAUM
03 Executive Vice President ... Mr. David A. GREENE
10 VP of Administration/CFO ... Mr. Nim CHINNIAH
86 Vice Pres Civic Engagement ... Ms. Ann Marie LIPINSKI
101 VP/Sec of the University ... Mr. David FITHIAN
46 VP for Research/Argonne Natl Lab ... Mr. Donald LEVY
17 EVP for Medical Affairs/Dean of BSD ... Dr. Kenneth POLONSKY
30 VP for Alumni Rel & Development ... Mr. Thomas J. FARRELL
43 Vice President & General Counsel ... Ms. Beth A. HARRIS
88 Vice Pres/Chief Investment Officer ... Mr. Mark SCHMIDT
84 VP/Dean Col Enroll/Financial Aid ... Mr. James NONDORF
42 Dean Rockefeller Memorial Chapel ... Ms. Elizabeth DAVENPORT
32 Vice President & Dean of Students ... Ms. Kimberley GOFF-CREWS
26 Vice Pres for Communications ... Ms. Julie PETERSON
18 Assoc Vice Pres Facilities Services ... Mr. Steve WIESENTHAL
16 Assoc VP Human Resources Mgmt ... Ms. Gwynne DILDAY
09 Assoc VP Rsrch/Dir Rsrch Admin ... Ms. Carol ZUICHES
21 Asst VP Risk Management & Audit ... Mr. Glenn KLINKSIEK
31 Assoc VP for Community Affairs ... Ms. Susan CAMPBELL
35 Ast VP Stdnt Life/Assoc Dean Col ... Ms. Eleanor DAUGHERTY
49 Dean of the College ... Mr. John W. BOYER
83 Dean of Social Sciences Division ... Mr. J. Mark HANSEN
79 Dean of Humanities Division ... Ms. Martha T. ROTH
61 Dean of the Law School ... Mr. Michael SCHILL
88 Dean Harris Sch Public Policy ... Mr. Colm O'MUIRCHEARTAIGH
81 Dean Physical Sciences Division ... Mr. Robert A. FEFFERMAN
88 Dean of the Divinity School ... Ms. Margaret MITCHELL
50 Dean of Booth School of Business ... Mr. Sunil KUMAR
70 Dean Social Svcs Admin ... Mr. Neil GUTERMAN
04 Associate Provost ... Ms. Ingrid E. GOULD
88 Deputy Provost for Research ... Mr. Roy WEISS
20 Deputy Provost for Grad Education ... Ms. Cathy COHEN
28 Deputy Provost for Minority Affairs ... Mr. William MCDADE
22 Assoc Provost/Affirm Action Ofcr ... Ms. Aneesah ALI
45 Assoc Provost for Planning ... Ms. Blair ARCHAMBEAU
20 Associate Provost ... Mr. Stephen H. GABEL
20 Associate Provost ... Ms. Mary J. HARVEY
21 AVP for Finance ... Mr. John R. KROLL
06 Registrar ... Mr. Gabriel G. OLSZEWSKI
07 Director of College Admissions ... Mr. Theodore A. O'NEILL
37 Director College Aid ... Ms. Alicia REYES
36 Co-Dir Career Adv & Planning Svcs ... Ms. Linda CHOI
36 Co-Dir Career Adv & Planning Svcs ... Ms. Meredith DAW
08 Director University Library ... Ms. Judith NADLER
38 Dir Stdnt Counseling/Resource Svc ... Dr. Thomas A M. KRAMER
96 Dir Central Procurement Services ... Mr. Gene SUWANSKI

*University of Illinois University Administration (E)

506 S Wright Street, Urbana IL 61801-3689
County: Champaign FICE Identification: 008001
Unit ID: 149587
Telephone: (217) 333-6400 Carnegie Class: N/A
FAX Number: (217) 333-5733
URL: www.uillinois.edu

01 President ... Dr. Michael J. HOGAN
10 CFO/VP and Comptroller ... Mr. Walter KNORR
05 Vice Pres of Academic Affairs ... Dr. MrinaLini C. RAO
88 Vice Pres for Health Affairs ... Dr. Joe GARCIA
09 Vice Pres for Research ... Dr. Lawrence SCHOOK
43 University Counsel ... Mr. Thomas R. BEARROWS
86 Exec Director for Govt Relations ... Ms. Katherine LAING
26 Exec Dir for University Relations ... Mr. Thomas P. HARDY
13 Executive CIO ... Dr. Michael HITES
16 Executive Director HR ... Ms. Maureen PARKS
101 Secretary Board of Trustees ... Dr. Michele M. THOMPSON
100 Exec Assistant to the President ... Dr. Lisa TROYER

*University of Illinois at Chicago (F)

601 S Morgan, M/C 102, Chicago IL 60607-7128
County: Cook FICE Identification: 001776
Unit ID: 145600
Telephone: (312) 996-7000 Carnegie Class: RU/VH
FAX Number: (312) 413-3393 Calendar System: Semester
URL: www.uic.edu
Established: 1896 Annual Undergrad Tuition & Fees (In-State): $13,464
Enrollment: 27,309 Coed
Affiliation or Control: State IRS Status: 501(c)3
Highest Offering: Doctorate
Program: Liberal Arts And General; Teacher Preparatory; Professional
Accreditation: NH, ART, BUS, BUSA, CEA, CLPSY, CS, DENT, DIETC, DIETD, ENG, ENGR, IPSY, MED, MIDWF, MIL, NURSE, OT, PH, PHAR, PLNG, PTA, SPAA, SW

02 Chancellor ... Dr. Paula ALLEN-MEARES
05 Int Vice Chanc Acad Affairs/Provost ... Dr. Jerry BAUMAN
32 Vice Chancellor Student Affairs ... Dr. Barbara HENLEY
11 Vice Chanc for Administrative Svcs ... Mr. Mark DONOVAN
46 Vice Chancellor for Research ... Dr. Skip GARCIA
26 Vice Chanc for External Affairs ... Dr. Warren CHAPMAN
17 CEO Healthcare System ... Mr. John DENARDO
29 Vice President Alumni Association ... Ms. Arlene NORSYM
30 Vice Chancellor for Development ... Ms. Penelepe C. HUNT
84 Int Vice Prov Acad/Enrollment Svcs ... Ms. Amy LEVANT
35 Assoc Vice Chanc/Dean Stdnt Affairs ... Dr. Linda DEANNA
27 Assoc Chancellor Public Affairs ... Mr. Mark ROSATI
23 Vice Pres for Health Affairs ... Dr. Skip GARCIA
10 Exec Asst VP Business/Finance ... Dr. Heather J. HABERAECKER
48 Dean College Arch & the Arts ... Ms. Judith RUSSI KIRSHNER
50 Int Dean College Business Admin ... Dr. Michael A. PAGANO
52 Dean College Dentistry ... Dr. Bruce GRAHAM
53 Dean College Education ... Dr. Victoria CHOU
54 Dean College Engineering ... Dr. Peter C. NELSON
76 Dean Col Applied Health Sciences ... Dr. Charlotte TATE
58 Interim Dean Graduate College ... Dr. Henri GILLET
92 Dean of the Honors College ... Dr. Bette L. BOTTOMS
49 Int Dean Liberal Arts & Sciences ... Dr. Astrida ORLE TANTILLO
63 Interim Dean College Medicine ... Dr. Dimitri AZAR
66 Dean College Nursing ... Dr. Terri E. WEAVER
67 Acting Dean College Pharmacy ... Dr. Steven SWANSON
70 Dean College Social Work ... Dr. Creasie HAIRSTON
69 Dean School of Public Health ... Dr. Paul BRANDT-RAUF
26 Dean Urban Planning/Public Affs ... Dr. Michael A. PAGANO
43 University Counsel ... Mr. Thomas R. BEARROWS

08 University Librarian ... Ms. Mary CASE
88 Asst Univ Librarian Health Sciences . Ms. Kathryn H. CARPENTER
07 Executive Director Admissions ... Mr. Thomas GLENN
41 Director Athletics ... Mr. James W. SCHMIDT
38 Director Student Counseling ... Dr. Joseph HERMES
37 Director Student Financial Aid ... Mr. Timothy OPGENORTH
09 Director of Institutional Research ... Ms. Mary LELIK
15 Director Faculty Affairs HR ... Ms. Angela L. YUDT
22 Director Access & Equity ... Ms. Caryn A. BILLS-WINDT
36 Director Career Services ... Mr. Andres GARZA
14 Interim Co-Director ... Ms. Cynthia E. HERRERA LINDSTROM
14 Interim Co-Director ... Mr. Robert F. GOLDSTEIN
56 Exec Director External Education ... Ms. Mary P. NIEMIEC
51 Director Continuing Education ... Ms. Cordelia MALONEY
06 Registrar ... Mr. Robert DIXON
96 Interim Director of Purchasing ... Mr. Eugene J. SUWANSKI
18 Director Operations & Maintenance ... Mr. Clarence E. BRIDGES

*University of Illinois at Springfield (A)

One University Plaza, Springfield IL 62703-5407

County: Sangamon — FICE Identification: 009333
Unit ID: 148654
Telephone: (217) 206-6600 — Carnegie Class: Master's L
FAX Number: (217) 206-6511 — Calendar System: Semester
URL: www.uis.edu
Established: 1969 — Annual Undergrad Tuition & Fees (In-State): $2,221
Enrollment: 5,174 — Coed
Affiliation or Control: State — IRS Status: 501(c)3
Highest Offering: Doctorate
Program: Liberal Arts And General; Teacher Preparatory; Professional
Accreditation: NH, BUS, CACREP, MT, SPAA, SW

02 Chancellor ... Dr. Susan KOCH
27 Assoc Chancellor/Constituent Rels ... Mr. Edward WOJCICKI
05 Interim Vice Chancellor Acad Affs ... Ms. Lynn PARDIE
32 Vice Chanc Student Affairs ... Dr. Timothy L. BARNETT
20 Vice Chanc Undergrad Education ... Ms. Karen MORANSKI
29 Vice President Alumni Relations ... Mr. Charles SCHRAGE
30 Associate Chancellor for Development ... Dr. Vicki MEGGINSON
18 Asc Chanc Admin/Exec Dir Facil Svcs ... Mr. David BARROWS
22 Asc Chanc Access/Equal Opportunity ... Ms. Deanie BROWN
49 Dean College Liberal Arts/Science ... Dr. James ERMATINGER
50 Dean College Business/Management ... Dr. Ronald D. MCNEIL
80 Dean College Public Affs/Admin ... Dr. Pinky S. WASSENBERG
53 Dean College Education/Human Svcs ... Dr. Larry D. STONECIPHER
15 Acting Director of Human Resources ... Mr. Robert LAEL
84 Director of Enrollment Management ... Vacant
43 Legal Counsel ... Dr. Mark HENSS
08 University Librarian ... Ms. Jane B. TREADWELL
26 Director Public Information ... Mr. Derek SCHNAPP
20 Associate Provost ... Mr. Aaron G. SHURES
19 Chief Campus Police Department ... Mr. Donald MITCHELL
06 Registrar ... Mr. Brian CLEVENGER
35 Director of Student Life ... Ms. Cynthia THOMPSON
41 Director of Athletics ... Dr. Rodger JEHLICKA
90 Director Campus Technology Service ... Vacant
09 Director Institutional Research ... Ms. Laura DORMAN
96 Director of Purchasing ... Mr. Michael BLOECHLE
37 Director Financial Assistance ... Dr. Gerard JOSEPH
38 Director Counseling Center ... Dr. Judith SHIPP
85 Director International Programs .. Dr. Jonathan GOLDBERGBELLE
24 Assoc Prov Educational Technology ... Mr. Farokh ESLAHI
39 Director Campus Housing ... Mr. John RINGLE

*University of Illinois at Urbana-Champaign (B)

601 E John Street, Champaign IL 61820-5711

County: Champaign — FICE Identification: 001775
Unit ID: 145637
Telephone: (217) 333-1000 — Carnegie Class: RU/VH
FAX Number: (217) 333-9758 — Calendar System: Semester
URL: www.illinois.edu
Established: 1867 — Annual Undergrad Tuition & Fees (In-State): $14,414
Enrollment: 31,253 — Coed
Affiliation or Control: State — IRS Status: 501(c)3
Highest Offering: Doctorate
Program: Occupational; Liberal Arts And General; Teacher Preparatory; Professional
Accreditation: NH, ART, AUD, BUS, BUSA, CLPSY, COPSY, CORE, CS, DANCE, DIETD, DIETI, ENG, FOR, IPSY, JOUR, LAW, LIB, LSAR, MUS, NRPA, PLNG, SP, SW, THEA, VET

02 Int VP and Chancellor ... Dr. Robert EASTER
05 Int Vice Chan Acad Affs & Provost ... Dr. Richard WHEELER
46 Interim Vice Chancellor Research ... Dr. Ravishankar K. IYER
32 Vice Chancellor Student Affairs ... Dr. C. Renee ROMANO
30 Vice Chanc for Inst Advancement ... Dr. James SCHROEDER
31 Int Vice Chanc Public Engagement ... Dr. Steven T. SONKA
20 Vice Provost Academic Affairs ... Dr. Barbara WILSON
88 Associate Chancellor ... Mr. Michael DELORENZO
88 Associate Chancellor ... Mr. William D. ADAMS
26 Associate Chanc Public Affairs ... Ms. Robin KALER
04 Associate Chancellor ... Dr. William E. BERRY
29 Int Assoc Chanc Alumni Relations ... Ms. Vanessa FAURIE
15 Associate Provost Human Resources ... Ms. Elyne COLE
07 Assoc Prov Enrollment Management ... Dr. Keith A. MARSHALL
82 Int Assoc Provost Intl Pgms/Studies ... Dr. Wolfgang SCHLOER
21 Assoc Provost Budgetary Planning ... Mr. Mike ANDRECHAK
09 Assoc Provost Management Info ... Dr. Carol J. LIVINGSTONE
49 Dean Liberal Arts & Sciences ... Dr. Ruth WATKINS
71 Dean Law ... Dr. Bruce SMITH
74 Dean Veterinary Medicine ... Dr. Herbert E. WHITELEY
54 Dean Engineering ... Dr. Ilesanmi ADESIDA
47 Dean Agric/Consumer/Environ Sci ... Dr. Robert HAUSER
50 Dean Business ... Dr. Larry DEBROCK
57 Dean Fine & Applied Arts ... Dr. Robert GRAVES
70 Dean School of Social Work ... Dr. Wynne S. KORR
68 Dean Col Applied Health Sciences ... Dr. Tanya M. GALLAGHER
60 Interim Dean College of Media ... Dr. Janet SLATER
58 Dean Graduate College ... Dr. Debasish DUTTA
62 Dean Grad Sch Library/Info Sci ... Dr. John M. UNSWORTH
53 Dean Education ... Dr. Mary KALANTZIS
63 Int Reg Dean Col Med/Urbana-Champ ... Dr. Uretz S. OLIPHANT
88 Dean School Labor & Employment Rels ... Dr. Joel CUTCHER-GERSHENFELD
08 University Librarian & Dean ... Dr. Paula KAUFMAN
88 Dir Acad Aff Institute of Aviation ... Mr. Tom EMANUEL
13 Interim Chief Information Officer ... Mr. Paul HIXSON
35 Dean of Students ... Dr. Kenneth BALLOM
56 Int Assoc Dean Extension & Outreach ... Dr. Robert HOEFT
41 Director Athletics ... Mr. Ronald E. GUENTHER
10 Asst Vice Pres Bus/Fin Affairs ... Ms. Maxine L. SANDRETTO
43 Campus Legal Counsel ... Mr. Scott RICE
88 Deputy CIO Information Technology ... Ms. Mona HEATH
22 Dir Equal Opportunity & Access ... Dr. Menah PRATT-CLARKE
19 Exec Director Public Safety ... Ms. Barbara R. O'CONNOR
18 Exec Director Facilities Services ... Dr. John G. DEMPSEY
23 Director McKinley Health Center ... Dr. Robert D. PALINKAS
36 Director Career Services Center ... Dr. Gail ROONEY
37 Director Student Financial Aid ... Mr. Daniel R. MANN
38 Director Counseling Center ... Dr. Carla MCCOWAN
39 Director Housing Division ... Mr. John E. COLLINS
51 Int Dir Cont Educ/Public Service ... Dr. Douglas BREWER
06 Registrar ... Ms. Carol E. MALMGREN

University of St. Francis (C)

500 N Wilcox Street, Joliet IL 60435-6188

County: Will — FICE Identification: 001664
Unit ID: 148584
Telephone: (815) 740-3400 — Carnegie Class: Master's L
FAX Number: (815) 740-4285 — Calendar System: Semester
URL: www.stfrancis.edu
Established: 1920 — Annual Undergrad Tuition & Fees: $25,932
Enrollment: 3,255 — Coed
Affiliation or Control: Roman Catholic — IRS Status: 501(c)3
Highest Offering: Doctorate
Program: Liberal Arts And General; Teacher Preparatory; Professional
Accreditation: NH, ACBSP, NRPA, NURSE, SW, TED

01 President ... Dr. Michael J. VINCIGUERRA
05 Provost/VP Academic Affairs ... Dr. Frank H. PASCOE
10 VP Finance & Administration ... Mr. Robert M. TENUTA
84 VP Admissions/Enrollment Svcs ... Mr. Charles M. BEUTEL
88 VP Mission Int & Ministry ... Sr. Mary Elizabeth IMLER
27 CIO ... Dr. Gerard H. KICKUL
30 Chief Advancement Officer ... Regina M. BLOCK
04 Executive Assistant to President ... Ms. Barbara S. INGOLD
26 Exec Dir Univ Rels/Pres Liaison ... Ms. Nancy A. POHLMAN
88 Exec Dir Student Acad Support Svcs ... Ms. Laura L. COLE
18 Exec Dir Operations & Facil Mgmt ... Mr. Lawrence R. BURICH
30 Exec Dir Development ... Ms. Jacquelyn A. BERSANO
21 Controller ... Mr. Mark MCCABE
49 Dean Col Arts & Sciences ... Dr. Robert KASE
50 Int Dean Col Business/Health Admin ... Dr. Anthony J. ZORDAN
53 Dean Col Education ... Dr. John S. GAMBRO
66 Dean Col Nursing ... Dr. Carol J. WILSON
32 Dean of Students ... Mr. Damon N. SLOAN
29 Dir Alumni Relations ... Ms. Aubrey L. DURISH
41 Dir Athletics ... Mr. Dave LAKETA
38 Dir Counseling Services ... Vacant
28 Dir Diversity ... Dr. Billie P. TERRELL
37 Dir Financial Aid ... Ms. Mary V. SHAW
07 Dir Grad/Degree Completion Admiss ... Ms. Sandra L. SLOKA
07 Dir Undergrad Admissions ... Ms. Julie R. MARLATT
15 Dir Human Resources ... Ms. Mary L. SPREITZER
09 Dir Institutional Effectiveness ... Ms. Janine M. HICKS
08 Dir Library Services ... Mr. Terrance L. COTTRELL
14 Dir Network Support Services ... Mr. Mark T. SNODGRASS
39 Dir Residence Life ... Ms. Christina M. AICHELE
19 Dir Security ... Mr. Thomas S. URASKI
35 Dir Student Development ... Ms. Dominique A. ANNIS
42 Dir University Ministry ... Vacant
06 Registrar ... Ms. Laura A. KOGA
23 Coordinator of Health Services ... Ms. Phyllis PETERSON
36 Asst Dir Career Services ... Ms. Kristi J. KELLY
24 Head of Tech Svcs ... Ms. Gail GAWLIK
105 Web Communications Manager ... Mr. Michael PLANETA

University of Saint Mary of the Lake-Mundelein Seminary (D)

1000 E Maple Avenue, Mundelein IL 60060-1174

County: Lake — FICE Identification: 001765
Unit ID: 148885
Telephone: (847) 566-6401 — Carnegie Class: Spec/Faith
FAX Number: (847) 566-7330 — Calendar System: Quarter
URL: www.usml.edu
Established: 1844 — Annual Graduate Tuition & Fees: $21,550
Enrollment: 160 — Male
Affiliation or Control: Roman Catholic — IRS Status: 501(c)3
Highest Offering: Doctorate; No Undergraduates
Program: Professional
Accreditation: THEOL

00 Chancellor ... Card. Francis GEORGE
01 Rector/President ... RevMgr. Dennis J. LYLE
03 Vice Rector ... Rev. James PRESTA
05 Vice President and Academic Dean ... Rev. Thomas A. BAIMA
73 Vice President/Ecclesiastical Dean ... Rev. John G. LODGE
32 Vice President/Dean of Formation ... Rev. Ronald HICKS
20 Vice President & Provost ... Rev. Thomas FRANZMAN
10 Vice President for Finance ... Mr. John F. LEHOCKY
30 Vice President for Inst Advancement ... Mr. Mark TERESI
18 Vice President for Facilities ... Mr. Stanley C. RYS
20 Assistant Academic Dean ... Mr. Christopher MCATEE
73 Director Pre-Theology Program ... Rev. August J. BELAUSKAS
08 Library Director ... Mrs. Lorraine OLLEY
06 Registrar ... Mrs. Mary Ann ULZ
88 Director of Pastoral Internships ... Rev. Raymond J. WEBB
88 Director of Liturgy ... Rev. John S. SZMYD
88 Director of Prayer Formation ... Rev. Marty BARNUM
39 Director of Seminary Residence Hall ... Rev. Jacque BELTRAN
14 Director Computer Services ... Mr. Nicholaus GREAZEL
28 Director of Diversity ... Rev. Martin BARNUM

VanderCook College of Music (E)

3140 S Federal Street, Chicago IL 60616-3731

County: Cook — FICE Identification: 001778
Unit ID: 149639
Telephone: (312) 225-6288 — Carnegie Class: Spec/Arts
FAX Number: (312) 225-5211 — Calendar System: Semester
URL: www.vandercook.edu
Established: 1909 — Annual Undergrad Tuition & Fees: $23,190
Enrollment: 380 — Coed
Affiliation or Control: Independent Non-Profit — IRS Status: 501(c)3
Highest Offering: Master's
Program: Teacher Preparatory; Professional; Music Emphasis
Accreditation: NH, MUS

01 President ... Dr. Charles T. MENGHINI
06 Registrar ... Mrs. Carolyn BERGHOFF
08 Head Librarian ... Mr. Robert DELAND
05 Dean of Undergraduate Division ... Ms. Kaye CLEMENTS
58 Dean of Graduate Studies ... Ms. Ruth RHODES
07 Director of Admissions ... Ms. Amy LENTING
10 Controller ... Ms. Diane KELLY
37 Director of Financial Aid ... Dr. D. DENNY
13 Director Information Technologies ... Mr. Rick MALIK
04 President's Assistant ... Ms. Cindy TOVAR
51 Director of Continuing Education ... Mr. Rick PALESE

Vatterott College-Quincy (F)

3609 North Marx Drive, Quincy IL 62305

County: Adams — FICE Identification: 020693
Unit ID: 148140
Telephone: (217) 224-0600 — Carnegie Class: Assoc/PrivFP
FAX Number: (217) 223-6771 — Calendar System: Other
URL: www.vatterott-college.edu
Established: 1995 — Annual Undergrad Tuition & Fees: $10,991
Enrollment: 515 — Coed
Affiliation or Control: Proprietary — IRS Status: Proprietary
Highest Offering: Associate Degree
Program: Occupational; 2-Year Principally Bachelor's Creditable
Accreditation: ACCSC

01 CEO & President ... Ms. Pam BELL
10 Chief Financial Officer ... Mr. Dennis BEAVERS
05 Vice President Academic Affairs ... Mr. Brandon SHEDRON
30 VP Regulatory Affs/Strategic Devel ... Mr. Aaron LACEY
43 General Counsel/Chief Administrator ... Mr. Scott CASANOVER
12 Campus Director ... Mr. Michael DENUM

Waubonsee Community College (G)

Route 47 at Waubonsee Drive,
Sugar Grove IL 60554-9799

County: Kane — FICE Identification: 006931
Unit ID: 149727
Telephone: (630) 466-7900 — Carnegie Class: Assoc/Pub-S-SC
FAX Number: (630) 466-7550 — Calendar System: Semester
URL: www.waubonsee.edu
Established: 1966 — Annual Undergrad Tuition & Fees (In-District): $2,450
Enrollment: 10,428 — Coed
Affiliation or Control: Local — IRS Status: 501(c)3
Highest Offering: Associate Degree
Program: Occupational; 2-Year Principally Bachelor's Creditable
Accreditation: NH, MAC, SURGT

01 President ... Dr. Christine J. SOBEK
05 Exec VP Educ Affs/Chief Lrng Ofcr ... Dr. Deborah F. LOVINGOOD
10 Vice President Finance & Operations ... Mr. David QUILLEN
09 VP Quality/Strategic Development ... Dr. Karen STEWART
31 Asst Vice Pres of Comm Development ... Dr. William MARZANO
56 Asst VP Pgm Devel/Distance Learning ... Ms. Jane REGNIER
20 Asst Vice President of Instruction ... Ms. Jill WOLD
32 Asst VP of Student Development ... Ms. Melinda L. JAMES
16 Director Human Resources ... Ms. Michele NEEDHAM
14 Chief Information Officer ... Mr. Edward F. LENINGER
76 Dean Health & Life Science ... Dr. Jess TOUSSAINT
83 Dean Social Sciences & Education ... Ms. Jacquelyn THOROUGHMAN
79 Dean Humanities/Fine Arts/Languages ... Ms. Cynthia FISHER

88 Dean Learning Enhancement .... Ms. Terri SAMUELSON
88 Dean Dist Learn/Instuc Tech .... Ms. Renee TONIONI
18 Director Campus Operations .... Mr. Dale WILLERTH
30 Director Fund Development .... Ms. Katharine RICHARDS
35 Dean Counseling/Student Support .... Ms. Kelli SINCLAIR
56 Dean Adult Education .... Ms. Jeri L. DIXON
72 Dean Tech/Math/Physical Science .... Dr. Paul HUMMEL
50 Dean Business/Information Systems .... Ms. Suzette LONG
103 Dean Workforce Development .... Ms. Lesa NORRIS
84 Dean Enrollment Mgmt/Student Life .... Ms. Faith LASHURE
26 Dir of Marketing/Communications .... Mr. Jeff NOBLITT
21 Asst Vice President of Finance .... Ms. Darla S. CARDINE
88 Construction Supt .... Mr. Al BOTA
04 Executive Assistant to President .... Ms. Teri D. LEATHERBURY
37 Director Student Fin Aid Services .... Dr. Charles BOUDREAU
28 Dir Governmental/Multicultural Affa .... Ms. Lourdes BLACKSMITH
31 Dean Community Education .... Mr. Douglas L. GRIER
88 Dean Campus Development .... Ms. Elizabeth E. BELL

Western Illinois University (A)

1 University Circle, Macomb IL 61455-1390
County: McDonough FICE Identification: 001780
Unit ID: 149772
Telephone: (309) 295-1414 Carnegie Class: Master's L
FAX Number: (309) 298-2400 Calendar System: Semester
URL: www.wiu.edu
Established: 1899 Annual Undergrad Tuition & Fees (In-State): $9,980
Enrollment: 12,585 Coed
Affiliation or Control: State IRS Status: 501(c)3
Highest Offering: Doctorate
Program: Liberal Arts And General; Teacher Preparatory; Nursing Emphasis
Accreditation: NH, ART, BUS, BUSA, CACREP, CEA, DIETD, MUS, NRPA, NURSE, SP, SW, TED, THEA

01 President .... Dr. Jack THOMAS
05 Interim Provost & Academic VP .... Dr. Kenneth HAWKINSON
20 Assoc Provost/Personnel .... Dr. Kathleen NEUMANN
20 Asst VP for Academic Affairs .... Dr. Ronald WILLIAMS
20 Asst Provost/Undergrad & Grad Stds .... Vacant
11 Interim VP Administrative Services .... Ms. Julie DEWEES
32 Vice President Student Services .... Dr. Gary M. BILLER
26 Vice Pres Advancement/Public Svcs .... Mr. Bradley BAINTER
29 Director Alumni Programs .... Ms. Amy SPELMAN
35 Assoc VP Student Support Svcs .... Mr. W. Earl BRACEY
39 Asst Vice Pres Student Services .... Vacant
45 VP for QC/Planning & Technology .... Dr. Joseph RIVES
86 Asst to Pres Government Relations .... Mr. David L. STEELMAN
49 Dean College Arts/
Sciences .... Dr. Susan MARTINELLI-FERNANDEZ
50 Dean College Business/Technology .... Dr. Thomas L. EREKSON
53 Dean College Ed & Human Svcs .... Dr. Sterling SADDLER
57 Interim Dean Fine Arts & Comm .... Dr. Sharon EVANS
08 Dean University Libraries .... Dr. Phyllis SELF
92 Dir Illinois Centennial Honors Col .... Vacant
64 Director School of Music .... Dr. Bart SHANKLIN
06 Registrar .... Dr. Angela LYNN
21 Director Business Services .... Ms. Dana BIERNBAUM
13 Dir Admin Information Mgmt Systems .... Ms. Brenda PARKS
90 Director of Academic Computing .... Vacant
27 Director University Relations .... Ms. Darcie R. SHINBERGER
09 Director Inst Research & Planning .... Ms. Rhonda K. KLINE
22 Director Equal Opportunity & Access .... Ms. Andrea HENDERSON
37 Director Financial Aid .... Mr. Robert ANDERSEN
36 Director Placement .... Mr. Martin J. KRAL
15 Director Human Resources .... Ms. Pamela L. BOWMAN
18 Director Physical Plant .... Dr. Charles G. DARNELL
19 Director Public Safety .... Mr. Robert E. FITZGERALD
23 Director Health Center .... Ms. Mary M. HARRIS
31 Dir Distance Learning and Outreach .... Dr. Richard CARTER
40 Director University Bookstore .... Mr. Jude KIAH
41 Director Athletics .... Dr. Tim VAN ALSTINE
102 Director WIU Foundation .... Mr. Bradley BAINTER
30 Director of Development .... Vacant
07 Director Admissions .... Dr. Andrew BORST
38 Director Student Counseling .... Dr. James E. DITULIO
96 Director of Purchasing .... Ms. Dana BIERNBAUM
85 Dir Center International Studies .... Dr. Richard CARTER

Westwood College-Chicago Loop (B)

17 North State Street, Suite 300, Chicago IL 60602
County: Cook Identification: 666424
Unit ID: 443687
Telephone: (312) 739-0850 Carnegie Class: Bac/Diverse
FAX Number: (312) 739-1004 Calendar System: Other
URL: www.westwood.edu
Established: 2003 Annual Undergrad Tuition & Fees: $25,028
Enrollment: 820 Coed
Affiliation or Control: Proprietary IRS Status: Proprietary
Highest Offering: Baccalaureate
Program: Occupational; Business Emphasis
Accreditation: ACICS

01 Campus President .... Debbie PLEMONS
05 Academic Dean .... Dillon RASMUSSEN
07 Admissions Director .... Jeff HILL

† Branch campus of Westwood College-Los Angeles, Los Angeles, CA.

Westwood College-DuPage (C)

7155 Janes Avenue, Woodridge IL 60517-2321
County: DuPage FICE Identification: 030792
Unit ID: 406194
Telephone: (866) 721-7646 Carnegie Class: Bac/Diverse
FAX Number: (630) 963-1420 Calendar System: Quarter
URL: www.westwood.edu
Established: N/A Annual Undergrad Tuition & Fees: $25,046
Enrollment: 491 Coed
Affiliation or Control: Proprietary IRS Status: Proprietary
Highest Offering: Baccalaureate
Program: Occupational; Liberal Arts And General
Accreditation: ACICS

01 Campus President .... Kelly T. MOORE
05 Campus Academic Dean .... Jennifer SHARP
11 Director of Campus Operations .... Diana GARCIA
07 Director of Admissions .... Scott KAWALL
32 Director of Student Services .... Kim QUINN
36 Assistant Director of Career Svcs .... Elliott REASONER
37 Director of Student Finance .... Pertrina BRIGGS

Westwood College-O'Hare Airport (D)

8501 W Higgins Road, Suite 100, Chicago IL 60631-2814
County: Cook FICE Identification: 023139
Unit ID: 178226
Telephone: (773) 380-6800 Carnegie Class: Bac/Diverse
FAX Number: (773) 380-6820 Calendar System: Other
URL: www.westwood.edu
Established: 2000 Annual Undergrad Tuition & Fees: $15,501
Enrollment: 811 Coed
Affiliation or Control: Proprietary IRS Status: Proprietary
Highest Offering: Baccalaureate
Program: Occupational; 2-Year Principally Bachelor's Creditable; Professional; Technical Emphasis
Accreditation: ACICS, MAC

01 President .... Mr. David BOSTICK
05 Academic Dean .... Dr. Ellen CROWE
32 Assistant Director of Student Svcs .... Ms. Staci CHAPMAN
10 Director of Campus Operations .... Ms. Zena WILLIAMS
07 Director of Admissions .... Mr. Lou BELLSOM
36 Director of Career Services .... Ms. Hope GREEN
37 Director of Student Finance .... Ms. Tracy WALKER

Westwood College-River Oaks (E)

80 River Oaks Center, Suite D-49,
Calumet City IL 60409-5555
County: Cook Identification: 666440
Unit ID: 440147
Telephone: (708) 832-1988 Carnegie Class: Bac/Diverse
FAX Number: (708) 862-6525 Calendar System: Other
URL: www.westwood.edu
Established: 2000 Annual Undergrad Tuition & Fees: $14,227
Enrollment: 631 Coed
Affiliation or Control: Proprietary IRS Status: Proprietary
Highest Offering: Baccalaureate
Program: Occupational
Accreditation: ACICS, MAC

01 Executive Director .... Bruce MCKENZIE

† Branch campus of Westwood College-Los Angeles, Los Angeles, CA.

Wheaton College (F)

501 College Avenue, Wheaton IL 60187-5593
County: DuPage FICE Identification: 001781
Unit ID: 149781
Telephone: (630) 752-5000 Carnegie Class: Bac/A&S
FAX Number: (630) 752-5555 Calendar System: Semester
URL: www.wheaton.edu
Established: 1860 Annual Undergrad Tuition & Fees: $28,960
Enrollment: 3,026 Coed
Affiliation or Control: Independent Non-Profit IRS Status: 501(c)3
Highest Offering: Doctorate
Program: Liberal Arts And General; Teacher Preparatory; Professional
Accreditation: NH, CLPSY, MUS, TED

01 President .... Dr. Philip G. RYKEN
05 Provost .... Dr. Stanton L. JONES
03 Vice President for Finance .... Mr. Dale A. KEMP
32 Vice President Student Development .... Mr. Paul O. CHELSEN
30 Vice Pres Advancement/Alumni Rels .... Dr. R. Mark DILLON
04 Exec Asst to the President .... Miss Marilee A. MELVIN
20 Assistant Provost/Dean of Grad Schl .... Dr. Jeffrey A. MOSHIER
79 Dean Humanities/Theol Studies .... Dr. Jill P. BAUMGAERTNER
49 Dean of the Conservatory of Music .... Dr. Michael WILDER
83 Dean Natural & Social Sciences .... Dr. Dorothy F. CHAPPELL
09 Dean Information and Technology .... Dr. Gary N. LARSON
35 Dean of Student Care and Services .... Dr. Melanie HUMPHREYS
06 Registrar .... Mrs. Peggy KING
20 Director Billy Graham Center .... Dr. Lon J. ALLISON
21 Business Manager .... Mr. Stephen W. MEAD
21 College Controller .... Mr. Patrick T. BROOKE
29 Director of Alumni
Relations .... Ms. Cindra STACKHOUSE TAETZCH
87 Director of Summer Session .... Dr. Terence H. PERCIANTE
24 Director of Media Resources .... Mr. J. R. SMITH
08 College Librarian .... Mrs. Lisa T. RICHMOND
36 Director of Career Services .... Mrs. Ita FISCHER
16 Director of Human Resources .... Mr. Chris E. WOODARD
13 Director of Computing Services .... Mr. Lowell W. BALLARD
07 Director Undergraduate Admissions .... Ms. Shawn B. LEFTWICH
07 Director Graduate Admissions .... Ms. Julie A. HUEBNER
37 Director of Student Financial Aid .... Ms. Karen BELLING
39 Associate Dean of Residence Life .... Mr. Justin HETH
104 Assoc Dean Global & Exper
Learning .... Dr. Laura M. MONTGOMERY
38 Director of Counseling .... Dr. Doug B. DEMERCHANT
42 Chaplain .... Dr. Stephen B. KELLOUGH
23 Director of Student Health Services .... Ms. Britt BLACK
27 Director of Media Relations .... Ms. LaTonya TAYLOR
18 Director of Physical Plant .... Mr. James M. JOHNSON
19 Chief of Public Safety .... Mr. Robert F. NORRIS
26 Director Marketing Communications .... Mrs. Georgia I. DOUGLAS
93 Director Multicultural Development .... Mr. Rodney K. SISCO
96 Director of Purchasing .... Mr. Gregory S. DOTY
88 Director Risk Management .... Mr. Vincent E. MORRIS
40 Manager of Bookstore .... Vacant

Worsham College of Mortuary Science (G)

495 Northgate Parkway, Wheeling IL 60090-2646
County: Cook FICE Identification: 001783
Unit ID: 369455
Telephone: (847) 808-8444 Carnegie Class: Assoc/PrivFP
FAX Number: (847) 808-8493 Calendar System: Quarter
URL: www.worshamcollege.com
Established: 1911 Annual Undergrad Tuition & Fees: $18,506
Enrollment: 122 Coed
Affiliation or Control: Proprietary IRS Status: Proprietary
Highest Offering: Associate Degree
Program: Occupational
Accreditation: FUSER

01 Director .... Ms. Stephanie J. KANN

Zarem/Golde ORT Technical Institute (H)

5440 W. Fargo Avenue, Skokie IL 60077
County: Cook FICE Identification: 041184
Unit ID: 393180
Telephone: (847) 324-5588 Carnegie Class: Not Classified
FAX Number: (847) 324-5580 Calendar System: Other
URL: www.chicagotrainingschool.com
Established: 1991 Annual Undergrad Tuition & Fees: $5,550
Enrollment: 5,000 Coed
Affiliation or Control: Independent Non-Profit IRS Status: 501(c)3
Highest Offering: Associate Degree
Program: Occupational; 2-Year Principally Bachelor's Creditable; Nursing Emphasis
Accreditation: CNCE

01 Director .... Marina CHUDNOVSKY

INDIANA

Ancilla College (I)

PO Box 1, Donaldson IN 46513-0001
County: Marshall FICE Identification: 001784
Unit ID: 150048
Telephone: (574) 936-8898 Carnegie Class: Assoc/PrivNFP
FAX Number: (574) 935-1773 Calendar System: Semester
URL: www.ancilla.edu
Established: 1937 Annual Undergrad Tuition & Fees: $13,650
Enrollment: 578 Coed
Affiliation or Control: Roman Catholic IRS Status: 501(c)3
Highest Offering: Associate Degree
Program: 2-Year Principally Bachelor's Creditable
Accreditation: NH

01 President .... Dr. Ron MAY
04 Assistant to the President .... Ms. Diana CALDWELL
05 Dean of Academic & Student Services .... Dr. Joanna BLOUNT
10 Exec Director Finance & Admin .... Mr. Mike BROWN
30 Exec Dir of Institutional Advance .... Mr. Todd ZELTWANGER
07 Executive Director of Admissions .... Mr. Tony BOOKER
42 Coord Mission Integration/Camp
Min .... Sr. Carleen WRASMAN, PHJC
21 Director of Business Affairs .... Mr. Raymond GIRRES
37 Director of Financial Aid .... Mrs. Katherine MILLS
41 Athletic Director .... Mr. Robert REESE
36 Director of Advising Center .... Mr. James CAWTHON
30 Assoc Dir Inst Advancement/Alumni .... Mr. Thomas SIBAL
13 Director of Information Technology .... Mr. John LINBACK
09 Interim Dir Inst Rsrch/Assessment .... Mr. Eric WIGNALL
18 Chief Facilities/Physical Plant .... Mr. Tom NOWAK
32 Director Student Development .... Mr. Gene REESE
06 Registrar .... Ms. Sharon BLUBAUGH
40 Bookstore Manager .... Ms. Nena HASKINS
08 Librarian .... Ms. Cassaundra BASH
17 Director Nursing & Health Science .... Ms. Ann FITZGERALD

Anderson University (A)

1100 E Fifth Street, Anderson IN 46012-3495
County: Madison   FICE Identification: 001785
Unit ID: 150066
Telephone: (765) 649-9071   Carnegie Class: DRU
FAX Number: (765) 641-3851   Calendar System: Semester
URL: www.anderson.edu
Established: 1917   Annual Undergrad Tuition & Fees: $24,540
Enrollment: 2,565   Coed
Affiliation or Control: Church Of God   IRS Status: 501(c)3
Highest Offering: Doctorate
Program: Liberal Arts And General; Teacher Preparatory; Professional
Accreditation: NH, ACBSP, MUS, NURSE, SW, TED, THEOL

01 President ... Dr. James L. EDWARDS
05 Vice President Academic Affairs ... Dr. Marie S. MORRIS
10 Vice President Finance/Treasurer ... Vacant
30 Vice President for Advancement ... Mr. Robert L. COFFMAN
32 VP Student Life & Dean of Students ... Dr. Brent A. BAKER
73 Dean School of Theology ... Dr. David L. SEBASTIAN
79 Dean College of the Arts ... Dr. Jeffrey E. WRIGHT
81 Dean College of Science/Humanities ... Dr. D. Blake JANUTOLO
50 Dean Falls School of Business ... Dr. Terry C. TRUITT
42 Campus Pastor ... Rev. J. Todd FAULKNER
06 University Registrar ... Mr. Arthur J. LEAK
26 Exec Director for Advancement ... Mr. Tom S. BRUCE
08 Director of Libraries ... Dr. Janet L. BREWER
07 Director of Admissions ... Mr. Joe M. DAVIS
21 Assistant Treasurer/Controller ... Mrs. Dana S. STUART
36 Dir Career Development/InVision AU ... Vacant
14 Director of Info Technology Svcs ... Mrs. Cynthia A. SMITH
37 Student Financial Services ... Mr. Kenneth F. NIEMAN
27 Dir Univ Communications/Cmty Rels ... Mr. Chris J. WILLIAMS
18 Exec Dir Facilities & Property Mgmt ... Mr. Joseph M. ROYER
16 Director of Human Resources ... Mrs. Denise A T. KRIEBEL
19 Director Police & Security Services ... Mr. Walter L. SMITH
24 Director of Ctr for Educ Technology ... Mr. Shelby D. CANTLEY
51 Dean School of Adult Learning ... Dr. Aleza D. BEVERLY
40 Bookstore Manager ... Mr. Antonio S. DELAROSA
41 Athletic Director ... Ms. Marcie J. TAYLOR
38 Director Counseling Services ... Ms. Christal R. HELVERING
29 Director of Alumni Relations ... Mr. Benjamin A. DAVIS

The Art Institute of Indianapolis (B)

3500 Depauw Boulevard Suite 1010,
Indianapolis IN 46268
County: Marion   Identification: 666247
Unit ID: 448345
Telephone: (317) 613-4800   Carnegie Class: Spec/Arts
FAX Number: (317) 613-4808   Calendar System: Quarter
URL: www.aii.edu/indianapolis
Established: 2006   Annual Undergrad Tuition & Fees: $17,416
Enrollment: 1,228   Coed
Affiliation or Control: Proprietary   IRS Status: Proprietary
Highest Offering: Baccalaureate
Program: Liberal Arts And General
Accreditation: ACICS

01 President ... Ms. Madeleine SLUTSKY
05 Dean of Academic Affairs ... Dr. Darrell BROWN

† Branch campus of The Art Institute of Las Vegas, Henderson, NV.

Associated Mennonite Biblical Seminary (C)

3003 Benham Avenue, Elkhart IN 46517-1999
County: Elkhart   FICE Identification: 001823
Unit ID: 151865
Telephone: (574) 295-3726   Carnegie Class: Spec/Faith
FAX Number: (574) 295-0092   Calendar System: 4/1/4
URL: www.ambs.edu
Established: 1946   Annual Graduate Tuition & Fees: $13,740
Enrollment: 141   Coed
Affiliation or Control: Mennonite Church   IRS Status: 501(c)3
Highest Offering: Master's; No Undergraduates
Program: Professional
Accreditation: NH, THEOL

01 President ... Dr. Sara W. SHENK
05 Academic Dean ... Dr. Rebecca SLOUGH
11 Administrative Vice President ... Mr. Ron RINGENBERG
30 Director of Development ... Ms. Missy K. SCHROCK
10 Chief Financial Officer ... Mr. Jeff MILLER
06 Registrar ... Ms. Irene KOOP
08 Librarian ... Ms. Eileen SANER
84 Director of Enrollment Services ... Mr. Bob ROSA
73 Director of Inst Mennonite Studies ... Dr. Mary H. SCHERTZ

Ball State University (D)

2000 W University Avenue, Muncie IN 47306-1099
County: Delaware   FICE Identification: 001786
Unit ID: 150136
Telephone: (765) 289-1241   Carnegie Class: RU/H
FAX Number: (765) 285-1461   Calendar System: Semester
URL: www.bsu.edu
Established: 1918   Annual Undergrad Tuition & Fees (In-State): $8,558
Enrollment: 22,083   Coed
Affiliation or Control: State   IRS Status: 501(c)3
Highest Offering: Doctorate
Program: Occupational; Liberal Arts And General; Teacher Preparatory; Professional
Accreditation: NH, DANCE, AAFCS, AAFCS, ART, AUD, BUS, BUSA, CACREP, CIDA, COPSY, CORE, DIETD, DIETI, ENGT, IPSY, JOUR, LSAR, MUS, NURSE, PLNG, RAD, SCPSY, SP, SW, TED, THEA

01 President ... Dr. Jo Ann M. GORA
05 Provost/Vice Pres Academic Affs ... Dr. Terry KING
84 VP Marketing/Comm/Enroll Mgmt ... Mr. Tom TAYLOR
10 VP Business Affairs & Treasurer ... Dr. Randy B. HOWARD
30 Vice Pres University Advancement ... Mr. Hudson AKIN
13 VP for Information Technology ... Mr. Philip C. REPP
32 VP Student Affairs/Dean of Students ... Dr. Kay BALES
41 Dir Intercollegiate Athletics ... Mr. Tom COLLINS
21 Assoc VP Business/Aux Svcs ... Ms. Leisa JULIAN
86 Assoc VP Governmental Relations ... Ms. Gretchen GUTMAN
21 Assoc VP Finance/Asst Treasurer ... Mr. Bernard HANNON
85 Dean Rinker Ctr for Intl Programs ... Dr. Kenneth M. HOLLAND
20 Assoc Provost/Dean Univ College ... Dr. Marilyn M. BUCK
18 Assoc VP Facilities Planning/Mgmt ... Mr. Kevin S. KENYON
07 Director Admissions & Orientation . Mr. Christopher T. MUNCHEL
32 Asc VP Student Affairs/Dir Housing ... Dr. Alan L. HARGRAVE
29 Exec Director Alumni Programs ... Vacant
26 Assoc VP Marketing & Communications .. Mr. Tony PROUDFOOT
38 Director Counseling/Health Services ... Dr. June P. PAYNE
14 Asst VP IT for Strategic/Fiscal Mgt ... Mr. Donald (Jr.) KING
88 Dir Unified Techonology Support ... Mr. Dan LUTZ
36 Director Career Center ... Mrs. Mollie FOUT
37 Director Scholarships/Financial Aid ... Dr. John MCPHERSON
22 Exec Director University Compliance ... Ms. Sali K. FALLING
06 Reg/Dir Registration/Acad Pgms ... Mrs. Nancy L. CRONK
09 Int Dir Inst Effectiveness ... Mrs. Andrea INGLE
30 Exec Director Univ Development ... Dr. Charles R. JAGGERS
96 Director of Purchasing Services ... Mrs. Rhodene UPCHURCH
24 Director of Teleplex ... Mr. William B. CAHOE
88 Asst to Vice Pres/Ombudsperson ... Mrs. Katie SLABAUGH
25 Director Contracts & Grants ... Ms. Kathy A. LUCAS
19 Director Public Safety ... Mr. Gene BURTON
15 Director of Human Resources Svcs ... Ms. Judith A. BURKE
28 Asst Provost Diversity ... Dr. Charles R. PAYNE
08 Dean University Libraries ... Dr. Arthur W. HAFNER
57 Dean College of Fine Arts ... Dr. Robert A. KVAM
50 Dean Miller College of Business ... Dr. Rajib N. SANYAL
48 Dean College Architecture/ Planning ... Dr. Guillermo P. VASQUEZ DE VELASCO
53 Dean of Teachers College ... Dr. John E. JACOBSON
58 Asc Provost/Research/Dean Grad Sch ... Dr. Robert J. MORRIS
88 AVP Econ Dev/Int Dean Scl Extend Ed ... Dr. Frank J. SABATINE
49 Dean Col of Science/Humanities ... Dr. Michael A. MAGGIOTTO
60 Dean Col of Comm/Info/Media ... Mr. Roger LAVERY
72 Dean Col Applied Science/Technology ... Dr. Mitchell H. WHALEY
92 Dean of Honors College ... Dr. James S. RUEBEL

Bethany Theological Seminary (E)

615 National Road W, Richmond IN 47374-4019
County: Wayne   FICE Identification: 001637
Unit ID: 143233
Telephone: (800) 287-8822   Carnegie Class: Spec/Faith
FAX Number: (765) 983-1840   Calendar System: Semester
URL: www.bethanyseminary.edu
Established: 1905   Annual Graduate Tuition & Fees: $11,610
Enrollment: 74   Coed
Affiliation or Control: Church Of The Brethren   IRS Status: 501(c)3
Highest Offering: Master's; No Undergraduates
Program: Professional
Accreditation: NH, THEOL

01 President ... Dr. Ruthann K. JOHANSEN
05 Academic Dean ... Dr. Steven J. SCHWEITZER
10 Exec Dir of Student/Business Svcs ... Ms. Brenda J. REISH
30 Exec Dir Institutional Advancement ... Mr. Lowell FLORY
20 Director of Academic Services ... Ms. April VANLONDEN
26 Director of Communications ... Ms. Jennifer L. WILLIAMS
32 Director of Student Development ... Ms. Amy S. GALL RITCHIE
12 Director Brethren Academy ... Ms. Julie M. HOSTETTER
88 Director Inst Ministry with Youth ... Mr. Russell HAITCH
07 Interim Director of Admissions ... Ms. Elizabeth KELLER

Bethel College (F)

1001 Bethel Circle, Mishawaka IN 46545-5509
County: Saint Joseph   FICE Identification: 001787
Unit ID: 150145
Telephone: (574) 259-8511   Carnegie Class: Bac/Diverse
FAX Number: (574) 257-3326   Calendar System: Semester
URL: www.bethelcollege.edu
Established: 1947   Annual Undergrad Tuition & Fees: $23,030
Enrollment: 2,152   Coed
Affiliation or Control: Missionary Church   IRS Status: 501(c)3
Highest Offering: Master's
Program: Liberal Arts And General; Teacher Preparatory; Professional; Nursing Emphasis
Accreditation: NH, ADNUR, IACBE, MUS, NUR, TED

01 President ... Dr. Steven CRAMER
03 Senior Vice President ... Dr. Dennis ENGBRECHT
05 Interim VP for Academic Services ... Dr. Bradley SMITH
30 VP for Development ... Mr. Terry ZEITLOW
10 VP & Chief Financial Officer ... Mr. Clair KNAPP
26 VP for College Relations ... Dr. Robert LAURENT
32 VP for Student Development ... Dr. Shawn HOLTGREN
36 VP for Life Calling/Stdnt Enrichmnt ... Dr. Kathy GRIBBIN
84 Asst VP for Enrollment/Marketng ... Mr. Randy BEACHY
13 Chief Technology Officer ... Mr. Wally NEHLS
66 Dean Division of Nursing ... Dr. Carol DOROUGH
49 Dean Division of Sciences ... Dr. Robert MYERS
88 Director of Non-Traditional Studies ... Mr. Dale GADD
79 Dean Arts & Humanities ... Dr. Thomas VISKER
58 Dean Professional & Graduate Pgm ... Dr. Bradley SMITH
39 Dean of Students ... Mrs. Julie BEAM
06 Registrar ... Mrs. Jeanne FOX
36 Director Student Enrichment ... Mrs. Michelle YAGER
37 Director Financial Aid ... Mr. Guy FISHER
26 Director Marketing & Communication ... Ms. Jaimee THIRION
41 Director Athletics ... Ms. Jody MARTINEZ
08 Director Library Services ... Dr. Clyde ROOT
24 Director Teacher Certification ... Mrs. Joyce LAURENT
18 Director Physical Plant ... Mr. Steve YAW
09 Director Institutional Research ... Dr. Ray WHITEMAN
19 Director Campus Safety ... Mr. Philip JEROME
85 Director International Students ... Mrs. Lori GONZALEZ
91 Director Administrative Computing ... Mr. Harold RODGERS
23 Director Wellness Center ... Mrs. Carol BEMIS
29 Director Alumni Services ... Mrs. Lois PANNABECKER
28 Director Intercultural Development ... Mr. Alex GONZALEZ
07 Director Admissions ... Vacant
15 Director Human Resources ... Mrs. Lisa MALKEWICZ

Brown Mackie College-Fort Wayne (G)

3000 E Coliseum Boulevard, Ste 100,
Fort Wayne IN 46805-1565
County: Allen   Identification: 666435
Unit ID: 408039
Telephone: (260) 484-4400   Carnegie Class: Assoc/PrivFP4
FAX Number: (260) 484-2678   Calendar System: Other
URL: www.brownmackie.edu
Established: 1882   Annual Undergrad Tuition & Fees: $11,124
Enrollment: 1,491   Coed
Affiliation or Control: Proprietary   IRS Status: Proprietary
Highest Offering: Baccalaureate
Program: 2-Year Principally Bachelor's Creditable; Business Emphasis
Accreditation: ACICS, MAC, OTA, #PTAA, SURGT, SURTEC

01 President ... Mr. Jim BISHOP
05 Dean of Academic Affairs ... Mr. Jeff GULLEY
32 Director of Student Services ... Ms. Kathy JUTT
07 Senior Director of Admissions ... Mr. Bob ALLEN
36 Director of Career Services ... Mr. Anthony DAVIS

† Branch campus of Brown Mackie-South Bend, South Bend, IN.

Brown Mackie College-Indianapolis (H)

1200 N. Meridian Street, Suite 100, Indianapolis IN 46204
County: Marion   Identification: 666394
Unit ID: 451699
Telephone: (317) 554-8300   Carnegie Class: Assoc/PrivFP4
FAX Number: (317) 632-4557   Calendar System: Quarter
URL: www.brownmackie.edu
Established: 2007   Annual Undergrad Tuition & Fees: $11,772
Enrollment: 1,385   Coed
Affiliation or Control: Proprietary   IRS Status: Proprietary
Highest Offering: Baccalaureate
Program: 2-Year Principally Bachelor's Creditable; Business Emphasis
Accreditation: ACICS, OTA

01 President ... Ms. Lisa RAMIREZ
05 Dean of Academic Affairs ... Ms. Terri FLEMING
07 Senior Director of Admissions ... Mr. James R. MILLS
06 Registrar ... Vacant
10 Student Account Advisor ... Ms. Marisa MALONE
37 Director of Financial Aid ... Vacant
08 Librarian ... Ms. Dawn LIPP

† Branch campus of Brown Mackie College-Findlay, Findlay, OH.

Brown Mackie College-Merrillville (I)

1000 E 80th Place, Suite 205M, Merrillville IN 46410-5602
County: Lake   FICE Identification: 021032
Unit ID: 151616
Telephone: (219) 769-3321   Carnegie Class: Assoc/PrivFP4
FAX Number: (219) 738-1076   Calendar System: Other
URL: www.brownmackie.edu
Established: 1890   Annual Undergrad Tuition & Fees: $11,124
Enrollment: 623   Coed
Affiliation or Control: Proprietary   IRS Status: Proprietary
Highest Offering: Associate Degree
Program: Occupational; 2-Year Principally Bachelor's Creditable; Business Emphasis
Accreditation: ACICS, MAAB, OTA, SURGT

01 President ... Ms. Shalisa POWELL
05 Dean of Academic Affairs ... Mr. Scott SENAK
07 Senior Director of Admissions ... Vacant
36 Director of Career Services ... Ms. Julie LYNCH
06 Registrar ... Ms. Tiffany BRACK

† Branch campus of Brown Mackie College-Cincinnati, Cincinnati, OH.

Brown Mackie College-Michigan City (A)

325 E US Highway 20, Michigan City IN 46360-7362
County: La Porte Identification: 666426
Unit ID: 151625
Telephone: (219) 877-3100 Carnegie Class: Assoc/PrivFP4
FAX Number: (219) 877-3110 Calendar System: Other
URL: www.cbcaec.com
Established: N/A Annual Undergrad Tuition & Fees: $11,124
Enrollment: 448 Coed
Affiliation or Control: Proprietary IRS Status: Proprietary
Highest Offering: Associate Degree
Program: Occupational; 2-Year Principally Bachelor's Creditable; Business Emphasis
Accreditation: ACICS, MAAB, SURGT

01 President .... Ms. Sheryl ELSTON
05 Dean of Academic Affairs .... Ms. Diane DIDONNA
07 Senior Director of Admissions .... Ms. Nancy SPENNY
06 Registrar .... Ms. Karry WIER
36 Director of Career Services .... Ms. Paula SCOTT

† Branch campus of Brown Mackie College-Cincinnati, Cincinnati, OH.

Brown Mackie College-South Bend (B)

3454 Douglas Road, South Bend IN 46635
County: Saint Joseph FICE Identification: 004583
Unit ID: 151944
Telephone: (574) 237-0774 Carnegie Class: Assoc/PrivFP4
FAX Number: (574) 237-3585 Calendar System: Other
URL: www.brownmackie.edu
Established: 1882 Annual Undergrad Tuition & Fees: $11,124
Enrollment: 1,004 Coed
Affiliation or Control: Proprietary IRS Status: Proprietary
Highest Offering: Baccalaureate
Program: 2-Year Principally Bachelor's Creditable; Business Emphasis
Accreditation: ACICS, MAC, OTA, PTAA

01 President .... Vacant
05 Dean of Academic Affairs .... Mr. Steve RICHARDS
07 Senior Director of Admissions .... Vacant
06 Registrar .... Ms. Heather RYAN
36 Director of Career Services .... Ms. Sheryl DECKER

Butler University (C)

4600 Sunset Avenue, Indianapolis IN 46208-3443
County: Marion FICE Identification: 001788
Unit ID: 150163
Telephone: (317) 940-8000 Carnegie Class: Master's M
FAX Number: (317) 940-9930 Calendar System: Semester
URL: www.butler.edu
Established: 1855 Annual Undergrad Tuition & Fees: $31,110
Enrollment: 4,640 Coed
Affiliation or Control: Independent Non-Profit IRS Status: 501(c)3
Highest Offering: Doctorate
Program: Liberal Arts And General; Teacher Preparatory; Professional
Accreditation: NH, ARCPA, BUS, CACREP, DANCE, IPSY, MUS, PHAR, TED, THEA

01 President .... Mr. James M. DANKO
05 Provost .... Dr. Jamie M. COMSTOCK
10 Vice President for Finance .... Mr. Bruce E. ARICK
30 VP University Advancement .... Mr. D. Mark HELMUS
84 Vice Pres Enrollment Management .... Mr. Thomas D. WEEDE
32 Vice President of Student Affairs .... Dr. Levester JOHNSON
18 Interim Vice President Operations .... Mr. Gerald CARLSON
20 Assoc Provost Student Acad Affs .... Dr. Mary M. RAMSBOTTOM
20 Assoc Prov Faculty Affs & Intl Pgms .... Dr. Laura L. BEHLING
57 Dean Jordan College Fine Arts .... Dr. Ronald CALTABIANO
50 Dean Business Administration .... Dr. Chuck R. WILLIAMS
49 Dean Liberal Arts & Science .... Dr. Jay R. HOWARD
53 Dean Education .... Dr. Ena M. SHELLEY
67 Dean Pharmacy & Health Sciences .... Dr. Mary H. ANDRITZ
60 Int Dean College of Communication .... Dr. William NEHER
35 Dean Student Services .... Dr. Sally E. CLICK
35 Dean Student Life .... Dr. Irene E. STEVENS
38 Asst Dean & Director Counseling Ctr .... Dr. Keith B. MAGNUS
08 Dean of Libraries .... Mr. Lewis R. MILLER
29 Exec Dir Alumni/Development Pgms .... Ms. M. Rachel STEPHEN BURT
15 Exec Dir HR/Chief Diversity Officer .... Mr. Jonathan A. SMALL
88 Exec Director Clowes Memorial Hall .... Ms. Elise J. KUSHIGIAN
37 Director Financial Aid .... Ms. Melissa J. SMURDON
21 Executive Budget Director .... Mr. Robert J. MARCUS
26 Exec Director University Relations .... Ms. Marcia A. DOWELL
07 Dean of Admission .... Mr. Scott D. HAM
31 Director Conference/Special Events .... Ms. Beth A. ALEXANDER
39 Director Residence Life .... Ms. Karla K. CUNNINGHAM
09 Director Institutional Research .... Dr. Nandini RAMASWAMY
85 Director International Programs .... Dr. C. Montgomery BROADED
06 Registrar .... Ms. Sondrea S. OZOLINS
36 Director Career Services .... Mr. Gary R. BEAULIEU
41 Director of Athletics .... Mr. Barry S. COLLIER
27 Chief Information Officer .... Mr. Scott A. KINCAID
19 Director Public Safety/Police Chief .... Mr. Ben D. HUNTER
21 Controller .... Ms. Susan M. WESTERMEYER
26 Dir Print Marketing/Communications .... Ms. Sally M. CUTLER
28 Director of Diversity Programs .... Ms. Valerie J. DAVIDSON
40 Manager Bookstore .... Ms. Janine L. FRAINIER
96 Manager of Purchasing .... Ms. Shelly S. RABIDEAU

Calumet College of Saint Joseph (D)

2400 New York Avenue, Whiting IN 46394-2195
County: Lake FICE Identification: 001834
Unit ID: 150172
Telephone: (219) 473-7770 Carnegie Class: Master's S
FAX Number: (219) 473-4259 Calendar System: Semester
URL: www.ccsj.edu
Established: 1951 Annual Undergrad Tuition & Fees: $14,680
Enrollment: 1,262 Coed
Affiliation or Control: Roman Catholic IRS Status: 501(c)3
Highest Offering: Master's
Program: Liberal Arts And General; Teacher Preparatory; Business Emphasis
Accreditation: NH

01 President .... Dr. Daniel LOWERY
05 Vice President Academic Affairs .... Dr. Joi PATTERSON
30 Vice President for Development .... Mr. James ADDUCI
32 Vice Pres Student Life .... Ms. Melisha HENDERSON
10 VP Business & Finance .... Ms. Deanne SHIMALA
35 Dean of Students .... Vacant
06 Registrar .... Ms. Diana FRANCIS
08 Librarian .... Ms. Virginia RODES
09 Institutional Researcher .... Mr. Darren HENDERSON
26 Director of Marketing & Pub Rel .... Ms. Linda GAJEWSKI
41 Athletic Director .... Mr. Peter HARING
42 Director of Campus Ministry .... Bro. Jerry SCHWIETERMAN
15 Director of Human Resources .... Ms. Jacqueline NALLS
18 Director of Facilities & Technology .... Mr. Gene KESSLER
36 Dir of Enrollment Services .... Ms. Mary SEVERA
37 Dir of Business Office & Fin Aid Op .... Ms. Gina PIRTLE
36 Director of Career Services .... Mr. Mike KENNY
13 Director of Computer Services .... Mr. Charles MYERS
105 Assoc Dir of Advertising/Webmaster .... Mr. Darren JASIENIECKI
29 Director Alumni Relations .... Mr. Herb YEKEL
40 Bookstore Manager .... Ms. Erren TAPIA

Christian Theological Seminary (E)

1000 W. 42nd Street, Indianapolis IN 46208-3301
County: Marion FICE Identification: 001789
Unit ID: 150215
Telephone: (317) 924-1331 Carnegie Class: Spec/Faith
FAX Number: (317) 923-1961 Calendar System: Semester
URL: www.cts.edu
Established: 1925 Annual Graduate Tuition & Fees: $14,400
Enrollment: 213 Coed
Affiliation or Control: Christian Church (Disciples Of Christ)
IRS Status: 501(c)3
Highest Offering: Doctorate; No Undergraduates
Program: Professional; Religious Emphasis
Accreditation: NH, MFCD, THEOL

01 President .... Dr. Matthew W. BOULTON
05 Int Vice President & Co- Acad Dean .... Dr. Holly HEARON
05 Int Vice President & Co-Acad Dean .... Dr. K. B. LYON
10 Vice President Finance .... Vacant
30 Vice President Development .... Ms. Melissa HICKMAN
32 Associate Dean for Student Services .... Rev. Mary HARRIS
16 Executive Admin/HR Director .... Ms. Kathleen BELL
44 Director Annual Fund .... Vacant
13 Information Technology Director .... Mr. Dean S. REYNOLDS
21 Director of Business Affairs .... Mrs. Shari CULLUMBER
42 Chaplain .... Dr. Tercio B. JUNKER
08 Director of Library .... Ms. Lorna SHOEMAKER
06 Registrar .... Mr. Matt SCHLIMGEN
75 Director of Field Education .... Dr. William KINCAID
18 Director of Physical Plant .... Mr. Richard DAVIS
37 Director of Student Financial Aid .... Mr. Ed DETAMORE
40 Director of Bookstore .... Mrs. Sarah EVANS
27 Communications Associate .... Mr. Chris VARNAU

College of Court Reporting, Inc. (F)

111 W 10th, Suite 111, Hobart IN 46342-5969
County: Lake FICE Identification: 026158
Unit ID: 150251
Telephone: (866) 294-3974 Carnegie Class: Assoc/PrivFP
FAX Number: (219) 942-1631 Calendar System: Semester
URL: www.ccr.edu
Established: 1984 Annual Undergrad Tuition & Fees: $12,875
Enrollment: 286 Coed
Affiliation or Control: Proprietary IRS Status: Proprietary
Highest Offering: Associate Degree
Program: Occupational
Accreditation: ACICS

01 President .... Mr. Jeff T. MOODY
03 Executive Director .... Mr. Jay VETTICKAL
07 Director of Admissions .... Ms. Nicky M. RODRIQUEZ
37 Director of Financial Aid .... Ms. Lisa MORTON
32 Director of Student Services .... Ms. Kathleen LAZART

Concordia Theological Seminary (G)

6600 N Clinton Street, Fort Wayne IN 46825-4996
County: Allen FICE Identification: 020876
Unit ID: 150288
Telephone: (260) 452-2100 Carnegie Class: Spec/Faith
FAX Number: (260) 452-2121 Calendar System: Quarter
URL: www.ctsfw.edu
Established: 1846 Annual Graduate Tuition & Fees: $23,856
Enrollment: 350 Male
Affiliation or Control: Lutheran Church - Missouri Synod
IRS Status: 501(c)3
Highest Offering: Doctorate; No Undergraduates
Program: Professional
Accreditation: NH, THEOL

01 President .... Dr. Lawrence R. RAST
05 Academic Dean .... Dr. Charles A. GIESCHEN
36 Dean Pastoral Education/ Placement .... Dr. Carl C. FICKENSCHER, II
32 Dean of Students .... Rev. Thomas P. ZIMMERMAN
10 Vice President Business Affairs .... Rev. Albert B. WINGFIELD
06 Registrar .... Mrs. Barbara A. WEGMAN
07 Director of Admissions .... Rev. Timothy R. PULS
08 Head Librarian .... Prof. Robert V. ROETHEMEYER

Crossroads Bible College (H)

601 N Shortridge Road, Indianapolis IN 46219-4912
County: Marion FICE Identification: 034567
Unit ID: 439613
Telephone: (317) 352-8736 Carnegie Class: Spec/Faith
FAX Number: (317) 352-9145 Calendar System: Semester
URL: www.crossroads.edu
Established: 1980 Annual Undergrad Tuition & Fees: $9,850
Enrollment: 221 Coed
Affiliation or Control: Independent Non-Profit IRS Status: 501(c)3
Highest Offering: Baccalaureate
Program: Religious Emphasis
Accreditation: BI

01 President .... Dr. A. Charles WARE
05 Chief Academic Officer .... Dr. John A. CRABTREE, JR.
06 Registrar .... Dr. Linda CHAVIS

DePauw University (I)

313 S Locust Street, Greencastle IN 46135-1772
County: Putnam FICE Identification: 001792
Unit ID: 150400
Telephone: (765) 658-4800 Carnegie Class: Bac/A&S
FAX Number: (765) 658-4177 Calendar System: 4/1/4
URL: www.depauw.edu
Established: 1837 Annual Undergrad Tuition & Fees: $36,500
Enrollment: 2,390 Coed
Affiliation or Control: United Methodist IRS Status: 501(c)3
Highest Offering: Baccalaureate
Program: Liberal Arts And General
Accreditation: NH, MUS, TED

01 President .... Dr. Brian W. CASEY
100 Senior Advisor to the President .... Mr. Christopher J. WELLS
45 VP for Comm & Strat Initiatives .... Mr. Christopher J. WELLS
05 Vice President for Academic Affairs .... Dr. David T. HARVEY
20 Dean of Faculty .... Dr. Kerry PANNELL
20 Dean of Academic Life .... Dr. Pedar W. FOSS
10 Vice Pres Finance/Administration .... Mr. Bradley A. KELSHEIMER
21 Assoc Vice Pres for Finance .... Mr. Kevin S. KESSINGER
30 VP for Advancement .... Dr. Marcia S. LATTA
07 Vice Pres Admissions/Financial Aid .... Mr. Daniel L. MEYER
32 VP Student Life/Dean of Students .... Dr. Cynthia BABINGTON
04 Executive Assistant to President .... Ms. Elizabeth DEMMINGS
06 Registrar .... Dr. Kenneth J. KIRKPATRICK
27 Chief Information Officer .... Ms. Carol L. SMITH
88 Executive Director of Development .... Mr. Jason G. PETROVICH
64 Dean of Music School .... Dr. Mark MCCOY
37 Director of Financial Aid .... Mr. Craig A. SLAUGHTER
29 Exec Director of Alumni Relations .... Ms. Jennifer C. SOSTER
41 Director of Athletics .... Mr. S. Page COTTON
36 Director of Career Services .... Mr. Steven LANGERUD
23 Director of Student Health Services .... Dr. Scott RIPPLE
88 Director of International Education .... Ms. Kathleen S. KNAUL
08 Director of Libraries .... Mr. Rick E. PROVINE
16 Director of Human Resources .... Ms. Patricia BACON
18 Director of Facilities .... Mr. Richard N. VANCE
19 Director of Public Safety .... Ms. Angela D. NALLY
09 Director of Institutional Research .... Dr. William M. TOBIN
91 Director of Application Systems .... Ms. Bonnie NEALON
42 University Chaplain .... Dr. Paul T. WILSON
38 Interim Director of Counseling .... Dr. Ethan L. BLISS
96 Director of Purchasing .... Mr. Richard SHUCK
21 Exec Director of Finance/Controller .... Mr. Keith ARCHER
26 Exec Director of Media Relations .... Mr. Ken OWEN
44 Director of the Annual Fund .... Vacant

DeVry University - Indianapolis (J)

9100 Keystone Crossing, Suite 350, Indianapolis IN 46240-2158
County: Marion Identification: 666556
Unit ID: 432214
Telephone: (317) 581-8854 Carnegie Class: Spec/Bus
FAX Number: (317) 581-8955 Calendar System: Semester
URL: www.devry.edu
Established: 1931 Annual Undergrad Tuition & Fees: $15,294
Enrollment: 545 Coed
Affiliation or Control: Proprietary IRS Status: Proprietary
Highest Offering: Master's
Program: Professional; Business Emphasis

Accreditation: &NH

01 Campus Director .... Bill COIT

† Regional accreditation is carried under the parent institution in Downers Grove, IL.

DeVry University - Merrillville Center (A)

1000 E 80th Place, Suite 222 Mall,
Merrillville IN 46410-5673

County: Lake — Identification: 666209
Unit ID: 432214
Telephone: (219) 736-7440 — Carnegie Class: Spec/Bus
FAX Number: (219) 736-7874 — Calendar System: Semester
URL: www.devry.edu
Established: 1997 — Annual Undergrad Tuition & Fees: $15,294
Enrollment: 437 — Coed
Affiliation or Control: Proprietary — IRS Status: Proprietary
Highest Offering: Master's
Program: Occupational; Professional; Business Emphasis
Accreditation: &NH

01 Center Dean .... Ms. Pam TAYLOR

† Regional accreditation is carried under the parent institution in Downers Grove, IL.

Earlham College and Earlham School of Religion (B)

801 National Road W, Richmond IN 47374-4095

County: Wayne — FICE Identification: 001793
Unit ID: 150455
Telephone: (765) 983-1200 — Carnegie Class: Bac/A&S
FAX Number: (765) 983-1304 — Calendar System: Semester
URL: www.earlham.edu
Established: 1847 — Annual Undergrad Tuition & Fees: $38,284
Enrollment: 1,135 — Coed
Affiliation or Control: Friends — IRS Status: 501(c)3
Highest Offering: Master's
Program: Liberal Arts And General; Teacher Preparatory; Professional; Religious Emphasis
Accreditation: NH, THEOL

01 President .... John David DAWSON
05 Vice President Academic Affairs .... Greg MAHLER
10 Vice President Business Affairs .... Sena LANDEY
30 Vice President Advancement .... Jim MCKEY
88 Vice President School of Religion .... Jay MARSHALL
31 Vice President for Community Rels .... Avis STEWART
44 Assoc VP for Institutional Advance .... Kim TANNER
32 Dean of Student Development .... Cheryl PRESLEY
07 Dean of Admissions/Financial Aid .... Vacant
04 Assistant to President .... JoBeth BUCKLEY
41 Athletic Director .... Frank CARR
21 Assistant VP for Business .... Dana NORTH
21 Controller .... Cathy HABSCHMIDT
88 Director Academic Support Services .... Donna KEESLING
29 Director of Alumni Relations .... Gail CLARK
42 Director of Religious Life .... Kelly BURK
36 Director of Career Services .... Vacant
14 Director of Computing Services .... Thomas STEFFES
37 Director of Financial Aid .... Robert ARNOLD
23 Director of Health Services .... Mary Ann STIENBARGER
16 Director of Human Resources .... Vacant
09 Director of Institutional Research .... Nelson BINGHAM
85 Director of International Programs .... Patty O'MALEY-LAMSON
18 Director of Physical Plant .... Vacant
26 Director of Public Affairs .... Vacant
27 Director of Public Information .... Mark BLACKMON
19 Director of Security .... Vacant
08 Librarian .... Scott SILVERMAN
40 Bookstore Manager .... Dee Dee CUMMINGS
06 Registrar .... Bonita WASHINGTON-LACEY
73 Admissions School of Religion .... Valerie HURWITZ
88 Registrar School of Religion .... April VANLONDON
35 Director Student Affairs .... Rich DORNBERGER
20 Associate Academic Officer .... Lyn MILLER
88 Provost .... Nelson BINGHAM
15 Director Personnel Services .... Vacant
28 Director of Diversity .... Trayce PETERSON
84 Director Enrollment Management .... Nancy SINEX
96 Director of Purchasing .... Alice LAFUZE

Franklin College of Indiana (C)

101 Branigin Boulevard, Franklin IN 46131-2623

County: Johnson — FICE Identification: 001798
Unit ID: 150604
Telephone: (317) 738-8000 — Carnegie Class: Bac/Diverse
FAX Number: (317) 736-6030 — Calendar System: 4/1/4
URL: www.franklincollege.edu
Established: 1834 — Annual Undergrad Tuition & Fees: $25,680
Enrollment: 1,106 — Coed
Affiliation or Control: American Baptist — IRS Status: 501(c)3
Highest Offering: Baccalaureate
Program: Liberal Arts And General; Teacher Preparatory
Accreditation: NH, TED

01 President .... Dr. James G. MOSELEY
04 Assistant to the President .... Ms. Janet D. SCHANTZ
10 Vice President Finance .... Mr. Bryan SPETTER
45 Vice Pres Planning/Plant/Technology .... Mrs. Lisa FEARS
30 Vice Pres Institutional Advancement .... Mr. Bart MEYER
05 Vice Pres Academic Affs/Dean of Col .... Dr. David G. BRAILOW
84 Vice Pres Enrollment and Marketing .... Mr. Alan P. HILL
32 Dean of Students .... Mr. Ellis F. HALL
20 Assoc Dean/Dir Faculty Development .... Dr. Timothy L. GARNER
20 Ast Dean Engaged Lrng/Dir Prof Dev .. Mrs. Brooke A. WORLAND
06 Registrar .... Mr. Matthew Robert JONES
18 Director of Plant Operations .... Mr. Mark LECHER
39 Director of Residence Life .... Ms. LaTika WEBSTER
38 Director of Counseling .... Dr. John R. SHAFER
35 Dir Stdnt Activities/Organizations .... Ms. Keri ELLINGTON
29 Director of Alumni Relations .... Mrs. Margee STAMPER
46 Dir of Devel Research & Records .... Ms. Betsy SCHMIDT
44 Dir Advancement/Leadership Giving .... Mr. Thomas W. ARMOR
37 Director of Financial Aid .... Mrs. Elizabeth SAPPENFIELD
42 Campus Minister .... Rev. David WEATHERSPOON
41 Athletic Director .... Mr. Kerry N. PRATHER
13 Dir of Information Tech Services .... Ms. Lisa E. MAHAN
36 Dir Career Svcs/Asst Dean Students .... Mr. Kirk J. BIXLER
88 Director of Leadership Development .... Mrs. Bonnie L. PRIBUSH
85 Director of Intercultural Studies .... Ms. Simone PILON
88 Director of Dining Services-Sodexo .... Mr. Les PETROFF
44 Dir Development/Donor Relations .... Mrs. Kristy BROWN
07 Director of Admissions .... Ms. Jacqueline ACOSTA
26 Director of Public Relations .... Ms. Deidra BAUMGARDNER
09 Director of Institutional Analysis .... Dr. Sara BRADLEY
08 Director of the Library .... Mr. Ronald L. SCHUETZ
19 Director of Campus Security .... Mr. Steve LEONARD
105 Webmaster .... Mr. Christopher J. MACNAUGHTON
44 Advancement Associate .... Mr. Daniel J. FRISCHE
15 Manager of Employee Resources .... Mrs. Maureen PINNICK
22 Proj Mgr Organization Devel/Safety .... Mr. Thomas PATZ
40 Bookstore Manager (Follett) .... Ms. Rhea CAIN
21 Business Office Manager .... Mr. Brad JONES
23 Coordinator of Health Services .... Ms. Theresa NIGH
28 Coord Multicultural/Diversity Svcs .... Ms. Chelsea S. REED
50 Head Business/Computing/Math Div .... Mr. James C. WILLIAMS
53 Head Education Division .... Mrs. Katherine M. REMSBURG
79 Head Humanities Division .... Dr. Sara COLBURN-ALSOP
60 Head Journalism Division .... Mr. Joel CRAMER
65 Head Natural Sciences Division .... Dr. Steven K. BROWDER
83 Head Social Sciences Division .... Dr. Denise M. BAIRD
57 Head Fine Arts Division .... Mr. Robin ROBERTS

Goshen College (D)

1700 S Main Street, Goshen IN 46526-4794

County: Elkhart — FICE Identification: 001799
Unit ID: 150668
Telephone: (574) 535-7000 — Carnegie Class: Bac/A&S
FAX Number: (574) 535-7060 — Calendar System: Semester
URL: www.goshen.edu
Established: 1894 — Annual Undergrad Tuition & Fees: $25,700
Enrollment: 857 — Coed
Affiliation or Control: Mennonite Church — IRS Status: 501(c)3
Highest Offering: Master's
Program: Liberal Arts And General; Teacher Preparatory; Professional
Accreditation: NH, NURSE, SW, TED

01 President .... Dr. James E. BRENNEMAN
05 Academic Dean/VP Academic Affairs .... Dr. Anita K. STALTER
10 Vice President for Finance .... Mr. James L. HISTAND
30 Vice Pres Institutional Advancement .... Mr. James K. CASKEY
84 Vice President for Enrollment .... Vacant
28 Director of Multicultural Affairs .... Dr. Odelet NANCE
32 Dean of Students/VP Student Life .... Mr. Bill BORN
20 Associate Academic Dean .... Dr. Ross PETERSON-VEATCH
66 Director of Nursing .... Ms. Vicki S. KIRKTON
70 Director of Social Work .... Dr. Robert M. BIRKEY
53 Director of Elementary Teacher Educ .... Dr. Kathryn MEYER REIMER
08 Librarian .... Ms. Lisa G. GUEDEA CARRENO
82 Director of International Education .... Dr. Tom J. MEYERS
14 Director of Information Tech Svcs .... Mr. Michael SHERER
09 Director of Institutional Research .... Mr. Scott BARGE
06 Registrar .... Mr. Stan W. MILLER
37 Director Student Financial Aid .... Ms. Judy S. MOORE
26 Director of Public Relations .... Mr. Richard AGUIRRE
29 Director of Alumni/Parent Relations .... Ms. Kelli B. KING
42 Campus Minister .... Mr. Robert E. YODER
36 Director of Career Services .... Ms. Anita R. YODER
18 Director of Facilities .... Mr. Clay E. SHETLER
15 Director of Human Resources .... Mr. Norm BAKHIT
88 Executive Director of Adult Pgms .... Mr. Randy GUNDEN
35 Director of Student Activities .... Ms. Michelle FANFAIR STEURY
88 Director of Special Programs .... Ms. Janette K. YODER
38 Director Student Counseling .... Mrs. Char HOCHSTETLER
04 Admin Assistant to the President .... Ms. Betty SCHRAG

Grace College and Seminary (E)

200 Seminary Drive, Winona Lake IN 46590-1294

County: Kosciusko — FICE Identification: 001800
Unit ID: 150677
Telephone: (574) 372-5100 — Carnegie Class: Bac/Diverse
FAX Number: (574) 372-5139 — Calendar System: Semester
URL: www.grace.edu
Established: 1948 — Annual Undergrad Tuition & Fees: $22,546
Enrollment: 1,773 — Coed
Affiliation or Control: Fellowship Of Grace Brethren Churches
IRS Status: 501(c)3
Highest Offering: Doctorate
Program: Liberal Arts And General; Teacher Preparatory; Religious Emphasis
Accreditation: NH, CACREP, IACBE, TED, THEOL

01 President .... Dr. Ronald E. MANAHAN
04 Exec Assistant to the President .... Mrs. Nancy L. WEIMER
05 Provost .... Dr. William J. KATIP
32 VP Student Affairs & Academic Svcs .... Dr. James E. SWANSON
10 Chief Financial Officer .... Mr. G. Stephen POPENFOOSE
30 Chief Advancement Officer .... Mr. John R. BOAL
11 Chief Operations Officer .... Mr. Thomas A. DUNN
73 Dean of the Seminary .... Dr. Jeffery A. GILL
13 Dir Information Technology .... Mr. Donald W. FLUKE
07 Dean of Admissions .... Mrs. Cindy N. SISSON
42 Dean of Chapel & Global Ministries .... Vacant
23 Director Student Health & Wellness .... Dr. Matthew A. MILLER
106 Dir Distance Ed & Online Learning .... Mr. Timothy J. ZIEBARTH
06 Registrar .... Mr. Steven T. CARLSON
08 Librarian .... Vacant
37 Director Student Financial Aid .... Mrs. Charlette R. SAUDERS
15 Director of Human Resource .... Mrs. Audrey L. RUSSELL
27 Dir of Marketing & Communication .... Mr. David GROUT
18 Director Physical Plant .... Mr. Randy KLEINHANS
29 Director Alumni Relations .... Vacant
41 Athletic Director .... Vacant
36 Director of Career Services .... Mrs. Denise TERRY
09 Director of Institutional Research .... Dr. Bradley K. LEMLER
88 Director Institutional Assessment .... Dr. James E. BOWLING
51 Dean of Adult & Community Educ .... Dr. Stephen A. GRILL

Hanover College (F)

PO Box 108, Hanover IN 47243-0108

County: Jefferson — FICE Identification: 001801
Unit ID: 150756
Telephone: (812) 866-7000 — Carnegie Class: Bac/A&S
FAX Number: (812) 866-2164 — Calendar System: Other
URL: www.hanover.edu
Established: 1827 — Annual Undergrad Tuition & Fees: $28,850
Enrollment: 1,005 — Coed
Affiliation or Control: Presbyterian Church (U.S.A.) — IRS Status: 501(c)3
Highest Offering: Baccalaureate
Program: Liberal Arts And General; Teacher Preparatory
Accreditation: NH, TED

01 President .... Dr. Sue DEWINE
04 Executive Asst to the President .... Mrs. Treva SHELTON
05 Vice Pres/Dean of the Faculty .... Dr. Steve JOBE
30 Vice President College Advancement .... Mr. Dennis HUNT
10 Vice President Business Affairs .... Mr. J. Michael BRUCE
32 Vice President Student Life .... Dr. David YEAGER
84 Dean of Enrollment Management .... Mr. Jon RIESTER
37 Director of Financial Aid .... Mr. Richard NASH
88 Exec Director-Rivers Institute .... Dr. Larry DEBUHR
88 Exec Director-Center for Bus Prep .... Mr. Jerry JOHNSON
36 Director of Placement .... Mrs. Margaret KRANTZ
06 Registrar .... Dr. Ken PRINCE
08 Director of College Libraries .... Mr. Ken GIBSON
18 Chief Facilities/Physical Plant .... Mr. Mike HUTCHINSON
26 Dir Communications & Marketing .... Mrs. Rhonda BURCH
29 Director of Alumni Relations .... Mrs. Ann INMAN
88 Director of Admission .... Mr. Chris GAGE
38 Director of Student Counseling .... Mrs. Katie DINE YOUNG
15 Director of Human Resources .... Ms. Shelley PREOCANIN
35 Coord Student Org/Leadership Trng .... Mrs. Kathryn LOWE-SCHNEIDER

Harrison College - Anderson Campus (G)

140 E 53rd Street, Anderson IN 46013-1717

County: Madison — Identification: 666030
Unit ID: 151157
Telephone: (765) 644-7514 — Carnegie Class: Assoc/PrivFP
FAX Number: (765) 644-5724 — Calendar System: Quarter
URL: www.harrison.edu
Established: 1902 — Annual Undergrad Tuition & Fees: $12,135
Enrollment: 280 — Coed
Affiliation or Control: Proprietary — IRS Status: Proprietary
Highest Offering: Baccalaureate
Program: Occupational; 2-Year Principally Bachelor's Creditable
Accreditation: &@NH, ACICS, MAC

01 President .... Mr. Jason T. KONESCO
12 Campus President .... Ms. Charlene STACY

† Regional accreditation is carried under the parent institution in Indianapolis (Downtown Campus), IN.

Harrison College - Columbus Indiana Campus (H)

2222 Poshard Drive, Columbus IN 47203-1843

County: Bartholomew — Identification: 666428
Unit ID: 151193
Telephone: (812) 379-9000 — Carnegie Class: Assoc/PrivFP
FAX Number: (812) 375-0414 — Calendar System: Quarter
URL: www.harrison.edu
Established: 1902 — Annual Undergrad Tuition & Fees: $12,135
Enrollment: 255 — Coed
Affiliation or Control: Proprietary — IRS Status: Proprietary
Highest Offering: Baccalaureate

Program: Occupational; 2-Year Principally Bachelor's Creditable
Accreditation: &@NH, ACICS, MAC

01 President .... Mr. Jason T. KONESCO
12 Campus President .... Ms. Angela SHAFER

† Regional accreditation is carried under the parent institution in Indianapolis (Downtown Campus), IN.

Harrison College - Elkhart Campus (A)

56075 Parkway Avenue, Elkhart IN 46516-9325
County: Elkhart Identification: 666143
Unit ID: 450386
Telephone: (574) 522-0397 Carnegie Class: Assoc/PrivFP
FAX Number: (574) 523-0829 Calendar System: Quarter
URL: www.ibcschools.edu
Established: 1902 Annual Undergrad Tuition & Fees: $12,135
Enrollment: 349 Coed
Affiliation or Control: Proprietary IRS Status: Proprietary
Highest Offering: Associate Degree
Program: Occupational; 2-Year Principally Bachelor's Creditable
Accreditation: ACICS, MAC

01 President .... Mr. Jason T. KONESCO
12 Campus President .... Mr. Justin ELLIOTT

† Branch campus of Harrison College, Indianapolis, IN.

Harrison College - Evansville Campus (B)

4601 Theater Drive, Evansville IN 47715-3901
County: Vanderburgh Identification: 666429
Unit ID: 423670
Telephone: (812) 476-6000 Carnegie Class: Bac/Assoc
FAX Number: (812) 471-8576 Calendar System: Quarter
URL: www.harrison.edu
Established: 1902 Annual Undergrad Tuition & Fees: $12,135
Enrollment: 233 Coed
Affiliation or Control: Proprietary IRS Status: Proprietary
Highest Offering: Baccalaureate
Program: Occupational; 2-Year Principally Bachelor's Creditable
Accreditation: &@NH, ACICS, MAC

01 President .... Mr. Jason T. KONESCO
12 Regional President .... Mr. Steve D. HARDIN

† Regional accreditation is carried under the parent institution in Indianapolis (Downtown Campus), IN.

Harrison College - Fort Wayne Campus (C)

6413 N Clinton Street, Fort Wayne IN 46825-4911
County: Allen Identification: 666029
Unit ID: 438966
Telephone: (260) 471-7667 Carnegie Class: Assoc/PrivFP4
FAX Number: (260) 471-6918 Calendar System: Quarter
URL: www.harrison.edu
Established: 1902 Annual Undergrad Tuition & Fees: $12,135
Enrollment: 497 Coed
Affiliation or Control: Proprietary IRS Status: Proprietary
Highest Offering: Baccalaureate
Program: Occupational; 2-Year Principally Bachelor's Creditable
Accreditation: &@NH, ACICS, MAC, SURGT

01 President .... Mr. Jason T. KONESCO
12 Regional President .... Ms. Janet HERMAN

† Regional accreditation is carried under the parent institution in Indianapolis (Downtown Campus), IN.

Harrison College - Indianapolis Downtown Campus (D)

550 E Washington Street, Indianapolis IN 46204-2611
County: Marion FICE Identification: 021584
Unit ID: 151166
Telephone: (317) 264-5656 Carnegie Class: Bac/Assoc
FAX Number: (317) 264-5650 Calendar System: Quarter
URL: www.harrison.edu
Established: 1902 Annual Undergrad Tuition & Fees: $12,135
Enrollment: 2,634 Coed
Affiliation or Control: Proprietary IRS Status: Proprietary
Highest Offering: Baccalaureate
Program: Occupational; 2-Year Principally Bachelor's Creditable
Accreditation: @NH, ACICS, ACFEI, MAC

01 President .... Mr. Jason T. KONESCO
12 Campus President .... Mr. Gregory P. REGER

Harrison College - Indianapolis East Campus (E)

8150 Brookville Road, Indianapolis IN 46239-8903
County: Marion Identification: 666430
Unit ID: 414850
Telephone: (317) 375-8000 Carnegie Class: Assoc/PrivFP
FAX Number: (317) 351-1871 Calendar System: Quarter
URL: www.harrison.edu
Established: 1902 Annual Undergrad Tuition & Fees: $12,135
Enrollment: 501 Coed
Affiliation or Control: Proprietary IRS Status: Proprietary
Highest Offering: Baccalaureate
Program: 2-Year Principally Bachelor's Creditable; Nursing Emphasis
Accreditation: &@NH, ACICS, ADNUR, MAC, MLTAD, SURGT

01 President .... Mr. Jason T. KONESCO
12 Campus President .... Mr. Gary A. MCGEE

† Regional accreditation is carried under the parent institution in Indianapolis (Downtown Campus), IN.

Harrison College - Indianapolis Northwest Campus (F)

6300 Technology Center Drive, Indianapolis IN 46278-6022
County: Hamilton Identification: 666388
Unit ID: 447397
Telephone: (317) 873-6500 Carnegie Class: Assoc/PrivFP
FAX Number: (317) 733-6266 Calendar System: Quarter
URL: www.harrison.edu
Established: 1902 Annual Undergrad Tuition & Fees: $12,135
Enrollment: 301 Coed
Affiliation or Control: Proprietary IRS Status: Proprietary
Highest Offering: Baccalaureate
Program: Occupational; 2-Year Principally Bachelor's Creditable
Accreditation: &@NH, ACICS

01 President .... Mr. Jason T. KONESCO
12 Campus President .... Mr. Marvin BAILEY

† Regional accreditation is carried under the parent institution in Indianapolis (Downtown Campus), IN.

Harrison College - Lafayette Campus (G)

4705 Meijer Court, Lafayette IN 47905-4859
County: Tippecanoe Identification: 666431
Unit ID: 151245
Telephone: (765) 447-9550 Carnegie Class: Assoc/PrivFP
FAX Number: (765) 447-0868 Calendar System: Quarter
URL: www.harrison.edu
Established: 1902 Annual Undergrad Tuition & Fees: $12,135
Enrollment: 297 Coed
Affiliation or Control: Proprietary IRS Status: Proprietary
Highest Offering: Baccalaureate
Program: Occupational; 2-Year Principally Bachelor's Creditable
Accreditation: &@NH, ACICS, MAC

01 President .... Mr. Jason T. KONESCO
12 Campus President .... Mr. Timothy I. PARSONS

† Regional accreditation is carried under the parent institution in Indianapolis (Downtown Campus), IN.

Harrison College - Muncie Campus (H)

411 West Riggin Road, Muncie IN 47303-6413
County: Delaware FICE Identification: 030097
Unit ID: 151209
Telephone: (765) 288-8681 Carnegie Class: Assoc/PrivFP4
FAX Number: (765) 288-8797 Calendar System: Quarter
URL: www.harrison.edu
Established: 1902 Annual Undergrad Tuition & Fees: $12,135
Enrollment: 229 Coed
Affiliation or Control: Proprietary IRS Status: Proprietary
Highest Offering: Baccalaureate
Program: Occupational; 2-Year Principally Bachelor's Creditable
Accreditation: @NH, ACICS, MAC

01 President .... Mr. Jason T. KONESCO
12 Campus President .... Ms. Charlene SAMPLE-PURTLEBAUGH

Harrison College - Terre Haute Campus (I)

1378 S State Road 46, Terre Haute IN 47803-9787
County: Vigo Identification: 666433
Unit ID: 151236
Telephone: (812) 877-2100 Carnegie Class: Assoc/PrivFP4
FAX Number: (812) 877-4440 Calendar System: Quarter
URL: www.harrison.edu
Established: 1902 Annual Undergrad Tuition & Fees: $12,135
Enrollment: 312 Coed
Affiliation or Control: Proprietary IRS Status: Proprietary
Highest Offering: Baccalaureate
Program: Occupational; 2-Year Principally Bachelor's Creditable
Accreditation: &@NH, ACICS, MAC

01 President .... Mr. Jason T. KONESCO
12 Campus President .... Ms. Pat J. MOZLEY

† Regional accreditation is carried under the parent institution in Indianapolis (Downtown Campus), IN.

Holy Cross College (J)

PO Box 308, Notre Dame IN 46556-0308
County: Saint Joseph FICE Identification: 007263
Unit ID: 150774
Telephone: (574) 239-8400 Carnegie Class: Bac/A&S
FAX Number: (574) 239-8323 Calendar System: Semester
URL: www.hcc-nd.edu
Established: 1966 Annual Undergrad Tuition & Fees: $21,700
Enrollment: 449 Coed
Affiliation or Control: Roman Catholic IRS Status: 501(c)3
Highest Offering: Baccalaureate
Program: Liberal Arts And General
Accreditation: NH

01 President .... Bro. John R. PAIGE, CSC
03 Senior Vice President .... Dr. Tina S. HOLLAND
11 VP for Operations .... Mr. Dan HAVERTY
30 VP for Mission Advancement .... Mr. Robert L. KLOSKA
04 Executive Assistant .... Ms. Jodie L. SWEET-PRZYBYSZ
20 Dean of Faculty .... Mr. Justin WATSON
32 Dean of Students .... Mr. Daniel J. COCHRAN
06 Registrar .... Mr. Richard J. SULLIVAN
84 Director of Enrollment Management .... Mrs. Marie BENSMAN
37 Director of Financial Aid .... Mr. Robert BENJAMIN
38 Director of Student Counseling Svcs . Bro. Chris J. DREYER, CSC
13 Director of Campus Technology ... Bro. Charles D. DREVON, CSC
18 Director of Building & Grounds .... Mr. Randy MCKINLEY
39 Director of Residence Life .... Dr. Christopher TORRIJAS
08 Director of Library Services .... Mrs. Mary Ellen HEGEDUS
36 Director of Discernment & Prep .... Mr. Charles BALL
42 Director of Campus Ministry .... Mr. Andrew POLANIECKI
41 Athletic Director .... Mr. Robert SCHERMERHORN

Huntington University (K)

2303 College Avenue, Huntington IN 46750-9986
County: Huntington FICE Identification: 001803
Unit ID: 150941
Telephone: (260) 356-6000 Carnegie Class: Bac/Diverse
FAX Number: (260) 359-4086 Calendar System: 4/1/4
URL: www.huntington.edu
Established: 1897 Annual Undergrad Tuition & Fees: $23,210
Enrollment: 1,278 Coed
Affiliation or Control: United Brethren Church IRS Status: 501(c)3
Highest Offering: Master's
Program: Liberal Arts And General; Teacher Preparatory; Professional
Accreditation: NH, MUS, NURSE, SW, TED

01 President .... Dr. G. Blair DOWDEN
05 Sr VP for Academic Affairs & Dean .... Dr. A. Norris FRIESEN
10 Sr VP for Ops & Finance/Treasurer .... Mr. Thomas W. AYERS
84 Sr VP Enrollment Mgmt & Marketing .. Mr. Jeffrey C. BERGGREN
45 Sr VP Strategy & Grad/Adult Program ... Dr. Ann C. MCPHERREN
30 Vice President for Advancement .... Mr. Vincent D. HAUPERT
32 Vice President for Student Life .... Dr. Ron L. COFFEY
45 VP for Strategy & Innovation .... Mr. Troy D. IRICK
26 Vice Pres for University Relations .... Mr. John W. PAFF
04 Admin Assistant to President .... Mrs. Barbara A. THOMPSON
42 Interim Campus Pastor .... Rev. Arthur L. WILSON
58 Dean Grad/Adult Pgm/Acad Effective ..... Dr. Stephen D. HOLTROP
36 Assoc Dean Student Life/Career Dev .... Ms. Martha J. SMITH
35 Associate Dean of Student Life .... Mr. Jesse M. BROWN
44 Senior Director of Gift Planning ...... Mr. Richard W. MCCONNELL
21 Controller/Dir Financial Services .... Mr. Scott A. BERRY
37 Director of Financial Aid .... Mrs. Sharon R. WOODS
06 Registrar .... Mrs. Sarah J. HARVEY
08 Director of Library Services .... Ms. Anita GRAY
13 Director of Technology Services .... Mr. Gary L. CAMPBELL
38 Director of Learning Assistance .... Mrs. Kristal L. CHAFIN
41 Interim Athletic Director .... Ms. Lori L. CULLER
18 Director of Physical Plant .... Mr. Jerry A. GRESSLEY
15 Dir Human Resources/Auxiliary Svcs .... Mrs. Julie A. HENDRYX
29 Director of Alumni .... Mrs. Margaret A. ROUSH
19 Director of Campus Police .... Mr. Barry A. COCHRAN
88 Dir Urban Scholarship & Mentoring .... Mr. Arthur L. WILSON
26 Assistant Director Media Relations .... Ms. Ashley SMITH
40 Bookstore Manager .... Mrs. Lisa M. SNYDER

Indiana Institute of Technology (L)

1600 E Washington Boulevard, Fort Wayne IN 46803-1297
County: Allen FICE Identification: 001805
Unit ID: 151290
Telephone: (260) 422-5561 Carnegie Class: Spec/Bus
FAX Number: (260) 420-1453 Calendar System: Semester
URL: www.indianatech.edu
Established: 1930 Annual Undergrad Tuition & Fees: $23,430
Enrollment: 4,420 Coed
Affiliation or Control: Independent Non-Profit IRS Status: 501(c)3
Highest Offering: Doctorate
Program: Professional; Business Emphasis
Accreditation: NH, ENG

01 President .... Dr. Arthur E. SNYDER
05 Vice President of Academic Affairs .... Dr. Douglas G. PERRY
03 Exec VP Finance & Administration .... Ms. Judy K. ROY
107 VP College of Professional Studies ...... Mr. Steve A. HERENDEEN
84 VP Enrollment Mgmt/Student Life ...... Ms. Allison G. CARNAHAN
30 Vice President of Inst Advancement .... Mr. Mark H. RICHTER
50 Dean of Business .... Dr. Jeffrey A. ZIMMERMAN
06 Registrar .... Ms. Lori L. BRUBAKER
97 Dean of General Studies .... Dr. Doty A. LATUSZEK
54 Dean of Engineering/Computer Sci .... Mr. David A. ASCHLIMAN
61 Dean of Law .... Vacant
37 Director of Financial Aid .... Ms. Jacki S. SWITZER
18 Director of Facilities Management .... Mr. R. Mike TOWNSLEY

13 Director of Information Technology ....Mr. Jeff S. LEICHTY
15 Human Resources Director ....Mr. Christopher B. BLACK
21 Controller ....Ms. Shelly R. MUSOLF
77 Assoc Dean of Computer Sciences ....Mr. Gary A. MESSICK
58 Director of PhD Program ....Dr. Kenneth E. RAUCH
20 Assoc Dean of CPS ....Dr. Andrew I. NWANNE
53 Director of Teacher Education ....Dr. Brad L. YODER
07 Assoc VP Enrollment Management ....Ms. Monica L. CHAMBERLAIN
26 Marketing Director ....Ms. Janet L. SCHUTTE
36 Dir of Career Planning & Devel Ctr ......Ms. Cynthia P. VERDUCE
11 Director of Operations-CPS ....Ms. Sharon LOKUTA
12 Operations Manager-Indianapolis ....Ms. Phyllis E. HOGAN
12 Operations Manager-Elkhart .... Ms. Janice M. CUNNINGHAM
08 Director McMillen Library ....Ms. Constance E. SCOTT
88 Director of Criminal Sciences .... Dr. Steven F. HUNDERSMARCK
106 Director of Online Learning ....Dr. Y. Ben LEE
89 Director of Freshman College & SSS .... Ms. Mary C. SCUDDER
39 Assoc VP Student Services ....Mr. Chris M. DICKSON
29 Dir Annual Fund & Alumni Relations .. Mr. Michael E. PETERSON
04 Executive Asst to the President ....Ms. Jennifer A. ROSS
42 Faith Services Coordinator ....Mr. Gregory P. BYMAN
102 Exec Dir U Communications ....Ms. Deborah S. AGLER
41 Athletic Director ....Mr. Martin C. NEUHOFF
32 Director Student Life ....Ms. Jessica M. INNIGER
35 Student Life Coordinator ....Ms. Andrea G. CHECK
84 Enrollment Manager-Fort Wayne .... Mr. Yiani DEMITSAS
84 Enrollment Manager-Indy .... Mr. Shayne D. ABRAHAMS
88 Associate VP Development .... Mr. Larry J. PIERKARSKI
88 CPS Development Manager ....Ms. A. Nicole SCOTT
88 Title III Director ....Ms. Danielle L. WITZIGREUTER

Indiana State University (A)

200 N 7th Street, Terre Haute IN 47809-1902
County: Vigo FICE Identification: 001807
Unit ID: 151324
Telephone: (812) 237-6311 Carnegie Class: DRU
FAX Number: (812) 237-2291 Calendar System: Semester
URL: web.indstate.edu
Established: 1865 Annual Undergrad Tuition & Fees (In-State): $7,782
Enrollment: 11,494 Coed
Affiliation or Control: State IRS Status: 501(c)3
Highest Offering: Doctorate
Program: Liberal Arts And General; Teacher Preparatory; Professional
Accreditation: NH, AAFCS, #ARCPA, ART, BUS, CACREP, CEA, CIDA, CLPSY, CONST, COPSY, DIETC, ENGT, MUS, NAIT, NRPA, NUR, SCPSY, SP, SW, TED

01 President ....Dr. Daniel J. BRADLEY
88 Spec Asst to the Pres Int Rel ....Ms. Teresa D. EXLINE
86 Spec Asst to the Pres Ext Rel ....Mr. Brian K. HASLER
88 Spec Asst to the Pres Strat Plng ....Dr. Karl BURGHER
05 Provost/Vice Pres Academic Affs .... Dr. C. Jack MAYNARD
10 VP Business Affs & Fin/Treas ....Ms. Diann E. MCKEE
84 VP Enrollment Mgmt/Mktg/Comm ....Mr. John BEACON
32 VP Student Affairs/Dean of Students ....Ms. Carmen TILLERY
43 General Council/Univ Secretary ....Ms. Melony A. SACOPULOS
20 Associate VP Academic Affairs ....Dr. Robert E. ENGLISH
20 Associate VP Academic Affairs ....Ms. Jennifer SCHRIVER
13 Assoc VP Chief Info Officer ....Dr. Edward R. KINLEY
18 Assoc VP Univ Facilities Management ....Mr. Kevin L. RUNION
26 Asst VP Communications/Marketing ....Ms. Tara SINGER
07 Asst VP Enrollment/Dir Admissions ....Mr. Richard J. TOOMEY
29 Interim Co-Dir of Alumni Affairs .... Mr. Gary BALLINGER
29 Interim Co-Dir of Alumni Affairs ....Ms. Jennifer LEWELLYN
15 Assoc VP Human Resources ....Mr. Wil DOWNS
14 Exec Dir Information Technology .... Mr. Yancy PHILLIPS
21 Business Officer ....Ms. Diann E. MCKEE
06 Registrar ....Ms. April HAY
22 Director of Affirm Action ....Ms. Sheila JOHNSON
28 University Diversity Officer ....Ms. Mary FERGUSON
41 Director of Athletics ....Mr. Ronald PRETTYMAN
36 Director of Career Center ....Vacant
88 AVP Community Engagement ....Dr. Nancy B. ROGERS
31 Director Community/Prof Pgm ....Vacant
25 Director Sponsored Programs .... Ms. Dawn UNDERWOOD
09 Director of Institutional Research ....Ms. Patty MCCLINTOCK
19 Director of Public Safety ....Mr. William C. MERCIER
96 Dir Purchasing/Central Receiving ....Mr. Kevin BARR
39 Director of Residential Life ....Mr. Rex KENDALL
38 Director of Student Counseling ....Dr. Kenneth CHEW
37 Director of Student Financial Aid ....Mr. Kim DONAT
49 Dean of Arts & Sciences ....Dr. John MURRAY
50 Dean of Business ....Dr. Nancy MERRITT
53 Dean of Education ....Dr. Bradley BALCH
68 Dean Nursing/Health & Human Svcs ....Dr. Richard (Biff) WILLIAMS
72 Dean of Technology ....Dr. Bradford (Brad) SIMS
58 Dean of Grad/Professional Studies .... Dr. Jay GATRELL
08 Dean of Library Services ....Ms. Alberta COMER
51 Dean of Extended Learning ....Dr. Ken BRAUCHLE

*Indiana University System (B)

Bryan Hall, Bloomington IN 47405-7000
County: Monroe FICE Identification: 008002
Telephone: (812) 332-0211 Carnegie Class: N/A
FAX Number: N/A
URL: www.indiana.edu

01 President ....Dr. Michael A. MCROBBIE
05 Exec Vice President/Provost IUB ....Dr. Karen HANSON
45 Exec Vice Pres/Chancellor IUPUI .... Dr. Charles BANTZ
45 Exec VP Univ Regional Affs/Plng/Pol .... Mr. John APPLEGATE
46 Vice Pres for Research ....Dr. George JOSE
28 VP Diversity/Equity/Multicultural .... Dr. Edwin MARSHALL
11 Vice Pres/Chief Admin Officer .... Mr. Thomas MORRISON
10 Vice Pres/Chief Financial Officer .... Dr. Neil THEOBALD
26 VP Public Affairs & Govt Relations .... Mr. Michael SAMPLE
100 Chief of Staff ....Dr. Karen H. ADAMS
13 Vice President Info Tech/CIO ....Dr. Brad C. WHEELER
43 Vice Pres and University Counsel ....Ms. Dorothy FRAPWELL
104 Vice Pres for International Affairs ....Dr. Patrick O'MEARA
88 Vice President for Engagement ....Mr. William B. STEPHAN
41 VP & Dir of Intercoll Athletics ....Mr. Fred GLASS
63 VP Univ Clinical Affs/Dean Sch Med .... Dr. Craig BRATER
21 University Treasurer ....Ms. Mary Frances MCCOURT
22 Director of Affirmative Action ....Ms. Julie KNOST
29 Exec Dir IU Alumni Association ....Mr. J. T FORBES
15 Director of Human Resources ....Mr. Dan RIVES
27 Director of Media Relations ....Mr. Lawrence MACINTYRE
102 President IU Foundation ....Vacant

*Indiana University Bloomington (C)

107 S. Indiana Ave., Bloomington IN 47405-7000
County: Monroe FICE Identification: 001809
Unit ID: 151351
Telephone: (812) 855-4848 Carnegie Class: RU/VH
FAX Number: (812) 855-5678 Calendar System: Semester
URL: www.iub.edu
Established: 1820 Annual Undergrad Tuition & Fees (In-State): $952
Enrollment: 42,464 Coed
Affiliation or Control: State IRS Status: 501(c)3
Highest Offering: Doctorate
Program: Liberal Arts And General; Teacher Preparatory; Professional
Accreditation: NH, ART, AUD, BUS, BUSA, CACREP, CIDA, CLPSY, COPSY, DIETD, IPSY, JOUR, LAW, LIB, MUS, NRPA, OPD, OPT, OPTR, OPTT, PH, SCPSY, SP, SPAA, TED, THEA

02 President ....Dr. Michael MCROBBIE
05 Exec Vice Pres & Provost IUB ....Dr. Karen HANSON
03 Exec Vice Pres & Chanc IUPUI ....Dr. Charles BANTZ
09 Exec VP Univ Reg Affs/Plng/Policy ....Mr. John S. APPLEGATE
88 Senior Advisor to Provost & Exec VP ... Dr. Maynard THOMPSON
10 Vice President & CFO .... Dr. Neil THEOBALD
63 VP Univ Clin Affrs/Dean Sch of Med .... Dr. D. Craig BRATER
18 Vice Pres Capital Proj/Facilities ....Dr. Tom MORRISON
28 VP Diversity/Equity & Multicul Affs .... Dr. Edwin MARSHALL
46 Vice President for Research ....Dr. Jorge JOSE
26 VP for Public Affs & Govt Relations ....Mr. Mike SAMPLE
88 Vice President for Engagement ....Mr. William B. STEPHAN
20 Vice Provost for Undergraduate Educ .... Dr. Sonya STEPHENS
20 Vice Prov Faculty & Academic Affs .... Dr. Thomas GIERYN
88 Assoc VP Rsrch/Vice Provost Rsrch ....Dr. P. Sarita SONI
84 Vice Provost Enrollment Mgmt .... Dr. David JOHNSON
30 Sr Vice Pres Development/IU Fdn ....Ms. Marti HEIL
15 Associate Vice Pres Human Resources ....Mr. Dan RIVES
09 Sr Advisor Univ Inst Rsrch & Rptg ....Dr. Vic BORDEN
91 Assoc VP Enterprise Infrastructure .... Mr. Dennis CROMWELL
21 Vice Chanc Budget & Admin/IUB .... Mr. James DONGES
27 Vice Pres Info Technology & CIO .... Dr. Brad WHEELER
58 Dean University Graduate School ....Dr. James WIMBUSH
102 Pres & CEO IU Foundation ....Dr. Eugene R. TEMPEL
20 Assoc Vice Prov Faculty & Acad Affs .... Dr. Michael WADE
20 Assoc Vice Prov Faculty & Acad Affs .... Dr. Anne MASSEY
85 Assoc VP for International Svcs .... Mr. Christopher VIERS
49 Dean College Arts & Sciences ....Dr. Larry SINGELL
08 Ruth Lilly Dean Univ Libraries .... Dr. Brenda JOHNSON
32 Dean of Students .... Dr. Pete GOLDSMITH
50 Dean Kelley School of Business .... Dr. Daniel SMITH
53 Dean School of Education .... Dr. Gerardo GONZALEZ
68 Int Dean Sch Health/Phys Ed/Recrtn ....Dr. Mo TORABI
88 Dean School of Optometry ....Dr. Joseph BONANNO
61 Dean School of Law ....Ms. Lauren ROBEL
64 Dean Jacobs School of Music .... Mr. Gwyn RICHARDS
60 Dean School of Journalism .... Dr. Brad HAMM
88 Dean School of Informatics ....Dr. Bobby SCHNABEL
80 Dean SPEA ....Dr. John D. GRAHAM
62 Intm Dean Sch Library/Info Science ....Dr. Debora SHAW
82 Vice Pres International Affairs ....Dr. David ZARET
51 Dean Sch Continuing Studies ....Dr. Daniel CALLISON
92 Dean Hutton Honors College .... Dr. Matthew AUER
94 Dean Women's Affairs ....Dr. Yvette ALEX-ASSENSOH
35 Assoc Dean of Students ....Ms. Carol MCCORD
29 Exec Dir IU Alumni Association ....Mr. J. T FORBES
39 Exec Dir Residential Pgm & Svcs ....Mr. Pat CONNOR
36 Director Career Dev Center ....Mr. Patrick DONAHUE
16 Director Human Resource Services ....Ms. Suzanne RYAN
06 Assoc Vice Provost/Registrar ....Mr. Roland COTE
23 Director Student Health Services ....Dr. Hugh JESSOP
43 VP & General Counsel ....Ms. Dorothy J. FRAPWELL
88 Director IU Press ....Dr. Janet RABINOWITCH
22 Director Affirmative Action ....Ms. Julie KNOST
40 Manager of IU Bookstore ....Mr. Joe BENDER
19 Chief of Police ....Mr. Keith CASH
88 Exec Dir Indiana Memorial Union .... Mr. Bruce JACOBS
88 Director Radio/TV Services ....Mr. Perry METZ
88 Director Campus Bus Service .... Mr. Perry MAULL
88 Director IU Auditorium ....Mr. Doug BOOHER
18 Asst VP Facilities Operations ....Mr. Hank HEWETSON
38 Director Counseling & Psych Svs ....Dr. Nancy STOCKTON
41 VP & Dir Intercollegiate Athletics ....Mr. Fred GLASS
96 Asst VP Purchasing .... Ms. Lorelei MEEKER
25 Exec Dir Grant & Contract Services .... Mr. Jim BECKER
90 Assoc Dean Research Technologies .... Dr. Craig STEWART
07 Director of Admissions .... Ms. Mary Ellen ANDERSON

*Indiana University East (D)

2325 Chester Boulevard, Richmond IN 47374-1289
County: Wayne FICE Identification: 001811
Unit ID: 151388
Telephone: (765) 973-8200 Carnegie Class: Bac/Diverse
FAX Number: (765) 973-8237 Calendar System: Semester
URL: www.iue.edu
Established: 1946 Annual Undergrad Tuition & Fees (In-State): $7,661
Enrollment: 3,365 Coed
Affiliation or Control: State IRS Status: 501(c)3
Highest Offering: Master's
Program: Liberal Arts And General; Teacher Preparatory
Accreditation: NH, ACBSP, NUR, TED

02 Chancellor .... Dr. Nasser H. PAYDAR
05 Exec Vice Chanc Academic Affairs .... Dr. Lawrence D. RICHARDS
26 Vice Chanc Exec Affairs/Marketing ....Mr. Rob ZINKAN
10 Vice Chancellor Admin & Finance ....Mr. Dan DOOLEY
32 Assoc Vice Chanc/Dean of Students .... Dr. Mary BLAKEFIELD
13 Director Information Technology ....Mr. Todd DUKE
30 Director of Gift Development ....Ms. Brindy ROOSA
06 Registrar .... Mr. Dennis HICKS
08 Director Library/Media Services .... Dr. Frances YATES
15 Director Human Resources .... Ms. Dianne S. CHANDLER
36 Director Career Services ....Vacant
07 Director of Admissions ....Ms. Molly VANDERPOOL
37 Asst Dir Fin Aid & Scholarships .... Ms. Sarah SOPER
20 Director University College .... Ms. Carrie HELLER
40 Manager of Barnes & Noble Bookstore ....Ms. Kristy FRASHER
35 Director of Campus Life .... Ms. Rebeckah SNODDY
21 Bursar ....Vacant
22 Interim Director Affirmative Action ....Ms. Dianne CHANDLER
70 Director Social Work/Human Services ....Mr. Ed FITZGERALD
27 Director Communications & Marketing ....Mr. John DALTON
51 Director Continuing Studies ....Vacant
29 Director Alumni Relations .... Ms. Terry WIESEHAN
28 Director of Multicultural Affairs ....Mr. Timothy WILLIAMS
50 Dean Business/Technology .... Dr. David FRANTZ
79 Dean Humanities & Social Sciences ....Dr. Joanne PASSET
81 Dean Natural Sciences & Mathematics ..Dr. Kumara JAYASURIYA
66 Dean of Nursing ....Ms. Karen CLARK
53 Dean Education .... Dr. Marilyn WATKINS

*Indiana University Kokomo (E)

2300 S Washington, Box 9003, Kokomo IN 46904-9003
County: Howard FICE Identification: 001814
Unit ID: 151333
Telephone: (765) 453-2000 Carnegie Class: Bac/Diverse
FAX Number: (765) 455-9444 Calendar System: Semester
URL: www.iuk.edu
Established: 1945 Annual Undergrad Tuition & Fees (In-State): $6,332
Enrollment: 3,109 Coed
Affiliation or Control: State IRS Status: 501(c)3
Highest Offering: Master's
Program: Occupational; Liberal Arts And General; Teacher Preparatory; Professional
Accreditation: NH, BUS, NURSE, RAD, TED

02 Chancellor ....Dr. Michael HARRIS
05 Exec Vice Chanc Academic Affairs ... Dr. Sue SCIAME-GIESECKE
10 Vice Chanc Admin/Finance ....Mr. Roy TAMIR
32 Vice Chancellor Student Affairs .... Dr. Jack A. THARP
30 Vice Chancellor for Advancement ....Ms. Penny LEE
20 Asst Vice Chanc Academic Affairs .... Dr. Kathy PARKISON
72 Director Division Purdue Tech ....Ms. Christy BOZIC
08 Dean of the Library ....Ms. Rhonda ARMSTRONG
37 Associate Director Financial Aid ....Ms. Karen GALLATIN
84 Director of Enrollment Management ....Ms. Tyana LANGE
15 Director Human Resources ....Vacant
06 Registrar ....Ms. Stacey THOMAS
38 Asst Vice Chanc Student Success ....Ms. Gerry G. STROMAN
36 Manager Career Services ....Ms. Tracy SPRINGER
29 Director Alumni Relations ....Ms. Catherine VALCKE
27 Director Communications & Marketing ....Ms. Marie RADEL
35 Dean of Students ....Ms. Sarah SARBER
18 Chief Facilities/Physical Plant ....Vacant
50 Dean School of Business ....Dr. Frank WADSWORTH
49 Interim Dean School Arts & Science .... Dr. Erv BOSCHMANN
66 Dean School of Nursing ....Dr. Linda WALLACE
53 Dean Division of Education ....Dr. Paul PAESE
81 Chair Natural/Info/Math Sciences ....Dr. Christian CHAURET
79 Chair Humanities ....Dr. Scott JONES

*Indiana University Northwest (F)

3400 Broadway, Gary IN 46408-1197
County: Lake FICE Identification: 001815
Unit ID: 151360
Telephone: (219) 980-6500 Carnegie Class: Master's M
FAX Number: (219) 980-6670 Calendar System: Semester
URL: www.iun.edu
Established: 1921 Annual Undergrad Tuition & Fees (In-State): $6,408
Enrollment: 5,969 Coed
Affiliation or Control: State IRS Status: 501(c)3
Highest Offering: Master's
Program: Occupational; Liberal Arts And General; Teacher Preparatory; Professional
Accreditation: NH, BUS, DA, DH, NUR, NURSE, RAD, RTT, SPAA, TED

02 Chancellor ... Dr. William J. LOWE
04 Exec Asst to the Chancellor ... Mrs. Kathy MALONE
05 Exec Vice Chanc Academic Affairs ... Dr. David J. MALIK
11 Vice Chancellor Administration ... Dr. Joseph PELLICCIOTTI
32 Vice Chancellor Student Services ... Dr. Diane HODGES
10 Campus Chief Financial Officer ... Mrs. Marianne MILICH
26 Executive Director External Rels ... Mr. K. Timothy WEIDMANN
27 Chief Information Officer ... Ms. Beth VAN GORDON
20 Assoc Vice Chanc Academic Affs ... Dr. Cynthia O'DELL
09 Asst VC Inst Effectiveness & Rsrch ... Mr. John NOVAK
49 Dean College of Arts & Sciences ... Dr. Mark HOYERT
88 Dean Col of Health & Human Svcs ... Dr. Patrick BANKSTON
50 Dean School of Business & Economics ... Dr. Anna ROMINGER
53 Dean School of Education ... Dr. Stanley WIGLE
51 Division Chair Continuing Studies ... Mr. Thomas SWIRSKI
80 Director Public & Environ Affs ... Dr. Barbara PEAT
70 Director Social Work ... Dr. Darlene LYNCH
06 Registrar ... Ms. Jo Anne BOWEN
51 Int Dir Extended/Continuing Study ... Dr. Atilla TUNCAY
07 Director Admissions ... Ms. Linda B. TEMPLETON
37 Director Financial Aid ... Mr. Harold BURTLEY
36 Director Career & Placement ... Ms. Sharese DUDLEY
35 Director Student Life ... Dr. Charles GARY, JR.
19 Director Security ... Mr. Denson CHATFIELD
29 Director Alumni Relations ... Ms. Paulette LAFATA-JOHNSON
66 Dean Division of Nursing ... Dr. Linda ROODA
24 Director Instructional Media Svcs ... Mr. Paul SHARPE
08 Director Library ... Mr. Timothy SUTHERLAND
18 Director Physical Plant ... Mr. Otto JEFIMENKO
21 Manager Student Accounts ... Ms. Sandra MENDOZA
25 Director Research/Sponsored Pgms ... Ms. T.J STOOPS
15 Director Human Resources ... Ms. Carolyn HARTLEY
28 Director of Diversity Programming ... Dr. Kenneth COOPWOOD
38 Director of Student Counseling Ctr ... Ms. Barbara A. BULLOCK
96 Dir of Purchasing & Campus Services ... Ms. Marianne MALYJ
22 Director Affirmative Action ... Ms. Ida GILLIS

*Indiana University-Purdue University Fort Wayne (A)

2101 E Coliseum Boulevard, Fort Wayne IN 46805-1499
County: Allen
FICE Identification: 001828
Unit ID: 151102
Telephone: (260) 481-6100
Carnegie Class: Master's L
FAX Number: (260) 481-6880
Calendar System: Semester
URL: www.ipfw.edu
Established: 1964
Annual Undergrad Tuition & Fees (In-State): $6,708
Enrollment: 14,192
Coed
Affiliation or Control: State
IRS Status: 501(c)3
Highest Offering: Master's
Program: Liberal Arts And General; Teacher Preparatory; Professional
Accreditation: NH, ADNUR, BUS, CS, DA, DH, DT, ENG, ENGT, MUS, NUR, RAD, SPAA, TED

02 Chancellor ... Dr. Michael A. WARTELL
05 Vice Chancellor Academic Affairs ... Dr. William J. MCKINNEY
10 Vice Chancellor Financial Affairs ... Mr. Walter J. BRANSON
32 Vice Chancellor Student Affairs ... Dr. George S. MCCLELLAN
45 Assoc Vice Chancellor Inst Research ... Dr. John C. DAHL
04 Admin Assistant to the Chancellor ... Ms. Kay FOLKS
30 Executive Director Development ... Ms. Linda L. RUFFOLO
26 Exec Dir Univ Relations/Commun ... Ms. Irene A. WALTERS
14 Director Information Tech Services ... Mr. Robert M. KOSTRUBANIC
18 Director Physical Plant ... Mr. Jay H. HARRIS
29 Director Alumni Relations ... Ms. Kimberly M. WAGNER
08 Library Dean ... Ms. Cheryl B. TRUESDELL
15 Director Human Resources ... Ms. Rose M. COSTELLO
41 Director of Athletics ... Mr. Tommy BELL
21 Comptroller ... Mr. Daniel L. GEBHART
06 Registrar ... Mr. Patrick A. MCLAUGHLIN
96 Director Purchasing ... Ms. Cynthia M. ELICK
19 Chief University Police ... Mr. Jeffrey W. DAVIS
22 Director Institutional Equity ... Vacant
85 Director International Program ... Mr. Brian MYLREA
37 Director Financial Aid ... Ms. Judith CRAMER
07 Director of Admissions ... Ms. Carol B. ISAACS
38 Assoc Vice Chanc Student Success ... Dr. Bruce BUSBY
84 Director Enrollment Management ... Mr. Mark A. FRANKE
49 Dean Arts & Sciences ... Dr. Carl N. DRUMMOND
76 Dean Health Sciences ... Vacant
51 Exec Director Continuing Stds ... Ms. Deborah M. CONKLIN
72 Dean Engr Tech/Computer Science ... Mr. S.C. Max YEN
53 Dean Education & Public Policy ... Dr. Barry W. KANPOL
50 Dean Business ... Dr. Otto H. CHANG
57 Dean Visual/Performing Arts ... Dr. Charles D. O'CONNOR
46 Assoc Vice Chanc Rsrch Ext Support ... Dr. J. ALBAYYARI
20 Associate Academic Officer ... Dr. Steve T. SARRATORE
35 Dean of Students ... Dr. Eric M. NORMAN
28 Assoc Vice Chancellor Diversity ... Mr. Kenneth C. CHRISTMON

*Indiana University-Purdue University Indianapolis (B)

355 N Lansing Street, Indianapolis IN 46202-2896
County: Marion
FICE Identification: 001813
Unit ID: 151111
Telephone: (317) 274-5555
Carnegie Class: RU/H
FAX Number: N/A
Calendar System: Semester
URL: www.iupui.edu
Established: 1969
Annual Undergrad Tuition & Fees (In-State): $6,756
Enrollment: 30,566
Coed
Affiliation or Control: State
IRS Status: 501(c)3
Highest Offering: Doctorate
Program: Occupational; Liberal Arts And General; Teacher Preparatory; Professional
Accreditation: NH, ADNUR, ART, CIDA, CLPSY, CS, CYTO, DA, DENT, DH, DIETI, EMT, ENG, ENGT, HSA, HT, IPSY, LAW, MED, MT, MUS, NMT, NUR, NURSE, OT, PA, PH, PTA, RAD, RADDOS, RTT, SPAA, SW

02 Chancellor ... Dr. Charles R. BANTZ
100 Chief of Staff ... Vacant
28 Asst Chanc Diversity/Equity/Incl ... Mr. Kenneth B. DURGANS
04 Assistant to Chancellor for Comm ... Ms. Sylvia M. PAYNE
05 Exec Vice Chanc/Dean Faculties ... Dr. Uday P. SUKHATME
10 Vice Chanc Administration & Finance ... Ms. Dawn M. RHODES
26 Vice Chancellor External Affairs ... Ms. Amy C. WARNER
32 Vice Chancellor Student Life ... Dr. Zebulun R. DAVENPORT
46 Vice Chancellor Research ... Dr. Kody VARAHRAMYAN
13 Dean Information Technologies ... Dr. Garland C. ELMORE
08 Dean University Library ... Mr. David W. LEWIS
84 Director Enrollment Services ... Dr. Rebecca E. PORTER
06 Registrar ... Ms. Mary Beth MYERS
21 Bursar ... Ms. Ingrid TOSCHLOG
22 Director Equal Opportunity ... Ms. Kim D. KIRKLAND
38 Director Student Counseling ... Dr. Julie LASH
39 Director Campus Housing ... Mr. Aaron HART
40 Bookstore Manager ... Ms. Michele G. CARTER
36 Director Placement ... Mr. Thomas T. COOK
41 Athletic Director ... Mr. Michael R. MOORE
29 Director Alumni Relations ... Mr. Stefan S. DAVIS
27 Director Communications/Marketing ... Mr. Troy D. BROWN
09 Director Institutional Research ... Dr. Gary PIKE
07 Dir of Undergraduate Admissions ... Mr. Chris J. FOLEY
37 Director Student Financial Aid ... Ms. Kathy PURVIS
15 Director Human Resources ... Vacant
23 Medical Director Student Health Svc ... Dr. Stephen F. WINTERMEYER
18 Director Campus Facility Services ... Ms. Emily C. WREN
19 Chief Campus Police ... Mr. Paul E. NORRIS
92 Dean Honors College ... Dr. E. Jane LUZAR
96 Director Purchasing ... Mr. Robert HALTER
45 Senior Advisor/Academic Planning ... Dr. Trudy W. BANTA
12 Dean Columbus Campus ... Dr. Marwan A. WAFA
76 Dean School Health/Rehab Sci ... Dr. Austin O. AGHO
57 Dean Herron School of Art ... Ms. Valerie EICKMEIER
51 Dean Sch of Continuing Studies ... Dr. Daniel J. CALLISON
52 Dean School of Dentistry ... Dr. John N. WILLIAMS
54 Dean School of Engr/Technology ... Dr. David J. RUSSOMANNO
88 Exec Assoc Dean of Informatics ... Dr. Anthony FAIOLA
61 Dean Sch of Law Indianapolis ... Mr. Gary R. ROBERTS
49 Dean School of Liberal Arts ... Dr. William A. BLOMQUIST
63 Dean School of Medicine ... Dr. D. Craig BRATER
66 Dean School of Nursing ... Dr. Marion E. BROOME
88 Interim Dean School of Optometry ... Dr. P. Sarita E. SONI
68 Dean School of Physical Education ... Dr. James M. GLADDEN
81 Dean School of Science ... Dr. Simon RHODES
70 Dean School of Social Work ... Dr. Michael PATCHNER
53 Exec Assoc Dean School of Education ... Dr. Patricia M. ROGAN
60 Dean Sch of Journalism ... Dr. Brad HAMM
62 Exec Assoc Dean Library/Info Sci ... Dr. Tomas A. LIPINSKI
80 Exec Assoc Dean Public/Environ Affs ... Dr. Terry BAUMER
85 Int Assoc Dean International Affs ... Dr. Sara K. ALLAEI
50 Assoc Dean School of Business ... Dr. Philip L. COCHRAN
58 Associate Dean Graduate School ... Dr. Sherry F. QUEENER

*Indiana University South Bend (C)

1700 Mishawaka Avenue, South Bend IN 46634-7111
County: Saint Joseph
FICE Identification: 001816
Unit ID: 151342
Telephone: (574) 520-4872
Carnegie Class: Master's M
FAX Number: (574) 520-4834
Calendar System: Semester
URL: www.iusb.edu
Established: 1940
Annual Undergrad Tuition & Fees (In-State): $6,467
Enrollment: 8,590
Coed
Affiliation or Control: State
IRS Status: 501(c)3
Highest Offering: Master's
Program: Occupational; Liberal Arts And General; Teacher Preparatory; Professional
Accreditation: NH, BUS, CACREP, DH, MACTE, NURSE, RAD, SPAA, TED

02 Chancellor ... Dr. Una Mae RECK
05 Exec Vice Chanc Academic Affairs ... Dr. Alfred J. GUILLAUME, JR.
10 Vice Chancellor Finance & Admin ... Mr. Bill J. O'DONNELL
26 Vice Chanc Public Affs/Univ Advance ... Dr. Ilene SHEFFER
32 Vice Chanc Student Affs/Enroll Mgmt ... Dr. Jeff JONES
13 Regional Chief Information Officer ... Ms. Elizabeth VAN GORDON
20 Assoc Vice Chanc Academic Affs ... Dr. John L. MCINTOSH
88 Assoc VC Student Acad Support Svcs ... Ms. Karen L. WHITE
84 Asst Vice Chanc for Enrollment Svcs ... Ms. Cathy M. BUCKMAN
06 Registrar ... Mr. Jeff JOHNSTON
36 Director Career Services Office ... Mr. Jeffery L. JACKSON
35 Dir Student Activit Ctr/Athletics ... Mr. Gary DEMSKI
37 Interim Director of Financial Aid ... Ms. Cyndi LANG
18 Director Facilities Management ... Mr. Michael PRATER
19 Director of Safety & Security ... Mr. Martin L. GERSEY
15 Director of Human Resources ... Ms. Sara ERMETI
24 Dir of Instructional Media Svcs ... Mr. Jim YOCOM
29 Dir Alumni Affs/Campus Ceremonies ... Ms. Jeanie METZGER
27 Director Communications/Marketing ... Mr. Kenneth W. BAIERL
52 Director of Dental Auxiliary Educ ... Ms. Kristyn QUIMBY
51 Director of Extended Learning ... Mr. Tim RYAN
97 Director of General Studies ... Dr. David A. VOLLRATH
85 Director of International Programs ... Dr. Scott SERNAU

38 Director Student Counseling Ctr ... Mr. James HURST
07 Director of Admissions ... Mr. Michael RENFROW
09 Director of Institutional Research ... Vacant
28 Director of Diversity ... Ms. Charlotte D. PFEIFFER
30 Director of Development ... Ms. Dina HARRIS
39 Director of Student Housing ... Mr. Paul KRIKAU
21 Director of Accounting ... Ms. Karen VARGO
49 Dean of Liberal Arts & Science ... Dr. Elizabeth E. DUNN
50 Dean of Business & Economics ... Dr. Robert DUCOFFE
53 Interim Dean of Education ... Dr. Karen CLARK
57 Dean of the Arts ... Dr. Marvin CURTIS
66 Dean of Nursing/Health Profess ... Dr. Mary Jo REGAN-KUBINSKI
08 Dean of Library Services ... Ms. Vicki BLOOM

*Indiana University Southeast (D)

4201 Grant Line Road, New Albany IN 47150-6405
County: Floyd
FICE Identification: 001817
Unit ID: 151379
Telephone: (812) 941-2000
Carnegie Class: Master's L
FAX Number: (812) 941-2475
Calendar System: Semester
URL: www.ius.edu
Established: 1941
Annual Undergrad Tuition & Fees (In-State): $6,422
Enrollment: 7,178
Coed
Affiliation or Control: State
IRS Status: 501(c)3
Highest Offering: Master's
Program: Occupational; Liberal Arts And General; Teacher Preparatory; Professional; Business Emphasis
Accreditation: NH, BUS, NURSE, TED

02 Chancellor ... Dr. Sandra R. PATTERSON-RANDLES
05 Vice Chancellor Academic Affairs ... Dr. Gilbert W. ATNIP
10 Vice Chanc Administration/Finance ... Mr. Dana C. WAVLE
32 Vice Chancellor Student Affairs ... Dr. Ruth C. GARVEY-NIX
29 Int Vice Chanc Alumni/Cmty Rels ... Mr. Jerry A. WAYNE
20 Assoc Vice Chanc Academic Affairs ... Vacant
13 Chief Information Officer ... Mr. Thomas SAWYER
84 Asst VC Enroll Mgmt/Dir Admissions ... Ms. Anne SKUCE
04 Admin Assistant to the President ... Ms. Debra A. EBERLE
32 Dean for Student Life ... Mr. Seuth CHALEUNPHONH
06 Registrar ... Vacant
37 Director Student Financial Aid ... Ms. Brittany HUBBARD
08 Director Library Services ... Mr. C. Martin ROSEN
14 Director IT Systems & Operations ... Mr. Kirk K. KLAPHAAK
36 Director Career Development Center ... Vacant
18 Director Physical Plant ... Mr. James WOLFE, JR.
14 Dir IT Communications & Support ... Mr. Nicholas T. RAY
21 Director Accounting Services ... Mr. Michael J. KERSTIENS
41 Director Athletics ... Mr. Joseph M. GLOVER
72 Purdue Pgms Site Administrator ... Dr. Andy SCHAFFER
15 Director Human Resources ... Ms. Ann B. LEE
09 Director Institutional Research ... Ms. Tanlee T. WASSON
19 Chief Safety & Security ... Mr. Charles EDELEN
38 Director Academic Success Center ... Mr. William G. MCGUIRE
22 Affirmative Action/Training Officer ... Ms. Darlene P. YOUNG
30 Director of Development ... Vacant
26 Dir of University Communication ... Ms. Jennifer J. WOLF
39 Director Residence Life & Housing ... Mr. Joshua DE WAR
51 Coord Continuing Studies-Credit ... Ms. Saundra E. BROWN
79 Dean School Arts & Letters ... Dr. Samantha EARLEY
81 Dean School Natural Sciences ... Dr. Emmanuel O. OTU
83 Dean School Social Sciences ... Dr. Joseph L. WERT
50 Dean School Business ... Dr. A. Jay WHITE
53 Dean School Education ... Dr. Gloria J. MURRAY
66 Dean School Nursing ... Dr. Marian A. MCKAY
46 Dean for Research ... Dr. Walter F. RYAN

Indiana Wesleyan University (E)

4201 S Washington Street, Marion IN 46953-4999
County: Grant
FICE Identification: 001822
Unit ID: 151801
Telephone: (765) 674-6901
Carnegie Class: Master's L
FAX Number: (765) 677-2499
Calendar System: 4/1/4
URL: www.indwes.edu
Established: 1920
Annual Undergrad Tuition & Fees: $29,104
Enrollment: 15,953
Coed
Affiliation or Control: Wesleyan Church
IRS Status: 501(c)3
Highest Offering: Doctorate
Program: Liberal Arts And General; Teacher Preparatory; Professional; Business Emphasis
Accreditation: NH, CACREP, MUS, NURSE, SW, TED

01 President ... Dr. Henry L. SMITH
03 Executive Vice President ... Dr. Keith NEWMAN
05 Provost ... Dr. David W. WRIGHT
10 Vice President Finance/CFO ... Dr. Duane KILTY
49 VP & Dean College of Arts & Science ... Dr. Darlene BRESSLER
51 VP & Dean Adult & Prof Studies ... Dr. Bridget AITCHISON
88 Vice President Wesley Seminary ... Dr. Wayne SCHMIDT
58 Dean Graduate School ... Dr. Jim FULLER
88 Dean of the Seminary ... Dr. Ken SCHENCK
66 Exec Director School of Nursing ... Dr. Barbara IHRKE
32 Vice Pres Student Development ... Dr. Michael MOFFITT
84 Vice Pres Enrollment Management ... Mrs. Kris DOUGLAS
13 Vice President Info Technology/CIO ... Mr. John JONES
20 Asst Provost Inst Research & Accred ... Dr. Don SPROWL
88 Assistant Provost for Scholarship ... Dr. Jerry PATTENGALE
20 Assistant Provost for Acad Svcs ... Mrs. Karen ROORBACH
37 Associate VP Financial Aid ... Mr. Thomas RATLIFF
08 Director Library Resources ... Mrs. Shelia CARLBLOM
08 Director Off-campus Library Svcs ... Mrs. Jule KIND

29 Director of Alumni ... Mr. Rick CARDER
07 Director Admissions ... Mr. Daniel SOLMS
15 Director Personnel Services ... Mr. Neil RUSH
06 University Registrar ... Mrs. Kim NICHOLSON
21 Controller ... Mr. Brian CAVIGGIOLA
36 Director Center for Life Calling ... Dr. Bill MILLARD
41 Athletic Director ... Mr. Mark DEMICHAEL
42 Dean of the Chapel ... Dr. Jim LO
44 Director Planned Giving ... Mr. Brian LEWIS
28 Director Intercultural Student Svcs ... Mrs. Latrese MOFFITT
92 Exec Director of Honors College ... Mr. David RIGGS
100 Chief of Staff ... Dr. Larry LINDSAY

International Business College (A)

5699 Coventry Lane, Fort Wayne IN 46804-9990
County: Allen FICE Identification: 004579
Unit ID: 151458
Telephone: (260) 459-4500 Carnegie Class: Bac/Assoc
FAX Number: (260) 436-1896 Calendar System: Semester
URL: www.ibcfortwayne.edu
Established: 1889 Annual Undergrad Tuition & Fees: $13,500
Enrollment: 616 Coed
Affiliation or Control: Proprietary IRS Status: Proprietary
Highest Offering: Baccalaureate
Program: Occupational; 2-Year Principally Bachelor's Creditable
Accreditation: ACICS, MAC

01 President ... Mr. Steve KINZER
05 Director of Education ... Ms. Debra PETERSEN
07 Director of Admissions ... Ms. Gena HOPKINS
32 Student Services Director ... Ms. Roxanna SHULL
51 Director Continuing Education ... Mr. Amee AUGENSPEIN
36 Director of Placement ... Ms. Heather WINGER
06 Registrar ... Ms. Cara CLAPPER

International Business College (B)

7205 Shadeland Station, Indianapolis IN 46256-3997
County: Marion Identification: 666929
Unit ID: 151467
Telephone: (317) 813-2300 Carnegie Class: Assoc/PrivFP
FAX Number: (317) 841-6419 Calendar System: Other
URL: www.intlbusinesscollege.com
Established: 1984 Annual Undergrad Tuition & Fees: $13,550
Enrollment: 405 Coed
Affiliation or Control: Proprietary IRS Status: Proprietary
Highest Offering: Associate Degree
Program: Occupational
Accreditation: ACICS, DA, MAC

01 President ... Ms. Kathy CHIUDIONI
05 Director of Education ... Ms. Scharme SMITH

ITT Technical Institute (C)

2810 Dupont Commerce Court,
Fort Wayne IN 46825-2393
County: Allen FICE Identification: 008329
Unit ID: 151500
Telephone: (260) 497-6200 Carnegie Class: Spec/Tech
FAX Number: (260) 497-6299 Calendar System: Quarter
URL: www.itt-tech.edu
Established: 1967 Annual Undergrad Tuition & Fees: N/A
Enrollment: 763 Coed
Affiliation or Control: Proprietary IRS Status: Proprietary
Highest Offering: Baccalaureate
Program: Technical Emphasis
Accreditation: ACICS

ITT Technical Institute (D)

9511 Angola Court, Indianapolis IN 46268-1119
County: Marion FICE Identification: 007329
Unit ID: 151519
Telephone: (317) 875-8640 Carnegie Class: Master's S
FAX Number: (317) 875-8641 Calendar System: Quarter
URL: www.itt-tech.edu
Established: 1956 Annual Undergrad Tuition & Fees: N/A
Enrollment: 7,619 Coed
Affiliation or Control: Proprietary IRS Status: Proprietary
Highest Offering: Master's
Program: Technical Emphasis
Accreditation: ACICS

ITT Technical Institute (E)

10999 Stahl Road, Newburgh IN 47630-7429
County: Warrick FICE Identification: 007327
Unit ID: 251251
Telephone: (812) 858-1600 Carnegie Class: Spec/Tech
FAX Number: (812) 858-0646 Calendar System: Quarter
URL: www.itt-tech.edu
Established: 1959 Annual Undergrad Tuition & Fees: N/A
Enrollment: 565 Coed
Affiliation or Control: Proprietary IRS Status: Proprietary
Highest Offering: Baccalaureate
Program: Technical Emphasis
Accreditation: ACICS

ITT Technical Institute (F)

17390 Dugdale Drive, Suite 100, South Bend IN 46635
County: St. Joseph Identification: 666700
Unit ID: 450270
Telephone: (574) 247-8300 Carnegie Class: Not Classified
FAX Number: (574) 247-8350 Calendar System: Quarter
URL: www.itt-tech.edu
Established: N/A Annual Undergrad Tuition & Fees: N/A
Enrollment: 512 Coed
Affiliation or Control: Proprietary IRS Status: Proprietary
Highest Offering: Baccalaureate
Program: Technical Emphasis
Accreditation: ACICS

† Branch campus of ITT Technical Institute, Fort Wayne, IN.

*Ivy Tech Community College of Indiana-Central Office (G)

50 W Fall Creek Parkway N Drive,
Indianapolis IN 46208-5752
County: Marion FICE Identification: 008546
Unit ID: 363563
Telephone: (317) 921-4882 Carnegie Class: N/A
FAX Number: (317) 921-4753
URL: www.ivytech.edu

01 President ... Mr. Thomas J. SNYDER
10 Vice President Finance/Treasurer ... Mr. Robert C. HOLMES
30 Vice President Development ... Dr. Joyce ROGERS
11 Vice President Administration ... Mr. William F. MORRIS
88 VP Program Analysis & Engagement ... Mr. Jeff TERP
32 Vice Pres Stdnt Affairs/Enrol Mgmt ... Dr. Benjamin YOUNG
103 Vice Pres Workforce & Econ Dev ... Dr. Rebecca NICKOLI
27 Vice Pres Marketing/Communications ... Mr. Jeff FANTER
05 Vice Provost Academic Affs/Provost ... Dr. Mary E. OSTRYE
43 Gen Counsel/Sr VP Wkfrc& Econ Dev ... Dr. Susan W. BROOKS
18 AVP Facilities Inst Planning ... Mr. Richard B. TULLY
53 Exec Dir Academic Policy/Assessment ... Dr. Cherry K. SMITH
88 Chief Finan Student Resources Offcr ... Mr. Ben BURTON
15 Executive Director Human Resources ... Mrs. Julie LORTON-ROWLAND
09 Exec Dir Institutional Research ... Mrs. Karen STANLEY
21 Assistant Treasurer ... Mr. Mark A. HUSK
13 Chief Technology Officer ... Mrs. Anne BRINSON

*Ivy Tech Community College of Indiana-Bloomington (H)

200 N Daniels Way, Bloomington IN 47404-9772
County: Monroe FICE Identification: 035213
Unit ID: 440244
Telephone: (812) 332-1559 Carnegie Class: Assoc/Pub-R-M
FAX Number: (812) 330-6106 Calendar System: Semester
URL: www.ivytech.edu/bloomington
Established: 1963 Annual Undergrad Tuition & Fees (In-State): $3,000
Enrollment: 6,500 Coed
Affiliation or Control: State IRS Status: 501(c)3
Highest Offering: Associate Degree
Program: Occupational; 2-Year Principally Bachelor's Creditable
Accreditation: &NH, ACBSP, ADNUR, EMT, NAIT, PNUR, RTT

02 Chancellor ... Mr. John R. WHIKEHART
05 Vice Chancellor Academic Affairs ... Dr. Jim O. SMITH
32 Vice Chancellor Student Affairs ... Ms. Jennie VAUGHAN
18 Director of Facilities ... Mr. Doug MATTICK
103 Interim Exec Dir Workfce/Econ Devel ... Ms. Katrina JONES
10 Executive Director Finance ... Mr. Doug GILES
30 Executive Director of Development ... Mr. John ZODY
13 Exec Dir of Campus Computing Svcs ... Mr. Ben ACKERMAN
26 Exec Director of Marketing ... Ms. Amanda BILLINGS
06 Registrar ... Ms. Rachel SKEENS
08 Library Director ... Ms. Susan CATT
28 Director of Outreach ... Ms. Debra VANCE
35 Director of Student Development ... Mr. Sam DEWEESE
21 Director Business Office ... Ms. Sherry DEIRTH
51 Director Continuing Education ... Ms. Susie GRAHAM
84 Director of Enrollment Services ... Ms. Beth PLESS
37 Director Student Financial Aid ... Ms. Patt MCCAFFERTY
36 Assistant Director Career Services ... Ms. Katie ANDERSON
29 Asst Dir Alumni Relations ... Ms. Jenny HUGGINS
09 Institutional Research Analyst ... Ms. Lindsey PANICCIA

*Ivy Tech Community College-Central Indiana (I)

50 W Fall Creek Parkway North Drive,
Indianapolis IN 46208-5752
County: Marion FICE Identification: 009917
Unit ID: 150987
Telephone: (317) 921-4882 Carnegie Class: Assoc/Pub-U-SC
FAX Number: (317) 921-4753 Calendar System: Semester
URL: www.ivytech.edu/indianapolis/
Established: 1966 Annual Undergrad Tuition & Fees (In-State): $3,355
Enrollment: 20,452 Coed
Affiliation or Control: State IRS Status: 501(c)3
Highest Offering: Associate Degree
Program: Occupational; 2-Year Principally Bachelor's Creditable
Accreditation: &NH, FUSER, ACBSP, ACFEI, ADNUR, MAC, NAIT, PNUR, RAD, SURGT

02 Chancellor ... Dr. B. Kaye WALTER
05 Vice Chanc of Academic Affairs ... Dr. Katherine LEE
32 Vice Chancellor of Student Affairs ... Dr. Darrell CAIN
35 Asst Vice Chanc Student Affairs ... Mr. Jerry H. HARRELL
103 Exec Dir Workforce & Economic Devel ... Mr. Scott HORVATH
20 Asst Vice Chanc Academic Affairs ... Mr. Gary PELLICO
09 Ex Dir Institutional Effectiveness ... Mr. Ken BOWEN
10 Executive Director of Finance ... Mr. Michael DAVIDSON
11 Exec Dir of Administrative Services ... Mr. James N. BARNEY
30 Exec Dir Institutional Advancement ... Mr. Randy ROGERS
15 Exec Director of Human Resources ... Mr. Ken BOWMAN
46 Exec Dir of Resource Development ... Mr. Paul ST. ANGELO
09 Director of Institutional Research ... Mr. Rick BENTLEY
37 Director of Financial Aid ... Ms. Lori J. HANDY
07 Director of Admissions ... Dr. Tracy FUNK
36 Director of Career Services ... Dr. Rebecca PATTEN-LEMONS
96 Director of Purchasing ... Mr. Jerry L. KOENIG
26 Director Marketing/Communications ... Ms. Shannon WILSON
06 Registrar ... Ms. Melanie HOUGH

*Ivy Tech Community College of Indiana-Columbus (J)

4475 Central Avenue, Columbus IN 47203-1868
County: Bartholomew FICE Identification: 010038
Unit ID: 150996
Telephone: (812) 372-9925 Carnegie Class: Assoc/Pub-R-M
FAX Number: (812) 372-0311 Calendar System: Semester
URL: www.ivytech.edu/columbus
Established: 1967 Annual Undergrad Tuition & Fees (In-State): $3,356
Enrollment: 6,523 Coed
Affiliation or Control: State IRS Status: 501(c)3
Highest Offering: Associate Degree
Program: Occupational; 2-Year Principally Bachelor's Creditable
Accreditation: &NH, ART, ACBSP, ADNUR, DA, EMT, MAC, NAIT, PNUR, SURGT

02 Chancellor ... Dr. John A. HOGAN
04 Assistant to the Chancellor ... Ms. Therese A. COPELAND
05 Int Vice Chancellor Academic Affs ... Ms. Catherine A. WOODWARD
32 Vice Chancellor for Student Affairs ... Mr. Roger B. BINGHAM
15 Exec Director of Human Resources ... Mr. John L. HATTER
103 Exec Dir Workforce/Economic Devel ... Ms. Teresa J. BEGLEY
26 Exec Dir Marketing/Communications ... Mr. Randall K. PROFFITT
30 Exec Dir of Resource Development ... Vacant
18 Executive Director of Facilities ... Mr. Floyd D. DONNELL
07 Director of Admissions ... Ms. Alisa DECK
37 Director of Financial Aid ... Mr. Paul R. JOHNSTON
14 Exec Director Computer Tech Svcs ... Mr. Dana STICKANS
06 Registrar ... Ms. Corrie A. MCGUCKIN
35 Dir Student Support & Development ... Ms. Rebecca A. ALLEN
36 Director Career/Employment Svcs ... Mr. Neil S. BAGADIONG
38 Int Dir Student Support/Development ... Ms. Janet M. SHARP

*Ivy Tech Community College of Indiana-East Central (K)

4301 Cowan Road, Muncie IN 47302-9448
County: Delaware FICE Identification: 009924
Unit ID: 151005
Telephone: (765) 289-2291 Carnegie Class: Assoc/Pub-R-L
FAX Number: (765) 289-2292 Calendar System: Semester
URL: www.ivytech.edu/eastcentral/
Established: 1968 Annual Undergrad Tuition & Fees (In-State): $2,707
Enrollment: 9,182 Coed
Affiliation or Control: State IRS Status: 501(c)3
Highest Offering: Associate Degree
Program: Occupational; 2-Year Principally Bachelor's Creditable
Accreditation: &NH, ACBSP, ACFEI, ADNUR, DA, DH, MAC, NAIT, PNUR, PTAA, RAD, SURGT

02 Chancellor ... Ms. Gail CHESTERFIELD
12 Vice Chancellor/Dean-Anderson ... Dr. Jim WILLEY
12 Vice Chancellor/Dean-Marion ... Dr. John LIGHTLE
05 Vice Chancellor Academic Affairs ... Dr. Ron SLOAN
32 Vice Chancellor Student Affairs ... Dr. Mary LEWELLEN
97 Dean General Education Division ... Mr. Neil ANTHONY
23 Dean Health Division ... Vacant
66 Dean School of Nursing ... Ms. Paula BOLEY
50 Dean Business Division ... Dr. Janet EVELYNDORSEY
72 Dean Technology Division ... Dr. Joyce WILKERSON
88 Dean Public Svcs/Academic Skills ... Mr. Jeff SCOTT
103 Exec Dir Workforce/Economic Devel ... Mr. Roy WINKLER
15 Exec Director of Human Resources ... Mr. Tim KELSEY
26 Exec Dir Mktg & Communications ... Ms. Betty WINGROVE
30 Exec Dir of Resource Development ... Ms. Tracey DANNER-ODENWELDER
21 Regional Dir Financial Affairs ... Mr. Mike EVANS
10 Director of Business Services ... Ms. Elda WILSFORD
35 Associate Dean of Student Affairs ... Vacant
06 Registrar ... Mr. Travis BLUME
07 Director of Admissions ... Dr. Mary LEWELLEN
18 Director of Facilities ... Mr. Harry MUELLER
11 Administrative Services Manager ... Ms. Sheila JOHNSON
37 Regional Director Financial Aid ... Ms. Tammy TOMFOHRDE
36 Coordinator Student Placement ... Vacant
84 Director Enrollment Management ... Mr. Corey SHARP

*Ivy Tech Community College of Indiana-Kokomo (A)

1815 E Morgan Street, Box 1373, Kokomo IN 46903-1373
County: Howard FICE Identification: 010041
Unit ID: 151014
Telephone: (765) 459-0561 Carnegie Class: Assoc/Pub-R-M
FAX Number: (765) 454-5121 Calendar System: Semester
URL: www.ivytech.edu/kokomo
Established: 1968 Annual Undergrad Tuition & Fees (In-State): $3,354
Enrollment: 5,401 Coed
Affiliation or Control: State IRS Status: 501(c)3
Highest Offering: Associate Degree
Program: Occupational; 2-Year Principally Bachelor's Creditable; Technical Emphasis
Accreditation: &NH, ACBSP, ADNUR, DA, EMT, MAC, NAIT, PNUR, SURGT

02 Chancellor .... Mr. Steve DAILY
05 Vice Chancellor of Academic Affairs .... Dr. Pamela LEWIS
32 Vice Chancellor Student Affairs .... Mrs. Michelle SIMMONS
12 Vice Chancellor of Logansport .... Mr. Kevin BOSTIC
12 Exec Dir Instructional Site Wabash .... Mrs. Pamella GUTHRIE
31 Exec Dir Corporate/Community Svcs .... Mrs. Janice BAILEY
10 Executive Director Finance .... Dr. Bradley THURMOND
45 Director Resource Development .... Mr. Gregory AARON
14 Exec Dir Instructional Technology .... Mr. Montaven HUGHES
16 Exec Director Human Resources .... Mrs. Celestine JOHNSON
37 Director Financial Aid .... Ms. Anjanetta POLK
26 Exec Dir Marketing/Communications .... Mrs. Marcia WORLAND
25 Director Grants/Projects .... Ms. Miriam THOMAS
06 Registrar .... Mr. David SCHEBLO
08 Library Director .... Ms. Julie DIESMAN
21 Business Office Manager .... Mrs. Cecilia (Jody) DAILY
75 Apprenticeship Coordinator .... Mrs. M. Nadine NEWSOM
18 Director Facilities .... Mr. Michael KARICKHOFF
40 Bookstore Manager .... Vacant
07 Director of Admissions .... Mr. Mike FEDERSPILL
36 Asst Director Career Services .... Ms. Jennifer NICHOLS
20 Asst Vice Chanc Academic Affairs .... Dr. Laurie PETERS

*Ivy Tech Community College of Indiana-Lafayette (B)

3101 S Creasy Lane, Box 6299, Lafayette IN 47903-6299
County: Tippecanoe FICE Identification: 010039
Unit ID: 151023
Telephone: (765) 269-5000 Carnegie Class: Assoc/Pub-R-L
FAX Number: (765) 772-9107 Calendar System: Semester
URL: www.ivytech.edu/lafayette
Established: 1968 Annual Undergrad Tuition & Fees (In-State): $3,355
Enrollment: 6,758 Coed
Affiliation or Control: State IRS Status: 501(c)3
Highest Offering: Associate Degree
Program: Occupational; 2-Year Principally Bachelor's Creditable
Accreditation: &NH, ACBSP, ADNUR, DA, MAC, NAIT, PNUR, SURGT

02 Chancellor .... Dr. David A. BATHE
05 Vice Chancellor of Academic Affairs .... Dr. Todd E. ROSWARSKI
32 Vice Chancellor of Student Affairs .... Dr. John LAWS
10 Exec Director of Administration .... Ms. Jane HARPER
15 Exec Director of Human Resources .... Ms. Carmen A. HURST
30 Exec Director Resource Development .... Ms. Pat COREY
103 Exec Dir of Work Force & Econ Devel .... Mr. Craig LAMB
26 Exec Dir Marketing & Communications .... Mr. Tom MCCOOL
20 Asst Vice Chanc Academic Affairs .... Dr. Victoria WACEK
09 Asst Vice Chanc Instnl Research .... Mr. William JONES
72 Dean School of Technology .... Mr. Glen ROBERSON
50 Dean School of Business .... Dr. Deborah SAKS
80 Dean Sch of Public & Social Svcs .... Mr. Bill COGHILL
76 Dean School of Health Sciences .... Ms. Jolene MILLER
49 Dean School of Lib Arts & Science .... Mr. David BERRY
54 Dean Sch of Applied Sci/Engr Tech .... Dr. Steven COMBS
12 Site Dir Montgomery Cnty Inst Ctr .... Mr. J. Geoff KNOWLES
12 Site Dir White Cnty Inst Ctr .... Ms. Judy DOPPELFELD
37 Director of Financial Aid .... Ms. Beverly COOPER
06 Registrar .... Dr. Susan STOKER
28 Exec Director Diversity/Engagement .... Mr. Andrew ANTONIO
18 Exec Director of Facilities .... Mr. Kenneth J. LARSON
35 Dir Student Life/Dev/Leadership .... Mr. Eric VANDEVOORDE
14 Exe Dir Computer/Technology Svcs .... Ms. Nikki LEBO
07 Director of Admissions .... Mr. Ivan HERNANDEZ
08 Library Director .... Ms. Cindy MITCHELL
36 Dir of Career Services .... Ms. Dottie LARSON
38 Dir of Academic Affairs & Support .... Ms. Nancy PEARSON
96 Dir Business Office/Cash Management .... Ms. Sandra PATCHETT
12 Site Manager Renaissance Inst Ctr .... Mr. Andrew MUFFETT
11 Asst Dir Internal Affairs/Outreach .... Ms. Laura KIRTLEY
04 Chancellor's Office Coordinator .... Ms. Jessica WALSH

*Ivy Tech Community College of Indiana-North Central (C)

220 Dean Johnson Boulevard, South Bend IN 46601-3415
County: Saint Joseph FICE Identification: 008423
Unit ID: 150978
Telephone: (574) 289-7001 Carnegie Class: Assoc/Pub-R-L
FAX Number: (574) 236-7165 Calendar System: Semester
URL: www.ivytech.edu/southbend
Established: 1967 Annual Undergrad Tuition & Fees (In-State): $3,355
Enrollment: 13,090 Coed
Affiliation or Control: State IRS Status: 501(c)3
Highest Offering: Associate Degree
Program: Occupational; 2-Year Principally Bachelor's Creditable
Accreditation: &NH, ART, ACBSP, ACFEI, ADNUR, DH, EMT, MAC, MLTAD, NAIT, PNUR

02 Chancellor .... Dr. Thomas G. COLEY
03 Vice Chancellor/Dean .... Mr. Randy MAXSON
03 Vice Chancellor/Dean .... Ms. Teresa SHAFFER
05 Vice Chancellor of Academic Affairs .... Dr. Chuck PHILIP
10 Exec Director of Finance .... Mr. Robert L. PLACEK
32 Vice Chanellor of Student Affairs .... Dr. Keith BRANHAM
16 Exec Director Human Resources .... Mr. Michael POPIELSKI
06 Registrar .... Mr. Ed J. GRAMS
07 Director of Admissions .... Ms. Janice AUSTIN
18 Director Facilities .... Mr. James JASIEWICZ
26 Exec Dir Marketing/Communications .... Ms. Tracie L. DAVIS
30 Executive Director Development .... Vacant
37 Director of Student Financial Aid .... Mr. Jeff A. FISHER
29 Director Alumni Relations .... Vacant

*Ivy Tech Community College of Indiana-Northeast (D)

3800 N Anthony Boulevard, Fort Wayne IN 46805-1489
County: Allen FICE Identification: 009926
Unit ID: 151032
Telephone: (260) 482-9171 Carnegie Class: Assoc/Pub-U-SC
FAX Number: (260) 480-4177 Calendar System: Semester
URL: www.ivytech.edu/fortwayne/
Established: 1968 Annual Undergrad Tuition & Fees (In-State): $3,257
Enrollment: 11,067 Coed
Affiliation or Control: State IRS Status: 501(c)3
Highest Offering: Associate Degree
Program: Occupational; 2-Year Principally Bachelor's Creditable
Accreditation: &NH, ACBSP, ACFEI, ADNUR, EMT, MAC, NAIT, PNUR

02 Chancellor .... Dr. Jerrilee K. MOSIER
05 Vice Chancellor Academic Affairs .... Dr. Russell D. BAKER
32 Vice Chancellor of Student Affairs .... Mr. John C. LEWTON
10 Executive Director of Finance .... Ms. Valerie EAKINS
13 Exec Dir Computer/Tech Svcs .... Mr. Clifford M. CLARKE
26 Exec Dir Marketing & Communications .... Mr. Edward J. REED
15 Exec Director of Human Resources .... Ms. Donna J. MARR
103 Exec Dir Workforce and Economic Dev .... Mr. James O. ASCHLIMAN
30 Exec Dir of Resource Development .... Mr. John MILENTIS
06 Registrar .... Ms. Amy J. JOHNSTON
37 Director of Financial Aid .... Mr. Norm NEWMAN
36 Director of Career Services .... Ms. Sheila BIGGS
18 Director of Facilities .... Mr. Everett L. LAWSON
08 Library Director .... Ms. Sharon S. HULTQUIST
07 Director of Admissions .... Mr. Steve M. SCHEER
51 Continuing Education Manager .... Ms. Amanda JONES

*Ivy Tech Community College of Indiana-Northwest (E)

1440 E 35th Avenue, Gary IN 46409-1499
County: Lake FICE Identification: 010040
Unit ID: 151087
Telephone: (219) 981-1111 Carnegie Class: Assoc/Pub-U-MC
FAX Number: (219) 981-4415 Calendar System: Semester
URL: www.ivytech.edu/northwest
Established: 1968 Annual Undergrad Tuition & Fees (In-State): $3,355
Enrollment: 9,412 Coed
Affiliation or Control: State IRS Status: 501(c)3
Highest Offering: Associate Degree
Program: Occupational; 2-Year Principally Bachelor's Creditable
Accreditation: &NH, ACBSP, ACFEI, ADNUR, FUSER, NAIT, PNUR, PTAA, SURGT

02 Chancellor .... Mr. J. Guadalupe VALTIERRA
04 Admin Assistant to the Chancellor .... Mrs. Jonetta C. ANTHONY
05 Vice Chanc of Academic Affairs .... Mrs. Deborah A. HALIK
32 Vice Chanc of Student Affairs .... Mr. R. Keith HOWARD
12 Vice Chancellor Valparaiso Campus .... Ms. Delores HAKLIN
12 Vice Chancellor East Chicago Campus .... Mr. R. Louie GONZALEZ
12 Vice Chanc Michigan City Campus .... Mr. Jerry HUDDLESTON
20 Asst Vice Chancellor Acad Affairs .... Mr. Ken ROSENBLUM
15 Exec Dir Regional Human Resources .... Mr. Rene VELA
103 Exec Dir Workforce/Economic Devel .... Mr. Forrest THON
10 Executive Director of Finance .... Mrs. Dawn THOSTESEN
18 Executive Director of Facilities .... Mr. Tony A. SKIMEHORN
26 Exec Dir Marketing/Communications .... Ms. Karen L. WILLIAMS
30 Exec Director Resource Development .... Ms. Cindy J. HALL
13 Exec Dir Computer Technology Svcs .... Mr. David GIDCUMB
18 Asst Director of Facilities .... Mr. Joseph PLESEK
37 Director of Financial Aid .... Mrs. Barbara JERZYK
06 Registrar .... Ms. Carol BOWRON
32 Dir of Student Life/Dev Leadership .... Ms. Jennifer KOCZUR-RICHARDSON
36 Director of Career Services .... Ms. Chandra GARY
08 Director of Library Services .... Mrs. Barbara WEAVER
07 Director of Admissions .... Mr. John JOHNSON
28 Director of Diversity Affairs .... Ms. Frances T. VEGA
25 Manager of Grant/Project .... Ms. Eugenia SACOPULOS

*Ivy Tech Community College of Indiana-Richmond (F)

2357 Chester Boulevard, Richmond IN 47374-1298
County: Wayne FICE Identification: 010037
Unit ID: 151078
Telephone: (765) 966-2656 Carnegie Class: Assoc/Pub-R-M
FAX Number: (765) 962-8741 Calendar System: Semester
URL: www.ivytech.edu/richmond
Established: 1968 Annual Undergrad Tuition & Fees (In-State): $3,354
Enrollment: 4,036 Coed
Affiliation or Control: State IRS Status: 501(c)3
Highest Offering: Associate Degree
Program: Occupational; 2-Year Principally Bachelor's Creditable
Accreditation: &NH, ACBSP, ADNUR, MAC, NAIT, PNUR

02 Chancellor .... Mr. James L. STECK
05 Vice Chancellor Academic Affairs .... Mr. Steve TINCHER
32 Vice Chanc Student Affs/Human Res .... Ms. Sabrina PENNINGTON
10 Exec Director Finance & Facilities .... Ms. Valerie RAY
103 Exec Dir Workforce & Economic Dev .... Ms. Kim THURLOW
30 Exec Dir Resource Development .... Ms. Diana J. PAPPIN
31 Exec Dir External Affairs .... Ms. Nancy L. GREEN
29 Alumni Relations .... Ms. Diana J. PAPPIN
26 Marketing Director .... Mr. Bruce MORGAN
07 Director of Admissions .... Ms. Christine SEGER
20 Dir Student Success/Retention .... Ms. Mary Louise EDWARDS
36 Dir Career/Employment Services .... Mr. Paul LUTTMAN
06 Registrar .... Ms. Jeannie HAMBLIN-FOX
37 Director Financial Aid .... Ms. Ann FRANZEN-ROHA
15 Director Human Resources .... Ms. Lindy COVALT
35 Director of Student Life .... Ms. Tiffany ERK
28 Director of Multicultural Affairs .... Vacant
24 Mgr Instructional Technology .... Mr. Curtis BLAKELY
22 Equal Opportunity Official .... Mr. Eugene AYTON
50 School Dean Bus/Tech/App Sci & Engr .... Ms. Peg J. TERRELL
76 School Dean Hlth Sci Ed/Public Svcs .... Ms. Jillene ANDERSON
49 School Dean Liberal Arts/Sciences .... Mr. William GRAESSER
66 School Dean Nursing .... Ms. Glenda CLINE

*Ivy Tech Community College of Indiana-Southeast (G)

590 Ivy Tech Drive, Madison IN 47250-1883
County: Jefferson FICE Identification: 009923
Unit ID: 151096
Telephone: (812) 265-2580 Carnegie Class: Assoc/Pub-R-M
FAX Number: (812) 265-4028 Calendar System: Semester
URL: www.ivytech.edu/southeast
Established: 1971 Annual Undergrad Tuition & Fees (In-State): $3,354
Enrollment: 3,343 Coed
Affiliation or Control: State IRS Status: 501(c)3
Highest Offering: Associate Degree
Program: Occupational; 2-Year Principally Bachelor's Creditable
Accreditation: &NH, ACBSP, ADNUR, MAC, PNUR

02 Chancellor .... Mr. Jim HELMS
05 Executive Dean .... Mr. Donald L. HEIDERMAN, JR.
12 Assoc VC Acad Affs Lawrenceburg .... Mr. Mark GRAVER
20 Vice Chancellor of Academic Affairs .... Dr. Joe MOORE
32 Vice Chancellor Student Affairs .... Mrs. Margaret STEWART
10 Exec Director of Business Affairs .... Mr. Jeff HOLLKAMP
15 Exec Director Resource Development .... Ms. Paula HEIDERMAN
103 Ex Dir Workforce/Economic Devel .... Mr. Randy JOHANN
23 ASN/PSN Program Chair .... Mrs. Georgia SIMMONS
06 Registrar .... Mr. Kevin L. BRADLEY
26 Exec Dir Marketing/Communication .... Mr. Hank BENTZ
37 Director of Financial Aid .... Mr. Richard HILL
36 Asst Dir Finan Aid/Career Svcs .... Ms. Anne CUSKER
07 Asst Dir Admiss/Career Counseling .... Mrs. Cindy HUTCHERSON

*Ivy Tech Community College of Indiana-Southern Indiana (H)

8204 Highway 311, Sellersburg IN 47172-1897
County: Clark FICE Identification: 010109
Unit ID: 151041
Telephone: (812) 246-3301 Carnegie Class: Assoc/Pub-S-SC
FAX Number: (812) 246-9905 Calendar System: Semester
URL: www.ivytech.edu/sellersburg/
Established: 1968 Annual Undergrad Tuition & Fees (In-State): $2,922
Enrollment: 5,171 Coed
Affiliation or Control: State IRS Status: 501(c)3
Highest Offering: Associate Degree
Program: Occupational; 2-Year Principally Bachelor's Creditable
Accreditation: &NH, ACBSP, ADNUR, MAC, MLTAD, NAIT, PNUR

02 Chancellor .... Dr. Rita H. SHOURDS
84 Vice Chancellor of Enroll Svcs .... Mr. Terry L. NOLOT
05 Vice Chancellor of Academic Affairs .... Ms. Catherine E. SHERRARD
07 Asst Vice Chanc of Enroll Svcs .... Mr. Benjamin G. HARRIS
30 Executive Director of Development .... Mr. Andrew B. TAKAMI
15 Executive Dir of Human Resources .... Ms. Lisa K. GENTNER
10 Executive Director of Finance .... Ms. Janet K. STALEY
37 Director Financial Aid .... Mr. Gary L. COTTRILL
21 Business Office Manager .... Ms. Mary E. LEAVITT
18 Director of Facilities .... Mr. Robert C. POFF
32 Asst Director of Campus Engagement .... Mr. Thomas W. EVANS
103 Director of Corporate College .... Ms. Sharon S. ALLEN

*Ivy Tech Community College of Indiana-Southwest (I)

3501 First Avenue, Evansville IN 47710-1881
County: Vanderburgh FICE Identification: 009925
Unit ID: 151050
Telephone: (812) 426-2865 Carnegie Class: Assoc/Pub-R-L
FAX Number: (812) 429-1483 Calendar System: Semester

URL: www.ivytech.edu/evansville/
Established: 1968 Annual Undergrad Tuition & Fees (In-State): $3,355
Enrollment: 6,813 Coed
Affiliation or Control: State IRS Status: 501(c)3
Highest Offering: Associate Degree
Program: Occupational; 2-Year Principally Bachelor's Creditable
Accreditation: &NH, ACBSP, ADNUR, ART, EMT, MAC, NAIT, PNUR, SURGT

02 Chancellor .... Dr. Daniel L. SCHENK
05 Vice Chancellor of Academic Affairs .... Dr. James AHERN
32 Vice Chancellor of Student Affairs .... Ms. Deborah ANDERSON
72 Dean Schs of Tech/Applied Sci/Eng .... Dr. Marvin D. BAUSMAN
50 Division Chair Business .... Dr. Mary Jo DENTINO
97 Div Chair General Ed/Support Svcs .... Dr. Michael E. PETTY
103 Exec Dir Workforce & Economic Devel .... Mr. Terry W. HUBER
15 Exec Director of Human Resources .... Ms. Mary MURPHY
11 Exec Director of Administration .... Mrs. Alisha AMAN
30 Exec Director of Development .... Vacant
26 Director Marketing/Communications .... Ms. Rachel RAWLINSON
06 Registrar .... Ms. Jennifer BRIGGS
07 Director of Admissions .... Mrs. Denise JOHNSON-KINCAID
37 Financial Aid Manager .... Ms. Kristi EIDSON
16 Career & Employment Svcs Manager .... Ms. Margie SCHENK

*Ivy Tech Community College of Indiana-Wabash Valley (A)

8000 S. Education Drive, Terre Haute IN 47802-4833
County: Vigo FICE Identification: 008547
Unit ID: 151069
Telephone: (812) 299-1121 Carnegie Class: Assoc/Pub-R-L
FAX Number: (812) 299-5723 Calendar System: Semester
URL: ivytech7.cc.in.us
Established: 1966 Annual Undergrad Tuition & Fees (In-State): $3,880
Enrollment: 7,332 Coed
Affiliation or Control: State IRS Status: 501(c)3
Highest Offering: Associate Degree
Program: Occupational; 2-Year Principally Bachelor's Creditable
Accreditation: &NH, ACBSP, ADNUR, EMT, MAC, MLTAD, NAIT, PNUR, RAD, SURGT

02 Chancellor .... Dr. Ann M. VALENTINE
05 Dean of Academic Affairs .... Ms. Deanna KING
32 Dean of Student Affairs .... Ms. Leah ALLMAN
11 Exec Director for Administration .... Mr. John R. ADKINS
103 Exec Dir Workforce & Economic Dev .... Ms. Lea Anne CROOKS
30 Executive Director of Resource Dev .... Ms. Becky MILLER
10 Executive Director of Finance .... Mr. Charles RUBEY
06 Registrar .... Mr. Wilson TURNER
37 Director of Financial Aid .... Ms. Julie WONDERLIN
07 Director of Admissions .... Mr. Michael FISHER
36 Director of Career Services .... Vacant
88 Asst Director of Admissions .... Ms. Brandy CANDLER
18 Director of Facilities .... Mr. Larry A. SWANK

Kaplan College (B)

7833 Indianapolis Boulevard, Hammond IN 46324-3347
County: Lake Identification: 666436
Unit ID: 152415
Telephone: (219) 844-0100 Carnegie Class: Assoc/PrivFP
FAX Number: (219) 844-0105 Calendar System: Quarter
URL: www.getinfo.kaplancollege.com
Established: 1969 Annual Undergrad Tuition & Fees: $14,697
Enrollment: 687 Coed
Affiliation or Control: Proprietary IRS Status: Proprietary
Highest Offering: Associate Degree
Program: Occupational
Accreditation: ACICS

01 Campus President .... Mr. Johnny CRAIG

† Branch campus of Kaplan College, Merrillville, IN.

Kaplan College (C)

7302 Woodland Drive, Indianapolis IN 46278-1736
County: Marion FICE Identification: 009777
Unit ID: 152220
Telephone: (317) 299-6001 Carnegie Class: Assoc/PrivFP
FAX Number: (317) 298-6342 Calendar System: Semester
URL: www.getinfo.kaplancollege.com
Established: 1967 Annual Undergrad Tuition & Fees: $9,900
Enrollment: 765 Coed
Affiliation or Control: Proprietary IRS Status: Proprietary
Highest Offering: Associate Degree
Program: Occupational
Accreditation: ACCSC, DA, MAC

01 Acting President .... Mr. Todd JENSEN

Kaplan College (D)

3803 E Lincoln Highway, Merrillville IN 46410-5809
County: Lake FICE Identification: 022018
Unit ID: 152424
Telephone: (219) 947-8400 Carnegie Class: Assoc/PrivFP
FAX Number: (219) 942-3762 Calendar System: Other
URL: www.kc-merrillville.com
Established: 1969 Annual Undergrad Tuition & Fees: $11,950
Enrollment: 345 Coed
Affiliation or Control: Proprietary IRS Status: Proprietary
Highest Offering: Associate Degree
Program: Occupational; 2-Year Principally Bachelor's Creditable
Accreditation: ACICS, DA

01 Executive Director .... Mr. Chris ARTIM
13 Director of Information Technology .... Mr. Richard MILLER
05 Director of Education .... Mrs. Kelley MANSFIELD
37 Financial Aid Director .... Mrs. Lisa GORDON
36 Career Service Director .... Ms. Jennifer ROSS-ANDERSON
07 Director Admissions .... Ms. Anitra JOHNSON
06 Registrar .... Ms. Dawn BOWMAN

Lincoln College of Technology (E)

7225 Winton Drive, Building 128, Indianapolis IN 46268-4198
County: Marion FICE Identification: 007938
Unit ID: 151661
Telephone: (317) 632-5553 Carnegie Class: Assoc/PrivFP
FAX Number: (317) 687-0475 Calendar System: Semester
URL: www.lincolntech.com
Established: 1962 Annual Undergrad Tuition & Fees: $27,200
Enrollment: 1,705 Coed
Affiliation or Control: Proprietary IRS Status: Proprietary
Highest Offering: Associate Degree
Program: Occupational
Accreditation: ACCSC

01 President .... Todd CLARK
05 Vice President of Education .... Dale SHEPPERSON
11 Director Administrative Services .... LaTrina JOHNSON
37 Director of Financial Aid .... Sherri HARMON
36 Director Student Placement .... Jennifer FINESILVER

Manchester College (F)

604 E College Avenue, North Manchester IN 46962-1225
County: Wabash FICE Identification: 001820
Unit ID: 151777
Telephone: (260) 982-5000 Carnegie Class: Bac/Diverse
FAX Number: (260) 982-5043 Calendar System: 4/1/4
URL: www.manchester.edu
Established: 1889 Annual Undergrad Tuition & Fees: $25,970
Enrollment: 1,278 Coed
Affiliation or Control: Church Of The Brethren IRS Status: 501(c)3
Highest Offering: Master's
Program: Liberal Arts And General; Teacher Preparatory; Professional
Accreditation: NH, SW, TED

01 President .... Dr. Jo YOUNG SWITZER
03 Executive Vice President .... Dr. David F. MCFADDEN
05 Vice President Academic Affairs .... Dr. Glenn R. SHARFMAN
10 Vice Pres Financial Affairs/Treas .... Mr. Jack A. GOCHENAUR
32 Vice President Student Development .... Dr. Beth E. SWEITZER-RILEY
30 Vice President College Advancement .... Mr. Michael EASTMAN
07 Director of Admissions .... Ms. Jamie GRANT
20 Associate Academic Dean .... Dr. Mark W. HUNTINGTON
29 Exec Director of Alumni Assocation .... Mr. Gary E. MONTEL
30 Executive Director of Development .... Ms. Melanie B. HARMON
15 Director Human Resources .... Mr. Dale E. CARPENTER
08 Director of the Library .... Mr. Robin J. GRATZ
06 Registrar .... Ms. Lila D. HAMMER
24 Director of Audio-Visual Services .... Mr. Stanley G. PITTMAN
38 Director of Counseling .... Ms. Danette NORMAN TILL
36 Director of Career Services .... Ms. Elizabeth J. BUSHNELL
39 Director of Residence Life .... Mr. Allen J. MACHIELSON
42 Campus Pastor .... Mr. Walt WILTSCHEK
41 Director of Athletics .... Mr. Rick ESPESET
13 Director of Mgmt Info Services .... Mr. Michael CASE
19 Director of Security .... Mr. Leslie L. GAHL
44 Director of the Manchester Fund .... Ms. Janeen W. KOOI
37 Director of Student Financial Aid .... Ms. Sherri L. SHOCKEY
88 Director of Multicultural Affairs .... Vacant
26 Director of Public Relations .... Ms. Jeri S. KORNEGAY
18 Director of Physical Plant .... Mr. Christopher W. GARBER
23 Director of Health Services .... Ms. Tara L. VOGEL
21 Senior Accountant .... Mr. Michael J. LECKRONE
35 Director Student Affairs .... Ms. Shanon L. FAWBUSH
96 Director of Purchasing .... Mr. Quentin J. MOUDY
40 Bookstore Manager .... Ms. Heather K. GOCHENAUR

Marian University (G)

3200 Cold Spring Road, Indianapolis IN 46222-1997
County: Marion FICE Identification: 001821
Unit ID: 151786
Telephone: (317) 955-6000 Carnegie Class: Bac/Diverse
FAX Number: (317) 955-6448 Calendar System: Semester
URL: www.marian.edu
Established: 1851 Annual Undergrad Tuition & Fees: $26,000
Enrollment: 2,357 Coed
Affiliation or Control: Roman Catholic IRS Status: 501(c)3
Highest Offering: Master's
Program: Liberal Arts And General; Teacher Preparatory; Professional
Accreditation: NH, IACBE, NURSE, TED

01 President .... Mr. Daniel J. ELSENER
05 Executive VP and Provost .... Dr. Thomas ENNEKING
10 VP for Finance & Business Opers .... Mr. Greg GINDER
26 VP for Marketing Communications .... Mr. Robert GOLOBISH
30 VP for Institutional Advancement .... Mr. John FINKE
32 VP Student Affairs/Dean of Students .... Ms. Ruth RODGERS
84 AVP Enrollment Management .... Dr. Jack P. POWELL
37 Dean Financial Aid/Enroll Mgmt .... Mr. Chad BIR
20 Dean for Academic Affairs .... Mr. William HARTING
18 Director of Facilities .... Mr. Neil LANGFERMAN
41 Director of Athletics .... Vacant
29 Director of Alumni Affairs .... Mrs. Barbara STUCKWISCH
06 Registrar .... Mr. John A. HILL
08 Librarian .... Ms. Kelley GRIFFITH
35 Director of Student Act/Orientation .... Ms. Angelia ZIELKE
19 Director of Safety & Police Svcs .... Mr. Scott RALPH
13 Director of Computer Services .... Mr. Daniel D. MILLER
27 Dir of Marketing Communications .... Mrs. Andrea FAGAN
36 Dir of Internships & Career Svcs .... Vacant
42 Director of Campus Ministry .... Vacant
38 Director Academic Support Services .... Mrs. Marjorie BATIC
07 Director of Enrollment .... Ms. Luann BRAMES
55 Exec Director Adult Programs .... Ms. Amy BENNETT
38 Director of Counseling Services .... Ms. Leanne MALLOY
88 Director of Advancement Information .... Mrs. Vida KOTARSKI
23 Director of Health & Wellness Svcs .... Ms. Jan CARNAGHI
09 Director of Institutional Research .... Mr. William HARTING
15 Director of Human Resources .... Ms. Anita HERBERTZ
21 Director of Business Services .... Ms. Alice SHELTON
40 Bookstore Manager .... Mr. Brian HOELLE

Martin University (H)

2171 Avondale Place, PO 18567, Indianapolis IN 46218-3878
County: Marion FICE Identification: 021408
Unit ID: 151810
Telephone: (317) 543-3235 Carnegie Class: Bac/A&S
FAX Number: (317) 543-3257 Calendar System: Semester
URL: www.martin.edu
Established: 1977 Annual Undergrad Tuition & Fees: $13,520
Enrollment: 909 Coed
Affiliation or Control: Independent Non-Profit IRS Status: 501(c)3
Highest Offering: Master's
Program: Liberal Arts And General
Accreditation: NH

01 Interim President .... Dr. Charlotte WESTERHAUS-RENFROW
05 Vice President Academic Affairs .... Dr. Martin GREENAN
09 VP of IR and Sponsored Programs .... Dr. Brian STEUERWALD
15 Vice President Human Resources .... Ms. Ruby BOWMAN
32 Vice President of Student Services .... Mrs. Charlesetta STALEY
32 Dean of Students .... Vacant
35 Chief of Staff .... Mr. James BELLAMY
10 Fiscal Officer .... Mr. Michael MOOS
37 Director Financial Aid .... Mrs. Berdia MARSHALL
30 Dir Institutional Advancement .... Mr. David VANDERSTEL
18 Director Facilities Management .... Mr. Andy LANE
31 Director of Community Relations .... Ms. Kim TEAGUE
13 Director of Informatics/Technology .... Mr. Anthony ADELEKE
06 Registrar .... Ms. Rudi MOORE
21 Bursar .... Mrs. Virginia GOODWIN
40 Manager Bookstore .... Ms. Tanya DOUGLAS
96 Purchasing Manager .... Ms. Pam HOOD

MedTech College (I)

7230 Engle Road, Suite 200, Fort Wayne IN 46804
County: Allen Identification: 666677
Unit ID: 456366
Telephone: (317) 845-0300 Carnegie Class: Not Classified
FAX Number: (317) 863-4895 Calendar System: Quarter
URL: www.medtechcollege.edu
Established: 2008 Annual Undergrad Tuition & Fees: $14,434
Enrollment: 498 Coed
Affiliation or Control: Proprietary IRS Status: Proprietary
Highest Offering: Associate Degree
Program: Occupational; 2-Year Principally Bachelor's Creditable
Accreditation: ACICS

01 Executive Director .... Mr. Luke KNOKE

† Branch campus of MedTech College, Indianapolis, IN.

MedTech College (J)

1500 American Way, Greenwood IN 46143
County: Johnson Identification: 666678
Unit ID: 456357
Telephone: (317) 534-0322 Carnegie Class: Not Classified
FAX Number: (317) 863-4895 Calendar System: Quarter
URL: www.medtechcollege.edu
Established: 2007 Annual Undergrad Tuition & Fees: N/A
Enrollment: 681 Coed
Affiliation or Control: Proprietary IRS Status: Proprietary
Highest Offering: Associate Degree
Program: Occupational; 2-Year Principally Bachelor's Creditable
Accreditation: ACICS, MAC

01 Executive Director .... Mr. Mike HARDING

† Branch campus of MedTech College, Indianapolis, IN.

MedTech College (K)

6612 East 75th Street Suite 300, Indianapolis IN 46250
County: Marion FICE Identification: 007362
Unit ID: 448415

- Telephone: (317) 845-0100 — Carnegie Class: Not Classified
- FAX Number: (317) 845-1800 — Calendar System: Quarter
- URL: www.medtechcollege.edu
- Established: 2004 — Annual Undergrad Tuition & Fees: $14,434
- Enrollment: 1,053 — Coed
- Affiliation or Control: Proprietary — IRS Status: Proprietary
- Highest Offering: Associate Degree
- Program: Occupational
- Accreditation: **ACICS**, MAC

- 01 Executive Director .... Mr. Simon LUMLEY

Mid-America College of Funeral Service (A)

3111 Hamburg Pike, Jeffersonville IN 47130-9630

- County: Clark — FICE Identification: 010618
- Unit ID: 151962
- Telephone: (812) 288-8878 — Carnegie Class: Spec/Other
- FAX Number: (812) 288-5942 — Calendar System: Quarter
- URL: www.mid-america.edu
- Established: 1905 — Annual Undergrad Tuition & Fees: $12,000
- Enrollment: 84 — Coed
- Affiliation or Control: Independent Non-Profit — IRS Status: 501(c)3
- Highest Offering: Associate Degree
- Program: Occupational
- Accreditation: **FUSER**

- 01 President .... Mr. John R. BRABOY
- 32 Dean of Students .... Mr. Richard D. NELSON
- 06 Registrar/Director of Admissions .... Mrs. Cathy DENISON
- 29 Director Alumni Relations .... Mr. Michael JOHNSON
- 37 Director Student Financial Aid .... Mr. Richard D. NELSON

Mid-America Reformed Seminary (B)

229 Seminary Drive, Dyer IN 46311-1069

- County: Lake — FICE Identification: 039893
- Unit ID: 373030
- Telephone: (219) 864-2400 — Carnegie Class: Not Classified
- FAX Number: (219) 864-2410 — Calendar System: Semester
- URL: www.midamerica.edu
- Established: 1981 — Annual Undergrad Tuition & Fees: $8,250
- Enrollment: 36 — Coed
- Affiliation or Control: Independent Non-Profit — IRS Status: 501(c)3
- Highest Offering: Master's
- Program: Religious Emphasis
- Accreditation: **THEOL**, TRACS

- 01 President .... Dr. Cornelius VENEMA
- 32 Dean of Students .... Rev. Alan STRANGE
- 06 Registrar .... Rev. Alan STRANGE
- 30 Director of Development .... Mr. Keith LEMAHIEU
- 96 Office Manager/Director Purchasing .... Ms. Florence KOOIMAN
- 36 Director of Apprenticeship Program .... Rev. Mark VANDERHART

National College (C)

6060 Castleway West Drive, Indianapolis IN 46250

- County: Marion — Identification: 666680
- Telephone: (317) 578 7353 — Carnegie Class: Not Classified
- FAX Number: (317) 578-7721 — Calendar System: Quarter
- URL: www.ncbt.edu
- Established: 1886 — Annual Undergrad Tuition & Fees: N/A
- Enrollment: N/A — Coed
- Affiliation or Control: Proprietary — IRS Status: Proprietary
- Highest Offering: Baccalaureate
- Program: Occupational
- Accreditation: **ACICS**, MAC, SURGT

- 01 Campus President .... Eileen TAYLOR

Oakland City University (D)

138 N Lucretia Street, Oakland City IN 47660-1099

- County: Gibson — FICE Identification: 001824
- Unit ID: 152099
- Telephone: (812) 749-4781 — Carnegie Class: Master's M
- FAX Number: (812) 749-1233 — Calendar System: Semester
- URL: www.oak.edu
- Established: 1885 — Annual Undergrad Tuition & Fees: $16,000
- Enrollment: 2,700 — Coed
- Affiliation or Control: Baptist — IRS Status: 501(c)3
- Highest Offering: Doctorate
- Program: Occupational; 2-Year Principally Bachelor's Creditable; Liberal Arts And General; Teacher Preparatory; Professional
- Accreditation: **NH**, IACBE, TED, THEOL

- 01 President .... Dr. Ray G. BARBER
- 11 Vice Pres Administration & Finance .... Dr. Robert E. YEAGER
- 05 Provost .... Dr. Michael J. ATKINSON
- 44 Vice Pres Planning & Research .... Dr. Bernard MARLEY
- 30 Director of Development .... Mr. Brian BAKER
- 32 Director Student Affairs/Housing .... Dr. James PRATT
- 12 Director Bedford College Center .... Dr. L. Kay COLLINS
- 42 Campus Chaplain .... Rev. Mark GRIMES
- 06 Registrar .... Ms. Betty BURNS
- 07 Director of Admissions .... Ms. Kim HELDT
- 37 Director Student Financial Aid .... Mrs. Caren RICHESON
- 09 Director of Institutional Research .... Dr. Morris PELZEL
- 15 Director Personnel Services .... Mrs. Kris PRATT
- 91 Director Information Technology .... Mr. Clint WOOLSEY
- 88 Director Institutional Assessment .... Mrs. Amy SATTERLY
- 08 Learning Resources Center .... Mrs. Denise PINNICK
- 29 Dir Alumni Rels/Chief Pub Rels Ofcr .... Ms. Susan SULLIVAN
- 36 Director Placement .... Dr. James PRATT
- 36 Dir Career & College Directions .... Mrs. Charity JULIAN
- 35 Director Student Support Services .... Mrs. Cinda K. PHILLIPS
- 88 Director Upward Bound Program .... Ms. Mary HEALY
- 10 Business Mgr/Chief Financial Ofcr .... Mrs. Elizabeth BARBER
- 88 Dean Sch Adult Degree/Prof Stds .... Dr. Micheal PELT
- 73 Dean Graduate School of Theology .... Dr. Douglas LOW
- 18 Chief Facilities/Physical Plant .... Mr. Wayne ROWLAND
- 53 Dean School of Education .... Dr. Mary Jo BEAUCHAMP
- 50 Dean School of Business .... Mr. Norman REYNOLDS
- 21 Assistant Chief Financial Officer .... Mrs. Elizabeth CARLISLE
- 49 Dean School of Arts & Sciences .... Dr. Claudine CUTCHIN
- 22 Compliance Officer .... Ms. Patricia ENDICOTT

Ottawa University Jeffersonville (E)

287 Quarter Master Court, Jeffersonville IN 47130-3669

- County: Clark — Identification: 666088
- Unit ID: 442897
- Telephone: (785) 242-5200 — Carnegie Class: Spec/Bus
- FAX Number: (812) 280-7269 — Calendar System: Semester
- URL: www.ottawa.edu
- Established: 2002 — Annual Undergrad Tuition & Fees: $10,560
- Enrollment: 144 — Coed
- Affiliation or Control: American Baptist — IRS Status: 501(c)3
- Highest Offering: Master's
- Program: Liberal Arts And General
- Accreditation: **&NH**

- 01 President .... Mr. Kevin EICHNER
- 03 Interim Campus Executive .... Mr. Walter CROX
- 05 Univ Provost/Chief Academic Officer .... Dr. Terry HAINES
- 10 Vice Pres Administration/CFO .... Mr. J. Clark RIBORDY
- 26 Mgr Public Relations & Publications .... Ms. Paula PAINE
- 30 Vice Pres University Advancement .... Mr. Paul BEAN
- 86 VP Regulatory/Governmental Affairs .... Dr. Donna LEVENE
- 88 Vice President for APOS .... Dr. Brian SANDUSKY
- 11 Administrative Manager .... Ms. Patrice FESS
- 07 Senior Enrollment Advisor .... Ms. Peg GERNAND
- 21 Director Finance/Controller .... Ms. Brenda GUENTHER
- 21 Director Business Operations .... Mr. Tom CORLEY
- 15 Director Human Resources .... Ms. Joanna WALTERS
- 06 University Registrar .... Ms. Karen ADAMS
- 37 Director Financial Aid .... Mr. Howard FISCHER
- 88 Vice President for APOS .... Mr. Brian MESSER

† Regional accreditation is carried under the parent institution in Ottawa, KS.

Purdue University Main Campus (F)

610 Purdue Mall, West Lafayette IN 47907-2040

- County: Tippecanoe — FICE Identification: 001825
- Unit ID: 243780
- Telephone: (765) 494-4600 — Carnegie Class: RU/VH
- FAX Number: N/A — Calendar System: Semester
- URL: www.purdue.edu
- Established: 1869 — Annual Undergrad Tuition & Fees (In-State): $9,470
- Enrollment: 39,726 — Coed
- Affiliation or Control: State — IRS Status: 501(c)3
- Highest Offering: Doctorate
- Program: Liberal Arts And General; Teacher Preparatory; Professional
- Accreditation: **NH**, AAB, ART, AUD, BUS, CACREP, CIDA, CLPSY, CONST, COPSY, CS, DIETC, DIETD, ENG, ENGR, ENGT, FOR, IPSY, LSAR, MFCD, NAIT, NURSE, PHAR, SP, TED, THEA, VET

- 01 President .... Dr. France A. CÓRDOVA
- 10 Exec Vice President & Treasurer .... Mr. Alphonso V. DIAZ
- 05 Exec VP Academic Affairs & Provost .... Dr. Timothy D. SANDS
- 30 Vice Pres for Development .... Ms. Lisa D. CALVERT
- 16 Vice President Ethics & Compliance .... Prof. Alysa C. ROLLOCK
- 10 Sr VP Business Svcs/Asst Treas .... Mr. James S. ALMOND
- 13 Vice Pres Information Technology .... Dr. William G. MCCARTNEY
- 15 Vice President Human Resources .... Mr. Luis E. LEWIN
- 18 Vice President Physical Facilities .... Mr. Robert E. MCMAINS
- 39 Assoc Vice Pres Housing/Food Serv .... Ms. Beth M. MCCUSKEY
- 26 Vice Pres Marketing & Media .... Ms. Teri THOMPSON
- 32 Vice President of Student Affairs .... Dr. Melissa E. EXUM
- 20 Vice Provost Undergrad Acad Affairs .... Dr. A. Dale WHITAKER
- 46 Vice President for Research .... Dr. Richard O. BUCKIUS
- 88 Vice Provost for Engagement .... Dr. Victor L. LECHTENBERG
- 86 Assoc VP Governmental Relations .... Mr. Timothy J. SANDERS
- 20 Vice Provost Faculty Affairs .... Dr. Beverly D. SYPHER
- 20 Assistant Provost .... Dr. Nancy A. BULGER
- 20 Assistant Provost/Financial Affairs .... Ms. Connie L. LAPINSKAS
- 47 Dean College of Agriculture .... Dr. Jay T. AKRIDGE
- 59 Dean College Health & Human Science .... Dr. Christine M. LADISCH
- 53 Dean College of Education .... Dr. Maryann SANTOS DE BARONA
- 54 Dean College of Engineering .... Dr. Leah H. JAMIESON
- 49 Dean College of Liberal Arts .... Dr. Irwin H. WEISER
- 50 Int Dean School of Management .... Dr. Gerald J. LYNCH
- 67 Dean College of Pharmacy .... Dr. Craig K. SVENSSON
- 81 Dean College of Science .... Dr. Jeffrey T. ROBERTS
- 72 Dean College of Technology .... Dr. Gary R. BERTOLINE
- 74 Dean School Veterinary Medicine .... Dr. Willie M. REED
- 58 Dean of Graduate School .... Dr. Mark J. SMITH
- 88 Int Vice Provost/Dean Intl Programs .... Dr. Michael A. BRZEZINSKI
- 08 Dean of Libraries .... Dr. James L. MULLINS
- 29 Exec Dir & CEO Alumni Association .... Mr. Kirk R. CERNY
- 45 Exec Dir Strateg Planning & Assess .... Prof. Rabindra N. MUKERJEA
- 41 Director Intercollegiate Athletics .... Mr. Morgan J. BURKE
- 09 Director of Institutional Research .... Dr. Jacque L. FROST
- 36 Director Center Career Opportunity .... Mr. Timothy B. LUZADER
- 31 Assistant VP External Relations .... Mr. Chris W. SIGURDSON
- 85 Dir Intl Students & Scholars .... Dr. Michael A. BRZEZINSKI
- 25 Director Sponsored Program Svcs .... Mr. Michael R. LUDWIG
- 94 Director Women's Studies .... Dr. Valentine M. MOGHADAM
- 07 Dean Admiss/Asst VP Enroll Mgmt .... Dr. Pamela T. HORNE
- 35 Dean of Students .... Ms. Danita M. BROWN
- 04 Executive Assistant to President .... Ms. Sharon K. WHITLOCK
- 37 Executive Director Financial Aid .... Ms. Joyce HALL
- 06 Registrar .... Mr. Robert A. KUBAT
- 28 Vice Provost Diversity & Inclusion .... Dr. G. Christine TAYLOR
- 38 Associate Dean Student Counseling .... Mr. Robert L. MATE
- 96 Director of Procurement Services .... Mr. James M. HUDSON
- 21 Comptroller .... Ms. Mary Catherine GAISBAUER
- 84 Asst VP/Dir Enroll Mgmt/Analys/Rep .... Mr. Brent M. DRAKE

Purdue University Calumet (G)

2200 169th Street, Hammond IN 46323-2094

- County: Lake — FICE Identification: 001827
- Unit ID: 152248
- Telephone: (219) 989-2993 — Carnegie Class: Master's L
- FAX Number: (219) 989-2581 — Calendar System: Semester
- URL: www.purduecal.edu
- Established: 1946 — Annual Undergrad Tuition & Fees (In-State): $7,759
- Enrollment: 9,807 — Coed
- Affiliation or Control: State — IRS Status: 501(c)3
- Highest Offering: Master's
- Program: Liberal Arts And General; Teacher Preparatory; Professional
- Accreditation: **NH**, ENG, ENGT, IACBE, MFCD, NUR, TED

- 01 Chancellor .... Thomas L. KEON
- 04 Exec Asst to Chancellor Engagement .... Regina D. BIDDINGS-MURO
- 05 Vice Chancellor Academic Affairs .... Ralph V. ROGERS
- 10 Vice Chanc Administrative Services .... James K. JOHNSTON
- 30 Vice Chancellor for Advancement .... Daniel HENDRICKS
- 13 Vice Chanc for Information Services .... Frank CERVONE
- 32 Interim Vice Chanc Student Services .... Sarah E. HOWARD
- 46 Interim Assoc VC Rsrch & Grad Stds .... Niaz LATIF
- 26 Assoc Vice Chancellor for Marketing .... Mark LACIEN
- 09 Asst VC Academic Quality & Outreach .... M. Beth PELLICCIOTTI
- 11 Asst Vice Chancellor for Admin Svcs .... Michael KULL
- 27 Asst Vice Chanc Advance/Univ Rels .... Wes K. LUKOSHUS
- 88 Asst Vice Chanc for ED OPP Programs .... Roy HAMILTON
- 20 Asst Vice Chanc Retention Strateg .... Ron KOVACH
- 21 Asst VC Business Svcs/Comptroller .... Linda BAER
- 15 Asst Vice Chanc Human Resources .... Mary Beth RINCON
- 84 Asst VC Enrollment Management .... Carol CORTILET-ALBRECHT
- 49 Dean Sch Liberal Arts/Social Sc .... Ronald CORTHEK
- 54 Interim Dean School Engr/Math/Sci .... Michael C. HENSON
- 72 Dean School of Technology .... Niaz LATIF
- 50 Dean School of Management .... Martine DUCHATELET
- 66 Dean School of Nursing .... Gerard S. PEGGY
- 53 Dean School of Educ/Teacher Educ .... Alice ANDERSON
- 06 Registrar .... Anne Agosto SEVERA
- 21 Asst Comptroller/Budget/Fiscal Plng .... Donna ADELSPERGER
- 07 Interim Exec Dir Admissions/Recruit .... Dorothy E. FRINK
- 37 Dir Financial Aid .... Mary Ann BISHEL
- 41 AVC Health/Recr/Sports/Athletic Dir .... Robert BUNNELL
- 38 Director Counseling Center .... Kenneth JACKSON
- 08 Dir Research/Learning & Res. Svcs .... Tammy GUERRERO
- 29 Dir Alumni Relations/Annual Giving .... Diana VIRIJEVICH
- 22 Assoc Director/AA/EEO/Diversity .... Linda KNOX
- 19 Chief University Police .... Anthony MARTIN
- 85 Exec Dir of International Programs .... Judith PENNYWELL
- 96 Dir of Procurement/General Services .... Phillip BROWN
- 39 Interim Director University Village .... Abbas HILL
- 92 Director of the Honors Program .... Bipin PAI

Purdue University North Central Campus (H)

1401 S US 421, Westville IN 46391-9542

- County: La Porte — FICE Identification: 001826
- Unit ID: 152266
- Telephone: (219) 785-5200 — Carnegie Class: Bac/Diverse
- FAX Number: (219) 785-5355 — Calendar System: Semester
- URL: www.pnc.edu
- Established: 1943 — Annual Undergrad Tuition & Fees (In-State): $6,872
- Enrollment: 4,614 — Coed
- Affiliation or Control: State — IRS Status: 501(c)3
- Highest Offering: Baccalaureate
- Program: Liberal Arts And General; Teacher Preparatory; Professional
- Accreditation: **NH**, ACBSP, ADNUR, ENGT, NUR, TED

- 01 Chancellor .... Dr. James B. DWORKIN
- 04 Executive Asst to the Chancellor .... Mrs. Debra A. NIELSEN
- 30 Exec Dir Advance/Engage & Cmty Rels .... Mr. Frederick C. MCNULTY
- 05 Vice Chanc Academic Affairs .... Dr. Karen L. SCHMID
- 20 Assoc Vice Chanc Acad Affairs .... Dr. Kumara JAYASURIYA
- 10 Vice Chanc for Admin .... Mr. Stephen R. TURNER
- 84 VC for Enroll Mgmt & Student Svcs .... Mr. Paul M. MCGUINNESS
- 32 Asst VC & Dean of Students .... Mr. John T. COGGINS
- 14 Asc VC Information Technology/CIO .... Mr. Daniel A. BURNS

10 Asc Vice Chanc Business Svcs/Budget ... Mr. Phillip E. JANKOWSKI
15 Assoc Vice Chanc Human Resources ... Mrs. Susan T. MILLER
50 Dean College of Business ... Dr. Alan G. KRABBENHOFT
72 Dean College of Engr & Tech ... Dr. Larryl K. MATTHEWS
49 Dean College of Liberal Arts ... Dr. S. Rex MORROW
88 Dean College of Science ... Dr. Keith E. SCHWINGENDORF
66 Chair Nursing Department ... Dr. Mario ORTIZ
83 Chair Social Sciences Department ... Dr. Michael LYNN
81 Chair Biology/Chem Department ... Dr. C. Kenneth HOLFORD
81 Chair Math/Physics/Statistics Dept ... Dr. Purna DAS
53 Chair Education Department ... Vacant
88 Int Chair English/Foreign Lang Dept ... Dr. Jerry HOLT
22 Asst Dir EEO & Training ... Ms. Laura ODOM
21 Bursar ... Mrs. Beverly J. PULLER
21 Accounting Manager ... Mr. Brock MARTIN
96 Dir Auxiliary Svcs & Resource Plng ... Mrs. Elizabeth DEPEW
08 Librarian ... Mr. Kent R. JOHNSON
07 Asst Dean Enroll & Student Outreach ... Mrs. Janice WHISLER
06 Assistant Registrar ... Mrs. Jennifer WOLSZCZAK
36 Director of Career Development ... Ms. Natalie CONNORS
37 Director Financial Aid & Compliance ... Mrs. Shelly BARNES
38 Director Student Counseling ... Ms. Diana MAROVICH
51 Dir Continuing Education Programs ... Ms. Phyllis DRANGER
19 Director of Public Safety ... Mr. Robert GAEKLE
27 Director Media & Comm Services ... Mrs. Carol CONNELLY
41 Director Student Athletics ... Mr. John WEBER
35 Director Student Activities ... Mrs. Keri MARRS DE BARRON
18 Director Facilities Management ... Mr. L. James SALLEE
09 Data Specialist ... Mrs. Madonna TRITLE
26 Asst VC of Mktg & Campus Relations ... Mrs. Judy N. JACOBI
88 Coord Special Events & Marketing ... Ms. Liz BERNEL
29 Director Alumni Relations ... Mrs. Amy NAVARDAUSKAS
58 Director Graduate Studies ... Dr. Kumara JAYASURIYA
50 Director MBA Program ... Mrs. Janet KNIGHT
88 Director of Food Service ... Mr. Keith PEFFERS
40 Bookstore Manager ... Mr. Richard EBHOTEMEN
88 Coord Service Learning ... Ms. Laura WEAVER
88 Dir School Partnerships ... Mrs. Susan WILSON
88 Dir Academic Advising ... Ms. Barbara AUSTIN
06 Asst Dean of Opers & Registrar ... Ms. Sandra CZEKAJ

Rose-Hulman Institute of Technology (A)

5500 Wabash Avenue, Terre Haute IN 47803-3920
County: Vigo — FICE Identification: 001830
Unit ID: 152318
Telephone: (812) 877-1511 — Carnegie Class: Spec/Engg
FAX Number: (812) 877-9925 — Calendar System: Quarter
URL: www.rose-hulman.edu
Established: 1874 — Annual Undergrad Tuition & Fees: $37,197
Enrollment: 1,980 — Coed
Affiliation or Control: Independent Non-Profit — IRS Status: 501(c)3
Highest Offering: Master's
Program: Professional; Technical Emphasis
Accreditation: NH, CS, ENG

01 President ... Mr. Matt BRANAM
05 InterimVP Acad Affs/Dean of Faculty ... Dr. William A. KLINE
30 Vice President Inst Advancement ... Mr. Rickey N. MCCURRY
13 Vice Pres Instruct/Admin/Info Tech ... Dr. Louis H. TURCOTTE
32 Vice President Student Affairs ... Mr. Peter A. GUSTAFSON
18 Sr Director Facilities Operations ... Mr. Michael A. TAYLOR
11 Vice Pres/Chief Administrative Ofcr ... Mr. Robert A. COONS
10 Controller ... Mr. Matt DAVIS
84 Vice President Enrollment Mgmt ... Mr. James A. GOECKER
20 Associate Dean of Faculty ... Dr. Daniel J. MOORE
36 Dir Career Services/Employer Rels ... Mr. Kevin L. HEWERDINE
26 VP Communications/Marketing ... Ms. Mary G. BARR
07 Director of Admissions ... Ms. Lisa M. NORTON
29 Director of Alumni Affairs ... Vacant
45 Exec Dir Inst Rsrch/Plng/Assessment ... Dr. Julia M. WILLIAMS
15 Director of Human Resources ... Ms. Kimberly D. MILLER
37 Director of Financial Aid ... Ms. Melinda L. MIDDLETON
41 Director of Athletics ... Mr. Jeffrey L. JENKINS
44 Director of Annual Giving ... Ms. Kim PERKINS
44 Director of Planned Giving ... Vacant
06 Registrar ... Mr. Timothy J. PRICKEL
08 Director & Institute Librarian ... Ms. Rachel C. CROWLEY
19 Director of Public Safety ... Mr. John S. WOLFE
40 Bookstore Manager ... Ms. Sheryl E. FULK
85 Dir Intl Stdnt Svcs/Special Pgms ... Ms. Karen A. DEGRANGE
100 Chief of Staff ... Mr. Michael DAVIDS
04 Exec Assistant to the President ... Ms. Tamera L. SHAFFER
25 Dir Fin Svcs/Sponsored Programs ... Ms. Linda L. PRICE
96 Director Administrative Services ... Mr. Dan WELLS
09 Director of Institutional Research ... Mr. Timothy CHOW
102 Director Corporate & Foundation Rel ... Mr. Richard D. BOYCE
39 Director of Residence Life ... Mr. Erik Z. HAYES
35 Dean of Student Affairs ... Mr. Thomas D. MILLER
35 Dean of Student Services ... Ms. Donna J. GUSTAFSON
20 Interim Assoc Dean Prof Experiences ... Dr. Richard E. STAMPER

Saint Joseph's College (B)

PO Box 870, US Highway 231, Rensselaer IN 47978-0870
County: Jasper — FICE Identification: 001833
Unit ID: 152363
Telephone: (219) 866-6000 — Carnegie Class: Bac/Diverse
FAX Number: (219) 866-6100 — Calendar System: Semester
URL: www.saintjoe.edu
Established: 1889 — Annual Undergrad Tuition & Fees: $26,330
Enrollment: 933 — Coed
Affiliation or Control: Roman Catholic — IRS Status: 501(c)3
Highest Offering: Master's
Program: Liberal Arts And General; Teacher Preparatory; Professional
Accreditation: NH, IACBE, TED

01 President ... Dr. F. Dennis RIEGELNEGG
04 Admin Asst to the President ... Mrs. Sheila K. HANEWICH
05 Vice President for Academic Affairs ... Dr. Daniel J. BLANKENSHIP
10 Vice President Business Affairs ... Mr. Randal J. FREEBOURN
30 Vice Pres Inst Advancement/Mrktng ... Dr. Maureen V. EGAN
84 Asst VP of Enrollment Management ... Mr. John WADELL
32 Dean of Students ... Dr. Leslie FRERE
06 Registrar ... Ms. Carol BURNS
08 Librarian ... Mrs. Catherine A. SALYERS
14 Director of Computer Center ... Mr. Vincent LUCAS
38 Director of Counseling Services ... Ms. Laura WAGNER
18 Chief Facilities/Physical Plant ... Vacant
15 Director Human Resources ... Ms. Nancy STUDER
26 Director of Integrated Marketing ... Mrs. Christine BABICK-SAQUI
29 Director Alumni Relations ... Mrs. Kendra ILLINGWORTH
37 Director Student Financial Services ... Mrs. Debra SIZEMORE
28 Director of Diversity ... Mr. Ernest WATSON
36 Director Career Development ... Dr. David BOOP
09 Director of Institutional Research ... Mrs. Elizabeth GRAF
41 Athletic Director ... Mr. William MASSOELS
40 Director Bookstore ... Mr. Vinse HERSHBERGER
42 Chaplain/Director Campus Ministry ... Fr. Kevin SCALF, CPPS

Saint Mary-of-the-Woods College (C)

St Mary of the Woods IN 47876-0067
County: Vigo — FICE Identification: 001835
Unit ID: 152381
Telephone: (812) 535-5151 — Carnegie Class: Bac/Diverse
FAX Number: (812) 535-5231 — Calendar System: Semester
URL: www.smwc.edu
Established: 1840 — Annual Undergrad Tuition & Fees: $25,690
Enrollment: 1,595 — Coed
Affiliation or Control: Roman Catholic — IRS Status: 501(c)3
Highest Offering: Master's
Program: Liberal Arts And General
Accreditation: NH, MUS, TED

01 President ... Dr. Dottie KING
30 Vice President for Advancement ... Mr. Chad LINZY
10 Vice Pres Finance & Administration ... Mr. Gordon AFDAHL
05 Vice President for Academic Affairs ... Dr. Janet CLARK
32 Vice President for Student Life ... Ms. Vicki KOSOWSKY
84 Vice Pres Enrollment Management ... Vacant
06 Registrar ... Ms. Susan MEIER
08 Director of the Library ... Ms. Judy TRIBBLE
29 Dir Alumnae Affairs/Annual Giving ... Ms. Chanel REEDER
26 Executive Dir of College Relations ... Ms. Dee REED
55 Dir Woods External Degree Pgm ... Ms. Gwen HAGEMEYER
13 Exec Dir Information Technology ... Vacant
21 Controller ... Ms. Missie SCHWAB
36 Director of Career Development ... Ms. Susan GRESHAM
15 Director Human Resources ... Ms. Diana WARREN
18 Chief Facilities/Physical Plant ... Mr. Bill ZINK
35 Director Campus Life ... Mr. Jeffrey MALLOY
37 Director Financial Aid ... Ms. Darla HOPPER
44 Dir Major and Planned Gifts ... Ms. April SIMMA
64 Dir Grad Pgm Music Therapy ... Ms. Tracy RICHARDSON
88 Dir Grad Pgm Art Therapy ... Ms. Kathy GOTSHALL
53 Dir Grad Pgm Education ... Dr. Annaliese PAYNE
88 Dir Grad Pgm Leadership Development ... Ms. Susan DECKER
106 Dir Woods On-Line Program ... Dr. Jennie MITCHELL

Saint Mary's College (D)

Notre Dame IN 46556
County: Saint Joseph — FICE Identification: 001836
Unit ID: 152390
Telephone: (574) 284-4000 — Carnegie Class: Bac/A&S
FAX Number: (574) 284-4716 — Calendar System: Semester
URL: www.saintmarys.edu
Established: 1844 — Annual Undergrad Tuition & Fees: $32,000
Enrollment: 1,555 — Female
Affiliation or Control: Roman Catholic — IRS Status: 501(c)3
Highest Offering: Baccalaureate
Program: Liberal Arts And General; Teacher Preparatory; Professional
Accreditation: NH, ART, MUS, NUR, SW, TED

01 President ... Dr. Carol Ann MOONEY
04 Executive Asst to the President ... Ms. Susan C. DAMPEER
05 Sr Vice President & Dean of Faculty ... Dr. Patricia A. FLEMING
26 Vice President College Relations ... Ms. Shari M. RODRIGUEZ
32 Vice President for Student Affairs ... Ms. Karen A. JOHNSON
10 Vice Pres Finance & Administration ... Mr. Richard SPELLER
84 Vice Pres for Enrollment Management ... Ms. Mona BOWE
88 Vice President for Mission ... Sr. Veronique WIEDOWER, CSC
89 Associate Dean for Advising ... Ms. Susan VANEK
06 Registrar ... Mr. Todd NORRIS
07 Director of Admission ... Ms. Kristin MCANDREW
08 Director of Library ... Ms. Janet S. FORE
09 Director of Institutional Research ... Ms. Jessica ICKES
29 Director of Alumnae Relations ... Ms. Kara O'LEARY
37 Director of Financial Aid ... Ms. Kathleen M. BROWN
27 Director of Publicity & Cmty Rels ... Ms. Gwen O'BRIEN
38 Director of Women's Health ... Ms. Catherine A. DECLEENE
13 Chief Information Officer ... Ms. Janice THOMASSON
15 Director of Human Resources ... Ms. Debra KELLY
19 Director of Safety & Security ... Mr. David GARIEPY
40 Manager Bookstore ... Mr. Michael G. HICKS
41 Director of Athletics ... Ms. Julie SCHROEDER-BIEK
42 Director of Campus Ministry ... Ms. Judith FEAN
18 Director of Facilities ... Mr. William HAMBLING
35 Dir Stdt Involvement/Multicult Pgm ... Ms. Stephanie STEWARD-BRIDGES
96 Director of Purchasing ... Mr. Daniel P. DEETER

Saint Meinrad Seminary and School of Theology (E)

200 Hill Drive, Saint Meinrad IN 47577-1030
County: Spencer — FICE Identification: 007276
Unit ID: 152451
Telephone: (812) 357-6611 — Carnegie Class: Spec/Faith
FAX Number: (812) 357-6964 — Calendar System: Semester
URL: www.saintmeinrad.edu
Established: 1861 — Annual Graduate Tuition & Fees: $20,542
Enrollment: 233 — Coed
Affiliation or Control: Roman Catholic — IRS Status: 501(c)3
Highest Offering: Master's; No Undergraduates
Program: Professional; Religious Emphasis
Accreditation: NH, THEOL

01 President & Rector ... Rev. Denis ROBINSON, OSB
03 Vice Rector ... Rev. Godfrey MULLEN, OSB
05 Academic Dean ... Dr. Robert ALVIS
84 Director of Enrollment ... Rev. Brendan MOSS, OSB
42 Director of Spiritual Formation ... Rev. Joseph MORIARTY
20 Director of Lay Degree Programs ... Mr. Kyle KRAMER
30 Vice President of Development ... Mr. Michael ZIEMIANSKI
10 Business Manager & Treasurer ... Rev. Adrian BURKE, OSB
08 Library Director ... Dr. Daniel KOLB
06 Registrar ... Mrs. Donna M. BALBACH
88 Dir Inst for Priests & Presbyterate ... Rev. Ronald KNOTT
21 Director of Budget ... Mrs. Pam DOWLAND
37 Director of Student Financial Aid ... Mrs. Ruth KRESS
26 Director of Communications ... Mrs. Mary Jeanne SCHUMACHER
29 Director of Alumni Relations ... Vacant
38 Director of Student Counseling Ctr ... Sr. Diane PHARO, SCN
88 Dir of Info & Instructional Tech ... Mr. Terry WAHL
09 Director of Institutional Research ... Rev. Bede CISCO, OSB
23 Director of Health Services ... Mrs. Ann ROHLEDER

Taylor University (F)

West 236 Reade Avenue, Upland IN 46989-1001
County: Grant — FICE Identification: 001838
Unit ID: 152530
Telephone: (765) 998-2751 — Carnegie Class: Bac/Diverse
FAX Number: (765) 998-4910 — Calendar System: 4/1/4
URL: www.taylor.edu
Established: 1846 — Annual Undergrad Tuition & Fees: $27,438
Enrollment: 2,589 — Coed
Affiliation or Control: Independent Non-Profit — IRS Status: 501(c)3
Highest Offering: Master's
Program: Liberal Arts And General; Teacher Preparatory; Fine Arts Emphasis
Accreditation: NH, ENG, MUS, SW, TED

01 President ... Dr. Eugene B. HABECKER
05 Provost ... Dr. Stephen S. BEDI
10 Vice Pres Business & Finance ... Mr. Ronald SUTHERLAND
30 Vice Pres University Advancement ... Dr. Ben SELLS
104 Dean International Programs ... Dr. Chris BENNETT
49 Dean Sch Liberal Arts ... Dr. Thomas JONES
58 Dean Sch Professional/Grad Studies ... Dr. Connie LIGHTFOOT
81 Dean Sch Natural & Applied Sciences ... Dr. Mark BIERMANN
20 Dean Faculty Development/Dir CTLE ... Dr. Faye CHECHOWICH
84 Dean of Enroll Mgmt & Marketing ... Mr. Stephen MORTLAND
32 Dean of Student Development/AVP ... Dr. Skip TRUDEAU
106 Dean of Online Learning ... Dr. Jeff GROELING
13 Chief Information Officer ... Mr. Rob LINEHAN
15 Director of HR Operations ... Ms. Toni NEWLIN
26 Assoc VP Univ Relations & Marketing ... Ms. Joyce WOOD
44 Assoc VP for Campaigns ... Mr. David RITCHIE
88 Assoc VP Business Develop & Svcs ... Mr. Stephen OLSON
29 Assoc VP Alumni & Parent Relations ... Mr. Brent RUDIN
44 Assoc VP for Major & Planned Gifts ... Mr. Mike FALDER
37 Assoc Dean Enroll Mgmt/Dir Fin Aid ... Mr. Timothy NACE
08 Assoc Dn Stdnt Support/Un Librarian ... Mr. Daniel BOWELL
06 Registrar ... Ms. Janet SHAFFER
42 Campus Pastor/Assoc Dean Students ... Rev. Randall GRUENDYKE
41 Director of Athletics ... Dr. Angie FINCANNON
36 Assoc Dean Students/Dir Career Dev ... Ms. Jill SMITH
39 Residence Life Pgm/Asc Dn Stdnt ... Mr. Steve MORLEY
18 Director of Physical Plant ... Mr. Greg ELEY
19 Chief of Police/Taylor Police ... Mr. Jeff WALLACE
38 Director of Counseling Center ... Mr. Robert NEIDECK
24 Director of Academic Technology ... Mr. Gary FRIESEN
88 Director Assessment/Quality Improv ... Mr. Brent MAHER
09 Institutional Research Analyst ... Mr. Stephen DAYTON
88 University Bursar ... Ms. Cathy MOORMAN
40 Bookstore Manager ... Mr. Matthew VOSS

TCM International Institute (G)

6337 Hollister Drive, Indianapolis IN 46224
Identification: 666333
Telephone: (317) 299-0333 — Carnegie Class: Not Classified
FAX Number: (317) 290-8607 — Calendar System: Semester
URL: www.tcmi.org

Established: 1991 Annual Graduate Tuition & Fees: N/A
Enrollment: N/A Coed
Affiliation or Control: Independent Non-Profit IRS Status: 501(c)3
Highest Offering: Master's; No Undergraduates
Program: Religious Emphasis
Accreditation: NH

01 President .... Dr. Tony TWIST

Trine University (A)

1 University Avenue, Angola IN 46703-1764
County: Steuben FICE Identification: 001839
Unit ID: 152567
Telephone: (260) 665-4100 Carnegie Class: Bac/Diverse
FAX Number: (260) 665-4292 Calendar System: Semester
URL: www.trine.edu
Established: 1884 Annual Undergrad Tuition & Fees: $26,600
Enrollment: 1,871 Coed
Affiliation or Control: Independent Non-Profit IRS Status: 501(c)3
Highest Offering: Master's
Program: Teacher Preparatory; Professional; Business Emphasis
Accreditation: NH, ACBSP, ENG, TED

01 President .... Dr. Earl D. BROOKS, II
03 Senior Vice President .... Mr. Mike BOCK
05 Vice President for Academic Affairs .... Dr. David FINLEY
10 Vice President Finance .... Ms. Jody GREER
30 Vice Pres for Alumni & Development .... Mr. Kent D. STUCKY
84 VP Enrollment Mgmt/Dean Admissions .... Mr. Scott GOPLIN
32 Vice President for Student Life .... Mr. Randy WHITE
51 Asst Vice Pres for Adult Learning .... Dr. Jean DELLER
107 Dean of Professional Studies .... Mr. David WOOD
15 Human Resources .... Ms. Cathy FAYE
41 Athletic Director .... Mr. Jeff POSENDEK
06 Registrar .... Ms. Debra F. HELMSING
27 Dir Integrated & Brand Marketing .... Ms. Jill BOGGS
04 Assistant to the President .... Ms. Dareen MCCLELLAND
37 Director Student Financial Planning .... Ms. Kim BENNETT
13 Chief Information Officer-IT .... Ms. Michelle DUNN
08 Director of the Library .... Ms. Kristina BREWER
36 Int Director of Placement/Coop Educ .... Ms. Linda BATEMAN
09 Director Inst Planning/Research .... Ms. Christina ZAMBRUN

University of Evansville (B)

1800 Lincoln Avenue, Evansville IN 47722-1586
County: Vanderburgh FICE Identification: 001795
Unit ID: 150534
Telephone: (812) 488-2000 Carnegie Class: Master's S
FAX Number: (812) 488-2320 Calendar System: Semester
URL: www.evansville.edu
Established: 1854 Annual Undergrad Tuition & Fees: $29,416
Enrollment: 2,961 Coed
Affiliation or Control: United Methodist IRS Status: 501(c)3
Highest Offering: Doctorate
Program: Liberal Arts And General; Teacher Preparatory; Professional
Accreditation: NH, BUS, CS, ENG, MUS, NUR, PTA, PTAA, TED

01 President .... Dr. Thomas A. KAZEE
05 Sr Vice President Academic Affairs .... Dr. John MOSBO
30 Vice Pres Institutional Advancement .... Mr. John C. BARNER
10 Vice President Fiscal Affairs/Admin .... Mr. Jeffery M. WOLF
32 VP Student Affairs/Dean of Students .... Ms. Dana CLAYTON
84 Vice President Enrollment Services .... Dr. Thomas E. BEAR
25 Assoc VP Academic Affs/Grants Dir .... Dr. Jennifer L. GRABAN
35 Asst VP Student Affs/Dir Res Life .... Mr. Michael A. TESSIER
21 Asst VP for Fiscal Affairs .... Ms. Donna O. TEAGUE
13 Asst VP & Chief Technology Office .... Mr. Donald HUDSON
49 Interim Dean of Arts & Sciences .... Dr. Jean BECKMAN
50 Dean of Business Administration .... Dr. Stephen STANDIFIRD
53 Dean of Education/Health Science .... Dr. Lynn R. PENLAND
54 Dean Engineering/Computer Science .... Dr. Phillip M. GERHART
41 Director of Athletics .... Mr. John STANLEY
26 Director of University Relations .... Ms. Lucy HIMSTEDT
06 Univ Registrar/Dir Inst Research .... Ms. Amy BRANDEBURY
08 University Librarian .... Mr. William F. LOUDEN
42 University Chaplain .... Rev. Tammy GIESELMAN
11 Director of Administrative Services .... Mr. Mark J. LOGEL
29 Director of Alumni/Parent Relations .... Ms. Sylvia Y. DEVAULT
44 Dir Gift Planning/Capital Support .... Ms. Abigail MILEY
36 Director of Career Svcs/Placement .... Mr. C. Gene WELLS
16 Director of Counseling/Health Educ .... Ms. Sylvia T. BUCK
37 Director of Financial Aid .... Ms. JoAnn E. LAUGEL
15 Director of Human Resources .... Mr. Keith GEHLHAUSEN
18 Director of Physical Plant .... Mr. Larry S. HORN
19 Director of Safety & Security .... Mr. Harold P. MATTHEWS
104 Director of Study Abroad/Harlaxton .... Mr. Earl D. KIRK
40 Director of Bookstore .... Mr. Douglas GUSTWILLER
28 Director of Diversity .... Ms. Latoya SMITH
44 Asst Director of Gift Giving .... Ms. Cathy RENNER
27 Coordinator of News Services .... Ms. Kristen LUND
07 Dean of Admissions .... Mr. Donald VOS

University of Indianapolis (C)

1400 E Hanna Avenue, Indianapolis IN 46227-3697
County: Marion FICE Identification: 001804
Unit ID: 151263
Telephone: (317) 788-3368 Carnegie Class: Master's L
FAX Number: (317) 788-3300 Calendar System: Other
URL: www.uindy.edu
Established: 1902 Annual Undergrad Tuition & Fees: $22,790
Enrollment: 5,240 Coed
Affiliation or Control: United Methodist IRS Status: 501(c)3
Highest Offering: Doctorate
Program: Occupational; Liberal Arts And General; Teacher Preparatory; Professional
Accreditation: NH, ACBSP, ADNUR, ART, CLPSY, MIDWF, MUS, NURSE, OT, PTA, PTAA, SW, TED

01 President .... Dr. Beverly J. PITTS
05 Provost/Vice Pres Academic Affairs .... Dr. Deborah Ware BALOGH
46 VP Research/Plng/Strategic Ptnrship .... Dr. Mary C. MOORE
10 Vice President Business & Finance .... Mr. Michael L. BRAUGHTON
32 Vice President for Student Affairs .... Mr. Mark T. WEIGAND
30 Vice President for Inst Advancement .... Mr. James E. SMITH
84 Vice President for Enrollment .... Mr. Mark T. WEIGAND
35 Assoc VP for Student Affairs .... Ms. Kory M. VITANGELI
49 Dean College of Arts & Sciences .... Dr. Daniel H. BRIERE
50 Dean School of Business .... Dr. Sheela N. YADAV
53 Dean School of Education .... Dr. Kathryn A. MORAN
66 Dean School of Nursing .... Dr. Anne C. THOMAS
76 Dean College of Health Sciences .... Dr. Stephanie KELLY
88 Dean School of Adult Learning .... Dr. Patricia A. JEFFERSON-BILBY
06 Registrar .... Dr. Mary Beth BAGG
27 Exec Dir Communications & Marketing .... Ms. Mary WADE ATTEBERRY
07 Director of Admissions .... Mr. Ronald W. WILKS
08 Librarian .... Dr. Chris LAMAR
15 Director Human Resources .... Mr. Stant CLARK
26 Director Marketing .... Mr. Joe P. SOLARI
36 Dir Career Svcs/Employer Relations .... Mr. Paul W. GABONAY
13 Chief Information Counselor .... Mr. Jeff L. RUSSELL
37 Director Student Financial Aid .... Mrs. Linda B. HANDY
58 Director Graduate Business Pgms .... Dr. Matthew W. WILL
18 Director Physical Plant .... Mr. Kenneth M. PIEPENBRINK
19 Director Safety & Police Services .... Mr. Michael REDDICK
29 Director Alumni & Parent Relations .... Vacant
31 Director Univ Cmty Bridge Program .... Dr. Mary E. BUSCH
41 Director Athletics .... Dr. Sue J. WILLEY
42 Co-Chaplain .... Rev. L. Lang BROWNLEE
42 Co-Chaplain .... Rev. Jeremiah GIBBS
44 Director Planned & Major Gifts .... Mr. Andy M. KOCHER
85 Director International Programs .... Ms. Marilyn O. CHASE
24 Director Media/Client Services .... Mr. Robert A. JONES
38 Senior Staff Counselor .... Ms. Kelly MILLER
72 Director Ctr for Instructional Tech .... Mrs. Elizabeth A. KIGGINS
09 Director Enrollment Research .... Ms. Mary E. GRANT
40 Bookstore Manager .... Ms. Lesley NORIEGA

University of Notre Dame (D)

400 Main Building, Notre Dame IN 46556
County: Saint Joseph FICE Identification: 001840
Unit ID: 152080
Telephone: (574) 631-5000 Carnegie Class: RU/VH
FAX Number: (574) 631-6947 Calendar System: Semester
URL: www.nd.edu
Established: 1842 Annual Undergrad Tuition & Fees: $55,260
Enrollment: 11,985 Coed
Affiliation or Control: Roman Catholic IRS Status: 501(c)3
Highest Offering: Doctorate
Program: Liberal Arts And General; Professional; Business Emphasis
Accreditation: NH, ART, BUS, BUSA, COPSY, CS, ENG, IPSY, LAW, THEOL

01 President .... Rev. John I. JENKINS, CSC
05 Provost .... Dr. Thomas G. BURISH
03 Executive Vice President .... Dr. John F. AFFLECK-GRAVES
20 Vice Pres/Associate Provost .... Dr. Christine M. MAZIAR
20 Vice Pres/Associate Provost .... Dr. Daniel J. MYERS
20 Vice Pres/Associate Provost .... Dr. Donald B. POPE-DAVIS
32 Vice President for Student Affairs .... Rev. Thomas DOYLE, CSC
30 VP for Public Affs/Communications .... Ms. Janet M. BOTZ
10 Vice President for Finance .... Mr. John A. SEJDINAJ
46 Vice President for Research .... Dr. Robert J. BERNHARD
43 Vice President & General Counsel .... Ms. Marianne CORR
11 Vice President Business Operations .... Mr. James J. LYPHOUT
88 Vice Pres/Chief Investment Ofcr .... Mr. Scott C. MALPASS
15 Assoc Vice Pres Human Resources .... Mr. Robert K. MCQUADE
26 Vice President University Relations .... Mr. Louis M. NANNI
13 VP & Chief Information Officer .... Mr. Ronald D. KRAEMER
100 Chief of Staff/Special Assistant .... Dr. Frances L. SHAVERS
04 Assoc VP/Counselor to President .... Rev. James E. MCDONALD, CSC
41 Director of Athletics .... Mr. John "Jack" B. SWARBRICK
84 Assoc VP Undergraduate Enrollment .... Mr. Donald BISHOP
82 Assoc Provost Internationalization .... Dr. Nicholas ENTRIKIN
06 Registrar .... Dr. Harold L. PACE
96 Director Procurement .... Mr. Rob M. KELLY
50 Dean of College of Business .... Dr. Carolyn Y. WOO
61 Dean of Law School .... Prof. Nell J. NEWTON
54 Dean College of Engineering .... Dr. Peter K. KILPATRICK
58 Dean of the Graduate School .... Dr. Greg E. STERLING
49 Dean of Arts & Letters .... Dr. John T. MCGREEVY
81 Dean of Science .... Dr. Gregory P. CRAWFORD
48 Dean of Architecture .... Dr. Michael N. LYKOUDIS
29 Assoc Exec Director Alumni Assoc .... Ms. Dolly DUFFY
88 Dean First Year of Studies .... Dr. Hugh R. PAGE
08 Interim Dir of University Libraries .... Ms. Susan OHMER
37 Director of Student Financial Aid .... Mr. Joseph A. RUSSO
36 Director of Career Center .... Mr. Lee J. SVETE
38 Director of Counseling Center .... Dr. Susan STEIBE-PASALICH
45 Assoc VP Strategic Planning .... Ms. Erin HOFFMAN-HARDING
19 Director of Security/Police .... Mr. Phillip A. JOHNSON

University of Saint Francis (E)

2701 Spring Street, Fort Wayne IN 46808-3994
County: Allen FICE Identification: 001832
Unit ID: 152336
Telephone: (260) 399-7700 Carnegie Class: Master's S
FAX Number: N/A Calendar System: Semester
URL: www.sf.edu
Established: 1890 Annual Undergrad Tuition & Fees: $3,150
Enrollment: 2,294 Coed
Affiliation or Control: Roman Catholic IRS Status: 501(c)3
Highest Offering: Master's
Program: Occupational; 2-Year Principally Bachelor's Creditable; Liberal Arts And General; Teacher Preparatory; Professional
Accreditation: NH, ADNUR, ARCPA, ART, NURSE, PTAA, RAD, SURGT, SW, TED

01 President .... Sr. M. Elise KRISS, OSF
05 Provost .... Dr. Rolf W. DANIEL
20 Assistant Provost .... Dr. J Andrew PRALL
03 Executive Vice President .... Dr. Stacy J. ADKINSON
11 Associate Vice President .... Mrs. Teresa SORDELET
10 Vice President Finance .... Mr. Richard BIENZ
30 Vice President University Relations .... Mr. Donald SCHENKEL
32 VP Student Life/Dean of Students .... Ms. Sharon K. MEJEUR
35 Associate Dean of Students .... Ms. Beth GROMAN
49 Dean School of Arts & Sciences .... Dr. Matthew SMITH
50 Dean Keith Busse School of Business .... Ms. Helen MURRAY
88 Assistant Dean School of Business .... Dr. Karen PALUMBO
57 Dean School of Creative Arts .... Mr. Rick E. CARTWRIGHT
17 Dean School of Health Sciences .... Dr. Nancy N. GILLESPIE
107 Dean School of Professional Studies .... Dr. Jane M. SWISS
06 Registrar .... Mr. Francis P. CONNOR
07 Director Admissions .... Mr. Jean Paul SPAGNOLO
29 Director Alumni .... Vacant
41 Interim Director Athletics .... Mr. Mike MCCAFFREY
88 Director Campaigns & Major Gifts .... Mr. William SLAYTON
42 Director Campus Ministry .... Mr. Joshua STAGNI
19 Director Campus Safety & Security .... Mr. Richard ROBBINS
36 Director Career Services .... Mr. William BRUNE
88 Dir Center for Service Engagement .... Ms. Katrina BOEDEKER
88 Director Co-Curricular Activities .... Ms. Melissa REESMAN
102 Dir Corp/Found Relations and Grants .... Ms. Lynn MCKENNA-FRAZIER
12 Interim Director Crown Point Site .... Ms. Margaret STOFFREGEN-DEYOUNG
30 Exec Dir Development/Alumni .... Mr. Jay NUSSEL
88 Director Development .... Ms. Kristen R. RIEBENACK
13 Dir Distance/Instruc/Educ Tech .... Mr. Robert SOULLIERE
37 Director Financial Aid .... Mrs. Jamie MCGRATH
21 Dir Financial Planning/Accounting .... Ms. Cathy CRAWFORD
88 Director Financial Reporting .... Ms. Mary HAFT
89 Dir 1st Yr Exper & Stdnt Acad Supp .... Ms. Jenny FAWBUSH
58 Director Graduate School .... Dr. Douglas BARCALOW
88 Director Health Sciences Sim Lab .... Dr. Dawn MABRY
88 Dir Hlth Sci Strategic Initiatives .... Dr. Lorene ARNOLD
92 Director Honors Program .... Dr. Mathew FISHER
39 Director Housing & Residence Life .... Mr. Andrew MCKEE
15 Director Human Resources .... Ms. Norma BOENKER
88 Dir Inst Effectiveness/Accredit .... Dr. Marcia K. SAUTER
09 Director Institutional Research .... Dr. Stephanie J. OETTING
08 Director Library Services .... Ms. Karla ALEXANDER
26 Director Marketing .... Ms. Trois HART
88 Asst to Pres for Mission Integra .... Sr. M. Mary Evelyn GOVERT, OSF
91 Dir Network & Information Mgmt .... Mr. Robbins MARK
88 Director Operations .... Mr. Thomas BUUCK
44 Director Planned Giving .... Sr. M. Marilyn OLIVER, OSF
88 Dir Retention and Academic Advising .... Ms. Michelle KUHLHORST
88 Director Sports Information .... Mr. Bill SCOTT
88 Dir Student Academic Support Svcs .... Mrs. Tricia BUGAJSKI
88 Dir Tech Security & Compliance .... Mr. Randy TROY
88 Director TRiO .... Mr. Tellis YOUNG
14 Dir Tech User Support Services .... Mr. A. Drew REPP
88 Mgr AVI Food Service .... Mr. Brian SMITH
40 Mgr Barnes & Noble Campus Shoppe .... Ms. Robin HUFFMAN

University of Southern Indiana (F)

8600 University Boulevard, Evansville IN 47712-3596
County: Vanderburgh FICE Identification: 001808
Unit ID: 151306
Telephone: (812) 464-8600 Carnegie Class: Master's L
FAX Number: (812) 464-1960 Calendar System: Semester
URL: www.usi.edu
Established: 1965 Annual Undergrad Tuition & Fees (In-State): $5,852
Enrollment: 10,702 Coed
Affiliation or Control: State IRS Status: 501(c)3
Highest Offering: Doctorate
Program: Liberal Arts And General; Teacher Preparatory; Professional
Accreditation: NH, BUS, BUSA, DA, DH, @DIETD, DMS, ENG, JOUR, NURSE, OT, OTA, RAD, SW, TED

01 President .... Dr. Linda L M. BENNETT
100 Assistant to the President .... Ms. Janel S. ALLEN
05 Provost .... Dr. Ronald S. ROCHON
10 Vice President Business Affairs .... Mr. Mark ROZEWSKI
86 Vice Pres Govt and Univ Relations .... Ms. Cynthia S. BRINKER
26 Asst VP Marketing/Communications .... Mr. Todd A. WILSON
56 Assoc Provost Outreach Engagement .... Dr. Mark C. BERNHARD
20 Asst Provost Undergraduate Studies .... Dr. Brian POSLER
32 Assoc Provost for Student Affairs .... Dr. Marcia K. KIESSLING

21 Asst Vice Pres Business Affairs ... Ms. Mary A. HUPFER
59 Exec Director Plng/Research/Assess . Dr. Katherine A. DRAUGHON
58 Director of Graduate Studies ... Dr. Peggy F. HARREL
06 Registrar ... Ms. Sandy K. FRANK
07 Director of Admission ... Mr. Eric H. OTTO
08 Director of Library Services ... Ms. Ruth H. MILLER
30 Director of Development/USI Fndtn ... Mr. David A. BOWER
92 Director Honors Program ... Dr. Antonia D. BAMBINA
38 Director of Counseling ... Dr. B. Thomas LONGWELL
36 Director of Career Counseling ... Mr. Timothy K. BUECHER
29 Director of Alumni Affairs ... Mrs. Nancy L. JOHNSON
37 Director of Student Financial Asst ... Ms. Mary J. HARPER
15 Director of Human Resources ... Ms. Donna J. EVINGER
36 Director Career Services/Placement ... Mr. Philip PARKER
35 Dean of Students ... Mr. Barry K. SCHONBERGER
85 Director of Intl Student Services ... Mrs. Heidi GREGORI-GAHAN
28 Director Multicultural Center ... Ms. Pamela F. HOPSON
14 Exec Dir of Information Technology ... Mr. Richard TOENISKOETTER
90 Academic Services Coordinator ... Mr. Juzar AHMED
18 Director of Facilities Operations ... Mr. Stephen P. HELFRICH
96 Director Procurement/Distribution ... Mr. David A. GOLDENBERG
27 Director of News & Information Svcs ... Ms. Kathy W. FUNKE
19 Director of Security ... Mr. Stephen WOODALL
39 Director of Residence Life ... Ms. Laurie M. BERRY
40 Bookstore Manager ... Mr. Michael J. GOELZHAUSER
41 Athletic Director ... Mr. Jon Mark HALL
24 Director Instructional Technology ... Vacant
50 Dean College of Business ... Dr. Mohammed KHAYUM
49 Dean College of Liberal Arts ... Mr. Michael K. AAKHUS
66 Dean College Nursing/Health Profess ... Dr. Nadine A. COUDRET
81 Dean College of Science/Engineering ... Dr. Scott A. GORDON
21 Asst Vice Pres Finance Admin Treas ... Mr. Steven J. BRIDGES
51 Director Continuing Education ... Ms. Linda L. CLEEK

Valparaiso University (A)

Valparaiso IN 46383-9978

County: Porter | FICE Identification: 001842 | Unit ID: 152600
Telephone: (219) 464-5000 | Carnegie Class: Master's L
FAX Number: (219) 464-5381 | Calendar System: Semester
URL: valpo.edu
Established: 1859 | Annual Undergrad Tuition & Fees: $31,040
Enrollment: 4,061 | Coed
Affiliation or Control: Lutheran | IRS Status: 501(c)3
Highest Offering: Doctorate
Program: Liberal Arts And General; Teacher Preparatory; Professional
Accreditation: NH, BUS, CACREP, ENG, LAW, MUS, NURSE, SW, TED

01 President ... Mr. Mark A. HECKLER
05 Provost/Exec Vice Pres Acad Affs ... Dr. Mark R. SCHWEHN
20 Senior Associate Provost ... Dr. Renu JUNEJA
32 Vice President for Student Affairs ... Dr. Bonnie L. HUNTER
11 VP for Administration & Finance ... Mr. Charley E. GILLISPIE
84 Vice Pres for Enrollment Management ... Vacant
26 VP Integrated Mktg/Communications ... Mr. Scott D. OCHANDER
58 Asc Provost/Dean Grad Sch/Cont Ed ... Dr. David L. ROWLAND
30 Vice Pres Institutional Advancement ... Ms. Lisa HOLLANDER
43 Vice President University Counsel ... Mr. Darron C. FARHA
92 Dean of Christ College ... Dr. Mel PIEHL
49 Dean College Arts & Sciences ... Dr. Jon T. KILPINEN
61 Dean School of Law ... Mr. Jay CONISON
54 Dean College of Engineering ... Dr. Kraig J. OLEJNICZAK
50 Int Dean College of Business Admin ... Dr. Roy A. AUSTENSEN
66 Dean College of Nursing ... Dr. Janet M. BROWN
08 Dean Library Services ... Dr. Bradford L. EDEN
35 Dean of Students ... Dr. Timothy S. JENKINS
07 Dean or Undergraduate Admission ... Mr. David FEVIG
42 Exec Dir of Campus Ministries ... Rev. Brian T. JOHNSON
13 Exec Dir Information Technology ... Mr. Mike TUCKER
06 Registrar ... Ms. Shelly KOOI
19 Chief University Police ... Ms. Rebecca A. WALKOWIAK
39 Asst Dean Students/Residential Life ... Mr. Ryan BLEVINS
104 Director of Study Abroad Programs ... Ms. Julie A. MADDOX
85 Dir International Students/Scholars ... Mr. Holly SINGH
37 Director Financial Aid ... Ms. Phyllis L. SCHROEDER
29 Director Alumni Relations ... Vacant
15 Dir Human Resource Services ... Ms. Nora WIERGACZ
88 Exec Dir for Capital Planning ... Mr. Fred W. PLANT
36 Director Career Center ... Mr. Tom CATH
38 Director of Counseling Services ... Dr. Stewart E. COOPER
41 Director Athletics ... Mr. Mark LABARBERA
20 Assistant Provost ... Dr. Rick GILLMAN
21 Controller ... Ms. Dianne M. WOODS
28 Director of Multicultural Programs ... Ms. Jane M. BELLO-BRUNSON
96 Director of Procurement ... Ms. Nancy K. MURRAY
09 Exec Dir Instnl Effectiveness ... Mr. Greg STINSON
42 University Pastor ... Rev. Charlene COX
42 University Pastor ... Rev. James WETZSTEIN

Vincennes University (B)

1002 N First Street, Vincennes IN 47591-1504

County: Knox | FICE Identification: 001843 | Unit ID: 152637
Telephone: (812) 888-8888 | Carnegie Class: Assoc/Pub4
FAX Number: (812) 888-5868 | Calendar System: Semester
URL: www.vinu.edu
Established: 1801 | Annual Undergrad Tuition & Fees (In-State): $4,705
Enrollment: 9,963 | Coed
Affiliation or Control: State | IRS Status: 501(c)3
Highest Offering: Baccalaureate
Program: Occupational; 2-Year Principally Bachelor's Creditable; Liberal Arts And General
Accreditation: NH, ACBSP, ADNUR, ART, EMT, FUSER, NUR, PNUR, PTAA, SURGA, SURGT, THEA

01 President ... Dr. Richard E. HELTON
05 Provost/Vice Pres Institutional Svc ... Vacant
10 Vice Pres Financial Svcs/Govt Rels ... Mr. Phillip S. RATH
103 VP Workforce Dev/Comm Services ... Mr. David C. TUCKER
12 Assistant VP/Dean Jasper Campus ... Dr. Alan D. JOHNSON
32 Asst Provost Student Affairs ... Ms. Lynn WHITE
20 Asst Provost Curriculum & Inst ... Dr. Carolyn K. JONES
35 Dean of Students ... Mr. John T. LIVERS
26 Sr Director External Relations ... Ms. Kristi R. DEETZ
07 Director of Admissions ... Mr. Christian BLOME
08 Director of Learning Resources/Tech ... Mr. David PETER
09 Director of Inst Research/Planning ... Vacant
13 Director of Mgmt Information Center ... Mr. Carmin A. SCHNARR
27 Director Public Information ... Mr. Duane H. CHATTIN
88 Director of University Events ... Ms. Brenda L. THOMPSON
36 Dir Ctr for Career & Empl Relations ... Mr. Richard A. COLEMAN
37 Director of Student Financial Aid ... Mr. Stanley J. WERNE
88 Director Disability Services ... Ms. Lynn S. MCCORMICK
38 Director of Student Counseling ... Dr. Lisa J. BISHOP
39 Director of Housing Facilities ... Ms. Patricia A. JOST
40 Manager of Bookstore ... Mr. Ronald L. KOTTER
102 President of VU Foundation ... Mr. Bumper R. HOSTETLER
41 Athletic Director ... Mr. Harry L. MEEKS
88 Director of Project Excel/Proj Link ... Ms. Heather MOFFAT
29 Director of Alumni Programs ... Ms. Jennifer D. GILMORE
85 Dir Multicultural/Intl Student Affs ... Mr. Daniel J. WHITMER
18 Director of Physical Plant ... Mr. James W. MINDERMAN
19 Director of Campus Police ... Mr. James M. JONES
21 Associate Vice President/Controller ... Ms. Linda L. WALDROUP
88 Bursar ... Ms. Lori J. HOSTETLER
23 Coordinator Student Health Office ... Ms. Margaret J. MILLIGAN
24 Director of Media Services ... Mr. Jay D. WOLF
06 Registrar/Veterans Affairs ... Ms. Donna Jo WEAVER
39 Director Residential Life ... Ms. Dawn M. BREWER
88 Director Marketing Services ... Ms. Andrea G. TSCHERTER
96 Director of Procurement ... Mr. Daniel R. MARTENS
38 Director Academic Advising ... Mr. Thomas E. KONKLE
88 Director Architectural Services ... Mr. Andrew YOUNG
16 Director Human Resources/AAO ... Ms. Lorethea H. POTTS-RUSK
76 Dean Health Sci/Human Perf ... Ms. Jana L. VIECK
50 Dean Business/Public Service Div ... Mr. Nicolas A. SPINA
72 Dean Technology Division ... Mr. Arthur H. HAASE
81 Dean Science/Math Division ... Dr. Peter A. IYERE
83 Dean Social Sci/Performing Arts ... Mr. Eric W. MARGERUM
51 Dean Extended Studies ... Mr. Donald E. KAUFMAN
79 Dean Humanities Div ... Dr. Charles W. REINHART
88 Dir Avia Tech Ctr Indianapolis ... Mr. Michael D. GEHRICH
88 Dir Marketing Communications ... Ms. Krystal F. SPENCER
88 Dir Institutional Effectiveness ... Mr. Michael GRESS

Wabash College (C)

301 W Wabash, PO Box 352,
Crawfordsville IN 47933-0352

County: Montgomery | FICE Identification: 001844 | Unit ID: 152673
Telephone: (765) 361-6100 | Carnegie Class: Bac/A&S
FAX Number: (765) 361-6461 | Calendar System: Semester
URL: www.wabash.edu
Established: 1832 | Annual Undergrad Tuition & Fees: $32,450
Enrollment: 871 | Male
Affiliation or Control: Independent Non-Profit | IRS Status: 501(c)3
Highest Offering: Baccalaureate
Program: Liberal Arts And General
Accreditation: NH, TED

01 President ... Dr. Patrick E. WHITE
05 Dean of the College ... Dr. Gary A. PHILLIPS
10 Chief Financial Officer & Treasurer ... Mr. Larry GRIFFITH
32 Dean of Students ... Mr. Michael P. RATERS
30 Dean for Advancement ... Mr. Joseph R. EMMICK
35 Associate Dean of Students ... Mr. George W. OPRISKO
06 Registrar and Assoc Dean ... Dr. Julie A. OLSEN
07 Dean of Admissions & Financial Aid ... Mr. Steven J. KLEIN
37 Director of Financial Aid ... Mr. R. Clinton GASAWAY
08 Head Librarian & Dir Lilly Library ... Mr. John E. LAMBORN
13 Director of IT Services ... Mr. Bradley K. WEAVER
36 Director of Career Development ... Mr. R. Scott CRAWFORD
29 Dir of Alumni & Parent Relations ... Mr. Thomas G. RUNGE
26 Dir of Public Affairs & Marketing ... Mr. James L. AMIDON
40 Director of Purchasing & Bookstore ... Mr. Thomas E. KEEDY
41 Dir of Athletics & Campus Wellness ... Mr. Joseph R. HAKLIN
44 Director of Development ... Ms. Alison KOTHE
15 Director of Human Resources ... Ms. Catherine A. METZ
18 Director of Campus Services ... Mr. David MORGAN
96 Director of Purchasing & Bookstore ... Mr. Thomas E. KEEDY
21 Controller ... Ms. Cathy VANARSDALL
38 Director of Counseling Services ... Mr. Kevin C. SWAIM
28 Dir of Malcolm X Inst & Assoc Dean ... Dr. Michael J. BROWN
88 Dir of Ctr of Inquiry in the LA ... Dr. Charles F. BLAICH
88 Dir Wabash Ctr Teaching/Learning ... Dr. Nadine S. PENCE
19 Director of Safety and Security ... Mr. Richard G. WOODS

IOWA

AIB College of Business (D)

2500 Fleur Drive, Des Moines IA 50321-1799

County: Polk | FICE Identification: 003963 | Unit ID: 152822
Telephone: (515) 244-4221 | Carnegie Class: Spec/Bus
FAX Number: (515) 244-6773 | Calendar System: Quarter
URL: www.aib.edu
Established: 1921 | Annual Undergrad Tuition & Fees: $13,740
Enrollment: 909 | Coed
Affiliation or Control: Independent Non-Profit | IRS Status: 501(c)3
Highest Offering: Baccalaureate
Program: Business Emphasis
Accreditation: NH

01 President ... Ms. Nancy WILLIAMS
05 Vice President for Academic Affairs ... Dr. M. Susan CIGELMAN
32 VP for Student Life & Athletics Dir ... Mr. Terry WILSON
20 Chief Academic Officer ... Ms. Christy ROLAND
07 Director of Admissions & Marketing ... Mr. Mark THOMPSON
30 Director of Advancement ... Ms. Maria` DAVIS
10 Chief Financial Officer ... Mr. Paul WINGET
15 Director of Human Resources ... Ms. Joan HITZEL
88 Faculty Assembly President ... Ms. Kelly SWINTON
04 Executive Assistant to President ... Ms. Ronette SMITH
50 Department Chair-Accounting ... Mr. Larry MURPHY
50 Dept Chair-Business Administration ... Ms. Ann WRIGHT
97 Dept Chair-Comm & General Studies ... Vacant
61 Dept Chair-Court Reporting ... Ms. Kay SMITH
14 Chief Information Officer ... Mr. Josh GLOVER
18 Chief Facilities Officer ... Mr. Chris SCHMIDT
36 Director of Career Services ... Ms. Jane DEHAVEN
21 Controller ... Ms. Janet CRUM
37 Director of Financial Aid Services ... Ms. Laurie SANDERS
88 Director of Facilities Management ... Mr. Mike LARSON
88 Director of Academic Advising ... Mr. Steve OLSEN
06 Registrar ... Mr. Randy TERRONEZ
88 Director of Activities ... Ms. Jennifer BEAL
38 Director of Student Counseling ... Ms. Sheila KEENE
35 Director of Student Life ... Ms. Kris PERALES
08 Library Director ... Ms. Leslie BINTNER
31 Director of Community Engagement ... Ms. Julie SPICER
90 Director of Academic Resources ... Ms. Suzanne HESS
29 Alumni Director ... Ms. Reonna SNYDER
88 Director of IT Application Services ... Mr. Mark ROLAND
105 Graphic/Web Designer ... Ms. Rachel SORENSEN
40 Bookstore Manager ... Ms. Michelle WHITE

Allen College (E)

1825 Logan Avenue, Waterloo IA 50703-1999

County: Black Hawk | FICE Identification: 030691 | Unit ID: 152798
Telephone: (319) 226-2000 | Carnegie Class: Spec/Health
FAX Number: (319) 226-2020 | Calendar System: Semester
URL: www.allencollege.edu
Established: 1989 | Annual Undergrad Tuition & Fees: $18,816
Enrollment: 477 | Coed
Affiliation or Control: Independent Non-Profit | IRS Status: 501(c)3
Highest Offering: Doctorate
Program: Professional
Accreditation: NH, MT, NUR, NURSE, RAD

01 Chancellor ... Dr. Jerry DURHAM
05 Vice Chancellor of Academic Affairs ... Dr. Nancy KRAMER
10 Dir Business/Administrative Svcs ... Ms. Denise HANSON
66 Dean School of Nursing ... Dr. Kendra WILLIAMS-PEREZ
76 Dean School of Health Sciences ... Dr. Peggy FORTSCH
06 Dir of Student Services/Registrar ... Ms. Joanna RAMSDEN-MEIER
37 Financial Aid Coordinator ... Ms. Kathie WALTERS
24 Media Specialist ... Ms. Robin NICHOLSON
07 Admissions Counselor ... Ms. Michelle KOEHN
08 Coordinator Library/Media Services ... Dr. Ruth YAN

Antioch School of Church Planting and Leadership Development (F)

2400 Oakwood Road, Ames IA 50014

County: Story | Identification: 667026
Telephone: (515) 292-9694 | Carnegie Class: Not Classified
FAX Number: (515) 292-1933 | Calendar System: Other
URL: www.antiochschool.edu
Established: 2006 | Annual Undergrad Tuition & Fees: $3,150
Enrollment: N/A | Coed
Affiliation or Control: Independent Non-Profit | IRS Status: 501(c)3
Highest Offering: Doctorate
Program: Religious Emphasis
Accreditation: DETC

01 President ... Jeff REED
05 Academic Dean ... Stephen KEMP

Ashford University (G)

400 N Bluff Boulevard, Clinton IA 52732-3997

County: Clinton | FICE Identification: 001881 | Unit ID: 154022
Telephone: (563) 242-4023 | Carnegie Class: Master's L
FAX Number: (563) 242-2003 | Calendar System: Semester
URL: www.ashford.edu

Established: 1918 Annual Undergrad Tuition & Fees: $16,270
Enrollment: 46,830 Coed
Affiliation or Control: Proprietary IRS Status: Proprietary
Highest Offering: Master's
Program: Liberal Arts And General; Teacher Preparatory; Business Emphasis
Accreditation: NH, IACBE

01 University President Dr. Elizabeth TICE
05 Provost Vacant
20 Vice President Academic Affairs Dr. James JEREMIAH
26 Director of Communications Mr. Larry LIBBERTON
07 Director of Admissions Mr. Jason WOODS
37 Director Financial Aid Ms. Lisa KRAMER
08 Library Director Ms. Flora LOWE
50 Dean Col Business/Professional Stds Dr. Charlie MINNICK
49 Dean College Arts & Sciences Dr. William LOWE
53 Dean College Education Dr. Joen ROTTLER
56 Center For External Studies Ms. Cynthia COMBS
39 Director of Residence Life Ms. Lettie CONNOLLY
41 Director of Athletics Ms. Meg SCHEBLER
06 University Registrar Mr. Kirk MORRISON
88 Director Prior Learning Assessment Dr. Karen CONZETT
19 Director of Security Mr. Kristopher SCHMIDT
09 Director of Institutional Research Mr. Kurt FOLKENDT

*Board of Regents, State of Iowa (A)

11260 Aurora Avenue, Urbandale IA 50322-7405
County: Polk FICE Identification: 033443
Telephone: (515) 281-3934 Carnegie Class: N/A
FAX Number: (515) 281-6420
URL: www.regents.iowa.gov

01 Executive Director Mr. Bob DONLEY
05 Chief Academic Officer Dr. Diana GONZALEZ
10 Chief Business Officer Mrs. Patrice M. SAYRE
43 General Counsel Mr. Thomas A. EVANS

*Iowa State University (B)

Ames IA 50011-0002
County: Story FICE Identification: 001869
Unit ID: 153603
Telephone: (515) 294-4111 Carnegie Class: RU/VH
FAX Number: (515) 294-2592 Calendar System: Semester
URL: www.iastate.edu
Established: 1858 Annual Undergrad Tuition & Fees (In-State): $7,486
Enrollment: 28,682 Coed
Affiliation or Control: State IRS Status: 501(c)3
Highest Offering: Doctorate
Program: Liberal Arts And General; Teacher Preparatory; Professional
Accreditation: NH, BUS, BUSA, CIDA, COPSY, CS, DIETD, DIETI, ENG, FOR, IPSY, JOUR, LSAR, MFCD, MUS, NAIT, PLNG, SPAA, VET

02 President Dr. Gregory L. GEOFFROY
05 Executive Vice President/Provost Dr. Elizabeth HOFFMAN
10 Vice President Business & Finance Mr. Warren R. MADDEN
32 Vice President Student Affairs Dr. Thomas L. HILL
46 Vice President Research/Econ Dev Dr. Sharon QUISENBERRY
56 Vice Pres Extension/Outreach Dr. Cathann KRESS
24 Vice Provost Info Technology & CIO Dr. James A. DAVIS
20 Associate Provost Academic Programs Dr. David K. HOLGER
28 Assoc Prov Acad Pers/Chief Div Off Dr. Dawn BRATSCH-PRINCE
21 Associate Vice President/Univ Sec Ms. Pam ELLIOTT CAIN
18 Assoc Vice Pres Facilities Mr. David J. MILLER
15 Assoc Vice Pres Human Resources Ms. Carla R. ESPINOZA
38 Asst VP for Counseling Service Dr. Terry W. MASON
04 Exec Asst to the President Dr. Tahira K. HIRA
102 President of ISU Foundation Mr. Daniel SAFTIG
29 President of Alumni Association Mr. Jeffrey W. JOHNSON
37 Director of Financial Aid Ms. Roberta L. JOHNSON
06 Registrar Ms. Kathleen M. JONES
07 Director of Admissions Mr. Marc HARDING
22 Director of Equal Oppty/Diversity Ms. Carla R. ESPINOZA
08 Dean of Library Services Ms. Olivia M. MADISON
09 Director of Institutional Research Dr. Gebre H. TESFAGIORGIS
19 Director of Public Safety Mr. Jerry D. STEWART
26 Director of University Relations Mr. John F. MCCARROLL
35 Dean of Students Vacant
23 Director of Student Health Ms. Michelle HENDRICKS
39 Director of Residence Dr. Peter D. ENGLIN
91 Associate CIO/Admin Info Systems Mr. Maury M. HOPE
25 Director of Sponsored Program Admin Ms. Joanne ALTIERI
41 Director of Athletics Mr. Jamie B. POLLARD
88 Director Ames Laboratory Dr. Alex H. KING
43 University Counsel Mr. Paul N. TANAKA
96 Director of Purchasing Ms. Nancy S. BROOKS
40 Director University Bookstore Ms. Rita M. PHILLIPS
58 Dean Graduate College Dr. David K. HOLGER
47 Dean College of Agriculture Dr. Wendy WINTERSTEEN
50 Dean College of Business Dr. Labh S. HIRA
48 Dean College of Design Mr. Luis C. RICO-GUTIERREZ
53 Dean College of Human Sciences Dr. Pamela WHITE
54 Dean College of Engineering Dr. Jonathan A. WICKERT
49 Int Dean Col of Lib Arts & Sciences Dr. David J. OLIVER
74 Dean College of Veterinary Medicine Dr. Lisa NOLAN

*University of Iowa (C)

Iowa City IA 52242-0001
County: Johnson FICE Identification: 001892
Unit ID: 153658
Telephone: (319) 335-3500 Carnegie Class: RU/VH
FAX Number: (319) 335-0807 Calendar System: Semester
URL: www.uiowa.edu
Established: 1847 Annual Undergrad Tuition & Fees (In-State): $7,765
Enrollment: 30,825 Coed
Affiliation or Control: State IRS Status: 501(c)3
Highest Offering: Doctorate
Program: Liberal Arts And General; Teacher Preparatory; Professional
Accreditation: NH, ANEST, ARCPA, AUD, BUS, BUSA, CACREP, CEA, CLPSY, COPSY, CORE, DANCE, DENT, DIETI, DMS, EMT, ENG, ENGR, HSA, IPSY, #JOUR, LAW, LIB, MED, MUS, NMT, NURSE, PERF, PH, PHAR, PLNG, PTA, RAD, RTT, SCPSY, SP, SW, THEA

02 President Dr. Sally MASON
05 Exec Vice President & Provost Dr. P. Barry BUTLER
46 Vice President Research Dr. Jordan L. COHEN
10 VP Finance/Operations/Univ Treas Mr. Douglas K. TRUE
32 VP Student Life Dr. Thomas R. ROCKLIN
17 Vice President for Medical Affairs Dr. Jean E. ROBILLARD
102 Vice Pres University Foundation Mr. David R. DIERKS
26 VP Strategic Communication Mr. Tysen KENDIG
20 Associate Provost Faculty Dr. Thomas W. RICE
51 Assoc Provost Continuing Education Dr. Chester S. RZONCA
28 Chief Diversity Officer/AP Dr. Georgina DODGE
88 Assoc Provost/Dean Univ College Dr. Beth INGRAM
45 Assoc Vice President Research Dr. Richard D. HICHWA
11 Assoc VP/Dir of Admin and Planning Mr. Donald J. SZESZYCKI
16 Assoc VP Finan/Univ Svcs/Dir HR Ms. Susan C. BUCKLEY
18 Assoc VP/Dir Facilities Management Mr. Donald J. GUCKERT
13 Assoc Vice President & CIO Mr. Steven R. FLEAGLE
23 Assoc VP/CEO Univ Hosp & Clinics Mr. Kenneth KATES
25 AVP Research/Dir Sponsored Pgms Ms. Twila REIGHLEY
19 Asst VP/Director Public Safety Mr. Charles D. GREEN
85 Dean International Programs Dr. Downing THOMAS
43 VP Legal Affairs & Gen Coun Ms. Carroll REASONER
08 University Librarian Ms. Nancy L. BAKER
29 Exec Director Alumni Association Mr. Vincent C. NELSON
30 President University Foundation Ms. Lynette L. MARSHALL
07 Director Admissions Mr. Michael BARRON
37 Director Student Financial Aid Mr. Mark S. WARNER
06 Registrar Mr. Lawrence J. LOCKWOOD
36 Director Career Center Mr. David A. BAUMGARTNER
38 Director Univ Counseling Services Dr. Sam V. COCHRAN, III
39 Director Residence Services Mr. Von STANGE
41 Director Athletics Administration Mr. Gary BARTA
49 Dean Col of Liberal Arts & Sciences Dr. Linda MAXSON
50 Dean College of Business Admin Dr. William (Curt) HUNTER
52 Dean College of Dentistry Dr. David C. JOHNSEN
53 Dean College of Education Dr. Sandra B. DAMICO
54 Interim Dean College of Engineering Dr. Alec SCRANTON
58 Dean Graduate College Dr. John C. KELLER
61 Dean College of Law Dr. Gail B. AGRAWAL
66 Dean College of Nursing Dr. Rita A. FRANTZ
67 Dean College of Pharmacy Dr. Donald E. LETENDRE
88 Assoc Dean Continuing Educ Programs Mr. Douglas J. LEE
69 Dean College of Public Health Dr. Susan CURRY
63 Dean College of Medicine Dr. Paul B. ROTHMAN
04 Special Assistant to President Dr. Thomas K. DEAN
22 Dir Equal Opportunity/Diversity Ms. Jennifer A. MODESTOU
86 Director State Relations Mr. Keith SAUNDERS
40 Director University Bookstore Mr. George E. HERBERT
96 Director Purchasing Ms. Deborah J. ZUMBACH
92 Director Honors Program Dr. Art L. SPISAK
87 Director Summer Session Mr. Douglas J. LEE
24 Manager Audiovisual Center Mr. Daniel G. LIND
35 Dean of Students Dr. David L. GRADY

*University of Northern Iowa (D)

1227 W 27th Street, Cedar Falls IA 50614-0001
County: Black Hawk FICE Identification: 001890
Unit ID: 154095
Telephone: (319) 273-2311 Carnegie Class: Master's L
FAX Number: (319) 273-2885 Calendar System: Semester
URL: www.uni.edu
Established: 1876 Annual Undergrad Tuition & Fees (In-State): $7,350
Enrollment: 13,201 Coed
Affiliation or Control: State IRS Status: 501(c)3
Highest Offering: Doctorate
Program: Liberal Arts And General; Teacher Preparatory
Accreditation: NH, BUS, CACREP, CEA, ENGT, MUS, NAIT, NRPA, SP, SW

02 President Dr. Benjamin J. ALLEN
05 Executive Vice President & Provost Dr. Gloria J. GIBSON
32 Vice Pres for Student Affairs Dr. Terrence HOGAN
11 Vice President for Admin & Finance Mr. Thomas G. SCHELLHARDT
18 Assoc VP for Facilities Management Mr. Morris E. MIKKELSEN
04 Spec Asst to Pres for Board/Gov Rel Dr. Patricia L. GEADELMANN
26 Exec Director University Relations Mr. James O'CONNOR
39 Asst VP & Executive Dir Residence Mr. Michael HAGER
20 Assoc Provost for Academic Affairs Dr. Michael J. LICARI
13 Chief Information Officer Dr. Shashidhar KAPARTHI
62 Dean of Library Services Vacant
06 Registrar Mr. Philip L. PATTON
37 Director of Financial Aid Ms. Joyce MORROW
15 Int Dir Human Resource Services Ms. Michelle C. BYERS
36 Director of Career Services Mr. Robert J. FREDERICK
83 Dean College Social/Behav Science Dr. Philip MAUCERI
53 Dean College of Education Dr. Dwight C. WATSON
49 Dean Col Humanities/Arts & Science Dr. Joel HAACK

51 Int Dean Cont Educ/Special Programs Dr. Kent M. JOHNSON
50 Dean College Business Admin Dr. Farzad MOUSSAVI
35 Dean of Students Dr. Jon BUSE
07 Director of Admissions Ms. Christie KANGAS
10 Controller/Secretary/Treasurer Mr. Gary B. SHONTZ
38 Counseling Director Dr. David C. TOWLE
22 Asst to Pres Compliance/Equity Mgmt Ms. Leah K. GUTKNECHT
41 Athletic Director Mr. Troy A. DANNEN
21 Director of Business Operations Ms. Kelly A. FLEGE

Briar Cliff University (E)

3303 Rebecca Street, Sioux City IA 51104-2100
County: Woodbury FICE Identification: 001846
Unit ID: 152992
Telephone: (712) 279-5321 Carnegie Class: Bac/Diverse
FAX Number: (712) 279-5410 Calendar System: 4/1/4
URL: www.briarcliff.edu
Established: 1929 Annual Undergrad Tuition & Fees: $23,600
Enrollment: 1,156 Coed
Affiliation or Control: Roman Catholic IRS Status: 501(c)3
Highest Offering: Master's
Program: Liberal Arts And General; Teacher Preparatory; Professional
Accreditation: NH, NUR, SW

01 President Mrs. Beverly A. WHARTON
05 Vice President Academic Affairs Dr. William MANGAN
10 Vice President Finance & Treasurer Mrs. Beth GRIGSBY
30 Vice Pres Institutional Advancement Mr. Jeff LAFAVOR
84 Vice Pres Enrollment Management Mrs. Sharisue WILCOXON
32 Vice President Student Development Mr. Steve JANOWIAK
06 Registrar Mrs. Deidre ENGEL
08 Librarian/Dir Information Services Ms. Debora ROBERTSON
14 Director Computer Center Ms. Leah WARD
29 Director Alumni Relations Ms. Jessica MURANO
36 Director Career Development Ms. Nancy MCGUIRE
37 Director Financial Aid Mr. Robert PIECHOTA
40 Director Bookstore Ms. Nancy WATSON
41 Athletic Director Mr. Steve GAST
42 Director Campus Ministry Sr. Janet MAY
18 Director Physical Plant Mr. Eric HOLMQUIST
26 Director Marketing & Communications Ms. Paula DAMON
44 Director Gift Planning Mr. Mike JORGENSEN
07 Director of Admissions Mr. Brian EBEN
15 Director Human Resources Mrs. JoAnn PETERSON
39 Director Residence Life Mr. Dave ARENS
38 Director Student Counseling Ms. Laurel MEINE
09 Director of Institutional Research Ms. Sally JACKSON

Brown Mackie College-Quad Cities (F)

2119 East Kimberly Road, Bettendorf IA 52722
County: Scott Identification: 666792
Unit ID: 373085
Telephone: (563) 344-1500 Carnegie Class: Not Classified
FAX Number: (563) 344-1501 Calendar System: Other
URL: www.brownmackie.edu
Established: N/A Annual Undergrad Tuition & Fees: $11,124
Enrollment: 359 Coed
Affiliation or Control: Proprietary IRS Status: Proprietary
Highest Offering: Baccalaureate
Program: Occupational; 2-Year Principally Bachelor's Creditable; Business Emphasis
Accreditation: ACICS

01 President Kao ODUKALE
07 Senior Director of Admissions Ann SANDOVAL
05 Dean of Academic Affairs Greg SMITH

Buena Vista University (G)

610 W Fourth Street, Storm Lake IA 50588-1798
County: Buena Vista FICE Identification: 001847
Unit ID: 153001
Telephone: (712) 749-2351 Carnegie Class: Bac/Diverse
FAX Number: (712) 749-2037 Calendar System: 4/1/4
URL: www.bvu.edu
Established: 1891 Annual Undergrad Tuition & Fees: $27,226
Enrollment: 1,039 Coed
Affiliation or Control: Presbyterian Church (U.S.A.) IRS Status: 501(c)3
Highest Offering: Master's
Program: Liberal Arts And General; Teacher Preparatory
Accreditation: NH, SW, @TEAC

01 President Dr. Frederick V. MOORE
04 Assistant to the President Ms. Donna L. SCHONEBOOM
05 VP Academic Affairs/Dean of Faculty Dr. David R. EVANS
10 Vice President Business Services Ms. Elizabeth MERTEN
84 Vice Pres for Enrollment Management Ms. Marcia NANCE
32 Int VP Student Svcs/Dean Students Dr. Mary GILL
30 Vice Pres for Inst Advancement Mr. Kenneth L. CONVERSE
81 Dean School of Science Mr. Ben DONATH
50 Int Dean HWS School of Business Dr. Elizabeth THROOP
53 Dean School of Education Vacant
60 Dean School Communication & Arts Dr. Michael D. WHITLATCH
83 Dean School Social Sci/Phil/Relig Dr. Dixee BARTHOLOMEW-FEIS
20 Associate Dean of Faculty Dr. Peter K. STEINFELD
20 AVP Acad Affs/Dn Graduate/Prof Stds Dr. Susan KALSOW
06 Registrar Ms. Nila HOUSKA
07 Director of Admissions Ms. Bridget KURKOWSKI

15 Human Resources Manager .... Ms. Beth MCNALLY
08 University Librarian .... Mr. James R. KENNEDY
27 Dir University Marketing & Comm .... Ms. Cathy GROTHE
29 Director of Alumni Rels/Annual Fund .... Ms. Amy J. JONES
13 Managing Director Univ Info Svcs .... Mr. Matt MORTON
18 Director of Physical Plant .... Mr. Keith E. SCHMIDT
36 Director of Career Services .... Ms. Carol J. LYTLE
37 Director of Financial Assistance .... Ms. Leanne VALENTINE
28 Director of Intercultural Programs .... Mr. Yorgun MARCEL
41 Athletic Director .... Vacant
42 Chaplain .... Rev. Ken MEISSNER
19 Director of Campus Security .... Mr. Mark KIRKHOLM
38 Director of Counseling Services .... Ms. Mandy BOOTHBY
09 Institutional Researcher .... Mr. James E. HEWETT
96 Purchasing Administrator .... Ms. Tanya LANDGRAF

Central College (A)

812 University, Pella IA 50219-1999
County: Marion FICE Identification: 001850
Unit ID: 153108
Telephone: (641) 628-9000 Carnegie Class: Bac/A&S
FAX Number: (641) 628-5316 Calendar System: Semester
URL: www.central.edu
Established: 1853 Annual Undergrad Tuition & Fees: $27,844
Enrollment: 1,648 Coed
Affiliation or Control: Reformed Church In America IRS Status: 501(c)3
Highest Offering: Baccalaureate
Program: Liberal Arts And General; Teacher Preparatory; Professional
Accreditation: NH, MUS

01 President .... Dr. Mark L. PUTNAM
05 VP Academic Affairs/Dean of Faculty .... Dr. Mary M. STREY
30 Vice President Advancement .... Mr. David B. SUTPHEN
32 Dean of Student Life .... Mr. Eric JONES
07 Dean of Admission .... Mrs. Carol WILLIAMSON
10 Interim Chief Financial Officer .... Dr. James F. GALBALLY, JR.
38 Director of Counseling .... Ms. Michelle KELLAR
39 Director of Residence Life .... Ms. Melissa SHARKEY
08 Director of Library .... Mrs. Natalie N. HUTCHINSON
20 Associate Dean for Global Education .... Ms. Lyn R. ISAACSON
36 Director of Career Center .... Mrs. Patricia JOACHIM KITZMAN
29 Director of Alumni Relations .... Ms. Ann VAN HEMERT
37 Director Financial Aid .... Mr. Wayne DILLE
104 Manager On-Campus Rels/Study Abroad .... Mr. Brian ZYLSTRA
14 Chief Information Officer .... Mr. Lee VANDE VOORT
90 Director of Academic Computing .... Ms. Debra BRUXVOORT
42 Chaplain .... Rev. Joe BRUMMEL
44 Director Planned Giving .... Mr. Don MORRISON
15 Director of Human Resources .... Mrs. Mona ROOZEBOOM
41 Director of Athletics .... Mr. Al DORENKAMP
18 Dir Facilities Planning/Management .... Mr. Mike LUBBERDEN
28 Director of Intercultural Life .... Mr. Brandyn WOODARD

Clarke University (B)

1550 Clarke Drive, Dubuque IA 52001-3198
County: Dubuque FICE Identification: 001852
Unit ID: 153126
Telephone: (563) 588-6300 Carnegie Class: Bac/Diverse
FAX Number: (563) 588-6789 Calendar System: Semester
URL: www.clarke.edu
Established: 1843 Annual Undergrad Tuition & Fees: $25,760
Enrollment: 1,107 Coed
Affiliation or Control: Roman Catholic IRS Status: 501(c)3
Highest Offering: Doctorate
Program: Liberal Arts And General; Teacher Preparatory; Professional
Accreditation: NH, MUS, NURSE, PTA, @SW

01 President .... Dr. Joanne M. BURROWS, SC
04 Assistant to the President .... Ms. Linda J. LAUFENBERG
05 Provost/Vice Pres Academic Affs .... Dr. Joan LINGEN, BVM
30 Vice Pres Institutional Advancement .... Mr. Bill BIEBUYCK
32 Vice President Student Life .... Ms. Kate ZANGER
10 Vice President Business & Finance .... Ms. Deanna MCCORMICK
84 Vice President Enrollment Mgmt .... Dr. Beth TRIPLETT
51 Director Adult & Continuing Educ .... Mr. Scott SCHNEIDER
06 Registrar .... Ms. Kristi BAGSTAD
08 Director of Library .... Ms. Susanne LEIBOLD
20 Academic Dean of Undergraduate Stds .... Dr. Graciela CANEIRO-LIVINGSTON
20 Academic Dean of Graduate Studies .... Dr. Kate HENDEL, BVM
37 Director of Financial Aid .... Ms. Amy NORTON
26 Exec Director of Marketing & Comm .... Mr. Mike CYZE
29 Director of Alumni Relations .... Ms. Katie BAHL
14 Director of Computer Center .... Ms. Karen GERHARD
18 Director of Facilities .... Mr. Brian SCHULTES
38 Director of Counseling Center .... Ms. Lorie MURPHY-FREEBOLIN
15 Director of Human Resources .... Ms. Megan LUCAS
41 Director of Athletics .... Mr. Curt LONG
42 Director of Campus Ministry .... Ms. Amy GOLM, BVM
40 Bookstore Manager .... Mr. James SPAULDING
23 Director of Health Services .... Ms. Julie BURGMEIER
90 Director of Academic Support Center .... Mr. Brian GOMOLL
85 International Students Advisor .... Ms. Evelyn NADEAU
07 Director of Admissions .... Ms. Emily KRUSE
44 Director of Annual Funds .... Ms. Wendy SCARDINO
09 Director of Institutional Research .... Mr. Glen LANTZ

Coe College (C)

1220 1st Avenue, NE, Cedar Rapids IA 52402-5092
County: Linn FICE Identification: 001854
Unit ID: 153144
Telephone: (319) 399-8000 Carnegie Class: Bac/A&S
FAX Number: (319) 399-8830 Calendar System: Semester
URL: www.coe.edu
Established: 1851 Annual Undergrad Tuition & Fees: $32,380
Enrollment: 1,357 Coed
Affiliation or Control: Independent Non-Profit IRS Status: 501(c)3
Highest Offering: Master's
Program: Liberal Arts And General; Teacher Preparatory; Professional
Accreditation: NH, MUS, NURSE

01 President .... Dr. James R. PHIFER
05 Vice Pres Acad Affs/Dean of Faculty .... Dr. Marie BAEHR
11 Vice President Administration .... Mr. Michael L. WHITE
32 Vice President Student Affairs .... Mr. Lou W. STARK
30 Vice President Advancement .... Mr. Richard E. MEISTERLING
07 Director of Admission .... Ms. Julia STAKER
21 Controller .... Mr. Richard E. RHEINSCHMIDT
06 Registrar .... Dr. Evelyn J. MOORE
08 Director Library Services .... Ms. Jill JACK
29 Director Alumni Programs .... Ms. Jean A. JOHNSON
09 Director of Institutional Research .... Dr. Wendy L. DUNN
26 Dir of Marketing/Public Relations .... Mr. Rod PRITCHARD
37 Director of Financial Aid .... Ms. Barbara HOFFMAN
20 Associate Dean .... Dr. Terry MCNABB
35 Dean of Students .... Mr. Erik ALBINSON
85 International Student Advisor .... Ms. Deanna L. JOBE
42 Chaplain .... Rev. Kristin E. HUTSON
23 Director of Health Services .... Ms. Melinda S. BROKAW
41 Director of Athletics .... Mr. John M. CHANDLER
18 Director of Physical Plant .... Ms. Lisa CIHA
36 Career Services Coordinator .... Ms. Michelle MCILLECE

Cornell College (D)

600 First Street SW, Mount Vernon IA 52314-1098
County: Linn FICE Identification: 001856
Unit ID: 153162
Telephone: (319) 895-4000 Carnegie Class: Bac/A&S
FAX Number: (319) 895-4492 Calendar System: Other
URL: www.cornellcollege.edu
Established: 1853 Annual Undergrad Tuition & Fees: $40,650
Enrollment: 1,183 Coed
Affiliation or Control: United Methodist IRS Status: 501(c)3
Highest Offering: Baccalaureate
Program: Liberal Arts And General; Teacher Preparatory
Accreditation: NH

01 President .... Mr. Jonathan BRAND
05 VP Acad Affairs/Dean of College .... Dr. R. Joseph DIEKER
10 Vice President Business Affairs .... Ms. Karen MERCER
84 VP Enroll/Dean of Finan Assistance .... Mr. Jonathan M. STROUD
32 Vice President Student Affairs .... Mr. John W. HARP
44 VP Alumni & College Advancement .... Mr. Peter WILCH
04 Special Asst to the President .... Dr. James W. BROWN
35 Dean of Students .... Dr. Heidi LEVINE
20 Associate Dean of the College .... Dr. Gayle LUCK
09 Director of Institutional Research .... Dr. Becki S. ELKINS
37 Director of Student Financial Asst .... Ms. Cindi P. REINTS
06 Registrar .... Ms. Jonna HIGGINS-FREESE
08 College Librarian .... Vacant
29 Director of Alumni Programs .... Ms. Lisa C. WHITE
30 Director College Advancement Svc .... Ms. Jennifer BOETTGER
27 Director of College Communications .... Ms. Dee A. REXROAT
96 Director of Purchasing/Admin Svcs .... Ms. Lisa M. LARSON
42 Chaplain .... Ms. Catherine M. QUEHL-ENGEL
22 Affirmative Action Officer .... Ms. Vickie L. FARMER
41 Athletics Director .... Mr. John T. COCHRANE
18 Director of Facilities .... Mr. Joel C. MILLER
36 Director Career Engagement Center .... Mr. RJ HOLMES
38 Director Student Counseling .... Dr. Brenda C. LOVSTUEN
15 Director of Human Resources .... Ms. Vickie L. FARMER
07 Director of Admissions .... Mr. Todd D. WHITE
28 Director of Intercultural Life .... Mr. Kenneth W. MORRIS
13 Director of Information Technology .... Mr. Mike J. CERVENY
40 Manager Bookstore .... Mr. Tyler WEDIG

Des Moines Area Community College (E)

2006 S Ankeny Boulevard, Ankeny IA 50023-3993
County: Polk FICE Identification: 007120
Unit ID: 153214
Telephone: (515) 964-6200 Carnegie Class: Assoc/Pub-R-L
FAX Number: N/A Calendar System: Semester
URL: www.dmacc.edu
Established: 1966 Annual Undergrad Tuition & Fees (In-District): $3,930
Enrollment: 26,648 Coed
Affiliation or Control: State/Local IRS Status: 501(c)3
Highest Offering: Associate Degree
Program: Occupational; 2-Year Principally Bachelor's Creditable
Accreditation: NH, FUSER, ACFEI, ADNUR, DA, DH, MAC, MLTAD, PNUR, SURGT

01 President/CEO .... Dr. Rob DENSON
05 Exec Vice Pres Academic Affairs .... Dr. Kim LINDUSKA
10 Vice President Business Svcs .... Mr. Doug WILLIAMS
103 Vice Pres Cmty/Workforce Partnershp .... Dr. Mary CHAPMAN
13 Vice Pres Information Solutions .... Mr. Greg MARTIN
12 Provost Urban Campus .... Dr. Laura DOUGLAS
12 Provost Boone Campus .... Mr. Tom LEE
12 Provost Carroll Campus .... Mr. Steve SCHULZ
12 Provost Newton Campus .... Ms. Mary ENTZ
12 Provost West Campus .... Dr. Tony PAUSTIAN
32 Exec Dean Student Services .... Dr. Laurie WOLF
15 Executive Director Human Resources .... Dr. Sandy TRYON
102 Executive Director Foundation .... Ms. Tara CONNOLLY
09 Exec Director Inst Effectiveness .... Dr. Joe DEHART
51 Exec Dir Continuing Education .... Ms. Jane HERRMANN
50 Exec Dir Business Resources .... Ms. Kim DIDIER
84 Exec Dir Enrollment Management .... Mr. Michael LENTSCH
37 Director Financial Aid .... Ms. DeLores HAWKINS
26 Director of Marketing .... Mr. Todd JONES
25 Director Grants/Contracts .... Ms. Deb KOUA
06 Registrar .... Ms. Rachel ERKKILA
18 Chief Facilities/Physical Plant .... Mr. Mark BAETHKE
38 Director Student Development .... Ms. Wendy ROBINSON
96 Director of Purchasing .... Mr. Tim HAGER
27 Media Liaison .... Mr. Dan IVIS
70 Dean Sciences & Humanities .... Mr. Jim STICK
72 Dean Industrial & Technology .... Mr. Scott OCKEN
76 Dean Health Service & Science .... Ms. Sally SCHROEDER
50 Dean Business/Mgmt/Information Tech .... Mr. Drew GOCKEN
55 Dean Evening & Weekend College .... Mr. Jeff KELLY

Des Moines University (F)

3200 Grand Avenue, Des Moines IA 50312-4198
County: Polk FICE Identification: 001855
Unit ID: 154156
Telephone: (515) 271-1400 Carnegie Class: Spec/Med
FAX Number: (515) 271-1532 Calendar System: Other
URL: www.dmu.edu
Established: 1898 Annual Graduate Tuition & Fees: N/A
Enrollment: 1,857 Coed
Affiliation or Control: Independent Non-Profit IRS Status: 501(c)3
Highest Offering: First Professional Degree; No Undergraduates
Program: Professional
Accreditation: NH, ARCPA, OSTEO, PH, POD, PTA

01 President/CEO .... Dr. Angela L. WALKER FRANKLIN
11 Vice President for Admin Services .... Mr. Stephen S. DENGLE
05 Provost .... Dr. Karen P. MCLEAN
32 Vice President Student Services .... Ms. Mary Ann ZUG
30 Vice Pres for Advancement .... Ms. Susan HUPPERT
46 Vice President for Research .... Vacant
06 Registrar .... Ms. Kathy L. SCAGLIONE
08 Director of Library .... Mr. Larry MARQUARDT
15 Director of Human Resources .... Ms. Becky LADE
27 Chief Information Officer .... Mr. Wayne BOWKER
37 Director of Financial Aid .... Ms. Mary PAYNE
18 Director of Facilities Management .... Mr. David MCNERNEY
19 Director University Services .... Mr. John BRUECKEN
43 University Counsel .... Mr. John PARMETER
21 Chief Financial Officer .... Mr. Mark J. PEIFFER
69 Director Public Health Program .... Dr. Mary Mincer HANSEN
76 Director Healthcare Administration .... Dr. Carla STEBBINS
26 Director Marketing & Communication .... Ms. Kendall DILLON
38 Director Educational Support Svcs .... Ms. Lynn MARTIN
84 Director Enrollment Management .... Ms. Margie GEHRINGER
76 Dean College Health Sciences .... Dr. Jodi CAHALAN
63 Dean Col Podiatric Medicine/Surg .... Dr. Robert YOHO
63 Dean Col Osteopathic Medicine/Surg .... Dr. Kendall REED
25 Director Sponsored Programs .... Ms. Kay COURTADE

† Tuition varies by program.

Divine Word College (G)

102 Jacoby Drive, SW, PO Box 380,
Epworth IA 52045-0380
County: Dubuque FICE Identification: 001858
Unit ID: 153241
Telephone: (563) 876-3353 Carnegie Class: Spec/Faith
FAX Number: (563) 876-3407 Calendar System: Semester
URL: www.dwci.edu
Established: 1918 Annual Undergrad Tuition & Fees: $11,600
Enrollment: 107 Male
Affiliation or Control: Roman Catholic IRS Status: 501(c)3
Highest Offering: Baccalaureate
Program: Religious Emphasis
Accreditation: NH

01 President .... Fr. Timothy A. LENCHAK
05 Academic Dean/Vice President .... Dr. Mathew KANJIRATHINKAL
10 Vice President for Finances .... Mrs. Linda WEIDEMANN
07 Director Admissions/VP Recruitment .... Mr. Len UHAL
30 Development Director .... Mr. Terrance SYKORA
32 Dean of Students .... Rev. Khien LUU
08 Librarian .... Mr. Daniel BOICE
37 Financial Aid Director .... Mrs. Linda WEIDEMANN
06 Registrar .... Mrs. Deborah HIRSCH
38 Counselor .... Mrs. Nan PECK
26 Public Relations Director .... Ms. Sandy WILGENBUSCH

Dordt College (H)

498 4th Avenue, NE, Sioux Center IA 51250-1697
County: Sioux FICE Identification: 001859
Unit ID: 153250
Telephone: (712) 722-6000 Carnegie Class: Bac/Diverse
FAX Number: (712) 722-1185 Calendar System: Semester
URL: www.dordt.edu
Established: 1955 Annual Undergrad Tuition & Fees: $24,300
Enrollment: 1,368 Coed
Affiliation or Control: Christian Reformed Church IRS Status: 501(c)3

Highest Offering: Master's
Program: 2-Year Principally Bachelor's Creditable; Liberal Arts And General; Teacher Preparatory
Accreditation: NH, ENG, NURSE, SW

01 President ... Dr. Carl E. ZYLSTRA
04 Assistant to the President ... Dr. Curtis J. TAYLOR
05 Provost ... Dr. Erik HOEKSTRA
10 Vice President Business ... Mr. Arlan NEDERHOFF
30 Vice President College Advancement ... Mr. John BAAS
20 Assoc Provost for Co-Curricular Pgm ... Ms. Bethany SCHUTTINGA
07 Executive Director Admissions ... Mr. Quentin VAN ESSEN
37 Director Financial Aid ... Mr. Michael EPEMA
06 Registrar ... Mr. James BOS
88 Dean for Research and Scholarship ... Dr. John H. KOK
20 Dean for Curriculum and Instruction ... Dr. Sherri LANTINGA
58 Director Graduate Education ... Dr. Timothy VAN SOELEN
36 Director of Career Services ... Mr. Chris DEJONG
26 Marketing and Public Relations ... Ms. Sonya JONGSMA KNAUSS
18 Director Physical Plant ... Mr. Stan OORDT
39 Director Resident Life ... Mr. Robert TAYLOR
42 Campus Pastor ... Rev. Aaron BAART
41 Director of Athletics ... Mr. Glenn BOUMA
40 Director Bookstore/Purchasing ... Ms. Lora DEVRIES
44 Director of Planned Giving ... Mr. Dave VANDER WERF
29 Director Alumni/Church Relations ... Mr. Wes FOPMA
15 Director Human Resources ... Mrs. Sue DROOG
96 Director of Purchasing ... Mr. Fred HAAN
91 Director of Computer Services ... Mr. Brian VAN DONSELAAR
44 Development Programs Coordinator ... Ms. Barbara J. MELLEMA
08 Director of Library Services ... Ms. Sheryl S. TAYLOR
23 Director of Health Sciences ... Ms. Pamela L. HULSTEIN
88 Director Academic Skills Center ... Ms. Pamala S. DE JONG

Drake University (A)

2507 University Avenue, Des Moines IA 50311-4505
County: Polk — FICE Identification: 001860
Unit ID: 153269
Telephone: (515) 271-2011 — Carnegie Class: Master's L
FAX Number: (515) 271-3016 — Calendar System: Semester
URL: www.drake.edu
Established: 1881 — Annual Undergrad Tuition & Fees: $28,250
Enrollment: 5,616 — Coed
Affiliation or Control: Independent Non-Profit — IRS Status: 501(c)3
Highest Offering: Doctorate
Program: Liberal Arts And General; Teacher Preparatory; Professional
Accreditation: NH, ART, BUS, BUSA, CORE, JOUR, LAW, MUS, PHAR

01 President ... Dr. David E. MAXWELL
05 Interim Provost ... Dr. Susan WRIGHT
10 Vice President Business & Finance ... Ms. Victoria F. PAYSEUR
30 Vice Pres Alumni and Development ... Mr. John SMITH
07 Vice Pres Admissions/Financial Aid ... Mr. Tom DELAHUNT
20 Associate Provost of Curriculum ... Mr. Art SANDERS
09 Associate Provost ... Dr. Raylene ROSPOND
32 Vice Prov Student Affs/Acad Success ... Dr. Wanda EVERAGE
35 Dean of Students ... Dr. Sentwali BAKARI
15 Human Resources Director ... Ms. Venessa MACRO
27 Chief Tech Information Officer ... Dr. Ann KOVALCHICK
04 Executive Asst to Pres/Secy of Univ ... Ms. Linda S. RYAN
18 Director Facility Services ... Ms. Jolene SCHMIDT
06 Director of Student Records ... Ms. Margie DAVIDSON
08 Dean Cowles Library ... Mr. Rodney N. HENSHAW
85 Director Intl Programs/Services ... Ms. Gretchen S. OLSON
91 Director Campus Information Svcs ... Ms. Angela EMBREE
19 Chief Campus Security Services ... Mr. Hans M. HANSON
26 Exec Dir Marketing & Communications ... Ms. Debra LUKEHART
29 Alumni/Parent Programs ... Mr. Blake CAMPBELL
49 Interim Dean Arts & Sciences ... Dr. Joe LENZ
53 Dean School Education ... Dr. Janet M. MCMAHILL
61 Dean Law School ... Mr. Allan VESTAL
50 Dean Business/Public Administration ... Mr. Charles EDWARDS, JR.
67 Dean Pharmacy/Health Science ... Dr. Raylene ROSPOND
60 Dean Journ/Mass Communications ... Mr. Charles EDWARDS, JR.
44 Director of Planned Giving ... Vacant
88 Assistant Dean of Students ... Ms. Melissa STURM-SMITH
41 Director Intercollegiate Athletics ... Ms. Sandy Hatfield CLUBB
37 Director Financial Aid ... Ms. Susan K. LADD
38 Director University Counseling Ctr ... Dr. Dee WRIGHT
92 Director Honors Program ... Ms. Angela BATTLE
94 Director Women's Studies ... Dr. Nancy REINCKE
31 Dir Community Outreach/Development ... Mr. Dolph PULLIAM
39 Director Office of Residence Life ... Vacant

*Eastern Iowa Community College District (B)

306 W River Drive, Davenport IA 52801-1221
County: Scott — FICE Identification: 004075
Unit ID: 153311
Telephone: (563) 336-3300 — Carnegie Class: N/A
FAX Number: (563) 336-3350
URL: www.eicc.edu

01 Chancellor ... Dr. Donald S. DOUCETTE
30 Exec Dir Resource Development ... Dr. Ellen KABAT LENSCH
51 Exec Dir Continuing Education ... Dr. Nancy KOTHENBEUTEL
31 Exec Dir Community & Econ Devel ... Mr. Mark KAPFER
26 Associate Director for Marketing ... Ms. Karen FARLEY
11 Exec Dir Administrative Services ... Ms. Lana J. DETTBARN
09 Dir Institutional Effectiveness ... Ms. Laurie R. HANSON
27 Associate Director Communications ... Mr. Alan CAMPBELL

*Clinton Community College (C)

1000 Lincoln Boulevard, Clinton IA 52732-6299
County: Clinton — FICE Identification: 001853
Unit ID: 153135
Telephone: (563) 244-7001 — Carnegie Class: Not Classified
FAX Number: (563) 244-7107 — Calendar System: Semester
URL: www.eicc.edu
Established: 1966 — Annual Undergrad Tuition & Fees (In-District): $128
Enrollment: 1,815 — Coed
Affiliation or Control: State/Local — IRS Status: 501(c)3
Highest Offering: Associate Degree
Program: Occupational; 2-Year Principally Bachelor's Creditable
Accreditation: &NH

02 President ... Dr. Karen VICKERS
05 Dean of the College ... Mr. Ron SERPLISS
32 Dean of Student Development ... Ms. Lisa MILLER
102 Asst to Pres/Exec Dir Sharar Found ... Ms. Ann EISENMAN
04 Assistant to President/Admin ... Ms. Deborah RICHTER

*Muscatine Community College (D)

152 Colorado Street, Muscatine IA 52761-5396
County: Muscatine — FICE Identification: 001882
Unit ID: 154040
Telephone: (563) 288-6001 — Carnegie Class: Not Classified
FAX Number: (563) 288-6074 — Calendar System: Semester
URL: www.eicc.edu
Established: 1929 — Annual Undergrad Tuition & Fees (In-District): $128
Enrollment: 1,969 — Coed
Affiliation or Control: State/Local — IRS Status: 501(c)3
Highest Offering: Associate Degree
Program: Occupational; 2-Year Principally Bachelor's Creditable
Accreditation: &NH

02 President ... Dr. Jeff ARMSTRONG
04 Assistant to the President ... Ms. Lisa WIEGEL
05 Dean of the College ... Dr. Gail SPIES
32 Dean of Student Development ... Ms. Shelly CRAM-RAHLF
31 Director Business/Industry Center ... Mr. Marvin SMITH
06 Registrar ... Ms. Robin MITCHELL
08 Library Specialist ... Ms. Nancy LUIKART

*Scott Community College (E)

500 Belmont Road, Bettendorf IA 52722-6804
County: Scott — FICE Identification: 001885
Unit ID: 154314
Telephone: (563) 441-4001 — Carnegie Class: Not Classified
FAX Number: (563) 441-4154 — Calendar System: Semester
URL: www.eicc.edu
Established: 1966 — Annual Undergrad Tuition & Fees (In-District): $128
Enrollment: 5,581 — Coed
Affiliation or Control: State/Local — IRS Status: 501(c)3
Highest Offering: Associate Degree
Program: Occupational; 2-Year Principally Bachelor's Creditable
Accreditation: &NH, DA, EEG, RAD

02 President ... Vacant
05 Dean of the College ... Dr. Teresa A. PAPER
32 Dean of Student Development/Affs ... Ms. Lisa BROWN
36 Dean Career Assistance Center ... Ms. Peg GARRISON
72 Dean Applied Technologies ... Ms. Janet COOGAN
49 Dean Arts & Sciences ... Dr. R. Andrew BURT
08 Librarian ... Ms. Michelle BAILEY
11 Asst to President Administration ... Mr. Matt SCHMIT
06 Registrar ... Mr. Arnold THODE
18 Chief Facilities/Physical Plant ... Mr. Ken MIROCHA
37 Director Student Financial Aid ... Ms. Jeannine INGELSON
36 Job Placement Specialist ... Mr. Wayne COLE

Emmaus Bible College (F)

2570 Asbury Road, Dubuque IA 52001-3096
County: Dubuque — FICE Identification: 023289
Unit ID: 153302
Telephone: (563) 588-8000 — Carnegie Class: Spec/Faith
FAX Number: (563) 588-1216 — Calendar System: Semester
URL: www.emmaus.edu
Established: 1941 — Annual Undergrad Tuition & Fees: $13,470
Enrollment: 250 — Coed
Affiliation or Control: Independent Non-Profit — IRS Status: 501(c)3
Highest Offering: Baccalaureate
Program: Liberal Arts And General; Teacher Preparatory; Professional
Accreditation: NH, BI

01 President ... Mr. Kenneth A. DAUGHTERS
11 VP for Administration & Finance ... Mr. Mark A. PRESSON
05 Vice President for Academic Affairs ... Mrs. Lisa L. BEATTY
32 VP for Student Development ... Mr. Jon W. GLOCK
30 Vice President for Advancement ... Dr. Steven R. WITTER
88 Dean for Biblical Studies ... Dr. David J. MACLEOD
06 Registrar ... Mrs. Kathryn L. VAN DINE
08 Librarian ... Mr. John H. RUSH
37 Financial Aid Officer ... Mr. Steve C. SEEMAN
10 Controller ... Mr. Steve M. JENSEN
07 Enrollment Services Manager ... Mr. Israel CHAVEZ

Faith Baptist Bible College and Seminary (G)

1900 NW 4th Street, Ankeny IA 50023-2152
County: Polk — FICE Identification: 007121
Unit ID: 153320
Telephone: (515) 964-0601 — Carnegie Class: Spec/Faith
FAX Number: (515) 964-1638 — Calendar System: Semester
URL: www.faith.edu
Established: 1921 — Annual Undergrad Tuition & Fees: $14,478
Enrollment: 364 — Coed
Affiliation or Control: Independent Non-Profit — IRS Status: 501(c)3
Highest Offering: First Professional Degree
Program: Liberal Arts And General; Teacher Preparatory; Religious Emphasis
Accreditation: NH, BI

01 President ... Dr. James D. MAXWELL, III
05 VP Academic Services/Librarian ... Dr. John HARTOG, III
73 Dean of Seminary ... Dr. Ernest SCHMIDT
10 VP for Business/CFO ... Mr. Daniel H. BJOKNE
84 VP for Enrollment & Student Life ... Mr. Patrick B. ODLE
34 Dean of Women ... Mrs. Sharon S. GUTWEIN
32 Dean of Students ... Mr. Shon R. LUNDBERG
33 Dean of Men ... Mr. Lance A. AUGSBURGER
27 Director of Communications ... Mr. Don K. ANDERSON
06 Registrar ... Mr. David L. STOUT
37 Director Student Financial Aid ... Mr. Breck H. APPELL

Graceland University (H)

1 University Place, Lamoni IA 50140-1699
County: Decatur — FICE Identification: 001866
Unit ID: 153366
Telephone: (641) 784-5000 — Carnegie Class: Master's L
FAX Number: (641) 784-5480 — Calendar System: 4/1/4
URL: www.graceland.edu
Established: 1895 — Annual Undergrad Tuition & Fees: $21,490
Enrollment: 2,267 — Coed
Affiliation or Control: Other — IRS Status: 501(c)3
Highest Offering: Doctorate
Program: Liberal Arts And General; Teacher Preparatory
Accreditation: NH, TED

01 President ... Dr. John SELLARS
05 Vice Pres Acad Affs/Dean of Faculty ... Dr. Parris R. WATTS
09 VP Institutional Effectiveness ... Dr. Kathleen M. CLAUSON
10 Vice Pres Business & Admin Svcs ... Ms. Janice TIFFANY
32 Dean of Students ... Mrs. Marian KILLPACK
84 Vice Pres Enrollment/Dean Admission ... Ms. Louise CUMMINGS-SIMMONS
30 Vice Pres Institutional Advancement ... Mr. Kelly EVERETT
51 Director for Graduate/Continuing Ed ... Mr. Paul BINNICKER
39 Director of Residence Life ... Ms. Deb SKINNER
13 Exec Dir for Information Services ... Mr. Kam MAHI
06 Registrar ... Mrs. M. Joyce LIGHTHILL
08 Librarian ... Mrs. Diane E. SHELTON
29 Director of Alumni Relations ... Mr. Paul DAVIS
37 Director of Financial Aid ... Mr. Jim WESENBERG
36 Director Career/Acad/CAP Couns Ctr ... Mrs. Michele MAGUIRE-BECK
23 Director Health Service ... Mrs. Benna EASTER
18 Director Facility Services ... Mr. Kurt REMMENGA
15 Director Human Resources ... Mrs. Ondrea DORY
26 Chief Public Relations Officer ... Mr. Randy MELINE
04 Executive Asst to President ... Ms. Jodi L. SEYMOUR
41 Athletic Director ... Mr. Jeff FALKNER
44 Director of Annual Fund/Stewardship ... Mrs. Peggy STURDEVANT
85 Director International Programs ... Ms. Diana JONES
86 Director Government Relations ... Dr. Tom MORAIN
50 Dean School of Business ... Dr. Steven ANDERS
53 Dean School of Education ... Dr. Tammy EVERETT
49 Dean Col Liberal Arts/Sciences ... Dr. Gary HEISSERER
66 Dean School of Nursing ... Dr. Claudia HORTON
07 Director of Admissions ... Mr. Kevin BROWN

Grand View University (I)

1200 Grandview Avenue, Des Moines IA 50316-1599
County: Polk — FICE Identification: 001867
Unit ID: 153375
Telephone: (515) 263-2800 — Carnegie Class: Bac/Diverse
FAX Number: (515) 263-6095 — Calendar System: Other
URL: www.grandview.edu
Established: 1896 — Annual Undergrad Tuition & Fees: $21,018
Enrollment: 2,108 — Coed
Affiliation or Control: Evangelical Lutheran Church In America
IRS Status: 501(c)3
Highest Offering: Master's
Program: Liberal Arts And General; Professional
Accreditation: NH, NURSE

01 President ... Mr. Kent L. HENNING
04 Executive Asst to the President ... Mr. Lucas J. CASEY
05 Provost/Vice Pres Academic Affairs ... Dr. Mary Elizabeth STIVERS
10 Vice Pres Administration & Finance ... Mr. Adam J. VOIGTS
30 Vice President Advancement ... Mr. William H. BURMA
84 Vice Pres Enrollment Management ... Ms. Debbie M. BARGER
26 Vice Pres Marketing/Communications ... Ms. Carol M. BAMFORD
32 Vice President Student Affairs ... Dr. Jay B. PRESCOTT
37 Director Financial Aid ... Ms. Michele A. DUNNE

20 Special Assistant to the Provost .... Ms. Pamela M. MILLOY
51 Acting Dean Col for Prof/Adult Lrng .... Dr. Patricia A. RINKE
35 Associate VP for Student Affairs .... Mr. Jason K. BAUER
06 Registrar .... Ms. Debbie K. GANNON
42 College Pastor .... Vacant
09 Director Inst Planning/Research .... Ms. Debbie M. BARGER
36 Director Career Center .... Ms. Susan M. STEARNS
91 Vice President Information Svcs/CIO .... Mr. Tim T. WHEELDON
08 Director of the Library .... Ms. Pamela D. REES
40 Director Bookstore & Campus Svcs .... Mr. Michael D. SHUPP
07 Director of Admissions .... Ms. Diane S. JOHNSON
18 Director Buildings & Grounds .... Ms. Kim I. BUTLER
38 Director Leadership & Counseling .... Mr. Kent A. SCHORNACK
28 Dir Multicultural & Cmty Outreach .... Mr. Alex H. PIEDRAS
41 Athletic Director .... Mr. Troy A. PLUMMER
15 Human Resources Manager .... Ms. Erica L. KLUVER

Grinnell College (A)

1121 Park Street, Grinnell IA 50112-1690
County: Poweshiek FICE Identification: 001868
Unit ID: 153384
Telephone: (641) 269-4000 Carnegie Class: Bac/A&S
FAX Number: (641) 269-3408 Calendar System: Semester
URL: www.grinnell.edu
Established: 1846 Annual Undergrad Tuition & Fees: $39,810
Enrollment: 1,624 Coed
Affiliation or Control: Independent Non-Profit IRS Status: 501(c)3
Highest Offering: Baccalaureate
Program: Liberal Arts And General; Teacher Preparatory
Accreditation: NH

01 President .... Raynard S. KINGTON
100 Special Assistant to the President .... Angela VOOS
05 Vice Pres Acad Affs/Dean of College .... Paula V. SMITH
26 Vice President College/Alumni Rels .... Beth HALLORAN
10 Chief Inves/Treasurer of College .... David S. CLAY
32 Vice Pres Student Services .... W. Houston DOUGHARTY
88 Vice President of College Services .... John KALKBRENNER
28 Vice Pres Diversity & Achievemnt .... Elena BERNAL
21 Vice President/Associate Treasurer .... Karen VOSS
20 Associate Dean of College .... Mark SCHNEIDER
20 Associate Dean of College .... Heather LOBBAN-VIRAVONG
07 Actg Dean of Admiss & Financial Aid .... Doug BADGER
30 Senior Director of Development .... Vacant
37 Director of Student Financial Aid .... Arnold A. WOODS, JR.
15 Director of Human Resources .... Kristin LOVIG
06 Registrar .... Cheryl CHASE
08 Librarian .... Richard FYFFE
29 Director of Alumni/Cmty Relations .... Vacant
14 Dir of Information Technology Svcs .... William FRANCIS
09 Director of Institutional Research .... Vacant
85 Director Intl Student Services .... Karen K. EDWARDS
40 Manager/Bookstore .... Cassandra J. WHERRY
41 Athletic Director .... Greg WALLACE
23 Director of Health Service .... Deb SHILL
38 Assoc Dean/Dir Academic Advising .... Joyce STERN
18 Director Facilities Management .... Mark E. GODAR
19 Director of Safety & Security .... Stephen A. BRISCOE
42 Chaplain .... Deanna SHORB
102 Director Corp/Founda/Govt Rels .... Karen WIESE
39 Asst Dean/Director Residence Life .... Andrea CONNER
35 Dean of Students .... Travis GREENE
27 Director of Communication .... Vacant
31 Coord Community Service Center .... Deanna SHORB

Hamilton Technical College (B)

1011 E 53rd Street, Davenport IA 52807-2616
County: Scott FICE Identification: 012064
Unit ID: 153427
Telephone: (563) 386-3570 Carnegie Class: Spec/Tech
FAX Number: (563) 386-6756 Calendar System: Semester
URL: www.hamiltontechcollege.com
Established: 1969 Annual Undergrad Tuition & Fees: $8,900
Enrollment: 359 Coed
Affiliation or Control: Proprietary IRS Status: Proprietary
Highest Offering: Baccalaureate
Program: Occupational; Technical Emphasis
Accreditation: ACCSC

01 President .... Mrs. Maryanne HAMILTON

Hawkeye Community College (C)

Box 8015, Waterloo IA 50704-8015
County: Black Hawk FICE Identification: 004595
Unit ID: 153445
Telephone: (319) 296-2320 Carnegie Class: Assoc/Pub-R-L
FAX Number: (319) 296-2874 Calendar System: Semester
URL: www.hawkeyecollege.edu
Established: 1966 Annual Undergrad Tuition & Fees (In-District): $4,170
Enrollment: 6,663 Coed
Affiliation or Control: State/Local IRS Status: 501(c)3
Highest Offering: Associate Degree
Program: Occupational; 2-Year Principally Bachelor's Creditable
Accreditation: NH, DA, DH, MLTAD, @PTAA

01 President .... Dr. Linda A. ALLEN
05 Interim Vice Pres Academic Affairs .... Dr. Patricia STANLEY
10 Vice Pres Administration & Finance .... Mr. Dan GILLEN
30 Vice Pres Institutional Advancement .... Ms. Kathy A. FLYNN
102 Executive Director Foundation .... Ms. Peg A. BROWN
15 Exec Dir Human Resource Services .... Mr. John D. CLOPTON
81 Dean Math & Sciences .... Dr. Cynthia BOTTRELL
79 Dean Humanities/Communication Arts .... Ms. Laurel KLINKENBERG
75 Dean Career & Technical Programs .... Mr. A. Ray BEETS
76 Dean Health Sciences & Nursing .... Ms. Sarah TURNER
50 Dean Business & Public Services .... Vacant
32 Dean of Students .... Ms. Nancy HENDERSON
07 Director Admissions & Recruitment .... Mr. Dave BALL
21 Director Business Services .... Ms. Denise BOUSKA
13 Director Communication/Info Systems .... Mr. Jared SHEFFIELD
62 Director Library Services .... Ms. Candace HAVELY
51 Director of Continuing Education .... Mr. Alan G. CLAUSEN
18 Director Plant & Facilities .... Mr. Dennis WESTENDORF
06 Dir Student Records & Registration .... Ms. Patricia A. EAST
24 Director Teaching/Learning Services .... Ms. D.J CORSON
09 Director Institutional Research .... Ms. Connie BUHR
26 Director Public Relations/Mktg .... Ms. Mary Pat MOORE
28 Assoc Dir of Multicultural Affairs .... Mr. Quentin HART
35 Student Life Coordinator .... Ms. Stephanie CHERRY
44 Development Officer .... Ms. Karen GEBEL
101 Board Secretary .... Ms. Denise A. DUNN

Indian Hills Community College (D)

525 Grandview, Ottumwa IA 52501-1398
County: Wapello FICE Identification: 008403
Unit ID: 153472
Telephone: (641) 683-5111 Carnegie Class: Assoc/Pub-R-M
FAX Number: (641) 683-5184 Calendar System: Quarter
URL: www.ihcc.cc.ia.us
Established: 1966 Annual Undergrad Tuition & Fees (In-District): $4,680
Enrollment: 4,280 Coed
Affiliation or Control: State/Local IRS Status: 501(c)3
Highest Offering: Associate Degree
Program: Occupational; 2-Year Principally Bachelor's Creditable
Accreditation: NH, ACFEI, PTAA, RAD

01 President .... Dr. Jim LINDENMAYER
10 Chief Financial Officer .... Ms. Sue PIXLEY
05 Vice President Academic Affairs .... Dr. Marlene SPROUSE
04 Asst to Pres/College & Industry Rel .... Mr. Mick LAWSON
86 Asst to Pres/Govt Affs & Comm Rels .... Dr. Bob MORRISSEY
49 Executive Dean Arts & Sciences .... Ms. Darlas SHOCKLEY
103 Exec Dean Reg Workforce/Econ Dev .... Mr. Tom RUBEL
32 Dean Student Services .... Mr. Kelly CONRAD
76 Dean Health Occupations .... Ms. Jill BUDDE
75 Assoc Dean Advanced Technologies .... Mr. Tom RUBEL
12 Dean Centerville Campus .... Mr. Joe STARCEVICH
15 Director Human Resources .... Ms. Bonnie CAMPBELL
20 Dean Academic Services .... Ms. Mary STEWART
18 Director Maintenance .... Mr. Rick FOSDYCK
06 Registrar .... Ms. Gail LOCKRIDGE
41 Athletic Director .... Mr. Terry CARLSON
26 Director for Media/Public Rels .... Mr. Kevin PINK
37 Director Student Financial Aid .... Mrs. Jo ALTHEIDE
88 Chair Aviation Programs .... Mr. Darrell DOWNING

INSTE Bible College (E)

2302 SW Third Street, Ankeny IA 50023-2453
County: Polk Identification: 666461
Telephone: (515) 289-9200 Carnegie Class: Not Classified
FAX Number: (515) 289-9201 Calendar System: Semester
URL: www.inste.edu
Established: 1982 Annual Undergrad Tuition & Fees: $1,744
Enrollment: 19 Coed
Affiliation or Control: Interdenominational IRS Status: 501(c)3
Highest Offering: Baccalaureate
Program: Liberal Arts And General; Religious Emphasis
Accreditation: DETC

01 President .... Dr. Nicholas VENDITTI
05 Vice President & Academic Dean .... Dr. Leona VENDITTI
20 Assistant Dean .... Rev. David DEL VALLE

Iowa Central Community College (F)

One Triton Circle, Fort Dodge IA 50501-5798
County: Webster FICE Identification: 001865
Unit ID: 153524
Telephone: (515) 576-7201 Carnegie Class: Assoc/Pub-R-M
FAX Number: (515) 576-7207 Calendar System: Semester
URL: www.iowacentral.edu
Established: 1966 Annual Undergrad Tuition & Fees (In-District): $4,200
Enrollment: 6,204 Coed
Affiliation or Control: Local IRS Status: 501(c)3
Highest Offering: Associate Degree
Program: Occupational; 2-Year Principally Bachelor's Creditable
Accreditation: NH, DH, MAC, MLTAD, RAD

01 President .... Dr. Daniel P. KINNEY
04 Assistant to the President .... Mrs. Karen L. LOMBARD
05 Vice President of Instruction .... Dr. Marlene A. MCCOMAS
32 Vice Pres Enroll Mgmt/Student Devel .... Mr. Thomas J. BENEKE
86 VP External Affairs/Govt Rels .... Mr. James B. KERSTEN
30 VP Development/Alumni Rels .... Mrs. Laurie M. HENDRICKS
10 Assoc VP Business Affairs .... Mrs. Angela A. MARTIN
50 Dean Business & Ind Technology .... Mr. Neale J. ADAMS
76 Dean Science/Health & Human Svcs .... Mrs. Connie K. BOYD
79 Dean Liberal Arts .... Mrs. Jennifer M. CONDON
106 Dean Distance Learning .... Mr. Timothy J. MARTIN
21 Director Business Office .... Mr. Luke J. GROVE
16 Director Human Resources .... Ms. Kimberly N. WHITMORE
15 Coordinator Human Resources .... Ms. Sandi J. PIEPER
06 Registrar .... Ms. Courtney A. KOPP
88 Assistant Registrar .... Mrs. Sarah J. RAMTHUN
84 Director Enrollment Management .... Ms. Sara A. CONDON
37 Director Financial Aid .... Mrs. Darci M. BANGERT
09 Director Institutional Effectivenes .... Mrs. Joni K. KELLEN
41 Director Intercollegiate Athletics .... Mr. Rick A. SANDQUIST
39 Director Housing .... Mr. Bob L. BRABENDER
35 Coord Student Life & Activities .... Mr. Anthony E. ACKLIN
08 Director Learning Resources .... Mr. Dan C. SCHIEFELBEIN
18 Director Physical Facilities .... Mr. Troy A. BRANDT
12 Director Storm Lake Center .... Mr. Dan J. ANDERSON
12 Director Webster City Center .... Mrs. Kelly J. WIRTZ
27 Director Public Information .... Mr. Paul A. DECOURSEY
13 Director Institutional Technology .... Mr. Jeff A. NELSEN
13 Director Institutional Technology .... Mr. Troy D. CRAMPTON
14 Computer System Analyst .... Mr. Warren K. BAUER
40 Bookstore Manager .... Mrs. Samantha E. MCCLAIN

Iowa Lakes Community College (G)

19 S Seventh Street, Estherville IA 51334-2234
County: Emmet FICE Identification: 001864
Unit ID: 153533
Telephone: (712) 362-2604 Carnegie Class: Assoc/Pub-R-M
FAX Number: (712) 362-8363 Calendar System: Semester
URL: www.iowalakes.edu
Established: 1967 Annual Undergrad Tuition & Fees (In-District): $5,004
Enrollment: 3,264 Coed
Affiliation or Control: State/Local IRS Status: 501(c)3
Highest Offering: Associate Degree
Program: Occupational; 2-Year Principally Bachelor's Creditable
Accreditation: NH, MAC, SURGT

01 President .... Ms. Valerie K. NEWHOUSE
03 Vice President of Administration .... Mr. Robert W. L'HEUREUX
12 Exec Dean Emmetsburg Campus .... Mr. Thomas S. BROTHERTON
27 Exec Director of Marketing .... Ms. Jane S. CAMPBELL
05 Exec Dean Instruction/Development .... Mr. Mark A. GRUWELL
18 Exec Dir of Facilities Management .... Ms. Delaine S. HINEY
51 Exec Dir Econ Development/Cont Educ .... Mr. Clark L. MARSHALL
12 Exec Dean Estherville Campus .... Mr. Darin D. MOELLER
30 Exec Director Inst Advancement .... Ms. Jolene R. ROGERS
32 Dean of Students .... Ms. Julie R. WILLIAMS

*Iowa Valley Community College District (H)

3702 S Center Street, Marshalltown IA 50158-4760
County: Marshall FICE Identification: 033436
Telephone: (641) 752-4643 Carnegie Class: N/A
FAX Number: (641) 754-1336
URL: www.ivccd.com

01 Chancellor .... Mr. Christopher DUREE
51 Vice Chanc Continuing Educ/Training .... Ms. Jacque GOODMAN
11 Vice Chanc Administrative Services .... Ms. Colleen SPRINGER
10 Chief Financial Officer .... Ms. Kathy PINK
12 Provost of ECC .... Dr. Nancy MUECKE
12 Provost of MCC .... Dr. Robin SHAFFER LILIENTHAL
12 Dean of Iowa Valley Grinnell .... Ms. Mary Anne NICKLE
26 Director of Marketing .... Ms. Robin ANCTIL
09 Institutional Researcher .... Dr. Lisa BREJA
04 Admin Assistant to the Chancellor .... Ms. Barbara JENNINGS
13 Dir Computing and Info Management .... Mr. Jim WILSON

*Ellsworth Community College (I)

1100 College Avenue, Iowa Falls IA 50126-1199
County: Hardin FICE Identification: 001862
Unit ID: 153296
Telephone: (641) 648-4611 Carnegie Class: Assoc/Pub-R-S
FAX Number: (641) 648-3128 Calendar System: Semester
URL: www.iavalley.cc.ia.us/ecc
Established: 1890 Annual Undergrad Tuition & Fees (In-District): $3,336
Enrollment: 1,078 Coed
Affiliation or Control: State/Local IRS Status: 501(c)3
Highest Offering: Associate Degree
Program: Occupational; 2-Year Principally Bachelor's Creditable
Accreditation: &NH, MAC

02 Provost .... Dr. Nancy MUECKE
05 District Chief Academic Officer .... Dr. Chris RUSSELL
08 Director of Libraries .... Ms. Sandra GREUFE
32 Dean of Student Serv/Athletic Dir .... Mr. Paul EBERHARDT
39 Director Student Housing .... Mr. O. J. PAYNE
37 Director Financial Aid .... Ms. Tara MILLER
44 Dir Annual Plan Giving/Dir Alum Rel .... Ms. Kaitlyn BARTLING
32 Associate Dean Student Services .... Ms. Annie KALOUS
84 Director Enrollment Mgmt/Registrar .... Ms. Barb KLEIN

*Marshalltown Community College (J)

3700 S Center Street, Marshalltown IA 50158-4760
County: Marshall FICE Identification: 001875
Unit ID: 153922
Telephone: (641) 752-7106 Carnegie Class: Assoc/Pub-R-S
FAX Number: (641) 752-8149 Calendar System: Semester
URL: www.iavalley.edu

Established: 1927 Annual Undergrad Tuition & Fees (In-District): $3,336
Enrollment: 2,078 Coed
Affiliation or Control: State/Local IRS Status: 501(c)3
Highest Offering: Associate Degree
Program: Occupational; 2-Year Principally Bachelor's Creditable
Accreditation: &NH, DA

02 Chancellor Dr. Christopher A. DUREE
05 Chief Academic Officer Dr. Chris A. RUSSELL
11 Vice Chanc Administrative Services Ms. Colleen SPRINGER
51 Vice Chancellor of Cont Educ/Trng Ms. Jacque GOODMAN
32 Dean of Student Services Mr. Neil HAYHURST
07 Assoc Dean Student Svcs/Dir Admiss Mrs. Deana INMAN
20 Assoc Dean of Learning Services Vacant
06 Registrar Ms. Molly M. OSMUN
76 Assoc Dean of Health Occupations Ms. Brenda KROGH DUREE
102 Executive Director of Foundation Ms. Barbara BEICHLEY
84 District Dean Enrollment Management Ms. Barb KLEIN
10 Chief Financial Officer Mr. Dan GILLEN
37 Director Student Financial Aid Ms. Chloe WEBB
26 Director of Marketing Ms. Robin ANCTIL
41 Athletic Director Mr. Neil HAYHURST
35 Supervisor Student Development Ms. Elaine PETERSON
38 Director of Student Counseling Ms. Barb KLEIN
39 Director of Student Housing Mr. John MCINTYRE
25 Dir of Grants Development Mr. Cort IVERSON
08 Library Supervisor Ms. Linda MOORE
40 Bookstore Supervisor Mr. Larry ROBERTS

Iowa Wesleyan College (A)

601 N Main, Mount Pleasant IA 52641-1398
County: Henry FICE Identification: 001871
Unit ID: 153621
Telephone: (319) 385-8021 Carnegie Class: Bac/Diverse
FAX Number: (319) 385-6296 Calendar System: Semester
URL: www.iwc.edu
Established: 1842 Annual Undergrad Tuition & Fees: $23,160
Enrollment: 771 Coed
Affiliation or Control: United Methodist IRS Status: 501(c)3
Highest Offering: Baccalaureate
Program: Liberal Arts And General; Teacher Preparatory; Professional
Accreditation: NH, NUR

01 President Dr. Jay K. SIMMONS
100 Special Assistant to the President Ms. Carol NEMITZ
10 Senior VP/Chief Financial Officer Ms. Phyllis WHITNEY
05 Vice President Academic Affairs Dr. Nancy ERICKSON
30 Vice Pres Institutional Relations Mr. Jerry THOMAS
32 Vice Pres and Dean for Student Life Dr. Linda R. BUCHANAN
51 Associate VP for Extended Learning Mr. David C. FILE
14 Assoc VP/Chief Information Officer Dr. Kit NIP
07 Assoc VP & Dean for Admissions Mr. Mark PETTY
06 Registrar Ms. Patty BROKKEN
37 Director of Financial Aid Ms. Renae ARMENTROUT
08 Librarian Mrs. Paula KINNEY
15 Director of Human Resources Ms. Kathy BLOOM
30 Director of Development Vacant
44 Director of Annual Fund Ms. Lori WILSON
26 Director of Marketing/Communication Ms. Martha POTTS-BELL
26 Publications Manager Ms. Sheri MICHAELS
29 Director of Alumni/Parent Relations Ms. Anita HAMPTON
42 Director of Church Relations Vacant
41 Athletic Director Mr. Mike HAMPTON
18 Director of Physical Plant Mr. Bob VITALE
35 Director of Student Activities Ms. Ashley LANG
36 Director of Career Development Ms. Heidi SEEGERS
40 Bookstore Director Mr. Mike SPRINGSTEEN
04 Senior Exec Asst to the President Ms. Rebecca ROWE

Iowa Western Community College (B)

2700 College Road, Council Bluffs IA 51503-0567
County: Pottawattamie FICE Identification: 004598
Unit ID: 153630
Telephone: (712) 325-3200 Carnegie Class: Assoc/Pub-S-MC
FAX Number: (712) 325-3424 Calendar System: Semester
URL: www.iwcc.edu
Established: 1966 Annual Undergrad Tuition & Fees (In-District): $3,960
Enrollment: 6,799 Coed
Affiliation or Control: State/Local IRS Status: 501(c)3
Highest Offering: Associate Degree
Program: Occupational; 2-Year Principally Bachelor's Creditable
Accreditation: NH, ACFEI, DA, DH, MAC, SURGT

01 President Dr. Dan KINNEY
04 Assistant to the President Ms. Kathryn A. SCHUSTER
10 Vice Pres of Finance & Operations Mr. Thomas JOHNSON
05 Vice President for Academic Affairs Dr. Dorothy DURAN
32 Vice President for Student Services Ms. Jeanine P. LARSEN
26 Vice Pres of Marketing/Public Rels Mr. Donald KOHLER
09 Dean of Institutional Research Ms. Karna LOEWENSTEIN
84 Dean Enrollment Services Ms. Tori CHRISTIE
35 Dean Student Support Services Ms. Sarah HOLLOWELL
12 Director of Clarinda Campus Mr. Chad WELLHAUSEN
06 Registrar Ms. Jill CLARK
15 Director of Personnel Services Ms. Joan RYAN
29 Director of Alumni Relations Ms. Rachel LENHARDT
37 Director of Student Financial Aid Mr. Blaine DUISTERMARS
21 Director Accounting Mr. Eddie HOLTZ
14 Director Computer Center Mr. James A. MAHLBERG
76 Area Nursing Coordinator Ms. Rita BERTHELSEN
88 Exec Dir Economic Development Mr. Mark STANLEY
41 Athletic Director Ms. Brenda HAMPTON
08 Librarian Ms. Ellen VANWAART
39 Director of Housing Ms. Kim HENRY
18 Chief Facilities/Physical Plant Mr. Greg CLAUSEN
07 Director of Admissions/Advising Mr. Christopher LEFERLA
96 Director of Purchasing Mrs. Diane OSBAHR
36 Dir Student Placement/Counseling Mr. Hugh IRWIN
40 Director Food Svcs/Bookstore Mgr Ms. Eddie HOLTZ

ITT Technical Institute (C)

1860 NW 118th Street, Suite 110, Clive IA 50325-8278
County: Polk Identification: 666596
Unit ID: 451954
Telephone: (515) 327-5500 Carnegie Class: Assoc/PrivFP4
FAX Number: (515) 327-5550 Calendar System: Quarter
URL: www.itt-tech.edu
Established: N/A Annual Undergrad Tuition & Fees: N/A
Enrollment: 280 Coed
Affiliation or Control: Proprietary IRS Status: Proprietary
Highest Offering: Baccalaureate
Program: Technical Emphasis
Accreditation: ACICS

† Branch campus of ITT Technical Institute, Thorton, CO.

Kaplan University (D)

3165 Edgewood Parkway SW,
Cedar Rapids IA 52404-2998
County: Linn FICE Identification: 004220
Unit ID: 153418
Telephone: (319) 363-0481 Carnegie Class: Bac/Assoc
FAX Number: (319) 363-3812 Calendar System: Quarter
URL: www.cedarrapids.kaplanuniversity.edu
Established: 1900 Annual Undergrad Tuition & Fees: $15,372
Enrollment: 916 Coed
Affiliation or Control: Proprietary IRS Status: Proprietary
Highest Offering: Baccalaureate
Program: Occupational; 2-Year Principally Bachelor's Creditable
Accreditation: &NH, MAC

01 Cedar Rapids Campus President Mrs. Susan M. SPIVEY
05 Academic Dean Dr. Steve BONNET
12 Mason City Campus Exec Director Mr. Joe ALBERS
12 Des Moines Campus President Ms. Colleen MCDERMOTT
12 Cedar Falls Campus President Ms. Connie REIDY

† Regional accreditation is carried under the parent institution in Davenport, IA.

Kaplan University (E)

1801 East Kimberly Road, Suite 1,
Davenport IA 52807-2095
County: Scott FICE Identification: 004586
Unit ID: 260901
Telephone: (563) 355-3500 Carnegie Class: Master's L
FAX Number: (563) 355-1320 Calendar System: Quarter
URL: www.kucampus.edu
Established: 1937 Annual Undergrad Tuition & Fees: $13,008
Enrollment: 23,490 Coed
Affiliation or Control: Proprietary IRS Status: Proprietary
Highest Offering: Doctorate
Program: Occupational
Accreditation: NH, MAC, NURSE

01 Campus President Dr. Mark GARLAND
04 Assistant to the Campus President Ms. Sara SKELTON
05 Director of Student Services Ms. Connie BONNE
37 Director of Financial Aid Ms. Sharon BARBER
07 Director of Admissions Mr. Jason WILEVSKI
36 Employment Search Coordinator Ms. Lisa ZERBONIA
08 Librarian Ms. Carole SWIFT
06 Registrar Ms. Janet GEHRLS

Kaplan University (F)

Plaza West 2570 4th Street, SW,
Mason City IA 50401-3102
County: Cerro Gordo Identification: 666438
Unit ID: 153409
Telephone: (641) 423-2530 Carnegie Class: Bac/Assoc
FAX Number: (641) 423-7512 Calendar System: Quarter
URL: www.KU-MasonCity.com
Established: 1900 Annual Undergrad Tuition & Fees: $15,327
Enrollment: 367 Coed
Affiliation or Control: Proprietary IRS Status: Proprietary
Highest Offering: Baccalaureate
Program: Occupational; 2-Year Principally Bachelor's Creditable; Professional; Business Emphasis
Accreditation: &NH, MAC

01 Interim Executive Director Mr. Todd W. ELLWEIN
84 Director of Admissions Mrs. Sara TURNBULL
32 Director of Student Services Mrs. Tamerah MCCREADY
37 Director of Financial Aid Mrs. Shari GARRISON
06 Registrar Mrs. Eden PATTI
36 Director of Career Services Mrs. Karen RIES
08 Director of Library Services Mrs. Kim MASHECK

† Regional accreditation is carried under the parent institution in Davenport, IA.

Kaplan University (G)

4655 121st Street, Urbandale IA 50323-2311
County: Polk Identification: 666437
Unit ID: 367024
Telephone: (515) 727-2100 Carnegie Class: Bac/Assoc
FAX Number: (515) 727-2115 Calendar System: Quarter
URL: www.kucampus.edu
Established: 1985 Annual Undergrad Tuition & Fees: $15,372
Enrollment: 1,258 Coed
Affiliation or Control: Proprietary IRS Status: Proprietary
Highest Offering: Baccalaureate
Program: Occupational
Accreditation: &NH, MAC

01 President Mr. Jeremy WELLS
05 Academic Dean Ms. Kacy WEBSTER
07 Director of Admissions Mr. Mark BANDY

† Regional accreditation is carried under the parent institution in Davenport, IA.

Kirkwood Community College (H)

PO Box 2068, Cedar Rapids IA 52406-2068
County: Linn FICE Identification: 004076
Unit ID: 153737
Telephone: (319) 398-5411 Carnegie Class: Assoc/Pub-R-L
FAX Number: (319) 398-1037 Calendar System: Semester
URL: www.kirkwood.edu
Established: 1966 Annual Undergrad Tuition & Fees (In-District): $3,968
Enrollment: 18,456 Coed
Affiliation or Control: Local IRS Status: 501(c)3
Highest Offering: Associate Degree
Program: Occupational; 2-Year Principally Bachelor's Creditable
Accreditation: NH, ACBSP, ACFEI, DA, DH, DT, EEG, EMT, MAC, OTA, PTAA, SURGT

01 President Dr. Mick STARCEVICH
51 Exec VP Cont Educ/Training Svcs Ms. Kim JOHNSON
10 Vice President/Chief Fin/Oper Ofcr Mr. Jim CHOATE
30 Vice President Resource Development Ms. Kathy HALL
05 Vice President Instruction Dr. Bill LAMB
84 Vice President Enrollment Dr. Kristie FISHER
20 Assoc Vice President Instruction Mr. John HENIK
12 Dean Iowa City Campus Dr. Dale SIMON
32 Dean of Students Mr. Bob E. BURNES
15 Director Human Resources Mr. Mike ROBERTS
13 Executive Director IT Mr. Jon NEFF
09 Exec Dir Institutional Research Mr. Al ROWE
86 Exec Director Governmental Rels Mr. Steven J. OVEL
56 Executive Director Secondary Pgm Mr. Todd PRUSHA
84 Director Enrollment Management Ms. Peg JULIUS
08 Director Library Mr. Aaron WINGS
07 Director Admissions Mr. Douglas F. BANNON
18 Executive Director Facilities Mr. Tom KALDENBERG
25 Director Grants & Fed Programs Ms. Chris O'BRIEN
41 Athletic Director Mr. Doug WAGEMESTER
26 Public Information Svs Director Mr. Steve CARPENTER
06 Registrar Ms. Dena RAUCH
29 Scholarship & Alumni Director Ms. Jody DONALDSON
37 Director Student Financial Aid Ms. Peg JULIUS
47 Dean Agriculture Mr. Scott ERMER
72 Dean Industrial Technology Mr. Jeff MITCHELL
88 Dean English Ms. Allison YORK
79 Dean Arts & Humanities Dr. Jennifer BRADLEY
76 Dean Health Sciences Ms. Nancy GLAB
83 Dean Social Sciences/Career Option Ms. Kathleen VAN STEENHUYSE
81 Dean Math/Science Dr. Bob DRIGGS
66 Dean Nursing Ms. Sandra COOPER
76 Dean Health Occupations Dr. Mike MCLAUGHLIN
50 Dean Business & Information Tech Mr. Chuck HINZ
88 Dean Learning Services Mr. Chuck HINZ
56 Dean Distance Learning Dr. Todd PRUSHA

Loras College (I)

1450 Alta Vista, Dubuque IA 52004-0178
County: Dubuque FICE Identification: 001873
Unit ID: 153825
Telephone: (563) 588-7100 Carnegie Class: Bac/Diverse
FAX Number: (563) 588-7964 Calendar System: Semester
URL: www.loras.edu
Established: 1839 Annual Undergrad Tuition & Fees: $27,258
Enrollment: 1,576 Coed
Affiliation or Control: Roman Catholic IRS Status: 501(c)3
Highest Offering: Master's
Program: Liberal Arts And General; Teacher Preparatory
Accreditation: NH, @SW

01 President Mr. James E. COLLINS
05 Provost & Academic Dean Dr. Cheryl R. JACOBSEN
10 Vice President Finance/Admin Svcs Mr. Stephen J. SCHMALL
84 Vice Pres Enrollment Management Dr. Lisa L. BUNDERS
30 Vice President Inst Advancement Ms. Pamela S. GERARD
04 Executive Assistant to President Vacant

20 Assoc Vice Pres Academic Affairs .... Dr. Mary E. CARROLL
32 Assoc Vice Pres/Dean of Students .... Mr. Arthur W. SUNLEAF
30 Assoc VP Institutional Advancement .... Mr. Michael H. DOYLE
42 Dean of Campus Spiritual Life .... Vacant
91 Sr Dir Technology Support Services .... Mr. Tom D. KRUSE
29 Exec Dir Alumni & Communications .... Ms. Bobbi L. EARLES
15 Dir Human/Organization Development .... Ms. Gloria A. BENTLEY
09 Director of Institutional Research .... Dr. Shaun E. COWMAN
38 Director Center for Counseling .... Dr. Michael J. BOYD
07 Director of Admissions .... Ms. Sharon K. LYONS
08 Director of Academic Resource Ctr .... Ms. Joyce A. MELDREM
19 Director of Safety/Security .... Vacant
44 Director of Major & Planned Giving .... Mr. Eric J. SOLBERG
41 Director of Athletics .... Mr. Robert E. QUINN
18 Director of Physical Plant .... Mr. John R. MCDERMOTT
40 Director of Bookstore .... Ms. Renee A. MENNE
23 Director of Health Center .... Mrs. Tammy S. MARTI
85 Director of Intercultural Office .... Mr. Alejandro J. PINO
42 Director of Campus Ministry .... Ms. Colleen M. KUHL
06 Registrar .... Mr. JT BROWN
39 Director of Residence Life .... Ms. Molly A. BURROWS-SCHUMACHER
35 Director of Student Life .... Ms. Kimberly A. WALSH
37 Director of Financial Planning .... Ms. Julie A. DUNN
25 Grant Writing Director .... Ms. Valorie A. WOERDEHOFF
26 Dir Communication/Media Relations .... Ms. Susan P. HAFKEMEYER
96 Controller for Business Office .... Ms. Sandy M. RECKER
36 Academic Internship Coordinator .... Ms. Faye A. FINNEGAN

Luther College (A)

700 College Drive, Decorah IA 52101-1045

County: Winneshiek FICE Identification: 001874

Unit ID: 153834

Telephone: (563) 387-2000 Carnegie Class: Bac/A&S

FAX Number: (563) 387-2158 Calendar System: 4/1/4

URL: www.luther.edu

Established: 1861 Annual Undergrad Tuition & Fees: $34,885

Enrollment: 2,481 Coed

Affiliation or Control: Evangelical Lutheran Church In America

IRS Status: 501(c)3

Highest Offering: Baccalaureate

Program: Liberal Arts And General; Teacher Preparatory; Professional

Accreditation: NH, MUS, NURSE, SW, TED

01 President .... Dr. Richard L. TORGERSON
05 Vice Pres Acad Affs/Dean of College .... Dr. Kevin KRAUS
20 Assistant Dean .... Ms. Arleen ORVIS
30 Vice President for Development .... Mr. Keith J. CHRISTENSEN
10 Vice President for Finance & Admin .... Ms. Diane L. TACKE
32 Vice Pres/Dean for Student Life .... Dr. Ann C. HIGHUM
84 Vice Pres Enrollment Management .... Mr. Scot SCHAEFFER
13 Exec Dir Library & Info Tech Svcs .... Vacant
91 Director Information Systems .... Ms. Marcia A. GULLICKSON
21 Controller .... Ms. Peggy LENSING
18 Exec Director Campus Services .... Mr. Richard J. TENNESON
44 Senior Development Officer .... Mr. Thomas K. MURRAY
06 Registrar .... Mr. Douglas KOSCHMEDER
20 Associate Dean .... Dr. Lori STANLEY
15 Director Human Resources .... Mr. Roy J. PRIGGE
41 Director Intercollegiate Athletics .... Dr. Joe H. THOMPSON
29 Director of Alumni Relations .... Ms. Sherry B. ALCOCK
26 Exec Dir Communications/Marketing .... Mr. Rob K. LARSON
26 Director of Public Information .... Mr. Jerrold JOHNSON
04 Assistant to the President .... Ms. Karen B. MARTIN-SCHRAMM
35 Associate Dean Student Life .... Ms. Jane HILDEBRAND
36 Director Career Center .... Ms. Keley SMITH-KELLER
38 Director Counseling Service .... Dr. Pamela C. TORRESDAL
37 Director Student Financial Planning .... Ms. Janice K. CORDELL
42 Dir Campus Ministry & Cong Rels .... Rev. Michael R. BLAIR
40 Director Book Shop/Union Services .... Vacant
27 Director of Publications .... Mr. Greg T. VANNEY
08 Head Librarian .... Ms. Christine FRANZEN
39 Assistant Dean & Dir Res Life .... Ms. Kristine FRANZEN
85 Exec Dir Ctr Glo Learning & Int Adm .... Mr. Jon LUND
44 Director of Planned Giving .... Mr. James ANDERSON
23 Director Health Services .... Ms. JoEllen ANDERSON
19 Director Security/Safety .... Mr. Robert HARRI
88 Director Campus Programing .... Ms. Tanya M. GERTZ
28 Exec Director of Diversity .... Dr. Sheila RADFORD-HILL
09 Director Assessment/Inst Research .... Dr. Jon A. CHRISTY
07 Director of Recruiting Services .... Mr. Kirk NEUBAUER
35 Coordinator Student Activities .... Ms. Trish NEUBAUER
88 Asst Dean & Health Res Adv .... Ms. Janet HUNTER

Maharishi University of Management (B)

1000 N 4th Street, Fairfield IA 52557-0001

County: Jefferson FICE Identification: 011113

Unit ID: 153861

Telephone: (641) 472-7000 Carnegie Class: Master's L

FAX Number: (641) 472-1179 Calendar System: Other

URL: www.mum.edu

Established: 1971 Annual Undergrad Tuition & Fees: $24,750

Enrollment: 1,090 Coed

Affiliation or Control: Independent Non-Profit IRS Status: 501(c)3

Highest Offering: Doctorate

Program: Liberal Arts And General; Teacher Preparatory

Accreditation: NH, IACBE

01 President .... Dr. Bevan H. MORRIS
03 Executive Vice President .... Dr. Craig PEARSON
05 Dean of Faculty .... Dr. Cathy GORINI
10 Treasurer .... Mr. Michael SPIVAK
88 International Vice President .... Dr. Michael DILLBECK
88 International Vice President .... Dr. Susan DILLBECK
11 Chief Administrative Officer .... Dr. David STREID
07 Dean of Admissions .... Mr. Bradford MYLETT
32 Dean of Student Life .... Ms. Ellen AKST JONES
33 Associate Dean of Men .... Mr. Lynwood KING
34 Associate Dean of Women .... Ms. Snezena PETROSKY
06 Registrar .... Mr. Tom ROWE
45 Director of Expansion .... Dr. David TODT
26 Media Director .... Mr. Ken CHAWKIN
51 Dir Distance Educ/Intl Programs .... Mr. Dennis HEATON
27 Director of Press .... Mr. Harry BRIGHT
39 Director of Housing .... Mr. Britt ZEIGER
37 Director of Student Financial Aid .... Mr. Bill CHRISTENSEN
14 Director of Information Services .... Mr. Tom HIRSCH
09 Director of Assessment .... Mr. Raoul CALDERON
15 Director of Personnel .... Mr. John KENNEDY
29 Director Alumni Relations .... Ms. Jennine FELLMER
30 Co-Director of Development .... Mr. Nick ROSANIA
30 Co-Director of Development .... Ms. Sandra ROSANIA
36 Director Student Placement .... Dr. Rachel GOODMAN
18 Chief Facilities/Physical Plant .... Mr. De Armond BRIGGS
49 Dean College of Arts & Sciences .... Mr. Kit HEALY
77 Dn College of Computer Sci & Math .... Mr. Gregory GUTHRIE
58 Dean of Graduate School .... Dr. Frederick TRAVIS

Mercy College of Health Sciences (C)

928 Sixth Avenue, Des Moines IA 50309-1239

County: Polk FICE Identification: 006273

Unit ID: 153977

Telephone: (515) 643-3180 Carnegie Class: Spec/Health

FAX Number: (515) 643-6698 Calendar System: Semester

URL: www.mchs.edu

Established: 1995 Annual Undergrad Tuition & Fees: $13,900

Enrollment: 792 Coed

Affiliation or Control: Roman Catholic IRS Status: 501(c)3

Highest Offering: Baccalaureate

Program: Liberal Arts And General; Professional

Accreditation: NH, ADNUR, DMS, EMT, MAC, MT, NMT, NURSE, POLYT, PTAA, RAD, SURGT

01 President .... Dr. Barbara Q. DECKER
05 Interim VP of Academic Affairs .... Dr. Steven D. LANGDON
26 VP of External Affairs .... Mr. Brian P. TINGLEFF
10 VP of Business & Regulatory Affairs .... Dr. Thomas LEAHY
66 Dean of Nursing .... Dr. Shirley BEAVER
49 Dean of Liberal Arts & Sciences .... Dr. Jeannine MATZ
76 Dean of Allied Health .... Ms. Theresa SMITH
09 Dean Inst Rsrch/Assess/Dist Educ .... Dr. Joan M. MCCLEISH
08 Dir of Library and Media Services .... Ms. Eileen HANSEN
06 Registrar .... Ms. Carolyn BUCKLIN
15 Human Resources Business Partner .... Ms. Anne DENNIS
37 Director of Financial Aid .... Ms. Lisa CROAT
38 Director of Student Success .... Dr. Mark KLOBERDANZ
13 Systems Technology Supervisor .... Mr. Tom IVERSON
18 Facilities Manager .... Mr. David STEENHOEK
07 Admissions Manager .... Ms. Kara DONOVAN
26 Marketing Manager .... Mr. Jim TAGYE
44 Dir Development Business Partner .... Ms. Angela JOENS
32 Director of Student Services .... Dr. Karen ANDERSON
88 Senior Finance Business Partner .... Mr. Warren TOWLES

Morningside College (D)

1501 Morningside Avenue, Sioux City IA 51106-1751

County: Woodbury FICE Identification: 001879

Unit ID: 154004

Telephone: (712) 274-5000 Carnegie Class: Bac/Diverse

FAX Number: (712) 274-5101 Calendar System: Semester

URL: www.morningside.edu

Established: 1894 Annual Undergrad Tuition & Fees: $24,050

Enrollment: 1,991 Coed

Affiliation or Control: United Methodist IRS Status: 501(c)3

Highest Offering: Master's

Program: Liberal Arts And General; Teacher Preparatory; Professional

Accreditation: NH, MUS, NURSE

01 President .... Mr. John C. REYNDERS
05 Vice President/Dean of College .... Dr. William C. DEEDS
10 Vice President Business & Finance .... Mr. Ronald A. JORGENSEN
32 Vice Pres Student Life & Enrollment .... Mrs. Terri A. CURRY
30 Vice Pres Institutional Advancement .... Mr. Thomas M. RICE
35 Dean for Advising/Assoc Dean Stdnts .... Dr. Mary LEIDA
84 Dean of Enrollment .... Ms. Robbie ROHLENA
20 Associate Dean for Acad Affairs .... Dr. Susan BURNS
09 Asc Dean Assessment/Inst Research .... Dr. John PINTO
06 Registrar .... Ms. Mary PESHEK
37 Director Student Financial Planning .... Ms. Karen GAGNON
14 Dir Info Tech/Dean Learning Center .... Mr. Andrew HEISER
26 Director Public Relations .... Mr. Rick WOLLMAN
29 Director of Alumni Relations .... Mr. Gene AMBROSON
58 Director of Graduate Studies .... Dr. Glenna J. TEVIS
18 Director of Physical Plant .... Mr. Kirk JOHNSON
19 Director of Security .... Mr. Jim CORNELIA
23 Director of Student Health .... Ms. Carol GARVEY
24 Media Center Supervisor .... Ms. Janet L. JACOBSON
36 Director of Career Services .... Ms. Stacie HAYS

40 Director of Bookstore .... Mr. Duane BENSON
41 Athletic Director .... Mr. Jerry SCHMUTTE
42 Campus Ministry .... Rev. Kathy MARTIN
44 Director of Gift Planning .... Mr. Fred S. ERBES
15 Director Human Resources .... Ms. Cindy WELP
38 Director Student Counseling .... Ms. Brenda CRAWFORD
21 Controller .... Mr. Paul TREFT

Mount Mercy University (E)

1330 Elmhurst Drive, NE, Cedar Rapids IA 52402-4797

County: Linn FICE Identification: 001880

Unit ID: 154013

Telephone: (319) 363-8213 Carnegie Class: Bac/Diverse

FAX Number: (319) 363-5270 Calendar System: 4/1/4

URL: www.mtmercy.edu

Established: 1928 Annual Undergrad Tuition & Fees: $24,360

Enrollment: 1,643 Coed

Affiliation or Control: Roman Catholic IRS Status: 501(c)3

Highest Offering: Master's

Program: Liberal Arts And General; Teacher Preparatory; Professional

Accreditation: NH, NURSE, SW

01 President .... Dr. Christopher R L. BLAKE
05 Acting Provost/VP Academic Affairs .... Dr. Melody GRAHAM
10 Vice President Finance .... Ms. Barbara D. PARKS POOLEY
84 Vice Pres Enrollment/Student Svcs .... Dr. Jennifer Sue OATEY
30 Interim Exec Dir for Development .... Ms. Kathy TOBORG
20 Vice Pres Academic Affairs .... Dr. Janet R. HANDLER
07 Dean of Admissions .... Mr. Scott BAUMLER
06 Registrar .... Mr. Jason CLAPP
08 Director of Library Services .... Mrs. Marilyn J. MURPHY
36 Director of Career Services .... Ms. Cheryl TABARELLA-REED
29 Assist VP for Alumni Development .... Ms. Lonna DREWELOW
37 Director of Financial Aid .... Ms. Bethany RINDERKNECHT
26 Asst VP Communications/Marketing .... Mr. Fritz MCDONALD
41 Director of Athletics .... Mr. Scot H. REISINGER
42 Director Campus Ministry .... Mr. William MULCAHEY
39 Director of Residence Life .... Ms. Jenifer A. HANSON
44 Director of Major & Planned Gifts .... Ms. Hilery LIVENGOOD
88 Director of Faculty Development .... Dr. Edy PARSONS
38 Director of Counseling Services .... Ms. Tricia BORELLI
13 Interim Director Info Technology .... Ms. Connie SNITKER
19 Director of Public Safety .... Mr. Raymond J. KESSENICH
24 Academic Technology Librarian .... Ms. Vicky MALOY
32 Director of Student Activities .... Ms. Sarah L. BOTKIN
15 Director Human Resources .... Ms. Vicky SMITH
18 Director Facilities/Physical Plant .... Mr. Dave D. DENNIS
92 Director Honors Program .... Dr. Joy E. OCHS
40 Bookstore Manager .... Ms. Janie A. MILLS
04 Exec Assistant to President .... Mrs. Dianne M. AUSTAD
09 Exec Dir of Institutional Research .... Ms. Lori HEYING

North Iowa Area Community College (F)

500 College Drive, Mason City IA 50401-7299

County: Cerro Gordo FICE Identification: 001877

Unit ID: 154059

Telephone: (641) 423-1264 Carnegie Class: Assoc/Pub-R-M

FAX Number: (641) 423-1711 Calendar System: Semester

URL: www.niacc.edu

Established: 1917 Annual Undergrad Tuition & Fees (In-District): $4,404

Enrollment: 3,744 Coed

Affiliation or Control: State/Local IRS Status: 501(c)3

Highest Offering: Associate Degree

Program: Occupational; 2-Year Principally Bachelor's Creditable

Accreditation: NH, ADNUR, MAC, PTAA

01 President .... Dr. Debra A. DERR
05 Vice Pres Academic/Student Affairs .... Vacant
10 Vice Pres Administrative Services .... Mrs. Kathy M. GROVE
32 Dean of Student Development .... Dr. Terri L. EWERS
06 Registrar .... Mrs. Michelle L. PETZNICK
07 Director of Admissions .... Mrs. Rachel L. MCGUIRE
55 Evening Dean .... Mr. William W. BACKLIN
51 Dean of Cont Ed & Economic Dev .... Mr. Terry W. SCHUMAKER
30 VP of Inst Advancement & JPEC .... Mr. Jamie T. ZANIOS
37 Director of Financial Aid .... Mrs. Mary E. BLOOMINGDALE
09 VP Inst Effectiveness & Organiz Dev .... Ms. Shelly M. SCHMIT
20 Director Learning Support Division .... Mrs. Jessica J. PUTNAM
14 Director of Technology Services .... Mr. Mark D. GREENWOOD
103 Ex Dir of Iowa Workforce Dev Center .... Ms. Angela A. KONIG
40 Bookstore Manager .... Mrs. Rhonda K. NESHEIM-KAUFFMAN
41 Director of Athletics .... Mr. Dan J. MASON
18 Director of Facilities Management .... Mr. Tony A. PAPPAS
21 Accountant/Business Office Manager .... Ms. Mindy R. EASTMAN
24 Instructional Technology Coord .... Mr. Bruce G. MCKEE
39 Director Student Housing .... Mr. Travis J. HERGERT
08 Librarian .... Ms. Karen F. DOLE
88 Director of Food Service .... Mr. Ken P. WEBBER
31 Dir Marketing/Cmty Rels/Govt Affs .... Mrs. Michele R. APPELGATE
88 Dir Incubation & Acceleration Svcs .... Mr. Mark C. OLCHEFSKE
88 Director of School Partnerships .... Mrs. Jean M. OSTRANDER
88 Director of Operations .... Mrs. Constance J. GLANDON
88 Director of Programming & Sales .... Mrs. Jody L. EAST

Northeast Iowa Community College (G)

Box 400, Calmar IA 52132-0400

County: Winneshiek FICE Identification: 004587

Unit ID: 154110

Telephone: (563) 562-3263 Carnegie Class: Assoc/Pub-R-M
FAX Number: (563) 562-3719 Calendar System: Semester
URL: www.nicc.edu
Established: 1966 Annual Undergrad Tuition & Fees (In-District): $5,056
Enrollment: 5,147 Coed
Affiliation or Control: Local IRS Status: 501(c)3
Highest Offering: Associate Degree
Program: Occupational; 2-Year Principally Bachelor's Creditable
Accreditation: NH, DA, RAD

01 Interim President .... Dr. Liang C. WEE
10 Vice Pres Finance & Administration .... Mr. John D. NOEL
05 Chief Acad Ofcr/VP Academic Affairs .... Mr. Curt E. OLDFIELD
46 Vice Pres Econ Development/ Services .... Dr. Wendy A. MIHM-HEROLD
12 Peosta Provost .... Ms. Amy H. ESTERHUIZEN
12 Calmar Provost .... Dr. Liang C. WEE
32 Dean Student Services .... Dr. Linda M. PETERSON
51 Exec Dir Town Clock/Dubuque Centers .... Ms. Wendy S. KNIGHT
51 Director Continuing Education .... Ms. Julie A. WURTZEL
21 Director Accounting Services .... Mr. Thomas M. RIDOUT
26 Director of External Relations .... Ms. Tracy L. KRUSE
15 Director Human Resources .... Dr. Julie G. HUISKAMP
106 Director Distance Learning .... Dr. Christopher M. OSTWINKLE
13 Director Computer Information Sys .... Mr. Leonard B. FIELDS
09 Director of Institutional Research .... Ms. Dolores M. MILLER
88 Director Economic Devel/Peosta .... Mr. Gregory A. WILLGING
37 Director of Financial Aid .... Mr. Jeff J. MURPHY
102 Associate Director NICC Foundation .... Ms. Barbara J. O'HEA
06 Registrar .... Ms. Karla R. WINTER
06 Registrar .... Ms. Sheila R. BECKER
07 Admissions Representative .... Ms. Brynn A. MCCONNELL
07 Admissions Representative .... Ms. Tierney M. HEIN
36 Employment & Career Svcs Manager .... Mr. Chris E. ENTRINGER

Northwest Iowa Community College (A)

603 W Park Street, Sheldon IA 51201-1046
County: Sioux FICE Identification: 004600
Unit ID: 154129
Telephone: (712) 324-5061 Carnegie Class: Assoc/Pub-R-S
FAX Number: (712) 324-4136 Calendar System: Semester
URL: www.nwicc.edu
Established: 1966 Annual Undergrad Tuition & Fees (In-District): $3,840
Enrollment: 1,654 Coed
Affiliation or Control: State/Local IRS Status: 501(c)3
Highest Offering: Associate Degree
Program: Occupational; 2-Year Principally Bachelor's Creditable; Technical Emphasis
Accreditation: NH

01 President .... Dr. Alethea F. STUBBE
05 VP Education & Learning Services .... Vacant
30 VP Inst Adv & Enrollment Services .... Dr. Jan E. SNYDER
10 VP Operations & Finance .... Mr. Mark BROWN
49 Dean Arts & Sci/Business/Health .... Dr. Rhonda R. PENNINGS
72 Dean Applied Technology .... Mr. Robert LEIFELD
53 Dean Extended Learning Services .... Ms. Gretchen G. BARTELSON
21 Director of Business Services .... Mr. Dan REEVES
37 Financial Aid Director .... Ms. Karna HOFMEYER
84 Director Enrollment Management .... Ms. Lisa L. STORY
08 Director of Library Services .... Ms. Molly D. GALM
13 Director of Technology & Info Svcs .... Mr. Mike OLDENKAMP
88 Director of TRIO .... Ms. Laurie L. EDWARDS
51 Exec Dir of Econ Dev & Cont Ed Trng .... Mr. Frank DE MILIA
06 Registrar .... Ms. Beth SIBENALLER-WOODALL
15 Director of Human Resources .... Ms. Sandy BRUNS
88 Director of Alt HS/Learning Center .... Ms. Susan SCHMIDT
26 Director Community Relations .... Ms. Kristin E. KOLLBAUM
18 Director Physical Facilities .... Mr. Doug RODGER

Northwestern College (B)

101 Seventh Street, SW, Orange City IA 51041-1996
County: Sioux FICE Identification: 001883
Unit ID: 154101
Telephone: (712) 707-7000 Carnegie Class: Bac/Diverse
FAX Number: (712) 707-7247 Calendar System: Semester
URL: www.nwciowa.edu
Established: 1882 Annual Undergrad Tuition & Fees: $24,480
Enrollment: 1,208 Coed
Affiliation or Control: Reformed Church In America IRS Status: 501(c)3
Highest Offering: Baccalaureate
Program: Liberal Arts And General; Teacher Preparatory; Professional
Accreditation: NH, IACBE, NURSE, SW, TED

01 President .... Mr. Gregory E. CHRISTY
05 Provost .... Dr. Jasper LESAGE
20 Dean of Faculty .... Dr. Adrienne M. FORGETTE
32 Dean of Students .... Dr. John J. BROGAN
10 Vice President Financial Affairs .... Mr. Doug D. BEUKELMAN
30 Vice President Advancement .... Mr. Jay WIELENGA
84 Dean of Enrollment Management .... Mr. Kenton PAULS
88 Assoc Dean of Spiritual Formation .... Ms. Barb DEWALD
104 Associate Dean for Global Education .... Dr. Douglas W. CARLSON
42 Chaplain .... Rev. Harlan VAN OORT
41 Director of Athletics .... Mr. Barry M. BRANDT
08 Director of the Library .... Mr. Tim SCHLAK
06 Registrar .... Ms. Sandy VAN KLEY
37 Director of Financial Aid .... Mr. Eric ANDERSON
14 Director of Computing Services .... Mr. Harlan R. JORGENSEN
26 Director of Public Relations .... Mr. Duane L. BEESON
36 Director of Career Development .... Mr. William C. MINNICK
38 Dir Student Counseling Services .... Dr. Sally EDMAN
18 Director of Maintenance/Operations .... Mr. Scott K. SIMMELINK
29 Director Alumni Relations .... Mr. Mark R. BLOEMENDAAL
15 Director of Human Resources .... Mrs. Deb SANDBULTE
09 Director of Institutional Research .... Vacant

Palmer College of Chiropractic (C)

1000 Brady Street, Davenport IA 52803-5287
County: Scott FICE Identification: 012300
Unit ID: 154174
Telephone: (563) 884-5000 Carnegie Class: Spec/Health
FAX Number: (563) 884-5409 Calendar System: Trimester
URL: www.palmer.edu
Established: 1897 Annual Undergrad Tuition & Fees: $29,925
Enrollment: 1,178 Coed
Affiliation or Control: Independent Non-Profit IRS Status: 501(c)3
Highest Offering: First Professional Degree
Program: Professional
Accreditation: NH, CHIRO

00 Chancellor .... Dr. Dennis M. MARCHIORI
01 Campus Provost .... Dr. Daniel J. WEINERT
05 Vice Chancellor for Academics .... Dr. Robert E. PERCUOCO
32 Vice Chancellor Student Success .... Dr. Kevin A. CUNNINGHAM
11 Vice Chancellor Support Services .... Mr. Robert E. LEE
84 Vice Chancellor for Enrollment .... Mr. J. Michael NOVAK
10 Vice Chancellor for Administration .... Mr. Thomas L. TIEMEIER
17 Vice Chancellor for Clinic Affairs .... Dr. Kurt W. WOOD
46 Vice Chancellor for Research .... Dr. Christine GOERTZ
26 Exec Dir for Marketing & PR .... Mr. Darren R. GARRETT
29 Executive Director for Alumni .... Dr. Mickey G. BURT
88 Exec Dir Office of Strategic Dev .... Dr. Judy M. SILVESTRONE
20 Dean of Academic Programs .... Vacant
88 Director of Undergrad Studies .... Ms. Cathy EBERHART
06 Senior Director/Registrar .... Ms. Mindy S. LEAHY
09 Sr Dir Institutional Plng/Research .... Dr. Dustin C. DERBY
21 Senior Dir for Financial Affairs .... Ms. Alexis A. VANDER HORN
13 Senior Director of IT .... Mr. Mike A. BENEDICT
15 Senior Director of Human Resources .... Ms. Michelle K. WALKER
18 Senior Director of Facilities .... Mr. Stanley E. CARLSON
07 Senior Director of Admissions .... Ms. Karen S. EDEN
37 Senior Dir of Financial Planning .... Ms. Jennifer L. RANDAZZO
88 Senior Director for Assessment .... Vacant
24 Sr Dir/Center for Teaching/Lrng .... Dr. Dana J. LAWRENCE
51 Senior Dir of Continuing Education .... Vacant
38 Senior Dir of Counseling Services .... Dr. Lori L. NEWMAN
08 Senior Director of Library .... Mr. Dennis R. PETERSON
40 Senior Director of Bookstores .... Ms. Carol A. HOYT
88 Sr Dir Quality Assurance/Sys Organ .... Ms. Earlye A. JULIEN
35 Dir of Student Academic Affairs .... Dr. Kevin W. PAUSTIAN
96 Purchasing Manager .... Ms. Cheryl L. KOFRON

St. Ambrose University (D)

518 W Locust Street, Davenport IA 52803-2898
County: Scott FICE Identification: 001889
Unit ID: 154235
Telephone: (563) 333-6000 Carnegie Class: Master's L
FAX Number: (563) 333-6243 Calendar System: Semester
URL: www.sau.edu
Established: 1882 Annual Undergrad Tuition & Fees: $24,920
Enrollment: 3,663 Coed
Affiliation or Control: Roman Catholic IRS Status: 501(c)3
Highest Offering: Doctorate
Program: Liberal Arts And General; Fine Arts Emphasis
Accreditation: NH, ACBSP, ENG, NURSE, OT, PTA, @SP, SW, TEAC

01 President .... Sr. Joan LESCINSKI, CSJ
05 Vice President for Academic Affairs .... Dr. Paul KOCH
10 Vice President Finance .... Mr. Michael C. POSTER
42 Chaplain .... Rev. Charles A. ADAM
30 Vice President Advancement .... Ms. Jeanne K. KOBUSZEWSKI
84 Vice Pres Enrollment Management .... Mr. John D. COOPER
88 Assoc Vice Pres for Advancement .... Mr. Edward J. FINN
46 Assoc Vice Pres Assess/ Research .... Dr. Tracy SCHUSTER-MATLOCK
21 Assistant Vice President Finance .... Ms. Carol A. GLINES
26 Asst Vice Pres Communications/Mktg .... Ms. Linda R. HIRSCH
32 Asst VP Student Svcs/Dean of Stdnts .... Mr. Timothy PHILLIPS
15 Director Human Resources .... Ms. Audrey D. HEIN
07 Director Admissions .... Ms. Meg F. HALLIGAN
14 Exec Dir of Information Resources .... Ms. Mary B. HEINZMAN
29 Director Alumni & Parent Rels .... Ms. Clare A. THOMPSON
37 Director Financial Aid .... Ms. Julie A. HAACK
38 Director Counseling .... Mr. Stephen TENDALL
18 Director Physical Plant .... Mr. Jim M. HANNON
06 Registrar .... Mr. Dan L. ZEIMET
23 Director of Health Services .... Ms. Nancy A. HINES
19 Director of Security .... Mr. Robert CHRISTOPHER
39 Director of Resident Life .... Mr. Matt B. HANSEN
08 Director Library .... Ms. Mary B. HEINZMAN
36 Director Career Development .... Ms. Angela P. ELLIOTT
44 Dir Planned Giving/Dir Annual Fund .... Ms. Sally E. CRINO
41 Athletic Director .... Mr. Raymond J. SHOVLAIN
94 Director of Women's Studies .... Dr. Beatrice F. JACOBSON
40 Manager of Bookstore .... Ms. Linda K. MACUMBER
85 Asst VP International Education .... Dr. Ryan D. DYE
88 Chair Masters Pastoral Studies .... Rev. Bud GRANT
88 Chair Masters Criminal Justice .... Mr. Waylyn C. MCCULLOH
49 Dean College Arts & Sciences .... Dr. Aron R. AJI
50 Dean College Business .... Dr. David J. O'CONNELL
71 Dean Education and Health Sciences .... Dr. Sandra L. CASSADY
88 Dean for Academic Adult Programming .... Dr. Regina M. MATHESON
54 Dir Ambrose Industrial Engineering .... Dr. Michael E. OPAR
57 Director Fine Arts .... Mr. Lance A. SADLEK
88 Director Occupational Therapy .... Ms. Phyllis J. WENTHE
88 Director Masters of Accounting .... Mr. Lew D. MARX
58 Director Academic Svcs MBA Pgm .... Ms. Allison S. AMBROSE
58 Director Graduate Student Recruit .... Ms. Elizabeth B. LOVELESS
28 Director of Diversity .... Dr. Paul C. KOCH

St. Luke's College (E)

2720 Stone Park Boulevard, Sioux City IA 51104-0010
County: Woodbury FICE Identification: 007291
Unit ID: 154262
Telephone: (712) 279-3149 Carnegie Class: Assoc/PrivNFP
FAX Number: (712) 233-8017 Calendar System: Semester
URL: www.stlukescollege.edu
Established: 1995 Annual Undergrad Tuition & Fees: $16,280
Enrollment: 197 Coed
Affiliation or Control: Independent Non-Profit IRS Status: 501(c)3
Highest Offering: Associate Degree
Program: Occupational; 2-Year Principally Bachelor's Creditable; Nursing Emphasis
Accreditation: NH, ADNUR, MT, RAD

01 Chancellor .... Mr. Michael D. STILES
05 Exec Dean/Chief Academic Officer .... Dr. Richard S. AYI
32 Dept Chair Student Services .... Ms. Danelle D. JOHANNSEN

Simpson College (F)

701 North C Street, Indianola IA 50125-1297
County: Warren FICE Identification: 001887
Unit ID: 154350
Telephone: (515) 961-6251 Carnegie Class: Bac/A&S
FAX Number: (515) 961-1498 Calendar System: Other
URL: www.simpson.edu
Established: 1860 Annual Undergrad Tuition & Fees: $27,568
Enrollment: 1,807 Coed
Affiliation or Control: United Methodist IRS Status: 501(c)3
Highest Offering: Master's
Program: Liberal Arts And General; Teacher Preparatory; Business Emphasis
Accreditation: NH, MUS

01 President .... Dr. John W. BYRD
05 Vice Pres/Dean Academic Affairs .... Dr. Steven J. GRIFFITH
10 Vice President Business/Finance .... Mr. Kenneth I. BIRKENHOLTZ
30 Vice President College Advancement .... Mr. Robert J. LANE
32 Vice President Student Development .... Mr. James D. THORIUS
84 Vice President Enrollment .... Ms. Deborah J. TIERNEY
91 VP Info Svcs/Chief Info Officer .... Ms. Kelley L. BRADDER
26 Executive Director College Rels .... Vacant
37 Asst VP Enrollment/Financial Aid .... Ms. Tracie PAVON
06 Registrar & Associate Dean .... Ms. Jody RAGAN
08 Director of Library .... Ms. Cynthia M. DYER
27 Director of Information Services .... Mr. Allan APPENZELLER
44 Director of Annual Giving .... Ms. Sherry FULLER
15 Director of Human Resources .... Ms. Mary E. BARTLEY
36 Director of Career Services .... Ms. Jennifer DEL PINO
07 Director of Admissions .... Ms. Alison SWANSON
41 Athletic Director .... Mr. John F. SIRIANNI
96 Director of Procurement .... Ms. Marilyn J. LEEK
35 Assistant Dean of Students .... Mr. Richard O. RAMOS
42 Chaplain .... Vacant
39 Director of Residence Life .... Vacant
18 Director Campus Services .... Mr. Jeff WAGNER
21 Controller .... Ms. Heather TRAVIS
19 Coordinator of Campus Security .... Mr. Chris FRERICHS
51 Associate Dean Adult Learning .... Dr. Rosemary J. LINK
28 International Educ Coordinator .... Mr. Jay WILKINSON

Southeastern Community College (G)

1500 W Agency Road, PO Box 180,
West Burlington IA 52655-0180
County: Des Moines FICE Identification: 001848
Unit ID: 154378
Telephone: (319) 752-2731 Carnegie Class: Assoc/Pub-R-M
FAX Number: (319) 752-4957 Calendar System: Semester
URL: www.scciowa.edu
Established: 1966 Annual Undergrad Tuition & Fees (In-District): $4,050
Enrollment: 3,601 Coed
Affiliation or Control: State/Local IRS Status: 501(c)3
Highest Offering: Associate Degree
Program: Occupational; 2-Year Principally Bachelor's Creditable
Accreditation: NH, MAC

01 President .... Dr. Beverly SIMONE
05 Vice Pres of Teaching & Learning .... Mr. Phil THOMAS
32 Vice President of Student Services .... Ms. Joan WILLIAMS
11 Vice Pres Admin Services/Human Res .... Mr. Bill MECK
20 Dean of Academic & Extended Svcs .... Vacant
30 Exec Director for Inst Advancement .... Ms. Rebecca RUMP
37 Financial Aid Officer .... Mr. Ean FREELS
84 Enrollment Coordinator .... Ms. Dana CHRISMAN

06 Registrar .... Mr. Tim GRAY
15 Director Human Resources .... Ms. Michelle FOSTER
49 Dean Humanities/Social Sciences .... Dr. Tim AHERN
12 Dean of Assessment & Keokuk Campus .... Dr. Ben DESPAIN
75 Dean Vocational-Technical Education .... Ms. Laura MENKE

Southwestern Community College (A)

1501 W Townline Street, Creston IA 50801-1098
County: Union FICE Identification: 001857
Unit ID: 154396
Telephone: (641) 782-7081 Carnegie Class: Assoc/Pub-R-S
FAX Number: (641) 782-3312 Calendar System: Semester
URL: www.swcciowa.edu
Established: 1966 Annual Undergrad Tuition & Fees (In-State): $4,230
Enrollment: 1,772 Coed
Affiliation or Control: State IRS Status: 501(c)3
Highest Offering: Associate Degree
Program: Occupational; 2-Year Principally Bachelor's Creditable
Accreditation: NH

01 Superintendent/President .... Dr. Barbara J. CRITTENDEN
10 Chief Financial Officer .... Mrs. Teresa KREJCI
05 Vice President Instruction .... Mr. Bill TAYLOR
88 Vice President Economic Development .... Mr. Thomas L. LESAN
32 Dean of Student Services .... Dr. Matt THOMPSON
20 Assoc Vice Pres of Instruction .... Mrs. Jane BRADLEY
30 Director Institutional Advancement .... Dr. Matt THOMPSON
26 Dir Marketing/Enrollment Management .... Mrs. Terri HIGGINS
08 Head Librarian .... Mrs. Ann COULTER
37 Director Financial Aid .... Mrs. Tracy DAVIS
15 Director of Human Resources .... Mrs. Jolene GRIFFITH

University of Dubuque (B)

2000 University Avenue, Dubuque IA 52001-5099
County: Dubuque FICE Identification: 001891
Unit ID: 153278
Telephone: (563) 589-3000 Carnegie Class: Master's S
FAX Number: (563) 589-3682 Calendar System: 4/1/4
URL: www.dbq.edu
Established: 1852 Annual Undergrad Tuition & Fees: $22,690
Enrollment: 1,974 Coed
Affiliation or Control: Presbyterian Church (U.S.A.) IRS Status: 501(c)3
Highest Offering: Doctorate
Program: Liberal Arts And General; Teacher Preparatory; Professional
Accreditation: NH, AAB, NURSE, THEOL

01 President .... Dr. Jeffrey F. BULLOCK
04 Exec Assistant to the President .... Mrs. Deborah L. BUOL
05 Vice President/Dean of the College .... Dr. Mark WARD
10 Vice President Finance & Treasurer .... Mr. James D. STEINER
84 Co-Vice Pres Enrollment/Univ Rels .... Mr. Peter L. SMITH
84 Co-Vice Pres Enrollment/Univ Rels .... Ms. Susan M. SMITH
20 Vice Pres/Dean of Seminary .... Dr. Bradley J. LONGFIELD
30 Vice President for Development .... Dr. Donald L. SALMON
32 Dean of Student Life .... Dr. Michael H. MIYAMOTO
13 Network Administrator .... Ms. Sherry CUSICK
07 Dean of Admission .... Mr. Jesse L. JAMES
06 Registrar .... Dr. Paul JOHNSON
08 Director of Libraries .... Ms. Mary Anne KNEFEL
16 Director of Human Resources .... Ms. Julie MACTAGGART
37 Dean of Student Financial Planning .... Mr. Timothy KREMER
09 Dir Institutional Research .... Ms. Janet SHEPHERD
36 Director of Career Services .... Dr. Amy BAUS
29 Director Alumni Relations .... Mr. David MOORE
40 Director Bookstore .... Ms. Margo KETELS
41 Athletic Director .... Mr. Dan RUNKLE
18 Director of Facilities .... Mr. Craig KLOFT
04 Special Assistant to the President .... Dr. John R. STEWART

Upper Iowa University (C)

605 Washington, Box 1857, Fayette IA 52142-1857
County: Fayette FICE Identification: 001893
Unit ID: 154493
Telephone: (563) 425-5200 Carnegie Class: Master's M
FAX Number: (563) 425-5271 Calendar System: Semester
URL: www.uiu.edu
Established: 1857 Annual Undergrad Tuition & Fees: $22,356
Enrollment: 6,802 Coed
Affiliation or Control: Independent Non-Profit IRS Status: 501(c)3
Highest Offering: Master's
Program: Liberal Arts And General; Teacher Preparatory
Accreditation: NH, NURSE

01 President .... Dr. Alan G. WALKER
05 Chief Academic Officer .... Dr. David CHOWN
10 Exec Vice President & CFO .... Mr. Donald AUNGST
20 Sr VP for Academic Extension .... Dr. William DUFFY
82 Sr VP International Programs .... Mr. Chris SANDERS
26 Sr VP/Chief Marketing Officer .... Mr. Melik KHOURY
07 VP of Admissions .... Ms. Jobyna JOHNSTON
30 VP for Development .... Mr. Wendell SNODGRASS
09 Dir of Instutional Effectiveness .... Ms. Janet SHEPHERD
32 Dean of Student Development .... Ms. Louise SCOTT
36 Assoc Dean Stdnts/Dir Res Life .... Ms. Jean MERKLE
12 Director South Central Region .... Mr. Wayne CONVERSE
12 Director North Central Region .... Mr. Fritz OPPENLANDER
06 Registrar .... Mrs. Holly STREETER
08 Director Library Services .... Mrs. Becky WADIAN
41 Athletic Director .... Mr. David MILLER
04 President's Assistant .... Dr. Adriel HILTON
56 Exec Dir Ctr for Distance Educ .... Dr. Peggy CHOWN
105 Director Internet Development .... Mr. Joel KUNZE
21 Associate Business Ofcr/Controller .... Ms. Laura MATT
36 Director of Career Development .... Vacant
35 Dir Student Leadership & Activities .... Mr. Daryl GROVE
26 Exec Dir of Comm & Marketing .... Ms. Monica HEATON
86 Director External Affairs .... Mr. Andrew WENTHE
13 Director Information Technology .... Mr. Terry SMID
15 Director Payroll & Benefits .... Ms. Tammy CAROLAN
88 Director Sports Info Services .... Mr. Howard THOMPSON
18 Chief Facilities/Physical Plant .... Mr. Bryan JOLLEY
40 Bookstore Manager .... Mr. Brett DEVORE

Vatterott College-Des Moines (D)

7000 Fleur Drive, Des Moines IA 50321-2414
County: Polk FICE Identification: 026092
Unit ID: 373058
Telephone: (515) 309-9000 Carnegie Class: Assoc/PrivFP
FAX Number: (515) 309-0366 Calendar System: Other
URL: www.vatterott-college.edu
Established: 1997 Annual Undergrad Tuition & Fees: $11,306
Enrollment: 565 Coed
Affiliation or Control: Proprietary IRS Status: Proprietary
Highest Offering: Associate Degree
Program: Occupational
Accreditation: ACCSC, DA, MAAB

01 CEO & President .... Ms. Pam BELL
10 Chief Financial Officer .... Mr. Dennis BEAVERS
05 Chief Academic Officer .... Dr. John TUCKER
11 Chief Administrative Officer .... Mr. Erio COMICI
12 Campus Director .... Mr. Dan NIELAND

Waldorf College (E)

106 S 6th Street, Forest City IA 50436-1713
County: Winnebago FICE Identification: 001895
Unit ID: 154518
Telephone: (641) 585-2450 Carnegie Class: Bac/Diverse
FAX Number: (641) 585-8194 Calendar System: Semester
URL: www.waldorf.edu
Established: 1903 Annual Undergrad Tuition & Fees: $18,876
Enrollment: 613 Coed
Affiliation or Control: Proprietary IRS Status: Proprietary
Highest Offering: Baccalaureate
Program: Liberal Arts And General
Accreditation: NH

01 President .... Dr. Joe MANJONE
05 Dean of Col/Vice Pres Acad Affs .... Dr. Robert ALSOP
30 Vice President Advancement .... Vacant
10 Vice President Business Affairs .... Mr. Mason HARMS
84 Vice President Admissions/Marketing .... Vacant
04 Assistant to the President .... Ms. Cindy CARTER
32 Dean of Students .... Mr. Jason RAMAKER
92 Dean of Honors Program .... Dr. Suzanne FALCK-YI
20 Associate Academic Dean .... Dr. Scott SEARCY
08 Library Director .... Ms. Amy HILL
29 Director of Alumni Affairs .... Ms. Rita GILBERTSON
06 Registrar .... Mrs. Twylah KRAGEL
37 Director of Financial Aid .... Mr. Duane POLSDOFER
18 Director of Facilities Services .... Mr. Allan EGGEBRAATEN
27 Director of Media .... Vacant
26 Communications Director .... Ms. Barbara BARROWS
44 Director of Annual Fund .... Ms. Nancy OLSON
38 Counselor .... Mr. James AMELSBERG
41 Athletic Director .... Mr. Michael SCARANO
39 Director of Residential Life .... Mr. Momo WOLAPAYE
42 Chaplain .... Vacant
36 Director Student Placement .... Ms. Mary REISETTER
91 Director Administrative Computing .... Vacant
40 Bookstore Manager .... Ms. Karla SCHAEFER
15 Director Human Resources .... Ms. Dawn RAMAKER

Wartburg College (F)

PO Box 1003, 100 Wartburg Boulevard,
Waverly IA 50677-0903
County: Bremer FICE Identification: 001896
Unit ID: 154527
Telephone: (319) 352-8200 Carnegie Class: Bac/A&S
FAX Number: (319) 352-8514 Calendar System: Other
URL: www.wartburg.edu
Established: 1852 Annual Undergrad Tuition & Fees: $30,960
Enrollment: 1,775 Coed
Affiliation or Control: Evangelical Lutheran Church In America
IRS Status: 501(c)3
Highest Offering: Baccalaureate
Program: Liberal Arts And General; Teacher Preparatory
Accreditation: NH, MUS, SW, TED

01 President .... Dr. Darrel D. COLSON
05 Interim VP Acad Affs/Dean Faculty .... Dr. Fred D. RIBICH
32 VP Student Life/Dean Students .... Dr. Deborah L. LOERS
10 Vice President for Administration .... Mr. Gary S. GRACE
30 Vice Pres Institutional Advancement .... Mr. Scott C. LEISINGER
84 Vice Pres Enrollment Management .... Dr. Edith J. WALDSTEIN
07 Asst VP Admiss/Alumni/Parent Pgms .... Mr. Jay T. COLEMAN
06 Registrar .... Ms. Sheree S. COVERT
26 Assoc VP for Mktg and Comm .... Mr. Graham GARNER
91 Dir of Info Technology Svcs/CIO .... Mr. Gary L. WIPPERMAN
08 College Librarian .... Ms. Christine L. SCHAFER
29 Director of Alumni/Parent Relations .... Mr. Jeff BECK
37 Director of Financial Aid .... Ms. Jen L. SASSMAN
41 Director of Athletics .... Mr. Eric R. WILLIS
42 Dean of the Chapel .... Rev. Ramona S. BOUZARD
18 Director of Physical Plant .... Mr. John A. WUERTZ
39 Asst Dean/Dir of Residential Life .... Mr. Wesley H. BROOKS
36 Assoc Dir of Pathways/Career Svcs .... Mr. Derek N. SOLHEIM
38 Director of Counseling Svcs .... Mrs. Stephanie R. NEWSOM
40 Bookstore Manager .... Mrs. Arlene K. SCHWARZENBACH
44 Director of Annual Fund .... Ms. Kendra S. MERFELD
85 Director of International Programs .... Mr. Kevin N. ROISELAND
35 Director of Campus Programming .... Ms. Sarah K. GLASCOCK
88 Campus Pastor .... Rev. Brian A. BECKSTROM
23 Dir of Health & Wellness Promotion .... Ms. Dawn R. WIEGMANN
21 Chief Business Officer & Treasurer .... Mr. Richard W. SEGGERMAN
15 Director of Human Resources .... Ms. Jane J. JUCHEMS
30 Director of Development .... Mr. Donald J. MEYER
09 Dir of Inst Research/Prof of Psych .... Dr. Fred D. RIBICH
92 Director Honors Program .... Dr. Mariah H. BIRGEN
04 Assistant to the President .... Ms. Janeen K. STEWART
20 Asst Dean for Academic Affairs .... Ms. Stephanie S. TEKIPPE

Wartburg Theological Seminary (G)

333 Wartburg Place, PO Box 5004,
Dubuque IA 52004-5004
County: Dubuque FICE Identification: 001897
Unit ID: 154536
Telephone: (563) 589-0200 Carnegie Class: Spec/Faith
FAX Number: (563) 589-0333 Calendar System: 4/1/4
URL: www.wartburgseminary.edu
Established: 1854 Annual Graduate Tuition & Fees: $13,800
Enrollment: 152 Coed
Affiliation or Control: Evangelical Lutheran Church In America
IRS Status: 501(c)3
Highest Offering: Master's; No Undergraduates
Program: Professional
Accreditation: NH, THEOL

01 President .... Dr. Stanley N. OLSON
05 Academic Dean of the Seminary .... Dr. Craig L. NESSAN
10 Vice Pres for Finance & Operations .... Mr. Andy B. WILLENBORG
30 Vice President for Mission Support .... Rev. Len HOFFMANN
15 Assistant to President & Dir of HR .... Ms. Eileen LEMAY
88 Dean for Vocation .... Rev. Amy L. CURRENT
08 Library Director .... Ms. Susan J S. EBERTZ
06 Registrar/Admin Assistant to Dean .... Dr. Kevin L. ANDERSON
13 Director of Information Technology .... Ms. Lori L. BRUFLODT

Western Iowa Tech Community College (H)

PO Box 5199, Sioux City IA 51102-5199
County: Woodbury FICE Identification: 007316
Unit ID: 154572
Telephone: (712) 274-6400 Carnegie Class: Assoc/Pub-R-L
FAX Number: (712) 274-6412 Calendar System: Semester
URL: www.witcc.edu
Established: 1966 Annual Undergrad Tuition & Fees (In-District): $4,185
Enrollment: 6,421 Coed
Affiliation or Control: State/Local IRS Status: 501(c)3
Highest Offering: Associate Degree
Program: Occupational; 2-Year Principally Bachelor's Creditable
Accreditation: NH, DA, EMT, MAC, PNUR, PTAA, SURGT

01 President .... Dr. Terry MURRELL
03 Executive Vice President .... Vacant
10 VP Finance/Administrative Svcs/CFO .... Mr. Troy JASMAN
31 Dean of Corporate College .... Mr. Martin REIMER
15 Exec Director of Human Resources .... Ms. Brenda BRADLEY
13 Dean of Information Technology .... Mr. Mike LOGAN
30 Exec Director College Development .... Ms. Carolyn ELLWANGER
32 Dean of Students .... Dr. Juline ALBERT
05 Dean of Instruction/Chief Acad Ofcr .... Dr. Mary MOHNI
31 Dean External Rels/Dir Job Trng Prt .... Dr. Julene STOIK
84 Dean of Enrollment Services .... Ms. Janet GILL
88 Director of Economic Development .... Ms. Angela LAWSON
08 Library Services Manager .... Ms. Sharon DYKSHOORN
88 KWIT/KOJI-FM General Manager .... Ms. Gretchen GONDEK
88 Director Small Business Devel Ctr .... Mr. Dan WUBBENA
18 Director Phys Plant/College Safety .... Mr. Kyle HUESER
09 Dir Instl Rsrch/Resource Dev Coord .... Mr. Larry OBERMEYER
07 Director of Recruitment .... Ms. Lora VANDER ZWAAG
06 Director of Records/Registration .... Vacant
26 Director Marketing/Publications .... Ms. Emma HEWITT
37 Director of Financial Aid .... Mr. Don DUZIK
29 Alumni Relations/Title III Director .... Vacant

William Penn University (I)

201 Trueblood Avenue, Oskaloosa IA 52577-1799
County: Mahaska FICE Identification: 001900
Unit ID: 154590
Telephone: (641) 673-1001 Carnegie Class: Bac/Diverse
FAX Number: (641) 673-1396 Calendar System: Semester
URL: www.wmpenn.edu
Established: 1873 Annual Undergrad Tuition & Fees: $21,720
Enrollment: 1,993 Coed

Affiliation or Control: Friends IRS Status: 501(c)3
Highest Offering: Master's
Program: Liberal Arts And General; Teacher Preparatory
Accreditation: NH

01 President Dr. Ann FIELDS
30 Vice President for Advancement Ms. Sherry TAYLOR
05 Vice President for Academic Affairs Dr. Noel STAHLE
32 VP Student Services/Enrollment Mgmt Mr. John OTTOSSON
10 VP Financial Operations Ms. Bonnie JOHNSON
41 VP Athletics Mr. Greg HAFNER
44 Assoc VP for Advancement Ms. Marsha RIORDAN
07 Director of Admissions Ms. Kira STRONG
06 Registrar Dr. Michael EDWARDS
37 Director of Financial Aid Ms. Cyndi PEIFFER
36 Career Services Coordinator Ms. Debbie STEVENS
08 Head Librarian Ms. Julie HANSEN
27 Director of Print Media Ms. Amber LAKE
29 Director of Alumni Relations Ms. Jodi GREINER
31 Director of Community Relations Ms. Jill DURSKY
15 Human Resource Manager Ms. Louise BLAINE
35 Director of Student Activities Mr. Levi TARBELL
38 Director Student Counseling Mr. Frank SIMS
09 Director of Institutional Research Vacant
42 Director of Campus Ministries Mr. Spencer THURY
40 Bookstore Manager Ms. Heidi PARKER
18 Director of Buildings & Grounds Mr. Milt CAMPBELL
83 Chair Div of Social/Behavioral Sci Dr. Michael COLLINS
72 Chair Div of Applied Technology Dr. Jim DROST
53 Chair Division of Education Dr. Pamela MARTIN
50 Chair Div of Business Admin Dr. Lonny L. WILSON
79 Chair Division of Humanities Dr. Jared PEARCE
76 Chair Div of Health & Life Sciences Dr. James A. NORTH

KANSAS

Allen County Community College (A)

1801 N Cottonwood, Iola KS 66749-1698
County: Allen FICE Identification: 001901
Unit ID: 154642
Telephone: (620) 365-5116 Carnegie Class: Assoc/Pub-R-M
FAX Number: (620) 365-7406 Calendar System: Semester
URL: www.allencc.edu
Established: 1923 Annual Undergrad Tuition & Fees (In-District): $2,080
Enrollment: 2,897 Coed
Affiliation or Control: State/Local IRS Status: 501(c)3
Highest Offering: Associate Degree
Program: Occupational; 2-Year Principally Bachelor's Creditable
Accreditation: NH

01 President Mr. John A. MASTERSON
05 Vice Pres for Academic Affairs Mr. Jon MARSHALL
10 Vice Pres for Finance & Operations Mr. Steve TROXEL
32 VP Student Affairs/Athletic Dir Dr. Randy WEBER
12 Dean for the Iola Campus Mrs. Tosca HARRIS
12 Dean for the Burlingame Campus Mr. Bob REAVIS
106 Dean for Online Learning Mrs. Regena BAILEY-AYE
08 Director of Library Mr. Steven ANDERSON
13 Director of MIS Mr. Doug DUNLAP
38 Director of Guidance Services Dr. Valis MCLEAN
37 Director of Financial Aid/Registrar Mrs. Vicki CURRY
30 Director of Development Mrs. Cynthia ADAMS
18 Director of Physical Plant Opers Mr. Don BAUER
07 Director of Admissions Ms. Rebecca BILDERBACK
40 Director of Bookstore Mrs. Donna CASON
17 Allied Health Director Mrs. April HENRY
85 Foreign Student Advisor Mr. John STEEL
90 Director Academic Computing Ms. Anna CATTERSON
09 Director Inst Research/Assessment Vacant
06 Registrar Mrs. Bobbie HAVILAND
26 Public Relations Coordinator Mrs. Nancy FORD

The Art Institutes International - Kansas City (B)

8208 Melrose Drive, Lenexa KS 66214
County: Johnson Identification: 666765
Unit ID: 452018
Telephone: (913) 217-4600 Carnegie Class: Not Classified
FAX Number: (913) 217-2690 Calendar System: Semester
URL: www.artinstitutes.edu
Established: N/A Annual Undergrad Tuition & Fees: $17,668
Enrollment: 595 Coed
Affiliation or Control: Proprietary IRS Status: Proprietary
Highest Offering: Baccalaureate
Program: Occupational
Accreditation: ACICS

01 President Ms. Cyndie SHADOW

† Branch campus of The Art Institutes International Minnesota, Minneapolis, MN.

Baker University (C)

618 Eighth Street, Baldwin City KS 66006-0065
County: Douglas FICE Identification: 001903
Unit ID: 154688
Telephone: (785) 594-6451 Carnegie Class: Master's L
FAX Number: (785) 594-2522 Calendar System: 4/1/4
URL: www.bakeru.edu
Established: 1858 Annual Undergrad Tuition & Fees: $23,310
Enrollment: 3,868 Coed
Affiliation or Control: United Methodist IRS Status: 501(c)3
Highest Offering: Doctorate
Program: Liberal Arts And General; Teacher Preparatory; Professional
Accreditation: NH, ACBSP, MUS, NURSE, TED

01 President Dr. Patricia N. LONG
11 Chief Operating Officer Dr. Susan LINDAHL
06 Registrar Ms. Ruth MILLER
58 VP/Dean Sch Prof/Grad Studies Dr. Peggy HARRIS
05 VP/Dean College Arts & Science Dr. Rand ZIEGLER
30 Vice President Advancement Ms. Lyn LAKIN
84 VP for Enrollment Mgmt/Student Svcs Mr. Mark BANDRE
26 Director of Marketing & Comm Mr. Neil KULBISKI
44 VP for Endowment/Planned Giving Mr. Jerry WEAKLEY
66 VP/Dean of School of Nursing Dr. Kathleen HARR
42 Minister to the University Dr. Ira L. DESPAIN
32 Dean of Students Ms. Cassy BAILEY
13 Vice President for Info Technology Mr. Simon MAXWELL
53 VP/Dean School of Education Dr. Peggy HARRIS
09 Director of Institutional Research Dr. Jean JOHNSON
88 Asst Dean Stdnt Engage & Success Dr. Judith SMRHA
97 Interim Asst Dean Liberal Studies Dr. Erin JOYCE
35 Associate Dean of Students Ms. Teresa CLOUNCH
20 Asst Dean College Arts & Sciences Dr. Rob FLAHERTY
08 Director of Libraries Ms. Kay BRADT
07 Director of Enrollment Management Mr. Kevin KROPF
37 Director of Financial Aid Mrs. Jeanne MOTT
36 Director of Career Development Ms. Susan WADE
41 Athletic Director Ms. Theresa YETMAR
23 Director of Health Services Ms. Ruth SARNA
18 Interim Director of Physical Plant Mr. Jeremy PORTLOCK
21 University Controller Ms. Melissa VAN LEIDEN
29 Director of Alumni Relations Mr. Doug BARTH
38 Director Student Counseling Dr. Tim HODGES
28 Director Multicultural Affairs Mr. Silas DULAN
44 Senior Director for Advancement Mr. Patrick MIKESIC
26 Director of Public Relations Mr. Steve ROTTINGHAUS
15 Director of Human Resources Ms. Connie DEEL
88 Consultant to Pres Health Svc Exp Dr. Kathryn BALLOU

Barclay College (D)

607 N Kingman, Haviland KS 67059-0288
County: Kiowa FICE Identification: 001917
Unit ID: 155070
Telephone: (620) 862-5252 Carnegie Class: Spec/Faith
FAX Number: (620) 862-5242 Calendar System: Semester
URL: www.barclaycollege.edu
Established: 1917 Annual Undergrad Tuition & Fees: $13,790
Enrollment: 245 Coed
Affiliation or Control: Independent Non-Profit IRS Status: 501(c)3
Highest Offering: Baccalaureate
Program: Liberal Arts And General; Religious Emphasis
Accreditation: BI

01 President Dr. Royce FRAZIER
05 VP Academics Dr. Adrian HALVERSTADT
10 VP Business Services Mr. Lee ANDERS
32 VP Student Services Mr. Kevin LEE
30 VP Institutional Advancement Mr. Steve TETER
06 VP Registration and Records Dr. Glenn W. LEPPERT
37 Director Student Financial Aid Mr. Ryan HAASE
07 Admissions Counselor Mr. Justin KENDALL
08 Librarian Mr. Pat HALL
29 Alumni Relations Dr. Herb FRAZIER

Barton County Community College (E)

245 NE 30th Road, Great Bend KS 67530-9107
County: Barton FICE Identification: 004608
Unit ID: 154697
Telephone: (620) 792-2701 Carnegie Class: Assoc/Pub-R-L
FAX Number: (620) 792-5624 Calendar System: Semester
URL: www.bartonccc.edu
Established: 1965 Annual Undergrad Tuition & Fees (In-District): $2,330
Enrollment: 4,770 Coed
Affiliation or Control: State/Local IRS Status: 501(c)3
Highest Offering: Associate Degree
Program: Occupational; 2-Year Principally Bachelor's Creditable
Accreditation: NH, ADNUR, EMT, MLTAD

01 President Dr. Carl R. HEILMAN
05 VP of Instruction & Student Svcs Dr. Penny QUINN
11 Dean of Administration Mr. Mark E. DEAN
32 Dean of Student Services Mrs. Angela M. MADDY
27 Dean of Information Services Mr. Charles PERKINS
20 Dean of Academics Dr. Richard L. ABEL
88 Dean Ft Riley Lrng Svcs/Mil Ops Mr. Gene KINGSLIEN
103 Dean Workforce Training & Cmty Educ Mrs. Elaine R. SIMMONS
30 Exec Dir Institutional Advancement Mrs. Darnell S. HOLOPIREK
76 Dir Healthcare/Pub Safety Ed Mr. Leonard BUNSELMEYER
13 Chief Information Technology Ofcr Mr. Charles W. PERKINS
26 Director of Public Relations Mr. Michael F. DAWES
04 Assistant to President Ms. Amy J. SCHNEIDER
41 Athletic Director Mr. Craig N. FLETCHALL
08 Director of Learning Resources Mrs. Mary L. HESTER
15 Director of Human Resources Mrs. Julie A. KNOBLICH
07 Director of Admissions & Marketing Mr. Todd B. MOORE
37 Director of Financial Aid Mrs. Myrna L. PERKINS
19 Coordinator of Facility Management Mr. Jim D. IRELAND
25 Director of Grants Ms. Cathie R. OSHIRO
06 Registrar Mrs. Lori D. CROWTHER
40 Bookstore Manager Mrs. Connie M. KERNS
09 Coordinator of Institution Research Mrs. Caicey L. CRUTCHER
39 Coordinator of Student Housing Mr. Dan MCFADDEN

Benedictine College (F)

1020 N 2nd Street, Atchison KS 66002-1499
County: Atchison FICE Identification: 010256
Unit ID: 154712
Telephone: (913) 367-5340 Carnegie Class: Bac/Diverse
FAX Number: (913) 367-6566 Calendar System: Semester
URL: www.benedictine.edu
Established: 1858 Annual Undergrad Tuition & Fees: $21,475
Enrollment: 1,909 Coed
Affiliation or Control: Roman Catholic IRS Status: 501(c)3
Highest Offering: Master's
Program: Liberal Arts And General; Teacher Preparatory; Business Emphasis
Accreditation: NH, MUS, TED

01 President Mr. Stephen D. MINNIS
05 Dean of the College Dr. Kimberly C. SHANKMAN
10 Chief Financial Officer Mr. Ronald J. OLINGER
30 Vice President Advancement Ms. Kelly J. VOWELS
84 Dean of Enrollment Management Mr. Pete HELGESEN
32 Vice President of Student Life Mrs. Linda HENRY
32 Dean of Students Mr. Joseph WURTZ
42 Director for Mission and Ministry Fr. Brendan ROLLING, OSB
41 Athletic Director Mr. Charles GARTENMAYER
26 Vice President for College Rels Mr. Tom HOOPES
20 Assoc Dean & Registrar Sr. Linda HERNDON, OSB
09 Assistant Dean of the College Ms. Sheri BARRETT
58 Exec Dir of Grad Business Programs Mr. Dave GEENENS
58 Director of MASL/Assoc Prof Educ Dr. Dianna HENDERSON
37 Director of Student Financial Aid Mr. Tony TANKING
27 Dir of Marketing & Communications Mr. Steve JOHNSON
38 Director of Counseling Center Mr. Kerry A. MARVIN
23 Director of Student Health Services Ms. Janet ADRIAN
18 Director of Operations Mr. Matt FASSERO
14 Dir of Tech & Information Sys Mr. Randy ROWLAND
88 Director of International Program Mr. Daniele MUSSO
08 Librarian Mr. Steven GROMATZKY
35 Director of Residence Life Mr. Sean MULCAHY
21 Bursar Ms. Becky MILLER
35 Student Activities Director Mr. Matt LITT
36 Director of Career Services Ms. Becky GILMORE
29 Director of Planned Giving & Alumni Mr. Tim ANDREWS

Bethany College (G)

335 E Swensson Street, Lindsborg KS 67456-1895
County: McPherson FICE Identification: 001904
Unit ID: 154721
Telephone: (785) 227-3311 Carnegie Class: Bac/Diverse
FAX Number: (785) 227-2004 Calendar System: 4/1/4
URL: www.bethanylb.edu
Established: 1881 Annual Undergrad Tuition & Fees: $21,677
Enrollment: 610 Coed
Affiliation or Control: Evangelical Lutheran Church In America
IRS Status: 501(c)3
Highest Offering: Baccalaureate
Program: Liberal Arts And General; Teacher Preparatory; Professional
Accreditation: NH, MUS, TED

01 President Dr. Edward F. LEONARD, III
05 Provost and Dean of the College Dr. Eugene F. BALES
30 Vice President of Advancement Mr. Jim RUBLE
10 VP for Finance and Operations Mr. Bob SCHMOLL
21 Controller Ms. Kimberly DEAL
32 Dean for Student Life Ms. Freda STRACK
84 Dean Recruitment & Marketing Ms. Tricia HAWK
44 Assoc Vice Pres for Advancement Mrs. Jayne NORLIN
88 Assoc Vice Pres for Development Mr. Warren OLSON
44 Exec Dir of Alumni & Advancement Mr. Galen B. BUNNING
06 Registrar Ms. Jill MEGREDY
08 Director of Library Mrs. Denise K. CARSON
41 Athletic Director Mr. Jon M. DANIELS
37 Director Financial Aid Ms. Amber MANETH
18 Director Campus Facilities Mr. Randal JIRAK
13 Director of Computer Services Mr. Brian RICHTER
26 Director of Communications Ms. Stephanie MCDOWELL
29 Director Alumni Development Ms. Molly B. JOHNSON
36 Director Career Services Ms. Jessica L. SCHIERLING
39 Residential Education Coordinator Ms. Trace TAYLOR
42 Campus Pastor Rev. Naomi M. STRAND
35 Director Student Programs Ms. Roxie L. SJOGREN
88 Program Dir Athletic Training Dr. David SLACK
53 Program Director Teacher Education Mr. Gail KONZEM
64 Program Director Music Dr. Jared CHASE
15 Director of Human Resources Mrs. Jo Ann M. MATTISON
09 Director of Assessment and Research Ms. Joanne GUNSOLLEY
40 Bookstore Manager Mrs. Brenda C. SMITH
92 Honors Program Coordinator Dr. Kristin VAN TASSEL
38 Student Counselor Ms. Valoree BARRETT
85 International Student Advisor Mr. David OLSON

Bethel College (H)

300 E 27th Street, North Newton KS 67117-0531
County: Harvey FICE Identification: 001905
Unit ID: 154749
Telephone: (316) 283-2500 Carnegie Class: Bac/Diverse

FAX Number: (316) 284-5286 Calendar System: 4/1/4
URL: www.bethelks.edu
Established: 1887 Annual Undergrad Tuition & Fees: $21,700
Enrollment: 476 Coed
Affiliation or Control: Mennonite Church IRS Status: 501(c)3
Highest Offering: Baccalaureate
Program: Liberal Arts And General; Teacher Preparatory; Professional
Accreditation: NH, NURSE, SW, TED

01 President .... Dr. Perry D. WHITE
04 Assistant to the President .... Ms. Rosa BARRERA
05 Vice President Academic Affairs .... Dr. Brad BORN
32 Interim Vice President Student Life .... Mr. Weldon MARTENS
41 Athletic Director .... Mr. Kent ALLSHOUSE
30 Vice President Advancement .... Ms. Sondra KOONTZ
10 Vice Presiden for Business Affairs .... Mr. Allen WEDEL
26 VP for Marketing and Communications .... Ms. Lori LIVENGOOD
06 Registrar .... Dr. Rodney FREY
44 Director of Development .... Mr. Fred GOERING
07 Vice President for Admissions .... Mr. Todd H. MOORE
37 Director of Financial Aid .... Mr. Tony GRABER
29 Director of Alumni Relations .... Mr. David LINSCHEID
08 Head Librarian .... Ms. Gail STUCKY
42 Director of Church Relations .... Mr. Dale SCHRAG
18 Chief Facilities/Physical Plant .... Mr. Les GOERZEN

Brown Mackie College-Kansas City (A)

9705 Lenexa Drive, Lenexa KS 66215-1345
County: Johnson Identification: 666091
Unit ID: 154767
Telephone: (913) 768-1900 Carnegie Class: Assoc/PrivFP
FAX Number: (913) 495-9555 Calendar System: Other
URL: www.brownmackie.edu
Established: 1984 Annual Undergrad Tuition & Fees: $11,124
Enrollment: 513 Coed
Affiliation or Control: Proprietary IRS Status: Proprietary
Highest Offering: Associate Degree
Program: Occupational; 2-Year Principally Bachelor's Creditable; Business Emphasis
Accreditation: &NH, OTA

01 President .... Vacant
05 Dean of Academic Affairs .... Ms. Connie BEENE
07 Senior Director of Admissions .... Vacant
06 Registrar .... Ms. Mary Lou WHITTON
36 Director of Career Services .... Ms. Mickie HOLLIDAY

† Branch campus of Brown Mackie College, Salina, KS.

Brown Mackie College-Salina (B)

2106 S 9th Street, Salina KS 67401-7307
County: Saline FICE Identification: 006755
Unit ID: 154776
Telephone: (785) 825-5422 Carnegie Class: Assoc/PrivFP
FAX Number: (785) 827-7623 Calendar System: Other
URL: www.brownmackie.edu
Established: 1892 Annual Undergrad Tuition & Fees: $11,124
Enrollment: 450 Coed
Affiliation or Control: Proprietary IRS Status: Proprietary
Highest Offering: Associate Degree
Program: Occupational; 2-Year Principally Bachelor's Creditable; Business Emphasis
Accreditation: NH, OTA

01 President .... Ms. Judy HOLMES
05 Dean of Academic Affairs .... Mr. Dennis RITTLE
07 Senior Director of Admissions .... Ms. Diann HEATH
06 Registrar .... Ms. Lisa GRAVES
36 Director of Career Services .... Ms. Garnett ZAMBONI

Bryan College (C)

1527 SW Fairlawn Road, Topeka KS 66604
County: Shawnee FICE Identification: 030662
Unit ID: 154794
Telephone: (785) 272-0889 Carnegie Class: Not Classified
FAX Number: (785) 272-4538 Calendar System: Other
URL: www.bryancolleges.edu
Established: N/A Annual Undergrad Tuition & Fees: N/A
Enrollment: 164 Coed
Affiliation or Control: Proprietary IRS Status: Proprietary
Highest Offering: Associate Degree
Program: Occupational
Accreditation: ACICS

01 Executive Director .... Mr. Wayne MAJOR

Butler Community College (D)

901 S. Haverhill Road, El Dorado KS 67042-3225
County: Butler FICE Identification: 001906
Unit ID: 154800
Telephone: (316) 321-2222 Carnegie Class: Assoc/Pub-S-MC
FAX Number: (316) 322-3109 Calendar System: Semester
URL: www.butlercc.edu
Established: 1927 Annual Undergrad Tuition & Fees (In-District): $1,776
Enrollment: 10,116 Coed
Affiliation or Control: Local IRS Status: 501(c)3
Highest Offering: Associate Degree
Program: Occupational; 2-Year Principally Bachelor's Creditable; Liberal Arts And General
Accreditation: NH, ACBSP, ADNUR, ENGT

01 President .... Dr. Jacqueline VIETTI
05 Vice President of Academics .... Dr. Karla FISHER
10 Vice President of Finance .... Mr. Kent WILLIAMS
32 Vice President of Student Services .... Mr. Bill RINKENBAUGH
08 Reference Librarian .... Ms. Judy BASTIN
06 Registrar .... Ms. Connie CRAFT
09 Director of Institutional Research .... Dr. Gene GEORGE
15 Director Personnel Services .... Ms. Vicki LONG
21 Associate Business Officer .... Ms. Edith WAUGH
26 Director Public Information/Rels .... Mr. Ryan ENTZ
29 Director Alumni Relations .... Ms. Keri MYERS
30 Chief Development .... Ms. Stacy COFER
35 Director Student Affairs/Counseling .... Ms. Karen GELVIN
36 Director Student Placement .... Ms. Loretta PATTERSON
37 Director Student Financial Aid .... Ms. Susie EDWARDS
84 Director Enrollment Management .... Vacant
18 Director Facilities .... Mr. Roger NEIFERT
28 Director of Diversity .... Vacant
96 Director of Purchasing .... Ms. Regina KIEFFER
07 Director of Admissions .... Ms. Kirsten ALLEN
38 Director Student Counseling .... Mr. Glenn LYGRISSE

Central Baptist Theological Seminary (E)

6601 Monticello Road, Shawnee KS 66226-3513
County: Johnson FICE Identification: 001907
Unit ID: 154837
Telephone: (913) 667-5700 Carnegie Class: Spec/Faith
FAX Number: (913) 371-8110 Calendar System: Semester
URL: www.cbts.edu
Established: 1901 Annual Graduate Tuition & Fees: $6,780
Enrollment: 179 Coed
Affiliation or Control: Baptist IRS Status: 501(c)3
Highest Offering: Doctorate; No Undergraduates
Program: Professional; Religious Emphasis
Accreditation: NH, THEOL

01 President .... Dr. Molly T. MARSHALL
05 Dean of the Seminary .... Dr. Robert E. JOHNSON
03 Executive Vice President .... Mr. George TOWNSEND
30 VP for Institutional Advancement .... Dr. John GRAVLEY
84 Director of Enrollment/Registrar .... Mr. Stephen GUINN
26 Director of Seminary Relations .... Ms. Robin SANDBOTHE
07 Director of Recruitment .... Rev. Debra SERMONS

Central Christian College of Kansas (F)

1200 S Main, PO Box 1403, McPherson KS 67460-5799
County: McPherson FICE Identification: 001908
Unit ID: 154855
Telephone: (620) 241-0723 Carnegie Class: Bac/Diverse
FAX Number: (620) 241-6032 Calendar System: 4/1/4
URL: www.centralchristian.edu
Established: 1884 Annual Undergrad Tuition & Fees: $18,400
Enrollment: 518 Coed
Affiliation or Control: Free Methodist IRS Status: 501(c)3
Highest Offering: Baccalaureate
Program: Liberal Arts And General
Accreditation: NH

01 President .... Mr. Hal V. HOXIE
05 Vice Pres of Academics .... Dr. Leonard FAVARA, JR.
10 Vice Pres of Finance & Enrollment .... Dr. David FERRELL
30 Vice President of Advancement .... Dr. Calvin H. HAWKINS
32 Dean of Student Development .... Rev. Chris M. SMITH
53 Dean of Professional Education .... Dr. Dean KROEKER
21 Director of Finance .... Mr. Dale L. BURGE
06 Registrar .... Mrs. Bev KELLEY
41 Athletic Director .... Mr. Melvin SANDERS
07 Director of Admissions .... Mr. Rick WYATT

Cleveland Chiropractic College - Kansas City (G)

10850 Lowell Avenue, Overland Park KS 66210
County: Johnson FICE Identification: 020907
Unit ID: 177038
Telephone: (913) 234-0600 Carnegie Class: Spec/Health
FAX Number: (913) 234-0904 Calendar System: Trimester
URL: www.cleveland.edu
Established: 1922 Annual Undergrad Tuition & Fees: $14,460
Enrollment: 593 Coed
Affiliation or Control: Independent Non-Profit IRS Status: 501(c)3
Highest Offering: First Professional Degree
Program: Professional
Accreditation: NH, CHIRO

01 President .... Dr. Carl S. CLEVELAND, III
10 Chief Operating Officer .... Mr. Jeff KARP
05 Provost .... Dr. Ashley CLEVELAND
29 Vice President of Alumni Services .... Dr. John NAB
26 Vice Pres of Campus Relations .... Dr. Clark BECKLEY
05 Academic Dean .... Dr. Paul BARLETT
21 Controller .... Ms. Marla COPE
27 Director of Communications .... Mr. Alan MORGAN
06 Director of Academic Records .... Mr. David FOOSE
37 Director of Financial Aid .... Ms. Caprice CALAMAIO
16 Director of Human Resources .... Mr. Dale MARRANT
09 Director Institutional Reporting .... Dr. Christena NICHOLSON
09 Director of Research .... Dr. Mark T. PFEFER
35 Director of Student Services .... Ms. Jalonna BOWIE
07 Director of Admissions .... Ms. Melissa DENTON
08 Library Director .... Ms. Marcia M. THOMAS
13 Systems Administrator .... Mr. Calvin DANIELS
04 Assistant to the President .... Ms. Marjorie BRADSHAW

Cloud County Community College (H)

2221 Campus Drive, Concordia KS 66901-1002
County: Cloud FICE Identification: 001909
Unit ID: 154907
Telephone: (785) 243-1435 Carnegie Class: Assoc/Pub-R-M
FAX Number: (785) 243-1459 Calendar System: Semester
URL: www.cloud.edu
Established: 1965 Annual Undergrad Tuition & Fees (In-District): $2,790
Enrollment: 3,010 Coed
Affiliation or Control: State/Local IRS Status: 501(c)3
Highest Offering: Associate Degree
Program: Occupational; 2-Year Principally Bachelor's Creditable
Accreditation: NH, ADNUR

01 President .... Dr. Danette TOONE
05 Vice President for Academic Affairs .... Dr. Kimberly KRULL
84 VP Enrollment Mgmt/Student Services .... Mr. Joel FIGGS
11 Vice Pres for Administrative Svcs .... Mr. Robert MAXSON
30 Director Institutional Advancement .... Vacant
07 Director of Admissions .... Ms. Kimberly REYNOLDS
08 Director of Library Services .... Ms. Jennifer SCHROEDER
41 Athletic Director .... Mr. Matthew BECHARD
06 Registrar .... Mrs. Linda PETERSEN
18 Chief Facilities/Physical Plant .... Mr. Rex E. SICARD
26 Chief Public Relations Officer .... Ms. Jenny ACREE
102 Ex Dir Cloud County Cmty Col Found .... Mr. James LUKACEVICH
37 Director Student Financial Aid .... Ms. Suzi KNOETTGEN
38 Director Advising & Retention .... Ms. Ashley DOUGLAS
15 Coordinator of Human Resources .... Ms. Christine WILSON

Coffeyville Community College (I)

400 W 11th Street, Coffeyville KS 67337-5064
County: Montgomery FICE Identification: 001910
Unit ID: 154925
Telephone: (620) 251-7700 Carnegie Class: Assoc/Pub-R-S
FAX Number: (620) 252-7098 Calendar System: Semester
URL: www.coffeyville.edu
Established: 1923 Annual Undergrad Tuition & Fees (In-District): $1,920
Enrollment: 2,037 Coed
Affiliation or Control: State/Local IRS Status: 501(c)3
Highest Offering: Associate Degree
Program: Occupational; 2-Year Principally Bachelor's Creditable
Accreditation: NH, EMT

01 President .... Ms. Linda MOLEY
05 Vice President for Learning .... Mrs. Alysia JOHNSTON
32 Vice President for Student Services .... Mr. Jill KOSLOSKY
10 Vice Pres for Operations & Finance .... Mr. Thomas A. SMART
88 VP for Innovation/Bus Initiatives .... Mr. Marlon THORNBURG
102 Exec Director-CCC Foundation .... Mr. Dickie ROLLS
26 Marketing Director/Grant Writer .... Mrs. Lisa KUEHN
06 Registrar .... Mrs. Deborah OESTMANN
08 Director Learning Resource Center .... Mr. Marty EVENSVOLD
37 Director of Financial Aid .... Mrs. Pam FEERER
18 Director of Buildings/Ground .... Ms. Vivian FROST
85 Director of International Students .... Mrs. Marla LARIMORE
51 Director of Continuing Education .... Vacant
106 Director of Distance Learning .... Mr. Brad WEBER
12 Director Columbus Technical Campus .... Mrs. Cindy HARROLD
35 Director of Student Life .... Mr. Andy MUNDAY
40 Bookstore Manager .... Mrs. Karen STRIMPLE
72 Dean of Technology .... Vacant
15 Director of Personnel .... Mrs. Cindy SUTHERLAND
41 Athletics Director .... Mr. Jeff LEIKER
36 Student Counselor/Academic Advisor .... Mrs. Delia NORTHRUP

Colby Community College (J)

1255 S Range, Colby KS 67701-4099
County: Thomas FICE Identification: 001911
Unit ID: 154934
Telephone: (785) 462-3984 Carnegie Class: Assoc/Pub-R-M
FAX Number: (785) 460-4699 Calendar System: Semester
URL: www.colbycc.edu
Established: 1964 Annual Undergrad Tuition & Fees (In-District): $2,944
Enrollment: 1,470 Coed
Affiliation or Control: State/Local IRS Status: 501(c)3
Highest Offering: Associate Degree
Program: Occupational; 2-Year Principally Bachelor's Creditable
Accreditation: NH, ADNUR, PTAA

01 President .... Dr. Stephen M. VACIK
05 Dean of Academic Affairs .... Mrs. Joyce WASHBURN
32 VP of Student Affairs .... Dr. Keegan NICHOLS
10 Vice President of Fiscal Affairs .... Mr. Alan WAITES
06 Registrar .... Ms. Brette PFEIFER
08 Librarian .... Mrs. Tara SCHROER

26 Director of Public Information ... Mrs. Deborah SCHWANKE
38 Director of Student Counseling ... Dr. Keegan NICHOLS
09 Director Institutional Research ... Vacant
07 Director of Admissions ... Mrs. Nikol NOLAN
15 Director of Human Resources ... Mr. Alan WAITES
18 Dean of External Affairs ... Mr. Barry KAAZ
37 Director of Student Financial Aid ... Mrs. Paula HALVORSON
29 Director Alumni Relations ... Mr. Nick WELLS
41 Athletic Director ... Mr. Ryan STURDY
14 Director of Computer Center ... Mr. Jess RANDEL

Cowley County Community College (A)

125 S Second, PO Box 1147,
Arkansas City KS 67005-1147

County: Cowley | FICE Identification: 001902 | Unit ID: 154952
Telephone: (620) 442-0430 | Carnegie Class: Assoc/Pub-R-M
FAX Number: (620) 441-5350 | Calendar System: Semester
URL: www.cowley.edu
Established: 1922 | Annual Undergrad Tuition & Fees (In-District): $2,220
Enrollment: 4,910 | Coed
Affiliation or Control: Local | IRS Status: 501(c)3
Highest Offering: Associate Degree
Program: Occupational; 2-Year Principally Bachelor's Creditable
Accreditation: NH, EMT

01 President ... Dr. Patrick J. MCATEE
10 Exec Vice Pres of Business Services ... Mr. Tony CROUCH
05 Vice President of Academic Affairs ... Mr. Slade GRIFFITHS
32 Vice President of Student Affairs ... Mrs. Sue SAIA
41 Athletic Director ... Mr. Tom V. SAIA
13 Vice Pres of Research & Technology ... Mr. Charles MCKOWN
30 Vice Pres Institutional Development ... Mr. Ben SCHEARS
06 Registrar ... Mr. Mark BRITTON
26 Dir Inst Comm/Public Relations ... Mr. Rama PEROO

Dodge City Community College (B)

2501 N 14th Avenue, Dodge City KS 67801-2399

County: Ford | FICE Identification: 001913 | Unit ID: 154998
Telephone: (620) 225-1321 | Carnegie Class: Assoc/Pub-R-M
FAX Number: (620) 227-9366 | Calendar System: Semester
URL: www.dc3.edu
Established: 1935 | Annual Undergrad Tuition & Fees (In-District): $1,584
Enrollment: 1,807 | Coed
Affiliation or Control: State/Local | IRS Status: 501(c)3
Highest Offering: Associate Degree
Program: Occupational; 2-Year Principally Bachelor's Creditable
Accreditation: NH, ADNUR, PNUR

01 President ... Dr. Don A. WOODBURN
05 Exec VP College Affairs/Learning ... Mr. Michael AHERN
10 Vice Pres of Operations & Finance ... Ms. Vada HERMON
103 VP Innovation/Workforce Development ... Mr. Danny GILLUM
35 VP of Student/Community Services ... Mr. Anthony LYONS
32 Dean of Student Services ... Mrs. Beverly TEMAAT
72 Dean Technology/Distance Education ... Mr. Thad RUSSELL
51 Dir Bus/Technology/Continuing Educ ... Ms. Melissa MCCOY
24 Director Adult Learning Center ... Mr. Ryan AUSMUS
26 Director Public Information Office ... Mr. Rick DRUSE
07 Dir Admissions Placement & Testing ... Mrs. Tammy TABOR
102 Exec Director of DCCC Foundation ... Mr. Roger PROFFITT
08 Director Learning Resource Center ... Mrs. Shelly HUELSMAN
66 Director Nursing Allied Health ... Mrs. Becky BREDFELDT
15 Director of Human Resources ... Ms. Sheila BERGKAMP
41 Athletic Director ... Mr. Casey MALEK
06 Registrar ... Ms. Stephanie LANNING
37 Director of Financial Aid ... Mr. Russ MCBEE
21 Director of Business Services ... Ms. Debbie BISCH
40 Director Bookstore ... Mrs. Debby MALEK
13 Director Information Technology ... Mrs. Judith MAXFIELD
39 Director of Residence Life ... Mr. Lewis MIZE
18 Facilities Maint/Operations Supv ... Mr. Greg PATEE
04 Exec Assistant to the President ... Mrs. Carla PATEE

Donnelly College (C)

608 N 18th Street, Kansas City KS 66102-4298

County: Wyandotte | FICE Identification: 001914 | Unit ID: 155007
Telephone: (913) 621-8700 | Carnegie Class: Bac/Assoc
FAX Number: (913) 621-8719 | Calendar System: Semester
URL: www.donnelly.edu
Established: 1949 | Annual Undergrad Tuition & Fees: $5,992
Enrollment: 652 | Coed
Affiliation or Control: Roman Catholic | IRS Status: 501(c)3
Highest Offering: Baccalaureate
Program: Occupational; 2-Year Principally Bachelor's Creditable; Liberal Arts And General
Accreditation: NH

01 President ... Dr. Steven M. LANASA
03 Vice President ... Mrs. Frances SANDERS
32 Vice President of Student Affairs ... Ms. Donette ALONZO
85 Dean of International Students ... Mr. Cyrus SHADFAR
88 Assoc VP of Student Success ... Mrs. Amy NEUFELD
06 Registrar ... Mrs. Amber BLOOMFIELD-MARTINEZ
26 Marketing Coordinator ... Mrs. Jennifer PRICE
30 Director of Development ... Mrs. Emily BUCKLEY
36 Career Center Coord/Library Dir ... Mrs. Jane BALLAGH DE TOVAR
37 Director of Financial Aid ... Mrs. Belinda OGAN
10 Dir Business Affairs/Personnel Svcs ... Mrs. Susan SERRANO
18 Director of Facilities ... Mr. Terry STARR
09 Dir Institutional Rsrch/Plng/Assess ... Mrs. Frances SANDERS
14 Director of Computer Services ... Mr. Wen Li SHU
07 Director of Admissions ... Mr. Edward MARQUEZ
29 Alumni Relations ... Mr. Roger BERG

Emporia State University (D)

1200 Commercial Street, Emporia KS 66801-5087

County: Lyon | FICE Identification: 001927 | Unit ID: 155025
Telephone: (620) 341-1200 | Carnegie Class: Master's L
FAX Number: (620) 341-5553 | Calendar System: Semester
URL: www.emporia.edu
Established: 1863 | Annual Undergrad Tuition & Fees (In-State): $4,952
Enrollment: 6,262 | Coed
Affiliation or Control: State | IRS Status: 501(c)3
Highest Offering: Doctorate
Program: Liberal Arts And General; Teacher Preparatory
Accreditation: NH, ART, BUS, CACREP, CORE, LIB, MUS, NUR, TED

01 Interim President ... Dr. H. Edward FLENTJE
05 Provost/VP for Academic Affairs ... Dr. Teresa A. MEHRING
11 Vice President Admin & Fiscal Affs ... Mr. Raymond A. HAUKE
32 VP Strategic Partnershps/Stdnt Life ... Dr. James E. WILLIAMS
14 Assoc Vice Pres Tech/Computing Svcs ... Mr. Michael ERICKSON
85 Asst Vice Pres for Internatl Educ ... Mr. Gonzalo BRUCE
35 Asst Vice Pres Student Affairs ... Ms. Lynn M. HOBSON
10 Assoc Vice Pres Fiscal Affairs ... Ms. Diana E. KUHLMANN
102 President ESU Foundation ... Mr. Timothy S. CLOTHIER
29 Director of Alumni/Govt Rels ... Mr. K. Tyler CURTIS
88 Director Natl Teachers Hall of Fame ... Ms. Jenny HARDER
22 Affirmative Action Officer ... Ms. Judy ANDERSON
53 Dean/The Teachers College ... Dr. J. Phillip BENNETT
49 Dean College of Liberal Arts/Sci ... Dr. Steven F. BROWN
50 Dean School of Business ... Dr. Joseph WEN
62 Dean School of Library/Info Mgmt ... Dr. Gwendolyn ALEXANDER
58 Dean Graduate Studies ... Dr. Kathy ERMLER
88 Exec Dir Jones Inst Educ Excel ... Dr. Larry D. CLARK
06 Registrar ... Ms. M. Elaine HENRIE
08 Dean University Libraries/Archives ... Mr. John SHERIDAN
88 Director Assessment/Measurements ... Dr. Anthony L. AMBROSIO
106 Director Distance Education ... Dr. Kathy ERMLER
37 Director Student Financial Aid ... Ms. M. Elaine HENRIE
07 Director Admissions ... Ms. Laura M. EDDY
36 Director Career Services ... Ms. June COLEMAN-HULL
38 Director Student Life & Counseling ... Dr. Jaqueline L. SCHMIDT
26 Director Marketing & Media Relation ... Mr. William NOBLITT
91 Director Computing & Telecom Svcs ... Vacant
41 Director Athletics ... Mr. Kent L. WEISER
18 Director Facilities/Physical Plant ... Mr. Mark S. RUNGE
15 Director Human Resources ... Ms. Judy ANDERSON
23 Director Health Services ... Dr. Jaqueline L. SCHMIDT
39 Dir Residential Life/Orientation ... Mr. Cass COUGHLEN
40 Manager Bookstore ... Mr. Michael MCRELL
19 Director Police & Safety ... Capt. Chris HOOVER
43 General Counsel ... Dr. Tracy A. GREENE
21 Controller ... Ms. Mary MINGENBACK
09 Director Institutional Research ... Dr. JoLanna KORD
92 Director Honors Program ... Dr. William H. CLAMURRO
28 Director of Diversity ... Ms. Elizabeth NELSON

Flint Hills Technical College (E)

3301 W 18th Avenue, Emporia KS 66801-5957

County: Lyon | FICE Identification: 005264 | Unit ID: 155052
Telephone: (620) 343-4600 | Carnegie Class: Assoc/Pub-R-S
FAX Number: (620) 343-4610 | Calendar System: Semester
URL: www.fhtc.edu
Established: 1965 | Annual Undergrad Tuition & Fees (In-District): $3,680
Enrollment: 675 | Coed
Affiliation or Control: State/Local | IRS Status: 501(c)3
Highest Offering: Associate Degree
Program: Occupational; Technical Emphasis
Accreditation: NH, DA, DH, EMT

01 President ... Dr. Dean HOLLENBECK
05 Dean of Instructional Services ... Mr. Steve LOEWEN
32 Dean of Student Services ... Ms. Lisa KIRMER
06 Registrar ... Ms. Brenda CARMICHAEL
10 Chief Business Officer ... Mrs. Nancy THOMPSON
15 Director Personnel Services ... Mrs. Sheri KNIGHT
37 Director Student Financial Aid ... Ms. Sandra SCHROEDER
84 Director Enrollment Management ... Ms. Brenda CARMICHAEL

Fort Hays State University (F)

600 Park Street, Hays KS 67601-4099

County: Ellis | FICE Identification: 001915 | Unit ID: 155061
Telephone: (785) 628-4000 | Carnegie Class: Master's L
FAX Number: (785) 628-4096 | Calendar System: Semester
URL: www.fhsu.edu
Established: 1902 | Annual Undergrad Tuition & Fees (In-State): $4,082
Enrollment: 11,883 | Coed
Affiliation or Control: State | IRS Status: 501(c)3
Highest Offering: Beyond Master's But Less Than Doctorate
Program: Liberal Arts And General; Teacher Preparatory; Professional
Accreditation: NH, MUS, NURSE, RAD, SP, SW, TED

01 President ... Dr. Edward H. HAMMOND
05 Provost ... Dr. Lawrence V. GOULD
10 Vice Pres Administration & Finance ... Mr. Mike BARNETT
32 Vice President Student Affairs ... Dr. Tisa MASON
35 Asst Vice Pres Student Affairs ... Ms. Shana MEYER
09 Asst Provost Quality Improvement ... Dr. Chris CRAWFORD
58 Dean Graduate Studies and Research ... Dr. Tim CROWLEY
04 Exec Assistant to the President ... Mr. Todd POWELL
04 Assistant to President ... Ms. Lisa M. KARLIN
06 Registrar ... Dr. Joseph G. LINN
07 Admissions Director ... Ms. Tricia CLINE
29 Exec Director Alumni & Govt Rels ... Ms. Debra K. PRIDEAUX
45 Director Budget & Planning ... Mr. Larry R. GETTY
36 Director Career Services ... Mr. Daniel B. RICE
37 Director Student Financial Aid ... Mr. Craig E. KARLIN
26 Director University Relations ... Mr. Kent L. STEWARD
14 Director Computing/Telecom Center ... Dr. David E. SCHMIDT
08 Director Library ... Mr. John A. ROSS
15 Director Personnel Services ... Mr. Tom KUHN
51 Dean Virtual College ... Mr. Dennis KING
53 Interim Dean College Education ... Dr. Robert F. SCOTT
49 Dean College Liberal Arts/Sciences ... Dr. Paul W. FABER
50 Dean College Business ... Dr. Mark BANNISTER
76 Dean Coll Health/Life Science ... Dr. Jeff BRIGGS
18 Co-Dir Chief Facil/Physical Plant ... Mr. Jim SCHREIBER
18 Co-Dir Chief Facil/Physical Plant ... Mr. Ken JACOBS
38 Dir Acad Advis/Career Exploration ... Dr. Patricia L. GRIFFIN
28 Diversity Coordinator ... Mr. George E. JACKSON, III

Fort Scott Community College (G)

2108 S Horton, Fort Scott KS 66701-3140

County: Bourbon | FICE Identification: 001916 | Unit ID: 155098
Telephone: (620) 223-2700 | Carnegie Class: Assoc/Pub-R-M
FAX Number: (620) 223-4927 | Calendar System: Semester
URL: www.fortscott.edu
Established: 1919 | Annual Undergrad Tuition & Fees (In-District): $2,430
Enrollment: 2,057 | Coed
Affiliation or Control: State/Local | IRS Status: 501(c)3
Highest Offering: Associate Degree
Program: Occupational; 2-Year Principally Bachelor's Creditable
Accreditation: NH, ADNUR

01 President ... Dr. Clayton TATRO
05 Dean of Inst/Academic/Tech Dept ... Dr. Donna ESTILL
32 Dean of Student Services ... Steve ARMSTRONG
10 Dean of Finance and Operations ... Karla FARMER
07 Director Admissions ... Mert BARROWS
08 Library Director ... Larry BAIN
06 Registrar ... Morgan BECK
26 Director Public Information ... Kathleen HINRICHS
66 Director Nursing ... Bill RHOADS
41 Athletic Director ... JD ETTORE
13 Information Technology Director ... Casey RUSSELL
12 Associate Dean Pittsburg ... Judy COLLINS
12 Associate Dean Paola ... Buddy Jo TANCK
38 Director Advising/Student Support ... Steve KRAMER
15 Director Personnel Services ... Juley MCDANIEL
18 Campus Services Director ... Joel RAMSEY
29 Director Alumni Rels/Development ... Gary PALMER
37 Director Student Financial Aid ... Lillie GRUBB
28 Director of Diversity ... Jill WARFORD
35 Director of Student Life ... Marci MYERS

Friends University (H)

2100 W University Avenue, Wichita KS 67213-3397

County: Sedgwick | FICE Identification: 001918 | Unit ID: 155089
Telephone: (316) 295-5000 | Carnegie Class: Master's L
FAX Number: (316) 295-5060 | Calendar System: Semester
URL: www.friends.edu
Established: 1898 | Annual Undergrad Tuition & Fees: $21,030
Enrollment: 2,800 | Coed
Affiliation or Control: Independent Non-Profit | IRS Status: 501(c)3
Highest Offering: Master's
Program: 2-Year Principally Bachelor's Creditable; Liberal Arts And General; Teacher Preparatory; Professional
Accreditation: NH, MFCD, MUS, TED

01 President ... Dr. TJ ARANT
04 Executive Secretary ... Ms. Nancy GRAF
10 Vice Pres Administration & Finance ... Mr. Randall C. DOERKSEN
32 Vice President of Student Life ... Dr. Carole OBERMEYER
30 Vice President University Relations ... Mr. Hervey WRIGHT, III
20 Assoc VP of Academic Affairs ... Dr. Darcy ZABEL
15 Assoc VP Admn Finance/Dir of HR ... Ms. Kelley WILLIAMS
06 Assoc VP Registrar/Enrollment Svcs ... Ms. Heidi HOSKINSON
49 Dean College of Bus/Art/Sci & Educ ... Dr. Steve PETERS
51 Dean Adult and Professional Studies ... Dr. Jo LOBERTINI
58 Dean Graduate School ... Dr. Evelyn HUME
50 Chair Business & IT ... Dr. Arlen HONTS
57 Chair Fine Arts ... Dr. Stephen EAVES
81 Chair Natural Science/Math ... Dr. Nora STRASSER
73 Chair Religion/Humanities ... Dr. Stan HARSTINE
53 Chair Teacher Education ... Dr. Jan WILSON
83 Chair Social/Behavioral Science ... Dr. Phillip WISELEY
46 Dir Inst Research & Assessment ... Dr. Stephanie J. HARGRAVE
08 Director Library ... Mr. Max BURSON

18 Chief Facilities/Physical Plant ... Mr. Paul WINCHESTER
16 Director of Purchasing/Aux Services ... Mr. Ryan ARCHER
88 Exec Dir Adult Student Recruitment ... Ms. Jeanette HANSON
07 Exec Dir Trad'l Undergrad Admiss ... Ms. Erin HANEBERG
41 Director Athletics ... Mr. Joe ZIMMERMAN
37 Director Financial Aid ... Mr. Brandon PIERCE
42 Chaplain ... Mr. Patrick SEHL, JR.
35 Director of Campus Life ... Mr. Gary RAPP
39 Director Residence Life ... Mr. Brian BOLLINGER
26 Director Communications ... Ms. Gisele MCMINIMY
29 Exec Dir Alumni/Annual Fund ... Ms. Lisa TILMA

Garden City Community College (A)

801 Campus Drive, Garden City KS 67846-6398

County: Finney | FICE Identification: 001919 | Unit ID: 155104
Telephone: (620) 276-7611 | Carnegie Class: Assoc/Pub-R-M
FAX Number: (620) 276-9573 | Calendar System: Semester
URL: www.gcccks.edu
Established: 1919 | Annual Undergrad Tuition & Fees (In-District): $2,272
Enrollment: 2,009 | Coed
Affiliation or Control: Local | IRS Status: 501(c)3
Highest Offering: Associate Degree
Program: Occupational; 2-Year Principally Bachelor's Creditable
Accreditation: NH, ADNUR, EMT

01 President ... Dr. Herbert SWENDER
05 Dean Academics ... Mr. Kevin BRUNGARDT
32 Dean Student Services ... Mr. Ryan RUDA
11 Exec Dean Administrative Services ... Ms. Dee WIGNER
08 Library Director ... Mr. Trent SMITH
06 Registrar ... Ms. Nancy UNRUH
07 Director of Admissions ... Ms. Nikki GEIER
09 Dean Institutional Effectiveness ... Ms. Deanna MANN
15 Director of Human Resources ... Ms. Cricket TURLEY
18 Physical Plant Director ... Mr. Larry JOHNSTON
26 Dir Information Svcs/Publication ... Mr. Steve QUAKENBUSH
37 Director Student Financial Aid ... Ms. Kathy BLAU
39 Director Residential Life ... Ms. Kate COVINGTON
38 Director Student Counseling ... Mr. Colin LAMB
75 Dean Technical Education ... Ms. Lenora COOK

Haskell Indian Nations University (B)

155 Indian Avenue, #5030, Lawrence KS 66046-4800

County: Douglas | FICE Identification: 010438 | Unit ID: 155140
Telephone: (785) 749-8404 | Carnegie Class: Tribal
FAX Number: (785) 749-8406 | Calendar System: Semester
URL: www.haskell.edu
Established: 1884 | Annual Undergrad Tuition & Fees: $430
Enrollment: 953 | Coed
Affiliation or Control: Federal | IRS Status: Exempt
Highest Offering: Baccalaureate
Program: 2-Year Principally Bachelor's Creditable; Liberal Arts And General; Teacher Preparatory
Accreditation: NH

01 President ... Mr. Chris REDMAN
05 Vice President for Academics ... Dr. Venida CHENAULT
11 Vice President University Services ... Mr. Clyde PEACOCK
10 Chief Finance Officer ... Mr. Michael LEWIS
27 Chief Information Officer ... Mr. Josh ARCE
08 Librarian/Dir Academic Support Ctr ... Dr. Marilyn RUSSELL
32 Dean of Student Life ... Mr. Jim TUCKER
37 Financial Aid Officer ... Ms. Reta BREWER
06 Registrar ... Mr. Manny KING
07 Admissions ... Ms. Patti GRANT-OROSCO
09 Dir Instl Research/Sponsored Pgms ... Ms. Freda GIPP
36 Director Student Placement ... Vacant
38 Director Student Counseling ... Ms. Brenda SCHILDT
15 Human Resources Liason ... Ms. Mona GONZALES
96 Acquisitions ... Ms. Janice BEGAY
26 Executive Asst/Public Relations ... Mr. Stephen PRUE
18 Facilities Manager ... Mr. Lee PAHCODDY, JR.

Hesston College (C)

Box 3000, Hesston KS 67062-2093

County: Harvey | FICE Identification: 001920 | Unit ID: 155177
Telephone: (620) 327-4221 | Carnegie Class: Assoc/PrivNFP
FAX Number: (620) 327-8300 | Calendar System: Semester
URL: www.hesston.edu
Established: 1909 | Annual Undergrad Tuition & Fees: $20,720
Enrollment: 448 | Coed
Affiliation or Control: Mennonite Church | IRS Status: 501(c)3
Highest Offering: Associate Degree
Program: Occupational; 2-Year Principally Bachelor's Creditable
Accreditation: NH, ADNUR

01 President ... Dr. Howard KEIM
05 Vice President of Academics ... Dr. Sandra ZERGER
30 Vice President of Advancement ... Mrs. Yvonne SIEBER
07 Vice President of Admissions ... Mrs. Rachel S. MILLER
10 Vice Pres of Finance & Auxil Svcs ... Mr. Don WEAVER
32 Vice President of Student Life ... Mr. Lamar ROTH
29 Director of Alumni & Church Rels ... Mr. Dallas STUTZMAN
06 Registrar ... Mr. Brent YODER
21 Business Manager ... Mr. Karl BRUBAKER

Highland Community College (D)

606 W Main, Highland KS 66035-0068

County: Doniphan | FICE Identification: 001921 | Unit ID: 155186
Telephone: (785) 442-6000 | Carnegie Class: Assoc/Pub-R-M
FAX Number: (785) 442-6100 | Calendar System: Semester
URL: www.highlandcc.edu
Established: 1858 | Annual Undergrad Tuition & Fees (In-District): $2,760
Enrollment: 3,845 | Coed
Affiliation or Control: Local | IRS Status: 501(c)3
Highest Offering: Associate Degree
Program: Occupational; 2-Year Principally Bachelor's Creditable
Accreditation: NH

01 President ... Mr. David REIST
05 Vice President for Academic Affairs ... Dr. Cia VERSCHELDEN
32 Vice President for Student Services ... Dr. Cheryl RASMUSSEN
10 Vice Pres for Finance/Operations ... Ms. Deborah FOX
88 Director of Technical Education ... Ms. Terri BALL
102 Exec Asst to Pres/Exec Dir HCC Foun ... Dr. Craig E. MOSHER
06 Registrar ... Ms. Alice HAMILTON
37 Financial Aid Director ... Ms. Kelly TWOMBLY
13 Director of Information Systems ... Mr. John NICHOLAS
09 Director of Institutional Research ... Dr. Harold ARNETT
38 Director Student Counseling ... Ms. Janette RUSHING
41 Athletic Director ... Mr. Greg DELZEIT
08 Library Director ... Ms. Penny DONALDSON
18 Supervisor of Buildings & Grounds ... Mr. Rick CROSSLAND
26 Chief Public Relations Officer ... Dr. Craig MOSHER
29 Director Alumni Relations ... Dr. Craig MOSHER
15 Human Resource Manager ... Ms. Eileen C. GRONNIGER
40 Bookstore Coordinator ... Ms. Sarah ALBERS
35 Coordinator of Student Activities ... Mr. Bradley DIXON

Highland Community College-Technical Center (E)

1501 W Riley Street, Atchison KS 66002-1537

County: Atchison | FICE Identification: 005266 | Unit ID: 155609
Telephone: (913) 367-6204 | Carnegie Class: Not Classified
FAX Number: (913) 367-3107 | Calendar System: Quarter
URL: www.highlandcc.edu
Established: 1967 | Annual Undergrad Tuition & Fees: $3,720
Enrollment: 340 | Coed
Affiliation or Control: Proprietary | IRS Status: Proprietary
Highest Offering: Associate Degree
Program: Occupational
Accreditation: &NH, COE

05 Dean of Curriculum & Instruction ... Mrs. Terri BALL

† Regional accreditation is carried under the parent institution in Highland, KS.

Hutchinson Community College and Area Vocational School (F)

1300 N Plum Street, Hutchinson KS 67501-5894

County: Reno | FICE Identification: 001923 | Unit ID: 155195
Telephone: (620) 665-3500 | Carnegie Class: Assoc/Pub-R-L
FAX Number: (620) 665-3310 | Calendar System: Semester
URL: www.hutchcc.edu
Established: 1928 | Annual Undergrad Tuition & Fees (In-District): $2,624
Enrollment: 5,588 | Coed
Affiliation or Control: State/Local | IRS Status: 501(c)3
Highest Offering: Associate Degree
Program: Occupational; 2-Year Principally Bachelor's Creditable
Accreditation: NH, ACBSP, ADNUR, EMT, PNUR, PTAA, RAD, SURGT

01 President ... Dr. Edward E. BERGER
05 Vice President of Academic Affairs ... Dr. Cindy HOSS
10 Vice President Finance/Operations ... Mr. Carter FILE
103 VP Workforce Development/Outreach ... Mr. Steve PORTER
32 Vice President of Students ... Mr. Randy E. MYERS
26 Director of Marketing & Info ... Mrs. M. L. HINKLE
13 Director of Data Processing ... Mr. Loren L. MORRIS
06 Registrar ... Mrs. Christina LONG
41 Athletic Director ... Mr. Randy STANGE
15 Director of Personnel ... Mr. Brooks E. MANTOOTH
37 Financial Aid Officer ... Mr. Ron MENEFEE
07 Director of Admissions ... Mr. Corbin STROBEL
18 Director of Plant Facilities ... Mr. Don ROSE
39 Director of Residence Life ... Ms. Dana HINSHAW
29 Director Alumni Relations ... Mrs. Cindy KEAST
08 Coordinator of Library Services ... Mr. Robert KELLY
09 Coord of Institutional Research ... Mr. Mike TONN

Independence Community College (G)

Brookside Drive and College Avenue,
Independence KS 67301-0708

County: Montgomery | FICE Identification: 001924 | Unit ID: 155201
Telephone: (620) 331-4100 | Carnegie Class: Assoc/Pub-R-S
FAX Number: (620) 331-5344 | Calendar System: Semester
URL: www.indycc.edu
Established: 1925 | Annual Undergrad Tuition & Fees (In-District): $1,950
Enrollment: 707 | Coed
Affiliation or Control: State/Local | IRS Status: 501(c)3
Highest Offering: Associate Degree
Program: Occupational; 2-Year Principally Bachelor's Creditable
Accreditation: NH

01 President ... Dr. Daniel BARWICK
05 Interim Dean Instructional Services ... Mr. Travis GITHENS
10 Chief Financial Officer ... Mr. Jan FISCHER
32 Dean Student Services ... Vacant
102 Foundation Director ... Ms. Lori SHAW
06 Registrar ... Ms. Sonja CONLEY
08 Director Library/Lrng Resource Ctr ... Ms. Lily MORGAN
41 Director Athletics ... Ms. Tammie GELDENHUYS
14 Chief Information and Facilities ... Mr. Greg EYTCHESON
18 Director Maintenance/Custodial ... Mr. Mario LOPEZ
12 Director William Inge Center ... Mr. Peter ELLENSTEIN
103 Workforce Development Generalist ... Vacant
07 Director of Admissions ... Ms. Sally CIUFULESCU
26 Public Relations/Marketing Director ... Ms. Lois LESSMAN
37 Financial Aid Coordinator ... Ms. Sheila SMITHER
13 MIS Coordinator ... Mr. Darrin MCFARLAND
09 Dir of Inst Effect/Retention ... Ms. Debbie PHELPS
04 Administrative Asst to President ... Ms. Beverly HARRIS
40 Bookstore Manager ... Ms. Teresa VESTAL
25 Grant Professional ... Ms. Misty GASCICH
88 Upward Bound Program Director ... Ms. Deatrea ROSE

ITT Technical Institute (H)

8111 E. 32nd St. N, Suite 103, Wichita KS 67226

County: Sedgwick | Identification: 666168 | Unit ID: 450234
Telephone: (316) 609-4100 | Carnegie Class: Not Classified
FAX Number: N/A | Calendar System: Quarter
URL: www.itt-tech.edu
Established: 2006 | Annual Undergrad Tuition & Fees: N/A
Enrollment: N/A | Coed
Affiliation or Control: Proprietary | IRS Status: Proprietary
Highest Offering: Baccalaureate
Program: Technical Emphasis
Accreditation: ACICS

† Branch campus of ITT Technical Institute, Seattle, WA.

Johnson County Community College (I)

12345 College Boulevard, Overland Park KS 66210-1299

County: Johnson | FICE Identification: 008244 | Unit ID: 155210
Telephone: (913) 469-8500 | Carnegie Class: Assoc/Pub-S-SC
FAX Number: (913) 469-2559 | Calendar System: Semester
URL: www.jccc.edu
Established: 1969 | Annual Undergrad Tuition & Fees (In-District): $1,215
Enrollment: 20,869 | Coed
Affiliation or Control: State/Local | IRS Status: 501(c)3
Highest Offering: Associate Degree
Program: Occupational; 2-Year Principally Bachelor's Creditable
Accreditation: NH, ACBSP, ACFEI, ADNUR, DH, EMT, IFSAC, POLYT

01 President ... Dr. Terry A. CALAWAY
04 Exec Asst to the President & Board ... Ms. Terri SCHLICHT
11 Exec Vice Pres Administrative Svcs ... Dr. Joseph M. SOPCICH
05 Exec Vice Pres Educational Planning ... Dr. Dana GROVE
20 Executive Vice Pres Academic Affair ... Dr. Marilyn RHINEHART
32 Vice President Student Services ... Dr. Dennis DAY
15 Executive Vice Pres HR & Comm/Econ ... Dr. Judy KORB
27 Vice President Information Services ... Ms. Denise MOORE
76 Dean Hlth Care Professions/Wellness ... Dr. Clarissa CRAIG
49 Dean Curriculum/Academic Quality ... Ms. Ruth RANDALL
35 Dean Student Services ... Mr. Paul KYLE
08 Director Library Services ... Mr. Mark DAGANAAR
72 Dean Technology ... Mr. Bill BROWN
88 Executive Director Academic Initiat ... Dr. Jason KOVAC
14 Director Admin Computing Services ... Ms. Sandra WARNER
26 AVPMarketing Communications ... Ms. Julie HAAS
10 AVP Financial Services ... Mr. Bob PRATER
18 Director Facilities Planning & Mgmt ... Vacant
37 Director Student Financial Aid ... Mr. Chris CHRISTENSEN
06 Registrar ... Ms. Leslie QUINN
36 Director Testing and Assessment ... Ms. Mary Ann DICKERSON
84 Asst Dean Enrollment Management ... Ms. MargE SHELLEY
35 Asst Dean Student Activ/Ldrshp Dev ... Ms. Pam VASSAR
68 Dir Physical Education/Athletics ... Mr. Carl HEINRICH
07 Director of Admissions ... Mr. Peter BELK
96 Executive Director Procurement ... Mr. Mitch BORCHERS
92 Program Facilitator Honors ... Dr. Pat DECKER

Kansas City Kansas Community College (J)

7250 State Avenue, Kansas City KS 66112-3003

County: Wyandotte | FICE Identification: 001925 | Unit ID: 155292
Telephone: (913) 334-1100 | Carnegie Class: Assoc/Pub-U-SC
FAX Number: (913) 288-7609 | Calendar System: Semester
URL: www.kckcc.edu
Established: 1923 | Annual Undergrad Tuition & Fees (In-District): $2,100
Enrollment: 7,540 | Coed
Affiliation or Control: State/Local | IRS Status: 501(c)3
Highest Offering: Associate Degree
Program: Occupational; 2-Year Principally Bachelor's Creditable

Accreditation: NH, ACBSP, ADNUR, EMT, FUSER, PTAA

01 President .... Dr. Doris F. GIVENS
11 VP Student & Administrative Svcs .... Mr. Brian BODE
05 Provost .... Dr. Tamara AGHA-JAFFAR
50 Dean Business & Continuing Educ .... Dr. Marvin HUNT
81 Dean Engineering/Math/Science .... Dr. Edward KREMER
84 Dean Enrollment Mgmt/Registrar .... Dr. Denise MCDOWELL
16 Dean Human Resources/Affirm Action .... Ms. Leota MARKS
79 Dean Humanities & Fine Arts .... Dr. Cherilee WALKER
13 Dean Information Services .... Mr. Baz ABOUELENEIN
45 Dean Institutional Services .... Dr. Sangki MIN
66 Dean Nursing Educ/Allied Health .... Dr. Shirley A. WENDEL
83 Dean Social & Behavioral Sciences .... Dr. Charles WILSON
32 Dean Student Services .... Vacant
75 Dean Technical Education Center .... Mr. Cliff SMITH
88 Exec Director Leavenworth Center .... Ms. Karalin ALSDURF
88 Director of Academic Resource Ctr .... Ms. Jaclyn ANDERSON
41 Director of Athletics .... Mr. Dan PRATT
40 Director of Bookstore Operations .... Mr. John BURRIGHT
18 Director of Buildings/Grounds .... Mr. Jeff SIXTA
19 Director of Campus Police .... Mr. Greg SCHNEIDER
36 Director of Career Planning/Plcmnt .... Ms. Linda L. WYATT
26 Director of College Advancement .... Mr. Jerry TONEY
14 Director of Computing .... Mr. James BENNETT
31 Director of Cont Educ & Cmty Svcs .... Ms. Rosemary L. LISCHKA
38 Director of Counseling .... Dr. Alda PRESTON
09 Director Ctr for Rsrch & Cmty Devel .... Ms. Kaaren FIFE
37 Director of Financial Aid .... Ms. Mary I. DORR
21 Director of Financial Records .... Ms. Marie BRANSTETTER
92 Director of Honors/Phi Theta Kappa .... Ms. Stacy TUCKER
28 Director of Intercultural Center .... Ms. Barbara CLARK-EVANS
08 Director of Library .... Ms. Cheryl POSTLEWAIT
24 Director Media Services Technology .... Mr. Michael J. KIMBROUGH
106 Director of Online Services .... Ms. Susan STUART
96 Director of Purchasing & Risk Mgr .... Mr. David ROOT
35 Director of Student Activities .... Ms. Linda SUTTON
07 Director of Admissions .... Ms. Sherri A. NEFF
06 Assistant Registrar .... Ms. Theresa HOLLIDAY
88 Director Community Outreach Counsel .... Ms. Andrea J. CHASTAIN
15 Director Human Resources .... Ms. Cheryl C. COLEMAN
88 Director Forensic Laboratory .... Mr. Alan H. COLEN
88 Director Wellness Center .... Mr. Rob M. CRANE
103 Director Emerging Workforce .... Ms. Jeanne CRANE-SMITH
88 Director Regional Prevention Center .... Ms. Carla D. GREEN
66 Director Nursing .... Ms. Anita M. KRONDAK
66 Director Practical Nursing .... Ms. Susan K. WHITE
88 Assistant Director Student Develop .... Ms. Tamara D. MILLER
88 Director EMT-MICT Program .... Ms. Donna OLAFSON
88 Director Technical Programs .... Mr. Richard PIPER
88 Director Technical Programs Perkins .... Ms. Donna S. SHAWN
88 Assistant Director Academic Resourc .... Ms. Amanda WILLIAMS
88 Director Performing Arts Center .... Mr. Bill YEAZEL

Kansas College of Chinese Medicine (A)

9235 East Harry, Bldg 200, Wichita KS 67207

County: Sedgwick — FICE Identification: 041453
Telephone: (316) 691-8822 — Carnegie Class: Not Classified
FAX Number: (316) 691-8868 — Calendar System: Semester
URL: www.kccm.edu
Established: 1997 — Annual Graduate Tuition & Fees: $5,850
Enrollment: 40 — Coed
Affiliation or Control: Proprietary — IRS Status: Proprietary
Highest Offering: Master's; No Undergraduates
Program: 2-Year Principally Bachelor's Creditable; Professional
Accreditation: @ACUP

01 President .... Dr. Qizhi GAO

Kansas State University (B)

Manhattan KS 66506

County: Riley — FICE Identification: 001928
Unit ID: 155399
Telephone: (785) 532-6250 — Carnegie Class: RU/H
FAX Number: (785) 532-2120 — Calendar System: Semester
URL: www.k-state.edu
Established: 1863 — Annual Undergrad Tuition & Fees (In-State): $7,657
Enrollment: 23,588 — Coed
Affiliation or Control: State — IRS Status: 501(c)3
Highest Offering: Doctorate
Program: Liberal Arts And General; Teacher Preparatory; Professional
Accreditation: NH, ART, BUS, BUSA, CACREP, CEA, CIDA, CONST, CS, DIETC, DIETD, ENG, IPSY, JOUR, LSAR, MFCD, MUS, NRPA, PLNG, SP, SPAA, SW, TED, THEA, VET

01 President .... Dr. Kirk H. SCHULZ
05 Provost and Senior Vice President .... Dr. April C. MASON
10 Vice Pres Administration & Finance .... Mr. Bruce SHUBERT
46 Vice President Research .... Dr. Ronald W. TREWYN
32 VP Student Life/Dean of Students .... Dr. Pat J. BOSCO
26 VP for Communications & Marketing .... Mr. Jeffery B. MORRIS
31 Dir of Community Rels/Asst to Pres .... Dr. Jackie L. HARTMAN
20 Senior Vice Provost .... Dr. Ruth DYER
86 Asst to Pres/Dir for Govt Relations .... Dr. Susan K. PETERSON
04 Admin Asst to the President .... Ms. Dana M. HASTINGS
13 Vice Provost Info Tech Svcs .... Mr. Kenneth STAFFORD
20 Associate Provost .... Dr. Brian A. NIEHOFF
88 Director Military Affairs .... LTC. Arthur S. DE GROAT
08 Dean of Libraries .... Dr. Lori A. GOETSCH
47 Interim Dean of Agriculture .... Dr. Gary PIERZYNSKI
48 Dean Architecture/Planning/Design .... Mr. Timothy DE NOBLE
49 Interim Dean of Arts & Sciences .... Dr. Joseph AISTRUP
50 Dean of Business Administration .... Dr. Ali R. MALEKZADEH
51 Dean of Continuing Education .... Dr. Sue C. MAES
53 Dean of Education .... Dr. Michael C. HOLEN
54 Dean of Engineering .... Dr. John R. ENGLISH
58 Dean of Graduate School .... Dr. Carol SHANKLIN
59 Dean of Human Ecology .... Dr. Virginia M. MOXLEY
72 Dean of Technology & Aviation .... Dr. Dennis K. KUHLMAN
74 Dean of Veterinary Medicine .... Dr. Ralph C. RICHARDSON
102 President/CEO of Foundation .... Dr. Fred A. CHOLICK
29 Alumni Association President .... Ms. Amy Button RENZ
41 Athletic Director .... Mr. John CURRIE
56 Interim Dir Research and Extension .... Dr. Gary PIERZYNSKI
21 Director of Budget .... Ms. Cindy A. BONTRAGER
37 Asst VP Student Financial Assist .... Mr. Lawrence E. MOEDER
36 Director Career & Employment Svcs .... Ms. Kerri D. KELLER
06 Registrar .... Dr. Monty E. NIELSEN
07 Asst VP/Director of Admissions .... Mr. Lawrence E. MOEDER
15 Asst VP for Human Resources .... Mr. Gary E. LEITNAKER
28 Asc Prov Diversity/Dual Career Dev .... Dr. Myra E. GORDON

Kansas State University-Salina, College of Technology and Aviation (C)

2310 Centennial Road, Salina KS 67401-8196

County: Saline — FICE Identification: 004611
Unit ID: 155405
Telephone: (785) 826-2601 — Carnegie Class: Not Classified
FAX Number: (785) 826-2998 — Calendar System: Semester
URL: www.salina.k-state.edu
Established: 1965 — Annual Undergrad Tuition & Fees (In-State): $5,900
Enrollment: 800 — Coed
Affiliation or Control: State — IRS Status: 501(c)3
Highest Offering: Baccalaureate
Program: Occupational; 2-Year Principally Bachelor's Creditable; Liberal Arts And General
Accreditation: &NH, AAB, ENGT

01 CEO and Dean .... Dr. Dennis K. KUHLMAN
05 Associate Dean of Academics .... Mr. David DELKER
32 Assoc Dean of Student Life .... Ms. Dixie SCHIERLMAN
10 Director of Fiscal Affairs .... Ms. Alyson ROME
37 Financial Aid Officer .... Ms. Cindy NEWELL
08 Librarian & Asst Dean of Academics .... Ms. Alysia STARKEY
06 Registrar .... Ms. Jackie DEAN
18 Chief Facilities/Physical Plant .... Mr. Ken KARY
26 Chief Public Rel/Dir Alum Relations .... Ms. Natalie BLAIR
36 Director Student Placement .... Vacant
38 Director Student Counseling .... Mr. Joel MATTHEWS
96 Director of Purchasing .... Ms. Alyson ROME

† Regional accreditation is carried under the parent institution in Manhattan, KS.

Kansas Wesleyan University (D)

100 E Claflin Avenue, Salina KS 67401-6196

County: Saline — FICE Identification: 001929
Unit ID: 155414
Telephone: (785) 827-5541 — Carnegie Class: Bac/Diverse
FAX Number: (785) 827-0927 — Calendar System: Semester
URL: www.kwu.edu
Established: 1886 — Annual Undergrad Tuition & Fees: $21,400
Enrollment: 825 — Coed
Affiliation or Control: United Methodist — IRS Status: 501(c)3
Highest Offering: Master's
Program: Liberal Arts And General; Teacher Preparatory; Professional
Accreditation: NH, NUR, TED

01 President and CEO .... Dr. Fletcher M. LAMKIN
10 Vice Pres Finance/Administration .... Mr. Wayne R. SCHNEIDER
30 Vice Pres Admiss & Inst Development .... Mr. William P. TANNER
32 VP for Student Development .... Dr. John N. BLACKWELL
21 Controller .... Ms. Cheri L. JOHNSON
44 Dir of Institutional Advancement .... Mr. Jeff CHAPMAN
84 Director Enrollment/Financial Svcs .... Ms. Glenna R. ALEXANDER
08 Director of Library Svcs .... Vacant
18 Director of Plant Operations .... Mr. Darrell D. VICTORY
41 Director of Athletic Programs .... Dr. Matthew J. WILLIAMS
29 Director of Alumni Relations .... Vacant
26 Director of Public Relations .... Vacant
13 Director of Information Systems .... Mr. Jay C. KROB
40 Bookstore Manager .... Mr. Steve CARRIER
66 Chair of Nursing Education .... Dr. Linda M. ADAMS-WENDLING
57 Dept Chair Communication & Theater .... Prof. Barbara J. MARSHALL
79 Division Chair Dept Humanities .... Prof. Marcia M. MACLENNAN
88 Div Chr Dept of Chemistry .... Dr. Dorothy A. HANNA
49 Div Chair Applied Art & Sciences .... Prof. Bryan MINNICH
83 Division Chair Dept Social Sciences .... Dr. Steve J. HOEKSTRA
53 Chair Department Teacher Education .... Dr. Kathleen A. BARRETT-JONES
64 Chair of Music Department .... Prof. Kensuke HAKODA
36 Director of Career Services .... Ms. Carla M. LARKIN
06 Registrar .... Ms. Glenna R. ALEXANDER
50 Director of MBA & Business Programs .... Dr. Monte SHADWICK
07 Director of Admissions .... Vacant
09 Dir Program Research/Assessment .... Dr. Susan K. MCDONALD
81 Dept Chair Mathematics & Physics .... Dr. Susan K. MCDONALD

Labette Community College (E)

200 S 14th, Parsons KS 67357-4299

County: Labette — FICE Identification: 001930
Unit ID: 155450
Telephone: (620) 421-6700 — Carnegie Class: Assoc/Pub-R-M
FAX Number: (620) 421-0921 — Calendar System: Semester
URL: www.labette.edu
Established: 1923 — Annual Undergrad Tuition & Fees (In-District): $2,400
Enrollment: 2,011 — Coed
Affiliation or Control: Local — IRS Status: 501(c)3
Highest Offering: Associate Degree
Program: Occupational; 2-Year Principally Bachelor's Creditable
Accreditation: NH, ADNUR, @PTAA, RAD

01 President .... Dr. George C. KNOX
04 Executive Assistant to President .... Ms. Megan A. FUGATE
05 Vice President Academic Affairs .... Mr. Joe BURKE
10 Vice President Finance & Operations .... Ms. Leanna J. NEWBERRY
32 Vice President Student Affairs .... Ms. Tammy FUENTEZ
20 Dean of Instruction .... Mrs. Sara HARRIS
13 Director of Information Technology .... Mrs. Jody BURZINSKI
30 Dir Resource Devel/Alumni Rels .... Mrs. Lindi D. FORBES
08 Director of Library Services .... Mr. Scott M. ZOLLARS
18 Director of Physical Plant .... Mr. Jim D. FISH
66 Director of Nursing .... Mrs. Delyna BOHNENBLUST
41 Athletic Director .... Mr. Aaron J. KEAL
31 Director of Community Services .... Mrs. MiChielle COOPER
26 Director of Public Relations .... Mrs. Bethany KENDRICK
06 Registrar/Dir Student Financial Aid .... Ms. Kathy JOHNSTON
07 Director of Admissions .... Ms. Kathy JOHNSTON
15 Director of Human Relations .... Ms. Janice S. GEORGE
37 Director Student Financial Aid .... Ms. Kathy JOHNSTON
35 Student Life Coordinator .... Ms. Tarah COCKRELL
40 Bookstore Specialist .... Mrs. Lois D. HEMBREE

Manhattan Area Technical College (F)

3136 Dickens Avenue, Manhattan KS 66503-2499

County: Riley — FICE Identification: 005500
Unit ID: 155487
Telephone: (785) 587-2800 — Carnegie Class: Assoc/Pub-R-S
FAX Number: (785) 587-2804 — Calendar System: Semester
URL: www.matc.net
Established: 1965 — Annual Undergrad Tuition & Fees (In-District): $3,400
Enrollment: 593 — Coed
Affiliation or Control: State/Local — IRS Status: 501(c)3
Highest Offering: Associate Degree
Program: Occupational; 2-Year Principally Bachelor's Creditable; Technical Emphasis
Accreditation: NH, ADNUR, DH

01 President/CEO .... Dr. Robert J. EDLESTON
05 Vice Pres of Instructional Services .... Ms. Marilyn MAHAN
32 Vice President of Student Services .... Mr. Justin PFEIFER
10 Vice President of Business Services .... Ms. Jane BLOODGOOD
30 Assoc VP Institutional Advancement .... Dr. Richard FOGG
15 Director Human Resources .... Ms. Trysta WILLIAMS
07 Director of Admissions .... Ms. Nicole FISCHER
37 Director Financial Aid .... Ms. Sarah SAUERESSIG

Manhattan Christian College (G)

1415 Anderson, Manhattan KS 66502-4081

County: Riley — FICE Identification: 001931
Unit ID: 155496
Telephone: (785) 539-3571 — Carnegie Class: Spec/Faith
FAX Number: (785) 539-0832 — Calendar System: Semester
URL: www.mccks.edu
Established: 1927 — Annual Undergrad Tuition & Fees: $12,400
Enrollment: 379 — Coed
Affiliation or Control: Christian Churches And Churches of Christ
IRS Status: 501(c)3
Highest Offering: Baccalaureate
Program: Liberal Arts And General; Professional; Religious Emphasis
Accreditation: NH, BI

01 President .... Mr. J. Kevin INGRAM
05 Vice President Academic Affairs .... Mr. Randall L. INGMIRE
10 Vice President Business Affairs .... Ms. Lori J. STANFIELD
30 Vice Pres Institutional Advancement .... Mr. Vern HENRICKS
32 Vice President Student Life .... Dr. Rick L. WRIGHT
06 Registrar .... Mrs. Lauren HESKETT
26 Asst to Institutional Advancement .... Mrs. Jolene K. RUPE
37 Director of Financial Aid .... Mrs. Margaret K. CARLISLE
08 Library Director .... Mrs. Mary Ann BUHLER
41 Athletic Director .... Mr. Shawn M. CONDRA
29 Alumni Relations Director .... Mrs. Genae DENVER
04 Admin Asst to President .... Ms. Juanita (Nita) M. PRICKETT

McPherson College (H)

1600 E Euclid, PO Box 1402, McPherson KS 67460-1402

County: McPherson — FICE Identification: 001933
Unit ID: 155511
Telephone: (620) 242-0400 — Carnegie Class: Bac/Diverse
FAX Number: (620) 241-8443 — Calendar System: 4/1/4
URL: www.mcpherson.edu
Established: 1887 — Annual Undergrad Tuition & Fees: $20,600
Enrollment: 622 — Coed
Affiliation or Control: Church Of The Brethren — IRS Status: 501(c)3
Highest Offering: Baccalaureate

Program: Liberal Arts And General; Teacher Preparatory
Accreditation: NH, TED

01 President Mr. Michael P. SCHNEIDER
05 Vice President Academic Affairs Dr. Kent EATON
30 Vice President for Advancement Ms. Amanda GUTIERREZ
10 Vice President for Finance Vacant
26 Vice President for Marketing Ms. Christi HOPKINS
07 Vice President for Admissions Mr. David BARRETT
32 Dean of Students Mr. LaMonte ROTHROCK
41 Athletic Director Mr. Doug QUINT
06 Assoc Dean of Academic Records Mrs. Karlene M. TYLER
88 Special Projects Coordinator Ms. Abbey ARCHER-RIERSON
37 Director of Financial Aid Ms. Brenda KREHBIEL
08 Director of Library Services Ms. Mary HESTER
36 Director of Career Services Mrs. Chris WIENS
26 Director Marketing & Communications Ms. Nancy YOUNG
40 Director of Bookstore Mrs. Linda BARRETT
42 Director of Campus Ministry Vacant
13 Director of Computer Services Mr. David GITCHELL

MidAmerica Nazarene University (A)

2030 E College Way, Olathe KS 66062-1899
County: Johnson FICE Identification: 007032
Unit ID: 155520
Telephone: (913) 782-3750 Carnegie Class: Master's M
FAX Number: (913) 971-3290 Calendar System: Semester
URL: www.mnu.edu
Established: 1966 Annual Undergrad Tuition & Fees: $20,500
Enrollment: 1,776 Coed
Affiliation or Control: Church Of The Nazarene IRS Status: 501(c)3
Highest Offering: Master's
Program: 2-Year Principally Bachelor's Creditable; Liberal Arts And General; Teacher Preparatory; Professional
Accreditation: NH, CACREP, MUS, NURSE, TED

01 Interim President Dr. Jim DIEHL
05 Vice President Academic Affairs Dr. Stephen W. RAGAN
10 Vice President Finance Mr. Kevin P. GILMORE
30 Vice Pres University Advancement Mr. Jon D. NORTH
32 Vice President Community Formation Dr. Randy BECKUM
42 University Chaplain Dr. Randy BECKUM
20 Associate Academic Vice President Dr. Mark C. FORD
27 Chief Technology Officer Dr. Martin CROSSLAND
88 Dean School Christian Min/Formation Dr. Bruce E. OLDHAM
66 Dean Sch Nursing/Health Sci Dr. Susan LARSON
50 Interim Dean School of Business Mrs. Jamie MYRTLE
53 Interim Dean School Educ/Counseling Dr. Linda ALEXANDER
49 Interim Dean College Arts & Science Dr. Cindy PETERSON
06 Registrar Mr. James R. GARRISON
08 Director of the Library Vacant
26 Assoc VP University Advancement Mr. Tim KEETON
07 Director of Admissions Mr. Warren W. ROGERS
39 Director of Residential Life Mrs. Kristi KEETON
29 Director of Alumni Mr. Kevin S. GARBER
37 Director of Student Financial Svcs Mr. Perry DIEHM
41 Athletic Director Mr. Kevin L. STEELE
14 Director of Information Technology Mr. Ruskin P. GOLDEN
15 Director of Human Resources Ms. Nancy S. MERIMEE
27 Director of Mktg & Communications Mr. Michael L. JOHNSON
18 Director of Facility Services Mr. Dennis JOHNSON
40 Bookstore Manager Mrs. Julie HARBOUR
19 Interim Director of Campus Safety Mr. Emil F. SCHELLACK

Neosho County Community College (B)

800 W 14th Street, Chanute KS 66720-2699
County: Neosho FICE Identification: 001936
Unit ID: 155566
Telephone: (620) 431-2820 Carnegie Class: Assoc/Pub-R-M
FAX Number: (620) 431-0082 Calendar System: Semester
URL: www.neosho.edu
Established: 1935 Annual Undergrad Tuition & Fees (In-District): $2,220
Enrollment: 2,805 Coed
Affiliation or Control: Local IRS Status: 501(c)3
Highest Offering: Associate Degree
Program: Occupational; 2-Year Principally Bachelor's Creditable
Accreditation: NH, ACBSP, ADNUR

01 President Dr. Brian L. INBODY
05 Vice President Student Learning Mr. James GENANDT
11 Vice President for Operations Mr. Benjamin J. SMITH
10 Chief Financial Officer Ms. Sondra K. SOLANDER
32 Dean Student Development Mr. Jason KEGLER
51 Dean of Outreach and Workforce Dev Ms. Brenda L. KRUMM
12 Dean Ottawa Campus Mr. Dale E. ERNST
30 Director of Development/Alumni Rels Ms. Claudia CHRISTIANSEN
13 Director of Technology Services/ CIO Mr. Kerry D. RANABARGAR
08 Director Library Services Ms. Susan D. WEISENBERGER
37 Director Student Financial Aid Ms. Kara B. HALE
66 Director of Nursing Ms. Pamela COVAULT
46 Director of Assessment/Research Ms. Sarah ROBB
15 Director Personnel Services Ms. Brenda S. ROWE
41 Athletic Director Ms. Amber BURDGE
07 Director of Admissions Ms. Sarah CADWALLADER
85 Coordinator/International Students Ms. Ann M. NEFF
06 Registrar Vacant
40 Director of Bookstore Ms. Selina WALLACE

26 Chief Public Relations Officer Ms. Nancy ISAAC
38 Director Student Counseling Vacant
39 Residence/Student Life Coordinator Mr. Jesse KEPPEN

Newman University (C)

3100 McCormick, Wichita KS 67213-2097
County: Sedgwick FICE Identification: 001939
Unit ID: 155335
Telephone: (316) 942-4291 Carnegie Class: Master's L
FAX Number: (316) 942-4483 Calendar System: Semester
URL: www.newmanu.edu
Established: 1933 Annual Undergrad Tuition & Fees: $21,716
Enrollment: 2,746 Coed
Affiliation or Control: Roman Catholic IRS Status: 501(c)3
Highest Offering: Master's
Program: Occupational; 2-Year Principally Bachelor's Creditable; Liberal Arts And General; Teacher Preparatory; Professional
Accreditation: NH, ANEST, NURSE, OTA, RAD, SW, TED

01 President Dr. Noreen CARROCCI
04 Exec Assistant to the President Ms. Tracy MCGAREY
05 Provost & Vice Pres Acad Affairs Dr. Michael AUSTIN
30 Vice Pres Institutional Advancement Mr. Tom BORREGO
10 Vice Pres Finance/Administration Mr. Mark DRESSELHAUS
15 Vice President Human Resources Ms. Rhonda CANTRELL
20 Assoc VP Acad Svcs/Student Dev Ms. Rosemary NIEDENS
42 Director of Campus Ministry Fr. Michael LINNEBUR
29 Director of Alumni Relations Ms. Ann FOX
26 Director of Communications Ms. Kelly SNEDDEN
14 Director of Information Technology Mr. Jim JONES
09 Director of Institutional Research Sr. JoAnn MARK, ASC
08 Library Director Mr. Joseph FORTE
06 Registrar Ms. Shirley RUEB
37 Director of Financial Aid Ms. Charly SMITH
41 Director of Athletics Mr. Victor TRILLI
40 Director of Bookstore Mr. Larry WILLIAMS
19 Director of Safety & Security Mr. Richard OLIVERSON
21 Controller Mr. Don WIESNER
07 Dean of Admissions Mr. John CLAYTON
32 Dean of Students Ms. Laura NICHOLAS HUPACH
58 Dean College of Grad/Cont Studies Dr. Audrey CURTIS HANE
49 Dean College of Undergrad Studies Dr. David SHUBERT

North Central Kansas Technical College (D)

PO Box 507, Beloit KS 67420-0507
County: Mitchell FICE Identification: 005265
Unit ID: 155593
Telephone: (785) 738-2276 Carnegie Class: Assoc/Pub-R-S
FAX Number: (785) 738-2903 Calendar System: Semester
URL: www.ncktc.edu
Established: 1964 Annual Undergrad Tuition & Fees (In-District): $4,312
Enrollment: 762 Coed
Affiliation or Control: State/Local IRS Status: 501(c)3
Highest Offering: Associate Degree
Program: Occupational; 2-Year Principally Bachelor's Creditable; Technical Emphasis
Accreditation: NH, ADNUR

01 President Mr. Clark COCO
05 Dean of Instruction Mr. Eric BURKS
11 Dean of Administrative Services Mrs. Brandi ZIMMER
66 Director of Nursing Mrs. Sandy GOTTSCHALK
06 Registrar Ms. Judy HEIDRICK
07 Director of Admissions Mr. David HUGHES
09 Coordinator Institutional Research Mrs. Jennifer BROWN
32 Dean of Student Services Mr. David HUGHES
37 Director Student Financial Aid Mr. Gary ODLE

Northwest Kansas Technical College (E)

1209 Harrison Street, PO Box 668,
Goodland KS 67735-3441
County: Sherman FICE Identification: 005267
Unit ID: 155618
Telephone: (785) 890-3641 Carnegie Class: Assoc/Pub-R-S
FAX Number: (785) 899-5711 Calendar System: Semester
URL: www.nwktc.edu
Established: 1964 Annual Undergrad Tuition & Fees (In-District): $8,525
Enrollment: 384 Coed
Affiliation or Control: State/Local IRS Status: 501(c)3
Highest Offering: Associate Degree
Program: Occupational; Technical Emphasis
Accreditation: NH, MAC

01 President Dr. Ed MILLS
05 Vice Pres Instructional Services Ms. Brenda L. CHATFIELD
32 Vice Pres Student Services Mr. Bill R. FINLEY
35 Asst Vice Pres of Student Affairs Ms. Diane STILES

Ottawa University (F)

1001 S Cedar Street, Ottawa KS 66067-3399
County: Franklin FICE Identification: 001937
Unit ID: 155627
Telephone: (785) 242-5200 Carnegie Class: Bac/Diverse
FAX Number: (785) 229-1020 Calendar System: Semester
URL: www.ottawa.edu
Established: 1865 Annual Undergrad Tuition & Fees: $21,680
Enrollment: 924 Coed
Affiliation or Control: American Baptist IRS Status: 501(c)3
Highest Offering: Master's
Program: Liberal Arts And General; Teacher Preparatory
Accreditation: NH, TED

01 President Mr. Kevin C. EICHNER
05 Univ Provost/Chief Academic Officer Dr. Terry HAINES
20 Vice Pres & Provost of the College Dr. Dennis J. TYNER
10 Vice Pres Administration/CFO Mr. J. Clark RIBORDY
26 Mgr Public Relations & Publications Ms. Paula PAINE
30 Vice Pres University Advancement Mr. Paul BEAN
86 VP Regulatory/Governmental Affairs Dr. Donna LEVENE
09 Assoc VP Governmental/Reg Affairs Ms. Jan STONE
88 Vice President for APOS Dr. Brian SANDUSKY
88 Vice President for APOS Mr. Brian MESSER
12 Campus Executive Arizona Dr. Mary VANIS
12 Interim Campus Executive Indiana Mr. Walter CROX
12 Campus Executive Wisconsin Dr. Wade MAULAND
12 Campus Executive Kansas Ms. Kristen MOORE
32 Dean Student Affairs Mr. Tom TALDO
84 Mgr New Student Enrollment Service Mr. Steed BELL
06 University Registrar Ms. Karen ADAMS
21 Director Finance/Controller Mrs. Brenda GUENTHER
21 Director Business Operations Mr. Thomas CORLEY
15 Director Human Resources Mrs. Joanna L. WALTERS
37 Director Financial Aid Mr. Howard FISCHER
13 Director Information Technology Dr. Jack MAXWELL
29 Director Alumni Programs Ms. Nori HALE
08 Director Library Services Ms. Gloria CREED-DIKEOGU
41 Director Athletics Ms. Arabie CONNER
36 Dir Career Svcs/Student Employment Mrs. Susan WEBB
18 Chief Facilities/Physical Plant Mr. Herb ORR
04 Executive Assistant to President Ms. Gaynia MENNINGER
11 Chief Operations Officer Mr. Keith JOHNSON
20 Dean of Instruction Dr. Karen OHNESORGE

Ottawa University Kansas City (G)

4370 W. 109th Street, Suite 200,
Overland Park KS 66211-1302
County: Johnson Identification: 666083
Unit ID: 155636
Telephone: (913) 266-8600 Carnegie Class: Bac/Diverse
FAX Number: (913) 451-0806 Calendar System: Semester
URL: www.ottawa.edu
Established: 1974 Annual Undergrad Tuition & Fees: $10,560
Enrollment: 366 Coed
Affiliation or Control: American Baptist IRS Status: 501(c)3
Highest Offering: Master's
Program: Liberal Arts And General; Teacher Preparatory
Accreditation: &NH

01 President Mr. Kevin EICHNER
03 Campus Executive Ms. Kristen MOORE
05 Univ Provost/Chief Academic Officer Dr. Terry HAINES
10 Vice Pres Administration/CFO Mr. J. Clark RIBORDY
26 Mgr Public Relations & Publications Ms. Paula PAINE
30 Vice Pres University Advancement Mr. Paul BEAN
86 VP Regulatory/Governmental Affairs Dr. Donna LEVENE
88 Vice President for APOS Dr. Brian SANDUSKY
20 Dean of Instruction Ms. Kristen MOORE
21 Director Finance/Controller Ms. Brenda GUENTHER
21 Director Business Operations Mr. Tom CORLEY
15 Director Human Resources Ms. Joanna WALTERS
06 University Registrar Ms. Karen ADAMS
07 Senior Enrollment Advisor Mr. Jake ASHLEY
21 Business Administrator Mr. Chad TALDO
88 Vice President for APOS Mr. Brian MESSER

† Regional accreditation is carried under the parent institution in Ottawa, KS.

Pinnacle Career Institute (H)

1601 W. 23rd Street, Ste 200, Lawrence KS 66046
County: Douglas FICE Identification: 026130
Unit ID: 367097
Telephone: (785) 841-9640 Carnegie Class: Not Classified
FAX Number: (785) 841-4854 Calendar System: Quarter
URL: www.pcitraining.edu
Established: 1953 Annual Undergrad Tuition & Fees: $13,715
Enrollment: 187 Coed
Affiliation or Control: Proprietary IRS Status: Proprietary
Highest Offering: Associate Degree
Program: Occupational
Accreditation: ACICS

01 Executive Director Mr. Jeremy COOPER

Pittsburg State University (I)

1701 S Broadway, Pittsburg KS 66762-7500
County: Crawford FICE Identification: 001926
Unit ID: 155681
Telephone: (620) 231-7000 Carnegie Class: Master's L
FAX Number: (620) 235-4080 Calendar System: Semester
URL: www.pittstate.edu
Established: 1903 Annual Undergrad Tuition & Fees (In-State): $5,162
Enrollment: 7,131 Coed
Affiliation or Control: State IRS Status: 501(c)3
Highest Offering: Beyond Master's But Less Than Doctorate

Program: Liberal Arts And General; Teacher Preparatory; Professional
Accreditation: NH, BUS, CACREP, ENGT, MUS, NRPA, NURSE, SW, TED

01 President .... Dr. Steven A. SCOTT
05 Provost & VP for Acad Affs .... Dr. Lynette OLSON
11 VP Administration & Campus Life .... Mr. John D. PATTERSON
30 Vice Pres University Advancement .... Dr. J. Bradford HODSON
06 Registrar .... Ms. Debbie GREVE
32 Assoc VP Campus Life/Auxil Svcs .... Dr. Steve ERWIN
88 Assoc VP for Communication & Mktg .... Mr. Chris KELLY
09 Director Analysis/Planning/Assess .... Dr. Robert B. WILKINSON
26 Director of Media Relations .... Mr. Ron WOMBLE
29 Dir Alumni Rels/Constituent Svcs ... Ms. Johnna M. SCHREMMER
27 Chief Information Officer .... Ms. Angela NERIA
15 Director Human Resource Svcs/Budget .... Dr. Michele D. SEXTON
51 Dean Continuing Graduate Studies .... Dr. Peggy J. SNYDER
49 Dean of Arts & Sciences .... Dr. Karl KUNKEL
50 Dean of Business .... Dr. Paul GRIMES
53 Dean of Education .... Dr. Howard W. SMITH
72 Dean of Technology .... Dr. Bruce D. DALLMAN
08 Dean of Learning Resources .... Dr. David BUNNELL
85 Director of International Affairs .... Mr. Charles A. OLCESE
04 Dir of Community & Govt Relations .... Vacant
18 Director of Trades & Landscape Svcs .... Mr. Tom AMERSHEK
18 Director Gen & Custodial Services .... Ms. Wanda ENDICOTT
19 Director of University Police .... Mr. Mike MCCRACKEN
22 Dir Equal Opportunity/Affirm Action .... Ms. Jamie JONES
37 Director of Financial Aid .... Ms. Tammy HIGGINS
41 Dir of Intercollegiate Athletics .... Mr. James JOHNSON
07 Director of Admissions .... Ms. Melinda A. ROELFS
36 Director Career Services .... Ms. Mindy E. CLONINGER
38 Dir University Counseling Services .... Dr. Steven MAYHEW
30 Director of University Development .... Ms. Kathleen FLANNERY
96 Director of Purchasing .... Mr. Jim HUGHES
28 Director of Diversity .... Vacant
10 Controller .... Ms. Barbara J. WINTER
84 Dean of Enrollment Management .... Dr. William IVY

Pratt Community College (A)

348 NE SR 61, Pratt KS 67124-8432
County: Pratt — FICE Identification: 001938
Unit ID: 155715
Telephone: (620) 672-5641 — Carnegie Class: Assoc/Pub-R-S
FAX Number: (620) 672-5288 — Calendar System: Semester
URL: www.prattcc.edu
Established: 1938 — Annual Undergrad Tuition & Fees (In-District): $2,805
Enrollment: 1,891 — Coed
Affiliation or Control: State/Local — IRS Status: 501(c)3
Highest Offering: Associate Degree
Program: Occupational; 2-Year Principally Bachelor's Creditable
Accreditation: NH, ACBSP, ADNUR

01 President .... Dr. William A. WOJCIECHOWSKI
05 Vice President Instruction .... Mr. James STRATFORD
10 Vice President Finance/Operations .... Mr. Kent ADAMS
84 Vice Pres Student Enroll Management .... Ms. Lisa MILLER
66 Dean of Allied Health/Nursing .... Ms. Gail WITHERS
41 Director of Athletics .... Mr. Kurt MCAFEE
20 Dean of Academic Instruction .... Vacant
75 Dean of Technical Instruction .... Mr. Jerry BURKHART
07 Director of Admissions .... Mr. Lynn PEREZ
06 Registrar .... Ms. Sally PROSSER
13 Director of Information Technology .... Mr. Jerry SANKO
37 Director of Financial Aid .... Ms. Leah BOWER
30 Director Development .... Ms. Jody JORNS
08 Dir Linda Hunt Memorial Library .... Ms. Pam DIETZ
16 Director of Personnel .... Ms. Rita PINKALL
38 Director Student Success Center .... Ms. Amy JACKSON
21 Controller .... Mr. Jay MIES
18 Director of Buildings & Grounds .... Mr. Dan PETZ
39 Director of Residence Life .... Vacant
26 Chief Public Relations Officer .... Ms. Megan SCHEUERMAN

Seward County Community College/Area Technical School (B)

1801 N Kansas Avenue, Liberal KS 67901-2054
County: Seward — FICE Identification: 008228
Unit ID: 155858
Telephone: (620) 624-1951 — Carnegie Class: Assoc/Pub-R-S
FAX Number: (620) 417-1169 — Calendar System: Semester
URL: www.sccc.edu
Established: 1967 — Annual Undergrad Tuition & Fees (In-District): $2,010
Enrollment: 1,870 — Coed
Affiliation or Control: State/Local — IRS Status: 501(c)3
Highest Offering: Associate Degree
Program: Occupational; 2-Year Principally Bachelor's Creditable
Accreditation: NH, ACBSP, ADNUR, MLTAD, SURGT

01 President .... Dr. Duane M. DUNN
05 Dean of Instruction .... Ms. Cynthia K. RAPP
10 Dean of Finance & Operations .... Mr. Dennis M. SANDER
32 Dean of Student Services .... Ms. Celeste DONOVAN
88 Dean of Outreach .... Mr. Dale K. REED
06 Registrar .... Ms. Donetta DREITZ
13 Director of Information Technology .... Mr. Mark W. MERRIHEW
37 Financial Aid Director .... Mrs. Donna M. FISHER
26 Dir of Public and Alumni Relations .... Mrs. Andrea G. YOXALL
50 Director of Business & Industry .... Mrs. Norma Jean DODGE
24 Director of Multi-media .... Mr. Doug BROWNE
08 Director of Library .... Mr. Matthew PANNKUK
41 Athletic Director .... Mr. Galen W. MCSPADDEN
18 Director of Buildings & Grounds .... Mr. Roger SCHEIB
40 Director of Bookstore .... Ms. Jerri L. LYDDON
30 Director of Development/Alumni Rels .... Ms. Tammy DOLL
39 Student Housing Manager .... Ms. Pam FREEMAN
09 Institutional Research/Data Analyst .... Ms. Teresa WEHMEIER
21 Fiscal Officer/Admin Assistant .... Mr. Mike BAILEY
19 Security Supervisor .... Mr. Kelly J. CAMPBELL
15 Director of Human Resources .... Ms. Deborah WEILERT
07 Admissions Coordinator .... Ms. Kylee J. HARRISON
38 Counselor/Coord of Student Develop .... Vacant
35 Director Student Activities .... Mr. Wade LYON
04 Adm Asst to Pres & Brd of Trustees .... Mrs. Pamela M. PERKINS
66 Dir of Nursing and Allied Health .... Mrs. Veda KING
75 Director of Area Technical School .... Mr. Bud SMITHSON
26 Director of Marketing .... Mr. J.R DONEY

Southwestern College (C)

100 College Street, Winfield KS 67156-2499
County: Cowley — FICE Identification: 001940
Unit ID: 155900
Telephone: (620) 229-6000 — Carnegie Class: Master's M
FAX Number: (620) 229-6224 — Calendar System: Semester
URL: www.sckans.edu
Established: 1885 — Annual Undergrad Tuition & Fees: $21,530
Enrollment: 1,791 — Coed
Affiliation or Control: United Methodist — IRS Status: 501(c)3
Highest Offering: Master's
Program: Liberal Arts And General; Teacher Preparatory; Professional
Accreditation: NH, MUS, NURSE, TED

01 President .... Dr. William R. MERRIMAN, JR.
05 Vice President Academic Affairs .... Dr. James A. SHEPPARD
10 Vice President Finance .... Ms. Sheila R. KRUG
32 Vice President Student Life .... Dr. Dawn E. PLEAS-BAILEY
107 Vice President Professional Studies .... Vacant
45 VP Planning/New Programs .... Dr. Stephen K. WILKE
30 Vice Pres Institutional Advancement .... Mr. Mike K. FARRELL
26 Vice President Communications .... Ms. Sara S. WEINERT
13 Vice Pres Information Technology .... Mr. Ben LIM
35 Dean of Student Life .... Mr. Dan FALK
29 Director Alumni Programs .... Ms. Susan G. LOWE
44 Director Development .... Ms. Jessica FALK
44 Director Major Gifts .... Mr. Ronnie D. JENKINS
20 Director Academic Affairs .... Ms. Gail CULLEN
08 Library Director .... Ms. Veronica MCASEY
88 Director Learner Services .... Ms. Joni RANKIN
07 Director Admission .... Ms. Marla SEXSON
37 Director Financial Aid .... Ms. Brenda D. HICKS
06 Registrar .... Ms. Stacy TOWNSLEY
35 Director Campus Life .... Ms. Lai-L CLEMONS
09 Director of Institutional Research .... Ms. Margaret A. ROBINSON
41 Director Athletics .... Mr. David DENLY
42 Campus Minister .... Ms. Ashlee E. ALLEY
87 Director Human Resources .... Ms. Lonnie BOYD
96 Director of Purchasing .... Mr. David H. DOLSEN
36 Director Advising/Student Success .... Ms. Tami P. PULLINS
04 Administrative Asst to President .... Ms. Skye BROWNING

Sterling College (D)

125 W Cooper Street, Sterling KS 67579-1533
County: Rice — FICE Identification: 001945
Unit ID: 155937
Telephone: (620) 278-2173 — Carnegie Class: Bac/Diverse
FAX Number: (620) 278-4411 — Calendar System: 4/1/4
URL: www.sterling.edu
Established: 1887 — Annual Undergrad Tuition & Fees: $19,950
Enrollment: 751 — Coed
Affiliation or Control: Presbyterian Church (U.S.A.) — IRS Status: 501(c)3
Highest Offering: Baccalaureate
Program: Liberal Arts And General; Teacher Preparatory
Accreditation: NH, TED

01 President .... Dr. Paul J. MAURER
05 Vice President Academic Affairs .... Dr. Greg KERR
30 Vice President for Inst Advancement .... Dr. Marvin DEWEY
10 Vice President Financial Services .... Mr. Scott RICH
32 VP Student Life & Student Affairs .... Mrs. Tina WOHLER
84 Vice Pres Enrollment & Marketing .... Mr. Dennis DUTTON
90 Vice Pres Innovation & Technology .... Vacant
06 Registrar .... Ms. Janet CAYWOOD
08 Head Librarian .... Mrs. Valorie STARR
37 Director of Financial Aid .... Vacant
29 Director of Alumni/Parent Services .... Vacant
41 Athletic Director .... Mr. Gary KEMPF
20 Director Academic Support .... Mr. Gentry SUTTON
44 Director of Annual Giving .... Mr. Don REED
18 Chief Facilities/Physical Plant .... Mr. Arlen NUEST
36 Director Student Placement .... Ms. Lisa PARSON
38 Director Student Counseling .... Ms. Teri ANDERSON
21 Associate Business Officer .... Ms. Michelle HALL
26 Chief Public Relations Officer .... Ms. Karin SWIHART

Tabor College (E)

400 S Jefferson Street, Hillsboro KS 67063-1753
County: Marion — FICE Identification: 001946
Unit ID: 155973
Telephone: (620) 947-3121 — Carnegie Class: Bac/Diverse
FAX Number: (620) 947-2607 — Calendar System: 4/1/4
URL: www.tabor.edu
Established: 1908 — Annual Undergrad Tuition & Fees: $21,740
Enrollment: 646 — Coed
Affiliation or Control: Mennonite Brethren Church — IRS Status: 501(c)3
Highest Offering: Master's
Program: Liberal Arts And General; Teacher Preparatory
Accreditation: NH, MUS, NURSE, TED

01 President .... Dr. Jules GLANZER
05 Vice President Academic Affairs .... Dr. Frank JOHNSON
10 Sr Vice President Business/Finance .... Mr. Kirby FADENRECHT
30 Vice President Advancement .... Mr. James ELLIOTT
41 Vice President of Athletics .... Mr. Rusty ALLEN
32 Vice President of Student Life .... Dr. Jim PAULUS
06 Registrar .... Ms. Deanne DUERKSEN
08 Director of Library Services .... Ms. Robin OTTOSON
84 Director Enrollment Management .... Mr. Rusty ALLEN
37 Dir of Student Financial Services .... Mr. Scott FRANZ
29 Director Alumni & Parent Relations .... Ms. Marlene FAST
27 Director of Communications .... Mrs. Beth RIFFEL
18 Director Facilities/Physical Plant .... Mr. Doug GRABER
35 Director Student Success .... Mr. Kevin HADDUCK
09 Institutional Research .... Mrs. Deborah PENN
13 Director of Information Services .... Mr. Chris GLANZER
27 Chief Information Officer .... Mrs. Joy MARK
15 Human Resources Coordinator .... Mrs. DJ FREEMAN

University of Kansas Main Campus (F)

1450 Jayhawk Boulevard, Room 230,
Lawrence KS 66045-7535
County: Douglas — FICE Identification: 001948
Unit ID: 155317
Telephone: (785) 864-2700 — Carnegie Class: RU/VH
FAX Number: N/A — Calendar System: Semester
URL: www.ku.edu
Established: 1866 — Annual Undergrad Tuition & Fees (In-State): $8,468
Enrollment: 29,462 — Coed
Affiliation or Control: State — IRS Status: 501(c)3
Highest Offering: Doctorate
Program: Liberal Arts And General; Teacher Preparatory; Professional
Accreditation: NH, ART, AUD, BUS, BUSA, CEA, CLPSY, COPSY, CS, ENG, HSA, IPSY, JOUR, LAW, MUS, PH, PHAR, PLNG, SCPSY, SP, SPAA, SW, TED

01 Chancellor .... Dr. Bernadette GRAY-LITTLE
05 Exec Vice Chancellor/Provost .... Dr. Jeffrey S. VITTER
12 Vice Chancellor/Dean Edwards Campus .... Dr. Robert M. CLARK
26 Vice Chancellor for Public Affairs .... Dr. Timothy CABONI
04 Executive Assistant to Chancellor .... Ms. Mary G. BURG
43 General Counsel .... Mr. James P. POTTORFF, JR.
20 Sr Vice Provost Academic Affairs .... Dr. Sara ROSEN
20 Vice Provost .... Dr. Mary Lee HUMMERT
20 Vice Provost .... Ms. Diane H. GODDARD
32 Vice Provost Student Success .... Dr. Marlesa A. RONEY
46 Vice Provost Research/Grad Studies .... Dr. Steven F. WARREN
28 Vice Provost Diversity & Equity .... Dr. Fred RODRIGUEZ
13 Chief Information Officer .... Mr. Bob LIM
45 Asst Vice Provost Research .... Ms. Joanne K. ALTIERI
58 Assoc VP/Dean Research & Grad Stds ... Dr. Sara Thomas ROSEN
104 Assoc VP International Programs .... Ms. Susan GRONBECK-TEDESCO
96 Assoc Vice Provost of Purchasing .... Mr. Barry K. SWANSON
84 AVP Recruitment/Enrollment .... Dr. Matt MELVIN
30 President Endowment Association .... Mr. Dale SEUFERLING
29 President Alumni Association .... Mr. Kevin J. CORBETT
07 Director Admissions .... Ms. Lisa P. KRESS
10 Chief Business/Financial Plng Ofcr .... Ms. Theresa K. GORDZICA
21 Comptroller .... Ms. Katrina M. YOAKUM
21 Director Budget Office .... Mr. Richard L. MCKINNEY
06 Interim University Registrar .... Ms. Marla HERRON
09 Univ Director Inst Research Plng .... Ms. Deborah J. TEETER
15 Director Human Resources .... Ms. Ola FAUCHER
85 Director International Student Svcs .... Dr. Joe POTTS
38 Director Counseling/Psych Services .... Dr. Michael LYNCH MAESTAS
18 Director Design & Construction Mgmt .... Mr. James E. MODIG
37 Director Student Financial Aid .... Ms. Brenda MAIGAARD
36 Director Career/Employment Svcs .... Mr. David GASTON
41 Director Intercollegiate Athletics .... Dr. Sheahon ZENGER
18 Director Facilities Operations .... Mr. Douglas A. RIAT
22 Director Equal Oppty/Recruitment .... Vacant
88 Int Director Multicultural Affairs .... Mr. Rueben PEREZ
23 Director Student Health Services .... Ms. Carol SEAGER
24 Director Media Services .... Dr. Susan M. ZVACEK
39 Director Housing .... Dr. Diana ROBERTSON
86 Director State Relations .... Ms. Kathy DAMRON
27 Director University Relations .... Mr. Todd COHEN
92 Director Honors Program .... Dr. Kathleen A. MCCLUSKEY-FAWCETT
40 Director Bookstores .... Ms. Estella MCCOLLUM
51 Exec Dir Continuing Education .... Mr. Frederick W. PAWLICKI
25 Manager Contract Negotiations .... Ms. Lucille MARINO
91 Project Coord Information Systems .... Mr. David M. GARDNER
49 Dean Liberal Arts/Science .... Dr. Danny J. ANDERSON
61 Dean of Law .... Mr. Stephen W. MAZZA
54 Dean of Engineering .... Dr. Stuart R. BELL
48 Dean Architecture/Design/Planning .... Mr. John C. GAUNT
50 Dean of Business .... Dr. Neeli BENDAPUDI
67 Dean of Pharmacy .... Dr. Kenneth L. AUDUS
60 Dean of Journalism .... Dr. Ann M. BRILL
53 Dean of Education .... Dr. Rick GINSBERG
64 Dean of Music .... Dr. Robert L. WALZEL, JR.
70 Dean of Social Welfare .... Dr. Mary Ellen KONDRAT
08 Dean of Library .... Ms. Lorraine J. HARICOMBE

57 Assoc Dean School of the Arts .... Ms. Elizabeth KOWALCHUK

† Medical Center and Main campus enrollments should be combined for the total Institution enrollment.

University of Kansas Medical Center (A)

3901 Rainbow Boulevard, Kansas City KS 66160-0001
County: Wyandotte FICE Identification: 024579
Unit ID: 155326
Telephone: (913) 588-5000 Carnegie Class: Not Classified
FAX Number: (913) 588-1412 Calendar System: Semester
URL: www.kumc.edu
Established: 1905 Annual Undergrad Tuition & Fees (In-State): $7,745
Enrollment: 2,431 Coed
Affiliation or Control: State IRS Status: 501(c)3
Highest Offering: Doctorate
Program: Professional
Accreditation: &NH, ANEST, CYTO, DIETI, DMOLS, DMS, MED, MIDWF, MT, NMT, NURSE, OT, PTA

01 Exec Vice Chanc/Exec Dean SOM .... Dr. Barbara F. ATKINSON
17 President & CEO Univ of Kansas Hosp .... Mr. Bob PAGE
05 Sr Vice Chan Acad Affs/Dean SON SAH .... Dr. Karen L. MILLER
11 Vice Chancellor for Administration .... Ms. Steffani WEBB
46 Vice Chan for Research/Pres KUMC RI .... Dr. Paul TERRANOVA
20 Vice Chanc Acad Affs/Dean Grad Stds .... Dr. Allen B. RAWITCH
25 Assoc Vice Chan Res Adm/Exec Dir RI .... Dr. Gregory S. KOPF
10 Assoc Vice Chancellor Finance .... Mr. Mike KEEBLE
13 Assoc VC Info Res/Chief Info Ofcr .Mr. James (Jim) L. BINGHAM
15 Assoc Vice Chanc Administration .... Mr. Chris LYON
09 Asst Vice Chan Enterprise Analytics .... Dr. Terry TURNER
88 Sr Assoc Dean for Clinical Affairs .... Dr. Doug GIROD
63 Dean School of Medicine Wichita .... Dr. H. David WILSON
43 Associate General Counsel .... Mr. Steve L. RUDDICK
66 Dir Acad Affairs Admin SON .... Mr. Edward WILSON
32 Dean of Student Services .... Dr. Dorothy A. KNOLL
63 Sr Assoc Dean for Medical Education .... Dr. Heidi CHUMLEY
88 Senior Associate Dean Finance .... Ms. Kimberly A. MEYER
100 Chf of Staff/Sr Assoc Dn Admin SOM .... Ms. Shelley GEBAR
06 Registrar/Asst Dean of Students .... Mr. Chris MEIERS
76 Asst Dean Administration SAH .... Ms. Lou LOESCHER-JUNGE
21 Controller .... Mr. Robert W. WESELOH
26 Director of Communications .... Ms. CJ JANOVY
08 Director Dykes Library .... Ms. Karen COLE
25 Director Sponsored Programs .... Ms. Mei-Shya CHEN
37 Director of Student Financial Aid .... Ms. Sara HONECK
38 Dir Student Counseling .... Dr. Larry LONG
35 Director of Student Engagement .... Mr. Ryan K. GOVE
29 Director Alumni Affairs .... Ms. Kim HUYETT
19 Dir Public Safety/Chief of Police .Mr. Richard (Rick) L. JOHNSON
105 Director Internet Development .... Mr. Jameson WATKINS
18 Director Facilities Management .... Mr. Don A. RAU
96 Director of Purchasing .... Mr. Stephen SCANLON
22 Director Equal Opportunity Office .... Ms. Danielle DEMPSEY-SWOPES
58 Director Graduate Studies .... Ms. Marcia A. JONES
85 Director International Programs .... Ms. Judith E. REAGAN
28 Diversity Coordinator .... Mr. Charles ROMERO

† Medical Center and Main campus enrollments should be combined for the total institution enrollment. Regional accreditation is carried under the parent institution in Lawrence, KS.

University of Saint Mary (B)

4100 S 4th Street Trafficway, Leavenworth KS 66048-5082
County: Leavenworth FICE Identification: 001943
Unit ID: 155812
Telephone: (913) 682-5151 Carnegie Class: Master's M
FAX Number: (913) 758-6140 Calendar System: Semester
URL: www.stmary.edu
Established: 1923 Annual Undergrad Tuition & Fees: $20,300
Enrollment: 993 Coed
Affiliation or Control: Roman Catholic IRS Status: 501(c)3
Highest Offering: Master's
Program: Liberal Arts And General; Teacher Preparatory; Professional
Accreditation: NH, IACBE, NURSE, TED

01 President .... Dr. Diane STEELE
05 Academic Vice President .... Dr. Bryan LEBEAU
10 Vice President for Finance .... Mr. Dale CULVER
30 Director of Development .... Mr. Andrew DAME
26 VP for Marketing & Communication .... Ms. Laura DAVIS
32 Dean of Students .... Dr. Lisa BECKENBAUGH
07 Director of Enrollment .... Mr. Ken WUERZEBERGER
06 Registrar .... Ms. Mary Pat DUTTON
08 Director of the Library .... Ms. Penny LONERGAN
09 Dir of Institutional Research/Plng .... Vacant
29 Director of Alumni & Annual Fund .... Vacant
37 Director of Financial Aid .... Mrs. Judith WIEDOWER
42 Campus Minister .... Sr. Julie MARSH
44 Major Gift/Planned Giving Director .... Ms. Pamela MCNALLY
41 Athletic Director .... Mr. Rob MILLER
15 Director Personnel Services .... Mr. Dale CULVER
39 Director of Residence Life .... Ms. Kristian JACKSON
21 Controller .... Ms. Sherry WELLS
38 Counselor .... Ms. Deborah SHADDY
18 Plant Manager .... Mr. Mark GIESEMAN
40 Bookstore Manager .... Ms. Terri MULLIS
12 Site Coordinator Johnson County .... Ms. Patricia HOWARD
14 Coordinator of Computer Operations .... Mr. Kevin GANTT

Vatterott College - Wichita (C)

8853 East 37th Street North, Wichita KS 67226-2018
County: Sedgwick Identification: 666583
Unit ID: 440891
Telephone: (316) 634-0066 Carnegie Class: Assoc/PrivFP
FAX Number: (316) 634-0002 Calendar System: Quarter
URL: www.vatterott-college.edu
Established: N/A Annual Undergrad Tuition & Fees: $11,000
Enrollment: 410 Coed
Affiliation or Control: Proprietary IRS Status: Proprietary
Highest Offering: Associate Degree
Program: Occupational; 2-Year Principally Bachelor's Creditable; Technical Emphasis
Accreditation: ACCSC

01 Campus Director .... Mr. Michael HARRIS

† Branch campus of Vatterott College-North Park, Berkeley, MO.

Washburn University (D)

1700 SW College Avenue, Topeka KS 66621-0001
County: Shawnee FICE Identification: 001949
Unit ID: 156082
Telephone: (785) 670-1010 Carnegie Class: Master's M
FAX Number: (785) 670-1089 Calendar System: Semester
URL: www.washburn.edu
Established: 1865 Annual Undergrad Tuition & Fees (In-District): $6,566
Enrollment: 7,230 Coed
Affiliation or Control: Local IRS Status: 501(c)3
Highest Offering: First Professional Degree
Program: Liberal Arts And General; Teacher Preparatory; Professional
Accreditation: NH, ART, BUS, DMS, LAW, MUS, NURSE, PTAA, RAD, SW, TED

01 President .... Dr. Jerry B. FARLEY
05 Vice President Acad Affairs .... Dr. Randall G. PEMBROOK
10 Vice Pres Admin & Treasurer .... Mr. Rick L. ANDERSON
32 Vice President for Student Life .... Dr. Denise OTTINGER
84 Director Enrollment Management .... Mr. Richard W. LIEDTKE
43 University Legal Counsel .... Ms. Lisa R. JONES
20 Assoc Vice Pres Acad Affairs .... Dr. Nancy A. TATE
30 President WU Foundation .... Dr. Juliann MAZACHEK
06 Registrar .... Dr. Carla RASCH
08 Dean of Libraries .... Dr. Alan BEARMAN
35 Dean of Students .... Mr. Meredith KIDD
37 Director Student Financial Aid .... Ms. Gail PALMER
07 Director of Admissions .... Mr. Morgan BOYACK
15 Director of Human Resources .... Ms. Deborah D. MOORE
90 Director Info Systems & Services .... Vacant
09 Director Institutional Research .... Ms. Melodie E. CHRISTAL
49 Dean College Arts & Sciences .... Dr. Gordon MCQUERE
88 Dean School Applied Studies .... Dr. William W. DUNLAP
61 Dean School of Law .... Mr. Thomas J. ROMIG
50 Dean School of Business .... Dr. David SOLLARS
66 Dean School of Nursing .... Dr. Monica S. SCHEIBMEIR
41 Athletic Director .... Mr. Loren FERRE
35 Director Student Services .... Ms. Jeanne D. KESSLER
22 Director Equal Opportunity .... Ms. Carol L. VOGEL
18 Director Facilities Services .... Mr. Bill GLATTS
23 Director Health Services .... Dr. Iris P. GONZALEZ
29 Alumni Director .... Ms. Susie HOFFMANN
96 Director of Purchasing .... Mr. Mel RAGAR
04 Special Assistant to the President ..Dr. Cynthia A. HORNBERGER
92 Dean Honors Program .... Dr. Michael J. MCGUIRE
39 Director Student Housing .... Ms. Mindy P. RENDON
40 Director Bookstore .... Ms. Kay FARLEY
35 Director Student Activities .... Ms. Jessica NEUMANN
38 Director Student Counseling .... Ms. Marilynn KOELLIKER

Wichita Area Technical College (E)

4004 N Webb Road, Wichita KS 67226-8101
County: Sedgwick FICE Identification: 005498
Unit ID: 156107
Telephone: (316) 677-9400 Carnegie Class: Assoc/Pub-U-MC
FAX Number: (316) 677-9510 Calendar System: Semester
URL: www.watc.edu
Established: 1965 Annual Undergrad Tuition & Fees (In-District): $2,178
Enrollment: 7,112 Coed
Affiliation or Control: State/Local IRS Status: 501(c)3
Highest Offering: Associate Degree
Program: 2-Year Principally Bachelor's Creditable; Technical Emphasis
Accreditation: NH, DA, MAC, PNUR, SURGT

01 President .... Dr. Anthony G. KINKEL
05 Vice Pres Academic Affairs .... Ms. Sheree UTASH
10 Chief Business Officer .... Mr. Doug BRANTNER
06 Registrar .... Ms. Willow DEAN
07 Director of Admissions .... Mr. Andy MCFAYDEN
09 Director of Institutional Research .... Dr. Scott LUCAS

Wichita State University (F)

1845 N Fairmount, Wichita KS 67260-0001
County: Sedgwick FICE Identification: 001950
Unit ID: 156125
Telephone: (316) 978-3456 Carnegie Class: RU/H
FAX Number: (316) 978-3770 Calendar System: Semester
URL: www.wichita.edu
Established: 1895 Annual Undergrad Tuition & Fees (In-State): $6,190
Enrollment: 14,577 Coed
Affiliation or Control: State IRS Status: 501(c)3
Highest Offering: Doctorate
Program: Liberal Arts And General; Teacher Preparatory; Professional
Accreditation: NH, ARCPA, ART, AUD, BUS, BUSA, CLPSY, DANCE, DENT, DH, ENG, IPSY, MT, MUS, NURSE, PTA, SP, SPAA, SW, TED

01 President .... Dr. Donald L. BEGGS
05 Provost/VP Academic Affs/Research .... Dr. Keith H. PICKUS
11 Vice Pres Administration & Finance .... Ms. Mary L. HERRIN
32 Vice Pres Campus Life/Un Relations .... Dr. Wade A. ROBINSON
43 Vice Pres/General Counsel/Dir EEO .... Mr. Ted D. AYRES
26 Assoc VP University Relations .... Ms. Barth A. HAGUE
09 Asst VP/Dir Institutional Research .... Dr. Donna J. HAWLEY
20 Senior Assoc Provost .... Dr. Richard D. MUMA
27 Assoc Provost/Chief Info Officer .... Dr. Ravi PENDSE
20 Associate Provost .... Dr. Linnea GLENMAYE
46 Asc Provost Research/Dir Rsch Admin ...Dr. J. David MCDONALD
49 Dean Liberal Arts & Sciences .... Dr. William D. BISCHOFF
50 Dean Barton School of Business .... Dr. Douglas A. HENSLER
53 Dean Education .... Dr. Sharon IORIO
54 Dean Engineering .... Dr. Zulma TORO-RAMOS
57 Dean Fine Arts .... Dr. Rodney E. MILLER
76 Dean Health Professions .... Dr. Peter A. COHEN
58 Dean Graduate School .... Dr. J. David MCDONALD
08 Dean Libraries .... Dr. Don GILSTRAP
84 Dean of Enrollment Services .... Ms. Christine SCHNEIKART-LUEBBE
86 Exec Director Government Relations .... Mr. Andrew SCHLAPP
24 Exec Dir Media Resources Center .... Mr. Michael A. WOOD
29 Exec Director Alumni Association .... Ms. Deborah KENNEDY
41 Athletic Director .... Dr. Eric L. SEXTON
88 Director Creative Services .... Mr. Craig LINDEMAN
15 Director Human Resources .... Ms. Frankie M. BROWN
21 Director Budgets .... Mr. Paul F. WERNER
06 Registrar .... Mr. William E. WYNNE
07 Director of Admissions .... Mr. Bobby GANDU
37 Director Financial Aid .... Ms. Deborah BYERS
36 Director Placement/Career Services .... Ms. Jill M. PLETCHER
38 Director Counseling & Testing ... Dr. Maureen DASEY-MORALES
18 Director Physical Plant .... Mr. Woodrow DEPONTIER
45 Director Facilities Planning .... Mr. John D. GIST
19 Campus Police Chief .... Mr. Paul W. DOTSON
23 Director Student Health Services .... Ms. Marilyn R. YOURDAN
39 Director Student Housing .... Ms. Vanessa RODRIGUEZ
28 Int Director Multicultural Affairs .... Mr. Victor COLLINS
40 Manager Bookstore .... Mr. Kevin J. KONDA
21 Controller .... Mr. Steven D. LAFEVER
42 Campus Minister .... Rev. Christopher ESHELMAN
96 Director of Purchasing .... Mr. Steven WHITE
102 Foundation CEO & President .... Dr. Elizabeth KING

Wright Career College (G)

10975 El Monte, Overland Park KS 66211
FICE Identification: 025909
Unit ID: 406200
Telephone: (913) 385-7700 Carnegie Class: Not Classified
FAX Number: (913) 647-8073 Calendar System: Other
URL: www.wrightcareercollege.com
Established: 1997 Annual Undergrad Tuition & Fees: N/A
Enrollment: 1,500 Coed
Affiliation or Control: Independent Non-Profit IRS Status: 501(c)3
Highest Offering: Associate Degree
Program: Occupational
Accreditation: ACICS

01 Campus Director .... Mr. Bradley VEITCH

KENTUCKY

Alice Lloyd College (H)

Purpose Road, Pippa Passes KY 41844-9703
County: Knott FICE Identification: 001951
Unit ID: 156189
Telephone: (606) 368-2101 Carnegie Class: Bac/A&S
FAX Number: (606) 368-6212 Calendar System: Semester
URL: www.alc.edu
Established: 1923 Annual Undergrad Tuition & Fees: $1,700
Enrollment: 598 Coed
Affiliation or Control: Independent Non-Profit IRS Status: 501(c)3
Highest Offering: Baccalaureate
Program: Liberal Arts And General; Teacher Preparatory
Accreditation: SC

01 President .... Dr. Joe A. STEPP
03 Executive Vice President .... Dr. Jim STEPP
05 Vice President Academic Affairs .... Dr. Claude CRUM
10 Vice President of Business Affairs .... Mr. David JOHNSON
32 Dean of Students & Community Life .... Mr. Scott CORNETT
07 Director of Admissions .... Ms. Angela PHIPPS
06 Registrar .... Mrs. Thelmarie THORNSBERRY
08 Director of Library .... Mr. Andrew BUSROE
37 Director of Financial Aid .... Mrs. Jacqueline STEWART
88 Director of Student Work Program .... Mr. Kerry RATLIFF
53 Director of Teacher Education .... Dr. Sherry LONG
18 Director of Physical Plant .... Mr. Ryan GIBSON
39 Director of Student Housing .... Mr. John MILLS
29 Director of Alumni Relations .... Mrs. Teresa GRENDER
35 Director of Student Activities .... Ms. Christine STUMBO
26 Director Marketing/Communications .... Mrs. Natalie GIBSON
09 Director of Institutional Research .... Mr. Gary GIBSON

† Cost of tuition is guaranteed for students from 108 county territories.

Asbury Theological Seminary (A)

204 N Lexington Avenue, Wilmore KY 40390-1199

County: Jessamine — FICE Identification: 001953
Unit ID: 156222
Telephone: (859) 858-3581 — Carnegie Class: Spec/Faith
FAX Number: N/A — Calendar System: 4/1/4
URL: www.asburyseminary.edu
Established: 1923 — Annual Graduate Tuition & Fees: $520
Enrollment: 1,534 — Coed
Affiliation or Control: Independent Non-Profit — IRS Status: 501(c)3
Highest Offering: Doctorate; No Undergraduates
Program: Professional
Accreditation: SC, THEOL

01 President .... Dr. Timothy C. TENNENT
05 Dean/Academic Affairs .... Dr. Leslie A. ANDREWS
10 Vice President Finance .... Mr. Bryan BLANKENSHIP
30 Vice President Seminary Advancement .... Mr. Jay MANSUR
31 Vice Pres Community Life .... Rev. John D. WALT
84 Vice Pres Enrollment Management .... Mr. Kevin BISH
08 Dean of Information Services .... Vacant
06 Registrar .... Mrs. Sheryl VOIGTS
07 Director of Admissions .... Mrs. Carolyn CLAYTON
37 Director of Student Financial Aid .... Mrs. Dawn TIPPEY
18 Chief Facilities/Physical Plant .... Mr. Lanny SPEARS
26 Chief Public Relations Officer .... Mrs. Amanda STAMPER
32 Chief Student Life Officer .... Mr. J. D. WALT
09 Director of Institutional Research .... Dr. Deborah COLWILL
15 Director Personnel Services .... Mrs. Barbara ANTROBUS
29 Director Alumni Relations .... Ms. Tammy CESSNA
73 Dean School of Theology of Ministry .... Dr. James THOBABEN
12 Dean Beeson Center .... Dr. Tom TUMBLIN
12 Dean E.S.J. School .... Dr. Terry MUCK

Asbury University (B)

1 Macklem Drive, Wilmore KY 40390-1198

County: Jessamine — FICE Identification: 001952
Unit ID: 156213
Telephone: (859) 858-3511 — Carnegie Class: Bac/Diverse
FAX Number: (859) 858-3921 — Calendar System: Semester
URL: www.asbury.edu
Established: 1890 — Annual Undergrad Tuition & Fees: $23,303
Enrollment: 1,623 — Coed
Affiliation or Control: Independent Non-Profit — IRS Status: 501(c)3
Highest Offering: Master's
Program: Liberal Arts And General; Teacher Preparatory
Accreditation: SC, MUS, SW, TED

01 President .... Dr. Sandra C. GRAY
05 Provost .... Dr. Jon S. KULAGA
10 Vice Pres Business Affairs & Treas .... Dr. Charlie D. FISKEAUX
32 Vice Pres Student Dev/Dean Students .... Dr. Mark J. TROYER
30 Vice President for Inst Advancement .... Dr. R. Gregory SWANSON
11 Asst Vice President Operations .... Mr. Glenn R. HAMILTON
44 Senior Advancement Director .... Rev. Stuart A. SMITH
37 Director Financial Aid .... Mr. Ronald M. ANDERSON
42 Assoc Dean for Campus Ministries .... Rev. Gregory K. HASELOFF
39 Assoc Dean for Residence Life .... Mr. Joe W. BRUNER
22 Asc Dean Stdnt Success/Intercult .... Mrs. Deborah L. VETTER
06 Registrar .... Mr. William A. HALL, JR.
29 Dir Alumni Relations/Parents Pgm .... Miss Carolyn L. RIDLEY
09 Institutional Research & Planning .... Dr. Gay L. HOLCOMB
08 Director Library Services .... Mr. Morgan A. TRACY
13 Director Information Services .... Mr. Paul J. DUPREE
07 Director of Admissions .... Mrs. Lisa D. HARPER
26 Director of Communications .... Mr. Frank GOAD
18 Director Physical Plant .... Mr. Eric C. MCMILLION
23 Supervisor of Clinic .... Miss Carol J. AMEY
36 Dir Center for Career & Calling .... Dr. Melanie NOBLE
38 Director of Counseling .... Ms. Judi KINLAW
96 Director of Purchasing .... Mr. Jerry MARCHAL
40 Manager of Bookstore .... Mr. C. David TRAMMELL
21 Associate Business Officer .... Mr. Gary E. HOWARD

ATA College (C)

10180 Linn Station Rd, Ste A-200, Louisville KY 40223

County: Jefferson — FICE Identification: 040383
Unit ID: 447935
Telephone: (502) 371-8330 — Carnegie Class: Not Classified
FAX Number: (502) 371-8598 — Calendar System: Quarter
URL: www.ata.edu
Established: 1994 — Annual Undergrad Tuition & Fees: N/A
Enrollment: 567 — Coed
Affiliation or Control: Proprietary — IRS Status: Proprietary
Highest Offering: Associate Degree
Program: Occupational
Accreditation: ABHES

01 President .... Mr. Donald A. JONES

Beckfield College (D)

16 Spiral Drive, Florence KY 41042-4866

County: Boone — FICE Identification: 024911
Unit ID: 247065
Telephone: (859) 371-9393 — Carnegie Class: Assoc/PrivFP4
FAX Number: (859) 371-5096 — Calendar System: Quarter
URL: www.beckfield.edu
Established: 1984 — Annual Undergrad Tuition & Fees: $15,120
Enrollment: 1,126 — Coed
Affiliation or Control: Proprietary — IRS Status: Proprietary
Highest Offering: Baccalaureate
Program: Professional; Business Emphasis
Accreditation: ACICS

01 President/CEO .... Ms. Diane G. WOLFER
05 Vice President of Academic Affairs .... Ms. Cindy GRIGGS
84 Corp Vice Pres Admissions/ Marketing .... Mr. Richard F. COSTA, JR.
12 Campus Director of Florence .... Mr. Keith GRANT
32 Director of Student Services .... Ms. Sarah CRABTREE
37 Director of Financial Aid .... Ms. Patricia A. NETTLETON
13 Director of Information Technology .... Mr. James BRUN
07 Director Admissions .... Ms. Kathy BENDER
36 Director Career Services .... Ms. Danielle FULLER
22 Director of Compliance .... Mr. Peter NETTLETON
06 Registrar .... Ms. Leah BOERGER
08 Librarian .... Ms. Emily STEELE
12 Interim Campus Dean-Florence .... Dr. Jerry LINGER, JR.
50 Dean of Business/Technology .... Ms. Amy M. HEDGES
66 Dean Division of Nursing .... Mr. Timothy D. CURL
76 Dean of Allied Health .... Ms. Ruth GABBARD
97 Dean of General Education .... Ms. Brittaney HARP
88 Dean of Criminal Justice .... Dr. Jack BROWN
04 Assistant to the President .... Ms. Cheryl A. KUNKEL

Bellarmine University (E)

2001 Newburg Road, Louisville KY 40205-0671

County: Jefferson — FICE Identification: 001954
Unit ID: 156286
Telephone: (502) 272-8000 — Carnegie Class: Master's L
FAX Number: (502) 272-8033 — Calendar System: Semester
URL: www.bellarmine.edu
Established: 1950 — Annual Undergrad Tuition & Fees: $32,140
Enrollment: 3,342 — Coed
Affiliation or Control: Independent Non-Profit — IRS Status: 501(c)3
Highest Offering: Doctorate
Program: Liberal Arts And General; Teacher Preparatory; Professional
Accreditation: SC, BUS, MT, NURSE, PTA, TED

01 President .... Dr. Joseph J. MCGOWAN
05 Provost .... Dr. Doris A. TEGART
10 Vice President Admin & Finance .... Mr. Robert L. ZIMLICH
32 Vice President Acad & Student Life .... Dr. Fred W. RHODES
30 Vice President Development & Alumni .... Mr. Glenn F. KOSSE
26 Vice President Comm/Public Affairs .... Mr. Hunt C. HELM
84 Vice President Enrollment Mgmt .... Mr. Sean J. RYAN
100 Exec Assistant to the President .... Ms. Marisa ZOELLER
20 Vice President Academic Affairs .... Dr. Carole PFEFFER
20 Asst VP Academic Affairs .... Dr. Graham ELLIS
20 Asst VP for Acadeic Affairs .... Dr. Cindy G. GNADINGER
66 Dn Lansing Sch of Nursing/Hlth Sci .... Dr. Susan H. DAVIS
50 Dean Rubel School of Business .... Dr. Daniel L. BAUER
107 Dean of Professional Studies .... Dr. Mike MATTEI
53 Dean Annsley Frazier Thornton Ed .... Dr. Robert B. COOTER
47 Dean Regional Environmental Studies .... Dr. Robert KINGSOLVER
49 Dean Bellarmine College .... Dr. William E. FENTON
15 Chief Human Resources Officer .... Ms. Lynn M. BYNUM
21 Asst VP for Admin and Finance .... Ms. Denise BROWN-CORNELIUS
28 Asst VP & Dir Multicultural Pgms .... Dr. Hannah CLAYBORNE
85 Director of International Programs .... Ms. Gabriele BOSLEY
35 Dean of Students .... Dr. Helen G. RYAN
89 Dean Academic Advising .... Dr. Catherine SUTTON
92 Director Honors Program .... Dr. Hank J. ROTHGERBER
41 Athletic Director .... Mr. Scott P. WIEGANDT
18 Chief Facilities/Physical Plant .... Mr. Thomas FISHER
07 Dean of Admission .... Mr. Timothy A. STURGEON
08 Director of the Library .... Mr. John K. STEMMER
19 Director Safety & Security .... Mr. Joseph FRYE
07 Dean of Graduate School Admission .... Dr. Sara YOUNT
06 Registrar .... Ms. Ann E. OLSEN
96 Purchasing Manager .... Mr. Patrick COONS
42 Director Campus Ministry .... Dr. Melanie P. SULLIVAN
39 Director Residence Life .... Ms. Leslie M. MAXIE-ASHFORD
13 Director Information Technology .... Mr. Fred LASSITER
37 Director Student Financial Aid .... Ms. Heather BOUTELL
09 Director of Institutional Research .... Mr. David M. MAHAN
88 Director of Academic Operations .... Ms. Beth O. DAVIS
36 Asst Dean Career Services .... Mr. Todd D. REALE
29 Executive Director Alumni Relations .... Mr. Peter W. KREMER
26 Director of News/Media/Social Netwk .... Mr. Jason A. CISSELL
38 Director Student Counseling .... Dr. Gary PETIPRIN
92 Director of Brown Scholars Program .... Dr. Matisa WILBON

Berea College (F)

101 Chestnut Street, Berea KY 40404-0003

County: Madison — FICE Identification: 001955
Unit ID: 156295
Telephone: (859) 985-3000 — Carnegie Class: Bac/A&S
FAX Number: (859) 985-3917 — Calendar System: Semester
URL: www.berea.edu
Established: 1855 — Annual Undergrad Tuition & Fees: $910
Enrollment: 1,613 — Coed
Affiliation or Control: Independent Non-Profit — IRS Status: 501(c)3
Highest Offering: Baccalaureate
Program: Liberal Arts And General; Teacher Preparatory; Professional
Accreditation: SC, NURSE, TED

01 President .... Dr. Larry D. SHINN
10 Vice President Finance .... Mr. Jeff S. AMBURGEY
30 Vice President Alumni College Rels .... Ms. Michelle JANSSEN
32 Vice President Labor & Student Life .... Ms. Gail WOLFORD
11 VP Operations & Sustainability .... Mr. Steve KARCHER
100 Assistant to Pres/Chief of Staff .... Ms. Tammy CLEMONS
35 Asst Vice Pres for Student Life .... Mr. Gus GERASSIMIDES
05 Academic VP/Dean of the Faculty .... Dr. Stephanie BROWNER
37 Dir of Student Financial Aid Svcs .... Ms. Nancy MELTON
38 Dir Counseling/Psychological Svcs .... Ms. Sue REIMONDO
44 Director of Gift Planning .... Ms. Amy SHEHEE
20 Dean of Curriculum/Student Learning .... Dr. Scott STEELE
13 Chief Information Officer .... Dr. John LYMPANY
84 Dean Enrollment/Academic Services .... Mr. Joe BAGNOLI
07 Director of Admissions Operations .... Mr. Luke HODSON
29 Director of Alumni Relations .... Ms. Mae SURAMEK
15 Director of People Services .... Ms. Carolyn CASTLE
18 Director of Facilities Management .... Mr. Jon METCALF
88 Director of Appalachian Center .... Dr. Chad BERRY
09 Director of Inst Rsrch/Assessment .... Ms. Judith WECKMAN
23 Director of College Health Service .... Dr. Miriam DAVID
26 Director of Public Relations .... Mr. Timothy W. JORDAN
08 Director of Library Services .... Ms. Anne CHASE
41 Dir Athletics/Seabury Ctr Complex .... Mr. Mark CARTMILL
42 Director Campus Christian Center .... Dr. Jeff B. POOL
43 General Counsel .... Mr. Judge WILSON
19 Director of Public Safety .... Mr. V. Lavoyed HUDGINS
28 Director Black Cultural Center .... Vacant
85 Director International Center .... Dr. Richard CAHILL
40 College Bookstore Director .... Ms. Marty WAYLAND
96 Purchasing Manager .... Ms. Aurelia BRANDENBURG
24 Media Services Coordinator .... Mr. Rob LEWIS
06 Director of Academic Services .... Mr. Curtis SANDBERG

Brescia University (G)

717 Frederica Street, Owensboro KY 42301-3023

County: Daviess — FICE Identification: 001958
Unit ID: 156356
Telephone: (270) 685-3131 — Carnegie Class: Bac/Diverse
FAX Number: (270) 686-6422 — Calendar System: Semester
URL: www.brescia.edu
Established: 1950 — Annual Undergrad Tuition & Fees: $17,700
Enrollment: 688 — Coed
Affiliation or Control: Roman Catholic — IRS Status: 501(c)3
Highest Offering: Master's
Program: Liberal Arts And General; Teacher Preparatory
Accreditation: SC, SW

01 President .... Rev. Larry HOSTETTER
05 Vice President & Academic Dean .... Dr. Cheryl CLEMONS
10 Vice President Business & Finance .... Mr. Dale CECIL
84 Vice President of Enrollment .... Mr. Christopher HOUK
30 Vice Pres Institutional Advancement .... Mr. Todd BROCK
32 Vice Pres/Dean Student Development .... Dr. James FITZPATRICK
39 Asst Dean Students Residence Life .... Mr. Jeffrey A. RUDNIK
35 Asst Dean Stdnts Act/Leadership Dev .... Mr. Lucas O. LANGDON
06 Registrar .... Sr. Helena FISCHER, OSU
71 Director of Weekend College .... Mr. Greg ALVEY
38 Director of Counseling Center .... Ms. Eva G. ATKINSON
08 Director of Library Services .... Sr. Judith N. RINEY, OSU
88 Director Student Support Services .... Dr. Dolores KIESLER
15 Director of Human Resources .... Vacant
13 Director of Information Technology .... Mr. Jack T. WILSON
18 Director of Physical Plant .... Mr. Larry J. YOUNGER
37 Director of Financial Aid .... Ms. Marcie TILLETT
41 Director of Athletics .... Mr. Patrick MROZOWSKI
26 Director of Public Relations .... Ms. Tina KASEY
29 Director of Alumni .... Mr. Jason COX
44 Director of Annual Giving .... Ms. Amy FRENCH
09 Director of Institutional Research .... Ms. Tracy NAYLOR
58 Director of Graduate Program-MBA .... Dr. Sandra O. OBILADE
58 Director of Graduate Program-MSCI .... Dr. Patricia A. AKOJIE
42 Director of Campus Ministry .... Sr. Pam MUELLER, OSU
21 Asst Director Business & Finance .... Ms. Nancy W. REYNOLDS
40 Bookstore Manager .... Ms. Beverly MCCANDLESS
36 Coordinator of Career Services .... Sr. Michele MOREK
20 Associate Academic Officer .... Mr. Keith HUDSON

Brown Mackie College-Hopkinsville (H)

4001 Fort Campbell Boulevard,
Hopkinsville KY 42240-4948

County: Christian — Identification: 666516
Unit ID: 421513
Telephone: (270) 886-1302 — Carnegie Class: Assoc/PrivFP
FAX Number: (270) 886-3544 — Calendar System: Other
URL: www.brownmackie.com
Established: 1995 — Annual Undergrad Tuition & Fees: $11,124
Enrollment: 282 — Coed
Affiliation or Control: Proprietary — IRS Status: Proprietary
Highest Offering: Associate Degree
Program: 2-Year Principally Bachelor's Creditable; Business Emphasis
Accreditation: ACICS, OTA

01 President .... Ms. Elaine CUE
06 Associate Registrar .... Ms. Belinda DOZIER
36 Director of Career Services .... Vacant
07 Senior Director of Admissions .... Ms. Delanda BYARS

† Branch campus of Brown Mackie College-Findlay, Findlay, OH.

rown Mackie College-Louisville (A)

3605 Fern Valley Road, Louisville KY 40219-1916
County: Jefferson FICE Identification: 021082
Unit ID: 157599
Telephone: (502) 810-6000 Carnegie Class: Assoc/PrivFP
FAX Number: (502) 357-9956 Calendar System: Other
URL: www.brownmackie.edu
Established: 1972 Annual Undergrad Tuition & Fees: $11,124
Enrollment: 1,948 Coed
Affiliation or Control: Proprietary IRS Status: Proprietary
Highest Offering: Baccalaureate
Program: Occupational; 2-Year Principally Bachelor's Creditable; Business Emphasis
Accreditation: ACICS, OTA, SURGT, SURTEC

01 President ...... Mr. Mike FONTAINE
05 Dean of Academic Affairs ...... Ms. Natalie HARRIS
07 Senior Director of Admissions ...... Mr. George NOSKO
06 Registrar ...... Ms. Shannon MITCHELL
36 Director of Career Services ...... Ms. Chasity TRZOP

† Branch campus of Brown Mackie College-Findlay, Findlay, OH.

Brown Mackie College-Northern Kentucky (B)

309 Buttermilk Pike, Fort Mitchell KY 41017-2191
County: Kenton Identification: 666446
Unit ID: 157696
Telephone: (859) 341-5627 Carnegie Class: Assoc/PrivFP
FAX Number: (859) 341-6483 Calendar System: Other
URL: www.brownmackie.edu
Established: 1981 Annual Undergrad Tuition & Fees: $11,124
Enrollment: 802 Coed
Affiliation or Control: Proprietary IRS Status: Proprietary
Highest Offering: Associate Degree
Program: Occupational; 2-Year Principally Bachelor's Creditable; Business Emphasis
Accreditation: ACICS, OTA

01 President ...... Ms. Christine KNOUFF
05 Dean of Academic Affairs ...... Ms. Marcia NEUDIGATE
07 Senior Director of Admissions ...... Ms. Amy WOLF
32 Director of Student Services ...... Ms. Jean SCHULTZ
36 Director of Career Services ...... Ms. Michelle DRENNEN

† Branch campus of Brown Mackie College, Cincinnati, OH.

Campbellsville University (C)

1 Universty Drive, Campbellsville KY 42718-2799
County: Taylor FICE Identification: 001959
Unit ID: 156365
Telephone: (270) 789-5000 Carnegie Class: Master's M
FAX Number: (270) 789-5050 Calendar System: Semester
URL: www.campbellsville.edu
Established: 1906 Annual Undergrad Tuition & Fees: $20,740
Enrollment: 3,431 Coed
Affiliation or Control: Baptist IRS Status: 501(c)3
Highest Offering: Master's
Program: Liberal Arts And General; Teacher Preparatory; Professional
Accreditation: SC, IACBE, MUS, SW, TED

01 President ...... Dr. Michael CARTER
10 Vice Pres Finance & Administration ...... Mr. Otto TENNANT
05 Vice President Academic Affairs ...... Dr. Frank CHEATHAM
30 Vice President for Development ...... Mr. Benji KELLY
26 VP for Church & External Rels ...... Mr. John E. CHOWNING
07 VP for Admissions/Student Svcs ...... Mr. Dave WALTERS
32 Dean of Student Services ...... Mr. Josh ANDERSON
20 Associate Academic Officer ...... Vacant
21 Comptroller ...... Mr. Tim JUDD
09 Director of Institutional Research ...... Mr. Paul DAMERON
38 Director of Student Counseling ...... Mrs. Jodi ALLEN
28 Director of Diversity ...... Mr. John E. CHOWNING
92 Director of Honors Program ...... Dr. Craig L. ROGERS
41 Director of Athletics ...... Mr. Rusty HOLLINGSWORTH
40 Director of Bookstore ...... Mrs. Donna WRIGHT
42 Director of Campus Ministries ...... Mr. Edwin C. PAVY
13 Director of Computing/Communication ...... Mr. Hermano QUEIROZ
37 Director of Financial Aid ...... Ms. Chris TOLSON
29 Director of Alumni Relations ...... Mrs. Paula SMITH
08 Director of Library Services ...... Mr. John BURCH
15 Director of Personnel Services ...... Mr. Terry VANMETER
18 Director of Maintenance ...... Mr. Steve MORRIS
27 Director of News Information ...... Mrs. Joan C. MCKINNEY
06 Director of Student Records ...... Mrs. Rita A. CREASON
04 Secretary to the President ...... Mrs. Kellie VAUGHN
96 Dir of Purchasing/Special Projects ...... Mr. Marion HALL
88 Director of Custodial Services ...... Mr. Bob STOTTS

Centre College (D)

600 W Walnut Street, Danville KY 40422-1394
County: Boyle FICE Identification: 001961
Unit ID: 156408
Telephone: (859) 238-5200 Carnegie Class: Bac/A&S
FAX Number: (859) 238-6977 Calendar System: Other
URL: www.centre.edu
Established: 1819 Annual Undergrad Tuition & Fees: $42,500
Enrollment: 1,241 Coed
Affiliation or Control: Independent Non-Profit IRS Status: 501(c)3
Highest Offering: Baccalaureate
Program: Liberal Arts And General; Teacher Preparatory
Accreditation: SC

01 President ...... Dr. John A. ROUSH
05 Vice President & Dean of College ...... Dr. Stephanie L. FABRITIUS
10 Vice Pres for Finance & Treasurer ...... Mr. John E. CUNY
26 Vice President College Relations ...... Dr. Richard W. TROLLINGER
32 Vice Pres/Dean of Student Life ...... Mr. Wm. Randy HAYS
30 Assoc VP Development/Alumni Affairs ...... Mr. Shawn LYONS
43 Assoc VP for Legal Affs/Gift Plng ...... Mr. James P. LEAHEY
53 Asst VP & Assoc Prof of Education ...... Mr. James H. ATKINS
07 Dean Admiss/Student Financial Plng ...... Mr. Robert M. NESMITH
20 Associate Dean of the College ...... Dr. Beth GLAZIER-MCDONALD
45 Asst to the President for Planning ...... Dr. Clarence R. WYATT
85 Director of International Programs ...... Dr. Milton M. REIGELMAN
08 Director of Library Services ...... Mr. Stanley R. CAMPBELL
04 Exec Assistant to the President ...... Ms. Yvonne Y. MORLEY
37 Director of Student Financial Plng ...... Mrs. Elaine E. LARSON
06 Registrar ...... Mr. Timothy P. CULHAN
15 Director Human Resources/Admin Svcs ...... Mrs. Kay L. DRAKE
27 Director of Communications ...... Dr. Michael P. STRYSICK
36 Director of Career Services ...... Ms. Deborah A. JONES
35 Director Student Life & Housing ...... Ms. Ann S. YOUNG
41 Director of Athletics & Recreation ...... Mr. Brian E. CHAFIN
19 Co-Director of Public Safety ...... Mr. Kevin S. MILBY
19 Co-Director of Public Safety ...... Mr. Gary D. BUGG
57 Mgr Director Norton Center for Arts ...... Mr. Steven A. HOFFMAN
09 Director of Institutional Research ...... Dr. J. Steven WINRICH
13 Director of Info Technology Service ...... Mr. Arthur L. MOORE
24 Int Dir Ctr for Teaching/Learning ...... Ms. Jami D. POWELL
18 Director of Facilities Management ...... Mr. D. Wayne KING
21 Controller ...... Mr. Steven A. JAMISON
42 College Chaplain ...... Dr. Richard D. AXTELL
38 Assoc Dean & Dir Residence Life ...... Ms. Sarah S. HALL
96 Dir Purchasing/Campus Interiors ...... Ms. Dorothy C. RINEHART
29 Director of Alumni Affairs ...... Ms. Megan L. HAAKE

Clear Creek Baptist Bible College (E)

300 Clear Creek Road, Pineville KY 40977-9754
County: Bell FICE Identification: 025356
Unit ID: 156417
Telephone: (606) 337-3196 Carnegie Class: Spec/Faith
FAX Number: (606) 337-2372 Calendar System: Semester
URL: www.ccbbc.edu
Established: 1926 Annual Undergrad Tuition & Fees: $5,822
Enrollment: 182 Coed
Affiliation or Control: Southern Baptist IRS Status: 501(c)3
Highest Offering: Baccalaureate
Program: Religious Emphasis
Accreditation: SC, BI

01 President ...... Dr. Donnie S. FOX
05 Academic Dean ...... Dr. Malcolm HESTER
32 Dean of Students ...... Rev. David WADE
11 Dean of Administrative Affairs ...... Vacant
30 Dean of Institutional Advancement ...... Dr. Jay SULFRIDGE
08 Librarian ...... Mrs. Marge CUMMINGS
42 Christian Service Director ...... Rev. Richard BARTELS
18 Dir of Maintenance and Facilities ...... Mr. Ronnie WASHAM
37 Director Financial Aid ...... Mr. Sam RISNER
06 Registrar ...... Mrs. Brenda HESTER
07 Admissions ...... Rev. Billy HOWELL
26 Director of College Relations ...... Rev. Richard L. WITHERITE
14 Director of Computer Operations ...... Mr. Michael BURNS
56 Director of Distance Education ...... Dr. Jay BARNETT

Daymar College-Bellevue (F)

119 Fairfield Avenue, Bellevue KY 41073
County: Campbell Identification: 666390
Unit ID: 447476
Telephone: (859) 291-0800 Carnegie Class: Assoc/PrivFP
FAX Number: (859) 491-7500 Calendar System: Quarter
URL: www.daymarcollege.edu
Established: 2005 Annual Undergrad Tuition & Fees: $16,610
Enrollment: 444 Coed
Affiliation or Control: Proprietary IRS Status: Proprietary
Highest Offering: Baccalaureate
Program: Technical Emphasis
Accreditation: ACICS

01 President ...... Mark A. GABIS
12 Campus President ...... Tina BARNES
05 Director of Education ...... James HUTCHINS
07 Director of Admissions ...... Cathy BARID
32 Director of Student Services ...... Raaven FLANIGAN

† Branch campus of Daymar College, Owensboro, KY.

Daymar College-Bowling Green (G)

2421 Fitzgerald Industrial Drive,
Bowling Green KY 42101-4071
County: Warren Identification: 666439
Unit ID: 363439
Telephone: (270) 843-6750 Carnegie Class: Assoc/PrivFP
FAX Number: (270) 843-6976 Calendar System: Quarter
URL: www.daymarcollege.edu
Established: 1954 Annual Undergrad Tuition & Fees: $16,610
Enrollment: 431 Coed
Affiliation or Control: Proprietary IRS Status: Proprietary
Highest Offering: Baccalaureate
Program: Technical Emphasis
Accreditation: ACICS

01 President ...... Mark GABIS
12 Campus President ...... Melva P. HALE
05 Director of Education ...... Duane DOYLE
07 Director of Admissions ...... Traci HENDERSON
37 Director of Financial Services ...... Janice CUTLIFF
32 Director of Student Services ...... Braden WILSON
36 Director or Career Services ...... Sarah ROSCOE

† Branch campus of Daymar Institute, Nashville, TN.

Daymar College-Louisville (H)

4112 Fern Valley Road, Louisville KY 40219-1973
County: Jefferson Identification: 666391
Unit ID: 406219
Telephone: (502) 495-1040 Carnegie Class: Assoc/PrivFP
FAX Number: (502) 495-1518 Calendar System: Quarter
URL: www.daymarcollege.edu
Established: 2001 Annual Undergrad Tuition & Fees: $16,610
Enrollment: 661 Coed
Affiliation or Control: Proprietary IRS Status: Proprietary
Highest Offering: Baccalaureate
Program: Technical Emphasis
Accreditation: ACICS

01 President ...... Mark GABIS
12 Campus President ...... Mark MANN
07 Senior Director of Admissions ...... Terry QUEENO
32 Director of Student Services ...... Jennifer BALL
08 Librarian ...... Jason ZARNDT

† Branch campus of Daymar College, Owensboro, KY.

Daymar College-Louisville East (I)

3309 Collins Lane, Louisville KY 40245
County: Jefferson Identification: 667081
Unit ID: 460473
Telephone: (502) 400-4075 Carnegie Class: Not Classified
FAX Number: N/A Calendar System: Quarter
URL: www.daymarcollege.edu
Established: N/A Annual Undergrad Tuition & Fees: $15,600
Enrollment: 187 Coed
Affiliation or Control: Proprietary IRS Status: Proprietary
Highest Offering: Baccalaureate
Program: Technical Emphasis
Accreditation: ACICS

01 President ...... Mark A. GABIS
12 Campus Director ...... Vacant

† Branch campus of Daymar College, Owensboro, KY.

Daymar College-Madisonville (J)

1105 National Mine Drive, Madisonville KY 42431
County: Hopkins Identification: 667079
Unit ID: 449302
Telephone: (270) 643-0312 Carnegie Class: Not Classified
FAX Number: N/A Calendar System: Quarter
URL: www.daymarcollege.edu
Established: N/A Annual Undergrad Tuition & Fees: $15,600
Enrollment: 25 Coed
Affiliation or Control: Proprietary IRS Status: Proprietary
Highest Offering: Baccalaureate
Program: Technical Emphasis
Accreditation: ACICS

01 President ...... Mark A. GABIS
12 Campus Director ...... Pat VINCENT

† Branch campus of Daymar College, Owensboro, KY.

Daymar College-Owensboro (K)

3361 Buckland Square, PO Box 22150,
Owensboro KY 42304-2150
County: Daviess FICE Identification: 009313
Unit ID: 157465
Telephone: (270) 926-4040 Carnegie Class: Assoc/PrivFP
FAX Number: (270) 685-4090 Calendar System: Quarter
URL: www.daymarcollege.edu
Established: 1963 Annual Undergrad Tuition & Fees: $16,610
Enrollment: 357 Coed
Affiliation or Control: Proprietary IRS Status: Proprietary
Highest Offering: Baccalaureate
Program: Technical Emphasis
Accreditation: ACICS

01 President ...... Mark A. GABIS
12 Campus President ...... Pamela MOON
05 Director of Education ...... Hany NASRALLAH
07 Director of Admissions ...... Latasha SHEMWELL
06 Registrar ...... Debi SWEEDEN
08 Librarian ...... Martha LUDWICZAK
36 Dir of Career Svc & Cmty Relations ...... Vacant

Daymar College-Paducah (A)

509 S 30th Street, Paducah KY 42002-4181
County: McCracken FICE Identification: 008425
Unit ID: 156903
Telephone: (270) 444-9676 Carnegie Class: Assoc/PrivFP
FAX Number: (270) 441-7202 Calendar System: Quarter
URL: www.daymarcollege.edu
Established: 1964 Annual Undergrad Tuition & Fees: $16,610
Enrollment: 308 Coed
Affiliation or Control: Proprietary IRS Status: Proprietary
Highest Offering: Baccalaureate
Program: Technical Emphasis
Accreditation: ACICS

01 President .... Mr. Mark A. GABIS
12 Campus President .... Mr. Brian CARROLL
07 Director of Admissions .... Ms. Connie HOLLEY
37 Director of Financial Services .... Ms. Jo Ann PRICE
32 Director of Student Services .... Ms. Peggy TIPPIN
05 Director of Education .... Mr. Greg WEBB
36 Dir of Career Svc & Cmty Relations .... Ms. Buffy BLANTON

Daymar College-Scottsville (B)

1138 Old Gallatin Road, Scottsville KY 42164
County: Allen Identification: 667080
Unit ID: 455646
Telephone: (270) 237-3577 Carnegie Class: Not Classified
FAX Number: N/A Calendar System: Quarter
URL: www.daymarcollege.edu
Established: N/A Annual Undergrad Tuition & Fees: $15,600
Enrollment: 171 Coed
Affiliation or Control: Proprietary IRS Status: Proprietary
Highest Offering: Baccalaureate
Program: Technical Emphasis
Accreditation: ACICS

01 President .... Mark A. GABIS
12 Campus Director .... David YOUNG

† Branch campus of Daymar College, Owensboro, KY.

DeVry University - Louisville (C)

10172 Linn Station Road, Suite 300,
Louisville KY 40223-3887
County: Jefferson Identification: 666588
Unit ID: 454209
Telephone: (502) 326-2860 Carnegie Class: Assoc/PrivFP4
FAX Number: (502) 329-5894 Calendar System: Semester
URL: www.devry.edu
Established: 1931 Annual Undergrad Tuition & Fees: $15,294
Enrollment: 162 Coed
Affiliation or Control: Proprietary IRS Status: Proprietary
Highest Offering: Baccalaureate
Program: Professional; Business Emphasis
Accreditation: &NH

01 Campus Director .... Mary HAWKINS

† Regional accreditation is carried under the parent institution in Downers Grove, IL.

Eastern Kentucky University (D)

521 Lancaster Avenue, Richmond KY 40475-3102
County: Madison FICE Identification: 001963
Unit ID: 156620
Telephone: (859) 622-1000 Carnegie Class: Master's L
FAX Number: (859) 622-1020 Calendar System: Semester
URL: www.eku.edu
Established: 1906 Annual Undergrad Tuition & Fees (In-State): $6,624
Enrollment: 16,567 Coed
Affiliation or Control: State IRS Status: 501(c)3
Highest Offering: Doctorate
Program: Occupational; Liberal Arts And General; Teacher Preparatory; Professional
Accreditation: SC, AAFCS, ADNUR, BUS, CACREP, CONST, CS, DIETD, DIETI, EMT, IFSAC, MAC, MLTAD, MT, MUS, NAIT, NRPA, NURSE, OT, PH, SP, SPAA, SW, TED

01 President .... Dr. Doug WHITLOCK
05 Provost/Vice Pres Academic Affairs .... Dr. Janna VICE
32 Assoc Provost & VP Student Affairs .... Dr. James CONNEELY
10 Vice Pres Financial Affs/Treasurer .... Ms. Debbie NEWSOM
30 Vice Pres Univ Advancement .... Mr. Joseph FOSTER
21 Associate Vice President Finance .... Mrs. Linda HERZOG
84 Assoc VP/Dean of Enrollment Mgmt .... Ms. Linda FOSSEN
45 Assoc VP University Programs .... Dr. Sara ZEIGLER
26 Assoc VP Public Relations/Marketing .... Mr. Marc WHITT
35 Assoc Vice Pres Student Affairs .... Dr. Mike REAGLE
76 Dean Health Sciences .... Dr. David D. GALE
49 Dean Arts & Sciences .... Dr. John WADE
50 Dean Business & Technology .... Dr. Robert ROGOW
53 Dean Education .... Dr. William PHILLIPS
88 Dean Justice & Safety .... Dr. Allen AULT
51 Dean Continuing Education/Outreach .... Dr. Charles HICKOX
86 Exec Dir Government Relations .... Mr. Jim CLARK
43 University Counsel .... Mrs. Judy SPAIN
19 Int Chief of Police .... Mr. Brian MULLINS
08 Director Libraries .... Ms. Carrie COOPER
06 Registrar .... Ms. Tina DAVIS
88 Director Advising .... Mr. Benton SHIREY
07 Director Admissions .... Mr. Keith GROB
36 Director Career Services .... Mrs. Laura MELIUS
25 Director Sponsored Programs .... Mr. Gus BENSON
92 Director Honors Program .... Dr. Linda FROST
09 Director Institutional Research .... Ms. Bethany MILLER
85 Director International Education .... Dr. Neil W. WRIGHT, III
38 Director Counseling Center .... Dr. Jen C. WALKER
39 Director Housing .... Mrs. Kenna MIDDLETON
88 Director Judicial Affairs/Disabled .... Mrs. Betsy BOHANNON
37 Director Student Financial Assist .... Mrs. Shelley S. PARK
23 Director Student Health Services .... Dr. Pradeep BOSE
40 Director Bookstore .... Ms. Lisa CROWE
15 Director Human Resources .... Mr. Gary BARKSDALE
90 Director Info Tech/Delivery Svcs .... Ms. Mona ISAACS
29 Director Alumni Relations .... Ms. Jackie COLLIER
88 Dir Student Involvement/Leadership .... Ms. April BARNES
24 Director Media Resources .... Ms. Jo BROSIUS
18 Director Facilities Services .... Mr. Rich MIDDLETON
28 Director of Diversity .... Ms. Sandra MOORE
96 Director of Purchasing .... Ms. Lora SNIDER
42 Chaplain .... Dr. Patrick C. NNOROMELE
04 Admin Asst to the President .... Ms. Lisa KELLEY
04 Admin Asst to the President .... Mrs. Dreidre ADAMS

Frontier Nursing University (E)

PO Box 528, Hyden KY 41749-0528
County: Leslie FICE Identification: 030070
Unit ID: 156727
Telephone: (606) 672-2312 Carnegie Class: Spec/Health
FAX Number: (606) 672-3776 Calendar System: Quarter
URL: www.frontier.edu
Established: 1939 Annual Graduate Tuition & Fees: $15,660
Enrollment: 1,044 Coed
Affiliation or Control: Independent Non-Profit IRS Status: 501(c)3
Highest Offering: Doctorate; No Undergraduates
Program: Professional; Nursing Emphasis
Accreditation: SC, MIDWF, NUR

01 President & Dean .... Dr. Susan STONE
11 Chief Operations Officer .... Ms. Shelley ALDRIDGE
10 Vice President of Finance .... Mr. Michael STEINMETZ
05 Associate Dean of Academic Affairs .... Dr. Joyce KNESTRICK
88 Assoc Dean Midwifery/Women's Health .... Dr. Suzan ULRICH
66 Assoc Dean of Family Nursing .... Dr. Julie MARFELL
88 Associate Dean of Research .... Dr. Janet ENGSTROM
88 DNP Program Director .... Dr. Barbara ANDERSON
88 Bridge Option Director .... Dr. Trish VOSS
29 Director of Development and Alumni .... Ms. Denise BARRETT
07 Director of Recruitment & Retention .... Ms. Stephanie BOYD
06 Registrar .... Ms. Sherri DAVIS
37 Director of Financial Aid .... Ms. Rainie BOGGS
08 Director of Library Services .... Ms. Billie Anne GEBB
13 Information Technology Manager .... Mr. Paul STACKHOUSE

Galen College of Nursing (F)

1031 Zorn Avenue, Suite 400, Louisville KY 40207-1064
County: Jefferson FICE Identification: 030837
Unit ID: 156471
Telephone: (502) 410-6200 Carnegie Class: Assoc/PrivFP
FAX Number: (502) 581-0425 Calendar System: Quarter
URL: www.galencollege.edu
Established: 1989 Annual Undergrad Tuition & Fees: $34,128
Enrollment: 948 Coed
Affiliation or Control: Proprietary IRS Status: Proprietary
Highest Offering: Associate Degree
Program: 2-Year Principally Bachelor's Creditable; Nursing Emphasis
Accreditation: COE

01 President .... Mr. Mark A. VOGT
05 Vice President of Academic Affairs .... Ms. Tracy A. ORTELLI
37 Financial Aid Director .... Ms. Joni M. PENLAND
07 Director of Admissions .... Ms. Brenda SKAGGS
20 Asst Vice Pres of Academic Affairs .... Ms. Louise DEBLOIS
12 President of the Cincinnati Campus .... Vacant
66 Dean of the Louisville Campus .... Ms. Joan L. FREY
66 Dean of the Tampa Bay Campus .... Ms. Sharon A. ROBERTS
66 Dean of the San Antonio Campus .... Dr. Judy STALEY

Georgetown College (G)

400 E College Street, Georgetown KY 40324-1696
County: Scott FICE Identification: 001964
Unit ID: 156745
Telephone: (502) 863-8000 Carnegie Class: Bac/A&S
FAX Number: (502) 868-8891 Calendar System: Semester
URL: www.georgetowncollege.edu
Established: 1787 Annual Undergrad Tuition & Fees: $29,300
Enrollment: 1,851 Coed
Affiliation or Control: Baptist IRS Status: 501(c)3
Highest Offering: Master's
Program: Liberal Arts And General; Teacher Preparatory
Accreditation: SC, TED

01 President .... Dr. William H. CROUCH, JR.
05 Provost/Dean of the College .... Dr. Rosemary ALLEN
10 Vice President/CFO/Treasurer .... Mr. James MOAK
43 General Counsel & Spec Asst to Pres .... Mr. Darryl CALLAHAN
30 VP Institutional Advancement .... Mr. Roy LOWDENBACK
32 VP Student Life/Dean of Students .... Dr. Todd GAMBILL
84 Vice President Enrollment Mgmt .... Mr. Garvel KINDRICK
13 Assoc VP for Info Tech Services .... Mr. Grover HIBBERD
26 Assoc VP Inst Adv/Dir Comm & Mktg .... Mr. Jim ALLISON
21 Controller .... Mr. David WILHITE
88 Bursar .... Mrs. Marianne RIDDLE
06 Registrar .... Mrs. Winnie BRATCHER
15 Director of Human Resources .... Mrs. Tracie SHAPIRO
28 Exec Dir Diversity Program .... Mr. Brian EVANS
53 Dean of Education .... Dr. Yolanda CARTER
07 Director of Admissions .... Mr. John LUCCHESI
37 Dir of Student Financial Planning .... Mrs. Tiffany HORNBERGER
09 Institutional Research Associate .... Mr. Jason TERWILLIGER
08 Director of Library Services .... Ms. Mary Margaret LOWE
29 Director of Alumni Affairs .... Mr. Mike CALHOUN
41 Athletic Director .... Mr. Eric WARD
42 Director of Religious Life .... Mr. H.K KINGKADE
36 Dir Graves Ctr for Calling & Career .... Vacant
19 Director Campus Safety .... Mr. Dan BROWN
38 Director of Counseling/Health Svcs .... Dr. Lloyd CLARK
18 Dir Facilities and Grounds .... Mr. Randall FRANCIS

ITT Technical Institute (H)

2473 Fortune Drive, Suite 180, Lexington KY 40509-4253
County: Fayette Identification: 666158
Unit ID: 448488
Telephone: (859) 246-3300 Carnegie Class: Assoc/PrivFP4
FAX Number: N/A Calendar System: Quarter
URL: www.itt-tech.edu
Established: 2006 Annual Undergrad Tuition & Fees: N/A
Enrollment: 559 Coed
Affiliation or Control: Proprietary IRS Status: Proprietary
Highest Offering: Baccalaureate
Program: Technical Emphasis
Accreditation: ACICS

† Branch campus of ITT Technical Institute, Newburgh, IN.

ITT Technical Institute (I)

9500 Ormsby Station Road, Suite 100,
Louisville KY 40223
County: Jefferson Identification: 666540
Unit ID: 413857
Telephone: (502) 327-7424 Carnegie Class: Spec/Tech
FAX Number: (502) 327-7624 Calendar System: Quarter
URL: www.itt-tech.edu
Established: 1993 Annual Undergrad Tuition & Fees: N/A
Enrollment: 993 Coed
Affiliation or Control: Proprietary IRS Status: Proprietary
Highest Offering: Baccalaureate
Program: Technical Emphasis
Accreditation: ACICS

† Branch campus of ITT Technical Institute, Newburgh, IN.

Kentucky Christian University (J)

100 Academic Parkway, Grayson KY 41143-2205
County: Carter FICE Identification: 001965
Unit ID: 157100
Telephone: (606) 474-3000 Carnegie Class: Bac/Diverse
FAX Number: (606) 474-3155 Calendar System: Semester
URL: www.kcu.edu
Established: 1919 Annual Undergrad Tuition & Fees: $16,138
Enrollment: 524 Coed
Affiliation or Control: Christian Churches And Churches of Christ
IRS Status: 501(c)3
Highest Offering: Master's
Program: Liberal Arts And General; Fine Arts Emphasis
Accreditation: SC, NURSE, SW

01 President/CEO .... Dr. Jeff K. METCALF
05 VP of Academic Affairs .... Dr. Perry L. STEPP
10 VP of Business & Finance .... Mr. William S. BONDURANT
84 VP of Enrollment Services .... Vacant
30 VP of University Advancement .... Mr. Larry D. MONROE
88 Director of Church Relations .... Mr. Jeff W. GREENE
06 Registrar .... Mrs. Andrea L. STAMPER
13 Director of Campus Technology .... Mr. Greg C. RICHARDSON
08 Librarian .... Mrs. Naulayne R. ENDERS
09 Assessment & SaBRE Director .... Mr. Kenneth L. BECK
32 Dean of Student Services .... Mr. Ron W. ARNETT
42 Campus Minister .... Mr. Larry W. MARSHALL
37 Director Financial Aid .... Mrs. Jennie M. BENDER
15 Human Resources Officer .... Mr. Terry L. YANKEY
38 Student Counseling Coordinator .... Mr. Jerry R. MORRIS
41 Athletic Director .... Mr. Bruce W. DIXON
39 Director of Residence Services .... Mr. Kris A. LANGSTAFF
18 Director of Maintenance .... Mr. Troy E. ROUSH
29 Alumni Relations Officer .... Vacant
58 Dean of the Graduate School .... Dr. David A. FIENSY
07 Director of Enrollment Services .... Mrs. Sheree D. GREER

Kentucky Community and Technical College System (A)

300 N Main Street, Versailles KY 40383-1245
County: Woodford — FICE Identification: 006724
Unit ID: 157854
Telephone: (859) 256-3100 — Carnegie Class: N/A
FAX Number: (859) 256-3119
URL: www.kctcs.edu

- 01 President ... Dr. Michael B. MCCALL
- 00 Chancellor ... Dr. Jay BOX
- 10 Vice President Finance ... Mr. Ken WALKER
- 46 Vice Pres Diversity/Strat Planning ... Dr. Gwen JOSEPH
- 13 Vice Pres of Technology Solutions ... Vacant
- 30 Vice Pres Devel & Public Relations ... Mr. Timothy R. BURCHAM, CFRE
- 04 Sr Exec Assistant to the President ... Ms. Beth HILLIARD

Ashland Community and Technical College (B)

1400 College Drive, Ashland KY 41101-3617
County: Boyd — FICE Identification: 001990
Unit ID: 156231
Telephone: (606) 326-2000 — Carnegie Class: Assoc/Pub-R-M
FAX Number: (606) 326-2187 — Calendar System: Semester
URL: www.ashland.kctcs.edu
Established: 1938 — Annual Undergrad Tuition & Fees (In-State): $3,120
Enrollment: 4,688 — Coed
Affiliation or Control: State — IRS Status: 501(c)3
Highest Offering: Associate Degree
Program: Occupational; 2-Year Principally Bachelor's Creditable
Accreditation: SC, ADNUR, IFSAC, SURGT

- 02 President ... Dr. Gregory ADKINS
- 05 Dean of Academic Affairs ... Dr. Janie KITCHEN
- 32 Dean of Student Affairs ... Ms. Willie G. MCCULLOUGH
- 10 Dean of Business Affairs ... Ms. Karen BLEVINS
- 11 Dean of Administrative Services ... Mr. Walter S. TAYLOR, III
- 08 Director of Library Services ... Mr. Matthew ONION
- 20 Assoc Dean Admissions/Registrar ... Mr. Chandra KUMAR
- 13 Assoc Dean Information Technology ... Mr. Farnoosh RAFIEE
- 30 Dean of Institutional Advancement ... Ms. Louise SHYTLE
- 28 Director of Cultural Diversity ... Mr. Alvin D. BAKER
- 15 Director of Human Resources ... Ms. Kellie L. ALLEN
- 25 Director of Grants & Contracts ... Ms. Sarah DIAMOND BURROWAY
- 26 Dean Mktg and Community Relations ... Mr. John K. MCGLONE
- 103 Dean of Workforce & Economic Devel ... Dr. Larry FERGUSON
- 36 Coordinator of Career Services ... Ms. Nancy L. MENSHOUSE
- 79 Division Chair Humanities ... Mr. Kevin COOTS
- 76 Division Chair Health Sciences ... Ms. Jennifer CARROLL
- 81 Div Chair Math & Natural Sciences ... Dr. Keith BRAMMELL
- 09 Dean of Inst Plng/Research/Effect ... Mr. Steve FLOUHOUSE
- 37 Director of Financial Aid ... Ms. Robin LEWIS
- 18 Chief Facilities/Physical Plant ... Mr. Emmett BLEVINS
- 18 Chief Facilities/Physical Plant ... Mr. Fred ROSEBERRY

Big Sandy Community and Technical College (C)

1 Bert T. Combs Drive, Prestonburg KY 41653-9502
County: Floyd — FICE Identification: 001996
Unit ID: 157553
Telephone: (606) 886-3863 — Carnegie Class: Assoc/Pub-R-M
FAX Number: (606) 886-2677 — Calendar System: Semester
URL: www.bigsandy.kctcs.edu
Established: 1964 — Annual Undergrad Tuition & Fees (In-State): $3,120
Enrollment: 5,360 — Coed
Affiliation or Control: State — IRS Status: 501(c)3
Highest Offering: Associate Degree
Program: Occupational; 2-Year Principally Bachelor's Creditable
Accreditation: SC, DH

- 02 President/CEO ... Dr. George EDWARDS
- 03 Vice Pres Institutional Services ... Mr. Bobby MCCOOL
- 05 Provost ... Dr. Nancy JOHNSON
- 10 Vice President of Business Affairs ... Mr. John HERALD
- 32 Interim Dean of Student Affairs ... Ms. Melinda JUSTICE
- 35 Assoc Dean of Student Affairs ... Mr. Jimmy WRIGHT
- 08 Director of Library Services ... Ms. Melissa FORSYTH
- 15 Director of Human Resources ... Mr. Jackie CECIL
- 06 Registrar ... Ms. Della PACK
- 37 Director of Financial Aid ... Ms. Denise TRUSTY
- 09 Int Dir Institutional Effectiveness ... Ms. Denese ATKINSON
- 13 Director of Information Technology ... Mr. John DOVE
- 40 Bookstore Manager ... Ms. Pam WILEY
- 26 Public Relations ... Mr. Randall ROBERTS
- 07 Director of Admissions ... Vacant
- 28 Director of Diversity ... Ms. Tina TERRY
- 103 Director Workforce Development ... Vacant

*Bluegrass Community and Technical College (D)

470 Cooper Drive, Lexington KY 40506-0001
County: Fayette — FICE Identification: 009707
Unit ID: 156392
Telephone: (859) 246-6200 — Carnegie Class: Assoc/Pub-R-L
FAX Number: (859) 246-4664 — Calendar System: Semester
URL: www.bluegrass.kctcs.edu
Established: 1965 — Annual Undergrad Tuition & Fees (In-State): $3,240
Enrollment: 14,164 — Coed
Affiliation or Control: State — IRS Status: 501(c)3
Highest Offering: Associate Degree
Program: Occupational; 2-Year Principally Bachelor's Creditable
Accreditation: SC, ADNUR, DA, DH, DT, IFSAC, MAC, NMT, POLYT, RAD, SURGT

- 02 President & CEO ... Dr. Augusta A. JULIAN
- 103 VP Workforce/Institutional Devel ... Mr. Mark MANUEL
- 13 Vice Pres of Information Technology ... Mr. Ren BATES
- 05 VP of Academics ... Dr. David M. HELLMICH
- 32 VP Student Dev/Enrollment Svcs ... Dr. Palisa WILLIAMS RUSHIN
- 10 VP Finance & Administration ... Ms. Lisa G. BELL
- 28 VP Multiculturalism & Inclusion ... Ms. Charlene WALKER
- 56 VP Regional Campuses/Outreach ... Mr. Francis (Tri) A. ROBERTS, III
- 20 Dean of Academic Affairs ... Dr. Sandra CAREY
- 20 Dean of Academic Affairs ... Ms. Bonnie NICHOLSON
- 06 Registrar ... Ms. Becky HARP-STEPHENS
- 37 Financial Aid Director ... Ms. Runan PENDERGRAST
- 07 Admissions Director ... Ms. Shelbie HUGLE
- 15 Director Human Resource/Payroll ... Ms. Deborrah L. COX
- 26 Chief Communications Officer ... Ms. Vernal L. KENNEDY
- 38 Advising/Assessment Int Director ... Ms. Lucinda WHITE
- 30 Chief Development Officer ... Ms. Linda EPLING
- 79 Assistant Dean Humanities ... Ms. Diana MARTIN
- 88 Assistant Dean Natural Sciences ... Ms. Tammy LILES
- 83 Asst Dean Behavioral Sciences ... Ms. Pat LEFLER
- 66 Assistant Dean Nursing ... Ms. Karen MAYO
- 76 Assistant Dean Allied Health ... Mr. Marty A. BAXTER
- 81 Asst Dean Mathematics/Statistics ... Ms. Vicki PARTIN
- 77 Asst Dean Computer Sci/Info Systems ... Ms. Debbie HOLT
- 72 Asst Dean Trades/Technologies/Equn ... Mr. Mike MCMILLEN
- 88 Asst Dean Mfg Industrial Technology ... Mr. Paul TURNER
- 50 Asst Dean Business/Education ... Ms. Jenny JONES
- 83 Asst Dean Comm/Hist/Lang/Social Sci ... Ms. Vicki WILSON
- 08 Asst Dean Learning Resources Center ... Mr. Charles JAMES
- 88 Asst Dean Adult Educ/Opportunity ... Dr. Rebecca SIMMS
- 106 Assistant Dean Distance Learning ... Mr. Ben WORTH
- 18 Director of Maintenance/Operations ... Mr. Michael BALL
- 96 Director of Purchasing ... Ms. Tammy HORN

*Bowling Green Technical College (E)

1845 Loop Drive, Bowling Green KY 42101-9202
County: Warren — FICE Identification: 005271
Unit ID: 156338
Telephone: (270) 901-1000 — Carnegie Class: Assoc/Pub-R-M
FAX Number: (270) 901-1145 — Calendar System: Semester
URL: www.bowlinggreen.kctcs.edu
Established: 1939 — Annual Undergrad Tuition & Fees (In-State): $3,240
Enrollment: 5,128 — Coed
Affiliation or Control: State — IRS Status: 501(c)3
Highest Offering: Associate Degree
Program: Occupational; 2-Year Principally Bachelor's Creditable
Accreditation: SC, ACFEI, DMS, IFSAC, POLYT, RAD, SURGT

- 02 President & CEO ... Dr. Nathan L. HODGES
- 03 Provost ... Dr. Phillip NEAL
- 05 Chief Academic Affairs ... Ms. Iris DOTSON
- 32 Chief Student Affairs ... Dr. Gerald NAPOLES
- 06 Registrar ... Ms. Brooke JUSTICE
- 10 Chief of Business Affairs ... Mr. Chris CUMENS
- 15 Director of Human Resources ... Ms. Sherri L. FORESTER
- 26 Director of Public Relations ... Mr. Mark D. BROOKS
- 30 Director of Advancement ... Ms. Donna P. MARTIN
- 37 Director of Financial Aid ... Mr. Rickie W. WILSON
- 09 Director Instituion Effectiveness ... Vacant
- 103 Director of Workforce Solutions ... Mr. Lewis BURKE, JR.

*Elizabethtown Community and Technical College (F)

600 College Street Road, Elizabethtown KY 42701-3081
County: Hardin — FICE Identification: 001991
Unit ID: 156648
Telephone: (270) 769-2371 — Carnegie Class: Assoc/Pub-R-M
FAX Number: (270) 769-0736 — Calendar System: Semester
URL: www.elizabethtown.kctcs.edu
Established: 1963 — Annual Undergrad Tuition & Fees (In-State): $135
Enrollment: 7,898 — Coed
Affiliation or Control: State — IRS Status: 501(c)3
Highest Offering: Associate Degree
Program: Occupational; 2-Year Principally Bachelor's Creditable
Accreditation: SC, ADNUR, IFSAC, RAD

- 02 President ... Dr. Thelma WHITE
- 05 Provost ... Dr. Cynthia CONE
- 32 Chief Student Affairs Officer ... Dr. Dale BUCKLES
- 11 Chief Operations ... Mr. Keith JOHNSON
- 12 Campus Education Center Director ... Mr. Darrin POWELL
- 103 Dean of Workforce Development ... Dr. Thomas DAVENPORT
- 10 Dean of Business Affairs ... Mr. Jonathan THOMPSON
- 08 Library Director ... Ms. Ann THOMPSON
- 15 Director of Human Resources ... Ms. Kris WOOD
- 06 Registrar ... Mr. Bryan SMITH
- 13 Director of Information Technology ... Mr. Chris LEE
- 37 Director of Financial Aid ... Mr. Michael BARLOW
- 30 Chief Development ... Mr. Ronald HARRELL
- 26 Director of Public Relations ... Ms. Mary Jo KING
- 24 Learning Center Coordinator ... Ms. Pam HARPER
- 36 Counselor ... Ms. Sharon SPRATT
- 38 Counselor ... Mr. Charles SPATARO
- 40 Bookstore Manager ... Ms. Pamela BENTLEY
- 46 Assoc Dean of Inst Effectiveness ... Dr. Jack DILBECK
- 18 Maintenance/Operations Supervisor ... Mr. Charles COBB
- 57 Chair Div of Arts/Humanities ... Ms. Carla HORNBACK
- 81 Chair Div of Biological Science ... Ms. Martha WOLFE
- 81 Chair Div of Physical Science ... Ms. Linda HOWARD
- 75 Chair Div Occupational Technology ... Mr. Mike HAZZARD
- 83 Chair Div of Social Science ... Dr. Diane OWSLEY
- 28 Director of Diversity ... Ms. Felicia TOLIVER

*Gateway Community and Technical College (G)

1025 Amsterdam Road, Covington KY 41011-2098
County: Kenton — FICE Identification: 005273
Unit ID: 157438
Telephone: (859) 441-4500 — Carnegie Class: Assoc/Pub-S-MC
FAX Number: (859) 292-6415 — Calendar System: Semester
URL: www.gateway.kctcs.edu
Established: 1961 — Annual Undergrad Tuition & Fees (In-State): $4,130
Enrollment: 4,797 — Coed
Affiliation or Control: State — IRS Status: 501(c)3
Highest Offering: Associate Degree
Program: Occupational; 2-Year Principally Bachelor's Creditable
Accreditation: SC, IFSAC

- 02 President/CEO ... Dr. Ed HUGHES
- 04 Assistant to the President ... Ms. Sharon POORE
- 05 Provost/Vice President Academic Aff ... Dr. Laura URBAN
- 30 VP Resource Devel/External Affairs ... Ms. Laura KROEGER
- 35 Vice President of Student Affairs ... Ms. Ingrid WASHINGTON
- 20 Associate Provost/Dean of Academic ... Ms. Teri VONHANDORF
- 20 Associate Provost/Dean of Academic ... Ms. Marinell BROWN
- 66 Assoc Prov/Dean Nursing/Allied Hlth ... Ms. Gail WISE
- 07 Admissions Counselor ... Ms. Linda S. CORNELL
- 07 Admissions Counselor ... Ms. Janet SAMPLES
- 06 Registrar ... Mr. Robin WRIGHT
- 10 Chief Business Affairs Officer ... Mr. Mike BAKER
- 15 Director of Human Resources ... Ms. Phyllis YEAGER
- 18 Director Maintenance & Operations ... Mr. George HALL
- 26 Director of Public Relations ... Ms. Margaret THOMSON
- 37 Director of Financial Aid ... Mr. Justin CRISTELLO
- 09 Dean Institutional Research & Plng ... Ms. Patricia GOODMAN
- 38 Director Student Advising ... Ms. Shelby KRENTZ
- 84 Director Enrollment Management ... Mr. Andre WASHINGTON
- 08 Director Library/Information Svcs ... Ms. Charlene MCGRATH
- 36 Director Student Placement ... Ms. Amy MONSON
- 103 VP Workforce Solutions ... Dr. Angie TAYLOR

*Hazard Community and Technical College (H)

One Community College Drive, Hazard KY 41701-2402
County: Perry — FICE Identification: 006962
Unit ID: 156790
Telephone: (606) 436-5721 — Carnegie Class: Assoc/Pub-R-M
FAX Number: (606) 439-2988 — Calendar System: Semester
URL: www.hazard.kctcs.edu
Established: 1968 — Annual Undergrad Tuition & Fees (In-State): $4,050
Enrollment: 4,796 — Coed
Affiliation or Control: State — IRS Status: 501(c)3
Highest Offering: Associate Degree
Program: Occupational; 2-Year Principally Bachelor's Creditable
Accreditation: SC, IFSAC, PTAA, RAD, SURGT

- 02 President/CEO ... Dr. Stephen GREINER
- 05 Vice Pres of Learning Services ... Dr. Kathy SMOOT
- 32 Vice President of Student Services ... Mr. Doug FRALEY
- 10 Vice President of Business Services ... Mr. Fred LANDRUM
- 04 Exec Admin Asst to President ... Ms. Delcie COMBS
- 86 Sr Dir of Advance & Govt Relations ... Mr. Ron DALEY
- 13 Chief Information Officer ... Ms. Donna ROARK
- 15 Senior Director of Human Resources ... Ms. Vickie COMBS
- 21 Dean of Business Services ... Ms. Connie WATTS
- 08 Director Library Services ... Mrs. Cathy BRANSON
- 20 Academic Dean Lees College Campus ... Ms. Leila SMITH
- 20 Academic Dean Technical Campus ... Mr. Neil BRASHAR
- 20 Academic Dean Hazard Campus ... Ms. Anna NAPIER
- 09 Coordinator of Inst Research ... Mrs. Anna L. PUFFER
- 18 Maintenance/Operations Supervisor ... Mr. Don CASTLE
- 26 Director of Public Relations ... Mrs. Evelyn WOOD
- 37 Director of Financial Aid ... Mr. Charles ANDERSON, JR.
- 35 Dean of Student Life/Engagement ... Mr. Cluster HOWARD
- 40 Bookstore Manager ... Mrs. Patricia CAUDILL
- 06 Registrar ... Ms. Libby PETERS
- 07 Director of Admissions ... Mr. Scott GROSS
- 88 Dean of Learner Success ... Ms. Germaine SHAFFER
- 28 Asst Director Cultural Diversity ... Mr. Elbert HAGANS
- 88 Director Radiology Program ... Mr. Homer TERRY
- 81 Div Chair Sciences & Mathematics ... Mr. Dell SASSER
- 88 Div Chair Occupational Technology ... Ms. Carolyn BUSH
- 76 Div Chair Allied Health Technology ... Ms. Gwen COLLINS
- 79 Div Chair Heritage/Humanities ... Mr. Thomas NEACE

*Henderson Community College (I)

2660 S Green Street, Henderson KY 42420-4699
County: Henderson — FICE Identification: 001993
Unit ID: 156851
Telephone: (270) 827-1867 — Carnegie Class: Assoc/Pub-R-M
FAX Number: (270) 831-9600 — Calendar System: Semester

URL: www.henderson.kctcs.edu
Established: 1960 Annual Undergrad Tuition & Fees (In-State): $3,240
Enrollment: 2,224 Coed
Affiliation or Control: State IRS Status: 501(c)3
Highest Offering: Associate Degree
Program: Occupational; 2-Year Principally Bachelor's Creditable
Accreditation: SC, ADNUR, DH, MAC, MLTAD

02 President/CEO .... Dr. Kris WILLIAMS
05 Dean of Academic Affairs .... Dr. David F. BRAUER
32 Dean Student Affairs .... Ms. Patricia MITCHELL
10 Dean of Business .... Mr. Jerry H. GENTRY
08 Library Director .... Mr. Mike W. KNECHT
13 Chief Information Technology Ofcr .... Ms. Kimberley S. CONLEY
15 Director of Human Resources .... Ms. Doris J. LAKE
57 Director of Fine Arts Center .... Ms. Rachael BAAR
06 Registrar .... Ms. Brenda L. KNIGHT
31 Dean Cmty Workforces/Economic Devel .. Ms. Pamala P. WILSON
28 Director of Cultural Diversity .... Mr. William DIXON
30 Chief Institutional Advance Ofcr .... Ms. Susanne WILSON
09 Asst Dean/Dir Plng & Rsrch .... Mr. Mike THURMAN
88 Coordinator Learning Skills Center .... Ms. Doris CHERRY
18 Maintenance/Oper Supervisor .... Mr. David CAMPBELL
35 Student Activities Coordinator .... Mr. Larry TUTT
36 Career Services Coordinator .... Ms. Angela WATSON
37 Director Financial Aid .... Vacant
103 Workforce Development Liaison .... Mr. Joe RAZZANO
07 Admissions Counselor .... Mr. Cary CONLEY
88 Professional Development Coord .... Ms. Cathy HUNT
57 Division Chair Arts/Humanities .... Mr. Mike A. KNECHT
81 Div Chair Physical Sciences .... Ms. Rebecca WELLS
83 Div Chair Social/Behavior Sciences .... Mr. Paul KASENOW
76 Div Chair Biological Sciences .... Dr. Mary Gail WILDER

*Hopkinsville Community College (A)

720 North Drive, PO Box 2100,
Hopkinsville KY 42241-2100
County: Christian FICE Identification: 001994
Unit ID: 156860
Telephone: (270) 707-3700 Carnegie Class: Assoc/Pub-R-M
FAX Number: (270) 886-0237 Calendar System: Semester
URL: www.hopkinsville.kctcs.edu
Established: 1965 Annual Undergrad Tuition & Fees (In-State): $3,240
Enrollment: 3,865 Coed
Affiliation or Control: State IRS Status: 501(c)3
Highest Offering: Associate Degree
Program: Occupational; 2-Year Principally Bachelor's Creditable
Accreditation: SC, ADNUR

02 President/CEO .... Dr. James E. SELBE
04 Executive Administrative Assistant .... Ms. Cheryle DYMEK
05 Acting Chief Acad Affairs Officer .... Ms. Alissa YOUNG
05 Acting Chief Acad Affairs Officer .... Dr. Randal H. WILSON
06 Registrar .... Ms. Melissa STEVENSON
08 Library Services Director .... Ms. Cynthia A. ATKINS
09 Institutional Effectiveness Dean .... Dr. Lance R. ANGELL
10 Chief Business Affairs Officer .... Ms. Beverly A. ATWOOD
12 Campus/Educ Center Director FTC .... Ms. Allisha LEE
13 Technology Solutions Director .... Mr. Terry DUNCAN
16 Human Resources Director .... Ms. Yvonne GLASMAN
18 Maintence/Operations Director .... Mr. Dan HAMBY
19 Safety Specialist .... Mr. Paul HATCHETT
21 Business Affairs Associate Dean .... Ms. Ann T. HOLLAND
26 Marketing & Communication Director .... Ms. Rena YOUNG
28 Cultural Diversity Director .... Ms. Tracey Y. WILLIAMS
30 Chief Institutional Advancement Ofc .... Ms. Yvette EASTHAM
32 Chief Student Affairs Officer .... Dr. Jason D. WARREN
36 Career & Transfer Director .... Ms. Kanya ALLEN
37 Financial Aid Director .... Ms. Janet GUNTHER
38 Advising Center Director .... Ms. Deloria SCOTT
40 Bookstore Director .... Ms. Diane CUNNINGHAM
51 Continuing Education Associate Dean .... Ms. Carol KIRVES
57 Fine Arts/Humanities Div Chair .... Mr. Thomas T. CARLISLE
72 Bus/Occupational Tech Div Chair .... Mr. Jerry GILLIAM
76 Allied Health Div Chair .... Ms. Peggy I. BOZARTH
81 Mathmatics & Sciences Div Chair .... Mr. Ted H. WILSON
83 Social & Behav Sciences Div Chair .... Dr. Vernell LARKIN
103 Acting Dean Cmty/Workforce/Econ Dev .... Mr. Jerry GILLIAM

*Jefferson Community and Technical College (B)

109 E Broadway, Louisville KY 40202-2000
County: Jefferson FICE Identification: 006961
Unit ID: 156921
Telephone: (502) 213-5333 Carnegie Class: Assoc/Pub-U-MC
FAX Number: N/A Calendar System: Semester
URL: www.jefferson.kctcs.edu
Established: 1967 Annual Undergrad Tuition & Fees (In-State): $4,090
Enrollment: 15,259 Coed
Affiliation or Control: State IRS Status: 501(c)3
Highest Offering: Associate Degree
Program: Occupational; 2-Year Principally Bachelor's Creditable
Accreditation: SC, ACFEI, ADNUR, DMS, IFSAC, MAC, NMT, OTA, PTAA, RAD, SURGT

02 President .... Dr. Anthony NEWBERRY
05 Provost/Chief Academic Affairs Ofcr .... Dr. Diane CALHOUN-FRENCH
10 Chief Business Officer .... Mr. Bill NOWAK
20 Dean Academic Affs Jefferson Tech .... Mr. Robert SILLIMAN
20 Dean Academic Affs Downtown .... Dr. Randy DAVIS
20 Dean Academic Affairs Southwest .... Dr. Katy VARNER
32 Dean of Student Affairs Southwest .... Dr. Denise GRAY-LACKEY
32 Dean Student Affairs Downtown .... Dr. Laura SMITH
21 Associate Dean of Business Affairs .... Ms. Ginny STRADLEY
08 Library Services Director .... Ms. Sheree WILLIAMS
08 Library Svcs Director Southwest .... Mr. Larry REES
13 Director Information Technology .... Mr. Thomas ROGERS
09 Director of Institutional Research .... Dr. Mary C. JONES
06 Registrar .... Ms. Amanda TINDALL
28 Director of Cultural Diversity .... Ms. Janet MULLER
26 Dir of Marketing/Public Relations .... Ms. Lisa BROSKY
15 Director of Human Resources .... Mr. Kent ROBINSON
18 Facilities Director .... Mr. Craig TURPIN
37 Director of Financial Aid .... Vacant
30 Dir Inst Advance/Development Coord .... Ms. Jo Carole DICKSON
88 Director CE/CS/Business/ Industry .... Ms. Mary Ann HYLAND-MURR
07 Director of Admissions .... Ms. Melanie VAUGHAN-COOKE
38 Director of Student Counseling .... Dr. Telly SELLARS
96 Director of Purchasing .... Ms. Pamela DUMM
12 Director of Carrolton Campus .... Ms. Susan CARLISLE
12 Director of Shelby Campus .... Dr. John WIELAND
12 Int Dir Bullitt County Campus .... Ms. Donna MILLER
44 Manager of Advancement .... Ms. Karla HALL
31 Coord Cont Education/Cmty Services .... Ms. Donna HILL
24 Learning Center Coord Downtown .... Ms. Reneau WAGGONER
79 Chairperson Humanities Southwest .... Dr. Donna ELKINS
50 Chairperson Business Downtown .... Dr. Pamela BESSER
65 Div Chair Natural Sci Downtown .... Ms. Caroline MARTINSON
66 Dean Nursing/Allied Health .... Dr. Carolyn O'DANIEL
76 Chair Allied Health Jefferson Tech .... Ms. Eva OLTMAN
83 Div Chair Behav/Soc Sci Downtown .... Mr. Ron WALFORD
83 Chair Behav/Soc Sci Southwest .... Ms. Cathy WRIGHT
50 Chairperson Business Southwest .... Mr. Pete RODSKI
79 Chairperson Humanities Downtown .... Ms. Marlisa AUSTIN
81 Chrpsn Natural Science Southwest .... Mr. Gerry JOHNSON
72 Chair Technology/Related Sci-SW .... Mr. Bruce JOST
72 Chair Technology & Industry .... Mr. Andrew KORNOWSKI

*Madisonville Community College (C)

2000 College Drive, Madisonville KY 42431-9199
County: Hopkins FICE Identification: 009010
Unit ID: 157304
Telephone: (270) 824-8573 Carnegie Class: Assoc/Pub-R-M
FAX Number: (270) 824-1864 Calendar System: Semester
URL: www.madisonville.kctcs.edu
Established: 1968 Annual Undergrad Tuition & Fees (In-State): $3,850
Enrollment: 4,883 Coed
Affiliation or Control: State IRS Status: 501(c)3
Highest Offering: Associate Degree
Program: Occupational; 2-Year Principally Bachelor's Creditable
Accreditation: SC, ADNUR, IFSAC, MLTAD, OTA, PTAA, RAD, SURGA, SURGT

02 President .... Dr. Judith L. RHOADS
05 Chief Academic Affairs Officer .... Dr. Deborah M. COX
32 Dean of Student Affairs .... Mr. Jonathan V. PARRENT
10 Chief Business Affairs Officer .... Mr. Ray GILLASPIE
72 Division Chair Applied Technology .... Ms. Darlena GALLEGOS
66 Div Chr Nursing/Related Tech .... Ms. Patricia SIMMONS
79 Div Chr Humanities/Related Tech .... Dr. Scott VANDER PLOEG
83 Div Chr Social Science/Related Tech .... Mr. Chester M. CUNNINGHAM
81 Div Chr Mathematics and Sciences .... Dr. John LOWBRIDGE
76 Div Chr Allied Health/Related Tech .... Ms. Karol A. CONRAD
08 Director of Library Services .... Ms. Cherry L. BERGES
06 Registrar .... Ms. Tiffanie WITT
15 Director of Human Resources .... Ms. May F. WRIGHT
36 Counselor .... Ms. Sherry D. HEWELL
30 Chief Development Officer .... Mr. John E. PETERS
37 Director of Financial Aid .... Ms. Martha PHELPS
26 Public Relations Officer .... Ms. Joyce RIGGS
56 Extended Campus Director .... Dr. George G. HUMPHREYS
40 Bookstore Manager .... Ms. Sonya L. BURNS
09 Dir Grants/Planning & Effectiveness ... Mr. David A. SCHUERMER
84 Coord of Enrollment Management .... Ms. Aimee J. WILKERSON
28 Director of Diversity .... Mr. James H. BOWLES
20 Associate Academic Officer .... Ms. Lisa A. HOWERTON
21 Associate Business Officer .... Mr. Michael L. JOHNSON
103 Director Workforce Solutions .... Mr. Mike DAVENPORT

*Maysville Community and Technical College (D)

1755 US 68, Maysville KY 41056-8910
County: Mason FICE Identification: 006960
Unit ID: 157331
Telephone: (606) 759-7141 Carnegie Class: Assoc/Pub-R-M
FAX Number: (606) 759-7174 Calendar System: Semester
URL: www.maysville.kctcs.edu
Established: 1966 Annual Undergrad Tuition & Fees (In-State): $4,050
Enrollment: 4,515 Coed
Affiliation or Control: State IRS Status: 501(c)3
Highest Offering: Associate Degree
Program: Occupational; 2-Year Principally Bachelor's Creditable
Accreditation: SC, IFSAC, MAC, SURGT

02 President .... Dr. Ed STORY
05 Chief Academic Officer .... Dr. Juston PATE
32 Chief Student Development Officer .... Mrs. Sandy SMALLWOOD
10 Chief Business Affairs Officer .... Mr. George A. JONES
06 Assoc Dean of Student Affairs .... Ms. Patricia MASSIE
08 Director Library Services .... Ms. Sonja EADS
13 Director Information Technology .... Mr. Henry JEFFERSON
24 Coordinator of Assessment/Testing .... Ms. Frances PETERSON
30 Dir Resource Development/Foundation .... Ms. Cara CLARKE
40 Bookstore Manager .... Ms. Kaye HIGH
103 Chief Officer Workforce Solutions .... Ms. Barbara CAMPBELL
50 Div Chr Bus/Inform Technologies .... Ms. Darla HUNT
60 Division Chair Humanities .... Mr. Russ WARD
81 Div Chair Math/Science/Agriculture .... Dr. Angela FULTZ
09 Director of Institutional Research .... Ms. Cindy WULFEKAMP
37 Director Student Financial Aid .... Ms. Leslie STORIE
26 Public Relations Director .... Ms. Tina CURTIS
20 Coordinator of Academic Programs .... Mr. Stanley CLICK
21 Associate Dean of Finance .... Mr. Steve WINFREY
28 Director of Diversity .... Mr. Noel WILLIAMS
15 Director of Human Resources .... Ms. Sandi L. ESTILL
66 Division Chair of Health Sciences .... Ms. Deborah NOLDER
72 Division Chair Industrial Tech .... Mr. Stanley W. CLICK

*Owensboro Community and Technical College (E)

4800 New Hartford Road, Owensboro KY 42303-1899
County: Daviess FICE Identification: 030345
Unit ID: 247940
Telephone: (270) 686-4400 Carnegie Class: Assoc/Pub-R-M
FAX Number: (270) 686-4594 Calendar System: Semester
URL: www.octc.kctcs.edu
Established: 1986 Annual Undergrad Tuition & Fees (In-State): $4,050
Enrollment: 7,061 Coed
Affiliation or Control: State IRS Status: 501(c)3
Highest Offering: Associate Degree
Program: Occupational; 2-Year Principally Bachelor's Creditable
Accreditation: SC, IFSAC, RAD, SURGT

02 Interim President .... Dr. J. Larry DURRENCE
04 Assistant to the President .... Ms. Kittridge DANT
05 VP of Academic Affairs .... Dr. Scott WILLIAMS
32 VP of Student Affairs .... Mr. Kevin BEARDMORE
30 VP of Advancement/Alumni Rels .... Mr. Larry S. MILLER
06 Registrar .... Ms. Sandy CARDEN
10 VP of Business Affairs .... Ms. Sarah PRICE
35 Associate Dean of Students .... Ms. Sandy CARDEN
08 Library Services Director .... Ms. Donna ABELL
13 Vice Pres Information Technology .... Mr. James HARTZ
15 Director of Human Resources .... Ms. Victoria HOHIEMER
09 Director of Institutional Research .... Mr. Kevin BEARDMORE
29 Dir Advancement/Alumni Relations .... Ms. Linda TAYLOR
37 Financial Aid Director .... Ms. Bernice AYER
26 Director of Public Relations .... Ms. Bernadette TOY-HALE
28 Director of Diversity .... Ms. Lorna HOLLOWELL
38 Director Student Counseling .... Ms. Barbara TIPMORE
84 Director Enrollment Management .... Mr. Kevin BEARDMORE
96 Director of Purchasing .... Ms. Sarah PRICE
24 Dir of Teaching & Learning Center .... Ms. Judy COOMES
40 Bookstore Manager .... Ms. Sonya SOUTHARD
88 TV Production Manager .... Mr. John BRYENTON
07 Senior Admissions Counselor .... Ms. Linda CALHOUN
55 Evening & Weekend Coordinator .... Mr. Barry STEPHENS
36 Career Resource/Placemnt Ctr Coord .... Ms. Katie BALLARD
79 Division Chair Humanities .... Dr. Julia LEDFORD
83 Div Chair Social Sci/Public Service .... Dr. Marc MALTBY
81 Div Chr Natural Sciences/Math .... Dr. Veena SALLAN
76 Division Chair Allied Health .... Ms. Peggy HOWARD
75 Div Chair Advanced Technologies .... Mr. James WATHEN
66 Associate Academic Dean Nursing .... Ms. Jessica ESTES
103 VP Workforce Solutions .... Ms. Cynthia FIORELLA

*Somerset Community College (F)

808 Monticello Street, Somerset KY 42501-2973
County: Pulaski FICE Identification: 001997
Unit ID: 157711
Telephone: (606) 679-8501 Carnegie Class: Assoc/Pub-R-L
FAX Number: (606) 679-3102 Calendar System: Semester
URL: www.somerset.kctcs.edu
Established: 1965 Annual Undergrad Tuition & Fees (In-State): $4,050
Enrollment: 9,247 Coed
Affiliation or Control: State IRS Status: 501(c)3
Highest Offering: Associate Degree
Program: Occupational; 2-Year Principally Bachelor's Creditable
Accreditation: SC, ADNUR, IFSAC, MLTAD, PTAA, RAD, SURGT

02 President/CEO .... Dr. Jo MARSHALL
05 Provost .... Dr. Tony L. HONEYCUTT
49 Dean of Arts and Sciences .... Ms. Sharon F. WHITEHEAD
09 Dean of Institutional Effectiveness .... Ms. Amy L. BEAUDOIN
32 Dean of Student Affairs .... Ms. Tracy L. CASADA
106 Assoc Dean for Distance Education .... Ms. Linda D. BOURNE
10 Chief Business Affairs Officer .... Mr. Timothy ZIMMERMAN
11 Chief Operations Officer .... Mr. Larry ABBOTT
30 Chief Institutional Advance Ofcr .... Ms. Ann O. ZWICK
103 Chief Cmty Wkfc & Economic Dev Ofc .... Mr. David A. WILES
76 Assoc Dean for Health Sciences .... Ms. Nancy L. POWELL
79 Assoc Dean Humanities/Fine Arts/SS .... Mr. Jon BURLEW
83 Assoc Dean Math/Natural Science .... Mr. Clint R. HAYES
88 Assoc Dean Const/Manuf/Trans .... Mr. Daniel C. BURNETT
50 Assoc Dean Bus/IT/Crim Just/ Ed&Cons .... Ms. Lois A. MCWHORTER
88 Dean Academic Support Services .... Mr. Bruce GOVER

46	Dir of Prof and Org Development	Ms. Karen M. WRIGHT
20	Assoc Dean for Learning	Ms. Shelley J. BURGETT
37	Commons Director of Financial Aid	Ms. Shawn R. ANDERSON
06	Registrar	Ms. Paula J. GUFFEY
15	Director of Human Resources	Ms. Jill N. MEECE
26	Director of Public Relations	Ms. Cindy D. CLOUSE
26	Director of Public Relations	Mr. David J. CAZALET, JR.
28	Director of Cultural Diversity	Ms. Elaine WILSON
12	McCreary Center Director	Ms. Gayle P. BORDERS
88	Dean of Applied Technology	Mr. Roger L. ANGERINE
12	Clinton Center Director	Ms. Dorothy E. PHILLIPS
12	Director of Casey Center	Ms. Judy SAPP
12	Director of Russell Center	Ms. Winfrey BATES
13	Director of Information Technology	Mr. Gary CUNNINGHAM

Southeast Kentucky Community and Technical College (A)

700 College Road, Cumberland KY 40823-1099

County: Harlan　FICE Identification: 001998
Unit ID: 157739
Telephone: (606) 589-2145　Carnegie Class: Assoc/Pub-R-M
FAX Number: (606) 589-4941　Calendar System: Semester
URL: www.southeast.kctcs.net
Established: 1960　Annual Undergrad Tuition & Fees (In-State): $3,120
Enrollment: 5,189　Coed
Affiliation or Control: State　IRS Status: 501(c)3
Highest Offering: Associate Degree
Program: Occupational; 2-Year Principally Bachelor's Creditable
Accreditation: SC, ADNUR, MLTAD, PNUR, PTAA, RAD, SURGT

02	President	Dr. W. Bruce AYERS
05	Chief Academic Officer	Dr. Wheeler CONOVER
10	Chief Business Affairs Officer	Ms. Susan CROUSHORN
12	Branch Campus Director	Ms. Deborah YOUNG
12	Campus/Education Center Director	Mr. Stephen STURGILL
06	Dean Student Affairs/Registrar	Ms. Karin GIBSON
21	Dean Administration Services	Mr. Tom POPE
103	Chief Community Workforce	Mr. Vic ADAMS
20	Chief Learning Officer	Mrs. Pam WHITEHEAD
26	Director of Public Relations	Mr. Chris JONES
16	Human Resources Director	Ms. Billie FRANKS
15	Human Resource Specialist	Ms. Jeannie HAYES
08	Head Librarian	Mr. Warren GRAY
37	Coordinator Financial Aid	Ms. Charlotte LOCKABY
13	Director of Information Technology	Mr. Merrill GALLOWAY
09	Director of Institutional Research	Dr. Rick MASON
11	Chief Operations Officer	Mr. Larry WARF
28	Director of Diversity	Ms. Carolyn SUNDY
30	Director of Advancement	Ms. Susan CALDWELL
35	Dean Student Affairs	Ms. Rebecca PARROTT-ROBBINS
96	Dean of Finance	Ms. Angela SIMPSON
07	Director of Admissions	Ms. Veria BALDWIN
40	Bookstore Manager	Ms. Tammy DEAL
81	Div Chr Allied Hlth/Coord Clin Lab	Ms. Kathy GUYN
83	Div Chair Soc Sci/Business/Rel Tech	Mr. Kevin LAMBERT
79	Div Chair Humanities/Comm/Fine Arts	Ms. Terry MACUILA
88	Div Chair Industrial Technology	Mr. Ronnie DANIELS
65	Div Chair Natural Sciences	Ms. Pat SCOPA

West Kentucky Community and Technical College (B)

4810 Alben Barkley Drive, Paducah KY 42002-7380

County: McCracken　FICE Identification: 001979
Unit ID: 157483
Telephone: (270) 554-9200　Carnegie Class: Assoc/Pub-R-L
FAX Number: (270) 554-6217　Calendar System: Semester
URL: www.westkentucky.kctcs.edu
Established: 1909　Annual Undergrad Tuition & Fees (In-State): $4,050
Enrollment: 7,364　Coed
Affiliation or Control: State　IRS Status: 501(c)3
Highest Offering: Associate Degree
Program: Occupational; 2-Year Principally Bachelor's Creditable
Accreditation: SC, ACFEI, ADNUR, DA, DMS, IFSAC, POLYT, PTAA, RAD, SURGT

02	President	Dr. Barbara VEAZEY
30	VP Economic Development	Dr. Deborah PAPE
05	VP of Academic Affairs	Dr. Tena PAYNE
32	Interim VP of Student Affairs	Dr. Belinda DALTON-RUSSELL
10	VP of Administrative Services	Mr. John CARRICO
88	VP Learning Initiatives	Ms. Sherry ANDERSON
09	VP Institutional Development	Dr. Steve FREEMAN
10	VP Business Affairs	Ms. Susan GRAVES
08	Interim Library Services Director	Mr. Ken BRADSHAW
37	Financial Aid Director	Ms. Sandy BARLOW
26	Public Relations Director	Ms. Janett BLYTHE
13	Director Information Technology	Ms. Ruby RODGERS
15	Director Human Resources	Ms. Bridget CANTER
30	Dir Institutional Advancement	Ms. Kay TRAVIS
40	Bookstore Manager	Mr. Todd MITCHELL
06	Registrar/Director of Admissions	Ms. Maria ROSA
35	Student Activities Coordinator	Mr. Rick TIPPIN
79	Dean Humanities/Fine Arts/Soc Sci	Ms. Sharla KRUPANSKY
66	Dean Nursing Division	Ms. Shari GHOLSON
50	Dean Business/Comp Related Tech Div	Ms. Tammy POTTER
76	Dean Allied Health Division	Ms. Peggy BLOCK
75	Dean Applied Tech Division	Ms. Stephanie MILLIKEN
81	Dean Science & Math Division	Dr. Karen HLINKA
97	Dean Transition Education Div	Ms. Maria FLYNN

88	Dean Institutional Effectiveness	Ms. Renea AKIN
07	Director of Admissions	Ms. Maria ROSA
28	Director of Diversity	Ms. Jipaum ASKEW-ROBINSON
36	Director Student Placement	Ms. Paula ARMON

Kentucky Mountain Bible College (C)

Box 10, Vancleve KY 41385-0010

County: Breathitt　FICE Identification: 030021
Unit ID: 157030
Telephone: (606) 693-5000　Carnegie Class: Spec/Faith
FAX Number: (606) 693-4884　Calendar System: Semester
URL: www.kmbc.edu
Established: 1931　Annual Undergrad Tuition & Fees: $6,600
Enrollment: 89　Coed
Affiliation or Control: Independent Non-Profit　IRS Status: 501(c)3
Highest Offering: Baccalaureate
Program: 2-Year Principally Bachelor's Creditable; Liberal Arts And General; Religious Emphasis
Accreditation: BI

01	President	Dr. Philip E. SPEAS
05	Exec Vice Pres/VP Academic Affs	Rev. Thomas H. LORIMER
30	Vice President Development	Dr. John E. NEIHOF, JR.
10	Chief Business Manager	Mr. Douglas R. DUNN
32	Dean of Student Affairs	Mr. Randall HUFF
13	Director IT	Mr. Stephen A. LORIMER
08	Head Librarian	Ms. Patricia A. BOWEN
06	Registrar	Mr. Richard ENGLEHARDT
07	Chief Admissions Counselor	Mr. David W. LORIMER
37	Director Student Financial Aid	Mrs. Carla FRAZIER
26	Dir PR/Foreign Stdnts/Dean of Men	Mr. James H. NELSON
34	Dean of Women	Ms. Jane HUFF

Kentucky State University (D)

400 E Main Street, Frankfort KY 40601-2355

County: Franklin　FICE Identification: 001968
Unit ID: 157058
Telephone: (502) 597-6000　Carnegie Class: Bac/A&S
FAX Number: (502) 597-6490　Calendar System: Semester
URL: www.kysu.edu
Established: 1886　Annual Undergrad Tuition & Fees (In-State): $7,837
Enrollment: 2,851　Coed
Affiliation or Control: State　IRS Status: 501(c)3
Highest Offering: Master's
Program: Liberal Arts And General; Teacher Preparatory
Accreditation: SC, ACBSP, ADNUR, MUS, NUR, SPAA, SW, TED

01	President	Dr. Mary E. SIAS
05	Int Provost/Vice Pres Academic Affs	Vacant
10	Chief Financial Officer	Ms. Alice JOHNSON
32	VP Stdnt Affs/Asc Prov Enroll Mgmt	Dr. Rubye JONES
30	VP External Relations & Development	Mr. Hinfred MCDUFFIE
07	Director of Admissions	Vacant
23	Director Student Health Services	Ms. Floarine WILSON
31	Int Director Educational Outreach	Ms. Irma JOHNSON
06	Director Records/Registrar	Mr. John MARTIN
08	Director Libraries	Ms. Sheila STUCKEY
100	Chief of Staff/Exec Asst to Pres	Mr. Stephen MASON
36	Int Dir Couns/Career Plng/Placement	Mr. Ronald BANKS
14	Director Computer Services	Mr. Edward FIELDS
15	Director Human Resources	Mr. Gary MEISELES
29	Director Alumni Affairs	Mr. Garland HIGGINS
39	Director Housing	Vacant
37	Director Student Financial Aid	Ms. Victoria OWENS
25	Int Director Land Grant Programs	Dr. Kimberley HOLMES
26	Director Public Relations	Ms. Felicia LEWIS
43	General Counsel	Ms. Lori A. DAVIS
21	Internal Auditor	Dr. Ralph KIMBROUGH
18	Director Physical Plant	Mr. Jack MCNEAR
41	Director Athletics	Dr. Denisha HENDRICKS
19	Chief University Police	Ms. Stephanie BASTIN
45	Budget Director	Ms. Claudine GEE
84	Director Enrollment Management	Dr. Roosevelt SHELTON
96	Director of Purchasing	Ms. Tonya MONTGOMERY
49	Dean Arts/Science/Interdiscip Stds	Dr. Sam OLEKA
88	Dean College of Prof Studies	Dr. Gashaw LAKE
09	Coord Instl Research/Effectivenes	Dr. Robin GEIGER

Kentucky Wesleyan College (E)

3000 Frederica Street, Owensboro KY 42301

County: Daviess　FICE Identification: 001969
Unit ID: 157076
Telephone: (270) 926-3111　Carnegie Class: Bac/Diverse
FAX Number: (270) 926-3196　Calendar System: Semester
URL: www.kwc.edu
Established: 1858　Annual Undergrad Tuition & Fees: $18,790
Enrollment: 802　Coed
Affiliation or Control: United Methodist　IRS Status: 501(c)3
Highest Offering: Baccalaureate
Program: Liberal Arts And General; Teacher Preparatory
Accreditation: SC, IACBE

01	President	Dr. Craig TURNER
05	VP Acad Affairs/Dean of the College	Dr. Paula DEHN
03	Executive Vice President	Vacant
10	Vice Pres for Finance/Treasurer	Ms. Cindra K. STIFF
30	VP for Development/Alumni Relations	Vacant
32	VP of Student Affairs	Mr. Scott E. KRAMER

07	Director of Admissions	Mr. Rashad SMITH
06	Registrar	Ms. Jennifer VAUGHN
09	Director of Institutional Research	Mr. Mark C. HEDGES
15	Director of Personnel Services	Mrs. Linda B. KELLER
37	Director of Student Financial Aid	Ms. Samantha HAYES
89	Director of the PLUS Center	Ms. Marisue S. COY
08	Director of Library Learning Center	Mrs. Patricia G. MCFARLING
41	Athletic Director	Vacant
21	Controller	Ms. Courtney LEMASTER
18	Physical Plant Director	Mr. David KNIGHT
29	Director of Alumni Relations	Vacant
26	Director of Public Relations	Ms. Kathy RUTHERMAN
42	Campus Minister	Mr. Kent LEWIS

Lexington Theological Seminary (F)

631 S Limestone, Lexington KY 40508-3288

County: Fayette　FICE Identification: 001971
Unit ID: 157207
Telephone: (859) 252-0361　Carnegie Class: Spec/Faith
FAX Number: (859) 281-6042　Calendar System: Semester
URL: www.lextheo.edu
Established: 1865　Annual Graduate Tuition & Fees: $9,600
Enrollment: 80　Coed
Affiliation or Control: Christian Church (Disciples Of Christ)
IRS Status: 501(c)3
Highest Offering: Doctorate; No Undergraduates
Program: Professional; Religious Emphasis
Accreditation: THEOL

01	President	Dr. James JOHNSON
05	Dean	Dr. Richard WEIS
30	Vice President for Advancement	Dr. James M. WRAY, JR.
10	Chief Financial Officer	Mrs. Laura DAVIS
06	Registrar	Ms. Windy KIDD
08	Librarian	Ms. Barbara PFEIFLE
36	Director Student Placement	Dr. Steve MONHOLLEN
13	Director Information Services	Mr. Ben WYATT
07	Director Admission	Dr. Charisse GILLETT

Lincoln College of Technology (G)

8095 Connector Drive, Florence KY 41042-1466

County: Boone　Identification: 666447
Unit ID: 245032
Telephone: (859) 282-9999　Carnegie Class: Assoc/PrivFP
FAX Number: (859) 282-7940　Calendar System: Quarter
URL: www.lincolnedu.com
Established: 1978　Annual Undergrad Tuition & Fees: $15,220
Enrollment: 633　Coed
Affiliation or Control: Proprietary　IRS Status: Proprietary
Highest Offering: Associate Degree
Program: Occupational; 2-Year Principally Bachelor's Creditable
Accreditation: ACICS, MAAB

01	Director	Mr. Peter MARTINELLO
05	Academic Dean	Ms. Laura CARNAGHI
07	Director of Admissions	Ms. Melissa DURKIN
37	Director of Financial Aid	Ms. Victoria HUBBARD

† Branch campus of Southwestern College, OH.

Lindsey Wilson College (H)

210 Lindsey Wilson Street, Columbia KY 42728-1298

County: Adair　FICE Identification: 001972
Unit ID: 157216
Telephone: (270) 384-2126　Carnegie Class: Master's M
FAX Number: (270) 384-8200　Calendar System: Semester
URL: www.lindsey.edu
Established: 1903　Annual Undergrad Tuition & Fees: $20,030
Enrollment: 2,554　Coed
Affiliation or Control: United Methodist　IRS Status: 501(c)3
Highest Offering: Master's
Program: 2-Year Principally Bachelor's Creditable; Liberal Arts And General; Teacher Preparatory
Accreditation: SC, CACREP, IACBE

01	President	Dr. William T. LUCKEY, JR.
03	Chancellor	Dr. John B. BEGLEY
05	Vice President Academic Affairs	Dr. Bettie C. STARR
10	Vice President Administration	Dr. Roger D. DRAKE
30	Vice President Advancement	Mr. Kevin A. THOMPSON
04	Executive Assistant	Mrs. Paula R. POWELL
32	Vice President Student Services	Dr. Dean ADAMS
37	VP Educ Outreach/Stdnt Finan Svcs	Mrs. Denise G. FUDGE
35	Dean of Students	Mr. Christopher SCHMIDT
38	Dean of Sch of Prof Counseling	Vacant
20	Associate Academic Dean	Ms. Lori SARGENT
88	Dean of Chapel	Dr. Terry W. SWAN
07	Dean of Admissions	Mrs. Traci M. POOLER
07	Director of Admissions	Mrs. Charity F. FERGUSON
55	Director of Evening College	Ms. Regina HAUGEN
41	Athletic Director	Mr. Willis POOLER, III
06	Registrar	Mrs. Sue B. COOMER
15	Director of Human Resources	Mrs. Karen F. WRIGHT
31	Dir of Civic Engagement & Std Ldrsp	Mrs. Amy C. THOMPSON-WELLS
36	Director Career Services	Mrs. Ashley MILLER
08	Librarian	Mr. C. Phil HANNA
18	Director of Physical Plant	Mr. Michael L. NEWTON
21	Director of Auxiliary Services	Mr. Jeff WILLIS

40 Bookstore Manager .... Mrs. Amy M. COOPER
35 Director of Student Activities .... Mrs. Jayne S. HOPKINS
85 Dir of International Stdnt Programs .... Mrs. Suzy MCALPINE
14 Director Information Services .... Mrs. Harriet B. GOLD
13 Director of Information Systems .... Mr. Anthony MOORE
26 Public Relations Officer .... Mr. Duane BONIFER
29 Assistant to Pres Alumni Affairs .... Mr. Randy BURNS
19 Director Safety/Security .... Mr. Darwin VICKERY
42 Chaplain .... Rev. Troy A. ELMORE
09 Dir Plng/Instl Effective/Research .... Vacant
37 Director Student Financial Services .... Ms. Marilyn RADFORD
38 Director Student Counseling .... Dr. Jeff CRANE
66 Director of Nursing .... Mrs. Suzette L. SCHEUERMANN

Louisville Bible College (A)

8013 Damascus Road, Louisville KY 40228
County: Jefferson FICE Identification: 041418
Unit ID: 157234
Telephone: (502) 231-5221 Carnegie Class: Spec/Faith
FAX Number: (502) 231-5222 Calendar System: Semester
URL: www.louisvillebiblecollege.org
Established: 1948 Annual Undergrad Tuition & Fees: $3,080
Enrollment: 112 Coed
Affiliation or Control: Independent Non-Profit IRS Status: 501(c)3
Highest Offering: Master's
Program: Religious Emphasis
Accreditation: @BI

01 President .... Dr. Tracy W. MARX
05 Academic Dean .... Ronald J. DOWNS
30 Director of Partnership Development .... Danny L. DYE
08 Director of Library .... John D. MERRITT
06 Registrar .... Angela MARX

Louisville Presbyterian Theological Seminary (B)

1044 Alta Vista Road, Louisville KY 40205-1798
County: Jefferson FICE Identification: 001974
Unit ID: 157298
Telephone: (502) 895-3411 Carnegie Class: Spec/Faith
FAX Number: (502) 895-1096 Calendar System: 4/1/4
URL: www.lpts.edu
Established: 1853 Annual Graduate Tuition & Fees: $10,546
Enrollment: 230 Coed
Affiliation or Control: Presbyterian Church (U.S.A.) IRS Status: 501(c)3
Highest Offering: Doctorate; No Undergraduates
Program: Professional; Religious Emphasis
Accreditation: SC, MFCD, THEOL

01 President .... Dr. Michael JINKINS
30 Vice Pres for Seminary Relations .... Mr. Dale MELTON
10 Vice President for Finance .... Mr. Patrick A. CECIL
05 Dean & Vice Pres Academic Affairs .... Dr. David C. HESTER
32 Dean of Students .... Rev. Kilen GRAY
06 Associate Dean & Registrar .... Rev. David E. GRAY
44 Director of Seminary Fund .... Ms. Judy JOHNSTON
29 Director Alum & Church Relations .... Rev. Leah J. BRADLEY
27 Director of Communications .... Ms. Michelle E. MELTON
08 Director of Library and IT Services .... Dr. Douglas L. GRAGG
21 Controller .... Ms. Marti F. MARSH
51 Director of Lifelong Learning .... Dr. David SAWYER
07 Director of Admissions .... Rev. Cheri HARPER
13 Systems Director .... Mr. Jack SHARER
18 Director of Facilities .... Mr. Tim WILLIAMS

Mid-Continent University (C)

99 Powell Road E, Mayfield KY 42066-9007
County: Graves FICE Identification: 025762
Unit ID: 157359
Telephone: (270) 247-8521 Carnegie Class: Bac/Diverse
FAX Number: (270) 247-3115 Calendar System: Semester
URL: www.midcontinent.edu
Established: 1949 Annual Undergrad Tuition & Fees: $13,350
Enrollment: 2,269 Coed
Affiliation or Control: Southern Baptist IRS Status: 501(c)3
Highest Offering: Master's
Program: Liberal Arts And General; Business Emphasis
Accreditation: SC

01 President .... Dr. Robert J. IMHOFF
04 Assistant to the President .... Mrs. Mitzi TURNER
03 Executive Vice President .... Mr. Charles W. FORD
05 Vice President Academic Affairs .... Dr. Stephen WILSON
10 Vice Pres Finance & Administration .... Col. Andrew B. STRATTON
32 Dean Students/International Affairs .... Ms. Kolby MILLER
55 VP Adult Pgms/Dir Advantage Pgm .... Mrs. Jacquelyn IMHOFF
20 Assoc VP Academic Affairs .... Dr. Debra HUDSON
08 Dean of the Markham Library .... Mr. Ray LYTLE
30 Acting Director External Relations .... Mr. David SMITH
06 University Registrar .... Mrs. Yvonne YATES
21 Director of Budget & Planning .... Col. Andrew B. STRATTON
07 Assoc Dean Admissions/Student Life .... Mr. Karl HATTON
37 Director Financial Aid Services .... Mr. Kent YOUNGBLOOD
45 Director Inst Effectiveness .... Ms. Darlene GIBSON
41 Athletic Director .... Mr. Larry LAMPKINS
18 Chief Facilities/Physical Plant .... Mr. Tim BLALOCK
14 Director of Computing Services .... Mr. David ROSS
15 Director of Human Resources .... Mr. Homer BURTON
21 Business Office Manager .... Mrs. Deborah NALL
49 Dean Baptist Col of Arts & Sci .... Dr. Jamie SUMMERVILLE
73 Dean Baptist College of Bible .... Dr. Larry ORANGE

Midway College (D)

512 E Stephens Street, Midway KY 40347-1120
County: Woodford FICE Identification: 001975
Unit ID: 157377
Telephone: (859) 846-4421 Carnegie Class: Bac/Diverse
FAX Number: (859) 846-5349 Calendar System: Semester
URL: www.midway.edu
Established: 1847 Annual Undergrad Tuition & Fees: $19,800
Enrollment: 1,606 Female
Affiliation or Control: Christian Church (Disciples Of Christ)
IRS Status: 501(c)3
Highest Offering: Doctorate
Program: 2-Year Principally Bachelor's Creditable; Liberal Arts And General; Teacher Preparatory; Professional
Accreditation: SC, ADNUR, NUR

01 President .... Dr. William B. DRAKE, JR.
05 Provost/Acad Dn Women's Col .... Dr. Sarah LAWS
04 Assistant to the President .... Ms. Sheila K. HOLSCLAW
106 VP Col Rels/Dn Mdwy Col Online .... Mrs. Judith W. MARCUM
30 Vice President Development .... Mr. Roy W. MUNDY, II
10 Vice Pres Business Affairs .... Mr. Lyen C. CREWS, II
36 Vice Pres/Dean Sch Career Dev .... Dr. William (Bill) BROWN
26 Vice Pres Marketing & Communication .... Mrs. Ellen D. GREGORY
84 Vice President Enrollment Managemen .... Dr. Johnie E. DEAN
32 Asst VP/Dean of Student Services .... Ms. Michelle PATRICK
06 Registrar .... Mrs. Linda P. ELDRIDGE
08 Director of Library Services .... Ms. Catherine L. REILENDER
41 Athletic Director .... Mrs. Wendy HOFFMAN
07 Director of Admissions Women's Col .... Mrs. Stacy M. SHARP
13 Director of Information Systems .... Mrs. C. Joan MCDANIEL
18 Director of Physical Plant .... Mr. Stephen D. GOODWIN
15 Director of Human Resources .... Mrs. Anne COCKLEY
37 Director of Student Financial Aid .... Ms. Katie A. CONRAD
39 Dir Residence Life/Stdnt Activities .... Ms. Leigh OAKLEY
21 Director of Student Accounts .... Mr. Robert L. NORTON
29 Director Devel/Alumni Relations .... Ms. Christy H. CLEVELAND

Morehead State University (E)

150 University Boulevard, Morehead KY 40351-1689
County: Rowan FICE Identification: 001976
Unit ID: 157386
Telephone: (606) 783-2221 Carnegie Class: Master's L
FAX Number: N/A Calendar System: Semester
URL: www.moreheadstate.edu
Established: 1887 Annual Undergrad Tuition & Fees (In-State): $6,942
Enrollment: 8,842 Coed
Affiliation or Control: State IRS Status: 501(c)3
Highest Offering: Doctorate
Program: Occupational; Liberal Arts And General; Teacher Preparatory; Professional
Accreditation: SC, ADNUR, BUS, DMS, MUS, NAIT, NURSE, RAD, SW, TED, THEA

01 President .... Dr. Wayne D. ANDREWS
05 Provost .... Dr. Karla HUGHES
10 Vice Pres Admin Fiscal Services .... Mr. Michael R. WALTERS
32 Vice President Student Life .... Ms. Madonna WEATHERS
30 Vice Pres for Univ Advancement .... Mr. James A. SHAW
45 Chief of Staff/VP Plng Budgets/Tech .... Ms. Beth PATRICK
20 Assoc VP Academic Affairs/Programs .... Dr. Dayna S. SEELIG
04 Assistant to the President .... Ms. Carol JOHNSON
06 Registrar .... Ms. Roslyn PERRY
46 Assoc VP for Research .... Dr. Bruce MATTINGLY
51 Asst VP Adult Ed & College Access .... Dr. Dan CONNELL
84 Asst Vice Pres Enrollment Services .... Mr. Jeffrey LILES
26 Asst VP Marketing & Communication .... Ms. Jami HORNBUCKLE
18 Asst VP Facilities Management .... Mr. Gene CAUDILL
40 Asst Vice Pres Auxiliary Services .... Mr. William REDWINE
08 Interim Dean of Library Services .... Vacant
09 Dir Inst Research & Analysis .... Dr. Timothy MILLARD
13 Director of Information Technology .... Mr. Drew HENDERSON
15 Director of Human Resources .... Mr. Phillip GNIOT
19 Director of Public Safety .... Mr. Matt SPARKS
88 Assistant to the Provost .... Mr. Bruce MAXWELL
21 Director Accounting/Budget Control .... Mrs. Kelli OWEN
21 Director of Budgets .... Ms. Teresa LINDGREN
28 Dir Multicultural Student Services .... Vacant
29 Director Alumni Relations .... Ms. Tami JONES
32 Dean of Students .... Mr. Kevin KOETT
37 Director Financial Aid .... Ms. Donna KING
36 Director Acad Advising/Career Svcs .... Ms. Julia HAWKINS
39 Director of Housing .... Ms. Dallas SAMMONS
41 Director of Athletics .... Mr. Brian A. HUTCHINSON
43 General Counsel .... Dr. Jane FITZPATRICK
44 Director of Development .... Ms. Melinda C. HIGHLEY
27 Media Relations Director .... Mr. Jason BLANTON
85 Director International Education .... Dr. Sam FAULKNER
96 Director Support Services .... Ms. Ladonna PURCELL
38 Director of Counseling & Health Svc .... Dr. Brenda WILBURN
50 Dean of Business .... Dr. Robert ALBERT
53 Dean Education .... Dr. Cathy GUNN
72 Dean Science & Technology .... Dr. Roger MCNEIL
79 Dean of Humanities .... Dr. Scott MCBRIDE
27 Asst VP Technology .... Mr. Gary HOLEMAN
20 Asst VP Academic Affairs .... Ms. Jill RATLIFF

Murray State University (F)

218 Wells Hall, Murray KY 42071-3318
County: Calloway FICE Identification: 001977
Unit ID: 157401
Telephone: (270) 809-3011 Carnegie Class: Master's L
FAX Number: (270) 809-3413 Calendar System: Semester
URL: www.murraystate.edu
Established: 1922 Annual Undergrad Tuition & Fees (In-State): $6,576
Enrollment: 10,416 Coed
Affiliation or Control: State IRS Status: 501(c)3
Highest Offering: Doctorate
Program: 2-Year Principally Bachelor's Creditable; Liberal Arts And General; Teacher Preparatory; Professional
Accreditation: SC, ANEST, ART, BUS, DIETD, DIETI, ENG, ENGR, ENGT, JOUR, MUS, NURSE, SP, SW, TED, THEA

01 President .... Dr. Randy J. DUNN
100 Chief of Staff .... Mr. Joshua E. JACOBS
101 Sr Exec Coord for Pres/Coord Bd Rel .... Ms. Jill HUNT LOVETT
05 Provost/VP Academic Affairs .... Dr. Bonnie S. HIGGINSON
10 VP Finance & Admin Svcs .... Mr. Tom W. DENTON
32 VP Student Affairs .... Dr. Don E. ROBERTSON
30 VP Institutional Advancement .... Mr. James F. CARTER
58 Assoc Provost/Grad Educ & Research .... Dr. Jay MORGAN
20 Assoc Prov/Undergrad Education .... Dr. Renae D. DUNCAN
88 Assoc VP Institutional Advancement .... Mr. Bob L. JACKSON
35 Asst VP Student Affairs .... Mr. Michael E. YOUNG
26 Asst VP Communications .... Ms. Catherine M. SIVILLS
43 General Counsel .... Mr. John P. RALL
50 Dean Business .... Dr. Timothy S. TODD
53 Int Dean Education .... Dr. Renee W. CAMPOY
76 Dean Health Sci & Human Svcs .... Dr. Susan M. MULLER
79 Dean Humanities & Fine Arts .... Dr. O. Ted BROWN
81 Dean Science/Engineering/Tech .... Dr. Stephen H. COBB
47 Dean Agriculture .... Dr. Tony L. BRANNON
66 Dean Nursing .... Dr. Marcia HOBBS
08 Dean University Libraries .... Mr. Adam L. MURRAY
51 Dn Cont Educ/Academic Outreach .... Dr. Brian W. VAN HORN
24 Asst Dn/Dir Dist Learn/Noncrdt Pgm .... Mr. Daniel A. LAVIT
97 Coordinator University Studies .... Dr. Peter F. MURPHY
92 Director Honors Program .... Dr. Warren EDMINSTER
85 Director Institute for Intl Studies .... Dr. Luis CANALES
104 Assoc Director Education Abroad .... Ms. Melanie C. MCCALLON
84 Exec Director Enrollment Mgmt .... Mr. Fred K. DIETZ
07 Dir Undgrad Admissions Svcs .... Ms. Lesa C. HARRIS
06 Registrar .... Ms. Tina L. COLLINS
37 Dir Student Fin Aid/Scholarships .... Ms. Lori A. MITCHUM
39 Director Housing .... Dr. J. David WILSON
38 Dir Counseling Wm's Ctr/Acad Enhanc .... Dr. William L. ALLBRITTEN
28 Dir African-American Student Svcs .... Mr. Sidney G. CARTHELL
36 Director Career Services .... Dr. Ross B. MELOAN
23 Director Health Services .... Ms. Roberta M. GARFIELD
16 Director Human Resources .... Mr. Thomas E. HOFFACKER
21 Sr Director Accounting & Fin Svcs .... Ms. Jacklyn K. DUDLEY
21 Dir Fiscal Plng/Analysis/Budget Ofc .... Mr. Carl F. PRESTFELDT
102 Executive Director MSU Foundation .... Dr. Tim I. MILLER
96 Director Procurement Services .... Mr. David T. BLACKBURN
22 Dir Office of Equal Opportunity .... Ms. Sabrina Y. DIAL
88 Exec Dir Regional Stwrdshp/Outreach .... Ms. Gina S. WINCHESTER
13 Chief Information Officer .... Ms. Linda G. MILLER
91 Manager Administrative Computing .... Mr. Brantly D. TRAVIS
90 Dir Ctr for Teaching/Learn/Tech .... Mr. Howard T. RICE
09 Coordinator Institutional Research .... Ms. Fugen MUSCIO
41 Athletic Director .... Mr. C. Allen WARD
18 VP Finance & Admin Svcs .... Mr. Tom W. DENTON
19 Dir Public Safety/Emergency Mgmt .... Mr. David V. DEVOSS
40 Director University Store .... Ms. R. Karol HARDISON
25 Interim Director Sponsored Programs .... Dr. Robert F. LONG
29 Assoc Director Alumni Affairs .... Ms. Sabrina K. MATHIS
105 Web Manager .... Mr. R. Tony A. POWELL

National College (G)

115 E Lexington Avenue, Danville KY 40422-1517
County: Boyle Identification: 666441
Unit ID: 433572
Telephone: (859) 236-6991 Carnegie Class: Not Classified
FAX Number: (859) 236-1063 Calendar System: Quarter
URL: www.ncbt.edu
Established: 1886 Annual Undergrad Tuition & Fees: $11,500
Enrollment: 450 Coed
Affiliation or Control: Proprietary IRS Status: Proprietary
Highest Offering: Associate Degree
Program: Occupational; 2-Year Principally Bachelor's Creditable
Accreditation: ACICS, MAC

01 Director .... Mr. Lee BOWLING
05 Vice President .... Ms. Charlotte BRINNEMAN

† Branch campus of National College, Lexington, KY.

National College (H)

7627 Ewing Boulevard, Florence KY 41042-1812
County: Boone Identification: 666442
Telephone: (859) 525-6510 Carnegie Class: Not Classified
FAX Number: (859) 525-8961 Calendar System: Quarter
URL: www.ncbt.edu
Established: 1970 Annual Undergrad Tuition & Fees: $10,704
Enrollment: 298 Coed
Affiliation or Control: Proprietary IRS Status: Proprietary
Highest Offering: Associate Degree

Program: Occupational; 2-Year Principally Bachelor's Creditable
Accreditation: ACICS, MAC, SURGT

01 Director ... Ms. Carole REED-MAHONEY
04 Assistant to the Director ... Mrs. Linda MERRELL
05 Vice President ... Ms. Charlotte BRINNEMAN

† Branch campus of National College, Lexington, KY.

National College (A)

2376 Sir Barton Way, Lexington KY 40509-2256
County: Fayette | FICE Identification: 010489 | Unit ID: 157021
Telephone: (859) 253-0621 | Carnegie Class: Assoc/PrivFP4
FAX Number: (859) 254-7664 | Calendar System: Quarter
URL: www.ncbt.edu
Established: 1941 | Annual Undergrad Tuition & Fees: $10,489
Enrollment: 2,418 | Coed
Affiliation or Control: Proprietary | IRS Status: Proprietary
Highest Offering: Baccalaureate
Program: Occupational; 2-Year Principally Bachelor's Creditable
Accreditation: ACICS, MAC, SURGT

01 President ... Mr. Frank LONGAKER
05 Campus Director ... Ms. Kim THOMASSON
03 Vice President ... Ms. Charlotte BRINNEMAN
37 Director of Financial Aid ... Ms. Pam COTTON
07 Regional Director of Admissions ... Ms. Donna STOUTENBOROUGH

National College (B)

4205 Dixie Highway, Louisville KY 40216-4147
County: Jefferson | Identification: 666443 | Unit ID: 433590
Telephone: (502) 447-7634 | Carnegie Class: Not Classified
FAX Number: (502) 447-7665 | Calendar System: Quarter
URL: www.national-college.edu
Established: 1886 | Annual Undergrad Tuition & Fees: $14,544
Enrollment: 641 | Coed
Affiliation or Control: Proprietary | IRS Status: Proprietary
Highest Offering: Baccalaureate
Program: Occupational; 2-Year Principally Bachelor's Creditable
Accreditation: ACICS, MAC, SURGT

01 Director ... Mr. Vincent TINEBRA
05 Assistant Director ... Ms. Vicki STRUNK

† Branch campus of National College, Lexington, KY.

National College (C)

50 National College Boulevard, Pikeville KY 41501-3176
County: Pike | Identification: 666444
Telephone: (606) 478-7200 | Carnegie Class: Not Classified
FAX Number: (606) 437-4952 | Calendar System: Quarter
URL: www.ncbt.edu
Established: 1970 | Annual Undergrad Tuition & Fees: $7,500
Enrollment: 285 | Coed
Affiliation or Control: Proprietary | IRS Status: Proprietary
Highest Offering: Associate Degree
Program: Occupational; 2-Year Principally Bachelor's Creditable
Accreditation: ACICS, MAC

01 Director ... Ms. Tammy RILEY

† Branch campus of National College, Lexington, KY.

National College (D)

125 S Killarney Lane, Richmond KY 40475-2309
County: Madison | Identification: 666445 | Unit ID: 433615
Telephone: (859) 623-8956 | Carnegie Class: Not Classified
FAX Number: (859) 624-5544 | Calendar System: Quarter
URL: www.ncbt.edu
Established: 1974 | Annual Undergrad Tuition & Fees: $9,450
Enrollment: 417 | Coed
Affiliation or Control: Proprietary | IRS Status: Proprietary
Highest Offering: Associate Degree
Program: Occupational; 2-Year Principally Bachelor's Creditable
Accreditation: ACICS, MAC

01 President ... Mr. Frank LONGAKER
03 Vice President ... Ms. Charlotte BRINNEMAN
05 Director ... Mrs. Keeley GADD

† Branch campus of National College, Lexington, KY.

Northern Kentucky University (E)

Nunn Drive, Highland Heights KY 41099-0000
County: Campbell | FICE Identification: 009275 | Unit ID: 157447
Telephone: (859) 572-5100 | Carnegie Class: Master's L
FAX Number: (859) 572-5566 | Calendar System: Semester
URL: www.nku.edu
Established: 1968 | Annual Undergrad Tuition & Fees (In-State): $7,488
Enrollment: 15,748 | Coed
Affiliation or Control: State | IRS Status: 501(c)3
Highest Offering: Doctorate
Program: 2-Year Principally Bachelor's Creditable; Liberal Arts And General; Teacher Preparatory; Professional
Accreditation: SC, BUS, CONST, ENGT, LAW, MUS, NUR, RAD, SPAA, SW, TED

01 President ... Dr. James C. VOTRUBA
04 Exec Asst to President ... Ms. Kathryn J. HERSCHEDE
05 Vice Pres Academic Affairs/Provost ... Dr. Gail W. WELLS
10 Vice Pres Admin & Finance ... Mr. Kenneth H. RAMEY
32 Interim Vice Pres Student Affairs ... Dr. Lisa RHINE
30 Vice Pres University Advancement ... Mr. Gerard A. ST. AMAND
45 Vice Pres Planning/Policy/Budget ... Dr. Sue HODGES MOORE
43 VP Legal Affairs & General Counsel ... Ms. Sara L. SIDEBOTTOM
86 Vice Pres Govt/Community Relations ... Mr. Joseph E. WIND
44 Asst VP University Development ... Mr. Donald A. GORBANDT
26 Asst VP Marketing & Communications ... Mr. Rick MEYERS
88 Assoc Provost for Reg Stewardship ... Dr. Jan HILLARD
20 Vice Provost University Programs ... Mr. J. Patrick MOYNAHAN
49 Dean College of Arts & Sciences ... Dr. Samuel ZACHARY
50 Dean College of Business ... Dr. Rick KOLBE
88 Dean College of Informatics ... Dr. Douglas PERRY
53 Dean College of Ed & Human Services ... Dr. Mark WASICSKO
61 Dean Chase College of Law ... Mr. Dennis HONABACH
66 Dean College of Health Professions ... Dr. Denise ROBINSON
11 Director of Administration ... Ms. Linda REYNOLDS
18 Asst VP Facilities Management ... Mr. Larry BLAKE
18 Director Operations & Maintenance ... Mr. Walter WELCH
21 Dir Fin & Operational Auditing ... Mr. Larry MEYER
21 Dir Business/Auxiliary Services ... Mr. Andy MEEKS
88 Dir Architecture & Construction ... Mr. Steve NIENABER
45 Director Campus Space and Planning ... Ms. Mary Paula SCHUH
15 Senior Director Human Resources ... Ms. Lori SOUTHWOOD
21 Comptroller ... Mr. Russell A. KERDOLFF
19 Director Public Safety ... Mr. Jason WILLIS
13 Director IT ... Ms. Kimberly HEIMBROCK
96 Director Procurement Services ... Mr. Jeffrey STRUNK
20 Assoc Provost Academic Affs/Admin ... Ms. Mary M. RYAN
13 Assoc Provost & CIO ... Mr. Timothy FERGUSON
08 Assoc Provost Library Services ... Mr. Arne J. ALMQUIST
92 Interim Director Honors Program ... Ms. Belle ZEMBRODT
84 Assoc VP Enrollment Management ... Mr. Joel L. ROBINSON
07 Director Admissions-Outreach ... Ms. Melissa GORBANDT
06 Registrar ... Ms. Michele HALL
37 Dir Student Financial Assistance ... Ms. Leah STEWART
78 Dir Center for Civ Engage ... Mr. Mark NEIKIRK
51 Director Community Connections ... Ms. Melinda SPONG
25 Director Research/Grants/Contracts ... Mr. William THOMPSON
89 Director First Year Programs ... Dr. Mei Mei BURR
88 Sr Director Office of the Budget ... Mr. Kenneth KLINE
45 Director Planning & Performance ... Vacant
09 Director Institutional Research ... Ms. Katherine A. BONTRAGER
00 Director Campus Recreation ... Mr. Matthew HACKETT
38 Dir Health/Counseling/Prevention ... Ms. Barbara SWEEN
35 Director Student Life ... Ms. Betty MULKEY
38 Dir Testing & Disability Services ... Ms. Lisa BESNOY
39 Director University Housing ... Mr. Peter TRENTACOSTE
36 Director Career Development ... Mr. Bill FROUDE
85 Director Intl Student & Scholars ... Ms. Elizabeth LEIBACH
41 Director Athletic Administration ... Dr. Scott EATON
102 Executive Director Foundation ... Ms. Karen ZERHUSEN KRUER
29 Director Alumni Programs ... Ms. Deidra FAJACK

St. Catharine College (F)

2735 Bardstown Road, Saint Catharine KY 40061-9499
County: Washington | FICE Identification: 001983 | Unit ID: 157632
Telephone: (859) 336-5082 | Carnegie Class: Bac/Assoc
FAX Number: (859) 336-5031 | Calendar System: Semester
URL: www.sccky.edu
Established: 1931 | Annual Undergrad Tuition & Fees: $16,950
Enrollment: 892 | Coed
Affiliation or Control: Roman Catholic | IRS Status: 501(c)3
Highest Offering: Master's
Program: Occupational; 2-Year Principally Bachelor's Creditable
Accreditation: SC, ADNUR, DMS, RAD, SURGT

01 President ... Mr. William D. HUSTON
03 Executive Vice President ... Mr. Roger L. MARCUM
05 Vice President for Academic Affairs ... Dr. Don GILES
10 Vice President Finance ... Mr. Gary ROBINSON
30 Vice President for Advancement ... Ms. Jenna COPPLE
84 VP Enrollment Mgt/Dean of Students ... Ms. Vicki GUTHRIE
06 Registrar ... Ms. Anita FOSTER
07 Director of Admissions ... Mr. Paul PRESTA
08 Head Librarian ... Ms. Ilona BURDETTE
37 Financial Aid Officer ... Ms. Laura DEAN
27 Director of Communications ... Mr. Jim EARLS
38 Director of Counseling ... Vacant
15 Director of Personnel Services ... Mrs. Carlotta BRUSSELL
18 Chief Facilities/Physical Plant ... Mr. Dwight COTTON
21 Associate Business Officer ... Mr. Jim SNYDER
26 Chief Public Relations Officer ... Mr. Jimmie EARLS
35 Director of Student Affairs ... Vacant
09 Director of Institutional Research ... Ms. Nora HATTON

Simmons College of Kentucky (G)

1018 South 7th Street, Louisville KY 40203-3322
County: Jefferson | Identification: 667011
Telephone: (502) 776-1443 | Carnegie Class: Not Classified
FAX Number: (502) 776-2227 | Calendar System: Semester
URL: www.simmonscollegeky.edu
Established: 1879 | Annual Undergrad Tuition & Fees: $7,650
Enrollment: N/A | Coed
Affiliation or Control: Baptist | IRS Status: 501(c)3
Highest Offering: Baccalaureate
Program: Religious Emphasis
Accreditation: @BI

01 President ... Mr. Kevin W. COSBY
05 Vice Pres Academic Affairs ... Dr. Brian J. WELLS
32 Vice Pres Student Affs/Dir Admiss ... Ms. Kathleen BROWN

The Southern Baptist Theological Seminary (H)

2825 Lexington Road, Louisville KY 40280-2899
County: Jefferson | FICE Identification: 001982 | Unit ID: 157748
Telephone: (502) 897-4011 | Carnegie Class: Spec/Faith
FAX Number: (502) 899-1770 | Calendar System: Other
URL: www.sbts.edu
Established: 1859 | Annual Undergrad Tuition & Fees: $8,785
Enrollment: 3,301 | Coed
Affiliation or Control: Southern Baptist | IRS Status: 501(c)3
Highest Offering: Doctorate
Program: Professional; Religious Emphasis
Accreditation: SC, MUS, THEOL

01 President ... Dr. R. Albert MOHLER, JR.
100 Chief of Staff to the President ... Mr. Matthew HALL
05 Sr VP Academic Administration ... Dr. Russell D. MOORE
11 Sr VP Institutional Administration ... Mr. Dan DUMAS
10 Vice Pres of Business Operations ... Mr. Craig PARKER
11 Vice President of Operations ... Mr. Andrew VINCENT
26 Vice President Communications ... Mr. Steve WATTERS
13 Vice Pres Information Technology ... Mr. Trevor WALLIS
30 VP Institutional Advancement ... Mr. Jason ALLEN
32 Vice President Student Services ... Dr. Randy STINSON
106 Assoc VP Online Learning ... Dr. Hayward ARMSTRONG
09 Director of Institutional Assessmnt ... Mr. Joseph C. HARROD
15 Interim Director Human Resources ... Mr. Edward HEINZE
18 Chief Facilities/Physical Plant ... Mr. Bob SNIP
96 Director of Procurement ... Mr. Andy DONAHOU
94 Director of Women's Leadership ... Mrs. Jaye MARTIN
41 Director of Health & Recreation ... Mr. Richard MCRAE
35 Dean of Students ... Mr. Lawrence A. SMITH
07 Director of Admissions ... Mr. Chuck HADDOX
08 Librarian ... Mr. Bruce L. KEISLING
29 Director Alumni Relations ... Mr. Benjamin DOCKERY
37 Manager of Financial Aid ... Mrs. Erin JOINER
73 Dean of School of Theology ... Dr. Russell D. MOORE
53 Dean School of Church Ministries ... Dr. Randy STINSON
88 Dean Missions Evang Ch Growth ... Vacant
88 Dean Boyce College ... Dr. Dan DEWITT

Spalding University (I)

845 S Third Street, Louisville KY 40203-2213
County: Jefferson | FICE Identification: 001960 | Unit ID: 157757
Telephone: (502) 585-9911 | Carnegie Class: DRU
FAX Number: (502) 585-7158 | Calendar System: Other
URL: www.spalding.edu
Established: 1814 | Annual Undergrad Tuition & Fees: $19,350
Enrollment: 2,349 | Coed
Affiliation or Control: Independent Non-Profit | IRS Status: 501(c)3
Highest Offering: Doctorate
Program: Liberal Arts And General; Teacher Preparatory; Professional
Accreditation: SC, CLPSY, IACBE, NURSE, OT, SW, TED

01 President ... Ms. Tori MURDEN MCCLURE
05 Provost ... Dr. Randy STRICKLAND
30 Dir of Advancement & Philanthropy ... Ms. Bobbie RAFFERTY
32 Dean of Students ... Dr. Richard HUDSON
10 Chief Financial Officer ... Dr. Mark HOHMANN
43 General Counsel ... Ms. Emily NORRIS
84 Dean of Enrollment Management ... Mr. Chris HART
53 Dean of College of Education ... Dr. Beverly C. KEEPERS
83 Dean College Social Science/Hum ... Dr. John JAMES
88 Chair Adult Accelerated Programs ... Dr. Linda BEATTIE
50 Dean Col Business & Communications ... Vacant
76 Dean College Health & Nat Science ... Ms. Joanne BERRYMAN
26 Ex Dir Marketing/Public Relations ... Mr. Rick BARNEY
20 Sr Dir Academic Resource Center ... Ms. Judith LUTHER
06 Registrar ... Ms. Jennifer GOHMANN
27 Chief Information Officer ... Mr. Ezra KRUMHANSL
08 Director Library ... Ms. Jackie YOUNG
37 Director Student Financial Aid ... Ms. Gina KUZUOKA
15 Human Resources Director ... Mrs. Melissa LOWE
09 Dir of Institutional Effectiveness ... Ms. Kay VETTER
26 Director of Executive Communication ... Ms. Beth NEWBERRY
88 Dir Student Achievement/Retention ... Ms. Judith LUTHER
41 Director of Athletics ... Mr. Roger BURKMAN
88 Admin Dir/Mstr Fin Arts in Writing ... Ms. Karen MANN
21 Business Manager ... Ms. Jamie PAGE
18 JLL Facilities Manager ... Mr. Kevin WEBER
40 Bookstore Manager ... Vacant
88 Director Applied Behavior Analysis ... Dr. Nicholas WEATHERLY

Spencerian College (J)

1575 Winchester Road, Lexington KY 40505-4520
County: Fayette | Identification: 666448 | Unit ID: 433563
Telephone: (859) 223-9608 | Carnegie Class: Assoc/PrivFP
FAX Number: (859) 224-7744 | Calendar System: Quarter
URL: www.spencerian.edu
Established: 1997 | Annual Undergrad Tuition & Fees: $20,000
Enrollment: 618 | Coed

Affiliation or Control: Proprietary IRS Status: Proprietary
Highest Offering: Associate Degree
Program: Occupational; 2-Year Principally Bachelor's Creditable
Accreditation: ACICS, MAC, MLTAB, RAD

01 Executive Director .... Mr. Buddy HOSKINSON
05 Academic Dean .... Mr. Chris DOUGLAS
20 Compliance Officer .... Mr. Brian HIGHLEY
07 Director of Admissions .... Mr. J.R ROMZEK
37 Director of Financial Planning .... Vacant
36 Dir of Career Services .... Ms. Reba CARROLL
06 Registrar .... Mr. Eric COMBS

† Branch campus of Spencerian College, Louisville, KY.

Spencerian College (A)

4627 Dixie Highway, Louisville KY 40216-2605
County: Jefferson FICE Identification: 004618
Unit ID: 157766
Telephone: (502) 447-1000 Carnegie Class: Assoc/PrivFP
FAX Number: (502) 447-4574 Calendar System: Quarter
URL: www.spencerian.edu
Established: 1892 Annual Undergrad Tuition & Fees: $15,870
Enrollment: 1,155 Coed
Affiliation or Control: Proprietary IRS Status: Proprietary
Highest Offering: Associate Degree
Program: Occupational
Accreditation: ACICS, CVT, MAC, MLTAB, RAD, SURGT

01 Executive Director .... Ms. Jan M. GORDON
05 Academic Dean .... Ms. Linda BLAIR
37 Director of Financial Planning .... Ms. Jill SCHULER
07 Director of Admissions .... Ms. Kathleen BELANGER
36 Director of Career Services .... Ms. Meredith AUSTIN
35 Associate Dean of Student Services .... Ms. Alice PHILLIPS

Sullivan College of Technology and Design (B)

3901 Atkinson Square Drive, Louisville KY 40218-4549
County: Jefferson FICE Identification: 012088
Unit ID: 157270
Telephone: (502) 456-6509 Carnegie Class: Spec/Arts
FAX Number: (502) 456-2341 Calendar System: Quarter
URL: www.sctd.edu
Established: 1961 Annual Undergrad Tuition & Fees: $16,890
Enrollment: 721 Coed
Affiliation or Control: Proprietary IRS Status: Proprietary
Highest Offering: Baccalaureate
Program: Occupational
Accreditation: ACICS

00 Chancellor .... Dr. A. R. SULLIVAN
01 President .... Mr. Glenn D. SULLIVAN
11 Senior Vice President .... Mr. Thomas F. DAVISSON
03 Executive Vice President .... Mr. Bill NOEL
05 Dean of Academic Affairs .... Dr. Sheree KOPPEL
10 Vice President Finance .... Mr. Shelton BRIDGES
84 Vice Pres Enrollment Management .... Mr. James CRICK
12 Executive Director .... Mr. David WINKLER
06 Registrar .... Ms. Cathy DRUIN
07 Director of Admissions .... Mr. Aamer CHAUHDRI
37 Dir of Student Financial Planning .... Mr. Andre DOWNING
08 Head Librarian .... Ms. Melinda MACCALL
36 Placement Director .... Mr. Sam MANNINO
55 Evening Division Dean .... Ms. Beverly LIVERS
96 Director of Purchasing .... Ms. Ann VEST
14 Chief Technology Officer .... Mr. Mike GROSSE
29 Director Alumni Relations .... Ms. Hazel MATTHEWS

Sullivan University (C)

3101 Bardstown Road, Louisville KY 40205-3000
County: Jefferson FICE Identification: 004619
Unit ID: 157793
Telephone: (502) 456-6504 Carnegie Class: Master's M
FAX Number: (502) 456-0040 Calendar System: Quarter
URL: www.sullivan.edu
Established: 1962 Annual Undergrad Tuition & Fees: $16,980
Enrollment: 6,069 Coed
Affiliation or Control: Proprietary IRS Status: Proprietary
Highest Offering: Doctorate
Program: Occupational; Professional
Accreditation: SC, ACFEI, MAC, PHAR

00 Chancellor .... Dr. A. R. SULLIVAN
01 President .... Mr. Glenn D. SULLIVAN
03 Vice President/Chief Executive Ofcr .... Dr. Eric HARTER
58 Exec Vice Pres/Dean Graduate School .... Mr. Bill NOEL
05 Chief Academic Officer .... Dr. Jay MARR
88 Senior Vice President .... Mr. Thomas F. DAVISSON
10 Vice President Finance .... Mr. Shelton BRIDGES
84 Vice Pres Enrollment Management .... Mr. James CRICK
32 Vice President of Student Services .... Mr. Chris ERNST
36 Vice President of Career Services .... Mr. Trace CHESSER
58 Associate Dean Graduate School .... Dr. Ken MILLER
35 Student Life Coordinator .... Ms. Kim RICHARDSON
88 Dir Natl Ctr Hospitality Studies .... Vacant
06 Registrar .... Ms. Kim MITCHELL
08 Librarian .... Mr. Charles BROWN
13 Chief Technology Officer .... Mr. Mike GROSSE
37 Director Student Financial Planning .... Ms. Sherry FITCHPATRICK
55 Director Evening Division .... Mr. James TAYLOR
40 Director Bookstore .... Ms. Brenda HOOKS
07 Director of Admissions .... Ms. Terri THOMAS
18 Manager Campus Facilities .... Mr. Mike FOWLER
12 Director Lexington Branch .... Mr. David KEENE
39 Director of Student Housing .... Mr. Chris WILLIAMS
20 Associate Dean of Students .... Mr. Bryan SHELANGOSKI
96 Director of Purchasing .... Ms. Ann VEST
56 Director of Extension Campus .... Ms. Barbara DEAN
88 Director of Enrollment Services .... Mr. Jim KLEIN
29 Director Alumni Relations .... Ms. Hazel MATTHEWS
09 Director Institutional Research .... Dr. Forrest HOULETTE
67 Dean College of Pharmacy .... Dr. Hieu TRAN
50 Dean College of Business Admin .... Mr. Ken MORAN
72 Dean College of Technology .... Dr. Thom LUCKETT

Thomas More College (D)

333 Thomas More Parkway,
Crestview Hills KY 41017-3495
County: Kenton FICE Identification: 002001
Unit ID: 157809
Telephone: (859) 341-5800 Carnegie Class: Master's S
FAX Number: (859) 344-3345 Calendar System: Semester
URL: www.thomasmore.edu/welcome.html
Established: 1921 Annual Undergrad Tuition & Fees: $25,000
Enrollment: 1,886 Coed
Affiliation or Control: Roman Catholic IRS Status: 501(c)3
Highest Offering: Master's
Program: Liberal Arts And General; Teacher Preparatory; Professional
Accreditation: SC, NUR

01 President .... Sr. Margaret A. STALLMEYER
04 Assistant to the President .... Ms. Charlene BARLOW
10 Vice President of Finance .... Mr. Peter W. AAMODT
05 Vice President for Academic Affairs .... Dr. Bradley A. BIELSKI
30 Vice Pres for Inst Advancement .... Ms. Cathy SILVERS
32 Vice Pres of Student Services .... Mr. Matthew H. WEBSTER
35 Dean of Students .... Ms. Ebony GRIGGS-GRIFFIN
09 Dir of Inst Planning/Effectiveness .... Ms. Genie M. WAMBAUGH
06 Registrar .... Ms. Kelly GOYETTE
08 Director of Library .... Mr. James M. MCKELLOGG
37 Director of Financial Aid .... Ms. Mary GIVHAN
13 Director of IT .... Mr. William K. SWISHER
26 Dir Communications/Media Relations .... Ms. Stacy ROGERS
38 Director of Counseling .... Ms. Veronica A. LUBBE
42 Chaplain .... Rev. Gerald E. TWADDELL
84 Director of Enrollment for TAP .... Dr. Bradley A. BIELSKI
41 Athletic Director .... Mr. Terry D. CONNOR
19 Director of Campus Safety .... Mr. Robert MARSHALL
15 Director of Human Resources .... Ms. Laura CUSTER
18 Director of Facilities .... Mr. Jeffrey KORDENBROCK
29 Director of Alumni .... Ms. Monica GINNEY
36 Dir of Career Planning/Coop Educ .... Mr. Shawn STOVALL
42 Director of Campus Ministry .... Sr. Patricia DOROBEK
21 Controller .... Ms. Debbie A. RAPIER
51 Director of Lifelong Learning .... Mr. Nathan HARTMAN
92 Director of Honors Program .... Dr. Catherine SHERRON
44 Dir Annual Giving/Special Events .... Ms. Beth MALEY
07 Assistant Director of Admissions .... Mr. Billy SARGE
35 Coordinator of Student Activities .... Vacant
39 Coordinator of Residence Life .... Mr. Brian SHEELEY

Transylvania University (E)

300 N Broadway, Lexington KY 40508-1797
County: Fayette FICE Identification: 001987
Unit ID: 157818
Telephone: (859) 233-8300 Carnegie Class: Bac/A&S
FAX Number: (859) 233-8797 Calendar System: Other
URL: www.transy.edu
Established: 1780 Annual Undergrad Tuition & Fees: $28,250
Enrollment: 1,110 Coed
Affiliation or Control: Christian Church (Disciples Of Christ)
IRS Status: 501(c)3
Highest Offering: Baccalaureate
Program: Liberal Arts And General; Teacher Preparatory
Accreditation: SC, TED

01 President .... Dr. R. Owen WILLIAMS
05 Vice President/Dean of College .... Dr. William F. POLLARD
20 Associate Dean/Assoc Vice President .... Dr. Kathleen JAGGER
10 Vice President Finance & Business .... Mr. Marc MATHEWS
30 Vice Pres Advancement .... Mr. Kirk PURDOM
32 Dean of Students .... Dr. Michael K. VETTER
06 Registrar .... Mr. James M. MILLS
09 Director of Institutional Research .... Mr. Rhyan M. CONYERS
07 Vice President for Enrollment .... Mr. Bradley L. GOAN
08 Librarian .... Ms. Susan M. BROWN
37 Director of Financial Aid .... Mr. David J. CECIL
26 Director of Public Relations .... Ms. Sarah EMMONS
36 Director of Placement Services .... Ms. Susan S. RAYER
13 Director of Information Technology .... Mr. Jason WHITAKER
104 Dir Study Abroad & Special Programs .... Ms. Kathryn C. SIMON
15 Director Personnel Services .... Mr. Jeff MUDRAK
18 Chief Facilities/Physical Plant .... Mr. Darrell L. BANKS
96 Director of Purchasing .... Ms. Shawn T. SINGLETON
29 Director Alumni Relations .... Ms. Natasa PAJIC

Union College (F)

310 College Street, Barbourville KY 40906-1499
County: Knox FICE Identification: 001988
Unit ID: 157863
Telephone: (606) 546-4151 Carnegie Class: Master's L
FAX Number: (606) 546-1217 Calendar System: Other
URL: www.unionky.edu
Established: 1879 Annual Undergrad Tuition & Fees: $20,004
Enrollment: 1,363 Coed
Affiliation or Control: United Methodist IRS Status: 501(c)3
Highest Offering: Master's
Program: Liberal Arts And General; Teacher Preparatory
Accreditation: SC, @SW

01 President .... Mr. Edward D. DE ROSSET
05 Vice President for Academic Affairs .. Dr. Thomas J. MCFARLAND
30 Vice President for Advancement .... Ms. Denise WAINSCOTT
84 Dean of Enrollment Management .... Dr. Jerry JACKSON
32 Dean of Students .... Ms. Deborah D' ANNA
53 Head of Educational Studies Dept .... Dr. Don MUSSELMAN
58 Dean of Graduate Studies .... Vacant
35 Associate Dean Student Life .... Ms. Barbara TEAGUE
21 Dir Purchasing/Act Pyable/Staff Act .... Vacant
06 Registrar .... Ms. Kathy WEBB
18 Director of Physical Plant (NMRC) .... Mr. Richard RICHARDSON
41 Athletic Director .... Dr. Darin WILSON
29 Director of Alumni Relations .... Ms. Melissa NEWMAN
09 Director of Institutional Research .... Vacant
10 Chief Business Officer .... Mr. Steve HOSKINS
26 Int Director of Public Relations .... Ms. Melissa REID
88 Director of Sports Information .... Mr. Jay STANCIL
88 Director of Special Programs .... Dr. Sarah HENDRIX
08 Head Librarian .... Ms. Tara L. COOPER
42 College Minister .... Rev. David MILLER
31 Director of Common Partners .... Ms. Gabrielle MELLENDORF
37 Assistant Director of Financial Aid .... Ms. Jessica COOK
38 Director of Counseling .... Mrs. Jodi CARROLL
15 Benefits Coordinator .... Ms. Lynn SMITH
19 Safety Team Leader .... Mr. Michael GRAY
50 Chair Department of Business .... Dr. Ella HENSLEY
88 Chair Dept Wellness/Human Perf/Rec .... Dr. Larry INKSTER
79 Chair Dept Engr/Comm/ Language .... Dr. Christine MARLEY-FREDERICK
57 Chr Dpt Hist/Relig Std/Fn/Perf Arts .... Dr. Russell SISSON
81 Chair Dept of Natural Sciences .... Dr. Dan COVINGTON
83 Chair Dept Social/Behav Science .... Dr. Robert ARMOUR
04 Executive Assistant for President .... Mrs. Margaret SENTERS
72 Director of Technology .... Mr. Brad JONES
88 Events Coordinator .... Ms. Bobbie DOOLIN

University of the Cumberlands (G)

6191 College Station Drive, Williamsburg KY 40769-4490
County: Whitley FICE Identification: 001962
Unit ID: 156541
Telephone: (606) 549-2200 Carnegie Class: Master's M
FAX Number: (606) 549-2820 Calendar System: Semester
URL: www.ucumberlands.edu
Established: 1888 Annual Undergrad Tuition & Fees: $18,000
Enrollment: 3,311 Coed
Affiliation or Control: Baptist IRS Status: 501(c)3
Highest Offering: Doctorate
Program: Liberal Arts And General; Teacher Preparatory
Accreditation: SC, #ARCPA

01 President .... Dr. James H. TAYLOR
30 Vice Pres Institutional Advancement .... Mrs. Sue WAKE
05 Vice President Academic Affairs .... Dr. Larry L. COCKRUM
32 Vice President Student Services .... Dr. Michael COLEGROVE
10 Vice President Business Services .... Mr. Steve MORRIS
21 Vice President Finance .... Ms. Jana K. BAILEY
11 Vice President Operations .... Mr. Kyle GILBERT
37 Vice Pres Student Financial Plng .... Mr. Steve ALLEN
07 Director of Admissions .... Mrs. Erica HARRIS
06 Registrar .... Ms. Emily J. MEADORS
20 Associate Dean .... Dr. Thomas E. FISH
09 Registrar Asst/Inst Research .... Mr. Charles DUPIER
26 Dir Multimedia/Sports Information .... Ms. Jennifer FLOYD
35 Dean Student Life .... Ms. Linda CARTER
15 Director of Human Resources .... Ms. Pearl BAKER
41 Athletic Director .... Mr. Randy VERNON
90 Director of Information Technology .... Mr. Donnie GRIMES
42 Dir International Pgm/Church Rels .... Dr. Rick FLEENOR
36 Director of Career Services .... Ms. Debbie HARP
08 Head Librarian .... Ms. Jan WREN
58 Director Graduate Program .... Dr. Robert HEFFERN
18 Director of Physical Plant .... Mr. David ROOT
21 Bursar .... Ms. Jo DUPIER
29 Director Alumni Relations .... Mr. Dave BERGMAN

University of Kentucky (H)

Lexington KY 40506-0003
County: Fayette FICE Identification: 001989
Unit ID: 157085
Telephone: (859) 257-9000 Carnegie Class: RU/VH
FAX Number: (859) 257-4000 Calendar System: Semester
URL: www.uky.edu
Established: 1865 Annual Undergrad Tuition & Fees (In-State): $9,128
Enrollment: 27,108 Coed
Affiliation or Control: State IRS Status: 501(c)3
Highest Offering: Doctorate

Program: Liberal Arts And General; Teacher Preparatory; Professional
Accreditation: SC, AAFCS, ARCPA, ART, BUS, BUSA, CIDA, CLPSY, COPSY, CORE, CS, DENT, DIETC, DIETD, DIETI, ENG, FOR, HSA, JOUR, LAW, LIB, LSAR, MED, MFCD, MT, MUS, NURSE, PH, PHAR, PTA, SCPSY, SP, SPAA, SW, TED

01 President ... Dr. Eli CAPILOUTO
46 Vice President Research ... Dr. James W. TRACY
05 Provost ... Dr. Kumble R. SUBBASWAMY
100 President's Chief of Staff ... Dr. Douglas BOYD
10 Exec VP Finance/Administration ... Mr. Frank A. BUTLER
17 Executive VP for Health Affairs ... Dr. Michael KARPF
13 Chief Information Technology Office ... Mr. Vincent J. KELLEN
46 VP Institutional Effectiveness ... Vacant
32 Vice Pres Student Affairs ... Dr. Robert C. MOCK, JR.
28 Vice Pres Institutional Diversity ... Dr. Judy J. JACKSON
30 Vice President for Development ... Dr. D. M. RICHEY
17 Vice Pres Health Care Operations ... Dr. Richard LOFGREN
10 VP Health Care Opers CFO ... Mr. Sergio MELGAR
45 VP Fin Operations and Treasurer ... Ms. Angela MARTIN
63 Dean Medic/VP Clinical Acad Affairs ... Dr. Fredrick C. DE BEER
18 Vice President Facilities Mgmt ... Mr. Bob WISEMAN
88 VP Commercialization/Econ Devel ... Dr. Leonard E. HELLER
88 Assoc VP Research Infrastructure ... Vacant
22 Assoc VP Institutional Equity ... Mr. Terry D. ALLEN
26 Associate VP External Affairs ... Mr. Thomas W. HARRIS
35 Assoc VP Stdnt Affs/Dean of Stdnts ... Dr. Victor A. HAZARD
15 Assoc VP Human Resource Services ... Ms. Kimberly R. WILSON
88 Asst Vice Pres Public Safety ... Mr. Anthany BEATTY
31 Assoc Vice Pres Auxiliary Services ... Mr. Ben CRUTCHER
25 Assoc VP Res Admin & Fiscal Affs ... Mr. Jack SUPPLEE, JR.
88 Assoc VP Res Spon Proj Acct ... Ms. Debbie DAVIS
44 Assoc VP University Engagement ... Dr. Philip GREASLEY
20 Assoc Provost Intl Affairs ... Dr. Susan CARVALHO
20 Assoc Prov Clncl Translational Sci ... Dr. William BALKE
17 Assoc VP Clinical Network Devel ... Mr. Joe CLAYPOOL
58 Assoc Prov Acad Adm/Dean Grad Sch . Dr. Jeannine BLACKWELL
88 Assoc Provost Educ Partnerships ... Dr. John YOPP
20 Assoc Provost Undergrad Educ ... Dr. Micheal D. MULLEN
20 Associate Provost Faculty Affairs ... Dr. Heidi M. ANDERSON
84 Assoc Provost Enroll Mgmt/Registrar ... Mr. Don WITT
08 Dean of Libraries ... Dr. Terry P. BIRDWHISTELL
27 Director University Press ... Dr. Stephen WRINN
43 General Counsel ... Ms. Barbara JONES
41 Director Athletics ... Mr. Mitch BARNHART
37 Director Student Financial Aid ... Ms. Lynda GEORGE
09 Director of Institutional Research ... Dr. Roger P. SUGARMAN
18 Chief Facilities/Physical Plant ... Vacant
36 Director Career Center ... Ms. Francene GILMER
38 Director Counseling & Testing ... Dr. Mary C. BOLIN-REECE
29 Director Alumni Relations ... Mr. Stan R. KEY
26 Exec Director Public Relations ... Mr. Jay BLANTON
90 Director Technical Academic Support ... Vacant
21 Controller ... Ms. Rhonda BECK
47 Dean of Agriculture ... Dr. M. Scott SMITH
19 Chief of Police ... Mr. Joseph W. MONROE
48 Dean College of Design ... Dr. Michael A. SPEAKS
88 Director Student Center ... Mr. John H. HERBST
49 Dean of Arts & Sciences ... Dr. Mark KORNBLUH
50 Dean of Business & Economics ... Dr. Devanathan SUDHARSHAN
53 Dean of Education ... Dr. Mary J. O'HAIR
54 Dean of Engineering ... Dr. Thomas W. LESTER
57 Dean of Fine Arts ... Dr. Michael TICK
60 Dean of Communication/Info Studies ... Dr. Dan O'HAIR
61 Dean of Law ... Mr. David BRENNEN
70 Dean of Social Work ... Dr. James P. ADAMS, JR.
76 Dean of Health Sciences ... Dr. Lori S. GONZALEZ
52 Dean of Dentistry ... Dr. Sharon P. TURNER
63 Dean of Medicine/VP Clinical Affs ... Vacant
66 Dean of Nursing ... Dr. Jane M. KIRSCHLING
67 Dean of Pharmacy ... Dr. Tim TRACY
69 Dean Public Health ... Dr. Stephen W. WYATT
96 Director of Purchasing ... Mr. William L. HARRIS
23 Director Univ Student Health Svcs ... Dr. Gregory R. MOORE

University of Louisville (A)

2301 S Third Street, Louisville KY 40292-0001
County: Jefferson — FICE Identification: 001999
Unit ID: 157289
Telephone: (502) 852-5555 — Carnegie Class: RU/VH
FAX Number: (502) 852-7013 — Calendar System: Semester
URL: www.louisville.edu
Established: 1798 — Annual Undergrad Tuition & Fees (In-State): $8,930
Enrollment: 22,290 — Coed
Affiliation or Control: State — IRS Status: 501(c)3
Highest Offering: Doctorate
Program: Occupational; 2-Year Principally Bachelor's Creditable; Liberal Arts And General; Teacher Preparatory; Professional
Accreditation: SC, AUD, BUS, BUSA, CIDA, CLPSY, COPSY, CS, DENT, DH, ENG, IPSY, LAW, MED, MFCD, MUS, NURSE, PH, PLNG, RTT, SP, SPAA, SW, TED, THEA

01 President ... Dr. James R. RAMSEY
05 Exec Vice Pres/University Prov ... Dr. Shirley C. WILLIHNGANZ
17 Exec Vice Pres for Health Affairs ... Dr. David DUNN
46 Interim Executive VP for Research ... Dr. Bill PIERCE
32 Vice President Student Affairs ... Dr. Tom JACKSON, JR.
11 Vice President for Business Affairs ... Mr. Larry L. OWSLEY
30 Vice Pres Univ Advancement ... Mr. Keith INMAN
13 Vice Pres Information Tech ... Dr. Priscilla HANCOCK
86 VP for Community Engagement ... Mr. Daniel HALL
10 Vice President for Finance ... Mr. Michael J. CURTIN
16 Vice Pres Human Resources ... Mr. Sam CONNALLY
41 Vice President for Athletics ... Mr. Tom JURICH
44 Sr Assoc VP Advancement ... Ms. Rebecca SIMPSON
18 Assoc VP Facilities/Physical Plant ... Mr. Larry DETHERAGE
29 Asst Vice Pres for Alumni Relations ... Mr. Jimmy FORD
100 Chief of Staff for the President ... Ms. Kathleen M. SMITH
43 University Counsel ... Ms. Angela D. KOSHEWA
20 Vice Prov Undergraduate Affairs ... Dr. Dale B. BILLINGSLEY
58 Int Dean Graduate School ... Dr. Beth A. BOEHM
28 Vice Prov for Diversity/Intl Affs ... Dr. Mordean TAYLOR-ARCHER
88 Assoc Prov Acad Acct/IR & Effect ... Mr. Robert S. GOLDSTEIN
106 Assoc Univ Provost Distance Ed/Delp ... Dr. Gale RHODES
88 Asst Prov for Accreditation ... Ms. Connie C. SHUMAKE
21 Controller ... Mr. Larry W. ZINK
07 Executive Director Admissions ... Ms. Jenny L. SAWYER
06 University Registrar ... Ms. Kathy L. OTTO
37 Exec Director Financial Aid ... Ms. Patricia O. ARAUZ
26 Director of Comm/Marketing ... Ms. Cindy HESS
25 Director Contract Admin/Risk Mgmt ... Mr. David MARTIN
15 Dir of Staff Dev/Employee Rel ... Ms. Mary E. MILES
19 Director Public Safety ... Mr. Wayne HALL
09 Director Inst Research and Planning ... Ms. Becky PATTERSON
45 Director Inst Effectiveness ... Ms. Cheryl B. GILCHRIST
39 Director Student Housing ... Ms. Shannon D. STATEN
105 Director of Digital Media ... Mr. Jeffery A. RUSHTON
27 Director Media Relations ... Mr. Mark HEBERT
88 Assoc Vice Pres for Audit Services ... Mr. David F. BARKER
14 Director IT Enterprise Security ... Ms. Brenda B. GOMBOSKY
92 Director of Honors Program ... Dr. John F. RICHARDSON
96 Director Purchasing ... Mr. David MARTIN
88 Dir Planning/Design & Construction ... Mr. Kenneth DIETZ
36 Director Career Services ... Ms. Leslye A. ERICKSON
38 Director Counseling Services ... Dr. Kathy J. PENDLETON
08 Dean of University Libraries ... Mr. Robert FOX
49 Dean College Arts & Sciences ... Dr. James B. HUDSON
50 Dean College of Business ... Dr. R. Charles MOYER
52 Dean School of Dentistry ... Dr. John J. SAUK
53 Int Dean Col of Educ/Human Develop ... Dr. Blake HASELTON
70 Dean Kent School Social Work ... Dr. Terry L. SINGER
64 Dean School of Music ... Dr. Christopher DOANE
61 Dean Brandeis School of Law ... Dr. James M. CHEN
66 Dean School of Nursing ... Dr. Marcia J. HERN
54 Dean Speed School of Engineering ... Dr. Neville PINTO
63 Dean of Medicine ... Dr. Edward C. HALPERIN
69 Dean Public Health/Information Sci ... Dr. Richard D. CLOVER
35 Dean of Students/Assoc VP Stdnt Aff ... Dr. Michael MARDIS
94 Chair Women's/Gender Studies ... Dr. Nancy M. THERIOT

University of Pikeville (B)

147 Sycamore Street, Pikeville KY 41501-1194
County: Pike — FICE Identification: 001980
Unit ID: 157535
Telephone: (606) 218-5250 — Carnegie Class: Bac/A&S
FAX Number: (606) 218-5269 — Calendar System: Semester
URL: www.pc.edu
Established: 1889 — Annual Undergrad Tuition & Fees: $16,250
Enrollment: 1,325 — Coed
Affiliation or Control: Presbyterian Church (U.S.A.) — IRS Status: 501(c)3
Highest Offering: Doctorate
Program: Liberal Arts And General; Teacher Preparatory
Accreditation: SC, OSTEO, @SW

01 President ... Mr. Paul E. PATTON
03 Vice Pres/Special Asst to President ... Mr. James HURLEY
05 VPAA/Dean College Arts/Sciences ... Mr. Thomas R. HESS
10 Vice Pres Finance/Business Affairs ... Mr. Douglas J. LANGE
30 Vice President for Development ... Mr. Eric BECHER
26 Asst Vice President for Marketing ... Mrs. Lucy HOLMAN
63 VP Health Affairs/Dean KYCOM ... Dr. Boyd R. BUSER
32 VP Student Svcs/Dean of Students ... Mr. Ron DAMRON
07 Director Admissions/Stdnt Fin Svcs ... Mr. Gary JUSTICE
08 Director of Library Services ... Ms. Karen S. CHAFIN-EVANS
06 Asst VP Academic Affairs/Registrar ... Mrs. Gia POTTER
09 Director of Institutional Research ... Dr. Meg SIDLE
14 Senior Info Services Administrator ... Mr. Randy SCARBERRY
18 Director of Facilities ... Mr. John HOLMAN
37 Asst Dean Student Financial Svcs ... Mrs. Judy BRADLEY
15 Director Personnel Services ... Ms. Rhonda MULLINS

Western Kentucky University (C)

1906 College Heights Blvd, Bowling Green KY 42101-3576
County: Warren — FICE Identification: 002002
Unit ID: 157951
Telephone: (270) 745-0111 — Carnegie Class: Master's L
FAX Number: (270) 745-5387 — Calendar System: Semester
URL: www.wku.edu
Established: 1906 — Annual Undergrad Tuition & Fees (In-State): $8,084
Enrollment: 20,897 — Coed
Affiliation or Control: State — IRS Status: 501(c)3
Highest Offering: Doctorate
Program: Occupational; Liberal Arts And General; Teacher Preparatory; Professional
Accreditation: SC, THEA, ADNUR, ART, BUS, BUSA, CACREP, DH, DIETD, ENG, JOUR, MUS, NAIT, NRPA, NURSE, PH, SP, SPAA, SW, TED

01 President ... Dr. Gary A. RANSDELL
05 Provost/Vice Pres Academic Affairs ... Dr. Gordon EMSLIE
46 VP for Research ... Dr. Gordon BAYLIS
26 Vice President for Public Affairs ... Ms. Robbin M. TAYLOR
30 Vice Pres Development & Alumni Rels ... Ms. Kathryn COSTELLO
13 Vice Pres Information Technology ... Dr. Bob OWEN
32 Vice President Student Affairs ... Mr. Howard E. BAILEY
10 Vice President Finance & Admin ... Ms. K. Ann MEAD
100 Chief of Staff/General Counsel ... Ms. Deborah T. WILKINS
20 Vice Provost Academic Affairs ... Dr. Richard C. MILLER
11 Vice Pres Campus Svcs & Facilities ... Mr. John N. OSBORNE
84 Interim Assoc VP for Enrollment Mgt ... Dr. Brian MEREDITH
55 Assoc VP Ext Learning & Outreach ... Dr. Beth LAVES
79 Dean Arts & Letters ... Dr. David D. LEE
50 Dean Business ... Dr. Jeffrey KATZ
53 Dean Education/Behavioral Sci ... Dr. Sam EVANS
81 Dean Science/Engineering ... Dr. Blaine R. FERRELL
58 Interim Dean Grad Studies & Researc ... Dr. Kinchel DOERNER
97 Dean University College ... Dr. Dennis K. GEORGE
62 Interim Dean Libraries ... Ms. Connie FOSTER
88 Assoc VP Enrichment & Effectiveness ... Dr. Doug MCELROY
88 Assoc VP Planning & Program Develop ... Dr. Sylvia GAIKO
21 Chief Financial Officer ... Mr. Jim CUMMINGS
21 Budget Director ... Ms. Kimberly REED
07 Director Admissions ... Mr. Scott S. GORDON
88 Assoc VP Academic Budgets & Admin ... Mr. Mike DALE
88 Assoc VP Research and Development ... Mr. Douglas ROHRER
06 Registrar ... Ms. Freida K. EGGLETON
91 Director Admin Systems/Applications ... Mr. Gordon L. JOHNSON
15 Director Human Resources ... Mr. Tony L. GLISSON
18 Director Facilities Management ... Mr. Charles E. JONES
12 Director and Assoc Dean Glasgow ... Dr. Sally RAY
12 Dir Elizabethtown & Assoc Dean ... Dr. Ronald STEPHENS
12 Dir Camp Owens & Assoc Dean ... Dr. Gene E. TICE
90 Director Academic Technology ... Mr. John BOWERS
88 Dir Acad Advising & Retention Ctr ... Mr. Kevin P. THOMAS
39 Director Housing & Residence Life ... Mr. Brian KUSTER
19 Chief of Police ... Mr. Robert DEANE
29 Asst VP WKU Alumni Association ... Mr. Donald SMITH
102 Director Corporate/Foundation Rels ... Mr. Richard A. DUBOSE
44 Assistant VP Major Gifts ... Mr. John P. BLAIR
36 Director Career Services Center ... Dr. Becky BENNETT
37 Dir Student Financial Assistance ... Ms. Cindy BURNETTE
38 Director Counseling & Testing Ctr ... Dr. Brian VAN BRUNT
40 Director Bookstore ... Ms. Shawna CAWTHORN
09 Director Institutional Research ... Dr. Tuesdi HELBIG
22 Equal Oppty/ADA/Compliance Director ... Ms. Huda N. MELKY
24 Director Educ Telecommunications ... Mr. Jack A. HANES
41 Athletics Director ... Mr. Ross BJORK
85 Director Intl Student & Sch Service ... Mr. Tarek EL SHAYEB
85 Exec Dir International Programs ... Dr. Richard C. SUTTON
92 Executive Director Honors College ... Dr. Craig COBANE
96 Director Purchasing/Accts Payable ... Mr. Ken BAUSHKE
28 Director Diversity Programs ... Mr. Ricardo NAZARIO-COLON
94 Director Women's Studies ... Dr. Jane OLMSTED
101 Senior Administrative Assistant ... Ms. Julia J. MCDONALD
104 Director Study Abroad/Global Lrng ... Mr. Thomas MILLINGTON
23 Assoc Director Health Services ... Mr. Jeffrey THOMAS
76 Dean Health & Human Services ... Dr. John A. BONAGURO
27 Director of Media Relations ... Mr. Bob SKIPPER
86 Dir Govt/Community Relations ... Ms. Jennifer B. SMITH
04 Executive Admininstrative Assistant ... Ms. Shelia E. HOUCHINS

LOUISIANA

Baton Rouge College (D)

1900 North Lobdell Boulevard,
Baton Rouge LA 70806-2246
County: East Baton Rouge — FICE Identification: 026171
Unit ID: 373447
Telephone: (225) 308-4588 — Carnegie Class: Assoc/PrivFP
FAX Number: (225) 292-5464 — Calendar System: Semester
URL: www.brc.edu
Established: 1981 — Annual Undergrad Tuition & Fees: $8,297
Enrollment: 39 — Coed
Affiliation or Control: Proprietary — IRS Status: Proprietary
Highest Offering: Associate Degree
Program: Occupational
Accreditation: CNCE

01 President ... Dr. Mohammad AJNAL

Baton Rouge School of Computers (E)

9352 Interline Avenue, Baton Rouge LA 70809-1909
County: East Baton Rouge — FICE Identification: 021975
Unit ID: 158343
Telephone: (225) 923-2524 — Carnegie Class: Assoc/PrivFP
FAX Number: (225) 923-2979 — Calendar System: Other
URL: www.brsc.edu
Established: 1979 — Annual Undergrad Tuition & Fees: $16,504
Enrollment: 50 — Coed
Affiliation or Control: Proprietary — IRS Status: Proprietary
Highest Offering: Associate Degree
Program: Occupational
Accreditation: ACCSC

01 President/Director ... Mrs. Betty D. TRUXILLO
05 Chief Academic Officer ... Ms. Pauline ROBERTS
37 Financial Aid Assistant ... Ms. Auburn DEGRAW
06 Registrar ... Vacant

Blue Cliff College (F)

100 Asma Boulevard, Suite 350, Lafayette LA 70508-3862
County: Lafayette — FICE Identification: 034226
Unit ID: 439491

Telephone: (337) 269-0620 Carnegie Class: Assoc/PrivFP
FAX Number: (337) 269-0688 Calendar System: Quarter
URL: www.bluecliffcollege.com
Established: 1987 Annual Undergrad Tuition & Fees: $14,344
Enrollment: 144 Coed
Affiliation or Control: Proprietary IRS Status: Proprietary
Highest Offering: Associate Degree
Program: Occupational
Accreditation: ACCSC

01 Director ... Ms. Teresa RICE
06 Registrar ... Ms. Tonya TRAHAN
07 Director of Admissions ... Mr. Dalton DURAL

Blue Cliff College (A)

3200 Cleary Avenue, Metairie LA 70002-5714
County: Jefferson FICE Identification: 032943
Unit ID: 434821
Telephone: (504) 456-3141 Carnegie Class: Assoc/PrivFP
FAX Number: (504) 456-7849 Calendar System: Quarter
URL: www.bluecliffcollege.com
Established: 1987 Annual Undergrad Tuition & Fees: N/A
Enrollment: 338 Coed
Affiliation or Control: Proprietary IRS Status: Proprietary
Highest Offering: Associate Degree
Program: Occupational
Accreditation: ACCSC

01 President/CEO ... Mr. Edward MOORE
05 Campus Director ... Mr. Doug ROBERTSON

Blue Cliff College (B)

8731 Park Plaza Drive, Shreveport LA 71105-5682
County: Caddo FICE Identification: 034225
Unit ID: 439482
Telephone: (318) 798-6868 Carnegie Class: Assoc/PrivFP
FAX Number: (318) 798-6880 Calendar System: Quarter
URL: www.bluecliffcollege.com
Established: 1995 Annual Undergrad Tuition & Fees: N/A
Enrollment: 423 Coed
Affiliation or Control: Proprietary IRS Status: Proprietary
Highest Offering: Associate Degree
Program: Occupational
Accreditation: ACCSC

01 Campus Director ... Mr. James POWELL
05 Director of Education ... Ms. Stacie BOLEY

Camelot College (C)

2618 Wooddale Boulevard, Suite A,
Baton Rouge LA 70805-7539
County: East Baton Rouge FICE Identification: 030235
Unit ID: 417549
Telephone: (225) 928-3005 Carnegie Class: Assoc/PrivFP
FAX Number: (225) 927-3794 Calendar System: Semester
URL: www.camelotcollege.com
Established: 1986 Annual Undergrad Tuition & Fees: $10,990
Enrollment: 260 Coed
Affiliation or Control: Proprietary IRS Status: Proprietary
Highest Offering: Associate Degree
Program: Occupational
Accreditation: ACICS

01 President & Academic Dean ... Rev. Ronnie L. WILLIAMS
10 Vice President/Accounting Officer ... Mr. Aaron SIMON, SR.
36 Placement Director ... Ms. Shaylon MOOREHEAD
07 Admissions Director ... Mr. Wesley GORDON
37 Financial Aid Director ... Ms. Connie WILLIAMS

Cameron College (D)

2740 Canal Street, New Orleans LA 70119-5500
County: Orleans FICE Identification: 022340
Unit ID: 158440
Telephone: (504) 821-5881 Carnegie Class: Assoc/PrivFP
FAX Number: (504) 822-3467 Calendar System: Other
URL: www.cameroncollege.com
Established: 1981 Annual Undergrad Tuition & Fees: $10,160
Enrollment: 275 Coed
Affiliation or Control: Proprietary IRS Status: Proprietary
Highest Offering: Associate Degree
Program: Occupational
Accreditation: COE

01 President ... Ms. Eleanor CAMERON SKOV

Career Technical College (E)

2319 Louisville Avenue, Monroe LA 71201-6126
County: Ouachita FICE Identification: 026068
Unit ID: 367112
Telephone: (318) 323-2889 Carnegie Class: Assoc/PrivFP
FAX Number: (318) 324-9883 Calendar System: Quarter
URL: www.careertc.edu
Established: 1988 Annual Undergrad Tuition & Fees: $14,160
Enrollment: 800 Coed
Affiliation or Control: Proprietary IRS Status: Proprietary
Highest Offering: Associate Degree
Program: Occupational; 2-Year Principally Bachelor's Creditable; Technical Emphasis
Accreditation: COE, MAC, RAD, SURGT

01 College Director ... Ms. Cheryl P. LOKEY

Centenary College of Louisiana (F)

PO Box 41188, Shreveport LA 71134-1188
County: Caddo FICE Identification: 002003
Unit ID: 158477
Telephone: (318) 869-5011 Carnegie Class: Bac/A&S
FAX Number: (318) 869-5010 Calendar System: Semester
URL: www.centenary.edu
Established: 1825 Annual Undergrad Tuition & Fees: $25,290
Enrollment: 904 Coed
Affiliation or Control: United Methodist IRS Status: 501(c)3
Highest Offering: Master's
Program: Liberal Arts And General; Teacher Preparatory
Accreditation: SC, MUS, TED

01 President ... Dr. B. David ROWE
04 Exec Assistant to the President ... Ms. Connie WHITTINGTON
05 Dean of the College & Provost ... Dr. Michael R. HEMPHILL
50 Dean of the School of Business ... Dr. Christopher L. MARTIN
64 Dean of the School of Music ... Dr. Gale ODOM
30 Vice President for Inst Advancement ... Mr. Scott RAWLES
84 Vice President of Enrollment Svcs ... Vacant
10 Vice President for Finance/Admin ... Mr. William H. BALLARD
42 Chaplain/VP Student Development ... Rev. Betsy EAVES
13 Director of Information Technology ... Mr. Scott MERRITT
21 Controller ... Mr. Mike PEARSON
41 Director of Athletics ... Dr. William BROUSSARD
32 Dean of Students ... Dr. Mark MILLER
38 Director of Counseling ... Ms. Tina FELDT
37 Director of Financial Aid ... Miss Mary Sue RIX
06 Registrar/Director Inst Research ... Dr. Gary R. YOUNG
08 Librarian ... Ms. Christy WRENN
26 Director Marketing & Communications ... Ms. Farrah REYNA
29 Director of Alumni Relations ... Ms. Saige WILHITE
38 Director of Career Services ... Mr. Dennis TAYLOR
18 Director of Facilities ... Mr. Chris SAMPITE
46 Director Sponsored Research ... Ms. Patty J. ROBERTS
88 Director of Church Relations ... Rev. Warren CLIFTON
44 Sr Director of Annual Giving ... Mr. Fred LANDRY
07 Director of Admissions ... Mr. Mickey QUINLAN
15 Human Resources Director ... Ms. Tracy MARANTO-PHILLIPS
19 Director of Public Safety ... Mr. Eddie WALKER

Delta College of Arts & Technology (G)

7380 Exchange Place, Baton Rouge LA 70806-3851
County: East Baton Rouge FICE Identification: 025383
Unit ID: 366270
Telephone: (225) 928-7770 Carnegie Class: Assoc/PrivFP
FAX Number: (225) 927-9096 Calendar System: Other
URL: www.deltacollege.com
Established: 1983 Annual Undergrad Tuition & Fees: $22,100
Enrollment: 635 Coed
Affiliation or Control: Proprietary IRS Status: Proprietary
Highest Offering: Associate Degree
Program: Occupational; 2-Year Principally Bachelor's Creditable; Nursing Emphasis
Accreditation: ACCSC

01 President ... Mr. Billy L. CLARK

Delta School of Business & Technology (H)

517 Broad Street, Lake Charles LA 70601-4334
County: Calcasieu FICE Identification: 020555
Unit ID: 158723
Telephone: (337) 439-5765 Carnegie Class: Assoc/PrivFP
FAX Number: (337) 436-5151 Calendar System: Quarter
URL: www.deltatech.edu
Established: 1970 Annual Undergrad Tuition & Fees: $9,590
Enrollment: 360 Coed
Affiliation or Control: Proprietary IRS Status: Proprietary
Highest Offering: Associate Degree
Program: Occupational; Business Emphasis
Accreditation: ACICS

01 Chief Executive Officer ... Mr. Jeff EDWARDS
10 Chief Fiscal Officer/Corp Secretary ... Mrs. Nina LEBLANC

Dillard University (I)

2601 Gentilly Boulevard, New Orleans LA 70122-3097
County: Orleans FICE Identification: 002004
Unit ID: 158802
Telephone: (504) 283-8822 Carnegie Class: Bac/A&S
FAX Number: N/A Calendar System: Semester
URL: www.dillard.edu
Established: 1869 Annual Undergrad Tuition & Fees: $15,520
Enrollment: 1,187 Coed
Affiliation or Control: United Methodist IRS Status: 501(c)3
Highest Offering: Baccalaureate
Program: Liberal Arts And General; Teacher Preparatory; Professional
Accreditation: SC, NUR

01 President ... Dr. Marvalene HUGHES
03 Executive Vice President ... Dr. Walter L. STRONG
05 Provost/Sr VP for Academic Affairs ... Dr. Phyllis W. DAWKINS
32 Vice President for Student Success ... Dr. Toya BARNES-TEAMER
43 VP for Legal Affairs ... Ms. Debra NEVEU
10 Interim VP for Business & Finance ... Ms. Wanda BROOKS
20 Associate Provost ... Vacant
07 Asst VP of Enrollment Management ... Dr. Alecia CYPRIAN
36 Director of Career/Prof Services ... Dr. Dawn WILLIAMS
06 Director of Records & Registration ... Ms. Pamela ENGLAND
37 Int Dir Financial Aid/Scholarships ... Ms. Shannon NEAL
102 Asst VP Research & Spons Programs ... Mr. Theodore CALLIER
30 Int Assistant VP for Development ... Dr. Troy BALDWIN
100 Assistant to the President ... Vacant
09 Director of Institutional Research ... Dr. Willie KIRKLAND
27 Asst Vice Pres Community Devel ... Mr. Nick L. HARRIS
19 Chief of Police ... Mr. Andre' MENZIES
16 Director of Human Resources ... Ms. Lori KNIGHT
26 Director of Mktg & Communications ... Ms. Mona DUFFEL-JONES
97 Dean of College of General Studies ... Dr. Dorothy SMITH
08 Interim Dean of Library/Learning ... Ms. Cynthia CHARLES
49 Dean of College of Arts & Sciences ... Dr. Robert COLLINS
18 Chief Facilities/Physical Plant ... Mr. Keith MCKENDALL
96 Purchasing Officer ... Ms. Anlatear KIRKLIN

Gretna Career College (J)

1415 Whitney Avenue, Gretna LA 70053-5835
County: Jefferson FICE Identification: 030951
Unit ID: 417567
Telephone: (504) 366-5409 Carnegie Class: Assoc/PrivFP
FAX Number: (504) 365-1005 Calendar System: Quarter
URL: www.gccla.edu
Established: 1991 Annual Undergrad Tuition & Fees: $12,300
Enrollment: 151 Coed
Affiliation or Control: Proprietary IRS Status: Proprietary
Highest Offering: Associate Degree
Program: Occupational
Accreditation: ACCSC

01 President ... Mr. Nick RANDAZZO

Herzing University (K)

2500 Williams Boulevard, Kenner LA 70062
County: Jefferson Identification: 666450
Unit ID: 433536
Telephone: (504) 733-0074 Carnegie Class: Bac/Assoc
FAX Number: (504) 733-0020 Calendar System: Semester
URL: www.herzing.edu
Established: 1996 Annual Undergrad Tuition & Fees: $14,200
Enrollment: 360 Coed
Affiliation or Control: Proprietary IRS Status: Proprietary
Highest Offering: Baccalaureate
Program: Occupational; 2-Year Principally Bachelor's Creditable; Technical Emphasis
Accreditation: &NH, MAAB, SURTEC

01 President ... Mr. Mark ASPIAZU
05 Academic Dean ... Ms. Stephanie BURNS
07 Director of Admissions ... Ms. Chrissy KALIVITIS
37 Director of Financial Services ... Ms. Ava B. GOMEZ
36 Director of Career Services ... Ms. Myeshia S. AMBROSE

† Regional accreditation is carried under the parent institution in Madison, WI.

ITI Technical College (L)

13944 Airline Highway, Baton Rouge LA 70817-5998
County: East Baton Rouge FICE Identification: 021662
Unit ID: 159197
Telephone: (225) 752-4230 Carnegie Class: Assoc/PrivFP
FAX Number: (225) 756-0903 Calendar System: Quarter
URL: www.iticollege.edu
Established: 1973 Annual Undergrad Tuition & Fees: $26,650
Enrollment: 453 Coed
Affiliation or Control: Proprietary IRS Status: Proprietary
Highest Offering: Associate Degree
Program: Occupational; Technical Emphasis
Accreditation: ACCSC

01 President ... Mr. Earl Joe MARTIN, III
03 Vice President ... Mr. Mark WORTHY
05 Dean of Education ... Mr. Louis BABIN

ITT Technical Institute (M)

14111 Airline Hwy, Suite 101,
Baton Rouge LA 70817-6241
County: East Baton Rouge Identification: 666164
Unit ID: 450216
Telephone: (225) 754-5800 Carnegie Class: Assoc/PrivFP4
FAX Number: N/A Calendar System: Quarter
URL: www.itt-tech.edu
Established: 2006 Annual Undergrad Tuition & Fees: N/A
Enrollment: 624 Coed
Affiliation or Control: Proprietary IRS Status: Proprietary
Highest Offering: Baccalaureate
Program: Technical Emphasis

Accreditation: ACICS

† Branch campus of ITT Technical Institute, Tucson, AZ.

ITT Technical Institute (A)

140 James Drive East, Saint Rose LA 70087-4005
County: Saint Charles Identification: 666031
Unit ID: 437042
Telephone: (504) 463-0338 Carnegie Class: Spec/Tech
FAX Number: (504) 463-0979 Calendar System: Quarter
URL: www.itt-tech.edu
Established: 1968 Annual Undergrad Tuition & Fees: N/A
Enrollment: 767 Coed
Affiliation or Control: Proprietary IRS Status: Proprietary
Highest Offering: Baccalaureate
Program: Technical Emphasis
Accreditation: ACICS

† Branch campus of ITT Technical Institute, Tucson, AZ.

Louisiana College (B)

1140 College Drive, Pineville LA 71359-0001
County: Rapides FICE Identification: 002007
Unit ID: 159568
Telephone: (318) 487-7011 Carnegie Class: Bac/Diverse
FAX Number: (318) 487-7191 Calendar System: Semester
URL: www.lacollege.edu
Established: 1906 Annual Undergrad Tuition & Fees: $13,380
Enrollment: 1,402 Coed
Affiliation or Control: Southern Baptist IRS Status: 501(c)3
Highest Offering: Master's
Program: Liberal Arts And General; Teacher Preparatory
Accreditation: SC, ACBSP, NURSE, PTAA, SW, TED

01 President .... Dr. Joe AGUILLARD
05 Vice Pres Academic Affairs .... Dr. Tim SEARCY
10 Vice President for Business Affairs .... Mr. Randall HARGIS
30 Vice President for Inst Advancement .... Mr. Tim JOHNSON
32 Dean of Students .... Mr. Eric JOHNSON
20 Assistant Dean of the College .... Dr. Wade WARREN
06 Registrar .... Ms. Carolyn DENNIS
84 Director Enrollment Mgmt/Admissions .... Mr. Byron MCGEE
37 Director of Financial Aid .... Mr. Eric GOSSETT
08 Director of the Library .... Mr. Terry MARTIN
26 Director of Marketing .... Ms. Allison BRACHHAUS
14 Director Computer Services .... Mr. Shane DAVIS
18 Director of Physical Plant .... Mr. Randall HARGIS
21 Director of Business Office .... Ms. Beverly INGRAM
39 Director of Housing .... Mr. Welson CESAR
41 Athletic Director .... Mr. Darrell PAYNE
42 Baptist Student Union Director .... Mr. Brandon ROBIN
44 Director Constituent Relations .... Mr. Danny MCVAY
35 Director Student Activities .... Ms. K. B THOMAS
36 Director Career Development .... Mrs. Leneil MERCER
09 Director of Institutional Research .... Mr. Mike MOFFETT
38 Director Student Counseling .... Ms. Leneil MERCER
07 Director of Admissions .... Mr. Byron MCGEE
15 Director Personnel Services .... Ms. Shannon TASSIN
40 Bookstore Manager .... Mrs. Linda BILLINGSLEY
29 Coord Alumni Affairs/Fdn Rels .... Ms. Luana CUNNINGHAM
19 Coordinator of Safety & Security .... Mr. Dwayne ROGERS
23 Coordinator of Health Services .... Ms. Carla MARTIN
04 Assistant to the President .... Ms. Susan NIXON

Louisiana Community & Technical College System (C)

265 S Foster Drive, Baton Rouge LA 70806-4104
County: East Baton Rouge Identification: 666188
Telephone: (225) 922-2800 Carnegie Class: N/A
FAX Number: (225) 922-2392
URL: www.lctcs.edu

01 President .... Dr. Joe MAY
03 Executive Vice President .... Dr. Monty SULLIVAN
10 Sr Vice Pres Finance & Admin .... Ms. Jan JACKSON
09 Asst VP of Institutional Research .... Dr. Albertha LAWSON
26 Director of Public Relations .... Ms. Kizzy PAYTON
30 Exec Director System Advancement .... Ms. Leah GOSS
04 Exec Assistant to the President .... Ms. Angel TETRICK
106 Executive Director of LCTCSOnline .... Dr. Robert JOHNSON

*Acadiana Technical College Lafayette Campus (D)

1101 Bertrand Drive, Lafayette LA 70506-4115
County: Lafayette FICE Identification: 022148
Unit ID: 159443
Telephone: (337) 262-5962 Carnegie Class: Assoc/Pub-R-S
FAX Number: (337) 262-5122 Calendar System: Semester
URL: www.acadiana.edu
Established: 1978 Annual Undergrad Tuition & Fees (In-State): $1,803
Enrollment: 1,398 Coed
Affiliation or Control: State IRS Status: 501(c)3
Highest Offering: Associate Degree
Program: Occupational; Technical Emphasis
Accreditation: COE, ACFEI, MLTAD, NAIT

02 Campus Dean .... Dr. Phyllis DUPUIS
05 Chief Acad Officer/Dir Stdnt Affs .... Ms. Christina DOOLEY
20 Assistant Dean .... Dr. Desiree HUGGINS
06 Registrar .... Ms. Toni AUCOIN
37 Director of Financial Aid .... Ms. Kelly CARUSO
09 Director of Institutional Research .... Ms. Judy HIGGINBOTHAM
10 Chief Business Officer .... Ms. Arlene HOAG
18 Chief Facilities/Physical Plant .... Mr. Willie SMITH
21 Associate Business Officer .... Ms. Paula LEJEUNE
38 Academic Counselor .... Ms. Connie CHOPIN

*Acadiana Technical College Charles B Coreil Campus (E)

1124 Vocational Dr Ward 1, IP, Ville Platte LA 70586-0296
County: Evangeline FICE Identification: 022402
Unit ID: 160816
Telephone: (337) 363-2197 Carnegie Class: Not Classified
FAX Number: (337) 363-7984 Calendar System: Semester
URL: www.ltc.edu
Established: 1976 Annual Undergrad Tuition & Fees (In-District): $1,474
Enrollment: 230 Coed
Affiliation or Control: State/Local IRS Status: 501(c)3
Highest Offering: Associate Degree
Program: Occupational; Technical Emphasis
Accreditation: COE

02 Campus Dean .... Mr. Willie SMITH

† Branch campus of Acadiana Technical College Lafayette Campus, Lafayette, LA.

*Acadiana Technical College Gulf Area Campus (F)

1301 Clover Street, Abbeville LA 70510-3811
County: Vermilion FICE Identification: 005482
Unit ID: 159018
Telephone: (337) 893-4984 Carnegie Class: Assoc/Pub-R-S
FAX Number: (337) 893-4991 Calendar System: Other
URL: www.ltc.edu
Established: 1952 Annual Undergrad Tuition & Fees (In-District): $1,489
Enrollment: 422 Coed
Affiliation or Control: State/Local IRS Status: 501(c)3
Highest Offering: Associate Degree
Program: Occupational; Technical Emphasis
Accreditation: COE

02 Campus Dean .... Ms. Annette FAULK
32 Dir Student Services/Financial Aid .... Ms. Tobi EDWARDS
10 Chief Business Officer .... Ms. Arlene HOAG

† Branch campus of Acadiana Technical College Lafayette Campus, Lafayette, LA.

*Acadiana Technical College T.H. Harris Campus (G)

332 East South Street, Opelousas LA 70570-6114
County: Saint Landry FICE Identification: 005466
Unit ID: 160676
Telephone: (337) 948-0239 Carnegie Class: Assoc/Pub-R-S
FAX Number: (337) 948-0243 Calendar System: Semester
URL: www.ltc.edu
Established: 1938 Annual Undergrad Tuition & Fees (In-District): $1,021
Enrollment: 666 Coed
Affiliation or Control: State/Local IRS Status: 501(c)3
Highest Offering: Associate Degree
Program: Occupational; 2-Year Principally Bachelor's Creditable; Technical Emphasis
Accreditation: COE

02 Director .... Mr. Willie SMITH
37 Financial Aid Officer .... Mrs. Kelly CARUSO
32 Student Affairs Officer .... Mrs. Twana BENOIT

† Branch campus of Acadiana Technical College Lafayette Campus, Lafayette, LA.

*Acadiana Technical College Teche Area Campus (H)

PO Box 11057, 609 Ember Drive,
New Iberia LA 70562-1057
County: Iberia FICE Identification: 005528
Unit ID: 160694
Telephone: (337) 373-0011 Carnegie Class: Assoc/Pub-R-S
FAX Number: (337) 373-0039 Calendar System: Semester
URL: www.techeareacampus.net
Established: 1951 Annual Undergrad Tuition & Fees (In-District): $1,489
Enrollment: 750 Coed
Affiliation or Control: State/Local IRS Status: 501(c)3
Highest Offering: Associate Degree
Program: Occupational; Technical Emphasis
Accreditation: COE

02 Associate Dean .... Mrs. Annette L. FAULK
05 Assistant Dean .... Dr. Camille L. JARRELL
06 Registrar .... Ms. Tammy B. FAULK

† Branch campus of Acadiana Technical College Lafayette Campus, Lafayette, LA.

*Baton Rouge Community College (I)

201 Community College Drive,
Baton Rouge LA 70806-4156
County: East Baton Rouge FICE Identification: 037303
Unit ID: 437103
Telephone: (225) 216-8000 Carnegie Class: Assoc/Pub-U-SC
FAX Number: (225) 216-8100 Calendar System: Semester
URL: www.mybrcc.edu
Established: 1998 Annual Undergrad Tuition & Fees (In-District): $2,832
Enrollment: 8,340 Coed
Affiliation or Control: State/Local IRS Status: 501(c)3
Highest Offering: Associate Degree
Program: Occupational; 2-Year Principally Bachelor's Creditable
Accreditation: SC, @ACBSP, ADNUR, NAIT

02 Interim Chancellor .... Dr. James F. HORTON
32 Int Vice Chancellor Student Affairs .... Dr. Kristine STRICKLAND
30 Vice Chanc Economic Development .... Ms. Phyllis MOUTON
05 Vice Chancellor Academic Affairs .... Dr. Bradley EBERSOLE
10 Vice Chanc Administration & Finance .... Ms. Pam DIEZ
30 Exec Director Inst Advancement .... Ms. Ann ZANDERS
07 Exec Director Admissions/Registrar .... Ms. Nancy CLAY
09 Director of Inst Effectiveness .... Ms. Jennifer DALY
15 Director of Human Resources/Payroll .... Mr. Larry REEHER
18 Chief of Facilities/Physical Plant .... Mr. Lloyd BAPTISTE
10 Chief Financial Officer .... Ms. Helen HARRIS
26 Exec Dir Pub Rels/Performing Arts .... Mr. Stephen MITCHELL
29 Director of External Resources .... Ms. Georgia SCOBEE
35 Dir Student Programs & Resources .... Ms. Stacia HARDY
36 Director Career and Job Placement .... Mr. Marvin BIRKS
37 Director Student Financial Aid .... Ms. Calaundra CLARKE
38 Exec Dir for Advising & Counseling .... Ms. Vinetta FRIE
96 Asst Director of Purchasing .... Mr. Michael CONSTANTIN

*Bossier Parish Community College (J)

6220 E Texas Street, Bossier City LA 71111-6922
County: Bossier FICE Identification: 020554
Unit ID: 158431
Telephone: (318) 678-6000 Carnegie Class: Assoc/Pub-R-M
FAX Number: (318) 678-6389 Calendar System: Semester
URL: www.bpcc.edu
Established: 1966 Annual Undergrad Tuition & Fees (In-District): $2,652
Enrollment: 6,473 Coed
Affiliation or Control: State/Local IRS Status: 501(c)3
Highest Offering: Associate Degree
Program: Occupational; 2-Year Principally Bachelor's Creditable
Accreditation: SC, ACFEI, EMT, MAC, OTA, PTAA, SURGT

02 Chancellor .... Mr. James B. HENDERSON
05 Vice Chanc for Academic Affairs .... Dr. Stan WILKINS
11 VC Business Affs/Economic Devel .... Mr. Tom WILLIAMS
32 Vice Chanc of Student Affairs .... Ms. Karen RECCHIA
10 Chief Financial Officer .... Ms. Michelle BREWER
20 Asc Vice Chanc Planning/Instruction .... Ms. Lesa TAYLOR-DUPREE
12 Dean of TLCM .... Mr. Larry POWELL
103 Dean of Workforce Develop/Cont Educ .... Ms. Lisa WARGO
08 Dean of Learning Resources .... Ms. Virginia S. BRYAN
88 Dean for Innovative Learning .... Ms. Donna WOMACK
21 Comptroller .... Ms. Michelle BREWER
38 Student Counselor .... Mr. Morris ROBINSON
37 Director Student Financial Aid .... Ms. Vickie TEMPLE
06 Registrar .... Ms. Patty H. STEWART
26 Director of Public Relations .... Ms. Karen MUSGROVE
16 Director of Human Resources .... Mrs. Teri BASHARA
35 Director of Student Activities .... Ms. Marjoree HARPER
13 Chief Information Officer .... Mr. Gary HOLLATZ
22 Director of Multicultural Affairs .... Ms. Cindy DARBY
72 Director of Educational Technology .... Ms. Kathleen GAY
18 Dir Physical Plant & Maintenance .... Mr. Joe ST. ANDRE
29 Director Alumni Relations .... Vacant
09 Dir Inst Research/Assessment/Grants .... Ms. Lisa WHEELER
96 Director of Purchasing .... Ms. Gayle DOUCET

*Capital Area Technical College Baton Rouge Campus (K)

3250 N Acadian Thruway E, Baton Rouge LA 70805-6699
County: East Baton Rouge FICE Identification: 005488
Unit ID: 158352
Telephone: (225) 359-9201 Carnegie Class: Assoc/Pub-U-MC
FAX Number: (225) 359-9306 Calendar System: Semester
URL: www.catc.edu
Established: 1944 Annual Undergrad Tuition & Fees (In-District): $1,060
Enrollment: 1,530 Coed
Affiliation or Control: State/Local IRS Status: 501(c)3
Highest Offering: Associate Degree
Program: Occupational; Technical Emphasis
Accreditation: COE, ACFEI, NAIT

02 Regional Director .... Dr. Kay MCDANIEL
05 Chief Academic Officer/Dn Instruct .... Mrs. Lynn HITCHCOCK
07 Senior Admissions Officer .... Ms. Enola MILLER
20 Assoc Chief Academic Officer .... Ms. Phyllis BECKMAN
10 Chief Business Officer .... Ms. Jodi BABIN
26 Chief Development/Public Rels Ofcr .... Mrs. Tammy BROWN
103 Chief Workforce Development Officer .... Mr. LaMoyne WILLIAMS
06 Records Officer .... Ms. Buffy BRINKLEY
37 Financial Aid Officer .... Ms. Latreva WALKER

38 Director Student Counseling ....Ms. Enola MILLER
09 Director of Institutional Research ....Mrs. Phyllis BECKMAN
96 Director of Purchasing ....Ms. Darlene HELM
15 Human Resources Manager ....Ms. Donna PEREZ
18 Facilities & Property Manager ....Mr. Mark VIGNES

*Capital Area Technical College Folkes Campus (A)

3337 Highway 10 E, Jackson LA 70748-6240
County: East Feliciana FICE Identification: 025099
Unit ID: 158945
Telephone: (225) 634-2636 Carnegie Class: Not Classified
FAX Number: (225) 634-4225 Calendar System: Semester
URL: www.catc.edu/folkes
Established: 1977 Annual Undergrad Tuition & Fees (In-District): $1,162
Enrollment: 475 Coed
Affiliation or Control: State/Local IRS Status: 501(c)3
Highest Offering: Associate Degree
Program: Occupational; Technical Emphasis
Accreditation: COE

02 Campus Administrator ....Mr. Johnny ARCENEAUX
18 Chf Facilities/Dir Security/Safety ....Mr. David MOFFAT
06 Registrar ....Mrs. Loretta PROFIT

† Branch campus of Capital Area Technical College Baton Rouge Campus.

*Capital Area Technical College Jumonville Campus (B)

PO Box 725, New Roads LA 70760-0725
County: Pointe Coupee FICE Identification: 005478
Unit ID: 160214
Telephone: (225) 638-8613 Carnegie Class: Not Classified
FAX Number: (225) 618-0157 Calendar System: Semester
URL: www.ltc.edu
Established: 1952 Annual Undergrad Tuition & Fees (In-District): $1,108
Enrollment: 259 Coed
Affiliation or Control: State/Local IRS Status: 501(c)3
Highest Offering: Associate Degree
Program: Occupational; Technical Emphasis
Accreditation: COE

02 Campus Dean ....Ms. Amy DAVIS

† Branch campus of Capital Area Technical College Baton Rouge Campus.

*Central Louisiana Technical College Alexandria Campus (C)

PO Box 5698, Alexandria LA 71307-5698
County: Rapides FICE Identification: 005489
Unit ID: 158088
Telephone: (318) 487-5443 Carnegie Class: Assoc/Pub-R-S
FAX Number: (318) 487-5970 Calendar System: Trimester
URL: www.region6.ltc.edu
Established: 1965 Annual Undergrad Tuition & Fees (In-State): $1,123
Enrollment: 3,139 Coed
Affiliation or Control: State IRS Status: 501(c)3
Highest Offering: Associate Degree
Program: Occupational; Technical Emphasis
Accreditation: COE

02 Campus Dean ....Mr. Mervin BIRDWELL
05 Assistant Campus Dean ....Dr. John R. MARTIN

*Central Louisiana Technical College Avoyelles Campus (D)

508 Choupique Street, Cottonport LA 71327-3743
County: Avoyelles FICE Identification: 008317
Unit ID: 158237
Telephone: (318) 876-2401 Carnegie Class: Not Classified
FAX Number: (318) 876-2634 Calendar System: Semester
URL: www.ltc.edu
Established: 1938 Annual Undergrad Tuition & Fees (In-District): $1,108
Enrollment: 378 Coed
Affiliation or Control: State/Local IRS Status: 501(c)3
Highest Offering: Associate Degree
Program: Occupational; Technical Emphasis
Accreditation: COE

02 Campus Dean ....Mr. Jude PITRE

*Central Louisiana Technical College Huey P. Long Campus (E)

304 S Jones Street, Winnfield LA 71483-3562
County: Winn FICE Identification: 005480
Unit ID: 159090
Telephone: (318) 628-4342 Carnegie Class: Not Classified
FAX Number: (318) 628-7768 Calendar System: Semester
URL: www.ltc.edu
Established: 1938 Annual Undergrad Tuition & Fees (In-District): $1,108
Enrollment: 310 Coed
Affiliation or Control: State/Local IRS Status: 501(c)3
Highest Offering: Associate Degree
Program: Occupational; Technical Emphasis
Accreditation: COE

02 Campus Dean ....Mr. Danny KEYES

*Central Louisiana Technical College Oakdale Campus (F)

117 Highway 1152, Oakdale LA 71463-3536
County: Allen FICE Identification: 030026
Unit ID: 160047
Telephone: (318) 335-3944 Carnegie Class: Assoc/Pub-R-S
FAX Number: (318) 335-3347 Calendar System: Quarter
URL: www.ltc.edu
Established: N/A Annual Undergrad Tuition & Fees (In-District): $1,474
Enrollment: 456 Coed
Affiliation or Control: State/Local IRS Status: 501(c)3
Highest Offering: Associate Degree
Program: Occupational; Technical Emphasis
Accreditation: COE

02 Campus Dean ....Mr. Darrell RODRIGUEZ
05 Assistant Campus Dean ....Dr. Randy ESTERS

*Delgado Community College (G)

615 City Park Avenue, New Orleans LA 70119-4399
County: Orleans FICE Identification: 004625
Unit ID: 158662
Telephone: (504) 671-5000 Carnegie Class: Assoc/Pub-U-MC
FAX Number: (504) 361-6699 Calendar System: Semester
URL: www.dcc.edu
Established: 1921 Annual Undergrad Tuition & Fees (In-District): $1,391
Enrollment: 18,767 Coed
Affiliation or Control: State/Local IRS Status: 501(c)3
Highest Offering: Associate Degree
Program: Occupational; 2-Year Principally Bachelor's Creditable
Accreditation: SC, ACBSP, ACFEI, ADNUR, DIETT, DMS, EMT, ENGT, FUSER, MLTAD, NAIT, NMT, OTA, PTAA, RAD, RTT, SURGT

02 Chancellor ....Dr. Ron WRIGHT
02 Acting Chancellor ....Ms. Deborah R. LEA
10 Vice Chanc Business/Admin Affairs ....Mr. A. C. EAGAN, III
05 Vice Chanc Learning & Student Devel ....Mr. Harold GASPARD
103 Vice Chanc Workforce Dev & Educ ....Ms. Kathleen MIX
66 Exec Dean School of Nursing Campus ....Dr. Cheryl MYERS
76 Dean of Allied Health ....Mr. Ray GISCLAIR
50 Dean Business & Technology ....Mr. Warren PUNEKY
49 Dean of Communication Division ....Mr. Lester ADELSBERG
81 Dean Science & Math ....Mr. Thomas GRUBER
79 Dean of Arts and Humanities ....Ms. Patrice MOORE
106 Dean of Dist Learn and Instr Tech ....Ms. Melissa LACOUR
12 Dean Northshore ....Ms. Ashley CHITWOOD
32 Asst VC of Student Affairs ....Ms. Arnel COSEY
12 Exec Dean West Bank Campus ....Ms. Larissa L. STEIB
15 Asst Vice Chanc for Human Resources ....Ms. Carmen WALTERS
14 Asst VC of Information Technology ....Mr. Thomas LOVINCE
21 Asst VC of Budget & Finance ....Mr. Steve CAZAUBON
18 Asst VC of Dir Facilities/Planning ....Mr. Adolfo GIRAU
103 Exec Dean for Workforce Dev & Educ ....Mr. Leroy KENDRICK
21 Comptroller ....Mr. Ronald RODRIGUEZ
88 Senior Compliance Officer ....Mr. Steve ZERINGUE
28 Executive Asst to the Chancellor ....Ms. Traci SMOTHERS
72 Asst Dean Business & Technology ....Mr. Rene CINTRON
55 Asst Dean Evening and Weekend Div ....Ms. Mercedes MUNSTER
26 Director of Public Relations ....Ms. Carol GNIADY
09 Director of Institutional Research ....Ms. Catherine SARRAZIN
29 Director Alumni Relations ....Ms. Nita HUTTER
08 Librarian ....Ms. Denise REPMAN
37 Director Financial Aid ....Ms. Germaine EDWARDS
41 Director of Athletics ....Mr. Tommy SMITH
06 Registrar ....Ms. Maria CISNEROS
07 Director Admissions/Enrollment Svcs ....Ms. Gwen BOUTTE
88 Director of Curriculum & Pgm Devel ....Mr. Timothy STAMM
25 Director of Grants Development ....Dr. Claudia SAUCIER
35 Director of Student Life ....Mrs. Michelle GRECO
88 Director Ofc of Advising & Testing ....Ms. Tania CARRADINE
96 Director of Purchasing ....Ms. Susan VARBLE
19 Director of Campus Police ....Mr. Ronald DOUCETTE
88 Director of Auxiliary Services ....Mr. Timothy GALLIANO

*L.E. Fletcher Technical Community College (H)

PO Box 5033, Houma LA 70361-5033
County: Terrebonne FICE Identification: 005761
Unit ID: 160481
Telephone: (985) 857-3655 Carnegie Class: Assoc/Pub-U-MC
FAX Number: (985) 857-3689 Calendar System: Semester
URL: www.ftcc.edu
Established: 1948 Annual Undergrad Tuition & Fees (In-State): $2,572
Enrollment: 2,395 Coed
Affiliation or Control: State IRS Status: Exempt
Highest Offering: Associate Degree
Program: Occupational; 2-Year Principally Bachelor's Creditable; Technical Emphasis
Accreditation: SC, COE, NAIT, PNUR

02 Chancellor ....Mr. F. Travis LAVIGNE, JR.
05 Vice Chancellor Instruction ....Mr. William H. TULAK
06 Registrar ....Ms. Lisa HIDALGO
09 Director of Institutional Research ....Mr. Stanton MCNEELY
10 Vice Chancellor Finance & Admin ....Mr. Bryan E. GLATTER
30 Director Institutional Development ....Ms. Marianne MCCRORY
32 Dean of Student Affairs ....Vacant
75 Dean of Technical Education ....Ms. Fathia WILLIAMS
66 Dean of Nursing and Allied Health ....Vacant
07 Director of Admissions ....Ms. Laci MELANCON
15 HR Manager ....Mrs. Dale SHAW
37 Director of Financial Aid ....Mrs. Shawn TRAVIS
04 Assistant to the Chancellor ....Ms. Brenda FAUCHEUX
08 Head Librarian ....Mrs. Suzanne MARTIN
26 Director of Public Relations ....Mrs. Elmy SAVOIE
49 Dean Art and Sciences ....Mrs. Donna ESTRADA
103 Director of Workforce Education ....Mrs. Catherine BARBER
75 Director of LAMPI ....Mr. Breck CHAISSON

*Louisiana Delta Community College (I)

7500 Millhaven Road, Monroe LA 71203
County: Ouachita Parish FICE Identification: 041301
Unit ID: 440624
Telephone: (318) 345-9000 Carnegie Class: Assoc/Pub-R-S
FAX Number: N/A Calendar System: Semester
URL: www.ladelta.edu
Established: 2001 Annual Undergrad Tuition & Fees (In-District): $2,662
Enrollment: 2,658 Coed
Affiliation or Control: State/Local IRS Status: 501(c)3
Highest Offering: Associate Degree
Program: Occupational; 2-Year Principally Bachelor's Creditable
Accreditation: SC

02 Chancellor ....Dr. Luke ROBINS
05 Vice Chancellor Academic/Stdnt Affs ....Mr. Barry DELCAMBRE
10 Vice Chancellor ....Dr. William GRAVES
20 Dean of Instruction ....Vacant
84 Dean of Enrollment Services ....Ms. Carey STICKNEY
32 Dean of Student Services ....Ms. Alvina THOMAS
30 Dir of Institutional Advancement ....Mr. Keith ADAMS
13 Assoc Dir of MIS/IT ....Mr. Bradley MASTERS

*Northeast Louisiana Technical College Delta-Ouachita Campus (J)

609 Vocational Parkway, West Monroe LA 71292-0128
County: Quachita FICE Identification: 005471
Unit ID: 158769
Telephone: (318) 397-6100 Carnegie Class: Assoc/Pub-R-S
FAX Number: (318) 397-6106 Calendar System: Semester
URL: www.myneltc.edu
Established: 1981 Annual Undergrad Tuition & Fees (In-District): $1,733
Enrollment: 850 Coed
Affiliation or Control: State/Local IRS Status: 501(c)3
Highest Offering: Associate Degree
Program: Occupational; Technical Emphasis
Accreditation: COE, NAIT

02 Interim Regional Director ....Dr. Luke ROBINS
05 Asst Dean/Chief Acad/S.Affairs Ofcr ....Ms. Margie F. MIXON
07 Director of Admissions ....Ms. Kathy GARDNER
15 Chief Human Resources Officer ....Ms. Dana ILIFF
10 Chief Financial Officer ....Ms. Margie BROWN
18 Asst Dean/Chief Facilities Officer ....Mr. Greg GROVES
21 Associate Business Officer ....Mr. Patrick TURNER
37 Director Student Financial Aid ....Mr. Adiran TURNER

*Northeast Louisiana Technical College Bastrop Campus (K)

PO Box 1120 Kammell Street, Bastrop LA 71221-1120
County: Morehouse Identification: 667030
Telephone: (318) 283-0836 Carnegie Class: Not Classified
FAX Number: (318) 283-0871 Calendar System: Semester
URL: www.region8.ltc.edu
Established: N/A Annual Undergrad Tuition & Fees (In-District): N/A
Enrollment: 321 Coed
Affiliation or Control: State/Local IRS Status: 501(c)3
Highest Offering: Associate Degree
Program: Occupational; Technical Emphasis
Accreditation: COE

02 Regional Director/Campus Director ....Norene R. SMITH
05 Interim Asst Campus Dean ....Loe DUNN

† Branch campus of Northeast Louisiana Technical College Delta-Ouachita Campus, West Monroe, LA.

*Northeast Louisiana Technical College Farmerville Campus (L)

605 W Boundary Street, Farmerville LA 71241-2067
County: Union FICE Identification: 005476
Unit ID: 159984
Telephone: (318) 368-3179 Carnegie Class: Not Classified
FAX Number: (318) 368-9180 Calendar System: Semester
URL: www.ltc.edu
Established: 1952 Annual Undergrad Tuition & Fees (In-District): $990
Enrollment: 95 Coed
Affiliation or Control: State/Local IRS Status: 501(c)3
Highest Offering: Associate Degree
Program: Occupational; Technical Emphasis

Accreditation: COE

2 Vice Chancellor .... Mrs. Norene R. SMITH
5 Dean .... Mr. Doug POSTEL
2 Asst Dean Student Affairs .... Ms. Lum FARR

† Branch campus Northeast Louisiana Technical College Delta-Ouachita Campus, West Monroe, LA.

Northeast Louisiana Technical College Northeast Campus (A)

1710 Warren Street, Winnsboro LA 71295-2940
County: Franklin　FICE Identification: 005475
Unit ID: 160001
Telephone: (318) 435-2163　Carnegie Class: Assoc/Pub-R-S
FAX Number: (318) 435-2166　Calendar System: Semester
URL: www.ltc.edu
Established: 1952　Annual Undergrad Tuition & Fees (In-District): $1,202
Enrollment: 377　Coed
Affiliation or Control: State/Local　IRS Status: 501(c)3
Highest Offering: Associate Degree
Program: Occupational; Technical Emphasis
Accreditation: COE

02 Campus Dean .... Mrs. Debbie M. PRICE

† Branch campus of Northeast Louisiana Technical College Delta-Ouachita Campus, West Monroe, LA.

Northeast Lousiana Technicial College Ruston Campus (B)

1010 James Street, PO Box 1070, Ruston LA 71273-1070
FICE Identification: 023404
Unit ID: 160366
Telephone: (318) 251-4145　Carnegie Class: Assoc/Pub-R-S
FAX Number: (318) 251-4159　Calendar System: Semester
URL: www.region8.ltc.edu
Established: 1977　Annual Undergrad Tuition & Fees (In-District): $861
Enrollment: 270　Coed
Affiliation or Control: State/Local　IRS Status: 501(c)3
Highest Offering: Associate Degree
Program: Occupational; Technical Emphasis
Accreditation: COE

02 Campus Dean .... Mr. Doug POSTEL

† Branch campus of Northeast Louisiana Technical College Delta-Ouachita Campus, West Monroe, LA.

Northshore Technical Community College (C)

1710 Sullivan Drive, Bogalusa LA 70427-5866
County: Washington　FICE Identification: 006756
Unit ID: 160667
Telephone: (985) 732-6640　Carnegie Class: Assoc/Pub-U-MC
FAX Number: (985) 732-6603　Calendar System: Trimester
URL: www.northshorecollege.edu
Established: 1930　Annual Undergrad Tuition & Fees (In-District): $1,946
Enrollment: 1,713　Coed
Affiliation or Control: State/Local　IRS Status: 501(c)3
Highest Offering: Associate Degree
Program: Occupational; Technical Emphasis
Accreditation: COE

02 Dean .... Mr. William S. WAINWRIGHT
05 Associate Dean .... Mr. William POTTER
20 Assistant Dean .... Ms. Gail LADNER
32 Student Services Officer .... Ms. Debra SHERMAN
09 Director of Institutional Research .... Ms. Shelia SINGLETARY
10 Chief Business Officer .... Mr. Marc CHAUVIN
15 Director of Personnel Services .... Ms. Marlise MCCAMMON
18 Chief Facilities/Physical Plant .... Mr. Gerald BLAPPERT
103 Chief Workforce Development .... Ms. Stephanie BADEAUX
37 Director of Financial Aid .... Mr. Mack JACKSON, III
96 Director of Purchasing .... Ms. Ann LUMPKIN

Northshore Technical College Florida Parishes Campus (D)

PO Box 1300, Greensburg LA 70441-0130
County: Saint Helena　FICE Identification: 005483
Unit ID: 158936
Telephone: (225) 222-4351　Carnegie Class: Assoc/Pub-R-S
FAX Number: (225) 222-6064　Calendar System: Semester
URL: www.northshorecollege.edu
Established: 1952　Annual Undergrad Tuition & Fees (In-District): $1,186
Enrollment: 1,045　Coed
Affiliation or Control: State/Local　IRS Status: 501(c)3
Highest Offering: Associate Degree
Program: Occupational; Technical Emphasis
Accreditation: COE

02 Campus Dean .... Mrs. Sharon G. HORNSBY
07 Director of Admissions .... Mr. Burke JONES

† Branch campus of Northshore Technical Community College, Bogalusa, LA.

*Northshore Technical College Hammond Area Campus (E)

111 Pride Drive, Hammond LA 70401
County: Tangipahoa　FICE Identification: 005481
Unit ID: 159045
Telephone: (985) 543-4120　Carnegie Class: Assoc/Pub-U-MC
FAX Number: (985) 543-4121　Calendar System: Semester
URL: www.northshorecollege.edu
Established: 1965　Annual Undergrad Tuition & Fees (In-District): $1,176
Enrollment: 554　Coed
Affiliation or Control: State/Local　IRS Status: 501(c)3
Highest Offering: Associate Degree
Program: Occupational; 2-Year Principally Bachelor's Creditable; Technical Emphasis
Accreditation: COE

02 Dean .... Mr. Mack JACKSON
37 Financial Aid Director .... Mrs. Shelly COLENDER
32 Student Affairs Officer .... Mr. Daniel A. ROBERTS

† Branch campus of Northshore Technical Community College, Bogalusa, LA.

*Northwest Louisiana Technical College Northwest Campus (F)

PO Box 835, Minden LA 71058-0835
County: Webster　FICE Identification: 009975
Unit ID: 160010
Telephone: (318) 371-3035　Carnegie Class: Assoc/Pub-R-S
FAX Number: (318) 371-3055　Calendar System: Trimester
URL: www.ltc.edu
Established: 1952　Annual Undergrad Tuition & Fees (In-District): $1,300
Enrollment: 3,020　Coed
Affiliation or Control: State/Local　IRS Status: 501(c)3
Highest Offering: Associate Degree
Program: Occupational; 2-Year Principally Bachelor's Creditable; Technical Emphasis
Accreditation: COE

02 Campus Dean .... Mr. Charles T. STRONG
32 Director of Student Services .... Ms. Helen DEVILLE
15 Director Personnel Services .... Ms. Lisa SNIDER
05 Assistant Dean .... Mr. David RHODES
05 Assistant Dean .... Ms. Diane CLARK
37 Director Student Financial Aid .... Ms. Annette CHANLER

*Northwest Louisiana Technical College Natchitoches Campus (G)

6587 Highway 1 Bypass (3110), Natchitoches LA 71458-0657
County: Natchitoches　FICE Identification: 021602
Unit ID: 159823
Telephone: (318) 357-3162　Carnegie Class: Assoc/Pub-R-S
FAX Number: (318) 352-2248　Calendar System: Semester
URL: www.ltc.edu
Established: 1938　Annual Undergrad Tuition & Fees (In-District): $1,390
Enrollment: 392　Coed
Affiliation or Control: State/Local　IRS Status: 501(c)3
Highest Offering: Associate Degree
Program: Occupational; Technical Emphasis
Accreditation: COE

02 Campus Dean .... Laurie MORROW
32 Asst Dean Student Affairs .... Moses BAINES

† Branch campus of Northwest Louisiana Technical College Northwest Campus, Minden, LA.

*Northwest Louisiana Technical College Shreveport Campus (H)

Box 78527, 2010 N Market Street, Shreveport LA 71137-8527
County: Caddo　FICE Identification: 005469
Unit ID: 160427
Telephone: (318) 676-7811　Carnegie Class: Assoc/Pub-R-S
FAX Number: (318) 676-7805　Calendar System: Semester
URL: www.nwltc.edu
Established: 1936　Annual Undergrad Tuition & Fees (In-District): $1,508
Enrollment: 1,500　Coed
Affiliation or Control: State/Local　IRS Status: 501(c)3
Highest Offering: Associate Degree
Program: Occupational; 2-Year Principally Bachelor's Creditable; Technical Emphasis
Accreditation: COE, ACFEI

02 Regional Director .... Mr. Charles STRONG
05 Campus Dean .... Ms. Angie RYMER
32 Director of Student Affairs .... Ms. Cindy MAGGIO
20 Assistant Campus Dean .... Mr. Don LUENSER
37 Student Financial Aid Officer .... Mr. Chris MOREE
84 Enrollment Data Base Management .... Ms. Theresa WIMBERLY
37 Student Financial Aid Officer .... Ms. Nakesha HALL
15 Admin Svcs Ofcr II/District Hum Res .... Ms. Amber SAUNDERS
21 Regional CFO .... Ms. Patti LANN
96 Procurement Specialist .... Ms. Kim HENRY

† Branch campus of Northwest Louisiana Technical College Northwest Campus, Minden, LA.

*Nunez Community College (I)

3710 Paris Road, Chalmette LA 70043-1297
County: Saint Bernard　FICE Identification: 021661
Unit ID: 158884
Telephone: (504) 278-6200　Carnegie Class: Assoc/Pub-S-SC
FAX Number: (504) 278-6480　Calendar System: Semester
URL: www.nunez.edu
Established: 1992　Annual Undergrad Tuition & Fees (In-District): $2,176
Enrollment: 2,413　Coed
Affiliation or Control: State/Local　IRS Status: 501(c)3
Highest Offering: Associate Degree
Program: Occupational; 2-Year Principally Bachelor's Creditable
Accreditation: SC, NAIT

02 Chancellor .... Dr. Thomas R. WARNER
05 Vice Chanc for Acad & Student Affs .... Dr. Steve BERRIEN
30 Ex Dir Inst Advanc/Ex Asst to Chanc .... Ms. Teresa L. SMITH
10 Chief Financial Officer .... Mr. Louis LEHR
32 Dean for Student Affairs .... Ms. Becky MAILLET
72 Dean of Business/Technology .... Vacant
45 Dir Planning/Inst Effectiveness .... Mr. Leonard UNBEHAGEN
08 Director of Library Services .... Mr. Richard DEFOE
15 Dir Human Res/Exec Asst to Chanc .... Dr. Carol MCLEOD
38 Student Counselor .... Mr. Tommie POWELL, III
06 Registrar .... Ms. Meg GREENFIELD
37 Director Financial Aid .... Ms. Glenda DESPENZA
103 Director Workforce Development .... Mr. Ernest T. FRAZIER, JR.
25 Director of Sponsored Programs .... Ms. Carly GERVAIS
29 Director Alumni Relations .... Vacant
18 Coordinator of Facilities .... Ms. Dawn HART-THORE
41 Coord Student Activities/Athletics .... Vacant
13 Computer Services Coordinator .... Mr. Jason HOSCH

*River Parishes Community College (J)

PO Box 310, Sorrento LA 70778-0310
County: Ascension　FICE Identification: 037894
Unit ID: 436304
Telephone: (225) 675-8270　Carnegie Class: Assoc/Pub-S-SC
FAX Number: (225) 675-5478　Calendar System: Semester
URL: www.rpcc.edu
Established: 1999　Annual Undergrad Tuition & Fees (In-District): $2,264
Enrollment: 2,151　Coed
Affiliation or Control: State/Local　IRS Status: 501(c)3
Highest Offering: Associate Degree
Program: 2-Year Principally Bachelor's Creditable
Accreditation: SC

02 Chancellor .... Dr. Joe Ben WELCH
03 Executive Vice Chancellor .... Dr. William MARTIN
10 VC Business/Finance/Administration .... Clen BURTON
84 Dean of Students/Enrollment Mgmt .... Allison D. VICKNAIR
05 Dean of Academic Studies .... Dr. Crystal LEE
21 Director of Accounting & Payroll .... Michael HUBBS
30 VC for Inst Advace & Effectiveness .... Dr. Lisa WATSON
06 Registrar .... LeAnn O. DETILLIER
37 Director Financial Aid .... Kim DUDLEY
38 Director Student Counseling .... Ashley GRAY
08 Director of Library Services .... Wendy JOHNSON
15 Human Resource Manager .... Donna WHITTINGTON
07 Admissions Counselor .... Jennifer KLEINPETER

*South Central Louisiana Technical College Young Memorial Campus (K)

900 Youngs Road, Morgan City LA 70380-2931
County: Saint Mary　FICE Identification: 005526
Unit ID: 160913
Telephone: (985) 380-2436　Carnegie Class: Assoc/Pub-S-MC
FAX Number: (985) 380-2440　Calendar System: Semester
URL: www.ltc.edu
Established: 1965　Annual Undergrad Tuition & Fees (In-District): $1,431
Enrollment: 3,018　Coed
Affiliation or Control: State/Local　IRS Status: 501(c)3
Highest Offering: Associate Degree
Program: Occupational; Technical Emphasis
Accreditation: COE

02 Campus Administrator .... Mr. Karl J. YOUNG, JR.
05 Chief Academic Officer .... Ms. Melanie HENRY
07 Dir of Admissions/Student Affairs .... Ms. Tanya J. ANDERSON
09 Director of Institutional Research .... Ms. Ann COOPER
10 Chief Business Officer .... Mr. Bill HEBERT
15 Director Human Resources .... Ms. Pam MILLER

*South Central Louisiana Technical College Lafourche Campus (L)

1425 Tiger Drive, Thibodaux LA 70301-4336
County: LaFourche　FICE Identification: 030091
Unit ID: 160719
Telephone: (985) 447-0924　Carnegie Class: Assoc/Pub-S-MC
FAX Number: (985) 447-0927　Calendar System: Semester
URL: www.ltc.edu
Established: 1976　Annual Undergrad Tuition & Fees (In-District): $1,200
Enrollment: 495　Coed

Affiliation or Control: State/Local IRS Status: 501(c)3
Highest Offering: Associate Degree
Program: Occupational; Technical Emphasis
Accreditation: COE, SURGT

02 Campus Administrator ... Mr. Anthony TRANCHINA
07 Director of Admissions & Records ... Mr. Anthony TRANCHINA
10 Campus Accountant ... Ms. Robin GEASON
11 Administrative Coordinator ... Ms. Patricia L. BAKER
12 Campus Coordinator Galliano Campus ... Ms. Donna PITRE

† Branch campus of South Central Louisiana Technical Colege Young Memorial Campus.

*South Central Louisiana Technical College River Parishes Campus (A)

PO Drawer AQ, 181 Regala Park Road, Reserve LA 70084-0542
County: Saint John the Baptist FICE Identification: 023334
Unit ID: 160311
Telephone: (985) 536-4418 Carnegie Class: Assoc/Pub-S-MC
FAX Number: (985) 536-7697 Calendar System: Quarter
URL: www.ltc.edu
Established: 1973 Annual Undergrad Tuition & Fees (In-District): $1,200
Enrollment: 1,427 Coed
Affiliation or Control: State/Local IRS Status: 501(c)3
Highest Offering: Associate Degree
Program: Occupational; Technical Emphasis
Accreditation: COE, NAIT

02 Campus Administrator ... Ms. Cynthia POSKEY
32 Director Student Affairs ... Ms. Annette THORNTON

† Branch campus of South Central Louisiana Technical Colege Young Memorial Campus.

*South Louisiana Community College (B)

320 Devalcourt Street, Lafayette LA 70506-4124
County: Lafayette FICE Identification: 039563
Unit ID: 434061
Telephone: (337) 521-8896 Carnegie Class: Assoc/Pub-R-M
FAX Number: (337) 262-2100 Calendar System: Semester
URL: www.southlouisiana.edu
Established: 1998 Annual Undergrad Tuition & Fees (In-District): $2,602
Enrollment: 4,197 Coed
Affiliation or Control: State/Local IRS Status: 501(c)3
Highest Offering: Associate Degree
Program: Occupational; 2-Year Principally Bachelor's Creditable
Accreditation: SC, EMT, NAIT

02 Interim Chancellor ... Dr. Phyllis DUPUIS
04 Assistant to the Chancellor ... Ms. Ziuta BLAES
05 Vice Chanc Student/Academic Affairs ... Dr. Theodore HANLEY
10 Vice Chanc Finance & Administration ... Mr. Rudy GONZALES
20 Dean Instruction & Effectiveness ... Ms. Annette ACCOMANDO
32 Dean of Students ... Ms. Meltida WILSON
09 Director of Institutional Research ... Dr. Charles MILLER
06 Registrar ... Mr. Arthur GILLIS
37 Director of Financial Aid ... Ms. Shonda ROSINSKI
08 Director of Library Services ... Ms. Katherine ROLFES
21 Business Manager ... Ms. Janet LAGRANGE
96 Financial Manager ... Ms. Gloria SMITH
18 Facilities Manager ... Mr. Ed LOPEZ
15 Human Resources Manager ... Ms. Alicia HULIN

*Sowela Technical Community College (C)

PO Box 16950, Lake Charles LA 70616-6950
County: Calcasieu FICE Identification: 005467
Unit ID: 160579
Telephone: (337) 491-2698 Carnegie Class: Assoc/Pub-R-S
FAX Number: (337) 491-2135 Calendar System: Semester
URL: www.sowela.edu
Established: 1938 Annual Undergrad Tuition & Fees (In-District): $3,564
Enrollment: 2,616 Coed
Affiliation or Control: State/Local IRS Status: 501(c)3
Highest Offering: Associate Degree
Program: 2-Year Principally Bachelor's Creditable; Technical Emphasis
Accreditation: COE

02 Chancellor ... Dr. Andrea Lewis MILLER
04 Assistant to the Chancellor ... Ms. Maria COTTO
05 Vice Chanc Acad Affs/Stdnt Success ... Dr. Rick BATEMAN, JR.
10 Vice Chancellor Finance ... Ms. Jeanine NEWMAN
46 Vice Chancellor Economic Devel ... Mr. Richard B. SMITH
27 Chief Info Resources & Tech Officer ... Dr. Charles NWANKWO
06 Exec Dean Enrollment Mgmt/Registrar ... Dr. Teresa JONES
21 Controller ... Mr. Francis PORCHE, JR.
37 Director of Financial Aid ... Ms. Anna DAIGLE
08 Director of Library Services ... Ms. Mary Frances SHERWOOD
15 Director of Human Resources ... Dr. Fitzpatrick U. ANYANWU
103 Director of Workforce Development ... Mr. William E. MAYO
35 Director of Student Support Service ... Ms. Christine COLLINS
18 Director Facilities Planning & Mgmt ... Mr. Davidson DARBONE
09 Exec Director Planning & Analysis ... Dr. Fitzpatrick U. ANYANWU

Louisiana Culinary Institute (D)

10550 Airline Highway, Baton Rouge LA 70816-4109
County: East Baton Rouge FICE Identification: 041123
Unit ID: 449612
Telephone: (225) 769-8820 Carnegie Class: Assoc/PrivFP
FAX Number: (225) 769-8792 Calendar System: Semester
URL: www.louisianaculinary.com
Established: 2002 Annual Undergrad Tuition & Fees: $28,075
Enrollment: 107 Coed
Affiliation or Control: Proprietary IRS Status: Proprietary
Highest Offering: Associate Degree
Program: Occupational
Accreditation: COE

01 Chief Executive Officer ... Keith RUSH

*Louisiana State University System Office (E)

3810 W Lakeshore Drive, Baton Rouge LA 70808-4600
County: East Baton Rouge FICE Identification: 002009
Unit ID: 159638
Telephone: (225) 578-2111 Carnegie Class: N/A
FAX Number: (225) 578-5524
URL: www.lsusystem.lsu.edu

01 President ... Dr. John V. LOMBARDI
03 Executive Vice President ... Vacant
05 VP Academic Affairs/Chief of Staff ... Dr. Carolyn H. HARGRAVE
20 VP Student and Academic Support ... Dr. Michael GARGANO
26 VP Communications/External Afairs ... Dr. Charles F. ZEWE
17 VP Health Care/Medical Education ... Dr. Fred P. CERISE
30 Asst VP Advancement Coordination ... Mr. Joseph CORSO
88 Asst Vice Pres for System Relations . Dr. Robert H. RASMUSSEN
10 CFO/Asst Vice Pres & Comptroller ... Mrs. Wendy SIMONEAUX
18 Asst VP Property/Facil/Univ Arch ... Mr. James HOWELL
09 Director Inst Research/Statistics ... Vacant
43 General Counsel to President ... Mr. P. Raymond LAMONICA
15 System Dir Human Resource/Risk Mgt ... Ms. Sharyon LIPSCOMB
21 System Director Internal Audit ... Mr. Chad BRACKIN

*Louisiana State University and Agricultural and Mechanical College (F)

Baton Rouge LA 70803-0100
County: East Baton Rouge FICE Identification: 002010
Unit ID: 159391
Telephone: (225) 578-3202 Carnegie Class: RU/VH
FAX Number: (225) 578-6400 Calendar System: Semester
URL: www.lsu.edu
Established: 1860 Annual Undergrad Tuition & Fees (In-State): $6,354
Enrollment: 28,771 Coed
Affiliation or Control: State IRS Status: 501(c)3
Highest Offering: Doctorate
Program: Liberal Arts And General; Teacher Preparatory; Professional
Accreditation: SC, AAFCS, ART, BUS, CACREP, CIDA, CLPSY, CONST, CS, DIETD, EMT, ENG, FOR, IPSY, JOUR, LIB, LSAR, MUS, SCPSY, SP, SPAA, SW, TED, THEA, VET

02 Chancellor ... Dr. Michael V. MARTIN
05 Exec Vice Chanc/Provost Acad Affs ... Dr. John M. HAMILTON
26 Assoc Vice Chan Comm & Univ Rel ... Mr. Herb VINCENT
10 Vice Chanc Fin & Admin/Controller ... Mr. Eric N. MONDAY
46 Vice Chanc Research & Econ Dev ... Dr. Thomas R. KLEI
45 Vice Chanc Strategic Initiatives ... Dr. Isiah M. WARNER
32 Vice Chanc Student Life/Enroll Svcs ... Dr. Kurt J. KEPPLER
102 Int President/CEO LSU Foundation ... MajGen. Lee G. GRIFFIN
28 Vice Prov Campus Equity/Diversity ... Dr. Katrice A. ALBERT
20 Vice Prov Academic Affairs ... Dr. Jane CASSIDY
20 Vice Provost Academics & Planning ... Dr. Gilmore REEVE
15 Assoc VC Human Resources Mgmt ... Mr. A. G. MONACO
84 Int Assoc VC Enrollment Management ... Dr. David KURPIUS
30 Exec Director Inst Advancement ... Ms. Bunnie CANNON
43 Legislative Affairs Director ... Dr. Jason DRODDY
27 Asst Vice Chanc Comm/Univ Relations ... Mrs. Holly CULLEN
85 Assoc VC International Programs ... Dr. Lakshman VELUPILLAI
37 Assoc Dir Student Aid/Scholarships ... Ms. Amy MARIX
08 Dean LSU Libraries ... Dr. Jennifer S. CARGILL
79 Int Dean College of Humanities ... Dr. Gaines FOSTER
58 Dean of Graduate School ... Dr. David CONSTANT
54 Dean College of Engineering ... Dr. Richard KOUBEK
47 Dean College of Agriculture ... Dr. Kenneth L. KOONCE
50 Dean Ourso College of Business ... Dr. Eli JONES
70 Dean School of Social Work ... Dr. Christian MOLIDOR
64 Dean College Music & Dramatic Arts ... Dr. Laurence KAPTAIN
81 Dean College of Science ... Dr. Kevin R. CARMAN
62 Dean Sch of Library & Info Science ... Dr. Beth M. PASKOFF
53 Interim Dean College of Education ... Dr. Laura F. LINDSAY
49 Int Dean College of Art & Design ... Mr. Kenneth CARPENTER
74 Dean Veterinary Medicine ... Dr. Peter F. HAYNES
60 Int Dean Manship Sch of Mass Comm ... Dr. Jerry CEPPOS
92 Dean Honors College ... Dr. Nancy L. CLARK
65 Dean Sch of Coast & Environ ... Dr. Christopher D'ELIA
88 Assoc Dean University College ... Mr. Paul IVEY
38 Assc Dean Advising & Counseling Ctr ... Mr. R. Paul IVEY
35 Assistant Dean Student Services ... Ms. Angela GUILLORY
88 Sr Ex Dir SN Ctr Security Rsch Trng ... Mr. Jim FERNANDEZ
88 Exec Director Center Energy Stds ... Dr. Allan G. PULSIPHER
51 Exec Director Continuing Education ... Mr. Doug WEIMER
29 President Alumni Association ... Dr. Charlie W. ROBERTS
59 Director School Human Ecology ... Dr. Roy J. MARTIN
88 Exec Director Museum of Art ... Mr. Thomas A. LIVESAY
18 Exec Director Facility Services ... Mr. Tony LOMBARDO
13 Int Chief Info Ofcr/Info Tech Svcs ... Mr. Brian NICHOLS
75 Dir Sch Human Res Ed/Workforce Dev .. Dr. Michael F. BURNETT
80 Director Public Admin Institute ... Dr. James A. RICHARDSON
88 Director LSU Press ... Ms. MaryKatherine CALLAWAY
41 Athletic Director ... Mr. Joe ALLEVA
06 Registrar ... Mr. Robert K. DOOLOS
36 Director Career Services ... Dr. Mary D. FEDUCCIA
09 Director of Institutional Research ... Ms. Sandy J. WALKER
93 Director Multicultural Affairs ... Ms. Chaunda ALLEN
94 Director Women's/Gender Studies ... Dr. Michelle MASSE
65 Director Museum of Natural Science ... Dr. Frederick H. SHELDON
88 Director Rural Life Museum ... Mr. David J W. FLOYD
96 Exec Dir of Purch & Property Mgmt ... Ms. Marie FRANK
07 Assoc Director of Admissions ... Ms. Lupe LAMADRID

*Louisiana State University at Alexandria (G)

8100 Highway 71 S, Alexandria LA 71302-9121
County: Rapides FICE Identification: 002011
Unit ID: 159382
Telephone: (318) 445-3672 Carnegie Class: Bac/A&S
FAX Number: (318) 473-6418 Calendar System: Semester
URL: www.lsua.edu
Established: 1959 Annual Undergrad Tuition & Fees (In-State): $4,129
Enrollment: 2,667 Coed
Affiliation or Control: State IRS Status: 501(c)3
Highest Offering: Baccalaureate
Program: Liberal Arts And General; Teacher Preparatory
Accreditation: SC, ADNUR, MLTAD, NUR, RAD, TED

02 Chancellor ... Dr. David P. MANUEL
05 Vice Chanc Academic & Student Affs ... Dr. Barbara S. HATFIELD
10 Vice Chanc Finance/Admin Services ... Mr. David WESSE
30 Director Institutional Advancement ... Ms. Melinda F. ANDERSON
20 Asst VC Academic/Student Affairs ... Dr. Eamon HALPIN
21 Asst VC Finance/Admin Services ... Ms. Belinda AARON
50 Dept Chair Business Administration ... Dr. Robert BUSH
49 Dept Chair Arts/English/Humanities ... Dr. Arthur RANKIN
83 Dept Chair Behavioral & Social Sci ... Dr. Jerry SANSON
81 Dept Chair Math & Physical Sciences ... Dr. Nathan PONDER
53 Deparment Chair Education ... Dr. Judy RUNDELL
76 Department Chair Allied Health ... Dr. Haywood JOINER
66 Department Chair Nursing ... Dr. Elizabeth BATTALORA
49 Dept Chair Biological Sciences ... Dr. Carol CORBAT
08 Director Library ... Dr. Bonnie HINES
18 Exec Director of Facility Services ... Mr. Robert KARAM
84 Exec Director Enrollment Management ... Ms. Teresa SEYMOUR
37 Director of Financial Aid ... Mr. Paul MONTELEONE
15 Director Human Resource Management ... Ms. Lynette BURLEW
14 Dir Information/Educ Technology ... Mr. Deron THAXTON
51 Director Continuing Education ... Mr. Robert S. SAVAGE
32 Director Student Services ... Dr. Eamon HALPIN
09 Dir Inst Research/Effectiveness ... Mr. Reed BLALOCK
96 Dir Procurement Svcs/Property Mgmt ... Mr. Larry WILLIAMS
27 Chief Information Officer ... Mr. Deron THAXTON
41 Director Athletics ... Mr. Dan PURVIS
07 Director of Admissions & Recruiting ... Ms. Shelly KIEFFER
06 Registrar ... Ms. Teresa SEYMOUR

*Louisiana State University at Eunice (H)

2048 Johnson Highway, Eunice LA 70535-6726
County: Acadia FICE Identification: 002012
Unit ID: 159407
Telephone: (337) 457-7311 Carnegie Class: Assoc/Pub2in4
FAX Number: (337) 546-6620 Calendar System: Semester
URL: www.lsue.edu
Established: 1964 Annual Undergrad Tuition & Fees (In-State): $2,500
Enrollment: 3,431 Coed
Affiliation or Control: State IRS Status: 501(c)3
Highest Offering: Associate Degree
Program: Occupational; 2-Year Principally Bachelor's Creditable
Accreditation: SC, ADNUR, DMS, RAD

02 Chancellor ... Dr. William J. NUNEZ, III
05 Vice Chancellor Academic Affairs ... Dr. Stephen GUEMPEL
32 Vice Chancellor Student Affairs ... Ms. Judy DANIELS
10 Vice Chancellor Business Affairs ... Ms. Arlene C. TUCKER
26 Director of Public Relations ... Mr. Van REED
08 Director of the Library ... Mr. Gerald PATOUT
06 Registrar/Director Admissions ... Vacant
37 Director of Financial Aid ... Ms. Jacqueline LA CHAPELLE
30 Director Institutional Development ... Ms. Madelaine LANDRY
51 Director of Continuing Education ... Mr. David PULLING
66 Director of Nursing ... Ms. Suzanne DUNBAR
20 Director Trio Programs ... Dr. Marvette J. THOMAS
13 Dir Info Tech/Instl Rsch/Effective ... Mr. Ron WRIGHT
18 Director Physical Plant ... Mr. Michael BROUSSARD
25 Director Grants ... Ms. Jane SPRADLING
15 Director Personnel Services ... Vacant
81 Head Division of Sciences ... Dr. Renee ROBICHAUX
50 Head Div Bus/Nursing/Allied Health ... Ms. Dotty MCDONALD
49 Head Division of Liberal Arts ... Dr. Luciane BERG
28 Director of Diversity ... Ms. Margaret YOUNG

*Louisiana State University Health Sciences Center-New Orleans (A)

433 Bolivar Street, New Orleans LA 70112-2223

County: Orleans — FICE Identification: 002014
Unit ID: 159373
Telephone: (504) 568-4808 — Carnegie Class: Spec/Med
FAX Number: N/A — Calendar System: Semester
URL: www.lsuhsc.edu
Established: 1931 — Annual Undergrad Tuition & Fees (In-State): $5,393
Enrollment: 2,699 — Coed
Affiliation or Control: State — IRS Status: 501(c)3
Highest Offering: Doctorate
Program: Occupational; 2-Year Principally Bachelor's Creditable; Liberal Arts And General; Professional
Accreditation: SC, ANEST, AUD, CORE, CVT, DENT, DH, DT, IPSY, MED, MT, NURSE, OT, PTA, SP

Code	Title	Name
00	Chancellor Emeritus	Dr. John ROCK
02	Chancellor	Dr. Larry H. HOLLIER
05	Vice Chanc Acad Aff/Dean Grad Stds	Dr. Joseph M. MOERSCHBAECHER
11	Vice Chancellor Admin & Finance	Mr. Ronald E. SMITH
17	Vice Chanc Clinic/Cmty/Security Aff	Mr. Ronald E. GARDNER
63	Dean Medicine NO	Dr. Steve NELSON
52	Dean School of Dentistry	Dr. Henry GREMILLION
66	Dean of Nursing	Dr. Demetrius PORCHE
69	Dean of Public Health	Dr. Elizabeth FONTHAM
76	Dean Allied Health Professions	Dr. Jim R. CAIRO
04	Assistant to the Chancellor	Mrs. Patricia MAGEE
85	Director of Government Programs	Ms. Rose D. CHATELAIN
14	Director Computer Services	Ms. Petina OWENS
13	Director Information Services	Ms. Leslie L. CAPO
08	Director Library Administration	Ms. Debra SIBLEY
15	Director Human Resource Mgmt	Mr. Duane LEBBE
06	Registrar	Mr. William Bryant FAUST
37	Director Student Financial Aid	Mr. Patrick J. GORMAN
09	Director of Institutional Research	Dr. Ken KRATZ
31	Director of Community Relations	Ms. Diane E. BAJOIE
18	Chief Facilities/Physical Plant	Mr. John BALL
96	Director of Purchasing	Mr. Brent HEROLD
26	Director of External Relations	Mr. Christopher VIDRINE

*Louisiana State University Health Sciences Center at Shreveport (B)

1501 Kings Highway, Shreveport LA 71103

County: Caddo — FICE Identification: 008067
Unit ID: 435000
Telephone: (318) 675-5000 — Carnegie Class: Not Classified
FAX Number: N/A — Calendar System: Semester
URL: www.lsuhscshreveport.edu
Established: N/A — Annual Undergrad Tuition & Fees (In-District): $823
Enrollment: 839 — Coed
Affiliation or Control: State/Local — IRS Status: 501(c)3
Highest Offering: Doctorate
Program: Professional
Accreditation: SC, DENT, MED, MT, OT, PTA, SP

Code	Title	Name
02	Chancellor	Dr. Robert A. BARISH
11	Vice Chancellor Administration	Mr. John T. DAILEY
06	Registrar	Ms. Kim CARMEN
10	Chief Financial Officer	Ms. Sheila FAOUR
63	Dean School of Medicine	Dr. Andrew L. CHESSON, JR.
76	Dean Sch Allied Health Professions	Dr. Joseph MCCULLOCH
58	Dean School of Graduate Studies	Dr. Sandra C. ROERIG

† Tuition varies by degree program.

*Louisiana State University Paul M. Hebert Law Center (C)

1 East Campus Drive, Baton Rouge LA 70803

County: East Baton Rouge — Identification: 667028
Telephone: (225) 578-8491 — Carnegie Class: Not Classified
FAX Number: (225) 578-8202 — Calendar System: Semester
URL: www.law.lsu.edu
Established: 1906 — Annual Graduate Tuition & Fees: $17,474
Enrollment: 695 — Coed
Affiliation or Control: State — IRS Status: 501(c)3
Highest Offering: Doctorate; No Undergraduates
Program: Professional
Accreditation: SC, LAW

Code	Title	Name
02	Chancellor	Jack M. WEISS
03	Vice Chancellor	Christopher PIETRUSZKIEWICZ
05	Vice Chancellor for Academic Affair	Cheney C. JOSEPH, JR.

*Louisiana State University in Shreveport (D)

1 University Place, Shreveport LA 71115-2399

County: Caddo — FICE Identification: 002013
Unit ID: 159416
Telephone: (318) 797-5000 — Carnegie Class: Master's M
FAX Number: (318) 797-5180 — Calendar System: Semester
URL: www.lsus.edu
Established: 1965 — Annual Undergrad Tuition & Fees (In-State): $4,124
Enrollment: 4,504 — Coed
Affiliation or Control: State — IRS Status: 501(c)3
Highest Offering: Beyond Master's But Less Than Doctorate
Program: Liberal Arts And General; Teacher Preparatory; Professional
Accreditation: SC, ARCPA, BUS, CS, TED

Code	Title	Name
02	Chancellor	Dr. Vincent J. MARSALA
05	Provost/Vice Chanc Academic Affairs	Dr. Paul D. SISSON
10	Vice Chancellor Business Affairs	Mr. Michael T. FERRELL
32	Vice Chancellor Student Affairs	Dr. Gloria W. RAINES
30	Interim Vice Chancellor Devel	Dr. Johnette H. MCCRERY
29	Director Alumni Affairs	Ms. Dianne B. HOWELL
09	Director Planning/Inst Research	Vacant
15	Director of Human Resource Mgt	Vacant
08	Librarian	Dr. Alan D. GABEHART
37	Director of Student Aid	Mrs. Betty M. MCCRARY
07	Director Admissions & Records	Mr. Mickey P. DIEZ
36	Director of Student Placement	Ms. Gina STARNES
38	Director Student Counseling	Mrs. Paula B. ATKINS
14	Director of Computing Services	Mr. Shelby C. KEITH
18	Director of Facility Services	Mr. Donald R. BLOXOM
40	Director of Bookstore	Ms. Brenda BARTLEBAUGH
96	Director of Purchasing	Mrs. Cynthia P. ARMSTRONG
26	Director of Media/Public Relations	Ms. Jennifer B. COOK
04	Assistant to the Chancellor	Vacant
19	Director of Security/Safety	Ms. Rebecca CHILES
41	Athletic Director	Mr. Charles D. ROBINSON
44	Director Annual/Planning Giving	Vacant
49	Dean of Arts and Sciences	Dr. Larry ANDERSON
58	Dean of Graduate Programs	Vacant
51	Dean Continuing Educ/Public Svcs	Vacant
53	Dean of Business/Educ/Human Devel	Dr. David B. GUSTAVSON

*University of New Orleans (E)

2000 Lakeshore Drive, New Orleans LA 70148-2000

County: Orleans — FICE Identification: 002015
Unit ID: 159939
Telephone: (504) 280-6000 — Carnegie Class: RU/H
FAX Number: (504) 280-5522 — Calendar System: Semester
URL: www.uno.edu/
Established: 1958 — Annual Undergrad Tuition & Fees (In-State): $4,758
Enrollment: 11,276 — Coed
Affiliation or Control: State — IRS Status: 501(c)3
Highest Offering: Doctorate
Program: Liberal Arts And General; Professional
Accreditation: SC, ART, BUS, BUSA, CACREP, CS, ENG, MUS, PLNG, TED, THEA

Code	Title	Name
02	Acting Chancellor	Dr. Joe M. KING
05	Provost/VC Acad & Student Affairs	Dr. Joe M. KING
58	VC Research & Dean of Grad School	Dr. Scott L. WHITTENBURG
11	Vice Chanc for Campus Services	Mr. Joel A. CHATELAIN
10	VC Fin Svcs/Bus Affs/Comptroller	Ms. Linda K. ROBISON
86	Vice Chanc for External Affairs	Ms. Rachel A. KINCAID
13	Chief Information Officer	Mr. Jim E. BURGARD
43	University/General Counsel	Ms. Patricia A. ADAMS
50	Dean of Business Administration	Dr. John WILLIAMS
53	Int Dean of Education & Human Dev	Dr. April BEDFORD
54	Dean of Engineering	Dr. Norma MATTEI
49	Dean of Liberal Arts	Dr. Susan E. KRANTZ
08	Dean of Library	Dr. Sharon B. MADER
81	Dean of Sciences	Dr. Steve JOHNSON
06	University Registrar	Ms. Kathleen G. PLANTE
32	Dean of Student Affairs	Dr. Janice LYN
29	Director Alumni Affairs	Ms. Pamela MEYER
26	Director of Public Relations	Mr. Adam NORRIS
27	Chief Marketing Officer	Mr. Mike RIVAULT
07	Director of Admissions	Mr. Andy J. BENOIT
15	Director of Human Resource Mgmt	Mr. Ronald P. BOUDREAUX
37	Director of Student Financial Aid	Ms. Emily LONDON-JONES
19	Asst Vice Chanc for Public Safety	Mr. Thomas HARRINGTON
19	Chief of UNO Police Operations	Mr. H. David ALLY
85	Director International Students	Ms. Christiana J. THOMAS
23	Director Student Health Services	Ms. Denise G. PEREZ
96	Director of Purchasing	Ms. Deborah K. BRIDGES
41	Director Intercollegiate Athletics	Ms. Amy CHAMPION
35	Associate Dean of Student Affairs	Dr. Pamela V. RAULT
39	Director Student Housing	Mr. Mike BRAUNINGER

Loyola University New Orleans (F)

6363 Saint Charles Avenue, New Orleans LA 70118-6195

County: Orleans — FICE Identification: 002016
Unit ID: 159656
Telephone: (504) 865-2011 — Carnegie Class: Master's L
FAX Number: (504) 865-3851 — Calendar System: Semester
URL: www.loyno.edu
Established: 1912 — Annual Undergrad Tuition & Fees: $33,552
Enrollment: 4,772 — Coed
Affiliation or Control: Roman Catholic — IRS Status: 501(c)3
Highest Offering: Doctorate
Program: Liberal Arts And General; Teacher Preparatory; Professional
Accreditation: SC, BUS, CACREP, LAW, MUS, NUR

Code	Title	Name
01	President	Rev. Kevin W. WILDES, SJ
101	Exec Asst to Pres for Board Rels	Ms. Kristine D. LELONG
05	Provost/Vice Pres Academic Affs	Dr. Edward J. KVET
10	Vice President for Business/Finance	Mr. John J. CALAMIA
30	Vice Pres Institutional Advance	Mr. William BISHOP
32	VP Student Affairs/Assoc Provost	Dr. Marcia L. PETTY
88	Vice Pres for Mission & Ministry	Rev. Ted DZIAK, SJ
13	Vice Prov Information Tech/CIO	Mr. Bret JACOBS
21	Assoc Vice Pres Financial Affairs	Mr. Leon MATHES
44	Assoc Vice Pres Development	Mr. Chris WISEMAN
27	Asst VP Marketing/Communications	Mr. Terrell F. FISHER
11	Asst Vice Pres Administration	Mr. Paul C. FLEMING
45	Asst Provost Inst Effective/Assess	Vacant
20	Asst Prov Teaching/Lrng/Faculty Dev	Dr. Brenda JOYNER
46	Spec Asst to Provost for Rsrch Dev	Dr. George E. CAPOWICH
84	Int Dean Admissions/Enrollment Mgmt	Ms. Lori A. ZAWISTOWSKI
42	Dean University Ministry	Mr. Kurt BINDEWALD
09	Assoc Dir of Institutional Research	Ms. Cynthia D. CAIRE
26	Dir Public Affairs/External Rels	Ms. Meredith HARTLEY
43	General Counsel	Ms. Gita BOLT
29	Director Alumni Relations	Ms. Monique G. GARDNER
06	Dir Stdnt Records/Registration Svcs	Ms. Kathy R. GROS
07	Director Admissions/Recruitment Ops	Mr. Keith E. GRAMLING
39	Director of Residential Life	Mr. Robert A. REED
15	Director of Human Resources	Mr. Ross D. MATTHEWS
40	Director Bookstore	Ms. Carol KNIGHT
41	Director Athletics & Wellness	Dr. Michael GIORLANDO
36	Director Career Services	Ms. Roberta KASKEL
23	Admin Director Student Health Svcs	Dr. Alicia BOURQUE
19	Director University Police	Mr. Patrick X. BAILEY
37	Director Scholarships/Financial Aid	Ms. Catherine SIMONEAUX
08	Director of the Law Library	Mr. P. Michael WHIPPLE
85	Director Ctr for International Ed	Ms. Debra DANNA
86	Dir Government Relations	Mr. Tommy SCREEN
38	Director Student Counseling	Dr. Alicia BOURQUE
96	Director of Purchasing	Mr. Bret PENNISON
28	Dir Intercultural Understanding	Ms. Lisa MARTIN
06	Director Student Records/Admn Svcs	Mr. Michael RACHAL
08	Dean of Libraries	Ms. Mary Lee SWEAT
49	Dean Humanities/Natural Science	Dr. Jo Ann Moran CRUZ
61	Dean of Law	Prof. Brian BROMBERGER
64	Dean of Music and Fine Arts	Dr. Anthony DECUIR
50	Dean of Business	Dr. William LOCANDER
83	Dean of Social Sciences	Dr. Luis MIRON
87	Dean of Summer Session	Vacant

MedVance Institute-Baton Rouge (G)

9255 Interline Avenue, Baton Rouge LA 70809

County: East Baton Rouge — FICE Identification: 034803
Unit ID: 439738
Telephone: (225) 248-1015 — Carnegie Class: Not Classified
FAX Number: (225) 248-9517 — Calendar System: Other
URL: www.medvance.edu/colleges/baton-rouge-la
Established: 1991 — Annual Undergrad Tuition & Fees: N/A
Enrollment: 797 — Coed
Affiliation or Control: Proprietary — IRS Status: Proprietary
Highest Offering: Associate Degree
Program: Occupational
Accreditation: ABHES, MLTAD, RAD, SURGT, SURTEC

Code	Title	Name
01	Campus Director	Mr. William PAUL

New Orleans Baptist Theological Seminary (H)

3939 Gentilly Boulevard, New Orleans LA 70126-4858

County: Orleans — FICE Identification: 002019
Unit ID: 159948
Telephone: (504) 282-4455 — Carnegie Class: Spec/Faith
FAX Number: (504) 283-3631 — Calendar System: Semester
URL: www.nobts.edu
Established: 1917 — Annual Undergrad Tuition & Fees: $4,150
Enrollment: 3,025 — Coed
Affiliation or Control: Southern Baptist — IRS Status: 501(c)3
Highest Offering: Doctorate
Program: Professional; Religious Emphasis
Accreditation: SC, MUS, THEOL

Code	Title	Name
01	President	Dr. Charles S. KELLEY, JR.
05	Provost	Dr. Steve W. LEMKE
10	Vice President for Business Affairs	Mr. Clay L. CORVIN
30	Vice President for Development	Vacant
58	Dean Graduate Studies	Dr. Jerry N. BARLOW
12	Dean Leavell College	Dr. L. Thomas STRONG, III
32	Dean of Students	Mr. J. Craig GARRETT
07	Dean of Admissions & Registrar	Dr. Paul E. GREGOIRE, JR.
08	Dean of Libraries	Dr. Jeff D. GRIFFIN
18	Associate VP of Facilities	Dr. Jim O. PARKER
73	Assoc Dean Prof Doctoral Pgms	Dr. Reggie R. OGEA
106	Associate Dean of Online Learning	Dr. W. Craig PRICE
20	Associate Dean of Graduate Studies	Dr. Michael H. EDENS
58	Assoc Dean Research Doctoral Pgms	Dr. Charles A. RAY, JR.
35	Assoc Dean of Students	Dr. Judy JACKSON
88	Director of Leavell Center	Dr. Preston L. NIX
15	Director of Human Resources	Ms. Pattie SHOENER
26	Chief Public Relations Officer	Mr. Gary D. MYERS
29	Director of Alumni Relations	Dr. Dennis L. PHELPS
36	Director of Student Enlistment	Dr. Page M. BROOKS
37	Director of Student Financial Aid	Mr. Owen NEASE
38	Director of Testing & Counseling	Dr. Jeffery W. NAVE

Notre Dame Seminary, Graduate School of Theology (I)

2901 S Carrollton Avenue, New Orleans LA 70118-4391

County: Orleans — FICE Identification: 002022
Unit ID: 160029
Telephone: (504) 866-7426 — Carnegie Class: Spec/Faith
FAX Number: (504) 866-3119 — Calendar System: Semester
URL: www.nds.edu
Established: 1923 — Annual Graduate Tuition & Fees: $18,582

Enrollment: 138 Coed
Affiliation or Control: Roman Catholic IRS Status: 501(c)3
Highest Offering: Master's; No Undergraduates
Program: Professional; Religious Emphasis
Accreditation: #SC, THEOL

01 President/Rector V.Rev. Jose I. LAVASTIDA
05 Academic Dean Rev. Minh PHAN
10 Business Manager Ms. Michelle W. KLEIN
08 Director of Library Mr. Thomas B. BENDER
06 Registrar Ms. Cynthia A. GARRITY
09 Director IE/Planning/Faculty Devel Dr. Rebecca S. MALONEY

Our Lady of Holy Cross College (A)

4123 Woodland Drive, New Orleans LA 70131-7399
County: Orleans FICE Identification: 002023
Unit ID: 160065
Telephone: (504) 394-7744 Carnegie Class: Master's S
FAX Number: (504) 391-2421 Calendar System: Semester
URL: www.olhcc.edu
Established: 1916 Annual Undergrad Tuition & Fees: $8,665
Enrollment: 1,260 Coed
Affiliation or Control: Roman Catholic IRS Status: 501(c)3
Highest Offering: Master's
Program: Liberal Arts And General; Teacher Preparatory; Professional; Nursing Emphasis
Accreditation: SC, CACREP, #IACBE, NUR, RAD, TED

01 President Rev. Anthony J. DE CONCILIIS, CSC
05 Vice Pres Academic Affairs Dr. James P. CURRY
10 Vice Pres for Finance & Operations Sr. Marjorie HEBERT, MSC
30 Vice Pres for Philanthropy/Planning Ms. Julie NICE
20 Assoc VP and Dean of Faculty Dr. Victoria DAHMES
07 Director of Admissions Ms. Katharine GONZALES
37 Coordinator of Financial Aid Mr. Theo WRIGHT
08 Director of Library Services Sr. Helen FONTENOT, MSC
107 Assoc Dean Professional Studies Dr. Patricia PRECHTER
06 Registrar Ms. Debora PANEPINTO
09 Director Inst Research & Planning Vacant
42 Director of Campus Ministry Vacant
15 Human Resources Manager Ms. Cathy WAGUESPACK
44 Director of Annual Fund Mr. David CATHERMAN
21 Director of Financial Management Ms. Arlean WEHLE
13 Director of Technology Services Mr. Wayne CLEMENT

Our Lady of the Lake College (B)

7434 Perkins Road, Baton Rouge LA 70808-4380
County: East Baton Rouge FICE Identification: 031062
Unit ID: 160074
Telephone: (225) 768-1700 Carnegie Class: Spec/Health
FAX Number: (225) 768-0811 Calendar System: Semester
URL: www.ololcollege.edu
Established: 1923 Annual Undergrad Tuition & Fees: $11,480
Enrollment: 1,860 Coed
Affiliation or Control: Roman Catholic IRS Status: 501(c)3
Highest Offering: Master's
Program: Occupational; 2-Year Principally Bachelor's Creditable; Liberal Arts And General; Professional
Accreditation: SC, ADNUR, ANEST, #ARCPA, MT, NUR, PTAA, RAD, SURGT

01 President Dr. Sandra S. HARPER
05 Exec VP for Academics and Students Dr. David ENGLAND
10 VP for Finance and Administration Mr. Hoa NGUYEN
45 VP for Planning and IE Vacant
51 Vice President Career Training Ms. Marie N. KELLEY
66 Dean School of Nursing Dr. Jennifer BECK
49 Dean School of A&S and Health Prof Dr. Katherine KRIEG
32 Dean Student Services Dr. Phyllis SIMPSON
08 Dean of Library Vacant
30 Director of Institutional Advance Ms. Denise DOKEY
37 Director Student Financial Aid Ms. Tiffany MAGEE
06 Registrar Mr. Ryan GARRITY
84 Director Enrollment Management Ms. Rebecca CANNON
88 Director Physician Asst Studies Mr. John ALLGOOD
58 Director Nurse Anesthetist Program Ms. Phyllis PEDERSEN
76 Director Radiologic Technology Ms. Dianne PHILLIPS
76 Director Clinical Lab Sciences Dr. Debbie FOX
76 Director Physical Therapist Asst Ms. Leah GEHEBER
76 Director Surgical Technology Ms. Alice COMISH
88 Dir Health Service Administration Ms. Elizabeth BERZAS
76 Director Respiratory Therapy Ms. Sue DAVIS
88 Director Engaged Learning/Writing Dr. Glenn BLALOCK
106 Director Distributed Education Mr. Eric SENECA
91 Manager Student Info System Mr. Janssen BURRIS

Remington College-Baton Rouge Campus (C)

10551 Coursey Boulevard, Baton Rouge LA 70816-4040
County: East Baton Rouge Identification: 666449
Unit ID: 440271
Telephone: (225) 236-3200 Carnegie Class: Assoc/PrivFP
FAX Number: (225) 922-9569 Calendar System: Quarter
URL: www.remingtoncollege.edu
Established: 1998 Annual Undergrad Tuition & Fees: $14,745
Enrollment: 463 Coed
Affiliation or Control: Proprietary IRS Status: Proprietary
Highest Offering: Associate Degree
Program: Occupational; 2-Year Principally Bachelor's Creditable
Accreditation: ACCSC

01 President Mr. Michael SMITH

† Branch campus of Remington College, Lafayette, LA.

Remington College-Lafayette Campus (D)

303 Rue Louis XIV, Lafayette LA 70508-5700
County: Lafayette FICE Identification: 005203
Unit ID: 160524
Telephone: (337) 981-4010 Carnegie Class: Assoc/PrivFP
FAX Number: (337) 983-7130 Calendar System: Quarter
URL: www.remingtoncollege.edu
Established: 1940 Annual Undergrad Tuition & Fees: $14,745
Enrollment: 392 Coed
Affiliation or Control: Proprietary IRS Status: Proprietary
Highest Offering: Associate Degree
Program: Occupational
Accreditation: ACCSC

01 President Ms. JoAnn BOUDREAUX
07 Director of Recruitment Mr. Joe HOWANSKY

Remington College-Shreveport (E)

2106 Bert Kouns Industrial Loop, Shreveport LA 71118
County: Caddo Identification: 666302
Unit ID: 451866
Telephone: (318) 671-4001 Carnegie Class: Assoc/PrivFP
FAX Number: (318) 671-4065 Calendar System: Semester
URL: www.remingtoncollege.edu
Established: 2007 Annual Undergrad Tuition & Fees: $14,745
Enrollment: 431 Coed
Affiliation or Control: Proprietary IRS Status: Proprietary
Highest Offering: Associate Degree
Program: Occupational
Accreditation: ACCSC

01 President Mr. Jerry DRISKILL

† Branch campus of Remington College, Cleveland, OH.

Saint Joseph Seminary College (F)

75376 River Road, Saint Benedict LA 70457-9999
County: Saint Tammany FICE Identification: 002027
Unit ID: 160409
Telephone: (985) 867-2225 Carnegie Class: Spec/Faith
FAX Number: (985) 867-2270 Calendar System: Semester
URL: www.sjasc.edu
Established: 1891 Annual Undergrad Tuition & Fees: $25,300
Enrollment: 114 Male
Affiliation or Control: Roman Catholic IRS Status: 501(c)3
Highest Offering: Baccalaureate
Program: Liberal Arts And General; Religious Emphasis
Accreditation: SC

01 President - Rector V.Rev. Gregory M. BOQUET, OSB
05 Academic Dean Dr. Jude LUPINETTI
03 Vice-Rector Rev. Matthew CLARK, OSB
08 Librarian Ms. Bonnie WOOD
56 Director Extension Programs Vacant
10 Business Officer Mrs. Judith GAUBERT
37 Director Financial Aid Mr. George BINDER
29 Director of Alumni Affairs Rev. Matthew CLARK, OSB
30 Director of Development Mrs. Vanessa CROUERE
27 Director of Communications Bro. Simon STUBBS, OSB
32 Dean of Students Rev. Killian TOLG, OSB

*Southern University and Agricultural & Mechanical College System Office (G)

JS Clark Admin Building, 4th Floor,
Baton Rouge LA 70813-0001
County: East Baton Rouge FICE Identification: 009637
Unit ID: 160533
Telephone: (225) 771-4680 Carnegie Class: N/A
FAX Number: (225) 771-5522
URL: www.sus.edu

01 President Dr. Ronald F. MASON, JR.
100 Chief of Staff Ms. Evola C. BATES
43 General Counsel to the System/Board Ms. Tracie J. WOODS
10 Vice Pres Finance/Business Affairs Mr. Kevin APPLETON
13 Vice Pres Information Technology Mr. Tony MOORE
05 System Officer for Academic Affairs Mr. Walter T. TILLMAN, JR.
30 VP Sys Advance/Exec Dir Foundation Dr. Ernie T. HUGHES
43 Exec Counsel/Legislative Liaison Mr. Byron C. WILLIAMS
29 Director of Alumni Affairs Ms. Robyn MERRICK
26 Director of Publications Mr. Henry TILLMAN
27 Director of Media Relations Dr. Katara A. WILLIAMS
18 Director of Facilities Planning Mr. Endas VINCENT
21 System Director of Internal Audit Ms. Linda H. CATALON

*Southern University and A&M College (H)

Baton Rouge LA 70813-0001
County: East Baton Rouge FICE Identification: 002025
Unit ID: 160621
Telephone: (225) 771-4500 Carnegie Class: Master's L
FAX Number: (225) 771-2018 Calendar System: Semester
URL: www.subr.edu
Established: 1880 Annual Undergrad Tuition & Fees (In-State): $5,074
Enrollment: 7,294 Coed
Affiliation or Control: State IRS Status: 501(c)3
Highest Offering: Doctorate
Program: Liberal Arts And General; Teacher Preparatory
Accreditation: SC, AAFCS, ART, BUS, CACREP, CORE, CS, DIETD, DIETI, ENG, ENGT, JOUR, LAW, MUS, NURSE, #SP, SPAA, SW, TED

02 Chancellor Dr. James LLORENS
05 Exec Vice Chancellor & Provost Dr. Mwalimu SHUJAA
32 Asst Vice Chanc Student Affairs Vacant
10 Vice Chanc of Finance & Admin Mr. Flandus MCCLINTON, JR.
46 VC Research/Strategic Initiative Dr. Michael STUBBLEFIELD
20 Assoc Vice Chan Academic Affairs Vacant
88 Asc VC for AA/University College Dr. Dana CARPENTER
84 Asst VC Enrollment Management Ms. Michelle L. HILL
26 Asst to Chanc for Media Relations Mr. Edward PRATT
45 Dir Planning Assess/Instnl Research Vacant
29 Director of Alumni Affairs Ms. Robyn MERRICK
15 Director Human Resources Ms. Ardene T. WRIGHT
21 Budget Director Vacant
06 Interim Registrar Ms. D'Andrea FRANK-LEE
07 Int Dir Admissions/Recruitment Mr. Nathaniel HARRISON
35 Director of Student Life Vacant
39 Int Director Residential Housing Mr. Shandon NEAL
37 Director of Financial Aid Ms. Ursula SHORTY
13 Director of Information System Ms. Willie L. FRANCOIS
51 Dir Intl Educ/Dir Svc Learning/CE Dr. Barbara CARPENTER
41 Interim Athletic Director Ms. LaSandra PUGH
18 Director Facilities Planning Mr. Endas VINCENT
88 Director School of Accountancy Ms. Mary A. DARBY
96 Director of Purchasing Mrs. Linda B. ANTOINE
38 Director Student Counseling Dr. ValaRay IRVIN
62 Dean of Libraries Mrs. Emma BRADFORD-PERRY
92 Dean of Honors College Dr. Ella KELLEY
58 Dean of the Graduate School Dr. Joseph MEYINSSE
54 Dean College of Engineering Dr. Habib P. MOHAMADIAN
50 Dean College of Business Dr. Donald R. ANDREWS
53 Dean College of Education Dr. Verjanis PEOPLES
47 Dean Col Agric/Family/Consum Sci Dr. Dewitt JONES
49 Dean College Arts/Humanities Dr. Joyce O'ROURKE
80 Dean School of Public Policy Dr. William ARP
48 Dean School Architecture Mr. Lonnie WILKINSON
66 Dean of School of Nursing Dr. Janet S. RAMI
81 Dean of College of Science Dr. Robert H. MILLER

*Southern University at New Orleans (I)

6400 Press Drive, New Orleans LA 70126-1009
County: Orleans FICE Identification: 002026
Unit ID: 160630
Telephone: (504) 286-5000 Carnegie Class: Master's M
FAX Number: (504) 286-5131 Calendar System: Semester
URL: www.suno.edu
Established: 1956 Annual Undergrad Tuition & Fees (In-State): $3,360
Enrollment: 3,165 Coed
Affiliation or Control: State IRS Status: 501(c)3
Highest Offering: Master's
Program: Liberal Arts And General; Teacher Preparatory; Business Emphasis
Accreditation: SC, SW, TED

02 Chancellor Dr. Victor UKPOLO
04 Exec Assoc to the Chancellor Mr. Harold E. CLARK
05 VC for Academic Affairs & SACS Dr. David S. ADEGBOYE
09 Dir IR & Strategic Initiatives Dr. Michael RALPH
09 Institutional Effectiveness Coord Ms. Ada KWANBUNBUMPEN
88 Learning Outcomes/Assessment Coord Vacant
10 VC for Admin & Finance Mr. Woodie WHITE
84 Int VC Student Affs & Enroll Svcs Dr. Donna GRANT
29 Vice Chan Cmty Outreach/Univ Advanc Mrs. Gloria B. MOULTRIE
21 Asst Vice Chanc Admin & Finance Mr. Robert B. CANNON
25 Dir Grants & Sponsored Programs Dr. William R. BELISLE
06 Registrar Ms. Gilda DAVIS
21 Comptroller Ms. Shawn M. GULLEY
08 Director of Library Mrs. Shatiqua A. MOSBY-WILSON
37 Director of Financial Aid Ms. Kathy G. WOODS
36 Dir Career Counseling & Vet Liaison Mr. Joseph MARION
14 Director of Information Technology Mr. Edmond M. CUMMINGS
15 Director of Human Resources Mr. Randy J. DUKES
19 Police Captain Campus Police Lt. Kevin BANKS
20 Assoc VC Academic Affairs Faculty Mr. Wesley T. BISHOP
41 Director of Athletics Mr. Elston H. KING
07 Int Dir Recruit Admission & Ret Ms. Leatrice D. LATIMORE
26 Director of Public Relations Mr. Eddie FRANCIS
96 Director of Purchasing Ms. Marilyn G. MANUEL
106 Interim Director of E-Learning Ms. Shelia WOOD
70 Dean School of Social Work Dr. Beverly C. FAVRE
50 Dean College of Business/Pub Admin Dr. Igwe E. UDEH
88 Director of Museum Studies Dr. Sara HOLLIS
58 Dean of Graduate Studies Dr. Ira NEIGHBORS
49 Dean College of Arts & Sciences Dr. Henry E. MOKOSSO

53 Int Dean College Educ & Human Dev .... Dr. Louise KALTENBAUGH
88 Dir Services for Students w/Disab .... Ms. Yolanda L. MIMS
35 Int Dir of Student Activities & Org .... Ms. Shawanda M. HOWARD
38 Dir of Student Development Center .... Mrs. Josephine OKORONKWO
39 Director of Residential Life .... Dr. Adrell L. PINKNEY
31 Coordinator of Community Outreach . Ms. Mary Ann J. FRANCOIS
88 Director of Title III Programs .... Dr. Brenda W. JACKSON
88 Dir Student Support Services Pgm .... Ms. Linda D. FREDERICK
88 Dir Ctr for African & American Stds .... Dr. Romanus EJIAGA

*Southern University at Shreveport-Louisiana (A)

3050 Martin Luther King Drive, Shreveport LA 71107-4795
County: Caddo FICE Identification: 007686
Unit ID: 160649
Telephone: (318) 670-6000 Carnegie Class: Assoc/Pub2in4
FAX Number: (318) 670-6374 Calendar System: Semester
URL: www.susla.edu
Established: 1964 Annual Undergrad Tuition & Fees (In-State): $3,195
Enrollment: 2,834 Coed
Affiliation or Control: State IRS Status: 501(c)3
Highest Offering: Associate Degree
Program: Occupational; 2-Year Principally Bachelor's Creditable
Accreditation: SC, ADNUR, DH, MLTAD, NAIT, RAD, SURGT

02 Chancellor .... Dr. Ray L. BELTON
26 Spec Asst to Chanc/Dir Univ Rels .... Mr. Theron J. JACKSON
04 Admin Assistant to the Chancellor .... Mrs. Carolyn S. WEBB
05 Vice Chanc Academic Affairs .... Dr. Orella BRAZILE
10 Vice Chanc for Fiscal Affairs .... Mr. Benjamin W. PUGH
21 Comptroller .... Mrs. Brandy JACOBSEN
21 Bursar .... Ms. LaSonia MORRIS
103 VC Cmty Outreach/Workforce Develop .... Mrs. Janice SNEED
32 Vice Chanc Student Affs/Athletics .... Dr. Sharon F. GREEN
84 Assoc Vice Chanc Enrollment Mgmt .... Vacant
06 Registrar .... Ms. Mahailier L. BROOM
08 Librarian .... Mrs. Jane O'RILEY
35 Asst Vice Chanc for Student Affairs .... Dr. Melva K. TURNER-WILLIAMS
20 Asst Vice Chanc for Academic Affs .... Dr. Regina ROBINSON
51 Director of Continuing Education .... Mrs. Beverly PARKER
07 Director of Admission & Recruitment ..... Mrs. Rhalanda JACKSON
37 Interim Director of Financial Aid .... Ms. Taishieka DAVIS
27 Director Ofc of Univ Comm/Marketing ..... Mr. William STROTHER
83 Div Chair Behavioral Sciences/Educ .... Mrs. Roslyn J. HOLT
50 Division Chair Business Studies .... Vacant
79 Division Chair for Humanities .... Mrs. June PHILLIPS
72 Div Chair Science & Technology .... Dr. Barry C. HESTER
76 Div Chair for Respiratory Therapy .... Mrs. JoAnn BROWN
46 Dir Inst Rsrch/Grants & Spnsrd Pgms .... Vacant
13 Director of Information Technology .... Dr. Gabriel FAGBEYIRO
88 Director Student Support Services .... Mrs. Valley C. PAYNE
75 Director Aerospace Technology .... Mr. David FOGLEMAN
38 Director Counseling Center .... Ms. Rubie J. SCERE
15 Director Human Resources .... Ms. Diane H. NEAL
96 Director of Purchasing .... Ms. Sophia JACKSON-LEE
18 Int Dir Physical Plant Facilities .... Mr. Tracy NELSON
88 Director of Testing Center .... Ms. Kaye WASHINGTON
21 University Budget Officer .... Ms. Regina WINN
72 Director Radiologic Technology .... Ms. Sheila SWIFT
88 Ex Dir TRIO Cmty Outrch/Talent Srch .... Mrs. Carrie ROBINSON
88 Director Dental Hygiene .... Mrs. Kheysia H. WASHINGTON
09 Director Inst Plng/Assessment/Rsrch .... Mr. Martin FORTNER
66 Dean of School of Nursing .... Dr. Sandra TUCKER
88 Director Biomedical Research Devel .... Dr. Joseph ORBAN
83 Dean Behav Sci/Educ/Bus Standards .... Vacant

Southwest University (B)

2200 Veterans Memorial Boulevard, Kenner LA 70062-4005
County: Jefferson Identification: 666310
Telephone: (504) 468-2900 Carnegie Class: Not Classified
FAX Number: (504) 468-3213 Calendar System: Semester
URL: www.southwest.edu
Established: 1982 Annual Undergrad Tuition & Fees: $9,000
Enrollment: 415 Coed
Affiliation or Control: Proprietary IRS Status: Proprietary
Highest Offering: Master's
Program: 2-Year Principally Bachelor's Creditable; Liberal Arts And General; Professional; Business Emphasis
Accreditation: DETC

01 President .... Dr. Grayce LEE
11 Administrative Officer .... Mr. Neil FESER
07 Admissions .... Mrs. Lydia OCMAND

Tulane University (C)

6823 St. Charles Avenue, New Orleans LA 70118-5698
County: Orleans FICE Identification: 002029
Unit ID: 160755
Telephone: (504) 865-5000 Carnegie Class: RU/VH
FAX Number: (504) 865-5202 Calendar System: Semester
URL: www.tulane.edu
Established: 1834 Annual Undergrad Tuition & Fees: $43,434
Enrollment: 12,144 Coed
Affiliation or Control: Independent Non-Profit IRS Status: 501(c)3
Highest Offering: Doctorate
Program: Liberal Arts And General; Teacher Preparatory; Professional
Accreditation: SC, BUS, DIETI, ENG, ENGR, HSA, IPSY, LAW, MED, PH, SCPSY, SW, TEAC

01 President .... Dr. Scott S. COWEN
05 Sr Vice Pres Acad Affairs/Provost .... Prof. Michael BERNSTEIN
26 COO/Sr VP External Affairs .... Ms. Yvette M. JONES
10 Sr Vice Pres for Operations & CFO .... Mr. Anthony P. LORINO
63 Sr Vice Pres/Dn School of Medicine .... Dr. Benjamin P. SACHS
17 Assoc Sr Vice Pres Health Sciences .... Dr. Alan MILLER
43 General Counsel .... Ms. Victoria D. JOHNSON
13 Vice Pres Information Tech/CIO .... Mr. Paul L. BARRON
20 Senior Associate Provost .... Ms. Ana LOPEZ
32 VP Student Affairs .... Mr. Michael HOGG
20 Associate Provost .... Dr. Brian MITCHELL
58 Assoc Prov Graduate Studies .... Dr. Brian S. MITCHELL
100 Chief of Staff & Vice President .... Ms. Anne BANOS
22 VP Inst Equity/Asst to Pres Dvrsity .... Ms. Deborah E. LOVE
32 Vice Pres Student Affs/Dn Students .... Dr. Cynthia CHERREY
84 Vice Pres Enrollment Mgmt/Registrar .... Mr. Earl RETIF
18 VP Operations & Facilities Services .... Dr. Earl F. BIHLMEYER
26 Vice Pres University Communications .... Ms. Deborah L. GRANT
46 Assoc Sr Vice President Research .... Ms. Laura LEVY
30 Vice President Development .... Ms. Luann D. DOZIER
86 Assoc VP Government Relations .... Ms. Sharon P. COURTNEY
35 Assoc VP Auxiliary Svcs/Student Ctr .... Mr. Robert C. HAILEY
18 Assoc Vice President Facilities .... Mr. Sylvester C. JOHNSON
44 Assoc Vice President Development .... Mr. Jeffrey A. BUSH
37 Asst Vice President Financial Aid .... Mr. Michael GOODMAN
90 Director End User Support Svcs .... Mr. Adam KROB
21 Director Budget .... Mr. Gene MEYERS
22 Exec Dir Empl Rels/Inst Equity .... Ms. Stephanie ALLWEISS
29 Director Alumni Affairs .... Ms. Charlotte TRAVIESO
21 Controller .... Mr. Frank (Doug) HARRELL
19 Director of Public Safety .... Mr. Kenneth DUPAQUIER
08 Dean Library & Academic Information .... Dr. Lance QUERY
38 Exec Dir Educ Resources/Couns .... Dr. Jillandra C. ROVARIS
36 Exec Director Career Svcs Ctr .... Dr. Amjad ANOUBI
12 Dir Tulane Natl Primate Res Ctr .... Mr. Andrew LACKNER
24 Executive Director Publications .... Ms. Carol J. SCHLUETER
39 Director Housing Services .... Mr. Marty BRANTLEY
96 Director Central Procurement Svcs .... Mr. William VAN CLEAVE
91 Dir Software Application Systems .... Ms. Mary T. WALSH
41 Director Athletics .... Mr. Richard P. DICKSON
51 Dean Sch Cont Stds/Summer Sch .... Dr. Rick MARKSBURY
49 Dean School of Liberal Arts .... Dr. Carol HABER
49 Dean Newcomb-Tulane College .... Dr. James MACLAREN
61 Dean School of Law .... Mr. Stephen GRIFFIN
69 Dean Sch Public Health/Trop Med .... Dr. Pierre BUEKENS
54 Dean School Science & Engineering .... Dr. Nicholas J. ALTIERO
48 Dean School of Architecture .... Mr. Kenneth SCHWARTZ
50 Dean School of Business .... Dr. Angelo S. DENISI
70 Dean School of Social Work .... Dr. Ronald MARKS
09 Director of Institutional Research .... Dr. Dave D. DAVIS

*University of Louisiana System Office (D)

1201 N Third Street, Suite 7-300, Baton Rouge LA 70802-5243
County: East Baton Rouge FICE Identification: 033444
Unit ID: 247083
Telephone: (225) 342-6950 Carnegie Class: N/A
FAX Number: (225) 342-6473
URL: www.ulsystem.net

01 President .... Dr. Randy MOFFETT
05 Provost & VP Acad & Student Affs .... Dr. Bradley O'HARA
10 VP Business & Finance .... Mr. Robbie ROBINSON
09 VP Research & Performance Assess .... Dr. Beatrice BALDWIN
21 Int Assoc VP for Budget & Finance .... Dr. Edwin LITOLFF

*Grambling State University (E)

Grambling LA 71245-3091
County: Lincoln FICE Identification: 002006
Unit ID: 159009
Telephone: (318) 247-3811 Carnegie Class: Master's M
FAX Number: (318) 274-6172 Calendar System: Semester
URL: www.gram.edu
Established: 1901 Annual Undergrad Tuition & Fees (In-State): $5,594
Enrollment: 4,994 Coed
Affiliation or Control: State IRS Status: 501(c)3
Highest Offering: Doctorate
Program: 2-Year Principally Bachelor's Creditable; Liberal Arts And General; Teacher Preparatory; Professional
Accreditation: SC, BUS, CS, ENGT, JOUR, MUS, NUR, SPAA, SW, TED, THEA

02 President .... Dr. Frank G. POGUE
05 Provost/Vice Pres Academic Affairs .... Dr. Connie WALTON
10 Vice President for Finance and Admn .... Mr. Leon SANDERS
32 Vice President Student Affairs .... Dr. Stacey DUHON
30 Vice President Inst Advancement .... Dr. Kenoye EKE
86 Exec Assoc VP of CIAP .... Mr. Mahmoud LAMADANIE
18 Director of Facilties Management .... Mr. Lavoyd R. DUDLEY
14 Assoc VP of Information Technology .... Mr. Winfred JONES
45 Assoc VP of Planning & Research .... Ms. Nettie DANIELS
19 University Police Chief .... Mr. Freddie PETERSON
15 AVP of Human Resources .... Mrs. Monica BRADLEY
53 Dean College of Education .... Dr. Wynetta Y. LEE
50 Dean College of Business .... Dr. Carl WRIGHT
58 Dean Division Grad Studies/Research .... Dr. Janet A. GUYDEN
88 Interim Dean Col of Prof Studies .... Dr. Rama TUNUGUNTLA
49 Interim Dean College of Arts & Sci .... Dr. Eveyln WYNN
92 Assistant Dean Honors College .... Dr. Ellen SMILEY
41 Director of Athletics .... Mr. J. Lin DAWSON
22 EEO Officer & Wage & Salary Officer .... Mrs. Monica BRADLEY
84 Interim VP for Mgmt/Ret .... Mr. Paul BRYANT
07 Director of Admissions .... Mrs. Annie MOSS
06 University Registrar .... Mrs. Patricia J. HUTCHERSON
37 Dir Student Financial Aid .... Mr. Albert TEZENO
91 Dir of Administrative Computing .... Mrs. Peggy HANLEY
04 Executive Asst to the President .... Dr. Ellen SMILEY
29 Director Alumni Relations .... Ms. Debra JOHNSON
08 Director of Library Services .... Dr. Felix UNAEZE
23 Director of Health Services .... Mrs. Patrice OUTLEY
38 Director Counseling Center .... Dr. Coleen SPEED
39 Dir of Residential Life and Housing .... Mr. Anthony JACKSON
42 Director of Campus Ministry .... Rev. Consuella BREAUX
96 Director of Purchasing .... Ms. Connie HAMPTON
40 Manager University Bookstore .... Ms. Rosalyn LEWIS
21 Dir Administrative Services .... Ms. Shakira M. HARDISON
106 Director of Distance Learning .... Mr. Eldrie HAMILTON
20 Special Assistant to Provost and VP .... Ms. Joann BROWN
36 Director of Career Services .... Mr. Johnny PATTERSON
44 Int Dir Annual Fund Coord .... Mr. Ralph WILSON

*Louisiana Tech University (F)

PO Box 3168, Ruston LA 71272-0001
County: Lincoln FICE Identification: 002008
Unit ID: 159647
Telephone: (318) 257-0211 Carnegie Class: RU/H
FAX Number: (318) 257-2928 Calendar System: Quarter
URL: www.latech.edu
Established: 1894 Annual Undergrad Tuition & Fees (In-State): $5,900
Enrollment: 11,804 Coed
Affiliation or Control: State IRS Status: 501(c)3
Highest Offering: Doctorate
Program: Liberal Arts And General; Teacher Preparatory; Professional
Accreditation: SC, AAB, AAFCS, ADNUR, ART, AUD, BUS, BUSA, CIDA, COPSY, CS, DIETD, DIETI, ENG, ENGT, FOR, MUS, SP, TED

02 President .... Dr. Daniel D. RENEAU
05 Vice President for Academic Affairs .... Dr. Kenneth W. REA
32 Vice President for Student Affairs .... Dr. Jim M. KING
11 Vice Pres Finance/Administration .... Mr. Joe R. THOMAS
30 Vice President for Univ Advancement .... Ms. Corre A. STEGALL
58 Exec VP & Dean of Graduate School .. Dr. Terry M. MCCONATHY
10 Comptroller .... Mrs. Lisa COLE
50 Dean of Business .... Dr. James LUMPKIN
49 Dean of Liberal Arts .... Dr. Ed C. JACOBS
53 Dean of Education .... Dr. David GULLATT
54 Dean of Engineering & Science .... Dr. Stan A. NAPPER
65 Dean of Applied & Natural Sciences ..... Dr. James D. LIBERATOS
84 Dean of Enrollment Management .... Mrs. Pamela R. FORD
07 Director of Admissions .... Mrs. Jan B. ALBRITTON
21 Business Officer .... Mr. Jerry S. DREWETT
14 Director of Computer Center .... Mr. Roy S. WATERS
37 Director Student Financial Aid .... Mr. Roger VICK
09 Director Institutional Research .... Mrs. Lori C. THEIS
06 Registrar .... Mr. Robert D. VENTO
08 Director of Libraries .... Mr. Michael DICARLO
15 Director of Personnel .... Mrs. Sheila TRAMMEL
26 Chief Public Relations Officer .... Mr. David GUERIN
29 Director of Alumni Relations .... Mr. Ryan RICHARD
36 Dir Career Ctr/Student Counseling .... Mr. Ron CATHEY
89 Director of Freshmen Studies .... Vacant
92 Director of Honors Program .... Dr. Rick SIMMONS
93 Director of Multicultural Affairs .... Vacant
96 Director of Purchasing .... Ms. Karen MURPHY
18 Int Chief Facilities/Physical Plant .... Mr. Doug WILLIS
35 Director Student Affairs .... Dr. Jim KING

*McNeese State University (G)

4205 Ryan Street, Lake Charles LA 70609-4510
County: Calcasieu FICE Identification: 002017
Unit ID: 159717
Telephone: (337) 475-5000 Carnegie Class: Master's L
FAX Number: (337) 475-5012 Calendar System: Semester
URL: www.mcneese.edu
Established: 1939 Annual Undergrad Tuition & Fees (In-State): $4,353
Enrollment: 8,941 Coed
Affiliation or Control: State IRS Status: 501(c)3
Highest Offering: Beyond Master's But Less Than Doctorate
Program: Liberal Arts And General; Teacher Preparatory; Professional
Accreditation: SC, AAFCS, ADNUR, ART, BUS, CS, DIETD, DIETI, ENG, ENGT, MT, MUS, NUR, NURSE, RAD, TED

02 President .... Dr. Philip C. WILLIAMS
05 Provost/VP Academic & Student Affs ..... Dr. Jeanne M. DABOVAL
10 Vice President for Business Affairs .... Mr. Eddie P. MECHE
30 Vice Pres University Advancement .... Mr. Richard H. REID
81 Dean College of Science .... Dr. George F. MEAD, JR.
58 Int Dean Dore Sch Graduate Studies ...... Dr. George F. MEAD, JR.
50 Interim Dean College Business .... Dr. Banamber MISHRA
53 Dean of College of Education .... Dr. Wayne R. FETTER
49 Dean College Liberal Arts .... Dr. Ray MILES
54 Dean Col of Engr & Engr Technology .... Dr. Nikos KIRITSIS
66 Dean of College of Nursing .... Dr. Peggy L. WOLFE
84 Dean Enrollment Management .... Ms. Stephanie B. TARVER
32 AVP Enrollment Mgt/Student Affairs .... Mr. Toby W. OSBURN
18 Director Facilities & Plant Opers .... Mr. Richard R. RHODEN
13 Director of Univ Computing Services .... Mr. Stanley HIPPLER

31 Dir Community Service and Outreach ... Mrs. Betty H. ANDERSON
15 Director of Human Resources ... Ms. Charlene R. ABBOTT
09 Director Institutional Research ... Ms. Kathleen S. DOUGAY
37 Director Student Financial Aid ... Ms. Taina J. SAVOIT
08 Director of Library ... Ms. Debbie L. JOHNSON-HOUSTON
19 Dir University Police/Info Center ... Ms. Cinnamon A. SALVADOR
29 Director Alumni Affairs ... Ms. Joyce D. PATTERSON
38 Director Scholarships/Testing ... Ms. Ralynn F. CASTETE
35 Assistant Dean Student Services ... Vacant
07 Dir of Admissions and Recruiting ... Ms. Kara SMITH
36 Director Career Services ... Ms. Kathy E. BOND
41 Athletic Director ... Mr. Thomas H. MCCLELLAND, II
45 Dir Inst Effectiveness/Acad Support ... Dr. Tom DVORSKE
96 Director Purchasing/Property Cntrl ... Ms. Pamela L. WATKINS
92 Director of Honors College ... Dr. Scott E. GOINS
14 Chief Information Technology ... Mr. Chad THIBODEAUX
46 Director of Research Services/LERC ... Ms. Janet R. WOOLMAN
85 International Student Advisor ... Ms. Christine M. KAY
26 Director Public Relations ... Ms. Candace V. TOWNSEND
23 RN Supervisor-Student Health ... Ms. Sharon E. GUILLORY
40 Bookstore Manager ... Ms. Sharamie T. MOORE
06 Coordinator Alternative Learning ... Mr. Matthew D. WELCH
90 Coord of Col of Science Computing ... Dr. William G. ALBRECHT
106 Director of Electronic Learning ... Ms. Helen B. WARE
28 Chief Diversity Officer ... Dr. Michael T. SNOWDEN

*Nicholls State University (A)

University Station, Thibodaux LA 70310-0001
County: Lafourche FICE Identification: 002005
Unit ID: 159966
Telephone: (985) 446-8111 Carnegie Class: Master's M
FAX Number: (985) 448-4920 Calendar System: Semester
URL: www.nicholls.edu
Established: 1948 Annual Undergrad Tuition & Fees (In-State): $4,819
Enrollment: 7,093 Coed
Affiliation or Control: State IRS Status: 501(c)3
Highest Offering: Beyond Master's But Less Than Doctorate
Program: 2-Year Principally Bachelor's Creditable; Liberal Arts And General; Teacher Preparatory
Accreditation: SC, AAFCS, ART, BUS, BUSA, CS, DIETD, ENGR, ENGT, JOUR, MUS, NAIT, NURSE, TED

02 President ... Dr. Stephen T. HULBERT
05 VP for Academic Affairs ... Dr. Allayne BARRILLEAUX
03 Executive Vice President ... Mr. Lawrence W. HOWELL
32 Vice Pres Student Affs/Enroll Svcs ... Dr. Eugene A. DIAL
30 Vice President for Inst Advancement ... Dr. David E. BOUDREAUX
21 Asst Vice Pres for Facilities ... Mr. Michael G. DAVIS
21 Asst Vice Pres for Finance/CFO ... Mr. Michael P. NAQUIN
45 Exec Dir of Planning/Effectiveness ... Mrs. Renee G. HICKS
49 Dean of Arts & Sciences ... Dr. B. ASRABADI
66 Dean of Nursing and Allied Health ... Dr. Velma S. WESTBROOK
50 Dean Business Administration ... Dr. Shawn MAULDIN
53 Dean of Education ... Dr. Steven WELSH
88 Dean of University College ... Dr. Albert DAVIS
32 Dean of Student Life ... Vacant
09 Dir Assess/Institutional Research ... Mrs. Leslie B. DISHMAN
08 Director of Library ... Ms. Carol A. MATHIAS
19 Director of University Police ... Mr. Craig M. JACCUZZO
36 Director of Student Placement ... Ms. Kristie R. TAUZIN
37 Director of Student Financial Aid ... Ms. Casie TRICHE
14 Director of Computing Center ... Mr. Charles R. ORDOYNE
15 Director of Human Resources ... Mr. John FORD
18 Dir Facility Plng/Special Projects ... Mr. Michael G. DAVIS
26 Director of University Relations ... Mrs. Renee PIPER
51 Assoc Dir of Continuing Education ... Ms. Simone HARRIS
41 Athletic Director ... Mr. Robert BERNARDI
29 Director of Alumni Affairs ... Miss Deborah A. RAZIANO
06 Director Records & Registration ... Mr. Kelly J. RODRIGUE
07 Assoc Director of Admissions ... Mrs. Becky L. DUROCHER
23 Director University Health Services ... Dr. Diane GARVEY
38 Director of Student Services ... Dr. Michele E. CARUSO
39 Director Residence Life ... Ms. Lisa GRUBBS
90 Director Academic Computing ... Mr. Thomas BONVILLAIN
84 Director of Enrollment Services ... Mrs. Courtney CASSARD
96 Director of Purchasing ... Mr. Terry G. DUPRE
88 Director Research & Sponsored Pgms ... Mrs. Debra BENOIT
58 Director of Graduate Programs ... Ms. Betty KLEEN
88 Director of Printing & Design ... Mr. Bruno RUGGIERO
88 Director of Auxiliary Services ... Mrs. Brenda HASKINS

*Northwestern State University (B)

140 Central Avenue, Natchitoches LA 71497-0002
County: Natchitoches FICE Identification: 002021
Unit ID: 160038
Telephone: (318) 357-6361 Carnegie Class: Master's L
FAX Number: (318) 357-4223 Calendar System: Semester
URL: www.nsula.edu
Established: 1884 Annual Undergrad Tuition & Fees (In-State): $6990.65
Enrollment: 9,244 Coed
Affiliation or Control: State IRS Status: 501(c)3
Highest Offering: Doctorate
Program: Liberal Arts And General; Teacher Preparatory; Professional
Accreditation: SC, AAFCS, ADNUR, ART, BUS, CACREP, ENGT, MUS, NURSE, RAD, SW, TED, THEA

02 President ... Dr. Randall J. WEBB
04 Exec Assistant to the President ... Mr. Robert CREW
05 Provost/VP Academic & Student Affs ... Dr. Lisa ABNEY
11 Vice Pres for University Affairs ... Dr. Marcus JONES

26 Vice President for External Affairs ... Mr. Jerry D. PIERCE
46 Vice Pres for Tech/Research/Eco Dev ... Dr. Darlene WILLIAMS
10 Vice President Business Affairs ... Mr. Carl JONES
20 Vice Provost ... Dr. Steve HORTON
32 Asst Provost & Dean of Students ... Dr. Chris MAGGIO
53 Dean Col of Education & Human Dev ... Dr. Vickie GENTRY
49 Dean Col of Arts/Letters/Grad Stds ... Dr. Steve HORTON
66 Dean Col of Nursing & Allied Health ... Dr. Norann PLANCHOCK
72 Dean Col of Science/Tech/Business ... Dr. Austin TEMPLE
88 Director Scholars College ... Dr. Davina MCCLAIN
12 Director Leesville Campus ... Mr. Joseph POPE
09 Director Institutional Research ... Vacant
06 Registrar ... Mrs. Lillie F. BELL
08 Director of Libraries ... Ms. Abbie LANDRY
29 Director Alumni Affairs & Devel ... Mr. Drake OWENS
37 Director Student Financial Aid ... Mrs. Misti ADAMS
27 Director Informational Services ... Mr. Don SEPULVADO
36 Director Counseling & Career Svcs ... Mrs. Rebecca BOONE
41 Athletic Director ... Mr. Greg BURKE
23 Director of Health Services ... Mrs. Stephanie CAMPBELL
07 Director of University Recruiting ... Mrs. Jana LUCKY
15 Director Human Resources ... Mr. Cecil KNOTTS
18 Physical Plant Director ... Mr. Chuck BOURG
96 Director of Purchasing ... Mr. Stan WRIGHT
21 Associate Business Officer ... Ms. Rita GRAVES

*Southeastern Louisiana University (C)

548 Western Avenue, Hammond LA 70402-0001
County: Tangipahoa FICE Identification: 002024
Unit ID: 160612
Telephone: (985) 549-2000 Carnegie Class: Master's L
FAX Number: (985) 549-2061 Calendar System: Semester
URL: www.selu.edu
Established: 1925 Annual Undergrad Tuition & Fees (In-State): $4,100
Enrollment: 15,351 Coed
Affiliation or Control: State IRS Status: 501(c)3
Highest Offering: Doctorate
Program: Liberal Arts And General; Teacher Preparatory; Professional
Accreditation: SC, AAFCS, ART, BUS, BUSA, CACREP, CS, MUS, NAIT, NURSE, SP, SW, TED

02 President ... Dr. John L. CRAIN
05 Provost/VP Academic Affairs ... Dr. Tammy BOURG
10 Vice Pres Administration/Finance ... Mr. Stephen M. SMITH
30 Vice Pres University Advancement ... Ms. Wendy JOHNS-LAUDERDALE
32 Vice President Student Affairs ... Dr. Marvin L. YATES
20 Asst VP Academic Affairs ... Dr. Josie WALKER
13 Asst Vice Pres for Technology ... Dr. Mike M. ASOODEH
21 Asst Vice Pres for Operations ... Mr. Sam B. DOMIANO
04 Exec Assistant to the President ... Ms. Erin K. MOORE
21 Controller ... Ms. Nettie L. BURCHFIELD
06 Director Records & Registration ... Ms. Paulette M. POCHE
08 Director of Library ... Mr. Eric W. JOHNSON
36 Director Career Development Svcs ... Mr. Ken W. RIDGEDELL
31 Interim Director Auxiliary Services ... Ms. Connie DAVIS
91 Director Admin Computing Services ... Mr. Julian D. KOCH
29 Director of Alumni Services ... Ms. Kathy L. PITTMAN
39 Dir Student Housing & Resident Svcs ... Vacant
15 Director Human Resources ... Ms. Jessie R. ROBERTS
19 Director University Police ... Mr. Michael L. PRESCOTT
46 Dir Sponsored Research/Programs ... Ms. Cheryl HALL
41 Athletic Director ... Mr. Bart BELLAIRS
18 Director Facility Planning ... Mr. Ken D. HOWE
92 Director Honors Program ... Dr. Kent NEUERBURG
23 Director Health Services ... Ms. Vera A. WILLIAMS
38 Director Counseling Center ... Dr. Barbara B. HEBERT
07 Director Admissions ... Vacant
37 Director Financial Aid ... Ms. Mary LACOUR
09 Director Inst Research/Assessment ... Dr. Michelle HALL
26 Director Public Information ... Mr. Rene G. ABADIE
96 Dir Purchasing/Property Control ... Mr. Ed E. GAUTIER
85 Dir Multicultural/Intl Stdnt Affs ... Mr. Eric J. SUMMERS
44 Annual Fund Coordinator ... Mr. Michael SISTRUNK
22 Coordinator EEO/ADA ... Mr. Gene E. PREGEANT
49 Int Dn Col Arts/Human/Soc Sciences ... Dr. Karen FONTENOT
50 Dean of College of Business ... Dr. Randy P. SETTOON
53 Interim Dean Col of Educ/Human Dev ... Dr. Bill NEAL
66 Interim Dean Col of Nurs/Health Sci ... Dr. Ann CARRUTH
72 Dean Col of Science & Technology ... Dr. Daniel MCCARTHY
56 Asst VP Extended Studies ... Ms. Joan GUNTER

*University of Louisiana at Lafayette (D)

104 University Circle, Lafayette LA 70503-0001
County: Lafayette FICE Identification: 002031
Unit ID: 160658
Telephone: (337) 482-1000 Carnegie Class: RU/H
FAX Number: (337) 482-6195 Calendar System: Semester
URL: www.louisiana.edu
Established: 1898 Annual Undergrad Tuition & Fees (In-State): $4,426
Enrollment: 16,763 Coed
Affiliation or Control: State IRS Status: 501(c)3
Highest Offering: Doctorate
Program: Liberal Arts And General; Teacher Preparatory; Professional
Accreditation: SC, ART, BUS, BUSA, CIDA, CS, DIETD, DIETI, ENG, JOUR, MUS, NAIT, NURSE, SP, TED

02 President ... Dr. E. Joseph SAVOIE
05 Provost and VP for Academic Affairs ... Dr. Carolyn BRUDER
10 VP Administration & Finance ... Mr. Jerry L. LEBLANC
32 Vice President for Student Affairs ... Mr. Edward PRATT
30 Vice Pres University Advancement ... Mr. Ken ARDOIN
46 Vice Pres for Research/Grad Studies ... Dr. Robert TWILLEY
84 VP for Enrollment Mgmt & Registrar ... Dr. DeWayne BOWIE
13 Chief Information Officer ... Mr. Gene FIELDS
11 Asst Vice Pres Business Services ... Mr. Wayne E. THERIOT
21 Asst Vice Pres Financial Services ... Mr. Ronald P. LAJAUNIE
45 Asst VP Institutional Planning ... Dr. Paula P. CARSON
20 Asst VP Academic Affairs ... Ms. Ellen D. COOK
35 Dean of Students ... Ms. Patricia F. COTTONHAM
88 Associate Dean of Students ... Ms. Dana BEKURS
25 Director Research/Sponsored Pgms ... Ms. Ruth LANDRY
91 Director of Information Systems ... Mr. Sam F. BULLARD
14 Director Computing Support Services ... Mr. Patrick LANDRY
08 Dean of University Libraries ... Dr. Charles W. TRICHE, III
07 Director of Admissions ... Mr. Leroy BROUSSARD, JR.
88 Director Information Networks ... Mr. Stephen J. MAHLER
09 Director of Institutional Research ... Ms. Lisa LORD
55 Director University College ... Ms. Amanda DOYLE
37 Director of Financial Aid ... Ms. Cindy SHOWS-PEREZ
96 Assistant Director Purchasing ... Ms. Lark CHARTIER
27 Assoc Director Publications ... Ms. Kathleen A. THAMES
36 Director Career Services ... Ms. Kim A. BILLEAUDEAU
19 Chief of Police ... Chief Joey STURM
23 Director Student Health Svcs ... Dr. Marelle YONGUE
49 Dean Liberal Arts ... Dr. A. David BARRY
54 Dean of Engineering ... Dr. Mark E. ZAPPI
53 Dean of Education ... Dr. Gerald P. CARLSON
66 Dean of Nursing ... Dr. Gail P. POIRRIER
58 Dean of Graduate School ... Dr. C. Eddie PALMER
50 Dean of Business Administration ... Dr. Joby JOHN
81 Dean of Sciences ... Dr. Bradd CLARK
97 Dean of General Studies ... Dr. Phebe A. HAYES
57 Dean College of the Arts ... Mr. H. Gordon BROOKS, II
77 Director Ctr Adv Computer Studies ... Dr. Magdy A. BAYOUMI
18 Director Physical Plant ... Mr. William J. CRIST
22 Director Operational Review/EEO Off ... Ms. Christine BRASHER
39 Director Housing ... Ms. Lisa L. LANDRY
40 Manager Bookstore ... Mr. Robert RICHARD
24 Director Univ Media/Printing Svcs ... Mr. Steve MAHLER
41 Athletic Director ... Mr. Scott FARMER
85 Director Office of Intl Affairs ... Dr. Rose HONEGGER
51 Director of Continuing Education ... Ms. Elaine D. LIVERS
31 Dean of Community Service ... Mr. David YARBROUGH
86 Coordinator Governmental Relations ... Vacant
26 Associate Director for Publications ... Ms. Kathleen THAMES
28 Asst to President for Campus Divers ... Dr. Jennifer JACKSON
29 Exec Director Alumni Affairs ... Mr. Dan W. HARE
44 Planned Giving Officer ... Mr. David P. COMEAUX
38 Director Counseling and Testing ... Mr. Brian FREDERICK
16 Director of Human Resources ... Ms. Charlene HAMILTON

*University of Louisiana at Monroe (E)

700 University Avenue, Monroe LA 71209-0001
County: Ouachita FICE Identification: 002020
Unit ID: 159993
Telephone: (318) 342-1000 Carnegie Class: Master's L
FAX Number: (318) 342-5161 Calendar System: Semester
URL: www.ulm.edu
Established: 1931 Annual Undergrad Tuition & Fees (In-State): $4,636
Enrollment: 8,801 Coed
Affiliation or Control: State IRS Status: 501(c)3
Highest Offering: Doctorate
Program: 2-Year Principally Bachelor's Creditable; Liberal Arts And General; Teacher Preparatory; Professional; Business Emphasis
Accreditation: SC, AAB, BUS, BUSA, CACREP, CONST, CS, DH, EXSC, MFCD, MT, MUS, NURSE, OTA, PHAR, RAD, SP, SW, TED

02 President ... Dr. Nick J. BRUNO
04 Executive Assistant to President ... Dr. Richard J. HOOD
05 Provost/VP for Academic Affairs ... Dr. Stephen P. RICHTERS
10 Vice President for Business Affairs ... Mr. David C. NICKLAS
32 Vice President for Student Affairs ... Dr. Wendell W. BRUMFIELD
30 VP Univ Advancement/External Affs ... Dr. Don A. SKELTON, SR.
20 Associate Provost Academic Officer ... Dr. Eric A. PANI
84 Assoc Provost Enrollment Mgmt ... Mrs. Lisa R. MILLER
35 Asst VP for Student Affairs ... Mr. Camile W. CURRIER
88 Director University Advancement ... Mr. Keith A. BROWN
41 Director of Athletics ... Mr. Robert H. STAUB
27 Director Media Relations ... Mrs. Laura J. WOODARD
88 Director Internal Audit ... Mr. Kirby D. CAMPBELL
49 Dean College of Arts & Sciences ... Dr. Jeffery CASS
57 Assoc Dn Sch Visual/Performing Arts ... Dr. Matthew H. JAMES
97 Director Program General Studies ... Dr. Richard B. CHARDKOFF
50 Dean Col Business Administration ... Dr. Ronald BERRY
88 Dir Ctr Business/Economic Research ... Dr. Robert C. EISENSTADT
53 Dean Col of Education/Human Devel ... Dr. Sandra M. LEMOINE
76 Dean College of Health Sciences ... Dr. Denny G. RYMAN
67 Dean College of Pharmacy ... Dr. Benny BLAYLOCK
58 Interim Dean of Graduate Programs ... Dr. William MCCOWN
92 Director Honors Program ... Dr. Christian RUBIO
92 Chair Honors Program ... Dr. Sandra B. HILL
88 Director Assessment and Evaluation ... Mrs. Allison L. THOMPSON
09 Exec Dir Univ Planning/Analysis ... Mr. Justin P. ROY
08 Dean of the Library ... Mr. Donald R. SMITH
51 Int Director Continuing Education ... Ms. Paula THORNHILL
106 Fac Electr & Off-Campus Learning ... Vacant
84 Dir of Mktg for Enroll Management ... Ms. Lauren BROWNELL
06 Registrar ... Mr. Anthony MALTA
37 Director of Financial Aid ... Ms. Teresa H. SMITH
88 Director Testing ... Ms. Denise M. DUPLECHIN

85	Dir Intl Student Program and Svcs	Dr. Mara C. LOEB
88	Director of University Retention	Mrs. Barbara MICHAELIDES
39	Director Residential Life	Ms. Tresea L. BUCKHAULTS
45	Budget Officer	Ms. Gail C. PARKER
21	Controller	Ms. Diane S. SINGLETARY
15	Director Human Resources	Mr. Larry M. ESTESS
96	Director Purchasing	Mr. Larry M. ESTESS
14	Director Computer Center	Mr. Thomas S. WHATLEY
88	Technology Support Manager	Mr. Chance W. EPPINETTE
88	Coordinator Auxiliary Enterprises	Mr. Michael R. TREVATHAN
40	Manager University Bookstore	Mr. Ricky GUERRERO
18	Director Physical Plant Admin	Mr. Lawrence B. THORN
88	Dir Facilities Mgmt & Ehs	Mr. Jason S. ROUBIQUE
35	Director of Student Services	Ms. Pamela JACKSON
88	Asst Dean Student Life/Leadership	Mr. Nathan HALL
38	Director Counseling Center	Ms. Karen FOSTER
23	Director Student Health Services	Ms. Yolanda CAMPER
19	Director University Police	Mr. Larry M. ELLERMAN
36	Assoc Director Career Services	Ms. Alberta GREEN
88	Dir Recreational Svcs/Facilities	Ms. Treina LANDRUM
88	Director of Development	Ms. Anne A. LOCKHART
105	Director of Web Services	Mr. Lindsey S. WILKERSON
102	Chief Finan Ofcr Univ Foundations	Mr. Mark S. LABUDE
29	Associate Director Alumni Relations	Mr. Tommy A. WALPOLE

Xavier University of Louisiana (A)

One Drexel Drive, New Orleans LA 70125-1098
County: Orleans — FICE Identification: 002032
Unit ID: 160904
Telephone: (504) 486-7411 — Carnegie Class: Bac/A&S
FAX Number: (504) 520-7904 — Calendar System: Semester
URL: www.xula.edu
Established: 1925 — Annual Undergrad Tuition & Fees: $16,900
Enrollment: 3,391 — Coed
Affiliation or Control: Roman Catholic — IRS Status: 501(c)3
Highest Offering: Doctorate
Program: Liberal Arts And General; Teacher Preparatory; Professional
Accreditation: SC, ACBSP, MUS, PHAR, TED

01	President	Dr. Norman C. FRANCIS
11	Sr Vice Pres for Administration	Mr. Calvin S. TREGRE
05	Sr Vice Pres for Academic Affairs	Dr. Loren BLANCHARD
30	Sr VP for Resource Development	Dr. Gene D'AMOUR
32	Vice President for Student Services	Mr. Joseph K. BYRD
30	Vice President for Inst Advancement	Dr. Kenneth ST.CHARLES
10	Vice President for Finance	Mr. Edward PHILLIPS
13	Interim VP for Office of Technology	Mrs. Melva WILLIAMS
45	Vice Pres Planning & Inst Research	Dr. Ronald R. DURNFORD
18	Vice President Facilities Planning	Mr. Marion BRACY
26	Assoc VP Public Affairs/Comm	Vacant
20	Assoc VP for Academic Affairs	Dr. Marguerite GIGUETTE
31	Assoc Vice Pres Auxiliary Services	Mr. William JEFFRION
07	Dean of Admissions	Mr. Winston D. BROWN
06	Registrar	Ms. Avis STUARD
42	Director of Campus Ministry	Mrs. Lisa L. MCCLAIN
21	Director of Accounting	Ms. Joyce SANDIFER
21	Director of Operations	Ms. Lori GIE
21	Dir Fin Reporting & External Audit	Mrs. Ingenue S. SCHEXNIDER-FIELDS
15	Director of Human Resources	Mr. Larry CALVIN
49	Dean of Arts & Sciences	Dr. Anil KUKREJA
67	Dean of College of Pharmacy	Dr. Kathleen KENNEDY
89	Dean of Freshmen Studies	Dr. Kenneth BOUTTE
09	Dir of Inst Effectiv & Assessment	Dr. Cecile BROOKOVER
09	Director of Institutional Research	Dr. Treva A. LEE
08	Director of the Library	Mr. Robert E. SKINNER
36	Director of Career Services	Mrs. Carolyn D. THOMAS
37	Director of Financial Aid	Mrs. Mildred HIGGINS
19	Director of Campus Police	Mr. Duane CARKUM
23	Director Student Health Services	Ms. Brenda MEDLEY
38	Director of Counseling Services	Ms. Eloise DOXIE-DIXON
29	Director of Alumni Relations	Ms. Kimberly REESE
40	Manager Bookstore	Ms. Rose NAQUIN
41	Athletic Director	Mr. Dennis COUSIN

MAINE

Bangor Theological Seminary (B)

PO Box 411, Bangor ME 04402-0411
County: Penobscot — FICE Identification: 002035
Unit ID: 160968
Telephone: (207) 942-6781 — Carnegie Class: Spec/Faith
FAX Number: (207) 990-1267 — Calendar System: Semester
URL: www.bts.edu
Established: 1814 — Annual Graduate Tuition & Fees: $11,760
Enrollment: 100 — Coed
Affiliation or Control: United Church Of Christ — IRS Status: 501(c)3
Highest Offering: Doctorate; No Undergraduates
Program: Professional; Religious Emphasis
Accreditation: EH, THEOL

01	Interim President	RevDr. Robert GROVE-MARKWOOD
30	Vice Pres of Advancement	Mrs. Lesley HEISER
26	Chief Public Relations Officer	Mrs. Lesley HEISER
05	Academic Dean	Dr. Steven LEWIS
07	Director of Admissions	Ms. Adrea JAEHNIG
06	Registrar	Ms. Danielle R. LAVINE
08	Librarian	Ms. Laurie MCQUARRIE
10	Controller	Mrs. Caroline HAMMOND
04	Assistant to the President	Mrs. Patricia O. ANNIS

Bates College (C)

2 Andrews Road, Lewiston ME 04240-6047
County: Androscoggin — FICE Identification: 002036
Unit ID: 160977
Telephone: (207) 786-6255 — Carnegie Class: Bac/A&S
FAX Number: (207) 786-6123 — Calendar System: Other
URL: www.bates.edu
Established: 1855 — Annual Undergrad Tuition & Fees: $55,300
Enrollment: 1,725 — Coed
Affiliation or Control: Independent Non-Profit — IRS Status: 501(c)3
Highest Offering: Baccalaureate
Program: Liberal Arts And General
Accreditation: EH

01	Interim President	Dr. Nancy J. CABLE
05	VP Academic Affairs/Dean of Faculty	Dr. Pamela J. BAKER
10	VP Finance & Admin/Treasurer	Ms. Terry J. BECKMANN
86	VP Enrollment and External Affairs	Dr. Nancy J. CABLE
08	VP Info & Libr Services/Librarian	Dr. Eugene L. WIEMERS
30	VP Advancement	Mr. Kelly KERNER
32	Dean of Students	Mr. Tedd GOUNDIE
21	Asst Vice Pres Financial Planning	Mr. Douglas W. GINEVAN
20	Associate Dean of Faculty	Dr. Matthew J. COTE
31	Acting Dir Community Partnerships	Dr. Georgia N. NIGRO
06	Registrar	Ms. Mary MESERVE
09	Dir Inst Rsch/Assessment	Ms. Ellen PETERS
15	Dir Human Resources	Ms. Mary MAIN
18	Dir Physical Plant Operations	Mr. Daniel F. NEIN
88	Dir Capital Planning/Construction	Ms. Pamela J. WICHROSKI
07	Acting Director of Admissions	Ms. Leigh WEISENBURGER
29	Dir Alumni & Parent Engagement	Ms. Marianne COWAN
22	Asst Dir Equity/Diversity Resources	Ms. Carmen PURDY
19	Dir Security & Campus Safety	Mr. Thomas P. CAREY
23	Dir Health Services	Ms. Christy TISDALE
26	Asst VP Communications/Media Rels	Ms. Margaret KIMMEL
37	Dir Student Financial Services	Ms. Wendy G. GLASS
40	Dir Bookstore/Contract Officer	Ms. Sarah POTTER
36	Dir of Career Services	Ms. Karen MCROBERTS
91	Dir Sys Development & Integration	Ms. Eileen P. ZIMMERMAN
24	Dir of Academic Technology Services	Mr. Andrew W. WHITE
41	Athletic Director	Mr. Kevin MCHUGH
42	College Chaplain	Mr. William BLAINE-WALLACE
39	Asst Dean of Students/Housing	Ms. Erin FOSTER ZSIGA
102	Dir Corp & Foundation Relations	Ms. Susan ORTON
104	Assoc Dean of Students/Study Abroad	Mr. Stephen SAWYER

† Tuition figure is a comprehensive fees figure. The comprehensive fee for 2011-2012 is $55,300.

Beal College (D)

99 Farm Road, Bangor ME 04401-6831
County: Penobscot — FICE Identification: 005204
Unit ID: 160995
Telephone: (207) 947-4591 — Carnegie Class: Assoc/PrivFP
FAX Number: (207) 947-0208 — Calendar System: Other
URL: www.bealcollege.edu
Established: 1891 — Annual Undergrad Tuition & Fees: $6,900
Enrollment: 552 — Coed
Affiliation or Control: Proprietary — IRS Status: Proprietary
Highest Offering: Associate Degree
Program: 2-Year Principally Bachelor's Creditable
Accreditation: ACICS, MAC

01	President	Mr. Allen T. STEHLE
05	Director of Education	Ms. Deborah CROCKETT
08	Chief Librarian	Mrs. Ann W. REA
37	Director Student Financial Aid	Ms. Maggie MAGEE
18	Superintendent Physical Plant	Mr. Kevin HARDY
10	Associate Business Officer	Ms. Pollyanne HEWES
88	Dir Early Child Ed/Hospitality Svcs	Ms. Susan XIRINACHS
76	Director Allied Health	Ms. Barbara MARCHELLETTA
88	Director Criminal Justice	Mr. Allen T. STEHLE
40	Director Bookstore	Mr. Corey LEIGHTON
36	Director Student Placement	Ms. Donna GILLETTE
06	Registrar	Ms. Ellen EDWARDS
07	Director of Admissions	Ms. Erin LEIGHTON
32	Director of Student Affairs	Ms. Debbie LEBLANC
88	Director Accounting	Ms. Joan TUKEY
88	Director Social & Human Svcs Asst	Ms. Susan POLYOT

Bowdoin College (E)

5700 College Station, Brunswick ME 04011-8448
County: Cumberland — FICE Identification: 002038
Unit ID: 161004
Telephone: (207) 725-3000 — Carnegie Class: Bac/A&S
FAX Number: (207) 725-3123 — Calendar System: Semester
URL: www.bowdoin.edu
Established: 1794 — Annual Undergrad Tuition & Fees: $42,386
Enrollment: 1,762 — Coed
Affiliation or Control: Independent Non-Profit — IRS Status: 501(c)3
Highest Offering: Master's
Program: Liberal Arts And General
Accreditation: EH

01	President	Dr. Barry MILLS
10	Sr VP Finance/Admin & Treasurer	Ms. S. Catherine LONGLEY
46	Sr VP Planning/Devel & Secy of Col	Vacant
32	Dean of Student Affairs	Mr. Timothy W. FOSTER
05	Dean for Academic Affairs	Dr. Cristle Collins JUDD
07	Dean of Admissions	Mr. Scott A. MEIKLEJOHN
26	VP/Dir Comm/Public Affairs	Mr. Scott W. HOOD
09	VP Institutional Planning & Assess	Mrs. Becky BRODIGAN
20	Assoc Dean for Academic Affairs	Dr. James A. HIGGINBOTHAM
35	Sr Associate Dean Student Affairs	Ms. Margaret L. HAZLETT
29	Director Alumni Relations	Ms. Rodie F. LLOYD
08	Librarian	Ms. Sherrie S. BERGMAN
37	Director of Student Aid	Mr. Stephen H. JOYCE
21	Controller	Mr. Matthew ORLANDO
06	Registrar	MS. Jan BRACKETT
15	Director of Human Resources	Ms. Tamara D. SPOERRI
19	Director of Security	Mr. Randall NICHOLS
36	Director of Career Planning	Mr. Timothy DIEHL
38	Director of Counseling Service	Dr. Bernie HERSHBERGER
41	Director of Athletics	Mr. Jeffrey H. WARD
13	Chief Information Officer	Mr. Mitchel W. DAVIS
23	Director of Health Services	Ms. Sandra J. HAYES
18	Director Facilities Ops/Maintenance	Mr. Theodore R. STAM
24	Instructional Media Librarian	Ms. Carmen M. GREENLEE
21	Director of Finance & Campus Svcs	Mr. Delwin C. WILSON
39	Director of Residential Life	Ms. Mary Pat MCMAHON
40	Dir Dining & Bookstore Services	Ms. Mary M. KENNEDY
35	Director of Student Activities	Dr. Allen W. DELONG
88	Dir of the Museum of Art	Dr. Kevin M. SALATINO
18	Director of Capital Projects	Mr. Donald V. BORKOWSKI

Central Maine Medical Center College of Nursing and Health Professions (F)

70 Middle Street, Lewiston ME 04240-7027
County: Androscoggin — FICE Identification: 006305
Unit ID: 161022
Telephone: (207) 795-2840 — Carnegie Class: Assoc/PrivNFP
FAX Number: (207) 795-2849 — Calendar System: Semester
URL: www.cmmcson.edu
Established: 1891 — Annual Undergrad Tuition & Fees: $7,590
Enrollment: 150 — Coed
Affiliation or Control: Independent Non-Profit — IRS Status: 501(c)3
Highest Offering: Associate Degree
Program: Occupational; 2-Year Principally Bachelor's Creditable; Nursing Emphasis
Accreditation: EH, ADNUR, NMT, RAD

01	President	Mrs. Susan C. BALTRUS
05	Director	Ms. Nancy J. ROSS
07	Chair Admissions	Mr. Peter R. MILLER
06	Registrar	Mrs. Kathleen C. JACQUES
37	Director Student Financial Aid	Mr. Keith R. BOURGAULT
24	Educational Media Coordinator	Mr. Peter R. MILLER

Colby College (G)

4000 Mayflower Hill, Waterville ME 04901-8840
County: Kennebec — FICE Identification: 002039
Unit ID: 161086
Telephone: (207) 859-4000 — Carnegie Class: Bac/A&S
FAX Number: (207) 859-4603 — Calendar System: 4/1/4
URL: www.colby.edu
Established: 1813 — Annual Undergrad Tuition & Fees: $53,800
Enrollment: 1,826 — Coed
Affiliation or Control: Independent Non-Profit — IRS Status: 501(c)3
Highest Offering: Baccalaureate
Program: Liberal Arts And General
Accreditation: EH

01	President	Dr. William D. ADAMS
05	Vice Pres Acad Affs/Dean of Faculty	Dr. Lori G. KLETZER
10	Vice President Admin & Treasurer	Mr. Douglas C. TERP
26	Vice Pres Development & Alumni Rels	Ms. Deborah DUTTON COX
03	Vice President/Secy of the Corp	Ms. Sally A. BAKER
32	VP Student Affairs/Dean of Students	Mr. James S. TERHUNE
88	Assoc Vice President Investments	Mr. Douglas E. REINHARDT
20	Assoc VP Acad Affs/Assoc Dn Faculty	Dr. Paul G. GREENWOOD
07	Vice Pres/Dean Admiss & Fin Aid	Dr. Terry E. COWDREY
35	Senior Associate Dean of Students	Mr. Paul E. JOHNSTON
06	Registrar	Ms. Elizabeth N. SCHILLER
08	Director of Libraries	Mr. Clement P. GUTHRO
36	Director of Career Center	Mr. Roger W. WOOLSEY
71	Director of Special Programs	Mr. Jacques MOORE
37	Director of Financial Aid	Ms. Lucia W. WHITTELSEY
29	Director of Alumni Relations	Ms. Margaret M. BOYD
35	Assoc Dean Stdnts/Dir Campus Life	Mr. Jed W. WARTMAN
16	Director Human Resources	Mr. Mark CROSBY
19	Director of Security	Mr. Peter S. CHENEVERT
13	Director of Info-Tech Services	Dr. Raymond B. PHILLIPS
18	Director of Physical Plant	Ms. Patricia C. WHITNEY
23	Medical Director	Dr. Paul D. BERKNER
38	Director of Counseling Services	Ms. Patricia N. NEWMEN
41	Director of Athletics	Ms. Marcella K. ZALOT
09	Dir Instnl Research & Assessment	Dr. William P. WILSON
21	Controller	Mr. Ruben L. RIVERA
40	Director of the Bookstore	Ms. Barbara C. SHUTT
104	Director of Off-Campus Study	Dr. Nancy DOWNEY
102	Dir Corp/Found/Govt Relations	Ms. Marcella J. BERNARD

College of the Atlantic (H)

105 Eden Street, Bar Harbor ME 04609-1198
County: Hancock — FICE Identification: 011385
Unit ID: 160959
Telephone: (207) 288-5015 — Carnegie Class: Bac/A&S

FAX Number: (207) 288-3780 Calendar System: Trimester
URL: www.coa.edu
Established: 1969 Annual Undergrad Tuition & Fees: $36,063
Enrollment: 370 Coed
Affiliation or Control: Independent Non-Profit IRS Status: 501(c)3
Highest Offering: Master's
Program: Liberal Arts And General; Teacher Preparatory
Accreditation: EH

01 President ... Dr. Darron COLLINS
05 Academic Dean ... Dr. Ken HILL
10 Administrative Dean ... Mr. Andy GRIFFITHS
32 Associate Dean for Student Life ... Ms. Sarah LUKE
06 Registrar ... Ms. Judy ALLEN
08 Library Director ... Ms. Jane HULTBERG
07 Dean of Admission ... Ms. Sarah BAKER
21 Comptroller ... Mrs. Melissa COOK
37 Director of Financial Aid ... Mr. Bruce HAZAM
30 Dean of Development ... Ms. Lynn BOULGER
26 Director Public Relations ... Ms. Donna GOLD
36 Internship Director ... Ms. Jill BARLOW-KELLEY

Husson University (A)

1 College Circle, Bangor ME 04401-2929
County: Penobscot FICE Identification: 002043
Unit ID: 161165
Telephone: (207) 941-7000 Carnegie Class: Master's M
FAX Number: (207) 941-7139 Calendar System: Semester
URL: www.husson.edu
Established: 1898 Annual Undergrad Tuition & Fees: $14,435
Enrollment: 3,111 Coed
Affiliation or Control: Independent Non-Profit IRS Status: 501(c)3
Highest Offering: Doctorate
Program: Liberal Arts And General; Professional
Accreditation: EH, IACBE, NURSE, OT, @PHAR, PTA

01 President ... Dr. Robert A. CLARK
05 Provost ... Dr. Lynne COY-OGAN
10 Vice Pres for Finance & Treasurer ... Craig HADLEY
30 Vice President for Advancement ... Thomas MARTZ
11 VP of Administration ... John RUBINO
32 Dean of Students ... Sharon WILSON-BARKER
50 Dean School of Business ... Ronald NYKIEL
67 Dean School of Pharmacy ... Rodney LARSON
66 Dean College of Health & Education ... Barbara HIGGINS
58 Dean of Graduate Studies ... Michael MULLANE
53 Director School of Education ... B. MOODY
07 Director of Admissions ... Carlena BEAN
37 Director of Financial Aid ... Linda HILL
08 Librarian ... Amy AVERRE
06 Registrar ... Nancy FENDERS
49 Dean Science/Humanities ... Francis HUBBARD
29 Director of Alumni Affairs ... Susan NUTTER
36 Director Career Services ... John WESTHOFF
41 Director of Athletics ... Robert REASSO
26 Dir of Public Affs/Govt Relations ... Julia GREEN
39 Director of Student Life ... Pamela KROPP-ANDERSON
16 Human Resources Director ... Mary DEMERS
14 Director of Institutional Research ... Gail TUDOR
18 Director of Maintenance ... Ed COSSETTE
13 Exec Dir of Information Resources ... Kevin CASEY

Institute for Doctoral Studies in the Visual Arts (B)

130 Neal Street, Portland ME 04102
County: Cumberland Identification: 667036
Telephone: (207) 879-8757 Carnegie Class: Not Classified
FAX Number: N/A Calendar System: Semester
URL: www.idsva.org
Established: 2007 Annual Graduate Tuition & Fees: $25,200
Enrollment: N/A Coed
Affiliation or Control: Independent Non-Profit IRS Status: 501(c)3
Highest Offering: Doctorate; No Undergraduates
Program: Professional
Accreditation: @EH

01 President ... George SMITH
03 Executive Vice President ... Amy CURTIS

Kaplan University-Maine (C)

265 Western Avenue, South Portland ME 04106
County: Cumberland FICE Identification: 009292
Unit ID: 160940
Telephone: (207) 774-6126 Carnegie Class: Assoc/PrivFP
FAX Number: (207) 774-1715 Calendar System: Other
URL: www.kucampus.edu
Established: 1966 Annual Undergrad Tuition & Fees: $11,057
Enrollment: 1,123 Coed
Affiliation or Control: Proprietary IRS Status: Proprietary
Highest Offering: Baccalaureate
Program: Occupational; 2-Year Principally Bachelor's Creditable; Business Emphasis
Accreditation: &NH

01 President ... Dr. Christopher QUINN
12 Lewiston Campus Director ... Matthew COTE
11 Director of Operations ... Lyndsey ERICKSON
05 Academic Dean ... Melanie BAAK
20 Associate Academic Dean-Lewiston ... Erin CONNOR
20 Associate Academic Dean-SoPortland ... Anne RYAN
32 Dean of Student Affairs-SoPortland ... Geraldine NEY
35 Director of Student Services-Lewist ... Karyn ESTES-LEWIS
08 Director of Library Services ... Martha OTT
14 KHE Team Leader/TS New England ... Stephen J. HORR
36 Director Career Services ... Robert KLAIBER
07 Director of Admissions-SoPortland ... Craig MACMUNN
07 Director of Admissions-Lewiston ... Kashina BRYANT
06 Registrar ... Lynsey WOOD
50 Director Business Administration ... Dr. Deborah WYMAN
88 Director of Criminal Justice ... Vacant
61 Director of Paralegal Studies ... Darren DEFOE
49 Director of Arts & Sciences ... Kevin KELLY
76 Director of Medical Assisting ... Dr. Peter NICKLESS
37 Director of Financial Aid ... Kelly KNIGHT
88 Director of Early Childhood Educ ... Lori LEVESQUE
88 Director of Travel & Hospitality ... Miriam GOUGH
40 Bookstore Manager ... Barbara VASSALLO
10 Business Office Manager ... Carol A. GAGNON

† Regional accreditation is carried under the parent institution in Davenport, IA.

The Landing School (D)

PO Box 1490, Kennebunkport ME 04046
County: York FICE Identification: 023613
Telephone: (207) 985-7976 Carnegie Class: Not Classified
FAX Number: (207) 985-7942 Calendar System: Other
URL: www.landingschool.edu
Established: 1978 Annual Undergrad Tuition & Fees: $19,000
Enrollment: 68 Coed
Affiliation or Control: Independent Non-Profit IRS Status: 501(c)3
Highest Offering: Associate Degree
Program: Occupational
Accreditation: ACCSC

01 President ... Mr. Robert DECOLFMACKER

Maine College of Art (E)

522 Congress St, Portland ME 04101
County: Cumberland FICE Identification: 011673
Unit ID: 161509
Telephone: (207) 775-3052 Carnegie Class: Spec/Arts
FAX Number: (207) 775-5087 Calendar System: Semester
URL: www.meca.edu
Established: 1882 Annual Undergrad Tuition & Fees: $29,345
Enrollment: 356 Coed
Affiliation or Control: Independent Non-Profit IRS Status: 501(c)3
Highest Offering: Master's
Program: Liberal Arts And General; Professional; Fine Arts Emphasis
Accreditation: EH, ART

01 President ... Mr. Donald TUSKI
05 Dean/Vice Pres Academic Affairs ... Mr. Christopher WHITTEY
03 Executive Vice President ... Ms. Beth ELICKER
30 VP Advancement & College Relations ... Mr. Tim KANE
07 Director of Admissions ... Ms. Grace HOPKINS-LISLE
32 Director of Student Affairs ... Mr. Melvin ADAMS
10 Director of Business Services ... Mr. Phil STEVENS
06 Registrar ... Ms. Anne DENNISON
37 Director of Financial Aid ... Ms. Adrienne AMARI
26 Dir Public Relations & Publications ... Ms. Jessica J. TOMLINSON
51 Director Continuing Studies ... Vacant
18 Chief Facilities/Physical Plant ... Mr. Douglas DOERING
08 Librarian ... Ms. Moira STEVENS
13 Director Technology Support ... Mr. David BRANSON

*Maine Community College System (F)

323 State Street, Augusta ME 04330-7131
County: Kennebec Identification: 666092
Unit ID: 409713
Telephone: (207) 629-4000 Carnegie Class: N/A
FAX Number: (207) 629-4048
URL: www.mccs.me.edu

01 President ... Dr. John FITZSIMMONS

*Central Maine Community College (G)

1250 Turner Street, Auburn ME 04210-6498
County: Androscoggin FICE Identification: 005276
Unit ID: 161077
Telephone: (207) 755-5100 Carnegie Class: Assoc/Pub-R-M
FAX Number: (207) 755-5491 Calendar System: Semester
URL: www.cmcc.edu
Established: 1964 Annual Undergrad Tuition & Fees (In-State): $3,324
Enrollment: 2,870 Coed
Affiliation or Control: State IRS Status: 501(c)3
Highest Offering: Associate Degree
Program: Occupational; 2-Year Principally Bachelor's Creditable
Accreditation: EH, ADNUR, ENGT

02 President ... Dr. Scott E. KNAPP
05 Dean Academic Affairs ... Dr. Judy WILDER
06 Registrar ... Mr. Ronald BOLSTRIDGE
10 Dean of Finance and General Service ... Ms. Pamela REMIERES-MORIN
37 Director of Financial Aid ... Mr. John BOWIE
31 Dean Corporate/Community Services ... Ms. Diane DOSTIE
32 Dean of Students ... Ms. Betsy LIBBY
30 Dean Planning/Development/PR ... Mr. Roger PHILIPPON
72 Director of Technology/Prep ... Mr. Walter RIDLON
08 Head Librarian ... Ms. Judith FROST
18 Chief Physical Plant ... Mr. Raymond MASSE
22 Affirmative Action Officer ... Ms. Barbara OWEN
39 Director of Housing/Athletic Dir ... Mr. David GONYEA
40 Director of Bookstore ... Ms. Christine MORIN
15 Director of Human Resources ... Ms. Barbara OWEN
07 Director of Admissions ... Mr. Marc GOSSELIN

*Eastern Maine Community College (H)

354 Hogan Road, Bangor ME 04401-4280
County: Penobscot FICE Identification: 005277
Unit ID: 161138
Telephone: (207) 974-4600 Carnegie Class: Assoc/Pub-R-M
FAX Number: (207) 974-4608 Calendar System: Semester
URL: www.emcc.edu
Established: 1966 Annual Undergrad Tuition & Fees (In-State): $3,720
Enrollment: 2,184 Coed
Affiliation or Control: State IRS Status: 501(c)3
Highest Offering: Associate Degree
Program: Occupational; 2-Year Principally Bachelor's Creditable; Liberal Arts And General
Accreditation: EH, ADNUR, MAC, RAD, SURGT

02 President ... Dr. Lawrence M. BARRETT
05 Academic Dean ... Dr. Pamela PROULX-CURRY
10 Dir Finance & Auxiliary Services ... Mr. Michael OSBORNE
09 Dean Inst Research/Enrollment Mgmt ... Mr. Daniel CROCKER
30 Dir Development & Business Services ... Mr. E. Michael BALLESTEROS
07 Director of Admissions ... Ms. Elizabeth RUSSELL
15 Director Personnel Services ... Mr. Noah LUNDY
08 Librarian ... Ms. Janet BLOOD
37 Director of Financial Aid ... Ms. Candace WARD
13 Dean of Communication/Info Tech ... Mr. Timothy CONROY
18 Dir Facilities Mgmt/Student Life ... Mr. Daniel BELYEA
20 Assistant Academic Dean ... Ms. Merlene SANBORN
26 Public Relations Officer ... Ms. CarolAnne DUBE

*Kennebec Valley Community College (I)

92 Western Avenue, Fairfield ME 04937-1367
County: Somerset FICE Identification: 009826
Unit ID: 161192
Telephone: (207) 453-5000 Carnegie Class: Assoc/Pub-R-M
FAX Number: (207) 453-5010 Calendar System: Semester
URL: www.kvcc.me.edu
Established: 1970 Annual Undergrad Tuition & Fees (In-State): $3,315
Enrollment: 2,564 Coed
Affiliation or Control: State IRS Status: 501(c)3
Highest Offering: Associate Degree
Program: Occupational; 2-Year Principally Bachelor's Creditable; Liberal Arts And General; Professional
Accreditation: EH, ACBSP, ADNUR, DMS, MAC, OTA, PTAA, RAD

02 President ... Dr. Barbara W. WOODLEE
05 Academic Dean/Vice President ... Mrs. Karen WHITE
13 Dean of Information Technology ... Mr. Ryan CONNON
32 Dean of Student Affairs ... Ms. Karen NORMANDIN
10 Dean of Finance & Administration ... Mr. John DELILE
06 Registrar ... Mrs. Lisa YORK-LEMELIN
30 Director of Development ... Ms. Michelle WEBB
07 Director of Admissions ... Mr. Jim BOURGOIN
37 Director Student Financial Aid ... Ms. Anne CONNORS

*Northern Maine Community College (J)

33 Edgemont Drive, Presque Isle ME 04769-2099
County: Aroostook FICE Identification: 005760
Unit ID: 161484
Telephone: (207) 768-2700 Carnegie Class: Assoc/Pub-R-S
FAX Number: (207) 768-2831 Calendar System: Semester
URL: www.nmcc.edu
Established: 1961 Annual Undergrad Tuition & Fees (In-State): $3,343
Enrollment: 1,116 Coed
Affiliation or Control: State IRS Status: 501(c)3
Highest Offering: Associate Degree
Program: Occupational; 2-Year Principally Bachelor's Creditable
Accreditation: EH, ACBSP, ADNUR

02 President ... Mr. Timothy D. CROWLEY
05 Interim Academic Dean ... Mr. Ronald FITZGERALD
32 Dean of Students ... Mr. William G. EGELER
10 Director of Finance ... Mr. Larry LAPLANTE
51 Dean of Continuing Education ... Vacant
30 Director Development & College Rels ... Mr. Jason PARENT
07 Director of Admissions ... Mr. Eugene MCCLUSKEY
20 Assistant Dean of Instruction ... Vacant
06 Registrar ... Ms. Betsy A. HARRIS
37 Asst Director for Financial Aid ... Ms. Norma M. SMITH
39 Director of Housing & Resident Life ... Mr. Thomas J. RICHARD
38 Director of Counseling ... Ms. Tammy NELSON
18 Director of Facilities ... Mr. Barry INGRAHAM
21 Business Manager ... Mr. Philip R. BROWN

15 Human Resource Manager ..... Mr. Thomas J. RICHARD
40 Bookstore Manager ..... Ms. Rebecca A. MAYNARD
88 Tech Prep Coordinator ..... Ms. Elizabeth M. MORGAN

*Southern Maine Community College (A)

Fort Road, South Portland ME 04106-1698
County: Cumberland FICE Identification: 005525
Unit ID: 161545
Telephone: (207) 741-5500 Carnegie Class: Assoc/Pub-R-M
FAX Number: (207) 741-5751 Calendar System: Semester
URL: www.smccme.edu
Established: 1946 Annual Undergrad Tuition & Fees (In-State): $3,961
Enrollment: 7,010 Coed
Affiliation or Control: State IRS Status: 501(c)3
Highest Offering: Associate Degree
Program: Occupational; 2-Year Principally Bachelor's Creditable; Liberal Arts And General
Accreditation: EH, ACFEI, ADNUR, DIETT, MAC, RAD, RTT

02 President/CEO ..... James O. ORTIZ
05 Vice President/Academic Dean ..... Janet M. SORTOR
32 Dean of Student Affairs ..... Diane M. VICKREY
26 Dean of Communications ..... Vacant
84 Associate Dean of Enrollment ..... Staci GRASKY
35 Associate Dean of Student Services ..... Mark A. KROGMAN
04 Exec Assistant to the President ..... Laura E. LIBBY
12 Asst to Vice Pres/Dir Bath Campus ..... Vacant
10 Dean of Finance ..... Robert COOMBS
11 Dean of Administration ..... Scott BEATTY
30 Dean of Advancement ..... Kaylene WAINDLE
37 Director of Financial Aid ..... Michel LUSSIER
36 Director of Student Development ..... Shane LONG
09 Director of Institutional Research ..... Diane VICKREY
19 Director Campus Security ..... Joseph MANHARDT
41 Director of Athletics ..... Matthew RICHARDS
72 Computer Technology Chair ..... Howard BURPEE
18 Plant Maintenance Engineer III ..... James RENY
88 Learning Assistance Chair ..... Joyce LESLIE
40 Manager Campus Store ..... Cherie BRYANT
21 Manager of Financial Services ..... Shaun GRAY
21 Business Manager of Student Billing ..... Irene FINCH
15 HR & Benefits Manager ..... Denise RENY

*Washington County Community College (B)

One College Drive, Calais ME 04619-9704
County: Washington FICE Identification: 009231
Unit ID: 161581
Telephone: (207) 454-1000 Carnegie Class: Assoc/Pub-R-S
FAX Number: (207) 454-1026 Calendar System: Semester
URL: www.wccc.me.edu
Established: 1968 Annual Undergrad Tuition & Fees (In-State): $3,400
Enrollment: 504 Coed
Affiliation or Control: State IRS Status: 501(c)3
Highest Offering: Associate Degree
Program: Occupational; 2-Year Principally Bachelor's Creditable
Accreditation: EH

02 President ..... Dr. Joyce B. HEDLUND
05 Dean of Academic & Student Affairs ..... Mr. David MARKOW
10 Dean of Finance & Admin Services ..... Ms. Desiree THOMPSON
04 Director of HR and Public Relations ..... Ms. Tina ERSKINE
84 Assoc Dean Enroll/Retention Svcs ..... Ms. Susan MINGO
31 Dean of Community Education ..... Mr. Darin L. MCGAW
07 Director of Admissions ..... Ms. Susan MINGO

*York County Community College (C)

112 College Drive, Wells ME 04090-0529
County: York FICE Identification: 031229
Unit ID: 420440
Telephone: (207) 646-9282 Carnegie Class: Assoc/Pub-R-S
FAX Number: (207) 646-9675 Calendar System: Semester
URL: www.yccc.edu
Established: 1994 Annual Undergrad Tuition & Fees (In-State): $3,315
Enrollment: 1,393 Coed
Affiliation or Control: State IRS Status: 501(c)3
Highest Offering: Associate Degree
Program: Occupational; 2-Year Principally Bachelor's Creditable
Accreditation: EH

02 President ..... Dr. Charles M. LYONS
05 Vice President/Academic Dean ..... Ms. Paula GAGNON
30 Dean of Institutional Advancement ..... Dr. John J. RAINONE
32 Dean of Students ..... Dr. Corinne KOWPAK
10 Dean of Finance & Administration ..... Ms. Nancy DROUIN
26 Dir of Marketing & Public Relations ..... Ms. Debra LAVOIE
51 Director of Continuing Education ..... Ms. Paulette MILLETTE
04 Admin Assistant to the President ..... Ms. Monica L. DUMONT
20 Associate Academic Dean ..... Ms. Doreen ROGAN
08 Director Library/Learning Resources ..... Ms. Amber TATNALL
88 Faculty Development Coordinator ..... Ms. Stefanie FORSTER
35 Assistant Dean of Students ..... Ms. Debra DUMOND
07 Director of Admissions ..... Mr. Fred QUISTGARD
84 Director of Enrollment Services ..... Ms. Jessica SHAFFER
37 Director Financial Aid ..... Mr. David DAIGLE
13 Director of Technology ..... Mr. Tim DUNNE

21 Business Manager ..... Mr. Samuel ELLIS
15 Human Resources & Benefits Manager ..... Ms. Ellen HARFORD
18 Manager of Facilities ..... Mr. Dana PETERSEN

Maine Maritime Academy (D)

Castine ME 04420-0001
County: Hancock FICE Identification: 002044
Unit ID: 161299
Telephone: (207) 326-4311 Carnegie Class: Bac/Diverse
FAX Number: (207) 326-2218 Calendar System: Semester
URL: www.mma.edu
Established: 1941 Annual Undergrad Tuition & Fees (In-State): $15,105
Enrollment: 923 Coed
Affiliation or Control: State IRS Status: 501(c)3
Highest Offering: Master's
Program: Professional
Accreditation: EH, ENG, ENGT

01 President ..... Dr. William J. BRENNAN
05 Academic Dean ..... Dr. John BARLOW
11 Vice Pres Administration & Finance ..... Mr. Richard R. ERICSON
84 Vice Pres of Enrollment Management ..... Mr. Jeffrey LOUSTAUNAU
30 Vice President for Advancement ..... Ms. Ellie WILLMANN
15 Human Resource Officer ..... Mr. James SOUCIE
32 Chief Student Life Officer ..... Ms. Lauren GARRETT
35 Dean of Student Services ..... Ms. Deidra DAVIS
36 Placement Director ..... Mr. John WORTH
07 Director of Admissions ..... Mr. Jeffrey WRIGHT
06 Registrar ..... Mr. Thomas SAWYER
29 Director Alumni Relations ..... Mr. Paul MERCER
37 Director Student Financial Aid ..... Ms. Kathy HEATH
38 Director Student Counseling ..... Mr. Paul FERREIRA
08 Head Librarian ..... Mr. H. Brent HALL
10 Chief Business Officer ..... Ms. Diana SNAPP
18 Chief Facilities/Physical Plant ..... Ms. Stacey ERICSON
20 Associate Academic Dean ..... Ms. Joceline BOUCHER
26 Chief Public Relations Officer ..... Ms. Janice ZENTER

New England School of Communications (E)

One College Circle, Bangor ME 04401-2999
County: Penobscot FICE Identification: 023471
Unit ID: 070027
Telephone: (207) 941-7176 Carnegie Class: Spec/Other
FAX Number: (207) 941-7139 Calendar System: Semester
URL: www.nescom.edu
Established: 1981 Annual Undergrad Tuition & Fees: $12,744
Enrollment: 514 Coed
Affiliation or Control: Independent Non-Profit IRS Status: 501(c)3
Highest Offering: Baccalaureate
Program: Occupational
Accreditation: ACCSC

01 President ..... Mr. Thomas C. JOHNSTON
03 Executive Vice President ..... Mr. Benjamin E. HASKELL
07 Director of Admissions ..... Mrs. Louise G. GRANT
06 Registrar ..... Ms. Anne E. REED
37 Director of Student Financial Aid ..... Ms. Nicole REDIKER
29 Director Alumni Relations ..... Mr. Mark NASON

Saint Joseph's College of Maine (F)

278 Whites Bridge Road, Standish ME 04084-5236
County: Cumberland FICE Identification: 002051
Unit ID: 161518
Telephone: (207) 892-6766 Carnegie Class: Master's M
FAX Number: (207) 893-7861 Calendar System: Semester
URL: www.sjcme.edu
Established: 1912 Annual Undergrad Tuition & Fees: $28,700
Enrollment: 2,775 Coed
Affiliation or Control: Roman Catholic IRS Status: 501(c)3
Highest Offering: Master's
Program: Liberal Arts And General; Teacher Preparatory; Professional
Accreditation: EH, NURSE

01 President ..... Dr. E. Joseph LEE
03 Executive Vice President ..... Mr. John ZERILLO
05 Vice President for Academic Affairs ..... Dr. Randall KRIEG
30 VP Institutional Advancement ..... Mr. Michael DEMPSEY
84 Vice Pres Enrollment Management ..... Ms. Kathleen DAVIS
88 Vice Pres for Sponsorship & Mission ..... Sr. Kathleen SULLIVAN
58 Dean Graduate/Prof Studies ..... Ms. Lynn OLSON
07 Dean of Admission ..... Mr. Vincent KLOSKOWSKI
37 Assoc Dean Student Financial Aid ..... Ms. Andrea CROSS
32 Dean of Student Life ..... Ms. Lynn BROWN
06 Director of Academic Records ..... Mr. Kevin PAQUETTE
08 Director of the Library ..... Ms. Richelle DAVIS
29 Director of Alumni ..... Ms. Kristen JEWETT
29 Dir Alumni & Parent Communications ..... Ms. Kristina GREEN
40 Director of Annual Giving ..... Ms. Heather PLATI
18 Chief Facilities/Physical Plant ..... Mr. Charles DAWES
41 Athletic Director ..... Mr. Brian CURTIN
26 Chief Public Relations Officer ..... Mr. William MCCARTHY
38 Director Student Counseling ..... Dr. Elizabeth WIESEN
13 Director Information Systems ..... Ms. Gayle LANGIS
23 Director Health Services ..... Vacant
36 Director Career Services ..... Mr. Thomas NOVAK
96 Director of Purchasing ..... Ms. Carlene P. LEMIEUX
39 Director Student Housing ..... Mr. Jon BLANCHARD

11 Chief Administration Officer ..... Ms. Janet LAFLAMME
20 Assistant Dean ..... Mr. David E. ROUSSEL

Thomas College (G)

180 W River Road, Waterville ME 04901-5097
County: Kennebec FICE Identification: 002052
Unit ID: 161563
Telephone: (207) 859-1111 Carnegie Class: Bac/Diverse
FAX Number: (207) 859-1114 Calendar System: Semester
URL: www.thomas.edu
Established: 1894 Annual Undergrad Tuition & Fees: $22,160
Enrollment: 984 Coed
Affiliation or Control: Independent Non-Profit IRS Status: 501(c)3
Highest Offering: Master's
Program: Liberal Arts And General; Teacher Preparatory; Professional
Accreditation: EH

01 President ..... Dr. George R. SPANN
05 Provost ..... Dr. Thomas EDWARDS
10 Senior Vice President/CFO/Treasurer ..... Ms. Beth B. GIBBS
13 Vice President Information Services ..... Mr. Christopher RHODA
84 Vice Pres Enrollment Management ..... Mr. Robert CALLAHAN
32 Vice President Student Affairs ..... Ms. Lisa DESAUTELS-POLIQUIN
30 Vice Pres Institutional Advancement ..... Mr. Robert M. MOORE
58 Asst Dean Continuing Ed/Grad School ..... Ms. Suzanne POOLER
07 Assoc Dean of Admissions ..... Ms. Wendy MARTIN
37 Director Student Financial Services ..... Ms. Jeannine BOSSE
36 Director Career Services ..... Mr. Richard GRANT
35 Assistant Dean of Students ..... Ms. Hannah GLADSTONE
18 Director of Physical Plant ..... Mr. James PARSONS
15 Director Human Resources ..... Ms. Michelle JOLER-LABBE
26 Director Public Relations ..... Ms. Jennifer BUKER
08 Director Library Services ..... Ms. Lisa AURIEMMA
06 Assistant Registrar ..... Ms. Meghan REITCHEL
29 Dir Annual Giving/Alumni Relations ..... Ms. Cathy DUMONT
40 Manager of Bookstore ..... Ms. Katie THOMAS

Unity College (H)

90 Quaker Hill Road, Unity ME 04988-9502
County: Waldo FICE Identification: 006858
Unit ID: 161572
Telephone: (207) 948-3131 Carnegie Class: Bac/Diverse
FAX Number: (207) 948-6277 Calendar System: Semester
URL: www.unity.edu
Established: 1966 Annual Undergrad Tuition & Fees: $21,850
Enrollment: 584 Coed
Affiliation or Control: Independent Non-Profit IRS Status: 501(c)3
Highest Offering: Baccalaureate
Program: Occupational; 2-Year Principally Bachelor's Creditable; Liberal Arts And General; Teacher Preparatory; Professional
Accreditation: EH

01 President ..... Dr. Stephen MULKEY
101 Exec Asst to President/Sec to Board ..... Ms. Chris MELANSON
05 Sr VP for Academic Affairs ..... Dr. Bill TRUMBALL
10 Vice Pres Finance & Administration ..... Ms. Eileen G. DRISCOLL
30 Vice Pres for College Advancement ..... Mr. Robert CONSTANTINE
32 Dean for Student Affairs ..... Mr. Gary ZANE
84 Dean of Enrollment Management ..... Ms. Alisa JOHNSON
06 Registrar ..... Ms. Holly A. HEIN
07 Director Admissions ..... Ms. Kay FIEDLER
88 Director Outdoor Adventure Center ..... Ms. Jessica STEELE
41 Director of Athletics ..... Mr. Chris KEIN
88 Director Dining Services ..... Ms. Sandy DONAHUE
18 Director Facilities & Public Safety ..... Mr. Roger DUVAL
37 Director Financial Aid ..... Mr. Rand E. NEWELL
23 Director Health & Wellness Center ..... Ms. Anna MCGALLIARD
16 Director Human Resources ..... Mrs. Kathleen HALE
13 Director Information Technology ..... Mr. Bill MORGAN
24 Director Learning Resource Center ..... Mr. James J. HORAN
08 Director Quimby Library ..... Mrs. Melora NORMAN
39 Director Residence Life ..... Mr. Stephen S. NASON
35 Director Student Accounts ..... Ms. Jeri ROBERTS
88 Director Writing Center ..... Ms. Judy WILLIAMS
26 Assoc Dir College Communications ..... Mr. Mark TARDIF
88 Sustainability Coordinator ..... Mr. Jesse PYLES
36 Career Consultant/Internship Coord ..... Ms. Nicole COLLINS
88 Community-Based Learning Coord ..... Ms. Jen OLIN
53 Co-Director of Teacher Education ..... Ms. Angela HARDY
19 Chief Public Safety Officer ..... Mr. Dean BESSEY
40 Manager Bookstore ..... Ms. Leigh JUSKEVICE

*University of Maine System Office (I)

16 Central Street, Bangor ME 04401-5106
County: Penobscot FICE Identification: 008012
Unit ID: 161280
Telephone: (207) 973-3200 Carnegie Class: N/A
FAX Number: (207) 973-3296
URL: www.maine.edu

01 Chancellor ..... Dr. Richard L. PATTENAUDE
05 Vice Chancellor Academic Affairs ..... Dr. James BREECE
10 CFO & Treasurer ..... Ms. Rebecca WYKE
43 University Counsel/Clerk of Board ..... Mr. J. Kelley WILTBANK
86 Asst to Chanc Governmental Rels ..... Mr. John LISNIK
15 Exec Director of Human Resources ..... Ms. Tracy BIGNEY
32 Exec Director of Student Affairs ..... Ms. Rosa REDONNETT
88 Director of Labor Relations ..... Mr. Frank GERRY
27 Chief Information Officer ..... Mr. Dick THOMPSON
18 Director of Facilities ..... Mr. M. F. Chip GAVIN

*University of Maine (A)

Orono ME 04469-0001
County: Penobscot FICE Identification: 002053
Unit ID: 161253
Telephone: (207) 581-1110 Carnegie Class: RU/H
FAX Number: (207) 581-1604 Calendar System: Semester
URL: www.umaine.edu
Established: 1865 Annual Undergrad Tuition & Fees (In-State): $10,588
Enrollment: 11,501 Coed
Affiliation or Control: State IRS Status: 501(c)3
Highest Offering: Doctorate
Program: Liberal Arts And General; Teacher Preparatory; Professional
Accreditation: EH, BUS, CLPSY, CS, DIETD, DIETI, ENG, ENGT, FOR, IPSY, MUS, NURSE, SP, SPAA, SW, TED

02 President ... Dr. Paul W. FERGUSON
05 Sr VP for Academic Affairs/Provost ... Dr. Susan J. HUNTER
10 Vice Pres Administration & Finance ... Ms. Janet WALDRON
30 Vice President for Development ... Mr. Eric F. ROLFSON
32 VP Student Affs/Dean of Students ... Dr. Robert DANA
46 Vice President for Research ... Dr. Michael ECKARDT
15 Asst Vice Pres for Human Resources ... Mr. Steve WEINBERGER
39 Int Asst VP of Auxiliary Services ... Mr. Daniel STURRUP
20 Assoc Provost/Dean Undergrad Educ ... Dr. Stuart L. MARRS
04 Senior Advisor to the President ... Vacant
08 Dean of Libraries ... Ms. Joyce RUMERY
13 Exec Dir of Information Technology ... Dr. John GREGORY
18 Ex Dir Facilities/Real Estate/Plng ... Ms. Elaine L. CLARK
26 Director University Relations ... Mr. Joseph CARR
25 Director Research & Sponsor Program ... Mr. Michael HASTINGS
06 Director Student Records ... Ms. Tammy LIGHT
07 Director of Admissions ... Ms. Sharon OLIVER
37 Director of Financial Aid ... Ms. Peggy L. CRAWFORD
36 Director of Career Center ... Ms. Patricia B. COUNIHAN
09 Director Institutional Studies ... Mr. Ted COLADARCI
85 Director International Pgms ... Ms. Karen BOUCIAS
41 Athletic Director ... Mr. Steven W. ABBOTT
28 Director Equal Employment Diversity ... Ms. Karen KEMBLE
19 Dir of Public Safety/Transportation ... Chief Roland LACROIX
29 Director Alumni Relations ... Mr. Todd SAUCIER
40 Interim Director of Bookstore ... Mr. Richard YOUNG
96 Dir Purchasing/Resource Efficiency ... Ms. June BALDACCI
21 Dir of Budget & Business Services ... Mrs. Claire STRICKLAND
38 Director Student Counseling ... Mr. Douglas JOHNSON
49 Dean Liberal Arts & Sciences ... Dr. Jeffrey E. HECKER
50 Int Dean Bus/Public Policy/Health ... Dr. Ivan MANEV
53 Dean Education/Human Development ... Dr. Anne POOLER
54 Dean Engineering ... Dr. Dana HUMPHREY
65 Dean Natural Science/Forestry/Agric ... Dr. Edward ASHWORTH
51 Interim Dean Lifelong Learning ... Dr. Lucille A. ZEPH
58 Dean Graduate School ... Dr. Daniel H. SANDWEISS

*University of Maine at Augusta (B)

46 University Drive, Augusta ME 04330-9410
County: Kennebec FICE Identification: 006760
Unit ID: 161217
Telephone: (207) 621-3000 Carnegie Class: Bac/Assoc
FAX Number: (207) 621-3116 Calendar System: Semester
URL: www.uma.edu
Established: 1965 Annual Undergrad Tuition & Fees (In-State): $7,125
Enrollment: 5,074 Coed
Affiliation or Control: State IRS Status: 501(c)3
Highest Offering: Baccalaureate
Program: 2-Year Principally Bachelor's Creditable; Liberal Arts And General; Professional
Accreditation: EH, ADNUR, DA, DH, MLTAD

02 President ... Dr. Allyson HUGHES HANDLEY
05 Executive Vice President/Provost ... Dr. Joe S. SZAKAS
10 Vice President of Finance and Admin ... Ms. Ellen SCHNEITER
11 Exec Director of Admin Services ... Ms. Sheri R. STEVENS
04 Executive Assistant to President ... Ms. Kathleen KING
08 Dean of Libraries ... Dr. Thomas E. ABBOTT
12 Dean Bangor Campus ... Ms. Gillian JORDAN
84 Dean of Enrollment Services ... Mr. Jon HENRY
32 Dean of Students ... Ms. Kathleen A. DEXTER
107 Interim Dean Prof Studies ... Ms. Brenda MCALEER
37 Director of Financial Aid ... Ms. Sherry MCCOLLETT
06 Registrar ... Ms. Ann CORBETT
15 Director Personnel Services ... Mr. David LANE
18 Chief Facilities/Physical Plant ... Mr. Peter ST. MICHEL
38 Dir of Cornerstone & Counseling ... Mr. William STONE
88 Director of Advising ... Ms. Sheri C. FRASER
35 Director of Student Life ... Mr. Warren NEWTON
40 Director Bookstore ... Mr. Jerry GARTHOFF
26 Dir of Communications & Marketing ... Mr. Bob STEIN
30 Director of University Advancement ... Ms. Joyce BLANCHARD

*University of Maine at Farmington (C)

224 Main Street, Farmington ME 04938-1911
County: Franklin FICE Identification: 002040
Unit ID: 161226
Telephone: (207) 778-7000 Carnegie Class: Bac/Diverse
FAX Number: (207) 778-7247 Calendar System: Semester
URL: www.umf.maine.edu
Established: 1864 Annual Undergrad Tuition & Fees (In-State): $9,374
Enrollment: 2,322 Coed
Affiliation or Control: State IRS Status: 501(c)3
Highest Offering: Master's
Program: Liberal Arts And General; Teacher Preparatory
Accreditation: EH, TED

02 President ... Dr. Theodora J. KALIKOW
05 Interim VP Academic Affairs/Provost ... Dr. Daniel P. GUNN
11 Interim Vice Pres Administration ... Mr. Ryan LOW
32 Vice Pres Student & Community Svcs ... Ms. Celeste BRANHAM
07 Director of Admissions ... Mr. Jamie E. MARCUS
84 Vice Pres Enrollmt Mgmt & Mktg ... Mr. Roberto NOYA
88 Sustainability Coordinator ... Ms. Valerie O. HUEBNER
53 Assoc Provost & Dean of Education ... Dr. Katherine W. YARDLEY
20 Assoc Provost & Dean of Acad Svcs ... Dr. Robert L. LIVELY
89 Asst to Dean First Yr Experience ... Mr. Douglas H. RAWLINGS
92 Director of Honors Program ... Dr. Mellisa A. CLAWSON
88 Dir of Learning Assistance Center ... Ms. Claire N. NELSON
08 Director of Library ... Mr. Franklin D. ROBERTS
37 Financial Aid Director ... Mr. Ronald P. MILLIKEN
15 Dir Human Res/Administrative Svcs ... Ms. Laurie A. GARDNER
06 Director Adm Sys/Student Records ... Ms. Sharon L. NADEAU
88 Dir Admin Svcs Stdnt Health Ctr ... Mr. Robert A. PEDERSON
44 Dir Gift Planning & Stewardship ... Ms. Patricia A. CARPENTER
27 Director of Media Relations ... Ms. April C. MULHERIN
14 Ex Dir Information Technolog Svcs ... Mr. Frederick L. BRITTAIN
41 Dir Athletics/Fitness & Recreation ... Ms. Julie A. DAVIS
88 Dir Fitness & Recreation Center ... Mr. James D. TONER
88 Coordinator of Outdoor Recreation ... Ms. Elizabeth E. BREIDENBACH
39 Interim Director Residential Life ... Mr. Brian K. UFFORD
35 Dir Center for Stdnt Involvement ... Ms. Kirsten SWAN
23 Dir Clinical Svcs Stdnt Health Ctr ... Dr. Susan E. COCHRAN
18 Director of Facilities Management ... Mr. Bernard PRATT
19 Director of Public Safety ... Mr. Edward J. BLAIS
29 Director of Alumni Relations ... Ms. Jennifer A. ERIKSEN
88 Director of Dining Services ... Mr. Patrick ANDERSON

*University of Maine at Fort Kent (D)

23 University Drive, Fort Kent ME 04743-1292
County: Aroostook FICE Identification: 002041
Unit ID: 161235
Telephone: (207) 834-7500 Carnegie Class: Bac/Diverse
FAX Number: (207) 834-7503 Calendar System: Semester
URL: www.umfk.maine.edu
Established: 1878 Annual Undergrad Tuition & Fees (In-State): $7,462
Enrollment: 1,073 Coed
Affiliation or Control: State IRS Status: 501(c)3
Highest Offering: Baccalaureate
Program: Occupational; 2-Year Principally Bachelor's Creditable; Liberal Arts And General; Teacher Preparatory; Professional; Nursing Emphasis
Accreditation: EH, IACBE, NURSE

02 President ... Mr. Wilson G. HESS
05 Vice President Academic Affairs ... Dr. Rachel E. ALBERT
11 Vice President for Administration ... Mr. John D. MURPHY
06 Registrar/Director Inst Research ... Mr. Donald M. RAYMOND
15 Exec Director of Human Resources ... Ms. Tamara J. MITCHELL
66 Nursing Division Director ... Ms. Erin SOUCY
08 Dir of Information Svcs/Library ... Ms. Leslie E. KELLY
07 Director of Admissions ... Ms. Jill CAIRNS
37 Director of Financial Aid ... Mr. Michael HUDDY
26 Dir University Relations/Alum Affs ... Mr. Terence KELLY
18 Director of Facilities Management ... Mr. Andrew C. JACOBS
31 Dean of Community Education ... Mr. Scott A. VOISINE
28 Assoc Dir Res Life & Diversity Pgms ... Mr. Raymond R. PHINNEY
09 Assoc Dir of Institutional Research ... Mr. Joseph R. BJERKLIE
21 Director of Business Systems ... Ms. Leslie A. NICHOLS
36 Student Success Coordinator ... Ms. Catherine FECINTA

*University of Maine at Machias (E)

116 O'Brien Avenue, Machias ME 04654-1397
County: Washington FICE Identification: 002055
Unit ID: 161244
Telephone: (207) 255-1200 Carnegie Class: Bac/A&S
FAX Number: (207) 255-4864 Calendar System: Semester
URL: www.umm.maine.edu
Established: 1909 Annual Undergrad Tuition & Fees (In-State): $7,480
Enrollment: 951 Coed
Affiliation or Control: State IRS Status: 501(c)3
Highest Offering: Baccalaureate
Program: Liberal Arts And General; Teacher Preparatory
Accreditation: EH, NRPA

02 President ... Dr. Cynthia E. HUGGINS
05 Vice Pres Academic Affairs/Provost ... Mr. Stuart G. SWAIN
10 Vice Pres Finance/Administration ... Mr. Thomas L. POTTER
32 Director Student Life ... Vacant
06 Registrar ... Ms. Mary STOVER
08 Director Library ... Ms. Angelynn KING
07 Director Admissions ... Mr. David DOLLINS
15 Director Human Resources ... Ms. Kim PAGE
37 Director Student Financial Aid ... Mrs. Stephanie D. LARRABEE
18 Director Physical Facilities ... Mr. Robert FARRIS
26 Director Public Relations ... Mr. Erik SMITH
13 Director Information Technology ... Mr. Michael MATIS
41 Director Athletics ... Mr. Brac BRADY

*University of Maine at Presque Isle (F)

181 Main Street, Presque Isle ME 04769-2888
County: Aroostook FICE Identification: 002033
Unit ID: 161341
Telephone: (207) 768-9400 Carnegie Class: Bac/Diverse
FAX Number: (207) 768-9608 Calendar System: Semester
URL: www.umpi.edu
Established: 1903 Annual Undergrad Tuition & Fees (In-State): $7,200
Enrollment: 1,434 Coed
Affiliation or Control: State IRS Status: 501(c)3
Highest Offering: Baccalaureate
Program: Liberal Arts And General; Teacher Preparatory; Professional
Accreditation: EH, MLTAD, SW

02 President ... Dr. Donald N. ZILLMAN
05 Vice President Academic Affairs ... Dr. Michael F. SONNTAG
11 Vice Pres Administration & Finance ... Mr. Charles G. BONIN
35 Dean of Students ... Ms. Christine CORSELLO
07 Director of Admissions ... Ms. Erin V. BENSON
15 Asst Director of Human Resources ... Ms. Jennie R. SAVAGE
38 Director of Counseling Services ... Mr. John D. HARRINGTON
08 Dir Library/Cmptr Tech/Media Svcs ... Vacant
06 Director of Student Records ... Ms. Kathy K. DAVIS
37 Director of Financial Aid ... Mr. Christopher A R. BELL
36 Director Student Placement ... Ms. Barbara J. DEVANEY
39 Director Residence Life ... Mr. James D. STEPP
41 Director of Athletics ... Ms. Christine CORSELLO
26 Director of Media Relations ... Ms. Rachel RICE
29 Director of Alumni Relations ... Mr. Keith L. MADORE
40 Bookstore Manager ... Mr. Greg DOAK
18 Manager of Physical Facilities ... Mr. David L. ST. PETER

*University of Southern Maine (G)

96 Falmouth Street, PO Box 9300,
Portland ME 04101-9300
County: Cumberland FICE Identification: 002054
Unit ID: 161554
Telephone: (207) 780-4141 Carnegie Class: Master's L
FAX Number: (207) 780-4933 Calendar System: Semester
URL: www.usm.maine.edu
Established: 1878 Annual Undergrad Tuition & Fees (In-State): $7,590
Enrollment: 9,654 Coed
Affiliation or Control: State IRS Status: 501(c)3
Highest Offering: Doctorate
Program: Liberal Arts And General; Teacher Preparatory; Professional
Accreditation: EH, ART, BUS, CACREP, CORE, CS, ENG, EXSC, HSA, LAW, MUS, NAIT, NURSE, OT, SW, TEAC

02 President ... Dr. Selma BOTMAN
04 Special Asst to the President ... Dr. Timothy STEVENS
11 Chief Operating Officer ... Ms. Katherine GREENLEAF
05 Interim Provost/VPAA ... Dr. John WRIGHT
10 Chief Financial Officer/VP Admin ... Mr. Richard CAMPBELL
27 Chief Information Officer ... Mr. William WELLS
32 Chief Student Affairs Officer ... Mr. Craig HUTCHINSON
88 Chief Student Success Officer ... Dr. Susan CAMPBELL
30 Vice President for Advancement ... Ms. Margaret WESTON
13 Director Information Reporting ... Ms. Patricia DAVIS
18 Exec Director Facilities Management ... Mr. Bob BERTRAM
21 Director of Business Services ... Mr. Gregg N. ALLEN
24 University Librarian/Director ITMS ... Mr. David NUTTY
88 Director Academic Assessment Ctr ... Ms. Susan L. KING
38 Director of Health & Counseling ... Dr. Kristine BERTINI
15 VP Human Res & Sr Adv to the Pres ... Ms. Judith RYAN
26 Executive Director Public Affairs ... Mr. Robert S. CASWELL
37 Director of Financial Aid ... Mr. Keith DUBOIS
88 Executive Director Student Success ... Ms. Elizabeth HIGGINS
07 Dean of Undergraduate Admissions ... Mr. Scott STEINBERG
06 Registrar ... Mr. Steven RAND
22 Director of Equity and Compliance ... Mr. Daryl MCLLWAIN
72 Director CTEL ... Dr. Ann Marie JOHNSON
25 Dir of Office of Sponsored Programs ... Mr. Lawrence WAXLER
31 Director of Community Standards ... Mr. Stephen NELSON
30 Director of Development ... Mr. David HUGHES
41 Director of Athletics & Rec Sports ... Mr. Al BEAN
51 Director of Continued Education ... Ms. Monique LAROCQUE
39 Director of Residential Life ... Ms. Denise NELSON
40 Director of USM Bookstore ... Ms. Nicole PIAGET
61 Dean School of Law ... Mr. Peter PITEGOFF
50 Dean College of Mgmt & Human Svcs ... Dr. Joseph MCDONNELL
88 Dean College of Sci/Tech & Health ... Dr. Andrew ANDERSON
88 Dean of Arts/Humanities & Soc Sci ... Dr. Lynn KUZMA
12 Dean Lewiston-Auburn College ... Dr. Joyce GIBSON
58 Dean for Graduate Studies ... Vacant
35 Executive Director Student Success ... Mr. Joseph M. AUSTIN
88 Manager Audiovisual/Media Services ... Ms. Angela COOK
94 Director of Women's Studies ... Dr. Wendy CHAPKIS
09 Director of Institutional Research ... Dr. Cristi CARSON
20 Associate Provost Academic Affairs ... Dr. Dahlia LYNN
88 Coordinator Multicultural Affairs ... Mr. Reza JALALI
29 Director of Alumni Relations ... Ms. Peggy SCHICK
88 Director of Marketing ... Ms. Traci ST. PIERRE
42 Director of Interfaith Chaplaincy ... Ms. Andrea THOMPSON-MCCALL
102 President USM Foundation ... Ms. Margaret WESTON

University of New England (H)

11 Hills Beach Road, Biddeford ME 04005-9988
County: York FICE Identification: 002050
Unit ID: 161457
Telephone: (207) 283-0171 Carnegie Class: Master's L
FAX Number: (207) 282-6379 Calendar System: Semester
URL: www.une.edu
Established: 1831 Annual Undergrad Tuition & Fees: $29,430
Enrollment: 5,168 Coed
Affiliation or Control: Independent Non-Profit IRS Status: 501(c)3
Highest Offering: Doctorate
Program: Occupational; Liberal Arts And General; Teacher Preparatory; Professional

Accreditation: EH, @ACBSP, ADNUR, ANEST, ARCPA, DH, NUR, OSTEO, OT, @PHAR, PTA, SW

01 President .... Dr. Danielle RIPICH
04 Executive Asst to the President .... Ms. MaryLou KADLIK
05 Vice Pres Academic Affairs/ Provost .... Dr. Williams JACK
23 Sr Vice Pres Health Services .... Dr. Marc HAHN
18 Vice Pres Campus Services .... Mr. William BOLA
88 Vice President Clinical Affairs .... Dr. Dora MILLS
10 Vice Pres Fiscal Services .... Ms. Nicole TRUFANT
30 Vice Pres Institutional Advancement .... Vacant
63 Director School of Nurse Anesthesia .... Ms. Maribeth MASSIE
32 Vice Pres Student Affairs .... Dr. Cynthia FORREST
46 Vice Pres Research .... Dr. Timothy FORD
26 VP of Communications .... Mr. Thomas WHITE
102 Asst VP Institutional Advancement .... Mr. Scott MARCHILDON
15 Assoc VP Human Resources .... Mr. Richard ROESLER
30 Assoc VP Institutional Advancement .... Mr. William CHANCE
88 Assoc Provost Global Initiatives .... Dr. Anouar MAJID
49 Dean College Arts & Sciences .... Dr. Christine BROWN
17 Dean College Health Professions .... Dr. David WARD
63 Dean College Osteopathic Medicine .... Dr. Marc HAHN
67 Dean College of Pharmacy .... Dr. Gayle BRAZEAU
84 Dean Enrollment Management .... Ms. Karen LUCAS
52 Dean College of Dental Medicine .... Dr. James J. KOELBL
58 Dean Graduate Studies .... Dr. Timothy FORD
62 Dean Library Services .... Mr. Andrew GOLUB
35 Asst Dean Students .... Mr. Ray HANDY
88 Asst Dean Student Support Svcs .... Mr. John LANGEVIN
17 Asst Dean College of Health Prof .... Mrs. Karen PARDUE@UNE.EDU
07 Assoc Director Admissions .... Mr. Robert PECCHIA
66 Assoc Director of Nursing .... Ms. Patricia MORGAN
49 Assoc Dean College Arts & Sciences .... Ms. Paulette ST. OURS
76 Assoc Dean Health Professions .... Dr. Clay GRAYBEAL
29 Director Alumni Relations .... Ms. Amy HAIL
41 Director Athletics & Recreation .... Ms. Kimberly ALLEN
88 Director Campus Planning .... Mr. Alan THIBEAULT
19 Director Campus Safety & Security .... Mr. Donald CLARK
104 Director Ctr Intl Education .... Ms. Trisha MASON
52 Director of Dental Hygiene .... Ms. Bernice MILLS
88 Dirctor Exercise & Sport Perf .... Mr. Wayne LAMARRE
09 Director Institutional Research .... Mr. Kuldeep PUPPALA
23 Director Medical U Health Care .... Dr. Christopher PEZZULLO
66 Director of Nursing HSM .... Ms. Bonnie DAVIS
63 Director Occupational Therapy .... Mr. Regi ROBNETT
63 Director of Physical Therapy .... Mr. Michael SHELDON
96 Director Purch/Risk Mgmt/Contract .... Mr. William BOLA
62 Director Reference Services .... Ms. Barbara SWARTZLANDER
39 Director Residence Life .... Ms. Jennifer DEBURRO
70 Director Social Work .... Dr. Martha WILSON
88 Director Sponsored Programs .... Mr. Nicholas GERE
38 Director Student Counseling .... Dr. John LANGEVIN
37 Exec Director Student Fiscal Svcs .... Mr. Paul HENDERSON

MARYLAND

Allegany College of Maryland (A)

12401 Willowbrook Road, SE,
Cumberland MD 21502-2596

County: Allegany | FICE Identification: 002057 | Unit ID: 161688
Telephone: (301) 784-5000 | Carnegie Class: Assoc/Pub-R-M
FAX Number: (301) 784-5050 | Calendar System: Semester
URL: www.allegany.edu
Established: 1961 | Annual Undergrad Tuition & Fees (In-District): $3,266
Enrollment: 4,069 | Coed
Affiliation or Control: Local | IRS Status: 501(c)3
Highest Offering: Associate Degree
Program: Occupational; 2-Year Principally Bachelor's Creditable
Accreditation: M, ADNUR, COMTA, DH, MAC, MLTAD, OTA, PTAA, RAD

01 President .... Dr. Cynthia S. BAMBARA
05 Int Vice Pres Instructional Affairs .... Mrs. Fran LEIBFREID
12 Vice President PA Campuses .... Dr. James M. SNIDER
10 Vice President Finance .... Mr. Dennis STEVENS
30 VP Col Advancement/Enroll Mgmt .... Mrs. Linda A. PRICE
11 VP Administrative Services .... Mrs. Mona CLITES
32 VP Student Services .... Dr. B. Renee CONNER
51 VP of Continuing Education .... Dr. Barbara R. BEEBE
14 Assoc Dean Computer Services .... Mr. Tim PELESKY
21 Associate Dean of Finance .... Vacant
25 Director Fundraising/Grant Writing .... Mr. David R. JONES
37 Director Student Financial Aid .... Mrs. Vicki SMITH
07 Director Admissions/Registration .... Mrs. Cathy M. NOLAN
18 Director of Physical Plant .... Mr. Nate EMORY
08 Director of Learning Resources .... Mr. Robert D. BALDWIN
26 Public Relations/Dir Recruitment .... Ms. Shauna N. MCQUADE
41 Athletic Director .... Mr. Robert D. KIRK
29 Secretary Alumni Association .... Mrs. Gail ROTRUCK
50 Director of Business/Indus Training .... Vacant
51 Director Professional Cont Educ .... Mrs. Becky L. HADRA
09 Director of Institutional Research .... Vacant
69 Director Health Prof Cont Education .... Ms. Linda ATKINSON
38 Director Student Counseling .... Vacant
15 Director Personnel .... Mrs. Rhonda WILES
04 Assistant to Vice President .... Mrs. Rebecca A. COOL

Anne Arundel Community College (B)

101 College Parkway, Arnold MD 21012-1895

County: Anne Arundel | FICE Identification: 002058 | Unit ID: 161767
Telephone: (410) 777-2222 | Carnegie Class: Assoc/Pub-S-SC
FAX Number: (410) 777-2489 | Calendar System: Semester
URL: www.aacc.edu
Established: 1961 | Annual Undergrad Tuition & Fees (In-District): $3,652
Enrollment: 17,665 | Coed
Affiliation or Control: State/Local | IRS Status: 501(c)3
Highest Offering: Associate Degree
Program: Occupational; 2-Year Principally Bachelor's Creditable
Accreditation: M, ACFEI, ADNUR, ARCPA, EMT, MAC, MLTAD, PTAA, RAD

01 President .... Dr. Martha A. SMITH
05 Vice President for Learning .... Dr. Andrew L. MEYER
10 VP Learning Resources Management .... Ms. Melissa A. BEARDMORE
03 VP for Learner Support Services .... Ms. Felicia L. PATTERSON
20 Associate Vice President Learning .... Ms. Patricia A. CASEY-WHITEMAN
106 Dean of Virtual Campus .... Ms. Jean M. RUNYON
30 Exec Dir Institutional Advancement .... Vacant
30 Director of Development .... Vacant
32 Dean of Student Services .... Dr. Ivan L. HARRELL
76 Dean School Health/Wellness/Phys Ed .... Dr. Claire L. SMITH
66 Director of Nursing .... Ms. Beth Anne BATTURS
49 Dean School Arts & Sciences .... Dr. Daniel F. SYMANCYK
72 Dean Sch Bus/Computing/Tech Stds .... Ms. Kelly A. KOERMER
51 Dean Sch of Continuing/Prof Studies .... Dr. Faith A. HARLAND-WHITE
103 Dean of Workforce Development .... Dr. Laura E. WEIDNER
22 Controller .... Ms. Martha D. ROTHSCHILD
21 Executive Director of Finance .... Mr. Andrew P. LITTLE
14 Chief Technology Officer/Info Svcs .... Ms. Shirin M. GOODARZI
08 Director of Library .... Ms. Cynthia K. STEINHOFF
06 Registrar .... Ms. Nancy A. BEIER
09 Dean Plng/Rsrch/Inst Assess .... Dr. Ricka K. FINE
15 Exec Director of Human Resources .... Ms. Suzanne L. BOYER
26 Exec Director PR & Marketing .... Mr. Daniel B. BAUM
37 Director of Financial Aid .... Mr. Richard C. HEATH
07 Dir Admissions/Enroll Development .. Mr. Thomas J. MCGINN, III
11 Exec Dir of Administrative Services .... Mr. Maury L. CHAPUT, JR.
35 Asst Dean Student Devel & Success .... Ms. Terry M. CLAY
84 Asst Dean Enrollment Services .... Dr. John F. GRABOWSKI
36 Dir Counseling/Advising/Reten Svcs .... Ms. Bonnie J. GARRETT
35 Director of Student Life .... Ms. Christine M. STORCK
22 Federal Compliance Officer .... Ms. Karen L. COOK
40 College Bookstore Manager .... Mr. Steven M. PEGG
19 Director Public Safety .... Mr. J. Gary LYLE
96 Director Purchasing/Contracting .... Ms. Debbie F. JACKSON
29 Coordinator Alumni Relations .... Ms. Leslie H. SALVAIL
23 Coordinator Health Services .... Ms. Beth A. MAYS
41 Intercollegiate Athletics Coordntor .... Mr. D. Bruce SPRINGER
28 Coordinator of Minority Recruitment .... Mr. James T. JACKSON, JR.
94 Coordinator of Women's Studies .... Dr. Suzanne J. SPOOR
88 Director of Environmental Center .... Dr. M. Stephen AILSTOCK
88 Director Center Study Local Issues .... Dr. Daniel D. NATAF
88 Dir Homeland Sec/Crim Justice Inst .... Dr. Tyrone POWERS
53 Director TEACH Institute .... Ms. Colleen K. EISENBEISER
88 Director Hosp/Cul Arts/Tourism Inst .... Ms. Mary Ellen MASON
38 Coordinator Inst for the Future .... Mr. Steven T. HENICK
88 Dir Sarbanes Center/Pub & Cmty Svc .... Ms. Cathleen H. DOYLE

Bais HaMedrash & Mesivta of Baltimore (C)

6823 Old Pimlico Road, Baltimore MD 21209

County: Baltimore | Identification: 667075
Telephone: (410) 486-0006 | Carnegie Class: Not Classified
FAX Number: (410) 602-9738 | Calendar System: Semester
Established: 1997 | Annual Undergrad Tuition & Fees: $49
Enrollment: 13,500 | Male
Affiliation or Control: Independent Non-Profit | IRS Status: 501(c)3
Highest Offering: First Talmudic Degree
Program: Professional
Accreditation: RABN

01 Rosh Yeshiva .... Rabbi Zvi Dov SLANGER

Baltimore City Community College (D)

2901 Liberty Heights Avenue, Baltimore MD 21215-7893

County: Baltimore City | FICE Identification: 002061 | Unit ID: 161864
Telephone: (410) 462-8300 | Carnegie Class: Assoc/Pub-U-MC
FAX Number: (410) 462-7795 | Calendar System: Semester
URL: www.bccc.edu
Established: 1947 | Annual Undergrad Tuition & Fees (In-District): $3,062
Enrollment: 6,953 | Coed
Affiliation or Control: State/Local | IRS Status: 501(c)3
Highest Offering: Associate Degree
Program: Occupational; 2-Year Principally Bachelor's Creditable
Accreditation: #M, ACBSP, ADNUR, DH, DIETT, PTAA, SURGT

01 President .... Dr. Carolane WILLIAMS
10 Vice President Business & Finance .... Ms. Kim JAMES
32 Vice President for Student Affairs ... Dr. Alicia B. HARVEY-SMITH
05 Vice Pres Academic Affairs .... Dr. Therese BUSHNER
51 Vice Pres Business & Cont Educ .... Mr. Lucious ANDERSON
84 Dean of Enrollment Management .... Ms. Julia PITTMAN
26 Exec Dir Communications/Research .... Ms. Vanessa G. CARROLL
18 Exec Dir Facilities/Plng/Operations .... Vacant
21 Controller/Chief of Accounting .... Ms. Kim JAMES
37 Director Student Financial Aid .... Ms. Vera BROOKS
13 Chief Information Tech Officer .... Mr. Levone T. WARD, SR.
08 Director Library/Media Services .... Ms. Stephanie REIDY
06 Exec Director Records/Registrar .... Ms. Kathleen STYLES
15 Exec Director of Human Resources .... Mr. Tony WARNER
09 Director Institutional Research .... Mr. Gerard REICHENBERG
102 Exec Director of Foundation .... Dr. Jim CHITWOOD
96 Chief Procurement Officer .... Mr. Dan COLMAN

Baltimore International College (E)

17 Commerce Street, Baltimore MD 21202-3230

County: Baltimore City | FICE Identification: 023148 | Unit ID: 161882
Telephone: (410) 752-4710 | Carnegie Class: Bac/Assoc
FAX Number: (410) 752-3730 | Calendar System: Semester
URL: www.bic.edu
Established: 1972 | Annual Undergrad Tuition & Fees: $28,560
Enrollment: 493 | Coed
Affiliation or Control: Independent Non-Profit | IRS Status: 501(c)3
Highest Offering: Master's
Program: 2-Year Principally Bachelor's Creditable; Liberal Arts And General
Accreditation: ACFEI

01 President .... Dr. Edgar B. SCHICK
05 Vice Pres Instruction/Student Svcs .... Vacant
10 Vice Pres & Chief Financial Officer .... Ms. Lorraine SELWAY
26 Director of Marketing .... Mr. Keith JONES
59 Director Culinary Arts Instruction .... Mr. Eric FRAUWIRTH
06 Director of Records/Registration .... Ms. Elizabeth ROGERS
37 Director Financial Planning .... Ms. Kim WITTLER
08 Director of Learning Resources .... Ms. Wendy BAKER
07 Director of Admissions .... Ms. Kim WHITTLER
09 Director of Institutional Research .... Dr. Shantell SAUNDERS
32 Director Student Svcs/Career Svcs .... Ms. Jarrette THOMAS
18 Director of Facilities Mgmt .... Mr. Jeff CHENOWETH
38 Director Student Counseling .... Ms. Georgia WILLIS

Capitol College (F)

11301 Springfield Road, Laurel MD 20708-9759

County: Prince Georges | FICE Identification: 001436 | Unit ID: 162061
Telephone: (301) 369-2800 | Carnegie Class: Spec/Engg
FAX Number: (301) 953-1442 | Calendar System: Semester
URL: www.capitol-college.edu
Established: 1927 | Annual Undergrad Tuition & Fees: $20,400
Enrollment: 756 | Coed
Affiliation or Control: Independent Non-Profit | IRS Status: 501(c)3
Highest Offering: Doctorate
Program: Technical Emphasis
Accreditation: M, ENG, ENGT, IACBE

01 President .... Dr. Michael T. WOOD
05 Vice President for Academic Affairs .... Dr. William MACONACHY
10 Vice President for Finance/Admin .... Derick A. VEENSTRA
46 Vice Pres for Planning/Assessment .... Dianne M. VEENSTRA
30 Vice President Advancement .... Dr. Michael GIBBS
20 Academic Dean .... Vacant
32 Dean Student Life & Retention .... Melinda A. BUNNELL-RHYNE
72 Dean Engineering/Computer Sci/Tech .... Dr. Robert WEILER
06 Director of Registration & Records .... Sallie MCKEVITT
08 Dir Library/Information Literacy .... Rick A. SAMPLE
11 Dir Administration/Human Resources .... Jacquelyn K. ENRIGHT
36 Dir Career Svcs/Community Relations .... Anthony G. MILLER
26 Director Marketing Communications .... Megan CAMPBELL
29 Dir Alumni Relations & Advancement .... Jason COPLEY
07 Director Recruiting & Admissions .... George WALLS
37 Director of Financial Aid .... Suzanne THOMPSON
21 Director of Finance .... Kathleen WERNER
51 Director of Continuing Education .... Vacant
91 Director Administrative Computing .... Jay HALL
18 Chief Facilities/Physical Plant .... Harry TRAPP

Carroll Community College (G)

1601 Washington Road, Westminster MD 21157-6913

County: Carroll | FICE Identification: 031007 | Unit ID: 405872
Telephone: (410) 386-8000 | Carnegie Class: Assoc/Pub-S-SC
FAX Number: (410) 386-8181 | Calendar System: Semester
URL: www.carrollcc.edu
Established: 1993 | Annual Undergrad Tuition & Fees (In-District): $3,589
Enrollment: 4,108 | Coed
Affiliation or Control: Local | IRS Status: 501(c)3
Highest Offering: Associate Degree
Program: Occupational; 2-Year Principally Bachelor's Creditable
Accreditation: M, PTAA

01 President .... Dr. Faye PAPPALARDO
11 Exec Vice Pres Administration .... Mr. Alan M. SCHUMAN
05 VP of Academic & Student Affairs .... Dr. James D. BALL
45 VP Planning Marketing & Assessment .... Dr. Craig A. CLAGETT
51 VP Continuing Education/Training .... Ms. Karen L. MERKLE
04 Executive Assistant to President .... Ms. Sylvia BLAIR
30 Exec Dir Inst Devel/College Found .... Mr. Steven WANTZ
88 Integrity & Judicial Affairs Advoca .... Mr. Joel M. HOSKOWITZ
88 Director Transfer .... Ms. Toyette SULLIVAN
35 Dean of Student Affairs .... Dr. Michael KIPHART
50 Dean of Business/Math/Sciences .... Mr. Robert BROWN
49 Dean of Arts/Letters & Soc Sci .... Mr. Steve GEPPI
38 Director of Advising/Counseling .... Ms. Janenne CORCORAN

07 Director of Admissions ....Ms. Candace EDWARDS
89 Dir Student Life/1st Yr Pgm/Honor ....Ms. Kristie CRUMLEY
06 Registrar ....Ms. Lauren SHIELDS
37 Director of Financial Aid ....Vacant
66 Director of Nursing ....Ms. Nancy PERRY
08 Sr Dir Library/Media/Dist Lrn ....Mr. Alan BOGAGE
106 Director Distance Lrng Programs ....Dr. Susan BIRO
26 Director Publications/Comm Design ....Ms. Eleni SWENGLER
09 Director Institutional Research ....Ms. Janet NICKELS
103 Sr Dir Cont Ed/Workforce/Bus Devel .Ms. Kathleen T. MENASCHE
31 Sr Dir Lifelong Lrng/Pgm Support ....Ms. Sally LONG
105 Director of Network & Tech Services ....Ms. Patti DAVIS
21 Director Fiscal Affairs ....Mr. Timothy LEAGUE
15 Director Human Resources ....Ms. Bridget S. LEIMBACH
18 Director Facilities Management ....Ms. Terry BOWEN

Cecil College (A)

One Seahawk Drive, North East MD 21901-1999
County: Cecil FICE Identification: 008308
Unit ID: 162104
Telephone: (410) 287-6060 Carnegie Class: Assoc/Pub-S-SC
FAX Number: (410) 287-1026 Calendar System: Semester
URL: www.cecil.edu
Established: 1968 Annual Undergrad Tuition & Fees (In-District): $3,080
Enrollment: 2,462 Coed
Affiliation or Control: State/Local IRS Status: 501(c)3
Highest Offering: Associate Degree
Program: Occupational; 2-Year Principally Bachelor's Creditable
Accreditation: M, ADNUR, MAC

01 President ....Dr. W. Stephen PANNILL
05 Vice President Academic Programs ....Dr. Mary WAY BOLT
11 Vice Pres Administrative Services ....Dr. Christine A. VALUCKAS
32 VP Students/Instit Effectiveness ....Dr. Diane C. LANE
13 VP/Chief Information Officer ....Mr. Steve DIFILIPO
30 Vice Pres Institutional Advancement ....Ms. Chris Ann SZEP
18 Director of Facilities ....Mr. Jeff BAUDER
09 Director of Institutional Research ....Mr. Dan STOICESCU
06 Registrar/Dir Admiss & Registration ....Vacant
37 Director of Financial Aid Services ....Mr. Stephen AMPERSAND
08 Director of Library Services ....Ms. Lorraine MARTORANA
15 Director Human Resources ....Dr. Jim WILBURN
26 Director of Marketing ....Ms. Charlene CONOLLY
29 Coordinator Alumni Relations ....Ms. Mary MOORE
93 Director Minority Student Services ....Ms. Laney HOXTER
66 Dean Nursing Ed/Alld Hlth/Hlth Sci ....Ms. Christy DRYER
41 Director Athletics ....Mr. Ed DURHAM
04 Assistant to the President ....Ms. Dawn KISNER

Chesapeake College (B)

PO Box 8, 1000 College Circle, Wye Mills MD 21679-0008
County: Queen Annes FICE Identification: 004650
Unit ID: 162168
Telephone: (410) 822-5400 Carnegie Class: Assoc/Pub-R-M
FAX Number: (410) 827-5875 Calendar System: Semester
URL: www.chesapeake.edu
Established: 1965 Annual Undergrad Tuition & Fees (In-District): $3,754
Enrollment: 2,956 Coed
Affiliation or Control: State/Local IRS Status: 501(c)3
Highest Offering: Associate Degree
Program: Occupational; 2-Year Principally Bachelor's Creditable
Accreditation: M, ADNUR, PTAA, RAD, SURGT

01 President ....Dr. Barbara A. VINIAR
05 VP Academic Affairs & Econ Develop ....Dr. Kathryn A. BARBOUR
11 Vice Pres for Administrative Svcs ....Mr. Michael D. KILGUS
32 VP Student Success/Enrollment Svcs ....Dr. Richard D. MIDCAP
18 Director of Facilities ....Mr. Monte W. GARRETTSON
51 Ex Dir Cont Educ Workforce Training ....Ms. Janet L. POTTER
49 Dean for Liberal Arts & Sciences ....Dr. Roger SMITTER
107 Dean for Career & Professional Stds ....Ms. Maureen A. GILMARTIN
72 VP Technology & Academic Support ....Mr. Douglass P. GRAY
08 Dean Lrng Res/Acad Sppt Svcs ....Ms. Chandra M. GIGLIOTTI-GURIDI
15 Director of Human Resources ....Ms. Susan A. CIANCHETTA
37 Director of Financial Aid ....Ms. Mindy M. SCHAFFER
30 Director Resource Development ....Ms. Lauren C. HALTERMAN
09 Dir Inst Planning/Research & Assmnt ....Ms. Kimberly A. MILLER
07 Dean for Recruitment Services ....Ms. Kathleen J. PETRICHENKO
26 Director of Public Information ....Ms. Marcie A. MOLLOY
06 Registrar ....Mr. James A. DAVIDSON
20 Dean for Retention Services ....Ms. Joan M. SEITZER

College of Southern Maryland (C)

PO Box 910, La Plata MD 20646-0910
County: Charles FICE Identification: 002064
Unit ID: 162122
Telephone: (301) 934-2251 Carnegie Class: Assoc/Pub-S-MC
FAX Number: (301) 934-7698 Calendar System: Semester
URL: www.csmd.edu
Established: 1958 Annual Undergrad Tuition & Fees (In-District): $3,948
Enrollment: 9,056 Coed
Affiliation or Control: Local IRS Status: 501(c)3
Highest Offering: Associate Degree
Program: Occupational; 2-Year Principally Bachelor's Creditable
Accreditation: M, ACBSP, ADNUR, PNUR, PTAA

01 President ....Dr. Bradley GOTTFRIED
05 Vice President Academic Affairs ....Dr. Debra TERVALA
12 Vice President Leonardtown Campus ....Dr. Frederico J. TALLEY
12 VP Prince Frederick Campus ....Dr. Richard FLEMING
102 VP Corporate/Cmty Training Inst ....Dr. Daniel MOSSER
10 VP Financial & Admin Services ....Mr. Tony JERNIGAN
32 VP Student/Instruc Support Svcs ....Dr. William COMEY
30 Vice President for Advancement ....Ms. Michelle GOODWIN
43 Vice President/General Counsel ....Mr. Craig PATENAUDE
20 Associate VP Academic Affairs ....Dr. Sue SUBOCZ
09 Assoc VP Plng/Inst Effective/Rsrch ....Ms. Kathleen ROTTIER
84 Assoc VP Enrollment Mgmt Team ....Ms. Joan MIDDLETON
41 Dir Wellness/Fitness/Rec ....Mr. LaRue COOK
18 Director of Facilities ....Mr. Buddy BROWN
15 Exec Director Human Resources ....Ms. Denise BAILEY CLARK
26 Exec Director Community Relations ....Ms. Karen SMITH-HUPP
37 Director Financial Assistance ....Mr. Christian ZIMMERMANN
06 Registrar ....Ms. Carol HARRISON
08 Director of Library ....Mr. Thomas REPENNING
66 Chair Nursing Dept ....Ms. Laura POLK
35 Director of Athletics/Student Life ....Ms. Michelle RUBLE
40 General Mgr College Store ....Ms. Marcy GANNON
07 Int Director Admissions Department ....Ms. Joan MIDDLETON
38 Director Advisement/Career Services ....Ms. Susan STRAUS
96 Director of Procurement ....Mr. Tom KELLEY

The Community College of Baltimore County (D)

7200 Sollers Point Road, Baltimore MD 21222-4649
County: Baltimore FICE Identification: 002063
Unit ID: 434672
Telephone: (443) 840-3700 Carnegie Class: Assoc/Pub-S-MC
FAX Number: (443) 840-1100 Calendar System: Semester
URL: www.ccbcmd.edu
Established: N/A Annual Undergrad Tuition & Fees (In-District): $3,742
Enrollment: 26,425 Coed
Affiliation or Control: Local IRS Status: 501(c)3
Highest Offering: Associate Degree
Program: Occupational; 2-Year Principally Bachelor's Creditable
Accreditation: M, ACBSP, ADNUR, COMTA, DH, EMT, FUSER, MLTAD, MUS, OTA, POLYT, RAD, SURGT, THEA

01 President ....Dr. Sandra L. KURTINITIS
30 Vice Pres Institutional Advancement ....Mr. Kenneth WESTARY
10 Vice Pres Finance/Administration ....Ms. Melissa HOPP
05 Vice Pres Instruction ....Dr. Mark MCCOLLOCH
84 VP Enrollment & Student Services ....Dr. Richard LILLEY
26 Sr Director for Public Relations ....Ms. Mary DELUCA
16 Senior Director Human Resources ....Ms. Penny MILSOM

DeVry University - Bethesda Center (E)

4550 Montgomery Avenue, Suite 100 N, Bethesda MD 20814-3304
County: Montgomery Identification: 666210
Unit ID: 439330
Telephone: (301) 652-8477 Carnegie Class: Spec/Bus
FAX Number: (301) 652-8577 Calendar System: Semester
URL: www.devry.edu
Established: 2001 Annual Undergrad Tuition & Fees: $15,294
Enrollment: 247 Coed
Affiliation or Control: Proprietary IRS Status: Proprietary
Highest Offering: Master's
Program: Occupational; Professional; Business Emphasis
Accreditation: &NH

01 Center Dean ....Mary Kay PORTER

† Regional accreditation is carried under the parent institution in Downers Grove, IL.

Faith Theological Seminary (F)

529 Walker Avenue, Baltimore MD 21212
County: Baltimore City Identification: 667016
Telephone: (410) 323-6211 Carnegie Class: Not Classified
FAX Number: (410) 323-6331 Calendar System: Semester
URL: www.faiththeological.org
Established: 1937 Annual Undergrad Tuition & Fees: $6,000
Enrollment: 110 Coed
Affiliation or Control: Non-denominational IRS Status: 501(c)3
Highest Offering: Doctorate; No Lower Division
Program: Religious Emphasis
Accreditation: @TRACS

01 President ....Dr. Norman J. MANOHAR
05 Academic Dean ....Dr. Stephen T. HAGUE

Frederick Community College (G)

7932 Opossumtown Pike, Frederick MD 21702-2097
County: Frederick FICE Identification: 002071
Unit ID: 162557
Telephone: (301) 846-2400 Carnegie Class: Assoc/Pub-S-SC
FAX Number: (301) 846-2498 Calendar System: Semester
URL: www.frederick.edu
Established: 1957 Annual Undergrad Tuition & Fees (In-District): $3,807
Enrollment: 6,285 Coed
Affiliation or Control: State/Local IRS Status: 501(c)3
Highest Offering: Associate Degree
Program: Occupational; 2-Year Principally Bachelor's Creditable
Accreditation: M, ADNUR, SURGT

01 Interim President ....Mr. Douglas D. BROWNING
05 Vice Pres for Learning ....Dr. Margaret F. BARTOW
11 Interim Vice Pres for Admn ....Mr. Donald FRANCIS
32 Vice Pres for Learning Support ....Dr. Debralee MCCLELLAN
30 Chief Development Officer ....Mr. Christopher A. MASSI
13 Chief Technology Officer ....Ms. Lori ROUNDS
84 Assoc VP Enrollment Management ....Ms. Laura MEARS
15 Interim Assoc VP Human Resources ....Ms. Diana OLIVER
10 Assoc VP for Fiscal & Aux Services ....Ms. Deborah JUDD
06 Assoc VP Stdnt Operations/Registrar ....Ms. Kathy FRAWLEY
51 Assoc VP Learning/Dean CE & WD ....Mr. David CROGHAN
88 Assoc VP Teaching & Learning ....Dr. Christine HELFRICH
35 Assoc VP/Dean of Students ....Dr. Irvin T. CLARK, III
20 Assoc VP Lrng/Dean Academic & Prof ....Dr. Gerald L. BOYD
18 Exec Dir Facilities Planning ....Mr. Sam YOUNG
08 Exec Dir Library ....Mr. Mick O'LEARY
09 Exec Dir Outcome Assess/Plng/Res ....Dr. Gohar FARAHANI
19 Exec Dir Risk Mgmt/Public Services ....Mr. Walter SMITH
26 Exec Dir Marketing/Public Relations . Mr. Michael H. PRITCHARD
38 Exec Dir Advising & Counseling ....Ms. Rachel NACHLAS
37 Exec Dir Financial Aid ....Ms. Brenda DAYHOFF
88 Exec Dir Academic Ops & Ext Lng ....Ms. Michelle HALL
04 Exec Asst to the President & Board ....Ms. Diane MORTON
88 Director Monroe Center ....Mr. James HARTSOCK
14 Director of Software Development ....Mr. Adam RENO
41 Director of Athletics ....Dr. Tom JANDOVITZ
88 Director Children's Center ....Ms. Teri BICKEL
88 Director Learning Technologies ....Mr. Alberto RAMIREZ
106 Director Distance Learning ....Mr. Jurgen HILKE
35 Dir Student Engagement/Student Life ....Ms. Jeanni WINSTON-MUIR
88 Dir Multicultural Student Services ....Mr. Chad ADERO
88 Director Office of Adult Services ....Ms. Sandra CAVALIER
88 Dir Svcs for Students w/ Disbilities ....Ms. Kate KRAMER-JEFFERSON
07 Director of Admissions ....Ms. Lisa FREEL
88 Dir Career & Transfer Services ....Ms. Lorraine DODSON
28 Director of Diversity ....Ms. Beverly HENDRIX
18 Director Plant Operations ....Mr. Curt SANDUSKY
14 Dir Network Info Security & Telecom ....Mr. Joe MARSHALL
105 Director Web Services ....Ms. Cindy OSBON
88 Dir Inst & Admin Support Services ....Ms. Kimberly FISHER
96 Director of Purchasing ....Mr. Robert GILL
40 Bookstore Director ....Mr. Frederick HOCKENBERRY
88 Dir Business Systems & Compliance ....Ms. Karen REILLY
88 Manager Food Services ....Ms. Donna S. SOWERS
29 Coord Annual Giving/Alumni Relation ....Ms. Akeembra GRADY

Garrett College (H)

687 Mosser Road, McHenry MD 21541-1265
County: Garrett FICE Identification: 010014
Unit ID: 162609
Telephone: (301) 387-3000 Carnegie Class: Assoc/Pub-R-S
FAX Number: (301) 387-3038 Calendar System: Semester
URL: www.garrettcollege.edu
Established: 1966 Annual Undergrad Tuition & Fees (In-District): $3,222
Enrollment: 850 Coed
Affiliation or Control: State/Local IRS Status: 501(c)3
Highest Offering: Associate Degree
Program: Occupational; 2-Year Principally Bachelor's Creditable
Accreditation: M

01 President ....Dr. Richard MACLENNAN
04 Executive Assistant to President ....Ms. Marcia KNEPP
10 Dean of Administration & Finance ....Ms. Josephine GILMAN
05 Interim Dean of Instruction ....Mr. James ALLEN, JR.
51 Dean of Cont Educ/Workforce Devel ....Ms. Julie YODER
13 Dean of Information Technology ....Ms. Cathy TOROK
26 Dean of Marketing & Enrollment Mgmt ....Ms. Ann WELLHAM
20 Associate Dean of Academic Affairs ....Mr. Philip RIVERA
32 Dean of Student Life ....Dr. George BRELSFORD
30 Dir Develop/Exec Dir Foundation ....Mr. Fred LEAREY
06 Director of Records & Registration ....Ms. Kim DEGIOVANNI
37 Director of Financial Aid ....Ms. Cissy VANSICKLE
08 Director of Library ....Mrs. Dana SHIMROCK
21 Director of Business Office ....Ms. Katherine BROWNING
18 Director of Campus Facilities ....Mr. Jerry ZIMMERMAN
15 Director of Human Resources ....Ms. Linda K. FIKE
65 Dir of Natural Res/Wildlife Tech ....Mr. Kevin DODGE
41 Director of Athletics ....Mr. Shawn NOEL
50 Director of Business/Info Tech ....Dr. Qing YUAN
36 Dir Acad Career & Trans Advising ....Ms. Judy CARBONE
96 Purchasing/Accounts Payable ....Ms. Bonnie BROADWATER
09 Institutional Research Analyst ....Ms. Kalie ASHBY
40 Bookstore Manager ....Ms. Margi L. PERFETTI
07 Director of Admissions ....Ms. Rachelle DAVIS
38 Coordinator of Counseling Services ....Ms. Madonna POOL
17 Coordinator of Health Services ....Ms. Jamie RESH-KAMP
24 Multimedia Support Technician ....Mr. Harry FIKE
39 Coordinator of Residential Services ....Ms. Mary Kate HEISER
45 Director of Institutional Planning ....Mr. James ALLEN, JR.
105 Webmaster ....Ms. Linda STEVANUS
49 Director of Liberal Arts & Sciences ....Ms. Elizabeth GRANT
88 Director of Adventure Sports ....Mr. Michael LOGSDON
53 Dir of Education & Teacher Prep ....Mr. Alexander TUEL

Goucher College (I)

1021 Dulaney Valley Road, Towson MD 21204-2780
County: Baltimore FICE Identification: 002073
Unit ID: 162654

Telephone: (410) 337-6000 Carnegie Class: Bac/A&S
FAX Number: (410) 337-6123 Calendar System: Semester
URL: www.goucher.edu
Established: 1885 Annual Undergrad Tuition & Fees: $36,011
Enrollment: 2,299 Coed
Affiliation or Control: Independent Non-Profit IRS Status: 501(c)3
Highest Offering: Master's
Program: Liberal Arts And General; Teacher Preparatory
Accreditation: M

01 President ..... Mr. Sanford J. UNGAR
05 Provost & Chief Academic Officer ..... Dr. Marc ROY
32 Vice Pres/Dean of Students ..... Dr. Gail N. EDMONDS
30 Actg Vice Pres Devel/Alumni Affs ..... Ms. Janet WILEY
84 Vice President Enrollment Mgmt ..... Mr. Michael O'LEARY
26 Vice President Communications ..... Vacant
13 VP for Technology and Planning ..... Mr. Bill LEIMBACH
43 General Counsel ..... Ms. Laura BURTON-GRAHAM
20 Associate Dean Academic Affairs ..... Ms. Janine BOWEN
82 Assoc Dean International Studies ..... Mr. Daniel NORTON
35 Assoc Dean for Student Engagement ..... Ms. Emily PERL
15 Asst VP Finance/Dir Human Resources ..... Ms. Deborah LUPTON
21 Controller ..... Mr. Alex ANTKOWIAK
07 Director of Admissions ..... Mr. Carlton E. SURBECK, III
08 Librarian ..... Ms. Nancy MAGNUSON
29 Exec Director of Alumnae/i ..... Ms. Margaret-Ann RADFORD-WEDEMEYER
36 Director of Career Development ..... Ms. Traci MARTIN
58 Director Grad Program in Education ..... Ms. Phyllis SUNSHINE
06 Registrar ..... Mr. Andrew WESTFALL
09 Asst Dir of Institutional Research ..... Ms. Pallabi ROY
10 Dir Business/Auxiliary Services ..... Mr. Calvin GLADDEN
18 Dir Facilities Management Services ..... Mr. Harold TINSLEY
37 Director Financial Aid ..... Ms. Ellen OSTENDORF
93 Asst Dean for Multicultural Stds ..... Ms. Mary TANDIA

Hagerstown Community College (A)

11400 Robinwood Drive, Hagerstown MD 21742-6590
County: Washington FICE Identification: 002074
Unit ID: 162690
Telephone: (301) 790-2800 Carnegie Class: Assoc/Pub-R-M
FAX Number: (301) 393-3682 Calendar System: Semester
URL: www.hagerstowncc.edu
Established: 1946 Annual Undergrad Tuition & Fees (In-District): $2,812
Enrollment: 4,898 Coed
Affiliation or Control: State/Local IRS Status: 501(c)3
Highest Offering: Associate Degree
Program: Occupational; 2-Year Principally Bachelor's Creditable
Accreditation: M, RAD

01 President ..... Dr. Guy ALTIERI
05 Vice President of Academic Affairs ..... Dr. Judith OLEKS
11 Vice Pres Administration/Finance ..... Ms. Anna M. BARKER
32 Dean of Students ..... Dr. Donna RUDY
09 Dean of Plng/Instl Effectiveness ..... Ms. Barbara E. MACHT
18 Dir Facilities Management & Plng ..... Dr. Robert SPONG
07 Dir Admissions/Records/Registration ..... Dr. Jennifer A. HAUGHIE
30 Director Institutional Advancement ..... Ms. Lieba J. COHEN
26 Director Marketing/Public Info ..... Ms. Elizabeth K. STULL
37 Director of Financial Aid ..... Ms. Carolyn S. COX
14 Dir Technology/Computer Studies ..... Ms. Margaret C. SPIVEY
51 Dean Continuing Educ/Extension Svcs ..... Ms. Theresa SHANK
21 Director of Business Services ..... Ms. Lita ORNER
66 Director of Nursing ..... Ms. Karen HAMMOND
15 Director of Human Resources ..... Ms. Donna MARRIOTT
41 Dir Athletics/Phys Ed/Leisure Stds ..... Mr. Robert MYERS
08 Director Library Svcs/Learning Tech ..... Mr. James R. FEAGIN
20 Director of Instruction ..... Mr. Gerald C. HAINES
13 Director of Information Technology ..... Mr. Craig M. FENTRESS
21 Director of Finance ..... Mr. David C. BITTORF
88 Dir Organization Devel/Special Proj ..... Vacant
76 Director of Health Sciences ..... Ms. Angela STOOPS

Harford Community College (B)

401 Thomas Run Road, Bel Air MD 21015-1698
County: Harford FICE Identification: 002075
Unit ID: 162706
Telephone: (443) 412-2000 Carnegie Class: Assoc/Pub-S-SC
FAX Number: (443) 412-2120 Calendar System: Semester
URL: www.harford.edu
Established: 1957 Annual Undergrad Tuition & Fees (In-District): $2,688
Enrollment: 7,135 Coed
Affiliation or Control: Local IRS Status: 501(c)3
Highest Offering: Associate Degree
Program: Occupational; 2-Year Principally Bachelor's Creditable
Accreditation: M, ADNUR, HT, MAC

01 President ..... Dr. Dennis GOLLADAY
05 Vice President Instruction ..... Dr. M. Annette HAGGRAY
10 VP Finance/Operations/Govt Rels ..... Dr. John L. COX
45 VP Student Dev & Inst Effectiveness ..... Dr. Deborah J. CRUISE
31 VP Mkting/Dev/Community Relations ..... Ms. Brenda M. MORRISON
13 VP Information Technology ..... Ms. Annie PAGURA
32 Assoc VP Student Development ..... Ms. Amanda A. KASTERN
32 Assoc VP Student Development ..... Dr. Diane L. RESIDES
21 Assistant Vice President Finance ..... Mr. Stephen S. PHILLIPS
51 Assoc VP Continuing Educ & Training ..... Ms. Marlene Y. LIEB
18 Assoc VP Campus Operations ..... Dr. Gregory A. DEAL
37 Director Financial Aid ..... Ms. D. Lynn LEE
06 Registrar ..... Ms. Sandra G. CLARK
96 Director for Purchasing ..... Mr. Victor H. DODSON
26 Dir Marketing & Public Relations ..... Ms. Nancy J. DYSARD
15 Dir Human Resources/Employee Dev ..... Ms. Cheryl E. HICKSON
29 Director College/Alumni Development ..... Ms. Denise M. DREGIER
08 Director Library & Info Resources ..... Ms. Carol M. ALLEN
09 Int Director Institutional Research ..... Mr. William M. EKEY
40 Manager College Store ..... Ms. Linda L. FIFE
07 Coordinator for Admissions ..... Mr. Brian J. HAMMOND
38 Dir Advising/Career/Transfer Svcs ..... Ms. J. Bonnie SULZBACH
81 Dean Science/Tech/Engr/Math ..... Ms. Deborah R. WROBEL
83 Dean Behavioral & Social Sciences ..... Mr. Avery W. WARD
79 Dean Humanities ..... Dr. Karry L. HATHAWAY
57 Dean Visual/Performing/Applied Arts ..... Mr. Paul E. LABE
50 Dean Business/Computer/Tech ..... Mr. John F. MAYHORNE
88 Dean Educ & Transitional Studies ..... Mr. Carl E. HENDERSON
66 Dean Nursing & Allied Health Profs ..... Ms. Laura C. PRESTON

Hood College (C)

401 Rosemont Avenue, Frederick MD 21701-8575
County: Frederick FICE Identification: 002076
Unit ID: 162760
Telephone: (301) 663-3131 Carnegie Class: Master's M
FAX Number: (301) 694-7653 Calendar System: Semester
URL: www.hood.edu
Established: 1893 Annual Undergrad Tuition & Fees: $31,060
Enrollment: 2,447 Coed
Affiliation or Control: Independent Non-Profit IRS Status: 501(c)3
Highest Offering: Master's
Program: Liberal Arts And General; Teacher Preparatory; Fine Arts Emphasis
Accreditation: M, SW, TED

01 President ..... Dr. Ronald J. VOLPE
05 Provost/Dean of Faculty ..... Dr. Katherine CONWAY-TURNER
10 Vice Pres Finance ..... Mr. Charles G. MANN
30 VP for Institutional Advancement ..... Ms. Nancy E. GILLECE
32 VP Student Life/Dean of Students ..... Dr. Olivia G. WHITE
84 VP Undergrad/Grad Enrollment ..... Dr. Kathleen BANDS
07 Director of Admissions ..... Mr. David ADAMS
58 Dean of Graduate School ..... Dr. Allen FLORA
20 Exec Dir Academic Svcs/Career Svcs ..... Mrs. Bonnie K. HAGERMAN
26 Exec Dir Marketing/Communications ..... Mr. Dave DIEHL
29 Director of Alumnae/i Programs ..... Ms. Linda HOFFMAN
06 Registrar ..... Mrs. Nanette MARKEY
08 Librarian ..... Mrs. Jan SAMET
37 Director of Financial Aid ..... Ms. Carol SCHROYER
15 Director of Human Resources ..... Ms. Carol M. WUENSCHEL
18 Director of Facilities Planning ..... Mr. Richard KAHLEY
13 Chief Technology Officer ..... Mr. Cornelius R. FAY, III
09 Director of Institutional Research ..... Ms. Cynthia EMORY

Howard Community College (D)

10901 Little Patuxent Parkway, Columbia MD 21044-3197
County: Howard FICE Identification: 008175
Unit ID: 162779
Telephone: (443) 518-1000 Carnegie Class: Assoc/Pub-S-SC
FAX Number: N/A Calendar System: Semester
URL: www.howardcc.edu
Established: 1966 Annual Undergrad Tuition & Fees (In-District): $4,063
Enrollment: 9,568 Coed
Affiliation or Control: State/Local IRS Status: 501(c)3
Highest Offering: Associate Degree
Program: Occupational; 2-Year Principally Bachelor's Creditable
Accreditation: M, ADNUR, CVT, EMT, MUS, PNUR

01 President ..... Dr. Kathleen B. HETHERINGTON
32 Vice President of Student Services ..... Dr. Cynthia J. PETERKA
05 Vice President of Academic Affairs ..... Dr. Sharon PIERCE
10 Vice Pres of Administration/Finance ..... Ms. Lynn C. COLEMAN
13 Vice President for Information Tech ..... Mr. Thomas J. GLASER
51 Assoc Vice Pres Cont Education ..... Ms. JoAnn HAWKINS
84 Assoc Vice Pres for Enroll Svcs ..... Ms. Barbara C. GREENFELD
35 Assoc Vice Pres for Student Devel ..... Ms. Janice L. MARKS
15 Associate Vice Pres Human Resources ..... Mr. Dave JORDAN
21 Associate VP of Finance ..... Ms. Janet L. CULLISON
09 Exec Dir Plng/Research & Org Dev ..... Ms. Zoe A. IRVIN
18 Exec Dir Capital Proj/Facilities ..... Mr. Charles NIGHTINGALE
101 Director of Board Rels/Special Proj ..... Ms. Erin YUN
06 Registrar ..... Mr. Camilo F. GARCIA
27 Director of Mktg & Communications ..... Mr. Randall R. BENGFORT
37 Director Financial Aid Services ..... Ms. Katherine M. ALLEN
30 Exec Director of Development ..... Ms. Melissa MATTEY
40 Director Auxiliary Services ..... Ms. Arla J. WEBB
19 Director of Security Services ..... Mr. Ken MCGLYNN
35 Director Student Life ..... Ms. Llatetra D. BROWN
04 Exec Assistant to the President ..... Ms. Farida GUZDAR
26 Executive Dir of Public Relations ..... Ms. Nancy S. GAINER
36 Director of Testing ..... Mr. Eli STAV
96 Director of Purchasing ..... Ms. Elizabeth H. MOSS

ITT Technical Institute (E)

11301 Red Run Boulevard, Owings Mills MD 21117-3246
County: Baltimore Identification: 666377
Unit ID: 446914
Telephone: (443) 394-7115 Carnegie Class: Assoc/PrivFP4
FAX Number: N/A Calendar System: Quarter
URL: www.itt-tech.edu
Established: N/A Annual Undergrad Tuition & Fees: N/A
Enrollment: 1,496 Coed
Affiliation or Control: Proprietary IRS Status: Proprietary
Highest Offering: Baccalaureate
Program: Technical Emphasis
Accreditation: ACICS

† Branch campus of ITT Technical Institute, Boise, ID.

Johns Hopkins University (F)

Charles and 34th Streets, Baltimore MD 21218-2680
County: Independent City FICE Identification: 002077
Unit ID: 162928
Telephone: (410) 516-8000 Carnegie Class: RU/VH
FAX Number: N/A Calendar System: Semester
URL: www.jhu.edu
Established: 1876 Annual Undergrad Tuition & Fees: $42,280
Enrollment: 21,363 Coed
Affiliation or Control: Independent Non-Profit IRS Status: 501(c)3
Highest Offering: Doctorate
Program: Liberal Arts And General; Teacher Preparatory; Professional
Accreditation: M, BBT, CS, DENT, DIETC, DIETI, DMS, ENG, ENGR, HSA, IPSY, MED, MIL, NMT, NURSE, PH, TED

01 President ..... Mr. Ronald J. DANIELS
100 Sr Vice President/Chief of Staff ..... Mr. Clayton D. ARMBRISTER
05 Provost & Sr VP Academic Affairs ..... Dr. Lloyd B. MINOR
10 Sr VP Finance & Administration ..... Mr. Daniel G. ENNIS
26 Vice President Comm/Public Affairs ..... Mr. Glenn M. BIELER
17 CEO Johns Hopkins Medicine ..... Dr. Edward D. MILLER, JR.
30 Sr VP for Development & Alumni Rels ..... Mr. Michael C. EICHER
43 Vice President/General Counsel ..... Mr. Stephen DUNHAM
86 Vice Pres Govt/Community Affairs ..... Mr. Thomas LEWIS
15 Vice President Human Resources ..... Ms. Charlene M. HAYES
32 Vice Provost for Student Affairs ..... Dr. Sarah STEINBERG
101 Secretary Board of Trustees ..... Mr. Jerome D. SCHNYDMAN
20 Vice Provost Faculty Affairs ..... Dr. Barbara LANDAU
20 Vice Provost Academic Services ..... Dr. Edgar E. ROULHAC
21 Vice President Finance & CFO ..... Vacant
58 Vice Provost Grad/Post-Doc Programs ..... Dr. Jonathan A. BAGGER
13 Vice Prov Info Technology/CIO ..... Ms. Stephanie REEL
22 Vice Provost Institutional Equity ..... Ms. Caroline LAGUERRE-BROWN
20 Vice Provost International Programs ..... Dr. Pam CRANSTON
46 Vice Provost Research ..... Dr. Scott L. ZEGER
09 Asst Provost Institutional Research ..... Dr. Cathy J. LEBO
21 Controller ..... Mr. Gregory S. OLER
18 Executive Director Operations ..... Mr. Lawrence R. KILDUFF
88 Executive Director Internal Audits ..... Mr. Francis X. BOSSLE
88 Executive Director JH Real Estate ..... Mr. Brian B. DEMBECK
88 Chief Investment Officer ..... Dr. Kathryn J. CRECELIUS
82 Dean Nitze School Adv Intl Studies ..... Dr. Jessica D. EINHORN
49 Dean Krieger School Arts & Sciences ..... Dr. Kathleen NEWMAN
50 Int Dean Carey Business School ..... Dr. Phil PHAN
53 Dean School of Education ..... Dr. David W. ANDREWS
54 Dean Whiting School of Engineering ..... Dr. Nicholas P. JONES
63 Dean of Faculty/School of Medicine ..... Dr. Edward D. MILLER, JR.
66 Dean School of Nursing ..... Dr. Martha N. HILL
64 Director Peabody Institute ..... Mr. Jeffrey SHARKEY
69 Dean Bloomberg School Public Health ..... Dr. Michael J. KLAG
81 Director Applied Physics Lab ..... Mr. Ralph SEMMEL
08 Dean Sheridan Libraries and Museums ..... Mr. Winston G. TABB
27 Executive Director Communications & ..... Mr. Dennis O'SHEA
96 Director Purchasing ..... Mr. Paul N. BEYER

Kaplan University (G)

18618 Crestwood Drive, Hagerstown MD 21742-2797
County: Washington FICE Identification: 007946
Unit ID: 162681
Telephone: (301) 766-3600 Carnegie Class: Assoc/PrivFP4
FAX Number: (301) 791-7661 Calendar System: Quarter
URL: www.hagerstown.kaplanuniversity.edu
Established: 1938 Annual Undergrad Tuition & Fees: $16,120
Enrollment: 1,150 Coed
Affiliation or Control: Proprietary IRS Status: Proprietary
Highest Offering: Baccalaureate
Program: Occupational; 2-Year Principally Bachelor's Creditable
Accreditation: &NH, MAC

01 President ..... Mr. W. Christopher MOTZ
05 Academic Dean ..... Dr. Samuel T. CROCKETT
32 Dean of Students ..... Ms. Lisa A. COPENHAVER
06 Registrar ..... Ms. Sheila R. GATES
10 Business Manager ..... Ms. Barbara A. KEESECKER
37 Director of Student Financial Aid ..... Ms. Kristin D. BREZLER
07 Director of Admissions ..... Mr. James W. KLEIN
36 Director of Career Services ..... Ms. Shannon N. CIANELLI
08 Director of Library Services ..... Mr. Thomas M. STATTON

† Regional accreditation is carried under the parent institution in Davenport, IA.

Lincoln College of Technology (H)

9325 Snowden River Parkway, Columbia MD 21046
County: Howard FICE Identification: 007936
Unit ID: 163028
Telephone: (410) 290-7100 Carnegie Class: Not Classified
FAX Number: (410) 290-7880 Calendar System: Quarter
URL: www.lincolntech.com
Established: 1978 Annual Undergrad Tuition & Fees: $25,920
Enrollment: 1,607 Coed
Affiliation or Control: Proprietary IRS Status: Proprietary
Highest Offering: Associate Degree

Program: Occupational
Accreditation: ACCSC, ACFEI

01 Director ... Ms. Susan SHERWOOD

Loyola University Maryland (A)

4501 N Charles Street, Baltimore MD 21210-2694
County: Independent City FICE Identification: 002078
Unit ID: 163046
Telephone: (410) 617-2000 Carnegie Class: Master's L
FAX Number: (410) 322-2768 Calendar System: Semester
URL: www.loyola.edu
Established: 1852 Annual Undergrad Tuition & Fees: $40,870
Enrollment: 6,061 Coed
Affiliation or Control: Roman Catholic IRS Status: 501(c)3
Highest Offering: Doctorate
Program: Liberal Arts And General; Teacher Preparatory
Accreditation: M, BUS, BUSA, CACREP, CLPSY, CS, ENG, SP, TED

01 President ... Rev. Brian F. LINNANE, SJ
04 Assistant to the President ... Ms. Vicki WELLER
05 Vice President for Academic Affairs ... Dr. Timothy L. SNYDER
10 Vice Pres for Finance & Treasurer ... Mr. Randall GENTZLER
11 Vice President for Administration ... Mr. Terrence M. SAWYER
30 Vice President Advancement ... Ms. Megan GILLICK
32 VP Student Devel/Dean of Students ... Dr. Susan M. DONOVAN
84 Vice Pres Enrollment Management ... Mr. Marc CAMILLE
20 Assoc Vice Pres Academic Affairs ... Ms. Jenny LOWRY
28 Asst VP Academic Affrs/Diversity ... Dr. Martha L. WHARTON
37 Asst Vice Pres of Financial Aid ... Mr. Mark L. LINDENMEYER
09 Asst VP of Institutional Research ... Ms. Terra SCHEHR
18 Assoc VP Facilities/Campus Services ... Ms. Helen SCHNEIDER
13 Asst VP of Technology Services/CIO ... Ms. Louise FINN
26 Director Public Relations ... Ms. Courtney JOLLEY
35 Asst Vice Pres Student Development ... Mr. Xavier COLE
15 Asst Vice Pres for Human Resources ... Mr. George CASEY
21 Asst Vice Pres for Administration ... Ms. Joan FLYNN
26 Asst VP Marketing/Communications ... Ms. Sharon HIGGINS
41 Asst VP/Director of Athletics ... Mr. James PAQUETTE
38 Dir Counsel Ctr/Ast VP Student Dev ... Dr. Donelda COOK
102 Dir Corporation & Foundation Rels ... Ms. Beth SCHRODER
07 Director Undergraduate Admissions ... Ms. Elena HICKS
07 Director of Graduate Admissions ... Ms. Maureen FAUX
06 Director of Records ... Ms. Rita L. STEINER
85 Director of International Programs ... Dr. Andre COLOMBAT
08 Director of Library ... Mr. John MCGINTY
42 Director of Campus Ministry ... Mr. Jack DENNIS
88 Dir Center Community Svc/Justice ... Sr. Catherine GUGERTY, SSND
36 Dir Career Devel/Placement Center ... Dr. CreSaundra Y. SILLS
88 Dir Alcohol/Drug Ed/Support Svcs ... Mr. Jan WILLIAMS
88 Director Recreational Sports ... Ms. Pamela WETHERBEE-METCALF
88 Dir Leadership/New Student Program ... Mr. Jeffrey KNIPLE
35 Director Student Activities ... Mr. Mark C. BRODERICK
88 Director Alana Services ... Mr. Rodney PARKER
23 Dir Health Svcs/Health Educ Pgms ... Ms. Eugenia A. LOMBARDI
21 Controller ... Ms. Kelly NELSON
45 Director of Resource Management ... Mr. David DAUGHADAY
88 Director of Facilities Operation ... Mr. Charles RIORDAN
31 Director Event Svcs/Auxiliary Mgmt ... Mr. Joseph BRADLEY
18 Dir Project Mgmt/Facilities Maint ... Mr. Laszlo PELY
88 Director Environment Health/Safety ... Mr. Thomas HETTLEMAN
19 Dir of Public Safety/Campus Police ... Mr. Timothy FOX
29 Director Alumni Relations ... Mr. Brian OAKES
44 Director of Annual Giving ... Ms. Jane Curley HOGGE
27 Director of Creative Services ... Mr. Brian HATCHER
88 Director Advancement Communications ... Mr. Carl LUTY
89 Dean First Yr Stdnts/Academic Svcs ... Dr. Ilona MCGUINESS
49 Dean College of Arts & Sciences ... Rev. James F. MIRACKY, SJ
50 Dean Sellinger Sch Business & Mgmt ... Ms. Karyl LEGGIO
49 Assistant Dean Arts & Sciences ... Dr. Suzanne KEILSON
50 Assistant Dean for Business Program ... Ms. Ann ATTANASIO
88 Associate Dean of Students ... Ms. Michelle CHEATEM

Maple Springs Baptist Bible College & Seminary (B)

4130 Belt Road, Capitol Heights MD 20743-5712
County: Prince Georges FICE Identification: 038224
Unit ID: 446394
Telephone: (301) 736-3631 Carnegie Class: Spec/Faith
FAX Number: (301) 735-6507 Calendar System: Semester
URL: www.msbbcs.edu
Established: 1986 Annual Undergrad Tuition & Fees: $3,620
Enrollment: 222 Coed
Affiliation or Control: Baptist IRS Status: 501(c)3
Highest Offering: Doctorate
Program: Religious Emphasis
Accreditation: TRACS

01 President ... Dr. Larry W. JORDAN
04 Executive Assistant to President ... Dr. Jerome S. TARVER
03 Executive Vice President ... Dr. Vivian E. BESS
05 Vice President Academic Affairs ... Dr. Emanuel D. CHATMAN
11 Vice Pres Administration & Finance ... Dr. Jerrye B. FELICIANA
73 Dean Bible College ... Dr. Carl KEELS
58 Dean Bible Seminary ... Dr. Daryl WATSON
06 Director Records/Admissions ... Mr. Percy COKER
10 Director Business Affairs ... Mrs. Fannie G. THOMPSON
32 Director Student Affairs ... Dr. James THOMPSON

08 Director Learning Resource Center ... Mr. Darren JONES
37 Financial Aid Coordinator ... Ms. Patricia JONES

Maryland Institute College of Art (C)

1300 Mount Royal Avenue, Baltimore MD 21217-4191
County: Independent City FICE Identification: 002080
Unit ID: 163295
Telephone: (410) 669-9200 Carnegie Class: Spec/Arts
FAX Number: (410) 669-9206 Calendar System: Semester
URL: www.mica.edu
Established: 1826 Annual Undergrad Tuition & Fees: $37,470
Enrollment: 2,102 Coed
Affiliation or Control: Independent Non-Profit IRS Status: 501(c)3
Highest Offering: Master's
Program: Fine Arts Emphasis
Accreditation: M, ART

01 President ... Mr. Fred LAZARUS, IV
05 Vice Pres Academic Affairs/Provost ... Mr. Ray ALLEN
10 Vice Pres Fiscal Affairs ... Mr. Douglas MANN
30 Vice Pres Advancement ... Mr. Michael R. FRANCO
32 Vice Pres/Dean Student Affairs ... Mr. J. Davidson (Dusty) PORTER
84 Vice Pres/Dean Admiss/Finan Aid ... Ms. Theresa BEDOYA
13 Vice Pres Technology Systems & Svcs ... Mr. Tom HYATT
11 Vice Pres Operations ... Mr. Mike MOLLA
46 Vice Provost Research ... Mr. Guna NADARAJAN
04 Executive Assistant to President ... Ms. Marian SMITH
37 Assoc VP Financial Aid ... Ms. Diane PRENGAMAN
44 Assoc VP Dev Constituent Rels ... Ms. Alison DAVITT
27 Assoc VP Institutnal Communication ... Mr. Cedric MOBLEY
44 Assoc VP Advancement/Plan/Sp Projct ... Ms. Mary Ann LAMBROS
14 Assoc VP Technology ... Ms. Susan MILTENBERGER
18 Assoc VP Facilities Management ... Mr. Timothy MILLNER
16 Assoc VP Human Resources ... Ms. Elizabeth ENSELEIN
20 Dean Undergrad Students/Fac ... Ms. Jan STINCHCOMB
20 Dean Academic Services ... Ms. Cynthia BARTH
58 Dean Graduate Studies ... Vacant
53 Dean Art Education ... Ms. Karen CARROLL
51 Dean Continuing Studies ... Mr. David GRACYALNY
35 Assoc Dean Stdnt Life/Judicial Affs ... Mr. Michael PATTERSON
35 Assoc Dean Student Development ... Ms. Cheryl GARNER
88 Assoc Dean Graduate Admission ... Mr. Scott KELLY
88 Assoc Dean Continuing Studies ... Mr. Peter DUBEAU
06 Assoc Dean Enrollment Svs/Registrar ... Ms. Christine PETERSON
88 Asst Dean Graduate Studies ... Ms. Erin JAKOWSKI
28 Asst Dean Diversity Intercultur Dev ... Mr. Clyde JOHNSON, JR.
21 Director Accounting ... Ms. Jessica RURKA
88 Director Budget ... Ms. Brigitte SULLIVAN
88 Director Student Accounts ... Mr. Chris SALONE
39 Director Residence Life ... Mr. Scott STONE
36 Director Career Development ... Ms. Megan MILLER
31 Director Community Engagement ... Ms. Karen STULTS
31 Director Community Art Partnerships ... Ms. Agnes MOON
38 Director Counseling Center ... Ms. Pat FARRELL
88 Director Student Activities ... Ms. Karol MARTINEZ
07 Director Undergraduate Admissions ... Ms. Christine SEESE
88 Director Admissions Operations ... Ms. Cheryl ISSOD
08 Director & Head Librarian ... Ms. Florence THORP
88 Director Annual Fund ... Ms. Carolyn STRATFORD-YOUNCE
88 Director Advancement Services ... Ms. Catherine BURRIER
88 Director Stewardships ... Ms. Erin CHREST
88 Director Exhibitions ... Mr. Gerald ROSS
85 Director International Affairs ... Ms. Petra VISSCHER
88 Director Writing St/Learn Res Ctr ... Mr. Daniel GUTSTEIN
88 Dir Data Mgmt/Registration Cont Std ... Ms. Kathy GREENBLATT
88 Director Marketing & Enrollment Svs ... Ms. Tracy JACOBS
09 Director Student Records & Research ... Mr. Hadley GARBART
19 Director of Campus Safety ... Mr. Stephen DAVIS
88 Director Events ... Ms. Anne SOUTH
88 Director Operation Services ... Mr. Chris BOHASKA
29 Interim Dir Alumni & Parent Rels ... Mr. David HART
102 Director Corp/Found/Govt Relations ... Ms. Sara WARREN
105 Director of Web Communications ... Mr. Gregory RAGO
24 Director Technical Support Services ... Mr. John RHODES
91 Director Administrative Systems ... Mr. Ted SIMPSON
88 Director Network Services ... Mr. David APAW
90 Academic Technology Specialist ... Mr. Paul IWANCIO
40 Manager College Store ... Ms. Kerri LITZ

McDaniel College (D)

2 College Hill, Westminster MD 21157-4390
County: Carroll FICE Identification: 002109
Unit ID: 164270
Telephone: (410) 848-7000 Carnegie Class: Bac/A&S
FAX Number: (410) 857-2279 Calendar System: Semester
URL: www.mcdaniel.edu
Established: 1867 Annual Undergrad Tuition & Fees: $34,780
Enrollment: 3,512 Coed
Affiliation or Control: Independent Non-Profit IRS Status: 501(c)3
Highest Offering: Master's
Program: Liberal Arts And General; Teacher Preparatory
Accreditation: M, SW, TED

01 President ... Dr. Roger N. CASEY
05 Provost/Dean of Faculty ... Dr. Thomas M. FALKNER
10 Vice Pres Administration & Finance ... Dr. Ethan A. SEIDEL
44 Vice Pres Institutional Advancement ... Mr. Richard G. KIEF
32 Vice Pres/Dean of Student Affairs ... Ms. Beth R. GERL
84 VP Enroll Mgt/Dean of Admissions ... Ms. Florence W. HINES
30 Assoc Vice Pres/Director Devel ... Mr. Lawrence JUNKIN
29 Assoc Vice Pres of Alumni Relations ... Ms. Robin A. BRENTON
27 Assoc Vice Pres Comm/Marketing ... Ms. Joyce D. MULLER
04 Exec Assistant to the President ... Ms. Tamara BOWEN
58 Dean Graduate/Professional Stds ... Dr. Henry B. REIFF
20 Associate Dean of Academic Affairs ... Dr. Debora JOHNSON-ROSS
88 Acting Assoc Dean Student Acad Life ... Ms. Lisa BRESLIN
102 Dir Corp & Foundation Relations ... Ms. Kathleen M. CURTIN
08 Director of Library ... Ms. Jessame E. FERGUSON
37 Director Financial Aid ... Ms. Patricia M. WILLIAMS
06 Registrar ... Ms. Jan A. KIPHART
41 Director Athletics ... Mr. Paul MOYER
36 Director Career Advising ... Vacant
38 Director Counseling ... Ms. Susan J. GLORE
35 Director Student Engagement ... Ms. Christine WORKMAN
21 Director Financial Services/Treas ... Mr. Arthur S. WISNER
15 Director Human Resources ... Mr. Thomas G. STEBACK
45 Dir Facility Plng/Capital Projects ... Mr. Edgar S. SELL, JR.
18 Director Physical Plant ... Mr. George W. BRENTON
19 Director of Campus Safety ... Mr. Michael N. WEBSTER
40 Manager Bookstore ... Mr. Kyle MELOCHE
18 Director Conferences/Auxil Svcs ... Ms. Mary J. COLBERT
13 Chief Information Officer ... Dr. Esther IGLICH
28 Director of Multicultural Services ... Ms. Mahlia JOYCE
92 Director of Honors Program ... Dr. Stephanie D. MADSEN
96 Director of Purchasing/Receiving ... Ms. Margaret G. BELL
88 Coord of Deaf Education Program ... Dr. Mark M. RUST
09 Director Institutional Research ... Dr. Brian AULT
101 Secretary of the Board of Trustees ... Ms. Mary Ann FRIDAY

Montgomery College (E)

900 Hungerford Drive, Rockville MD 20850-1733
County: Montgomery FICE Identification: 006911
Unit ID: 163426
Telephone: (240) 567-5000 Carnegie Class: Assoc/Pub-S-MC
FAX Number: (240) 567-6397 Calendar System: Semester
URL: www.montgomerycollege.edu
Established: 1946 Annual Undergrad Tuition & Fees (In-District): $4,380
Enrollment: 26,015 Coed
Affiliation or Control: Local IRS Status: 501(c)3
Highest Offering: Associate Degree
Program: Occupational; 2-Year Principally Bachelor's Creditable
Accreditation: M, ADNUR, DMS, MUS, PTAA, RAD, SURGT

01 President ... Dr. DeRionne P. POLLARD
05 Int Sr VP for Academic Affairs ... Ms. Paula MATUSKEY
32 Sr VP for Student Services ... Dr. Beverly WALKER-GRIFFEA
11 Sr VP Admin & Fiscal Services ... Ms. Cathy JONES
12 Vice Pres/Provost Rockville Campus ... Dr. Judy ACKERMAN
12 Vice Pres/Provost Germantown Campus ... Dr. Sanjay RAI
12 Vice Pres/Prov Takoma Park Campus ... Dr. Brad J. STEWART
103 VP for Workforce Dev & Contuing Ed ... Mr. George M. PAYNE
100 Chief of Staff/Chief Strategy Ofcr ... Dr. Stephen D. CAIN
30 Vice Pres of Advancement ... Mr. David SEARS
45 VP for Planning and Inst Effective ... Ms. Kathleen WESSMAN
13 VP of Instructional & IT/CIO ... Dr. Mike RUSSELL
09 Dir Institutional Rsrch & Analysis ... Dr. Robert LYNCH
86 Chief Government Relations Officer ... Ms. Susan MADDEN
43 General Counsel ... Mr. Clyde H. SORRELL
15 Chief Human Resource Officer ... Ms. Vivian M. LAWYER
18 Chief Facilities Officer ... Mr. David J. CAPP
28 Chief Diversity Officer ... Dr. Michelle T. SCOTT
37 College Dir Student Financial Aid ... Ms. Melissa GREGORY
07 Dir of Admissions/Enrollment Mgmt ... Ms. Rochelle I. MOORE
21 Director of Budget ... Ms. Donna L. DIMON
31 Director of Auxiliary Services ... Dr. Kathi CAREY-FLETCHER
26 Director of Communications ... Vacant
29 Director Alumni Relations ... Vacant
96 Director of Procurement ... Dr. Janet WORMACK
10 Chief Business Officer ... Mr. Thomas SHEERAN

Morgan State University (F)

1700 East Cold Spring Lane, Baltimore MD 21251-0001
County: Independent City FICE Identification: 002083
Unit ID: 163453
Telephone: (443) 885-3333 Carnegie Class: DRU
FAX Number: (443) 885-3698 Calendar System: Semester
URL: www.morgan.edu
Established: 1867 Annual Undergrad Tuition & Fees (In-State): $6,928
Enrollment: 7,805 Coed
Affiliation or Control: State IRS Status: 501(c)3
Highest Offering: Doctorate
Program: Liberal Arts And General; Teacher Preparatory; Professional
Accreditation: M, BUS, BUSA, DIETD, ENG, LSAR, MT, MUS, PH, PLNG, SW, TED

01 President ... Dr. David WILSON
05 Provost/Vice Pres Academic Affairs ... Dr. T. Joan ROBINSON
11 Vice President for Operations ... Dr. Maurice TAYLOR
10 Vice President Finance & Management ... Mr. Raymond VOLLMER
45 Vice President Planning ... Dr. Joseph POPOVICH
32 Acting Vice Pres Student Affairs ... Ms. Tanya RUSH
30 Vice Pres Institutional Advancement ... Ms. Cheryl Y. HITCHCOCK
20 Assoc VP for Academic Affairs ... Dr. Kara TURNER
21 Asst Vice President for Finance ... Mr. Bickram JANAK
35 Associate VP Student Affairs ... Ms. Tanya RUSH
04 Executive Assistant to President ... Dr. Willie LARKIN
49 Dean College of Liberal Arts ... Dr. Adele NEWSON-HORST
50 Dean School Busines & Management ... Dr. Otis THOMAS
53 Dean School of Education ... Dr. Patricia WELCH

54 Dean School of Engineering .... Dr. Eugene DELOATCH
58 Acting Dean of the Graduate School .... Dr. Mark GARRISON
48 Dean School of Architecture .... Dr. Mary Anne AKERS
70 Dean School of Social Work .... Dr. Anna MCPHATTER
69 Dean School of Community Health .... Dr. Allan NOONAN
37 Acting Director of Financial Aid .... Ms. Tanya WILKERSON
38 Director of Counseling Services .... Ms. Nina DOBSON-HOPKINS
08 Director of Library .... Dr. Richard BRADBERRY
06 Director of Records/Registration .... Mr. Paul THOMPSON
07 Director of Admissions .... Ms. Shonda GRAY
36 Director of Placement .... Mr. William CARSON
15 Director Human Resources .... Mrs. Armada GRANT
29 Director Alumni Association .... Mrs. Joyce BROWN
14 Director Computer Center .... Mr. Gilbert MORGAN
86 Director State Relations .... Mr. Claude E. HITCHCOCK
09 Director of Institutional Research .... Ms. Cheryl ROLLINS
18 Director Physical Plant .... Mr. Kenneth ELLIS
26 Director Public Relations .... Mr. Clinton R. COLEMAN
84 Exec Dir Enrollment Management .... Mr. Joseph C. BOZEMAN
96 Director of Purchasing .... Mr. Churchill B. WORTHERLY
28 Director of Diversity .... Vacant

Mount St. Mary's University (A)

16300 Old Emmitsburg Road,
Emmitsburg MD 21727-7799
County: Frederick FICE Identification: 002086
Unit ID: 163462
Telephone: (301) 447-6122 Carnegie Class: Master's M
FAX Number: (301) 447-5634 Calendar System: Semester
URL: www.msmary.edu
Established: 1808 Annual Undergrad Tuition & Fees: $31,536
Enrollment: 2,112 Coed
Affiliation or Control: Roman Catholic IRS Status: 501(c)3
Highest Offering: Master's
Program: Liberal Arts And General; Teacher Preparatory; Professional; Religious Emphasis
Accreditation: M, IACBE, TED, THEOL

01 President .... Dr. Thomas H. POWELL
03 Vice President/Rector .... Msgr. Steven ROHLFS
03 Executive Vice President .... Mr. Dan SOLLER
88 Vice President University Affairs .... Ms. Pauline ENGLESTATTER
05 Provost .... Dr. David B. REHM
10 Vice Pres for Business & Finance .... Mr. Michael MALEWICKI
30 Vice President for Advancement .... Mr. Robert J. BRENNAN
84 Vice Pres Enrollment Management .... Mr. Michael POST
20 Assoc Provost .... Dr. Leona SEVICK
50 Dean Richard J Bolte Sr Sch of Bus .... Dr. William FORGANG
53 Dean Sch Education & Human Services .... Dr. Barbara MARTIN PALMER
81 Dean School Natural Science & Math .... Dr. David BUSHMAN
79 Dean College of Liberal Arts .... Dr. Joshua HOCHSCHILD
41 Director of Athletics .... Ms. Lynne P. ROBINSON
42 Chaplain .... Fr. Brian NOLAN
32 Dean of Students .... Mr. Michael TABERSKI
51 Director Professional/Cont Studies .... Mr. Joe LEBHERZ
08 Dean of the Library .... Mr. Charles KUHN
09 Director Institutional Research .... Ms. Linda K. JUNKER
06 Registrar .... Ms. Margot RHOADES
50 Director of MBA Program .... Vacant
88 Director Conferences/Special Pgms .... Ms. Marianne DEMPSEY
23 Director of Health Services .... Dr. Bonnie PORTIER
24 Director of the Media Center .... Mr. John B. BREWER, JR.
37 Director of Financial Aid .... Mr. David C. REEDER
36 Director Career Center .... Ms. Sabira VOHRA
13 Chief Information Officer .... Mr. Bobby L. FLACK
26 Director of Communications .... Ms. Linda SHERMAN
44 Director of Annual Giving .... Ms. Marie CACACE
16 Director of Human Resources .... Ms. Barbara R. MILLER
19 Director of Public Safety .... Mr. R. Barry TITLER
29 Director of Alumni Relations .... Ms. Maureen C. PLANT
18 Director of Physical Plant .... Mr. Bruce NORMAN
88 Director Community Services .... Mr. Jeff ABEL
28 Director Ctr for Student Diversity .... Ms. Chianti BLACKMON
35 Dir Campus Activ/Student Ldrshp .... Mr. Kenneth MCVEARRY
92 Director of the Honors Program .... Vacant
40 Manager of College Store .... Mr. Joseph KNORR
96 Purchasing Agent .... Ms. Maria L. TOPPER

National Labor College (B)

10000 New Hampshire Avenue,
Silver Spring MD 20903-1706
County: Montgomery FICE Identification: 034555
Unit ID: 434034
Telephone: (301) 431-6400 Carnegie Class: Spec/Bus
FAX Number: (301) 434-5411 Calendar System: Semester
URL: www.nlc.edu
Established: 1997 Annual Undergrad Tuition & Fees: $4,200
Enrollment: 695 Coed
Affiliation or Control: Independent Non-Profit IRS Status: 501(c)3
Highest Offering: Baccalaureate
Program: Liberal Arts And General
Accreditation: M

01 President & CEO .... Dr. Paula PEINOVICH
05 Provost/VP Academic Affairs .... Dr. Tom KRIGER
11 Vice Pres Operations .... Beth SHANNON
06 Registrar .... Toni RILEY
10 Controller .... Antonio DENICOLIS
15 Int Human Resources Manager .... Annette PIECORA

Ner Israel Rabbinical College (C)

400 Mount Wilson Lane, Baltimore MD 21208-1198
County: Baltimore FICE Identification: 002087
Unit ID: 163532
Telephone: (410) 484-7200 Carnegie Class: Spec/Faith
FAX Number: (410) 484-3060 Calendar System: Semester
Established: 1933 Annual Undergrad Tuition & Fees: $9,400
Enrollment: 562 Male
Affiliation or Control: Independent Non-Profit IRS Status: 501(c)3
Highest Offering: Doctorate
Program: Teacher Preparatory; Professional; Religious Emphasis
Accreditation: RABN

01 President .... Rabbi Sheftel M. NEUBERGER
05 Chief Academic Officer .... Rabbi Aharon FELDMAN
03 Executive Director .... Mr. Jerome H. KADDEN
04 Assistant to the President .... Rabbi Boruch NEUBERGER
07 Director of Admissions .... Rabbi Beryl WEISBORD
13 Director of Administrative Services .... Mr. Larry RIBAKOW
06 Registrar .... Rabbi Chaim D. LAPIDUS
37 Director Student Financial Aid .... Rabbi Shmuel SCHACHTER
85 Foreign Student Advisor .... Rabbi Eliyahu HAKKAKIAN
11 Senior Administrator .... Rabbi Abraham PELBERG
30 Director of Development .... Rabbi Louis HOFFMAN
45 Director of Planning .... Rabbi Leonard OBERSTEIN
26 Director Community Relations .... Rabbi Jonathan SEIDEMANN
18 Chief Physical Plant .... Mr. David FRIEDMAN
08 Head Librarian .... Rabbi Avrohom SHNIDMAN
39 Director of Student Housing .... Rabbi Emanuel GOLDFEIZ
29 Associate Director Alumni Relations .... Rabbi Eli GREENGART

Notre Dame of Maryland University (D)

4701 N Charles Street, Baltimore MD 21210-2404
County: Independent City FICE Identification: 002065
Unit ID: 163578
Telephone: (410) 435-0100 Carnegie Class: Master's L
FAX Number: (410) 532-5791 Calendar System: Semester
URL: www.ndm.edu
Established: 1873 Annual Undergrad Tuition & Fees: $28,700
Enrollment: 501 Female
Affiliation or Control: Roman Catholic IRS Status: 501(c)3
Highest Offering: Doctorate
Program: Liberal Arts And General; Teacher Preparatory; Professional
Accreditation: M, NUR, @PHAR, TED

01 President .... Dr. Mary Pat SEURKAMP
05 Vice President Academic Affairs .... Sr. Christine DE VINNE
32 Vice President Student Development .... Dr. Patricia SWATFAGER-HANEY
30 Vice Pres Institutional Advancement .... Ms. Patricia A. BOSSE
84 Vice Pres Enrollment Management .... Ms. Heidi L. FLETCHER
10 Vice Pres Finance & Administration .... Mr. Thomas MAHER
20 Associate VP Academic Affairs .... Dr. Anne HENDERSON
35 Dean of Students .... Ms. Pauline WILLIAMSON
04 Special Assistant to the President .... Ms. Candace CARACO
06 Assoc VP Enrollment/Registrar .... Ms. Sharon BOGDAN
37 Director of Financial Aid .... Ms. Zhanna GOLTSER
36 Dir Academic & Career Enrichment .... Ms. Diane MCCANN
13 Director Information Technology .... Mr. Warren SZELISTOWSKI
29 Director of Alumnae Relations .... Ms. Emilia POITER
08 Librarian .... Mr. John W. MCGINTY
85 Director International Program .... Sr. Miriam JANSEN
07 Director of Admissions .... Mr. Lucas J. SIFUENTES
09 Director of Institutional Research .... Mr. Shuang LIU
15 Director of Human Resources .... Ms. Geri LARSEN
18 Director of Facility Management .... Mr. Mario CANDIELLO
21 Director Business Officer .... Ms. Barbara MORRIS
38 Director Counseling Center .... Ms. Amy PROVAN
19 Director of Public Safety .... Mr. Jeff MUNCHEL
40 Bookstore Manager .... Ms. Ashley ROENIGK
41 Athletic Director .... Ms. Erin FOLEY
42 Director Campus Ministry .... Ms. Melissa LEES
67 Dean School of Pharmacy .... Dr. Anne LIN
07 Director Pharmacy Admissions .... Mr. Larry SHATTUCK

Peabody Institute of Johns Hopkins University (E)

1 E Mount Vernon Place, Baltimore MD 21202-2397
County: Independent City FICE Identification: 002088
Unit ID: 163611
Telephone: (410) 234-4500 Carnegie Class: Not Classified
FAX Number: (410) 659-8129 Calendar System: Semester
URL: www.peabody.jhu.edu
Established: 1857 Annual Undergrad Tuition & Fees: $37,000
Enrollment: 744 Coed
Affiliation or Control: Independent Non-Profit IRS Status: 501(c)3
Highest Offering: Doctorate
Program: Teacher Preparatory; Professional; Music Emphasis
Accreditation: &M, MUS

01 Director of the Institute .... Mr. Jeffrey SHARKEY
05 Dean of Conservatory/Deputy Dir .... Dr. Mellasenah MORRIS
20 Assoc Dean Academic Affairs .... Dr. Paul MATHEWS
32 Assoc Dean Student Affairs .... Ms. Katsura KURITA
11 Assoc Dean for Administration .... Ms. Maureen HARRIGAN
26 Assoc Dean External Relations .... Ms. Andrea TRISCIUZZI
27 Director of Communications .... Mr. Richard SELDEN
06 Registrar .... Mr. James DOBSON
07 Director of Admissions .... Mr. David H. LANE
08 Head Librarian .... Ms. Jennifer OTTERVIK
37 Director of Financial Aid .... Mr. Thomas MCDERMOTT
88 Director of Constituent Engagement .... Ms. Rebecca POLGAR
18 Director Facilities Management .... Mr. Joseph BRANT
15 Manager Human Resources & Payroll .... Ms. Laura BROOKS
36 Dir Career Counseling & Placement .... Vacant

† Regional accreditation is carried under the parent institution, Johns Hopkins University, MD.

Prince George's Community College (F)

301 Largo Road, Largo MD 20774-2199
County: Prince Georges FICE Identification: 002089
Unit ID: 163657
Telephone: (301) 336-6000 Carnegie Class: Assoc/Pub-S-SC
FAX Number: (301) 808-0960 Calendar System: Semester
URL: www.pgcc.edu
Established: 1958 Annual Undergrad Tuition & Fees (In-District): $3,146
Enrollment: 14,814 Coed
Affiliation or Control: Local IRS Status: 501(c)3
Highest Offering: Associate Degree
Program: Occupational; 2-Year Principally Bachelor's Creditable
Accreditation: M, ADNUR, ENGT, NMT, RAD

01 President .... Dr. Charlene M. DUKES
05 Vice Pres Academic Affairs .... Dr. Sandra F. DUNNINGTON
32 Vice Pres Student Services .... Dr. Tyjaun A. LEE
10 Vice Pres Administrative Services .... Mr. Tom E. KNAPP
103 Interim VP Workforce Devel/Cont Ed . Mr. Joseph L. MARTINELLI
14 Vice Pres Technology Services .... Dr. Joseph G. ROSSMEIER
38 Dean Student Development Svcs ... Dr. Scheherazade W. FORMAN
84 Dean of Enrollment Services .... Dr. Tracy A. HARRIS
51 Dean Wrkfrce Dev/Cont Educ Pgms .... Vacant
04 Chief of Staff .... Ms. Alonia C. SHARPS
08 Interim Dir Library/Learning Res .... Ms. Priscilla C. THOMPSON
09 Dean Planning/Institutional Rsrch .... Dr. Andrea A. LEX
06 Director Admissions & Records .... Ms. Vera L. BAGLEY
07 Director Recruitment .... Ms. Jennifer M. PRICE
18 Dean Facilities Management .... Dr. David C. MOSBY
41 Director Physical Facilities .... Mr. Gilberto HINOJOSA
86 Dir Community & Government Affairs ... Dr. Jacqueline L. BROWN
30 Exec Dir Institutional Advancement .... Ms. Brenda S. MITCHELL
26 Director Marketing & Creative Svcs .... Dr. Deidra W. HILL
13 Chief Technology Officer .... Mr. William L. ANDERSON
15 Dean Human Resources .... Ms. Lark T. DOBSON
37 Director Financial Aid .... Ms. Sharon E. HASSAN
79 Dean of Liberal Arts .... Dr. Carolyn F. HOFFMAN
35 Dean College Life Services .... Mr. Malverse A. NICHOLSON, JR.
76 Dean of Health Science .... Ms. Angela D. ANDERSON
81 Dean Science/Tech/Engr/Math .... Dr. Christine E. BARROW
83 Dean Social Sci & Bus Studies Div .... Dr. John A. ROSICKY
88 Dean Educ Development .... Dr. Beverly S. REED
21 Dean Financial Affairs .... Ms. Nancy E. BURGESS
20 Sr Acad Admin to VP for Acad Affs .... Ms. Catherine LAPALOMBARA
36 Manager Career & Job Services .... Ms. Stephanie S. PAIR-CUNNINGHAM
96 Procurement Officer .... Vacant

St. John's College (G)

PO Box 2800, Annapolis MD 21404-2800
County: Anne Arundel FICE Identification: 002092
Unit ID: 163976
Telephone: (410) 263-2371 Carnegie Class: Bac/A&S
FAX Number: (410) 626-2886 Calendar System: Semester
URL: www.sjca.edu
Established: 1784 Annual Undergrad Tuition & Fees: $43,656
Enrollment: 538 Coed
Affiliation or Control: Independent Non-Profit IRS Status: 501(c)3
Highest Offering: Master's
Program: Liberal Arts And General
Accreditation: M

01 President .... Mr. Christopher B. NELSON
30 Vice Pres Advancement Annapolis .... Ms. Barbara GOYETTE
05 Dean .... Ms. Pamela KRAUS
10 Treasurer .... Ms. Bronte JONES
06 Registrar .... Mr. Daniel CROWE
07 Director of Admissions .... Mr. John M. CHRISTENSEN
102 Director Corporate/Foundation Rels .... Ms. Susan BORDEN
37 Director of Financial Aid .... Ms. Dana KENNEDY
08 Librarian .... Ms. Cathy DIXON
15 Director of Personnel .... Ms. Deborah ANAWALT
18 Supt of Buildings & Grounds .... Mr. Sid PHIPPS
19 Chief of Security .... Mr. Timon LINN
23 Director of Student Health .... Ms. Nancy CALABRESE
27 Director of Communications .... Ms. Patricia DEMPSEY
32 Director of Student Services .... Ms. Taylor WATERS
20 Assistant Dean .... Ms. Susan PAALMAN
36 Director of Career Services .... Ms. Jaime DUNN
40 Bookstore Manager .... Mr. Robin DUNN
41 Director of Athletics .... Mr. Leo PICKENS
58 Director of Graduate Institute .... Mr. Jeff BLACK
21 Controller .... Ms. Diane SAWYER
29 Director of Alumni Relations .... Ms. Jo Ann MATTSON

† See Affiliate: St. John's College at Santa Fe, NM.

St. Mary's College of Maryland (A)

18952 E Fisher Road, Saint Mary's City MD 20686-3001

County: Saint Mary's — FICE Identification: 002095
Unit ID: 163912

Telephone: (240) 895-2000 — Carnegie Class: Bac/A&S
FAX Number: (240) 895-4462 — Calendar System: Semester
URL: www.smcm.edu
Established: 1840 — Annual Undergrad Tuition & Fees (In-State): $14,445
Enrollment: 2,017 — Coed
Affiliation or Control: State — IRS Status: 501(c)3
Highest Offering: Master's
Program: Liberal Arts And General
Accreditation: M

01	President	Dr. Joseph R. URGO
05	Dean of Faculty/VP for Acad Affairs	Dr. Beth RUSHING
10	VP Business & Finance	Dr. Thomas J. BOTZMAN
30	Vice President for Advancement	Dr. Maureen C. SILVA
44	Asst Vice Pres for Development	Vacant
26	Assoc VP for Marketing/Public Rels	Vacant
29	Director Alumni Relations	Mr. David M. SUSHINSKY
09	Assist Dir Institutional Research	Vacant
06	Registrar	Ms. Susan A. BENNETT
20	Assoc Dean of Faculty	Dr. Rich PLATT
20	Dean of the Core Curric/1st-yr Exp	Dr. Elizabeth N. WILLIAMS
07	Dean Admissions/Financial Aid	Vacant
37	Director of Financial Aid	Ms. Caroline O. BRIGHT
88	Asst VP for Academic Administration	Mr. Mark W. HEIDRICH
35	Dean of Students	Dr. Laura BAYLESS
38	Director of Counseling Services	Dr. Mary-Jeanne RALEIGH
41	Director of Athletics/Recreation	Mr. Scott W. DEVINE
83	Chair Anthropology	Dr. Iris C. FORD
57	Chair of Arts & Art History	Dr. Joe E. LUCCHESI
88	Chair of Biology	Dr. Rachel MYEROWITZ
88	Chair of Chemistry	Dr. Andrew S. KOCH
88	Chair of Economics	Dr. Michael H. YE
83	Chair Educational Studies	Dr. Lois T. STOVER
79	Chair of English	Dr. Ben A. CLICK
83	Chair of History	Dr. Thomas M. BARRETT
79	Chair of Intl Languages/Cultures	Dr. Laine DOGGETT
81	Chair of Math/Computer Science	Dr. Simon READ
64	Acting Chair of Music	Dr. Deborah LAWRENCE
79	Chair Philosophy/Religious Studies	Dr. Bjorn H. KRONDORFER
77	Chair of Physics	Dr. Charles L. ADLER
82	Chair of Political Science	Dr. Sahar SHAFQAT
83	Chair of Psychology	Dr. Eric J. HIRIS
83	Chair of Sociology	Dr. Elizabeth A. OSBORN
57	Chair of Theatre/Film/Media Stds	Dr. Joanne R. KLEIN
51	Asst Vice Pres Lifelong Learning	Vacant
20	Asst Vice Pres Academic Services	Dr. William L. HOWARD
18	Assoc Vice President of Facilities	Mr. Charles C. JACKSON
19	Interim Director of Public Safety	Mr. David D. ZYLAK
40	Director of the Campus Store	Mr. Richard T. WAGNER
15	Associate Vice President of HR	Ms. Sally A. MERCER
23	Director of Health Services	Ms. Linda WALLACE
35	Associate Dean of Students	Ms. Joanne A. GOLDWATER
13	Dir Campus Technology Support Svcs	Mr. George W. WAGGONER
44	Donor Relations and Comm Officer	Ms. Karen C. RALEY
08	Director of the Library/Media Svcs	Dr. Celia E. RABINOWITZ
102	Senior Development Officer	Ms. Liisa E. FRANZEN
21	Comptroller/Director of Accounting	Mr. Gabriel A. MBOMEH
43	Assistant Attorney General	Ms. Sara SLAFF
22	Affirm Act/Equal Opportunity Office	Mr. Melvin A. MCCLINTOCK
25	Director of Sponsored Research	Vacant
28	Fair Practices Officer	Ms. Sally A. MERCER
84	Director Enrollment Management	Vacant
96	Procurement Officer	Mr. Patrick G. HUNT

Saint Mary's Seminary and University (B)

5400 Roland Avenue, Baltimore MD 21210-1994

County: Independent City — FICE Identification: 002096
Unit ID: 163842

Telephone: (410) 864-4000 — Carnegie Class: Spec/Faith
FAX Number: (410) 864-4278 — Calendar System: Semester
URL: www.stmarys.edu
Established: 1791 — Annual Undergrad Tuition & Fees: $28,316
Enrollment: 258 — Coed
Affiliation or Control: Roman Catholic — IRS Status: 501(c)3
Highest Offering: First Professional Degree
Program: Liberal Arts And General; Professional; Religious Emphasis
Accreditation: M, THEOL

01	President/Rector	Rev. Thomas R. HURST
30	Vice Pres Institutional Advancement	Mrs. Elizabeth L. VISCONAGE
05	Dean School Theology	Rev. Timothy A. KULBICKI, OFM CONV
73	Dean Ecumenical Institute Theology	Dr. Michael J. GORMAN
73	Dean Ecclesiastical Faculty	Mr. Timothy A. KULBICKI, OFM CONV
10	University Treasurer	Mr. Richard G. CHILDS
06	University Registrar	Ms. Paula M. THIGPEN
37	Director Financial Aid	Mrs. Victoria F. GAUNT
08	Director of Library	Mr. Thomas RASZEWSKI

The SANS Technology Institute (C)

8120 Woodmont Avenue, Suite 205, Bethesda MD 20814

County: Montgomery — Identification: 667006
Telephone: (301) 654-7267 — Carnegie Class: Not Classified
FAX Number: (301) 951-0140 — Calendar System: Semester
URL: www.sans.edu
Established: N/A — Annual Graduate Tuition & Fees: $17,800
Enrollment: N/A — Coed
Affiliation or Control: Independent Non-Profit — IRS Status: 501(c)3
Highest Offering: Master's; No Undergraduates
Program: Professional
Accreditation: @M

01	President	Mr. Stephen NORTHCUTT
05	Dean of the Faculty	Dr. Johannes ULLRICH
07	Dean of Admissions/Student Svcs	Dr. Debbie SVOBODA

Sojourner-Douglass College (D)

200 North Central Avenue, Baltimore MD 21202

County: Baltimore — FICE Identification: 021279
Unit ID: 163921

Telephone: (410) 276-0306 — Carnegie Class: Bac/Diverse
FAX Number: (410) 675-1810 — Calendar System: Trimester
URL: www.sdc.edu
Established: 1980 — Annual Undergrad Tuition & Fees: $12,540
Enrollment: 1,251 — Coed
Affiliation or Control: Independent Non-Profit — IRS Status: 501(c)3
Highest Offering: Master's
Program: Liberal Arts And General
Accreditation: M, @SW

01	President	Dr. Charles W. SIMMONS
03	Executive Vice President	Dr. Howard L. SIMMONS
05	Provost/Vice Pres Academic Affairs	Dr. Marian STANTON
10	Vice Pres for Admin & Fiscal Affs	Mr. Donald L. HUTCHINS
44	Ex Asst to Pres/Spon Pgms/Appld Res	Dr. Alice THOMAS
04	Special Assistant to the President	Ms. Carolyn J. ECHOLS
15	Department Chair Human Services	Ms. Monica KERR-POINDEXTER
36	Dept Chair Human Growth/Development	Ms. Deborah KING
20	Dean of Academic Affairs	Ms. Shirley EVANS
12	Dean of Lanham Campus	Dr. Bernard M. GROSS
12	Dean of Annapolis Campus	Dr. Charlestine FAIRLEY
12	Dean of Salisbury Campus	Ms. Constance STEWART
12	Dean of Cambridge Campus	Dr. Vivian FULLER
12	Dean of Nassau Bahamas Campus	Hon. Theresa MOXEY-INGRAHAM
12	Dean of Owings Mills Campus	Ms. Doris W. CARROLL
06	Registrar	Ms. Mary ROBINSON
51	Director of Continuing Education	Dr. Ann BOSTIC
37	Director of Financial Aid	Ms. Rebecca CHALK
04	Spec Asst to Pres Institution	Mr. Benjamin MASON
31	Director Community Outreach	Mr. Jamal MUBDI-BEY
18	Director Facilities/Physical Plant	Mr. Gilbert RAWLINGS
08	Director of Library	Mr. Omowali ALI
19	Director Security/Safety	Col. Mahdi EL-HAQQ
21	Bursar	Mr. Bert LEE
29	Director Alumni Relations	Ms. Marshear MARSH
58	Director of Graduate Studies	Dr. Linda FASSETT
09	Dir of Institutional Research/Plng	Mr. Kareem AZIZ
35	Chief Admin Stdt Dev/Stdt Sppt Svcs	Dr. John BARBER
38	Director Student Counseling	Ms. Chantaye HAUGHTON
07	Director of Admissions	Ms. Diana SAMUELS
13	Information Technology Director	Mr. Tacuma SIMMONS

Stevenson University (E)

1525 Greenspring Valley Road,
Stevenson MD 21153-0641

County: Baltimore — FICE Identification: 002107
Unit ID: 164173

Telephone: (410) 486-7000 — Carnegie Class: Master's S
FAX Number: (410) 486-3552 — Calendar System: Semester
URL: www.stevenson.edu
Established: 1947 — Annual Undergrad Tuition & Fees: $23,636
Enrollment: 3,941 — Coed
Affiliation or Control: Independent Non-Profit — IRS Status: 501(c)3
Highest Offering: Master's
Program: Liberal Arts And General; Teacher Preparatory
Accreditation: M, MT, NUR, NURSE, TED

01	President	Dr. Kevin J. MANNING
04	Assistant to President	Ms. Ruth HUBBARD
03	Exec Vice President/Academic Dean	Dr. Paul D. LACK
10	Exec Vice Pres/Chief Financial Ofcr	Mr. Timothy M. CAMPBELL
05	Chief Academic Officer	Dr. Paul D. LACK
30	Vice Pres University Advancement	Mr. Steve CLOSE
84	Vice Pres Enrollment Management	Mr. Mark J. HERGAN
32	Vice Pres Student Affairs	Ms. Claire E. MOORE
27	VP Marketing & Public Relations	Ms. Glenda G. LE GENDRE
15	Vice Pres for Human Resources	Ms. Brenda BALZER
100	Chief of Staff	Ms. Sue KENNEY
20	Asst Vice Pres for Academic Affairs	Dr. Jo-Ellen ASBURY
88	Asst Vice Pres for Exp Learning/Ca	Ms. Christine A. NOYA
58	Dean Graduate/Professional Studies	Ms. Joyce K. BECKER
50	Dean School of Business	Vacant
81	Dean School of Science	Dr. Susan GORMAN
83	Dean Sch of Humanities/Social Sci	Dr. James SALVUCCI
88	Dean School of Design	Mr. Keith KUTCH
53	Interim Dean School of Education	Dr. Deborah KRAFT
18	Asst VP Fac & Campus Svcs	Mr. Leland BEITEL
21	Asst VP Finan Affs/Controller	Ms. Melanie M. EDMONDSON
07	Asst VP Enrollment Management	Mr. Robert HERR
37	Director of Financial Aid	Ms. Barbara MILLER
35	Dean of Students	Mr. Robert MIKUS
14	Chief Information Officer/Asst VP	Mr. Tom ALLEN
88	Assistant VP for Acad Supp Svcs	Dr. Jeff KELLY
09	Assoc Dean Inst Rsrch & Assess	Ms. Nicole C. MARANO
23	Assoc Dean/Dir of Wellness Center	Ms. Linda REYMANN
35	Assoc Dean/Dir of Stdnt Activities	Mr. Daniel BARNHART
88	Associate Dean GPS UG Programs	Ms. Patricia ELLIS
66	Associate Dean Nursing Education	Dr. Judith FEUSTLE
66	Associate Dean for Nursing Educ	Dr. Denise SEIGART
106	Associate Dean Distance Education	Dr. Barbara ZIRKIN
08	Director of Library Services	Ms. Maureen A. BECK
36	Exec Director of Career HQ	Mr. Art TAGUDING
06	Registrar	Ms. Tracy L. BOLT
19	Director of Safety & Security	Vacant
41	Athletic Director	Mr. Brett C. ADAMS
40	Director Auxiliary Service	Mr. Robert REED
28	Director of Multicultural Affairs	Ms. Cheryl HINTON
29	Director Alumni Rels	Ms. Frances GUNSHOL
88	Director Acad Link and PASS	Ms. Christine FLAX
88	Director of Developmental Studies	Ms. Esther ROSENSTOCK

Tai Sophia Institute (F)

7750 Montpelier Road, Laurel MD 20723-6010

County: Howard — FICE Identification: 025784
Unit ID: 164085

Telephone: (410) 888-9048 — Carnegie Class: Master's S
FAX Number: (410) 888-9004 — Calendar System: Trimester
URL: www.tai.edu
Established: 1981 — Annual Graduate Tuition & Fees: $26,500
Enrollment: 427 — Coed
Affiliation or Control: Independent Non-Profit — IRS Status: 501(c)3
Highest Offering: Master's; No Undergraduates
Program: Professional
Accreditation: M, ACUP

01	President & CEO	Mr. Frank VITALE
05	Provost/Vice Pres Academic Affairs	Dr. Judith BROIDA
11	VP Administration/General Counsel	Ms. Louise GUSSIN
30	Vice Pres Institutional Advancement	Mr. Timothy J. AMBROSE
26	VP Marketing/Enrollment Mgmt	Ms. Lisa L. CONNELLY-DUGGAN
10	Vice Pres Business/Financial Svcs	Mr. Marc LEVIN
04	Assistant to the President	Vacant
06	Assoc VP Student Svcs/Registrar	Mr. Reginald GARCON
07	Director of Graduate Admissions	Ms. Gabrielle JULIEN-MOLINEAUX
29	Coordinator Alumni Relations	Ms. Patricia DELORENZO
37	Director Student Financial Aid	Mr. John GAY
08	Director of Library Services and IT	Ms. Jenifer KIRIN
32	Academic & Student Affairs Advisor	Ms. Sara COMEAU

TESST College of Technology (G)

1520 S Caton Avenue, Baltimore MD 21227-1063

County: Baltimore City — FICE Identification: 007491
Unit ID: 163736

Telephone: (410) 644-6400 — Carnegie Class: Assoc/PrivFP
FAX Number: (410) 644-6481 — Calendar System: Quarter
URL: www.tesst.com
Established: 1956 — Annual Undergrad Tuition & Fees: N/A
Enrollment: 1,007 — Coed
Affiliation or Control: Proprietary — IRS Status: Proprietary
Highest Offering: Associate Degree
Program: Occupational
Accreditation: ACCSC

01	President	Mr. Jake ELSEN
11	Director of Operations	Vacant

TESST College of Technology (H)

4600 Powder Mill Road, Suite 500,
Beltsville MD 20705-2649

County: Prince Georges — FICE Identification: 020836
Unit ID: 164058

Telephone: (301) 937-8448 — Carnegie Class: Assoc/PrivFP
FAX Number: (301) 937-5327 — Calendar System: Quarter
URL: www.tesst.com
Established: 1956 — Annual Undergrad Tuition & Fees: N/A
Enrollment: 660 — Coed
Affiliation or Control: Proprietary — IRS Status: Proprietary
Highest Offering: Associate Degree
Program: Occupational
Accreditation: ACCSC

01	President	Ms. Shartoyea SCOTT DIXON
06	Registrar	Mrs. LaDonna DAVIS
07	Director of Admissions	Ms. Cathy MCKINNEY
36	Director of Career Services	Ms. Marsha D. HUNT
37	Director of Financial Aid	Ms. Carmenita Renee CLARK
35	Director of Student Service	Vacant
10	Finance Manager	Vacant
05	Director of Education	Vacant

TESST College of Technology (I)

803 Glen Eagles Court, Towson MD 21286-2201

County: Baltimore — FICE Identification: 010410
Unit ID: 161776

Telephone: (410) 296-5350 — Carnegie Class: Assoc/PrivFP
FAX Number: (410) 296-5356 — Calendar System: Quarter
URL: www.tesst.com
Established: 1956 — Annual Undergrad Tuition & Fees: $12,900
Enrollment: 360 — Coed

Affiliation or Control: Proprietary IRS Status: Proprietary
Highest Offering: Associate Degree
Program: Occupational
Accreditation: ACCSC

01 President .... Vacant
11 Acting Executive Director .... Ms. Sandra UGOL

*The University System of Maryland Office (A)

3300 Metzerott Road, Adelphi MD 20783-1690
County: Prince Georges FICE Identification: 007959
Unit ID: 164146
Telephone: (301) 445-1901 Carnegie Class: N/A
FAX Number: (301) 445-1931
URL: www.usmd.edu

01 Chancellor .... Dr. William KIRWAN
12 Pres Univ of Md Ctr Environment Sci .... Dr. Donald F. BOESCH
05 Sr VC Academic Affairs .... Dr. Irwin L. GOLDSTEIN
11 COO/Vice Chanc Admin & Finance .... Mr. Joseph F. VIVONA
30 Vice Chancellor Advancement .... Mr. Leonard R. RALEY
100 USM Chief of Staff .... Ms. Janice B. DOYLE
10 Assoc VC Financial Affairs .... Mr. James E. SANSBURY
86 Assoc VC Governmental Relations .... Mr. Patrick J. HOGAN
20 Assoc Vice Chanc Academic Affairs .... Ms. Teri HOLLANDER
26 Associate Vice Chanc Communications .... Ms. Anne MOULTRIE
13 Assoc VC Information Technology .... Mr. Donald Z. SPICER
21 Asst VC Administration & Finance .... Ms. JoAnn GOEDERT
21 Director Internal Audit .... Mr. David MOSCA
21 Director Budget Analysis .... Ms. Monica WEST

*University of Maryland College Park (B)

College Park MD 20742-0001
County: Prince Georges FICE Identification: 002103
Unit ID: 163286
Telephone: (301) 405-1000 Carnegie Class: RU/VH
FAX Number: (301) 314-9560 Calendar System: Semester
URL: www.umd.edu
Established: 1856 Annual Undergrad Tuition & Fees (In-State): $8,415
Enrollment: 37,200 Coed
Affiliation or Control: State IRS Status: 501(c)3
Highest Offering: Doctorate
Program: Liberal Arts And General; Teacher Preparatory; Professional
Accreditation: M, AUD, BUS, CACREP, CEA, CLPSY, COPSY, CORE, DIETD, DIETI, ENG, IACBE, IPSY, JOUR, LIB, LSAR, MFCD, MUS, PH, PLNG, SCPSY, SP, SPAA, TED

02 President .... Dr. Wallace D. LOH
05 Sr Vice Pres and Provost .... Dr. Ann G. WYLIE
11 Vice President Administrative Affs .... Mr. Frank BREWER
43 General Counsel .... Mr. J. Terrance ROACH
26 Vice President University Relations .... Mr. William B. REMINGTON
32 Vice President Student Affairs .... Dr. Linda M. CLEMENT
13 Vice President & CIO .... Mr. Brian D. VOSS
46 Vice President Research .... Dr. Patrick G. O'SHEA
47 Dean Col Agric/Natural Resources .... Dr. Cheng-I WEI
48 Dean Sch Architecture/Plng/Preserv .... Mr. David CRONRATH
79 Dean College Arts & Humanities .... Dr. Bonnie T. DILL
83 Dean Col Behavioral/Social Sciences .... Dr. John R. TOWNSHEND
50 Dean Smith School of Business .... Dr. G. Anand ANANDALINGAM
81 Dean Computer/Math/Natural Science .... Dr. Jayanth R. BANAVAR
53 Dean of College of Education .... Dr. Donna WISEMAN
54 Dean Clark School of Engineering .... Dr. Darryll J. PINES
69 Dean School of Public Health .... Dr. Robert S. GOLD
60 Dean Merrill College of Journalism .... Mr. Kevin KLOSE
62 Dean College Info Studies .... Dr. Jennifer J. PREECE
80 Dean School Public Policy .... Dr. Donald F. KETTL
20 Dean Undergraduate Studies .... Dr. Donna B. HAMILTON
58 Dean Graduate School .... Dr. Charles A. CARAMELLO
08 Dean of Libraries .... Dr. Patricia A. STEELE
88 Assoc Provost International Affairs .... Dr. Jonathan WILKENFELD
20 Professor/Assoc Prov Faculty Affs .... Dr. Juan URIAGEREKA
09 Assoc VP/Inst Research & Planning .... Dr. Mona LEVINE
18 Associate VP Facilities/Management .... Mr. J. Frank BREWER
28 Int Assoc VP Equity Affs/Diversity .... Dr. Lee THORNTON
39 Asst VP/Director Resident Life .... Dr. Deborah F. GRANDNER
25 Asst VP/Dir Research Adv & Admin .... Ms. Denise CLARK
35 Asst Vice Pres Student Affairs .... Mr. John ZACKER
07 Asst VP Admissions .... Ms. Barbara A. GILL
06 Asst VP Records/Registration .... Mr. Chuck A. WILSON
36 Executive Director Career Center .... Mr. Rick HEARIN
29 Asst VP Alumni Relation/Devel .... Vacant
64 Director School of Music .... Dr. Robert L. GIBSON
37 Director Student Financial Aid .... Ms. Sarah J. BAUDER
85 Int Dir International Services .... Ms. Barbara VARSA
41 Director Athletics .... Mr. Kevin ANDERSON
40 Director University Book Center .... Mr. Mike GORE
23 Director Health Center .... Dr. Sacared A. BODISON
38 Director Counseling Center .... Dr. Sharon E. KIRKLAND-GORDON
19 Chief Campus Police .... Mr. David B. MITCHELL
27 Director University Communications .... Mr. Millree WILLIAMS
15 Director University Human Resources .... Mr. Dale O. ANDERSON
92 Director University Honors Program .... Dr. William DORLAND
96 Director Procurement & Supply .... Mr. James S. STIRLING
31 Asst Director Community Service .... Mr. Craig SLACK

*University of Maryland Baltimore (C)

620 W. Lexington Street, Baltimore MD 21201-1508
County: Independent City FICE Identification: 002104
Unit ID: 163259
Telephone: (410) 706-7004 Carnegie Class: Spec/Med
FAX Number: (410) 706-5483 Calendar System: 4/1/4
URL: www.umaryland.edu
Established: 1807 Annual Undergrad Tuition & Fees (In-State): $8,966
Enrollment: 6,349 Coed
Affiliation or Control: State IRS Status: 501(c)3
Highest Offering: Doctorate
Program: Professional
Accreditation: M, ANEST, DENT, DH, DIETI, IPSY, LAW, MED, MT, NURSE, PA, PH, PHAR, PTA, RADDOS, SW

02 President .... Dr. Jay A. PERMAN
05 Int Vice President Academic Affairs .... Dr. Roger J. WARD
17 Vice President Medical Affairs/Dean .... Dr. E. Albert REECE
86 Vice President Government Affairs .... Ms. T. Sue GLADHILL
11 Vice Pres Administration & Finance .... Ms. Kathleen M. BYINGTON
13 Vice President and CIO .... Dr. Peter J. MURRAY
46 Vice Pres Research & Development .... Mr. James L. HUGHES
26 Vice President Communications .... Ms. Jennifer B. LITCHMAN
88 Senior VP Planning/Accountability .... Mr. Peter N. GILBERT
30 Vice President Development .... Vacant
43 Senior University Counsel .... Ms. Susan GILLETTE
18 Assoc VP Facilities Management .... Mr. Robert M. ROWAN
16 Assoc VP Human Resource Svc .... Ms. Marjorie L. POWELL
86 Assoc VP Govt & Community Affairs .... Ms. Barbara A. KLEIN
45 Asst VP Resource Management .... Dr. Judith S. BLACKBURN
21 Asst Vice Pres Budget & Finance .... Mr. John E. GEIMAN
25 Assistant Vice President Research .... Ms. Marjorie FORSTER
14 Asst VP Information Technology .... Mr. Christopher G. PHILLIPS
24 Asst VP Technology Svcs & Support .... Mr. Paul S. PETROSKI
22 Asst Vice President for Compliance .... Mr. Joseph J. GIFFELS
09 Asst VP Institutional Research .... Mr. Gregory C. SPENGLER
37 Asst VP Student Financial Assist .... Ms. Patricia A. SCOTT
27 Int Asst Vice Pres Communications .... Ms. Laura KOZAK
08 Exec Dir Health Sci/Human Svc Libr .... Ms. Mary J. TOOEY
06 Director Records & Registration .... Mr. Thomas C. DAY
19 Director of Public Safety .... Mr. Antonio WILLIAMS
41 Dir Recreation Wellness Services .... Mr. William P. CROCKETT
39 Director Auxiliary Services .... Ms. Marion A. LIPINSKI
88 Director Compensation .... Ms. Mary L. DIGIACINTO
31 Coordinator Community Affairs .... Mr. Brian C. STURDIVANT
15 Exec Dir Human Resource Services .... Mr. Joseph T. SMITH
38 Director Counseling .... Ms. Emilia PETRILLO
15 Director Staffing & HR Svc Center .... Ms. Mary L. DIGIACINTO
35 Director Student Services .... Ms. Cynthia E. RICE
88 Director of Financial Services .... Ms. Susan E. MCKECHNIE
96 Director of Procurement Services .... Mr. Joseph EVANS
52 Dean Dental School .... Dr. Christian S. STOHLER
58 Interim Dean Graduate School .... Dr. Roger J. WARD
61 Dean School of Law .... Ms. Phoebe A. HADDON
63 Dean School of Medicine .... Dr. Albert REECE
66 Dean School of Nursing .... Dr. Janet D. ALLAN
67 Dean School of Pharmacy .... Dr. Natalie D. EDDINGTON
70 Dean School of Social Work .... Dr. Richard BARTH
84 Asst Dean Grad Admin/Enrollment Mgt .... Mr. Keith BROOKS

*University of Maryland Baltimore County (D)

1000 Hilltop Circle, Baltimore MD 21250-0001
County: Baltimore FICE Identification: 002105
Unit ID: 163268
Telephone: (410) 455-1000 Carnegie Class: RU/H
FAX Number: (410) 455-1210 Calendar System: 4/1/4
URL: www.umbc.edu
Established: 1966 Annual Undergrad Tuition & Fees (In-State): $9,466
Enrollment: 12,888 Coed
Affiliation or Control: State IRS Status: 501(c)3
Highest Offering: Doctorate
Program: Liberal Arts And General; Teacher Preparatory
Accreditation: M, CLPSY, CS, DMS, EMT, ENG, SPAA, SW, TED

02 President .... Dr. Freeman A. HRABOWSKI
05 Int Provost/Sr Vice Pres Acad Affs .... Dr. Philip ROUS
10 Vice Pres Finance/Administration .... Ms. Lynne SCHAEFER
32 Vice President Student Affairs .... Dr. Nancy YOUNG
30 Vice Pres Institutional Advancement .... Mr. Gregory SIMMONS
27 Vice Pres Information Technology .... Mr. Jack J. SUESS
46 Vice President of Research .... Dr. Geoffrey P. SUMMERS
49 Dean Col of Arts/Humanities/Soc Sci .... Dr. John JEFFRIES
81 Int Dean Col Natural/Math Sciences .... Dr. William LACOURSE
54 Dean College of Engr/Info Tech .... Dr. Warren R. DEVRIES
84 Asst Dean Graduate Enrollment Mgmt .... Ms. K. Jill BARR
20 Vice Provost/Dean Undergrad Educ .... Dr. Diane M. LEE
51 VP Cont/Prf Std/Ex Dir Shriver Ctr .... Dr. John S. MARTELLO
20 Vice Provost Academic Affairs .... Dr. Antonio R. MOREIRA
58 Dean/Vice Provost for Graduate Educ .... Dr. Janet RUTLEDGE
15 Vice Provost Faculty Affairs .... Dr. Patrice MCDERMOTT
84 Assistant Provost Enrollment Mgmt .... Ms. Yvette MOZIE-ROSS
21 Assoc VP Financial Services .... Mr. Benjamin LOWENTHAL
26 Assistant to Pres/Assoc VP Mktg/PR .... Ms. Lisa G. AKCHIN
11 Assoc VP Administrative Services .... Ms. Terry COOK
15 Associate VP for Human Resources .... Ms. Valerie A. THOMAS
29 Asst VP for Alumni Relations/Devel .... Ms. Susan EMFINGER
88 Asst VP New Media/Instruction Tech .... Mr. John FRITZ
18 Asst VP Facilities Management .... Mr. Rusty POSTLEWATE
04 Assistant to the President .... Mr. Douglas R. PEAR
96 Director of Procurement .... Ms. Sharon QUINN
92 Acting Director Honors College .... Dr. Simon STACEY
41 Director Physical Educ & Athletics .... Dr. Charles R. BROWN
19 Director University Police .... Mr. Mark SPARKS
36 Director Career Services Cntr .... Ms. Anne SCHOLL-FIEDLER
23 Director Health Services .... Ms. Jennifer LEPUS
37 Director Financial Aid .... Ms. Stephanie JOHNSON
27 Director of Communications .... Ms. Elyse ASHBURN
28 Director of Human Relations .... Vacant
25 Director Sponsored Programs .... Ms. Jocelyn CHASIS
40 Director of UMBC Bookstore .... Mr. Robert J. SOMERS
85 Director International Educ Svcs .... Dr. Arlene V. WERGIN
08 Director Library .... Dr. Larry M. WILT
06 Registrar .... Mr. Steven SMITH
35 Director Student Life .... Ms. Lee CALIZO
43 General Counsel .... Mr. David GLEASON
07 Dir Undergrd Admissions .... Mr. Dale BITTINGER
39 Director Residential Life .... Ms. Katherine B. BOONE
09 Director of Institutional Research .... Dr. Michael DILLON
38 Director Student Counseling .... Dr. J. LaVelle INGRAM

*University of Maryland Eastern Shore (E)

Princess Anne MD 21853-1299
County: Somerset FICE Identification: 002106
Unit ID: 163338
Telephone: (410) 651-2200 Carnegie Class: Master's S
FAX Number: (410) 651-6105 Calendar System: Semester
URL: www.umes.edu
Established: 1886 Annual Undergrad Tuition & Fees (In-State): $6,482
Enrollment: 4,540 Coed
Affiliation or Control: State IRS Status: 501(c)3
Highest Offering: Doctorate
Program: Liberal Arts And General; Teacher Preparatory; Professional
Accreditation: M, ARCPA, BUS, CONST, CORE, DIETD, DIETI, @PHAR, PTA, TED

02 Interim President .... Dr. Mortimer H. NEUFVILLE
04 Sr Exec Asst to Pres/Exec Dir IP .... Dr. Emmanuel T. ACQUAH
05 Vice President Academic Affairs .... Dr. Charles WILLIAMS
10 Vice Pres Administrative Affairs .... Dr. Ronnie E. HOLDEN
30 Vice President Inst Advancement .... Mr. Gains B. HAWKINS
32 Vice President Student Affairs .... Dr. Anthony L. JENKINS
88 Vice Pres Tech/Commercialization .... Dr. Ronald G. FORSYTHE, JR.
20 Asst Vice Pres Academic Affairs .... Dr. Jacqueline BRICE-FINCH
20 Int Asst VP Academic Affairs .... Dr. Bernita M. SIMS-TUCKER
11 Asst Vice President Admin Affairs .... Mr. Alverne W. CHESTERFIELD
21 Asst VP Admin Affs/Budget Director .... Ms. Nelva G. COLLIER-WHITE
84 Assoc VP Student Life/Enroll Mgt .... Dr. James M. WHITE
88 Asst to VP Administrative Affairs .... Dr. Maurice C. NGWABA
04 Special Assistant to the President .... Ms. Rolanda C. BURNEY
91 Director Administrative Computing .... Mr. Kenneth GASTON
56 Assoc Dir Cooperative Extension .... Dr. Henry M. BROOKS
29 Director Alumni Affairs .... Dr. Kimberly C. DUMPSON
15 Director Human Resources .... Ms. Marie H. BILLIE
08 Dean Library Services .... Dr. Ellis B. BETECK
37 Director Financial Aid .... Mr. James W. KELLAM
23 Director Student Health Services .... Ms. Sharone V. GRANT
96 Director Procurement .... Ms. Jacqueline M. COLLINS
88 Director Univ Dining Services .... Mr. David SCOTT
07 Director Admissions .... Mr. Tyrone YOUNG
06 Registrar .... Ms. Cheryl HOLDEN-DUFFY
12 Director Richard A Henson Center .... Mr. Corey J. BOWEN
36 Director Career Services .... Ms. Theresa QUEENAN
09 Director Inst Research/Plng/Assess .... Dr. Stanley M. NYIRENDA
19 Director Public Safety .... Mr. Warner I. SUMPTER
18 Director Physical Plant .... Mr. Leon J. BIVENS
39 Director Residence Life .... Mr. Marvin L. JONES
41 Athletic Director .... Mr. Keith S. DAVIDSON
21 Comptroller .... Ms. Bonita E. BYRD
46 Director Sponsored Research .... Ms. Catherine BOLEK
88 Director Student Retention & Svcs .... Ms. Wanda ANDERSON
88 Director Rural Development .... Mr. Daniel S. KUENNEN
88 Director Upward Bound .... Mr. Norman G. TILGHMAN
35 Director Student Activities .... Mr. James G. LUNNERMON, JR.
88 Director Title III Program .... Dr. Frances H. MCKINNEY
26 Director Public Relations .... Mr. William ROBINSON
44 Director Development .... Dr. Veronique L. DIRIKER
88 Director Advancement Services .... Mrs. Chenita R. KOLLOCK
51 Coordinator Continuing Education .... Ms. Gretchen M. BOGGS
38 Coordinator Counseling Services .... Dr. Patricia E. TILGHMAN
58 Dean Graduate Studies .... Dr. Jennifer M. KEANE-DAWES
47 Int Dean Sch Agric/Natural Sciences .... Dr. Jurgen G. SCHWARZ
49 Dean School of Arts & Professions .... Dr. Timothy H. BAUGHMAN
50 Dean School Business & Technology .... Dr. Ayodele J. ALADE
67 Dean Sch Pharmacy/Health Profession .... Dr. Nicholas R. BLANCHARD

*University of Maryland University College (F)

3501 University Boulevard East, Adelphi MD 20783-7998
County: Prince Georges FICE Identification: 011644
Unit ID: 163204
Telephone: (301) 985-7000 Carnegie Class: Master's L
FAX Number: (301) 985-7678 Calendar System: Semester
URL: www.umuc.edu
Established: 1947 Annual Undergrad Tuition & Fees (In-State): $6,000
Enrollment: 39,577 Coed
Affiliation or Control: State IRS Status: 501(c)3

Highest Offering: Doctorate
Program: Liberal Arts And General; Professional
Accreditation: M

02 President .... Dr. Susan C. ALDRIDGE
03 Chief Operating Officer .... Mr. George SHOENBERGER
10 Vice Pres Chief Financial Officer .... Mr. Eugene D. LOCKETT, JR.
05 Provost .... Dr. Greg VON LEHMEN
15 Vice President Human Resources .... Ms. Nadine PORTER
26 VP Marketing and Communications .... Vacant
45 Sr VP Institutional Effectiveness .... Mr. Javier MIYARES
86 Vice President Military Operations .... Mr. James H. SELBE
43 Vice President & General Counsel .... Ms. Nancy WILLIAMSON
49 Vice President & Dean SUS .... Dr. Marie CINI
58 Sr VP Acad Pgm/Dn Grad Sch Mgt/Tech .... Dr. Michael FRANK
13 Vice Pres for IT & CIO .... Mr. Peter C. YOUNG
84 Vice Pres Enrollment Management .... Mr. Sean CHUNG
08 Assoc Provost of Library Services .... Mr. Stephen MILLER
18 Associate Vice President Facilities .... Mr. George TRUJILLO
88 Associate VP Government Relations .... Mr. Benjamin BIRGE
37 AVP Student Financial Aid .... Ms. Cheryl STORIE
09 Director Institutional Research .... Wei ZHOU
06 Int Assoc Provost/Univ Registrar .... Ms. Michelle SAMUELS-JONES
28 Director of Diversity Initiatives .... Dr. Blair HAYES
07 Director of Admissions .... Ms. Insiya JIWANJI

*Bowie State University (A)

14000 Jericho Park Road, Bowie MD 20715-3318
County: Prince Georges
FICE Identification: 002062
Unit ID: 162007
Telephone: (301) 860-4000
Carnegie Class: DRU
FAX Number: (301) 860-3510
Calendar System: Semester
URL: www.bowiestate.edu
Established: 1865
Annual Undergrad Tuition & Fees (In-State): $6,347
Enrollment: 5,578
Coed
Affiliation or Control: State
IRS Status: 501(c)3
Highest Offering: Doctorate
Program: Liberal Arts And General; Teacher Preparatory
Accreditation: M, ACBSP, CS, NUR, SW, TED

02 President .... Dr. Mickey L. BURNIM
05 Int Provost/Vice Pres Academic Affs .... Ms. Karen JOHNSON SHAHEED
10 Vice Pres Finance & Administration .... Dr. Karl B. BROCKENBROUGH
30 Vice Pres Institutional Advancement .... Dr. Richard LUCAS, JR.
32 VP Student Affairs/Campus Life .... Dr. Artie L. TRAVIS
43 Int Vice Pres & General Counsel .... Ms. Antoinette J. MARBRAY
35 Student Code of Conduct .... Mrs. Thomaice BOARDLEY
13 VP Office of Information Technology .... Dr. Al VALBUENA
84 Asst VP Enrollment Management .... Mr. Donald L. KIAH
88 Asst to Prov Institutional Effec .... Ms. Gayle M. FINK
06 University Registrar .... Ms. Patricia MITCHELL
08 Assoc Library Dir/Interim Dean .... Ms. Marian RUCKER-SHAMU
36 Director Career Services .... Ms. April JOHNSON
15 Sr Director of Human Resources .... Ms. Sheila HOBSON
19 Chief of Campus Police .... Mr. Ernest WAITERS
58 Int Dean Sch of Grad Stds/Research .... Dr. Cosmos NWOKEAFOR
49 Dean School of Arts & Sciences .... Dr. George ACQUAAH
53 Dean Sch of Education .... Dr. Traki TAYLOR-WEBB
107 Int Dean Sch Professional Studies .... Dr. Elliott PARRIS
92 Director UCE Honors Program .... Dr. Monika GROSS
23 Director University Wellness Center .... Dr. Rita WUTHO
41 Director Athletics .... Mr. Anton GOFF
26 Dir University Relations/ Marketing .... Ms. Cassandra M. ROBINSON
88 Director University Wiseman Centre .... Mr. Frank WALLER
37 Director Financial Aid .... Ms. Deborah STANLEY
18 Director Facilities .... Mr. Darryl WILLIFORD
07 Director Undergraduate Admissions .... Mr. Lonnie MORRIS
29 Director of Alumni Relations .... Ms. Anette WEDDERBURN
88 Dir of Model Inst for Excellence .... Dr. Elaine DAVIS
96 Director of Purchasing .... Mr. Steve A. JOST
09 Director of Institutional Research .... Dr. Doug NUTTER

*Coppin State University (B)

2500 W North Avenue, Baltimore MD 21216-3698
County: Baltimore City
FICE Identification: 002068
Unit ID: 162283
Telephone: (410) 951-3000
Carnegie Class: Master's S
FAX Number: (410) 523-7238
Calendar System: Semester
URL: www.coppin.edu
Established: 1900
Annual Undergrad Tuition & Fees (In-State): $5,732
Enrollment: 3,800
Coed
Affiliation or Control: State
IRS Status: 501(c)3
Highest Offering: Doctorate
Program: Liberal Arts And General; Teacher Preparatory; Professional
Accreditation: M, CORE, NUR, NURSE, SW, TED

02 President .... Dr. Reginald S. AVERY
05 Interim Provost/VP Academic Affairs .... Dr. Ronnie L. COLLINS, SR.
30 Int VP Institutional Advancement .... Mr. James ROBERTS
10 VP Administration & Finance .... Mr. Richard SIEMER
32 VP Student Affairs .... Dr. Franklin D. CHAMBERS
13 VP Information Systems/CIO .... Dr. Ahmed EL-HAGGAN
84 VP Enrollment Management .... Dr. Reginald ROSS
45 Assoc VP Planning/Assessment .... Dr. Scott J. DANTLEY
20 Assoc Vice Pres for Academic Affs .... Dr. Linda NIXON HUDSON
21 Assoc Vice Pres Admin/Finance .... Vacant
32 Associate VP Student Affairs .... Dr. Joann CHRISTOPHER-HICKS
18 Assoc VP Capital Plng/Constr & Cont .... Mr. Maqbool PATEL
86 Assoc VP of Pub Policy & Govt Rel .... Dr. Monica RANDALL
07 Director of Admissions .... Ms. Michelle GROSS
06 Registrar .... Dr. Margaret TURNER
21 Controller .... Mr. Vincent BLACKBURN
08 Director of the Library .... Dr. Mary WANZA
09 Director of Institutional Research .... Dr. Oyebanjo LAJUBUTU
37 Director of Financial Aid .... Mr. Mose CARTIER
36 Director of Career Services .... Mrs. Linda BOWIE
15 Director of Human Resorces .... Mrs. Lisa EARLY
19 Chief of Public Safety .... Chief Leonard HAMM
39 Director of Housing/Residence Life .... Mr. Patrick E. BAILEY
41 Director of Athletics .... Mr. Derrick RAMSEY
35 Director Student Support Services .... Ms. Leila WASHINGTON
88 Director Academic Resource Center .... Ms. Juanita GILLIAM
88 Director of Academic Advisement .... Ms. Jackie KNIGHT
29 Director Alumni Relations .... Ms. Tara TURNER
96 Director of Purchasing .... Mr. Thomas E. DAWSON, JR.
26 Director of University Relations .... Vacant
88 Director Client Computing Services .... Mr. Emmanuel OWUSU-SEKYERE
88 Director Coppin Academy .... Mr. Frank WHORLEY
35 Director of Student Activities .... Mrs. Jocelyn BRYANT-WEBB
88 Chair Interdisciplinary Studies .... Ms. Tondelaya BLACKSTONE
27 Director Telecommunications .... Mr. Claude K. RADER
105 Director Web & Multimedia .... Mr. Andrew C. BAIN
31 Exec Dir of Community Partnerships .... Mr. Albert ROBINSON
49 Interim Dean Arts & Sciences .... Dr. Alcott ARTHUR
92 Dean Honors College & McNair Pgms .... Mr. Ronnie L. COLLINS, SR.
58 Dean Graduate School .... Dr. Mary E. OWENS
66 Dean of Nursing .... Dr. Marcella COPES
53 Dean of Education .... Dr. Edna SIMMONS
04 Executive Assistant to President .... Mrs. Sherie JOHNSON
97 General & Adult Education .... Dr. Jacqueline H. WILLIAMS
88 Applied Psych/Rehab Counsel .... Dr. Judith KEHE
61 Criminal Justice/ Law Enforcement .... Dr. Dilip DAS
53 Curriculum & Instruction .... Dr. Glynis BARBER
57 Fine Arts .... Dr. Garey HYATT
82 History Geography/Intl Studies .... Dr. Katherine BANKOLE-MEDINA
79 Interim Chair Humanities .... Dr. Elaine SYKES
50 Mgmt Sci & Economics (Business) .... Dr. Habtu BRAHA
77 Math & Computer Science .... Dr. Genevieve KNIGHT
65 Natural Sciences .... Dr. Gilbert OGONJI
83 Social Sciences .... Dr. John HUDGINS
70 Social Work .... Dr. Shirley R. NEWTON-GUEST
68 Health/Physical Education .... Dr. Edna SIMMONS
88 Special Education .... Dr. George R. TAYLOR
88 Exec Dir Local to Global Engagement .... Dr. York BRADSHAW

*Frostburg State University (C)

101 Braddock Road, Frostburg MD 21532-2303
County: Allegany
FICE Identification: 002072
Unit ID: 162584
Telephone: (301) 687-4000
Carnegie Class: Master's L
FAX Number: (301) 687-4737
Calendar System: Semester
URL: www.frostburg.edu
Established: 1898
Annual Undergrad Tuition & Fees (In-State): $7,128
Enrollment: 5,470
Coed
Affiliation or Control: State
IRS Status: 501(c)3
Highest Offering: Master's
Program: Liberal Arts And General; Teacher Preparatory; Business Emphasis
Accreditation: M, BUS, NRPA, SW, TED

02 President .... Dr. Jonathan GIBRALTER
05 Provost & Vice Pres Acad Affs .... Dr. Stephen J. SIMPSON
32 Vice Pres Student/Education Svcs .... Dr. Thomas L. BOWLING
10 Vice President for Admin & Finance .... Mr. David C. ROSE
30 Vice Pres University Advancement .... Mr. Bernard J. DAVISSON
84 Assoc VP for Enrollment Management .... Mr. Wray BLAIR
86 Chief of Staff/VP for Govt Relation .... Mr. Steven SPAHR
43 University Counsel .... Ms. Karen A. TREBER
20 Associate Provost .... Dr. Mary GARTNER
21 Assoc VP Finance & Controller .... Mr. Richard A. REPAC
35 Asst VP for Student Services .... Dr. Jesse KETTERMAN
35 Asst Vice Pres Student Services .... Mr. Bernard WYNDER
45 Assoc Director Budget & Planning .... Ms. Denise MURPHY
20 Vice Provost .... Dr. John BOWMAN
49 Dean Col Liberal Arts & Science .... Dr. Joseph M. HOFFMAN
50 Dean College of Business .... Dr. Ahmad TOOTOONCHI
53 Acting Dean College of Education .... Dr. Clarence GOLDEN
08 Director of the Library .... Dr. David M. GILLESPIE
37 Director of Financial Aid .... Mrs. Angela L. HOVATTER
88 Asst Vice Pres Planning and Assess .... Mr. Robert E. SMITH
09 Director of Institutional Research .... Vacant
15 Director Human Resources .... Ms. Katherine SNYDER
58 Director of Graduate Services .... Ms. Vicki MAZER
18 Director Facilities/Physical Plant .... Mr. Robert BOYCE
27 Director News & Media Services .... Ms. Elizabeth MEDCALF
36 Director Career Services .... Dr. Robbie L. CORDLE
38 Director Student Counseling .... Dr. Spenser F. DEAKIN
40 Director Bookstore & ID Services .... Ms. Melissa HILLER
41 Athletic Director .... Mr. Troy DELL
19 Chief University Police .... Ms. Cynthia SMITH
90 Director of Academic Computing .... Ms. Beth KENNEY
91 Director of Admin Computing .... Mr. Bruce LEHMAN
44 Director Annual Giving .... Ms. Leslie K. REED
22 Director of AA/EEO .... Mrs. Beth HOFFMAN
25 Dir Research/Sponsored Programs .... Vacant
07 Director of Admissions .... Ms. Trisha GREGORY
28 Director of Diversity .... Ms. Robin WYNDER
29 Director Alumni Programs .... Ms. Shannon L. GRIBBLE
13 Dir Networking/Telecommunications .... Vacant
96 Coord Procurement/Material Handling .... Mr. Alan R. SNYDER
23 Director Health Services .... Ms. Mary A. TOLA
39 Director Residence Life .... Mr. Dana A. SEVERANCE

*Salisbury University (D)

1101 Camden Avenue, Salisbury MD 21801-6860
County: Wicomico
FICE Identification: 002091
Unit ID: 163851
Telephone: (410) 543-6000
Carnegie Class: Master's L
FAX Number: (410) 548-2587
Calendar System: Semester
URL: www.salisbury.edu
Established: 1925
Annual Undergrad Tuition & Fees (In-State): $7,332
Enrollment: 8,397
Coed
Affiliation or Control: State
IRS Status: 501(c)3
Highest Offering: Master's
Program: Liberal Arts And General; Teacher Preparatory; Professional
Accreditation: M, BUS, EXSC, MT, MUS, NURSE, SW, TED

02 President .... Dr. Janet E. DUDLEY-ESHBACH
05 Provost/VPAA .... Dr. Diane D. ALLEN
100 Chief of Staff .... Ms. Amy S. HASSON
10 Vice Pres Administration/Finance .... Mrs. Betty P. CROCKETT
32 Int Vice Pres of Student Affairs .... Dr. Dane R. FOUST
30 Vice Pres Institutional Advancement .... Dr. Rosemary M. THOMAS
28 Chief Diversity Officer .... Vacant
35 Associate VP of Student Affairs .... Dr. Dane R. FOUST
86 Asst to Pres Government/Cmty Rels .... Mr. Scott R. JENSEN
20 Associate Provost .... Dr. Melanie L. PERREAULT
20 Asst Vice Pres Academic Affairs .... Vacant
21 Assistant Vice President of Finance .... Vacant
84 Dean of Enrollment Management .... Ms. Jane H. DANE
35 Dean of Students .... Mr. Edwin A. COWELL
27 Chief Information Officer .... Mr. Jerome F. WALDRON
26 Director of Public Relations .... Mr. Richard W. CULVER
31 Director of Auxiliary Services .... Mr. Paul W. LAND
41 Athletics Director .... Dr. Michael P. VIENNA
92 Int Director Honors Program .... Dr. Jay R. CARLANDER
06 Registrar .... Ms. Jacqueline M. MAISEL
07 Director of Admissions .... Mr. Aaron M. BASKO
09 Dir Univ Analysis/Rpt/Assessment .... Dr. Kara O. SIEGERT
08 Dean of Library & Info Resources .... Dr. Alice H. BAHR
38 Director Student Counseling Service .... Dr. Kathleen J. SCOTT
36 Director Career Services .... Dr. Rebecca A. EMERY
37 Director of Financial Aid .... Ms. Barri ZIMMERMAN
15 Director Human Resources .... Mr. Marvin L. PYLES
29 Int Director of Alumni Relations .... Mr. Jayme E. BLOCK
23 Director of Student Health Services .... Ms. Jennifer R. BERKMAN
35 Director of Student Activities .... Ms. Jennifer D. BLACKWELL
39 Director Housing/Residence Life .... Mr. David P. GUTOSKEY
19 Director of Public Safety .... Mr. Edwin L. LASHLEY
40 Director of Bookstore .... Ms. Lisa G. GRAY
18 Director Facilities/Physical Plant .... Mr. Kevin J. MANN
96 Director of Purchasing .... Ms. Joyce L. FALKINBURG
75 Dean Henson Sch Science/Tech .... Dr. Karen L. OLMSTEAD
50 Dean Perdue School of Business .... Dr. Bob G. WOOD
49 Dean Fulton School of Liberal Arts .... Dr. Maarten L. PEREBOOM
53 Dean Seidel Sch Educ/Prof Studies .... Dr. Dennis A. PATANICZEK
58 Dean Graduate Studies/Research .... Dr. Clifton P. GRIFFIN
88 Dir Ctr for Student Achievement .... Dr. Heather W. HOLMES

*Towson University (E)

8000 York Road, Baltimore MD 21252-0001
County: Baltimore
FICE Identification: 002099
Unit ID: 164076
Telephone: (410) 704-2000
Carnegie Class: Master's L
FAX Number: N/A
Calendar System: 4/1/4
URL: www.towson.edu
Established: 1866
Annual Undergrad Tuition & Fees (In-State): $7,906
Enrollment: 21,840
Coed
Affiliation or Control: State
IRS Status: 501(c)3
Highest Offering: Doctorate
Program: Liberal Arts And General; Teacher Preparatory; Professional
Accreditation: M, ARCPA, AUD, BUS, BUSA, CS, DANCE, IPSY, MUS, NURSE, OT, SP, TED, THEA

02 Interim President .... Dr. Marcia G. WELSH
05 Provost/VP Academic Affairs .... Dr. Marcia G. WELSH
10 Vice Pres/Chief Fiscal Officer .... Mr. James P. SHEEHAN
30 Vice Pres University Advancement .... Dr. Gary N. RUBIN
32 Vice President Student Affairs .... Dr. Debra MORIARTY
31 VP Economic/Community Outreach .... Ms. Dyan L. BRASINGTON
100 Interim Chief of Staff .... Mr. Laslo BOYD
04 Spec Asst to the Pres Div & Equ Opp .... Ms. Debra SEEBERGER
20 Associate Provost .... Dr. James DILISIO
84 Sr Assoc VP Enrollment Mgmt .... Mr. G. Lonnie MCNEW
06 Registrar/Assoc VP Academic Affairs .... Mr. Robert GIORDANI
44 Assoc Vice President Development .... Ms. Donna MAYER
26 Assoc VP University Marketing .... Ms. Ellen E. STOKES
29 Assoc Vice Pres Alumni Relations .... Ms. Lori B. ARMSTRONG
13 Assoc Vice President OTS/CIO .... Mr. Jeffrey SCHMIDT
31 Assoc Vice Pres Auxiliary Services .... Mr. Joseph OSTER
18 Int Assoc Vice Pres Facilities Mgmt .... Mr. Roger HAYDEN
21 Assoc VP Fiscal Planning & Svcs .... Mr. James D. WILLIAMSON
15 Associate Vice Pres Human Resources .... Mr. Phillip ROSS, III
35 Assoc Vice Pres Student Affairs .... Dr. Jana VARWIG
45 Assoc Prov Academic Res & Plng .... Dr. Gary LEVY
88 Assoc Vice President Campus Life .... Dr. Teresa HALL

28 Asst VP Ctr for Student Diversity .... Mr. Art KING
39 Asst VP/Dir Housing/Residence Life .... Mr. Jerome T. DIERINGER
37 AVP Cmty College Rels/Financial Aid ...... Mr. Vincent C. PECORA
25 Asst VP University Research Svcs .... Ms. Mary Louise HEALY
07 Asst VP & Director of Admissions .... Mr. Brian HAZLETT
19 Asst VP Public Sfty/Chief of Police .... Chief Bernard GERST
53 Dean College of Education .... Dr. Raymond LORION
50 Dean College of Business/Economics ....Dr. Shohreh KAYNAMA
49 Dean College of Liberal Arts .... Dr. Terry COONEY
81 Dean J&M Fisher Col of Science/Math ....Dr. David VANKO
57 Dean Col Fine Arts/Communications .... Ms. Susan PICINICH
76 Dean College of Health Professions ....Dr. Charlotte E. EXNER
92 Dean Honors College .... Dr. Joseph MCGINN
43 University Counsel .... Mr. Michael A. AMSELMI
08 Dean of University Libraries .... Ms. Deborah NOLAN
104 Director Study Abroad .... Dr. Rebecca L. PISANO
94 Chair Women's Studies ....Dr. Karen DUGGER
09 Director Institutional Research .... Ms. Laura BAGEANT
26 Director University Relations .... Ms. Carol DUNSWORTH
41 Director of Athletics .... Mr. Michael WADDELL
23 Director of Health Services .... Dr. Jane L. HALPERN
40 Director of University Bookstore .... Ms. Stacey ELOFIR
96 Director of Procurement .... Ms. Lucy SLAICH
88 Exec Dir Technology Support Svcs .... Vacant
38 Director Counseling Center .... Dr. James SPIVACK
36 Director of Career Services .... Ms. Lorie LOGAN-BENNETT

University of Baltimore (A)

1420 N Charles Street, Baltimore MD 21201-5779
County: Independent City FICE Identification: 002102
Unit ID: 161873
Telephone: (410) 837-4200 Carnegie Class: Master's L
FAX Number: N/A Calendar System: Semester
URL: www.ubalt.edu
Established: 1925 Annual Undergrad Tuition & Fees (In-State): $7,494
Enrollment: 6,501 Coed
Affiliation or Control: State IRS Status: 501(c)3
Highest Offering: Doctorate
Program: Liberal Arts And General; Professional
Accreditation: M, BUS, LAW, SPAA

02 President .... Mr. Robert L. BOGOMOLNY
05 Provost .... Dr. Joseph S. WOOD
10 Chief Financial Officer .... Ms. Kristen MCCARTHY
100 Exec Dir Pres Operations & Projects .... Ms. Susan SCHUBERT
04 Sr Vice Pres Enrollment Management ....Ms. Miriam E. KING
11 Vice Pres Administration .... Mr. Harry SCHUCKEL
30 Vice Pres Institutional Advancement .... Ms. Theresa SILANSKIS
45 Vice Pres Planning/External Affairs .... Mr. Peter TORAN
86 VP Government & Community Relations .... Ms. Anita THOMAS
18 Vice Pres Real Estate & Facilities .... Mr. Steve CASSARD
13 Vice Pres Technology/CIO .... Mr. David BOBART
15 Asst Vice Pres Human Resources .... Mr. Bill NELSON
20 Associate Provost .... Mr. Jeffrey SAWYER
20 Asst Provost Institutional Research .... Mr. Paul MONIODIS
35 Assoc Vice Pres Student Affairs .... Ms. Shelia BURKHATTER
32 Dean of Students .... Ms. Kathleen ANDERSON
35 Director Center Student Involvement .... Ms. Susan LUCHEY
28 Dir Intl/Multicultural Student Svcs .... Ms. Karla M. SHEPHERD
07 Actg Executive Director Admissions .... Ms. Janet WHELAN
08 Director of Library .... Ms. Lucy HOLMAN
19 Chief of Police .... Mr. Samuel D. TRESS
37 Director Financial Aid .... Ms. Anne HAMILL
96 Director of Procurement & Supply .... Mr. Blair BLANKINSHIP
44 Dir Annual Giving/Alumni Relations .... Ms. Kate CRIMMINS
38 Director Counseling Services .... Dr. Myra WATERS
36 Director Career Center .... Ms. Carol VELLUCCI
06 Registrar .... Mr. Richard MORRELL
09 Director Institutional Research .... Dr. Merrill R. PRITCHETT
27 Manager Public Information .... Mr. Chris HART
80 Dean College of Public Affairs .... Dr. Steve PERCY
49 Dean College of Arts & Sciences .... Dr. Diedre L. BADEJO
61 Dean of the School of Law .... Dr. Phil CLOSIUS
50 Dean School of Business .... Dr. Darlene SMITH

Washington Adventist University (B)

7600 Flower Avenue, Takoma Park MD 20912-7794
County: Montgomery FICE Identification: 002067
Unit ID: 162210
Telephone: (301) 891-4000 Carnegie Class: Bac/Diverse
FAX Number: (301) 270-1618 Calendar System: Semester
URL: www.wau.edu
Established: 1904 Annual Undergrad Tuition & Fees: $18,900
Enrollment: 1,298 Coed
Affiliation or Control: Seventh-day Adventist IRS Status: 501(c)3
Highest Offering: Master's
Program: Liberal Arts And General; Teacher Preparatory; Professional
Accreditation: M, NUR

01 President .... Dr. Weymouth SPENCE
10 Vice Pres Financial Administration .... Mr. Patrick FARLEY
32 VP for Student Life & Retention .... Ms. Jean WARDEN
13 Assoc VP for Info Tech Systems .... Mr. Gregory INGRAM
58 Dean Sch Grad/Professional Studies .... Dr. Davenia LEA
33 Dean of Men .... Mr. Tim NELSON
34 Dean of Women .... Ms. Adrienne MATTHEWS
08 Librarian .... Ms. Lee Marie WISEL
30 Director of Development .... Vacant
06 Director of Records/Admissions .... Vacant
19 Director Safety & Security .... Mr. Steve LAPHAM
40 Manager the College Bookstore .... Mr. Lloyd YUTUC
42 Chaplain .... Pastor Gary WIMBISH
41 Athletic Director .... Vacant
84 Director of Student Recruiting .... Vacant
29 Director of Alumni .... Vacant
15 Director of Human Resources .... Ms. Estevanny JIMENEZ
21 Comptroller .... Vacant
27 Director Marketing & Communications ......Ms. Angela ABRAHAM
78 Dir Coop Educ/Acad Support & Test .... Mr. Fitzroy THOMAS
18 Chief Facilities/Physical Plant .... Mr. Steve LAPHAM
37 Director Student Financial Aid .... Ms. Sharon CONWAY
38 Director Student Counseling .... Ms. Lauri PRESTON
09 Director of Institutional Research .... Ms. Janette NEUFVILLE

Washington Bible College/Capital Bible Seminary (C)

6511 Princess Garden Parkway, Lanham MD 20706-3599
County: Prince Georges FICE Identification: 001462
Unit ID: 164207
Telephone: (301) 552-1400 Carnegie Class: Spec/Faith
FAX Number: (301) 552-2775 Calendar System: Semester
URL: www.bible.edu
Established: 1938 Annual Undergrad Tuition & Fees: $14,119
Enrollment: 540 Coed
Affiliation or Control: Independent Non-Profit IRS Status: 501(c)3
Highest Offering: First Professional Degree
Program: Teacher Preparatory; Religious Emphasis
Accreditation: M, BI, THEOL

01 President .... Dr. Larry MERCER
05 Associate Academic Dean .... Dr. Ed CURTIS
20 Vice Pres Academic Affairs .... Dr. B. Gerard DAVIS
11 Vice President Administration .... Ms. Barbara R. FOX
32 Vice President Student Afairs .... Vacant
04 Spec Asst to Pres Inst Effective .... Mrs. Marilyn SKEMP
45 Spec Asst to Pres Resource Devel .... Ms. Rita CARVER
35 Acting Dean of Students .... Ms. Barbara FOX
37 Financial Aid Administrator .... Ms. Nicky SESIANE
08 Librarian .... Ms. Sue KOLODZEJSKI
41 Athletic Director .... Rev. Brian P. SMITH
07 Director of Admissions .... Mr. Carlos HOLLIDAY
15 Special Asst to Pres/Human Res Dir .....Ms. Vornadette SIMPSON
22 Compliance Officer .... Rev. Lynwood DAVIS
18 Maintenance Manager .... Mr. Brian SHIELDS

Washington College (D)

300 Washington Avenue, Chestertown MD 21620-1197
County: Kent FICE Identification: 002108
Unit ID: 164216
Telephone: (410) 778-2800 Carnegie Class: Bac/A&S
FAX Number: (410) 778-7850 Calendar System: Semester
URL: www.washcoll.edu
Established: 1782 Annual Undergrad Tuition & Fees: $38,542
Enrollment: 1,450 Coed
Affiliation or Control: Independent Non-Profit IRS Status: 501(c)3
Highest Offering: Master's
Program: Liberal Arts And General; Teacher Preparatory; Fine Arts Emphasis
Accreditation: M

01 President .... Dr. Mitchell B. REISS
05 Provost/Dean of College .... Dr. John B. TAYLOR
100 Chief of Staff .... Mr. Joseph L. HOLT
10 Senior Vice Pres Finance & Mgmt .... Mr. James V. MANARO
30 Vice Pres for College Advancement .... Vacant
07 Vice Pres Admiss/Enrollment Mgmt .... Mr. Kevin C. COVENEY
26 VP College Relations/ Marketing .... Ms. Meredith DAVIES HADAWAY
32 Vice President & Dean of Students .... Dr. Mela DUTKA
30 Director of Development .... Mr. Mark P. GADSON
44 AVP Ldrshp Gifts/Int VP Col Plcmt .... Ms. Barbara H. HECK
29 Asst Vice Pres for Alumni Relations .... Mrs. Lorraine K. POLVINALE
46 Asst Provost/Instl Research & Assmt ...... Mr. Dale W. TRUSHEIM
20 Asst Dean Academic Resources .... Dr. Kathryn W. SACK
31 Director of Campus Special Events .... Mrs. Laura J. WILSON
41 Director of Athletics .... Dr. Bryan L. MATTHEWS
06 Registrar .... Mrs. Jennifer L. BERSHON
08 Director of Miller Library .... Dr. Ruth C. SHOGE
27 Chief Information Officer .... Mrs. Billie S. DODGE
91 Asst Director of Admin Computing .... Mr. Kenneth W. SUTTON
58 Director of Graduate Program .... Dr. Christopher AMES
21 Controller .... Ms. Penelope L. FARLEY
18 Director of Physical Plant .... Mr. Reid C. RAUDENBUSH
15 Director of Human Resources .... Dr. Alan P. CHESNEY
19 Director of Public Safety .... Mr. Gerald K. RODERICK
37 Director of Financial Aid .... Ms. Jeani M. NARCUM
35 Dir of Student Development Programs . Dr. Sarah R. FEYERHERM
39 Dir Resid Life/Assoc Dean of Stdnts .... Mr. Carl CROWE
85 Director International Programs .... Vacant
23 Clinical Director Health Services .... Mrs. Dawn NORDHOFF
38 Director of Counseling Center .... Dr. Bonnie MICHAELSON FISHER
36 Director of Career Development ....Mr. James M. ALLISON, JR.
28 Director of Multi-Cultural Affairs .... Mr. Darnell PARKER
27 Director of Media Relations .... Ms. Kay MACINTOSH
40 Bookstore Manager .... Ms. Shannon WYBLE

Wor-Wic Community College (E)

32000 Campus Drive, Salisbury MD 21804-1486
County: Wicomico FICE Identification: 020739
Unit ID: 164313
Telephone: (410) 334-2800 Carnegie Class: Assoc/Pub-R-M
FAX Number: (410) 334-2951 Calendar System: Semester
URL: www.worwic.edu
Established: 1975 Annual Undergrad Tuition & Fees (In-District): $2,927
Enrollment: 4,150 Coed
Affiliation or Control: Local IRS Status: 501(c)3
Highest Offering: Associate Degree
Program: Occupational; 2-Year Principally Bachelor's Creditable
Accreditation: M, RAD

01 President .... Dr. Murray K. HOY
05 Vice Pres Academic & Student Affs .... Dr. Stephen L. CAPELLI
11 Vice Pres Administrative Services .... Mr. Mark V. RUDNICK
26 Vice Pres Institutional Affairs .... Dr. Reenie MCCORMICK
32 Dean Student Development .... Dr. Lynn M. WILJANEN
51 Dean Continuing Education .... Mrs. Ruth E. BAKER
97 Dean General Education .... Dr. Colleen C. DALLAM
75 Dean Occupational Education .... Dr. Trevor H. JONES
07 Director Admissions .... Mr. Richard C. WEBSTER
14 Director Information Technology .... Ms. Anne TURNER
36 Director Career Services .... Ms. Lori SMOOT
37 Director Financial Aid .... Ms. Deborah D. JENKINS
21 Director Accounting .... Mr. Thomas N. TYSON
15 Director Human Resources .... Ms. Jennifer A. SANDT
38 Director Counseling .... Ms. Suzanne T. ALEXANDER
27 Director Marketing .... Ms. Janet S. KENNINGTON
09 Director Institutional Research .... Ms. Carol A. MENZEL
30 Director Development .... Ms. Janice MURPHY
06 Registrar .... Ms. Kelly HEWETT
88 Dir Retention & Student Success .... Ms. Deirdra G. JOHNSON
35 Director Student Activities .... Ms. Tricia G. SMITH
08 Media Center Director .... Ms. Cheryl MICHAEL
18 Director Plant Management .... Mr. Paul MACE
96 Director Purchasing .... Ms. Allison M. CANADA
105 Webmaster .... Mr. Joshua W. TOWNSEND

Yeshiva College of the Nation's Capital (F)

1216 Arcola Avenue, Silver Spring MD 20902-3408
County: Montgomery FICE Identification: 039373
Unit ID: 434937
Telephone: (301) 593-2534 Carnegie Class: Spec/Faith
FAX Number: (301) 593-2534 Calendar System: Semester
Established: 1995 Annual Undergrad Tuition & Fees: $9,500
Enrollment: 54 Male
Affiliation or Control: Independent Non-Profit IRS Status: 501(c)3
Highest Offering: Second Talmudic Degree
Program: Teacher Preparatory; Professional; Religious Emphasis
Accreditation: RABN

01 President .... Rabbi Yitzchok MERKIN
05 Rosh Yeshiva .... Rabbi Aaron LOPIANSKY
37 Financial Aid Director .... Ms. Irene LAWSON

MASSACHUSETTS

American International College (G)

1000 State Street, Springfield MA 01109-3155
County: Hampden FICE Identification: 002114
Unit ID: 164447
Telephone: (413) 737-7000 Carnegie Class: Master's L
FAX Number: (413) 205-3943 Calendar System: Semester
URL: www.aic.edu
Established: 1885 Annual Undergrad Tuition & Fees: $27,500
Enrollment: 3,509 Coed
Affiliation or Control: Independent Non-Profit IRS Status: 501(c)3
Highest Offering: Doctorate
Program: Liberal Arts And General; Teacher Preparatory; Professional
Accreditation: EH, IACBE, NURSE, OT, PTA

01 President .... Dr. Vincent M. MANIACI
05 Executive VP for Academics .... Dr. Gregory T. SCHMUTTE
11 Executive VP for Administration .... Mr. Richard F. BEDARD
09 Associate VP for Inst Effectiveness .... Dr. John W. ROGERS
10 Exec VP Finance/Admin .... Mr. Mark R. BERMAN
32 VP Student Affairs .... Dr. Blaine K. STEVENS
51 Assoc VP Educational Enterprise .... Ms. Ellen R. NOONAN
07 VP for Admissions Services .... Mr. Peter J. MILLER
76 Dean Health Sciences .... Dr. Carol A. JOBE
06 Registrar .... Ms. Diane H. FURTEK
08 Librarian .... Ms. Estelle H. SPENCER
18 Plant Director (Sodexo) .... Mr. Henry NOEL
37 Assoc VP Student Financial Svcs .... Ms. Linda DAGRADI
38 Director Counseling Center .... Dr. Rose L. ANDREJCZYK
36 Dir Career Dev/Placement/Employment .... Ms. Abby MAHONEY
14 Chief Information Officer .... Mr. Bill SERETTA
49 Dean Arts/Education & Sciences .... Dr. Vickie HESS
50 Dean Business Administration .... Dr. Lea JOHNSON
66 Director Division of Nursing .... Ms. Carol S. JOBE
41 Director of Athletics .... Mr. Richard F. BEDARD
96 Director Auxiliary Svcs/Purchasing .... Ms. Katherine M. TOOHEY
88 Director Occupational Therapy Pgm ... Ms. Cathy A. DOW-ROYER
88 Director Physical Therapy Program .... Ms. Carol JOBE

60 Director Communications Center ... Vacant
21 Comptroller ... Vacant
15 Director of Human Resources ... Ms. Nicolle CESTERO
29 Director Alumni Relations ... Ms. Heather CAHILL

Amherst College (A)

PO Box 5000, Amherst MA 01002-5000
County: Hampshire
FICE Identification: 002115
Unit ID: 164465
Telephone: (413) 542-2000
Carnegie Class: Bac/A&S
FAX Number: (413) 542-2621
Calendar System: Semester
URL: www.amherst.edu
Established: 1821
Annual Undergrad Tuition & Fees: $42,898
Enrollment: 1,794
Coed
Affiliation or Control: Independent Non-Profit
IRS Status: 501(c)3
Highest Offering: Baccalaureate
Program: Liberal Arts And General
Accreditation: EH

01 President ... Dr. Carolyn A. MARTIN
04 Exec Assistant to the President ... Ms. Susan PIKOR
05 Dean of the Faculty ... Dr. Gregory S. CALL
20 Associate Dean of the Faculty ... Dr. John CHENEY
20 Associate Dean of the Faculty ... Dr. Fredrick GRIFFITHS
10 Treasurer ... Mr. Peter J. SHEA
21 Assoc Treasurer/Dir of the Budget ... Mrs. Shannon D. GUREK
30 Chief Advancement Officer ... Ms. Megan MOREY
43 Legal & Admin Counsel/AAO ... Mr. Paul MURPHY
29 Exec Director Alumni/Parent Pgms ... Ms. Elizabeth CANNON SMITH
32 Dean of Students ... Dr. Allen HART
07 Dean Admission/Financial Aid ... Mr. Thomas H. PARKER
06 Registrar ... Ms. Kathleen GOFF
37 Director of Financial Aid ... Mr. Joe P. CASE
15 Director of Human Resources ... Ms. Maria-Judith RODRIGUEZ
21 Comptroller ... Mr. Stephen M. NIGRO
09 Director of Institutional Research ... Ms. Marian F. MATHESON
26 Director of Public Affairs ... Mr. Peter J. ROONEY
08 College Librarian ... Mr. Bryn GEFFERT
13 Director of Information Technology ... Vacant
22 Affirmative Action Officer ... Vacant
23 Director of Student Health Services ... Dr. Warren H. MORGAN
38 Director of Counseling Center ... Dr. Jacqueline S. BEARCE
36 Director of Career Center ... Vacant
39 Director of Resident Life ... Mr. Torin Y. MOORE
41 Director of Athletics ... Dr. Suzanne R. COFFEY
18 Director Facilities/Planning/Mgmt ... Mr. James D. BRASSORD
19 Chief of Campus Police ... Mr. John B. CARTER
88 Director of Dining Services ... Mr. Charles G. THOMPSON

Andover Newton Theological School (B)

210 Herrick Road, Newton Centre MA 02459-2243
County: Middlesex
FICE Identification: 002116
Unit ID: 164474
Telephone: (617) 964-1100
Carnegie Class: Spec/Faith
FAX Number: (617) 965-9756
Calendar System: Semester
URL: www.ants.edu
Established: 1807
Annual Graduate Tuition & Fees: $14,856
Enrollment: 300
Coed
Affiliation or Control: Independent Non-Profit
IRS Status: 501(c)3
Highest Offering: Doctorate; No Undergraduates
Program: Professional; Religious Emphasis
Accreditation: EH, THEOL

01 President ... Dr. Nick CARTER
05 Dean of the Faculty ... Dr. Sarah B. DRUMMOND
10 Vice President for Finance ... Ms. Susan HUNT
30 Int Vice Pres Institutional Advance ... Dr. Nick CARTER
29 Director of the Annual Fund ... Rev. Ruth EDENS
06 Registrar ... Ms. Nayda G. AGUILA
84 Director of Recruitment ... Ms. Alison MCCARTY
08 Co-Director of the Library ... Ms. Diana YOUNT
08 Co-Director of the Library ... Mr. Jeffrey BRIGHAM
32 Dean of Students ... Dr. Nancy E. NIENHUIS
04 Assistant to the President ... Ms. Rose L. COSTAS
18 Director Physical Plant ... Mr. Frank CAVACO
27 Director Information Office ... Mr. Tim SWANSEY
37 Coordinator Financial Aid ... Ms. Rosemary TURANO
39 Director Housing & Events Planning ... Mr. Frank NOVO

Anna Maria College (C)

50 Sunset Lane, Paxton MA 01612-1198
County: Worcester
FICE Identification: 002117
Unit ID: 164492
Telephone: (508) 849-3300
Carnegie Class: Master's M
FAX Number: (508) 849-3334
Calendar System: 4/1/4
URL: www.annamaria.edu
Established: 1946
Annual Undergrad Tuition & Fees: $29,860
Enrollment: 1,498
Coed
Affiliation or Control: Roman Catholic
IRS Status: 501(c)3
Highest Offering: Beyond Master's But Less Than Doctorate
Program: Liberal Arts And General; Teacher Preparatory; Professional
Accreditation: EH, ADNUR, MUS, NUR, SW

01 President ... Dr. Jack P. CALARESO
03 Executive Vice President ... Ms. Mary Louise RETELLE
10 Vice President Finance & Admin ... Ms. Cheryl SLEBODA
21 Controller ... Ms. Yvonnie MALCOLM
05 Vice President for Academic Affairs ... Dr. Billye W. AUCLAIR
32 Vice President for Student Affairs ... Mr. Andrew O. KLEIN
84 VP for Marketing & College Relation ... Ms. Paula L. GREEN
09 Director of Institutional Research ... Ms. Irene IRUDAYAM
06 Registrar ... Ms. Barbara ZAWALICH
30 Director Institutional Advancement ... Mr. Eric P. GUSTAFSON
38 Director Counseling Services ... Mr. Dennis VANASSE
23 Director of Health Services ... Ms. Linda ARONSON
08 Director of Library ... Ms. Ruth PYNE
29 Director Alumni Relations ... Ms. Ann E. THOMPSON
26 VP of Marketing/Community Rels ... Ms. Paula L. GREEN
36 Director Career Counsel/Placement ... Ms. Judith M. SPARANGES
37 Director Financial Aid ... Ms. Sandra PEREIRA
13 Director of Information Technology ... Mr. Michael MIERS
04 Administrative Assistant ... Ms. Renee J. MARKIEWICZ
04 Executive Asst to the President ... Mrs. Kay PRENTISS
18 Director Physical Plant ... Mr. Mark COLLETTE
66 Director of Assoc Nursing Program ... Dr. Carol GABRIELE
39 Assoc Dean of Campus Life ... Ms. Elizabeth BONNEAU
41 Athletic Director ... Mr. David SHEA
42 Director Campus Ministry ... Ms. Maria BARI
15 Director of Human Resources ... Ms. Lisa DRISCOLL
44 Director of Annual Fund ... Ms. Meghan HALLOCK
88 Dean of Mission Effectiveness ... Sr. Rollande QUINTAL

The Art Institute of Boston at Lesley University (D)

700 Beacon Street, Boston MA 02215-2598
County: Suffolk
FICE Identification: 008174
Unit ID: 164526
Telephone: (617) 585-6600
Carnegie Class: Not Classified
FAX Number: (617) 437-1226
Calendar System: Semester
URL: www.aiboston.edu
Established: 1912
Annual Undergrad Tuition & Fees: $28,750
Enrollment: 530
Coed
Affiliation or Control: Independent Non-Profit
IRS Status: 501(c)3
Highest Offering: Master's
Program: Professional; Fine Arts Emphasis
Accreditation: &EH, ART

01 President ... Dr. Joseph B. MOORE
05 Provost ... Dr. Selase W. WILLIAMS
03 Dean ... Mr. Stan TRECKER
20 Senior Associate Dean ... Mr. Matthew CHERRY
84 Vice Pres Enrollment Management ... Mr. Jeffrey HANDLER
30 Vice President of Advancement ... Mr. Randy STABILE
32 Dean of Student Life & Academic Dev ... Dr. Nathaniel MAYS
07 Director of Admissions ... Mr. Bob GIELOW
08 Head Librarian ... Ms. Patricia PAYNE
90 Director of Academic Computing ... Mr. Fred LEVY
20 Director of Academic Advising ... Ms. Julie STANWOOD
88 Director of Exhibitions ... Ms. Bonnell ROBINSON
09 Dir Assessment/Institutional Rsrch ... Ms. Linda PURSLEY
10 Chief Financial Officer ... Ms. Bernice BRADIN
06 Registrar ... Ms. Melissa JANOT
29 Director Alumni Relations ... Ms. Pattyanne LYONS
39 Director of Residence Life ... Ms. Nancy GALVIN
18 Director of Facilities & Operations ... Mr. Kevin MURPHY
35 Student Activities Director ... Ms. Amanda MEREAU
36 Assoc Dir Career Resource Center ... Mr. Francis ALIX
37 Director of Financial Aid ... Mr. Scott JEWELL
38 Director of Student Counseling ... Ms. Magi MCKINNIES
26 Public Affairs Manager ... Mr. Bill DONCASTER
15 Director of Human Resources ... Ms. Jane JOYCE
22 Dir Equal Opportunity & Inclusion ... Ms. Barbara ADDISON REID
96 Director of Purchasing ... Mr. William HOYT

† Regional accreditation carried under the parent institution, Lesley University in Cambridge, MA.

Assumption College (E)

500 Salisbury Street, Worcester MA 01609-1296
County: Worcester
FICE Identification: 002118
Unit ID: 164562
Telephone: (508) 767-7000
Carnegie Class: Master's M
FAX Number: (508) 756-1780
Calendar System: Semester
URL: www.assumption.edu
Established: 1904
Annual Undergrad Tuition & Fees: $32,545
Enrollment: 2,724
Coed
Affiliation or Control: Roman Catholic
IRS Status: 501(c)3
Highest Offering: Beyond Master's But Less Than Doctorate
Program: Liberal Arts And General; Teacher Preparatory; Professional
Accreditation: EH, CORE

01 President ... Dr. Francesco C. CESAREO
03 Executive Vice President ... Mr. Christian MCCARTHY
05 Provost/Academic Vice Pres ... Dr. Francis M. LAZARUS
32 Vice President for Student Affairs ... Dr. Catherine M. WOODBROOKS
30 Vice Pres Institutional Advancement ... Mr. Thomas E. RYAN
42 Vice President Mission ... Rev. Dennis M. GALLAGHER, AA
84 Vice Pres for Enrollment Management ... Mr. Evan E. LIPP
43 General Counsel ... Dr. Michael H. RUBINO
20 Associate Provost ... Dr. Louise CARROLL KEELEY
51 Dir of Career and Continuing Ed ... Mr. Dennis BRAUN
07 Dean of Admissions ... Ms. Kathleen M. MURPHY
20 Dean of Undergraduate Studies ... Dr. Eloise KNOWLTON
58 Dean of Graduate Studies ... Vacant
89 Associate Dean for the First Year ... Dr. Jennifer K. MORRISON
42 Director of Campus Ministry ... Mr. James RIZZA
35 Dean of Student Development ... Dr. Neil R. CASTRONOVO
08 Director of Library Services ... Ms. Doris Ann SWEET
10 Director of Finance ... Mr. John F. KOMPEL
21 Dir of Facilities Planning & Projs ... Vacant
09 Director Inst Research and Ac Asst ... Mr. Stuart J. MUNRO
58 Director Grad Enrollment/Mgmt/Svcs ... Ms. Barbara BENOIT
06 Registrar ... Mr. David W. AALTO
13 Exec Dir Info Tech & Media Svcs ... Dr. Dawn M. THISTLE
15 Director of Human Resources/AAO ... Ms. Grace BLUNT
26 Director of Public Affairs ... Ms. Renee BUISSON
29 Director of Alumni Relations ... Ms. Diane LASKA-NIXON
44 Director of Annual Giving ... Mr. Timothy R. MARTIN
88 Director of Academic Support Center ... Dr. Allen A. BRUEHL
35 Dean of Campus Life ... Ms. Nancy P. CRIMMIN
39 Assoc Dean Campus Life/Dir Res Life ... Mr. Conway CAMPBELL
41 Director of Athletics ... Mr. Ted PAULAUSKAS
19 Director of Public Safety ... Mr. Robert MURPHY
23 Director of Health Services ... Ms. Christine ZANFINI-PARKER
24 Director of Media Services ... Mr. Ted HALEY
37 Director of Financial Aid ... Ms. Linda MULARCZYK
88 Director of Auxiliary Services ... Mr. John LANGLOIS
25 Director of Grant Development ... Dr. Landy C. JOHNSON
35 Dean of Students ... Mr. Robert G. RAVENELLE
28 Director of Multicultural Affairs ... Vacant
96 Director of Purchasing ... Ms. Gail M. RACINE
86 Exec Asst for Govt/Cmty Relations ... Mr. Paul BELSITO

Atlantic Union College (F)

PO Box 1000, South Lancaster MA 01561-1000
County: Worcester
FICE Identification: 002119
Unit ID: 164571
Telephone: (978) 368-2000
Carnegie Class: Bac/Diverse
FAX Number: (978) 368-2015
Calendar System: Semester
URL: www.auc.edu
Established: 1882
Annual Undergrad Tuition & Fees: $17,500
Enrollment: 478
Coed
Affiliation or Control: Seventh-day Adventist
IRS Status: 501(c)3
Highest Offering: Master's
Program: Occupational; 2-Year Principally Bachelor's Creditable; Teacher Preparatory; Professional; Religious Emphasis
Accreditation: ADNUR, MUS, NUR

01 President ... Dr. Norman WENDTH
05 Senior Vice President Academics ... Dr. Clarence (Chip) ATES
10 Senior Vice President Finance ... Mr. Lloyd BROWN
84 Vice Pres Enrollment/Retention ... Dr. Bordes HENRY-SATURNE
32 Vice President for Student Services ... Mr. Jack MENTGES
30 Int VP Advancement/Alumni Affairs ... Dr. Clarence (Chip) ATES
26 CIO/Public Relations Director ... Ms. Cynthia A. KURTZHALS
27 Assistant VP for Marketing ... Dr. Lois KING
09 Asst VP of Inst Research/Assessment ... Dr. Issumael NZAMUTUMA
06 Director of Academic Records ... Ms. Lynn Marie ZABALETA
08 Library Director ... Mrs. Jacqueline NEATH-FOSTER
34 Asst Dean of Women ... Ms. Opal FORRESTER
33 Dean of Men ... Mr. Andrew FRANCIS
37 Director of Financial Aid ... Vacant
13 Director of Information Technology ... Vacant
18 Plant Services Manager ... Mr. Leslie AHO
19 Director of Security ... Mr. Robert BRAND
39 Director Housing ... Mrs. Paula RAMOS
23 Director Health Services ... Mrs. Joan MITCHELL
40 Director of Bookstore ... Ms. Blanche CASTLE
41 Recreation Director ... Mr. Sandy SMITH
42 Chaplain/Director Campus Ministry ... Mr. Daniel Israel SIERRA
15 Director Personnel Services/HR ... Mr. Roberto REYNA
21 Comptroller ... Mr. Donovan KURTZ
35 Director Student Accounts ... Ms. Carolyn WOODS
84 Enrollment Manager ... Ms. Kallie KIRCHBERG

Babson College (G)

231 Forest Street, Babson Park MA 02457-0310
County: Norfolk
FICE Identification: 002121
Unit ID: 164580
Telephone: (781) 235-1200
Carnegie Class: Spec/Bus
FAX Number: (781) 239-5231
Calendar System: Semester
URL: www.babson.edu
Established: 1919
Annual Undergrad Tuition & Fees: $40,400
Enrollment: 3,300
Coed
Affiliation or Control: Independent Non-Profit
IRS Status: 501(c)3
Highest Offering: Master's
Program: Professional; Business Emphasis
Accreditation: EH, BUS

01 President ... Dr. Leonard A. SCHLESINGER
05 Provost ... Dr. Shahid ANSARI
11 VP of Administration ... Ms. Mary ROSE
29 VP Alumni and Friends Network ... Ms. Carol J. HACKER
30 Executive Director Development ... Ms. Diana P. ZAIS
10 VP for Finance and CFO ... Mr. Philip SHAPIRO
15 VP Human Resources ... Ms. Donna BONAPARTE
43 VP and General Counsel ... Mr. Jonathan MOLL
20 Vice Provost ... Dr. Henry DENEAULT
18 Assoc VP Facilities/Services ... Mr. Shelley KAPLAN
13 Chief Information Officer ... Mr. Samuel DUNN
32 Dean of Student Affairs ... Ms. Elizabeth NEWMAN
20 Dean of Faculty ... Ms. Carolyn HOTCHKISS
100 Chief of Staff ... Ms. Tracee PETRILLO
58 Dean of Graduate School ... Dr. Raghu TADEPALLI

50 Dean of Undergraduate School ... Dr. Dennis HANNO
51 Dean of Babson Exec Education ... Ms. Elaine EISENMAN
07 Dean Undergraduate Admissions ... Mr. Grant GOSSELIN
37 Assoc Dean UG Sch/Dir Std Fin Svcs ... Ms. Melissa J. SHAAK
06 Registrar ... Ms. Linda KEAN
07 Director Graduate Admissions ... Ms. Barbara J. SELMO
36 Dir Graduate Career Svcs ... Ms. Cheri PAULSON
36 Dir Undergraduate Career Services ... Ms. Megan HOULKER
09 Director of Institutional Research ... Ms. Anne Marie DELANEY
26 Director Public Relations ... Mr. Michael CHMURA
21 Assoc VP Fin Services/Controller ... Mr. Richard BOWMAN
96 Director of Business Services ... Ms. Teresa PITARO
28 Chief Diversity Officer ... Ms. Elizabeth THORNTON

Bard College at Simon's Rock (A)

84 Alford Road, Great Barrington MA 01230-9702
County: Berkshire | FICE Identification: 009645 | Unit ID: 167792
Telephone: (413) 644-4400 | Carnegie Class: Bac/Assoc
FAX Number: (413) 528-7365 | Calendar System: Semester
URL: www.simons-rock.edu
Established: 1964 | Annual Undergrad Tuition & Fees: $43,000
Enrollment: 480 | Coed
Affiliation or Control: Independent Non-Profit | IRS Status: 501(c)3
Highest Offering: Baccalaureate
Program: Liberal Arts And General
Accreditation: EH

01 President ... Dr. Leon BOTSTEIN
03 Executive Vice President ... Mr. Dimitri PAPADIMITRIOU
05 Vice President/Provost ... Dr. Peter LAIPSON
04 Asst to Vice President & Provost ... Ms. Jackie GENTILE
84 VP Early College Policies/Programs ... Mr. U. Ba WIN
32 Dean of the College ... Ms. Leslie DAVIDSON
20 Dean of Academic Affairs ... Dr. Anne O'DWYER
88 Dean of New Students ... Dr. Rebecca FISKE
35 Assoc Dean of Student Affairs ... Mr. Robert GRAVES
27 Director of College Relations ... Mr. Christopher SINK
06 Registrar ... Ms. Rochelle DUFFY
08 Head Librarian ... Mr. Brian MIKESELL
37 Director of Financial Aid ... Ms. Ann MURTAGH GITTO
18 Director Physical Plant ... Mr. Steven CARIGNAN
10 Dir of Finance/Administration/HR ... Mr. Jon A. MACCLAREN
38 Dir Counsel/Post Degree Counseling ... Dr. Judith WIN
23 Director of Student Health Services ... Ms. Jodi TULLER, RN
90 Director of Academic Computing ... Ms. Janice GILDAWIE
19 Director of Security ... Mr. Kenneth GEREMIA
26 Director of External Affairs ... Ms. Susan EMERSON CLAPP
44 Director of Annual Fund ... Mr. Richard MONTONE
40 Director of Bookstore ... Vacant
41 Athletic Center Manager ... Mr. David COLLOPY
57 Division Head Arts & Aesthetics ... Dr. John MYERS
81 Division Head Math/Natural Science ... Dr. Michael BERGMAN
83 Division Head Social Studies ... Dr. Chris COGGINS
79 Division Head Language & Literature ... Dr. Mileta ROE

Bay Path College (B)

588 Longmeadow Street, Longmeadow MA 01106-2292
County: Hampden | FICE Identification: 002122 | Unit ID: 164632
Telephone: (413) 565-1000 | Carnegie Class: Bac/A&S
FAX Number: (413) 565-1105 | Calendar System: Semester
URL: www.baypath.edu
Established: 1897 | Annual Undergrad Tuition & Fees: $27,045
Enrollment: 2,116 | Female
Affiliation or Control: Independent Non-Profit | IRS Status: 501(c)3
Highest Offering: Master's
Program: Liberal Arts And General; Teacher Preparatory; Professional
Accreditation: EH, OT

01 President ... Dr. Carol A. LEARY
05 Vice Pres Academic Affairs/ Provost ... Dr. Melissa MORRISS-OLSON
10 VP Finance/Administrative Services ... Mr. Michael GIAMPIETRO
30 VP for Institutional Advancement ... Ms. Kathleen BOURQUE
45 Vice Pres Plng/Student Development ... Ms. Caron T. HOBIN
88 VP Academic & Adminstrative Tech ... Dr. David DEMERS
04 Assistant to the President ... Ms. Barbara KOCHON
21 Associate Vice President Finance ... Ms. Donna GUERTIN
20 Assoc Vice Pres Academic Affairs ... Ms. Ann DOBMEYER
12 Director of the Burlington Campus ... Dr. Cristy SUGARMAN
12 Director CMC Campus ... Ms. Kathy JARRETT
26 Director of Communications ... Ms. Kathleen WROBLEWSKI
07 Dean of Admissions ... Ms. Diane RANALDI
37 Director of Student Financial Svcs ... Ms. Stephanie KING
36 Exec Dir Career & Life Planning ... Vacant
07 Director of Graduate Admissions ... Ms. Lisa ADAMS
08 Director of the Library ... Mr. Michael MORAN
06 Registrar ... Ms. Laura LANDER
36 Director Career Services ... Ms. Sally J. SCHIRMER-SMITH
29 Dir of Alumni Relations ... Ms. Kathleen COTNOIR
23 Director of Health Services ... Ms. Margaret ANDERSON
19 Director of Campus Public Safety ... Vacant
15 Director Human Resources ... Ms. Kathleen HALPIN-ROBBINS
14 Information Systems Administrator ... Mrs. Linda A. SIMONDS
18 Director Facilities/Campus Svcs ... Mr. Paul E. STANTON
41 Director of Athletics ... Mr. Steven J. SMITH
88 Dir Masters of Sci Commun/Info Mgmt ... Dr. Elizabeth RIVET
32 Director of Student Life ... Mr. Peter AXTMANN
88 Dir Business Pgms for One-Day Pgm ... Dr. Sandi COYNE
88 Dir MBA Entrepr Thnkg/Innov Practic ... Mr. Mo SATTAR
88 Dir Grad Pgms Nonprofit Mgmt/Philan ... Mr. Jeffrey GREIM
09 Dir Institutional Research & Data ... Ms. Amanda GOULD
88 Director of Life Skills Program ... Ms. Katie JONES
88 Dir Center for Teaching & Learning ... Vacant
17 Director of Clinical Education ... Mr. Anthony PELLEGRINO
96 Director of Purchasing/Office Svcs ... Vacant
102 Dir Foundation/Corporate Relations ... Ms. Janine MCVAY
49 Dean College of Arts & Sciences ... Dr. Michael KONIG
53 Dean School of Education ... Dr. Elizabeth FLEMING
88 Dean School of Mgmt/Social Justice ... Dr. Geofrey MILLS
107 Fndng Dean Sch Adult & Profess Stds ... Dr. Gina JOSEPH-COLLINS
88 Dean of Student Success ... Mr. Dave YELLE
83 Fndg Dean Sch Health Sci/Hum Behav ... Vacant
50 Chair Business Department ... Ms. Lauren WAY
88 Chair Criminal Justice Department ... Atty. Elizabeth DINEEN
88 Chair Occupational Therapy Dept ... Dr. Lori VAUGHN
88 Chair Psychology Department ... Ms. Kathy WIEZBICKI-STEVENS
61 Chair Legal Studies Department ... Atty. John WOODRUFF
51 Dean Cont Educ & Grad Recruitment ... Ms. Diane RANALDI
79 Chair Liberal Studies ... Dr. Thomas SCHORLE
81 Chair Science ... Dr. Gina SEMPREBON
81 Chair Math & Information Systems ... Dr. Farrokh SABA
88 Chair Creative and Performing Arts ... Vacant
88 Director PA Program ... Dr. Jennifer HIXON

Bay State College (C)

122 Commonwealth Avenue, Boston MA 02116-2975
County: Suffolk | FICE Identification: 003965 | Unit ID: 164641
Telephone: (617) 217-9000 | Carnegie Class: Assoc/PrivFP4
FAX Number: (617) 249-0400 | Calendar System: Semester
URL: www.baystate.edu
Established: 1946 | Annual Undergrad Tuition & Fees: $21,930
Enrollment: 1,200 | Coed
Affiliation or Control: Proprietary | IRS Status: Proprietary
Highest Offering: Baccalaureate
Program: Occupational; 2-Year Principally Bachelor's Creditable
Accreditation: EH, MAAB, PTAA

01 President ... Craig PFANNENSTIEHL
05 Vice President of Academic Affairs ... Dr. William CARROLL
32 Vice President of Student Services ... Sylvia REIFLER
10 Vice Pres Administration & Finance ... Meg TRANT
37 Director of Financial Aid ... Jeani DEVANI
84 Vice Pres of Enrollment & Marketing ... Chip BERGSTROM
06 Registrar ... Lynn DUNHAM
08 Librarian ... Jessica NEAVE
32 Chief Student Life Officer ... Michelle BROKAW
35 Director Student Affairs ... Kate ACKERMAN
07 Director of Admissions ... Kim OLDS
18 Chief Facilities/Physical Plant ... Kate AKERMAN
21 Bursar ... Jeff MCMASTER
36 Director Student Placement ... Tom CORRIGAN
38 Director Student Counseling ... Cheryl RAICHE

Becker College-Worcester (D)

61 Sever Street, Worcester MA 01609-2165
County: Worcester | FICE Identification: 002123 | Unit ID: 164720
Telephone: (508) 791-9241 | Carnegie Class: Bac/Diverse
FAX Number: (508) 831-7505 | Calendar System: Semester
URL: www.becker.edu
Established: 1887 | Annual Undergrad Tuition & Fees: $28,490
Enrollment: 1,751 | Coed
Affiliation or Control: Independent Non-Profit | IRS Status: 501(c)3
Highest Offering: Baccalaureate
Program: 2-Year Principally Bachelor's Creditable; Liberal Arts And General
Accreditation: EH, ADNUR

01 President ... Dr. Robert E. JOHNSON
30 Vice President Development ... Mr. Dean HICKEY
30 Vice Pres Institutional Advancement ... Mr. Gerald N. TUORI
32 Vice President of Student Affairs ... Mr. Ken CAMERON
10 Vice President of Finance ... Mr. George LEAR
15 Assoc Vice Pres of Human Resources ... Mrs. Kathleen M. GARVEY
05 Dean of Academic Affairs ... Ms. Elizabeth FULLER
66 Dean of Nursing/Health Stds ... Ms. Linda ESPER
62 Dean of the Libraries ... Ms. Jean COLLINS
07 Dean of Admissions ... Ms. Karen SCHEDIN
27 Chief Information officer ... Ms. Patty PATRIA
06 Registrar ... Ms. Tonya LABROSSE
29 Assistant Director Alumni Affairs ... Ms. Caitlin VISSCHER
35 Director Student Services-Worcester ... Ms. Jean BLACKMER
35 Dir of Student Services - Leicester ... Ms. Michelle FATCHERIC
37 Asst Dir Student Financial Services ... Ms. Kim STELMACH
38 Director of Counseling ... Ms. Wendy MILES
20 Dir Center for Academic Success ... Ms. Dolores RADLO
88 Director for BA in Design ... Mr. Paul COTNOIR
41 Director of Athletics ... Mr. Frank MILLERICK
74 Director Animal Science Programs ... Dr. James KNIGHT
27 Communications Director ... Ms. Sandy LASHIN-CUREWITZ
96 Director of Business Services ... Mr. Mike MONGEON
26 Director of Marketing ... Mr. Robert FERNANDEZ
21 Controller ... Mr. Richard NAYLOR
19 Campus Police Chief ... Mr. David BOUSQUET
36 Director of Career Services ... Mr. Eric SACZAWA

Benjamin Franklin Institute of Technology (E)

41 Berkeley Street, Boston MA 02116-6296
County: Suffolk | FICE Identification: 002151 | Unit ID: 165884
Telephone: (617) 423-4630 | Carnegie Class: Spec/Tech
FAX Number: (617) 482-3706 | Calendar System: Semester
URL: www.bfit.edu
Established: 1908 | Annual Undergrad Tuition & Fees: $15,950
Enrollment: 540 | Coed
Affiliation or Control: Independent Non-Profit | IRS Status: 501(c)3
Highest Offering: Baccalaureate
Program: Occupational; 2-Year Principally Bachelor's Creditable; Technical Emphasis
Accreditation: EH

01 President ... George C. CHRYSSIS
05 Dean of Academic Affairs ... Anthony BENOIT
32 Dean of Students ... Brian BICKNELL
10 Chief Financial Officer ... Keith DROPKIN
11 Chief Operating Officer ... Stephen LOZEN
06 Registrar ... James KLASEN
08 Librarian ... Sharon B. BONK
84 Dean of Enrollment Management ... Mike BOSCO
19 Director Security ... Myftar MYRTAJ
07 Director of Admissions ... Marvin LOISEAU
30 Director of Development ... Juliana FIELD
20 Director Academic Support Services ... Rachel ARNO
13 Director Computing & Info Mgmt ... Vacant

Bentley University (F)

175 Forest Street, Waltham MA 02452-4705
County: Middlesex | FICE Identification: 002124 | Unit ID: 164739
Telephone: (781) 891-2000 | Carnegie Class: Master's L
FAX Number: (781) 891-2569 | Calendar System: Semester
URL: www.bentley.edu
Established: 1917 | Annual Undergrad Tuition & Fees: $36,840
Enrollment: 5,695 | Coed
Affiliation or Control: Independent Non-Profit | IRS Status: 501(c)3
Highest Offering: Doctorate
Program: Liberal Arts And General; Professional; Business Emphasis
Accreditation: EH, BUS, BUSA

01 President ... Ms. Gloria C. LARSON
43 General Counsel ... Ms. Judith A. MALONE
102 Director Foundation Relations ... Mr. Paul K. CARBERRY
05 VP Academic Affairs/Provost ... Dr. Michael J. PAGE
10 VP Business/Finance/Treas ... Mr. Paul CLEMENTE
30 VP University Advancement ... Mr. John PINI
32 VP Student Affairs ... Dr. Andrew J. SHEPARDSON
13 COO & VP for Information Technology ... Ms. Traci A. LOGAN
84 VP Enrollment Management ... Ms. Joann C. MCKENNA
49 Dean of Arts and Sciences ... Dr. Daniel L. EVERETT
50 Dean of Business/McCallum Grad Sch ... Dr. Michael J. PAGE
09 Reporting Specialist/Inst Research ... Ms. Lindsey C. LEWIS
49 Assoc Dean of Arts and Sciences ... Dr. Juliet GAINSBOROUGH
44 Senior Director of Special Gifts ... Mr. John A. PINI
29 Mng Dir Alumni/Parents & Friends ... Ms. Leigh GASPAR
27 Exec Director Mktg/Communication ... Ms. Katherine H. BLAKE
16 Exec Director of Human Resources ... Ms. Ann DEXTER
11 Assoc Dean of Administration ... Ms. Judy KAMM
21 Exec Dir Financial Operations ... Ms. Marianne F. CWALINA
06 Registrar ... Ms. Patricia A. ROGERS
22 Pres Assistant Equal Opportunity ... Dr. Earl L. AVERY
38 Assoc Dean/Dir Couns & Student Dev ... Dr. Roger A. DANCHISE
41 Director of Athletics ... Mr. Robert A. DEFELICE
37 Exec Dir Enroll Mgmt & Fin Assist ... Ms. Donna M. KENDALL
39 Dir Housing & Student Systems ... Mr. Ronald M. ARDIZZONE
90 Dir Academic Tech/Library/Rsch Svcs ... Dr. Phillip G. KNUTEL
31 Director Service-Learning Center ... Mr. Franklyn P. SALIMBENE
19 Executive Director of Public Safety ... Mr. Ernest H. LEFFLER
26 Director Public & Media Relations ... Ms. Michele M. WALSH
88 Mng Dir Corp Fin & Sponsored Pgms ... Mr. Leonard MORRISON
23 Asst Dean/Dir Health & Wellness ... Ms. Geraldine S. TAYLOR
25 Director of Sponsored Programs ... Ms. Mary Louise PAULI
88 Director of Conference Services ... Mr. Robert L. WEBB
07 Asst Dean/Dir of Grad Admission ... Ms. Sharon F. HILL
58 Director of MBA Programs ... Vacant
88 Senior Associate Dir Reunion Pgms ... Mr. Gary E. KELLY
18 Director Facilities Management ... Mr. Thomas W. KANE
96 Director Purchasing/Contract Svcs ... Ms. Julianne BRITT
28 Director of Diversity ... Vacant
35 Dean of Student Affairs ... Dr. J. Andrew SHEPARDSON

Berklee College of Music (G)

1140 Boylston Street, Boston MA 02215-3693
County: Suffolk | FICE Identification: 002126 | Unit ID: 164748
Telephone: (617) 266-1400 | Carnegie Class: Spec/Arts
FAX Number: (617) 247-6878 | Calendar System: Semester
URL: www.berklee.edu
Established: 1945 | Annual Undergrad Tuition & Fees: $33,460
Enrollment: 4,275 | Coed
Affiliation or Control: Independent Non-Profit | IRS Status: 501(c)3
Highest Offering: Baccalaureate
Program: Music Emphasis
Accreditation: EH

01 President .... Roger H. BROWN
05 Sr Vice Pres Academic Affs/Provost .... Lawrence J. SIMPSON
32 Vice Pres Student Affs/Dean Stdnts .... Lawrence E. BETHUNE
102 Sr VP Institutional Advancement .... Deborah GROZEN BIERI
10 Chief Financial Officer .... Richard M. HISEY
11 Vice President Administration .... John ELDERT
21 Vice President Finance .... Amelia KOCH
30 Vice Pres Institutional Advancement .... David MCKAY
13 Vice Pres Technology/Educ Outreach .... David MASH
28 Vice Pres for Cultural Diversity .... Myra HINDUS
88 Assoc VP for Administration .... Nancy EAGEN
84 Vice President Enrollment .... Mark CAMPBELL
14 Assoc VP Information Technology .... Scott V. STREET
15 Vice Pres Human Res/Diversity/Incl .... Christine M. CONNORS
88 Assoc Ed Outreach/Ex Dir BC Music .... J. Curtis WARNER, JR.
82 Asst Vice Pres Intl Programs .... Greg BADOLATO
35 Asst VP Student Affs/Student Devel .... Steven LIPMAN
20 Assoc VP Academic Affs/Assoc Prov .... Jay S. KENNEDY
27 Asst VP for Public Information .... Rob HAYES
88 Asst VP Academic Technology .... Matt MARVUGLIO
88 Dean of Prof Writing Division .... Kari JUUSELA
53 Dean of Prof Education Division .... Darla S. HANLEY
64 Dean of Music Technology .... Stephen CROES
08 Dean of Learning Resources .... Gary HAGGERTY
09 Director Inst Reseach & Assessment .... Susan Coia GAILEY
91 Director Telecom/Networking Svcs .... Norman E. SILVER
06 Registrar .... Michael HAGERTY
39 Director of Housing .... William M. MACKAY
37 Director of Financial Aid .... Julie POORMAN
38 Director of Counseling .... Sara REGAN
07 Director of Admissions .... Damien S. BRACKEN
29 Director Alumni Relations .... Karen BELL
36 Director Career Development Center .... Peter SPELLMAN
18 Assoc Director of Physical Plant .... George O'MEARA

Blessed John XXIII National Seminary (A)

558 South Avenue, Weston MA 02493-2699
County: Middlesex FICE Identification: 002202
Unit ID: 167464
Telephone: (781) 899-5500 Carnegie Class: Spec/Faith
FAX Number: (781) 899-9057 Calendar System: Semester
URL: www.blessedjohnxxiii.edu
Established: 1964 Annual Graduate Tuition & Fees: $22,750
Enrollment: 56 Male
Affiliation or Control: Roman Catholic IRS Status: 501(c)3
Highest Offering: Master's; No Undergraduates
Program: Professional
Accreditation: THEOL

01 Rector and President .... Rev. William B. PALARDY
05 Academic Dean/Registrar .... Dr. Anthony KEATY
08 Librarian .... Sr. Jacqueline MILLER
10 Business Manager .... Mrs. Kyle RYAN

Boston Architectural College (B)

320 Newbury Street, Boston MA 02115-2795
County: Suffolk FICE Identification: 003966
Unit ID: 164872
Telephone: (617) 262-5000 Carnegie Class: Spec/Arts
FAX Number: (617) 585-0111 Calendar System: Semester
URL: www.the-bac.edu
Established: 1889 Annual Undergrad Tuition & Fees: $16,826
Enrollment: 1,045 Coed
Affiliation or Control: Independent Non-Profit IRS Status: 501(c)3
Highest Offering: Master's
Program: Liberal Arts And General; Professional
Accreditation: EH, CIDA, LSAR

01 President/CEO .... Dr. Theodore C. LANDSMARK
03 Executive Vice President .... Mr. James DUNN
04 Assistant to the President .... Ms. Kristin KOCHANCZYK
04 Assistant to the Exec VP & Board .... Ms. Amyjo HOFNER
05 Provost .... Ms. Julia HALEVY
10 Vice President for Finance/Admin .... Ms. Kathleen C. ROOD
30 VP Institutional Advancement .... Mr. Christopher COX
48 Head School of Architecture & Dean .... Vacant
88 Head School of Interior Design .... Mr. Crandon GUSTAFSON
88 Head School of Landscape Architect .... Ms. Maria BELLALTA
88 Head School of Design Studies .... Mr. Donald HUNSICKER
51 Head Continuing Ed Pgms/Curriculum .... Ms. Jane TOLAND
88 Head of Practice .... Mr. Len CHARNEY
46 Dean Research and Assessment .... Mr. Herb CHILDRESS
32 Assoc Provost/Dean of Students .... Mr. Richard M. GRISWOLD
51 Director of Continuing Education .... Mr. Adam MAGUIRE
20 Exec Dir of Educational Initiatives .... Mr. Curt LAMB
88 Director of Technical Operations .... Mr. Timothy OGAWA
36 Director of Student Placement .... Ms. Susan S. BRODY
88 Dir of Master's Thesis Arch .... Mr. Ian TABERNER
88 Director of Design Computing .... Mr. Diego L. MATHO
88 Director of Media Arts .... Mr. Luis MONTALVO
88 Director of Distance M Arch .... Mr. Tom PARKS
88 Dir of Special Projects/Practice .... Mr. Gabe BERGERON
88 Asst Dir of Practice Component .... Ms. Cat CRAFT
08 Library Director .... Ms. Susan A. LEWIS
06 Registrar .... Ms. Ann ROYALL
07 Director Admissions .... Mr. Richard MOYER
37 Director Financial Aid Operations .... Mr. James RYAN
86 Director of External/Gov Relations .... Ms. Janet OBERTO
35 Director of Student Development .... Ms. Kara PEET
18 Director of Facilities .... Mr. Arthur BYERS
11 Dir of Administrative Operations .... Ms. Patti VAUGHN
88 Director of Academic Services .... Mr. Joshua WHITE
88 Director of Faculty Development .... Ms. Tina BLYTHE
20 Director of Educational Services .... Mr. Christopher RAICHLE
88 Director of Foundation Education .... Ms. Chala J. HADIMI
88 Acting Head School of Architecture .... Ms. Karen L. NELSON
88 Director of Foundation Studies .... Mr. Lee PETERS

Boston Baptist College (C)

950 Metropolitan Avenue, Boston MA 02136-4000
County: Suffolk FICE Identification: 032483
Unit ID: 164614
Telephone: (617) 364-3510 Carnegie Class: Spec/Faith
FAX Number: (775) 245-1498 Calendar System: Semester
URL: www.boston.edu
Established: 1976 Annual Undergrad Tuition & Fees: $10,491
Enrollment: 124 Coed
Affiliation or Control: Baptist IRS Status: 501(c)3
Highest Offering: Baccalaureate
Program: Religious Emphasis
Accreditation: TRACS

00 Chancellor .... Dr. Harry R. BOYLE
01 President .... Rev. David V. MELTON
05 Vice President for Academics .... Rev. Kenneth D. GILLMING
32 Vice President for Student Affairs .... Mr. James THOMASSON
11 Vice President for Operations .... Mr. Randall WARD
84 Director of Enrollment Services .... Mrs. Grace N. SNAVELY
07 Director of Admissions .... Mrs. Karen FOX
08 Head Librarian .... Mr. Fred TATRO
31 Community Relations Officer .... Mr. Joseph SAWYER

Boston College (D)

140 Commonwealth Avenue, Chestnut Hill MA 02467-3934
County: Middlesex FICE Identification: 002128
Unit ID: 164924
Telephone: (617) 552-8000 Carnegie Class: RU/H
FAX Number: (617) 552-8828 Calendar System: Semester
URL: www.bc.edu
Established: 1863 Annual Undergrad Tuition & Fees: $42,204
Enrollment: 14,640 Coed
Affiliation or Control: Roman Catholic IRS Status: 501(c)3
Highest Offering: Doctorate
Program: Liberal Arts And General; Teacher Preparatory; Professional
Accreditation: EH, THEOL, ANEST, BUS, COPSY, LAW, NURSE, SW, TEAC

01 President .... Rev. William P. LEAHY, SJ
00 Chancellor .... Rev. J. Donald MONAN, SJ
05 Provost/Dean of Faculties .... Dr. Cutberto GARZA
03 Executive Vice President .... Dr. Patrick J. KEATING
26 Senior Vice President .... Dr. James P. MCINTYRE
30 Sr Vice Pres University Advancement .... Mr. James J. HUSSON
04 Executive Assistant to President .... Mr. Kevin J. SHEA
100 Chief of Staff Provost's Office .... Dr. Anita TIEN
10 Financial Vice President/Treasurer .... Mr. Peter C. MCKENZIE
101 Vice President/University Secretary .... Mrs. Mary Lou DELONG
32 Vice Pres Student Affairs .... Dr. Patrick H. ROMBALSKI
16 Vice President for Human Resources .... Mr. Leo V. SULLIVAN
44 Vice Pres for Development .... Mr. Thomas P. LOCKERBY
13 Vice Pres Information Technology .... Mr. Michael J. BOURQUE
88 Vice Pres Univ Mission & Ministry .... Rev. John T. BUTLER, SJ
86 Vice Pres Govt/Community Affairs .... Mr. Thomas J. KEADY
18 Vice Pres Facilities Management .... Mr. Daniel F. BOURQUE
04 Vice Pres/Special Asst to President .... Rev. William B. NEENAN, SJ
20 Vice Provost for Undergrad Affairs .... Dr. Donald L. HAFNER
58 Vice Provost Graduate Education .... Dr. Gilda MORELLI
46 Vice Provost for Research .... Dr. Kevin BEDELL
20 Vice Provost for Faculties .... Dr. Patricia DE LEEUW
14 Assoc VP Information Technology .... Mrs. Mary C. CORCORAN
44 Assoc Vice Pres Annual Giving .... Mr. Matthew EYNON
90 Exec Director Academic Technology .... Mrs. Rita OWENS
20 Assoc Vice Provost Undergrad Acad .... Dr. J. Joseph BURNS
09 AVP Inst Rsrch/Plng/Assess .... Dr. Kelli J. ARMSTRONG
18 Assoc VP Capital Projects .... Ms. Mary S. NARDONE
29 Associate VP for Alumni Relations .... Mr. John A. FEUDO
49 Dean College Arts & Sciences .... Dr. David QUIGLEY
87 Dean Col Adv Stds/Summer Session .... Rev. James A. WOODS, SJ
53 Dean School of Education .... Vacant
61 Dean Law School .... Mr. Vincent D. ROUGEAU
50 Dean School of Management .... Dr. Andrew C. BOYNTON
66 Dean of School of Nursing .... Dr. Susan GENNARO
70 Dean Grad School of Social Work .... Dr. Alberto A. GODENZI
84 Dean of Enrollment Management .... Mr. Robert S. LAY
35 Sr Assoc Dean Student Development .... Mr. Paul J. CHEBATOR
07 Director of Admission .... Mr. John L. MAHONEY, JR.
08 University Librarian Emeritus .... Dr. Thomas WALL
28 Exec Dir Institutional Diversity .... Mr. Richard P. JEFFERSON
06 Exec Director Student Services .... Dr. Louise M. LONABOCKER
26 Exec Dir/Special Asst to Pres/Mktg .... Mr. Ben BIRNBAUM
27 Dir Office of News & Public Affairs .... Mr. John B. DUNN
102 Director Corp & Foundation Rels .... Mrs. Ginger SAARIAHO
41 Director Athletic Department .... Mr. Eugene B. DEFILIPPO
36 Director of Career Center .... Ms. Theresa A. HARRIGAN
42 Director Campus Ministry .... Rev. Anthony PENNA
31 Director of Community Affairs .... Mr. William R. MILLS
38 Director Univ Counseling Services .... Dr. Thomas P. MCGUINNESS
37 Director Financial Aid .... Mrs. Mary S. MCGRANAHAN
23 Director Health Services .... Dr. Thomas I. NARY
39 Director of Residential Life .... Mr. George A. AREY
25 Director Sponsored Programs .... Mrs. Joanne SCIBILIA
19 Dir Public Safety/Chief of Police .... Mr. John M. KING
40 Director Bookstore .... Mr. Robert STEWART
43 General Counsel .... Mr. Joseph M. HERLIHY
24 Director Media Technology Services .... Mr. David CORKUM
85 Director International Programs .... Dr. Bernd WIDDIG
92 Director Honors Program A & S .... Dr. Mark F. O'CONNOR
93 Director AHANA Student Programs .... Dr. Ines MATURANA SENDOYA
86 Director Governmental Relations .... Ms. Jeanne LEVESQUE
94 Director of Women's Studies .... Dr. Sharlene HESSE-BIBER
96 Director Procurement Services .... Mr. Paul MCGOWAN
09 Director Institutional Research .... Dr. Jessica A. GREENE

The Boston Conservatory (E)

8 The Fenway, Boston MA 02215-4006
County: Suffolk FICE Identification: 002129
Unit ID: 164933
Telephone: (617) 536-6340 Carnegie Class: Spec/Arts
FAX Number: (617) 912-9101 Calendar System: Semester
URL: www.bostonconservatory.edu
Established: 1867 Annual Undergrad Tuition & Fees: $45,000
Enrollment: 725 Coed
Affiliation or Control: Independent Non-Profit IRS Status: 501(c)3
Highest Offering: Master's
Program: Teacher Preparatory; Professional; Music Emphasis
Accreditation: EH, MUS

01 President .... Mr. Richard ORTNER
05 VP for Academic Affairs .... Dr. Patricia HOY
10 VP for Finance and Planning .... Mr. Eric NORMAN
21 Chief Financial Officer .... Mr. Charles P. PETIT
32 Vice Pres Admin & Dean of Students .... Dr. Carmen S. GRIGGS
20 Associate Dean of the Conservatory .... Mr. James O'DELL
84 Director of Admissions .... Ms. Meghan CADWALLADER
30 Director of Development .... Ms. Eileen M. MENY
64 Director Music Division .... Dr. Karl PAULNACK
57 Director Dance Division .... Ms. Cathy YOUNG
57 Director Theater Division .... Mr. Neil DONOHOE
06 Registrar .... Mr. Gregory KARAS
37 Director Student Financial Aid .... Ms. Nicole BRENNAN
08 Director of the Library .... Ms. Jennifer HUNT
13 Director of Information Technology .... Mr. Bob XAVIER
18 Director Facilities & Plant .... Mr. Dan CORSETTI
39 Asst Dean Housing & Resident Life .... Ms. Kim RUSSELL
26 Director Marketing & Communications .... Ms. Karen FOGERTY
85 Director International Student Svcs .... Mr. Gordon HOMANN
15 Director Human Resources .... Mr. Rob ELKIN
29 Dir of Alumni and Parent Relations .... Ms. Tracy SMITH
35 Dir of Student & Community Programs .... Ms. Kim HAACK
38 Director of Counseling .... Ms. Melanie DUARTE

Boston Graduate School of Psychoanalysis (F)

1581 Beacon Street, Brookline MA 02446-4602
County: Norfolk FICE Identification: 031943
Unit ID: 164915
Telephone: (617) 277-3915 Carnegie Class: Spec/Health
FAX Number: (617) 277-0312 Calendar System: Semester
URL: www.bgsp.edu
Established: 1973 Annual Graduate Tuition & Fees: $13,920
Enrollment: 152 Coed
Affiliation or Control: Independent Non-Profit IRS Status: 501(c)3
Highest Offering: Doctorate; No Undergraduates
Program: Professional
Accreditation: EH

01 President .... Dr. Jane SYNDER
05 Vice President/Provost .... Dr. Jane SNYDER
10 Vice President Finance .... Dr. Carol PANETTA
58 Dean of Graduate Studies .... Dr. Lynn PERLMAN
07 Director of Admissions .... Dr. Mara WAGNER
26 Director of Marketing .... Ms. Paula BERMAN
06 Registrar .... Ms. Arianne PNIOWER
37 Director of Financial Aid .... Ms. Stephanie WOOLBERT
21 Controller .... Ms. Gayle DOLAN

Boston University (G)

One Silber Way, Boston MA 02215-1700
County: Suffolk FICE Identification: 002130
Unit ID: 164988
Telephone: (617) 353-2000 Carnegie Class: RU/VH
FAX Number: (617) 353-2053 Calendar System: Semester
URL: www.bu.edu
Established: 1839 Annual Undergrad Tuition & Fees: $41,420
Enrollment: 32,727 Coed
Affiliation or Control: Independent Non-Profit IRS Status: 501(c)3
Highest Offering: Doctorate
Program: Liberal Arts And General; Teacher Preparatory; Professional
Accreditation: EH, BUS, CEA, CLPSY, DENT, DIETD, DIETI, ENG, HSA, IPSY, LAW, MED, MUS, OT, PH, PTA, SP, SW, THEOL

01 President .... Robert A. BROWN
03 Executive Vice President .... Joseph P. MERCURIO
05 University Provost .... Jean MORRISON
17 Provost Medical Campus .... Karen H. ANTMAN
11 Vice Pres Administrative Services .... Peter FIEDLER
10 Vice Pres/CFO & Treasurer .... Martin J. HOWARD

Code	Title	Name
88	VP Global Ops/Dpty Gen Counsel	Willis G. WANG
30	Vice Pres Devel/Alumni Relations	Scott G. NICHOLS
21	Vice Pres Auxiliary Services	Peter CUSATO
84	VP Enrollment & Student Affairs	Laurie POHL
86	Vice Pres Government & Cmty Affairs	Edward M. KING
18	Vice President Operations	Gary W. NICKSA
43	VP/General Counsel & Board Secy	Todd L C. KLIPP
90	VP Information Systems & Technology	Tracy SCHROEDER
26	Vice President Marketing & Comm	Stephen P. BURGAY
88	Assoc VP BUMC Business Affairs	William GASPER
21	Exec Vice President Administration	Peter SMOKOWSKI
20	Associate Provost	Hannelore GLASER
88	Assoc Provost Global Health	Gerald T. KEUSCH
21	Sr Assoc Vice Pres Financial Affs	John IMBERGAMO
18	Sr Assoc VP Real Estate Management	Michael DONOVAN
29	Assoc VP Development & Alumni Rels	Steven A. HALL
18	Assoc VP Facilities Mgmt & Planning	Thomas DALEY
25	Assoc Provost Sponsored Programs	Joan KIRKENDALL
56	Assoc Provost Intl Education	Urbain DE WINTER
46	Assoc Provost & VP Research	Andrei E. RUCKENSTEIN
46	Associate Provost Research	Mark S. KLEMPNER
44	Assoc VP Development & Alumni Rels	Christopher J. MENARD
44	Assoc VP Sch-based Dev & Alum Rels	Adam K. WISE
45	Asst VP Budget/Institutional Rsrch	Joseph P. GROSSI
15	Asst Vice Pres Human Resources	Manuel P. MONTEIRO
32	Dean of Students	Kenneth ELMORE
42	Dean of Marsh Chapel	Robert A. HILL
55	Dean Metropolitan Col/Extended Educ	Jay HALFOND
73	Dean School of Theology	Mary E. MOORE
49	Dean Col/Grad Sch Arts & Sciences	Virginia SAPIRO
61	Dean of School of Law	Maureen A. O'ROURKE
63	Dean School of Medicine	Karen H. ANTMAN
52	Dean Sch of Dental Medicine	Jeffery W. HUTTER
54	Dean College of Engineering	Kenneth R. LUTCHEN
70	Dean School of Social Work	Gail STEKETEE
60	Dean College of Communication	Thomas FIEDLER
53	Dean School of Education	Hardin COLEMAN
57	Dean College of Fine Arts	Benjamin JUAREZ
76	Dean Health & Rehab Science	Gloria S. WATERS
50	Dean School Management	Louis LATAIF
97	Dean College General Studies	Linda S. WELLS
69	Dean School of Public Health	Robert F. MEENAN
88	Dean School of Hospitality Admin	Christopher MULLER
87	Assistant Dean Summer Term	Donna SHEA
88	Dir University Professors Program	Sir Hans KORNBERG
06	Registrar	Florence BERGERON
68	Director Physical Education	Warin DEXTER
41	Exec Dir Department of Athletics	Jack PARKER
08	Director Mugar Library	Robert HUDSON
37	Director Financial Assistance	Christine MCGUIRE
39	Director of Housing	Marc ROBILLARD
07	Exec Dir Undergraduate Admissions	Kelly WALTER
23	Director Student Health Services	David R. MCBRIDE
09	Exec Dir of Institutional Research	Melanie MADAIO-O'BRIEN
27	Director Campus Information	Amy HOOK
44	Director of Annual Giving	Lindsey MCCULLOUGH
85	Director Intl Student/Scholars Ofc	Jeanne KELLEY
19	Chief of Police	Thomas G. ROBBINS
36	Director Career Planning Services	Richard LEGER
35	Director of Student Activities	Melinda STROH
40	General Manager Bookstore	Stephen TURCO
96	Director Purchasing Services	Richard STACK
28	Director Thurman Center	Katherine KENNEDY
88	Director Judicial Affairs	Daryl DELUCA
39	Director Residence Life	David ZAMOJSKI
88	Director of Stewardship DAR	Maureen D. DONNELLY
38	Asst Dir Wellness & Residential Ed	Laura A. DEVEAU
100	Chief of Staff Office of the Pres	Elizabeth B. GREEN

Brandeis University (A)

415 South Street, Waltham MA 02454-9110
County: Middlesex
FICE Identification: 002133
Unit ID: 165015
Telephone: (781) 736-2000
Carnegie Class: RU/VH
FAX Number: (781) 736-8699
Calendar System: Semester
URL: www.brandeis.edu
Established: 1948
Annual Undergrad Tuition & Fees: $41,860
Enrollment: 5,642
Coed
Affiliation or Control: Independent Non-Profit
IRS Status: 501(c)3
Highest Offering: Doctorate
Program: Liberal Arts And General; Professional
Accreditation: EH, BUS

Code	Title	Name
00	Chairman of the Board	Mr. Malcolm SHERMAN
01	President	Mr. Frederick M. LAWRENCE
04	Executive Asst to the President	Ms. Celia D. HARRIS
05	Provost/Sr Vice Pres for Acad Affs	Dr. Steve GOLDSTEIN
20	Vice Provost for Academic Affairs	Dr. Michaele WHELAN
30	Sr Vice Pres Inst Advancement	Ms. Nancy K. WINSHIP
29	Vice President of Development	Mr. Myles E. WEISENBERG
102	Sr Director Corporate & Foundations	Mr. Robert SILK
84	Sr Vice Pres for Students/Enroll	Vacant
26	Sr VP Communication & External Affs	Mr. Andrew GULLY
43	Sr VP and General Counsel	Ms. Judith R. SIZER
100	Chief of Staff	Mr. David A. BUNIS
88	Chief Investment Officer	Mr. Nicholas WARREN
10	Sr VP for Finance and CFO	Ms. Frances DROLETTE
90	VP for IT/Vice Provost for Library	Mr. Perry HANSON
11	Senior VP for Administration	Mr. Mark COLLINS
18	Associate VP for Facilities	Mr. Peter C. SHIELDS
19	Director of Public Safety	Mr. Edward CALLAHAN
15	Vice Pres Human Resources	Mr. Scot R. BEMIS
18	VP for Planning & Inst Research	Mr. Dan FELDMAN
58	Exec Director Div Grad Prof Studies	Ms. Sybil SMITH
49	Dean of Arts & Sciences	Dr. Susan J. BIREN
58	Dean Grad School/Arts & Sciences	Dr. Malcolm W. WATSON
70	Dean Heller School Social Pol & Mgt	Dr. Lisa LYNCH
50	Dean International Business School	Dr. Bruce R. MAGID
32	Assoc VP & Dean of Student Life	Mr. Rick SAWYER
35	Associate Dean of Student Life	Mr. Jamele ADAMS
35	Associate Dean of Student Life	Ms. Maggie BALCH
41	Director of Athletics	Ms. Sheryl A. SOUSA
07	Director of Admissions	Mr. Mark SPENCER
37	Dean of Student Financial Svcs	Mr. Peter M. GIUMETTE
08	Chief University Librarian	Vacant
06	University Registrar	Dr. Mark S. HEWITT
88	Asst Provost for Research Admin	Mr. Paul O'KEEFE
36	Director Hiatt Career Center	Mr. Joseph DUPONT
38	Director Psych Counseling Center	Mr. Robert Y. BERLIN
96	Director of Procurement	Mr. Edward PERKINS
42	Coordinator Interfaith Chaplaincy	Fr. Walter CUENIN
104	Asst Dean/Director of Study Abroad	Mr. J. Scott VAN DER MEID

Cambridge College (B)

1000 Massachusetts Avenue, Cambridge MA 02138-5304
County: Middlesex
FICE Identification: 021829
Unit ID: 165167
Telephone: (617) 868-1000
Carnegie Class: Master's L
FAX Number: (617) 349-3545
Calendar System: Trimester
URL: www.cambridgecollege.edu
Established: 1971
Annual Undergrad Tuition & Fees: $13,140
Enrollment: 4,293
Coed
Affiliation or Control: Independent Non-Profit
IRS Status: 501(c)3
Highest Offering: Doctorate
Program: Liberal Arts And General; Professional
Accreditation: EH, @TEAC

Code	Title	Name
01	President	Deborah JACKSON
03	Executive Vice President	Dr. Joseph DAISY
05	Provost/VP Academic Affairs	Dr. Joe LEE
10	VP for Finance and Administration	Kim GAZZOLA
43	General Counsel	R. Yvette CLARK
30	Vice President Instnl Advancement	Patricia DENN
16	Director of Human Resources	Vacant
37	Director of Financial Aid	Frank LAUDER
21	Controller	Lynn WOOD
06	Registrar	Mark SLAWSON
84	Dean of Enrollment Management	Elaine LAPOMARDO
90	Director of Information Technology	Richard PAPAZIAN
18	Director of Business Operations	Michael PIERCE
12	Director Chesapeake VA Reg Ctr	Dr. Ella BENSON
12	Director of Merrimack Valley Center	Linda RICHELSON
12	Director Springfield Center	Teresa (Terrie) FORTE
12	Director Inland Empire Center	Dr. Ellie KAUCHER
12	Interim Director Puerto Rico Center	Sandra GARCIA-SANCHEZ
12	Director Memphis Regional Center	Lee JONES
12	Director Augusta Regional Center	Sharlotte EVANS
56	Exec Dir Regional Centers/NITE	Dr. Kristin POPPO

Clark University (C)

950 Main Street, Worcester MA 01610-1477
County: Worcester
FICE Identification: 002139
Unit ID: 165334
Telephone: (508) 793-7711
Carnegie Class: RU/H
FAX Number: (508) 793-7780
Calendar System: Semester
URL: www.clarku.edu
Established: 1887
Annual Undergrad Tuition & Fees: $37,350
Enrollment: 3,451
Coed
Affiliation or Control: Independent Non-Profit
IRS Status: 501(c)3
Highest Offering: Doctorate
Program: Liberal Arts And General; Teacher Preparatory; Professional
Accreditation: EH, BUS, CLPSY

Code	Title	Name
01	President	Dr. David P. ANGEL
05	Provost & Vice Pres Academic Affs	Dr. Davis BAIRD
03	Executive Vice President	Mr. James E. COLLINS
30	Vice Pres University Advancement	Mr. C. Andrew MCGADNEY
26	Vice Pres Marketing & Communication	Ms. Paula DAVID
10	Vice President Budget & Planning	Ms. Andrea P. MICHAELS
13	Vice Pres for Information Tech/CIO	Ms. Pennie TURGEON
86	VP Government/Cmty Affs/Campus Svcs	Mr. John FOLEY
32	VP Student Affairs/Dean of Students	Ms. Denise M. DARRIGRAND
46	Assoc Provost/Dean of Research	Dr. Nancy BUDWIG
58	Assoc Provost/Dean Graduate Studies	Dr. Priscilla ELSASS
49	Assoc Provost/Dean of College	Dr. Walter WRIGHT
35	Associate Dean of Students	Mr. Jason ZELESKY
38	Associate Dean Academic Advising	Dr. Kevin M. MCKENNA
50	Int Dean Graduate School Mgmt	Dr. Joseph SARKIS
51	Dean Col Profess & Cont Education	Dr. Thomas P. MASSEY
07	Dean of Admissions & Financial Aid	Mr. Donald HONEMAN
37	Director of Financial Aid	Ms. Mary Ellen SEVERANCE
08	University Librarian	Dr. Gwendolynne ARTHUR
21	Controller	Ms. Katherine CANNON
36	Director of Career Services	Mr. David MCDONOUGH
29	Director of Alumni Affairs	Ms. Aixa L. KIDD
06	Registrar	Ms. Rebecca HUNTER
15	Dir of Human Resources/Affirm Act	Ms. Lynn F. OLSON
18	Director of Physical Plant	Mr. Michael DAWLEY
41	Director of Athletics	Mr. Sean SULLIVAN
19	Chief of Campus Police	Mr. Stephen P. GOULET
23	Director of Health Service	Ms. Robin MCNALLY
04	Assistant to the President	Ms. Joanne MILLER
21	Business Manager	Mr. Paul WYKES

College of the Holy Cross (D)

1 College Street, Worcester MA 01610-2322
County: Worcester
FICE Identification: 002141
Unit ID: 166124
Telephone: (508) 793-2011
Carnegie Class: Bac/A&S
FAX Number: (508) 793-3030
Calendar System: Semester
URL: www.holycross.edu
Established: 1843
Annual Undergrad Tuition & Fees: $41,488
Enrollment: 2,862
Coed
Affiliation or Control: Roman Catholic
IRS Status: 501(c)3
Highest Offering: Baccalaureate
Program: Liberal Arts And General
Accreditation: EH, THEA

Code	Title	Name
01	President	Rev. Michael C. MCFARLAND, SJ
03	Senior Vice President	Dr. Frank VELLACCIO
10	Treasurer/VP Admin & Finance	Mr. Michael LOCHHEAD
10	Chief Investment Officer	Mr. Timothy JARRY
88	Dir of Finance/Asst Treasurer	Ms. Dottie HAUVER
32	VP Student Affairs/Dean of Students	Ms. Jacqueline D. PETERSON
30	Vice President Development	Vacant
05	VP Academic Affairs/Dean of College	Dr. Timothy R. AUSTIN
20	Associate Dean of the College	Ms. Margaret FREIJE
20	Associate Dean of the College	Dr. Amy WOLFSON
06	Registrar	Vacant
07	Director of Admissions	Ms. Ann B. MCDERMOTT
08	Director of Library Services	Ms. Karen CARNEY
37	Director of Financial Aid	Ms. Lynne M. MYERS
25	Director Grants/Found & Corp Giving	Dr. Charles S. WEISS
42	Director Ofc of College Chaplains	Ms. Marybeth KEARNS-BARRETT
71	Director Ctr Interdisc/Spec Studies	Dr. Richard E. MATLAK
36	Director of Career Planning	Ms. Amy MURPHY
13	Director Information Tech Services	Ms. Ellen J. KEOHANE
26	Director of Public Affairs	Ms. Ellen RYDER
29	Director of Alumni Relations	Ms. Kristyn M. DYER
19	Director of Public Safety	Mr. Robert HART
35	Director of Campus Center	Mr. Jeremiah O'CONNOR
16	Human Resources Director	Ms. Donna C. WRENN
18	Director of Physical Plant	Mr. Scott M. MERRILL
41	Director of Athletics	Mr. Richard M. REGAN
21	Controller	Mr. Charles F. ESTAPHAN
45	Director of Planning	Ms. Judy A. HANNUM
38	Director Counseling Center	Dr. Paul GALVINHILL
23	Director Student Health Services	Ms. Martha SULLIVAN
11	Director Administrative Services	Mr. William J. CONLEY
96	Manager of Purchasing	Ms. Joan E. ANDERSON
09	Ofc of Assessment/Research	Ms. Denise BELL
86	Dir of Government/Cmty Relations	Mr. Edward AUGUSTUS

College of Our Lady of the Elms (E)

291 Springfield Street, Chicopee MA 01013-2839
County: Hampden
FICE Identification: 002140
Unit ID: 167394
Telephone: (413) 594-2761
Carnegie Class: Bac/Diverse
FAX Number: (413) 592-4871
Calendar System: Semester
URL: www.elms.edu
Established: 1928
Annual Undergrad Tuition & Fees: $27,157
Enrollment: 1,259
Coed
Affiliation or Control: Roman Catholic
IRS Status: 501(c)3
Highest Offering: Master's
Program: Liberal Arts And General; Teacher Preparatory; Professional
Accreditation: EH, IACBE, NURSE, SW

Code	Title	Name
01	President	Dr. Mary REAP
05	Vice President of Academic Affairs	Dr. Walter C. BREAU
10	Vice Pres Finance/Administration	Mr. Brian E. DOHERTY
32	Vice Pres of Student Affairs	Mr. John KELLER
30	Vice Pres of Instl Advancement	Mr. Kevin M. EDWARDS
35	Associate Dean of Students	Ms. Teresa WINTERS-DUNN
20	Assoc Acad Dean Grad Studies/CE	Dr. Elizabeth HUKOWICZ
44	Senior Director of Development	Ms. Deborah K. BAKER
07	Director of Admissions	Mr. Joseph WAGNER
42	Director of Campus Ministry	Sr. Carol ALLAN
06	Registrar	Ms. Frances BLISS
08	Director of Library	Ms. Patricia BOMBARDIER
18	Director Operations & Campus Svcs	Mr. Stephen SCHWARTZ
19	Director of Public Safety	Mr. Michael SULLIVAN
26	Director of Institutional Marketing	Mr. John M. GUIMOND
37	Director of Financial Aid	Mr. Troy DAVIS
36	Director of Career Services	Ms. Karen ANTI
14	Director Information Technology	Mr. Tom MANLEY
38	Director Student Counseling Svcs	Mr. John COAN
41	Director of Athletics	Ms. Louise MCCLEARY
15	Director Human Resources/Personnel	Ms. Marie PHILLIPS
35	Director of Student Activities	Mr. Joseph TOLSON
85	Dir of ESL/International Program	Ms. Joyce HAMPTON

Conway School of Landscape Design (F)

332 S Deerfield Road, PO Box 179,
Conway MA 01341-0179
County: Franklin
FICE Identification: 022743
Unit ID: 165495
Telephone: (413) 369-4044
Carnegie Class: Spec/Arts
FAX Number: (413) 369-4032
Calendar System: Trimester

URL: www.csld.edu
Established: 1972 Annual Graduate Tuition & Fees: $31,450
Enrollment: 18 Coed
Affiliation or Control: Independent Non-Profit IRS Status: 501(c)3
Highest Offering: Master's; No Undergraduates
Program: Professional
Accreditation: EH

01 President/Director ....Mr. Paul C. HELLMUND
32 Assoc Dir Student Svcs/Fin/Fac ....Mr. David NORDSTROM
07 Assoc Dir Admissions/Comm ....Ms. Mollie BABIZE
30 Director of Development ....Ms. Lynn BARCLAY

Curry College (A)

1071 Blue Hill Avenue, Milton MA 02186-2395
County: Norfolk FICE Identification: 002143
Unit ID: 165529
Telephone: (617) 333-0500 Carnegie Class: Master's M
FAX Number: (617) 979-3540 Calendar System: Semester
URL: www.curry.edu
Established: 1879 Annual Undergrad Tuition & Fees: $32,210
Enrollment: 2,887 Coed
Affiliation or Control: Independent Non-Profit IRS Status: 501(c)3
Highest Offering: Master's
Program: Liberal Arts And General; Professional
Accreditation: EH, NURSE

01 President ....Mr. Kenneth K. QUIGLEY, JR.
05 Chief Academic Officer ....Dr. David POTASH
30 Vice Pres Institutional Advancement ....Mr. Christopher LAWSON
10 Chief Financial Officer ....Mr. Richard F. SULLIVAN, JR.
07 Dean of Admission ....Ms. Jane P. FIDLER
32 Dean of Student Affairs ....Ms. Maryellen M. KILEY
45 Dean for Institutional Planning ....Dr. Susan W. PENNINI
04 Assistant to the President ....Ms. Amy M. BIANCHI
08 Interim Librarian ....Mr. David P. MILLER
14 Chief Information Officer ....Mr. Dennis THIBEAULT
15 Director of Human Resources ....Ms. Mary E. DUNN
20 Associate Dean Academic Affairs ....Dr. Lisa IJIRI
84 Asst Dean Enrollment Mgt/Registrar ....Ms. Sally A. BUCKLEY
18 Chief Facilities/Physical Plant ....Mr. Robert G. O'CONNELL
26 Chief Public Relations Officer ....Ms. Frances L. JACKSON
29 Director of Alumni Relations ....Vacant
36 Director of Student Placement ....Ms. Maureen A. ASHBURN
37 Dir of Student Financial Services ....Ms. Stephanny J. ELIAS
38 Director of Student Counseling ....Dr. Alison W. MARKSON
51 Dean of Continuing Ed/Graduate Stds ....Dr. Ruth D. SHERMAN

Dean College (B)

99 Main Street, Franklin MA 02038-1994
County: Norfolk FICE Identification: 002144
Unit ID: 165574
Telephone: (508) 541-1508 Carnegie Class: Assoc/PrivNFP4
FAX Number: (508) 541-8726 Calendar System: Semester
URL: www.dean.edu
Established: 1865 Annual Undergrad Tuition & Fees: $30,570
Enrollment: 1,266 Coed
Affiliation or Control: Independent Non-Profit IRS Status: 501(c)3
Highest Offering: Baccalaureate
Program: 2-Year Principally Bachelor's Creditable; Liberal Arts And General
Accreditation: EH

01 President ....Dr. Paula M. ROONEY
04 Assistant to the President ....Ms. Sandra CAIN
05 Vice President Academic Affairs ....Dr. Linda RAGOSTA
84 VP Enrollment Services/Marketing ....Mr. John MARCUS
10 Vice Pres Financial Svcs/Treasurer ....Mr. Dan MODELANE
32 VP Student Development & Retention ....Ms. Cindy T. KOZIL
16 Vice President Human Resources ....Mr. Peter MARTEL
30 Vice Pres Institutional Advancement ....Ms. Coleen RESNICK
44 Asst Vice Pres Leadership Gifts ....Ms. Renee VACHON DANHO
07 Asst VP Enrollment/Dean Admission ....Mr. James FOWLER
20 Dean Academic Support Services ....Ms. Wendy ADLER
35 Dean of Students ....Mr. David DRUCKER
20 Dean for Curriculum & Assessment ....Ms. Melissa P. READ
51 Assoc Dean Professional/Cont Stds ....Ms. Ida M. LAMOTHE
27 Chief Information Officer ....Mr. Darrell KULESZA
11 Dir College Operations/Facilities ....Mr. Brian KELLY
26 Director Public Rels/Communications ....Mr. Gregg CHALK
06 Registrar ....Ms. Nancy SULLIVAN
19 Director of Public Safety ....Mr. Kenneth F. CORKRAN
08 Director of the Library ....Mr. Ted BURKE
29 Director Alumni Relations ....Ms. Maureen RIDINGS
41 Athletic Director ....Mr. John A. JACKSON
39 Director Residence Life ....Ms. Shannon OVERCASH
35 Dir Orientation/Student Activities ....Ms. Jennifer BOTHWELL
40 Director of Bookstore ....Ms. Kathleen EKBOLM
37 Director of Financial Aid ....Ms. Jenny AGUIAR
21 Controller/Assistant Treasurer ....Ms. Kathleen MCGUIRE
84 Director Enrollment Operations ....Ms. Kathleen RYAN

Eastern Nazarene College (C)

23 E Elm Avenue, Quincy MA 02170-2999
County: Norfolk FICE Identification: 002145
Unit ID: 165644
Telephone: (617) 745-3000 Carnegie Class: Bac/A&S
FAX Number: (617) 745-3907 Calendar System: 4/1/4
URL: www.enc.edu
Established: 1918 Annual Undergrad Tuition & Fees: $24,361
Enrollment: 1,016 Coed
Affiliation or Control: Church Of The Nazarene IRS Status: 501(c)3
Highest Offering: Master's
Program: Liberal Arts And General; Teacher Preparatory
Accreditation: EH, SW

01 President ....Dr. Corlis A. MCGEE
05 Provost & Dean of the College ....Dr. Timothy T. WOOSTER
10 Vice President Financial Affairs ....Mr. Jan G. WEISEN
32 Vice Pres Student Devel & Retention ....Dr. Vernon L. WESLEY
07 VP of Admissions/Financial Aid ....Dr. Timothy T. WOOSTER
26 Vice President Inst Advancement ....Dr. Scott TURCOTT
32 Assoc Dean Students/Residence Life ....Vacant
06 Registrar ....Mrs. Margaret BALLARD
37 Director Student Financial Aid ....Mr. Lerick FANFANX
08 Director of Library Services ....Ms. Susan J. WATKINS
19 Director Safety/Security/Risk Mgmt ....Mr. Jan G. WEISEN
38 Dir Counseling & Career Services ....Mr. Bradford E. THORNE
58 Dean of Div of Graduate/Prof Stds ....Vacant
41 Athletic Director ....Dr. Nancy DETWILER
18 Director of Facilities Management ....Mr. Jim HARDING
45 Director of Instructional Resources ....Ms. Patricia VASQUEZ
21 Controller ....Mrs. Myrna GIBERTSON
42 Chaplain/VP Spiritual Development ....Dr. Corey MACPHERSON
22 Dir Affirm Action/Dir Human Res ....Mrs. Fran WRIGHT
40 Director Bookstore ....Vacant
13 Director of Information Technology ....Mr. Charles BURT
51 Director Adult Education ....Dr. William DRISCOLL
04 Admin Assistant to the President ....Mrs. Sheryl WEISEN
28 Director of Multicultural Affairs ....Mr. Robert BENJAMIN

Emerson College (D)

120 Boylston Street, Boston MA 02116-4624
County: Suffolk FICE Identification: 002146
Unit ID: 165662
Telephone: (617) 824-8500 Carnegie Class: Master's L
FAX Number: (617) 824-8511 Calendar System: Semester
URL: www.emerson.edu
Established: 1880 Annual Undergrad Tuition & Fees: $32,728
Enrollment: 4,566 Coed
Affiliation or Control: Independent Non-Profit IRS Status: 501(c)3
Highest Offering: Doctorate
Program: Liberal Arts And General; Professional
Accreditation: EH, SP

01 President ....Dr. Jacqueline W. LIEBERGOTT
43 Vice President & General Counsel ....Ms. Christine HUGHES
11 Vice President for Admin & Finance ....Ms. Maureen MURPHY
05 Vice President for Academic Affairs ....Dr. Linda MOORE
13 VP for Information Technology ....Dr. William GILLIGAN
26 Vice Pres Communications/Marketing ....Mr. Andrew TIEDEMANN
04 Special Asst to the President ....Mr. David ROSEN
10 AVP for Finance/Int Chf Fin Ofcr ....Mr. John DONOHOE
15 Assoc Vice Pres for Human Resources ....Ms. Alexa JACKSON
29 AVP Inst Advance/Dir Alumni Affrs ....Ms. Barbara RUTBERG
22 Assoc VP Diversity & Inclusion ....Ms. Gwendolyn BATES
86 Assoc Vice Pres Govt/Community Rels ....Ms. Margaret Ann INGS
32 Dean of Students ....Dr. Ronald LUDMAN
107 Exec Director Professional Studies ....Mr. Henry W. ZAPPALA
08 Exec Director of Library Services ....Mr. Robert FLEMING
58 Director of Graduate Studies ....Dr. Donna J. SCHROTH
07 Director of Graduate Admission ....Ms. Kristin BURKE
36 Director of Career Services ....Ms. Sheri A. ZICCARDI
38 Director Counseling Center ....Dr. Cheryl ROSENTHAL
19 Deputy Director of Public Safety ....Mr. Scott BORNSTEIN
41 Director of Athletics/Head Coach ....Mr. Henry SMITH
85 Director International Student Affs ....Ms. Virga MOHSINI
96 Director Purchasing/Risk Management ....Ms. Margaret ROGAN
28 Exec Director Center for Diversity ....Dr. William H. SMITH
39 Assoc Dean Housing/Residence Life ....Mr. David W. HADEN
21 Controller ....Ms. Kristin BURNS
06 Registrar ....Mr. William DEWOLF
42 Chair Center for Spiritual Life ....Mr. Albert S. AXELRAD
101 Exec Asst to the Board of Trustees ....Ms. Anne SHAUGHNESSY
18 Director of Facilities ....Mr. Neal A. LESPASIO, JR.
37 Director Financial Services ....Ms. Michelle B. SMITH
07 Director of Admissions ....Ms. Sara RAMIREZ
09 Director of Institutional Research ....Mr. Eric SYKES

Emmanuel College (E)

400 The Fenway, Boston MA 02115-5798
County: Suffolk FICE Identification: 002147
Unit ID: 165671
Telephone: (617) 277-9340 Carnegie Class: Master's S
FAX Number: (617) 735-9877 Calendar System: Semester
URL: www.emmanuel.edu
Established: 1919 Annual Undergrad Tuition & Fees: $32,100
Enrollment: 2,810 Coed
Affiliation or Control: Roman Catholic IRS Status: 501(c)3
Highest Offering: Master's
Program: Liberal Arts And General; Teacher Preparatory; Professional
Accreditation: EH, NURSE

01 President ....Sr. Janet EISNER, SND
03 Exec Asst to the President ....Ms. Michelle H. ERICKSON
04 Senior Assistant to President ....Ms. Kathleen PHALEN
05 Vice President Academic Affairs ....Dr. Joyce DE LEO
10 Exec Vice Pres & Chief Oper Ofcr ....Mr. Neil G. BUCKLEY
26 Vice President Govt/Cmty Relations ....Ms. Sarah WELSH
32 Vice President of Student Affairs ....Dr. Patricia RISSMEYER
37 Assoc VP Student Financial Services ....Ms. Jennifer C. PORTER
26 Assoc Vice President of Mktg/Comm ....Ms. Molly HONAN
07 Dean of Enrollment ....Ms. Sandra ROBBINS
35 Dean of Students ....Dr. Joseph ONOFRIETTI
49 Dean of Arts & Sciences ....Dr. William LEONARD
06 Associate Dean & Registrar ....Ms. Elizabeth ROSS
38 Director of Academic Advising ....Sr. Susan THORNELL
08 Director of Library ....Ms. Susan VON DAUM THOLL
15 Director Human Resources ....Ms. Erin FARMER NOONAN
41 Director of Athletics ....Ms. Pamela ROECKER
42 Director of Campus Ministry ....Fr. John SPENCER
24 Director Academic Program Support ....Ms. Cindy O'CALLAGHAN
38 Director Counseling Services ....Dr. Linda JURGELA
90 Assoc Director Academic Resource ....Ms. Virginia MULLIN
89 Asst Dean & Dir Student Ctr Svcs ....Ms. Mary Beth THOMAS

Endicott College (F)

376 Hale Street, Beverly MA 01915-2098
County: Essex FICE Identification: 002148
Unit ID: 165699
Telephone: (978) 927-0585 Carnegie Class: Master's M
FAX Number: (978) 927-0084 Calendar System: 4/1/4
URL: www.endicott.edu
Established: 1939 Annual Undergrad Tuition & Fees: $26,730
Enrollment: 2,096 Coed
Affiliation or Control: Independent Non-Profit IRS Status: 501(c)3
Highest Offering: Master's
Program: Liberal Arts And General; Professional
Accreditation: EH, CIDA, NUR

01 President ....Dr. Richard E. WYLIE
05 Vice President & Academic Dean ....Dr. Laura ROSSI-LE
03 Executive VP/Vice President Finance ....Ms. Lynne B. O'TOOLE
84 Vice Pres Admissions/Financial Aid ....Mr. Thomas J. REDMAN
58 VP/Dean Graduate & Prof Stds ....Dr. Mary HUEGEL
32 Vice President Student Affairs ....Ms. Beverly DOLINSKY
30 Vice Pres Institutional Advancement ....Mr. David VIGNERON
11 Vice Pres Special Proj/Omudsperson ....Ms. Denise BILODEAU
04 Assistant to the President ....Ms. Joanne L. WALDNER
90 Assoc Dean of Academic Computing ....Mr. Kent BARCLAY
07 Associate Dean of Admission ....Mr. George M. SHERMAN
45 Executive Director of Research ....Mr. Peter L. HART
15 Director Human Resources ....Ms. Sally ARNOLD
21 Treasurer ....Ms. Donna L. COUTURE
06 Registrar ....Ms. Anita L. MCFARLANE
08 Library Director ....Mr. Brian COURTEMANCHE
29 Director Alumni Relations ....Ms. Erin NEUHARDT
37 Director Financial Aid ....Ms. Marcia D. TOOMEY
41 Athletic Director ....Mr. Brian WYLIE
91 Chief Information Systems Officer ....Mr. Gary F. KELLEY
19 Director Campus Safety ....Mr. Gary DERICKSON
38 Senior Counselor ....Mr. Scott RUSSELL
39 Director of Residence Life ....Ms. Erica HEDRICK
18 Director of Physical Plant ....Mr. Dennis MONACO
26 Director Communications ....Ms. Carol RAICHE
36 Director of Career Services ....Ms. Dale MCLENNAN
09 Assoc Dir of Institutional Research ....Mr. Donald FEMINO
96 Purchasing Agent ....Mr. Terry SCHWENK
85 Dean of Undergrad International Ed ....Dr. April BURRISS
20 Dean of Academic Resources ....Dr. Kathleen BARNES
49 Dean of Arts & Sciences ....Vacant
53 Dean of Education ....Dr. Sara QUAY
57 Dean of Art & Design ....Mr. Mark TOWNER
59 Dean of Hospitality Management ....Dr. William H. SAMENFINK
68 Dean of Sports Science ....Dr. Deborah SWANTON
76 Dean of Health Sciences ....Dr. Kelly FISHER
50 Dean of Business & Technology ....Ms. Amy ROSS
60 Dean of Communication ....Dr. Laurel HELLERSTEIN

Episcopal Divinity School (G)

99 Brattle Street, Cambridge MA 02138-3494
County: Middlesex FICE Identification: 002149
Unit ID: 165705
Telephone: (617) 868-3450 Carnegie Class: Spec/Faith
FAX Number: (617) 864-5385 Calendar System: Semester
URL: www.eds.edu
Established: 1857 Annual Graduate Tuition & Fees: $13,781
Enrollment: 93 Coed
Affiliation or Control: Protestant Episcopal IRS Status: 501(c)3
Highest Offering: Doctorate; No Undergraduates
Program: Professional; Religious Emphasis
Accreditation: THEOL

01 President and Dean ....Rev Dr. Katherine H. RAGSDALE
05 Academic Dean ....Dr. Angela BAUER-LEVESQUE
100 Dean of Student & Dep for Admin ....Rev. Miriam GELFER
30 Director of Institutional Advancmnt ....Vacant
08 Director of the Library ....Ms. Pat PAYNE
27 Director of Communications & Mktg ....Vacant
10 Chief Financial and Planning Office ....Mr. William JUDGE
21 Comptroller ....Ms. Joanne MANNING
07 Director Admission/Enrollment Mgmt ....Mr. Christopher J. MEDEIROS
06 Registrar/Manager Academic Affairs ....Ms. Cecelia CULL
88 Director Congregational Studies ....Vacant
88 Director Field Education ....Dr. William KONDRATH
18 Superintendent Buildings & Grounds ....Mr. Frank DASILVA
04 Exec Assistant to President & Dean ....Ms. Jane WAGNER
37 Director Student Financial Aid ....Ms. Valeria PATERSON
15 Director of Human Resources ....Ms. Samaria WILSON-STALLINGS

FINE Mortuary College (A)

150 Kerry Place, Norwood MA 02062
County: Norfolk FICE Identification: 033164
Unit ID: 436599
Telephone: (781) 762-1211 Carnegie Class: Assoc/PrivFP
FAX Number: (781) 762-7177 Calendar System: Quarter
URL: www.fine-ne.com
Established: 1996 Annual Undergrad Tuition & Fees: $18,495
Enrollment: 64 Coed
Affiliation or Control: Proprietary IRS Status: Proprietary
Highest Offering: Associate Degree
Program: Occupational; Business Emphasis
Accreditation: FUSER

01	President	Dr. Louis MISANTONE
03	Executive Vice President	Dr. Jocelyn PRENDERGAST
37	Director Financial Aid	Ms. Brenda SWANSON

Fisher College (B)

118 Beacon Street, Boston MA 02116-1500
County: Suffolk FICE Identification: 002150
Unit ID: 165802
Telephone: (617) 236-8800 Carnegie Class: Bac/Assoc
FAX Number: (617) 236-8858 Calendar System: Semester
URL: www.fisher.edu
Established: 1903 Annual Undergrad Tuition & Fees: $24,783
Enrollment: 1,402 Coed
Affiliation or Control: Independent Non-Profit IRS Status: 501(c)3
Highest Offering: Baccalaureate
Program: Occupational; 2-Year Principally Bachelor's Creditable; Liberal Arts And General; Business Emphasis
Accreditation: EH

01	President	Dr. Thomas MCGOVERN
05	Chief Academic Officer	Ms. Janet KUSER
10	VP for Finance	Mr. Steven RICH
11	VP for Administration	Ms. Rhonda PIERONI
30	VP for Institutional Advancement	Mr. Richard LEVITT
51	VP for Development and Outreach	Ms. Janet HARRINGTON
07	Dean of Admissions	Mr. Robert MELARAGNI
32	Dean of Students	Ms. Shiela LALLY
104	Dean Intl Acad Oper/Curriculum Dev	Ms. Nancy PITHIS
49	Chairman Div of Arts & Sciences	Dr. Dean WALTON
50	Chairwoman Div of Management	Ms. Janet KUSER
06	College Registrar	Ms. Rosa CADENA
41	Director of Athletics	Mr. Scott DULIN
21	Director of Accounting	Mr. Jeffrey CONRAD
13	Director of Information Services	Mr. Jonathan BARTSCH
18	Director of Facilities	Mr. Paul MCBRINE
37	Director of Financial Aid	Ms. Anne SYLVAIN
23	Director of Nursing Services	Ms. Linda OATES
100	Chief of Staff	Ms. Melinda COOK
89	Dir of Acad Center for Enrichment	Mrs. Jennifer MANDOLESE
35	Director of Student Activities	Ms. Margarita ASCENCIO
42	Director of Spiritual Life	Dr. Ann CLARKE
19	Chief of Campus Police	Mr. Timothy CALLAHAN
26	Dir Communications/Special Projects	Ms. Jennie MOORE
36	Director of Career Services	Ms. Heather CARPENTER
88	Director of Accessibility Service	Ms. Michele ALMEIDA
15	Director of Human Resources	Mr. Gary PARNHAM
21	College Bursar	Ms. Joy NELSON
08	College Librarian	Mr. Joshua MCKAIN
29	Director Alumni Relations	Ms. Kristen SHERMAN
51	Dir Continuing Education Operations	Mr. Neil TROTTA

Franklin W. Olin College of Engineering (C)

Olin Way, Needham MA 02492-1200
County: Norfolk FICE Identification: 039463
Unit ID: 441982
Telephone: (781) 292-2300 Carnegie Class: Spec/Engg
FAX Number: (781) 292-2210 Calendar System: Semester
URL: www.olin.edu
Established: 2002 Annual Undergrad Tuition & Fees: $39,000
Enrollment: 348 Coed
Affiliation or Control: Independent Non-Profit IRS Status: 501(c)3
Highest Offering: Baccalaureate
Program: Professional
Accreditation: EH, ENG

01	President	Dr. Richard K. MILLER
10	Executive Vice President/Treasurer	Mr. Stephen P. HANNABURY
26	VP External Rels/Dean of Admission	Dr. Charles S. NOLAN
05	Provost/Dean of Faculty	Dr. Vincent P. MANNO
13	VP IT Operations/Chief Info Officer	Ms. Joanne KOSSUTH
32	Dean of Student Life	Dr. Roger C. CRAFTS, JR.
27	AVP Ext Relations/Dir Communication	Mr. Joseph A. HUNTER
29	Director Family & Alumni Relations	Ms. Kristina RAPOSA
30	Director of Development	Ms. Synthia WAYNE

† All admitted students who enroll at Olin College receive an Olin Scholarship covering half tuition during the eight semesters of the baccalaureate program.

Gibbs College of Boston, Inc. (D)

126 Newbury Street, Boston MA 02116-2904
County: Suffolk FICE Identification: 007481
Unit ID: 166276
Telephone: (617) 578-7100 Carnegie Class: Assoc/PrivFP
FAX Number: (617) 262-6210 Calendar System: Other
URL: www.gibbsboston.edu
Established: 1917 Annual Undergrad Tuition & Fees: $23,500
Enrollment: 215 Coed
Affiliation or Control: Proprietary IRS Status: Proprietary
Highest Offering: Associate Degree
Program: Occupational; 2-Year Principally Bachelor's Creditable; Business Emphasis
Accreditation: ACICS, MAAB

01	President	Dr. Richard FARMER
05	Academic Dean	Ms. Debra HESSELL
08	Librarian	Mr. William GREALISH
07	Director of Admissions	Ms. Jaimee TYLER
37	Director of Financial Aid	Mr. Jay BEIRNE
06	Registrar	Ms. Elisa ADAMS
36	Associate Director Career Services	Ms. Laura MEYER

Gordon College (E)

255 Grapevine Road, Wenham MA 01984-1899
County: Essex FICE Identification: 002153
Unit ID: 165936
Telephone: (978) 927-2300 Carnegie Class: Bac/A&S
FAX Number: (978) 867-4659 Calendar System: Semester
URL: www.gordon.edu
Established: 1889 Annual Undergrad Tuition & Fees: $30,606
Enrollment: 1,476 Coed
Affiliation or Control: Independent Non-Profit IRS Status: 501(c)3
Highest Offering: Master's
Program: Liberal Arts And General
Accreditation: EH, MUS, SW

01	President	Dr. D. Michael LINDSAY
05	Provost	Dr. Mark L. SARGENT
10	Vice President for Finance/CFO	Mr. Michael J. AHEARN
27	EVP Advancement/Communications/Tech	Mr. Daniel TYMANN
84	Vice President Enrollment	Ms. June BODONI
32	Vice President/Dean of Students	Mr. Barry J. LOY
20	Academic Dean	Dr. Daniel RUSS
45	Dean College Planning/Legal Counsel	Dr. Stephen C. MACLEOD
42	Dean of the Chapel	Dr. Gregory W. CARMER
08	Director Library	Mr. Myron SCHIRER-SUTER
06	Registrar	Ms. Carol A. HERRICK
13	Dir of Ctr for Education Technology	Mr. Christopher JONES
37	Dir of Student Financial Services	Mr. Daniel O'CONNELL
15	Director Human Resources	Ms. Nancy ANDERSON
18	Chief Facilities/Physical Plant	Mr. Paul HELGESEN
21	Controller	Ms. Kim MATHER
26	Assoc Dir of College Communications	Ms. Cyndi MCMAHON
29	Director Alumni & Parent Relations	Ms. Adrienne COOK
36	Director Student Placement	Ms. Pam LAZARAKIS
96	Director of Purchasing	Mr. Ken EBERSOLE

Gordon-Conwell Theological Seminary (F)

130 Essex Street, South Hamilton MA 01982-2317
County: Essex FICE Identification: 009747
Unit ID: 165945
Telephone: (978) 468-7111 Carnegie Class: Spec/Faith
FAX Number: (978) 468-6691 Calendar System: Semester
URL: www.gordonconwell.edu
Established: 1884 Annual Graduate Tuition & Fees: $16,530
Enrollment: 1,895 Coed
Affiliation or Control: Independent Non-Profit IRS Status: 501(c)3
Highest Offering: Doctorate; No Undergraduates
Program: Professional
Accreditation: EH, THEOL

01	President	Dr. Dennis HOLLINGER
10	Executive Vice President & CFO	Mr. Robert S. LANDREBE
30	Vice President of Advancement	Mr. Kurt W. DRESCHER
05	Provost	Mr. Frank A. JAMES, III
12	Academic Dean - Hamilton	Dr. Carol M. KAMINSKI
12	Int Academic Dean - Boston (CUME)	Dr. Dwight JESSUP
12	Academic Dean - Charlotte	Dr. Timothy S. LANIAK
32	Dean of Students/Dir Stdnt Life Svc	Mrs. Lita SCHLUETER
16	Director of Human Resources	Ms. Susan M. BESSE
13	Chief Information Officer	Mrs. Amy E. DONOVAN
84	Dean Enrollment Mgmt	Mr. Scott B. POBLENZ
18	Director of Physical Plant	Mr. Timothy INGRAHAM
08	Director of Goddard Library	Mr. Meredith KLINE
88	Director of the Ockenga Institute	Dr. David G. HORN
37	Director of Financial Aid	Mr. Stacey T. GLIDDEN
40	Director of Support Services	Mr. David SHOREY
19	Director of Campus Safety	Mr. Cabot W. DODGE
26	Dir of Communications & Marketing	Mr. Michael L. COLARERI
07	Director of Admissions & Marketing	Ms. Jill M. BARLOW
21	Controller & Dir Financial Svcs	Mr. Gregg HANSEN
30	Director Institutional Advancement	Mr. William M. FISHER
42	Sr Administrator Mentored Ministry	Mrs. Katherine K. HORVATH

Hampshire College (G)

893 West Street, Amherst MA 01002-3372
County: Hampshire FICE Identification: 004661
Unit ID: 166018
Telephone: (413) 549-4600 Carnegie Class: Bac/A&S
FAX Number: (413) 559-5584 Calendar System: 4/1/4
URL: www.hampshire.edu
Established: 1965 Annual Undergrad Tuition & Fees: $42,880
Enrollment: 1,529 Coed
Affiliation or Control: Independent Non-Profit IRS Status: 501(c)3
Highest Offering: Baccalaureate
Program: Liberal Arts And General
Accreditation: EH

01	President	Dr. Jonathan LASH
101	Secretary of the College	Ms. Beth I. WARD
05	Vice President & Dean of Faculty	Dr. Alan GOODMAN
32	Dean of Student Services	Ms. Dawn ELLINWOOD
10	Vice Pres for Finance & Admin	Mr. Mark SPIRO
15	Assoc Vice Pres Human Resources	Ms. Ann Michele RUOCCO
30	Chief Advancement Officer	Mr. Clay BALLANTINE
07	Dean of Admissions & Financial Aid	Ms. Julie RICHARDSON
08	Director of Library/Info Services	Ms. Susan DAYALL
06	Director of Central Records	Ms. Roberta P. STUART
37	Director of Financial Aid	Ms. Jennifer G. LAWTON
09	Director of Institutional Research	Ms. Carol TROSSET
18	Director of Facilities and Grounds	Mr. Mark CAPPELLO
20	Associate Dean of Faculty	Ms. Yaniris FERNANDEZ
26	Chief Public Relations Officer	Ms. B. Elaine THOMAS
29	Director Alumni Relations	Ms. Killara BURN
36	Director Student Placement	Ms. Carin RANK
38	Director Student Counseling	Dr. Eliza MCARDLE
100	Chief of Staff	Ms. Diana FERNANDEZ
28	Director of Diversity	Mr. Jaime DAVILA

Harvard University (H)

1350 Massachusetts Ave, Cambridge MA 02138-3800
County: Middlesex FICE Identification: 002155
Unit ID: 166027
Telephone: (617) 495-1000 Carnegie Class: RU/VH
FAX Number: (617) 495-0500 Calendar System: Semester
URL: www.harvard.edu
Established: 1636 Annual Undergrad Tuition & Fees: $39,849
Enrollment: 27,594 Coed
Affiliation or Control: Independent Non-Profit IRS Status: 501(c)3
Highest Offering: Doctorate
Program: Liberal Arts And General; Teacher Preparatory; Professional
Accreditation: EH, BUS, CLPSY, DENT, ENG, IPSY, LAW, LSAR, MED, PH, PLNG, SPAA, THEOL

01	President	Drew G. FAUST
05	Provost	Alan M. GARBER
03	Executive Vice President	Katherine N. LAPP
88	Treasurer	James ROTHENBERG
49	Dean Faculty Arts & Sciences	Michael D. SMITH
20	Dean of Harvard College	Evelynn M. HAMMONDS
58	Dean Grad School of Arts & Science	Allan M. BRANDT
54	Dean of Engineering/Applied Science	Cherry A. MURRAY
50	Dean of Harvard Business School	Nitin NOHRIA
52	Dean of Dental Medicine	R. Bruce DONOFF
48	Dean Graduate School of Design	Mohsen MOSTAFAVI
73	Dean of the Divinity School	William A. GRAHAM
51	Dean of Continuing Education	Michael SHINAGEL
53	Dean Graduate School of Education	Kathleen MCCARTNEY
61	Dean of the Law School	Martha MINOW
63	Dean of the Medical School	Dr. Jeffrey S. FLIER
80	Dean of Government	David ELLWOOD
69	Dean of Public Health	Julio FRENK
88	Int Dean Radcliffe Inst Advance Std	Lizabeth COHEN
88	Vice President for Policy	A. Clayton SPENCER
10	Vice President for Finance and CFO	Daniel SHORE
11	Vice President for Campus Services	Lisa HOGARTY
43	Vice President & General Counsel	Robert W. IULIANO
26	Vice Pres Public Aff/Communications	Christine HEENAN
29	Vice Pres Alumni Affs & Development	Tamara E. ROGERS
15	Vice President for Human Resources	Marilyn HAUSAMMANN
28	Sr Vice Prov Fac Devel & Diversity	Judith SINGER
18	Vice President for Campus Services	Lisa HOGARTY
25	Director Sponsored Programs	Catherine BREEN
28	Chief Diversity Ofc/Sp Asst to Pres	Lisa M. COLEMAN
13	Univ Chief Information Officer	Anne MARGULIES
07	Dean of Admissions/Financial Aid	William R. FITZSIMMONS
06	Registrar/Faculty Arts & Sciences	Michael P. BURKE
08	Exec Director for Harvard Library	Helen SHENTON
23	Director Health Services	David S. ROSENTHAL
19	Dir Police/Security/Chief of Police	Francis D. RILEY
09	Director of Institutional Research	Erin DRIVER-LINN
37	Director Student Financial Aid	Sally C. DONAHUE

Hebrew College (I)

160 Herrick Road, Newton Centre MA 02459-2237
County: Middlesex FICE Identification: 002157
Unit ID: 166045
Telephone: (617) 559-8600 Carnegie Class: Spec/Faith
FAX Number: (617) 559-8601 Calendar System: Semester
URL: www.hebrewcollege.edu
Established: 1921 Annual Undergrad Tuition & Fees: $17,480
Enrollment: 200 Coed
Affiliation or Control: Independent Non-Profit IRS Status: 501(c)3
Highest Offering: Beyond Master's But Less Than Doctorate
Program: Professional; Religious Emphasis
Accreditation: EH

01	President	Rabbi Daniel LEHMANN
10	Vice Pres Finance & Administration	Mr. Leon ZAIMES
05	Provost	Dr. Barry MESCH
84	Director of Enrollment Management	Ms. Sara SHALVA
06	Registrar/Financial Aid Services	Ms. Marilyn JAYE
30	Director of Development	Mr. Lowell LUSTIG

15 Director Personnel Services .... Ms. Steffi BOBBIN
04 Assistant to the President .... Ms. Annette ASHIN

Hellenic College-Holy Cross Greek Orthodox School of Theology (A)

50 Goddard Avenue, Brookline MA 02445-7496
County: Norfolk FICE Identification: 002154
Unit ID: 166054
Telephone: (617) 731-3500 Carnegie Class: Spec/Faith
FAX Number: (617) 850-1460 Calendar System: Semester
URL: www.hchc.edu
Established: 1937 Annual Undergrad Tuition & Fees: $20,450
Enrollment: 217 Coed
Affiliation or Control: Greek Orthodox IRS Status: 501(c)3
Highest Offering: Master's
Program: Teacher Preparatory; Professional
Accreditation: EH, THEOL

01 President .... Rev. Nicholas C. TRIANTAFILOU
73 Dean School of Theology .... Rev Dr. Thomas FITZGERALD
05 Dean Hellenic College .... Dr. Demetrios KATOS
32 Dean of Students .... Dean Nicholas BELCHER
11 Chief Operating Officer .... Mr. James D. KARLOUTSOS
10 Chief Financial Officer .... Mr. Charles KROLL
07 Director of Admissions & Records .... Mr. Gregory FLOOR
08 Director Library .... Rev. Joachim COTSONIS
37 Financial Aid Officer .... Mr. George GEORGENES
06 Registrar .... Ms. Alba PAGAN
40 Bookstore Manager .... Ms. Tanya CONTOS
13 Director Computing/Information Mgmt .... Mr. Mugur ROZ
42 Chaplain .... Rev. Peter CHAMBERAS
38 Director Student Counseling .... Ms. Athina-Eleni MAVROUDHIS
30 Director Institutional Advancement .... Rev. James KATINAS
29 Director of Alumni Office .... Mr. Gregory FLOOR
04 Administrator of President's Office .... Mrs. Joanna BAKAS

Hult International Business School (B)

One Education Street, Cambridge MA 02141-1805
County: Middlesex FICE Identification: 020727
Unit ID: 164368
Telephone: (617) 746-1990 Carnegie Class: Not Classified
FAX Number: (617) 746-1991 Calendar System: Trimester
URL: www.hult.edu
Established: 1964 Annual Undergrad Tuition & Fees: $55,500
Enrollment: 810 Coed
Affiliation or Control: Proprietary IRS Status: Proprietary
Highest Offering: Master's
Program: Professional; Business Emphasis
Accreditation: EH

01 President .... Dr. Stephen HODGES
05 Provost .... Dr. Richard JOSEPH
12 Dean Boston Campus .... Mr. Henrik TOTTERMAN
12 Dean San Francisco Campus .... Mr. Luis TIMMS
32 Associate Dean Boston Campus .... Mr. Farhoud KAFI
32 Assistant Dean San Francisco .... Ms. Mona DHILLON
20 Assistant Dean Boston Campus .... Ms. Katherine STEBBINS
84 Director of Recruiting .... Mr. Steve WYNN
36 Director of Career Services Boston .... Mr. James MORRISON
35 Director Student Services Boston .... Mr. David HIETT
06 Registrar Boston Campus .... Ms. Nicole GREGOIRE
06 Registrar San Francisco Campus .... Ms. Ewa NOWICKI

ITT Technical Institute (C)

333 Providence Highway, Norwood MA 02062
County: Norfolk Identification: 666541
Unit ID: 366580
Telephone: (781) 278-7200 Carnegie Class: Spec/Tech
FAX Number: (781) 278-0766 Calendar System: Quarter
URL: www.itt-tech.edu
Established: 1990 Annual Undergrad Tuition & Fees: N/A
Enrollment: 597 Coed
Affiliation or Control: Proprietary IRS Status: Proprietary
Highest Offering: Baccalaureate
Program: Technical Emphasis
Accreditation: ACICS

† Branch campus of ITT Technical Institute, Newburgh, IN.

ITT Technical Institute (D)

200 Ballardvale Street, Suite 200, Wilmington MA 01887
County: Middlesex Identification: 666119
Unit ID: 439136
Telephone: (978) 658-2636 Carnegie Class: Assoc/PrivFP
FAX Number: (781) 937-3402 Calendar System: Quarter
URL: www.itt-tech.edu
Established: 2000 Annual Undergrad Tuition & Fees: N/A
Enrollment: 547 Coed
Affiliation or Control: Proprietary IRS Status: Proprietary
Highest Offering: Baccalaureate
Program: Technical Emphasis
Accreditation: ACICS

† Branch campus of ITT Technical Institute, Newburgh, IN.

Laboure College (E)

2120 Dorchester Avenue, Boston MA 02124-5698
County: Suffolk FICE Identification: 006324
Unit ID: 165264
Telephone: (617) 296-8300 Carnegie Class: Assoc/PrivNFP
FAX Number: (617) 296-7947 Calendar System: Semester
URL: www.laboure.edu
Established: 1892 Annual Undergrad Tuition & Fees: $25,495
Enrollment: 717 Coed
Affiliation or Control: Roman Catholic IRS Status: 501(c)3
Highest Offering: Baccalaureate
Program: Occupational; 2-Year Principally Bachelor's Creditable
Accreditation: EH, ADNUR, DIETT, EEG, RTT

01 Interim President .... Dr. Maureen A. SMITH
10 Vice Pres Administration & Finance .... Mr. Mark VIRELLO
05 Dean Academic Affairs .... Ms. Paula VOSBURGH
32 Vice Pres/Dean Student Affairs .... Mrs. Karen MASTERS
08 Director Learning Resources Center .... Mr. Andrew CALO
06 Registrar .... Mr. John SACCO
84 Director of Enrollment Services .... Ms. Gina MORRISSETTE
30 Director Institutional Advancement .... Vacant
26 Director Public Relations/Marketing .... Ms. Katelyn DWYER
37 Director Student Financial Aid .... Ms. Erin HANLON
66 Int Dir Nursing Division .... Ms. Denise EDINGER
88 Chair of Dietetic Division .... Mrs. Anne MANION
76 Div Chair Health Info Tech .... Vacant
88 Div Chair Radiation Technology .... Mrs. Pauline CLANCY
88 Div Chair Electroneuro Technology .... Mrs. Jean FARLEY

Lasell College (F)

1844 Commonwealth Avenue, Newton MA 02466-2716
County: Middlesex FICE Identification: 002158
Unit ID: 166391
Telephone: (617) 243-2000 Carnegie Class: Bac/Diverse
FAX Number: (617) 243-2389 Calendar System: Semester
URL: www.lasell.edu
Established: 1851 Annual Undergrad Tuition & Fees: $27,500
Enrollment: 1,613 Coed
Affiliation or Control: Independent Non-Profit IRS Status: 501(c)3
Highest Offering: Master's
Program: Liberal Arts And General
Accreditation: EH

01 President .... Michael B. ALEXANDER
04 Exec Assistant to the President .... Pamela FARIA
05 VP Academic Affairs .... James OSTROW
10 VP Business & Finance .... Michael HOYLE
84 VP Enrollment Management .... Kathleen O'CONNOR
88 VP Lasell Village .... Paula PANCHUCK
32 VP of Student Affairs .... Diane AUSTIN
30 Dean of Institutional Advancement .... Ruth SHUMAN
07 Dean of Undergraduate Admission .... James TWEED
53 Dean of Undergraduate Education .... Steven BLOOM
58 Dean of Grad & Prof Studies .... Joan DOLAMORE
89 Dean of Advis & First Year Programs .... Helena SANTOS
35 Assoc Dean of Student Affairs .... David HENNESSEY
21 Dir of Business Operations .... Diane PARKER
37 Dir of Financial Aid .... Michele KOSBOTH
09 Dir of Institutional Research .... Vacant
06 Registrar .... Dianne POLIZZI
44 Dir of Annual Giving/Const Rel .... Haegan FORREST
18 Dir of Plant Ops/Public Safety .... Thomas KOERBER
27 Dir of Communications .... Michelle GASSEAU
30 Dir of Development .... Mark LAFRANCE
30 Senior Advancement Officer .... Katharine URNER-JONES
29 Assoc Dir of Alumni Relations .... Lauren MCCAUSLIN
35 Dir of Student Act & Orientation .... Jennifer GRANGER
23 Dir of Health Services .... Ann SHERMAN
08 Dir of Library .... Marilyn NEGIP
41 Dir of Athletics .... Kristy WALTER
15 Dir of Human Resources .... Kathryn BRYNE
38 Dir of Counseling Center .... Janice FLETCHER
07 Dir of Graduate Admission .... Adrienne FRANCIOSI
42 Dir of Center for Spirtual Life .... Thomas SULLIVAN
13 Chief Information Officer .... Deborah GELCH
39 Dir of Residential Life .... Scott LAMPHERE

Lesley University (G)

29 Everett Street, Cambridge MA 02138-2790
County: Middlesex FICE Identification: 002160
Unit ID: 166452
Telephone: (617) 868-9600 Carnegie Class: Master's L
FAX Number: (617) 349-8717 Calendar System: Semester
URL: www.lesley.edu
Established: 1909 Annual Undergrad Tuition & Fees: $30,420
Enrollment: 5,999 Coed
Affiliation or Control: Independent Non-Profit IRS Status: 501(c)3
Highest Offering: Doctorate
Program: Liberal Arts And General; Teacher Preparatory; Professional
Accreditation: EH, TEAC

01 President .... Dr. Joseph B. MOORE
05 Provost .... Dr. Selase W. WILLIAMS
11 Vice President for Administration .... Ms. Marylou BATT
10 Vice President/CFO .... Ms. Bernice BRADIN
30 Vice President of Advancement .... Mr. Randy STABILE
84 VP Enrollment Mgmt .... Mr. Jeffrey HANDLER
21 VP for Budgeting & Fin Planning .... Ms. M. L. DYMSKI
43 General Counsel .... Ms. Shirin PHILIPP
100 Chief of Staff .... Dr. MaryPat LOHSE
20 Associate Provost .... Ms. Gene DIAZ
22 Dir Equal Opportunity & Inclusion .... Dr. Barbara ADDISON REID
58 Dean Grad Sch Arts & Social Sci .... Dr. Catherine KOVEROLA
53 Dean School of Education .... Dr. Jack GILLETTE
32 Dean of Student Life & Academic Dev .... Dr. Nathaniel MAYS
88 Dean Art Institute of Boston .... Mr. Stan TRECKER
88 Dean Lesley College .... Dr. Mary COLEMAN
18 Dir Operations & Campus Planning .... Mr. George SMITH
13 Chief Information Officer .... Ms. Karen BOUDREAU-SHEA
07 Director of Graduate Admissions .... Ms. Martha SHEEHAN
91 Director Admin Applications UT .... Mr. Scott BOULET
90 Assoc VP Acad Tech/Program Planning .. Ms. Karen MUNCASTER
15 Director of Human Resources .... Ms. Jane JOYCE
37 Director of Financial Aid .... Mr. Scott JEWELL
19 Captain of Security .... Ms. Nicole O'LEARY
88 Budget Director .... Ms. Anne GROGAN
88 Director Student Accounts .... Ms. Heather CLANG
21 Controller .... Ms. Karen BAYTCH
40 Manager of Bookstore/Campus Shop .... Ms. Lee-Ann LANZILLO
44 Dir of Annual Giving & Alumni Rels .... Ms. Pattyanne LYONS
08 Director of Libraries .... Ms. Patricia PAYNE
06 Registrar .... Ms. Melissa JANOT
36 Assoc Dean Career/Community Service .... Ms. Alice DIAMOND
41 Director of Athletics .... Mr. Stanley VIEIRA
07 Dir Undergrad Admissions Lesley Col .... Ms. Deb KOCAR
88 Director of Admissions AIB .... Mr. Robert GIELOW
39 Director Residence Life .... Ms. Nancy GALVIN
38 Director Counseling Center .... Ms. Magi MCKINNIES
85 Dir International Student Services .... Ms. Janie BESS
09 Dir of Assessment/Inst Research .... Dr. Linda PURSLEY
26 Director Public Affairs .... Mr. Bill DONCASTER
88 Director of Marketing Comm .... Mr. Leo RICE
27 Dir of Advancement Communications .... Ms. Anya WOODS
96 Director of Purchasing .... Mr. William HOYT

Longy School of Music of Bard College (H)

1 Follen Street, Cambridge MA 02138-3502
County: Middlesex FICE Identification: 021430
Unit ID: 166489
Telephone: (617) 876-0956 Carnegie Class: Spec/Arts
FAX Number: (617) 876-9326 Calendar System: Semester
URL: www.longy.edu
Established: 1915 Annual Graduate Tuition & Fees: $29,700
Enrollment: 252 Coed
Affiliation or Control: Independent Non-Profit IRS Status: 501(c)3
Highest Offering: Master's; No Undergraduates
Program: Music Emphasis
Accreditation: EH, MUS

01 President .... Ms. Karen ZORN
04 Executive Asst to the President .... Ms. Anne BOVENGA
05 Dean of the Conservatory .... Mr. Wayman CHIN
30 Interim Director of Development .... Ms. Kimberlee LABONTE
10 Chief Financial Officer .... Mr. Howard LEVY
100 Chief of Staff .... Mr. Kalen RATZLAFF
26 Director of Communications .... Vacant
31 Director of Community Programs .... Ms. Miriam ECKELHOEFER
20 Associate Dean for Academic Affairs .... Mr. James MOYLAN
07 Director of Admissions .... Mr. Alex POWELL
37 Director of Student Financial Aid .... Ms. Elvira REYES
08 Library Director .... Mr. Roy RUDOLPH

† Partner of Bard College, NY.

Marian Court College (I)

35 Littles Point Road, Swampscott MA 01907-2896
County: Essex FICE Identification: 006873
Unit ID: 166601
Telephone: (781) 595-6768 Carnegie Class: Assoc/PrivNFP
FAX Number: (781) 595-3560 Calendar System: Semester
URL: www.mariancourt.edu
Established: 1964 Annual Undergrad Tuition & Fees: $16,400
Enrollment: 174 Coed
Affiliation or Control: Roman Catholic IRS Status: 501(c)3
Highest Offering: Associate Degree
Program: Occupational; 2-Year Principally Bachelor's Creditable
Accreditation: EH

01 President .... Dr. Ghazi DARKAZALLI
10 Chief Financial Officer .... Ms. Maribeth FORBES
30 VP Development and Marketing .... Ms. Michele L. AHOUSE
05 Dean of Academic & Student Affairs .... Dr. Denise HAMMON
06 Registrar .... Ms. Linda LUNDSTROM
07 Sr Assoc Director of Admissions .... Mr. Peter SCHILLING
88 Assoc Director Admissions .... Ms. Danielle MORSE
08 Librarian & Career Info Specialist .... Ms. Mia MORGAN
38 Dir of Academic & Career Services .... Ms. Megan PENYACK
37 Director of Financial Aid .... Ms. Stacy BONSANG
50 Chair Business Dept .... Ms. Joan THOMPSON
79 Chair Liberal Studies .... Dr. Tom HALLORAN
13 Director of Information Technology .... Mr. Jorge CORREIA
88 Chair Criminal Justice .... Mr. Fran BRENNAN

Massachusetts Board of Higher Education (A)

One Ashburton Place, Room 1401,
Boston MA 02108-1696
County: Suffolk FICE Identification: 029283
Unit ID: 166531
Telephone: (617) 994-6950 Carnegie Class: N/A
FAX Number: (617) 727-6397
URL: www.mass.edu

01 Commissioner ... Dr. Richard M. FREELAND
103 Assoc Comm of Workforce Development ... Mr. David C. CEDRONE
05 Deputy Comm Academic Policy ... Ms. Aundrea KELLEY
43 General Counsel ... Ms. Constantia PAPANIKOLAOU
10 Dep Comm Administration and Finance ... Mr. Steven LENHARDT
09 Assoc Comm Institutional Research ... Dr. Jonathan KELLER
37 Sr Dep Comm Student Financial Aid ... Dr. Clantha MCCURDY

University of Massachusetts Central Office (B)

225 Franklin Street, 33rd Floor, Boston MA 02110
County: Suffolk FICE Identification: 008017
Unit ID: 166665
Telephone: (617) 287-7000 Carnegie Class: N/A
FAX Number: (617) 287-7196
URL: www.massachusetts.edu

01 President ... Dr. Robert L. CARET
03 Exec VP/Chief Operating Officer ... Mr. James R. JULIAN
05 Sr VP Acad Affs/Stdnt & Intl Affs ... Dr. Marcellette WILLIAMS
11 Sr VP Admin/Finance & Tech ... Mr. David J. GRAY
102 Exec VP UMass Foundation ... Mr. Robert M. GOODHUE
46 Vice President Economic Development ... Mr. Thomas J. CHMURA
30 Vice Pres for Advancement & Comm ... Vacant
26 VP Strategic Comm/Univ Spokesperson ... Mr. Robert P. CONNOLLY
104 Asst Vice Pres International Rels ... Ms. Susan M. KELLY
04 AVP Admin Svcs to Pres/Exec Asst ... Ms. Virginia O'SULLIVAN
43 General Counsel ... Ms. Deirdre HEATWOLE
20 Assoc VP for Academic Affairs ... Dr. Kate HARRINGTON
21 Assoc VP for Budget & Admin ... Mr. Brian DOUGLAS
27 Assoc VP and Chief Info Officer ... Mr. Robert SOLIS
101 Secretary to Board of Trustees ... Ms. Barbara F. DEVICO
21 Director for University Auditing ... Mr. Robert HARRISON
15 Univ Director of Human Resources ... Mr. Roy S. MILBURY
106 CEO UMass Online ... Dr. Ken UDAS

University of Massachusetts (C)

Amherst MA 01003-0001
County: Hampshire FICE Identification: 002221
Unit ID: 166629
Telephone: (413) 545-0111 Carnegie Class: RU/VH
FAX Number: N/A Calendar System: Semester
URL: www.umass.edu
Established: 1863 Annual Undergrad Tuition & Fees (In-State): $12,612
Enrollment: 27,569 Coed
Affiliation or Control: State IRS Status: 501(c)3
Highest Offering: Doctorate
Program: Liberal Arts And General; Teacher Preparatory; Professional
Accreditation: EH, AUD, BUS, BUSA, CLPSY, DIETD, DIETI, ENG, FOR, IPSY, LSAR, MUS, NURSE, PH, PLNG, SCPSY, SP, TED

02 Chancellor ... Dr. Robert C. HOLUB
03 Deputy Chancellor ... Dr. Todd DIACON
10 Vice Chancellor Admin/Finance ... Ms. Joyce M. HATCH
30 Vice Chancellor Univ Advancement ... Mr. Michael LETO
46 Vice Chancellor Research ... Dr. Michael F. MALONE
32 VC Student Affairs & Campus Life ... Dr. Jean KIM
31 Vice Chanc University Relations ... Mr. John KENNEDY
41 Director of Athletics ... Mr. John F. MCCUTCHEON
43 Associate Counsel ... Mr. Brian W. BURKE
13 Special Asst to Chancellor & CIO ... Dr. John F. DUBACH
15 Asst Vice Chanc Human Resources ... Mr. Juan A. JARRETT
04 Asst to the Chancellor ... Ms. Becky DEAN
05 Provost/Sr Vice Chancellor ... Dr. James V. STAROS
88 Vice Provost/Dean of Faculty ... Dr. Joel W. MARTIN
98 Associate Chancellor ... Ms. Susan PEARSON
45 Assoc Provost Academic Plng/Assess ... Dr. Bryan C. HARVEY
09 Director of Institutional Research ... Dr. Marilyn H. BLAUSTEIN
84 Director of Enrollment Management ... Dr. James ROCHE
37 Director Financial Aid Services ... Ms. Suzanne PETERS
07 Director Undergraduate Admissions ... Mr. Kevin KELLY
20 Vice Provost ... Dr. Carol BARR
06 Registrar ... Mr. John LENZI
35 Dean Student Affairs ... Ms. Enku GELAYE
21 Assoc VC/Budget Director/Controller ... Mr. Andrew P. MANGELS
18 Assoc VC Facilities Planning ... Ms. Juanita M. HOLLER
23 Exec Director Univ Health Services ... Ms. Bernette A. MELBY
27 News Director ... Mr. Edward F. BLAGUSZEWSKI
51 Director Continuing/Education ... Mr. William S. MCCLURE
87 Assistant Provost Summer Programs ... Dr. Ed FERSZT
92 Dean Commonwealth College ... Dr. Priscilla M. CLARKSON
85 Assoc Provost Internatl Programs ... Dr. Jack AHERN
08 Director of Libraries ... Mr. Jay SCHAFER
20 Asst Provost Advising/Acad Support ... Dr. Pamela R. MARSH-WILLIAMS
22 Assoc Chanc Equal Oppty/Diversity ... Ms. Debora D. FERREIRA
25 Director Grant & Contract Admin ... Ms. Carol SPRAGUE
39 Director Housing Svcs & Res Life ... Mr. Edward C. HULL
19 Director Public Safety/Chief Police ... Mr. Johnny C. WHITEHEAD
58 Graduate Dean ... Dr. John R. MULLIN
79 Dean Col Humanities & Fine Arts ... Dr. Julie C. HAYES
81 Dean Col Natural Science ... Dr. Steve GOODWIN
83 Dean Col Social & Behavioral Sci ... Mr. Robert S. FELDMAN
53 Dean School of Education ... Dr. Christine B. MCCORMICK
54 Dean College of Engineering ... Mr. Theodore E. DJAFERIS
50 Dean School of Management ... Dr. Mark A. FULLER
66 Dean School of Nursing ... Dr. Stephen CAVANAGH
69 Dean Sch Public Health/Health Sci ... Dr. C. Marjorie AELION
56 Director of Extension ... Ms. Nancy GARRABRANTS
47 Dir Stockbridge School Agriculture ... Mr. William MITCHELL
40 Manager Univ Store/Retail Services ... Mr. Phillip OLSON
90 Director OIT Academic Computing ... Ms. Copper F. GILOTH
102 Director Corporate/Foundation Rels ... Ms. Linda SOPP
36 Director Career Services ... Mr. Jeffrey I. SILVER
38 Director Mental Health/Health Svcs ... Dr. Harry S. ROCKLAND-MILLER
44 Director Annual Giving ... Mr. Thomas P. NAVIN
96 Director of Purchasing ... Mr. John O. MARTIN
29 Exec Director Alumni Relations ... Ms. Deb GOODHIND
24 Director Educational Media ... Mr. Stephen PIELOCK
86 Dir Public/Constituent Relations ... Mr. Christopher DUNN
105 Web Manager ... Ms. Nina SOSSEN
31 Dir Cmty Relations/Special Events ... Dr. Nancy BUFFONE
91 Associate CIO/Dir Admin Applics ... Ms. Heidi DOLLARD

*University of Massachusetts Boston (D)

100 Morrissey Boulevard, Boston MA 02125-3393
County: Suffolk FICE Identification: 002222
Unit ID: 166638
Telephone: (617) 287-5000 Carnegie Class: RU/H
FAX Number: (617) 265-7173 Calendar System: Semester
URL: www.umb.edu
Established: 1964 Annual Undergrad Tuition & Fees (In-State): $11,405
Enrollment: 15,454 Coed
Affiliation or Control: State IRS Status: 501(c)3
Highest Offering: Doctorate
Program: Liberal Arts And General; Teacher Preparatory; Professional; Business Emphasis
Accreditation: EH, BUS, CLPSY, CORE, CS, MFCD, NURSE, @TEAC

02 Chancellor ... Dr. J. Keith MOTLEY
88 Assistant Chancellor ... Dr. Theresa MORTIMER
100 Chief of Staff ... Mr. Christopher HOGAN
05 Provost ... Dr. Winston LANGLEY
10 Vice Chanc for Admin & Finance ... Ms. Ellen O'CONNOR
30 Int VC Chanc for Univ Advancement ... Ms. Gina CAPPELLO
84 Vice Chanc Enrollment Management ... Ms. Kathleen TEEHAN
32 Vice Chancellor Student Affairs ... Mr. Patrick K. DAY
41 VC for Athletics & Special Projects ... Mr. Charlie TITUS
86 VC for Govt Rel/Public Aff ... Mr. Arthur BERNARD
14 Vice Provost Information Tech/CIO ... Ms. Anne S. AGEE
84 Assoc Vice Chanc Enrollment Mgmt ... Dr. Lisa JOHNSON
15 Asst Vice Chanc for Human Resources ... Mr. Jeff MCCUE
29 Asst VC Family & Alumni Relations ... Mr. Joe DEMEDERIOS
31 Asst Vice Chanc Community Relations ... Ms. Gail HOBIN
23 Ast VC Std Aff/Ex Dir Univ Hlth Svc ... Dr. Kathleen GOLDEN MCANDREW
20 Associate Provost ... Ms. Kristine ALSTER
20 Assoc Provost Assess and Planning ... Dr. Peter LANGER
53 Int Dean Col of Educ & Human Dev ... Ms. Felicia WILCZENSKI
51 Dean of University College ... Dr. Philip DISALVIO
81 Dean of Math & Science ... Dr. Andrew GROSOVSKY
79 Int Dean of Liberal Arts ... Dr. Emily MCDERMOTT
50 Dean College of Management ... Dr. Philip L. QUAGLIERI
66 Dean College of Nursing ... Dr. Greer GLAZER
80 Int Dean of CPCS ... Dr. Anna MADISON
35 Dean of Students ... Vacant
43 Interim General Counsel ... Ms. Deirdre HEATWOLE
26 Director of Communications ... Mr. DeWayne LEHMAN
38 Director Univ Advising Center ... Ms. Gail STUBBS
09 Director Institutional Research ... Dr. Jennifer A. BROWN
06 Director of Registration & Records ... Mr. David R. CESARIO
07 Director of Undergrad Admissions ... Mr. John DREW
37 Director Financial Aid Services ... Ms. Judy KEYES
08 Director of Libraries ... Dr. Daniel ORTIZ
22 Chief Diversity Officer-ODI ... Mr. Juan NUNEZ
18 Director of Facilities Devel & Mgmt ... Ms. Dorothy RENAGHAN
19 Director of Public Safety ... Mr. James OVERTON
40 Director of Campus Services ... Ms. Diane D'ARRIGO
41 Senior Assoc Director of Athletics ... Ms. Terry CONDON
36 Director of Career Services ... Mr. Len KONARSKI
24 Media Services Manager ... Mr. John POTTER
96 Director of Procurement ... Mr. Darryl MAYERS
92 Director of Honors Programs ... Ms. Rajini SRIKANTH
20 Asst Vice Provost Undergrad Studies ... Ms. Maura MAST

*University of Massachusetts Dartmouth (E)

285 Old Westport Road, North Dartmouth MA 02747-2300
County: Bristol FICE Identification: 002210
Unit ID: 167987
Telephone: (508) 999-8000 Carnegie Class: Master's L
FAX Number: (508) 999-8901 Calendar System: Semester
URL: www.umassd.edu
Established: 1895 Annual Undergrad Tuition & Fees (In-State): $11,135
Enrollment: 9,432 Coed
Affiliation or Control: State IRS Status: 501(c)3
Highest Offering: Doctorate
Program: Liberal Arts And General; Teacher Preparatory; Professional
Accreditation: EH, ART, BUS, CS, ENG, MT, NUR

02 Chancellor ... Dr. Jean F. MACCORMACK
05 Prov/Vice Chanc Academic/Stdnt Affs ... Dr. Anthony J. GARRO
10 Vice Chanc Admin/Fiscal Services ... Ms. Deborah MCLAUGHLIN
30 Asst Chancellor Advancement ... Mr. Michael EATOUGH
04 Executive Office Director ... Ms. Clare POIRIER
51 Asst VC/Director of PCE ... Dr. Joy MCGUIRL-HADLEY
09 Asst Chanc Inst Rsrch & Assessment ... Dr. Richard J. PANOFSKY
20 Assoc Provost Undergad Studies ... Dr. Magali CARRERA
20 Assoc Provost Graduate Studies ... Dr. Alex FOWLER
84 Assc VC Enrollment Management ... Ms. Teresa MAUK
21 Associate Vice Chancellor Finance ... Mr. William A. MITCHELL
11 Assoc VC Admin & Fiscal Services ... Mr. Salvatore FILARDI
58 Dir Graduate Studies/Admissions ... Mr. Scott WEBSTER
22 Asst Chanc Eq Oppty/Divers/Outrch ... Dr. George S. SMITH
31 Asst Chanc Economic Development ... Mr. Paul VIGEANT
88 Assistant VC Academic Affairs ... Dr. Bruce ROSE
35 Assoc Vice Chanc Student Affairs ... Dr. David M. MILSTONE
13 CIO & Assoc VC IT ... Ms. Donna R. MASSANO
91 Dir Information Technology Devel ... Ms. Carolyn HAMEL
46 Asst VC Research Development ... Dr. Louis PETROVIC
25 Director Research Administration ... Ms. Joanne ZANELLA-LITKE
49 Dean College Arts & Science ... Dr. William HOGAN
50 Dean Charlton College of Business ... Dr. Susan ENGELKEMEYER
54 Dean College of Engineering ... Dr. Robert PECK
66 Dean College of Nursing ... Dr. James FAIN
57 Dean College Visual Perform Arts ... Mr. Adrian TIO
88 Dean School Marine Science/Tech ... Dr. Steven LOHRENZ
53 Int Dean Sch Educ/Pub Pol & Civic ... Dr. Ismael RAMIREZ-SOTO
96 Asst VC for Administrative Services ... Mr. Michael LAGRASSA
21 Controller ... Ms. Suzanne AUDET
92 Director Honors Program ... Dr. Robert DARST
94 Director Women's Studies Program ... Dr. Jeannette E. RILEY
88 Int Dir Academic Advising Center ... Ms. Suzanne MELLONI
06 University Registrar ... Dr. Carnell JONES, JR.
07 Director of Admissions ... Mr. Michael LYNCH
09 Director of Institutional Research ... Ms. Tammy A. SILVA
08 Dean Library Services ... Mr. Terrance BURTON
19 Dir Public Safety/Chief of Police ... Col. Emil FIORAVANTI
36 Director Career Development Center ... Dr. Gail L. BERMAN-MARTIN
37 Director Financial Aid ... Mr. Bruce H. PALMER
38 Dir Counseling/Stdnt Develop Ctr ... Dr. D. Christine FRIZZELL
90 Exec Dir IT Service Assurance ... Ms. Margaret S. DIAS
29 AVC Alumni Relations ... Ms. Lori JACQUES
29 Director of Alumni Relations ... Mr. C. Chad ARGOSINGER
15 Asst VC Human Resources ... Ms. Carol SANTOS
15 Deputy Dir Human Resources ... Ms. Michellle RODERICK
18 Director Facilities/Physical Plant ... Mr. David FERGUSON
41 Director of Athletics ... Mr. Ian DAY
23 Director of Health Services ... Ms. Sheila DORGAN
39 Director of Housing/Residence Life ... Ms. Lucinda POUDRIER-AARONSON
40 Director Campus Store ... Ms. Catherine M. HICKEY
44 Director Annual Giving/Development ... Vacant
26 Asst Chancellor/Public Info ... Mr. John T. HOEY
88 Bursar ... Ms. Kathleen L. EUBANKS
35 Asst VC Student Affairs ... Ms. Cynthia CUMMINGS
35 Associate Dean of Students ... Ms. Shelly METIVIER SCOTT
104 Dir Intl Exch/Study Abroad Programs ... Ms. Kristen KALBRENER
85 Dir International Student Center ... Ms. Christina M. BRUEN
93 Dir FD Unity House/Asst Dean Stdnts ... Mr. Keith WILDER
88 Director Academic Resource Center ... Mr. Thomas DAIGLE
88 Ombudsman ... Mr. William KING
105 Webmaster ... Mr. Don KING

*University of Massachusetts Lowell (F)

1 University Avenue, Lowell MA 01854-2881
County: Middlesex FICE Identification: 002161
Unit ID: 166513
Telephone: (978) 934-4000 Carnegie Class: RU/H
FAX Number: (978) 934-3000 Calendar System: Semester
URL: www.uml.edu
Established: 1894 Annual Undergrad Tuition & Fees (In-State): $11,297
Enrollment: 14,702 Coed
Affiliation or Control: State IRS Status: 501(c)3
Highest Offering: Doctorate
Program: 2-Year Principally Bachelor's Creditable; Liberal Arts And General; Teacher Preparatory
Accreditation: EH, ART, BUS, ENG, ENGR, ENGT, MT, MUS, NURSE, PTA, TED

02 Chancellor ... Mr. Martin T. MEEHAN
03 Executive Vice Chancellor ... Dr. Jacqueline MOLONEY
05 Provost ... Dr. Ahmed ABDELAL
10 Vice Chancellor Adm & Finance ... Ms. Joanne YESTRAMSKI
31 Executive Dir Community Outreach ... Mr. Paul MARION
30 Vice Chanc University Advancemant ... Mr. Edward CHIU
46 Vice Provost for Research ... Dr. Julie CHEN
49 Dean Col Arts/Sciences H/SS ... Dr. Nina COPPENS
81 Dean College Math/Science ... Dr. Robert H. TAMARIN
53 Int Dean College of Education ... Dr. Anita GREENWOOD
20 Exec Dir Academic Svcs/Cont Educ ... Ms. Pauline CARROLL
54 Dean of College of Engineering ... Dr. John TING
76 Dean College Health & Environment ... Dr. Shortie MCKINNEY
50 Dean College Management ... Dr. Kathryn CARTER
88 Dean School of Marine Sci & Tech ... Dr. Robert GAMACHE
13 Chief Information Officer ... Mr. Richard ZERA
09 Director of Institutional Research ... Vacant
08 Dir of Libraries & Info Resources ... Ms. Patricia NOREAU

06 Registrar ... Ms. Patricia DUFF
37 Director of Financial Aid ... Ms. Joyce MCLAUGHLIN
35 Dean of Students ... Mr. Larry SIEGEL
38 Director of Counseling ... Dr. John PAKSTIS
36 Director of Career Services ... Ms. Patricia A. YATES
41 Director of Athletics ... Mr. Dana SKINNER
44 Associate Director of Development ... Vacant
29 Dir of Alumni Programs & Gifts ... Ms. Diane EARL
15 Director of Human Resources ... Mr. John GIARUSSO
19 Chief Univ Police Dir Public Safe ... Mr. Randolph BRASCHERS
23 Exec Director Health Services ... Ms. Nancy QUATTROCCHI
88 Director of Reporting ... Ms. Laura PRUDDEN
88 Dir Graduate Admissions ... Ms. Linda SOUTHWORTH
96 Dir Purchasing & Campus Services ... Mr. Thomas HOOLE
88 Dir Outreach & Recruitment ... Mr. Michael BELCHER
07 Director of Undergrad Admissions ... Ms. Kerrie JOHNSTON
13 Associate Dir U Card Services ... Mr. Joh VICTORINE
21 Comptroller ... Vacant
28 Dir Equal Opportunity & Outreach ... Ms. Oneida BLAGG
84 Dean Enrollment & Student Success ... Mr. Thomas TAYLOR
26 Chief Public Affairs Officer ... Ms. Patricia MCCAFFERTY
21 Assoc Vice Chancellor for Finance ... Mr. Steven O'RIORDAN
88 Director of Disabilities ... Ms. Chandrika SHARMA
39 Dir of Student Residence Life ... Mr. John KOHL

*University of Massachusetts at Worcester (A)

55 Lake Avenue N, Worcester MA 01655-0001
County: Worcester
FICE Identification: 009756
Unit ID: 166708
Telephone: (508) 856-8989
Carnegie Class: Spec/Med
FAX Number: (508) 856-8181
Calendar System: Semester
URL: www.umassmed.edu
Established: 1962
Annual Graduate Tuition & Fees: $18,593
Enrollment: 1,158
Coed
Affiliation or Control: State
IRS Status: 501(c)3
Highest Offering: Doctorate; No Undergraduates
Program: Professional
Accreditation: EH, DENT, IPSY, MED, NMT, NURSE, PDPSY, RTT

02 Chancellor & SVP Health Sciences ... Dr. Michael F. COLLINS
05 Exec Dep Chanc Provost & Dean ... Dr. Terence R. FLOTTE
10 VC Administration & Finance ... Mr. Robert E. JENAL
30 Vice Chancellor for Development ... Mr. Charles J. PAGNAM
88 Int Exec Director UMass Biologics ... Dr. Terence R. FLOTTE
88 Deputy Chanc Com Med ... Mr. Thomas D. MANNING
11 Vice Chancellor & COO Comm Med ... Ms. Joyce MURPHY
88 Vice Provost Faculty Affairs ... Dr. Luanne THORNDYKE
16 Assoc Vice Chanc & Chief HR officer ... Vacant
86 Vice Chanc Government/Cmty Relation ... Mr. James LEARY
22 Assoc VC Diversity/Equal Opportunity . Ms. Deborah L. PLUMMER
26 Vice Chancellor of Communications ... Mr. Edward J. KEOHANE
18 Assoc Vice Chanc Facilities Mgmt ... Mr. John T. BAKER
88 Vice Provost School Services ... Dr. Deborah-Harmon HINES
43 General Counsel ... Mr. James HEALY
46 Vice Provost for Research ... Dr. John L. SULLIVAN
53 Sr Assoc Dean Educational Affairs ... Dr. Michele P. PUGNAIRE
63 Sr Assc Dean Clin Aff/Assc Dean GME ... Dr. Deborah DEMARCO
66 Dean Graduate School of Nursing ... Dr. Paulette SEYMOUR-ROUTE
32 Associate Dean Student Affairs ... Dr. Mai-Lan A. ROGOFF
58 Dean Grad School Biomedical Science ... Dr. Anthony CARRUTHERS
06 Registrar ... Mr. Michael F. BAKER
13 Chief Information Officer ... Mr. Robert P. PETERSON
07 Assoc Dean for Admissions ... Dr. John A. PARASKOS
37 Director Financial Aid ... Ms. Betsy A. GROVES
08 Director of Library ... Ms. Elaine R. MARTIN
100 Sr Director Chief of Staff ... Mr. Brendan H. CHISHOLM
04 Exec Assistant to the Chancellor ... Ms. Jill ALMY
17 Sr Assoc Dean UMass Medical Group ... Dr. Eric DICKSON
88 Assoc Provost for Global Health ... Dr. Katherine LUZURIAGA
88 Asst Dean for Admin/Chief of Staff ... Ms. Lisa B. BEITTEL
09 Institutional Research Officer ... Dr. Mary L. ZANETTI

*Bridgewater State University (B)

Bridgewater MA 02325-0001
County: Plymouth
FICE Identification: 002183
Unit ID: 165024
Telephone: (508) 531-1000
Carnegie Class: Master's L
FAX Number: N/A
Calendar System: Semester
URL: www.bridgew.edu
Established: 1840
Annual Undergrad Tuition & Fees (In-State): $7,553
Enrollment: 11,201
Coed
Affiliation or Control: State
IRS Status: 501(c)3
Highest Offering: Master's
Program: Liberal Arts And General; Teacher Preparatory; Professional
Accreditation: EH, CACREP, MUS, SPAA, SW, TED

02 President ... Dr. Dana MOHLER-FARIA
05 Provost & VP Academic Affairs ... Dr. Howard LONDON
11 Vice Pres Administration/Finance ... Mr. Miguel GOMES
32 Vice President Student Affairs ... Dr. David OSTROTH
30 VP Univ Advance/Strategic Planning ... Mr. Bryan BALDWIN
26 Vice President for External Affairs ... Dr. Ed MINNOCK
10 Assoc VP for Fiscal Affs/Controller . Ms. Darlene COSTA-BROWN
15 Assoc Vice Pres Human Resources ... Ms. Keri POWERS
22 Asst to Pres Affirm Action/Min Affs ... Dr. Alan COMEDY
32 Asst Vice Pres Student Affairs ... Mr. Brian SALVAGGIO
32 Asst Vice Pres Student Affairs ... Dr. Anthony M. ESPOSITO
35 Assoc Vice Pres Student Affairs ... Ms. Catherine HOLBROOK
84 Assoc Vice Pres for Enrollment Svcs ... Dr. Heather SMITH
20 Assoc Provost for Academic Affairs ... Dr. Andrew HARRIS
45 Assoc Provost Academic Plng/Admin ... Dr. Michael YOUNG
79 Actg Dean Col Humanities/Social Sci ... Dr. Howard LONDON
53 Dean Col Education/Allied Studies ... Dr. Anna BRADFIELD
50 Dean College of Business ... Dr. Marian EXTEJT
100 Chief of Staff ... Dr. Brenda MOLIFE
13 Chief Information Officer ... Mr. Patrick CRONIN
06 Director Student Records/Registrar ... Ms. Irene C. CHECKOVICH
07 Director of Admissions ... Mr. Gregg MEYER
38 Director Academic Achievement Ctr ... Dr. Peggy SMITH
29 Dir Alumni/Development Programs ... Vacant
30 Senior Development Officer ... Mr. Todd AUDYATIS
41 Director Athletics ... Mr. John C. HARPER
21 Director Admin Support Svcs ... Mrs. Margarida VIEIRA
19 Chief Campus Police ... Mr. David H. TILLINGHAST
36 Director Career Services ... Mr. John PAGANELLI
88 Director Day Care Center ... Ms. Jane DOYON
18 Director Facilities ... Mr. Keith MACDONALD
37 Director of Financial Aid ... Ms. Janet GUMBRIS
23 Director Counseling/Health Services ... Ms. Mary Lou FRIAS
08 Director Library Services ... Mr. Michael SOMERS
51 Dir Continuing/Distance Education ... Dr. Mary W. FULLER
22 Director Multicultural Affairs ... Ms. Andrea GARR-BARNES
27 Dir of Marketing & Publications ... Ms. Eva GAFFNEY
25 Director Grants/Sponsored Projects ... Ms. Mia ENRIGHT
96 Director of Purchasing ... Ms. Jean ZONA
28 Director of Institutional Diversity .. Dr. Sabrina GENTLEWARRIOR

*Fitchburg State University (C)

160 Pearl Street, Fitchburg MA 01420-2697
County: Worcester
FICE Identification: 002184
Unit ID: 165820
Telephone: (978) 345-2151
Carnegie Class: Master's L
FAX Number: (978) 665-3693
Calendar System: Semester
URL: www.fitchburgstate.edu
Established: 1894
Annual Undergrad Tuition & Fees (In-State): $8,300
Enrollment: 6,771
Coed
Affiliation or Control: State
IRS Status: 501(c)3
Highest Offering: Master's
Program: Liberal Arts And General; Teacher Preparatory; Professional
Accreditation: EH, CS, IACBE, NURSE, TED

02 President ... Dr. Robert V. ANTONUCCI
05 Vice President Academic Affairs ... Dr. Robin E. BOWEN
10 Vice Pres Finance & Administration ... Ms. Sheila SYKES
20 Associate VP Academic Affairs ... Dr. Shirley WAGNER
11 Chief Operating Officer ... Mr. Jay D. BRY
26 Exec Asst to Pres for External Affs ... Mr. Michael V. SHANLEY
32 Dean of Student & Academic Life ... Dr. Stanley BUCHOLC
84 Dean Enrollment Mgmt/Financial Aid .. Ms. Pamela MCCAFFERTY
51 Dean of Graduate Cont Educ ... Ms. Catherine E. CANNEY
53 Interim Dean of Education ... Dr. Pamela HILL
30 Exec Director of Advancement ... Vacant
35 Director of Student Development ... Dr. Henry C. PARKINSON, III
06 Registrar ... Ms. Linda DUPELL
09 Director of Institutional Research ... Mr. Terrance J. CARROLL
08 Director Library ... Mr. Robert A. FOLEY
41 Director Athletics ... Ms. Sue M. LAUDER
07 Director of Admissions ... Ms. Kay REYNOLDS
36 Director of Career Services ... Ms. Erin C. KELLEHER
38 Director Counseling ... Dr. Robert HYNES
23 Director Student Health Services ... Ms. Martha FAVRE
29 Asst Director of Alumni Relations ... Mr. Michael KUSHMEREK
19 Director of Campus Police ... Chief James HAMEL
44 Director of Annual Fund ... Vacant
96 Director of Procurement ... Ms. Doreen ARES
15 Asst VP of Human Resources/Payroll ... Ms. Jessica MURDOCH
18 Dir Capital Planning/Maintenance ... Mr. Eric HANSEN

*Framingham State University (D)

100 State Street, PO Box 9101,
Framingham MA 01701-9101
County: Middlesex
FICE Identification: 002185
Unit ID: 165866
Telephone: (508) 620-1220
Carnegie Class: Master's L
FAX Number: (508) 626-4592
Calendar System: Semester
URL: www.framingham.edu
Established: 1839
Annual Undergrad Tuition & Fees (In-State): $7,580
Enrollment: 5,953
Coed
Affiliation or Control: State
IRS Status: 501(c)3
Highest Offering: Master's
Program: Liberal Arts And General; Teacher Preparatory
Accreditation: EH, DIETC, DIETD, NURSE

02 President ... Dr. Timothy J. FLANAGAN
03 Executive Vice President ... Dr. Dale M. HAMEL
05 Vice President Academic Affairs ... Dr. Linda VADEN-GOAD
84 Vice Pres Enrollment & Student Dev ... Dr. Susanne H. CONLEY
30 Vice Pres Univ Advancement ... Mr. Christopher HENDRY
100 Chief of Staff/General Counsel ... Ms. Rita COLUCCI
20 Assoc Vice Pres Academic Affairs ... Dr. Ellen ZIMMERMAN
20 Assoc Vice President and Dean ... Dr. Scott B. GREENBERG
13 Assoc Vice President & CITO ... Mr. Patrick LAUGHRAN
07 Dean of Admissions ... Mr. Jeremy SPENCER
32 Dean of Student Affairs ... Dr. Melinda K. STOOPS
39 Assoc Dean & Dir Residence Life ... Mr. Glenn COCHRAN
28 Assoc Dean & Dir Multicultural ... Mr. David N. BALDWIN
88 Asst Dean & Director of Advising ... Dr. Christopher GREGORY
15 Assoc Director of Human Resources ... Ms. Erin NECHIPURENKO
09 Chief Inst Research Officer ... Ms. Ann CASO
19 Chief Public Safety Police Services ... Mr. Brad MEDEIROS
88 Director of Academic Support ... Ms. LaDonna BRIDGES
91 Director Student Info Systems ... Ms. Marsha BRYAN
29 Assistant Director Alumni Relations ... Mr. Robert WALMSLEY
41 Director of Athletics ... Mr. Thomas KELLEY
18 Director Capital Plng & Facil Ops ... Mr. Warren FAIRBANKS
36 Director Career Services ... Mr. Rich DAVINO
106 Director of Education Technology ... Ms. Robin ROBINSON
37 Director Financial Aid ... Ms. Susan LANZILLO
21 Director Financial Services ... Mr. Joseph P. CALAPA
89 Director First Year Programs ... Mr. Benjamin J. TRAPANICK
23 Director of Health Services ... Ms. Ilene HOFRENNING
104 Director International Education ... Ms. Jane DECATUR
90 Director of User Services ... Ms. Deborah MOSCHELLA
08 Director of Library Services ... Mrs. Bonnie MITCHELL
38 Director Counseling Center ... Dr. Paul WELCH
35 Director Student Involvement ... Ms. Rachel LUCKING
06 Registrar ... Mr. Mark R. POWERS
88 Director of Student Accounts ... Ms. Deborah DALTON
44 Director of Annual Giving ... Ms. Maria QUIRAY
04 Special Assistant to the President ... Ms. Kathleen BROSNIHAN
86 External Relations/Communications ... Mr. Daniel MAGAZU
88 Network and Telecom ... Mr. Michael ZINKUS

*Massachusetts College of Art and Design (E)

621 Huntington Avenue, Boston MA 02115-5882
County: Suffolk
FICE Identification: 002180
Unit ID: 166674
Telephone: (617) 879-7000
Carnegie Class: Spec/Arts
FAX Number: (617) 566-4034
Calendar System: Semester
URL: www.massart.edu
Established: 1873
Annual Undergrad Tuition & Fees (In-State): $9,700
Enrollment: 2,012
Coed
Affiliation or Control: State
IRS Status: 501(c)3
Highest Offering: Master's
Program: Teacher Preparatory; Professional
Accreditation: EH, ART

02 President ... Ms. Dawn BARRETT
05 Senior Vice Pres Academic Affairs ... Dr. Maureen KELLY
10 Vice Pres Finance/CFO ... Mr. Kurt STEINBERG
32 Vice President Student Development ... Dr. Maureen KEEFE
30 Vice Pres Institutional Advancement ... Mr. Hunter O'HANIAN
09 Assoc VP of Planning/Research ... Ms. Kathleen KEENAN
20 Associate VP Academic Affairs ... Ms. Michele FURST
21 Asst Vice Pres of Fiscal Affairs ... Mr. Donald ARPINO
100 Exec Assistant to the President ... Ms. Julianne WALSH
86 Asst to Pres Government/Cmty Rels ... Mr. Robert CHAMBERS
07 Dean of Admissions ... Ms. Karen TOWNSEND
35 Dean Students/Multi-Cultural Affrs ... Dr. Jamie COSTELLO
58 Dean Graduate Programs ... Mr. George CREAMER
06 Registrar ... Mr. Frank CALLAHAN
37 Director of Financial Aid ... Mr. Aurelio RAMIREZ
88 Dir Curatorial Pgms/Prof Galleries ... Ms. Lisa TUNG
08 Director Library ... Mr. Paul DOBBS
16 Director Human Resources ... Ms. Elaine O'SULLIVAN
26 Director of Communications ... Ms. Darlene GILLAN
22 Dir Civil Rights Compliance/Dvrsty ... Ms. Mercedes EVANS
18 Director Facilities/Physical Plant ... Mr. Howie LAROSEE
96 Director of Administrative Services ... Mr. James MCDAID
27 Chief Information Officer ... Mr. Eric BIRD
88 Director of Public Art ... Mr. Jeffrey KEOUGH
29 Director of Alumni Relations ... Ms. Emily FOSTER-DAY
26 Exec Dir Marketing/Communications ... Ms. Ana DAVIS

*Massachusetts College of Liberal Arts (F)

375 Church Street, North Adams MA 01247-4100
County: Berkshire
FICE Identification: 002187
Unit ID: 167288
Telephone: (413) 662-5000
Carnegie Class: Bac/A&S
FAX Number: (413) 662-5010
Calendar System: Semester
URL: www.mcla.edu
Established: 1894
Annual Undergrad Tuition & Fees (In-State): $8,075
Enrollment: 1,974
Coed
Affiliation or Control: State
IRS Status: 501(c)3
Highest Offering: Master's
Program: Liberal Arts And General; Teacher Preparatory; Professional
Accreditation: EH

02 President ... Dr. Mary K. GRANT
05 VP Academic Affairs ... Dr. Cynthia F. BROWN
10 VP Administration & Finance ... Dr. James M. STAKENAS
84 VP Enrollment & External Relations ... Ms. Denise RICHARDELLO
30 Chief Advancement Officer ... Ms. Marianne DRAKE
32 Dean of Students ... Ms. Charlotte DEGEN
20 Dean Academic Affairs ... Dr. Monica JOSLIN
04 Executive Assistant to President ... Mr. Thomas BERNARD
26 Coord of Marketing & Communications ... Ms. Bernadette LUPO
27 Chief Information Officer ... Mr. Mark BERMAN
21 Treasurer ... Mr. Gerald DESMARAIS
45 Assoc Dean Assessment & Planning ... Dr. Kristina BENDIKAS
08 Assoc Dean Library Services ... Ms. Maureen HORAK
90 Assoc Dean Information Technology ... Mr. Peter ALLMAKER
06 Asst Dean Enrollment Services ... Mr. Steven KING
35 Asst Dean of Students ... Ms. Theresa M. O'BRYANT

37 Director Financial Aid .... Ms. Elizabeth PETRI
39 Director Residential Programs .... Ms. Dianne M. MANNING
41 Director Athletics .... Mr. Scott NICHOLS
21 Director Student Accounts/
Bursar .... Ms. Jennifer MACKSEY-ETHIER
44 Dir Annual Fund & Alumni Relations .... Ms. Jocelyn MERRICK
36 Director Career Services .... Ms. Sharron ZAVATTARO
23 Director Health Services .... Ms. JoAnn TIERNEY
15 Director Human Resources .... Ms. Marilyn C. TRUSKOWSKI
19 Director Public Safety .... Mr. Joseph CHARON
07 Assoc Director Admissions .... Mr. Joshua MENDEL
09 Staff Asst Institutional Research .... Mr. Jason G. CANALES
28 Coord ALANA & International Program . Mr. Thomas ALEXANDER

Massachusetts Maritime Academy (A)

101 Academy Drive, Buzzards Bay MA 02532-3400
County: Barnstable — FICE Identification: 002181
Unit ID: 166692
Telephone: (508) 830-5000 — Carnegie Class: Bac/Diverse
FAX Number: (508) 830-5004 — Calendar System: Semester
URL: www.maritime.edu
Established: 1891 — Annual Undergrad Tuition & Fees (In-State): $6,951
Enrollment: 1,296 — Coed
Affiliation or Control: State — IRS Status: 501(c)3
Highest Offering: Master's
Program: Professional
Accreditation: EH

02 President .... RADM. R. G. GURNON
05 Vice President/Dean .... CAPT. Brad LIMA
26 Vice Pres External Relations .... Mr. Michael A. JOYCE
30 Vice Pres Advancement .... Ms. Holly KNIGHT
32 Dean of Students .... CAPT. Edward ROZAK
36 Assoc Dir Career/Professional Svcs ... CDR. Maryanne RICHARDS
84 Director Enrollment Management ..... CAPT. Elizabeth STEVENSON
06 Director Student Records/Registrar .... Mr. Michael CUFF
08 Director Library .... Ms. Susan BERTEAUX
15 Director Personnel Services .... Mrs. Elizabeth BENWAY
18 Chief Facilities/Physical Plant .... Mr. Paul O'KEEFE
21 Associate Business Officer .... Mrs. Rose CASS
26 Chief Public Relations Officer .... Mr. Christopher RYAN
29 Director Alumni Relations .... Ms. Kristine ESDALE
37 Director Student Financial Aid .... Mrs. Cathy KEDSKI
96 Director of Purchasing .... Mr. Brian CHURCHILL

Salem State University (B)

352 Lafayette Street, Salem MA 01970-5353
County: Essex — FICE Identification: 002188
Unit ID: 167729
Telephone: (978) 542-6000 — Carnegie Class: Master's L
FAX Number: (978) 542-6970 — Calendar System: Semester
URL: www.salemstate.edu
Established: 1854 — Annual Undergrad Tuition & Fees (In-State): $7,960
Enrollment: 9,993 — Coed
Affiliation or Control: State — IRS Status: 501(c)3
Highest Offering: Master's
Program: Liberal Arts And General; Teacher Preparatory; Professional
Accreditation: EH, ART, CS, MUS, NMT, NURSE, OT, SW, TED, THEA

02 President .... Dr. Patricia M. MESERVEY
03 Executive Vice President .... Dr. Stanley CAHILL
05 Provost & Academic VP .... Dr. Kristin ESTERBERG
10 VP Finance & Facilities .... Mr. Andy SOLL
30 VP Institutional Advancement .... Ms. Cynthia MCGURREN
08 Dean Library & Instr/Learning Supp .... Dr. Susan CIRILLO
70 Dean School of Human Services .... Dr. Neal DECHILLO
50 Dean School of Business .... Dr. K. Brewer DORAN
58 Dean Graduate School .... Dr. Carol A. GLOD
51 Dean Continuing Education .... Dr. Arlene T. GREENSTEIN
49 Dean School of Arts & Sciences .... Dr. Jude NIXON
26 Assoc VP Marketing & Communications .... Ms. Karen CADY
21 Assoc VP Financial Svcs .... Mr. Joseph DONOVAN
84 Assoc VP Enrollment Management .... Dr. Scott JAMES
32 Assoc VP & Dean of Student Life .... Dr. James G. STOLL
15 Assistant VP for HR&EEO .... Ms. Beth MARSHALL
44 Asst VP Alumni Affairs/Annual Giv .... Ms. Eileen O'BRIEN
13 CIO Information Technology Svcs .... Mrs. Patricia AINSWORTH
19 Director Public Safety .... Mr. William G. ANGLIN
86 Special Assistant to President .... Ms. Beth BOWER
100 Exec Asst to President/Secy to BOT .... Ms. Jean FLEISCHMAN
41 Director Athletics .... Mr. Timothy P. SHEA

*Westfield State University (C)

577 Western Avenue, Westfield MA 01086-1630
County: Hampden — FICE Identification: 002189
Unit ID: 168263
Telephone: (413) 572-5300 — Carnegie Class: Master's M
FAX Number: (413) 572-8147 — Calendar System: Semester
URL: www.westfield.ma.edu
Established: 1838 — Annual Undergrad Tuition & Fees (In-State): $7,886
Enrollment: 5,868 — Coed
Affiliation or Control: State — IRS Status: 501(c)3
Highest Offering: Beyond Master's But Less Than Doctorate
Program: Liberal Arts And General; Teacher Preparatory
Accreditation: EH, MUS, CS, EXSC, SW, TED

02 President .... Dr. Evan S. DOBELLE
05 Vice Pres Academic Affairs .... Dr. Elizabeth PRESTON
32 Vice Pres Student Affairs .... Dr. Carlton PICKRON
84 Vice Pres Enrollment Management .... Dr. Carol PERSSON
10 Vice Pres Administration & Finance .... Mr. Jerry HAYES
30 Vice Pres Advancement/College Rels ..... Hon. Kenneth LEMANSKI
20 Dean of Faculty .... Dr. Andrew BONACCI
49 Dean of Undergraduate Programs .... Dr. Marsha MAROTTA
51 Dean Graduate/Continuing Educ .... Dr. Kimberly TOBIN
53 Dean of Education .... Dr. Cheryl STANLEY
35 Dean Student Affairs .... Ms. Susan LAMONTAGNE
06 Registrar .... Mr. John OHOTNICKY
09 Assoc Dean Institutional Reseach .... Dr. Lisa PLANTEFABER
22 Director Multicult Affairs/AA/EO .... Ms. Waleska LUGO-DEJESUS
08 Director Library .... Mr. Thomas RAFFENSPERGER
11 Asst Vice Pres Administration .... Dr. Curt D. ROBIE
39 Exec Director Residential Life .... Dr. Jon CONLOGUE
19 Interim Director Public Safety .... Mr. Michael NOCKUNAS
27 Asst to President Communications .... Mr. Robert PLASSE
36 Director Career Services .... Mr. Junior DELGADO
13 Exec Dir Information Technology .... Mr. Christopher HIRTLE
91 Director Admin Systems .... Mr. Rudolph HEBERT
44 Associate VP Advancement/College .... Mr. Don BOWMAN
18 Asst Dir Facilities/Physical Plant .... Mr. Terry FENSTAD
41 Director Athletics .... Mr. Richard LENFEST
24 Director Media Services .... Mr. Robert MAILLOUX
38 Director Counseling Center .... Ms. Tammy BRINGAZE
23 Director Health Services .... Ms. Patricia BERUBE
37 Director of Financial Aid .... Ms. Catherine RYAN
07 Director of Admissions .... Dr. Kelly HART
21 Director Administrative Services .... Ms. Elizabeth MOKRZECKI
21 Director of Finance .... Ms. Lisa FREEMAN
29 Assoc VP Alumni Relations .... Ms. Nanci SALVIDIO
96 Director of Purchasing .... Mr. Chris RAYMOND
16 Director of Human Resources .... Mr. Rafael BONES
102 Director of Corporate Relations .... Mr. Olen BIELSKI
25 Director Faculty Grants Spons Rsrch .... Ms. Louann D'ANGELO

*Worcester State University (D)

486 Chandler Street, Worcester MA 01602-2597
County: Worcester — FICE Identification: 002190
Unit ID: 168430
Telephone: (508) 929-8000 — Carnegie Class: Master's M
FAX Number: (508) 929-8191 — Calendar System: Semester
URL: www.worcester.edu
Established: 1874 — Annual Undergrad Tuition & Fees (In-State): $7,725
Enrollment: 5,708 — Coed
Affiliation or Control: State — IRS Status: 501(c)3
Highest Offering: Master's
Program: Occupational; Liberal Arts And General; Teacher Preparatory; Professional
Accreditation: EH, NMT, NURSE, OT, SP

02 President .... Mr. Barry M. MALONEY
05 Provost/Vice President Academic Aff .... Dr. Charles CULLUM
10 Vice President of Fiscal Affairs .... Ms. Kathleen EICHELROTH
32 Vice President Student Affairs .... Dr. Sibyl M. BROWNLEE
30 Vice Pres Institutional Advancement .... Mr. Thomas MCNAMARA
04 Exec Assistant to the President .... Ms. Judith A. ST. AMAND
58 Assoc VP CE/Out & Dean Grad Stds .... Dr. William H. WHITE
93 Asst Dean/Dir Multicultural
Affairs .... Ms. Marcela A. URIBE-JENNINGS
55 Assoc Dean of Graduate/Cont Educ .... Dr. Roberta KYLE
22 Director of Affirmative Action .... Dr. Calvin HILL
13 Vice President Information Technogy . Dr. Donald W. VESCIO, JR.
20 Asst VP for Assessment & Planning .... Dr. Carol LERCH
20 Assoc Vice President for
Academics .... Dr. Maureen SHAMGOCHIAN
35 Associate VP/Dean of Students .... Ms. Julie KAZARIAN
21 Assoc VP for Fiscal Affairs .... Ms. Robin QUILL
17 Exec Dir Center for Health Profess .... Vacant
07 Director of Admissions .... Ms. Beth AXELSON
26 Asst VP of PR/Marketing .... Ms. Lea Ann ERICKSON
37 Director of Financial Aid .... Ms. Jayne MCGINN
08 Director Library .... Dr. Donald HOCHSTETLER
18 Director of Facilities .... Ms. Sandra OLSON
15 Director Human Resources .... Mr. Russell E. VICKSTROM
19 Chief of Campus Police .... Ms. Rosemary NAUGHTON
27 Director Publications/Printing Svcs .... Vacant
36 Director Career Services .... Ms. Marcia EAGLESON
06 Registrar .... Ms. Julie CHAFEE
41 Director Athletics & Rec Sports .... Ms. Susan E. CHAPMAN
39 Assistant Director of Life/Housing .... Mr. James MOURNIGHAN
35 Dir Student Center/Stdnt Activities .... Mr. Timothy J. SULLIVAN
38 Director Student Counseling .... Ms. Laura BRUNELLE
42 Chaplain .... Fr. Robert LOFTUS
85 Int Dir of International Students .... Ms. Katey PALUMBO
96 Director of Procurement/Bus Mgr .... Ms. Brenda BUSSEY
88 Manager of Student Accounts .... Ms. Julie CARMEL
09 Director of Institutional Research .... Mr. Kenneth SMITH

*Berkshire Community College (E)

1350 West Street, Pittsfield MA 01201-5786
County: Berkshire — FICE Identification: 002167
Unit ID: 164775
Telephone: (413) 499-4660 — Carnegie Class: Assoc/Pub-R-M
FAX Number: (413) 447-7840 — Calendar System: Semester
URL: www.berkshirecc.edu
Established: 1960 — Annual Undergrad Tuition & Fees (In-State): $5,965
Enrollment: 2,730 — Coed
Affiliation or Control: State — IRS Status: 501(c)3
Highest Offering: Associate Degree
Program: Occupational; 2-Year Principally Bachelor's Creditable
Accreditation: EH, ADNUR, PTAA

02 President .... Dr. Paul E. RAVERTA
05 Vice President for Academic Affairs .... Dr. Frances FEINERMAN
10 Vice President Admin/Finance .... Ms. Ellen KENNEDY
32 Vice Pres Student Affs/Enroll Svcs .... Mr. Michael BULLOCK
30 Vice Pres Institutional Advancement .... Mr. Jeffrey DOSCHER
79 Dean Humanities .... Mr. Thomas CURLEY
54 Dean Engineering/Sciences .... Dr. Charles KAMINSKI
66 Dean Nursing/Allied Hlth .... Ms. Anna FOSS
103 VP Lifelong Lrng/Workforce Dev .... Mr. William MULHOLLAND
37 Director Student Financial Aid .... Ms. Anne MOORE
13 Director Information Technology .... Mr. Richard WIXSOM
06 Registrar .... Mr. Donald PFEIFER
08 Director of Library .... Ms. Nancy WALKER
15 VP Human Res/Affirm Action Officer .... Ms. Deborah COTE
88 Student Advisor Transfer .... Mr. Geoff TABOR
26 Director Public Relations .... Ms. Christina BARRETT
12 Director of So County Center .... Ms. Phylene FARRELL
18 Director of Facilities .... Mr. Scott RICHARDS
40 Manager Bookstore .... Ms. Kristen SCALA
32 Director of Student Life .... Mr. Dane WESTED
24 Dir of Instructional Technology .... Vacant
09 Dir Institutional Rsrch/Plng/Grants .... Mr. John PASKUS
31 Dir Development/Community Outreach .... Ms. Jennifer KERWOOD

*Bristol Community College (F)

777 Elsbree Street, Fall River MA 02720-7395
County: Bristol — FICE Identification: 002176
Unit ID: 165033
Telephone: (508) 678-2811 — Carnegie Class: Assoc/Pub-U-MC
FAX Number: (508) 730-3270 — Calendar System: Semester
URL: www.bristolcc.edu
Established: 1965 — Annual Undergrad Tuition & Fees (In-State): $4,058
Enrollment: 8,893 — Coed
Affiliation or Control: State — IRS Status: 501(c)3
Highest Offering: Associate Degree
Program: Occupational; 2-Year Principally Bachelor's Creditable
Accreditation: EH, ADNUR, DH, MAC, MLTAD, OTA

02 President .... Dr. John J. SBREGA
03 Executive Vice President .... Mr. David F. FEENEY
05 Vice President of Academic Affairs .... Dr. Sarah GARRETT
50 Dean of Business & Info Tech .... Mr. William BERARDI
79 Dean of Humanities & Education .... Ms. Joanne PRESTON
83 Dean of Behavioral & Soc Sciences .... Dr. Vernon HARLAN
76 Dean of Health Sciences .... Ms. Patricia DENT
81 Dean of Math/Science & Engineering .... Dr. Peter SCHUYLER
10 VP of Administration & Finance .... Mr. Steven KENYON
30 VP of Resource Development .... Ms. Elizabeth K. MCCARTHY
84 VP of Students and Enrollment Mgt .... Mr. Steve OZUG
91 VP of Information Technology .... Ms. Jo-Ann M. PELLETIER
32 Director Student Engagement .... Ms. Kathleen BURNS
07 Dean of Admissions .... Mr. Rodney CLARK
12 Dean of New Bedford Campus .... Ms. Theresa ROMANOVITCH
12 Acting Dean of Attleboro Center . Ms. Kathy TORPEY GARGANTA
06 Registrar .... Mr. Milton CLEMENT
08 Assistant Dean of the Library .... Mr. Sainath CHINNASWAMY
25 Dean of Grant Development .... Ms. Marianne TAYLOR
37 Director Student Financial Aid .... Mr. David ALLEN
38 Director Counseling Services .... Mr. Michael BENSINK
15 VP of Human Resources/Affirm Action .... Mr. Tafa AWOLAJU
18 Director of Facilities Management .... Mr. Leo RACINE
19 Director of Public Safety .... Mr. Wayne WOOD
21 Comptroller .... Mr. Keith TONI
11 Associate VP of Administration .... Ms. Linda DANZELL
20 Assoc VP Academic Affairs .... Dr. Michael VIEIRA
20 Assoc VP of Academic Affairs .... Dr. Frederick ROCCO
84 Assoc VP Enrollment
Services .... Ms. Kathleen TORPEY GARGANTA
27 VP College Communications .... Ms. Sally C. CAMERON
29 Dir Alumni Relations/Special Events .... Ms. Jane L H. ASH
88 Dean Disability Svcs & Student
Engm .... Ms. Susan BOISSONEAULT
78 Director Coop Education .... Ms. Margaret (Peg) CURRO
50 Dean Center for Business & Industry .... Ms. Carmen AGUILAR
23 Health Services Coordinator .... Ms. Carol CONSTANTINE
56 Asst Dean Instructional Lrng Tech .... Ms. April BELLAFIORE
09 VP Inst Research/Plng & Assessment .. Ms. Rhonda GABOVITCH
92 Director Honors Program .... Mr. J. Thomas GRADY
96 Director of Purchasing .... Ms. Philicia PACHECO
36 Career Services - Sr Acad Counselor .... Ms. Patricia CONDON
41 Athletic Director .... Mr. Derek VIVEIROS
04 Executive Assistant to President .... Ms. Karen L. GIGLIO
88 Dean Developmental Educ .... Ms. Sarah MORRELL

*Bunker Hill Community College (G)

250 New Rutherford Avenue, Boston MA 02129-2925
County: Suffolk — FICE Identification: 011210
Unit ID: 165112
Telephone: (617) 228-2000 — Carnegie Class: Assoc/Pub-U-MC
FAX Number: (617) 228-2082 — Calendar System: Semester
URL: www.bhcc.mass.edu
Established: 1973 — Annual Undergrad Tuition & Fees (In-State): $3,384
Enrollment: 12,000 — Coed
Affiliation or Control: State — IRS Status: 501(c)3
Highest Offering: Associate Degree
Program: Occupational; 2-Year Principally Bachelor's Creditable
Accreditation: EH, ADNUR, DMS, RAD, SURGT

02 President .... Dr. Mary L. FIFIELD

03 Executive Vice President & CFO ....Mr. Jesse M. THOMPSON
05 VP Academic Affairs/Student Service ....Dr. James F. CANNIFF
28 Director Diversity & Inclusion .... Mr. Thomas L. SALTONSTALL
09 Exec Dean Inst Effectiveness ....Dr. Emily DIBBLE
20 Associate Academic Dean ....Ms. Judith GRAHAM
35 Dean of Students ....Ms. Janice M. BONANNO
26 Exec Director of Communications ....Dr. Colleen ROACH
18 Dir Facil Mgmt & Engineering Svcs ....Vacant
81 Dean of Mathematics/Behav Sciences ..... Dr. S. Leonard MHLABA
79 Dean of Humanities ....Ms. Lori A. CATALLOZZI
54 Dean Science/Engineering ....Dr. Laurie K. MCCORRY
107 Dean of Professional Studies ...... Dr. Bogusia WOJCIECHOWSKA
66 Dean Nurse Education ....Dr. Roxanne E. MIHAL
12 Dean Chelsea Campus ....Ms. MaryAnne MILLER
21 Comptroller ....Mr. Weusi A. TAFAWA
25 Director of Grants Development ....Mr. Steven A. ROLLER
06 Registrar ....Ms. Debra A. BOYER
08 Director Library/Info Center ....Vacant
91 Chief Information Officer ....Mr. Bret MOELLER
15 Dir Human Resources/Labor Relations .... Ms. Molly B. AMBROSE
19 Director of Public Safety ....Mr. Robert BARROWS
37 Director of Financial Aid ....Ms. Melissa HOLSTER
96 Director of Purchasing ....Mr. Richard J. PISHKIN
38 Dir Advising/Counseling/Assessment ....Ms. Anne BROWN
30 Executive Director of Development ....Ms. Anne HYDE

*Cape Cod Community College (A)

2240 Iyannough Road, West Barnstable MA 02668-1599
County: Barnstable FICE Identification: 002168
Unit ID: 165194
Telephone: (508) 362-2131 Carnegie Class: Assoc/Pub-R-M
FAX Number: (508) 362-3988 Calendar System: Semester
URL: www.capecod.edu
Established: 1960 Annual Undergrad Tuition & Fees (In-State): $4,792
Enrollment: 4,482 Coed
Affiliation or Control: State IRS Status: 501(c)3
Highest Offering: Associate Degree
Program: Occupational; 2-Year Principally Bachelor's Creditable
Accreditation: EH, ADNUR, DH, MAC

02 President ....Dr. Kathleen SCHATZBERG
05 Vice Pres Academic/Student Affairs ....Ms. Susan MILLER
10 Vice President Admin & Finance ....Ms. Dixie K. NORRIS
21 Asst VP Administration & Finance ....Ms. Cynthia CROSSMAN
18 Asst VP Sustainability/Facil Mgmt ....Mr. John LEBICA
13 Asst VP Information Technology ....Mr. Gregory BANWARTH
49 Dean Arts & Humanities ....Dr. Lore DEBOWER
81 Dean Science/Tech/Math/Business ....Vacant
08 Dean Learning Res & Student Success ....Mr. David ZIEMBA
84 Dean Enroll Mgmt/Advising Services ....Ms. Roseanna PENA-WARFIELD
83 Dean Health/Social Sci/Human Svcs ....Ms. Susan MADDIGAN
15 Dean Human Resources & Admin ....Mr. Chester W. YACEK
08 Assoc Dean Learning Resources ....Ms. Jeanmarie FRASER
07 Director Admissions ....Ms. Susan K. SYMINGTON
37 Director of Financial Aid ....Ms. Sherry ANDERSEN
27 Director College Communications ....Mr. Michael GROSS
06 Registrar ....Ms. Sandra BRITO
19 Director Public Safety ....Mr. Philip RYAN
04 Staff Assoc to President ....Ms. Linda HOULE
36 Coord Career Plng & Placement ....Ms. Kristina IERARDI
09 Dir Institutional Research & Effec ....Dr. Elizabeth O'CONNOR-JOHNSTON

*Greenfield Community College (B)

1 College Drive, Greenfield MA 01301-9739
County: Franklin FICE Identification: 002169
Unit ID: 165981
Telephone: (413) 775-1000 Carnegie Class: Assoc/Pub-S-SC
FAX Number: (413) 774-4676 Calendar System: Semester
URL: www.gcc.mass.edu
Established: 1962 Annual Undergrad Tuition & Fees (In-State): $5,238
Enrollment: 2,583 Coed
Affiliation or Control: State IRS Status: 501(c)3
Highest Offering: Associate Degree
Program: Occupational; 2-Year Principally Bachelor's Creditable
Accreditation: EH, ADNUR, COMTA

02 President ....Dr. Robert L. PURA
05 Chief Academic/Student Affairs Ofcr ....Mr. David RAM
10 Chief Financial Officer ....Mr. Barry BRAIM
45 Chief Inst Support/Advancement Ofcr ....Dr. Martha FIELD
31 Dean of Community Education ....Mr. Robert BARBA
84 Dean Enrollment Services ....Mr. Shane HAMMOND
20 Dean Learning Resources ....Ms. Judi GREENE-CORVEE
79 Dean Humanities ....Mr. Leo HWANG-CARLOS
81 Dean Soc & Nat Sci/Math/Bus/Tech ....Dr. Peter ROSNIK
76 Dean Professional Studies ....Dr. Terence LYNN
15 Executive Dir of Human Resources ....Dr. Rita HARDIMAN
30 Exec Director Resource Development ....Ms. Regina CURTIS
102 Executive Director Annual Giving ....Dr. Allen DAVIS
13 Chief Information Officer ....Mr. Michael ASSAF
28 Chief Diversity Officer ....Dr. Rita HARDIMAN
18 Director Physical Plant ....Mr. Jeffrey MARQUES
07 Director Admissions ....Mr. Herbert E. HENTZ
37 Director Financial Aid ....Ms. Linda DESJARDINS
19 Director Public Safety ....Mr. William MAYROSE
96 Director of Purchasing ....Mr. Ryan AIKEN
08 Director Library ....Ms. Deborah CHOWN
21 Comptroller ....Ms. Karen PHILLIPS

06 Registrar ....Ms. Heather HOYT
38 Co-Coord Learning Asst Programs ....Ms. Mary Ellen KELLY
38 Co-Coord Learning Asst Programs ....Mr. Norman BEEBE
36 Coordinator of Student Assessment ....Ms. Jean BOUCIAS
08 Coordinator Library ....Mr. Eric POULIN
23 Coordinator of Health Services ....Ms. Donna M. LARSON
35 Coordinator of Student Life ....Ms. Melissa EICH

*Holyoke Community College (C)

303 Homestead Avenue, Holyoke MA 01040-1099
County: Hampden FICE Identification: 002170
Unit ID: 166133
Telephone: (413) 538-7000 Carnegie Class: Assoc/Pub-S-SC
FAX Number: (413) 552-2045 Calendar System: Semester
URL: www.hcc.edu
Established: 1946 Annual Undergrad Tuition & Fees (In-State): $227
Enrollment: 7,325 Coed
Affiliation or Control: State IRS Status: 501(c)3
Highest Offering: Associate Degree
Program: Occupational; 2-Year Principally Bachelor's Creditable
Accreditation: EH, ACFEI, ADNUR, MUS, RAD

02 President ....Dr. William F. MESSNER
11 Vice Pres Administration & Finance ....Mr. William FOGARTY
05 Vice President Academic Affairs ....Dr. Matthew REED
32 Vice President Student Affairs ....Ms. Yanina VARGAS
30 Vice Pres Institutional Development ....Ms. Erica BROMAN
28 Assistant Vice Pres of Diversity ....Ms. Idelia SMITH
08 Interim Dean Library ....Ms. Kathleen MCDONOUGH
15 Dean Human Resources ....Ms. Clara ELLIOTT
36 Dean Coop Education & Career Svcs ....Dr. Theresa HOWARD
06 Registrar ....Mr. Anthony SBALBI
07 Director of Admissions ....Ms. Marcia ROSBURY-HENNE
37 Director of Financial Aid ....Ms. Karen DEROUIN
91 Director Administrative Computing ....Vacant
18 Director of Facilities ....Mr. Michael CICHONSKI
10 Comptroller ....Mr. Johan LETH-STEENSEN
13 Chief Information Officer ....Ms. Linda SZALANKIEWICZ
21 Dir Business Services/Purchasing ....Ms. Tara WOLMAN
09 Director Institutional Research ....Ms. Michelle RIBERDY
26 Dir of Marketing/Public Relations ....Ms. JoAnne ROME
29 Director of Alumni Relations ....Ms. Joanna BROWN
35 Dean of Student Services ....Vacant
20 Director of Academic Administration ....Ms. Idelia SMITH
38 Dir Retention & Adult Support Svcs ....Vacant

*Massachusetts Bay Community College (D)

50 Oakland Street, Wellesley Hills MA 02481-5357
County: Norfolk FICE Identification: 002171
Unit ID: 166647
Telephone: (781) 239-3000 Carnegie Class: Assoc/Pub-S-MC
FAX Number: (781) 237-1061 Calendar System: Semester
URL: www.massbay.edu
Established: 1961 Annual Undergrad Tuition & Fees (In-State): $4,600
Enrollment: 5,635 Coed
Affiliation or Control: State IRS Status: 501(c)3
Highest Offering: Associate Degree
Program: Occupational; 2-Year Principally Bachelor's Creditable
Accreditation: EH, ADNUR, COMTA, RAD, SURGT

02 President ....Dr. John O'DONNELL
05 Interim Provost/VP Academic Affairs ....Dr. Lisa GANSON
10 VP Admin & Finance/CFO ....Mr. Richard HASKELL
45 Int VP Planning & Inst Effectivens ....Dr. Lynn HUNTER
26 Associate VP for Public Affairs ....Mr. Jeremy SOLOMON
84 Asst Provost Enrol Mgt/Student Aff ....Ms. Marva PERRY
15 Assistant VP of Human Resources ... Ms. Robin NELSON-BAILEY
30 Director Institutional Advancement ....Mr. David FAULKNER
76 Dean Health Sciences Division ....Dr. JoAnn MACKEY
79 Dean Humanities Division ....Dr. David COLEMAN
88 Dean Transportation & Energy ....Mr. Howard FERRIS
107 Dean Social Sci & Profess Studies ....Dr. Jane O'BRIEN FRIEDERICHS
81 Dean STEM Division ....Dr. Hemant PENDHARKAR
55 Dean Evening & Weekend Programming .... Ms. Carol STAFFIER
09 Dean Inst Planning Res & Assessment ....Dr. Yves SALOMON-FERNÁNDEZ
51 Dean Corporate/Community Education ....Mr. Diego PORTILLO MAZAL
32 Dean of Students (Wellesley Hills) .... Dr. Elizabeth BLUMBERG
32 Dean of Students (Framingham) ....Mr. Craig MACK
07 Director of Admissions ....Ms. Donna RAPOSA
20 Director of Academic Advising ....Ms. Sarah READING
37 Director of Financial Aid ....Ms. Elizabeth ENOS
06 Registrar ....Mr. Ali GUVENDIREN
88 Interim Dir Acad Achievement Ctr ....Ms. Barbara HATCH
16 Director of Career Services ....Ms. Julie KOMACK
38 Director of Counseling ....Mr. Jon EDWARDS
85 Director of International Education ....Ms. Marie Lourdes ELGIRUS
90 Dir Ctr for Teaching & Learning ....Dr. Linda GRISHAM
08 Director of Learning Services ....Mr. Timothy RIVARD
41 Dir Athletics Recreat'n & Wellness ....Mr. Bill RAYNOR
35 Coordinator of Student Activities ....Ms. Julie SCHLEICHER
21 Controller ....Ms. Linda FAZIO
96 Budget Analyst/Purchasing Manager ....Mr. Kevin FLYNN
96 Purchasing Supervisor ....Ms. Lauren CURLEY
88 Director of Grants Development ....Dr. Cheryl WEST
13 Technical Director ....Mr. Michael LYONS
91 Director Administrative Computing ....Mr. Terry KRAMER

18 Director of Facilities ....Mr. Marco BRANCATO
19 Manager of Public Safety ....Ms. Deborah CRAFTS
04 Exec Assistant to the President ....Ms. Vivian ORTIZ

*Massasoit Community College (E)

1 Massasoit Boulevard, Brockton MA 02302-3996
County: Plymouth FICE Identification: 002177
Unit ID: 166823
Telephone: (508) 588-9100 Carnegie Class: Assoc/Pub-R-L
FAX Number: (508) 427-1202 Calendar System: Semester
URL: www.massasoit.mass.edu
Established: 1966 Annual Undergrad Tuition & Fees (In-State): $4,650
Enrollment: 8,053 Coed
Affiliation or Control: State IRS Status: 501(c)3
Highest Offering: Associate Degree
Program: Occupational; 2-Year Principally Bachelor's Creditable
Accreditation: EH, ADNUR, DA, MAC, RAD

02 President ....Dr. Charles WALL
05 Senior VP Faculty & Instruction .... Dr. Barbara E. FINKELSTEIN
10 Chief Financial Officer ....Ms. Betty Ann LEARNED
32 Vice Pres Student Svcs/Enroll Mgmt ....Mr. David TRACY
12 Vice Pres/Dean of Canton Campus ...... Mr. Nicholas PALANTZAS
15 VP & Director of Human Resources ....Mr. Peter AKEKE
04 Exec Dir Extrnl Affs/Asst to Pres ....Mr. Phillip SHEPPARD
26 Public Relations Director ....Ms. Laurie MAKER
84 Dean of Enrollment Management ....Vacant
35 Dean Student Affairs ....Ms. Maureen THAYER
07 Director of Admissions ....Ms. Michelle HUGHES
37 Director Student Financial Aid .... Ms. Mary Beth COURTRIGHT
06 Registrar ....Ms. Elizabeth COLLINS
09 Director of Institutional Research ....Ms. Mary GOODHUE LYNCH
38 Director Student Counseling ....Ms. Christine DYMENT
28 Director of Diversity ....Ms. Joyce ZYMARIS
13 CIO ....Mr. Albert B. AYERS
21 Comptroller ....Ms. Sophie LEE
36 Director of Career Placement ....Ms. Kathyrn PRYLES
18 Director Facilities/Physical Plant ....Mr. Rocco RICHARDI
41 Director of Athletics ....Ms. Julie MULVEY
29 Director Alumni Relations ....Ms. Sheryl SAVAGE
25 Director of Grants ....Ms. Hollyce STATES
50 Acting Dean Business & Technology .... Ms. Lynda THOMPSON
79 Dean Humanities/Social Science ....Ms. Deanna YAMEEN
76 Dean Allied Health ....Dr. Anne SCALZO-MCNEIL
83 Dean Public Svc/Social Science ....Ms. Karyn BOUTIN
81 Acting Dean Science & Math ....Ms. Fran MCCUTCHEON
72 Dean of Emergent Technologies ....Mr. Felix DEVITO
88 Dean of Academic Advising ....Mr. Peter JOHNSTON

*Middlesex Community College (F)

591 Springs Road, Bedford MA 01730-1197
County: Middlesex FICE Identification: 009936
Unit ID: 166887
Telephone: (781) 280-3200 Carnegie Class: Assoc/Pub-S-MC
FAX Number: (781) 275-0741 Calendar System: Semester
URL: www.middlesex.mass.edu
Established: 1969 Annual Undergrad Tuition & Fees (In-State): $4,200
Enrollment: 9,712 Coed
Affiliation or Control: State IRS Status: 501(c)3
Highest Offering: Associate Degree
Program: Occupational; 2-Year Principally Bachelor's Creditable
Accreditation: EH, ADNUR, DA, DH, DMS, DT, MAC, RAD

02 President ....Dr. Carole A. COWAN
05 Provost/VP of Academic Affairs ....Mr. Philip SISSON
11 VP for Administration/Finance ....Mr. James F. LINNEHAN, JR.
84 VP Enrollment Svcs/Rsrch & Plng ....Dr. Lois A. ALVES
04 Assistant to the President ....Ms. Lura SMITH
20 Associate Provost ....Ms. Clea ANDREADIS
32 Dean of Students ....Ms. Pamela FLAHERTY
88 Dean of International Arts ....Mr. Kent H. MITCHELL
79 Dean Humanities/Soc Sci/Cmty Engage ....Mr. Matthew OLSON
72 Dean of Business/Engineering/Tech ....Ms. Judith HOGAN
17 Dean of Health Careers ....Ms. Kathleen J. SWEENEY
24 Dean of Academic Resources Div ....Mr. Michael BADOLATO
36 Int Exec Director Career Placement . Mr. Christopher J. BRENNAN
88 Dean Professional/Instructional Dev ....Ms. Mary Anne DEAN
22 Dean Multicult Affairs/Affirm Act ....Ms. Darcy ORELLANA
12 Dean of Lowell Campus ....Dr. Molly H. SHEEHY
12 Dean Fac Mgmt/Bedford Campus Mgr ....Mr. Matt SEPE
84 Dean of Enrollment Services ....Ms. Eileen M. FAGAN
26 Dean External Affs/Col Advancement ....Mr. Dennis MALVERS
07 Dean of Admissions ....Ms. Marilynn GALLAGAN
60 Dean College Communication ....Ms. Brenda C. LOUCKS
35 Associate Dean of Student Life ....Vacant
09 Assoc Dean Institutional Planning ....Vacant
16 Director Human Resources ....Mr. Gary R. MCPHEE
37 Director of Financial Aid ....Mr. Robert BAUMAL
21 Director of Financial Affairs ....Ms. Kathy RICH
21 Bursar ....Mr. Christopher FIORI
08 Director Library Services ....Ms. Maryann NILES
23 Director of Health Services ....Ms. Dorothy J. O'CONNELL
15 Director Human Resources ....Mr. Gary MCPHEE
06 Registrar ....Mr. Kevin GATELY
96 Coordinator of Purchasing ....Ms. Maureen HUDSON

*Mount Wachusett Community College (G)

444 Green Street, Gardner MA 01440-1000
County: Worcester FICE Identification: 002172
Unit ID: 166957

Telephone: (978) 632-6600 Carnegie Class: Assoc/Pub-R-M
FAX Number: (978) 632-6155 Calendar System: Semester
URL: www.mwcc.mass.edu
Established: 1963 Annual Undergrad Tuition & Fees (In-State): $5,840
Enrollment: 4,893 Coed
Affiliation or Control: State IRS Status: 501(c)3
Highest Offering: Associate Degree
Program: Occupational; 2-Year Principally Bachelor's Creditable; Business Emphasis
Accreditation: EH, ADNUR, DH, MAC, MLTAD, PNUR, PTAA

02 President ... Dr. Daniel M. ASQUINO
03 Exec VP & VP of Enrollment Services ... Ms. Ann M. MCDONALD
05 Vice Pres of Academic Affairs ... Dr. Melissa FAMA
51 VP Lifelong Learning/Workforce Dev ... Ms. Jacqueline FELDMAN
26 Sr VP Advancement & External Affs ... Ms. Sharyn RICE
30 Assoc VP Institutional Advancement ... Mr. Joseph STISO
11 VP Finance & Administration ... Mr. Robert LABONTE
15 VP HR/Affirmative Action Officer ... Ms. Diane RUKSNAITIS
12 Dean Leominster Campus ... Mr. John WALSH
79 Dean School of Liberal Arts/Math ... Dr. Vincent BATES
72 Dean Academic & Inst Technology ... Mr. Vincent IALENTI
76 Dean School of Health Sciences ... Ms. Eileen COSTELLO
08 Dean Library and Academic Support ... Ms. Heidi MCCANN
36 Dir North Central Career Services ... Ms. Cynthia KRUSEN
27 Director of Marketing ... Ms. Nichole CARTER
07 Director of Admissions ... Vacant
18 Director Maintenance/Mechanical Sys ... Mr. William SWIFT
09 Dir Institutional Research ... Ms. Veena DHANKHER
37 Dir Student Records/Financial Mgmt ... Vacant
68 Director Fitness & Wellness Center ... Mr. Stephen WASHKEVICH
19 Chief Public Safety & Security ... Ms. Karen KOLIMAGA
35 Assistant Dean of Student Services ... Mr. Gregory CLEMENT
38 Director of Counseling ... Vacant
84 Assoc Dean Enrollment Services ... Mr. Glenn ROBERTS
29 Dir Alumni Affairs/Annual Giving ... Vacant
06 Registrar ... Ms. Rebecca FOREST

North Shore Community College (A)

1 Ferncroft Road, PO Box 3340, Danvers MA 01923-0840
County: Essex FICE Identification: 002173
Unit ID: 167312
Telephone: (978) 762-4000 Carnegie Class: Assoc/Pub-S-MC
FAX Number: (978) 762-4020 Calendar System: Semester
URL: www.northshore.edu
Established: 1965 Annual Undergrad Tuition & Fees (In-State): $3,888
Enrollment: 7,985 Coed
Affiliation or Control: State IRS Status: 501(c)3
Highest Offering: Associate Degree
Program: Occupational; 2-Year Principally Bachelor's Creditable
Accreditation: EH, AAB, ADNUR, MAC, OTA, PTAA, RAD, SURGT

02 President ... Dr. Wayne M. BURTON
05 Vice President of Academic Affairs ... Mr. Paul M. FRYDRYCH
84 Vice Pres Enrollment Mgmt/Students ... Dr. Donna L. RICHEMOND
30 Vice Pres Institutional Advancement ... Dr. Sandra B. EDWARDS
11 Vice President of Administration ... Ms. Janice M. FORSSTROM
15 Vice President Human Res/Affirm Act ... Ms. Madeline WALLIS
31 Dean of Community Svcs/Corp Ed ... Ms. Dianne PALTER-GILL
90 Dean Academic Technology ... Ms. Tina LEMOI
84 Dean of Enrollment ... Dr. Joanne LIGHT
32 Dean of Students ... Dr. Lloyd A. HOLMES
20 Assistant Dean Academic Affairs ... Dr. Laura VENTIMIGLIA
08 Director of Learning Resources ... Ms. Karen PANGALLO
14 Dir of Networking/Info Services ... Mr. Gary HAM
37 Dean of Financial Aid ... Mr. Stephen CREAMER
09 Director Inst Research/Planning ... Ms. Laurie LACHAPELLE
18 Director of Facilities Mgmt ... Mr. Richard RENEY
19 Campus Police Chief ... Mr. Douglas P. PUSKA
21 Comptroller ... Ms. Helen CLEMENTS
26 Director Public Relations/Marketing ... Ms. Linda BRANTLY
29 Director Alumni Relations ... Ms. Sandra ROCHON
35 Chief Student Life Officer ... Ms. Lisa MILSO
36 Director Student Placement ... Ms. Lynn MARCUS
07 Director of Recruitment ... Ms. Jennifer KIRK
38 Director Student Support Center ... Mr. Daniel O'NEILL
40 Bookstore Manager ... Mr. Shawn CRONIN

*Northern Essex Community College (B)

100 Elliott Street, Haverhill MA 01830-2399
County: Essex FICE Identification: 002174
Unit ID: 167376
Telephone: (978) 556-3000 Carnegie Class: Assoc/Pub-S-MC
FAX Number: (978) 556-3723 Calendar System: Semester
URL: www.necc.mass.edu
Established: 1960 Annual Undergrad Tuition & Fees (In-State): $4,410
Enrollment: 7,439 Coed
Affiliation or Control: State IRS Status: 501(c)3
Highest Offering: Associate Degree
Program: Occupational; 2-Year Principally Bachelor's Creditable; Fine Arts Emphasis
Accreditation: EH, ADNUR, DA, MAC, PNUR, POLYT, RAD

02 President ... Dr. Lane A. GLENN
30 Vice Pres Institutional Advancement ... Ms. Jean C. POTH
05 Vice President of Academic Affairs ... Dr. William HEINEMAN
84 Exec VP Enroll Mgmt/Student Svcs ... Ms. Mary Ellen ASHLEY
11 Vice President of Administration ... Mr. David GINGERELLA
103 Dean Workforce Devel/Continuing Ed ... Mr. Kelly OSMER
27 Chief Information Officer ... Mr. Jeffrey BICKFORD
12 Dean of Lawrence Campus ... Ms. Mary Ellen ASHLEY
15 Dean of Human Resources ... Mr. Stephen W. FABBRUCCI
09 Dean of Institutional Research ... Mr. Thomas FALLON
44 Assistant Dean of Development ... Ms. Wendy SHAFFER
38 Asst Dean/Dir Counseling Center ... Vacant
07 Assoc VP Enroll Svcs/Admissions ... Ms. Nora SHERIDAN
06 Registrar ... Vacant
37 Director of Financial Aid ... Ms. Brittany DEBITY
26 Director of Public Relations ... Ms. Ernestine GREENSLADE
29 Director Alumni Relations ... Ms. Libby JENSEN
32 Chief Student Life Officer ... Ms. Nita LAMBORGHINI
35 Director Student Affairs ... Ms. Dina BROWN
18 Chief Facilities/Physical Plant ... Mr. Richard GOULET
96 Director of Purchasing ... Vacant

*Quinsigamond Community College (C)

670 W Boylston Street, Worcester MA 01606-2092
County: Worcester FICE Identification: 002175
Unit ID: 167534
Telephone: (508) 853-2300 Carnegie Class: Assoc/Pub-U-SC
FAX Number: (508) 852-6943 Calendar System: Semester
URL: www.qcc.mass.edu
Established: 1963 Annual Undergrad Tuition & Fees (In-State): $5,340
Enrollment: 8,922 Coed
Affiliation or Control: State IRS Status: 501(c)3
Highest Offering: Associate Degree
Program: Occupational; 2-Year Principally Bachelor's Creditable; Business Emphasis
Accreditation: EH, ADNUR, DA, DH, MAC, OTA, PNUR, RAD, SURGT

02 President ... Dr. Gail E. CARBERRY
05 Vice President of Academic Affairs ... Ms. Patricia A. TONEY
11 Vice President of Administration ... Mr. Todd C. EMMONS
32 Vice Pres Enrollment/Student Svcs ... Mr. Stephen B. SULLIVAN
26 Vice Pres of Community Engagement ... Mr. Dale ALLEN
88 Asst VP to the President & Trustees ... Ms. Susan LAPRADE
20 Assistant VP Academic Affairs ... Ms. Jane SHEA
04 Executive Assistant to President ... Ms. Patricia A. SOLITRO
21 Comptroller ... Ms. Debra A. LAFLASH
81 Dean Instruction Math/Social Sci ... Mr. James BROWN
79 Dean Humanities ... Ms. Nicole CURRIER
76 Dn Instruction Health Care/Hum Svcs ... Dr. Jane JUNE
84 Assoc VP of Enrollment Management ... Ms. Iris GODES
15 Assoc VP of Human Resources ... Mr. William DARING
06 Associate Dean/Registrar ... Ms. Tara F. JENKINS
62 Dean of Library Services ... Ms. Andrea MACRITCHIE
42 Campus Minister ... Vacant
09 Director of Institutional Research ... Dr. Ingrid SKADBERG
07 Director of Admissions ... Ms. Michelle TUFAU-AFRIYIE
13 Chief Technology Officer ... Mr. Ken DWYER
26 Director of Public Affs ... Mr. Victor SOMMA
35 Director Student Life ... Mr. Jonathan MILLER
18 Director of Facilities ... Mr. Donny HALL
37 Director Student Financial Aid ... Ms. Paula OGDEN
96 Director of Purchasing ... Ms. Paula CAREY
19 Director Of Public Safety ... Mr. Kevin RITACCO
28 Director of Diversity ... Vacant
29 Director Alumni Relations ... Vacant
88 Director of Institutuinal Communica ... Mr. Joshua MARTIN
22 Director Affirm Action/Equal Opp ... Ms. Anita BOWDEN
38 Coordinator Student Counseling ... Ms. Karen COX

*Roxbury Community College (D)

1234 Columbus Avenue,
Roxbury Crossing MA 02120-3423
County: Suffolk FICE Identification: 011930
Unit ID: 167631
Telephone: (617) 427-0060 Carnegie Class: Assoc/Pub-S-MC
FAX Number: (617) 541-5351 Calendar System: Semester
URL: rcc.mass.edu
Established: 1973 Annual Undergrad Tuition & Fees (In-State): $3,962
Enrollment: 2,672 Coed
Affiliation or Control: State IRS Status: 501(c)3
Highest Offering: Associate Degree
Program: Occupational; 2-Year Principally Bachelor's Creditable
Accreditation: EH, ADNUR, RAD

02 President ... Dr. Terrence A. GOMES
04 Executive Asst to the President ... Ms. Shirley Y. LESLIE
05 Vice President of Academic Affairs ... Dr. Brenda W. MERCOMES
10 Vice President of Admin & Finance ... Dr. Alane K. SHANKS
84 VP Enrollment Mgmt/Student Affairs ... Dr. Stephanie C. JANEY
13 Chief Information Tech Officer ... Mr. Patrick JEAN-LOUIS
81 Dean of Science/Tech/Eng/Math ... Dr. Tala KHUDAIRI
66 Dean of Health Sciences ... Dr. Gloria H. CATER
49 Dean of Liberal Arts ... Dr. Nancy A. TEEL
09 Dean of Inst Research & Planning ... Mr. Mike WALKER
90 Dean of Academic Technology ... Ms. Jenene COOK
07 Dean of Enroll Mgmt/Stdnt Jud Affs ... Mr. Walter CLARK
88 Dean of Student Success ... Mr. Mark GARTH
51 Asst Dean Continuing Education ... Mr. Morisset ST. PREUX
20 Assoc Dean of Academic Affairs ... Dr. Jose ALICEA
41 Director of RLTAC & Athletics ... Mr. A. Keith MCDERMOTT
29 Director of Alumni Affairs ... Ms. Carol BLISS-FURR
Comptroller ... Mr. Chuks OKOLI
21 Budget Director ... Mr. Craig ZAEHRING
88 Bursar ... Ms. Nicole V. KULIG
37 Director Financial Aid ... Mr. Raymond O'ROURKE
08 Director of Library ... Mr. Mark LAWRENCE
23 Director of Health Services ... Ms. Ruth HINES
06 Registrar ... Mr. Gib PORNKITTICHOTCHAROEN
88 Associate Registrar ... Vacant
35 Director of Student Life ... Ms. Elizabeth CLARK
18 Director of Facilities ... Mr. Thomas GALVIN
15 Director of Human Resources/AA ... Mr. P. Paul ALEXANDER
26 Director Marketing/Communications ... Mr. Milton SAMUELS
36 Director Testing & Assessment ... Ms. Colleen SPENCE
25 Director of Grants Development ... Ms. Theresa BREWER
103 Dir of Corp & Community Education ... Mr. Freddy GONZALES
57 Dir of Visual/Performing/Media Arts ... Mr. Marshall HUGHES
88 Director of the Writing Center Lab ... Ms. Judith KAHALAS
88 Director of Academic Advising ... Ms. Lisa CARTER
88 Director of Upward Bound ... Mr. Mark JACKSON
88 Program Coord Mentoring/Success ... Ms. Lise HAGEN

*Springfield Technical Community College (E)

Armory Square, Springfield MA 01105-1296
County: Hampden FICE Identification: 008078
Unit ID: 167905
Telephone: (413) 781-7822 Carnegie Class: Assoc/Pub-U-SC
FAX Number: (413) 755-6309 Calendar System: Semester
URL: www.stcc.edu
Established: 1967 Annual Undergrad Tuition & Fees (In-State): $4,776
Enrollment: 6,888 Coed
Affiliation or Control: State IRS Status: 501(c)3
Highest Offering: Associate Degree
Program: Occupational; 2-Year Principally Bachelor's Creditable; Technical Emphasis
Accreditation: EH, ADNUR, COMTA, DA, DH, DMS, ENGT, MAC, MLTAD, NMT, OTA, PTAA, RAD, SURGT

02 President ... Dr. Ira H. RUBENZAHL
05 Vice President Academic Affairs ... Mr. Stephen H. KELLER
10 VP of Finance/CFO ... Mr. Joseph DASILVA
84 Vice Pres Enroll Mgmt/Student Affs ... Dr. Patrick TIGUE
50 Vice President Econ/Business Devel ... Vacant
20 Asst Vice Pres Academic Affairs ... Mr. Richard C. PARKIN
15 VP Human Res/Multi-Cultural Affairs ... Mrs. Myra D. SMITH
88 Asst VP Ctr for Business/Technology ... Vacant
04 Assistant to the President ... Mr. Michael J. SUZOR
50 Dean Business ... Dr. Leona R. ITTLEMAN
66 Dean of Nursing ... Ms. Mary TARBELL
72 Dean Engineering Technologies ... Ms. Adrienne SMITH
76 Dean School of Health ... Mr. Michael C. FOSS
79 Dean Arts/Humanities/Social Sci ... Dr. Arlene RODRIGUEZ
81 Dean Math/Science/Engineering ... Dr. Robert DICKERMAN
51 Dean School Continuing Education ... Dr. Debbie BELLUCCI
97 Dean General Stds/Lib Arts Transfer ... Ms. Teresa A. BURR
32 Dean of Student Affairs ... Mr. Ray BLAIR
07 Dean of Admissions ... Ms. Louisa M. DAVIS FREEMAN
06 Registrar ... Mr. Matthew GRAVEL
09 Director of Institutional Research ... Vacant
41 Director of Athletics ... Mr. J. Vincent GRASSETTI
102 Exec Director STCC Foundation ... Mr. William A. KWOLEK
19 Director of Security & Safety ... Ms. Wendy MASIUK
18 Director of Facilities ... Mr. Michael FERN
90 Chief Information Technology ... Ms. Eileen CUSICK
24 Director of Media Production ... Vacant
38 Director of Counseling ... Vacant
23 Director of Health Services ... Mr. Jonathan L. MILLER
26 Dir Public Relations & Publications ... Ms. Setta MCCABE
35 Coord Student Activities/Devel ... Ms. Andrea TARPEY
36 Director of Coop/Career Placement ... Ms. Pamela WHITE
26 Director of Marketing ... Ms. Joan THOMAS
15 Director of Human Resources ... Ms. Michelle CAPDEVILLE
28 Director of Diversity ... Ms. Myra SMITH

Massachusetts College of Pharmacy and Health Sciences (F)

179 Longwood Avenue, Boston MA 02115-5896
County: Suffolk FICE Identification: 002165
Unit ID: 166656
Telephone: (617) 732-2800 Carnegie Class: Spec/Health
FAX Number: (617) 732-2801 Calendar System: Semester
URL: www.mcphs.edu
Established: 1823 Annual Undergrad Tuition & Fees: $26,460
Enrollment: 4,636 Coed
Affiliation or Control: Independent Non-Profit IRS Status: 501(c)3
Highest Offering: Doctorate
Program: Professional
Accreditation: EH, ARCPA, DH, NMT, NURSE, PHAR, @PTA, RAD, RTT

01 President ... Mr. Charles F. MONAHAN, JR.
05 VP Academic Affairs/Provost ... Dr. George E. HUMPHREY
10 Exec Vice Pres Finance & Admin/COO ... Mr. Richard J. LESSARD
30 VP for Development & Chief of Staff ... Ms. Marguerite JOHNSON
12 Vice President Wor/Manch Campuses ... Mr. Dennis LYONS
20 Assoc Provost for Academic Affairs ... Dr. Lily HSU
20 Assoc Provost for Undergraduate Ed ... Dr. David TANNER
106 Assoc Provost Online Education/CEO ... Dr. Barbara MACAULAY
43 Legal Counsel ... Ms. Deborah A. O'MALLEY
32 Dean of Students-Boston ... Dr. Jean JOYCE-BRADY
32 Dean of Students-W/M ... Dr. Shuli XU
67 Dean Pharmacy Boston ... Dr. Douglas J. PISANO
67 Dean Pharmacy Worcester ... Dr. Michael J. MALLOY

08 Dean Library & Learning Resources ... Mr. Richard KAPLAN
49 Dean School of Arts and Sciences ... Dr. Delia C. ANDERSON
66 Dean School of Nursing ... Dr. Carol ELIADI
52 Dean Forsyth School for Dental Hyg ... Dr. Linda D. BOYD
88 Dean School of Phys Asst Studies ... Vacant
88 Dean School of Physical Therapy ... Dr. Linda J. TSOUMAS
88 Dean Sch Medical Imaging & Therap ... Ms. Frances KEECH
37 Exec Dir Student Enrollment Svcs ... Ms. Carrie GLASS
15 Director of Human Resources ... Ms. Mary LILLY
06 Registrar ... Ms. Stacey TAYLOR
13 Director of Information Services ... Mr. Tom SCANLON
21 Chief Business Officer ... Mr. Keith BELLUCCI
12 Exec Director Manchester Campus ... Mr. Seth P. WALL
29 Exec Director Alumni Relations ... Ms. Dawn BALLOU
07 Executive Director of Admissions ... Ms. Kathleen RYAN
96 Director of Purchasing ... Ms. Margaret EATON-CRAWFORD
38 Director Counseling Services ... Ms. Molly PAYNE
27 Director of Communications ... Mr. Michael RATTY
39 Director of Residence Life ... Ms. Jennifer KOSSES
35 Asst Dean Campus Life & Leadership ... Ms. Jennifer MICHAEL
18 Director of Facilities ... Mr. Michael O'NEIL
19 Chief of Public Safety ... Mr. Jack KELLY
105 Director of Web Services ... Ms. Linda DANGELO
21 Dean of Optometry ... Dr. Lesley WALLS

Massachusetts Institute of Technology (A)

77 Massachusetts Avenue, Cambridge MA 02139-4307
County: Middlesex FICE Identification: 002178
Unit ID: 166683
Telephone: (617) 253-1000 Carnegie Class: RU/VH
FAX Number: N/A Calendar System: 4/1/4
URL: web.mit.edu
Established: 1861 Annual Undergrad Tuition & Fees: $40,732
Enrollment: 10,566 Coed
Affiliation or Control: Independent Non-Profit IRS Status: 501(c)3
Highest Offering: Doctorate
Program: Technical Emphasis
Accreditation: EH, BUS, CS, ENG, PLNG

01 President ... Dr. Susan HOCKFIELD
00 Chairman of the Corporation ... Mr. John REED
05 Provost ... Dr. L. Rafael REIF
88 Chancellor ... Prof. W. Eric L. GRIMSON
03 Exec Vice President & Treasurer ... Ms. Theresa M. STONE
101 VP Institute Affairs & Secy of Corp . Dr. Kirk D. KOLENBRANDER
30 Vice Pres for Resource Development ... Mr. Jeffrey L. NEWTON
43 Vice President & General Counsel ... Mr. R. Gregory MORGAN
10 Vice President for Finance ... Mr. Israel RUIZ
15 Vice President for Human Resources ... Dr. Alison ALDEN
46 VP for Research & Associate Provost ... Prof. Claude R. CANIZARES
29 Exec VP & CEO Alumni Association ... Ms. Judith M. COLE
88 President MIT Investment Mgmt Co ... Mr. Seth ALEXANDER
20 Associate Provost ... Prof. Martin A. SCHMIDT
20 Associate Provost ... Prof. Philip S. KHOURY
20 Associate Provost Faculty Equity ... Prof. Barbara LISKOV
20 Associate Provost Faculty Equity ... Prof. Wesley L. HARRIS
48 Dean Sch of Architecture & Planning ... Prof. Adele N. SANTOS
54 Dean School of Engineering ... Prof. Ian A. WAITZ
79 Dean Sch Hum/Arts/Soc Sciences . Prof. Deborah K. FITZGERALD
50 Dean Sloan School of Management ... Prof. David C. SCHMITTLEIN
81 Dean School of Science ... Prof. Marc A. KASTNER
58 Dean Graduate for Education ... Dr. Christine ORTIZ
88 Dean for Undergraduate Education ... Prof. Daniel E. HASTINGS
32 Dean for Student Life ... Mr. Costantino 'Chris' COLOMBO
08 Director of Libraries ... Ms. Ann J. WOLPERT
88 Director Lincoln Laboratory ... Dr. Eric D. EVANS
86 Director MIT Washington Office ... Mr. William B. BONVILLIAN
27 Dir of MIT Communications ... Mr. Nate NICKERSON
07 Dean of Admissions ... Mr. Stuart SCHMILL
37 Exec Dir Student Financial Services ... Ms. Elizabeth M. HICKS
23 Medical Dir & Head MIT Medical ... Dr. William M. KETTYLE
13 Head of Info Services & Technology ... Ms. Marilyn T. SMITH
18 Dir Facilities Operations&Security ... Chief John DI FAVA
45 Director Campus Planning & Design ... Ms. Pamela DELPHENICH
102 Director Foundation Relations ... Ms. Lindley HUEY
25 Dir Office of Sponsored Programs ... Ms. Michelle D. CHRISTY
96 Asst Dir of Strategic Sourcing ... Ms. Sara MALCONIAN
41 Director of Athletics ... Ms. Julie SORIERO
09 Director of Institutional Research ... Mrs. Lydia S. SNOVER
85 Dir International Students Office ... Ms. Danielle GUICHARD-ASHBROOK
36 Exec Dir Global Educ/Career Dev Ctr ... Ms. Melanie L. PARKER
93 Associate Dean and Director OME ... Ms. DiOnetta JONES
06 Registrar ... Ms. Mary CALLAHAN
40 Director MIT Press ... Ms. Ellen W. FARAN
39 Director of Housing ... Mr. Dennis COLLINS
42 Chaplain to the Institute ... Dr. Robert M. RANDOLPH
38 Assoc Dean Student Support Services ... Mr. Arnold R. HENDERSON, JR.
94 Women's and Gender Studies Director ... Prof. Sally HASLANGER
104 Associate Dean Global Education ... Ms. Malgorzata HEDDERICK
105 Web Manager ... Mr. Patrick GILLOOLY
24 Manager Audio Visual ... Mr. Louis W. GRAHAM, JR.

Massachusetts School of Law at Andover (B)

500 Federal Street, Andover MA 01810-1094
County: Essex FICE Identification: 032353
Unit ID: 369002
Telephone: (978) 681-0800 Carnegie Class: Spec/Law
FAX Number: (978) 681-6330 Calendar System: Semester
URL: www.mslaw.edu
Established: 1988 Annual Graduate Tuition & Fees: $15,739
Enrollment: 672 Coed
Affiliation or Control: Independent Non-Profit IRS Status: 501(c)3
Highest Offering: Doctorate; No Undergraduates
Program: Professional
Accreditation: EH

01 Dean ... Mr. Lawrence R. VELVEL
05 Chief Acad Ofcr/Dir Personnel Svc ... Prof. Michael COYNE
10 Chief Business Officer ... Prof. Paula KALDIS
37 Director Student Financial Aid ... Ms. Lynn BOWAB
06 Registrar ... Ms. Louise ROSE
07 Director of Admissions ... Ms. Paula COLBY CLEMENTS
26 Chief Public Relations Officer ... Vacant
29 Director Alumni Relations ... Ms. Michelle HEBERT

Massachusetts School of Professional Psychology (C)

221 Rivermoor Street, Boston MA 02132-4935
County: Suffolk FICE Identification: 021636
Unit ID: 166717
Telephone: (617) 327-6777 Carnegie Class: Spec/Health
FAX Number: (617) 327-4447 Calendar System: Semester
URL: www.mspp.edu
Established: 1974 Annual Graduate Tuition & Fees: $32,972
Enrollment: 529 Coed
Affiliation or Control: Independent Non-Profit IRS Status: 501(c)3
Highest Offering: Doctorate; No Undergraduates
Program: Professional
Accreditation: EH, CLPSY

01 President ... Dr. Nicholas COVINO
04 Executive Asst to the President ... Mrs. Julie M. ROWLINGS
05 Vice President Academic Affairs ... Dr. Dan KING
10 VP Finance and Operations ... Mr. Patrick CAPOBIANCO
21 Assoc VP Finance ... Mr. Daniel BRENT
46 Assoc VP for Research ... Dr. Edward DEVOS
06 Director of Student Services ... Ms. Eileen O'DONNELL
28 Dir Diversity Educ & Inclusion ... Dr. Stacey LAMBERT
37 Director Financial Aid ... Mrs. Elaine TOOMEY
32 Dean of Students ... Dr. Frances MERVYN
88 Director of Multicultural Affairs ... Mrs. Gretchen NASH
07 Director of Admissions ... Mr. Mario MURGA
51 Director Continuing Prof Education ... Mr. Dean ABBY
36 Director Career Services ... Mrs. Tricia KRZYWICKI
27 Director of Marketing ... Mrs. Katie O'HARE
13 Dir Information Technology ... Mr. Jeff CHOO
78 Assoc Dir Community Education ... Mrs. Beth BASNIGHT
24 Manager of Classroom/Media Support ... Ms. Tracy CHEN
08 Head Librarian ... Mr. Matt KRAMER
15 Human Resource Manager ... Mrs. Ellen COLLINS
18 Facilities Manager ... Mr. Kevin COSTELLO

Merrimack College (D)

315 Turnpike Street, North Andover MA 01845-5800
County: Essex FICE Identification: 002120
Unit ID: 166850
Telephone: (978) 837-5000 Carnegie Class: Bac/Diverse
FAX Number: (978) 837-5222 Calendar System: Semester
URL: www.merrimack.edu
Established: 1947 Annual Undergrad Tuition & Fees: $32,865
Enrollment: 2,168 Coed
Affiliation or Control: Roman Catholic IRS Status: 501(c)3
Highest Offering: Master's
Program: Liberal Arts And General; Teacher Preparatory; Professional
Accreditation: EH, ENG

01 President ... Dr. Christopher E. HOPEY
100 Chief of Staff ... Mr. Jeffrey DOGGETT
04 Director Office of the President ... Ms. Lisa JEBALI
43 Vice President Admin & Gen Counsel ... Ms. Alexa ABOWITZ
05 Vice President for Academic Affairs ... Vacant
30 VP Col Advancement & Ext Relations ... Mr. Michael ACCARDI
84 Vice Pres for Enrollment Management ... Ms. Kristin GREENE
88 Vice Pres Mission/Student Affairs .. Rev. Raymond DLUGOS, OSA
13 Interim Chief Information Officer ... Mr. Chip STILES
20 Vice Provost ... Dr. Raymond SHAW
09 Asst VP Inst Research & Planning ... Ms. Kim BRIDGEO
15 Asst VP of Personnel & Payroll Svs ... Ms. Linda MURPHY
10 Interim CFO & Asst VP for Finance ... Mr. Mark VADALA
06 Interim Registrar ... Ms. Elaine GRELLE
07 Dean of Admissions ... Vacant
50 Dean Girard Sch Business/Intl Comm ... Dr. Mark CORDANO
54 Interim Provost & Dean Sci & Eng ... Dr. Josephine MODICA-NAPOLITANO
49 Dean of Liberal Arts ... Dr. Michael J. ROSSI
51 Dean School for Advanced Studies ... Ms. Jane LARKIN
53 Dean School of Education ... Dr. Dan BUTIN
08 Director of the Library ... Ms. Bridget RAWDING
15 Director of Human Resources ... Vacant
18 Director of Physical Plant ... Mr. Robert COPPOLA
19 Director of Police Services ... Mr. Ronald GUILMETTE
26 VP Communications and Marketing ... Ms. Sue THORN
29 Director of Alumni Relations ... Vacant
102 Dir Corp Found & Govt Relations ... Ms. Theresa ALLEN
23 Director Counseling & Health Svcs ... Dr. Gerald M. DUGAL

41 Director of Athletics ... Mr. Glenn HOFMANN
42 Director of Campus Ministry ... Vacant
32 Dean of Campus Life ... Dr. Donna L. SWARTWOUT
36 Director Career Services/Co-op Educ ... Vacant
37 Director of Student Financial Aid ... Ms. Christine A. MORDACH
96 Dir of Procurement & Risk Mgmnt ... Ms. Donna TOMBARELLI
28 Director Diversity Education ... Mr. J. Scott GAGE
24 Dir of Media Instructional Services ... Mr. Kevin SALEMME
35 Assistant Dean of Campus Life ... Ms. Allison GILL
104 Director of International Programs ... Ms. Lauren GANNON
39 Associate Director of Res Life ... Ms. Sara HICKS

MGH Institute of Health Professions (E)

36 1st Avenue, Boston MA 02129-4557
County: Suffolk FICE Identification: 022316
Unit ID: 166869
Telephone: (617) 726-2947 Carnegie Class: Spec/Health
FAX Number: (617) 726-3716 Calendar System: Semester
URL: www.mghihp.edu
Established: 1977 Annual Graduate Tuition & Fees: $1,000
Enrollment: 1,039 Coed
Affiliation or Control: Independent Non-Profit IRS Status: 501(c)3
Highest Offering: Doctorate; No Undergraduates
Program: Professional
Accreditation: EH, NURSE, PTA, RAD, SP

01 President ... Dr. Janis P. BELLACK
05 Provost/VP of Academic Affairs ... Dr. Alex F. JOHNSON
10 VP for Finance & Administration ... Mr. Atlas D. EVANS
26 Chief Information Officer ... Mr. Denis G. STRATFORD
30 Chief Development Officer ... Ms. Harriet S. KORNFELD
32 Dean of Student Affairs ... Ms. Carolyn LOCKE
66 Dean of Nursing ... Dr. Margery CHISHOLM
76 Int Dean School of Hlth & Rehab Sci ... Dr. Leslie PORTNEY
88 Chair Comm Sciences & Disorders ... Dr. Gregory LOF
76 Director of Medical Imaging ... Mr. Richard TERRASS
20 Assoc Provost for Acad Affairs ... Dr. Bette Ann HARRIS
06 Asst Dean of Students/Registrar ... Mr. James V. VITAGLIANO
04 Executive Assistant to President ... Ms. Elizabeth D. CAMELO
37 Director Student Financial Aid ... Vacant
09 Director of Inst Effectiveness ... Ms. Cynthia P. KING
84 Manager of Admissions ... Mr. Brett DIMARZO
21 Student Accounts Manager ... Ms. Joyce DESANCTIS
07 Director of Admissions ... Ms. Maureen JUDD
27 Director of Communications ... Mr. Paul W. MURPHY

Montserrat College of Art (F)

23 Essex Street, Box 26, Beverly MA 01915-4508
County: Essex FICE Identification: 020630
Unit ID: 166911
Telephone: (978) 922-8222 Carnegie Class: Spec/Arts
FAX Number: (978) 922-4268 Calendar System: Semester
URL: www.montserrat.edu
Established: 1970 Annual Undergrad Tuition & Fees: $24,990
Enrollment: 339 Coed
Affiliation or Control: Independent Non-Profit IRS Status: 501(c)3
Highest Offering: Baccalaureate
Program: Liberal Arts And General
Accreditation: EH, ART

01 President ... Dr. Stephen D. IMMERMAN
05 Dean Faculty/Academic Affairs ... Ms. Laura TONELLI
84 Dean Admissions/Enrollment Mgmt ... Mr. Rick LONGO
32 Interim Dean of Student Services ... Ms. Barbara FIENMAN
30 Dean of Development ... Mr. Howard AMIDON
26 Dean College Rels/Spec Asst to Pres ... Ms. Jo BRODERICK
21 Controller ... Ms. Susan JACOBS
13 Director of Information Technology ... Mr. David KWOK
08 Library Director ... Ms. Cheri COE
06 Registrar ... Mrs. Theresa SKELLY
37 Director of Financial Aid ... Ms. Creda CAMACHO
15 Human Resources Director ... Ms. Jennifer THOMAS TROUPE

Mount Holyoke College (G)

50 College Street, South Hadley MA 01075-1424
County: Hampshire FICE Identification: 002192
Unit ID: 166939
Telephone: (413) 538-2000 Carnegie Class: Bac/A&S
FAX Number: (413) 538-2391 Calendar System: Semester
URL: www.mtholyoke.edu
Established: 1837 Annual Undergrad Tuition & Fees: $41,270
Enrollment: 2,344 Female
Affiliation or Control: Independent Non-Profit IRS Status: 501(c)3
Highest Offering: Master's
Program: Liberal Arts And General; Teacher Preparatory
Accreditation: EH

01 President ... Lynn PASQUERELLA
05 Dean of Faculty/Vice Pres Acad Affs ... Christopher BENFEY
10 Vice Pres Finance/Administration ... Ben HAMMOND
84 Interim Vice Pres Enrollment ... Diane ANCI
30 Vice President for Development ... Charles HAIGHT
32 Dean of the College/VP Student Affs ... Cerri BANKS
07 Dean of Admission ... Diane ANCI
04 Chief of Staff ... Jennifer SANBORN
26 Dir Comm and Marketing ... Patricia VANDENBERG
06 Registrar ... Elizabeth PYLE

36 Dir of Career Development Center .... Steve KOPPI
37 Director of Financial Assistance .... Kathryn BLAISDELL
29 Exec Director Alumnae Association .... Jane E. ZACHARY
15 Director of Human Resources .... Vacant
08 Executive Director Library & IT .... Charlotte PATRIQUIN
09 Director of Institutional Research .... Alison K. DONTA-VENMAN

Mount Ida College (A)

777 Dedham Street, Newton MA 02459
County: Middlesex FICE Identification: 002193
Unit ID: 166948
Telephone: (617) 928-4500 Carnegie Class: Bac/Diverse
FAX Number: (617) 928-4746 Calendar System: Semester
URL: www.mountida.edu
Established: 1899 Annual Undergrad Tuition & Fees: $25,650
Enrollment: 1,481 Coed
Affiliation or Control: Independent Non-Profit IRS Status: 501(c)3
Highest Offering: Master's
Program: Liberal Arts And General; Professional
Accreditation: EH, ART, CIDA, DH, FUSER

01 President .... Dr. Lance CARLUCCIO
05 Vice Pres Academic Affairs .... Dr. Ellen BEAULIEU
30 Vice President for Development .... Dr. Deborah HIRSCH
10 Vice President for Finance/Admin .... Mr. David HEALY
84 Actg Vice Pres Enrollment Mgmt/Mktg . Ms. Maureen MORIARTY
32 Vice President of Student Affairs .... Dr. Elizabeth TRUE
07 Dean of Admissions .... Mr. Jay TITUS
35 Associate Dean of Students .... Mr. William CRIBBY
06 Registrar .... Ms. Maureen MORIARTY
08 Director of Learning Resources .... Ms. Margaret LIPPINCOTT
29 Director of Alumni Relations .... Vacant
37 Director Financial Aid .... Ms. Dyan TEEHAN
21 Controller .... Mr. Edward MOLLER
36 Director of Career Services .... Mr. Robert BROOKS
15 Director of Human Resources .... Ms. Omaira ROY
26 Director of Mkting & Communications .. Ms. Annmarie FARRETTA
85 Director of Intl Student Affairs .... Ms. Jane HOWARD
41 Athletic Director .... Mr. Matthew BURKE
19 Director Campus Security .... Mr. Ben KATZ
18 Director Physical Plant .... Mr. Kevin KELLY
09 Director of Institutional Research .... Mr. Jerome DEAN
88 Dean of College Academic Services .... Ms. Alyce CURTIS
24 Director of Educational Media .... Mr. Manouche MADANIPOUR
96 Director of Business Services .... Ms. Leah WEBBER
28 Director of Diversity .... Vacant
42 College Chaplain .... Rev. Lynne PHIPPS
14 Director Network Services .... Mr. Walter GEER
23 Director Health Services .... Ms. Marsha WELBURN
35 Director Student Activities .... Ms. Adebimpe DARE
58 Dean Graduate Studies/Cont Educ .... Ms. Lois NUNEZ

The National Graduate School of Quality Systems Management (B)

186 Jones Road, Falmouth MA 02540-2908
County: Barnstable FICE Identification: 035043
Unit ID: 441478
Telephone: (508) 457-1313 Carnegie Class: Spec/Bus
FAX Number: (508) 457-5347 Calendar System: Other
URL: www.ngs.edu
Established: 1993 Annual Undergrad Tuition & Fees: $19,800
Enrollment: 393 Coed
Affiliation or Control: Independent Non-Profit IRS Status: 501(c)3
Highest Offering: Doctorate
Program: Business Emphasis
Accreditation: EH

01 President .... Dr. Robert GEE
84 Vice Pres Enrollment Management .... Ms. Virginia C. PETISCE
88 Director Regulatory Affairs .... Ms. Maureen REARDON
06 Registrar .... Ms. Marie CALDER
10 Comptroller .... Ms. Mary ORLANDO

New England College of Business and Finance (C)

10 High Street, Suite 204, Boston MA 02110
County: Suffolk FICE Identification: 039653
Unit ID: 164438
Telephone: (617) 951-2350 Carnegie Class: Assoc/PrivFP4
FAX Number: (617) 951-2533 Calendar System: Other
URL: www.necb.edu
Established: 1909 Annual Undergrad Tuition & Fees: $9,875
Enrollment: 1,146 Coed
Affiliation or Control: Proprietary IRS Status: Proprietary
Highest Offering: Master's
Program: 2-Year Principally Bachelor's Creditable; Business Emphasis
Accreditation: EH

01 President .... Mr. Howard E. HORTON
05 Vice President Academic Affairs .... Dr. Carol ANDERSON
106 VP of E-Learning/Instr Design .... Ms. Paula BRAMANTE
10 Controller .... Mr. William MCDONALD
04 Asst to the President/Office Mgr .... Ms. Kathy CANTALUPA
06 Registrar .... Mr. Robert WAGSTAFF
07 Dir of Admissions/Student Services ... Ms. Pamela DELLA PORTA
37 Director of Financial Aid .... Ms. Maria MORELLI
88 Asst Dean E-Learning & Instr Des .... Mr. Jonathan SMALL
97 Department Chair General Education .... Dr. Christian BROCATO
50 Department Chair Business/Finance .... Dr. Christopher WEIR

The New England College of Optometry (D)

424 Beacon Street, Boston MA 02115-1129
County: Suffolk FICE Identification: 002164
Unit ID: 167093
Telephone: (617) 266-2030 Carnegie Class: Spec/Health
FAX Number: (617) 424-9202 Calendar System: Semester
URL: www.neco.edu
Established: 1894 Annual Undergrad Tuition & Fees: $36,389
Enrollment: 466 Coed
Affiliation or Control: Independent Non-Profit IRS Status: 501(c)3
Highest Offering: Doctorate
Program: Professional
Accreditation: EH, OPT, OPTR

01 President .... Dr. Clifford SCOTT
05 VP & Dean of Academic Affairs .... Dr. Barry FISCH
10 VP Business Development .... Mr. Robert GORDON
17 VP Clinical Affairs & CEO of NEEI .... Ms. Jody FLEIT
30 VP of Philanthropy .... Ms. Nancy BROUDE
32 Assoc Dean Students/Dir Stdnt Svcs .... Ms. Barbara MCGINLEY
07 Assoc Dean of Admissions .... Dr. Taline FARRA
37 Director Student Financial Aid .... Ms. Carol RUBEL
15 Director of Human Resources .... Ms. Patricia DAHILL
06 Registrar .... Ms. Glenda UNDERWOOD
08 Director of Library Services .... Ms. Kristin MOTTE
04 Executive Asst to the President .... Ms. Marie HILL

New England Conservatory of Music (E)

290 Huntington Avenue, Boston MA 02115-5018
County: Suffolk FICE Identification: 002194
Unit ID: 167057
Telephone: (617) 585-1100 Carnegie Class: Spec/Arts
FAX Number: (617) 262-0500 Calendar System: Semester
URL: www.necmusic.edu
Established: 1867 Annual Undergrad Tuition & Fees: $36,700
Enrollment: 798 Coed
Affiliation or Control: Independent Non-Profit IRS Status: 501(c)3
Highest Offering: Doctorate
Program: Liberal Arts And General; Teacher Preparatory; Professional
Accreditation: EH, MUS

01 President .... Mr. Tony WOODCOCK
05 Dean of the College .... Mr. Thomas NOVAK
30 Vice Pres Institutional Advancement .... Mr. Don JONES
10 Sr Vice Pres Finance/Operations .... Mr. Edward R. LESSER
100 Chief of Staff .... Ms. Suzanne WILSON
56 Dean of Extension Division .... Mr. Mark CHURCHILL
32 Dean of Students .... Mr. Tom HANDEL
11 Head of Operations/Inst Planning .... Ms. Hilary FIELD
18 Director of Facilities & Operations .... Mr. Michael RYAN
06 Registrar .... Mr. Robert WINKLEY
08 Director of Libraries .... Ms. Jean MORROW
37 Director Financial Aid .... Ms. Lauren URBANEK
35 Director Student Activities .... Ms. Colleen PALMER
36 Director of Career Services .... Dr. Angela Myles BEECHING
29 Director of Alumni Relations .... Ms. Cheryl WEBER
15 Director of Human Resources .... Ms. Elise COMEAU
13 Director ITS .... Mr. Charles MEMBRINO
26 Dir of Marketing/Public Relations .... Ms. Carol PHELAN
07 Director of Admissions .... Ms. Christina DALY
09 Director of Institutional Research .... Ms. Sarah DOW
20 Asst Dean of Academic Studies .... Vacant
38 Director Student Counseling .... Ms. Jan LERBINGER
51 Director of Continuing Education .... Mr. Sean P. HAGON

The New England Institute of Art (F)

10 Brookline Place W, Brookline MA 02445-7295
County: Norfolk FICE Identification: 007486
Unit ID: 167321
Telephone: (617) 739-1700 Carnegie Class: Spec/Arts
FAX Number: (617) 582-4500 Calendar System: Semester
URL: www.artinstitutes.edu/boston
Established: 1952 Annual Undergrad Tuition & Fees: $25,740
Enrollment: 1,483 Coed
Affiliation or Control: Proprietary IRS Status: Proprietary
Highest Offering: Baccalaureate
Program: Occupational; Fine Arts Emphasis
Accreditation: EH

01 President .... Dr. David WARREN
04 Assistant to the President .... Ms. Carolyn WILSON
05 Interim Dean of Academic Affairs .... Ms. Laurie WHITE
32 Dean of Student Affairs .... Ms. Michele TRACIA
06 Registrar .... Ms. Dawn NORRIS
07 Senior Director of Admissions .... Vacant
08 Library Director .... Dr. Mary Ann TRICARICO
10 Director of Admin & Financial Svcs .... Mr. Ross SORACI
13 Campus Technology Manager .... Ms. Connie BURKE
15 Human Resources Manager .... Ms. Lauren ROWE
36 Director of Career Services .... Mr. John LAY
37 Director Student Financial Services .... Mr. Michael CARDENAS
20 Associate Dean of Academic Affairs .... Mr. Jeremy GOODMAN
40 Bookstore Manager .... Ms. Stephanie VINCENT

New England Law | Boston (G)

154 Stuart Street, Boston MA 02116-5687
County: Suffolk FICE Identification: 008916
Unit ID: 167215
Telephone: (617) 451-0010 Carnegie Class: Spec/Law
FAX Number: (617) 422-7333 Calendar System: Semester
URL: www.nesl.edu
Established: 1908 Annual Undergrad Tuition & Fees: $40,904
Enrollment: 1,132 Coed
Affiliation or Control: Independent Non-Profit IRS Status: 501(c)3
Highest Offering: First Professional Degree
Program: Professional
Accreditation: LAW

01 Dean .... Mr. John F. O'BRIEN
05 Associate Dean .... Ms. Judith G. GREENBERG
11 Associate Dean of Administration .... Ms. Susan S. CALAMARE
07 Director of Admission .... Ms. Michelle L'ETOILE
10 Chief Financial Officer .... Mr. Fred COVELLE
08 Librarian .... Ms. Anne ACTON
36 Director Career Services .... Ms. Mandie R. ARAUJO
37 Director Financial Aid .... Mr. Eric A. KRUPSKI
26 Dir Marketing/Communication .... Mr. Michael FISCH
06 Registrar .... Mr. David M. BERTI
18 Director of Facilities/Security .... Mr. Anthony GIORDANO
35 Director of Student Services .... Ms. Cornelia B. GODFREY
13 Chief Information Officer .... Mr. Charles KILLAM

New England School of Acupuncture (H)

150 California Street, Newton MA 02458-1005
County: Middlesex FICE Identification: 025798
Unit ID: 167181
Telephone: (617) 558-1788 Carnegie Class: Spec/Health
FAX Number: (617) 558-1789 Calendar System: Trimester
URL: www.nesa.edu
Established: 1975 Annual Undergrad Tuition & Fees: $19,885
Enrollment: 200 Coed
Affiliation or Control: Independent Non-Profit IRS Status: 501(c)3
Highest Offering: Master's; No Lower Division
Program: Professional
Accreditation: ACUP

01 President .... Vacant
03 Executive Dean .... Susan L. GORMAN
05 Academic Dean .... Meredith ST. JOHN
07 Admissions Director .... Catherine HAMILTON

Newbury College (I)

129 Fisher Avenue, Brookline MA 02445-5796
County: Norfolk FICE Identification: 007484
Unit ID: 167251
Telephone: (617) 730-7000 Carnegie Class: Bac/Diverse
FAX Number: (617) 731-9618 Calendar System: Semester
URL: www.newbury.edu
Established: 1962 Annual Undergrad Tuition & Fees: $26,600
Enrollment: 1,018 Coed
Affiliation or Control: Independent Non-Profit IRS Status: 501(c)3
Highest Offering: Baccalaureate
Program: Liberal Arts And General
Accreditation: EH, CIDA

01 President .... Ms. Hannah M. MCCARTHY
05 Dean of College/VP Academic Affairs .... Dr. Hannah LEVERTOV
10 Vice President Finance/CFO .... Ms. Joyce HANLON
03 Executive Vice President .... Mr. Joseph CHILLO
32 Vice President of Student Affairs .... Mr. Paul MARTIN
30 VP for Development .... Ms. Clare MCCULLY
35 Dean of Student Affairs .... Ms. Amy SHIRLEY
20 Assoc Dean for Academic Services .... Ms. Sara D'ANJOU
08 Director of Library Services .... Mr. Peter G. OBUCHAN
37 Int Dir Student Financial Services .... Ms. Jennifer ROBERTS
06 Registrar .... Ms. Rachelle E. MAZZA
27 Chief Information Officer .... Mr. Gary HAMMON
15 Director Human Resources .... Ms. Amy DOWNING
36 Director of Career Services .... Ms. Sara SHECKELLS
38 Director Counseling/Health Educ .... Ms. Susan CHAMANDY
18 Director of Facilities .... Mr. Ron MINERVINI
55 Asst VP for Adult Enrollment .... Ms. Eileen SHERIDAN
41 Director of Athletics .... Ms. Jessica GOULD

Nichols College (J)

Center Road, PO Box 5000, Dudley MA 01571-5000
County: Worcester FICE Identification: 002197
Unit ID: 167260
Telephone: (508) 213-1560 Carnegie Class: Bac/Diverse
FAX Number: N/A Calendar System: Semester
URL: www.nichols.edu
Established: 1815 Annual Undergrad Tuition & Fees: $30,400
Enrollment: 1,088 Coed
Affiliation or Control: Independent Non-Profit IRS Status: 501(c)3
Highest Offering: Master's
Program: Liberal Arts And General; Teacher Preparatory; Professional; Business Emphasis
Accreditation: EH, IACBE

01 President ....Susan WEST ENGELKEMEYER
05 Provost and Senior Vice President ....Alan J. REINHARDT
10 Vice President Administration ....Michael J. STANTON
30 Vice President for Advancement ....William C. PIECZYNSKI
84 Vice Pres Enrollment & Marketing ....Thomas R. CAFARO
32 Vice Pres Student Affairs & Dean ....Brian T. MCCOY
13 Vice Pres for Information Services ....Kevin F. BRASSARD
55 Dean Graduate & Prof Studies ....Dawn C. SHERMAN
21 Assoc Vice Pres for Finance ....Patricia A. HERTZFELD
04 Exec Assistant to the President ....Cynthia L. BROWN
09 Assoc Dean Academic Admin/Records ....Peter M. ENGH
41 Assoc Dn Stdt Svcs/Dir Athletics ....Charlyn A. ROBERT
07 Director Admissions ....Paul O. BROWER
06 Registrar ....Betin ROBICHAUD
08 Director of Library ....Jim DOUGLAS
15 Director of Human Resources ....Rick WOODS
29 Director of Alumni Relations ....Brianne S. CALLAHAN
35 Dir Student Activities/Orientation ....Joseph GINESE
36 Director of Career Services ....Vacant
37 Director of Financial Aid ....Denise BRINDLE
38 Director Mental Health Services . Monica GOODRICH PELLETIER
26 Director of Communications ....Dorothy J. MILLHOFER
18 Assoc VP for Facilities Management ....Robert W. LAVIGNE
07 Associate Director of Admissions ....Paul A. MAY
96 Director of Purchasing ....Kay F. YOUNG
19 Director Public Safety ....Jack CAULFIELD
23 Director Health Services ....Katherine NICOLETTI
39 Dir Res Life & Judicial Affairs ....P. J. BOGGIO
42 Director Spiritual Life & Chaplain ....Wayne-Daniel S. BERARD

Northeastern University (A)

360 Huntington Avenue, Boston MA 02115-0195
County: Suffolk FICE Identification: 002199
Unit ID: 167358
Telephone: (617) 373-2000 Carnegie Class: RU/H
FAX Number: N/A Calendar System: Semester
URL: www.northeastern.edu
Established: 1898 Annual Undergrad Tuition & Fees: $38,252
Enrollment: 29,519 Coed
Affiliation or Control: Independent Non-Profit IRS Status: 501(c)3
Highest Offering: Doctorate
Program: Liberal Arts And General; Teacher Preparatory; Professional
Accreditation: EH, ANEST, ARCPA, AUD, BUS, CS, ENG, ENGT, LAW, NURSE, PHAR, PSPSY, PTA, SP, SPAA

01 President ....Dr. Joseph E. AOUN
04 Exec Assistant to the President ....Ms. Susie C. GUSZCZA
100 Chief of Staff ....Ms. Elisabeth A. WERBY
05 Sr Vice Pres Academic Affs/Provost ....Dr. Stephen W. DIRECTOR
84 Sr Vice Pres Enroll Mgmt/Stdnt Affs ....Dr. Philomena V. MANTELLA
10 Sr Vice Pres Admin & Finance ....Mr. John H. MCCARTHY
88 Sr Vice Pres and General Counsel ....Mr. Ralph C. MARTIN II
26 Sr Vice Pres External Affairs ....Mr. Michael A. ARMINI
30 Sr Vice President Advancement ....Ms. Diane N. MACGILLIVRAY
43 Vice President & University Counsel ....Mr. Vincent J. LEMBO
10 Vice President & Chief Fin Ofc ....Mr. Thomas NEDELL
84 Vice President Enrollment Mgmt ....Ms. Jane B. BROWN
32 Int Vice President Student Affairs .Ms. Madeleine A. ESTABROOK
18 Vice President Facilities ....Ms. Nancy S. MAY
16 Vice President Human Resources ....Ms. Katherine N. PENDERGAST
29 Vice President Alumni Relations ....Mr. Jack MOYNIHAN
88 Vice Pres Public Affairs ....Mr. Robert P. GITTENS
86 Vice President Government Relations ....Mr. Tim E. LESHAN
13 Vice President Information Systems ....Vacant
31 Vice Pres City & Community Affairs ....Mr. John M. TOBIN
46 Sr Vice Prov Rsch & Grad Education ....Dr. Melvin BERNSTEIN
20 Vice Provost for Undergrad Educ ....Dr. Bruce E. RONKIN
20 Vice Provost Academic Affairs ....Dr. Mary LOEFFELHOLZ
21 Vice Provost Budget/Planning/Admin ....Dr. Anthony RINI
92 Vice Provost Honors & FY Programs ....Dr. Susan G. POWERS-LEE
104 Vice Provost International Affairs ....Dr. Robert P. LOWNDES
58 Vice Provost Graduate Education ....Vacant
76 Dean Bouve Col Health Science ....Dr. Stephen R. ZOLOTH
77 Dean Col Computer and Info Science ..Dr. Larry A. FINKELSTEIN
54 Dean College of Engineering ....Dr. David E. LUZZI
81 Dean College of Science ....Dr. J. Murray GIBSON
50 Acting Dean Col of Business Admin ....Dr. Harry W. LANE
61 Dean School of Law ....Ms. Emily A. SPIELER
49 Dean College of Arts/Media & Design ....Dr. Xavier COSTA
83 Dean Col of Soc Sci & Humanities ....Dr. Georges VAN DEN ABBEELE
107 Int Dean College of Prof Studies ....Dr. John G. LABRIE
08 Dean University Libraries ....Mr. William M. WAKELING
07 Assoc Vice Pres Enroll/Dean Admiss ....Ms. Ronne PATRICK-TURNER
36 Assoc VP/Dean Enroll & Career Svcs ..Mr. M. Seamus HARREYS
39 Assoc Dean Cultural & Res Life ....Mr. Robert O. JOSE
23 Exec Director of Health Services ...Ms. Madeleine A. ESTABROOK
06 University Registrar ....Ms. Linda D. ALLEN
88 Dir Inst Rsch & Data Administration ....Dr. Nancy M. LUDWIG
22 Dir Inst Diversity & Equity ....Vacant
42 Director Spiritual Life ....Ms. Shelli M. JANKOWSKI-SMITH
92 Director Honors Program ....Dr. Maureen E. KELLEHER
36 Director Career Services ....Ms. Maria K. STEIN
21 Director of Finance & Treasurer ....Mr. Samuel B. SOLOMON
19 Director Public Safety ....Mr. D. Joseph GRIFFIN
27 Director of Communications ....Ms. Renata NYUL
41 Director Athletics ....Mr. Peter P. ROBY

Pine Manor College (B)

400 Heath Street, Chestnut Hill MA 02467-2332
County: Norfolk FICE Identification: 002201
Unit ID: 167455
Telephone: (617) 731-7000 Carnegie Class: Bac/A&S
FAX Number: (617) 731-7199 Calendar System: Semester
URL: www.pmc.edu
Established: 1911 Annual Undergrad Tuition & Fees: $22,042
Enrollment: 478 Female
Affiliation or Control: Independent Non-Profit IRS Status: 501(c)3
Highest Offering: Master's
Program: Liberal Arts And General; Teacher Preparatory
Accreditation: EH

01 President ....Dr. Alane K. SHANKS
05 Dean of College ....Dr. William VOGELE
32 Interim Dean of Students ....Ms. Whitney RETALLIC
84 Director of Enrollment ....Vacant
10 Director of Finance ....Mr. Timothy JOHNSON
06 Registrar ....Mr. Jeffrey MEI
26 Dir Publications/Media Relations ....Mr. Peter WOLOSCHUK
08 Library Director ....Ms. Marilyn BREGOLI
44 Mgr Annual Giving/Alumnae Relations ....Ms. Rose DIXON

Quincy College (C)

24 Saville Avenue, Quincy MA 02169-4324
County: Norfolk FICE Identification: 002205
Unit ID: 167525
Telephone: (617) 984-1700 Carnegie Class: Assoc/Pub-S-MC
FAX Number: (617) 984-1779 Calendar System: Semester
URL: www.quincycollege.edu
Established: 1956 Annual Undergrad Tuition & Fees (In-District): $4,970
Enrollment: 4,505 Coed
Affiliation or Control: Local IRS Status: 501(c)3
Highest Offering: Associate Degree
Program: Occupational; 2-Year Principally Bachelor's Creditable
Accreditation: EH, ADNUR, PNUR, SURGT

01 President ....Mr. Peter H. TSAFFARAS
05 Vice Pres Academic Affairs ....Ms. Anna WILLIAMS-COTE
11 Vice Pres Administration/Finance ....Mr. Pushap R. KAPOOR
04 Assistant to the President ....Mr. Robert BAKER
10 Chief Financial Officer ....Vacant
04 Admin Asst to President ....Ms. Donna M. BRUGMAN
84 Exec Dean Enrollment Svcs/Registrar ....Ms. Paula M. SMITH
66 Dean of Nursing ....Ms. Kimberly CROCKER-CROWTHER
49 Dean Liberal Arts ....Dr. Kenneth BINDSEIL
50 Dean Business & Public Service ....Dr. Sandra SMALES
81 Dean of Science ....Dr. Laura CORINA
21 Senior Director Accounts/Finance ....Mr. Martin AHERN
13 Exec Dir Admin Network Systems ....Mr. Tom C. PHAM
12 Dean of Plymouth Campus ....Ms. Mary BURKE
37 Exec Director of Financial Aid ....Ms. Rose M. DE VITO
18 Ex Dir Campus Facilities & Security ....Mr. William C. HALL
36 Exec Dir Student Support Services ....Ms. Susan G. BOSSA
15 Exec Director Human Resources ....Ms. Lorri A. MAYER
26 Exec Dir Strategic Mktng/Brand Mgmt ....Mr. Taggart BOYLE
07 Dir of Admissions and Enrollment ....Ms. Lisa J. STACK
85 Director International Student Svcs ....Mr. Pushap KAPOOR
103 Dir Career Svcs & Workforce Educ ....Mr. Gary G. WALLRAPP
09 Director Institutional Research ....Dr. Kimberly PUHALA
32 Director Student Affairs ....Ms. Kathi SCHAEFFER

Regis College (D)

235 Wellesley Street, Weston MA 02493-1571
County: Middlesex FICE Identification: 002206
Unit ID: 167598
Telephone: (781) 768-7000 Carnegie Class: Spec/Health
FAX Number: (781) 768-8339 Calendar System: Semester
URL: www.regiscollege.edu
Established: 1927 Annual Undergrad Tuition & Fees: $31,785
Enrollment: 1,737 Coed
Affiliation or Control: Independent Non-Profit IRS Status: 501(c)3
Highest Offering: Doctorate
Program: Liberal Arts And General; Teacher Preparatory; Professional
Accreditation: EH, ADNUR, NMT, NUR, RAD, SW

01 President ....Dr. Antoinette M. HAYS
10 Vice President Finance/Business ....Mr. Thomas G. PISTORINO
84 Vice Pres Enrollment & Marketing ....Mr. Paul VACCARO
20 Assoc Vice Pres Academic Affairs ....Ms. Sarah BARRETT
07 Director of Admission ....Ms. Wanda SURIEL
37 Director of Financial Aid ....Ms. Pamela GILLIGAN
06 Registrar ....Ms. Esther A. GHAZARIAN
09 Director of Institutional Research ....Sr. Margaret MCGARRY
15 Director of Human Resources ....Ms. Joan D. SULLIVAN
18 Director of Physical Plant ....Mr. Joseph SHAUGHNESSY
21 Director Finance & Business ....Mr. Steven SAVAS
29 Director of Alumni Relations ....Ms. Barbara CLANCY
32 Dean of Students ....Ms. Kara KOLOMITZ
36 Co-Dir Experiential Lrng/Career Svc ....Mr. John CONWAY
36 Co-Dir Experiential Lrng/Career Svc ....Ms. Karen SINGLE
23 Director of Health Services ....Ms. Dianna JONES
04 Special Assistant to President ....Ms. Mary Jane DOHERTY
08 Director of Library ....Ms. Lynn TRIPLETT
13 Director ITS ....Ms. Marla BOTELHO
19 Director Campus Services ....Mr. Robert NAUGHTON
41 Director Athletics & Physical Ed ....Ms. Marybeth LAMB
42 Director Campus Ministry ....Sr. Rosemary MULVIHILL

90 Director Academic Computing ....Mr. Mark LEWIS
96 Director of Purchasing ....Ms. Diep SHEEHAN
31 Director of Community Living ....Mr. Shawn EDIE
44 Director Annual Fund ....Ms. Tara BRADY
40 Bookstore Manager ....Mr. Daegan VON SWEARINGEN
35 Director of Student Programs ....Ms. Jessica HOMER
30 Chief Development Officer ....Ms. Miriam FINN-SHERMAN

Saint John's Seminary (E)

127 Lake Street, Brighton MA 02135-3898
County: Suffolk FICE Identification: 002214
Unit ID: 167677
Telephone: (617) 254-2610 Carnegie Class: Spec/Faith
FAX Number: (617) 787-2336 Calendar System: Semester
URL: www.sjs.edu
Established: 1884 Annual Undergrad Tuition & Fees: $20,000
Enrollment: 280 Male
Affiliation or Control: Roman Catholic IRS Status: 501(c)3
Highest Offering: Master's
Program: Professional; Religious Emphasis
Accreditation: EH, THEOL

01 Rector ....M.Rev. Arthur A. KENNEDY
03 Vice Rector ....Rev. Christopher K. O'CONNOR
05 Dean of Faculty ....Rev. Stephen E. SALOCKS
32 Dean of Students ....Rev. Edward RILEY
07 Director of Admissions & Records ...Mrs. Maureen DEBERNARDI
08 Librarian ....Rev. Raymond VAN DE MOORTELL
10 Director Finance and Operations ....Mr. Richard A. FLAHERTY
73 Director Pre-Theology Program ....Rev. Joseph SCORZELLO
21 Associate Business Officer ....Ms. Susan MOLNAR

Salter College (F)

184 West Boylston Street, West Boylston MA 01583
County: Worcester FICE Identification: 004666
Unit ID: 167738
Telephone: (508) 853-1074 Carnegie Class: Not Classified
FAX Number: (508) 853-1674 Calendar System: Semester
URL: www.saltercollege-us.com
Established: 1937 Annual Undergrad Tuition & Fees: N/A
Enrollment: 1,120 Coed
Affiliation or Control: Proprietary IRS Status: Proprietary
Highest Offering: Associate Degree
Program: Occupational; 2-Year Principally Bachelor's Creditable
Accreditation: ACICS, COMTA

01 President ....Ms. Charlene KEEFE

School of the Museum of Fine Arts-Boston (G)

230 The Fenway, Boston MA 02115-5518
County: Suffolk FICE Identification: 004667
Unit ID: 166984
Telephone: (617) 267-6100 Carnegie Class: Spec/Arts
FAX Number: (617) 424-6271 Calendar System: Semester
URL: www.smfa.edu
Established: 1876 Annual Undergrad Tuition & Fees: $35,760
Enrollment: 758 Coed
Affiliation or Control: Independent Non-Profit IRS Status: 501(c)3
Highest Offering: Master's
Program: Liberal Arts And General; Teacher Preparatory; Fine Arts Emphasis
Accreditation: ART

01 President ....Chris BRATTON
04 Executive Assistant ....Christina MANSDORF
03 VP for Academic Affairs ....Vacant
05 Dean of Faculty ....Fritz BUEHNER
06 Registrar ....Dan JOHNSON
30 VP for Development & Ext Relations ....Anne COWIE
84 VP for Enrollment ....Eric THOMPSON
10 Chief Financial Officer ....Mark KERWIN
21 Director of Business Operations ....Barbara DONNELLAN
09 Assoc VP Operations and Research ....Mary ROETZEL
32 Dean of Students ....Ernest PLOWMAN
45 Budget and Planning Officer ....Christopher FOX
51 Director Artist's Res Ctr/Cont Educ ....Debra SAMDPERIL
20 Assoc VP Academic Administration ....Greg D'ANGELO
58 Assoc Dean Graduate Studies ....David BROWN
37 Director of Financial Aid ....Beth GOREHAM
20 Assoc Dean Undergraduate Studies ....Susan LUSH
88 Bursar ....Kelly LANE
07 Associate Dean of Admissions ....Robyn REED
27 Dir of Marketing & Communications ....Sarah JENNINGS
44 Senior Development Officer ....Nicole FREEMAN
26 Press Coordinator ....Brooke WITKOWSKI
29 Director of Alumni Relations ....Vacant
08 Librarian ....Darin MURPHY
90 Mgr of Instructional Technology ....Matthew GIRARD
40 School Store Manager ....Terri NORDONE
88 Asst Dir Artist Resource Center ....Catherine TUTTER
35 Asst Coordinator Student Life ....Christy CORNETT
39 Asst Dir of Residential Housing ....Holly GOULD
18 Director of Facilities ....David GELDART
15 Director Human Resources ....Jane O'REILLY
96 Director of Purchasing ....Brendan MULLIGAN
19 Director of Protective Services ....Craig MCQUATE
88 Curator ....Joanna SOLTAN

Simmons College (A)

300 The Fenway, Boston MA 02115-5898
County: Suffolk FICE Identification: 002208
Unit ID: 167783
Telephone: (617) 521-2000 Carnegie Class: Master's L
FAX Number: (617) 521-3199 Calendar System: Semester
URL: www.simmons.edu
Established: 1899 Annual Undergrad Tuition & Fees: $32,230
Enrollment: 4,983 Coordinate
Affiliation or Control: Independent Non-Profit IRS Status: 501(c)3
Highest Offering: Doctorate
Program: Liberal Arts And General; Teacher Preparatory; Professional
Accreditation: EH, BUS, DIETD, DIETI, HSA, LIB, NURSE, PTA, SW

01 President .... Helen G. DRINAN
10 Sr VP Finance/Admin/Treasurer .... Stefano FALCONI
05 Provost .... Charlena SEYMOUR
20 Deputy Provost .... Carol E. BONNER
30 Vice President of Advancement .... Kristina G. SCHAEFER
26 Vice Pres Mktg/Undergrad Admiss .... Cheryl HOWARD
43 General Counsel .... Kathleen R. ROGERS
21 Assistant Vice President Finance .... Patricia C. FALLON
11 Asst Vice President Administration .... Janet FISHSTEIN
32 Dean for Student Life .... Sarah NEILL
49 Int Dean College of Arts & Sciences .... Laurie CRUMPACKER
50 Int Dean School of Management .... Deborah MERLINO
62 Dean Grad Sch Library/Info Science .... Michele CLOONAN
70 Dean School of Social Work .... Stefan KRUG
76 Dean School of Health Sciences .... Judy BEAL
13 Executive Director Technology .... Debra ORR
06 Registrar .... Donna M. DOLAN
08 Director of Library .... Daphne HARRINGTON
37 Director Student Financial Services .... Diane M. HALLISEY
41 Athletic Director .... Ali KANTOR
35 Dir Student Ldrshp/Activities/Advng .... Erin O'CONNOR
39 Director of Residence Life .... Vacant
25 Director Sponsored Programs .... Jon KIMBALL
07 Director Undergraduate Admissions .... Catherine CAPULUPO
96 Dir Purchasing/Procurement .... Kathy PERONI-CALLAHAN
36 Director Career Education Center .... Andrea WOLF

Smith College (B)

Northampton MA 01063-0001
County: Hampshire FICE Identification: 002209
Unit ID: 167835
Telephone: (413) 584-2700 Carnegie Class: Bac/A&S
FAX Number: (413) 585-2123 Calendar System: Semester
URL: www.smith.edu
Established: 1871 Annual Undergrad Tuition & Fees: $39,800
Enrollment: 3,113 Female
Affiliation or Control: Independent Non-Profit IRS Status: 501(c)3
Highest Offering: Doctorate
Program: Liberal Arts And General; Teacher Preparatory; Professional
Accreditation: EH, ENG, SW

01 President .... Carol T. CHRIST
04 Secretary to the President .... Jackie SCALZO
10 Vice Pres Finance & Administration .... Ruth H. CONSTANTINE
05 Provost & Dean of the Faculty .... Marilyn R. SCHUSTER
20 Dean for Academic Development .... John DAVIS
32 Dean of the College .... Maureen A. MAHONEY
35 Dean of Students .... Julianne OHOTNICKY
70 Dean School for Social Work .... Carolyn JACOBS
39 Director of Residence Life .... Becky SHAW
85 Assoc Dean International Students .... Lisa D. JOHNSON
30 Associate VP for Development .... Sandra DOUCETT
38 Assoc Dir Health Svcs/Stdnt Counsel .... Pamela MCCARTHY
26 VP for Public Affairs .... Laurie FENLASON
29 Exec Director Alumnae Association .Carrie S. CADWELL BROWN
13 Exec Director Info Technology Svcs .... Herb L. NICKLES
09 Dir Inst Research and Edu Assess .... Cate ROWEN
08 Director of Libraries .... Christopher LORING
15 Assoc VP for Human Resources .... Lawerence HUNT
07 Director of Admission .... Debra D. SHAVER
58 Director of Graduate Study .... Danielle D. RAMDATH
37 Dir Student Financial Services .... David J. BELANGER
06 Registrar .... Patricia A. O'NEIL
36 Director Career Development Office .... Stacie HAGENBAUGH
28 Advisor for Equity .... Adrianne ANDREWS
88 Associate Dean of the Faculty .... Danielle D. RAMDATH
18 Assoc VP for Facilities Management .... John SHENETTE
23 Director of Health Services .... Leslie R. JAFFE
41 Director of Athletics .... Lynn OBERBILLIG
42 Dean of Religious Life .... Jennifer L. WALTERS
43 Office of General Counsel .... Vacant
84 Assoc VP for Enrollment .... Audrey Y. SMITH
96 Procurement Manager .... Linda HIESIGER

Springfield College (C)

263 Alden Street, Springfield MA 01109-3788
County: Hampden FICE Identification: 002211
Unit ID: 167899
Telephone: (413) 748-3000 Carnegie Class: Master's L
FAX Number: (413) 748-3746 Calendar System: Semester
URL: www.spfldcol.edu
Established: 1885 Annual Undergrad Tuition & Fees: $30,660
Enrollment: 5,367 Coed
Affiliation or Control: Independent Non-Profit IRS Status: 501(c)3
Highest Offering: Doctorate
Program: Liberal Arts And General; Professional
Accreditation: EH, ARCPA, CORE, EXSC, IACBE, NRPA, OT, PTA, SW

01 President .... Dr. Richard B. FLYNN
45 Executive Vice President .... Dr. Jill F. RUSSELL
04 Special Assistant to President .... Ms. Mary Lou DYJAK
05 Vice President Academic Affairs .... Dr. Jean A. WYLD
29 Vice President Devel & Alumni Rels .... Mr. John A. WHITE
10 VP for Administration/Finance .... Mr. John MAILHOT
32 VP Student Affairs/Dean of Students .... Dr. David BRAVERMAN
20 Assistant VP Academic Affairs .... Dr. Mary Ann COUGHLIN
84 Dir Enrollment Management .... Ms. Mary DEANGELO
15 Asst Vice President Admin/Finance .... Ms. Rosanne CAPTAIN
21 Treasurer .... Mr. Michael DOBISE
30 Associate VP Development .... Mr. Scott M. BERG
06 Registrar .... Mr. Keith INGALLS
07 Dir Undergrad Admission .... Mr. Richard VERES
08 Director Library .... Ms. Andrea S. TAUPIER
29 Director Alumni Programs .... Ms. Tamie KIDESS LUCEY
37 Director of Financial Aid .... Mr. Edward CIOSEK
36 Director Career Services .... Ms. Barbara K. KAUTZ
13 Chief Information Officer .... Mr. Danny DAVIS
90 Director Academic Computer Center .... Mr. Thomas F. LARKIN
26 Director of Marketing/Communication .... Ms. Amy DEAN
38 Director of Counseling Center .... Vacant
19 Director Campus Police Department .... Ms. L. Judy JACKSON
88 Director YMCA Programs .... Mr. Harry ROCK
85 Director of International Center .... Dr. Deborah ALM
42 Director Campus Ministry .... Mr. David MCMAHON
18 Director of Facilities & Campus Svc .... Mr. Stephen LEFEVER
39 Director of Residence Life .... Mr. Tarome ALFORD
41 Director of Athletics .... Dr. Cathie SCHWEITZER
96 Director of Purchasing .... Ms. Lita ADAMS
28 Director Multicultural Affairs .... Mr. John WILSON

Stonehill College (D)

320 Washington Street, Easton MA 02357-6110
County: Bristol FICE Identification: 002217
Unit ID: 167996
Telephone: (508) 565-1000 Carnegie Class: Bac/A&S
FAX Number: (508) 565-1500 Calendar System: Semester
URL: www.stonehill.edu
Established: 1948 Annual Undergrad Tuition & Fees: $46,780
Enrollment: 2,567 Coed
Affiliation or Control: Roman Catholic IRS Status: 501(c)3
Highest Offering: Master's
Program: Liberal Arts And General; Teacher Preparatory; Professional
Accreditation: EH

01 President .... Rev. Mark T. CREGAN, CSC
05 Provost and VP for Academic Affairs .... Dr. Katie CONBOY
10 Vice Pres for Finance & Treasurer .... Ms. Jeanne FINLAYSON
30 Vice President for Advancement .... Mr. Francis X. DILLON
32 Vice President for Student Affairs .... Rev. John DENNING, CSC
88 Vice President for Mission .... Mr. Paul DAPONTE
84 VP for Enrollment Mgmt & Marketing .... Vacant
21 Assoc Vice President for Finance .... Mr. Craig BINNEY
35 Assoc VP for Students Affairs .... Ms. Pauline DOBROWSKI
20 Assoc VP for Academic Affairs .... Dr. Joseph FAVAZZA
18 Assoc VP for Operations .... Vacant
37 Asst VP/Dir of Student Aid/Finance .... Mrs. Eileen K. O'LEARY
04 Sr Executive Asst to the President .... Vacant
43 General Counsel .... Mr. Thomas V. FLYNN
21 Controller .... Ms. Jennifer MATHEWS
07 Dean of Admissions .... Mr. Daniel MONAHAN
06 Registrar .... Mr. John PESTANA
09 Director Planning/Inst Research .... Ms. Laura J. UERLING
08 Director of College Library .... Vacant
26 Dir of Media Rels & Communications .... Mr. Martin P. MCGOVERN
29 Director of Alumni Affairs .... Ms. Anne M. SANT
15 Director of Human Resources .... Ms. Maryann B. PERRY
38 Dir of Counseling & Testing Center .... Ms. Maria A. KAVANAUGH
27 Chief Information Officer .... Ms. Tamara ANDERSON
19 Chief of Police .... Mr. Peter CARNES
42 Director Campus Ministry .... Rev. Hugh CLEARY, CSC
90 Manager of Instructional Technology .... Ms. Janice HARRISON
45 Director of Academic Development .... Ms. Bonnie L. TROUPE
88 Dir of Enterprise Infrastructure .... Ms. Lauri DONIGER
23 Director of Health Services .... Ms. Diane LEARY
36 Director of Career Services .... Ms. Heather HEERMAN
41 Dir of Intercollegiate Athletics .... Mr. Brendan SULLIVAN
92 Director of Honors Program .... Rev. George PIGGFORD, CSC
44 Director of Development .... Mr. Douglas J. SMITH
20 Director of Academic Services .... Mr. Richard J. GRANT
96 Director of Purchasing .... Mr. Gregory WOLFE
45 Asst VP for Planning .... Mr. Stephen BEAUREGARD
39 Director of Residence Life .... Ms. Ali HICKS
24 Dir of Media/Videography Services .... Mr. Michael PIETROWSKI
40 Manager of College Bookstore .... Ms. Mary CULLINANE
88 Dean of Academic Achievement .... Dr. Craig ALMEIDA
97 Dir Gen Educ/First Year Experience .... Dr. Todd S. GERNES
18 Dir of Facilities Management .... Mr. Bruce BOYER
88 Dir of Ctr for Teaching & Learning .... Ms. Stacy GROOTERS
104 Director International Programs .... Ms. Alice CRONIN
31 Campus Minister for Community Svc .... Ms. Mary Anne CAPPELLERI
88 Dir Ctr for Academic Achievement .... Dr. Martha UCCI
28 Director of Intercultural Affairs .... Ms. Liza TALUSAN

Suffolk University (E)

Beacon Hill, Boston MA 02108-2770
County: Suffolk FICE Identification: 002218
Unit ID: 168005
Telephone: (617) 573-8000 Carnegie Class: Master's L
FAX Number: (617) 573-8353 Calendar System: Semester
URL: www.suffolk.edu
Established: 1906 Annual Undergrad Tuition & Fees: $29,894
Enrollment: 9,068 Coed
Affiliation or Control: Independent Non-Profit IRS Status: 501(c)3
Highest Offering: Doctorate
Program: Liberal Arts And General; Teacher Preparatory; Professional
Accreditation: EH, ART, BUS, BUSA, CIDA, CLPSY, ENG, IPSY, LAW, RTT, SPAA

01 Acting President .... Mr. Barry BROWN
05 Provost .... Mr. Barry BROWN
10 Vice President/Treasurer .... Vacant
84 VP Enrollment/International Pgms .... Ms. Marguerite J. DENNIS
30 Vice Pres of Advancement .... Mr. Chris MOSHER
32 Vice President of Student Services .... Dr. Nancy C. STOLL
20 Vice Pres Academic Affairs .... Ms. Janice C. GRIFFITH
26 Vice President External Affairs .... Mr. John A. NUCCI
50 Dean Sawyer Business School .... Mr. William J. O'NEILL
61 Dean of the Law School .... Ms. Camile NELSON
49 Dean College Arts & Science .... Dr. Kenneth S. GREENBERG
84 Assoc VP Enrollment/Retention .... Mr. Walter CAFFEY
37 Dean of Financial Aid .... Ms. Christine M. PERRY
93 Asst to Pres/Dir Minority Affairs .... Dr. Eric LEE
07 Director Undergraduate Admission .... Mr. John HAMEL
07 Director Graduate Admission .... Ms. Judith L. REYNOLDS
08 Director of Sawyer Library .... Mr. Robert E. DUGAN
06 College Registrar .... Miss Mary LALLY
36 Director Career Plng & Placement .... Mr. Paul TANKLEFSKY
15 Director of Human Resources .... Ms. Judy MINARDI
29 Director of Alumni Affairs/Law Sch .... Ms. Diane SCHOENFELD
13 Chief Information Officer .... Mr. Fouad YATIM
19 Captain University Police .... Mr. John PAGLIARULO
35 Director of Student Activities .... Mr. John SILVERIA
41 Director of Athletics .... Mr. James E. NELSON
18 Sr Dir Facilites Plng & Mgmt .... Mr. Gordon B. KING
07 Director of Law School Admission .... Ms. Gail ELLIS
06 Law School Registrar .... Ms. Lorraine D. COVE
36 Director of Law School Placement .... Mr. David JAMES
08 Law Librarian .... Ms. Elizabeth MCKENZIE
09 Director of Institutional Research .... Mr. Michael B. DUGGAN
38 Director of Student Counseling .... Dr. Kenneth F. GARNI
21 Associate Business Officer .... Mr. Gregory HARRIS

Tufts University (F)

Medford MA 02155-5555
County: Middlesex FICE Identification: 002219
Unit ID: 168148
Telephone: (617) 628-5000 Carnegie Class: RU/VH
FAX Number: N/A Calendar System: Semester
URL: www.tufts.edu
Established: 1852 Annual Undergrad Tuition & Fees: $42,962
Enrollment: 10,026 Coed
Affiliation or Control: Independent Non-Profit IRS Status: 501(c)3
Highest Offering: Doctorate
Program: Liberal Arts And General; Teacher Preparatory; Professional
Accreditation: EH, CS, DENT, ENG, IPSY, MED, OT, PH, PLNG, VET

01 President .... Dr. Anthony P. MONACO
03 Executive Vice President .... Ms. Patricia CAMPBELL
05 Interim Sr Vice President/Provost .... Ms. Peggy NEWELL
26 Vice President University Relations .... Ms. Mary R. JEKA
30 Vice Pres University Advancement .... Mr. Brian LEE
11 Vice President Operations .... Mr. Richard REYNOLDS
10 Vice President Finance/Treasurer .... Mr. Thomas S. MCGURTY
16 Vice President Human Resources .... Ms. Kathe CRONIN
13 VP & Chief Info Tech Officer .... Mr. David J. KAHLE
20 Associate Provost .... Dr. Mary Y. LEE
09 Assoc Provost Inst Research .... Dr. Dawn G. TERKLA
20 Vice Provost .... Ms. Peggy NEWELL
20 Assistant Provost .... Mr. Gary ROBERTS
23 Sr Director Health/Wellness Svcs .... Ms. Michelle D. BOWDLER
42 Chaplain .... Rev. David M. O'LEARY
43 Senior Legal Counsel .... Mr. Martin OPPENHEIMER
06 Registrar Arts & Sciences .... Ms. Jo Ann JACK
07 Dean Undergrad Admiss/Enroll Mgt .... Mr. Lee A. COFFIN
20 Dean of Student Services/Art & Sci .... Mr. Paul STANTON
08 Director Tisch Library .... Ms. Laura WOOD
37 Director of Financial Aid .... Ms. Patricia REILLY
88 Interim Dean Friedman School Nutri .... Dr. Robin KANAREK
32 Dean of Student Affairs .... Mr. Bruce REITMAN
49 Dean Arts & Sciences .... Dr. Joanne E. BERGER-SWEENEY
53 Interim Dean of Undergraduate Ed .... Dr. Carmen LOWE
54 Dean of Engineering .... Dr. Linda ABRIOLA
58 Dean Grad School of Arts & Science .... Dr. Lynne PEPALL
82 Dean Fletcher Law & Diplomacy .... Mr. Stephen BOSWORTH
52 Dean of Dental Medicine .... Dr. Huw F. THOMAS
74 Dean Cummings Sch of Veterinary Med .Dr. Deborah KOCHEVAR
63 Interim Dean Medical School .... Dr. Harris BERMAN
88 Dean Sackler School .... Dr. Naomi ROSENBERG
88 Interim Dean Tisch College .... Ms. Nancy WILSON
29 Exec Director Alumni Relations .... Mr. Tim BROOKS
22 Exec Director Inst Diversity .... Vacant
45 Exec Dir Planning & Administration .... Ms. Martha POKRAS
15 Director Human Res & Talent Mgmt .... Ms. Alison A. BLACKBURN
26 Director Public Relations-Medford .... Ms. Kimberly M. THURLER
28 Director Equal Opportunity .... Vacant
96 Purchasing Director .... Ms. Diane M. DEVLIN
94 Director Women's Center .... Ms. Steph L. GAUCHEL
19 Senior Director Public Safety .... Vacant
41 Director Athletics .... Mr. William GEHLING

100 Chief of Staff ... Mr. Michael BAENEN
18 Director of Facilities Services ... Mr. Bob BURNS
36 Director Career Services ... Ms. Jean M. PAPALIA
38 Director Mental Health Services ... Dr. Julie S. ROSS
43 Senior Legal Counsel ... Mr. Dickens MATHIEU

Urban College of Boston (A)

178 Tremont Street, Boston MA 02111-1093

County: Suffolk
FICE Identification: 031305
Unit ID: 429128
Telephone: (617) 348-6359
Carnegie Class: Assoc/PrivNFP
FAX Number: (617) 423-4758
Calendar System: Semester
URL: www.urbancollege.edu
Established: 1993
Annual Undergrad Tuition & Fees: $5,880
Enrollment: 602
Coed
Affiliation or Control: Independent Non-Profit
IRS Status: 501(c)3
Highest Offering: Associate Degree
Program: 2-Year Principally Bachelor's Creditable
Accreditation: EH

01 President ... Dr. Linda EDMONDS TURNER
05 Interim Academic Dean ... Ms. Hanna GEBRETENSAE
84 Dean Enrollment Svcs & Registrar ... Dr. Henry J. JOHNSON
08 Dir of Learning Resource Center ... Ms. Nancy DANIEL
11 VP/Dean of Administration ... Mr. Tom H. NEEL
37 Director of Financial Aid ... Ms. Mia TAYLOR
26 Assoc Dir Communication/Spec Proj ... Ms. Tina CABRAL
29 Alumni Association Advisor ... Ms. Olivia DYBING
20 Director Academic Support Services ... Mr. Josie HATUEY
30 Director Institutional Advancement ... Ms. Christa JONES

Wellesley College (B)

106 Central Street, Wellesley MA 02481-8203

County: Norfolk
FICE Identification: 002224
Unit ID: 168218
Telephone: (781) 283-1000
Carnegie Class: Bac/A&S
FAX Number: (781) 283-3639
Calendar System: Semester
URL: www.wellesley.edu
Established: 1875
Annual Undergrad Tuition & Fees: $53,250
Enrollment: 2,411
Female
Affiliation or Control: Independent Non-Profit
IRS Status: 501(c)3
Highest Offering: Baccalaureate
Program: Liberal Arts And General
Accreditation: EH

01 President ... Kim BOTTOMLY
05 Provost & Dean of the College ... Andrew SHENNAN
30 VP for Resources & Public Affairs ... Cameran MASON
10 Vice President Finance & Treasurer ... Andrew EVANS
18 Asst VP Facilities Management/Plng ... Peter ZURAW
27 Chief Information Officer ... Ganesan RAVISHANKER
07 Dean of Admission ... Jennifer DESJARLAIS
32 Dean of Students ... Debra DEMEIS
42 Dn Intercult Educ/Relig/Spirit Life ... Victor H. KAZANJIAN
20 Dean of Academic Affairs ... Richard G. FRENCH
20 Dean of Faculty Affairs ... Kathryn LYNCH
06 Registrar ... Carol SHANMUGARATNAM
29 Executive Director Alumnae Assn ... Susan CHALLENGER
37 Director of Student Financial Svcs ... Scott JUEDES
15 Director Human Resources ... Eloise MCGAW
36 Director Center for Work & Service ... Joanne S. MURRAY
26 Chief Public Relations Officer ... Elizabeth T. GILDERSLEEVE
35 Assoc Director Student Involvement ... Megan K. JORDAN
38 Administrative Counseling Svcs ... Robin COOK-NOBLES
101 Clerk Board of Trustees ... Marianne B. COOLEY
09 Director of Institutional Research ... Vacant
96 Purchasing Manager ... Tina M. DOLAN

Wentworth Institute of Technology (C)

550 Huntington Avenue, Boston MA 02115-5998

County: Suffolk
FICE Identification: 002225
Unit ID: 168227
Telephone: (617) 989-4590
Carnegie Class: Bac/Diverse
FAX Number: (617) 989-4591
Calendar System: Semester
URL: www.wit.edu
Established: 1904
Annual Undergrad Tuition & Fees: $24,000
Enrollment: 3,390
Coed
Affiliation or Control: Independent Non-Profit
IRS Status: 501(c)3
Highest Offering: Master's
Program: Professional; Technical Emphasis
Accreditation: EH, ART, CIDA, CONST, ENG, ENGT, IACBE

01 President ... Dr. Zorica PANTIC
100 Chief of Staff ... Ms. Amy INTILLE
05 Sr VP Academic Affairs/Provost ... Dr. Russell PINIZZOTTO
10 Vice Pres Finance ... Mr. Robert TOTINO
21 Vice President Business ... Mr. David A. WAHLSTROM
30 Vice Pres Institutional Advancement ... Ms. Brenda CROSS-SANCHEZ
32 VP Enrollment Mgmt/Student Affairs ... Ms. Keiko BROOMHEAD
15 Vice Pres Human Resources ... Ms. Anne M. GILL
13 VP of Information Technology ... Vacant
04 Exec Assistant to the President ... Ms. Nancy BANDOIAN
20 Assoc Provost ... Mr. Charles HOTCHKISS
35 Assoc Vice Pres of Student Affairs ... Ms. Annamaria WENNER
21 Assoc Vice President Finance ... Mr. Peter MADDOCKS
84 Assoc VP of Enrollment Management ... Ms. Dianne PLUMMER
31 Assoc VP Community Affairs ... Ms. Sandra E. PASCAL
91 Assoc VP Information Technology ... Mr. Leslie VAUGHAN
90 Assoc VP Learning & Development ... Ms. Monique FUCHS
20 Assoc Provost for Acad. Operations ... Ms. Susan PARIS
51 Dean of College of Prof & Cont Educ ... Mr. Larry CARR
07 Executive Director of Admissions ... Ms. Maureen DISCHINO
06 Registrar ... Mr. Matthew BURKE
08 Director of Library ... Mr. Walter PUNCH
35 Dir Student Financial Services ... Ms. Wen-Hsin CHEN
18 Associate VP Physical Facilities ... Mr. Michael PANKIEVICH
29 Director of Alumni Programs ... Ms. Kelleyrobin MULVIHILL
27 Director of Publications ... Mr. Daniel MORRELL
35 Assistant Dean of Students ... Mr. Peter FOWLER
102 Director of Corporate Relations ... Mr. Jonathan CARROLL
25 Grants Manager ... Vacant
37 Director Financial Aid ... Ms. Anne-Marie CARUSO
38 Director of Counseling ... Ms. Maura MULLIGAN
26 Associate Vice Pres Public Affairs ... Mr. Jamie KELLY
19 Director of Public Safety ... Mr. Charlie NOYES
41 Associate Athletic Director ... Mr. William P. GORMAN
36 Director of Career Services ... Mr. Gregory DENON
39 Director Housing & Residential Life ... Mr. Philip BERNARD
41 Director of Athletics ... Mr. Lee CONRAD
09 Director of Institutional Research ... Mr. Bradford WILD
96 Director of Purchasing ... Mr. Gerald INMAN
09 Institutional Researcher ... Mr. Alan T. WHITEMORE
49 Dean for Arts & Sciences ... Mr. Patrick HAFFORD
48 Dean for Arch/Design & Const Mgmt ... Dr. Glenn WIGGINS
54 Dean for Engineering & Technology ... Mr. Frederick DRISCOLL
88 Director of Marketing & Comm ... Mr. Robert YEE
18 Director of Physical Plant ... Mr. Robert FERRO
88 Dir of Stdnt Lead Pgm & Camp Ctr ... Ms. Carissa DURFEE

Western New England University (D)

1215 Wilbraham Road, Springfield MA 01119-2684

County: Hampden
FICE Identification: 002226
Unit ID: 168254
Telephone: (413) 782-3111
Carnegie Class: Master's M
FAX Number: (413) 782-1746
Calendar System: Semester
URL: www.wnec.edu
Established: 1919
Annual Undergrad Tuition & Fees: $30,844
Enrollment: 3,723
Coed
Affiliation or Control: Independent Non-Profit
IRS Status: 501(c)3
Highest Offering: Doctorate
Program: Liberal Arts And General; Professional; Fine Arts Emphasis
Accreditation: EH, BUS, ENG, LAW, @PHAR, SW

01 President ... Dr. Anthony S. CAPRIO
05 Provost/Vice Pres Academic Affairs ... Dr. Jerry A. HIRSCH
26 Vice Pres Marketing & External Affs ... Mrs. Barbara A. CAMPANELLA
10 Vice Pres Finance & Administration ... Mr. William J. KELLEHER
84 Vice President for Enrollment Mgmt ... Dr. Charles R. POLLOCK
32 VP Student Affairs/Dean of Students ... Dr. Jeanne S. STEFFES
30 Vice President Advancement ... Ms. Beverly J. DWIGHT
14 Asst Vice Pres Information Tech ... Mr. Scott J. COOPEE
88 Vice Pres for Strategic Initiatives ... Dr. Richard S. KEATING
61 Dean of Law ... Prof. Arthur R. GAUDIO
54 Dean of Engineering ... Dr. S. Hossein CHERAGHI
50 Dean School of Business ... Dr. Julie SICILIANO
49 Dean of Arts & Sciences ... Dr. Saeed GHAHRAMANI
89 Dean Freshmen/Transfer Students ... Ms. Kerri P. JARZABSKI
39 Assistant Dean for Residence Life ... Mr. Thomas P. WOZNIAK
15 Exec Dir Human Res/Career Ctr ... Mr. Gregory C. MICHAEL
09 Director Inst Research & Planning ... Dr. Richard A. WAGNER
29 Dir Alumni Relations/Annual Giving ... Ms. Kathrine PAPPAS
20 Academic Schdl Contr/Info Analyst ... Ms. Linda M. CHOJNICKI
08 Director of D'Amour Library ... Mrs. Priscilla L. PERKINS
37 Director of Student Admin Services ... Mr. Rodney W. PEASE
38 Director of Counseling Services ... Dr. Wayne D. CARPENTER
18 Director of Facilities Management ... Mr. Michael C. DUNCAN
41 Director of Athletics ... Dr. Michael THEULEN
31 Cultural Liaison Coordinator ... Rabbi Jerome S. GURLAND
08 Assoc Dean Library/Info Resources ... Ms. Barbara A. WEST
23 Director of Health Services ... Mrs. Kathleen A. REID
19 Director of Public Safety ... Mr. Adam WOODROW
28 Director of Diversity Programs ... Mrs. Yvonne BOGLE
11 Director Administrative Services ... Ms. Arlene M. ROCK

Wheaton College (E)

26 E Main Street, Norton MA 02766-2322

County: Bristol
FICE Identification: 002227
Unit ID: 168281
Telephone: (508) 285-7722
Carnegie Class: Bac/A&S
FAX Number: (508) 286-8270
Calendar System: Semester
URL: www.wheatonma.edu
Established: 1834
Annual Undergrad Tuition & Fees: $41,894
Enrollment: 1,635
Coed
Affiliation or Control: Independent Non-Profit
IRS Status: 501(c)3
Highest Offering: Baccalaureate
Program: Liberal Arts And General
Accreditation: EH

01 President ... Dr. Ronald A. CRUTCHER
05 Provost ... Dr. Linda EISENMANN
10 Vice President Finance/Admin ... Vacant
30 Vice President College Advancement ... Ms. Mary M. CASEY
84 Vice President Enrollment/Marketing ... Ms. Gail BERSON
32 VP Student Affairs/Dean of Students ... Ms. Lee B. WILLIAMS
37 Asst VP Enroll/Stdnt Finan Svcs ... Ms. Robin RANDALL
26 Asst Vice Pres for Communications ... Mr. Michael GRACA
06 Registrar/Dean Academic Systems ... Ms. Patricia SANTILLI
29 Dir Alumni Rels/Annual Giving ... Ms. Jill LAWLOR
105 Director College Web Strategy ... Mr. David CALDWELL
15 Asst VP/Director Human Resources ... Ms. Barbara LEMA
38 Director College Counseling ... Ms. Martha LAMB
07 Director of Admissions ... Ms. Lynne STACK
18 Asst VP Business Svcs/Phys Plant ... Mr. John M. SULLIVAN
96 Director of Purchasing ... Vacant
26 Director Public Affairs ... Vacant
09 Director of Institutional Research ... Ms. Audrey ADAM
39 Assoc Dean Stdnt Affs/Dir Res Life ... Ms. Kathryn E. MCCAFFREY
35 Assoc Director Student Life ... Vacant
19 Director Public Safety ... Mr. Charles A. FURGAL

Wheelock College (F)

200 The Riverway, Boston MA 02215-4176

County: Suffolk
FICE Identification: 002228
Unit ID: 168290
Telephone: (617) 879-2000
Carnegie Class: Master's M
FAX Number: (617) 566-7369
Calendar System: Semester
URL: www.wheelock.edu
Established: 1888
Annual Undergrad Tuition & Fees: $29,900
Enrollment: 908
Coed
Affiliation or Control: Independent Non-Profit
IRS Status: 501(c)3
Highest Offering: Beyond Master's But Less Than Doctorate
Program: Liberal Arts And General; Teacher Preparatory
Accreditation: EH, SW, TED

01 President ... Ms. Jackie JENKINS-SCOTT
04 Executive Assistant to President ... Ms. Valerie THORNHILL-HUDSON
32 VP Campus Life and IT ... Mr. Roy SCHIFILLITI
05 Vice Pres for Academic Affairs ... Dr. Julie WOLLMAN
30 Vice Pres for Devel & Inst Advance ... Ms. Linda WELTER
10 Vice Pres/Chief Financial Officer ... Ms. Anne Marie MARTORANA
84 VP Enrollment Mgt/Student Success ... Dr. Adrian K. HAUGABROOK
35 Dean of Students ... Ms. Barbara MORGAN
49 Dean of Arts & Sciences ... Dr. Shirley MALONE-FENNER
53 Int Dean of Education/Social Work ... Dr. Donna MCKIBBENS
07 Senior Dir of Undergrad Admissions ... Ms. Kristen HARRINGTON
07 Director of Graduate Admissions ... Mr. Brian MINCHELLO
06 Interim Registrar ... Ms. Michelle ORMEROD
08 Director of Academic Resc & Library ... Ms. Brenda ECSEDY
15 Director of Human Resources ... Ms. Michele CREWS
13 Director of Information Technology ... Mr. Jonathan LAPIERRE
37 Director Financial Aid ... Ms. Roxanne DUMAS
36 Dir Center for Career Development ... Ms. Mary SULLIVAN
85 Int Director Center for Intl Educ ... Dr. Linda DAVIS
18 Chief Facilities/Physical Plant ... Mr. Ed JACQUES
38 Director Counseling Center ... Ms. Eileen THOMPSON
26 Interim Director of Marketing Comm ... Mr. Stephen DILL
86 Dir of Government and Ext Affairs ... Ms. Marta ROSA
29 Dir of Development/Alumni Relations ... Ms. Lauren MARQUIS
41 Athletic Director ... Ms. Diana CUTAIA

Williams College (G)

Williamstown MA 01267

County: Berkshire
FICE Identification: 002229
Unit ID: 168342
Telephone: (413) 597-3131
Carnegie Class: Bac/A&S
FAX Number: N/A
Calendar System: 4/1/4
URL: www.williams.edu
Established: 1793
Annual Undergrad Tuition & Fees: $42,938
Enrollment: 2,083
Coed
Affiliation or Control: Independent Non-Profit
IRS Status: 501(c)3
Highest Offering: Master's
Program: Liberal Arts And General
Accreditation: EH

01 President ... Adam F. FALK
05 Dean of Faculty ... Peter T. MURPHY
45 Provost ... William C. DUDLEY
10 VP for Finance and Administration ... Frederick W. PUDDESTER
32 Vice President for Campus Life ... Stephen P. KLASS
30 Vice Pres Development/Alumni Rels ... John M. MALCOLM
28 VP Strategic Plng/Inst Diversity ... Michael E. REED
04 Asst to Pres/Secretary of the Col ... Keli A. KAEGI
20 Dean of the College ... Sarah R. BOLTON
26 Asst to Pres for Public Affairs ... James G. KOLESAR
18 Assoc VP of Facilities ... Diana E. PRIDEAUX-BRUNE
06 Registrar ... Charles R. TOOMAJIAN, JR.
07 Director of Admission ... Richard L. NESBITT
37 Director of Financial Aid ... Paul J. BOYER
08 Librarian ... David M. PILACHOWSKI
21 Controller ... Susan S. HOGAN
29 Director Alumni Relations ... Brooks L. FOEHL
15 Director of Human Resources ... Martha R. TETRAULT
36 Director of Career Counseling ... John H. NOBLE
88 Director of Dining Services ... Robert P. VOLPI
14 Chief Technology Officer ... Dinny S. TAYLOR
09 Director of Institutional Research ... Vacant
23 Director of Health Services ... Ruth G. HARRISON
35 Director of Campus Life ... Douglas J. SCHIAZZA
41 Director of Athletics/PE ... Lisa M. MELENDY
42 Chaplain ... Richard E. SPALDING

Woods Hole Oceanographic Institution (A)

266 Woods Hole Road, Woods Hole MA 02543-1535
County: Barnstable FICE Identification: 002230
Unit ID: 166610
Telephone: (508) 289-2252 Carnegie Class: Not Classified
FAX Number: N/A Calendar System: 4/1/4
URL: www.whoi.edu
Established: 1930 Annual Graduate Tuition & Fees: $53,940
Enrollment: 130 Coed
Affiliation or Control: Independent Non-Profit IRS Status: 501(c)3
Highest Offering: Doctorate; No Undergraduates
Program: Professional
Accreditation: EH

01 President and Director ... Dr. Susan AVERY
09 Director of Research ... Dr. Laurence P. MADIN
05 VP of Academic Programs and Dean ... Dr. James A. YODER
10 Vice Pres of Finance & Admin/ CFO ... Mr. Christopher J. WINSLOW
20 Associate Dean ... Dr. Margaret K. TIVEY
06 Registrar ... Ms. Julia WESTWATER
08 Research Librarian ... Ms. Catherine N. NORTON

Worcester Polytechnic Institute (B)

100 Institute Road, Worcester MA 01609-2280
County: Worcester FICE Identification: 002233
Unit ID: 168421
Telephone: (508) 831-5000 Carnegie Class: DRU
FAX Number: (508) 831-5753 Calendar System: Semester
URL: www.wpi.edu
Established: 1865 Annual Undergrad Tuition & Fees: $40,300
Enrollment: 4,522 Coed
Affiliation or Control: Independent Non-Profit IRS Status: 501(c)3
Highest Offering: Doctorate
Program: Liberal Arts And General; Professional; Technical Emphasis
Accreditation: EH, BUS, CS, ENG

01 President ... Dr. Dennis D. BERKEY
05 Interim Provost ... Dr. Eric OVERSTROM
10 Executive Vice President & CFO ... Mr. Jeffrey S. SOLOMON
30 Interim VP Develop/Alumni Relations ... Ms. Jo-Ann G. ALESSANDRINI
32 VP Student Affairs/Campus Life . Ms. Janet BEGIN-RICHARDSON
26 Exec Director Mktg & Communication ... Ms. Amy M. MORTON
13 CIO ... Ms. Deborah C. SCOTT
84 Sr VP Enrollment & Instnl Strategy ... Ms. Kristin R. TICHENOR
18 Asst Vice President for Facilities ... Mr. Alfred DIMAURO, JR.
15 Vice President of Human Resources ... Ms. A. Tracy HASSETT
20 Assoc Provost/VP Acad & Corp Devel ... Mr. Stephen P. FLAVIN
35 Dean of Students ... Mr. Philip N. CLAY
22 University Compliance Officer ... Mr. Michael J. CURLEY
36 Director of Career Devel Services ... Ms. Jeanette M. DOYLE
08 Dean of Library Services ... Dr. Tracey LEGER-HORNBY
100 Chief of Staff ... Ms. Stephanie PASHA
07 Dean of Admissions ... Mr. Edward J. CONNOR
06 Registrar ... Ms. Heather JACKSON
27 Director of Research/Communications ... Mr. Michael W. DORSEY
44 Assoc Director Annual Giving ... Mr. Patrick T. MALONEY
96 Manager of Procurement Services ... Ms. Laurie COLELLA
21 Acting Controller ... Ms. Charlene M. BELLOWS
09 Assistant VP of Budget Planning ... Ms. Judith L. TRAINOR
38 Director Student Counseling ... Mr. Charles C. MORSE
88 Dir WPI Bioengineering Institute ... Mr. Donald D. EASSON
37 Director Student Financial Aid ... Ms. Monica M. BLONDIN
19 Mgr Env Occupational Safety ... Mr. David H. MESSIER
28 Director of Diversity ... Ms. NaTonia TRAMMELL
29 Exec Director of Alumni Relations ... Mr. Peter A. THOMAS

Zion Bible College (C)

320 South Main Street, Haverhill MA 01835
County: Essex FICE Identification: 035705
Unit ID: 217606
Telephone: (978) 478-3400 Carnegie Class: Spec/Faith
FAX Number: (978) 478-3406 Calendar System: Semester
URL: www.zbc.edu
Established: 1924 Annual Undergrad Tuition & Fees: $10,093
Enrollment: 302 Coed
Affiliation or Control: Assemblies Of God Church IRS Status: 501(c)3
Highest Offering: Baccalaureate
Program: Religious Emphasis
Accreditation: BI

01 President ... Rev Dr. Charles CRABTREE
03 Executive Vice President ... Rev Dr. Patrick G. GALLAGHER
32 Vice President of Student Affairs ... Ms. Donna Jo SCRUGGS
10 Director of Finance ... Mr. Edward LAUGHLIN
07 Director of Admissions ... Rev. David HODGE
08 Head Librarian ... Miss Ginger MCDONALD
37 Director of Financial Aid ... Miss Patricia STAUFFER

MICHIGAN

Adrian College (D)

110 S Madison Street, Adrian MI 49221-2575
County: Lenawee FICE Identification: 002234
Unit ID: 168528
Telephone: (517) 265-5161 Carnegie Class: Bac/Diverse
FAX Number: (517) 264-3331 Calendar System: Semester
URL: www.adrian.edu
Established: 1859 Annual Undergrad Tuition & Fees: $27,050
Enrollment: 1,652 Coed
Affiliation or Control: United Methodist IRS Status: 501(c)3
Highest Offering: Master's
Program: Liberal Arts And General; Teacher Preparatory
Accreditation: NH, SW, @TEAC

01 President ... Dr. Jeffrey R. DOCKING
03 Executive Vice President ... Vacant
05 Vice Pres/Dean for Academic Affairs ... Dr. Agnes CALDWELL
30 Vice Pres Institutional Advancement ... Mr. Ron REEVES
84 Vice President of Enrollment ... Mr. Frank J. HRIBAR
32 Dean of Student Life ... Mrs. Kristi HOTTENSTEIN
20 Asst Dean of Academic Affairs ... Dr. Keith MCCLEARY
21 Asst Vice Pres of Business Affairs ... Mr. David DREWS
44 Asst Vice President for Development ... Mr. James A. MAHONY
07 Associate Director of Admissions ... Ms. Mallory FRAILING
42 Chaplain/Director Church Relations .. Dr. Christopher P. MOMANY
26 Director of Public Relations ... Ms. Jennifer COMPTON
06 Registrar ... Ms. Bridgette WINSLOW
35 Associate Dean for Student Life ... Vacant
88 Controller ... Ms. Nicole MEGALE
86 Dir of Govt & Foundation Relations ... Ms. Katie F. HAMMOND
15 Director of Human Resources ... Mrs. Ann FORRISTER
40 Bookstore Manager ... Ms. Rachelle M. DUFFY
93 Dir Multicultural Cultural Programs ... Ms. Idali FELICIANO
29 Director Alumni Relations ... Mrs. Marsha FIELDER
41 Director of Athletics ... Mr. Michael DUFFY
19 Director of Campus Safety ... Mr. Charley DECKER
36 Director of Career Planning ... Mrs. Janna D'AMICO
88 Director of Conferences ... Ms. Lesley CARSON
38 Director of Counseling ... Ms. Monique J. SAVAGE
08 Head Librarian ... Mr. David CRUSE
23 Director of Health Center ... Ms. Dawn MARSH
96 Director of Purchasing ... Ms. Heather HOLSOPPLE
37 Director of Financial Aid ... Mr. Andy SPOHN
18 Director of Facilities ... Mr. John E. JOHNSTON
09 Director of Institutional Research ... Dr. Jason M. HARTZ
88 Director of Academic Services ... Ms. Linda JACOBS
88 Assoc Director of Academic Services ... Ms. Carolyn QUINLAN
27 Asst Dir of Information Services ... Mr. Bradley MAGGARD

Albion College (E)

611 E Porter Street, Albion MI 49224-1831
County: Calhoun FICE Identification: 002235
Unit ID: 168546
Telephone: (517) 629-1000 Carnegie Class: Bac/A&S
FAX Number: (517) 629-0509 Calendar System: Semester
URL: www.albion.edu
Established: 1835 Annual Undergrad Tuition & Fees: $32,100
Enrollment: 1,582 Coed
Affiliation or Control: United Methodist IRS Status: 501(c)3
Highest Offering: Baccalaureate
Program: Liberal Arts And General; Teacher Preparatory
Accreditation: NH, MUS, @TEAC

01 President ... Dr. Donna M. RANDALL
10 Int Vice Pres Business & Finance ... Mr. Michael FRANDSEN
05 Provost ... Dr. Susan CONNER
30 Vice Pres Institutional Advancement ... Mr. Joshua MERCHANT
84 Vice Pres Enrollment Mgmt ... Vacant
32 Vice Pres & Dean Student Affairs ... Dr. Sally J. WALKER
13 Assoc Vice Pres Info Svcs/CIO ... Mr. Scott STEPHAN
07 Director of Admissions ... Vacant
39 Director Residential Life ... Mr. Michael WADSWORTH
08 Director of Libraries ... Dr. Michael VAN HOUTEN
26 Director of Communications ... Ms. Sarah F. BRIGGS
29 Director of Alumni Engagement ... Mr. Mark BACZEWSKI
38 Director of Counseling ... Dr. Frank KELEMAN
37 Director of Financial Aid ... Ms. Ann WHITMER
06 Registrar ... Dr. Andrew DUNHAM
88 Director Dining & Hospitality Svcs ... Mr. Todd TEKIELE
18 Director of Facilities Operations ... Mr. Donald MASTERNAK
19 Director of Campus Safety ... Mr. Kenneth SNYDER
41 Athletic Director ... Mr. Matthew AREND
42 College Chaplain ... Rev. Daniel MCQUOWN
15 Director of Human Resources ... Mrs. Lisa LOCKE
09 Director of Institutional Research ... Dr. Andrew DUNHAM
20 Associate Academic Officer ... Dr. Beth LINCOLN
28 Assoc Director Multicultural Affs ... Vacant
40 Manager of Bookstore ... Mr. Nick ANGLE

Alma College (F)

614 W Superior, Alma MI 48801-1599
County: Gratiot FICE Identification: 002236
Unit ID: 168591
Telephone: (989) 463-7111 Carnegie Class: Bac/A&S
FAX Number: (989) 463-7277 Calendar System: Other
URL: www.alma.edu
Established: 1886 Annual Undergrad Tuition & Fees: $29,230
Enrollment: 1,401 Coed
Affiliation or Control: Independent Non-Profit IRS Status: 501(c)3
Highest Offering: Baccalaureate
Program: Liberal Arts And General; Teacher Preparatory
Accreditation: NH, MUS, @TEAC

01 President ... Dr. Jeff ABERNATHY
05 Provost & Vice Pres for Acad Affs ... Dr. Michael L. SELMON
10 Vice Pres for Business Affairs ... Mr. David V. BUHL
30 Vice President for Advancement ... Ms. Carol F. HYBLE
84 Vice President for Enrollment ... Dr. Karen S. KLUMPP
32 Vice President for Student Life ... Dr. Nicholas A. PICCOLO
04 Executive Asst to the President ... Ms. Sandee A. GADDE
20 Assistant Provost ... Ms. Julie WILLIAMS
06 Registrar ... Ms. Susan M. DEEL
42 Chaplain ... Dr. Carol M. GREGG
37 Director of Financial Aid ... Mr. Chris A. BROWN
08 Director of Library ... Ms. Carol ZEILE
26 Director of College Communications ... Mr. Mike SILVERTHORN
14 Chief Technology Officer ... Dr. Keith R. NELSON
18 Director Facilities & Service Mgmt ... Mr. Douglas DICE
15 Director Human Resources ... Mr. Kenneth L. BORGMAN
21 Controller ... Mr. Dan HENRIS
29 Director Alumni Relations ... Ms. Lou ECKEN
20 Special Assistant to President ... Ms. Ann HALL
35 Director Campus Life ... Mr. David K. BLANDFORD
38 Director Counseling & Wellness ... Ms. Anne K. LAMBRECHT
07 Director Admissions ... Mr. Bob GARCIA
09 Director of Institutional Research ... Mr. Robert ROE

Alpena Community College (G)

665 Johnson Street, Alpena MI 49707-1495
County: Alpena FICE Identification: 002237
Unit ID: 168607
Telephone: (989) 356-9021 Carnegie Class: Assoc/Pub-R-M
FAX Number: (989) 358-7553 Calendar System: Semester
URL: www.alpenacc.edu
Established: 1952 Annual Undergrad Tuition & Fees (In-District): $3,510
Enrollment: 2,081 Coed
Affiliation or Control: Local IRS Status: 501(c)3
Highest Offering: Associate Degree
Program: Occupational; 2-Year Principally Bachelor's Creditable
Accreditation: NH, MAC

01 President ... Dr. Olin JOYNTON
10 Vice President Admin & Finance ... Mr. Richard SUTHERLAND
05 Vice President of Instruction ... Dr. Mark CURTIS
21 Controller ... Ms. Lyn KOWALEWSKY
32 Dean of Student Affairs ... Mr. Max P. LINDSAY
20 Dean Learning Resource Center ... Ms. Wendy BROOKS
103 Dean Workplace Partnership Program .. Mr. Donald MACMASTER
13 Co-Director Computing/Info Mgmt ... Ms. Vicky KROPP
13 Co-Director Computing/Info Mgmt ... Mr. Mark GRUNDER
26 Director Public Information ... Mr. Jay WALTERREIT
40 Director Bookstore ... Mr. William MATZKE
12 Director Huron Shores Campus ... Mr. George FALKENHAGEN
102 Foundation Director ... Ms. Penny BOLDREY
18 Director Buildings & Grounds ... Mr. Thomas LUDWIG
88 Director Volunteer Center ... Ms. Kathleen BRUSKI
06 Registrar ... Ms. Lori DZIESINSKI
15 Director Personnel Services ... Ms. Carolyn THOMAS
07 Director of Admissions ... Mr. Mike KOLLIEN
04 Assistant to President ... Ms. Elizabeth SPRAGG
09 Director of Institutional Research ... Mr. Donald MACMASTER
37 Director Student Financial Aid ... Mr. Robert ROOSE

Andrews University (H)

Berrien Springs MI 49104-0001
County: Berrien FICE Identification: 002238
Unit ID: 168740
Telephone: (269) 471-7771 Carnegie Class: DRU
FAX Number: (269) 471-6900 Calendar System: Semester
URL: www.andrews.edu
Established: 1874 Annual Undergrad Tuition & Fees: $23,428
Enrollment: 3,487 Coed
Affiliation or Control: Seventh-day Adventist IRS Status: 501(c)3
Highest Offering: Doctorate
Program: Liberal Arts And General; Teacher Preparatory; Professional
Accreditation: NH, CACREP, DIETD, DIETI, ENG, IACBE, MT, MUS, NUR, PTA, SW, TED, THEOL

01 President ... Dr. Niels-Erik A. ANDREASEN
05 Provost ... Dr. Andrea T. LUXTON
20 Associate Provost ... Dr. Emilio GARCIA-MARENKO
04 Asst to Pres for Spiritual Life ... Mr. Ronald H. WHITEHEAD
10 Vice President for Financial Admin ... Mr. Lawrence E. SCHALK
32 Vice President for Student Life ... Dr. Frances M. FAEHNER
84 Vice Pres of Enrollment & Marketing ... Mr. Stephen D. PAYNE
30 Vice President for Advancement ... Dr. David A. FAEHNER
43 General Counsel ... Mr. Brent G T. GERATY
06 Registrar ... Dr. Emilio GARCIA-MARENKO
49 Dean College Arts & Sciences ... Dr. Keith E. MATTINGLY
50 Dean School of Business Admin ... Dr. Allen F. STEMBRIDGE
53 Dean School of Education ... Dr. James R. JEFFERY
72 Dean College of Technology ... Dr. Verlyn R. BENSON
48 Dean School of Architecture ... Mr. Carey CARSCALLEN
73 Dean of Theological Seminary ... Dr. Denis FORTIN
58 Dean School of Grad Studies ... Dr. Christon ARTHUR
106 Dean School of Distance Education ... Dr. Alayne THORPE
08 Dean of Libraries ... Mr. Lawrence W. ONSAGER
21 Associate Business Officer ... Mr. Glenn A. MEEKMA
90 Chief Information Officer ... Ms. Lorena L. BIDWELL
39 Dir of University Apartment Life ... Mr. Alfredo RUIZ
34 Dir of the Women's Residence Halls ... Ms. Jennifer R. BURRILL
33 Dir of the Men's Residence Halls ... Mr. Spencer D. CARTER
85 Dir of International Student Svcs ... Dr. Najeeb W. NAKHLE
92 Director of Honors Program ... Dr. L. Monique PITTMAN
15 Director of Human Resources ... Mr. Daniel E. AGNETTA

37 Director Student Financial Aid .... Ms. Elynda A. BEDNEY
27 Director of Campus Relations .... Mrs. Rebecca L. MAY
26 Media Relations Specialist .... Ms. Keri SUAREZ
29 Director of Alumni Services .... Ms. Tami CONDON
38 Dir of Counseling/Testing Center .... Dr. Judith FISHER
40 Manager of Bookstore .... Ms. Cheryl KEAN
19 Director of Campus Safety .... Mr. Dale B. HODGES
23 Director of Medical Services .... Dr. Dan REICHERT
42 Chaplain .... Mr. Timothy P. NIXON
09 Director Institutional Research .... Mr. James R. MASSENA
18 Director of Facilities Management .... Mr. Richard L. SCOTT

Aquinas College (A)

1607 Robinson Road, SE, Grand Rapids MI 49506-1799
County: Kent FICE Identification: 002239
Unit ID: 168786
Telephone: (616) 632-8900 Carnegie Class: Master's M
FAX Number: (616) 732-4469 Calendar System: Semester
URL: www.aquinas.edu
Established: 1886 Annual Undergrad Tuition & Fees: $24,286
Enrollment: 2,186 Coed
Affiliation or Control: Roman Catholic IRS Status: 501(c)3
Highest Offering: Master's
Program: Liberal Arts And General; Teacher Preparatory; Professional
Accreditation: NH, @TEAC

01 President .... Dr. Juan OLIVAREZ
05 Provost/Dean of Faculty .... Dr. Charles GUNNOE, JR.
45 Vice Pres Planning/Research .... Vacant
30 Vice President Advancement .... Mr. Greg MCALEENAN
10 Vice President Finance & Operations .... Mr. Stephen WONCH
84 Vice Pres Enrollment Management .... Ms. Paula T. MEEHAN
04 Assistant to President .... Ms. Jan SOMMERVILLE
102 Assoc VP for Inst Advancement .... Mr. Gregory MEYER
06 Registrar .... Mrs. Cecelia MESLER
07 Dean of Admissions .... Mr. Thomas MIKOWSKI
20 Associate Provost .... Ms. Nanette CLATTERBUCK
32 Dean of Student Services .... Mr. Brian MATZKE
35 Associate Dean of Student Affairs .... Dr. Jennifer DAWSON
38 Director of Career/Counseling Svcs .... Ms. Sharon SMITH
104 Dir International Education Pgms .... Ms. Joelle BALDWIN
94 Director of Women's Studies . Dr. Susan HAWORTH-HOEPPNER
92 Director of Honors Program .... Dr. Michelle DEROSE
58 Director of Graduate Management .... Mr. Brian DIVITA
08 Co-Director Woodhouse Library .... Ms. Shelly JEFFRIES
08 Co-Director Woodhouse Library .... Ms. Francine PAOLINI
24 Media Coordinator .... Ms. Francine PAOLINI
21 Controller .... Ms. Cathy LUCK
15 Director of Human Resources .... Mr. Stephen WOLF
14 Director College Computing .... Ms. Joyce L. LAFLEUR
18 Director of Maintenance .... Mr. Dale HAISMA
23 Manager of Health and Wellness .... Ms. Veronica BEITNER
39 Director Residence Life .... Vacant
07 Director of Admissions .... Ms. Angela SCHLOSSER-BACON
37 Director of Financial Aid .... Mr. David J. STEFFEE
41 Director Athletics .... Mr. Terry M. BOCIAN
42 Director Campus Ministry .... Ms. Mary CLARK-KAISER
29 Director of Alumni Relations .... Ms. Brigid AVERY
35 Director of Campus Life .... Ms. Heather HALL
44 Director of Major Gifts .... Ms. Cecelia CUNNINGHAM
44 Director of Corporate Giving .... Dr. Ali ERHAN
26 Assoc VP Marketing & Communication .... Ms. Meg DERRER
20 Director of Academic Advising .... Ms. Cecelia MESLER
28 Director of Diversity .... Ms. Marnika BROWN
40 Director Bookstore .... Ms. Marian TODISH

The Art Institute of Michigan (B)

28125 Cabot Drive, Novi MI 48377
County: Oakland Identification: 666692
Unit ID: 451796
Telephone: (248) 675-3800 Carnegie Class: Not Classified
FAX Number: (248) 489-3961 Calendar System: Semester
URL: www.artinstitutes.edu/detroit
Established: 2007 Annual Undergrad Tuition & Fees: $43,470
Enrollment: 751 Coed
Affiliation or Control: Proprietary IRS Status: Proprietary
Highest Offering: Baccalaureate
Program: Fine Arts Emphasis
Accreditation: &NH, ACFEI

01 President .... Dr. Ted BLASHAK

† Regional accreditation is carried under the parent institution The Illinois Institute of Art, Chicago, IL.

*Baker College System (C)

1050 W Bristol Road, Flint MI 48507-5508
County: Genesee Identification: 666923
Unit ID: 419572
Telephone: (810) 766-4280 Carnegie Class: N/A
FAX Number: (810) 766-4279
URL: www.baker.edu

00 Chairman of the Board .... Mr. Edward J. KURTZ
01 CEO/President of System .... Mr. F. James CUMMINS
05 Vice President for Academics .... Dr. Denise A. BANNAN
13 Vice President for Computer Systems .... Mr. Joel P. HOITENGA
32 Vice President for Student Services .... Mr. Ellis P. SALIM
15 Vice President of Human Resources .... Ms. Rosemary ZAWACKI
26 Vice Pres Marketing/Admissions/PR .... Mr. Richard DELONG
10 Vice President for Finance .... Ms. Tiffany DAVIS
12 Campus Director-Cass City .... Ms. Karen EASTERLING
12 Campus Director-West Branch .... Ms. Karen EASTERLING
07 System Director for Admissions .... Mr. Bruce LUNDEEN
35 Director of Student Life .... Vacant
45 Director of Assessment .... Ms. Debra BILLINGS
20 Director Curriculum .... Ms. Kim L. LUTZ
36 Director of Career Services .... Mr. Michael HELSEN
13 Director Computer Programming .... Mr. Michael A. ANDRITSIS
14 Director Computer Operations .... Mrs. Sheryl L. DEAN
08 Director of Library Services .... Mr. Eric PALMER
58 President Graduate Studies .... Dr. Michael HEBERLING

*Baker College of Allen Park (D)

4500 Enterprise Drive, Allen Park MI 48101-3033
Identification: 666996
Unit ID: 444167
Telephone: (313) 425-3700 Carnegie Class: Bac/Assoc
FAX Number: (313) 425-3777 Calendar System: Quarter
URL: www.baker.edu
Established: 2003 Annual Undergrad Tuition & Fees: $7,560
Enrollment: 3,926 Coed
Affiliation or Control: Independent Non-Profit IRS Status: 501(c)3
Highest Offering: Baccalaureate
Program: Occupational; 2-Year Principally Bachelor's Creditable; Liberal Arts And General
Accreditation: &NH, IACBE, MAC, MLTAD, OTA, PTAA, SURGT

02 Campus President .... Mr. Aaron J. MAIKE
05 Chief Academic Officer .... Dr. Karen BRATUS
06 Registrar .... Ms. Kimberly BLAIR-CHAMBERS
07 Vice President of Admissions .... Mr. Steven PETERSON
10 Chief Business Officer .... Ms. Kristine BARANN
37 Director Student Financial Aid .... Ms. Candi RUFFNER

*Baker College of Auburn Hills (E)

1500 University Drive, Auburn Hills MI 48326-2642
County: Oakland Identification: 666940
Unit ID: 404073
Telephone: (248) 340-0600 Carnegie Class: Bac/Assoc
FAX Number: (248) 340-0608 Calendar System: Quarter
URL: www.baker.edu
Established: 1992 Annual Undergrad Tuition & Fees: $7,560
Enrollment: 4,179 Coed
Affiliation or Control: Independent Non-Profit IRS Status: 501(c)3
Highest Offering: Baccalaureate
Program: Occupational; 2-Year Principally Bachelor's Creditable; Liberal Arts And General
Accreditation: &NH, DA, DH, DMS, IACBE

02 President .... Mr. Jeffrey M. LOVE
07 Vice President of Admissions .... Ms. Jan BOHLEN
05 Vice President of Academics .... Dr. Susan D. CATHCART
10 Vice President of Finance .... Mr. Jim MARTIN
06 Registrar/Student Counseling .... Mr. Tim M. YOUNT
18 Director of Facilities .... Mr. Jim DELASHMIT
36 Director of Career Services .... Ms. Beth NUCCIO
37 Director of Financial Aid .... Mr. Greg LITTLE

*Baker College of Cadillac (F)

9600 E 13th Street, Cadillac MI 49601-9600
County: Wexford Identification: 666941
Unit ID: 404648
Telephone: (231) 876-3100 Carnegie Class: Bac/Assoc
FAX Number: (231) 775-8505 Calendar System: Quarter
URL: www.baker.edu
Established: 1986 Annual Undergrad Tuition & Fees: $7,560
Enrollment: 2,094 Coed
Affiliation or Control: Independent Non-Profit IRS Status: 501(c)3
Highest Offering: Baccalaureate
Program: Occupational; 2-Year Principally Bachelor's Creditable; Technical Emphasis
Accreditation: &NH, IACBE, MAC, SURGT

02 Campus President .... Dr. Kelly SMITH
05 Chief Academic Officer .... Ms. Nancy FOSTER
07 Director of Admissions .... Ms. Audrey CHARMOLI
06 Registrar/Academic Advisor .... Mr. Cliff REDES
10 Business Manager .... Ms. Ami MCBRIDE
36 Director of Career Services .... Ms. Jackie SOLTMAN
37 Director of Financial Aid .... Ms. Kristin BONNEY
08 Librarian .... Ms. Melissa MCPHERSON
53 Dean of Education .... Vacant
76 Dean of Health .... Ms. Gail BALLARD
97 Dean of General Education .... Mr. David DARROW
13 Dean Computer Info Systems/Tech .... Vacant

*Baker College of Clinton Township (G)

34950 Little Mack Avenue,
Clinton Township MI 48035-4701
County: Macomb Identification: 666942
Unit ID: 404082
Telephone: (586) 791-6610 Carnegie Class: Bac/Assoc
FAX Number: (586) 791-6611 Calendar System: Quarter
URL: www.baker.edu
Established: 1990 Annual Undergrad Tuition & Fees: $7,560
Enrollment: 6,265 Coed
Affiliation or Control: Independent Non-Profit IRS Status: 501(c)3
Highest Offering: Baccalaureate
Program: Occupational; 2-Year Principally Bachelor's Creditable; Liberal Arts And General
Accreditation: &NH, IACBE, MAC, RAD, SURGT

02 President .... Mr. Donald R. TORLINE
07 Vice President of Admissions .... Ms. Annette LOOSER
32 Vice President of Student Services .... Ms. Lisa HARVENER
10 Vice President of Finance .... Ms. Marsha ADAMKIEWICZ
05 Vice President of Academics .... Mr. James KOENIG
50 Dean of Business .... Mr. Joseph PEPOY
72 Dean of CIS/Technology .... Ms. Pauline DUEWEKE
76 Dean of Allied Health Sciences .... Ms. Anna CZUBATYJ
06 Registrar .... Mr. Shaun STEVENS
38 Director Student Counseling .... Ms. Barbara KRYGEL
08 Head Librarian .... Ms. Kathy HARGER
36 Director Student Placement .... Ms. Marilyn WOODS
19 Director Security/Safety .... Mr. Dan OSBORN

*Baker College of Flint (H)

1050 W Bristol Road, Flint MI 48507-5508
County: Genesee FICE Identification: 004673
Unit ID: 168847
Telephone: (810) 766-4000 Carnegie Class: Bac/Assoc
FAX Number: (810) 766-4293 Calendar System: Quarter
URL: www.baker.edu
Established: 1911 Annual Undergrad Tuition & Fees: $7,560
Enrollment: 7,166 Coed
Affiliation or Control: Independent Non-Profit IRS Status: 501(c)3
Highest Offering: Doctorate
Program: Occupational; 2-Year Principally Bachelor's Creditable; Liberal Arts And General; Business Emphasis
Accreditation: NH, ENG, ENGT, IACBE, MAC, OT, POLYT, PTAA, SURGT

02 President .... Dr. Julianne T. PRINCINSKY
05 Vice President of Academics .... Dr. Candace JOHNSON
07 Vice President of Admissions .... Ms. Jodi CUNEAZ
15 Vice President of Human Resources .... Ms. Rosemary ZAWACKI
32 Vice President of Student Services .... Mr. Gerald MCCARTY, II
08 Director of Library Services .... Mr. Eric PALMER
06 Registrar .... Mr. Robert MARTIN
88 Dean of Developmental Education .... Mrs. Connie WARNER
50 Dean of Business Administration .... Dr. John C. COTE
97 Dean of General Education .... Dr. Mary Ann THAYER
76 Dean of Health/Human Services .... Ms. Clementine RICE
72 Dean of Technical Division .... Mr. James RIDDELL
13 Director of Computer Operations .... Mr. Michael MEYERS
18 Director of Facilities .... Mr. Marvin DEAN
38 Director of Counseling/Assessment .... Mr. Paul ZANG
19 Director of Safety/Security .... Mr. Thomas POKORA
40 Director of Bookstore .... Mr. James ROTTA
54 Dir Engineering/Computer Science .... Mr. James RIDDELL
26 Actg Director Community Relations .. Dr. Julianne T. PRINCINSKY
10 Business Officer .... Mrs. Rebecca AYRE-BOGGS
36 Director of Career Services .... Mrs. Janie STEWART
37 Director Student Financial Aid .... Ms. Veta NORRIS
31 Director Corporate/Community Svcs .... Ms. Karen EASTERLING
23 Director of Health and Fitness .... Ms. Maureen PARMANN
39 Housing Coordinator .... Mr. Leon CARTER

*Baker College of Jackson (I)

2800 Springport Road, Jackson MI 49202-1290
County: Jackson FICE Identification: 004680
Unit ID: 414160
Telephone: (517) 788-7800 Carnegie Class: Bac/Assoc
FAX Number: (517) 789-7331 Calendar System: Quarter
URL: www.baker.edu
Established: 1994 Annual Undergrad Tuition & Fees: $7,560
Enrollment: 2,917 Coed
Affiliation or Control: Independent Non-Profit IRS Status: 501(c)3
Highest Offering: Baccalaureate
Program: Occupational; 2-Year Principally Bachelor's Creditable; Technical Emphasis
Accreditation: &NH, IACBE, MAC, OPD, RTT, SURGT

02 President/Chief Academic Officer .... Dr. Patty KAUFMAN
07 Vice President of Admissions .... Mr. Kevin M. PNACEK
10 Vice President of Finance .... Vacant
32 VP Student Affs/Dir Stdnt Placment .... Ms. Michelle SHIELDS
20 Dean of Developmental Education .... Ms. Cindy VAN GIESON
15 Dean of Education/Human Services .... Mr. Blaine GOODRICH
37 Financial Aid Director .... Ms. Jenni SAMONS
06 Registrar .... Ms. Jill M. DUTTON
18 Director Facilities/Physical Plant .... Mr. Ryan SMITHSOM
50 Dean Business & Technology .... Mr. Jack JORDAN
76 Dean Allied Health .... Ms. Marie BONKOWSKI
97 Dean General Education .... Ms. Nancy HILL
38 Director of Student Counseling .... Vacant
21 Business Officer & Personnel Svcs .... Ms. Lisa GOWDY

*Baker College of Muskegon (J)

1903 Marquette Avenue, Muskegon MI 49442-1590
County: Muskegon FICE Identification: 002296
Unit ID: 171298
Telephone: (231) 777-5200 Carnegie Class: Bac/Assoc
FAX Number: (231) 777-5265 Calendar System: Quarter
URL: www.baker.edu
Established: 1911 Annual Undergrad Tuition & Fees: $7,560

Enrollment: 5,810 Coed
Affiliation or Control: Independent Non-Profit IRS Status: 501(c)3
Highest Offering: Baccalaureate
Program: Occupational; 2-Year Principally Bachelor's Creditable; Liberal Arts And General
Accreditation: &NH, ACFEI, IACBE, MAC, OTA, PTAA, RAD, SURGT

02 President ... Dr. Lee COGGIN
05 Vice President for Academics ... Dr. DeAnna BURT
10 Vice President for Finance ... Ms. Manifa DENNISON
32 Vice President for Student Services ... Mr. Michael L. HELSEN
07 Vice President Admissions ... Ms. Kathy JACOBSON
06 Registrar ... Ms. Christine FOGG
50 Dean for Business & Office Admin ... Vacant
97 Dean for General Education ... Ms. Kijm PILIECI
77 Dean for CIS Technical ... Mr. Gary VERSALLE
15 Dean for Health ... Mr. Eric SURGE
37 Financial Aid Director ... Mrs. Leslie JOLMAN
08 Director of Library Services ... Ms. Gail POWERS-SCHAUB
18 Director of Facilities ... Mr. David STURGEON
19 Director of Campus Safety ... Mr. Joe STAPEL
38 Director of Counseling & Assessment ... Ms. Christine BULTEMA

Baker College of Owosso (A)

1020 S Washington Street, Owosso MI 48867-4400
County: Shiawassee Identification: 666937
Unit ID: 168838
Telephone: (989) 729-3370 Carnegie Class: Bac/Assoc
FAX Number: (989) 729-3429 Calendar System: Quarter
URL: www.baker.edu
Established: 1983 Annual Undergrad Tuition & Fees: $7,560
Enrollment: 3,532 Coed
Affiliation or Control: Independent Non-Profit IRS Status: 501(c)3
Highest Offering: Baccalaureate
Program: Occupational; 2-Year Principally Bachelor's Creditable; Liberal Arts And General
Accreditation: &NH, ADNUR, DMS, IACBE, MAC, MLTAD, RAD

02 President ... Mr. Peter KARSTEN
05 Vice President of Academics ... Dr. Carol DOWSETT
32 Vice President of Student Services ... Mrs. Lisa A. LYNCH
10 Vice President of Finance ... Mr. Michael MOORE
07 Vice President of Admissions ... Mr. Michael KONOPACKE
37 Director of Financial Aid ... Ms. Nicole BOELK
06 Registrar ... Ms. Christy VERITY
18 Chief Facilities/Physical Plant ... Mr. Pat PRASKI
26 Chief Public Relations Officer ... Vacant
38 Director Student Counseling ... Mr. James BAUER

Baker College of Port Huron (B)

3403 Lapeer Road, Port Huron MI 48060-2597
County: Saint Clair Identification: 666943
Unit ID: 381617
Telephone: (810) 985-7000 Carnegie Class: Bac/Assoc
FAX Number: (810) 985-7066 Calendar System: Quarter
URL: www.baker.edu
Established: 1990 Annual Undergrad Tuition & Fees: $7,560
Enrollment: 1,776 Coed
Affiliation or Control: Independent Non-Profit IRS Status: 501(c)3
Highest Offering: Baccalaureate
Program: Occupational; 2-Year Principally Bachelor's Creditable; Liberal Arts And General
Accreditation: &NH, DA, DH, IACBE, MAC, MLTAD, SURGT

02 President ... Dr. Connie HARRISON
05 Chief Academic Officer ... Dr. Laura TREANOR
07 Vice President of Admissions ... Mr. Dan KENNY
32 Vice President of Student Services ... Ms. Betsy WHITE
06 Registrar ... Ms. Judi LANGOLF
97 Dean General Education ... Ms. Louise WANG-WELDON
88 Dean of Developmental Education ... Ms. Marjorie BEAUDRY
50 Dean Business Administration ... Ms. Susan PORRETT
72 Dean Technical ... Ms. Jean HALL
76 Dean Health Science ... Dr. Pamela GOLL
53 Dean Education & Human Services ... Dr. Janelle MCGUIRE
08 Director of Library ... Ms. Dora MARSHALL-TURNER
37 Senior Officer of Financial Aid ... Ms. Barbara MALCOLM
38 Director Academic Counseling ... Mr. Greg RUMPZ
18 Director of Facilities ... Mr. Shane HENSLEY
10 Business Manager ... Mr. Charles DECKER

Bay Mills Community College (C)

12214 W Lakeshore Drive, Brimley MI 49715-9750
County: Chippewa FICE Identification: 030666
Unit ID: 380359
Telephone: (906) 248-3354 Carnegie Class: Tribal
FAX Number: (906) 248-3351 Calendar System: Semester
URL: www.bmcc.edu
Established: 1984 Annual Undergrad Tuition & Fees: $2,850
Enrollment: 607 Coed
Affiliation or Control: Tribal Control IRS Status: 501(c)3
Highest Offering: Associate Degree
Program: Occupational; 2-Year Principally Bachelor's Creditable; Business Emphasis
Accreditation: NH

01 President ... Michael C. PARISH
05 Vice President of Academic Affairs ... Samantha CAMERON
14 Technology Director ... Chet KASPER
10 VP of Business & Finance ... Laura POSTMA
32 Dean of Student Services ... Debra J. WILSON
06 Registrar ... Sherri SCHOFIELD
37 Director Student Financial Aid ... Tina MILLER

Bay Noc Community College (D)

2001 N Lincoln Road, Escanaba MI 49829-2510
County: Delta FICE Identification: 002240
Unit ID: 168883
Telephone: (906) 786-5802 Carnegie Class: Assoc/Pub-R-M
FAX Number: (906) 789-6952 Calendar System: Semester
URL: www.baycollege.edu
Established: 1962 Annual Undergrad Tuition & Fees (In-District): $3,347
Enrollment: 2,811 Coed
Affiliation or Control: Local IRS Status: 501(c)3
Highest Offering: Associate Degree
Program: Occupational; 2-Year Principally Bachelor's Creditable
Accreditation: NH, ADNUR

01 President ... Dr. Laura L. COLEMAN
05 VP Instructional/Student Lrng ... Dr. Wendolyn E. TETLOW
10 VP Administrative Svcs ... Mr. Tom J. SABOR
12 Vice President West Campus ... Dr. Patrick KENNEDY
32 Exec Dean of Student Services ... Mr. Matthew R. SOUCY
49 Dean of Arts and Sciences ... Dr. Deborah ANDERSON
72 Dean of Business and Tech ... Mr. Dan M. WOODWARD
30 Exec Dir Institutional Advancement ... Ms. Kim CARNE
13 Executive Dir of Information Tech ... Ms. Christine WILLIAMS
37 Director of Financial Aid ... Ms. Susan K. HEBERT
07 Director of Admissions ... Ms. Cynthia A. CARTER
15 Director of Human Resources ... Mr. Thomas J. GRIGGS
18 Superintendent Buildings/Grounds ... Mr. Ralph W. CURRY
76 Interim Dean Allied Health/Wellness ... Ms. Patti HENNING
51 Manager Continuing Educ & Prof Dev ... Ms. Lori L. SHEA
09 Exec Dir of Institutional Research ... Mr. Mark KINNEY
36 Career/Academic Advisor ... Ms. Annette M. JOHNSON
38 Director Student Counseling ... Mr. Douglas S. KENDRICK
103 Director of Workforce Development ... Ms. Barbara A. WALDEN

Calvin College (E)

3201 Burton Street, SE, Grand Rapids MI 49546-4388
County: Kent FICE Identification: 002241
Unit ID: 169080
Telephone: (616) 526-6000 Carnegie Class: Bac/A&S
FAX Number: (616) 526-8551 Calendar System: 4/1/4
URL: www.calvin.edu
Established: 1876 Annual Undergrad Tuition & Fees: $25,340
Enrollment: 3,991 Coed
Affiliation or Control: Christian Reformed Church IRS Status: 501(c)3
Highest Offering: Master's
Program: Liberal Arts And General; Teacher Preparatory
Accreditation: NH, CS, ENG, MUS, NURSE, @SP, SW, @TEAC

01 President ... Dr. Gaylen J. BYKER
04 Senior Executive Associate ... Mr. Robert A. BERKHOF
04 Executive Associate ... Ms. Darlene K. MEYERING
05 Provost ... Dr. Claudia BEVERSLUIS
10 Vice Pres Admin/Finance/Info Tech ... Dr. Henry E. DEVRIES, II
30 Vice President for Advancement ... Mr. Kenneth ERFFMEYER
84 Vice Pres Enrollment Management ... Mr. Russell J. BLOEM
32 Vice President Student Life ... Dr. Shirley VOGELZANG HOOGSTRA
21 Director of Finance ... Mr. Samuel L. WANNER
08 Director of the Library ... Mr. Glenn A. REMELTS
29 Director Alumni/Parent Relations ... Mr. Michael J. VAN DENEND
06 Director Academic Svcs/Registrar ... Mr. Thomas L. STEENWYK
07 Director Enrollment Policy/Planning ... Mr. Dale D. KUIPER
39 Dean of Residence Life ... Mr. John WITTE
35 Dean of Student Development ... Mr. C. Robert CROW
88 Dean of Students for Judicial Affs ... Ms. Jane E. HENDRIKSMA
46 Dean of Research & Scholarship ... Dr. Matthew WALHOUT
20 Dean for Institutional Effectivenes ... Dr. Michael STOB
83 Academic Dean Soc Sci/Context Disc ... Dr. Cheryl BRANDSEN
79 Acad Dean Arts/Language/Education ... Dr. Mark WILLIAMS
81 Academic Dean Natural Science/Math ... Dr. Stanley L. HAAN
28 Dean of Multicultural Academic Affs ... Dr. Michelle LOYD-PAIGE
15 Director of Human Resources ... Mr. Todd K. HUBERS
36 Director of Career Development ... Mr. Glenn E. TRIEZENBERG
09 Dir Institutional/Enroll Research ... Mr. Thomas A. VAN ECK
31 Director Conferences/Campus Events ... Mr. Jeffrey A. STOB
26 Director of Communic & Marketing ... Mr. Timothy L. ELLENS
88 Director Social Research Center ... Vacant
19 Director of Campus Safety ... Mr. William T. CORNER
18 Director Physical Plant ... Mr. Philip D. BEEZHOLD
24 Director Instruc Resources Center ... Mr. Randal G. NIEUWSMA
38 Director Broene Counseling Center ... Dr. Cynthia KOK
23 Director Health Services ... Dr. Laura CHAMPION
92 Director Honors Program ... Dr. Kenneth D. BRATT
42 College Chaplain ... Dr. Mary HULST
40 Manager of the College Store ... Mr. Thomas J. VAN WINGERDEN
41 Athletic Director Men ... Dr. James TIMMER, JR.
41 Athletic Director Women ... Dr. Nancy L. MEYER

Calvin Theological Seminary (F)

3233 Burton Street, SE, Grand Rapids MI 49546-4387
County: Kent FICE Identification: 002242
Unit ID: 169099
Telephone: (616) 957-6036 Carnegie Class: Spec/Faith
FAX Number: (616) 957-8621 Calendar System: Semester
URL: www.calvinseminary.edu
Established: 1876 Annual Graduate Tuition & Fees: $12,903
Enrollment: 275 Coed
Affiliation or Control: Christian Reformed Church IRS Status: 501(c)3
Highest Offering: Doctorate; No Undergraduates
Program: Professional
Accreditation: THEOL

01 President ... Rev. Julius T. MEDENBLIK
05 Dean of Academic Programs ... Dr. Ronald J. FEENSTRA
20 Dean of the Faculty ... Dr. Lyle D. BIERMA
06 Registrar ... Ms. Joan BEELEN
32 Dean of Students/Intl Stdnt Advisor ... Rev. Richard SYTSMA
08 Theological Librarian ... Rev. Lugene L. SCHEMPER
10 Chief Financial Officer ... Mr. Philip VANDEN BERGE
30 Director of Development ... Mr. Robert KNOOR
36 Coordinator Field Education ... Rev. Alvern GELDER
37 Financial Aid Ofcr/Coord Recruitmnt ... Mr. Matthew COOKE

Central Michigan University (G)

Mount Pleasant MI 48859-0001
County: Isabella FICE Identification: 002243
Unit ID: 169248
Telephone: (989) 774-4000 Carnegie Class: DRU
FAX Number: (989) 774-3537 Calendar System: Semester
URL: www.cmich.edu
Established: 1892 Annual Undergrad Tuition & Fees (In-State): $10,740
Enrollment: 28,292 Coed
Affiliation or Control: State IRS Status: 501(c)3
Highest Offering: Doctorate
Program: Liberal Arts And General; Teacher Preparatory; Professional
Accreditation: NH, ART, ARCPA, AUD, BUS, BUSA, CIDA, CLPSY, DIETD, DIETI, ENG, JOUR, MUS, NAIT, NRPA, PTA, SCPSY, SP, SPAA, SW, TEAC

01 President ... Dr. George E. ROSS
05 Executive VP/Provost ... Dr. E. Gary SHAPIRO
10 Vice Pres Finance/Admin Svcs ... Mr. David A. BURDETTE
30 Vice Pres Development/Ext Relations ... Ms. Kathleen M. WILBUR
107 VP/Executive Director Prof Educ ... Dr. Merodie A. HANCOCK
14 Vice President Information Tech/CIO ... Dr. Roger E. REHM
21 AVP Fin Svcs & Reporting/Controller ... Mr. Barrie J. WILKES
26 Assoc VP University Communications ... Ms. Renee T. WALKER
18 Assoc Vice Pres Facilities Mgmt ... Mr. Stephen P. LAWRENCE
39 Assoc VP Residence/Auxiliary Svcs ... Mr. John S. FISHER
88 Assoc VP Faculty Personnel Svcs ... Mr. Robert C. MARTIN
28 Assoc VP Institutional Diversity ... Dr. Denise O. GREEN
15 Interim Assoc VP Human Resources ... Ms. Lori L. HELLA
88 Assoc VP Academic Pgm/Prof Educ ... Mr. Peter G. ROSS
20 Interim Vice Provost Acad Affairs ... Dr. Claudia B. DOUGLASS
88 Vice Provost Academic Admin ... Dr. Ray L. CHRISTIE
46 Interim Vice Provost Research ... Dr. James H. HAGEMAN
44 Asst VP Major/Planned Giving Pgm ... Mr. Edward A. TOLCHER
08 Dean of Libraries ... Mr. Thomas J. MOORE
32 Dean of Students ... Dr. Bruce K. ROSCOE
35 Asst Dean/Director Student Life ... Mr. Tony A. VOISIN
88 Asst Dean/Dir Acad Advis/Assistance ... Ms. Michelle L. HOWARD
29 Exec Dir of Alumni Relations ... Ms. Marcie OTTEMAN
09 Director Institutional Research ... Dr. Wei ZHOU
22 Director Civil Rights/Inst Equity ... Ms. Jeannie JACKSON
07 Director of Admissions ... Ms. Betty J. WAGNER
43 General Counsel ... Dr. Manuel R. RUPE
06 Registrar ... Ms. Karen E. HUTSLAR
37 Director Scholarships/Financial Aid ... Mr. Kirk M. YATS
36 Director Career Services ... Ms. Julia B. SHERLOCK
41 Assoc VP/Athletics Director ... Mr. David HEEKE, JR.
38 Director Counseling Center ... Mr. Ross J. RAPAPORT
45 Director Financial Plan & Budgets ... Ms. Carol A. HAAS
88 Director Internal Audit ... Mr. Michael J. ROETHLISBERGER
27 Director Public Relations ... Mr. Steven F. SMITH
19 Chief of Police ... Mr. William YEAGLEY
40 Director CMU Bookstore ... Mr. Barry D. WATERS
72 Dean College of Sci & Tech ... Dr. Ian R. DAVISON
76 Dean Col of Health Professions ... Dr. Chris INGERSOLL
63 Dean College of Medicine ... Dr. Ernest YODER
79 Dean Col Hum/Soc/Behav Sci ... Dr. Pamela S. GATES
57 Dean College Comm/Fine Arts ... Dr. Salma I. GHANEM
50 Dean College of Business Admin ... Dr. Charles T. CRESPY
53 Interim Dean Education/Human Svcs ... Dr. Kathryn E. KOCH
58 Interim Dean Graduate Studies ... Dr. Roger L. COLES
04 Executive Assistant to President ... Ms. Mary Jane FLANAGAN
88 General Manager Public Broadcasting ... Dr. Edward B. GRANT
85 Exec Dir International Affairs ... Dr. Mark POINDEXTER
88 Asst VP Univ Rec/Events & Confs ... Mr. Stan L. SHINGLES
96 Director Contract & Purchasing Svcs ... Mr. Thomas P. TRIONFI
92 Dir University Honors/Centralis ... Dr. Phame M. CAMARENA
93 Director of Minority Students Svcs ... Ms. Traci L. GUINN
88 Associate Dean Libraries ... Dr. Richard M. COCHRAN
88 Assoc Dean/Administration & Finance ... Deborah L. BIGGS
88 Interim Assoc Dean Educ/Human Svcs ... Dr. Raymond W. FRANCIS
88 Assoc Dean Clin Affairs & Hosp Rel ... Sean K. KESTERSON
88 Assoc Dean Science & Technology ... Dr. Jane M. MATTY
88 Int Assoc Dean Business Admin ... Dr. Karl L. SMART
88 Assoc Dean Health Professions ... Dr. Thomas J. MASTERSON
88 Int Assc Dean Human/Soc/Behav Sci ... Dr. Rick S. KURTZ
88 Associate Dean Comm/Fine Arts ... Dr. Shelly S. HINCK
88 Sr Assoc Dean Business Admin ... Dr. Daniel E. VETTER
31 Exec Asst to Pres-Detroit Outreach ... Mr. Tyrone JORDAN
86 Director Government Relations ... Mr. Toby ROTH

Cleary University (H)

3601 Plymouth Road, Ann Arbor MI 48105-2659
County: Washtenaw FICE Identification: 002246
Unit ID: 169327

Telephone: (800) 686-1886 Carnegie Class: Spec/Bus
FAX Number: (734) 332-4646 Calendar System: Quarter
URL: www.cleary.edu
Established: 1883 Annual Undergrad Tuition & Fees: $370
Enrollment: 769 Coed
Affiliation or Control: Independent Non-Profit IRS Status: 501(c)3
Highest Offering: Master's
Program: Occupational; Professional; Business Emphasis
Accreditation: NH

01 President & CEO .... Mr. Thomas P. SULLIVAN
05 Provost & VP Academic Affairs .... Dr. Vincent P. LINDER
10 VP Finance & Administration .... Ms. Judy WALKER
06 Asst VP Academic Svcs/Registrar .... Ms. Dawn M. FISER
04 Exec Asst to Pres/Board of Trustees .... Ms. Linda T. RENTZ
12 Dean Livingston Campus .... Mr. Roy COONS
32 Dean Ann Arbor Campus .... Ms. Donna M. FRANKLIN
88 Dean Col Applied Business Science .... Mr. Clyde RIVARD
50 Dean College of Management .... Mr. Dave CASTLEGRANT
72 Dn Col Bus Innovation/Applied Tech .... Ms. Dawn MARKELL
58 Dean College of Graduate Studies .... Ms. Sadhana ALANGAR
13 Exec Director/Chief Info Officer .... Mr. David G. BOWERS
09 Dir Institutional Research/Analysis .... Mr. Tim VEENSTRA
18 Director Facilities .... Mr. Gary BACHMAN
88 Director Institutional Improvement .... Ms. Monica MOSES
30 Exec Dir Development/Alumni Rel .... Mr. Dennis PURDY
37 Director Financial Aid .... Ms. Vesta SMITH-CAMPBELL
36 Dir Career Services & Placement .... Ms. Tonya MCFEE
40 Director Bookstore Services .... Ms. Sheila THOMPSON
07 Director of Admissions .... Ms. Carrie BONOFIGLIO
26 Chief Public Relations Officer .... Ms. Amanda HOLDSWORTH
29 Director Alumni Relations .... Ms. Kathy SPRING

College for Creative Studies (A)

201 E Kirby, Detroit MI 48202-4034
County: Wayne FICE Identification: 006771
Unit ID: 169442
Telephone: (313) 664-7400 Carnegie Class: Spec/Arts
FAX Number: (313) 872-8377 Calendar System: Semester
URL: www.collegeforcreativestudies.edu
Established: 1906 Annual Undergrad Tuition & Fees: $32,785
Enrollment: 1,351 Coed
Affiliation or Control: Independent Non-Profit IRS Status: 501(c)3
Highest Offering: Master's
Program: Teacher Preparatory; Professional; Fine Arts Emphasis
Accreditation: NH, ART, CIDA

01 President .... Mr. Richard L. ROGERS
100 Executive Assistant/Chief of Staff .... Ms. Sandra BRADEN
04 Admin Assistant to the President .... Ms. Brigette NEAL
10 Vice Pres Administration & Finance .... Ms. Anne D. BECK
30 Vice Pres Institutional Advancement .... Ms. Nina HOLDEN
05 Dean of the College .... Mr. Imre MOLNAR
84 Dean of Enrollmnt and Student Svcs .... Ms. Julie HINGELBERG
07 Director of Admissions .... Ms. Lori WATSON
28 Director of Multicultural Affairs .... Mr. Cliff HARRIS
20 Assoc Dean Academic Affairs .... Ms. Sharon PROCTER
51 Director Continuing Education .... Ms. Carla GONZALEZ
31 Dir Community Arts Partnerships .... Mr. Mikel BRESEE
13 Director Information Technology .... Mr. Greg FRASER
90 Director of Academic Technologies .... Ms. Laurie EVANS
08 Director Library .... Ms. Beth WALKER
21 Director Business Services .... Ms. Kerri MCKAY
32 Director Student Life .... Mr. Michael COLEMAN
85 Director Intl Student Services .... Ms. Jennifer DICKEY
37 Director Financial Aid .... Ms. Kristin MOSKOVITZ
15 Director Human Resources .... Mr. Gregory KNOFF
18 Director Facilities & Admin Svcs .... Mr. Geoffrey SLEEMAN
26 Director Marketing & Communications .... Mr. Marcus POPIOLEK
29 Alumni Coordinator .... Ms. Ingrida KAMIS
06 Registrar & Acad Advising Director .... Ms. Nadine ASHTON
102 Director Corp/Foundation Relations .... Ms. Shannon MCPARTLON
44 Dir Annual Giving/Donor Services .... Ms. Elizabeth KLOS
38 Personal Counselor .... Mr. James BAUER
36 Director Career Services .... Ms. Cathy KARRY
40 Manager Bookstore .... Mr. Robert KOLINSKI
35 Assistant Director Student Life .... Mr. Daniel LONG
19 Director of Security .... Mr. Garrett OCHALEK

Concordia University (B)

4090 Geddes Road, Ann Arbor MI 48105-2797
County: Washtenaw FICE Identification: 002247
Unit ID: 169363
Telephone: (734) 995-7300 Carnegie Class: Bac/Diverse
FAX Number: (734) 995-4610 Calendar System: Semester
URL: www.cuaa.edu
Established: 1962 Annual Undergrad Tuition & Fees: $21,600
Enrollment: 668 Coed
Affiliation or Control: Lutheran Church - Missouri Synod
IRS Status: 501(c)3
Highest Offering: Master's
Program: Liberal Arts And General; Teacher Preparatory
Accreditation: NH, TED

00 Interim Chief Executive Officer .... Dr. Russell NICHOLS
01 Acting President .... Mr. Randall LUECKE
05 Vice President Academics .... Dr. Dennis GENIG
10 Vice Pres/Chief Operating Officer .... Mr. Randall LUECKE
07 Director of Admissions .... Mr. Benjamin LIMBACK
13 Int Director Information Technology .... Mr. Woodrow HOLBERT
06 Registrar .... Ms. Colleen CLELAND
32 Executive Director Student Services .... Mr. Eric CHAMBERS
08 Librarian .... Mrs. Brenda BURROUGHS
37 Director Financial Aid .... Mrs. Karen NEUENDORF
42 Director of Spiritual Life .... Mr. Robert MCKINNEY
30 Director of Development .... Mr. Martin MORO
19 Director Security/Safety .... Mr. Kevin TANNER
26 Director Marketing & Communication .... Mr. Joel IVERSON
38 Director Student Counseling .... Mrs. Gina VERSEMAN
29 Director of Alumni Relations .... Mrs. Shannon MACLELLAN
39 Director Residence Life .... Ms. Elizabeth HENKE
41 Director of Athletics .... Mr. Ben LIMBACK
18 Chief Facilities/Physical Plant .... Mr. Jerry NOVAK
21 Controller .... Mr. Rocky MAZZARO
36 Director Student Placement .... Mrs. Susan GRESE
96 Director of Purchasing .... Mr. Dean ROE
09 Director of Institutional Research .... Vacant
15 Director Personnel Services .... Mrs. Barb WALTHER

Cornerstone University (C)

1001 E Beltline Avenue, NE, Grand Rapids MI 49525-5897
County: Kent FICE Identification: 002266
Unit ID: 170037
Telephone: (616) 949-5300 Carnegie Class: Master's L
FAX Number: (616) 222-1540 Calendar System: Semester
URL: www.cornerstone.edu
Established: 1941 Annual Undergrad Tuition & Fees: $21,818
Enrollment: 2,852 Coed
Affiliation or Control: Independent Non-Profit IRS Status: 501(c)3
Highest Offering: Master's
Program: Liberal Arts And General; Teacher Preparatory; Professional
Accreditation: NH, MUS, SW, @TEAC, THEOL

01 President .... Dr. Joseph M. STOWELL
03 Executive Vice President .... Mr. Marc FOWLER
05 Provost .... Dr. Richard OSTRANDER
30 Exec Vice President Advancement .... Mr. William KNOTT
88 Vice President of Broadcasting .... Mr. Chris LEMKE
42 Vice Pres Spiritual Formation .... Mr. Gerald LONGJOHN
58 Assoc Prov/Professional & Grad Stds .... Dr. Robert SIMPSON
97 Assoc Provost Undergraduate Pgms .... Dr. Timothy DETWILER
73 Dean Grand Rpds Theol Seminary .... Mr. John VER BERKMOES
32 Dean of Student Engagement .... Mr. Chip HUBER
55 Dir Acad Excel/Qual Assurance Pgms .... Miss Colleen SMITH
35 Director of Student Services .... Mr. Keith DEBOER
08 Director of Miller Library .... Mr. Fred SWEET
37 Director Financial Services .... Mr. Scott STEWART
21 Controller .... Mr. Scott STEWART
88 Director of Retention .... Mrs. Kay LANDRUM
41 Athletic Director .... Mr. Dave GRUBE
15 Director of Human Resources .... Mrs. Emilie AZKOUL
18 Director of Campus Services .... Mr. Chris LOWE
19 Director of Campus Safety .... Mr. Richard HONHOLT
36 Director of Career Services .... Mr. John WARREN
29 Director of Alumni .... Mrs. Darci IRWIN
06 Registrar .... Mrs. Gail DUHON
24 Director of Technical Support .... Vacant
38 Director of the Counseling Center .... Ms. Dana MARINO
92 Director of Honors Program .... Mr. Michael STEVENS
07 Director of Admissions .... Mrs. Lisa LINK
09 Director of Institutional Research .... Dr. Tim DETWILER
10 Chief Financial Officer .... Mrs. Nancy SCHOONMAKER
26 Chief Public Relations Officer .... Mr. Bob SACK

Cranbrook Academy of Art (D)

39221 Woodward Avenue, PO Box 801,
Bloomfield Hills MI 48303-0801
County: Oakland FICE Identification: 002248
Unit ID: 169424
Telephone: (248) 645-3300 Carnegie Class: Spec/Arts
FAX Number: (248) 646-0046 Calendar System: Semester
URL: www.cranbrook.edu
Established: 1932 Annual Graduate Tuition & Fees: $29,604
Enrollment: 154 Coed
Affiliation or Control: Independent Non-Profit IRS Status: 501(c)3
Highest Offering: Master's; No Undergraduates
Program: Professional
Accreditation: NH, ART

01 Director .... Mr. Reed KROLOFF
07 Dean of Admissions .... Mrs. Katharine WILLMAN

Davenport University (E)

6191 Kraft Ave., S.E., Grand Rapids MI 49512
County: Kent FICE Identification: 002249
Unit ID: 169479
Telephone: (616) 698-7111 Carnegie Class: Master's M
FAX Number: N/A Calendar System: Semester
URL: www.davenport.edu
Established: 1866 Annual Undergrad Tuition & Fees: $11,894
Enrollment: 13,025 Coed
Affiliation or Control: Independent Non-Profit IRS Status: 501(c)3
Highest Offering: Master's
Program: Professional; Business Emphasis
Accreditation: NH, ADNUR, IACBE, MAC, NUR, PNUR

01 President .... Dr. Richard J. PAPPAS
30 Exec VP Advancement .... Mr. Dennis C. WASHINGTON
26 Exec VP Univ Relations & Communic .... Ms. Kimberly A. BRUYN
46 Exec VP of Quality & Effectiveness .... Dr. Scott EPSTEIN
15 Exec VP Human/Organizational Devel .... Mr. Dave VENEKLASE
07 Exec VP Admission & Student Svcs .... Dr. Larry POLSELLI
10 Exec Vice President for Finance/CFO .... Mr. Michael S. VOLK
05 Exec VP Academics/Provost .... Dr. Linda RINKER
13 Vice Pres Information Technology .... Mr. Brian MILLER
09 VP for Institutional Research .... Dr. Kathy ABOUFADEL
18 Vice President for Plant & Security .... Mr. Duane TERPSTRA
32 Vice President Student Services .... Ms. Tammy LOUD
50 Dean of School of Business .... Vacant
72 Dean of School of Technology .... Mr. Michael CLANCY
76 Dean of School Health Professions .... Dr. Karen DALEY
37 Exec Director Financial Aid .... Mr. David DE BOER
29 Director of Alumni Relations .... Ms. Cathie ROGG
21 Controller .... Mr. Michael SLEVA
06 University Registrar .... Ms. Donna MILHAM
96 Director of Purchasing .... Mr. Bruce RENTZ
41 Director of Athletics .... Mr. Paul LOWDEN
26 Executive Dir of Communications .... Mr. Robyn LUYMES

Delta College (F)

1961 Delta Drive, University Center MI 48710-0001
County: Bay FICE Identification: 002251
Unit ID: 169521
Telephone: (989) 686-9000 Carnegie Class: Assoc/Pub-R-L
FAX Number: (989) 667-0620 Calendar System: Semester
URL: www.delta.edu
Established: 1961 Annual Undergrad Tuition & Fees (In-District): $3,431
Enrollment: 11,529 Coed
Affiliation or Control: Local IRS Status: 501(c)3
Highest Offering: Associate Degree
Program: Occupational; 2-Year Principally Bachelor's Creditable
Accreditation: NH, ADNUR, DA, DH, DMS, PTAA, RAD, SURGT

01 President .... Dr. Jean GOODNOW
10 Vice President Finance/Treasurer .... Ms. Debra K. LUTZ
32 Vice President Student & Educ Svcs .... Dr. Trevor A. KUBATZKE
05 Vice Pres Instruction/Learning Svcs .... Dr. Thomas LANE
20 Dean of Teaching & Learning .... Dr. Gail HOFFMAN-JOHNSON
20 Dean of Student and Acad Services .... Ms. Judy MILLER
36 Dean Career Educ/Learning Part .... Ms. Ginny PRZYGOCKI
26 Marketing & Public Info Director .... Ms. Leanne GOVITZ
24 Exec Dir Broadcasting/General Mgr .... Mr. Barry BAKER
30 Ex Dir Delta Col Found/Inst Advance .... Ms. Pam CLARK
11 Asst to Pres/Dir Strategic Planning .... Ms. Andrea L. URSUY
25 Exec Dir Corp Services & Res Devel .... Dr. Patricia A. GRAVES
43 General Counsel and Board Secretary .... Ms. Leslie MYLES-SANDERS
13 Chief Information Officer .... Mr. Jason STAHL
37 Director of Student Financial Aid .... Mr. David URBANIAK
15 Director of Human Resources .... Ms. Tamie L. GRUNOW
18 Director of Facilities Management .... Mr. Larry E. RAMSEYER
22 Dean Stdnt & Educ Svc Eqty Ofcr .... Ms. Margaret MOSQUEDA
40 Bookstore Manager .... Ms. Barbara POWERS
07 Director of Admissions .... Mr. Gary BRASSEUR
06 Registrar .... Mr. Keith MALKOWSKI
19 Director Law Enforce & Training Ctr .... Mr. Mike WILTSE
08 Library Learning Info Center Dir .... Mr. Jack WOOD
38 Dir Counseling Advising/Career Svcs .... Ms. Diana GUTIERREZ
21 Business Services Director .... Ms. Barbara WEBB
09 Director of Institutional Research .... Mr. Wm. Michael WOOD
44 Coordinator of Development .... Ms. Mary HARDING
31 Assoc Dean of Community Develop .... Ms. Teresa STITT

DeVry University - Southfield (G)

26999 Central Park Blvd, Suite 125,
Southfield MI 48076-4174
County: Oakland Identification: 666557
Unit ID: 450508
Telephone: (248) 213-1610 Carnegie Class: Bac/Assoc
FAX Number: (248) 353-1804 Calendar System: Semester
URL: www.devry.edu
Established: 1931 Annual Undergrad Tuition & Fees: $15,294
Enrollment: 199 Coed
Affiliation or Control: Proprietary IRS Status: Proprietary
Highest Offering: Baccalaureate
Program: Professional; Business Emphasis
Accreditation: &NH

01 Campus Director .... Georgianna BAILEY

† Regional accreditation is carried under the parent institution in Downers Grove, IL.

Eastern Michigan University (H)

Ypsilanti MI 48197-2207
County: Washtenaw FICE Identification: 002259
Unit ID: 169798
Telephone: (734) 487-1849 Carnegie Class: Master's L
FAX Number: (734) 481-1095 Calendar System: Semester
URL: www.emich.edu
Established: 1849 Annual Undergrad Tuition & Fees (In-State): $8,683
Enrollment: 23,579 Coed
Affiliation or Control: State IRS Status: 501(c)3
Highest Offering: Doctorate
Program: Liberal Arts And General; Teacher Preparatory; Professional
Accreditation: NH, BUS, CACREP, CIDA, CLPSY, CONST, DIETC, MT, MUS, NURSE, OPE, OT, PLNG, SP, SPAA, SW, TED

01 President ... Dr. Susan MARTIN
04 Special Asst to President ... Ms. Linda MCGILL
05 Provost/Executive Vice President ... Vacant
10 Chief Financial Officer ... Mr. John LUMM
26 Vice President for Communications ... Mr. Walter KRAFT
30 Vice Pres Advancement ... Mr. Thomas STEVICK
32 VP Student Affairs/Enrollment Mgmt ... Ms. Bernice LINDKE
20 Interim Assoc Provost ... Dr. James CARROLL
58 Interim Dean Graduate School ... Dr. Deborah DE LASKI-SMITH
26 Assoc VP Marketing & Communications ... Mr. Theodore G. COUTILISH
15 Chief Human Resources Officer ... Dr. James GALLAHER
35 Assoc Vice Pres Student Affairs ... Mr. Kevin KUCERA
21 Associate Vice President Finance ... Ms. Andrea JAECKEL
21 Dir Financial Svcs/Controller ... Ms. Doris CELIAN
18 Chief of Operations ... Mr. John P. DONEGAN
69 Dean Col Health & Human Svcs ... Dr. Murali NAIR
51 Dean Extended Programs ... Dr. Byron D. BOND
49 Dean of Art & Sciences ... Dr. Thomas VENNER
50 Dean of Business ... Dr. David E. MIELKE
53 Dean of Education ... Dr. Jann JOSEPH
72 Dean of Technology ... Dr. Morell BOONE
43 University Attorney ... Ms. Gloria HAGE
13 Chief Information Officer ... Dr. Carl POWELL
09 Exec Dir Inst Research/Info Mgmt ... Mr. Bin NING
102 Exec Dir Foundation Operations/CFO ... Ms. Laura WILBANKS
07 Director of Admissions ... Ms. Kathryn B. ORSCHELN
36 Interim Director Career Service Ctr ... Ms. Sarah KERSEY OTTO
88 Ombudsman ... Mr. Gregory A. PEOPLES
46 Int Director Research Development ... Ms. Caryn CHARTER
29 Director Alumni Relations ... Ms. Vicki REAUME
19 Director of Public Safety ... Mr. Greg O'DELL
28 Director of Diversity/Affirm Action ... Ms. Sharon ABRAHAM
23 Exec Director Student Wellbeing ... Ms. Ellen GOLD
39 Director Housing ... Ms. Rebecca FIGURA
41 Director Intercollegiate Athletics ... Dr. Derrick L. GRAGG, JR.
85 Director International Students Ofc ... Ms. Esther GUNEL
27 Executive Director Media Relations ... Mr. Geoff LARCOM
96 Director Purchasing ... Mr. Dean BACKOS
38 Director Counseling Services ... Dr. Lisa LAUTERBACH
06 Registrar ... Ms. Chris SHELL
37 Director Student Financial Aid ... Ms. Cynthia VAN PELT

Ecumenical Theological Seminary (A)

2930 Woodward Avenue, Detroit MI 48201-3035
County: Wayne FICE Identification: 040024
Unit ID: 247162
Telephone: (313) 831-5200 Carnegie Class: Spec/Faith
FAX Number: (313) 831-1353 Calendar System: Quarter
URL: www.etseminary.edu
Established: 1980 Annual Undergrad Tuition & Fees: $12,300
Enrollment: 127 Coed
Affiliation or Control: Independent Non-Profit IRS Status: 501(c)3
Highest Offering: Doctorate
Program: Professional; Religious Emphasis
Accreditation: THEOL

01 President ... Dr. Marsha FOSTER BOYD
05 Vice Pres Academic Affs/Acad Dean ... Dr. Anneliese SINNOTT
11 Vice President of Administration ... Rev. Margaret PRIEST
30 Director of Advancement ... Ms. Cathy MAHER
06 Registrar ... Ms. Jean D. MURPHY
08 Head Librarian ... Rev. Dianne VAN MARTER

Ferris State University (B)

1201 S. State Street, Big Rapids MI 49307-2295
County: Mecosta FICE Identification: 002260
Unit ID: 169910
Telephone: (231) 591-2000 Carnegie Class: Master's L
FAX Number: (231) 591-2990 Calendar System: Semester
URL: www.ferris.edu
Established: 1884 Annual Undergrad Tuition & Fees (In-State): $10,440
Enrollment: 14,381 Coed
Affiliation or Control: State IRS Status: 501(c)3
Highest Offering: First Professional Degree
Program: Occupational; 2-Year Principally Bachelor's Creditable; Liberal Arts And General; Teacher Preparatory; Professional
Accreditation: NH, @ACBSP, ART, CIDA, CONST, DH, DMS, ENG, ENGT, MLTAD, MT, NMT, NRPA, NUR, OPT, OPTR, PHAR, RAD, SW, @TEAC

01 President ... Dr. David L. EISLER
05 Provost & VP for Academic Affairs ... Dr. Fritz J. ERICKSON
43 Vice President & General Counsel ... Mr. Miles J. POSTEMA
10 VP of Administration & Finance ... Mr. Jerry L. SCOBY
30 VP Univ Advancement and Marketing ... Mr. John H. WILLEY
32 Vice President Student Affairs ... Dr. Daniel BURCHAM
12 President/Vice Chancellor KCAD ... Dr. Oliver EVANS
88 Vice Chancellor Admin & Fin KCAD ... Ms. Sandra DAVISON-WILSON
12 VP External/Intl Operations/Dean ... Dr. Donald GREEN
28 VP for Diversity and Inclusion ... Dr. David PILGRIM
20 Associate Provost ... Dr. Roberta TEAHEN
20 Associate Provost ... Mr. Donald FLICKINGER
21 Assoc Vice President Finance ... Mr. Richard CHRISTNER
35 Assoc Vice Pres Student Affairs ... Dr. Michael A. CAIRNS
26 Assoc Vice Pres Marketing & Comm ... Ms. Shelly ARMSTRONG
16 Assoc Vice Pres Human Resources ... Dr. Warren HILLS
30 Assoc Vice Pres for Advancement ... Ms. Carla MILLER
18 Assoc Vice Pres Plant Management ... Mr. Mike HUGHES
84 Associate Dean Enrollment Services ... Ms. Kathy LAKE
06 Dean Enroll Svc/Dir Admiss & Rec ... Dr. Kristen SALOMONSON
88 Associate VP Auxiliary Enterprises ... Vacant
45 Director Budget Planning/Analysis ... Ms. Sally DEPEW
84 Dean of Enrollment Services ... Dr. Kristen SALOMONSON
14 Chief Technology Officer ... Mr. John URBANICK
22 Director of Equal Opportunity ... Vacant
19 Director of Public Safety ... Mr. Martin BLEDSOE
36 Mgr Stdnt Employment & Career Svcs ... Mr. John RANDLE
88 Director Rankin Student Center ... Mr. Mark SCHUELKE
23 Interim Director Counseling Center ... Ms. Renee DOUGLAS
23 Director of Birkam Health Center ... Dr. Paul SULLIVAN
32 Dean of Student Life ... Mr. Leroy WRIGHT
88 Dir Multicultural Student Svcs ... Dr. Matthew CHANEY
88 Dir Student Leadership/Activities ... Vacant
88 Director University Recreation ... Ms. Cindy HORN
29 Dir Alumni Relations/Annual Giving ... Mr. Jeremy MISHLER
09 Director of Institutional Research ... Dr. Kristen SALOMANSON
39 Director Residential Life ... Mr. Jon SHAFFER
40 Director Bookstore ... Ms. Karen BOHREN
41 Director of Athletics ... Mr. Perk WEISENBURGER
44 Director Planned Giving ... Mr. Todd JACOBS
96 Director Purchasing ... Mr. Michael PETHICK
49 Interim Dean of Arts & Sciences ... Dr. Karen STRASSER
50 Dean of Business ... Dr. David NICOL
51 Dean of Professional & Tech Studies ... Dr. Donald GREEN
53 Dean of Education & Human Services ... Dr. Michelle JOHNSTON
67 Interim Dean of Pharmacy ... Dr. Steve DURST
76 Interim Dean AHS ... Dr. Jule COON
63 Dean Michigan College Optometry ... Dr. Michael CRON
72 Interim Dean Engineering Technology ... Dr. Ron MCKEAN
92 Dean University College ... Dr. William POTTER
08 Interim Dean Library ... Dr. Leah MONGER

Finlandia University (C)

601 Quincy Street, Hancock MI 49930-1882
County: Houghton FICE Identification: 002322
Unit ID: 172440
Telephone: (906) 482-5300 Carnegie Class: Bac/Diverse
FAX Number: (906) 487-7366 Calendar System: Semester
URL: www.finlandia.edu
Established: 1896 Annual Undergrad Tuition & Fees: $19,898
Enrollment: 672 Coed
Affiliation or Control: Evangelical Lutheran Church In America
IRS Status: 501(c)3
Highest Offering: Baccalaureate
Program: Liberal Arts And General; Professional
Accreditation: NH, NURSE, PTAA

01 President ... Dr. Philip JOHNSON
10 Exec Vice Pres Business/Finance ... Mr. Nick STEVENS
05 Executive Vice Pres/Provost ... Ms. TyAnn LINDELL
26 Exec VP External Relations/CAO ... Mr. Duane AHO
04 Executive Administrative Assistant ... Ms. Doreen KORPELA
27 Executive Director Communications ... Ms. Karen JOHNSON
84 Dean Enrollment Management ... Vacant
20 Assistant Provost ... Ms. Carol BATES
102 Director Foundation Relations ... Ms. Robin BONINI
08 Librarian ... Ms. Elizabeth MARTIN
35 Director of Student Affairs ... Ms. Kelley MARTIN
42 University Chaplain ... Mr. Soren SCHMIDT
06 Registrar ... Ms. Evelyn GOKE
29 Director Alumni Relations ... Ms. Cheryl RIES
38 Director Student Support Services ... Mr. Rob MCTAGGART
13 Director Information Technology ... Mr. Scott BLAKE
41 Athletic Director ... Mr. Chris SALANI
44 Advancement Officer ... Mr. Ross RINKINEN
18 Director of Plant and Facilities ... Mr. Curt HAHKA
21 Controller ... Vacant
37 Director Student Financial Aid ... Ms. Sandra TURNQUIST
36 Career Services Manager ... Mr. Mark CAVIS
09 Institutional Research Analyst ... Mr. Hannu LEPPANEN
40 Bookstore Manager ... Ms. Alana EVANS
96 Purchaser ... Ms. Janine NOTTKE
15 Director of Human Resources ... Ms. Ann TESTINI
07 Assoc Director of Admissions ... Ms. Kitti LOUKUS
19 Director of Campus Safety/Security ... Mr. Jim HARDEN
39 Residence Life Coordinator ... Ms. Kelly HOLSAPPLE
49 Dean College of Arts & Sciences ... Dr. Christine O'NEIL
57 Dean Intl School of Art & Design ... Ms. Denise VANDEVILLE
76 Co-Dean College of Health Science ... Dr. Fredi DE YAMPERT
76 Co-Dean College of Health Science ... Dr. Cameron WILLIAMS
104 Dean Intl School of Business ... Dr. Terry MONSON

Glen Oaks Community College (D)

62249 Shimmel Road, Centreville MI 49032-9719
County: Saint Joseph FICE Identification: 002263
Unit ID: 169974
Telephone: (269) 467-9945 Carnegie Class: Assoc/Pub-R-S
FAX Number: (269) 467-4114 Calendar System: Semester
URL: www.glenoaks.edu
Established: 1965 Annual Undergrad Tuition & Fees (In-District): $3,346
Enrollment: 1,453 Coed
Affiliation or Control: Local IRS Status: 501(c)3
Highest Offering: Associate Degree
Program: Occupational; 2-Year Principally Bachelor's Creditable
Accreditation: NH, MAC

01 President ... Dr. Gary WHEELER
05 Dean of the College ... Dr. Ana GAILLAT
11 Chief Operations Officer ... Ms. Marilyn WIESCHOWSKI
32 Dean of Student/Community Services ... Dr. Margaret HALE-SMITH
66 Asst Dean of Nursing ... Ms. Karen GANGER
08 Director Learning Resources Center ... Ms. Betsy S. MORGAN
35 Ast Dean Enrol Svcs/Dir Stdnt Svcs ... Ms. Beverly ANDREWS
21 Accountant ... Ms. Jennifer DODSON
18 Director of Buildings/Grounds ... Mr. Nick MILLIMAN
07 Director of Admissions ... Ms. Tonya HOWDEN
06 Registrar ... Ms. Bev ANDREWS
37 Dir of Financial Aid/Scholarships ... Ms. Jean ZIMMERMAN
09 Dir Grants/Institutional Research ... Ms. Alissa SHEFTIC
41 Director of Athletics ... Mr. Steve PROEFROCK
15 Personnel Coordinator ... Ms. Candy BOHACZ
26 Public Relations/Marketing ... Mr. Lon HUFFMAN
20 Associate Dean of Instruction ... Ms. Patricia MORGENSTERN

Gogebic Community College (E)

E4946 Jackson Road, Ironwood MI 49938-1366
County: Gogebic FICE Identification: 002264
Unit ID: 169992
Telephone: (906) 932-4231 Carnegie Class: Assoc/Pub-R-S
FAX Number: (906) 932-5541 Calendar System: Semester
URL: www.gogebic.edu
Established: 1931 Annual Undergrad Tuition & Fees (In-District): $3,380
Enrollment: 1,228 Coed
Affiliation or Control: Local IRS Status: 501(c)3
Highest Offering: Associate Degree
Program: Occupational; 2-Year Principally Bachelor's Creditable
Accreditation: NH

01 President ... Mr. James A. LORENSON
05 Dean of Instruction/Dir Exten Pgm ... Mr. Ken J. TRZASKA
10 Dean of Business Services ... Mr. Erik M. GUENARD
32 Interim Dean Student Services ... Ms. Jeanne GRAHAM
37 Dir Financial Aid/Veterans Svcs ... Ms. Suzetta R. FORBES
76 Director of Allied Health Program ... Ms. Kari LUOMA
18 Director of Buildings & Grounds ... Vacant
88 Director of Ski Area Management ... Mr. James VANDERSPOEL
08 Dir Learning Resource/Instruct Tech ... Mr. Walter LESSUN
14 Director of Computer Services ... Mrs. Kathie A. MUNN
07 Dir of Admission/Public Information ... Ms. Jeanne P. GRAHAM
30 Dir of Institutional Development ... Ms. Kelly MARZCAK
88 Transfer Coordinator ... Mrs. Therese PAWLAK

Grace Bible College (F)

1011 Aldon Street, SW, Grand Rapids MI 49509-1998
County: Kent FICE Identification: 002265
Unit ID: 170000
Telephone: (616) 538-2330 Carnegie Class: Bac/Diverse
FAX Number: (616) 538-0599 Calendar System: Semester
URL: www.gbcol.edu
Established: 1939 Annual Undergrad Tuition & Fees: $14,850
Enrollment: 207 Coed
Affiliation or Control: Independent Non-Profit IRS Status: 501(c)3
Highest Offering: Baccalaureate
Program: Liberal Arts And General; Teacher Preparatory; Religious Emphasis
Accreditation: NH, BI

01 President ... Dr. Kenneth B. KEMPER
05 Vice President/Academic Dean ... Mr. Paul R. SWEET
10 Vice President for Business/Finance ... Mr. Gregory HEATH
32 Vice Pres Cmty Life/Student Svcs ... Mr. Brian P. SHERSTAD
44 Vice President for Fund Development ... Mr. Steve HILBRANDS
106 Vice Pres Adult & Online Education ... Mr. Mike STOWELL
04 Admin Assistant to President ... Mrs. Joyce A. STORMS
06 Registrar ... Ms. Linda K. SILER
08 Librarian ... Mrs. Kathy L. MOLENKAMP
37 Director of Financial Aid ... Mr. Kurt POSTMA
84 Director of Enrollment ... Mr. Kevin E. GILLIAM
13 Information Technology Director ... Mr. James PETERS
18 Director of Maintenance ... Mr. Nathan JOHNSON
41 Athletic Director ... Mr. Rich RENZEMA
42 Director of Campus Ministries ... Mr. John SPOONER
39 Director of Residence Life ... Mrs. Michelle LOVERIN
88 Dir Recruitment Online & Adult Stds ... Mr. Zak SORENSEN

Grand Rapids Community College (G)

143 Bostwick Avenue, NE, Grand Rapids MI 49503-3295
County: Kent FICE Identification: 002267
Unit ID: 170055
Telephone: (616) 234-4000 Carnegie Class: Assoc/Pub-U-SC
FAX Number: (616) 234-4005 Calendar System: Semester
URL: www.grcc.edu
Established: 1914 Annual Undergrad Tuition & Fees (In-District): $3,124
Enrollment: 17,920 Coed
Affiliation or Control: Local IRS Status: 501(c)3
Highest Offering: Associate Degree
Program: Occupational; 2-Year Principally Bachelor's Creditable
Accreditation: NH, ACFEI, ADNUR, ART, DA, DH, MUS, OTA, PNUR, RAD

01 President ... Dr. Steven C. ENDER
05 Exec Vice Pres Academic Affairs ... Dr. Gilda G. GELY
10 Exec VP Business/Financial Services ... Ms. Lisa FREIBURGER
13 VP & CIO Lrng Res/Tech Solutions ... Mr. Kevin O'HALLA
30 Assoc VP College Advancement ... Mr. Andy BOWNE
88 Dean of Adult & Developmental Educ ... Ms. Cindy MARTIN
103 Director Workforce Training ... Ms. Julie PARKS
21 Exec Director Financial Services ... Mr. James PETERSON

75 Dean Sch Workforce Development .... Ms. Fiona HERT
32 Dean Student Affairs .... Ms. Tina OEN-HOXIE
09 Dean Inst Research & Planning .... Ms. Donna KRAGT
49 Dean School of Arts & Science .... Dr. Laurie CHESLEY
72 Dean Instruct Design/Info Tech .... Ms. Patti TREPKOWSKI
07 Assoc Dean Admiss/Enrollment Mgmt .... Ms. Diane D. PATRICK
26 Director of Communications .... Mr. Raul ALVAREZ, JR.
37 Exec Dir Student Financial Services .... Ms. Jill M. NUTT
16 Executive Director Human Resources .... Ms. Cathy WILSON
06 Registrar .... Ms. Diane PATRICK
35 Director Student Activities .... Mr. Eric MULLEN
36 Assoc Director Student Employment .... Ms. Luann WEDGE
08 Director of Library Services .... Ms. Pat INGERSOLL
18 Executive Director of Facilities .... Mr. Thomas J. SMITH
88 Director MTEC/Employment Training .... Mr. George WAITE
19 Chief of Campus Police .... Ms. Rebecca R. WHITMAN
43 General Counsel .... Ms. Kathy KEATING
96 Director Purchasing .... Mr. Mansfield MATTHEWSON
12 Dean of Lakeshore Campus & Outreach .... Mr. Daniel CLARK
22 Exec Dir Equity/Community/Legis .... Mr. Eric WILLIAMS
28 Dir Diversity Learning Center .... Ms. Christina ARNOLD

Grand Valley State University (A)

1 Campus Drive, Allendale MI 49401-9403
County: Ottawa FICE Identification: 002268
Unit ID: 170082
Telephone: (616) 331-5000 Carnegie Class: Master's L
FAX Number: (616) 331-3503 Calendar System: Semester
URL: www.gvsu.edu
Established: 1960 Annual Undergrad Tuition & Fees (In-State): $9,088
Enrollment: 24,541 Coed
Affiliation or Control: State IRS Status: 501(c)3
Highest Offering: Doctorate
Program: Liberal Arts And General; Teacher Preparatory; Professional
Accreditation: NH, ARCPA, ART, BUS, BUSA, CS, DMS, ENG, IPSY, MT, MUS, NURSE, OT, PTA, RTT, SPAA, SW, TED

01 President .... Dr. Thomas J. HAAS
05 Provost & Vice Pres Academic Affs .... Dr. Gayle R. DAVIS
10 Vice President Finance/Admin .... Mr. James BACHMEIER
26 Vice President University Relations .... Mr. Matthew E. MCLOGAN
30 Vice President of Development .... Ms. Maribeth WARDROP
22 VP Inclusion and Equity .... Dr. Jeanne J. ARNOLD
04 Special Assistant to President .... Ms. Teri L. LOSEY
32 Vice Provost/Dean Student Services .... Dr. H. Bart MERKLE
20 Vice Provost/Dean Academic Svcs .... Ms. Lynn BLUE
20 Assoc Vice Pres Academic Affairs .... Mr. Jon A. JELLEMA
20 Assoc Vice Pres Academic Affairs .... Dr. Joseph H. GODWIN
20 Asst Vice Pres Academic Affairs .... Dr. Nancy GIARDINA
20 Asst Vice Pres Academic Affairs .... Dr. Julia GUEVARA
21 Associate VP Business/Finance .... Mr. Brian COPELAND
21 Asst VP for University Budgets .... Mr. Jeff MUSSER
15 Assoc Vice Pres Human Resources .... Mr. D. Scott RICHARDSON
26 Asst VP Institutional Marketing .... Ms. Rhonda LUBBERTS
27 Asst VP News & Information Svcs .... Ms. Mary Eilleen LYON
18 Asst Vice Pres Facilities Services .... Mr. Timothy THIMMESCH
88 Asst VP for Facilities Planning .... Mr. James MOYER
88 Asst VP for Pew Campus Operations .... Ms. Lisa HAYNES
49 Dean Col of Liberal Arts & Sciences .... Dr. Frederick ANTCZAK
50 Dean Seidman College of Business .... Dr. H. James WILLIAMS
70 Dean College of Cmty/Public Service .... Dr. George GRANT
53 Dean College of Education .... Dr. Elaine COLLINS
54 Dean Padnos Col Engr & Computing .... Dr. Paul PLOTKOWSKI
76 Dean College of Health Professions .... Dr. Roy OLSSON
66 Dean Kirkhof College of Nursing .... Dr. Cynthia MCCURREN
58 Dean Graduate Studies .... Dr. Jeffrey POTTEIGER
25 Dir Grants Administration .... Ms. Christine CHAMBERLAIN
07 Director of Admissions .... Ms. Jodi CHYCINSKI
08 Dean University Libraries .... Dr. Lee VAN ORSDEL
43 University Counsel .... Mr. Thomas A. BUTCHER
37 Director of Financial Aid .... Ms. Michelle RHODES
06 Registrar .... Mr. Jerry MONTAG
36 Director Career Services .... Mr. Troy FARLEY
14 Director of Information Technology .... Ms. Sue KORZINEK
29 Director Alumni Relations .... Mr. Chris W. BARBEE
09 Director of Institutional Analysis .... Mr. Philip BATTY
39 Dir of Housing and Residence Life .... Dr. Andrew J. BEACHNAU
85 Exec Dir International Educ .... Dr. Mark SCHAUB
28 Director Multicultural Affairs .... Ms. Connie DANG
19 Director of Public Safety Services .... Ms. Barbara BERGERS
88 Exec Dir Van Andel Global Trade Ctr .... Ms. Sonja JOHNSON
88 Dir Pew Faculty Teaching/Lrng Ctr .... Dr. Christine RENER
88 Dir Sm Business/Technology Dev Ctr .... Ms. Carol LOPUCKI
96 Director of Procurement Services .... Mr. Kim PATRICK
41 Athletic Director .... Mr. Tim SELGO
40 Bookstore Manager .... Mr. Jerrod NICKELS
88 General Manager WGVU TV & Radio .... Mr. Michael WALENTA
88 Spec Asst for Charter Schools .... Mr. Tim WOOD
88 Dean College Interdisciplin Studies .... Dr. Wendy WENNER
88 Director Annis Water Resources Inst .... Dr. Alan STEINMAN
88 Dir Michigan Alt/Renwble Energy Ctr .... Mr. Arn BOEZAART
88 Int Dir W MI Sci/Tech Initiative .... Mr. Rich COOK
38 Dir Counseling/Career Development .... Dr. Barbara PALOMBI
88 Director of Hauenstein Center .... Mr. Gleaves WHITNEY
22 Asst VP for Affirmative Action .... Mr. Dwight HAMILTON

Great Lakes Christian College (B)

6211 Willow Highway, Lansing MI 48917-1299
County: Eaton FICE Identification: 002269
Unit ID: 170091
Telephone: (517) 321-0242 Carnegie Class: Spec/Faith
FAX Number: (517) 321-5902 Calendar System: Semester
URL: www.glcc.edu
Established: 1949 Annual Undergrad Tuition & Fees: $13,000
Enrollment: 273 Coed
Affiliation or Control: Christian Churches And Churches of Christ
IRS Status: 501(c)3
Highest Offering: Baccalaureate
Program: Professional; Religious Emphasis
Accreditation: NH, BI

01 President .... Mr. Lawrence L. CARTER
10 Vice President Finance/Operations .... Mr. William D. BROSSMANN
05 Vice President of Academic Affairs .... Mr. David J. RICHARDS
30 Vice Pres Institutional Advancement .... Mr. Philip E. BEAVERS
84 Vice Pres of Enrollment Management .... Mr. Lloyd S. SCHARER
32 Dean of Student Affairs .... Mrs. Betsy L. CARTER
06 Registrar .... Mr. Brian SLENSKI
27 Publications Coordinator .... Mrs. Robyn ORME
08 Director of Library Services .... Mr. James ORME
37 Financial Aid Director .... Mr. Tedd C. KEES
18 Maintenance Supervisor .... Mr. Brian SMITH
35 Director of Student Life .... Mr. Kris BARGEN
41 Athletic Director .... Mr. Scott AEDER
88 Director of Outreach Ministries .... Mrs. Judy BEAVERS

Griggs University (C)

8903 N US Highway 31, Suite 2,
Berrien Springs MI 49104-1900
County: Berrien FICE Identification: 009454
Telephone: (800) 782-4769 Carnegie Class: Not Classified
FAX Number: (269) 471-2804 Calendar System: Semester
URL: www.griggs.edu
Established: 1990 Annual Undergrad Tuition & Fees: $10,760
Enrollment: 2,756 Coed
Affiliation or Control: Seventh-day Adventist IRS Status: 501(c)3
Highest Offering: Master's
Program: Religious Emphasis
Accreditation: DETC

01 President .... Dr. Alayne D. THORPE
03 Vice President .... Dr. Janine LIM
32 Director of Student Services .... Dr. Glynis BRADFIELD
07 Director of Admissions/Registrar .... Dr. Emilio GARCIA-MARENKO
10 Chief Financial Officer .... Mr. Nantoo BANERJEE
07 Graduate Admissions .... Ms. M. Angelica MUNOZ
21 Administrative Services Manager .... Vacant
15 Human Resources Manager .... Mr. Daniel AGNETTA
05 Chief Academic Office .... Dr. Janine LIM
09 Director of Institutional Research .... Ms. Charlotte CONWAY
26 Chief Public Relations Officer .... Mr. Stephen D. PAYNE

Henry Ford Community College (D)

5101 Evergreen Road, Dearborn MI 48128-1495
County: Wayne FICE Identification: 002270
Unit ID: 170240
Telephone: (313) 845-9615 Carnegie Class: Assoc/Pub-S-MC
FAX Number: (313) 845-9658 Calendar System: Semester
URL: www.hfcc.edu
Established: 1938 Annual Undergrad Tuition & Fees (In-District): $2,772
Enrollment: 18,525 Coed
Affiliation or Control: Local IRS Status: 501(c)3
Highest Offering: Associate Degree
Program: Occupational; 2 Year Principally Bachelor's Creditable
Accreditation: NH, ACFEI, ADNUR, MAC, PTAA, RAD, SURGT

01 President .... Dr. Gail C. MEE
10 Vice President/Controller .... Ms. Marjorie SWAN
32 Vice Pres/Dean Student Service .... Dr. Lisa JONES-HARRIS
05 Vice Pres/Dean Academic Education .... Dr. Reg GERLICA
75 Vice Pres/Dean Career Education .... Dr. William BARBER
30 Exec Director of Development .... Mr. John LEWANDOWSKI
18 Director Buildings & Grounds .... Mr. T. Allen GIGLIOTTI
06 Director of Registration and Record .... Ms. Holly DIAMOND
38 Division Director Counseling .... Ms. Dianne GREEN
51 Director Corporate Training .... Mr. Gary SAGANSKI
66 Director of Nursing .... Ms. Katherine HOWE
08 Director Library .... Ms. Barbara LUKASIEWICZ
13 Director Data & Voice .... Mr. Sandro SILVESTRI
84 Director of Enrollment Development .... Mr. Douglas A. FREED
21 Director Financial Services .... Dr. David CUNNINGHAM
26 Communications Director .... Mr. Gary ERWIN
37 Director Student Financial Aid .... Mr. Kevin J. CULLER
15 Director Human Resources .... Ms. Elizabeth DAVIS
92 Director Honors Program .... Dr. Nabeel ABRAHAM
94 Director Women's Studies .... Vacant
96 Director Purchasing .... Mr. Fred STEINER
09 Director Research Planning Effectiv .... Ms. Becky J. CHADWICK
40 Manager of College Store .... Ms. Pamela HALL
24 Instructional Technologist .... Dr. Vivian BEATY
19 Coordinator of Security .... Mr. Gary MCBAIN

Hillsdale College (E)

33 East College Street, Hillsdale MI 49242-1298
County: Hillsdale FICE Identification: 002272
Unit ID: 170286
Telephone: (517) 437-7341 Carnegie Class: Not Classified
FAX Number: (517) 437-3923 Calendar System: Semester
URL: www.hillsdale.edu
Established: 1844 Annual Undergrad Tuition & Fees: $20,950
Enrollment: 1,377 Coed
Affiliation or Control: Independent Non-Profit IRS Status: 501(c)3
Highest Offering: Baccalaureate
Program: Liberal Arts And General; Teacher Preparatory
Accreditation: NH

01 President .... Dr. Larry P. ARNN, III
05 Provost .... Dr. David WHALEN
30 Vice Pres Institutional Advancement .... Mr. John CERVINI
10 Chf Admin Ofcr/VP Fin Affs & Treas .... Mr. Patrick FLANNERY
11 VP Admin & Sec of Board of Trustees .... Mr. Richard P. PEWE
26 VP of External Affairs .... Mr. Douglas JEFFREY
32 VP Student Affairs/Dean of Women .... Mrs. Diane PHILIPP
88 Vice Pres for Dow Leadership Center .... Mr. Jack OXENRIDER
100 Chief of Staff/Asst to President .... Mr. Mike HARNER
20 Associate Provost .... Dr. Mark MAIER
33 Dean of Men .... Mr. Aaron PETERSEN
07 Director of Admissions .... Mr. Jeffrey S. LANTIS
27 Exec Director of Media Relations .... Mr. Douglas JEFFREY
37 Director of Financial Aid .... Mr. Richard MOEGGENBERG
41 Athletic Director .... Mr. Don BRUBACHER
06 Registrar .... Mr. Douglas MCARTHUR
29 Director of Alumni Affairs .... Mr. Grigor HASTED
36 Director Career Planning .... Mrs. Joanna S. WISELEY
08 Librarian .... Mr. Daniel L. KNOCH
40 Bookstore Manager .... Mrs. Vicki NASH
42 Chaplain .... R.Rev. Peter BECKWITCH
18 Physical Plant Director .... Mr. Todd CLOW
90 Director of Academic Computing .... Mr. David M. ZENZ
15 Director Personnel Services .... Mrs. Jill PULLY

Hope College (F)

141 E 12th Street, Holland MI 49423-3607
County: Ottawa FICE Identification: 002273
Unit ID: 170301
Telephone: (616) 395-7000 Carnegie Class: Bac/A&S
FAX Number: (616) 395-7922 Calendar System: Semester
URL: www.hope.edu
Established: 1866 Annual Undergrad Tuition & Fees: $27,020
Enrollment: 3,202 Coed
Affiliation or Control: Reformed Church In America IRS Status: 501(c)3
Highest Offering: Baccalaureate
Program: Liberal Arts And General; Teacher Preparatory; Professional
Accreditation: NH, ART, DANCE, ENG, MUS, NURSE, SW, @TEAC, THEA

01 President .... Dr. James E. BULTMAN
05 Provost .... Dr. R. Richard RAY, JR.
10 Vice Pres and Chief Fiscal Officer .... Mr. Thomas W. BYLSMA
07 Vice President for Admissions .... Mr. William VANDERBILT
30 Interim VP for College Advancement .... Mr. David VANDERWEL
32 VP Student Devel/Dean of Students .... Dr. Richard A. FROST
20 Associate Provost .... Mr. Alfredo M. GONZALES
26 Assoc VP Public & Community Rels .... Mr. Tom L. RENNER
08 Librarian .... Ms. Kelly G. JACOBSMA
39 Dir of Residential Life & Housing .... Dr. John E. JOBSON
22 Director of Multicultural Life .... Ms. Vanessa GREENE
94 Director of Women's Studies .... Dr. Annie G. DANDAVATI
81 Dean for Natural Sciences .... Dr. Moses LEE
79 Dean for Arts & Humanities .... Dr. William D. REYNOLDS
83 Dean for Social Sciences .... Dr. Carol SIMON
88 Dean of the Chapel .... Rev. Trygve D. JOHNSON
06 Registrar .... Ms. Carol DEJONG
37 Director of Financial Aid .... Ms. Phyllis K. HOOYMAN
36 Director Career Services .... Mr. Dale F. AUSTIN
21 Director of Finance & Business Svcs .... Mr. Douglas VAN DYKEN
13 Director of Operations & Technology .... Mr. Greg MAYBURY
14 Director of Computing & Info Tech .... Mr. Carl E. HEIDEMAN
15 Director Human Resources .... Mrs. Lori MULDER
18 Director Physical Plant .... Mr. Greg MAYBURY
40 Manager of Bookstore .... Mr. Mark COOK
29 Dir of Parent & Alumni Relations .... Mr. Scott TRAVIS
41 Co-Director of Athletics .... Mr. Tim SCHOONVELD
41 Co-Director of Athletics .... Mrs. Eva Dean FOLKERT
42 Senior Chaplain .... Rev. Paul H. BOERSMA
42 Chaplain .... Rev. Kate DAVELAAR
38 Asst Dean/Director Counseling Ctr .... Dr. Kristen GRAY

International Academy of Design and Technology (G)

1850 Research Drive, Troy MI 48083
County: Oakland Identification: 666632
Unit ID: 445124
Telephone: (248) 457-2700 Carnegie Class: Not Classified
FAX Number: (248) 526-1710 Calendar System: Quarter
URL: www.iadt.edu/detroit
Established: 2003 Annual Undergrad Tuition & Fees: $17,280
Enrollment: 980 Coed
Affiliation or Control: Proprietary IRS Status: Proprietary
Highest Offering: Baccalaureate
Program: Liberal Arts And General; Fine Arts Emphasis
Accreditation: ACICS, CIDA

01 President .... Ms. Cynthia BECHILL
05 Director of Education .... Dr. Julia SMETANKA
07 Director of Admissions .... Ms. Roslyn WHITE
10 Regional Controller .... Mr. Michael THAYER
37 Director of Student Finance .... Mr. Donald STEVENS
32 Student Services Manager .... Mr. Giovannie THOMAS
13 Director IT .... Mr. Jordan KOTUBEY
36 Director Career Services .... Ms. Cheryl HARVEY

† Branch campus of International Academy of Design and Technology, Chicago, IL.

ITT Technical Institute (A)

1905 S Haggerty Road, Canton MI 48188-2025
County: Wayne Identification: 666323
Unit ID: 442338
Telephone: (734) 397-7800 Carnegie Class: Assoc/PrivFP
FAX Number: (734) 397-1945 Calendar System: Quarter
URL: www.itt-tech.edu
Established: 2003 Annual Undergrad Tuition & Fees: N/A
Enrollment: 809 Coed
Affiliation or Control: Proprietary IRS Status: Proprietary
Highest Offering: Baccalaureate
Program: Technical Emphasis
Accreditation: ACICS

† Branch campus of ITT Technical Institute, Grand Rapids, MI.

ITT Technical Institute (B)

1980 Metro Court S.W., Grand Rapids MI 49519
County: Kent FICE Identification: 010627
Unit ID: 170417
Telephone: (616) 406-1200 Carnegie Class: Spec/Tech
FAX Number: (616) 956-5606 Calendar System: Quarter
URL: www.itt-tech.edu
Established: 1968 Annual Undergrad Tuition & Fees: N/A
Enrollment: 985 Coed
Affiliation or Control: Proprietary IRS Status: Proprietary
Highest Offering: Baccalaureate
Program: Technical Emphasis
Accreditation: ACICS

ITT Technical Institute (C)

6359 Miller Road, Swartz Creek MI 48473-1520
County: Genesee Identification: 666146
Unit ID: 448479
Telephone: (810) 628-2500 Carnegie Class: Assoc/PrivFP
FAX Number: N/A Calendar System: Quarter
URL: www.itt-tech.edu
Established: 2006 Annual Undergrad Tuition & Fees: N/A
Enrollment: 978 Coed
Affiliation or Control: Proprietary IRS Status: Proprietary
Highest Offering: Baccalaureate
Program: Technical Emphasis
Accreditation: ACICS

† Branch campus of ITT Technical Institute, Earth City, MO.

ITT Technical Institute (D)

1522 E Big Beaver Road, Troy MI 48083-1905
County: Oakland Identification: 666542
Unit ID: 261472
Telephone: (248) 524-1800 Carnegie Class: Assoc/PrivFP
FAX Number: (248) 524-1965 Calendar System: Quarter
URL: www.itt-tech.edu
Established: 1987 Annual Undergrad Tuition & Fees: N/A
Enrollment: 1,434 Coed
Affiliation or Control: Proprietary IRS Status: Proprietary
Highest Offering: Baccalaureate
Program: Technical Emphasis
Accreditation: ACICS

† Branch campus of ITT Technical Institute, Fort Wayne, IN.

Jackson Community College (E)

2111 Emmons Road, Jackson MI 49201-8399
County: Jackson FICE Identification: 002274
Unit ID: 170444
Telephone: (517) 787-0800 Carnegie Class: Assoc/Pub-R-L
FAX Number: (517) 789-1623 Calendar System: Semester
URL: www.jccmi.edu
Established: 1928 Annual Undergrad Tuition & Fees (In-District): $3,156
Enrollment: 7,870 Coed
Affiliation or Control: Local IRS Status: 501(c)3
Highest Offering: Associate Degree
Program: Occupational; 2-Year Principally Bachelor's Creditable
Accreditation: NH, ACBSP, DMS, MAC, RAD

01 President/CEO .... Dr. Daniel J. PHELAN
11 Vice Pres Finance & College Opers .... Mr. Thomas VAINNER
32 Executive Dean of Students .... Dr. Michelle SHIELDS
05 Executive Dean of Instruction .... Dr. Rebekah WOODS
31 Exec Dir Cmty Rels/Perf Arts .... Ms. Cindy ALLEN
46 Exec Dir Quality/Inst Effectiveness .... Ms. Nancy MILLER
102 Exec Dir JCC Foundation/Grants .... Mr. Jason VALENTE
15 Exec Director of HR & Org Develop .... Vacant

Kalamazoo College (F)

1200 Academy Street, Kalamazoo MI 49006-3295
County: Kalamazoo FICE Identification: 002275
Unit ID: 170532
Telephone: (269) 337-7000 Carnegie Class: Bac/A&S
FAX Number: (269) 337-7251 Calendar System: Quarter
URL: www.kzoo.edu
Established: 1833 Annual Undergrad Tuition & Fees: $43,899
Enrollment: 1,369 Coed
Affiliation or Control: Independent Non-Profit IRS Status: 501(c)3
Highest Offering: Baccalaureate
Program: Liberal Arts And General
Accreditation: NH

01 President .... Dr. Eileen B. WILSON-OYELARAN
05 Provost .... Dr. Michael A. MCDONALD
10 Vice President Business & Finance .... Mr. James E. PRINCE
30 Vice President College Advancement .... Mr. Albert J. DESIMONE
32 VP Student Devel & Dean of Students .... Dr. Sarah B. WESTFALL
20 Associate Provost .... Dr. Paul R. SOTHERLAND
85 Associate Provost for Intl Pgms .... Dr. Joseph L. BROCKINGTON
13 Associate Provost for Info Services .... Mr. Gregory S. DIMENT
09 Asst Provost Inst Support/Research .... Ms. Anne T. DUEWEKE
89 Dean of First Year & Advising .... Dr. Zaide E. PIXLEY
06 Registrar .... Mr. Ted WITRYK
15 Human Resources Manager .... Ms. Laura A. ANDERSEN
07 Dean of Admission and Financial Aid .... Mr. Eric P. STAAB
37 Director of Financial Aid .... Ms. Marian STOWERS
27 Director of College Communication .... Mr. James A. VANSWEDEN
18 Director of Facilities Management .... Mr. Paul W. MANSTROM
40 Director Bookstore .... Ms. Deborah L. THOMPSON
29 Director of Alumni Relations .... Ms. Kimberly J. ALDRICH
38 Director of Student Counseling .... Dr. Patricia A. PONTO
36 Dir Ctr Career/Professional Devel .... Ms. Joan HAWXHURST
20 Associate Provost .... Dr. Amy L. SMITH

Kalamazoo Valley Community College (G)

6767 West O Avenue, PO Box 4070,
Kalamazoo MI 49003-4070
County: Kalamazoo FICE Identification: 006949
Unit ID: 170541
Telephone: (269) 488-4400 Carnegie Class: Assoc/Pub-R-L
FAX Number: (269) 488-4555 Calendar System: Semester
URL: www.kvcc.edu
Established: 1966 Annual Undergrad Tuition & Fees (In-District): $2,422
Enrollment: 13,500 Coed
Affiliation or Control: Local IRS Status: 501(c)3
Highest Offering: Associate Degree
Program: Occupational; 2-Year Principally Bachelor's Creditable
Accreditation: NH, DH, EMT, MAC

01 President .... Dr. Marilyn J. SCHLACK
05 Vice President Academic Services .... Dr. Bruce KOCHER
10 Vice President Financial Services .... Ms. Louise ANDERSON
32 VP for College & Student Relations .... Mr. Michael COLLINS
15 Vice President of Human Resources .... Ms. Sandra BOIINET
13 Vice Pres Information Technologies .... Mr. Terrel F. HUTCHINS
50 VP Econ & Business Development .... Mr. James DEHAVEN
20 Asst VP for Academic Services .... Mr. Dennis BERTCH
86 Exec Dir of Governmental Relations .... Ms. Kathy JOHNSON
12 Dean Arcadia Commons Campus .... Mr. Grant CHANDLER
19 Director of Public Safety .... Mr. Ken COLBY
62 Director of Libraries .... Ms. Janet ALM
07 Dir Admissions/Records/Registrar .... Mr. Michael MCCALL
09 Director of Institutional Research .... Mr. Stephen CANNELL
30 Director Development .... Mr. Steve DOHERTY
37 Director Financial Aid .... Mr. Roger MILLER
49 Dean Liberal Arts & Business .... Dr. Nora EVERS
76 Dean Health/Science & Technology .... Mr. James W. TAYLOR
18 Chief Facilities/Physical Plant .... Mr. Daniel MALEY
96 Director of Purchasing .... Ms. Kathy CAMPBELL
21 Business Manager .... Ms. Muriel HICE
35 Director of Student Success .... Ms. Laura COSBY
101 Asst to President and Plng Coord .... Ms. Patricia NIEWOONDER

Kellogg Community College (H)

450 North Avenue, Battle Creek MI 49017-3397
County: Calhoun FICE Identification: 002276
Unit ID: 170550
Telephone: (269) 965-3931 Carnegie Class: Assoc/Pub-R-L
FAX Number: (269) 962-4260 Calendar System: Semester
URL: www.kellogg.edu
Established: 1956 Annual Undergrad Tuition & Fees (In-District): $2,625
Enrollment: 6,150 Coed
Affiliation or Control: Local IRS Status: 501(c)3
Highest Offering: Associate Degree
Program: Occupational; 2-Year Principally Bachelor's Creditable
Accreditation: NH, DH, MLTAD, PTAA, RAD

01 President .... Dr. Dennis BONA
05 Vice President Instruction .... Ms. Catherine HENDLER
11 Vice Pres Administration/Finance .... Mr. Mark O'CONNELL
10 Chief Financial Officer .... Mr. Richard SCOTT
13 Chief Information Officer .... Ms. Catherine HENDLER
32 Vice President Student Services .... Ms. Kay KECK
49 Dean Arts/Sciences/Regional Educ .... Dr. Kevin RABINEAU
102 Executive Director KCC Foundation .... Ms. Ginger CUTSINGER
96 Director Purchasing .... Ms. Angela COCHRAN
06 Registrar .... Dr. Kay KECK
57 Chair Arts & Communication .... Ms. Barbara SUDEIKIS
08 Director Library Services .... Ms. Martha STILWELL
41 Director Athletics & PE .... Mr. Tom SHAW
12 Director of Grahl Center .... Ms. Roberta GAGNAN
12 Director Fehsenfeld Center .... Mr. Timothy SLEEVI
12 Director Eastern Academic Center .... Mr. Colin MCCALEB
15 Director Human Resources .... Ms. Alice ROBERTSON
18 Dir Inst Facilities/Public Safety .... Mr. John DIPIERRO
51 Director Lifelong Learning .... Ms. Mary GREEN
09 Director Institutional Research .... Ms. Doris LEWIS
21 Director of Finance .... Ms. Tracy BEATTY
84 Director Enrollment Services .... Ms. Denise NEWMAN
12 Dir Reg Manufacturing Tech Center .... Ms. Laura DEPOMPOLO
40 Bookstore Manager .... Ms. Catherine JAMES
35 Dir Student Life/Academic Advising .... Ms. Terah ZAREMBA
26 Dir Public Information & Marketing .... Ms. Nicole FINKBEINER
07 Director of Admissions .... Ms. Meredith STRAVERS

Kettering University (I)

1700 University Avenue, Flint MI 48504-6214
County: Genesee FICE Identification: 002262
Unit ID: 169983
Telephone: (810) 762-9500 Carnegie Class: Master's M
FAX Number: (810) 762-9837 Calendar System: Semester
URL: www.kettering.edu
Established: 1919 Annual Undergrad Tuition & Fees: $29,978
Enrollment: 2,187 Coed
Affiliation or Control: Independent Non-Profit IRS Status: 501(c)3
Highest Offering: Master's
Program: Professional
Accreditation: NH, ACBSP, CS, ENG

01 President .... Dr. Robert K. MCMAHAN
04 Assistant to President .... Ms. Susan M. FLECKENSTEIN
05 Provost & VP Academic Affairs .... Dr. Robert L. SIMPSON
10 VP Administration/Finance .... Ms. Susan K. BOLT
84 VP Enrollment Services .... Vacant
16 VP Human Resources .... Ms. Linda K. PETERSON
30 Interim VP University Advancement .... Mr. Darryl A. SCZEPANSKI
20 Vice Provost/Assoc VP Acad Services .... Dr. Jacqueline A. EL-SAYED
58 Int Assoc Prov Grad Stds/Cont Educ .... Mr. Tony HAIN
32 Assoc Prov Stdnt Affs/Dean of Stdnt .... Ms. Betsy E. HOMSHER
26 Chief Public Relations Officer .... Ms. Pat A. MROCZEK
102 Exec Dir Corp Foundation Relations .... Ms. Peggy A. SIMPSON
88 Exec Dir Individual/Major Gifts .... Mr. Jack P. STOCK
19 Chief Campus Safety .... Mr. James R. BENFORD
37 Director Student Financial Aid .... Ms. Diane K. BICE
21 Controller .... Ms. Beth A. COVERS
09 Director Institution Effectiveness .... Dr. William A. MAHLER
58 Director Grad Ops & Corp Activities .... Mr. Todd J. STEELE
18 Director Physical Plant .... Ms. Patricia A. ENGLE
08 Director Library Services .... Dr. Charles D. HANSON
07 Director Intl & Undergrad Admiss .... Ms. Karen A. FULL
41 Director Athletics/Rec Service .... Mr. Michael L. SCHAAL
93 Director Minority Student Affairs .... Mr. Dwight L. TAVADA
104 Director International Office .... Vacant
88 Director Environment Health/Safety .... Ms. Nadine L. THOR
27 Director of Marketing .... Ms. Julie A. ULSETH
06 Registrar .... Ms. Sheila R. RUPP
23 Director Wellness Center .... Ms. Deborah WILLIAMS-ROBERTS
88 Director Greek Life .... Vacant
39 Director Residence Life .... Ms. Katherine BOSIO
86 Dir External Affs/Assoc to Pres .... Mr. Robert M. NICHOLS
88 Director Thesis & Academic Services .... Ms. Caron S. WILSON
36 Director Coop Educ & Career Svcs .... Ms. Venetia S. PETTEWAY
88 Director Academic Advising .... Ms. Carol A. BROOKS
88 MI SBTDC Regional Director .... Ms. Marsha J. LYTTLE
96 Purchasing Manager .... Ms. Kathleen A. REMENDER
13 Director of Information Technology .... Ms. Viola M. SPRAGUE
44 Director of Annual Giving .... Ms. Michelle D. LOPER
88 Director Adv Technology Incubator .... Mr. Neil G. SHERIDAN
29 Director of Alumni Events .... Ms. Melinda S. TRIPLETT
25 Contract/Grant Specialist .... Ms. Jodi L. DORR

Keweenaw Bay Ojibwa Community College (J)

111 Beartown Rd, PO Box 519, Baraga MI 49908
County: Baraga Identification: 667037
Telephone: (906) 353-4600 Carnegie Class: Not Classified
FAX Number: N/A Calendar System: Semester
URL: www.kbocc.org
Established: 1975 Annual Undergrad Tuition & Fees (In-District): $1,055
Enrollment: N/A Coed
Affiliation or Control: Local IRS Status: 501(c)3
Highest Offering: Associate Degree
Program: Occupational; 2-Year Principally Bachelor's Creditable
Accreditation: @NH

01 President .... Ms. Debra J. PARRISH
05 Dean of Instruction .... Ms. Kristin TEPSA
07 Admissions Officer .... Ms. Robin CHOSA
10 Business Officer .... Ms. Megan SHANAHAN
32 Dean of Student Services .... Ms. Cherie DAKOTA
37 Director Financial Aid/Enroll Coord .... Ms. Elizabeth JULIO
88 Cultural Advisor .... Ms. Debra WILLIAMSON

Kirtland Community College (K)

10775 N Saint Helen Road, Roscommon MI 48653-9721
County: Roscommon FICE Identification: 007171
Unit ID: 170587
Telephone: (989) 275-5000 Carnegie Class: Assoc/Pub-R-M
FAX Number: (989) 275-8210 Calendar System: Semester
URL: www.kirtland.edu
Established: 1966 Annual Undergrad Tuition & Fees (In-District): $3,195
Enrollment: 2,349 Coed
Affiliation or Control: Local IRS Status: 501(c)3
Highest Offering: Associate Degree
Program: Occupational; 2-Year Principally Bachelor's Creditable

Accreditation: NH

01 President Dr. Thomas QUINN
05 Dean of Instruction Ms. Kathy MARSH
32 Dean of Student Services Ms. Michelle VYSKOCIL
76 Associate Dean Health Sciences Vacant
20 Associate Dean Instruction Vacant
08 Director of Library Ms. Deb SHUMAKER
37 Director of Financial Aid Ms. Christin HORNDT
10 Chief Financial Officer Mr. Jason BROGE
26 Director of Institutional Services Mr. Tim SCHERER
18 Director of Physical Plant Ms. Evelyn SCHENK
06 Registrar Ms. Michelle VYSKOCIL
15 Director of Human Resources Mr. Dale SHANTZ
09 Director of Institutional Research Mr. Nick BAKER
30 Chief Development Mr. Tim HAGEN-FOLEY
07 Admissions Coordinator Ms. Michelle DEVINE

Kuyper College (A)

3333 East Beltline Avenue, NE,
Grand Rapids MI 49525-9749

County: Kent FICE Identification: 002311
Unit ID: 171881
Telephone: (616) 222-3000 Carnegie Class: Bac/Diverse
FAX Number: (616) 988-3608 Calendar System: Semester
URL: www.kuyper.edu
Established: 1939 Annual Undergrad Tuition & Fees: $17,526
Enrollment: 341 Coed
Affiliation or Control: Independent Non-Profit IRS Status: 501(c)3
Highest Offering: Baccalaureate
Program: Professional; Religious Emphasis
Accreditation: NH, BI, SW

01 President Dr. Nicholas V. KROEZE
05 Provost Dr. Melvin J. FLIKKEMA
30 Vice President College Advancement Mr. Ken CAPISCIOLTO
10 Vice Pres Business Administration Mr. Duane BRAS
04 Assistant to the President Ms. Dawn A. LYNEMA
20 Dean for Academic Programs Dr. Tamara ROSIER
08 Librarian Ms. Dianne V. ZANDBERGEN
06 Registrar Ms. Joy MILANO
07 Director of Admissions Ms. Sung-Ae REED
35 Director of Student Life Mr. Cisco GONZALEZ
37 Financial Aid Director Ms. Agnes M. RUSSELL
29 Director of Alumni/Public Relations Ms. Marrilee CHAMBERLAIN
39 Resident Director Vacant
13 Director Computing/Info Management Mr. Keith TORNO
19 Supervisor of Physical Plant Mr. Lance EBENSTEIN
18 Director of Plant Mr. Tim CHUPP
40 Bookstore Manager Vacant

Lake Michigan College (B)

2755 E Napier, Benton Harbor MI 49022-1899

County: Berrien FICE Identification: 002277
Unit ID: 170620
Telephone: (269) 927-3571 Carnegie Class: Assoc/Pub-R-M
FAX Number: (269) 927-6656 Calendar System: Semester
URL: www.lakemichigancollege.edu
Established: 1946 Annual Undergrad Tuition & Fees (In-District): $1,392
Enrollment: 4,832 Coed
Affiliation or Control: Local IRS Status: 501(c)3
Highest Offering: Associate Degree
Program: Occupational; 2-Year Principally Bachelor's Creditable
Accreditation: NH, ADNUR, DA, RAD

01 President Dr. Robert HARRISON
05 Vice President of Instruction Ms. Sarah DEMPSEY
11 VP Admin Svcs/Special Asst to Pres Ms. Anne C. ERDMAN
30 VP Institutional Advance/Planning Mr. Greg A. KOROCH
10 Vice President Financial Services Ms. Deanna COLEMAN
04 Exec Assistant to the President Ms. Kerri LEROUX
49 Exec Dean Arts & Sciences Mr. Chris RODDY
50 Dean Tech/Health Sciences/Business Ms. Leslie KELLOGG
12 Exec Dean South Haven Campus Ms. Janice VARNEY
12 Exec Dean Bertrand Crossing Mrs. Barbara CRAIG
32 Interim Exec Dean Student Services Mr. Danny SLEDGE
88 Director Mainstage Services Ms. Cindy KINNEY
18 Director Facilities Management Mr. Lee H. VAN GINHOVEN
21 Director Financial Services Mr. Bruce ZAKRZEWSKI
13 Exec Dir Info Tech/Inst Rsrch Mr. Randall MELTON
26 Director Marketing Services Ms. Laura KRAKLAU
37 Director of Financial Aid Ms. Anne TEWS
06 Registrar Vacant
51 Dir Cmty Outreach/Continuing Educ Vacant
102 Director Foundations & Grants Ms. Charmaine KIBLER
96 Dir Purchasing and Support Services Ms. Linda MARUTZ
88 Dir Conference and Event Services Mr. Larry ERDMAN
91 Network Systems/Database Admin Ms. Alecia LIN
90 Activity Dir/Instruction Technology Mr. Mark KELLY

Lake Superior State University (C)

650 W Easterday Avenue,
Sault Sainte Marie MI 49783-1699

County: Chippewa FICE Identification: 002293
Unit ID: 170639
Telephone: (906) 632-6841 Carnegie Class: Bac/Diverse
FAX Number: (906) 635-2111 Calendar System: Semester
URL: www.lssu.edu
Established: 1946 Annual Undergrad Tuition & Fees (In-State): $9,264
Enrollment: 2,662 Coed
Affiliation or Control: State IRS Status: 501(c)3
Highest Offering: Master's
Program: Liberal Arts And General; Teacher Preparatory; Professional
Accreditation: NH, ENG, ENGT, IFSAC, NUR, @TEAC

01 President Dr. Tony L. MCLAIN
05 Vice President/Provost Mr. Maurice WALWORTH
32 Vice President Student Affairs Dr. Kenneth PERESS
10 Vice President Finance Ms. Sherry L. BROOKS
84 Vice President Enrollment Services Mr. William EILOLA
49 Dean Arts/Letters/Social Science Dr. Gary BALFANTZ
20 Dean Academic Services Dr. Fredrick A. MICHELS
13 Act Director Information Technology Mr. Scott OLSON
18 Director Physical Plant Ms. Sherry BROOKS
06 Registrar Ms. Nancy NEVE
07 Director of Admissions Ms. Susan K. CAMP
16 Dir Human Resources/Affirm Act Ofcr Ms. Beverly E. WHITE
36 Director of Career Services Ms. Theresa WEAVER
37 Director of Financial Aid Ms. Deborah FAUST
38 Director of Counseling Mr. David H. CASTNER
39 Director Housing/Residential Life Mr. Scott M. KORB
26 Director of Public Affairs Mr. Thomas A. PINK
29 Director Alumni Relations Ms. Susan FITZPATRICK
102 Director of Foundation Mr. Tom COATES
96 Director of Purchasing Ms. Colleen RYE
23 Director Health Services Ms. Karen STOREY
28 Dir Native American Ctr/Diversity Ms. Stephanie SABATINE
41 Athletic Director Ms. Kristin DUNBAR
35 Director Student Life Mr. Scott KORB
40 Bookstore Manager Ms. Amber MCLEAN
09 Institutional Research Analyst Ms. Cynthia F. MERKEL

Lansing Community College (D)

419 N Capitol Avenue, Lansing MI 48901-7211

County: Ingham FICE Identification: 002278
Unit ID: 170657
Telephone: (517) 483-1957 Carnegie Class: Assoc/Pub-R-L
FAX Number: (517) 483-1845 Calendar System: Semester
URL: www.lcc.edu
Established: 1957 Annual Undergrad Tuition & Fees (In-District): $2,654
Enrollment: 22,164 Coed
Affiliation or Control: Local IRS Status: 501(c)3
Highest Offering: Associate Degree
Program: Occupational; 2-Year Principally Bachelor's Creditable
Accreditation: NH, ADNUR, COMTA, DH, DMS, EMT, HT, IFSAC, RAD, SURGT

01 President Dr. Brent KNIGHT
05 Provost Dr. Stephanie SHANBLATT
11 Sr VP Finance/Admin & Advancement Ms. Lisa WEBB SHARPE
10 Chief Financial Officer Ms. Catherine FISHER
13 Chief Information Officer Mr. Kevin BUBB
88 Exec Dir Administrative Services Mr. Chris STRUGAR-FRITSCH
20 Associate VP Academic Affairs Mr. Jack BERGERON
88 Associate VP Strategic Initiatives Ms. Judith BERRY
56 Dean Ext Learning & Prof Studies Dr. Jean MORCIGLIO
88 Dean Health & Human Services Ms. Margie CLARK
49 Dean Arts & Sciences Dr. Michael NEALON
32 Dean Student Services Dr. Evan MONTAGUE
72 Dean Technical Careers Mr. George BERGHORN
26 Director Public Affairs Ms. Ellen JONES
15 Exec Director Human Resources Ms. Ann KRONEMAN

Lawrence Technological University (E)

21000 W Ten Mile Road, Southfield MI 48075-1058

County: Oakland FICE Identification: 002279
Unit ID: 170675
Telephone: (248) 204-4000 Carnegie Class: Master's L
FAX Number: (248) 204-3727 Calendar System: Semester
URL: www.ltu.edu
Established: 1932 Annual Undergrad Tuition & Fees: $26,300
Enrollment: 4,489 Coed
Affiliation or Control: Independent Non-Profit IRS Status: 501(c)3
Highest Offering: Doctorate
Program: Liberal Arts And General; Professional
Accreditation: NH, ACBSP, ART, CIDA, ENG, IACBE

01 President Dr. Lewis N. WALKER
04 Exec Assistant to the President Ms. Louise M. GARRETT
05 Provost Dr. Maria J. VAZ
10 Vice Pres Finance/Admin Ms. Linda L. HEIGHT
30 VP of University Advancement Mr. Stephen E. BROWN
88 Assoc VP Advance/Chief Dev Officer Mr. Dennis J. HOWIE
58 Assoc Provost/Dean Grad Program Dr. S. Alan MCCORD
84 Asst Provost Enrollment Management Ms. Lisa R. KUJAWA
48 Dean of Architecture & Design Mr. Glen S. LEROY
49 Dean of Arts & Sciences Dr. Hsiao-Ping H. MOORE
54 Dean of Engineering Dr. Nabil F. GRACE
50 Interim Dean of Management Dr. S. Alan MCCORD
32 Dean of Students Mr. Kevin FINN
26 Exec Dir Marketing & Public Affs Mr. Bruce J. ANNETT, JR.
10 Director Business Services Vacant
07 Director Admissions Ms. Jane T. ROHRBACK
06 Interim Registrar Ms. Noreen FERGUSON
08 Director Library Mr. Gary R. COCOZZOLI
18 Director Campus Facilities Mr. Carey G. VALENTINE
14 Ex Dir IT Svc Delivery Organization Mr. Tim CHAVIS
37 Dir Student Financial Aid/Vet Affs Mr. Mark A. MARTIN
35 Dir Stdnt Rec/Athletics & Wellness Mr. Scott TRUDEAU
36 Director of Career Services Ms. Peg PIERCE
44 Asst Vice Pres/Campaign Director Mr. Dino M. HERNANDEZ
85 Director of International Programs Ms. Cyndi MCMICHAEL
24 Director Audio Visual Media Svcs Mr. Walter G. BIZON
39 Director Residence Life Ms. Kimberly OSANTOWSKI
86 Exec Dir Econ Dev & Govt Relations Mr. Mark J. BRUCKI
102 Dir of Corp & Foundation Relations Mr. Howard DAVIS
44 Director Major Gifts Ms. Julie VULAJ
13 Director Help Desk/Services Ms. Charlene RAMOS
28 Director of Diversity Mr. Kevin FINN
89 Director of Freshman Studies Vacant
15 Director of Human Resources Ms. Deshawn WARRICK-JOHNSON
40 Manager Campus Bookstore Mr. Carl CAMPANELLA
88 Manager Dining Services Ms. Nancy THOMAS
27 Managing Editor News Bureau Mr. Eric POPE
19 Director of Campus Safety Mr. Harry P. BUTLER
29 Manager Alumni Rels/Alumni Giving Ms. Mary RANDAZZO
31 Dir of University Special Events Ms. Robin LECLERC
26 Dir Univ Comm & Academic Editor Ms. Anne M G. ADAMUS
88 Banner Project Manager Vacant
44 Mgr Advancement Svcs/Annual Giving Vacant
88 University Architect Mr. Joseph C. VERYSER
88 Director of Student Engagement Ms. Leslie WILSON
88 Dir of Academic Achievement Center Dr. Gladys M. AVILES
09 Dir of Inst Research/Academic Plng Ms. Mary E. THOMAS
96 Purchasing Agent Ms. Michelle BUTKOVICH

Macomb Community College (F)

14500 Twelve Mile Road, Warren MI 48088-9838

County: Macomb FICE Identification: 008906
Unit ID: 170790
Telephone: (586) 445-7999 Carnegie Class: Assoc/Pub-S-MC
FAX Number: (586) 445-7886 Calendar System: Semester
URL: www.macomb.edu
Established: 1954 Annual Undergrad Tuition & Fees (In-District): $2,520
Enrollment: 24,750 Coed
Affiliation or Control: Local IRS Status: 501(c)3
Highest Offering: Associate Degree
Program: Occupational; 2-Year Principally Bachelor's Creditable
Accreditation: NH, ACFEI, ADNUR, MAC, MLTAD, NMT, OTA, PTAA, SURGA, SURGT

01 President Dr. James JACOBS
05 Vice Pres/Provost Learning Unit Dr. James SAWYER
10 Vice President for Business Ms. Elizabeth ARGIRI
16 Vice President for Human Resources Mr. F. Jack WITT
26 VP College Adv/Community Relations Ms. Casandra ULBRICH
18 Vice President Facilities/Operation Ms. Libby ARGIRI
88 Director University Relations Ms. Donna PETRAS
32 Vice President for Student Services Ms. Jill M. LITTLE
49 Dean Arts & Sciences Ms. Katherine GRENDA
49 Dean Arts & Sciences Ms. Carole A. DEYER
76 Dean Health/Human Services Ms. Charlene MCPEAK
54 Dean Engineering & Adv Tech Mr. Joseph PETROSKY
50 Dean Info/Technology/Business Mr. David CORBA
35 Dean of Student Success Ms. Susan BOYD
31 Dean Student & Cmty Services Mr. Geary MAIURI
45 Exec Director Planning & Research Ms. Gerri Lynn PAVONE
21 Director Finance & Investments Ms. Roberta REMIAS
19 Captain College Police Mr. Thomas WILK
88 Director Public Service Institute Mr. Michael METZ
26 Director Marketing & Recruitment Ms. Audrey TAKACS
09 Director Institutional Research Mr. Randall HICKMAN
102 Director Foundation Ms. Gayle GOOD
06 Registrar/Dir Enrollment Services Mr. Ronald HUGHES
29 Director Alumni Relations Ms. Gayle GOOD
38 Dir Counseling & Academic Advising Mr. Gerald KNESEK
96 Director of Purchasing Mr. Dennis COSTELLO
41 Dir Athletics/Sports Clubs Mr. Brent BIEBUYCK
18 Director of Plant Operations Mr. Stevan ALTON
37 Director of Financial Aid Mr. Douglas LEVY
36 Dir Student Dev/Career Services Mr. Robert PENKALA
51 Dir Center for Continuing Education Ms. Elise JOHNSON
27 Chief Information Officer Mr. Michael ZIMMERMAN
08 Director Libraries/Info Resources Mr. Michael BALSAMO
43 General Counsel Mr. Hunter WENDT

Madonna University (G)

36600 Schoolcraft Road, Livonia MI 48150-1176

County: Wayne FICE Identification: 002282
Unit ID: 170806
Telephone: (734) 432-5300 Carnegie Class: Master's M
FAX Number: (734) 432-5333 Calendar System: Semester
URL: www.madonna.edu
Established: 1947 Annual Undergrad Tuition & Fees: $14,700
Enrollment: 4,571 Coed
Affiliation or Control: Roman Catholic IRS Status: 501(c)3
Highest Offering: Doctorate
Program: Liberal Arts And General; Teacher Preparatory; Professional
Accreditation: NH, DIETD, NURSE, SW, TED

01 President Sr. Rose Marie KUJAWA
30 Vice President for Advancement Ms. Andrea NODGE
05 Provost and VP for Academic Admin Dr. Ernest NOLAN
10 Vice Pres for Finance/Operations Mr. Leonard WILHELM
32 Vice President for Student Affairs Dr. Connie TINGSON-GATUZ
84 Vice Pres Planning/Enrollment Mgmt Mr. Michael KENNEY
12 Dean Outreach and Distance Learning Dr. James NOVAK
42 Director of Campus Ministry Sr. Anita Marie TADDONIO
06 Registrar Ms. Dina DUBUIS

07 Director of Admissions ... Mr. Mike QUATTRO
28 Director Diversity/Multicultural ... Mr. Glenn BROOKS
08 Director of Library Services ... Ms. Joanne LUMETTA
37 Director of Financial Aid ... Mr. Chris ZIEGLER
13 Director Information Systems ... Sr. Serafina Marie DIXON
15 Director of Human Resources ... Ms. Cheryl FREDRICKSON
36 Director of Career Services ... Ms. Christine BRANT
30 Director Corp Devel/Special Events ... Ms. Ann CLEARY
19 Director Public Safety ... Mr. David HAMMERSCHMIDT
41 Director Athletics ... Mr. Bryan RIZZO
40 Bookstore Manager ... Ms. Debbie MITCHELL
39 Director Residence Hall ... Ms. Tanisha MCINTOSH
24 Director Media Services ... Ms. Patricia DERRY
23 Director Instruction Center ... Dr. Patricia VINT
09 Director of Institutional Research ... Dr. Edith RALEIGH
18 Chief Facilities/Physical Plant ... Mr. Craig FLICKINGER
29 Director Alumni Relations ... Ms. Carole BOOMS
26 Director of Marketing ... Ms. Karen SANBORN
79 Dean Arts & Humanities ... Dr. Kathleen O'DOWD
50 Dean Business ... Dr. Stuart ARENDS
58 Dean Graduate Studies ... Dr. Edith RALEIGH
66 Dean Nursing & Health ... Dr. Teresa THOMPSON
72 Dean Science & Mathematics ... Dr. Theodore BIERMANN
83 Dean Social Sciences ... Dr. Karen ROSS
53 Dean Education ... Dr. Karen OBSNIUK

Marygrove College (A)

8425 W McNichols Road, Detroit MI 48221-2599
County: Wayne FICE Identification: 002284
Unit ID: 170842
Telephone: (313) 927-1200 Carnegie Class: Master's L
FAX Number: (313) 927-1345 Calendar System: Semester
URL: www.marygrove.edu
Established: 1905 Annual Undergrad Tuition & Fees: $18,020
Enrollment: 2,702 Coed
Affiliation or Control: Roman Catholic IRS Status: 501(c)3
Highest Offering: Master's
Program: 2-Year Principally Bachelor's Creditable; Liberal Arts And General; Teacher Preparatory; Professional
Accreditation: NH, SW, @TEAC

01 President ... Dr. David J. FIKE
05 VP Academic Affairs ... Ms. Jane HAMMANG-BUHL
32 VP Student Affs & Enrollment Svcs ... Dr. Juliana MOSLEY
30 Vice Pres Institutional Advancement ... Mr. Kenneth MALECKE
10 VP Finance/Admin & CFO ... Mr. William L. JOHNSON
53 Dean of Education ... Dr. Chris KOENIG SEGUIN
49 Dean of Arts and Sciences ... Dr. Judith HEINEN
31 Dean of Community Based Learning ... Dr. Brenda BRYANT
57 Dean of Visual & Performing Arts ... Ms. Rose DESLOOVER
51 Asst Dean of Continuing Education ... Ms. Sherry LEFTON
06 Registrar ... Ms. Gladys SMITH
07 Dir of Grad & Undergrad Admissions ... Ms. Sherry QUINN
09 Director of Institutional Research ... Mr. John SENKO
29 Director of Alumni Relations ... Ms. Diane PUHL
84 Dir Enrollment Svcs & Financial Aid ... Ms. Patricia CHAPLIN
41 Athletic Director ... Mr. David SICHTERMAN
42 Director of Campus Ministry ... Mr. Jesse COX
15 Director of Human Resources ... Ms. Anne JOHNSON
38 Director of Student Counseling ... Dr. Carolyn ROBERTS
39 Director Housing & Residence Life ... Mr. Timothy JOHNSTON
104 Director of International Programs ... Ms. Michelle CADE
19 Dir of Campus Security & Services ... Mr. Horace DANDRIDGE
35 Director of Student Life ... Mr. Garth HOWARD

Michigan Jewish Institute (B)

6890 West Maple, West Bloomfield MI 48322
County: Oakland FICE Identification: 032843
Unit ID: 434414
Telephone: (248) 414-6900 Carnegie Class: Bac/A&S
FAX Number: (248) 414-6907 Calendar System: Semester
URL: www.mji.edu
Established: 1994 Annual Undergrad Tuition & Fees: $10,900
Enrollment: 79 Coed
Affiliation or Control: Independent Non-Profit IRS Status: 501(c)3
Highest Offering: Baccalaureate
Program: Business Emphasis
Accreditation: ACICS

01 President/CFO/VP Financial Affs ... Rabbi Kasriel SHEMTOV
05 VP Inst Adv & Dean Academic Admin ... Dr. T. Hershel GARDIN
06 Registrar ... Ms. Karen R-HENRY
26 Director of Marketing/Student Dev ... Mr. Dov STEIN
104 Study Abroad ... Ms. Fran HERMAN
105 Web & Lan Services ... Mr. Kerry SANDERS

Michigan School of Professional Psychology (C)

26811 Orchard Lake Road,
Farmington Hills MI 48334-4512
County: Oakland FICE Identification: 021989
Unit ID: 169220
Telephone: (248) 476-1122 Carnegie Class: Spec/Health
FAX Number: (248) 476-1125 Calendar System: Semester
URL: www.mispp.edu
Established: 1981 Annual Graduate Tuition & Fees: $26,963
Enrollment: 138 Coed
Affiliation or Control: Independent Non-Profit IRS Status: 501(c)3
Highest Offering: Doctorate; No Undergraduates
Program: Professional
Accreditation: NH

01 President/Chief Academic Officer ... Dr. Kerry MOUSTAKAS
03 Vice President ... Ms. Diane ZALAPI
10 Chief Financial/Business Officer ... Mr. Tom HRZEK
58 Academic Program Chair ... Dr. Lee BACH
88 Director of Clinical Training ... Dr. Fran BROWN
13 Information Systems Coordinator ... Mr. Jeffrey CROSS
37 Director of Financial Aid ... Ms. Sandra BUTTERWORTH
08 Head Academic Librarian ... Ms. Michelle WHEELER
06 Registrar ... Ms. Heather RIGBY
07 Admissions/Recruitment Coordinator ... Ms. Amanda MING
04 Special Assistant ... Ms. Laura LANE

Michigan State University (D)

East Lansing MI 48824-1046
County: Ingham FICE Identification: 002290
Unit ID: 171100
Telephone: (517) 355-1855 Carnegie Class: RU/VH
FAX Number: N/A Calendar System: Semester
URL: www.msu.edu
Established: 1855 Annual Undergrad Tuition & Fees (In-State): $12,768
Enrollment: 47,137 Coed
Affiliation or Control: State IRS Status: 501(c)3
Highest Offering: Doctorate
Program: Liberal Arts And General; Teacher Preparatory; Professional
Accreditation: NH, ANEST, BUS, BUSA, CACREP, CEA, CIDA, CLPSY, CONST, CORE, DIETD, DIETI, DMOLS, ENG, FOR, IPSY, JOUR, LAW, LSAR, MED, MFCD, MT, MUS, NURSE, OSTEO, PLNG, SCPSY, SP, SW, TEAC, VET

01 President ... Dr. Lou Anna K. SIMON
05 Provost/Vice Pres Academic Affairs ... Dr. Kim A. WILCOX
10 Vice Pres Finance Opers/Treasurer ... Dr. Fred L. POSTON
32 Interim VP Student Affairs & Svcs ... Dr. Denise B. MAYBANK
46 Vice President Research & Grad Stds ... Dr. J. Ian GRAY
86 Vice President Governmental Affairs ... Mr. Mark A. BURNHAM
30 Vice Pres Univ Advancement ... Mr. Robert GROVES
26 Interim Vice Pres Univ Relations ... Ms. Heather C. SWAIN
43 General Counsel/VP Legal Affairs ... Mr. Robert A. NOTO
13 Assoc VP Research/Graduate Studies ... Dr. Paul M. HUNT
35 Sr Assoc VP and Dir Student Life ... Vacant
101 Secy Board Trust/Exec Asst to Pres ... Mr. William R. BEEKMAN
20 Senior Associate Provost ... Dr. June P. YOUATT
51 Assoc Prov Univ Outreach/Engagement ... Dr. Hiram E. FITZGERALD
88 Assoc Prov Academic Student Svcs ... Vacant
88 Assoc Provost Academic Svcs ... Dr. Linda O. STANFORD
58 Assoc Prov Grad Stds/Dean Grad Sch ... Dr. Karen L. KLOMPARENS
88 Asc Prov Ugrad Educ/Dn Ugrad Stds ... Dr. Douglas ESTRY
17 Assoc Provost Human Health Affairs ... Dr. James Randolph HILLARD
15 Assoc Prov/VP Academic Human Res ... Mr. Theodore H. CURRY, II
15 Asst Vice Pres Human Resources ... Mr. Brent BOWDITCH
88 Vice Prov Libraries/Computing/Tech ... Mr. David GIFT
21 Asst Vice Pres Finance/Operations ... Ms. Kathryn E. LINDAHL
45 Asst VP & Director of Plng/Budgets ... Mr. David S. BYELICH
18 Asst Vice Pres Physical Plant Admin ... Mr. Ronald T. FLINN
39 Asst VP Housing & Food Service ... Mr. Vennie GORE
21 Asst Vice Pres CFO & Controller ... Mr. David BROWER
91 Director Admin Information Services ... Mr. Scott D. MCGILL
21 Director Invest/Financial Mgmt ... Mr. Glen J. KLEIN
07 Director of Admissions ... Mr. James W. COTTER
22 Dir Incl/Intrcult Init/Sr Adv P Dvr ... Ms. Paulette GRANBERRY-RUSSELL
29 Assoc VP University Advancement ... Mr. W. Scott WESTERMAN, III
36 Director Career Services/Placement ... Mr. Kelley D. BISHOP
90 Dir Academic Technology Services ... Mr. Thomas D. DAVIS
25 Director Contract & Grant Admin ... Mr. Daniel T. EVON
38 Director Counseling Center ... Dr. Jan T. COLLINS-EAGLIN
88 Dir Michigan AGR Experiment Stn ... Dr. Steven G. PUEPPKE
56 Director MSU Extension ... Dr. Thomas G. COON
37 Director of Financial Aid ... Mr. Richard SHIPMAN
06 Registrar ... Dr. Nicole ROVIG
85 Director Intl Students/Scholars ... Mr. Peter F. BRIGGS
23 Director MSU Student Health Ctr ... Dr. Glynda M. MOORER
92 Dean Honors College ... Dr. Cynthia JACKSON-ELMOORE
41 Director Intercollegiate Athletics ... Mr. Mark J. HOLLIS
08 Director of Libraries ... Mr. Clifford H. HAKA
88 Director National Cyclotron Lab ... Dr. Konrad GELBKE
19 Police Chf/Dir Police & Pub Safety ... Mr. James H. DUNLAP
88 Director Undergraduate Univ Div ... Dr. Bonita P. CURRY
96 Actg Dir University Svc/Purchasing ... Mr. Nathan MAHER
47 Interim Dean Col Ag & Nat Resources ... Dr. Douglas BUHLER
79 Dean College Arts & Letters ... Dr. Karin A. WURST
79 Dean Res Col Arts/Humanities ... Dr. Stephen L. ESQUITH
50 Dean Eli Broad Col of Business ... Dr. Stefanie A. LENWAY
60 Dean Col Commun Arts & Science ... Dr. Pamela WHITTEN
53 Dean College of Education ... Dr. Carole AMES
54 Dean College of Engineering ... Dr. Satish S. UDPA
63 Dean College Human Medicine ... Dr. Marsha D. RAPPLEY
82 Dean James Madison College ... Dr. Sherman W. GARNETT
61 Dean College of Law ... Ms. Joan W. HOWARTH
81 Dean Lyman Briggs College ... Dr. Elizabeth H. SIMMONS
64 Dean College of Music ... Mr. James FORGER
81 Dean College Natural Science ... Dr. R. James KIRKPATRICK
66 Dean College of Nursing ... Dr. Mary H. MUNDT
63 Dean College Osteopathic Medicine ... Dr. William D. STRAMPEL
83 Dean College of Social Science ... Dr. Marietta BABA
74 Dean College Veterinary Medicine ... Dr. Christopher M. BROWN
82 Dean Intl Studies & Programs ... Dr. Jeffrey M. RIEDINGER

Michigan Technological University (E)

1400 Townsend Drive, Houghton MI 49931-1295
County: Houghton FICE Identification: 002292
Unit ID: 171128
Telephone: (906) 487-1885 Carnegie Class: RU/H
FAX Number: (906) 487-2935 Calendar System: Semester
URL: www.mtu.edu
Established: 1885 Annual Undergrad Tuition & Fees (In-State): $12,615
Enrollment: 6,957 Coed
Affiliation or Control: State IRS Status: 501(c)3
Highest Offering: Doctorate
Program: Liberal Arts And General; Teacher Preparatory; Professional
Accreditation: NH, BUS, ENG, ENGT, FOR, @TEAC

01 President ... Dr. Glenn D. MROZ
05 Provost/Vice Pres Academic Affairs ... Dr. Max SEEL
86 Vice Pres Governmental Relations ... Dr. Dale R. TAHTINEN
11 Vice President for Administration ... Ms. Ellen S. HORSCH
46 Vice President for Research ... Dr. David D. REED
32 Vice President for Student Affairs ... Dr. Les P. COOK
30 Vice President Michigan Tech Fund ... Mr. Shea MCGREW
84 Asst VP for Enrollment Services ... Mr. John B. LEHMAN
35 Dean of Students ... Ms. Bonnie GORMAN
10 Chief Financial Officer ... Mr. Daniel D. GREENLEE
26 Director Marketing/Communications ... Vacant
08 Director of the Library ... Ms. Ellen MARKS
09 Institutional Analysis ... Mr. Richard ELENICH
29 Director Alumni Association ... Ms. Brenda RUDIGER
06 Registrar ... Ms. Theresa K. JACQUES
07 Director Undergraduate Recruitment ... Ms. Allison A. CARTER
15 Director Human Resources ... Ms. Anita QUINN
37 Director of Financial Aid ... Mr. William R. ROBERTS
36 Director University Career Center ... Mr. James TURNQUIST
18 Director Facilities/Physical Plant ... Mr. John ROVANO
21 Director Planning & Budgeting ... Ms. Deborah L. LASSILA
38 Director Counseling Services ... Mr. Donald S. WILLIAMS
19 Director Public Safety ... Mr. Daniel P. BENNETT
22 Director Affirmative Programs ... Vacant
28 Director Institutional Diversity ... Ms. Chris S. ANDERSON
96 Director of Purchasing ... Mr. Raymond E. LASANEN
58 Dean Graduate School ... Dr. Jacqueline E. HUNTOON
50 Dean Business & Economics ... Dr. Darrell RADSON
54 Dean of Engineering ... Dr. Timothy J. SCHULZ
65 Dean of Forestry ... Dr. Margaret R. GALE
49 Dean Sciences/Arts ... Dr. Bruce E. SEELY
72 Dean of Technology ... Dr. James FRENDEWEY, JR.

Mid Michigan Community College (F)

1375 S Clare Avenue, Harrison MI 48625-9447
County: Clare FICE Identification: 006768
Unit ID: 171155
Telephone: (989) 386-6622 Carnegie Class: Assoc/Pub-R-M
FAX Number: (989) 386-2411 Calendar System: Semester
URL: www.midmich.edu
Established: 1965 Annual Undergrad Tuition & Fees (In-District): $3,213
Enrollment: 5,219 Coed
Affiliation or Control: State/Local IRS Status: 501(c)3
Highest Offering: Associate Degree
Program: Occupational; 2-Year Principally Bachelor's Creditable
Accreditation: NH, MAC, PTAA, RAD

01 President ... Ms. Carol A. CHURCHILL
05 Vice President of Academic Services . Dr. Michael W. JANKOVIAK
32 VP Community/Student Relations ... Mr. Matt MILLER
10 Vice President for Admin & Finance ... Ms. Lillian K. FRICK
04 Executive Assistant to President ... Ms. Sherry L. KYLE
15 Exec Director of Human Resources ... Ms. Gail NUNAMAKER
13 Director IT ... Mr. Kirk A. LEHR
81 Dean of Math & Science ... Mr. Peter VELGUTH
09 Dir of Inst Research/Grants Mgr ... Ms. Carol DARLINGTON
07 Director of Admissions ... Mr. Scott MERTES
21 Director of Accounting ... Mr. Gene SCHMIDT
96 Purchasing Manager ... Mr. Jeffery PUNCHES
88 Title III/Acad Advising Director ... Ms. Carol SHANNON
84 General/Occupational Recruiter ... Mr. Chris PELLERITO
88 SBTDC Director ... Mr. Anthony FOX
26 Director of Marketing ... Ms. Jessica GORDON
08 Dir Library/Learning Services ... Mr. Corey GOETHE
37 Director of Financial Aid ... Mr. Gale M. CRANDELL
40 Director Auxiliary Services ... Ms. Kelly KOCH
18 Director of Facilities ... Mr. William D. WHITMAN
88 Hospitality Services Manager ... Ms. Cathy STARKWEATHER
76 Director Radiology ... Mr. John B. SKINNER
25 Title III Coordinator ... Ms. Lori CORTEZ
88 Radiology Tech Clinical Coordinator ... Mr. Galen P. MILLER
27 College Info/Org Dev Officer ... Mr. Anthony FREDS
14 Systems Programmer ... Mr. Chris KLIEWONEIT
66 Dean of Academics ... Mr. Chris GOFFNETT
50 Associate Dean Business ... Mr. Shawn TROY
103 Exec Dir Econ/Workforce Dev ... Mr. Scott GOVITZ
35 Exec Dean of Student Services ... Ms. Kimberly BARNES

Monroe County Community College (G)

1555 S Raisinville Road, Monroe MI 48161-9746
County: Monroe FICE Identification: 002294
Unit ID: 171225
Telephone: (734) 242-7300 Carnegie Class: Assoc/Pub-S-SC
FAX Number: (734) 242-9711 Calendar System: Semester
URL: www.monroeccc.edu

Established: 1964 Annual Undergrad Tuition & Fees (In-District): $2,490
Enrollment: 4,723 Coed
Affiliation or Control: Local IRS Status: 170(c)1
Highest Offering: Associate Degree
Program: Occupational; 2-Year Principally Bachelor's Creditable
Accreditation: NH, ADNUR

01 President ... Dr. David E. NIXON
05 Vice President of Instruction ... Dr. Grace B. YACKEE
10 Vice Pres of Admin & Exec Dir Fdn ... Ms. Suzanne M. WETZEL
32 Vice Pres Student & Information Svc ... Mr. Randell W. DANIELS
50 Dean of Business ... Mr. Paul L. KNOLLMAN
76 Dean of Health Sciences ... Dr. Cynthia ROMAN
79 Dean of Humanities/Social Science ... Mr. Vincent MALTESE
72 Dean of Industrial Technology ... Mr. Parmeshwar COOMAR
81 Dean of Science/Mathematics ... Mr. Vincent MALTESE
31 Dean of Corporate/Cmty Svcs ... Mr. John A. JOY
08 Director Learning Resources ... Ms. Barbara MCNAMEE
06 Registrar ... Ms. Tracy VOGT
07 Director of Admissions/Guidance ... Mr. Mark HALL
88 Director of Upward Bound ... Mr. Anthony QUINN
88 Director of Respiratory Therapy ... Ms. Bonnie B. BOGGS
21 Business Manager and Treasurer ... Mr. Daniel J. SCHWAB
18 Director Physical Plant ... Mr. James J. BLUMBERG
96 Dir Auxiliary Services/Purchasing ... Ms. Jean FORD
14 Director Data Processing Services ... Mr. James A. ROSS
37 Director of Financial Aid ... Vacant
36 Dir Business Devel/Employment Svcs ... Mr. Barry C. KINSEY
56 Director of Extension Centers ... Ms. Sandy KOSMYNA
88 Director of Lifelong Learning ... Ms. Tina PILLARELLI
13 Manager Information Services ... Mr. Brian K. LAY
27 Director of Marketing ... Mr. Joseph VERKENNES
15 Director of Human Resources ... Ms. Molly M. MCCUTCHAN

Montcalm Community College (A)

2800 College Drive, Sidney MI 48885-9723
County: Montcalm FICE Identification: 002295
Unit ID: 171234
Telephone: (989) 328-2111 Carnegie Class: Assoc/Pub-R-M
FAX Number: (989) 328-2950 Calendar System: Semester
URL: www.montcalm.edu
Established: 1965 Annual Undergrad Tuition & Fees (In-District): $2,760
Enrollment: 2,113 Coed
Affiliation or Control: Local IRS Status: 501(c)3
Highest Offering: Associate Degree
Program: Occupational; 2-Year Principally Bachelor's Creditable; Liberal Arts And General
Accreditation: NH, MAC

01 President ... Mr. Robert C. FERRENTINO
11 Vice Pres Administrative Services ... Mr. James D. LANTZ
05 Vice Pres for Academic Affairs ... Mr. Robert SPOHR
32 Dean of Student Services ... Ms. Denise NEWMAN
31 Dean of Community Outreach ... Ms. Susan HATTO
37 Director of Financial Aid ... Ms. Traci NICHOLS
21 Director of Accounting ... Ms. Margery E. FORIST
18 Director of Facilities ... Mr. George F. GERMAIN
13 Information Systems Director ... Mr. Rodney C. MIDDLETON
66 Director of Nursing & Allied Health ... Ms. Beth MOWATT
08 Director of the Library ... Mr. Richard L. PARKER
103 Dir of Workforce Training Solutions ... Ms. Leslie A. WOOD
84 Director of Enrollment Services ... Ms. Denise E. EDWARDS
30 Dir of Institutional Advancement ... Ms. Therese A. SMITH
40 Bookstore Director ... Ms. Janet M. CAMPBELL
07 Dir Admissions/Asc Dn Student Svcs ... Ms. Debra ALEXANDER
09 Dir of Assessment & Inst Research ... Dr. Maria A. SUCHOWSKI
26 Public Information Coordinator ... Ms. Shelly STRAUTZ-SPRINGBORN
20 Dean of Instruction & Faculty ... Mr. Gary HAUCK
06 Registrar ... Ms. Denise E. EDWARDS
10 Chief Business Officer ... Mr. James D. LANTZ
15 Director of Human Resources ... Ms. Connie STEWART

Moody Theological Seminary-Michigan (B)

41550 E Ann Arbor Trail, Plymouth MI 48170-4308
County: Wayne FICE Identification: 031353
Unit ID: 429076
Telephone: (734) 207-9581 Carnegie Class: Spec/Faith
FAX Number: (734) 207-9582 Calendar System: Trimester
URL: www.mts.edu
Established: 1993 Annual Graduate Tuition & Fees: $13,680
Enrollment: 171 Coed
Affiliation or Control: Independent Non-Profit IRS Status: 501(c)3
Highest Offering: Master's; No Undergraduates
Program: Religious Emphasis
Accreditation: &NH, THEOL

01 President ... Dr. Paul NYQUIST
05 Associate Academic Dean ... Dr. John RESTUM
06 Registrar ... Mr. George MOSHER
08 Director of Library Services ... Mr. Micah JELINAK
42 Chaplain ... Dr. Paul WILSON
18 Facilities Operations ... Mr. Brian L. MOLLENKAMP

† Regional accreditation is carried under the parent institution Moody Bible Institute, Chicago, IL.

Mott Community College (C)

1401 E Court Street, Flint MI 48503-2089
County: Genesee FICE Identification: 002261
Unit ID: 169275
Telephone: (810) 762-0200 Carnegie Class: Assoc/Pub-R-L
FAX Number: (810) 762-0257 Calendar System: Semester
URL: www.mcc.edu
Established: 1923 Annual Undergrad Tuition & Fees (In-District): $3,254
Enrollment: 12,345 Coed
Affiliation or Control: Local IRS Status: 501(c)3
Highest Offering: Associate Degree
Program: Occupational; 2-Year Principally Bachelor's Creditable; Business Emphasis
Accreditation: NH, ACBSP, ADNUR, DA, DH, OTA, PTAA

01 President ... Dr. Dick SHAINK
30 Exec Dir Inst Developmnt/Foundation ... Ms. Lennetta CONEY
05 Vice Pres Academic Affairs ... Dr. Amy FUGATE
11 VP Student & Administrative Svcs ... Mr. Scott JENKINS
10 Chief Financial Officer ... Mr. Larry GAWTHROP
16 Chief Human Resources Officer ... Mr. Mark KENNEDY
88 Exec Dean Regional Tech Ctr Project ... Mr. Tom CRAMPTON
51 Exec Dir Corporate Svcs & Cont Educ ... Mr. Chuck THIEL
35 Dean Student Services ... Dr. Delores DEEN
37 Exec Dir Student Fin Svcs ... Ms. Jennifer DOW-MCDONALD
81 Dean of Math & Science ... Dr. Johanna BROWN
32 Dean Counseling & Student Devlop ... Mr. Troy BOQUETTE
83 Dean Social Sciences & Fine Arts ... Ms. Mary CUSACK
50 Dean of Business ... Mr. Chuck HAYES
72 Dean of Technology ... Mr. Clark HARRIS
26 Exec Director Marketing & PR ... Mr. Michael KELLY
27 Chief Technology Officer ... Ms. Cheryl BASSETT
06 Registrar ... Mr. Chris ENGLE
36 Exec Dir Career Ctr/Job Placement ... Mrs. Cindy MCDANIEL
62 Executive Director Library ... Mrs. Kathy IRWIN
18 Exec Dir Physical Plant/Architect ... Mr. Larry KOEHLER
41 Director Athletics/Campus Rec ... Mr. Tom HEALEY
09 Exec Dir Institutional Research ... Mrs. Gail IVES
32 Director Student Life ... Ms. Dawn VANNIMAN
96 Director of Purchasing ... Ms. Jody MICHAEL

Muskegon Community College (D)

221 S Quarterline Road, Muskegon MI 49442-1493
County: Muskegon FICE Identification: 002297
Unit ID: 171304
Telephone: (231) 773-9131 Carnegie Class: Assoc/Pub-U-SC
FAX Number: (231) 777-0255 Calendar System: Semester
URL: www.muskegoncc.edu
Established: 1926 Annual Undergrad Tuition & Fees (In-District): $2,813
Enrollment: 5,311 Coed
Affiliation or Control: Local IRS Status: Exempt
Highest Offering: Associate Degree
Program: Occupational; 2-Year Principally Bachelor's Creditable
Accreditation: NH, ADNUR

01 President ... Dr. Dale K. NESBARY
05 Vice President of Academic Affairs ... Ms. Teresa STURRUS
11 Vice Pres Administrative Service ... Ms. Rosemary ZINK
32 Vice President Student Services ... Dr. John SELMON
20 Dean of Academic Svcs/Registrar ... Ms. Joan ROBERTS
20 Dean of Instruction & Assessment ... Mr. Ed BREITENBACH
51 Dean Continuing Ed/Program Outreach ... Ms. Trynette Lottie HARPS
84 Dean of Enrollment Services ... Mr. George MANIATES
10 Director of Finance ... Ms. Beth DICK
13 Chief Information Officer ... Mr. Mike ALSTROM
37 Director Financial Aid ... Mr. Bruce WIERDA
26 Director of Public Information ... Vacant
06 Registrar ... Ms. Jean ROBERTS
09 Director of Institutional Research ... Ms. Anne MEILOF
31 Director of Community Relations ... Ms. Tina DEE
15 Director of Human Resources ... Mr. Aaron HILLIARD
41 Athletic Director ... Mr. Marty MCDERMOTT

North Central Michigan College (E)

1515 Howard Street, Petoskey MI 49770-8717
County: Emmet FICE Identification: 002299
Unit ID: 171395
Telephone: (231) 348-6600 Carnegie Class: Assoc/Pub-R-M
FAX Number: (231) 348-6628 Calendar System: Semester
URL: www.ncmich.edu
Established: 1958 Annual Undergrad Tuition & Fees (In-District): $1,161
Enrollment: 3,123 Coed
Affiliation or Control: Local IRS Status: 501(c)3
Highest Offering: Associate Degree
Program: Occupational; 2-Year Principally Bachelor's Creditable
Accreditation: NH

01 President ... Dr. Cameron BRUNET-KOCH
05 Dean of Instruction ... Dr. Christine HAMMOND
10 Dean Finance & Facilities ... Mr. Todd MCDONALD
32 Dean of Students ... Mrs. Naomi DEWINTER
102 Executive Director Foundation ... Mr. Sean POLLION
08 Librarian ... Mrs. Eunice TEEL
37 Director of Financial Aid ... Mrs. Virginia PANOFF
18 Director of Physical Plant ... Mr. Jeff GARDNER
84 Dir Enrollment Services/Registrar ... Ms. Renee DEYOUNG
15 Human Resources ... Ms. Diana SOUZA

21 Controller ... Mrs. Nancy ALLISON
26 Director Public Relations ... Mr. Charlie MACINNIS
29 Director Alumni Relations ... Mr. Sean POLLION
35 Dir Student Activities/Camp Housing ... Mr. Scott POWELL
40 Bookstore Manager ... Ms. Julie WEAVER

Northern Michigan University (F)

1401 Presque Isle Avenue, Marquette MI 49855-5301
County: Marquette FICE Identification: 002301
Unit ID: 171456
Telephone: (906) 227-1000 Carnegie Class: Master's M
FAX Number: (906) 227-2204 Calendar System: Semester
URL: www.nmu.edu
Established: 1899 Annual Undergrad Tuition & Fees (In-State): $8,414
Enrollment: 9,417 Coed
Affiliation or Control: State IRS Status: 501(c)3
Highest Offering: Beyond Master's But Less Than Doctorate
Program: Occupational; 2-Year Principally Bachelor's Creditable; Liberal Arts And General; Teacher Preparatory; Professional
Accreditation: NH, BUS, DMOLS, ENGT, MLTAD, MT, MUS, NURSE, SURGT, SW, TEAC

01 President ... Dr. Leslie E. WONG
10 VP for Finance & Administration ... Mr. R. Gavin LEACH
05 Interim Provost/VP Academic Affairs ... Dr. Paul L. LANG
32 Assoc Prov Student Svcs/Enrollment ... Mr. William A. BERNARD
20 Associate Provost Academic Affairs ... Dr. Terrance L. SEETHOFF
09 Assoc VP for Inst Research ... Dr. Paul B. DUBY
21 Assoc VP Business & Auxiliary Svcs ... Mr. Arthur J. GISCHIA
90 Dean Academic Information Services ... Ms. Darlene M. WALCH
35 Dean of Students ... Ms. Christine G. GREER
49 Dean of Arts & Sciences ... Dr. Michael J. BROADWAY
50 Dean Walker L. Cisler Col Bus ... Dr. Jamal A. RASHED
107 Interim Dean College Prof Studies ... Dr. Harvey A. WALLACE
58 Dean Graduate Studies & Research ... Dr. Terrance L. SEETHOFF
30 Exec Director of Advancement ... Ms. Martha B. HAYNES
06 Registrar ... Ms. Kim M. ROTUNDO
43 General Counsel ... Ms. Catherine L. DEHLIN
102 Director of Foundation Operations ... Ms. Amy M. HUBINGER
27 Director Communications & Marketing ... Ms. Cindy L. PAAVOLA
36 Dir of Acad & Career Advisement ... Mr. James G. GADZINSKI
37 Director of Financial Aid ... Mr. Michael R. ROTUNDO
38 Head Counseling Center ... Ms. Marie M. AHO
88 Admin Sports Training Center ... Vacant
88 Director Glenn T. Seaborg Center ... Ms. Debra L. HOMEIER
41 Athletic Director ... Mr. Kenneth G. GODFREY
19 Interim Dir Public Safety/Pol, Svcs ... Mr. Michael J. BATH
39 Director Housing/Residence Life ... Mr. Carl D. HOLM
07 Director of Admissions ... Ms. Gerri L. DANIELS
23 Chief of Staff/Physician ... Vacant
15 Director of Human Resources ... Ms. Ann M. SHERMAN
26 Marketing Director ... Ms. Anne M. STARK
28 Dir Multicult Educ/Resource Center ... Vacant
85 Exec Dir International Programs ... Dr. Marcelo E. SILES
92 Director of Honors Program ... Dr. David H. WOOD
88 Director of Support/Consulting Svcs ... Ms. Felecia J. FLACK
24 Director Broadcast & AV Services ... Mr. Eric L. SMITH
29 Director Alumni Operations ... Ms. Deanna K. HEMMILA
40 Bookstore Manager ... Mr. Michael J. KUZAK
18 Associate VP Eng & Plan/Facilities ... Ms. Kathy A. RICHARDS
13 Chief Technology Officer ... Mr. David W. MAKI

Northwestern Michigan College (G)

1701 E Front Street, Traverse City MI 49686-3061
County: Grand Traverse FICE Identification: 002302
Unit ID: 171483
Telephone: (231) 995-1000 Carnegie Class: Assoc/Pub-R-M
FAX Number: (231) 995-1339 Calendar System: Semester
URL: www.nmc.edu
Established: 1951 Annual Undergrad Tuition & Fees (In-District): $5,452
Enrollment: 5,440 Coed
Affiliation or Control: Local IRS Status: 501(c)3
Highest Offering: Associate Degree
Program: Occupational; 2-Year Principally Bachelor's Creditable
Accreditation: NH, ACFEI, DA

01 President ... Mr. Timothy J. NELSON
05 Vice Pres for Educational Services ... Dr. Stephen N. SICILIANO
88 VP Lifelong/Professional Learning ... Ms. Marguerite C. COTTO
10 Interim VP of Fin & Administration ... Ms. Vicki COOK
04 Exec Assistant to President & Board ... Ms. Holly J. GORTON
08 Exec Director Lrng Res/Technologies ... Mr. Craig A. MULDER
15 Director of Human Resources ... Ms. Christine M. KEENAN
88 Director of Dennos Museum Center ... Mr. Eugene A. JENNEMAN
32 Dean for Enrollment & Student Svcs ... Dr. Chris WEBER
24 Director Educational Media Tech ... Ms. Janet W. OLIVER
12 Supt Great Lakes Maritime Academy ... RAdm. Gerard ACHENBACH, USMS
20 Dir Academic Affairs/Business Chair ... Ms. Susan DECAMILLIS
31 Director Extended Educ Services ... Ms. Carol A. EVANS
06 Registrar ... Ms. Carol J. TABERSKI
23 Director of Health Services ... Ms. Renee R. JACOBSON
09 Dir Research Planning Effectiveness ... Dr. Darby L. HILLER-FREUND
18 Director of Facilites ... Mr. Paul PERRY
26 Interim Dir of PR & Communications ... Mr. John PARKER
44 Director of Development ... Ms. Rebecca TEAHEN
62 Library Director ... Ms. Tina ULRICH
88 Director Great Lakes Culinary Inst ... Mr. Fredrick L. LAUGHLIN
88 Director Upward Bound ... Ms. Patty ROTH

88 Director of Training/Research .... Mr. Richard R. WOLIN
21 Controller .... Ms. Cheryl SULLIVAN
96 Manager of Purchasing .... Mr. Stephen A. WESTPHAL
19 Campus Security .... Mr. Jim WHITE
07 Director of Admissions .... Mr. James S. BENSLEY
37 Director of Financial Aid .... Ms. Pam PALERMO
36 Director of Learning Services .... Ms. Kari L. KAHLER
68 Coordinator Physical Education .... Mr. Peter W. LACOURSE
60 Communications Chair .... Ms. Bronwyn R. JONES
75 Director of Technical Division .... Mr. Ed BAILEY
88 Director of Aviation .... Mr. Aaron COOK
79 Humanities Chair .... Mr. Jim PRESS
81 Science & Math Chair .... Mr. Anthony L. JENKINS
76 Health Occupations Chair .... Ms. Jean ROKOS

Northwood University (A)

4000 Whiting Drive, Midland MI 48640-2398
County: Midland FICE Identification: 004072
Unit ID: 171492
Telephone: (989) 837-4200 Carnegie Class: Spec/Bus
FAX Number: (989) 837-4111 Calendar System: Semester
URL: www.northwood.edu
Established: 1959 Annual Undergrad Tuition & Fees: $20,140
Enrollment: 6,326 Coed
Affiliation or Control: Independent Non-Profit IRS Status: 501(c)3
Highest Offering: Master's
Program: Liberal Arts And General; Business Emphasis
Accreditation: NH

01 President & Chief Executive Officer .... Dr. Keith A. PRETTY
05 Exec VP/Chief Academic Officer .... Dr. Kristin STEHOUWER
10 Vice President Finance & Treasurer .... Mr. W. Karl STEPHAN
30 Vice President Advancement .... Mr. Arnold D'AMBROSIO
88 VP Strategic/Corporate Alliances .... Dr. Timothy G. NASH
84 VP Marketing/Enrollment Mgmt .... Mr. John O. YOUNG
12 Provost-Michigan Campus .... Dr. William K. BATEMAN
12 Provost-Florida Campus .... Dr. Rose B. BELLANCA
12 Provost-Texas Campus .... Dr. Kevin G. FEGAN
51 Associate Dean Adult Degree Program .... Ms. Rhonda C. ANDERSON
07 Dean of Admissions .... Mr. Daniel F. TOLAND
32 Dean of Students .... Mr. Larry J. LINDSEY
85 Dean International Programs .... Dr. Daniel K. LIECHTY
45 Director of Asset Management .... Mr. David L. BENDER
26 Director of Communications .... Mr. Michael D. CURRY
06 Registrar .... Ms. Marisa L. TOSCHKOFF
09 Dir of Institutional Effectiveness .... Ms. Stacy A. SMITH
37 System Financial Aid Director .... Mr. Mark A. MARTIN
15 Director of Human Resources .... Ms. Pamela L. CHRISTIE
21 System Bussines Officer .... Ms. Susan M. RIDGWAY
29 Executive Director Alumni Relations .... Ms. Julie L. FELSKE

Oakland Community College (B)

2480 Opdyke Road, Bloomfield Hills MI 48304-2266
County: Oakland FICE Identification: 002303
Unit ID: 171535
Telephone: (248) 341-2000 Carnegie Class: Assoc/Pub-S-MC
FAX Number: (248) 341-2118 Calendar System: Semester
URL: www.oaklandcc.edu
Established: 1964 Annual Undergrad Tuition & Fees (In-District): $2,106
Enrollment: 28,944 Coed
Affiliation or Control: State/Local IRS Status: 501(c)3
Highest Offering: Associate Degree
Program: Occupational; 2-Year Principally Bachelor's Creditable
Accreditation: NH, ACFEI, ADNUR, DH, DMS, MAC, RAD, SURGT

01 Chancellor .... Dr. Timothy R. MEYER
05 Vice Chanc Academic Affairs .... Dr. Richard E. HOLCOMB
45 Vice Chanc for Planning & Devel .... Vacant
11 Vice Chanc Administrative Services .... Mr. Clarence E. BRANTLEY
04 Exec Assistant to Chancellor .... Ms. Cherie A. FOSTER
12 President Highland Lakes Campus .... Dr. Gordon F. MAY
12 President Royal Oak/Southfield Camp .... Dr. Steven J. REIF
12 President Auburn Hills Campus .... Dr. Patricia A. DOLLY
12 President Orchard Ridge Campus .... Dr. Jacqueline SHADKO
16 Chief Human Resources Officer .... Ms. Catherine J. RUSH
27 Director College Communication .... Mr. George A. CARTSONIS
13 Chief Information Officer .... Mr. Andrew R. HILLBERRY
84 Dean Enrollment Services .... Mrs. Carla R. MATHEWS
76 Dean Allied Health .... Vacant
26 Executive Director Marketing .... Vacant
72 Exec Director Tech Infrastructure .... Mr. Robert J. MONTGOMERY
88 Director of Training .... Ms. Pamela L. DORRIS
20 Dean Academic Services .... Vacant
06 Interim Registrar .... Mr. Stephen M. LINDEN
18 Director Physical Facilities .... Mr. Daniel P. CHEREWICK
14 Exec Director Tech Applications .... Mr. David M. DUNSHEE
19 Director Public Safety .... Mr. Terry L. MCCAULEY
30 Actg Chief Strategic Devel Officer .... Ms. Sharon MILLER
21 Controller .... Mrs. Gail S. PITTS
22 Director Employee Relations .... Mr. Gary S. CASEY
102 Director of OCC Foundation .... Ms. Cynthia A. TANNER
36 Director Placement/Coop Education .... Mr. Willie L. LLOYD
41 Interim Athletic Director .... Ms. Laurie G. HUBER
96 Director Purchasing/Auxiliary Svcs .... Ms. Gheretta R. HARRIS
09 Director Assessment & Effectiveness .... Mr. Martin A. ORLOWSKI
21 Director Financial Services .... Ms. Sharon K. CONVERSE
37 Director Financial Res/Scholarships .... Ms. Wilma B. PORTER
15 Director of Personnel Services .... Mrs. Margaret R. CARROLL
35 Exec Director Student Services .... Vacant
29 Coordinator Alumni Association .... Vacant

Oakland University (C)

2200 N. Squirrel Road, Rochester MI 48309-4401
County: Oakland FICE Identification: 002307
Unit ID: 171571
Telephone: (248) 370-2100 Carnegie Class: DRU
FAX Number: (248) 370-2286 Calendar System: Semester
URL: www.oakland.edu
Established: 1957 Annual Undergrad Tuition & Fees (In-State): $10,398
Enrollment: 19,053 Coed
Affiliation or Control: State IRS Status: 501(c)3
Highest Offering: Doctorate
Program: Liberal Arts And General; Teacher Preparatory; Professional
Accreditation: NH, ANEST, BUS, BUSA, CACREP, CS, DANCE, ENG, ENGR, #MED, MUS, NURSE, PTA, SPAA, SW, TEAC, THEA

01 President .... Dr. Gary D. RUSSI
04 Executive Asst to the President .... Ms. Karen S. KUKUK
05 Sr VP Academic Affairs & Provost .... Dr. Virinder K. MOUDGIL
32 VP Student Affs & Enrollment Mgmt .... Dr. Mary Beth SNYDER
30 VP for Community Engagement .... Mr. Eric BARRITT
10 VP Finance & Administration .... Mr. John W. BEAGHAN
43 VP Legal Affairs & General Counsel .... Mr. Victor A. ZAMBARDI
86 VP Government Relations .... Ms. Rochelle A. BLACK
12 Assc VP Outreach/Exec Dir OU Macomb .... Dr. Betty YOUNGBLOOD
66 Dean of Nursing .... Dr. Kerri SCHUILING
54 Dean Engineer & Computer Science .... Dr. Louay M. CHAMRA
76 Dean School Health Sciences .... Dr. Kenneth R. HIGHTOWER
53 Dean Educ & Human Services .... Dr. Louis B. GALLIEN
49 Dean College Arts & Sciences .... Dr. Ronald A. SUDOL
50 Dean School of Business Admin .... Dr. Mohan R. TANNIRU
63 Dean School of Medicine .... Dr. Robert FOLBERG
62 Dean of the Library .... Ms. Adriene LIM
20 Senior Associate Provost .... Dr. Susan M. AWBREY
46 Vice Provost Research .... Dr. Bradley ROTH
27 Chief Information Officer .... Ms. Theresa M. ROWE
09 Dir Inst Research & Assessment .... Ms. Laura A. SCHARTMAN
24 Asst VP Classrm Spprt/Instruct Tech .... Mr. George T. PREISINGER
90 Asst VP E-Learning/Instr Support .... Dr. Catheryn L. CHEAL
20 Asst VP Academic Affairs .... Ms. Peggy S. COOKE
88 Int Dir Ctr Excellence Tchg Lrng .... Dr. David LAU
88 Dir Eye Research Institute .... Dr. Frank GIBLIN
88 Director FAJRI .... Dr. Sayed NASSAR
21 Asst VP Finance & Administration .... Mr. Stephen W. ROBERTS
18 Assoc VP Facilities Mgmt .... Mr. Terry STOLLSTEIMER
15 Asst VP University Human Resources .... Mr. Ronald P. WATSON
102 Asst VP & Campaign Director .... Ms. Bernice LOPATA
07 Asst VP Student Affs Admissions .... Ms. Eleanor L. REYNOLDS
35 Asst VP & Dean Student Life .... Mr. Glenn MCINTOSH
19 Chief of Police .... Mr. Samuel C. LUCIDO
06 Registrar .... Mr. Steven J. SHABLIN
44 Director Annual Giving Programs .... Ms. Starr CORNELL
37 Director of Financial Aid .... Ms. Cindy L. HERMSEN
29 Director of Alumni Relations .... Vacant
27 Director Communications & Marketing .... Vacant
41 Director of Athletics .... Mr. Tracy A. HUTH
28 Dir Inclus Intercu Initiatives/Atty .... Ms. Joi M. CUNNINGHAM
39 Director of University Housing .... Mr. James R. ZENTMEYER
36 Director Career Services .... Mr. Wayne J. THIBODEAU
38 Director Counseling Center .... Dr. David J. SCHWARTZ
85 Director International Students .... Mr. David John J. ARCHBOLD
88 Director Disability Support Svcs .... Ms. Linda G. SISSON
96 Purchasing Manager .... Ms. Maria E. EBNER-SMITH

Olivet College (D)

320 S Main Street, Olivet MI 49076-9406
County: Eaton FICE Identification: 002308
Unit ID: 171599
Telephone: (269) 749-7000 Carnegie Class: Bac/Diverse
FAX Number: (269) 749-7600 Calendar System: Semester
URL: www.olivetcollege.edu
Established: 1844 Annual Undergrad Tuition & Fees: $21,118
Enrollment: 1,136 Coed
Affiliation or Control: Independent Non-Profit IRS Status: 501(c)3
Highest Offering: Master's
Program: Liberal Arts And General; Teacher Preparatory
Accreditation: NH, @TEAC

01 President .... Dr. Steven M. COREY
05 Provost and Dean of the College .... Dr. Maria DAVIS
10 Sr Vice Pres/Chief Financial Ofcr .... Mr. William KURTZ
11 Vice President Admin/Physical Plant .... Mr. Larry COLVIN
84 Vice Pres Enrollment Management .... Vacant
32 Vice President/Dean Student Life .... Dr. Linda LOGAN
30 Vice Pres Development/Inst Advance .... Vacant
06 Registrar .... Ms. Leslie SULLIVAN
41 Athletic Director .... Ms. Heather BATEMAN
42 Director of Church Relations .... Mr. Michael F. FALES
36 Int Dir Career Services Network .... Ms. Joanne WILLIAMS
37 Director of Student Financial Aid .... Ms. Libby JEAN
07 Director of Admissions .... Ms. Melissa CASAREZ
94 Director of Women's Resource Center .... Ms. Dianne THOMAS
39 Student Housing .... Ms. Tamyra WALTERS
13 Information & Technology Manager .... Mr. Suresh ACHARYA
15 Human Resources Specialist .... Mrs. Therese WOOD
29 Alumni Relations Coordinator .... Ms. Martha MASON JENNINGS

Robert B. Miller College (E)

450 North Avenue, Battle Creek MI 49017-3397
County: Calhoun FICE Identification: 040943
Unit ID: 448804
Telephone: (269) 660-8021 Carnegie Class: Bac/Diverse
FAX Number: (269) 565-2180 Calendar System: Semester
URL: www.millercollege.edu
Established: 2002 Annual Undergrad Tuition & Fees: $9,990
Enrollment: 350 Coed
Affiliation or Control: Independent Non-Profit IRS Status: 501(c)3
Highest Offering: Baccalaureate
Program: Liberal Arts And General; Teacher Preparatory; Business Emphasis
Accreditation: NH, NURSE, @TEAC

01 President .... Dr. David J. HARRIS
11 Director of Administrative Services .... Ms. Lorene E. FRISBIE
05 Provost .... Ms. Gloria ROBERTSON
32 Dean of Student Services .... Ms. Kimberly F. CVITKOVIC

Rochester College (F)

800 W Avon Road, Rochester Hills MI 48307-2764
County: Oakland FICE Identification: 002288
Unit ID: 170967
Telephone: (248) 218-2000 Carnegie Class: Bac/Diverse
FAX Number: (248) 218-2025 Calendar System: Semester
URL: www.rc.edu
Established: 1959 Annual Undergrad Tuition & Fees: $17,394
Enrollment: 1,045 Coed
Affiliation or Control: Independent Non-Profit IRS Status: 501(c)3
Highest Offering: Master's
Program: Liberal Arts And General
Accreditation: NH

01 President .... Dr. Thomas R. SHELLY
05 Vice President Academic Affairs .... Dr. John D. BARTON
84 Vice President Enrollment .... Mr. Klint PLEASANT
10 Chief Financial Officer .... Mr. Mark VANRHEENEN
30 Assoc Vice Pres Inst Advancement .... Mr. Scott SAMUELS
20 Academic Dean .... Dr. Katrina VANDERWOUDE
21 Controller .... Ms. Kim WILLIAMS
14 Director Operational Support .... Mr. Mark JOHNSON
50 Chair Div Col of Bus/Prof Studies .... Mr. Larry NORMAN
49 Chair Div Col of Arts & Sciences .... Dr. David KELLER
15 Director of Human Resources .... Ms. Lindsey M. DUNFEE
26 Director of Mktg & Design .... Mr. Elliot JONES
32 Dean of Students .... Mr. Brian COLE
37 Director of Student Financial Svcs .... Ms. Kara MILLER
08 Director of Library Services .... Ms. Alison KELLER
06 Registrar .... Ms. Julie HARPER
88 Director of Assessment .... Mr. John M. MANRY
29 Director of Alumni/Bookstore Mgr .... Mr. Larry STEWART
35 Assoc Dean of Students/Campus Life .... Mr. Terrill HALL
41 Director of Athletics .... Mr. Klint PLEASANT
42 Campus Minister .... Mr. Adam HILL
19 Director of Safety & Security .... Mr. Shawn WESTAWAY
04 Assistant to the President .... Ms. Karen HART

Sacred Heart Major Seminary/ College and Theologate (G)

2701 Chicago Boulevard, Detroit MI 48206-1799
County: Wayne FICE Identification: 002313
Unit ID: 172033
Telephone: (313) 883-8500 Carnegie Class: Spec/Faith
FAX Number: (313) 868-6440 Calendar System: Semester
URL: www.shms.edu
Established: 1919 Annual Undergrad Tuition & Fees: $11,270
Enrollment: 412 Coed
Affiliation or Control: Roman Catholic IRS Status: 501(c)3
Highest Offering: Master's
Program: Liberal Arts And General; Professional
Accreditation: NH, THEOL

01 Rector & President .... V.Rev. Jeffrey M. MONFORTON
32 Vice Rector/Dean of Seminarians .... Rev. Gerard BATTERSBY
05 Dean of Studies .... Rev. Todd LAJINESS
73 Dean of the Institute for Ministry .... Mrs. Janet DIAZ
10 Director Finance/Treasurer .... Ms. Ann Marie CONNOLLY
06 Registrar .... Mr. John MELDRUM
35 Director Undergraduate Seminarians .... Rev. Stephen BURR
38 Graduate Spiritual Director .... Rev. Daniel TRAPP
08 Librarian .... Mr. Christopher SPILKER
38 Undergraduate Spiritual Director .... Rev. Robert SPEZIA
58 Dir Graduate Pastoral Formation .... Mr. Douglas BIGNALL

Saginaw Chippewa Tribal College (H)

2274 Enterprise Drive, Mount Pleasant MI 48858-2335
County: Isabella FICE Identification: 037723
Unit ID: 441070
Telephone: (989) 775-4123 Carnegie Class: Tribal
FAX Number: (989) 775-4528 Calendar System: Semester
URL: www.sagchip.edu
Established: 1998 Annual Undergrad Tuition & Fees: $2,040
Enrollment: 153 Coed
Affiliation or Control: Tribal Control IRS Status: 501(c)3
Highest Offering: Associate Degree
Program: 2-Year Principally Bachelor's Creditable

Accreditation: NH

01	President	Dr. Betty REDLEAF-COLLETT
05	Dean of Instruction/Student Svcs	Ms. Carla SINEWAY
20	Academic Support Services Manager	Ms. Kathryn DENHEETEN
07	Admissions Officer/Registrar	Ms. Tracy REED

Saginaw Valley State University (A)

7400 Bay Road, University Center MI 48710-0001
County: Saginaw FICE Identification: 002314
Unit ID: 172051
Telephone: (989) 964-4000 Carnegie Class: Master's L
FAX Number: (989) 964-0180 Calendar System: Semester
URL: www.svsu.edu
Established: 1963 Annual Undergrad Tuition & Fees (In-State): $7,815
Enrollment: 10,656 Coed
Affiliation or Control: State IRS Status: 501(c)3
Highest Offering: Master's
Program: Liberal Arts And General; Teacher Preparatory; Professional
Accreditation: NH, BUS, ENG, MT, MUS, NURSE, OT, SW, TED

01	President	Dr. Eric R. GILBERTSON
05	Provost/VP Academic Affairs	Dr. Donald J. BACHAND
10	Exec VP Admin & Business Affairs	Mr. James G. MULADORE
84	Vice Pres Enrollment Mgmt	Mr. James P. DWYER
32	VP Student Affairs/Dean of Students	Ms. Merry Jo BRANDIMORE
86	Spec Asst to Pres/Government Rels	Dr. Eugene J. HAMILTON
28	Spec Asst to Pres/Diversity Pgms	Dr. Mamie T. THORNS
04	Exec Asst Pres/Dir Public Affairs	Dr. Carlos RAMET
45	Assoc Provost	Dr. Marc PERETZ
88	Assoc VP Enrollment Mgmt	Dr. Clifford DORNE
09	Asst VP/Registrar/Dir Inst Rsrch	Mr. Chris LOONEY
21	Asst VP Business Services	Mr. Ronald E. PORTWINE
18	Asst Vice Pres Campus Facilities	Mr. Stephen L. HOCQUARD
13	Exec Dir Information Tech Svcs	Mr. Kenneth A. SCHINDLER
85	Director International Programs	Ms. Stephanie SIEGGREEN
07	Director Admissions	Ms. Jennifer PAHL
88	Director Intergrated Marketing	Ms. Jan R. POPPE
36	Dir Career Planning & Placement	Mr. Michael MAJOR
21	University Controller	Ms. Susan L. CRANE
21	Director Business Services	Ms. Connie J. SCHWEITZER
88	University Ombudsman	Mr. Richard P. THOMPSON
29	Director Alumni	Mr. Kevin J. SCHULTZ
14	Director Information Tech Svcs	Mr. Patrick C. SAMOLEWSKI
31	Dir Media & Community Relations	Mr. J. J. BOEHM
08	Director Library/Learning Resources	Ms. Linda J. FARYNK
25	Director Spnsrd/Acad Pgms Support	Ms. Janet D. RENTSCH
15	Director Human Resources	Dr. Jack VANHOORELBEKE
19	Chief University Police	Mr. Ronald E. TREPKOWSKI
37	Director Scholarships/Financial Aid	Mr. Robert L. LEMUEL
51	Director Continuing Education	Ms. Monica B. REYES
38	Dir Student Counseling Center	Ms. Jennifer N. ORDWAY
41	Director of Athletics	Mr. Michael E. WATSON
44	Director Annual & Planned Giving	Mr. Joseph A. VOGL
88	Dir Sch & University Partnerships	Mr. Joseph ROUSSEAU
88	Dir Enviornmental Health & Safety	Mr. Robert J. TUTSOCK
40	Bookstore Manager	Mr. Chris J. PAWLOSKI
06	Registrar	Mr. Chris LOONEY
88	Exec Dir Ctr for Business/Econ Dev	Mr. Harold L. LEAVER
93	Director Multicultural Services	Vacant
20	Associate Provost	Mr. Marc H. PERETZ
26	Dir Media & Community Relations	Mr. J. J. BOEHM
102	Executive Director SVSU Foundation	Mr. Andrew J. BETHUNE
96	Purchasing Manager	Mr. Joshua M. WEBB
35	Director Student Life	Ms. Kimberly BRANDIMORE
49	Dean Arts & Behavioral Science	Dr. Mary A. HEDBERG
50	Dean Business & Management	Dr. Jill WETMORE
53	Int Dean College of Education	Dr. Susie EMOND
76	Dean of Health & Human Services	Vacant
54	Dean Science Engr & Technology	Dr. Deborah HUNTLEY

St. Clair County Community College (B)

323 Erie Street, PO Box 5015, Port Huron MI 48061-5015
County: St. Clair FICE Identification: 002310
Unit ID: 172291
Telephone: (810) 984-3881 Carnegie Class: Assoc/Pub-S-SC
FAX Number: (810) 984-4730 Calendar System: Semester
URL: www.sc4.edu
Established: 1923 Annual Undergrad Tuition & Fees (In-District): $3,183
Enrollment: 4,914 Coed
Affiliation or Control: Local IRS Status: 501(c)3
Highest Offering: Associate Degree
Program: Occupational; 2-Year Principally Bachelor's Creditable
Accreditation: NH

01	President	Dr. Kevin A. POLLOCK
04	Executive Assistant to President	Ms. Mary L. HAWTIN
10	Vice Pres Administrative Services	Mr. Kirk A. KRAMER
05	Vice President Academic Services	Mrs. Denise M. MCNEIL
32	Vice President Student Services	Mr. Pete LACEY
15	Exec Director Human Resources/LR	Mr. Kenneth M. LORD
103	Dean Workforce Training	Ms. Michelle K. MUELLER
35	Dean of Students & Grants	Dr. Patricia Y. LEONARD
23	Director of Health/Human Services	Ms. Cindy NICHOLSON
37	Dir of Financial Assistance/Svcs	Ms. Josephine R. CASSAR
06	Registrar	Ms. Carrie BEARSS
18	Director of Physical Plant	Mr. Thomas R. DONOVAN
21	Controller	Ms. Mary K. BRUNNER

09	Exec Dir of Inst Effectiveness	Vacant
26	Exec Dir PR/Mktg/Legis Affairs	Mr. Shawn M. STARKEY
41	Dir Campus Activities/Athletics	Mr. Dale R. VOS
106	Dean of eLearning/Instr Technology	Ms. Linda DAVIS
30	Dir Advancement/Alumni Relations	Mr. David GOETZE
20	Associate Dean of Instruction	Dr. Suzanne O'BRIEN
08	Director of Library Services	Mr. Christopher RENNIE

Schoolcraft College (C)

18600 Haggerty Road, Livonia MI 48152-2696
County: Wayne FICE Identification: 002315
Unit ID: 172200
Telephone: (734) 462-4400 Carnegie Class: Assoc/Pub-S-SC
FAX Number: (734) 462-4507 Calendar System: Semester
URL: www.schoolcraft.edu
Established: 1961 Annual Undergrad Tuition & Fees (In-District): $2,604
Enrollment: 13,579 Coed
Affiliation or Control: Local IRS Status: 501(c)3
Highest Offering: Associate Degree
Program: Occupational; 2-Year Principally Bachelor's Creditable
Accreditation: NH, ACFEI, MAC

01	President	Dr. Conway A. JEFFRESS
10	Vice Pres/Chief Financial Officer	Mr. Glenn CERNY
05	Vice Pres of Instruction	Mr. Richard WEINKAUF
32	Dean of Student Services	Ms. Cheryl M. HAGEN
49	Dean Liberal Arts & Sciences	Ms. Cheryl HAWKINS
75	Dean Occupational Prog/Econ Dev	Mr. William DUNBAR
45	Assoc Dean Learning Support Svcs	Dr. Deborah DAIEK
88	Asst Dean College Centers	Dr. Todd SCOTT
56	Assoc Dean Distance Learning	Ms. Cheri HOLMAN
72	Asst Dean Occupational Programs	Dr. Mark POGLIANO
51	Dir Cont Educ/Prof Development	Dr. Leslie PETTY
30	Exec Director Devel/Govt Relations	Dr. James RYAN
15	Exec Director of Human Resources	Ms. Cindy J. KOENIGSKNECHT
21	Exec Dir Business Services/Risk Mgt	Mr. James R. POLKOWSKI
18	Exec Dir Construction and Design	Mr. Robert A. WIELECHOWSKI
46	Exec Director Planning & Research	Ms. Susan LUPO
27	Chief Information Officer	Mr. Frank WILTRAKIS
12	Director of College Centers	Dr. Bonnie HECKARD
09	Director of Institutional Research	Mr. Rob STIRTON
84	Dir of Enrollment Svcs/Registrar	Ms. Nicole WILSON-FENNELL
38	Dir Counseling & Career Services	Vacant
37	Director of Financial Aid	Ms. Regina MOSLEY
26	Director of Marketing	Mr. Martin HEATOR
19	Director of Campus Security Police	Mr. John A. MONGE
21	Director of Finance	Mr. Jeffrey LILLEY
96	Director of Purchasing	Mr. Matthew WILSON

Siena Heights University (D)

1247 Siena Heights Drive, Adrian MI 49221-1796
County: Lenawee FICE Identification: 002316
Unit ID: 172264
Telephone: (517) 263-0731 Carnegie Class: Master's M
FAX Number: (517) 264-7704 Calendar System: Semester
URL: www.sienaheights.edu
Established: 1919 Annual Undergrad Tuition & Fees: $20,554
Enrollment: 2,389 Coed
Affiliation or Control: Roman Catholic IRS Status: 501(c)3
Highest Offering: Beyond Master's But Less Than Doctorate
Program: Occupational; Liberal Arts And General; Teacher Preparatory; Professional
Accreditation: NH, ART, NURSE, SW, @TEAC

01	President	Dr. Peg ALBERT, OP
10	Sr Vice Pres for Business/Finance	Dr. J. Lee JOHNSON
30	Vice President for Advancement	Mr. Mitchell P. BLONDE
05	Vice President for Academic Affairs	Dr. Sharon R. WEBER, OP
84	Vice Pres of Enrollment Mgmt Svcs	Mr. C. Patrick PALMER
26	Assoc Vice Pres Advancement	Mrs. Jennifer H. CHURCH
58	Dean of Graduate Studies	Mrs. Anne HOOGHART
107	Dean College Professional Studies	Mrs. Deborah CARTER
32	Dean for Students	Mr. Michael ORLANDO
06	Registrar	Mrs. Brenda K. DOREMUS
08	Library Director	Dr. Robert W. GORDON
13	Director Computer Systems/Services	Mr. Robert C. METZ
41	Director of Athletics	Mr. Frederick M. SMITH
15	Human Resource Director	Mr. Michael L. KARABETSOS
42	Director of Campus Ministry	Mr. Thomas PUSZCZEWICZ
38	Director of Counseling Services	Ms. Joan EBBITT
20	Director of Academic Advising	Mrs. Rene L. TEATER
18	Supt of Buildings & Grounds	Mr. Brian BERTRAM
39	Director of Residence Life	Vacant
19	Director of Campus Security	Mrs. Cindy A. BIRDWELL
23	Director of Health Services	Ms. Marlene WALDVOGEL
29	Director of Alumni Relations	Mrs. Jennifer H. CHURCH
36	Director of Career Services	Mrs. Melissa A. GROWDEN
44	Director of Donor Relations	Mrs. Jenn BROOKET
88	Dir of Integrated Univ Marketing	Mr. Doug GOODNOUGH
37	Director Student Financial Aid	Mr. Christian HOWARD
21	Controller	Ms. Mary KRUSE
07	Director of Admissions	Ms. Sara JOHNSON
44	Coordinator of Annual Fund	Mrs. Kate HAMILTON
49	Dean College of Arts and Science	Dr. Mark SCHERSTEN

Southwestern Michigan College (E)

58900 Cherry Grove Road, Dowagiac MI 49047-9793
County: Cass FICE Identification: 002317
Unit ID: 172307
Telephone: (269) 782-1000 Carnegie Class: Assoc/Pub-R-M
FAX Number: (269) 782-8414 Calendar System: Semester
URL: www.swmich.edu
Established: 1964 Annual Undergrad Tuition & Fees (In-District): $4,118
Enrollment: 3,262 Coed
Affiliation or Control: State/Local IRS Status: 501(c)3
Highest Offering: Associate Degree
Program: Occupational; 2-Year Principally Bachelor's Creditable
Accreditation: NH

01	President	Dr. David M. MATHEWS
100	Chief of Staff	Mr. John A. FANNIN
03	Exec Vice Pres/Chief Operating Ofcr	Dr. Diane CHADDOCK
10	Interim Chief Business Officer	Ms. Susan COULSTON
27	Chief Information Officer	Mr. Ronald YOUNG
05	Vice President of Instruction	Dr. David FLEMING
88	Vice President of Academic Support	Dr. Margaret HAY
26	Exec Dir of Mktg Enrollment Mgmt	Mr. Gregory DERUE
32	Exec Dir Student Housing/Camp Life	Ms. Eileen CROUSE
88	Director of Developmental Studies	Dr. Naomi LUDMAN
88	Dean of Academic Studies	Dr. Scott TOPPING
66	Dean School Nursing/Human Services	Dr. Elaine FOSTER
103	Dean of Workforce Ed/Bus Solutions	Mr. Thomas BUSZEK
09	Director of Institutional Research	Dr. Angela CARRICO
18	Director of Buildings & Grounds	Mr. George DIERICKX
37	Director of Financial Aid	Ms. Susan FINTZE
15	Director of Human Resources	Ms. Diana CLARK
88	Senior Budget Analyst	Ms. Breighan BROWN
88	Manager of Accounting	Ms. Christy MANGUS
44	Director of Development	Ms. Eileen TONEY
103	Director of Workforce Training	Mr. Tim CHILDS
35	Associate Dean of Students	Ms. Angela PALSAK
88	Assistant Dean of Academic Support	Mr. Shane VARGA
08	Director of Library Services	Ms. Colleen WELSCH
06	Director of Records/Registrar	Ms. Kathy PETERSON
35	Director Student Support Services	Ms. Laura SKILLINGS
88	Director of Teaching & Learning Ctr	Ms. Annette MILESKI
88	Dir of Educational Talent Srch Prgm	Ms. Amy ANDERSON
88	Dir of Acad Assess & Testing Svcs	Ms. Charlotte MCGOWAN
84	Director of Enrollment Management	Mr. Brent BREWER
88	Director of Museum	Mr. Steve ARSENEAU
39	Director of Housing	Mr. Jason WILT
35	Director of Student Activity Center	Mr. Shawn RAWSON

Spring Arbor University (F)

106 E Main Street, Spring Arbor MI 49283-9799
County: Jackson FICE Identification: 002318
Unit ID: 172334
Telephone: (517) 750-1200 Carnegie Class: Master's L
FAX Number: (517) 750-6620 Calendar System: Semester
URL: www.arbor.edu
Established: 1873 Annual Undergrad Tuition & Fees: $21,520
Enrollment: 4,195 Coed
Affiliation or Control: Free Methodist IRS Status: 501(c)3
Highest Offering: Master's
Program: Liberal Arts And General
Accreditation: NH, NURSE, SW, @TEAC

01	President	Dr. Charles H. WEBB
05	Provost/Chief Academic Officer	Dr. Betty J. OVERTON-ADKINS
10	Vice Pres Finance & Administration	Mr. Jerry L. WHITE
30	Vice Pres University Advancement	Dr. Brent ELLIS
32	VP Student Development/Learning	Mrs. Kimberly K. HAYWORTH
84	VP for Enrollment Services	Mr. Matthew S. OSBORNE
13	VP Technology Services/CIO	Mr. Jeff E. EDWARDS
20	Assoc VP for Academic Affairs	Mr. Rod S. STEWART
100	Chief of Staff	Mr. Damon M. SEACOTT
58	Interim Dean Sch Grad/Prof Studies	Mrs. Natalie GIANETTI
58	Associate Dean Graduate Programs	Dr. Carl E. PAVEY
107	Associate Dean Professional Studies	Mrs. Tamara L. DINDOFFER
49	Int Dean School Arts & Sciences	Mr. Roger M. VARLAND
50	Dean Gainey School of Business	Dr. James G. COE
53	Dean School of Education	Dr. Linda G. SHERRILL
106	Dean SAU Online	Mr. Todd MARSHALL
06	Registrar	Mr. Tim WIEGERT
21	Controller	Mrs. Janet M. TJEPKEMA
41	Athletic Director	Mr. John S. RIGGLEMAN
91	Asst VP Technology Services	Mr. Michael K. DEVER
26	Asst VP for Univ Communications	Mrs. Ann M. TSCHIRHART
105	Director of Web Development	Mrs. Rebecca M. NEGRON
88	Director of Support Services	Mrs. Christina E. RANDALL
106	Director Content and eLearning	Mr. John R. MEREDITH
44	Executive Director of Development	Mrs. Linda SCHAUB
07	Executive Director of Admissions	Mr. Randy C. COMFORT
15	Assistant VP for Human Resources	Mr. Randy S. ROSSMAN
08	Director Library	Mr. Roy MEADOR
37	Director Student Financial Aid	Mr. Geoff A. MARSH
29	Director Alumni Relations	Mrs. Irene L. PRICE
09	Director Institutional Research	Mr. Thomas P. KORMAN
18	Director of Physical Plant	Mr. Larry OUSLEY
35	Asst VP Student Development	Mr. Dan VANDERHILL
39	Asst Dean Students/Dir of Housing	Mr. Robert C. PRATT
31	Asst Dean Students/Dir of Outreach	Mr. Steven D. NEWTON
89	Director Retention & Freshman Pgms	Mrs. Robin R. SMITH
36	Director Career Svcs/Acad Advising	Mr. John BECK
42	Chaplain	Mr. Ronald L. KOPICKO
19	Director Campus Safety	Mr. Tom D. FIERO
104	Director Cross Cultural Studies	Mrs. Diane L. KURTZ
23	Director Student Health Services	Mrs. Mary A. RICK
40	Bookstore Supervisor	Vacant

SS. Cyril and Methodius Seminary (A)

3535 Indian Trail, Orchard Lake MI 48324-1623
County: Oakland FICE Identification: 037384
Unit ID: 260211
Telephone: (248) 683-0310 Carnegie Class: Not Classified
FAX Number: (248) 738-6735 Calendar System: Semester
URL: www.sscms.edu
Established: 1885 Annual Graduate Tuition & Fees: $12,400
Enrollment: 44 Coed
Affiliation or Control: Roman Catholic IRS Status: 501(c)3
Highest Offering: Master's; No Undergraduates
Program: Professional
Accreditation: THEOL

01 Rector/President ....RevCan. Thomas MACHALSKI
05 Academic Dean .... Msgr. John KASZA

Thomas M. Cooley Law School (B)

300 S Capitol Avenue, Lansing MI 48933
County: Ingham FICE Identification: 012627
Unit ID: 172477
Telephone: (517) 371-5140 Carnegie Class: Spec/Law
FAX Number: (517) 334-5718 Calendar System: Semester
URL: www.cooley.edu
Established: 1972 Annual Graduate Tuition & Fees: $42,360
Enrollment: 4,001 Coed
Affiliation or Control: Independent Non-Profit IRS Status: 501(c)3
Highest Offering: First Professional Degree; No Undergraduates
Program: Professional
Accreditation: NH, LAW

01 President .... Don LEDUC
04 Executive Asst to the President .... Cherie BECK
05 Dean .... Don LEDUC
10 Chief Financial Officer ....Kathleen CONKLIN
11 Chief Operating Officer .... William SCHOETTLE
08 Associate Dean Library/Info Svcs .... Duane STROJNY
20 Associate Dean for Faculty .... Charles CERCONE
45 Associate Dean Planning/Programs .... M. Ann WOOD
36 Assoc Dean Career Prof Development .... Charles TOY
32 Assoc Dean Students/Professionalism .... Amy TIMMER
30 Associate Dean for Development .... James ROBB
13 Associate Dean for Information Tech ....Charles MICKENS
84 Assoc Dean for Enrollment Services .... Paul ZELENSKI
26 Assoc Dean for Community Relations ....Helen MICKENS
12 Associate Dean Auburn Hills .... John NUSSBAUMER
12 Associate Dean Grand Rapids ....Nelson MILLER
23 Assoc Dean Ann Arbor .... Joan VESTRAND
104 Assoc Dean International Programs .... William WEINER
88 Assistant Dean Auburn Hills .... Lauren ROUSSEAU
88 Assistant Dean Ann Arbor .... Martha MOORE
88 Assistant Dean Grand Rapids .... Tracey BRAME
06 Registrar & Assistant Dean .... Sherida WYSOCKI
07 Director Admissions/Assistant Dean .... Stephanie GREGG
37 Director Financial Aid .... Richard BORUSZEWSKI
40 Director Bookstore .... Joelle TOPP
21 Controller .... Ronda BECK
29 Director Alumni Donor Relations .... Pamela HEOS
27 Director Communications .... Terry CARRELLA
15 Director Human Resources .... Scott HARRISON
96 Purchasing Manager .... Theresa ISKRA
35 Director Student Services .... Christopher LEWIS

University of Detroit Mercy (C)

4001 W McNichols Road, Detroit MI 48221-3038
County: Wayne FICE Identification: 002323
Unit ID: 169716
Telephone: (313) 993-1000 Carnegie Class: Master's L
FAX Number: (313) 993-1011 Calendar System: Semester
URL: www.udmercy.edu
Established: 1877 Annual Undergrad Tuition & Fees: $32,500
Enrollment: 5,534 Coed
Affiliation or Control: Roman Catholic IRS Status: 501(c)3
Highest Offering: Doctorate
Program: Liberal Arts And General; Teacher Preparatory; Professional
Accreditation: NH, ANEST, ARCPA, BUS, CACREP, CLPSY, DENT, DH, ENG, LAW, NURSE, SW, @TEAC

01 President ....Dr. Antoine M. GARIBALDI
05 VP for Academic Affairs .... Ms. Pamela ZARKOWSKI
03 Executive Vice President ....Mr. Michael JOSEPH
10 VP for Business & Finance and CFO . Mr. Vincent ABATEMARCO
44 VP Dev/Major/Plan Gift Campn .... Mr. Gregory CASCIONE
07 Vice President Enrollment/ Admission ....Ms. Denise WILLIAMS MALLETT
101 Corporate Council/Univ Secretary .... Ms. Monica BARBOUR
11 Assoc Vice Pres Facil Management .....Ms. Tamara BATCHELLER
15 Associate Vice Pres Human Resources ...... Mr. Steven J. NELSON
27 Assoc VP Marketing & Public Affairs .... Ms. Liz PATTERSON
14 Associate Vice President ITS ....Mr. Edward TRACY, II
06 Associate VP/Registrar ....Ms. Diane M. PRAET
29 Assoc VP Annual Giving & Alumni Rel ....Ms. Linda SMALL
32 Dean of Students .... Ms. Monica WILLIAMS
08 Dean of Libraries .... Ms. Margaret AUER
09 Director Institutional Research .... Ms. Elaine BELL
37 Director Scholarships & Aid ....Ms. Jenny MCALONAN
35 Director of Student Life ....Ms. Dorothy STEWART
41 Director of Athletics ....Ms. Karen L. GAITHER
42 Director University Ministry .... Mr. David NANTAIS
49 Interim Dean Col Lib Arts/Education .... Dr. Roy FINKENBINE
61 Dean School of Law ....Mr. Lloyd SEMPLE
54 Dean College Engineering & Science .... Dr. Leo E. HANIFIN
48 Dean School of Architecture .... Mr. William WITTIG
50 Dean Col Business Admin .... Dr. Joseph EISENHAUER
52 Dean School of Dentistry .... Dr. Mert AKSU
76 Dean CHP/Nursing ....Dr. Christine PACINI
88 Dean Coop Education/Career Ctr ....Ms. Sheryl MCGRIFF
39 Director Residence Life .... Ms. Lanae GILL
04 Exec Asst to the President ....Ms. Lisa MACDONNELL
88 Executive Assistant to the Acad VP ....Mr. John THOMSON
85 Director International Students .... Ms. Claire OFIARA
36 Director Student Placement .... Vacant
38 Director Student Counseling .... Ms. Natalie WICKS
92 Director of Honors Program .... Mr. Jason ROCHE
96 Director of Purchasing .... Ms. Tina A. MAITLAND
18 Director of Facility Ops/Const Mgmt .... Mr. David VANDELINDER
30 Coordinator of Advancement .... Ms. Stephanie LANDERS

University of Michigan-Ann Arbor (D)

Ann Arbor MI 48109-1318
County: Washtenaw FICE Identification: 002325
Unit ID: 170976
Telephone: (734) 764-1817 Carnegie Class: RU/VH
FAX Number: N/A Calendar System: Trimester
URL: www.umich.edu
Established: 1817 Annual Undergrad Tuition & Fees (In-State): $12,634
Enrollment: 41,480 Coed
Affiliation or Control: State IRS Status: 501(c)3
Highest Offering: Doctorate
Program: Liberal Arts And General; Teacher Preparatory; Professional
Accreditation: NH, DANCE, ART, BUS, CLPSY, CS, DENT, DH, DIETD, DIETI, ENG, ENGR, HSA, IPSY, LAW, LIB, LSAR, MED, MIDWF, MUS, NURSE, PDPSY, PH, PHAR, PLNG, SW, TEAC

01 President ....Dr. Mary Sue COLEMAN
05 Provost/Exec VP Academic Affs ....Dr. Philip J. HANLON
10 Exec VP/Chief Financial Officer .... Mr. Timothy P. SLOTTOW
17 Exec VP for Medical Affairs .... Dr. Ora H. PESCOVITZ
30 Vice President Development .... Mr. Jerry A. MAY
32 Vice President Student Affairs .... Dr. E. Royster HARPER
46 Vice President for Research .... Dr. Stephen R. FORREST
06 Vice Pres Governmental Relations .... Ms. Cynthia H. WILBANKS
26 Vice Pres Global Communications .... Ms. Lisa M. RUDGERS
43 Vice President/General Counsel .... Ms. Suellyn SCARNECCHIA
35 Assoc VP for Student Affairs .... Mr. Loren J. RULLMAN
101 Vice Pres/Sec of the University ....Ms. Sally J. CHURCHILL
20 Sr Vice Provost Academic Affairs ....Dr. Lester P. MONTS
04 Deputy Asst to the President .... Ms. Erika J. HRABEC
100 Chief of Staff .... Ms. Karen L. GIBBONS
20 Vice Provost Acad/Budget Affairs ....Dr. Martha E. POLLACK
20 Vice Provost for Strategy .... Dr. John L. KING
20 Vice Provost Acad/Faculty Affairs ....Dr. Lori J. PIERCE
20 Vice Provost Acad & Faculty Affairs .... Dr. Chris WHITMAN
58 Vice Provost Acad Affs Grad Stds ....Dr. Janet A. WEISS
104 Vice Provost Intl Affairs .... Dr. Mark A. TESSLER
09 Assoc Vice Provost & Exec Dir OBP ....Ms. Glenna L. SCHWEITZER
07 Assoc VP/Exec Dir UG Admissions .... Mr. Theodore L. SPENCER
88 Assoc Vice Provost/Exec Dir OAMI ....Dr. John H. MATLOCK
88 Assoc Vice Provost/Exec Dir CRLT .... Dr. Constance E. COOK
15 Assoc VP & Sr Dr Acad HR ....Mr. Jeffery R. FRUMKIN
22 Assoc VP/Sr Dir Ofc Inst Equity ....Mr. Anthony J. WALESBY
18 Assoc VP Facilities/Operations ....Mr. Henry D. BAIER
21 Assoc VP Finance ....Dr. Rowan A. MIRANDA
88 Chief Investment Officer .... Mr. Erik LUNDBERG
30 Assoc VP for Development .... Mr. Jefferson PORTER
17 Assoc VP for Medical Affairs .... Dr. John E. BILLI
46 Assoc VP for Research ....Dr. Mark M. BANASZAK HOLL
46 Assoc VP for Research ....Dr. James A. SHAYMAN
46 Assoc VP for Research ....Dr. Toni C. ANTONUCCI
46 Assoc VP for Research .... Mr. Marvin G. PARNES
35 Assoc VP Student Affs/Dean Stdnts ....Ms. Laura B. JONES
35 Assoc VP Student Affairs ....Ms. Anjali N. ANTURKAR
35 Assoc VP Student Affairs .... Dr. Simone HIMBEAULT-TAYLOR
16 Assoc VP for Human Resources ....Ms. Laurita E. THOMAS
27 Assoc VP/Chief Information Officer .....Ms. Laura M. PATTERSON
06 University Registrar .... Mr. Paul A. ROBINSON
44 Director Annual Giving Program ....Ms. Kristina L. MEYER
96 Director Procurement Services .... Ms. Nancy A. HOBBS
38 Director Counseling & Psych Service ....Dr. Todd D. SEVIG
39 Director University Housing ....Ms. Linda L. NEWMAN
23 Director University Health Service ....Dr. Robert A. WINFIELD
19 Exec Dir Public Safety/Security .... Mr. Kenneth W. MAGEE
37 Exec Director Financial Aid ....Ms. Pamela W. FOWLER
18 Executive Director Plant Operations ....Mr. Richard W. ROBBEN
41 Athletic Director .... Mr. David A. BRANDON
48 Dean Col Architecture & Urban Plng ......Ms. Monica P. DE LEON
49 Dean Col Literature/Science/Arts .... Dr. Terrence J. MCDONALD
54 Dean College of Engineering ....Dr. David C. MUNSON
61 Dean Law School ....Mr. Evan H. CAMINKER
63 Dean Medical School .... Dr. James O. WOOLLISCROFT
67 Dean College of Pharmacy .... Dr. Frank J. ASCIONE
65 Dean Sch Natural Resrc/Environ .... Dr. Rosina M. BIERBAUM
64 Dean School Music Theatre & Dance ....Mr. Christopher W. KENDALL
57 Dean School of Art & Design ....Dr. Bryan L. ROGERS
50 Dean School of Business .... Dr. Alison DAVIS-BLAKE
52 Dean School of Dentistry .... Dr. Peter J. POLVERINI
53 Dean School of Education ....Dr. Deborah L. BALL
62 Dean School of Information ....Dr. Jeffrey K. MACKIE-MASON
68 Dean School of Kinesiology ....Dr. Ronald F. ZERNICKE
66 Dean School of Nursing .... Dr. Kathleen M. POTEMPA
80 Dean School of Public Policy .... Dr. Susan M. COLLINS
70 Dean School of Social Work .... Dr. Laura LEIN
69 Dean School of Public Health .... Dr. Martin A. PHILBERT
29 President Alumni Association ....Mr. Steve C. GRAFTON

University of Michigan-Dearborn (E)

4901 Evergreen Road, Dearborn MI 48128-1491
County: Wayne FICE Identification: 002326
Unit ID: 171137
Telephone: (313) 593-5000 Carnegie Class: Master's L
FAX Number: (313) 593-5452 Calendar System: Trimester
URL: www.umd.umich.edu
Established: 1959 Annual Undergrad Tuition & Fees (In-State): $9,885
Enrollment: 8,885 Coed
Affiliation or Control: State IRS Status: 501(c)3
Highest Offering: Doctorate
Program: Liberal Arts And General; Teacher Preparatory; Professional
Accreditation: NH, BUS, CS, ENG, @TEAC

01 Chancellor .... Dr. Daniel LITTLE
05 Prov/Vice Chanc Academic Affs ....Dr. Catherine A. DAVY
10 Vice Chancellor Business Affairs ....Mr. Jeffrey L. EVANS
84 Vice Chanc Enrollment Management .Mr. Stanley E. HENDERSON
30 Vice Chanc Inst Advancement .... Mr. Thomas A. BAIRD
86 Vice Chanc for Govt Relations ....Mr. Edward J. BAGALE
21 Assoc Vice Chancellor Finance .... Mr. Robert K. GASSEL
06 Registrar .... Ms. Janice LEWIS-BOYD
100 Chief of Staff .... Mr. Ray METZ
26 Director of Communications .... Mr. Ken KETTENBEIL
15 Director of Human Resources .... Ms. Ginny ZARRAS
29 Alumni Engagement .... Ms. Cecile AITCHISON
20 Associate Provost .... Mr. Ismael AHMED
20 Associate Provost .... Dr. Malayppan SHRIDHAR
20 Associate Provost ....Dr. Martin HERSHOCK
13 Chief Technology Officer .... Ms. Violetta OGILVY
08 Interim Director of Library .... Ms. Barbara KRIIGEL
09 Director of Institutional Research .... Ms. Roma E. HEANEY
84 Exec Director Enrollment Management .... Mr. Christopher W. TREMBLAY
07 Director of Admissions ....Ms. Deb PEFFER
37 Director of Financial Aid ....Ms. Katherine ALLEN
38 Director of Counseling .... Dr. David SCHROAT
36 Director of Career Services ....Ms. Regina M. STORRS
35 Director Student Activities .... Ms. Kristine L. DAY
18 Director of Facilities Management .... Mr. Lawrence HICKS
19 Director of Campus Safety ....Mr. Richard GORDON
22 Institutional Equity Officer .... Vacant
28 Multicultural Affairs .... Dr. Ann LAMPKIN-WILLIAMS
49 Dean Col Arts/Science/Letters .... Dr. Jerold HALE
54 Dean Col of Engr/Computer Science .... Dr. Subrata SENGUPTA
50 Dean College of Business .... Dr. Kim SCHATZEL
53 Dean School of Education ....Dr. Edward SILVER

University of Michigan-Flint (F)

303 E Kearsley Street, Flint MI 48502-1950
County: Genesee FICE Identification: 002327
Unit ID: 171146
Telephone: (810) 762-3000 Carnegie Class: Master's L
FAX Number: (810) 762-5725 Calendar System: Semester
URL: www.umflint.edu
Established: 1956 Annual Undergrad Tuition & Fees (In-State): $8,565
Enrollment: 8,138 Coed
Affiliation or Control: State IRS Status: 501(c)3
Highest Offering: Doctorate
Program: Liberal Arts And General; Teacher Preparatory; Professional
Accreditation: NH, ANEST, BUS, MUS, NURSE, PTA, RTT, SW

01 Chancellor ....Dr. Ruth J. PERSON
05 Provost/VC Academic Affairs .... Dr. Gerard VOLAND
32 Vice Chancellor for Student Affairs ....Dr. Mary Jo S. SEKELSKY
11 Vice Chanc for Business and Finance ... Mr. David BARTHELMES
35 Asst VC for Student Affairs .... Dr. Johnny YOUNG
21 Asst Vice Chanc Business & Finance ..Mr. William C. WEBB, JR.
58 Assoc Provost/Dean Grad Pgms .... Dr. Vahid LOTFI
20 Asst Prov/Dean Undergrad Studies .... Ms. Christine WATERS
26 Exec Director University Relations ....Ms. Jennifer HOGAN
86 Director Government Relations ....Mr. David E. LOSSING
28 Exec Director Educational Oppty .... Mr. Tendaji W. GANGES
08 Director of Library ....Mr. Robert L. HOUBECK, JR.
06 Registrar .... Ms. Karen A. ARNOULD
07 Interim Admissions Director .... Mr. Jon DAVIDSON
37 Director Financial Aid .... Ms. Lori VEDDER
15 Director Human Res/Affirm Action ....Ms. Diana T. CURRAN
49 Dean College Arts & Sciences .... Dr. D. J. TRELA
50 Interim Dean School of Management .... Dr. Vahid LOTFI
66 Director Nursing Program .... Dr. Margaret ANDREWS
76 Dean Sch Health Prof & Studies .... Dr. David GORDON
53 Dean Sch Education & Human Svcs .... Dr. Robert BARNETT
51 Director of Extended Learning ....Ms. Deborah WHITE
19 Interim Director of Public Safety .... Mr. Allen COZART
18 Director Facilities Mgmt/Auxil Svcs .... Mr. George HAKIM
14 Director Info Technology Services .... Mr. Scott ARNST
36 Director Acad Advis & Career Center .... Ms. Aimi MOSS
46 Director of Research ....Dr. Terry VAN ALLEN
21 Director of Financial Svcs & Budget .... Mr. Gerald GLASCO
88 Int Director University Outreach .... Mr. Jonathan JAROSZ
29 Exec Dir of Dev and Alumni Relation .... Mr. Scott BERTSCHY
96 Director of Purchasing ....Mr. Gregory J. SNYDER
09 Director of Institutional Analysis .... Ms. Fawn SKARSTEN

Walsh College of Accountancy and Business Administration (A)

3838 Livernois Road, Box 7006, Troy MI 48007-7006
County: Oakland FICE Identification: 004071
Unit ID: 172608
Telephone: (248) 689-8282 Carnegie Class: Spec/Bus
FAX Number: (248) 689-9066 Calendar System: Semester
URL: www.walshcollege.edu
Established: 1922 Annual Undergrad Tuition & Fees: $10,425
Enrollment: 3,199 Coed
Affiliation or Control: Independent Non-Profit IRS Status: 501(c)3
Highest Offering: Doctorate
Program: Professional; Business Emphasis
Accreditation: NH, ACBSP, IACBE

01 President & CEO .... Ms. Stephanie W. BERGERON
05 Int Exec VP/Chief Academic Officer .... Dr. Michael LEVENS
10 Vice President/CFO/Treasurer . Ms. Helen C. KIEBA-TOLKSDORF
84 VP/Chief Mktg & Enrollment Mgt Ofcr .... Mr. John W. LICHTENBERG
16 VP/Chief Human Resources/Admin Ofcr .... Ms. Elizabeth A. BARNES
30 Vice President/Chief Devel Officer .... Ms. Audrey OLMSTEAD
04 Exec Assistant to the President .... Ms. Rosemarie E. ZOOK
08 Assoc VP Acad Admin/Librarian .... Dr. Jonathan CAMPBELL
32 Asst VP Student Services/Marketing .... Ms. Victoria R. SCAVONE
20 Asst VP Academic Administration .... Ms. Terri WASHBURN
106 Dean Office of Online Learning .... Dr. Karen RHODA
20 Director Academic Administration .... Vacant
37 Director Financial Aid .... Mr. Howard THOMAS
18 Director Facilities/Auxiliary Svcs .... Ms. Chris STOUT
21 Director Accounting/Business Ofcr .... Mr. Brant WRIGHT
07 Director Admissions/Acad Advising .... Mr. Jeremy GUC
06 Director of Records/Registrar .... Ms. Karen HILLEBRAND
13 Exec Dir Ofc of Info Technology .... Mr. Joseph ESDALE
12 Director Novi Campus .... Ms. Hamsa DAHER
36 Director Career Services .... Ms. Laurie SIEBERT
72 Int Chair Business Info Tech/IA .... Ms. Terri WASHBURN
88 Chair Accounting .... Mr. Richard BERSCHBACK
88 Chair Taxation & Business Law .... Mr. Mark R. SOLOMON
88 Chair Economics & Finance .... Dr. Linda WIECHOWSKI
88 Director of MBA/MSM Program .... Dr. Sheila R. RONIS
88 Director Doctoral Program .... Dr. Linda HAGAN
88 Int Dir Undergrad Business Program .... Dr. Linda HAGAN
26 Public Relations Coordinator .... Ms. Donna MIRABITO
88 Director Corporate Rel/BLI .... Ms. Janet HUBBARD
29 Manager of Alumni Rels .... Ms. Savannah LEE
88 Director Information Assurance .... Ms. Nanette POULIOS
88 Dir Center for Entrepreneurship .... Ms. Michelle LANGE

Washtenaw Community College (B)

4800 E Huron River Dr, Ann Arbor MI 48105-4800
County: Washtenaw FICE Identification: 002328
Unit ID: 172617
Telephone: (734) 973-3300 Carnegie Class: Assoc/Pub-U-SC
FAX Number: (734) 677-5413 Calendar System: Semester
URL: www.wccnet.edu
Established: 1965 Annual Undergrad Tuition & Fees (In-District): $2,852
Enrollment: 14,189 Coed
Affiliation or Control: Local IRS Status: 501(c)3
Highest Offering: Associate Degree
Program: Occupational; 2-Year Principally Bachelor's Creditable
Accreditation: NH, ACFEI, ADNUR, DA, PTAA, RAD

01 President .... Dr. Rose BELLANCA
11 Vice President Admin & Finance .... Mr. Steven HARDY
05 Vice President for Instruction .... Dr. Stuart BLACKLAW
16 Assoc VP Human Resources Mgmt .... Mr. Douglas KRUZEL
32 Associate VP Student Services .... Ms. Linda S. BLAKEY
18 Assoc VP Facilities Devel & Opers .... Mr. Damon FLOWERS
30 Assoc Vice Pres Dev/Grant/Govt .... Ms. Wendy LAWSON
45 Exec Associate to the President .... Ms. Julie MORRISON
79 Dean Humanities & Social Science .... Dr. William ABERNETHY
20 Dean Supp Svcs & Student Advocacy .... Dr. Patricia TAYLOR
62 Interim Dean Learning Resources .... Mr. Victor LIU
50 Dean Business & Computer Tech .... Ms. Rosemary WILSON
81 Dean Math/Natural & Behavioral Sci .... Ms. Martha SHOWALTER
51 Dean Continuing Ed/Community Svcs .... Ms. Marilyn DONHAM
75 Interim Dean Vocational Technology .... Mr. Ross GORDON
106 Dean Distance Learning .... Mr. James EGAN
07 Dean Admissions & Student Life .... Mr. Arnett CHISHOLM
13 Chief Information Officer .... Mr. Amin LADHA
10 Controller .... Ms. Lynn MARTIN
21 Dir Budget Purchasing Aux Svcs .... Ms. Barbara FILLINGER
15 Director Compensation/Benefits .... Ms. Christine MIHALY
37 Director Financial Aid .... Ms. Lori TRAPP
09 Director Institutional Research .... Dr. Roger MOURAD
20 Director Educational Services .... Ms. Kathleen A. STADTFELD
19 Director Safety & Security .... Mr. Jacque DESROSIERS
26 Director Public Relations & Mktg .... Ms. Catherine SMILLIE
43 General Counsel .... Ms. Sarah STITT
35 Dir Student Development/Activities .... Mr. Pete LESHKEVICH
88 Ombudsman .... Mr. Larry AEILTS
88 Enrollment Svcs Info Officer .... Ms. Kathryn STAFFORD

Wayne County Community College District (C)

801 W Fort Street, Detroit MI 48226-3010
County: Wayne FICE Identification: 009230
Unit ID: 172635
Telephone: (313) 496-2600 Carnegie Class: Assoc/Pub-U-MC
FAX Number: (313) 961-9439 Calendar System: Semester
URL: www.wcccd.edu
Established: 1967 Annual Undergrad Tuition & Fees (In-District): $1,882
Enrollment: 72,667 Coed
Affiliation or Control: State/Local IRS Status: 501(c)3
Highest Offering: Associate Degree
Program: Occupational; 2-Year Principally Bachelor's Creditable
Accreditation: NH, DA, DH, DIETT, OTA, SURGA, SURGT

01 Chancellor .... Dr. Curtis L. IVERY
03 Dist Executive Vice Chancellor .... Mr. John BOLDEN
05 Dist Vice Chanc Educational Affairs .... Dr. Stephanie BULGER
31 Dist Vice Chanc External Affairs .... Dr. George SWAN
32 Vice Chanc Student Services .... Mr. Brian SINGLETON
51 Dist Vice Chanc Sch Continuing Educ .... Ms. Shawna FORBES
10 Dist Vice Chanc Admin/Finance .... Ms. Kim DICARO
15 Dist Vice Chanc HR/Accountability .... Mr. Mirza F. AHMED
13 Dist Vice Chance/Chief Info Officer .... Ms. Kiran SEKHRI
96 Dist Assoc Vice Chanc Procurement .... Ms. Tami D. STANZA
20 Dist AVC Adjunct Faculty/Curriculum .... Ms. CharMaine HINES
09 District VC IE/Info Management .... Ms. Johnesa HODGE
88 Dist Assoc VC Transfer Programs .... Ms. Karen JACKSON
35 Dist Assoc Vice Chanc Student Svcs .... Mr. Adrian PHILLIPS
12 Campus President Downriver .... Mr. Anthony ARMINIAK
12 Campus President Downtown .... Ms. Shawna FORBES
12 Campus President Western .... Mr. Michael P. DOTSON
12 Campus Pres NW/Exec Prov Hlth Sci .... Dr. Debraha WATSON
12 Campus President Eastern/Corp Col .... Dr. Sandra T. ROBINSON
30 Dist VC Comm/Inst Advancement .... Ms. Muna KHOURY
18 Dist COO Physical Plant/Facilities .... Mr. Sammie RICE
88 Asst to Chanc Instruct/Stdnt Succes .... Dr. Patrick MCNALLY

Wayne State University (D)

Detroit MI 48202-4095
County: Wayne FICE Identification: 002329
Unit ID: 172644
Telephone: (313) 577-2424 Carnegie Class: RU/VH
FAX Number: (313) 577-8154 Calendar System: Semester
URL: www.wayne.edu
Established: 1868 Annual Undergrad Tuition & Fees (In-State): $9,809
Enrollment: 31,505 Coed
Affiliation or Control: State IRS Status: 501(c)3
Highest Offering: Doctorate
Program: Occupational; Liberal Arts And General; Teacher Preparatory; Professional
Accreditation: NH, ANEST, ARCPA, AUD, BUS, CACREP, CLPSY, CORE, DANCE, DIETC, ENG, ENGR, ENGT, FUSER, IPSY, LAW, LIB, MED, MIDWF, MT, MUS, NURSE, OT, PA, PH, PHAR, PLNG, PTA, RAD, RTT, SP, SPAA, SW, @TEAC, THEA

01 President .... Mr. Allan GILMOUR
100 VP Marketing & Comm/Chief of Staff .... Mr. Michael G. WRIGHT
05 Sr Vice Pres Acad Affairs & Provost .... Dr. Ronald T. BROWN
10 VP Finance & Business/Treasurer/CFO .... Mr. Rick NORK
43 Vice President & General Counsel .... Mr. Louis A. LESSEM
46 Vice Pres Res/Interim Dean Grad Sch .... Dr. Hilary H. RATNER
30 Vice Pres Devel/Alumni Affairs .... Mr. David RIPPLE
86 Vice Pres Govt & Community Affairs .... Mr. Harvey HOLLINS, III
20 Assoc VP Undergrad Pgms/Gen Ed .... Dr. Howard N. SHAPIRO
101 Sec to the BOG & Exec Asst to Pres .... Ms. Julie H. MILLER
04 Assistant to the President .... Ms. Carol L. BALDWIN
29 Asst Vice Pres Alumni Relations .... Mr. Christopher S. POLK
15 Assoc Vice Pres Human Resources .... Mr. Mark K. ANKENBAUER
18 Assoc VP Facilities/Planning/Mgmt .... Mr. James R. SEARS
21 Assoc Vice Pres University Budget .... Mr. Robert KOHRMAN
32 Dean of Students .... Dr. David J. STRAUSS
07 Sr Dir of UG Admiss/New Stdnt Ornt .... Ms. Judy B. TATUM
26 Director Corporate/Public Affairs .... Ms. Francine WUNDER
25 Sr Dir Sponsored Programs Admin .... Ms. Gail L. RYAN
37 Director Student Financial Aid .... Mr. Albert G. HERMSEN
38 Director Counseling & Placement Svc .... Dr. Ronald H. KENT
08 Dean University Libraries .... Dr. Sandra G. YEE
06 Registrar .... Ms. Linda K. FALKIEWICZ
09 Asst VP for Institutional Research .... Mr. Mark A. BYRD
49 Dean Liberal Arts & Sciences .... Dr. Robert L. THOMAS
61 Dean of the Law School .... Mr. Robert M. ACKERMAN
63 Dean School of Medicine .... Dr. Valarie M. PARISI
66 Dean College of Nursing .... Dr. Barbara K. REDMAN
54 Dean College of Engineering .... Dr. Farshad FOTOUHI
50 Dean Sch Business Administration .... Dr. David L. WILLIAMS
70 Dean School of Social Work .... Dr. Phyllis I. VROOM
67 Dean Pharmacy & Health Sciences .... Dr. Lloyd Y. YOUNG
53 Dean College of Education .... Dr. Carolyn C. SHIELDS
57 Dean Col Fine/Performing/Comm Arts .... Mr. Mat SEEGER
92 Dean Honors College .... Dr. Jerry HERRON
96 Senior Director of Purchasing .... Ms. Joan M. GOSSMAN

West Shore Community College (E)

3000 N. Stiles Rd., Scottville MI 49454-0277
County: Mason FICE Identification: 007950
Unit ID: 172671
Telephone: (231) 845-6211 Carnegie Class: Assoc/Pub-R-S
FAX Number: (231) 845-0207 Calendar System: Semester
URL: www.westshore.edu
Established: 1967 Annual Undergrad Tuition & Fees (In-District): $2,493
Enrollment: 1,565 Coed
Affiliation or Control: Local IRS Status: 501(c)3
Highest Offering: Associate Degree
Program: Occupational; 2-Year Principally Bachelor's Creditable
Accreditation: NH

01 President .... Dr. Charles T. DILLON
11 VP of Administrative Services .... Mr. Scott WARD
05 VP of Academic and Student Services .... Ms. Lisa STICH
32 Dean of Student Services .... Mr. Chad E. INABINET
40 Director of Bookstore & Food Svcs .... Ms. Cheryl HOGAN
04 Executive Assistant to President .... Ms. Lisa STANKOWSKI
07 Director of Admissions .... Ms. Wendy FOUGHT
37 Director Financial Aid .... Ms. Julianne MURPHY
91 Manager of Adm Computing Systems .... Mr. Stephen VON PFAHL
88 Director of Criminal Justice .... Mr. Dan DELLAR
88 Director of Recreational Services .... Mr. Michael A. MOORE
30 Director of Development .... Mr. Mark A. BERGSTROM
15 Director of Human Resources .... Ms. Debbie CAMPBELL
88 Director of Women's Resource Center .... Ms. Carla E. SHAY
26 Director of College Relations .... Mr. Thomas A. HAWLEY
23 Director of Wellness Center .... Ms. Julie PAGE-SMITH
10 Director of Accounting .... Ms. Kristen BIGGS
106 Director Distance Learning & Info .... Mr. John GERTS

Western Michigan University (F)

1903 W Michigan Avenue, Kalamazoo MI 49008-5202
County: Kalamazoo FICE Identification: 002330
Unit ID: 172699
Telephone: (269) 387-1000 Carnegie Class: RU/H
FAX Number: (269) 387-0958 Calendar System: Semester
URL: www.wmich.edu
Established: 1903 Annual Undergrad Tuition & Fees (In-State): $9,606
Enrollment: 25,045 Coed
Affiliation or Control: State IRS Status: 501(c)3
Highest Offering: Doctorate
Program: Occupational; Liberal Arts And General; Teacher Preparatory; Professional
Accreditation: NH, AAB, ARCPA, ART, AUD, BUS, BUSA, CACREP, CEA, CIDA, CLPSY, COPSY, CORE, CS, DANCE, DIETD, DIETI, ENG, ENGT, IPSY, MUS, NURSE, OT, SP, SPAA, SW, TED, THEA

01 President .... Dr. John M. DUNN
05 Provost/Vice Pres Academic Affairs .... Dr. Timothy J. GREENE
10 Vice President Business & Finance .... Ms. Jan VAN DER KLEY
32 VP Student Affairs/Dean of Students .... Dr. Diane K. ANDERSON
46 Vice President Research .... Dr. Daniel M. LITYNSKI
13 Vice Provost Acad Operations & CIO .... Dr. James A. GILCHRIST
30 VP Development & Alumni Relations .... Mr. James THOMAS
09 Vice Provost Inst Effectiveness .... Dr. Eileen B. EVANS
84 Int Vice Provost Enrollment Mgmt .... Dr. Keith M. HEARIT
43 VP Legal Affairs/General Counsel .... Ms. Carol L J. HUSTOLES
86 VP Governmental Affs/University Rel .... Mr. Greg J. ROSINE
15 Director Human Resources Services .... Ms. Felicia CRAWFORD
21 Assoc Vice President of Finance .... Vacant
28 Assoc Vice Pres Diversity/Inclusion .... Dr. Martha B. WARFIELD
18 Assoc Vice Pres Facilities Mgmt .... Mr. Peter J. STRAZDAS
26 Exec Dir of University Relations .... Ms. Cheryl ROLAND
101 Secretary Board of Trustees .... Ms. Betty A. KOCHER
51 Assoc Prov Extended Univ Pgms .... Dr. Dawn GAYMER
58 Interim Dean Graduate College .... Dr. Gene FREUDENBURG
49 Dean of Arts & Sciences .... Dr. Alexander ENYEDI
50 Dean of Business .... Dr. Kay PALAN
53 Dean of Education .... Dr. John J. WHEELER
54 Dean of Engr & Applied Sciences .... Dr. Anthony J. VIZZINI
57 Dean of Fine Arts .... Dr. Margaret M. MERRION
76 Dean Health & Human Services .... Dr. Earlie WASHINGTON
63 Dean School of Medicine .... Dr. Hal B. JENSON
92 Dean of Honors College .... Dr. Nicholas ANDREADIS
88 Dean of Aviation .... Capt. Dave POWELL
08 Dean of Libraries .... Dr. Joseph G. REISH
35 Associate Dean of Students .... Ms. Suzie NAGEL
29 Executive Director Alumni Relations .... Ms. M. Jamie JEREMY
82 Dir Haenicke Inst for Global Educ .... Dr. Donald MCCLOUD
07 Director Admissions/Orientation .... Ms. Penny BUNDY
45 Vice Provost Budget Personnel/CIO .... Dr. James A. GILCHRIST
06 Registrar .... Vacant
37 Director Student Financial Aid .... Mr. Mark J. DELOREY
36 Director Career & Employment Svcs .... Ms. Lynn KELLY-ALBERTSON
38 Dir Univ Counseling & Testing Ctr .... Vacant
96 Dir Logistical Svcs (Purchasing) .... Mr. Donald PENSKAR

Western Theological Seminary (G)

101 E 13th Street, Holland MI 49423-3622
County: Ottawa FICE Identification: 002331
Unit ID: 172705
Telephone: (616) 392-8555 Carnegie Class: Spec/Faith
FAX Number: (616) 392-7717 Calendar System: Semester
URL: www.westernsem.edu
Established: 1866 Annual Graduate Tuition & Fees: $11,904
Enrollment: 239 Coed
Affiliation or Control: Reformed Church In America IRS Status: 501(c)3
Highest Offering: Doctorate; No Undergraduates
Program: Professional; Religious Emphasis
Accreditation: THEOL

01 President .... Dr. Timothy BROWN
05 Dean/Vice Pres Academic Affairs .... Dr. Leanne VAN DYK
30 Vice President Advancement/Comm .... Mr. Ken NEEVEL
10 Vice President of Finance .... Mr. Norman DONKERSLOOT
08 Director of the Library .... Rev. Paul M. SMITH

Yeshiva Beth Yehuda - Yeshiva Gedolah of Greater Detroit (A)

24600 Greenfield, Oak Park MI 48237-1544
County: Oakland
FICE Identification: 023638
Unit ID: 247773
Telephone: (248) 968-3360
Carnegie Class: Spec/Faith
FAX Number: (248) 968-8613
Calendar System: Semester
Established: 1985
Annual Undergrad Tuition & Fees: $6,100
Enrollment: 88
Male
Affiliation or Control: Independent Non-Profit
IRS Status: 501(c)3
Highest Offering: Doctorate
Program: Professional
Accreditation: RABN

01 Dean .... Rabbi Y. BAKST
05 Assistant Dean .... Rabbi M. S. BAKST
11 Executive Administrator .... Rabbi P. RUSHNAWITZ
37 Director of Financial Aid .... Rabbi Y. BLITZ

MINNESOTA

Academy College (B)

1101 E 78th Street, Suite 100,
Minneapolis MN 55420-1402
County: Hennepin
FICE Identification: 020503
Unit ID: 172866
Telephone: (952) 851-0066
Carnegie Class: Bac/Assoc
FAX Number: (952) 851-0094
Calendar System: Quarter
URL: www.academycollege.edu
Established: 1936
Annual Undergrad Tuition & Fees: $19,708
Enrollment: 238
Coed
Affiliation or Control: Proprietary
IRS Status: Proprietary
Highest Offering: Baccalaureate
Program: 2-Year Principally Bachelor's Creditable
Accreditation: ACICS, MAC

01 Director .... Ms. Mary ERICKSON

Adler Graduate School (C)

1550 E 78th Street, Richfield MN 55423
County: Hennepin
FICE Identification: 030519
Unit ID: 374024
Telephone: (612) 861-7554
Carnegie Class: Spec/Health
FAX Number: (612) 861-7559
Calendar System: Quarter
URL: www.alfredadler.edu
Established: 1969
Annual Graduate Tuition & Fees: $23,280
Enrollment: 435
Coed
Affiliation or Control: Independent Non-Profit
IRS Status: 501(c)3
Highest Offering: Master's; No Undergraduates
Program: Professional
Accreditation: NH

01 President .... Dr. Daniel HAUGEN
05 Chief Academic Officer .... Vacant
04 Assistant to the President .... Ms. Margie MCGOVERN
07 Director of Admissions/Student Svcs .... Ms. Evelyn HAAS
37 Director of Student Financial Aid .... Ms. Jeanette MAYNARD NELSON

American Academy of Acupuncture and Oriental Medicine (D)

1925 W County Road B2, Roseville MN 55113-2703
County: Ramsey
FICE Identification: 038333
Unit ID: 446002
Telephone: (651) 631-0204
Carnegie Class: Spec/Health
FAX Number: (651) 631-0361
Calendar System: Trimester
URL: www.aaaom.org
Established: 1997
Annual Graduate Tuition & Fees: $11,212
Enrollment: 105
Coed
Affiliation or Control: Proprietary
IRS Status: Proprietary
Highest Offering: Master's; No Undergraduates
Program: Professional
Accreditation: ACUP

01 President .... Dr. Changzhen GONG
05 Academic Dean .... Dr. Yubin LU
11 Administrative Director .... Leila NIELSEN
37 Financial Aid Officer .... Lillian CHEUNG

Argosy University, Twin Cities (E)

1515 Central Parkway, Eagan MN 55121-1756
County: Dakota
FICE Identification: 007619
Unit ID: 173984
Telephone: (888) 844-2004
Carnegie Class: Master's S
FAX Number: (651) 994-0895
Calendar System: Semester
URL: www.argosy.edu/twincities
Established: 1961
Annual Undergrad Tuition & Fees: $14,580
Enrollment: 2,580
Coed
Affiliation or Control: Proprietary
IRS Status: Proprietary
Highest Offering: Doctorate
Program: Professional
Accreditation: &NH, CLPSY, DH, DMS, HT, MAC, MFCD, MLTAD, RAD, RTT

01 Campus President .... Dr. Scott TJADEN
05 Vice President of Academic Affairs .... Dr. Kristin BENSON
07 Senior Director of Admissions .... Janet ZIMPRICH
32 Director of Student Services .... Aprile EICH
08 Director of Library Services .... Carl RALSTON
10 Dir of Admin & Financial Services .... Irene AYERS
15 Director of Human Resources .... Melissa JONES
36 Director of Career Services .... Andrew SYKES
07 Director of Admissions .... Cate WEBER
07 Director of Admissions .... Mike BELZ
06 Registrar .... Amy SUDBECK
18 Facilites Manager .... Joe MIKE
37 Dir Student Financial Services .... Larry WERNER

† Regional accreditation is carried under the parent institution in Chicago, IL.

The Art Institutes International Minnesota (F)

15 S 9th Street, Minneapolis MN 55402-2808
County: Hennepin
FICE Identification: 010248
Unit ID: 173887
Telephone: (612) 332-3361
Carnegie Class: Spec/Arts
FAX Number: (612) 904-1541
Calendar System: Quarter
URL: www.artinstitutes.edu/minneapolis
Established: 1964
Annual Undergrad Tuition & Fees: $23,788
Enrollment: 2,018
Coed
Affiliation or Control: Proprietary
IRS Status: Proprietary
Highest Offering: Baccalaureate
Program: Occupational
Accreditation: @NH, ACICS, ACFEI

01 President .... Dr. Jeffrey ALLEN
05 Dean of Academic Affairs .... Dr. Susan TARNOWSKI
32 Dean of Student Affairs .... Pam BOERSIG
36 Director of Career Services .... Becky BATES
07 Director of Admissions .... Mary STRAND
26 Director of Communications .... Anj KOZEL

Augsburg College (G)

2211 Riverside Avenue, Minneapolis MN 55454-1398
County: Hennepin
FICE Identification: 002334
Unit ID: 173045
Telephone: (612) 330-1000
Carnegie Class: Master's L
FAX Number: (612) 330-1649
Calendar System: Semester
URL: www.augsburg.edu
Established: 1869
Annual Undergrad Tuition & Fees: $30,418
Enrollment: 3,997
Coed
Affiliation or Control: Evangelical Lutheran Church In America
IRS Status: 501(c)3
Highest Offering: Doctorate
Program: Liberal Arts And General; Teacher Preparatory; Professional
Accreditation: NH, ARCPA, MUS, NURSE, SW, TED

01 President .... Dr. Paul C. PRIBBENOW
100 Vice President and Chief of Staff .... Ms. Christine M. SZAJ
88 Exec Dir Center Faith & Learning .... Dr. Thomas F. MORGAN
05 VP Academic Affs/Dean of College .... Dr. Barbara FARLEY
10 CFO/Vice Pres Finance/Admin .... Ms. Tammy MCGEE
44 Vice President Advancement .... Mr. Jeremy WELLS
84 Vice Pres Enrollment Management .... Ms. Julie A. EDSTROM
32 Vice President Student Affairs .... Ms. Anne L. GARVEY
30 Asst Vice President Development .... Ms. Cassidy TITCOMB
58 Asst VP/Dean of Grad & Prof Stds .... Dr. Lori PETERSON
12 Director Rochester Program .... Dr. Karl WOLFE
26 Director Marketing/Communications .... Ms. Rebecca JOHN
42 Campus Pastor .... Rev. David T. WOLD
37 Director Student Financial Services .... Mr. Paul L. TERRIO
06 Registrar .... Mr. Wayne H. KALLESTAD
07 Asst VP for Admissions .... Ms. Carrie M. CARROLL
09 Dir Enrollment Plng/Systems Devel .... Mr. James C. ERCHUL
18 Director Facilities Management .... Mr. David A. DRAUS
25 Director Sponsored Programs .... Ms. Carol M. FORBES
29 Director Alum & Constituent Rels .... Ms. Kim STONE
36 Director Ctr Service/Work/Learning .... Ms. Lois A. OLSON
13 VP & Chief Information Officer .... Mr. Leif B. ANDERSON
38 Director Counseling & Health Promo .... Ms. Nancy G. GUILBEAULT
15 Asst VP for Human Resources .... Ms. Andrea TURNER
35 Dean of Students .... Dr. Sarah GRIESSE
35 Dir Campus Activities/Orientation .... Ms. Joanne REECK-IRBY
08 Director Library Services .... Ms. Jane A. NELSON
86 Dir Government Relations .... Mr. Jay BENANAV
19 Director Public Safety .... Vacant
102 Dir Corporate/Foundation Relations .... Ms. Laura ROLLER
31 Director Community Relations .... Mr. Steve PEACOCK
88 Director Parent/Family Relations .... Ms. Sally DANIELS
55 Dir Augsburg for Adults .... Vacant
88 Director StepUp Program .... Ms. Patrice SALMERI
88 Director Advancement Services .... Mr. Kevin HEALY
88 Dir Center for Teaching/Learning .... Ms. Velma J. LASHBROOK
40 Bookstore Manager .... Ms. Laura FORGEY
96 Director Purchasing/Central Support .... Mr. Matthew RUMPZA
85 Asst Vice Pres Intl Programs .... Mr. Orval J. GINGERICH
49 Asst Vice Pres/Dean of Arts & Sci .... Dr. Amy GORT
41 Athletic Director .... Mr. Jeffrey F. SWENSON

Bethany Lutheran College (H)

700 Luther Drive, Mankato MN 56001-6163
County: Blue Earth
FICE Identification: 002337
Unit ID: 173142
Telephone: (507) 344-7000
Carnegie Class: Bac/A&S
FAX Number: (507) 344-7376
Calendar System: Semester
URL: www.blc.edu
Established: 1911
Annual Undergrad Tuition & Fees: $22,410
Enrollment: 608
Coed
Affiliation or Control: Evangelical Lutheran Synod
IRS Status: 501(c)3
Highest Offering: Baccalaureate
Program: Liberal Arts And General
Accreditation: NH

01 President .... Dr. Dan R. BRUSS
42 Dir Campus Spiritual Life/Chaplain .... Rev. Donald L. MOLDSTAD
05 Dean of Academic Affairs .... Dr. Eric K. WOLLER
32 Vice President for Student Affairs .... Mr. Steven C. JAEGER
10 Chief Financial/Administrative Ofcr .... Mr. Daniel L. MUNDAHL
30 Chief Advancement Officer .... Mr. Arthur P. WESTPHAL
35 Dean of Student Services .... Dr. Theodore E. MANTHE
37 Director of Financial Aid .... Mr. Jeffrey W. YOUNGE
06 Registrar .... Ms. Mary Jo H. STARKSON
07 Dean of Admissions .... Mr. Donald M. WESTPHAL
16 Manager of Employee Relations .... Mrs. Paulette L. TONN BOOKER
08 Director of Library Services .... Mr. Orrin J. AUSEN
13 Director of Information Technology .... Mr. John M. SEHLOFF
26 Director of Marketing/Public Rels .... Mr. Lance W. SCHWARTZ
57 Director of Fine Arts .... Mrs. Lois A. JAEGER
41 Director of Athletics .... Mr. Karl E. FAGER
29 Manager of Alumni Relations .... Mr. Jacob C. KRIER
19 Manager of Security Services .... Mr. Jonathan L. MOLDSTAD
91 Manager of Administrative Computing .... Ms. Lisa A. SHUBERT
90 Manager of Academic Computing .... Mr. Mark S. MEYER
40 Bookstore Manager .... Mr. Paul G. WOLD
21 Controller .... Mr. Gregory W. COSTELLO
28 Coord Ctr for Intercultural Develop .... Mr. Thomas G. FLUNKER
36 Coord Career Svcs & Internships .... Ms. Sarah A. HARSTAD
38 Coord of Student Counseling .... Mrs. Patricia J. REAGLES
18 Director of Facilities .... Mr. Juel O. MERSETH

Bethel University (I)

3900 Bethel Drive, Saint Paul MN 55112-6999
County: Ramsey
FICE Identification: 009058
Unit ID: 173160
Telephone: (651) 638-6400
Carnegie Class: Master's L
FAX Number: (651) 638-6001
Calendar System: Semester
URL: www.bethel.edu
Established: 1871
Annual Undergrad Tuition & Fees: $29,460
Enrollment: 5,451
Coed
Affiliation or Control: Baptist
IRS Status: 501(c)3
Highest Offering: Doctorate
Program: Liberal Arts And General; Teacher Preparatory
Accreditation: NH, MFCD, NURSE, SW, TEAC, THEOL

01 President .... Dr. James H. BARNES, III
100 Executive Assistant to President .... Dr. Richard J. SHERRY
05 Executive Vice Pres and Provost .... Dr. David K. CLARK
10 Sr Vice Pres Business Affs .... Ms. Kathleen J. NELSON
46 Sr VP Strategic Planning & Research .... Mr. Joseph LALUZERNE
26 Sr VP Communications/Marketing .... Ms. Sherie J. LINDVALL
30 Sr VP University Relations .... Mr. Patrick MAZOROL
44 Vice President Development .... Mr. Bruce W. ANDERSON
07 VP for Admiss/Fin Aid & Retention .... Mr. Daniel NELSON
90 Vice President Information Tech .... Dr. William H. DOYLE
29 Vice Pres Constituent Relations .... Mr. Ralph GUSTAFSON
32 Vice President Student Life .... Dr. Edee SCHULZE
49 Vice Pres/Dean of Arts & Sciences .... Dr. Debra HARLESS
58 Vice Pres Dean Cont Stds/Grad Pgm .... Mr. Richard CROMBIE
51 Dean Acad of Cont Studies/Grad Pgm .... Dr. Lori JASS
73 Interim VP and Dean BSSP .... Dr. David CLARK
20 Associate Dean Arts and Sciences .... Dr. Barrett FISHER
20 Assoc Dean Gen Educ & Fac Develop .... Dr. Deborah SULLIVAN-TRAINOR
46 Actg Assoc Dean Inst Assess Accred .... Dr. Joel FREDERICKSON
81 Acting Assoc Dean Nat Behav Sci .... Dr. Jeffery L. PORT
88 Acting Assoc Dean for the Faculty .... Dr. Katherine J. NEVINS
12 Dean/Exec Ofcr Bethel Sem San Diego .... Dr. John R. LILLIS
12 Dean/Exec Ofcr Bethel Sem East .... Dr. Douglas W. FOMBELLE
35 Dean of Students .... Mr. James A. FEREIRA
35 Dean of Students .... Dr. Marie WISNER
08 Director of Libraries .... Mr. David R. STEWART
15 Director of Human Resources .... Mr. William L. GOODMAN
41 Athletic Director .... Mr. Robert B. BJORKLUND
37 Financial Aid Officer .... Mr. Jeffery D. OLSON
42 Dean Campus Ministrs/Campus Pastor .... Ms. Laurel BUNKER
07 Director of Admissions .... Mr. Jay T. FEDJE
07 Director of Seminary Admissions .... Mr. Joseph V. DWORAK
06 University Registrar .... Ms. Katrina CHAPMAN
36 Acting Dir Career Counsel/Placement .... Mr. Dave BROZA
19 Chief of Security and Safety .... Mr. Andrew LUCHSINGER
40 Director Campus Stores .... Ms. Jill SONSTEBY
23 Director of Health Services .... Mrs. Elizabeth K. MILLER
96 Director of Purchasing .... Mr. Bill KIDDER
21 Associate Business Officer .... Mr. John BERGESON
38 Director Student Counseling .... Dr. James KOCH
28 Chief Diversity Officer .... Dr. Leon RODRIGUES

† The marriage and family therapy master's program at Bethel Seminary San Diego is accredited by the Commission on Accreditation for Marriage and Family Therapy Education (COAMFTE) of the American Association for Marriage and Family Therapy (AAMFT)

Brown College (J)

1340 Mendota Heights Road, Mendota Heights MN 55120
County: Dakota
FICE Identification: 007351
Unit ID: 174394

Telephone: (651) 905-3400 Carnegie Class: Bac/Assoc
FAX Number: (651) 905-3550 Calendar System: Other
URL: www.browncollege.edu
Established: 1946 Annual Undergrad Tuition & Fees: $19,850
Enrollment: 1,081 Coed
Affiliation or Control: Proprietary IRS Status: Proprietary
Highest Offering: Baccalaureate
Program: Occupational; 2-Year Principally Bachelor's Creditable; Professional; Business Emphasis
Accreditation: ACCSC, MAAB

01 President ....Dr. Michelle ERNST
05 Dean of Education ....Ms. Lisa THOMAS
07 Vice President of Admissions ....Ms. May THAO-FEHUK
10 Business Office Manager ....Mr. Calvin OLSTAD
12 Director of Brooklyn Center Campus ....Mr. Timothy PETERSON
15 Director of Human Resources ....Mr. Ross REYNOLDS
20 Assistant Dean ....Mr. Kirk GALLUP
36 Director of Career Services ....Mr. Paul KRAIMER
37 Director of Financial Aid ....Ms. Molly USSATIN
13 Director of Information Technology ....Mr. John HANS
06 Registrar ....Ms. Debra NEWGARD
08 Librarian ....Mr. Philip DUDAS
29 Director of Alumni Affairs ....Vacant

Capella University (A)

225 S 6th Street, 9th Floor, Minneapolis MN 55402-4319
County: Hennepin FICE Identification: 032673
Unit ID: 413413
Telephone: (888) 227-3552 Carnegie Class: DRU
FAX Number: (612) 977-5066 Calendar System: Other
URL: www.capella.edu
Established: 1993 Annual Undergrad Tuition & Fees: $12,720
Enrollment: 24,150 Coed
Affiliation or Control: Proprietary IRS Status: Proprietary
Highest Offering: Doctorate
Program: Professional
Accreditation: NH, CACREP, TED

00 Chancellor ....Dr. Michael J. OFFERMAN
01 President ....Mr. Larry A. ISAAK
03 Interim President ....Dr. Deborah BUSHWAY
05 Vice Pres Academic Affs/Provost ....Dr. Deborah BUSHWAY
04 Executive Asst Supervisor ....Ms. Cristy SIEDE
27 Vice President Chief Info Officer ....Mr. Scott HENKEL
84 Vice President Enrollment Services ....Ms. Leslie BRONK
15 Vice President Human Resources ....Ms. Sally CHIAL
43 VP Govrnmt Affs/Gen Counsel/Sec ....Mr. Greg THOM
79 Dean School of Human Services ....Dr. Deborah BUSHWAY
72 Act Dean School of Business/Tech ....Dr. William REED
53 Dean School of Education ....Dr. Barbara BUTTS WILLIAMS
88 Dean School of Psychology ....Dr. Deb BUSHWAY
09 Assessment & Inst Rsch Director ....Ms. Kim PEARCE
06 Registrar ....Ms. Nancy PENNA
10 Chief Financial Officer ....Ms. Lois MARTIN
21 Corporate Controller ....Ms. Amy DRIFKA
21 Director of Finance ....Mr. Andy WATT
88 Director Next Generation Learning ....Mr. Keith KOCH
27 Director Marketing/Communications ....Mr. Brad FRANK
31 Director Events & Outreach ....Mr. Tom CLEMENS
26 Director of Public Relations ....Ms. Irene SILBER
46 Director Academic Research ....Dr. Tsuey-Hwa CHEN
18 Director of Facilities ....Ms. Carla BUSTROM
08 Manager Library Services ....Ms. Kathe PELLETIER
88 Licensing Specialist ....Mr. Dick BUTALA
07 Asst Registr/Mgr Opertnl Strategies ....Ms. Debra NEWGARD
43 Corp Attorney/Govt Affs/Compliance ....Ms. Priscilla MCNULTY

Carleton College (B)

1 N College Street, Northfield MN 55057-4001
County: Rice FICE Identification: 002340
Unit ID: 173258
Telephone: (507) 222-4000 Carnegie Class: Bac/A&S
FAX Number: (507) 222-4204 Calendar System: Trimester
URL: www.carleton.edu
Established: 1866 Annual Undergrad Tuition & Fees: $42,942
Enrollment: 1,991 Coed
Affiliation or Control: Independent Non-Profit IRS Status: 501(c)3
Highest Offering: Baccalaureate
Program: Liberal Arts And General; Teacher Preparatory
Accreditation: NH

01 President ....Mr. Steven G. POSKANZER, JR.
05 Dean of the College ....Ms. Beverly NAGEL
10 VP Business & Finance/Treasurer ....Mr. Frederick A. ROGERS
30 Vice President External Relations ....Vacant
100 Assoc Vice President/Chief of Staff ....Ms. Elise ESLINGER
26 AVP & Int VP for External Relations ....Ms. Gayle MCJUNKIN
26 AVP & Int VP for External Relations ....Mr. Joe HARGIS
32 Dean of Students ....Ms. Hudlin WAGNER
07 Dean of Admissions ....Mr. Paul THIBOUTOT
45 Dean for Budget & Planning ....Vacant
35 Associate Dean of Students ....Ms. Julie THORNTON
35 Associate Dean of Students ....Mr. Joseph BAGGOT
39 Director of Residential Life ....Mr. Steve WISENER
42 Chaplain ....Rev. Carolyn FURE-SLOCUM
06 Registrar ....Mr. Roger LASLEY
08 Interim College Librarian ....Ms. Jennifer EDWINS
29 Director of Alumni Affairs ....Ms. Becky ZRIMSEK
36 Director Career Center ....Mr. Richard BERMAN
13 Information Technology Svc Director ....Mr. Joel COOPER
90 Assoc Director Academic Computing ....Ms. Andrea NIXON
91 Assoc Director Admin Computing ....Ms. Sue TRAXLER
27 Director of Media Relations ....Mr. Eric SIEGER
37 Assoc Dean Admiss/Dir Stdnt Fin Svc ....Mr. Rod M. OTO
15 Director of Human Resources ....Ms. Kerstin CARDENAS
88 Dir Intercult/International Life ....Ms. Joy KLUTTZ
88 Director of The Wellness Center ....Ms. Cathy CARLSON
18 Director of Facilities/Capital Plng ....Mr. Steven SPEHN
40 Director Book Store/Central Service ....Mr. David SCHLOSSER
41 Athletic Director ....Mr. Gerald YOUNG
19 Director of Security Services ....Mr. Wayne EISENHUTH
20 Associate Academic Officer ....Mr. Nathan GRAWE
20 Associate Academic Officer ....Mr. Arjendu PATTANAYAK

Central Baptist Theological Seminary of Minneapolis (C)

900 Forestview Lane N, Plymouth MN 55441-5934
County: Hennepin Identification: 666050
Telephone: (763) 417-8250 Carnegie Class: Not Classified
FAX Number: (763) 417-8258 Calendar System: Semester
URL: www.centralseminary.edu
Established: 1956 Annual Undergrad Tuition & Fees: $6,720
Enrollment: 90 Coed
Affiliation or Control: Baptist IRS Status: 501(c)3
Highest Offering: Doctorate
Program: Religious Emphasis
Accreditation: TRACS

01 President ....Dr. Samuel E. HORN
05 VP of Academic Affairs ....Dr. Jonathan R. PRATT
06 Registrar ....Jason STAMPER

*College of Medicine, Mayo Clinic (D)

200 First Street, Rochester MN 55905-3712
County: Olmsted Identification: 666719
Telephone: (507) 284-2511 Carnegie Class: N/A
FAX Number: (507) 284-0999
URL: www.mayo.edu

01 Chief Executive Officer ....Dr. John H. NOSEWORTHY
05 Exec Dean for Education Mayo Clinic ....Dr. Torrence CASCINO
46 Exec Dean for Research Mayo Clinic ....Dr. Robert A. RIZZA
22 Affirmative Action Administrator ....Mr. Kenneth J. SCHNEIDER
27 Head Communications Division ....Mr. John LAFORGIA
43 Immigration Attorney ....Mr. Bruce R. LARSON
37 Financial Aid Officer ....Mr. David L. DAHLEN
08 Director of Libraries ....Mr. J. Michael HOMAN
29 Director Mayo Clinic Alumni Center ....Ms. Karen D. HERMAN
30 Director of Development ....Dr. Michael CAMILLERI
86 Director Government Relations ....Vacant

*Mayo Clinic College of Medicine-Mayo Graduate School (E)

200 First Street, SW, Rochester MN 55905-0001
County: Olmsted FICE Identification: 011516
Unit ID: 365426
Telephone: (507) 538-1160 Carnegie Class: DRU
FAX Number: (507) 293-0838 Calendar System: Quarter
URL: www.mayo.edu/mgs/
Established: 1915 Annual Graduate Tuition & Fees: $24,500
Enrollment: 177 Coed
Affiliation or Control: Independent Non-Profit IRS Status: 501(c)3
Highest Offering: Doctorate; No Undergraduates
Program: Professional
Accreditation: &NH

02 Dean ....Dr. Diane F. JELINEK
05 Associate Dean Academic Affairs ....Dr. L. James MAHER
32 Assoc Dean Student Affairs ....Dr. Bruce F. HORAZDOVSKY
20 Assistant Dean ....Ms. Kim WOLFGRAM SALZ

† Regional accreditation is carried under College of Medicine, Mayo Clinic.

*Mayo Medical School (F)

200 1st Street, SW, Rochester MN 55905-0001
County: Olmsted FICE Identification: 011732
Unit ID: 173957
Telephone: (507) 538-4897 Carnegie Class: Spec/Med
FAX Number: (507) 284-2634 Calendar System: Other
URL: www.mayo.edu/mms
Established: 1971 Annual Undergrad Tuition & Fees: $29,355
Enrollment: 186 Coed
Affiliation or Control: Independent Non-Profit IRS Status: 501(c)3
Highest Offering: First Professional Degree
Program: Professional
Accreditation: &NH, MED

02 Dean ....Dr. Keith D. LINDOR
05 Assoc Dean Academic Affairs ....Dr. Joseph GRANDE
32 Assoc Dean Student Affairs ....Dr. Patricia A. BARRIER
20 Assoc Dean Faculty Affairs ....Dr. Thomas R. VIGGIANO
35 Assistant Dean ....Mr. Jonathan TORRENS-BURTON
22 Chief Human Resources ....Ms. Jill RAGSDALE
26 Chief Mrktng Ofcr/Chair Public Affs ....Mr. John W. LAFORGIA
85 International Personnel Advisor ....Ms. Ann H. LANCE
37 Financial Aid Officer ....Mr. David L. DAHLEN
08 Head Librarian ....Mr. J. Michael HOMAN

† Regional accreditation is carried under college of Medicine, Mayo Clinic.

*Mayo School of Health Sciences (G)

200 First St. SW, Siebens Bldg 11, Rochester MN 55905-0001
County: Olmsted FICE Identification: 008182
Unit ID: 173966
Telephone: (507) 284-3678 Carnegie Class: Spec/Health
FAX Number: (507) 284-0656 Calendar System: Semester
URL: www.mayo.edu/mshs/
Established: 1973 Annual Undergrad Tuition & Fees: N/A
Enrollment: 1,000 Coed
Affiliation or Control: Independent Non-Profit IRS Status: 501(c)3
Highest Offering: Doctorate
Program: Occupational; Professional
Accreditation: &NH, ANEST, CYTO, DENT, DIETI, DMS, EEG, HT, MT, NMT, PTA, RAD, RTT

02 Dean ....Dr. Claire E. BENDER
05 Associate Dean ....Dr. Michael H. SILBER
05 Associate Dean ....Dr. David C. AGERTER
20 Associate Dean Jacksonville ....Dr. Galen PERDIKIS
20 Associate Dean Scottsdale ....Dr. Catherine C. ROBERTS
88 Administrator/Assistant Dean ....Ms. Bethany KROM
12 Operations Manager Jacksonville ....Ms. Kate RAY
12 Operations Manager Scottsdale ....Ms. Nancy GRAY
11 Operations Manager Rochester ....Mr. Troy TYNSKY
11 Operations Manager Rochester ....Ms. Virginia WRIGHT-PETERSON
32 Operations Manager/Student Svcs ....Mr. Troy KEACH
06 Director of Financial Aid/Registrar ....Mr. David DAHLEN
37 Asst Director Financial Aid ....Ms. Marcy LANSWERK

† Regional accreditation is carried under College of Medicine, Mayo Clinic.

College of Saint Benedict (H)

37 S College Avenue, Saint Joseph MN 56374-2099
County: Stearns FICE Identification: 002341
Unit ID: 174747
Telephone: (320) 363-5011 Carnegie Class: Bac/A&S
FAX Number: (320) 363-6099 Calendar System: Other
URL: www.csbsju.edu
Established: 1887 Annual Undergrad Tuition & Fees: $34,308
Enrollment: 2,031 Coordinate
Affiliation or Control: Roman Catholic IRS Status: 501(c)3
Highest Offering: Baccalaureate
Program: Liberal Arts And General; Teacher Preparatory
Accreditation: NH, DIETD, MUS, NURSE, TED

01 President ....Dr. MaryAnn BAENNINGER
05 Provost Academic Affairs ....Dr. Rita KNUESEL
32 Vice President Student Development ....Ms. Mary A. GELLER
30 Vice Pres Institutional Advancement ....Ms. Kimberly FERLAAK MOTES
84 VP Planning and Public Affairs ....Mr. Jon D. MCGEE
10 Vice Pres Finance/Administration ....Ms. Susan M. PALMER
07 VP Admission & Financial Aid ....Dr. Calvin MOSLEY
18 Exec Dir Facilities and Safety ....Mr. James E. SCHUMANN
20 Academic Dean & Assoc Provost ....Dr. Joseph DES JARDINS
26 Assoc VP of Institutional Advance ....Ms. Kolleen E. KELLOM
27 Exec Dir Comm & Marketing Svcs ....Mr. Greg A. HOYE
34 Dean of Students ....Ms. Jody L. TERHAAR
06 Registrar ....Ms. Julie E. GRUSKA
08 Director Library ....Ms. Kathleen PARKER
37 Exec Director Financial Aid ....Ms. Jane A. HAUGEN
15 Director Human Resources ....Ms. Carol ABELL
38 Director of Counseling ....Dr. Mike J. EWING
42 Director of Campus Ministry ....Vacant
41 Athletic Director ....Ms. Carol HOWE-VEENSTRA
13 Director of Info Technology Svc ....Mr. Jim J. KOENIG
19 Director of Security ....Mr. Darren SWANSON
21 Controller ....Ms. Anne OBERMAN
44 Director of Gift Planning ....Mr. Bill HICKEY
36 Director of Career Services ....Dr. Heidi HARLANDER
09 Assoc Dir of Institutional Research ....Ms. Karen KNUTSON
40 Director of Bookstores ....Mr. Don L. FORBES
100 Chief of Staff/Exec Asst to Pres ....Ms. Emily L. COOK
44 Director of Annual Giving ....Ms. Heather PIEPER-OLSON
28 Director Intercultural Center ....Ms. BernaDette W. SUWAREH
29 Director Alumnae Relations ....Ms. Jessie SANDOVAL
22 Human Resources Coordinator ....Ms. Marlene ERGEN
96 Purchasing Coordinator ....Ms. Doris GANGL

The College of Saint Scholastica (I)

1200 Kenwood Avenue, Duluth MN 55811-4199
County: Saint Louis FICE Identification: 002343
Unit ID: 174899
Telephone: (218) 723-6000 Carnegie Class: Master's M
FAX Number: (218) 723-6290 Calendar System: Semester
URL: www.css.edu
Established: 1912 Annual Undergrad Tuition & Fees: $29,328
Enrollment: 3,898 Coed
Affiliation or Control: Roman Catholic IRS Status: 501(c)3
Highest Offering: Doctorate
Program: Liberal Arts And General; Teacher Preparatory; Professional
Accreditation: NH, NURSE, OT, PTA, SW, TEAC

01 President .... Dr. Larry GOODWIN
10 Vice President Finance .... Mr. Patrick FLATTERY
05 Vice Pres Academic Affairs .... Dr. Elizabeth DOMHOLDT
30 Vice Pres College Advancement .... Ms. Margot ZELENZ
32 Vice President for Student Affairs .... Mr. Steve LYONS
84 Vice Pres for Enrollment Management .... Mr. Eric BERG
15 Vice President for Human Resources .... Ms. Lori COLLARD
26 Vice President for Marketing .... Mr. Jeffrey RICH
88 Assoc Vice Pres College Advancement .... Ms. Janet S. ROSEN
06 Registrar .... Mr. George A. BEATTIE
26 Exec Dir Mktg/Communic/Public Rels .... Mr. Robert J. ASHENMACHER
13 Chief Information Officer .... Dr. Lynne HAMRE
08 Director of Library .... Mr. Kevin MCGREW
09 Director of Institutional Research .... Dr. Iwalani ELSE
18 Director of Facilities Services .... Mr. Tom BREKKE
21 Director Business Office .... Ms. Linda ROGENTINE
29 Director Alumni Relations .... Ms. Lisa ROSETH
07 Director of Freshman Admissions .... Mr. Joe WICKLUND
07 Director of Transfer Admissions .... Mr. Clarence SHARPE
41 Athletic Director .... Mr. Don OLSON
42 Director of Campus Ministry .... Mr. Nathan LANGER
37 Director Student Financial Aid .... Mr. Jon ERICKSON
38 Dir Stdnt Ctr Health/Well-Being .... Mr. Tad SEARS
96 Purchasing Manager .... Ms. Lisa ANDERSON
79 Dean School of Arts & Letters .... Dr. Tammy OSTRANDER
50 Dean Sch of Business & Technology .... Mr. Kurt LINBERG
53 Dean School of Education .... Dr. Jo OLSEN
76 Dean School of Health Sciences .... Dr. Rondell BERKELAND
66 Dean School of Nursing .... Dr. Marty WITRAK
81 Interim Dean School of Sciences .. Dr. Gerald HENKEL-JOHNSON
85 International Student Advisor .... Ms. Alison CHAMPEAUX
104 Director of International Eduction .... Mr. Thomas HOMAN
56 Executive Director of Extended Sds .... Mr. Donald WORTHAM
04 Exec Admin Asst to President .... Ms. Joan HOLTER
19 Safety and Security Manager .... Mr. Michael TURNER
39 Asst Dean of Students-Campus Life .... Ms. Elizabeth KNEEPKENS
92 Director Honors Program .... Dr. Debra SCHROEDER
44 Exec Dir of Dev/Planned Giving .... Mr. Gary GARLIE
40 Bookstore Manager .... Ms. Ksenia OLSON
97 Director of General Education .... Dr. Darryl DIETRICH
88 Assoc Vice Pres of Mission Integrat .... Sr. Mary ROCHEFORT
88 Exec Dir Ctr for Healthcare Innovat .... Ms. Tami LICHTENBERG

College of Visual Arts (A)

344 Summit Avenue, Saint Paul MN 55102-2199
County: Ramsey FICE Identification: 007462
Unit ID: 174932
Telephone: (651) 757-4000 Carnegie Class: Spec/Arts
FAX Number: (651) 757-4010 Calendar System: Semester
URL: www.cva.edu
Established: 1924 Annual Undergrad Tuition & Fees: $24,810
Enrollment: 209 Coed
Affiliation or Control: Independent Non-Profit IRS Status: 501(c)3
Highest Offering: Baccalaureate
Program: Fine Arts Emphasis
Accreditation: NH

01 President & Academic Dean .... Ms. Ann LEDY
09 Vice President Inst Research/COO .... Dr. Susan SHORT
37 Director of Financial Aid .... Mr. David WOODWARD
13 Exec Director of Technology Support .... Ms. Barbara SZUREK
26 Director of External Relations .... Ms. Demeri C. MULLIKIN
06 Registrar .... Ms. Lois CANEDAY
10 Controller .... Ms. Sibyl ROCHE
08 Library Director .... Ms. Kathy HEUER

Concordia College (B)

901 8th Street S, Moorhead MN 56562-0001
County: Clay FICE Identification: 002346
Unit ID: 173300
Telephone: (218) 299-4000 Carnegie Class: Bac/A&S
FAX Number: (218) 299-3947 Calendar System: Semester
URL: www.cord.edu
Established: 1891 Annual Undergrad Tuition & Fees: $29,360
Enrollment: 2,810 Coed
Affiliation or Control: Evangelical Lutheran Church In America
IRS Status: 501(c)3
Highest Offering: Master's
Program: Liberal Arts And General; Teacher Preparatory
Accreditation: NH, DIETD, DIETI, MUS, NURSE, SW, @TEAC

01 President .... Dr. William J. CRAFT
05 Provost and Dean of the College .... Dr. Mark J. KREJCI
10 Vice Pres Finance/Treasurer .... Ms. Linda J. BROWN
84 Vice President for Enrollment .... Vacant
88 VP Concordia Language Villages .... Dr. Christine L. SCHULZE
30 Vice Pres Advancement .... Ms. Teresa L. HARLAND
04 Senior Associate to the President .... Ms. Tracey A. MOORHEAD
32 Interim Dean of Students .... Mr. Bruce W. VIEWEG
07 Director of Admissions .... Mr. Scott D. ELLINGSON
06 Registrar .... Ms. Nancy PENNA
37 Director Financial Aid .... Mrs. Jane A. WILLIAMS
08 Librarian .... Mrs. Sharon R. HOVERSON
36 Director of Career Center .... Mr. Jay H. THORESON
15 Director Human Resources .... Ms. Peggy L. TORRANCE
29 Director Alumni Relations .... Ms. Karen A. CARLSON
27 Sr Dir of Communications/Marketing .... Mr. Roger E. DEGERMAN
13 Chief Information Ofcr/Asc Provost .... Mr. Bruce W. VIEWEG
09 Director of Institutional Research .... Dr. Polly A. FASSINGER
18 Director of Facilities Management .... Mr. Wayne R. FLACK
38 Director of Student Counseling .... Ms. Monica R. KERSTING
41 Athletic Director .... Dr. Larry A. PAPENFUSS
42 Campus Pastor .... Rev. Timothy M. MEGORDEN
85 Director Intercultural Affairs .... Dr. Per ANDERSON

Concordia University, St. Paul (C)

275 Syndicate Street N, Saint Paul MN 55104-5494
County: Ramsey FICE Identification: 002347
Unit ID: 173328
Telephone: (651) 641-8278 Carnegie Class: Master's L
FAX Number: (651) 659-0207 Calendar System: Semester
URL: www.csp.edu
Established: 1893 Annual Undergrad Tuition & Fees: $28,400
Enrollment: 2,842 Coed
Affiliation or Control: Lutheran Church - Missouri Synod
IRS Status: 501(c)3
Highest Offering: Master's
Program: Liberal Arts And General; Teacher Preparatory
Accreditation: NH, ACBSP, TED

01 President .... Rev. Thomas Karl RIES
03 Executive Vice President .... Dr. Cheryl T. CHATMAN
05 Vice President Academic Affairs .... Mr. Lonn D. MALY
10 Vice President for Finance .... Rev. Michael H. DORNER
32 Vice President Student Services .... Dr. Miriam E. LUEBKE
30 Vice President for Advancement .... Mr. Paul SELTZ
11 Sr Vice Pres for Administration .... Dr. Eric E. LAMOTT
35 Associate VP for Student Life .... Mr. Jason M. RAHN
53 Dean College of Education .... Dr. Donald W. HELMSTETTER
49 Dean College of Arts & Sciences .... Vacant
58 Dean of Graduate School .... Dr. Michael WALCHESKI
73 Dean College of Vocation/Ministry .... Dr. David A. LUMPP
50 Dean College of Bus/Org Leadership .... Dr. Bruce P. CORRIE
28 Dean of Diversity .... Dr. Cheryl T. CHATMAN
39 Associate Dean of Residence Life .... Ms. Sharon R. SCHEWE
06 Registrar .... Mrs. Toni SQUIRES
23 Director Health Services .... Mrs. Cher A. RAFFTERY
08 Director of Library Services .... Dr. Charlotte M. KNOCHE
07 Director Undergraduate Admission .... Mrs. Kristin M. SCHOON
26 Director of Marketing .... Ms. Jill D. JOHNSON
102 Dir Foundation/Corporate Relations .... Dr. Alan D. WINEGARDEN
15 Director of Human Resources .... Mrs. Mary M. ARNOLD
37 Director of Financial Aid .... Ms. Jeanie PECK
04 Executive Assistant to President .... Mrs. Jill K. SIMON
42 Campus Chaplain .... Rev. Todd STOCKER
88 Director of Traditional Advising .... Ms. Renee L. RERKO
09 Director of Institutional Research .... Ms. Beth C. PETER
29 Director of Alumni Relations .... Mrs. Rhonda K. BEHM
41 Director of Athletics .... Mr. Thomas J. RUBBELKE
19 Risk Manager .... Mrs. Sara K. MULSO
18 Director of Operations .... Mr. James P. ORCHARD
36 Director of Placement/Prof .... Ms. Mary LEWIS
40 Bookstore Manager .... Mr. Anthony J. ROSS
90 Director of Computer Services .... Mr. Jonathan S. BREITBARTH
91 Director Administrative Computing .... Ms. Beth C. PETER
38 Director of Counseling Services .... Vacant
24 Help Desk Coordinator .... Mr. Jason T. DEBOER-MORAN

Crossroads College (D)

920 Mayowood Road, SW, Rochester MN 55902-2382
County: Olmsted FICE Identification: 002366
Unit ID: 174206
Telephone: (507) 288-4563 Carnegie Class: Spec/Faith
FAX Number: (507) 288-9046 Calendar System: Semester
URL: www.crossroadscollege.edu
Established: 1913 Annual Undergrad Tuition & Fees: $15,280
Enrollment: 177 Coed
Affiliation or Control: Christian Churches And Churches of Christ
IRS Status: 501(c)3
Highest Offering: Baccalaureate
Program: 2-Year Principally Bachelor's Creditable; Religious Emphasis
Accreditation: #BI

01 President .... Michael KILGALLIN
05 Vice President of Academics .... Claudio DIVINO
11 Vice Pres Administration & Finance .... Roger LANGSETH
32 Vice President Student Development .... Tim MCKINNEY
30 VP of Institutional Advancement .... Vacant
06 Registrar .... Robert DAMON
08 Director of the Library .... Jim GODSEY
07 Director of Admissions .... Christopher WILLIAMS
37 Director of Financial Aid .... Polly KELLOGG-BRADLEY
10 Business Manager .... Roger W. LANGSETH

Crown College (E)

8700 College View Drive, Saint Bonifacius MN 55375-9001
County: Carver FICE Identification: 002383
Unit ID: 174862
Telephone: (952) 446-4100 Carnegie Class: Bac/Diverse
FAX Number: (952) 446-4149 Calendar System: Semester
URL: www.crown.edu
Established: 1916 Annual Undergrad Tuition & Fees: $28,850
Enrollment: 1,176 Coed
Affiliation or Control: The Christian And Missionary Alliance
IRS Status: 501(c)3
Highest Offering: Master's
Program: Liberal Arts And General; Teacher Preparatory
Accreditation: NH, NURSE

01 President .... Dr. Richard P. MANN
04 Exec Assistant to the President .... Mrs. Shirley M. GRANLUND
10 VP Finance .... Mr. David TARRANT
05 VP Academic Affairs .... Dr. Scott MOATS
32 VP Student Development .... Mr. Michael SOHM
84 VP Enrollment & Marketing Services .... Mr. Mike PRICE
30 VP Advancement .... Mrs. Wendy EDGAR
11 Director of Operations .... Mr. Benjamin WAURMS
20 Dean for Undergraduate Pgms .... Dr. Scott MOATS
66 Interim Director of Nursing .... Mrs. Teresa NEWBY
21 Controller .... Mr. Ronald STRAKA
41 Athletic Director .... Mr. Joshua DUNWOODY
08 Director of Media Services .... Dr. Dennis INGOLFSLAND
06 Registrar .... Mrs. Cheryl FISK
37 Director of Financial Aid .... Vacant
35 Dir Leadership Dev/Student Activit .... Mrs. Brittany PETERSON
18 Director of Facilities Services .... Mr. Rick LARSON
40 Director of Bookstore Services .... Mr. Leroy JAURIGUI
50 Director/Adult & Graduate Studies .... Mr. Matt NEWBY
44 Director of Development .... Mrs. Karen ROSE
42 Chaplain .... Mr. Bill KUHN
84 Director Undergraduate Enrollment .... Mr. Greg WYMER
15 Director of Human Resources .... Mrs. Amy LUESSE
36 Dir Career Svcs/Academic Advising .... Mr. Donald TALBERT
13 Director of Technology Services .... Mr. Jeff AUNE
26 Interim Director of Marketing .... Mr. Mike PRICE
29 Director Alumni Relations .... Mr. Michael WOOD

DeVry University - Edina (F)

7700 France Avenue South, Suite 575,
Edina MN 55435-5876
County: Hennepin Identification: 666558
Unit ID: 445407
Telephone: (952) 838-1860 Carnegie Class: Spec/Bus
FAX Number: (952) 838-3737 Calendar System: Semester
URL: www.devry.edu
Established: 1931 Annual Undergrad Tuition & Fees: $15,294
Enrollment: 297 Coed
Affiliation or Control: Proprietary IRS Status: Proprietary
Highest Offering: Master's
Program: Liberal Arts And General; Professional; Business Emphasis
Accreditation: &NH

01 Campus Director .... Gina QUINN

† Regional accreditation is carried under the parent institution in Downers Grove, IL.

DeVry University - St. Louis Park (G)

400 Highway 169 S, Suite 100,
Saint Louis Park MN 55426-1105
County: Hennepin Identification: 666559
Telephone: (952) 738-3100 Carnegie Class: Not Classified
FAX Number: (952) 738-9114 Calendar System: Semester
URL: www.devry.edu
Established: 1931 Annual Undergrad Tuition & Fees: $15,294
Enrollment: 523 Coed
Affiliation or Control: Proprietary IRS Status: Proprietary
Highest Offering: Master's
Program: Teacher Preparatory; Business Emphasis
Accreditation: &NH

01 Center Dean .... Cassandra TABOR

† Regional accreditation is carried under the parent institution in Downers Grove, IL.

Duluth Business University, Inc. (H)

4724 Mike Colalillo Drive, Duluth MN 55807-2723
County: Saint Louis FICE Identification: 009892
Unit ID: 173489
Telephone: (218) 722-4000 Carnegie Class: Assoc/PrivFP
FAX Number: (218) 628-2127 Calendar System: Quarter
URL: www.dbumn.edu
Established: 1891 Annual Undergrad Tuition & Fees: $11,100
Enrollment: 325 Coed
Affiliation or Control: Proprietary IRS Status: Proprietary
Highest Offering: Baccalaureate
Program: Occupational; 2-Year Principally Bachelor's Creditable; Technical Emphasis
Accreditation: ACICS, MAC

01 President .... Mr. James R. GESSNER
03 Campus Director .... Mrs. Bonnie L. KUPCZYNSKI
05 Director of Education .... Mrs. LaVonne R. TUCCI
91 Dir Info Technology/Dist Educ Oper .... Mr. David R. LUTZKA
06 Registrar .... Ms. Lisa E. NAGURSKI
08 Librarian .... Ms. Joyce C. PETERSON
36 Career Services Manager .... Mr. David E. COOK
37 Financial Aid Advisor .... Mrs. Gloria G. COOLE

Dunwoody College of Technology (I)

818 Dunwoody Boulevard, Minneapolis MN 55403-1192
County: Hennepin FICE Identification: 004641
Unit ID: 175227
Telephone: (612) 374-5800 Carnegie Class: Assoc/PrivNFP4
FAX Number: (612) 381-9620 Calendar System: Quarter
URL: www.dunwoody.edu
Established: 1914 Annual Undergrad Tuition & Fees: $17,800

Enrollment: 1,409 Coed
Affiliation or Control: Independent Non-Profit IRS Status: 501(c)3
Highest Offering: Baccalaureate
Program: Occupational; Technical Emphasis
Accreditation: NH, RAD

01 President .... Mr. Rich WAGNER
32 Dean/Chief Student Affairs Officer .... Mr. Jeff YLINEN
05 Dean/Chief Academic Affairs Officer .... Ms. Ann IVERSON
10 Chief Financial Officer .... Ms. Nancy J. FUCHS
30 VP Development/Alumni Relations .... Mr. Mark SKIPPER
15 Director of Human Resources .... Ms. Patricia EDMAN

Globe University (A)

8089 Globe Drive, Woodbury MN 55125-3388
County: Washington FICE Identification: 004642
Unit ID: 173629
Telephone: (651) 730-5100 Carnegie Class: Bac/Assoc
FAX Number: (651) 730-5151 Calendar System: Quarter
URL: www.globeuniversity.edu
Established: 1885 Annual Undergrad Tuition & Fees: $20,575
Enrollment: 1,032 Coed
Affiliation or Control: Proprietary IRS Status: Proprietary
Highest Offering: Master's
Program: Occupational
Accreditation: ACICS, MAAB, MAC

01 Campus Director .... Ms. Lisa PALERMO
05 Dean of Faculty .... Ms. Denise RADCLIFFE
32 Dean of Students .... Mr. Brian RAICHE
37 Director of Financial Aid .... Mr. Ben FLIKEID
07 Director of Admissions .... Ms. Jessica MCCABE
36 Director of Career Services .... Ms. Teresa DYE

Gustavus Adolphus College (B)

800 W College Avenue, Saint Peter MN 56082-1498
County: Nicollet FICE Identification: 002353
Unit ID: 173647
Telephone: (507) 933-8000 Carnegie Class: Bac/A&S
FAX Number: (507) 933-7041 Calendar System: Semester
URL: www.gustavus.edu
Established: 1862 Annual Undergrad Tuition & Fees: $35,100
Enrollment: 2,424 Coed
Affiliation or Control: Evangelical Lutheran Church In America
IRS Status: 501(c)3
Highest Offering: Baccalaureate
Program: Liberal Arts And General; Teacher Preparatory
Accreditation: NH, MUS, NURSE, TED

01 President .... Mr. Jack R. OHLE
05 Provost and Dean of the College .... Dr. Mark BRAUN
10 VP for Finance and Treasurer .... Mr. Kenneth C. WESTPHAL
07 VP for Enrollment Management .... Mr. Tom CRADY
30 VP for Institutional Advancement .... Mr. Tom YOUNG
32 VP for Student Life .... Ms. JoNes VANHECKE
26 VP Marketing & Communication .... Vacant
28 Dir Multicultural/Asst Dean of Stdn .... Mr. Virgil E. JONES
09 Director Institutional Research .... Dr. David A. MENK
08 Head Librarian .... Ms. Barbara FISTER
88 Director Church Relations .... Rev. Grady I. ST. DENNIS
29 Director Alumni Relations .... Mr. Randall M. STUCKEY
36 Director Career Center .... Ms. Cynthia L. FAVRE
06 Registrar .... Ms. Kristianne WESTPHAL
13 Dir Gustavus Technology Services .... Mr. Bruce N. AARSVOLD
18 Director Physical Plant .... Mr. Warren P. WUNDERLICH
37 Director Student Financial Aid .... Mr. Doug MINTER
39 Director Residential Life .... Vacant
42 Chaplain .... Vacant
42 Chaplain .... Rev. Rachel S. LARSON
35 Associate Dean of Students .... Mr. Steve BENNETT
41 Athletic Director .... Dr. Alan I. MOLDE
15 Director Human Resources .... Dr. Kirk D. BEYER
19 Director Campus Security .... Mr. Raymond H. THROWER
40 Manager Bookstore .... Ms. Molly YONKERS
27 Media Relations Manager .... Mr. Matthew D. THOMAS
04 Asst to the Pres & Sec to the Board .... Ms. Jolene D. CHRISTENSEN

Hamline University (C)

1536 Hewitt Avenue, Saint Paul MN 55104-1284
County: Ramsey FICE Identification: 002354
Unit ID: 173665
Telephone: (651) 523-2800 Carnegie Class: Master's L
FAX Number: (651) 523-2899 Calendar System: 4/1/4
URL: www.hamline.edu
Established: 1854 Annual Undergrad Tuition & Fees: $31,652
Enrollment: 5,003 Coed
Affiliation or Control: United Methodist IRS Status: 501(c)3
Highest Offering: Doctorate
Program: Liberal Arts And General; Teacher Preparatory; Professional
Accreditation: NH, LAW, MUS, TED

01 President .... Dr. Linda N. HANSON
05 VP Academic & Student Affairs .... Dr. David STERN
10 Vice President Finance .... Mr. Douglas P. ANDERSON
84 VP Enrollment & Marketing .... Dr. John PYLE
30 VP Development & Alumni Relations .. Mr. Tony GRUNDHAUSER
32 Dean of Students .... Dr. Alan A. SICKBERT
43 VP HR/General Counsel .... Ms. Catherine WASSBERG
13 Assoc VP/Dir IT .... Mr. Mark KONDRAK
26 Assoc VP Marketing Communications .... Ms. Breanne HANSON HEGG
84 Assoc VP of Enrollment Services .... Ms. Pamela JOHNSON
28 Assoc VP/Dir Diversity Integration .... Dr. Poonam ARORA
18 Assoc VP Facilities/Physical Plant .... Mr. Lowell BROMANDER
61 Dean School of Law .... Mr. Donald M. LEWIS
50 Dean School of Business .... Ms. Anne MCCARTHY
53 Dean School of Education .... Vacant
49 Dean College Liberal Arts .... Dr. John MATACHEK
28 Ast Dn/Dir Multicult/Intl Stdt Affs .... Mr. Carlos SNEED
06 Registrar Undergrad/Grad Schools .... Mr. Tim TRAFFIE
29 Exec Director Assoc of Hamline Alum .... Ms. Elizabeth L. RADTKE
37 Director Financial Aid .... Ms. Lynette WAHL
06 Registrar Law School .... Ms. Colleen CLISH
07 Director Law School Admissions .... Ms. Robin C. INGLI
07 Director of Admissions .... Mr. Milyon TRULOVE
15 Director Human Resources .... Ms. Dorcas M. MICHAELSON
36 Interim Dir Career Development .... Mr. Terry MIDDENDORF
41 Athletic Director .... Mr. Robert BEEMAN
19 Director of Safety & Security .... Ms. Shirleen A. HOFFMAN
23 Director Counseling & Health Center .... Ms. Barbara BESTER
35 Dir Student Leadership & Activities .... Ms. Wendy BURNS
42 Chaplain & Director .... Ms. Nancy M. VICTORIN-VANGERUD
96 Director of Purchasing .... Ms. Susan BORNUS
04 Exec Assistant to the President .... Ms. Jane A. TELLEEN

Hazelden Graduate School of Addiction Studies (D)

PO Box 11 (CO9), Center City MN 55012-0011
County: Chisago FICE Identification: 040443
Unit ID: 173683
Telephone: (651) 213-4175 Carnegie Class: Spec/Health
FAX Number: (651) 213-4411 Calendar System: Semester
URL: www.hazelden.edu
Established: 1999 Annual Graduate Tuition & Fees: $28,014
Enrollment: 107 Coed
Affiliation or Control: Independent Non-Profit IRS Status: 501(c)3
Highest Offering: Master's; No Undergraduates
Program: Professional
Accreditation: NH

01 President and CEO .... Mr. Mark MISHEK
05 Chief Academic Officer & Provost .... Dr. Valerie SLAYMAKER
88 Asst to the Chief Academic Officer .... Ms. Heidi SOLOMONSON
20 Dean .... Dr. Dan FRIGO
07 Admissions Specialist .... Ms. Nancy KAMINSKI
06 Registrar .... Ms. Debra MATTISON
09 Dir of Institutional Effectiveness .... Dr. Timothy SHEEHAN
06 Registrar of Administrative Service .... Ms. Twyla RAMSDELL

Herzing University (E)

5700 West Broadway, Minneapolis MN 55428
County: Hennepin FICE Identification: 011017
Unit ID: 174154
Telephone: (763) 535-3000 Carnegie Class: Spec/Health
FAX Number: (763) 535-9205 Calendar System: Semester
URL: www.herzing.edu
Established: 1961 Annual Undergrad Tuition & Fees: $10,909
Enrollment: 373 Coed
Affiliation or Control: Proprietary IRS Status: Proprietary
Highest Offering: Baccalaureate
Program: Professional
Accreditation: &NH, DA, DH, MAC

01 Chief Executive Officer .... Mr. John SLAMA
07 Director of Admissions .... Ms. Shelly LARSON
10 Director Financial Services .... Mr. Larry DOTY
37 Director Student Financial Aid .... Mr. Larry DOTY

† Regional accreditation is carried under the parent institution in Madison, WI.

Institute of Production and Recording (F)

312 Washington Avenue North, Minneapolis MN 55401
County: Hennepin FICE Identification: 041302
Unit ID: 454616
Telephone: (612) 375-1900 Carnegie Class: Not Classified
FAX Number: (612) 375-1919 Calendar System: Other
URL: www.ipr.edu
Established: 2002 Annual Undergrad Tuition & Fees: $19,500
Enrollment: 385 Coed
Affiliation or Control: Proprietary IRS Status: Proprietary
Highest Offering: Associate Degree
Program: Occupational
Accreditation: ACCSC

01 Campus Director .... Brian JACOBY
03 Vice President .... Lance SABIN
05 Dean of Faculty .... Madeline HENGEL
07 Director of Admissions .... Suzanne FERKINGSTAD
32 Director of Student Services .... Erica WEST
08 Librarian .... Tina HALFMANN

ITT Technical Institute (G)

8911 Columbine Road, Eden Prairie MN 55347-4143
County: Hennepin Identification: 666319
Unit ID: 445081
Telephone: (952) 914-5300 Carnegie Class: Spec/Tech
FAX Number: (952) 914-5350 Calendar System: Quarter
URL: www.itt-tech.edu
Established: 2004 Annual Undergrad Tuition & Fees: N/A
Enrollment: 704 Coed
Affiliation or Control: Proprietary IRS Status: Proprietary
Highest Offering: Baccalaureate
Program: Technical Emphasis
Accreditation: ACICS

† Branch campus of ITT Technical Institute, Greenfield, WI.

Le Cordon Bleu College of Culinary Arts in Minneapolis/St Paul (H)

1315 Mendota Heights Road,
Mendota Heights MN 55120-1129
County: Dakota Identification: 666370
Unit ID: 446844
Telephone: (651) 675-4700 Carnegie Class: Assoc/PrivFP
FAX Number: (651) 452-5282 Calendar System: Quarter
URL: www.chefs.edu/minneapolis-st-paul
Established: 1999 Annual Undergrad Tuition & Fees: $17,550
Enrollment: 800 Coed
Affiliation or Control: Proprietary IRS Status: Proprietary
Highest Offering: Associate Degree
Program: Occupational; Technical Emphasis
Accreditation: ACICS, ACFEI

01 President .... Mr. Kevin L. SANDERSON
10 Business Operations Manager .... Ms. Pamela TRANDAHL
05 Executive Chef .... Mr. Steven SHAPLEY
07 Senior Director of Admissions .... Mr. David PETERSON
36 Director of Career Services .... Ms. Kianna RAMOS
22 Director of Compliance .... Ms. Barbara BUBNIKOVICH
88 Lead Instructor Patisserie-Baking .... Ms. Amy SHIPSHOCK
88 Lead Instructor Culinary Arts .... Ms. Farley KAISER
06 Associate Registrar .... Ms. Cindy THOMPSON

† Branch campus of Le Cordon Bleu College of Culinary Arts, Portland, OR.

Leech Lake Tribal College (I)

P.O. Box 180, Cass Lake MN 56633-0180
County: Cass FICE Identification: 030964
Unit ID: 413626
Telephone: (218) 335-4200 Carnegie Class: Tribal
FAX Number: (218) 335-4282 Calendar System: Semester
URL: www.lltc.edu
Established: 1990 Annual Undergrad Tuition & Fees: $4,432
Enrollment: 259 Coed
Affiliation or Control: Tribal Control IRS Status: 501(c)3
Highest Offering: Associate Degree
Program: Occupational, 2-Year Principally Bachelor's Creditable
Accreditation: NH

01 President .... Dr. Ginny CARNEY
03 Vice President .... Dr. Beverly RODGERS
05 Dean of Academics .... Dr. Sharon MARCOTTE
10 Chief Financial Officer .... Rochelle PEMBERTON
30 Director Institutional Advancement .... Kyle ERICKSON

Luther Seminary (J)

2481 Como Avenue, Saint Paul MN 55108-1496
County: Ramsey FICE Identification: 002357
Unit ID: 173896
Telephone: (651) 641-3456 Carnegie Class: Spec/Faith
FAX Number: (651) 641-3425 Calendar System: Semester
URL: www.luthersem.edu
Established: 1869 Annual Graduate Tuition & Fees: $14,000
Enrollment: 796 Coed
Affiliation or Control: Evangelical Lutheran Church In America
IRS Status: 501(c)3
Highest Offering: Doctorate; No Undergraduates
Program: Professional; Religious Emphasis
Accreditation: NH, THEOL

01 President .... Dr. Richard BLIESE
05 Dean of Academic Affairs .... Dr. Roland MARTINSON
11 VP Admininstration & Finance .... Mr. Donald LEWIS
26 VP Seminary Relations .... Mr. Thomas JOLIVETTE
32 VP Student Affairs & Enrollment .... Ms. Carrie CARROLL
15 VP Human Resources .... Ms. Sandra MIDDENDORF
42 Seminary Pastor .... Rev. Paul HARRINGTON
07 Director of Admissions .... Vacant
06 Registrar .... Ms. Diane DONCITS

Lutheran Brethren Seminary (K)

815 West Vernon Avenue, Fergus Falls MN 56537-2676
County: Otter Tail Identification: 666644
Telephone: (218) 739-3375 Carnegie Class: Not Classified
FAX Number: (218) 739-1259 Calendar System: Semester

URL: www.lbs.edu
Established: 1903 Annual Undergrad Tuition & Fees: $10,206
Enrollment: 19 Coed
Affiliation or Control: Other IRS Status: 501(c)3
Highest Offering: Master's
Program: Liberal Arts And General; Religious Emphasis
Accreditation: @TRACS

01 President .... Dr. David VEUM
05 Dean .... Dr. Eugene BOE
06 Registrar .... Dr. Gaylan MATHIESEN

Macalester College (A)

1600 Grand Avenue, Saint Paul MN 55105-1801
County: Ramsey FICE Identification: 002358
Unit ID: 173902
Telephone: (651) 696-6000 Carnegie Class: Bac/A&S
FAX Number: (651) 696-6689 Calendar System: Semester
URL: www.macalester.edu
Established: 1874 Annual Undergrad Tuition & Fees: $42,021
Enrollment: 2,033 Coed
Affiliation or Control: Presbyterian Church (U.S.A.) IRS Status: 501(c)3
Highest Offering: Baccalaureate
Program: Liberal Arts And General
Accreditation: NH

01 President .... Dr. Brian C. ROSENBERG
05 Dean of the Faculty & Provost .... Dr. Kathleen M. MURRAY
88 Chief Investment Officer .... Mr. Mansco PERRY
30 Vice President College Advancement .... Mr. Thomas P. BONNER
32 Vice President Student Affairs .... Ms. Laurie B. HAMRE
11 Vice President for Admin/Finance .... Mr. David M. WHEATON
08 Associate Vice President ITS .... Mr. Jerry R. SANDERS
07 Dean of Admissions/Financial Aid .... Mr. Lorne T. ROBINSON
85 Inst for Global Citizenship .... Dr. Ahmed I. SAMATAR
20 Director of Academic Programs .... Ms. Ann M. MINNICK
28 Dean of Multicultural Life .... Mr. Tommy L. WOON
09 Assoc Provost/Inst Research .... Mr. Daniel J. BALIK
35 Dean of Students .... Mr. Jim HOPPE
37 Director Student Financial Aid .... Mr. Brian LINDEMAN
06 Registrar .... Ms. Jayne L. NIEMI
36 Assoc Dean for Student Services .... Ms. Denise WARD
15 Director Human Resources .... Mr. Chuck STANDFUSS
18 Director Facilities Management .... Mr. Mark D. DICKINSON
41 Athletic Director .... Ms. Kim CHANDLER
04 Assistant to the President .... Ms. Cynthia L. HENDRICKS
21 Assistant Vice President Finance .... Ms. Kate WALKER
26 Interim Director College Relations .... Mr. David P. WARCH
29 Director Alumni Relations .... Ms. Gabrielle S. LAWRENCE
38 Director Health and Wellness Center .... Ms. Denise WARD
96 Dir Purchasing/Accounts Payable .... Ms. Kathleen L. JOHNSON

Martin Luther College (B)

1995 Luther Court, New Ulm MN 56073-3300
County: Brown FICE Identification: 002361
Unit ID: 173452
Telephone: (507) 354-8221 Carnegie Class: Bac/Diverse
FAX Number: (507) 354-8225 Calendar System: Semester
URL: www.mlc-wels.edu
Established: 1995 Annual Undergrad Tuition & Fees: $11,320
Enrollment: 724 Coed
Affiliation or Control: Wisconsin Evangelical Lutheran Synod
IRS Status: 501(c)3
Highest Offering: Master's
Program: Liberal Arts And General; Teacher Preparatory
Accreditation: NH

01 President .... Rev. Mark G. ZARLING
05 Vice President for Academics .... Dr. David O. WENDLER
11 Vice President for Administration .... Prof. Steven R. THIESFELDT
84 Vice President for Enrollment Mgmt .... Vacant
32 Vice President Student Life .... Prof. Jeffrey L. SCHONE
53 Academic Dean Educational Ministry .... Prof. Kurt A. WITTMERSHAUS
73 Academic Dean Pastoral Ministry .... Prof. Daniel N. BALGE
10 Director of Finance .... Mrs. Carla J. HULKE
08 Librarian .... Prof. David M. GOSDECK
37 Director of Financial Aid .... Mr. Gene A. SLETTEDAHL
07 Director of Admissions .... Prof. Mark A. STEIN
51 Director of Continuing Education .... Prof. David T. BAUER
88 Director of Clinical Experiences .... Prof. Paul A. TESS
41 Director of Athletics .... Prof. James M. UNKE
42 Campus Pastor .... Rev. John C. BOEDER
14 Director of Technology .... Mr. James A. RATHJE
26 Director of Public Relations .... Prof. William A. PEKRUL
40 Bookstore Manager .... Mrs. Valerie J. BOVEE
90 Director of Academic Computing .... Dr. James R. GRUNWALD
29 Director Alumni Relations .... Mr. Stephen J. BALZA

McNally Smith College of Music (C)

19 Exchange Street, Saint Paul MN 55101-2220
County: Ramsey FICE Identification: 030012
Unit ID: 367194
Telephone: (651) 291-0177 Carnegie Class: Spec/Arts
FAX Number: (651) 291-0366 Calendar System: Semester
URL: www.mcnallysmith.edu
Established: 1985 Annual Undergrad Tuition & Fees: $24,500
Enrollment: 641 Coed
Affiliation or Control: Proprietary IRS Status: Proprietary
Highest Offering: Baccalaureate
Program: Occupational; Liberal Arts And General; Professional; Music Emphasis
Accreditation: MUS

01 President .... Harry CHALMIERS
37 Financial Aid Director .... Jeffrey R. AALBERS
07 Admissions Director .... Kathy HAWKS

Minneapolis Business College (D)

1711 W County Road B, Roseville MN 55113-4056
County: Ramsey FICE Identification: 004645
Unit ID: 174118
Telephone: (651) 636-7406 Carnegie Class: Assoc/PrivFP
FAX Number: (651) 636-8185 Calendar System: Semester
URL: www.minneapolisbusinesscollege.edu
Established: 1874 Annual Undergrad Tuition & Fees: $14,090
Enrollment: 377 Coed
Affiliation or Control: Proprietary IRS Status: Proprietary
Highest Offering: Associate Degree
Program: Occupational
Accreditation: ACICS, MAC

01 President .... Mr. David WHITMAN
05 Director of Education .... Mr. Jon BLUMENTHAL
32 Director of Student Services .... Mrs. Marie MARTIN
36 Placement Coordinator .... Mrs. Suzanne ERICKSON

Minneapolis College of Art Design (E)

2501 Stevens Avenue, Minneapolis MN 55404-4343
County: Hennepin FICE Identification: 002365
Unit ID: 174127
Telephone: (612) 874-3700 Carnegie Class: Spec/Arts
FAX Number: (612) 874-3704 Calendar System: Semester
URL: www.mcad.edu
Established: 1886 Annual Undergrad Tuition & Fees: $30,386
Enrollment: 727 Coed
Affiliation or Control: Independent Non-Profit IRS Status: 501(c)3
Highest Offering: Master's
Program: Liberal Arts And General; Professional; Fine Arts Emphasis
Accreditation: NH, ART

01 President .... Mr. Jay COOGAN
04 Executive Assistant to President .... Ms. Kate MOHN
05 Vice President Academic Affairs .... Mr. Vince LEO
30 Vice Pres Institutional Advancement .... Ms. Joan G. OLSON
11 Vice President Administration .... Ms. Pam NEWSOME
32 Vice President Student Affairs .... Ms. Susan P. CALMENSON
84 Vice Pres Enrollment Management .... Mr. William MULLEN
20 Assoc Vice Pres Academic Affairs .... Ms. Karen RUSKIN
18 Assoc VP Facilities/Public Safety .... Mr. Brock RASMUSSEN
13 Assoc Vice President Technology .... Mr. R. Hal WELLS
10 Chief Financial Officer/Treasurer .... Mr. Dan SJOQUIST
06 Registrar .... Ms. Jacki L. CHESTNUT
51 Director of Continuing Studies .... Ms. Lara ROY
08 Library Director .... Ms. Suzanne C. DEGLER
24 Director of Media Center .... Mr. Scott BOWMAN
36 Director of Career Services .... Ms. Christine DAVES
29 Director Major and Alumni Giving .... Mr. Brian GIOIELLI
39 Director Student Housing .... Mr. Nate K. LUTZ
26 Director Communications .... Mr. Rob DAVIS
37 Director Student Financial Aid .... Ms. Laura LINK
40 Manager of Bookstore .... Ms. Allyson R. HARPER

Minnesota School of Business (F)

5910 Shingle Creek Parkway, #200,
Brooklyn Center MN 55430-2319
County: Hennepin Identification: 666453
Unit ID: 407285
Telephone: (763) 566-7777 Carnegie Class: Bac/Assoc
FAX Number: (763) 566-7030 Calendar System: Quarter
URL: www.msbcollege.edu
Established: 1877 Annual Undergrad Tuition & Fees: $15,660
Enrollment: 620 Coed
Affiliation or Control: Proprietary IRS Status: Proprietary
Highest Offering: Baccalaureate
Program: Occupational
Accreditation: ACICS, MAAB, MAC

01 Director .... Ms. Jana GYMER-KOCH

† Branch campus of Minnesota School of Business, Richfield, MN.

Minnesota School of Business (G)

1401 W 76th Street, Suite 500, Richfield MN 55423-3846
County: Hennepin FICE Identification: 004646
Unit ID: 174279
Telephone: (612) 861-2000 Carnegie Class: Master's S
FAX Number: (612) 861-5548 Calendar System: Quarter
URL: www.msbcollege.edu
Established: 1877 Annual Undergrad Tuition & Fees: $15,390
Enrollment: 1,850 Coed
Affiliation or Control: Proprietary IRS Status: Proprietary
Highest Offering: Master's
Program: Occupational
Accreditation: ACICS, MAAB, MAC, NURSE

01 Campus Director .... Mr. Robert M. HENDRICKSON
05 Dean of Faculty .... Ms. Tamara MATTISON
32 Dean of Students .... Ms. Tabitha HORNE
07 Director of Admissions .... Mr. Chad PETERSON
36 Director of Career Services .... Ms. Sara SHORE
37 Director of Financial Aid .... Ms. Nicole PAULSON

*Minnesota State Colleges and Universities System Office (H)

WellsFargo Pl, Ste 350, 30 7th St,E,
Saint Paul MN 55101-4901
County: Ramsey FICE Identification: 009346
Unit ID: 428453
Telephone: (651) 201-1800 Carnegie Class: N/A
FAX Number: (651) 297-5550
URL: www.mnscu.edu

01 Chancellor .... Steven J. ROSENSTONE
05 Int Vice Chanc Academic/Stdnt Affs .... Vacant
09 System Director for Research .... Craig V. SCHOENECKER
10 Vice Chancellor Finance/CFO .... Laura M. KING
16 Vice Chancellor Human Resources .... Loretta M. LAMB
13 Vice Chanc/Chief Information Ofcr .... Darrel S. HUISH
18 Assoc Vice Chancellor Facilities .... Brian D. YOLITZ
26 Assoc Vice Chanc Public Affairs .... Linda Y. KOHL
46 Assoc Vice Chanc Research/Planning .... Leslie K. MERCER
35 Assoc Vice Chanc Student Affairs .... Mike LOPEZ
22 Exec Dir Diversity/Multiculturalism .... Whitney Stewart HARRIS
102 Exec Dir System/Foundation Rels .... Maria R. MCLEMORE
43 General Counsel .... Gail M. OLSON
86 Director Governmental Relations .... Mary E. DAVENPORT
21 Director of Internal Auditing .... Beth H. BUSE

*Alexandria Technical & Community College (I)

1601 Jefferson Street, Alexandria MN 56308-2796
County: Douglas FICE Identification: 005544
Unit ID: 172918
Telephone: (320) 762-0221 Carnegie Class: Assoc/Pub-R-M
FAX Number: (320) 762-4501 Calendar System: Semester
URL: www.alextech.edu
Established: 1961 Annual Undergrad Tuition & Fees (In-State): $5,882
Enrollment: 2,347 Coed
Affiliation or Control: State IRS Status: 501(c)3
Highest Offering: Associate Degree
Program: Occupational; 2-Year Principally Bachelor's Creditable; Technical Emphasis
Accreditation: NH, MLTAD

02 President .... Dr. Kevin KOPISCHKE
05 Exec VP Academic/Student Affairs .... Dr. Jan DOEBBERT
41 Vice Pres/Athletic Director .... Vacant
51 Vice Pres Custom Services .... Dr. Chad COAUETTE
10 Chief Financial Officer .... Mr. David BJELLAND
05 Dean of Academic Affairs .... Mr. Gregg RAISANEN
32 Dean of Student Affairs .... Vacant
72 Dean of Technology .... Mr. Steve RICHARDS
20 Associate Dean of Academic Affairs .... Ms. Kellie TATGE
19 Associate Dean of Law Enforcement .... Mr. Scott BERGER
37 Financial Aid Director .... Mr. Steve RICHARDS
22 Human Rights Officer .... Ms. Tamzin BUKOWSKI
36 Director of Employment Services .... Ms. Stephanie ANDERSON
30 Exec Dir Advancement/Foundation .... Ms. Kathy NOHRE
06 Registrar .... Ms. Debra LE DOUX
18 Director of Facilities .... Mr. Tim TOUGAS
15 Chief Human Resources Officer .... Ms. Shari MALONEY
27 Director Institutional Marketing .... Ms. Kathy JOSEPHSON
28 Director of Diversity .... Vacant
35 Director of Student Activities .... Ms. Michelle AHLQUIST
38 Dir Testing Center/PSEO Specialist .... Ms. Mary LENZ
04 Asst to Pres/Dir of Office Services .... Ms. Annette PAVEK
21 Accounting Supervisor .... Ms. Joan STICH
40 Bookstore Manager .... Ms. Karen SLACK
29 Alumni Coordinator .... Ms. Linda DOLAN
88 Support Services Coordinator .... Ms. Mary ACKERMAN
07 Director of Admissions .... Mr. Charles (Tex) CLAYMORE

*Anoka-Ramsey Community College (J)

11200 Mississippi Boulevard NW,
Coon Rapids MN 55433-3499
County: Anoka FICE Identification: 002332
Unit ID: 172963
Telephone: (763) 433-1100 Carnegie Class: Assoc/Pub-S-MC
FAX Number: (763) 433-1121 Calendar System: Semester
URL: www.anokaramsey.edu
Established: 1965 Annual Undergrad Tuition & Fees (In-State): $4,773
Enrollment: 9,419 Coed
Affiliation or Control: State IRS Status: 501(c)3
Highest Offering: Associate Degree
Program: Occupational; 2-Year Principally Bachelor's Creditable
Accreditation: NH, ADNUR, PTAA

02 Interim President .... Dr. Jessica STUMPF
10 VP Finance & Administration .... Mr. Michael SEYMOUR
05 VP Academic/Student Affairs .... Ms. Deidra PEASLEE
32 Dean/Chief Student Affairs Officer .... Dr. Mary RAEKER-REBEK
18 Physical Plant Manager .... Mr. Roger FREEMAN

16 Chief HR Director ... Mr. Darren HOFF
57 Dean of Arts & Letters ... Ms. Dana IRGENS
88 Dean CE/CT/Bus/Tech/Wellness ... Ms. Luanne KANE
35 Interim Dean Student Life ... Ms. Lisa HARRIS
76 Dean of Allied Health ... Vacant
21 Director Fiscal & Auxiliary Svcs ... Vacant
46 Dean of Innovative Teaching ... Ms. Kim LYNCH
09 Dean of Research & Assessment ... Ms. Nora MORRIS
28 Director of Multicultural Affairs ... Mr. Marcellus DAVIS
102 Director of Foundations ... Mr. Marc JOHNSON
26 Director of Mktg/Public Relations ... Ms. Mary JACOBSON
19 Director of Safety & Security ... Mr. Orrin NYHUS
35 Director of Student Life ... Ms. Joyce TRACZYK
13 Interim Director of Technology ... Mr. Tim ZONDLO
21 Business Manager ... Ms. Kim BIENFANG

*Anoka Technical College (A)

1355 W Highway 10, Anoka MN 55303-1590

County: Anoka | FICE Identification: 007350 | Unit ID: 172954
Telephone: (763) 576-4700 | Carnegie Class: Assoc/Pub-S-MC
FAX Number: (763) 576-4715 | Calendar System: Semester
URL: www.anokatech.edu
Established: 1967 | Annual Undergrad Tuition & Fees (In-District): $5,426
Enrollment: 2,580 | Coed
Affiliation or Control: State/Local | IRS Status: 501(c)3
Highest Offering: Associate Degree
Program: Occupational; 2-Year Principally Bachelor's Creditable
Accreditation: NH, MAC, OTA, SURGT

02 Interim President ... Shari L. OLSON
05 Int Vice Pres of Acad/Student Affs ... Chad COAUETTE
13 Chief Information/Facilities Ofcr ... David JEFFREY
10 Chief Business Ofcr/Facil/Phys Plnt ... Wendy MEYER
04 Assistant to the President ... Carol LARSON
15 Chief Human Res Ofcr/Dir Diversity ... Marybeth CHRISTENSON-JONES
26 Director of Marketing/Diversity ... Bobbie DAHLKE
06 Registrar ... Kimberly ROAN
07 Director of Admissions ... Vacant
37 Financial Aid Director ... Lucy ROSS

*Bemidji State University (B)

1500 Birchmont Drive, NE, Bemidji MN 56601-2699

County: Beltrami | FICE Identification: 002336 | Unit ID: 173124
Telephone: (218) 755-2001 | Carnegie Class: Master's S
FAX Number: (218) 755-2749 | Calendar System: Semester
URL: www.bemidjistate.edu
Established: 1919 | Annual Undergrad Tuition & Fees (In-State): $7,856
Enrollment: 5,365 | Coed
Affiliation or Control: State | IRS Status: 501(c)3
Highest Offering: Master's
Program: Liberal Arts And General; Teacher Preparatory
Accreditation: NH, IACBE, MUS, NAIT, NURSE, SW

02 President ... Dr. Richard A. HANSON
05 Interim VP for Academic Affairs ... Mr. Robert J. GRIGGS
10 VP for Finance & Administration ... Mr. William D. MAKI
84 VP for Development & Enrollment ... Dr. Lisa A. ERWIN
20 Assoc VP for Extended Lrng/Library ... Vacant
50 Dean Col Business/Tech/Commun ... Dr. James R. MAXWELL
49 Dean of Arts & Sciences ... Dr. P. J. POOR
76 Dean Col Health Sci/Human Ecology ... Dr. Patricia L. ROGERS
20 Int Assoc VP for Academic Affairs ... Dr. Patrick G. GUILFOILE
07 Int Director of Admissions ... Ms. MaryJo CHIRPICH
06 Registrar ... Ms. Michelle FRENZEL
37 Director Financial Aid ... Mr. Paul G. LINDSETH
09 Director Inst Rsrch/Effectiveness ... Dr. Douglas P. OLNEY
26 Chief Public Relations Officer ... Dr. Rose L. JONES
36 Director of Career Services ... Ms. Margie T. GIAUQUE
29 Director Alumni Relations ... Ms. Marla H. PATRIAS
92 Director Honors Program ... Dr. Marsha DRISCOLL
88 Dir American Indian Resource Ctr ... Dr. Donald R. DAY
94 Director Women's Studies ... Dr. Colleen R. GREER
96 Director of Logistical Services ... Ms. Belinda S. LINDELL
15 Dir Human Resources/Affirm Action ... Ms. Linda J. GILSRUD
21 Business Manager ... Vacant
18 Physical Plant Director ... Mr. Jeff A. SANDE
19 Director of Security/Safety ... Mr. Casey J. MCCARTHY
41 Athletic Director ... Dr. Rick A. GOEB
39 Director of Residential Life ... Mr. R. D. LADIG
30 Exec Dir for University Advancement ... Mr. Robert D. BOLLINGER
27 Chief Information Officer ... Mr. Mitch D. DAVIDSON

*Central Lakes College (C)

501 W College Drive, Brainerd MN 56401-3900

County: Crow Wing | FICE Identification: 002339 | Unit ID: 173203
Telephone: (218) 855-8000 | Carnegie Class: Assoc/Pub-R-M
FAX Number: (218) 855-8057 | Calendar System: Semester
URL: www.clcmn.edu
Established: 1938 | Annual Undergrad Tuition & Fees (In-State): $5,712
Enrollment: 5,092 | Coed
Affiliation or Control: State | IRS Status: 501(c)3
Highest Offering: Associate Degree
Program: Occupational; 2-Year Principally Bachelor's Creditable
Accreditation: NH, DA

02 President ... Dr. Larry A. LUNDBLAD
05 Vice Pres Academic & Student Affs ... Dr. Suresh TIWARI
11 VP Administrative Svcs/Facilities ... Ms. Kari CHRISTIANSEN
103 Dean Workforce/Econ & Regional Dev ... Ms. Rebecca BEST
84 Dean of Enrollment/Student Services ... Ms. Beth ADAMS
12 Dean Technical Pgms/Staples Campus ... Mr. Jeff WIG
32 Dean of Students ... Ms. Judy RICHER
13 Dean of Academic/Technology Svcs ... Mr. Michael AMICK
49 Dean of Liberal Arts ... Mr. Kelly MCCALLA
30 Dir Resource Development/CLC Fndtn ... Ms. Pamela THOMSEN
15 Director of Human Resources ... Ms. Nancy PAULSON
07 Director Admissions ... Ms. Charlotte DANIELS
06 Registrar ... Mr. Nick HEISSERER
08 Librarian ... Mr. Larry KELLERMAN
37 Director Financial Aid ... Mr. Mike BARNABY
27 Public Information Officer ... Mr. Steve WALLER
21 Director of Business Services ... Ms. Christina VOPATEK
18 Physical Plant Director ... Mr. Rick OTTESON
28 Director of Diversity ... Ms. Mary SAM

*Century College (D)

3300 Century Avenue N, White Bear Lake MN 55110-1894

County: Ramsey | FICE Identification: 010546 | Unit ID: 175315
Telephone: (651) 779-3200 | Carnegie Class: Assoc/Pub-S-SC
FAX Number: (651) 779-3417 | Calendar System: Semester
URL: www.century.edu
Established: 1967 | Annual Undergrad Tuition & Fees (In-State): $502,3.8
Enrollment: 10,775 | Coed
Affiliation or Control: State | IRS Status: 501(c)3
Highest Offering: Associate Degree
Program: Occupational; 2-Year Principally Bachelor's Creditable
Accreditation: NH, ADNUR, DA, DH, EMT, MAC, OPE, RAD

02 President ... Dr. Ron ANDERSON
05 VP Academic Affs/Finance/Admin ... Vacant
32 VP Student Services/Facilities ... Dr. Michael BRUNER
51 VP Continuing Educ/Customized Train ... Ms. Jeralyn JARGO
10 VP Finance & Administration ... Dr. Patrick OPATZ
96 Purchasing & Auxiliary Svcs Suprvr ... Mr. Todd OSEBY
21 Director of Finance ... Ms. Bonnie MEYERS
13 Assoc VP Information Tech/Admn Svcs ... Mr. John ROHLEDER
102 Executive Director Foundation ... Mr. Nick MARAS
06 Registrar ... Ms. Susan DICKENS
15 Director of Human Resources ... Ms. Betty MAYER
07 Director of Admissions ... Ms. Christine PAULOS
45 Director of Resource Development ... Mr. Donald LONG
37 Director of Financial Aid ... Ms. Pam ENGEBRETSON
18 Mgr of Facilities Svcs/Super of Bld ... Mr. Ron FIELDS
28 Director of Diversity ... Mr. Herbert KING
26 Dir Cmty Rels/College Advanc/Alumni ... Ms. Nancy LIVINGSTON
66 Dean Nursing/Allied Health ... Ms. Kathleen BELL
75 Dean Trades/Public Safety/Svcs ... Dr. James GROSS
72 Dean Science/Technology ... Ms. Brenda LYSENG
81 Dean English/ESOL/Reading/Math ... Dr. Susan EHLERS
83 Dean Social & Behav Sci/Lang/Com ... Ms. Pakou VANG
84 Dean Students/Enrollment Mgmt ... Vacant
36 Dean Student Support Services ... Ms. Andrea RYSTROM
35 Dean of Student Life ... Ms. Kristin HAGEMAN
51 Dean Cont Educ/Customized Trng ... Ms. Jane NICHOLSON
19 Director of Public Safety ... Mr. Mark HOLPER

*Dakota County Technical College (E)

145th Street E, Rosemount MN 55068-2999

County: Dakota | FICE Identification: 010402 | Unit ID: 173416
Telephone: (651) 423-8000 | Carnegie Class: Assoc/Pub-S-SC
FAX Number: (651) 423-8775 | Calendar System: Semester
URL: www.dctc.edu
Established: 1970 | Annual Undergrad Tuition & Fees (In-District): $5,700
Enrollment: 3,668 | Coed
Affiliation or Control: State/Local | IRS Status: 501(c)3
Highest Offering: Associate Degree
Program: Occupational; 2-Year Principally Bachelor's Creditable; Technical Emphasis
Accreditation: NH, DA, MAC

02 President ... Dr. Ron THOMAS
05 VP Academic & Student Affairs ... Dr. Kelly MURTAUGH
10 Vice President Finance & Operations ... Ms. Vicki PLAISTOW
88 Dean Transportation Indust Careers ... Mr. Mike OPP
50 Dn Bus/Design/Tech/Hlth/Svc Careers ... Ms. Sherralyn COX
97 Dean of General Education ... Ms. Christine PIGSLEY
06 Registrar ... Ms. Jodie SWEARINGEN
15 Human Resources Director ... Ms. Susan RADDATZ
18 Chief Facilities/Physical Plant ... Mr. Paul DEMUTH
32 Chief Student Life Officer ... Ms. Nicole MEULEMANS
36 Director of Employment/Training ... Vacant
07 Admissions Coordinator ... Mr. Patrick LAIR
30 Director Institutional Advancement ... Ms. Erin LARSEN
37 Financial Aid Coordinator ... Mr. Scott ROELKE
09 Director of Institutional Research ... Ms. Carrie SCHNEIDER

*Fond du Lac Tribal and Community College (F)

2101 14th Street, Cloquet MN 55720-2984

County: Carlton | FICE Identification: 031291 | Unit ID: 380368
Telephone: (218) 879-0800 | Carnegie Class: Tribal
FAX Number: (218) 879-0814 | Calendar System: Semester
URL: www.fdltcc.edu
Established: 1987 | Annual Undergrad Tuition & Fees (In-State): $5,035
Enrollment: 2,362 | Coed
Affiliation or Control: State | IRS Status: 501(c)3
Highest Offering: Associate Degree
Program: Occupational; 2-Year Principally Bachelor's Creditable; Liberal Arts And General
Accreditation: NH

02 President ... Mr. Larry ANDERSON
05 Vice President of Instruction ... Dr. Anna FELLEGY
10 Director of Fiscal Operations ... Ms. Stephanie HAMMITT
27 Director of Public Information ... Mr. Tom URBANSKI
06 Registrar ... Ms. Leah LENO
88 Disability Services Student Service ... Ms. Anita HANSON
13 Information Technology Specialist ... Mr. Loran WAPPES
37 Director of Financial Aid ... Mr. David SUTHERLAND
07 Director of Admissions ... Ms. Kathie JUBIE
09 Director of Institutional Research ... Ms. Diann LOWINSKI
32 Dir of Student Support Services ... Ms. Roberta TORGERSON
62 Library Services ... Ms. Nancy BROUGHTON
30 Director of Development ... Mr. Reid HAGLIN
39 Director of Housing ... Mr. Jesse STIREWALT
15 Director of Human Resources ... Ms. Louise LIND
18 Chief Facilities/Physical Plant ... Mr. Mark BERNHARDSON
40 Bookstore Coordinator ... Ms. Bonnie BERNHARDSON
04 Executive Assistant to President ... Ms. Mary SOYRING

*Hennepin Technical College (G)

9000 Brooklyn Boulevard, Brooklyn Park MN 55445-2399

County: Hennepin | FICE Identification: 010491 | Unit ID: 173708
Telephone: (952) 995-1300 | Carnegie Class: Assoc/Pub-S-MC
FAX Number: (763) 488-2956 | Calendar System: Semester
URL: www.hennepintech.edu
Established: 1972 | Annual Undergrad Tuition & Fees (In-District): $4,530
Enrollment: 6,728 | Coed
Affiliation or Control: State/Local | IRS Status: 501(c)3
Highest Offering: Associate Degree
Program: Occupational
Accreditation: NH, ACFEI, DA, IFSAC

02 President ... Dr. Cecillia Y M. CERVANTES
05 Vice President Academic Affairs ... Ms. Lisa LARSON
11 Vice Pres Administrative Services ... Ms. Diane PAULSON
32 Vice President Student Affairs ... Mr. Mark FELSHEIM
06 Registrar ... Ms. Julie HIGDEM
15 Chief Human Resources Officer ... Ms. Sharon MOHR
30 Dir Development/Alumni Relations ... Ms. Jeanne MORPHEW
28 Director of Diversity ... Ms. Colette Campbell STUART

*Hibbing Community College, A Technical and Community College (H)

1515 E 25th Street, Hibbing MN 55746-3300

County: Saint Louis | FICE Identification: 002355 | Unit ID: 173735
Telephone: (218) 262-7200 | Carnegie Class: Assoc/Pub-R-S
FAX Number: (218) 262-6717 | Calendar System: Semester
URL: www.hibbing.edu
Established: 1916 | Annual Undergrad Tuition & Fees (In-State): $5,067
Enrollment: 1,346 | Coed
Affiliation or Control: State | IRS Status: 501(c)3
Highest Offering: Associate Degree
Program: Occupational; 2-Year Principally Bachelor's Creditable
Accreditation: NH, DA, MLTAD

02 President ... Dr. M. Sue COLLINS
03 Provost ... Dr. Ken SIMBERG
05 Dean of Acad Affairs & Student Svcs ... Mr. Mike RAICH
35 Associate Dean of Student Services ... Ms. Heidi KIPPENHAN
10 Chief Fiscal Officer ... Mr. Bill MANNEY
09 Institutional Research ... Ms. Tracey ROY
37 Director Student Financial Aid ... Mr. Paul HATCH
18 Plant Maintenance Engineer ... Vacant
26 Director of Public Information ... Ms. Susan DEGNAN

*Inver Hills Community College (I)

2500 80th Street E, Inver Grove Heights MN 55076-3224

County: Dakota | FICE Identification: 009740 | Unit ID: 173799
Telephone: (651) 450-8500 | Carnegie Class: Assoc/Pub-S-SC
FAX Number: (651) 450-8679 | Calendar System: Semester
URL: www.inverhills.edu
Established: 1970 | Annual Undergrad Tuition & Fees (In-State): $5,958
Enrollment: 6,370 | Coed
Affiliation or Control: State | IRS Status: 501(c)3
Highest Offering: Associate Degree
Program: Occupational; 2-Year Principally Bachelor's Creditable
Accreditation: NH, ACBSP, ADNUR, EMT

02 President ... Mr. Timothy WYNES
05 Prov/VP Academic Affs & Student Dev ... Dr. Joan COSTELLO
10 Vice Pres Administrative Services ... Dr. Dee BERNARD
32 Interim Dean of Student/Enroll Svcs ... Mr. Tom WILLIAMSON
81 Dean of Math/Science/Technology ... Dr. Kevin GYOLAI
79 Dean of Fine Arts and Humanities ... Dr. Douglas BINSFELD
76 Dean of Allied Health Sciences ... Dr. Doris HILL
51 Dean of Continuing Education ... Mr. David ANDERSON

37 Director of Financial Aid ... Mr. Steve YANG
83 Dean of Social Sciences & Business ... Ms. Anne JOHNSON
90 Director Acad Tech/Computing Svcs ... Mr. Mark PETERSON
15 Director of Human Resources ... Ms. Elizabeth NEWBERRY
08 Librarian ... Ms. Julie BENOLKEN
84 Director of Enrollment Services ... Mr. Matt TRAXLER
88 Dir Paralegal Pgm/Office Sys-Legal ... Ms. Sally DAHLQUIST
18 Director Facilities Plng/Management ... Mr. Pat BUHL
28 Director of Multicultural Affairs ... Mr. Tadael EMIRU
88 Interim Dir of Emerg Health Svcs ... Ms. Tia RADANT

*Itasca Community College (A)

1851 E Highway 169, Grand Rapids MN 55744-3397
County: Itasca FICE Identification: 002356
Unit ID: 173805
Telephone: (800) 996-6422 Carnegie Class: Assoc/Pub-R-S
FAX Number: (218) 322-2332 Calendar System: Semester
URL: www.itascacc.edu
Established: 1922 Annual Undergrad Tuition & Fees (In-State): $5,119
Enrollment: 1,300 Coed
Affiliation or Control: State IRS Status: 501(c)3
Highest Offering: Associate Degree
Program: 2-Year Principally Bachelor's Creditable
Accreditation: NH

02 Provost ... Dr. Michael JOHNSON
05 Academic Dean ... Dr. Barbara MCDONALD
10 Director of Finance & Facilities ... Ms. Patricia LEISTIKOW
84 Dir of Enrollment Mgmt/Admissions ... Ms. Candace PERRY
06 Registrar ... Ms. Gwen LITCHKE
29 Director of Alumni Relations ... Ms. Beth ANDERSON
30 Director of College Development ... Vacant
37 Director of Student Financial Aid ... Mr. Nathan WRIGHT
08 Head Librarian ... Mr. Steve BEAN
18 Chief Facilities/Physical Plant ... Mr. Chad HAATVEDT
40 Director of Bookstore ... Ms. Cheryl BENNETT
28 Director of Diversity ... Mr. Harold ANNETTE

*Lake Superior College (B)

2101 Trinity Road, Duluth MN 55811-3399
County: Saint Louis FICE Identification: 005757
Unit ID: 173461
Telephone: (218) 733-7600 Carnegie Class: Assoc/Pub-R-L
FAX Number: (218) 733-4921 Calendar System: Semester
URL: www.lsc.edu
Established: 1995 Annual Undergrad Tuition & Fees (In-State): $4,360
Enrollment: 4,966 Coed
Affiliation or Control: State IRS Status: 501(c)3
Highest Offering: Associate Degree
Program: Occupational; 2-Year Principally Bachelor's Creditable
Accreditation: NH, DH, MAC, MLTAD, PTAA, RAD, SURGT

02 President ... Dr. Patrick JOHNS
05 Vice President of Academic Affairs ... Mr. Mark MAGNUSON
10 Vice President of Finance & Admin ... Mr. Mark WINSON
103 Vice Pres Workforce/Cmty Develop ... Mr. Steve WAGNER
49 Dean of Liberal Arts & Sciences ... Ms. Hanna ERPESTAD
75 Dean of Industrial Programs ... Vacant
76 Dean of Allied Health & Nursing ... Ms. Pamela ELSTAD
09 Int Dir IR/Accred Assessment ... Mr. Kent RICHARDS
15 Director of Human Resources ... Ms. Mary Kay NIENABER
26 Dir of Public Affairs/Advancement ... Mr. Gary KRUCHOWSKI
06 Registrar ... Ms. Jean STOJEVICH
07 Director of Admissions ... Ms. Melissa LENO
18 Director Physical Plant ... Mr. Gary ADAMS
28 Dir Diversity & Stdnt Support Svcs ... Mr. Wade GORDON
36 Director Student Placement ... Ms. Betsy JACOBSON
37 Director Student Financial Aid ... Ms. LaNita ROBINSON
29 Director Alumni Relations ... Ms. LuAnne ANDERSON
35 Director Student Life ... Mr. Roger JOHNSON
96 Director of Purchasing ... Ms. Joyce CLOCK
21 Director Business Services ... Ms. Kathy DUGDALE
102 Foundation Director ... Mr. Paul DAMBERG

*Mesabi Range Community & Technical College (C)

1001 Chestnut Street West, Virginia MN 55792-3401
County: Saint Louis FICE Identification: 005739
Unit ID: 173993
Telephone: (218) 741-3095 Carnegie Class: Assoc/Pub-R-S
FAX Number: (218) 748-2419 Calendar System: Semester
URL: www.mesabirange.edu
Established: 1963 Annual Undergrad Tuition & Fees (In-State): $4,844
Enrollment: 1,218 Coed
Affiliation or Control: State IRS Status: Exempt
Highest Offering: Associate Degree
Program: Occupational; 2-Year Principally Bachelor's Creditable
Accreditation: NH

02 President ... Dr. Sue COLLINS
05 Provost ... Dr. Tina ROYER
32 Dean of Students ... Mr. David DAILEY
10 Chief Finance and Facilities Office ... Mr. Keith HARVEY
15 Director Human Resources ... Ms. Carmen BRADACH
37 Director Student Financial Aid ... Ms. Jodi PONTINEN
06 Registrar ... Ms. Shar ANDERSON
07 Director of Admissions ... Ms. Brenda KOCHEVAR
09 Director of Institutional Research ... Ms. Tracey ROY
26 Chief Public Relations Officer ... Ms. Brenda KOCHEVAR
38 Director Student Counseling ... Ms. Sara MATUSZAK
36 Director Student Placement ... Mr. Toby ANDERSON
84 Director Enrollment Management ... Ms. Brenda KOCHEVAR

*Metropolitan State University (D)

700 E 7th Street, Saint Paul MN 55106-5000
County: Ramsey FICE Identification: 010374
Unit ID: 174020
Telephone: (651) 793-1212 Carnegie Class: Master's M
FAX Number: (651) 793-1721 Calendar System: Semester
URL: www.metrostate.edu
Established: 1971 Annual Undergrad Tuition & Fees (In-State): $6,340
Enrollment: 7,787 Coed
Affiliation or Control: State IRS Status: 501(c)3
Highest Offering: Doctorate
Program: Liberal Arts And General; Teacher Preparatory; Professional
Accreditation: NH, NURSE, SW

02 President ... Dr. Sue K. HAMMERSMITH
05 Int Provost/Vice Pres Academic Affs ... Dr. Gary SEILER
11 Vice Pres Administrative Affairs ... Mr. Martuza SIDDIQUI
32 Vice President Student Affairs ... Dr. Trenda BOYUM-BREEN
30 Vice Pres University Advancement ... Mr. Robert HEUERMANN
35 Dean of Students ... Ms. Cecilia STANTON
18 Assoc Vice Pres Admin Affairs ... Mr. Daniel HAMBROCK
13 Assoc VP Info/Telecom/Tech/CIO ... Vacant
10 Assoc VP Financial Management ... Vacant
15 Director Human Resources ... Ms. Stephanie MILLER
06 Registrar ... Mr. Daryl JOHNSON
37 Director Financial Aid ... Ms. Lois LARSON
26 Dir of Communications and Marketing ... Mr. John HENDRICKSON
27 Publication/News Services Director ... Ms. Susan M. AMOS PALMER
29 Director Alumni Relations ... Ms. Vicki LOFQUIST
22 Int Director Affirmative Action ... Ms. Truly WEBB
09 Director Institutional Research ... Ms. Cynthia DEVORE
07 Director of Admissions ... Mr. Daryl JOHNSON
49 Dean College of Arts & Sciences ... Dr. Becky OMDAHL
58 Dean of College of Management ... Dr. Y. Paul HUO
107 Int Dean Col Professional Studies ... Dr. Leah HARVEY
88 Interim Dean First College ... Dr. Leah HARVEY
66 Interim Dean School of Nursing ... Dr. Ann LEJA
88 Dean Sch Law Enforce/Crim Justice ... Ms. Ginny LANE

*Minneapolis Community and Technical College (E)

1501 Hennepin Avenue, Minneapolis MN 55403-9810
County: Hennepin FICE Identification: 002362
Unit ID: 174136
Telephone: (612) 659-6000 Carnegie Class: Assoc/Pub-U-SC
FAX Number: (612) 659-6210 Calendar System: Semester
URL: www.minneapolis.edu
Established: 1996 Annual Undergrad Tuition & Fees (In-State): $5,192
Enrollment: 10,542 Coed
Affiliation or Control: State IRS Status: 501(c)3
Highest Offering: Associate Degree
Program: Occupational; 2-Year Principally Bachelor's Creditable
Accreditation: NH, ADNUR, DA, EEG, PNUR, POLYT

02 President ... Mr. Phillip L. DAVIS
05 Vice Pres Academic/Student Affairs ... Dr. Lois BOLLMAN
10 Vice President Finance/Operations ... Mr. Scott ERICKSON
46 Int VP Strategy/Plng/Accountability ... Dr. Gail O'KANE
30 Exec Director College Advancement ... Mr. Reede O. WEBSTER
43 Director Legal Affairs ... Ms. Dianna CUSICK
84 Dean of Enroll Mgmt/Assoc Vice Pres ... Ms. Laura FEDOCK
20 Dean Liberal Arts & Assoc Vice Pres ... Dr. Linnea STENSON
81 Dean of Science & Math ... Mr. Chuck PAULSON
103 Dean of Workforce Development ... Ms. Jess NIEBUHR
35 Dean of Students ... Ms. Cheryl SAUNDERS
66 Dean of Nursing & Allied Health ... Mr. Robert MUSTER
88 Dean of Academic Development ... Ms. Karen HYNICK
50 Dean of Business & Technology ... Mr. Mike MCGEE
72 Dean of Technical Programs ... Mr. Mick COLEMAN
16 Director of Human Resources ... Mr. Keith BALASKI
13 Chief Information Officer ... Mr. Jim DILLEMUTH
07 Director of Admissions ... Ms. Kerri CARLSON
06 Registrar ... Ms. Elizabeth ERREDGE
08 Librarian ... Mr. Tom ELAND
37 Financial Aid Director ... Ms. Angela CHRISTENSEN
09 Director of Institutional Research ... Dr. Elizabeth YEH
18 Director Facilities ... Mr. Roger BROZ
19 Director of Public Safety ... Mr. Curt SCHMIDT
26 Chief Public Relations Officer ... Ms. Dawn SKELLY
32 Chief Student Life Officer ... Ms. Tara MARTINEZ

*Minnesota State College - Southeast Technical (F)

1250 Homer Road, PO Box 409, Winona MN 55987-4897
County: Winona FICE Identification: 002393
Unit ID: 175263
Telephone: (507) 453-2700 Carnegie Class: Assoc/Pub-R-M
FAX Number: (507) 453-2795 Calendar System: Semester
URL: www.southeastmn.edu
Established: 1949 Annual Undergrad Tuition & Fees (In-District): $4,650
Enrollment: 2,865 Coed
Affiliation or Control: State/Local IRS Status: 501(c)3
Highest Offering: Associate Degree
Program: Occupational; 2-Year Principally Bachelor's Creditable
Accreditation: NH, RAD

02 President ... Mr. James J. JOHNSON
04 Assistant to President ... Ms. Casie JOHNSON
05 Vice President Academic Affairs ... Dr. Jessica STUMPF
32 Vice Pres Student Affs/Inst Rsrch ... Mr. Nate EMERSON
20 Interim CAO/Dean of Technology ... Mr. Ron SELLNAU
20 Dean of Academic Affairs ... Dr. Nancee WOZNEY
66 Dean of Nursing/Allied Health ... Ms. Laurie BECKER
49 Dean of Liberal Arts & Sciences ... Ms. Jolene PONCELET
10 Chief Finance Officer/Purchasing ... Mr. Mike KROENING
15 Chief Human Resource Officer ... Ms. Deanna VOTH
26 Director of Public Relations ... Ms. Peggy WHALEN
13 Chief Information Officer ... Vacant
06 Registrar ... Ms. Mary JOHNSON
37 Director Financial Aid ... Ms. Anne DAHLEN
09 Director of Institutional Research ... Ms. Bunny NOVAK
84 Dir of Enrollment Svcs/Stdnt Plcmt ... Vacant
30 Exec Dir Institutional Advancement ... Mr. Kent SPAULDING
38 Director Student Counseling ... Vacant
07 Admissions Counselor ... Ms. Melissa CARRINGTON-IRWIN
07 Admissions Counselor ... Mr. Gale LANNING
18 Chief Facilities/Physical Plant ... Mr. Thomas HOFFMAN
51 Dir Continuing/Workforce Education ... Vacant

*Minnesota State Community and Technical College (G)

1414 College Way, Fergus Falls MN 56537-1000
County: Otter Tail FICE Identification: 005541
Unit ID: 173559
Telephone: (218) 736-1500 Carnegie Class: Assoc/Pub-R-L
FAX Number: (218) 736-1510 Calendar System: Semester
URL: www.minnesota.edu
Established: 1960 Annual Undergrad Tuition & Fees (In-State): $5,033
Enrollment: 6,925 Coed
Affiliation or Control: State IRS Status: 501(c)3
Highest Offering: Associate Degree
Program: Occupational; 2-Year Principally Bachelor's Creditable; Liberal Arts And General
Accreditation: NH, DA, MLTAD, RAD

02 Interim President ... Dr. Peggy KENNEDY
05 Chief Academic Officer ... Ms. Kathy BROCK
30 Vice President of Advancement ... Vacant
32 Dean Student Svcs and Financial Aid ... Mr. Robert ANDERSON
16 Director of Human Resources ... Mrs. Dacia JOHNSON
13 Chief Information Officer ... Mr. Dave OVERBY
10 Chief Financial Officer ... Mr. Pat NORDICK
84 Interim Dean of Enrollment ... Mr. Anthony SCHAFFHAUSER
26 Dir of Communications & Marketing ... Ms. Mary DEVINE
09 Assoc VP Inst Effectiveness ... Dr. Barry LANE
18 Supt of Buildings & Grounds ... Mr. Matt SHEPPARD
06 Stdnt Svcs Dean and Registrar ... Mr. Shawn ANDERSON
12 Interim Provost - Detroit Lakes ... Mr. Tom WHELIHAN
12 Interim Provost - Fergus Falls ... Ms. Carrie BRIMHALL
12 Provost - Moorhead ... Dr. Jerry MIGLER
12 Provost - Wadena and CSSO ... Dr. Peter WIELINSKI
20 Assoc Dean of Academics ... Dr. Jill ABBOTT
20 Academic & Student Svcs Dean - DL ... Ms. Helene HEDLUND
20 Academic Dean - Fergus Falls ... Dr. Gary HENRICKSON
20 Academic Dean - Moorhead ... Mr. John CENTKO
20 Academic Dean - Moorhead ... Ms. Trish SCHROM
20 Academic & Stdnt Svcs Dean - Wadena ... Mr. Monty JOHNSON

*Minnesota State University, Mankato (H)

228 Wiecking Center, Mankato MN 56001-6062
County: Blue Earth FICE Identification: 002360
Unit ID: 173920
Telephone: (507) 389-1866 Carnegie Class: Master's L
FAX Number: (507) 389-2227 Calendar System: Semester
URL: www.mnsu.edu
Established: 1868 Annual Undergrad Tuition & Fees (In-State): $7,148
Enrollment: 15,435 Coed
Affiliation or Control: State IRS Status: Exempt
Highest Offering: Doctorate
Program: Liberal Arts And General; Teacher Preparatory; Professional
Accreditation: NH, ART, BUS, CACREP, CONST, CORE, DH, DIETD, ENG, ENGT, MUS, NRPA, NURSE, SP, SW, TED

02 President ... Dr. Richard DAVENPORT
05 VP Academic & Student Affairs ... Dr. Scott R. OLSON
10 Vice Pres Finance & Administration ... Mr. Richard STRAKA
30 VP Univ Advance/Chief Dev Ofcr ... Mr. Douglas MAYO
13 VP Technolgy/CIO ... Mr. Ed CLARK
88 VP Strategic/Busnss/Ed/Reg Prtrshps ... Dr. Robert HOFFMAN
28 Interm Dean Institutional Diversity ... Mr. Henry MORRIS
32 Assoc VP for Student Affairs ... Dr. David JONES
20 Asso Vice Pres for Academic Affairs ... Dr. Warren SANDMANN
04 Assistant to the President ... Ms. Carol STALLKAMP
20 Asst VP for Undergrad Stds Intl Ed ... Dr. Maria-Claudia TOMANY
27 Asst VP Integrated Marketing/Comm ... Mr. Jeff ISEMINGER
18 Int Asst Vice Pres Facilities Mgmt ... Mr. David COWAN
06 Registrar ... Mr. Marcius BROCK
07 Director of Admissions ... Mr. Brian JONES
08 Dean Library Services ... Dr. Joan ROCA
15 Director of Human Resources ... Ms. Becky BARKMEIER
36 Director Career Development ... Ms. Pamela WELLER-DENGEL

26 Director Media Relations .... Mr. Michael COOPER
41 Director of Athletics .... Mr. Kevin BUISMAN
29 Director of Alumni Relations .... Ms. Jennifer GUYER- WOOD
22 Affirmative Action Officer .... Ms. Linda HANSON
37 Student Financial Services .... Ms. Jan MARBLE
58 Int Dean Graduate Studies/Research .... Dr. Barry RIES
79 Dean of Arts & Humanities .... Dr. Walter ZAKAHI
53 Interim Dean of Education .... Dr. Jean HAAR
50 Dean of Business .... Dr. Brenda FLANNERY
76 Interim Dean Allied Health/Nursing .... Dr. Harry KRAMPF
81 Dean Science/Engineering/Technology .... Dr. Vijendra AGARWAL
83 Dean Social/Behavioral Science .... Dr. Kimberly GREER
38 Director Student Counseling .... Ms. Kari MUCH

*Minnesota State University Moorhead (A)

1104 7th Avenue S, Moorhead MN 56563-2996
County: Clay FICE Identification: 002367
Unit ID: 174358
Telephone: (218) 477-4000 Carnegie Class: Master's M
FAX Number: (218) 477-2168 Calendar System: Semester
URL: www.mnstate.edu
Established: 1887 Annual Undergrad Tuition & Fees (In-State): $7,352
Enrollment: 7,497 Coed
Affiliation or Control: State IRS Status: 501(c)3
Highest Offering: Doctorate
Program: Liberal Arts And General; Teacher Preparatory; Professional
Accreditation: NH, ART, BUS, CACREP, CONST, DH, MUS, NAIT, NURSE, SP, SW, TED

02 President .... Dr. Edna M. SZYMANSKI
05 Provost & Sr VP Academic Affairs .... Dr. Anne E. BLACKHURST
10 VP Finance & Administration .... Ms. Janet L. MAHONEY
32 VP Student Affairs .... Mr. Warren K. WIESE
29 VP Alumni Foundation .... Ms. Laura L. HUTH
84 VP Enrollment Management .... Ms. Diane P. SOLINGER
45 AVP F&A/Univ Plng & Budget Ofcr .... Ms. Jean R. HOLLAAR
04 Assistant to the President .... Vacant
20 AVP Acad Affairs .... Ms. Ginny V. BAIR
41 Director of Athletics .... Mr. Doug D. PETERS
14 Chief Information Officer .... Mr. Daniel A. HECKAMAN
21 Comptroller .... Mr. Mark P. RICE
28 AVP Student Affairs for Diversity .... Dr. Donna L. BROWN
50 Dean Business & Industry .... Dr. Marsha L. WEBER
79 Dean Arts & Humanities .... Dr. Timothy A. BORCHERS
53 Dean Education & Human Services .... Dr. Teri L. WALSETH
83 Dean Social & Natural Sciences .... Dr. Michelle L. MALOTT
08 Dean Instructional Resources .... Ms. Brittney G. GOODMAN
89 Dean University College .... Ms. Denise M. GORSLINE
15 Director Human Resources .... Mr. Corey A. MORIYAMA
06 AVP Records & Inst Effectiveness .... Dr. Russell L. CURLEY
22 Affirmative Action Officer .... Dr. Donna L. BROWN
26 Int Director of Marketing .... Mr. Jeremy JOHNSON
19 Director of Security .... Mr. Gregory J. LEMKE
37 Dir Financial Aid & Scholarships .... Ms. Carolyn F. ZEHREN
23 Dir Health/Wellness/Counseling Ctrs .... Ms. Carol M. GRIMM
38 Dir Disabilities & Career Services .... Mr. Greg A. TOUTGES
07 Director of Admissions .... Mr. Jeremy R. JOHNSON
44 AVP Fundraising .... Ms. Laurie J. WIGTIL
35 Exec Dir Student Union .... Ms. Karen B. MEHNERT-MELAND
39 Dir Housing & Residential Life .... Ms. Heather PHILLIPS
40 Bookstore Supervisor .... Ms. Kim M. SAMSON
18 Director Physical Plant .... Mr. Jeffrey D. GOEBEL
85 Int Director Intl Student Affs .... Ms. Janet M. HOHENSTEIN

*Minnesota West Community and Technical College (B)

1450 Collegeway, Worthington MN 56187
County: Nobles FICE Identification: 005263
Unit ID: 173638
Telephone: (507) 372-3400 Carnegie Class: Assoc/Pub-R-M
FAX Number: (507) 372-5801 Calendar System: Semester
URL: www.mnwest.edu
Established: 1985 Annual Undergrad Tuition & Fees (In-State): $5,424
Enrollment: 3,465 Coed
Affiliation or Control: State IRS Status: 501(c)3
Highest Offering: Associate Degree
Program: Occupational; 2-Year Principally Bachelor's Creditable
Accreditation: NH, ADNUR, DA, MAC, MLTAD, RAD, SURGT

02 President .... Dr. Richard SHRUBB
05 College Provost .... Dr. Jeff WILLIAMSON
11 Vice President of Administration .... Ms. Lori VOSS
106 Dean Technology/Distance Learning .... Ms. Kayla WESTRA
84 Director of Enrollment Management .... Vacant
37 Director of Student Financial Aid .... Ms. Jodi LANDGAARD
18 Chief Facilities/Physical Plant .... Mr. Jeff HARMS
06 Registrar .... Ms. Crystal STROUTH
15 Director Human Resources .... Ms. Karen MILLER
102 Foundation Director .... Mr. James SMALLEY

*Normandale Community College (C)

9700 France Avenue S, Bloomington MN 55431-4399
County: Hennepin FICE Identification: 007954
Unit ID: 174428
Telephone: (952) 358-8200 Carnegie Class: Assoc/Pub-S-SC
FAX Number: (952) 487-8101 Calendar System: Semester
URL: www.normandale.mnscu.edu
Established: 1968 Annual Undergrad Tuition & Fees (In-State): $5,448
Enrollment: 10,169 Coed
Affiliation or Control: State IRS Status: 501(c)3
Highest Offering: Associate Degree
Program: Occupational; 2-Year Principally Bachelor's Creditable
Accreditation: NH, ACBSP, ADNUR, ART, DH, DIETT, MUS, THEA

02 President .... Dr. Joe OPATZ
10 Vice Pres Finance & Operations .... Mr. Ed WINES
05 Vice President Academic Affairs .... Ms. Julie GUELICH
32 Vice President Student Affairs .... Dr. Lisa WHEELER
35 Dean of Students .... Dr. Orinthia MONTAGUE
50 Dean Bus/Tech/Library/Social Sci .... Vacant
79 Dean of Humanities/Col Readiness .... Mr. Jeff JUDGE
81 Dean Natural Science/Mathematics .... Ms. Tina WADE
76 Dean of Health Sciences .... Dr. Colleen BRICKLE
10 Director Fiscal Services .... Mr. Craig ERICKSON
15 Director Human Resources .... Ms. Michelle THOM
35 Associate Dean of Students .... Ms. Catherine L. BREUER
13 Director of Information Tech Svcs .... Ms. Andrea KODNER-WENZEL
18 Director of Building Services .... Mr. Michael KOREEN
102 Director of Foundation Office .... Mr. Chuck WALETZKO
84 Dean of Enroll/Marketing/Multicul .... Mr. Matt CRAWFORD
26 Chief Public Relations Officer .... Mr. Geoffrey JONES
06 Registrar .... Ms. Tonya HANSON HUBER
07 Director of Admissions .... Vacant
09 Assoc VP Planning & Inst Research .... Mr. Michael BERNDT

*North Hennepin Community College (D)

7411 85th Avenue N, Brooklyn Park MN 55445-2299
County: Hennepin FICE Identification: 002370
Unit ID: 174376
Telephone: (763) 424-0702 Carnegie Class: Assoc/Pub-S-SC
FAX Number: (763) 424-0929 Calendar System: Semester
URL: www.nhcc.edu
Established: 1966 Annual Undergrad Tuition & Fees (In-State): $5,186
Enrollment: 7,505 Coed
Affiliation or Control: State IRS Status: 501(c)3
Highest Offering: Associate Degree
Program: Occupational; 2-Year Principally Bachelor's Creditable
Accreditation: NH, ACBSP, ADNUR, HT, MLTAD

02 President .... Dr. John O'BRIEN
05 Vice Pres Academic/Student Affs .... Ms. Jane REINKE
32 Chief Student Academic Officer .... Dr. Landon PIRIUS
09 Dean of Institutional Services .... Dr. Lisa SCHLOTTERHAUSEN
72 Dean Academic & Technology Services .... Vacant
20 Assoc Dean Student Success .... Mr. Jim BORER
37 Assoc Dean Financial Aid .... Ms. Jackie OLSSON
08 Librarian .... Mr. Craig LARSON
06 Director Records & Registration .... Ms. Lori KIRKEBY
07 Director Admissions & Outreach .... Ms. Jennifer SUMMER-LAMBRECHT
15 Chief Human Resources Officer .... Ms. Sue APPELQUIST
10 Chief Finance/Facilities Officer .... Ms. Dawn REIMER
45 Director Planning & Research .... Ms. Sheryl OLSON
38 Dir Counseling/Advising/Career Plng .... Ms. Sarah MILLER
18 Director of Plant Services .... Mr. Larry MEYERS
30 Director of Development .... Vacant
28 Director Diversity/Multiculturalism .... Mr. Matthew Antonio BOSCH
26 Director of Communications .... Ms. Carmen SHOQUIST
21 Business Manager .... Ms. Dawn BELKO
49 Dean Liberal Arts .... Ms. Suellen RUNDQUIST
50 Dean Business & Career Programs .... Ms. Renae FRY
76 Dean Health Careers/Science .... Dr. Elaina BLEIFIELD
51 Dean of Cont Educ/Custom Trng .... Vacant

*Northland Community and Technical College (E)

1101 Highway 1 E, Thief River Falls MN 56701-2598
County: Pennington FICE Identification: 002385
Unit ID: 174473
Telephone: (218) 683-8800 Carnegie Class: Assoc/Pub-R-M
FAX Number: (218) 683-8980 Calendar System: Semester
URL: www.northlandcollege.edu
Established: 1965 Annual Undergrad Tuition & Fees (In-State): $5,060
Enrollment: 5,712 Coed
Affiliation or Control: State IRS Status: 501(c)3
Highest Offering: Associate Degree
Program: Occupational; 2-Year Principally Bachelor's Creditable; Technical Emphasis
Accreditation: NH, ADNUR, CVT, EMT, OTA, PTAA, RAD, SURGT

02 President .... Dr. Anne T. TEMTE
05 VP Academic Affairs/Student Svcs .... Mr. Kent HANSON
04 Assistant to the President .... Ms. Cindy CEDERGREN
20 Dean of Academic Affairs .... Ms. Norma KONSCHAK
20 Dean of Academic Affairs .... Vacant
32 Dean of Student Development .... Mr. Steve CRITTENDEN
32 Dean of Students East Grand Forks .... Ms. Mary FONTES
103 Dean Workforce & Econ Development .... Mr. James RETKA
08 Learning Center Director .... Mr. Dean DALEN
10 Chief Business Officer .... Mr. Dennis PAESLER
38 Counselor .... Ms. Kelsy BLOWERS
38 Counselor .... Ms. Kate SCHMALENBERG
66 Director of Nursing .... Ms. Susan FIELD
66 Director of Nursing .... Ms. Barb FORREST
84 Director of Enrollment Management .... Mr. Gene KLINKE
37 Director Student Financial Aid .... Mr. Gerald SCHULTE
09 Director of Institutional Research .... Mr. Rocky AMMERMAN
15 Director Personnel Services .... Ms. Becky LINDSETH
18 Chief Facilities/Physical Plant .... Mr. Clinton CASTLE
26 Director Marketing/Communication .... Mr. Jason TRAINER
44 Dir Annual Giving/Alumni Relations .... Mr. Dustin BUSE
06 Registrar .... Mr. Rocky AMMERMAN
07 Director of Admissions .... Mr. Gene KLINKE
28 Director of Diversity .... Vacant
30 Chief Development Officer .... Mr. Dan KLUG
13 Director Computing/Information Mgmt .... Ms. Stacey HRON
27 Chief Information Officer .... Ms. Becky LINDSETH
41 Athletic Director .... Mr. Paul PETERSON

*Northwest Technical College (F)

905 Grant Avenue, SE, Bemidji MN 56601-4907
County: Beltrami FICE Identification: 005759
Unit ID: 173115
Telephone: (218) 333-6600 Carnegie Class: Assoc/Pub-R-S
FAX Number: (218) 333-6694 Calendar System: Semester
URL: www.ntcmn.edu
Established: 1966 Annual Undergrad Tuition & Fees (In-State): $5,468
Enrollment: 1,424 Coed
Affiliation or Control: State IRS Status: 501(c)3
Highest Offering: Associate Degree
Program: Occupational; 2-Year Principally Bachelor's Creditable
Accreditation: NH, DA

05 Dean of Academics .... Mr. James CLARK

*Pine Technical College (G)

900 Fourth Street, SE, Pine City MN 55063-2198
County: Pine FICE Identification: 005535
Unit ID: 174570
Telephone: (320) 629-5100 Carnegie Class: Assoc/Pub-R-S
FAX Number: (320) 629-5101 Calendar System: Semester
URL: www.pinetech.edu
Established: 1965 Annual Undergrad Tuition & Fees (In-State): $3,728
Enrollment: 1,047 Coed
Affiliation or Control: State IRS Status: 501(c)3
Highest Offering: Associate Degree
Program: Occupational; 2-Year Principally Bachelor's Creditable; Business Emphasis
Accreditation: NH

02 President .... Dr. Robert MUSGROVE
05 Chief Academic Officer .... Dr. Joan BLOEMENDAAL-GRUETT
13 Chief Information Officer .... Mr. Kenneth RIES
32 Dean Student Affairs .... Ms. Nancy MACH
51 Dean of Continuing Education .... Mr. Jason SPAETH
06 Registrar .... Mr. Robert BAKER
15 Chief Human Resources Officer .... Mrs. Penny HUDLOW
07 Director of Admissions .... Mr. James STUMNE
37 Director Student Financial Aid .... Ms. Susan PIXLEY
10 Business Manager .... Ms. Janis WEGNER
18 Physical Plant Supervisor .... Mr. Steven LANGE

*Rainy River Community College (H)

1501 Highway 71, International Falls MN 56649-2187
County: Koochiching FICE Identification: 006775
Unit ID: 174604
Telephone: (218) 285-7722 Carnegie Class: Assoc/Pub-R-S
FAX Number: (218) 285-2239 Calendar System: Semester
URL: www.rrcc.mnscu.edu
Established: 1967 Annual Undergrad Tuition & Fees (In-State): $5,141
Enrollment: 315 Coed
Affiliation or Control: State IRS Status: 501(c)3
Highest Offering: Associate Degree
Program: Occupational; 2-Year Principally Bachelor's Creditable
Accreditation: NH

02 Provost .... Dr. Kenneth SIMBERG
06 Registrar .... Ms. Berta HAGEN
37 Dir of Financial Aid/Housing .... Mr. Scott T. RILEY
13 Dir Information Technology .... Mr. James BUJOLD

*Ridgewater College (I)

PO Box 1097, 2101 15th Ave NW, Willmar MN 56201-1097
County: Kandiyohi FICE Identification: 005252
Unit ID: 175236
Telephone: (320) 222-5200 Carnegie Class: Assoc/Pub-R-M
FAX Number: (320) 222-5212 Calendar System: Semester
URL: www.ridgewater.edu
Established: 1961 Annual Undergrad Tuition & Fees (In-State): $5,173
Enrollment: 4,373 Coed
Affiliation or Control: State IRS Status: 501(c)3
Highest Offering: Associate Degree
Program: Occupational; 2-Year Principally Bachelor's Creditable
Accreditation: NH, ADNUR, EMT, MAC

02 President .... Dr. Douglas W. ALLEN
05 Vice Pres Acad Affs/Student Svcs .... Ms. Betty J. STREHLOW
10 Vice President Finance & Operations .... Mr. Daniel F. HOLTZ
51 Dean of Cust Trng & Cont Education .... Ms. Kathy M. SCHWANTES
20 Dean of Instruction .... Mr. Michael J. BOEHME

20 Dean of Instruction ... Vacant
20 Dean of Instruction ... Dr. Ronald L. PRIBBLE
32 Dean of Student Services ... Ms. Heidi L. OLSON
21 Director of Business Services ... Ms. Cheryl A. NORLIEN
15 Chief Human Resource Officer ... Ms. Jodi L. KNAUS
66 Director of Nursing ... Ms. C. Lynn JOHNSON
37 Director of Financial Aid ... Mr. James W. RICE
07 Director of Admissions ... Ms. Sally KERFELD
41 Athletic Director ... Mr. Todd M. THORSTAD
06 Registrar ... Ms. Kelli S. KIENITZ
13 Chief Information Officer ... Mr. Timothy L. FURR
26 Director of Communication/Marketing ... Mr. Samuel J. BOWEN
102 Foundation Executive Director ... Ms. Kelly J. MAGNUSON
47 Director of Management Programs ... Mr. James H. MOLENAAR
09 Director of Institutional Research ... Dr. Mary L. MYERS
28 Director of Multicultural Affairs ... Mr. Edelgard FERNANDEZ MEJIA
18 Physical Plant Director ... Mr. Kip R. OVESON

Riverland Community College (A)

1900 8th Avenue, NW, Austin MN 55912-1473

County: Mower FICE Identification: 002335
Unit ID: 173063
Telephone: (507) 433-0600 Carnegie Class: Assoc/Pub-R-M
FAX Number: (507) 433-0665 Calendar System: Semester
URL: www.riverland.edu
Established: 1940 Annual Undergrad Tuition & Fees (In-State): $5,331
Enrollment: 4,015 Coed
Affiliation or Control: State IRS Status: 501(c)3
Highest Offering: Associate Degree
Program: Occupational; 2-Year Principally Bachelor's Creditable; Liberal Arts And General
Accreditation: NH, ADNUR, RAD

02 President ... Dr. Terrence LEAS
05 Exec Vice Pres/Chief Academic Ofcr ... Dr. Ron LANGRELL
10 Chief Financial Officer ... Mr. Brad DOSS
16 Vice Pres Employee/Public Relations ... Ms. Celeste RUBLE
09 Dean Institutional Advancement ... Mr. Steve BOWRON
76 Dean Health Sciences & Services ... Ms. Kari BUSCH
49 Dean Liberal Arts & Sciences ... Ms. Jan WALLER
36 Dean Academic Affs/Career Tech Educ ... Mr. Steve BOWRON
32 Dean of Student Affairs ... Mr. Gary SCHINDLER
102 Executive Director of Foundation ... Ms. Julie ANDERSON
06 Registrar ... Ms. Sue JECH
07 Director of Admissions ... Ms. Danielle HEINY
26 Director of Communications ... Mr. James DOUGLASS
37 Director of Financial Aid ... Ms. Judy ROBECK
36 Director of Placement & Grad Svcs ... Ms. Tricia WHALEN
04 Executive Assist to the President ... Ms. Marijo ALEXANDER
13 Director of Technology ... Mr. Dan HARBER
18 Facilities Supervisor ... Ms. Judy ENRIGHT
96 Purchasing Agent ... Ms. Page PETERSEN
28 Regional Diversty Trainer/Investgtr ... Ms. Ricki WALTERS

*Rochester Community and Technical College (B)

851 30th Avenue, SE, Rochester MN 55904-4999

County: Olmsted FICE Identification: 002373
Unit ID: 174738
Telephone: (507) 285-7210 Carnegie Class: Assoc/Pub-R-M
FAX Number: (507) 285-7496 Calendar System: Semester
URL: www.rctc.edu
Established: 1915 Annual Undergrad Tuition & Fees (In-State): $5,400
Enrollment: 6,263 Coed
Affiliation or Control: State IRS Status: 501(c)3
Highest Offering: Associate Degree
Program: Occupational; 2-Year Principally Bachelor's Creditable; Liberal Arts And General
Accreditation: NH, ADNUR, DA, DH, EMT, PNUR, SURGT

02 President ... Mr. Don D. SUPALLA
05 Vice President Teaching & Learning ... Dr. Michael BEQUETTE
10 Vice Pres Finance and Facilities ... Ms. Marilyn HANSMANN
76 Dean Allied Health ... Dr. Nirmala KOTAGAL
49 Dean ... Dr. Barbara J. MOLLBERG
75 Dean ... Ms. Michelle PYFFEROEN
15 Chief Human Resources Officer ... Mrs. Renee ENGELMEYER
13 Chief Information Technology Ofcr ... Mr. Scott SAHS
45 Chief Strategic Operations Officer ... Mr. Dave N. WEBER
51 Dir of Business/Econ Development ... Ms. Michelle PYFFEROEN
32 Student Life Coordinator ... Mr. Scott KROOK
06 Registrar ... Ms. Nancy SHUMAKER
07 Director Admissions ... Ms. Holly BIGELOW
37 Director Financial Aid ... Ms. Rosemary HICKS
09 Director of Institutional Research ... Ms. Christine MILLER
04 Assistant to President ... Mrs. Judy K. KINGSBURY
21 Business Office Supervisor ... Ms. Ruth SIEFERT
26 Chief Public Relations Officer ... Mr. Dave WEBER
19 Security Officer ... Vacant
40 Bookstore Coordinator ... Ms. Michelle PETERSON
102 Foundation Executive Director ... Ms. Lisa BALDUS
96 Director of Purchasing ... Ms. June MEITZNER
29 Director of Alumni Relations ... Ms. Lisa BALDUS

*St. Cloud State University (C)

720 4th Avenue S, Saint Cloud MN 56301-4498

County: Stearns FICE Identification: 002377
Unit ID: 174783
Telephone: (320) 308-0121 Carnegie Class: Master's L
FAX Number: N/A Calendar System: Semester
URL: www.stcloudstate.edu
Established: 1869 Annual Undergrad Tuition & Fees (In-State): $6,285
Enrollment: 18,650 Coed
Affiliation or Control: State IRS Status: 501(c)3
Highest Offering: Doctorate
Program: Liberal Arts And General; Teacher Preparatory
Accreditation: NH, AAB, ART, BUS, CACREP, CORE, CS, ENG, ENGR, #JOUR, MFCD, MUS, NAIT, NURSE, SP, SW, TED, THEA

02 President ... Dr. Earl H. POTTER, III
05 Provost/Vice Pres Academic Affairs ... Dr. Devinder MALHOTRA
88 Assoc Provost for Organizat ... Dr. John PALMER
46 Interim Assoc Provost for Research ... Dr. Dan GREGORY
20 Assoc Provost Undergraduate ... Dr. Miguel SAENZ
88 Interim Asst Provost Student Supp ... Dr. Freddie WALKER
32 Vice Pres Student Life Development ... Dr. Wanda OVERLAND
11 Vice Pres Administrative Affairs ... Mr. Steven LUDWIG
30 Vice Pres University Advancement ... Mr. Craig WRUCK
85 Assoc VP International Studies ... Dr. Ann B. RADWAN
84 Assoc VP Enrollment Management ... Dr. Mahmoud SAFFARI
10 Assoc VP Financial Mgmt/Budget ... Ms. Diana K. BURLISON
45 Asst VP for Inst Effectiveness ... Ms. Lisa FOSS
27 Asst VP Marketing & Communications ... Mr. Loren BOONE
43 Special Advisor to the President ... Dr. Judith P. SIMINOE
50 Dean of Business ... Dr. Diana LAWSON
51 Dean of Continuing Studies ... Dr. John BURGESON
53 Dean of Education ... Dr. Osman ALAWIYE
57 Dean Fine Arts & Humanities ... Dr. Todd DEVRIESE
72 Dean Science & Engineering ... Dr. David K. DEGROOTE
83 Dean of Social Sciences ... Dr. Francis B. HARROLD
08 Dean Learning Resources/Tech Svcs ... Dr. Kristi TORNQUIST
07 Director of Admissions ... Mr. Richard SHEARER
22 Equity and Affirmative Action Ofc ... Ms. Ellyn BARTGES
06 Registrar ... Ms. Sue BAYERL
29 Director of Constituent Engagement ... Ms. Terri MISCHE
41 Athletic Director ... Dr. Morris KURTZ
18 Interim Facilities Management ... Mr. John FRISCHMANN
36 Director Career Services ... Ms. Addie TURKOWSKI
91 Dir Admin Computer Svcs/Info System ... Dr. Ilya V. YAKOVLEV
38 Director of Counseling ... Dr. John M. EGGERS
37 Director of Financial Aid ... Mr. Mike T. URAN
39 Director of Student Housing ... Mr. Daniel T. PEDERSEN
09 Director Institutional Research ... Mr. Kim OREN
15 Director Human Resources ... Dr. Larry N. CHAMBERS
19 Director Public Safety ... Mr. Miles J. HECKENDORN
40 Bookstore Manager ... Mr. Ted MEARS

*Saint Cloud Technical and Community College (D)

1540 Northway Drive, Saint Cloud MN 56303-1240

County: Stearns FICE Identification: 005534
Unit ID: 174756
Telephone: (320) 308-5000 Carnegie Class: Assoc/Pub-R-M
FAX Number: (320) 308-5981 Calendar System: Semester
URL: www.sctcc.edu
Established: 1948 Annual Undergrad Tuition & Fees (In-State): $5,149
Enrollment: 3,661 Coed
Affiliation or Control: State IRS Status: 501(c)3
Highest Offering: Associate Degree
Program: 2-Year Principally Bachelor's Creditable; Technical Emphasis
Accreditation: NH, CVT, DA, DH, DMS, EMT, SURGT

02 President ... Ms. Joyce M. HELENS
05 VP of Academic Affairs ... Ms. Margaret (Peg) SHROYER
88 Exec Dir Custom Training/Dev ... Vacant
04 Assistant to the President ... Ms. Karen A. HIEMENZ
32 Vice President of Student Affairs ... Mr. Phillip SCHROEDER
10 Vice Pres Admin/Chief Finan Officer ... Ms. Lori KLOOS
75 Dean Trade/Industry ... Mr. Bruce A. PETERSON
76 Dean Health/Human Services ... Ms. Janet STEINKAMP
49 Dean of Liberal Arts & Sciences ... Mr. Jason TETZLOFF
50 Dean of Business/Comp Science ... Ms. Kristina KELLER
06 Registrar ... Ms. Lana L. FEDDEMA
15 Dir Personnel Services/Aff Action ... Ms. Deb A. HOLSTAD
84 Dir of Enroll Management/Admissions ... Ms. Jodi M. ELNESS
08 Head Librarian ... Ms. Patricia AKERMAN
19 Security/Safety Officer ... Ms. Joni AKERSON
37 Director Student Financial Aid ... Ms. Anita G. BAUGH
20 Curriculum/Faculty Development ... Ms. Margaret (Peg) SHROYER
36 Director Student Placement ... Ms. Jackie BAUER
40 Director Bookstore ... Mr. James SCHOLLA
38 Director Student Counseling ... Ms. Judy JACOBSON-BERG
35 Activ Dir/Chief Student Life Ofcr ... Mr. John R. HALLER
18 Chief Facilities/Physical Plant ... Mr. Jason THEISEN
27 Chief Information Officer ... Ms. Lynette OLSON
09 Director of Institutional Research ... Ms. Lynette OLSON
21 Associate Business Officer ... Mr. Duane DAHLSTROM
28 Director of Diversity ... Vacant
96 Director of Purchasing ... Ms. Susan MEYER
106 Online Education/E-learning ... Mr. James FALKOFSKE
13 Director Library & Info Technology ... Ms. Viola BERGQUIST
22 Director Affirm Action/Equal Oppty ... Ms. Deb HOLSTAD
30 Chief Devel/Dir Annual/Planned Giv ... Ms. Kristina GEORGE

*Saint Paul College-A Community & Technical College (E)

235 Marshall Avenue, Saint Paul MN 55102-1800

County: Ramsey FICE Identification: 005533
Unit ID: 175041
Telephone: (651) 846-1600 Carnegie Class: Assoc/Pub-U-SC
FAX Number: (651) 846-1451 Calendar System: Semester
URL: www.saintpaul.edu
Established: 1910 Annual Undergrad Tuition & Fees (In-State): $4,806
Enrollment: 9,625 Coed
Affiliation or Control: State IRS Status: 501(c)3
Highest Offering: Associate Degree
Program: Occupational; 2-Year Principally Bachelor's Creditable
Accreditation: NH, ACBSP, ACFEI, MLTAD, PNUR

02 President ... Dr. Rassoul DASTMOZD
05 Sr VP Academic Affs/Student Devel ... Dr. Peggy D. KENNEDY
102 VP Corporate Foundation/Cmty Rels ... Mr. Craig ANDERSON
10 Vice President Finance & Operations ... Ms. Shaan HAMILTON
06 Registrar ... Ms. Katie YEP
09 Dean Research/Plng/Effectiveness ... Dr. Margie TOMSIC
15 Director of Human Resources ... Ms. Rachelle M. SCHMIDT
18 Director Facilities/Physical Plant ... Mr. Tom DOODY
07 Director Admissions/Enrollment Mgmt ... Ms. Sarah CARRICO
21 Business Manager ... Mr. John PALMER
26 Director of Marketing ... Mr. Jim STUMNE
35 Dean Student Development/Services ... Mr. Thomas MATOS
36 Director of Student Placement ... Mr. Brian MOGREN
37 Director of Student Financial Aid ... Ms. Susan PIXLEY
29 Director Alumni Relations ... Ms. Laura SAVIN
13 Chief Information Officer ... Mr. Najam SAEED
30 Chief Development Officer ... Ms. Laura SAVIN
32 Chief Student Life Officer ... Ms. Lisa CHRISTENSEN
17 Dean Health & Services ... Dr. Marilyn KRASOWSKI
49 Dean Liberal Arts & Sciences ... Dr. Linda KINGSTON
50 Dean Business & Computer Careers ... Dr. Cathie PETERSON
75 Dean Trade & Technical ... Dr. Gary HERTEL
90 Assoc Dean Instruct Tech/Prof Dev ... Ms. Shelley BIBEAU

*South Central College (F)

1920 Lee Boulevard, PO Box 1920,
North Mankato MN 56002-1920

County: Nicollet FICE Identification: 005537
Unit ID: 173911
Telephone: (507) 389-7200 Carnegie Class: Assoc/Pub-R-M
FAX Number: (507) 388-9951 Calendar System: Semester
URL: www.southcentral.edu
Established: 1946 Annual Undergrad Tuition & Fees (In-District): $5,109
Enrollment: 4,268 Coed
Affiliation or Control: State/Local IRS Status: 501(c)3
Highest Offering: Associate Degree
Program: Occupational; 2-Year Principally Bachelor's Creditable
Accreditation: NH, DA, EMT, MLTAD

02 President ... Mr. Keith STOVER
04 Exec Assistant to the President ... Ms. Carol FREED
05 Vice President of Academic Affairs ... Dr. Nancy GENELIN
10 Vice President Finance & Operations ... Ms. Karen SNOREK
45 Director of Research & Planning ... Ms. Dena COLEMER
32 Dean of Student Affairs ... Ms. Linda BEER
54 Dn Engineering & Construction Tech ... Dr. Suzanne NORDBLOM
50 Dean of Health & Business ... Mr. W. C. SANDERS
49 Dean of Liberal Arts & Sciences ... Dr. Brian FORS
27 Public Information Officer ... Ms. Ann SPLINTER
06 Registrar/Dir Enrollment Management ... Ms. Donna MARZOLF
09 Director of Institutional Research ... Ms. Dena COLEMER
28 Director of Diversity ... Dr. Brian FORS
15 Dir Human Resource/Personnel Svcs ... Ms. Laural KUBAT
37 Director Student Financial Aid ... Ms. Jayne DINSE
18 Chief Facilities/Physical Plant ... Ms. Karen SNOREK
07 Director of Admissions ... Mr. David MILLER
08 Director of Library/Media Services ... Ms. Johnna HORTON
13 Dean of Technology ... Mr. Wes TAYLOR

*Southwest Minnesota State University (G)

1501 State Street, Marshall MN 56258-1598

County: Lyon FICE Identification: 002375
Unit ID: 175078
Telephone: (507) 537-7678 Carnegie Class: Master's M
FAX Number: (507) 537-7154 Calendar System: Semester
URL: www.smsu.edu
Established: 1963 Annual Undergrad Tuition & Fees (In-State): $7,743
Enrollment: 6,618 Coed
Affiliation or Control: State IRS Status: 501(c)3
Highest Offering: Master's
Program: Liberal Arts And General; Teacher Preparatory; Professional
Accreditation: NH, MUS, SW

02 Interim President ... Dr. Ronald A. WOOD
05 Provost ... Dr. Beth WEATHERBY
10 Interim VP Finance and Admin ... Ms. Debra KERKAERT
30 Vice President for Advancement ... Vacant
32 AVP Stdnt Affairs/Dean of Students ... Mr. Scott CROWELL
102 AVP Advance/Dir Devel/Foundation ... Mr. William MULSO
49 Interim Dean Arts/Letters/Sciences ... Dr. Jan LOFT
50 Interim Dean Bus/Ed/Grad/Prof Stud ... Dr. Raphael ONYEAGHALA
20 Assoc Dean Academics/Student Svcs ... Vacant
41 Athletic Director ... Mr. Christopher HMIELEWSKI
27 Chief Information Officer ... Mr. Dan BAUN
07 Director Admissions ... Mr. Andrew HLUBEK
14 Director of Computer Services ... Mr. Shawn HEDMAN
06 Registrar ... Ms. Patricia CARMODY
19 Director University Public Safety ... Mr. Michael MUNFORD
28 Director Cultural Diversity ... Mr. Don ROBERTSON

15 Director Human Resources ......Ms. Deb ALMER
29 Director of Alumni ......Mr. Tyler BOWEN
18 Director of Facilities ......Ms. Cyndi HOLM
36 Director of Career Services ......Ms. Sheila RISACHER
35 Director of Student Center ......Mr. Paul LAMANTIA
37 Director of Student Financial Aid ......Mr. David VIKANDER
38 Director of Student Counseling ......Mr. Robert LARSEN
96 Director of Purchasing ......Mr. Jeff KUIPER
21 Business Manager ......Vacant

*Vermilion Community College (A)

1900 E Camp Street, Ely MN 55731-1998
County: Saint Louis FICE Identification: 002350
Unit ID: 175157
Telephone: (218) 235-2101 Carnegie Class: Assoc/Pub-R-S
FAX Number: (218) 235-2173 Calendar System: Semester
URL: www.vcc.edu
Established: 1922 Annual Undergrad Tuition & Fees (In-State): $4,113
Enrollment: 708 Coed
Affiliation or Control: State IRS Status: 501(c)3
Highest Offering: Associate Degree
Program: Occupational; 2-Year Principally Bachelor's Creditable
Accreditation: NH

02 Provost/Chief Academic Officer ......Mr. Shawn BINA
06 Registrar ......Ms. Nadine FORSMAN
07 Director of Admissions/Student Affs ......Mr. Jeff NELSON
09 Director of Institutional Research ......Ms. Tracey ROY
10 Business Manager ......Ms. Nicole SQUIRES
15 Director of Personnel Services ......Ms. Patti DELICH
32 Dir Student Life/Facil/Phy Plant ......Mr. Dave MARSHALL
36 Director of Student Placement ......Mr. Doug FURNSTAHL
37 Director of Student Financial Aid ......Ms. Kristi L'ALLIER
38 Director of Student Counseling ......Ms. Cindy ANDERSON-BINA
29 Director Alumni Relations ......Ms. Patti ZUPANCICH
28 Director of Diversity ......Ms. Donna PRICHARD
26 Chief Public Relations Officer ......Mr. Doug FURNSTAHL

*Winona State University (B)

PO Box 5838, Winona MN 55987-0838
County: Winona FICE Identification: 002394
Unit ID: 175272
Telephone: (507) 457-5000 Carnegie Class: Master's M
FAX Number: (507) 457-5586 Calendar System: Quarter
URL: www.winona.edu
Established: 1858 Annual Undergrad Tuition & Fees (In-State): $8,200
Enrollment: 8,539 Coed
Affiliation or Control: State IRS Status: 501(c)3
Highest Offering: Doctorate
Program: Liberal Arts And General; Teacher Preparatory; Professional
Accreditation: NH, BUS, CACREP, ENG, MUS, NURSE, SW, TED, THEA

02 President ......Dr. Judith A. RAMALEY
05 Provost/Vice Pres Academic Affairs ......Dr. Sally JOHNSTONE
10 Vice Pres Finance & Administration ......Mr. Kurt LOHIDE
30 Vice Pres University Advancement ......Dr. James SCHMIDT
32 Vice President Student Life & Dev ......Dr. Connie GORES
13 Assoc Vice Pres/CIO Tech Svcs ......Mr. Kenneth JANZ
21 Assoc VP for Finance/Admin Svcs/ CFO ......Mr. Scott ELLINGHUYSEN
20 Assoc Vice Pres Academic Affairs ......Dr. Nancy JANNIK
26 Assistant VP Marketing & Communicat ......Ms. Cristeen CUSTER
38 Chairperson of Counseling Services ......Ms. Patricia FERDEN
54 Dean Col of Science/Engineering ......Dr. Walter ORNES
49 Dean Liberal Arts ......Dr. Ralph TOWNSEND
50 Dean of Business ......Dr. Bill MURPHY
53 Dean of Education ......Dr. Henry RUBIN
66 Dean Nursing/Health Science ......Dr. William MCBREEN
35 Dean of Students ......Ms. Karen JOHNSON
06 Registrar ......Mr. Glenn PETERSEN
09 Director Institutional Research ......Ms. Teri HINDS
37 Director of Financial Aid ......Mr. Greg PETERSON
36 Director Career Services ......Ms. Vicki DECKER
07 Director of Admissions ......Mr. Carl STANGE
39 Director Residential College ......Mr. Ron ELCOMBE
31 Director of Auxiliary Services ......Vacant
29 Director of Alumni Affairs ......Mr. Michael SWENSON
40 Director of Bookstore ......Ms. Karen KRAUSE
44 Director Major Gifts ......Ms. Mary ROHRER
88 Director of International Svcs ......Mr. Jay SKRANKA
19 Director of Security ......Mr. Don WALSKI
41 Athletic Director ......Mr. Larry HOLSTAD
18 Chief Facilities/Physical Plant ......Mr. Richard LANDE
27 Director University Communications ......Ms. Andrea MIKKELSEN
94 Director of Women's Studies ......Dr. Tamara BERG
96 Director of Purchasing ......Ms. Deborah BENZ
28 Director of Cultural Diversity ......Mr. Alexander HINES
15 Director of Human Resources ......Ms. Lori REED

North Central University (C)

910 Elliot Avenue, Minneapolis MN 55404-1391
County: Hennepin FICE Identification: 002369
Unit ID: 174437
Telephone: (612) 343-4400 Carnegie Class: Bac/Diverse
FAX Number: (612) 343-4778 Calendar System: Semester
URL: www.northcentral.edu
Established: 1930 Annual Undergrad Tuition & Fees: $15,660
Enrollment: 2,165 Coed
Affiliation or Control: Assemblies Of God Church IRS Status: 501(c)3
Highest Offering: Baccalaureate
Program: Liberal Arts And General
Accreditation: NH

01 President ......Dr. Gordon L. ANDERSON
10 Vice President Finance ......Mrs. Cheryl A. BOOK
05 Vice Pres Academic Affs/Acad Dean ......Dr. Tom A. BURKMAN
30 Vice President Advancement ......Dr. Paul A. FREITAG
32 Vice President Student Development ......Mr. Mike A. NOSSER
26 VP University Rels/Enrollment ......Mr. Nate P. RUCH
57 Executive Director Fine Arts ......Mr. Larry C. BACH
39 Dean of Residence Life ......Mr. Jake SMITH
31 Dean of Community Life ......Ms. Jolene A. CASSELIUS
41 Athletic Director ......Mr. Jon HIGH
37 Director of Financial Aid ......Ms. Donna JAGER
08 Library Director ......Ms. Melody REEDY
07 Exec Director Enrollment/Admissions ......Mr. Troy PEARSON
13 Director of Information Technology ......Mr. Michael CAPPELLI
06 Registrar ......Mr. Cody SCHMITZ
18 Director of Plant/Operations ......Mr. Vern KISSNER
44 Director Plannned Giving ......Mr. Wes BOOK
36 Director Student Placement ......Mr. Tracy PAINO

Northwest Technical Institute (D)

950 Blue Gentian Road, Suite 500, Eagan MN 55121-1626
County: Dakota FICE Identification: 008267
Unit ID: 174482
Telephone: (952) 944-0080 Carnegie Class: Assoc/PrivFP
FAX Number: (952) 944-9274 Calendar System: Semester
URL: www.nti.edu
Established: 1957 Annual Undergrad Tuition & Fees: $16,950
Enrollment: 67 Coed
Affiliation or Control: Proprietary IRS Status: Proprietary
Highest Offering: Associate Degree
Program: Occupational; 2-Year Principally Bachelor's Creditable; Technical Emphasis
Accreditation: ACCSC

00 Chairman of the Board ......Mr. Norris J. NELSON
01 President ......Mr. Keith A. FOSSEN
05 Chief Academic Officer ......Dr. Amy NELSON
36 Placement ......Mrs. Theres HEIMEL
07 Director of Admissions ......Mr. Keith FOSSEN

Northwestern College (E)

3003 Snelling Avenue N, Saint Paul MN 55113-1598
County: Ramsey FICE Identification: 002371
Unit ID: 174491
Telephone: (651) 631-5100 Carnegie Class: Bac/Diverse
FAX Number: (651) 628-3339 Calendar System: Semester
URL: www.nwc.edu
Established: 1902 Annual Undergrad Tuition & Fees: $25,055
Enrollment: 3,062 Coed
Affiliation or Control: Independent Non-Profit IRS Status: 501(c)3
Highest Offering: Master's
Program: Liberal Arts And General; Teacher Preparatory
Accreditation: NH, MUS

01 President ......Dr. Alan S. CURETON
05 Senior Vice Pres Academic Affairs ......Dr. Janet B. SOMMERS
30 Vice President Advancement ......Mrs. Amy B. CAREY
10 Vice President Finance/CFO ......Mr. Douglas R. SCHROEDER
27 Senior Vice President Media ......Dr. Paul H. VIRTS
51 Vice President Grad/Continuing Educ ......Dr. Don F. JOHNSON
32 Vice Pres Student Life & Athletics ......Dr. Mathew B. HILL
00 President Emeritus ......Dr. Donald O. ERICKSEN
21 Director of Business Services ......Mrs. Marla K. DENNISON
20 Dean of Faculty ......Dr. Mark D. BADEN
88 Dean of Retention ......Ms. Monica R. GROVES
35 Dean of Student Development ......Mr. Paul A. BRADLEY
35 Assoc Dean Student Development ......Dr. Katie J. SMITH
06 Registrar ......Mr. Andrew L. SIMPSON
09 Institutional Researcher Rprt Spec ......Mr. Russell E. ERICKSON
29 Dir of Alumni & Parent Relations ......Mr. James E. BENDER
37 Director of Financial Aid ......Mr. Richard L. BLATCHLEY
58 Asst Dean Acad Pgm/Grad Cont Educ ......Dr. Erin L. HEATH
13 Vice Pres for Campus Technology/CIO ......Mr. Ray C. KUNTZ
88 Controller ......Mr. Bryon D. KRUEGER
08 Director of Library Services ......Mrs. Ruth A. MCGUIRE
15 Director of Human Resources ......Mr. Timothy A. RICH
24 Director of Academic Technology ......Ms. Susie A. BROOKS
23 Director of Health Services ......Mrs. Cynthia P. REEDSTROM
42 Senior Dir of Campus Ministries ......Mr. James K. JOHNSON
18 Assoc VP Facility Ops & Planning ......Mr. Brian L. HUMPHRIES
36 Director of Career Development ......Ms. Linda F. MAYES
26 Dir of Mktg & Communications ......Ms. Marita K. MEINERTS
40 Manager Campus Store ......Ms. Andrea R. HALVERSON
19 Director of Public Safety ......Mr. Peter L. SOLA
38 Director of Counseling/Student Svcs ......Ms. Dannette C. WILFAHRT
44 Director of Planned Giving ......Mr. David D. DANIELSON
96 Purchasing Manager ......Mrs. Lindy J. STANKEY
07 Senior Director of Admissions ......Mr. Ken K. FAFFLER
88 Asst to Pres for ADA Initiatives ......Dr. Yvonne R. BANKS
88 Assoc Dean Commuter Life/Transition ......Mr. Jeff B. SNYDER
102 Senior Director/Development ......Ms. Alisha J. CORA
101 Exec Secy to Pres & Bd of Trustees ......Ms. Mona S. GRELLSON
39 Associate Dean for Residence Life ......Mr. Jerod L. CORNELIUS

Northwestern Health Sciences University (F)

2501 W 84th Street, Bloomington MN 55431-1599
County: Hennepin FICE Identification: 012328
Unit ID: 174507
Telephone: (952) 888-4777 Carnegie Class: Spec/Health
FAX Number: (952) 888-6713 Calendar System: Trimester
URL: www.nwhealth.edu
Established: 1941 Annual Undergrad Tuition & Fees: $9,630
Enrollment: 852 Coed
Affiliation or Control: Independent Non-Profit IRS Status: 501(c)3
Highest Offering: First Professional Degree
Program: Professional
Accreditation: NH, ACUP, CHIRO, COMTA

01 President ......Dr. Mark T. ZEIGLER
03 Senior Vice President ......Dr. Charles E. SAWYER
05 Provost ......Dr. Michael WILES
11 Vice Pres Administrative Affairs ......Mr. Ross DUGAS
32 Dean Student Affs/Enrollment Mgmt ......Dr. Emily TWEED
07 Director of Admissions ......Vacant
08 Director of Library Services ......Ms. Della SHUPE
29 Director Alumni Relations/Dev Svcs ......Ms. Deborah A. PETERSON
06 Chief Records Officer & Registrar ......Ms. RuthAnn MARKS
15 Director of Human Resources ......Ms. Deborah HOGENSON
37 Director of Financial Aid ......Mr. Andrew S. HOPPIN
51 Director Continuing Education ......Ms. Diana BERG
26 Director of Communications ......Mr. John W. HEALY
30 Chief Development Officer ......Mr. Scott PALMER
13 Chief Information Systems Officer ......Mr. Don PRILL
38 University Counselor ......Ms. Becky LAWYER
18 Director Physical Plant ......Mr. Kevin WOLPERN
96 Director of Purchasing ......Ms. Jan HALLEEN

Oak Hills Christian College (G)

1600 Oak Hills Road, SW, Bemidji MN 56601-8826
County: Beltrami FICE Identification: 009992
Unit ID: 174525
Telephone: (218) 751-8670 Carnegie Class: Spec/Faith
FAX Number: (218) 751-8825 Calendar System: Semester
URL: www.oakhills.edu
Established: 1946 Annual Undergrad Tuition & Fees: $14,670
Enrollment: 140 Coed
Affiliation or Control: Interdenominational IRS Status: 501(c)3
Highest Offering: Baccalaureate
Program: Religious Emphasis
Accreditation: BI

01 President ......Dr. Steve J. HOSTETTER
05 Dean of the College ......Dr. Steven J. WARE
30 Vice President for Advancement ......Mrs. Joan L. BERNTSON
10 Business Manager ......Mrs. Carol NELSON
06 Registrar ......Mrs. Mary HANNAH
08 Library Director ......Mr. Keith BUSH
07 Dean of Student Enrollment ......Mr. John ENGQUIST
37 Director of Financial Aid ......Mr. Daniel HOVESTOL

*Rasmussen College - Lake Elmo/ Woodbury (H)

8550 Hudson Blvd, Suite 110, Lake Elmo MN 55042
County: Washington Identification: 667034
Unit ID: 17501405
Telephone: (651) 636-3305 Carnegie Class: N/A
FAX Number: (651) 636-3375
URL: www.rasmussen.edu

01 Campus Director ......Mr. Phillip KAGOL

*Rasmussen College - Blaine (I)

3629 95th Avenue Northeast, Blaine MN 55014
County: Anoka Identification: 667061
Unit ID: 17501406
Telephone: (763) 795-4720 Carnegie Class: Not Classified
FAX Number: (763) 795-4721 Calendar System: Quarter
URL: www.rasmussen.edu
Established: 1900 Annual Undergrad Tuition & Fees: $16,340
Enrollment: 204 Coed
Affiliation or Control: Proprietary IRS Status: Proprietary
Highest Offering: Baccalaureate
Program: Occupational; 2-Year Principally Bachelor's Creditable
Accreditation: &NH

02 Campus Director ......Patty SAGERT

† Regional accreditation is carried under the parent institution in Lake Elmo, MN.

*Rasmussen College - Bloomington (J)

4400 W 78th St, 6th Floor, Bloomington MN 55435
County: Hennepin FICE Identification: 011686
Unit ID: 174464
Telephone: (952) 545-2000 Carnegie Class: Assoc/PrivFP4
FAX Number: (952) 545-7038 Calendar System: Quarter
URL: www.Rasmussen.edu
Established: 1963 Annual Undergrad Tuition & Fees: $16,340
Enrollment: 701 Coed
Affiliation or Control: Proprietary IRS Status: Proprietary

Highest Offering: Baccalaureate
Program: Occupational; 2-Year Principally Bachelor's Creditable
Accreditation: &NH, MAC

02 Campus Director .... Mr. Jeff BROSZ

† Regional accreditation carried under the parent institution in Lake Elmo, MN.

Rasmussen College - Brooklyn Park (A)

3301 93rd Avenue North, Brooklyn Park MN 55445-1512
County: Hennepin — Identification: 666769
Unit ID: 17501404
Telephone: (763) 493-4500 — Carnegie Class: Not Classified
FAX Number: N/A — Calendar System: Semester
URL: www.rasmussen.edu
Established: N/A — Annual Undergrad Tuition & Fees: $16,340
Enrollment: 1,203 — Coed
Affiliation or Control: Proprietary — IRS Status: Proprietary
Highest Offering: Baccalaureate
Program: Occupational; 2-Year Principally Bachelor's Creditable
Accreditation: &NH, MAC

02 Campus Director .... Ms. Naomi MOGARD

† Regional accreditation carried under the parent institution in Lake Elmo, MN.

Rasmussen College - Eagan (B)

3500 Federal Drive, Eagan MN 55122-1346
County: Dakota — FICE Identification: 004648
Unit ID: 174622
Telephone: (651) 687-9000 — Carnegie Class: Bac/Assoc
FAX Number: (651) 687-0507 — Calendar System: Quarter
URL: www.Rasmussen.edu
Established: 1900 — Annual Undergrad Tuition & Fees: $16,340
Enrollment: 1,016 — Coed
Affiliation or Control: Proprietary — IRS Status: Proprietary
Highest Offering: Baccalaureate
Program: Occupational; 2-Year Principally Bachelor's Creditable
Accreditation: &NH, MAC

02 Campus Director .... Ms. Tammy JACKSON

† Regional accreditation carried under the parent institution in Lake Elmo, MN.

Rasmussen College - Mankato (C)

130 Saint Andrews Drive, Mankato MN 56001
County: Blue Earth — FICE Identification: 025033
Unit ID: 174631
Telephone: (507) 625-6556 — Carnegie Class: Bac/Assoc
FAX Number: (507) 625-6557 — Calendar System: Quarter
URL: www.Rasmussen.edu
Established: 1900 — Annual Undergrad Tuition & Fees: $16,340
Enrollment: 935 — Coed
Affiliation or Control: Proprietary — IRS Status: Proprietary
Highest Offering: Baccalaureate
Program: Occupational; 2-Year Principally Bachelor's Creditable
Accreditation: &NH, MAC, MLTAD

02 Campus Director .... Ms. Kathy SANGER

† Regional accreditation carried under the parent institution in Lake Elmo, MN.

Rasmussen College - St. Cloud (D)

226 Park Avenue South, Saint Cloud MN 56301-3713
County: Stearns — FICE Identification: 008694
Unit ID: 175014
Telephone: (320) 251-5600 — Carnegie Class: Assoc/PrivFP4
FAX Number: (320) 251-3702 — Calendar System: Quarter
URL: www.Rasmussen.edu
Established: 1902 — Annual Undergrad Tuition & Fees: $16,340
Enrollment: 1,251 — Coed
Affiliation or Control: Proprietary — IRS Status: Proprietary
Highest Offering: Baccalaureate
Program: Occupational; 2-Year Principally Bachelor's Creditable
Accreditation: &NH, MAC, MLTAD, SURGT

02 Campus Director .... Mr. John SMITH-COPPES

† Regional accreditation carried under the parent institution in Lake Elmo, MN.

St. Catherine University (E)

2004 Randolph Avenue, Saint Paul MN 55105-1789
County: Ramsey — FICE Identification: 002342
Unit ID: 175005
Telephone: (651) 690-6000 — Carnegie Class: Master's L
FAX Number: (651) 690-6024 — Calendar System: 4/1/4
URL: www.stkate.edu
Established: 1905 — Annual Undergrad Tuition & Fees: $31,640
Enrollment: 5,328 — Female
Affiliation or Control: Roman Catholic — IRS Status: 501(c)3
Highest Offering: Doctorate
Program: Liberal Arts And General; Teacher Preparatory; Professional
Accreditation: NH, ADNUR, DIETD, DMS, EXSC, LIB, MACTE, NUR, OT, OTA, PTA, PTAA, RAD, SW

01 President .... Dr. Andrea J. LEE, IHM
03 Senior Vice President .... Ms. Colleen HEGRANES
10 Vice Pres Finance/Administration .... Mr. Thomas ROONEY
26 Vice Pres for External Relations ..... Ms. Marjorie Mathison HANCE
84 VP Enrollment Mgmt/Student Affairs .... Dr. Brian BRUESS
05 Chief Academic Officer .... Ms. Colleen HEGRANES
06 Registrar .... Ms. Cynthia EGENESS
08 Library Director .... Ms. Carol JOHNSON
30 Chief Development .... Ms. Marjorie MATHISON HANCE
32 Chief Student Life Officer .... Dr. Brian BRUESS
29 Director Alumnae Relations .... Ms. Ruth C. BROMBACH
26 Dir of Marketing & Communications .... Ms. Amy GAGE
37 Director of Financial Aid .... Ms. Elizabeth STEVENS
36 Director of Career Development .... Ms. Kimberly BETZ
14 Director of Computing Services .... Mr. John JERIES
21 Business Manager .... Ms. Tracey GRAN
04 Exec Assistant to the President .... Ms. Stacy JACOBSON
15 Director of Personnel Services .... Ms. Susan SEXTON
38 Director of Student Counseling .... Ms. Heide MALAT
92 Director of Honors Program .... Dr. Gayle GASKILL
94 Director of Women's Studies .... Dr. Sharon DOHERTY
96 Director of Purchasing .... Ms. Gail BLIVEN
09 Dir Instl Rsrch/Plng/Assessment .... Dr. Jennifer ROBINSON KLOOS
18 Chief Facilities/Physical Plant .... Mr. James MANSHIP
49 Dean Sch Humanities/Arts/Sciences .... Dr. Alan SILVA
107 Dean of Professional Studies .... Dr. MaryAnn JANOSIK
76 Dean Henrietta Schmoll Sch Health .... Dr. Penelope MOYERS
07 Associate Dean of Admissions .... Ms. Marlene MOHS
27 Assoc Dean Admiss/Market Devel .... Mr. Greg STEENSON
28 Asc Dean Students/Multicultural Ed .... Mr. Wachen Bedell ANDERSON
35 Associate Dean for Student Affairs .... Mr. Curt GALLOWAY
88 Dean Business & Leadership .... Dr. Paula KING
20 Associate Dean Academic Affairs .... Ms. Bonnie LADUCA
20 Associate Dean of Academic Affairs .... Dr. Lynda SZYMANSKI
53 Associate Dean of Education .... Dr. Lori MAXFIELD

Saint John's University (F)

Box 2000, Collegeville MN 56321-2000
County: Stearns — FICE Identification: 002379
Unit ID: 174792
Telephone: (320) 363-2011 — Carnegie Class: Bac/A&S
FAX Number: (320) 363-2504 — Calendar System: Semester
URL: www.csbsju.edu
Established: 1857 — Annual Undergrad Tuition & Fees: $33,606
Enrollment: 1,906 — Coordinate
Affiliation or Control: Roman Catholic — IRS Status: 501(c)3
Highest Offering: Master's
Program: Liberal Arts And General; Teacher Preparatory; Professional
Accreditation: NH, DIETD, MUS, NURSE, TED, THEOL

01 President .... Fr. Robert J. KOOPMANN, OSB
05 Provost Academic Affairs .... Dr. Rita KNUESEL
20 Associate Provost/Academic Dean .... Dr. Joseph DES JARDINS
30 Vice President for Inst Advancement .... Mr. Rob CULLIGAN
32 Vice President Student Development ... Fr. Douglas MULLIN, OSB
10 Vice Pres Finance/Admin Services .... Mr. Richard ADAMSON
46 VP Inst Plng/Research/Communication .... Mr. Jon MCGEE
07 Vice Pres Admissions/Financial Aid .... Mr. Cal MOSLEY
73 Dean School Theology .... Dr. William CAHOY
88 Int Dean Intl/Experimental Educ .... Mr. Joseph ROGERS
35 Dean of Students .... Mr. Michael CONNOLLY
45 Associate Dean Planning/Budget .... Mr. David LYNDGAARD
26 Exec Director of Comm & Marketing .... Mr. Greg HOYE
08 Director of Library .... Ms. Kathleen PARKER
06 Registrar .... Ms. Julie GRUSKA
38 Director Counseling/Career Services .... Ms. Heidi HARLANDER
37 Director of Financial Aid .... Mr. Stuart PERRY
90 Director of Computing Services .... Mr. Jim KOENIG
29 Director of Alumni Relations .... Mr. Thom William WOODWARD
15 Director Human Resources .... Ms. Carol ABELL
41 Athletic Director .... Mr. Tom STOCK
19 Director Life Safety Services .... Mr. Shawn VIERZBA
42 Director of Campus Ministry .... Fr. William SCHIPPER, OSB
18 Director Facilities/Physical Plant .... Mr. Bill BOOM
40 Director Bookstore .... Mr. Donald FORBES
09 Assoc Director Inst Research .... Ms. Karen G. KNUTSON

Saint Mary's University of Minnesota (G)

700 Terrace Heights, Winona MN 55987-1399
County: Winona — FICE Identification: 002380
Unit ID: 174817
Telephone: (507) 452-4430 — Carnegie Class: DRU
FAX Number: (507) 457-1633 — Calendar System: Semester
URL: www.smumn.edu
Established: 1912 — Annual Undergrad Tuition & Fees: $27,250
Enrollment: 6,058 — Coed
Affiliation or Control: Roman Catholic — IRS Status: 501(c)3
Highest Offering: Doctorate
Program: Liberal Arts And General; Teacher Preparatory
Accreditation: NH, ANEST, IACBE, MFCD, MUS, NMT, SURGT

00 Chancellor .... Bro. Louis DETHOMASIS, FSC
01 President .... Bro. William MANN, FSC
03 Vice President of the College .... Mr. James BEDTKE
07 Vice President Admissions .... Mr. Anthony M. PISCITIELLO
30 Sr Vice Pres University Advancement .... Dr. Steve TITUS
32 Vice President Student Development .... Mr. Chris KENDALL
10 Vice President Financial Affairs .... Ms. Cynthia MAREK
43 Exec Vice Pres/General Counsel .... Ms. Ann E. MERCHLEWITZ
26 VP for Communication & Marketing .... Mr. Robert CONOVER
05 Vice President for Academic Affairs .... Dr. Donna ARONSON
58 VP Schs of Graduate/Professnl Pgms .... Dr. Marcel DUMESTRE
20 Academic Dean/Assoc Vice President .... Ms. Linka HOLEY
35 Dean of Students/Dir Resident Life .... Mr. Tim GOSSEN
04 Assistant to the President .... Ms. Mary BECKER
06 Registrar .... Ms. Yunge H K. DUTTON
13 Director of Information Technology .... Mr. Francis SPECK
37 Director of Financial Aid .... Ms. Jayne WOBIG
88 Director of Toner Student Center .... Ms. Terrie LUECK
36 Dir Career Services & Internships .... Ms. Jackie BAKER
38 Director of Counseling Center .... Dr. Ann E. GIBSON
08 Director of Library .... Ms. Laura OANES
22 Affirmative Action Officer .... Ms. Ann E. MERCHLEWITZ
21 Assistant Controller .... Mr. Paul J. WILDENBORG
19 Director of Security .... Ms. Andrea ESSAR
18 Director of Buildings/Grounds .... Mr. John SCHOLLMEIER
42 Director of Campus Ministry .... Mr. Dennis GALLAGHER
23 Director of Health Services .... Ms. Angela WEISBROD
29 Director Alumni Relations .... Ms. Margaret RICHTMAN
41 Director of Athletics .... Ms. Nicole FENNERN
15 Director of Human Resources .... Ms. Genelle GROH BECK
09 Institutional Researcher .... Ms. Kara WENER
53 Dean School Education .... Dr. Jane ANDERSON
79 Dean School of the Arts .... Mr. Michael CHARRON

St. Olaf College (H)

1520 St. Olaf Avenue, Northfield MN 55057-1098
County: Rice — FICE Identification: 002382
Unit ID: 174844
Telephone: (507) 786-2222 — Carnegie Class: Bac/A&S
FAX Number: (507) 786-3549 — Calendar System: 4/1/4
URL: www.stolaf.edu
Established: 1874 — Annual Undergrad Tuition & Fees: $46,950
Enrollment: 3,105 — Coed
Affiliation or Control: Evangelical Lutheran Church In America
IRS Status: 501(c)3
Highest Offering: Baccalaureate
Program: Liberal Arts And General; Teacher Preparatory; Professional
Accreditation: NH, DANCE, MUS, NURSE, SW, TED, THEA

01 President .... Dr. David R. ANDERSON
05 Provost & Dean of the College .... Dr. Marci J. SORTOR
10 Vice President & Treasurer .... Dr. Alan J. NORTON
30 Vice Pres Advancement/College Rels . Mr. Michael STITSWORTH
32 VP Student Affs/Dean of Students .... Mr. Greg KNESER
84 Vice President/Dean for Enrollment .... Mr. Michael KYLE
88 VP Liaison to the Board of Regents .... Dr. Paula J. CARLSON
18 Asst Vice President for Facilities .... Mr. Peter SANDBERG
31 Asst to the Pres for Inst Diversity .... Mr. Bruce KING
20 Assistant Provost .... Vacant
06 Asst VP Registrar .... Dr. Mary CISAR
89 Assoc Dean Interdisciplin/Gen Stds .... Dr. Phyllis LARSON
81 Assoc Dean Natural Sciences & Math .... Dr. Matthew RICHEY
79 Assoc Dean Humanities .... Dr. Corliss SWAIN
57 Assoc Dean Fine Arts .... Dr. Dan DRESSEN
83 Assoc Dean Social Sciences .... Dr. Dan HOFRENNING
88 Assoc VP for Advancement/College .... Ms. Janet K. THOMPSON
21 Asst VP/Chief Investment Officer .... Mr. Mark GELLE
37 Asst VP Enroll/Dean Financial Aid .... Ms. Katharine RUBY
35 Associate Dean of Students .... Ms. Rosalyn EATON-NEEB
35 Assoc Dean & Dir Buntrock Commons ..... Mr. Timothy SCHROER
42 Campus Pastor .... Vacant
36 Sr Assoc Dir of Career Connections .... Ms. Kirsten CAHOON
44 Senior Director of Development .... Mr. Enoch BLAZIS
13 Dir Information/Instructional Tech .... Ms. Roberta LEMBKE
08 Interim Director Library Services .... Ms. Roberta LEMBKE
44 Director Annual Giving .... Ms. Tracy FOSSUM
29 Director of Alumni Parent Relations .... Mr. Nathan SOLAND
07 Dean of Admissions .... Mr. Derek GUELDENZOPH
15 Director of Human Resources .... Mr. Roger LOFTUS
19 Director of Public Safety .... Mr. Fred C. BEHR
41 Director of Athletics .... Mr. Matt C. MCDONALD
38 Director of Counseling .... Dr. Stephen O'NEILL
26 Dir of Marketing & Communications .... Mr. Steve BLODGETT
88 Dir Center for Experiential Lrng .... Dr. Steve MCKELVEY
09 Director of Institutional Research .... Ms. Susan CANON
39 Director of Residence Life .... Ms. Pamela MCDOWELL
40 Bookstore Director .... Ms. Victoria BEUSSMAN
93 Dir Multicultural Cmty Outreach .... Mr. William GREEN
96 Director of Auxiliary Operations .... Mr. Steve ABBOTT
37 Director of Student Financial Aid .... Ms. Sandra SUNDSTROM
102 Dir of Govt & Foundation Relations .... Ms. Patricia MARTIN
104 Dir of Intl & Off Campus Studies .... Dr. Eric LUND
85 International Student Advisor .... Ms. Christy HALL-HOLT
04 Exec Assistant to the President .... Ms. Pat HESS

United Theological Seminary of the Twin Cities (I)

3000 Fifth Street, NW, New Brighton MN 55112-2598
County: Ramsey — FICE Identification: 002386
Unit ID: 175139
Telephone: (651) 633-4311 — Carnegie Class: Spec/Faith
FAX Number: (651) 633-4315 — Calendar System: 4/1/4
URL: www.unitedseminary.edu
Established: 1962 — Annual Graduate Tuition & Fees: $14,845
Enrollment: 171 — Coed

Affiliation or Control: United Church Of Christ IRS Status: 501(c)3
Highest Offering: Doctorate; No Undergraduates
Program: Professional; Religious Emphasis
Accreditation: NH, THEOL

01 President .... Rev. Mary E. MCNAMARA
05 Dean of the Seminary .... Ms. Susan EBBERS
10 VP for Finance and Administration .... Mr. Tom LOCKHART
30 VP for Development .... Mr. Jim OLSEN
44 Director of Development .... Ms. Julie BROWN
07 Director of Admissions .... Rev. Glen HERRINGTON-HALL
04 Admin Assistant to the President .... Ms. Gretchen MILLOY
06 Registrar .... Ms. Susan HASTINGS
37 Director Student Financial Aid .... Ms. Michelle TURNAU
08 Librarian .... Ms. Susan EBBERS
51 Director Continuing Education .... Dr. Cindi Beth JOHNSON
42 Chaplain/Assc Prof Spirit Formation .... Rev. Martha POSTLETHWAITE
18 Director Physical Plant .... Mr. Brandon KROSCH

University of Minnesota-Crookston (A)

2900 University Avenue, Crookston MN 56716-5001
County: Polk FICE Identification: 004069
Unit ID: 174075
Telephone: (218) 281-6510 Carnegie Class: Bac/Diverse
FAX Number: (218) 281-8040 Calendar System: Semester
URL: www.crk.umn.edu
Established: 1965 Annual Undergrad Tuition & Fees (In-State): $11,096
Enrollment: 1,460 Coed
Affiliation or Control: State IRS Status: 501(c)3
Highest Offering: Baccalaureate
Program: Liberal Arts And General
Accreditation: NH

01 Chancellor .... Dr. Charles H. CASEY
05 Sr VC Academic/Student Affairs .... Dr. Thomas BALDWIN
32 Assoc VC Student Affs/Enrollment .... Dr. Peter PHAIAH
18 Director Facilities/Operations .... Vacant
10 Dir of Finance/University Services .... Ms. Tricia SANDERS
15 Director Human Resources .... Mr. Les JOHNSON
37 Director Financial Aid .... Ms. Melissa DINGMANN
26 Director of Communications .... Mr. Andrew SVEC
30 Dir Development/Alumni Relations .... Mr. Corby KEMMER
08 Director Library .... Mr. Owen WILLIAMS
36 Director Career/Counseling .... Mr. Donald R. CAVALIER
49 Head of Arts/Humanities/Soc Sci .... Dr. Jack GELLER
47 Head Agriculture & Nat Resources .... Dr. Ron DEL VECCHIO
72 Head Math/Science/Technology .... Dr. Adel ALI
50 Head Business .... Dr. Susan BRORSON
51 Director Center for Adult Learning .... Ms. Michelle CHRISTOPHERSON
06 Registrar .... Dr. Bob NELSON
07 Director of Admissions .... Ms. Amber EVANS-DAILEY
28 Director of Diversity .... Mr. Thomas WILLIAMS
85 Dir of International Programs .... Dr. Kimberly GILLETTE

University of Minnesota Duluth (B)

1049 University Drive, Duluth MN 55812-3011
County: Saint Louis FICE Identification: 002388
Unit ID: 174233
Telephone: (218) 726-8000 Carnegie Class: Master's M
FAX Number: (218) 726-6254 Calendar System: Semester
URL: www.d.umn.edu
Established: 1947 Annual Undergrad Tuition & Fees (In-State): $12,782
Enrollment: 11,729 Coed
Affiliation or Control: State IRS Status: 501(c)3
Highest Offering: Doctorate
Program: Liberal Arts And General; Teacher Preparatory; Professional
Accreditation: NH, BUS, CS, ENG, MUS, SP, SW, TED

01 Chancellor .... Dr. Lendley C. BLACK
05 Interim Exec Vice Chanc Acad Admin .... Dr. Bilin TSAI
32 Vice Chancellor Student Life .... Dr. Jackie MILLSLAGLE
10 Int Vice Chanc Finance/Operations .... Mr. John KING
26 Vice Chanc University Relations .... Mr. William WADE
06 Registrar .... Ms. Brenda H. HERZIG
08 Director of Library .... Mr. Basil W. SOZANSKY, JR.
37 Director Financial Aid .... Ms. Brenda H. HERZIG
36 Director Career Services .... Ms. Julie A. WESTLUND
13 Director Info Tech Systems/Services .... Dr. Linda DENEEN
09 Director Institutional Research .... Dr. Giljae LEE
25 Senior Grant Administrator .... Vacant
51 Director Continuing Education .... Dr. Robert KRUMWIEDE
41 Athletic Director .... Mr. Robert NIELSON
15 Director Personnel Services .... Ms. Judith S. KARON
07 Director Admissions .... Ms. Beth ESSELSTROM
18 Director Facilities/Physical Plant .... Mr. John KING
29 Director Alumni Relations .... Ms. Patty DELANO
30 Director Development .... Ms. Tricia BUNTEN
63 Associate Dean School of Medicine .... Dr. Gary DAVIS
81 Interim Dean Col Science/Engr .... Dr. Penny MORTON
49 Dean College Liberal Arts .... Dr. Susan MAHER
53 Dean Col Education/Human Svc Prof .... Dr. Paul DEPUTY
50 Dean School of Business & Economics .... Dr. Kjell KNUDSEN
57 Interim Dean School Fine Arts .... Mr. William PAYNE
58 Director of Graduate Programs .... Dr. Tim HOLST

University of Minnesota-Morris (C)

600 E 4th Street, Morris MN 56267-2132
County: Stevens FICE Identification: 002389
Unit ID: 174251
Telephone: (320) 589-2211 Carnegie Class: Bac/A&S
FAX Number: (320) 589-6399 Calendar System: Semester
URL: www.morris.umn.edu
Established: 1959 Annual Undergrad Tuition & Fees (In-State): $11,168
Enrollment: 1,811 Coed
Affiliation or Control: State IRS Status: 501(c)3
Highest Offering: Baccalaureate
Program: Liberal Arts And General; Teacher Preparatory
Accreditation: NH, TED

01 Chancellor .... Dr. Jacqueline JOHNSON
05 Int Vice Chanc Academic Affs/Dean .... Dr. Bart FINZEL
32 Vice Chanc for Student Affairs .... Ms. Sandra OLSON-LOY
30 Assoc VC for External Relations .... Ms. Maddy MAXEINER
18 Assoc VC Physical Plant/Master Plng .... Mr. Lowell C. RASMUSSEN
10 Director for Finance .... Ms. Colleen MILLER
08 Head Librarian .... Ms. LeAnn DEAN
06 Registrar .... Ms. Clare DINGLEY
26 Chief Public Relations Officer .... Ms. Christine MAHONEY
29 Director of Alumni Relations .... Ms. Carla RILEY
09 Director of Institutional Research .... Ms. Nancy HELSPER
36 Director Career Center .... Mr. Gary L. DONOVAN
14 Director of Information Technology .... Mr. James HALL
38 Director of Counseling .... Dr. Henry FULDA
37 Director of Financial Aid .... Ms. Jill BEAUREGARD
93 Dir Multi Ethnic Student Program .... Ms. Hilda LADNER
24 Director Educational Media .... Mr. Roger P. BOLEMAN
07 Director of Admissions .... Mr. Bryan HERRMANN
53 Chair of Education Division .... Dr. Gwen RUDNEY
81 Chair of Science/Math Division .... Dr. Peh Peh NG
79 Chair of Humanities Division .... Dr. Janet ERICKSEN
83 Chair of Social Science Division .... Dr. Leslie MEEK

University of Minnesota-Twin Cities (D)

100 Church Street, SE, Minneapolis MN 55455-0213
County: Hennepin FICE Identification: 003969
Unit ID: 174066
Telephone: (612) 625-5000 Carnegie Class: RU/VH
FAX Number: (612) 624-6369 Calendar System: Semester
URL: www.umn.edu
Established: 1851 Annual Undergrad Tuition & Fees (In-State): $12,902
Enrollment: 51,721 Coed
Affiliation or Control: State IRS Status: 501(c)3
Highest Offering: Doctorate
Program: Occupational; Liberal Arts And General; Teacher Preparatory; Professional
Accreditation: NH, ANEST, AUD, BUS, CIDA, CLPSY, COPSY, DANCE, DENT, DH, DIETC, DIETD, DIETI, ENG, ENGR, FOR, FUSER, HSA, IPSY, JOUR, LAW, LSAR, MED, MFCD, MIDWF, MT, MUS, NURSE, OT, PH, PHAR, PLNG, PTA, RAD, RTT, SCPSY, SP, SPAA, SW, TED, THEA, VET

01 President .... Dr. Eric W. KALER
100 Chief of Staff .... Ms. Amy PHENIX
05 Sr VP for Academic Affairs/Provost .... Mr. E. Thomas SULLIVAN
17 Vice President for Health Sciences .... Dr. Aaron FRIEDMAN
11 Sr Vice Pres for System Acad Admin .... Dr. Robert J. JONES
10 Vice President/Chief Financial Ofcr .... Mr. Richard H. PFUTZENREUTER
26 Vice Pres for University Relations .... Vacant
46 Vice President for Research .... Dr. R. Timothy MULCAHY
58 Vice Prov/Dean Graduate Education .... Dr. Henning SCHROEDER
20 Vice Prov/Dean Undergrad Education .... Dr. Robert MCMASTER
15 Vice President Human Resources .... Ms. Kathryn F. BROWN
45 VP Statewide Strategic Res Develop .... Dr. Charles C. MUSCOPLAT
88 Vice Pres for University Services .... Ms. Kathleen A. O'BRIEN
28 Acting VP for Equity and Diversity .... Ms. Kristin LOCKHART
43 General Counsel .... Mr. Mark B. ROTENBERG
27 Acting Vice President/CIO .... Ms. Ann HILL DUIN
88 Vice Pres Scholarly/Cultural Affs .... Vacant
102 President Univ Minnesota Foundation .... Mr. L. Steven GOLDSTEIN
25 Assoc VP Sponsored Projects Admin .... Mr. Edward F. WINK
86 Assoc Vice Pres for Govt Relations .... Ms. Donna C. PETERSON
18 Associate VP/Chief of Facilities .... Mr. Mike BERTHELSEN
32 Vice Provost for Student Affairs .... Mr. Gerald D. RINEHART
19 Asst VP Pub Safety/Chief of Police .... Mr. Gregory S. HESTNESS
30 Chief Development Officer .... Mr. L. Steven GOLDSTEIN
08 University Librarian .... Dr. Wendy P. LOUGEE
06 Registrar .... Ms. Sue N. VAN VOORHIS
07 Director of Admissions .... Dr. Wayne SIGLER
09 Director of Institutional Research .... Dr. Richard D. HOWARD
22 Director Equal Oppty/Affirm Action .... Ms. Kimberly HEWITT BOYD
37 Director of Student Finance .... Ms. Kristine A. WRIGHT
40 Director of the U of M Bookstores .... Mr. Robert J. CRABB
39 Director of Student Housing .... Ms. Laurie L. MCLAUGHLIN
48 Dean of the College of Design .... Dr. Thomas R. FISHER
86 Director of Federal Relations .... Ms. Channing RIGGS
29 CEO Alumni Association .... Dr. Phil L. ESTEN
38 Director of Counseling Services .... Dr. Harriett C. HAYNES
87 Director of the Summer Session .... Dr. Jack K. JOHNSON
21 Associate VP for Budget/Finance .... Ms. Julie A. TONNESON
36 Director of Student Placement .... Ms. Jennifer A. ENGLER
96 Director of Purchasing .... Ms. Karen TRIPLETT
35 Chief Student Life Officer .... Mr. Gerald D. RINEHART
49 Dean of the College of Liberal Arts .... Mr. James A. PARENTE, JR.
51 Dean College of Continuing Educ .... Dr. Mary L. NICHOLS
61 Dean of the Law School .... Mr. David WIPPMAN
74 Dean College of Veterinary Medicine .... Dr. Trevor R. AMES
63 Dean of the Medical School .... Dr. Aaron FRIEDMAN
66 Dean of the School of Nursing .... Dr. Connie J. DELANEY
53 Dean College Education/Human Devel .... Dr. Jean K. QUAM
52 Dean of the School of Dentistry .... Mr. Patrick M. LLOYD
69 Dean of the School Public Health .... Dr. John FINNEGAN
72 Dean College of Science/Engineering .... Dr. Steven CROUCH
67 Dean of the College Pharmacy .... Dr. Marilyn K. SPEEDIE
50 Dean Carlson School of Management .... Dr. Alison DAVIS-BLAKE
80 Int Dean Humphrey Sch of Pub Aff .... Dr. Greg LINDSEY
81 Dean College of Biological Science .... Dr. Robert P. ELDE
47 Dean Col Food/Agric/Nat Resourc Sci .... Dr. Allen LEVINE
41 Director Intercollegiate Athletics .... Mr. Joel MATURI

University of Saint Thomas (E)

2115 Summit Avenue, Saint Paul MN 55105-1096
County: Ramsey FICE Identification: 002345
Unit ID: 174914
Telephone: (651) 962-5000 Carnegie Class: DRU
FAX Number: (651) 962-6360 Calendar System: 4/1/4
URL: www.stthomas.edu
Established: 1885 Annual Undergrad Tuition & Fees: $31,504
Enrollment: 10,839 Coed
Affiliation or Control: Roman Catholic IRS Status: 501(c)3
Highest Offering: Doctorate
Program: Liberal Arts And General; Teacher Preparatory; Professional
Accreditation: NH, COPSY, ENG, HSA, IPSY, LAW, MUS, SW, TED, THEOL

01 President .... Rev. Dennis J. DEASE
04 Executive Advisor to President .... Dr. Susan L. ALEXANDER
03 Exec Vice Pres/Chief Admin Officer .... Dr. Mark C. DIENHART
05 Int Exec VP/Chief Academic Officer .... Dr. Susan J. HUBER
88 Rector/Vice Pres School of Divinity .... Msgr. Aloysius R. CALLAGHAN
88 Vice President for Mission .... Fr. John MALONE
32 Vice President for Student Affairs .... Ms. Jane W. CANNEY
10 Vice Pres for Business Affairs/CFO .... Mr. Mark D. VANGSGARD
26 Vice President University Relations .... Mr. Doug E. HENNES
13 VP Information Resources & Tech .... Dr. Samuel J. LEVY
20 Assoc Vice Pres Academic Affairs .... Dr. Joseph L. KREITZER
20 Assoc Vice Pres Academic Affs .... Dr. Eleni ROULIS
84 Assoc VP Enrollment Services .... Ms. Marla J. FRIEDERICHS
15 Assoc VP for Human Resources .... Vacant
21 Assoc VP/Finance & Controller .... Mr. Gary L. THYEN
18 Associate Vice Pres Facilities .... Mr. Gerald M. ANDERLEY
88 Associate VP for Auxiliary Services .... Mr. Bruce VAN DEN BERGHE
49 Int Dean College Arts & Sciences .... Dr. Terrence G. LANGAN
50 Dean Opus College of Business .... Dr. Christopher P. PUTO
53 Int Dean of School of Education .... Dr. Bruce H. KRAMER
83 Dean of School of Social Work .... Dr. Barbara W. SHANK
73 Dean St Paul Seminary School of Div .... Dr. Christopher J. THOMPSON
61 Dean School of Law .... Mr. Thomas M. MENGLER
35 Dean of Student Life .... Ms. Karen M. LANGE
88 Assoc Dean Grad Prof Psychology .... Dr. Christopher VYE
88 Director Grad Pgm/Business Comm .... Dr. Michael PORTER
88 Sr Assoc Dean College of Business .... Dr. Michael GARRISON
54 Dean School of Engineering .... Dr. Donald H. WEINKFAUF
30 Executive Director for Development .... Mr. Stephen A. HOEPPNER
06 Registrar .... Mr. Paul M. SIMMONS
07 Director Admissions & Financial Aid .... Ms. Kris A. GETTING
09 Director of Institutional Research .... Dr. Michael F. COGAN
35 Executive Director Campus Life .... Ms. Mary A. RYAN
36 Director of Career Services .... Ms. Diane G. CRIST
27 Director of the News Service .... Mr. James C. WINTERER
29 Exec Dir Alumni/Constituent Rels .... Ms. Rachel A. WOBSCHALL
41 Athletic Director .... Mr. Stephen J. FRITZ
40 Director Bookstore .... Mr. Tony W. ERICKSON
42 Director Campus Ministry .... Fr. Erich RUTTEN
19 Director Safety/Security .... Mr. Daniel J. MEUWISSEN
39 Director Campus Life .... Ms. Margaret D. CAHILL
38 Director Student Counseling .... Dr. Jeri M. ROCKETT
96 Director Purchasing Services .... Ms. Karen M. HARTHORN
88 Director Recruit/Admis MBA Pgms .... Dr. William WOODSON
28 Director of Diversity .... Dr. MariAnn GRAHAM

Walden University (F)

155 Fifth Avenue S, Suite 100,
Minneapolis MN 55401-2597
County: Hennepin FICE Identification: 025042
Unit ID: 125231
Telephone: (612) 338-7224 Carnegie Class: DRU
FAX Number: (612) 338-5092 Calendar System: Other
URL: www.waldenu.edu
Established: 1970 Annual Undergrad Tuition & Fees: $12,720
Enrollment: 47,456 Coed
Affiliation or Control: Proprietary IRS Status: Proprietary
Highest Offering: Doctorate
Program: Teacher Preparatory
Accreditation: NH, ACBSP, CACREP, NURSE

01 President .... Mr. Jonathan A. KAPLAN
05 Chief Academic Officer .... Dr. David CLINEFELTER
69 Exec VP & VP College Health Sci .... Dr. Cynthia BAUM
53 VP RWR College of Education .... Ms. Victoria REID
83 Int VP College Soc & Behav Sciences .... Dr. Melanie STORMS
50 VP College of Mgmt & Tech .... Mr. Paul THOMAS
53 Dean RWR College of Education .... Dr. Kate STEFFENS
46 Exec Dir Office of IR & Assesment .... Dr. Eric RIEDEL
32 Exec Dir Ctr for Student Success .... Ms. Susanna DAVIDSEN
45 Exec Dir Ctr for Fac Excellence .... Dr. Donna LILJEGREN
88 Exec Dir Center for UG Studies .... Dr. David J. MATHIEU

88 Exec Dir Ctr for Research Support .... Dr. Laura LYNN
88 Exec Dir International Programs .... Ms. Lauren STONE
20 VP of Undergraduate Programs .... Ms. Susan B. DREIFUSS
10 COO and CFO .... Mr. Rick PATRO
15 Director of Human Resources .... Ms. Sherine HIGH
26 VP Marketing .... Mr. Christian SCHINDLER
13 IT Director .... Mr. Jason ROWLEY
07 Director of Admissions .... Ms. Devon LOETZ
21 Bursar .... Ms. Linda ANTHONY
37 National Director of Financial Aid .... Ms. Ernestine WHITING
06 Registrar .... Ms. Eve DAUER
88 Special Asst for Univ Initiatives .... Dr. Denise DEZOLT
43 VP and Assistant General Counsel .... Ms. Deborah L. ZIMIC
88 Div VP for Inst Quality & Integrity .... Dr. John A. SABATINI, JR.

White Earth Tribal and Community College (A)

PO Box 478, Mahnomen MN 56557-0478
County: Mahnomen　FICE Identification: 039214
Unit ID: 434751
Telephone: (218) 935-0417　Carnegie Class: Tribal
FAX Number: (218) 936-5614　Calendar System: Semester
URL: www.wetcc.org
Established: 1997　Annual Undergrad Tuition & Fees: $3,285
Enrollment: 119　Coed
Affiliation or Control: Tribal Control　IRS Status: 501(c)3
Highest Offering: Associate Degree
Program: 2-Year Principally Bachelor's Creditable
Accreditation: NH

01 President .... Wannetta BENNETT
05 Academic Dean .... Greg VAN DOREN
32 Dean of Student Services .... Lisa HANDLEY
10 Director of Finance .... Denise WARREN
21 Finance Assistant .... George BASS
45 Director of Special Projects .... Deborah MCARTHUR
37 Director Student Financial Aid .... Doreen STONE

William Mitchell College of Law (B)

875 Summit Avenue, Saint Paul MN 55105-3076
County: Ramsey　FICE Identification: 002391
Unit ID: 175281
Telephone: (651) 227-9171　Carnegie Class: Spec/Law
FAX Number: (651) 290-6414　Calendar System: Semester
URL: www.wmitchell.edu
Established: 1900　Annual Graduate Tuition & Fees: $35,660
Enrollment: 1,013　Coed
Affiliation or Control: Independent Non-Profit　IRS Status: 501(c)3
Highest Offering: First Professional Degree; No Undergraduates
Program: Professional
Accreditation: LAW

01 President & Dean .... Mr. Eric S. JANUS
04 Exec Asst to President & Board .... Ms. Deb CALVERT
05 Vice Dean of Faculty .... Mr. Niels B. SCHAUMANN
05 Vice Dean of Academic Programs .... Ms. Nancy M. VER STEEGH
30 VP of Institutional Advancement .... Ms. Linda K. BERG
16 Vice President Human Resources .... Ms. Mary E. GALE
13 Vice Pres Information Technology .... Mr. James VILLARS
10 Vice President Finance .... Ms. Kathy PANCIERA
32 Dean Student Affairs/Student Life .... Mr. Daniel J. THOMPSON
08 Assoc Dean/Director of Library .... Mr. Simon CANICK
28 Asst Dean/Dir Multicultural Affairs .... Ms. Lawrencina ORAMALU
36 Asst Dean for Career Development .... Ms. Bridgid E. DOWDAL
07 Asst Dean/Director of Admissions .... Ms. Kendra DANE
06 Registrar .... Mr. Jim STEVENS
26 Director of Marketing/Alumni Rels .... Ms. Louise COPELAND
37 Director of Financial Aid .... Ms. Patty HARRIS
18 Director of Facilities .... Mr. Larry EVELAND
30 Director of Development .... Mr. Brian NELSON
96 Purchasing Manager .... Ms. Paula B. MERTH

MISSISSIPPI

Alcorn State University (C)

1000 ASU Drive, #359, Alcorn State MS 39096-7500
County: Claiborne　FICE Identification: 002396
Unit ID: 175342
Telephone: (601) 877-6100　Carnegie Class: Master's M
FAX Number: (601) 877-2975　Calendar System: Semester
URL: www.alcorn.edu
Established: 1871　Annual Undergrad Tuition & Fees (In-State): $5,256
Enrollment: 3,682　Coed
Affiliation or Control: State　IRS Status: 501(c)3
Highest Offering: Beyond Master's But Less Than Doctorate
Program: 2-Year Principally Bachelor's Creditable; Liberal Arts And General; Teacher Preparatory; Professional
Accreditation: SC, AAFCS, ADNUR, DIETD, MUS, NAIT, NUR, @SW, TED

01 President .... Dr. M.Christopher BROWN, II
05 VP for Academic Affairs .... Dr. Samuel L. WHITE
100 Chief of Staff .... Mr. Marcus D. WARD
04 Admin Asst to the President .... Ms. Karen R. SHEDRICK
88 Special Asst to the President .... Dr. Josephine M. POSEY
88 Director of Internal Audit .... Mr. Permy K. THUHA
10 Acting VP for Finance & Admin Svcs .... Ms. Carolyn HINTON
32 VP for Student Affairs .... Dr. Gerald C. PEOPLES
30 VP Development and Marketing .... Mr. Stephen L. MCDANIEL
20 Assoc VP for Academic Affs .... Vacant
21 Assoc VP/Comptroller .... Vacant
35 Assoc VP of Student Affairs .... Vacant
18 Assoc VP for Facilities Management .... Mr. Jessie STEPHNEY
39 Director Housing .... Ms. Jessica L. FOXWORTH
21 Director of Accounting .... Mrs. Cassandra B. LEWIS
96 Purchasing Agent .... Ms. George V. MERTHA
07 Director of Admissions/Recruiting .... Mr. Emanuel BARNES
37 Director Student Financial Aid .... Mrs. Juanita RUSSELL
06 Registrar .... Mr. Jimmy L. SMITH
08 Dean University Libraries .... Dr. Blanche SANDERS
47 Dean School of Agriculture .... Dr. Barry BEQUETTE
49 Actg Dean School of Arts & Science .... Dr. Norris EDNEY
50 Int Dean School of Business .... Dr. Vivek BHARGAVA
53 Dean School of Education .... Dr. Robert CARR
66 Dean School of Nursing .... Dr. Linda GODLEY
88 Dir Academic Student Support Svcs .... Dr. Edward L. VAUGHN
91 Actg CIO for Ctr for Info Tech Svcs .... Ms. Donna G. HAYDEN
26 Assoc VP for University Relations .... Ms. Clara R. STAMPS
15 Acting Director of Human Resources .... Ms. Carla WILLIAMS
36 Director Career Services .... Ms. Adrienne WILLIS
23 Director of Health Services .... Ms. Dorothy G. JACKSON
41 Acting Director of Athletics .... Dr. Malvin A. WILLIAMS, SR.
40 Bookstore Manager .... Mrs. Classie O. JOHNSON
38 Director of Counseling & Testing .... Mrs. Dyann W. MOSES
09 Director Institutional Res/Assess .... Dr. Ramesh MADDALI
88 Dir Institutional Effectiveness .... Dr. Milanda BUTLER
19 Chief of Campus Police .... Mr. Melvin MAXWELL
88 General Manager Sodexo .... Mr. Brian LEE
102 Exec Dir ASU Foundation .... Mr. Stephen L. MCDANIEL
31 Dir Ctr Rural Life/Econ Dev .... Dr. Samuel L. WHITE
92 Director of Pre-Prof/Honors Program .... Dr. Thomas C. STURGIS
58 Dean Graduate Studies .... Dr. Donzell LEE
25 Grants/Contract Administrator .... Ms. Sallie GRIFFIN

Antonelli College (D)

1500 N 31st Avenue, Hattiesburg MS 39401-3056
County: Forrest　Identification: 666517
Unit ID: 383950
Telephone: (601) 583-4100　Carnegie Class: Assoc/PrivFP
FAX Number: (601) 583-0839　Calendar System: Quarter
URL: www.antonellic.com
Established: 1996　Annual Undergrad Tuition & Fees: $15,550
Enrollment: 460　Coed
Affiliation or Control: Proprietary　IRS Status: Proprietary
Highest Offering: Associate Degree
Program: Occupational
Accreditation: ACCSC

01 President .... Mr. Steve BRYANT

† Branch campus of Antonelli College, OH.

Antonelli College (E)

2323 Lakeland Drive, Jackson MS 39208-9549
County: Rankin　Identification: 666518
Unit ID: 175528
Telephone: (601) 362-9991　Carnegie Class: Assoc/PrivFP
FAX Number: (601) 362-2333　Calendar System: Quarter
URL: www.antonellicollege.edu
Established: 1996　Annual Undergrad Tuition & Fees: $11,050
Enrollment: 365　Coed
Affiliation or Control: Proprietary　IRS Status: Proprietary
Highest Offering: Associate Degree
Program: Occupational
Accreditation: ACCSC

01 Director .... Ms. Debra J. MOORE

† Branch campus of Antonelli College, OH.

Belhaven University (F)

1500 Peachtree, Jackson MS 39202-1798
County: Hinds　FICE Identification: 002397
Unit ID: 175421
Telephone: (601) 968-5919　Carnegie Class: Master's M
FAX Number: (601) 968-9998　Calendar System: Semester
URL: www.belhaven.edu
Established: 1883　Annual Undergrad Tuition & Fees: $18,420
Enrollment: 3,099　Coed
Affiliation or Control: Presbyterian Church (U.S.A.)　IRS Status: 501(c)3
Highest Offering: Master's
Program: Liberal Arts And General; Teacher Preparatory; Professional
Accreditation: SC, ART, DANCE, IACBE, MUS, THEA

01 President .... Dr. Roger PARROTT
05 Exec Vice President & Provost .... Dr. Dan FREDERICKS
30 Vice Pres Institutional Advancement .... Mr. Kevin RUSSELL
03 VP of Adult & Graduate Marketing .... Dr. Audrey KELLEHER
10 Chief Financial Officer .... Mrs. Virginia HENDERSON
32 VP for Student Affairs and Athletic .... Mr. Scott LITTLE
11 Asst Vice Pres Campus Operations .... Mr. David POTVIN
20 Vice Provost and Dean of Art & Sci .... Dr. Glenn SUMRALL
44 Asst VP Institutional Advancement .... Mrs. Linda PHILLIPS
51 Asst Vice Pres of Adult Studies .... Dr. Richard HARRIS
88 Dean of Academic Enhancement .... Dr. Lee SKINKLE
12 Academic Dean/Texas .... Dr. Marguerite P. JOYCE
12 Academic Dean/Mississippi .... Dr. Kay OWEN
12 Academic Dean/Tennessee .... Dr. Charles DEWITT
12 Academic Dean/Chattanooga-Atlanta .... Dr. Curt BECK
53 Dean of the School of Education .... Dr. Sandra RASBERRY
50 Dean of the School of Business .... Dr. Chip MASON
08 Librarian .... Mrs. Susan SPRINGER
07 Director of Admissions .... Mrs. Suzanne SULLIVAN
06 Registrar .... Mrs. Donna WEEKS
27 Director of Integrated Marketing .... Mr. Bryant BUTLER
35 Director of Student Leadership .... Ms. JoBeth PETTY
29 Director Alumni Relations .... Mr. Michael DUKES
13 Director Institutional Technology .... Mr. Bo MILLER
19 Director Security/Safety .... Mr. Steve FARMER
40 Bookstore Manager .... Mrs. Sheila LYONS
36 Dean of Student Development .... Mr. Ron PIRTLE
35 Dean of Student Life .... Mr. Greg HAWKINS

Blue Cliff College (G)

12251 Bernard Parkway, Gulfport MS 39503-5086
County: Harrison　FICE Identification: 035253
Unit ID: 441502
Telephone: (228) 896-9727　Carnegie Class: Assoc/PrivFP
FAX Number: (228) 896-7238　Calendar System: Quarter
URL: www.bluecliffcollege.com
Established: 1987　Annual Undergrad Tuition & Fees: $13,100
Enrollment: 240　Coed
Affiliation or Control: Proprietary　IRS Status: Proprietary
Highest Offering: Associate Degree
Program: Occupational
Accreditation: ACCSC

01 Director .... Ms. Sharon L. ANSLEY

Blue Mountain College (H)

201 W Main Street, PO Box 160,
Blue Mountain MS 38610-0160
County: Tippah　FICE Identification: 002398
Unit ID: 175430
Telephone: (662) 685-4771　Carnegie Class: Bac/Diverse
FAX Number: (662) 685-4776　Calendar System: Semester
URL: www.bmc.edu
Established: 1873　Annual Undergrad Tuition & Fees: $9,130
Enrollment: 553　Coed
Affiliation or Control: Southern Baptist　IRS Status: 501(c)3
Highest Offering: Master's
Program: Liberal Arts And General; Teacher Preparatory; Fine Arts Emphasis
Accreditation: SC

01 President .... Dr. Bettye R. COWARD
05 Vice President for Academic Affairs .... Dr. Sharon B. ENZOR
32 Executive VP Stdnt Affs/Graduate .... Dr. Janice I. NICHOLSON
04 Admin Assistant to the President .... Mrs. Pam BOWMAN
06 Registrar .... Mrs. Sheila D. FREEMAN
08 Librarian for Information Services .... Miss Sherry N. DIXON
37 Director of Financial Aid .... Mrs. Michelle HALL
07 Director of Admissions .... Miss Maria TEEL
40 Director Bookstore .... Mrs. Dot M. LOCKE
41 Athletic Director .... Mr. Lavon DRISKELL
42 Director Baptist Student Union .... Mrs. Tracy S. MOSER
09 Director of Institutional Research .... Mr. Robert E. RUCKER
36 Director Career Services .... Dr. Teresa R. ARRINGTON
13 Director of Information Services .... Mr. Kevin BAREFIELD
26 Dir of PR/Publications .... Ms. Emma L. AINSWORTH
29 Director of Alumnae/Alumni Affairs .... Mrs. Lea S. BENNETT
10 Chief Financial Officer .... Mrs. Joyce PETERS

Coahoma Community College (I)

3240 Friars Point Road, Clarksdale MS 38614-9700
County: Coahoma　FICE Identification: 002401
Unit ID: 175519
Telephone: (662) 627-2571　Carnegie Class: Assoc/Pub-R-S
FAX Number: (662) 627-9451　Calendar System: Semester
URL: www.ccc.cc.ms.us
Established: 1949　Annual Undergrad Tuition & Fees (In-District): $2,040
Enrollment: 2,742　Coed
Affiliation or Control: State/Local　IRS Status: 501(c)3
Highest Offering: Associate Degree
Program: Occupational; 2-Year Principally Bachelor's Creditable
Accreditation: SC, POLYT

01 President .... Dr. Vivian M. PRESLEY
05 Vice President for Academic Affairs .... Dr. Rosetta HOWARD
10 Vice Pres for Finance & Operations .... Ms. Deborah MCNEAL
32 Vice Pres Student Affs/Support Svcs .... Dr. Gregory HUDSON
09 VP Inst Effectiveness/SACS Liaison .... Ms. Rosemary DILL
30 VP Instnl Advance/Federal Programs .... Mrs. Marilyn STARKS
75 VP Career & Technical Education .... Mrs. Anne SHELTON-CLARK
07 Dean of Admissions .... Mrs. Delores RICHARD
08 Dean Library/Instructionl Resources .... Mrs. Yvonne STANFORD
14 Director Computer Service .... Mr. Leandrew PRESLEY
19 Director of Safety/Transportation .... Mr. William HOUSTON
26 Director of Public Relations .... Ms. Panny MAYFIELD
37 Director of Financial Aid .... Mrs. Patricia BROOKS
15 Director Accounting/Human Resources .... Mr. Michael HOUSTON
18 Chief Facilities/Physical Plant .... Mr. Jerone SHAW
51 Director of Educational Outreach .... Ms. Cynthia WILLIAMS
06 Registrar .... Mrs. Delores RICHARD
29 Director Alumni Relations .... Mr. Eddie C. SMITH

36 Director Student Placement ....Mr. Orlando PADEN
38 Director Student Counseling ....Vacant
96 Director of Purchasing ....Mrs. Deborah MCNEAL

Copiah-Lincoln Community College (A)

PO Box 649, Wesson MS 39191-0649

County: Copiah — FICE Identification: 002402
Unit ID: 175573
Telephone: (601) 643-5101 — Carnegie Class: Assoc/Pub-R-M
FAX Number: (601) 643-8212 — Calendar System: Semester
URL: www.colin.edu
Established: 1928 — Annual Undergrad Tuition & Fees (In-State): $5,000
Enrollment: 3,799 — Coed
Affiliation or Control: State — IRS Status: 501(c)3
Highest Offering: Associate Degree
Program: Occupational; 2-Year Principally Bachelor's Creditable
Accreditation: SC, ADNUR, MLTAD, RAD

01 President ....Dr. Ronald E. NETTLES
04 Assistant to the President ....Mrs. Brenda J. PARRETT
10 Vice President Business Affairs ....Mr. Michael TANNER
05 Vice Pres of Instructional Services ....Dr. Jane HULON
12 VP of the Simpson County Center ....Dr. John DICKERSON
12 Vice Pres of the Natchez Campus ....Ms. Teresa BUSBY
32 Dean of Student Services ....Mrs. Brenda SMITH
75 Dean Career &Technical Educ ....Dr. Gail BALDWIN
41 Athletic Director ....Mr. Gwyn YOUNG
38 Director Student Counseling ....Mrs. Lea Ann KNIGHT
35 Assistant Dean of Students ....Mr. Bryan NOBILE
37 Director Student Financial Aid ....Mrs. Leslie SMITH
40 Director Bookstore ....Mr. Charles HART
08 Librarian ....Mr. Kendall P. CHAPMAN
26 Director of Public Relations ....Mrs. Natalie DAVIS
14 Director of Computer Center ....Mr. Danny DYKES
19 Director of Security ....Mr. Wayne ROBERTS
09 Director of Institutional Research ....Mr. Jeff POSEY
07 Director of Admissions ....Mr. Chris WARREN
30 Chief Devel/Fdn & Alumni Aff Dir ....Mr. David CAMPBELL
18 Chief Facilities ....Mr. Daniel CASE
66 Director of Assoc Degree Nursing . Mrs. Mary Ann CANTERBURY
06 Student Records Manager ....Mrs. Gay LANGHAM
57 Chair Fine Arts Division ....Mrs. Janet SMITH
50 Chair Business Division ....Mr. Michael MCINTYRE
68 Chair Physical Education Division ....Dr. Stephanie DUGUID
81 Chair Math/Computer Science Div ....Mrs. Carol FORD
79 Chair Humanities Division ....Vacant
82 Chair Social Science Division ....Mr. David HIGGS
88 Chair Science Division ....Dr. Kevin MCKONE
96 Director of Purchasing ....Mrs. Erin LIKENS

Delta State University (B)

1003 W. Sunflower Rd., Cleveland MS 38733

County: Bolivar — FICE Identification: 002403
Unit ID: 175616
Telephone: (662) 846-3000 — Carnegie Class: Master's L
FAX Number: (662) 846-4014 — Calendar System: Semester
URL: www.deltastate.edu
Established: 1924 — Annual Undergrad Tuition & Fees (In-State): $5,288
Enrollment: 4,327 — Coed
Affiliation or Control: State — IRS Status: 501(c)3
Highest Offering: Doctorate
Program: Liberal Arts And General; Teacher Preparatory; Professional
Accreditation: SC, AAFCS, ACBSP, ART, CACREP, DIETC, MUS, NURSE, SW, TED

01 President ....Dr. John M. HILPERT
05 Provost/VP Academic Affairs ....Dr. Ann C. LOTVEN
32 Vice President for Student Affairs ....Dr. H. Wayne BLANSETT
10 Vice President for Finance ....Mr. Greg REDLIN
11 Vice President University Relations ....Dr. Michelle A. ROBERTS
21 Assoc Vice President for Finance ....Dr. Myrtis TABB
41 Director of Athletics ....Mr. Jeremy MCCLAIN
29 Exec Dir of Alumni/Foundation ....Mr. D. Keith FULCHER
04 Exec Assistant to the President ....Ms. Leigh S. KORB
49 Dean College of Arts & Sciences ....Dr. Paul HANKINS
50 Dean College of Business ....Dr. Billy MOORE
53 Dean College of Education ....Dr. Leslie GRIFFIN
66 Dean School of Nursing ....Dr. Libby L. CARLSON
08 Dean Library Services ....Mr. Jeff SLAGELL
58 Dean Graduate/Continuing Studies ....Dr. Albert NYLANDER
07 Dean Enrollment Management ....Dr. Debbie S. HESLEP
46 Dean Research/Assessment/Planning ....Dr. Beverly MOON
88 Internal Auditor ....Ms. Vicki WILLIAMS
88 Associate Dean Delta Regional Devel ....Dr. Luther BROWN
13 Chief Information Officer ....Mr. Edwin CRAFT
20 Director Academic Support Services ....Ms. Diane BLANSETT
25 Director Institutional Grants ....Ms. Robin BOYLES
09 Director Institutional Research ....Ms. Suzanne SIMPSON
06 Registrar ....Mr. John ELLIOTT
106 Director of E-Learning ....Vacant
31 Director Ctr for Community/Econ Dev ....Dr. Paulette MEIKLE
88 Director Coahoma County Higher Educ ....Ms. Jennifer WALLER
88 Director Small Bus Devel Center ....Vacant
88 Director Field Experiences ....Dr. Cheryl CUMMINS
21 Comptroller ....Mr. James RUTLEDGE
18 Director of Facilities Management ....Ms. Linda SMITH
88 Director Student Business Services ....Ms. Teresa HOUSTON
96 Manager Procurement & Accts Payable ....Ms. Beverly LINDSEY
35 Ast to VP Stdnt Affs/Dir Stdnt Life ....Ms. Elsie L. ERVIN
38 Director Counsel/Stdnt Health Svcs ....Dr. Richard HOUSTON
37 Director Student Financial Assist ....Ms. Ann M. MULLINS
19 Director of Police Department ....Mr. N. Lynn BUFORD
36 Director Career Services/Placement ....Ms. Christy MONTESI
39 Director of Housing ....Ms. Julie JACKSON
30 Director of Development ....Ms. Sarah D. AYLWARD
29 Director of Alumni Affairs ....Mr. Jeffery FARRIS
26 Director of Communications & Mktg ....Mr. Michael GANN
88 Executive Director BPAC ....Ms. Roseann BUCK
40 Manager of Bookstore ....Ms. Coameca WILLIAMS

East Central Community College (C)

PO Box 129, Decatur MS 39327-0129

County: Newton — FICE Identification: 002404
Unit ID: 175643
Telephone: (601) 635-2111 — Carnegie Class: Assoc/Pub-R-M
FAX Number: (601) 635-4011 — Calendar System: Semester
URL: www.eccc.edu
Established: 1928 — Annual Undergrad Tuition & Fees (In-District): $1,980
Enrollment: 2,720 — Coed
Affiliation or Control: Local — IRS Status: 501(c)3
Highest Offering: Associate Degree
Program: Occupational; 2-Year Principally Bachelor's Creditable
Accreditation: SC, ADNUR, EMT, SURGT

01 President ....Dr. Phil A. SUTPHIN
05 Vice President for Instruction ....Dr. Lavinia B. SPARKMAN
10 Vice Pres for Business Operations ....Mr. Mickey VANCE
32 Vice President for Student Services ....Mr. Randall LEE
102 Vice Pres Foundation/Alumni Rels ....Vacant
26 Vice Pres for Public Information ....Mr. E. Bubby JOHNSTON
51 Director of ABE/GED ....Mr. Ryan CLARKE
75 Director of Career Tech Instruction ....Mr. Wayne EASON
07 Director Admission/Records/Research ....Mr. David CASE
41 Athletic Dir/Dir of Personnel Svcs ....Mr. Chris HARRIS
18 Director of Physical Plant ....Mr. Artie FOREMAN
103 Dean Workforce Educ & Development ....Mr. Roger WHITLOCK
72 Director for Technology Management ....Mr. Derek PACE
38 Academic Counselor ....Mr. Michael D. ALEXANDER
37 Director of Financial Aid ....Mrs. Brenda B. CARSON
08 Library Director ....Mr. Leslie HUGHES
13 Assoc Director for Technology Mgmt ....Mrs. Regena BOYKIN
19 Chief of Police ....Mr. Mitch MCCLEON
35 Director of Student Activities ....Mr. Scott HILL
29 Director Alumni Relations ....Dr. Stacey HOLLINGSWORTH
57 Chairperson Fine Arts Division ....Mr. Tom CARSON
83 Chairperson Social Sciences ....Mrs. Wanda HURLEY
81 Chrpn Mathematics/Computer Science ....Dr. Lisa MCMILLIN
76 Dean of Healthcare Education ....Dr. Betsy MANN
81 Chairperson Science ....Mr. Curt SKIPPER
60 Chairperson Communications/ Language ....Mrs. Carol SHACKELFORD

East Mississippi Community College (D)

PO Box 158, Scooba MS 39358-0158

County: Kemper — FICE Identification: 002405
Unit ID: 175652
Telephone: (662) 476-8442 — Carnegie Class: Assoc/Pub-R-M
FAX Number: (662) 476-5058 — Calendar System: Semester
URL: www.eastms.edu
Established: 1927 — Annual Undergrad Tuition & Fees (In-District): $2,350
Enrollment: 5,433 — Coed
Affiliation or Control: State/Local — IRS Status: 501(c)3
Highest Offering: Associate Degree
Program: Occupational; 2-Year Principally Bachelor's Creditable
Accreditation: SC, EMT, FUSER

01 President ....Dr. F. Rick YOUNG
05 Vice Pres for Instruction ....Dr. Andrea MAYFIELD
12 Vice President for GT Campus ....Dr. Paul MILLER
03 Vice President for Scooba Campus ....Dr. Jackie STENNIS
10 Vice President for Finance ....Vacant
41 Vice Pres Athletics/SC Operations ....Mr. Mickey E. STOKES
09 VP for Research/Effectiveness ....Dr. Andrea MAYFIELD
103 VP of Workforce & Cmty Services ....Dr. Raj SHAUNAK
37 Vice Pres for Financial Aid ....Mr. James GIBSON
04 Administrative Asst to President ....Mrs. Doreen BRYAN
08 District Librarian ....Ms. Donna BALLARD
13 Dist Director of Info Technology ....Mr. Michael TVARKUNAS
18 Physical Plant Director-Scooba ....Mr. Bobby JONES
21 District Business Manager ....Mrs. Melissa MOSLEY
37 Director of Financial Aid GT ....Mr. Garry JONES
30 Director of Development ....Mr. Nick CLARK
06 Registrar-Scooba ....Mrs. Melinda SCIPLE
07 Director of Admissions-SC ....Mrs. Karen BRIGGS
56 Director of MNAS Extension ....Mr. James MCMULLAN
40 District Bookstore Manager ....Ms. Vickie TURNER
27 Director of Public Information ....Ms. Suzanne MONK
39 Director of Housing ....Ms. Kate NEELY

Hinds Community College (E)

PO Box 1100, Raymond MS 39154-1100

County: Hinds — FICE Identification: 002407
Unit ID: 175786
Telephone: (601) 857-5261 — Carnegie Class: Assoc/Pub-R-L
FAX Number: (601) 857-3392 — Calendar System: Semester
URL: www.hindscc.edu
Established: 1917 — Annual Undergrad Tuition & Fees (In-District): $1,710
Enrollment: 18,888 — Coed
Affiliation or Control: State/Local — IRS Status: 501(c)3
Highest Offering: Associate Degree
Program: Occupational; 2-Year Principally Bachelor's Creditable
Accreditation: SC, ADNUR, DA, DMS, EMT, MAC, MLTAD, PTAA, RAD, SURGT

01 President ....Dr. Clyde MUSE
11 VP Admin Svcs/VP Utica/Vicksburg ....Dr. George BARNES
10 Vice President Business Services ....Mr. Russell SHAW
12 VP Raymond/NSG/AH/Parallel Pgm ....Dr. Theresa HAMILTON
12 VP Rankin/Jackson/Dir Occup Pgm ....Dr. Sue POWELL
31 Vice Pres Community Relations ....Ms. Colleen C. HARTFORD
88 VP for Economic Dev & Training ....Mr. John J. WOODS
18 VP Physical Plant & Aux Services ....Mr. Thomas WASSON
30 Vice Pres Institutional Advancement ....Ms. Jacqueline M. GRANBERRY
84 Director of Enrollment Services ....Ms. Kathryn B. COLE
32 Dean of Student Affairs ....Dr. Barbara BLANKENSHIP
07 Director of Admissions & Records ....Mr. Randall HARRIS
08 Dean of Learning Resources ....Ms. Mary Beth APPLIN
20 Academic Dean ....Dr. Thomas KELLY
15 Director of Human Resources ....Ms. Christina NELSON
37 Dir of Financial Aid & VA Affairs ....Ms. Carrie COOPER
38 Director of Counseling Services ....Ms. Mary Lee MCDANIEL
41 Athletic Director ....Mr. Gene MURPHY
09 Director of Institutional Research ....Ms. Carley DEAR
26 Public Relations Director ....Ms. Cathy C. HAYDEN
96 Director of Purchasing ....Mr. Samuel LEMONIS

Holmes Community College (F)

Hill Street, PO Box 369, Goodman MS 39079-0369

County: Holmes — FICE Identification: 002408
Unit ID: 175810
Telephone: (662) 472-2312 — Carnegie Class: Assoc/Pub-R-L
FAX Number: (662) 472-9152 — Calendar System: Semester
URL: www.holmescc.edu
Established: 1925 — Annual Undergrad Tuition & Fees (In-District): $3,990
Enrollment: 6,416 — Coed
Affiliation or Control: Local — IRS Status: 501(c)3
Highest Offering: Associate Degree
Program: Occupational; 2-Year Principally Bachelor's Creditable
Accreditation: SC, ADNUR, EMT, FUSER, NAIT, OTA, SURGT

01 President ....Dr. Glenn F. BOYCE
04 Asst to President/Dir Inst Rsch ....Dr. Lindy MCCAIN
10 Exec VP Finance/Admin & Stdnt Svcs ....Mr. Steve CALDWELL
05 Vice Pres for Academic Programs ....Dr. Fran COX
12 Vice President Ridgeland Campus ....Dr. Don BURNHAM
12 Vice President Grenada Center ....Dr. Jim HAFFEY
07 Vice Pres of Admissions & Records ....Mr. Joshua GUEST
72 Vice Pres Career/Technical Educ ....Mrs. Sherrie CHEEK
08 Librarian ....Mrs. Joan TIERCE
26 District Director of Communications ....Mr. Steve DIFFEY
32 Dn Goodman Cam/Dist Coord Stdt Svcs ....Mr. Andy WOOD
31 Director Community/Workforce Devel ....Mr. Mike BLANKENSHIP
37 Director Student Financial Aid ....Mr. Sonny SPARKS
15 Director Personnel Services ....Ms. Julia BROWN
29 Dir Alumni Relations/Communication ....Mr. Steve DIFFEY
18 Chief Facilities/Physical Plant ....Vacant
96 Director of Purchasing ....Ms. Roxanne CHISOLM
21 Business Manager ....Mr. Matt SURRELL
09 Director of Institutional Research ....Dr. Lindy MCCAIN

Itawamba Community College (G)

602 W Hill Street, Fulton MS 38843-1022

County: Itawamba — FICE Identification: 002409
Unit ID: 175829
Telephone: (662) 862-8000 — Carnegie Class: Assoc/Pub-R-M
FAX Number: (662) 862-8036 — Calendar System: Semester
URL: www.icc.cc.ms.us
Established: 1948 — Annual Undergrad Tuition & Fees (In-District): $1,900
Enrollment: 7,756 — Coed
Affiliation or Control: Local — IRS Status: 501(c)3
Highest Offering: Associate Degree
Program: Occupational; 2-Year Principally Bachelor's Creditable
Accreditation: SC, ADNUR, DMS, EMT, OTA, PTAA, RAD, SURGT

01 President ....Dr. David C. COLE
05 Vice President of Instruction ....Dr. Sara JOHNSON
10 Vice President of Business Services ....Mr. Jerry SENTER
32 Vice President of Student Services ....Mr. Buddy COLLINS
30 Vice Pres Dev/Plng/Telecom/Info Svc ....Mr. Wayne SULLIVAN
07 Dir Admiss/Registration ....Ms. Cay LOLLAR
26 Dir Pub Rel/Mktg/Sports Info ....Mr. Will KOLLMEYER
37 Director of Financial Aid ....Mr. Robert WALKER
24 Director of Learning Resources ....Dr. Glenda SEGARS
08 Librarian/Tupelo ....Ms. Janet Y. ARMOUR
51 Director of Adult & Continuing Educ ....Vacant
41 Athletic Director ....Ms. Carrie BALL-WILLIAMSON
44 Dir of Institutional Advancement ....Mr. Jim INGRAM
18 Chief Facilities/Physical Plant ....Mr. Thomas BONDS
35 Director Stdnt Affs/Counseling ....Mr. Larry BOGGS
09 Director of Institutional Research ....Mrs. Elizabeth EDWARDS
15 Director Personnel Services ....Mr. Timothy C. SENTER

ITT Technical Institute (H)

382 Galleria Parkway, Suite 100, Madison MS 39110

County: Madison — Identification: 666701
Unit ID: 456393
Telephone: (601) 607-4500 — Carnegie Class: Not Classified
FAX Number: (601) 607-4550 — Calendar System: Quarter
URL: www.itt-tech.edu

Established: N/A Annual Undergrad Tuition & Fees: N/A
Enrollment: 214 Coed
Affiliation or Control: Proprietary IRS Status: Proprietary
Highest Offering: Baccalaureate
Program: Technical Emphasis
Accreditation: ACICS

† Branch campus of ITT Technical Institute, Boise, ID.

Jackson State University (A)

1400 J. R. Lynch Street, Jackson MS 39217
County: Hinds FICE Identification: 002410
Unit ID: 175856
Telephone: (601) 979-2100 Carnegie Class: RU/H
FAX Number: (601) 979-2358 Calendar System: Semester
URL: www.jsums.edu
Established: 1877 Annual Undergrad Tuition & Fees (In-State): $5,504
Enrollment: 8,687 Coed
Affiliation or Control: State IRS Status: 501(c)3
Highest Offering: Doctorate
Program: Liberal Arts And General; Teacher Preparatory; Professional
Accreditation: SC, ART, BUS, CACREP, CLPSY, CORE, CS, ENG, JOUR, MUS, NAIT, PH, PLNG, SP, SPAA, SW, TED

01 President ....Dr. Carolyn MEYERS
100 Exec Assistant to the President ....Dr. James RENICK
05 Int Prov/VP Acad Affairs/Stdnt Life ....Dr. Quinton WILLIAMS
10 Int VP for Business & Finance ....Mr. Michael THOMAS
46 VP for Federally Funded Research ....Dr. Felix A. OKOJIE
13 VP for Information & Process Mgmt ....Dr. Willie BROWN
43 Legal Counsel ....Mrs. Regina QUINN
21 Internal Auditor ....Ms. Ella HOLMES
18 Assoc VP for Facil/Construct/ Mgmt ....Mr. Wayne GOODWIN
21 Assoc VP for Business & Finance ....Ms. Sherry WILSON
20 Assoc Provost for Academic Affairs ....Dr. James MADDIRALA
20 Assoc VP for Academic Affairs ....Dr. Della POSEY
32 Assoc VP for Student Life ....Dr. Marcus A. CHANAY
84 Assoc VP for Enrollment Management ....Dr. Bettye GRAVES
09 Assoc VP Inst Research/Plng/ Effect ....Dr. Nicole EDWARDS- EVANS
13 Assoc VP for Information Technology ..Dr. Idehen M. OMOREGIE
46 Assoc VP for Research & Development ....Ms. Ethel R. PRESLEY
53 Dean College Educ/Human Devel ....Dr. Daniel WATKINS
58 Dean Division of Graduate Studies ....Dr. Dorris R. ROBINSON-GARDNER
20 Dean Division Undergrad Studies ....Dr. Evelyn LEGGETTE
49 Dean College of Liberal Arts ....Dr. Dollye M E. ROBINSON
88 Dean Division of Internat Studies ....Dr. Ally MACK
50 Dean College of Business ....Dr. Glenda B. GLOVER
80 Int Dean College of Public Service ....Dr. Mario AZEVEDO
72 Dean College of Sci/Engr/Tech ....Dr. Mark G. HARDY
51 Dean College of Lifelong Learning ....Dr. Johnnie MILLS-JONES
08 Int Dean Div of Library & Info Res ....Dr. Melissa DRUCKREY
20 Assoc Dean University College ..Dr. Marie O'BANNER-JACKSON
88 Assoc Dean Div of Undergrad Stds ....Dr. Maria HARVEY
46 Dir of JSU RTRNDTCC/Prof Chem ....Dr. Jim PERKINS
88 Dir Ofc of Strategic Initiatives ....Dr. Shelton SWANIER
88 Dir Comm Planning/Development ....Dr. Kimberly HILLIARD
88 Director of Development ....Dr. Linda DANIELS
88 Director Testing & Assessment ....Dr. Arthur JEFFERSON
88 Exe Dir Ctr Svc & Comm/Eng Learning ....Dr. Valerie J. SHELBY
29 Dir Alumni/Constituency Relations ....Mrs. Gwendolyn CAPLES
88 Exec Dir Financial Operations ....Mr. Edwin QUINN
15 Executive Director Human Resources ....Mrs. Sandra SELLERS
07 Director of Student Recruitment ....Mrs. Linda RUSH
30 Exec Dir Institutional Advancement ....Ms. Evangeline W. ROBINSON
39 Director of Residence Life ....Ms. Vera JACKSON
88 Director of Payroll ....Mrs. Rita SINGLETON
18 Director of Facilities Operations ....Ms. Jennie GRIFFIN
37 Director of Financial Aid ....Mrs. Betty MONCURE
21 Dir Budget & Financial Analysis ....Mrs. Tammiko HARRISON
06 Registrar ....Mr. Alfred B. JACKSON
23 Dir/Head Nurse Student Hlth Center ....Mrs. Ollie HARPER
88 Dir Mississippi Learning Inst ....Mrs. Nikisha GREEN WARE
20 Executive Dir of Academic Integrity ....Dr. Alisa MOSLEY
89 Director of First Year Experience ....Mrs. Patricia SHERIFF-TAYLOR
07 Director Undergraduate Admissions ....Mrs. Stephanie CHATMAN
41 Director of Athletics ....Vacant
88 Director of Title III ....Dr. Mary MYLES
96 Dir Univ Strategic Sourcing Svcs ....Vacant
88 Director MS Urban Research Ctr ....Dr. Melvin DAVIS
19 Interim Director Public Safety ....Mr. Tyrone KIDD
26 Director University Communications ....Mr. Anthony DEAN
22 ADA Coordinator ....Mr. Vinson BALLARD
88 Exec Dir Auxiliary Enterprises ....Mr. Alfred CARTER
88 Director Human Capital Development ....Ms. Angela GOBAR
13 Director of Process Management ....Mr. Jerry DANNER
88 Director of Capital Improvement ....Mr. Walter JOHNSON
28 Director of Communications/Outreach ....Mrs. Lori STEWART
40 Manager Bookstore ....Mr. Mark PERSON

Jones County Junior College (B)

900 S Court Street, Ellisville MS 39437-3999
County: Jones FICE Identification: 002411
Unit ID: 175883
Telephone: (601) 477-4000 Carnegie Class: Assoc/Pub-R-M
FAX Number: (601) 477-4017 Calendar System: Semester
URL: www.jcjc.edu
Established: 1927 Annual Undergrad Tuition & Fees (In-District): $2,320
Enrollment: 5,386 Coed
Affiliation or Control: State/Local IRS Status: Exempt
Highest Offering: Associate Degree
Program: Occupational; 2-Year Principally Bachelor's Creditable
Accreditation: SC, ACBSP, ADNUR, EMT, RAD

01 President ....Dr. Jesse R. SMITH
05 VP Instructional Affrs/Assessment ....Dr. Laverne C. ULMER, JR.
10 Vice President of Business Affairs ....Mr. Rick YOUNGBLOOD
32 Vice President of Student Affairs ....Mr. Ed SMITH
88 Vice President of External Affairs ....Mr. Jim WALLEY
30 VP of Institutional Advancement ....Ms. Caroline RAMAGOS
13 VP of Information Technology ....Mr. Casey MERCIER
26 Vice President of Marketing ....Ms. Marlo DORSEY
04 Assistant to the President ....Mr. John M. CARTER
20 Academic Dean ....Dr. Shannon CAMPBELL
35 Dean of Student Affairs ....Dr. Sam JONES
88 Director of the Adv Tech Center ....Mr. Greg BUTLER
09 Dir of Inst Effectiveness/Planning ....Dr. Laverne ULMER
92 Dean of Honors College/Campus Life ....Dr. Mark TAYLOR
07 Director of Admissions & Records ....Mr. Rick HAMILTON
38 Dir of Student Success Center ....Mr. Andrew SHARP
37 Director of Student Financial Aid ....Ms. Jennifer SUBER
75 Dean Career/Technical Education ....Ms. Candace WEAVER
39 Director of Housing-Women ....Ms. Ashley HILL
39 Director of Housing-Men ....Mr. Van TUGGLE
40 Bookstore Manager ....Mr. Kevin KUHN
41 Athletic Director ....Ms. Katie HERRINGTON
18 Chief Physical Plant ....Mr. Roy BARNETT
25 Director of Grants ....Mr. Jason DEDWYLDER
15 Director of Human Resources ....Ms. Christy HILBUN
96 Director of Purchasing ....Ms. LeAnne NIXON
106 eLearning Coordinator ....Ms. Jennifer POWELL

Meridian Community College (C)

910 Highway 19 N, Meridian MS 39307-5890
County: Lauderdale FICE Identification: 002413
Unit ID: 175935
Telephone: (601) 483-8241 Carnegie Class: Assoc/Pub-R-M
FAX Number: (601) 481-1305 Calendar System: Semester
URL: www.mcc.cc.ms.us
Established: 1937 Annual Undergrad Tuition & Fees (In-District): $2,140
Enrollment: 4,146 Coed
Affiliation or Control: Local IRS Status: 501(c)3
Highest Offering: Associate Degree
Program: Occupational; 2-Year Principally Bachelor's Creditable
Accreditation: SC, ADNUR, DA, DH, MLTAD, PNUR, PTAA, RAD, SURGT

01 President ....Dr. Scott D. ELLIOTT
10 Assoc Vice President for Finance ....Mrs. Amy BRAND
03 Vice President of Operations ....Mrs. Barbara JONES
07 Director of Admissions ....Mrs. Angela PAYNE
09 Dir Institutional Effectiveness ....Mrs. Cathy PARKER
32 Dean of Students ....Mrs. Soraya WELDEN
05 Dean of Academic Affs/General Educ ....Mr. Michael THOMPSON
62 Dean of Learning Resources ....Mr. Billy BEAL
30 Dir Institutional Advancement ....Mrs. Kathy BROOKSHIRE
18 Director Physical Plant ....Mr. Terry WILLIAMS
37 Director Financial Aid ....Ms. Nedra BRADLEY
15 Director Human Resources ....Ms. Shellye ESPEY
41 Athletic Director ....Mr. Hilary ALLEN
19 Chief of Security ....Mr. Shane WILLIAMS
40 Bookstore Manager ....Mrs. Martha WILLIAMS
27 College Promotions Coordinator ....Mrs. Kay THOMAS
36 Career Center Development Director ....Mrs. Darlene MAYATT
75 Assoc Vice Pres for Workforce Educ ....Dr. Richie MCALISTER

Millsaps College (D)

1701 N State Street, Jackson MS 39210-0001
County: Hinds FICE Identification: 002414
Unit ID: 175980
Telephone: (601) 974-1000 Carnegie Class: Bac/A&S
FAX Number: (601) 974-1059 Calendar System: Semester
URL: www.millsaps.edu
Established: 1890 Annual Undergrad Tuition & Fees: $29,482
Enrollment: 1,060 Coed
Affiliation or Control: United Methodist IRS Status: 501(c)3
Highest Offering: Master's
Program: Liberal Arts And General; Teacher Preparatory
Accreditation: SC, BUS, TED

01 President ....Dr. Rob PEARIGEN
05 VP/Dean of the College ....Dr. Keith DUNN
10 Vice President for Finance ....Ms. Louise BURNEY
30 VP for Institutional Advancement ....Dr. Charles LEWIS
32 VP Student Life/Dean Students ....Dr. Brit KATZ
50 Dean of the School of Management ....Dr. Howard MCMILLAN
84 Dean of Enrollment ....Mr. Michael THORP
79 Assoc Dean Arts & Letters ....Dr. David DAVIS
49 Associate Dean Sciences Division ....Dr. Timothy J. WARD
82 Assoc Dean International Education ....Dr. George J. BEY
26 Dir of Communications & Marketing ....Ms. Patti P. WADE
37 Director of Financial Aid ....Mr. Patrick JAMES
20 Director Academic Support Services ....Ms. Janet R. LANGLEY
51 Director of Continuing Education ....Dr. Nola R. GIBSON
08 College Librarian ....Mr. Thomas W. HENDERSON
36 Director of Career Center ....Ms. Tonya CRAFT
41 Director of Athletics ....Mr. Tim WISE
15 Dir of Payroll & Employee Services ....Ms. Patricia S. BRUCE
42 Chaplain ....Rev. Rwth ASHTON
28 Director of Multicultural Affairs ....Ms. Sherryl E. WILBURN
21 Assistant Controller ....Ms. Allison ROOKER
06 Coordinator of Records ....Ms. Katherine ADAMS
09 Institutional Research Analyst ....Ms. Katherine S. LANDRUM
18 Director of Physical Plant ....Mr. W. David WILKINSON

Mississippi College (E)

200 W College Street, Clinton MS 39058-0001
County: Hinds FICE Identification: 002415
Unit ID: 176053
Telephone: (601) 925-3000 Carnegie Class: Master's L
FAX Number: (601) 925-3276 Calendar System: Semester
URL: www.mc.edu
Established: 1826 Annual Undergrad Tuition & Fees: $14,038
Enrollment: 4,963 Coed
Affiliation or Control: Southern Baptist IRS Status: 501(c)3
Highest Offering: Doctorate
Program: Liberal Arts And General; Teacher Preparatory; Professional
Accreditation: SC, ACBSP, #ARCPA, CACREP, LAW, MUS, NURSE, SW, TED

01 President ....Dr. Lee G. ROYCE
04 Sr Exec Assistant to President ....Mrs. Patty TADLOCK
10 Chief Financial Officer ....Mrs. Donna LEWIS
05 Vice President Academic Affairs ....Dr. Ronald HOWARD
32 VP Enrollment Mgmt/ Student Affairs ....Dr. Jim TURCOTTE
45 Vice President Planning/Assessment ....Dr. Debbie NORRIS
42 Vice Pres Christian Development ....Dr. Eric PRATT
30 VP Inst Advan/Alum/Leg Coun to Pres ....Dr. Bill TOWNSEND
11 Vice Pres Admin/Government Rels ....Dr. Steve STANFORD
84 Director Enrollment Services ....Mr. Mark HUGHES
06 Registrar ....Mrs. Ginger ROBBINS
09 Director of Institutional Research ....Ms. Cassandra SESSUMS
08 Librarian ....Ms. Kathleen HUTCHISON
21 Comptroller ....Mrs. Cheryl MOBLEY
27 Chief Information Officer ....Mr. Bill CRANFORD
38 Director Counseling/Testing Center ....Dr. Morgan BRYANT
15 Director Human Resources ....Ms. Donna SMITH
29 Director Alumni Affairs ....Mr. Ross AVEN
26 Director Public Relations ....Mrs. Tracey HARRISON
18 Director of Physical Plant ....Mr. Glenn WORLEY
39 Director of Residence Life ....Mr. Rick HARTFIELD
37 Director Student Financial Aid ....Mrs. Karon MCMILLAN
07 Director of Admissions ....Mr. Kyle BRANTLEY
35 Director Student Affairs ....Ms. Cam ARMSTRONG
19 Director of Public Safety ....Mr. Steven MCCRANEY
41 Director of Athletics ....Mr. Michael JONES
96 Director of Purchasing ....Mrs. Dana ELMORE
40 Manager Bookstore ....Ms. Karen BARNES
36 Coordinator of Career Services ....Mrs. Karen LINDSEY-LLOYD
81 Dean School of Science/Mathematics ....Dr. Stan BALDWIN
50 Dean School of Business Admin ....Dr. Marcelo EDUARDO
79 Dean School of Humanities ....Dr. Gary MAYFIELD
53 Dean School of Education ....Dr. Don LOCKE
73 Dean Sch Christian Studies/Fine Art ....Dr. Wayne VAN HORN
61 Dean School of Law ....Dr. Jim ROSENBLATT
58 Dean Grad School/Special Programs ....Dr. Debbie NORRIS
66 Dean School of Nursing ....Dr. Mary Jean PADGETT

Mississippi Delta Community College (F)

PO Box 668, Moorhead MS 38761-0668
County: Sunflower FICE Identification: 002416
Unit ID: 176008
Telephone: (662) 246-6322 Carnegie Class: Assoc/Pub-R-M
FAX Number: (662) 246-6321 Calendar System: Semester
URL: www.msdelta.edu
Established: 1926 Annual Undergrad Tuition & Fees (In-District): $2,330
Enrollment: 3,521 Coed
Affiliation or Control: Local IRS Status: 501(c)3
Highest Offering: Associate Degree
Program: Occupational; 2-Year Principally Bachelor's Creditable
Accreditation: SC, ADNUR, DH, MLTAD, PNUR, RAD

01 President ....Dr. Larry G. BAILEY
11 VP of Admin Svcs/IE/GHEC Operations ....Dr. Mary Jean LUSH
05 Vice President of Instruction ....Ms. Magdalene ABRAHAM
10 Vice President of Business Services ....Mr. Don GARRETT
32 Vice President of Student Services ....Dr. Edward RICE
21 Associate VP of Business Services ....Mrs. Marsha LEE
88 Assoc VP GHEC Operations ....Dr. MaryAnne BROCATO
84 Associate Vice Pres of Enrollment ....Dr. Brent GREGORY
102 Assoc VP College Rels/Development ....Mr. Reed ABRAHAM
04 Admin Asst to President/Coord of HR ....Ms. Brenda VANLANDINGHAM
37 Director of Financial Aid ....Mrs. Mary P. RODGERS
07 Director of Admissions ....Mr. Joe F. RAY
13 Director Computer & Info Tech Svcs ....Mr. Jimmy H. FREE
08 Director of Library Services ....Mrs. Kristi BARIOLA
07 Director Counseling/Recruiting ....Mrs. Stacy UPTON
18 Director of Maintenance ....Mr. Rick DAVIS
26 Director of Public Relations ....Mrs. Corey SMITH
09 Director of Institutional Research ....Dr. Sharon FREEMAN

Mississippi Gulf Coast Community College (G)

PO Box 609, Perkinston MS 39573-0012
County: Stone FICE Identification: 002417
Unit ID: 176071
Telephone: (601) 928-5211 Carnegie Class: Assoc/Pub-R-L
FAX Number: (601) 928-6386 Calendar System: Semester
URL: www.mgccc.edu

Established: 1911 Annual Undergrad Tuition & Fees (In-District): $2,712
Enrollment: 10,073 Coed
Affiliation or Control: Local IRS Status: 501(c)3
Highest Offering: Associate Degree
Program: Occupational; 2-Year Principally Bachelor's Creditable
Accreditation: SC, ADNUR, EMT, FUSER, MLTAD, NAIT, PNUR, RAD, SURGT

01 President ... Dr. Mary S. GRAHAM
05 Vice Pres Instruction/Student Svcs ... Dr. Jason PUGH
10 Vice Pres Administration/Finance ... Dr. Billy W. STEWART
12 Vice President Perkinston Campus ... Dr. Jay ALLEN
12 Vice Pres Jefferson Davis Campus ... Dr. Susan SCAGGS
12 Vice President Community Campus ... Ms. Anna Faye KELLEY-WINDERS
12 Vice Pres Jackson County Campus ... Dr. Michael HEINDL
30 Assoc Vice Pres for Development ... Mr. F. Russell YOUNG
09 College Director of Inst Research ... Ms. Lynn TINCHER-LADNER
14 Director of Information Technology ... Mr. David BESANCON
41 Athletic Director ... Mr. Ladd TAYLOR
106 Director of E-Learning ... Ms. Jennifer LEIMER
103 Director Workforce Dev JD Campus ... Mr. Wayne KUNTZ
103 Director Workforce Dev JC Campus ... Mr. Mark LANDRY
21 Comptroller ... Ms. Debbie BORGMAN
06 Records Clerk Perkinston Campus ... Ms. Latrice MCDONALD
06 Records Clerk Jackson Co Campus ... Ms. Kay ROSONET
06 Records Clerk Jeff Davis Campus ... Ms. Mary JOYCE
20 Int Dean Instruct Jackson Co Campus ... Mr. Jonathan WOODWARD
05 Dean of Instruction Jeff Davis Camp ... Mr. Larry MILLER
05 Dean of Instruction Perkinston Camp ... Dr. Jan MOODY
21 Dn Business Svcs Perkinston Campus ... Ms. Sheree BOND
21 Dn Business Svcs Jackson Co Campus ... Ms. Tammy FRANKS
21 Dn Business Svcs Jeff Davis Campus ... Ms. Stacy CARMICHAEL
75 Asst Dean Vo-Tec Instruc Perk Camp ... Ms. Cheryl BOND
75 Asst Dean Vo-Tec Instruc JD Camp ... Dr. Beverly CLARK
75 Asst Dean Vo-Tec Instruc JC Camp ... Mr. Brock CLARK
08 Librarian Perkinston Campus ... Dr. Brenda RIVERO
08 Librarian Jackson County Campus ... Dr. Pam LADNER
08 Librarian Jefferson Davis Campus ... Mr. Charles CLARK
32 Dean Student Svcs Perkinston Campus ... Ms. Michelle SEKUL
32 Dean Student Svcs Jackson Co Campus ... Dr. Bill YATES
32 Dean Student Svcs Jeff Davis Campus ... Dr. Tyrone JACKSON
07 Dir Admissions Perkinston Campus ... Ms. Nichol GREEN
07 Dir Admissions Jack County Campus ... Vacant
07 Dir Admissions Jeff Davis Campus ... Mr. Bruce LAYTON
29 Director Alumni Relations ... Vacant
35 Director Student Affairs ... Vacant
75 Dean of Career/Technical Education ... Mr. John SHOWS
37 Financial Aid Director Jeff Davis ... Ms. Searcy TAYLOR
37 Financial Aid Director Perkinston ... Ms. Saadia RIDGLE
37 Financial Aid Dir Jackson County ... Ms. LaShanda CHAMBERLAIN
15 Director Human Resources ... Mr. Glen MOORE
96 Dir Purchasing/Property Control ... Ms. Lynn DEEGEN
18 Construction Manager ... Mr. Lavell BOND
26 Coord Institutional Development ... Ms. Brenda DAVIS

Mississippi State University (A)

Mississippi State MS 39762-5708
County: Oktibbeha FICE Identification: 002423
Unit ID: 176080
Telephone: (662) 325-2323 Carnegie Class: RU/VH
FAX Number: (662) 325-7455 Calendar System: Semester
URL: www.msstate.edu
Established: 1878 Annual Undergrad Tuition & Fees (In-State): $5,805
Enrollment: 19,644 Coed
Affiliation or Control: State IRS Status: 501(c)3
Highest Offering: Doctorate
Program: Liberal Arts And General; Teacher Preparatory; Professional
Accreditation: SC, AAFCS, ART, BUS, BUSA, CACREP, CIDA, CORE, CS, DIETD, DIETI, ENG, FOR, LSAR, MUS, SCPSY, SPAA, SW, TED, VET

01 President ... Dr. Mark E. KEENUM
05 Provost/Executive Vice President ... Dr. Jerome A. GILBERT
32 Vice President for Student Affairs ... Dr. William L. KIBLER
30 VP for Development and Alumni ... Mr. John P. RUSH
10 VP for Budget and Planning ... Mr. Don ZANT
46 Vice Pres Research & Economic Devel ... Dr. David SHAW
47 Vice Pres Agricult/Forestry/Vet Med ... Dr. Gregory BOHACH
35 Assoc Vice Pres of Student Affairs ... Vacant
20 Assoc Provost Academic Affairs ... Dr. Peter RYAN
21 Assoc VP for Budget and Planning ... Mr. J. Wayne BLAND
04 Assistant to the President ... Mr. Joe R. FARRIS
41 Athletic Director ... Mr. Scott STRICKLIN
43 General Counsel ... Ms. Joan LUCAS
21 Director Internal Audit ... Ms. Leisa BRYANT
48 Dean of Architecture/Art/Design ... Mr. James L. WEST
49 Dean College Arts & Sciences ... Dr. Gary L. MYERS
50 Dean College Business ... Dr. Sharon OSWALD
53 Dean of Education ... Dr. Richard L. BLACKBOURN
58 Dean of Graduate Studies ... Dr. Louis D'ABRAMO
54 Dean College of Engineering ... Dr. Sarah A. RAJALA
65 Dean of Forest Resources ... Dr. George M. HOPPER
74 Dean of Veterinary Medicine ... Dr. Kent H. HOBLET
12 Int Dean of Meridian Campus ... Dr. Dennis MITCHELL
08 Dean of Libraries ... Ms. Frances N. COLEMAN
35 Dean of Students ... Dr. Thomas BOURGEOIS
51 Director Academic Outreach/Cont Ed ... Dr. Mark BINKLEY
09 Director Institutional Research ... Dr. Tim CHAMBLEE
06 Registrar ... Mr. Butch STOKES
07 Director Admissions/Scholarships ... Dr. Philip BONFANTI
38 Director of Counseling Center ... Dr. Leigh JENSEN
37 Director Student Financial Aid ... Vacant
39 Director Housing/Residence Life ... Dr. Ann BAILEY
36 Director Career Services/Coop Educ ... Mr. Scott MAYNARD
85 Asst Dir International Services ... Mr. Stephen E. COTTRELL
35 Director Student Life ... Dr. Edwin M. KEITH
13 Head Information Technology Svcs ... Mr. J. Mike RACKLEY
14 Dir Enterprise Information Systems ... Ms. Rene HUNT
23 Director Student Health Center ... Dr. Robert K. COLLINS
16 Director Human Resources Mgmt ... Ms. Judith SPENCER
28 Dir Diversity/Equity Programs ... Dr. Tommy STEVENSON, JR.
29 Director of Alumni Association ... Dr. Jimmy ABRAHAM
26 Director University Relations ... Ms. Maridith W. GEUDER
44 Director of Planned Giving ... Mr. Vance BRISTOW
86 Director Government Relations ... Mr. John A. TOMLINSON
25 Director Sponsored Programs ... Mr. Richard SWANN
24 Director of Television Center ... Mr. Michael R. GODWIN
19 Police Chief ... Ms. Georgia LINDLEY
18 Exec Director Campus Operations ... Ms. Amy TUCK
56 Dir Univ Extension Service ... Dr. Gary JACKSON
88 Dir Agricultural Experiment Station ... Dr. George M. HOPPER
96 Director Procurement/Contracts ... Mr. Don BUFFUM

Mississippi University for Women (B)

1100 College Street, Columbus MS 39701-5800
County: Lowndes FICE Identification: 002422
Unit ID: 176035
Telephone: (877) 462-8439 Carnegie Class: Master's S
FAX Number: (662) 329-7297 Calendar System: Semester
URL: www.muw.edu
Established: 1884 Annual Undergrad Tuition & Fees (In-State): $4,876
Enrollment: 2,587 Coed
Affiliation or Control: State IRS Status: 501(c)3
Highest Offering: Master's
Program: Liberal Arts And General; Teacher Preparatory; Professional
Accreditation: SC, ACBSP, ADNUR, ART, MUS, NURSE, SP, TED

01 Interim President ... Ms. Allegra BRIGHAM
05 Interim Provost/VP Academic Affairs ... Dr. Everett CASTON
10 Vice President for Finance & Admin ... Ms. Nora R. MILLER
30 Int Vice Pres Inst Advancement ... Mr. Ken KENNEDY
32 Vice Pres for Student Services ... Dr. Jennifer MILES
20 Assoc Vice Pres Academic Affairs ... Dr. Martin HATTON
04 Assistant to the President ... Mr. Perry SANSING
49 Dean College Arts/Sciences ... Dr. Thomas C. RICHARDSON
107 Dean of Professional Studies ... Dr. William MAYFIELD
53 Dean College Educ/Human Sciences ... Dr. Sue JOLLY-SMITH
66 Dean College Nursing/Speech ... Dr. Sheila V. ADAMS
08 Dean of Library Services ... Ms. Gail P. GUNTER
58 Director Graduate Studies ... Dr. Martin HATTON
51 Director Continuing Education ... Dr. Barbara MOORE
06 Registrar ... Ms. Tammy PRATHER
88 Dir Center for Academic Excellence ... Dr. Quiteya WALKER
88 Director Advising ... Ms. Rhonda THOMAS
92 Dir Honors College/Study Abroad ... Dr. Thomas VELEK
88 Director Sponsored Programs ... Mr. James DENNEY
29 Director Alumni Relations ... Ms. Mary Margaret ROBERTS
30 Executive Director Development ... Ms. Andrea N. STEVENS
44 Director Annual Giving ... Ms. Kristin M. BARNER
26 Director Public Affairs ... Ms. Anika M. PERKINS
105 Director Web Development ... Mr. Bryant COOK
21 Comptroller ... Ms. Tonya G. MOAK
88 Director Internal Audit ... Ms. Eileen VAN DER WEELE
13 Director Information Tech Services ... Mr. Larry W. JONES
07 Director Admissions ... Ms. Cassie DERDEN
37 Director Financial Aid ... Mr. Dan MILLER
15 Director Human Resources ... Ms. Melanie H. FREEMAN
09 Director Institutional Research ... Ms. Carla LOWERY
19 Chief of Police ... Mr. Kennedy MEADERS
18 Director of Facilities Management ... Mr. Dewey BLANSETT
96 Director Resources Management ... Ms. Angie S. ATKINS
28 Director Student Life ... Mr. Phillip COCKRELL
39 Director Community Living ... Ms. Sirena PARKER
41 Exec Director Campus Recreation ... Ms. Suzanne RIES
40 Director Bookstore ... Ms. Lana ALLEN
85 Coord of International Programs ... Mr. Kevin PATRICK

Mississippi Valley State University (C)

14000 Highway 82 W, Itta Bena MS 38941-1400
County: Leflore FICE Identification: 002424
Unit ID: 176044
Telephone: (662) 254-9041 Carnegie Class: Master's M
FAX Number: (662) 254-6709 Calendar System: Other
URL: www.mvsu.edu
Established: 1946 Annual Undergrad Tuition & Fees (In-State): $5,791
Enrollment: 2,636 Coed
Affiliation or Control: State IRS Status: 501(c)3
Highest Offering: Master's
Program: Liberal Arts And General; Teacher Preparatory; Professional
Accreditation: SC, ACBSP, ART, CS, MUS, SW, TED

01 President ... Dr. Donna H. OLIVER
05 Executive Vice President/Provost ... Dr. Anna HAMMOND
10 Vice Pres for Business and Finance ... Mr. James B. WASHBURN
32 Vice Pres for Student Affairs ... Dr. Jerald ADLEY
35 Assoc VP for Student Affairs ... Ms. Dallas REED
20 Assoc Provost for Academic Affairs ... Dr. Samuel D. SHINGLES
20 Asst Provost Academic Affairs ... Vacant
35 Asst VP for Student & Enroll Svcs ... Vacant
21 Asst Vice Pres Business & Finance ... Ms. Joyce DIXON
100 Chief of Staff/Spec Asst to Pres ... Dr. A. Zachary FAISON, JR.
30 Vice Pres for Univ Advancement ... Ms. Angela GETTER
12 Director Greenwood Center ... Vacant
53 Int Dean Professionanl Stds/Educ ... Vacant
51 Director of Continuing Education ... Dr. Ronald LOVE
88 Director Renaissance Programs ... Dr. Glenell LEE-PRUITT
58 Dean of Graduate College ... Dr. Curressia BROWN
41 Interim Director of Athletics ... Mr. Donald R. SIMS
06 Director of Student Records ... Mrs. Maxcine B. RUSH
07 Actg Asst Dir Admission/Recruitment ... Ms. Ann WILLIAMS
08 Head Librarian ... Ms. Mantra HENDERSON
15 Director of Human Resources ... Mr. Frank SOWELL
14 Director of Computer Center ... Mr. Edgar BLAND
37 Director of Financial Aid ... Dr. Torrence MCKNIGHT
29 Director of Alumni Relations ... Vacant
26 Acting Dir of University Relations ... Ms. Maxine BOWEN
19 Director University Police ... Mr. Robert SANDERS
18 Director Facilities/Physical Plant ... Mr. Tommy VERDELL
39 Director Residential Life ... Mr. Byrce LOWE
36 Director Career Development ... Ms. Tiffany WALLACE
38 Director Student Counseling ... Ms. Yolanda JONES
50 Chair of Business Department ... Dr. Lawrence GULLEY
53 Int Chair of Education Department ... Dr. Chuck AHANONU
65 Int Chair Nat Sci/Env Health Dept ... Dr. Louis J. HALL
49 Dean College of Arts & Sciences ... Dr. Tazinski LEE
88 Chair English/Foreign Language ... Dr. John ZHENG
57 Chair Fine Arts Department ... Dr. Alphonso SANDERS
68 Chair Health/Phys Ed/Rec Dept ... Mr. James WILKINSON
81 Chair of Math/Computer Science Dept ... Dr. Constance BLAND
54 Act Chair of Industrial Tech Dept ... Dr. Richard MAXWELL
60 Chair Mass Communication Dept ... Dr. Samuel OSUNDE
70 Interim Chair Crim Justice ... Dr. Emmanuel AMADI
70 Chair Social Work Department ... Dr. Vincent VENTURINI
96 Director of Purchasing ... Mr. Billy SCOTT
28 Director of Cultural Diversity ... Vacant
84 Director Enrollment Management ... Vacant

Northeast Mississippi Community College (D)

101 Cunningham Boulevard, Booneville MS 38829-1731
County: Prentiss FICE Identification: 002426
Unit ID: 176169
Telephone: (662) 728-7751 Carnegie Class: Assoc/Pub-R-M
FAX Number: (662) 728-1165 Calendar System: Semester
URL: www.nemcc.edu
Established: 1948 Annual Undergrad Tuition & Fees (In-District): $1,920
Enrollment: 3,633 Coed
Affiliation or Control: State/Local IRS Status: 501(c)3
Highest Offering: Associate Degree
Program: Occupational; 2-Year Principally Bachelor's Creditable
Accreditation: SC, ADNUR, DH, MAC, MLTAD, RAD

01 President ... Johnny L. ALLEN
03 Executive Vice President ... Larry J. NABORS
10 Vice President Finance/Operations ... Cheryl H. RAGAN
103 Vice Pres Wrkfrce Training/Econ Dev ... Nadara L. COLE
26 Assoc Vice Pres of Public Info ... Tony FINCH
09 Assoc Vice Pres Planning/Research ... Rilla C. JONES
05 Dean of Instruction ... Charlie BARNETT
35 Assoc Dean of Student Activities ... Angie LANGLEY
08 Director Learning Resources ... Glenice STONE
96 Director of Purchasing ... Amanda DOWNS
37 Director of Financial Aid ... Greg WINDHAM
38 Director Student Counseling ... Joey WILLIFORD
14 Director Computer Center ... Gregory SMITH
18 Director Facilities/Maintenance ... William MCKINNEY
39 Director Residential Housing ... Rod COGGIN
32 Dean of Students/Athletic Director ... Ricky FORD
75 Director of Vocational Tech Educ ... Ritchie WILLIAMS
84 Dir of Enrollment Svcs/Registrar ... Lynn GIBSON
15 Human Resources Officer ... Lynn VUNCANNON
35 Director Student Affairs ... Kenneth POUNDERS
29 Dir Alumni Relations/Devel Found ... Barbara SHACKELFORD

Northwest Mississippi Community College (E)

4975 Highway 51 N, Senatobia MS 38668-1703
County: Tate FICE Identification: 002427
Unit ID: 176178
Telephone: (662) 562-3200 Carnegie Class: Assoc/Pub-R-L
FAX Number: (662) 562-3911 Calendar System: Semester
URL: www.northwestms.edu
Established: 1927 Annual Undergrad Tuition & Fees (In-State): $1,950
Enrollment: 6,607 Coed
Affiliation or Control: State IRS Status: 501(c)3
Highest Offering: Associate Degree
Program: Occupational; 2-Year Principally Bachelor's Creditable
Accreditation: SC, ADNUR, EMT, FUSER

01 President ... Dr. Gary Lee SPEARS
10 Vice President for Fiscal Affairs ... Mr. Gary MOSLEY
32 VP Student Affs/Chief of Staff ... Mr. Dan SMITH
05 Vice Pres for Educational Affairs ... Dr. Chuck STRONG
20 Academic Dean ... Dr. Matthew S. DOMAS
75 Dean Career Tech Ed/Wrkfce Dev Trng ... Mr. Jerry NICHOLS
51 Dir Division of Continuing Educ ... Ms. Pam WOOTEN
84 Dean Enrollment Mgmt & Registrar ... Mr. Larry SIMPSON
35 Director of Student Personnel ... Mr. Mike DOTTOREY
27 Director of Communications ... Mrs. Sarah SAPP
37 Director of Financial Aid ... Mr. Joe BOYLES

6	Dir Student Development Center	Ms. Meg ROSS
8	Director of Learning Resources	Mrs. Maggie MORAN
3	Director Management Information Sys	Mrs. Amy LATHAM
7	Director of Recruiting	Mrs. Jere HERRINGTON
9	Director Planning/Inst Research	Dr. Matthew DOMAS
8	Director of Physical Plant Building	Mr. Mike ROBISON
9	Chief of Campus Security	Mr. Al DODSON
0	Director of Development/Alumni Rels	Mrs. Sybil CANON
9	Director of Campus Life and Housing	Mrs. Aime ANDERSON
0	Director Bookstore	Mr. Joel BOYLES
1	Director of Athletics/Intramurals	Mr. Cameron BLOUNT
6	Director of Purchasing	Mrs. Barbara YOUNG
5	Personnel Officer	Mrs. Rita DOWDLE
9	Director Alumni Relations	Mrs. Dolores WOOTEN
1	Business Manager	Ms. Ruthie CASTLE

Pearl River Community College (A)

101 Highway 11 N, Poplarville MS 39470-2298

County: Pearl River — FICE Identification: 002430 — Unit ID: 176239
Telephone: (601) 403-1000 — Carnegie Class: Assoc/Pub-R-M
FAX Number: (601) 403-1129 — Calendar System: Semester
URL: www.prcc.edu
Established: 1909 — Annual Undergrad Tuition & Fees (In-District): $2,000
Enrollment: 5,540 — Coed
Affiliation or Control: State/Local — IRS Status: 501(c)3
Highest Offering: Associate Degree
Program: Occupational; 2-Year Principally Bachelor's Creditable
Accreditation: SC, ADNUR, DA, DH, MLTAD, OTA, PTAA, RAD, SURGT

01	President	Dr. William A. LEWIS
05	VP for General Education	Dr. Martha L. SMITH
32	VP Poplarville Campus/Hancock Ctr	Dr. Adam BREERWOOD
10	VP for Business/Admn Services	Mr. Roger A. KNIGHT
08	Director of College Libraries	Ms. Jeanne DYAR
26	Director of Public Relations	Mr. Chuck ABADIE
84	VP for Enrollment Management	Mr. Dow FORD
12	VP of Forrest County Operations	Dr. Cecil BURT
14	Chief Technology Officer	Mr. Steve HOWARD
18	Director of Physical Plant	Mr. Craig TYNES
30	Director Development/Alumni Rels	Mr. Ernest L. LOVELL, JR.
37	Director Student Financial Aid	Ms. Valerie HORNE
41	Director of Athletics	Mr. Richard MATHIS
07	Director of Recruitment/Orientation	Vacant
09	VP for Planning & Research	Dr. Rebecca ASKEW
36	Dir Student Placement/Counselor	Dr. Ann MOORE
31	VP Econ/Comm Development	Dr. David S. ALSOBROOKS

Reformed Theological Seminary (B)

5422 Clinton Boulevard, Jackson MS 39209-3099

County: Hinds — FICE Identification: 009193 — Unit ID: 176284
Telephone: (601) 923-1600 — Carnegie Class: Not Classified
FAX Number: (601) 923-1654 — Calendar System: 4/1/4
URL: www.rts.edu
Established: 1965 — Annual Graduate Tuition & Fees: $14,150
Enrollment: 329 — Coed
Affiliation or Control: Independent Non-Profit — IRS Status: 501(c)3
Highest Offering: Doctorate; No Undergraduates
Program: Professional
Accreditation: SC, MFCD, THEOL

00	Chancellor-Elect	Dr. Mike MILTON
01	Chancellor & CEO	Dr. Robert C. CANNADA, JR.
03	Chief Operations Officer	Mr. Steve WALLACE
12	President Charlotte Campus	Dr. Mike MILTON
12	President Orlando Campus	Dr. Don SWEETING
10	Chief Financial Officer	Mr. Bradley TISDALE
05	Chief Academic Officer	Dr. Robert CARA
12	President Jackson Campus	Dr. Guy L. RICHARDSON
12	President Virtual Campus	Dr. Andrew J. PETERSON
12	President Atlanta Campus	Mr. John T. SOWELL
12	Executive Director Washington DC	Mr. Hugh WHELCHEL
84	Senior VP Enrollment Management	Vacant
44	Vice President for Development	Mr. Robert PENNY
30	Chief Development Officer	Dr. Lynwood C. PEREZ
06	Registrar Jackson Campus	Ms. Kim LEE
08	Library Director	Mr. John MUETHER
32	Dean of Student Affairs/Admissions	Mr. Brian C. GAULT
29	Dir Alum Rels/Dev/Supt Svcs Jackson	Mrs. Stephanie J. HARTLEY
04	Assistant to Pres Jackson Campus	Mrs. Wanda RUSHING
88	Dir Marriage & Fam Ther Jackson	Dr. James B. HURLEY
18	Maintenance Director Jackson Campus	Mr. Joe MORRIS
26	Dir of Institutional Communications	Dr. Lynwood C. PEREZ
09	Director of Institutional Research	Ms. Polly STONE
15	Director Personnel Svcs Jackson	Ms. Linda COCHRAN

Rust College (C)

150 Rust Avenue, Holly Springs MS 38635-2328

County: Marshall — FICE Identification: 002433 — Unit ID: 176318
Telephone: (662) 252-8000 — Carnegie Class: Bac/A&S
FAX Number: (662) 252-6107 — Calendar System: Semester
URL: www.rustcollege.edu
Established: 1866 — Annual Undergrad Tuition & Fees: $8,100
Enrollment: 960 — Coed
Affiliation or Control: United Methodist — IRS Status: 501(c)3
Highest Offering: Baccalaureate
Program: Liberal Arts And General
Accreditation: SC, SW, @TEAC

01	President	Dr. David L. BECKLEY
30	Vice President Development	Dr. Ishmell H. EDWARDS
10	Vice President for Finance/ Business	Mr. Donald MANNING-MILLER
09	Asst to the Pres for Assessment	Dr. Tequecie MEEK
05	VP for Academic Affairs	Dr. Paul C. LAMPLEY
06	Registrar	Mr. Clarence E. SMITH
08	Head Librarian	Mrs. Anita W. MOORE
14	Director Computer Center	Ms. Barbara NAYLOR MOORE
32	Dean of Student Affairs	Mrs. Carolyn HYMON
35	Director Student Activities	Mrs. Priscilla FISHER
37	Director of Financial Aid	Mrs. Helen STREET
25	Director Contracts & Grants	Mrs. Christine L. RATCLIFF
27	Director of Public Information	Ms. Adrienne PHILLIPS
29	Director Alumni Development	Vacant
38	Inst Counselor/Dir 1st Yr Exper	Dr. Juanita M. SEALS-JONES
26	Director of Public Relations	Vacant
21	Comptroller	Vacant
84	Director Enrollment Services	Ms. JoAnn SCOTT
23	Director Student Health Services	Dr. Dianna HUGHES
39	Director Student Housing	Mrs. Dorothy DONNELL
36	Director of Career Development	Mr. John PEACHES
18	Director Physical Plant	Mr. Robert CURRY
83	Division Chair Social Science	Dr. Alfred J. STOVALL
15	Director Personnel Services	Ms. Patricia PEGUES
19	Chief of Security	Mr. Claude GLEETON
30	Director of Development	Vacant
40	Bookstore Manager	Mrs. Patricia HARRIS
42	College Chaplain	Rev. Annie TRAVIS
96	Director of Purchasing	Ms. Ollie BOWENS
28	Director of Diversity	Miss Patricia PEGUES
50	Division Chair Business	Mr. Richard FREDERICK
53	Division Chair Education	Dr. Leon HOWARD
79	Division Chair Humanities	Dr. Sylvester W. OLIVER
81	Chair Division Science & Math	Dr. Frank YEH
70	Chair Department of Social Work	Dr. Gemma BECKLEY

Southeastern Baptist College (D)

4229 Highway 15 N, Laurel MS 39440-1096

County: Jones — FICE Identification: 002435 — Unit ID: 176336
Telephone: (601) 426-6346 — Carnegie Class: Spec/Faith
FAX Number: (601) 426-6347 — Calendar System: Semester
URL: www.southeasternbaptist.edu
Established: 1948 — Annual Undergrad Tuition & Fees: $4,000
Enrollment: 65 — Coed
Affiliation or Control: Baptist — IRS Status: 501(c)3
Highest Offering: Baccalaureate
Program: 2-Year Principally Bachelor's Creditable; Liberal Arts And General; Religious Emphasis
Accreditation: BI

01	President	Dr. Medrick H. SAVELL
03	Executive Vice President	Mr. Joseph HARRIS
05	Academic Dean	Dr. Aaron L. PARKER
32	Director of Student Services	Mr. Greg HILLMAN
07	Director of Admissions/Recruitment	Mr. Ronnie KITCHENS
06	Registrar	Mrs. Emma BOND
37	Financial Aid Administrator	Ms. Ginny SINGLETON
08	Director of Library	Mrs. Amy E. HINTON
38	Director of Student Counseling	Mr. Greg HILLMAN

Southwest Mississippi Community College (E)

1156 College Drive, Summit MS 39666-9029

County: Pike — FICE Identification: 002436 — Unit ID: 176354
Telephone: (601) 276-2000 — Carnegie Class: Assoc/Pub-R-S
FAX Number: (601) 276-3888 — Calendar System: Semester
URL: www.smcc.edu
Established: 1918 — Annual Undergrad Tuition & Fees (In-District): $2,090
Enrollment: 2,143 — Coed
Affiliation or Control: Local — IRS Status: 501(c)3
Highest Offering: Associate Degree
Program: Occupational; 2-Year Principally Bachelor's Creditable
Accreditation: SC, ADNUR

01	President	Dr. Steve BISHOP
05	Vice President of Academic Affairs	Ms. Alicia SHOWS
10	Vice President of Financial Affairs	Mr. Grady SMITH
32	Vice President of Student Affairs	Mr. Bill ASHLEY
06	Registrar/Vice President Admissions	Mr. Matthew CALHOUN
75	Vice Pres Career & Tech Education	Mr. Jeremy SMITH
37	Director Student Financial Aid	Mrs. Stacey HODGES
09	Director of Institutional Research	Dr. Bill TUCKER
08	Librarian	Mrs. Natalie MCMAHON

Tougaloo College (F)

Tougaloo MS 39174-9999

County: Madison — FICE Identification: 002439 — Unit ID: 176406
Telephone: (601) 977-7730 — Carnegie Class: Bac/A&S
FAX Number: (601) 977-7739 — Calendar System: Semester
URL: www.tougaloo.edu
Established: 1869 — Annual Undergrad Tuition & Fees: $9,740
Enrollment: 918 — Coed
Affiliation or Control: United Church Of Christ — IRS Status: 501(c)3
Highest Offering: Baccalaureate
Program: Liberal Arts And General
Accreditation: #SC

01	President	Dr. Beverly W. HOGAN
05	Provost/Vice Pres Academic Affairs	Vacant
32	Vice President Student Affairs	Mr. Fred ALEXANDER
30	Int Vice Pres Institutional Advance	Mrs. Sandra A M. BOWIE
10	Vice Pres Finance Administration	Dr. Cynthia MELVIN
18	Vice Pres for Facilities Management	Mr. Kelle MENOGAN
20	Asst Provost/VP Academic Affairs	Dr. Ollye W. JOHNSON
84	Asst VP for Enrollment Management	Mr. Steven SMITH
35	Asst Vice Pres for Student Affairs	Mrs. Gladys J. JONES
88	Ex Dir Ntnl Transp Sec Ctr of Excel	Mr. Eduardo MARTINEZ
08	Director of Library Services	Mrs. Orthella P. MOMAN
13	Chief Information Officer	Mr. Terry J. JORDAN
37	Director of Student Financial Aid	Ms. Maria THOMAS
09	Director Inst Research/Assess/Plng	Dr. Larry JOHNSON
06	Registrar	Ms. Carolyn L. EVANS
15	Director Human Resources	Ms. Doretha PRESLEY
26	Dir Communications/Public Affairs	Mr. Danny L. JONES
29	Director of Alumni Affairs	Mrs. Doris BRIDGEMAN
07	Director of Admissions	Ms. Junoesque JACOBS
36	Director of Career Services	Mrs. Gladys J. JONES
44	Director of Advancement Services	Mrs. Sanette LANGSTON-SMITH
46	Dir of Sponsored Programs/Research	Dr. Connie RICHARDSON
88	Director of TRiO	Dr. Valvia WILSON
38	Director of Counseling Services	Dr. Rosie HARPER
96	Purchasing Agent	Ms. Easter COMMON
102	Dir Corporation & Foundation Rels	Vacant

University of Mississippi (G)

University MS 38677-9999

County: Lafayette — FICE Identification: 002440 — Unit ID: 176017
Telephone: (662) 915-7211 — Carnegie Class: RU/H
FAX Number: (662) 915-7010 — Calendar System: Semester
URL: www.olemiss.edu
Established: 1844 — Annual Undergrad Tuition & Fees (In-State): $5,790
Enrollment: 17,085 — Coed
Affiliation or Control: State — IRS Status: 501(c)3
Highest Offering: Doctorate
Program: Liberal Arts And General; Teacher Preparatory; Professional
Accreditation: SC, ART, BUS, BUSA, CACREP, CLPSY, CS, DIETC, DIETD, ENG, JOUR, LAW, MUS, NRPA, PHAR, SP, SW, TED, THEA

01	Chancellor	Dr. Daniel W. JONES
26	Chief Marketing Officer	Vacant
05	Provost/Vice Chanc Academic Affairs	Dr. Morris H. STOCKS
10	Vice Chanc Finance & Administration	Mr. Larry D. SPARKS
32	Vice Chancellor Student Life	Dr. Larry RIDGEWAY
46	Vice Chanc Research/Sponsored Pgms	Dr. Alice M. CLARK
30	Sr Executive Dir of Development	Ms. Deborah S. VAUGHN
20	Associate Provost	Dr. Maurice R. EFTINK
20	Associate Provost	Dr. Noel E. WILKIN
20	Associate Provost	Dr. Ann CANTY
85	Ast Prov/Ast to Chanc Multicul Affs	Dr. Donald R. COLE
08	Dean of Libraries	Ms. Julia RHOLES
35	Asst Vice Chanc Student Affairs	Dr. Thomas J. REARDON
13	Chief Information Officer	Dr. Kathryn F. GATES
87	Asst Provost Summer School/Outreach	Dr. Timothy R. ANGLE
36	Director Career Center	Ms. Toni D. AVANT
29	Exec Director of Alumni Affairs	Mr. Timothy L. WALSH
37	Director of Financial Aid	Ms. Laura DIVEN-BROWN
41	Director Intercollegiate Athletics	Mr. James T. BOONE
15	Director of Human Resources	Mr. Clayton H. JONES
18	Interim Director of Physical Plant	Mr. Ashton PEARSON
19	Director Univ Police/Campus Safety	Chief Calvin SELLERS
38	Director of Counseling Center	Dr. Marc K. SHOWALTER
23	Director University Health Service	Ms. Barbara COLLIER
39	Dir of Student Housing/Res Life	Ms. Lorinda S. KRHUT
09	Director Institutional Research	Ms. Mary M. HARRINGTON
22	Exec Dir Equal Oppty/Reg Compliance	Ms. Wilma F. WEBBER-COLBERT
100	Chief of Staff to the Chancellor	Dr. Andrew P. MULLINS
04	Assistant to the Chancellor	Ms. Sue T. KEISER
43	Univ Attorney/Spec Asst to Chanc	Dr. Lee TYNER
35	Asst Vice Chancellor Student Affs	Dr. Charlotte FANT
96	Director of Procurement Services	Mr. James R. WINDHAM
50	Dean School of Business Admin	Dr. Kendall B. CYREE
49	Dean College of Liberal Arts	Dr. Glenn W. HOPKINS
81	Dean School of Applied Sciences	Dr. Linda F. CHITWOOD
53	Dean School of Education	Dr. David ROCK
54	Dean School of Engineering	Dr. Alex CHENG
61	Dean School of Law	Dr. I. Richard GERSHON
67	Dean of the School of Pharmacy	Dr. Barbara G. WELLS
88	Dean School of Accountancy	Dr. W. Mark WILDER
60	Dean Journalism & New Media	Dr. H. Will NORTON
06	Registrar	Mrs. Denise KNIGHTON
21	Controller	Mr. Sam THOMAS
84	Director of Enrollment Services	Mr. Whitman SMITH

University of Mississippi Medical Center (H)

2500 N State Street, Jackson MS 39216-4505

County: Hinds — FICE Identification: 004688 — Unit ID: 176026
Telephone: (601) 984-1000 — Carnegie Class: Spec/Med
FAX Number: (601) 984-1013 — Calendar System: Semester
URL: www.umc.edu
Established: 1955 — Annual Undergrad Tuition & Fees (In-State): $5,792
Enrollment: 2,461 — Coed

Affiliation or Control: State IRS Status: 501(c)3
Highest Offering: Doctorate
Program: Professional; Nursing Emphasis
Accreditation: SC, CYTO, DENT, DH, IPSY, MED, MT, NMT, NURSE, OT, PTA, RAD

01 Vice Chancellor Health Affairs ... Dr. James E. KEETON
63 Assoc VC Health Affs/Vice Dean SOM .. Dr. LouAnn WOODWARD
100 Chief of Staff to Vice Chancellor ... Vacant
10 Associate Vice Chanc Financial Affs ... Mr. J. Michael LIGHTSEY
21 Associate Business Officer ... Mr. Sam E. SMITH
11 Associate Vice Chanc Admin Affairs ... Dr. David L. POWE
46 Associate Vice Chanc Research ... Dr. John E. HALL
05 Assoc Vice Chanc Academic Affairs ... Dr. Helen TURNER
20 Deputy Chief Academic Officer ... Dr. Robin ROCKHOLD
28 Assoc Vice Chanc Multicultural Affs ... Dr. Jasmine P. TAYLOR
23 Assoc Vice Chanc Clinical Affairs ... Dr. Scott STRINGER
17 CEO University Hosp and Clinics ... Mr. David G. PUTT
43 Chief Legal Officer ... Mr. John T. NEWSOME
26 Chief Public Affs & Comm Officer ... Mr. Tom FORTNER
27 Chief Information Officer ... Mr. Charles R. ENICKS
15 Chief Human Resources Officer ... Mr. Michael ESTES
66 Dean School of Nursing ... Dr. Kim HOOVER
58 Dean Sch Grad Stds Health Sciences ... Dr. Joey GRANGER
76 Dean School Health Rel Profession ... Dr. Ben L. MITCHELL
52 Interim Dean of School of Dentistry ... Dr. Gary W. REEVES
63 Assoc Dean-Graduate Medical Educ .. Dr. Shirley SCHLESSINGER
09 Interim Dir Institutional Research ... Dr. David G. FOWLER
45 Director Strategic Res Alliances ... Dr. David J. DZIELAK
19 Director Police & Logistical Svcs ... Mr. Arty E. GIROD
18 Director Physical Facilities ... Mr. Ivory BOGAN
30 Director Development ... Vacant
88 Director of Accreditation ... Dr. Mitzi NORRIS
96 Director Supply Chain ... Mr. Edward SMITH
29 Assoc Director Alumni Affairs ... Mr. Geoffrey MITCHELL
38 Director Academic Counseling ... Dr. Natalie W. GAUGHF
37 Director Student Financial Aid ... Ms. Stacy MATHEWS
32 Chief Student Affairs Officer ... Dr. Jerry CLARK
06 Dir Student Records & Registrar . Ms. Barbara M. WESTERFIELD
08 Director Rowland Medical Library ... Ms. Susan B. CLARK

University of Southern Mississippi (A)

118 College Drive, #5001, Hattiesburg MS 39406-0001
County: Forrest FICE Identification: 002441
Unit ID: 176372
Telephone: (601) 266-1000 Carnegie Class: RU/H
FAX Number: (601) 266-5756 Calendar System: Semester
URL: www.usm.edu
Established: 1910 Annual Undergrad Tuition & Fees (In-State): $5,834
Enrollment: 15,778 Coed
Affiliation or Control: State IRS Status: 501(c)3
Highest Offering: Doctorate
Program: Liberal Arts And General; Teacher Preparatory; Professional
Accreditation: SC, AAFCS, ART, AUD, BUS, BUSA, CIDA, CLPSY, CONST, COPSY, CS, DANCE, DIETD, DIETI, ENGT, JOUR, KIN, LIB, MFCD, MT, MUS, NRPA, NURSE, PH, SCPSY, SP, SW, TED, THEA

01 President ... Dr. Martha SAUNDERS
04 Assistant to the President ... Ms. Mary D. GREGG
05 Provost ... Dr. Bob LYMAN
20 Assoc Provost Academic Affairs ... Dr. Cynthia EASTERLING
12 Vice Pres for Gulf Coast Campus ... Dr. Frances LUCAS
20 Associate Provost Academic Affairs ... Dr. William W. POWELL
20 Asst Provost Academic Affairs ... Dr. Brett KEMKER
46 Vice Pres Research ... Dr. Denis WIESENBURG
11 Vice Pres for Admin Affairs ... Mr. Russ WILLIS
32 Vice President for Student Affairs ... Dr. Joseph S. PAUL
37 Asst VP Student Affs & Finan Aid ... Dr. Kristi MOTTER
35 Asc Vice President Student Affairs ... Mr. Sid GONSOULIN
30 Vice President Advancement ... Mr. Bob PIERCE
53 Dean College Education/Psychology ... Dr. Ann BLACKWELL
49 Int Dean College Arts & Letters ... Dr. Steven MOSER
50 Dean College Business ... Dr. Lance NAIL
72 Dean College Science/Technology ... Dr. Joe WHITEHEAD
92 Dean of Honors College ... Dr. David DAVIES
76 Dean College Health ... Dr. Michael FORSTER
58 Dean Graduate School ... Dr. Susan SILTANEN
08 Dean/University Librarian ... Dr. Carole KIEHL
18 Director Physical Plant ... Mr. Chris CRENSHAW
14 Chief Information Technology Ofcr ... Mr. Homer COFFMAN
41 Athletic Director ... Mr. Richard GIANNINI
06 Registrar ... Mr. Greg PIERCE
25 Dir Research & Sponsored Programs ... Ms. Constance V. WYLDMON
09 Director of Institutional Research ... Mrs. Michelle ARRINGTON
45 Dir of Institutional Effectiveness ... Mrs. Kathryn LOWERY
29 Alumni Activities/Exec Director ... Mr. Jerry DEFATTA
36 Director Career Planning/Placement ... Mr. Russell ANDERSON
21 Controller ... Ms. Allyson EASTERWOOD
22 Director of Affirmative Action ... Ms. Rebecca WOODRICK
38 Director of Counseling Center ... Dr. Deena CRAWFORD
23 Director of Health Services ... Dr. Virginia CRAWFORD
39 Director of Residence Life ... Dr. Scott BLACKWELL
15 Director of Human Resources ... Mr. Russ WILLIS
94 Director of Women's Studies ... Dr. Kay HARRIS
96 Director Purchasing/Procuremnt Svcs ... Mr. Michael HERNDON
07 Int Director of Admissions ... Ms. Amanda KING

Virginia College (B)

920 Cedar Lake Road, Biloxi MS 39532-2107
County: Harrison Identification: 666073
Unit ID: 450191
Telephone: (228) 546-9100 Carnegie Class: Assoc/PrivFP
FAX Number: (228) 392-2039 Calendar System: Quarter
URL: www.vc.edu
Established: 2005 Annual Undergrad Tuition & Fees: $15,616
Enrollment: 470 Coed
Affiliation or Control: Proprietary IRS Status: Proprietary
Highest Offering: Associate Degree
Program: Occupational
Accreditation: ACICS

01 Campus President ... Ms. Edna HIGGINS
05 Academic Dean ... Mr. Richard SCHNORBUS
36 Director of Career Services ... Ms. Hilde FLYNT
37 Director of Financial Planning ... Mr. Leo HUNSINGER
06 Registrar ... Ms. Patti L. COSKIE
07 Director of Admissions ... Ms. Betina D. YURKUS
08 Librarian ... Ms. Alana CREAR

† Branch campus of Virginia College, Birmingham, AL.

Virginia College (C)

4795 I-55 North, Jackson MS 39206
County: Hinds Identification: 666032
Unit ID: 441919
Telephone: (601) 977-0960 Carnegie Class: Assoc/PrivFP
FAX Number: (601) 956-4325 Calendar System: Quarter
URL: www.vc.edu
Established: 1999 Annual Undergrad Tuition & Fees: $19,258
Enrollment: 958 Coed
Affiliation or Control: Proprietary IRS Status: Proprietary
Highest Offering: Associate Degree
Program: Occupational
Accreditation: ACICS

01 Campus President ... Mr. Milton ANDERSON
05 Vice President & Academic Dean ... Mr. Jorge GONZALEZ
07 Director of Admissions ... Ms. Ellie DENMAN
06 Registrar ... Ms. Gina S. PHELPS
37 Director of Financial Aid ... Ms. Judy S. STOTT
36 Director of Career Services ... Mr. Stephen STEED

† Branch campus of Virginia College, Birmingham, AL.

Wesley Biblical Seminary (D)

787 E Northside Drive, Jackson MS 39206-4945
County: Hinds FICE Identification: 025162
Unit ID: 176451
Telephone: (601) 366-8880 Carnegie Class: Spec/Faith
FAX Number: (601) 366-8832 Calendar System: Semester
URL: www.wbs.edu
Established: 1974 Annual Graduate Tuition & Fees: $11,500
Enrollment: 137 Coed
Affiliation or Control: Interdenominational IRS Status: 501(c)3
Highest Offering: Master's; No Undergraduates
Program: Professional; Religious Emphasis
Accreditation: THEOL

01 President ... Dr. James L. PORTER
05 Vice President Academic Affairs ... Dr. Daniel L. BURNETT
32 VP of Business/Student Development ... Rev. Tom HALFORD
08 Director of Library Services ... Dr. Daniel L. BURNETT
10 Business Officer ... Mrs. Leigh THOMAS
18 Director of Operations ... Vacant

William Carey University (E)

498 Tuscan Avenue, Hattiesburg MS 39401-5461
County: Forrest FICE Identification: 002447
Unit ID: 176479
Telephone: (601) 318-6051 Carnegie Class: Master's L
FAX Number: (601) 318-6494 Calendar System: Trimester
URL: www.wmcarey.edu
Established: 1906 Annual Undergrad Tuition & Fees: $10,350
Enrollment: 3,626 Coed
Affiliation or Control: Southern Baptist IRS Status: 501(c)3
Highest Offering: Doctorate
Program: Liberal Arts And General; Teacher Preparatory; Professional
Accreditation: SC, MUS, NURSE, @OSTEO

01 President/Chief Executive Officer ... Dr. Tommy KING
05 Vice President of Academic Affairs ... Dr. Garry M. BRELAND
10 Vice Pres Business Affs/CFO ... Mr. Grant GUTHRIE
32 Vice President Student Services ... Ms. Brenda WALDRIP
46 Vice President Inst Effectiveness ... Dr. Bennie R. CROCKETT
30 VP Advancement/Church Relations ... Dr. Scott HUMMEL
63 VP/Dean Col Osteopathic Medicine ... Dr. Darrell LOVINS
12 Admin Dean Tradition Campus ... Mr. Gerald BRACEY
04 Executive Assistant to President ... Ms. Barbara HAMILTON
50 Dean School of Business ... Dr. Cheryl DALE
53 Dean School of Education ... Dr. Barry MORRIS
83 Dean Sch Natural/Behavioral Science ... Dr. Frank BAUGH
66 Dean School of Nursing ... Dr. Janet WILLIAMS
49 Dean School of Arts & Letters ... Dr. Myron NOONKESTER
64 Dean Winters School of Music ... Dr. Don ODOM
73 Dean School of Missions ... Dr. Daniel CALDWELL
84 Dean of Enrollment Management ... Mr. William N. CURRY
58 Dean of Graduate Studies/Admission ... Dr. Frank BAUGH
20 Assoc Dean of Academic Services ... Dr. Les STEVERSON
09 Director Institutional Research ... Dr. William T. RIVERO
06 Registrar ... Mrs. Gayle KNIGHT
08 Director of Libraries ... Mrs. Sherry LAUGHLIN
29 Alumni Director ... Mrs. Cindy COFIELD
26 Chief Public Relations Officer ... Vacant
13 Director of Information Technology ... Mr. Jeff ANDREWS
92 Director of Honors Program ... Dr. Read M. DIKET
21 Director of Budget Management ... Mr. Grant GUTHRIE
41 Athletic Director ... Mr. Steven H. KNIGHT
18 Dir Facilities/Grounds/Maintenance ... Mr. Robert BLEVINS
32 Dir Student Svcs Tradition Campus ... Mr. James M. HARRISON
66 Associate Dean Nursing NO Campus ... Dr. Marilyn COOKSEY
21 Dir Business Svcs Tradition Campus ... Mr. Gerald BRACEY
12 Director of Keesler Center ... Ms. Amanda KNESAL
15 Director Personnel Services ... Ms. Deidre SHOWS
19 Director Campus Security ... Vacant
88 Coord of Instructional Technology ... Mr. David J. BROCKWAY
12 Coordinator New Orleans Campus ... Mr. Jeffrey ANDREWS

MISSOURI

A. T. Still University of Health Sciences (F)

800 W Jefferson Street, Kirksville MO 63501-1497
County: Adair FICE Identification: 002477
Unit ID: 177834
Telephone: (660) 626-2391 Carnegie Class: Spec/Med
FAX Number: (660) 626-2672 Calendar System: Quarter
URL: www.atsu.edu
Established: 1892 Annual Graduate Tuition & Fees: N/A
Enrollment: 3,624 Coed
Affiliation or Control: Independent Non-Profit IRS Status: 501(c)3
Highest Offering: First Professional Degree; No Undergraduates
Program: Professional
Accreditation: NH, OSTEO, OT

01 President ... Dr. Jack MAGRUDER
05 Senior VP Academic Affairs ... Dr. Doug WOOD
63 Interim Dean of KCOM ... Dr. Jeffrey SUZEWITS
32 VP Student & Alumni Affairs ... Mr. Ron GABER
30 VP for Institutional Advancement ... Mr. Robert BASHAM
43 General Counsel ... Mr. Matthew HEEREN
46 Vice Pres Inst Research & Grants ... Dr. John HEARD
26 VP Comm & Spec Asst to President ... Dr. Heinz WOEHLK
88 Exec VP for Strategic Initiatives ... Dr. Craig PHELPS
58 Dean School of Health Managemnt ... Dr. Kimberly O'REILLY
52 Dean AZ Sch of Dentistry/Oral Hlth ... Dr. Jack DILLENBERG
76 Dean Arizona Sch of Health Sciences ... Dr. Barbara MAXWELL
63 Dean School of Osteo Med in Arizona ... Dr. Thomas MCWILLIAMS
10 Vice President for Finance/CFO ... Mrs. Monnie HARRISON
07 Assoc VP Admissions & Alumni Svcs ... Mrs. Lori HAXTON
31 Asst VP Community Developments ... Vacant
13 Asst VP Info Technologies/Services ... Mr. Bryan KRUSNIAK
20 Associate Dean Academic Affairs ... Dr. Stephen LAIRD
20 Assoc Dean Clinical Regional Affs ... Dr. Jeff SUZEWITS
51 Asst Dean/Cont Osteopathic Med Educ ... Dr. Lloyd CLEAVER
04 Assistant to the President ... Mrs. Tracey J. LANTZ
06 Registrar ... Dr. Deanna HUNSAKER
08 Director of Library ... Mr. Doug BLANSIT
15 Director of Human Resources ... Mrs. Donna BROWN
18 Director Facilities/Plant Operation ... Mr. Robert EHRLICH
22 Affirmative Action Officer ... Mrs. Donna BROWN
37 Dir Student Financial Assistance ... Mr. Steven JORDEN
38 Director of Student Counseling ... Mr. Thomas VAN VLECK
96 Director of Purchasing ... Mr. Corey LOUDER

† Arizona campus accreditation includes ARPCA, AUD, DENT, OT, PTA.

Anthem College (G)

13723 Riverport Drive, Suite 103, Maryland Heights MO 63043-4819
County: Saint Louis FICE Identification: 022392
Unit ID: 176549
Telephone: (314) 595-3400 Carnegie Class: Assoc/PrivFP
FAX Number: (314) 739-5133 Calendar System: Other
URL: www.anthemcollege.edu
Established: 1981 Annual Undergrad Tuition & Fees: $22,072
Enrollment: 539 Coed
Affiliation or Control: Proprietary IRS Status: Proprietary
Highest Offering: Associate Degree
Program: Occupational
Accreditation: ABHES, SURTEC

01 President ... Ms. Heidi WIND

American College of Technology (H)

2300 Frederick Avenue, Saint Joseph MO 64506
County: Buchanan FICE Identification: 041187
Unit ID: 457688
Telephone: (816) 279-7000 Carnegie Class: Not Classified
FAX Number: (800) 908-9329 Calendar System: Other
URL: www.acot.edu
Established: 2001 Annual Undergrad Tuition & Fees: $8,950
Enrollment: 77 Coed
Affiliation or Control: Proprietary IRS Status: Proprietary
Highest Offering: Associate Degree
Program: Occupational; 2-Year Principally Bachelor's Creditable; Technical Emphasis
Accreditation: DETC

01 President ... Mr. Sam ATIEH
05 Director of Technology ... Mr. Lute ATIEH
37 Financial Aid Administrator ... Ms. Justine MCMULLEN

Aquinas Institute of Theology (A)

23 S Spring Avenue, Saint Louis MO 63108-3323
County: City of Saint Louis FICE Identification: 001632
Unit ID: 176600
Telephone: (314) 256-8800 Carnegie Class: Spec/Faith
FAX Number: (314) 256-8888 Calendar System: Semester
URL: www.ai.edu
Established: 1951 Annual Graduate Tuition & Fees: $15,750
Enrollment: 192 Coed
Affiliation or Control: Roman Catholic IRS Status: 501(c)3
Highest Offering: Doctorate; No Undergraduates
Program: Professional; Religious Emphasis
Accreditation: NH, THEOL

01 President ... Rev. Richard A. PEDDICORD
05 Academic Dean ... Rev. Gregory HEILLE
10 Director of Finance ... Mr. Thomas BARBARAK
06 Registrar ... Ms. Julie QUINT
30 Director of Inst Advancement ... Mrs. Barbara MAYNARD
32 Dean of Students ... Rev. George BOUDREAU
07 Director Admissions/Financial Aid ... Mr. David WERTHMANN
26 Director of Marketing ... Mr. Thomas BARBARAK

Assemblies of God Theological Seminary (B)

1435 N Glenstone Avenue, Springfield MO 65802-2131
County: Greene FICE Identification: 012120
Unit ID: 176619
Telephone: (417) 268-1000 Carnegie Class: Spec/Faith
FAX Number: (417) 268-1001 Calendar System: Semester
URL: www.agts.edu
Established: 1972 Annual Graduate Tuition & Fees: $12,672
Enrollment: 426 Coed
Affiliation or Control: Assemblies Of God Church IRS Status: 501(c)3
Highest Offering: Doctorate; No Undergraduates
Program: Professional; Religious Emphasis
Accreditation: NH, THEOL

01 President ... Dr. Byron D. KLAUS
05 Academic Dean ... Dr. Stephen LIM
58 Dir Intercultural Doctoral Studies ... Dr. DeLonn L. RANCE
58 Director DMin Program ... Dr. Cheryl A. TAYLOR
10 Director of Business ... Rev. David W. WILLEMSEN
26 Director of Institutional Relations ... Mrs. Dorothea J. LOTTER
08 Director of Library Services ... Mr. Joseph F. MARICS
30 Director of Development ... Vacant
27 Promotions Coordinator ... Mrs. Jennifer S. HALL
73 Chair Bible/Theology Department ... Dr. Roger D. COTTON
88 Chair Global Missions Department ... Dr. DeLonn L. RANCE
88 Chair Prac Theology Department ... Dr. Jay P. TAYLOR
42 Director of Spiritual Formation ... Dr. Jay P. TAYLOR
51 Director of Continuing Education ... Dr. Randy C. WALLS
84 Director of Enrollment Management ... Dr. Mario H. GUERREIRO

Avila University (C)

11901 Wornall Road, Kansas City MO 64145-9990
County: Jackson FICE Identification: 002449
Unit ID: 176628
Telephone: (816) 942-8400 Carnegie Class: Master's M
FAX Number: (816) 942-3362 Calendar System: Semester
URL: www.avila.edu
Established: 1916 Annual Undergrad Tuition & Fees: $22,250
Enrollment: 1,876 Coed
Affiliation or Control: Roman Catholic IRS Status: 501(c)3
Highest Offering: Master's
Program: Liberal Arts And General; Teacher Preparatory; Professional
Accreditation: NH, #IACBE, NURSE, RAD, SW

01 President ... Dr. Ron SLEPITZA
05 Provost/Vice Pres Academic Affairs ... Sr. Marie Joan HARRIS
20 Vice Provost for Academic Affairs ... Dr. Sue KING
10 Vice Pres for Finance/Admin Svcs ... Mr. Paul G. BOOKMEYER
26 Chief Marketing/Commnications Ofcr ... Mrs. Linda SHAFFER
32 Dean of Students ... Ms. Darby GOUGH
30 Director of Development ... Ms. Molly SIRRIDGE
06 Registrar ... Mrs. Dana R. SHIRLEY
07 Director of Admission ... Mr. Brandon JOHNSON
08 Librarian ... Ms. Kathleen FINEGAN
37 Director of Financial Aid ... Ms. Crystal BRUNTZ
13 Director of IT Operations ... Mr. Jared BANKS
42 Dir Mission Effect & Campus Ministr ... Mr. David M. ARMSTRONG
21 Controller ... Mr. Joseph H. SJUTS
29 Director Alumni & Donor Relations ... Mrs. Susan RANDOLPH
41 Athletic Director ... Mr. Gary GALLUP
15 Director of Human Resources ... Ms. Janet MCMANUS
18 Exec Dir Operations/Campus Devel ... Mr. Len CARTEE
40 Bookstore Manager ... Mr. John A. TARANTO
38 Coord Counseling & Career Services ... Ms. Susan WULFF

Baptist Bible College (D)

628 E Kearney St, Springfield MO 65803-3498
County: Greene FICE Identification: 013208
Unit ID: 176664
Telephone: (417) 268-6013 Carnegie Class: Spec/Faith
FAX Number: (417) 268-6694 Calendar System: Semester
URL: www.gobbc.edu
Established: 1950 Annual Undergrad Tuition & Fees: $6,500
Enrollment: 580 Coed
Affiliation or Control: Baptist IRS Status: 501(c)3
Highest Offering: First Professional Degree
Program: Teacher Preparatory; Professional; Religious Emphasis
Accreditation: NH, BI

01 President ... Mr. James N. EDGE
05 Vice President of Academic Affairs ... Dr. Greg T. CHRISTOPHER
10 Chief Financial Officer ... Mrs. Krista L. CORCORAN
32 Dean of Students ... Mr. Ray L. ADAMS
18 Chief Facilities/Physical Plant ... Mr. Jeff C. BUCKLEW
20 Director of Academic Advising ... Dr. Joseph K. GLEASON
06 Registrar ... Mr. Terry A. ALLCORN
07 Director of Enrollment Services ... Mr. Jon N. SLAYDEN
37 Director of Financial Aid ... Mr. Bob L. KOTULSKI
35 Senior Director Student Development ... Mr. Bill W. LEVERGOOD
38 Campus Counselor ... Mr. Bill A. PIATT
36 Director of Career Success ... Mrs. Linda R. RUDE
39 Director of Resident Life ... Mrs. Brenda J. CORRELL
15 Director of Human Resources ... Mrs. Angel M. SARVER
23 Director Health Services ... Mrs. Gay Nell CRANOR
19 Director Security/Safety ... Mr. James C. CLATWORTHY
41 Athletic Director ... Mr. Dan ELLIOTT
40 Bookstore ... Mrs. Ethyl HARE
08 Director of Library Services ... Mr. Jon JONES
09 Director of Institutional Research ... Mrs. Lesa M. CHASTAIN
106 Dean of Online Education ... Ms. Cheryl PAGE
72 Director of Technology ... Mr. Landon GHAN

Bolivar Technical College (E)

2001 W Broadway Street, PO Box 592,
Bolivar MO 65613-1861
County: Polk Identification: 667033
Telephone: (417) 777-5062 Carnegie Class: Not Classified
FAX Number: (417) 777-8908 Calendar System: Semester
URL: www.bolivarcollege.org
Established: 1996 Annual Undergrad Tuition & Fees: N/A
Enrollment: 153 Coed
Affiliation or Control: Independent Non-Profit IRS Status: 501(c)3
Highest Offering: Associate Degree
Program: Occupational; 2-Year Principally Bachelor's Creditable
Accreditation: ACICS

01 President/Campus Director ... Ms. Charlotte GRAY
03 Vice President ... Dr. William GRAY
05 Academic Director ... Mr. Dave THOMPSON

Brown Mackie College-St. Louis (F)

2 Soccer Park Road, Fenton MO 63026-2564
County: St. Louis Identification: 666793
Unit ID: 460048
Telephone: (636) 651-3290 Carnegie Class: Not Classified
FAX Number: (636) 651-3349 Calendar System: Other
URL: www.brownmackie.edu
Established: N/A Annual Undergrad Tuition & Fees: $10,188
Enrollment: 376 Coed
Affiliation or Control: Proprietary IRS Status: Proprietary
Highest Offering: Baccalaureate
Program: Occupational; 2-Year Principally Bachelor's Creditable; Business Emphasis
Accreditation: ACICS

01 President ... Terri LEAP
07 Senior Director of Admissions ... Phyllis HUTTO
05 Dean of Academic Affairs ... Lisa CASIMERE

† Branch campus of Brown Mackie College, Tucson, AZ.

Bryan College (G)

4255 Nature Center Way, Springfield MO 65804
County: Greene FICE Identification: 030663
Unit ID: 369516
Telephone: (417) 862-5700 Carnegie Class: Assoc/PrivFP
FAX Number: (417) 865-7144 Calendar System: Other
URL: www.bryancolleges.edu
Established: 1982 Annual Undergrad Tuition & Fees: $17,500
Enrollment: 348 Coed
Affiliation or Control: Proprietary IRS Status: Proprietary
Highest Offering: Associate Degree
Program: Occupational; 2-Year Principally Bachelor's Creditable; Business Emphasis
Accreditation: ACICS

01 Executive Director ... Mr. Scott HAAR

Calvary Bible College and Theological Seminary (H)

15800 Calvary Road, Kansas City MO 64147-1341
County: Cass FICE Identification: 002450
Unit ID: 176789
Telephone: (816) 322-0110 Carnegie Class: Spec/Faith
FAX Number: (816) 331-4474 Calendar System: Semester
URL: www.calvary.edu
Established: 1932 Annual Undergrad Tuition & Fees: $9,664
Enrollment: 332 Coed
Affiliation or Control: Independent Non-Profit IRS Status: 501(c)3
Highest Offering: First Professional Degree
Program: Teacher Preparatory; Religious Emphasis
Accreditation: NH, BI

01 President ... Dr. James L. CLARK
11 Vice President of Operations ... Mr. Randy GRIMM
05 Academic Dean of the College ... Dr. Teddy BITNER
20 Seminary Academic Dean ... Dr. Thomas S. BAURAIN
32 Dean of Students ... Vacant
34 Dean of Women ... Mrs. Kim BAILEY
06 Dean Enrollment Mgmt/Registrar ... Mr. Larry SPRY
08 Head Librarian ... Miss Hannah BITNER
29 Director of Alumni ... Miss Dorothy JEFFREY
07 Director Admissions ... Mr. Robert CRANK
18 Director Buildings & Grounds ... Mr. Caleb ARNETT
41 Athletic Director ... Miss Jeanette REGIER
91 Director Administrative Computing ... Mr. Aaron HEATH
38 Director Biblical Counsel/Educ Ctr ... Mrs. Patricia A. MILLER
30 Director of Development ... Mr. Jeff CAMPA
19 Director of Security ... Mr. Cory D. TROWBRIDGE
37 Director of Financial Aid ... Mr. Ryan LOWE
26 Coordinator of Public Relations ... Vacant
09 Institutional Research Coordinator ... Mr. Cory D. TROWBRIDGE
15 Human Resources Coordinator ... Mrs. Jolayne ROGERS

Central Bible College (I)

3000 N Grant, Springfield MO 65803-1096
County: Greene FICE Identification: 002452
Unit ID: 176938
Telephone: (417) 833-2551 Carnegie Class: Spec/Faith
FAX Number: (417) 833-5141 Calendar System: Semester
URL: www.cbcag.edu
Established: 1922 Annual Undergrad Tuition & Fees: $12,050
Enrollment: 742 Coed
Affiliation or Control: Assemblies Of God Church IRS Status: 501(c)3
Highest Offering: Baccalaureate
Program: Liberal Arts And General; Religious Emphasis
Accreditation: NH, BI

01 President ... Dr. Gary A. DENBOW
05 Vice President Academic Affairs ... Dr. David ARNETT
32 Vice President Student Development ... Dr. Jim VIGIL
08 Librarian ... Mr. Lynn ANDERSON
06 Registrar/Dir Student Records ... Dr. Leo THERIOT
18 Chief Facilities/Physical Plant ... Mr. Dwayne HUFF
29 Director Alumni Relations ... Mrs. Kathy ARNETT
36 Director Student Placement ... Rev. Philip GOCKE
37 Director Student Financial Services ... Mr. William A. TATE
38 Director Student Counseling ... Rev. Deonna CRABTREE
84 Director Enrollment Services ... Mr. Joshua MARTIN
15 Director Human Resources ... Mr. Nathan HALL

Central Christian College of the Bible (J)

911 E Urbandale Drive, Moberly MO 65270-1997
County: Randolph FICE Identification: 022664
Unit ID: 176910
Telephone: (660) 263-3900 Carnegie Class: Spec/Faith
FAX Number: (660) 263-3936 Calendar System: Semester
URL: www.cccb.edu
Established: 1957 Annual Undergrad Tuition & Fees: $8,725
Enrollment: 318 Coed
Affiliation or Control: Christian Churches And Churches of Christ
IRS Status: 501(c)3
Highest Offering: Baccalaureate
Program: 2-Year Principally Bachelor's Creditable; Liberal Arts And General; Professional; Religious Emphasis
Accreditation: BI

01 President ... Dr. Ronald L. OAKES
05 Vice President of Academics ... Dr. David B. FINCHER
32 Vice President Student Development ... Mr. Richard R. REXRODE
30 VP of Institutional Advancement ... Mr. Phillip MARLEY
10 Chief Financial Officer ... Mrs. Lara LAWRENCE
20 Associate Dean of Assessment ... Mr. Richard A. FORDYCE
07 Director of Admissions Programs ... Mr. Andrew KOVAR
07 Director of Admissions Services ... Mr. Rocky CHRISTENSEN
44 Asst Director of Development ... Mr. Alan G. WILSON
04 Executive Asst to the President ... Mrs. Loretta L. KELCHNER
33 Dean of Men ... Mr. Jason LYKINS
34 Dean of Women ... Ms. Anne P. MENEAR
41 Athletic Director ... Ms. Anne P. MENEAR
08 Head Librarian ... Mrs. Patty A. AGEE
06 Registrar ... Mrs. Faith M. AXTON
37 Director of Financial Aid ... Mrs. Rhonda J. DUNHAM
13 Director of Information Systems ... Mr. Tracy ROACH
18 Physical Plant Manager ... Mr. Mark E. DUNHAM
40 Bookstore Manager ... Mrs. Kelly HARDING
29 Public and Alumni Relations ... Mrs. Sherry WALLIS
35 Director of Student Services ... Mrs. Lori PETER
39 Residence Director - Women ... Mrs. April CHRISTENSEN
39 Residence Director - Men ... Mr. Rocky CHRISTENSEN
21 Accounting Manager ... Mrs. Theresa BARTHOLMEY
102 Foundation & Corporate Relations ... Mrs. Veronica HAMBLIN
04 Administrative Executive Assistant ... Mrs. Cindy MEYER

Central Methodist University (K)

411 Central Methodist Square, Fayette MO 65248-1198
County: Howard FICE Identification: 002453
Unit ID: 445267

Telephone: (660) 248-3391 Carnegie Class: Bac/Diverse
FAX Number: (660) 248-2287 Calendar System: 4/1/4
URL: www.centralmethodist.edu
Established: 1854 Annual Undergrad Tuition & Fees: $20,130
Enrollment: 5,897 Coed
Affiliation or Control: United Methodist IRS Status: 501(c)3
Highest Offering: Master's
Program: Liberal Arts And General; Teacher Preparatory
Accreditation: NH, MUS, NURSE

01 President .... Dr. Marianne E. INMAN
05 Vice Pres & Dean of the University .... Dr. Rita GULSTAD
10 Vice Pres Finance & Administration .... Ms. Julee SHERMAN
30 Vice President Advancement .... Ms. Donna MERRELL
32 VP Campus Life/Dean of Students .... Mr. James N. WEBSTER
49 Asc Dean Col Liberal Arts & Science .... Dr. Jack HEALY
27 Vice President Information Services .... Mr. Chad GAINES
20 Asst Dean Inst Rsrch/Dean LA & Sci .... Ms. Amy DYKENS
07 Director of Admission .... Mr. Larry ANDERSON
41 Athletic Director .... Mr. James N. WEBSTER
29 Director of Alumni Affairs .... Mr. Alan G. MARSHALL
06 Registrar .... Ms. Kathryn WINEGARD
37 Student Aid Administrator .... Ms. Linda MACKEY
18 Chief Facilities/Physical Plant .... Mr. Derry WISWALL
26 Chief Public Relations Officer .... Mr. Kent PROPST
36 Director Student Placement .... Ms. Linda LORENZ

Chamberlain College of Nursing - St. Louis (A)

11830 Westline Industrial Dr, #106, Saint Louis MO 63146
County: Saint Louis FICE Identification: 006385
Unit ID: 177153
Telephone: (314) 991-6200 Carnegie Class: Spec/Health
FAX Number: (314) 991-6283 Calendar System: Semester
URL: www.chamberlain.edu
Established: 1889 Annual Undergrad Tuition & Fees: $15,600
Enrollment: 7,002 Coed
Affiliation or Control: Proprietary IRS Status: Proprietary
Highest Offering: Master's
Program: Nursing Emphasis
Accreditation: NH, ADNUR, NUR

01 President .... Ms. Susan L. GROENWALD
05 Campus Dean .... Dr. DeLois WEEKES
106 Director of Online Programs .... Ms. Margaret WHEELER
88 Director Accreditation .... Ms. Kathleen R. MODENE
32 National Student Services Director .... Ms. June MARLOWE
26 Director of Marketing .... Ms. Stephanie L. GALLO

† Part of Devry University, IL.

City Vision College (B)

712 E 31st Street, P.O. Box 413188,
Kansas City MO 64141-3188
County: Jackson FICE Identification: 041191
Unit ID: 457697
Telephone: (816) 960-2008 Carnegie Class: Not Classified
FAX Number: (816) 569-0223 Calendar System: Other
URL: www.cityvision.edu
Established: 1998 Annual Undergrad Tuition & Fees: $6,000
Enrollment: 119 Coed
Affiliation or Control: Other IRS Status: 501(c)3
Highest Offering: Baccalaureate
Program: Professional; Religious Emphasis
Accreditation: DETC

01 President .... Rev. Michael K. LIIMATTA
05 Academic Dean .... Dr. Fletcher L. TINK

College of the Ozarks (C)

PO Box 17, Point Lookout MO 65726-0017
County: Taney FICE Identification: 002500
Unit ID: 178697
Telephone: (417) 334-6411 Carnegie Class: Bac/Diverse
FAX Number: (417) 335-2618 Calendar System: Semester
URL: www.cofo.edu
Established: 1906 Annual Undergrad Tuition & Fees: $430
Enrollment: 1,371 Coed
Affiliation or Control: Independent Non-Profit IRS Status: 501(c)3
Highest Offering: Baccalaureate
Program: Liberal Arts And General
Accreditation: NH, DIETD, NURSE

01 President .... Dr. Jerry C. DAVIS
03 Vice President .... Dr. Howell W. KEETER
05 Dean of the College .... Dr. Eric BOLGER
30 Dean of Development .... Mr. Timothy HUDDLESTON
10 Treasurer .... Mr. Charles F. HUGHES
11 Dean of Administration .... Dr. Marvin SCHOENECKE
78 Dean of the Work Program .... Dr. Chris LARSEN
32 Dean of Student Services .... Mr. Nick SHARP
07 Dean Director of Admissions .... Dr. Marci LINSON
06 Registrar .... Mrs. Fran FORMAN
29 Director of Alumni Affairs .... Mrs. Angela WILLIAMSON
36 Director of Career Placement .... Mr. Ron MARTIN
37 Director Student Financial Aid .... Mrs. Kyla MCCARTY
26 Director Public Relations .... Mrs. Elizabeth B. HUGHES
96 Director of Purchasing .... Mr. Kurt MCDONALD
38 Student Counseling .... Mrs. Pat MCLEAN

Colorado Technical University, Kansas City (D)

520 E 19th Avenue, North Kansas City MO 64116-3614
County: Clay Identification: 666457
Unit ID: 409838
Telephone: (816) 303-7799 Carnegie Class: Bac/Assoc
FAX Number: (816) 472-0688 Calendar System: Quarter
URL: www.ctukansascity.com
Established: 1965 Annual Undergrad Tuition & Fees: $25,800
Enrollment: 947 Coed
Affiliation or Control: Proprietary IRS Status: Proprietary
Highest Offering: Baccalaureate
Program: Occupational; Business Emphasis
Accreditation: &NH, MAAB, RAD, SURGT

01 President .... Mr. Tim GRAMLING

† Regional accreditation is carried under the parent institution in Colorado Springs, CO.

Columbia College (E)

1001 Rogers Street, Columbia MO 65216-0001
County: Boone FICE Identification: 002456
Unit ID: 177065
Telephone: (573) 875-8700 Carnegie Class: Master's M
FAX Number: (573) 875-7209 Calendar System: Semester
URL: www.ccis.edu
Established: 1851 Annual Undergrad Tuition & Fees: $16,532
Enrollment: 1,050 Coed
Affiliation or Control: Christian Church (Disciples Of Christ)
IRS Status: 501(c)3
Highest Offering: Master's
Program: Liberal Arts And General; Teacher Preparatory; Professional
Accreditation: NH

01 President .... Dr. Gerald T. BROUDER
04 Exec Assistant to the President .... Ms. Lori K. EWING
05 Exec Vice Pres/Dean of Academic Affs .... Dr. Terry B. SMITH
56 Vice Pres of Adult Higher Education .... Mr. Mike RANDERSON
84 Assistant VP for Enrollment Mgmt .... Mr. Tery DONELSON
32 Dean for Campus Life .... Ms. Faye C. BURCHARD
10 Controller/Chief Financial Officer .... Mr. Bruce E. BOYER
30 Exec Director of Devel/Alumni Svcs .... Mr. Mike KATEMAN
18 Exec Director of Admin Services .... Mr. Bob C. HUTTON
88 Executive Director of Marketing .... Ms. Lana POOLE
27 Chief Information Officer .... Mr. Kevin PALMER
07 Director of Admissions .... Ms. Samantha WHITE
06 Registrar .... Ms. Sue M. KOOPMANS
29 Senior Director of Alumni Services .... Ms. Susan Y. DAVIS
26 Senior Director of Public Relations .... Ms. Joanne TEDESCO
37 Director of Financial Aid .... Ms. Sharon A. ABERNATHY
08 Director of Stafford Library .... Ms. Janet CARUTHERS
35 Director of Student Activities .... Ms. Elizabeth BALL
36 Director Career Services Center .... Mr. Don G. MALSON
16 Director Human Resources .... Ms. Patty FISCHER
23 Director of Wellness Center .... Ms. Kim J. KINYON
13 Director of Technology Services .... Mr. Rick POWELL
55 Assoc Dean Adult Higher Education .... Mr. Eric CUNNINGHAM
58 Associate Dean Graduate Studies .... Dr. Steve C. WIEGENSTEIN
41 Athletic Director .... Mr. Bob P. BURCHARD
09 Institutional Research Analyst .... Ms. Misty HASKAMP
19 Director of Campus Safety .... Mr. Robert KLAUSMEYER
21 Associate Controller .... Mr. Randal SCHENEWERK
51 Dean for Adult Higher Education .... Mr. Gary MASSEY

Conception Seminary College (F)

37174 State Highway VV, PO Box 502,
Conception MO 64433-0502
County: Nodaway FICE Identification: 002467
Unit ID: 177083
Telephone: (660) 944-3105 Carnegie Class: Spec/Faith
FAX Number: (660) 944-2829 Calendar System: Semester
URL: www.conception.edu
Established: 1883 Annual Undergrad Tuition & Fees: $16,860
Enrollment: 116 Male
Affiliation or Control: Roman Catholic IRS Status: 501(c)3
Highest Offering: Baccalaureate
Program: Liberal Arts And General; Religious Emphasis
Accreditation: NH

01 Rector & President .... Rev. Samuel J. RUSSELL
11 Director of Administration .... Mrs. Amy K. SCHIEBER
32 Dean of Students .... Rev. Ralph O'DONNELL
05 Dean of Academic Affairs .... Dr. Elizabeth Z. MCGRATH
10 Business Manager/Dir Auxiliary Svcs .... Rev. Benedict T. NEENAN
30 Development Director .... Rev. Adam RYAN
07 Director of Admissions .... Bro. Etienne HUARD
37 Director of Student Financial Aid .... Bro. Justin J. HERNANDEZ
06 Registrar .... Mrs. Jeanette SCHIEBER
29 Director of Alumni .... Rev. Daniel PETSCHE
08 Librarian .... Bro. Thomas SULLIVAN
26 Director of Communications .... Mrs. Jenny HUARD
13 Director of Information Technology .... Mr. Tony MEISTER
38 Director of Counseling Services .... Rev. Duane REINERT
41 Director of Wellness Program .... Mr. Skip SHEAR

Concorde Career College (G)

3239 Broadway Boulevard, Kansas City MO 64111-2407
County: Jackson FICE Identification: 023616
Unit ID: 155283
Telephone: (816) 531-5223 Carnegie Class: Assoc/PrivFP
FAX Number: (816) 756-3231 Calendar System: Other
URL: www.concordecareers.com/kansas/
Established: 1986 Annual Undergrad Tuition & Fees: $9,800
Enrollment: 472 Coed
Affiliation or Control: Proprietary IRS Status: Proprietary
Highest Offering: Associate Degree
Program: Occupational
Accreditation: ACCSC, DA, DH, @PTAA

01 President .... Debra CROW
05 Academic Dean .... James KRALICEK
07 Director Student Recruitment .... Aaron GRAY

Concordia Seminary (H)

801 Seminary Place, Saint Louis MO 63105-3168
County: Saint Louis FICE Identification: 002457
Unit ID: 177092
Telephone: (314) 505-7000 Carnegie Class: Spec/Faith
FAX Number: (314) 505-7001 Calendar System: Quarter
URL: www.csl.edu
Established: 1839 Annual Graduate Tuition & Fees: $24,450
Enrollment: 623 Coed
Affiliation or Control: Lutheran Church - Missouri Synod
IRS Status: 501(c)3
Highest Offering: Doctorate; No Undergraduates
Program: Professional; Religious Emphasis
Accreditation: NH, THEOL

01 President .... Dr. Dale A. MEYER
03 Provost .... Dr. Arthur D. BACON
05 Vice President for Academic Affairs .... Dr. Andrew H. BARTELT
10 Sr VP for Financial Planning/Admin .... Mr. Michael A. LOUIS
84 Sr VP of Enrollment Management .... Rev. Michael REDEKER
30 Senior VP for Advancement .... Dr. Paul DEVANTIER
21 VP of Financial Planning/Admin .... Mr. Chad CATTOOR
58 Dean of Advanced Studies .... Dr. Bruce G. SCHUCHARD
06 Registrar .... Mrs. Beth R. MENNEKE
08 Director of Library Services .... Prof. David O. BERGER
51 Director Continuing Education .... Dr. Jeffrey KLOHA
26 Director of Communications .... Dr. Paul DEVANTIER
88 Director Center for Hispanic Study .... Dr. Leopoldo A. SANCHEZ
15 Director of Human Resources .... Mr. Thomas MYERS
18 Director Facilities/Physical Plant .... Mr. Stephen B. MUDD
36 Dir Student Placement/Alumni Activ .... Rev. Robert HOEHNER
37 Director of Student Financial Aid .... Mrs. Kerry R. HALLAHAN
27 Chief Information Officer .... Mr. John KLINGER

Cottey College (I)

1000 W Austin Boulevard, Nevada MO 64772-2763
County: Vernon FICE Identification: 002458
Unit ID: 177117
Telephone: (417) 667-8181 Carnegie Class: Assoc/PrivNFP
FAX Number: (417) 667-8103 Calendar System: Semester
URL: www.cottey.edu
Established: 1884 Annual Undergrad Tuition & Fees: $15,900
Enrollment: 304 Female
Affiliation or Control: Independent Non-Profit IRS Status: 501(c)3
Highest Offering: Baccalaureate
Program: 2-Year Principally Bachelor's Creditable; Liberal Arts And General
Accreditation: NH, MUS

01 President .... Dr. Judy R. ROGERS
05 Vice President for Academic Affairs .... Dr. Cathryn PRIDAL
88 Exec Dir Women's Leadership .... Ms. Sonia COWEN
36 Student Success Coordinator .... Ms. Renee HAMPTON
04 Assistant to the President .... Mrs. Tricia BOBBETT
10 VP for Administration & Finance .... Mrs. Mary S. HAGGANS
26 Interim VP for Inst Advancement .... Mr. Stuart LANG
32 VP for Student Life .... Dr. Mari Anne PHILLIPS
42 Dir Spiritual Life & Diversity .... Ms. Erica SIGAUKE
84 VP for Enrollment Management .... Mr. Richard EBER
06 Registrar .... Ms. Marcia MORTON
21 Controller .... Ms. Amy RUETTEN
08 Library Director .... Ms. Rebecca J. KIEL
18 Director Physical Plant/Security .... Mr. Neal R. SWARNES
27 Director of Public Information .... Mr. Steve E. REED
15 Director of Human Resources .... Ms. Betsy A. MCREYNOLDS
91 Director Administratrive Computing .... Mr. Keith J. SPENCER
37 Director of Financial Aid .... Mrs. Sherry R. PENNINGTON
90 Director Academic Computing .... Mr. Adam S. DEAN
88 Director Center Women's Leadership .... Mrs. Denise C. HEDGES
39 Director of Student Housing .... Ms. Helen LODGE
41 Director of Athletics .... Mr. Dave V. KETTERMAN
30 Director of Development .... Ms. Terri FALLIN
21 Asst to VP Admin & Finance .... Mrs. Tina BUCKNER
40 Bookstore Manager .... Mrs. Lois J. WITTE
09 Coordinator Institutional Research .... Mrs. Nancy KERBS
29 Coordinator Alumnae Relations .... Ms. Courtney MAJORS
38 Coordinator of Counseling .... Ms. Jeanna BRAUER
88 Campaign Manager .... Ms. Carla FARMER
88 Director of Food Service .... Mr. Michael RICHARDSON
88 Coordinator of PEO Relations .... Ms. Tracy H. CORDOVA

Covenant Theological Seminary (A)

12330 Conway Road, Saint Louis MO 63141-8697
County: Saint Louis FICE Identification: 004707
Unit ID: 177126
Telephone: (314) 434-4044 Carnegie Class: Spec/Faith
FAX Number: (314) 434-4819 Calendar System: 4/1/4
URL: www.covenantseminary.edu
Established: 1956 Annual Graduate Tuition & Fees: $14,400
Enrollment: 788 Coed
Affiliation or Control: Presbyterian Church In America IRS Status: 501(c)3
Highest Offering: Doctorate; No Undergraduates
Program: Professional; Religious Emphasis
Accreditation: NH, THEOL

01 President ... Dr. Bryan CHAPELL
03 Executive Vice President ... Vacant
05 Vice President of Academics ... Dr. Mark DALBEY
10 Vice President of Business Admin ... Mr. Al LI
32 Dean of Students ... Rev. Michael HIGGINS
30 Vice President of Student Develop ... Vacant
26 Vice President of Advancement ... Vacant
20 Assoc Dean of Academic Admin ... Rev. Christopher FLORENCE
07 Director of Admissions ... Mr. Jeremy KICKLIGHTER
21 Controller ... Miss Jean LEHMKUHL
13 Director of Information Technology ... Mr. Richard HIERS
18 Director Facilities & Operations ... Mr. David BROWN
08 Librarian ... Rev. James C. PAKALA
37 Director of Financial Aid ... Miss Melinda CONN
29 Director Alumni Relations ... Mr. Joel HATHAWAY
06 Registrar ... Miss Betsy GASOSKE
44 Interim Director of Development ... Mr. John RANHEIM

Cox College (B)

1423 N Jefferson Avenue, Springfield MO 65802-1917
County: Greene FICE Identification: 020682
Unit ID: 176770
Telephone: (417) 269-3401 Carnegie Class: Spec/Health
FAX Number: (417) 269-3581 Calendar System: Semester
URL: www.coxcollege.edu
Established: 1995 Annual Undergrad Tuition & Fees: $13,750
Enrollment: 710 Coed
Affiliation or Control: Independent Non-Profit IRS Status: 501(c)3
Highest Offering: Master's
Program: Occupational; 2-Year Principally Bachelor's Creditable; Professional
Accreditation: NH, ADNUR, DIETI, NURSE

01 President ... Dr. Anne BRETT
11 Vice President of Operations ... Vacant
05 Vice President of Academic Affairs ... Dr. Martin SELLERS
08 Director Library Services ... Wilma C. BUNCH
66 Dean Department of Nursing ... Dr. Tricia WAGNER
76 Dean Health Sciences Department ... Sonya HAYTER
06 Dean of Enrollment Mgmt/Registrar ... David SCHOOLFIELD
09 Director of Institutional Research ... Vacant
10 Business Manager ... Deborah ADKINS
37 Financial Aid Counselor ... Angela KEENER
37 Financial Aid Coordinator ... Steve NICHOLS
07 Director of Admissions ... Lindy BIGLIENI
29 Director of Alumni Relations & Mktg ... Todd RUTLEDGE

Crowder College (C)

601 Laclede Avenue, Neosho MO 64850-9165
County: Newton FICE Identification: 002459
Unit ID: 177135
Telephone: (417) 451-3223 Carnegie Class: Assoc/Pub-R-M
FAX Number: (417) 455-5702 Calendar System: Semester
URL: www.crowder.edu
Established: 1963 Annual Undergrad Tuition & Fees (In-District): $2,550
Enrollment: 5,219 Coed
Affiliation or Control: Local IRS Status: 501(c)3
Highest Offering: Associate Degree
Program: Occupational; 2-Year Principally Bachelor's Creditable
Accreditation: NH, NAIT

01 President ... Dr. Alan D. MARBLE
10 Vice President of Finance ... Mr. Ron GRANGER
05 Vice President of Academic Affairs ... Dr. Herb SCHADE
06 Vice President of Student Affairs ... Dr. Nicole STRIEGEL
20 Assoc VP of Academic Affairs ... Mrs. Amy RAND
75 Assoc VP of Careers & Tech Ed ... Mr. Ken RHUEMS
07 Director of Admissions ... Mr. Jim RIGGS
09 Director of Institutional Research ... Mrs. Mickie MAHAN
08 Director of Lee Library ... Mrs. Mary LARGENT
27 Director of Public Information ... Mrs. Cindy BROWN
41 Athletic Director ... Mrs. Millie GILION
37 Director of Financial Aid ... Mrs. Michelle PAUL
15 Director of Human Resources ... Mrs. Gale MARSH
25 Director of Grants & Development ... Mrs. Pam HUDSON
40 Bookstore Manager ... Ms. Colleen HOLLAND
36 Career & Retention Svcs Coordinator ... Ms. Jolene SULLIVAN
13 Director of Information Technology ... Mr. Chris WOITOWITZ

Culver-Stockton College (D)

1 College Hill, Canton MO 63435-1257
County: Lewis FICE Identification: 002460
Unit ID: 177144
Telephone: (573) 288-6000 Carnegie Class: Bac/Diverse
FAX Number: (573) 288-6611 Calendar System: Semester
URL: www.culver.edu
Established: 1853 Annual Undergrad Tuition & Fees: $22,550
Enrollment: 771 Coed
Affiliation or Control: Christian Church (Disciples Of Christ)
IRS Status: 501(c)3
Highest Offering: Baccalaureate
Program: Liberal Arts And General; Teacher Preparatory
Accreditation: NH, IACBE, MUS

01 President ... Mr. Richard D. VALENTINE
05 Vice Pres Academic Affs/Dean of Col ... Dr. David W. WILSON
32 Dean of Student Life ... Mr. D. Christopher GILL
84 Sr Associate Director of Admission ... Mrs. Misty MCBEE
30 Director of Advancement/Alumni Pgm ... Mr. Eric BARKLEY
06 Registrar/Director Inst Research ... Mrs. Chris HUEBOTTER
08 Librarian ... Mrs. Sharon K. UPCHURCH
26 Director of College Communications ... Mr. Kyle TRUDELL
37 Director Financial Aid ... Mrs. Tina WISEMAN
29 Director of Alumni Programs ... Mr. Jeffrey MCREYNOLDS
91 Exec Dir Admin Systems & Service ... Mr. Joseph LIESEN
21 Controller ... Mrs. Diane BOZARTH
10 Chief Financial Officer ... Mr. Lewin B. DAVIS
35 Coordinator of Student Activities ... Mr. Devon OSSORIO
42 Chaplain ... Rev. Brent REYNOLDS
41 Athletic Director ... Mr. Greg MCVEY
40 Logo Shop Manager ... Mrs. Sharon FARR
04 Assistant to the President ... Mrs. Doris BRISCOE
19 Director Campus Security & Facil ... Mr. Michael BRINGER
81 Chair Natural & Math Sciences Div ... Dr. Lauren SCHELLENBERGER
50 Chair Business Division ... Dr. Dell Ann JANNEY
53 Chair Education/Applied Arts Div ... Ms. Ann E. HAMMER
57 Chair Fine Arts Division ... Mr. Kent MILLER
79 Chair Humanities/Social Sci Div ... Dr. C. Patrick HOTLE
92 Director of Honors Program ... Dr. Steven LONG
93 Director of Minority Students ... Dr. Mohamed EL-BERMAWY
24 Media Coordinator ... Mrs. Julie WRIGHT
44 Director of the Annual Fund ... Mr. Scott MCGAUGHEY
36 Coord of Career Services/Internship ... Mrs. Nancy NISH
39 Director of Residential Life ... Ms. Heather KELLER
20 Director of Advising/Retention/FY ... Ms. Holly ANDRESS-MARTIN
38 Dir Counseling/Student Wellness ... Ms. Susan MOON
09 Director of Institutional Research ... Mrs. Karla MCREYNOLDS
88 Director of Advancement Operations ... Mrs. Marjorie ELLISON
35 Asst Director of Student Life ... Mr. Robert DUDOLSKI

DeVry University - Kansas City Campus (E)

11224 Holmes Road, Kansas City MO 64131-3626
County: Jackson FICE Identification: 002455
Unit ID: 177162
Telephone: (816) 943-7300 Carnegie Class: Master's S
FAX Number: N/A Calendar System: Semester
URL: www.devry.edu
Established: 1969 Annual Undergrad Tuition & Fees: $15,294
Enrollment: 1,484 Coed
Affiliation or Control: Proprietary IRS Status: Proprietary
Highest Offering: Master's
Program: Occupational; Professional; Business Emphasis
Accreditation: &NH, ENGT

01 Metro President ... Mr. Shane SMEED
05 Registrar ... Mr. Ryan MEADOR
58 Dean of Graduate Studies ... Ms. Cynthia FULKS
08 Director of Library Services ... Ms. Beth CALDARELLO
31 Director of Community Relations ... Ms. Adele LISKO
15 Human Resources Business Partner ... Ms. Maria LEVIT
97 Dean of General Education & Busines ... Mr. John STRANGE
36 Director of Career Services ... Mr. Gerald ELLIS
07 Senior Director of Admissions ... Ms. Kena WOLF
54 Dean of Engineering ... Mr. Don WEISS

† Regional accreditation is carried under the parent institution in Downers Grove, IL.

DeVry University - Kansas City Downtown Center (F)

1100 Main Street, Suite 118, Kansas City MO 64105-2112
County: Jackson Identification: 666211
Unit ID: 437370
Telephone: (816) 221-1300 Carnegie Class: Not Classified
FAX Number: (816) 474-0318 Calendar System: Semester
URL: www.devry.edu
Established: 1990 Annual Undergrad Tuition & Fees: $15,294
Enrollment: 301 Coed
Affiliation or Control: Proprietary IRS Status: Proprietary
Highest Offering: Master's
Program: Occupational; Professional; Business Emphasis
Accreditation: &NH

01 Center Dean ... Cass BUTLER

† Regional accreditation is carried under the parent institution in Downers Grove, IL.

DeVry University - St. Louis (G)

11830 Westline Industrial Dr., Saint Louis MO 63146-4157
County: Saint Louis Identification: 666214
Unit ID: 432180
Telephone: (314) 991-6400 Carnegie Class: Not Classified
FAX Number: N/A Calendar System: Semester
URL: www.devry.edu
Established: 1993 Annual Undergrad Tuition & Fees: $15,294
Enrollment: 446 Coed
Affiliation or Control: Proprietary IRS Status: Proprietary
Highest Offering: Master's
Program: Occupational; Professional; Business Emphasis
Accreditation: &NH

01 Campus Dean ... Jennifer MATHES

† Regional accreditation is carried under the parent institution in Downers Grove, IL.

Drury University (H)

900 N Benton Avenue, Springfield MO 65802-3791
County: Greene FICE Identification: 002461
Unit ID: 177214
Telephone: (417) 873-7879 Carnegie Class: Master's M
FAX Number: (417) 873-7529 Calendar System: Semester
URL: www.drury.edu
Established: 1873 Annual Undergrad Tuition & Fees: $20,500
Enrollment: 5,625 Coed
Affiliation or Control: Independent Non-Profit IRS Status: 501(c)3
Highest Offering: Master's
Program: Liberal Arts And General; Teacher Preparatory; Professional
Accreditation: NH, ACBSP, BUS, MUS, TED

01 President ... Mr. Todd PARNELL
10 Chief Financial Officer ... Mr. Rob FRIDGE
11 Vice President for Administration ... Mr. Bill SCORSE
32 Vice President for Student Services ... Dr. Tijuana S. JULIAN
18 VP Campus Oper/Sustainability ... Mr. Pete RADECKI
05 Vice President for Academic Affairs ... Dr. Charles TAYLOR
30 Vice Pres Alumni & Development ... Dr. Krystal COMPAS
84 Vice Pres of Enrollment Management ... Ms. Dawn HILES
58 Dean of Graduate & Cont Studies ... Dr. Brian HOLLOWAY
20 Associate Dean of College ... Dr. Bruce CALLEN
06 Registrar ... Mrs. Gale M. BOUTWELL
26 Dir of Marketing & Communications ... Ms. Jann HOLLAND
37 Director of Financial Aid ... Mrs. Annette AVERY
88 Director of Facilities Services ... Mr. Ron CUSHMAN
08 Director of Library/Info Services ... Ms. Polly BORUFF-JONES
36 Director of Career Development ... Ms. Jill WIGGINS
15 Director of Human Resources ... Ms. Scotti SIEBERT
29 Director Alumni Relations ... Ms. Meleah SPENCER
09 Director of Institutional Research ... Vacant
38 Dir of Counseling/Student Devel ... Mr. Ed DERR
19 Director Safety/Security ... Ms. Sarene DEEDS
28 Director of Diversity ... Mr. L. A. ANDERSON
35 Director Student Affairs ... Ms. Emily GIVENS

East Central College (I)

1964 Prairie Dell Road, Union MO 63084-0529
County: Franklin FICE Identification: 008862
Unit ID: 177250
Telephone: (636) 583-5193 Carnegie Class: Assoc/Pub-S-MC
FAX Number: (636) 583-1897 Calendar System: Semester
URL: www.eastcentral.edu
Established: 1968 Annual Undergrad Tuition & Fees (In-District): $2,280
Enrollment: 4,471 Coed
Affiliation or Control: Local IRS Status: 501(c)3
Highest Offering: Associate Degree
Program: Occupational; 2-Year Principally Bachelor's Creditable
Accreditation: NH, ACFEI, NAIT, OTA

01 President ... Dr. Edward D. JACKSON, JR.
10 Vice Pres Finance/Administration ... Dr. Carl J. BAUER
05 Vice President Instruction ... Ms. Jean A. MCCANN
32 Vice President Student Development ... Ms. Ina R. HAYS
75 VP Career and Outreach Education ... Ms. Brenda A. BOUSE
12 Director of Rolla Campus ... Ms. Christina M. AYRES
30 Dir of Institutional Development ... Ms. Shannon M. GRUS
18 Director Facilities & Grounds ... Mr. Mark A. EATON
08 Director of Library Services ... Ms. Kathleen T. SCHLUMP
96 Purchasing Manager ... Ms. Melissa D. GARRISON
83 Div Chair Educ/Business/Soc Science ... Ms. Mary B. HUXEL
57 Div Chair Fine & Performing Arts ... Mr. Vincent T. NIEHAUS
79 Div Chair English/For Language ... Mr. John M. HARDECKE
81 Div Chair Science/Mathematics ... Vacant
15 Director Human Resources ... Ms. Wendy HARTMANN
66 Director of Nursing/Allied Health ... Ms. Robyn C. WALTER
37 Director Financial Aid ... Ms. Karen KOENIG-GRIFFIN
06 Registrar ... Ms. Karen S. WIEDA
21 Director Financial Svcs/Comptroller . Ms. Shirley A. HOFSTETTER
09 Director of Institutional Research ... Ms. Bethany L. LOHDEN
26 Director of Public Relations ... Ms. Dorothy A. SCHOWE
13 Director Information Technology ... Vacant
40 Bookstore/Mail/Imaging Coordinator ... Mr. Doug A. AGEE
36 Coordinator Advisement Services ... Ms. Tammy A. WEINHOLD
103 Executive Director Workforce Devel ... Ms. Gretchen A. PETTIT
51 Coordinator Adult Educ & Literacy ... Ms. Micki D. HOFFMAN
24 Coordinator Instructional Design ... Mr. R. Chad BALDWIN
31 Coordinator Community Partnerships ... Vacant
35 Coordinator Student Activities ... Mr. Bradley J. BRUNS

Eden Theological Seminary (J)

475 E Lockwood Avenue,
Webster Groves MO 63119-3192
County: Saint Louis FICE Identification: 002462
Unit ID: 177278

Telephone: (314) 961-3627 Carnegie Class: Spec/Faith
FAX Number: (314) 918-2626 Calendar System: 4/1/4
URL: www.eden.edu
Established: 1850 Annual Graduate Tuition & Fees: $13,500
Enrollment: 200 Coed
Affiliation or Control: United Church Of Christ IRS Status: 501(c)3
Highest Offering: Doctorate; No Undergraduates
Program: Professional; Religious Emphasis
Accreditation: NH, THEOL

01 President .... Dr. David M. GREENHAW
03 Executive Vice President .... Mr. Richard WALTERS
30 Vice Pres Institutional Advancement .. Mr. James SCHNURBUSCH
05 Academic Dean .... Dr. Deborah KRAUSE
11 Director of Administration .... Mr. Al SCHON
44 Director of Development .... Ms. Jackie HAMILTON
06 Registrar .... Ms. Michelle WOBBE
08 Director Eden Library .... Mr. Michael BODDY
07 Director of Recruitment/Admissions .... Rev. Carol SHANKS
40 Director Eden Bookstore .... Ms. Mary BRACKE
10 Director of Finance .... Mrs. Wendy ENKE
105 Video & Web Services .... Mr. James SCHNURBUSCH
04 Executive Asst to the President .... Ms. Denise STAUFFER

Evangel University (A)

1111 N Glenstone, Springfield MO 65802-2191
County: Greene FICE Identification: 002463
Unit ID: 177339
Telephone: (417) 865-2811 Carnegie Class: Bac/Diverse
FAX Number: (417) 865-9599 Calendar System: Semester
URL: www.evangel.edu
Established: 1955 Annual Undergrad Tuition & Fees: $17,900
Enrollment: 2,072 Coed
Affiliation or Control: Assemblies Of God Church IRS Status: 501(c)3
Highest Offering: Master's
Program: Liberal Arts And General; Teacher Preparatory
Accreditation: NH, MUS, SW, TED

01 President .... Dr. Robert H. SPENCE
10 Vice President for Business/Finance .... Mr. George F. CRAWFORD
32 Vice Pres for Student Development .... Dr. David R. BUNDRICK
30 Vice Pres Institutional Advancement .... Mr. James WILLIAMS
05 Vice President for Academic Affairs .... Dr. Glenn H. BERNET
84 Vice Pres Enrollment Management .... Mr. Andy DENTON
18 Director of Physical Plant .... Mr. Tom KELTNER
41 Director of Athletics .... Dr. David L. STAIR
06 Registrar .... Mrs. Cathy WILLIAMS
14 Director Computer Svcs/Acad Comput .... Mr. Brett WEIMER
08 Librarian .... Mr. Dale JENSEN
19 Director of Security .... Mr. Gene THOMLINSON
38 Director of Counseling Services .... Mr. Brian UPTON
29 Director Alumni Relations .... Mr. Chuck COX
37 Dir of Student Financial Services .... Mrs. Dorynda CARPENTER
36 Career Development/Placement .... Mrs. Sheri PHILLIPS
42 Campus Pastor .... Rev. John PLAKE
26 Director of Public Relations .... Mr. Paul LOGSDON
07 Director Undergraduate Admissions .... Mr. Jeff BURNETT
23 Director of Health Services .... Mrs. Susan BRYAN
21 Controller .... Mr. John KRAUS
35 Director Student Life .... Miss Gina RENTSCHLER
15 Supervisor Human Resources .... Mrs. Ocki HAAS
39 Housing Coordinator .... Mrs. Pamela SMALLWOOD
09 Director of Institutional Research .... Dr. Linda WELLBORN

Everest College (B)

1010 W Sunshine, Springfield MO 65807-2488
County: Greene FICE Identification: 022506
Unit ID: 179070
Telephone: (417) 864-7220 Carnegie Class: Bac/Assoc
FAX Number: (417) 864-5697 Calendar System: Quarter
URL: www.everestcollege.com
Established: 1976 Annual Undergrad Tuition & Fees: $35,000
Enrollment: 451 Coed
Affiliation or Control: Proprietary IRS Status: Proprietary
Highest Offering: Baccalaureate
Program: Occupational; 2-Year Principally Bachelor's Creditable; Business Emphasis
Accreditation: ACICS, MAC

01 President .... Mr. Gary L. MYERS
05 Academic Dean .... Mr. Brian J. HARVEY
07 Director of Admissions .... Ms. Wendy WOOSLEY
06 Registrar .... Ms. Annette THOMAS
04 Senior Administrative Assistant .... Ms. Beth HAWLEY
37 Financial Aid Director .... Ms. Brenda GROOVER
36 Director of Placement .... Ms. Dorothy ROBBINS
10 Director of Student Accounts .... Ms. Jennifer RUMLEY
07 High School Director of Admissions .... Mr. Tully LALE
08 Librarian .... Mr. Trenton TUBBS

Fontbonne University (C)

6800 Wydown Boulevard, Saint Louis MO 63105-3098
County: Saint Louis FICE Identification: 002464
Unit ID: 177418
Telephone: (314) 862-3456 Carnegie Class: Master's L
FAX Number: (314) 889-1451 Calendar System: Semester
URL: www.fontbonne.edu
Established: 1923 Annual Undergrad Tuition & Fees: $20,860
Enrollment: 2,532 Coed
Affiliation or Control: Roman Catholic IRS Status: 501(c)3
Highest Offering: Master's
Program: Liberal Arts And General; Teacher Preparatory; Professional
Accreditation: NH, ACBSP, DIETD, SP, @SW, TED

01 President .... Dr. Dennis C. GOLDEN
03 Executive Vice Pres Strat/Oper .... Mr. Gregory TAYLOR
05 Vice Pres/Dean Academic Affairs .... Dr. John BRUNO
30 Vice President Inst Advancement .... Ms. Marilyn SHEPERD
32 Vice President Student Affairs .... Ms. Randi WILSON
10 Vice President Finance & Admin/CFO .... Dr. Gary L. ZACK
84 Vice President Enrollment Mgt .... Vacant
13 Vice Pres Information Technology .... Mr. Mark FRANZ
35 Associate Vice Pres Student Affairs .... Ms. Carla HICKMAN
20 Interim Associate Academic Dean .... Dr. Joyce STARR JOHNSON
97 Dean of Undergraduate Studies .... Dr. Genevieve ROBINSON
58 Director of Graduate Studies/MAED .... Dr. James MUSKOPF
53 Dean of Education .... Dr. William FREEMAN
50 Dean of Global Business & Prof Stds .... Ms. Linda MAURER
88 Asst to the Pres for Mission Integ .... Dr. Mary Beth GALLAGHER
06 Registrar .... Ms. Mazie MOORE
15 Director of Human Resources .... Ms. Linda PIPITONE
08 University Librarian .... Ms. Sharon MCCASLIN
45 Director of Academic Resources .... Dr. Jane SNYDER
09 Dir of Inst Research & Assessment .... Dr. Laurie A. RODGERS
26 Director Communications/Marketing .... Mr. Mark JOHNSON
106 Director of Online Program .... Ms. Amanda (Ame) MEAD
37 Director of Financial Aid .... Ms. Nicole MOORE
88 Director of Academic Advising .... Ms. Lee DELAET
85 Director of International Affairs .... Ms. Rebecca GRANT BAHAN
29 Director of Alumni Relations .... Ms. Carrie WENBERG
41 Interim Director of Athletics .... Ms. Maria EFTINK
28 Director of Multicultural Affairs .... Ms. Leslie DOYLE
88 Director of Student Development .... Mr. Chris GILL
42 Director of Campus Ministry .... Ms. Sarah BOUL
19 Director of Public Safety .... Mr. Bob KRAEUCHI
21 Controller .... Mr. Dennis JOHNSON
07 Director of Admissions .... Ms. Dorothy DAVIS
18 Director Physical Plant .... Mr. Brent SPIES

Global University (D)

1211 South Glenstone Avenue,
Springfield MO 65804-1894
County: Greene Identification: 666687
Unit ID: 247296
Telephone: (800) 443-1083 Carnegie Class: Not Classified
FAX Number: (417) 865-7167 Calendar System: Other
URL: www.globaluniversity.edu
Established: 1948 Annual Undergrad Tuition & Fees: $3,750
Enrollment: 5,000 Coed
Affiliation or Control: Assemblies Of God Church IRS Status: 501(c)3
Highest Offering: Master's
Program: Occupational; 2-Year Principally Bachelor's Creditable; Liberal Arts And General; Professional; Religious Emphasis
Accreditation: NH, DETC

01 President .... Dr. Gary SEEVERS, JR.
03 Executive Vice President .... Rev. Keith HEERMANN
05 Provost .... Dr. Jack NILL
20 Vice Provost .... Dr. Robert LOVE
58 Graduate School Dean .... Dr. Carl CHRISNER
88 Berean School of the Bible Dean .... Dr. Randy HEDLUN
73 UG School of Bible & Theology .... Dr. Willard TEAGUE
13 VP Info Tech/Media Dept .... Dr. Mark BARCLIFT
09 Director Research/Evaluation .... Rev. Brad AUSBURY
07 Director of Enrollment Services .... Rev. Todd WAGGONER
06 Registrar .... Mrs. Lynne KROH
10 Chief Financial Officer .... Mr. Mark PERRY
15 Director of Human Resources .... Rev. Bob ARMONT

Goldfarb School of Nursing at Barnes-Jewish College (E)

4483 Duncan Avenue, Saint Louis MO 63110-1111
County: Saint Louis FICE Identification: 006389
Unit ID: 177719
Telephone: (314) 454-7055 Carnegie Class: Spec/Health
FAX Number: (314) 362-9250 Calendar System: Semester
URL: www.barnesjewishcollege.edu
Established: 1902 Annual Undergrad Tuition & Fees: $25,000
Enrollment: 700 Coed
Affiliation or Control: Independent Non-Profit IRS Status: 501(c)3
Highest Offering: Doctorate
Program: Professional; Nursing Emphasis
Accreditation: NH, ANEST, NURSE

01 Dean .... Dr. Michael L. EVANS
05 Associate Dean of Academic Programs .... Dr. Connie KOCH
11 Assoc Dean for Administration .... Mr. Thomas EDLER
20 Assoc Dean for Student Programs .... Dr. Michael WARD
46 Associate Dean for Research .... Dr. Donna TALIAFERRO
88 Asst Dean Post-Licensure Programs .... Dr. Gretchen DRINKARD
88 Asst Dean Pre-Licensure Programs .... Dr. Gail REA
88 Asst Dean for Educ Partnerships .... Dr. Cynthia BILLMAN
08 Library & Info Services Director .... Ms. Renee GORRELL
13 Information System Director .... Mr. Wade LEHDE
37 Financial Aid Director .... Mr. Jason CROWE
32 Student & Support Services Director .. Ms. June COWELL-OATES
29 Director Alumni Relations .... Mrs. Betsy DENNIS
84 Enrollment Manager .... Ms. Margaret O'CONNOR

Graceland University (F)

1401 West Truman Road, Independence MO 64050-3434
County: Jackson Identification: 666262
Unit ID: 15336601
Telephone: (816) 833-0524 Carnegie Class: Not Classified
FAX Number: (816) 833-2990 Calendar System: Semester
URL: www.graceland.edu
Established: 1895 Annual Undergrad Tuition & Fees: $21,950
Enrollment: 884 Coed
Affiliation or Control: Other IRS Status: 501(c)3
Highest Offering: Master's
Program: Liberal Arts And General; Professional
Accreditation: &NH, NURSE

01 President .... Dr. John D. SELLARS
05 Vice Pres Acad Affairs/Dean of Fac .... Dr. Parris R. WATTS
51 Exec Dir for Grad & Continuing Educ .... Dr. Taul BINNICKER
66 Dean of Nursing .... Dr. Claudia D. HORTON

† Regional accreditation is carried under the parent institution in Lamoni, IA.

Grantham University (G)

7200 NW 86th Street, Kansas City MO 64153-2262
FICE Identification: 004283
Unit ID: 442569
Telephone: (800) 955-2527 Carnegie Class: Master's S
FAX Number: (816) 595-5757 Calendar System: Other
URL: www.grantham.edu
Established: 1951 Annual Undergrad Tuition & Fees: $7,950
Enrollment: 8,750 Coed
Affiliation or Control: Proprietary IRS Status: Proprietary
Highest Offering: Master's
Program: Occupational; Professional; Technical Emphasis
Accreditation: DETC

01 President .... Dr. Fredrick SNOW
05 Provost/Chief Academic Officer .... Dr. Cynthia HOSS
06 Registrar .... Ms. Rachelle FREESE
26 Vice President of Marketing .... Mr. Shahid BUTT
84 Vice President of Enrollment Mgmt .... Mr. Matthew HAWES
10 Vice President of Finance .... Mr. Ed SAMMARCO
30 Vice Pres Strategic Initiatives .... Dr. Jeffrey CROPSEY
15 Vice President of Human Resources .... Mr. Kip ESRY
32 Dean of Student Services .... Ms. Cindy OTTS
13 Chief Technology Officer .... Mr. Robert WALKER
37 Director of Financial Aid .... Mr. Chris LEE
20 Dean of Curriculum Dev/Acad Svcs .... Dr. Carol FAGAN
08 University Librarian .... Ms. Linda CATLIN
49 Dean College of Arts & Sciences .... Dr. Paul ILLIAN
50 Dean School of Business .... Ms. Rhonda CORWIN

Hannibal-La Grange University (H)

2800 Palmyra Road, Hannibal MO 63401-1999
County: Marion FICE Identification: 009089
Unit ID: 177542
Telephone: (573) 221-3675 Carnegie Class: Bac/Diverse
FAX Number: (573) 221-6594 Calendar System: Semester
URL: www.hlg.edu
Established: 1858 Annual Undergrad Tuition & Fees: $16,800
Enrollment: 1,180 Coed
Affiliation or Control: Southern Baptist IRS Status: 501(c)3
Highest Offering: Master's
Program: Liberal Arts And General
Accreditation: NH, ADNUR

01 President .... Dr. Woodrow W. BURT
05 VP for Academic Affairs .... Dr. David J. PELLETIER
84 VP for Enrollment Management .... Dr. Raymond W. CARTY
30 VP for Institutional Advancement .... Mr. Steve T. MILLER
32 Dean of Student Development .... Mr. Kyle R. BRENNEMANN
10 Dean of Business & Finance .... Mrs. Betty L. ANDERSON
26 Director Public Relations .... Mrs. Carolyn A. CARPENTER
06 Director of Records/Student Accts .... Mrs. Mary E. FORD
37 Director of Financial Aid .... Mr. Brice D. BAUMGARDNER
29 Director Alumni Services .... Ms. Lauren YOUSE
35 Director Student Affairs .... Mrs. Margaret F. STREET
36 Director Student Placement .... Dr. Karry D. RICHARDSON
08 Librarian .... Mrs. Julie A. ANDRESEN
18 Chief Facilities/Physical Plant .... Mr. James P. MILLER
19 Director Security/Safety .... Mr. Lucas R. HIRTZEL
39 Director Student Housing .... Mrs. Sara E. KECK
40 Director Bookstore .... Mrs. Susan A. BOOTH
41 Athletic Director .... Mr. Jason D. NICHOLS
42 Director Campus Ministry .... Dr. Jeffrey D. BROWN

Harris-Stowe State University (I)

3026 Laclede Avenue, Saint Louis MO 63103-2199
County: Independent City FICE Identification: 002466
Unit ID: 177551
Telephone: (314) 340-3380 Carnegie Class: Bac/Diverse
FAX Number: (314) 340-3399 Calendar System: Semester
URL: www.hssu.edu
Established: 1857 Annual Undergrad Tuition & Fees (In-State): $5,586
Enrollment: 1,716 Coed
Affiliation or Control: State IRS Status: 501(c)3
Highest Offering: Baccalaureate
Program: Teacher Preparatory; Professional; Business Emphasis

Accreditation: **NH**, ACBSP, #IACBE, TED

President ... Dr. Henry GIVENS, JR.
1 VP for Admin and Exec Adm Asst Pres ... Vacant
5 Vice President Academic Affairs ... Dr. Dwayne SMITH
0 Exec VP Business/Financial Affairs ... Mrs. Constance G. GULLY
1 Asst VP Business/Financial Affairs ... Ms. Rochelle TILGHMAN
6 Int Dir Communication/Marketing ... Mrs. Nisa SCHMITZ
6 Registrar ... Ms. Chauvette MCELMURRY
7 Exec Dir Admissions/Enrollment Mgmt .. Ms. LaShanda R. BOONE
8 Director of Academic Advisement ... Ms. Carla LEE
8 Director Library Services ... Mrs. Barbara NOBLE
7 Director of Financial Aid ... Ms. Regina BLACKSHEAR
5 Director Human Resources ... Mrs. Virginia J. MALONE
3 Director Counseling Services ... Mrs. Vicki BERNARD
6 Director Title III/Sponsored Pgms ... Mrs. Heather BOSTIC
0 Director Special Acad Support Pgms ... Vacant
1 Director of Athletics ... Mr. Don KAVERMAN
8 Director of Physical Plant ... Mr. Paul KENNON
0 Dir Development & Alumni Affairs ... Vacant
8 Director of Business Services ... Ms. Barbara A. MORROW
9 Director of Institutional Research ... Vacant
6 Director of Career Services ... Mrs. Wanda MCNEIL
1 Comptroller/Grants Officer ... Mrs. Andrea DAVIS
8 Coord Student Counseling/Wellness ... Vacant
3 Dean College of Education ... Dr. LaTisha T. SMITH
0 Dean Busch School of Business Admin ... Ms. Fatemeh ZAKERY
2 Dean Student Affairs ... Mr. Charles H. GOODEN
8 Chair Urban Specializations ... Vacant
9 Chair College of Arts & Sciences ... Dr. Lateef ADELANI

Heritage College (A)

1200 E 104th Street, Suite 300,
Kansas City MO 64131-4557
County: Jackson — Identification: 666155
Unit ID: 445814
Telephone: (816) 942-5474 — Carnegie Class: Assoc/PrivFP
FAX Number: (816) 942-5405 — Calendar System: Other
URL: www.heritage-education.com
Established: 2002 — Annual Undergrad Tuition & Fees: $23,388
Enrollment: 852 — Coed
Affiliation or Control: Proprietary — IRS Status: Proprietary
Highest Offering: Associate Degree
Program: Occupational
Accreditation: **ABHES**

01 Director ... Mr. Larry CARTMILL

† Branch campus of Heritage College, Denver, CO.

Hickey College (B)

940 W Port Plaza, Suite 101, Saint Louis MO 63146-3127
County: Saint Louis — FICE Identification: 010279
Unit ID: 177579
Telephone: (314) 434-2212 — Carnegie Class: Bac/Assoc
FAX Number: (314) 434-1974 — Calendar System: Other
URL: www.hickeycollege.edu
Established: 1933 — Annual Undergrad Tuition & Fees: $13,380
Enrollment: 372 — Coed
Affiliation or Control: Proprietary — IRS Status: Proprietary
Highest Offering: Baccalaureate
Program: Business Emphasis
Accreditation: **ACICS**

01 President ... Mr. Christopher A. GEARIN
11 Director of Operations ... Mr. Patrick M. GLYNN
05 Director of Education ... Ms. Connie L. SCOTT
32 Director of Student Services ... Ms. Deanna L. PECORONI
07 Director of Admissions ... Mr. Bill E. LEWIS

IHM Academy of EMS (C)

2500 Abbott Place, Saint Louis MO 63143
County: Saint Louis — Identification: 667021
Telephone: (314) 768-1234 — Carnegie Class: Not Classified
FAX Number: (314) 768-1595 — Calendar System: Other
URL: www.ihmacademyofems.net
Established: N/A — Annual Undergrad Tuition & Fees: $4,351
Enrollment: N/A — Coed
Affiliation or Control: Proprietary — IRS Status: Proprietary
Highest Offering: Associate Degree
Program: Occupational; 2-Year Principally Bachelor's Creditable
Accreditation: **EMT**

01 Chief Administrator ... Jessica L. TOTH
05 Dean ... Charlene CORLEY

ITT Technical Institute (D)

1930 Meyer Drury Drive, Arnold MO 63010-6004
County: Jefferson — Identification: 666033
Unit ID: 434548
Telephone: (636) 464-6600 — Carnegie Class: Spec/Tech
FAX Number: (636) 464-6611 — Calendar System: Quarter
URL: www.itt-tech.edu
Established: 1997 — Annual Undergrad Tuition & Fees: N/A
Enrollment: 848 — Coed
Affiliation or Control: Proprietary — IRS Status: Proprietary
Highest Offering: Baccalaureate
Program: Technical Emphasis
Accreditation: **ACICS**

† Branch campus of ITT Technical Institute, Newburgh, IN.

ITT Technical Institute (E)

3640 Corporate Trail Drive, Earth City MO 63045-1122
County: Saint Louis — FICE Identification: 007557
Unit ID: 176637
Telephone: (314) 298-7800 — Carnegie Class: Spec/Tech
FAX Number: (314) 298-0559 — Calendar System: Quarter
URL: www.itt-tech.edu
Established: 1936 — Annual Undergrad Tuition & Fees: N/A
Enrollment: 1,082 — Coed
Affiliation or Control: Proprietary — IRS Status: Proprietary
Highest Offering: Baccalaureate
Program: Technical Emphasis
Accreditation: **ACICS**

ITT Technical Institute (F)

9150 East 41st Terrace, Kansas City MO 64133-1448
County: Jackson — Identification: 666380
Unit ID: 446899
Telephone: (816) 276-1400 — Carnegie Class: Spec/Tech
FAX Number: N/A — Calendar System: Quarter
URL: www.itt-tech.edu
Established: N/A — Annual Undergrad Tuition & Fees: N/A
Enrollment: 827 — Coed
Affiliation or Control: Proprietary — IRS Status: Proprietary
Highest Offering: Baccalaureate
Program: Technical Emphasis
Accreditation: **ACICS**

† Branch campus of ITT Technical Institute, Torrance, CA.

ITT Technical Institute (G)

3216 South National Avenue, Springfield MO 65807
County: Greene — Identification: 666702
Unit ID: 456409
Telephone: (417) 877-4800 — Carnegie Class: Not Classified
FAX Number: (417) 877-4800 — Calendar System: Quarter
URL: www.itt-tech.edu
Established: N/A — Annual Undergrad Tuition & Fees: N/A
Enrollment: 303 — Coed
Affiliation or Control: Proprietary — IRS Status: Proprietary
Highest Offering: Baccalaureate
Program: Technical Emphasis
Accreditation: **ACICS**

† Branch campus of ITT Technical Institute, Grand Rapids, MI.

Jefferson College (H)

1000 Viking Drive, Hillsboro MO 63050-2441
County: Jefferson — FICE Identification: 002468
Unit ID: 177676
Telephone: (636) 797-3000 — Carnegie Class: Assoc/Pub-S-MC
FAX Number: (636) 789-4012 — Calendar System: Semester
URL: www.jeffco.edu
Established: 1963 — Annual Undergrad Tuition & Fees (In-District): $2,700
Enrollment: 6,203 — Coed
Affiliation or Control: State/Local — IRS Status: 501(c)3
Highest Offering: Associate Degree
Program: Occupational; 2-Year Principally Bachelor's Creditable
Accreditation: **NH**

01 President ... Dr. Raymond V. CUMMISKEY
05 VP Academic Affairs & Student Svcs ... Dr. Joyce BANJAC
75 Dean Career/Technical Education ... Ms. Elizabeth CHECK
32 Dean Student Services ... Ms. Julie FRASER
49 Dean of Arts & Sciences ... Dr. Melinda K. SELSOR
10 VP Finance & Administration ... Dr. Richard T. TURLEY
30 Executive Director of Advancement ... Vacant
15 Director of Human Resources ... Ms. Tasha D. WELSH
26 Director of PR & Marketing ... Mr. Roger A. BARRENTINE
09 Director Research & Planning ... Vacant
74 Director Veterinary Technology ... Ms. Dana A. NEVOIS
76 Acting Director Health Technologies ... Ms. Marybeth OTTINGER
06 Registrar ... Ms. Kim M. HARVEY
07 Director Admissions/Financial Aid ... Vacant
35 Director Student Support Services ... Ms. Barbara FLESH
21 Controller ... Mr. Richard H. HARDIN
41 Director Athletics ... Mr. Doug STOTLER
31 Director Business & Community Devel ... Mr. Bryan D. HERRICK
12 Director Arnold & Northwest ... Ms. Dena M. MCCAFFREY
08 Director Library Services ... Ms. Lisa C. WOLFE
90 Dir Inst Support/Academic Computing ... Mr. Allan A. WAMSLEY
18 Director Buildings & Grounds ... Mr. Ed TOMASZKIEWICZ
96 Dir Purchasing & Contract Admin ... Mr. Gary D. ALEXANDER
13 Director Telecomm & Networking ... Mr. Tracy JAMES
91 Director Administrative Computing ... Mr. Brian E. BOLLE
88 Director Child Care Center ... Ms. Sandra K. BASLER
75 Div Chair Business/Technical Educ ... Ms. Marybeth OTTINGER
81 Division Chair Math/Science ... Mr. Ryan GROENEMAN
83 Division Chair Social Sciences ... Ms. Sandy FREY
60 Division Chair Communication ... Ms. Shirley DUBMAN

Kansas City Art Institute (I)

4415 Warwick Boulevard, Kansas City MO 64111-1874
County: Jackson — FICE Identification: 002473
Unit ID: 177746
Telephone: (816) 472-4852 — Carnegie Class: Spec/Arts
FAX Number: (816) 472-3439 — Calendar System: Semester
URL: www.kcai.edu
Established: 1885 — Annual Undergrad Tuition & Fees: $30,762
Enrollment: 739 — Coed
Affiliation or Control: Independent Non-Profit — IRS Status: 501(c)3
Highest Offering: Baccalaureate
Program: Fine Arts Emphasis
Accreditation: **NH**, ART

01 President ... Ms. Jacqueline CHANDA
11 Executive Vice Pres Administration ... Mr. Ronald E. CATTELINO
05 Vice President for Academic Affairs ... Mr. Mark SALMON
30 Vice President for Advancement ... Ms. Pamela SIBERT
84 VP Enroll Mgt & Student Achievement ... Ms. Bambi BURGARD
26 Vice President for Communications ... Ms. Anne CANFIELD
13 Vice Pres/Chief Information Officer ... Mr. Larry DICKERSON
51 Dir Continuing/Professional Studies ... Ms. Tabitha SCHMIDT
06 Registrar ... Ms. Andrea KHAN
15 Director of Human Resources ... Ms. Barbara FINKE
18 Facilities Director/Plant Services ... Mr. Larry STUCKEY
29 Director of Alumni Relations ... Ms. Andrea ADAMS
37 Executive Director of Financial Aid ... Ms. Christal D. WILLIAMS
21 Controller ... Ms. Suzette NAYLOR
36 Director of Career Services ... Ms. Julie METZLER
08 Director of Library ... Ms. M. J. POEHLER
39 Dir Residence Life/Campus Activity ... Ms. Gina GOLBA
24 Director of Media Center ... Mr. Aldo BACCHETTA
19 Director of Safety & Security ... Mr. Robert BAYLESS
40 Director of Auxiliary Services ... Mr. Ed RODRIGUEZ
88 Director of Block Artspace Gallery ... Ms. Raechell SMITH
104 Study Abroad Coordinator ... Ms. Emily BRATTIN
04 Exec Admin Asst to the President ... Ms. Susan KLEIN

Kansas City University of Medicine & Biosciences (J)

1750 Independence Avenue, Kansas City MO 64106-1453
County: Jackson — FICE Identification: 002474
Unit ID: 179812
Telephone: (816) 654-7000 — Carnegie Class: Spec/Med
FAX Number: (816) 654-7101 — Calendar System: Semester
URL: www.kcumb.edu
Established: 1916 — Annual Graduate Tuition & Fees: $42,039
Enrollment: 41,013 — Coed
Affiliation or Control: Independent Non-Profit — IRS Status: 501(c)3
Highest Offering: First Professional Degree; No Undergraduates
Program: Professional
Accreditation: **NH**, OSTEO

01 President & CEO ... Dr. H. Danny WEAVER
03 Exec VP Acad & Med Affairs/Dean COM ... Dr. Darin L. HAUG
10 Chief Financial Officer ... Mr. Joseph MASSMAN
30 Vice Pres for Advancement ... Ms. Beth DOLLASE
11 Vice President Finance & Admin ... Mr. James E. PARK
43 Interim EVP Adm & Legal Affairs ... Mr. Nelson T. MANN
20 Assoc Dean for Clin Educ & Med Affs ... Dr. John DOUGHERTY
20 Assoc Dean for Curric Affairs ... Ms. Linda ADKISON
32 Assoc Dean for Student Affairs ... Dr. Maurice OELKLAUS
35 Asst Dean for Student Affairs ... Ms. LeAnn K. CARLTON
88 Exec Director University Events ... Ms. Nancy A. JONES
26 Vice Pres Marketing/Univ Relations ... Ms. Natalie LUTZ
08 Director of Libraries ... Miss Marilyn J. DEGEUS
15 Vice Pres Human Resources ... Ms. Dawn M. ROHRS
18 Director Physical Facilities ... Mr. Walter W. SNYDER
96 Director of Purchasing ... Ms. Carrie L. SIMSHEUSER
88 Director Clinical Research ... Dr. Patrick G. CLAY
27 Chief Information Officer ... Ms. Rebecca G. TALKEN
37 Director of Financial Aid ... Ms. Sharon S. HERMAN
30 Director of Development ... Ms. Christine A. WAHLERT
84 VP Enrollment & Registrar ... Ms. Heidi TERRY
88 Adm Dir Community Clin Educ ... Ms. Valorie L. MILLICAN
19 Director Security ... Mr. Freddy D. POINDEXTER
28 Director Learning Enhancement ... Mr. Stan VIEBROCK
44 Dir Alumni & Major Gift Development ... Mr. Ted P. PLACE
35 Exec Dir Comm of Student Affairs ... Ms. Sara E. SELKIRK
76 Dean of College of Biosciences ... Dr. Douglas R. RUSHING
63 Assoc Dean Basic Medical Sciences ... Dr. Alan G. GLAROS
20 Asst Dean Curricular Affairs ... Dr. Gary O. BALLAM
76 Assoc Dean College of Biosciences ... Dr. Robert E. STEPHENS
24 Instructional Tech Media Technician ... Mr. Wade W. GLOSSER
04 Assistant to the President ... Mr. Brian T. REESE
07 Director Admissions ... Ms. Patricia HARPER
36 Coordinator Placement ... Ms. Allison O. MOORE

Kenrick-Glennon Seminary-Kenrick School of Theology (K)

5200 Glennon Drive, Saint Louis MO 63119-4399
County: Saint Louis — FICE Identification: 002476
Unit ID: 177816
Telephone: (314) 792-6100 — Carnegie Class: Spec/Faith
FAX Number: (314) 792-6500 — Calendar System: Semester
URL: www.kenrick.edu
Established: 1893 — Annual Undergrad Tuition & Fees: $20,608
Enrollment: 120 — Male
Affiliation or Control: Roman Catholic — IRS Status: 501(c)3
Highest Offering: Master's

Program: Professional
Accreditation: NH, THEOL

01 Interim President/Rector ... Rev. Michael J. WITT
42 Dir Pre-Theology/Vice Rector ... Rev. Edward J. RICHARD, M.S.
05 Academic Dean ... Rev. Donald HENKE
10 Chief Business Officer ... Mr. Michael J. BASLER
32 Dean of Students ... Rev. Paul ROTHSCHILD
08 Librarian ... Dr. John J. GRESHAM
38 Director of Formation ... Rev. Edward J. RICHARD, M.S.
30 Director of Development ... Mr. Seth JANSEN
06 Registrar/Financial Aid ... Ms. Mary Ann AUBIN
18 Chief Facilities/Physical Plant ... Mr. Tracy LATO
20 Associate Academic Officer ... Rev. Donald E. HENKE
26 Chief Public Relations Officer ... Mr. Seth JANSEN

L'Ecole Culinaire (A)

9811 South Outer Forty Drive, Saint Louis MO 63124
Identification: 666275
Unit ID: 445726
Telephone: (314) 587-2433 Carnegie Class: Assoc/PrivFP
FAX Number: (314) 587-2430 Calendar System: Semester
URL: www.lecoleculinaire.com
Established: 2004 Annual Undergrad Tuition & Fees: N/A
Enrollment: 604 Coed
Affiliation or Control: Proprietary IRS Status: Proprietary
Highest Offering: Associate Degree
Program: Occupational
Accreditation: ACCSC, ACFEI

01 President ... Ms. Pamela BELL
11 Director ... Ms. Jane MCNAMEE

† Branch campus of Vatterott College, Des Moines, IA.

Lincoln University (B)

820 Chestnut Street, Jefferson City MO 65101-3537
County: Cole FICE Identification: 002479
Unit ID: 177940
Telephone: (573) 681-5000 Carnegie Class: Master's S
FAX Number: (573) 681-5566 Calendar System: Semester
URL: www.lincolnu.edu
Established: 1866 Annual Undergrad Tuition & Fees (In-State): $6,800
Enrollment: 3,159 Coed
Affiliation or Control: State IRS Status: 501(c)3
Highest Offering: Beyond Master's But Less Than Doctorate
Program: 2-Year Principally Bachelor's Creditable; Liberal Arts And General; Teacher Preparatory; Professional; Music Emphasis
Accreditation: NH, ACBSP, ADNUR, MUS, NUR, SURGT, TED

01 President ... Dr. Carolyn R. MAHONEY
05 Interim VP Academic Affairs/Provost ... Dr. Ann HARRIS
32 Vice President Student Affairs ... Mrs. Theressa FERGUSON
30 VP University Advancement ... Mrs. Benecia R. WILLIAMS
10 Vice President Administration ... Mr. Curtis CREAGH
20 Asst to Pres Acad Success/Stdnt Ret ... Vacant
83 Dean Col Behavioral\Technical Sci ... Dr. Ruthie STURDEVANT
107 Dean Col of Professional Studies ... Dr. Linda S. BICKEL
49 Interim Dean College of Art/Letters ... Dr. Ruthie STURDEVANT
47 Dean College of Ag/Natural Sciences ... Dr. Steven MEREDITH
08 University Librarian ... Vacant
21 Controller ... Mrs. Sandy KOETTING
45 Institutional Planner ... Vacant
51 Director Continuing Education ... Ms. Kathy PABST
15 Director Human Resources ... Mr. James MARCANTONIO
88 Director Design and Construction ... Mrs. Sheila GASSNER
19 Director Public Safety ... Mr. Bill NELSON
41 Director of Athletics ... Mrs. Betty KEMNA
29 Director Alumni Affairs ... Ms. Benecia WILLIAMS
26 Director Public Info/Univ Relations ... Ms. Misty YOUNG
06 Director of Records/Registrar ... Ms. Liz MORROW
38 Director Counseling/Career Services ... Mrs. Cheryl AVANT
84 Int Exec Dir Enroll Mgmt/Dir Admiss ... Mrs. Wanda HARPER
09 Director Ctr Assess/Inst Rsrch/Plng ... Vacant
23 Director Student Health Services ... Mrs. Barbara BLACK
35 Director of Student Life ... Ms. Tammy NOBLES
43 Director Legal Svcs/Genl Counsel ... Mr. Kent BROWN
37 Dir Financial Aid/Stdnt Employment ... Mr. Alfred L. ROBINSON
88 Director Educ Opportunity Program ... Vacant
96 Director of Purchasing ... Ms. Debra KIDWELL
18 Director of Buildings and Grounds ... Mr. Mark FRIEDMAN
13 Chief Information Officer ... Mrs. Ruth CAMPBELL
39 Director of Student Housing ... Mr. Carlos GRAHAM
12 Director Fort Leonard Wood Site ... Mrs. Millie GREER
86 Director of Government Relations ... Mr. Ken FERGUSON
24 Coord Center for Teaching/Learning ... Mr. Jamere BROWN
40 Manager LU Bookstore ... Mr. James HOWARD
101 Exec Asst to President & Curators ... Ms. Rose Ann ORTMEYER
85 International Student Advisor ... Mrs. Mary BEZA
105 Web Content Manager ... Ms. Cherryl JONES

Lindenwood University (C)

209 S Kingshighway, Saint Charles MO 63301-1695
County: Saint Charles FICE Identification: 002480
Unit ID: 177968
Telephone: (636) 949-2000 Carnegie Class: Master's L
FAX Number: (636) 949-4910 Calendar System: Semester
URL: www.lindenwood.edu
Established: 1827 Annual Undergrad Tuition & Fees: $14,360
Enrollment: 17,317 Coed
Affiliation or Control: Independent Non-Profit IRS Status: 501(c)3
Highest Offering: Doctorate
Program: Liberal Arts And General; Teacher Preparatory; Professional
Accreditation: NH, @ACBSP, SW, @TEAC

01 President ... Dr. James D. EVANS
04 Executive Assistant ... Ms. Judy SHANAHAN
05 Provost & Vice Pres Acad Affairs ... Dr. Jann RUDD WEITZEL
11 Vice Pres Operations/Finance & COO ... Ms. Julie MUELLER
30 Vice Pres Institutional Advancement ... Dr. Lucy S. MORROS
32 Vice President Student Development ... Dr. John OLDANI
16 Vice Pres Human Res/Dean Faculty ... Dr. Richard A. BOYLE
09 Dean of Institutional Research ... Dr. Donald HEIDENREICH
06 Registrar ... Ms. Christine HANNAR
10 Chief Financial Officer ... Mr. David KANDEL
29 Director Alumni Relations ... Ms. Whitney FRAIER
26 Dir Communications/Public Relations ... Mr. Scott QUEEN
31 Director Community Development ... Ms. Charlsie FLOYD
13 Director of Information Services ... Mr. Shawn HAGHIGHI
08 Director of Library Services ... Ms. Elizabeth MACDONALD
37 Director of Financial Aid ... Ms. Lori BODE
35 Director of Student Activites ... Ms. Kerry COX
39 Director of Residential Operations ... Mr. Terry RUSSELL
39 Director of Residential Life ... Ms. Michelle GIESSMAN
92 Director of Honors Program ... Dr. Michael WHALEY
44 Dir Planned Giving/Internal Counsel ... Mr. Eric STUHLER
102 Dir Corporate/Foundation Relations ... Vacant
86 Dir of Outreach & Govt Relations ... Vacant
85 Director International Programs ... Mr. Ryan GUFFEY
40 Director of Auxiliary Services ... Mr. David DICKHERBER
22 Director of Compliance ... Ms. Christine REBORI
84 Dean of Enrollment Management ... Ms. Christie RODGERS
07 Dean of Undergraduate Admissions ... Mr. Joseph PARISI
12 Dean of Boone Campus ... Dr. David KNOTTS
20 Dean Academic Services ... Mr. Barry FINNEGAN
55 Dean Evening/Ext Campus Admissions ... Mr. Brett BARGER
36 Director of Student Placement ... Ms. Dana WEHRLI
41 Athletic Director ... Mr. John CREER
42 Chaplain ... Dr. Michael MASON
15 Personnel Officer ... Ms. Joyce TOWNSEND
20 Coordinator of Academic Services ... Vacant
79 School Dean Humanities ... Dr. Michael WHALEY
81 School Dean Sciences ... Dr. Marilyn ABBOTT
53 School Dean Education ... Dr. Cynthia BICE
57 School Dean Arts ... Mr. Donnell WALSH
50 Sch Dean Business/Entrepreneurship ... Dr. Roger ELLIS
60 School Dean Communications ... Mr. Mike WALL
88 School Dean Human Services ... Ms. Carla MUELLER
51 School Dean LCIE(Adult Learning) ... Mr. Dan KEMPER

Linn State Technical College (D)

One Technology Drive, Linn MO 65051-0479
County: Osage FICE Identification: 004711
Unit ID: 177977
Telephone: (573) 897-5000 Carnegie Class: Assoc/Pub-R-S
FAX Number: (573) 897-4656 Calendar System: Semester
URL: www.linnstate.edu
Established: 1961 Annual Undergrad Tuition & Fees (In-State): $4,440
Enrollment: 2,733 Coed
Affiliation or Control: State IRS Status: 501(c)3
Highest Offering: Associate Degree
Program: Occupational; 2-Year Principally Bachelor's Creditable
Accreditation: NH, ENGT, NAIT, PTAA

01 President ... Dr. Donald M. CLAYCOMB
11 Vice Pres Administration/Finance ... John NILGES
05 Dean Academic Affairs/Student Svcs ... Victoria SCHWINKE
13 Dean Information Technology ... Don LLOYD
09 Dean Institutional Research/Plng ... Dr. Rick MIHALEVICH
30 Executive Director Development ... Carla MCDANIEL
12 Int Exec Dir Adv Technology Center ... A. J PROBST
08 Int College Librarian ... Fran STUMPF
37 Director Student Financial Aid ... Becky WHITHAUS
06 Registrar ... Elaine BRANDT
07 Director Admissions/Enroll Mgmt ... Kathy SCHEULEN
15 Dir Personnel Serv/Chief Facilities ... John NILGES
20 Associate Academic Officer ... Janet CLANTON
21 Associate Business Officer ... Kim STALEY
29 Dir Alumni Relations/Chief PR Ofcr ... Carla MCDANIEL
35 Director Student Affairs ... Vacant
36 Director Student Placement ... Glenda WHITNEY
28 Director of Diversity ... Richard PEMBERTON
18 Chief Facilities/Physical Plant ... Dennis SALLIN
26 Chief Public Relations Officer ... Carla MCDANIEL
38 Student Counselor ... Ronda THOMPSON

Logan College of Chiropractic (E)

1851 Schoettler Road, PO Box 1065,
Chesterfield MO 63006-1065
County: Saint Louis FICE Identification: 004703
Unit ID: 177986
Telephone: (636) 227-2100 Carnegie Class: Spec/Health
FAX Number: (636) 207-2424 Calendar System: Trimester
URL: www.logan.edu
Established: 1935 Annual Undergrad Tuition & Fees: $5,790
Enrollment: 1,104 Coed
Affiliation or Control: Independent Non-Profit IRS Status: 501(c)3
Highest Offering: First Professional Degree
Program: Professional
Accreditation: NH, CHIRO

01 President ... Dr. George A. GOODMAN
05 Acting VP Academic Affairs ... Dr. Carl W. SAUBERT, IV
10 Chief Financial Officer ... Ms. Pat MARCELLA
84 VP Enrollment Management ... Dr. Boyd BRADSHAW
11 Vice Pres Administrative Affairs ... Ms. Sharon K. KEHRER
30 Vice Pres Institutional Advancement ... Ms. Patricia C. JONES
49 Dean University Programs ... Dr. Elizabeth A. GOODMAN
43 General Counsel ... Ms. Laura MCLAUGHLIN
17 VP Chiropractic Affairs/PostGrad Ed ... Dr. Ralph BARALLE
32 Dean of Student Services ... Mr. James PAINE
26 Associate VP Public Relations ... Mr. Thomas KELLER
23 Chief of Clinical Services ... Dr. Michael WITTMER
20 Assistant VP Academic Affairs ... Dr. Angela R. MCCALL
46 Dean of Research and Development ... Dr. Rodger E. TEPE
07 Director of Admissions ... Mr. Steve HELD
06 Registrar ... Ms. Alva ROZAR
37 Director Student Financial Aid ... Ms. Linda HAMAN
08 Director Learning Resource Center ... Ms. Chabha TEPE
24 Director of Media ... Mr. Vince MCGEE
15 Director of Human Resources ... Mr. Les LEXOW
13 Director Information Systems ... Ms. Ginger JACKSON
96 Director of Purchasing ... Mr. Charles FELTMANN
18 Physical Plant Superintendent ... Mr. Bill WHARTON
29 Alumni Director ... Ms. Valerie MCLENDON
28 Multicultural Advisor ... Ms. Felicia LINEAR

Maryville University of Saint Louis (F)

650 Maryville University Drive,
Saint Louis MO 63141-7299
County: Saint Louis FICE Identification: 002482
Unit ID: 178059
Telephone: (314) 529-9300 Carnegie Class: DRU
FAX Number: (314) 542-9085 Calendar System: Semester
URL: www.maryville.edu
Established: 1872 Annual Undergrad Tuition & Fees: $21,922
Enrollment: 3,676 Coed
Affiliation or Control: Independent Non-Profit IRS Status: 501(c)3
Highest Offering: Doctorate
Program: Liberal Arts And General; Teacher Preparatory; Professional
Accreditation: NH, ACBSP, ART, CIDA, CORE, MUS, NURSE, OT, PTA, TED

01 President ... Dr. Mark LOMBARDI
05 Vice Pres Academic Affairs ... Dr. Mary Ellen FINCH
45 Exec Dir of Planning/Research/Tech ... Mr. Jerry BRISSON
10 Vice Pres Administration & Finance ... Dr. Larry HAYS
84 Vice President Enrollment ... Mr. Jeffrey MILLER
30 VP Inst Advancemnt & Chief Dev Ofcr ... Mr. Thomas ESCHEN
32 VP for Student Life & Dn of Stdnts ... Dr. Nina CALDWELL
20 Associate VP Academic Affairs ... Dr. Tammy GOCIAL
100 Chief of Staff ... Ms. Kathy LUNAN
50 Dean School of Business ... Dr. Pamela HORWITZ
53 Dean School of Education ... Dr. Sam HAUSFATHER
76 Dean School Health Professions ... Dr. Charles GULAS
49 Dean College of Arts & Sciences ... Dr. Daniel SPARLING
08 Dean University Library ... Dr. Eugenia MCKEE
06 Registrar ... Ms. Stephanie ELFRINK
88 Director of Academic Success Center ... Ms. Kelly MOCK
07 Director of Admissions ... Ms. Shani LENORE-JENKINS
29 Director of Alumni Affairs ... Ms. Erin VERRY
41 Director of Athletics ... Mr. Marcus MANNING
42 Dir Campus Ministry & Comm Service ... Mr. Stephen DISALVO
35 Assoc Dean of Students ... Ms. Kathy QUINN
36 Director Career Education ... Ms. Lynn WILLITS
35 Director Student Involvement ... Mr. Zach LEWIS
21 Controller/Dir Finance/Aux Enterpr ... Mr. Charles BARNES
102 Director of Development/Foundations ... Ms. Megan OVER
37 Director of Financial Aid ... Ms. Martha HARBAUGH
23 Director of Health & Wellness ... Ms. Pamela CULLITON
15 Dir HR/Affirm Action Officer ... Ms. Jackie PLUNKETT
14 Director Administrative Technology ... Mr. Richard KUBB
91 Dir Administrative Applications ... Mr. David SCHULTE
09 Institutional Research Analyst ... Ms. Mary MERRIFIELD
90 Dir Acad Comp & Instr Tech ... Ms. Julie BERGFELD
26 Dir Marketing & Community Rels ... Mr. Marty PARKES
28 Director of Multicultural Programs ... Ms. Christie CRUISE-HARPER
18 Director of Physical Plant ... Mr. Tom BENNING
44 Director of Planned Gifts ... Mr. Mark ROOCK
19 Director of Public Safety ... Mr. Michael PARKINSON
39 Director of Residential Life ... Ms. Kimberly WATSON
88 Assoc VP/Dir Acad Success & FYE ... Dr. Jennifer MCCLUSKEY
104 Assoc VP/Dir Ctr for Global Educ ... Dr. James HARF
44 Assoc VP for Inst Advancement ... Ms. Beth ALBES
88 Director Sports Information ... Ms. Katie Jo KUHENS
53 Director Teacher Education Programs ... Dr. Nancy WILLIAMS
21 Director Student Accounts ... Ms. Karen SCHOLBE
88 Director Fresh Ideas Food Services ... Ms. Linda THACKER
38 Director Personal Counseling ... Ms. Jennifer HENRY
44 Director of Development ... Ms. Fay FETICK
105 Director Web Services ... Ms. Ronnie GAUBATZ
88 Assoc VP Ctr for Civic Engage & Dem ... Dr. Alden CRADDOCK

Messenger College (G)

300 E 50th Street, Joplin MO 64804-4909
County: Newton FICE Identification: 030926
Unit ID: 417752
Telephone: (417) 624-7070 Carnegie Class: Spec/Faith
FAX Number: (417) 624-5070 Calendar System: Semester
URL: www.messengercollege.edu
Established: 1987 Annual Undergrad Tuition & Fees: $8,290
Enrollment: 89 Coed
Affiliation or Control: Pentecostal Church of God IRS Status: 501(c)3

Highest Offering: Baccalaureate
Program: Liberal Arts And General; Religious Emphasis
Accreditation: TRACS

01 President .... Dr. Daniel P. DAVIS
05 Exec VP/VP Academic Affairs .... Dr. Jason BRYANT
10 Vice President Business Affairs .... Ms. Angela HEPPNER
32 Vice President Student Services .... Ms. Rhonda DAVIS
56 Director of External Studies .... Vacant
07 Dir of Admissions/Financial Aid .... Ms. Pat PENTACOST
08 Director of Library Services .... Ms. Jackie HARRIS

Metro Business College (A)

1732 N Kingshighway, Cape Girardeau MO 63701-2122
County: Cape FICE Identification: 021802
Unit ID: 178110
Telephone: (573) 334-9181 Carnegie Class: Assoc/PrivFP
FAX Number: (573) 334-0617 Calendar System: Quarter
URL: www.metrobusinesscollege.edu
Established: 1981 Annual Undergrad Tuition & Fees: $9,750
Enrollment: 170 Coed
Affiliation or Control: Proprietary IRS Status: Proprietary
Highest Offering: Associate Degree
Program: Occupational; 2-Year Principally Bachelor's Creditable; Business Emphasis
Accreditation: ACICS

01 President .... Ms. Mary BUCKLEY
12 Campus Director .... Mrs. Jan REIMANN
05 Academic Dean .... Mrs. Pat SCHWAB
37 Financial Aid Director .... Mrs. Janie WARNE
36 Career Services Coordinator .... Ms. Diane JORDAN

Metro Business College (B)

1407 Southwest Boulevard, Jefferson City MO 65109-5508
County: Cole Identification: 666454
Unit ID: 245430
Telephone: (573) 635-6600 Carnegie Class: Not Classified
FAX Number: (573) 635-6999 Calendar System: Quarter
URL: www.metrobusinesscollege.edu
Established: 1979 Annual Undergrad Tuition & Fees: $9,875
Enrollment: 243 Coed
Affiliation or Control: Proprietary IRS Status: Proprietary
Highest Offering: Associate Degree
Program: Occupational
Accreditation: ACICS

01 Director .... Mrs. Cheri CHOCKLEY
36 Career Services Coordinator .... Mr. Daniel NICHOLS
14 IT Coordinator .... Mr. Randy CHOCKLEY

† Branch campus of Metro Business College, Cape Girardeau, MO.

Metro Business College (C)

1202 E Highway 72, Rolla MO 65401-3938
County: Phelps Identification: 666455
Unit ID: 245421
Telephone: (573) 364-8464 Carnegie Class: Not Classified
FAX Number: (573) 364-8077 Calendar System: Quarter
URL: www.metrobusinesscollege.edu
Established: 1984 Annual Undergrad Tuition & Fees: $9,680
Enrollment: 106 Coed
Affiliation or Control: Proprietary IRS Status: Proprietary
Highest Offering: Associate Degree
Program: Occupational
Accreditation: ACICS

01 Director .... Ms. Mary GACSEH

† Branch campus of Metro Business College, Cape Girardeau, MO.

*Metropolitan Community College - Kansas City Administrative Center (D)

3200 Broadway, Kansas City MO 64111-2429
County: Jackson FICE Identification: 009137
Unit ID: 178129
Telephone: (816) 604-1000 Carnegie Class: N/A
FAX Number: (816) 759-1158
URL: www.mcckc.edu

01 Chancellor .... Mr. Mark S. JAMES
101 Chancellor's Asst/Board Secretary .... Ms. Cindy K. JOHNSON
05 Vice Chanc Acad Affairs/Technology .... Mr. Paul D. LONG
10 Vice Chanc Admin Svcs/Student Dev .... Dr. Tuesday L. STANLEY
100 Chief of Staff .... Ms. Kathy WALTER-MACK
27 Assoc VC College/Cmty Relations .... Dr. Tom M. VANSAGHI
15 Assoc VC Human Resources .... Ms. Carolyn R. BASKETT
88 Performance Director Resource Dev .... Ms. Carolyn S. BROWN
88 Director Management/Auxiliary Svcs .... Mr. Reinhard WEGLARZ
14 Director Computer Services .... Mr. Gary W. SCHIEBER
102 Director MCC Foundation .... Mr. Vincent M. ANCH
96 Director Purchasing .... Ms. Dorothy A. MILLER
18 Director Physical Facilities .... Mr. Darrel W. MEYER
103 Exec Dir Workforce Dev/HSI .... Ms. Margaret E. BOYD
88 Director Community Engagement .... Mr. Juan M. RANGEL
88 Director Educational Services .... Ms. Fran A. PADOW
106 Director Distance Education .... Dr. Leo J. HIRNER
88 Director Educ Progams/Employee Dev .... Dr. Rich HIGGASON
09 Director Inst Research/Assessment .... Dr. Kristy A. BISHOP
88 Director Student Development .... Dr. Susan B. WILSON
37 Director Student Financial Aid .... Ms. Cindy A. BUTLER
84 Director of Enrollment Services .... Ms. Kathy M. HALE
21 Director Financial Services .... Ms. Jane A. SMELTZER
88 Director Mgmt Advisory Services .... Ms. Patricia A. AMICK
19 Assoc Director Public Safety .... Mr. Domenick R. BROUILLETTE
88 Chief of Campus Police .... Mr. Bill HUDSON
13 Director of Technology Services .... Mr. Bill E. ANKER
88 Director Tech Prep .... Ms. Teresa A. LONEY
88 Director Business Development .... Mr. Stan D. FIELDS
21 Director Finance & Business Service .... Mr. Mark A. BURNS

*Metropolitan Community College - Blue River (E)

20301 E 78 Highway, Independence MO 64057-2053
County: Jackson FICE Identification: 032613
Unit ID: 440305
Telephone: (816) 604-6550 Carnegie Class: Assoc/Pub-U-MC
FAX Number: (816) 759-6582 Calendar System: Semester
URL: www.mcckc.edu
Established: 1997 Annual Undergrad Tuition & Fees (In-District): $2,520
Enrollment: 4,211 Coed
Affiliation or Control: State/Local IRS Status: 501(c)3
Highest Offering: Associate Degree
Program: Occupational; 2-Year Principally Bachelor's Creditable
Accreditation: &NH

02 President .... Dr. Joseph SEABROOKS, JR.
04 Assistant to the President .... Mrs. Kimberly A. MORICONI
05 Dean of Instruction .... Dr. Cheryl CARPENTER-DAVIS
32 Dean of Student Development .... Dr. Jonathan L. BURKE
51 Assoc Dean of Instruction .... Mr. Basil M. LISTER
88 Director Western Missouri PSTI .... Mr. Mike W. HENDERSHOT
08 Head Librarian .... Mr. Jared RINCK
35 Assoc Dean of Student Development .... Mrs. Karen GOOS
18 Facilities Superintendent .... Mr. Bob L. SHRAUNER
38 Lead Counselor .... Mr. Jeff WILT
84 Enrollment Manager .... Mr. Rowdy PYLE
14 Campus Network Coordinator .... Mr. Jeffrey M. EUBANK
19 Campus Police Captain .... Mr. Booker S. ARMSTRONG
26 Marketing Coordinator .... Mr. Bob K. FLORENCE

*Metropolitan Community College - Business and Technology (F)

1775 Universal Avenue, Kansas City MO 64120-2429
Identification: 666295
Unit ID: 442000
Telephone: (816) 604-5200 Carnegie Class: Assoc/Pub-U-MC
FAX Number: (816) 482-5256 Calendar System: Semester
URL: www.mcckc.edu/btc
Established: 1995 Annual Undergrad Tuition & Fees (In-District): $2,088
Enrollment: 976 Coed
Affiliation or Control: Local IRS Status: 501(c)3
Highest Offering: Associate Degree
Program: Occupational; 2-Year Principally Bachelor's Creditable; Technical Emphasis
Accreditation: &NH

02 President .... Ms. Debbie GOODALL
05 Dean of Instruction .... Dr. Thomas WHEELER
32 Dean of Student Development .... Ms. Karen MOORE
84 Enrollment Manager .... Ms. Rene BENNETT
04 Assistant to the President .... Vacant

*Metropolitan Community College - Longview (G)

500 SW Longview Road, Lee's Summit MO 64081-2105
County: Jackson FICE Identification: 009140
Unit ID: 177995
Telephone: (816) 604-2000 Carnegie Class: Assoc/Pub-U-MC
FAX Number: (816) 672-2025 Calendar System: Semester
URL: www.mcckc.edu
Established: 1969 Annual Undergrad Tuition & Fees (In-District): $2,610
Enrollment: 8,095 Coed
Affiliation or Control: Local IRS Status: 501(c)3
Highest Offering: Associate Degree
Program: Occupational; 2-Year Principally Bachelor's Creditable
Accreditation: &NH

02 President .... Dr. Fred L. GROGAN
05 Dean of Instruction .... Vacant
32 Dean Student Devel/Support Services .... Ms. Janet H. CLINE
20 Associate Dean Instruction .... Ms. Karen B. DEXTER
35 Assoc Dean Student Dev/Support Svcs .... Dr. Marvin R. AARON
07 Director of Admissions/Registrar .... Mr. David A. FRITZ
37 Manager of Student Financial Aid .... Ms. Lisa L. FANNAN
10 Business Office Supervisor .... Vacant
18 Physical Facilities Superintendent .... Mr. Steve B. GREIFE
36 Coordinator Student Employment Svcs .... Ms. Linda S. ANDERSON
38 Director Student Counseling .... Mrs. Gretchen S. BLYTHE

*Metropolitan Community College - Maple Woods (H)

2601 NE Barry Road, Kansas City MO 64156-1299
County: Clay FICE Identification: 009139
Unit ID: 178022
Telephone: (816) 604-3000 Carnegie Class: Assoc/Pub-U-MC
FAX Number: (816) 437-3049 Calendar System: Semester
URL: www.mcckc.edu
Established: 1968 Annual Undergrad Tuition & Fees (In-District): $2,610
Enrollment: 6,213 Coed
Affiliation or Control: Local IRS Status: 501(c)3
Highest Offering: Associate Degree
Program: Occupational; 2-Year Principally Bachelor's Creditable
Accreditation: &NH

02 President .... Dr. Merna S. SALIMAN
05 Dean Instruction .... Dr. Arminda MCCALLUM
32 Dean Student Services .... Ms. Shelli ALLEN
20 Associate Dean .... Mrs. Dawn K. HATTERMAN
20 Associate Dean .... Dr. Brian BECHTEL
08 Librarian .... Mrs. Linda CARTER
41 Athletic Director .... Dr. Brian BECHTEL
37 Manager Student Financial Aid .... Mrs. Robin STIMAC
40 College Bookstore Manager .... Ms. Beth AUSTIN
18 Physical Facilities Superintendent .... Mr. Jeff ALLEN
10 Business Office Supervisor .... Ms. Emily THOMPSON
31 Community Relations Coordinator .... Mrs. Heather K. PEREZ
36 Student Employment Service Coord .... Ms. Mary Lynn MUNGER
38 Lead Counselor .... Ms. Barbara COOKE

*Metropolitan Community College - Penn Valley (I)

3201 Southwest Trafficway, Kansas City MO 64111-2764
County: Jackson FICE Identification: 002484
Unit ID: 178785
Telephone: (816) 604-4000 Carnegie Class: Assoc/Pub-U-MC
FAX Number: (816) 759-4010 Calendar System: Semester
URL: www.mcckc.edu
Established: 1915 Annual Undergrad Tuition & Fees (In-District): $2,610
Enrollment: 6,669 Coed
Affiliation or Control: Local IRS Status: 501(c)3
Highest Offering: Associate Degree
Program: Occupational; 2-Year Principally Bachelor's Creditable; Nursing Emphasis
Accreditation: &NH, ADNUR, DA, OTA, PNUR, PTAA, RAD

02 President .... Dr. Joe SEABROOKS
05 Dean Instructional Services .... Dr. Al DIMMITT
32 Dean of Student Services .... Dr. Elizabeth MINIS
35 Associate Dean of Student Services .... Mrs. Carroll O'NEAL
20 Director of Health Sciences .... Ms. Sandy MCILNAY
06 Registrar/Director of Admissions .... Mr. Carlton FOWLER
14 Campus Network Coordinator .... Vacant
18 Maintenance Supervisor .... Mr. Jon HOPKINS
19 Campus Police Captain .... Cpt. Gary WILSON
41 Athletic Programs Manager .... Mr. Marcus HARVEY
37 Student Financial Aid Manager .... Ms. Rossann DOWNING
40 College Bookstore Manager .... Selin GAONA
10 Business Office Supervisor .... Ms. Michele ALLEN
38 Lead Counselor .... Vacant
08 Librarian .... Ms. Gloria MAXWELL
27 Community & Public Relations Coord .... Ms. Kimberly RILEY
36 Student Employment Service Coord .... Ms. Melanie BOWMAN

Midwest Institute (J)

10910 Manchester Road, Kirkwood MO 63122
County: St. Louis FICE Identification: 021211
Unit ID: 178183
Telephone: (314) 965-8363 Carnegie Class: Not Classified
FAX Number: (314) 965-1558 Calendar System: Other
URL: www.midwestinstitute.com
Established: 1965 Annual Undergrad Tuition & Fees: $14,280
Enrollment: 191 Coed
Affiliation or Control: Proprietary IRS Status: Proprietary
Highest Offering: Associate Degree
Program: Occupational
Accreditation: ABHES

Midwest Institute-Earth City (K)

4260 Shoreline Drive Suite 100, Earth City MO 63045
County: Saint Louis Identification: 667074
Telephone: (314) 344-4440 Carnegie Class: Not Classified
FAX Number: (314) 344-0495 Calendar System: Other
URL: www.midwestinstitute.com
Established: 1970 Annual Undergrad Tuition & Fees: N/A
Enrollment: N/A Coed
Affiliation or Control: Proprietary IRS Status: Proprietary
Highest Offering: Associate Degree
Program: Occupational
Accreditation: ABHES

01 President .... Ms. Christine SHREFFLER

Midwestern Baptist Theological Seminary (A)

5001 N Oak Trafficway, Kansas City MO 64118-4697
County: Clay FICE Identification: 002485
Unit ID: 178208
Telephone: (816) 414-3700 Carnegie Class: Spec/Faith
FAX Number: (816) 414-3724 Calendar System: Semester
URL: www.mbts.edu
Established: 1957 Annual Undergrad Tuition & Fees: $6,520
Enrollment: 1,065 Coed
Affiliation or Control: Southern Baptist IRS Status: 501(c)3
Highest Offering: Doctorate
Program: Professional; Religious Emphasis
Accreditation: NH, THEOL

01 President ... Dr. R. Philip ROBERTS
05 VP Academic Dev & Academic Dean ... Dr. Jerry SUTTON
10 Interim VP of Business Services ... Mr. Dennis ERICKSON
32 Vice President Student Development ... Dr. David M. MCALPIN
30 Sr VP of Institutional Advancement ... Dr. Anthony W. ALLEN
09 Vice President Inst Effectiveness ... Dr. Rodney A. HARRISON
06 Registrar ... Dr. Steven THOMPSON
08 Librarian ... Dr. Craig KUBIC
73 Chairman of Doctoral Studies ... Dr. Rodney A. HARRISON
10 Director Financial Services ... Mrs. Cheryl HICKS
15 Human Resources ... Mr. Gary CRUTCHER
04 Exec Assistant to the President ... Mrs. Shanna GUMMIG
18 Director of Campus Operations ... Mr. Larry HEADLEY
37 Int Financial Aid Coordinator ... Mrs. Raschelle JOHNSTON
84 Dir Student Recruitment & Admission ... Mr. Rusty MARRIOTT
13 Director of Information Technology ... Vacant
26 Director Communications/Public Rels ... Mr. Pat HUDSON

Mineral Area College (B)

5270 Flat River Drive, Park Hills MO 63601-2224
County: Saint Francois FICE Identification: 002486
Unit ID: 178217
Telephone: (573) 431-4593 Carnegie Class: Assoc/Pub-R-M
FAX Number: (573) 518-2164 Calendar System: Semester
URL: www.mineralarea.edu
Established: 1922 Annual Undergrad Tuition & Fees (In-District): $2,610
Enrollment: 3,991 Coed
Affiliation or Control: Local IRS Status: 501(c)3
Highest Offering: Associate Degree
Program: Occupational; 2-Year Principally Bachelor's Creditable
Accreditation: NH, @PTAA, RAD

01 President ... Dr. Steve KURTZ
03 Vice Pres/Dean Career/Tech Educ ... Mr. John (Gil) KENNON
49 Dean of Arts & Sciences ... Ms. Carolyn CRECELIUS
32 Dean Student Services ... Ms. Jean MERRILL-DOSS
10 Business Manager ... Mr. Rusty STRAUGHAN
13 Director of Computer Services ... Mr. Kent KAMP
06 Registrar ... Ms. Linda HUFFMAN
07 Director of Admissions ... Ms. Julie SHEETS
09 Director of Institutional Research ... Ms. Lisa EDBURG
18 Chief Facil/Phys Plnt/Purchasing ... Mr. Rusty STRAUGHAN
26 Chief Public Relations Officer ... Ms. Sarah HAAS
29 Director Alumni Relations ... Ms. Julia DILL
15 Chief Human Resource Officer ... Ms. Kathryn NEFF
37 Director Student Financial Aid ... Ms. Denise SEBASTIAN
38 Director Student Counseling ... Mr. Michael EASTER
88 General Services Supervisor ... Mr. Tom BOWYER
21 Director Payroll ... Ms. Lisa CLAUSER

Missouri Baptist University (C)

One College Park Drive, Saint Louis MO 63141-8698
County: Saint Louis FICE Identification: 007540
Unit ID: 178244
Telephone: (314) 434-1115 Carnegie Class: Master's L
FAX Number: (314) 434-7596 Calendar System: Semester
URL: www.mobap.edu
Established: 1964 Annual Undergrad Tuition & Fees: $18,700
Enrollment: 5,062 Coed
Affiliation or Control: Baptist IRS Status: 501(c)3
Highest Offering: Doctorate
Program: Liberal Arts And General; Teacher Preparatory
Accreditation: NH, EXSC, MUS, TED

01 President ... Dr. R. Alton LACEY
04 Assistant to the President ... Mrs. Susan RUTLEDGE
05 Senior VP of Academic Affs/Provost ... Dr. Arlen R. DYKSTRA
30 Senior VP of Inst Advancement ... Mr. Keith ROSS
32 Senior VP of Student Development ... Dr. Andy CHAMBERS
10 Senior VP for Business Affairs ... Mr. Ken REVENAUGH
58 VP of Grad Stds/Academic Pgm Review ... Dr. Clark TRIPLETT
84 VP of Enrollment Services ... Mr. Terry Dale CRUSE
29 Director for Alumni Relations ... Mrs. Jennifer BLACK
85 Director of International Services ... Mrs. Kari SAUNDERS
09 Director Institutional Research ... Mrs. Heather BRASE
08 Librarian ... Ms. Nitsa HINDELEH
37 Director Financial Services ... Vacant
26 Director University Communications ... Mr. Bryce CHAPMAN
36 Dir Career Svcs/Assoc Dean Students ... Ms. Kimberly GREY
41 Athletic Director ... Dr. Thomas SMITH
20 Associate Academic Dean ... Vacant
18 Director Campus Operations ... Mr. Stu LINDLEY
06 Director of Records ... Mrs. Linda CHRISOPE
15 Director Personnel Services ... Mrs. Barb BURNS
14 Director of Information Systems ... Mr. Chris SANDERS
19 Director Public Safety ... Mr. Stephen HEIDKE
35 Director Student Activities ... Mrs. Lara HINES
21 Associate Business Officer ... Mrs. Mindi OKAI
30 Director of Development ... Mr. Jon VESTAL
07 Director of Admissions ... Mr. Aaron BLACK

Missouri College (D)

1405 South Hanley Road, Brentwood MO 63144-2902
County: St. Louis FICE Identification: 009795
Unit ID: 178305
Telephone: (314) 768-7800 Carnegie Class: Bac/Assoc
FAX Number: (314) 768-7900 Calendar System: Semester
URL: www.missouricollege.com
Established: 1963 Annual Undergrad Tuition & Fees: $14,850
Enrollment: 1,051 Coed
Affiliation or Control: Proprietary IRS Status: Proprietary
Highest Offering: Baccalaureate
Program: Occupational; 2-Year Principally Bachelor's Creditable
Accreditation: ACCSC, ACICS, DA, DH, MAAB

01 President ... Mr. Karl PETERSEN
05 Dean of Academics ... Mrs. Nicole GRAMLICH
07 Admissions Director ... Ms. Heidi HOLMES
06 Registrar ... Ms. Katie FERRY

Missouri Southern State University (E)

3950 E Newman Road, Joplin MO 64801-1595
County: Jasper FICE Identification: 002488
Unit ID: 178341
Telephone: (417) 625-9300 Carnegie Class: Bac/Diverse
FAX Number: (417) 625-3121 Calendar System: Semester
URL: www.mssu.edu
Established: 1965 Annual Undergrad Tuition & Fees (In-State): $5,090
Enrollment: 5,802 Coed
Affiliation or Control: State IRS Status: 501(c)3
Highest Offering: Master's
Program: Liberal Arts And General; Teacher Preparatory; Professional
Accreditation: NH, ACBSP, DH, ENGT, NUR, NURSE, RAD, TED

01 President ... Dr. Bruce SPECK
05 Vice Pres Academic Affairs ... Dr. A. J ANGLIN
32 Vice President for Student Affairs ... Mr. Darren S. FULLERTON
10 Asst Vice Pres Business Affairs ... Mr. Rob YUST
13 Dir of Information Technology Svcs ... Mr. Albert (Al) STADLER
09 Asst VP Assessment/Inst Research ... Dr. Delores HONEY
20 Asst Vice Pres Academic Affairs ... Vacant
35 Dean of Students ... Vacant
06 Registrar ... Ms. Cheryl DOBSON
84 Director of Admissions ... Mr. Derek S. SKAGGS
92 Director of Honors Program ... Dr. Michael GAROUTTE
08 Library Director ... Mrs. Wendy MCGRANE
30 Vice Pres for Development ... Dr. Mark PARSONS
27 Director Univ Relations & Marketing ... Mr. Rod E. SURBER
36 Director of Career Services ... Vacant
29 Director Alumni Association ... Mrs. Lee Eliff POUND
37 Director Student Financial Aid ... Mrs. Becca L. DISKIN
38 Director of ACTS ... Mrs. Kelly WILSON
39 Director Student Housing ... Mr. Josh DOAK
21 Treasurer ... Mrs. Linda EIS
15 Director Human Resources ... Ms. Debbie D. KELLEY
18 Director Facilities/Physical Plant ... Mr. Robert HARRINGTON
32 Director of Student Activities ... Ms. Malorie CASHEL
96 Director of Purchasing ... Ms. Hiedi CARLIN
26 Chief Public Relations Officer ... Mr. Rod SURBER
72 Dean School Technology ... Dr. Tia STRAIT
49 Dean School of Arts & Sciences ... Dr. Richard B. MILLER
53 Dean School Education ... Dr. Glenn COLTHARP
50 Int Dean School Business Admin ... Dr. Beverly BLOCK

Missouri State University (F)

901 S National Avenue, Springfield MO 65897-0027
County: Greene FICE Identification: 002503
Unit ID: 179566
Telephone: (417) 836-8500 Carnegie Class: Master's L
FAX Number: (417) 836-7669 Calendar System: Semester
URL: www.missouristate.edu
Established: 1905 Annual Undergrad Tuition & Fees (In-State): $6,598
Enrollment: 20,472 Coed
Affiliation or Control: State IRS Status: 501(c)3
Highest Offering: Doctorate
Program: Liberal Arts And General; Teacher Preparatory; Professional
Accreditation: NH, ADNUR, ANEST, ARCPA, AUD, BUS, BUSA, CEA, CONST, CS, DIETD, MUS, NAIT, NRPA, NURSE, PLNG, PTA, SP, SPAA, SW, TED, THEA

01 President ... Mr. Clifton M. SMART, III
05 Provost ... Dr. Belinda R. MCCARTHY
12 Chancellor West Plains Campus ... Dr. Drew A. BENNETT
46 VP for Research/Economic Devel ... Dr. James P. BAKER
11 Vice Pres Administrative/Info Svcs ... Mr. Ken MCCLURE
30 Vice Pres University Advancement ... Mr. W. Brent DUNN
32 VP Student Affairs & Dean of Stdts ... Dr. Earle F. DOMAN
28 Int Vice Pres Diversity/Inclusion ... Dr. Leslie ANDERSON
20 Associate Provost ... Dr. John C. CATAU
58 Assoc Provost/Dean of Grad College ... Dr. Frank A. EINHELLIG
10 Chief Financial Officer ... Mrs. Nila HAYES
84 Asst VP Stdnt Affs/Enrollment Svcs ... Mr. Donald E. SIMPSON
08 Dean Library Services ... Ms. Neosho MACKEY
09 Director of Institutional Research ... Dr. Katherine C. COY
29 Exec Dir of Alumni Relations ... Ms. Julie A. EBERSOLD
15 Director of Human Resources ... Mr. Edward CHOATE
37 Director of Student Financial Aid ... Ms. Vicki S. MATTOCKS
19 Director of Safety & Transportation ... Mr. Donald A. CLARK
36 Director of the Career Center ... Mr. Jack M. HUNTER
14 Director of Computer Services ... Mr. Jeff P. MORRISSEY
22 Equal Opportunity Officer ... Mr. Harold PRATT
100 Chief of Staff ... Mr. Paul K. KINCAID
23 Director of Health & Wellness Svcs ... Mr. Burnie L. SNODGRASS
92 Director Honors College ... Dr. Arthur L. SPISAK
18 Director Facilities Management ... Mr. Robert T. ECKELS
96 Director of Procurement ... Mr. Mike WILLS
07 Director of Admissions ... Mr. Andrew WRIGHT
06 Enrollment Services Systems Coord ... Mr. Rob HORNBERGER
49 Dean College Arts & Letters ... Dr. Carey H. ADAMS
79 Dean Col Humanities/Public Affairs ... Dr. Victor MATTHEWS
76 Dean Col Health/Human Services ... Dr. Helen C. REID
81 Dean Col Natural/Applied Science ... Dr. Tamera S. JAHNKE
53 Dean College of Education ... Dr. Dennis J. KEAR
50 Dean Col of Business Administration ... Dr. Phil HARSHA
51 Asst Provost Extended Campus ... Mr. Stephen H. ROBINETTE
105 Director of Web Services ... Ms. Sara M. CLARK

Missouri State University - West Plains (G)

128 Garfield, West Plains MO 65775-2715
County: Howell FICE Identification: 031060
Unit ID: 179344
Telephone: (417) 255-7255 Carnegie Class: Assoc/Pub2in4
FAX Number: (417) 255-7962 Calendar System: Semester
URL: www.wp.missouristate.edu
Established: 1963 Annual Undergrad Tuition & Fees (In-State): $3,504
Enrollment: 2,229 Coed
Affiliation or Control: State IRS Status: 501(c)3
Highest Offering: Associate Degree
Program: Occupational; 2-Year Principally Bachelor's Creditable
Accreditation: NH

05 Chief Academic Officer ... Dr. Chris DYER
32 Dean of Student Services ... Dr. Herbert LUNDAY
10 Director of Business Services ... Mr. Matt MORRIS
30 Director of Development ... Mrs. Elizabeth GRISHAM
27 Director of Univ Communications ... Mrs. Cheryl CALDWELL
31 Director of Univ/Community Pgms ... Mrs. Brenda MALKOWSKI
14 Director of Computer Services ... Mrs. Sue INGRAM
06 Registrar ... Mrs. Shanna DALE
07 Coordinator of Admissions ... Mrs. Melissa JETT
09 Coord of Institutional Research ... Mrs. Patricia J. WALSH
26 Chief Public Relations Officer ... Mrs. Cheryl CALDWELL
36 Coordinator of Student Placement ... Mrs. Pam TATE
37 Coord of Student Financial Aid ... Mrs. Donna BASSHAM
84 Director Enrollment Management ... Dr. Herbert LUNDAY
18 Chief Facilities/Physical Plant ... Mr. Ron HENSLEY

Missouri Tech (H)

1690 Country Club Plaza Drive, Saint Charles MO 63303
County: Saint Louis FICE Identification: 023040
Unit ID: 178350
Telephone: (636) 573-9300 Carnegie Class: Spec/Tech
FAX Number: (636) 573-9398 Calendar System: Semester
URL: www.motech.edu
Established: 1932 Annual Undergrad Tuition & Fees: $14,330
Enrollment: 150 Coed
Affiliation or Control: Proprietary IRS Status: Proprietary
Highest Offering: Baccalaureate
Program: Technical Emphasis
Accreditation: ACCSC

01 President ... Ms. Cynthia DODGE
05 Dean of Education ... Dr. Mark STINSON
37 Director Financial Aid ... Ms. Cindy Ann SINNOTT

Missouri Valley College (I)

500 E College, Marshall MO 65340-3197
County: Saline FICE Identification: 002489
Unit ID: 178369
Telephone: (660) 831-4000 Carnegie Class: Bac/Diverse
FAX Number: (660) 831-4039 Calendar System: Semester
URL: www.moval.edu
Established: 1889 Annual Undergrad Tuition & Fees: $17,780
Enrollment: 1,461 Coed
Affiliation or Control: Presbyterian Church (U.S.A.) IRS Status: 501(c)3
Highest Offering: Baccalaureate
Program: Liberal Arts And General; Teacher Preparatory
Accreditation: NH

01 President ... Dr. Bonnie HUMPHREY
00 Chancellor Emeritus ... Dr. Earl J. REEVES
10 Vice Pres of Business & Finance ... Mrs. Amy ROE
30 Vice Pres Institutional Advancement ... Mr. Eric SAPPINGTON
05 Chief Academic Officer ... Dr. Sharon WEISER
07 Dean of Admissions ... Ms. Tennille LANGDON
06 Registrar ... Ms. Marsha LASHLEY
21 Business Officer ... Mrs. Tonia BARTEL
08 Head Librarian ... Mrs. Pamela K. REEDER
41 Athletic Director/Dir of Operations ... Mr. Tom FIFER

42 Director Campus Ministry ... Rev. Pam SEBASTIAN
18 Director Maintenance ... Mr. Tim SCHULTE
32 Dean of Students ... Mr. Heath MORGAN
09 Director of Institutional Research ... Ms. Marilyn BELWOOD
15 Dir Personnel Svcs/Dir Purchasing ... Mrs. Amy ROE
37 Director Student Financial Aid ... Mr. Buddy MAYFIELD
38 Director Student Counseling ... Mrs. Rachel MAYFIELD
13 Director of Systems Administration ... Mr. Jason RINNE
29 Director Alumni Relations ... Mr. Eric SAPPINGTON
26 Dir of Marketing & Media Relations ... Mr. Chad JAECQUES

Missouri Western State University (A)

4525 Downs Drive, Saint Joseph MO 64507-2294
County: Buchanan FICE Identification: 002490
Unit ID: 178387
Telephone: (816) 271-4200 Carnegie Class: Bac/Diverse
FAX Number: N/A Calendar System: Semester
URL: www.missouriwestern.edu
Established: 1915 Annual Undergrad Tuition & Fees (In-State): $4,833
Enrollment: 6,134 Coed
Affiliation or Control: State IRS Status: 501(c)3
Highest Offering: Master's
Program: Liberal Arts And General; Teacher Preparatory
Accreditation: NH, BUS, ENGT, MUS, NURSE, PTAA, SW, TED

01 President ... Dr. Robert A. VARTEBEDIAN
05 Provost/VP Academic Affairs ... Dr. Jeanne DAFFRON
30 Vice Pres University Advancement ... Mr. Dan NICOSON
10 VP Financial Plng/Administration ... Mr. Melvin KLINKNER
35 Vice President for Student Affairs ... Dr. Esther PERALEZ
20 Assoc Vice Pres Academic Affairs ... Dr. Cindy HEIDER
21 Assoc VP Finan Plng/Administration ... Mr. Rick GILMORE
32 Dean of Students ... Dr. Judith GRIMES
49 Dean Liberal Arts & Science ... Dr. Murray NABORS
75 Dean Professional Studies ... Vacant
51 Dean of Western Institute ... Dr. Gordon MAPLEY
06 Registrar ... Ms. Susan BRACCIANO
07 Director of Admissions ... Mr. Howard MCCAULEY
08 Director of Library ... Ms. Julia SCHNEIDER
37 Director Student Financial Aid ... Ms. Marilyn BAKER
13 Director of Information Technology ... Mr. Mark MABE
38 Director Student Counsel & Testing ... Mr. H. David BROWN
18 Director Physical Plant ... Mr. Lonnie JOHNSON
41 Director of Athletics ... Vacant
15 Director of Human Resources ... Ms. Sally SANDERS
24 Director of Instructional Media ... Vacant
26 Dir of Public Relations & Marketing ... Mr. Roger SWAFFORD
29 Director of Alumni Services ... Ms. Colleen KOWICH
44 Director of Development ... Mr. Jerry PICKMAN
96 Director of Purchasing ... Ms. Carey MCMILLIAN

Moberly Area Community College (B)

101 College Avenue, Moberly MO 65270-1304
County: Randolph FICE Identification: 002491
Unit ID: 178448
Telephone: (660) 263-4110 Carnegie Class: Assoc/Pub-R-M
FAX Number: (660) 263-6252 Calendar System: Semester
URL: www.macc.edu
Established: 1927 Annual Undergrad Tuition & Fees (In-District): $2,430
Enrollment: 5,446 Coed
Affiliation or Control: State/Local IRS Status: 501(c)3
Highest Offering: Associate Degree
Program: Occupational; 2-Year Principally Bachelor's Creditable
Accreditation: NH, MLTAD, OTA

01 President ... Dr. Evelyn E. JORGENSON
05 Vice President for Instruction ... Dr. Jeffery LASHLEY
10 Vice President for Finance ... Mr. Gary STEFFES
75 Dean of Career/Technical Educ ... Mr. Greg MOSIER
32 Dean of Student Services ... Dr. James GRANT
12 Dean Off-Camp Pgms/Instr Tech ... Ms. Michele MCCALL
20 Dean of Academic Affairs ... Ms. Paula GLOVER
09 Director Inst Effectiveness/Plng ... Mrs. Deanne K. FESSLER
21 Director Business/Accounting Svcs ... Ms. Sandra MAREK
26 Dir of Inst Devel/Mktg/Public Rels ... Mrs. Jaime MORGANS
18 Director of Plant Operations ... Mr. Eric ROSS
14 Director Technology/Computer Svcs ... Mr. Lloyd MARCHANT
08 Director of Library Services ... Ms. Valerie DARST
15 Director of Human Resources ... Ms. Ann PARKS
40 Director of Inst Svcs/Bookstore Mgr ... Ms. Virginia GEBHARDT
37 Director of Financial Aid ... Mrs. Amy HAGER
06 Registrar ... Ms. Lynn WALKER
29 Director Alumni Services ... Mr. Scott MCGARVEY
36 Dir of Career and Technical Pgms ... Ms. Susan BROUK
35 Associate Dean of Student Services ... Vacant

Nazarene Theological Seminary (C)

1700 E Meyer Boulevard, Kansas City MO 64131-1263
County: Jackson FICE Identification: 002494
Unit ID: 178518
Telephone: (816) 268-5400 Carnegie Class: Spec/Faith
FAX Number: (816) 268-5500 Calendar System: Semester
URL: www.nts.edu
Established: 1945 Annual Graduate Tuition & Fees: $7,830
Enrollment: 297 Coed
Affiliation or Control: Church Of The Nazarene IRS Status: 501(c)3
Highest Offering: Doctorate; No Undergraduates
Program: Professional
Accreditation: THEOL

01 President ... Dr. David BUSIC
05 Dean of the Faculty ... Dr. Roger HAHN
11 Dean for Administration ... Dr. D. Martin BUTLER
08 Director Library Service ... Mrs. Debra BRADSHAW
06 Registrar & Director of Admissions ... Mrs. Pamela ASHER
37 Financial Aid Coordinator ... Mr. Derek DAVIS

North Central Missouri College (D)

1301 Main Street, Trenton MO 64683-1824
County: Grundy FICE Identification: 002514
Unit ID: 179715
Telephone: (660) 359-3948 Carnegie Class: Assoc/Pub-R-S
FAX Number: (660) 359-2211 Calendar System: Semester
URL: www.ncmissouri.edu
Established: 1925 Annual Undergrad Tuition & Fees (In-District): $2,928
Enrollment: 1,701 Coed
Affiliation or Control: Local IRS Status: 501(c)3
Highest Offering: Associate Degree
Program: Occupational; 2-Year Principally Bachelor's Creditable
Accreditation: NH, DH

01 President ... Dr. Neil NUTTALL
05 VP Instruction/Student Services ... Dr. James GARDNER
11 Vice Pres Administrative Services ... Ms. Sharon BARNETT
32 Dean of Student Services ... Dr. Kristen ALLEY
20 Dean of Instruction ... Dr. Jamie HOOYMAN
76 Dean Allied Health Sciences ... Ms. Janet VANDERPOOL
06 Registrar ... Ms. Linda BROWN
27 Chief Information Officer ... Mr. Alan BARNETT
08 Librarian ... Ms. Ann SAMPSON
37 Director of Financial Aid ... Ms. Melissa GUESS
30 Director Development ... Mr. Steve MAXEY
40 Director Bookstore ... Ms. Cecilia GRISWOLD
39 Director Student Housing ... Mr. Donnie HILLERMAN
41 Athletic Director ... Mr. Steve RICHMAN
18 Director of Facilities ... Mr. Randy YOUNG
15 Director Human Resources ... Ms. Donna CALLIHAN
101 Sec of Inst/Board of Governors ... Ms. Vicki WEAVER
105 Director Web Services ... Mr. Anthony ALEXANDER
09 Director of Institutional Research ... Ms. Tara NOAH

Northwest Missouri State University (E)

800 University Drive, Maryville MO 64468-6015
County: Nodaway FICE Identification: 002496
Unit ID: 178624
Telephone: (660) 562-1212 Carnegie Class: Master's L
FAX Number: (660) 562-1900 Calendar System: Trimester
URL: www.nwmissouri.edu
Established: 1905 Annual Undergrad Tuition & Fees (In-State): $7,434
Enrollment: 7,142 Coed
Affiliation or Control: State IRS Status: 501(c)3
Highest Offering: Beyond Master's But Less Than Doctorate
Program: Liberal Arts And General; Teacher Preparatory
Accreditation: NH, AAFCS, ACBSP, DIETD, MUS, TED

01 President ... Dr. John JASINSKI
05 Provost ... Dr. Doug DUNHAM
10 Vice Pres for Finance ... Ms. Stacy CARRICK
32 Vice President for Student Affairs ... Vacant
13 Vice Pres for Information Systems ... Dr. Jon T. RICKMAN
26 Vice President University Relations ... Vacant
15 VP Human Resources/Org Effective ... Ms. Mary E. THROENER
35 Dean of Students ... Mr. Matthew BAKER
84 Dean Enrollment Management ... Ms. Beverly S. SCHENKEL
09 Director Strategic Research ... Mr. Nate J. BLACKFORD
08 Dir of Academic & Library Services ... Ms. Leslie GALBREATH
06 Registrar ... Ms. Terri VOGEL
37 Director Financial Aid ... Mr. Del MORLEY
36 Director of Career Services ... Ms. Joan SCHNEIDER
29 Director Alumni Relations ... Mr. Steve SUTTON
19 Chief University Police Department ... Mr. Clarence GREEN
41 Director Athletics/HPERD ... Mr. Wren BAKER
23 Director Wellness Services ... Dr. Gerald WILMES
96 Director of Purchasing ... Ms. Ann MARTIN
18 Director Environmental Services ... Dr. Paul MCGRAW
58 Dean of Graduate School ... Dr. Gregory HADDOCK
53 Dean Col of Education & Human Svcs ... Dr. Joyce PIVERAL
49 Dean Col of Arts & Sciences ... Dr. Charles MCADAMS
50 Dean Col of Business/Prof Studies ... Dr. Thomas BILLESBACH
38 Director Student Counseling Center ... Vacant

Ozark Christian College (F)

1111 N Main Street, Joplin MO 64801-4804
County: Jasper FICE Identification: 022027
Unit ID: 178679
Telephone: (417) 626-1234 Carnegie Class: Spec/Faith
FAX Number: (417) 624-0090 Calendar System: Semester
URL: www.occ.edu
Established: 1942 Annual Undergrad Tuition & Fees: $9,000
Enrollment: 657 Coed
Affiliation or Control: Independent Non-Profit IRS Status: 501(c)3
Highest Offering: Baccalaureate
Program: Religious Emphasis
Accreditation: BI

01 President ... Matt PROCTOR
03 Executive Vice President ... Greg HAFER
04 Assistant to the President ... Kathy BOWERS
05 Interim Academic Dean ... Doug ALDRIDGE
06 Registrar ... Jennifer MCMILLIN
32 Exec Director of Student Devel ... Monte SHOEMAKE
34 Dean of Women ... Lisa WHITE
10 Exec Dir of Business Operations ... David MCMILLIN
07 Executive Director Admissions ... Troy NELSON
09 Dir of Inst Research/ Gen Counsel ... Doug MILLER
26 Director College Events ... Lisa WITTE
29 Dir Alumni/Publications/Conventions ... Meredith WILLIAMS
42 Director Campus Ministry ... Kevin GREER
88 Director of Christian Services ... Doug WELCH
88 Director Youth Minister Relations ... Bob WITTE
08 Director of Library Services ... John HUNTER
37 Director of Student Financial Aid ... Kim BALENTINE
40 Director of Bookstore ... Bob HEATH
41 Athletic Director ... Chris LAHM
90 Director Academic Computing ... David FISH
18 Director Physical Plant ... Bob RASMUSSEN
38 Director Student Counseling ... Sharon ENGELBRECHT
88 Director of Food Services ... Rita PEABODY
13 Director of College Technology Dept ... Mitchell PIERCY
105 Web Developer/Network Admin ... Matt DICKEY
64 Coordinator of Music Department ... Scott HANDLEY
14 Coordinator of Data Processing ... Gary WHEAT

Ozarks Technical Community College (G)

1001 E Chestnut Expressway, Springfield MO 65802-3625
County: Greene FICE Identification: 030830
Unit ID: 177472
Telephone: (417) 447-7500 Carnegie Class: Assoc/Pub-R-L
FAX Number: N/A Calendar System: Semester
URL: www.otc.edu
Established: 1990 Annual Undergrad Tuition & Fees (In-District): $3,180
Enrollment: 13,907 Coed
Affiliation or Control: State/Local IRS Status: 501(c)3
Highest Offering: Associate Degree
Program: Occupational; 2-Year Principally Bachelor's Creditable
Accreditation: NH, ACFEI, ADNUR, DA, DH, IFSAC, MLTAD, OTA, PTAA, SURGT

01 Chancellor ... Dr. Hal L. HIGDON
04 Exec Secretary to Chancellor ... Ms. Karen CREIGHTON
05 Vice Chancellor Academic Affairs ... Dr. Shirley LAWLER
11 Vice Chancellor Admin Services ... Mr. Rob RECTOR
13 Vice Chancellor IT ... Mr. Joel LAREAU
30 Vice Chancellor Inst Advancement ... Mr. Cliff DAVIS
10 Vice Chancellor Finance ... Ms. Marla MOODY
12 President Richwood Valley Campus ... Dr. Jeff JOCHEMS
32 Assoc Chancello Student Services ... Ms. Joan BARRETT
20 Dean of Academic Services ... Dr. Kathy PERKINS
76 Dean of Allied Health Programs ... Dr. Steve BISHOP
97 Interim Dean of General Education ... Dr. Steve BISHOP
56 Dean Extended Campus/Col Outreach ... Ms. Sue MOORE
72 Dean of Technical Education ... Mr. Layton CHILDRESS
08 Dean of Learning Resources ... Mr. Mike MADDEN
103 Exec Dir Ctr Workforce Development ... Ms. Dawn BUSICK
38 Director of Counseling & Advising ... Ms. Joyce THOMAS
26 College Dir Comm & Marketing ... Mr. Joel DOEPKER
18 Director of College Facilities ... Mr. Rick TAYLOR
13 Asst Vice Chancellor IT ... Mr. Gerald BRYANT
14 Director of Computer Services ... Mr. Jack DOZIER
28 Asst Dean Disabilities Support Svcs ... Ms. Julie EDWARDS
37 College Director of Financial Aid ... Mr. Jeff FORD
15 College Director of Human Resources ... Ms. Alice RAMEY
88 Director of Learning Resources Ctr ... Mr. Corky MCCORMACK
36 Director of Career Employment Svcs ... Ms. Kathy CHRISTY
102 Exec Director of OTC Foundation ... Mr. Cliff DAVIS
09 Dir Research/Strategic Planning ... Mr. John CLAYTON
19 Director of Safety & Security ... Mr. Peter ROTHROCK
84 Dir of Recruitment/Enrollment Mgmt ... Ms. Vicki MACDONALD
29 Director of Alumni Relations ... Ms. Stephanie BROWN
56 Coord Dual Credit/Tech Prep Program ... Ms. Cindy PHILLIPS

Park University (H)

8700 River Park Drive, Parkville MO 64152-3795
County: Platte FICE Identification: 002498
Unit ID: 178721
Telephone: (816) 741-2000 Carnegie Class: Master's M
FAX Number: (816) 746-6423 Calendar System: Semester
URL: www.park.edu
Established: 1875 Annual Undergrad Tuition & Fees: $9,240
Enrollment: 12,022 Coed
Affiliation or Control: Independent Non-Profit IRS Status: 501(c)3
Highest Offering: Master's
Program: Liberal Arts And General; Teacher Preparatory; Professional
Accreditation: NH, ADNUR, SW

01 President ... Dr. Michael DROGE
05 Provost & VP Acad Affairs ... Dr. Jerry JORGENSEN
10 Vice President for Finance & Admin ... Ms. Dorla WATKINS
30 Vice Pres University Advancement ... Ms. Laurie MCCORMACK
84 VP Enrollment Mgt/Student Services ... Mr. Alan J. LIEBRECHT
27 Vice President for Communication ... Ms. Rita WEIGHILL
20 Associate VP for Academic Affairs ... Dr. Dan DONALDSON
11 Assoc VP for Administration ... Mr. Brian DAVIS
32 Associate VP for Student Services ... Ms. Clarinda CREIGHTON
44 Asst Vice Pres for Development ... Vacant
32 Dean of Student Life ... Dr. Diana MCELROY

58	Dean School of Grad & Prof Studies	Dr. Laurie DIPADOVA-STOCKS
06	Registrar	Ms. Eileen WEST
07	Assoc Dean Admissions and SFS	Ms. Cathy COLAPIETRO
08	Director of Library Systems	Ms. Ann SCHULTIS
12	Director Park Accelerated Programs	Mr. S. L. SARTAIN
88	Director of Advancement Services	Mrs. Sandra SANDERS
15	Director of Human Resources	Mr. Roger DUSING
29	Directoer of Alumni Relations	Ms. Julie MCCOLLUM
96	Dir or Budget and Purchasing	Ms. Donna BAKER
18	Director of Environmental Services	Mr. Randy BAILEY
41	Director of Athletics	Mr. Claude ENGLISH
66	Director of Nursing Program	Ms. Gerry WALKER
85	Director of Foreign Students	Mr. Michael HERNANDEZ
37	Director Student Financial Services	Ms. Carla BOREN
13	CIO Technical Services	Mr. David MONCHUSIE
09	Director Inst Research & Assessment	Dr. John TEW, JR.
50	Director MBA Program	Dr. Nick KOUDOU
96	Asst Director Purchasing Services	Ms. Alicia THIESSEN
04	Exec Asst to the President	Ms. Laure CHRISTENSEN
26	Director of Marketing	Vacant
25	Director Sponsored Programs	Mr. Edmund BRACKETT
50	Dean School of Business/Mgmt	Dr. Brad KLEINDL
106	Dean Park Distance Learning	Vacant
49	Dean Liberal Arts & Sciences	Dr. Jane WOOD
53	Dean School for Education	Dr. Michelle MYERS
80	Associate Dean HSPA	Dr. Rebekkah STUTEVILLE

Pinnacle Career Institute (A)

1001 E 101st Terrace, Suite 325,
Kansas City MO 64131-3368

County: Jackson — FICE Identification: 010405
Unit ID: 177302
Telephone: (816) 331-5700 — Carnegie Class: Assoc/PrivFP
FAX Number: (816) 331-2026 — Calendar System: Quarter
URL: www.pcitraining.edu
Established: 1952 — Annual Undergrad Tuition & Fees: $13,700
Enrollment: 1,185 — Coed
Affiliation or Control: Proprietary — IRS Status: Proprietary
Highest Offering: Associate Degree
Program: Occupational
Accreditation: **ACCSC**, ACICS

01	Executive Director	Mr. Monte SCHAICH
05	Director of Education	Dr. Guy COGNET
20	Academic Dean	Mr. Larry FAJEN
36	Director Student Placement	Ms. Allison JOHNSON
07	Director of Admissions	Ms. Allison JOHNSON

Ranken Technical College (B)

4431 Finney Avenue, Saint Louis MO 63113-2898

County: Saint Louis — FICE Identification: 012500
Unit ID: 178891
Telephone: (314) 371-0236 — Carnegie Class: Assoc/PrivNFP4
FAX Number: (314) 371-0241 — Calendar System: Semester
URL: www.ranken.edu
Established: 1907 — Annual Undergrad Tuition & Fees: $12,348
Enrollment: 1,938 — Coed
Affiliation or Control: Independent Non-Profit — IRS Status: 501(c)3
Highest Offering: Baccalaureate
Program: Occupational; 2-Year Principally Bachelor's Creditable; Technical Emphasis
Accreditation: **NH**

01	President	Mr. Stan SHOUN
10	Vice President for Finance & Admin	Mr. Peter T. MURTAUGH
05	Vice President for Education	Mr. Don POHL
30	Vice President for Development	Mr. Timothy J. WILLARD
32	Vice President for Student Success	Mr. John WOOD
51	Dean of Continuing Education	Mr. Keyvan GERAMI
20	Dean Academic Affairs	Ms. Crystal HERRON
07	Admissions Director	Mr. Michael E. HAWLEY
06	Registrar	Ms. Carol J. WINKLER
08	Head Librarian	Ms. Barbara EDWARDS
18	Director Buildings & Grounds	Mr. Steve P. HARTGE
29	Director of Alumni Relations	Ms. Kathy T. FERN
37	Director Financial Aid	Ms. Michelle L. WILLIAMS
21	Business Office Manager	Ms. Seletha R. CURTIS
36	Career Services Coordinator	Ms. Janie K. SUMMERS
15	Human Resources Coordinator	Ms. Janice A. BOLLMANN

Research College of Nursing (C)

2525 E Meyer Boulevard, Kansas City MO 64132-1133

County: Jackson — FICE Identification: 006392
Unit ID: 178989
Telephone: (816) 995-2800 — Carnegie Class: Spec/Health
FAX Number: (816) 995-2817 — Calendar System: Semester
URL: www.researchcollege.edu
Established: 1980 — Annual Undergrad Tuition & Fees: $27,770
Enrollment: 463 — Coed
Affiliation or Control: Proprietary — IRS Status: Proprietary
Highest Offering: Master's
Program: Liberal Arts And General; Professional; Nursing Emphasis
Accreditation: **NH**, NURSE

01	President/Dean	Dr. Nancy O. DEBASIO
05	Assoc Dean Academic Programs	Dr. Janet ANDREWS
24	Director LRC	Ms. Tobey STOSBERG
32	Director Student Affairs	Ms. Lori VITALE

Rockhurst University (D)

1100 Rockhurst Road, Kansas City MO 64110-2561

County: Jackson — FICE Identification: 002499
Unit ID: 179043
Telephone: (816) 501-4000 — Carnegie Class: Master's L
FAX Number: (816) 501-4588 — Calendar System: Semester
URL: www.rockhurst.edu
Established: 1910 — Annual Undergrad Tuition & Fees: $28,510
Enrollment: 2,895 — Coed
Affiliation or Control: Roman Catholic — IRS Status: 501(c)3
Highest Offering: Doctorate
Program: Liberal Arts And General; Teacher Preparatory; Professional; Business Emphasis
Accreditation: **NH**, BUS, OT, PTA, SP, TEAC

01	President	Rev. Thomas B. CURRAN, OSFS
30	Vice Pres University Advancement	Mr. Robert GRANT
10	Vice Pres Finance & Administration	Mr. Guy SWANSON
05	Vice Pres for Academic Affairs	Dr. Sharon HOMAN
88	Vice Pres for Mission & Ministry	Vacant
32	VP Student Developmnt/Athletics	Dr. Matthew D. QUICK
11	Assoc VP Facilities & Technology	Mr. Matt W. HEINRICH
84	Associate Vice Pres Enrollment	Mr. Lane RAMEY
35	Director of Student Life	Ms. Angie CARR
88	Assistant Dean of Students	Mrs. Sandy WADDELL
39	Assistant Dean of Students	Mr. Sean GRUBE
04	Assistant to the President	Ms. Kathy J. SOLODUCHA
50	Dean Helzberg School of Management	Dr. James M. DALEY
49	Dean Arts & Sciences	Dr. Timothy MCDONALD
58	Dean School Graduate/Prof Studies	Dr. Jeffrey BREESE
66	Pres/Dean Research Col of Nursing	Dr. Nancy DEBASIO
08	Director Library	Ms. Laurie E. HATHMAN
06	Registrar	Ms. Minda THROWER
37	Director Student Financial Aid	Ms. Angela KARLIN
41	Director of Athletics	Mr. Richard KONZEM
15	Director of Human Resources	Ms. Mary R. BURNETT
14	Director of Infrastructure Services	Mr. Michael CRAIG
36	Director of Career Center	Mr. Michael J. THEOBALD
26	Exec Dir Marketing/Communications	Vacant
29	Director Alumni Rels & Constituent	Mrs. Mary LANDERS
42	Director of Campus Ministry	Ms. Maureen E. HENDERSON
19	Director Security/Safety	Mr. William G. EVANS
38	Director of Student Counseling	Dr. Rick D. HANSON
44	Director of Gift Planning	Mr. Ed FREDENBERG
31	Director Community Relations	Ms. Alicia R. DOUGLAS
40	Director Bookstore	Mr. James GARBARINO
92	Director Honors Program	Dr. Mindy WALKER
45	Assessment Coordinator	Ms. Keli BRAITMAN
44	Senior Development Officer	Ms. Amy DROUIN
09	Institutional Research Coordinator	Ms. Wendy PICKEL
28	Area & Diversity Coordinator	Ms. Emily J. KEMPF
24	Coordinator AV and Media	Mr. Darnell JONES
88	Controller	Ms. Rachel LIERZ

St. Charles Community College (E)

4601 Mid Rivers Mall Drive, Cottleville MO 63376-2865

County: Saint Charles — FICE Identification: 025306
Unit ID: 262031
Telephone: (636) 922-8000 — Carnegie Class: Assoc/Pub-S-SC
FAX Number: (636) 922-8352 — Calendar System: Semester
URL: www.stchas.edu
Established: 1986 — Annual Undergrad Tuition & Fees (In-District): $2,550
Enrollment: 8,290 — Coed
Affiliation or Control: State/Local — IRS Status: 501(c)3
Highest Offering: Associate Degree
Program: Occupational; 2-Year Principally Bachelor's Creditable
Accreditation: **NH**, ADNUR, OTA

01	President	Dr. John M. MCGUIRE
05	Vice Pres Academic/Student Affairs	Dr. Michael L. BANKS
11	Vice Pres for Administrative Svcs	Mr. Todd GALBIERZ
45	Vice Pres for IT/Research/Planning	Dr. Barbara KEIM
15	Vice President for Human Resources	Ms. Donna DAVIS
20	Asst Vice Pres for Academic Affairs	Dr. Michael B. DOMPIERRE
26	Vice President for Marketing & Comm	Ms. Heather MCDORMAN
57	Dean Arts & Humanities	Dr. Denise KING
50	Dean Business & Social Science	Mr. Bill STRECKER
81	Dean Mathematics/Science/Health	Mr. Chris BREITMEYER
31	Dean Corporate & Community Dev	Ms. Yvonne WILLS
08	Dean Learning Resources	Dr. Stephanie TOLSON
04	Exec Assistant to the President	Ms. Julie PARCEL
102	Exec Dir Foundation/Alumni Rels	Ms. Kasey MCKEE
21	Director of Financial Services	Ms. Susan RUBEMEYER
06	Registrar/Director of Admissions	Ms. Kathy BROCKGREITENS
40	Director of Bookstore	Ms. Patricia A. HAYNES
91	Director of Admin Computing	Ms. Floretha J. JOHNSON
07	Director of Admissions	Ms. Kathy BROCKGREITENS
09	Director of Institutional Research	Dr. Ronald PENNINGTON
96	Director of Purchasing	Ms. Christine E. ROMER
41	Athletic Director	Mr. Chris G. GOBER
38	Dean of Student Development	Ms. Yvette M. SWEENEY
51	Assoc Dean Continuing Education	Vacant
103	Director of Workforce Development	Ms. Amanda SIZEMORE
36	Job Placement Coordinator	Ms. Martha A. TOEBBEN
18	Director of Facilities	Mr. Al KOEHLER
37	Director Student Financial Aid	Ms. Kathy BROCKGREITENS
35	Student Activities Coordinator	Ms. Kelley PFEIFFER
84	Dean of Enrollment Services	Ms. Kathy BROCKGREITENS
91	Manager of Academic Computing	Ms. Lisa MOUSER
19	Director of Public Safety	Mr. Bob RONKOSKI

Saint Louis Christian College (F)

1360 Grandview Drive, Florissant MO 63033-6499

County: Saint Louis — FICE Identification: 012580
Unit ID: 179256
Telephone: (314) 837-6777 — Carnegie Class: Spec/Faith
FAX Number: (314) 837-8291 — Calendar System: Semester
URL: www.slcconline.edu
Established: 1956 — Annual Undergrad Tuition & Fees: $650
Enrollment: 337 — Coed
Affiliation or Control: Other Protestant — IRS Status: 501(c)3
Highest Offering: Baccalaureate
Program: 2-Year Principally Bachelor's Creditable; Religious Emphasis
Accreditation: **BI**

00	Chancellor	Mr. Thomas W. MCGEE
01	President	Dr. Guthrie VEECH
05	Academic Dean	Dr. Michael CHAMBERS
10	Vice President of Finance	Dr. Judy LINCOLN
32	Dean of Students	Ms. Christine CABLE
08	Librarian	Mr. Matt DEWITT
41	Athletic Director	Mr. John-Michael BROWN
06	Registrar	Ms. Cindy BINGAMON
07	Director of Admissions	Ms. Carrie CHAPMAN
37	Financial Aid Director	Ms. Cathy WILHOIT
40	Bookstore Co-Manager	Ms. Dawn OTTWELL
40	Bookstore Co-Manager	Ms. Melissa RABIDEAU

Saint Louis College of Health Careers-Fenton Campus (G)

1297 N Highway Drive, Fenton MO 63026-1909

County: Saint Louis — Identification: 666274
Unit ID: 442426
Telephone: (636) 529-0000 — Carnegie Class: Assoc/PrivFP
FAX Number: (636) 529-0430 — Calendar System: Semester
URL: www.slchc.com
Established: 1981 — Annual Undergrad Tuition & Fees: $25,750
Enrollment: 261 — Coed
Affiliation or Control: Proprietary — IRS Status: Proprietary
Highest Offering: Associate Degree
Program: Occupational
Accreditation: **ABHES**

01	Chief Executive Officer	Mr. Steven N. BARSAM
05	Dean of Nursing & Allied Health	Ms. Nancy K. KAUFMANN

† Branch campus of Saint Louis College of Health Careers-South Taylor, Saint Louis, MO.

Saint Louis College of Health Careers-South Taylor (H)

909 S Taylor Avenue, Saint Louis MO 63110-1511

County: Saint Louis — FICE Identification: 023405
Unit ID: 179511
Telephone: (314) 652-0300 — Carnegie Class: Assoc/PrivFP
FAX Number: (314) 652-2125 — Calendar System: Semester
URL: www.slchc.com
Established: 1981 — Annual Undergrad Tuition & Fees: $14,750
Enrollment: 529 — Coed
Affiliation or Control: Proprietary — IRS Status: Proprietary
Highest Offering: Associate Degree
Program: Occupational
Accreditation: **ABHES**

01	Associate Dean	Lou VIDOVIC
05	Director of Education	Michelle YEAGER

St. Louis College of Pharmacy (I)

4588 Parkview Place, Saint Louis MO 63110-1088

County: Independent City — FICE Identification: 002504
Unit ID: 179265
Telephone: (314) 367-8700 — Carnegie Class: Spec/Health
FAX Number: (314) 446-8304 — Calendar System: Semester
URL: www.stlcop.edu
Established: 1864 — Annual Undergrad Tuition & Fees: $26,334
Enrollment: 1,241 — Coed
Affiliation or Control: Independent Non-Profit — IRS Status: 501(c)3
Highest Offering: First Professional Degree
Program: Professional
Accreditation: **NH**, PHAR

01	President	Dr. John A. PIEPER
30	Vice Pres Devel/Alumni Relations	Mr. Brett T. SCHOTT
10	VP Finance/Administration/CFO	Mr. Gary G. TORRENCE
07	Vice Pres of Enrollment Services	Ms. Gloria J. VERTREES
90	Vice Pres Info Technology & CIO	Mr. Chad SHEPHERD
49	Dean Arts & Science/Student Affairs	Dr. Kimberly J. KILGORE
67	Dean of Pharmacy	Dr. Wendy DUNCAN
15	Director of Human Resources	Mr. Daniel C. BAUER
06	Registrar	Ms. Penny J. BRYANT
08	Library Director	Ms. Jill NISSEN
37	Director of Financial Aid	Mr. Daniel J. STIFFLER
36	Director of Placement Services	Vacant
18	Chief Facilities/Physical Plant	Mr. Al FARROW
26	Vice President Mktg/Communications	Mr. Marcus LONG
29	Director Devel/Alumni Relations	Ms. Necole POWELL
41	Director of Athletics	Ms. Jill JOKERST-HARTER
04	Special Assistant to the President	Sr. Mary Louise DEGENHART

Saint Louis Community College Center (A)

300 S Broadway, Saint Louis MO 63102-2820
County: Saint Louis | FICE Identification: 002469
Unit ID: 179283
Telephone: (314) 539-5000 | Carnegie Class: N/A
FAX Number: (314) 539-5170
URL: www.stlcc.edu

01 Chancellor ... Dr. Myrtle E B. DORSEY
05 Vice Chanc Academic & Stdnt Affairs ... Dr. Donna DARE
10 Vice Chanc Finance/Business Svcs ... Ms. Carla S. CHANCE
13 Vice Chancellor Technology ... Dr. Craig KLIMCZAK
103 Vice Chanc Workforce & Cmty Develop ... Mr. Rod NUNN
102 Executive Director Foundation ... Ms. Jo-Ann DIGMAN
84 Director Enrollment Management ... Dr. Joanie FRIEND
21 Controller ... Mr. Bruce VOGELGESANG
15 Acting Director Human Resources ... Mr. Roy SHANEBERGER
26 Director Communications ... Mr. DeLancey SMITH
09 Director of Institutional Research ... Mr. John J. COSGROVE
20 Director Instructional Resources ... Vacant
30 Director Institutional Development ... Ms. Castella HENDERSON
06 Manager Central Student Records ... Ms. Lauren ROBERDS

Saint Louis Community College at Florissant Valley (B)

3400 Pershall Road, Saint Louis MO 63135-1499
County: Saint Louis | FICE Identification: 002470
Unit ID: 179292
Telephone: (314) 513-4200 | Carnegie Class: Assoc/Pub-U-MC
FAX Number: N/A | Calendar System: Semester
URL: www.stlcc.edu
Established: 1962 | Annual Undergrad Tuition & Fees (In-District): $1,992
Enrollment: 7,438 | Coed
Affiliation or Control: Local | IRS Status: 501(c)3
Highest Offering: Associate Degree
Program: Occupational; 2-Year Principally Bachelor's Creditable
Accreditation: &NH, ADNUR, ART, DIETT, ENGT

02 President ... Dr. Marcia F. PFEIFFER
05 Vice President Academic Affairs ... Mr. Ashok AGRAWAL
32 Vice President Student Affairs ... Ms. Laura F. STERMAN
50 Dean Business/Human Development ... Ms. Ruby CURRY
49 Dean Liberal Arts ... Dr. Nancy LINZY
81 Interim Dean Math/Sci/Engineering ... Ms. Ellene LYONS
04 Executive Assistant to President ... Ms. Adria WERNER
31 Community Relations Director ... Ms. Kedra TOLSON
06 Registrar ... Ms. Brenda DAVENPORT
21 Manager Business Services ... Mr. Douglas MAHONEY
18 Manager Facilities/Physical Plant ... Mr. John FERLISI
37 Manager of Student Aid ... Ms. Khaneetah CUNNINGHAM
35 Manager Campus Life ... Ms. Gwen NIXON
36 Coordinator Career & Employment ... Ms. Michela WALSH
84 Coordinator Enrollment Management ... Ms. Janice FITZGERALD
29 Coordinator Alumni Relations ... Vacant
38 Department Chair Counseling ... Dr. Joe WORTH

*Saint Louis Community College at Forest Park (C)

5600 Oakland Avenue, Saint Louis MO 63110-1393
County: Independent City | FICE Identification: 002471
Unit ID: 179308
Telephone: (314) 644-9100 | Carnegie Class: Assoc/Pub-U-MC
FAX Number: (314) 644-9752 | Calendar System: Semester
URL: www.stlcc.edu
Established: 1962 | Annual Undergrad Tuition & Fees (In-District): $2,112
Enrollment: 8,721 | Coed
Affiliation or Control: Local | IRS Status: 501(c)3
Highest Offering: Associate Degree
Program: Occupational; 2-Year Principally Bachelor's Creditable
Accreditation: &NH, ACFEI, ADNUR, DA, DH, DMS, FUSER, MLTAD, RAD, SURGT

02 President ... Dr. Cindy K. HESS
05 Vice President Academic Affairs ... Dr. Tracy HALL
32 Vice President Student Affairs ... Dr. Thomas WALKER, JR.
83 Dean Hum/Social Sci/Soc Pgms ... Vacant
76 Dean Allied Health/Natural Science ... Ms. Patricia MCEWEN
50 Dean Business/Math/Technology ... Ms. Brenda RUSSELL
38 Chair of Counseling ... Ms. Marlene RHODES
27 Manager Campus Community Relations ... Ms. Claudia PERRY
19 College Police Chief ... Mr. Richard BANAHAN
10 Manager Campus Business Office ... Ms. Chitra SUBRAMANIAN
36 Manager Career & Employment Svcs ... Mr. Davis MOORE
37 Manager of Student Aid ... Ms. Paulette JOHNSON
51 Manager Continuing Education ... Ms. Kim PORTER

*Saint Louis Community College at Meramec (D)

11333 Big Bend Rd., Kirkwood MO 63122-5799
County: Saint Louis | FICE Identification: 002472
Unit ID: 179113
Telephone: (314) 984-7500 | Carnegie Class: Assoc/Pub-U-MC
FAX Number: (314) 984-7006 | Calendar System: Semester
URL: www.stlcc.edu
Established: 1962 | Annual Undergrad Tuition & Fees (In-District): $2,112
Enrollment: 11,439 | Coed
Affiliation or Control: Local | IRS Status: 501(c)3
Highest Offering: Associate Degree
Program: Occupational; 2-Year Principally Bachelor's Creditable
Accreditation: &NH, ADNUR, ART, OTA, PTAA

02 President ... Mr. George WASSON
05 Acting VP Academic Affairs ... Dr. Vernon M. KAYS
32 VP Student Affairs ... Ms. Linden G. CRAWFORD
50 Dean Business Administration ... Ms. Donna SNEED
81 Acting Dean Communications & Math ... Dr. Angela GRUPAS
79 Dean Humanities/Social Sciences ... Dr. Yvonne J. JOHNSON
72 Dean Science & Technology ... Dr. Andrew M. LANGREHR
26 Coordinator Community Relations ... Ms. Toni L. OPLT
21 Manager Business Office ... Mr. Ron L. ROMER
37 Manager Financial Aid ... Mr. Michael T. SMITH
08 Sr Mgr Library/Instruct Resources ... Ms. Bonnie K. SANGUINET
12 Manager South County Educ Center ... Ms. Claudia J. POTTS
35 Manager Student Activities ... Mr. Steven D. BRADY
19 College Police Chief ... Mr. Paul J. BANTA
40 Manager Auxiliary Services ... Mr. Kevin P. METZLER
36 Manager Career/Employ Services ... Ms. Jacqueline D. MEADERS-BOOTH
18 Manager Buildings & Grounds ... Mr. Willie WRIGHT
06 Manager Admissions/Registration ... Dr. Michael CUNDIFF
38 Acting Chair Dept of Counseling ... Ms. Donna ZUMWINKEL
91 Mgr Technology Support Svcs ... Ms. Sharon K. SWAN

*Saint Louis Community College at Wildwood (E)

2645 Generations Drive, Wildwood MO 63040-1168
County: Saint Louis | Identification: 667084
Unit ID: 450137
Telephone: (636) 422-2000 | Carnegie Class: Assoc/Pub-U-MC
FAX Number: (636) 422-2020 | Calendar System: Semester
URL: www.stlcc.edu
Established: 1962 | Annual Undergrad Tuition & Fees (In-District): $2,112
Enrollment: 1,500 | Coed
Affiliation or Control: Local | IRS Status: 501(c)3
Highest Offering: Associate Degree
Program: Occupational; 2-Year Principally Bachelor's Creditable
Accreditation: &NH

02 President ... Ms. Pam MCINTYRE
05 Vice President Academic Affairs ... Dr. Patrick VAUGHN
32 Director of Student Affairs ... Ms. Marilyn TARAS
26 Coordinator of Community Relations ... Ms. Trish AUMANN
18 Manager of Physical Facilities ... Mr. John TETSTILL
40 Manager of Campus Auxiliary Svcs ... Ms. Ellen GOUGH
04 Executive Asst to the President ... Ms. Judy BROUK

Saint Louis University (F)

One Grand Boulevard, Saint Louis MO 63103-2097
County: Independent City | FICE Identification: 002506
Unit ID: 179159
Telephone: (314) 977-2500 | Carnegie Class: RU/H
FAX Number: (314) 977-3874 | Calendar System: Semester
URL: www.slu.edu
Established: 1818 | Annual Undergrad Tuition & Fees: $33,986
Enrollment: 17,709 | Coed
Affiliation or Control: Roman Catholic | IRS Status: 501(c)3
Highest Offering: Doctorate
Program: Liberal Arts And General; Teacher Preparatory; Professional
Accreditation: NH, AAB, ARCPA, BUS, CLPSY, CYTO, DENT, DIETD, DIETI, ENG, HSA, LAW, MED, MFCD, MT, NMT, NURSE, OT, PH, PTA, RTT, SP, SPAA, SW, TED

01 President ... Rev. Lawrence BIONDI, SJ
12 Vice President for Frost Campus ... Dr. Manoj PATANKAR
10 Vice Pres/Chief Financial Officer ... Mr. Bob WOODRUFF
88 Vice Pres Facilities Mgt/Civic Affs ... Ms. Kathleen BRADY
12 Rector Madrid Campus ... Rev. Frank REALE, SJ
16 Vice Pres Human Resources ... Mr. Kenneth FLEISCHMANN
30 VP Advancement/Univ Relations ... Mr. Jeffrey FOWLER
43 Vice President/General Counsel ... Mr. William R. KAUFFMAN
32 Vice President Student Development ... Dr. Kent PORTERFIELD
42 Vice President Mission & Ministry ... Rev. Frank REALE, SJ
13 Vice Pres Information Tech Svcs/CIO ... Mr. Tim BROOKS
23 Vice President for Health Sciences ... Dr. Philip O. ALDERSON
26 Assoc VP University Mtkg/Communicat ... Mr. Jeffrey L. FOWLER
29 Assoc VP for Alumni Relations ... Ms. Meg CONNOLLY
21 Controller ... Mr. David HELMBURGER
35 Associate VP and Dean of Students ... Vacant
54 Assoc Dean Parks Col Engr/Aviation ... Dr. Krishnaswamy RAVINDRA
76 Dean Doisy College of Health Scis ... Dr. Charlotte ROYEEN
49 Dean Arts & Sciences ... Rev. Michael BARBER, SJ
50 Dean Cook School of Business ... Dr. Ellen F. HARSHMAN
61 Dean of Law ... Ms. Annette CLARK
63 Dean of Medical School ... Dr. Philip O. ALDERSON
79 Dean Philosophy & Letters ... Rev. Michael D. BARBER, SJ
69 Interim Dean of Public Health ... Dr. Homer SCHMITZ
53 Int Dean Col of Educ & Public Svc ... Dr. Gerard FOWLER
08 University Librarian ... Dr. Gail STAINES
88 Exec Dir Ctr for Health Care Ethics ... Dr. Jeffrey BISHOP
52 Exec Dir Ctr Advanced Dental Educ ... Dr. Rolf G. BEHRENTS
46 Vice President for Research ... Dr. Raymond TAIT
19 Director Public Safety ... Mr. Michael LAUER
06 Int University Registrar ... Ms. Cari S. WICKLIFFE
07 Dean of Undergraduate Admission ... Ms. Jean GILMAN
37 Director Financial Aid ... Ms. Cari S. WICKLIFFE
39 Int Director Housing & Res Life ... Dr. Scott SMITH
41 Athletics Director ... Mr. Christopher V. MAY
36 Director Career Services ... Ms. Kim REITTER
28 Dir Diversity/Affirmative Action ... Ms. Jennifer SCHEESSELE
85 Director International Center ... Dr. Robert BARRY
92 Director Honors Program ... Dr. Elizabeth CALLAHAN
23 Director Student Health Center ... Ms. Deborah M. SCHEFF
31 Pgm Mgr Leadership Community Svcs ... Mr. Robert WASSEL
88 Director Internal Audit ... Ms. Elizabeth A. WINCHESTER
04 Assistant to the President ... Ms. Bridget FLETCHER
88 Director Univ Museums/Galleries ... Dr. Petruta LIPAN
44 Director Planned Giving ... Mr. Kent G. LEVAN
40 Manager Bookstore ... Ms. Debbie SCHNEIDER
96 Manager of Purchasing ... Ms. Janice CRAWFORD
09 Assistant Vice President ... Dr. Steven SANCHEZ

Saint Luke's College of Health Sciences (G)

8320 Ward Parkway, Suite 300,
Kansas City MO 64114-2042
County: Jackson | FICE Identification: 009782
Unit ID: 179450
Telephone: (816) 932-2367 | Carnegie Class: Spec/Health
FAX Number: (816) 932-9064 | Calendar System: Semester
URL: www.saintlukescollege.edu
Established: 1991 | Annual Undergrad Tuition & Fees: $12,982
Enrollment: 127 | Coed
Affiliation or Control: Independent Non-Profit | IRS Status: 501(c)3
Highest Offering: Baccalaureate
Program: Nursing Emphasis
Accreditation: NH, NURSE

01 President ... Dr. Dean L. HUBBARD
10 Chief Financial Officer ... Ms. Marcia LADAGE
09 Director of Institutional Research ... Ms. Tere E. NAYLOR
05 Academic Dean ... Dr. Jim HAUSCHILDT
07 Director Admissions ... Mr. Josh RICHARDS
06 Registrar ... Ms. Jean SUMMERS

Saint Paul School of Theology (H)

5123 E. Truman Road, Kansas City MO 64127-2499
County: Jackson | FICE Identification: 002509
Unit ID: 179317
Telephone: (816) 483-9600 | Carnegie Class: Spec/Faith
FAX Number: (816) 483-9605 | Calendar System: Other
URL: www.spst.edu
Established: 1958 | Annual Graduate Tuition & Fees: $16,650
Enrollment: 272 | Coed
Affiliation or Control: United Methodist | IRS Status: 501(c)3
Highest Offering: Doctorate; No Undergraduates
Program: Professional; Religious Emphasis
Accreditation: NH, THEOL

01 President ... Dr. Myron F. MCCOY
03 VP Support Services ... Rev. Larry WILLIAMS
05 VP Academic Affairs/Dean ... Dr. Don COMPIER
20 Associate Dean ... Dr. Suzanne MCLAUGHLIN
30 Vice President for Development ... Vacant
10 Chief Financial Officer ... Ms. Laura SNOW
12 Academic Dean for OCU Extens Site ... Dr. Elaine ROBINSON
08 Librarian ... Dr. Logan S. WRIGHT
07 Director of Admissions ... Rev. Lee JOHNSON
04 Executive Assistant to President ... Ms. Leigh PRECISE
26 Director of Communications ... Ms. Heather CHAMBERLIN

Sanford-Brown College (I)

1345 Smizer Mill Road, Fenton MO 63026-3400
County: Saint Louis | FICE Identification: 022052
Unit ID: 179201
Telephone: (636) 651-1600 | Carnegie Class: Bac/Assoc
FAX Number: (636) 651-1732 | Calendar System: Quarter
URL: www.sanfordbrown.edu/Fenton
Established: 1866 | Annual Undergrad Tuition & Fees: $24,220
Enrollment: 2,705 | Coed
Affiliation or Control: Proprietary | IRS Status: Proprietary
Highest Offering: Baccalaureate
Program: Occupational; 2-Year Principally Bachelor's Creditable; Liberal Arts And General
Accreditation: ACICS, DMS, MAAB, POLYT, RAD

01 Campus President ... Ms. Melissa MANGOLD
10 Vice President of Finance ... Mr. Jim REICH
12 Campus President-Collinsville ... Ms. Tina SEIDEL
12 Campus President-Hazelwood ... Ms. Phyllis FORNEY
12 Campus President-St. Peters ... Ms. Julia LEEMAN
27 Information Technology Manager ... Mr. Wade THURMOND
07 Director of Admissions ... Mr. Henry GAMEL
37 Director Student Financial Aid ... Ms. Amy KETTS

Sanford-Brown College (J)

75 Village Square, Hazelwood MO 63042-1817
County: Saint Louis | Identification: 666456
Unit ID: 406264
Telephone: (314) 687-2900 | Carnegie Class: Assoc/PrivFP
FAX Number: (314) 731-0550 | Calendar System: Quarter
URL: www.sanfordbrown.edu/Hazelwood
Established: 1982 | Annual Undergrad Tuition & Fees: $10,220
Enrollment: 942 | Coed

Affiliation or Control: Proprietary IRS Status: Proprietary
Highest Offering: Associate Degree
Program: Occupational
Accreditation: **ACICS**, MAAB, OTA

01 Director .... Dr. Phyllis FORNEY
07 Vice Presidnet Admissions .... Eric STONEKING

Sanford-Brown College (A)

100 Richmond Center Boulevard,
Saint Peters MO 63376-5950
County: Saint Charles Identification: 666458
Unit ID: 409829
Telephone: (636) 696-2300 Carnegie Class: Spec/Health
FAX Number: (636) 696-2067 Calendar System: Quarter
URL: www.sanfordbrown.edu/St-Peters
Established: 1982 Annual Undergrad Tuition & Fees: $10,578
Enrollment: 748 Coed
Affiliation or Control: Proprietary IRS Status: Proprietary
Highest Offering: Baccalaureate
Program: Occupational
Accreditation: **ACICS**, MAAB, SURTEC

01 Campus President .... Ms. Lisa MANCINI

† Branch campus of Sanford-Brown College, Fenton, MO.

The School of Professional Psychology at Forest Institute (B)

2885 West Battlefield Road, Springfield MO 65807-1445
County: Greene FICE Identification: 021642
Unit ID: 177427
Telephone: (800) 424-7793 Carnegie Class: Spec/Health
FAX Number: (417) 823-3442 Calendar System: Semester
URL: www.forest.edu
Established: 1979 Annual Graduate Tuition & Fees: $28,000
Enrollment: 260 Coed
Affiliation or Control: Independent Non-Profit IRS Status: 501(c)3
Highest Offering: Doctorate; No Undergraduates
Program: Professional
Accreditation: **NH**, #CLPSY, IPSY, MFCD

01 President .... Dr. Mark SKRADE
05 Director of Clinical Training .... Dr. Michael LEFTWICH
08 Director of Library Services .... Ms. Nan HADLEY
32 Director Student & Alumni Services .... Vacant
06 Registrar .... Ms. Carolyn SMITH
07 Vice Pres of Enrollment Services .... Ms. Dawn MEDLEY

Southeast Missouri Hospital College of Nursing and Health Sciences (C)

2001 William Street, 2nd Floor,
Cape Girardeau MO 63703-5815
County: Cape Girardeau FICE Identification: 030709
Unit ID: 417734
Telephone: (573) 334-6825 Carnegie Class: Assoc/PrivNFP
FAX Number: (573) 339-7805 Calendar System: Other
URL: www.southeastmissourihospitalcollege.edu
Established: 1990 Annual Undergrad Tuition & Fees: $145
Enrollment: 140 Coed
Affiliation or Control: Independent Non-Profit IRS Status: 501(c)3
Highest Offering: Associate Degree
Program: 2-Year Principally Bachelor's Creditable; Nursing Emphasis
Accreditation: **NH**, ADNUR, MT, RAD

01 President .... Dr. Tonya BUTTRY

Southeast Missouri State University (D)

One University Plaza, Cape Girardeau MO 63701-4799
County: Cape Girardeau FICE Identification: 002501
Unit ID: 179557
Telephone: (573) 651-2000 Carnegie Class: Master's L
FAX Number: (573) 651-2200 Calendar System: Semester
URL: www.semo.edu
Established: 1873 Annual Undergrad Tuition & Fees (In-State): $6,555
Enrollment: 11,112 Coed
Affiliation or Control: State IRS Status: 501(c)3
Highest Offering: Beyond Master's But Less Than Doctorate
Program: Liberal Arts And General; Teacher Preparatory; Professional
Accreditation: **NH**, BUS, CACREP, CS, DIETD, DIETI, ENG, ENGT, #JOUR, MUS, NAIT, NRPA, NURSE, SP, SW, TED

01 President .... Dr. Kenneth W. DOBBINS
05 Provost .... Dr. Ronald ROSATI
10 VP Finance & Administration .... Mrs. Kathy M. MANGELS
84 VP Enrollment Mgmt & Stdnt Success .... Dr. Dennis HOLT
30 Vice Pres University Advancement .... Mr. Bill HOLLAND
20 Sr Associate Provost .... Dr. Bill EDDLEMAN
04 Assistant to the President .... Ms. Diane O. SIDES
22 Int Asst to Pres Equity & Div Iss .... Ms. Sophia SCOTT
13 Asst Vice Pres Information Tech .... Mr. Archie SPRENGEL
56 Interim Dean Online & Ext Lrng .... Dr. Allen GATHMAN
58 Dean Sch of Grad Studies .... Dr. Bill EDDLEMAN
72 Int Dean Sch of Polytech Studies .... Dr. Chris MCGOWAN
50 Dean DL Harrison College Business .. Dr. Gerald S. MCDOUGALL
53 Interim Dean College of Education .... Dr. Tamela RANDOLPH
76 Dean College Health & Human Svc .... Dr. Loretta PRATER
79 Dean College of Liberal Arts .... Dr. Francisco BARRIOS
72 Dean College of Science & Math .... Dr. Chris MCGOWAN
32 Dean of Students .... Dr. Dennis HOLT
88 Dean Univ Studies & Acad Info Svcs .... Dr. David STARRETT
07 Asst VP & Director of Admissions .... Dr. Debbie BELOW
35 Director of Campus Life .... Ms. Michele IRBY
26 Director Marketing & Univ Relations .... Ms. Karen GREBING
41 Interim Director of Athletics .... Ms. Cindy GANNON
29 Director Alumni Services .... Mr. Shad BURNER
85 Exec Dir Intl Education & Svcs .... Mr. Zahir AHMED
51 Dir Extended & Continuing Education .... Ms. Joyce D. BECKER
12 Director Malden Campus .... Dr. Rick HUX
12 Director Kennett Campus .... Ms. Marsha L. BLANCHARD
12 Director Sikeston Campus .... Ms. Judith K. BUCK
18 Director of Facilities Management .... Ms. Angela MEYER
37 Director of Financial Aid .... Ms. Karen WALKER
09 Director of Institutional Research .... Dr. Patricia C. RYAN
27 Director of News Bureau .... Ms. Ann K. HAYES
15 Director of Human Resources .... Mr. Jim COOK
19 Director of Public Safety/Transit .... Mr. Doug RICHARDS
06 Registrar .... Ms. Sandy L. HINKLE
39 Director of Housing & Dining .... Dr. Bruce SKINNER
88 Director of Show Me Center .... Mr. David B. ROSS
21 Director of Business Operations .... Ms. Laura D. STOCK
89 Director of Student Transitions .... Ms. Theresa HAUG-BELVIN
92 Director University Honors Program .... Dr. Craig W. ROBERTS
38 Dir Counseling & Disability Svcs .... Mr. Bob LEFEBVRE
96 Director of Purchasing .... Ms. Sarah STEINNERD

Southwest Baptist University (E)

1600 University Avenue, Bolivar MO 65613-2597
County: Polk FICE Identification: 002502
Unit ID: 179326
Telephone: (417) 328-5281 Carnegie Class: Master's L
FAX Number: (417) 328-1514 Calendar System: Semester
URL: www.sbuniv.edu
Established: 1878 Annual Undergrad Tuition & Fees: $17,400
Enrollment: 3,669 Coed
Affiliation or Control: Southern Baptist IRS Status: 501(c)3
Highest Offering: Doctorate
Program: Liberal Arts And General; Teacher Preparatory; Professional
Accreditation: **NH**, ACBSP, ADNUR, MUS, NUR, PTA, @SW

01 President .... Dr. Pat TAYLOR
05 Provost .... Dr. Bill BROWN
11 Vice President Administration .... Mr. Ron MAUPIN
30 Vice President University Relations .... Vacant
84 Vice Pres Enrollment Management .... Dr. Stephanie MILLER
13 Vice Pres Computer/Info Services .... Dr. Robert MCGLASSON
20 Associate Provost .... Dr. Allison LANGFORD
44 Director Estate Planning .... Vacant
29 Director Alumni & Church Relations .... Mrs. Lindsay SCHINDLER
07 Director Admissions .... Mr. Darren CROWDER
41 Athletic Director .... Mr. Mike PITTS
06 Registrar .... Mr. John CREDILLE
32 Dean Student Development .... Mr. Rob HARRIS
35 Director Student Activities .... Mr. Nathan PENLAND
39 Director Residence Life .... Ms. Landee NEVILLS
42 Director University Ministries .... Mr. Kurt CADDY
15 Director of Human Resources .... Mr. David PIERCE
18 Director Physical Plant .... Mr. Bob GLIDWELL
19 Director Campus Security .... Mr. Mark GRABOWSKI
08 Director of Library Services .... Mr. Ed WALTON
50 Dean College Business/Computer Sci .... Dr. Kenneth BANDY
73 Dean College Theology/Ministry .... Dr. Rodney REEVES
53 Dean Education/Social Sciences .... Dr. Linda WOODERSON
57 Dean Music/Arts/Letters .... Dr. Jeff WATERS
81 Dean Science/Math .... Dr. Perry TOMPKINS
36 Director of Career Services .... Mrs. Suzanne POWERS
14 Director Computer Services .... Mr. Kevin KELLEY
90 Director Institutional Computing .... Mr. Jeffery H. HOGUE
91 Director Administrative Computing .... Mr. David BOLTON
38 Director Counseling Services .... Mrs. Pearlene BRESHEARS
37 Director Student Financial Planning .... Mr. Brad GAMBLE
26 Chief Public Relations Officer .... Mrs. Sharina SMITH
09 Director of Institutional Research .... Mr. Jason VAUGHN
96 Director of Purchasing .... Vacant
40 Book Store Manager .... Mr. Walter TREDWAY

State Fair Community College (F)

3201 W 16th Street, Sedalia MO 65301-2199
County: Pettis FICE Identification: 008080
Unit ID: 179539
Telephone: (660) 530-5800 Carnegie Class: Assoc/Pub-R-M
FAX Number: (660) 530-5820 Calendar System: Semester
URL: www.sfccmo.edu
Established: 1966 Annual Undergrad Tuition & Fees (In-District): $2,700
Enrollment: 4,823 Coed
Affiliation or Control: Local IRS Status: 501(c)3
Highest Offering: Associate Degree
Program: Occupational; 2-Year Principally Bachelor's Creditable
Accreditation: **NH**, CONST, DH, NAIT, OTA, RAD

01 President .... Dr. Marsha K. DRENNON
05 VP for Educ/Student Support Svcs .... Dr. Brent BATES
10 VP for Finance/Administration & HR .... Mr. Garry SORRELL
32 VP for Institutional Advancement .... Dr. Michael Lee ASH
13 CIO Information Systems & Tech .... Mr. Mark HAVERLY
20 Dean of Academic Affairs .... Dr. Craig KLEIN
30 Exec Director for Development .... Ms. Jackie ALMQUIST
09 Director Institutional Planning .... Mrs. Patricia GILLMAN
06 Registrar .... Mrs. Jennifer WILBANKS
37 Director of Financial Aid .... Mr. John MATTHEWS
18 Chief Facilities/Physical Plant .... Mr. Steve KUCYNDA
21 Associate Business Officer .... Mrs. Diane BROCKMAN
26 Director of Marketing/Communication .... Mrs. Dana KELCHNER
38 Interm Dean Student Support .... Mr. Joe GILGOUR
07 Director of Admissions .... Mr. Mark CARTER

Stephens College (G)

1200 E Broadway, Columbia MO 65215-0001
County: Boone FICE Identification: 002512
Unit ID: 179548
Telephone: (573) 442-2211 Carnegie Class: Bac/Diverse
FAX Number: (573) 876-7248 Calendar System: Semester
URL: www.stephens.edu
Established: 1833 Annual Undergrad Tuition & Fees: $26,420
Enrollment: 1,123 Female
Affiliation or Control: Independent Non-Profit IRS Status: 501(c)3
Highest Offering: Master's
Program: Liberal Arts And General; Teacher Preparatory; Professional
Accreditation: **NH**, IACBE

01 President .... Dr. Dianne LYNCH
10 Vice Pres Finance/Business/CFO .... Ms. Lindi OVERTON
05 Vice President Academic Affairs .... Dr. Mary C. HASSINGER
30 Vice President of Philanthropy .... Ms. Shannon WALLS
32 Vice President for Student Services .... Ms. Deborah DUREN
26 VP of Marketing/Public Relations .... Ms. Amy GIPSON
84 Vice Pres Enrollment Management .... Mr. Chris COLLIER
49 Dean of Liberal Arts .... Ms. Mimi HEDGES
51 Dean of Grad & Continuing Studies .... Ms. Suzanne SHARP
29 Director of Alumnae/Board Relations .... Ms. Kathryn ADAMS
06 Registrar .... Ms. Linda SHARP
13 IT Director .... Mr. Mark BRUNNER
16 Director Human Resources .... Mr. Richard ENYARD
36 Director Career Development .... Ms. Amanda ROBERTS
41 Athletic Director .... Ms. Deborah DUREN
44 Director Annual/Planned Giving .... Vacant
07 Director of Recruitment .... Ms. Jennifer DEAVER
21 Controller .... Ms. Mary HAYDEN
37 Financial Aid Coordinator .... Ms. Gena BOLING
09 Dir of Institutional Research .... Ms. Ann ROGERS
39 Director of Residence Life .... Ms. Lory ARNOLD
23 Director of Health Services .... Ms. Brenda MCSHERRY
08 Library Dir/Tech Svcs Librarian .... Ms. Corrie HUTCHINSON

Stevens Institute of Business & Arts (H)

1521 Washington Avenue, Saint Louis MO 63103
County: Saint Louis FICE Identification: 008552
Unit ID: 178767
Telephone: (314) 421-0949 Carnegie Class: Bac/Diverse
FAX Number: (314) 421-0304 Calendar System: Quarter
URL: www.siba.edu
Established: 1947 Annual Undergrad Tuition & Fees: $16,200
Enrollment: 200 Coed
Affiliation or Control: Proprietary IRS Status: Proprietary
Highest Offering: Baccalaureate
Program: Occupational
Accreditation: **ACICS**

01 President .... Ms. Cynthia A. MUSTERMAN
05 Academic Dean & Registrar .... Ms. Ruth Ann HOLTMANN
37 Director of Financial Aid .... Mr. Gregory M. ELSENRATH
07 Director of Admissions .... Mr. John WILLMON

Texas County Technical College (I)

6915 S Highway 63 PO Box 314, Houston MO 65483
County: Texas FICE Identification: 035793
Unit ID: 441487
Telephone: (417) 967-5466 Carnegie Class: Not Classified
FAX Number: (417) 967-4604 Calendar System: Semester
URL: www.texascountytech.edu
Established: 1986 Annual Undergrad Tuition & Fees: $16,979
Enrollment: 222 Coed
Affiliation or Control: Independent Non-Profit IRS Status: 501(c)3
Highest Offering: Associate Degree
Program: Occupational; 2-Year Principally Bachelor's Creditable
Accreditation: **ACICS**

01 President .... Ms. Charlotte GRAY
07 Director of Admissions/Registrar .... Ms. Clarice CASEBEER
37 Acting Financial Aid Director .... Ms. Clarice CASEBEER

Three Rivers Community College (J)

2080 Three Rivers Boulevard,
Poplar Bluff MO 63901-2350
County: Butler FICE Identification: 004713
Unit ID: 179645
Telephone: (573) 840-9600 Carnegie Class: Assoc/Pub-R-M
FAX Number: (573) 840-9604 Calendar System: Semester
URL: www.trcc.edu
Established: 1966 Annual Undergrad Tuition & Fees (In-State): $2,670

Enrollment: 3,732 Coed
Affiliation or Control: State IRS Status: 501(c)3
Highest Offering: Associate Degree
Program: Occupational; 2-Year Principally Bachelor's Creditable
Accreditation: NH, ACBSP, ADNUR, MLTAD

01 President .... Dr. Devin STEPHENSON
10 Chief Financial Officer .... Ms. Charlotte EUBANK
32 Vice President for Student Success .... Mr. Jason HOSENEY
05 Vice President for Learning .... Dr. Wesley A. PAYNE
08 Director Library Services .... Mr. Gordon T. JOHNSTON
37 Director Financial Aid .... Ms. Laura MILLIGAN
06 Registrar .... Ms. Marcia C. FIELDS
35 Director of Student Services .... Ms. Marcia C. FIELDS
09 Director of Institutional Research .... Ms. Melanie HAMANN
18 Chief Facilities/Physical Plant .... Mr. Derick A. ALLEN
15 Director Human Resources .... Ms. Kristina D. MCDANIEL

Truman State University (A)

100 E Normal, Kirksville MO 63501-4221
County: Adair FICE Identification: 002495
Unit ID: 178615
Telephone: (660) 785-4000 Carnegie Class: Master's M
FAX Number: (660) 785-4030 Calendar System: Semester
URL: www.truman.edu
Established: 1867 Annual Undergrad Tuition & Fees (In-State): $7,008
Enrollment: 6,002 Coed
Affiliation or Control: State IRS Status: 501(c)3
Highest Offering: Master's
Program: Liberal Arts And General; Teacher Preparatory; Professional
Accreditation: NH, BUS, BUSA, MUS, NURSE, SP, TED

01 President .... Dr. Troy D. PAINO
05 Int Provost/VP for Academic Affairs .... Mr. Richard COUGHLIN
30 Vice Pres University Advancement .... Mr. Mark GAMBAIANA
11 VP for Admin Finance & Planning .... Mr. David RECTOR
84 Assoc VP for Enrollment Management .... Mrs. Regina MORIN
32 Dean of Student Affairs .... Dr. Lou Ann GILCHRIST
43 General Counsel .... Mr. Warren WELLS
21 Comptroller .... Mrs. Judy MULLINS
41 Athletic Director .... Mr. Jerry WOLLMERING
15 Exec Dir HR/EEO Compliance Ofcr .... Ms. Sally DETWEILER
07 Director of Admissions .... Mrs. Melody CHAMBERS
37 Financial Aid Director .... Mrs. Kathy ELSEA
06 Registrar .... Mrs. Margaret HERRON
20 Director of Public Relations .... Mrs. Heidi TEMPLETON
88 Director of Truman Institute .... Dr. Kevin MINCH
38 Dir Student Health/Counseling Svcs .... Dr. Brenda HIGGINS
88 Dean of Social & Cultural Studies .... Dr. Douglas DAVENPORT
49 Dean of School of Arts & Letters .... Dr. Priscilla RIGGLE
81 Dean Sch of Science & Mathematics .... Dr. Jon GERING
53 Dean Sch of Health Sciences & Educ .... Dr. Janet GOOCH
08 Dean of Libraries & Museums .... Mr. Richard COUGHLIN
50 Dean School of Business .... Dr. Debra KERBY
88 Dean New Student Programs .... Dr. Marty EISENBERG

University of Central Missouri (B)

101 Administration Building, Warrensburg MO 64093-5299
County: Johnson FICE Identification: 002454
Unit ID: 176965
Telephone: (660) 543-4255 Carnegie Class: Master's L
FAX Number: (660) 543-4200 Calendar System: Semester
URL: www.ucmo.edu
Established: 1871 Annual Undergrad Tuition & Fees (In-State): $6,759
Enrollment: 11,323 Coed
Affiliation or Control: State IRS Status: 501(c)3
Highest Offering: Beyond Master's But Less Than Doctorate
Program: Liberal Arts And General; Teacher Preparatory; Professional
Accreditation: NH, AAB, ART, BUS, BUSA, CACREP, CEA, CONST, DIETD, ENGR, MUS, NAIT, NURSE, SP, SW, TED

01 President .... Dr. Charles M. AMBROSE
101 Spec Asst to Pres for Board Affs .... Ms. Monica R. HUFFMAN
05 Provost/VP for Academic Affairs .... Dr. George W. WILSON
32 Vice President for Student Affairs .... Dr. Rich MORRELL
05 Vice Provost Student Experience/Eng .. Dr. Sharlene GARBER BAX
45 Vice Provost Institutional Effectiv .... Dr. Michael GRELLE
35 Asst Vice Pres Student Affairs .... Mr. Corey L. BOWMAN
84 Vice Provost Enrollment Management .... Dr. Richard D. SLUDER
08 Dean of Library Services .... Ms. Mollie D. DINWIDDIE
58 Dean Graduate Sch & Extended Stds .... Dr. Joseph VAUGHN
49 Dean College of Arts/Humanities/Sci .... Dr. Gersham NELSON
72 Dean College of Health/Science/Tech .... Dr. Alice L. GREIFE
50 Dean Harmon Col Business/Prof Stds .... Dr. Roger J. BEST
92 Dean of the Honors College .... Dr. Joseph LEWANDOWSKI
53 Dean of College of Education .... Dr. Michael WRIGHT
10 Controller .... Mr. John MERRIGAN
30 University Director Development .... Vacant
13 Vice Provost for Technology .... Dr. James F. GRAHAM
43 General Counsel .... Mr. Henry SETSER
41 Athletic Director .... Mr. Jerry M. HUGHES
06 Director of Registrar .... Ms. Teri BOWMAN
26 University Director Communications .... Vacant
09 Director Testing & Assess Services ... Ms. Cynthia A. BERTALOTT
36 Director Career Services .... Ms. Teresa Fine ALEWEL
37 Dir Student Financial Assistance .... Mr. Phillip SHREVES
19 Director of Public Safety .... Ms. Kimberly VANSELL
39 Sr Dir Univ Housing/Res Dining Svcs ..... Mr. Patrick J. BRADLEY
21 Director Accounting Services .... Ms. Toni L. KREKE
18 Dir Facilities & Planning Op .... Mr. Christopher WELLMAN

96 Director Purchasing .... Vacant
15 Director Human Resources .... Mr. Rick DIXON
40 Director of Univ Store & Textbooks .... Mr. Charles D. RUTT
85 Director of International Center .... Dr. Joy STEVENSON
88 Director User Services .... Mr. Matthew C. LINK
45 Planning Officer .... Ms. Carole E. NIMMER
07 Director Admissions .... Ms. Ann A. NORDYKE
15 Asst Director of Human Resources .... Ms. Cheryl D. TRELOW
29 Director Alumni Relations .... Mrs. Jenne VANDERBOUT
38 Asst Dir Counseling Center .... Dr. Paul D. POLYCHRONIS
44 Manager Annual Fund .... Mr. Scott ALVESTED
24 Coord of Academic Media Services .... Ms. Mary E. GRIFFIS

*University of Missouri System Administration (C)

321 University Hall, Columbia MO 65211-3020
County: Boone FICE Identification: 002515
Unit ID: 178439
Telephone: (573) 882-2011 Carnegie Class: N/A
FAX Number: (573) 882-2721
URL: www.umsystem.edu

01 Interim President .... Mr. Stephen J. OWENS
100 Chief of Staff .... Ms. Kathleen M. MILLER
10 Vice Pres Finance & Administration .... Ms. Natalie KRAWITZ
05 Sr Assoc Vice Pres Academic Affairs .... Dr. Steven W. GRAHAM
13 Vice President Info Technology .... Dr. Gary K. ALLEN
86 Vice President Government Relations .... Mr. Stephen C. KNORR
15 Vice Pres Human Resource Services ... Ms. Elizabeth RODRIGUEZ
46 Vice President Research & Econ Dev ..... Mr. Michael F. NICHOLS
43 Acting General Counsel .... Mr. Phillip J. HOSKINS
26 Assoc VP Strategic Communications .... Ms. Cindy POLLARD
17 Executive Director UM Health Care .... Mr. James H. ROSS
23 Vice Chancellor for Health Sciences .. Dr. Harold A. WILLIAMSON
21 Treasurer .... Mr. Thomas RICHARDS
21 Controller .... Ms. Jane E. CLOSTERMAN

*University of Missouri - Columbia (D)

Columbia MO 65211-0001
County: Boone FICE Identification: 002516
Unit ID: 178396
Telephone: (573) 882-2121 Carnegie Class: RU/VH
FAX Number: (573) 882-0007 Calendar System: Semester
URL: www.missouri.edu
Established: 1839 Annual Undergrad Tuition & Fees (In-State): $8,989
Enrollment: 32,415 Coed
Affiliation or Control: State IRS Status: 501(c)3
Highest Offering: Doctorate
Program: Liberal Arts And General; Teacher Preparatory; Professional; Business Emphasis
Accreditation: NH, BUS, BUSA, CIDA, CLPSY, COPSY, DIETC, DMS, ENG, FOR, HSA, IPSY, JOUR, LAW, LIB, MED, MUS, NMT, NRPA, NURSE, OT, PH, PTA, RAD, SCPSY, SP, SPAA, SW, @TEAC, VET

02 Chancellor .... Dr. Brady J. DEATON
03 Deputy Chancellor .... Mr. Michael A. MIDDLETON
05 Provost .... Dr. Brian L. FOSTER
20 Deputy Provost .... Mr. Kenneth D. DEAN
20 Vice Provost Undergrad Studies .... Dr. James SPAIN
32 Vice Chancellor Student Affairs .... Dr. Catherine C. SCROGGS
11 VC Administrative Services .... Ms. Jacquelyn K. JONES
10 Vice Chancellor Administrative Svcs .... Ms. Jacquelyn K. JONES
58 VP Adv Studies/Dean Grad Sch .... Mr. George JUSTICE
58 Associate Graduate Dean .... Dr. Sheryl TUCKER
04 Asst to Chanc for University Affs .... Ms. Christine H. KOUKOLA
30 VC Development/Alumni Relations .... Mr. David P. HOUSH
29 Assoc VC Alumni Relations/Devel .... Mr. Todd A. MCCUBBIN
17 Vice Chancellor for Health Sciences .... Dr. Harold A. WILLIAMSON, JR.
57 Director School of Music .... Dr. Robert SHAY
84 Vice Provost for Enrollment Mgmt .... Dr. Ann J. KORSCHGEN
56 Vice Provost for Extension .... Dr. Michael D. OUART
85 Vice Provost International Pgms .... Dr. Handy WILLIAMSON
46 Vice Chancellor for Research .... Mr. Robert DUNCAN
88 Director of Budget .... Mr. Timothy R. ROONEY
13 Chief Information Officer .... Dr. Gary K. ALLEN
15 Asst Vice Chanc Human Resources .... Ms. Karen E. TOUZEAU
18 Assoc Vice Chanc Campus Facilities .... Mr. Gary L. WARD
46 Spec Asst to Vice Chanc of Research .... Dr. Michael WARNOCK
35 Asst Vice Chanc Student Affairs .... Dr. Jeffrey ZEILENGA
06 University Registrar .... Ms. Brenda V. SELMAN
09 Director Institutional Research .... Dr. Mardy T. EIMERS
08 Director of Libraries .... Mr. James A. COGSWELL
37 Assoc Dir Student Financial Aid .... Mr. Nick PREWETT
47 Vice Chan & Dean Agric/Food/Nat Res .... Dr. Thomas L. PAYNE
49 Dean Arts & Science .... Dr. Michael J. O'BRIEN
50 Dean of Business .... Ms. Joan GABEL
88 Director School of Accountancy .... Dr. Vairam ARUNACHALAM
53 Dean of Education .... Dr. Daniel CLAY
54 Dean of Engineering .... Dr. James E. THOMPSON
65 Dir School of Natural Resources .... Dr. Mark R. RYAN
76 Dean School of Health Professions .... Dr. Richard E. OLIVER
59 Dean Human Environmental Science . Dr. Stephen R. JORGENSEN
60 Dean of Journalism .... Dr. R. Dean MILLS
61 Dean of Law .... Dr. R. Lawrence DESSEM
63 Dean of Medicine .... Dr. Robert CHURCHILL
66 Dean of Nursing .... Dr. Judith FITZGERALD MILLER
70 Director School of Social Work .... Dr. Marjorie SABLE
74 Dean of Veterinary Medicine .... Dr. Neil OLSON
19 Director of University Police .... Mr. Jack W. WATRING

27 Director News Services .... Ms. Mary Jo BANKEN
41 Intercollegiate Athletic Director .... Mr. Michael F. ALDEN
39 Director Residential Life .... Mr. Frankie D. MINOR
25 Director Sponsored Program Admin .... Ms. Jennifer DUNCAN
40 Regional Director Retail Operations .... Ms. Sherry POLLARD
38 Director Counseling Services .... Dr. David WALLACE
88 Assoc Vice Provost Intl Initiatives .... Dr. James K. SCOTT
36 Director Career Services .... Dr. Matthew REISKE
23 Director Student Health Services .... Dr. Susan E. EVEN
92 Director Honors College .... Dr. Stuart B. PALONSKY
94 Director Women's/Gender Studies .... Dr. Jacquelyn S. LITT
88 Director Info Science Learning Tech .... Dr. John WEDMAN
80 Director Truman Schl Public Affairs ...... Dr. Barton J. WECHSLER
07 Director of Admissions .... Ms. Barbara A. RUPP
26 Assistant to Chancellor Univ Affs .... Ms. Christine H. KOUKOLA
35 Director Student Life .... Dr. Mark L. LUCAS
28 Chief Diversity Officer .... Dr. Roger L. WORTHINGTON
96 Manager of Campus Procurement .... Ms. Sherri L. WOOD

*University of Missouri - Kansas City (E)

5100 Rockhill Road, Kansas City MO 64110-2499
County: Jackson FICE Identification: 002518
Unit ID: 178402
Telephone: (816) 235-1000 Carnegie Class: RU/H
FAX Number: (816) 235-1717 Calendar System: Semester
URL: www.umkc.edu
Established: 1929 Annual Undergrad Tuition & Fees (In-State): $7,406
Enrollment: 15,277 Coed
Affiliation or Control: State IRS Status: 501(c)3
Highest Offering: Doctorate
Program: Liberal Arts And General; Teacher Preparatory; Professional
Accreditation: NH, DANCE, AA, ANEST, BUS, CLPSY, COPSY, CS, DENT, DH, ENG, IPSY, LAW, MED, MUS, NURSE, OTA, PHAR, SPAA, SW, TED, THEA

02 Chancellor .... Mr. Leo E. MORTON
100 Chief of Staff .... Dr. Margaret BROMMELSIEK
28 Deputy Chancellor for Diversity .... Dr. Karen L. DACE
05 Exec Vice Chanc and Provost .... Dr. Gail HACKETT
32 Vice Chanc Stdnt Affs/Enroll Mgmt .... Mr. Melvin C. TYLER
11 Vice Chanc for Admin Services .... Ms. Sharon LINDENBAUM
21 Director Budgeting and Planning .... Ms. Karen D. WILKERSON
30 Vice Chanc for Univ Advancement .... Mr. Curt J. CRESPINO
41 Athletic Director .... Mr. Timothy W. HALL
20 CIO & Vice Prov for Acad Pgms . Dr. Mary Lou A. HINES-FRITTS
20 Vice Prov for Academic Affairs .... Dr. Cynthia L. PEMBERTON
20 Vice Prov for Faculty Affairs .... Dr. Denis M. MEDEIROS
49 Int Dean College of Arts & Sciences .... Dr. Wayne VAUGHT
50 Dean Bloch School Bus Public Admin .... Dr. Teng-Kee TAN
81 Dean School Biological Sciences .... Dr. Lawrence A. DREYFUS
64 Dean Conservatory of Music .... Mr. Peter T. WITTE
52 Dean School of Dentistry .... Dr. Marsha A. PYLE
53 Dean School of Education .... Dr. Wanda J. BLANCHETT
54 Dean Sch of Computing/Engineering .... Dr. Kevin Z. TRUMAN
61 Dean School of Law .... Ms. Ellen Y. SUNI
63 Dean School of Medicine .... Dr. Betty M. DREES
66 Dean School of Nursing .... Dr. Lora LACEY-HAUN
67 Dean School of Pharmacy .... Dr. Russell B. MELCHERT
62 Dean University Libraries .... Dr. Sharon L. BOSTICK
58 Dean of School of Graduate Studies ...... Dr. Denis M. MEDEIROS
09 Director Institutional Research .... Dr. Larry BUNCE
16 Asst Vice Chanc Human Resources .... Ms. Carol HINTZ
84 Asst Vice Chanc Enrollment Mgmt ...... Ms. Jennifer DEHAEMERS
88 Asst Vice Chanc for Auxiliary Svcs .... Mr. Paris SAUNDERS
35 Assistant Dean of Students .... Dr. Eric GROSPITCH
35 Assistant Dean of Students .... Dr. Jeff TRAIGER
35 Director Student Involvement .... Dr. Angela COTTRELL
88 Asst VC Univ Communications .... Ms. Sarah L. MORRIS
26 Associate Director Public Relations .... Ms. Wandra B. GREEN
102 Asst VC for Development .... Ms. Jenea OLIVER
29 Asst VC AlumniConstituent Relations .... Ms. Lisen TAMMEUS
44 Director Planned Giving .... Mr. Phil WATSON
86 Legislative Liaison .... Mr. Troy LILLEBO
22 Director Affirmative Action .... Mr. Michael D. BATES
88 Int Dir Center for Academic Develop .... Dr. Marion STONE
07 Director of Admissions .... Mr. W. C. VANCE
85 Director Internatl Student Affairs .... Ms. Sandra GAULT
28 Director Multicultural Affairs .... Ms. Tiffany S. WILLIAMS
37 Director Student Financial Aid .... Ms. Nancy MERZ
06 Registrar .... Mr. Doug SWINK
19 Director Campus Police .... Mr. Michael BONGARTZ
40 Director Bookstore .... Mr. Pete EISENTRAGER
38 Director Counseling/Health Test Ctr .... Dr. Marita BARKIS
88 Director Womens Center .... Dr. Brenda BETHMAN
36 Director Career Services .... Mr. Greg HAYES
39 Associate Director Residential Life .... Ms. Kristen ABELL
96 Manager Campus Procurement .... Ms. Catherine A. BARKER
25 Asst to VC for Admin Services .... Mr. Colin C. GAGE
18 Director Campus Facilities .... Mr. Robert A. SIMMONS
104 Director International Acad Pgms .... Dr. Linna F. PLACE

*University of Missouri - Saint Louis (F)

One University Boulevard, Saint Louis MO 63121-4400
County: Saint Louis FICE Identification: 002519
Unit ID: 178420
Telephone: (314) 516-5000 Carnegie Class: RU/H
FAX Number: (314) 516-5378 Calendar System: Semester
URL: www.umsl.edu
Established: 1963 Annual Undergrad Tuition & Fees (In-State): $9,038
Enrollment: 12,692 Coed

Affiliation or Control: State IRS Status: 501(c)3
Highest Offering: Doctorate
Program: Liberal Arts And General; Teacher Preparatory; Professional
Accreditation: NH, BUS, BUSA, CACREP, CLPSY, ENG, IPSY, MUS, NURSE, OPT, OPTR, SPAA, SW, TED

02 Chancellor ... Dr. Thomas F. GEORGE
05 Provost/Vice Chanc Academic Affairs ... Dr. Glen H. COPE
10 Vice Chanc Managerial/Tech Svcs ... Dr. James M. KRUEGER
30 Vice Chancellor Univ Advancement ... Mr. Martin F. LEIFELD
22 Dir of Equal Opportunity/Diversity ... Ms. Deborah J. BURRIS
46 Vice Provost Research Admin ... Dr. Nasser ARSHADI
32 Vice Provost Student Affairs ... Mr. Curtis C. COONROD
58 Vice Prov Acad Affs/Dean Grad Sch ... Dr. Judith WALKER DE FELIX
13 Assoc VC Information Technology/ CIO ... Mr. Lawrence W. FREDERICK
88 Dir Center for Teaching & Learning ... Dr. Margaret W. COHEN
85 Director International Studies ... Dr. Joel N. GLASSMAN
49 Dean College Arts & Sciences ... Dr. Ronald YASBIN
50 Dean College of Business Admin ... Dr. N. Keith WOMER
53 Dean College of Education ... Dr. Carole G. BASILE
57 Int Dean College of Fine Arts/Comm ... Dr. James E. RICHARDS
66 Dean College of Nursing ... Dr. Juliann G. SEBASTAIN
92 Dean Honors College ... Dr. Robert M. BLISS
88 Dean College of Optometry ... Dr. Larry J. DAVIS
08 Int Dean of Libraries ... Mr. Christopher DAMES
54 Dean Engineering Program ... Dr. Joseph O'SULLIVAN
51 Dean Continuing Education ... Dr. Wm Thomas WALKER
88 Assistant to Provost Public Affairs ... Ms. Elizabeth VAN UUM
23 Asst Vice Provost Hlth/Wellness ... Dr. Nancy M. MAGNUSON
88 Asst Dean of Students/Stdnt Conduct ... Mr. D'Andre BRADDIX
93 Asst Dean of Stdnts/MultiCultural ... Ms. Natissia SMALL
35 Asst Dean of Students/Student Life ... Ms. Miriam I. HUFFMAN
41 Director of Athletics ... Ms. Lori FLANAGAN
07 Director of Admissions ... Mr. Alan BYRD
40 Manager Bookstore ... Ms. Stephanie EATON
36 Director Career Services ... Ms. Teresa A. BALESTRERI
38 Director Counseling Services ... Dr. M. Sharon BIEGEN
06 Registrar ... Ms. Linda C. SILMAN
39 Director Residential Life ... Mr. Jonathan A. LIDGUS
37 Director Student Financial Aid ... Dr. Anthony C. GEORGES
88 Vice Pres Ctr Emerging Technologies ... Mr. William SIMON
88 Director Ctr Nanoscience ... Dr. Jingyue (Jimmy) LIU
88 Director Center Neurodynamics ... Dr. Sonya BAHAR
88 Dir Scientific & Computing/ITE ... Mr. William J. LEMON
88 Dir MO Institute of Mental Health ... Mr. Joseph PARKS
25 Manager Bus/Fiscal/Research Admin ... Ms. Karen O. BOYD
88 Director Business Services ... Ms. Gloria J. LEONARD
18 Director Engr/Planning & Const ... Mr. H. Sam DARANDARI
18 Director Facilities Services ... Mr. Frank S. KOCHIN
21 Director of Finance ... Mr. Ernest A. CORNFORD
15 Assoc VC Human Resources ... Mr. Peter A. HEITHAUS
19 Director Institutional Safety ... Mr. Forrest L. VAN NESS
09 Director Institutional Research ... Mr. Lawrence W. WESTERMEYER
26 Chief Marketing Officer ... Mr. Ronald H. GOSSEN
102 Assoc VC Dev Corporation/Foundation ... Dr. Brenda M. MCPHAIL
88 Sr Dir Development Colleges/Units ... Ms. Lily AYALA BERLYN
88 Sr Dir University Campaigns ... Mr. Mark A. BERLYN
88 Director KWMU-FM Radio/Gen Mgr ... Mr. Tim J. EBY
29 Dir Alumni Relations/Annual Giving ... Ms. Deborah L. GRAHAM
27 Chief Information Officer ... Mr. Robert D. SAMPLES
44 Director of Planned Giving ... Mr. Kent KROBER
94 Director Women's & Gender Studies ... Dr. Kathy J. GENTILE
70 Director Social Work ... Dr. Lois PIERCE
79 Director Center for the Humanities ... Dr. Diane H. TOULIATOS-MILES
88 Dir Gateway Writing Project ... Dr. Nancy SINGER
88 Dir Public Policy Administration ... Dr. Deborah B. BALSER
88 Director Public Policy Research Ctr ... Dr. Mark TRANEL
88 Dir Women in Public Life ... Ms. Vivian EVELOFF
31 Director Community College Relation ... Ms. Melissa HATTMAN
88 Managing Dir Performing Arts Center ... Mr. John R. CATTANACH
88 Dir Des Lee Collaborative Vision ... Ms. Patricia ZAHN

*Missouri University of Science & Technology (A)

300 W 13th Street, Rolla MO 65409-0001
County: Phelps FICE Identification: 002517
Unit ID: 178411
Telephone: (573) 341-4111 Carnegie Class: Spec/Engg
FAX Number: (573) 341-4307 Calendar System: Semester
URL: www.mst.edu
Established: 1870 Annual Undergrad Tuition & Fees (In-State): $9,193
Enrollment: 7,206 Coed
Affiliation or Control: State IRS Status: 501(c)3
Highest Offering: Doctorate
Program: Professional; Technical Emphasis
Accreditation: NH, CS, ENG

02 Chancellor ... Dr. John F. CARNEY, III
05 Provost/Exec Vice Chanc Acad Affs ... Dr. Warren K. WRAY
11 Vice Chanc Administrative Services ... Mr. F. Stephen MALOTT
30 Vice Chance University Advancement ... Ms. Joan M. NESBITT
32 Vice Chancellor Student Affairs ... Dr. Debra A G. ROBINSON
46 Vice Provost for Research Services ... Dr. K. KRISHNAMURTHY
20 Vice Provost Academic Affairs ... Dr. Robert W. SCHWARTZ
20 Vice Prov Undergrad Studies ... Dr. Harvest L. COLLIER
58 Vice Provost Graduate Studies ... Dr. Venkata ALLADA
56 Vice Provost of Global Learning ... Dr. Henry A. WIEBE
84 Vice Prov & Dean of Enrollment Mgmt ... Mr. Jay W. GOFF
08 Director of Library ... Mr. J. Andrew STEWART
13 Chief Information Officer/Asoc VP-R ... Ms. Margaret CLINE
06 Registrar ... Ms. Laura K. STOLL
38 Asst Vice Chanc Stdnt Affs/Supp Svc ... Dr. Carl F. BURNS
41 Director of Athletics ... Mr. Mark E. MULLIN
15 Dir Human Resource/Affirm Action ... Ms. Shenethia MANUEL
36 Dir Career Opportunities Center ... Ms. Lea-Ann MORTON
85 Director Intl/Cultural Affairs ... Ms. Jeanie H. HOFER
35 Director Student Life/Univ Center-R ... Mr. Mark POTRAFKA
39 Director Residential Life ... Ms. Tina F. SHEPPARD
09 Director Inst Research & Assessment ... Dr. Thulasi KUMAR
07 Director of Admissions ... Mr. Rance LARSEN
29 Director Alumni/Constit Relations ... Ms. Marianne A. WARD
37 Director of Student Financial Aid ... Ms. Lynn K. STICHNOTE
26 Director of Communications ... Mr. Andrew P. CAREAGA
18 Director of Physical Facilities ... Mr. James PACKARD
28 Dir Ctr Pre-College Pgms/Stdnt Divr ... Mr. Will PERKINS
88 Dir of Womens Leadership Institute ... Ms. Cecilia ELMORE
40 Asst Director of Univ Bookstore ... Mr. Mark GALLARDO

Urshan Graduate School of Theology (B)

704 Howdershell Road, Florissant MO 63031-7526
County: St. Louis Identification: 666406
Unit ID: 455099
Telephone: (314) 921-9290 Carnegie Class: Spec/Faith
FAX Number: (314) 921-9203 Calendar System: Semester
URL: www.ugst.edu
Established: 2001 Annual Undergrad Tuition & Fees: $8,500
Enrollment: 77 Coed
Affiliation or Control: Other Protestant IRS Status: 501(c)3
Highest Offering: Master's
Program: Professional; Religious Emphasis
Accreditation: THEOL

01 President ... Dr. David K. BERNARD
05 Chief Academic Officer/Dean Admin ... Daniel L. SEGRAVES

Vatterott College-Joplin (C)

809 Illinois, Joplin MO 64801-9538
County: Jasper Identification: 666060
Unit ID: 404374
Telephone: (417) 781-5633 Carnegie Class: Assoc/PrivFP
FAX Number: (417) 781-6437 Calendar System: Other
URL: www.vatterott-college.edu
Established: 1969 Annual Undergrad Tuition & Fees: $21,420
Enrollment: 494 Coed
Affiliation or Control: Proprietary IRS Status: Proprietary
Highest Offering: Associate Degree
Program: Occupational; Business Emphasis
Accreditation: ACCSC

01 CEO & President ... Ms. Pam BELL
05 Vice President Academic Affairs ... Mr. Brandon SHEDRON
10 Chief Financial Officer ... Mr. Dennis BEAVERS
43 Associate Counsel ... Mr. Mike HODGE
12 Campus Director ... Ms. Jacqueline O'DELL

† Branch campus of Vatterott College-North Park, Berkeley, MO.

Vatterott College-Kansas City (D)

8955 East 38th Terrace, Kansas City MO 64129-1692
County: Jackson Identification: 666519
Unit ID: 404383
Telephone: (816) 861-1000 Carnegie Class: Assoc/PrivFP
FAX Number: (816) 861-1400 Calendar System: Other
URL: www.vatterott-college.edu
Established: 1969 Annual Undergrad Tuition & Fees: $11,890
Enrollment: 977 Coed
Affiliation or Control: Proprietary IRS Status: Proprietary
Highest Offering: Associate Degree
Program: Occupational; Technical Emphasis
Accreditation: ACCSC

01 CEO & President ... Ms. Pam BELL
10 Chief Financial Officer ... Mr. Dennis BEAVERS
05 Chief Academic Officer ... Dr. John TUCKER
11 Chief Administrative Officer ... Mr. Erio COMICI
12 Campus Director ... Mr. Brian SCHUMANN

† Branch campus of Vatterott College-North Park, Berkeley, MO.

Vatterott College-NorthPark (E)

8580 Evans Avenue, Berkeley MO 63134-2900
County: Saint Louis FICE Identification: 025997
Unit ID: 245342
Telephone: (314) 264-1000 Carnegie Class: Assoc/PrivFP4
FAX Number: (314) 522-6174 Calendar System: Other
URL: www.vatterott-college.edu
Established: 1969 Annual Undergrad Tuition & Fees: $17,338
Enrollment: 1,707 Coed
Affiliation or Control: Proprietary IRS Status: Proprietary
Highest Offering: Baccalaureate
Program: Occupational; 2-Year Principally Bachelor's Creditable; Technical Emphasis
Accreditation: ACCSC

01 Campus Director ... Robert DONNELL
10 Chief Financial Officer ... Dennis BEAVERS
05 Director of Education ... Al WASHINGTON
05 Director of Education ... Samuel BOYD, III
06 Registrar ... Brenda LINCOLN-PENZEL
07 Director of Admissions ... Harvey CHAMBERLAIN

Vatterott College-O'Fallon (F)

3550 West Clay, St. Charles MO 63301
County: Saint Charles Identification: 666584
Unit ID: 445559
Telephone: (636) 978-7488 Carnegie Class: Assoc/PrivFP
FAX Number: (636) 978-5121 Calendar System: Semester
URL: www.vatterott.edu
Established: 1969 Annual Undergrad Tuition & Fees: N/A
Enrollment: 374 Coed
Affiliation or Control: Proprietary IRS Status: Proprietary
Highest Offering: Associate Degree
Program: Occupational
Accreditation: ACCSC

01 Campus Director ... Ms. Jessie BAILEY

† Branch campus of Vatterott College-North Park, Berkeley, MO.

Vatterott College-Saint Joseph (G)

3131 Frederick Avenue, Saint Joseph MO 64506
County: Buchanan Identification: 666520
Unit ID: 436182
Telephone: (816) 364-5399 Carnegie Class: Assoc/PrivFP
FAX Number: (816) 364-1593 Calendar System: Other
URL: www.vatterott-college.edu
Established: 1969 Annual Undergrad Tuition & Fees: $17,500
Enrollment: 341 Coed
Affiliation or Control: Proprietary IRS Status: Proprietary
Highest Offering: Associate Degree
Program: Occupational; Technical Emphasis
Accreditation: ACCSC

01 CEO & President ... Ms. Pam BELL
10 Chief Financial Officer ... Mr. Dennis BEAVERS
05 Vice President Academic Affairs ... Dr. Brandon SHEDRON
30 VP Regulatory Affs/Strategic Devel ... Mr. Aaron LACEY
43 General Counsel/Chief Administrator ... Mr. Scott CASANOVER
12 Campus Director ... Ms. Shawn RIGGINS

† Branch campus of Vatterott College-Des Moines, Des Moines, IA.

Vatterott College-Springfield (H)

3850 S Campbell Avenue, Springfield MO 65807-5340
County: Greene Identification: 666521
Unit ID: 404365
Telephone: (417) 831-8116 Carnegie Class: Assoc/PrivFP
FAX Number: (417) 831-5099 Calendar System: Other
URL: www.vatterott-college.edu
Established: 1969 Annual Undergrad Tuition & Fees: $10,250
Enrollment: 609 Coed
Affiliation or Control: Proprietary IRS Status: Proprietary
Highest Offering: Associate Degree
Program: Occupational; Technical Emphasis
Accreditation: ACCSC

01 CEO & President ... Ms. Pam BELL
43 Vice Pres of HR/General Counsel ... Mr. D. Scott CASANOVER
10 Chief Financial Officer ... Mr. Dennis BEAVERS
05 Chief Academic Officer ... Mr. Brandon SHEDRON
12 Campus Director ... Ms. Marcia JOHNSON

† Branch campus of Vatterott College-North Park, Berkeley, MO.

Vatterott College-Sunset Hills (I)

12970 Maurer Industrial Drive,
Sunset Hills MO 63127-1516
County: Saint Louis Identification: 666522
Unit ID: 436191
Telephone: (314) 843-4200 Carnegie Class: Bac/Assoc
FAX Number: (314) 843-1709 Calendar System: Other
URL: www.vatterott-college.com
Established: 1969 Annual Undergrad Tuition & Fees: $36,900
Enrollment: 805 Coed
Affiliation or Control: Proprietary IRS Status: Proprietary
Highest Offering: Baccalaureate
Program: Occupational; Technical Emphasis
Accreditation: ACCSC

01 CEO & President ... Ms. Pam BELL
10 Chief Financial Officer ... Mr. Dennis BEAVERS
05 Vice President Academic Affairs ... Dr. Brandon SHEDRON
45 VP Regulatory Affs/Strategic Devel ... Mr. Aaron LACEY
43 General Counsel/Chief Administrator ... Mr. Scott CASANOVER
12 Campus Director ... Ms. Denise K. JONES
106 Online Director ... Mrs. Jamie ORF

† Branch campus of Vatterott College-North Park, Berkeley, MO.

Washington University in St. Louis (J)

One Brookings Drive, Saint Louis MO 63130-4899
County: Saint Louis FICE Identification: 002520
Unit ID: 179867

Telephone: (314) 935-5000　Carnegie Class: RU/VH
FAX Number: N/A　Calendar System: Semester
URL: www.wustl.edu
Established: 1853　Annual Undergrad Tuition & Fees: $41,992
Enrollment: 13,995　Coed
Affiliation or Control: Independent Non-Profit　IRS Status: 501(c)3
Highest Offering: Doctorate
Program: Liberal Arts And General; Professional
Accreditation: NH, ART, AUD, BUS, CLPSY, ENG, LAW, MED, OT, PTA, SW

01 Chancellor .... Prof. Mark S. WRIGHTON
05 Exec VC Academic Affairs/Provost .... Prof. Edward S. MACIAS
11 Exec VC Administration .... Mr. Henry S. WEBBER
63 Exec Vice Chanc/Dean of Medicine .... Dr. Larry J. SHAPIRO
43 Exec Vice Chanc/General Counsel .... Mr. Michael R. CANNON
30 Exec VC Alumni & Development .... Mr. David T. BLASINGAME
10 Vice Chancellor for Finance/CFO .... Ms. Barbara A. FEINER
46 VC for Research .... Prof. Evan D. KHARASCH
16 Vice Chanc for Human Resources .... Ms. Ann B. PRENATT
32 VC for Students/Dean College A&S .... Mr. James E. MCLEOD
26 Vice Chanc for Public Affairs .... Mr. M. Fredric VOLKMANN
08 VC Scholarly Res/Dean of Libraries .... Ms. Shirley K. BAKER
86 VC Government & Community Relations . Ms. Pamela S. LOKKEN
88 Chief Investment Officer .... Ms. Kimberly G. WALKER
21 Assoc VC for Finance and Treasurer .... Ms. Amy B. KWESKIN
49 Dean Arts & Sciences .... Prof. Gary S. WIHL
61 Dean School of Law .... Prof. Kent D. SYVERUD
54 Dean Engineering & Applied Science ..... Dr. Ralph S. QUATRANO
57 Dean Sam Fox Sch Design Visual Arts .... Prof. Carmon COLANGELO
57 Dean College & Graduate Sch of Art .... Prof. Franklin SPECTOR
50 Dean Olin Business School .... Prof. Mahendra R. GUPTA
58 Dean Graduate School of A & S .... Prof. Richard J. SMITH
70 Dean Brown School of Social Work .... Prof. Edward F. LAWLOR
55 Dean University College .... Prof. Robert E. WILTENBURG
48 Dean Architecture .... Prof. Bruce M. LINDSEY
04 Assistant to Chancellor .... Dr. Robert M. WILD
101 Secretary to the Board of Trustees .... Ms. Ida H. EARLY
84 Assoc VC Undergraduate Admissions .... Mr. John A. BERG
20 Assoc VC Spec Asst Academic Affs .... Prof. Gerhild S. WILLIAMS
88 Assoc VC for Development .... Mr. William S. STOLL
29 Assoc VC Alumni & Development Pgm .. Ms. Pamella A. HENSON
26 Assoc VC/Exec Dir Med Public Affs .... Mr. Donald E. CLAYTON
28 Vice Provost .... Prof. Adrienne D. DAVIS
85 Assoc VC International Affairs .... Prof. James V. WERTSCH
39 Assoc VC Students/Dean Students .... Mr. Justin X. CARROLL
13 Assoc VC Info Services & Tech .... Mr. Andrew D. ORTSTADT
35 Assoc VC Students/Dean Campus Life .... Dr. Jill E. CARNAGHI
89 Assoc VC Students/Dean First Yr Ctr .... Dr. Sharon STAHL
27 Assoc VC for Public Affairs/U News .... Mr. Steven J. GIVENS
85 Asst VC/Dir International Students .... Ms. Kathy STEINER-LANG
96 Asst Vice Chanc Resource Management ..... Mr. Alan S. KUEBLER
36 Asst VC/Dir Career Planning & Plcmt .... Mr. Mark W. SMITH
18 Asst VC Facilities Planning/Mgmt ...... Mr. Arthur J. ACKERMANN
88 Asst VC Environ Health & Safety .... Mr. Bruce D. BACKUS
88 Asst VC Real Estate .... Ms. Mary B. CAMPBELL
72 Asst VC/Co-Dir Tech Management .... Dr. Bradley J. CASTANHO
72 Asst VC/Co-Dir Tech Management .... Mr. Michael T. MARRAH
14 Asst VC App Development & Support .... Ms. Denise R. HIRSCHBECK
23 Asst VC/Dir Student Health Services .... Dr. Alan I. GLASS
37 Director of Student Financial Svcs ...... Mr. William H. WITBRODT
41 Director of Athletics .... Mr. John M. SCHAEL
19 Director of Campus Police .... Mr. Donald STROM
07 Director of Admissions .... Ms. Julie SHIMABUKURO
06 Director Student Records/Registrar .... Ms. Susan E. HOSACK
38 Assoc Director of Student Health .... Dr. Thomas M. BROUNK

Webster University (A)

470 E Lockwood, Webster Groves MO 63119-3141
County: Saint Louis　FICE Identification: 002521
Unit ID: 179894
Telephone: (314) 968-6900　Carnegie Class: Master's L
FAX Number: (314) 968-7112　Calendar System: Semester
URL: www.webster.edu
Established: 1915　Annual Undergrad Tuition & Fees: $22,340
Enrollment: 19,342　Coed
Affiliation or Control: Independent Non-Profit　IRS Status: 501(c)3
Highest Offering: Doctorate
Program: Liberal Arts And General
Accreditation: NH, ANEST, MUS, NUR, TED

01 President .... Dr. Elizabeth J. STROBLE
04 Special Assistant to President .... Dr. Oren YAGIL
00 Chancellor .... Dr. Neil J. GEORGE
05 Provost .... Dr. Julian Z. SCHUSTER
30 Vice Pres Development/Alumni Pgms .... Ms. Faith D. MADDY
84 VP Students & Enrollment Mgmt .... Dr. Paul CARNEY
10 VP/Finance/Administration .... Dr. Greg GUNDERSON
13 Interim VP Information Technology .... Mr. Kenneth FREEMAN
20 AVP Academic Affairs .... Dr. Carol J. ADAMS
20 AVP Academic Affairs .... Dr. Elizabeth RUSSEL
20 AVP Academic Affairs .... Mr. Randy WRIGHT
21 AVP Resource Planning & Budget .... Mr. Dan HITCHELL
44 AVP Development/Alumni Pgms .... Mr. Matt ANDREW
32 Associate VP/Dean of Students .... Dr. Ted HOEF
106 AVP Acad Affs/Dir OnLine Learning .... Mr. Dan VIELE
82 AVP Academic Affairs/Dir Intl Pgms .... Dr. Grant CHAPMAN
15 AVP Human Resources .... Ms. Betsy SCHMUTZ
07 AVP/Dean of Admissions .... Dr. Matt NOLAN
29 AVP Alumni Programs .... Ms. Jennifer JEZEK-TAUSSIG
50 Dean School Business & Technology .... Dr. Benjamin O. AKANDE
53 Dean School of Education .... Dr. Brenda S. FYFE
57 Dean Leigh Gerdine Col of Fine Arts .... Mr. Peter E. SARGENT
49 Dean Col of Arts & Sciences .... Dr. David C. WILSON
60 Dean School of Communication .... Ms. Debra CARPENTER
08 Act Dean of University Library .... Ms. Eileen CONDON
39 Assoc Dean Stdts/Housing/Res Life .... Dr. John BUCK
20 Director of Academic Advising .... Dr. Tom NICKOLAI
19 Director Public Safety .... Mr. Dan PESOLD
06 Registrar .... Mr. Don MORRIS
27 Director News & Public Information .... Ms. Polly BURTCH
24 Director of Media Center .... Mr. Greg LITTLE
88 Director International Recruitment .... Mr. Calvin SMITH
41 Director Athletics .... Mr. Tom HART
36 Director Career Center .... Ms. Tamara GEGG-LAPLUME
23 Director Student Health Svcs .... Ms. Ann BROPHY
35 Director Student Activities .... Mr. John GINSBURG
37 Director Financial Aid .... Mr. Jon GRUETT
38 Director Counsel & Life Development .... Dr. Patrick STACK
96 Director of Procurement Services .... Mr. Kenneth CREEHAN
18 Director Facility Planning/Mgmt .... Mr. David STONE
09 Director Institutional Effectivenes .... Dr. Julie WEISSMAN

Wentworth Military Academy and Junior College (B)

1880 Washington Avenue, Lexington MO 64067-1799
County: Lafayette　FICE Identification: 002522
Unit ID: 179919
Telephone: (800) 962-7682　Carnegie Class: Assoc/PrivNFP
FAX Number: (660) 259-2677　Calendar System: Semester
URL: www.wma.edu
Established: 1880　Annual Undergrad Tuition & Fees: $5,325
Enrollment: 687　Coed
Affiliation or Control: Independent Non-Profit　IRS Status: 501(c)3
Highest Offering: Associate Degree
Program: Liberal Arts And General
Accreditation: NH

01 President .... Col. William W. SELLERS
03 Superintendent .... Col. Michael LIERMAN
05 Chief Academic Officer .... Col. Timothy CASEY
11 Chief of Operations/Admin .... Col. Rick COTTRELL
30 Chief Development .... Mr. Dan RYAN
32 Commandant of Cadets .... 1Sgt. Gary WILLIS
84 Director Enrollment Managment .... LtCol. Steve PUCK
41 Athletic Director .... LtCol. Tom HUGHES
10 CFO .... LtCol. Glenn MILLER
21 Director of Business Services .... Maj. Jacki WORTHINGTON
81 Professor of Military Science .... LtCol. Darren FITZGERLAD
29 Alumni Director .... LtCol. Al MCCORMICK
04 Executive Assistant .... Ms. Rebecca MARKLEY
06 Registrar .... Ms. Cheney PARRISH
08 Librarian .... Capt. Linda CHRISTIAN
37 Director Student Financial Aid .... Mrs. Cindy HOWARD
13 Director Information Technology .... Maj. Logan SEALS
85 Director Foreign Students .... Maj. Christhina STARKE
23 Director Health Services .... Capt. Carol LAJAUNIE
42 Chaplain .... Vacant
19 Director Safety and Security .... Maj. Fred FAILING
40 Director Bookstore .... Capt. Chris FIORA
35 Director Student Affairs .... Capt. Lindsey MESNER

Westminster College (C)

501 Westminster Avenue, Fulton MO 65251-1230
County: Callaway　FICE Identification: 002523
Unit ID: 179946
Telephone: (573) 642-3361　Carnegie Class: Bac/A&S
FAX Number: (573) 592-5227　Calendar System: Semester
URL: www.westminster-mo.edu
Established: 1851　Annual Undergrad Tuition & Fees: $20,570
Enrollment: 1,124　Coed
Affiliation or Control: Independent Non-Profit　IRS Status: 501(c)3
Highest Offering: Baccalaureate
Program: Liberal Arts And General; Teacher Preparatory
Accreditation: NH

01 President .... Dr. George B. FORSYTHE
05 VP Academic Affairs/Dean of Faculty .... Dr. Carolyn J. PERRY
30 VP for Advancement .... Dr. John COMERFORD
10 VP for Business and Finance .... Mr. Terry BOWMASTER
26 Director of College Relations .... Mr. Robert CROUSE
84 Dean of Enrollment Services .... Mr. George WOLF
32 VP & Dean of Student Life .... Ms. Christina RAJMAIRA
20 Associate Dean .... Dr. Linda WEBSTER
08 Director of Library Services .... Ms. Angela GERLING
06 Registrar .... Mrs. Phyllis J. MASEK
13 VP & Chief Information Officer .... Mr. Scott LOWE
37 Director of Financial Aid .... Ms. Aimee BRISTOW
15 Director of Human Resources .... Mr. Carl MARRIOTT
39 Director of Residential/Greek Life .... Ms. Jacqueline J. WEBER
41 Athletic Director .... Mr. Matt MITCHELL
38 Asst Director Counseling Services .... Ms. Kate HARRISON
23 Exec Director Wellness Center .... Vacant
88 Exec Dir Marketing/Communications .... Ms. Kris LENSMEYER
29 Dir Alumni Engagement/Events .... Ms. Melanie BARGER
36 Director of Career Services .... Ms. Meg LANGLAND
18 Exec Dir Plant Ops/Auxiliary Svcs .... Mr. Daniel HASLAG
07 Director of Admissions .... Ms. Kelle SILVEY
09 Director of Institutional Research .... Dr. Ray BROWN
19 Dir Campus Safety & Security .... Mr. Jack BENKE
42 Chaplain .... Vacant

William Jewell College (D)

500 College Hill, Liberty MO 64068-1896
County: Clay　FICE Identification: 002524
Unit ID: 179955
Telephone: (816) 781-7700　Carnegie Class: Bac/A&S
FAX Number: (816) 415-5027　Calendar System: Semester
URL: www.jewell.edu
Established: 1849　Annual Undergrad Tuition & Fees: $29,600
Enrollment: 1,060　Coed
Affiliation or Control: Independent Non-Profit　IRS Status: 501(c)3
Highest Offering: Baccalaureate
Program: Liberal Arts And General; Teacher Preparatory; Professional
Accreditation: NH, MUS, NURSE

01 President .... Dr. David L. SALLEE
05 Provost .... Dr. Anne C. DEMA
10 Vice Pres for Finance & Operations .... Mr. Brian CLEMONS
30 Vice Pres Institutional Advancement .... Dr. Chad J. JOLLY
42 Chaplain/Vice Pres Rel Ministries .... Dr. Andrew L. PRATT
84 VP Enrollment & Student Affairs .... Dr. Richard P. WINSLOW
32 Dean of Student Affairs .... Ms. Shelly KING
07 Dean of Admissions .... Mr. Clint CHAPMAN
06 Registrar .... Dr. Edwin H. LANE
08 Director of the Library .... Ms. Stephanie DECLUE
21 Controller .... Mr. Ron DEMPSEY
13 Manager of Information Services .... Ms. Lan GUO
97 Assoc Dean Core Curriculum .... Dr. Ron WITZKE
37 Director of Financial Aid .... Ms. Susan J. KARNES
15 Assoc Director of Human Resources .... Ms. Penny OWENS
18 Director of Facilities Mgmt .... Mr. Steve ANDERSON
57 Executive Director Harriman-Jewell .... Mr. Clark W. MORRIS
41 Director of Athletics .... Dr. Darlene BAILEY
36 Director of Career Services .... Ms. Judith A. RYCHLEWSKI
38 Director of Counseling Services .... Dr. Beth GENTRY-EPLEY
29 Exec Director Alumni Relations .... Mr. Kent HUYSER
104 Coordinator of International Stds .... Ms. Sara ROUND

William Woods University (E)

One University Avenue, Fulton MO 65251-1098
County: Callaway　FICE Identification: 002525
Unit ID: 179964
Telephone: (573) 642-2251　Carnegie Class: Master's L
FAX Number: (573) 592-1146　Calendar System: Other
URL: www.williamwoods.edu
Established: 1870　Annual Undergrad Tuition & Fees: $18,450
Enrollment: 2,185　Coed
Affiliation or Control: Christian Church (Disciples Of Christ)
IRS Status: 501(c)3
Highest Offering: Beyond Master's But Less Than Doctorate
Program: Liberal Arts And General; Teacher Preparatory; Professional
Accreditation: NH, SW, TEAC

01 President .... Dr. Jahnae H. BARNETT
03 Vice President .... Scott GALLAGHER
05 Vice President & Academic Dean .... Dr. Sherry MCCARTHY
11 Vice President Administration .... Dr. Robert FESSLER
04 Executive Assistant to President .... Kenda E G. SHINDLER
07 Dean of Admissions .... Sarah MUNNS
58 VP and Dean of Grad Studies .... Dr. Michael W. WESTERFIELD
32 Dean of Student Life .... Venita MITCHELL
41 Director of Athletics .... Amber COX
10 Chief Financial Officer .... Cale FESSLER
20 Assoc Dean Academic Services .... Tom FRANKMAN
88 Assoc Dean Assessment .... Dr. Susan JONES
44 Assoc VP of Advancement .... D. Scott MINIEA
08 Director Libraries .... Erlene DUDLEY
26 Director of Marketing .... Kristina BRIGHT
18 Director of Buildings & Grounds .... Mike DILLON
06 Director of Records/Registrar .... Tara DEIERLING
15 Director Human Resources & Benefits .... Kathy GROVES
21 Controller .... Marie BEAVER
37 Director Student Financial Services .... Deana READY
27 Director of University Relations .... Mary Ann BEAHON
29 Director of Alumni Activities .... Becky STINSON
50 Chair Business & Economics Division .... David FORSTER
53 Chair Education Division .... Dr. Betty R. TUTT
49 Chair Art Division .... Dr. Aimee SAPP
88 Chair Equestrian Studies Division .... Vacant
88 Chair Human Performance Division .... Anthony LUNGSTRUM
83 Chair Behavioral/Soc Sciences Div .... Shawn HULL
88 Director Graduate Education Pgms .... Dr. E. Douglas EBERSOLD
39 Dir Residential Life/Campus Safety .... Mike WILLS
13 Director of Technology .... Jim LONG
09 Director of Institutional Research .... Dr. Erin M. HANSMAN
36 Dir Career Svcs/Student Success .... Michelle KEMP
35 Coord Greek Life/Student Involvemnt .... Neil STANGLEIN
42 Chaplain/Faith & Service Director .... Travis TAMERIUS
88 ADA Coordinator/Interpreter .... Margie WHITE
28 Coordinator Multicultural Affairs .... Tamara CARTER
38 Counselor .... Rebecca SEITZ

MONTANA

Blackfeet Community College (F)

Box 819, Browning MT 59417-0819
County: Glacier　FICE Identification: 025106
Unit ID: 180054
Telephone: (406) 338-5441　Carnegie Class: Tribal
FAX Number: (406) 338-3272　Calendar System: Semester
URL: www.bfcc.org

Established: 1976 Annual Undergrad Tuition & Fees: $2,280
Enrollment: 536 Coed
Affiliation or Control: Independent Non-Profit IRS Status: 501(c)3
Highest Offering: Associate Degree
Program: Occupational; 2-Year Principally Bachelor's Creditable
Accreditation: NW

01 President ....Dr. Lee E. THORTON
05 Int Dean of Academic Affairs ....Ms. Anne RACINE
32 Dean Student Services ....Mr. Robert TAILFEATHERS
10 Director of Finance ....Ms. Debra DAVIS
37 Director of Financial Aid ....Ms. Margaret BIRD
06 Registrar/Admissions Officer ....Ms. Deana M. MCNABB
15 Director Human Resources ....Ms. Dana L. PEMBERTON

Carroll College (A)

1601 N Benton Avenue, Helena MT 59625-0002
County: Lewis And Clark FICE Identification: 002526
Unit ID: 180106
Telephone: (406) 447-4300 Carnegie Class: Bac/Diverse
FAX Number: (406) 447-4533 Calendar System: Semester
URL: www.carroll.edu
Established: 1909 Annual Undergrad Tuition & Fees: $25,198
Enrollment: 1,477 Coed
Affiliation or Control: Roman Catholic IRS Status: 501(c)3
Highest Offering: Baccalaureate
Program: Occupational; Liberal Arts And General; Teacher Preparatory; Professional
Accreditation: NW, ENG, NURSE

01 President ....Dr. Thomas J. TREBON
05 Sr Vice President Academic Affairs ....Dr. Paula MCNUTT
10 Interim VP for Finance & Admin ....Ms. Lori PETERSON
30 VP Advancement & Community Rels . Mr. Thomas J. MCCARVEL
32 Vice President for Student Life ....Dr. James D. HARDWICK
84 Assoc Vice Pres of Enrollment Mgmt ....Ms. Nina LOCOCO
30 VP for Institutional Advancement ....Vacant
42 Chaplain/Director ....Rev. Marc LENNEMAN
26 Dir Integrated Mktg & Communication ....Vacant
06 Registrar ....Ms. Catherine D. DAY
08 Director of Library ....Mr. Christian FRAZZA
37 Financial Aid Director ....Ms. Janet RIIS
36 Director of Career Services ....Ms. Rosalie K. WALSH
07 Director Admissions/Enrollment Ops ....Ms. Cynthia J. THORNQUIST
15 Director of Human Res & Adm Svcs ....Ms. Renee M. MCMAHON
18 Director of Facilities ....Mr. Walter H. BISKUPIAK
39 Director of Community Living ....Mr. Ben MACINTYRE
38 Director of Counseling ....Mr. K. Mike FRANKLIN
21 Interim Controller ....Ms. Lori LADAS
13 Director Information Technology ....Ms. Loretta ANDREWS
29 Director Alumni Relations ....Ms. Kathy RAMIREZ
09 Director of Institutional Effective ....Dr. Dawn GALLINGER

Chief Dull Knife College (B)

PO Box 98, Lame Deer MT 59043-0098
County: Rosebud FICE Identification: 025452
Unit ID: 180160
Telephone: (406) 477-6215 Carnegie Class: Tribal
FAX Number: (406) 477-6219 Calendar System: Semester
URL: www.cdkc.edu
Established: 1975 Annual Undergrad Tuition & Fees: $2,260
Enrollment: 433 Coed
Affiliation or Control: Independent Non-Profit IRS Status: 501(c)3
Highest Offering: Associate Degree
Program: Occupational; 2-Year Principally Bachelor's Creditable
Accreditation: NW

01 President ....Dr. Richard LITTLEBEAR
03 Vice President ....Mr. William WERTMAN
05 Dean Academic Affairs ....Ms. Michelle CURLEE
32 Dean Student Affairs ....Mr. Zane SPANG
37 Director Student Financial Aid ....Mr. Devin WERTMAN
08 Head Librarian ....Mrs. Joan HANTZ

Dawson Community College (C)

Box 421, Glendive MT 59330-0421
County: Dawson FICE Identification: 002529
Unit ID: 180151
Telephone: (406) 377-3396 Carnegie Class: Assoc/Pub-R-S
FAX Number: (406) 377-8132 Calendar System: Semester
URL: www.dawson.cc.mt.us
Established: 1940 Annual Undergrad Tuition & Fees (In-District): $3,050
Enrollment: 1,470 Coed
Affiliation or Control: State/Local IRS Status: 501(c)3
Highest Offering: Associate Degree
Program: Occupational; 2-Year Principally Bachelor's Creditable
Accreditation: NW

01 President ....Dr. Jim A. CARGILL
05 Dean of Instructional Services ....Dr. Jackie SCHULTZ
32 Dean of Student Services ....Vacant
11 Dean of Administrative Services ....Mr. Justin CROSS
06 Registrar ....Mr. Lane HOLTE
31 Director Special Services ....Mr. Kent DION
08 Librarian ....Mr. Todd KNISPEL
07 Director Admissions/Financial Aid ....Ms. Jolene MYERS
13 Technology Specialist ....Vacant
26 Chief Public Relations Officer ....Ms. Jane WYNNE

Flathead Valley Community College (D)

777 Grandview Drive, Kalispell MT 59901
County: Flathead FICE Identification: 006777
Unit ID: 180197
Telephone: (406) 756-3822 Carnegie Class: Assoc/Pub-R-M
FAX Number: (406) 756-3815 Calendar System: Semester
URL: www.fvcc.edu
Established: 1967 Annual Undergrad Tuition & Fees (In-District): $3,657
Enrollment: 2,539 Coed
Affiliation or Control: Local IRS Status: 501(c)3
Highest Offering: Associate Degree
Program: Occupational; 2-Year Principally Bachelor's Creditable
Accreditation: NW, MAC, SURGT

01 President ....Dr. Jane A. KARAS
05 Vice President Instruction ....Dr. Kristen JONES
10 Vice Pres Administration & Finance ....Mr. Chuck JENSEN
12 Director Lincoln County Campus ....Mr. Patrick PEZZELLE
20 Director Educational Services ....Ms. Mary JORDT
32 Dean of Students ....Ms. Brenda HANSON
06 Registrar/Coord/Admissions/Records ....Ms. Marlene STOLTZ
51 Director Economic Dev/Continuing Ed ....Ms. Susan BURCH
20 Director TRIO ....Ms. Lynn L. FARRIS
13 Director Mgmt Information Services ....Mr. Bill E. BOND
37 Director Student Financial Aid ....Ms. Cindy KIEFER
15 Director of Human Resources ....Mr. Warren D. TOLLEY
88 Director of Adult Basic Education ....Ms. Margaret L. GIRKINS
18 Director Maintenance Service ....Mr. Jack ROARK
21 Controller ....Mr. Kirk ZANDER
26 Asst Dir Marketing/Communications ....Ms. Tara E. ROTH
24 Coord Instructional Media Services ....Ms. Malinda CRAWFORD
36 Director Student Placement ....Ms. Karen DARROW
96 Director of Purchasing ....Mr. Steve LARSON
30 Director Institutional Advancement ....Ms. Coleen UNTERREINER
09 Director of Institutional Research ....Dr. Brad ELDREDGE

Fort Belknap College (E)

PO Box 159, Harlem MT 59526-0159
County: Blaine FICE Identification: 025175
Unit ID: 180203
Telephone: (406) 353-2607 Carnegie Class: Tribal
FAX Number: (406) 353-2898 Calendar System: Semester
URL: www.fbcc.edu
Established: 1984 Annual Undergrad Tuition & Fees: $2,410
Enrollment: 214 Coed
Affiliation or Control: Tribal Control IRS Status: 501(c)3
Highest Offering: Associate Degree
Program: Occupational; 2-Year Principally Bachelor's Creditable
Accreditation: NW

01 President ....Dr. Carole FALCON-CHANDLER
05 Interim Dean of Academic Affairs ....Vacant
32 Dean of Student Affairs ....Ms. Clarena BROCKIE
10 Comptroller ....Ms. Debra EVE
06 Registrar/Admissions Officer ....Mrs. Dixie BROCKIE
37 Financial Aid Officer ....Mrs. Mildred KINSEY
08 Director of Library Services ....Ms. Eva ENGLISH
13 Information Systems Manager ....Mr. Harold H. HEPPNER
40 Interim Bookstore Manager ....Ms. Kimberly BROCKIE

Fort Peck Community College (F)

PO Box 398, Poplar MT 59255-0398
County: Roosevelt FICE Identification: 023430
Unit ID: 180212
Telephone: (406) 768-6300 Carnegie Class: Tribal
FAX Number: (406) 768-6301 Calendar System: Semester
URL: www.fpcc.edu
Established: 1978 Annual Undergrad Tuition & Fees: $2,250
Enrollment: 452 Coed
Affiliation or Control: Tribal Control IRS Status: 501(c)3
Highest Offering: Associate Degree
Program: Occupational; 2-Year Principally Bachelor's Creditable; Business Emphasis
Accreditation: NW

01 President ....Dr. James E. SHANLEY
05 Academic Vice President ....Dr. Florence GARCIA
32 Vice President Student Services ....Ms. Haven GOURNEAU
09 Vice Pres Institutional Research ....Mr. Craig SMITH
31 Vice President Community Services ....Mr. Larry WETSIT
10 Business Manager ....Ms. Rose ATKINSON
06 Registrar/Admissions ....Ms. Linda L. HANSEN
37 Financial Aid Officer ....Ms. Lanette CLARKE
40 Bookstore Manager ....Ms. Jackie AZURE
08 Head Librarian ....Mrs. Anita A. SCHEETZ

Little Big Horn College (G)

PO Box 370, Crow Agency MT 59022-0370
County: Big Horn FICE Identification: 022866
Unit ID: 180328
Telephone: (406) 638-3104 Carnegie Class: Tribal
FAX Number: (406) 638-3169 Calendar System: Semester
URL: www.lbhc.edu
Established: 1980 Annual Undergrad Tuition & Fees: $2,760
Enrollment: 410 Coed
Affiliation or Control: Tribal Control IRS Status: 501(c)3
Highest Offering: Associate Degree
Program: Occupational; 2-Year Principally Bachelor's Creditable
Accreditation: #NW

01 President ....Dr. David YARLOTT, JR.
05 Academic Dean ....Miss Frederica LEFT HAND
32 Dean of Student Services ....Miss Te-Atta OLD BEAR
11 Dean of Administration ....Mr. David SMALL
08 Director of Library ....Mr. Tim BERNARDIS
13 Chief Information Officer ....Mr. Franklin COOPER
10 Chief Finance Officer ....Ms. Aldean GOOD LUCK
15 Director Human Resources ....Ms. Natalie COLIFLOWER
97 Dept Head/General Stds/Crow Stds ....Dr. Tim MCCLEARY
81 Dept Head/Math/Science/Technology ....Ms. Dianna HOOKER

Miles Community College (H)

2715 Dickinson, Miles City MT 59301-4799
County: Custer FICE Identification: 002528
Unit ID: 180373
Telephone: (406) 874-6100 Carnegie Class: Assoc/Pub-R-S
FAX Number: (406) 874-6282 Calendar System: Semester
URL: www.milescc.edu
Established: 1939 Annual Undergrad Tuition & Fees (In-District): $2,130
Enrollment: 582 Coed
Affiliation or Control: State/Local IRS Status: 501(c)3
Highest Offering: Associate Degree
Program: Occupational; 2-Year Principally Bachelor's Creditable
Accreditation: NW, ADNUR

01 President ....Dr. Stefani G. HICSWA
11 VP Administration & Finance ....Mr. Tad H. TORGERSON
05 Vice Pres of Academic Affairs ....Ms. Shelly WEIGHT
32 VP Student Success/Instl Research ....Mr. Darren PITCHER
08 Director of Library ....Ms. Ann O. RUTHERFORD
13 Director Information Technology ....Mr. Donald D. WARNER
37 Director Student Financial Aid ....Mr. Loren LANCASTER
18 Chief Facilities/Physical Plant ....Mr. Ross LAWRENCE
21 Controller ....Ms. Laura BENNETT
06 Registrar ....Ms. Lisa BLUNT
09 Dir Institutional Rsrch/Pub Rels ....Mrs. Carol HUDSON
15 Director Human Resources ....Ms. Kylene PHIPPS
66 Director Nursing ....Ms. Karla LUND
20 Associate Academic Officer ....Mr. Garth SLEIGHT
26 Chief Public Relations Officer ....Mrs. Carol I. HUDSON
40 Manager Bookstore ....Mrs. Judy STROBEL
38 Student Counselor ....Ms. Sheila SEIFERT

Montana Bible College (I)

3625 South 19th Avenue, Bozeman MT 59718-9108
County: Gallatin FICE Identification: 041403
Telephone: (406) 586-3585 Carnegie Class: Not Classified
FAX Number: (406) 586-3585 Calendar System: Semester
URL: www.montanabiblecollege.edu
Established: 1987 Annual Undergrad Tuition & Fees: $9,000
Enrollment: 120 Coed
Affiliation or Control: Independent Non-Profit IRS Status: 501(c)3
Highest Offering: Baccalaureate
Program: Religious Emphasis
Accreditation: @BI

01 President ....Mr. Jim CARLSON
05 Academic Dean ....Dr. Gale HEIDE
06 Registrar ....Mrs. Louise TURNER
07 Admissions Coordinator ....Mrs. Susan JACKSON
08 Head Librarian ....Mr. Micah FORSYTHE
32 Dean of Students ....Mr. Scott MORNINGSTAR
10 Business Manager ....Mrs. Leota FRED
21 Office Manager ....Mrs. Jeanie TYPOLT
18 Facilities Manager ....Mr. Ty TYPOLT
30 Advancement ....Ms. Barbara HANNO
26 Recruitment ....Mr. Ryan WARD

*Montana University System Office (J)

2500 Broadway, Helena MT 59601-3201
County: Lewis And Clark FICE Identification: 029072
Unit ID: 180470
Telephone: (406) 444-6570 Carnegie Class: N/A
FAX Number: (406) 444-1469
URL: www.mus.edu

01 Commissioner Higher Education ....Dr. Sheila M. STEARNS
05 Deputy Comm Academic/Student Affs ....Dr. Sylvia MOORE
10 Assoc Comm for Fiscal Affairs ....Mr. Mick ROBINSON
45 Assoc Comm for Plng & Public Policy ....Mr. Tyler TREVOR
43 Chief Legal Counsel ....Ms. Catherine SWIFT
15 Director Labor Relations/Personnel ....Mr. Kevin MCRAE
88 Director of Benefits ....Mrs. Connie WELSH
37 Director Guaranteed Student Loans ....Mr. Bruce MARKS
21 Director Accounting & Budget ....Ms. Frieda HOUSER
88 Director of Work Comp Risk Mgmt ....Ms. Leah Jo TIETZ
88 Dir of Distance Learning/Bus Devel ....Dr. Tom GIBSON
88 Dir of Transferability Initiatives ....Dr. Bill MACGREGOR
103 Deputy Comm Two-Year Educ ....Mr. John CECH
88 Dir Talent Search/Partners for Acce ....Ms. Rene DUBAY
93 Dir Minority/Amer Ind Achievement ....Vacant
88 Gear UP Director ....Ms. Sandy MERDINGER
88 IT Manager ....Ms. Edwina MORRISON

The University of Montana - Missoula (A)

32 Campus Drive, Missoula MT 59812-0001
County: Missoula FICE Identification: 002536
Unit ID: 180489
Telephone: (406) 243-0211 Carnegie Class: RU/H
FAX Number: (406) 243-2797 Calendar System: Semester
URL: www.umt.edu
Established: 1893 Annual Undergrad Tuition & Fees (In-State): $5,722
Enrollment: 15,036 Coed
Affiliation or Control: State IRS Status: 501(c)3
Highest Offering: Doctorate
Program: Liberal Arts And General; Teacher Preparatory; Professional
Accreditation: NW, ART, BUS, BUSA, CACREP, CLPSY, CS, FOR, JOUR, LAW, MUS, PHAR, PTA, @SP, SW, TED, THEA

02 President .... Dr. Royce C. ENGSTROM
03 Unversity Exec Vice President .... Mr. Jim FOLEY
05 Provost/Vice Pres Academic Affairs .... Mr. Perry BROWN
10 Vice President Finance/Admin .... Mr. Robert A. DURINGER
32 Vice President for Student Affairs .... Dr. Teresa S. BRANCH
46 Vice President Research/Devel .... Dr. Daniel J. DWYER
84 Asst Vice Pres Enrollment Services .... Mr. Jed LISTON
45 AVP for Planning/Budget Analysis .... Mr. William MUSE
20 Associate Provost .... Dr. Arlene WALKER-ANDREWS
104 Assoc Prov International Programs .... Dr. Mehrdad KIA
58 Assoc Provost Graduate Educ .... Dr. Perry J. BROWN
35 Dean of Students .... Dr. Charles COUTURE
43 Legal Counsel .... Dr. David J. ARONOFSKY
12 Director Mansfield Center .... Dr. Terry M. WEIDNER
88 Director Broadcast Media Center .... Mr. William MARCUS
22 Dir Equal Opportunity/Affirm Action .... Ms. Lucy FRANCE
15 Director Human Resource Services .... Vacant
06 Registrar .... Mr. Edwin JOHNSON
18 Director Facilities Services .... Mr. Hugh A. JESSE
13 Senior Assoc CIO .... Mr. Stephen S. HENRY
38 Director Counseling .... Dr. Brian KRYLOWICZ
36 Director Career Services .... Mr. Michael HEURING
37 Director of Financial Aid .... Mr. Myron L. HANSON
26 Director University Relations .... Ms. Rita MUNZENRIDER
29 Director of Alumni Association .... Mr. William S. JOHNSTON
102 President & CEO/UM Foundation .... Ms. Laura BREHM
19 Director of Public Safety .... Mr. Jim R. LEMCKE
23 Director Curry Health Center .... Dr. David E. BELL
24 Director Presentation Tech Services .... Mr. Randy GOTTFRIED
39 Director Residence Life .... Ms. Sandra CURIOONOVER
40 General Manager Univ Bookstore .... Mr. Bryan C. THORNTON
41 Director Intercollegiate Athletics .... Mr. Jim O'DAY
85 Dir Foreign Student & Scholar Svcs .... Ms. Effie F. KOEHN
21 Director Business Services .... Mr. Mark H. PULLIUM
07 Director Marketing Recruitment .... Ms. Juana J. ALCALA
62 Dean Library Services .... Dr. Bonnie ALLEN
51 Dean Continuing Education .... Dr. Sharon E. ALEXANDER
49 Dean College Arts & Sciences .... Dr. Christopher COMER
61 Dean School of Law .... Dr. Irma RUSSELL
65 Dean Col Forestry/Conservation .... Dr. James BURCHFIELD
50 Dean School of Business Admin .... Dr. Larry D. GIANCHETTA
76 Dean Col Hlth Prof & Biomed Sci .... Dr. David FORBES
60 Dean School of Journalism .... Ms. Peggy KUHR
53 Dean College of Educ & Human Svcs .... Dr. Roberta EVANS
57 Dean College Visual Performing Arts .... Mr. Stephen KALM
75 Dean College of Technology .... Dr. Barry GOOD
92 Dean Honors College .... Dr. James MCKUSICK

*The University of Montana Western (B)

710 S Atlantic St, Dillon MT 59725-3598
County: Beaverhead FICE Identification: 002537
Unit ID: 180692
Telephone: (406) 683-7011 Carnegie Class: Bac/Diverse
FAX Number: (406) 683-7493 Calendar System: Other
URL: www.umwestern.edu
Established: 1893 Annual Undergrad Tuition & Fees (In-State): $3,945
Enrollment: 1,365 Coed
Affiliation or Control: State IRS Status: 501(c)3
Highest Offering: Baccalaureate
Program: 2-Year Principally Bachelor's Creditable; Liberal Arts And General; Teacher Preparatory
Accreditation: NW, IACBE, TED

02 Chancellor .... Dr. Richard D. STOREY
05 Provost/Vice Chanc Academic Affairs .... Dr. Karl ULRICH
10 Vice Chanc Administration/Finance .... Ms. Susan BRIGGS
26 Director Marketing/Univ Relations .... Mr. Kent J. ORD
06 Registrar .... Mr. Jason KARCH
07 Director of Admissions .... Ms. Catherine REDHEAD
08 Librarian .... Mr. Michael SCHULZ
36 Director of Field Learning .... Mr. Michael MILLER
24 Director of Media Relations .... Mr. David NOLT
41 Director of Athletics .... Mr. Mark DURHAM
14 Director of Computer Center .... Mr. Jim EFTA
18 Director of Facilities Services .... Mr. Dan PAYNE
32 Dean of Students .... Ms. Nicole HAZELBAKER
09 Director of Institutional Research .... Ms. Anneliese RIPLEY
30 Director of Devel/Alumni Relations .... Ms. Amberly PAHUT
37 Director Student Financial Aid .... Ms. Erica JONES
38 Director Student Counseling .... Ms. Lynn MEIER WELTZIEN
15 Director Personnel Services .... Ms. Susan BRIGGS

*The University of Montana - Helena College of Technology (C)

1115 N Roberts, Helena MT 59601-3098
County: Lewis and Clark FICE Identification: 007570
Unit ID: 180276
Telephone: (406) 444-6800 Carnegie Class: Assoc/Pub2in4
FAX Number: (406) 444-6892 Calendar System: Semester
URL: www.umhelena.edu
Established: 1939 Annual Undergrad Tuition & Fees (In-State): $1,552
Enrollment: 1,500 Coed
Affiliation or Control: State IRS Status: 501(c)3
Highest Offering: Associate Degree
Program: Occupational; 2-Year Principally Bachelor's Creditable; Technical Emphasis
Accreditation: NW, ADNUR

02 Dean/CEO .... Dr. Daniel BINGHAM
04 Assistant to the Dean/CEO .... Ms. Winnie STRAINER
05 Associate Dean of Academic Affairs .... Ms. Brandi FOSTER
103 Exec Dir of Acad & Workforce Dev .... Mr. Kevin BROCKBANK
06 Registrar .... Ms. Sarah DELLWO
08 Director of Library Services .... Ms. Janice BACINO
51 Director of Continuing Education .... Ms. Mary LANNERT
18 Assistant Dean of Fiscal & Plant .... Mr. Russ FILLNER
13 Information Systems Support Manager .... Mr. Jeff BLOCK
40 Bookstore Manager .... Ms. Joanne JOHNSON
32 Assistant Dean of Student Services .... Mr. Michael S. BROWN
26 Marketing & Comm Coordinator .... Ms. Barb MCALMOND
37 Director Student Financial Aid .... Ms. Valerie LAMBERT
32 Director of Retention & Advising .... Ms. Suzanne HUNGER
88 Dir Learning Ctr & Disability Svcs .... Ms. Cindy YARBERRY
15 Director of Human Resources .... Ms. Kila SHEPHERD
36 Career Services Coordinator .... Mr. Alan THOMPSON

*The University of Montana - College of Technology (D)

909 South Avenue W, Missoula MT 59801-7910
County: Missoula FICE Identification: 007561
Unit ID: 180382
Telephone: (406) 243-7811 Carnegie Class: Not Classified
FAX Number: (406) 243-7899 Calendar System: Semester
URL: www.cte.umt.edu
Established: 1907 Annual Undergrad Tuition & Fees (In-State): $3,368
Enrollment: 2,444 Coed
Affiliation or Control: State IRS Status: 501(c)3
Highest Offering: Associate Degree
Program: Occupational; 2-Year Principally Bachelor's Creditable; Professional; Technical Emphasis
Accreditation: &NW, ACFEI, ADNUR, SURGT

02 Dean .... Dr. Barry GOOD
05 Associate Dean .... Ms. Lynn STOCKING
05 Associate Dean .... Mr. Alan FUGLEBERG
11 Administrative Officer .... Ms. Jacqueline HOFMANN

† Regional accreditation is carried under the parent institution The University of Montana-Missoula, Missoula, MT.

*Montana State University (E)

PO Box 172190, Bozeman MT 59717-2190
County: Gallatin FICE Identification: 002532
Unit ID: 180461
Telephone: (406) 994-2452 Carnegie Class: RU/VH
FAX Number: (406) 994-1923 Calendar System: Semester
URL: www.montana.edu
Established: 1893 Annual Undergrad Tuition & Fees (In-State): $6,410
Enrollment: 13,559 Coed
Affiliation or Control: State IRS Status: 501(c)3
Highest Offering: Doctorate
Program: Occupational; 2-Year Principally Bachelor's Creditable; Liberal Arts And General; Teacher Preparatory; Professional
Accreditation: NW, ART, BUS, CACREP, CS, DIETD, @DIETI, ENG, ENGT, IPSY, MT, MUS, NURSE, TEAC

02 President .... Dr. Waded CRUZADO
05 Provost/Vice Pres Academic Affairs .... Dr. Martha POTVIN
10 Interim Vice Pres Admin/Finance .... Mr. Terry LEIST
32 Vice Pres Student Success .... Dr. Allen L. YARNELL
86 Vice Pres Ext Rels/Dir Extension .... Dr. Douglas STEELE
13 VP Planning & Analysis/CIO .... Dr. Jim RIMPAU
46 VP Rsrch/Creativity/Tech Transfer .... Dr. Thomas MCCOY
04 Assistant to the President .... Dr. Henrietta MANN
18 Assoc Vice Pres University Services .... Mr. Robert V. LASHAWAY
88 Assoc VP Res/Creativity/Tch Trnsfer .... Dr. Lee SPANGLER
15 Asst Vice Pres Human Resources .... Ms. Jo PACKHAM
21 Asst Vice Pres Financial Services .... Ms. Laura HUMBERGER
102 President/CEO MSU Foundation .... Mr. Michael STEVENSON
104 Exec Dir International Education .... Dr. Norman PETERSON
27 Exec Director Univ Communications .... Mr. Thomas CALCAGNI
88 Exec Director Museum of the Rockies .... Ms. Sheldon MCKAMEY
50 Interim Dean Business .... Dr. Susan DANA
53 Dean Education/Health/Human Dev .... Dr. Larry BAKER
54 Dean Engineering .... Dr. Robert MARLEY
49 Dean Letters & Science .... Dr. Paula LUTZ
66 Dean Nursing .... Dr. Helen MELLAND
08 Dean Libraries .... Ms. Tamara MILLER
88 Dean Students .... Dr. Matthew CAIRES
58 Dean Graduate School .... Dr. Carl FOX
47 Dean Agriculture .... Dr. Jeffrey JACOBSEN
48 Interim Dean Arts/Architecture .... Dr. Joseph FEDOCK
70 Dean Gallatin College Programs .... Mr. Robert HIETALA
07 Director Admissions .... Ms. Ronda RUSSELL
22 Interim Dir Affirmative Action/HR .... Ms. Diane LETENDRE
29 Director Alumni Relations .... Ms. Jaynee GROSETH
41 Director Athletics .... Mr. Peter FIELDS
88 Director Auxiliary Services .... Mr. Tom STUMP
36 Director Career Services .... Dr. Carina BECK
38 Director Counseling/Psych Services .... Dr. Patrick DONAHOE
88 Dir Disability/Re-ent/Veteran Svcs .... Ms. Brenda YORK
56 Director Extended University .... Dr. Kim OBBINK
37 Director Financial Aid .... Ms. Brandi PAYNE
43 Legal Counsel .... Dr. Leslie TAYLOR
45 Assoc Director Planning & Analysis .... Dr. Chris FASTNOW
96 Director Purchasing .... Dr. Shawna LANPHEAR
06 Registrar .... Ms. Bonnie ASHLEY
26 Director Marketing/Creative Service .... Ms. Julie KIPFER
19 Director University Police .... Mr. Robert PUTZKE

*Montana State University - Billings (F)

1500 University Drive, Billings MT 59101-0245
County: Yellowstone FICE Identification: 002530
Unit ID: 180179
Telephone: (406) 657-2011 Carnegie Class: Master's M
FAX Number: (406) 657-2302 Calendar System: Semester
URL: www.msubillings.edu
Established: 1927 Annual Undergrad Tuition & Fees (In-State): $5,241
Enrollment: 5,335 Coed
Affiliation or Control: State IRS Status: 501(c)3
Highest Offering: Master's
Program: Occupational; Liberal Arts And General; Teacher Preparatory; Business Emphasis
Accreditation: NW, ART, BUS, CORE, EMT, MUS, TED

02 Chancellor .... Dr. Rolf S. GROSETH
11 Administrative Vice Chancellor .... Ms. Terrie IVERSON
05 Int Provost/VC for Acad Affairs .... Dr. Gary YOUNG
32 Vice Chancellor for Student Affairs .... Dr. Stacy KLIPPENSTEIN
102 President/CEO Foundation .... Ms. Marilynn MILLER
08 Director Library Services .... Mr. Brent ROBERTS
84 Director Enrollment Management .... Dr. Stacy KLIPPENSTEIN
07 Director Admiss/Records/Registrar .... Ms. Cheri JOHANNES
15 Director Human Resources/EEO AA .... Ms. Janet SIMON
36 Director Career Services .... Ms. Patricia B. REUSS
27 Chief Information Officer .... Dr. Michael J. BARBER
25 Assoc Dir Grants & Sponsored Pgms .... Ms. Heather CONLEY
25 Assoc Dir Grants & Sponsored Pgms .... Ms. Deborah PETERS
26 Director University Relations .... Mr. Dan CARTER
09 Office Institutional Planning .... Vacant
18 Director Facility Services .... Mr. Eakle BARFIELD
58 Director Graduate Programs .... Dr. Gary YOUNG
41 Athletic Director .... Dr. Gary GRAY
19 Chief of Campus Police .... Mr. Scott FORSHEE
29 Director Alumni Relations .... Ms. Julie SEEDHOUSE
37 Director Student Financial Aid .... Ms. Judy CHAPMAN
40 Director Bookstore .... Mr. Dennis REA
39 Dir Stdnt Union/Housing/Res Life .... Ms. Jeannie MCISAAC-TRACY
31 Director of Community Involvement .... Ms. Kathy KOTECKI
35 Dir Student Svcs/Assoc Registrar .... Dr. Rita KRATKY
21 University Budget Director .... Ms. Liz TOOLEY
96 Director of Business Services .... Mr. Jim NIELSEN
20 Dir Academic Support Center .... Mr. Benjamin BARCKHOLTZ
20 Dir Ctr for Applied Econ Research .... Dr. Scott RICKARD
28 Dir Montana Center on Disabilities .... Ms. Marsha SAMPSON
89 Director New Student Services .... Ms. Shelly ANDERSEN
38 Interim Assistant Director Advising .... Ms. Becky LYONS
88 Director American Indian Outreach .... Ms. Reno CHARETTE
85 Exec Dir International Outreach .... Dr. Kirk LACY
106 Director eLearning Services .... Dr. Michael BARBER
92 Director of Honors Program .... Ms. Tami HAALAND
104 Program Mgr Intl Studies & Outreach .... Ms. Janese CARSTENS
12 Executive Director MSUB Downtown .... Mr. Bob CARR
49 Dean of Arts & Sciences .... Dr. Tasneem KHALEEL
53 Dean of Education .... Dr. Mary Susan FISHBAUGH
50 Int Dean College of Business .... Dr. Tim WILKINSON
72 Int Dean College of Technology .... Dr. Gary YOUNG
76 Dean Col of Allied Health Prof .... Dr. Diane DUIN
88 Assoc Dean College of Technology .... Ms. Tammi MILLER

*Montana State University - Northern (G)

PO Box 7751, Havre MT 59501-7751
County: Hill FICE Identification: 002533
Unit ID: 180522
Telephone: (406) 265-3700 Carnegie Class: Bac/Diverse
FAX Number: N/A Calendar System: Semester
URL: www.msun.edu
Established: 1929 Annual Undergrad Tuition & Fees (In-State): $4,476
Enrollment: 1,275 Coed
Affiliation or Control: State IRS Status: 501(c)3
Highest Offering: Master's
Program: Liberal Arts And General; Teacher Preparatory; Professional; Music Emphasis
Accreditation: NW, ADNUR, ENGT, NUR

02 Interim Chancellor .... Dr. Joseph CALLAHAN
05 Provost/Vice Chanc Academic Affairs .... Dr. Rosalyn TEMPLETON
10 Director of Business Services .... Ms. Sue OST

102 Executive Director of Foundation .... Ms. Shauna ALBRECHT
72 Dean College Technical Sciences .... Mr. Gregory KEGEL
32 Assistant Dean of Students .... Mr. William LANIER
53 Dean Col Educ/Arts & Sci/Nursing ....Vacant
06 Dean of Students/Registrar ....Ms. Lindsey BROWN
66 Director of Nursing .... Ms. Mary PAPPAS
41 Athletic Director .... Mr. Mark SAMSON
36 Director Career Planning/Placement .... Ms. Tracey JETTE
13 Int Director Info Technology Svcs ....Mr. Rock BROWN
37 Director of Financial Aid ....Ms. Cindy SMALL
26 Director of University Relations .... Mr. James POTTER
08 Interim Director of Library ....Ms. Vicki GIST
38 Director Student Support Services ....Mr. John A. DONALDSON
15 Director Human Resources .... Ms. Kathy JAYNES
29 Alumni Coordinator .... Ms. Autumn ELLIOT
07 Assoc Director New Student Services ....Vacant
18 Interim Facilities Manager .... Mr. Dan ULMEN

*Montana State University - Billings College of Technology (A)

3803 Central Avenue, Billings MT 59102-4398

County: Yellowstone FICE Identification: 010166
Unit ID: 180045
Telephone: (406) 247-3000 Carnegie Class: Assoc/Pub2in4
FAX Number: (406) 652-1729 Calendar System: Semester
URL: www.cot.msubillings.edu
Established: 1969 Annual Undergrad Tuition & Fees (In-State): $10,194
Enrollment: 1,531 Coed
Affiliation or Control: State IRS Status: 501(c)3
Highest Offering: Associate Degree
Program: Occupational
Accreditation: &NW

02 Dean ....Vacant
05 Associate Dean .... Ms. Tammi MILLER
10 Chief Business Officer .... Ms. Susan STEWART
07 Admissions and Registrar ....Dr. Rita KRATKY
08 Co-Librarian .... Ms. Shelly LOVELESS
08 Co-Librarian ....Ms. Gail BINFORD
20 Associate Academic Officer ....Vacant

† Regional accreditation is carried under the parent institution Montana State University-Billings, Billings, MT.

*Montana State University - Great Falls College of Technology (B)

2100 16th Avenue South, Great Falls MT 59405-4909

County: Cascade FICE Identification: 009314
Unit ID: 180249
Telephone: (406) 771-4300 Carnegie Class: Assoc/Pub2in4
FAX Number: (406) 771-4317 Calendar System: Semester
URL: www.msugf.edu
Established: 1969 Annual Undergrad Tuition & Fees (In-State): $3,012
Enrollment: 1,229 Coed
Affiliation or Control: State IRS Status: 501(c)3
Highest Offering: Associate Degree
Program: Occupational; 2-Year Principally Bachelor's Creditable
Accreditation: NW, DA, DH, SURGT

02 Dean/CEO .... Dr. Joseph SCHAFFER
04 Executive Assistant to the Dean ....Mrs. Heather PALERMO
05 Assoc Dean Academic Affairs .... Dr. Heidi PASEK
10 Assoc Dean Administration & Finance .... Ms. Mary Ellen BAUKOL
26 Exec Dir College Rel/Advancement ....Ms. Pamela PARSONS
06 Registrar/Admissions Officer .... Mrs. Dena WAGNER-FOSSEN
07 Director of Admissions ....Mr. Tom DEGEL
15 Exec Director Human Resources .... Ms. Mary Kay BONILLA
30 Director of Development .... Mr. Thomas FIGARELLE
37 Director Student Financial Aid ....Ms. Leah HABEL
36 Director Student Placement .... Ms. Courtney JOHNSRUD
35 Assistant Dean Student Services ....Ms. Judy HAY
40 Bookstore Manager .... Mr. Steve HALSTED
96 Budget & Purchasing Officer ....Ms. Deby GUNTER
18 Director of Facilities Services .... Mr. Scott KARAFFA
08 Director of Weaver Library ....Mr. Ken WARDINSKY
09 Director of Institutional Research ....Ms. Wendy DOVE

*Montana Tech of The University of Montana (C)

1300 W Park Street, Butte MT 59701-8997

County: Silver Bow FICE Identification: 002531
Unit ID: 180416
Telephone: (406) 496-4101 Carnegie Class: Bac/Diverse
FAX Number: (406) 496-4133 Calendar System: Semester
URL: www.mtech.edu
Established: 1893 Annual Undergrad Tuition & Fees (In-State): $6,420
Enrollment: 2,864 Coed
Affiliation or Control: State IRS Status: 501(c)3
Highest Offering: Master's
Program: 2-Year Principally Bachelor's Creditable; Liberal Arts And General; Professional; Technical Emphasis
Accreditation: NW, ADNUR, CS, ENG, ENGR

02 Chancellor .... Dr. Donald M. BLACKKETTER
05 Vice Chanc Acad Affs/Research .... Dr. Douglas M. ABBOTT
10 Business Officer/Controller .... Mr. John C. BADOVINAC
11 VC for Administration & Finance ....Ms. Maggie PETERSON
30 Interim Vice Chanc Dev/Alumni Aff .... Ms. Traci O'NEILL
32 Assoc VC for Student Affairs ....Mr. Paul V. BEATTY
20 Assoc VC AA/Research/Dean Grad Sch ....Dr. Joseph F. FIGUEIRA
65 Director Bureau of Mines & Geology .... Dr. Edmond G. DEAL
84 Director of Enrollment Management .... Mr. Tony CAMPEAU
31 Director of Technical Outreach ....Ms. Amy VERLANIC
36 Director Career Services ....Ms. Sarah RAYMOND
08 Director Library ....Ms. Ann F. ST. CLAIR
37 Director of Financial Aid .... Mr. Michael W. RICHARDSON
18 Director of Physical Facilities .... Mr. Art ANDERSON
29 Director Alumni Affairs .... Ms. Peggy S. MCCOY
41 Athletic Director .... Mr. Joe MCCLAFFERTY
21 Dir Financial Planning/Analysis .... Mr. Daniel FAUGHT
72 Dean College of Technology ....Mr. John GARIC
81 Dean Col Letters/Sci/Prof Studies ....Dr. Douglas A. COE
88 Dean School of Mines & Engineering ....Dr. H. Peter KNUDSEN
44 Director of Development ....Mr. Michael BARTH
39 Director Residence Life ....Mr. Jacob FLOCH
26 Director Public Relations ....Ms. Amanda BADOVINAC
40 Bookstore Director .... Ms. Jeni L. LUFT
09 Director Institutional Research .... Ms. Melissa HARRINGTON

*Montana Tech College of Technology (D)

25 Basin Creek Road, Butte MT 59701-9704

County: Silver Bow FICE Identification: 009282
Unit ID: 180081
Telephone: (406) 496-3701 Carnegie Class: Assoc/Pub-R-S
FAX Number: (406) 496-3710 Calendar System: Semester
URL: www.mtech.edu
Established: 1969 Annual Undergrad Tuition & Fees (In-State): $3,141
Enrollment: 560 Coed
Affiliation or Control: State IRS Status: Exempt
Highest Offering: Associate Degree
Program: Occupational; 2-Year Principally Bachelor's Creditable
Accreditation: &NW

02 Dean ....Dr. John M. GARIC
05 Vice Chancellor of Academic Affairs ....Dr. Douglas ABBOTT
10 Vice Chancellor Admin & Finance .... Mrs. Margaret PETERSON
30 Vice Chancellor Devel & Student Svc .... Mr. Michael JOHNSON
32 Assoc Vice Chancellor Student Svcs ....Mr. Paul BEATTY
37 Financial Aid Officer .... Mr. Michael W. RICHARDSON
08 Director of Library ....Ms. Ann ST CLAIR
38 Counselor .... Ms. Joyce O'NEIL
38 Counselor .... Ms. Cricket PIETSCH
06 Director of Enrollment Services ....Mr. Tony CAMPEAU
09 Director of Institutional Research .... Ms. Melissa HARRINGTON
18 Director of Physical Facilities .... Mr. Arthur ANDERSON
21 Controller .... Mr. John BADOVINAC
26 Director of Public Relations .... Mrs. Amanda BADOVINAC
29 Director of Alumni Affairs ....Ms. Peggy MCCOY
84 Director of Enrollment Services ....Mr. Tony CAMPEAU
96 Associate Director Budgets .... Mr. Daniel FAUGHT

Rocky Mountain College (E)

1511 Poly Drive, Billings MT 59102-1796

County: Yellowstone FICE Identification: 002534
Unit ID: 180595
Telephone: (406) 657-1000 Carnegie Class: Bac/Diverse
FAX Number: (406) 259-9751 Calendar System: Semester
URL: www.rocky.edu
Established: 1878 Annual Undergrad Tuition & Fees: $22,134
Enrollment: 984 Coed
Affiliation or Control: Interdenominational IRS Status: 501(c)3
Highest Offering: Master's
Program: Liberal Arts And General; Teacher Preparatory
Accreditation: NW, AAB, ARCPA

01 President .... Mr. Michael R. MACE
05 Academic Vice President/Provost ....Mr. Anthony PILTZ
32 Vice President of Student Services .... Mr. Bradley A. NASON
84 Vice Pres Enrol Svcs/Dir Admissions .... Ms. Kelly EDWARDS
10 Chief Financial Officer .... Ms. Carol JENSEN
35 Associate Dean of Students .... Ms. Katie CARPENTER
16 Vice President for Human Resources ....Mr. Gregory N. KOHN
56 Dir Dist Lrng & Degree Completion ....Ms. Stevie SCHMITZ
08 Director of the Library .... Mr. Bill KEHLER
44 Director of Planned Giving ....Mr. Obert UNDEM
26 Director News and Information ....Mr. Dan BURKHART
91 Dir of Administrative Computing .... Ms. Kellee PIERCE
18 Director of Facilities Management .... Mr. Terry STEINER
41 Director of Athletics ....Mr. Robert BEERS
30 Director of Major Gifts ....Ms. Vickie DAVISON
09 Institutional Research Analyst ....Mr. Erik WILLBORG
06 Registrar ....Dr. Leslie G. EDWARDS
37 Director of Financial Assistance ...... Ms. Jessica FRANCISCHETTI
39 Director of Residence Life .... Ms. April STEVENSON
42 Chaplain Dir Campus Ministries ....Ms. Kristi FOSTER
04 Executive Assistant to the Pres ....Ms. Pam ERICKSON

Salish Kootenai College (F)

PO Box 70, Pablo MT 59855-0070

County: Lake FICE Identification: 021434
Unit ID: 180647
Telephone: (406) 275-4800 Carnegie Class: Tribal
FAX Number: (406) 275-4801 Calendar System: Quarter
URL: www.skc.edu
Established: 1977 Annual Undergrad Tuition & Fees: $6,141
Enrollment: 1,170 Coed
Affiliation or Control: Independent Non-Profit IRS Status: 501(c)3
Highest Offering: Baccalaureate
Program: Occupational; 2-Year Principally Bachelor's Creditable; Liberal Arts And General
Accreditation: NW, ADNUR, DA, NUR, SW

01 President ....Dr. Luana ROSS
05 Academic Vice President .... Ms. Carmen TAYLOR
10 Vice President Business Affairs .... Mr. Lon WHITAKER
06 Registrar .... Ms. Cleo KENMILLE
37 Financial Aid Director .... Ms. Jackie SWAIN
09 Director of Institutional Research ....Dr. Robert PEREGOY
15 Director Personnel Services ....Mrs. Dawn BENSON
30 Development Director ....Mrs. Lois SLATER
32 Chief Student Life Officer ....Mr. Juan PEREZ
13 Director of Information Technology ....Mr. Al ANDERSON
18 Facilities/Physical Plant Manager ....Mr. Fred WEBSTER
35 Inter Campus Coordinator .... Mr. Corky CLAIRMONT

Stone Child College (G)

8294 Upper Box Elder Road, Box Elder MT 59521-9796

County: Hill FICE Identification: 026109
Unit ID: 366340
Telephone: (406) 395-4313 Carnegie Class: Tribal
FAX Number: (406) 395-4836 Calendar System: Semester
URL: www.stonechild.edu/
Established: 1984 Annual Undergrad Tuition & Fees: $2,450
Enrollment: 1,049 Coed
Affiliation or Control: Tribal Control IRS Status: 501(c)3
Highest Offering: Associate Degree
Program: 2-Year Principally Bachelor's Creditable
Accreditation: NW

01 President ....Ms. Melody HENRY
05 Dean of Instruction ....Ms. Cory SANGREY-BILLY
32 Dean of Student Services ....Ms. Clarice MORSETTE
10 Business Manager ....Ms. Jewel L. WHITFORD
04 Admin Asst to the President ....Ms. Wanda ST. MARKS
06 Registrar ....Mrs. Gaile TORRES
13 Management Information Specialist ....Mr. Jeffery HENRY
40 Bookstore Manager .... Ms. Jennifer RAINING BIRD
37 Financial Aid Officer .... Ms. Tiffany GALBAVY
18 Plant Manager .... Mr. Frank HENRY
08 Head Librarian .... Ms. Helen WINDY BOY

University of Great Falls (H)

1301 Twentieth Street S, Great Falls MT 59405-4996

County: Cascade FICE Identification: 002527
Unit ID: 180258
Telephone: (800) 856-9544 Carnegie Class: Bac/Diverse
FAX Number: (406) 791-5209 Calendar System: Semester
URL: www.ugf.edu
Established: 1932 Annual Undergrad Tuition & Fees: $18,480
Enrollment: 884 Coed
Affiliation or Control: Roman Catholic IRS Status: 501(c)3
Highest Offering: Master's
Program: Liberal Arts And General; Teacher Preparatory; Professional
Accreditation: NW, NURSE

01 President .... Dr. Eugene J. MCALLISTER
05 VP for Academic Affairs/Provost ....Dr. Richard MCDOWELL
10 Vice President for Finance ....Ms. Stacey EVE
32 Dean of Student Development .... Ms. Twila CROFT
30 VP for Philanthropy ....Mr. Tenis TENNYSON
84 VP for Enrollment Management .... Ms. Charlene BROWN
20 Academic Dean .... Fr. James SIKORA
37 Director Financial Aid .... Ms. Sandra BAUMAN
06 Registrar .... Ms. Kerri KOTESKEY
14 Director Administrative Computing .... Ms. Kathryn CARBIS
26 Director of Marketing and PR ....Ms. Kristi GOLIK
18 Director Physical Plant ....Mr. Chet PIETRYKOWSKI
29 Director Alumni Relations .... Mr. Brian JOHNSON
38 Director Student Counseling ....Ms. Linda FAGENSTROM
41 Director of Athletics .... Mr. Gary EHNES
21 Director of the Business Office .... Ms. Amber OBRESLEY
51 Director of Continuing Education .... Ms. Sonja BICKFORD
106 Director of Distance Learning ....Mr. Jim GRETCH
15 Director of Human Resources ....Ms. Kristen RANTZ
09 Director of Institutional Research ....Mr. Greg MADSON
40 Campus Store Manger ....Ms. Theresa HILL
88 Director of Mission Integration .... Sr. Mary Kaye NEALEN
13 Operations Manager/IT Services ....Mr. John KOEHLER
88 Director Student Support Services ....Ms. LaTosha WILLIAMS

NEBRASKA

Alegent Health School of Radiologic Technology (I)

7500 Mercy Road, Omaha NE 68124

County: Douglas FICE Identification: 008492
Unit ID: 181145
Telephone: (402) 398-5527 Carnegie Class: Not Classified
FAX Number: (402) 398-6650 Calendar System: Semester
URL: www.alegent.com
Established: 1953 Annual Undergrad Tuition & Fees: $4,590
Enrollment: 22 Coed
Affiliation or Control: Independent Non-Profit IRS Status: 501(c)3
Highest Offering: Associate Degree
Program: Occupational; 2-Year Principally Bachelor's Creditable

Accreditation: RAD

01 Program Director ... Robert A. HUGHES

Bellevue University (A)

1000 Galvin Road S, Bellevue NE 68005-3098

County: Sarpy FICE Identification: 009743
Unit ID: 180814
Telephone: (402) 293-2000 Carnegie Class: Master's L
FAX Number: (402) 293-2020 Calendar System: Other
URL: www.bellevue.edu
Established: 1965 Annual Undergrad Tuition & Fees: $7,320
Enrollment: 10,407 Coed
Affiliation or Control: Independent Non-Profit IRS Status: 501(c)3
Highest Offering: Doctorate
Program: Liberal Arts And General
Accreditation: NH, IACBE

01 President ... Dr. Mary B. HAWKINS
00 Chancellor ... Dr. John B. MULLER
11 Vice President Administration ... Mr. Jerry A. BLASIG
05 Vice President Academic Affairs ... Ms. Donna N. MCDANIEL
45 Exec VP Strategic Initiatives ... Dr. Mike ECHOLS
15 Asst VP Human Resources ... Mr. Michael WARNER
107 Interim Dean College Prof Studies ... Ms. Donna N. MCDANIEL
88 Dean Ctr Learning Innovation ... Ms. Cathy ERION
88 Dean of College of Information Tech ... Ms. Mary DOBRANSKY
20 Asst VP of Academic Services ... Ms. Michelle EPPLER
49 Dean College Arts & Sciences ... Dr. Therese MICHELS
26 Sr Research Analyst/PR ... Mr. John WATSON
14 Asst VP of Information Technology ... Mr. James S. VEREBELY
07 Asst VP Enrollment Management ... Mr. Matthew DAVIS
21 Controller ... Mr. Craig ERWIN
04 Exec Assistant to the President ... Ms. Christine DOOCY
06 Registrar ... Ms. Cheri JOHNSON
37 Director Student Financial Svcs ... Ms. Janet YALE
08 Library Director ... Ms. Robin BERNSTEIN
102 Foundation CEO ... Mr. Russ RUPIPER
41 Director of Athletics ... Mr. Ed LEHOTAK
40 Director Bookstore ... Mr. Mark RIGGERT
18 Director of Facilities ... Mr. Ralph J. BORER
29 Director Alumni Relations ... Ms. Dorothy MORROW
50 Dean College of Business ... Dr. Rod HEWLETT
88 Dean Center for Academic Excellence ... Dr. Linda WILD

Bryan LGH College of Health Sciences (B)

5035 Everett Street, Lincoln NE 68506-1315

County: Lancaster FICE Identification: 006399
Unit ID: 180878
Telephone: (402) 481-8697 Carnegie Class: Spec/Health
FAX Number: N/A Calendar System: Semester
URL: www.bryanlghcollege.edu
Established: 2001 Annual Undergrad Tuition & Fees: $10,900
Enrollment: 495 Coed
Affiliation or Control: Independent Non-Profit IRS Status: 501(c)3
Highest Offering: Master's
Program: Professional; Nursing Emphasis
Accreditation: NH, ANEST, CVT, DMS, NUR

01 President ... Dr. Elizabeth WALL
05 Provost ... Dr. Kay MAIZE
97 Dean of General Education ... Vacant
11 Dean of Administration ... Ms. June SMITH
66 Dean of Nursing ... Dr. Theresa DELAHOYDE
76 Dean of Allied Health ... Ms. Diane KATHOL
88 Dean of Nurse Anesthesia ... Mr. James CUDDEFORD
106 Dean of Instructional Technology ... Dr. Kim LEIGHTON
32 Dean of Students ... Ms. Debra BORDER
08 Director of Library Services ... Ms. Anne HEIMANN
84 Director of Enrollment Management ... Ms. Sara MALSBURY
06 Registrar ... Ms. Nancy SCHLIZ

Central Community College (C)

PO Box 4903, Grand Island NE 68802-4903

County: Hall FICE Identification: 020995
Unit ID: 180902
Telephone: (308) 398-4222 Carnegie Class: Assoc/Pub-R-L
FAX Number: (308) 398-7398 Calendar System: Semester
URL: www.cccneb.edu
Established: 1966 Annual Undergrad Tuition & Fees (In-District): $2,580
Enrollment: 7,527 Coed
Affiliation or Control: Local IRS Status: 501(c)3
Highest Offering: Associate Degree
Program: Occupational; 2-Year Principally Bachelor's Creditable
Accreditation: NH, ADNUR, DA, DH, MAC, MLTAD, OTA

01 College President ... Dr. Greg P. SMITH
05 Exec Vice Pres/Chief Academic Ofcr ... Dr. Deb BRENNAN
12 Columbus Campus President ... Dr. Matt R. GOTSCHALL
12 Grand Island Campus President ... Dr. Lynn C. BLACK
12 Hastings Campus President ... Mr. Bill HITESMAN
26 Public Relations/Marketing Director ... Mr. James E. STRAYER
10 College Business Officer ... Mr. Larry C. GLAZIER
13 Dir Information Technology Services ... Mr. Tom D. PETERS
102 Foundation Director ... Mr. Dean MOORS
15 Human Resource Manager ... Mr. Douglas L. ADLER
06 Registrar ... Ms. Barb LARSON
29 Director Alumni Relations ... Mr. Dean MOORS
37 Director Student Financial Aid ... Mr. Steve MILLNITZ
84 Director Enrollment Management ... Mr. Ken REZAC
09 Director Institutional Research ... Mr. Brian MCDERMOTT
28 Director Diversity ... Mr. Doug ADLER
32 Director Student Affairs ... Mr. Ken REZAC
96 Director of Purchasing ... Ms. Alicia HAUSSLER
29 Alumni Coordinator ... Ms. Pat STANGE

Clarkson College (D)

101 S 42nd Street, Omaha NE 68131-2739

County: Douglas FICE Identification: 009862
Unit ID: 180832
Telephone: (402) 552-3100 Carnegie Class: Spec/Health
FAX Number: (402) 552-3369 Calendar System: Semester
URL: www.clarksoncollege.edu
Established: 1888 Annual Undergrad Tuition & Fees: $13,770
Enrollment: 989 Coed
Affiliation or Control: Independent Non-Profit IRS Status: 501(c)3
Highest Offering: Master's
Program: Liberal Arts And General; Professional; Nursing Emphasis
Accreditation: NH, ANEST, IACBE, NUR, PTAA, RAD

01 President ... Dr. Louis W. BURGHER
05 VP of Academic Affairs ... Dr. Jody WOODWORTH
84 VP of Enroll Mgt/Campus Life Ops ... Tony M. DAMEWOOD
10 Controller ... Megan WICKLESS
06 Registrar ... Michele D. STIRTZ
15 Director Human Resources ... Deb TOMEK
13 Director Technology ... Larry J. VINSON
26 Director of Marketing ... Jina PAUL
28 Director Diversity Services ... Aubray D. ORDUNA
37 Director Student Financial Services ... Margie R. HARRIS
08 Director Library Services ... Nancy M. RALSTON
38 Director Success Center ... Chuck C. MACDONELL
97 Director General Education ... Lori BACHLE
66 Dir Grad Nursing/Dean of Nursing ... Dr. Aubray ORDUNA
66 Director Bachelor of Sci in Nursing ... Aubray ORDUNA
50 Dir of Business & HIM ... Carla DIRKSCHNEIDER
76 Dir Medical Imaging/Radiologic Tech ... Ellen COLLINS
76 Dir Physical Therapist Asst Pgm ... Andreia NEBEL
07 Director Admissions ... Denise WORK
51 Director of Professional Dev ... Judi B. DUNN
29 Director Alumni Relations ... Rita VANFLEET
88 Dir Basic and Advanced Life Support ... Liz A. SVATOS
106 Coordinator Online Education ... Linda A. NIETO
00 Dir Center of Teaching Excellence ... Mark WHITE

College of Saint Mary (E)

7000 Mercy Road, Omaha NE 68106-2606

County: Douglas FICE Identification: 002540
Unit ID: 181604
Telephone: (402) 399-2400 Carnegie Class: Master's S
FAX Number: (402) 399-2647 Calendar System: Semester
URL: www.csm.edu
Established: 1923 Annual Undergrad Tuition & Fees: $24,350
Enrollment: 1,070 Female
Affiliation or Control: Roman Catholic IRS Status: 501(c)3
Highest Offering: Doctorate
Program: Liberal Arts And General; Teacher Preparatory; Professional
Accreditation: NH, ADNUR, IACBE, NUR, OT

01 President ... Dr. Maryanne STEVENS, RSM
32 Vice President Student Development ... Dr. Tara KNUDSON-CARL
05 Vice Pres Academic Affairs/Dean ... Dr. Christine PHARR
30 Vice Pres Institutional Advancement ... Verlyn SCHUELER
07 Vice President Enrollment/Marketing ... Mr. Joe SZEJK
10 Vice Pres Financial Services/CFO ... Ms. Sarah KOTTICH
04 Executive Asst to the President ... Ms. Shirley GUNDERSON
06 Registrar ... Mrs. Deb NUGEN
08 Director of Library ... Ms. Sarah WATKINS
14 Director of Computer Center ... Mr. Jason DEGN
29 Director of Alumnae ... Ms. Diane PROULX
37 Director Student Financial Aid ... Ms. Beth SISK
26 Public Relations Director ... Mr. Glen SISK
35 Director Student Affairs ... Mrs. Katty PETAK
39 Director Student Housing ... Ms. Emily BENNETT
40 Director Bookstore ... Mr. Steve WESTENBROEK
41 Athletic Director ... Mr. Jim KRUEGER
42 Director Campus Ministry ... Ms. Vicki ZOBRIST
84 Director Enrollment Management ... Mr. Joe SZEJK
85 Director Foreign Students ... Ms. Jennifer WITTSTOCK
18 Director Physical Plant ... Mr. Dan SPARGEN
44 Director Annual Giving ... Ms. Keli OFFERMAN
09 Director of Institutional Research ... Ms. Ellen JACOBS
21 Associate Business Officer ... Ms. Bridgette RENBARGER
15 Director Personnel Services ... Ms. Sarah M. LIVINGSTON

Concordia University (F)

800 N Columbia Avenue, Seward NE 68434-1599

County: Seward FICE Identification: 002541
Unit ID: 180984
Telephone: (402) 643-3651 Carnegie Class: Master's S
FAX Number: (402) 643-4073 Calendar System: Other
URL: www.cune.edu
Established: 1894 Annual Undergrad Tuition & Fees: $23,060
Enrollment: 2,146 Coed
Affiliation or Control: Lutheran Church - Missouri Synod
IRS Status: 501(c)3
Highest Offering: Master's
Program: Liberal Arts And General; Teacher Preparatory
Accreditation: NH, IACBE, MUS, TED

01 President ... Rev Dr. Brian L. FRIEDRICH
05 Provost ... Dr. Jenny MUELLER-ROEBKE
30 Vice President Inst Advancement ... Vacant
84 VP Enroll Mgt/Stdnt Svcs/Athletics ... Mr. Scott SEEVERS
20 Associate Provost ... Dr. Lisa ASHBY
10 Chief Financial Officer ... Mr. David KUMM
53 Dean of College of Education ... Dr. Ronald BORK
49 Dean of Arts & Sciences ... Dr. Brent ROYUK
13 Co-Dean Information Technology ... Dr. Donald SYLWESTER
13 Co-Dean Information Technology ... Dr. Kent EINSPAHR
08 Director of Library Services ... Mr. Philip HENDRICKSON
06 University Registrar ... Mr. Ed SIFFRING
36 Synodical & Education Placement Dir ... Mr. William SCHRANZ
29 Director Alumni/University Rels ... Mrs. Jan KOOPMAN
35 Director Student Life ... Vacant
36 Career Counselor ... Mr. Corey GRAY
41 Athletic Director ... Mr. Devin SMITH
42 Campus Pastor ... Rev. Ryan MATTHIAS
37 Director of Financial Aid ... Mrs. Gloria HENNIG
18 Chief Facilities/Physical Plant ... Mr. David RYAN
15 Director of Human Resources ... Mrs. Connie BUTLER
07 Director Undergraduate Admissions ... Mr. Aaron ROBERTS
26 Director of Marketing ... Mr. Andrew SWENSON
21 Dir Invest/Student Admin Svcs ... Mr. Curt SHERMAN
44 Coord of Resource Devel Ops ... Mrs. Janet TONJES
38 Director of Counseling ... Ms. Dina CRITEL-RATHJE

The Creative Center (G)

10850 Emmet Street, Omaha NE 68164-2911

County: Douglas FICE Identification: 031643
Unit ID: 430485
Telephone: (402) 898-1000 Carnegie Class: Spec/Arts
FAX Number: (402) 898-1301 Calendar System: Semester
URL: www.creativecenter.edu
Established: 1993 Annual Undergrad Tuition & Fees: N/A
Enrollment: 115 Coed
Affiliation or Control: Proprietary IRS Status: Proprietary
Highest Offering: Baccalaureate
Program: Occupational; 2-Year Principally Bachelor's Creditable; Fine Arts Emphasis
Accreditation: ACCSC

01 President ... Mr. Ray DOTZLER
05 Director ... Ms. Kim GUYER

Creighton University (H)

2500 California Plaza, Omaha NE 68178-0001

County: Douglas FICE Identification: 002542
Unit ID: 181002
Telephone: (402) 280-2700 Carnegie Class: Master's L
FAX Number: N/A Calendar System: Semester
URL: www.creighton.edu
Established: 1878 Annual Undergrad Tuition & Fees: $31,894
Enrollment: 7,662 Coed
Affiliation or Control: Roman Catholic IRS Status: 501(c)3
Highest Offering: Doctorate
Program: Liberal Arts And General; Teacher Preparatory; Professional
Accreditation: NH, BUS, BUSA, DENT, EMT, LAW, MED, NURSE, OT, PHAR, PTA, SW, TED

01 President ... Rev. Timothy R. LANNON, SJ
05 Vice President Academic Affairs ... Mr. Patrick J. BORCHERS
32 Vice President for Student Services ... Dr. John C. CERNECH
11 Vice President for Administration ... Mr. John L. WILHELM
17 Vice President Health Sciences ... Dr. Donald FREY
03 Sr Vice President for Operations ... Mr. Daniel E. BURKEY
26 Vice Pres for University Relations ... Vacant
13 Vice President Information Systems ... Mr. Brian A. YOUNG
42 Vice President University Ministry ... Rev. Andrew F. ALEXANDER, SJ
43 VP and General Legal Counsel ... Vacant
30 Sr Assoc VP Devel/Campaign Dir ... Ms. Laura SIMIC
39 Assoc Vice President Resident Life ... Dr. Richard E. ROSSI
22 Assoc VP Affirm Act/Divrsty Outrch ... Mr. John E. PIERCE
84 Assoc VP Enrollment Management ... Ms. Mary E. CHASE
20 Assoc VP Academic Affairs ... Ms. Tricia A. BRUNDO-SHARRAR
20 Assoc VP for Acad Excel ... Dr. Mary Ann DANIELSON
35 Assoc VP Student Services ... Dr. Tanya WINEGARD
27 Asst VP Marketing/Public Relations ... Ms. Kim B. MANNING
90 Assoc VP Information Technology ... Ms. Colette L. O'MEARA
30 Asst VP Advancement ... Vacant
46 Assoc VP for Research/Compliance ... Mrs. Kathleen J. TAGGART
29 Assistant VP for Alumni Relations ... Ms. Anna NUBEL
15 Exec Director Human Resources ... Mr. Jeffrey C. BRANSTETTER
10 Chief Business Officer ... Ms. Jan D. MADSEN
06 Registrar ... Vacant
07 Dir Admissions/Scholarships ... Vacant
08 Director Reinert Alumni Library ... Mr. Michael J. LACROIX
85 Director International Programs ... Dr. Maria C. KRANE
18 Director Facility Planning/Mgmt ... Mr. Lennis D. PEDERSON
19 Director of Public Safety ... Mr. Richard J. MCAULIFFE
38 Director of Univ Counseling Center ... Dr. Michael KELLEY
37 Director Student Financial Aid ... Mr. Robert D. WALKER
36 Director Career Services ... Mr. Jim BRETL
41 Director Athletics ... Mr. Bruce D. RASMUSSEN
27 Director Public Relations ... Ms. Deborah DALEY
21 Budget Director ... Ms. Tara MCGUIRE

92 Interim Director Honors Program ... Dr. Jeffrey HAUSE
96 Director of Purchasing ... Mr. Joseph J. ZABOROWSKI
87 Director of the Summer Session ... Ms. Debra DALY
28 Director of Multicultural Affairs ... Mr. Ricardo ARIZA
40 Bookstore Manager ... Mr. Calvin PETERSEN
09 Sr Analyst Institutional Research ... Dr. Stephanie WERNIG
49 Dean Arts & Sciences ... Dr. Robert LUEGER
58 Dean of Graduate School ... Dr. Gail JENSEN
61 Dean of Law ... Ms. Marianne B. CULHANE
63 Dean of Medicine ... Dr. Rowen ZETTERMAN
52 Interim Dean of Dentistry ... Dr. Mark A. LATTA
50 Dean Business Administration ... Dr. Anthony HENDRICKSON
67 Dean Pharm/Allied Health Profession ... Dr. J. Chris BRADBERRY
66 Dean of Nursing ... Dr. Eleanor V. HOWELL
51 Dean of University College ... Dr. Gail JENSEN

Doane College (A)

1014 Boswell Avenue, Crete NE 68333
County: Saline — FICE Identification: 002544
Unit ID: 181020
Telephone: (402) 826-2161 — Carnegie Class: Bac/A&S
FAX Number: (402) 826-8600 — Calendar System: 4/1/4
URL: www.doane.edu
Established: 1872 — Annual Undergrad Tuition & Fees: $23,590
Enrollment: 2,787 — Coed
Affiliation or Control: United Church Of Christ — IRS Status: 501(c)3
Highest Offering: Master's
Program: Liberal Arts And General; Teacher Preparatory
Accreditation: NH, TED

01 President ... Dr. Jacque CARTER
05 Vice President Academic Affairs ... Dr. John BURNEY
10 Vice President Financial Affairs ... Ms. Julie SCHMIDT
30 Vice Pres Institutional Advancement ... Dr. Jerry WOOD
32 Vice President Student Leadership ... Ms. Kim JACOBS
13 VP for Information Technology ... Mr. Mike CARPENTER
07 Vice President Admission ... Mr. Joel WEYAND
88 Dean of Educational Leadership ... Dr. Jed JOHNSTON
20 Dean of Curriculum & Instruction ... Dr. Lyn FORESTER
58 Dean of Grad Studies in Mgmt ... Ms. Janice M. HADFIELD
51 Dean Adult Undergraduate Studies ... Ms. Janice M. HADFIELD
88 Director of Hansen Leadership Pgm ... Ms. Carrie PETR
06 Registrar ... Ms. Denise ELLIS
37 Director of Financial Aid ... Ms. Peggy TVRDY
08 Director of the Library ... Ms. Donna JURENA
21 Controller ... Mr. Ned TUCKER
36 Director Career Development ... Ms. Carolyn ERSLAND
26 Director of Public Relations ... Ms. Jacque POMAJZL
29 Director of Alumni Relation ... Ms. Anne GOLDEN
29 Director of Advancement Operation ... Ms. Jennifer JORGENSEN
15 Director of Human Resources ... Ms. Laura SEARS
18 Interim Chief of Fac/Phys Plant ... Mr. Brian FLESNER
58 Dean of Grad Studies in Counseling ... Dr. Thomas J. GILLIGAN
41 Athletic Director ... Mr. Greg HEIER
42 Chaplain ... Ms. Karla COOPER
40 Bookstore Manager ... Ms. Lynette NEWTON
28 Director of Multicultural Pgm & Edu ... Ms. Wilma JACKSON
23 Director of Health and Wellness ... Ms. Kelly JIROVEC
35 Director of Student Support Service ... Ms. Sherri HANIGAN
09 Director of Institutional Research ... Ms. Raja TAYEH
19 Interim Director of Campus Safety ... Mr. Christopher LOOS

Grace University (B)

1311 S 9th Street, Omaha NE 68108-3629
County: Douglas — FICE Identification: 002547
Unit ID: 181093
Telephone: (402) 449-2800 — Carnegie Class: Bac/Diverse
FAX Number: (402) 341-9587 — Calendar System: Semester
URL: www.graceu.edu
Established: 1943 — Annual Undergrad Tuition & Fees: $16,616
Enrollment: 481 — Coed
Affiliation or Control: Independent Non-Profit — IRS Status: 501(c)3
Highest Offering: Master's
Program: Liberal Arts And General; Teacher Preparatory; Religious Emphasis
Accreditation: NH, BI, IACBE

01 President ... Dr. James P. ECKMAN
03 Executive Vice President ... Mr. Michael F. JAMES
05 Academic Dean ... Dr. John D. HOLMES
32 Student Services Dean ... Mrs. Deb OSMANSON
84 Enrollment Management Dean ... Mr. Chris PRUITT
10 Director of Finance ... Ms. Anita RODRIGUEZ
06 Registrar ... Mr. Kris J. UDD
88 Director of Adult Education ... Dr. Martin (Dick) R. DAHLQUIST
07 Manager TUG Admissions ... Ms. Tara KOTH
09 Dir of Assessment & Inst Research ... Dr. Ronald J. SHOPE
37 Director of Financial Aid ... Mr. Ray MILLER
15 Director Human Resources ... Mr. Steve R. WIEMEYER
26 Development & Marketing Officer ... Vacant
29 Alumni Director ... Vacant
08 Librarian ... Mr. Harold (Ben) B. BRICK, III
04 Admin Assistant to the President ... Ms. Joanne R. FAST
11 Director of Operations ... Mrs. Deb OSMANSON
33 Dean of Men ... Mr. Jon T. MCNEEL
34 Dean of Women ... Ms. Marilyn AMSTUTZ
41 Athletic Director ... Mr. Jon HOOD
13 Director Information Services ... Vacant
88 Director Christian Formation & SLT ... Mr. Wesley WILMER

Hastings College (C)

710 N Turner Avenue, Box 269, Hastings NE 68902-0269
County: Adams — FICE Identification: 002548
Unit ID: 181127
Telephone: (402) 463-2402 — Carnegie Class: Bac/Diverse
FAX Number: (402) 461-7490 — Calendar System: 4/1/4
URL: www.hastings.edu
Established: 1882 — Annual Undergrad Tuition & Fees: $22,784
Enrollment: 1,193 — Coed
Affiliation or Control: Presbyterian Church (U.S.A.) — IRS Status: 501(c)3
Highest Offering: Master's
Program: Liberal Arts And General; Teacher Preparatory
Accreditation: NH, MUS, TED

01 President of the College ... Mr. Dennis C. TROTTER
00 Chairman of the Board ... Mr. Harold "Hal" E. DITTMER
30 Interim Pres of the Foundation ... Mr. Bill ASBURY
10 Vice Pres for Financial Affairs ... Ms. Kay LANGSETH
84 VP for Enrollment Management ... Ms. Maryjo "MJ" HUEBNER
05 Interim VP Acad Affrs/Dean Faculty ... Dr. W. Clark HENDLEY
32 VP Student Affs/Dean of Students ... Mr. Ronald D. CHESBROUGH
26 Assoc VP for Mkting/Communications ... Ms. Susan MEESKE
20 Assoc VP for Academic Affairs ... Dr. Anne FAIRBANKS
41 Assoc VP for Admin/Athletic Dir ... Mr. Ian ROBERTS
35 Assoc VP for Student Affairs ... Rev. Joan MCCARTHY
07 Assoc VP Admissions & Enrollment ... Ms. Mary MOLLICONI
44 VP for Planned & Major Gifts ... Mr. Michael KARLOFF
88 VP of Scholarship Development ... Ms. Patty SITORIUS
00 Development President Emeritus ... Dr. Phillip L. DUDLEY, JR.
102 Assoc VP for Development ... Ms. Judee L. KONEN
06 Registrar ... Mr. Daniel J. PETERS
37 Director of Financial Aid ... Ms. Terri GRAHAM
39 Director of Housing ... Mrs. Lori HERGOTT
15 Director of Human Resources ... Ms. Margo BUSBOOM
105 Web Content Manager ... Mr. Christopher FRUEHLING
08 Director of Libraries ... Mr. Robert M. NEDDERMAN
24 Director Educ Media/Librarian ... Ms. Susan FRANKLIN
29 Director of Alumni Relations ... Ms. Hauli SABATKA
13 Director Computing & Info Mgmt ... Vacant
105 Network Administrator ... Mr. Jim MACKIN
90 Acad Computer Support Specialist ... Mr. Erik NIELSEN
18 Director Physical Plant Services ... Mr. James RUZICKA
93 Minority Students ... Dr. Moses DOGBEVIA
28 International Studies/Diversity Pgm ... Dr. Anne FAIRBANKS
36 Director of Career Services ... Ms. Kimberly K. GRAVIETTE
23 Director Campus Health Services ... Ms. Beth LITTRELL
42 Chaplain ... Rev Dr. David B. MCCARTHY
21 Director of Accounting ... Mr. Dan LAUX
35 Director Student Activities ... Mr. Pat MCCAULEY
19 Director of Security/Safety ... Mr. John SILVESTER
38 Director of Counseling Services ... Mr. Jon LOETTERLE
40 Bookstore Manager ... Mrs. Monica LLOYD
27 News Service/Writer/Editor ... Ms. Amber MEDINA
88 Graphic Designer/Publisher ... Ms. Camille KIRCHHOFF
85 Foreign Students/Student Life ... Dr. Antje ANDERSON

ITT Technical Institute (D)

9814 M Street, Omaha NE 68127-2056
County: Douglas — Identification: 666543
Unit ID: 407319
Telephone: (402) 331-2900 — Carnegie Class: Spec/Tech
FAX Number: (402) 331-9495 — Calendar System: Quarter
URL: www.itt-tech.edu
Established: 1991 — Annual Undergrad Tuition & Fees: N/A
Enrollment: 732 — Coed
Affiliation or Control: Proprietary — IRS Status: Proprietary
Highest Offering: Baccalaureate
Program: Technical Emphasis
Accreditation: ACICS

† Branch campus of ITT Technical Institute, Earch City, MO.

Kaplan University (E)

1821 K Street, PO Box 82826, Lincoln NE 68501-2826
County: Lancaster — FICE Identification: 004721
Unit ID: 181242
Telephone: (402) 474-5315 — Carnegie Class: Assoc/PrivFP4
FAX Number: (402) 474-0896 — Calendar System: Quarter
URL: www.lincoln.kaplanuniversity.edu
Established: 1884 — Annual Undergrad Tuition & Fees: $21,300
Enrollment: 690 — Coed
Affiliation or Control: Proprietary — IRS Status: Proprietary
Highest Offering: Baccalaureate
Program: Occupational; 2-Year Principally Bachelor's Creditable; Professional
Accreditation: &NH, MAC

01 Campus President ... Ms. Kathleen NOBLE
05 Dean of Education ... Mr. Timothy SCHOLL
07 Director of Admissions ... Mr. Michael KLACIK
10 Director of Finance ... Ms. Valerie STANDEVEN
36 Director of Career Services ... Mr. Jason LEMON
06 Registrar ... Ms. Christina RUHGE
32 Director of Student Services ... Ms. Jill MATHERS
08 Director Library/Bookstore Services ... Ms. Kathleen KELLER

† Regional accreditation is carried under the parent institution in Davenport, IA.

Kaplan University (F)

5425 N. 103rd Street, Omaha NE 68134-1002
County: Douglas — FICE Identification: 008491
Unit ID: 181400
Telephone: (402) 431-6100 — Carnegie Class: Assoc/PrivFP4
FAX Number: (402) 573-1341 — Calendar System: Other
URL: www.omaha.kaplanuniversity.edu
Established: 1891 — Annual Undergrad Tuition & Fees: $20,750
Enrollment: 782 — Coed
Affiliation or Control: Proprietary — IRS Status: Proprietary
Highest Offering: Associate Degree
Program: Occupational; 2-Year Principally Bachelor's Creditable
Accreditation: &NH, DA, MAC

01 President ... Mr. Jeremy BRUNSSEN
05 Campus Academic Dean ... Dr. George ARNOLD
06 Registrar ... Ms. Linda SMITH
07 Director of Admissions ... Mr. Mike BAUM
36 Director Student Placement ... Ms. Gayle MCCONNELL
37 Director of Financial Aid ... Ms. Crystal FAXON

† Regional accreditation is carried under the parent institution in Davenport, IA.

Little Priest Tribal College (G)

PO Box 270, Winnebago NE 68071-0270
County: Thurston — FICE Identification: 033233
Unit ID: 434016
Telephone: (402) 878-2380 — Carnegie Class: Tribal
FAX Number: (402) 878-2355 — Calendar System: Semester
URL: www.littlepriest.edu
Established: 1996 — Annual Undergrad Tuition & Fees: $2,985
Enrollment: 141 — Coed
Affiliation or Control: Independent Non-Profit — IRS Status: 501(c)3
Highest Offering: Associate Degree
Program: Occupational; 2-Year Principally Bachelor's Creditable
Accreditation: NH

01 President ... Mr. Paul ROBERTSON
05 Academic Dean ... Ms. Brigid QUINN
10 Controller ... Mr. Robert BAXTER
37 Director of Financial Aid ... Ms. Billie KITCHEYAN
13 IT Director ... Mr. Brandon STOUT
31 Coordinator of Community Education ... Ms. Sharon REDHORN-CHAMBERLAIN

Metropolitan Community College (H)

PO Box 3777, Omaha NE 68103-0777
County: Douglas — FICE Identification: 012586
Unit ID: 181303
Telephone: (402) 457-2400 — Carnegie Class: Assoc/Pub-U-MC
FAX Number: (402) 457-2395 — Calendar System: Quarter
URL: www.mccneb.edu
Established: 1974 — Annual Undergrad Tuition & Fees (In-District): $2,385
Enrollment: 18,523 — Coed
Affiliation or Control: Local — IRS Status: 501(c)3
Highest Offering: Associate Degree
Program: Occupational; 2-Year Principally Bachelor's Creditable
Accreditation: NH, ACBSP, ACFEI, ADNUR, DA, EMT

01 President ... Mr. Randy SCHMAILZL
03 Executive Vice President ... Mr. James GROTRIAN
05 Vice President Academic Affairs ... Mr. David HO
11 VP Technology/Administrative Svcs ... Dr. Mary K. WISE
32 VP of Campuses/Student Affairs ... Dr. Arthur RICH
28 Assoc Vice Pres Equity/Diversity ... Dr. Cynthia GOOCH
16 Assoc Vice Pres of Human Resources ... Ms. Maureen MOEGLIN
30 Assoc Vice Pres of Development ... Ms. Pat CRISLER
20 Associate Dean of Academic Affairs ... Ms. Cathy HEFFERNAN
84 Asst Vice Pres for Student Affairs ... Ms. Marie VAZQUEZ
10 Executive College Business Officer ... Mr. Dave KOEBEL
26 Exec Director of Public Affairs ... Ms. Sheila O'CONNOR
18 Director Facilities Management ... Mr. Bernard SEDLACEK
37 Director of Financial Aid ... Ms. Wilma HJELLUM
13 Dir Management Information Svcs ... Mr. Mick GAHAN
96 Director Administrative Management ... Mr. Richard HANNEMAN
19 Dir Public Safety/Emergency Mgmt ... Mr. David FRIEND

Mid-Plains Community College (I)

601 W State Farm Road, North Platte NE 69101-9491
County: Lincoln — FICE Identification: 002557
Unit ID: 181312
Telephone: (308) 535-3600 — Carnegie Class: Assoc/Pub-R-M
FAX Number: (308) 535-3790 — Calendar System: Semester
URL: www.mpcc.edu
Established: 1926 — Annual Undergrad Tuition & Fees (In-District): $2,670
Enrollment: 2,988 — Coed
Affiliation or Control: State/Local — IRS Status: 501(c)3
Highest Offering: Associate Degree
Program: Occupational; 2-Year Principally Bachelor's Creditable; Technical Emphasis
Accreditation: NH, ADNUR, DA, MLTAD

01 President ... Dr. Michael CHIPPS
12 VP North Platte Community College ... Mr. Marcus GARSTECKI
12 VP McCook Community College ... Dr. Richard TUBBS
11 Assoc VP Administrative Services ... Mr. Ryan PURDY

32 Area VP Educ Svcs/Student Devel .... Ms. Jody TOMANEK
09 Area Dir Instl Research & Planning .... Mr. Tad PFEIFER
32 Area Dean of Student Life ....Ms. Michele GILL
31 Dean of Community Services .... Vacant
56 Dean of Outreach & Training ....Mr. Bruce DOWSE
36 Area Dean of Career Services ....Mr. Bill EAKINS
84 Area Dean of Enrollment Management .... Vacant
06 Area Registrar ....Ms. Mari Jo WIDGER
26 Area Dir Public Inform/Marketing ....Mr. Charles SALESTROM
15 Area Director of Human Resources ....Mr. Bruce BERGMAN
21 Area Accounting Director ....Mr. Bruce BERGMAN
13 Area Director of Info Technology .... Mr. Tim HALL
37 Area Dir of Student Financial Aid ....Mr. Dale BROWN
07 Area Admissions Coord/Recruiter ....Ms. Kelly RIPPEN

Midland University (A)

900 N Clarkson, Fremont NE 68025-4395

County: Dodge FICE Identification: 002553
Unit ID: 181330
Telephone: (402) 721-5480 Carnegie Class: Bac/Diverse
FAX Number: (402) 721-0250 Calendar System: 4/1/4
URL: www.midlandu.edu
Established: 1883 Annual Undergrad Tuition & Fees: $24,410
Enrollment: 962 Coed
Affiliation or Control: Evangelical Lutheran Church In America
IRS Status: 501(c)3
Highest Offering: Master's
Program: Occupational; Liberal Arts And General; Teacher Preparatory; Professional; Business Emphasis
Accreditation: NH, NUR

01 President ....Dr. Benjamin SASSE
05 Chief Academic Officer ....Dr. Steven BULLOCK
10 Vice Pres for Administration & CFO .... Ms. Jodi BENJAMIN
32 Vice Pres Student Dev & Retention .... Mr. Greg FRITZ
84 Chief Enrollment Officer ....Ms. Eliza FERZELY
26 Director of Public Relations ....Ms. Ashley CRADDUCK
06 Registrar & Institutional Research ....Ms. Jenifer JOST
37 Director of Financial Aid ....Mr. Doug WATSON
21 Controller ....Ms. Jessie COMBS
36 Director of Career Resource Devel ....Ms. Connie M. BOTTGER
41 Director of Athletic Operations ....Mr. Jason DANNELLY
66 Chair of Nursing ....Ms. Linda QUINN
14 Director Informational Technology .... Mr. Ken CLIPPERTON
18 Director of Physical Plant ....Mr. Roger SONGSTER
30 Director of Development ....Ms. Kari RIDDER
07 Director of Student Recruitment ....Mr. Jason BLOHM
53 Education Department Chair ....Dr. Keith ROHWER

Myotherapy Institute (B)

6020 S 58th Street, Building D, Lincoln NE 68516-3641

County: Lancaster FICE Identification: 032793
Unit ID: 434432
Telephone: (402) 421-7410 Carnegie Class: Assoc/PrivFP
FAX Number: (402) 421-6736 Calendar System: Other
URL: www.myotherapy.edu
Established: 1992 Annual Undergrad Tuition & Fees: $12,300
Enrollment: 45 Coed
Affiliation or Control: Proprietary IRS Status: Proprietary
Highest Offering: Associate Degree
Program: Occupational
Accreditation: ACCSC

01 Director .... Ms. Sue KOZISEK

Nebraska Christian College (C)

12550 S 114th Street, Papillion NE 68046-4256

County: Sarpy FICE Identification: 012976
Unit ID: 181376
Telephone: (402) 935-9400 Carnegie Class: Spec/Faith
FAX Number: (402) 935-9500 Calendar System: Semester
URL: www.nechristian.edu
Established: 1945 Annual Undergrad Tuition & Fees: $11,760
Enrollment: 141 Coed
Affiliation or Control: Christian Churches And Churches of Christ
IRS Status: 501(c)3
Highest Offering: Baccalaureate
Program: Religious Emphasis
Accreditation: BI

01 President ....Mr. Richard MILLIKEN
05 Academic Dean/Registrar ....Dr. Mark KRAUSE
30 Director of Development ....Mr. James HARDY
32 Dean of Students/Chief Stdnt Ofcr ....Mr. Dave HUSKEY
10 Business Manager ....Mr. Tony CLARK
07 Director of Admissions ....Mr. Brian TAYLOR
08 Head Librarian .... Ms. Linda LLOYD
37 Financial Aid Officer ....Mrs. Tina LARSEN

Nebraska Indian Community College (D)

1111 Hwy 75 - PO Box 428, Macy NE 68039-0428

County: Thurston FICE Identification: 025508
Unit ID: 181419
Telephone: (402) 494-2311 Carnegie Class: Tribal
FAX Number: (402) 837-4183 Calendar System: Semester
URL: www.thenicc.edu
Established: 1973 Annual Undergrad Tuition & Fees: $4,080
Enrollment: 138 Coed
Affiliation or Control: Federal IRS Status: 501(c)3
Highest Offering: Associate Degree
Program: Occupational; 2-Year Principally Bachelor's Creditable
Accreditation: #NH

01 President ....Dr. Michael OLTROGGE
30 Business Office Director .... Vacant
32 Student Support Services ....Dawne PRICE

Nebraska Methodist College (E)

720 N 87th Street, Omaha NE 68114-2852

County: Douglas FICE Identification: 006404
Unit ID: 181297
Telephone: (402) 354-7000 Carnegie Class: Spec/Health
FAX Number: (402) 354-7090 Calendar System: Semester
URL: www.methodistcollege.edu
Established: 1891 Annual Undergrad Tuition & Fees: $11,640
Enrollment: 765 Coed
Affiliation or Control: Independent Non-Profit IRS Status: 501(c)3
Highest Offering: Master's
Program: Professional; Nursing Emphasis
Accreditation: NH, DMS, MAC, NURSE, PTAA, RAD, SURGT

01 President ....Dr. Dennis A. JOSLIN
05 Vice President Academic Affairs ....Dr. Kenneth R. RYALLS
32 Vice President Student Affairs ....Dr. Kristine M. HESS
26 VP Business Dev & Communication ....Ms. Danielle DUBUC-PEDERSEN
35 Dean of Students .... Dr. Melissa HOFFMAN
66 Associate Dean Nursing .... Dr. Marilyn VALERIO
58 Program Director Master's Nursing .... Dr. Linda FOLEY
66 Pgm Director Undergrad Nursing .... Dr. Linda HUGHES
76 Associate Dean Health Professions .... Dr. Patricia SULLIVAN
97 Associate Dean General Education .... Dr. Mary Lee LUSBY
76 Pgm Director Phys Therapist Asst .... Ms. Shannon STRUBY
76 Program Director Respiratory Care .... Dr. Chris HAMILTON
88 Program Director Radiography ....Ms. Jane SIMS
88 Program Director Sonography .... Ms. Rebecca MATHIASEN
88 Pgm Director Surgical Technology .... Ms. Christy GRANT
08 Director of Library Services .... Ms. Beverly SEDLACEK
42 Dir Spiritual Dev/Campus Ministry .... Rev. Daniel JOHNSTON
29 Director Alumni Relations ....Ms. Denise M. CARLSON
07 Director Enrollment Services .... Ms. Sara HANSON
06 Director Registration & Records ....Ms. Melinda STONER
37 Director Financial Aid ....Ms. Penny JAMES
88 Assoc Dean Professional Development .... Ms. Rose LEAVITT
09 Director of Institutional Research .... Dr. Deborah CARLSON
10 Director Business Office ....Ms. Beth FRIEDMAN

*Nebraska State College System (F)

PO Box 94605, Lincoln NE 68509-4605

County: Lancaster FICE Identification: 033441
Telephone: (402) 471-2505 Carnegie Class: N/A
FAX Number: (402) 471-2669
URL: www.nscs.edu

01 Chancellor .... Mr. Stan CARPENTER
43 General Counsel & VC for Emp Rel ....Ms. Kristin PETERSEN
10 Vice Chancellor Finance/Admin .... Ms. Carolyn MURPHY
05 Vice Chanc for Acad & Student Affs ....Ms. Korinne TANDE
18 Vice Chanc Facil/Plng/Info Tech ....Mr. Ed HOFFMAN
26 Assoc VC for Comm/Mktg/Sys Relation .... Vacant
13 Network Specialist/Accountant ....Ms. Becky KOHRS

*Chadron State College (G)

1000 Main Street, Chadron NE 69337-2690

County: Dawes FICE Identification: 002539
Unit ID: 180948
Telephone: (308) 432-6000 Carnegie Class: Bac/Diverse
FAX Number: (308) 432-6464 Calendar System: Semester
URL: www.csc.edu
Established: 1911 Annual Undergrad Tuition & Fees (In-State): $5,330
Enrollment: 2,841 Coed
Affiliation or Control: State IRS Status: 501(c)3
Highest Offering: Master's
Program: Liberal Arts And General; Teacher Preparatory; Professional
Accreditation: NH, ACBSP, SW, TED

02 President .... Dr. Janie C. PARK
30 Executive Director CS Foundation ... Ms. Connie A. RASMUSSEN
05 Vice President Academic Affairs .... Dr. Lois VEATH
84 Vice Pres Enrollment/Student Svcs .... Dr. Randy RHINE
11 Vice Pres Administration & Finance ....Mr. Dale E. GRANT
09 Asst VP Enroll Mgmt/Inst Research ....Ms. Theresa R. DAWSON
26 Assoc VP for Market Development ....Mr. Steve M. TAYLOR
06 Registrar ....Mr. Dale E. WILLIAMSON
07 Director of Admissions ....Ms. Tena COOK
10 Comptroller ....Ms. Julie GOODMAN
88 Dean of Professional Licensure .... Dr. Margaret CROUSE
49 Dean of Teaching and Learning ....Dr. Charles SNARE
88 Dean of Curriculum & Academic Advmt ....Dr. Joel HYER
08 Director Library/Learning Resources .... Mr. Milton WOLF
14 Director of Computer Services .... Ms. Ann M. BURK
37 Director of Financial Aid ....Ms. Sherry L. DOUGLAS
16 Director Human Resources ....Ms. Kara VOGT
29 Director of Alumni & Annual Giving ....Ms. Karen K. POPE
39 Director of Housing ....Ms. Sherri J. SIMONS
41 Director of Athletics .... Mr. Bradley R. SMITH
12 Director Extended Campus Sites ....Ms. Deann BAYNE
36 Director of Student Placement ....Ms. Deena KENNELL
21 Budget Director ....Ms. Melany HUGHES
26 Chief Public Relations Officer ....Mr. Justin HAAG
18 Coordinator of Physical Facilities .... Mr. Blair BRENNAN

*Peru State College (H)

PO Box 10, Peru NE 68421-0010

County: Nemaha FICE Identification: 002559
Unit ID: 181534
Telephone: (402) 872-3815 Carnegie Class: Master's L
FAX Number: (402) 872-2375 Calendar System: Semester
URL: www.peru.edu
Established: 1867 Annual Undergrad Tuition & Fees (In-State): $5,371
Enrollment: 2,518 Coed
Affiliation or Control: State IRS Status: 501(c)3
Highest Offering: Master's
Program: Liberal Arts And General; Teacher Preparatory
Accreditation: NH, TED

02 President ....Dr. Daniel HANSON
05 Vice Pres Academic Affairs .... Dr. Todd DREW
10 Vice Pres Administration & Finance .... Mr. Bruce BATTERSON
84 VP Enrollment Mgmt/Student Services ....Ms. Michaela WILLIS
32 Dean of Student Life .... Vacant
102 Executive Director Foundation .... Mr. Todd SIMPSON
41 Athletic Director ....Mr. Steve SCHNEIDER
26 Dir of Marketing & Media Services ....Ms. Regan ANSON
06 Registrar .... Ms. Dixie TETEN
37 Director of Financial Aid .... Ms. Janice VOLKER
08 Director of Library ....Mr. Roger BECKER
15 Human Resources Director .... Ms. Eulanda CADE
18 Director Campus Services .... Vacant
09 Dir Student Assess & Success Svcs .... Dr. Ursula WALN
21 Director of Business Services ....Ms. Kathy TYNON

*Wayne State College (I)

1111 Main Street, Wayne NE 68787-1172

County: Wayne FICE Identification: 002566
Unit ID: 181783
Telephone: (402) 375-7000 Carnegie Class: Master's L
FAX Number: (402) 375-7204 Calendar System: Semester
URL: www.wsc.edu
Established: 1909 Annual Undergrad Tuition & Fees (In-State): $5,317
Enrollment: 3,571 Coed
Affiliation or Control: State IRS Status: 501(c)3
Highest Offering: Beyond Master's But Less Than Doctorate
Program: Liberal Arts And General; Teacher Preparatory; Professional; Business Emphasis
Accreditation: NH, ART, IACBE, MUS, TED

02 President .... Mr. Curt FRYE
05 Vice President Academic Affairs ....Dr. Robert MCCUE
10 Vice Pres Admin/Finance ....Ms. Jean DALE
30 Vice Pres Institutional Advancement ....Ms. Phyllis CONNER
32 Vice President & Dean Students .... Dr. Jeffrey CARSTENS
20 Assoc VP Acad Affs/Graduate Dean ....Vacant
37 Director Financial Aid ....Ms. Kyle ROSE
07 Director of Admissions .... Mr. Kevin HALLE
38 Director of Counseling .... Ms. Lin BRUMMELS
39 Director Housing/Residence Life .... Mr. Matt WEEKLEY
36 Director of Career Services .... Ms. Jason BARELMAN
14 Director of Computer Center .... Ms. Janell SCARDINO
26 Director College Relations ....Mr. Jay COLLIER
41 Director of Athletics ....Mr. Eric SCHOH
18 Director of Physical Plant ....Mr. Chad ALTWINE
08 Director of Library Services .... Mr. David GRABER
51 Director of Continuing Education ....Vacant
06 Registrar ....Ms. Lynette LENTZ
29 Dir Development & Alumni Relations .... Ms. Deb LUNDAHL
15 Director Personnel Services ....Dr. Cheryl WADDINGTON
79 Dean School of Arts & Humanities .... Dr. James O'DONNELL
50 Dean Sch of Business & Technology .... Dr. Vaughn BENSON
53 School of Education & Counseling ....Dr. Neal SCHNOOR
83 Dean School of Natural/Social Sci .... Dr. Jon DALAGER

Nebraska Wesleyan University (J)

5000 St. Paul Avenue, Lincoln NE 68504-2794

County: Lancaster FICE Identification: 002555
Unit ID: 181446
Telephone: (402) 466-2371 Carnegie Class: Bac/A&S
FAX Number: (402) 465-2179 Calendar System: Semester
URL: www.nebrwesleyan.edu
Established: 1887 Annual Undergrad Tuition & Fees: $24,656
Enrollment: 2,083 Coed
Affiliation or Control: United Methodist IRS Status: 501(c)3
Highest Offering: Master's
Program: Liberal Arts And General
Accreditation: NH, ACBSP, MUS, NUR, SW, TED

01 President .... Dr. Frederik OHLES
05 Provost .... Dr. Judy A. MUYSKENS
10 Vice Pres Finance/Administration .... Mr. Clark T. CHANDLER
26 Vice President External Relations ....Ms. Patricia F. KARTHAUSER
30 Vice President Advancement .... Mr. John GREVING
58 Dean of University College .... Dr. Jack E. SIEMSEN
32 Dean of Students .... Mr. Peter ARMSTRONG
49 Dean College of Lib Arts & Sciences ....Dr. Katherine J. WOLFE

88 Asst Provost Experiential Learning ... Dr. Kelly E. EATON
06 Registrar & Asst Dean ... Ms. Bette OLSON
35 Asst Dean of Students ... Ms. Geri E. COTTER
15 Asst Vice Pres for Human Resources ... Ms. Nancy B. COOKSON
18 Asst Vice Pres for Physical Plant ... Mr. Matthew T. KADAVY
07 Director of Admissions ... Mr. David B. DUZIK
27 Director of Public Relations ... Ms. Sara M. OLSON
08 Director of Library ... Mr. John J. MONTAG
37 Director of Financial Aid ... Mr. Tom J. OCHSNER
29 Director of Alumni/Special Programs . Ms. Natalie A. CUMMINGS
41 Athletic Director ... Dr. Ira A. ZEFF
13 Director of Computer Services ... Mr. Steven R. DOW
26 Director of Marketing ... Ms. Peggy S. HAIN
36 Director Career & Counseling Ctr ... Ms. Janelle S. ANDREINI
39 Director Residential Education ... Ms. Brandi SESTAK
104 Director of Global Engagement ... Ms. Sarah BARR
92 Director Wesleyan Honors Academy ... Dr. Marian BORGMANN-INGWERSEN
102 Director of Foundation Relations ... Ms. Nancy WEHRBEIN
23 Director Student Health Services ... Ms. Nancy J. NEWMAN
88 Asst to President Church Relations ... Rev. Mel LUETCHENS
42 University Minister ... Rev. Mara Z. BAILEY

Northeast Community College (A)

801 E Benjamin, PO Box 469, Norfolk NE 68702-0469
County: Madison FICE Identification: 011667
Unit ID: 181491
Telephone: (402) 371-2020 Carnegie Class: Assoc/Pub-R-M
FAX Number: (402) 844-7400 Calendar System: Semester
URL: www.northeast.edu
Established: 1973 Annual Undergrad Tuition & Fees (In-District): $2,754
Enrollment: 5,377 Coed
Affiliation or Control: Local IRS Status: 501(c)3
Highest Offering: Associate Degree
Program: Occupational; 2-Year Principally Bachelor's Creditable; Technical Emphasis
Accreditation: NH, ADNUR, PTAA

01 President ... Dr. Bill R. PATH
30 Vice President of Inst Advancement ... Mrs. Mary J. HONKE
05 Vice President Educational Services ... Mr. John V. BLAYLOCK
43 Gen Counsel/VP of Human Res ... Mr. David H. PTAK
32 Vice President of Student Services ... Dr. Karen J. SEVERSON
10 Vice Pres of Administrative Svcs ... Ms. Lynne D. KOSKI
75 Dean of Applied Technology ... Mr. Lyle J. KATHOL
47 Dean Agriculture/Health/Sciences ... Mr. Chuck M. POHLMAN
51 Dean of Cont Educ/Distance Lrng ... Mr. Wayne ERICKSON
49 Dean Humanities/Arts/Social Sci ... Mrs. Donna A. NIEMEYER
50 Dean of Business/Math/Tech ... Mr. Eric JOHNSON
11 Dean of Administrative Services ... Mrs. Coleen BRESSLER
30 Executive Director of Development ... Mrs. Courtney KLEIN-FAUST
84 Director of Enrollment Management ... Mrs. Tammy LANGAN-YOUNG
21 Director of Business Services ... Mrs. Mary J. MEYER
06 Registrar ... Mrs. Kathy J. STOVER
37 Financial Aid Director ... Ms. Stacy DIECKMAN
12 Dean of College Center ... Mrs. Pamela MILLER
18 Director of Physical Plant ... Mr. Brandon MCLEAN
36 Director of Career Services ... Mrs. Terri HEGGEMEYER
24 Director of Technology Support ... Mr. Tom A. LARSEN
66 Director of Nursing Programs ... Mrs. Karen K. WEIDNER
21 Director of Accounting Services ... Mr. John ROBERTSON
15 Human Resources Coordinator ... Mrs. Jennifer HAPPOLD
96 Director of Purchasing ... Mrs. Nell VOTRUBA
41 Athletic Director ... Mr. Kurt PYTLESKI
07 Advisor/Recruiter ... Mrs. Shelley LAMMERS
105 Web Development Manager ... Mr. Derik BIERMAN
14 Communications Supervisor ... Mrs. Janet HEBERER
26 Director of Media Relations ... Mrs. Janelle GERHARTER
29 Alumni & Resource Development Coord ... Mrs. Connie L. SIXTA
07 Recruiter/Advisor ... Vacant
13 Director of Information Services ... Ms. Karen I. GUY
38 Advisor/Recruiter ... Mr. Anthony FAUST
39 Director Residence & Student Life ... Mr. Pete RIZZO
35 Student Activities Coordinator ... Ms. Carissa KOLLATH
08 Director of Library Services ... Mrs. Mary Louise FOSTER
50 Director Econ Dev/Business Industry ... Mr. Joe C. FERGUSON
40 Bookstore Manager ... Mrs. Shirley A. POWERS
09 Director of Institutional Research ... Ms. Julie MELNICK
35 Dean of Students ... Mrs. Maureen BAKER
76 Director of Allied Health Services ... Ms. Mary MARSTON

Saint Gregory the Great Seminary (B)

800 Fletcher Road, Seward NE 68434-8145
County: Seward Identification: 667027
Telephone: (402) 643-4052 Carnegie Class: Not Classified
FAX Number: (402) 643-6964 Calendar System: Semester
URL: www.stgregoryseminary.edu
Established: 1998 Annual Undergrad Tuition & Fees: $8,000
Enrollment: 44 Male
Affiliation or Control: Roman Catholic IRS Status: 501(c)3
Highest Offering: Baccalaureate
Program: Liberal Arts And General; Religious Emphasis
Accreditation: NH

01 Rector ... Msgr. John T. FOLDA

Southeast Community College (C)

301 S 68 Street Place, Lincoln NE 68510-2449
County: Lancaster FICE Identification: 025083
Unit ID: 181640
Telephone: (402) 323-3400 Carnegie Class: Assoc/Pub-R-L
FAX Number: (402) 323-3420 Calendar System: Quarter
URL: www.southeast.edu
Established: 1973 Annual Undergrad Tuition & Fees (In-District): $2,351
Enrollment: 12,242 Coed
Affiliation or Control: State/Local IRS Status: 501(c)3
Highest Offering: Associate Degree
Program: Occupational; 2-Year Principally Bachelor's Creditable
Accreditation: NH, ACBSP, ACFEI, ADNUR, DA, DIETT, MAC, MLTAD, PNUR, POLYT, PTAA, RAD, SURGT

01 President ... Dr. Jack J. HUCK
05 Vice President Instruction ... Dr. Dennis HEADRICK
22 Vice Pres Access/Equity/Diversity ... Mr. Jose SOTO
11 Vice Pres Administrative Services ... Mr. Theodore G. SUHR
12 VP Student Svcs/Campus Director ... Ms. Jeanette VOLKER
12 VP Technology/Campus Director ... Mr. Lyle NEAL
15 Vice President for Human Resources ... Mr. Bruce TANGEMAN
37 Dean Student Svcs/Dir Financial Aid ... Mr. Dave SONENBERG
35 Dean Student Svcs/Dir Stdnt Support ... Dr. Thomas CARDWELL
84 Dean Student Svcs/Dir Enrollment ... Ms. Robin MOORE
26 Dir of Public Information/Marketing ... Mr. Stu OSTERTHUN
90 Information Services Manager ... Mr. Alan BRUNKOW

Union College (D)

3800 S 48th, Lincoln NE 68506-4300
County: Lancaster FICE Identification: 002563
Unit ID: 181738
Telephone: (402) 486-2600 Carnegie Class: Bac/Diverse
FAX Number: (402) 486-2895 Calendar System: Semester
URL: www.ucollege.edu
Established: 1891 Annual Undergrad Tuition & Fees: $18,780
Enrollment: 901 Coed
Affiliation or Control: Seventh-day Adventist IRS Status: 501(c)3
Highest Offering: Master's
Program: Liberal Arts And General; Teacher Preparatory; Professional
Accreditation: NH, ARCPA, NURSE, SW, TED

01 President ... Vacant
05 Vice President for Academic Admin ... Dr. Malcolm RUSSELL
10 Vice President for Financial Admin ... Mr. Gary BOLLINGER
32 Vice President Student Services ... Dr. Linda BECKER
30 Vice President for Advancement ... Ms. LuAnn DAVIS
07 Vice President Enrollment Services ... Ms. Nadine NELSON
42 Vice President for Spiritual Life ... Dr. Rich CARLSON
08 Library Director ... Ms. Sabrina RILEY
14 Director of Information Systems ... Mr. Tom BECKER
34 Dean of Women ... Ms. LeAnn MERTH
33 Dean of Men ... Mr. Doug TALLMAN
06 Dir Records/Registrar ... Ms. Michelle YOUNKIN
26 Director of Public Relations ... Mr. Ryan TELLER
29 Director Alumni Relations ... Ms. Janya MEKELBURG
37 Director Student Financial Aid ... Ms. Elina CAMARINA
15 Director for Human Resources ... Mr. Jonathan SHIELDS
18 Director of Plant Service ... Mr. Don MURRAY
21 Associate Business Officer ... Mr. Harvey MEIER
36 Career Center Coordinator ... Ms. Teresa EDGERTON
38 Director Student Counseling ... Dr. Linda BECKER

Universal College of Healing Arts (E)

8702 N 30th Street, Omaha NE 68112-1810
County: Douglas FICE Identification: 038214
Unit ID: 446598
Telephone: (402) 556-4456 Carnegie Class: Assoc/PrivFP
FAX Number: (402) 561-0635 Calendar System: Semester
URL: www.ucha.com
Established: 1995 Annual Undergrad Tuition & Fees: $11,802
Enrollment: 62 Coed
Affiliation or Control: Proprietary IRS Status: Proprietary
Highest Offering: Associate Degree
Program: Occupational
Accreditation: ABHES

01 Director ... Ms. Paulette GENTHON

*University of Nebraska Central Administration (F)

3835 Holdrege, Lincoln NE 68583-0745
County: Lancaster FICE Identification: 008025
Unit ID: 181747
Telephone: (402) 472-2111 Carnegie Class: N/A
FAX Number: (402) 472-1237
URL: www.nebraska.edu

01 President ... Mr. James B. MILLIKEN
05 Exec Vice President & Provost ... Dr. Linda PRATT
10 Vice President Business & Finance ... Mr. David LECHNER
43 Vice President General Counsel ... Mr. Joel D. PEDERSEN
47 VP Agriculture/Natural Resources ... Dr. Ronnie GREEN
88 Vice Provost for Global Engagement ... Mr. Thomas FARRELL
04 Senior Associate to the President ... Ms. Dara L. TROUTMAN
13 Chief Information Officer ... Mr. Walter G. WEIR
20 Interim Corporation Secretary ... Ms. Carmen K. MAURER
86 Assoc VP/Director Govt Relations ... Mr. Ron WITHEM
16 Asst VP/Dir HR/Acad Affs/Diversity ... Mr. Edward D. WIMES
04 Sr Assoc to Pres Innov/Econ Compet ... Dr. Jim LINDER
18 Asst VP/Dir Facility Plng/Mgmt ... Ms. Rebecca H. KOLLER
26 Assoc VP Communications/Marketing ... Ms. Sharon R. STEPHAN
09 Asst VP/Dir Inst Research/Planning ... Dr. Kristin YATES

*University of Nebraska at Kearney (G)

905 W 25th Street, Kearney NE 68849
County: Buffalo FICE Identification: 002551
Unit ID: 181215
Telephone: (308) 865-8208 Carnegie Class: Master's L
FAX Number: (308) 865-8665 Calendar System: Semester
URL: www.unk.edu
Established: 1903 Annual Undergrad Tuition & Fees (In-State): $6,199
Enrollment: 6,753 Coed
Affiliation or Control: State IRS Status: 501(c)3
Highest Offering: Beyond Master's But Less Than Doctorate
Program: Liberal Arts And General; Teacher Preparatory; Professional
Accreditation: NH, BUS, CACREP, CIDA, MUS, NAIT, SP, SW, TED

02 Chancellor ... Dr. Douglas A. KRISTENSEN
05 Sr VC Academic & Student Affairs ... Dr. Charles J. BICAK
10 Vice Chanc Business & Finance ... Ms. Barbara L. JOHNSON
26 Vice Chanc University Relations ... Mr. Curtis K. CARLSON
30 Vice President Development ... Mr. Peter KOTSIOPULOS
13 Asst Vice Chanc Info Technology ... Ms. Debbie SCHROEDER
21 Assistant Vice Chancellor Business ... Mr. John LAKEY
83 Dean Natural/Social Science ... Dr. John C. LA DUKE
50 Dean Business/Technology ... Dr. Timothy J. BURKINK
53 Dean of Education ... Dr. Edgar (Ed) L. SCANTLING
57 Dean Fine Arts & Humanities ... Dr. William JURMA
58 Dean Graduate Studies & Research ... Dr. Kenya S. TAYLOR
32 Dean of Student Affairs ... Dr. Joseph A. ORAVECZ
04 Exec Assistant to the Chancellor ... Vacant
06 Registrar ... Ms. Kim SCHIPPOREIT
08 Dean of the Library ... Ms. Janet S. WILKE
15 Director Human Resources ... Ms. Cheryl BRESSINGTON
36 Director Academic & Career Services ... Ms. Mary DAAKE
07 Director of Admissions ... Mr. Dusty NEWTON
18 Director Facilities ... Mr. Lee MCQUEEN
19 Director Police & Parking Services ... Ms. Michelle HAMAKER
22 Dir Affirm Action/Equal Opportunity ... Ms. Cheryl BRESSINGTON
09 Director Institutional Research ... Ms. Kathy LIVINGSTON
27 Director University Communications ... Ms. Glennis NAGEL
29 Director Alumni Services ... Mr. Peter KOTSIOPULOS
88 Director Student Union ... Ms. Sharon PELC
38 Director Counseling Center ... Dr. LeAnn OBRECHT
39 Director Residential Life ... Dr. C. Anthony EARLS
40 Interim Director Bookstore ... Ms. Jill EICKHOFF
41 Athletic Director ... Mr. Jon MCBRIDE
21 Director Finance ... Mr. Larry RIESSLAND
23 Director Student Health Service ... Dr. LeAnn OBRECHT
104 Director International Education ... Dr. Keith (Dallas) KENNY
21 Budget Director ... Mrs. Jean MATTSON
96 Director Business Services ... Mrs. Jane SHELDON
37 Director Financial Aid ... Ms. Mary SOMMERS
28 Director of Diversity ... Mr. Juan GUZMAN

*University of Nebraska - Lincoln (H)

14th and R Streets, Lincoln NE 68588-0002
County: Lancaster FICE Identification: 002565
Unit ID: 181464
Telephone: (402) 472-7211 Carnegie Class: RU/VH
FAX Number: (402) 472-2410 Calendar System: Semester
URL: www.unl.edu
Established: 1869 Annual Undergrad Tuition & Fees (In-State): $7,631
Enrollment: 24,610 Coed
Affiliation or Control: State IRS Status: 501(c)3
Highest Offering: Doctorate
Program: Liberal Arts And General; Teacher Preparatory; Professional
Accreditation: NH, ART, AUD, BUS, BUSA, CIDA, CLPSY, CONST, COPSY, CS, DIETD, DIETI, ENG, IPSY, JOUR, LAW, MFCD, MUS, PLNG, SCPSY, SP, TEAC, THEA

02 Chancellor ... Mr. Harvey PERLMAN
05 Senior Vice Chanc Academic Affairs ... Ms. Ellen WEISSINGER
10 Vice Chanc Business & Finance ... Ms. Christine JACKSON
32 Vice Chancellor Student Affairs ... Dr. Juan FRANCO
65 Vice Chanc Agric/Nat Resources ... Dr. Ronnie D. GREEN
46 VC Research & Economic Development ... Dr. Prem S. PAUL
13 Chief Information Officer ... Mr. Mark ASKREN
04 Associate to Chancellor ... Mr. William NUNEZ
31 Asst to Chanc Community Relations ... Ms. Michelle WAITE
15 Asst Vice Chanc for Human Resources ... Mr. Bruce A. CURRIN
18 Asst VC Facilities Mgt/Planning ... Dr. Ted WEIDNER
07 Dean Admissions ... Dr. Alan CERVENY
08 Dean University Libraries ... Dr. Joan R. GIESECKE
58 Dean Graduate Studies ... Dr. Patrick H. DUSSAULT
49 Dean Arts & Sciences ... Dr. David C. MANDERSCHEID
54 Dean Engineering ... Dr. Timothy WEI
61 Dean of Law ... Dr. Susan POSER
47 Dean Agric Scienc/Nat Resources ... Dr. Steven S. WALLER
50 Dean Business Administration ... Dr. Donde PLOWMAN
60 Dean Journalism/Mass Communic ... Mr. Gary KEBBEL
53 Dean Education & Human Sciences ... Dr. Marjorie KOSTELNIK
48 Dean College Architecture ... Mr. R. Wayne DRUMMOND
47 Dean Agricultural Research Division ... Dr. Susan M. FRITZ
56 Dean & Dir Cooperative Extens ... Dr. Elbert C. DICKEY
93 Director Educ Access & TRIO Pgms .. Ms. Catherine YAMAMOTO
57 Dean Fine & Performing Arts ... Dr. Giacomo M. OLIVA
37 Director Scholarships/Financial Aid ... Mr. Craig D. MUNIER
09 Director Inst Research & Planning ... Dr. William J. NUNEZ
87 Director of Summer Sessions ... Dr. Paul A. SAVORY
92 Director Honors Program ... Dr. Patrice BERGER
94 Director Women's Studies ... Dr. Joy RITCHIE
06 Director Registrar & Records ... Dr. Earl W. HAWKEY

36 Director Career Services Center Dr. Larry R. ROUTH
19 Chief University Police Services Mr. Owen YARDLEY
22 Director Affirm Action/Diversity Ms. Linda CRUMP
23 Director University Health Center Dr. James GUEST
39 Director Housing Office Dr. Douglas S. ZATECHKA
41 Director of Athletics Dr. Tom OSBORNE
25 Director Research Grants/Contract Mr. Norm BRAATEN
55 Dir Distance Education Services Dr. Nancy ADEN-FOX
29 Exec Director Alumni Association Ms. Diane MENDENHALL
26 Director University Communications Dr. Meg LAUERMAN
20 Associate Academic Officer Dr. Evelyn M. JACOBSON
30 Chief Development Mr. Clarey CASTNER
38 Director Student Counseling Dr. Robert N. PORTNOY
84 Director Enrollment Management Dr. Rita KEAN
96 Associate Director of Purchasing Mr. Carl HUTCHISON
28 Director of Diversity Ms. Linda CRUMP

University of Nebraska Medical Center (A)

987020 Nebraska Medical Center, Omaha NE 68198-7020
County: Douglas　FICE Identification: 006895
Unit ID: 181428
Telephone: (402) 559-4000　Carnegie Class: Spec/Med
FAX Number: (402) 559-4396　Calendar System: Semester
URL: www.unmc.edu
Established: 1869　Annual Undergrad Tuition & Fees (In-State): $7,925
Enrollment: 3,493　Coed
Affiliation or Control: State　IRS Status: 501(c)3
Highest Offering: Doctorate
Program: Professional
Accreditation: NH, ARCPA, CYTO, DENT, DH, DIETI, DMS, MED, MT, NMT, NURSE, PERF, PH, PHAR, PTA, RAD, RTT

02 Chancellor Dr. Harold M. MAURER
05 Int Vice Chancellor Acad Affairs Dr. David CROUSE
10 Vice Chanc Business & Finance Mr. Donald LEUENBERGER
46 Vice Chancellor for Research Dr. Jennifer LARSEN
86 Vice Chanc for External Affairs Mr. Robert D. BARTEE
20 Assoc Vice Chanc Academic Affairs Dr. James TURPEN
20 Int Asst Vice Chanc Acad Affairs Dr. Cheryl THOMPSON
20 Assoc Vice Chanc Acad Affs/Reg Comp Dr. Ernest D. PRENTICE
45 Assoc Vice Chanc for Research Vacant
21 Assoc Vice Chanc Business/Finance Ms. Deborah THOMAS
21 Assoc Vice Chanc Bus Development Dr. Rodney MARKIN
18 Assistant Vice Chancellor for FMP Mr. Kenneth HANSEN
21 Interim Asst VC for Budget & Plng Ms. Pamela BATAILLON
14 Exec Dir Information Tech Services Ms. Yvette A. HOLLY
58 Interim Dean Graduate Studies Dr. David CROUSE
52 Dean College of Dentistry Dr. John W. REINHARDT
63 Dean College of Medicine Dr. Bradley E. BRITIGAN
66 Acting Dean College of Nursing Dr. Janet CUDDIGAN
67 Dean College of Pharmacy Dr. Courtney FLETCHER
69 Dean College of Public Health Dr. Ayman EL MOHANDES
76 Assoc Dean Allied Health Profession Dr. Kyle MEYER
88 Dir Eppley Cancer Research Inst Dr. Kenneth H. COWAN
88 Director Munroe-Meyer Inst Dr. J. Michael LEIBOWITZ
08 Director Library of Medicine Dr. Nancy N. WOELFL
37 Exec Dir Financial Aid Office Ms. Judith D. WALKER
26 Director of Public Relations Mr. William O'NEILL
15 Exec Director Human Resources Mr. John P. RUSSELL
29 Director Alumni Affairs Ms. Roxana JOKELA
38 Director Student Counseling Dr. David S. CARVER
28 Director of Diversity Vacant
96 Director of Purchasing Mr. Thomas P. KEENAN
09 Director Institutional Research Ms. Jeanne FERBRACHE

*University of Nebraska at Omaha (B)

6001 Dodge Street, Omaha NE 68182-0001
County: Douglas　FICE Identification: 002554
Unit ID: 181394
Telephone: (402) 554-2200　Carnegie Class: DRU
FAX Number: (402) 554-3555　Calendar System: Semester
URL: www.unomaha.edu
Established: 1908　Annual Undergrad Tuition & Fees (In-State): $6,895
Enrollment: 15,448　Coed
Affiliation or Control: State　IRS Status: 501(c)3
Highest Offering: Doctorate
Program: Liberal Arts And General; Teacher Preparatory; Professional
Accreditation: NH, AAB, ART, BUS, CACREP, CS, MUS, PH, SP, SPAA, SW, TED

02 Chancellor Dr. John E. CHRISTENSEN
05 Int Sr Vice Chanc Acad/Student Affs Dr. Burton J. REED
10 Vice Chanc Business & Finance Mr. Bill CONLEY
04 Exec Assistant to the Chancellor Ms. Nancy CASTILOW
20 Assoc Vice Chanc Acad Affs-Tech Mr. John L. FIENE
21 Assoc Vice Chanc Business & Finance Ms. Julie TOTTEN
32 Assoc Vice Chanc Student Affairs Dr. Thomas WALLACE
58 Dean Graduate Studies Dr. Deb SMITH-HOWELL
57 Dean Fine Arts/Communication/Media Dr. Gail BAKER
53 Dean of Education Dr. Nancy EDICK
50 Dean of Business Administration Dr. Lou POL
49 Dean of Arts & Sciences Dr. David BOOCKER
82 Dean of International Studies Mr. Thomas E. GOUTTIERRE
72 Dean Info Science/Technology Dr. Hesham ALI
80 Dean Public Affairs/Community Vacant
62 Dean of Library Services Mr. Stephen SHORB
09 Acting Dir Institutional Research Dr. Russell SMITH
35 Chief Student Life Officer Ms. Rita HENRY
15 Director Human Resources Ms. Molllie ANDERSON
18 Director Facilities Mgmt/Planning Mr. John AMEND
06 Registrar Mr. Mark GOLDSBERRY
07 Director of Admissions Vacant
37 Director Financial Aid Mr. Randall L. SELL
88 Director Student Testing Center Ms. Marion FORTIN-WAVRA
41 Director of Athletics Mr. Trev ALBERTS
29 Director of Alumni Association Mr. Lee DENKER
26 Director Communications Mr. Tim KALDAHL
96 Director of Purchasing Mr. Ken HULTMAN
40 Manager Book Store Mr. Michael E. SCHMIDT
19 Manager Campus Security Mr. Paul KOSEL

*University of Nebraska - Nebraska College of Technical Agriculture (C)

404 E 7th Street, Curtis NE 69025-9502
County: Frontier　FICE Identification: 007358
Unit ID: 181765
Telephone: (308) 367-4124　Carnegie Class: Assoc/Pub2in4
FAX Number: (308) 367-5203　Calendar System: Semester
URL: www.ncta.unl.edu
Established: 1912　Annual Undergrad Tuition & Fees (In-State): $4,810
Enrollment: 383　Coed
Affiliation or Control: State　IRS Status: 501(c)3
Highest Offering: Associate Degree
Program: Occupational; 2-Year Principally Bachelor's Creditable; Technical Emphasis
Accreditation: NH

02 Dean Dr. Weldon SLEIGHT
03 Associate Dean Dr. Scott MICKELSEN
10 Business Officer Ms. Jan GILBERT

Vatterott College-Omaha (D)

11818 I Street, Omaha NE 68137-1237
County: Douglas　FICE Identification: 030233
Unit ID: 181756
Telephone: (402) 891-9411　Carnegie Class: Assoc/PrivFP
FAX Number: (402) 891-9413　Calendar System: Quarter
URL: www.vatterott-college.edu
Established: 1996　Annual Undergrad Tuition & Fees: $19,500
Enrollment: 755　Coed
Affiliation or Control: Proprietary　IRS Status: Proprietary
Highest Offering: Baccalaureate
Program: Occupational; 2-Year Principally Bachelor's Creditable; Technical Emphasis
Accreditation: ACCSC, DA, MAAB

01 CEO & President Ms. Pam BELL
10 Chief Financial Officer Mr. Dennis BEAVERS
05 Vice President Academic Affairs Dr. Brandon SHEDRON
45 VP Regulatory Affs/Strategic Devel Mr. Aaron LACEY
43 General Counsel/Chief Administrator Mr. Scott CASANOVER
12 Campus Director Ms. Roberta WORM

Western Nebraska Community College (E)

1601 E 27th Street, Scotts Bluff NE 69361-1815
County: Scotts Bluff　FICE Identification: 002560
Unit ID: 181817
Telephone: (308) 635-3606　Carnegie Class: Assoc/Pub-R-L
FAX Number: (308) 635-6100　Calendar System: Semester
URL: www.wncc.edu
Established: 1926　Annual Undergrad Tuition & Fees (In-District): $2,760
Enrollment: 2,417　Coed
Affiliation or Control: State/Local　IRS Status: 501(c)3
Highest Offering: Associate Degree
Program: Occupational; 2-Year Principally Bachelor's Creditable
Accreditation: NH, PNUR

01 President Dr. Todd R. HOLCOMB
05 Vice President Educational Services Mr. Terry B. GAALSWYK
16 Vice President Human Resources Mr. David E. GROSHANS
32 Vice President Student Services Ms. Susan K. YOWELL
11 Dean Administrative Services Mr. William D. KNAPPER
20 Dean of Educational Services Mr. Garry R. ALKIRE
103 Dean of Workforce Development Mr. Jason L. STRATMAN
50 Dean Business & Individual Training Ms. Judith L. AMOO
36 Ast Dn Stdt Svc/Career/Intrnshp Dir Mrs. Carla M. STEIN
12 Sidney Campus Director Ms. Paula J. ABBOTT
12 Alliance Campus Director Dr. John D. CORUM
102 Foundation Executive Director Ms. Dayle L. WALLIEN
06 Registrar Mr. Roger S. HOVEY
37 Financial Aid Director Ms. Sheila R. JOHNS
26 College Relations Director Ms. Erin STINNER
38 Counseling Director Mr. Norman J. STEPHENSON
08 Information Services Director Mrs. Valetta L. SCHNEIDER
21 Accounting Services Director Mr. David KOEHLER
41 Athletic Director Mr. Ryan C. BURGNER
88 Bus & Individual Training Director Ms. Lori S. STROMBERG
07 Admissions Director Ms. Amy WINTERS
39 Residence Life Director Mr. Mario J. CHAVEZ
13 Exec Dir Information Technology Dr. Paul G. JACOBSEN
40 Bookstore Operations Director Ms. Suzane KARBOWSKI
19 Safety/Environmental Mgmt Director Mr. Robert L. HESSLER
09 Director of Institutional Research Mrs. Mary E. BARKELOO
88 ILAC Coordinator Ms. Tammie KLEICH
39 Residence Life/Activities Coord Mr. Yahosh BONNER
39 Residence Life/Activities Coord Ms. Molly A. BONUCHI
50 Division Chair Business Mr. Tom ROBINSON
81 Division Chair Math/Sciences/PE Ms. Judy SCHNELL
83 Division Chair Social Sciences Dr. Guy WYLIE
88 Division Chair Language & Arts Mr. Andy NEWMAN
72 Division Chair Applied Technology Mr. Willie QUINDT
76 Div Chair Health/Acad Enrichment Mr. Garry R. ALKIRE

York College (F)

1125 E 8th Street, York NE 68467-2699
County: York　FICE Identification: 002567
Unit ID: 181853
Telephone: (402) 363-5600　Carnegie Class: Bac/Diverse
FAX Number: (402) 363-5623　Calendar System: Semester
URL: www.york.edu
Established: 1890　Annual Undergrad Tuition & Fees: $15,300
Enrollment: 481　Coed
Affiliation or Control: Churches Of Christ　IRS Status: 501(c)3
Highest Offering: Master's
Program: Liberal Arts And General; Business Emphasis
Accreditation: NH, TED

01 President Dr. Steven W. ECKMAN
05 Vice President for Academic Affairs Dr. Tracey L. WYATT
10 Vice President Finance & Operations Mr. Todd SHELDON
30 Vice Pres Advancement Mr. Brent MAGNER
32 Vice Pres for Student Development Dr. Shane MOUNTJOY
21 Business Manager Mr. Dan COLE
06 Registrar Mr. Tod J. MARTIN
07 Vice President of Admissions Mr. Willie SANCHEZ
08 Director of Library Mr. Ken GUNSELMAN
26 Director of Publications Mr. Steddon L. SIKES
37 Financial Aid Director Mr. Brien ALLEY
40 Bookstore Director Mr. Ronald SHIELDS
41 Athletic Director Mr. Jared A. STARK
18 Supervisor Buildings & Grounds Mr. Bob GAVER
91 Director Administrative Computing Mr. Joel COEHOORN
36 Director Student Placement Vacant
42 Campus Minister Mr. Tim D. LEWIS
50 Chair Business Mr. Mark MOORE
53 Chair Education Dr. Kathleen B. WHEELER
73 Chair Bible Dr. Frank E. WHEELER
88 Chair History Mr. Tim D. MCNEESE
50 Chair English Mrs. Beverly MCNEESE
81 Chair Math/Sciences Dr. Ray MILLER
57 Chair Performing Arts/Communication Dr. Clark A. ROUSH
29 Dir Alumni & Community Relations Mrs. Sue ROUSH

NEVADA

The Art Institute of Las Vegas (G)

2350 Corporate Circle, Henderson NV 89074-7737
County: Clark　FICE Identification: 030846
Unit ID: 182111
Telephone: (702) 369-9944　Carnegie Class: Spec/Arts
FAX Number: (702) 992-8564　Calendar System: Quarter
URL: www.ailv.artinstitutes.edu
Established: 1983　Annual Undergrad Tuition & Fees: $27,316
Enrollment: 1,210　Coed
Affiliation or Control: Proprietary　IRS Status: Proprietary
Highest Offering: Baccalaureate
Program: Occupational; 2-Year Principally Bachelor's Creditable; Liberal Arts And General
Accreditation: ACICS, ACFEI, CIDA

01 President Ms. Kris DIGIACOMO
32 Dean of Student Affairs Ms. Sallie PALMER
05 Dean of Academic Affairs Mr. Francisco VIRELLA

Career College of Northern Nevada (H)

1421 Pullman Drive, Sparks NV 89434
County: Washoe　FICE Identification: 026215
Unit ID: 181941
Telephone: (775) 856-2266　Carnegie Class: Assoc/PrivFP
FAX Number: (775) 856-0935　Calendar System: Quarter
URL: www.ccnn.edu
Established: 1984　Annual Undergrad Tuition & Fees: $23,415
Enrollment: 665　Coed
Affiliation or Control: Proprietary　IRS Status: Proprietary
Highest Offering: Associate Degree
Program: Occupational
Accreditation: ACCSC

01 President Mr. L. Nathan N. CLARK

DeVry University - Henderson (I)

2490 Paseo Verde Parkway, Suite 150, Henderson NV 89074-7120
County: Clark　Identification: 666560
Unit ID: 443997
Telephone: (702) 933-9700　Carnegie Class: Bac/Diverse
FAX Number: (803) 933-9717　Calendar System: Semester
URL: www.devry.edu
Established: 1931　Annual Undergrad Tuition & Fees: $15,294
Enrollment: 550　Coed
Affiliation or Control: Proprietary　IRS Status: Proprietary

Highest Offering: Master's
Program: Professional; Business Emphasis
Accreditation: &NH

01 Interim Campus Dean .... Bill WORTH

† Regional accreditation is carried under the parent institution in Downers Grove, IL.

Everest College (A)

170 North Stephanie Street, Henderson NV 89074
FICE Identification: 022375
Unit ID: 182148
Telephone: (702) 567-1920 Carnegie Class: Assoc/PrivFP
FAX Number: (702) 566-9725 Calendar System: Semester
URL: www.everest.edu
Established: 2004 Annual Undergrad Tuition & Fees: N/A
Enrollment: 1,263 Coed
Affiliation or Control: Proprietary IRS Status: Proprietary
Highest Offering: Associate Degree
Program: Occupational
Accreditation: ACICS, MAAB

01 President .... Mr. Dave FRITZ

ITT Technical Institute (B)

168 N Gibson Road, Henderson NV 89014-6712
County: Clark Identification: 666544
Unit ID: 429599
Telephone: (702) 558-5404 Carnegie Class: Spec/Tech
FAX Number: (702) 558-5412 Calendar System: Quarter
URL: www.itt-tech.edu
Established: 1997 Annual Undergrad Tuition & Fees: N/A
Enrollment: 907 Coed
Affiliation or Control: Proprietary IRS Status: Proprietary
Highest Offering: Baccalaureate
Program: Technical Emphasis
Accreditation: ACICS

† Branch campus of ITT Technical Institute, Murray, UT.

Kaplan College (C)

3535 West Sahara Ave, Las Vegas NV 89102
County: Clark FICE Identification: 030432
Unit ID: 374875
Telephone: (702) 368-2338 Carnegie Class: Assoc/PrivFP
FAX Number: (702) 368-3853 Calendar System: Other
URL: www.kaplancollege.com
Established: 1991 Annual Undergrad Tuition & Fees: $29,350
Enrollment: 557 Coed
Affiliation or Control: Proprietary IRS Status: Proprietary
Highest Offering: Associate Degree
Program: Occupational; 2-Year Principally Bachelor's Creditable; Technical Emphasis
Accreditation: ACCSC, MAAB, PNUR

01 Executive Director .... Mr. Rob DILLMAN
11 Director of Operations .... Mr. Jason SALMONSON
05 Director of Education .... Ms. Pam LIVINGSTON
07 Director of Admissions .... Mrs. Queena FULLER
06 Registrar .... Ms. Kassy PINDAR
10 Director of Finance .... Ms. Carmen TORRES
36 Director of Career Services .... Mr. Ryan GUNDERSEN
20 Assistant Director of Education .... Mr. Jeffrey FOUNTAIN
77 Dir Computer Service Technician .... Mr. Joseph RYAN
61 Dept Chair Criminal Justice .... Mr. John NORTON
76 Dept Chr Med Coder & Biller .... Mrs. Phyllis ECKERT
67 Dept Chair Pharmacy Technician .... Mr. Mark BRUNTON
88 Dept Chair Medical Assistant .... Mrs. Renee CANAS

Le Cordon Bleu College of Culinary Arts in Las Vegas (D)

1451 Center Crossing Road, Las Vegas NV 89144-7047
County: Clark Identification: 666303
Unit ID: 445115
Telephone: (702) 365-7690 Carnegie Class: Assoc/PrivFP
FAX Number: (702) 365-7911 Calendar System: Other
URL: www.chefs.edu/las-vegas
Established: 2003 Annual Undergrad Tuition & Fees: N/A
Enrollment: 814 Coed
Affiliation or Control: Proprietary IRS Status: Proprietary
Highest Offering: Associate Degree
Program: Occupational
Accreditation: ACCSC, ACFEI

01 President .... Mr. Robert WOY

† Branch campus of Le Cordon Bleu College of Culinary Arts, Scottsdale, AZ.

Morrison University (E)

10315 Professional Circle, Ste 201, Reno NV 89521-4826
County: Washoe FICE Identification: 010098
Unit ID: 182430
Telephone: (775) 850-0700 Carnegie Class: Bac/Diverse
FAX Number: (775) 850-0711 Calendar System: Quarter
URL: www.morrisonuniversity.com
Established: 1902 Annual Undergrad Tuition & Fees: $9,975
Enrollment: 295 Coed
Affiliation or Control: Proprietary IRS Status: Proprietary
Highest Offering: Master's
Program: Occupational; Liberal Arts And General; Professional
Accreditation: ACICS

01 Campus Director .... Mr. Dave HECKELER
05 Director of Education .... Mr. Joel NELSON
08 Library Director .... Ms. Usha MEHTA
37 Director Financial Aid .... Mr. Jim HADWICK
06 Registrar .... Ms. Gina AKAO
36 Director Career Services .... Ms. Emily AVILA

*Nevada System of Higher Education (F)

2601 Enterprise Road, Reno NV 89512-1666
County: Washoe FICE Identification: 008026
Unit ID: 182519
Telephone: (775) 784-4901 Carnegie Class: N/A
FAX Number: (775) 784-1127
URL: www.nevada.edu

01 Chancellor .... Mr. Daniel J. KLAICH
05 VC Academic & Student Affairs .... Dr. Jane A. NICHOLS
10 Vice Chancellor of Finance .... Mr. Mark STEVENS
88 Chief Exec Ofcr Board of Regents .... Mr. Scott WASSERMAN

*College of Southern Nevada (G)

6375 W Charleston Boulevard, Las Vegas NV 89146-1139
County: Clark FICE Identification: 010362
Unit ID: 182005
Telephone: (702) 651-5000 Carnegie Class: Assoc/Pub4
FAX Number: (702) 651-4835 Calendar System: Semester
URL: www.csn.edu
Established: 1971 Annual Undergrad Tuition & Fees (In-State): $1,944
Enrollment: 44,088 Coed
Affiliation or Control: State IRS Status: 501(c)3
Highest Offering: Baccalaureate
Program: Occupational; 2-Year Principally Bachelor's Creditable
Accreditation: NW, ACBSP, ACFEI, ADNUR, CEA, COMTA, DA, DH, DMS, EMT, ENGT, MAC, MLTAD, OPD, OTA, PNUR, PTAA, RTT, SURGT

02 President .... Dr. Michael D. RICHARDS
04 Exec Assistant to the President .... Ms. Francine WOODHOUSE
10 Sr Vice Pres Finance & Facilities .... Ms. Patricia A. CHARLTON
05 Vice Pres Academic Affairs .... Dr. Darren D. DIVINE
32 Int VP for Student Affairs .... Dr. Chemene L. CRAWFORD
12 Sr Advsr to Pres/Chf Admin-Cheyenne .... Mr. Thomas BROWN
12 Campus Manager Charleston .... Dr. Joan MCGEE
12 Campus Manager Henderson .... Vacant
20 Assoc VP Academic Affairs .... Dr. Hyla WINTERS
21 Asst Vice Pres Fin Svcs/Controller .... Ms. Mary Kaye BAILEY
18 Assoc VP Facilities/Oper/Maint .... Ms. Sherri PAYNE
43 Legal Counsel .... Mr. Richard HINCKLEY
12 Interim Dean Charleston Campus .... Dr. Bradley W. GRUNER
06 Registrar .... Ms. Pat ZOZAYA
21 Exec Director Business Services .... Mr. Dan MORRIS
75 Exec Dir Apprenticeship Studies .... Mr. Dan GOUKER
36 Director Student Services .... Ms. Kelly WUEST
102 Exec Dir CSN Foundation .... Ms. Jacque MATTHEWS
30 Operations Manager CSN Foundation .... Ms. Shirley CARTON
72 Dean Adv & Applied Technologies .... Dr. Michael SPANGLER
81 Dean Science & Mathematics .... Ms. Sally JOHNSTON
83 Dean Social Sciences & Education .... Dr. Charles OKEKE
88 Dean Arts & Letters .... Dr. Wendy WEINER
76 Dean Health Sciences .... Dr. Patricia CASTRO
103 Exec Dir Workforce/Economic Devel .... Ms. Rebecca METTY-BURNS
96 Int Director of Purchasing .... Mr. Mark CAHILL
41 Director of Athletics .... Mr. Marc MORSE
27 Director of Communications & Events .... Ms. Kathryn C. BREKKEN
35 Director of Student Activities .... Mr. Vitaliano FIGUEROA
45 Int Dir Admin/Resource Development .... Ms. Diane WARYAS
88 Director of Budget Services .... Ms. Lisa BAKKE
09 Director of Institutional Research .... Mr. John BEARCE
62 Director Library Services .... Ms. Clarissa ERWIN
88 Director of Scheduling .... Dr. Joe WEST
37 Asst Director Student Financial Aid .... Ms. Katharyn VAN DE CAR
19 Chief of Police .... Mr. Darryl CARABALLO
85 Director International Student Ctr .... Ms. Tammy SILVER
13 Technology CIO .... Mr. Mugunth VAITHYLINGAM
105 Webmaster .... Mr. Taylor C. GRAY

*Great Basin College (H)

1500 College Parkway, Elko NV 89801-5032
County: Elko FICE Identification: 006977
Unit ID: 182306
Telephone: (775) 738-8493 Carnegie Class: Bac/Assoc
FAX Number: (775) 738-8771 Calendar System: Semester
URL: www.gbcnv.edu
Established: 1967 Annual Undergrad Tuition & Fees (In-State): $2,512
Enrollment: 3,581 Coed
Affiliation or Control: State IRS Status: 501(c)3
Highest Offering: Baccalaureate
Program: Occupational; 2-Year Principally Bachelor's Creditable
Accreditation: NW, ADNUR, NUR, RAD

02 President .... Mr. Carl DIEKHANS
32 Vice President Student Services .... Mrs. Lynn M. MAHLBERG
05 Vice President Academic Affairs .... Dr. Mike MCFARLANE
04 Assistant to the President .... Ms. Mardell WILKINS
07 Director of Admissions & Registrar .... Ms. Janice KING
09 Dir Institutional Rsrch/Effective .... Ms. Cathy FULKERSON
30 Chief Development Officer .... Dr. John RICE
08 Library Director .... Mr. David ELLEFSON
37 Director Financial Aid .... Mr. Scott NIELSEN
10 Chief Business Officer .... Ms. Sonja SIBERT
26 Public Information Officer .... Dr. John RICE
84 Director Enrollment Management .... Ms. Julie BYRNES
75 Dean Academic Support/Applied Sci .... Mr. Brett MURPHY
66 Director of Nursing .... Dr. Kris MILLER
12 Director Ely Center .... Ms. Mary SWETICH
12 Director Winnemucca Center .... Ms. Lisa CAMPBELL
12 Director Pahrump Valley Center .... Vacant
21 Controller .... Mr. Wayne OLMSTEAD
51 Director Continuing Education .... Mrs. Angie DEBRAGA
56 Dean of Extended Studies .... Vacant
06 Registrar .... Ms. Janice KING
88 Director Child & Family Center .... Ms. Connie ZELLER
102 Director Foundation .... Dr. John RICE
19 Director Safety and Security .... Ms. Patricia ANDERSON

*Nevada State College (I)

1125 Nevada State Drive, Henderson NV 89002-9455
County: Clark FICE Identification: 041143
Unit ID: 441900
Telephone: (702) 992-2000 Carnegie Class: Bac/Diverse
FAX Number: (702) 992-2226 Calendar System: Semester
URL: www.nsc.nevada.edu
Established: 2002 Annual Undergrad Tuition & Fees (In-District): $3,563
Enrollment: 2,988 Coed
Affiliation or Control: State/Local IRS Status: 501(c)3
Highest Offering: Master's
Program: Liberal Arts And General; Teacher Preparatory; Professional; Nursing Emphasis
Accreditation: NW, NURSE

02 President .... Dr. Lesley Ann DI MARE
05 Provost .... Ms. Erika BECK
06 Registrar .... Ms. Patricia RING

*Truckee Meadows Community College (J)

7000 Dandini Boulevard, Reno NV 89512-3999
County: Washoe FICE Identification: 021077
Unit ID: 182500
Telephone: (775) 673-7000 Carnegie Class: Assoc/Pub-R-L
FAX Number: (775) 673-7108 Calendar System: Semester
URL: www.tmcc.edu
Established: 1971 Annual Undergrad Tuition & Fees (In-State): $2,258
Enrollment: 13,139 Coed
Affiliation or Control: State IRS Status: 501(c)3
Highest Offering: Associate Degree
Program: Occupational; 2-Year Principally Bachelor's Creditable
Accreditation: NW, ACFEI, ADNUR, DA, DH, DIETT

02 President .... Dr. Maria C. SHEEHAN
04 Executive Assistant to President .... Ms. Anne TISCARENO
05 Vice President Academic Affairs .... Dr. John TUTHILL
10 Vice Pres Finance & Admin Services .... Ms. Delores A. SANFORD
32 Dean of Student Services .... Vacant
72 Dean Math/Science/Engr/Technology .... Mr. Ted PLAGGEMEYER
50 Act Dean Social Science & Business .... Ms. Armida FRUZZETTI
88 Dean External Funding/Grants .... Dr. Barbara SANDERS
79 Arts & Humanities Chair .... Ms. Nancy FAIRES
51 Dean Workforce Devel/Cont Education .... Vacant
20 Assoc Dean Office of the President .... Ms. Pat SLAVIN
102 Executive Director Foundation .... Ms. Paula Lee HOBSON
07 Director Admissions & Records .... Ms. Mona CONCHA-BUCKHEART
21 Controller .... Mr. Earl AULSTON
37 Director Financial Aid .... Ms. Sharon WURM
08 Director Learning Resources Center .... Ms. Michelle NOEL
15 Director Human Resources .... Ms. Michele MEADOR
18 Director Facilities Services .... Mr. Dave ROBERTS
26 Dir Public Info/Publications .... Dr. J. Kyle DALPE
103 Dir Workforce Devel/Cont Education .... Ms. Deb O'GORMAN
38 Director Counseling .... Ms. Estela LEVARIO-GUTIERREZ
45 Budget & Planning Technician .... Vacant
13 Director Information Tech Services .... Mr. Chris WINSLOW
35 Dir Educ Center/Student Services .... Vacant
88 Dir Student Outreach & Testing Svcs .... Vacant
88 Director Re-Entry & Womens Center .... Mrs. Barbara TWITCHELL
19 Chief of Police/Campus Police .... Mr. Randy FLOCCHINI
09 Director Institutional Research .... Ms. Elena BUBNOVA
28 Director of Equity & Diversity .... Vacant
29 Donor & Alumni Coordinator .... Ms. Tara HAWKINS

*University of Nevada, Las Vegas (K)

4505 S Maryland Parkway, Las Vegas NV 89154-1001
County: Clark FICE Identification: 002569
Unit ID: 182281
Telephone: (702) 895-3011 Carnegie Class: RU/H
FAX Number: (702) 895-3850 Calendar System: Semester
URL: www.unlv.edu
Established: 1957 Annual Undergrad Tuition & Fees (In-State): $5,303
Enrollment: 28,203 Coed

Affiliation or Control: State IRS Status: 501(c)3
Highest Offering: Doctorate
Program: Liberal Arts And General; Teacher Preparatory; Professional
Accreditation: NW, ART, BUS, BUSA, CACREP, CIDA, CLPSY, CONST, CS, DENT, DIETD, DIETI, ENG, ENGR, LAW, LSAR, MFCD, MT, MUS, NMT, NURSE, PTA, RAD, SPAA, SW, TED, THEA

02 President ... Dr. Neal SMATRESK
100 Chief of Staff ... Dr. Fred TREDUP
05 Executive Vice President & Provost ... Dr. Michael W. BOWERS
10 Senior Vice Pres Finance & Business ... Mr. Gerry BOMOTTI
41 Dir Intercollegiate Athletics ... Mr. Jim LIVENGOOD
32 Vice President for Student Affairs ... Dr. Juanita FAIN
58 Int VP Research & Graduate Studies ... Dr. Ron SMITH
88 Sr Advisor to the President ... Dr. Marta MEANA
30 VP Advancement ... Dr. William BOLDT
86 VP Diversity & Govt Relations ... Mr. Luis VALERA
43 VP & General Counsel ... Mr. Richard LINSTROM
11 Assoc Vice Pres for Administration ... Dr. Mike SAUER
35 Assoc VP for Student Affairs ... Ms. Karen STRONG
31 Assoc VP Alumni Relations ... Mr. Jim RATIGAN
26 Assoc Vice Pres Community Relations ... Ms. Lucy KLINKHAMMER
15 Chief Human Resources Officer ... Mr. Larry HAMILTON
87 Int Vice Prov Educational Outreach ... Dr. Margaret REES
13 Vice Provost Info Technology ... Dr. Lori TEMPLE
50 Dean Business ... Dr. Paul JARLEY
49 Dean Liberal Arts ... Dr. Chris HUDGINS
53 Interim Dean of Education ... Dr. William SPEER
54 Dean of Engineering ... Dr. Rama VENKAT
52 Dean School of Dental Medicine ... Dr. Karen P. WEST
61 Dean School of Law ... Mr. John V. WHITE
81 Dean of Sciences ... Dr. Timothy PORTER
88 Dean Hotel Administration ... Dr. Donald SNYDER
57 Dean Fine Arts ... Dr. Jeffrey KOEP
08 Dean of Libraries ... Ms. Patricia IANNUZZI
88 Interim Dean Urban Affairs ... Dr. Lee BERNICK
92 Dean Honors College ... Dr. Peter STARKWEATHER
88 Dean Academic Success Ctr ... Dr. Ann MCDONOUGH
88 Founding Dean Community Health ... Dr. Mary GUINAN
76 Dean Sch Allied Health Sciences ... Dr. Carolyn YUCHA
06 Exec Dir of Admissions & Recruiting ... Mr. Luke SCHULTHEIS
37 Financial Aid & Scholarships ... Mr. Norm BEDFORD
27 Assoc VP Univ Communications ... Mr. Earnest PHILLIPS
19 Director Public Safety ... Mr. Jose ELIQUE
09 Director Inst Analysis/Planning ... Mrs. Kari C. COBURN
39 Exec Dir Residential Life ... Mr. Richard CLARK
38 AVP Student Wellness ... Dr. Jamie DAVIDSON
23 Director Student Health ... Ms. Kathy A. UNDERWOOD
96 Director Purchasing ... Ms. Sharrie MAYDEN
85 Director Intl Students & Scholars ... Ms. Kristen YOUNG
25 Director Sponsored Programs ... Ms. Rochelle ATHEY
46 AVP for Research ... Dr. Stan SMITH
102 Sr Assoc VP & Exec Dir UNLV Found ... Ms. Nancy STROUSE
44 Assoc VP Development ... Mr. Scott ROBERTS

*University of Nevada, Reno (A)

Reno NV 89557-0095
County: Washoe FICE Identification: 002568
Unit ID: 182290
Telephone: (775) 784-1110 Carnegie Class: RU/H
FAX Number: (775) 784-1300 Calendar System: Semester
URL: www.unr.edu
Established: 1874 Annual Undergrad Tuition & Fees (In-State): $4,841
Enrollment: 17,679 Coed
Affiliation or Control: State IRS Status: 501(c)3
Highest Offering: Doctorate
Program: Liberal Arts And General; Teacher Preparatory; Professional
Accreditation: NW, BUS, BUSA, CACREP, CLPSY, CS, DIETD, DIETI, ENG, JOUR, MED, MUS, NURSE, PH, SP, SW, TED

02 Interim President ... Dr. Marc JOHNSON
05 Interim Exec Vice Pres & Provost ... Dr. Heather HARDY
11 Vice Pres Administration & Finance ... Mr. Ronald M. ZUREK
63 Vice President Health Sciences ... Vacant
30 Vice President Devel/Alumni Rels ... Mr. John CAROTHERS
32 Vice President for Student Services ... Dr. Shannon ELLIS
46 Vice President for Research ... Dr. Marsha READ
08 Interim Dean of Libraries ... Dr. Kathlin D. RAY
20 Vice Prov Instr/Undergrad Programs ... Dr. William N. CATHEY
20 Vice Provost/Sec of Univ ... Dr. Jannet VREELAND
51 Vice Provost for Extended Studies ... Dr. Fred B. HOLMAN
10 Assoc VP Business & Finance ... Mr. Thomas L. JUDY
84 Assoc VP Enrollment Services ... Dr. Melisa N. CHOROSZY
38 Assoc VP Student Success Services ... Dr. Jerry MARCZYNSKI
45 Asst VP Planning/Budget/Analysis ... Mr. Bruce L. SHIVELY
18 Int Asst Vice Pres Facilities Svcs ... Mr. John WALSH
21 Controller ... Ms. Philomena MCCAFFREY
41 Director Athletics ... Ms. Cary GROTH
96 Director Purchasing ... Mr. Garth KWIECHIEN
19 Director University Police Svcs ... Mr. Adam GARCIA
22 Director Affirmative Action ... Vacant
37 Director Student Financial Svcs ... Mr. Timothy WOLFF
39 Director Resident Life & Housing ... Mr. Rodney L. AESCHLIMANN
23 Director Student Health Svcs ... Dr. Cheryl HUG-ENGLISH
09 Director Institutional Analysis ... Dr. Serge HERZOG
86 Dir Govt Relations & Economic Dev ... Dr. Robert E. DICKENS
65 Dir Mackay Sch Mines/Earth Science ... Vacant
66 Director of Nursing ... Dr. Patsy L. RUCHALA
57 Director School of the Arts ... Dr. Larry ENGSTROM
25 Int Director Sponsored Projects ... Dr. Richard BJUR
40 Manager Bookstore ... Ms. Marie STEWART
49 Dean Liberal Arts ... Dr. Heather HARDY
47 Dean Agriculture/Biotech/Nat Res ... Dr. Ron PARDINI
50 Dean Business Admininistration ... Dr. Gregory MOSIER
53 Interim Dean of Education ... Dr. Christine CHENEY
54 Dean Engineering ... Dr. Emmanuel MARAGAKIS
60 Interim Dean School of Journalism ... Mr. William WINTER
63 Dean School of Medicine ... Dr. Ole THIENHAUS
81 Dean College of Science ... Dr. Jeffrey S. THOMPSON
65 Director Academy for Environment ... Dr. Jen HUNTLEY-SMITH
07 Director of Admissions ... Dr. Stephen MAPLES
29 Director Alumni Relations ... Ms. Amy CAROTHERS

*Western Nevada College (B)

2201 W College Parkway, Carson City NV 89703-7316
County: Carson FICE Identification: 010363
Unit ID: 182564
Telephone: (775) 445-3000 Carnegie Class: Assoc/Pub4
FAX Number: (775) 887-3051 Calendar System: Semester
URL: www.wnc.edu
Established: 1971 Annual Undergrad Tuition & Fees (In-State): $2,243
Enrollment: 5,567 Coed
Affiliation or Control: State IRS Status: 501(c)3
Highest Offering: Baccalaureate
Program: Occupational; 2-Year Principally Bachelor's Creditable
Accreditation: NW, ADNUR, SURGT

02 President ... Dr. Carol A. LUCEY
04 Assistant to the President ... Ms. Bonnie M. BERTOCCHI
05 Int Vice Pres Academic/Student Affs ... Ms. Connie CAPURRO
15 VP Human Resources/Dir Diversity ... Mr. Mark GHAN
20 Dean of Instruction ... Vacant
32 Dean Student Services ... Mr. John KINKELLA
21 Interim Controller ... Ms. Coral LOPEZ
88 Director Child Development Center ... Ms. Andrea DORAN
38 Director of Counseling/Advising ... Ms. Deborah CASE
18 Director Facilities Mgmt/Planning ... Mr. Dave ROLLINGS
37 Director Financial Aid ... Ms. Lori TIEDE
27 Director Information & Marketing ... Ms. Anne P. HANSEN
08 Director Library & Media Services ... Mr. Kenneth A. SULLIVAN
06 Registrar/Director of Admissions ... Ms. Dianne HILLIARD
30 Director of Development ... Ms. Amy GINDER
13 Administrator Computing Services ... Ms. Susan SCHOEFFLER
10 Interim Senior Fiscal Analyst ... Ms. Darla DODGE
15 Asst Director Human Resources ... Ms. Irene TUCKER
51 Outreach Coordinator ... Ms. Katie LEAO
35 Student Life Coordinator ... Ms. Katie LEAO
81 Div Chair Science Math/Engr ... Dr. Brigette DILLET
83 Div Chair Soc Sci/Educ/Hum/Publ Svc ... Dr. Robert MORIN
57 Div Chair Communications/Fine Arts ... Ms. Maxine CIRAC
76 Div Chair Nursing/Allied Health ... Dr. Judith CORDIA
72 Division Chair Technology ... Mr. Edward MARTIN

Pima Medical Institute-Las Vegas (C)

3333 E Flamingo Road, Las Vegas NV 89121-4329
County: Clark Identification: 666273
Unit ID: 445230
Telephone: (702) 458-9650 Carnegie Class: Assoc/PrivFP
FAX Number: (702) 458-9653 Calendar System: Quarter
URL: www.pmi.edu
Established: 2003 Annual Undergrad Tuition & Fees: $10,150
Enrollment: 1,144 Coed
Affiliation or Control: Proprietary IRS Status: Proprietary
Highest Offering: Associate Degree
Program: Occupational
Accreditation: ABHES, RAD

01 Director ... Mr. Sam A. GENTILE

† Branch campus of Pima Medical Institute, Tucson, AZ.

Roseman University of Health Sciences (D)

11 Sunset Way, Henderson NV 89014-2333
County: Clark FICE Identification: 040653
Unit ID: 445735
Telephone: (702) 990-4433 Carnegie Class: Spec/Health
FAX Number: (702) 990-4435 Calendar System: Other
URL: www.usn.edu
Established: 1999 Annual Undergrad Tuition & Fees: $38,587
Enrollment: 1,082 Coed
Affiliation or Control: Independent Non-Profit IRS Status: 501(c)3
Highest Offering: Doctorate
Program: Professional
Accreditation: NW, DENT, IACBE, NUR, PHAR

01 President ... Dr. Harry ROSENBERG
03 Executive VP Quality Assurance ... Dr. Renee COFFMAN
12 Chancellor Henderson Campus ... Dr. Eucharia E. NNADI
12 Chancellor South Jordan Campus ... Vacant
10 Chief Operating Officer & Treasurer ... Mr. Stuart A. WIENER
18 Vice President Facilities & Mgmt ... Ms. Marlene R. MILLER
13 Vice President Info Technologies ... Mr. Raymond PEREZ
03 Vice President Executive Affairs ... Dr. Charles F. LACY
26 Vice President Communications & PR ... Mr. Jason ROTH
67 Dean College of Pharmacy ... Dr. Renee E. COFFMAN
67 Campus Dean College of Pharmacy UT ... Dr. Larry FANNIN
66 Dean College of Nursing Henderson ... Dr. Mable H. SMITH
66 Dean College of Nursing UT ... Dr. Marlene LUNA
52 Dean College of Dental Medicine ... Dr. Richard BUCHANAN
52 Dean College of Dental Medicine Hen ... Dr. Jaleh POURHAMIDI
50 Director MBA Program ... Dr. Okeleke NZEOGWU
09 Dir of Inst Research/Assessment ... Dr. Thomas METZGER
88 Assoc Dean Admissions Pharmacy ... Dr. Michael DEYOUNG
37 Director of Financial Aid ... Mr. Jesse STASHER
88 Assoc Dean Clinical Programs Pharm ... Dr. Gary M. LEVIN
51 Director of Continuing Education ... Dr. Katherine SMITH
52 Assoc Dean Academic Affairs Dental ... Dr. Victor A. SANDOVAL
52 Assoc Dean Clinical Affairs ... Dr. Leslie KARNS
07 Assoc Dean Admissions/Student Svcs ... Dr. William HARMAN
15 Director of Human Resources ... Dr. G. Benjamin WILLS
62 Director of Library Services ... Ms. Karen CANEPI
30 Director of University Relations ... Ms. Barbara WOOD
44 Director of Development ... Ms. Brenda GRIEGO
06 Registrar/Director of Student Svcs ... Ms. Angela D. BIGBY
88 Marketing Director South Jordan ... Ms. Tracy HERNANDEZ

Sierra Nevada College (E)

999 Tahoe Boulevard, Incline Village NV 89451-9500
County: Washoe FICE Identification: 009192
Unit ID: 182458
Telephone: (775) 831-1314 Carnegie Class: Master's M
FAX Number: (775) 832-1696 Calendar System: Semester
URL: www.sierranevada.edu
Established: 1969 Annual Undergrad Tuition & Fees: $3,400
Enrollment: 1,034 Coed
Affiliation or Control: Independent Non-Profit IRS Status: 501(c)3
Highest Offering: Master's
Program: Liberal Arts And General
Accreditation: NW

00 Chairman Board of Trustees ... Dr. Barry MUNITZ
01 President ... Dr. Richard RUBSAMEN
05 Executive Vice President/Provost ... Dr. Lynn GILLETTE
30 VP Development & College Relations ... Dr. Deborah PROUT
84 Dean Enrollment Services & Student ... Ms. Julie FOSTER
07 Director of Admissions ... Ms. Amye COLE
20 Director Academic Support Services ... Mr. Henry CONOVER
37 Director of Financial Aid ... Ms. Nicole FERGUSON
08 Director of Library ... Dr. Elizabeth MARKLE
06 Registrar ... Ms. Rose BEENK
53 Statewide Dir Teacher Education ... Ms. Beth BOUCHARD
13 Director Information Technology ... Ms. Nicole FERGERSON
10 Chief Financial Officer ... Mr. Dan RUSHIN
15 Director Human Resources ... Mr. David WEBB
21 Controller ... Ms. Lynda ODELL
04 Executive Asst to the President ... Ms. Kristine YOUNG

NEW HAMPSHIRE

Antioch University New England (F)

40 Avon Street, Keene NH 03431-3516
County: Cheshire Identification: 666992
Unit ID: 245865
Telephone: (800) 553-8920 Carnegie Class: Master's L
FAX Number: (603) 357-0718 Calendar System: Other
URL: www.antiochne.edu
Established: 1964 Annual Graduate Tuition & Fees: $24,650
Enrollment: 908 Coed
Affiliation or Control: Independent Non-Profit IRS Status: 501(c)3
Highest Offering: Doctorate; No Undergraduates
Program: Professional
Accreditation: &NH, CACREP, CLPSY, MFCD

01 President ... Dr. David A. CARUSO
05 Vice Pres Academic Affairs ... Dr. Stephen NEUN
30 Vice Pres Institutional Advancement ... Ms. Tracey THOMPSON
10 Vice Pres Finance/Administration ... Mr. Timothy G. JORDAN
06 Registrar ... Ms. Susan CHAMBERLIN
07 Director of Admissions ... Ms. Laura B. ANDREWS
21 Controller ... Ms. Kathleen M. CURTISS
29 Int Dir of Development/Alumni Rels ... Ms. Faith LINSKY
37 Director Student Financial Aid ... Ms. Susan L. HOWARD
18 Director Facilities/Security/Safety ... Mr. Paul R. WHICKER
15 Director of Human Resources ... Ms. Andrea HODSON
27 Dir of Marketing & Communications ... Ms. Janet FIDERIO
96 Director of Purchasing ... Ms. Joan A. NELSON
20 Assoc Acad Ofcr/Chf Stdnt Svcs Ofcr ... Ms. Leatrice ORAM

† Regional accreditation is carried under the parent institution in Yellow Springs, OH.

Chester College of New England (G)

40 Chester Street, Chester NH 03036-4331
County: Rockingham FICE Identification: 004733
Unit ID: 183345
Telephone: (603) 887-4401 Carnegie Class: Bac/A&S
FAX Number: (603) 887-1777 Calendar System: Semester
URL: www.chestercollege.edu
Established: 1965 Annual Undergrad Tuition & Fees: $19,730
Enrollment: 164 Coed
Affiliation or Control: Independent Non-Profit IRS Status: 501(c)3
Highest Offering: Baccalaureate
Program: Liberal Arts And General; Fine Arts Emphasis
Accreditation: EH

01 President & CEO ... Mr. Robert A. BAINES

05 VP Academic Affairs & Student Svcs .... Ms. Laura IVES
04 Exec Assistant to the President ....Mrs. Sandra L. BOULDRY
10 VP for Operations & Finance ....Mr. Richard P. BENOIT
08 Interim Director Library Services ....Mr. Eric CRAPO
32 Director of Student Services ....Ms. Jenna GAWNE
06 Registrar ....Mrs. Barbara GILL
21 Director of the Business Office ....Ms. Susan SCHWIEGER
13 Director of Information Technology .... Mr. Kenneth MAILLOUX
18 Interim Director Physical Plant ....Mr. William RHOR
07 VP for Admission and Enrollment ....Mr. Anthony PADILLA
37 Director Student Financial Aid ....Mr. Roger ILLESCAS

Colby-Sawyer College (A)

541 Main Street, New London NH 03257-7835
County: Merrimack FICE Identification: 002572
Unit ID: 182634
Telephone: (603) 526-3000 Carnegie Class: Bac/Diverse
FAX Number: (603) 526-2135 Calendar System: Semester
URL: www.colby-sawyer.edu
Established: 1837 Annual Undergrad Tuition & Fees: $34,110
Enrollment: 1,156 Coed
Affiliation or Control: Independent Non-Profit IRS Status: 501(c)3
Highest Offering: Baccalaureate
Program: Liberal Arts And General; Teacher Preparatory
Accreditation: EH, NURSE

01 President ....Mr. Thomas C. GALLIGAN
05 Academic Vice Pres/Dean of Faculty ....Dr. Deborah A. TAYLOR
11 Vice President Administration .... Mr. Douglas G. ATKINS
10 Treasurer ....Mr. Douglas W. LYON
32 VP Stdnt Devel/Dean of Students ....Mr. David A. SAUERWEIN
30 Vice President Advancement .... Ms. Elizabeth A. CAHILL
84 Vice Pres Enrollment Management ... Mr. Gregory W. MATTHEWS
101 Secretary of the College ....Ms. Linda J. VARNUM
04 Assistant to the President ....Ms. Lisa F. TEDESCHI
20 Academic Dean ....Dr. Elizabeth C. CROCKFORD
35 Assoc Dean Stdnt/Dir Citizenship Ed ....Ms. Robin BURROUGHS-DAVIS
39 Director Residential Education .... Ms. Mary MCLAUGHLIN
37 Director of Financial Aid ....Mr. Ted W. CRAIGIE
30 Director of Development ....Ms. Kathleen A. CARROLL
08 College Librarian ....Ms. Carrie THOMAS
06 Registrar ....Ms. Carole H. PARSONS
07 Director of Admission Counseling ....Ms. Tracey G. PERKINS
13 Director Information Resources ....Mr. Kenneth G. KOCHIEN
41 Director of Athletics ....Ms. Deborah F. MCGRATH
18 Director of Facilities ....Mr. Robert MORSE
23 Director of Health & Counseling .... Ms. Jacqueline F. WEBB
27 Exec Director of Publications ....Vacant
36 Director of Career Development ....Ms. Kathy J. TAYLOR
88 Asst Dir Acad Development Ctr ...... Ms. Caren BALDWIN-DIMEO
85 Dir English Lang/Amer Culture Pgm ....Mr. David ELLIOTT
44 Dir Annual Giving ....Mr. Christopher S. REED
29 Dir Alumni Relations ....Ms. Tracey M. AUSTIN
19 Director of Campus Safety ....Mr. Peter L. BERTHIAUME
15 Director of Human Resources ....Ms. Sharon L. BEAUDRY
35 Director of Campus Activities .... Ms. Sharon WILLIAMSON
09 Director Institutional Research ....Dr. Yi NI
21 Controller ....Ms. Karen I. BONEWALD
26 Director of Communications ....Ms. Kimberly S. SLOVER
40 Bookstore Manager ....Ms. Mairim KILMISTER
92 Coordinator of the Honors Program ....Ms. Ann Page STECKER
28 Associate Dean of Intl & Diversity ....Dr. Pamela SEROTA COTE

*Community College System of New Hampshire (B)

26 College Drive, Concord NH 03301-7407
County: Merrimack Identification: 666462
Telephone: (603) 271-2722 Carnegie Class: N/A
FAX Number: (603) 271-2725
URL: www.ccsnh.edu

01 Chancellor ....J. Bonnie NEWMAN
03 Vice Chancellor ....Dr. Charles ANNAL
10 Director of Financial Management ....Michael MARR
15 Director of Human Resources ....Sara SAWYER
27 Director of Communications ....Shannon REID

*Great Bay Community College (C)

320 Corporate Drive, Portsmouth NH 03801-2879
County: Rockingham FICE Identification: 002583
Unit ID: 183150
Telephone: (603) 427-7600 Carnegie Class: Assoc/Pub-R-M
FAX Number: (603) 334-6308 Calendar System: Semester
URL: www.greatbay.edu
Established: N/A Annual Undergrad Tuition & Fees (In-State): $6,320
Enrollment: 1,595 Coed
Affiliation or Control: State IRS Status: 501(c)3
Highest Offering: Associate Degree
Program: Occupational; 2-Year Principally Bachelor's Creditable
Accreditation: EH, ACBSP, ADNUR, SURGT

02 President ....Mr. Wildolfo ARVELO
05 Vice President Academic Affairs ....Ms. Diane CHIN
84 Vice Pres Enrollment Mgmt/Students ....Dr. Bruce BAKER
06 Registrar ....Ms. Sandra HO
10 Chief Financial Officer ....Ms. Joanne BERRY

*Lakes Region Community College (D)

379 Belmont Road, Laconia NH 03246-1364
County: Belknap FICE Identification: 007555
Unit ID: 183123
Telephone: (603) 524-3207 Carnegie Class: Assoc/Pub-R-S
FAX Number: (603) 527-2042 Calendar System: Semester
URL: www.lrcc.edu
Established: 1967 Annual Undergrad Tuition & Fees (In-District): $6,840
Enrollment: 1,628 Coed
Affiliation or Control: State/Local IRS Status: 501(c)3
Highest Offering: Associate Degree
Program: Occupational; 2-Year Principally Bachelor's Creditable
Accreditation: EH

02 Interim President ....Dr. Scott KALICKI
05 VP of Academic & Community Affairs ..... Mr. Thomas GOULETTE
32 VP of Student & Corporate Affairs . Dr. James VANDER HOOVEN
10 Chief Financial Officer ....Ms. Alice MOWERY

*Manchester Community College (E)

1066 Front Street, Manchester NH 03102-8518
County: Hillsborough FICE Identification: 002582
Unit ID: 183132
Telephone: (603) 668-6706 Carnegie Class: Assoc/Pub-R-M
FAX Number: (603) 668-5354 Calendar System: Semester
URL: www.manchestercommunitycollege.edu
Established: 1945 Annual Undergrad Tuition & Fees (In-State): $5,226
Enrollment: 2,842 Coed
Affiliation or Control: State IRS Status: 501(c)3
Highest Offering: Associate Degree
Program: Occupational; 2-Year Principally Bachelor's Creditable
Accreditation: EH, ACBSP, ADNUR, MAC

02 President ....Dr. Susan D. HUARD
05 Vice President Academic Affairs ....Dr. Mary SCERRA
32 VP Student/Community Services ....Kim KEEGAN
20 Associate Vice President Academics ....Joan ACORACE
84 Assoc VP Enrollment Management ....Dr. Larissa BAIA
26 Dir of Marketing/Public Info Ofcr ....Janet PHELPS
37 Financial Aid Officer ....Stephanie J. WELDON
06 Registrar ....Evelyn R. PERRON
08 Librarian ....Mary MARKS
09 Director of Institutional Research ....Dr. David FLINT
10 Chief Officer Financial/Admin Svcs ....Timothy FONTAINE
22 Director AA/EO ....Alicia CUTTING
40 Bookstore Manager ....Vacant
66 Nursing Director .... Charlene WOLFE-STEPRO
21 Accountant I ....Carol DESPATHY
13 Dir of Academic/Admin Computing ....Naim SYED
35 Director Student Life ....Aileen CLAY

*Nashua Community College (F)

505 Amherst Street, Nashua NH 03063-1092
County: Hillsborough FICE Identification: 009236
Unit ID: 183141
Telephone: (603) 882-6923 Carnegie Class: Assoc/Pub-R-M
FAX Number: (603) 882-8690 Calendar System: Semester
URL: www.nashuacc.edu
Established: 1967 Annual Undergrad Tuition & Fees (In-State): $5,424
Enrollment: 2,296 Coed
Affiliation or Control: State IRS Status: 501(c)3
Highest Offering: Associate Degree
Program: Occupational; 2-Year Principally Bachelor's Creditable
Accreditation: EH, ADNUR, ENGT

02 President ....Ms. Lucille JORDAN
05 VP Academic Affs/Chief Campus Ofcr .... Mr. Brian PELLINEN
32 Vice Pres Student Services ....Ms. Patricia GOODMAN
10 Chief Financial Officer ....Ms. Amber WHEELER
06 Registrar-Nashua ....Ms. Jennifer LEITNER
08 Librarian-Nashua ....Mr. William A. MCINTYRE
37 Financial Aid Officer-Nashua ....Ms. Lizbeth GONZALEZ

*NHTI-Concord's Community College (G)

31 College Drive, Concord NH 03301-7412
County: Merrimack FICE Identification: 002581
Unit ID: 183099
Telephone: (603) 271-6484 Carnegie Class: Assoc/Pub-R-M
FAX Number: (603) 271-7734 Calendar System: Semester
URL: www.nhti.edu
Established: 1965 Annual Undergrad Tuition & Fees (In-State): $6,890
Enrollment: 4,556 Coed
Affiliation or Control: State IRS Status: 501(c)3
Highest Offering: Associate Degree
Program: Occupational; 2-Year Principally Bachelor's Creditable
Accreditation: EH, ACBSP, ADNUR, DA, DH, DMS, EMT, ENGT, PNUR, RAD, RTT

02 President .... Ms. Lynn KILCHENSTEIN
32 Vice President Student Affairs ....Mr. Stephen P. CACCIA
05 Vice President Academic Affairs ....Ms. Pamela LANGLEY
51 Vice Pres Continuing/Corp Education .... Mr. Thomas FOULKES
20 Assoc Vice Pres of Academic Affairs ....Vacant
09 Assoc VP of Acad Affairs/Inst Rsrch ... Ms. Beth BLANKENSTEIN
84 Assoc VP of Enrollment Management ....Vacant

10 Chief Financial Officer ....Ms. Melanie KIRBY
08 Director Learning Resources .... Mr. Stephen AMBRA
07 Director of Admissions ....Mr. Francis P. MEYER
06 Registrar .... Ms. Michele KARWOCKI
13 Director of Computer Services .... Mr. Thomas TOWLE
18 Director of Facilities Maintenance .... Mr. Michael THERRIEN
27 Director of Communications ....Mr. Alan BLAKE
36 Dir Residence Life/Career Counsel ....Ms. Trish GODINO
38 Director Student Counseling ....Vacant
37 Financial Aid Director ....Ms. Sheri GONTHIER
19 Chief of Campus Safety ....Ms. Anne L. BREEN
41 Athletic Director ....Mr. Paul HOGAN
15 Director Human Resources ....Ms. Alyssa LABELLE
28 Dir Cross-Cultural Education/ESOL ....Ms. Dawn HIGGINS
96 Director of Purchasing ....Ms. Irene AUBUT
21 Bursar ....Ms. Jessica BRYAN
105 Website Coordinator ....Ms. Christine METCALF
35 Coordinator of Campus Activities ....Mr. Chuck LLOYD

*River Valley Community College (H)

1 College Drive, Claremont NH 03743-9707
County: Sullivan FICE Identification: 007560
Unit ID: 183114
Telephone: (603) 542-7744 Carnegie Class: Assoc/Pub-R-S
FAX Number: (603) 543-1844 Calendar System: Semester
URL: www.rivervalley.edu
Established: N/A Annual Undergrad Tuition & Fees (In-State): $5,040
Enrollment: 1,168 Coed
Affiliation or Control: State IRS Status: 501(c)3
Highest Offering: Associate Degree
Program: Occupational; 2-Year Principally Bachelor's Creditable
Accreditation: EH, ACBSP, ADNUR, MAC, MLTAD, OTA, PTAA

02 President ....Dr. Steven G. BUDD
05 Vice President Academic Affairs ....Ms. Andrea GORDON
32 VP Student Svcs/Cmty Relations ....Ms. Valerie MAHAR
20 Assoc Vice Pres Academic Affairs ..... Dr. Lisa HAYWARD-WYZIK
37 Financial Aid Officer ....Ms. Julia DOWER
06 Registrar ....Ms. Sharon GILBERT
10 Chief Financial Officer ....Ms. Marie MARCUM

*White Mountains Community College (I)

2020 Riverside Drive, Berlin NH 03570-3799
County: Coos FICE Identification: 005291
Unit ID: 183105
Telephone: (603) 752-1113 Carnegie Class: Assoc/Pub-R-S
FAX Number: (603) 752-6335 Calendar System: Semester
URL: www.wmcc.edu
Established: 1966 Annual Undergrad Tuition & Fees (In-State): $7,374
Enrollment: 1,037 Coed
Affiliation or Control: State IRS Status: 501(c)3
Highest Offering: Associate Degree
Program: Occupational; 2-Year Principally Bachelor's Creditable
Accreditation: EH, MAC

02 President ....Katharine ENEGUESS
05 Vice Pres Academic Affairs ....Frank CLULOW
32 Vice President Student Affairs ....Martha LAFLAMME
37 Financial Aid Officer ....Tyler BERGMEIER
10 Business Administrator ....Lynn MOORE
06 Registrar ....Marie BLY
08 Librarian ....Katharine DOHERTY
18 Chief Facilities/Physical Plant ....Stephen DEROSIER
14 Director Computer Center ....Jeffrey SCHALL
91 Director Administrative Computing ....Donald WEEKS
38 Director Student Counseling ....Emily ELLIOTT
22 Dir Affirmative Action/Equal Oppty ....Margaret HEANEY
40 Director Bookstore ....Karen SEVIER
07 Director of Admissions ....Mark DESMARAIS

Daniel Webster College (J)

20 University Drive, Nashua NH 03063-1300
County: Hillsborough FICE Identification: 004731
Unit ID: 182661
Telephone: (603) 577-6000 Carnegie Class: Bac/Diverse
FAX Number: (603) 577-6001 Calendar System: Semester
URL: www.dwc.edu
Established: 1965 Annual Undergrad Tuition & Fees: $14,845
Enrollment: 767 Coed
Affiliation or Control: Proprietary IRS Status: Proprietary
Highest Offering: Master's
Program: Liberal Arts And General; Technical Emphasis
Accreditation: EH, AAB, ENG

01 President ....Dr. Michael E. DIFFILY
05 VP Academic Affairs ....Dr. Richard KETTNER-POLLEY
10 Vice Pres for Finance & Operations ....Vacant
32 Vice President Student Services .... Ms. Susan C. ELSASS
04 Exec Assistant to the President ....Ms. Cherie HOVEY
49 Dean School of Arts and Sciences ....Dr. Kathleen HIPP
88 Dean School of Aviation Science ....Mr. Jonathan PROHASKA
50 Dean School of Business Management ...Dr. Roland LIVINGSTON
54 Dean School Engineering & Comp Sci ....Mr. Nicholas BERTOZZI
07 Director of Admissions ....Mr. Martin NILSSON
88 Director of Flight Operations .... Mr. Aidan SELTSAM-WILPS
08 Library Director ....Ms. Susan WAGNER
06 Registrar ....Ms. Marilyn NIEUWEBOER

35	Dean of Students	Ms. Michelle O'MALLEY
20	Dean Acad Support & Faculty Affairs	Ms. Kimberly BLANCHETTE
36	Director Career Planning/Placement	Ms. Katie MCAULIFFE
41	Director of Athletics	Vacant
19	Director of Campus Safety	Mr. John CLARK
21	Director of Finance	Mr. Sean LATTIMER
15	Director Human Resources	Vacant

Dartmouth College (A)

Hanover NH 03755-4030

County: Grafton — FICE Identification: 002573

Unit ID: 182670

Telephone: (603) 646-1110 — Carnegie Class: RU/VH

FAX Number: N/A — Calendar System: Quarter

URL: www.dartmouth.edu

Established: 1769 — Annual Undergrad Tuition & Fees: $41,736

Enrollment: 6,141 — Coed

Affiliation or Control: Independent Non-Profit — IRS Status: 501(c)3

Highest Offering: Doctorate

Program: Liberal Arts And General; Professional

Accreditation: EH, BUS, ENG, IPSY, MED, PH

01	President	Dr. Jim Y. KIM
03	Executive Vice President and CFO	Mr. Steven N. KADISH
101	Secretary to Board of Trustees	Ms. Marcia J. KELLY
05	Provost	Dr. Carol L. FOLT
46	Vice Provost for Research	Dr. Martin N. WYBOURNE
10	Vice Pres Finance	Mr. Michael F. WAGNER
30	Sr Vice President for Advancement	Ms. Carolyn A. PELZEL
26	Vice Pres for Communications	Mr. Roddy O. YOUNG
28	Vice Pres for Inst Diversity/Equity	Dr. Evelynn ELLIS
15	Vice Pres Human Resources	Mr. Myron S. MCCOO
29	Vice President Alumni Relations	Ms. Martha J. BEATTIE
100	Chief of Staff	Mr. David P. SPALDING
43	General Counsel	Mr. Robert B. DONIN
20	Dean of the College	Ms. Charlotte H. JOHNSON
06	Registrar	Ms. Meredith BRAZ
07	Dean Admiss/Finan Aid/Assoc Provost	Ms. Maria LASKARIS
37	Director of Financial Aid	Ms. Virginia S. HAZEN
13	Chief Information Officer	Ms. Ellen J. WAITE-FRANZEN
08	Dean of Libraries/Librarian of Col	Mr. Jeffrey L. HORRELL
49	Dean of Faculty of Arts & Sciences	Dr. Michael MASTANDUNO
50	Dean of Amos Tuck School	Dr. Paul DANOS
54	Dean of the Thayer School	Dr. Joseph HELBLE
63	VP Hlth Affs/Dean Dartmouth Med Sch	Dr. Wiley W. SOUBA, JR.
58	Dean of Graduate Studies	Dr. Brian W. POGUE
88	Dean of Tucker Foundation	Dr. Richard R. CROCKER
41	Director of Athletics	Mr. Harry SHEEHY
21	Director Integrated Risk Mgmt/Insur	Ms. Catherine LARK
23	Director of Health Services	Dr. John H. TURCO
36	Acting Co-Director Career Services	Ms. Kathryn DOUGHTY
36	Acting Co-Director Career Services	Ms. Monica WILSON
25	Dir Office of Sponsored Projects	Ms. Jill M. MORTALI
35	Assoc Dean Student Acad Spprt Svcs	Dr. Inge-Lise AMEER
19	Director Safety & Security	Mr. Harry C. KINNE, III
09	Actg Dir of Institutional Research	Ms. Lynn FOSTER-JOHNSON
38	Dir Counseling/Human Development	Dr. Mark H. REED
22	Dir Equal Opportunity/Affirm Action	Dr. Evelynn ELLIS
96	Director of Procurement	Ms. Tammy L. MOFFATT
88	Chief Investment Officer	Ms. Pamela L. PEEDIN

Franklin Pierce University (B)

40 University Drive, Rindge NH 03461-5046

County: Cheshire — FICE Identification: 002575

Unit ID: 182795

Telephone: (603) 899-4000 — Carnegie Class: Master's S

FAX Number: (603) 899-6448 — Calendar System: Semester

URL: www.franklinpierce.edu

Established: 1962 — Annual Undergrad Tuition & Fees: $29,450

Enrollment: 2,396 — Coed

Affiliation or Control: Independent Non-Profit — IRS Status: 501(c)3

Highest Offering: Doctorate

Program: Liberal Arts And General; Teacher Preparatory; Professional

Accreditation: EH, #ARCPA, NUR, PTA

01	President	Dr. James F. BIRGE
05	VP Academic Affairs/Provost	Dr. Kim MOONEY
41	Vice President/Athletic Director	Mr. Bruce M. KIRSH
10	Vice Pres Finance & Planning	Mr. Richard MARSHALL
32	Vice President for Student Affairs	Dr. James P. EARLE
84	Vice Pres Enrollment Management	Mr. William HAWKINS
11	Vice Pres Student Admin Svcs/CIO	Vacant
26	Vice Pres for College Relations	Mr. Ahmad BOURA
58	Dean Grad/Professional Studies	Dr. Thomas SABBAGH
35	Dean Student Affairs	Mr. Jules TETREAULT
07	Director of Admissions	Ms. Linda QUIMBY
09	Director of Institutional Research	Ms. Dawn K. STEVENSON
15	Director of Human Resources	Ms. Sharon T. BURKE
06	Registrar	Ms. Tonya B. LABROSSE
08	Director of Library Resource Center	Ms. Carissa DELIZIO
37	Director of Financial Aid	Mr. Ken FERREIRA
29	Director of Alumni Affairs	Mrs. Shirley ENGLISH-WHITMAN
12	Academic Dean Rindge Campus	Dr. Paul M. KOTILA
12	Director Concord Center	Mrs. Paula SMYKIL
12	Director Portsmouth Center	Ms. Heather THIBODEAU
12	Director Manchester Campus	Mr. Brian EGO
12	Asst Dean Goodyear (AZ) Campus	Mrs. Andrea M. BRODE
27	Dir of Marketing & Communication	Ms. Patricia GARRITY
36	Director of Career Development	Ms. Rosemary NICHOLS
20	Dir Center for Academic Excellence	Ms. Teresa DOWNING
42	Chaplain	Rev. Bill BEARDSLEE
23	Director Health Services	Ms. Aletha E. POTTER
19	Director Campus Safety	Vacant
39	Director Residential Life	Mr. Kenneth ERVIN
85	Director Int'l Student Services	Ms. Susan OEHLSCHLAEGER
18	Chief Facilities/Physical Plant	Mr. Doug LEAR
21	Director of Financial Services	Ms. Sandra QUAYE
96	Director of Purchasing	Mr. Robert ST. JEAN
104	Director Study Abroad	Mrs. Stella WALLING
40	Manager Follett's Bookstore	Ms. Kate BROWN

Hesser College (C)

3 Sundial Avenue, Manchester NH 03103-7245

County: Hillsborough — FICE Identification: 004729

Unit ID: 182865

Telephone: (603) 668-6660 — Carnegie Class: Bac/Assoc

FAX Number: (603) 666-4722 — Calendar System: Semester

URL: www.hesser.edu

Established: 1900 — Annual Undergrad Tuition & Fees: $14,997

Enrollment: 4,148 — Coed

Affiliation or Control: Proprietary — IRS Status: Proprietary

Highest Offering: Baccalaureate

Program: Occupational; 2-Year Principally Bachelor's Creditable

Accreditation: EH, MAC, PTAA

01	President	Dr. Jacquelyn ARMITAGE
05	Int Vice Pres for Academic Affairs	Ms. Mary WELLS
12	Dean of Manchester	Ms. Mary WELLS
32	Dean of Student Services	Vacant
20	Academic Dean	Dr. Marc WILSON
10	Director of Finance	Ms. Mary GORMAN
37	Director Financial Aid	Mr. Shaman QUINN
06	Registrar	Ms. Susan PROVENCHER
08	Director of Library Services	Ms. Ada KEMP
18	Director of Operations/Security	Vacant
36	Director of Career Services	Mr. Rudy RACINE
37	Director Student Financial Aid	Vacant
04	Assistant to the President	Mrs. Carol DEWALT

Lebanon College (D)

15 Hanover Street, Lebanon NH 03766-1312

County: Grafton — FICE Identification: 007025

Unit ID: 182008

Telephone: (603) 448-2445 — Carnegie Class: Not Classified

FAX Number: (603) 448-2491 — Calendar System: Trimester

URL: www.lebanoncollege.edu

Established: 1956 — Annual Undergrad Tuition & Fees: $6,600

Enrollment: 684 — Coed

Affiliation or Control: Independent Non-Profit — IRS Status: 501(c)3

Highest Offering: Associate Degree

Program: Occupational; 2-Year Principally Bachelor's Creditable

Accreditation: ACICS, RAD

01	President	Dr. Graziella SACCON
05	Academic Dean	Dr. Bruce GORDON

New England College (E)

98 Bridge Street, Henniker NH 03242-3244

County: Merrimack — FICE Identification: 002579

Unit ID: 182980

Telephone: (603) 428-2211 — Carnegie Class: Master's M

FAX Number: (603) 428-7230 — Calendar System: Semester

URL: www.nec.edu

Established: 1946 — Annual Undergrad Tuition & Fees: $30,400

Enrollment: 2,043 — Coed

Affiliation or Control: Independent Non-Profit — IRS Status: 501(c)3

Highest Offering: Doctorate

Program: Liberal Arts And General; Teacher Preparatory; Professional

Accreditation: EH

01	President	Dr. Michele D. PERKINS
05	VP for Academic Affairs	Dr. Hilton HALLOCK
84	VP of Enrollment and Marketing	Dr. Barbara LAYNE
10	VP for Finance and Administration	Ms. Paula AMATO
30	VP Strategic Priorities Advancement	Dr. James GARVEY
08	Director of Danforth Library	Ms. Kathy VAN WEELDEN
32	Dean of Students	Dr. Eric BRAUN
58	Dean Graduate School	Dr. Nelly LEJTER
20	Associate Dean of Academic Services	Mr. Mark WATMAN
04	Admin Assistant to President	Ms. Melissa K. STEPHENSON
15	Human Resources Manager	Ms. Holly COLE
91	Director of Information Technology	Mr. Greg SCHOLZ
07	Dean of Admissions	Ms. Diane RAYMOND
06	Registrar	Mr. Frank L. HALL
37	Director Student Financial Svcs	Ms. Kristen BLASE
21	Controller	Ms. Betty FARR
18	Chief Facilities/Physical Plant	Mr. Jay BURGESS
41	Athletic Director	Ms. Lori RUNKSMEIER
26	Director of Public Information	Ms. Kathleen WILLIAMS

New Hampshire Institute of Art (F)

148 Concord Street, Manchester NH 03104-4858

County: Hillsborough — FICE Identification: 031823

Unit ID: 430810

Telephone: (603) 623-0313 — Carnegie Class: Spec/Arts

FAX Number: (603) 641-1832 — Calendar System: Semester

URL: www.nhia.edu

Established: 1898 — Annual Undergrad Tuition & Fees: $21,120

Enrollment: 490 — Coed

Affiliation or Control: Independent Non-Profit — IRS Status: 501(c)3

Highest Offering: Baccalaureate

Program: Fine Arts Emphasis

Accreditation: @EH, ART

01	President	Mr. Roger WILLIAMS
03	Executive Vice President	Mr. Richard STRAWBRIDGE
10	Vice President for Finance	Mr. Jim CHATTERTON
04	Executive Assistant to President	Ms. Melissa SULLIVAN
05	Dean of Academic Affairs	Mr. Patrick MCCAY
08	Library Director	Ms. Anastasia WEIGLE
88	Director of Advising	Vacant
06	Registrar	Ms. Gail SORA
20	Academic Affairs Administrator	Ms. Kathy TRAYNOR
88	Bursar	Ms. Cathy CONSENTINO
30	Director of Development	Ms. Suzanne LENZ
84	Director of Enrollment	Mr. Liam SULLIVAN
32	Director of Student Affairs	Vacant
37	Director Financial Aid	Ms. Cami CZOHARA
51	Continuing Education Director	Ms. Karen FRANCIS
15	Director of Human Resources	Mr. Bill SCIMONE
21	Accounting Manager	Ms. Mary Anne LA BRIE
21	Business Services Manager	Ms. Kelly LEVIS
18	Facilities Manager	Mr. Jonathan WOODCOCK
40	Retail Manager	Mr. Joe VIVILECCHIA
13	Manager of Information Technologies	Mr. Drew ROYER
88	IT Specialist	Mr. Erwan DE BECKERS
38	Counselor	Ms. Tanya POPOLOSKI
88	Academic Support Center Coordinator	Ms. Liza OPPENHEIM

Rivier College (G)

420 S Main Street, Nashua NH 03060-5086

County: Hillsborough — FICE Identification: 002586

Unit ID: 183211

Telephone: (603) 888-1311 — Carnegie Class: Master's L

FAX Number: (603) 897-8811 — Calendar System: Semester

URL: www.rivier.edu

Established: 1933 — Annual Undergrad Tuition & Fees: $25,410

Enrollment: 851 — Coed

Affiliation or Control: Roman Catholic — IRS Status: 501(c)3

Highest Offering: Doctorate

Program: Liberal Arts And General; Teacher Preparatory; Professional; Nursing Emphasis

Accreditation: EH, ADNUR, NUR

01	President	Sr. Paula Marie BULEY
05	Vice President for Academic Affairs	Sr. Therese LAROCHELLE
10	Vice Pres Finance & Administration	Mr. Joseph A. FAGAN
32	Vice President Student Development	Ms. Linda JANSKY
84	Vice Pres Enrollment Management	Mr. David BOISVERT
35	Asst Vice Pres Student Development	Ms. Paula RANDAZZA
13	Exec Director Info Technologies	Mr. H. William SCHLEIFER
30	Exec Director Development/Marketing	Ms. Karen COOPER
21	Controller	Ms. Jennifer YEOMANS
06	Registrar	Mr. Kevin GATELY
08	Librarian	Mr. Daniel SPEIDEL
36	Director Career Placement	Ms. Marie SULLIVAN
37	Director Student Financial Aid	Ms. Valerie PATNAUDE
15	Director Human Resources	Ms. Diana STRANO
18	Director Facilities Management	Mr. Richard PERRINE
14	Director Computer Center	Sr. Martha VILLENEUVE
41	Athletic Director	Ms. Joanne MERRILL
42	Chaplain Campus Ministry	Bro. Paul DEMERS
28	Director Multicultural Affairs	Ms. Sharron ROWLETT
29	Asst Director Alumni Relations	Ms. Mary BOLLINGER

Saint Anselm College (H)

100 Saint Anselm Drive, Manchester NH 03102-1310

County: Hillsborough — FICE Identification: 002587

Unit ID: 183239

Telephone: (603) 641-7000 — Carnegie Class: Bac/A&S

FAX Number: (603) 641-7116 — Calendar System: Semester

URL: www.anselm.edu

Established: 1889 — Annual Undergrad Tuition & Fees: $32,365

Enrollment: 1,870 — Coed

Affiliation or Control: Roman Catholic — IRS Status: 501(c)3

Highest Offering: Baccalaureate

Program: Liberal Arts And General; Teacher Preparatory

Accreditation: EH, NURSE

01	President	Rev. Jonathan P. DEFELICE, OSB
03	Executive Vice President	Dr. Suzanne K. MELLON
30	Vice President College Advancement	Mr. James P. FLANAGAN
11	Vice President for Administration	Ms. Patricia SHUSTER
84	VP College Mktg & Enrollment Mgmt	Mr. Brad F. POZNANSKI
32	Vice President Student Affairs	Dr. Joseph M. HORTON
26	Asst VP of College Comm & Mktg	Vacant
05	Dean of the College	Rev. Augustine KELLY, OSB
10	Treasurer	Rev. Mark A. COOPER, OSB
06	Registrar	Ms. MaryAnn ERICSON
07	Dean of Admissions	Ms. Nancy DAVIS GRIFFIN
08	Librarian	Dr. Joseph W. CONSTANCE, JR.
37	Director of Financial Aid	Ms. Elizabeth KEUFFEL
35	Dean of Students	Dr. Alicia A. FINN
36	Director of Career Planning	Mr. Samuel ALLEN, JR.
20	Director of Academic Advisement	Ms. Anne E. HARRINGTON
87	Director Summer Sessions	Dr. Dennis SWEETLAND
66	Dean of Nursing	Dr. Sharon A. GEORGE

04 Assistant to the President .... Ms. Janet L. POIRIER
18 Director of Maintenance .... Mr. Donald MOREAU
23 Director of Health Services .... Ms. Maura MARSHALL
29 Asst VP of Alum/Advanc Programming .... Ms. Patricia GUANCI-THERRIEN
41 Director of Athletics .... Vacant
42 Director of Campus Ministry .... Ms. Susan S. GABERT
09 Director of Institutional Research .... Dr. Hui-Ling CHEN
27 Chief Information Officer .... Mr. Adam R. ALBINA
15 Director Human Resources .... Vacant
19 Director Security/Safety .... Mr. Donald DAVIDSON
53 Director Education Planning .... Dr. Laura WASIELEWSKI
28 Director Multicultural Center .... Ms. Oluyemi MAHONEY
39 Director Student Housing .... Ms. Susan WEINTRAUB

St. Joseph School of Nursing (A)

5 Woodward Avenue, Nashua NH 03060
County: Hillsborough FICE Identification: 021404
Unit ID: 183248
Telephone: (603) 594-2567 Carnegie Class: Not Classified
FAX Number: (603) 578-5028 Calendar System: Semester
URL: www.sjhacademiccenter.org
Established: 1964 Annual Undergrad Tuition & Fees: $13,615
Enrollment: 82 Coed
Affiliation or Control: Independent Non-Profit IRS Status: 501(c)3
Highest Offering: Associate Degree
Program: Occupational; 2-Year Principally Bachelor's Creditable; Nursing Emphasis
Accreditation: ACCSC, PNUR

01 Director .... Dr. Camilie TWISS

Southern New Hampshire University (B)

2500 N River Road, Manchester NH 03106-1045
County: Hillsborough FICE Identification: 002580
Unit ID: 183026
Telephone: (603) 668-2211 Carnegie Class: Master's L
FAX Number: (603) 645-9665 Calendar System: Semester
URL: www.snhu.edu
Established: 1932 Annual Undergrad Tuition & Fees: $27,234
Enrollment: 8,034 Coed
Affiliation or Control: Independent Non-Profit IRS Status: 501(c)3
Highest Offering: Doctorate
Program: Liberal Arts And General; Teacher Preparatory; Professional
Accreditation: EH, ACBSP, ACFEI

01 President .... Dr. Paul LEBLANC
05 Provost/Sr Vice Pres Academic Affs .... Dr. Patricia LYNOTT
10 Sr Vice Pres Opers/Finance/Treas .... Mr. William D. MCGARRY
30 Vice Pres Institutional Advancement .... Mr. Donald BREZINSKI
84 Sr VP Student Recruitment/Marketing ... Mr. Stephen HODOWNES
27 VP Marketing & Communications .. Ms. Martha RUSH-MUELLER
15 VP Human Resources & Development .... Ms. Pamela HOGAN
51 Sr VP Continuing/Online Education .... Ms. Yvonne SIMON
43 General Counsel/Secretary to Board .... Ms. Karen D. ABBOTT
50 Dean School of Business .... Mr. William GILLETT
35 Interim Dean of Student Affairs .... Ms. Heather LORENZ
08 Dean of the Library .... Ms. Kathy GROWNEY
20 Associate VP for Academic Affairs .... Dr. Nicholas HUNT-BULL
06 Registrar .... Ms. Jennifer DISTEFANO
35 Director of Student Activities .... Mr. Scott TIERNO
37 Interim Director Financial Aid .... Ms. Robin GAGNON
23 Director Wellness Center .... Ms. Jet GOLDBERG
14 Director of Computer Center .... Mr. Daryl A. DREFFS
18 Director Facilities/Physical Plant .... Mr. Robert VACHON
04 Exec Asst to the President .... Ms. Nancy RICHARDSON
26 Chief Public Relations Officer .... Mr. Gregory MAZZOLA
07 Director of Admissions .... Mr. Steven SOBA
28 Dir Cultural Outreach & Involvement .... Ms. Louisa MARTIN
09 Director of Institutional Research .... Mr. Thomas BERALDI

The Thomas More College of Liberal Arts (C)

6 Manchester Street, Merrimack NH 03054-4805
County: Hillsborough FICE Identification: 030431
Unit ID: 183275
Telephone: (603) 880-8308 Carnegie Class: Bac/A&S
FAX Number: (603) 880-9280 Calendar System: Semester
URL: www.thomasmorecollege.edu
Established: 1978 Annual Undergrad Tuition & Fees: $16,100
Enrollment: 77 Coed
Affiliation or Control: Independent Non-Profit IRS Status: 501(c)3
Highest Offering: Baccalaureate
Program: Liberal Arts And General; Religious Emphasis
Accreditation: #EH

01 President .... Dr. William E. FAHEY
11 Vice President Administration .... Mr. Clint HANSON
30 Vice Pres Institutional Advancement .... Mr. Charlie MCKINNEY
05 Academic Dean .... Dr. Christopher BLUM
32 Dean of Students .... Mr. Walter J. THOMPSON
07 Director of Admission .... Mr. Mark SCHWERDT
06 Registrar .... Ms. Pamela BERNSTEIN
35 Direct Student Life .... Ms. Annie CLARK
04 Executive Asst President's Office .... Ms. Valerie BURGESS

*University System of New Hampshire (D)

Dunlap Center, 25 Concord Road, Durham NH 03824-3545
County: Strafford FICE Identification: 008027
Unit ID: 183327
Telephone: (603) 862-1800 Carnegie Class: N/A
FAX Number: (603) 862-0908
URL: usnh.edu

01 Chancellor .... Dr. Edward R. MACKAY
03 Vice Chancellor & Treasurer .... Mr. Ken CODY
15 Director Human Resource Services .... Ms. Joan M. TAMBLING
43 General Counsel .... Mr. Ronald F. RODGERS
04 USNH Secretary .... Mr. Ronald F. RODGERS
86 Assoc Vice Chanc Government Affs ..... Ms. Kathleen SALISBURY
26 Assoc Vice Chanc for External Affs .... Vacant
05 Assoc Vice Chanc Academic & Student .... Vacant

*University of New Hampshire (E)

Durham NH 03824
County: Strafford FICE Identification: 002589
Unit ID: 183044
Telephone: (603) 862-1234 Carnegie Class: RU/H
FAX Number: N/A Calendar System: Semester
URL: www.unh.edu
Established: 1866 Annual Undergrad Tuition & Fees (In-State): $14,600
Enrollment: 14,469 Coed
Affiliation or Control: State IRS Status: 501(c)3
Highest Offering: Doctorate
Program: Occupational; 2-Year Principally Bachelor's Creditable; Liberal Arts And General; Teacher Preparatory; Professional
Accreditation: EH, BUS, CS, DIETD, DIETI, DIETT, ENG, ENGT, FOR, IPSY, MFCD, MT, MUS, NRPA, NURSE, OT, PH, SP, SW, TEAC

02 President .... Dr. Mark W. HUDDLESTON
100 Chief of Staff .... Ms. Megan W. DAVIS
05 Prov & VP Academic Affairs .... Dr. John D. ABER
10 VP Finance/Administration .... Mr. Richard J. CANNON
46 Sr Vice Provost Research .... Dr. Jane A. NISBET
32 VP Student & Academic Services .... Dr. Mark RUBINSTEIN
26 Assoc VP Univ Communications .... Mr. Justin HARMON
43 General Counsel .... Mr. Ronald F. RODGERS
88 Assoc Prov Academic Administration .... Ms. Leigh Anne MELANSON
28 Vice Prov & Chief Diversity Officer .... Dr. Wanda S. MITCHELL
20 Sr Vice Prov Academic Affairs .... Dr. Lisa MACFARLANE
20 Asst Prov & MPA Program Dir .... Mr. James S. VARN
20 Assoc VP Rsrch & Outreach Scholar .... Dr. Julie E. WILLIAMS
21 Assc VP Financial Planning & Budget .... Mr. David R. PROULX
13 Assoc VP Computing/Info Svcs .... Ms. Joanna C. YOUNG
16 Asst VP Human Resources .... Vacant
11 Assoc VP Operations .... Mr. Anthony ZIZOS
21 Asst VP Business Affairs .... Mr. David J. MAY
18 Asst VP Energy & Campus Development .... Mr. Paul D. CHAMBERLIN
35 Dean of Students .... Dr. Martha A. LAWING
35 Asst VP Stdnt/Acad Svc/Dir Res Life .... Mr. Scott CHESNEY
23 Asst VP SAS/Exec Dir Health Svcs .... Dr. Kevin E. CHARLES
36 Assoc Prov Acad Achievement/Support .... Dr. Judith SPILLER
25 Exec Dir Sponsored Research .... Mr. Victor SOSA
30 VP Advancement .... Mr. Peter B. WEILER
47 Dean Life Sciences/Agriculture .... Dr. Thomas E. BRADY
49 Dean Liberal Arts .... Dr. Kenneth FULD
50 Dean Whittemore Sch Business/Econ .... Dr. Daniel E. INNIS
58 Dean Graduate School .... Dr. Harry J. RICHARDS
76 Dean Health & Human Services .... Dr. Barbara A. ARRINGTON
54 Dean Engineering/Physical Sciences .... Dr. Samuel MUKASA
12 Dean UNH at Manchester .... Dr. Kristin R. WOOLEVER
08 Dean of the University Library .... Dr. Sherry VELLUCCI
56 Dean/Dir Cooperative Extension .... Dr. John E. PIKE
88 Dir Thompson School Appl Science .... Dr. Regina A. SMICK-ATTISANO
22 Dir Affirmative Action & Equity ... Ms. Donna Marie SORRENTINO
07 Asst VP Stdnt & Acad Svc/Dir Admiss .... Mr. Robert P H. MCGANN
06 Registrar .... Ms. Kathryn P. FORBES
37 Dir Financial Aid .... Ms. Susan K. ALLEN
41 Dir Intercollegiate Athletics .... Mr. Martin SCARANO
38 Dir Counseling Center .... Dr. David CROSS
29 Asst VP Advanc/Exec Dir Alumni Assc .... Mr. Stephen J. DONOVAN
39 Dir Housing/Conf Services .... Ms. Kathy IRLA-CHESNEY
19 Chief University Police .... Chief Nicholas J. HALIAS
85 Dir Intl Students & Scholars .... Ms. Leila L. PAJE-MANALO
42 University Chaplain .... Pastor Larry BRICKNER-WOOD
96 Dir Purchasing & Contract Svcs .... Ms. Denise M. SMITH
92 Dir Honors Program .... Dr. Sean MOORE
09 Dir Inst Research & Assessment .... Dr. John D. KRAUS, JR.
18 Director of Facility Operations .... Ms. Michelle HAYES
104 Dir Center International Education .... Dr. Claire L. MALARTE-FELDMAN
94 Coord Women's Studies Program .... Dr. Marla B. BRETTSCHNEIDER
40 Manager of UNH Bookstore .... Ms. Sarah HUTZ

*University of New Hampshire at Manchester (F)

400 Commerical Street, Manchester NH 03101-1113
County: Hillsborough FICE Identification: 009009
Unit ID: 183071
Telephone: (603) 641-4321 Carnegie Class: Bac/A&S
FAX Number: (603) 641-4305 Calendar System: Semester
URL: www.unhm.unh.edu
Established: 1967 Annual Undergrad Tuition & Fees (In-State): $10,725
Enrollment: 1,437 Coed
Affiliation or Control: State IRS Status: 501(c)3
Highest Offering: Master's
Program: Liberal Arts And General
Accreditation: &EH

02 Interim Dean .... Dr. Sally K. WARD
05 Associate Dean Academic Affairs .... Dr. Daniel W. REAGAN
10 Director of Administration & Financ .... Ms. Kathy E. BRAUN
32 Asst Dean of Academic Student Svcs .. Ms. Regina K. MCCARTHY
91 Dir of UNHM Information Technology .... Mr. Sean P. EMBREE
19 Supervisor of Security Services .... Mr. Gary W. SEARS
62 Director Library Services .... Ms. Ann E. DONAHUE
28 Director Center Academic Enrichment .... Dr. Margaret F. POBYWAJLO
26 Dir of Marketing & Cmty Relations .... Ms. Virginia H. LEVER
37 Associate Director Financial Aid .... Ms. Jodi A. ABAD
07 Assistant Director of Admissions .... Ms. Miho S. BEAN
06 Associate Registrar .... Ms. Doreen E. PALMER
38 Director of Academic Counseling .... Ms. Carol A. SWIECH
15 Human Resources Partner .... Ms. Stacey J. SILVA

*University of New Hampshire School of Law - formerly Franklin Pierce Law Center (G)

Two White Street, Concord NH 03301-4197
County: Merrimack FICE Identification: 020979
Unit ID: 182829
Telephone: (603) 228-1541 Carnegie Class: Spec/Law
FAX Number: (603) 228-1074 Calendar System: Semester
URL: www.law.unh.edu
Established: 1973 Annual Graduate Tuition & Fees: $39,900
Enrollment: 451 Coed
Affiliation or Control: Independent Non-Profit IRS Status: 501(c)3
Highest Offering: Doctorate; No Undergraduates
Program: Professional
Accreditation: EH, LAW

02 Dean/President .... Mr. John T. BRODERICK, JR.
05 Associate Dean .... Prof. Jordan BUDD
00 Chairman of the Board .... Ms. Cathy GREEN
10 Vice President Financial Affairs .... Ms. Linda LUGG
32 Assistant Dean for Student Affairs .... Ms. Fran CANNING
06 Assistant Dean Registration/Records .... Ms. Lory ATTALLA
84 Chair Admissions Committee .... Prof. Albert SCHERR
08 Law Librarian .... Prof. Judith A. GIRE
88 Director of Accreditation .... Prof. Margaret S. MCCAPE
88 Director of Clinical Programs .... Prof. Peter WRIGHT
88 Director Inst for Health/Law/Ethics .... Prof. Tom BUNNELL
36 Assistant Dean for Career Services .... Ms. Donna MILLER
58 Director of Graduate Programs .... Ms. Debbie BEAUREGARD
07 Assistant Dean for Admissions .... Ms. Katie MCDONALD
30 Director of Development .... Ms. Angel COLARUSSO
29 Director of Alumni Relations .... Ms. Mary SHEFFER
37 Director of Financial Aid .... Ms. Susan AHERN
26 Director of Communications .... Mr. Peter DAVIES
04 Executive Assistant to The Dean .... Ms. Linda L. LUGG

*Granite State College (H)

8 Old Suncook Road, Concord NH 03301-7317
County: Merrimack FICE Identification: 031013
Unit ID: 183257
Telephone: (603) 228-3000 Carnegie Class: Bac/A&S
FAX Number: (603) 513-1389 Calendar System: Trimester
URL: www.granite.edu
Established: 1972 Annual Undergrad Tuition & Fees (In-State): $6,810
Enrollment: 1,798 Coed
Affiliation or Control: State IRS Status: 501(c)3
Highest Offering: Master's
Program: Liberal Arts And General; Teacher Preparatory; Professional
Accreditation: EH

02 President .... Dr. Todd LEACH
05 Dean of Academic Affairs .... Dr. Sheila TAYLOR-KING
13 Dean of Education Tech/Computing .... Mr. Mike MOROUKIAN
10 Dean of Finance and Administration .... Ms. Lisa SHAWNEY
100 Special Assistant to the President .... Dr. Kathi MULLEN
20 Dean of Students/External Engage .... Ms. Teresa H. MCDONNELL
56 Dean of External Programs .... Mr. Bernard J. KEENAN
53 Assoc Dean of Education Programs .... Dr. Mary FORD
20 Assoc Dean of Academic Affairs .... Dr. Laurie QUINN
11 Dean of Center Operations .... Dr. Elaine MILLEN
26 Director Marketing/Enrollment Mgmt .... Ms. Mary Beth LUFKIN
06 Registrar .... Ms. Karen R. KING
24 Director of Educational Technology .... Ms. Reta CHAFFEE
37 Director of Financial Aid .... Mr. Kevin PIOTROWSKI
15 Director of Human Resources .... Ms. Beth DALZELL
09 Director of Institutional Research .... Mr. Jim MILLER

18 Dir of Facilities/Safety/Sustain .... Mr. Peter CONKLIN
08 Director Library/Info Services .... Vacant
07 Associate Director of Admissions .... Ms. Ruth NAWN
21 Director of Financial Operations .... Mr. Steve PERROTTA
21 Bursar .... Ms. Jodi WOLBERT
04 Exec Assistant to the President .... Ms. Mary YOUNG

Keene State College (A)

229 Main Street, Keene NH 03435-0001
County: Cheshire FICE Identification: 002590
Unit ID: 183062
Telephone: (603) 352-1909 Carnegie Class: Master's S
FAX Number: (603) 358-2257 Calendar System: Semester
URL: www.keene.edu
Established: 1909 Annual Undergrad Tuition & Fees (In-State): $10,590
Enrollment: 5,390 Coed
Affiliation or Control: State IRS Status: 501(c)3
Highest Offering: Master's
Program: Liberal Arts And General; Teacher Preparatory; Professional
Accreditation: EH, DIETD, DIETI, MUS, TED

02 President .... Dr. Helen F. GILES-GEE
05 Provost/Vice Pres Academic Affairs .... Dr. Emile NETZHAMMER
32 Vice President Student Affairs .... Dr. Andrew ROBINSON
10 Vice President Finance & Planning .... Dr. Jay V. KAHN
30 Vice President Advancement .... Ms. Maryann LINDBERG
04 Sr Exec Asst & Legislative Liaison .... Ms. Misha J. CHARLES
04 Executive Asst to the President .... Ms. Ann M. GAGNON
20 Assoc Provost Academic Affairs .... Dr. Ann RANCOURT
35 Dean of Students .... Dr. Gail ZIMMERMAN
08 Dean of Library .... Ms. Irene HEROLD
07 Director of Admissions .... Ms. Margaret RICHMOND
06 Registrar .... Mr. Thomas RICHARD
27 Chief Information Officer .... Ms. Laura SERAICHICK
30 Director of Development .... Mr. Ken GOEBEL
15 Human Resources Director .... Ms. Kim HARKNESS
26 Interim Dir of Marketing & Comm .... Ms. Eve ALINTUCK
37 Director Financial Aid .... Ms. Patricia A. BLODGETT
18 Director Physical Plant .... Mr. Frank MAZZOLA
39 Director of Residential Life .... Mr. Kent DRAKE-DEESE
09 Director of Institutional Research .... Vacant
29 Director of Alumni Relations .... Ms. Patricia FARMER
38 Director Student Counseling .... Dr. Brian QUIGLEY
21 Associate Business Officer .... Ms. Karen HOUSE
96 Purchasing Agent .... Mr. James DRAPER
81 Dean of Sciences .... Dr. Gordon LEVERSEE
58 Dean Professional/Graduate Studies .. Dr. Melinda D. TREADWELL
79 Dean Arts & Humanities .... Dr. Nona FIENBERG
28 Chief Officer Diversity/Multicult .... Dr. Dottie MORRIS

*Plymouth State University (B)

17 High Street, Plymouth NH 03264-1595
County: Grafton FICE Identification: 002591
Unit ID: 183080
Telephone: (603) 535-5000 Carnegie Class: Master's L
FAX Number: (603) 535-2654 Calendar System: Semester
URL: www.plymouth.edu
Established: 1871 Annual Undergrad Tuition & Fees (In-State): $11,518
Enrollment: 5,831 Coed
Affiliation or Control: State IRS Status: 501(c)3
Highest Offering: Doctorate
Program: Liberal Arts And General; Teacher Preparatory; Business Emphasis
Accreditation: EH, ACBSP, CACREP, SW, TED

02 President .... Dr. Sara Jayne STEEN
05 Vice Pres Academic Affairs/Provost .... Dr. Julie N. BERNIER
10 VP for Finance & Administration .... Mr. Stephen TAKSAR
32 Vice President for Student Affairs .... Vacant
20 VP for Undergraduate Studies .... Mr. David ZEHR
20 Vice Provost .... Mr. Daniel MOORE
58 Associate VP Graduate Studies .... Dr. George F. TUTHILL
35 Dean of Students .... Mr. Timothy C. KEEFE
09 Assoc Dean Inst Resources/Assessmnt .... Dr. Scott MANTIE
06 Registrar .... Vacant
08 Director of Lamson Library .... Mr. David BERONA
07 Senior Assoc Director of Admissions .... Mr. Eugene D. FAHEY
26 Exec Director University Relations .... Mr. Steve BARBA
29 Director of Alumni Relations .... Vacant
36 Director Career Services .... Vacant
37 Director of Financial Aid .... Ms. June SCHLABACH
15 Director of Human Resources .... Vacant
19 Chief of Campus Police .... Mr. Creig DOYLE
41 Athletic Director .... Mr. John P. CLARK
13 Director of Information Technology .... Vacant
18 Director of Physical Plant .... Ms. Ellen SHIPPEE
30 Exec Dir University Advancement .... Vacant
38 Director of Counseling .... Dr. Michael L. FISCHLER
40 Bookstore Manager .... Mr. Steve RHEAUME
39 Dir of Residential Life & Dining ..... Mr. Frank L. COCCHIARELLA
88 Director Hartman Union Building .... Ms. Teri L. POTTER
96 Manager of Purchasing .... Ms. Heather HUCKINS

NEW JERSEY

Assumption College for Sisters (C)

350 Bernardsville Road, Mendham NJ 07945-2923
County: Morris FICE Identification: 002595
Unit ID: 183600
Telephone: (973) 543-6528 Carnegie Class: Assoc/PrivNFP
FAX Number: (973) 543-1738 Calendar System: Semester
URL: www.acs350.org
Established: 1953 Annual Undergrad Tuition & Fees: $10,000
Enrollment: 54 Female
Affiliation or Control: Roman Catholic IRS Status: 501(c)3
Highest Offering: Associate Degree
Program: 2-Year Principally Bachelor's Creditable; Religious Emphasis
Accreditation: M

01 President/Chief of Development .... Sr. Joseph SPRING, SCC
05 Dean/Registrar/Admissions .... Sr. Gerardine TANTSITS, SCC
10 Treasurer .... Mrs. Patricia MCGRADY
08 Librarian/Technology .... Sr. Theresa BOWER, SCC

Atlantic Cape Community College (D)

5100 Black Horse Pike, Mays Landing NJ 08330-2699
County: Atlantic FICE Identification: 002596
Unit ID: 183655
Telephone: (609) 343-4900 Carnegie Class: Assoc/Pub-R-L
FAX Number: (609) 343-4917 Calendar System: Semester
URL: www.atlantic.edu
Established: 1964 Annual Undergrad Tuition & Fees (In-District): $3,667
Enrollment: 7,655 Coed
Affiliation or Control: State/Local IRS Status: 501(c)3
Highest Offering: Associate Degree
Program: Occupational; 2-Year Principally Bachelor's Creditable
Accreditation: M, ACFEI, ADNUR, SURGT

01 President .... Dr. Peter L. MORA
05 Vice President Academic Affairs .... Dr. Arthur WEXLER
12 Dean Atlantic Cty Ctr/Cmty Affs .... Mr. Bobby L. ROYAL, SR.
51 Dean Cape May Camp/Cont Ed/Res Dev ...... Dr. Patricia GENTILE
46 Dean Facilities/Planning/Research .... Dr. Richard PERNICIARO
10 Dean Finance and Administration .... Ms. Catherine SKINNER
35 Dean of Students .... Ms. Carmen ROYAL
14 Dean Information Tech Services .... Mr. Douglas HEDGES
15 Dean Human Resources & Compliance ... Ms. Eileen CURRISTINE
20 Dean of Instruction .... Dr. Ronald MCARTHUR
88 Dean Academy of Culinary Arts .... Ms. Kelly MCCLAY
32 Dir of Stdnt Dev & Judical Officer .... Ms. Nancy PORFIDO
88 Assoc Dean Academic Support Svcs .... Mr. Grant WILINSKI
88 Assoc Dean Aviation/Tech Inst & GIS .... Mr. Otto HERNANDEZ
09 Asst Dean Research & Assessment .... Ms. Paula PITCHER
101 Exec Asst to Pres/Dir of Board Svcs .... Mr. Sean FISCHER
21 Exec Director Business Services .... Ms. Theresa SAMPSON
84 Director Enrollment Services .... Ms. Heather PETERSON
26 Exec Director College Relations .... Ms. Kathleen J. CORBALIS
37 Director Financial Aid .... Ms. Linda DESANTIS
06 Registrar .... Ms. Heather PETERSON
07 Director of Admissions .... Ms. Regina SKINNER
18 Director Facil Plng & Capital Proj .... Mr. Mark STRECKENBEIN
38 Director of Student Counseling .... Ms. Paula DAVIS

Bais Medrash Toras Chesed (E)

910 Monmouth Avenue, Lakewood NJ 08701-1921
County: Ocean FICE Identification: 040813
Unit ID: 449658
Telephone: (732) 364-1220 Carnegie Class: Spec/Faith
FAX Number: (732) 886-2323 Calendar System: Semester
Established: 1999 Annual Undergrad Tuition & Fees: $8,700
Enrollment: 113 Male
Affiliation or Control: Independent Non-Profit IRS Status: 501(c)3
Highest Offering: Baccalaureate
Program: Professional
Accreditation: RABN

01 Dean .... Rabbi N. STEIN
37 Director of Financial Aid .... Mrs. A. R. STEIN
10 Bursar .... Rabbi M. GELFAND

Bergen Community College (F)

400 Paramus Road, Paramus NJ 07652-1595
County: Bergen FICE Identification: 004736
Unit ID: 183743
Telephone: (201) 447-7100 Carnegie Class: Assoc/Pub-S-SC
FAX Number: (201) 444-7036 Calendar System: Semester
URL: www.bergen.edu
Established: 1965 Annual Undergrad Tuition & Fees (In-District): $3,937
Enrollment: 17,197 Coed
Affiliation or Control: State/Local IRS Status: 501(c)3
Highest Offering: Associate Degree
Program: Occupational; 2-Year Principally Bachelor's Creditable
Accreditation: M, ADNUR, DH, DMS, MAC, RAD, RTT, SURGT

01 President .... Dr. G. Jeremiah RYAN
05 Academic Vice President .... Dr. Jose ADAMES
32 Vice President Student Services .... Mr. Raymond SMITH
11 Int Vice Pres of Admin Services .... Mr. Dennis MILLER
51 VP of Cont Ed/Outreach & Grants Dev .... Dr. Ronald MILON
09 VP Research/Plng/Assess & Quality .... Dr. Peter DLUGOS
81 Dean Business/Social Sci/Pub Svc .... Mr. Raymond WELCH
79 Dean Arts/Humanities & Wellness .... Prof. Amparo CODDING
17 Dean Health Professions .... Dr. Susan BARNARD
57 Dean English .... Dr. Carol MIELE
106 Dn Pgm Dev/Lrng Tech/Process Improv . Mr. Edward PITTARELLI
81 Dean Math & Science .... Mr. Pascal J. RICATTO
51 Asst Dean Cont Ed/Comm Outreach Pgm .... Ms. Sandra SROKA
35 Dean of Student Svcs/Retention Svcs .... Dr. Denise JERMAN LIGUORI
32 Assoc Dean Student Services .... Dr. Ralph CHOONOO
15 Chief Human Resources Officer .... Mr. James MILLER
18 Director Physical Plant .... Mr. Norman SHAPIRO
19 Director Public Safety .... Mr. William CORCORAN
80 Int Dir Civic Engage/Govt Relations .... Mr. Andre SAYEGH
13 Director of Technologies .... Mr. Evan KOBOLAKIS
10 Controller .... Ms. Diane MANDRAFINA
06 Dir Registration/Student Services .... Ms. Jacqueline OTTEY
88 Director Community/Cultural Affairs .... Vacant
36 Director Career Dev/Transfer Svcs .... Ms. Jennifer REYES
101 Secretary to Board of Trustees .... Ms. Wendy DODGE
29 Director Alumni Relations .... Ms. Laurie FRANCIS
51 Dir Cont Educ/Cmty Outreach Pgms .... Ms. Ilene KLEINMAN
37 Dir Financial Ops/Stdnt Assistance .... Ms. Caroline OFODILE
38 Director Student Development .... Ms. Darlene MCGRATH FLORANCE
08 Dean Library Services .... Ms. Patricia DENHOLM
102 Director Foundation/Development .... Ms. Laurie FRANCIS
31 Chief of Community Relations .... Ms. Angela HARRINGTON
25 Director of Grants .... Dr. William YAKOWICZ
96 Director of Purchasing .... Ms. Barbara HAMILTON-GOLDEN
04 Int Exec Assistant to the President .... Ms. Ann LOTA

Berkeley College (G)

44 Rifle Camp Road, Woodland Park NJ 07424-3367
County: Passaic FICE Identification: 007502
Unit ID: 183789
Telephone: (973) 278-5400 Carnegie Class: Spec/Bus
FAX Number: (973) 278-0080 Calendar System: Quarter
URL: www.berkeleycollege.edu
Established: 1931 Annual Undergrad Tuition & Fees: $21,750
Enrollment: 3,772 Coed
Affiliation or Control: Proprietary IRS Status: Proprietary
Highest Offering: Baccalaureate
Program: Business Emphasis
Accreditation: M

00 Chairman of the Board .... Mr. Kevin L. LUING
01 President .... Dr. Dario A. CORTES
100 Chief of Staff & Assoc VP Planning .... Ms. Linda LUCIANO
04 Special Assistant to the President .... Dr. Rose Mary HEALY
05 Provost .... Dr. Glen ZEITZER
10 Sr Vice President Finance & Admin .... Ms. Lee S. MIARA
36 Vice President Advisement .... Dr. Beth COYLE
84 Sr Vice Pres Enrollment Mgmt .... Ms. Diane RECINOS
26 Senior Vice President Marketing .... Mr. Don CHALLIS
20 Assoc Provost for Faculty Affairs .... Dr. Marianne VAKALIS
20 Assoc Provost Academic Admin .... Dr. Troy ADAIR
32 VP Stdnt Development & Campus Life .... Dr. Edwin HUGHES
20 Vice President Academic Admin .... Ms. Tia DELOUISE
07 Vice President Enrollment .... Ms. Christine G. RICHARD
07 VP International Enrollment Svcs .... Ms. Cynthia C. MARCHESE
22 Vice Pres & Compliance Officer .... Mr. William BRANDT
08 Vice President Library Services .... Ms. Marlene DOTY
12 Garret Mountain Campus Oper Ofcr .... Ms. Linda PINSKY
12 Middlesex Campus Operating Officer . Ms. Debra L. MALLAMACE
12 Newark Campus Operating Officer .... Mr. W. Stan HOLLAND
12 Paramus Campus Operating Officer .... Mr. Evan MILLER
12 Online Campus Operating Officer .... Ms. Sharon GOLDSTEIN
09 Asst VP Assessment & Inst Research .... Dr. Ross MILLER
50 Dean School of Business .... Dr. John RAPANOS
49 Dean School Liberal Arts .... Dr. Don KIEFFER
107 Dean School Professional Studies .... Dr. Judith KORNBERG
51 Dean School Continuing Education .... Mr. Ricardo ORTEGON
106 Assistant Provost & Dean of Online .... Ms. Carol SMITH
86 Senior Vice Pres External Affairs .... Ms. Teri DUDA
84 Assoc Vice President Enrollment .... Ms. Carol ALLEN-COVINO
38 Sr Director Personal Counseling .... Ms. Sandra COPPOLA
35 Director Student Devel/Campus Life .... Ms. Amy YOUNG
21 Assoc VP Student Accounts .... Ms. Ursula BISCONTI
37 Senior Director Financial Aid .... Ms. Barbara SYLVESTER
09 Director Institutional Research .... Mr. Christopher J. VINGER
26 Director Media Relations .... Ms. Ilene LUMPKIN
36 VP Advisement .... Ms. Gail OKUN
41 Athletic Director .... Mr. Brian MAHER

Beth Medrash Govoha (H)

617 Sixth Street, Lakewood NJ 08701-2797
County: Ocean FICE Identification: 007947
Unit ID: 183804
Telephone: (732) 367-1060 Carnegie Class: Spec/Faith
FAX Number: (732) 367-7487 Calendar System: Semester
URL: www.bmg.edu
Established: 1943 Annual Undergrad Tuition & Fees: $16,316
Enrollment: 6,206 Male
Affiliation or Control: Independent Non-Profit IRS Status: 501(c)3
Highest Offering: Beyond Master's But Less Than Doctorate
Program: Teacher Preparatory; Professional
Accreditation: RABN

00 President .... Rabbi A. Malkiel KOTLER
01 Chief Executive Officer .... Rabbi Aaron KOTLER
10 VP Finance/Technology Compliance .... Mr. Isaac LEVINE
43 VP Finance/Corporate/Legal Affairs .... Rabbi Eli KUPERMAN
11 Vice President Admin/Campus Life ...... Rabbi Yitzchok S. KOTLER
33 Dean of Students .... Rabbi Mattisyahu SALOMON
58 Dean of Graduate Studies .... Rabbi Yisroel NEUMAN
05 Executive Administrator .... Rabbi Mordechai HERSKOWITZ

86 Director Government Affairs ... Mrs. Chanie JACOBOWITZ
06 Registrar ... Rabbi Jacob BURSZTYN
07 Director of Admissions ... Rabbi Avraham FEUER
08 Director Library/Research Programs ... Rabbi Benjamin SPIEGEL
36 Director of Field Services ... Rabbi Jacob SHULMAN
39 Director Residence Halls ... Rabbi Yosef SLOMOVITS

Bloomfield College (A)

467 Franklin Street, Bloomfield NJ 07003-3425
County: Essex FICE Identification: 002597
Unit ID: 183822
Telephone: (973) 748-9000 Carnegie Class: Bac/A&S
FAX Number: (973) 743-3998 Calendar System: Semester
URL: www.bloomfield.edu
Established: 1868 Annual Undergrad Tuition & Fees: $22,500
Enrollment: 2,180 Coed
Affiliation or Control: Presbyterian Church (U.S.A.) IRS Status: 501(c)3
Highest Offering: Master's
Program: Liberal Arts And General; Teacher Preparatory; Professional
Accreditation: M, NURSE, TEAC

01 President ... Richard A. LEVAO
10 Senior Vice Pres of Admin/Finance ... John G. CROSS
04 Administrative Asst to President ... Christina NOLAN
05 Vice President Academic Affairs ... Marion TERENZIO
07 Interim VP Enroll Mgmt/Admission ... Adam CASTRO
32 VP Student Affairs/Dean of Students ... Patrick J. LAMY
30 VP for Advancement ... Kwi BRENNAN
72 VP Inst of Tech & Prof Studies ... Peter JEONG
21 AVP for Finance and Administration ... William A. MCDONALD
20 AVP for Academic Development ... Josephine COHN
06 Registrar and Director of Advising ... Eileen M. POLAZZI
09 Director Instnl Research/Assessment ... Eugene W. MULLER
20 Associate Dean for Faculty ... Carolyn I. SPIES
79 Chair Div of Humanities ... Paul GENEGA
83 Chair Div Social/Behavioral Science ... Denise BANE
66 Chair Div of Nursing ... Neddie SERRA
81 Chair Div of Natural Science/Math ... Jim MURPHY
57 Chair Div Creative Arts Technology ... Nancy BACCI
50 Chair Div Accounting/Business/CIS ... Robert COLLMIER
53 Chair Div of Education ... Nora KRIEGER
88 Assoc Dean Inst Educ Support Svcs ... Leonard ROBERTS
08 Library Director ... Danilo H. FIGUEREDO
13 Director of Information Services ... Erzsebet FELSOVALYI
36 Director of Career Services ... Carol RUIZ
37 Director of Financial Aid ... Stacy SALINAS
31 Director Center for Adult Learning ... John MWAURA
06 Associate Registrar ... Annette RAYMOND
35 Associate Dean Student Development ... Rose MITCHELL
15 Assoc Director Human Resources ... Janice CECERE
18 Super of Buildings & Grounds ... Jack V. MCGRANE
07 Coordinator of Intl Admissions ... Ninah PRETTO
44 Director Annual Giving/Alumni Rels ... Carrie BENNETT
38 Director Personal Counseling ... Jessica DISLA
26 Director Public Rels/Advancemnt Mkt ... Jill ALEXANDER
42 Dir Spirtual Life/Col Chaplain ... Cynthia BETZ-BOGOLY
88 Director Teacher Education ... Dayna HASSELL
41 Director of Athletics ... Sheila WOOTEN
88 Director Center Academic Develop ... Patricia ARTEAGA
19 Director of Security ... Jack CORTEZ
39 Director Res Educ & Housing ... Rochelle GABRIEL
105 Webmaster ... Rob KRIEGER
24 Director of Media Center ... Barbara ISACSON
88 Director Office for Instnl Tech ... Yifeng BAI
40 Store Manager ... Roberta STEVENSON

Brookdale Community College (B)

Newman Springs Road, Lincroft NJ 07738-1597
County: Monmouth FICE Identification: 008404
Unit ID: 183859
Telephone: (732) 842-1900 Carnegie Class: Assoc/Pub-S-SC
FAX Number: (732) 224-2242 Calendar System: Other
URL: www.brookdalecc.edu
Established: 1967 Annual Undergrad Tuition & Fees (In-District): $4,408
Enrollment: 15,783 Coed
Affiliation or Control: State/Local IRS Status: 501(c)3
Highest Offering: Associate Degree
Program: Occupational; 2-Year Principally Bachelor's Creditable
Accreditation: M, ADNUR, RAD

01 Interim President ... Dr. William M. TOMS
03 Executive Vice President ... Dr. Dianna PHILLIPS
10 Int Vice Pres Business & Finance ... Ms. Maureen LAWRENCE
11 Exec VP Admin/Oprtns/Info Tech Svcs ... Dr. James SULTON
04 Executive Assistant to President ... Ms. Louise M. HORGAN
46 Vice Pres Plng/Dev/Govt & Comm Rels ... Dr. Webster B. TRAMMELL
31 Vice Pres Outreach Bus & Cmty Devel ... Dr. Linda MILSTEIN
13 Executive Director/OIT ... Dr. Patricia KAHN
84 Act Dean Enroll Dev/Student Affrs ... Mr. Richard PFEFFER
05 Dean of Academic Affairs ... Ms. Nancy KEGELMAN
15 Dean Human Resources ... Ms. Patricia SENSI
08 Executive Director Library ... Mr. David MURRAY
45 Exec Dir Planning/Assessment/Rsrch ... Mr. Arnold J. GELFMAN
26 Int Exec Director College Relations ... Ms. Avis MCMILLON
102 Exec Dir Foundation/Alumni Affs ... Mr. Timothy ZEISS
18 Exec Dir Facilities Plng/Engnrng ... Mr. Richard FRANK
32 Director Stdnt Affs/Support Svcs ... Mr. Richard J. PFEFFER
88 Assoc Director/Creative Services ... Ms. Barbara PETERSON
37 Director of Financial Aid ... Ms. Stephanie FITZSIMMONS

28 Diversity Management Officer ... Ms. Sylvia GOLDEN
25 Director Grants & Institutional Dev ... Ms. Laura V. QAISSAUNEE
38 Director Student Development Svcs ... Dr. Stephen A. CURTO
06 Registrar ... Ms. Kimberly TOOMEY
09 Dir of Institutional Research/Evalu ... Ms. Laura LONGO
27 Manager Marketing ... Ms. Laurie BENDER
96 Director Material & Printing Svcs ... Mr. Raimondi OTTO

Burlington County College (C)

601 Pemberton-Browns Mills Road,
Pemberton NJ 08068-1599
County: Burlington FICE Identification: 007730
Unit ID: 183877
Telephone: (609) 894-9311 Carnegie Class: Assoc/Pub-S-MC
FAX Number: (609) 894-0183 Calendar System: Semester
URL: www.bcc.edu
Established: 1966 Annual Undergrad Tuition & Fees (In-District): $3,615
Enrollment: 10,091 Coed
Affiliation or Control: State/Local IRS Status: 501(c)3
Highest Offering: Associate Degree
Program: Occupational; 2-Year Principally Bachelor's Creditable
Accreditation: M, ADNUR, DH, ENGT, RAD

01 President ... Dr. Robert C. MESSINA, JR.
05 Vice President Academic Programs ... Dr. David SPANG
10 Vice Pres Fiscal/Admin Services ... Mr. Ronald BRAND
32 VP Student Svcs/Dean Cmty Enrich ... Dr. Kris DIXON
04 Executive Asst to the President ... Dr. Stephen DIPIETRO
16 VP of Human Resources ... Mr. Dennis HAGGERTY
26 Dir of Marketing and Col Relations ... Ms. Valerie WINTER
09 Exec Dir of Institutional Research ... Mr. Max SLUSHER
14 Chief Information Technology ... Mr. Mark MEARA
81 Asst Dean Science/Math & Tech ... Ms. Anne EDWARDS
79 Dean of Liberal Arts ... Mr. David LONGENBACH
07 Director of Student Recruitment ... Ms. Dotti PURSLEY
88 Dean of Corporate College ... Mr. Ketan GANDHI
08 Director of the Library ... Ms. Michelle MARTIN
37 Financial Aid Director ... Mr. Michael CIOCE
38 Director Academic Advising/Transfer ... Dr. Robert ARIOSTO
25 Director of Grants Administration ... Ms. Barbara WITKOWSKI
06 Registrar ... Ms. Nyambura M. PHILLIPS
35 Dir of Stdnt Activities/Campus Pgms ... Ms. Catherine BRIGGS
19 Director of Security & Safety ... Mr. Hector GONZALEZ
66 Dean of Nursing/Allied Health ... Ms. Charlotte MCCARRAHER
21 Director Admin & Auxiliary Svcs ... Mr. Matthew FARR
24 Educational Tech Spec Distance Lrng ... Mr. Martin HOFFMAN
88 Director Construction Management ... Mr. Donald HUDSON
84 Exec Dir of Enroll Mgmt/Resrch/Plng ... Ms. Mary Louise MASCARIN
18 Manager of Physical Plant ... Mr. Jay FALKENSTEIN
103 Assoc Dean Business Development ... Ms. Sharon ROGERS
30 Exec Dir Development/Foundation ... Ms. Rebecca CORBIN
96 Asst Director of Purchasing ... Mr. Chester HEINLEIN

Caldwell College (D)

120 Bloomfield Avenue, Caldwell NJ 07006-5310
County: Essex FICE Identification: 002598
Unit ID: 183910
Telephone: (973) 618-3000 Carnegie Class: Master's M
FAX Number: (973) 618-3300 Calendar System: Semester
URL: www.caldwell.edu
Established: 1939 Annual Undergrad Tuition & Fees: $26,090
Enrollment: 2,290 Coed
Affiliation or Control: Roman Catholic IRS Status: 501(c)3
Highest Offering: Doctorate
Program: Liberal Arts And General; Teacher Preparatory
Accreditation: M, ACBSP, TEAC

01 President ... Dr. Nancy BLATTNER
05 Vice President for Academic Affairs ... Dr. Patrick R. PROGAR
10 Vice President for Finance & Admin ... Mr. Jack T. RAINEY
16 VP Institutional Effectiveness ... Mrs. Sheila N. O'ROURKE
32 Vice President for Student Affairs ... Sr. Kathleen TUITE
84 Vice President for Enrollment Mgmt ... Mr. Joseph J. POSILLICO
30 Vice Pres Development/Alumni Affs ... Mr. Kevin BOYLE
50 Associate Dean Business Division ... Dr. Bernard C. O'ROURKE
53 Associate Dean Education Division ... Dr. Janice STEWART
35 Assistant Dean Student Life ... Ms. Heather EATON-DWYER
88 Exec Director Student Success ... Ms. Joann GONZALEZ-GENERALS
44 Director Development ... Ms. Beth GORAB
29 Director Alumni Affairs & Grants ... Ms. Kathleen BUSE
06 Registrar & Director Inst Research ... Mr. Michael E. MAYSILLES
08 College Librarian ... Dr. Peter PANOS
07 Executive Director Admissions ... Mr. Stephen QUINN
58 Director Graduate Studies ... Ms. Vilma MUELLER
88 Assoc Dean External Partnerships ... Dr. Lisa DIBISCEGLIE
38 Director of Counseling ... Ms. Robin DAVENPORT
39 Director Residence Life ... Ms. Sandra GILOT
13 Exec Director Information Techn ... Mr. Robert PESCINSKI
36 Dir Career Plng & Development ... Ms. Geraldine PERRET
37 Director Financial Aid ... Mr. Hayato SUZUKI
42 Chaplain ... Fr. Albert J. BERNER
41 Executive Director of Athletics ... Mr. Mark A. CORINO
88 Director Technical Support Services ... Ms. Roselle LAZA-SCHMITZ
27 Dir Media Relations and Advertising ... Ms. Colette LIDDY
19 Director Campus Safety ... Mr. William B. ORTMAN
91 Director Administrative Technology ... Mr. David BOHNY
15 Dir Recruitment and Development ... Mrs. Michelle STAUSS
35 Director Student Activities ... Ms. Michele DEVOE

Camden County College (E)

PO Box 200, Blackwood NJ 08012-0200
County: Camden FICE Identification: 006865
Unit ID: 183938
Telephone: (856) 227-7200 Carnegie Class: Assoc/Pub-S-MC
FAX Number: (856) 374-4894 Calendar System: Semester
URL: www.camdencc.edu
Established: 1967 Annual Undergrad Tuition & Fees (In-District): $4,050
Enrollment: 15,493 Coed
Affiliation or Control: State/Local IRS Status: 501(c)3
Highest Offering: Associate Degree
Program: Occupational; 2-Year Principally Bachelor's Creditable
Accreditation: M, DA, DH, DIETT, MLTAD, OPD

01 President ... Dr. Raymond YANNUZZI
05 Vice Pres Academic Affairs ... Dr. Margaret HAMILTON
30 VP for Institutional Advancement ... Mr. William THOMPSON
41 Athletic Director ... Mr. Peter DILORENZO
15 Executive Director Human Resources ... Ms. Rose COSTON-MCHUGH
26 Dean Communications/Enroll Dev ... Ms. Rosemary SCHAMP
84 Dean of Enrollment Svcs ... Ms. Jackie BALDWIN
96 Executive Director of Finance ... Mr. Steve BLATHERWICK
21 Manager Business Office Operations ... Ms. Danielle POWERS
08 Library Refer & Instr Coordinator ... Ms. Miriam MLYNARSKI
15 Chief Fiscal Officer ... Ms. Patricia MEEHAN
37 Director of Financial Aid ... Ms. Felicia BRYANT
09 Dean Inst Research/Planning/Grants ... Dr. Marilyn FEINGOLD
18 Exec Dir Safety and Facilities ... Mr. Edward CARNEY
35 Exec Dean Enrollment/Student Svcs ... Dr. James CANONICA
83 Exec Dean William G Rohrer Center ... Dr. Robert KACZOROWSKI
81 Dean Div Math/Sci/Health Careers ... Dr. Wendy BLUME
50 Dean Div Business/Comptr/Tech Stds ... Dr. Melvin ROBERTS
12 Exec Dean Camden City Campus ... Mr. Gary DIVENS
36 Director Testing/Assessment ... Ms. Eve HIGHSTREET

Centenary College (F)

400 Jefferson Street, Hackettstown NJ 07840-2100
County: Warren FICE Identification: 002599
Unit ID: 183974
Telephone: (908) 852-1400 Carnegie Class: Master's M
FAX Number: (908) 850-9508 Calendar System: Semester
URL: www.centenarycollege.edu
Established: 1867 Annual Undergrad Tuition & Fees: $26,200
Enrollment: 3,109 Coed
Affiliation or Control: Independent Non-Profit IRS Status: 501(c)3
Highest Offering: Master's
Program: Liberal Arts And General; Teacher Preparatory
Accreditation: M, IACBE, SW, TEAC

01 President ... Dr. Barbara-Jayne LEWTHWAITE
05 Provost & Chief Academic Officer ... Dr. James PATTERSON
10 Chief Operating Officer ... Mr. Roger ANDERSON
26 Sr VP College Relations/Marketing ... Ms. Diane P. FINNAN
32 VP Student Engagement/Service ... Rev. David JONES
07 Dean of Admissions ... Ms. Glenna WARREN
09 Dean of Institutional Research ... Mr. Rob MILLER
06 Registrar ... Ms. Elise BAYSE
37 Director of Financial Aid ... Ms. Chanel GREENE
08 Director Learning Resources ... Ms. Nancy MADACSI
36 Director Career Development ... Ms. Patricia MAHAFFEY
15 Director of Human Resources ... Vacant
18 Exec Director of Facilities ... Mr. Todd MILLER
23 Director of Health Services ... Ms. Jean ROBERT
41 Director of Athletics ... Ms. Billie Jo BLACKWELL
42 Chaplain ... Rev. David JONES
44 Director of Strategic Advancement ... Ms. Roxanne THOMPSON
19 Director of Security ... Mr. Leonard CUNZ
38 Director of Counseling ... Ms. Lorna FARMER
29 Director of Alumni ... Ms. Deana CYNAR
13 Information Technology Manager ... Ms. Chris STRUBE
85 International Academic Coordinator ... Mr. Joe SPAYD
40 Manager of the Bookstore ... Ms. Heidi MCDONNELL

The College of New Jersey (G)

2000 Pennington Road, Ewing NJ 08628-1104
County: Mercer FICE Identification: 002642
Unit ID: 187134
Telephone: (609) 771-1855 Carnegie Class: Master's L
FAX Number: (609) 637-5191 Calendar System: Semester
URL: www.tcnj.edu
Established: 1855 Annual Undergrad Tuition & Fees (In-State): $13,867
Enrollment: 7,115 Coed
Affiliation or Control: State IRS Status: 501(c)3
Highest Offering: Master's
Program: Liberal Arts And General; Teacher Preparatory; Professional
Accreditation: M, BUS, CACREP, CS, ENG, MUS, NURSE, TED

01 President ... Dr. R. Barbara GITENSTEIN
05 Interim Provost ... Dr. Susan BAKEWELL-SACHS
11 Vice Pres of Administration ... Mr. Curt HEURING
10 Treasurer ... Mr. Lloyd RICKETTS
43 General Counsel ... Mr. Thomas MAHONEY
30 Vice Pres College Rels/Advancement ... Dr. Matthew GOLDEN
32 Vice President Student Affairs ... Mr. James NORFLEET
15 Vice Pres Human Resources ... Dr. Gregory POGUE
101 Exec Asst to Pres/Secy to Board ... Ms. Heather FEHN
18 Assoc VP Facilities & Admin Svcs ... Ms. Kathryn LEVERTON
44 Assoc Vice President of Development ... Mr. Peter MANETAS

35 Asst VP Student Affs/Dn of Students .... Ms. Magda MANETAS
20 Interim Vice Provost .... Dr. William BEHRE
84 Assoc Provost Enrollment Management .... Ms. Lisa ANGELONI
57 Dean School of The Arts & Comm .... Dr. John LAUGHTON
50 Dean School of Business .... Dr. John KEEP
79 Dean School Culture & Society .... Dr. Benjamin RIFKIN
53 Int Dean School of Education .... Dr. Mark KISELICA
54 Dean School of Engineering .... Dr. Steven SCHREINER
66 Int Dean Nursing/Hlth/Exercise Sci .... Dr. Marcia BLICHARZ
81 Dean School of Science .... Dr. Jeffrey OSBORN
58 Asst Dean Graduate Global Programs .... Dr. Susan HYDRO
21 Assistant Treasurer .... Ms. Amy MERCOGLIANO
37 Dir of Student Financial Services .... Vacant
09 Dir Center for Inst Effectiveness .... Dr. Paula MAAS
41 Director of Athletics .... Mr. John CASTALDO
36 Dir Career Ctr/Asc Dn Student Affs ... Ms. Cecelia O'CALLAGHAN
29 Director Alumni Affairs .... Ms. Lisa MCCARTHY
102 Dir Corp & Foundation Relations .... Vacant
18 Director of Campus Construction .... Mr. William RUDEAU
23 Assoc Director for Health Services ...... Ms. Janice VERMEYCHUK
38 Director for Student Counseling .... Dr. Marc CELENTANA
06 Director of Records/Registration .... Mr. Frank COOPER
19 Chief of Police .... Chief John COLLINS
96 Director of Purchasing .... Mr. Mark MEHLER
26 Exec Director College Relations .... Ms. Stacy SCHUSTER
28 Director of EEO/AA/Diversity .... Ms. Kerry TILLETT

College of Saint Elizabeth (A)

2 Convent Road, Morristown NJ 07960-6989

County: Morris FICE Identification: 002600
Unit ID: 186618
Telephone: (973) 290-4000 Carnegie Class: Master's L
FAX Number: (973) 290-4488 Calendar System: Semester
URL: www.cse.edu
Established: 1899 Annual Undergrad Tuition & Fees: $28,221
Enrollment: 2,112 Coed
Affiliation or Control: Roman Catholic IRS Status: 501(c)3
Highest Offering: Doctorate
Program: Liberal Arts And General; Teacher Preparatory
Accreditation: M, DIETD, DIETI, NUR, TEAC

01 President .... Sr. Francis RAFTERY
05 VP Academic Affairs/Dean of Studies .... Dr. James DLUGOS
32 VP Student Affairs/Dean of Students .... Ms. Katherine BUCK
10 VP Finance/Administration/Treasurer . Ms. Maria R. CAMMARATA
30 VP Inst Advancement/Development .... Vacant
07 Dean of Admission .... Ms. Donna TATARKA
58 Dean of Graduate Programs .... Dr. Jacqueline MCGLADE
20 Dean Women's College/Undergrad Stds .... Dr. Carol STROBECK
06 Registrar .... Ms. Laura Lee BOWENS GELLMAN
21 Controller .... Mr. Anthony COLABRARO
19 Securitas Site Manager .... Mr. Donald GREEN
13 Chief Technology Officer .... Mr. Brad MORTON
09 Director Institutional Research .... Dr. Louise MURRAY
73 Act Dir Ctr Theol/Spiritual Devel .... Ms. Carol PISANI
08 Director of Library .... Ms. Amira UNVER
42 Campus Minister .... Mr. Roger PISANI
18 Director of Facilities .... Mr. Frank A. NEGLIA
37 Director of Financial Aid .... Ms. Debra WULFF
27 Director Marketing/ Communications .... Ms. Donna M. LINDEMEYER
22 Director EOF Program .... Ms. Carolina E. GONZALEZ
36 Director Career Services .... Ms. Teri CORSO
39 Director of Residence Life .... Ms. Meredith NOVKOVIC
38 Director of Counseling .... Ms. Sharon MCNULTY
88 Director of Volunteer Services .... Ms. Nanette SPEDDEN
35 Director of Student Activities .... Ms. Leigh Anne WALTERS
41 Director of Athletics .... Ms. Juliene SIMPSON
90 Director of Academic Computing .... Ms. Kathy DAINO-MARINO
91 Dir Application Devel & Support .... Ms. Ana M. FIGUEROA
44 Director of Annual Fund .... Ms. Tanya SORCE
51 Asst Director Continuing Studies .... Sr. Gabriel M. DONAHUE
24 Director Media Services .... Mr. Ronald LONEKER
29 Exec Director Alumnae Association .... Ms. Debbie MARTIN
15 Director Human Resources .... Ms. Dianna SOFO
84 Director of Recruitment .... Vacant
85 Director Intl/Multicultural Affairs .... Ms. Lenee WOODSON
28 Asst Dir Intl/Multicultural Affairs .... Ms. Maya BLEY
40 College Store Manager .... Mr. David STALKER
04 Spec Asst to Pres Mission/Values .... Ms. Carol PISANI

County College of Morris (B)

214 Center Grove Road, Randolph NJ 07869-2086

County: Morris FICE Identification: 007729
Unit ID: 184180
Telephone: (973) 328-5000 Carnegie Class: Assoc/Pub-S-SC
FAX Number: (973) 328-1282 Calendar System: Semester
URL: www.ccm.edu
Established: 1965 Annual Undergrad Tuition & Fees (In-District): $4,088
Enrollment: 8,705 Coed
Affiliation or Control: State/Local IRS Status: 501(c)3
Highest Offering: Associate Degree
Program: Occupational; 2-Year Principally Bachelor's Creditable
Accreditation: M, ACBSP, ADNUR, ENGT, RAD

01 President .... Dr. Edward J. YAW
05 Vice President of Academic Affairs .... Dr. Dwight L. SMITH
10 Vice President of Business/Finance .... Ms. Karen VANDERHOOF
32 VP of Student Dev/Enrollment Mgmt .... Dr. Bette M. SIMMONS
30 Exec Dir Col Advancement/Planning .... Mr. Joseph VITALE
15 Dir Human Resources & Labor Rels .... Mr. Thomas BURK
09 Director Inst Research & Planning .... Dr. Charles SECOLSKY
21 Director Budget & Business Services .... Mr. John YOUNG
25 Director Resource Development .... Dr. Kevin KEEFE
07 Admissions Officer .... Ms. Jessica CHAMBERS
37 Director Financial Aid .... Mr. Harvey WILLIS
06 Associate Registrar .... Ms. Karen WHITMORE
06 Registrar .... Ms. Michelle DUNN
26 Chief Public Relations Officer .... Ms. Kathleen BRUNET EAGAN
29 Director Alumni Office .... Ms. Barbara CAPSOURAS
13 Director Information Systems .... Mr. Roger FLAHIVE
08 Director of Library Services .... Vacant
36 Director Career Svcs/Coop Education .... Ms. Denise SCHMIDT
38 Counseling Services Coordinator .... Dr. Lorna JOASIL
79 Dean Liberal Arts .... Dr. Keith SMITH
76 Dean Health/Natural Sciences .... Ms. Joan CUNNINGHAM
81 Dean Business/Math/Engr/Technology .... Mr. Patrick ENRIGHT
31 Dean Corp & Community Programs .... Dr. Jane ARMSTRONG
19 Director Security & Safety .... Mr. Harvey JACKSON
41 Director Athletics .... Mr. Jack SULLIVAN
23 Health Services Coordinator .... Ms. Elizabeth HOBAN
18 Director of Plant & Maintenance .... Mr. Joseph PONTURO
96 Director of Purchasing .... Ms. Joanne KEARNS
40 Bookstore Manager .... Mr. Abdelilan ENNASSEF

Cumberland County College (C)

3322 College Drive, PO Box 1500,
Vineland NJ 08362-1500

County: Cumberland FICE Identification: 002601
Unit ID: 184205
Telephone: (856) 691-8600 Carnegie Class: Assoc/Pub-R-M
FAX Number: (856) 691-3876 Calendar System: Semester
URL: www.cccnj.edu
Established: 1963 Annual Undergrad Tuition & Fees (In-District): $4,020
Enrollment: 4,291 Coed
Affiliation or Control: State/Local IRS Status: 501(c)3
Highest Offering: Associate Degree
Program: Occupational; 2-Year Principally Bachelor's Creditable
Accreditation: M, ADNUR, RAD

01 President .... Dr. Thomas A. ISEKENEGBE
05 VP Academic Affairs/Enrollment Svcs .... Dr. Jacqueline GALBIATI
10 Vice President Finance & Admin Svcs .... Mr. John K. PITCHER
30 Exec Dir Grant Develop/Trustee Rels .... Ms. Anne M. BERGAMO
21 Director Finance & Budget .... Ms. Sherri L. WELCH
32 Exec Dir Student Life/Campus Svcs .... Mr. Joseph L. HIBBS
08 Director Library Services .... Ms. Patti A. SCHMID
88 Ex Dir Ctr for Acad & Student Succ .... Dr. Maud FRIED-GOODNIGHT
26 Director Public Relations .... Mr. John S. NICHOLS
29 Exec Dir Foundation & Alumni .... Ms. Sue A. PERRY
35 Director Student Affairs .... Mr. Joseph L. HIBBS
37 Director Student Financial Aid .... Ms. Kim HENRY-MITCHELL
88 Director University Ctr .... Dr. Terrence HARDEE
50 Dean Business/Educ/Social Sciences .... Dr. Charles KOCHER
51 Exec Dir Prof & Community Education .... Ms. Vicki SIMEK
76 Dean STEM/Health .... Ms. MaryAnn WESTERFIELD
57 Dean Arts & Humanities .... Mr. James PICCONE
04 Assistant to the President .... Ms. Anne M. BERGAMO
15 Executive Director Human Resources .... Ms. Patricia N. BRINING
72 Chief Technology Officer .... Mr. Douglas WHITE
18 Supt Facilities & Grounds .... Mr. Anthony F. ABRIOLA
96 Director of Purchasing .... Ms. Dorothy M. ZILA
09 ExDir Planning, Research & Inst. Ef .... Dr. Sandra D. VADEN
38 Director Adv/Trans & Career Svcs .... Dr. Steven M. STOLAR
07 Director of Admissions .... Ms. Anne M. DALY-EIMER

DeVry University - North Brunswick Campus (D)

630 US Highway One, North Brunswick NJ 08902-3362

County: Middlesex FICE Identification: 009228
Unit ID: 184269
Telephone: (732) 729-3532 Carnegie Class: Bac/Assoc
FAX Number: (732) 729-3806 Calendar System: Semester
URL: www.devry.edu
Established: 1931 Annual Undergrad Tuition & Fees: $15,294
Enrollment: 1,905 Coed
Affiliation or Control: Proprietary IRS Status: Proprietary
Highest Offering: Baccalaureate
Program: Occupational; Professional; Business Emphasis
Accreditation: &NH, EEG, ENGT

01 Metro President .... Mr. Chris GREVESEN
05 Dean of Academic Affairs .... Mr. Joseph KONOPKA
07 Senior Director of Admissions .... Mr. Gerald WARGO
36 Director of Career Services .... Ms. Florence HERMAN
37 Director of Student Finance .... Mr. Albert CAMA
15 Human Resources Business Partner .... Ms. Sarah MADDEN
72 Dean Technology Programs .... Mr. Tom KIST
06 Registrar .... Ms. Janine EMMA
08 Director of Library Services .... Mr. Joseph LOUDERBACK
38 Student Services Manager .... Ms. Lisa LYLE

† Regional accreditation is carried under the parent institution in Downers Grove, IL.

DeVry University - Paramus (E)

81 East State Route 4, Suite 102,
Paramus NJ 07652-2634

County: Bergen Identification: 666561
Telephone: (201) 556-2840 Carnegie Class: Not Classified
FAX Number: (201) 556-2863 Calendar System: Semester
URL: www.devry.edu
Established: 1931 Annual Undergrad Tuition & Fees: $15,294
Enrollment: 500 Coed
Affiliation or Control: Proprietary IRS Status: Proprietary
Highest Offering: Master's
Program: Liberal Arts And General; Business Emphasis
Accreditation: &NH

01 Center Dean .... Pavi JALLOH

† Regional accreditation is carried under the parent institution in Downers Grove, IL.

Drew University (F)

36 Madison Avenue, Madison NJ 07940-1493

County: Morris FICE Identification: 002603
Unit ID: 184348
Telephone: (973) 408-3000 Carnegie Class: Bac/A&S
FAX Number: (973) 408-3939 Calendar System: 4/1/4
URL: www.drew.edu
Established: 1866 Annual Undergrad Tuition & Fees: $40,704
Enrollment: 2,697 Coed
Affiliation or Control: Independent Non-Profit IRS Status: 501(c)3
Highest Offering: Doctorate
Program: Liberal Arts And General; Professional
Accreditation: M, @TEAC, THEOL

01 President .... Dr. Robert WEISBUCH
05 Provost & Academic Vice President .... Dr. Pamela J. GUNTER-SMITH
11 Vice President Admin/Univ Relations .... Mrs. Margaret HOWARD
30 Vice Pres Devel/Alumni/ae Affairs .... Mr. Christopher M. BIEHN
10 Vice Pres Finance/Business Affairs .... Mr. Howard B. BUXBAUM
20 Vice President & Dean of College .... Dr. Jonathan LEVIN
73 Vice Pres/Dean Theological School .... Dr. Maxine C. BEACH
29 Assoc VP Devel/Alumni/ae Affs .... Mr. Kenneth ALEXO
13 Asst VP University Technology .... Dr. Alan CANDIOTTI
07 Dean Col Admissions/Financial Asst .... Ms. Alyssa MCCLOUD
08 Dean of the Libraries .... Dr. Andrew SCRIMGEOUR
32 Dean Campus Life & Student Affs .... Dr. Sara WALDRON
26 Chief Communications Officer .... Mr. David MUHA
29 Director Alumni Affairs .... Ms. Melissa FUEST
15 Director of Human Resources .... Ms. Deborah RAIKES-COLBERT
22 Affirmative Action Officer .... Dr. George-Harold JENNINGS
90 Dir Instructional Technology Svcs .... Ms. Gamin BARTLE
91 Director Administrative Computing .... Ms. Marsha A. HUBER
21 Controller .... Mr. Frank MALTINO
96 Director Purchasing .... Mr. Harry C. SCARPA
18 Director Facilities Operations .... Mr. Michael KOPAS
37 Dir Finan Assistance/Col Admissions .... Ms. Renee VOLAK
19 Director Public Safety .... Mr. Thomas EVANS
23 Director Health Services .... Ms. Joyce MAGLION
39 Director Housing/Conf/Hospitality .... Ms. Patricia NAYLOR
40 Manager Bookstore .... Ms. Liz GALLO
35 Director Student Activities .... Ms. Michelle BRISSON
38 Director Counseling Services .... Dr. Jim MANDALA
36 Director Career Planning/Placement .... Ms. Patricia LAPREY
07 Director Theological Admissions .... Mr. Kevin D. MILLER
07 Director Graduate Admissions .... Ms. Carla BURNS
58 Dean of Casperson Sch Grad Stdy .... Dr. Richard GREENWALD
42 University Chaplain .... Rev. Tanya Lynn BENNETT
09 Director Institutional Research .... Dr. Christopher VAN WYK
41 Director Athletics .... Mr. Jason FEIN
06 Registrar .... Mr. Horace TATE
28 Special Asst to Prov for Diversity .... Dr. Carlos YORDAN

Eastern International College (G)

3000 Kennedy Blvd, Ste 310, Jersey City NJ 07306

County: Hudson FICE Identification: 031226
Unit ID: 421878
Telephone: (201) 216-9901 Carnegie Class: Not Classified
FAX Number: (201) 216-9225 Calendar System: Semester
URL: www.eicollege.edu
Established: 1990 Annual Undergrad Tuition & Fees: $7,500
Enrollment: 269 Coed
Affiliation or Control: Proprietary IRS Status: Proprietary
Highest Offering: Associate Degree
Program: Occupational
Accreditation: ACCSC

01 President .... Bashir MOHSEN
05 Vice President of Academic Affairs .... Dr. Mustafa MUSTAF
11 Vice President of Operations .... Dr. James M. CATALANO

Eastwick College (H)

10 South Franklin Turnpike, Ramsey NJ 07446

FICE Identification: 020537
Unit ID: 184959
Telephone: (201) 327-8877 Carnegie Class: Not Classified
FAX Number: (201) 327-9054 Calendar System: Other
URL: www.eastwick.edu
Established: 1968 Annual Undergrad Tuition & Fees: $14,500
Enrollment: 1,000 Coed
Affiliation or Control: Proprietary IRS Status: Proprietary
Highest Offering: Associate Degree
Program: Occupational; 2-Year Principally Bachelor's Creditable; Nursing Emphasis
Accreditation: ACICS, SURGT

01 Corporate Systems Administrator .... Antonio JEREZ
05 Vice President Academic Affairs .... Rafael CASTILLA
32 Dean of Students .... Bobby DAVIES
37 Director of Financial Aid .... Viviana FLORES

Essex County College (A)

303 University Avenue, Newark NJ 07102-1798
County: Essex FICE Identification: 007107
Unit ID: 184481
Telephone: (973) 877-3000 Carnegie Class: Assoc/Pub-U-MC
FAX Number: (973) 877-3044 Calendar System: Other
URL: www.essex.edu
Established: 1966 Annual Undergrad Tuition & Fees (In-District): $3,384
Enrollment: 13,424 Coed
Affiliation or Control: State/Local IRS Status: 501(c)3
Highest Offering: Associate Degree
Program: Occupational; 2-Year Principally Bachelor's Creditable
Accreditation: M, ADNUR, ENGT, OPD, PTAA, RAD

01 President .... Dr. Edythe M. ABDULLAH
03 Exec Vice President .... Dr. Vernell PATRICK
101 Asst to Pres/Director Board Affairs .... Ms. June PERSAUD
10 Comptroller .... Mr. Louis GENOVESE
45 Dean Planning/Inst Research .... Dr. Stephen KIESTER
20 Dean of Faculty .... Dr. Ladylease WHITE
20 Dean of Educational Services .... Dr. Felix LINFANTE
51 Dean Community & Cont Education .... Mr. Charles G. LOVALLO
13 Dean Information Technology/CIO .... Mr. Mohamed SEDDIKI
32 Dean of Student Affairs .... Dr. Susan C. MULLIGAN
09 Assoc Dean Plng/Research/Assessment .. Dr. J. Scott DRAKULICH
35 Asst Dean Student Affs/Enroll Svcs .... Ms. Marva MACK
12 Assoc Dean West Essex Campus .... Ms. Elvira VIEIRA
08 Director Learning Resource Center .... Mrs. Gwendolyn SLATON
35 Director Student Life & Activities .... Ms. Patricia SLADE
18 Asst to Vice Pres Facilities Mgmt .... Mr. Jeff SHAPIRO
19 Asst to Exec VP Public Safety .... Mr. Cromartie ANTHONY
26 Director of Public Relations .... Ms. Karen TINEBRA
30 Director of Development .... Ms. Annette WEIS
15 Director of Human Resources .... Ms. Jeannette ROBINSON
96 Director Purchasing .... Ms. Marylyn RUTHERFORD
37 Director Financial Aid .... Mrs. Mildred COFER
84 Asst Dean Student Affs/Enroll Svcs .... Ms. Zewdnesh KASSA
21 Director Office of Bursar .... Ms. Darlene MILLER
36 Director Career Resource Center .... Ms. Pamela MAYNARD
88 Director Child Development Center .... Ms. Deloris GRIMSLEY
41 Director Athletics .... Mr. Melvin KNIGHT
24 Dir Media Prod Technology (MPT) .... Ms. Nadine SHAW
78 Director Cooperative Education .... Ms. Marcia HOSPEDALES
55 Director of Evening/Weekend Svcs .... Mr. Ronald ROSS

Fairleigh Dickinson University (B)

1000 River Road, Teaneck NJ 07666-1996
County: Bergen FICE Identification: 002607
Unit ID: 184603
Telephone: (201) 692-2000 Carnegie Class: Master's L
FAX Number: N/A Calendar System: Semester
URL: www.fdu.edu
Established: 1942 Annual Undergrad Tuition & Fees: $32,538
Enrollment: 12,436 Coed
Affiliation or Control: Independent Non-Profit IRS Status: 501(c)3
Highest Offering: Doctorate
Program: Occupational; 2-Year Principally Bachelor's Creditable; Liberal Arts And General; Teacher Preparatory; Professional
Accreditation: M, BUS, CLPSY, CS, ENG, ENGT, NURSE, TEAC

01 President .... Dr. J. Michael ADAMS
43 University Counsel/Secretary .... Mr. Wayne M. RICHARDSON
05 Univ Provost/VPAA .... Dr. Christopher CAPUANO
30 Sr Vice Pres University Advancement .... Mr. Richard REISS
03 Senior Vice President & CEO .... Mr. Sheldon DRUCKER
10 Vice Pres for Finance & Treasurer .... Ms. Hania FERRARA
11 Vice President for Administration .... Mr. Richard A. RICCIO
84 Vice Pres for Enrollment Management .... Mr. Jon WEXLER
13 VP/Chief Information Officer .... Mr. Neal M. STURM
26 Assistant VP for University Advance .... Mr. Angelo CARFAGNA
16 Univ Director for Human Resources .... Ms. Rose D'AMBROSIO
29 Director Alumni Affairs .... Mr. Okang MCBRIDE
12 Dean Petrocelli Col of Cont Stds .... Mr. Kenneth T. VEHRKENS
49 Dean Becton Col of Arts & Sci .... Dr. Geoffrey WEINMAN
50 Dean College Business Admin .... Dr. William MOORE
20 Dean University College .... Dr. Patti MILLS
32 Dean of Students-Teaneck Campus .... Ms. Michelle MCCROY-HEINS
32 Dean of Students-Madison Campus .... Dr. Brian MAURO
08 Associate University Librarian-Flor .... Ms. Maria WEBB
08 Associate University Librarian-Met .... Ms. Kathy STEIN-SMITH
51 Director Continuing Education .... Dr. Thomas SWANZEY
26 Dir Public Administration Institute .... Dr. William ROBERTS
38 Director Psychology .... Dr. Ronald DUMONT
21 Director Internal Audit .... Mr. Peter FORMAN
53 Director School of Education .... Dr. Vicki COHEN
66 Director Sch of Nurs/Allied Health .... Dr. Minerva GUTTMAN
88 Director Sch Hotel/Restaurant Mgmt .... Dr. Richard WISCH
41 Director of Athletics-Teaneck .... Mr. David LANGFORD
41 Director of Athletics-Madison .... Mr. William KLIKA
07 University Dir of Enrollment Svcs .... Ms. Carol CREEKMORE
09 Director of Institutional Research .... Ms. Indira GOVINDAN
37 University Director Financial Aid .... Mr. Vincent TUNSTALL
19 Campus Dir Public Safety/F/M Campus .... Ms. Willie THORNTON
12 Provost Metropolitan Campus .... Dr. Joseph KIERNAN
12 Provost Florham/Madison Campus .... Dr. Kenneth GREENE
19 Univ Dir Public Safety/T/H Campus .... Mr. David A. MILES
96 Director of Purchasing .... Ms. Juliette BROOKS

Felician College (C)

262 S Main Street, Lodi NJ 07644-2198
County: Bergen FICE Identification: 002610
Unit ID: 184612
Telephone: (201) 559-6000 Carnegie Class: Master's S
FAX Number: (201) 559-6188 Calendar System: Semester
URL: www.felician.edu
Established: 1942 Annual Undergrad Tuition & Fees: $27,925
Enrollment: 2,249 Coed
Affiliation or Control: Roman Catholic IRS Status: 501(c)3
Highest Offering: Master's
Program: Liberal Arts And General; Teacher Preparatory; Professional
Accreditation: M, IACBE, NURSE, TEAC

01 President .... Sr. Theresa M. MARTIN
03 Senior Exec Vice President .... Dr. Charles J. ROONEY
05 Provost/Vice Pres Acad Affairs .... Sr. Mary Rosita BRENNAN
20 Asst VP Academic Support Services .... Dr. Ann V. GUILLORY
30 Vice Pres Institutional Advancement ... Ms. Celeste A. ORANCHAK
10 Exec Vice Pres for Admin & Finance .... Mr. Marc J. CHALFIN
18 Vice President of College Services .... Mr. Robert W. DECKER
32 Vice President for Student Affairs ... Sr. Tarcilia M. JUCHNIEWICZ
32 VP Stdnt Svcs/Admin Ruth Campus .... Ms. Susan M. CHALFIN
11 Interim VP for Admin Operations .... Mr. Arthur D. GOON
04 Admin Assistant to the President .... Ms. Rita A. PETERSEN
06 Registrar .... Ms. June FINN
07 Assoc VP Undergrad Enroll Services .... Mr. Alexander SCOTT
07 Assoc VP Adult/Grad Enroll Svc .... Dr. Wendy LIN-COOK
08 Director of the Library .... Mr. Paul GLASSMAN
09 Director Institutional Research .... Dr. Jerry TROMBELLA
15 Coordinator Human Resources .... Ms. Diane DEPADOVA
31 Director Community Svc Facilities .... Ms. Maria MALLIA
37 Director Student Financial Aid .... Ms. Janet MERLI
29 Director of Alumni Relations .... Ms. Lori WALKER
42 Director Campus Ministry/Chaplain .... Rev. Damian COLICCHIO
39 Director of Residence Life .... Ms. Laura BARRY
36 Director of Career Counseling .... Ms. Cristiana DAMIAO
11 Director of Administrative Services .... Ms. Meggan O'NEILL
13 Director of Information Technology .... Mr. Christopher FINCH
24 Director A-V Center .... Mr. Anthony KLYMENKO
88 Assoc Director Center for Learning .... Mr. Hamdi SHAHIN
26 Director of Public Relations .... Ms. Teri GATTO
26 Dir Inst Marketing & Publications . Ms. Barbara PURDUE-LYNCH
40 Manager College Bookstore .... Ms. Beth LIGNOWSKI
76 Dean Div Nurs/Health Mgmt Sciences .... Dr. Muriel SHORE
53 Dean Division of Teacher Educ .... Vacant
49 Dean Division of Arts & Science .... Dr. Edward KUBERSKY
50 Dean Div of Business Mgmt Sciences .... Dr. Beth CASTIGLIA
88 Dean Assessment/Fac Excellence .... Dr. Dolores HENCHY
88 Director EOF Program .... Ms. Dinelia GARDNER
104 Director Study Abroad Program .... Ms. Maureen BRADY COYLE
85 Director of International Programs .... Ms. Cristiana KUNYCZKA
23 Director Health Services .... Ms. Carolyn LEWIS
41 Director of Athletics .... Mr. Benjamin DI NALLO
92 Director Honors Program .... Dr. Maria VECCHIO
91 Director Administrative Computing .... Mr. John PANNEGGIANTE

Georgian Court University (D)

900 Lakewood Avenue, Lakewood NJ 08701-2697
County: Ocean FICE Identification: 002608
Unit ID: 184773
Telephone: (732) 987-2200 Carnegie Class: Master's L
FAX Number: N/A Calendar System: Semester
URL: www.georgian.edu
Established: 1908 Annual Undergrad Tuition & Fees: $28,194
Enrollment: 2,885 Female
Affiliation or Control: Roman Catholic IRS Status: 501(c)3
Highest Offering: Master's
Program: Liberal Arts And General; Teacher Preparatory; Professional
Accreditation: M, ACBSP, SW, TEAC

01 President .... Sr. Rosemary JEFFRIES
05 Provost .... Ms. Evelyn QUINN
10 Chief Financial Officer .... Mr. Ronald RECK
30 Spec Asst to Pres for Advancement .... Ms. Cynthia WHITNEY
20 Assoc Provost Academic Pgm Devel .... Dr. Michael GROSS
84 Dean of Enrollment Management .... Mr. John MCAULIFFE
32 Dean of Students .... Ms. Karen GOFF
88 Director of Advising .... Mrs. Carol A. LIPPIN
42 Director of Campus Ministry .... Sr. Mariann MAHON
41 Director Athletics/Recreation .... Ms. Laura LIESMAN
88 Dir Academic Development Center .... Ms. Phyllis KREMEN
50 Dean School of Business .... Mr. Joseph MONAHAN
53 Dean of School of Education .... Dr. Jacqueline KRESS
49 Dean School of Arts & Sciences .... Dr. Linda JAMES
09 Director of Institutional Research .... Mr. Wayne S. ARNDT
08 Director of Library Services .... Ms. Jacqueline DA COSTA
06 Registrar .... Ms. Jill RILEY
21 Controller .... Mrs. Maureen RYAN-HOFFMAN
15 Director of Human Resources .... Dr. Carol KONTOS-COHEN
13 Chief Information Officer .... Ms. Christine MEHOLIC
07 Asst Dir Undergraduate Admissions .... Ms. Maria COLON
37 Director of Financial Aid .... Ms. Judith SCHNEIDER
26 Dir Public Rels/Col Communications .... Ms. Gail TOWNS
31 Dir Conferences & Special Events .... Ms. Mary E. CRANWELL
29 Director of Alumni Engagement .... Ms. Lauren TRAYLOR
36 Director Career Development .... Mr. Steven FUSCO
38 Director of Counseling .... Dr. Robin SOLBACH
23 Director Student Health Services .... Mrs. Patricia DORITY
22 Affirmative Action Officer .... Dr. Carol KONTOS-COHEN
18 Director of Facilities .... Mr. Mark BIANCHI
96 Director of Purchasing .... Mr. Thomas BARANOWSKI
19 Director of Security .... Mr. Thomas ZAMBRANO
09 Dir Ofc Assessment/Intl Research .... Dr. Pamela SCHNEIDER
07 Asst Director Graduate Admissions .... Mr. Patrick GIVENS
44 Director of Annual Giving .... Ms. Cynthia BARTHOLE
39 Coordinator Residence Life .... Ms. Crystal LOPEZ

Gloucester County College (E)

1400 Tanyard Road, Sewell NJ 08080-9518
County: Gloucester FICE Identification: 006901
Unit ID: 184791
Telephone: (856) 468-5000 Carnegie Class: Assoc/Pub-S-SC
FAX Number: N/A Calendar System: 4/1/4
URL: www.gccnj.edu
Established: 1966 Annual Undergrad Tuition & Fees (In-District): $3,390
Enrollment: 6,609 Coed
Affiliation or Control: State/Local IRS Status: 501(c)3
Highest Offering: Associate Degree
Program: Occupational; 2-Year Principally Bachelor's Creditable
Accreditation: M, ADNUR, DMS, NMT

01 Interim President .... Mr. Frederick KEATING
05 Provost and VP Academic Svcs .... Mr. John HENZY
03 Vice President College Operations .... Mr. Dominick BURZICHELLI
32 Vice President Student Svcs .... Vacant
10 Exec Director Financial Services .... Mrs. Elizabeth HALL
16 Exec Director Human Resource .... Ms. Danielle MORGANTI
04 Exec Assistant to the President .... Mrs. Karen SITARSKI
22 Exec Dir Diversity and Equity .... Mrs. Almarie JONES
09 Exec Dir Inst Research & Assessment .... Ms. Karen DURKIN
13 Exec Director Technology .... Mr. Josh R. PIDDINGTON
66 Dean Nursing & Allied Health .... Mrs. Susan HALL
49 Dean Liberal Arts .... Ms. Barbara NIENSTEDT
81 Dean Mathematics and Science .... Ms. Barbara TURNER
50 Dean Business & Technologies .... Mr. C. Joseph NACE
68 Dean Health/Physical Educ/Rec .... Mr. Ron CASE
88 Dean Public Safety & Security .... Mr. Fred H. MADDEN
51 Dean Continuing Ed & Inst Advanc .... Ms. Patricia CLAGHORN
06 Registrar .... Ms. Judith ATKINSTON
07 Director Admissions .... Ms. Sandra HOFFMAN
36 Director Advising .... Mr. Richard BROWN
35 Director Student Affairs .... Ms. Hilda SANTIAGO
08 Director Library Services .... Mrs. Jane S. CROCKER

Hudson County Community College (F)

25 Journal Square, 14th Floor, Jersey City NJ 07306-4301
County: Hudson FICE Identification: 012954
Unit ID: 184995
Telephone: (201) 714-7100 Carnegie Class: Assoc/Pub-U-SC
FAX Number: (201) 656-1799 Calendar System: Semester
URL: www.hccc.edu
Established: 1974 Annual Undergrad Tuition & Fees (In-District): $4,240
Enrollment: 9,331 Coed
Affiliation or Control: State/Local IRS Status: 501(c)3
Highest Offering: Associate Degree
Program: Occupational; 2-Year Principally Bachelor's Creditable
Accreditation: M, ACFEI

01 President .... Dr. Glen E. GABERT
05 Vice President Academic Affairs .... Dr. Abegail DOUGLAS-JOHNSON
10 Vice President for Finance .... Mr. John SOMMER
30 VP Development/Asst to President .... Mr. Joseph SANSONE
11 Vice President College Operations .... Mr. Frank MERCADO
32 VP North Hudson Ctr/Student Affairs .... Ms. Paula ADELHOCH
31 Dean Community Education .... Mr. Eric FRIEDMAN
09 Assoc Dean Institutional Rsrch/Plng .... Mr. Kris KRISHNAN
20 Assistant Dean Academic Affairs .... Dr. Chanida KATKANANT
84 Assoc Dean Enrollment Services .... Mr. Peter VIDA
50 Assoc Dean Business and Science .... Ms. Catherine SIRANGELO-ELBADAWY
79 Associate Dean English/Humanities .... Ms. Linda RODRIQUES
37 Assoc Dean Student Financial Asst .... Ms. Pamela F. NORRIS-LITTLES
35 Associate Dean for Student Services .... Mr. Michael REIMER
88 Assoc Dean ESL/Bilingual & Dev Educ .... Mr. Christopher WAHL
06 Registrar .... Ms. Victoria ORELLANA
13 Chief Information Officer .... Mr. Vincent ZICOLELLO
07 Director of Admissions .... Mr. Nelson VIEIRA
12 Dean North Hudson Center .... Dr. Carlos TONCHE
20 Dean of Instruction .... Mr. David EDWARDS
88 Director Testing & Assessment .... Mr. Larry FRANCO
88 Director EOF .... Mr. Ruben MELENDEZ
88 Director SSSP .... Ms. Syokwaa MULUMBA
88 Executive Director Culinary Arts .... Mr. Paul DILLON
76 Director Health Related Programs .... Ms. Susanne SANSEVERE
88 Ex Dir Ctr Bus/Industry/Cntrct Trng .... Mr. Nicholas MICUCCI
45 Director Academic Foundations .... Vacant
18 Director of Facilities .... Mr. Joseph TORTURELLI
21 Controller .... Mr. Robert CRUZ
25 Acting Director of Grants .... Mr. Ryan MARTIN
08 Director Learning Resource Center .... Ms. P. J. REILLY
35 Director Student Activities .... Ms. Ophelia MORGAN
26 Director of Communications .... Ms. Jennifer CHRISTOPHER

28 Director of Diversity .... Ms. Randi MILLER
29 Director Alumni Relations/Devel .... Mr. Joseph SANSONE
15 Director Human Resources .... Ms. Randi MILLER
38 Director Advisement & Counseling .... Ms. Rose CUNNINGHAM
40 Manager HCCC Bookstore .... Ms. Christine SALZMAN
96 Manager Purchasing .... Mr. Alus GREEN
88 Coordinator Medical Assisting .... Ms. Judith A. BENDER
36 Coordinator Career & Transfer Svc .. Ms. Karine PIERRE-PIERRE

Immaculate Conception Seminary of Seton Hall University (A)

400 S Orange Avenue, South Orange NJ 07079-2646
County: Essex FICE Identification: 002611
Unit ID: 185004
Telephone: (973) 761-9575 Carnegie Class: Not Classified
FAX Number: (973) 761-9577 Calendar System: Semester
URL: www.shu.edu
Established: 1861 Annual Undergrad Tuition & Fees: $31,090
Enrollment: 251 Coed
Affiliation or Control: Roman Catholic IRS Status: 501(c)3
Highest Offering: Master's
Program: Professional
Accreditation: &M, THEOL

01 Rector/Dean .... Msgr. Robert F. COLEMAN
10 Vice Rector/Bus Mgr/Formation Dir .... Rev. Robert K. SUSZKO
05 Associate Dean .... Rev. Christopher M. CICCARINO
20 Associate Dean .... Dr. Dianne M. TRAFLET
88 Assoc Dean Undergraduate Program .. Rev. Douglas J. MILEWSKI
42 Spiritual Director .... Msgr. Gerard H. MCCARREN
08 Director of Seminary Library .... Rev. Lawrence B. PORTER
30 Director of Development .... Mrs. Catherine A. CUNNING
07 Academic Svcs & Admissions Coord .... Mrs. Diane M. CARR

† Regional accreditation is carried under the parent institution in South Orange, NJ.

Kean University (B)

1000 Morris Avenue, Union NJ 07083-0411
County: Union FICE Identification: 002622
Unit ID: 185262
Telephone: (908) 737-5326 Carnegie Class: Master's L
FAX Number: (908) 737-4636 Calendar System: Semester
URL: www.kean.edu
Established: 1855 Annual Undergrad Tuition & Fees (In-State): $10199.5
Enrollment: 15,939 Coed
Affiliation or Control: State IRS Status: 501(c)3
Highest Offering: Doctorate
Program: Liberal Arts And General; Teacher Preparatory; Professional
Accreditation: M, ART, CACREP, CIDA, MUS, NUR, OT, SP, SPAA, SW, TED, THEA

01 President .... Dr. Dawood FARAHI
10 Exec VP for Operations .... Mr. Philip CONNELLY
101 Exec Asst Board/Exec Dir Media/Pub .... Ms. Audrey KELLY
05 Vice Pres Academic Affairs .... Vacant
30 Vice Pres Institutional Advancement .... Dr. Kristie REILLY
32 Vice President for Student Affairs ... Ms. Janice MURRAY-LAURY
20 Assoc VP for Academic Affairs .... Dr. Ken SANDERS
12 Assoc VP/Dean Kean Ocean .... Dr. Robert CIRASA
58 Dean Nathan Weiss Grad Col .... Dr. Steven LORENZET
53 Dean Col Education .... Dr. Susan POLIRSTOK
79 Dean Col Humanities/SocialSciences ... Dr. Kenneth DOLLARHIDE
81 Dean Col Natural & Applied Hlth Sci .... Dr. Jeffrey TONEY
50 Dean Col Business & Public Admin .... Dr. Kathryn MARTELL
57 Acting Dean Col Visual/Perform Arts .... Dr. Holly LOGUE
15 Director Human Resources .... Mr. Faruque CHOWDHURY
07 Director for Undergrad Admissions .... Ms. Valerie WINSLOW
06 Registrar .... Mr. Ken WOLPIN
08 University Librarian .... Mr. Luis RODRIGUEZ
27 Dir Media & Publications .... Mr. Matt CARUSO
21 Dir Student Financial Services .... Mr. Charlie XU
25 Director Research & Sponsored Pgms .... Ms. Susan GANNON
09 Director Institutional Research .... Dr. Shiji SHEN
88 Director for Accredit & Assessment .... Mr. Lamonte ROUSE
37 Director Financial Aid .... Ms. Sharon AUDET
39 Director Residence Life .... Ms. Maximina RIVERA
38 Dir Counselng/Disabil/Intl Students .... Vacant
41 Director for Athletics .... Vacant
29 Director Alumni Relations .... Ms. Adriana BRENNAN
96 Director for Purchasing .... Mr. George THORN
18 Dir Facilities & Campus Planning .... Ms. Phyllis DUKE
88 Director for Sustainability .... Dr. Nicholas SMITH-SEBASTO
23 Director for Health Services .... Ms. Lori PURWIN
22 Director Affirmative Action .... Dr. Charlie WILLIAMS
14 Dir Office for Computer/Inform Svcs .... Mr. Anthony SANTORA
35 Dir Center for Leadership & Service .... Vacant
36 Dir Career Development & Adv .... Dr. Steven KUBOW
104 Dir Ctr for International Studies .... Mr. Timothy TORRE
88 Director Veterans Affairs .... Vacant
19 Chief Campus Police .... Dr. Dave PARKS
43 University Counsel .... Mr. Michael TRIPODI
42 Chaplain for Ministry .... Fr. Thomas BLIND

Mercer County Community College (C)

1200 Old Trenton Road, PO Box B,
Trenton NJ 08690-1099
County: Mercer FICE Identification: 004740
Unit ID: 185509
Telephone: (609) 586-4800 Carnegie Class: Assoc/Pub-R-L
FAX Number: (609) 570-3870 Calendar System: Semester
URL: www.mccc.edu
Established: 1966 Annual Undergrad Tuition & Fees (In-District): $3,990
Enrollment: 9,697 Coed
Affiliation or Control: State/Local IRS Status: 501(c)3
Highest Offering: Associate Degree
Program: Occupational; 2-Year Principally Bachelor's Creditable
Accreditation: M, AAB, ADNUR, FUSER, MLTAD, PTAA, RAD

01 President .... Dr. Patricia C. DONOHUE
30 Vice President College Advancement .... Ms. Mellissia ZANJANI
05 Vice President Academic Affairs .... Dr. Donald GENERALS
11 Vice President for Admin & CBO .... Mr. Jacob EAPEN
32 Exec Dean for Student Affairs .... Dr. Diane CAMPBELL
76 Dean Sciences/Health Professions .... Dr. Linda MARTIN
49 Dean Liberal Arts .... Dr. Robin SCHORE
50 Dean Business and Technology .... Ms. Judith A. EHRESMAN
31 Ast Dean-JKC-Acad Pgm/Evening Svcs .... Mr. Edward W. FREDERICK
35 Asst Dean Student Services .... Mr. John SIMONE
13 Exec Dir for Info Technology Svcs .... Ms. Susan BOWEN
21 Exec Dir of Finance .... Mr. Walter BROOKS
26 Dir Marketing/Public Information .... Ms. Lynn HOLL
15 Exec Dir for Compliance & Human Res ..... Mr. Jose FERNANDEZ
06 Registrar .... Ms. Joan GUGGENHEIM
37 Director of Financial Aid .... Mr. Reginald PAGE
09 Director Institutional Research .... Ms. Nina MAY
18 Chief Facilities/Physical Plant .... Mr. Bryon MARSHALL
96 Director of Purchasing .... Mr. Stephen GREGOROWICZ
07 Director of Admissions & Outreach .... Ms. Savita BAMBHROLIA
38 Director Student Counseling .... Ms. Laurene JONES
84 Director Enrollment Management .. Ms. Latonya ASHFORD-LIGON
29 Director of Alumni Relations .... Ms. Kay EATON

Mesivta Keser Torah (D)

503 Eleventh Avenue, Belmar NJ 07719-2407
County: Monmouth Identification: 666779
Telephone: (732) 367-4259 Carnegie Class: Not Classified
FAX Number: (732) 681-7171 Calendar System: Semester
Established: 1991 Annual Undergrad Tuition & Fees: $11,250
Enrollment: 48 Male
Affiliation or Control: Independent Non-Profit IRS Status: 501(c)3
Highest Offering: Baccalaureate
Program: Liberal Arts And General, Professional, Religious Emphasis
Accreditation: RABN

01 President .... Rabbi Dovid HEINEMANN

Middlesex County College (E)

2600 Woodbridge Avenue, Edison NJ 08818-3050
County: Middlesex FICE Identification: 002615
Unit ID: 185536
Telephone: (732) 548-6000 Carnegie Class: Assoc/Pub-S-SC
FAX Number: (732) 494-8244 Calendar System: Semester
URL: www.middlesexcc.edu
Established: 1964 Annual Undergrad Tuition & Fees (In-District): $4,065
Enrollment: 12,903 Coed
Affiliation or Control: State/Local IRS Status: 501(c)3
Highest Offering: Associate Degree
Program: Occupational; 2-Year Principally Bachelor's Creditable
Accreditation: M, ADNUR, DH, DIETT, ENGT, MLTAD, RAD

01 President .... Dr. Joann LA PERLA-MORALES
05 Vice President Academic Affairs .... Dr. Karen HAYS
10 VP Pres Finance & Administration .... Ms. Susan K. PERKINS
30 VP for Institutional Advancement .... Mr. Patrick MADAMA
84 Dean Enrollment Management .... Ms. Marla BRINSON
107 Dean Professional Studies .... Ms. Marilyn LASKOWSKI-SACHNOFF
49 Dean Arts and Sciences .... Mr. David EDWARDS
31 Dean Corporate & Commuity Education .Ms. Mary Ann CONNERS
18 Exec Director Facilities Management .... Mr. Donald DROST
14 Exec Director Information Tech .... Mr. Neil SACHNOFF
21 Controller .... Ms. Lori WILKIN
07 Asst Dean of Admissions .... Ms. Aretha WATSON
06 Registrar .... Mr. Richard COLE
36 Director of Counseling/Career Svcs .... Dr. John R. HERRLING
37 Financial Aid Director .... Ms. Gail SCOTT-BEY
08 Director Learning Resources .... Mr. Mark THOMPSON
26 Chief Public Relations Officer .... Mr. Thomas PETERSON
96 Director of Purchasing .... Mr. David FRICKE

Monmouth University (F)

400 Cedar Avenue, West Long Branch NJ 07764-1898
County: Monmouth FICE Identification: 002616
Unit ID: 185572
Telephone: (732) 571-3400 Carnegie Class: Master's L
FAX Number: (732) 571-3629 Calendar System: Semester
URL: www.monmouth.edu
Established: 1933 Annual Undergrad Tuition & Fees: $28,000
Enrollment: 6,507 Coed
Affiliation or Control: Independent Non-Profit IRS Status: 501(c)3
Highest Offering: Master's
Program: 2-Year Principally Bachelor's Creditable; Liberal Arts And General; Teacher Preparatory; Professional
Accreditation: M, BUS, CACREP, ENG, NURSE, SW, TED

01 President .... VADM. Paul G. GAFFNEY, II
04 Executive Assistant to President .... Mrs. Annette GOUGH
101 Special Asst Board of Trustees .... Ms. Janet FELL
05 Vice Pres Academic Affs/Provost .... Dr. Thomas PEARSON
58 Vice Provost/Dean Graduate School .... Dr. Datta V. NAIK
49 Dean Sch Humanities/Social Science .... Dr. Stanton GREEN
50 Dean Leon Hess Business Sch .... Prof. Donald MOLIVER
53 Dean School of Education .... Dr. Lynn ROMEO
72 Dean School of Science .... Dr. Michael PALLADINO
66 Dean School of Nursing/Health Stds .... Dr. Janet MAHONEY
70 Dean School of Social Work .... Dr. Robin MAMA
92 Dean Honors School .... Dr. Kevin DOOLEY
08 Dean of Library .... Dr. Ravindra SHARMA
10 Vice President Finance .... Mr. William G. CRAIG
21 Assoc VP for Finance/Budgets .... Mr. Jack GAVIN
96 Director of Purchasing .... Mr. Mark MIRANDA
43 Vice President & General Counsel .... Mr. Grey DIMENNA
88 Director of Compliance .... Ms. Melissa DALE
22 Dir Affirm Action/Human Relations .... Mr. Julian WILLIAMS
11 Vice President Administrative Svcs .... Mrs. Patricia SWANNACK
18 Assoc VP Campus Plng/Construction .... Mr. Robert CORNERO
19 Director/Chief of Police .... Capt. William MCELRATH
15 Director of Human Resources .... Ms. Maureen COFFEY
32 Vice President Student Services .... Mrs. Mary Anne NAGY
35 Assoc VP for Student Services .... Mr. James PILLAR
35 Dir Student Activities/Student Ctr .... Ms. Amy BELLINA
26 Director of Public Affairs .... Ms. Petra LUDWIG
30 Vice Pres University Advancement .... Dr. Jeffery MILLS
29 Director of Alumni Affairs .... Ms. Marilynn PERRY
84 Vice Pres Enrollment Management .... Dr. Robert MC CAIG
37 Assoc VP/Director Financial Aid .... Ms. Claire ALASIO
07 Assistant VP Undergrad Admissions .Ms. Lauren VENTO-CIFELLI
07 Director Graduate Admission .... Mr. Kevin ROANE
41 Vice Pres & Director of Athletics .... Dr. Marilyn MCNEIL
13 Vice Pres Information Management .....Dr. Edward CHRISTENSEN
09 Assoc VP Acad & Inst Assessment .... Dr. David STROHMETZ
09 Director of Institutional Research .... Dr. Eleanor SWANSON
06 Assoc VP Academic Admin/Registrar .... Ms. Susan O'KEEFE
38 Dean of the Center for Student Succ .... Dr. Mercy AZEKE
36 Assistant Dean for Career Services .... Mr. William HILL
20 Assoc VP for Global Initiatives .... Dr. Saliba SARSAR

Montclair State University (G)

1 Normal Avenue, Montclair NJ 07043-9987
County: Essex and Passaic FICE Identification: 002617
Unit ID: 185590
Telephone: (973) 655-4000 Carnegie Class: Master's L
FAX Number: N/A Calendar System: Semester
URL: www.montclair.edu
Established: 1908 Annual Undergrad Tuition & Fees (In-State): $10,800
Enrollment: 18,402 Coed
Affiliation or Control: State IRS Status: 501(c)3
Highest Offering: Doctorate
Program: Liberal Arts And General; Teacher Preparatory; Professional
Accreditation: M, ART, AUD, BUS, CACREP, CS, DANCE, DIETD, DIETI, MUS, SP, TED, THEA

01 President .... Dr. Susan A. COLE
05 Provost/Vice Pres Academic Affairs .... Dr. Willard P. GINGERICH
10 Vice President Finance & Treasurer .... Mr. Donald D. CIPULLO
32 Vice Pres Student Devel/Campus Life .Dr. Karen L. PENNINGTON
30 Vice Pres University Advancement .... Mr. John T. SHANNON
16 Vice President Human Resources .... Ms. Judith E. HAIN
18 Vice Pres Univ Facilities .... Mr. Gregory W. BRESSLER
13 VP Information Technology .... Dr. Edward V. CHAPEL
43 University Counsel .... Ms. Valerie L. VAN BAAREN
86 Director Government Relations .... Ms. Shivaun P. GAINES
45 Exec Director Budget and Planning .... Mr. David JOSEPHSON
101 Special Asst to the President .... Dr. Frank J. SCHWARTZ
79 Dean College Humanities/Soc Scis .... Dr. Marietta MORRISSEY
81 Dean College Science & Math .... Dr. Robert S. PREZANT
53 Dean Col Education & Human Svcs .... Dr. Ada Beth CUTLER
57 Dean College of the Arts .... Dr. Geoffrey W. NEWMAN
50 Dean School of Business .... Dr. E. LaBrent CHRITE
08 Dean of Library Services .... Dr. Judith L. HUNT
20 Dean of Grad School .... Dr. Joan C. FICKE
35 Dean of Students .... Dr. Rose Mary HOWELL
84 Assoc VP Enrollment/Stdnt Acad Sup .... Dr. Bryan J. TERRY
20 Vice Provost for Learning and Teach .... Dr. Kenneth R. BAIN
58 Vice Provost for Research .... Dr. Constantine THEODOSIOU
20 Assoc Provost Acad Pgm/Assessment .... Dr. Joanne F. COTE-BONANNO
18 Assoc Vice Pres Facilities Svcs .... Dr. Timothy CAREY
18 Assoc VP Design & Construction .... Mr. Charles SARAJIAN
18 Exec Dir Facil Maintnc/Engineering .... Mr. Walter D. EDDY
91 Asso VP Enterprise Software/Dep CIO .... Ms. Carolyn M. ORTEGA
35 Assoc VP Student Dev/Campus Life .... Ms. Kathleen E. RAGAN
15 Asst VP Univ Staffing Services .... Ms. Catherine N. BONGO
15 Asst VP Employee Relations .... Mr. Michael G. OWEN
64 Director School of Music .... Dr. Robert CART
09 Director Institutional Research .... Dr. Steven L. JOHNSON
06 Registrar .... Ms. Denise M. DEBLASIO
07 Director Undergraduate Admissions .... Ms. Lisa A. KASPER
26 Exec Dir University Communications .... Ms. Paula MALIANDI
26 Dir Marketing and Graphic Svcs .... Ms. Claudia BOGRIS
30 Assoc VP Univ Advancement .... Ms. Jane M. BOYLE
30 Assoc VP Univ Advancement .... Ms. Carol A. BLAZEJOWSKI
31 Exec Dir Community Rel/Univ Events .... Ms. Julie ADAMS
29 Exec Dir Alumni Relations .... Ms. Jeanne MARANO
19 Chief of University Police .... Mr. Paul M. CELL
22 Dir EO/Affirmative Action/Diversity .... Ms. Barbara J. MILTON

38 Director Counseling/Psych Services ....Dr. Jaclyn FRIEDMAN-LOMBARDO
39 Exec Director Residential Ed/Svcs .Mr. Dominic A. PETRUZZELLI
40 General Mgr University Bookstore ....Mr. Richard AMMERMAN
41 Director Intercollegiate Athletics ....Ms. Holly P. GERA
37 Director Financial Aid ....Mr. James T. ANDERSON
87 Dir Summer Sessions/Special Pgms ....Mr. Jamieson A. BILELLA
36 Exec Dir Ctr Career Svcs/Coop Educ ....Ms. Carolyn D. JONES
96 Dir Procurement/Fin Div Admin ....Ms. Nancy G. CARVER
89 Dir New Student Experience Pgm ....Ms. Michele CAMPAGNA
92 Director Honors Program ....Dr. Gregory L. WATERS
21 Asst VP for Finance & Controller ....Ms. Catherine A. CORYAT
21 Director of Student Accounts ....Ms. Marion CAGGIANO
23 Director University Health Center ....Ms. Donna M. BARRY
104 Exec Director International Affairs ....Ms. Marina CUNNINGHAM
28 Director Equity and Diversity ....Ms. Esmilda M. ABREU
25 Dir Research & Sponsored Programs ....Vacant
88 Asst Dean for Student Life ....Ms. Fatima DECARVALHO
105 Dir Web Services ....Ms. Cindy L. MENEGHIN
04 Exec Asst to the President ....Ms. Phyllis L. WOOSTER
42 Chaplain ....Fr. James CHERN
88 Director Fin Systems Administration ....Ms. Catherine I. RUSH
88 Dir Construction Procurement ....Mr. Daniel ROCHE
88 Asst VP Enterprise Tech Services ....Mr. Jeff GIACOBBE
88 Exec Dir Advancement Services ....Ms. Jeanette HANLEIN
88 Dir Campus Planning ....Mr. Michael ZANKO
88 Dir Tech Training and Integration ....Ms. Yanling SUN
88 Dir Environmental Health and Safety ....Ms. Amy FERDINAND

New Brunswick Theological Seminary (A)

17 Seminary Place, New Brunswick NJ 08901-1196
County: Middlesex FICE Identification: 002619
Unit ID: 185758
Telephone: (732) 247-5241 Carnegie Class: Spec/Faith
FAX Number: (732) 249-5412 Calendar System: Semester
URL: www.nbts.edu
Established: 1784 Annual Graduate Tuition & Fees: $10,296
Enrollment: 205 Coed
Affiliation or Control: Reformed Church In America IRS Status: 501(c)3
Highest Offering: Doctorate; No Undergraduates
Program: Professional; Religious Emphasis
Accreditation: THEOL

01 President ....Dr. Gregg A. MAST
04 Assistant to the President ....Ms. Yasha PEOPLE
05 Dean of the Seminary ....Dr. Renee HOUSE
10 Director Finance & Administration ....Mr. Allan BENISH
21 Controller ....Mr. Kenneth TERMOTT
32 Dean of Students ....Dr. Jessica DAVIS
30 Director of Development ....Mrs. Catherine PROCTOR
08 Director of Library ....Mr. Christopher BRENNAN
06 Registrar & Assistant Dean of AA ....Ms. Sharon A. WATTS
07 Admissions Committee Chair ....Dr. Beth L. TANNER

New Jersey City University (B)

2039 Kennedy Boulevard, Jersey City NJ 07305-1597
County: Hudson FICE Identification: 002613
Unit ID: 185129
Telephone: (201) 200-2000 Carnegie Class: Master's L
FAX Number: (201) 200-2352 Calendar System: Semester
URL: www.njcu.edu
Established: 1927 Annual Undergrad Tuition & Fees (In-State): $9,347
Enrollment: 8,517 Coed
Affiliation or Control: State IRS Status: 501(c)3
Highest Offering: Master's
Program: Liberal Arts And General; Teacher Preparatory; Professional
Accreditation: M, ACBSP, ART, MUS, NUR, @TEAC, TED

01 President ....Dr. Carlos HERNANDEZ
05 Vice Pres Academic Affairs ....Dr. Joanne Z. BRUNO
32 Vice Pres for Student Affairs ....Dr. John MELENDEZ
11 Vice Pres Administration/Finance ....Mr. Aaron ASKA
44 Vice Pres University Advancement ....Vacant
21 Controller ....Ms. Mary BOLOWSKI
13 Assoc VP Computer Inform Systems ....Mr. Robert MCBRIDE
18 Assoc VP Facil/Construction Mgmt ....Mr. Andrew CHRIST
20 Act Asst Vice Pres Academic Affs ....Dr. Debra WOO
30 Interim VP University Advancement ....Mr. William FELLENBERG
07 Asst VP Admissions/Enrollment Mgmt ....Ms. Carmen PANLILIO
26 Asst VP Pub Info/Community Rel .Ms. Ellen WAYMAN-GORDON
14 Asst VP Information Technology ....Ms. Phyllis SZANI
101 Exec Asst to Pres/Sec for Board ....Ms. Gayle FORD
04 Executive Asst to the President ....Ms. Maria COBARRUBIAS
49 Dean Arts & Sciences ....Dr. Barbara FELDMAN
58 Dean of Graduate Studies ....Dr. Richard HENDRIX
53 Dean Education ....Dr. Allan DE FINA
107 Dean Professional Studies ....Dr. Sandra BLOOMBERG
35 Dean of Students ....Dr. Lyn HAMLIN
08 Director of University Library ....Ms. Grace F. BULAONG
06 Registrar ....Ms. Miriam LARIA
36 Director Career Planning/Placement ....Dr. Jennifer JONES
09 Director Institutional Research ....Dr. Arthur KRAMER
15 Director Human Resources ....Mr. Robert PIASKOWSKY
19 Director Public Safety ....Mr. Bruce HARMAN
41 Director Athletics/Recreation ....Ms. Alice DE FAZIO
22 Dir Affirmative Action/Equal Oppty ....Ms. Lisa NAZARIO
29 Interim Director Alumni Relations ....Ms. Jane MCCLELLAN
78 Director Cooperative Education ....Dr. Jennifer JONES
44 Director Annual Giving ....Vacant
38 Director Student Counseling ....Dr. Abisola GALLAGHER
96 Director of Purchasing ....Ms. Edie DELVECCHIO
90 Director of Academic Computing ....Dr. Charles PRATT
85 Foreign Student Advisor ....Mr. Craig KATZ
43 University Counsel ....Mr. Alfred RAMEY
37 Director Student Financial Aid ....Vacant
30 Director of Development ....Ms. Lori SUMMERS

New Jersey Institute of Technology (C)

University Heights, Newark NJ 07102-1982
County: Essex FICE Identification: 002621
Unit ID: 185828
Telephone: (973) 596-3000 Carnegie Class: RU/H
FAX Number: (973) 642-4380 Calendar System: Semester
URL: www.njit.edu
Established: 1881 Annual Undergrad Tuition & Fees (In-State): $13,524
Enrollment: 8,934 Coed
Affiliation or Control: State IRS Status: 501(c)3
Highest Offering: Doctorate
Program: Professional
Accreditation: M, BUS, CS, ENG, ENGT, PH

01 Interim President ....Dr. Joel BLOOM
05 Provost/Sr VP for Academic Affairs ....Dr. Ian GATLEY
10 Senior Vice Pres Admin & Treasurer ....Mr. Henry A. MAUERMEYER
30 Vice Pres University Advancement ....Dr. Charles DEES
46 Vice President Research & Devel ....Dr. Donald H. SEBASTIAN
22 VP HR/Ex Dir Cmplnce/Trng/Cmty Rels ....Dr. Theodore T. JOHNSON
48 Dean of Architecture ....Mr. Urs P. GAUCHAT
54 Dean of Engineering ....Dr. Sunil SAIGAL
49 Dean College Science/Liberal Arts ....Dr. Fadi P. DEEK
50 Dean School of Management ....Dr. Pius J. EGBELU
92 Dean A Dorman Honors College ....Dr. Joel S. BLOOM
77 Dean College Computing Science ....Dr. Narain GEHANI
21 Asst Vice Pres Finance & Controller ....Mr. William GARCIA
18 Assoc VP Facilities Management ....Mr. Joseph F. TARTAGLIA
58 Assoc Provost Graduate Studies ....Dr. Marino XANTOS
13 Assoc Provost Information Svcs Tech ....Mr. David F. ULLMAN
51 Assoc VP Cont/Distance Education ....Dr. Gale T. SPAK
07 Assoc VP Enroll Svcs/Dean Admiss ....Ms. Kathryn KELLY
88 Asst Vice Pres Pre-College Programs ....Dr. Howard S. KIMMEL
32 Dean Student Services ....Dr. Jack GENTUL
89 Assoc Dean/Ctr for First Yr Stdnts ....Dr. Sharon E. MORGAN
20 Associate Dean Academic Affairs ..Dr. Shanti GOPALAKRISHNAN
27 Executive Director Communications ....Ms. Jean M. LLEWELLYN
29 Exec Director of Alumni Affairs ....Mr. Robert A. BOYNTON
04 Executive Assistant to President ....Ms. Renee WATKINS
78 Exec Director Career Devel Svcs ....Mr. Gregory MASS
26 Director of Public Relations ....Ms. Sheryl M. WEINSTEIN
105 University Webmaster ....Vacant
09 Director Inst Research/Planning ....Dr. Eugene P. DEESS
08 University Librarian ....Mr. Richard T. SWEENEY
06 Registrar ....Mr. Joseph F. THOMPSON
37 Director of Financial Aid ....Ms. Ivon NUNEZ
38 Director of Counseling Center ....Dr. Phyllis BOLLING
19 Director of Public Safety ....Mr. Robert G. SABATTIS
24 Dir Instructional Tech/Media Svcs ....Mr. William F. REYNOLDS
41 Sr Admin Physical Educ/Athletics ....Mr. Leonard I. KAPLAN
85 Director International Students/Fac ....Mr. Jeffrey W. GRUNDY
35 Director Student Activities ....Ms. Donna MINNICH
96 Director Purchasing/Office Services ....Ms. Eugenia REGENCIO

Ocean County College (D)

PO Box 2001, Toms River NJ 08754-2001
County: Ocean FICE Identification: 002624
Unit ID: 185873
Telephone: (732) 255-0400 Carnegie Class: Assoc/Pub-S-SC
FAX Number: (732) 255-0444 Calendar System: Semester
URL: www.ocean.edu
Established: 1964 Annual Undergrad Tuition & Fees (In-District): $3,700
Enrollment: 10,367 Coed
Affiliation or Control: State/Local IRS Status: 501(c)3
Highest Offering: Associate Degree
Program: Occupational; 2-Year Principally Bachelor's Creditable
Accreditation: M, ADNUR

01 President ....Dr. Jon H. LARSON
11 Executive VP Operational ....Dr. James J. MCGINTY
05 Executive VP Instructional ....Mr. Richard STRADA
32 VP Student Affairs ....Mr. Donald DORAN
10 VP of Finance ....Ms. Sara WINCHESTER
26 VP of College Advancement ....Ms. Tara B. KELLY
04 Senior Asst to the President ....Mr. David WOLFE
04 Asst to Pres for Inst Quality ....Ms. Janet HUBBS
20 Assoc VP of Academic Affairs ....Dr. Carolyn LAFFERTY
20 Asst VP for Instructional Services ..Dr. Antoinette M. CLAY-HALL
18 Asst VP Facilities/Planning/Constr ....Mr. Kenneth E. OLSEN
57 Actg Dean Language and the Arts ....Mr. Kleinschmidt ROBERT
81 Acting Dean Math/Science & Tech ....Dr. Yehia ELMOGZHZY
66 Actg Dean for the School of Nursing ....Ms. Colleen MANZETTI
106 Dean of E-learning and Adj Faculty ....Dr. Maysa HAYWARD
83 Actg Dean Soc Sci & Off Campus Svc ....Ms. Eileen SCHILLING
102 Exec Dir OCC Foundation ....Ms. Sandy S. BROUGHTON
106 Exec Director of E-learning ....Ms. Patricia FENN
51 Director of Cont & Prof Educ ....Ms. Deborah ROBINSON
08 Director of Library Services ....Mr. Joseph TOTH
13 CIO ....Mr. August STOLL
37 Director of Financial Aid ....Dr. Norma BETZ
88 Director of Academic Planning ....Ms. Mary KELLER
19 Director of Security Operations ....Mr. Robert KUMPF
88 Dir Broadcast/Instructional Tech ....Mr. Lee KOBUS
88 Director of College Relations ....Ms. Jan KIRSTEN
15 Director of Human Resourses ....Ms. Karen BLYSKAL
06 Director of Registration/Records ....Ms. Mary FENNESSY
93 Director of EOF & OMS ....Ms. Laura RICKARDS
18 Dir of Facilities/Engr & Ops ....Mr. Fulvio CESCO-CANCIAN
41 Director of Athletics ....Ms. Ilene COHEN
09 Dir of Inst Research ....Vacant
40 Dir of Auxiliary Svcs ....Ms. Carol KAUNITZ
44 Manager OCC Foundation/Alumni ....Ms. Kathy H. BUFFUM

Passaic County Community College (E)

1 College Boulevard, Paterson NJ 07509-1179
County: Passaic FICE Identification: 009994
Unit ID: 186034
Telephone: (973) 684-6868 Carnegie Class: Assoc/Pub-S-SC
FAX Number: (973) 684-5843 Calendar System: Semester
URL: www.pccc.edu
Established: 1968 Annual Undergrad Tuition & Fees (In-District): $3,954
Enrollment: 9,548 Coed
Affiliation or Control: State/Local IRS Status: 501(c)3
Highest Offering: Associate Degree
Program: Occupational; 2-Year Principally Bachelor's Creditable
Accreditation: M, ADNUR, ENGT, RAD

01 President ....Dr. Steven ROSE
05 Vice Pres Academic/Student Affairs ....Dr. Jacqueline KINEAVY
10 Vice Pres Finance/Administration ....Mr. Maurice FEIGENBAUM
12 Vice Pres Passaic Academic Center . Ms. Josephine HERNANDEZ
13 Vice Pres Information Technology ....Mr. Robert MONDELLI
15 Vice Pres Human Resources ....Mr. Gilbert RIVERA
20 Dean Academic Affairs ....Dr. Bassel STASSIS
09 Exec Dir Institutional Rsrch/Plng ....Dr. Gurvinder KHANEJA
88 Ex Dir Cultural Affs/The Poetry Ctr ....Ms. Maria GILLAN
30 Exec Dir of Institutional Devel ....Mr. Todd SORBER
84 Exec Dir of Enrollment Management ....Ms. Betsy MARINACE
08 Associate Dean Learning Resources ....Mr. Greg FALLON
66 Asst Dean Nurse Educ/Health Scis ....Ms. Donna STANKIEWICZ
37 Director Financial Aid ....Ms. Linda GAYTON
06 Registrar ....Ms. Donna FISCHER
19 Director Security ....Mr. John MORGAN
18 Exec Dir Facilities Mgmt/Planning ....Mr. Brian EGAN
35 Director Student Activities ....Ms. Doris ALCIVAR
41 Athletic Director ....Mr. Bernard JOHNSON
07 Director of Admissions ....Ms. Stephanie DECKER
29 Director Alumni Relations ....Ms. Maria MEDINA
32 Chief Student Life Officer ....Ms. Sharon GOLDSTEIN
36 Director Student Placement ....Vacant
26 Chief Public Relations Officer ....Ms. Betsy MARINACE
96 Director of Purchasing ....Ms. Marge HOLLINGSWORTH
88 Coordinator of Testing ....Mr. Tom CONN
04 Administrative Asst to President ....Ms. Evelyn DEFEIS

Princeton Theological Seminary (F)

PO Box 821, Princeton NJ 08542-0803
County: Mercer FICE Identification: 002626
Unit ID: 186122
Telephone: (609) 921-8300 Carnegie Class: Spec/Faith
FAX Number: (609) 924-2973 Calendar System: Semester
URL: www.ptsem.edu
Established: 1812 Annual Graduate Tuition & Fees: $11,000
Enrollment: 606 Coed
Affiliation or Control: Presbyterian Church (U.S.A.) IRS Status: 501(c)3
Highest Offering: Doctorate; No Undergraduates
Program: Professional; Religious Emphasis
Accreditation: M, THEOL

01 President ....Dr. Iain R. TORRANCE
10 Sr Vice Pres/Chief Oper Ofcr/Treas ....Mr. John W. GILMORE
45 Vice Pres Strategy ....Dr. Charles F. KALMBACH
26 Vice President Seminary Relations ..Rev. Rosemary C. MITCHELL
13 Vice Pres Information Technology ....Mr. Adrian BACKUS
05 Dean of Academic Affairs ....Dr. James F. KAY
32 Dean of Student Life ....Dr. Nancy L. GROSS
20 Associate Dean of Curricula ....Dr. Shawn OLIVER
73 Dir Sch of Christian/Voc/Mission ....Dr. Charles F. KALMBACH
21 Controller ....Mr. Barry L. GRUVER
29 Director Alumni/ae Relations/ Giving ....Rev. W. Robert SHARMAN, III
06 Registrar ....Mr. David H. WALL
07 Director Admissions/Financial Aid ....Mr. Matthew R. SPINA
08 Chief Librarian ....Dr. Stephen D. CROCCO
30 Director Development ....Ms. Claire A. NOON
35 Director Stdnt Rels/Sr Placement ....Dr. Catherine C. DAVIS
15 Director of Human Resources ....Ms. Sandra J. MALEY
27 Director Communications/Publication ....Rev. Barbara A. CHAAPEL
18 Director of Facilities ....Mr. German MARTINEZ
14 Dir Telecomm/Network/Suport Svcs ....Mr. William R. FRENCH
24 Director Educational Media ....Rev. Joicy BECKER-RICHARDS
39 Director of Housing/Auxiliary Svcs ....Mr. Stephen CARDONE
44 Director of Planned Giving ....Mr. John S. MCANLIS
36 Director of Student Placement ....Dr. Catherine C. DAVIS
38 Director of Student Counseling ....Rev. Nancy L. SCHONGALLA-BOWMAN
42 Minister of the Chapel ....Rev. Janice S. AMMON
28 Director Multicultural Relations ....Rev. Victor ALOYO, JR.

Princeton University (A)

Princeton NJ 08544-1098
County: Mercer FICE Identification: 002627
Unit ID: 186131
Telephone: (609) 258-3000 Carnegie Class: RU/VH
FAX Number: N/A Calendar System: Semester
URL: www.princeton.edu
Established: 1746 Annual Undergrad Tuition & Fees: $37,000
Enrollment: 7,802 Coed
Affiliation or Control: Independent Non-Profit IRS Status: 501(c)3
Highest Offering: Doctorate
Program: Liberal Arts And General; Teacher Preparatory; Professional
Accreditation: M, ENG, TEAC

01 President .... Shirley M. TILGHMAN
03 Executive Vice President .... Mark BURSTEIN
05 Provost .... Christopher L. EISGRUBER
04 Vice President & Secretary .... Robert K. DURKEE
10 Vice Pres for Finance & Treasurer .... Carolyn N. AINSLIE
30 Vice President for Development .... Elizabeth B. WOOD
26 Vice President for Public Affairs .... Robert K. DURKEE
32 Vice President of Campus Life .... Cynthia CHERREY
18 Vice President for Facilities .... Michael E. MCKAY
13 Vice President Info Technology/CIO .... Betty LEYDON
16 Vice President for Human Resources .... Lianne C. SULLIVAN-CROWLEY
20 Vice Provost Academic Affairs .... Katherine ROHRER
22 Vice Provost Instl Equity/Diversity .... Terri HARRIS REED
09 Vice Provost Institutional Research .... Jed MARSH
25 Vice Prov Space Programming/Plan .... Paul LAMARCHE
21 Budget Dir/Vice Provost Finance .... Steven GILL
20 Vice Provost Intl Initiatives .... Diana K. DAVIES
26 Asst Vice President Communications .... Lauren D. UGORJI
29 Asst Vice President Alumni Affairs .... Margaret M. MILLER
44 Asst Vice President Annual Giving .... William M. HARDT
19 Asst VP Safety/Administration .... Charlotte Treby WILLIAMS
11 Asst VP for University Services .... Paul BREITMAN
88 Asst VP for Facilities Services .... Chad L. KLAUS
88 AVP Facilities Design/Construction .... Anne ST. MAURO
18 Asst Vice Pres Facilities Plant .... Roger DEMARESKI
46 Chair Univ Rsrch Bd/Dean Research .... A. J. Stewart SMITH
43 General Counsel .... Peter G. MCDONOUGH
88 President PRINCO .... Andrew K. GOLDEN
88 Dean of the Faculty .... David P. DOBKIN
58 Dean of Graduate School .... William B. RUSSEL
49 Dean of the College .... Valerie SMITH
54 Dean of School of Engineering .... H. Vincent POOR
82 Dean of Woodrow Wilson School .... Christina H. PAXSON
48 Dean of School of Architecture .... Stanley T. ALLEN
42 Dean of Religious Life .... Alison BODEN
35 Dean of Undergraduate Students .... Kathleen DEIGNAN
07 Dean of Admission .... Janet L. RAPELYE
17 Exec Director Health Services .... John KOLLIGIAN
08 University Librarian .... Karin TRAINER
06 Registrar .... Polly WINFREY GRIFFIN
37 Dir Undergraduate Financial Aid .... Robin A. MOSCATO
86 Director Government Affairs .... Joyce A. RECHTSCHAFFEN
31 Dir Community & Regional Affairs .... Kristin APPELGET
41 Director of Athletics .... Gary D. WALTERS
96 Director of Purchasing .... Donald E. WESTON, JR.
38 Dir of Counseling & Psych Services .... Anita MCLEAN
15 Director Human Resources .... Claire JACOBS ELSON
85 Director Davis International Center .... Jackie LEIGHTON
36 Director Career Services .... Beverly HAMILTON-CHANDLER
90 Assoc CIO/Dir Academic Services OIT .... Serge J. GOLDSTEIN
14 Assoc CIO/Dir Support Services OIT .... Steven M. SATHER
91 Dir Enterprise Infrastructure OIT .... Donna E. TATRO
27 Director of News and Editorial Svcs .... Cass CLIATT
105 Director of Web Communications .... Thomas J. BARTUS
28 Manager Diversity & Inclusion .... Vacant
88 AVP for Development Relations .... Justin HARMON
44 AVP for Capital Giving .... Vacant
104 Sr Asc Dn of Col/Dir Ofc Intl Pgms .... Nancy A. KANACH
39 Director Housing .... Andrew KANE

Rabbi Jacob Joseph School (B)

1 Plainfield Avenue, Edison NJ 08817-4494
County: Middlesex FICE Identification: 030775
Unit ID: 384421
Telephone: (732) 985-6533 Carnegie Class: Spec/Faith
FAX Number: (732) 985-6553 Calendar System: Semester
URL: www.jfgmc.org/rjjy/htm
Established: 1982 Annual Undergrad Tuition & Fees: $10,900
Enrollment: 76 Male
Affiliation or Control: Independent Non-Profit IRS Status: 501(c)3
Highest Offering: Baccalaureate
Program: Teacher Preparatory; Professional
Accreditation: @RABN

01 President .... Dr. Marvin SCHICK
03 Rosh Yeshiva .... Rabbi Yaakov BUSEL
05 Rosh Yeshiva .... Rabbi Joseph EICHENSTEIN
37 Financial Aid Director .... Rabbi Yitzchok WEINTRAUB

Rabbinical College of America (C)

226 Sussex Avenue, Morristown NJ 07960-3600
County: Morris FICE Identification: 008609
Unit ID: 186186
Telephone: (973) 267-9404 Carnegie Class: Spec/Faith
FAX Number: (973) 267-5208 Calendar System: Trimester
URL: www.rca.edu
Established: 1956 Annual Undergrad Tuition & Fees: $10,000
Enrollment: 270 Male
Affiliation or Control: Independent Non-Profit IRS Status: 501(c)3
Highest Offering: Baccalaureate
Program: Teacher Preparatory
Accreditation: RABN

00 Chairman of the Board .... David T. CHASE
01 Dean .... Rabbi Moshe HERSON
04 Admin Assistant to the Dean .... Shoshana SOLOMON
26 Public Relations Officer .... Rabbi Mendel SOLOMON
06 Registrar .... Ms. Sharon MILLER
20 Director New Direction Program .... Rabbi Zalman DUBINSKY
33 Director Ordination Program .... Rabbi Sholom SPALTER
10 Chief Business Officer .... Rabbi Hershel LIPSKIER
29 Director Alumni Relations .... Vacant
37 Director Student Financial Aid .... Rabbi Moshe WEISBERG
08 Chief Librarian .... Rabbi Sholom SPALTER
51 Director Continuing Education .... Rabbi Boruch HECHT
88 Director Semicha Program .... Rabbi Chaim SCHAPIRO

Ramapo College of New Jersey (D)

505 Ramapo Valley Road, Mahwah NJ 07430-1680
County: Bergen FICE Identification: 009344
Unit ID: 186201
Telephone: (201) 684-7500 Carnegie Class: Master's M
FAX Number: (201) 684-7508 Calendar System: Semester
URL: www.ramapo.edu
Established: 1969 Annual Undergrad Tuition & Fees (In-State): $12,758
Enrollment: 6,008 Coed
Affiliation or Control: State IRS Status: 501(c)3
Highest Offering: Master's
Program: Liberal Arts And General; Teacher Preparatory; Professional
Accreditation: M, BUS, NUR, SW, TEAC

01 President .... Dr. Peter P. MERCER
05 Provost/VP Academic Affairs .... Dr. Beth BARNETT
10 Vice Pres Administration & Finance .... Vacant
32 Assoc VP of Student Affairs .... Ms. Miki CAMMARATA
84 Assoc VP of Enrollment Mgmt .... Mr. Christopher ROMANO
46 Chief Planning Officer .... Dr. Dorothy ECHOLS TOBE
20 Vice Provost for Academic Affairs .... Dr. Eric DAFFRON
21 Assoc Vice Pres Admin/Finance .... Mr. Richard ROBERTS
08 College Librarian/Dean .... Ms. Elizabeth SIECKE
102 Exec Director Ramapo Found/VPIA .... Ms. Cathleen DAVEY
06 Registrar .... Ms. Cynthia BRENNAN
07 Director of Admissions .... Mr. Peter RICE
37 Director of Financial Aid .... Mr. Mark SINGER
21 Controller .... Mr. August DAQUILA
13 Chief Information Officer .... Mr. George TABBACK
26 Asst VP Marketing & Communications .... Ms. Anna FARNESKI
15 Director of Human Resources .... Mr. Bill STOVALL
78 Dir Exper Learning/Career Svcs .... Ms. Beth RICCA
39 Director Residence Life .... Ms. Linda DIAZ
41 Acting Director of Athletics .... Ms. Kathleen FINNEGAN
18 Director Campus Facilities .... Mr. Ronald MARTUCCI
19 Director Security & Safety .... Mr. Vincent MARKOWSKI
88 Director Educ Opportunity Program .... Mr. Lorne WEEMS
50 Dean Anisfield School of Business .... Dr. Lewis CHAKRIN
82 Dean Sch Amer Intern Studies .... Dr. Hassan NEJAD
57 Dean Sch of Contemporary Arts .... Mr. Steven PERRY
83 Dean Sch Soc Science & Human Svc .... Dr. Samuel ROSENBERG
81 Actg Dn Sch Theoretical/Applied Sci .... Dr. Edward SAIFF
53 Coordinator of Teacher Education .... Dr. Alexander URBIEL
38 Director Ctr for Health/Counseling .... Dr. Judith GREEN
29 Asst Director Alumni Relations .... Ms. Purvi PAREKH
24 Asst Manager Academic Media Svcs .... Mr. Michael SAVIANESO
04 Executive Assistant to President .... Ms. Patricia KOZAKIEWICZ
25 Int Director Grants Administration .... Dr. Ronald KASE
23 Coordinator Health Services .... Ms. Debbie LUKACSKO
09 Asst VP Inst Effect & Plng/Inst Res .... Ms. Babette VARANO
22 Dir Affirm Action/Equal Opportunity .... Ms. Lorraine EDWARDS
35 Assoc VP Student Affairs .... Dr. Patrick CHANG
42 Bookstore Manager .... Ms. Theresa KING
85 Exec Director of Intl Education .... Mr. Ben LEVY
36 Asst Dir Career Dev & Placement .... Ms. Debra STARK
96 Director of Purchasing .... Mr. Stephen SONDEY
04 Special Assistant to President .... Ms. Brittany WILLIAMS-GOLDSTEIN

Raritan Valley Community College (E)

PO Box 3300, Somerville NJ 08876-1265
County: Somerset FICE Identification: 007731
Unit ID: 186645
Telephone: (908) 526-1200 Carnegie Class: Assoc/Pub-S-SC
FAX Number: (908) 526-0253 Calendar System: Semester
URL: www.raritanval.edu
Established: 1966 Annual Undergrad Tuition & Fees (In-District): $3,965
Enrollment: 8,484 Coed
Affiliation or Control: State/Local IRS Status: 501(c)3
Highest Offering: Associate Degree
Program: Occupational; 2-Year Principally Bachelor's Creditable
Accreditation: M, ADNUR, OPD

01 President .... Dr. Casey CRABILL
05 Sr Vice Pres Academic Affairs .... Dr. Eileen ABEL
10 Vice President Finance/Facilities .... Mr. John TROJAN
20 Vice Pres Learning/Technology Svcs .... Mr. Charles E. CHULVICK
15 VP for Human Resources .... Ms. Nancy MOORE
30 Dean of College Advancement .... Ms. Jackie BELIN
20 Dean of Instruction .... Dr. Maxwell STEVENS
45 Dean Academic Resource Development .... Ms. Nancy E. JORDAN
51 Dean of Corporate & Continuing Educ .... Ms. Janet L. PERANTONI
20 Dean of Faculty .... Mr. Thomas VALASEK
38 Dean Student Affairs/Dir Counsel .... Ms. Diane LEMCOE
12 Associate Dean Franklin Center .... Vacant
18 Exec Director Facilities/Grounds .... Mr. Brian O'ROURKE
84 Exec Dir of Enrollment Services .... Ms. Mary O'MALLEY
07 Exec Dir Mrktng/Acad Recruitment .... Ms. Janet THOMPSON
88 Conference Services Director .... Ms. Karen VAUGHAN
72 Executive Director Inst Technology .... Mr. Michael E. MACHNIK
102 Executive Director Foundation .... Vacant
13 Director Management Info Services .... Mr. Warren RUTE
21 Controller/Exec Dir of Finance .... Ms. Violet J. WILLENSKY
57 Director of Theatre .... Mr. Alan C. LIDDELL
09 Dir of Inst Research/Assessment .... Mr. Keith GUERIN
88 Director of Planetarium .... Mr. Jerome VINSKI
88 Director of Child Care Center .... Ms. Cathy GRIFFIN
37 Director of Financial Aid .... Mr. Lenny MESONAS
08 Library Director .... Ms. Julie MAGINN
06 Registrar .... Mr. Dan PALUBNIAK
96 Director of Purchasing .... Mr. Lester MILLER
32 Director of Student Life .... Ms. Mary SULLIVAN
36 Director Transfer/Career Services .... Mr. Paul MICHAUD

The Richard Stockton College of New Jersey (F)

101 Vera King Farris Drive, Pomona NJ 08205-9441
County: Atlantic FICE Identification: 009345
Unit ID: 186876
Telephone: (609) 652-1776 Carnegie Class: Master's M
FAX Number: (609) 652-0275 Calendar System: Semester
URL: www.stockton.edu
Established: 1969 Annual Undergrad Tuition & Fees (In-State): $11,963
Enrollment: 7,879 Coed
Affiliation or Control: State IRS Status: 501(c)3
Highest Offering: Doctorate
Program: Liberal Arts And General; Teacher Preparatory; Professional
Accreditation: M, NURSE, OT, PTA, @SP, SW, TEAC

01 President .... Dr. Herman J. SAATKAMP, JR.
05 Provost/Exec Vice Pres of Acad Affs .... Dr. Harvey KESSELMAN
100 Chief of Staff .... Mr. Brian K. JACKSON
10 Int VP Administration and Finance .... Mr. Robert D'AUGUSTINE
32 Vice President Student Affairs .... Dr. Thomasa GONZALEZ
45 Chief Planning Officer .... Dr. Claudine KEENAN
20 Associate Provost .... Dr. Marc LOWENSTEIN
20 Assistant Provost .... Dr. Debra DAGAVARIAN
96 Asst Supervisor Purchasing .... Ms. Annette HAMM
13 Assoc VP Computing/Communication .... Mr. James MCCARTHY
21 Assoc VP Administration & Finance .... Mr. Donald MOORE
22 Sp Ast to Pres Affirm Act/Ethcl Std .... Ms. Nancy W. HICKS
26 Spec Asst to Pres for External Affs .... Ms. Sharon SCHULMAN
30 Chief Dev Ofcr/Exec Dir Foundation .... Mr. Philip T. ELLMORE
84 Dean of Enrollment Management .... Mr. John IACOVELLI
07 Associate Dean of Admissions .... Ms. Alison HENRY
35 Dean of Students .... Mr. Pedro SANTANA
06 Assoc Dean Records/Registration .... Mr. Joseph LO SASSO
53 Interim Dean School of Education .... Dr. Joseph MARCHETTI
97 Dean School of General Studies .... Dr. G. Jan COLIJN
79 Dean School of Arts & Humanities .... Dr. Robert GREGG
50 Dean School of Business .... Dr. Janet M. WAGNER
58 Dean School of Graduate Studies .... Dr. Lewis LEITNER
81 Dean School of Natural Science/Math .... Dr. Dennis WEISS
83 Dean Sch Social/Behavioral Sciences .... Dr. Cheryl KAUS
76 Dean School of Health Sciences .... Dr. Brenda STEVENSON-MARSHALL
15 Director Human Resource Management .... Ms. Natalie M. HAVRAN
09 Director Institutional Research .... Dr. Xiangping KONG
08 Director of Library Services .... Dr. David PINTO
88 Director South Regional ETTC .... Ms. Patricia WEEKS
37 Director of Financial Aid .... Ms. Jeanne LEWIS
19 Dir Campus Security/Chief of Police .... Chief Glenn MILLER
88 Director Performing Arts Center .... Mr. Michael COOL
41 Dir of Athletics and Recreations .... Mr. Lonnie FOLKS
39 Director of Residential Life .... Vacant
36 Director of Career Services .... Mr. Walter L. TARVER, III
43 General Counsel .... Ms. Melissa HAGER
38 Dir Counseling and Health Services .... Ms. Frances H. BOTTONE
88 Director Academic Advising .... Dr. Peter HAGEN
21 Director Budget & Fiscal Planning .... Mr. Michael WOOD
29 Director Alumni Relations .... Ms. Sara FAUROT-CROWLEY
44 Director Major Gifts .... Ms. Peg FIORE

Rider University (G)

2083 Lawrenceville Road, Lawrenceville NJ 08648-3099
County: Mercer FICE Identification: 002628
Unit ID: 186283
Telephone: (609) 896-5000 Carnegie Class: Master's L
FAX Number: (609) 896-8029 Calendar System: Semester
URL: www.rider.edu
Established: 1865 Annual Undergrad Tuition & Fees: $31,330
Enrollment: 5,776 Coed
Affiliation or Control: Independent Non-Profit IRS Status: 501(c)3
Highest Offering: Master's
Program: Liberal Arts And General; Teacher Preparatory; Professional
Accreditation: M, BUS, BUSA, CACREP, MUS, TED

01 President .... Dr. Mordechai ROZANSKI
05 Vice Pres Academic Affairs/Provost .... Dr. Donald A. STEVEN

10 Vice President Finance/Treasurer .... Ms. Julie A. KARNS
30 Vice Pres University Advancement ....Mr. Jonathan D. MEER
32 VP Student Affairs/Dean of Students .... Dr. Anthony CAMPBELL
84 Vice Pres Enrollment Management ....Mr. James P. O'HARA
14 Assoc VP Information Technology ....Ms. Carol S. KONDRACH
21 Associate Vice President/Controller ....Mr. William ROELL
09 Assoc Vice Pres Institutional Rsrch ....Mr. Ronald WALKER
20 Associate Provost .... Dr. James O. CASTAGNERA
18 Associate Vice President ....Mr. Michael F. RECA
45 Associate Vice President Planning ....Ms. Debbie STASOLLA
12 Dean Westminster ....Mr. Robert L. ANNIS
07 Dean of Enrollment ....Ms. Susan C. CHRISTIAN
51 Dean College of Cont Studies ....Mr. Boris VILIC
49 Dean Liberal Arts & Science/Educ ....Dr. Pat MOSTO
53 Dean School of Education ....Dr. Sharon SHERMAN
50 Dean Business Administration ....Dr. Larry M. NEWMAN
06 Registrar ....Ms. Susan A. STEFANICK
36 Director of Career Placement ....Ms. Gwendolyn J. TYLER
08 Director of Library Services ....Mr. F. William CHICKERING
15 Dir Human Resources/Affirm Action ....Mr. Robert STOTO
40 Manager College Store ....Mr. Joseph JUDGE
19 Director of Public Safety ....Ms. Vickie L. WEAVER
26 Exec Director Univ Communications ....Mr. Daniel E. HIGGINS
29 Director of Alumni Relations ....Ms. Natalie M. POLLARD
41 Director of Athletics ....Mr. Donald P. HARNUM
37 Director Student Financial Svcs ....Mr. Drew C. AROMANDO
04 Executive Asst to the President ....Ms. Christine ZELENAK

Rowan University (A)

201 Mullica Hill Road, Glassboro NJ 08028-1700

County: Gloucester | FICE Identification: 002609 | Unit ID: 184782
Telephone: (856) 256-4000 | Carnegie Class: Master's L
FAX Number: (856) 256-4929 | Calendar System: Semester
URL: www.rowan.edu
Established: 1923 | Annual Undergrad Tuition & Fees (In-State): $12,018
Enrollment: 11,392 | Coed
Affiliation or Control: State | IRS Status: 501(c)3
Highest Offering: Doctorate
Program: Liberal Arts And General; Teacher Preparatory; Professional
Accreditation: M, ART, BUS, CS, ENG, #MED, MUS, TED, THEA

01 Interim President ....Dr. Ali A. HOUSHMAND
05 Interim Provost ....Dr. James NEWELL
26 VP Univ Rels/Pres Chief of Staff ....Dr. Thomas J. GALLIA
10 Vice Pres of Finance/CFO ....Mr. Joseph F. SCULLY
30 Vice Pres University Advancement ....Vacant
32 Vice President for Student Life ....Mr. Richard JONES
86 Vice Pres Civic/Governmental Rels ....Vacant
18 VP for Operations & Facilities ....Mr. Michael HARRIS
44 Asst VP University Advancement ....Mr. Ronald J. TALLARIDA
20 Int Assoc Provost Academic Affairs .... Dr. Roberta HARVEY
16 Assoc Provost Employee & Labor Rels .... Mr. Robert ZAZZALI
13 Assoc Provost Information Resources .... Mr. Anthony A. MORDOSKY
46 Assoc Provost Research ....Dr. Shreekanth MANDAYAM
09 Assoc Prov Inst Effectiveness/Plng .... Dr. Mira LALOVIC-HAND
26 Assoc VP for University Relations ....Dr. Jose CARDONA
84 Assoc Prov Strategic Enroll Mgmt ....Dr. Jeffrey HAND
31 AVP Campus Recreation/Stdnt Ctr/CES ....Ms. Tina M. PINOCCI
19 AVP Public Safety/Emergency Mgmt ....Mr. Michael KANTNER
38 Dir Counseling/Psych Services ....Dr. David RUBENSTEIN
91 Director of EIS ....Mr. James HENDERSON
37 Director of Financial Aid ....Mr. Luis A. TAVAREZ
06 Registrar ....Ms. Muriel FRIERSON
63 Dean of Cooper Medical School of RU .... Dr. Paul KATZ
08 Dean of the Library ....Mr. Bruce WHITHAM
50 Dean Rohrer College of Business ....Dr. Niranjan PATI
49 Dean of Liberal Arts & Science ....Dr. Parviz ANSARI
53 Dean of Education ....Dr. Carol SHARP
57 Int Dean of Fine/Performing Arts ....Dr. John R. PASTIN
58 Dean Graduate & Continuing Educ ....Dr. Horacio SOSA
54 Dean of Engineering ....Vacant
60 Dean of Communication ....Dr. Lorin ARNOLD
12 Asst Provost/Dean Camden Campus ....Dr. Tyrone MCCOMBS
15 Sr Director of Human Resources ....Ms. Eileen SCOTT
22 Affirmative Action Officer ....Ms. Johanna VELEZ-YELIN
41 Director of Athletics ....Ms. Joy SOLOMEN
29 Director Alumni Relations ....Ms. Kathy ROZANSKI
07 Director of Admissions ....Mr. Albert BETTS
36 Dir Career & Academic Planning Ctr ....Ms. Lizziel SULLIVAN-WILLIAMS
96 Sr Dir Contracting & Procurement ......Ms. Christina BRASTETER
27 Director University Publications ....Ms. Lori MARSHALL
105 Director Web Services ....Ms. Jennifer BELL
85 Director International Center ....Vacant
28 Director of EOF/MAP ....Ms. Penny MCPHERSON-BARNES
04 Spec Asst Plng/Campus Initiatives ....Dr. Christy FAISON

*Rutgers the State University of New Jersey Central Office (B)

83 Somerset Street, New Brunswick NJ 08901-1281

County: Middlesex | FICE Identification: 002629 | Unit ID: 186362
Telephone: (732) 932-4636 | Carnegie Class: N/A
FAX Number: (732) 932-8060
URL: www.rutgers.edu

01 President ....Dr. Richard L. MCCORMICK
05 Interim Exec VP for Acad Affairs .... Dr. Richard EDWARDS
10 Senior VP for Admin & CFO ....Mr. Bruce C. FEHN
21 Vice President Budgeting .... Dr. Nancy S. WINTERBAUER
46 VP Research & Grad Professional Ed ....Dr. Michael J. PAZZANI
14 Vice President Info Tech ....Mr. Donald E. SMITH
26 Vice President University Relations ....Ms. Kimberly M. MANNING
32 Vice President Student Affairs ....Dr. Gregory S. BLIMLING
51 Vice Pres Continuous Educ/Outreach ....Dr. Raphael CAPRIO
18 Vice Pres Univ Facil/Capital Plng ....Mr. Antonio CALCADO
43 Senior VP & General Counsel ....Mr. Jonathan ALGER
29 Asst VP Alumni Relations ....Mr. Brian R. PERILLO
04 Exec Assistant to the President ....Ms. Carol KONCSOL
20 Assoc Vice Pres Academic Affairs ....Dr. Karen R. STUBAUS
15 Vice Pres of Fac & Staff Resources .... Ms. Vivian FERNANDEZ
102 Pres RU Found/Exec VP Dev/Alum Rels ... Ms. Carol P. HERRING
08 VP Info Services & Univ Librarian ....Ms. Marianne I. GAUNT
101 Secretary of the University ....Mrs. Leslie A. FEHRENBACH
19 Vice Pres Admin & Public Safety ....Mr. Jay KOHL
23 Exec Director Student Health Svcs ....Ms. Melodee S. LASKY
06 University Registrar ....Mr. Kenneth J. IUSO
07 Director Grad/Prof Admiss ....Ms. Linda J. COSTA
37 University Dir Financial Aid ....Mr. Jean MCDONALD-RASH
39 Executive Director of Housing ....Mr. Michael C. IMPERIALE
41 Director Intercollegiate Athletics ....Mr. Tim R. PERNETTI
22 Dir Employment Equity ....Ms. Jayne M. GRANDES
36 Dir Career Devel/Placement Services ....Mr. Richard L. WHITE
09 Director Institutional Research ....Dr. Robert J. HEFFERNAN
14 U Dir & Deputy Chief Inform Officer ....Ms. Bernice GINDER
86 Vice President Public Affairs ....Mr. Peter J. MCDONOUGH, JR.
84 Vice President Enrollment Mgmt ....Dr. Courtney MCANUFF
88 VP Undergrad Education ....Dr. Barry V. QUALLS
29 VP Alumni Relations ....Ms. Donna THORNTON
28 Dir Inst Diversity & Equity ....Dr. Karen R. STUBAUS
86 Asst VP Federal Relations ....Ms. Francine PFEIFFER
86 Senior Director State Relations ....Vacant

*Rutgers the State University of New Jersey Camden Campus (C)

303 Cooper Street, Camden NJ 08102-1461

County: Camden | FICE Identification: 004741 | Unit ID: 186371
Telephone: (856) 225-6026 | Carnegie Class: Master's M
FAX Number: (856) 225-6495 | Calendar System: Semester
URL: www.camden.rutgers.edu
Established: 1927 | Annual Undergrad Tuition & Fees (In-State): $12,294
Enrollment: 6,158 | Coed
Affiliation or Control: State | IRS Status: 501(c)3
Highest Offering: Doctorate
Program: Liberal Arts And General; Teacher Preparatory; Professional
Accreditation: &M, BUS, LAW, NURSE, PTA, SPAA, TEAC

02 Chancellor .... Dr. Wendell PRITCHETT
11 Assoc Chancellor Admin & Finance ....Mr. Larry GAINES
32 Assoc Chancellor Student Life ....Ms. Mary Beth DAISEY
84 Assoc Chancellor Enrollment Mgmt ....Dr. Rodney MORRISON
88 Director Economic Development ....Mr. Gregory GAMBLE
61 Dean School of Law ....Dr. Rayman L. SOLOMON
58 Executive Dean Grad School ....Dr. Margaret MARSH
50 Dean School of Business .... Dr. Jaishankar GANESH
49 Exec Dean Fac Arts & Sci/Univ Col ....Dr. Margaret MARSH
26 Assoc Chancellor for External Rels ......Mr. Michael J. SEPANIC
06 Registrar .... Ms. Theresa R. CRISTOFARO
37 Director Financial Aid ....Ms. Linda J. TAYLOR
10 Director Campus Financial Services ....Ms. Rosa RIVERA
19 Chief Campus Police ....Chief Guy M. STILL
29 Director Alumni Relations ....Mr. Charles J. MANNELLA
96 Supplier Diversity Manager .. Ms. Pamela Y. MCMELLON-WELLS
15 Human Resources Consultant ....Ms. Carol C. FISHER
18 Director Facilities/Physical Plant ...... Mr. Bernard V. DELGUIDICE
21 Business Manager ....Ms. Marlene DRUDING
28 Director of Diversity ....Dr. Nancy G. ROSOFF
41 Dir Athletics & Rec Services .... Mr. Jeffrey L. DEAN
36 Asst Dean/Director Stdnt Career Ctr .... Mr. James MARINO
38 Assoc Director Student Counseling ....Dr. N. Maria SERRA
30 Director of Development .... Ms. Akua ASIAMAH-ANDRADE
08 Library Director .... Dr. Gary GOLDEN
23 Director Health Services ....Dr. Paul P. BROWN
39 Director of Housing ....Ms. Allison A. WISNIEWSKI

*Rutgers the State University of New Jersey New Brunswick Campus (D)

New Brunswick NJ 08901-1281

County: Middlesex | FICE Identification: 006964 | Unit ID: 186380
Telephone: (732) 932-4636 | Carnegie Class: RU/VH
FAX Number: (732) 932-8060 | Calendar System: Semester
URL: www.rutgers.edu
Established: 1766 | Annual Undergrad Tuition & Fees (In-State): $12,754
Enrollment: 38,912 | Coed
Affiliation or Control: State | IRS Status: 501(c)3
Highest Offering: Doctorate
Program: Liberal Arts And General; Teacher Preparatory; Professional
Accreditation: M, CACREP, CLPSY, DANCE, DIETD, ENG, LIB, LSAR, MUS, PH, PHAR, PLNG, SCPSY, SW, TEAC

02 Acting Dean Graduate School ....Dr. Jerome J. KUKOR
80 Dean EJB School Plng/Public Policy .... Dr. James W. HUGHES
81 Exec Dean Sch Enviro/Biological Sci ....Dr. Robert M. GOODMAN
12 Dean Douglass Residential College ....Dr. Jacquelyn LITT
12 Dean Livingston Campus ....Dr. Lea P. STEWART
12 Dean Busch Campus ....Dr. Thomas V. PAPATHOMAS
49 Executive Dean of SAS ....Dr. Douglas GREENBERG
12 Dean College Avenue Campus ....Dr. Matthew K. MATSUDA
12 Dean Cook Campus ....Dr. Richard D. LUDESCHER
12 Dean Univ College/Comm/NB .... Dr. Susan J. SHURMAN
54 Dean School of Engineering ....Dr. Thomas N. FARRIS
67 Dean Ernest Mario Sch Pharmacy ...... Dr. Christopher J. MOLLOY
57 Dean Mason Gross School of Art ....Dr. George B. STAUFFER
62 Dean Sch Communication & Info ....Dr. Jorge R. SCHEMENT
83 Dean Grad School Applied/Prof Psych ......Dr. Stanley B. MESSER
53 Dean Grad School of Education .... Dr. Richard DELISI
66 Dean Rutgers College of Nursing ....Dr. William L. HOLZEMER
70 Dean School of Social Work ....Dr. Richard L. EDWARDS
50 Int Dean School of Business-UG NB ....Dr. Glenn R. SHAFER
88 Dean School of Mgmt/Labor Relations ......Dr. David L. FINEGOLD
06 University Registrar ....Mr. Kenneth J. IUSO
104 Rutgers Study Abroad Dean ....Dr. Stephen L. REINERT

*Rutgers the State University of New Jersey Newark Campus (E)

249 University Avenue, Newark NJ 07102-1897

County: Essex | FICE Identification: 002631 | Unit ID: 186399
Telephone: (973) 353-5568 | Carnegie Class: RU/H
FAX Number: (973) 353-1048 | Calendar System: Semester
URL: www.newark.rutgers.edu
Established: 1892 | Annual Undergrad Tuition & Fees (In-State): $12,560
Enrollment: 11,798 | Coed
Affiliation or Control: State | IRS Status: 501(c)3
Highest Offering: Doctorate
Program: Liberal Arts And General; Teacher Preparatory; Professional
Accreditation: &M, BUS, LAW, NURSE, SPAA, SW, TEAC

02 Chancellor/Graduate School Dean .... Dr. Steven J. DINER
10 Exec Vice Chancellor Administration ....Mr. Kemel W. DAWKINS
32 Vice Chancellor Stdnt/Cmty Outreach ....Dr. Marcia W. BROWN
15 Assoc Chancellor Human Resources .... Ms. Carol MARTANCIK
18 Assoc Vice Chancellor Facilities ....Mr. Martin B. RYAN
30 Vice Chancellor for Development .... Ms. Irene O'BRIEN
05 Vice Chancellor Acad Pgms & Svcs .... Dr. Gary ROTH
11 Asst Chanc Admin Services/Budget ....Ms. Mary TAMASCO
35 Asst Chancellor for Student Life ....Mr. Gerald MASSENBURG
06 Registrar ....Dr. Miguel A. ESTREMERA
14 Director Information Technology ....Ms. Marie J. BOTTICELLI
07 Director of Admissions ....Mr. Jason HAND
19 Director Campus Safety Newark ....Mr. Michael P. LATTIMORE
27 Director Campus Communications ....Ms. Helen S. PAXTON
08 Asst Chancellor Dana Library ....Dr. Mark D. WINSTON
37 Manager of Financial Aid ....Mr. Melvin L. BROWN
49 Dean Faculty of Arts & Science ....Dr. Philip L. YEAGLE
61 Dean of School of Law ....Dr. John J. FARMER, JR.
50 Int Dean Business Newark/New Bruns ....Dr. Glenn SHAFER
66 Dean College of Nursing ....Dr. William L. HOLZEMER
88 Acting Dean School Criminal Justice .... Dr. Bonita VEYSEY
38 Director Student Counseling ....Dr. Pamela K. HEARD
96 Director of Purchasing ....Mr. Joseph PANDUR
88 Dean Sch of Public Affairs & Admin ....Dr. Marc HOLZER
39 Director Housing & Residence Life ....Mr. Timothy J. JOHNSON
23 Director Health Services ....Ms. Sandra SAMUELS
41 Director of Athletics ....Mr. Mark GRIFFIN

Saint Peter's College (F)

2641 Kennedy Boulevard, Jersey City NJ 07306-5997

County: Hudson | FICE Identification: 002638 | Unit ID: 186432
Telephone: (201) 761-6000 | Carnegie Class: Master's L
FAX Number: (201) 761-7801 | Calendar System: Semester
URL: www.spc.edu
Established: 1872 | Annual Undergrad Tuition & Fees: $29,800
Enrollment: 3,010 | Coed
Affiliation or Control: Roman Catholic | IRS Status: 501(c)3
Highest Offering: Doctorate
Program: Liberal Arts And General; Teacher Preparatory; Professional
Accreditation: M, NURSE, TEAC

01 President .... Dr. Eugene J. CORNACCHIA
05 Provost/Vice Pres Academic Affairs .... Dr. Marylou YAM
10 Interim VP of Finance & Business ....Mr. Denton L. STARGEL
30 Vice President Advancement ....Mr. Michael A. FAZIO
32 Assoc VP Student Life & Develop .... Fr. Stephen HESS, SJ
42 Vice Pres for Mission & Ministry ....Fr. Michael L. BRADEN, SJ
84 VP Enrollment Mgmt & Marketing .... Mr. Terence PEAVY
04 Special Assistant to the President .... Dr. Virginia BENDER
20 Academic Dean Day Session .... Dr. Velda GOLDBERG
51 Assoc Dean & Director of JC SPCS ....Ms. Elizabeth KANE
78 Assoc Dean of Experiential Lrng .... Dr. Peter M. GOTLIEB
88 Associate Dean of Undergraduates .... Dr. Anna CICIRELLI
35 Interim Dean of Students .... Ms. Carla THARP
26 Director of College Communications ...... Ms. Sarah MALINOWSKI
84 Director Enrollment/Research/Tech ....Mr. Ben SCHOLZ
07 Director of Admissions ....Vacant
08 Director of the Libraries ....Mr. David I. ORENSTEIN
88 Director Special Events & Projects ....Mr. William KNAPP
37 Director of Student Fin Aid ....Ms. Jennifer RAGSDALE
06 Registrar & Dir of Student Accounts .... Ms. Irma WILLIAMS
27 Chief Information Officer ....Ms. Dale HOCHSTEIN
09 Director of Institutional Research ....Mr. Lamberto C. NIEVES
66 Director BSN/MSN Nursing Program ....Dr. Ann TRITAK
19 Director of Campus Safety ....Mr. Art YOUMANS
24 Instructional Design Specialist ....Ms. Renee EVANS

15 Director of Human Resources .... Mr. Joseph A. DESCISCIO
29 Director Alumni Relations .... Ms. Gloria MERCURIO
30 Director of Gift/Planning .... Ms. Ana M. CRAVO
38 Director Personal Development .... Mr. Ron BECKER
39 Director of Residence Life .... Mr. David SURRATT
41 Director of Athletics .... Mr. Patrick ELLIOTT
42 Director of Campus Ministry ...... Ms. Mary Sue CALLAN-FARLEY
36 Director of Career Services .... Mr. Crescenzo FONZO
13 Director of Network Services .... Mr. Bert VABRE
85 Foreign Studies Adviser .... Mr. Tushar TRIVEDI
18 Manager of College Services .... Ms. Anna DE PAULA
58 Admin Coord Graduate Educ Pgm .... Ms. Joan SHIELDS
50 Admin Coord of MBA Programs .... Ms. Carmela BEUTEL

Salem Community College (A)

460 Hollywood Avenue, Carneys Point NJ 08069-2799
County: Salem FICE Identification: 005461
Unit ID: 186469
Telephone: (856) 299-2100 Carnegie Class: Assoc/Pub-S-SC
FAX Number: (856) 351-2634 Calendar System: Semester
URL: www.salemcc.edu
Established: 1972 Annual Undergrad Tuition & Fees (In-District): $3,924
Enrollment: 1,499 Coed
Affiliation or Control: State/Local IRS Status: 501(c)3
Highest Offering: Associate Degree
Program: Occupational; 2-Year Principally Bachelor's Creditable
Accreditation: M, ADNUR, PNUR

01 President .... Dr. Peter B. CONTINI
05 Provost/Chief Academic Officer .... Ms. Joan BAILLIE
26 Exec Asst to Pres/Dir Public Rels .... Mr. William CLARK
32 Dean of Student Affairs .... Dr. Joanne DAMMINGER
11 Dean of Administrative Services .... Mr. John DESERABLE
35 Director of Student Succes Programs .... Dr. Cherita G. WEATHERSPOON
20 Dean of Academic Affairs .... Mr. Mark MCCORMICK
66 Director Nursing .... Mrs. Michelle O'NEAL
41 Athletic Director .... Ms. Karen FREED
29 Director Alumni Relations .... Mr. William CLARK
84 Director Enrollment Management .... Vacant
102 Chief Foundation Officer .... Ms. Linda P. SMITH
96 Manager of Purchasing .... Ms. Janet CROUSE
09 Director Inst Rsrch/Planning/Devel .... Ms. Amy E. SHEW
21 Manager of Finance .... Ms. Catherine PRIEST
37 Director of Financial Aid .... Mr. Maurice THOMAS

Seton Hall University (B)

400 S Orange Avenue, South Orange NJ 07079-2697
County: Essex FICE Identification: 002632
Unit ID: 186584
Telephone: (973) 761-9000 Carnegie Class: DRU
FAX Number: N/A Calendar System: Semester
URL: www.shu.edu
Established: 1856 Annual Undergrad Tuition & Fees: $33,490
Enrollment: 9,836 Coed
Affiliation or Control: Roman Catholic IRS Status: 501(c)3
Highest Offering: Doctorate
Program: Liberal Arts And General; Teacher Preparatory; Professional
Accreditation: M, ARCPA, BUS, BUSA, COPSY, MFCD, NURSE, OT, PTA, SP, SPAA, SW, TED

01 President .... Dr. A. Gabriel ESTEBAN
05 Provost & Executive Vice President .... Dr. Larry ROBINSON
11 Assoc Prov Finance/Administration .... Dr. Nicholas SNOW
10 Vice Pres for Finance & Technology .... Mr. Dennis J. GARBINI
43 Vice President & General Counsel ...... Ms. Catherine A. KIERNAN
30 Int Vice Pres Univ Advancement .... Mr. G. Gregory TOBIN
32 Vice President Student Affairs .... Dr. Laura A. WANKEL
84 Vice President of Enrollment Mgmt .... Dr. Alyssa MCCLOUD
42 Vice Pres for Mission & Ministry ...... Msgr. C. Anthony ZICCARDI
16 Assoc Vice Pres Human Resources .... Vacant
29 Assoc VP Alumni/Government Rels .... Mr. Matthew BOROWICK
44 Int Assoc Vice Pres Univ Advance .... Mr. Joseph GUASCONI
26 Assoc VP Public Relations & Mktg .... Vacant
18 Assoc VP for Facilities & Operation .... Mr. John SIGNORELLO
88 Asst VP Finance & Technology .... Mr. David MIDDLETON
35 Asst VP Student Affs/Dir Pub Safety .... Mr. Patrick LIFANTE
31 Asc VP/Dean of Students/Cmty Dev ..... Ms. Karen VAN NORMAN
20 Int Vice Provost Academic Affairs .... Ms. Kathleen BOOZANG
45 Assoc Provost/Dean Rsrch/Grad Stds .... Dr. Gregory A. BURTON
104 Asc Prov Intl Pgms/Acad Support Svc .... Mrs. Mary K. RAWN
49 Interim Dean of Arts & Sciences .... Dr. Joan GUETTI
50 Acting Dean School of Business .... Dr. Joyce A. STRAWSER
66 Dean of Nursing .... Dr. Phyllis HANSELL
53 Acting Dean College Education Svcs .... Dr. Grace MAY
73 Dean School of Theology .... Msgr. Robert F. COLEMAN
63 Dean School of Health & Med.Science .... Dr. Brian SHULMAN
82 Dean Diplomacy/Intl Relations .... Dr. John K. MENZIES
61 Dean of Law School .... Mr. Patrick J. HOBBS
08 Dean of University Libraries .... Dr. Chrysanthy M. GRIECO
51 Dean Cont Educ/Professional Studies .... Vacant
88 Assoc Dean/Director of EOP .... Dr. Hasani CARTER
88 Assoc Dean/Exec Dir of Special Pgms .... Ms. Cassandra E. DAVIS
21 Director of Business Affairs .... Ms. Theresa L. DEEHAN
13 Chief Information Officer .... Dr. Stephen LANDRY
28 Director Compliance & Risk Mgmt .... Ms. Lori A. BROWN
37 Sr Assoc Director for Financial Aid .... Ms. Ruth NOVELLO
39 Director of Housing/Residence Life .... Ms. Tara HART
06 University Registrar .... Ms. Mary Ellen FARRELL
07 Recruitment/Compensation Manager .... Ms. Jane JACOBS
36 Director of the Career Center .... Ms. Jacquline CHAFFIN
41 Dir Athletics/Recreational Services .... Mr. Patrick G. LYONS
46 Director of Grants & Research .... Vacant
18 Director of Physical Plant .... Mr. Steve KURTYKA
23 Acting Director of Counseling .... Dr. Katherine EVANS
42 Director of Campus Ministry .... Rev. Stanley GOMES
88 Minister to Priest Community .... Msgr. James M. CAFONE
09 Dir Planning Inst Research & Asses .... Ms. Connie L. BEALE
96 Director of Procurement .... Mr. Martin E. KOELLER
38 Director Health Services .... Ms. Mary Elizabeth COSTELLO
88 Director Core Curriculum .... Dr. Anthony C. SCIGLITANO, JR.
15 Manager Employer & Labor Relations .... Mr. Thomas DEL CORE

Seton Hall University School of Law (C)

One Newark Center, Newark NJ 07102-5210
County: Essex FICE Identification: 009986
Telephone: (973) 642-8500 Carnegie Class: Not Classified
FAX Number: (973) 642-8031 Calendar System: Semester
URL: law.shu.edu
Established: 1951 Annual Graduate Tuition & Fees: $46,840
Enrollment: 1,090 Coed
Affiliation or Control: Roman Catholic IRS Status: 501(c)3
Highest Offering: First Professional Degree; No Undergraduates
Program: Professional
Accreditation: &M, LAW

01 Dean .... Patrick E. HOBBS
05 Senior Associate Dean .... Erik R. LILLQUIST
20 Associate Dean .... Claudette L. ST. ROMAIN
17 Associate Dean .... Kathleen M. BOOZANG
84 Dean of Enrollment Management .... Gisele JOACHIM
07 Director of Admissions .... David T. WEINBERG
32 Dean of Students .... Cara Herrick FOERST
20 Asst Dean Academic Affairs/Policy .... Gary S. BAVERO
11 Asst Dean Administration/Finance .... Terry DE ALMEIDA
30 Asst Dean Alumni/Development .... Vicki FLEISCHER
13 Asst Dean Leg Comp/Info Tech/Comm .... Carmelo LUBRANO
88 Asst Dean Special Projects .... Rosa ALVES
36 Asst Dean of Career Services .... Janice MANGANELLO
36 Director of Career Services .... Sonia CUNHA
08 Director Law Library .... Charles SULLIVAN
09 Director of Institutional Research .... Vacant
96 Director Special Programs .... Gina FONDETTO
37 Director of Financial Resource Mgmt .... Karen A. SOKOL
37 Associate Director of Financial Aid .... Tai GEDEON
42 Chaplain .... Rev. Nicholas GENGARO
06 Registrar & Bursar .... Jo Ann MALDONADO
18 Facilities Engineer .... John FLANAGAN
90 Director PC Support .... Michael J. MCBRIDE
90 PC Support Specialist .... Kwok-Shui LIU
91 Director IT Projects .... Eric D. WINCH
19 Security Manager .... Gerald LENIHAN
88 Director Legal Educ Oppty Pgms .... Christina L. BENNETT
102 Director Corp & Foundation Relation .... Denise M. PINNEY
43 Director Center for Social Justice .... Lori A. NESSEL
29 Director Alumni Relations .... Lori THIMMEL
44 Director of Annual Giving .... Anthony BELLUCCI
35 Director Student Affairs .... Cindy B. WILSON
44 Director of Major Gift .... Bryan STEROS
20 Director Academic Services .... Gwenda R. DAVIS
26 Director of Communications .... Janet LEMONNIER
28 Director of Diversity .... Malikah FULTON
86 Assoc Director for Government Empl .... James G. ANDREWS
23 Exec Director Healthcare Compl Pgm .... Simone HANDLER-HUTCHINSON
58 Administrator of Graduate Pgm .... Helen CUMMINGS
30 Development & Scholarship Coord .... Andrea DECHELLIS
30 Development & Reunion Coord .... Carrie SHARPE
105 Webmaster/Web Coordinator .... Ana L. SANTOS
36 Career Counselor .... Joseph STEINBERG

† Regional accreditation is carried under the parent institution in South Orange, NJ.

Somerset Christian College (D)

10 College Way, Zarephath NJ 08890-9998
County: Somerset FICE Identification: 036663
Unit ID: 440794
Telephone: (732) 356-1595 Carnegie Class: Spec/Faith
FAX Number: (732) 356-4846 Calendar System: Semester
URL: www.somerset.edu
Established: 1908 Annual Undergrad Tuition & Fees: $15,000
Enrollment: 312 Coed
Affiliation or Control: Wesleyan Church IRS Status: 501(c)3
Highest Offering: Baccalaureate
Program: Professional; Business Emphasis
Accreditation: M, BI

01 President .... Dr. David E. SCHROEDER
05 VP Academic Affairs .... Vacant
10 VP Finance and Operations .... Mrs. Elizabeth MINTZ
30 VP Institutional Advancement .... Dr. Kobie Blair MORGAN
20 Dean of the Faculty .... Dr. Beverly BUSCH
04 Executive Assistant to President .... Ms. Linda SCHMITT
06 Registrar .... Mrs. Amy HUBER
88 Director of Adult Degree Program .... Mrs. Marsha GRIFFIN
07 Director of Admissions .... Ms. Keyla GUZMAN
37 Director of Financial Aid .... Mrs. Betzi SCHROEDER
32 Director of Student Life .... Dr. Joanne NOEL

Stevens Institute of Technology (E)

Castle Point on Hudson, Hoboken NJ 07030-5991
County: Hudson FICE Identification: 002639
Unit ID: 186867
Telephone: (201) 216-5000 Carnegie Class: RU/H
FAX Number: (201) 216-8341 Calendar System: Semester
URL: www.stevens.edu
Established: 1870 Annual Undergrad Tuition & Fees: $41,782
Enrollment: 5,929 Coed
Affiliation or Control: Independent Non-Profit IRS Status: 501(c)3
Highest Offering: Doctorate
Program: Liberal Arts And General; Technical Emphasis
Accreditation: M, CS, ENG

01 President .... Dr. Nariman FARVARDIN
04 Exec Assistant to the President .... Ms. Diana COLOMBO
03 Provost/University Vice President .... Dr. George P. KORFIATIS
30 Vice Pres Development .... Mr. Edward EICHHORN
10 Vice Pres for Finance/Treasurer .... Mr. Randy GREENE
07 VP Univ Enrollment/Administration .... Dr. Maureen WEATHERALL
18 VP Facilities/Community Relations .... Mr. Henry DOBBELAAR
15 Vice President Human Resources .... Mr. Mark SAMOLEWICZ
32 Asst VP Stdnt Dev/Dir Coop Educ .... Mr. Joseph STAHLEY
13 Asst VP for Information Technology .... Mr. Eric ROSENBERG
27 AVP Mktg & Univ Communications .... Mr. Michael SCHINELLI
05 Dean Undergraduate Academics .... Mr. Larry RUSS
35 Dean of Student Life .... Mr. Kenneth NILSEN
39 Dean of Residence Life .... Ms. Trina BALLANTYNE
84 Dean of University Enrollment .... Mr. Daniel GALLAGHER
20 Assoc Dean Undergraduate Academics .... Dr. Erol CESMEBASI
29 Exec Director Alumni Association .... Miss Anita LANG
36 Director of Career Services .... Ms. Lynn INSLEY
19 Chief/Director of Security .... Mr. Timothy GRIFFIN
41 Athletic Director .... Mr. Russell ROGERS
85 Dir of Intl Student/Scholar Svcs .... Mr. Alan J. JOSS
06 Associate Registrar .... Ms. Sherra JONES
96 Director of Business Services .... Mr. James NEWMAN
37 Director Student Financial Aid .... Mr. Shawn O'NEILL
38 Director Student Counseling .... Vacant
08 Director of Library .... Ourida OUBRAHAM
40 Manager Campus Bookstore .... Ms. Teresa TRIDENTE
25 Director Sponsored Research .... Ms. Barbara DEHAVEN
58 Dean of Graduate Academics .... Dr. Charles SUFFEL
54 Dean School of Engineering & Scienc ...... Dr. Michael S. BRUNO
72 Int Dean School Technology Mgmt .... Dr. C. Timothy KOELLER
49 Dean College of Arts & Letters .... Dr. Lisa DOLLING
88 Dean School of Systems & Enterprise .... Dr. Dinesh VERMA
09 Director of Institutional Research .... Ms. Agata WOLFE
26 Chief Public Relations Officer .... Ms. Danielle WOODRUFFE

Sussex County Community College (F)

One College Hill Road, Newton NJ 07860-1146
County: Sussex FICE Identification: 025688
Unit ID: 247603
Telephone: (973) 300-2100 Carnegie Class: Assoc/Pub-S-SC
FAX Number: (973) 579-9351 Calendar System: Semester
URL: www.sussex.edu
Established: 1982 Annual Undergrad Tuition & Fees (In-District): $4,470
Enrollment: 4,122 Coed
Affiliation or Control: State/Local IRS Status: 501(c)3
Highest Offering: Associate Degree
Program: Occupational; 2-Year Principally Bachelor's Creditable
Accreditation: M, MAC, SURGT

01 President .... Dr. Paul MAZUR
04 Asst to President/Board of Trustees .... Wendy FULLEM
05 Sr VP of Academic & Student Affairs .... Harold DAMATO
10 VP of Finance and Operations .... Frank NOCELLA
16 Exec Dir of Human Res/Legal Matters .... Claudia OLIVO
26 Exec Dir of Marketing/Public Info .... Kathleen SCOTT
30 Exec Director of the Foundation .... Barbara WORTMANN
20 Sr Dean of Business/Law/Math/Scienc .... William WAITE
20 Dean of Lib Arts/Social Sci/Educati .... Dr. Marian EBERLY
24 Assoc Dean of Learning Resources .... Dr. Kathleen OKAY
20 Asst Dean of Academic Affairs .... Alberta JAEGER
103 Asst Dean of Community Ed/Workf Dev .... Kathleen NELSON
38 Asst Dean of Counseling/Fin Aid/Reg .... Deborah MCFADDEN
41 Asst Dean of Athletics/Student Affs .... John KUNTZ
21 Exec Director of Finance .... Kristine PERRY
18 Exec Dir Facilities/Campus Security .... Anthony VALENTI
13 Dir of Management Info Systems .... Craig MACKEY
88 Director of Bursar Office .... Catherine WINTERFIELD
106 Dir of Media Services/Distance Educ .... Tony SELIMO
08 Director of Library .... Stephanie COOPER
07 Director of Admissions .... Todd POLTERSDORF
88 Director of Health Sciences .... Barbara COOK
88 Director of Instructional Design .... Anthony SORRENTO
37 Director of Financial Aid .... Michael CORSO
88 Director of Accounting .... Patricia NOBLIN
09 Assoc Dir of Institutional Research .... Matthew MILLER
06 Assoc Registrar .... Solweig DIMINO
35 Assoc Dir of Student Activities .... Heidi GREGG

Talmudical Academy of New Jersey (G)

Route 524, Adelphia NJ 07710-9999
County: Monmouth FICE Identification: 011989
Unit ID: 186900
Telephone: (732) 431-1600 Carnegie Class: Spec/Faith

FAX Number: (732) 431-3951 Calendar System: Semester
Established: 1971 Annual Undergrad Tuition & Fees: $10,750
Enrollment: 60 Male
Affiliation or Control: Independent Non-Profit IRS Status: 501(c)3
Highest Offering: Baccalaureate
Program: Teacher Preparatory; Professional
Accreditation: RABN

01 President ... Mr. Charles SEMAH
05 Dean ... Rabbi Yeruchim SHAIN

Thomas Edison State College (A)

101 W State Street, Trenton NJ 08608-1176
County: Mercer FICE Identification: 021922
Unit ID: 187046
Telephone: (609) 984-1100 Carnegie Class: Master's S
FAX Number: (609) 292-9000 Calendar System: Other
URL: www.tesc.edu
Established: 1972 Annual Undergrad Tuition & Fees (In-State): $5,176
Enrollment: 20,251 Coed
Affiliation or Control: State IRS Status: 501(c)3
Highest Offering: Master's
Program: Liberal Arts And General; Professional
Accreditation: M, NUR, NURSE, TEAC

01 President ... Dr. George A. PRUITT
05 Vice President & Provost ... Mr. William J. SEATON
10 Vice President & Treasurer ... Mr. Michael J. SCHEIRING
26 Vice President Public Affairs ... Mr. John P. THURBER
45 Vice President Planning & Research ... Dr. Penelope BROUWER
84 VP Enrollment Mgmt/Learner Services ... Dr. Mary Ellen CARO
106 Vice Prov Directed Indp Adult Lrng ... Dr. Henry VAN ZYL
51 Vice Prov/Dean Watson Sch Cont Educ ... Dr. Joseph YOUNGBLOOD
88 AVP Enroll Mgmt/Strategic Partnrshp ... Ms. Sylvia HAMILTON
32 Assoc VP and Dean of Learner Svcs ... Dr. Raymond YOUNG
26 Assoc Vice President Marketing .. Ms. Marie R. POWER-BARNES
21 Associate Vice President/Treasurer ... Mr. Farouk HASSIEB
35 Asst Vice Prov Learner Services ... Mr. Dave ANDERSON
100 Chief of Staff ... Ms. Linda M. VASBINDER
101 Executive Asst to the President ... Dr. Terri T. HAMMILL
86 Dir Communications/Govt Affairs ... Ms. Robin WALTON
43 General Counsel ... Ms. Barbara KLEVA
09 Director Inst Res/Outcomes Assess ... Dr. Ann Marie SENIOR
66 Dean School of Nursing ... Dr. Susan M. O'BRIEN
49 Dean Heavin Sch of Arts & Sciences .. Dr. Susan C. DAVENPORT
50 Dean School of Business & Mgmt ... Dr. Susan GILBERT
06 Registrar ... Ms. Sharon SMITH
72 Dean School of Applied Sci/Tech ... Vacant
21 Controller ... Mr. Christopher STRINGER
13 Chief Information Officer ... Mr. Drew W. HOPKINS
88 Dir Center for Acad Program Reviews ... Vacant
07 Director Admissions ... Mr. David HOFTIEZER
16 Director Human Resources ... Ms. Mindi SHALITA
29 Director of Alumni Affairs ... Ms. Roxanne GLOBIS
37 Director of Financial Aid ... Mr. James OWENS
11 Director Administrative Services ... Ms. Mary C. HACK
21 Director Budget and Analysis ... Ms. Diane KOYE
21 Bursar ... Mr. Philip SANDERS
30 Director of Development ... Ms. Misty ISAK
102 Director Corporate/Foundation Rels ... Mr. Frederick BRAND
88 Dir Military & Veteran Education ... Mr. Louis MARTINI
27 Director of Communications ... Mr. Joseph GUZZARDO
08 State Librarian ... Ms. Norma E. BLAKE
88 ADA Coordinator ... Ms. Barbara AIKENS
105 Director Website & Multimedia Produ .... Mr. Jeffery LUSHBAUGH
88 Director of Advancement Services ... Ms. Erica SPIZZIRRRI
44 Asc Dir Annual Fund/Donor Relations ... Ms. Jennifer GUERRERO
88 Executive Director Watson Institute ... Ms. Barbara JOHNSON
88 Director Instr Design & Course Dev ... Mr. Matthew COOPER
88 Director of Outcomes Assessment ... Ms. Cynthia MACMILLAN

Union County College (B)

1033 Springfield Avenue, Cranford NJ 07016-1598
County: Union FICE Identification: 002643
Unit ID: 187198
Telephone: (908) 709-7000 Carnegie Class: Assoc/Pub-S-MC
FAX Number: (908) 709-0527 Calendar System: Semester
URL: www.ucc.edu
Established: 1933 Annual Undergrad Tuition & Fees (In-District): $431,7.5
Enrollment: 12,774 Coed
Affiliation or Control: State/Local IRS Status: 501(c)3
Highest Offering: Associate Degree
Program: Occupational; 2-Year Principally Bachelor's Creditable
Accreditation: M, PNUR, PTAA

01 President ... Dr. Margaret M. MCMENAMIN
05 Vice President Academic Affairs ... Dr. Maris LOWN
10 Vice Pres Financial Affs/Treasurer ... Mr. Bernard LENIHAN
32 Vice President Student Services ... Dr. Ralph FORD
11 Vice Pres Administrative Services ... Dr. Stephen NACCO
12 Provost Elizabeth Campus ... Dr. Barbara GABA
12 Provost Plainfield Campus ... Dr. Negar FARAKISH
84 Dean of Enrollment Management ... Mr. David SHERIDAN
26 Exec Director College Relations ... Ms. Ellen DOTTO
13 Director of Information Tech ... Mr. Thomas CHERUBINO
06 Dir Admissions/Records/Registrar ... Ms. Joann DAVIS-WAYNE
08 Acting Director Libraries ... Ms. Dena LEITER
38 Director of Counseling ... Vacant
37 Director of Financial Aid ... Ms. Evelyn BLATT
21 Director of Student Accounts ... Mr. Larry GOLDMAN
51 Dean Continuing Educ/Econ Dev ... Vacant
09 Exec Dir Assessment Plng & Research ... Dr. Patricia S. BIDDAR
15 Dir Human Res/Purch/Aux Enterpr ... Mr. Robert A. WEAKLEY
18 Director Facilities ... Mr. Henry KEY
45 Director Resource Development ... Ms. Barbara GAVIN-WILLIAMS
102 Executive Director Foundation ... Mr. Michael DRISCOLL
20 Director Academic Testing ... Mr. Douglas GREENWOOD
28 Director EOF ... Ms. Sharon JOHNSON
41 Acting Director Athletics ... Ms. Tamalea SMITH
19 Director Public Safety ... Vacant
24 Director Media Technologies ... Mr. Stephen KATO
20 Director Academic Learning Center ... Ms. Gail HEIN
21 Controller ... Ms. Lynne WELCH
96 Director of Purchasing ... Ms. Sandra AULD
40 Manager Bookstore ... Mr. Carl BRUSS
44 Coordinator Annual Giving ... Vacant

*University of Medicine and Dentistry of New Jersey (C)

65 Bergen Street, Newark NJ 07101-1709
County: Essex FICE Identification: 010394
Unit ID: 187222
Telephone: (973) 972-4400 Carnegie Class: N/A
FAX Number: (973) 972-4429
URL: www.umdnj.edu

01 President ... Dr. William F. OWEN, JR.
05 Exec VP Academic/Clinical Affairs ... Dr. Denise V. RODGERS
10 University Chief Financial Officer ... Vacant
43 Senior Vice Pres/General Counsel ... Mr. Lester ARON
30 Sr VP Univ Advancemt\Communication ... Ms. Diane WEATHERS
10 Senior Vice President for Finance ... Ms. Denise MULKERN
11 Sr VP Admin/Pres & CEO/UBHC ... Mr. Christopher O. KOSSEFF
86 Sr VP Gov and Community Affairs ... Ms. Julane MILLER-ARMBRISTER
88 Sr VP Chief Ethics & Compliance ... Mr. Bret S. BISSEY
100 Chief of Staff ... Mr. James ROWAN, JR.
88 VP Academic & Clinical Initiatives ... Vacant
21 Vice President Finance/Treasurer ... Mr. Francis X. COLFORD
17 Acting Pres/CEO University Hosp ... Ms. Robin WITTENSTEIN
15 Acting VP Human Resources ... Mr. Gerard GARCIA
88 Vice Pres Supply Chain Management ... Mr. Thomas W. KENYON, JR.
20 VP for Academic Affairs ... Ms. Freda ZACKIN
46 Vice President Research ... Dr. Kathleen W. SCOTTO
13 VP for IS&T ... Ms. Denise ROMANO
88 VP Investigations Group ... Mr. Neil SCHORR
102 Vice Chairman/CEO UMDNJ Foundation ... Dr. George F. HEINRICH
102 Pres & COO UMDNJ Foundation ... Mr. James M. GOLUBIESKI
22 Assoc VP Workplace Diversity ... Ms. Catherine M. BOLDER
08 Assoc VP Scholarly Resour/Univ Lib ... Ms. Judith S. COHN
51 Assoc VP/CEO Continuing Education ... Vacant
18 Executive Director of Construction ... Mr. David C. SCHULZ
96 Asst VP Supplier Diversity/Vendors ... Ms. Ernestine WATSON
09 Exec Dir Faculty Affairs/Inst Rsch ... Dr. Sheila EDER
06 University Registrar ... Ms. Susan E. NELSON
37 Director University Financial Aid ... Ms. Elaine P. VARAS
19 Director Public Safety ... Mr. Carmelo V. HUERTAS

*UMDNJ-New Jersey Dental School (D)

110 Bergen Street, Room B-830, Newark NJ 07101-1709
County: Essex FICE Identification: 024635
Telephone: (973) 972-4633 Carnegie Class: Not Classified
FAX Number: (973) 972-3689 Calendar System: Semester
URL: dentalschool.umdnj.edu/
Established: 1954 Annual Graduate Tuition & Fees: N/A
Enrollment: 481 Coed
Affiliation or Control: State IRS Status: 501(c)3
Highest Offering: First Professional Degree; No Undergraduates
Program: Professional
Accreditation: &M, DENT

02 Dean ... Dr. Cecile A. FELDMAN
05 Interim Assoc Dean Academic Affairs ... Dr. Kim FENESY
32 Assoc Dean Student Affairs ... Dr. Kim E. FENESY
46 Acting Associate Dean Research ... Dr. Barbara L. GREENBERG
11 Assoc Dean Administration/Finance ... Vacant
17 Assoc Dean Clinical Affairs ... Dr. Michael CONTE
07 Acting Dir Predoc Admiss & Recruit ... Dr. Rosa M. CHAVIANO-MORAN
84 Dir Enrollment/Student Services ... Ms. Joanne LAMETTA

*UMDNJ-Graduate School of Biomedical Sciences (E)

185 South Orange Avenue, MSB C-696, Newark NJ 07107-1709
County: Essex FICE Identification: 011174
Telephone: (973) 972-5332 Carnegie Class: Not Classified
FAX Number: (973) 972-7148 Calendar System: Semester
URL: gsbs.umdnj.edu/
Established: 1970 Annual Undergrad Tuition & Fees (In-State): N/A
Enrollment: 1,262 Coed
Affiliation or Control: State IRS Status: 501(c)3
Highest Offering: Doctorate
Program: Professional
Accreditation: &M

02 Interim Dean ... Dr. Kathleen W. SCOTTO
12 Senior Associate Dean NJMS ... Dr. Andrew P. THOMAS
12 Senior Associate Dean RWJMS ... Dr. Terri G. KINZY
12 Senior Associate Dean SOM ... Dr. Carl E. HOCK
06 Manager ... Ms. Barbara COLEMAN-LEE
04 Exec Asst to the Interim Dean ... Ms. Susan M. LOMANTO

*UMDNJ-New Jersey Medical School (F)

185 S Orange Avenue, Newark NJ 07101-1709
County: Essex FICE Identification: 002620
Telephone: (973) 972-4538 Carnegie Class: Not Classified
FAX Number: (973) 972-7104 Calendar System: Semester
URL: njms.umdnj.edu/
Established: 1954 Annual Undergrad Tuition & Fees (In-State): N/A
Enrollment: 754 Coed
Affiliation or Control: State IRS Status: 501(c)3
Highest Offering: First Professional Degree; No Lower Division
Program: Professional
Accreditation: &M, MED

02 Dean ... Dr. Robert L. JOHNSON
05 Vice Dean ... Dr. Maria L. SOTO-GREENE
17 Sr Assoc Dean Clinical Affairs ... Dr. Kendell R. SPROTT
10 Associate Dean/CFO ... Mr. David L. ROE
46 Senior Associate Dean Research ... Dr. William C. GAUSE
32 Assoc Dean Student Affairs ... Dr. James M. HILL
07 Assoc Dean Admissions/Special Pgms ... Dr. George F. HEINRICH
35 Assistant Dean Student Affairs ... Ms. Julie FERGUSON
21 Business Manager ... Mr. Ron JENKINS

*UMDNJ-Robert Wood Johnson Medical School (G)

675 Hoes Lane, Piscataway NJ 08854-5635
County: Middlesex FICE Identification: 024549
Telephone: (732) 235-6300 Carnegie Class: Not Classified
FAX Number: (732) 235-6315 Calendar System: Semester
URL: rwjms.umdnj.edu/
Established: 1962 Annual Undergrad Tuition & Fees (In-State): N/A
Enrollment: 665 Coed
Affiliation or Control: State IRS Status: 501(c)3
Highest Offering: First Professional Degree
Program: Professional
Accreditation: &M, IPSY, MED

02 Dean ... Dr. Peter S. AMENTA
05 Senior Associate Dean Education ... Vacant
88 Senior Assoc Dean Community Health ... Dr. Eric G. JAHN
46 Interim Senior Assoc Dean Research ... Dr. Terri KINZY
17 Sr Assoc Dean Clinical Aff ... Dr. Anthony T. SCARDELLA
32 Assoc Dean Student Affairs ... Dr. David SEIDEN
07 Associate Dean Admissions ... Dr. Carol A. TERREGINO
11 Chief Operating Officer ... Ms. Alice LUSTIG
06 Registrar ... Mr. Daniel OSTIN

*UMDNJ-School of Nursing (H)

65 Bergen Street, Room 1126, Newark NJ 07101-1709
County: Essex Identification: 666970
Telephone: (973) 972-4276 Carnegie Class: Not Classified
FAX Number: (973) 972-3225 Calendar System: Semester
URL: sn.umdnj.edu/
Established: 1992 Annual Undergrad Tuition & Fees (In-State): N/A
Enrollment: 1,390 Coed
Affiliation or Control: State IRS Status: 501(c)3
Highest Offering: Doctorate
Program: Nursing Emphasis
Accreditation: &M, ANEST, MIDWF, NUR

02 Dean ... Dr. Susan W. SALMOND
46 Associate Dean Research ... Vacant
05 Associate Dean For Academic Affairs ... Dr. Marie T. O'TOOLE
31 Assoc Dean Community/Clinical Affs ... Vacant
11 Assistant Dean for Administration ... Ms. Wendy A. RITCH
17 Assistant Dean Clinical Affairs ... Mr. David W. UNKLE
32 Assistant Dean for Student Affairs ... Dr. Donna CILL
58 Assistant Dean Graduate Studies ... Dr. Patricia K. KINDIN
12 Associate Dean Stratford Campus ... Dr. Marie T. O'TOOLE
88 Asst Dean Pre-Licensure Programs ... Vacant
06 Registrar ... Ms. Bianca THOMPSON

*UMDNJ-School of Osteopathic Medicine (I)

One Medical Center Drive, Stratford NJ 08084-1501
County: Camden FICE Identification: 024540
Telephone: (856) 566-6764 Carnegie Class: Not Classified
FAX Number: (856) 566-6895 Calendar System: Semester
URL: som.umdnj.edu/
Established: 1976 Annual Undergrad Tuition & Fees (In-State): N/A
Enrollment: 510 Coed
Affiliation or Control: State IRS Status: 501(c)3
Highest Offering: First Professional Degree
Program: Professional
Accreditation: &M, OSTEO

02 Dean ... Dr. Thomas A. CAVALIERI
11 Chief Operating Officer ... Ms. Vivian LUBIN

10 Chief Financial Officer .... Mr. Robert J. SCHIERI
05 Assoc Dean Academic Affairs .... Dr. Paul M. KRUEGER
17 Assoc Dean Clinical Affairs .... Dr. Vincent J. DERISIO
46 Assoc Dean Research .... Dr. Carl E. HOCK
32 Assistant Dean Student Affairs .... Dr. Kathryn C. LAMBERT
06 Associate Registrar .... Ms. Regina WILMES

*UMDNJ-School of Public Health (A)

683 Hoes Lane W, Room 235, Piscataway NJ 08854-8021
County: Middlesex — Identification: 666991
Telephone: (732) 445-9700 — Carnegie Class: Not Classified
FAX Number: (732) 445-9755 — Calendar System: Semester
URL: sph.umdnj.edu/
Established: 1998 — Annual Undergrad Tuition & Fees (In-State): N/A
Enrollment: 380 — Coed
Affiliation or Control: State — IRS Status: 501(c)3
Highest Offering: Doctorate
Program: Professional
Accreditation: &M, PH

02 Interim Dean .... Dr. George RHOADS
12 Associate Dean Pisc/NB .... Dr. Pamela STRICKLAND
12 Associate Dean Newark .... Dr. Lois A. GRAU
12 Asst Dean Stratford/Camden .... Dr. Bernadette WEST
05 Assoc Dean Acad and Faculty Affairs .... Dr. Alan C. MONHEIT
46 Associate Dean Research .... Dr. Patrick CLIFFORD
32 Asst Dean Student/Alumni Affairs .... Dr. Shou-En LU
10 Business Manager .... Mr. Alexander ZAROS
06 Assistant Registrar .... Ms. Vanessa J. JAGO

*UMDNJ-School of Health Related Professions (B)

65 Bergen Street, Room 149, Newark NJ 07101-1709
County: Essex — FICE Identification: 020668
Telephone: (973) 972-5454 — Carnegie Class: Not Classified
FAX Number: (973) 972-7028 — Calendar System: Semester
URL: shrp.umdnj.edu/
Established: 1976 — Annual Undergrad Tuition & Fees (In-State): N/A
Enrollment: 1,467 — Coed
Affiliation or Control: State — IRS Status: 501(c)3
Highest Offering: Doctorate
Program: Professional
Accreditation: &M, ARCPA, CACREP, CORE, CVT, CYTO, DA, DH, DIETC, DIETI, DMS, MIDWF, MT, NMT, PTA

02 Interim Dean .... Dr. Julie O'SULLIVAN-MAILLET
11 Assoc Dean Administrative Service .... Dr. Gwendolyn MAHON
05 Interim Assoc Dean Academic Affairs .... Dr. Ann W. TUCKER
12 Assoc Dean Southern New Jersey .... Dr. Ann W. TUCKER
12 Administrator Scotch Plains .... Mr. Vernon CABALFIN
32 Assoc Dean Acad & Student Services .... Vacant
46 Interim Associate Dean for Research .... Dr. Robert M. DENMARK
06 Registrar .... Ms. Bianca THOMPSON

Warren County Community College (C)

475 Route 57 W, Washington NJ 07882-4343
County: Warren — FICE Identification: 025039
Unit ID: 245625
Telephone: (908) 835-9222 — Carnegie Class: Assoc/Pub-S-SC
FAX Number: (908) 689-9262 — Calendar System: Semester
URL: www.warren.edu
Established: 1981 — Annual Undergrad Tuition & Fees (In-District): $3,900
Enrollment: 2,338 — Coed
Affiliation or Control: State/Local — IRS Status: 501(c)3
Highest Offering: Associate Degree
Program: Occupational; 2-Year Principally Bachelor's Creditable
Accreditation: M, ADNUR, MAC

01 President .... Dr. William AUSTIN
05 Vice Pres Academics/Student Svcs .... Dr. Lisa SUMMINS
10 Vice Pres Finance & Operations .... Ms. Barbara PRATT
51 Vice Pres Corporate/Continuing Educ .... Ms. Eve AZAR
11 Dean of Administration .... Mr. Dennis FLORENTINE
08 Director of Library/CIO .... Mr. David ORENSTEIN
37 Director of Financial Aid .... Ms. Jessica LEEPER
32 Asst Dean of Academic & Stdnt Svcs .... Mr. Jeremy BEELER
09 Dir Inst Rsrch/Plng/Assessment .... Mr. Lamont ROUSE
15 Director Human Resources .... Ms. Sharon HINTZ
35 Director Student Activities .... Ms. Rose LYNCH
21 Director Business Services .... Mr. Jay ALEXANDER
13 Information Technology .... Mr. Jeff CAROLLA
36 Coord Stdnt Acad Outcomes/Success .... Ms. Fae GUERIN
07 Coord Stdnt Recruit/Acad Admissions .... Ms. Laurel ATTANASIO

William Paterson University of New Jersey (D)

300 Pompton Road, Wayne NJ 07470-2152
County: Passaic — FICE Identification: 002625
Unit ID: 187444
Telephone: (973) 720-2000 — Carnegie Class: Master's L
FAX Number: (973) 720-2399 — Calendar System: Semester
URL: www.wpunj.edu
Established: 1855 — Annual Undergrad Tuition & Fees (In-State): $11,464
Enrollment: 11,361 — Coed
Affiliation or Control: State — IRS Status: 501(c)3
Highest Offering: Doctorate
Program: Liberal Arts And General; Teacher Preparatory; Professional
Accreditation: M, ART, BUS, CACREP, CS, MUS, NURSE, SP, TED

01 President .... Dr. Kathleen WALDRON
05 Senior Vice President/Provost .... Dr. Edward WEIL
101 Chf of Staff to Pres/Board of Trust .... Dr. Robert SEAL
11 Vice Pres Administration/Finance .... Mr. Stephen BOLYAI
30 Vice Pres Institutional Advancement .... Ms. Pamela FERGUSON
32 Vice President Student Development .... Dr. John MARTONE
84 VP of Enrollment Management .... Ms. Kristin COHEN
58 Assoc VP Acad Affs/Dean Grad Stds .... Dr. Nina JEMMOTT
21 Assoc VP for Administration .... Mr. Richard STOMBER
26 Assoc VP Mkting & Public Relations .... Mr. Stuart GOLDSTEIN
16 Associate Vice Pres Human Resources .... Mr. John POLDING
08 Assoc VP Library Services/Info Tech .... Vacant
35 Associate VP for Campus Life .... Mr. Roland WATTS
19 Dir Public Safety & Univ Police .... Mr. Robert FULLEMAN
35 Asst Vice Pres for Campus Life .... Mr. Francisco DIAZ
35 Assoc VP/Dean Student Development .... Dr. Glen SHERMAN
60 Acting Dean Col Arts/Comm .... Dr. Stephen HAHN
53 Dean College of Education .... Dr. Candace BURNS
66 Dean College of Science & Health .... Dr. Sandra DEYOUNG
79 Dean Human & Social Science .... Dr. Kara M. RABBITT
50 Dean College of Business .... Dr. Sam N. BASU
08 Dean D & L Cheng Library .... Dr. Anne CILIBERTI
21 Assoc VP Finance & Comptroller .... Ms. Rosemarie GENCO
28 Dir Employment Equity & Diversity .... Mr. John SIMS
46 Exec Director Academic Development .... Ms. Janet DAVIS-DUKES
51 Exec Dir Cont Educ/Distance Lrng .... Ms. Bernadette TIERNAN
20 Associate Provost .... Dr. Stephen HAHN
26 Director External Relations .... Mr. Patrick DEDEO
29 Executive Director Alumni .... Ms. Janis SCHWARTZ
45 Director Inst Research & Assessment .... Dr. Jane ZEFF
13 Chief Information Officer .... Mr. Leonard BOGDON
15 Director of Human Resources .... Ms. Denise ROBINSON-LEWIS
07 Director of Undergrad Admissions .... Ms. Colleen M. O'CONNOR
37 Director Financial Aid .... Ms. Elizabeth RIQUEZ
06 Registrar .... Ms. Nina TRELISKY
41 Director Athletics .... Ms. Sabrina GRANT
36 Director of Career Dev & Advisement .... Ms. Sharon ROSENGART
39 Director of Residence Life .... Mr. Joseph CAFFARELLI
23 Director Health & Wellness Center .... Dr. Eileen LUBECK
90 Director Instruction/Research Tech .... Dr. Sandra MILLER
09 Dir Institutional Research/Assess .... Dr. Jane ZEFF
40 Director Bookstore .... Mr. Scott DUNLAP
27 Director Public Information .... Ms. Mary Beth ZEMAN
24 Head Audio Visual-Library .... Ms. Jane HUTCHISON
18 Director Capital Plng/Design/Constr .... Vacant
85 Director International Student Svcs .... Ms. Cinzia RICHARDSON
94 Director of Women's Center .... Ms. Librada SANCHEZ
96 Director of Purchasing .... Mr. Lirse JONES
38 Director Student Counseling .... Dr. Eileen LUBECK
89 Director of Freshmen Studies .... Dr. Kim DANIEL-ROBINSON
92 Director of Honors College .... Dr. Susan DINAN

Yeshiva Gedolah Zichron Leyma (E)

1000 Orchard Terrace, Linden NJ 07036
County: Union — Identification: 667078
Telephone: (908) 587-0502 — Carnegie Class: Not Classified
FAX Number: N/A — Calendar System: Semester
Established: 1999 — Annual Undergrad Tuition & Fees: $10,000
Enrollment: 52 — Male
Affiliation or Control: Independent Non-Profit — IRS Status: 501(c)3
Highest Offering: First Talmudic Degree
Program: Professional
Accreditation: RABN

Yeshiva Toras Chaim (F)

1027 Ridge Avenue, Lakewood NJ 08701-2120
County: Ocean — FICE Identification: 041311
Unit ID: 451398
Telephone: (732) 414-2834 — Carnegie Class: Spec/Faith
FAX Number: (732) 358-0220 — Calendar System: Semester
Established: 2000 — Annual Undergrad Tuition & Fees: $11,650
Enrollment: 167 — Male
Affiliation or Control: Independent Non-Profit — IRS Status: 501(c)3
Highest Offering: Baccalaureate
Program: Teacher Preparatory; Professional
Accreditation: RABN

05 Chief Academic Officer .... Rabbi Mendel SLOMOVITS
06 Registrar .... Mrs. Devoiry DURST
21 Bookkeeper .... Mrs. Rachel REINER

Yeshivas Be'er Yitzchok (G)

1391 North Avenue, Elizabeth NJ 07208-2480
County: Union — FICE Identification: 041234
Unit ID: 451370
Telephone: (908) 354-6057 — Carnegie Class: Spec/Faith
FAX Number: (908) 820-0431 — Calendar System: Semester
Established: 1999 — Annual Undergrad Tuition & Fees: $11,000
Enrollment: 53 — Male
Affiliation or Control: Independent Non-Profit — IRS Status: 501(c)3
Highest Offering: Baccalaureate
Program: Professional
Accreditation: RABN

01 Chief Executive Officer .... Rabbi Avrohom SCHULMAN
37 Director of Student Financial Aid .... Rabbi Meyer RUBIN
11 Chief of Administration .... Chani MILLER

NEW MEXICO

Brookline College (H)

4201 Central Avenue NW Ste J, Albuquerque NM 87105-1649
County: Bernalillo — Identification: 666724
Unit ID: 444088
Telephone: (505) 880-2877 — Carnegie Class: Not Classified
FAX Number: (505) 352-0199 — Calendar System: Other
URL: www.brooklinecollege.edu
Established: 1979 — Annual Undergrad Tuition & Fees: $13,750
Enrollment: 599 — Coed
Affiliation or Control: Proprietary — IRS Status: Proprietary
Highest Offering: Baccalaureate
Program: Occupational; Liberal Arts And General
Accreditation: ACICS

01 Campus Director .... Mr. Andrew WEBB
05 Director of Education .... Mr. David GOULD

† Branch campus of Brookline College, Phoenix, AZ

Carrington College - Albuquerque (I)

1001 Menaul Boulevard NE, Albuquerque NM 87107-1642
County: Bernalillo — Identification: 666014
Unit ID: 442602
Telephone: (505) 254-7777 — Carnegie Class: Not Classified
FAX Number: (505) 254-1101 — Calendar System: Other
URL: www.apollocollege.com
Established: 1976 — Annual Undergrad Tuition & Fees: $13,295
Enrollment: 1,116 — Coed
Affiliation or Control: Proprietary — IRS Status: Proprietary
Highest Offering: Associate Degree
Program: Occupational; 2-Year Principally Bachelor's Creditable
Accreditation: ACICS, @PTAA

01 Executive Campus Director .... Mr. Mark E. LUCERO

† Branch campus of Carrington College, Phoenix, AZ.

Central New Mexico Community College (J)

525 Buena Vista, SE, Albuquerque NM 87106-4096
County: Bernalillo — FICE Identification: 004742
Unit ID: 187532
Telephone: (505) 224-4412 — Carnegie Class: Assoc/Pub-U-MC
FAX Number: (505) 224-4417 — Calendar System: Semester
URL: www.cnm.edu
Established: 1965 — Annual Undergrad Tuition & Fees (In-District): $1,857
Enrollment: 29,948 — Coed
Affiliation or Control: State/Local — IRS Status: 501(c)3
Highest Offering: Associate Degree
Program: 2-Year Principally Bachelor's Creditable
Accreditation: NH, ACBSP, ACFEI, ADNUR, CONST, DA, DMS, EMT, MLTAD, PNUR, SURGT

01 President .... Dr. Katharine W. WINOGRAD
05 Vice President for Academic Affairs .... Mrs. Beth PITONZO
11 Vice President Administrative Svcs .... Mr. Robert BROWN
35 Vice President for Student Services .... Mr. Phillip BUSTOS
10 Vice Pres for Finance & Operations .... Mrs. Katherine ULIBARRI
84 Assoc Vice Pres Enrollment Mgmt .... Mr. Eugene PADILLA
08 Director Learning Resources .... Ms. Xeturah WOODLEY
23 Director Student Health Center .... Ms. Marti BRITTENHAM
19 Director Security .... Mr. Ernest CHAVEZ
13 Director Info Technology Services .... Mr. Joe GIERI
103 Director Workforce Training Center .... Ms. Evelyn DOW-SIMPSON
36 Director of Job Connection Center .... Ms. Tammy STRICKLER
30 Director of Development .... Mrs. Lisa MCCULLOCH
07 Director Enrollment Services .... Ms. Jane E. CAMPBELL
26 Dir Marketing & Public Relations .... Ms. Alexis KERSCHNER
27 Dir Communications & Media Relation .... Mr. Brad MOORE
37 Director Student Financial Aid .... Mr. Lee CARRILLO
15 Director Human Resources .... Mrs. Carol ADLER
81 Dean School of Math/Sci/Engineering .... Mr. Richard CALABRO
50 Dean School of Bus/Info Technology .... Mr. Sydney GUNTHORPE
72 Dean School of Applied Technologies .... Ms. Diane BURKE
53 Dean School of Adult & General Edu .... Dr. Pam ETRE-PEREZ
83 InterimDean Comm/Humanities/Soc Sci .... Ms. Xeturah WOODLEY
76 Dean Health/Wellness/Public Safety .... Mr. Nicholas SPEZZA
06 Registrar .... Ms. Yvonne MARTINEZ
18 Exec Dir Facilities/Physical Plant .... Mr. Luis CAMPOS
21 Comptroller .... Mr. Martin SERNA
29 Director of Alumni Relations .... Mrs. Anna SANCHEZ
32 Dean of Student Services .... Mr. Rudy GARCIA
38 Director of Student Counseling .... Ms. Tammy STRICKLER
96 Director of Purchasing .... Mrs. Charlotte GENSLER

Clovis Community College (K)

417 Schepps Boulevard, Clovis NM 88101-8381
County: Curry — FICE Identification: 004743
Unit ID: 187639
Telephone: (575) 769-2811 — Carnegie Class: Assoc/Pub-R-M
FAX Number: (575) 769-4190 — Calendar System: Semester
URL: www.clovis.edu
Established: 1971 — Annual Undergrad Tuition & Fees (In-State): $936
Enrollment: 4,175 — Coed
Affiliation or Control: State — IRS Status: 501(c)3

Highest Offering: Associate Degree
Program: Occupational; 2-Year Principally Bachelor's Creditable
Accreditation: **NH**, ADNUR, RAD

01 President — Dr. Becky ROWLEY
03 Executive Vice President — Dr. Robin JONES
10 Vice President Finance — Mrs. Theresa FOX
05 Chief Academic Officer — Dr. Becky K. ROWLEY
13 VP of Information Technology — Vacant
09 Vice Pres Instl Effectiveness — Vacant
32 Dean of Student Services — Dr. Michelle SCHMIDT
21 Director of Business Affairs — Ms. Jayne CRAIG
07 Dir Admissions/Records/Registrar — Ms. Rosie CORRIE
37 Director of Financial Aid — Ms. April CHAVEZ
08 Director Library/Learning Resources — Ms. Deborah ANDERSON
40 Bookstore Manager — Mrs. Jacque OCHS
35 Dir Center for Student Success — Mrs. Mona Lee NORMAN-ARMSTRONG
38 Dir of Counseling/Testing/Advisemnt — Mrs. Bonnie MILLER
15 Director of Human Resource Services — Mrs. Rhonda JESKO
88 Director Small Business Development — Mrs. Sandra TAYLOR-SAWYER
91 Director of Administrative Info Sys — Ms. Teresa WHITEHEAD
86 Exec Dir Business/Government Rels — Mr. Tom DRAKE
103 Director Workforce Training Center — Vacant
75 Director Vocational Pgm/TCC — Mrs. Jean MORROW
36 Director Student Placement — Vacant
30 Chief Development Officer — Ms. Stephanie SPENCER
18 Director of Physical Plant — Ms. Brenda DIXON
26 Director of Marketing/Cmty Rels — Ms. Lisa SPENCER
76 Dean of Allied Health Programs — Dr. Robin JONES
83 Div Chair Soc/Behav Sci/Humanities — Mr. Paul NAGY
50 Div Chair of Business Admin & Tech — Mrs. Becky CARRUTHERS
81 Division Chair of Math/Science — Mr. Larry POWELL

Eastern New Mexico University Main Campus (A)

1500 S Avenue K, Portales NM 88130-7400
County: Roosevelt — FICE Identification: 002651
Unit ID: 187648
Telephone: (575) 562-1011 — Carnegie Class: Master's S
FAX Number: (575) 562-2256 — Calendar System: Semester
URL: www.enmu.edu
Established: 1927 — Annual Undergrad Tuition & Fees (In-State): $4,147
Enrollment: 5,080 — Coed
Affiliation or Control: State — IRS Status: 501(c)3
Highest Offering: Master's
Program: Liberal Arts And General; Teacher Preparatory
Accreditation: **NH**, ACBSP, MUS, NUR, SP, SW, TED

01 President — Dr. Steven GAMBLE
05 Vice President Academic Affairs — Dr. Jamie LAURENZ
10 Vice President Business Affairs — Mr. Scott SMART
32 Vice President for Student Affairs — Dr. Judith HAISLETT
26 VP University Relations/Enroll Svcs — Ms. Ronnie BIRDSONG
45 Exec Dir Planning/Analysis/Inst Ren — Dr. Patrice CALDWELL
20 Asst Vice Pres for Academic Affairs — Dr. Renee NEELY
20 Asst Vice Pres Academic Affairs — Dr. John MONTGOMERY
21 Comptroller — Mrs. Kathy KNOLL
53 Dean Education/Technology — Dr. Jerry HARMON
50 Interim Dean Business — Dr. Christopher TAYLOR
57 Dean Fine Arts — Dr. Joseph KLINE
49 Dean Liberal Arts & Science — Dr. Mary AYALA
58 Dean Graduate School — Dr. Linda WEEMS
22 Affirmative Action Officer — Ms. Teresa VILLANUEVA
08 Director of Library — Ms. Melveta WALKER
06 Registrar — Ms. Crystal CREEKMORE
37 Director Student Financial Aid — Mr. Brent SMALL
07 Director Enrollment Services — Mr. Cody SPITZ
30 Director Development — Ms. Noelle BARTL
13 Dir Computing/Information Mgmt — Mr. Clark ELSWICK
15 Director of Human Resources — Vacant
88 Director of Broadcasting — Mr. Duane RYAN
18 Director Physical Plant — Mr. Ted FARES
41 Athletic Director — Dr. Jeff GEISER
19 Chief of University Police — Mr. Brad MAULDIN
23 Director of Health Services — Vacant
36 Dir Counseling Ctr/Career Svcs — Ms. Susan LARSON
39 Director Student Housing — Mr. Steven ESTOCK
09 Assoc Dir Institutional Research — Ms. Amy HOLT
96 Director of Purchasing — Ms. Jane BLAKELEY
27 Director of Publications — Vacant
29 Coordinator of Alumni — Vacant
56 Dir of Distance Learning/Outreach — Ms. Trish MAGUIRE
25 Director Grant Activities — Ms. Jo LANEY
84 Director Enrollment Management — Ms. Ronnie BIRDSONG
38 Director Student Counseling — Ms. Susan LARSON
35 Director Campus Life — Ms. Barbara JAMES

Eastern New Mexico University-Roswell (B)

PO Box 6000, Roswell NM 88202-6000
County: Chaves — FICE Identification: 002661
Unit ID: 187666
Telephone: (575) 624-7000 — Carnegie Class: Assoc/Pub2in4
FAX Number: (575) 624-7119 — Calendar System: Semester
URL: www.roswell.enmu.edu
Established: 1958 — Annual Undergrad Tuition & Fees (In-State): $1,339
Enrollment: 4,374 — Coed
Affiliation or Control: State — IRS Status: 501(c)3
Highest Offering: Associate Degree
Program: Occupational; 2-Year Principally Bachelor's Creditable
Accreditation: **NH**, ADNUR, DH, EMT, MAC, OTA

01 President — Dr. John MADDEN
05 Provost Academic/Stdnt Affs — Dr. Martyn CLAY
10 VP for Business Affairs — Mr. Eric JOHNSTON-ORTIZ
32 VP for Student Affairs — Mr. Robert BOWMAN
20 Asst VP for Academic Affairs — Ms. Cherryl KILNESS
20 Asst VP for Academic Affairs/CTE — Ms. Dusty MANION
21 Controller — Ms. Karen FRANKLIN
35 Asst VP for Student Affairs — Mr. Mike MARTINEZ
08 Director Learning Resource Center — Mr. Rollah ASTON
37 Director Financial Aid — Ms. Jessie SJUE
30 Director College Development — Ms. Donna ORACION
07 Director Admissions and Records — Ms. Lilia QUEZADA
13 Director of Computer Services — Mr. Tillman CROCKER
15 Director of Human Resources — Dr. Steve CHAMBERS
18 Director of Physical Plant — Mr. Darryl WARD
19 Director of Security — Mr. Robert NEWBERRY
96 Director of Purchasing — Ms. Roberta BRUCE
09 Institutional Research Professional — Ms. Rhonda CROCKER

Institute of American Indian and Alaska Native Culture and Arts Development (C)

83 Avan Nu Po Road, Santa Fe NM 87508-1300
County: Santa Fe — FICE Identification: 021464
Unit ID: 187745
Telephone: (505) 424-2300 — Carnegie Class: Tribal
FAX Number: (505) 424-3900 — Calendar System: Semester
URL: www.iaia.edu
Established: 1962 — Annual Undergrad Tuition & Fees: $2,840
Enrollment: 325 — Coed
Affiliation or Control: Federal — IRS Status: 501(c)3
Highest Offering: Baccalaureate
Program: Fine Arts Emphasis
Accreditation: **NH**, ART

01 President — Dr. Robert MARTIN
05 Dean Instruct Ctr Art & Cult Stds — Dr. Ann FILEMYR
32 Dean of Student Life — Ms. Carmen HENAN
08 Director of Library Programs — Ms. Sarah KOSTELECKY
10 Dir of Finance & Administration — Mr. David RIVARD
26 Communications/Marketing Dir — Ms. Staci GOLAR
84 Dir Admission/Records/Enroll Mgmt — Mr. Nena MARTINEZ ANAYA
30 Dir of Institutional Advancement — Ms. Kirsten JASNA
37 Director of Financial Aid — Ms. LaLa GALLEGOS
18 Facilities Management — Mr. David AIGNER
15 Human Resources Director — Ms. Maria HIDALGO
44 Deputy Director Development — Ms. Susan CROW

ITT Technical Institute (D)

5100 Masthead Street NE, Albuquerque NM 87109-4366
County: Bernalillo — Identification: 666545
Unit ID: 369084
Telephone: (505) 828-1114 — Carnegie Class: Spec/Tech
FAX Number: (505) 828-1849 — Calendar System: Quarter
URL: www.itt-tech.edu
Established: 1989 — Annual Undergrad Tuition & Fees: N/A
Enrollment: 934 — Coed
Affiliation or Control: Proprietary — IRS Status: Proprietary
Highest Offering: Baccalaureate
Program: Technical Emphasis
Accreditation: **ACICS**

† Branch campus of ITT Technical Institute, Phoenix, AZ.

Luna Community College (E)

366 Luna Drive, Las Vegas NM 87701-1510
County: San Miguel — FICE Identification: 009962
Unit ID: 363633
Telephone: (505) 454-2500 — Carnegie Class: Assoc/Pub-R-M
FAX Number: (505) 454-2519 — Calendar System: Semester
URL: www.luna.cc.nm.us
Established: 1970 — Annual Undergrad Tuition & Fees (In-District): $960
Enrollment: 2,379 — Coed
Affiliation or Control: State/Local — IRS Status: 501(c)3
Highest Offering: Associate Degree
Program: Occupational; Liberal Arts And General; Teacher Preparatory; Professional
Accreditation: **NH**, ADNUR, DA

01 President — Dr. Pete CAMPOS
10 Exec Director for Budget & Finance — Ms. Donna FLORES-MEDINA
09 Exec Dir Inst Research/Development — Dr. Peter MANTHEI
05 Vice Pres Academic/Student Affairs — Dr. Vidal MARTINEZ
07 Int Director of Admissions — Mr. Moses MARQUEZ
06 Registrar — Mr. Johnathan ORTIZ
18 Chief Facilities/Physical Plant — Mr. Ron GONZALES
37 Director Student Financial Aid — Ms. Regina MADRID
15 Director Human Resources — Mr. Lawrence QUINTANA
08 Director Learning Resource Center — Vacant
30 Chief Development — Ms. Mary WARD
13 Director of Computer Services — Mr. Michael ADAMS

Mesalands Community College (F)

911 S 10th Street, Tucumcari NM 88401-3352
County: Quay — FICE Identification: 032063
Unit ID: 188261
Telephone: (505) 461-4413 — Carnegie Class: Assoc/Pub-R-S
FAX Number: (505) 461-1901 — Calendar System: Semester
URL: www.mesalands.edu
Established: 1980 — Annual Undergrad Tuition & Fees (In-District): $1,740
Enrollment: 1,108 — Coed
Affiliation or Control: State/Local — IRS Status: 501(c)3
Highest Offering: Associate Degree
Program: Occupational; 2-Year Principally Bachelor's Creditable
Accreditation: **NH**

01 President — Dr. Mildred P. LOVATO
04 Executive Asst to President — Ms. Connie CHAVEZ
11 Dean of Administrative Services — Mr. David PLUMMER
32 Dean Student Services — Dr. Aaron KENNEDY
05 Dean of Academic Affairs — Ms. Natalie GILLARD
37 Director Financial Aid — Ms. Amanda HAMMER
26 Director Public Relations — Ms. Kimberly HANNA
72 Director of NAWRTC — Mr. Jim MORGAN
84 Director of Enrollment Management — Ms. Robin ALDEN
15 Director of Personnel — Vacant
14 Coord of Institutional Computing — Mr. Larry WICKMAN

National College of Midwifery (G)

209 State Road 240, Taos NM 87571-6834
County: Taos — Identification: 666251
Telephone: (575) 758-8914 — Carnegie Class: Not Classified
FAX Number: (575) 758-0302 — Calendar System: Other
URL: www.midwiferycollege.org
Established: 1989 — Annual Undergrad Tuition & Fees: $5,000
Enrollment: 160 — Coed
Affiliation or Control: Independent Non-Profit — IRS Status: 501(c)3
Highest Offering: Doctorate
Program: Professional; Nursing Emphasis
Accreditation: **MEAC**

01 President — Pres. Elizabeth GILMORE

Navajo Technical College (H)

PO Box 849, Crownpoint NM 87313-0849
County: McKinley — FICE Identification: 023576
Unit ID: 187596
Telephone: (505) 786-4100 — Carnegie Class: Tribal
FAX Number: (505) 786-5644 — Calendar System: Semester
URL: www.navajotech.edu
Established: 1979 — Annual Undergrad Tuition & Fees: $1,140
Enrollment: 972 — Coed
Affiliation or Control: Tribal Control — IRS Status: 501(c)3
Highest Offering: Baccalaureate
Program: Occupational; 2-Year Principally Bachelor's Creditable; Technical Emphasis
Accreditation: **NH**

01 President — Mr. Elmer GUY
05 Chief Academic Office — Mr. Tom DAVIS
06 Registrar/Director of Admissions — Ms. Deloris BECENTI
09 Data Assessment Director — Mr. Roy TRACY
10 Contracts & Grant Officer — Mr. Kenneth PETERSON
32 Director of Student Affairs — Dr. Lawrence ISAAC, JR.
37 Director of Student Financial Aid — Mr. Tyrrell HARDY
15 Director Personnel Services — Mr. Steven BENALLY
18 Chief Facilities/Physical Plant — Mr. McKeever CURLEY
21 Associate Business Officer — Mrs. April CHISCHILLY
96 Director of Purchasing — Vacant

† Tuition figure is for a student enrolled in a federally recognized Indian tribe; for students who are not members of a federally recognized Indian tribe, tuition, including fees, is $2,280.

New Mexico Highlands University (I)

PO Box 9000, Las Vegas NM 87701-9000
County: San Miguel — FICE Identification: 002653
Unit ID: 187897
Telephone: (505) 425-7511 — Carnegie Class: Master's L
FAX Number: N/A — Calendar System: Semester
URL: www.nmhu.edu
Established: 1893 — Annual Undergrad Tuition & Fees (In-State): $3,264
Enrollment: 3,809 — Coed
Affiliation or Control: State — IRS Status: 501(c)3
Highest Offering: Master's
Program: Liberal Arts And General; Teacher Preparatory
Accreditation: **NH**, ACBSP, CORE, NURSE, SW

01 President — Dr. James FRIES
05 VP for Academic Affairs — Dr. Gilbert RIVERA
10 VP Finance & Administration — Vacant
32 Vice Pres of Student Affairs/Dean — Dr. Fidel J. TRUJILLO
20 Associate VP of Academic Affairs — Dr. Linda LAGRANGE
07 Registrar/Director of Admissions — Mr. John COCA
08 Library Director — Mr. Ruben ARAGON
09 Dir Inst Effectiveness & Research — Dr. Jean HILL
14 Director of Information Technology — Mr. Max BACA
15 Director Human Resources — Ms. Donna CASTRO
18 Director of Facilities Management — Ms. Marisol GREENE

19 Chief Police/Security .... Mr. Donato SENA
21 Comptroller .... Mr. Nesbitt HAGOOD
26 Director of University Relations .... Mr. Sean WEAVER
29 Coordinator of Alumni Affairs .... Mr. James MANDARINO
30 Executive Dir for Advancement .... Dr. Sharon CABALLERO
36 Director of Career Services .... Mr. Ron GARCIA
37 Director of Financial Aid .... Ms. Eileen SEDILLO
40 Bookstore Manager .... Vacant
41 Athletic Director .... Mr. Ed MANZANARES
49 Dean College of Arts & Sci .... Dr. Roy LUJAN
50 Dean School of Business .... Dr. Margaret YOUNG
70 Dean School of Social Work .... Dr. Alfredo GARCIA
96 Director of Purchasing .... Mr. Michael SAAVEDRA

New Mexico Institute of Mining and Technology (A)

801 Leroy Place, Socorro NM 87801-4796
County: Socorro　FICE Identification: 002654
Unit ID: 187967
Telephone: (575) 835-5434　Carnegie Class: Master's M
FAX Number: (575) 835-6329　Calendar System: Semester
URL: www.nmt.edu
Established: 1889　Annual Undergrad Tuition & Fees (In-State): $5,302
Enrollment: 1,928　Coed
Affiliation or Control: State　IRS Status: 501(c)3
Highest Offering: Doctorate
Program: Professional; Technical Emphasis
Accreditation: NH, CS, ENG

01 President .... Dr. Daniel H. LOPEZ
10 Vice Pres Administration & Finance .... Mr. Lonnie G. MARQUEZ
05 Vice President Academic Affairs .... Dr. Peter F. GERITY
26 VP Student & University Relations .... Ms. Melissa JARAMILLO FLEMING
46 Vice Pres Research/Economic Devel .... Dr. Van D. ROMERO
20 Assoc Vice Pres Academic Affairs .... Dr. Mary DEZEMBER
35 Asst VP Student & University Rels .... Vacant
32 Dean of Students .... Ms. Melissa JARAMILLO-FLEMING
08 Librarian .... Ms. Lisa BEINHOFF
15 Director of Human Resources .... Ms. Joann SALOME
06 Registrar .... Ms. Sara GRIJALVA
07 Director of Admission .... Mr. Michael KLOEPPEL
37 Director of Financial Aid .... Ms. Annette KAUS
30 Director Office for Advancement .... Ms. Colleen GUENGERICH
22 Director Affirm Action & Compliance .... Ms. Joann SALOME
14 Director Computer Center .... Dr. Michael L. TOPLIFF
13 Director of Information Services .... Mr. Joseph FRANKLIN
65 Director Bur Geology & Mineral Res .... Dr. Peter A. SCHOLLE
12 Director Petro Recovery Res Ctr .... Dr. Robert L. LEE
58 Interim Dean of Graduate Studies .... Dr. David WESTPFAHL
18 Director Facilities Management .... Ms. Yvonne MANZANO-BROWN
21 Director of Finance .... Ms. Arleen VALLES
36 Director Career Services .... Ms. Chelsea BUFFINGTON
38 Dir Counseling/Disabilities Svcs .... Ms. Janet WARD
96 Director of Purchasing .... Ms. Kimela MILLER

New Mexico Junior College (B)

1 Thunderbird Circle, Hobbs NM 88240-9123
County: Lea　FICE Identification: 002655
Unit ID: 187903
Telephone: (575) 392-4510　Carnegie Class: Assoc/Pub-R-M
FAX Number: (575) 492-2732　Calendar System: Semester
URL: www.nmjc.edu
Established: 1965　Annual Undergrad Tuition & Fees (In-District): $1,056
Enrollment: 3,082　Coed
Affiliation or Control: Local　IRS Status: 501(c)3
Highest Offering: Associate Degree
Program: Occupational; 2-Year Principally Bachelor's Creditable
Accreditation: NH, ADNUR

01 President .... Dr. Steve MCCLEERY
05 Vice President Instruction .... Dr. John GRATTON
10 Vice President Finance .... Dan HARDIN
32 Vice President Student Services .... Dr. Regina ORGAN
103 Vice President Training & Outreach .... Dr. Robert RHODES
84 Dean Enrollment Management .... Dr. A. Michele CLINGMAN
14 Dir Computer Information System .... Bill KUNKO
26 Director PR/Marketing .... Vicki VARDEMAN
04 Executive Asst to the President .... Jerri SHIELDS
37 Director Financial Aid .... A. Laura MARQUEZ
09 Director of Inst Effectiveness .... Dr. Larry SANDERSON
66 Director of Nursing .... Delores THOMPSON
18 Chief Facilities/Physical Plant .... Dr. Charley CARROLL
81 Dean Business/Math & Sciences .... Kelly HOLLADAY
79 Dean Arts/Humanities & Career Tech .... Dr. Mickey BEST
40 Director of Bookstore Services .... Elisa AUTRY
106 Dean of Training & Outreach .... Jeffery MCCOOL
75 Dean of Public Safety & Industry .... Dr. August FONS
08 Director of Library Services .... Mary TUYTSCHAEVERS
96 Coordinator of Purchasing .... Regina CHOATE
41 Director of Athletics .... Donald WORTH
102 Acct/Controller-NMJC Foundation .... Christina KUNKO
11 Director of Administrative Services .... Bill MORRILL
88 Controller .... Joshua MORGAN
39 Director Student Housing .... Sandy HARDIN

New Mexico Military Institute (C)

101 W College, Roswell NM 88201-5173
County: Chaves　FICE Identification: 002656
Unit ID: 187912
Telephone: (575) 622-6250　Carnegie Class: Assoc/Pub-Spec
FAX Number: (575) 624-8058　Calendar System: Semester
URL: www.nmmi.edu
Established: 1891　Annual Undergrad Tuition & Fees (In-State): $3,669
Enrollment: 480　Coed
Affiliation or Control: State　IRS Status: 501(c)3
Highest Offering: Associate Degree
Program: 2-Year Principally Bachelor's Creditable
Accreditation: NH

01 Superintendent/President .... MGen. Jerry W. GRIZZLE
32 Commandant .... BGen. Richard V. GERACI
100 Chief of Staff .... Col. Frank COGGINS
10 Asst Vice President of Finance .... LtCol. Charles HENDRICKSON
05 Dean .... BGen. Douglas J. MURRAY
07 Director of Admissions .... LtCol. Jeffery SAVAGE
41 Athletic Director/Dir Physical Educ .... Col. Reginald FRANKLIN
30 Director of Development .... LtCol. Nickie VIGIL-GARCIA
29 Director Alumni Association .... LtCol. Lee JONES, JR.
21 Internal Auditor .... LtCol. David GRAY
88 Professor of Military Science .... LtCol. Jonathan GRAFF
20 Asst Dean & High School Princ .... LtCol. George BRICK
35 Associate Dean Leadership .... Vacant
50 Assoc Dean Social Science/Business .... Col. Walter T. HITCHCOCK
81 Assoc Dean Science/Mathematics .... LtCol. John R. MCVAY
79 Associate Dean Humanities .... Major Joel DYKSTRA
64 Director of Music .... LtCol. Stephen M. THORP
08 Director of the Library .... Col. Jerome J. KLOPFER
26 Public Relations Officer .... CWO3 Carl K. HANSEN
18 Chief Facilities/Physical Plant .... Mr. David W. WEST
06 Registrar .... Maj. Edwin G. PREBLE
37 Director Student Financial Aid .... Maj. Sonya F. RODRIGUEZ
38 Dir College Acad Advising/Placement .... Maj. Donald HANAK
19 Director Security/Safety .... Mr. Jerrold LONOWSKI
42 Chaplain/Director Campus Ministry .... Maj. Dan MUSGRAVE

New Mexico State University Main Campus (D)

Box 30001, Las Cruces NM 88003-8001
County: Dona Ana　FICE Identification: 002657
Unit ID: 188030
Telephone: (575) 646-2035　Carnegie Class: RU/H
FAX Number: (575) 646-6334　Calendar System: Semester
URL: www.nmsu.edu
Established: 1888　Annual Undergrad Tuition & Fees (In-State): $5,827
Enrollment: 18,552　Coed
Affiliation or Control: State　IRS Status: 501(c)3
Highest Offering: Doctorate
Program: Liberal Arts And General; Teacher Preparatory; Professional
Accreditation: NH, BUS, BUSA, CACREP, COPSY, DIETD, @DIETI, ENG, ENGT, MUS, NURSE, PH, SP, SPAA, SW, TED

01 President .... Dr. Barbara COUTURE
05 Provost & Executive Vice President .... Dr. Wendy K. WILKINS
10 Int Sr VP Administration/Finance .... Ms. Angela THRONEBERRY
100 Sr VP External Rel/Chief of Staff .... Mr. Benjamin E. WOODS
30 VP Univ Advance/Pres NMSU Found. .... Mr. Dennis PRESCOTT
85 Vice Provost Internationl Programs .... Vacant
26 Assoc VP Univ Comm/Marketing .... Ms. Maureen HOWARD
21 Int Assoc VP Admin & Finance .... Ms. D'Anne STUART
20 VP Student Affairs/Enroll Mgmt .... Dr. Bernadette MONTOYA
20 Asst VP/Deputy Provost .... Dr. Greg FANT
47 Dean College of Agric & Home Econ .... Dr. Lowell CATLETT
49 Dean College of Arts & Sciences .... Dr. Christa D. SLATON
50 Dean Business College .... Dr. Garrey E. CARRUTHERS
53 Dean College of Education .... Dr. Michael A. MOREHEAD
54 Dean College of Engineering .... Dr. Ricardo JACQUEZ
58 Dean Graduate School .... Dr. Linda LACEY
76 Dean Col of Health & Social Svcs .... Dr. Tilahuan ADERA
35 Interim Dean of Students .... Dr. Susan WALDO
37 Int Dir Fin Aid/Scholarship Svcs .... Ms. Janie MERCHANT
27 Chief Information Officer .... Dr. Shaun COOPER
06 Registrar .... Mr. Michael ZIMMERMAN
43 General Counsel .... Mr. Bruce KITE
08 Dean University Library .... Dr. Elizabeth TITUS
29 Assoc VP Alumni Outreach .... Ms. Deborah WIDGER
25 Assoc Controller Sponsored Projects .... Ms. Norma NOEL
39 Director Student Housing .... Ms. Julie WEBER
09 Asst VP Institutional Analysis .... Dr. Judy BOSLAND
45 Assoc Dir Institutional Analysis .... Ms. Candice GUZIE
23 Director Student Health Center .... Ms. Lori MCKEE
38 Director Counseling Center .... Dr. Karen D. SCHAEFER
86 Asst VP Government Relations .... Mr. Ricardo REL
41 Director Athletics .... Dr. McKinley BOSTON
36 Int Dir Placement/Career Services .... Dr. Susan WALDO
96 Dir Purchasing/Risk Management .... Mr. Michael J. ABERNETHY
28 Dir Institutional Equity/EEO .... Mr. Gerard NEVAREZ
07 Director Admissions .... Ms. Valerie PICKETT
15 Int Dir Personnel Services .... Ms. Dorothy ANDERSON

New Mexico State University at Alamogordo (E)

2400 N Scenic Drive, Alamogordo NM 88310-4239
County: Otero　FICE Identification: 002658
Unit ID: 187994
Telephone: (575) 439-3600　Carnegie Class: Assoc/Pub2in4
FAX Number: (575) 439-3643　Calendar System: Semester
URL: www.nmsua.edu
Established: 1958　Annual Undergrad Tuition & Fees (In-State): $1,824
Enrollment: 3,946　Coed
Affiliation or Control: State　IRS Status: 501(c)3
Highest Offering: Associate Degree
Program: Occupational; 2-Year Principally Bachelor's Creditable
Accreditation: NH, ADNUR

01 President .... Dr. Cheri A. JIMENO
05 Vice President for Academic Affairs .... Dr. Debra TEACHMAN
32 Vice President for Student Services .... Mrs. Sharon G. FISCHER
10 Vice President for Business/Finance .... Mr. Antonio SALINAS
26 Campus Public Information Officer .... Ms. Hope PATTERSON
08 Librarian .... Mr. Eric GREEN
07 Director of Admissions/Registrar .... Ms. Tina TRUONG
37 Director Student Financial Aid .... Ms. Darlene DUVALL
09 Director of Institutional Research .... Dr. Bruce MARTIN
06 Registrar .... Ms. Tina TRUONG
15 Director Human Resources .... Mrs. Brenda W. GARCIA
18 Director Facilities/Physical Plant .... Mrs. Nancy MONTGOMERY
36 Director Student Placement .... Mr. Jeremy PATTON
38 Director Student Counseling .... Mrs. Barbara E. MCDONALD
56 Assoc Vice Pres Extended Programs .... Mrs. Donna L. COOK
96 Buyer Specialist 1 .... Mr. Lee M. KINNEY

New Mexico State University at Carlsbad (F)

1500 University Drive, Carlsbad NM 88220-3598
County: Eddy　FICE Identification: 002659
Unit ID: 188003
Telephone: (575) 234-9200　Carnegie Class: Assoc/Pub2in4
FAX Number: (575) 885-4951　Calendar System: Semester
URL: www.cavern.nmsu.edu
Established: 1950　Annual Undergrad Tuition & Fees (In-State): $1,036
Enrollment: 1,887　Coed
Affiliation or Control: State　IRS Status: 501(c)3
Highest Offering: Associate Degree
Program: Occupational; 2-Year Principally Bachelor's Creditable
Accreditation: NH, ADNUR

01 President .... Mr. Russell F. HARDY
05 Vice Pres Academic Affairs .... Dr. Bruce F. PETRIE
32 Vice Pres Student Services .... Mr. Michael J. CLEARY
10 Vice Pres Business & Finance .... Ms. Catherine DYCK
38 Director Student Counseling .... Ms. Karla K. THOMPSON
37 Director Financial Aid .... Ms. Judith SEARS
15 Human Resources Specialist .... Ms. Melinda WILSON
09 Senior Institutional Researcher .... Mr. Biniam TESFAMARIAM

New Mexico State University Dona Ana Community College (G)

Box 30001, MSC 3DA, Las Cruces NM 88003-8001
County: Dona Ana　Identification: 666649
Unit ID: 187620
Telephone: (575) 527-7500　Carnegie Class: Assoc/Pub2in4
FAX Number: (575) 527-7515　Calendar System: Semester
URL: dacc.nmsu.edu
Established: 1973　Annual Undergrad Tuition & Fees (In-State): $1,776
Enrollment: 9,797　Coed
Affiliation or Control: State　IRS Status: 501(c)3
Highest Offering: Associate Degree
Program: Occupational; 2-Year Principally Bachelor's Creditable
Accreditation: NH, ACBSP, ADNUR, DA, DH, DMS, EMT, IFSAC, RAD

01 President .... Dr. Margie C. HUERTA
05 VP for Academic Affairs .... Vacant
10 VP for Business & Finance .... Mr. Andrew J. BURKE
32 VP for Student Services .... Mr. Amadeo LEDESMA
20 Assoc VP for Academic Affairs .... Dr. John WALKER
50 Division Dean Business/Info Systems .... Ms. Lydia BAGWELL
97 Division Dean General Studies .... Dr. Bernard PINA
76 Div Dean Health/Public Services .... Ms. Evelyn HOBBS
72 Division Dean Technical Studies .... Vacant
55 Exec Director Adult Basic Education .... Ms. Sylvia NICKERSON
51 Exec Director Continuing Education .... Dr. William GLENN
62 Director Library Services .... Ms. Tammy WELCH
09 Campus Inst Effectiveness/Plng Ofcr .... Dr. Fred LILLIBRIDGE
26 Chief Public Relations/Devel Ofcr .... Mr. Kenneth TELLEZ
31 Director Community Education .... Vacant
40 Bookstore Manager .... Mr. Marvin PAZ
21 Business Manager .... Ms. Nancy RITTER
15 Human Resources Manager .... Vacant
90 Computer Support Manager .... Ms. Lori ALLEN
18 Facilities Manager .... Ms. Kathleen REDDINGTON
07 Coordinator Admissions & Records .... Ms. Geraldine MARTINEZ
37 Financial Aid Coordinator .... Ms. Gladys CHAIREZ
28 Coord Disabled Student Services .... Vacant
78 Coord Cooperative Educ/ Placement .... Ms. Rosa DE LA TORRE-BURMEISTER

New Mexico State University Grants (H)

1500 Third Street, Grants NM 87020-2025
County: Cibola　FICE Identification: 008854
Unit ID: 188021
Telephone: (505) 287-6678　Carnegie Class: Assoc/Pub2in4
FAX Number: (505) 287-2329　Calendar System: Semester
URL: www.grants.nmsu.edu
Established: 1968　Annual Undergrad Tuition & Fees (In-State): $1,704
Enrollment: 1,568　Coed
Affiliation or Control: State　IRS Status: 501(c)3
Highest Offering: Associate Degree
Program: Occupational; 2-Year Principally Bachelor's Creditable

Accreditation: &NH

01 President ... Ms. Felicia CASADOS
05 Vice Pres Academic Affairs ... Dr. Harry SHESKI
32 Vice Pres Student Services ... Ms. Beth ARMSTEAD
10 Vice Pres Business/Finance ... Ms. Gaylyn YANKE
08 Librarian ... Ms. Cecilia STAFFORD
09 Director of Institutional Research ... Ms. Rose CARLSON
18 Chief Facilities/Physical Plant ... Mr. Dan CHRISTMANN

† Regional accreditation is carried under the parent institution in Las Cruces, NM.

Northern New Mexico College (A)

921 N Paseo de Onate, Espanola NM 87532-2649
County: Rio Arriba — FICE Identification: 020839
Unit ID: 188058
Telephone: (505) 747-2100 — Carnegie Class: Bac/Assoc
FAX Number: (505) 747-2170 — Calendar System: Semester
URL: www.nnmc.edu
Established: 1909 — Annual Undergrad Tuition & Fees (In-State): $1,413
Enrollment: 2,126 — Coed
Affiliation or Control: State — IRS Status: 501(c)3
Highest Offering: Baccalaureate
Program: Occupational; 2-Year Principally Bachelor's Creditable; Liberal Arts And General; Teacher Preparatory
Accreditation: NH, ACBSP, RAD

01 President ... Dr. Nancy (Rusty) BARCELO
03 Executive Vice President ... Vacant
10 Int Vice Pres Administration ... Mr. David SCHUTZ
05 Provost ... Dr. Anthony SENA
32 Dean of Student Services ... Mr. Frank ORONA
30 Director of Development ... Vacant
12 Director El Rito Campus ... Vacant
06 Registrar ... Dr. Jan DAWSON
08 Head Librarian ... Ms. Isabel RODARTE
84 Director of Recruitment ... Mr. Frank ORONA
37 Director of Financial Aid ... Mr. Alfredo MONTOYA
13 Director of Management Info Systems ... Mr. Jorge LUCERO
15 Director of Human Resources ... Ms. Nancy O'ROURKE
18 Director of Facilities ... Mr. David SCHUTZ
26 Director of Public Information ... Vacant
35 Director of TRIO Programs ... Mr. Hilario ROMERO
09 Director of Inst Effectiveness ... Ms. Carmella MARTINEZ
96 Director of Purchasing ... Ms. Linda ATENCIO
38 Coordinator Student Advisement ... Ms. Paula REID
25 Dean Grants Devel/Spec Initiatives ... Vacant
51 Director Continuing Education ... Mr. Matt PUMPHREY
41 Athletic Director/Coach ... Mr. Ryan CORDOVA
53 Dean College of Teacher Education ... Dr. Cathy BERRYHILL
49 Dean College of Arts and Sciences ... Dr. Mellis SCHMIDT
103 Dn Col Cmty Wrkfrce/Career Tech Ed ... Dr. Camilla BUSTAMANTE

Pima Medical Institute-Albuquerque (B)

4400 Cutler Avenue NE, Albuquerque NM 87110-3935
County: Bernalillo — FICE Identification: 036783
Unit ID: 105543
Telephone: (505) 881-1234 — Carnegie Class: Assoc/PrivFP
FAX Number: (505) 881-5329 — Calendar System: Other
URL: www.pmi.edu
Established: 1985 — Annual Undergrad Tuition & Fees: N/A
Enrollment: 755 — Coed
Affiliation or Control: Proprietary — IRS Status: Proprietary
Highest Offering: Associate Degree
Program: Occupational; 2-Year Principally Bachelor's Creditable
Accreditation: ABHES, DH, PTAA, RAD

01 Campus Director ... Dr. Voytek PANAS

St. John's College (C)

1160 Camino de la Cruz Blanca,
Santa Fe NM 87505-4599
County: Santa Fe — FICE Identification: 002093
Unit ID: 245652
Telephone: (505) 984-6000 — Carnegie Class: Master's S
FAX Number: (505) 984-6003 — Calendar System: Semester
URL: www.stjohnscollege.edu
Established: 1964 — Annual Undergrad Tuition & Fees: $43,256
Enrollment: 41,792 — Coed
Affiliation or Control: Independent Non-Profit — IRS Status: 501(c)3
Highest Offering: Master's
Program: Liberal Arts And General
Accreditation: NH

01 President ... Mr. Michael P. PETERS
05 Dean ... Mr. Walter J. STERLING
30 Vice President for Advancement ... Mr. James OSTERHOLT
10 Treasurer ... Mr. Bryan VALENTINE
06 Registrar ... Mrs. Marline MARQUEZ-SCALLY
08 Library Director ... Ms. Jennifer SPRAGUE
07 Director of Admissions ... Mr. Larry CLENDENIN
58 Director of Graduate Institute ... Mr. Matt DAVIS
09 Director of Institutional Research ... Mr. Nick GIACONA
15 Director of Human Resources ... Ms. Lois RAEL
18 Chief Facilities/Physical Plant ... Mr. Pat HOLMAN
26 Dir of Communications/External Rels ... Ms. Anna SOCHOCKY
29 Assoc Director Alumni Relations ... Ms. Nancie WINGO
36 Director Student Placement ... Ms. Margaret ODELL
37 Director Student Financial Aid ... Mr. Mike RODRIQUEZ

† Affiliated with St. John's College, Maryland.

San Juan College (D)

4601 College Boulevard, Farmington NM 87402-4699
County: San Juan — FICE Identification: 002660
Unit ID: 188100
Telephone: (505) 326-3311 — Carnegie Class: Assoc/Pub-R-L
FAX Number: (505) 566-3385 — Calendar System: Semester
URL: www.sanjuancollege.edu
Established: 1956 — Annual Undergrad Tuition & Fees (In-District): $1,128
Enrollment: 11,239 — Coed
Affiliation or Control: Local — IRS Status: 501(c)3
Highest Offering: Associate Degree
Program: Occupational; 2-Year Principally Bachelor's Creditable
Accreditation: NH, ACBSP, ADNUR, DH, MLTAD, PTAA, SURGT

01 Interim President ... Mr. Michael TACHA
13 Vice Pres for Technology Services ... Mr. Tim WARREN
05 Vice Pres for Learning ... Dr. Sher HRUSKA
10 Vice Pres Administrative Services ... Vacant
32 Vice Pres for Student Services ... Mr. David EPPICH
04 Administrative Asst to President ... Ms. MaryAnne FACIO
20 Assoc Vice Pres for Learning ... Dr. Pamela MILLER
102 Executive Director Foundation ... Ms. Gayle DEAN
21 Assoc Vice Pres Administrative Svcs ... Ms. Dianne GARCIA
31 Chief Community Relations Officer ... Ms. Nancy SHEPHERD
21 Controller ... Mr. Russell LITKE
26 Sr Dir Marketing/Public Relations ... Ms. Linda BAKER
88 Dir Ctr for Student Engagement ... Mr. Tim SCHROEDER
84 Sr Dir Enrollment Management ... Mr. Jon BETZ
50 Dean Sch Business/Sciences ... Dr. Merrill ADAMS
79 Dean School of Humanities ... Ms. Lisa WILSON
76 Dean School of Health Sciences ... Mr. Oliver BORDEN
65 Dean School of Energy ... Mr. Randy PACHECO
72 Dean School Trades & Technology ... Mr. Bill LEWIS
22 Director Affirmative Action/EEO ... Ms. Stacey ALLEN
88 Director Native American Programs ... Ms. Michele PETERSON
08 Director Library Services ... Mr. Chris SCHIPPER
37 Director of Financial Aid ... Mr. Jerry MCKEEN
18 Director Physical Plant ... Mr. Steve BIERNACKI
19 Director Security/Safety ... Mr. Billy NEWTON
35 Director Student Activities ... Ms. Marcia STERLING
96 Director Purchasing ... Mr. Damian VIGIL
38 Director Student Advising Center ... Mr. Ken KERNAGIS
74 Director Vet-Tech Program ... Dr. David WRIGHT
36 Coordinator Job Placement ... Ms. Marie SCHUMACHER
06 Registrar ... Ms. Sherri GAUGH
09 Director of Institutional Research ... Ms. Candace GILFILLAN

Santa Fe Community College (E)

6401 Richards Avenue, Santa Fe NM 87508-4887
County: Santa Fe — FICE Identification: 022781
Unit ID: 188137
Telephone: (505) 428-1000 — Carnegie Class: Assoc/Pub-R-L
FAX Number: (505) 428-1296 — Calendar System: Semester
URL: www.sfcc.edu
Established: 1983 — Annual Undergrad Tuition & Fees (In-State): $1,689
Enrollment: 6,586 — Coed
Affiliation or Control: State — IRS Status: 501(c)3
Highest Offering: Associate Degree
Program: Occupational; 2-Year Principally Bachelor's Creditable
Accreditation: NH, ADNUR, DA, EMT, MAC

01 President ... Dr. Sheila ORTEGO
05 VP of Academic & Student Affairs ... Dr. Ron LISS
10 Vice Pres Finance & Administration ... Ms. Meridee WALTERS
09 VP Planning & Inst Effectiveness ... Dr. Jacqueline VIRGINT
21 Associate Vice President Finance ... Ms. Gilda ESPINOZA
20 Asst VP of Student Retention ... Ms. Jill DOUGLASS
84 Asst VP Enrollment & Student Svcs ... Dr. Cheryl DRANGMEISTER
51 Asst VP Cont Educ Customized Trng ... Mr. Randy GRISSOM
53 Asst VP for School of Education ... Ms. Michelle STOBNICKE
26 Exec Dir Marketing/Public Rels ... Ms. Janet WISE
30 Grow SFCC Foundation ... Ms. Deborah BOLDT
06 Registrar ... Ms. Barbara TUCCI
13 Chief Information Officer ... Mr. Wayne KELLER
37 Financial Aid Director ... Mr. Scott WHITAKER
66 Director of Nursing ... Ms. Kathleen MATTA
08 Library Director ... Ms. Peg JOHNSON
15 Director of Human Resources ... Ms. Karla QUINTANA
88 Director Small Business Development ... Mr. Michael MYKRIS
18 Director of Plant Operations ... Mr. Frank JOY
24 Media Technician ... Vacant
49 Dean Sch Liberal Arts/Core Studies ... Dr. Bruno GAGNON
76 Dean Sch Health and Sciences ... Dr. Julie GOOD
57 Int Dean School of Arts and Design ... Dr. Mechele HESBROOK
50 Dean Sch Business & Applied Tech ... Mr. Albert REED
101 Executive Asst to the President ... Ms. Rosemarie M. GARCIA
96 Director of Purchasing ... Mr. Michael CLOKEY

Santa Fe University of Art and Design (F)

1600 St. Michael's Drive, Santa Fe NM 87505-7634
County: Santa Fe — FICE Identification: 002649
Unit ID: 188146
Telephone: (505) 473-6011 — Carnegie Class: Spec/Arts
FAX Number: (505) 473-6127 — Calendar System: Semester
URL: www.santafeuniversity.edu
Established: 1947 — Annual Undergrad Tuition & Fees: $32,472
Enrollment: 302 — Coed
Affiliation or Control: Proprietary — IRS Status: Proprietary
Highest Offering: Master's
Program: Liberal Arts And General; Professional; Fine Arts Emphasis
Accreditation: NH

01 Interim President ... Mr. Laurence A. HINZ
05 Vice President for Academic Affairs ... Mr. Gerry SNYDER
32 Sr Director of Student Life ... Ms. Laura NUNNELLY
13 Dir Campus Technology Services ... Mr. Jeff PEARCE
10 Dir of Finance & Operations ... Mr. James VIGIL
84 Regional Director of Enrollment ... Mr. Richard FERGUSON
06 Registrar ... Ms. Mary ANGELL
09 Dir Inst Research & Assessment ... Ms. Sarah DENNISON
88 Mgr Academic Program Development ... Ms. Susan PENCE
88 Director Campus-Based Facilities ... Mr. Thomas OLMSTEAD
18 Dir Facilities & Security ... Mr. Peter ROMERO
08 Director of Fogelson Library ... Ms. Valerie NYE
15 Director of Human Resources ... Mr. Todd SPILMAN
39 Director of Campus Life ... Mr. Kristiaan RAWLINGS
37 Director of Financial Aid ... Ms. Amy KEARNS
07 Director of Admissions ... Ms. Christine GUEVARA
85 Dir International Student Support ... Mr. John RODRIGUEZ
29 Director of Alumni Affairs ... Ms. Maria VELEZ
26 Marketing Manager ... Mr. Daniel MILLER
35 Student Activities Coordinator ... Ms. Anne RITCHIE

Southwest University of Visual Arts (G)

5000 Marble Avenue, NE, Albuquerque NM 87110-6344
County: Bernalillo — Identification: 666524
Unit ID: 402776
Telephone: (505) 254-7575 — Carnegie Class: Spec/Arts
FAX Number: (505) 254-4754 — Calendar System: Trimester
URL: www.theartcenter.edu
Established: 1989 — Annual Undergrad Tuition & Fees: $18,360
Enrollment: 292 — Coed
Affiliation or Control: Proprietary — IRS Status: Proprietary
Highest Offering: Baccalaureate
Program: Occupational
Accreditation: &NH, CIDA

01 Assoc Dean of Instruction ... Ms. Amy BOLDT

† Branch campus of Southwest University of Visual Arts, AZ.

Southwest Acupuncture College (H)

1622 Galisteo Street, Santa Fe NM 87505-6351
County: Santa Fe — FICE Identification: 026220
Unit ID: 366605
Telephone: (505) 438-8884 — Carnegie Class: Spec/Health
FAX Number: (505) 438-8883 — Calendar System: Trimester
URL: www.acupuncturecollege.edu
Established: 1980 — Annual Undergrad Tuition & Fees: $13,945
Enrollment: 264 — Coed
Affiliation or Control: Proprietary — IRS Status: Proprietary
Highest Offering: Master's; No Lower Division
Program: Professional
Accreditation: ACUP

01 President ... Dr. Anthony ABBATE
03 Executive Director ... Dr. Skya ABBATE
10 Fiscal Officer ... Ms. Piper KING
12 Campus Director Albuquerque ... Dr. Li XU
12 Campus Director Boulder ... Dr. Valerie HOBBS
12 Campus Director Santa Fe ... Ms. Latricia GONZALES-MCKOSKY
12 Administrative Director Albuquerque ... Mrs. Toni MEEKS
12 Administrative Director Boulder ... Ms. Heather LANG
17 Clinical Director Santa Fe ... Dr. Mary Ellen MARINO
17 Clinical Director Albuquerque ... Dr. Hilary BROADBENT
17 Clinic Director Boulder ... Ms. Joanne NIVELE
05 Academic Dean Santa Fe ... Dr. Maya YU
05 Academic Dean Albuquerque ... Dr. Dawei SHAO
05 Academic Dean Boulder ... Ms. Melanie CRANE
37 Director of Financial Aid ... Ms. Angela ANAYA

Southwest Acupuncture College-Albuquerque (I)

7801 Academy Blvd N Town Bdg #1 NE,
Albuquerque NM 87109
County: Bernalillo — Identification: 666666
Unit ID: 413644
Telephone: (505) 888-8898 — Carnegie Class: Not Classified
FAX Number: (505) 888-1380 — Calendar System: Other
URL: www.acupuncturecollege.edu
Established: 1980 — Annual Graduate Tuition & Fees: $12,893
Enrollment: 79 — Coed
Affiliation or Control: Proprietary — IRS Status: Proprietary
Highest Offering: Master's; No Undergraduates
Program: Professional
Accreditation: ACUP

01 Campus Director ... Dr. Li XU

† Branch campus of Southwest Acupuncture College, Santa Fe, NM.

Southwestern College (A)

PO Box 4788, Santa Fe NM 87502-4788
County: Santa Fe　FICE Identification: 030761
Unit ID: 188207
Telephone: (505) 471-5756　Carnegie Class: Assoc/PrivNFP4
FAX Number: (505) 471-4071　Calendar System: Quarter
URL: www.swc.edu
Established: 1979　Annual Graduate Tuition & Fees: $16,200
Enrollment: 126　Coed
Affiliation or Control: Independent Non-Profit　IRS Status: 501(c)3
Highest Offering: Master's; No Undergraduates
Program: Professional
Accreditation: NH

01 President .... Dr. Jim NOLAN
03 Vice Pres/Dir Community Educ Pgms .... Ms. Katherine NINOS
05 Academic Dean .... Dr. Antonio NUNEZ
07 Director of Admissions .... Ms. Dru PHOENIX

Southwestern Indian Polytechnic Institute (B)

9169 Coors Blvd., NW, Albuquerque NM 87120
County: Bernalillo　FICE Identification: 025110
Unit ID: 188216
Telephone: (505) 346-2347　Carnegie Class: Tribal
FAX Number: (505) 346-2343　Calendar System: Trimester
URL: www.sipi.edu
Established: 1971　Annual Undergrad Tuition & Fees: $280
Enrollment: 657　Coed
Affiliation or Control: Federal　IRS Status: 501(c)3
Highest Offering: Associate Degree
Program: Occupational; 2-Year Principally Bachelor's Creditable; Technical Emphasis
Accreditation: @NH, OPD, OPLT

01 President .... Dr. Sherry ALLISON
10 Acting Vice Pres College Operations .... Mr. Monte MONTEITH
05 Vice President Academic Programs .... Ms. Valerie MONTOYA
39 Director of Residential Life .... Mr. Raymond GACHUPIAN
07 Director Admiss/Finan Aid/Registrar .... Mr. Joseph CARPIO
09 Director of Institutional Research .... Mr. Edward HUMMINGBIRD
15 Human Resources Specialist .... Ms. Bernadine FISHERMAN
18 Facilities Director .... Ms. Carlisa SHOMOUR
37 Director Student Financial Aid .... Mr. Joseph CARPIO

University of New Mexico Main Campus (C)

1 University of New Mexico, Albuquerque NM 87131-0001
County: Bernalillo　FICE Identification: 002663
Unit ID: 187985
Telephone: (505) 277-0111　Carnegie Class: RU/VH
FAX Number: (505) 277-6019　Calendar System: Semester
URL: www.unm.edu
Established: 1889　Annual Undergrad Tuition & Fees (In-State): $5,809
Enrollment: 28,757　Coed
Affiliation or Control: State　IRS Status: 501(c)3
Highest Offering: Doctorate
Program: Liberal Arts And General; Teacher Preparatory; Professional
Accreditation: NH, ARCPA, BUS, BUSA, CACREP, CLPSY, CONST, CS, DANCE, DENT, DH, DIETD, DIETI, EMT, ENG, IPSY, JOUR, LAW, LSAR, MED, MIDWF, MT, MUS, NURSE, OT, PH, PHAR, PLNG, PTA, SP, SPAA, TED, THEA

01 President .... Dr. David J. SCHMIDLY
05 Int Provost/Exec VP Academic Affs .... Dr. Chaouki ABDALLAH
17 Chancellor of Health Sciences Ctr .... Dr. Paul B. ROTH
10 Exec Vice Pres Administration .... Dr. David W. HARRIS
100 Chief of Staff .... Dr. Breda BOVA
20 Deputy Provost Academic Affairs .... Vacant
20 Vice Provost Academic Affairs .... Dr. Wynn M. GOERING
106 Vice Provost Extended University ... Dr. Jeronimo C. DOMINGUEZ
46 Vice President for Research .... Dr. Julia FULGHUM
32 Vice President Student Affairs .... Dr. Eliseo S. TORRES
28 Vice President Equity & Inclusion .... Dr. Josephine DE LEON
28 Vice President HSC Diversity .... Dr. Valerie ROMERO-LEGGOTT
84 Vice Pres Enrollment Management .... Vacant
15 Vice Pres Human Resources .... Helen GONZALES
41 Vice President for Athletics .... Paul R. KREBS
21 VP HSC/UNM Finance/Controller .... Ava LOVELL
13 Chief Information Officer .... Gilbert GONZALES
43 University Counsel .... K. Lee PEIFER
29 AVP Alumni Relations .... Karen A. ABRAHAM
20 AVP Bdgt/Plng Analysis for Provost .... Curtis R. PORTER
21 AVP Ofc of Budget Plng & Analysis .... Andrew CULLEN
35 AVP Student Life .... Dr. Walter C. MILLER
35 AVP Student Services .... Dr. Tim GUTIERREZ
50 Dean Anderson School of Management .... Doug M. BROWN
48 Dean Sch of Architecture/Planning ... Dr. Geraldine FORBES ISAIS
49 Dean of Arts & Sciences .... Vacant
53 Dean of Education .... Dr. Richard HOWELL
54 Interim Dean of Engineering .... Dr. Arup MAJI
57 Interim Dean of Fine Arts .... Dr. Jim LINNELL
61 Dean School of Law .... Kevin WASHBURN
63 Exec Vice Dean School of Medicine .... Dr. Jeffrey GRIFFITH
66 Dean of Nursing .... Dr. Nancy A. RIDENOUR
67 Interim Dean of Pharmacy .... Dr. Donald GODWIN
80 Director Public Administration .... Dr. Uday DESAI
97 Acting Dean University College .... Dr. Wynn GOERING
58 Dean Graduate Studies .... Dr. Amy WOHLERT
51 Dean of Continuing Education .... Dr. Rita MARTINEZ PURSON
08 Dean University Libraries .... Dr. Martha BEDARD
12 Int Exec Director UNM West .... Dr. Beth MILLER
45 Consultant for Strategy & Goals .... Carolyn J. THOMPSON
26 University Marketing Director .... Cinnamon BLAIR
27 Director University Communications .... Susan B. MCKINSEY
86 Director Government Affairs .... Marc SAAVEDRA
09 Director Institutional Research .... Mark P. CHISHOLM
18 University Planning Officer .... Mary W. KENNEY
19 Chief of Police .... Kathy A. GUIMOND
96 Chief Procurement Officer .... Bruce E. CHERRIN
23 Director Student Health Center .... Dr. Beverly KLOEPPEL
22 Acting Dir Ofc Equal Opportunity .... Theresa RAMOS
24 Dir New Media & Extended Learning .... Debby KNOTTS
35 Interim Dean of Students .... Kimmerly KLOEPPEL
07 Director Admissions and Recruitment .... Matt HULETT
06 Interim Registrar .... Alex GONZALEZ
37 Director Student Financial Aid .... Brian MALONE
36 Director Career Services .... Jenna S. CRABB
39 Director Housing & Food Svcs/Bus .... Patrick CALL
104 Director International Programs .... Dr. Thomas BOGENSCHILD
40 Director Bookstore .... Melanie SPARKS
102 UNM Foundation President and CEO .... Henry NEMCIK
30 VP Development Academics .... Larry RYAN
30 VP Development Health Sciences Ctr .... Bill UHER
88 CEO UNM Hospital .... Steve MCKERNAN

University of New Mexico-Gallup (D)

200 College Road, Gallup NM 87301-5697
County: McKinley　FICE Identification: 006881
Unit ID: 187958
Telephone: (505) 863-7500　Carnegie Class: Assoc/Pub2in4
FAX Number: (505) 863-7532　Calendar System: Semester
URL: www.gallup.unm.edu
Established: 1968　Annual Undergrad Tuition & Fees (In-State): $1,704
Enrollment: 2,800　Coed
Affiliation or Control: State　IRS Status: 501(c)3
Highest Offering: Associate Degree
Program: Occupational; 2-Year Principally Bachelor's Creditable
Accreditation: &NH, DA, MLTAD

01 Executive Director .... Dr. Sylvia R. ANDREW
05 Dean of Instruction .... Dr. Neal MANGHAM
10 Director Business Operations .... Vacant
32 Interim Director Student Services .... Zeke GARCIA
07 Manager of Admissions Advisor .... Pearl A. MORRIS
26 Sr Public Affairs Representative .... Linda THORNTON
06 Registrar .... Suzette WYACO
13 Manager Information Technology .... Jim BLACKSHEAR
40 Manager Bookstore .... Vacant
37 Manager Financial Aid .... Vacant
18 Manager Maintenance/Construction .... Ron PETRANOVICH
84 Enrollment Representative .... Anthony BILLY

† Regional accreditation is carried under the parent institution in Albuquerque, NM.

University of New Mexico-Los Alamos (E)

4000 University Drive, Los Alamos NM 87544-2233
County: Los Alamos　Identification: 666742
Unit ID: 187976
Telephone: (505) 662-5919　Carnegie Class: Assoc/Pub2in4
FAX Number: (505) 662-0344　Calendar System: Semester
URL: www.unm.edu
Established: 1980　Annual Undergrad Tuition & Fees (In-State): $1,548
Enrollment: 747　Coed
Affiliation or Control: State　IRS Status: 501(c)3
Highest Offering: Associate Degree
Program: Occupational; 2-Year Principally Bachelor's Creditable; Liberal Arts And General; Technical Emphasis
Accreditation: &NH

01 Executive Director .... Dr. Cedric D. PAGE
05 Dean of Instruction .... Dr. Kathy MASSENGALE
10 Campus Resources Director .... Ms. Lisa CLOUGH
13 Manager Computing Services .... Mr. William C. GILSON
32 Student Affairs Director .... Dr. Patricia BOYER
06 Branch Registrar .... Ms. Kathryn VIGIL
08 Library Director .... Mr. Dennis DAVIES-WILSON
25 Accountant II/C&G/Personnel .... Ms. Denise SERNA
37 Branch Financial Aid .... Ms. Lolita MARTINEZ
40 Manager Branch Bookstore .... Mr. Steve A. CIDDIO
18 Manager Facilities Services .... Mr. Eugene ORTIZ
27 Communications & Marketing Services .... Ms. Bonnie GORDON
09 Institutional Researcher .... Ms. Valida DUSHDUROVA
15 Student Housing Coordinator .... Ms. Betsy SUAZO
106 Manager UNM Distance Educ Program .... Ms. Cindy LEYBA

† Regional accreditation is carried under the parent institution in Albuquerque, NM.

University of New Mexico-Taos (F)

115 Civic Plaza Drive, Taos NM 87571-6401
County: Taos　Identification: 666743
Unit ID: 188225
Telephone: (575) 737-6200　Carnegie Class: Assoc/Pub2in4
FAX Number: (575) 758-5898　Calendar System: Semester
URL: www.taos.unm.edu
Established: 1993　Annual Undergrad Tuition & Fees (In-State): $1,406
Enrollment: 1,523　Coed
Affiliation or Control: State　IRS Status: 501(c)3
Highest Offering: Associate Degree
Program: Occupational; 2-Year Principally Bachelor's Creditable
Accreditation: &NH

01 Exec Director/Branch Campus .... Catherine O'NEILL
05 Dean of Instruction .... Jim GILROY
45 Campus Resource Director .... Mario SPUAZO
35 Academic Student Success Director .... Antonia Amie CHAVEZ-AGUILAR
84 Student Enrollment Director .... Patricia GONZALES

† Regional accreditation is carried under the parent institution in Albuquerque, NM.

University of New Mexico-Valencia (G)

280 La Entrada Road, Los Lunas NM 87031-7633
County: Valencia　Identification: 666741
Unit ID: 188049
Telephone: (505) 925-8500　Carnegie Class: Assoc/Pub2in4
FAX Number: (505) 925-8501　Calendar System: Semester
URL: www.unm.edu/~unmvc/
Established: 1981　Annual Undergrad Tuition & Fees (In-State): $1,561
Enrollment: 2,338　Coed
Affiliation or Control: State　IRS Status: 501(c)3
Highest Offering: Associate Degree
Program: Occupational; 2-Year Principally Bachelor's Creditable
Accreditation: &NH

01 Executive Director .... Alice V. LETTENEY
05 Interim Dean of Instruction .... Dr. Julie DEPREE
45 Director Campus Resources .... Andrew E. SANCHEZ
32 Associate Director Student Affairs .... Vigil HANK
88 Mgr Small Business Devel Center .... Wayne ABRAHAM
26 Sr Public Affairs Representative .... Chad L. PERRY
15 Human Resources Representative .... Shireen E. MCDONALD
18 Manager Facilities Services .... William BOWDICH
08 Manager Library Operations .... Barbara LOVATO
40 Manager Bookstore .... Tracy PERALTA
21 Business Manager .... Sally HEBERT
30 Manager Development/Donor Relations .... Ann-Mary MACLEOD
84 Manager Enrollment Services .... Duran FRANCES
37 Br/Div Mgr Student Financial Aid .... Bill BLOOM

† Regional accreditation is carried under the parent institution in Albuquerque, NM.

University of the Southwest (H)

6610 Lovington Highway, Hobbs NM 88240-9129
County: Lea　FICE Identification: 002650
Unit ID: 188182
Telephone: (575) 392-6561　Carnegie Class: Bac/Diverse
FAX Number: (575) 392-6006　Calendar System: Semester
URL: www.usw.edu
Established: 1962　Annual Undergrad Tuition & Fees: $11,664
Enrollment: 538　Coed
Affiliation or Control: Independent Non-Profit　IRS Status: 501(c)3
Highest Offering: Master's
Program: Liberal Arts And General; Teacher Preparatory
Accreditation: NH

01 President .... Dr. Gary DILL
10 VP for Administration & CFO .... Dr. Dee MOONEY
05 VP of Academics/Dean of Faculty .... Dr. James SMITH
07 Dean of Enrollment Mgmt/Student Sup .... Mrs. Jordan BODINE
18 Campus Steward .... Mr. David ARNOLD
41 Dean of Athletics .... Mr. Michael GALVAN
32 Dean of Students .... Mr. Tom MULKEY
49 Dean School of Arts & Sciences .... Vacant
50 Dean School of Business .... Dr. Tom WILSON
53 Dean School of Education .... Dr. Mary HARRIS
35 Assoc Dean of Campus Life .... Mrs. Evelyn RISING
42 Campus Minister .... Rev. Kenneth REED
08 Director of Library .... Mr. John MCCANCE
15 Director of Personnel Services .... Mrs. Melody ARNOLD
37 Financial Aid Director .... Mrs. Kerrie MITCHELL
13 Technology Services Director .... Mrs. Charlotte SMITH
44 Director Develop Opers/Alumni Rels .... Ms. Laurie DEAN
26 Webmaster/Dir of Public Relations .... Mrs. Brenda HENNING
88 Maintenance Supervisor .... Mr. Lonnie HARRISON

Western New Mexico University (I)

PO Box 680, Silver City NM 88062-0680
County: Grant　FICE Identification: 002664
Unit ID: 188304
Telephone: (505) 538-6011　Carnegie Class: Master's M
FAX Number: (505) 538-6364　Calendar System: Semester
URL: www.wnmu.edu
Established: 1893　Annual Undergrad Tuition & Fees (In-State): $3,812
Enrollment: 3,506　Coed
Affiliation or Control: State　IRS Status: 501(c)3
Highest Offering: Master's
Program: Liberal Arts And General; Teacher Preparatory
Accreditation: NH, ACBSP, ADNUR, NURSE, OT, SW, TED

01 President .... Dr. John E. COUNTS
05 Provost/Vice Pres Academic Affairs .... Dr. Faye VOWELL
32 VP Student Affairs/Enrollment Mgmt .... Dr. Chris FARREN

10 Vice President Business Affairs .... Ms. Sherri A. BAYS
30 VP Instl Advancement/Economic Devel .... Ms. Linda Kay JONES
20 Assoc Vice Pres Academic Affairs .... Ms. Marcia BOURDETTE
35 Assoc Vice Pres Student Affairs .... Ms. Peggy LANKFORD
06 Registrar .... Ms. Betsy MILLER
08 University Librarian .... Ms. Gilda BAEZA-ORTEGO
37 Director Student Financial Aid .... Ms. Onorina FRANCO
07 Director Admissions .... Mr. Dan TRESSLER
09 Director of Institutional Research .... Mr. Paul LANDRUM
15 Director of Human Resources .... Ms. Charlene ASHBURN
18 Chief Facilities/Physical Plant .... Mr. Henry SANCHEZ
26 Chief Public Relations Officer .... Mr. Abe VILLARREAL
29 Director of Alumni Relations .... Ms. Arlene SCHADEL
44 Chief Development Officer .... Mr. Vance REDFERN
36 Director of Career Services .... Ms. Marie LECK
28 Dir Multi-Cultural Affs/Student Act .... Ms. Maria DOMINGUEZ
96 Director of Purchasing .... Ms. Amy BACA

NEW YORK

Adelphi University (A)

1 South Avenue, PO Box 701,
Garden City NY 11530-0701
County: Nassau FICE Identification: 002666
Unit ID: 188429
Telephone: (516) 877-3000 Carnegie Class: DRU
FAX Number: (516) 877-3545 Calendar System: Semester
URL: www.adelphi.edu
Established: 1896 Annual Undergrad Tuition & Fees: $28,460
Enrollment: 7,917 Coed
Affiliation or Control: Independent Non-Profit IRS Status: 501(c)3
Highest Offering: Doctorate
Program: Liberal Arts And General; Teacher Preparatory; Professional
Accreditation: M, AUD, BUS, CLPSY, NURSE, SP, SW, TED

01 President .... Dr. Robert A. SCOTT
03 Provost .... Dr. Gayle D. INSLER
05 Senior Assoc Provost for Acad Affs .... Dr. Audrey S. BLUMBERG
11 Senior Associate Provost for Admin .... Dr. Lawrence HOBBIE
20 Associate Provost Academic Affairs .... Dr. Lester BALTIMORE
56 Ex Dir Off Campus Adm Enrol/Std Afs .... Mr. James MCGOWAN
32 Vice Pres Admin/Student Scvs .... Mr. Angelo B. PROTO
10 Senior Vice President & Treasurer .... Mr. Timothy P. BURTON
30 Vice Pres University Advancement .... Mr. Chris VAUPEL
26 Vice President for Communications .... Ms. Lori DUGGAN-GOLD
84 Assoc VP Enrollment Mgt/Stdnt Affs .... Ms. Esther GOODCUFF
21 Assoc VP for Finance & Co-Treasurer .... Mr. Robert L. DECARLO
15 Asst VP Human Resource/Labor Rel .... Ms. Lisa ARAUJO
49 Dean of Arts & Sciences .... Dr. Sam L. GROGG
53 Dean School of Education .... Dr. Jane ASHDOWN
66 Dean School of Nursing .... Dr. Patrick R. COONAN
70 Dean School of Social Work .... Dr. Andrew SAFYER
58 Dean Derner Inst Advanc Psych Std .... Dr. Jacques BARBER
50 Dean School of Business .... Mr. Rakesh GUPTA
92 Dean of Honors College .... Dr. Richard GARNER
32 Dean Student Affairs .... Mr. Jeffrey A. KESSLER
19 Exec Director of Public Safety .... Mr. Eugene PALMA
18 Exec Dir Facilities/Physical Plant .... Mr. James KOSLOSKI
12 Director Manhattan Center .... Ms. June TRIZZINO-PECOR
09 Director Research/Assessment/Plng .... Dr. Nava LERER
14 Communication Admin Info Tech .... Mr. Steve FILIPELLI
13 Chief Information Officer/CIO .... Mr. Jack CHEN
41 Asst VP/Director of Athletics .... Mr. Robert E. HARTWELL
35 Associate Dean Student Affairs .... Ms. Della HUDSON-TOMLIN
58 Asc Dn Derner Inst Advanc Psych Std .... Dr. Christopher J. MURAN
37 Director Student Financial Aid .... Ms. Sheryl L. MIHOPULOS
36 Exec Dir Career Plng & Placement .... Mr. Thomas J. WARD
23 Director Health Services .... Ms. Jacqueline CARTABUKE
39 Director Residential Life/Housing .... Mr. Guy SENEQUE
06 Registrar .... Ms. Rita ARMENIA
29 Director Alumni Relations .... Mr. Joseph GERACI
38 Director Student Counseling Center .... Ms. Carol PHELAN
96 Purchasing Manager .... Ms. Elizabeth F. KASH
13 Dir Info Technology & Resources .... Mr. Joseph BATTAGLIA
07 Director of Admissions .... Ms. Christine MURPHY
88 Budget Director .... Mr. Michael J. MCLEOD
88 Director Business Affairs .... Mr. Russell A. PALMER
40 Bookstore Manager .... Vacant

Adirondack Community College (B)

640 Bay Road, Queensbury NY 12804-1498
County: Warren FICE Identification: 002860
Unit ID: 188438
Telephone: (518) 743-2200 Carnegie Class: Assoc/Pub-R-M
FAX Number: (518) 745-1433 Calendar System: Semester
URL: www.sunyacc.edu
Established: 1960 Annual Undergrad Tuition & Fees (In-District): $3,556
Enrollment: 4,020 Coed
Affiliation or Control: State/Local IRS Status: 501(c)3
Highest Offering: Associate Degree
Program: Occupational; 2-Year Principally Bachelor's Creditable
Accreditation: M, ADNUR

01 President .... Dr. Ronald C. HEACOCK
04 Assistant to the President .... Ms. Dari L. NORMAN
05 Int VP Academic/Student Affairs .... Mr. Brian DURANT
11 Vice Pres Admin Services/Treasurer .... Mr. William LONG, III
30 Exec Dir Dev/Alumni Rels/ACC Fndtn .... Mr. Joseph CUTSHALL-KING
51 Dean of Cont & External Stds .... Ms. Denise BRUCKER
20 Dean for Special Academic Svcs .... Ms. Diane DALTO
32 Int Dean for Student Affairs .... Ms. Barbara GREEN
26 Director Marketing & Cmty Rels .... Mr. Mark PARFITT
09 Director of Inst Research/Planning .... Mr. David SMITH
27 Chief Information Officer .... Ms. Susan A. TRUMPICK
15 Director of Human Resources .... Ms. Marjorie KELLY
40 Director Bookstore .... Mr. Tom KENT
10 Chief Financial Officer .... Mr. Kevin B. RIELLY
21 Director of Business Affairs .... Ms. Ann Marie SOMMA
18 Director Facilities .... Mr. Anthony PALANGI
37 Director Student Financial Aid .... Ms. Maureen REILLY
06 Director of Records .... Ms. Sarah LEVIN
84 Director of Enrollment Management .... Ms. Sarah J. LINEHAN
90 Director Academic Computer Services .... Ms. Roseann ANZALONE
08 Director of Library Services .... Ms. Teresa RONNING
35 Coordinator of Student Activities .... Ms. Heather CHARPENTIER
41 Athletic Director .... Ms. Darla BELEVICH

Albany College of Pharmacy and Health Sciences (C)

106 New Scotland Avenue, Albany NY 12208-3492
County: Albany FICE Identification: 002885
Unit ID: 188526
Telephone: (518) 694-7200 Carnegie Class: Spec/Health
FAX Number: (518) 694-7202 Calendar System: Semester
URL: www.acphs.edu
Established: 1881 Annual Undergrad Tuition & Fees: $25,700
Enrollment: 1,597 Coed
Affiliation or Control: Independent Non-Profit IRS Status: 501(c)3
Highest Offering: Doctorate
Program: Professional
Accreditation: M, CYTO, MT, PHAR

01 President .... James GOZZO
05 Provost .... Mehdi BOROUJERDI
46 Vice Provost for Research .... Shaker MOUSA
35 Dean of Students .... John DENIO
12 Associate Dean for Vermont Campus .... Robert HAMILTON
43 General Counsel .... Gerald KATZMAN
10 VP of Finance .... Michele VIEN
30 VP of Institutional Advancement .... Vicki DILORENZO
84 VP of Enrollment Management .... Tiffany GUTIERREZ
32 VP of Campus Life .... Jose RODRIGUEZ
13 Chief Technology Officer .... Pamela SMITH
11 AVP of Administrative Operations .... Packy MCGRAW
09 AVP of Institutional Effectiveness .... Angela DOMINELLI
100 Special Assistant to the President .... Michael SASS
07 Director of Admissions .... Matthew STEVER
06 Registrar .... Judy SCHMONSKY
08 Director of Library Services .... Sue IWANOWICZ
26 Exec Director of Marketing/Comm .... Gil CHORBAJIAN
41 Athletic Director .... Ryan VENTER
15 Director of Human Resources .... Casey DIMARCO

Albany Law School (D)

80 New Scotland Avenue, Albany NY 12208-3494
County: Albany FICE Identification: 002886
Unit ID: 188535
Telephone: (518) 445-2311 Carnegie Class: Spec/Law
FAX Number: (518) 445-2315 Calendar System: Semester
URL: www.albanylaw.edu
Established: 1851 Annual Undergrad Tuition & Fees: $41,720
Enrollment: 702 Coed
Affiliation or Control: Independent Non-Profit IRS Status: 501(c)3
Highest Offering: First Professional Degree
Program: Professional
Accreditation: LAW

01 Acting President & Dean .... Prof. Connie M. MAYER
05 Acting Assoc Dean Academic Affs .... Prof. Helane DAVIS
10 Vice President Finance & Business .... Mr. Victor E. RAUSCHER
30 Vice Pres Institutional Advancement .... Ms. Helen ADAMS-KEANE
32 Assistant Dean for Student Affairs .... Ms. Susan FEATHERS
06 Assistant Dean and Registrar .... Ms. Joanne FITZSIMMONS
36 Assistant Dean Career Planning .... Ms. Sandra MANS
08 Acting Director Law Library .... Mr. Robert EMERY
26 Assoc Dean External Affairs .... Ms. Patricia E. SALKIN
09 Assoc Dean for Rsrch & Scholarship .... Mr. James GATHII
27 Director Communications .... Mr. David SINGER
04 Executive Assistant to the Dean .... Ms. Barbara JORDAN-SMITH
07 Assistant Dean of Admissions .... Ms. Gail BENSEN
88 Director Clinical Program .... Prof. Joseph CONNOR
13 Director Enterprise Tech Services .... Mr. Christopher CASEY
30 Director Development .... Mr. James KELLERHOUSE
29 Director Alumni Affairs .... Ms. Christina SEBASTIAN
15 Director Human Resources .... Ms. Sherri DONNELLY
37 Director Student Financial Aid .... Ms. Andrea WEDLER
28 Director of Diversity .... Ms. Pershia WILKINS
18 Facilities Manager .... Mr. Brian LA PLANTE
44 Annual Giving Coordinator .... Ms. Morgan MORRISSEY
36 Career Services Coordinator .... Mrs. Joanne CASEY

Albany Medical College (E)

47 New Scotland Avenue, Mail #34,
Albany NY 12208-3479
County: Albany FICE Identification: 002887
Unit ID: 188580
Telephone: (518) 262-6008 Carnegie Class: Spec/Med
FAX Number: (518) 262-6515 Calendar System: Other
URL: www.amc.edu
Established: 1839 Annual Graduate Tuition & Fees: $45,310
Enrollment: 813 Coed
Affiliation or Control: Independent Non-Profit IRS Status: 501(c)3
Highest Offering: Doctorate; No Undergraduates
Program: Professional
Accreditation: M, ANEST, ARCPA, IPSY, MED

01 Dean .... Dr. Vincent P. VERDILE
05 Vice Dean for Academic Admin .... Dr. Henry S. POHL
32 Assoc Dean for Acad & Student Affs .... Dr. Elizabeth HIGGINS
63 Assoc Dean Graduate Medical Educ .... Dr. Joel BARTFIELD
90 Assoc Dean Info Resources & Tech .... Ms. Enid GEYER
88 Assoc Dean Undergrad Medical Educ .... Dr. Jonathan M. ROSEN
22 Assoc Dean Cmty Outreach/Medical Ed .... Ms. Ingrid ALLARD
08 Asc Dn Info Resrcs/Tech/Dir Library .... Ms. Enid GEYER
88 Asst Dean Undergrad Medical Educ .... Dr. Rebecca KELLER
88 Asst Dean Undergrad Medical Educ .... Dr. Kimberly KILBY
06 Registrar .... Mr. Len SCHLEGEL
63 Director Graduate Medical Education .... Ms. Catherine RIDDLE
76 Director Physician Asst Program .... Mr. David IRVINE
07 Dir Admissions & Student Records .... Ms. Joanne NANOS
29 Executive Director Alumni Relations .... Ms. Maura MACK-HISGEN
26 Director Public Relations .... Mr. Gregory J. MCGARRY
30 Chief Development .... Ms. Terri CERVENY
51 Director Cont Medical Education .... Ms. Jennifer PRICE
15 Director Human Resources .... Ms. Cathy HALAKAN
37 Director Student Financial Aid .... Ms. Ann LOUGHMAN
96 Director of Purchasing .... Ms. Patricia MARINO

Alfred University (F)

One Saxon Drive, Alfred NY 14802-1205
County: Allegany FICE Identification: 002668
Unit ID: 188641
Telephone: (607) 871-2111 Carnegie Class: Master's L
FAX Number: (607) 871-2339 Calendar System: Semester
URL: www.alfred.edu
Established: 1836 Annual Undergrad Tuition & Fees: $26,884
Enrollment: 2,306 Coed
Affiliation or Control: Independent Non-Profit IRS Status: 501(c)3
Highest Offering: Doctorate
Program: Liberal Arts And General; Teacher Preparatory; Professional
Accreditation: M, ART, BUS, ENG, SCPSY, TEAC

01 President .... Dr. Charles M. EDMONDSON
05 Provost/VP for Academic Affairs .... Dr. William HALL
10 VP for Business & Finance/Treasurer .... Ms. Giovina LLOYD
30 VP for University Relations .... Mr. Stanley A. COLLA, JR.
84 VP for Enrollment Management .... Mr. Earl E. PIERCE, JR.
32 VP for Student Affairs .... Mrs. Kathy WOUGHTER
57 Dean School of Art & Design .... Ms. Leslie BELLAVANCE
49 Dean Col of Lib Arts & Sciences .... Dr. Mary MCGEE
50 Acting Dean College of Business .... Dr. Nancy EVANGELISTA
54 Dean School of Engineering .... Dr. Doreen EDWARDS
29 Exec Dir Annual Giv/Alum Relations .... Mr. Mark SHARDLOW
37 Director of Student Financial Aid .... Mr. Earl E. PIERCE, JR.
07 Director of Admissions .... Mr. Corry D. UNIS
06 Registrar .... Mr. Lawrence J. CASEY
19 Chief of Public Safety .... Mr. John M. DOUGHERTY
09 Dir Enrollment Operations & Rsch .... Ms. Karen L. JOHNSON
27 Director of Communications .... Mrs. Susan C. GOETSCHIUS
39 Director of Residence Life .... Mrs. Brenda I. PORTER
13 Director Information Tech Svcs .... Mr. Gary O. ROBERTS
36 Director Career Development Ctr .... Mr. Mark MCFADDEN
41 Director of Athletics .... Mr. James M. MORETTI
23 Dir Counseling & Wellness Center .... Ms. Cathie L. CHESTER
18 Director of Physical Plant .... Mr. Dave PECKHAM
08 Dir Herrick Lib/Dean of Libraries .... Mr. Stephen S. CRANDALL
08 Director of Scholes Library .... Mr. Mark SMITH
16 Director of Human Resources .... Mr. Mark A. GUINAN, JR.
21 Controller .... Mrs. Tammara RAUB
92 Director of the Honors Program .... Dr. Gordan ATLAS
94 Dir of Women's Leadership Center .... Ms. Julia OVERTON-HEALY
35 Director of Student Activities .... Mr. Daniel NAPOLITANO
96 Director of Office Services .... Ms. Susan M. PECK
43 Dir Capital Operations/Leg Affairs .... Mr. Michael A. NEIDERBACH
101 Secretary to the Corporation .... Ms. Laura J. CRAIN
104 Acting Dir International Programs .... Dr. Vicky WESTACOTT
40 Bookstore Manager .... Mrs. Marcy K. BRADLEY
88 Assistant VP for Statutory Affairs .... Dr. Linda E. JONES

AMDA College and Conservatory of the Performing Arts (G)

211 West 61st Street, New York NY 10023-7832
County: New York FICE Identification: 007572
Unit ID: 188854
Telephone: (212) 787-5300 Carnegie Class: Not Classified
FAX Number: (212) 247-0488 Calendar System: Semester
URL: www.amda.edu
Established: 1964 Annual Undergrad Tuition & Fees: $29,960
Enrollment: 1,183 Coed
Affiliation or Control: Independent Non-Profit IRS Status: 501(c)3
Highest Offering: Baccalaureate
Program: Liberal Arts And General; Fine Arts Emphasis
Accreditation: THEA

01 President/Artistic Director .... Mr. David MARTIN
11 Executive Director .... Ms. Jan MARTIN
07 Director of Admissions .... Ms. Charlotte FRANCOVALLE

American Academy of Dramatic Arts (A)

120 Madison Avenue, New York NY 10016-7089

County: New York | FICE Identification: 007465 | Unit ID: 188678

Telephone: (212) 686-9244 | Carnegie Class: Assoc/PrivNFP

FAX Number: (212) 545-7934 | Calendar System: Other

URL: www.aada.edu

Established: 1884 | Annual Undergrad Tuition & Fees: $29,900

Enrollment: 422 | Coed

Affiliation or Control: Independent Non-Profit | IRS Status: 501(c)3

Highest Offering: Associate Degree

Program: Occupational; 2-Year Principally Bachelor's Creditable

Accreditation: M, NY, THEA

Code	Title	Name
01	Acting President/COO	Ms. Susan ZECH
10	Chief Financial Officer	Mr. John POLSKY
05	Director of Instruction	Mr. Constantine SCOPAS
07	Director of Admissions	Ms. Karen HIGGINBOTHAM
37	Director Financial Aid	Mr. Roberto LOPEZ
08	Librarian	Ms. Deborah PICONE
21	Controller	Ms. Linda VIALA
04	Assistant to the President	Ms. Lynette BELARDO
26	Director External Affairs	Mrs. Elizabeth LAWSON
18	Superintendent	Mr. Oliver SULLIVAN

American Academy McAllister Institute of Funeral Service (B)

619 W 54th Street, 6th Floor, New York NY 10019

County: New York | FICE Identification: 010813 | Unit ID: 188687

Telephone: (212) 757-1190 | Carnegie Class: Assoc/PrivNFP

FAX Number: (212) 765-5923 | Calendar System: Semester

URL: www.funeraleducation.org

Established: 1926 | Annual Undergrad Tuition & Fees: $11,560

Enrollment: 312 | Coed

Affiliation or Control: Independent Non-Profit | IRS Status: 501(c)3

Highest Offering: Associate Degree

Program: Occupational

Accreditation: FUSER

Code	Title	Name
01	President/CEO	Ms. Meg DUNN
05	Academic Dean/CAO	Ms. Regina SMITH
43	Legal Counsel	Mr. Charles MAURER
10	Bursar/Director of Admissions	Mr. Norman PROVOST
06	Registrar	Ms. Kerriann WILLIAMS
07	Dir Admissions/Enrollment Mgmt	Mr. Juan LOPEZ
08	Librarian	Ms. Mary MOON
37	Financial Aid Administrator	Mr. Jaway TSO
20	Academic Advisor	Ms. Anna Marie LANZA

The Art Institute of New York City (C)

11 Beach Street, New York NY 10013-1917

County: New York | FICE Identification: 025256 | Unit ID: 365055

Telephone: (212) 625-6000 | Carnegie Class: Assoc/PrivFP

FAX Number: (212) 226-5644 | Calendar System: Quarter

URL: www.ainyc.aii.edu

Established: 1980 | Annual Undergrad Tuition & Fees: $30,282

Enrollment: 1,413 | Coed

Affiliation or Control: Proprietary | IRS Status: Proprietary

Highest Offering: Associate Degree

Program: 2-Year Principally Bachelor's Creditable; Fine Arts Emphasis

Accreditation: ACICS

Code	Title	Name
01	President	Mr. Tad GRAHAM-HANDLEY
05	Dean of Academic Affairs	Mr. David MOUGHALIAN
07	Director of Admissions	Mrs. Mary Ann GRILLO
10	Director Admin & Financial Svcs	Vacant
37	Director of Student Financial Svcs	Mr. Fred HAMILTON
36	Director of Career Services	Mr. Marc SCOLERI
32	Dean of Student Affairs	Mr. Joe PIRRELLO
06	Registrar	Mr. Giovanni PALOMO

ASA Institute of Business & Computer Technology (D)

81 Willoughby Street, Brooklyn NY 11201

County: Kings | FICE Identification: 030955 | Unit ID: 404994

Telephone: (718) 522-9073 | Carnegie Class: Assoc/PrivFP

FAX Number: (718) 532-1430 | Calendar System: Semester

URL: www.asa.edu

Established: 1994 | Annual Undergrad Tuition & Fees: $11,950

Enrollment: 3,182 | Coed

Affiliation or Control: Proprietary | IRS Status: Proprietary

Highest Offering: Associate Degree

Program: Occupational; 2-Year Principally Bachelor's Creditable

Accreditation: M, ACICS, MAC

Code	Title	Name
01	President	Mr. Alex SHCHEGOL
05	Sr Vice President Academic Affairs	Dr. Alexander AGAFONOV
07	Vice President Marketing/Admissions	Ms. Victoria KOSTYUKOV
36	Vice Pres Placement/Alumni Svcs	Ms. Lesia WILLIS-CAMPBELL
86	Vice Pres Govt & Community Rels	Mr. Roberto DUMAUAL

Bank Street College of Education (E)

610 W 112 Street, New York NY 10025-1898

County: New York | FICE Identification: 002669 | Unit ID: 189015

Telephone: (212) 875-4400 | Carnegie Class: Spec/Other

FAX Number: (212) 875-4759 | Calendar System: Semester

URL: www.bankstreet.edu

Established: 1916 | Annual Graduate Tuition & Fees: $23,329

Enrollment: 1,112 | Coed

Affiliation or Control: Independent Non-Profit | IRS Status: 501(c)3

Highest Offering: Master's; No Undergraduates

Program: Teacher Preparatory; Professional

Accreditation: M

Code	Title	Name
01	President	Elizabeth D. DICKEY
10	Chief Operating Officer	Frank NUARA
30	Vice Pres Institutional Advancement	John S. BORDEN
05	Dean of the College	Jon D. SNYDER
58	Dean of the Graduate School	Virginia ROACH
88	Dean of Childrens Programs	Alexis S. WRIGHT
88	Associate Dean for IPR	Farhad ASGHAR
11	Associate Dean Administration	Barbara COLEMAN
20	Associate Dean Academic Affairs	Virginia CASPER
07	Director of Admissions	Ann MORGAN
06	Registrar	Sandra SCLAFANI
37	Director Student Financial Aid	Lou PALEFSKY
29	Director of Alumni Relations	Linda REING
15	Director of Human Resources	Carol SAMBERG
13	Director Information Services	Arlen RAUSCHKOLB
18	Director of Facilities	Lesly PIERRE
08	Director of Library Services	Kristin FREDA
36	Director Student Placement	Susan LEVINE
09	Director of Institutional Research	Ian BECKFORD

Bard College (F)

PO Box 5000, Annandale-On-Hudson NY 12504-5000

County: Dutchess | FICE Identification: 002671 | Unit ID: 189088

Telephone: (845) 758-6822 | Carnegie Class: Bac/A&S

FAX Number: (845) 758-4294 | Calendar System: Semester

URL: www.bard.edu

Established: 1860 | Annual Undergrad Tuition & Fees: $43,306

Enrollment: 2,264 | Coed

Affiliation or Control: Independent Non-Profit | IRS Status: 501(c)3

Highest Offering: Doctorate

Program: Liberal Arts And General

Accreditation: M, @TEAC

Code	Title	Name
01	President	Dr. Leon BOTSTEIN
03	Executive Vice President	Dr. Dimitri B. PAPADIMITRIOU
30	Vice Pres Alumni/ae Affairs/Devel	Ms. Debra PEMSTEIN
11	Vice President for Administration	Dr. James BRUDVIG
20	Vice President/Dean of the College	Dr. Michele DOMINY
05	Vice President Academic Affairs	Dr. Robert MARTIN
82	AVP/Dn Intl Aff/Civ Engmt/Dir IILE	Dr. Jonathan BECKER
58	Dean of Graduate Studies	Dr. Norton BATKIN
08	Dean Information Svcs/Dir Libraries	Mr. Jeffrey KATZ
39	Dean of Campus Life	Ms. Gretchen PERRY
32	Dean of Students	Ms. Erin CANNAN
13	CTO/Assoc Dean Information Svcs	Mr. Bill TERRY
88	Associate Dean of the College	Dr. Mark D. HALSEY
88	Asst Dean College/Asc Dean Std Affs	Dr. David SHEIN
35	Assistant Dean of Students	Ms. Bethany NOHLGREN
53	Dir Master of Arts in Teaching Pgm	Mr. Ric CAMPBELL
57	Dir Milton Avery Grad Sch of Arts	Mr. Arthur GIBBONS
88	Dir Bard Grad Ctr Decorative Arts	Dr. Susan WEBER
88	Exec Dir Ctr Curatorial Studies	Mr. Tom ECCLES
88	Director of Institutional Support	Ms. Karen UNGER
88	Director Ctr Environmental Policy	Dr. Eban GOODSTEIN
07	Director of Admissions	Ms. Mary I. BACKLUND
37	Director Financial Aid	Ms. Denise ACKERMAN
06	Registrar	Mr. Peter GADSBY
26	Director of Communications	Mr. Mark PRIMOFF
15	Director of Human Resources	Ms. Patricia P. WALKER
21	Controller	Mr. Kevin PARKER
88	Director Inst Writing/Thinking	Ms. Theresa J. VILARDI
18	Director of Buildings & Grounds	Mr. Chuck SIMMONS
13	Director of Mgmt Info Systems	Mr. Michael TOMPKINS
29	Director Alumni/ae Affairs	Ms. Jane BRIEN
36	Director Career Development	Ms. April KINSER
19	Director Safety & Security	Mr. Kenneth COOPER
09	Director of Institutional Research	Mr. Joseph F. AHERN
24	Audio/Video Engineer Fisher Ctr	Mr. Paul LABARBERA
28	Director of Multicultural Affairs	Dr. Ann SEATON
41	Director of Athletics	Ms. Kristin HALL
42	Chaplain	Dr. Bruce D. CHILTON
40	Bookstore Manager	Ms. Merry MEYER
23	Director Health Services	Ms. Marsha DAVIS
38	Director Student Counseling	Vacant
96	Director of Purchasing	Ms. Julie K. MYERS

Barnard College (G)

3009 Broadway, New York NY 10027-6598

County: New York | FICE Identification: 002708 | Unit ID: 189097

Telephone: (212) 854-5262 | Carnegie Class: Bac/A&S

FAX Number: (212) 854-6220 | Calendar System: Semester

URL: www.barnard.edu

Established: 1889 | Annual Undergrad Tuition & Fees: $42,184

Enrollment: 2,456 | Female

Affiliation or Control: Independent Non-Profit | IRS Status: 501(c)3

Highest Offering: Baccalaureate

Program: Liberal Arts And General

Accreditation: M, DANCE, @TEAC

Code	Title	Name
01	President	Debora L. SPAR
05	Provost & Dean of the Faculty	Elizabeth S. BOYLAN
11	Vice President Administration	Lisa GAMSU
26	Vice President Communications	Joanne KWONG
10	Chief Operating Officer	Gregory N. BROWN
30	Vice President Development	Bobbi MARK
08	Vice Pres Information Technology	Carol KATZMAN
20	Dean of the College	Avis HINKSON
32	Dean of Studies	Karen J. BLANK
07	Dean of Admissions	Jennifer FONDILLER
39	Director Residential Life & Housing	Ann AVERSA
06	Registrar	Constance BROWN
29	Director of Alumnae Affairs	Erin FREDRICK
37	Director of Financial Aid	Nanette DILAURO
36	Director of Career Development	Robert EARL
15	Director of Human Resources	Lori MCFARLAND
19	Director of Safety/Security	Dianna PENNETTI
23	Director of Health Services	Brenda SLADE
96	Director of Purchasing & Stores	Douglas MAGET
21	Associate Business Officer	Eileen M. DIBENEDETTO
09	Director of Institutional Research	Sean BIXLER

† Affiliated with Columbia University in the City of New York.

Be'er Yaakov Talmudic Seminary (H)

12 Jefferson Avenue, Spring Valley NY 10977

County: Rockland | Identification: 667076

Telephone: (845) 362-3053 | Carnegie Class: Not Classified

FAX Number: (845) 406-9699 | Calendar System: Semester

Established: 1995 | Annual Undergrad Tuition & Fees: $6,000

Enrollment: 199 | Male

Affiliation or Control: Independent Non-Profit | IRS Status: 501(c)3

Highest Offering: First Talmudic Degree

Program: Professional

Accreditation: RABN

Code	Title	Name
01	CEO	Mr. Jacob UNGAR
05	Dean	Rabbi Yosef Yisioel EISENBERGER
06	Registrar/Administrator	Rabbi Yitzchok SOIFER
37	Financial Aid Administrator	Rabbi Yosef BRAILOFSKY

Beis Medrash Heichal Dovid (I)

211 Beach 17th Street, Far Rockaway NY 11691-4433

County: Queens | FICE Identification: 037133 | Unit ID: 444413

Telephone: (718) 868-2300 | Carnegie Class: Spec/Faith

FAX Number: (718) 868-0517 | Calendar System: Semester

Established: 1999 | Annual Undergrad Tuition & Fees: $6,900

Enrollment: 116 | Male

Affiliation or Control: Independent Non-Profit | IRS Status: 501(c)3

Highest Offering: Second Talmudic Degree

Program: Teacher Preparatory; Professional

Accreditation: RABN

Code	Title	Name
01	Dean	Rabbi Yaakov BENDER
05	Rosh Yeshiva	Rabbi Shlomo Avidgor ALTUSKY
37	Financial Aid Officer	Mrs. Amy KURTZ

Berkeley College (J)

3 E 43rd Street, New York NY 10017-4604

County: New York | FICE Identification: 007394 | Unit ID: 189228

Telephone: (212) 986-4343 | Carnegie Class: Spec/Bus

FAX Number: (212) 818-1169 | Calendar System: Quarter

URL: www.berkeleycollege.edu

Established: 1931 | Annual Undergrad Tuition & Fees: $21,750

Enrollment: 5,202 | Coed

Affiliation or Control: Proprietary | IRS Status: Proprietary

Highest Offering: Baccalaureate

Program: Business Emphasis

Accreditation: M

Code	Title	Name
00	Chairman of the Board	Mr. Kevin L. LUING
01	President	Dr. Dario CORTES
100	Chief of Staff & Director Planning	Ms. Linda LUCIANO
04	Special Assistant to the President	Dr. Rose Mary HEALY
05	Provost	Dr. Glen ZEITZER
10	Sr Vice President Finance & Admin	Ms. Lee S. MIARA
11	Assoc Provost Acad Support & Admin	Dr. Beth COYLE
84	Sr Vice President Enrollment Mgmt	Ms. Diane RECINOS
20	Associate Provost Academic Admin	Dr. Troy ADAIR
26	Senior Vice President Marketing	Mr. Don CHALLIS
20	Assoc Provost Faculty Affairs	Dr. Marianne VAKALIS
37	Vice President Financial Aid	Mr. Howard LESLIE
32	VP Student Development/Campus Life	Dr. Edwin HUGHES
36	Vice President Advisement	Ms. Tia DELOUISE
07	Vice President Enrollment	Ms. Christine G. RICHARD
07	VP International Enrollment Svcs	Ms. Cynthia C. MARCHESE
22	Vice Pres & Compliance Officer	Mr. William BRANDT
88	Vice President External Affairs	Mr. Kevin HILL
88	Vice President Student Accounts	Ms. Eileen LOFTUS-BERLIN
08	Vice President Library Services	Ms. Marlene DOTY
12	NYC Campus Operating Officer	Ms. Kristin ROWE
12	Westchester Campus Operatng Officer	Ms. Cynthia RUBINO
09	Asst VP Assessment & Inst Research	Dr. Ross MILLER

50	Dean School of Business	Dr. John RAPANOS
49	Dean School of Liberal Arts	Dr. Don KIEFFER
107	Dean School of Professional Studies	Dr. Judith KORNBERG
51	Dean School of Continuing Education	Mr. Ricardo ORTEGON
106	Dean Berkeley College Online	Ms. Carol SMITH
88	Associate VP Advisement	Ms. Gail OKUN
84	Assoc Vice President Enrollment	Ms. Linda PINSKY
38	Asst Dean Dir Personal Counseling	Ms. Katherine WU
07	Sr Dir International Division	Ms. Nori JAFFER
37	Senior Director Financial Aid	Ms. Christine DESOUSA
21	Associate VP Student Accounts	Ms. Ursula BISCONTI
09	Director Institutional Research	Mr. Christopher J. VINGER
26	Director Media Relations	Ms. Ilene GREENFIELD
41	Athletic Director	Mr. Brian MAHER

Beth Hamedrash Shaarei Yosher Institute (A)

4102-10 16th Avenue, Brooklyn NY 11204-1099

County: Kings FICE Identification: 011192
Unit ID: 189273

Telephone: (718) 854-2290 Carnegie Class: Spec/Faith
FAX Number: (718) 436-9045 Calendar System: Semester
Established: 1962 Annual Undergrad Tuition & Fees: $6,010
Enrollment: 40 Male
Affiliation or Control: Independent Non-Profit IRS Status: 501(c)3
Highest Offering: Second Talmudic Degree
Program: Teacher Preparatory; Professional
Accreditation: RABN

05	Chief Academic Officer	Rabbi Yosef ROSENBLUM
10	Chief Business Officer	Rabbi Eliezer REICHMAN
30	Chief Development Officer	Rabbi Moses GRUENBERGER
45	Chief Planning Officer	Rabbi Chaim BLAU
26	Public Relations Officer	Mr. Zelig MAYER
29	Director Alumni Association	Rabbi Chaim ROSENBERG
15	Director Personnel Services	Rabbi Mordechai MARGULIES
37	Director Student Financial Aid	Mr. Menachem STEINBERG
06	Registrar	Rabbi Nusyn P. ERLICH

Beth Hatalmud Rabbinical College (B)

2127 82nd Street, Brooklyn NY 11214-2594

County: Kings FICE Identification: 011922
Unit ID: 189264

Telephone: (718) 259-2525 Carnegie Class: Spec/Faith
FAX Number: (718) 256-5592 Calendar System: Semester
Established: 1950 Annual Undergrad Tuition & Fees: $6,150
Enrollment: 56 Male
Affiliation or Control: Independent Non-Profit IRS Status: 501(c)3
Highest Offering: Second Talmudic Degree
Program: Teacher Preparatory; Professional
Accreditation: RABN

01	President	Rabbi Chaim STEFANSKY
10	Fiscal Officer	Rabbi C. L. PERKOWSKI
08	Librarian	Mr. Shimon HESS

Boricua College (C)

3755 Broadway, New York NY 10032-1599

County: New York FICE Identification: 013029
Unit ID: 189413

Telephone: (212) 694-1000 Carnegie Class: Bac/Diverse
FAX Number: (212) 694-1015 Calendar System: Semester
URL: www.boricuacollege.edu
Established: 1974 Annual Undergrad Tuition & Fees: $10,110
Enrollment: 1,208 Coed
Affiliation or Control: Independent Non-Profit IRS Status: 501(c)3
Highest Offering: Master's
Program: Liberal Arts And General; Professional
Accreditation: M, @TEAC

01	President	Dr. Victor G. ALICEA
04	Admin Assistant to the President	Ms. Sandra BELLAMY
12	VP/Dn Acad Affs/Dn Brklyn Camp Ctr	Prof. Maria MONTES-MORALES
05	VP/Chief Acad Ofcr Manhattan Campus	Dr. Shivaji SENGUPTA
13	Vice Pres Information Technology	Mr. Irving RAMIREZ
43	Legal Counsel	Mr. Dasil VELEZ
10	Director Finance	Mr. Elias OYOLA
07	Director Admissions Northside Ctr	Ms. Miriam PFEFFER
07	Director Admissions Manhattan Ctr	Mr. Abraham CRUZ
07	Director Admissions Graham	Miss Aurea MORALES
06	Director Registration & Assessment	Dr. Mercedes ALICEA
37	Dir Finan Aid Res/Academic Support	Ms. Rosalia CRUZ
15	Director Personnel/Human Resources	Ms. Francia L. CASTRO
08	Director Library/Learning Resources	Ms. Liza RIVERA
18	Director Environmental Services	Mr. Angel REYES
41	Director of Athletics	Mr. Robert GUILBE
30	Director of Development	Vacant

Bramson O R T College (D)

69-30 Austin Street, Forest Hills NY 11375-4239

County: Queens FICE Identification: 021068
Unit ID: 189422

Telephone: (718) 261-5800 Carnegie Class: Assoc/PrivNFP
FAX Number: (718) 575-5119 Calendar System: Semester
URL: www.bramsonort.edu
Established: 1977 Annual Undergrad Tuition & Fees: $10,610
Enrollment: 1,021 Coed
Affiliation or Control: Independent Non-Profit IRS Status: 501(c)3
Highest Offering: Associate Degree
Program: Occupational; 2-Year Principally Bachelor's Creditable
Accreditation: NY

01	Director	Dr. Ephraim BUHKS
05	Dean of Academic Services	Dr. Robert ADELBERG
07	Recruitment/Admissions	Ms. Dashia SILVA
10	Chief Financial Officer	Mr. Leonard SCHWARTZ
08	Librarian	Ms. Rivka BURKOS
21	Bursar	Ms. Marina SHALAMOV
37	Financial Aid Coordinator	Ms. Angelina MARRA
60	ESL/English Coordinator	Ms. Leslie AARONS
36	Job Development Advisor	Ms. Beth MORGANLANDER
50	Business Technology & Account Coord	Mr. Robert ADELBERG
56	Computer Tech/Distance Learn Coord	Mr. Damindra PERSAUD
56	Coordinator Extension Site	Mr. Yair ROSENRAUCH
76	Medical Assistant Program Coord	Dr. Emil ASDURIAN
96	Director of Purchasing	Ms. Svetlana NISENBOYM
06	Registrar	Ms. Aleksandra KAGAN
09	Assistant Director	Ms. Jean VITALE
88	Controller	Ms. Mary C. RICKEY

Briarcliffe College (E)

1055 Stewart Avenue, Bethpage NY 11714-3545

County: Nassau FICE Identification: 020757
Unit ID: 189459

Telephone: (516) 918-3600 Carnegie Class: Bac/Assoc
FAX Number: (516) 470-6020 Calendar System: Semester
URL: www.briarcliffe.edu
Established: 1966 Annual Undergrad Tuition & Fees: $18,360
Enrollment: 1,922 Coed
Affiliation or Control: Proprietary IRS Status: Proprietary
Highest Offering: Baccalaureate
Program: Business Emphasis
Accreditation: M

01	President	Dr. George SANTIAGO
10	VP Finance & Oper/Chief Fin Ofcr	Mr. Louis COMMISSO
84	Vice Pres Enrollment Management	Mr. C. Gabriel CASTANO
32	Vice President Student Affairs	Ms. Kathy GENUA
05	Provost	Mr. David COHEN
22	Director Regulatory Operations	Ms. Susan PESCADOR
35	Director of Student Management	Ms. Georgette OSTROSKE
15	Director of Human Resources	Mr. Mel LYONS
14	Director of Information Systems	Mr. Michael HALBREICH
18	Dir Facilities/Security Management	Mr. Jerry MOSES
37	Director Financial Aid	Ms. Cindy ROYS
06	Senior Registrar	Ms. Vikki LEVINE
36	Director of Career Services	Ms. Stacy ZAGER
41	Athletic Director	Ms. Gina D'AMARO
08	Librarian	Ms. Jennifer DEVITO

Brooklyn Law School (F)

250 Joralemon Street, Brooklyn NY 11201-3798

County: Kings FICE Identification: 002677
Unit ID: 189501

Telephone: (718) 625-2200 Carnegie Class: Spec/Law
FAX Number: (718) 780-0393 Calendar System: Semester
URL: www.brooklaw.edu
Established: 1901 Annual Graduate Tuition & Fees: $48,416
Enrollment: 1,461 Coed
Affiliation or Control: Independent Non-Profit IRS Status: 501(c)3
Highest Offering: First Professional Degree; No Undergraduates
Program: Professional
Accreditation: LAW

01	President	Ms. Joan G. WEXLER
00	Chairman of the Board of Trustees	Mr. Stuart SUBOTNICK
05	Interim Dean	Dean Michael A. GERBER
20	Assoc Dean for Academic Affairs	Dean Michael T. CAHILL
32	Assoc Dean for Student Affairs	Dean Beryl R. JONES-WOODIN
10	Chief Financial Officer	Ms. Laurie H. NEWITZ
21	Treasurer	Ms. Shoshanna M. CAMPBELL
07	Dean of Admissions & Financial Aid	Dean Henry W. HAVERSTICK, III
08	Director of Library	Prof. Victoria SZYMCZAK
30	Director of Development	Ms. Jean SMITH
29	Director of Alumni Relations	Ms. Caitlin MONCK-MARCELLINO
36	Director of Career Services	Ms. Camille CHIN KEE FATT
06	Registrar	Ms. Suzanne DENNIS
37	Director of Financial Aid	Ms. Nancy L. ZAHZAM
26	Asst Dean of External Affairs	Ms. Linda HARVEY
39	Director of Residence Life	Ms. Jennifer LANG
07	Director of Admissions	Mr. Myron B. CHAITOVSKY
18	Facilities Manager	Mr. Steven OLEKSIW
15	Human Resources Manager	Ms. Christina WALLACE

Broome Community College (G)

PO Box 1017, Binghamton NY 13902-1017

County: Broome FICE Identification: 002862
Unit ID: 189547

Telephone: (607) 778-5000 Carnegie Class: Assoc/Pub-R-L
FAX Number: (607) 778-5310 Calendar System: Semester
URL: www.sunybroome.edu
Established: 1946 Annual Undergrad Tuition & Fees (In-District): $3,909
Enrollment: 6,950 Coed
Affiliation or Control: State/Local IRS Status: 501(c)3
Highest Offering: Associate Degree
Program: Occupational; 2-Year Principally Bachelor's Creditable
Accreditation: M, ADNUR, DH, ENGT, MAC, MLTAD, PTAA, RAD

01	President	Dr. Kevin DRUMM
05	Vice President Academic Affairs	Ms. Julia E. PEACOCK
11	Actg Vice Pres Admin/Financial Affs	Ms. Regina LOSINGER
32	Acting VP Student/CommunityAffairs	Ms. Debra MORELLO
50	Dean of Business/Public Services	Mr. Gregory TALLEY
76	Dean of Health Sciences	Dr. Andrea WADE
49	Dean of Liberal Arts/Human Services	Ms. Mary DICKSON
51	Dean Continuing Education	Ms. Debra MORELLO
81	Dean Science/Tech/Engr/Math	Dr. Kelli LIGEIKIS
102	Executive Director BCC Foundation	Dr. Judy U. SIGGINS
08	Director Learning Resource Center	Ms. Robin PETRUS
07	Director of Admissions	Ms. Jenae SCHMIDT-NORRIS
15	Human Resources Officer	Ms. Elizabeth A. WOOD
06	Acting Registrar	Ms. Cynthia MOWRY
36	Director of Placement Services	Mr. Lawrence T. TRUILLO
09	Director Institutional Res/Plan	Vacant
18	Campus Operations Director	Mr. Richard ARMSTRONG
21	Controller	Ms. Jeanette TILLOTSON
37	Director of Financial Aid	Mr. Douglas S. LUKASIK
14	Dir Information Technology Services	Mr. John PETKASH
23	Director of Health Services	Ms. Margaret SMITH
25	Director of Sponsored Programs	Mr. Cliff BALLIET
41	Director of Athletics	Mr. Daniel J. MINCH
19	Dir of Campus Safety & Security	Mr. Joseph O'CONNOR
29	Director Alumni Affairs	Ms. Natalie THOMPSON
35	Director Student Activities	Mr. David R. MASLAR
40	Director Bookstore	Ms. Donna M. FIRENZE
88	Dir Educational Opportunity Pgm	Ms. Claudia CLARKE
96	Director of Purchasing	Mr. John HASTIE
26	Public Affairs Officer	Mr. Richard DAVID
85	Asst Counselor Foreign Students	Ms. Beverly PLOWUCHA
38	Student Counseling	Ms. Mary MCCARTHY

*Bryant & Stratton College System Office (H)

2350 N Forest Road, Suite 12A, Getzville NY 14068-1296

County: Erie Identification: 666828
Telephone: (716) 250-7500 Carnegie Class: N/A
FAX Number: (716) 250-7510
URL: www.bryantstratton.edu

01	President & CEO	Mr. John J. STASCHAK
03	Executive Vice President	Dr. Francis J. FELSER
05	Vice Pres Chief Academic Officer	Ms. Beth A. TARQUINO
10	VP/Chief Financial Ofcr/Treasurer	Mr. David VADEN

*Bryant & Stratton College (I)

1259 Central Avenue, Albany NY 12205-5230

County: Albany FICE Identification: 004749
Unit ID: 188517

Telephone: (518) 437-1802 Carnegie Class: Assoc/PrivFP
FAX Number: (518) 437-1048 Calendar System: Semester
URL: www.bryantstratton.edu
Established: 1857 Annual Undergrad Tuition & Fees: $15,570
Enrollment: 845 Coed
Affiliation or Control: Proprietary IRS Status: Proprietary
Highest Offering: Associate Degree
Program: Occupational; 2-Year Principally Bachelor's Creditable
Accreditation: &M, MAC

02	Campus Director	Mr. Michael GUTIERREZ
05	Dean of Instruction	Mr. David DENOFIO
32	Dean of Student Services	Ms. Amy MORI
07	Director of Admissions	Mr. Bryan GREGORY
36	Director of Career Services	Ms. Gina CASSIDY

*Bryant & Stratton College (J)

465 Main Street, Suite 400, Buffalo NY 14203-1795

County: Erie FICE Identification: 002678
Unit ID: 189583

Telephone: (716) 884-9120 Carnegie Class: Assoc/PrivFP4
FAX Number: (716) 884-0091 Calendar System: Semester
URL: www.bryantstratton.edu
Established: 1854 Annual Undergrad Tuition & Fees: $15,570
Enrollment: 956 Coed
Affiliation or Control: Proprietary IRS Status: Proprietary
Highest Offering: Associate Degree
Program: 2-Year Principally Bachelor's Creditable; Liberal Arts And General; Business Emphasis
Accreditation: &M, MAC

02	Campus Director	Dr. Marvel E. ROSS-JONES
05	Dean of Instruction	Ms. Adiam TSEGAI
07	Director of Admissions	Mr. Phil J. STRUEBEL
36	Director of Career Services	Ms. Diane WESTBROOK
10	WNY Business Office Director	Ms. Kathleen OWCZARCZAK

*Bryant & Stratton College (K)

3650 Millersport Highway, Getzville NY 14068

County: Erie Identification: 666114
Unit ID: 189556

Telephone: (716) 625-6300 Carnegie Class: Bac/Assoc
FAX Number: N/A Calendar System: Semester
URL: www.bryantstratton.edu
Established: 1854 Annual Undergrad Tuition & Fees: $15,570
Enrollment: 567 Coed
Affiliation or Control: Proprietary IRS Status: Proprietary

Highest Offering: Baccalaureate
Program: Liberal Arts And General; Business Emphasis
Accreditation: &M

02 Campus Director .... Mr. Michael A. MARIANI
05 Dean of Instruction .... Ms. Janice Y. FERGUSON
07 Director of Admissions .... Mr. Brian K. DIOGUARDI
36 Director of Career Services .... Mr. Stephen G. MAKOSY
10 Western NY Business Office Director .... Ms. Kathleen OWCZARCZAK

Bryant & Stratton College (A)

8687 Carling Road, Liverpool NY 13090-1315
County: Onondaga Identification: 666115
Unit ID: 189565
Telephone: (315) 652-6500 Carnegie Class: Assoc/PrivFP
FAX Number: (315) 652-5500 Calendar System: Semester
URL: www.bryantstratton.edu
Established: 1854 Annual Undergrad Tuition & Fees: $15,605
Enrollment: 624 Coed
Affiliation or Control: Proprietary IRS Status: Proprietary
Highest Offering: Associate Degree
Program: 2-Year Principally Bachelor's Creditable
Accreditation: &M

02 Campus Director .... Ms. Susan K. CUMOLETTI
05 Dean of Instruction .... Ms. Kathleen M. ZAKRI
10 Market Business Director .... Ms. Mary CLIFTON
07 Director of Admissions .... Ms. Heather MACKNIK
32 Dean of Student Services .... Mr. Terry PUDNEY, JR.
36 Market Director of Career Services .... Ms. Kristen AUST

*Bryant & Stratton College (B)

Sterling Park 200 Red Tail, Orchard Park NY 14127-1562
County: Erie Identification: 666460
Unit ID: 374972
Telephone: (716) 677-9500 Carnegie Class: Assoc/PrivFP4
FAX Number: (716) 677-9599 Calendar System: Semester
URL: www.bryantstratton.edu
Established: 1854 Annual Undergrad Tuition & Fees: $15,570
Enrollment: 2,272 Coed
Affiliation or Control: Proprietary IRS Status: Proprietary
Highest Offering: Baccalaureate
Program: Occupational; 2-Year Principally Bachelor's Creditable; Liberal Arts And General
Accreditation: &M

02 Campus Director .... Mr. Paul BAHR
05 Dean of Instruction .... Mr. James WESOLOWSKI
07 Director of Admissions .... Mrs. Tracy DOMINIAK
36 Director of Career Services .... Mr. Steve MAKOSY
10 WNY Business Office Director .... Ms. Kathleen OWCZARCZAK

*Bryant & Stratton College (C)

150 Bellwood Drive, Rochester NY 14606-4227
County: Monroe FICE Identification: 012470
Unit ID: 189592
Telephone: (585) 720-0660 Carnegie Class: Assoc/PrivFP
FAX Number: (585) 720-9226 Calendar System: Semester
URL: www.bryantstratton.edu
Established: 1973 Annual Undergrad Tuition & Fees: $15,570
Enrollment: 395 Coed
Affiliation or Control: Proprietary IRS Status: Proprietary
Highest Offering: Associate Degree
Program: Occupational; 2-Year Principally Bachelor's Creditable
Accreditation: &M

02 Campus Director .... Mr. Marc D. AMBROSI
05 Dean of Instruction .... Mr. Paul PETRITUS
32 Dean of Student Services .... Mr. John C. SCHIFANO
36 Director of Career Services .... Ms. Kelly K. HENRY
10 Market Business Director .... Ms. Marie D'ALESSANDRO
07 Director of Admissions .... Mr. Brandon DINELL

*Bryant & Stratton College (D)

1225 Jefferson Road, Rochester NY 14623-3136
County: Monroe Identification: 666116
Unit ID: 410496
Telephone: (585) 292-5627 Carnegie Class: Assoc/PrivFP
FAX Number: (585) 292-6015 Calendar System: Semester
URL: www.bryantstratton.edu
Established: 1973 Annual Undergrad Tuition & Fees: $15,605
Enrollment: 436 Coed
Affiliation or Control: Proprietary IRS Status: Proprietary
Highest Offering: Associate Degree
Program: Occupational; 2-Year Principally Bachelor's Creditable
Accreditation: &M, MAC

02 Associate Campus Director .... Mr. Robert P. FERRELL
05 Dean of Instruction .... Mr. Kennan T. BECKSTRAND
32 Dean of Student Services .... Mr. Robert SLEBODNIK
07 Market Director of Admissions .... Mr. Kevin M. LEONARD
10 Market Business Director .... Ms. Marie A. D'ALESSANDRO
36 Market Director of Career Services .... Ms. Kelly K. HENRY

*Bryant & Stratton College (E)

953 James Street, Syracuse NY 13203-2502
County: Onondaga FICE Identification: 008276
Unit ID: 189574
Telephone: (315) 472-6603 Carnegie Class: Assoc/PrivFP
FAX Number: (315) 474-4383 Calendar System: Semester
URL: www.bryantstratton.edu
Established: 1854 Annual Undergrad Tuition & Fees: $15,570
Enrollment: 802 Coed
Affiliation or Control: Proprietary IRS Status: Proprietary
Highest Offering: Associate Degree
Program: Occupational; 2-Year Principally Bachelor's Creditable
Accreditation: &M, MAC

02 Campus Director .... Mr. Michael SATTLER
05 Dean of Instruction .... Mr. Richard FOWLER
32 Dean of Student Services .... Mrs. Susan SCHILLING
07 Director of Admissions .... Mr. Jon BRISTOL
26 Market Business Director .... Ms. Mary CLIFTON

Business Informatics Center, Inc. (F)

134 S Central Avenue, Valley Stream NY 11580-5418
County: Nassau FICE Identification: 025729
Unit ID: 189653
Telephone: (516) 561-0050 Carnegie Class: Assoc/PrivFP
FAX Number: (516) 561-0074 Calendar System: Quarter
URL: www.thecollegeforbusiness.com
Established: 1983 Annual Undergrad Tuition & Fees: $11,250
Enrollment: 200 Coed
Affiliation or Control: Proprietary IRS Status: Proprietary
Highest Offering: Associate Degree
Program: Occupational
Accreditation: ACCSC

01 President .... Ms. Constance BROWN
05 Academic Dean .... Dr. Eugene ALEXANDER
07 Admissions Director .... Mr. Hank MEANEY
37 Financial Aid Director .... Mr. Salvatore FERRO

Canisius College (G)

2001 Main Street, Buffalo NY 14208-1098
County: Erie FICE Identification: 002681
Unit ID: 189705
Telephone: (716) 883-7000 Carnegie Class: Master's L
FAX Number: (716) 888-2525 Calendar System: Semester
URL: www.canisius.edu
Established: 1870 Annual Undergrad Tuition & Fees: $30,657
Enrollment: 5,111 Coed
Affiliation or Control: Roman Catholic IRS Status: 501(c)3
Highest Offering: Master's
Program: Liberal Arts And General; Teacher Preparatory; Professional; Business Emphasis
Accreditation: M, BUS, CACREP, TED

01 President .... Mr. John J. HURLEY
43 Special Counsel to President .... Mr. George M. MARTIN
05 Interim VP Academic Affairs .... Dr. Richard A. WALL
10 Vice President Business & Finance .... Mr. Patrick E. RICHEY
32 Vice President Student Affairs .... Dr. Ellen O. CONLEY
30 VP of Advancement .... Mr. Craig T. CHINDEMI
20 Assoc VP for Academic Affairs .... Dr. Jerome L. NEUNER
13 Assoc VP Library/Information Svcs .... Dr. Joel A. COHEN
07 Dean of Admissions .... Ms. Donna L. SHAFFNER
44 Director of Principal Gifts .... Mr. J. Patrick GREENWALD
06 Assoc VP of Acad Affairs/Registrar .... Mr. Blair W. FOSTER
35 Dean of Students .... Dr. Terri L. MANGIONE
87 Director of Summer Sessions .... Mr. Blair W. FOSTER
49 Dean College of Arts & Sciences .... Dr. David W. EWING
50 Dean School of Business .... Dr. Antone F. ALBER
37 Director of Student Financial Aid .... Mr. Curtis C. GAUME
36 Director of Career Center .... Mr. James V. JONES
27 Assoc VP of Public Relations .... Ms. Debra S. PARK
15 Director of Human Resourses .... Ms. Deborah J. WINSLOW-SCHABER
53 Dean School Education/Human Svcs .... Dr. Michael J. PARDALES
107 Exec Dir of Professional Studies .... Dr. Khalid W. BIBI
25 Director of Sponsored Programs .... Ms. Mary Ann LANGLOIS
18 Director Facilities Management .... Mr. Edward P. COGAN
19 Director of Public Safety .... Mr. Gary M. EVERETT
88 Associate VP of Finance/Controller .... Mr. Michael J. EADIE
23 Director Student Health Center .... Ms. Patricia H. CREAHAN
29 Director Alumni Relations .... Ms. Eileen L. HUDSON
38 Director Counseling Center .... Ms. Eileen A. NILAND
39 Dir Res Life/Assoc Dean of Stdnts .... Mr. Matthew H. MULVILLE
85 Director Intl/Student Programs .... Ms. Esther A. NORTHMAN
40 Manager Bookstore .... Mr. Bhagbat KARKI
41 Director Athletics .... Mr. William J. MAHER
42 Director Campus Ministry .... Rev. John P. BUCKI, SJ
88 Director of Creative Services .... Ms. Andolyn M. COURTNEY
88 Director of Development Services .... Ms. Francine R. MERGL
90 Director of Academic Computing .... Ms. Estelle M. SIENER
88 Associate Controller .... Mr. Ronald J. HABERER
94 Director of Women Studies .... Dr. Jane E. FISHER
92 Director of All College Honors Pgm .... Dr. Bruce J. DIERENFIELD
86 Director of Government Relations .... Mr. Kenneth C. KRULY
09 Director of Institutional Research .... Dr. Pat MIZAK
88 Director of Multi Cultural Programs .... Mr. Sababu C. NORRIS
08 Head Librarian .... Dr. Barbara BOEHNKE
14 Dir Computer Infrastructure/Opers .... Mr. Frank W. KIRSTEIN
24 Director Media Center .... Mr. Daniel J. DREW
44 Director Canisius Fund .... Ms. Jeanmarie O. CIESLICA
91 Director Administrative Computing .... Mr. Walter J. DRABEK
96 Facilities Operations Manager .... Mr. Gary B. LEW
102 Director Corp/Foundation Relations .... Dr. Jennifer KOCH
105 Director of Web Services .... Mr. Chuck PUSTELNIK
04 Assistand to the President .... Ms. Erica C. SAMMARCO

Cayuga Community College (H)

197 Franklin Street, Auburn NY 13021-3099
County: Cayuga FICE Identification: 002861
Unit ID: 189839
Telephone: (315) 255-1743 Carnegie Class: Assoc/Pub-S-SC
FAX Number: (315) 255-2117 Calendar System: Semester
URL: www.cayuga-cc.edu
Established: 1953 Annual Undergrad Tuition & Fees (In-District): $3,820
Enrollment: 4,967 Coed
Affiliation or Control: State/Local IRS Status: 501(c)3
Highest Offering: Associate Degree
Program: Occupational; 2-Year Principally Bachelor's Creditable
Accreditation: M, ADNUR

01 President .... Dr. Daniel P. LARSON
04 Assistant to President/Board .... Ms. Carolyn L. GUARIGLIA
05 Vice Pres Academic/Student Affairs .... Dr. Anne HERRON
10 Vice Pres Administration/Treasurer .... Ms. Diane L. HUTCHINSON
12 Assoc VP & Dean Fulton Campus .... Ms. Margaret KILLORAN
30 Executive Director Foundation .... Mr. Jeffrey L. HOFFMAN
103 Dean Cmty Educ & Workforce Develop .... Ms. Carla DESHAW
84 Dean Enrollment Management .... Ms. Cheryl A. ANDERSON
14 Dean Information Technology .... Mr. John TAYLOR
07 Director of Admissions .... Mr. Bruce M. BLODGETT
29 Director Alumni Association .... Ms. Louise B. WILSON
18 Director Buildings & Grounds .... Mr. Kevin S. DRAYER
21 Dir Business Services & Comptroller .... Ms. Marie A. NELLENBACK
106 Director Distance Learning .... Mr. Edward J. KOWALSKI, JR.
37 Director Financial Aid .... Ms. Judith G. MILADIN
92 Director Honors Program .... Vacant
09 Director Institutional Research .... Ms. Carol E. RUNGE
08 Director Library & Learn Resources .... Mr. Marc W. WILDMAN
41 Director Athletics .... Mr. Peter E. LIDDELL
88 Director Academic Support Center .... Mr. Jeffrey E. ROSENTHAL
88 Director Adult Learning Program .... Ms. Janet A. NELSON
66 Director Nursing .... Ms. Linda L. ALFIERI
15 Director HR & Affirm Action .... Mr. Scott WHALEN
27 Director Public Rel & Inst Commun .... Ms. Margaret SPILLETT
06 Registrar .... Mr. Michael A. PASTORE
32 Director Student Development .... Mr. Patrick MCPEAK
36 Director Career Services .... Ms. Margaret H. OSBORNE
19 Director Campus Safety and Security .... Mr. William J. MARVENTANO
88 Director Assessment .... Ms. Maureen ERICKSON

Cazenovia College (I)

Cazenovia NY 13035-1085
County: Madison FICE Identification: 002685
Unit ID: 189848
Telephone: (800) 654-3210 Carnegie Class: Bac/Diverse
FAX Number: (315) 655-4143 Calendar System: Semester
URL: www.cazenovia.edu
Established: 1824 Annual Undergrad Tuition & Fees: $26,736
Enrollment: 955 Coed
Affiliation or Control: Independent Non-Profit IRS Status: 501(c)3
Highest Offering: Baccalaureate
Program: Liberal Arts And General; Professional
Accreditation: M, IACBE, @TEAC

01 President .... Dr. Mark J. TIERNO
03 Executive Vice President .... Ms. Susan A. BERGER
05 VP Academic Affs/Dean of Faculty .... Dr. Donald A. MCCRIMMON
10 Chief Finan Ofcr/VP Financial Affs .... Mr. Mark H. EDWARDS
84 VP Enrol Mgmt/Dean Admiss/Fin Aid .... Mr. Robert A. CROOT
30 VP for Institutional Advancement .... Ms. Carol SATCHWELL
32 VP Student Devel/Dean of Students .... Mr. C. Joseph BEHAN
51 Director of Extended Learning .... Ms. Lesley C. OWENS-PELTON
08 Director of Library Services .... Mr. Stanley KOZACZKA
37 Director of Financial Aid .... Ms. Christine MANDEL
26 Director of Communications .... Mr. Wayne WESTERVELT
15 Director Human Resources .... Ms. Janice ROMAGNOLI
23 Director Health Services .... Ms. Susan A. BERGER
36 Dir Career Svcs/Internship Pgms .... Ms. Christine RICHARDSON
41 Int Dir Intercollegiate Athletics .... Mr. Robert F. KENNA
13 Director of Technology Development .... Vacant
06 Registrar .... Mr. Zachary KELLEY
09 Dir Institutional Rsrch/Assessment .... Ms. Bridget MILLER
18 Dir of Physical Plant Operations .... Mr. Jeff SLOCUM
29 Director Alumni Relations .... Ms. Shari WHITAKER
38 Director of Counseling Services .... Dr. Todd SPANGLER

Central Yeshiva Tomchei Tmimim Lubavitch America (J)

841-853 Ocean Parkway, Brooklyn NY 11230-2798
County: Kings FICE Identification: 004776
Unit ID: 189857
Telephone: (718) 434-0784 Carnegie Class: Spec/Faith
FAX Number: (718) 434-1519 Calendar System: Semester
Established: 1941 Annual Undergrad Tuition & Fees: $5,700
Enrollment: 695 Male

Affiliation or Control: Independent Non-Profit IRS Status: 501(c)3
Highest Offering: Second Talmudic Degree
Program: Teacher Preparatory; Professional
Accreditation: RABN

01 President .... Rabbi David RASKIN
05 Dean .... Rabbi Zalman LABKOWSKI
06 Registrar .... Rabbi Joseph WILMOWSKY
37 Financial Aid Director .... Rabbi Moshe M. GLUCKOWSKY
26 Director Public Relations .... Mr. Shaya BOYMELGREEN
10 Treasurer .... Rabbi Moshe BOGOMILSKY

Christ the King Seminary (A)

711 Knox Road, Box 607, East Aurora NY 14052-0607
County: Erie FICE Identification: 002822
Unit ID: 189981
Telephone: (716) 652-8900 Carnegie Class: Spec/Faith
FAX Number: (716) 652-8903 Calendar System: Semester
URL: www.cks.edu
Established: 1974 Annual Graduate Tuition & Fees: $7,110
Enrollment: 94 Coed
Affiliation or Control: Roman Catholic IRS Status: 501(c)3
Highest Offering: Master's; No Undergraduates
Program: Religious Emphasis
Accreditation: M, THEOL

01 Rector/President .... Rev. Peter DRILLING
03 Vice Rector .... Rev. Gregory M. FAULHABER
05 Academic Dean .... Dr. Dennis A. CASTILLO
10 Comptroller .... Mrs. Nancy M. EHLERS
11 Chief of Operations .... Mr. Michael SHERRY
30 Director Institutional Advancement .... Mr. David J. KERSTEN
18 Director of Facilities .... Vacant
08 Library Director .... Ms. Teresa LUBIENECKI
38 Director of Ministry Development .... Mr. Douglas J. GEORGE
26 Chief Public Relations Officer .... Ms. Susan LANKES

Christie's Education, Inc. (B)

11 West 42nd Street, 8th Floor, New York NY 10036
County: New York FICE Identification: 036654
Telephone: (212) 355-1501 Carnegie Class: Not Classified
FAX Number: (212) 355-7370 Calendar System: Other
URL: www.christieseducation.com
Established: N/A Annual Graduate Tuition & Fees: N/A
Enrollment: N/A Coed
Affiliation or Control: Proprietary IRS Status: Proprietary
Highest Offering: Master's; No Undergraduates
Program: Professional
Accreditation: NY

01 Director of Studies .... Dr. Veronique CHAGNON-BURKE
08 Librarian .... Ms. Karen MAGUIRE

*City University of New York (C)

535 E 80th Street, New York NY 10075
County: New York FICE Identification: 025061
Unit ID: 190035
Telephone: (212) 794-5555 Carnegie Class: N/A
FAX Number: (212) 794-5549
URL: www.cuny.edu

01 Chancellor .... Dr. Matthew GOLDSTEIN
03 Exec Vice Chanc/Chief Oper Officer .... Mr. Allan H. DOBRIN
05 Exec VC/University Provost .... Dr. Alexandra LOGUE
26 Sr Vice Chanc University Relations .... Mr. Jay HERSHENSON
43 Sr Vice Chancellor Legal Affairs .... Mr. Frederick P. SCHAFFER
10 Sr Vice Chancellor Budget/Finance .... Mr. Marc SHAW
45 Vice Chanc Facility Plng/Constr Mgt .... Ms. Iris WEINSHALL
15 Vice Chanc for Human Resources Mgmt ... Ms. Gloriana WATERS
88 Vice Chancellor for Labor Relations .... Ms. Pamela S. SILVERBLATT
09 Vice Chancellor for Research .... Dr. Gillian SMALL
32 Vice Chancellor Student Affairs .... Dr. Frank SANCHEZ
88 Vice Chancellor Community Colleges .... Dr. Eduardo MARTI
27 Assoc VC/Chief Information Officer .... Mr. Brian COHEN
21 Assoc Vice Chanc Budget/Finance .... Mr. Matthew SAPIENZA

*Baruch College/City University of New York (D)

One Bernard Baruch Way, New York NY 10010-5526
County: New York FICE Identification: 007273
Unit ID: 190512
Telephone: (646) 312-1000 Carnegie Class: Master's L
FAX Number: N/A Calendar System: Semester
URL: www.baruch.cuny.edu
Established: 1968 Annual Undergrad Tuition & Fees (In-District): $4,600
Enrollment: 16,189 Coed
Affiliation or Control: State/Local IRS Status: 501(c)3
Highest Offering: Master's
Program: Liberal Arts And General; Teacher Preparatory; Professional; Business Emphasis
Accreditation: M, BUS, BUSA, HSA, SPAA

02 President .... Dr. Michael B. WALLERSTEIN
05 Provost/SVP Academic Affairs .... Dr. James MCCARTHY
11 Vice Pres Administration/Finance .... Mr. Gabriel ESZTERHAS
32 Vice Pres Student Affs/Enroll Mgmt .... Dr. Ben CORPUS
30 Vice Pres for College Advancement .... Mr. Mark GIBBEL
50 Vice Pres/Dean Zicklin Sch Business .... Dr. John ELLIOTT
45 Asst VP Campus Facilities/Ops .... Mr. Jim LLOYD
84 Asst VP Enrollment Mgmt/Fin Aid .... Ms. Marybeth MURPHY
13 Asst VP Info Tech/Chief Librarian .... Mr. Arthur DOWNING
35 Asst Vice President Student Affairs .... Dr. Corlisse THOMAS
21 Asst Vice President Finance .... Ms. Mary FINNEN
49 Dn Sch Arts & Sci/V Prov Glob Strat .... Dr. Jeffrey M. PECK
20 Associate Provost .... Dr. Barbara LAWRENCE
20 Associate Provost .... Dr. Dennis SLAVIN
80 Dean School Public Affairs .... Dr. David BIRDSELL
20 Dean Faculty & Staff Relations .... Mr. John DUGAN
58 Executive Officer Doctoral Program .... Dr. Joseph WEINTROP
100 Chief of Staff .... Ms. Mary GORMAN-HETHERINGTON
25 Director of Sponsored Programs .... Mr. Alan EVELYN
15 Director of Human Resources .... Ms. Liz ROBINSON
36 Director Career Development Center .... Dr. Patricia IMBIMBO
90 Asst Dir Client Svcs/Fac Liais .... Mr. Frank WERBER
85 Director Intl Student Office .... Ms. Marisa DELACRUZ
19 Director Public Safety .... Mr. Henry J. MCLAUGHLIN
06 Registrar .... Ms. Phyllis BAGLEY
09 Dir Institutional Rsrch/Pgm Assess .... Mr. John CHOONOO
26 Chief Communications Officer .... Ms. Christina LATOUF
29 Director Alumni Relations .... Ms. Lisa POULLARD-BURTON
96 Director of Purchasing .... Dr. David GARLOCK
22 Director Affirmative Action .... Ms. Carmen PEDROGO
41 Athletic Director .... Dr. William ENG
86 Director Government Relations .... Mr. Eric LUGO

*City University of New York Borough of Manhattan Community College (E)

199 Chambers Street, New York NY 10007-1047
County: New York FICE Identification: 002691
Unit ID: 190521
Telephone: (212) 220-1230 Carnegie Class: Assoc/Pub-U-MC
FAX Number: (212) 220-1244 Calendar System: Semester
URL: www.bmcc.cuny.edu
Established: 1963 Annual Undergrad Tuition & Fees (In-District): $3,783
Enrollment: 21,560 Coed
Affiliation or Control: State/Local IRS Status: 501(c)3
Highest Offering: Associate Degree
Program: Occupational; 2-Year Principally Bachelor's Creditable
Accreditation: M, ADNUR, EMT

02 President .... Dr. Antonio PEREZ
05 Senior Vice Pres Academic Affairs .... Dr. Sadie BRAGG
11 Vice President Administration/Plng .... Mr. G. Scott ANDERSON
43 VP Legal Affs/Faculty & Staff Rels .... Dr. Robert DIAZ
32 Vice President of Student Affairs .... Dr. Marva CRAIG
30 Vice President of Development .... Ms. Karen WENDEROFF
10 Asst Vice Pres of Finance .... Ms. Elena SAMUELS
51 Dean Ctr for Cont Ed/ Workforce Dev .... Dr. Sunil GUPTA
25 Dean Grants & Development .... Mr. John MONTANEZ
20 Dean for Instruction/Curriculum .... Dr. Erwin WONG
88 Assoc Dean Academic Support Svcs .... Dr. Michael GILLESPIE
37 Deputy Director Financial Aid .... Mr. Ralph W. BUXTON
15 Deputy Director Human Resources .... Ms. Gloria CHAO
07 Assoc Director of Admissions .... Ms. Antoinette MIDDLETON
84 Director Enrollment Management .... Mr. Eugenio BARRIOS
06 Senior Registrar .... Mr. Gregory WIST
08 Director Learning Resource Center .... Mr. James TYNES
09 Director Institutional Research .... Dr. Jane Lee DELGADO
22 Affirmative Action Officer .... Ms. Iyana TITUS
18 Campus Facilities Officer .... Mr. Edward SULLIVAN
26 Public Relations Officer .... Mr. Barry ROSEN
41 Director of Athletics .... Mr. Stephen KELLY
102 Dir Foundation/Corporate Relations .... Mr. Bryan HALLER
36 Dir Acad Advisement/Transfer Ctr .... Ms. Freda MCCLEAN
38 Director Counseling Center .... Dr. Ardie DEWALT
96 Director of Procurement .... Mr. Robert RAFFERTY

*City University of New York Bronx Community College (F)

2155 University Avenue, Bronx NY 10453-2895
County: Bronx FICE Identification: 002692
Unit ID: 190530
Telephone: (718) 289-5100 Carnegie Class: Assoc/Pub-U-MC
FAX Number: (718) 289-6011 Calendar System: Semester
URL: www.bcc.cuny.edu
Established: 1957 Annual Undergrad Tuition & Fees (In-District): $3,954
Enrollment: 10,740 Coed
Affiliation or Control: State/Local IRS Status: 501(c)3
Highest Offering: Associate Degree
Program: Occupational; 2-Year Principally Bachelor's Creditable
Accreditation: M, ACBSP, ADNUR, ENGT, MLTAD, NMT, RAD

02 President .... Dr. Carole M. BEROTTE JOSEPH
05 VP of Academic Affairs .... Dr. Howard WACH
11 SVP of Administration & Finance .... Ms. Mary E. COLEMAN
26 Special Asst to Pres for Cmty Rels .... Ms. Carol WHITE
04 Exec Asst to the Pres .... Ms. Carmen VAZQUEZ
32 VP of Student Dev & Enroll Mgmt .... Dr. Peter BARBATIS
30 Asst Vice Pres of Institutional Dev .... Ms. Carin SAVAGE
84 Dean of Enrollment Management .... Mr. Bernard GANTT
45 Assoc Dean Inst Research & Planning .... Dr. Nancy RITZE
20 Dean of Faculty & Academic Affairs .... Dr. Alice FULLER
10 Chief Business Officer .... Mr. Donovan THOMPSON
06 Registrar .... Mr. Bernard GANTT
14 Exec Dir of Information Technology .... Mr. James KENNELLY
37 Director of Financial Aid .... Ms. Maria BARLAAM
07 Admissions Officer .... Ms. Alba CANCETTY
15 Personnel Officer .... Mrs. Shelley LEVY
08 Chief Librarian .... Ms. Teresa MCMANUS
19 Director of Security .... Mr. James VERDICCHIO
35 Director Student Life .... Ms. Melissa KIRK
41 Director of Athletics .... Mr. Eric MERCADO
18 Chief Superintendnt Phys Plant Svcs .... Mr. Wayne MURPHY
29 Director of Alumni Relations .... Mr. Robert WHELAN
36 Assoc Dir for Career/Transfer Svcs .... Ms. Aurora BRITO
38 Director of Student Counseling .... Dr. Jennifer MISICK
43 Labor Designee/Legal Counsel .... Ms. Mary T. ROGAN
96 Director of Purchasing .... Ms. Sharon LUCKIE

*City University of New York Brooklyn College (G)

2900 Bedford Avenue, Brooklyn NY 11210-2889
County: Kings FICE Identification: 002687
Unit ID: 190549
Telephone: (718) 951-5000 Carnegie Class: Master's L
FAX Number: N/A Calendar System: Semester
URL: www.brooklyn.cuny.edu
Established: 1930 Annual Undergrad Tuition & Fees (In-District): $5,051
Enrollment: 16,912 Coed
Affiliation or Control: State/Local IRS Status: 501(c)3
Highest Offering: Master's
Program: Liberal Arts And General; Teacher Preparatory; Professional
Accreditation: M, AUD, CACREP, DIETD, DIETI, PH, SP, TED

02 President .... Dr. Karen L. GOULD
05 Provost/Vice Pres Acad Affairs .... Dr. William A. TRAMONTANO
84 VP for Enrollment Management .... Dr. Stephen E. JOYNER
10 VP for Finance & Administration .... Mr. Steve G. LITTLE
30 Vice Pres Institutional Advancement .... Dr. Andrew SILLEN
32 VP for Student Affairs .... Dr. Milga MORALES
100 Acting Chief of Staff to President .... Ms. Nicole HOSTEN-HAAS
26 Senior Dir Communicat & Marketing .... Mr. Jeremy THOMPSON
20 Associate Provost .... Dr. Jerrold MIROTZNIK
20 Assoc Provost for Academic Programs .... Dr. Donna WILSON
45 Asst Provost Plng & Spec Projects .... Ms. Colette WAGNER
57 Dean School Visual Media & Perf Art .... Dr. Maria A. CONELLI
50 Dean of School of Business .... Dr. Willie HOPKINS
83 Dean School Humanities & Social Sci .... Dr. Kimberley L. PHILLIPS
81 Dean School Natural & Behav Science .... Dr. Kleanthis PSARRIS
53 Dean School of Education .... Dr. Deborah A. SHANLEY
18 Asst VP Facilities Plng/Operations .... Mr. Steve G. CZIRAK
21 AVP Finance/Budget & Planning/Compt .... Mr. Alan GILBERT
13 Asst VP Information Technology Svcs .... Mr. Mark GOLD
15 Asst VP Human Resource Services .... Mr. Michael HEWITT
86 Dir Government & External Affairs .... Vacant
35 Assoc Dean for Student Affairs .... Dr. Jacqueline WILLIAMS
88 Asst Dean for School of Education .... Dr. Geraldine FARIA
35 Asst Dean Student Development .... Ms. Vannessa GREEN
51 Asst Dean Enroll Effica & Adult Lit .... Ms. Lillian O'REILLY
08 Chief Librarian .... Ms. Stephanie WALKER
88 Deputy Comptroller .... Ms. Beatrice GILLING RAYNOR
21 Bursar .... Ms. Yasmin ALI
44 Assoc Director Annual Funds .... Ms. Patricia ALLEN
09 Dir Inst Plng/Research & Assess .... Dr. Michael AYERS
88 Director of Women's Center .... Ms. Sau Fong AU
88 Director of Speech & Hearing Center .... Mr. Michael BERGEN
104 Sen Dir Int Ed & Global Engagement .... Dr. Alice G. BIER
88 Student Center Administrator/Dir .... Mr. Hyan BUCK
25 Dir Research & Sponsored Programs .... Ms. Sabrina CEREZO
40 Bookstore Manager .... Mr. Michael D'ACIERNO
37 Director Financial Aid .... Mr. Ahad FARHANG
41 Dir Rec Intramurals/Intercol Athl .... Mr. Bruce FILOSA
85 Dir International Student Services .... Mr. Kenneth FORSH
88 General Mgr Media/Perform Arts Ctr .... Mr. Richard GROSSBERG
88 Dir Scholarships & Honors Recruit .... Ms. Evelyn GUZMAN
38 Director of Personal Counseling .... Dr. Gregory KUHLMAN
30 Assoc Exec Director of Development .... Ms. Beth F. LEVINE
94 Coordinator of Women's Studies .... Dr. Namita MANOHAR
22 Dir Diversity & Equity Program .... Ms. Natalie L. MASON-KINSEY
36 Dir Magner Ctr Career Dev/Intrn .... Mr. Robert OLIVA
96 Dir of Purchasing & Contracting .... Ms. Diane OQUENDO
88 Dir Academic Advise & Stdnt Success .... Mr. Jesus PEREZ
43 Director of Legal Services .... Ms. Pamela POLLACK
29 Director Alumni Affairs .... Ms. Marla H. SCHREIBMAN
92 Dir Scholars Pgm & Honors Academy .... Dr. Lisa SCHWEBEL
90 Dir Acad Computer & Library Systems .... Dr. Howard SPIVAK
88 Director of Testing .... Ms. Althea STERLING
88 Dir Ctr for Stdnt Disability Svcs .... Ms. Valerie M. STEWART-LOVELL
105 Web Content Manager .... Ms. Nancy STREIN
23 Director Health Clinic .... Ms. Ilene TANNENBAUM
07 Dir Undergrad Admiss & Recruitment .... Ms. Penelope TERRY
19 Director Safety & Security .... Mr. Donald A. WENZ

*City University of New York The City College (H)

160 Convent Avenue, New York NY 10031-9198
County: New York FICE Identification: 002688
Unit ID: 190567
Telephone: (212) 650-7000 Carnegie Class: Master's L
FAX Number: (212) 650-7680 Calendar System: Semester
URL: www1.ccny.cuny.edu
Established: 1847 Annual Undergrad Tuition & Fees (In-District): $5,179
Enrollment: 15,416 Coed

Affiliation or Control: State/Local IRS Status: 501(c)3
Highest Offering: Doctorate
Program: Liberal Arts And General; Teacher Preparatory; Professional
Accreditation: M, ARCPA, #CLPSY, CS, ENG, LSAR, TED

02 President .... Dr. Lisa STAIANO-COICO
05 Provost .... Dr. Martin MOSKOVITS
27 Vice Pres Communication/ Marketing .... Ms. Mary Lou EDMONDSON
30 VP Development/Inst Advancement .... Ms. Rachelle BUTLER
10 Vice Pres Finance & Administration .... Mr. Jerold POSMAN
84 Vice Pres Enrollment Management .... Ms. Celia LLOYD
45 VP Campus Planning/Facilities Mgmt .... Mr. Robert SANTOS
26 VP Urban & Governmental Affairs .... Ms. Karen WITHERSPOON
32 Asst Vice Pres for Student Affairs .... Mr. Robert RODRIGUEZ
18 Asst Vice Pres for Facilities .... Mr. Richard SLAWSKI
13 Interim Chief Information Officer .... Mr. Ken IHRER
15 Asst VP Human Resources .... Ms. Sabrina ELLIS
100 Sr Advisor to Pres/Chief of Staff .... Ms. Deborah HARTNETT
29 Executive Director Alumni Affairs .... Mr. Donald K. JORDAN
63 Dean Sophie Davis Medical School .... Dr. Maurizio TREVISAN
54 Dean of Engineering .... Dr. Barba A. JOSEPH
53 Acting Dean of Education .... Dr. Doris CINTRON
47 Dean School of Architecture .... Dr. George RANALLI
88 Dean of CWE .... Dr. Juan Carlos MERCADO
81 Acting Dean of Science .... Dr. Ruth STARK
83 Dean of Social Science .... Dr. Marilyn HOSKIN
79 Dean of Humanities & The Arts .... Dr. Geraldine MURPHY
04 Counsel to President .... Mr. Paul F. OCCHIOGROSSO
06 Senior Registrar .... Vacant
35 Executive Director Student Affairs .... Dr. Beth LESEN
08 Chief Librarian .... Ms. Pamela GILLESPIE
46 Director Research Administration .... Ms. Regina MASTERSON
09 Director of Institutional Research .... Mr. Edward SILVERMAN
37 Director of Financial Aid .... Ms. Thelma MASON
26 Director of Public Relations .... Mr. Ellis SIMON
22 Int Director of Affirmative Action .... Mr. Robert RODRIGUEZ
90 Director of IT & Computer Services .... Mr. Curtis RIAS
23 Dir Access/Wellness/Counseling Ctr .... Dr. Beth LESEN
36 Director of Career Services .... Dr. Sophia DEMETRIOU
19 Director Public Safety & Security .... Mr. John MCKEE
11 Administrative Superintendent .... Mr. Gerry MILLER
24 Director of Instructional Media .... Mr. Nana ABEYIE
07 Director of Admissions .... Mr. Joseph FANTOZZI
28 Director of Diversity .... Mr. Robert RODRIGUEZ
38 Director Student Counseling .... Dr. Sarah HAHN
96 Director of Purchasing .... Mr. Mario CRESCENZO
21 Controller .... Ms. Donna Lee DIANE
21 Budget Director .... Mr. Andreas AARBO

*City University of New York College of Staten Island (A)

2800 Victory Boulevard, Staten Island NY 10314-6600
County: Richmond FICE Identification: 002698
Unit ID: 190558
Telephone: (718) 982-2000 Carnegie Class: Master's L
FAX Number: N/A Calendar System: Semester
URL: www.csi.cuny.edu
Established: 1955 Annual Undergrad Tuition & Fees (In-District): $5,208
Enrollment: 13,894 Coed
Affiliation or Control: State/Local IRS Status: 501(c)3
Highest Offering: Beyond Master's But Less Than Doctorate
Program: 2-Year Principally Bachelor's Creditable; Liberal Arts And General; Teacher Preparatory; Professional
Accreditation: M, ADNUR, CS, ENG, ENGT, NUR, PTA, TED

02 President .... Dr. Tomás D. MORALES
05 Sr Vice Pres Acad Affairs/Provost .... Dr. William J. FRITZ
10 Interim VP President Finance/Admin .... Mr. Ira PERSKY
32 Vice President for Student Affairs .... Ms. A. R. BROWN
30 VP Inst Advance/External Affairs .... Ms. Barbara R. ESHOO
72 Vice Pres for Technology Systems .... Dr. Michael KRESS
91 Deputy to VP Technology Systems .... Ms. Joyce TAYLOR
100 Actg Deputy to Pres/Chief of Staff .... Mr. Kenichi IWAMA, ESQ.
84 Asst VP Enrollment Management .... Ms. MaryBeth REILLY
18 AVP for Campus Planning/Facilities .... Mr. James PEPE
20 Associate Provost .... Dr. Susan L. HOLAK
81 Dean Science & Technology .... Dr. Alex CHIGOGIDZE
79 Dean Humanities/Social Science .... Dr. Christine FLYNN SAULNIER
35 Assoc Dean for Student Affairs .... Vacant
06 Registrar .... Ms. Neila GREEN
08 Chief Librarian .... Dr. Wilma L. JONES
21 AVP for Fin & Business Services .... Mr. Ed RIOS
16 Director of Human Resources .... Ms. Hope BERTE
26 Dir Communications & Marketing .... Mr. Kenneth BACH
89 Director of New Student Orientation .... Mr. Brian DELONG
88 Director of CSI Association .... Ms. Marianne MCLAUGHLIN
88 Director of Disability Svcs .... Mr. Christopher CRUZ-CULLARI
25 Director of Spons Grants & Research .... Ms. Lisa EBERT
07 Director Recruitment/Admissions .... Mr. Emmanuel ESPERANCE
37 Director of Financial Aid .... Mr. Philippe MARIUS
19 Director of Public Safety .... Mr. Paul MURTHA
29 Assoc Director of Alumni Relations .... Ms. Jennifer LYNCH
36 Dir Career & Scholarship Center .... Ms. Caryl WATKINS
51 Executive Dir of Continuing Educ .... Dr. Hugo KIJNE
85 Director Center for Intl Services .... Ms. Ann HELM
43 Special Assistant for Legal Affairs .... Ms. Kathleen F. GALVEZ
41 Director Athletics & Recreation .... Mr. Vernon MUMMERT
38 Director of Counseling .... Dr. Ann BOOTH
23 Nurse Manager of Health Center .... Ms. Terianne DARRAGH
88 Budget Director .... Mr. Nicholas SACCONE

90 Assoc Dir Computer Labs/LAN Sys .... Ms. Linda JOHN
92 Acting Director of Honors College .... Dr. Deborah POPPER
28 Actg Dir of Compliance & Diversity .... Ms. Danielle E. DIMITROV
45 Director of Campus Planning .... Mr. George TARGOWNIK
96 Director of Purchasing .... Ms. Kiesha STEWART
24 Director Media & Library Tech .... Mr. Mark LEWENTAL
88 Director Academic Advisement .... Ms. Paulette BROWER-GARRETT
88 Director of Student Life .... Ms. Carol BROWER
27 Director of Design & Publications .... Ms. Janice AWERBUCH
88 Executive Director Aux Svcs .... Mr. Ira PERSKY
88 Network Director .... Mr. George CONCEPCION
88 Asst Director Graduate Admissions .... Ms. Sasha SPENCE
88 Director of Telecommunications .... Mr. Avi GANNON
88 Director Center for the Arts .... Mr. John JANKOWSKI
88 Director College Testing Office .... Mr. Alan HOFFNER
09 Director of Institutional Research .... Mr. Sam MICHALOWSKI
102 Director Corporate Foundation .... Ms. Maryann LAURIA
88 SEEK Director .... Ms. Gloria GARCIA
40 Manager of Bookstore .... Ms. Carmela BALESTRIERI
44 Development Director .... Ms. Enrica CHRETIEN
20 Acting Asst Provost Academic Pgms .... Dr. Ann LUBRANO
88 Asst VP Inst Advance/Ext Affairs .... Dr. Kenneth BOYDEN
88 Director Academic Support .... Ms. Linda SHARIB

*City University of New York Graduate Center (B)

365 Fifth Avenue, New York NY 10016-4309
County: New York FICE Identification: 004765
Unit ID: 190576
Telephone: (212) 817-7000 Carnegie Class: RU/VH
FAX Number: (212) 817-1624 Calendar System: Semester
URL: www.gc.cuny.edu
Established: 1961 Annual Undergrad Tuition & Fees (In-District): $6,910
Enrollment: 4,504 Coed
Affiliation or Control: State/Local IRS Status: 501(c)3
Highest Offering: Doctorate
Program: Professional
Accreditation: M, PH, SCPSY

02 President .... Dr. William P. KELLY
05 Provost/Senior Vice President .... Dr. Chase F. ROBINSON
10 Sr VP Finance and Administration .... Dr. Sebastian T. PERSICO
20 Assoc Provost/Dean Human & Soc Sci .... Dr. Louise LENNIHAN
88 Actg Assc Prov/Dean Doc Sciences .... Dr. Ann S. HENDERSON
32 Vice President Student Affairs .... Mr. Matthew G. SCHOENGOOD
46 Exec Dir Research & Sponsored Pgm .... Dr. Edith GONZALEZ DE SCOLLARD
30 Vice Pres Institutional Advancement .... Mr. Raymond C. SOLDAVIN
13 VP Information Technology .... Mr. Robert D. CAMPBELL
21 Asst Vice President Finance .... Mr. Stuart B. SHOR
15 Asst VP for Faculty & Staff Rels .... Ms. Yosette JONES JOHNSON
25 Director Sponsored Research .... Ms. Hilry FISHER
27 Director Media Relations .... Vacant
08 Chief Librarian .... Prof. Julie CUNNINGHAM
07 Director Admissions .... Mr. Les GRIBBEN
06 Dir Student Svcs/Senior Registrar .... Mr. Vincent J. DELUCA
09 Assoc Dir Inst Research .... Ms. Marie BURRAGE
88 Dir Bldg Design/Exhibits .... Mr. Ray RING
28 Executive Officer Educ Opp/Div Pgm .... Dr. Donald ROBOTHAM
85 Director International Students .... Mr. Douglas EWING
88 Dir Well Ctr/Psy Coun Svc/Adult Dev .... Dr. Robert HATCHER
23 Director Student Health Services .... Ms. Adraenne BOWE
37 Director of Financial Aid .... Mr. John WILLIAMS
22 Affirmative Action Officer .... Ms. Edith RIVERA
16 Director of Human Resources .... Ms. Ella KISELYUK
31 Dir Special Events/Events Planning .... Mr. Eric BLOMQUIST
18 Director Facilities/Physical Plant .... Mr. Michael BYERS
96 Director of Purchasing .... Mr. Ronald PAYNTER
35 Director Student Affairs .... Ms. Sharon LERNER
19 Dir of Security & Public Safety .... Mr. John FLAHERTY
94 Coordinator Women's Studies .... Dr. Victoria PITTS-TAYLOR

*City University of New York Herbert H. Lehman College (C)

250 Bedford Park Boulevard W, Bronx NY 10468-1589
County: Bronx FICE Identification: 007022
Unit ID: 190637
Telephone: (718) 960-8000 Carnegie Class: Master's L
FAX Number: N/A Calendar System: Semester
URL: www.lehman.cuny.edu
Established: 1968 Annual Undergrad Tuition & Fees (In-District): $2,415
Enrollment: 12,115 Coed
Affiliation or Control: State/Local IRS Status: 501(c)3
Highest Offering: Master's
Program: Liberal Arts And General; Teacher Preparatory; Professional
Accreditation: M, CACREP, DIETD, DIETI, NURSE, PH, SP, SW, TED

02 President .... Dr. Ricardo R. FERNANDEZ
100 Chief of Staff .... Ms. Dawn EWING-MORGAN
43 Sp Coun to Pres Legal Affs/Lab Rels .... Mr. Esdras TULIER
88 Deputy to Pres for HS & Educ Init .... Ms. Sandra LERNER
05 Provost/Vice Pres Academic Affs .... Dr. Mary A. PAPAZIAN
11 Vice President for Administration .... Mr. Vincent W. CLARK
32 Vice President Student Affairs .... Mr. Jose MAGDALENO
30 Vice President for Inst Advancement .... Mr. Mario DELLAPINA
27 Vice Pres/Chief Info Officer .... Mr. Ronald BERGMANN
84 Assoc Provost/VP Enroll Mgmt .... Dr. Robert C. TROY
18 Asst VP of Campus Planning & Facil .... Ms. Rene M. ROTOLO

30 Asst Vice President Inst Advance .... Mr. Fredrick GILBERT
88 Exec Asst to Vice Pres Student Affs .... Mr. Vincent ZUCCHETTO
79 Dean for Arts/Humanities .... Dr. Timothy ALBORN
53 Dean School of Education .... Dr. Harriet FAYNE
83 Dean Natural & Social Sciences .... Dr. Edward JARROLL
51 Dean Adult & Cont Education .... Dr. Marzie A. JAFARI
35 Dean of Student Affairs .... Mr. John HOLLOWAY
21 Business Manager .... Mr. J. Edward ROBINSON
08 Chief Librarian .... Dr. Kenneth SCHLESINGER
06 Registrar .... Mr. John CAPOCCI
07 Director of Admissions .... Ms. Laurie AUSTIN
29 Director of Alumni Relations .... Ms. Cristina NECULA
88 Director of the Art Gallery .... Ms. Susan HOELTZEL
36 Director Career Services .... Ms. Nancy A. CINTRON
38 Director Counseling Center .... Ms. Norma COFRESI
37 Director Financial Aid .... Mr. David MARTINEZ
89 Director Freshman Year Initiative .... Dr. Steven WYCKOFF
25 Director of Grants & Contracts .... Ms. Stephanie ENDY
92 Director of Honors College Program .... Dr. Gary SCHWARTZ
15 Director of Human Resources .... Mr. Eric WASHINGTON
14 Director Info Tech Resources .... Mr. Joseph MIDDLETON
09 Director of Institutional Research .... Dr. Susanne M. TUMELTY
38 Dir Instruct Support Services Pgm .... Ms. Althea FORDE
26 Director Media Rels/Publications .... Ms. Margaret RICE
88 Director Performing Arts Center .... Ms. Eva BORNSTEIN
19 Director of Public Safety .... Mr. Domenick LAPERUTA
96 Director of Purchasing .... Mr. Sunny VIRK
41 Athletic Director .... Dr. Martin ZWIREN
40 Bookstore Manager .... Vacant

*Hostos Community College-City University of New York (D)

500 Grand Concourse, Bronx NY 10451-5323
County: Bronx FICE Identification: 008611
Unit ID: 190585
Telephone: (718) 518-4300 Carnegie Class: Assoc/Pub-U-MC
FAX Number: (718) 518-4294 Calendar System: Semester
URL: www.hostos.cuny.edu
Established: 1970 Annual Undergrad Tuition & Fees (In-District): $3,505
Enrollment: 6,700 Coed
Affiliation or Control: State/Local IRS Status: 501(c)3
Highest Offering: Associate Degree
Program: 2-Year Principally Bachelor's Creditable
Accreditation: M, DH, RAD

02 President .... Dr. Felix MATOS
05 Provost/Sr VP for Academic Affairs .... Dr. Carmen COBALLES-VEGA
10 Senior Vice Pres for Admin/ Finance .... Ms. Esther RODRIGUEZ-CHARDAVOYNE
32 Int Vice Pres Student Development .... Mr. Nathaniel CRUZ
100 Deputy to President .... Ms. Dolly MARTINEZ
30 Vice Pres Institutional Advancement .... Ms. Ana M. CARRION-SILVA
13 Asst Vice Pres Info Technology .... Mr. Varun SEHGAL
04 Special Assistant to the President .... Ms. Ana I. GARCIA-REYES
88 Dean for Special Programs .... Dr. Carlos MOLINA
21 Assistant Dean Budget & Finance .... Mr. Jagdish PATEL
18 Asst Dean Admin/Director Facility .... Mr. Steve DELGADO
20 Assoc Dean of Academic Support .... Ms. Christine MANGINO
35 Assistant Dean of Student Life .... Ms. Johanna GOMEZ
88 Executive Counsel & Labor Designee .... Ms. Glenda GRACE
27 Dir of Publications Development .... Mr. Don BRASWELL
38 Director of Counseling .... Ms. Linda ALEXANDER-WALLACE
15 College Personnel Officer .... Ms. Shirley SHEVACH
86 Dir Intergovernmental Relations .... Vacant
06 Registrar .... Ms. Nelida PASTORIZA
07 Director of Admissions .... Mr. Ronald VELEZ
37 Director of Financial Aid .... Mr. Joseph ALICEA
19 Director of Campus Security .... Mr. Arnaldo BERNABE
25 Director Grants & Contracts .... Ms. Lourdes TORRES
09 Director Institutional Research .... Dr. Richard GAMPERT
08 Head Librarian .... Ms. Madeline FORD
22 Affirmative Action Officer .... Mr. Eugene SOHN
29 Director Alumni Relations .... Ms. Nydia EDGECOMBE
36 Director Career Services .... Ms. Rebecca HODA
35 Director Student Activities .... Mr. Jerry ROSA
96 Director of Purchasing .... Mr. Kevin CARMINE

*City University of New York Hunter College (E)

695 Park Avenue, New York NY 10065
County: New York FICE Identification: 002689
Unit ID: 190594
Telephone: (212) 772-4000 Carnegie Class: Master's L
FAX Number: N/A Calendar System: Semester
URL: www.hunter.cuny.edu
Established: 1870 Annual Undergrad Tuition & Fees (In-District): $5,729
Enrollment: 22,407 Coed
Affiliation or Control: State/Local IRS Status: 501(c)3
Highest Offering: Master's
Program: Liberal Arts And General; Teacher Preparatory; Professional
Accreditation: M, AUD, CACREP, CORE, DIETD, DIETI, ENGR, NURSE, PH, PLNG, PTA, SP, SW, TED

02 President .... Ms. Jennifer J. RAAB
100 Chief of Staff/Exec Asst to Pres .... Ms. Judith ALPERT
11 Vice Pres Administration/COO .... Mr. Len ZINNANTI
05 Provost/Vice Pres Academic Affairs .... Dr. Vita RABINOWITZ

32 VP Student Affs/Dean of Stdnts .... Ms. Eija AYRAVAINEN
43 Counsel to the President ....Ms. Gail A. SCOVELL
13 Asst Vice Pres Information Tech .... Dr. Franklin STEEN
28 Dean Diversity and Compliance ....Mr. John ROSE
70 Dean School of Social Work .... Dr. Jacqueline MONDROS
53 Dean School of Education ....Dr. David STEINER
66 Acting Dean School of Nursing .... Dr. Joyce GRIFFIN-SOBEL
49 Dean School of Arts & Sciences .... Dr. Robert GREENBERG
18 Asst Vice Pres of Facilities ....Mr. Rick CHANDLER
30 Executive Director Development .... Ms. Jayne ROSENGARTEN
26 Ex Dir Communication/Marketing ....Ms. Meredith HALPERN
10 Chief Business Officer ....Mr. Giancarlo BONAGURA
08 Chief Librarian .... Mr. Daniel CHERUBIN
06 Registrar ....Ms. Marilyn DALY-WESTON
07 Director of Admissions .... Mr. William ZLATA
09 Director of Institutional Research .... Ms. Joan LAMBE
15 Director of Human Resources ....Ms. Serafina DOLAN
35 Director Student Advising ....Mr. Case WILLOUGHBY
36 Director Student Placement .... Ms. Susan MCCARTY
37 Director Student Financial Aid .... Ms. Aristalia RODRIGUEZ
38 Director Student Counseling ....Ms. Madlyn STOKELY
29 Director Alumni Relations ....Ms. Deborah DAVIS
96 Director of Purchasing ....Mr. John ALBIN
19 College Security Director ....Mr. Louis MADER

*City University of New York John Jay College of Criminal Justice (A)

899 Tenth Avenue, New York NY 10019-1093
County: New York FICE Identification: 002693
Unit ID: 190600
Telephone: (212) 237-8000 Carnegie Class: Master's L
FAX Number: (212) 237-8901 Calendar System: Semester
URL: www.jjay.cuny.edu
Established: 1964 Annual Undergrad Tuition & Fees (In-District): $2,730
Enrollment: 15,288 Coed
Affiliation or Control: State/Local IRS Status: 501(c)3
Highest Offering: Master's
Program: Liberal Arts And General; Professional
Accreditation: M, SPAA

02 President .... Mr. Jeremy TRAVIS
05 Prov/Sr Vice Pres Academic Affairs .... Dr. Jane BOWERS
11 Sr Vice Pres Administrative Affairs .... Mr. Robert PIGNATELLO
32 Vice President Student Development ....Dr. Berenecea JOHNSON-EANES
30 Int Asst Vice Pres Marketing/Dev .... Ms. Mayra NIEVES
84 Vice Pres Enrollment Management ....Dr. Richard SAULNIER
45 Assoc Provost for Effect/Assessment .... Dr. James LLANA
04 Executive Assistant to President .... Vacant
100 Interim Chief of Staff .... Dr. Rulisa GALLOWAY-PERRY
58 Graduate & Professional Studies .... Dr. Jannette DOMINGO
46 Int Asc Prov/Dn Rsrch/Strat Partner .... Dr. Karen TERRY
32 Dean of Students ....Dr. Wayne EDWARDS
15 Dean Human Resources .... Mr. Donald GRAY
20 Dean of Undergraduate Studies ....Dr. Anne LOPES
10 Exec Dir Financial/Business Svcs .... Ms. Patricia KETTERER
08 Chief Librarian .... Dr. Lawrence SULLIVAN
37 Director of Financial Aid .... Ms. Sylvia CRESPO-LOPEZ
44 Director of Development .... Vacant
35 Director Student Activities ....Mr. Jerrell W. ROBINSON
25 Director of Funded Research ....Mr. Jacob MARINI
09 Director of Institutional Research .... Mr. Ricardo ANZALDVA
89 Director of First Year Experience ....Ms. Katalin SZUR
06 Interim Registrar .... Mr. Cheuk LEE
88 Director of CRJ Research & Eval ....Dr. Jeffrey BUTTS
07 Director of Admissions .... Ms. Sandra PALLEJA
13 Chief Information Officer ....Mr. Praveen PANCHAL
19 Director of Public Safety ....Mr. Stephen HOLLOWELL
90 Director Technology Services ....Mr. William PANGBURN
22 Affirmative Action Officer ....Ms. Silvia MONTALBAN
24 Director of Media Services .... Mr. Paul BRENNER
27 Executive Director Communications .... Ms. Christine GODEK
36 Director of Career Development Svcs .... Mr. Will SIMKINS
38 Director of Counseling ....Dr. Calvin CHIN
41 Athletic Director ....Mr. Daniel PALUMBO
21 Associate Business Officer ....Ms. Emily KARP
29 Director Alumni Relations ....Ms. Jerylle KEMP
96 Director of Purchasing ....Mr. Daniel DOLAN
04 Assistant to the President ....Ms. Bettina MUENSTER
18 Director Facilities/Physical Plant ....Mr. Elmer PHELON
43 Assistant Vice President & Counsel ....Hon. Rosemarie MALDONADO
86 Director of Government Relations .... Vacant
88 Director of Academic Advisement ....Dr. Sumaya VILLANUEVA
88 Int Dir of Accessibility Services .... Ms. Danielle OFFICER

*City University of New York Kingsborough Community College (B)

2001 Oriental Boulevard, Brooklyn NY 11235-2333
County: Kings FICE Identification: 002694
Unit ID: 190619
Telephone: (718) 368-5000 Carnegie Class: Assoc/Pub-U-MC
FAX Number: (718) 368-5003 Calendar System: Other
URL: www.kbcc.cuny.edu
Established: 1963 Annual Undergrad Tuition & Fees (In-District): $4,285
Enrollment: 18,606 Coed
Affiliation or Control: State/Local IRS Status: 501(c)3
Highest Offering: Associate Degree
Program: Occupational; 2-Year Principally Bachelor's Creditable
Accreditation: M, ADNUR, PTAA, SURGT

02 President ....Dr. Regina S. PERUGGI
05 Vice Pres Academic Affs/Provost .... Dr. Stuart SUSS
10 Vice Pres Finance/Administration ....Mr. Bill KELLER
04 Exec Assistant to the President .... Mr. Peter POBAT
32 Dean of Student Affairs .... Dr. Paulette DALPES
51 Dean Continuing Educ/Dir Cmty Rels ....Dr. Saul W. KATZ
35 Dean of Student Life .... Ms. Tasheka YOUNG
20 Dean of Instructional Services .... Dr. David GOMEZ
84 Dean Enrollment Management .... Mr. Thomas FRIEBEL
09 Dean Inst Effective/Strategic Plng ....Dr. Richard FOX
30 Assoc Dean College Advancement .... Dr. Elizabeth BASILE
15 Director of Human Resources .... Ms. Micheline DRISCOLL
22 Dir Affirmative Action/EO Officer .... Vacant
19 Actg Director of Security & Safety ....Mr. Pat MORENA
08 Chief Librarian .... Vacant
06 Registrar .... Ms. Sonia SALADUCHIN
18 Campus Facilities Officer .... Mr. Anthony CORAZZA
37 Financial Aid Officer .... Mr. Wayne H. HAREWOOD
27 Chief Information Officer .... Mr. Asif HUSSAIN
36 Dir Career Couns/Placement/Transfer ....Mr. Brian MITRA
23 Director of Health Services .... Vacant
24 Director of Educational Media .... Mr. Michael ROSSON
41 Director of Athletics ....Ms. Gina KRANWINKLE
26 Chief Public Relations Officer .... Ms. Ruby RYLES
96 Director of Purchasing .... Ms. Lyn RELAY
07 Director of Admissions ....Ms. Rosalie FAYAD
29 Director Alumni Relations .... Mr. Michael GOLDSTEIN
38 Director Student Counseling .... Dr. Maria BARTOLOMEO
14 Assoc Director of Computer Center .... Vacant
21 Business Manager .... Mr. Anthony IMPERATO
88 Deputy Business Officer ....Mr. Bill CORRENTI

*La Guardia Community College/ City University of New York (C)

31-10 Thomson Avenue, Long Island City NY 11101-3083
County: Queens FICE Identification: 010051
Unit ID: 190628
Telephone: (718) 482-7200 Carnegie Class: Assoc/Pub-U-SC
FAX Number: (718) 609-2000 Calendar System: Semester
URL: www.lagcc.cuny.edu
Established: 1971 Annual Undergrad Tuition & Fees (In-District): $3,790
Enrollment: 17,028 Coed
Affiliation or Control: State/Local IRS Status: 501(c)3
Highest Offering: Associate Degree
Program: Occupational; 2-Year Principally Bachelor's Creditable
Accreditation: M, ADNUR, DIETT, OTA, PTAA

02 President ....Dr. Gail O. MELLOW
05 Vice President Academic Affairs .... Dr. Peter KATOPES
04 Executive Associate to President .... Ms. Rosemary TALMADGE
11 Vice President of Administration ....Mr. Richard ELLIOTT
30 Vice Pres Institutional Advancement .... Mr. E. Ramone SEGREE
13 Vice Pres Information Technology .... Mr. Henry SALTIEL
32 Act VP Enrollment Mgmt/Student Dev .... Dr. Michael BASTON
51 Vice Pres Adult/Continuing Educ ....Ms. Jane SCHULMAN
20 Dean of Academic Affairs ....Mr. Paul ARCARIO
84 Asst Dean Enrollment Services .... Ms. Reine SARMIENTO
18 Exec Dir Facilities Mgmt/Planning ....Mr. Shahir ERFAN
15 Exec Director of Human Resources .... Ms. Diane DARCY
10 Exec Director Finance & Business .... Mr. Thomas HLADEK
86 Exec Dir for Government Relations .... Mr. Jose L. ORENGO
35 Sr Administrator Student Devel .... Ms. Renee BUTLER
08 Chief Librarian ....Ms. Jane DEVINE
37 Director Student Financial Services ..... Ms. Gail BAKSH-JARRETT
29 Director Alumni/Community Outreach .... Ms. Maria RIGGS
25 Director Grants Development .... Mr. Robert KAHN
38 Dir Ctr Counseling/Advis/Acad Spprt ....Dr. Mitchell A. LEVY
07 Director of Admissions ....Ms. LaVora DESVIGNE
26 Dir Marketing/Communications ....Ms. Susan LYDDON
43 Legal & Labor Relations Officer .. Ms. Jemma ROBAIN LACAILLE
22 Director of Affirmative Action .... Ms. April TUCKER
09 Director of Institutional Research ....Mr. Nathan DICKMEYER
21 Associate Business Manager ....Ms. Carmen LUONG
36 Director Employment/Career Svc Ctr .... Ms. Claudia BALDONEDO
96 Director Procurement & Contracts ....Mr. Mitchell HENDERSON
06 Associate Registrar ....Mr. Thomas F. MURASSO

*City University of New York Medgar Evers College (D)

1650 Bedford Avenue, Brooklyn NY 11225-2010
County: Kings FICE Identification: 010097
Unit ID: 190646
Telephone: (718) 270-4900 Carnegie Class: Bac/Assoc
FAX Number: (718) 270-5126 Calendar System: Semester
URL: www.mec.cuny.edu
Established: 1969 Annual Undergrad Tuition & Fees (In-District): $4,965
Enrollment: 7,016 Coed
Affiliation or Control: State/Local IRS Status: 501(c)3
Highest Offering: Baccalaureate
Program: Liberal Arts And General; Teacher Preparatory; Professional
Accreditation: M, ACBSP, ADNUR, NUR, @SW, TED

02 President ....Dr. William L. POLLARD
05 Provost/Senior Vice President ....Dr. Howard C. JOHNSON
100 Interim Sr VP for Operations .... Mr. Earl CABBELL
32 Vice President of Student Affairs ....Dr. Vincent BANREY
51 VP Sch Professional & Community Dev ....Mrs. Simone RODRIGUEZ-DORESTANT
20 Assistant Provost ....Dr. Claudia SCHRADER

18 Asst VP Facilities Management ....Ms. Lisa K. EDWARDS
50 Int Dean of the School of Business .... Dr. John GRAHAM
89 Dean College of Freshman Studies ....Dr. Gale E. GIBSON
49 Actg Dean Sch of Lib Arts & Educ ....Dr. Carlyle THOMPSON
72 Dean School of Science/Health/Tech .... Dr. Mohsin PATWARY
09 Exec Dean Accred/Inst Effectiveness .... Dean Richard JONES
21 Comptroller .... Mr. Donal CHRISTIAN
43 Counsel to President ....Mrs. Valerie KENNEDY
04 Exec Assistant to the President ....Ms. Lisa YOUNG
22 Director of Affirmative Action ....Dr. Sylvia KINARD
06 Registrar .... Ms. Johana RIVERA
91 Chief Information Officer .... Ms. Claudia COLBERT
37 Director of Financial Aid .... Mr. Conley JAMES
38 Director of Counseling .... Dr. JoAnn JOYNER-GRAHAM
19 Director of Security ....Mr. Elvert MILLER
41 Director of Athletics ....Mr. Tyler D. HACK
25 Grants Officer ....Mr. Chi KOON
89 Dir Freshman Year Program ....Dr. Jeffrey SIGLER
55 Director Evening/Weekend Programs ....Ms. Yvette WALL
36 Director of Career Development ....Ms. Deborah YOUNG
30 Exec Director of Development .... Vacant
09 Office of External Relations .... Dr. Moses NEWSOME
26 Coordinator of College Relations .... Vacant
18 Supt of Buildings & Grounds ....Mr. Cory WRIGHT
07 Director of Admissions ....Ms. Julie AUGUSTINE
29 Director of Alumni Relations ....Mr. Fred PRICE
21 Chief Independent Financial Auditor ....Mr. Bruno DEGEN
96 Director of Purchasing ....Ms. Goldene LEWIS
84 Director Enrollment Management ....Mr. Warren HEUSNER
09 Director of Institutional Research ....Dr. Eva CHAN
62 Actg Chair Dept of Library Services .... Ms. Vanrea THOMAS
66 Chair Dept of Nursing .... Dr. Jean GUMBS
88 Chair Dept Interdisciplinary Stds .... Vacant
50 Chair Dept of Business Admin ....Dr. Evelyn MAGGIO
53 Chair Department of Education ....Dr. Nancy LESTER
60 Chair Dept of Mass Communications .... Ms. Elendar BARNES
88 Chair Department Accounting ....Dr. Rosemary WILLIAMS
81 Chair Department of Mathematics ....Dr. Umesh NAGARKATTE
77 Chair Dept Physical/Computer Sci .... Dr. Kwesi AMOA
81 Chair Department of Biology .... Dr. Anthony UDEOGALANYA
83 Chair Dept of Social/Behavioral Sci ....Dr. Sallie CUFFEE
88 Chair Department of Psychology ....Dr. Ethan GOLOGOR
88 Chair Dept of Public Administration ....Dr. Zulema BLAIR
13 Chair Computer Info Systems ....Dr. Adesina FADARIO
66 Chair Department BS Nursing .... Vacant
88 Chair Department Economics/Finance .... Dr. Emmanuel EGBE
88 Chair Department of English ....Dr. Augustine OKEREKE
88 Chair Dept of Philosophy & Religion .... Dr. Darryl TRIMIEW
88 Chair Dept of Foreign Languages ....Dr. Jesus BOTTARO
35 Director of Student Life .... Mr. Kevin ADAMS

*New York City College of Technology/City University of New York (E)

300 Jay Street, Brooklyn NY 11201-1909
County: Kings FICE Identification: 002696
Unit ID: 190655
Telephone: (718) 260-5000 Carnegie Class: Bac/Assoc
FAX Number: (718) 260-5198 Calendar System: Semester
URL: www.citytech.cuny.edu
Established: 1946 Annual Undergrad Tuition & Fees (In-District): $4,830
Enrollment: 15,368 Coed
Affiliation or Control: State/Local IRS Status: 501(c)3
Highest Offering: Baccalaureate
Program: Professional; Technical Emphasis
Accreditation: M, ADNUR, DH, DT, ENGT, NUR, OPD, RAD, TED

02 President ....Dr. Russell K. HOTZLER
05 Provost ....Dr. Bonne AUGUST
10 Vice Pres Finance/Administration ....Dr. Miguel CAIROL
84 VP Enrollment/Student Affairs ....Dr. Marcela ARMOZA
22 Counsel/Affirmative Action Officer ....Ms. Gilen CHAN
07 Director of Admissions .... Ms. Alexis CHACONIS
06 Registrar .... Mr. Jerry M. BERROL
37 Director of Financial Aid .... Ms. Sandra HIGGINS
08 Librarian .... Mr. Darrow WOOD
14 Director of Computer Center .... Ms. Rita UDDIN
107 Dean of Professional Studies .... Dr. Barbara GRUMET
54 Dean of Technology .... Vacant
49 Interim Dean of Arts & Science ....Dr. Pamela BROWN
51 Dean Continuing Education .... Dr. Carol SONNENBLICK
55 Director Evening Session .... Mr. James LAP
15 Director of Human Resources ....Ms. Marie TINSLEY
25 Grants Officer .... Ms. Barbara BURKE
24 Director of Inst Tech/Media Svcs ....Ms. Karen LUNDSTREM
09 Director of Assessment .... Dr. Tammie CUMMING
26 Chief Public Relations Officer ....Ms. Michele FORSTEN
29 Director Alumni Relations .... Vacant
36 Director Student Placement ....Mr. Adrian GRIFFIN
38 Director Student Counseling ....Ms. Cynthia BINK
96 Director of Purchasing .... Mr. Wayne ROBINSON
18 Chief Facilities/Physical Plant .... Mr. James VASQUEZ
30 Chief Development/Spec Asst to Pres ....Dr. Stephen SOIFFER
35 Director Student Life .... Mr. Daniel FICTUM
35 Administrator Student Affairs ....Mr. Joseph LENTO
21 Business Manager .... Mr. Wayne ROBINSON

*City University of New York Queens College (F)

65-30 Kissena Boulevard, Flushing NY 11367-1597
County: Queens FICE Identification: 002690
Unit ID: 190664

Telephone: (718) 997-5000 Carnegie Class: Master's L
FAX Number: (718) 997-5598 Calendar System: Semester
URL: www.qc.cuny.edu
Established: 1937 Annual Undergrad Tuition & Fees (In-District): $5,068
Enrollment: 20,906 Coed
Affiliation or Control: State/Local IRS Status: 501(c)3
Highest Offering: Master's
Program: Liberal Arts And General; Teacher Preparatory; Professional
Accreditation: M, AAFCS, DIETD, DIETI, LAW, LIB, SP, TED

02 President .... Dr. James L. MUYSKENS
05 Provost .... Dr. James STELLAR
10 Vice Pres Finance/Administration .... Ms. Katharine COBB
30 Vice Pres Institutional Advancement .... Ms. Sue HENDERSON
32 Vice President for Student Affairs .... Dr. Joe BERTOLINO
91 Asst Vice Pres Converging Tech .... Mr. Naveed HUSAIN
20 Assoc Provost Academic Plng/Pgms .... Dr. Steven SCHWARZ
43 Asst Vice Pres for Labor Relations .... Ms. Meryl KAYNARD
27 Asst Vice Pres of Communications .... Ms. Maria TERRONE
21 Assistant VP Business Affairs .... Mr. Brian MURPHY
26 Asst VP Institutional Advancement .... Ms. Laurie DORF
88 Assistant Provost .... Dr. June BOBB
57 Dean Arts & Humanities .... Dr. Tamara EVANS
81 Dean Math & Natural Sciences .... Dr. Larry LIEBOVITCH
53 Dean Education .... Dr. Francine PETERMAN
58 Dean of Research/Grad Studies .... Dr. Richard BODNAR
83 Dean Social Sciences .... Dr. Elizabeth HENDREY
15 Director Human Resources/Payroll .... Ms. Reinalda MEDINA
41 Assistant Vice President Athletics .... Dr. Richard WETTAN
88 Director of Events .... Ms. Wendy LEE
07 Executive Director Admissions .... Mr. Vincent ANGRISANI
38 Dir of Counseling and Advisement .... Dr. Elizabeth MCCAFFREY
06 Director Registrar's Office .... Mr. Ramon RIVERA
09 Director of Institutional Research .... Dr. Margaret MCAULIFFE
08 Chief Librarian .... Dr. Robert SHADDY
37 Director Financial Aid Services .... Ms. Rena SMITH-KIAWU
29 Manager Alumni Affairs .... Mr. Christopher GREAVES
19 Director Security/Safety .... Mr. Pedro PINEIRO
22 Director Affirmative Action .... Ms. Cynthia ROUNTREE
96 Director of Purchasing .... Ms. Lorraine PRASAD

*City University of New York Queensborough Community College (A)

222-05 56th Avenue, Bayside NY 11364-1497
County: Queens FICE Identification: 002607
Unit ID: 190673
Telephone: (718) 631-6262 Carnegie Class: Assoc/Pub-U-MC
FAX Number: N/A Calendar System: Semester
URL: www.qcc.cuny.edu
Established: 1958 Annual Undergrad Tuition & Fees (In-District): $3,640
Enrollment: 15,502 Coed
Affiliation or Control: State/Local IRS Status: 501(c)3
Highest Offering: Associate Degree
Program: Occupational; 2-Year Principally Bachelor's Creditable
Accreditation: M, ACBSP, ADNUR, ENGT

02 Interim President .... Dr. Diane CALL
05 Vice President Academic Affairs .... Dr. Karen B. STEELE
10 Vice Pres Finance & Administration .... Ms. Sherri NEWCOMB
30 Vice Pres Institutional Advancement .... Ms. Rosemary S. ZINS
32 Vice President Student Affairs .... Ms. Ellen HARTIGAN
15 Dean Human Resource/Labor Rels .... Ms. Liza LARIOS
51 Dean Continuing Ed/Workforce Devel .... Ms. Denise WARD
20 Assoc Dean Acad Affs/Inst Research .... Dr. Paul MARCHESE
35 Assoc Dean of Student Affairs .... Dr. Paul JEAN-PIERRE
20 Assoc Dean for Academic Affairs .... Ms. Michele CUOMO
88 Assoc Dean Accred Assessment .... Dr. Arthur CORRADETTI
21 Assoc Dean Bus Admin/Comptroller .... Mr. William FAULKNER
13 Chief Information Technology Ofcr .... Mr. George SHERMAN
08 Chief Librarian .... Ms. Jeanne GALVIN
06 Registrar .... Ms. Ann TULLIO
37 Financial Aid Director .... Ms. Veronica LUKAS
07 Director Admissions & Recruitment .... Mr. Winston YARDE
09 Director of Institutional Research .... Ms. Elisabeth LACKNER
15 Personnel Officer .... Ms. Ellen ADAMS
26 Director of Marketing .... Vacant
19 Director of Safety & Security .... Mr. Edward LOCKE
22 Affirmative Action Officer .... Ms. Mavis HALL
04 Executive Assistant to President .... Ms. Millie CONTE
104 Dir Ctr for Intl Stds/Study Abroad .... Mr. Juan Carlos FAJARDO
90 Exec Dir Academic Computing Center .... Mr. Bruce NAPLES
96 Director of Purchasing .... Mr. MacArthur MARSHALL
18 Chief Facilities/Physical Plant .... Mr. Joseph CARTOLANO
36 Director of Career Services .... Ms. Constance PELUSO
38 Director of Student Counseling .... Dr. Jannette URCIUOLI
30 Chief Devel/Dir Alumni Relations .... Vacant
84 Director Enrollment Management .... Ms. Veronica LUKAS
44 Director Annual Giving/Major Gifts .... Vacant

*City University of New York York College (B)

94-20 Guy Brewer Boulevard, Jamaica NY 11451-0001
County: Queens FICE Identification: 004759
Unit ID: 190691
Telephone: (718) 262-2000 Carnegie Class: Bac/Diverse
FAX Number: (718) 262-2730 Calendar System: Semester
URL: www.york.cuny.edu
Established: 1966 Annual Undergrad Tuition & Fees (In-District): $4,911
Enrollment: 7,821 Coed
Affiliation or Control: State/Local IRS Status: 501(c)3
Highest Offering: Master's
Program: Liberal Arts And General; Teacher Preparatory; Professional
Accreditation: M, ARCPA, MT, NUR, #OT, SW, TED

02 President .... Dr. Marcia V. KEIZS
05 Provost & Sr VP for Academic Affs .... Dr. Ivelaw L. GRIFFITH
10 COO & Senior Vice Pres .... Vacant
11 Interim VP Administrative Affairs .... Mr. Ronald C. THOMAS
32 Vice Pres for Student Development .... Vacant
20 Assistant Provost .... Dr. Holger HENKE
100 Dean for the Executive Office .... Dr. William V. DINELLO
49 Dean School of Arts & Sciences .... Dr. Panayiotis MELETIES
83 Dean Sch of Health & Behavioral Sci .... Vacant
50 Dean Sch of Business & Info Systems .... Dr. Alfred NTOKO
35 Associate Dean Student Development .... Vacant
43 Exec Dir Compliance & Legal Affairs .... Ms. Olga DAIS
15 Int Assc Exec Dir HR & Labor Design .... Ms. Barbara MANUEL
13 Chief Information Officer .... Mr. Peter TIGHE
09 Director Institutional Research .... Dr. Aghajan MOHAMMADI
06 Registrar .... Ms. Sharon DAVIDSON
08 Chief Librarian .... Mr. John DROBNICKI
90 Director of Academic Computing .... Dr. Che-Tsao HUANG
86 Dir of Govt and Community Relations .... Mr. Earl G. SIMONS
19 Acting Director of Security .... Lt. Tyrone FORTE
37 Director of Financial Aid .... Ms. Cathy MICHAELS
26 Director Marketing/Communications .... Vacant
18 Director Campus Planning .... Mr. Noel GAMBOA
35 Director Student Activites .... Dr. Jean PHELPS
36 Director Career Services .... Ms. Linda H. CHESNEY
25 Dir Research/Sponsored Programs .... Ms. Dawn HEWITT
38 Director of Counseling .... Dr. Susan LINDNER
07 Acting Director of Admissions .... Ms. Laura BRUNO
41 Athletic Director .... Mr. Ronald ST. JOHN
10 Confidential Business Manager .... Ms. Jacqueline CLARK
04 Executive Asst to the President .... Ms. Sandra BELL ADAMS
84 Asst VP for Enrollment Management .... Mr. Michel A. HODGE
96 Director of Purchasing .... Mr. Marlon TORRES
29 Dir of Development & Alumni Rel .... Ms. Mondell A. SEALY

Clarkson University (C)

8 Clarkson Avenue, Potsdam NY 13699-5500
County: St. Lawrence FICE Identification: 002699
Unit ID: 190044
Telephone: (315) 268-6400 Carnegie Class: RU/H
FAX Number: N/A Calendar System: Semester
URL: www.clarkson.edu
Established: 1896 Annual Undergrad Tuition & Fees: $36,780
Enrollment: 3,330 Coed
Affiliation or Control: Independent Non-Profit IRS Status: 501(c)3
Highest Offering: Doctorate
Program: Liberal Arts And General; Professional
Accreditation: M, BUS, ENG, PTA

01 President .... Dr. Anthony G. COLLINS
10 Chief Financial Officer .... Mr. James FISH
05 Provost .... Mr. Thomas C. YOUNG
32 VP University Outreach/Stdnt Affs .... Ms. Kathryn B. JOHNSON
26 VP External Relations .... Mrs. Kelly O. CHEZUM
30 VP Philanthropy/Alumni Relations .... Mr. Richard W. JOHNSON
29 Assoc Vice Pres Alumni Relations .... Mr. Stephen NEWKOFSKY
88 Assoc VP of Philanthropy/Alumni Rel .... Mr. Paul JULIN
54 Dean of Engineering .... Dr. Goodarz AHMADI
49 Dean of Arts & Sciences .... Mr. Peter TURNER
50 Dean of School of Business .... Dr. Timothy F. SUGRUE
35 Dean of Students .... Mr. Kurt W. STIMELING
18 Director of Facilities & Services .... Mr. Gard MESERVE
85 Dir International Students/Scholars .... Mrs. Tess C. CASLER
06 Registrar .... Ms. Karen J. BURKUM
07 Dean of Admissions .... Mr. Brian T. GRANT
04 Assistant to the President .... Mrs. Barbara PARKER
15 Executive Dir of Human Resources .... Mrs. Marilyn ARDITO
28 Assoc VP Inst Diversity Initiatives .... Ms. Jennifer DE COSTE
13 Director of OIT .... Mr. Kevin P. LYNCH
08 Librarian .... Ms. Michelle L. YOUNG
24 Sr Communications Specialist .... Mr. Daniel E. DULLEA
44 Director of Gift Planning .... Mr. Salvatore J. CANIA
88 Associate Director Clarkson Fund .... Ms. Nichole E. THOMAS
88 Assoc Director Clarkson Fund .... Mrs. Ashley J. BRESSETT
45 Director of Budgets Planning .... Ms. Allison S. ALDRICH
44 Director of Principal Gifts .... Mr. Peter A. BEEKMAN
25 Contract & Grant Administrator .... Ms. Constance M. FERGUSON
41 Director of Athletics & Recreation .... Mr. Steven J. YIANOUKOS
19 Director Campus Safety & Security .... Mr. David W. DELISLE
86 Director Government Relations .... Mr. Robert H. WOOD
23 Director Student Health Center .... Sunhee SOHN-ROBENSON
37 Director of Financial Aid .... Ms. Pamela NICHOLS
46 Director of Research/Tech Transfer .... Mr. Gregory C. SLACK
96 Dir Payroll/Purchasing/Risk Mgmt .... Mr. George GIORDANO
38 Director of Counseling .... Mr. David C. BOWEN

Clinton Community College (D)

136 Clinton Point Drive, Plattsburgh NY 12901-9573
County: Clinton FICE Identification: 006787
Unit ID: 190053
Telephone: (518) 562-4200 Carnegie Class: Assoc/Pub-R-M
FAX Number: (518) 561-4890 Calendar System: Semester
URL: www.clintoncc.suny.edu
Established: 1966 Annual Undergrad Tuition & Fees (In-District): $3,794
Enrollment: 2,256 Coed
Affiliation or Control: State/Local IRS Status: 501(c)3
Highest Offering: Associate Degree
Program: Occupational; 2-Year Principally Bachelor's Creditable
Accreditation: M, ADNUR

01 President .... Mr. John E. JABLONSKI
05 Vice President for Academic Affairs .... Dr. Cheryl REAGAN
10 Vice Pres for Admin/Business Affs .... Mr. Thomas MOFFETT
32 Vice President for Student Affairs .... Dr. Steven ST. ONGE
30 Assoc Vice Pres Inst Advancement .... Mr. Steven G. FREDERICK
08 Dean Learning Resource Center .... Vacant
84 Assoc Dean Student Retention Svcs .... Vacant
09 Assoc Dean Inst Research/Planning .... Vacant
37 Director of Financial Aid .... Mrs. Cheryl SEYMOUR
07 Director Admissions .... Mrs. Tobi MAY
06 Registrar .... Vacant
13 Mgmt Information Systems Director .... Mr. Rick BATCHELDER
15 Human Resource/Affirm Act Officer .... Ms. Adrienne BOYD-WILEY
26 College Relations Officer .... Vacant
18 Chief Facilities/Physical Plant .... Mr. John CONLEY

Cochran School of Nursing (E)

967 North Broadway, Yonkers NY 10701-1399
County: Westchester FICE Identification: 006443
Unit ID: 190071
Telephone: (914) 964-4282 Carnegie Class: Not Classified
FAX Number: (914) 964-4266 Calendar System: Other
URL: www.cochranschoolofnursing.us
Established: N/A Annual Undergrad Tuition & Fees: $10,800
Enrollment: 342 Coed
Affiliation or Control: Independent Non-Profit IRS Status: 501(c)3
Highest Offering: Associate Degree
Program: Nursing Emphasis
Accreditation: ADNUR

05 Vice Pres Education & Dean .... Dr. Kathleen M. DIRSCHEL
08 Learning Resources Director .... Ms. Wanda LAMONT
06 Registrar .... Ms. Janee MCCOY

Cold Spring Harbor Laboratory/ Watson School of Biological Sciences (F)

PO Box 100, One Bungtown Road,
Cold Spring Harbor NY 11724-0100
County: Suffolk FICE Identification: 034563
Unit ID: 436377
Telephone: (516) 367-6890 Carnegie Class: Not Classified
FAX Number: (516) 367-6919 Calendar System: Other
URL: www.cshl.edu
Established: 1890 Annual Graduate Tuition & Fees: N/A
Enrollment: 7 Coed
Affiliation or Control: Independent Non-Profit IRS Status: 501(c)3
Highest Offering: Doctorate; No Undergraduates
Program: Professional
Accreditation: NY

00 Chancellor Emeritis .... Dr. James D. WATSON
01 President .... Dr. Bruce STILLMAN
05 Dean .... Dr. Leemor JOSHUA-TOR

Colgate Rochester Crozer Divinity School (G)

1100 S Goodman Street, Rochester NY 14620-2589
County: Monroe FICE Identification: 002700
Unit ID: 190080
Telephone: (585) 271-1320 Carnegie Class: Spec/Faith
FAX Number: (585) 271-8013 Calendar System: Semester
URL: www.crcds.edu
Established: 1817 Annual Graduate Tuition & Fees: $10,075
Enrollment: 126 Coed
Affiliation or Control: Independent Non-Profit IRS Status: 501(c)3
Highest Offering: Doctorate; No Undergraduates
Program: Religious Emphasis
Accreditation: THEOL

01 President .... Dr. Marvin A. MCMICKLE
05 VP Academic Life & Dean of Faculty .... Prof. Stephanie L. SAUVE
10 Chief Financial Officer .... Mr. Gerald E. VANSTRYDONCK
84 Vice Pres of Enrollment Services .... Ms. Melissa MORRAL
94 Dean of Women & Gender Studies .... Dr. Barbara MOORE
06 Registrar .... Ms. Andrea MASON
18 Director of Facilities .... Mr. Mark DEVINCENTIS
08 Librarian .... Vacant
73 Dean Black Church Studies .... Prof. Gay BYRON
40 Director Bookstore .... Ms. Margaret A. NEAD
37 Director of Financial Aid .... Ms. Andrea MASON
44 Dir of Dev/Alumni & Chruch Rels .... Mr. W. Thomas MCDADE-CLAY

Colgate University (H)

13 Oak Drive, Hamilton NY 13346-1386
County: Madison FICE Identification: 002701
Unit ID: 190099
Telephone: (315) 228-1000 Carnegie Class: Bac/A&S
FAX Number: (315) 228-7798 Calendar System: Semester
URL: www.colgate.edu
Established: 1819 Annual Undergrad Tuition & Fees: $42,920
Enrollment: 2,876 Coed
Affiliation or Control: Independent Non-Profit IRS Status: 501(c)3

Highest Offering: Master's
Program: Liberal Arts And General
Accreditation: M, TEAC

01 President .... Jeffrey HERBST
101 VP/Sr Advisor/Sec Board of Trustees .... Robert L. TYBURSKI
05 Interim Provost & Dean of Faculty .... Bruce S. SELLECK
10 Vice President Finance & Admin .... David HALE
26 VP Communications/Public Relations .... Debra TOWNSEND
30 Vice President Inst Advancement .... Murray DECOCK
07 Vice President & Dean of Admissions .... Gary L. ROSS
20 Interim VP & Dean of the College .... Scott BROWN
21 Associate Vice Pres/Controller .... Thomas O'NEILL
18 Assoc Vice Pres for Facilities .... Paul FICK
21 Assoc VP for Finance/Asst Treasurer .... Carolee WHITE
15 Assoc VP for Human Resources .... Pamela PRESCOD-CAESAR
89 Dean of First Year Students .... Beverly LOW
20 Associate Dean of the Faculty .... Ian HELFANT
06 Registrar .... Gretchen HERRINGER
08 University Librarian .... Joanne SCHNEIDER
13 Chief Information Technology Offcr .... David GREGORY
29 Director of Alumni Affairs .... Tim MANSFIELD
37 Director of Financial Aid .... Marcelle TYBURSKI
19 Director of Campus Safety .... William FERGUSON
36 Director of Career Services .... Ursula HIBBERT OLENDER
41 Director of Athletics .... David ROACH
40 Director of Bookstore .... Victoria BONDUM
42 University Chaplain .... Mark SHINER
44 Director of Planned Giving .... Andrew CODDINGTON
38 Director Counseling/Psych Services .... Mark THOMPSON
96 Director of Purchasing .... Art PUNSONI
23 Director Student Health Services .... Merrill MILLER
94 Director Women's Studies .... Ulla GRAPARD
44 Director Annual Fund Operations .... Sara GROH
39 Director of Residential Life .... Vacant
09 Dir Institutional Planning/Research .... Brendt SIMPSON

College of Mount Saint Vincent (A)

6301 Riverdale Avenue, Riverdale NY 10471-1093
County: Bronx FICE Identification: 002703
Unit ID: 193399
Telephone: (718) 405-3200 Carnegie Class: Master's S
FAX Number: (718) 601-6392 Calendar System: Semester
URL: www.mountsaintvincent.edu
Established: 1847 Annual Undergrad Tuition & Fees: $26,500
Enrollment: 1,889 Coed
Affiliation or Control: Independent Non-Profit IRS Status: 501(c)3
Highest Offering: Master's
Program: Liberal Arts And General; Teacher Preparatory; Professional
Accreditation: M, ACBSP, NURSE, TEAC

01 President .... Dr. Charles L. FLYNN
05 Provost/Dean of Faculty .... Dr. Guy LOMETTI
20 Dean Undergraduate College .... Dr. Paul DOUILLARD
30 VP Inst Advancement/External Rels . Mrs. Madeleine MELKONIAN
10 Executive VP/Treasurer .... Mr. Abed ELKESHK
10 VP for Business .... Mr. Matthew MCDEVITT
32 VP Student Affs/Dean of Students .... Dr. Dianna DALE
88 Executive Director/Mission .... Dr. Jean FLANNELY, SC
88 Assoc VP Institutional Advancement .... Sr. Kathleen TRACEY, SC
84 VP for Admissions/Financial Aid .... Mr. Timothy NASH
51 Dean School Professional/Cont Stds .... Dr. Edward MEYER
06 Registrar .... Mrs. Jeanette PICHARDO
20 Director of Academic Advisement .... Ms. Sandra JENNINGS
08 Director of Library .... Mr. Sebastian DERRY
13 VP Information Technology/CIO .... Mr. Adam WICHERN
09 Director of Institutional Research .... Sr. Carol M. FINEGAN, SC
36 Director Internships/Career Devel .... Mrs. Diane MACHADO
37 Director of Financial Aid .... Mrs. Monica SIMOTAS
42 Director of Campus Ministry .... Sr. Cecilia HARRIENDORF, SC
39 Director of Residence Life .... Mr. Travaras GETER
41 Director of Athletics .... Vacant
38 Director Counseling Services .... Ms. Vicki HALLAS
23 Director of Health Services .... Mrs. Eileen MCCABE
29 Director Alumnae Relations .... Ms. Christina WESOLEK
26 Director College Relations .... Ms. Erin WALSH
31 Director Campus Events/Admin Svcs .... Ms. Jessy ORTIZ
19 Dir Campus Safety/Security .... Mr. Paul RUNG
66 Director of Nursing .... Dr. Carol VICINO
44 Director of Annual Giving .... Ms. Jennifer PORTER
15 Director of Human Resources .... Mr. William BECHMAN
21 Controller .... Mr. Murray GENEE
04 Assistant to the President .... Ms. Catherine MCKENNA
18 Director of Facilities .... Mr. Timothy DRURY
07 Director of Admissions .... Vacant
92 Director of Honors Program .... Dr. Daniel HRUBES
97 Director of Core Curriculum .... Dr. Sarah STEVENSON

The College of New Rochelle (B)

29 Castle Place, New Rochelle NY 10805-2338
County: Westchester FICE Identification: 002704
Unit ID: 193645
Telephone: (914) 654-5000 Carnegie Class: Master's L
FAX Number: (914) 654-5554 Calendar System: Semester
URL: www.cnr.edu
Established: 1904 Annual Undergrad Tuition & Fees: $28,002
Enrollment: 4,819 Coed
Affiliation or Control: Independent Non-Profit IRS Status: 501(c)3
Highest Offering: Master's
Program: Liberal Arts And General; Teacher Preparatory; Professional
Accreditation: M, NURSE, SW, @TEAC

01 President .... Mrs. Judith HUNTINGTON
03 Executive Vice President .... Dr. Ellen R. CURRY DAMATO
05 Senior Vice Pres Academic Affairs .... Dr. Dorothy A. ESCRIBANO
10 Vice President Financial Affairs .... Mr. Keith BORGE
32 Vice President Student Services .... Dr. Colette GEARY
30 Vice President College Advancement .... Ms. Brenna S. MAYER
84 Associate VP for Enrollment Mgmt .... Ms. Ellen LOCKAMY
49 Dean School of Arts & Sciences .... Dr. Richard H. THOMPSON
58 Dean of the Graduate School .... Dr. Marie RIBARICH
51 Dean School of New Resources .... Ms. Elza DINWIDDIE-BOYD
66 Dean School of Nursing .... Dr. Mary Alice DONIUS
06 Registrar .... Ms. Tania QUINN
08 Dean of the Library .... Ms. Ana FONTOURA
37 Director of Financial Aid .... Ms. Anne C. PELAK
36 Dir Counseling & Career Services .... Ms. Lynda L. MAGRATH
29 Director Alumnae/i Relations .... Ms. Kelly BRENNAN
44 Exec Director of Capital Campaigns .... Ms. Linda V. DAVID
15 Director of Human Resources .... Ms. JoEllen L. VAVASOUR
18 Director of Facilities Management .... Mr. Fred SULLO
96 Director of Purchasing .... Ms. Silvana BAJANA
09 Coordinator Institutional Research ... Mr. Lambros G. STAMOULIS

The College of Saint Rose (C)

432 Western Avenue, Albany NY 12203-1490
County: Albany FICE Identification: 002705
Unit ID: 195234
Telephone: (518) 454-5111 Carnegie Class: Master's L
FAX Number: (518) 438-3293 Calendar System: Semester
URL: www.strose.edu
Established: 1920 Annual Undergrad Tuition & Fees: $35,866
Enrollment: 5,130 Coed
Affiliation or Control: Independent Non-Profit IRS Status: 501(c)3
Highest Offering: Master's
Program: Liberal Arts And General; Teacher Preparatory
Accreditation: M, ACBSP, ART, MUS, SP, SW, TED

01 President .... Dr. R. Mark SULLIVAN
88 Asst to Pres Donor Rels/Spec Proj .... Vacant
04 Assistant to President .... Ms. Debra LIBERATORE
05 Provost/VP Academic Affairs .... Dr. David SZCZERBACKI
10 Vice Pres Finance/Administration .... Mr. Marcus BUCKLEY
30 Vice President for Inst Advancement .... Ms. Karin CARR
32 Vice President Student Services .... Mr. Dennis MCDONALD
84 Vice Pres of Enroll Mgmt/Admissions . Mrs. Mary M. GRONDAHL
15 Asst Vice Pres Human Res/Risk Mgt .... Mr. Jeffrey KNAPP
35 Assoc Dn Stdnt Affs/Dir Stdnt Life .... Ms. Mary R. MCLAUGHLIN
42 Dean of Spiritual Life .... Rev. Christopher DEGIOVINE
86 Exec Dir of Govt Community Affairs .... Mr. Michael D'ATTILIO
90 Exec Dir of Info Technology Service .... Mr. John ELLIS
44 Director Development/Annual Fund .... Ms. Lisa MCKENZIE
21 Comptroller .... Ms. Debra Lee POLLEY
06 Registrar .... Ms. Judith KELLY
07 Asst VP of Undergrad Admissions .... Mr. Jeremy BOGAN
07 Asst VP of Graduate Admissions .... Ms. Susan PATTERSON
08 Director of Library .... Mr. Peter KOONZ
39 Director Residence Life .... Ms. Jennifer RICHARDSON
36 Director Career Development Center .... Ms. Michelle OSBORNE
37 Asst VP of Financial Aid .... Mr. Steven W. DWIRE
38 Director Counsel/Psychological Svcs .... Mr. Ronald J. HAMER
41 Director Athletics & Recreation .... Ms. Catherine A. HAKER
91 Director Administrative Info Sys .... Mr. William TRAVER
29 Dir Alumni Relations/Annual Giving .... Mr. Jason MANNING
27 Asst VP of Public Information .... Mrs. Lisa HALEY-THOMSON
31 Director Community Services .... Mr. Kenneth SCOTT
42 Director of Campus Ministry .... Ms. Joan HORGAN
23 Director of Health Services .... Ms. Sandra FREHSE
19 Director of Safety/Security .... Mr. Steven STELLA
85 Director of Multicultural Affairs .... Vacant
09 Exec Dir Budget & Inst Research .... Ms. Gail A. GARDNER
09 Manager of Institutional Research .... Mr. Patrick CONNELL
28 Director of Diversity .... Ms. Shai BUTLER
38 Director of Advisement .... Dr. Kelly MEYER
88 Art Gallery Director .... Ms. Jeanne FLANAGAN
23 Director of Clinical Services .... Ms. Kimberly LAMPARELLI
96 Director Purchasing/Auxiliary Svcs .... Ms. Patricia BUCKLEY
26 Assoc Dir Media Relations .... Mr. Benjamin MARVIN
18 Dir of Facilities Planning & Mgmt .... Mrs. Nancy MACDONALD
40 Manager of Campus Store .... Mr. Chris WILSON
24 Coord of Academic Media Technology .... Mr. Michael STRATTON

The College of Westchester (D)

PO Box 710, White Plains NY 10602-0710
County: Westchester FICE Identification: 005208
Unit ID: 197285
Telephone: (914) 948-4442 Carnegie Class: Assoc/PrivFP4
FAX Number: (914) 948-5441 Calendar System: Semester
URL: www.cw.edu
Established: 1915 Annual Undergrad Tuition & Fees: $20,070
Enrollment: 1,219 Coed
Affiliation or Control: Proprietary IRS Status: Proprietary
Highest Offering: Baccalaureate
Program: Business Emphasis
Accreditation: M

00 Chairman .... Mr. Ernest H. SUTKOWSKI
01 President .... Mrs. Karen J. SMITH
03 Vice President .... Mrs. Mary Beth DEL BALZO
26 Vice President Marketing .... Mr. Dale T. SMITH
05 Chief Academic Officer .... Dr. Joann MULQUEEN
20 Dean of Student Academic Services .... Ms. Jean CARLSON
84 Senior Dir New Student Enrollment .... Mr. Robert CATANESE
36 Director of Career Services .... Ms. Joann SONDEY
88 Dir of Student Success/Retention .... Dr. Judith LILLESTON
37 Dir of Student Financial Services .... Mrs. Dianne PEPITONE

Columbia-Greene Community College (E)

4400 Route 23, Hudson NY 12534-9543
County: Columbia FICE Identification: 006789
Unit ID: 190169
Telephone: (518) 828-4181 Carnegie Class: Assoc/Pub-R-S
FAX Number: (518) 828-8543 Calendar System: Semester
URL: www.sunycgcc.edu
Established: 1966 Annual Undergrad Tuition & Fees (In-District): $3,978
Enrollment: 2,031 Coed
Affiliation or Control: State/Local IRS Status: 501(c)3
Highest Offering: Associate Degree
Program: Occupational; 2-Year Principally Bachelor's Creditable
Accreditation: M, ADNUR

01 President .... Mr. James R. CAMPION
05 VP & Dean of Academic Affairs .... Ms. Phyllis CARITO
11 Vice Pres & Dean of Administration .... Mr. A. Joseph MATTIES
32 VP/Dean of Students/Enrollment Mgmt .... Dr. Joseph WATSON
38 Counselor .... Ms. Diane JOHNSON
18 Director Building & Grounds .... Mr. James FOLZ
26 Director Public Information .... Mr. Allen KOVLER
37 Dir Stndt Fin Aid/Asst Dean Stdnts .... Mr. Earl TRETHEWAY
21 Assistant Dean of Administration .... Ms. Dianne TOPPLE
06 Registrar .... Ms. Catherine TRETHEWAY
14 Director Information Systems .... Mr. Gino RIZZI
15 Director of Human Resources .... Ms. Melissa FANDOZZI
22 Affirmative Action Officer .... Ms. Melissa FANDOZZI
09 Director of Institutional Research .... Mr. Thomas WRIGHT
31 Director of Community Services .... Mr. Robert BODRATTI
41 Athletic Director .... Mr. Walter RICKARD
88 Director Academic Support Center .... Dr. Mary-Teresa HEATH
103 Director of Workforce Development .... Ms. Mary Alane WILTSE
07 Director of Admissions .... Ms. Christine PEPITONE
30 Dir of Development & Alumni Svcs .... Ms. Joan KOWEEK
20 Assistant Dean of Academic Affairs .... Ms. Carol DOERFER
21 Bursar .... Ms. Kathleen DALLAS
19 Director of Security .... Mr. Raymond TROWBRIDGE
96 Purchasing Officer .... Ms. Patricia DAY
62 Department Chair Library Services .... Ms. Geralyn DEMAREST
83 Div Chair Behavioral/Social Science .... Mr. Thomas GERRY
81 Div Chair Compuer Science/Math .... Mr. Stewart DUTFIELD
57 Division Chair Arts & Humanities .... Mr. Michael ALLARD
66 Division Chair Nursing .... Ms. Dawn WRIGLEY
72 Division Chair Technology .... Vacant

Columbia University in the City of New York (F)

615 West 131st Street, New York NY 10027-6902
County: New York FICE Identification: 002707
Unit ID: 190150
Telephone: (212) 851-0627 Carnegie Class: RU/VH
FAX Number: (212) 851-7022 Calendar System: Semester
URL: www.columbia.edu
Established: 1754 Annual Undergrad Tuition & Fees: $44,806
Enrollment: 25,208 Coed
Affiliation or Control: Independent Non-Profit IRS Status: 501(c)3
Highest Offering: Doctorate
Program: Liberal Arts And General; Professional; Business Emphasis
Accreditation: M, ANEST, BUS, DENT, ENG, HSA, IPSY, JOUR, LAW, MED, MIDWF, NURSE, OT, PH, PLNG, PTA, SW

01 President .... Mr. Lee C. BOLLINGER
05 Interim Provost .... Mr. John COATSWORTH
03 Senior Exec Vice President .... Mr. Robert KASDIN
10 Exec Vice President of Finance .... Ms. Anne R. SULLIVAN
76 Exec VP Health/Biomed Sciences .... Dr. Lee GOLDMAN
30 Exec VP Univ Devel/Alumni Rels ... Mr. Frederick M. VAN SICKLE
88 Special Advisor to the President .... Ms. Susan K. FEAGIN
18 Exec Vice Pres Univ Facilities .... Mr. Joe A. IENUSO
32 Exec Vice Pres Student/Admin Svcs .... Mr. Jeffrey F. SCOTT
27 Exec Vice Pres Communications .... Mr. David M. STONE
88 University Secretary .... Mr. Jerome DAVIS
07 Executive Director of Admissions .... Ms. Jessica MARINACCIO
09 Exec Vice President Research .... Dr. David I. HIRSH
26 Exec Vice Pres Govt Rels/Cmty Affs .... Ms. Maxine F. GRIFFITH
20 Sr Vice Provost for Acad Personnel .... Mr. Stephen RITTENBERG
28 Vice Provost for Diversity .... Ms. Geraldine DOWNEY
21 Treasurer .... Ms. Gail HOFFMAN
49 Vice President Arts & Sciences .... Mr. Nicholas B. DIRKS
08 Vice Pres Info Svcs Univ Libraries .... Dr. James NEAL
88 Pres IMC Ofc of Univ Investments .... Mr. Nirmal P. NARVEKAR
15 Vice President Human Resources .... Ms. Lucinda DURNING
96 Vice President Procurement Svcs .... Mr. Joseph HARNEY
43 General Counsel .... Ms. Jane E. BOOTH
06 Registrar .... Mr. John P. CARTER
37 Director Admissions/Financial Aid .... Ms. Nanette M. DILAURO
29 Director Alumni Relations .... Vacant
38 Director of Student Counseling .... Dr. Richard EICHLER
84 Director of Enrollment Management .... Ms. Jessica MARINACCIO
48 Dean Grad School Arch/Plng/Preserv .... Mr. Mark A. WIGLEY
57 Dean School of the Arts .... Ms. Carol BECKER
50 Dean Graduate School of Business .... Dr. R. Glenn HUBBARD
49 Dean Columbia College .... Vacant

52 Dean School Dental & Oral Surgery ... Dr. Ira B. LAMSTER
54 Act Dean Sch Engr/Applied Science ... Dr. Gerald NAVRATIL
97 Dean School General Studies ... Dr. Peter AWN
49 Dean Grad School of Arts & Science ... Dr. Carlos J. ALONSO
82 Dean School of Intl/Public Affairs ... Mr. John COATSWORTH
60 Dean Graduate School Journalism ... Mr. Nicholas LEMANN
61 Dean School of Law ... Mr. David M. SCHIZER
63 Dean Faculty of Medicine ... Dr. Lee GOLDMAN
66 Dean School of Nursing ... Dr. Mary MUNDINGER
69 Dean School of Public Health ... Dr. Linda P. FRIED
70 Dean School of Social Work ... Dr. Jeanette C. TAKAMURA

† Parent institution of Barnard College and Teachers College, Columbia University.

Concordia College (A)

171 White Plains Road, Bronxville NY 10708-1923
County: Westchester FICE Identification: 002709
Unit ID: 190248
Telephone: (914) 337-9300 Carnegie Class: Bac/Diverse
FAX Number: (914) 395-4500 Calendar System: Semester
URL: www.concordia-ny.edu
Established: 1881 Annual Undergrad Tuition & Fees: $25,560
Enrollment: 186 Coed
Affiliation or Control: Lutheran Church - Missouri Synod
IRS Status: 501(c)3
Highest Offering: Master's
Program: Liberal Arts And General; Teacher Preparatory; Professional
Accreditation: M, NURSE, SW, TED

01 President ... Dr. Viji D. GEORGE
10 Chief Financial Officer ... Mr. William W. ZAMBELLI
11 Vice Pres Administration ... Mr. Lloyd WARDLEY
30 Vice Pres Advancement ... Mr. Paul D. GRAND PRE
04 Special Assistant to the President ... Ms. Eloise L. MORGAN
05 Dean of the College ... Prof. Sherry J. FRASER
20 Dean of Faculty ... Ms. Mandana NAKHAI
66 Dean of Nursing ... Dr. Susan M. APOLD
88 Dean of Adult Education ... Mr. William M. SALVA
42 Dean of Worship ... Rev. Patrick J. BAYENS
20 Dean Experiential Learning ... Mr. John M. BAHR
32 Asst Dean of Student Development ... Mr. Christopher S. KOUTSOVITIS
06 Registrar ... Mr. Mark E. BLANCO
08 Library Director ... Mr. William L. PERRENOD
38 Director of Counseling ... Ms. Betty C. GEILING
41 Athletic Director ... Mr. Ivan MARQUEZ
23 Director Health Services ... Ms. Mindy WARNKEN
37 Director Financial Aid ... Mr. Kenneth T. FICK
18 Director Support Services ... Mr. Paul A. SCHULZ
26 Director of Marketing ... Mr. North CALLAHAN
42 Director of Church Relations ... Rev. Gregory DWYER
07 Director of Admissions ... Mr. Robert C. PIUROWSKI
39 Dir Residence Life/Student Act ... Ms. Tara HANNA
92 Director of Honors Program ... Dr. Kate E. BEHR
15 Director Personnel Services ... Ms. Kathleen D. CLARKE
13 Manager of Information Services ... Mr. Aaron J. MEYER
21 Business Manager ... Mr. Edward J. MCPARTLAN
44 Manager Annual Giving ... Ms. Nancy PETRIE
35 Coord Student Support/Career Devel ... Ms. Johanna L. PERRY
36 Director Student Placement ... Ms. Lois DIERLAM

Cooper Union (B)

30 Cooper Square, New York NY 10003-7120
County: New York FICE Identification: 002710
Unit ID: 190372
Telephone: (212) 353-4100 Carnegie Class: Bac/Diverse
FAX Number: (212) 353-4244 Calendar System: Semester
URL: www.cooper.edu
Established: 1859 Annual Undergrad Tuition & Fees: $35,000
Enrollment: 990 Coed
Affiliation or Control: Independent Non-Profit IRS Status: 501(c)3
Highest Offering: Master's
Program: Liberal Arts And General; Professional
Accreditation: M, ART, ENG

01 President ... Jamshed BHARUCHA
10 Vice President Finance and Admin ... Theresa C. WESTCOTT
26 Vice President of External Affairs ... Vacant
30 Vice President Development ... Derek WITTNER
101 Secy Board of Trustees/Dir of Opers ... Lawrence CACCIATORE
07 Dean Admissions/Records/Registrar ... Mitchell LIPTON
32 Dean of Students ... Linda LEMIESZ
57 Dean of Art ... Saskia BOS
48 Dean of Architecture ... Anthony VIDLER
54 Acting Dean of Engineering ... Simon BEN-AVI
79 Dean Human & Social Sciences ... William GERMANO
08 Head Librarian ... Ulla VOLK
21 Dir Budget/Personnel/Inst Research ... Vacant
44 Dir Major Gifts & Donor Relations ... Jeanne LUNIN
29 Director Alumni Relations ... Susan MOYLE LYNCH
44 Director of Institutional Giving ... Gerald FETNER
37 Director Financial Aid ... Mary RUOKONEN
06 Registrar ... Ellen DORSEY
46 Director of Research ... Vacant
26 Director of Public Affairs ... Claire H. MCCARTHY
14 Chief Technology Officer ... Robert P. HOPKINS
09 Director Assessment & Innovation ... Gerardo DEL CERRO
88 Director of Off Campus Programming ... Margaret MORTON
18 Director of Facilities Management ... Jody GRAPES
51 Director of Continuing Education ... David GREENSTEIN
41 Director of Athletics ... Stephen BAKER
36 Director of Career Services ... Robert THILL
24 Director of Audiovisual/Media ... Paul TUMMOLO
39 Residence Hall Manager ... Natasha CORNELL-POKU
91 Director of Administrative Database ... Sue MCCOY

† Every student receives a full-tuition scholarship.

Cornell University (C)

Ithaca NY 14853-2801
County: Tompkins FICE Identification: 002711
Unit ID: 190415
Telephone: (607) 255-2000 Carnegie Class: RU/VH
FAX Number: (607) 255-5396 Calendar System: Semester
URL: www.cornell.edu
Established: 1865 Annual Undergrad Tuition & Fees: $41,541
Enrollment: 20,939 Coed
Affiliation or Control: Independent Non-Profit IRS Status: 501(c)3
Highest Offering: Doctorate
Program: Liberal Arts And General; Teacher Preparatory; Professional
Accreditation: M, BUS, CIDA, DIETD, DIETI, ENG, HSA, LAW, LSAR, PLNG, @TEAC, VET

01 President ... David J. SKORTON
05 Provost ... W. Kent FUCHS
63 Provost/Medical Affairs ... Antonio M. GOTTO, JR.
20 Sr Vice Provost Academic Affairs ... John A. SILICIANO
20 Vice Provost Undergrad Educ ... Laura S. BROWN
46 Senior Vice Provost Research ... Robert A. BUHRMAN
58 Vice Prov & Dean Graduate School ... Barbara A. KNUTH
88 Vice Prov International Relations ... Alice N. PELL
88 Sr Vice Provost Land Grant Affairs ... Ronald SEEBER
45 Vice Pres Planning & Budget ... Elmira MANGUM
30 VP Alumni Affairs & Development ... Charles D. PHLEGAR
16 Vice President Human Resources ... Mary George OPPERMAN
32 VP Student & Academic Services ... Susan H. MURPHY
26 Vice Pres for University Relations ... Glenn C. ALTSCHULER
86 VP Government & Community Rels ... Stephen P. JOHNSON
27 Vice President Univ Communications ... Thomas W. BRUCE
43 University Counsel & Secretary Corp ... James J. MINGLE
10 VP Financial Affs/CFO ... Joanne M. DESTEFANO
13 CIO and VP for Info Technology ... Thomas E. DODDS
18 Vice President Facilities/Services ... Kyu-Jung WHANG
21 University Controller ... Anne SHAPIRO
21 Assoc Vice President/Treasurer ... Patricia A. JOHNSON
21 University Auditor ... Michael B. DICKINSON
20 Dean of Faculty ... William E. FRY
47 Dean Col Agriculture/Life Sciences ... Kathryn J. BOOR
48 Dean College Arch/Art/Planning ... Kent KLEINMAN
49 Dean College Arts & Science ... G. Peter LEPAGE
54 Dean College of Engineering ... Lance R. COLLINS
88 Dean School Hotel Administration ... Michael D. JOHNSON
59 Dean College Human Ecology ... Alan D. MATHIOS
50 Dean Johnson Graduate School Mgmt ... L. Joseph THOMAS
50 Dean School Industrial/Labor Rels ... Harry C. KATZ
61 Dean Law School ... Stewart J. SCHWAB
74 Dean College Veterinary Medicine ... Michael I. KOTLIKOFF
77 Dean Faculty of Computing and Info ... Daniel P. HUTTENLOCHER
51 Dean Cont Education/Summer Session ... Glenn C. ALTSCHULER
08 University Librarian ... Anne R. KENNEY
88 Director Africana Studies/Research ... Robert L. HARRIS
07 Director Undergraduate Admissions ... Jason C. LOCKE
37 Dir Financial Aid/Student Employ ... Susan HITCHCOCK
35 Dean of Students ... Kent L. HUBBELL
41 Director Athletics/Physical Educ ... J. Andrew NOEL, JR.
36 Director of Cornell Career Services ... Rebecca M. SPARROW
22 Assoc VP Wrkfrce Dvrsty & Inclusion ... Lynette CHAPPELL-WILLIAMS
23 Exec Dir University Health Services ... Janet L. CORSON-RIKERT
28 Assoc Vice Provost Acad Diversity ... Andrew T. MILLER
93 Assoc Dean Intercultural Programs ... Renee T. ALEXANDER
42 Dir Cornell United Religious Works ... Kenneth J. CLARKE
25 Assoc Vice Pres Research Admin ... Catherine E. LONG
25 Sr Director Sponsored Programs Svcs ... Jeffrey A. SILBER
19 Chief Cornell Police ... Kathy R. ZONER
96 Sr Dir Supply Channel Management ... Thomas W. ROMANTIC
44 Sr Assoc VP University Development ... Patricia A. WATSON
29 Assoc Vice Pres Alumni Affairs ... Christopher V. MARSHALL
09 Director Inst Research/Planning ... Marin E. CLARKBERG

† Parent institution of Weill Medical College of Cornell University.

Corning Community College (D)

One Academic Drive, Corning NY 14830-3297
County: Steuben FICE Identification: 002863
Unit ID: 190442
Telephone: (607) 962-9011 Carnegie Class: Assoc/Pub-R-M
FAX Number: (607) 962-9456 Calendar System: Semester
URL: www.corning-cc.edu
Established: 1956 Annual Undergrad Tuition & Fees (In-District): $4,670
Enrollment: 5,396 Coed
Affiliation or Control: State/Local IRS Status: 501(c)3
Highest Offering: Associate Degree
Program: Occupational; 2-Year Principally Bachelor's Creditable
Accreditation: M, ADNUR

01 President ... Dr. Katherine P. DOUGLAS
05 Vice Pres & Dean Academic Affairs ... Ms. Andrea RUBIN
11 Vice President Administrative Svcs ... Mr. Thomas F. CARR
32 Vice Pres & Dean of Student Devel ... Mr. Donald HEINS
30 Vice Pres Institutional Advancement ... Vacant
08 Director Learning Resources Center ... Ms. Sarah WEISMAN
06 Registrar ... Ms. Karen BOULAS
07 Director of Admissions ... Ms. Karen BROWN
14 Director of Computer Center ... Mr. Barry GARRISON
15 Director Human Resources ... Ms. Nannette NICHOLAS
10 Chief Business Officer ... Mr. Thomas F. CARR
18 Chief Facilities/Physical Plant ... Mr. Calvin WILLIAMS
37 Director Student Financial Aid ... Mrs. Barbara SNOW
09 Research Analyst ... Ms. Monica DEFENDORF

Crouse Hospital College of Nursing (E)

736 Irving Avenue, Syracuse NY 13210
County: Onondaga FICE Identification: 006445
Unit ID: 190451
Telephone: (315) 470-7481 Carnegie Class: Not Classified
FAX Number: (315) 470-5774 Calendar System: Semester
URL: www.crouse.org/nursing
Established: 1913 Annual Undergrad Tuition & Fees: $9,366
Enrollment: 277 Coed
Affiliation or Control: Independent Non-Profit IRS Status: 501(c)3
Highest Offering: Associate Degree
Program: 2-Year Principally Bachelor's Creditable; Nursing Emphasis
Accreditation: ADNUR

01 Director ... Dr. Ann SEDORE

Culinary Institute of America (F)

1946 Campus Drive, Hyde Park NY 12538-1499
County: Dutchess FICE Identification: 007304
Unit ID: 190503
Telephone: (845) 452-9600 Carnegie Class: Spec/Other
FAX Number: (845) 452-0165 Calendar System: Semester
URL: www.ciachef.edu
Established: 1946 Annual Undergrad Tuition & Fees: $26,180
Enrollment: 2,785 Coed
Affiliation or Control: Independent Non-Profit IRS Status: 501(c)3
Highest Offering: Baccalaureate
Program: Occupational; 2-Year Principally Bachelor's Creditable; Technical Emphasis
Accreditation: M

01 President ... Dr. Tim RYAN
10 Sr VP of Finance/Administration ... Mr. Charles A. O'MARA
30 Vice President for Advancement ... Ms. Nancy HARVIN
88 VP/Dean of Culinary Education ... Mr. Mark ERICKSON
26 VP Marketing/Strat/Enroll Planning ... Mr. Bruce HILLENBRAND
15 Vice President of Human Resources ... Mr. Richard MIGNAULT
05 Vice President of Academic Affairs ... Dr. Peter RAINSFORD
09 Assoc VP Plng/Research/Accred ... Dr. Ann A. WEEKS
49 Dean of Liberal Arts & Business Mgt ... Dr. Kathleen MERGET
32 Dean of Students ... Ms. Alice-Ann SCHUSTER
35 Assoc Dean Student Activities ... Mr. David WHALEN
06 Registrar ... Vacant
07 Director of Admissions ... Ms. Rachel BIRCHWOOD
19 Director of Safety ... Mr. Richard T. CULLEN
08 Library Director ... Ms. Eileen A. DEVRIES
36 Director of Career Services ... Mr. Chester KOULIK
37 Director of Financial Aid ... Ms. Kathleen GAILOR
18 Director of Facilities ... Mr. Thomas M. HIRST
29 Senior Alumni Relations Officer ... Ms. Patti HAMILTON
21 Director of Finance & Accounting ... Mr. Steven STROM
38 Director Student Counseling ... Dr. Daria PAPALIA
96 Director of Purchasing ... Mr. Brad MATTHEWS

Daemen College (G)

4380 Main Street, Amherst NY 14226-3592
County: Erie FICE Identification: 002808
Unit ID: 190725
Telephone: (716) 839-3600 Carnegie Class: Master's L
FAX Number: (716) 839-8516 Calendar System: Semester
URL: www.daemen.edu
Established: 1947 Annual Undergrad Tuition & Fees: $22,310
Enrollment: 2,958 Coed
Affiliation or Control: Independent Non-Profit IRS Status: 501(c)3
Highest Offering: Doctorate
Program: Liberal Arts And General; Teacher Preparatory; Professional
Accreditation: M, ARCPA, IACBE, NUR, PTA, SW, @TEAC

01 President ... Dr. Edwin G. CLAUSEN
05 Vice Pres Academic Affairs/Dean ... Dr. Michael S. BROGAN
10 VP for Business Affairs & Treasurer ... Mr. Robert C. BEISWANGER
30 Vice President External Relations ... Dr. David A. CRISTANTELLO
84 VP of Enrollment Management ... Dr. Patricia R. BROWN
32 VP Student Affairs/Dean of Students ... Dr. Richanne C. MANKEY
20 Assoc VP Academic Affairs ... Dr. Kathleen C. BOONE
07 Dean of Admissions ... Mr. Frank WILLIAMS
21 Controller & Assistant Treasurer ... Mr. Michael E. LOOKER
91 Director Information Resources Mgmt ... Mr. Brian J. WILKINS
90 Director Academic Computing Service ... Mr. Christopher F. WILSON
09 Director of Institutional Research ... Dr. Patricia L. BEAMAN
88 Dir of Institutional Assessment ... Dr. Mimi H. STEADMAN
08 Head Librarian ... Mr. Francis J. CAREY
06 Registrar ... Ms. Paulette A. ANZELONE
88 Exec Dir for Academic Support Svcs ... Dr. Blake THURMAN
51 Director of Educational Technology ... Mr. Anthony J. KLEJNA

37 Director Financial Aid ... Mr. Jeffrey M. PAGANO
15 Director of Personnel ... Mrs. Pamela R. NEUMANN
07 Assoc Director Grad Admissions ... Mr. Scott T. ROWE
26 Director of College Relations ... Mr. Michael G. ANDREI
44 Dir Annual Giving/Alumni Relations ... Ms. Lauren METZGER
78 Director of Career Services ... Ms. Maureen MILLANE
39 Director of Residence Life ... Ms. Sara C. ANDERSON
35 Director of Student Activities ... Mr. Christopher P. MALIK
24 Director Instruct Technology Svcs ... Mr. James J. BACHRATY
18 Director of Physical Plant ... Mr. Frank X. SWEITZER, JR.
19 Director Security & Fire Safety ... Mr. Craig HUGHES
42 Director Campus Ministry ... Rev. Cassandra L. SALTER-SMITH
41 Director of Athletics ... Mr. Donald V. SILVERI
96 Dir of Purchasing/Central Services ... Ms. Gwendolyn M. WALKER
92 Director of Honors Program ... Dr. Matthew WARD
40 Bookstore Manager ... Mrs. Julie MILLER
31 Coordinator Service Learning ... Ms. Susan M. MARCHIONE

Davis College (A)

400 Riverside Drive, Johnson City NY 13790-2714
County: Broome FICE Identification: 021691
Unit ID: 194569
Telephone: (607) 729-1581 Carnegie Class: Spec/Faith
FAX Number: (607) 729-2962 Calendar System: Semester
URL: www.davisny.edu
Established: 1900 Annual Undergrad Tuition & Fees: $11,940
Enrollment: 375 Coed
Affiliation or Control: Independent Non-Profit IRS Status: 501(c)3
Highest Offering: Baccalaureate
Program: Religious Emphasis
Accreditation: M, BI

01 President ... Dr. Dino J. PEDRONE
84 Director of Enrollment Management ... Mr. Rick CRAMER
05 Chief Academic Officer ... Dr. Gilbert A. PARKER
32 Director of Student Development ... Mrs. Nichole POST
30 VP Inst Advancement ... Vacant
10 Chief Financial Officer ... Mrs. Shelly WILCOX
04 Assistant to the President ... Mr. Daniel RATHMELL
06 Registrar ... Mr. Spencer KEY
08 Library Manager ... Mr. Jeremy MCGINNISS
37 Director Financial Aid ... Mr. Larry ELLIS
04 Executive Assistant ... Ms. Jenny GREEN

DeVry College of New York (B)

180 Madison Avenue, Suite 900, New York NY 10016
County: New York Identification: 666979
Unit ID: 432199
Telephone: (212) 312-4301 Carnegie Class: Master's M
FAX Number: N/A Calendar System: Semester
URL: www.devry.edu
Established: 1931 Annual Undergrad Tuition & Fees: $15,294
Enrollment: 1,784 Coed
Affiliation or Control: Proprietary IRS Status: Proprietary
Highest Offering: Master's
Program: Occupational; Professional; Business Emphasis
Accreditation: &NH, ENGT

01 Metro President ... Anthony STANZIANI
10 Sr Director Finance & Admin ... Helen FIALKOFF
97 Dean of General Education ... Michael GOOCH
05 Dean of Academic Affairs ... John GIBBONS
26 Director of Community Outreach ... Kristina DELAS
08 Director of Library Services ... Emily TURNER
15 Human Resources Manager ... Dorothy HUTCHERSON
07 Senior Director of Admissions ... Patricia CAPALDO
36 Director of Career Services ... Scott PASSESER

† Regional accreditation is carried under the parent institution in Downers Grove, IL.

Dominican College of Blauvelt (C)

470 Western Highway, Orangeburg NY 10962-1210
County: Rockland FICE Identification: 002713
Unit ID: 190761
Telephone: (845) 848-7800 Carnegie Class: Master's S
FAX Number: (845) 359-2313 Calendar System: Semester
URL: www.dc.edu
Established: 1952 Annual Undergrad Tuition & Fees: $22,940
Enrollment: 2,070 Coed
Affiliation or Control: Independent Non-Profit IRS Status: 501(c)3
Highest Offering: Doctorate
Program: Liberal Arts And General; Teacher Preparatory; Professional
Accreditation: M, IACBE, NURSE, OT, PTA, SW, TEAC

01 President ... SrDr. Mary Eileen O'BRIEN
00 Chancellor ... Sr. Kathleen SULLIVAN
05 Vice Pres/Dean Academic Affairs ... Dr. Thomas S. NOWAK
84 Vice Pres of Enrollment Management ... Mr. Brian FERNANDES
32 Dean of Students ... Mr. John BURKE
10 Director of Fiscal Affairs ... Mr. Anthony CIPOLLA
06 Registrar ... Ms. Mary MCFADDEN
07 Director of Admissions ... Ms. Joyce ELBE
08 Librarian ... Mr. John BARRIE
30 Director of Inst Advancement ... Ms. Dorothy FILORAMO
15 Director Human Resources ... Ms. Marybeth BRODERICK
26 Chief Public Relations Officer ... Mr. Brett BEKRITSKY
29 Director Alumni Relations ... Ms. Samira ALLEN
35 Director Student Activities ... Vacant
09 Inst Research/Plng/Assessment Ofcr ... Dr. William J. STEGMAYER
37 Director Student Financial Aid ... Mr. Daniel SHIELDS
36 Director Student Placement ... Ms. Evelyn FISKAA
38 Director Student Couseling ... Ms. Alise COHEN
21 Controller ... Ms. Joanne PORETTE
13 Director Information Technology ... Mr. Russell DIAZ
18 Chief Facilities/Physical Plant ... Mr. Michael DEMPSEY
20 Associate Academic Officer ... Ms. Ann VAVOLIZZA
39 Director Student Housing ... Mr. Ryan O'GORMAN
41 Athletic Director ... Mr. Joseph CLINTON
42 Director Campus Ministry ... Sr. Barbara MCENEANY
96 Director of Purchasing ... Ms. Amy BIANCO
28 Director of Diversity ... Vacant
19 Director of Security/Safety ... Mr. John LENNON
42 Chaplain ... Fr. Ronald STANLEY, OP

Dowling College (D)

Idle Hour Boulevard, Oakdale NY 11769-1999
County: Suffolk FICE Identification: 002667
Unit ID: 190770
Telephone: (631) 244-3000 Carnegie Class: Master's L
FAX Number: (631) 563-7831 Calendar System: Semester
URL: www.dowling.edu
Established: 1959 Annual Undergrad Tuition & Fees: $25,013
Enrollment: 5,900 Coed
Affiliation or Control: Independent Non-Profit IRS Status: 501(c)3
Highest Offering: Doctorate
Program: Liberal Arts And General; Teacher Preparatory; Professional
Accreditation: M, IACBE, TED

01 President ... Dr. Jeremy D. BROWN
05 Interim Provost ... Dr. Elana ZOLFO
11 VP Col Administration/Student Svcs ... Dr. David RING
32 VP Enrollment and Student Services ... Ms. Ronnie MACDONALD
26 VP for Marketing & Communications ... Ms. Amy NEIL
51 VP Corporate Programs/Cont Educ ... Dr. Elana ZOLFO
10 CFO and Treasurer ... Vacant
29 Associate VP of Alumni Relations ... Vacant
21 Associate VP Business and Finance ... Ms. Lisa DIIORIO
84 Asst VP for Enrollment/Student Svcs ... Ms. Jennifer A. KUHL
07 Dean of Admissions ... Vacant
26 Dir Communications/Public Relations ... Ms. Heather SHIVOKEVICH
41 Director of Athletics ... Mr. Richard COLE
09 Director Inst Research/Assessment ... Mr. Robert MCMANUS
15 Exec Director Human Resources ... Ms. Anne DIMOLA
18 Director of Facilities Services ... Mr. Tom DOWNS
06 Registrar ... Ms. Jennifer A. KUHL
37 Director of Student Financial Svcs ... Ms. Denise SCALZO
96 Director of Purchasing ... Ms. Stephanie SWEET
13 Dir of Information Technology Svcs ... Mr. Thomas FRANZA

Dutchess Community College (E)

53 Pendell Road, Poughkeepsie NY 12601-1595
County: Dutchess FICE Identification: 002864
Unit ID: 190840
Telephone: (845) 431-8000 Carnegie Class: Assoc/Pub-R-L
FAX Number: (845) 431-8984 Calendar System: Semester
URL: www.sunydutchess.edu
Established: 1957 Annual Undergrad Tuition & Fees (In-District): $3,305
Enrollment: 10,319 Coed
Affiliation or Control: State/Local IRS Status: 501(c)3
Highest Offering: Associate Degree
Program: Occupational; 2-Year Principally Bachelor's Creditable; Business Emphasis
Accreditation: M, ADNUR, EMT, MLTAD

01 President ... Dr. D. David CONKLIN
05 Dean of Academic Affairs ... Mr. Carl DENTI
20 Associate Dean of Academic Affairs ... Ms. Ellen GAMBINO
20 Associate Dean of Academic Affairs ... Ms. Carla MAZZARELLI
32 Dean Student Svcs/Enroll Mgmt ... Dr. Sandra MILLER HOLST
11 Dean of Administration ... Mr. W. John DUNN
31 Dean Community Svcs/Special Pgms ... Dr. Carol STEVENS
21 Associate Dean Administration ... Ms. Donna ROCAP
88 Assoc Dean Cmty Svcs/Special Pgms ... Ms. Virginia STOEFFEL
06 Registrar ... Vacant
07 Director of Admissions ... Vacant
08 Director of the Library ... Ms. Cathy CARL
14 Director Information Systems ... Mr. Patrick GRIFFIN
30 Director Institutional Advancement ... Ms. Patricia PRUNTY
09 Director Planning/Inst Research ... Ms. Donna JOHNSON
24 Director Telecomm/Instructnl Media ... Vacant
37 Director Financial Aid ... Ms. Susan MEAD
36 Director Counseling/Career Svcs ... Vacant
15 Director Human Resources Mgmt ... Mr. George BUCHANAN
18 Assoc Dean of Admin Facilities Mgmt ... Ms. Bridgette ANDERSON
19 Interim Director Campus Security ... Mr. Ed COX
13 Assoc Dean Admin Info Technology ... Mr. Klaus GESSLER
35 Director of Student Activities ... Vacant
26 Chief Public Relations Officer ... Ms. Judi STOKES
88 Assoc Dir Teaching Learning Center ... Ms. Chrisie MITCHELL
88 Director of Scheduling ... Ms. Susan MOORE
12 Director DCC South Branch ... Mr. Timothy DECKER
04 Admin Assistant to the President ... Ms. Linda M. BEASIMER

D'Youville College (F)

320 Porter Avenue, Buffalo NY 14201-1084
County: Erie FICE Identification: 002712
Unit ID: 190716
Telephone: (716) 829-8000 Carnegie Class: Master's L
FAX Number: (716) 829-7820 Calendar System: Semester
URL: www.dyc.edu
Established: 1908 Annual Undergrad Tuition & Fees: $21,450
Enrollment: 3,152 Coed
Affiliation or Control: Independent Non-Profit IRS Status: 501(c)3
Highest Offering: Doctorate
Program: Liberal Arts And General; Teacher Preparatory; Professional
Accreditation: M, CHIRO, ARCPA, DIETC, IACBE, NURSE, OT, @PHAR, PTA

01 President ... Sr. Denise A. ROCHE
05 Vice President for Academic Affairs ... Dr. Arup SEN
10 Vice President Financal Affairs ... Mr. Edward JOHNSON
32 VP Student Affairs & Enroll Mgmt ... Mr. Robert P. MURPHY
30 Vice Pres Institutional Advancement ... Mr. Timothy G. BRENNAN
11 Vice President Operations ... Mr. Donald G. KELLER
88 VP Admin Svcs & External Relations ... Dr. William MARIANI
06 Registrar ... Dr. Dion DALY
66 Dean School of Nursing ... Dr. Judith LEWIS
53 Dean School of Education ... Vacant
67 Dean School of Pharmacy ... Dr. Gary STOEHR
88 Artistic Director Kavinoky Theater ... Mr. David LAMB
35 Associate VP for Student Affairs ... Mr. Jeffrey PLATT
35 Assistant VP for Student Affairs ... Mr. Anthony SPINA
21 Bursar ... Mrs. Mary POTTER
18 Director of Facilities ... Mr. Leonard OSEEKEY
21 Controller ... Ms. Laurie HALL
09 Dir Inst Rsrch & Assessment Support ... Mr. Mark ECKSTEIN
90 Director Academic Computing ... Dr. John T. MURPHY
91 Director Administrative Computing ... Mr. Robert HALL
29 Director Alumni Relations ... Ms. Mary PFEIFFER
44 Director Annual Giving ... Mrs. Aimee PEARSON
41 Director Athletics ... Mr. Brian CAVAHAUGH
42 Director Campus Ministry ... Fr. Paterick O'KEEFE
36 Director Career Services Center ... Ms. Christine DEMCIE
88 Director College Center ... Ms. Deborah E. OWENS
13 Director Computer & Network Svcs ... Ms. Mary SPENCE
102 Director Foundation Relations ... Mr. William P. MCKEEVER
25 Director Government Grants ... Ms. Molly FLYNN
23 Director Health Center ... Mrs. Susan NIERENBERG
15 Director Human Resources ... Ms. Linda MORETTI
85 Director International Stdnt Svcs ... Mrs. Laryssa PETRYSHYN
88 Director Learning Center ... Sr. Mary B. CONNORS
08 Director Library Services ... Mr. Rand BELLAVIA
44 Director Major & Planned Gifts ... Ms. Patricia VAN DYKE
28 Director Multicultural Affairs ... Mrs. Yolanda WOOD
38 Director Personal Counseling ... Ms. Kimberly ZITTEL
26 Director Public Relations ... Mr. D. John BRAY
19 Director Security ... Mr. Mark GRIFFITH
37 Director Student Financial Aid ... Ms. Lorraine METZ
07 Director Undergraduate Admissions ... Dr. Steve SMITH
07 Director Graduate Admissions ... Ms. Linda FISHER
07 Director Intl Admiss & Marketing ... CMDR. Ronald DANNECKER
88 Director Veterans Affairs Office ... Mr. Benjamin RANDLE

Ellis School of Nursing (G)

1101 Nott Street, Schenectady NY 12308
County: Schenectady FICE Identification: 006448
Unit ID: 190956
Telephone: (518) 243-4471 Carnegie Class: Not Classified
FAX Number: (518) 243-4470 Calendar System: Other
URL: www.ellisschoolofnursing.org
Established: 1903 Annual Undergrad Tuition & Fees: $8,297
Enrollment: 119 Coed
Affiliation or Control: Independent Non-Profit IRS Status: 501(c)3
Highest Offering: Associate Degree
Program: Nursing Emphasis
Accreditation: ADNUR

01 Director ... Dr. Marilyn STAPLETON

The Elmezzi Graduate School of Molecular Medicine (H)

350 Community Drive, Manhasset NY 11030-3828
County: Nassau Identification: 666671
Telephone: (516) 562-3467 Carnegie Class: Not Classified
FAX Number: (516) 562-1022 Calendar System: Other
URL: www.elmezzigraduateschool.org
Established: 2008 Annual Graduate Tuition & Fees: N/A
Enrollment: N/A Coed
Affiliation or Control: Independent Non-Profit IRS Status: 501(c)3
Highest Offering: Doctorate; No Undergraduates
Program: Professional
Accreditation: NY

01 President ... Dr. Kevin J. TRACEY
05 Dean ... Dr. Bettie STEINBERG

Elmira Business Institute (I)

Langdon Plaza, 303 N Main Street, Elmira NY 14901-3086
County: Chemung FICE Identification: 009043
Unit ID: 190974
Telephone: (607) 733-7177 Carnegie Class: Assoc/PrivFP
FAX Number: (607) 733-7178 Calendar System: Semester
URL: www.ebi-college.com
Established: 1858 Annual Undergrad Tuition & Fees: $11,650
Enrollment: 589 Coed
Affiliation or Control: Proprietary IRS Status: Proprietary
Highest Offering: Associate Degree
Program: Occupational

Accreditation: ACICS, MAC

01 President .... Mr. Brad C. PHILLIPS
03 Vice President .... Mrs. Kathleen M. HAMILTON
32 Director of Student Services .... Mrs. Lisa A. ROAN
37 Financial Aid Director .... Mrs. Sue REINBOLD

Elmira College (A)

One Park Place, Elmira NY 14901-2099
County: Chemung FICE Identification: 002718
Unit ID: 190983
Telephone: (607) 735-1800 Carnegie Class: Bac/Diverse
FAX Number: (607) 735-1758 Calendar System: Other
URL: www.elmira.edu
Established: 1855 Annual Undergrad Tuition & Fees: $35,550
Enrollment: 1,785 Coed
Affiliation or Control: Independent Non-Profit IRS Status: 501(c)3
Highest Offering: Master's
Program: Liberal Arts And General; Teacher Preparatory; Professional; Business Emphasis
Accreditation: M, NUR, @TEAC

01 President .... Dr. Thomas K. MEIER
10 Vice President & Treasurer .... Dr. Robert W. RUBLE
05 Academic Vice President .... Dr. Stephen F. COLEMAN
30 Vice President of Development .... Ms. Sherry M. TROCINO
32 Vice Pres/Dean of Student Life .... Ms. Julianne D. BAUMANN
41 Vice President Athletics .... Ms. Patricia A. THOMPSON
51 Dean of Continuing Education .... Ms. Elizabeth A. LAMBERT
07 Director of Admissions .... Mr. Brett C. MOORE
37 Dean of Financial Aid .... Ms. Kathleen L. COHEN
06 Registrar .... Mr. Michael HALPERIN
08 Dean of Library & IT .... Ms. Elizabeth M. WAVLE
36 Director Counsel/Career Services .... Dr. William D. COUCHON
26 Director Public Relations .... Mr. Michael B. ROGERS
50 Chair Business Programs .... Dr. Mariam KHAWAR
57 Chair Fine Arts Program .... Prof. George DEFALUSSY
79 Chair of Humanities .... Dr. Heidi DIERCKX
81 Chair Math/Natural Sciences .... Dr. Christine BEZOTTE
83 Chair Social/Behavioral Sciences .... Dr. Charles MITCHELL
88 Chair of Professional Programs .. Dr. Maureen DONOHUE-SMITH
29 Director of Alumni Relations .... Ms. Adriana F. GIANCOLI
66 Director Nursing Program .... Prof. Lois SCHOENER
18 Superintendent of B&G .... Mr. Donald L. BRIMMER
27 Director of Communications .... Mr. Daniel A. BAROODY
39 Director of Campus Life .... Mr. Benjamin J. CURTIS
40 Director Business Operations .... Mrs. Shannon MOYLAN
15 Director Personnel Services .... Ms. Carey L. IPPINECA
09 Director of Development Research .... Ms. Ellen BURKE

Erie Community College City Campus (B)

121 Ellicott Street, Buffalo NY 14203-2698
County: Erie FICE Identification: 010684
Unit ID: 191083
Telephone: (716) 842-2770 Carnegie Class: Assoc/Pub-U-MC
FAX Number: (716) 851-1129 Calendar System: Semester
URL: www.ecc.edu
Established: 1971 Annual Undergrad Tuition & Fees (In-District): $4,110
Enrollment: 3,833 Coed
Affiliation or Control: State/Local IRS Status: 501(c)3
Highest Offering: Associate Degree
Program: Occupational; 2-Year Principally Bachelor's Creditable
Accreditation: M, ADNUR, RTT

01 President .... Mr. Jack F. QUINN
05 Associate Vice President Academics .... Dr. Edward J. HOLMES
88 Assoc VP Academic Transition Pgms .... Vacant
32 Associate VP Student Services .... Dr. Marsha D. JACKSON
19 Assoc Vice President Security .... Mr. John MCDONNELL
10 Chief Admin & Financial Officer .... Mr. William D. REUTER
35 Dean of Students .... Ms. Petrina HILL-CHEATOM
103 Exec Dean Workforce Dev/Cmty Svcs .... Ms. Carrie W. KAHN
102 Executive Director Foundation .... Vacant
49 Asst Academic Dean Liberal Arts .... Dr. Marcia A. GELLIN
50 Asst Academic Dean Business .... Dr. Kenneth J. BARNES
28 Director of Equity & Diversity .... Ms. Darley WILLIS
06 Registrar .... Ms. Susan I. DUKE
08 Librarian .... Ms. Kathleen MCGRIFF-POWERS
40 Bookstore Manager .... Ms. Teresa KALINOWSKI
23 Health Services Nurse .... Vacant
26 Director of Public Relations .... Mr. Lance R. KONKLE
27 Public Information Officer .... Ms. Katharine M. MCLAUGHLIN
41 Director of Athletics .... Mr. Peter J. JEREBKO
37 Financial Aid Coordinator .... Ms. Charlotte M. COSTON
24 Audio Visual Coordinator .... Mr. Gregg S. FILIPPONE
36 Career Resource Center Coordinator .... Ms. Barbara S. HOUSE
92 Coordinator Honors Program .... Dr. Jill N. KEARNS-BODKIN
88 Coordinator of Corporate Training .... Mr. John P. SLISZ
29 Coordinator of Alumni Affairs .... Ms. Mary Jo R. DENNEE
55 Asst Coordinator Evening Activities .... Vacant
04 Assistant to the President .... Mr. Charles W. ESTOFF
07 Admissions Counselor .... Ms. Heather A. CRUZ
07 Admissions Counselor .... Ms. Deborah M. MEDINA

Erie Community College North Campus (C)

6205 Main Street, Williamsville NY 14221-7095
County: Erie FICE Identification: 002865
Unit ID: 191065
Telephone: (716) 634-0800 Carnegie Class: Not Classified
FAX Number: (716) 851-1429 Calendar System: Semester
URL: www.ecc.edu
Established: 1946 Annual Undergrad Tuition & Fees (In-District): $4,110
Enrollment: 6,760 Coed
Affiliation or Control: State/Local IRS Status: 501(c)3
Highest Offering: Associate Degree
Program: Occupational; 2-Year Principally Bachelor's Creditable
Accreditation: &M, ADNUR, DH, DIETT, ENGT, MAC, MLTAD, OPD, OTA

01 President .... Mr. Jack F. QUINN
05 Exec Vice Pres Academic Affairs .... Mr. Richard C. WASHOUSKY
84 Asst VP Enrollment Mgmt/Marketing .... Vacant
23 Associate Vice Pres Health Sciences .... Mr. Patrick J. WILES
32 Dean of Students .... Ms. Barbara M. RIEMAN
45 Director Assessment/Accreditation .... Dr. Marilou C. BLAIR
09 Director of Institutional Research .... Ms. Marlene ARNO
14 Director of ERP Sys & Info Svcs .... Mr. David L. ARLINGTON
72 Assistant Academic Dean-Technology .... Mr. Mark S. HOEBER
50 Assistant Academic Dean-Business .... Vacant
49 Assistant Academic Dean-Lib Arts .... Ms. Mary A. BEARD
06 Director of Registration .... Mr. Paul A. LAMANNA
08 Librarian .... Ms. Jane E. ASHWILL
07 Director of Admissions/Call Center .... Mr. Erik D'AQUINO
36 Career Resource Center Coordinator .... Mr. Joseph P. ABBARNO
25 Grants Coordinator .... Dr. William G. FALKOWSKI
37 Financial Aid Assistant Coordinator .... Ms. Sarah E. IZZO
24 Audio Visual Coordinator .... Vacant
23 Health Services Nurse .... Ms. Rita A. BELZER
11 Coordinator Institutional Services .... Mr. Joel J. DAMIANI
41 Assistant Director Athletics .... Mr. Steve L. MULLEN
85 Foreign Student Advisor .... Mr. John DANNA
88 Advanced Studies Coordinator .... Ms. Deborah F. SCHMITT
40 Bookstore Manager .... Ms. Teresa KALINOWSKI
92 Coordinator Honors Program .... Ms. Lisa A. MATTHIES-WIZA
55 Asst Coordinator Evening Services .... Vacant
25 Grants Coordinator .... Mr. Michael J. BIGGANE
19 Coordinator of Public Safety .... Vacant
37 Financial Aid Asst Coordinator .... Ms. Robin FILIPPONE

† Regional accreditation is carried under the parent institution in Buffalo, NY.

Erie Community College-South Campus (D)

4041 Southwestern Boulevard, Orchard Park NY 14127-2199
County: Erie FICE Identification: 012427
Unit ID: 191074
Telephone: (716) 648-5400 Carnegie Class: Not Classified
FAX Number: (716) 851-1629 Calendar System: Semester
URL: www.ecc.edu
Established: 1974 Annual Undergrad Tuition & Fees (In-District): $4,110
Enrollment: 4,597 Coed
Affiliation or Control: State/Local IRS Status: 501(c)3
Highest Offering: Associate Degree
Program: Occupational; 2-Year Principally Bachelor's Creditable
Accreditation: &M, DT

01 President .... Mr. Jack F. QUINN
32 Exec Vice President Student Affairs .... Ms. Monica RASCOE
05 Associate Vice Pres Academics .... Vacant
13 Assoc Vice Pres/Chief Info Officer .... Mr. Joseph W. STEWART
10 Associate VP Finance/Controller .... Mr. Richard G. SCHOTT
35 Dean of Students .... Vacant
15 Human Resources Director .... Ms. Eileen P. FLAHERTY
37 Director of Financial Aid .... Mr. Scott WELTJEN
08 Librarian .... Ms. Melissa E. PETERSON
18 Director Buildings & Grounds .... Mr. Anthony NESCI
49 Assistant Academic Dean-Lib Arts .... Mr. Richard D. WOLCOTT
56 Director Distance Learning .... Ms. Martha J. DIXON
72 Assistant Academic Dean-Technology .... Vacant
06 Registrar .... Mr. Samuel P. PALUMBO
07 Admissions Counselor .... Ms. Kathleen E. SAKO
07 Admissions Counselor .... Ms. Roslyn M. CANTY
21 Business Manager .... Mr. Paul F. DANIEU
24 Audio Visual Coordinator .... Mr. David G. MALLORY
88 Coordinator Special Services .... Ms. Kathy S. HOFFMAN
23 Health Services Nurse .... Ms. Sally STEPHENSON
36 Career Resource Center Director .... Mr. Michael M. GOLEBIEWSKI
55 Asst Coordinator Evening Services .... Vacant
92 Coordinator of Honors Program .... Mr. Rene L. ROJAS
40 Bookstore Supervisor .... Mr. Ryan SNYDER
15 Assistant Director Human Resources .... Vacant
78 Coordinator Internships/Coop .... Ms. Margaret ARCADI

† Regional accreditation is carried under the parent institution in Buffalo, NY.

Everest Institute (E)

1630 Portland Avenue, Rochester NY 14521-3007
County: Monroe FICE Identification: 004811
Unit ID: 194967
Telephone: (585) 266-0430 Carnegie Class: Assoc/PrivFP
FAX Number: (585) 266-8243 Calendar System: Quarter
Established: 1863 Annual Undergrad Tuition & Fees: $16,992
Enrollment: 875 Coed
Affiliation or Control: Proprietary IRS Status: Proprietary
Highest Offering: Associate Degree
Program: Occupational; 2-Year Principally Bachelor's Creditable; Business Emphasis

Accreditation: ACICS, MAC

01 President .... Mr. Carl A. SILVIO
05 Academic Dean .... Ms. Eva WILCOX
07 Director of Admissions .... Ms. Deanna PFLUKE
37 Director Student Finance .... Mrs. Kandace REID
10 Director of Student Accounts .... Ms. Maureen GILMORE
36 Director of Career Services .... Ms. Annette PERRIN
12 East Campus Director .... Mr. James TEAL
04 Admin Asst to the President .... Ms. Karen M. BAFFORD
08 Librarian .... Mr. Kyle DANIELS
106 Online Coordinator .... Ms. Tanisha SEWELL
06 Registrar .... Ms. Gail BRUENGINSEN

Excelsior College (F)

7 Columbia Circle, Albany NY 12203-5156
County: Albany FICE Identification: 002834
Unit ID: 196680
Telephone: (518) 464-8500 Carnegie Class: Master's M
FAX Number: (518) 464-8777 Calendar System: Other
URL: www.excelsior.edu
Established: 1971 Annual Undergrad Tuition & Fees: N/A
Enrollment: 29,939 Coed
Affiliation or Control: Independent Non-Profit IRS Status: 501(c)3
Highest Offering: Master's
Program: Liberal Arts And General; Professional
Accreditation: M, ADNUR, ENGT, IACBE, NUR

01 President .... Dr. John F. EBERSOLE
05 Chief Academic Officer/Provost .... Dr. Mary Beth HANNER
10 VP Finance & Administration .... Mr. John M. PONTIUS, JR.
43 VP and General Counsel .... Mr. Joseph B. PORTER
26 VP Institutional Advancement .... Ms. Cathy KUSHNER
88 VP Outcomes Assess/Faculty Devel .... Vacant
16 VP Human Resources & Facilities .... Mr. Edmund MCTERNAN
84 VP Enrollment Management .... Mr. Craig MASLOWSKY
13 VP Information Technology .... Ms. Susan O'HERN
37 Asst VP/Director of Financial Aid .... Mr. Thomas DALTON
07 Exec Director of Admissions .... Mr. Roberto FIGUEROA
30 Asst VP Institutional Advancement .... Mr. William M. STEWART
86 Asst VP for Government Relations .... Dr. Paul SHIFFMAN
21 Asst VP and Controller .... Ms. Michele AURICCHIO
106 Dean Online Education/Learning Svcs .... Dr. George TIMMONS
21 AVP/Dir Budgets/Financial Analysis .... Mr. Todd S. THOMAS
13 AVP Information Technology .... Mr. Ronald MARZITELLI
88 AVP Outcomes Assessment & Inst .... Dr. Lisa DANIELS
102 Director of Grants and Research .... Ms. Patricia CROOP
30 Director of Development .... Ms. Marcy STRYKER
06 Registrar .... Ms. Lori MORANO
20 Vice Provost .... Dr. Patrick JONES
66 Dean of Nursing .... Dr. Mary Lee POLLARD
50 Dean of Business & Technology .... Dr. Jane LECLAIR
49 Dean of Liberal Arts .... Dr. Scott DALRYMPLE
76 Dean of Health Sciences .... Dr. Debbie SOPCZYK

Fashion Institute of Technology (G)

Seventh Avenue at 27 Street, New York NY 10001-5992
County: New York FICE Identification: 002866
Unit ID: 191126
Telephone: (212) 217-7999 Carnegie Class: Master's S
FAX Number: N/A Calendar System: Semester
URL: www.fitnyc.edu
Established: 1944 Annual Undergrad Tuition & Fees (In-District): $5,168
Enrollment: 10,386 Coed
Affiliation or Control: State/Local IRS Status: 501(c)3
Highest Offering: Master's
Program: 2-Year Principally Bachelor's Creditable; Professional
Accreditation: M, ART, CIDA

01 President .... Dr. Joyce F. BROWN
10 Treas/VP Finance/Administration .... Ms. Sherry F. BRABHAM
101 Secy of College/General Counsel .... Vacant
05 Vice President Academic Affairs .... Dr. Giacomo OLIVA
26 Vice Pres Comm/External Rels ... Ms. Loretta LAWRENCE KEANE
84 VP Enrollment Mgmt/Student Success .... Ms. Marybeth MURPHY
15 Vice President Human Res/Labor Rels .... Mr. Arthur E. BROWN
13 VP for Information Technology/CIO .... Mr. Gregg CHOTTINER
30 Vice Pres Development & Exec Dir .... Ms. Dawn B. DUNCAN
20 Assoc Vice Pres Academic Affairs .... Mr. Howard DILLON
88 Asst Vice Pres Human Res/Labor Rels .... Ms. Laura SOLOMON
21 Asst Vice Pres Finance .... Mr. Mark BLAIFEDER
21 Assistant VP of Administration .... Ms. Rebecca CORRADO
88 Asst VP Software Svcs/Info Access .... Mr. Van Buren WINSTON
27 Asst Vice Pres for Communications .... Ms. Carol LEVEN
04 Exec Asst to the President .... Ms. Shari PRUSSIN
20 Dean Curriculum/Instruction .... Dr. Dympna BOWLES
32 Dean Student Development .... Mr. Erik KNEUBUEHL
51 Dean Continuing & Prof Studies .... Dr. Lisa R. BRAVERMAN
57 Dean Art & Design .... Ms. Joanne ARBUCKLE
58 Dean Graduate Studies .... Dr. W. Taylor JOHNSON
49 Dean Liberal Arts .... Dr. Scott F. STODDART
50 Dean Business & Technology .... Vacant
07 Dir of Admissions/Strat Recruiting .... Ms. Laura ARBOGAST
88 Director Special Events .... Ms. Vicki GURANOWSKI
11 Director Operational Services .... Mr. John WILSON
18 Executive Director of Facilities .... Mr. George JEFREMOW
22 Affirmative Action Officer .... Ms. Griselda GONZALEZ
38 Director of the Counseling Center .... Ms. Terry GINDER
37 Director of Financial Aid .... Ms. Mina FRIEDMANN
08 Dir of the Gladys Marcus Library .... Mr. N. J. WOLFE
06 Director of Registration & Records .... Ms. Young-Ja KIM

39 Director of Residental Life .... Ms. Ann Marie GRAPPO
36 Director Career & Internship .... Mr. Andrew CRONAN
35 Acting Director of Student Life ...... Ms. Suzanne MCGILLICUDDY
23 Director of Health Services .... Ms. Anne MILLER
19 Director of Security .... Mr. Curtis DIXON
88 Director of The Museum at FIT .... Dr. Valerie STEELE
09 Director of Institutional Research .... Mr. Jason CASEY
86 Dir Government/Community Relations .... Ms. Lisa WAGER
27 Exec Director of Public & Media Rel .... Ms. Cheri FEIN
104 Director of International Programs ...... Dr. Georgianna APPIGNANI
41 Director of Athletics & Recreation ...... Ms. Kerri-Ann MCTIERNAN
96 Director of Budget .... Ms. Nancy SU
88 Dir of Education Opportunity Pgms .... Ms. Taur D. ORANGE
21 Controller/Assistant Treas .... Mr. John JOHNSTON
88 Dir Envir Health/Safety Compliance .... Mr. Joseph J. ARCOLEO
92 Coord Presidential Scholars Pgm .... Dr. Irene BUCHMAN
96 Director of Purchasing .... Mr. Robert OTTO
105 Manager of Web Communications .... Ms. Donna LEHMANN
55 Dir Evening/Weekend/Pre-College .... Ms. Michele NAGEL
29 Director of Alumni Relations .... Ms. Allison OLDEHOFF
44 Director of Development .... Mr. Terry CULVER
102 Director of Corporate & Foundation .... Mr. Kevin HERVAS

Finger Lakes Community College (A)

3325 Marvin Sands Drive, Canandaigua NY 14424-8405
County: Ontario FICE Identification: 007532
Unit ID: 191199
Telephone: (585) 394-3500 Carnegie Class: Assoc/Pub-S-SC
FAX Number: (585) 394-5005 Calendar System: Semester
URL: www.flcc.edu
Established: 1965 Annual Undergrad Tuition & Fees (In-District): $3,484
Enrollment: 6,935 Coed
Affiliation or Control: State/Local IRS Status: 501(c)3
Highest Offering: Associate Degree
Program: Occupational; 2-Year Principally Bachelor's Creditable
Accreditation: M, ADNUR

01 President .... Dr. Barbara G. RISSER
05 Vice Pres Academic/Student Affairs .... Dr. Thomas E. TOPPING
10 Vice President of Admin/Treasurer .... Mr. James R. FISHER
84 Vice Pres Enrollment Management .... Ms. Carol S. URBAITIS
32 Assoc Vice Pres of Student Affairs .... Ms. Kerry L. LEVETT
20 Assoc VP Instruction & Assessment .... Mr. Milton L. JOHNSON
20 Assoc VP Academic Initiatives .... Ms. Nancy H. PURDY
16 Director of Human Resources .... Ms. Grace H. LOOMIS
30 Development Officer .... Ms. Amy I. PAULEY
19 Campus Safety Officer .... Mr. Jason R. MAITLAND
21 Controller .... Mr. Joseph L. DELFORTE
18 Director of Building & Grounds .... Ms. Jan J. JUNE
06 Registrar .... Ms. Elaine S. BENNETT
07 Director of Admissions .... Ms. Bonnie B. RITTS
15 Director Personnel Services .... Ms. Kathryn A. BOLLEN
25 Director of Grants Development .... Ms. Karen A. VAN KEUREN
37 Director of Financial Aid .... Ms. Susan M. ROMANO
35 Director of Student Life .... Ms. Sarah E. WHIFFEN
13 Director Information Technology .... Dr. Richard W. EVANS
38 Director Career Services .... Ms. Corrine M. CANOUGH
36 Career Services Coordinator .... Ms. Laura A. RAKOCZY
08 Director of Library .... Mr. Frank R. QUEENER
26 Director of Marketing .... Ms. Heidi C. MARCIN
23 Director of Student Health .... Ms. Karen P Z. STEIN
24 Director of Educational Technology .... Mr. Daniel P. FARSACI
29 Director of Alumni Relations .... Ms. Susan P. MORGAN
96 Director of Business Services .... Mr. Bruce J. TREAT
72 Chair Science & Technology .... Dr. Melissa A. MILLER
50 Chair Business .... Ms. Mary M. WILSEY
65 Chair Environment Conservation Hort .... Ms. Ann B. SCHNELL
64 Chair Visual/Performing Arts .... Dr. Inez DRASKOVIC
66 Chair Nursing .... Ms. Nancy E. CLARKSON
68 Chair Physical Education .... Mr. Dennis T. MOORE
81 Chair Computer Science .... Ms. April A. DEVAUX
79 Chair Humanities .... Mr. Jon A. PALZER
83 Chair Social Science .... Mr. Joshua W. HELLER
81 Chair Mathematics .... Mr. Jacob E. AMIDON

Five Towns College (B)

305 North Service Road, Dix Hills NY 11746-6055
County: Suffolk FICE Identification: 012561
Unit ID: 191205
Telephone: (631) 656-2157 Carnegie Class: Bac/Diverse
FAX Number: (631) 656-2172 Calendar System: Semester
URL: www.ftc.edu
Established: 1972 Annual Undergrad Tuition & Fees: $19,570
Enrollment: 1,101 Coed
Affiliation or Control: Proprietary IRS Status: Proprietary
Highest Offering: Doctorate
Program: Occupational; 2-Year Principally Bachelor's Creditable; Liberal Arts And General
Accreditation: M, TED

01 President .... Dr. Stanley G. COHEN
05 Dean of Academic Affairs/Provost .... Dr. Roger H. SHERMAN
11 Dean of Administration .... Dr. Martin L. COHEN
84 Dean of Enrollment .... Mr. Jerry L. COHEN
11 Assoc Dean of Administration .... Mr. Jerome KOHN
06 Registrar .... Ms. Riva MEYER
21 Business Officer .... Mr. Robert A. SHERMAN
07 Director of Recruitment Services .... Ms. Kelly HAYES
08 Head Librarian .... Mr. John VANSTEEN
38 College Counselor .... Ms. Carolyn NEWMAN

64 Chair of Music Division .... Prof. Jeffrey LIPTON
50 Chair of Business Division .... Ms. Darlene DECICCO
49 Chair of Liberal Arts Division .... Dr. Richard D. KELLEY
53 Chair of Education Division .... Dr. Patricia SCHMIDT
88 Chair of Film/Video .... Mr. Robert DIGIACOMO
88 Chair of Theatre Arts .... Prof. Jeffrey LIPTON

Fordham University (C)

441 East Fordham Road, Bronx NY 10458-9993
County: Bronx FICE Identification: 002722
Unit ID: 191241
Telephone: (718) 817-1000 Carnegie Class: RU/H
FAX Number: (718) 817-4925 Calendar System: Semester
URL: www.fordham.edu
Established: 1841 Annual Undergrad Tuition & Fees: $39,235
Enrollment: 15,158 Coed
Affiliation or Control: Independent Non-Profit IRS Status: 501(c)3
Highest Offering: Doctorate
Program: Liberal Arts And General; Teacher Preparatory; Professional
Accreditation: M, BUS, CLPSY, COPSY, DANCE, LAW, SCPSY, SW, TED

01 President .... Rev. Joseph M. MCSHANE, SJ
04 Exec Assistant to the President .... Ms. Dorothy MARINUCCI
04 Assistant to the President .... Dr. Rosemary A. DEJULIO
05 Provost .... Dr. Stephen FREEDMAN
10 Sr VP & Chief Financial Officer .... Mr. John J. LORDAN
21 Vice President for Finance .... Mr. Frank SIMIO
32 Vice President Student Affairs .... Mr. Jeffrey L. GRAY
13 VP for Information Technology .... Dr. Frank SIRIANNI
84 Vice President for Enrollment .... Dr. Peter A. STACE
12 Vice President for Lincoln Center .... Dr. Brian J. BYRNE
30 Vice President for Development .... Mr. Roger MILICI
88 Vice President for Mission/Ministry .... Msgr. Joseph G. QUINN
86 Vice President for Government Rels .... Mr. Thomas A. DUNNE
18 VP Facilities/Physical Plant .... Mr. Marc VALERA
11 Vice President for Administration .... Mr. Thomas A. DUNNE
20 Assoc Vice Pres Academic Affairs .... Dr. Benjamin CROOKER
20 Assoc Vice Pres Academic Affairs .... Dr. Ron JACOBSON
26 AVP Univ Marketing Communications ..... Ms. Catherine SPENCER
29 Director of Alumni Relations .... Ms. Caitlin TRAMEL
07 Asst Vice Pres Undgrad Enrollment .... Mr. John W. BUCKLEY
06 Asst Vice Pres Enrollment/Registrar .... Mr. Stephen J. BORDAS
37 Asst VP Student Financial Services .... Ms. Angela VAN DEKKER
86 Assoc Vice Pres for Government Rels .... Mr. Joseph P. MURIANA
101 Secretary of the University .... Ms. Margaret T. BALL
43 General Counsel .... Mr. Thomas E. DEJULIO
35 Dean of Students .... Mr. Christopher RODGERS
35 Dean of Student Services .... Mr. Gregory J. PAPPAS
12 Dean Fordham College at Rose Hill .... Dr. Michael LATHAM
58 Dean Graduate Arts & Science .... Dr. Nancy BUSCH
73 Dean Graduate Religious Education .... Rev. Anthony J. CIORRA
50 Dean College Business Admin .... Dr. Donna RAPACCIOLI
88 Dean Fordham College of Lib Studies .... Dr. Isabel FRANK
12 Dean Fordham College Lincoln Center .... Rev. Robert GRIMES
88 Dean Graduate Business Admin LC .... Dr. David GAUTSCHI
53 Dean Graduate Education LC .... Dr. James HENNESSY
61 Dean School of Law LC .... Mr. Michael MARTIN
70 Dean Graduate Social Service LC .... Dr. Peter VAUGHAN
15 Exec Director of Human Resources .... Mr. Michael MINEO
09 Director Institutional Research .... Dr. Donald A. GILLESPIE
42 Director Campus Ministry .... Rev. Philip J. FLORIO, SJ
21 Controller .... Mr. Anthony GRONO
19 Director of Security .... Mr. John CARROLL
22 Administrative Policies Monitor .... Dr. Georgina N. CALIA
46 Dir Research/Sponsored Programs .... Dr. Nancy BUSCH
08 Director of University Libraries .... Dr. James P. MCCABE
24 Director Media Center .... Mr. Jerry GREEN
23 Director of Health Center .... Ms. Kathleen MALARA
35 Assistant Dean of Students .... Dr. Greer JASON
41 Director of Athletics .... Mr. Francis X. MCLAUGHLIN
96 Director of Procurement .... Mr. Frank A. DEORIO
38 Director of Psychological Svcs .... Dr. Jennifer NEUHOF
28 Director of Multicultural Programs .... Ms. Sofia BAUSTISTA PERTUZ
36 Director Career Services .... Ms. Stefany FATTOR

Fulton-Montgomery Community College (D)

2805 State Highway 67, Johnstown NY 12095-3790
County: Montgomery FICE Identification: 002867
Unit ID: 191302
Telephone: (518) 762-4651 Carnegie Class: Assoc/Pub-R-M
FAX Number: (518) 762-4334 Calendar System: Semester
URL: www.fmcc.suny.edu
Established: 1963 Annual Undergrad Tuition & Fees (In-District): $3,738
Enrollment: 2,833 Coed
Affiliation or Control: State/Local IRS Status: 501(c)3
Highest Offering: Associate Degree
Program: Occupational; 2-Year Principally Bachelor's Creditable
Accreditation: M

01 President .... Dr. Dustin SWANGER
05 Provost/Vice Pres Academic Affairs ... Dr. Greg TRUCKENMILLER
10 Vice Pres Finance & Administration .... Mr. David M. MORROW
32 Vice President of Student Affairs .... Ms. Jane KELLEY
49 Dean of Arts & Sciences .... Dr. Greg TRUCKENMILLER
75 Dean Business/Tech/Health Prof .... Ms. Diana PUTNAM
21 Controller .... Vacant
14 Director of Computer Center .... Mr. Paul PUTMAN
18 Superintendent Building & Grounds .... Mr. Gregory HILLIER

07 Director of Admissions .... Ms. Laura LAPORTE
06 Registrar .... Mrs. Susan CHRISTIANO
08 Librarian .... Mrs. Mary DONOHUE
103 Director Workforce Development .... Vacant
36 Director of Career Planning .... Ms. Rebecca HAUST
38 Director Advisement/Counseling/Test .... Ms. Mary-Jo FERRAUILO-DAVIS
30 Chief Development .... Ms. Lesley LANZI
09 Director of Institutional Research .... Mr. Eric KIMMELMAN
37 Coordinator Financial Aid .... Ms. Rebecca COZZOCREA

General Theological Seminary (E)

440 West 21st Street, New York NY 10011-2981
County: New York FICE Identification: 002726
Unit ID: 191320
Telephone: (212) 243-5150 Carnegie Class: Spec/Faith
FAX Number: (212) 727-3907 Calendar System: Semester
URL: www.gts.edu
Established: 1817 Annual Graduate Tuition & Fees: $15,200
Enrollment: 149 Coed
Affiliation or Control: Protestant Episcopal IRS Status: 501(c)3
Highest Offering: Doctorate; No Undergraduates
Program: Professional
Accreditation: THEOL

01 President .... Rev. Lang LOWREY
05 Interim Dean .... Rt.Rev. Peter LEE
10 VP for Finance and Operations .... Ms. Sandra JOHNSON
30 VP for Institutional Advancement .... Ms. Donna ASHLEY
08 Head Librarian .... Rev. Andrew KADEL
07 Director of Admissions .... Mr. William C. WEBSTER
27 Exec Director of Communications .... Mr. Bruce PARKER
32 Director of Campus Services .... Ms. Helen ALLADIN
06 Registrar .... Mr. Stephen HAGERTY
04 Exec Asst to the President .... Mr. Christopher MCFADDEN

Genesee Community College (F)

One College Road, Batavia NY 14020-9704
County: Genesee FICE Identification: 006782
Unit ID: 191339
Telephone: (585) 343-0055 Carnegie Class: Assoc/Pub-R-M
FAX Number: (585) 343-4541 Calendar System: Semester
URL: www.genesee.edu
Established: 1966 Annual Undergrad Tuition & Fees (In-District): $3,703
Enrollment: 7,365 Coed
Affiliation or Control: State/Local IRS Status: 501(c)3
Highest Offering: Associate Degree
Program: Occupational; 2-Year Principally Bachelor's Creditable
Accreditation: M, ADNUR, PTAA

01 President .... Dr. James SUNSER
05 Exec Vice Pres Academic Affairs .... Dr. Eunice BELLINGER
10 Vice Pres for Finance & Operations .... Mr. Kevin HAMILTON
32 VP for Student & Enrollment Svcs .... Dr. Virginia TAYLOR
45 Vice Pres Human Resources/Planning .... Dr. Larene L. HOELCLE
103 Assoc VP for Workforce Development ... Mr. Jerry A. KOZLOWSKI
15 Assoc VP for Human Resources .... Ms. Gina WEAVER
20 Asc Dean Accelerated Col Enrol Pgms ... Mr. Edward LEVINSTEIN
81 Dean Math/Science/Career Education .... Dr. Rafael ALICEA-MALDONADO
83 Dean Human Communication/Behavior .... Dr. Katharina E. KOVACH-ALLEN
56 Dean Educ Tech/Distance Learning .... Mr. Robert G. KNIPE
35 Dean of Students .... Ms. Jennifer M. NEWELL
06 Registrar .... Mr. Terrence REDING
07 Director of Admissions .... Ms. Tanya LANE-MARTIN
14 Director of Computer Services .... Ms. Cindy DELMAR
37 Director of Financial Aid .... Mr. Joseph A. BAILEY
26 Director Devel & External Affairs .... Mr. Richard G. ENSMAN, JR.
88 Director of Student Activities .... Mr. Clifford M. SCUTELLA
21 Controller .... Ms. Kristin L. YUNKER
41 Director of Athletics .... Ms. Margaret SISSON
18 Director of Buildings & Grounds .... Mr. Timothy M. LANDERS
88 Director Business Skills Training .... Mr. Ramon C. CHAYA
09 Assoc Dean Inst Rsrch & Assessment .... Ms. Carol MARRIOTT
57 Director Fine & Performing Arts .... Ms. Maryanne ARENA
90 Manager of Academic Computing .... Mrs. Mary Jane HEIDER
91 Manager of Administrative Computing .... Vacant
40 Manager of Bookstore .... Mr. Robert PUMA
35 Assoc Dean for Student Development .... Ms. Margaret HEATER
88 Director of Health and Phys Ed .... Ms. Rebecca DZIEKAN
88 Director Business Skills Training .... Ms. Lina LAMATTINA

Globe Institute of Technology (G)

500 Seventh Avenue, New York NY 10018
County: New York FICE Identification: 025408
Unit ID: 188465
Telephone: (212) 349-4330 Carnegie Class: Spec/Bus
FAX Number: (212) 227-5920 Calendar System: Semester
URL: www.globe.edu
Established: 1985 Annual Undergrad Tuition & Fees: $11,120
Enrollment: 580 Coed
Affiliation or Control: Proprietary IRS Status: Proprietary
Highest Offering: Baccalaureate
Program: Occupational
Accreditation: NY

01 President .... Mr. Martin OLINER

05 Academic Dean ... Ms. Elena ESTRIN
11 Dean of Administrative Services ... Mr. Alex OLINER
32 Dean of Student Services ... Ms. Andrea MOSLEY
08 Director of Information Services ... Mr. Boris KAMENETSKIY
13 Director of Information Technology ... Mr. Jacob KUPERSHTEYN
07 Director of Admissions ... Mr. Michael SCALICE
37 Director of Financial Aid ... Ms. Tatiana NUSENBAUM
06 Registrar ... Ms. Vivian PAGAN
41 Athletic Director ... Mr. Mark MORSE
38 Coord Student Counseling/Placement ... Ms. Nellie CHEN

Hamilton College (A)

198 College Hill Road, Clinton NY 13323-1218
County: Oneida FICE Identification: 002728
Unit ID: 191515
Telephone: (315) 859-4011 Carnegie Class: Bac/A&S
FAX Number: (315) 859-4991 Calendar System: Semester
URL: www.hamilton.edu
Established: 1812 Annual Undergrad Tuition & Fees: $42,640
Enrollment: 1,843 Coed
Affiliation or Control: Independent Non-Profit IRS Status: 501(c)3
Highest Offering: Baccalaureate
Program: Liberal Arts And General
Accreditation: M

01 President ... Joan H. STEWART
05 VPAA/Dean of Faculty ... Patrick D. REYNOLDS
11 Vice Pres Administration/Finance ... Karen L. LEACH
30 Vice President Commun/Development ... Richard C. TANTILLO
13 Vice Pres Information Technology ... David L. SMALLEN
07 VP/Dean Admission & Financial Aid ... Monica C. INZER
32 Dean of Students ... Nancy R. THOMPSON
20 Associate Dean of Faculty ... Margaret GENTRY
41 Athletic Director ... Jonathan T. HIND
39 Director Residential Life ... Travis R. HILL
10 Controller ... Shari K. WHITING
08 Interim Director of the Library ... David L. SMALLEN
27 Director Strategic Communications ... Stacey J. HIMMELBERGER
37 Director of Financial Aid ... Melissa ROSE
36 Interim Exec Director Career Center ... Mary EVANS
06 Registrar ... Kristin M. FRIEDEL
15 Director of Human Resources ... Stephen STEMKOSKI
23 Director Student Health Services ... Christine C. MERRITT
18 Director Physical Plant ... Steven J. BELLONA
19 Director of Campus Safety ... Francis A. MANFREDO
38 Director Counseling/Psych Services ... Robert KAZIN
42 Newman Chaplain ... John CROGHAN
24 Director Audiovisual Services ... Timothy J. HICKS
09 Director of Institutional Research ... Gordon J. HEWITT
27 Exec Director of Communications ... Michael J. DEBRAGGIO
28 Chief Diversity Officer ... Donald M. CARTER
29 Director Alumni Relations ... Sharon T. RIPPEY
96 Director of Purchasing ... Irene K. CORNISH
40 Manager College Store ... Jennifer PHILLIPS

Hartwick College (B)

One Hartwick Drive, Oneonta NY 13820-1790
County: Otsego FICE Identification: 002729
Unit ID: 191533
Telephone: (607) 431-4000 Carnegie Class: Bac/A&S
FAX Number: (607) 431-4206 Calendar System: 4/1/4
URL: www.hartwick.edu
Established: 1797 Annual Undergrad Tuition & Fees: $36,040
Enrollment: 1,531 Coed
Affiliation or Control: Independent Non-Profit IRS Status: 501(c)3
Highest Offering: Baccalaureate
Program: Liberal Arts And General; Teacher Preparatory; Professional
Accreditation: M, ART, MUS, NURSE, TEAC

01 President ... Dr. Margaret L. DRUGOVICH
05 Executive Vice President & Provost ... Dr. Michael TANNENBAUM
10 Vice President Finance/CFO ... Mr. George J. ELSBECK
30 Vice Pres Institutional Advancement ... Mr. Jim BROSCHART
32 Vice President for Student Life ... Dr. Meg NOWAK
84 Vice Pres for Enrollment Management ... Mr. David CONWAY
04 Exec Assistant to the President ... Ms. Ashley MCCARTHY
15 Director Human Resources ... Ms. Suzanne JANITZ
88 Dean of Global Studies ... Vacant
36 Dean Experiential Integrative Lrng ... Vacant
39 Director Residence Life ... Mr. Zachary BROWN
06 Registrar ... Mr. Matthew SANFORD
20 Dean of Academic Affairs ... Dr. Gerald HUNSBERGER
37 Director of Financial Aid ... Ms. Melissa ALLEN
08 Director of Libraries ... Mr. F. Paul COLEMAN
88 Coord Yager Museum of Art & Culture ... Ms. Donna ANDERSON
85 Director International Pgms ... Ms. Jenifer CHAMBERS
46 Exec Dir of Info Technology ... Mr. Davis B. CONLEY
13 Director Inst Info Systems Services ... Ms. Deb B. HILTS
91 Director Technologies Services ... Ms. Suzanne GAYNOR
18 Director of Facilities Services ... Mr. Joseph MACK
41 Director of Athletics ... Dr. Kimberly FIERKE
38 Director of Counseling Services ... Mr. Gary ROBINSON
23 Director of Student Health Center ... Ms. Elizabeth MORLEY
27 Exec Dir Marketing & Communications ... Mr. James JOLLY
26 Director of College Relations ... Vacant
44 Director of Annual Giving ... Ms. Emily ERNSBERGER
07 Director Admissions ... Mr. Jonathan KENT
12 Director Pine Lake Campus ... Dr. Brian HAGENBUCH
21 Director Financial Svcs/Controller ... Ms. Nancy LEHTONEN
09 Director of Institutional Research ... Ms. Minghui WANG

29 Director of Alumni Relations ... Mr. Duncan MACDONALD
19 Director of Security ... Mr. Thomas KELLY
40 Manager of Bookstore ... Mr. Frank WERDANN
96 Manager of Purchasing ... Ms. Marilyn NIENART
44 Major Gifts Officer ... Ms. Kathryn GIBSON

Hebrew Union College-Jewish Institute of Religion (New York Branch) (C)

1 West 4th Street, New York NY 10012-1186
County: New York FICE Identification: 004054
Unit ID: 203067
Telephone: (212) 674-5300 Carnegie Class: Spec/Faith
FAX Number: (212) 388-1720 Calendar System: Semester
URL: www.huc.edu
Established: 1875 Annual Graduate Tuition & Fees: $21,000
Enrollment: 112 Coed
Affiliation or Control: Jewish IRS Status: 501(c)3
Highest Offering: Doctorate; No Undergraduates
Program: Professional; Religious Emphasis
Accreditation: M

05 Dean/Dir Graduate Programs ... Rabbi Shirley IDELSON
73 Assoc Dean/Dir Rabbinical Program ... Rabbi Renni ALTMAN
53 Director of School of Education ... Ms. Jo KAY
64 Director of School of Sacred Music ... Dr. Bruce RUBEN
30 Director of Development-East ... Ms. Eve STARKMAN
08 Librarian ... Dr. Phillip E. MILLER
10 Director of Operations ... Ms. Paula DWOSKIN-SITZER

† See other campus listings in California and Ohio.

Helene Fuld College of Nursing (D)

1879 Madison Avenue, New York NY 10035-2709
County: New York FICE Identification: 010153
Unit ID: 191597
Telephone: (212) 616-7299 Carnegie Class: Assoc/PrivNFP
FAX Number: (212) 427-2453 Calendar System: Quarter
URL: www.helenefuld.edu
Established: 1945 Annual Undergrad Tuition & Fees: $15,176
Enrollment: 443 Cood
Affiliation or Control: Independent Non-Profit IRS Status: 501(c)3
Highest Offering: Associate Degree
Program: Occupational; 2-Year Principally Bachelor's Creditable
Accreditation: M, ADNUR

01 President ... Dr. Margaret WINES
10 Chief Financial Officer ... Mrs. Adenike ABOYADE-COLE
05 Vice President Academic Affairs ... Ms. Wendy ROBINSON
11 Director of Administration ... Ms. Celeste WALLIN
32 Director Student Services ... Ms. Sandra SENIOR
08 Director of Learning Center ... Mr. Indrajeet SINGH CHAUHAN
35 Associate Director Student Services ... Ms. Gladys PINEDA
26 Director of External Affairs ... Ms. Michelle HERNANDEZ

Herkimer County Community College (E)

100 Reservoir Road, Herkimer NY 13350-1598
County: Herkimer FICE Identification: 004788
Unit ID: 191612
Telephone: (315) 866-0300 Carnegie Class: Assoc/Pub-R-M
FAX Number: (315) 866-7253 Calendar System: Semester
URL: www.herkimer.edu
Established: 1966 Annual Undergrad Tuition & Fees (In-District): $4,100
Enrollment: 3,774 Coed
Affiliation or Control: State/Local IRS Status: 501(c)3
Highest Offering: Associate Degree
Program: Occupational; 2-Year Principally Bachelor's Creditable
Accreditation: M, EMT, PTAA

01 President ... Dr. Ann Marie MURRAY
11 Vice Pres Administration & Finance ... Mr. Nicholas LAINO
05 Dean of Academic Affairs ... Mr. Michael ORIOLO
32 Dean of Students ... Dr. Matthew HAWES
30 Director of Development ... Vacant
20 Associate Dean Academic Affairs ... Vacant
27 Director of Information Services ... Mrs. AnneMarie AMBROSE
84 Assoc Dean for Enrollment ... Mr. Robert PALMIERI
83 Assoc Dean Academic Affairs Soc Sci ... Mr. Robert MOSCHGAT
51 Assoc Dean of Continuing Education ... Mrs. Linda LAMB
35 Assoc Dean of Student Services ... Ms. Janet TAMBURRINO
20 Asst Dean of Academic Affairs ... Mrs. Jackie SNYDER
15 Director of Human Resources ... Mr. James SALAMY
41 Director of Athletics ... Mr. Donald DUTCHER
08 Director of Library Services ... Mr. Andrew URBANEK
09 Director Institutional Research ... Ms. Marie MIKNAVICH
31 Director of Community Education ... Mr. William MCDONALD
18 Director of Facilities Operations ... Mr. Tom STOCK
37 Director Student Financial Aid ... Mrs. Susan TRIPP
26 Director of Public Relations ... Ms. Rebecca RUFFING
06 Registrar ... Mr. Craig DEWAN
36 Career Services Counselor ... Mrs. Suzanne PADDOCK
36 Transfer Counselor ... Ms. Katie SCHWABACH
40 Bookstore Manager ... Mr. Brian MARHAVER
96 Purchasing Agent ... Mr. Robert NEARY

Hilbert College (F)

5200 S Park Avenue, Hamburg NY 14075-1597
County: Erie FICE Identification: 002735
Unit ID: 191621
Telephone: (716) 649-7900 Carnegie Class: Bac/Diverse
FAX Number: (716) 649-0702 Calendar System: Semester
URL: www.hilbert.edu
Established: 1957 Annual Undergrad Tuition & Fees: $18,900
Enrollment: 1,056 Coed
Affiliation or Control: Independent Non-Profit IRS Status: 501(c)3
Highest Offering: Master's
Program: Liberal Arts And General; Professional
Accreditation: M

01 President ... Dr. Cynthia A. ZANE
05 Provost/Vice Pres Academic Affairs ... Dr. Christopher L. HOLOMAN
30 Vice Pres Institutional Advancement ... Vacant
10 Vice President Business/Finance ... Mr. Richard J. PINKOWSKI, JR.
27 Vice President Information Services ... Mr. Michael MURRIN
84 VP Enrollment Mgmt/Dean of Students ... Mr. Peter S. BURNS
32 Vice Prov Leadership Development ... Mr. James P. STURM
49 Chair Arts & Sciences ... Dr. Amy E. SMITH
26 Director Public Relations ... Ms. Paula WITHERELL
92 Director Honors Program ... Dr. Amy E. SMITH
39 Dir Residence Life/Judicial Affairs ... Mr. Jason LANKER
41 Athletic Director ... Ms. Susan VISCOMI
19 Director Security/Safety ... Mr. Matthew SCHAMANN
30 Director of Development ... Mr. Craig HARRIS
42 Dir Mission Intgrtn/Campus Ministry ... Ms. Barbara BONANNO
08 Director of McGrath Library ... Mr. Wilson PROUT
07 Director of Admissions ... Mr. Timothy LEE
36 Director Placement/Career Services ... Ms. Denise HARRIS
37 Director Financial Aid ... Ms. Beverly CHUDY
06 Director of Student Records ... Ms. Georgina ADAMCHICK
38 Director Student Counseling ... Ms. Phyllis K. DEWEY
09 Director of Institutional Research ... Vacant
15 Director of Human Resources ... Ms. Maura FLYNN
28 Director of Multicultural Affairs ... Ms. Tara JABBAAR-GYAMBRAH
35 Director of Student Activities ... Ms. Jean MACDONALD
96 Director of Purchasing ... Mr. Gary DILLSWORTH
21 Associate Business Officer ... Mr. Anthony WIERTEL
18 Chief Facilities/Physical Plant ... Mr. Gary DILLSWORTH

Hobart and William Smith Colleges (G)

300 Pulteney Street, Geneva NY 14456-3397
County: Ontario FICE Identification: 002731
Unit ID: 191630
Telephone: (315) 781-3000 Carnegie Class: Bac/A&S
FAX Number: (315) 781-3654 Calendar System: Semester
URL: www.hws.edu
Established: 1822 Annual Undergrad Tuition & Fees: $42,014
Enrollment: 2,173 Coordinate
Affiliation or Control: Independent Non-Profit IRS Status: 501(c)3
Highest Offering: Master's
Program: Liberal Arts And General; Teacher Preparatory
Accreditation: M, @TEAC

01 President ... Mr. Mark D. GEARAN
05 Acting Dean of Faculty/Provost ... Dr. Patrick MCGUIRE
10 Vice President for Finance ... Mr. Peter POLINAK
30 Vice Pres Institutional Advancement ... Mr. Bob O'CONNOR
32 Vice President for Student Affairs ... Mr. Robert FLOWERS
84 VP for Enrollment/Dean of Admission ... Mr. Robert MURPHY
13 Vice Pres for Information Tech/CIO ... Mr. Fred DAMIANO
35 Assistant VP for Student Affairs ... Mr. Jeffrey VANLONE
26 Director of Communicatons ... Ms. Cathy WILLIAMS
33 Dean of Hobart College ... Dr. Eugen BAER
34 Acting Dean William Smith College ... Dr. Susanne MCNALLY
19 Assoc Dn Campus Sfty/Stdnt Conduct ... Dr. Montrose STREETER
42 Chaplain ... Rev. Lesley ADAMS
101 Secretary to the Board Of Trustees ... Mr. Michael HOEPP
20 Associate Dean of Faculty ... Dr. Paul KEHLE
20 Associate Dean of Faculty ... Dr. Christine DE DENUS
16 Director of Human Resources ... Ms. Sandra BISSELL
08 Director of the Library ... Mr. Vincent BOISSELLE
06 Registrar ... Mr. Peter SARRATORI
36 Director Center for Career Services ... Ms. Brandi FERRARA
21 Controller ... Mr. Michael PAPARO
40 Director of the College Store ... Ms. Lucille SMART
07 Director of Admissions ... Mr. John YOUNG
37 Director of Financial Aid ... Ms. Beth TURNER
39 Director of Residential Education ... Ms. Stacey PIERCE
41 Director of Hobart Athletics ... Mr. Michael HANNA
41 Director of William Smith Athletics ... Ms. Deborah STEWARD
29 Director of Alumni Relations ... Mr. Jared WEEDEN
29 Director of Alumnae Relations ... Ms. Kathleen REGAN
44 Director of Annual Giving ... Ms. Kristen EINSTEIN
25 Director of Grants ... Ms. Martha BOND

Hofstra University (H)

Hempstead NY 11549-1000
County: Nassau FICE Identification: 002732
Unit ID: 191649
Telephone: (516) 463-6600 Carnegie Class: DRU
FAX Number: (516) 463-4848 Calendar System: Semester
URL: www.hofstra.edu
Established: 1935 Annual Undergrad Tuition & Fees: $34,150
Enrollment: 11,579 Coed

Affiliation or Control: Independent Non-Profit IRS Status: 501(c)3
Highest Offering: Doctorate
Program: Liberal Arts And General; Teacher Preparatory; Professional
Accreditation: M, ARCPA, AUD, BUS, BUSA, CLPSY, CORE, ENG, JOUR, LAW, #MED, SCPSY, SP, TEAC

01 President .... Mr. Stuart RABINOWITZ
05 Provost/Sr VP for Academic Affairs .... Dr. Herman A. BERLINER
45 Sr VP for Planning and Admin .... Ms. M. Patricia ADAMSKI
10 VP Financial Affairs/Treasurer .... Ms. Catherine HENNESSY
32 Vice President for Student Affairs .... Ms. Sandra JOHNSON
30 Vice President for Development .... Mr. Alan J. KELLY
26 Vice President University Relations .... Ms. Melissa A. CONNOLLY
43 VP Legal Affairs & General Counsel .... Ms. Dolores FREDRICH
13 Vice Pres Information Technology .... Mr. Robert W. JUCKIEWICZ
18 VP for Facilities and Operations .... Mr. Joseph BARKWILL
84 Vice Pres Enrollment Management .... Ms. Jessica L. EADS
86 Vice President Business Dev Ctr .... Mr. Richard V. GUARDINO
91 Asst VP for Information Technology .... Ms. Linda J. HANTZSCHEL
09 Asst VP Inst Research/Admin Assess .... Ms. Stephanie BUSHEY
20 Vice Provost for Academic Affairs .... Dr. Liora P. SCHMELKIN
21 Assoc Provost Budget & Planning .... Mr. Richard M. APOLLO
25 Assoc Provost Rsrch/Sponsored Pgms .... Ms. Sofia KAKOULIDIS
07 Dean Admissions & Financial Aid .... Ms. Jessica L. EADS
50 Dean Frank G Zarb Sch of Business .... Dr. Patrick J. SOCCI
60 Dean School of Communication .... Dr. Evan W. CORNOG
53 Dean School of Education .... Dr. Nancy E. HALLIDAY
49 Dean College Liberal Arts/Science .... Dr. Bernard J. FIRESTONE
08 Dean Library & Info Services .... Dr. Daniel R. RUBEY
88 Dean for University Advisement .... Ms. Anne M. MONGILLO
07 Dean Graduate Admissions .... Ms. Carol J. DRUMMER
61 Dean of Law School .... Ms. Nora V. DEMLEITNER
63 Dean Medical School .... Dr. Lawrence SMITH
35 Dean of Students .... Mr. Peter LIBMAN
84 Asst Dean Law Sch Enrollment Mgmt .... Mr. John CHALMERS
29 Senior Director Alumni Relations .... Mr. Robert SALTZMAN
39 Assoc Director Residential Programs .... Ms. Novia P. WHYTE
38 Dir Student Counseling Services .... Dr. John C. GUTHMAN
22 Equal Rights/Opportunity Ofcr .... Ms. Jennifer MONE
23 Director Health & Wellness Center .... Ms. Maureen B. HOUCK
41 Director Intercollegiate Athletics .... Mr. Jack W. HAYES
15 Director of Human Resources .... Ms. Evelyn V. MILLER-SUBER
90 Director Faculty Computing Services .... Ms. Judith L. TABRON
40 Manager Bookstore .... Mr. Steven BABBITT
19 Director Public Safety .... Ms. Karen O'CALLAGHAN
96 Director of Purchasing .... Mr. Richard FRANCOS
92 Dean Honors College .... Dr. Warren FRISINA
06 Registrar/Executive Director .... Ms. Lynne DOUGHERTY
04 Admin Assistant to the President .... Ms. Isabel D. FREY
37 Director Student Financial Aid .... Ms. Sandra FILBRY

Holy Trinity Orthodox Seminary (A)

PO Box 36, Jordanville NY 13361-0036
County: Herkimer FICE Identification: 002733
Unit ID: 191658
Telephone: (315) 858-0945 Carnegie Class: Not Classified
FAX Number: (315) 858-0945 Calendar System: Semester
URL: www.hts.edu
Established: 1948 Annual Undergrad Tuition & Fees: $5,500
Enrollment: 31 Male
Affiliation or Control: Russian Orthodox IRS Status: 501(c)3
Highest Offering: Baccalaureate
Program: Professional; Religious Emphasis
Accreditation: NY

01 Rector .... V.Rev. Luke MURIANKA
05 Dean .... V.Rev. Vladimir A. TSURIKOV
06 Registrar .... Rev. Theophylact CLAPPER-DEWELL
32 Dean of Students .... Rev. Cyprian ALEXANDROU
20 Assistant Dean .... Mr. Sergey S. KIRYUKHIN

Houghton College (B)

One Willard Avenue, Houghton NY 14744-0128
County: Allegany FICE Identification: 002734
Unit ID: 191676
Telephone: (585) 567-9200 Carnegie Class: Bac/A&S
FAX Number: (585) 567-9572 Calendar System: Semester
URL: www.houghton.edu
Established: 1883 Annual Undergrad Tuition & Fees: $25,994
Enrollment: 1,272 Coed
Affiliation or Control: Wesleyan Church IRS Status: 501(c)3
Highest Offering: Master's
Program: Liberal Arts And General; Teacher Preparatory
Accreditation: M, MUS, TEAC

01 President .... Dr. Shirley A. MULLEN
05 Interim Academic Dean .... Dr. Linda MILLS WOOLSEY
32 Vice President of Student Life .... Ms. Sharra HYNES
10 Chief Business Officer .... Mr. Dale F. WRIGHT
30 Vice President Advancement .... Mr. Bob VAN WICKLIN
06 Registrar .... Ms. Margery L. AVERY
37 Director of Financial Aid .... Mr. Troy R. MARTIN
08 Director of the Library .... Mr. David STEVICK
29 Executive Director Alumni Relations .... Mr. Daniel NOYES
07 Director of Admissions .... Mr. Matthew REITNOUR
09 Assoc Dean Institutional Research .... Dr. Daryl H. STEVENSON
20 Associate Academic Dean .... Dr. Mark HIJLEH
36 Coordinator of Career Services .... Mr. Brian REITNOUR
15 Director of Human Resources .... Mr. Dale F. WRIGHT
26 Dir Marketing & Communications .... Ms. Elaine TOOLEY
14 Director of Technology .... Mr. Donald HAINGRAY
18 Director of Facilities .... Mr. Charles SMITH
19 Chief Security Officer .... Mr. Ray M. PARLETT
23 Director of Health Services .... Dr. David BRUBAKER
41 Athletic Director .... Mr. Harold W. LORD
21 Controller .... Mr. David M. MERCER
39 Director Residence Life .... Mr. Gabriel JACOBSON
38 Director Student Counseling .... Dr. Michael D. LASTORIA
92 Director of Honors Program .... Vacant
31 Director Community Relations .... Mrs. Phyllis E. GAERTE
35 Dean of Students .... Mr. Dennis STACK

Hudson Valley Community College (C)

80 Vandenburgh Avenue, Troy NY 12180-6096
County: Rensselaer FICE Identification: 002868
Unit ID: 191719
Telephone: (518) 629-4822 Carnegie Class: Assoc/Pub-U-SC
FAX Number: (518) 629-4576 Calendar System: Semester
URL: www.hvcc.edu
Established: 1953 Annual Undergrad Tuition & Fees (In-District): $3,700
Enrollment: 14,011 Coed
Affiliation or Control: State/Local IRS Status: 501(c)3
Highest Offering: Associate Degree
Program: Occupational; 2-Year Principally Bachelor's Creditable
Accreditation: M, ADNUR, DH, DMS, EMT, ENGT, FUSER

01 President .... Dr. Andrew J. MATONAK
04 Exec Assistant to the President .... Dr. Michael S. GREEN
04 Assistant to the President .... Ms. Suzanne K. KALKBRENNER
11 Int Vice Pres for Administration .... Mr. James J. LAGATTA
05 Vice President for Academic Affairs .... Dr. Carolyn G. CURTIS
32 VP Enrol Mgmt/Stdnt Development .... Dr. Alexander J. POPOVICS
10 Vice President for Finance .... Mr. Joel R. FATATO
49 Dean Sch Liberal Arts/Health Sci .... Dr. Margaret M. GEEHAN
72 Dean Engr/Indus Tech/Business .... Mr. P. Phillip WHITE
51 Assoc Dean Cmty/Professional Pgms .... Ms. Christine A. HELWIG
08 Director of Learning Resources Ctr .... Mr. David CLICKNER
07 Director of Admissions .... Ms. Mary Claire BAUER
06 Registrar .... Ms. Kathleen PETLEY
14 Chief Information Officer .... Dr. Steve CHEN
18 Interim Director Physical Plant .... Ms. Karen SEWARD
38 Director Student Development .... Dr. Kathleen SWEENER
37 Director of Financial Aid .... Ms. Lisa VAN WIE
36 Dir Center For Careers/Employment .... Ms. Gayle HEALY
15 Director of Human Resources .... Mr. John TIBBETTS
19 Director of Public Safety .... Mr. Fred ALIBERTI
23 Coordinator Health Services .... Ms. Claudine POTVIN-GIORDANO
88 Director of Disability Resources .... Mr. Pablo E. NEGRON
09 Director Planning & Research .... Mr. James F. MACKLIN
35 Director of Student Life .... Mr. Louis COPLIN
85 International Student Advisor .... Mr. Jay DEITCHMAN
40 Director of Bookstore .... Mr. Stephen J. STEGMAN
41 Director of Athletics .... Ms. Kristan M. PELLETIER
72 Assistant to VP of Academics .... Dr. Sondra E. VALLE
88 Asoc Dean Instruct Spprt Svcs/Reten .... Ms. Karen FERRER-MUNIZ
50 Director of Business Services .... Ms. Mary Ellen LAJEUNESSE
21 Comptroller .... Ms. Debra D. STORY
26 Exec Dir Communications/Marketing .... Mr. Dennis KENNEDY
29 Dir Annual Giving/Donor Rels .... Ms. Kimberley PEABODY
44 Dir Advancement Operations .... Vacant
102 Exec Director Foundation .... Ms. Rachel KIMMELBLATT

Institute of Design and Construction (D)

141 Willoughby Street, Brooklyn NY 11201-5317
County: Kings FICE Identification: 012107
Unit ID: 191764
Telephone: (718) 855-3661 Carnegie Class: Assoc/PrivNFP
FAX Number: (718) 852-5889 Calendar System: Semester
URL: www.idc.edu
Established: 1947 Annual Undergrad Tuition & Fees: $8,225
Enrollment: 245 Coed
Affiliation or Control: Independent Non-Profit IRS Status: 501(c)3
Highest Offering: Associate Degree
Program: Occupational; 2-Year Principally Bachelor's Creditable
Accreditation: NY

01 Executive Director .... Mr. Vincent C. BATTISTA
11 Administrator .... Mr. John ANSELMO
18 Chairman Building Construction .... Mr. Richard L. MITCHELL
07 Director of Admissions .... Mr. Kevin GIANNETTI
27 Dir Communications/Inst Development .... Ms. Elizabeth BATTISTA
08 Head Librarian .... Mrs. Eleanor J. BROWN

Iona College (E)

715 North Avenue, New Rochelle NY 10801-1890
County: Westchester FICE Identification: 002737
Unit ID: 191931
Telephone: (914) 633-2000 Carnegie Class: Master's L
FAX Number: (914) 633-2642 Calendar System: Semester
URL: www.iona.edu
Established: 1940 Annual Undergrad Tuition & Fees: $30,192
Enrollment: 4,123 Coed
Affiliation or Control: Independent Non-Profit IRS Status: 501(c)3
Highest Offering: Master's
Program: Liberal Arts And General; Teacher Preparatory; Professional
Accreditation: M, BUS, CS, JOUR, MFCD, SW, TED

01 President .... Dr. Joseph E. NYRE
05 Interim Provost .... Dr. Brian J. NICKERSON
07 Assistant VP for College Admissions .... Mr. Kevin CAVANAGH
10 Vice President Finance .... Mr. Jonathan C. IVEC
30 Acting VP Advance/External Affs .... Ms. Marilyn WILKIE
13 Vice Provost Info Technology/CIO .... Ms. Joanne STEELE
32 Vice Provost Student Development .... Mr. Charles CARLSON
37 Asst VP Student Fin Svcs .... Ms. Nancy BUCHANAN
91 Asst Vice Provost for Info Tech .... Mr. Dimitris HALARIS
20 Assistant VP Academic Affairs .... Dr. Tresmaine GRIMES
49 Dean School Arts & Sciences .... Dr. Brain J. NICKERSON
50 Dean Hagan School of Business .... Dr. Vincent CALLUZZO
04 Spec Exec Asst to the President .... Sr. Patricia MCGINLEY
18 Director of Facilities Management .... Mr. Mark MURPHY
15 Director of Human Resources .... Ms. Mary Ellen CALLAGHAN
38 Director of Counseling Center .... Dr. Ingrid GRIEGER
36 Director of Career Development .... Ms. Christina BARBERO
08 Director of Libraries .... Mr. Richard PALLADINO
42 Director of Campus Ministries .... Mr. Carl PROCARIO-FOLEY
06 Registrar .... Ms. Nancy MILLS
41 Director of Athletics .... Mr. Eugene MARSHALL
86 Director of Govt Relations/Grants .... Mr. Daniel KONOPKA
29 Asst VP for Advancement & Alumni .... Ms. Nancy PATOTA
39 Asst Vice Provost Residential Life .... Mr. Derek ZUCKERMAN
12 Director of Rockland Campus .... Sr. Patricia MCGINLEY
09 Programmer Analyst/Inst Research .... Ms. Gigi KULANGARA
21 Director of Business Services .... Ms. Joan CLARK
26 Director of Public Relations .... Ms. Dawn INSANALLI
19 Dir Campus Safety and Securities .... Mr. Dominic LOCATELLI
23 Director of Health Services .... Ms. Jacqueline AGNELLO-VAZQUEZ
44 Director of Annual Giving .... Ms. Kara BRENNAN
96 Purchasing Coordinator .... Ms. Margarita FONG
35 Asst Vice Provost Student Develop .... Ms. Elizabeth OLIVIERI-LENAHAN

Island Drafting and Technical Institute (F)

128 Broadway, Amityville NY 11701-2704
County: Suffolk FICE Identification: 007375
Unit ID: 191959
Telephone: (631) 691-8733 Carnegie Class: Assoc/PrivFP
FAX Number: (631) 691-8738 Calendar System: Semester
URL: www.idti.edu
Established: 1957 Annual Undergrad Tuition & Fees: $14,850
Enrollment: 196 Coed
Affiliation or Control: Proprietary IRS Status: Proprietary
Highest Offering: Associate Degree
Program: Occupational
Accreditation: ACCSC

01 President .... Mr. James G. DILIBERTO
03 Vice President .... Mr. John G. DILIBERTO

Ithaca College (G)

953 Danby Road, Ithaca NY 14850-7001
County: Tompkins FICE Identification: 002739
Unit ID: 191968
Telephone: (607) 274-3011 Carnegie Class: Master's L
FAX Number: N/A Calendar System: Semester
URL: www.ithaca.edu
Established: 1892 Annual Undergrad Tuition & Fees: $35,278
Enrollment: 6,949 Coed
Affiliation or Control: Independent Non-Profit IRS Status: 501(c)3
Highest Offering: Doctorate
Program: Liberal Arts And General; Teacher Preparatory; Professional
Accreditation: M, BUS, MUS, NRPA, OT, PTA, SP, THEA

01 President .... Dr. Thomas R. ROCHON
04 Exec Assistant to President .... Ms. Diane VERONEAU
05 Provost/Vice Pres Academic Affairs .... Ms. Marisa KELLY
10 VP of Finance & Administration .... Mr. Carl E. SGRECCI
32 VP Student Affairs/Campus Life .... Mr. Brian J. MCAREE
26 Vice Pres Institutional Advancement .... Ms. Shelley S. SEMMLER
43 Vice President & General Counsel .... Ms. Nancy E. PRINGLE
84 VP Enrollment Management .... Mr. Eric MAGUIRE
20 Asst Prov/Dean Interdis/Intl Stds .... Dr. Tanya R. SAUNDERS
13 Assoc VP for Info Tech Svcs .... Mr. Edwin W. FULLER
15 Assoc VP for Human Resources .... Mr. Mark COLDREN
18 Assoc VP for Facilities Management .... Mr. Richard COUTURE
30 Assoc VP Institutional Advancement .... Vacant
35 Assoc Vice Pres Student Affairs .... Dr. Roger RICHARDSON
35 Assoc Vice Pres Student Affairs .... Mr. Rory ROTHMAN
20 Associate Provost .... Ms. Carol HENDERSON
58 Dean of Grad & Prof Studies .... Mr. Rob GEARHART
49 Dean School Humanities/Science .... Dr. Leslie LEWIS
64 Dean of School of Music .... Dr. Gregory WOODWARD
76 Dean Sch Health Sciences/Human Perf .... Mr. John SIGG
50 Dean School of Business .... Mr. Mark CORDANO
60 Dean School of Communications .... Ms. Diane GAYESKI
29 Director Alumni Relations .... Ms. Gretchen VAN VALEN
44 Executive Director of Development .... Ms. Kate LARRABEE
27 Int Dir Marketing Communications .... Ms. Laurie WARD
06 Registrar .... Mr. Brian SCHOLTEN
22 Asst Counsel & Dir EO Compliance .... Ms. Traevena BYRD
09 Director Institutional Research .... Ms. Martha D. GRAY
07 Director of Admission .... Mr. Gerard TURBIDE
12 Director London Center .... Mr. William SHEASGREEN
51 Program Dir/Graduate & Prof Studies .... Ms. Madelyn WILLIAMS
35 Dir Std Engagement/Multicult Affair .... Ms. Terry MARTINEZ
36 Director Career Services .... Mr. John P. BRADAC

38 Director for Counseling Svcs .... Dr. Deborah HARPER
07 Dir of Student Financial Services .... Mrs. Lisa HOSKEY
23 Director Health Center .... Dr. David E. NEWMAN
39 Dir Res Life/Judicial Affairs .... Ms. Bonnie S. PRUNTY
08 College Librarian .... Ms. Lisabeth CHABOT
41 Dir Intercol Athletics/Rec Sports .... Mr. Ken KUTLER
21 Director of Budget .... Ms. Sally DIETZ
90 Dir Technology/Inst Support Svcs .... Mr. Michael E. TAVES
91 Director Information Systems/Svcs .... Mr. Michael E. TAVES
19 Director Public Safety .... Ms. Terri STEWART
88 Director of Academic Funding .... Dr. Paul J. HAMILL
96 Director of Purchasing .... Vacant
27 Assoc Dir for Campus Communication .... Mr. David C. MALEY
40 Manager of College Stores .... Mr. Rick WATSON
42 Coordinator of Chaplains .... Rev. Meredith ELLIS

ITT Technical Institute (A)

13 Airline Drive, Albany NY 12205-1003

County: Albany　Identification: 666138
Unit ID: 434566
Telephone: (518) 452-9300　Carnegie Class: Assoc/PrivFP
FAX Number: (518) 452-9393　Calendar System: Quarter
URL: www.itt-tech.edu
Established: 1998　Annual Undergrad Tuition & Fees: N/A
Enrollment: 518　Coed
Affiliation or Control: Proprietary　IRS Status: Proprietary
Highest Offering: Associate Degree
Program: Technical Emphasis
Accreditation: **ACICS**

† Branch campus of ITT Technical Institute, Boise, ID.

ITT Technical Institute (B)

2295 Millersport Hwy, PO Box 327,
Getzville NY 14068-1219

County: Erie　Identification: 666609
Unit ID: 420404
Telephone: (716) 689-2200　Carnegie Class: Assoc/PrivFP
FAX Number: (716) 689-2828　Calendar System: Quarter
URL: www.itt-tech.edu
Established: 1995　Annual Undergrad Tuition & Fees: N/A
Enrollment: 668　Coed
Affiliation or Control: Proprietary　IRS Status: Proprietary
Highest Offering: Baccalaureate
Program: Technical Emphasis
Accreditation: **ACICS**

† Branch campus of ITT Technical Institute, Grand Rapids, MI.

ITT Technical Institute (C)

235 Greenfield Parkway, Liverpool NY 13088-6653

County: Onondaga　Identification: 666137
Unit ID: 434575
Telephone: (315) 461-8000　Carnegie Class: Assoc/PrivFP
FAX Number: (315) 461-8008　Calendar System: Quarter
URL: www.itt-tech.edu
Established: 1998　Annual Undergrad Tuition & Fees: N/A
Enrollment: 386　Coed
Affiliation or Control: Proprietary　IRS Status: Proprietary
Highest Offering: Associate Degree
Program: Technical Emphasis
Accreditation: **ACICS**

† Branch campus of ITT Technical Institute, Thornton, CO.

Jamestown Business College (D)

7 Fairmount Avenue, Box 429, Jamestown NY 14702-0429

County: Chautauqua　FICE Identification: 008495
Unit ID: 192004
Telephone: (716) 664-5100　Carnegie Class: Assoc/PrivFP4
FAX Number: (716) 664-3144　Calendar System: Quarter
URL: www.jbcny.org
Established: 1886　Annual Undergrad Tuition & Fees: $10,900
Enrollment: 386　Coed
Affiliation or Control: Proprietary　IRS Status: Proprietary
Highest Offering: Baccalaureate
Program: Occupational; 2-Year Principally Bachelor's Creditable
Accreditation: **M**

01 President/Academic Dean .... Mr. David CONKLIN
32 Dean of Student Affairs .... Ms. Rosanne JOHANSON
07 Director Admissions .... Ms. Brenda SALEMME
37 Director of Financial Aid .... Mrs. Diane STURZENBECKER
26 Director of Communications .... Ms. Jessica GOLLEY
04 Assistant to Academic Dean .... Ms. Cindy CARTWRIGHT

Jamestown Community College (E)

525 Falconer Street, Jamestown NY 14701-1999

County: Chautauqua　FICE Identification: 002869
Unit ID: 191986
Telephone: (716) 338-1000　Carnegie Class: Assoc/Pub-R-M
FAX Number: (716) 338-1466　Calendar System: Semester
URL: www.sunyjcc.edu
Established: 1950　Annual Undergrad Tuition & Fees (In-District): $4,380
Enrollment: 4,182　Coed
Affiliation or Control: State/Local　IRS Status: 501(c)3
Highest Offering: Associate Degree
Program: Occupational; 2-Year Principally Bachelor's Creditable
Accreditation: **M, ADNUR, OTA**

01 President .... Dr. Gregory T. DECINQUE
05 VP/Dean of Academic Affairs .... Dr. Marilyn A. ZAGORA
32 VP/Dean of Student Development .... Dr. Eileen J. GOODLING
12 VP/Dean Catt County Campus .... Mr. Jean J. SAYEGH
11 VP/Dean of Administration .... Mr. John R. GARFOOT
06 Registrar .... Mr. Kreig ELICKER
07 Director Admission/Recruitment .... Ms. Wendy PRESENT
26 Executive Director of Marketing .... Mr. Nelson J. GARIFI
08 Library Director .... Mr. Dennis BENAMATI
36 Placement Coordinator .... Mr. Ronald A. TURAK
37 Director of Financial Aid .... Ms. Laurie A. VORP
15 Director Human Resources .... Ms. Susan BRONSTEIN
09 Director Institutional Research .... Ms. Barbara RUSSELL
41 Athletic Director .... Mr. William BURK
43 Legal Counsel .... Mr. Stephen ABDELLA
18 Director Facilities/Physical Plant .... Mr. David JOHNSON

Jefferson Community College (F)

Outer Coffeen Street, Watertown NY 13601-1897

County: Jefferson　FICE Identification: 002870
Unit ID: 192022
Telephone: (315) 786-2200　Carnegie Class: Assoc/Pub-R-M
FAX Number: (315) 786-0158　Calendar System: Semester
URL: www.sunyjefferson.edu
Established: 1961　Annual Undergrad Tuition & Fees (In-District): $3,648
Enrollment: 3,861　Coed
Affiliation or Control: State/Local　IRS Status: 501(c)3
Highest Offering: Associate Degree
Program: Occupational; 2-Year Principally Bachelor's Creditable
Accreditation: **M, ADNUR**

01 President .... Dr. Carole A. MCCOY
05 Vice President Academic Affairs .... Mr. Thomas FINCH
10 Vice President Admin/Finance .... Mr. Daniel DUPEE
32 Vice President of Students .... Ms. Betsy S. PENROSE
20 Dean Curriculum/Instruction .... Ms. Jerilyn FAIRMAN
51 Dean for Continuing Education .... Ms. Jill BETTINGER
21 Dean for Business .... Ms. Vicki QUIGLEY
04 Assistant to the President .... Ms. Karen A. CARR
08 Library Director .... Ms. Connie HOLBERG
07 Director of Admissions .... Ms. Roseanne N. WEIR
37 Director Financial Aid .... Mr. James AMBROSE
06 Registrar .... Ms. Natalie M. SPOONER
88 Director Small Business Center .... Mr. Eric F. CONSTANCE
09 Director of Institutional Research .... Ms. Mary A. PERRINE
18 Chief Facilities/Physical Plant .... Mr. Adam POTTER
29 Director Alumni Relations .... Ms. Mary KINNE
35 Director Student Devel/Activities .... Mr. Frank DOLDO
36 Director Student Placement .... Ms. Michele D. GEFELL
38 Director Student Counseling .... Mr. Matthew LAMBERT
26 Chief Public Relations Officer .... Ms. Karen J. FREEMAN
15 Exec Dir Finance/Human Resources .... Ms. Kerry A. YOUNG
30 College Development Officer .... Ms. Christina RIZZO
31 Coordinator Community Services .... Ms. Andrea PEDRICK

Jewish Theological Seminary of America (G)

3080 Broadway, New York NY 10027-4649

County: New York　FICE Identification: 002740
Unit ID: 192040
Telephone: (212) 678-8023　Carnegie Class: Spec/Faith
FAX Number: (212) 678-8947　Calendar System: Semester
URL: www.jtsa.edu
Established: 1886　Annual Undergrad Tuition & Fees: $16,740
Enrollment: 465　Coed
Affiliation or Control: Independent Non-Profit　IRS Status: 501(c)3
Highest Offering: Doctorate
Program: Liberal Arts And General; Teacher Preparatory; Professional; Religious Emphasis
Accreditation: **M**

01 Chancellor .... Dr. Arnold M. EISEN
03 Vice Chanc/Chief Operating Officer . Dr. Michael B. GREENBAUM
30 Vice Chanc/Chief Development Office .... Rabbi Marc WOLF
43 Counsel .... Ms. Ann H. APPELBAUM
05 Provost .... Dr. Alan COOPER
10 Chief Financial Officer .... Mr. Fred SCHNUR
49 Dean List College Jewish Studies .... Dr. Shuly SCHWARTZ
53 Dean Davidson School of Education .... Dr. Barry HOLTZ
58 Dean The Graduate School .... Dr. Shuly SCHWARTZ
64 Director Miller Cantorial School .... Cantor Nancy ABRAMSON
73 Dean of Religious Leadership .... Rabbi Daniel NEVINS
32 Dean of Student Life .... Ms. Sara HOROWITZ
08 Librarian .... Dr. David KRAEMER
09 Director Institutional Research .... Miss Girija V. GHOLKAR
15 Director of Human Resources .... Ms. Diana TORRES-PETRILLI
18 Director of Operations .... Mr. James ESPOSITO
13 Director Information Technology .... Mr. Hal POLLENZ
27 Chief Communications Officer .... Ms. Elise DOWELL
06 Registrar/Director Financial Aid .... Ms. Linda LEVINE
84 Director of Enrollment Management .... Vacant
39 Director of Residence Life .... Mr. Bradley MOOT
07 Director List College Admissions .... Mrs. Melissa PRESENT
35 Director of Student Life .... Ms. Ruth DECALO
38 Director Student Counseling .... Mr. David DAVAR
29 Director of Alumni Affairs .... Mrs. Melissa FRIEDMAN
20 Associate Provost .... Dr. Stephen GARFINKEL
26 Chief Communications Officer .... Ms. Elise DOWELL
37 Director of Financial Aid .... Ms. Linda LEVINE

The Juilliard School (H)

60 Lincoln Center Plaza, New York NY 10023-6588

County: New York　FICE Identification: 002742
Unit ID: 192110
Telephone: (212) 799-5000　Carnegie Class: Spec/Arts
FAX Number: (212) 724-0263　Calendar System: Semester
URL: www.juilliard.edu
Established: 1905　Annual Undergrad Tuition & Fees: $33,630
Enrollment: 846　Coed
Affiliation or Control: Independent Non-Profit　IRS Status: 501(c)3
Highest Offering: Doctorate
Program: Professional
Accreditation: **M**

01 President .... Dr. Joseph W. POLISI
05 Provost & Dean .... Mr. Ara GUZELIMIAN
10 Vice Pres/Chief Operating Officer .... Mr. Jon ROSENHEIN
30 Vice Pres for Dev/Public Affairs .... Mr. Riccardo SALMONA
20 Vice Pres/Dean Academic Affairs .... Ms. Karen WAGNER
43 Vice President & General Counsel .... Ms. Laurie A. CARTER
08 VP for Library/Info Resources .... Ms. Jane GOTTLIEB
18 Vice Pres for Facilities Management .... Mr. Joseph MASTRANGELO
21 Vice Pres for Finance & Controller .... Ms. Christine TODD
84 Vice Pres for Enrollment Management .... Ms. Joan D. WARREN
27 Associate VP for Communications .... Ms. Janet KESSIN
28 Asc VP for Diversity & Campus Life .... Ms. Alison SCOTT-WILLIAMS
88 AVP Strategic/Artistic Initiatives .... Mr. Christopher MOSSEY
88 Assoc VP for Executive Projects .... Ms. Tricia ROSS
07 Associate Dean for Admissions .... Ms. Lee CIOPPA
11 Assoc Dean for Administration .... Mr. Adam MEYER
64 Asst Dean/Dir of Chamber Music .... Ms. Barli NUGENT
57 Artistic Director of Drama Division .... Mr. James HOUGHTON
57 Artistic Director of Dance Division .... Mr. Lawrence RHODES
88 Artistic Director of Vocal Arts .... Mr. Brian ZEGER
88 Artistic Dir Historical Performance .... Ms. Monica HUGGETT
88 Artistic Dir Pre-College Division .... Ms. Yoheved KAPLINSKY
06 Registrar .... Ms. Katherine GERTSON
16 Director of Human Resources .... Ms. Caryn G. DOKTOR
32 Director of Student Affairs .... Ms. Sabrina TANBARA
38 Director of Counseling Services .... Mr. William BUSE
37 Director Student Financial Aid .... Ms. Tina GONZALEZ
29 Dir of Natl Advance/Alumni Rels .... Ms. Jamee ARD
88 Artistic Director of Jazz Studies .... Mr. Carl ALLEN
96 Director of Office Services .... Mr. Scott A. HOLDEN
36 Director Career Services .... Ms. Courtney BLACKWELL
13 Director Information Technology .... Mr. Tunde GIWA

Kehilath Yakov Rabbinical Seminary (I)

638 Bedford Avenue, Brooklyn NY 11211-8007

County: Kings　FICE Identification: 010549
Unit ID: 192165
Telephone: (718) 963-1212　Carnegie Class: Spec/Faith
FAX Number: (718) 387-8586　Calendar System: Semester
Established: 1948　Annual Undergrad Tuition & Fees: $6,350
Enrollment: 116　Male
Affiliation or Control: Independent Non-Profit　IRS Status: 501(c)3
Highest Offering: First Talmudic Degree
Program: Teacher Preparatory; Professional
Accreditation: **RABN**

01 President .... Mr. Sandor SCHWARTZ

Keller Graduate School of Management (J)

120 W 45th Street, 6th Floor, New York NY 10036-4041

County: New York　Identification: 666258
Telephone: (212) 556-0002　Carnegie Class: Not Classified
FAX Number: (212) 556-0040　Calendar System: Semester
URL: www.keller.edu
Established: 2003　Annual Graduate Tuition & Fees: $26,355
Enrollment: 175　Coed
Affiliation or Control: Proprietary　IRS Status: Proprietary
Highest Offering: Master's; No Undergraduates
Program: Occupational; Business Emphasis
Accreditation: **&NH**

01 Campus Dean .... Ms. Patricia CAPALDO

† Regional accreditation is carried under the parent institution, DeVry University, Downers Grove, IL.

Keuka College (K)

Keuka Park NY 14478-0098

County: Yates　FICE Identification: 002744
Unit ID: 192192
Telephone: (315) 279-5000　Carnegie Class: Master's S
FAX Number: (315) 279-5216　Calendar System: Semester
URL: www.keuka.edu
Established: 1890　Annual Undergrad Tuition & Fees: $24,310
Enrollment: 1,867　Coed
Affiliation or Control: Independent Non-Profit　IRS Status: 501(c)3

Highest Offering: Master's
Program: Liberal Arts And General; Teacher Preparatory; Professional
Accreditation: M, IACBE, NUR, NURSE, OT, SW, @TEAC

01 President ... Dr. Jorge L. DIAZ-HERRERA
05 Vice President Academic Affairs ... Dr. Anne WEED
03 Executive Vice President/COO ... Dr. Carolanne MARQUIS
32 Vice Pres of Student Development ... Dr. James BLACKBURN
20 Asc Vice Pres of Academic Programs ... Dr. Timothy SELLERS
10 VP Finance/Chief Financial Officer ... Mr. Jerry HILLER
08 Director of Library ... Ms. Linda PARK
29 Director of Alumni/Family Relations ... Ms. Kathy WAYE
27 Exec Director of Communications ... Mr. Doug LIPPINCOTT
30 Asc Vice Pres for Devlopment ... Mr. Larry LELNER
37 Director Financial Aid ... Ms. Jennifer BATES
07 Dir of Admissions & Marketing ... Mr. Fred HOYLE
09 Director of Institutional Research ... Mr. Mark PALMIERI
14 Director of Computer Services ... Mr. Brad TURNER
18 Director of Facilities ... Mr. Dennis HOINS
21 Controller ... Ms. Carol N. GROVER
19 Director of Security ... Mr. Kevin TIERNEY
23 Director of Health Services ... Ms. Martha RICH
38 Director of Counseling Services ... Ms. Claudia WELBOURNE
35 Director of Student Life Activities ... Ms. Jennifer FURNER
26 Director of Marketing ... Mr. Fred HOYLE
41 Director of Athletics ... Mr. David M. SWEET
36 Asst Dean for Experiential Educ ... Dr. Anne Marie GUTHRIE
58 Assoc VP for Prof & Intl Programs ... Mr. Gary SMITH
88 Dir Administrative/Adult Learning ... Ms. Anne KILLEN
42 Chaplain ... Mr. Eric DETAR
06 Registrar ... Ms. Linda M. FLEISCHMAN
88 Marketing Manager Adult Learning ... Mr. Jack FARRELL
96 Purchasing Agent ... Ms. Audrey FAULKNER
15 Personnel Coordinator ... Ms. Susan DELYSER
76 Div Chair OT & Dir OT Grad Studies ... Ms. Victoria SMITH
83 Div Chrm Basic Social & Applied Sci ... Dr. Steve HALLAM
50 Div Chrm Business & Management ... Mr. Neil SEIBENHAR
53 Div Chrm Ed & Dir Ed Grad Studies ... Ms. Diane M. BURKE
79 Div Chrm Humanities/Fine Arts ... Dr. Alexis HAYNES
81 Div Chrm Natural Sciences/Math/PE ... Dr. Michael KECK
75 Division Chairman OT ... Ms. Vicki SMITH
44 Asst Director Dev/Donor Relations ... Ms. Billie Jo JAYNE
44 Asst Dir Devel/Annual Giving Pgms ... Ms. Andi LIPPINCOTT

The King's College (A)

350 Fifth Avenue, Suite 1500, New York NY 10118-1500
County: New York FICE Identification: 040953
Unit ID: 454184
Telephone: (212) 659-7200 Carnegie Class: Bac/A&S
FAX Number: (212) 659-7210 Calendar System: Semester
URL: www.tkc.edu
Established: 1938 Annual Undergrad Tuition & Fees: $29,240
Enrollment: 408 Coed
Affiliation or Control: Independent Non-Profit IRS Status: 501(c)3
Highest Offering: Baccalaureate
Program: Liberal Arts And General; Business Emphasis
Accreditation: M

00 Chairman of the Board of Trustees ... Mr. Andrew MILLS
01 President ... Mr. Dinesh J. D'SOUZA
07 Vice President of Admissions ... Mr. Brian PARKER
32 Vice President Student Development ... Mr. Eric BENNETT
30 Vice President of Advancement ... Mr. Jamey NORDBY
05 Vice President Academic Affairs ... Dr. Marvin OLASKY
35 Dean of Students ... Mr. David LEEDY
10 Chief Financial Officer ... Vacant
21 Controller ... Ms. Judy BARRINGER
06 Registrar ... Ms. Paula THIGPEN
37 Director of Financial Services ... Ms. Anna PETERS

Le Moyne College (B)

1419 Salt Springs Road, Syracuse NY 13214-1301
County: Onondaga FICE Identification: 002748
Unit ID: 192323
Telephone: (315) 445-4100 Carnegie Class: Master's L
FAX Number: (315) 445-4540 Calendar System: Semester
URL: www.lemoyne.edu
Established: 1946 Annual Undergrad Tuition & Fees: $28,380
Enrollment: 3,502 Coed
Affiliation or Control: Independent Non-Profit IRS Status: 501(c)3
Highest Offering: Master's
Program: Liberal Arts And General; Teacher Preparatory; Professional; Business Emphasis
Accreditation: M, ARCPA, BUS, NURSE, TEAC

01 President ... Dr. Fred P. PESTELLO
05 Provost & VP for Academic Affairs ... Dr. Linda M. LEMURA
84 Vice Pres Enrollment Management ... Dr. Dennis R. DEPERRO
10 Vice Pres Finance & Administration . Mr. Roger W. STACKPOOLE
30 Vice Pres Institutional Advancement ... Dr. Gregory J. STAHL
32 Vice Pres Student Development ... Dr. Deborah M. CADY MELZER
88 Director of Mission & Identity ... Rev. David C. MCCALLUM, SJ
88 Rector of the Jesuit Community ... Rev. William S. DOLAN, SJ
22 EEO/Affirmative Action Officer ... Mr. Timothy M. BARRETT
28 Director of Diversity ... Ms. Barbara M. KARPER
49 Interim Dean of Arts & Sciences ... Dr. J. Barron BOYD
50 Dean of Management ... Dr. Wally J. ELMER
20 Assoc Provost New Program Develop ... Dr. Mary K. COLLINS
08 Director of the Library ... Dr. Robert C. JOHNSTON
07 Dean of Admission ... Mr. Dennis J. NICHOLSON
26 Director of Communications ... Mr. Joseph B. DELLA POSTA
51 Director of Continuing Education ... Ms. Patricia J. BLISS
37 Director of Financial Aid ... Mr. William C. CHEETHAM
06 Registrar ... Ms. Mary M. CHANDLER
21 Assoc VP for Finance & Controller ... Mr. Brian M. LOUCY
41 Asst VP & Director of Athletics ... Mr. Matthew D. BASSETT
18 Asst VP Facilities Mgmt & Planning ... Mr. Jed S. SCHNEIDER
15 Director of Human Resources ... Mr. Timothy M. BARRETT
13 Acting Director of Info Technology ... Mr. Shaun C. BLACK
09 Director of Institutional Research ... Dr. Daniel L. SKIDMORE
40 Bookstore Manager ... Ms. Jessica L. HAMMOND
88 Assoc VP Institutional Advancement ... Ms. Juliahn GALLER SIMMS
29 Director Alumni & Parent Programs ... Ms. Kimberly B. MCAULIFF
44 Director of Annual Giving ... Ms. Monica M. MERANTE
86 Director Govt/Foundation Relations ... Mr. Steven W. KULICK
88 Director of Stewardship ... Ms. Katherine COGSWELL
88 Asst VP for Student Development ... Ms. Barbara M. KARPER
88 Asst Dean for Academic Advising ... Ms. Susan E. AMES
35 Asst Dean for Student Development ... Mr. Mark G. GODLESKI
42 Director of Campus Ministry ... Rev. Louis P. SOGLIUZZO, SJ
36 Director of Career Services ... Ms. Linda J. MCGRAW
38 Director Health/Counseling Center ... Ms. Anne E. KEARNEY
19 Director of Security ... Mr. John P. O BRIEN

LIM College (C)

12 E 53rd Street, New York NY 10022-5268
County: New York FICE Identification: 007466
Unit ID: 192271
Telephone: (212) 752-1530 Carnegie Class: Spec/Bus
FAX Number: (212) 832-6109 Calendar System: Semester
URL: www.limcollege.edu
Established: 1939 Annual Undergrad Tuition & Fees: $22,225
Enrollment: 1,508 Coed
Affiliation or Control: Proprietary IRS Status: Proprietary
Highest Offering: Master's
Program: Professional; Business Emphasis
Accreditation: M

01 President ... Elizabeth S. MARCUSE
04 Special Assistant to the President ... Linda HARRIS PAOLILLO
10 Senior Vice Pres Finance/Operations ... Michael DONOHUE
05 Senior VP for Academic/Student Affs ... Jo Ann ROLLE
88 Vice Pres for Student Development ... Michael FERRY
20 Associate VP for Academic Affairs ... Jacqueline LEBLANC
32 Assoc VP for Student Affairs ... Michael SACHS
07 Assistant Dean of Admissions ... Kristina ORTIZ
88 Asst Director of Academic Advising ... Lauren BAZHDARI
88 Asst Dean of Stdnt Academic Affairs ... Patricia FITZMAURICE
37 Dean of Student Financial Services ... Christopher BARTO
36 Director of Career Development ... Mariela TORRES
21 Accounting Manager ... Hubert STACHURA
96 Purchasing Agent ... Eric MARTIN
08 Director of Library Services ... Louis ACERNO
26 Director of Communications ... Meredith FINNIN
15 Associate Director of HR ... Andrea GRANVILLE
88 Sr Dir of Strategic Initiatives ... Pamela LINTON
13 Chief Technology Officer ... Maurice MORENCY
88 President Emeritus ... Adrian G. MARCUSE
38 Dir of Counseling/Wellness Svcs ... Jodi LICHT
06 Registrar ... Carolyn DISNEW
18 Director of Facilities ... Aldo TORTORELLI
30 Sr Dir Institutional Advancement ... Gail NARDIN
58 Vice President of Graduate Studies ... Milan MILASINOVIC
04 Assistant to the President ... Paula HOWELL
39 Dir of Housing & Residence Life ... Samara SCHINDLER
105 Web Content Manager/Administrator ... Lola REPHANN
09 Assoc Dean Recruit/Inst Research ... William IMBRIALE
35 Assoc Dean Student Affairs ... Charles PRYOR
88 Assoc Dean Continuing Education ... Lisa M. DECKER
88 Dean of Academic Affairs ... Rick LESTER
35 Director of Student Life ... Michael PALLADINO
07 Graduate Admissions Coordinator ... Paul MUCCIARONE

Long Island Business Institute (D)

136-18 39th Avenue, Flushing NY 11354
County: Queens FICE Identification: 020937
Unit ID: 192509
Telephone: (718) 939-5100 Carnegie Class: Assoc/PrivFP
FAX Number: (718) 939-9235 Calendar System: Trimester
URL: www.libi.edu
Established: 1968 Annual Undergrad Tuition & Fees: $14,073
Enrollment: 1,040 Coed
Affiliation or Control: Proprietary IRS Status: Proprietary
Highest Offering: Associate Degree
Program: Occupational; Business Emphasis
Accreditation: ACICS

01 President ... Ms. Monica W. FOOTE
12 Asst Campus Program Director ... Ms. Michelle HOUSTON
11 Dean of Administration ... Mr. Enos CHEUNG
37 Financial Aid Director ... Mr. Nazaret KIREGIAN
08 Librarian Commack Campus ... Ms. Terry CANAVAN
08 Librarian Flushing Campus ... Ms. Adrianna ARGUELLES
05 Chief Academic/Student Svcs Officer ... Ms. Stacey JOHNSON

Long Island College Hospital School of Nursing (E)

350 Henry Street, 7th Floor, Brooklyn NY 11201-6011
County: Kings FICE Identification: 021187
Unit ID: 192475
Telephone: (718) 780-1953 Carnegie Class: Assoc/PrivNFP
FAX Number: (718) 780-1936 Calendar System: Semester
URL: www.futurenurselich.org
Established: 1883 Annual Undergrad Tuition & Fees: $13,394
Enrollment: 147 Coed
Affiliation or Control: Independent Non-Profit IRS Status: 501(c)3
Highest Offering: Associate Degree
Program: Occupational; 2-Year Principally Bachelor's Creditable; Nursing Emphasis
Accreditation: ADNUR

01 Acting President/CEO ... Debra CAREY
05 Dean ... Nancy DIMAURO
37 Senior Director Financial Aid ... Ivette ROSA
32 Manager of Student Svcs/Registrar ... Johanna SANCHEZ
66 Vice President for Nursing ... Catherine GALLOGLY
88 Director School of Radiologic Tech ... Sergeo GUILBAUD
04 Assistant to the Dean ... Linda RUBINO

*Long Island University (F)

700 Northern Boulevard, Brookville NY 11548-1326
County: Nassau FICE Identification: 002751
Unit ID: 192457
Telephone: (516) 299-1926 Carnegie Class: N/A
FAX Number: (516) 299-2072
URL: www.liu.edu

01 President ... Dr. David J. STEINBERG
05 Vice President Academic Affairs ... Dr. Jeffrey KANE
88 Academic Budget Officer ... Ms. M. Peggy RIGGS
10 Vice President Finance & Treasurer ... Mr. Robert N. ALTHOLZ
20 Exec Asst to VP Acad Affairs ... Ms. Rachel CAVANAUGH
45 VP Planning & Human Resources ... Dr. Daniel J. RODAS
30 Vice President University Relations ... Mr. Richard W. GORMAN
43 Vice Pres Legal Svcs/Univ Counsel ... Ms. Lynette PHILLIPS
88 Sr Advisor & Teasurer Emerita ... Mrs. Mary M. LAI
04 Exec Assistant to the President ... Ms. Kathleen CAMPO
20 Associate VP Academic Affairs ... Dr. Lori KNAPP
13 Chief Business Process Mgr & CIO ... Mr. George BAROUDI
18 Assoc VP for Capital Projects ... Mr. Peter TYMUS
21 Assoc Vice Pres/Controller ... Mr. Mark SCHMOTZER
29 Assoc VP Delevop/Alumni Relations ... Ms. Jennifer GOODWIN
30 Assoc Vice Pres Development ... Ms. Melodee GANDIA
20 Asst VP Instr Tech/Faculty Develop ... Dr. Elizabeth CIABOCCHI
100 Asst Vice Pres Office of President ... Ms. Heather GIBBS
25 Asst Vice Pres Sponsored Research ... Ms. Kathryn S. ROCKETT
86 Assoc VP Public Policy/Govt/Found ... Mr. Christopher WILLIAMS
16 Assoc Vice Pres Human Resources ... Ms. Lisa CONZA
22 Asst VP for Employee Relations ... Ms. Gail WEINER
14 Assoc VP Information Systems ... Mr. Sal GRECO
62 Dean of University Libraries ... Ms. Valeda DENT
26 Assoc VP Mktg & Public Rels ... Vacant
21 Assoc VP Finance and Budget Dir ... Mr. Christopher FEVOLA
88 Assoc Controller Accounting Svcs ... Mr. Joseph PELIO, JR.
88 Associate Counsel ... Ms. Catherine MURPHY
88 Assoc Controller Comp Operations ... Ms. Linda NOYES
21 Dir of Student Financial Services ... Ms. Lorraine CELLI
88 Exec Dir Tilles Ctr/Inst Arts & Cul ... Vacant
88 Director Devel Svcs/Campaign Assoc ... Ms. Susan SHEBAR
15 Director Univ Fringe Benefits Pgm ... Ms. Nancy SISSONS
09 Director of Institutional Research ... Mr. Claude CHEEK
88 Univ Director Network Services ... Mr. Carlos SIVERIO
96 Director of Purchasing ... Ms. Margaret NATALIE
37 Univ Director Financial Aid ... Mr. David MAINENTI
88 Univ Dir Develop Bus Operations ... Vacant

*Long Island University Brentwood Campus (G)

100 Second Avenue, Brentwood NY 11717-5300
County: Suffolk Identification: 666076
Unit ID: 192563
Telephone: (631) 273-5112 Carnegie Class: Master's L
FAX Number: (631) 952-0809 Calendar System: Semester
URL: www.liu.edu
Established: 1959 Annual Undergrad Tuition & Fees: $30,046
Enrollment: 450 Coed
Affiliation or Control: Independent Non-Profit IRS Status: 501(c)3
Highest Offering: Master's
Program: Liberal Arts And General; Teacher Preparatory; Professional
Accreditation: &M

07 Director of Admissions ... Mr. John METCALFE

*Long Island University Brooklyn Campus (H)

1 University Plaza, Brooklyn NY 11201-5301
County: Kings FICE Identification: 004779
Unit ID: 192439
Telephone: (718) 488-1000 Carnegie Class: Master's L
FAX Number: (718) 780-4045 Calendar System: Semester
URL: www.liu.edu
Established: 1926 Annual Undergrad Tuition & Fees: $27,854
Enrollment: 8,574 Coed
Affiliation or Control: Independent Non-Profit IRS Status: 501(c)3
Highest Offering: Doctorate
Program: Occupational; Liberal Arts And General; Teacher Preparatory; Professional

Accreditation: &M, ARCPA, CLPSY, DMS, NURSE, OT, PHAR, PTA, SP, SPAA, SURGT, SW, TEAC

02 Provost ....Ms. Gale STEVENS HAYNES
05 Associate Provost ....Dr. Gladys SCHRYNEMAKERS
20 Assistant Provost ....Ms. Hazel SEIVWRIGHT
11 Associate Provost Campus Services ....Mr. Brad COHEN
06 Registrar ....Mr. Thomas CASTIGLIONE
37 Associate Provost Student Fin Svcs ....Ms. Patricia CONNORS
84 Dean of Admissions & Records ....Ms. Elizabeth STORINGE
49 Dean Conolly Col Arts & Science ....Dr. David COHEN
67 Dean Col Pharmacy/Sch Health Prof ....Dr. David TAFT
62 Dean of the Library ....Ms. Valeda DENT
66 Dean School of Nursing ....Vacant
72 Dean of IT/Deputy CIO ....Dr. Kamel LECHEHEB
46 Dean of Research ....Dr. Carol MAGAI
53 Dean School of Education ....Dr. Cecelia TRAUGH
51 Executive Director Continuing Educ ....Mr. George ROSALES
50 Dean Business/Public Admin/Info Sci ....Dr. Mohammed GHRIGA
30 Dean Inst Advance & Student Affairs ....Ms. Kimberly WILLIAMS
23 University Health Manager ....Ms. Virginia SMALL
85 Director International Students ....Mr. Steve CHIN
88 Director Academic Reinforcement Ctr ....Mr. Courtney FREDERICK
26 Director of Public Relations ....Mr. Brian HARMON
36 Asst Dean Career Dev & Coop Educ ....Ms. Stephanie STEINBERG
39 Director Residence Life & Housing ....Dr. Rodney PINK
89 Assistant Dean First Year Programs ....Mr. Shaun MCGUIRE
09 Director of Institutional Research ....Mr. Claude CHEEK
29 AVP Develpment & Alumni Relations ....Mr. Drew KAIDEN
41 Director of Athletics ....Mr. John SUAREZ
35 Director Student Life & Leader Dev ....Ms. Karlene JACKSON THOMPSON
18 Director Public Safety ....Mr. Selvin LIVINGSTON
88 Dir Spec Svcs & Achievement Studies ....Vacant
88 Co-Director Higher Educ Oppty Pgms ....Ms. Diana VOELKER
88 Co-Director Higher Educ Oppty Pgms ....Ms. Okarita STEVENS
88 Dean of Student Devel & Retention ....Ms. Michelle RELYEA
86 Director Comm Outreach & Arts Prom ....Ms. Fatima KAFELE
15 Human Resources Officer ....Ms. Raquel COLLADO
92 Co-Director of Honors Program ....Ms. Cris GLEICHER
92 Co-Director of Honors Program ....Dr. James CLARKE

*Long Island University C.W. Post Campus (A)

720 Northern Boulevard, Brookville NY 11548-1300

County: Nassau FICE Identification: 002754
Unit ID: 192448
Telephone: (516) 299-2000 Carnegie Class: Master's L
FAX Number: (516) 299-4020 Calendar System: Semester
URL: www.liu.edu/cwpost
Established: 1954 Annual Undergrad Tuition & Fees: $31,646
Enrollment: 10,964 Coed
Affiliation or Control: Independent Non-Profit IRS Status: 501(c)3
Highest Offering: Doctorate
Program: Occupational; Liberal Arts And General; Teacher Preparatory; Professional; Business Emphasis
Accreditation: M, BUS, CACREP, CLPSY, DIETD, DIETI, LIB, MT, NURSE, PERF, RAD, SP, SPAA, SW, TEAC

02 Provost ....Dr. Paul FORESTELL
04 Executive Asst to the Provost ....Ms. Stephanie ARCHER
10 Sr Asst Prov Budget Mgmt/Aux Svcs ....Ms. Dana WEISS
27 Assoc Provost/Director Public Rels ....Ms. Rita LANGDON
84 Assoc Provost Enrollment Services ....Vacant
51 Asst Provost Continuing Ed ....Dr. Kay SATO
32 Asst Provost for Student Affairs ....Ms. Amy URQUHART
36 Associate Provost Student Success ....Mr. William GUSTAFSON
07 Assist Prov/Exec Dir Admiss/Recruit ....Ms. Joanne GRAZIANO
29 Assoc VP of Development/Alumni Rels ....Ms. Lisa MULVEY
06 Registrar ....Ms. Beth CARSON
21 Bursar ....Mr. Edward A. BOSS, JR.
66 Dean School Health Prof/Nursing ....Dr. MaryAnn CLARK
57 Dean School Visual/Performing Arts ....Vacant
53 Dean Col Education & Info Sciences ....Dr. Robert HANNAFIN
50 Dean College of Management ....Mr. Francis BONSIGNORE
49 Dean College Arts & Sci ....Dr. Katherine HILL-MILLER
15 Human Resources Officer ....Mr. Ronald EDWARDS
88 Dir Higher Educ Opportunity Pgms ....Mr. William CLYDE, JR.
92 Director Honors Program ....Dr. Joan DIGBY
88 Director of Conference Services ....Ms. Theresa DUGGAN
88 Dir Life Leadership Development ....Ms. Alerie TIRSCH
90 Deputy Chief Information Officer ....Ms. Nancy MARKSBURY
88 Director NonTraditional Students ....Ms. Rita JORGENSEN
18 Director of Facilities ....Mr. William KIRKER
19 Director of Public Safety ....Mr. Paul RAPESS
38 Dir Student Health & Counseling ....Mr. William MILFORD
41 Director of Athletics ....Mr. Bryan COLLINS
85 Asst Provost Intl Student Services ....Dr. Jessica HAYES
37 Director Student Financial Aid ....Ms. Karen URDAHL
88 Director of Athletic Fundraising ....Vacant
88 Director of SCALE/ACE Programs ....Ms. Ann WALSH
88 Director of English Lang Programs ....Mr. Joseph GRANITTO
42 Director of Religious Life ....Fr. Ted BROWN
88 Dir Student Conduct & Community Ed ....Mr. Adam GROHMAN
45 Assistant Provost Inst Effectiv ....Mr. John MCLOUGHLIN
88 Director Student Information Center ....Vacant
88 Director Recreational Sports ....Ms. Mary NIGRO
88 Director Learning Support Center ....Ms. Susan ROCK
30 Assoc Director of Development ....Ms. Jennifer GREISOFE
36 Exec Dir Prof Exper & Placement ....Vacant
39 Associate Provost - ISS ....Dr. Jessica HAYES
29 Director Alumni Relations ....Ms. Katherine HOWLETT

07 Director of Graduate Admission ....Ms. Carol ZERAH
88 Director of Academic & Career Plng ....Mr. John MCLOUGHLIN
07 Director of Freshman Admissions ....Mr. David FOLLICK
07 Director of Transfer Admissions ....Ms. Denise SEIGEL
88 Director of Admissions Mktg ....Ms. Catherine CALAME
88 Director Veteran Services ....Mr. Adam GROHMAN

*Long Island University Riverhead Campus (B)

121 Speonk-Riverhead Road, Riverhead NY 11901-3499

County: Suffolk Identification: 666174
Unit ID: 450766
Telephone: (631) 287-8010 Carnegie Class: Master's S
FAX Number: (631) 287-8130 Calendar System: Semester
URL: www.liu.edu
Established: 2007 Annual Undergrad Tuition & Fees: $31,426
Enrollment: 262 Coed
Affiliation or Control: Independent Non-Profit IRS Status: 501(c)3
Highest Offering: Master's
Program: Liberal Arts And General; Teacher Preparatory
Accreditation: &M, TEAC

02 Associate Provost ....Ms. Jennifer BROWNE
07 Director of Admissions ....Ms. Andrea BORRA

*Long Island University Hudson Graduate Center at Rockland (C)

70 Route 340, Orangeburg NY 10962-2219

County: Rockland Identification: 666077
Unit ID: 192554
Telephone: (845) 359-7200 Carnegie Class: Spec/Other
FAX Number: (845) 359-7248 Calendar System: Semester
URL: www.liu.edu
Established: 1980 Annual Graduate Tuition & Fees: $24,432
Enrollment: 350 Coed
Affiliation or Control: Independent Non-Profit IRS Status: 501(c)3
Highest Offering: Master's; No Undergraduates
Program: Teacher Preparatory; Professional
Accreditation: &M

02 CEO/Dean of Education ....Dr. Sylvia BLAKE

*Long Island University Hudson Graduate Center at Westchester (D)

735 Anderson Hill Road, Purchase NY 10577-1400

County: Westchester Identification: 666078
Unit ID: 432357
Telephone: (914) 831-2700 Carnegie Class: Spec/Other
FAX Number: (914) 251-5959 Calendar System: Semester
URL: www.liu.edu/westchester
Established: 1975 Annual Graduate Tuition & Fees: $24,672
Enrollment: 350 Coed
Affiliation or Control: Independent Non-Profit IRS Status: 501(c)3
Highest Offering: Master's; No Undergraduates
Program: Liberal Arts And General; Teacher Preparatory; Professional
Accreditation: &M, TEAC

02 Dean and Chief Operating Officer ....Dr. Sylvia BLAKE
07 Director of Marketing & Enrollment ....Ms. Cindy PAGNOTTA

Louis V. Gerstner Jr. Graduate School of Biomedical Sciences at Memorial Sloan-Kettering Cancer Ctr (E)

1275 York Avenue, P.O. Box 441, New York NY 10065

County: New York Identification: 666643
Telephone: (646) 888-6639 Carnegie Class: Not Classified
FAX Number: N/A Calendar System: Other
URL: www.sloankettering.edu
Established: 2004 Annual Graduate Tuition & Fees: $33,950
Enrollment: 52 Coed
Affiliation or Control: Independent Non-Profit IRS Status: 501(c)3
Highest Offering: Doctorate; No Undergraduates
Program: Professional
Accreditation: NY

01 President ....Dr. Craig THOMPSON
05 Provost ....Dr. Thomas J. KELLY
20 Dean ....Dr. Kenneth J. MARIANS
88 Associate Dean ....Dr. Linda BURNLEY

Machzikei Hadath Rabbinical College (F)

5407 16th Avenue, Brooklyn NY 11204-1805

County: Kings FICE Identification: 013026
Unit ID: 192624
Telephone: (718) 854-8777 Carnegie Class: Spec/Faith
FAX Number: (718) 851-1265 Calendar System: Semester
Established: 1956 Annual Undergrad Tuition & Fees: $8,050
Enrollment: 115 Male
Affiliation or Control: Independent Non-Profit IRS Status: 501(c)3
Highest Offering: Second Talmudic Degree
Program: Teacher Preparatory
Accreditation: RABN

01 President ....Mr. Alexander SCHAECHTER

Mandl School (G)

254 W 54th Street, 9th Floor, New York NY 10019

County: New York FICE Identification: 007401
Unit ID: 192688
Telephone: (212) 247-3434 Carnegie Class: Assoc/PrivFP
FAX Number: (212) 247-3617 Calendar System: Semester
URL: www.mandl.edu
Established: 1924 Annual Undergrad Tuition & Fees: $24,000
Enrollment: 716 Coed
Affiliation or Control: Proprietary IRS Status: Proprietary
Highest Offering: Associate Degree
Program: Occupational; 2-Year Principally Bachelor's Creditable
Accreditation: ABHES, SURTEC

01 President ....Mr. Melvyn P. WEINER
05 Vice President of Academic Affairs ....Ms. Shanthi KONKOTH
37 VP/Director of Financial Aid ....Mr. Stuart WEINER
88 Director of Compliance ....Ms. Maritza E M. MERCADO
15 Director of Human Resources ....Ms. Phylis STAGNO
55 Dean of Evening/Weekend College ....Ms. Allison WRIGHT
36 Director of Career Services ....Mr. James FLANAGAN
06 Dean of Records & Registration ....Mr. Marc WEINER
84 Director of Enrollment Management ....Ms. Randie SENSER
08 Head Librarian ....Ms. Clover STEELE
07 Director of Recruitment ....Ms. Racquel GARCIA

Manhattan College (H)

Manhattan College Parkway, Bronx NY 10471-4099

County: Bronx FICE Identification: 002758
Unit ID: 192703
Telephone: (718) 862-8000 Carnegie Class: Master's M
FAX Number: (718) 862-8014 Calendar System: Semester
URL: www.manhattan.edu
Established: 1853 Annual Undergrad Tuition & Fees: $30,200
Enrollment: 3,069 Coed
Affiliation or Control: Independent Non-Profit IRS Status: 501(c)3
Highest Offering: Master's
Program: Liberal Arts And General; Teacher Preparatory; Professional
Accreditation: M, BUS, ENG, TEAC

01 President ....Dr. Brennan O'DONNELL
05 Executive Vice President & Provost ....Dr. William CLYDE
10 VP for Finance & Capital Projects ....Mr. Thomas J. RYAN
32 Vice President Student Life ....Dr. Richard SATTERLEE
30 Vice President College Advancement ....Mr. Thomas MAURIELLO
15 Vice President for Human Resources ....Mrs. Barbara A. FABE
18 Vice Pres Facilities Management ....Mr. Robert A. MAHAN
84 Vice President Enrollment Mgmt ....Mr. William J. BISSET
88 Vice President for Mission ....Br. James WALLACE
20 Assoc Prov Res/Fac/Computer System ....Mr. Walter F. MATYSTIK
35 Dean of Students ....Dr. Michael CAREY
39 Director Residence Life ....Mr. Jack GORMLEY
06 Registrar ....Mrs. Luz TORRES
84 Director of Enrollment Operations ....Ms. Paula D'ORIO
35 Director Student Development ....Ms. Elaine T. WHITE
08 Director of Libraries ....Ms. Maire I. DUCHON
14 Director of Computer Services ....Ms. Janice A. MELINO
19 Director of Security ....Mr. Juan E. CEREZO
29 Director of Alumni Relations ....Vacant
26 Director of College Relations ....Mrs. Lydia E. GRAY
36 Director Career Svcs/Coop Education ....Ms. Marjorie APEL
38 Dir of Counseling & Health Services ....Dr. Terence HANNIGAN
41 Director of Athletics ....Mr. Robert J. BYRNES
42 Director of Campus Ministry ....Ms. Lois HARR
44 Director of Development/Advancement ....Mr. Stephen WHITE
78 Director Academic Support Services ....Ms. Marilyn CARTER-STEVENS
40 Director of Campus Bookstore ....Mr. Paul QUILLIN
22 Dir of Personnel/Affirm Action Ofcr ....Ms. Vickie M. COWAN
09 Director of Assessment ....Ms. Judith SLISZ
21 Controller ....Mr. Dennis LONERGAN
21 Business Manager ....Mr. George KUZMA
85 International Student Advisor ....Ms. Debra L. DAMICO
21 Bursar ....Ms. Lisa JUNCAJ
49 Dean of Arts ....Dr. Richard K. EMMERSON
50 Dean of Business ....Dr. Salwa AMMAR
53 Dean of Education ....Dr. William J. MERRIMAN
54 Dean of Engineering ....Dr. Tim WARD
81 Dean of Science ....Dr. Constantine THEODOSIOU

Manhattan School of Music (I)

120 Claremont Avenue, New York NY 10027-4698

County: New York FICE Identification: 002759
Unit ID: 192712
Telephone: (212) 749-2802 Carnegie Class: Spec/Arts
FAX Number: (212) 749-5471 Calendar System: Semester
URL: www.msmnyc.edu
Established: 1917 Annual Undergrad Tuition & Fees: $32,815
Enrollment: 926 Coed
Affiliation or Control: Independent Non-Profit IRS Status: 501(c)3
Highest Offering: Doctorate
Program: Professional; Music Emphasis
Accreditation: M

01 President ....Dr. Robert SIROTA

00 Vice President Emeritis .... Mr. Richard E. ADAMS
10 VP Finance & Administration .... Mr. Paul D. KELLERHER
30 Vice Pres External Affairs .... Ms. Susan EBERSOLE
05 Vice Pres Academics & Performance .... Dr. Marjorie MERRYMAN
64 Vice Pres Instrument Performance .... Mr. David GEBER
32 Dean of Students .... Ms. Elsa Jean DAVIDSON
07 Associate Dean for Enrollment Mgt .... Ms. Amy A. ANDERSON
26 Dir Public Rel/Mrktng/Publications .... Ms. Debra KINZLER
15 Director Admin & Human Relations .... Ms. Carol MATOS
06 Registrar .... Mr. David MCDONAGH
39 Dir of Student & Residential Life .... Mr. Scott LATIOLAIS
31 Director of Educational Outreach .... Ms. Rebecca CHARNOW
36 Assoc Dir Career Devel/Alumni Affs .... Mr. Ar ADLER
37 Assoc Dir Student Financial Aid .... Ms. Angela PASQUINI
18 Director of Facilities .... Mr. Frank GRAUPE
29 Director Alumni Affairs .... Mr. John BLANCHARD
08 Director of Library Services .... Mr. Peter CALEB

Manhattanville College (A)

2900 Purchase Street, Purchase NY 10577-2132
County: Westchester FICE Identification: 002760
Unit ID: 192749
Telephone: (914) 694-2200 Carnegie Class: Master's L
FAX Number: (914) 694-2386 Calendar System: Semester
URL: www.mville.edu
Established: 1841 Annual Undergrad Tuition & Fees: $34,350
Enrollment: 2,695 Coed
Affiliation or Control: Independent Non-Profit IRS Status: 501(c)3
Highest Offering: Doctorate
Program: Liberal Arts And General; Teacher Preparatory
Accreditation: M, IACBE, TED

01 Acting President .... Mr. Robert C. HALL
04 Exec Admin Asst to the President .... Ms. Deborah A. FALLONE
05 Provost/VP of Academic Affairs .... Dr. Gail SIMMONS
10 Int VP Finance/Administration .... Ms. Marina VASARHELYI
84 Vice Pres Enrollment Management .... Ms. Kathy FITZGERALD
30 Vice Pres Institutional Advancement .... Mr. Jose GONZALEZ
32 Vice President for Student Life .... Dr. Douglas GEIGER
11 Vice President of Operations .... Mr. Gregory PALMER
58 Dean Graduate/Professional Studies .... Dr. Anthony DAVIDSON
53 Dean School of Education .... Dr. Shelley WEPNER
26 Mng Dir Media/PR/ Communications .... Ms. Jennifer JAMES PRYOR
06 Registrar .... Mr. Thomas MURASSO
85 Director of English Lang Institute .... Ms. Judith H. LEWIS
08 Director of the Library .... Ms. Rhonna GOODMAN
37 Interim Director of Financial Aid .... Mr. Robert GILMORE
23 Director Hlth Svcs/Counseling Svcs .... Dr. Pamela DUNCAN
35 Dean of Students .... Mr. Brandon DAWSON
41 Director of Athletics .... Mr. Keith LEVINTHAL
42 Int Catholic Chpln/Interfaith Coord .... Fr. Wil TYRRELL
36 Director Center for Career Devel .... Ms. Rosalie SHEMMER
29 Dir Alumni Relations/Annual Giving .... Ms. Teresa WEBER
19 Director of Security .... Mr. Anthony HERRMANN
30 Director of Development .... Ms. Nancy KINGSTON
07 Director of Undergrad Admissions .... Vacant
09 Director of Institutional Research .... Ms. Noreen O'HARA
15 Director of Human Resources .... Mr. Don DEAN
35 Director of Student Activities .... Ms. Pascha MCTYSON
18 Chief Facilities/Physical Plant .... Mr. Gregory PALMER
96 Director of Purchasing .... Ms. Marsha KIRCHOFF

Maria College of Albany (B)

700 New Scotland Avenue, Albany NY 12208-1798
County: Albany FICE Identification: 002763
Unit ID: 192785
Telephone: (518) 438-3111 Carnegie Class: Assoc/PrivNFP
FAX Number: (518) 438-7170 Calendar System: 4/1/4
URL: www.mariacollege.edu
Established: 1958 Annual Undergrad Tuition & Fees: $9,800
Enrollment: 834 Coed
Affiliation or Control: Independent Non-Profit IRS Status: 501(c)3
Highest Offering: Baccalaureate
Program: Occupational; 2-Year Principally Bachelor's Creditable
Accreditation: M, ADNUR, OTA

01 President .... Sr. Laureen A. FITZGERALD
05 Vice President for Academic Affairs .... Dr. Margie L. BYRD
10 Director of Business Affairs .... Mrs. Frances BERNARD
51 Director of Continuing Education .... Sr. Ellen BOYLE
06 Director of Student Records .... Dr. Kenneth CLOUGH
07 Director of Admissions .... Ms. Laurie A. GILMORE
08 Librarian .... Sr. Rose HOBBS
32 Dean of Student Services .... Ms. Deborah CORRIGAN
13 Director of Academic Computing .... Mr. Stephen F. DELORENZO
18 Chief Physical Plant .... Mr. Andrew PEREZ
36 Director Placement/Alumni .... Sr. Renee M. CUDHEA
30 Chief Development .... Mrs. Martha FASHOUER

Marist College (C)

3399 North Road, Poughkeepsie NY 12601-1387
County: Dutchess FICE Identification: 002765
Unit ID: 192819
Telephone: (845) 575-3000 Carnegie Class: Master's L
FAX Number: (845) 471-6213 Calendar System: Semester
URL: www.marist.edu
Established: 1929 Annual Undergrad Tuition & Fees: $28,300
Enrollment: 6,140 Coed
Affiliation or Control: Independent Non-Profit IRS Status: 501(c)3
Highest Offering: Master's
Program: Liberal Arts And General; Teacher Preparatory; Professional
Accreditation: M, BUS, MT, SW

01 President .... Dr. Dennis J. MURRAY
03 Executive Vice President .... Dr. Roy H. MEROLLI
03 Executive Vice President .... Dr. Geoffrey L. BRACKETT
05 Vice President for Academic Affairs .... Dr. Thomas S. WERMUTH
84 VP Admission & Enrollment Planning .... Mr. Sean P. KAYLOR
30 Vice President College Advancement .... Mr. Christopher M. DELGIORNO
13 VP Information Technology/ CIO .... Mr. William T. THIRSK
32 VP/Dean of Student Affairs .... Mrs. Deborah A. DICAPRIO
10 Vice President Business Affairs/CFO .... Mr. John P. PECCHIA
20 Assoc VP/ Dean Academic Affairs .... Dr. John RITSCHDORFF
07 Dean of Undergraduate Admission .... Mr. Kenton W. RINEHART
88 Dean of Grad and Adult Enrollment .... Mr. Sean-Michael GREEN
35 Assoc Dean of Student Affairs .... Mr. Steve SANSOLA
29 Executive Director Alumni Relations .... Ms. Amy K. WOODS
09 Director Inst Research & Planning .... Mrs. Susan H. DUNCAN
20 Assoc Dean of Academic Affairs .... Mrs. Judith IVANKOVIC
37 Exec Dir Student Financial Services .... Mr. Joseph R. WEGLARZ
08 Director Library .... Mr. Verne NEWTON
38 Director Counseling Services .... Ms. Naomi A. FERLEGER
90 Director Academic Technology .... Mr. Joshua D. BARON
18 Director of Physical Plant .... Mr. Justin BUTWELL
26 Chief Public Affairs Officer .... Mr. Timmian MASSIE
15 Asst VP for Human Resources .... Mr. Michael J. SILVESTRO
96 Director of Purchasing .... Mr. Stephen J. KOCHIS
36 Director Career Services .... Mr. Stephen W. COLE

Marymount Manhattan College (D)

221 E 71st Street, New York NY 10021-4597
County: New York FICE Identification: 002769
Unit ID: 192864
Telephone: (212) 517-0400 Carnegie Class: Bac/A&S
FAX Number: (212) 517-0541 Calendar System: Semester
URL: www.mmm.edu
Established: 1936 Annual Undergrad Tuition & Fees: $24,708
Enrollment: 2,095 Coed
Affiliation or Control: Independent Non-Profit IRS Status: 501(c)3
Highest Offering: Baccalaureate
Program: Liberal Arts And General
Accreditation: M

01 President .... Dr. Judson R. SHAVER
88 Assoc to the Pres for Operations .... Ms. Melissa G. RICHMAN
05 VP Acad Affairs/Dean of Faculty .... Dr. David PODELL
10 Exec Vice Pres Admin & Finance .... Mr. Paul CIRAULO
30 VP Col Relations/Chief Advance Ofcr .... Mr. Derek C. BELLIN
09 VP Institutional Research/Planning .... Dean Peter H. BAKER
32 VP Student Affairs/Dean of Students .... Dr. Carol JACKSON
21 Associate Vice Pres & Controller .... Mr. Wayne SANTUCCI
07 Dean of Admissions .... Mr. James ROGERS
20 Associate Dean for Academic Affairs .... Dr. Kathleen LEBESCO
06 Registrar .... Ms. Regina CHAN
15 Director of Human Resources .... Ms. Bree BULLINGHAM
08 Librarian .... Ms. Donna HURWITZ
13 Director Information Technology .... Ms. Patricia HANSEN
37 Director Student Financial Svcs .... Ms. Maria DEINNOCENTIIS
38 Dir Counseling & Psychological Svcs .... Dr. Paul GRAYSON
18 Director of Facilities .... Mr. Pete ROMAIN
35 Asst Dean/Dir Student Activities .... Ms. Rosemary AMPUERO
36 Director Career Svcs & Internships .... Ms. Melissa BENCA
96 Director of Purchasing .... Ms. Maria MARZANO
88 Asst Controller .... Ms. Melissa SAVINO
29 Dir of Annual and Alumni Programs .... Ms. Carolyn BOLT

Medaille College (E)

Agassiz Circle, Buffalo NY 14214-2695
County: Erie FICE Identification: 002777
Unit ID: 192925
Telephone: (716) 880-2000 Carnegie Class: Master's L
FAX Number: (716) 884-0291 Calendar System: Semester
URL: www.medaille.edu
Established: 1875 Annual Undergrad Tuition & Fees: $21,598
Enrollment: 2,736 Coed
Affiliation or Control: Independent Non-Profit IRS Status: 501(c)3
Highest Offering: Master's
Program: Liberal Arts And General; Teacher Preparatory
Accreditation: M, IACBE, TEAC

01 President .... Dr. Richard T. JURASEK
05 Vice President for Academic Affairs .... Dr. Douglas W. HOWARD
10 Vice President Business/Finance .... Mr. Matthew J. CARVER
30 Vice Pres for College Relations .... Ms. Paula R. VALENTE
84 VP Enroll Mgmt/Sch Adult & Grad Ed .... Ms. Jacqueline S. MATHENY
07 VP Enroll Mgmt/Undergrad Admissions .... Mr. Gregory P. FLORCZAK
32 Dean for Student Affairs .... Ms. Amy M. DEKAY
44 Dir of Major Gifts & Planned Giving .... Ms. Sara B. FLUSKEY
41 Athletic Director .... Mr. Peter E. LONERGAN
36 Director Career Planning/Placement .... Ms. Carol CULLINAN
27 Chief Information Officer .... Mr. Robert D. CHYKA
06 Registrar .... Ms. Kathleen LAZAR
09 Dir of Institutional Research .... Mr. Patrick S. MCDONALD
08 Library Director .... Ms. Pamela R. JONES
37 Director Financial Aid .... Ms. Catherine BUZANSKI
15 Director of Human Resources .... Ms. Barbara J. BILOTTA
20 Sr Dir Special Academic Services .... Vacant
18 Director Facilities/Physical Plant .... Mr. Nate R. MARTON
29 Coordinator of Alumni Relations .... Vacant
35 Director Ofc of Student Involvement .... Ms. Melisa L. WILLIAMS
38 Director Counseling Services .... Ms. Jeannine D. SUK
96 Manager of Purchasing .... Vacant
26 Director of Communications .... Ms. Kara M. KANE
19 Director of Campus Public Safety .... Mr. Ronald J. CHRISTOPHER

Memorial Hospital School of Nursing (F)

600 Northern Boulevard, Albany NY 12204-1004
County: Albany FICE Identification: 012203
Unit ID: 192961
Telephone: (518) 471-3260 Carnegie Class: Not Classified
FAX Number: N/A Calendar System: Semester
URL: www.nehealth.com
Established: N/A Annual Undergrad Tuition & Fees: $8,033
Enrollment: 110 Coed
Affiliation or Control: Independent Non-Profit IRS Status: 501(c)3
Highest Offering: Associate Degree
Program: Nursing Emphasis
Accreditation: NY

01 Executive Director .... Ms. Linda D'ARCANGELIS

Mercy College (G)

555 Broadway, Dobbs Ferry NY 10522-1189
County: Westchester FICE Identification: 002772
Unit ID: 193016
Telephone: (800) 637-2969 Carnegie Class: Master's L
FAX Number: N/A Calendar System: Semester
URL: www.mercy.edu
Established: 1950 Annual Undergrad Tuition & Fees: $17,360
Enrollment: 10,851 Coed
Affiliation or Control: Independent Non-Profit IRS Status: 501(c)3
Highest Offering: Doctorate
Program: 2-Year Principally Bachelor's Creditable; Liberal Arts And General; Teacher Preparatory; Professional
Accreditation: M, ART, ARCPA, NURSE, OT, OTA, PTA, SP, SW

01 President .... Dr. Kimberly R. CLINE
05 Provost & Vice Pres Acad Affairs .... Dr. Michael SPERLING
50 Dean School of Business .... Dr. Lucretia MANN
53 Dean School of Education .... Dr. Alfred POSAMENTIER
83 Dean School Social/Behavioral Sci .... Dr. Lois WIMS
76 Dean School Health/Natural Science .... Dr. William SUSMAN
97 Dean School Liberal Arts .... Dr. Miriam GOGOL
11 Chief Operating Officer .... Mr. Joseph SCHAEFER
84 Vice Pres for Enrollment Management .... Ms. Deirdre WHITMAN
10 Vice President for Finance .... Ms. Jeanne PLECENIK
30 Exec Dir Institutional Advancement .... Mr. William MARTINOV
88 Chief Compliance Officer .... Mr. James MCCUE
20 Exec Dean Academic Engagement/Plng .... Ms. Carolyn TRAGNI
37 AVP for Student Financial Services .... Ms. Margaret MCGRAIL
09 Dir Institutional Research/Planning .... Ms. Victoria TYLER
32 Student Success and Engagement .... Mr. Andy PERSON
90 Director of Information Technology .... Vacant
06 Exec Director of Registrar .... Ms. Debra KENNEY
21 Controller .... Ms. Samantha CHRISTIAN
21 Director Budget & Planning .... Mr. Dommick BUMBACO
08 Dean of Libraries/Acad Tech & OL .... Dr. BRADDLEE
15 Associate Dir of Human Resources .... Mr. David VERNON
19 Director of Security .... Mr. Kenneth GABELMAN
41 Director of Athletics .... Ms. Patricia KENNEDY
27 Associate Director Public Relations .... Ms. Melissa CORTELLINI
04 Assistant to the President .... Ms. Irene BUCKLEY
21 Director of Business Operations .... Vacant
39 Deputy Director PACT/Residence Life .... Ms. Patricia CHRISTIANO
07 Senior Director of Admissions .... Ms. Tara FAY-REILLY
96 Director of Purchasing .... Ms. Patricia SABATINO
29 Director of Alumni Relations .... Mr. Drew BROWN
18 Director of Facilities .... Ms. Elaine TREFFILETTI

Mesivta of Eastern Parkway Rabbinical Seminary (H)

510 Dahill Road, Brooklyn NY 11218-5559
County: Kings FICE Identification: 009335
Unit ID: 193061
Telephone: (718) 438-1002 Carnegie Class: Spec/Faith
FAX Number: (718) 438-2591 Calendar System: Semester
Established: 1947 Annual Undergrad Tuition & Fees: $11,825
Enrollment: 38 Male
Affiliation or Control: Independent Non-Profit IRS Status: 501(c)3
Highest Offering: Second Talmudic Degree
Program: Teacher Preparatory; Professional
Accreditation: RABN

01 President .... Rabbi Issac HEIMOVITZ
32 Dean of Students .... Rabbi Chaim L. EPSTEIN
37 Director of Student Financial Aid .... Rabbi Ira LIBERMAN
46 Director of Research .... Rabbi Hersch BASCH
10 Chief Fiscal Officer .... Rabbi Joseph HALBERSTADT

Mesivta Tifereth Jerusalem of America (I)

141-7 E Broadway, New York NY 10002-6301
County: New York FICE Identification: 003974
Unit ID: 193070

Telephone: (212) 964-2830 Carnegie Class: Spec/Faith
FAX Number: (212) 349-5213 Calendar System: Semester
Established: 1907 Annual Undergrad Tuition & Fees: $8,900
Enrollment: 81 Male
Affiliation or Control: Independent Non-Profit IRS Status: 501(c)3
Highest Offering: Second Talmudic Degree
Program: Teacher Preparatory; Professional
Accreditation: RABN

01 President & Dean Faculties .... Rabbi David FEINSTEIN

Mesivta Torah Vodaath Seminary (A)

425 E Ninth Street, Brooklyn NY 11218-5299
County: Kings FICE Identification: 007264
Unit ID: 193052
Telephone: (718) 941-8000 Carnegie Class: Spec/Faith
FAX Number: (718) 941-8032 Calendar System: Semester
Established: 1918 Annual Undergrad Tuition & Fees: $8,600
Enrollment: 250 Male
Affiliation or Control: Independent Non-Profit IRS Status: 501(c)3
Highest Offering: Second Talmudic Degree
Program: Teacher Preparatory; Professional
Accreditation: RABN

01 Dean .... Rabbi Moshe WOLFSON
03 Executive Director .... Rabbi Yitzchok GOTTDIENER
06 Registrar .... Rabbi Yonason SHAPIRO
33 Dean of Men .... Rabbi Elya KATZ
31 Director Community Services .... Rabbi Ezriel ROVT

Metropolitan College of New York (B)

431 Canal Street, New York NY 10013-1919
County: New York FICE Identification: 009769
Unit ID: 190114
Telephone: (212) 343-1234 Carnegie Class: Master's L
FAX Number: (212) 343-7399 Calendar System: Semester
URL: www.metropolitan.edu
Established: 1964 Annual Undergrad Tuition & Fees: $16,720
Enrollment: 1,193 Coed
Affiliation or Control: Independent Non-Profit IRS Status: 501(c)3
Highest Offering: Master's
Program: Professional
Accreditation: M, TED

01 President .... Dr. Vinton THOMPSON
10 Exec Vice President and CFO .... Mr. Vincent MASSARO
84 Vice Pres for Enrollment Management .... Dr. Collette GARRITY
88 Dean Enrollment Services .... Mr. Steven LENHART
58 Dean School of Management .... Dr. Humphrey CROOKENDALE
88 Dean Audrey Cohen School Human Svcs .... Dr. Ruth E. LUGO
35 Dean of Students .... Ms. Dona SOSA
37 Interim Director Financial Aid .... Ms. Andrea DAMAR
06 Registrar .... Ms. Noreen SMITH
08 Director of Library Services .... Mr. Lou ACIERNO
09 Dir Institutional Rsrch/Assessment .... Vacant
15 Director Human Resources .... Ms. Judith SANTIAGO
18 Chief Facilities/Physical Plant .... Ms. Mercedes MELENDEZ
30 Director of Development .... Ms. Didi LACHER
26 Chief Public Relations Officer .... Vacant
96 Director of Purchasing .... Vacant
13 Information Systems Manager .... Mr. Naftaly KLEINMAN

Mildred Elley (C)

855 Central Avenue, Albany NY 12206
County: Albany FICE Identification: 022195
Unit ID: 193201
Telephone: (518) 786-0855 Carnegie Class: Assoc/PrivFP
FAX Number: (518) 786-0890 Calendar System: Other
URL: www.mildred-elley.edu
Established: 1917 Annual Undergrad Tuition & Fees: $12,900
Enrollment: 881 Coed
Affiliation or Control: Proprietary IRS Status: Proprietary
Highest Offering: Associate Degree
Program: Occupational
Accreditation: ACICS

01 President .... Ms. Faith A. TAKES

Mirrer Yeshiva Central Institute (D)

1795 Ocean Parkway, Brooklyn NY 11223-2010
County: Kings FICE Identification: 004798
Unit ID: 193247
Telephone: (718) 645-0536 Carnegie Class: Spec/Faith
FAX Number: (718) 645-9251 Calendar System: Semester
Established: 1947 Annual Undergrad Tuition & Fees: $4,700
Enrollment: 305 Male
Affiliation or Control: Independent Non-Profit IRS Status: 501(c)3
Highest Offering: Second Talmudic Degree
Program: Teacher Preparatory; Professional
Accreditation: RABN

00 Chancellor .... Rabbi Avrohom Yaakov NELKENBAUM
01 President and Dean .... Rabbi Osher KALMANOWITZ
05 Vice President & Dean .... Rabbi Osher BERENBAUM
33 Dean of Men .... Rabbi Esrael ERLANGER
03 Executive Director .... Rabbi Pinchas HECHT
06 Registrar-Administrator .... Mrs. Devorah BERENBAUM
08 Director of the Library .... Rabbi Jacob FELDMANN
38 Director of Guidance .... Rabbi Yisroel FISHMAN
37 Financial Aid Director .... Mrs. Rachel BERENBAUM

Mohawk Valley Community College (E)

1101 Sherman Drive, Utica NY 13501-5394
County: Oneida FICE Identification: 002871
Unit ID: 193283
Telephone: (315) 792-5400 Carnegie Class: Assoc/Pub-R-L
FAX Number: (315) 792-5666 Calendar System: Semester
URL: www.mvcc.edu
Established: 1946 Annual Undergrad Tuition & Fees (In-District): $4,010
Enrollment: 7,151 Coed
Affiliation or Control: State/Local IRS Status: 501(c)3
Highest Offering: Associate Degree
Program: Occupational; 2-Year Principally Bachelor's Creditable
Accreditation: M, ADNUR, ENGT

01 President .... Dr. Randall J. VAN WAGONER
04 Assistant to the President .... Ms. Jill HEINTZ
88 Exec Dir Organizational Development .... Mr. John BULLIS
88 Director of Strategic Initiatives .... Mrs. Patricia FOX
09 Dir Institutional Research/Analysis .... Mr. Mark E. RADLOWSKI
05 Vice Pres Learning/Academic Affairs .... Dr. Maryrose EANNACE
20 Director of Academic Systems .... Mr. Richard PUCINE
79 Dean of Arts & Humanities .... Mr. Lewis KAHLER
88 Dean of Language & Learn Design .... Ms. Jennifer BOULANGER
88 Dean of Life & Health Sciences .... Vacant
88 Dean of STEM .... Mr. Donald WILLNER
50 Dean of Business/Soc Sci & Info Sci .... Ms. Marianne BUTTENSCHON
08 Director College Libraries .... Mr. Stephen FRISBEE
24 Dir of Educational Technologies .... Mr. James LYNCH
11 Vice Pres Administrative Services .... Mr. Ralph J. FEOLA
32 VP Student Svcs/Dean of Students ..Ms. Stephanie C. REYNOLDS
84 Asst Dean Enrollment & Advisement .... Mrs. Jennifer DEWEERTH
36 Director Career & Transfer Service .... Mr. James MAIO
39 Asst Dean of Student Life .... Mr. Dennis GIBBONS
12 Assoc Vice Pres/Dean Rome Campus .... Dr. Ronald G. CANTOR
30 Exec Dir Institutional Advancement .... Mr. Frank DUROSS
44 Dir of Donor & Resource Development .... Ms. Deanna FERRO
96 Coord Expend/Fixed Asset Procure .... Ms. Joyce PALMER
13 Exec Dir of Information Technology .... Mr. Paul KATCHMAR
31 Exec Dir Ctr Community/Economic Dev .... Ms. Franca ARMSTRONG
15 Director of Human Resources .... Mrs. Kimberly EVANS-DAME
26 Director Marketing/Communications .... Mr. Matthew SNYDER
07 Director of Admissions .... Mr. Daniel IANNO
37 Director of Financial Aid .... Mrs. Annette BROSKI
06 Dir of Student Records/Registrar .... Mrs. Rosemary V. SPETKA
18 Dir of Facilities and Operations .... Mr. Michael MCHARRIS
19 Director Campus Safety & Security .... Mr. Joseph PALMER
21 Business Office Controller .... Mr. Brian MOLINARO
29 Coord Annual Funds/Alumni Relations .... Ms. Marie KOHL
35 Asst Dean of Student Support .... Vacant
31 Dir of Community/Student Engagement .... Vacant

Molloy College (F)

1000 Hempstead Avenue, PO Box 5002,
Rockville Centre NY 11571-5002
County: Nassau FICE Identification: 002775
Unit ID: 193292
Telephone: (516) 678-5000 Carnegie Class: Master's L
FAX Number: (516) 256-2247 Calendar System: 4/1/4
URL: www.molloy.edu
Established: 1955 Annual Undergrad Tuition & Fees: $22,290
Enrollment: 4,188 Coed
Affiliation or Control: Independent Non-Profit IRS Status: 501(c)3
Highest Offering: Doctorate
Program: Liberal Arts And General; Teacher Preparatory; Professional
Accreditation: M, CVT, NMT, NURSE, @SP, SW, TED

01 President .... Dr. Drew BOGNER
05 VP Academic Affairs/Dean of Faculty .... Dr. Valerie COLLINS
10 Vice Pres for Finance & Treasurer .... Mr. Michael MC GOVERN
84 Vice Pres Enrollment Management .... Ms. Linda ALBANESE
30 Vice President for Advancement .... Mr. Edward J. THOMPSON
32 Vice President Student Svcs .... Mr. Robert HOULIHAN
45 VP Planning/Research/Info Tech .... Dr. Robert PATERSON
88 Vice President for Mission .... Sr. Dorothy Anne FITZGIBBONS
42 Director of Campus Ministries .... Mr. Scott SALVATO
37 Director Student Financial Services .... Ms. Sharion SCOTT
36 Director of Career Services Center .... Ms. June HINTON-DOYLE
41 Director of Athletics .... Ms. Susan CASSIDY
07 Director of Admissions .... Ms. Marguerite LANE
37 Director of Financial Aid .... Mrs. Ana C. LOCKWARD
21 Assistant Treasurer .... Mr. Anthony PERFETTI
44 Director of Development .... Ms. Catherine MUSCENTE
06 Registrar .... Ms. Susan FORTMAN
09 Director of Institutional Research .... Mr. Michael TORRES
15 Director of Human Resources .... Ms. Lisa MILLER
18 Director of Facilities .... Mr. James MULTARI
26 Dir Public Affairs & Commnications .... Mr. Kenneth YOUNG
96 Director of Purchasing .... Ms. Lorraine JACKSON
35 Director of Campus Life .... Ms. Janine MCELROY
29 Alumni Relations Officer .... Dr. Marion FLOMENHAFT
32 Director of Residential Life .... Mr. Stephen OSTENDORFF

Monroe College (G)

2501 Jerome Avenue, Bronx NY 10468-5407
County: Bronx FICE Identification: 004799
Unit ID: 193308
Telephone: (718) 933-6700 Carnegie Class: Master's S
FAX Number: (718) 295-5861 Calendar System: Semester
URL: www.monroecollege.edu
Established: 1933 Annual Undergrad Tuition & Fees: $12,440
Enrollment: 7,143 Coed
Affiliation or Control: Proprietary IRS Status: Proprietary
Highest Offering: Master's
Program: Liberal Arts And General; Business Emphasis
Accreditation: M

01 President .... Stephen J. JEROME
12 Exec VP/Director of Branch Campus .... Marc M. JEROME
03 Sr Vice Pres Student Financial Svcs .... James GATHARD
05 Vice President Academics .... Dr. W. Jeff WALLIS
11 Vice President Administration .... David DIMOND
10 Sr Vice President for Finance .... Alan E. MINTZ
84 Vice Pres Enroll Mgmt/Campus Dean .... Anthony ALLEN
32 Vice President Student Affairs .... Roberta GREENBERG
97 Dean School of General Studies .... Alex CANALS
20 Assoc Vice President for Academics .... Dr. Karenann CARTY
20 Dean of Academics New Rochelle Camp .... Dr. Janice GIRARDI
86 Asst Vice Pres Governmental Affairs .... Dr. Donald E. SIMON
09 Dean Institutional Research .... Dr. Edward S. SCHNEIDERMAN
55 Director of Evening Division .... Barry GORDON
106 Exec Dir of Online Learning .... Craig PATRICK
06 Registrar .... Dr. Edward S. SCHNEIDERMAN
09 Dir Institutional Research .... Peter NWAKEZE
21 Bursar/Branch Campus .... Michael NIEDZWIECKI
21 Bursar/Branch .... Daniel SHARON
35 Dean of Student Services - Branch .... Stephen SCHULTHEIS
21 Bursar .... Villan CRUZ
88 Assistant Dean for Student Services .... Mark SONNENSTEIN
31 Director Auxiliary Services .... Nivia CAMARA
07 Dean of Admissions Branch .... Gersom LOPEZ
07 Vice President Admissions .... Evan JEROME
88 Director Student Fin Aid Compliance .... Erdene KIMS
36 Assoc VP Ofc of Career Advancement .... Carol GENESE
36 Dir Ofc of Career Advancement-NR .... Hillary SULLIVAN
08 Director of Library Services .... Shawn KABAB
08 Director of Library Services/Branch .... Angela LAURETANO
24 Director of Learning Center .... Marie LOFTUS
39 Exec Director of Residential Life .... Walter EDDIE
29 Director of Alumni Relations .... Leslie JEROME

Monroe Community College (H)

1000 E Henrietta Road, Rochester NY 14623-5780
County: Monroe FICE Identification: 002872
Unit ID: 193326
Telephone: (585) 292-2000 Carnegie Class: Assoc/Pub-U-MC
FAX Number: (585) 427-2749 Calendar System: Semester
URL: www.monroecc.edu
Established: 1961 Annual Undergrad Tuition & Fees (In-District): $3,060
Enrollment: 18,995 Coed
Affiliation or Control: State/Local IRS Status: 501(c)3
Highest Offering: Associate Degree
Program: Occupational; 2-Year Principally Bachelor's Creditable
Accreditation: M, ADNUR, DA, DH, EMT, ENGT, RAD

01 President .... Dr. Anne M. KRESS
05 Provost & VP Academic Services ....Dr. Michael J. MCDONOUGH
72 Vice President Educational Tech Svc . Dr. Jeffrey P. BARTKOVICH
32 Vice President Student Services .... Dr. Susan M. SALVADOR
10 CFO and VP Administrative Svcs .... Mr. Hezekiah N. SIMMONS
103 VP Econ Dev/Workforce Svc .... Mr. Todd M. OLDHAM
102 Exec Director MCC Foundation .... Ms. Diane L. SHOGER
35 Assoc Vice Pres Student Services .... Mr. Richard H. RYTHER
12 Exec Dean Damon City Campus .... Dr. Emeterio M. OTERO
26 Asst to the Pres College Relations .... Ms. Cynthia L. COOPER
35 Asst Vice Pres Student Services .... Dr. Susan D. BAKER
88 Asst VP Educational Technology Svcs .... Mr. Dale E. MALLORY
18 Assistant Vice President Facilities .... Mr. David A. SCHOTTLER
20 Int Dean Curriculum/Program Devel .... Mrs. Charlotte DOWNING
37 Director Financial Aid .... Mr. Jerome S. ST. CROIX
09 Director Research .... Mr. Angel E. ANDREU
08 Director ETS Libraries .... Mr. Thaddeus J. CIAMBOR
36 Director Career Center .... Mr. G. Christopher BELLE-ISLE
21 Asst Vice President Admin Svcs ..Mr. Darrell K. JACHIM-MOORE
06 Director Registration and Records .... Ms. Elizabeth R. RIPTON
30 Director of Development .... Mr. Mark J. PASTORELLA
38 Dir Counseling & Advising .... Ms. Peggy A. HARVEY-LEE
19 Director Public Safety .... Mr. Lee E. STRUBLE
41 Director Athletics .... Mr. Dudley (Skip) L. BAILEY
25 Director Grants .... Ms. Patricia R. WILLIAMS
35 Director of Student Life .... Ms. Elizabeth J. STEWART
23 Director of Health Services .... Ms. Donna G. MUELLER
21 Controller .... Mr. Michael G. QUINN
79 Interim Dean Liberal Arts .... Ms. Kristen M. FRAGNOLI
50 Int Dean Science/Health/Business .... Ms. Laurel T. SANGER
75 Interim Dean Technical Education .... Mr. James A. PETROSINO
88 Dean Interdisciplinary Programs .... Ms. Carol H. ADAMS
19 Dean Public Safety Training Ctr .... Mr. Michael S. KARNES
32 Dean Student Services-DCC .... Dr. Ann V. TOPPING
88 Dean Acad Svcs DCC .... Ms. Kate M. SCHIEFEN
13 Assoc Dean/Director ETS Computing .... Mr. Robert G. BERTRAM
16 Asst to President Human Resources .... Ms. Alberta G. LEE
40 Manager Bookstore .... Ms. Carol M. FISHER

22 Affirmative Action Officer ... Ms. Diane M. CECERO
07 Director of Admissions ... Mr. Andrew W. FREEMAN
88 Director Educ Opportunity Program ... Ms. Brenda A. SMITH
32 Assoc Director Student Svcs-DCC ... Mr. Rick F. SADWICK
78 Director Adult/Experiential Lrng ... Mr. William D. SIGISMOND
43 Legal Counsel ... Ms. Diane M. CECERO
88 Assoc Director Master Scheduling ... Ms. Kimberley D. WILLIS
96 Director of Purchasing ... Mr. Patrick M. BATES
39 Director Housing/Residence Life ... Ms. Shelitha W. DICKERSON
88 Director of Planning ... Ms. Valarie L. AVALONE
28 Chief Diversity Officer ... Ms. Diane M. CECERO

Mount Saint Mary College (A)

330 Powell Avenue, Newburgh NY 12550-3412
County: Orange FICE Identification: 002778
Unit ID: 193353
Telephone: (845) 561-0800 Carnegie Class: Master's L
FAX Number: (845) 562-6762 Calendar System: Semester
URL: www.msmc.edu
Established: 1959 Annual Undergrad Tuition & Fees: $24,400
Enrollment: 2,700 Coed
Affiliation or Control: Independent Non-Profit IRS Status: 501(c)3
Highest Offering: Master's
Program: Liberal Arts And General; Teacher Preparatory; Professional; Nursing Emphasis
Accreditation: M, NURSE, TED

01 President ... Fr. Kevin MACKIN, OFM
05 Vice President Academic Affairs ... Dr. Iris TURKENKOPF
10 Vice Pres Finance & Admin/Treasurer ... Mrs. Cathleen KENNY
30 Vice Pres for College Advancement ... Mr. Joseph VALENTI
45 Vice Pres for Planning & Assessment ... Dr. Mary HINTON
18 Vice Pres Facilities ... Mr. James RAIMO
32 Vice President for Student Affairs ... Mr. Harry R. STEINWAY
84 VP for Enrollment Management ... Mr. Art CRISS
38 Dir Counseling/Coord Prsns w/Disab ... Dr. Orin STRAUCHLER
20 Associate Dean for Academic Affairs ... Dr. Alice WALTERS
06 Registrar ... Ms. Darlene BENZENBERG
07 Director of Admissions ... Mrs. Michelle TAYLOR
08 Director of the Library ... Mrs. Barbara W. PETRUZZELLI
37 Director of Financial Aid ... Ms. Barbra WINCHELL
09 Director of Planning and Research ... Mr. Ryan WILLIAMS
15 Director of Human Resources ... Mr. Lee ZAWISTOWSKI
42 Chaplain ... Fr. Francis AMODIO
35 Director of Student Activities ... Ms. Sandra CEFALONI
39 Exec Dir of Operations and Housing ... Mrs. Elaine O'GRADY
29 Director of Alumni Affairs ... Ms. Michelle A. IACUESSA
41 Director of Athletics & Recreation ... Mr. John WRIGHT
36 Exec Director of the Career Center ... Mrs. Janet ZEMAN
27 Chief Information Officer ... Mr. Dennis RUSH
96 Purchasing Manager ... Mr. Brian MOORE

Mount Sinai School of Medicine (B)

One Gustave L. Levy Place, New York NY 10029-6500
County: New York FICE Identification: 007026
Unit ID: 193405
Telephone: (212) 241-6500 Carnegie Class: Not Classified
FAX Number: (212) 241-7146 Calendar System: Other
URL: www.mountsinai.org/education
Established: N/A Annual Graduate Tuition & Fees: $35,750
Enrollment: 1,086 Coed
Affiliation or Control: Independent Non-Profit IRS Status: 501(c)3
Highest Offering: Doctorate; No Undergraduates
Program: Professional
Accreditation: M, DENT, IPSY, MED, PH

01 Dean ... Dr. Dennis S. CHARNEY
05 Dean for Medical Education ... Dr. David MULLER

Nassau Community College (C)

1 Education Drive, Garden City NY 11530-6793
County: Nassau FICE Identification: 002873
Unit ID: 193478
Telephone: (516) 572-7501 Carnegie Class: Assoc/Pub-S-SC
FAX Number: (516) 572-7750 Calendar System: Semester
URL: www.ncc.edu
Established: 1959 Annual Undergrad Tuition & Fees (In-District): $4,200
Enrollment: 23,468 Coed
Affiliation or Control: State/Local IRS Status: 501(c)3
Highest Offering: Associate Degree
Program: Occupational; 2-Year Principally Bachelor's Creditable
Accreditation: M, ADNUR, ENGT, FUSER, MLTAD, MUS, PTAA, RTT, SURGT

01 President ... Dr. Donald P. ASTRAB
03 Executive Vice President ... Dr. Kenneth K. SAUNDERS
05 Vice President Academic Affairs ... Dr. Roberta SCHRODER
11 Vice President Administration/Plng ... Dr. Joseph MUSCARELLA
10 Vice President Finance ... Mr. James BEHRENS
32 Vice Pres Academic/Student Svcs ... Ms. Maria CONZATTI
22 AVP Equity & Inclusion/AA Officer ... Mr. Craig J. WRIGHT
43 Spec Asst to Pres/College Counsel ... Ms. Donna M. HAUGEN
16 Assoc Vice Pres Human Resources ... Mr. Fred DOWNS
103 Asst Vice Pres Workforce Devel ... Ms. Janet CARUSO
21 Comptroller ... Ms. Inna REZNIK
13 Dean Management Info Svcs ... Mr. Dennis E. GAI
18 Asst VP Maintenance/Operations ... Mr. Masoom ALI
15 Asst Vice Pres Human Resources . Ms. Deborah REED-SEGRETTI
96 Asst Vice President Procurement ... Mr. Gary HOMKOW

35 Dean of Students ... Ms. Charmian SMITH
09 Assc VP Institutional Effectiveness ... Mr. Frank BILLINGS
37 Dean Financial Aid ... Ms. Patricia NOREN
07 Dean of Admissions ... Ms. Tika ESLER
25 Resource Devel/Grants Fiscal Mgr ... Mr. Edmund KOEPPEL
86 General Counsel for Govt Relations ... Mr. Chuck CUTOLO
26 AVP Marketing/Communications ... Mr. Reginald TUGGLE
08 Director of Library ... Ms. Nancy WILLIAMSON
41 Director Special Pgm Athletics/PED ... Mr. Michael C. PELLICCIA
06 Acting Registrar ... Ms. Tika ESLER
19 Director of Public Safety ... Mr. Martin RODDINI
23 Director Health Services ... Ms. Ethel FRITZ
36 Director of Placement Testing ... Ms. Noreen WADE
38 Dir Advisement/Special Programs ... Mr. John SPIEGEL
27 Chief Information Officer ... Mr. Richard LAWLESS

Nazareth College of Rochester (D)

4245 East Avenue, Rochester NY 14618-3790
County: Monroe FICE Identification: 002779
Unit ID: 193584
Telephone: (585) 389-2525 Carnegie Class: Master's L
FAX Number: (585) 586-2452 Calendar System: Semester
URL: www.naz.edu
Established: 1924 Annual Undergrad Tuition & Fees: $27,222
Enrollment: 2,919 Coed
Affiliation or Control: Independent Non-Profit IRS Status: 501(c)3
Highest Offering: Doctorate
Program: Liberal Arts And General; Teacher Preparatory; Professional
Accreditation: M, MUS, NURSE, PTA, SP, SW, TEAC

01 President ... Dr. Daan BRAVEMAN
04 Assistant to President ... Ms. Patricia GENTHNER
04 Executive Secretary to President ... Ms. Cathleen M. STEVENS
05 Vice President Academic Affairs ... Dr. Sara VARHUS
30 Vice Pres Institutional Advancement ... Ms. Kelly GAGAN
10 Vice President Finance & Treasurer ... Ms. Maragaret C. FERBER
32 Vice President Student Development ... Mr. Kevin WORTHEN
07 Vice Pres Enrollment Management ... Mr. Thomas R. DARIN
29 Director of Alumni Relations ... Mr. Kerry GOTHAM
22 Director Multicultural Affairs ... Ms. Gaynelle WETHERS
15 Assoc VP Human Resources ... Mrs. JoEllen PINKHAM
20 Asst VP Academic Affairs ... Dr. Robert MARINO
06 Registrar ... Mr. Andrew MORRIS
37 Director Student Financial Aid ... Ms. Samantha VEEDER
26 Director Marketing & Communications ... Ms. Kathleen PHILBIN
13 Director Information Tech Svcs ... Ms. Karen KUPPINGER
08 Director of Library ... Ms. Catherine DOYLE
19 Director of Security ... Mr. Robert MALDONADO
39 Director of Residential Life ... Ms. Joan ANDERSON
41 Director of Athletics ... Mr. Peter G. BOTHNER
38 Director of Counseling ... Dr. Frederica AMSTEY
42 Director Center for Spirituality ... Ms. Lynne BOUCHER
36 Director of Career Services ... Mr. Michael D. KAHL
18 Director Buildings/Grounds ... Mr. Peter LANA
09 Director of Institutional Research ... Ms. Nancy C. GREAR
23 Director of Health Services ... Ms. Donna WILLOME
20 Director of Academic Advisement ... Ms. Linda SEARING
88 Director of the Arts Center ... Ms. Susan C. LUSIGNAN
21 Bursar ... Mr. John GARBE
88 Dir Patricia Carter Child Care Ctr ... Ms. Mimi BERRY
35 Director of Student Affairs ... Mrs. Jane E. KELLY
92 Director Honors Program ... Dr. Susan NOWAK
94 Director Women's Studies Program ... Dr. Sekile NZINGA-JOHNSON
49 Dean of Col of Arts and Sciences ... Dr. Deborah DOOLEY
76 Dean School of Health & Human Svcs ... Dr. Shirley SZEKERES
53 Dean School of Education ... Dr. Timothy GLANDER
88 Dean School of Management ... Mr. Gerard ZAPPIA
88 Director of the Casa Italiana ... Dr. Stella PLUTINO-CALABRESE
88 Exec Dir of Ctr International Educ ... Dr. George EISEN
88 Dir the Ctr for Teaching Excellence ... Dr. Diane ENERSON
88 Dir of Center for Service Learning ... Dr. Marie WATKINS
89 Dir Stdnt Transition/First Year Ctr ... Ms. Marrlee BURGESS
96 Director of Purchasing ... Ms. Tracy MORAN
88 Exec Dir Center 4 Civic Engagement ... Ms. Nuala BOYLE

The New School (E)

66 W 12th Street, New York NY 10011-8603
County: New York FICE Identification: 020662
Unit ID: 193654
Telephone: (212) 229-5600 Carnegie Class: DRU
FAX Number: (212) 229-5330 Calendar System: Semester
URL: www.newschool.edu
Established: 1919 Annual Undergrad Tuition & Fees: $39,350
Enrollment: 10,678 Coed
Affiliation or Control: Independent Non-Profit IRS Status: 501(c)3
Highest Offering: Doctorate
Program: 2-Year Principally Bachelor's Creditable; Liberal Arts And General
Accreditation: M, ART, CLPSY, SPAA

01 President ... Dr. David VAN ZANDT
05 Provost and Chief Academic Officer ... Mr. Tim MARSHALL
10 CFO & Sr VP for Finance & Business ... Mr. Frank BARLETTA
20 Vice Provost Academic Services ... Dr. Elizabeth ROSS
13 Sr VP for Information Technology ... Ms. Shelley REED
30 Sr VP of Development & Alumni ... Ms. Pamela BESNARD
32 Sr Vice President Student Services ... Ms. Linda REIMER
84 VP of Enrollment Management ... Mr. Bob GAY
26 VP for Communications/External Affs ... Ms. Nancy DONNER
43 General Counsel/VP Legal Affairs ... Mr. Roy P. MOSKOWITZ
49 Dean Eugene Lang College ... Ms. Stephanie BROWNER
51 Exec Dean School for Public Engage ... Mr. David SCOBEY
57 Dean Parsons School for Design ... Mr. Joel TOWERS
58 Dean New School for Social Research ... Dr. Michael SCHOBER
88 VP and Secretary of the Corporation ... Ms. Doris SUAREZ
21 Vice President and Treasurer ... Mr. Craig BECKER
20 Dep Provost & Sr VP Academic Affs ... Dr. Bryna SANGER
64 Dean Mannes College of Music ... Mr. Richard KESSLER
82 Senior VP for International Affairs ... Dr. Ben LEE
88 Vice Pres for Design & Construction ... Ms. Lia GARTNER
20 Vice Provost Acad Planning ... Ms. Pat BAXTER
88 Director The New School for Drama ... Mr. Pippin PARKER
88 Executive Director Jazz Program ... Mr. Martin MUELLER
58 Dean Milano School of Intl Affairs ... Dr. Neil GRABOIS
15 Sr VP for HR & Labor Relations ... Ms. Carol CANTRELL
35 Asst VP for Student & Campus Life ... Mr. Tom MCDONALD
21 Asst Vice Pres of Budget & Planning ... Mr. Steve STABILE
46 Assoc Provost Research Sp Projects ... Dr. Ronald KASSIMIR
21 Asst Vice Pres & Controller ... Ms. Natalie PRESSEY
07 Asst VP for Enrollment Operations ... Ms. Christy KALAN
21 Asst VP Student Financial Services ... Ms. Eileen DOYLE
37 Director Financial Aid ... Vacant
96 Sr Director of Business Operations ... Mr. Ed VERDI
18 Sr Director Facilities Management ... Mr. Tim SHELDON
08 University Librarian ... Mr. Ed SCARCELLE
09 Assoc Provost Inst & Market Rsrch ... Vacant
106 Director The New School Online ... Mr. James O'CONNOR
06 University Registrar ... Mr. William KIMMEL
23 LCSW/Asst VP Student Health ... Ms. Tracy ROBIN
36 Director Student Development ... Ms. Shannon LOGAN
28 Director of Intercultural Support ... Ms. Keisha DAVENPORT-RAMIREZ
29 Director Alumni Relations ... Vacant
39 Director University Housing ... Mr. Robert LUTOMSKI
88 Director of Student Disability Svcs ... Mr. Jason LUCHS
85 Dir International Student Services ... Ms. Monique N. NRI

New York Academy of Art (F)

111 Franklin Street, New York NY 10013-2911
County: New York FICE Identification: 026001
Unit ID: 366368
Telephone: (212) 966-0300 Carnegie Class: Spec/Arts
FAX Number: (212) 966-3217 Calendar System: Semester
URL: www.nyaa.edu
Established: 1982 Annual Graduate Tuition & Fees: $29,700
Enrollment: 113 Coed
Affiliation or Control: Independent Non-Profit IRS Status: 501(c)3
Highest Offering: Master's; No Undergraduates
Program: Professional; Fine Arts Emphasis
Accreditation: NY

01 President ... Mr. David KRATZ
05 Dean of Academic Affairs ... Mr. Peter DRAKE
37 Director of Student Financial Aid ... Mr. Andrew MUELLER
32 Director of Student Affairs ... Mr. Elvin R. FREYTES
08 Librarian & Archivist ... Ms. Holly FRISBEE

New York Career Institute (G)

11 Park Place, 4th Floor, New York NY 10007
County: New York FICE Identification: 021634
Unit ID: 195845
Telephone: (212) 962-0002 Carnegie Class: Assoc/PrivFP
FAX Number: (212) 385-7574 Calendar System: Trimester
URL: www.nyci.edu
Established: 1941 Annual Undergrad Tuition & Fees: $12,120
Enrollment: 805 Coed
Affiliation or Control: Proprietary IRS Status: Proprietary
Highest Offering: Associate Degree
Program: Occupational; 2-Year Principally Bachelor's Creditable
Accreditation: NY

01 CEO ... Ivan LONDA
05 Chief Academic Officer ... Lois CITRON
32 Director of Student Services ... Cindy MCMAHON
37 Director Financial Aid ... Dennis BYRNS

New York Chiropractic College (H)

2360 State Route 89, Seneca Falls NY 13148-0800
County: Seneca FICE Identification: 012277
Unit ID: 193751
Telephone: (315) 568-3000 Carnegie Class: Spec/Health
FAX Number: (315) 568-3012 Calendar System: Trimester
URL: www.nycc.edu
Established: 1919 Annual Undergrad Tuition & Fees: $30,873
Enrollment: 811 Coed
Affiliation or Control: Independent Non-Profit IRS Status: 501(c)3
Highest Offering: First Professional Degree
Program: Professional
Accreditation: M, ACUP, CHIRO

01 President ... Dr. Frank J. NICCHI
05 Exec Vice President & Provost ... Dr. Michael A. MESTAN
10 Vice Pres of Finance/Admin Svcs ... Mr. Sean ANGLIM
20 Dean Academic Affairs ... Dr. Rose REINHART
20 Dean of Chiropractic Education ... Dr. Karen A. BOBAK
20 Dean Health Centers ... Dr. Wendy L. MANERI
88 Vice Pres Inst Quality/Assessment ... Dr. David R. ODIORNE
06 Registrar ... Mr. Kevin MCCARTHY

84 Vice Pres Enrollment Management ... Ms. Diane DIXON
07 Director of Admissions ... Mr. Michael LYNCH
37 Director Financial Aid ... Mr. Darrin ROOKER
88 Director of Bachelor Prof Studies ... Dr. Kristina L. PETROCCO-NAPULI
46 Dean of Research ... Dr. Jeanmarie R. BURKE
12 Depew Health Center Chief of Staff ... Dr. Lorraine A. KOCHANOWSKI-SUTTER
12 Levittown Health Ctr Chief of Staff ... Dr. Charles HEMSEY
17 Seneca Falls Hlth Ctr Chf of Staff ... Dr. Wendy L. MANERI
51 Dean Post Grad & Cont Educ ... Dr. Thomas VENTIMIGLIA
08 Director of the Library ... Ms. Bethyn BONI
38 Assoc Director Counseling Services ... Ms. Eve ABRAMS
88 Dir Academy Admc Excl Stdnt Success ... Ms. Kara KREINHEDER
39 Secretary Housing ... Mrs. Janette ELSTER
41 Dir Health & Fitness Education ... Mr. Anthony M. PETROCCIA
35 Director Student Life ... Ms. Holly Anne WAYE
36 Director of Career Development Ctr ... Ms. Susan D. PITTENGER
30 Exec Director Devel & Govt Rels ... Vacant
29 Director of Alumni Relations ... Ms. Diane ZINK
30 Vice President of Inst Advancement ... Mr. Peter R. VANTYLE
45 Director Accreditation ... Dr. Beth DONOHUE
09 Quality Engineer ... Ms. Patricia MERKLE
15 Human Resources Manager ... Ms. Christine MCDERMOTT
91 Network Administrator ... Mr. Shane SHOWERS
19 Director Facilities/Security ... Mr. William WAYNE
96 Assoc VP Admin Svcs/Dir Purchasing ... Mr. Richard B. WORDEN
40 Bookstore Manager ... Mr. Chris BYRNE
63 Dir MS Clinical Anatomy Pgm ... Dr. Karen GANA
76 Dir Applied Clinical Nutrition Pgm ... Dr. Anna KELLES
88 Dean of FL Sch Acup/Oriental Med ... Mr. Jason WRIGHT
88 Dir MS Diagnostic Imaging Program ... Dr. Jean-Nicholas POIRIER
88 Dir Academy for Teaching Excellence ... Dr. Kristina L. PETROCCO-NAPULI
12 Campus Health Ctr Chief of Staff ... Dr. Jonathon EGAN
12 Rochester Hlth Ctr Chf of Staff ... Dr. Wendy L. MANERI
90 Systems Administrator ... Ms. Shelly STUCK
24 Educational Tech Administrator ... Mr. Bernard CECCHINI
23 Administrative Dir of the Hlth Ctrs ... Ms. Jennifer VONHAHMANN
21 Controller ... Ms. Karen QUEST
88 Director Academy for Prof Success ... Dr. Theresa M. HOBAN
88 Dir MS Hum Anat Phys Instructn Pgm ... Dr. Robert A. CROCKER

New York College of Health Professions (A)

6801 Jericho Turnpike, Syosset NY 11791-4413
County: Nassau FICE Identification: 025994
Unit ID: 418126
Telephone: (516) 364-0808 Carnegie Class: Spec/Health
FAX Number: (516) 364-6645 Calendar System: Trimester
URL: www.nycollege.edu
Established: 1981 Annual Undergrad Tuition & Fees: $11,880
Enrollment: 722 Coed
Affiliation or Control: Independent Non-Profit IRS Status: 501(c)3
Highest Offering: Master's
Program: Professional; Technical Emphasis
Accreditation: NY, ACUP

01 President ... Ms. Lisa PAMINTUAN
04 Executive Assistant to President ... Mr. Alex BRESALIER
26 Sr VP Mktg/Comm/Business Oper ... Ms. Barbara CARVER
07 Acting Dean of Admissions ... Ms. Barbara CARVER
05 Vice Pres Professional Programs ... Mr. Hugh MAYBRAY
10 Chief Financial Officer ... Mr. Errol VIRASAWMI
63 Dean Grad Sch Oriental Medicine ... Dr. A. Li SONG
88 Dean Sch of Massage Therapy ... Mr. Hugh MAYBRAY
06 Registrar ... Mr. Daniella BROWN
07 Senior Admissions Counselor ... Ms. Mary RODAS
84 Acting Director Enrollmnt Services ... Mr. Chester BARKAN
08 Dir Library/Information Services ... Ms. Erin CLARK
21 Bursar ... Ms. Jacqueline MCINTYRE
13 Manager Information Technology ... Mr. Joe FOX
36 Director Career Services ... Ms. Erin CLARK
32 Manager Student Services ... Ms. daniella BROWN
09 Institutional Research Analyst ... Ms. Rajbir KAUR
20 Chief Academic Officer ... Mr. King CHEEK

New York College of Podiatric Medicine (B)

53 E 124th Street, New York NY 10035-1815
County: New York FICE Identification: 002749
Unit ID: 194073
Telephone: (212) 410-8000 Carnegie Class: Spec/Health
FAX Number: (212) 876-7670 Calendar System: Semester
URL: www.nycpm.edu
Established: 1911 Annual Undergrad Tuition & Fees: $27,530
Enrollment: 386 Coed
Affiliation or Control: Independent Non-Profit IRS Status: 501(c)3
Highest Offering: First Professional Degree
Program: Professional
Accreditation: POD

01 President ... Mr. Louis L. LEVINE
05 Dean/Chief Academic Officer ... Dr. Michael J. TREPAL
11 Chief Operating Officer ... Mr. Joel STURM
10 Chief Financial Officer ... Mr. Greg ONAIFO
13 Vice Pres Info Systems & Technology ... Mr. William GRAHAM
32 Dean Student Affairs ... Dr. Laurence LOWY
63 Dean Medical Education/Medical Dir ... Dr. Mark SWARTZ
81 Dean Basic Sciences ... Dr. Eileen CHUSID
51 Dean Post-Doctorate Education ... Dr. Robert ECKLES
20 Dean Clinical Educ/Dir Res Pgms ... Dr. Robert ECKLES
09 Dean Institutional Research ... Dr. Eileen CHUSID
07 Assoc Dean Admissions/Student Svcs ... Ms. Lisa LEE
30 Director Institutional Advancement ... Mr. Stanley KORNHAUSER
26 Director Public Affairs/Development ... Mr. Roger GREENE
15 Dir Human Resources/Risk Management ... Mr. Joel STURM
08 Director of Library ... Mr. Thomas WALKER
18 Director Safety ... Mr. James WARREN
37 Director Financial Aid ... Ms. Eve TRAUBE
06 Registrar ... Ms. Vernese PANNELL

New York College of Traditional Chinese Medicine (C)

155 First Street, Mineola NY 11501-4005
County: Nassau FICE Identification: 034433
Unit ID: 439783
Telephone: (516) 739-1545 Carnegie Class: Spec/Health
FAX Number: (516) 873-9622 Calendar System: Trimester
URL: www.nyctcm.edu
Established: 1996 Annual Undergrad Tuition & Fees: $15,315
Enrollment: 142 Coed
Affiliation or Control: Independent Non-Profit IRS Status: 501(c)3
Highest Offering: Master's
Program: Professional
Accreditation: ACUP

01 President ... Mr. Yemeng CHEN
11 Administrative Dean ... Dr. James S. BARE
05 Academic Dean ... Dr. Sunny SHEN
07 Admissions Manager ... Ms. Gail AURICCHIO

New York Institute of Technology (D)

Northern Boulevard, Old Westbury NY 11568-8000
County: Nassau FICE Identification: 004804
Unit ID: 194091
Telephone: (516) 686-7516 Carnegie Class: Master's L
FAX Number: (516) 686-7613 Calendar System: Semester
URL: www.nyit.edu
Established: 1955 Annual Undergrad Tuition & Fees: $26,430
Enrollment: 8,607 Coed
Affiliation or Control: Independent Non-Profit IRS Status: 501(c)3
Highest Offering: Doctorate
Program: Liberal Arts And General; Teacher Preparatory; Professional
Accreditation: M, ARCPA, CIDA, ENG, ENGT, NURSE, OSTEO, OT, PTA, TED

01 President ... Dr. Edward GUILIANO
05 Provost/Vice Pres Academic Affairs ... Dr. Rahmat SHOURESHI
100 Chief of Staff ... Mr. Peter KINNEY
30 Vice President for Development ... Mr. John ELIZANDRO
17 Vice Pres Health Sci & Medical Affs ... Dr. Barbara ROSS-LEE
32 VP Stdnt Affs/Chief Stdnt Affs Ofcr ... Mr. Joseph FORD
11 Vice Pres of IT & Infrastructure ... Dr. Niyazi BODUR
45 Vice Pres for Planning/Assessment ... Dr. Harriet ARNONE
84 Vice President Enrollment Services ... Dr. Jacquelyn NEALON
10 CFO & Treasurer ... Mr. Leonard AUBREY
21 Comptroller ... Mr. Daniel MCGOVERN
43 General Counsel ... Ms. Catherine FLICKINGER
06 Registrar ... Mr. Guy HILDEBRANDT
76 Dean School of Health Professions ... Dr. Patricia CHUTE
48 Dean Sch Architecture & Design ... Ms. Judith DIMAIO
53 Dean School of Education ... Dr. Michael UTTENDORFER
54 Dean School of Engr & Comp Sciences ... Dr. Nada ANID
49 Dean School Arts & Sciences ... Dr. Roger YU
50 Dean School of Management ... Dr. Jess BORONICO
63 Dean NY Col of Osteopathic Medicine ... Dr. Thomas SCANDALIS
75 Dean Voc Independence Program ... Dr. Ernst VAN BERGEIJK
09 Director Inst Research & Assessment ... Dr. Carol DEVICTORIA
07 Associate Dean of Admissions ... Vacant
88 Director Branch Services ... Dr. Gerri FLANZRAICH
27 Director Publications & Advertising ... Ms. Susan WARNER
29 Director of Alumni Relations ... Mr. Joe FORTINE
18 Director of Facilities Operations ... Mr. William MARCHAND
37 Associate Dean of Financial Aid ... Ms. Rosemary FERRUCCI
37 Director of Financial Aid ... Ms. Doreen MEYER
19 Director Security ... Mr. Denis MCGUCKIN
41 Director Athletics & Recreation ... Mr. Clyde DOUGHTY, JR.
25 Asst Provost Spnsrd Pgms & Research ... Dr. Allison ANDORS
13 Director Plng & Business Affairs ... Ms. Ajisa DERVISEVIC
96 Director Purchasing ... Mr. David UDKOW
88 Director of Internal Audit ... Ms. Jessica JONES-NAGLE
38 Director Counseling & Wellness Svcs ... Ms. Alice HERON-BURKE
88 Dir Advising & Enrichment Pgms ... Ms. Monika SCHUEREN
15 Director of Human Resources ... Ms. Carol JABLONSKY
90 Director Client Services ... Ms. Laurie HARVEY
91 Director Systems & Network ... Mr. Brian MAROLDO
91 Director Enterprise Systems & Svcs ... Ms. Chuqian ZHANG
35 Associate Dean for Campus Life ... Ms. Marcia SINGER
35 Assoc Dean Student Development ... Ms. Zennabelle SEWELL
40 Bookstore Manager ... Ms. Jayne MO
88 Dir Events Planning & Hospitality ... Mr. Jerry LIMONCELLI
26 Director of Media/Public Relations ... Mr. Dave MARCUS

New York Law School (E)

185 West Broadway, New York NY 10013-2959
County: New York FICE Identification: 002783
Unit ID: 193821
Telephone: (212) 431-2100 Carnegie Class: Spec/Law
FAX Number: (212) 965-8838 Calendar System: Semester
URL: www.nyls.edu
Established: 1891 Annual Graduate Tuition & Fees: $46,640
Enrollment: 1,923 Coed
Affiliation or Control: Independent Non-Profit IRS Status: 501(c)3
Highest Offering: Doctorate; No Undergraduates
Program: Professional
Accreditation: LAW

01 Dean ... Dean Matasar A. RICHARD
26 Vice Pres Communications/Mrktng ... Ms. Nancy J. GUIDA
88 Vice President Academic Publishing ... Prof. Jethro K. LIEBERMAN
30 Assc Dean/Vice Pres Devel/Alum Rels ... Dean Suzanne DAVIDSON
29 Assistant Vice Pres Alumni Rels ... Ms. Tara REGIST-TOMLINSON
10 Asst Vice Pres Business Operations ... Ms. Catherine MACLEOD
21 Asst VP Financial Planning & Mgmt ... Ms. Susan REDLER
15 Assistant Vice Pres Human Resources ... Mr. Kevin HAUSS
19 Assist Vice Pres Security & Safety ... Mr. George HAYES
44 Assistant Vice Pres Development ... Mr. Seth ROSEN
09 Asst VP Institutional Research ... Dr. Joanne INGHAM
05 Assoc Dean for Academic Affairs ... Dean Carol BUCKLER
21 Assoc Dean for Finance & Admin ... Dean Fred DEJOHN
45 Assoc Dean for Special Projects ... Dean Joan R. FISHMAN
45 Assoc Dean for Special Projects ... Dean Harry ALTHAUS
07 Asst Dean Admissions/Financial Aid ... Dean Perez WILLIAM
32 Assoc Dean Professional Devel ... Dean Marianna HOGAN
36 Asst Dean for Career Planning ... Dean Meg REUTER
08 Director of Law Library ... Prof. Camille BROUSSARD
20 Assistant Dean Academic Affairs ... Ms. Victoria EASTUS
20 Assoc Director Academic Affairs ... Ms. Haley MEADE
20 Assoc Director Academic Affairs ... Ms. Danielle FRIEDMAN
37 Sr Dir Admissions/Financial Aid ... Ms. Susan GROSS
18 Chief of Maintenance/Operations ... Mr. Donald BLANCHARD
06 Assistant Dean and Registrar ... Mr. Oral HOPE
35 Sr Director of Student Life ... Ms. Sally HARDING
88 Assistant Dean for Students ... Ms. Helena PRIGAL
20 Assistant Dean for Curriculum ... Vacant
38 Director Student Counseling ... Ms. Sally HARDING
84 Director Enrollment Management ... Ms. Susan GROSS
96 Purchasing Coordinator ... Mr. Norman DAWKINS

New York Medical College (F)

Valhalla NY 10595-1690
County: Westchester FICE Identification: 002784
Unit ID: 193830
Telephone: (914) 594-4000 Carnegie Class: Spec/Med
FAX Number: (914) 594-4541 Calendar System: Other
URL: www.nymc.edu
Established: 1860 Annual Graduate Tuition & Fees: $46,496
Enrollment: 1,475 Coed
Affiliation or Control: Independent Non-Profit IRS Status: 501(c)3
Highest Offering: Doctorate; No Undergraduates
Program: Professional
Accreditation: M, DENT, MED, PH, PTA, SP

01 President ... Dr. Alan KADISH
01 Chief Executive Officer ... Dr. Karl P. ADLER
05 Provost of Univ/Dean Medical School ... Dr. Ralph A. O'CONNELL
10 Sr VP/CFO/Vice Prov Admin & Finance ... Mr. Stephen PICCOLO, JR.
58 Dean Grad Sch Basic Medical Science ... Dr. Francis L. BELLONI
43 Vice President/General Counsel ... Mr. Waldemar A. COMAS
30 Vice President Univ Dev/Alumni Rels ... Ms. Julie KUBASKA
86 Vice President Government Affairs ... Dr. Robert W. AMLER
15 Assoc Vice Pres Human Resources ... Mr. Peter M. BROWN
21 Assoc Vice Pres/Controller ... Mr. George NESTLER
43 Assoc Vice Pres Legal Affairs ... Ms. Dana LEE
26 Assoc Vice Pres Communications ... Ms. Donna E. MORIARTY
11 Vice Prov/Sr Assoc Dean Acad Admin ... Mr. William A. STEADMAN, II
88 Chief Affiliation Officer ... Mr. Howard NELSON
27 Chief Information Officer ... Dr. Sandra SHIVERS
76 Dean Sch Health Sciences & Practice ... Dr. Robert W. AMLER
63 Vice Dean Grad Med Ed/Affiliations ... Dr. Richard G. MCCARRICK
63 Vice Dean Medical Education ... Dr. Paul M. WALLACH
09 Assoc Dean Research Administration ... Ms. Catharine CREA
32 Sr Assoc Dean Student Affairs ... Dr. Gladys M. AYALA
37 Asc Dn Stdnt Affs/Dir Finan Plng ... Mr. Anthony M. SOZZO
88 Sr Assoc Dean Pre-Internship Pgm ... Dr. Saverio S. BENTIVEGNA
07 Sr Associate Dean Admissions ... Dr. Fern R. JUSTER
51 Assoc Dean Continuing Med Education ... Dr. Joseph F. DURSI
08 Assoc Dean/Dir Health Sci Library ... Ms. Diana J. CUNNINGHAM
07 Director of Admissions ... Ms. Robin BAUM
06 University Registrar/Assoc Provost ... Ms. Judith A. EHREN
39 Director Student Housing ... Ms. Amy SCHACK
18 Director Facilities Management ... Mr. Michael J. SHALLO
19 Director of Security ... Mr. William ALLISON
85 Intl Student/Scholar Advisor ... Ms. Elizabeth WARD
51 Director of Continuing Medical Educ ... Ms. Kathy J. KAVANAGH
04 Asst to Pres & Board of Trustees ... Ms. Patricia J. TRAVIS
23 Director Health Services ... Dr. Joseph F. DURSI
38 Director Student Counseling ... Dr. Mark SINGER
105 Director Web Services ... Mr. Kevin R. CUMMINGS
40 Director Bookstore ... Ms. Liz REYNOLDS
24 Head Educational Media ... Mr. Michael COTTER
14 Coord of Instruct Computing Tech ... Mr. Jason DI NARDI
96 Purchasing Manager ... Mr. John STEIN

New York School of Interior Design (G)

170 E 70th Street, New York NY 10021-5110
County: New York FICE Identification: 020690
Unit ID: 194116

Telephone: (212) 472-1500 Carnegie Class: Spec/Arts
FAX Number: (212) 472-3800 Calendar System: 4/1/4
URL: www.nysid.edu
Established: 1916 Annual Undergrad Tuition & Fees: $23,500
Enrollment: 818 Coed
Affiliation or Control: Independent Non-Profit IRS Status: 501(c)3
Highest Offering: Master's
Program: Professional
Accreditation: ®M, ART, CIDA

01 President ... Dr. Christopher J. CYPHERS
05 Dean ... Dr. Ellen FISHER
10 VP for Finance & Administration ... Ms. Jane CHEN
84 Vice Pres for Enrollment Management ... Mr. David SPROULS
04 Assistant to the President ... Ms. Jeanne KO
36 Academic Advisor/Dir Career Place ... Ms. Patricia ZIEGLER
06 Registrar ... Ms. Susan LOVELL
08 Director of the Library ... Ms. Sarah FALLS
07 Director of Admissions ... Mr. David SPROULS
37 Financial Aid Administrator ... Ms. Rashmi WADHVANI
15 Director of Personnel Services ... Ms. Balbina CALO
18 Chief Facilities/Physical Plant ... Mr. Zeke KOLENOVIC
26 Chief Public Relations Officer ... Mr. Brent PETERSON
30 Chief Development/Dir Alumni Rels ... Ms. Monica CHESLAK
20 Associate Academic Officer ... Ms. Veronica WHITLOCK
29 Director Alumni Relations ... Vacant
32 Chief Student Life Officer ... Mr. Douglas DAVEE
13 Dir Computing/Information Mgmt ... Mr. Tomasz SOWINSKI
90 Director Academic Computing ... Mr. Richard T. CLASS
40 Director Bookstore ... Mr. Daniel TERCHEK
38 Director Student Counseling ... Dr. Penny MORGANSTEIN

New York Theological Seminary (A)

475 Riverside Drive, Suite 500, New York NY 10115-0083
County: New York FICE Identification: 002674
Unit ID: 193894
Telephone: (212) 870-1211 Carnegie Class: Not Classified
FAX Number: (212) 870-1236 Calendar System: Semester
URL: www.nyts.edu
Established: 1900 Annual Graduate Tuition & Fees: $12,400
Enrollment: 323 Coed
Affiliation or Control: Independent Non-Profit IRS Status: 501(c)3
Highest Offering: Doctorate; No Undergraduates
Program: Professional
Accreditation: THEOL

01 President ... Dr. Dale T. IRVIN
30 VP Development/Institutional Advanc ... Vacant
05 Academic Dean ... Dr. Eleanor MOODY-SHEPHERD
08 Librarian ... Mr. Jerry REISIG
06 Registrar ... Ms. Lydia R. BUMGARDNER
37 Director Financial Aid ... Ms. Tamisia WHITE

New York University (B)

70 Washington Square S, New York NY 10012-1092
County: New York FICE Identification: 002785
Unit ID: 193900
Telephone: (212) 998-1212 Carnegie Class: RU/VH
FAX Number: N/A Calendar System: Semester
URL: www.nyu.edu
Established: 1831 Annual Undergrad Tuition & Fees: $41,606
Enrollment: 43,797 Coed
Affiliation or Control: Independent Non-Profit IRS Status: 501(c)3
Highest Offering: Doctorate
Program: Occupational; 2-Year Principally Bachelor's Creditable; Liberal Arts And General; Teacher Preparatory; Professional
Accreditation: M, BUS, COPSY, DENT, DH, DIETD, DIETI, DMS, HSA, IPSY, JOUR, LAW, MED, MIDWF, NURSE, OT, PH, PLNG, PTA, SCPSY, SP, SPAA, SURGT, SW, TEAC

01 President ... Dr. John SEXTON
05 Provost ... Dr. David MCLAUGHLIN
03 Executive VP ... Dr. Michael ALFANO
17 Executive VP for Health ... Dr. Robert BERNE
100 Chief of Staff/Deputy to President ... Ms. Diane YU
43 Sr VP General Counsel & Secretary ... Ms. Bonnie BRIER
26 Sr VP for Univ Rels/Pub Affairs ... Dr. Lynne BROWN
10 Sr VP for Finance & Budget ... Dr. Martin DORPH
20 Sr Vice Provost Academic Policies ... Dr. Pierre HOHENBERG
46 Sr Vice Provost for Research ... Dr. Paul HORN
30 Sr VP Development/Alumni Relations ... Ms. Debra LAMORTE
18 Sr VP for Operations ... Ms. Alison LEARY
32 Sr Vice Provost Ugrad Ed/Univ Life ... Dr. Linda MILLS
20 Provost Polytech Inst at NYU ... Dr. Dianne REKOW
18 VP Construction Management ... Mr. David ALONSO
26 VP for Public Affairs ... Mr. John BECKMAN
45 VP Public Resource Admin & Devel ... Dr. Richard BING
15 VP for Human Resources ... Ms. Catherine CASEY
84 VP Enrollment Management ... Dr. Randall DEIKE
13 VP for Global Technology ... Mr. Thomas DELANEY
11 VP for Admin/Chief of Staff ... Mr. A. Steven DONOFRIO
86 VP Gov Affairs/Community Engagement ... Dr. Alicia HURLEY
21 VP Budget & Planning ... Mr. Anthony JIGA
40 VP for Auxiliary Services ... Dr. Robert KIVETZ
21 VP Finance Operations ... Ms. Rosemarie LOFFREDO
19 VP Global Security & Crisis Mgmt ... Mr. Jules MARTIN
13 VP IT and CITO for NYU NY Campus ... Ms. Marilyn MCMILLAN
06 University Registrar ... Dr. Roger PRINTUP
21 Acting Chief Investment Officer ... Ms. Tina SURH
35 VP for Student Affairs ... Dr. Marc WAIS
26 Assoc VP for Marketing Comm ... Ms. Deborah BRODERICK
21 Assoc VP for Finance ... Ms. Catherine DELONG
88 Assoc Vice Provost Rsrch Compliance ... Dr. Martha DUNNE
96 Assoc VP Administrative Services ... Mr. Stephen HELLER
88 Assoc VP Planning and Design ... Ms. Lori MAZOR
20 Assoc Vice Provost Acad Initiatives ... Dr. Nancy MORRISON
20 Assoc Provost Academic Operations ... Dr. Carol KLAPERMAN MORROW
88 Assoc VP Real Estate Services ... Mr. David SOLES
07 Asst VP for Undergrad Admissions ... Mr. Shawn ABBOTT
20 Asst Provost Academic Pgm Review ... Mr. Barnett HAMBERGER
28 Asst VP Diversity/Stdnt Comm Devel ... Mr. Allen MCFARLANE
21 Asst Treasurer/Bursar ... Mr. James SORANNO
21 Asst VP/Controller ... Ms. Kerri TRICARICO
41 Dir Athletics/Recreation/Intr Sport ... Mr. Christopher BLEDSOE
23 Deputy Exec Dir & Medical Dir ... Dr. Carlo CIOTOLI
09 Dir Institutional Research ... Mr. Fredric COHEN
37 Dir Financial Aid ... Ms. Lynn HIGINBOTHAM
102 Dir Office of Sponsored Programs ... Mr. Richard LOUTH
88 Dir Internal Audit ... Mr. Eugene PAWLOWSKI
22 Exec Dir Ofc of Equal Opportunity ... Ms. Mary SIGNOR
36 Exec Dir Career Services ... Ms. Trudy STEINFELD

Niagara County Community College (C)

3111 Saunders Settlement Road, Sanborn NY 14132-9460
County: Niagara FICE Identification: 002874
Unit ID: 193946
Telephone: (716) 614-6200 Carnegie Class: Assoc/Pub-S-SC
FAX Number: (716) 614-6700 Calendar System: Semester
URL: www.niagaracc.suny.edu
Established: 1962 Annual Undergrad Tuition & Fees (In-District): $3,958
Enrollment: 7,435 Coed
Affiliation or Control: State/Local IRS Status: 501(c)3
Highest Offering: Associate Degree
Program: Occupational; 2-Year Principally Bachelor's Creditable
Accreditation: M, ADNUR, MAC, PTAA, RAD, SURGT

01 President ... Dr. James KLYCZEK
05 Vice President Academic Affairs ... Dr. Gregory LAMONTAGNE
103 VP Workforce Development ... Mr. Randy BOWEN
10 Vice President of Finance/Info Tech ... Mr. William SCHICKLING
32 Vice President of Student Services ... Dr. Bassam DEEB
11 Vice President of Operations ... Mr. Dennis DRAGICH
09 Director Planning and Research ... Dr. Mary Jane FELDMAN
20 Associate Dean ... Vacant
15 Interim Director of Human Resources ... Mr. Donald ARMSTRONG
07 Director of Admissions ... Ms. Kathy SAUNDERS
21 Director of Business Services ... Ms. Theresa DIGREGORIO
04 Assistant to President ... Ms. Nancy DEDARIO
06 Registrar ... Ms. Julie SPEER
35 Director of Student Development ... Mrs. Allison ARMUSEWICZ
30 Chief Development Officer ... Ms. Deborah BREWER
37 Director of Financial Aid ... Mr. James TRIMBOLI
26 Interim Director Public Relations ... Mr. Robert KOSHINSKI
18 Assistant Director of Facilities ... Mr. James LOBDELL
28 Director of Diversity ... Ms. Beverly DAVID-LEWIS

Niagara University (D)

Niagara University NY 14109-9999
County: Niagara FICE Identification: 002788
Unit ID: 193973
Telephone: (716) 285-1212 Carnegie Class: Master's L
FAX Number: (716) 286-8710 Calendar System: Semester
URL: www.niagara.edu
Established: 1856 Annual Undergrad Tuition & Fees: $26,400
Enrollment: 4,273 Coed
Affiliation or Control: Independent Non-Profit IRS Status: 501(c)3
Highest Offering: Doctorate
Program: Liberal Arts And General; Teacher Preparatory; Professional
Accreditation: M, BUS, NURSE, SW, TED

01 President ... Rev. Joseph LEVESQUE, CM
03 Exec Vice President ... Dr. Bonnie ROSE
05 Vice President for Academic Affairs ... Dr. Timothy M. DOWNS
32 Vice President for Student Life ... Dr. Kevin HEARN
10 Vice Pres Business Aff & Treasurer ... Mr. Michael S. JASZKA
30 Vice Pres Institutional Advancement ... Mr. Donald P. BIELECKI
20 Asc VP Academic Affs/Pgms & Policy ... Dr. Marilynn P. FLECKENSTEIN
20 Assoc VP Acad Affs/Ops/Outreach ... Ms. Mary E. BORGOGNONI
44 Assoc VP for Institutional Advance ... Mr. J Patrick HULSMAN
45 Asst to the President for Planning ... Dr. Judith A. WILLARD
43 General Counsel ... Ms. Stephanie A. COLE
06 Registrar/Dean of Enrollment Mgmt ... Mr. Michael J. KONOPSKI
09 Director Institutional Research ... Ms. Catherine E. SERIANNI
07 Director of Admissions ... Mr. Harry GONG
08 Director of Libraries ... Mr. David SCHOEN
19 Director of Campus Safety ... Mr. John F. BARKER
35 Dean of Student Affairs ... Vacant
37 Director Student Financial Aid ... Ms. Maureen SALFI
39 Director of Residence Life ... Ms. Kimberly J. ZUKOWSKI
26 Director of Comm/Public Relations ... Mr. Thomas BURNS
29 Director of Alumni Association ... Mr. Arthur V. CARDELLA
13 Director Information Technology ... Mr. Richard P. KERNIN
49 Dean College of Arts & Science ... Dr. Nancy E. MCGLEN
53 Dean College of Education ... Dr. Debra A. COLLEY
50 Interim Dean College Business Admin ... Dr. Tenpao LEE
88 Dean Col Hospitality/Tourism Mgmt ... Dr. Gary D. PRAETZEL
57 Director of Art Museum ... Ms. Kate KOPERSKI
15 Director of Human Resources ... Mr. Robert PFEIL
23 Supervisor of Health Services ... Ms. Lori SOOS
41 Athletic Director ... Mr. Ed MCLAUGHLIN
18 Director of Facility Services ... Mr. Daniel M. GUARIGLIA
44 Director Annual Fund ... Ms. Christine S. O'HARA
42 Assoc VP of Campus Ministry ... Rev. Kevin KREAGH, CM
88 Director Academic Support Services ... Mrs. Patricia KINNER
51 Dir Continuing/Community Education ... Mr. Jon Jay STOCKSLADER
38 Director Counseling Services ... Monica ROMEO
21 Controller ... Mr. Donald E. SMITH
96 Director of Business Services ... Ms. Christy FERGUSON
88 Assoc Dean for Graduate Recruitment ... Mr. Carlos TEJADA
88 Assoc Dean for Transfer Recruitment ... Mr. Mark WOJNOWSKI
36 Director Career/Academic & Service ... Ms. Antonia KNIGHT
88 Director of Instructional Support ... Ms. Jennifer HERMAN
85 Dir Multicultural & Intl Stdnt Affs ... Mr. David BLACKBURN
06 Director of Records & Operations ... Ms. Lenora ANDREWS
88 Director of Student Accounts ... Ms. Martie HOWELL
25 Dir of Sponsored Programs & Rsrch ... Ms. Adrienne LEIBOWITZ
102 Dir Corporate & Foundations ... Ms. Denise Z. RIVERS

North Country Community College (E)

23 Santanoni Avenue, PO Box 89,
Saranac Lake NY 12983-0089
County: Essex FICE Identification: 007111
Unit ID: 194028
Telephone: (518) 891-2915 Carnegie Class: Assoc/Pub-R-S
FAX Number: (518) 891-2915 Calendar System: Semester
URL: www.nccc.edu
Established: 1967 Annual Undergrad Tuition & Fees (In-District): $4,565
Enrollment: 2,252 Coed
Affiliation or Control: State/Local IRS Status: 501(c)3
Highest Offering: Associate Degree
Program: Occupational; 2-Year Principally Bachelor's Creditable
Accreditation: M, RAD

01 President ... Ms. Carol BROWN
05 Vice Pres of Academic Affairs ... Dr. Carole RICHARDSON
10 Vice Pres for Fiscal Operations/CFO ... Mr. William CHAPIN
84 VP Enroll/Stdnt Svcs/Asst to Pres ... Mr. Edwin TRATHEN
06 Registrar/Records Officer ... Ms. Sandra BAKER
09 Asst Dean Inst Rsrch/Spprt ... Mr. Scott HARWOOD
18 Asst Dean Facilities/Spec Projects ... Mr. Shane CHATELLE
07 Dir Admiss/Alumni Rels/Chf PR Ofcr ... Mr. Edwin TRATHEN
35 Director of Campus & Student Life ... Mrs. Roberta KARP
28 Asst Dir Campus & Student Diversity ... Ms. Ashley ANDREWS

Northeastern Seminary (F)

2265 Westside Drive, Rochester NY 14624-1932
County: Monroe FICE Identification: 034194
Unit ID: 439817
Telephone: (585) 594-6800 Carnegie Class: Spec/Faith
FAX Number: (585) 594-6801 Calendar System: Semester
URL: www.nes.edu
Established: 1998 Annual Graduate Tuition & Fees: $7,910
Enrollment: 136 Coed
Affiliation or Control: Independent Non-Profit IRS Status: 501(c)3
Highest Offering: Doctorate; No Undergraduates
Program: Professional
Accreditation: M, NY, THEOL

01 President ... Dr. John A. MARTIN
05 Academic Vice President and Dean ... Dr. Douglas CULLUM

† The Seminary is affiliated with Roberts Wesleyan College.

Nyack College (G)

1 South Boulevard, Nyack NY 10960-3698
County: Rockland FICE Identification: 002790
Unit ID: 194161
Telephone: (845) 675-4400 Carnegie Class: Master's L
FAX Number: (845) 358-1751 Calendar System: Semester
URL: www.nyack.edu
Established: 1882 Annual Undergrad Tuition & Fees: $20,500
Enrollment: 3,305 Coed
Affiliation or Control: The Christian And Missionary Alliance
IRS Status: 501(c)3
Highest Offering: Doctorate
Program: 2-Year Principally Bachelor's Creditable; Liberal Arts And General; Teacher Preparatory; Professional
Accreditation: M, MUS, SW, TED, THEOL

01 President ... Dr. Michael G. SCALES
04 Assistant to the President ... Mrs. Carol Ann FREEMAN
05 Provost/VP for Academic Affairs ... Dr. David F. TURK
10 Exec Vice President & Treasurer ... Mr. David C. JENNINGS
84 Vice President for Enrollment ... Dr. Andrea HENNESSY
30 Vice President of Advancement ... Mr. Jeff CORY
20 Assistant Provost ... Dr. Bennett SCHEPENS
73 Dean Seminary ... Dr. Ronald WALBORN
50 Dean School of Business & Ldrshp ... Dr. Anita UNDERWOOD
64 Dean School of Music ... Dr. Glenn KOPONEN
53 Dean School of Education ... Dr. JoAnn LOONEY
49 Assoc Dean College of Arts & Sci ... Dr. Fernando ARZOLA
04 Asst to Pres/Dean of NCDC ... Dr. Richard GATHRO
08 Dean of Library Services ... Mrs. Linda K. POSTON
89 Assoc Dean Student Success ... Dr. Gwen PARKER AMES

73 Assoc Dean Seminary (NYC) .... Dr. Luis CARLO
73 Asst Dean Seminary (Puerto Rico) .... Dr. Julio APONTE
32 Dean of Students .... Mrs. Wanda VELEZ
06 Undergraduate Registrar .... Ms. Evangeline COUCHEY
06 Graduate Registrar .... Ms. Rebecca NOSS
07 Dir of Admissions Undergrad .... Mr. Dinesh MAHTANI
07 Dir of Admissions Undergrad (NYC) .... Mrs. Leslie ROSADO
07 Dir of Admissions Seminary .... Mrs. Traci PIESCKI
21 Assistant Treasurer .... Mrs. Dona P. SCHEPENS
37 Dir of Fin Svcs Undergrad .... Mr. Steve PHILLIPS
37 Dir of Fin Svcs Undergrad (NYC) .... Mr. Isaac FOSTER
31 Executive Director of Community Rel .... Mr. Earl MILLER
41 Director of Athletics .... Mr. Keith A. DAVIE
36 Director of Career Services .... Ms. Tiffany AUSTIN
15 Director of Human Resources .... Mrs. Karen DAVIE
13 Director of Information Technology .... Mr. Kevin A. BUEL
09 Director of Institutional Research .... Mr. Greg BEEMAN
18 Director of Operations/Aramark .... Mr. Douglas WALKER
26 Director of Pub & Media Relations .... Ms. Deborah WALKER
42 Director of Spiritual Formation .... Mrs. Wanda F. WALBORN
38 Director of Wellness Services .... Mrs. Drusila F. NIEVES
29 Coordinator of Alumni Services .... Mrs. Melissa HICKEY
105 Webmaster .... Mr. Joshua WAY

Ohr Hameir Theological Seminary (A)

141 Furnace Woods Road,
Cortlandt Manor NY 10567-6112

County: Westchester — FICE Identification: 011984
Unit ID: 194189
Telephone: (914) 736-1500 — Carnegie Class: Spec/Faith
FAX Number: (914) 736-1055 — Calendar System: Semester
Established: 1962 — Annual Undergrad Tuition & Fees: $8,100
Enrollment: 127 — Male
Affiliation or Control: Independent Non-Profit — IRS Status: 501(c)3
Highest Offering: Second Talmudic Degree
Program: Teacher Preparatory; Professional
Accreditation: RABN

01 President .... Rabbi E. KANAREK
30 Chief Devel Ofcr/Dir Financial Aid .... Mr. Naftoly KEMPLER
06 Registrar .... Rabbi Berel KANAREK

Ohr Somayach Tanenbaum Educational Center (B)

244 Route 306, Monsey NY 10952-0334

County: Rockland — FICE Identification: 023201
Unit ID: 243805
Telephone: (845) 425-1370 — Carnegie Class: Not Classified
FAX Number: (845) 425-8865 — Calendar System: Trimester
URL: www.os.edu
Established: 1979 — Annual Undergrad Tuition & Fees: $7,000
Enrollment: 70 — Coordinate
Affiliation or Control: Independent Non-Profit — IRS Status: 501(c)3
Highest Offering: First Professional Degree
Program: Professional
Accreditation: RABN

01 Director .... Rabbi Abraham BRAUN
05 Dean .... Rabbi Israel ROKOWSKY
06 Registrar .... Mrs. Miriam GROSSMAN
10 Chief Business Officer .... Rabbi Naftali REICH

Olean Business Institute (C)

301 N Union Street, Olean NY 14760-2691

County: Cattaraugus — FICE Identification: 009003
Unit ID: 194204
Telephone: (716) 372-7978 — Carnegie Class: Assoc/PrivFP
FAX Number: (716) 372-2120 — Calendar System: Semester
URL: www.obi.edu
Established: 1961 — Annual Undergrad Tuition & Fees: $11,600
Enrollment: 86 — Coed
Affiliation or Control: Proprietary — IRS Status: Proprietary
Highest Offering: Associate Degree
Program: Occupational; 2-Year Principally Bachelor's Creditable; Business Emphasis
Accreditation: ACICS

01 President/Academic Dean .... Mrs. Jennifer L. MADISON
37 Director of Financial Aid .... Mrs. Valerie A. GOODWIN
07 Director of Admissions & Placement .... Mr. Carl J. ENGLISH
08 Librarian .... Ms. Charlotte STOUGHTON
10 Business Manager .... Mrs. Debra J. RALSTON

Onondaga Community College (D)

4585 West Seneca Turnpike, Syracuse NY 13215-4585

County: Onondaga — FICE Identification: 002875
Unit ID: 194222
Telephone: (315) 498-2622 — Carnegie Class: Assoc/Pub-U-MC
FAX Number: (315) 492-9208 — Calendar System: Semester
URL: www.sunyocc.edu
Established: 1962 — Annual Undergrad Tuition & Fees (In-District): $4,544
Enrollment: 11,783 — Coed
Affiliation or Control: State/Local — IRS Status: 501(c)3
Highest Offering: Associate Degree
Program: Occupational; 2-Year Principally Bachelor's Creditable
Accreditation: M, ADNUR, ENGT, PTAA, SURGT

01 President .... Dr. Debbie L. SYDOW
05 Provost and Senior Vice President .... Dr. Cathleen C. MCCOLGIN
10 Sr VP Administration & Finance .... Mr. William EMM
30 Vice Pres Institutional Advancement .... Mr. Thomas BURTON
26 VP HR & External Affairs .... Ms. Amy KREMENEK
09 Chief Inst Plng/Assess/Resrch Ofcr .... Dr. Agatha AWUAH
14 Chief Information Officer .... Ms. Andrea VENUTI
20 Int VP Instructional Services .... Dr. Emmanuel AWUAH
84 VP Enrollment Mgmt & Student Dev .... Dr. Kristine DUFFY
28 Vice Pres Diversity Services .... Ms. Eunice WILLIAMS
18 VP Facilities Management .... Mr. John PADDOCK
37 Acting Director of Student Finance .... Ms. Kate BELLEFEUILLE
41 Interim Athletic Director .... Mr. David PASIAK
88 Director Student Svcs Initiatives .... Ms. Nancy J. HAZZARD
08 Chair Library .... Ms. Pauline SHOSTACK
38 Chair Counseling Department .... Ms. Janet HAMLY
19 VP Campus Safety & Security .... Mr. Douglas KINNEY
88 Disability Services Specialist .... Ms. Nancy CARR
06 Dir Student Certification/Records .... Ms. Tracey GREEN
21 Bursar .... Ms. Shawn GILLEN-CARYL
29 Alumni Coordinator .... Ms. Anita MURPHY
36 Director Student Life & Development .... Ms. Lysa SIMMONS
96 Director Management Services .... Mr. Michael MCMULLEN
39 Residence Life Director .... Ms. Cathy DOTTERER
35 Director of Student Activities .... Mr. Monty FLYNN
07 Director of Admissions .... Ms. Katherine PERRY

Orange County Community College (E)

115 South Street, Middletown NY 10940-6437

County: Orange — FICE Identification: 002876
Unit ID: 194240
Telephone: (845) 344-6222 — Carnegie Class: Assoc/Pub-R-L
FAX Number: (845) 343-1228 — Calendar System: Semester
URL: www.sunyorange.edu
Established: 1950 — Annual Undergrad Tuition & Fees (In-District): $3,900
Enrollment: 7,223 — Coed
Affiliation or Control: State/Local — IRS Status: 501(c)3
Highest Offering: Associate Degree
Program: Occupational; 2-Year Principally Bachelor's Creditable
Accreditation: M, ACBSP, ADNUR, DH, MLTAD, OTA, PTAA, RAD

01 President .... Dr. William RICHARDS
05 Vice President Academic Affairs .... Ms. Heather PERFETTI
32 Vice President Student Development .... Mr. Paul BROADIE, II
11 Vice Pres Administration/Finance .... Ms. Roslyn SMITH
30 Vice Pres Institutional Advancement .... Mr. Vinnie CAZZETTA
12 Vice President Newburgh Campus .... Ms. Mindy ROSS
13 Assoc Vice Pres Information Tech .... Vacant
84 Assoc VP for Enrollment Management .... Ms. Gerianne BRUSATI
76 Assoc VP Health Professions .... Mr. Michael GAWRONSKI, JR.
49 Int Assoc Vice Pres of Liberal Arts .... Ms. Mary WARRENER
50 Assoc VP Business/Math/Sci/Tech .... Ms. Stacey MOEGENBURG
88 Assoc Vice Pres Newburgh Campus .... Ms. Rosana REYES-ROSELLO
15 Assoc Vice Pres Human Resources .... Ms. Wendy HOLMES
08 Director Learning Resource .... Ms. Susan PARRY
20 Director Academic Services .... Mr. Neil FOLEY
51 Dir Continuing/Professional Educ .... Mr. David KOHN
19 Director Campus Security/Safety .... Mr. John AHERNE
09 Inst Plng/Assessment/Research Ofcr .... Ms. Christine WORK
18 Dir Facilities Administrative Svcs .... Mr. Michael WORDEN
21 Comptroller .... Ms. Jo Ann HAMBURG
37 Director of Financial Aid .... Mr. John IVANKOVIC
06 Registrar .... Mr. Neil FOLEY
26 Director of Communications .... Mr. Mike ALBRIGHT
38 Director Advising and Counseling .... Ms. Crystal SCHACHTER
07 Director of Admissions/Recruitment .... Mr. Michael ROE
35 Director Student Activities .... Mr. Steve HARPST
37 Asst Director of Financial Aid .... Ms. Rosemary BARRETT

Pace University (F)

1 Pace Plaza, New York NY 10038-1598

County: New York — FICE Identification: 002791
Unit ID: 194310
Telephone: (212) 346-1200 — Carnegie Class: DRU
FAX Number: (212) 346-1933 — Calendar System: Semester
URL: www.pace.edu
Established: 1906 — Annual Undergrad Tuition & Fees: $35,032
Enrollment: 12,752 — Coed
Affiliation or Control: Independent Non-Profit — IRS Status: 501(c)3
Highest Offering: Doctorate
Program: Liberal Arts And General; Teacher Preparatory; Professional
Accreditation: M, ARCPA, BUS, BUSA, CS, IPSY, LAW, NURSE, PSPSY, TED

01 President .... Mr. Stephen J. FRIEDMAN
10 Exec VP/Chief Financial Officer .... Mr. Robert ALMON
05 Int Provost/Exec VP Academic Affs .... Ms. Harriet FELDMAN
11 Sr Vice Pres/Chief Admin Ofcr .... Mr. William MCGRATH
21 Sr Vice President Finance/Treasurer .... Mr. Toby R. WINER
84 Vice Pres Enrollment Management .... Ms. Robina C. SCHEPP
30 VP Development/Alumni Relations .... Ms. Christine MEOLA
13 VP Information Tech/Chief Info Ofcr .... Mr. Frank J. MONACO
26 Vice Pres for University Relations .... Mr. Tom TORELLO
15 Int Vice Pres Human Resources .... Mr. Matt RENNA
09 Asst Vice Pres Plng/Assess/Inst Res .... Ms. Barbara S. PENNIPEDE
86 Asst Vice Pres Govt/Community Rels .... Ms. Meghan Q. FRENCH
32 AVP Ofc Student Assistance .... Mr. Matthew F. BONILLA
27 Asst VP Marketing/Communications .... Ms. Susan W. KAYNE
21 Assoc VP Finance/Asst Treasurer .... Mr. Ronald NAHUM
19 Associate VP General Services .... Mr. Frank MCDONALD
35 Assoc Provost for Student Success .... Dr. Mark Allen POISEL
20 Associate Provost for Academic Affs .... Dr. Sheying CHEN
50 Dean Lubin School of Business .... Mr. Neil BRAUN
49 Dean Dyson College Arts/Sci .... Dr. Nira HERRMANN
53 Dean School of Education .... Dr. Andrea M. SPENCER
66 Int Dean Lienhard School of Nursing .... Dr. Geraldine COLOMBRARO
77 Dean School of CSIS .... Dr. Susan M. MERRITT
32 Dean of Students New York .... Dr. Marijo RUSSELL O'GRADY
32 Dean of Students Westchester .... Dr. Lisa BARDILL MOSCARITOLO
61 Dean School of Law .... Ms. Michelle S. SIMON
06 Assoc VP Stdnt Svcs/Univ Registrar .... Mr. Steven L. JOHNSON
06 Graduate Registrar .... Ms. Margaret JONES
06 Registrar Pleasantville .... Ms. Annmarie MCGRAIL
06 Law School Registrar .... Ms. Nilda RODRIGUEZ
88 Associate University Registrar .... Ms. Barbara MCCARTHY
36 Exec Director Career Svcs/Coop Educ .... Ms. Jody QUEEN-HUBERT
88 Asst Director Adult Education NY .... Ms. Nicola FOSTER
21 Interim Comptroller .... Mr. William VOLL
44 Manager Annual Fund .... Ms. Nicole L. SOUZA
29 Director of Alumni Relations .... Ms. Sheri GIBSON
43 University Counsel .... Mr. Stephen BRODSKY
08 Associate Director Library .... Mr. Melvin ISAACSON
21 University Bursar .... Ms. Susan WEYGANT
37 Director Financial Aid .... Mr. Steven JOHNSON
07 Dir of Admissions NY/Westchester .... Ms. Joanna BRODA
45 Director Budget/Planning/Analysis .... Mr. Len CERTA
22 Affirmative Action Officer .... Ms. Arletha MILES
14 Univ Director Computer Systems .... Mr. Gerard TARPEY
24 Univ Director Educational Media Svc .... Mr. Frank MANNLE
84 Director Adult Enroll Svcs/New York .... Ms. Janet KIRTMAN
23 Assoc Director Health Care Unit .... Ms. Jamesetta NEWLAND
27 Director of Media Relations .... Mr. Christopher CORY
88 Director Pace Adult Resource Center .... Ms. Tamra PLOTNICK
35 Director of Student Devel New York .... Dr. David CLARK
38 Director Counseling Services .... Dr. Richard SHADICK
39 Director of Residential Life .... Mr. A. Patrick ROGER-GORDON
40 Executive Director Bookstore .... Ms. Mary LIETO
85 Assoc Dir Intl Pgms & Services .... Mr. Kraig WALKUP
96 Director of Purchasing - Contracts .... Ms. Alice SEIFERT
18 Director Facilities/Physical Plant .... Mr. Abdul JABAR
28 Director of Diversity .... Ms. Shanelle HENRY ROBINSON

Pacific College of Oriental Medicine (G)

915 Broadway, Second Floor, New York NY 10107-8243

County: New York — Identification: 666139
Unit ID: 414595
Telephone: (212) 982-3456 — Carnegie Class: Spec/Health
FAX Number: (212) 982-6514 — Calendar System: Semester
URL: www.pacificcollege.edu/
Established: 1993 — Annual Graduate Tuition & Fees: $17,150
Enrollment: 502 — Coed
Affiliation or Control: Proprietary — IRS Status: Proprietary
Highest Offering: Master's; No Undergraduates
Program: Professional
Accreditation: ACCSC, ACUP

01 Dean/Chief Operating Officer .... Ms. Gina LEPORE
06 Head Registrar/Dean of Admin .... Ms. Shana GARWOOD
05 Academic Dean .... Dr. Belinda ANDERSEN

† Branch campus of Pacific College of Oriental Medicine, San Diego CA.

Paul Smith's College of Arts and Sciences (H)

PO Box 265, Paul Smiths NY 12970-0265

County: Franklin — FICE Identification: 002795
Unit ID: 194392
Telephone: (518) 327-6000 — Carnegie Class: Bac/Diverse
FAX Number: (518) 327-6060 — Calendar System: Trimester
URL: www.paulsmiths.edu
Established: 1937 — Annual Undergrad Tuition & Fees: $22,940
Enrollment: 1,007 — Coed
Affiliation or Control: Independent Non-Profit — IRS Status: 501(c)3
Highest Offering: Baccalaureate
Program: 2-Year Principally Bachelor's Creditable; Technical Emphasis
Accreditation: M, ACFEI, ENGT, FOR

01 President .... Dr. John W. MILLS
04 Assistant to the President .... Ms. Kathleen A. KECK
05 Provost .... Dr. Richard NELSON
10 Vice President Business/Finance .... Vacant
30 Vice President Inst Advancement .... Mr. F. Raymond AGNEW
84 Vice Pres Enrollment Management .... Vacant
18 VP Facilities Mgmt/Capital Project .... Mr. Steven W. MCFARLAND
13 Vice Pres Information Services .... Mr. James BUYEA
29 Director of Alumni Relations .... Vacant
38 Director of Student Development .... Ms. Cheryl C. CULOTTA
37 Director of Financial Aid .... Ms. Mary Ellen M. CHAMBERLAIN
23 Director of Health Services .... Ms. Reiko REXILIUS-TUTHILL
24 Director Education Support Services .... Mr. Neil SURPRENANT
15 Director of Human Resources .... Ms. Susan Y. SWEENEY
26 Director of Communications .... Mr. Kenneth AARON
06 Registrar .... Dr. Loralyn TAYLOR
07 Director of Admissions .... Ms. Lynn GILBERT
19 Lead Campus Safety Officer .... Mr. Phil FIACCO

09 Director Institutional Research ....Dr. Loralyn TAYLOR
22 Director HEOP ....Ms. Kate MULLEN
41 Int Dir of Athletics/Physical Educ ....Mr. James TUCKER
21 Comptroller ....Ms. Laura ROZELL
32 Chief Student Affairs Officer ....Mr. Matthew SETON-SCHUR
40 Manager of College Store ....Ms. Diana L. LYNG-GLIDDI
96 Purchasing Coordinator ....Ms. Cynthia LEMERY
36 Career Coordinator ....Ms. Debra DUTCHER
49 Dean Science/Liberal Arts/Bus Mgmt ....Dr. Phillip TAYLOR
65 Dean Forestry/Natural Res/Recreat ....Dr. Jeffrey T. WALTON
88 Dean Culinary Arts and Service Mgt ....Mr. James MILLER

Phillips Beth Israel School of Nursing (A)

776 Sixth Avenue, 4th Floor, New York NY 10001-6354
County: New York FICE Identification: 006438
Unit ID: 189282
Telephone: (212) 614-6110 Carnegie Class: Assoc/PrivNFP
FAX Number: (212) 614-6109 Calendar System: Semester
URL: www.futurenursebi.org
Established: 1904 Annual Undergrad Tuition & Fees: $19,200
Enrollment: 271 Coed
Affiliation or Control: Independent Non-Profit IRS Status: 501(c)3
Highest Offering: Associate Degree
Program: Occupational; 2-Year Principally Bachelor's Creditable; Nursing Emphasis
Accreditation: ADNUR

01 Dean ....Dr. Janet MACKIN
05 Assistant Dean ....Mrs. Bernice PASS-STERN
32 Manager Student Services ....Ms. Linda FABRIZIO

Plaza College (B)

74-09 37th Avenue, Jackson Heights NY 11372-6391
County: Queens FICE Identification: 012358
Unit ID: 194499
Telephone: (718) 779-1430 Carnegie Class: Bac/Assoc
FAX Number: (718) 779-7423 Calendar System: Semester
URL: www.plazacollege.edu
Established: 1916 Annual Undergrad Tuition & Fees: $12,350
Enrollment: 793 Coed
Affiliation or Control: Proprietary IRS Status: Proprietary
Highest Offering: Baccalaureate
Program: Occupational; 2-Year Principally Bachelor's Creditable
Accreditation: M, MAC

01 President ....Charles E. CALLAHAN, SR.
03 Provost ....Charles E. CALLAHAN, III
10 Vice Pres of Financial Services ....Elizabeth K. CALLAHAN
05 Academic Dean ....Marie DOLLA
06 Registrar ....Carol GARCIA
21 Comptroller ....Linda ROCKHILL
07 Dean of Admissions ....Rose Ann BLACK
20 Dean Curriculum Development ....Marianne C. ZIPF
08 College Librarian ....Eva BABALIS
23 Director Health Services ....Candice CALLAHAN
37 Financial Aid Coord/Dir Fin Svcs ....Peggy CHUNG
29 Alumni Relations/Internship Coord ....Jonathan HOWLE
100 Chief of Staff/HR Officer/Placement ....Correne CAVALIERI
09 Assoc Dean Institutional Research ....Edward DEE
27 Chief Information Officer ....Dean DEBEER
32 Director of Student Services ....Dawn VETRANO
62 Director of Library/LRC ....Kathleen D'APRIX
13 Director Information Technology ....Norman ALVARADO
45 Director Strategic Initiatives ....Charles CALLAHAN, IV
76 Program Director Medical Assisting ....Daryl ANDERSON

Polytechnic Institute of New York University (C)

6 Metrotech Center, Brooklyn NY 11201-3840
County: Kings FICE Identification: 002796
Unit ID: 194541
Telephone: (718) 260-3600 Carnegie Class: RU/H
FAX Number: (718) 260-3136 Calendar System: Semester
URL: www.poly.edu
Established: 1854 Annual Undergrad Tuition & Fees: $36,684
Enrollment: 4,432 Coed
Affiliation or Control: Independent Non-Profit IRS Status: 501(c)3
Highest Offering: Doctorate
Program: Liberal Arts And General; Professional
Accreditation: M, ENG

01 President ....Mr. Jerry M. HULTIN
03 Provost ....Dr. Dianne REKOW
10 Vice Pres Finance & Administration ....Mr. Dennis DINTINO
30 VP Development and Alumni Relations ....Ms. Barbara NOSEWORTHY
27 VP of Marketing and Communications ....Vacant
88 VP of Enterprise Learning ....Mr. Robert N. UBELL
100 Chief of Staff/VP Strat Initiatives ....Ms. Ji Mi CHOI
21 Asst VP for Financial Operations ....Vacant
05 Assoc Provost Research/PhD Programs ....Dr. Kurt BECKER
84 Assoc Provost Enrollment Services ....Ms. Barbara HALL
45 Assoc Provost Pgms/Plng/Development ....Dr. Mary COWMAN
54 Assoc Provost Abu Dhabi Engineering ....Dr. Sunil KUMAR
58 Assoc Provost Graduate Academics ....Dr. Walter ZURAWSKY
05 Assoc Provost Undergrad Academics ....Dr. Iraj KALKHORAN
32 Dean of Student Affairs ....Ms. Anita FARRINGTON
26 Director Marketing & Communications ....Ms. Kathleen HAMILTON
08 Director of Libraries ....Ms. Jana STEVENS-RICHMAN
06 Registrar ....Ms. Beth KIENLE-GRANZO
36 Director of Career Services ....Mr. James SILLCOX
88 Director of Special Services ....Ms. Haang FUNG
37 Director Financial Aid ....Ms. Christine FALZERANO
15 Director Human Resources ....Mr. Suong IVES
29 Director Alumni Relations ....Mr. Andthony D. KAPP
46 Director Sponsored Research ....Ms. Christine VILLANI
18 Director Facilities ....Ms. Annie CARINO
41 Director of Athletics ....Ms. Maureen BRAZIEL
88 Director Student Financial Services ....Mr. Anthony BONANO
09 Director of Institutional Research ....Mr. Michael A. MAINIERO
30 Director of Development ....Ms. Erica MARKS
84 Director Grad Enrollment Mgmt ....Mr. J. C BONILLA
88 Director K-12 Stem Education ....Mr. Ben ESNER

Pratt Institute (D)

200 Willoughby Avenue, Brooklyn NY 11205-3899
County: Kings FICE Identification: 002798
Unit ID: 194578
Telephone: (718) 636-3600 Carnegie Class: Master's L
FAX Number: (718) 636-3670 Calendar System: Semester
URL: www.pratt.edu
Established: 1887 Annual Undergrad Tuition & Fees: $39,310
Enrollment: 4,733 Coed
Affiliation or Control: Independent Non-Profit IRS Status: 501(c)3
Highest Offering: Doctorate
Program: Liberal Arts And General; Professional
Accreditation: M, ART, CIDA, LIB, PLNG, @TEAC

01 President ....Dr. Thomas F. SCHUTTE
05 Provost ....Mr. Peter BARNA
32 Vice President for Student Life ....Dr. Helen MATUSOW-AYRES
10 Vice Pres Finance/Administration ....Mr. Edmund RUTKOWSKI
30 Vice President Development ....Mr. Todd GALITZ
84 Vice President for Enrollment ....Ms. Judith AARON
11 Assistant to Pres Administration ....Ms. Josie CAPORUSCIO
06 Registrar ....Mr. Lisle HENDERSON
08 Acting Director of the Library ....Mr. Russ ABELL
20 Associate Provost ....Dr. Marianthi ZIKOPOULOS
15 Director Human Resources ....Mr. Tom GREENE
51 Dir Ctr for Continuing & Prof Stds ....Mr. Charles MUNSTER
21 Comptroller ....Ms. Sylvia ACUESTA
26 Executive Director Public Relations ....Ms. Mara MCGINNIS
29 Director Alumni Relations ....Vacant
36 Director Student Placement ....Ms. Judith NYLEN
37 Actg Director Student Financial Aid ....Ms. Fiona APPROO
09 Director of Institutional Research ....Mr. Vladimir BRILLER
07 Director of Undergraduate Admission ....Mr. William SWAN
96 Director of Purchasing ....Vacant
57 Dean Art & Design ....Ms. Concetta STEWART
49 Dean Liberal Arts/Science ....Dr. Andrew BARNES
48 Dean School of Architecture ....Mr. Thomas HANRAHAN
62 Dean Information/Library Sci ....Dr. Tula GIANNINI

Professional Business College (E)

125 Canal Street, New York NY 10002-5056
County: New York FICE Identification: 023065
Unit ID: 194611
Telephone: (212) 226-7300 Carnegie Class: Assoc/PrivNFP
FAX Number: (212) 431-8294 Calendar System: Semester
URL: www.pbcny.edu
Established: 2004 Annual Undergrad Tuition & Fees: $14,707
Enrollment: 744 Coed
Affiliation or Control: Independent Non-Profit IRS Status: 501(c)3
Highest Offering: Associate Degree
Program: Occupational; 2-Year Principally Bachelor's Creditable; Business Emphasis
Accreditation: ACICS

01 President ....Mr. Leon LEE
03 Academic Vice President ....Mr. Richard SLUSARCZYK
05 Academic Dean ....Ms. Lynne BEJOIAN
32 Asst Vice President for Students ....Ms. Ellen RICHMOND
20 Director of Academic Success Pgm ....Ms. Trang LE-CHAN
36 Placement Director ....Ms. Judith RODRIGUEZ
06 Registrar ....Mr. David RODRIGUEZ
08 Head Librarian ....Mr. James CAMELLA
07 Admissions Director ....Mr. David WANG
37 Financial Aid Director ....Ms. Cheryl ZHANG

Rabbi Isaac Elchanan Theological Seminary (F)

2540 Amsterdam Avenue, New York NY 10033-9986
County: New York FICE Identification: 033104
Unit ID: 194727
Telephone: (212) 960-5310 Carnegie Class: Not Classified
FAX Number: (212) 960-0055 Calendar System: Semester
URL: riets.edu
Established: 1886 Annual Graduate Tuition & Fees: $15,200
Enrollment: 320 Male
Affiliation or Control: Jewish IRS Status: 501(c)3
Highest Offering: Beyond Master's But Less Than Doctorate; No Undergraduates
Program: Professional
Accreditation: NY

01 Chancellor ....Rabbi Norman LAMM
05 Max & Marion Grill Dean ....Rabbi Yonah REESE
64 Director Belz School Jewish Music ....Cantor Bernard BEER
06 Registrar ....Ms. Frances FISHER
07 Director of Admissions ....Mr. Michael KRANZLER
37 Director of Student Finances ....Mr. Robert FRIEDMAN
08 Librarian ....Ms. Pearl BERGER
11 Administrator ....Rabbi Chaim BRONSTEIN
30 Director Institutional Advancement ....Mr. Dan FORMAN

Rabbinical Academy Mesivta Rabbi Chaim Berlin (G)

1605 Coney Island Avenue, Brooklyn NY 11230-4715
County: Kings FICE Identification: 003976
Unit ID: 194657
Telephone: (718) 377-0777 Carnegie Class: Spec/Faith
FAX Number: (718) 338-5578 Calendar System: Semester
Established: 1939 Annual Undergrad Tuition & Fees: $10,850
Enrollment: 321 Male
Affiliation or Control: Independent Non-Profit IRS Status: 501(c)3
Highest Offering: Second Talmudic Degree
Program: Teacher Preparatory; Professional
Accreditation: RABN

01 Provost ....Rabbi Abraham H. FRUCHTHANDLER
05 President of the Faculty ....Rabbi Aaron M. SCHECHTER
03 Executive Director ....Rabbi Y. Mayer LASKER
29 Director of Alumni Association ....Mendel SCHECHTER
45 Chief Planning Officer ....Rabbi Tuvia M. OBERMEISTER
20 Associate Director ....Eli RABINOWITZ
37 Financial Aid Administrator ....Michael A. REISS

Rabbinical College Beth Shraga (H)

28 Saddle River Road, Monsey NY 10952-3035
County: Rockland FICE Identification: 010943
Unit ID: 194693
Telephone: (845) 356-1980 Carnegie Class: Spec/Faith
FAX Number: (845) 425-2604 Calendar System: Semester
Established: 1965 Annual Undergrad Tuition & Fees: $10,050
Enrollment: 43 Male
Affiliation or Control: Independent Non-Profit IRS Status: 501(c)3
Highest Offering: Second Talmudic Degree
Program: Teacher Preparatory; Professional
Accreditation: RABN

01 President ....Rabbi Sidney SCHIFF

Rabbinical College Bobover Yeshiva B'nei Zion (I)

1577 48th Street, Brooklyn NY 11219-3293
County: Kings FICE Identification: 008614
Unit ID: 194666
Telephone: (718) 438-2018 Carnegie Class: Spec/Faith
FAX Number: (718) 871-9031 Calendar System: Semester
Established: 1947 Annual Undergrad Tuition & Fees: $8,960
Enrollment: 321 Male
Affiliation or Control: Independent Non-Profit IRS Status: 501(c)3
Highest Offering: Second Talmudic Degree
Program: Teacher Preparatory; Professional
Accreditation: RABN

01 President ....Rabbi Boruch Avrohom HOROWITZ

Rabbinical College Ch'san Sofer (J)

1876 50th Street, Brooklyn NY 11204-0304
County: Kings FICE Identification: 003977
Unit ID: 194675
Telephone: (718) 236-1171 Carnegie Class: Spec/Faith
FAX Number: (718) 236-1119 Calendar System: Semester
Established: 1940 Annual Undergrad Tuition & Fees: $8,500
Enrollment: 47 Male
Affiliation or Control: Independent Non-Profit IRS Status: 501(c)3
Highest Offering: Second Talmudic Degree
Program: Teacher Preparatory; Professional
Accreditation: RABN

01 Executive Vice President ....Rabbi A. EHRENFELD
05 Dean of the College ....Rabbi S. B. EHRENFELD
10 Treasurer ....Mr. Samuel FISCHER
06 Registrar ....Rabbi William GREENWALD

Rabbinical College of Long Island (K)

205 W Beech Street, Long Beach NY 11561-0630
County: Nassau FICE Identification: 010378
Unit ID: 194736
Telephone: (516) 255-4700 Carnegie Class: Spec/Faith
FAX Number: (516) 255-4701 Calendar System: Semester
Established: 1965 Annual Undergrad Tuition & Fees: $11,000
Enrollment: 120 Male
Affiliation or Control: Independent Non-Profit IRS Status: 501(c)3
Highest Offering: First Talmudic Degree
Program: Teacher Preparatory; Professional
Accreditation: RABN

01 President .... Rabbi Yitzchok FEIGELSTOCK
06 Registrar .... Rabbi Dovid N. ROTHSCHILD
32 Dean of Students .... Rabbi Yeruchem PITTER
07 Director of Admissions .... Rabbi Chaim HOBERMAN
37 Financial Aid Administrator .... Rabbi Shlomo TEICHMAN

Rabbinical College Ohr Shimon Yisroel (A)

215-217 Hewes Street, Brooklyn NY 11211-8102
County: Kings FICE Identification: 031292
Unit ID: 405854
Telephone: (718) 855-4092 Carnegie Class: Spec/Faith
FAX Number: (718) 855-8479 Calendar System: Semester
Established: N/A Annual Undergrad Tuition & Fees: $9,600
Enrollment: 176 Male
Affiliation or Control: Independent Non-Profit IRS Status: 501(c)3
Highest Offering: First Talmudic Degree
Program: Professional
Accreditation: @RABN

01 President .... Rabbi Shulem WALTER

Rabbinical Seminary of America (B)

76-01 147th Street, Flushing NY 11367-3148
County: Queens FICE Identification: 003978
Unit ID: 194763
Telephone: (718) 268-4700 Carnegie Class: Spec/Faith
FAX Number: (718) 268-4684 Calendar System: Semester
Established: 1933 Annual Undergrad Tuition & Fees: $8,000
Enrollment: 466 Male
Affiliation or Control: Independent Non-Profit IRS Status: 501(c)3
Highest Offering: Second Talmudic Degree
Program: Teacher Preparatory; Professional
Accreditation: RABN

01 Executive Director .... Rabbi Meir GLAZER
03 Executive Vice President .... Rabbi Hayim SCHWARTZ
05 Vice President .... Rabbi David HARRIS
20 Vice President .... Rabbi Akiva GRUNBLATT
04 Assistant to the Dean .... Rabbi Abraham GINZBERG
06 Registrar .... Rabbi Abraham SEMMEL
30 Director Development .... Rabbi Yossi SINGER
37 Director of Financial Aid .... Mrs. Laya EISENSTEIN
18 Chief Physical Plant .... Mr. David COHEN
88 Director of Special Projects .... Vacant
91 Director of Admin Computing .... Mr. Michael WEINSTOCK
39 Director Student Housing .... Rabbi Aryeh GOLDMAN
46 Director Research & Development .... Vacant

Rabbinical Seminary M'kor Chaim (C)

1571 55th Street, Brooklyn NY 11219-4300
County: Kings FICE Identification: 008617
Unit ID: 194718
Telephone: (718) 851-0183 Carnegie Class: Spec/Faith
FAX Number: (718) 853-2967 Calendar System: Semester
Established: 1965 Annual Undergrad Tuition & Fees: $5,940
Enrollment: 53 Male
Affiliation or Control: Independent Non-Profit IRS Status: 501(c)3
Highest Offering: Second Talmudic Degree
Program: Teacher Preparatory; Professional
Accreditation: RABN

01 President .... Rabbi Benjamin LEDERER

Rensselaer Polytechnic Institute (D)

110 8th Street, Troy NY 12180-3590
County: Rensselaer FICE Identification: 002803
Unit ID: 194824
Telephone: (518) 276-6000 Carnegie Class: RU/VH
FAX Number: N/A Calendar System: Semester
URL: www.rpi.edu
Established: 1824 Annual Undergrad Tuition & Fees: $42,704
Enrollment: 7,144 Coed
Affiliation or Control: Independent Non-Profit IRS Status: 501(c)3
Highest Offering: Doctorate
Program: Liberal Arts And General; Professional
Accreditation: M, BUS, ENG

01 President .... Dr. Shirley A. JACKSON
05 Provost .... Dr. Robert PALAZZO
11 Vice President for Administration .... Mr. Claude ROUNDS
10 Vice President for Finance .... Ms. Virginia GREGG
30 Vice Pres Institute Advancement .... Ms. Brenda WILSON-HALE
32 Vice President Student Life .... Dr. Timothy E. SAMS
15 VP Human Resources/Inst Diversity .... Mr. Curtis N. POWELL
45 Vice Pres for Research .... Dr. Francine BERMAN
13 Vice Pres for Info Services & CIO .... Mr. John E. KOLB
21 Asst Vice Pres for Administration .... Mr. Paul MARTIN
26 Asst VP for Govt & Ext Relations .... Ms. Allison NEWMAN
29 Asst Vice Pres Alumni Relations .... Mr. Jeff SCHANZ
54 Dean School of Engineering .... Dr. David ROSOWSKY
81 Dean School of Science .... Dr. Laurie LESHIN
79 Dean Sch of Humanities/Social Sci .... Dr. Mary SIMONI
50 Dean Lally School of Mgmt/Tech .... Dr. Thomas BEGLEY
48 Dean School of Architecture .... Mr. Evan DOUGLIS
43 Secy of the Inst/General Counsel .... Mr. Charles F. CARLETTA
20 Associate Dean for Information Tech .... Mr. David SPOONER
84 Dean Enrollment Management .... Dr. Paul MARTHERS
32 Dean of Students .... Mr. Mark SMITH
06 Dir Stdnt Records/Fin Svcs/Registr .... Ms. Sharon L. KUNKEL
37 Director Financial Aid .... Mr. Larry CHAMBERS
09 Director of Institutional Research .... Mr. Jack MAHONEY
08 Acting Director of Libraries .... Mr. Bob MAYO
25 Director Office Contracts & Grants .... Mr. Richard E. SCAMMELL
36 Director Career Development Center .... Mr. Thomas L. TARANTELLI
07 Director of Graduate Admissions .... Mr. George ROBBINS
100 Chief of Staff .... Mr. Laban COBLENTZ
18 Director Physical Plant .... Mr. Mark FROST
86 Director of Federal Relations .... Ms. Deborah E. ALTENBURG
23 Director Student Health Center .... Dr. Leslie LAWRENCE
38 Director Student Counseling .... Dr. Benjamin MARTE
96 Manager Purchasing Systems .... Mr. Craig MCINTOSH

Richard Gilder Graduate School at the American Museum of Natural History (E)

Central Park West at 79th Street, New York NY 10024
County: New York Identification: 667003
Unit ID: 458548
Telephone: (212) 769-5055 Carnegie Class: Not Classified
FAX Number: N/A Calendar System: Other
URL: rggs.amnh.org
Established: 2006 Annual Graduate Tuition & Fees: N/A
Enrollment: 13 Coed
Affiliation or Control: Independent Non-Profit IRS Status: 501(c)3
Highest Offering: Doctorate; No Undergraduates
Program: Professional
Accreditation: NY

01 Dean .... Dr. John J. FLYNN

Roberts Wesleyan College (F)

2301 Westside Drive, Rochester NY 14624-1997
County: Monroe FICE Identification: 002805
Unit ID: 194958
Telephone: (585) 594-6000 Carnegie Class: Master's L
FAX Number: (585) 594-6371 Calendar System: Semester
URL: www.roberts.edu
Established: 1866 Annual Undergrad Tuition & Fees: $25,322
Enrollment: 1,835 Coed
Affiliation or Control: Independent Non-Profit IRS Status: 501(c)3
Highest Offering: Master's
Program: Liberal Arts And General; Teacher Preparatory; Professional
Accreditation: M, ART, IACBE, MUS, NURSE, SW, @TEAC

01 President .... Dr. John A. MARTIN
03 Sr VP & Provost .... Dr. Robert ZWIER
45 Sr VP Advancement & External Rels .... Dr. S. Jack CONNELL
10 Sr Vice President & Treasurer .... Mr. James E. CUTHBERT
05 VP for Academic & Student Support .... Dr. Nelson W. HILL
11 Vice President for Administration .... Mrs. Ruth LOGAN
07 Vice President for Admissions .... Vacant
44 Vice President for Planned Giving .... Mr. Lawrence J. GREENO
40 Director of Bookstore Services .... Mr. Arnoldo DEJESUS
41 Director of Athletics .... Mr. Michael E. FARO
37 Director of Student Financial Svcs .... Mr. Stephen G. FIELD
09 Dir Institutional Research/Assess .... Dr. Paul W. KENNEDY
42 Chaplain .... Rev. Jonathan BRATT
06 Registrar .... Mrs. Lesa J. KOHR
08 Director of Library Services .... Mr. Alfred C. KROBER
13 Chief Information Officer .... Mr. Pradeep SAXENA

† Parent institution of Northeastern Seminary.

Rochester Institute of Technology (G)

1 Lomb Memorial Drive, Rochester NY 14623-5604
County: Monroe FICE Identification: 002806
Unit ID: 195003
Telephone: (585) 475-2411 Carnegie Class: Master's L
FAX Number: (585) 475-7049 Calendar System: Quarter
URL: www.rit.edu
Established: 1829 Annual Undergrad Tuition & Fees: $31,854
Enrollment: 17,206 Coed
Affiliation or Control: Independent Non-Profit IRS Status: 501(c)3
Highest Offering: Doctorate
Program: Liberal Arts And General; Teacher Preparatory; Professional; Technical Emphasis
Accreditation: M, ARCPA, ART, BUS, CIDA, CS, DIETD, DMS, ENG, ENGR, ENGT, TEAC

01 President .... Dr. William W. DESTLER
05 Provost & Sr VP for Acad Affs .... Dr. Jeremy A. HAEFNER
100 Chief of Staff .... Mrs. Karen A. BARROWS
10 Sr Vice Pres Finance/Administration .... Dr. James H. WATTERS
84 Sr VP Enroll Mgmt/Career Svcs .... Dr. James G. MILLER
32 Sr Vice President Student Affairs .... Dr. Mary-Beth COOPER
12 President NTID/RIT Vice Pres & Dean .... Dr. Gerard BUCKLEY
30 VP for Development & Alumni Rels .... Ms. Lisa CAUDA
86 Vice President Govt/Cmty Relations .... Ms. Deborah M. STENDARDI
20 Senior Assoc Provost .... Dr. Christine M. LICATA
36 Assoc VP/Dir Coop Ed/Career Svcs .... Dr. Emanuel CONTOMANOLIS
21 Controller & Asst Treasurer .... Ms. Lyn KELLY
27 Chief Communications Officer .... Mr. Robert FINNERTY
46 Vice President Research .... Dr. Ryne RAFFAELLE
20 Asst Provost and Director CIMS .... Dr. Nabil NASR
08 Director of RIT Libraries .... Ms. Shirley BOWER
20 Assoc Provost for Faculty Success .... Dr. Lynn A. WILD
18 Int Director Facilities Managment .... Mr. Jan REICH
12 Pres/Dean Amer Col Mgt/Tech RIT .... Mr. Donald HUDSPETH
29 Asst VP Alumni Relations .... Ms. Kelly REDDER
06 Asst VP/Registrar .... Mr. Joe LOFFREDO
07 Asst VP/Dir Undergrad Admissions .... Dr. Daniel SHELLEY
37 Asst VP & Dir Fin Aid & Scholarship .... Ms. Verna J. HAZEN
88 Asst VP and Dir Grad/PT Enroll Svc .... Ms. Diane ELLISON
44 Asst VP for Principal/Planned Gift .... Ms. Heather ENGEL
09 Asst VP Inst Rsrch/Policy Studies .... Dr. Joan E. GRAHAM
15 Asst VP/Director Human Resources .... Ms. Judy BENDER
44 Exec Dir Fund for RIT .... Ms. Marisa PSAILA
35 Sr Director Center for Campus Life .... Ms. Karey PINE
89 Int Director First Year Enrichment .... Mr. Joshua BAUROTH
85 Assoc Dir International Student Svc .... Mr. Jeffrey W. COX
96 Exec Director Procurement Services .... Ms. Debra KUSSE
28 Chief Diversity Officer .... Mr. Kevin MCDONALD
12 Director Academic Affs AUK Kosovo .... Dr. Shawn STURGEON
102 Exec Director Foundation Relations .... Ms. Susan WATSON MOLINE
102 Dir Corporate Relations .... Mr. Paul HARRIS
26 Chief Public Relations Officer .... Mr. Robert FINNERTY
38 Director Student Counseling .... Mr. John WEAS
101 Secretary of the Institution .... Mrs. Karen A. BARROWS
50 Dean of Business .... Dr. Ashok RAO
54 Dean of Engineering .... Dr. Harvey J. PALMER
72 Dean Applied Science/Technology .... Dr. H. Fred WALKER
49 Dean of Liberal Arts .... Dr. James J. WINEBRAKE
81 Dean of Science .... Dr. Sophia MAGGELAKIS
57 Dean College Imaging Arts/Sci .... Ms. Lorraine JUSTICE
77 Dean B Golisano Col Comp/Info Sci .... Dr. Andrew L. SEARS
58 Dean Graduate Studies .... Dr. Hector FLORES
12 President & Dean RIT Dubai .... Dr. Mustafa ABUSHAGUR

Rockefeller University (H)

1230 York Avenue, New York NY 10065-6399
County: New York FICE Identification: 002807
Unit ID: 195049
Telephone: (212) 327-8000 Carnegie Class: RU/VH
FAX Number: (212) 327-8699 Calendar System: Other
URL: www.rockefeller.edu
Established: 1901 Annual Graduate Tuition & Fees: N/A
Enrollment: 196 Coed
Affiliation or Control: Independent Non-Profit IRS Status: 501(c)3
Highest Offering: Doctorate; No Undergraduates
Program: Professional
Accreditation: NY

01 President .... Dr. Marc TESSIER-LAVIGNE
43 Vice President & General Counsel .... Ms. Harriet RABB
05 Vice President Academic Affairs .... Mr. Michael W. YOUNG
10 Vice President Finance .... Mr. James H. LAPPLE
30 Vice President Development .... Ms. Maren E. IMHOFF
17 Vice President for Medical Affairs .... Dr. Barry S. COLLER
20 Dean & Vice Pres of Educ Affairs .... Dr. Sidney STRICKLAND
88 Vice Pres Scientific/Fac Oper .... Dr. John TOOZE
15 Vice President Human Resources .... Ms. Virginia A. HUFFMAN
18 Assoc Vice Pres Plant Operations .... Mr. Alexander KOGAN
45 Assoc Vice Pres Plng & Constr .... Mr. George B. CANDLER
13 Chief Information Officer .... Mr. Gerald LATTER
25 Dir Pgm Dev & Sponsored Research .... Dr. Gila BUDESCU
08 University Librarian .... Ms. Carol FELTES
19 Director Security .... Mr. James ROGERS

Rockland Community College (I)

145 College Road, Suffern NY 10901-3699
County: Rockland FICE Identification: 002877
Unit ID: 195058
Telephone: (845) 574-4000 Carnegie Class: Assoc/Pub-S-SC
FAX Number: (845) 574-4463 Calendar System: Semester
URL: www.sunyrockland.edu
Established: 1959 Annual Undergrad Tuition & Fees (In-District): $3,815
Enrollment: 7,395 Coed
Affiliation or Control: State/Local IRS Status: 501(c)3
Highest Offering: Associate Degree
Program: Occupational; 2-Year Principally Bachelor's Creditable
Accreditation: M, ADNUR, OTA

01 President .... Dr. Cliff L. WOOD
03 Executive Vice President .... Mr. Morton MEYERS
05 Vice President Academic Affairs .... Dr. Susan DEER
32 Int Vice Pres Student Development .... Ms. Karen GUALTIERI
10 Assoc VP Finance/Administration .... Mr. Larry FERRIER
88 Dean CTR Personal/Prof Development .... Mr. Richard SYREK
35 Dean Students/Stdnt Personnel Svcs .... Dr. James SIEGEL
84 Int Dean of Enrollment Management .... Ms. Dana STILLEY
37 Director Financial Aid .... Ms. Debra BOUABIDI
06 Registrar .... Ms. Robin CONKLIN
14 Director of Information Services .... Dr. Steven FERRES
08 Director of Library/Learning Res .... Mr. Timothy DOMICK
38 Director Student Counseling .... Vacant
18 Chief Facilities/Physical Plant .... Vacant
28 Dir Equity/Compliance/Affirm Act .... Ms. Melissa ROY
09 Director of Institutional Research .... Mr. Michael LIPKIN
20 Asst to Vice Pres Academic Affairs .... Ms. Patricia KOBES
26 Chief Public Relations Officer .... Ms. Zipora REITMAN

The Sage Colleges (A)

65 First Streeet, Troy NY 12180-4199
County: Rensselaer
FICE Identification: 002810
Unit ID: 195128
Telephone: (518) 244-2000
Carnegie Class: Master's L
FAX Number: (518) 244-2460
Calendar System: Semester
URL: www.sage.edu
Established: 1916
Annual Undergrad Tuition & Fees: $28,000
Enrollment: 2,966
Coed
Affiliation or Control: Independent Non-Profit
IRS Status: 501(c)3
Highest Offering: Baccalaureate
Program: Liberal Arts And General; Teacher Preparatory; Professional
Accreditation: M, ART, DIETD, DIETI, NURSE, OT, PTA, TED

01 President .... Dr. Susan C. SCRIMSHAW
05 Provost .... Dr. Terry WEINER
30 Vice President Development .... Mr. Daniel LUNDQUIST
12 Dean Sage College of Albany .... Ms. Sarolta TAKACS
10 VP for Finance & Treasurer .... Mr. Peter D. HUGHES
84 VP Marketing/Enrollment Mgmt .... Mr. Daniel LUNDQUIST
32 Vice Pres for Campus Life .... Ms. Patricia CELLEMME
13 VP Administration & Planning .... Ms. Deirdre ZARRILLO
12 Dean Russell Sage College .... Dr. Sharon ROBINSON
35 Dean of Students - RSC .... Mr. David MILFORD
35 Dean of Students - SCA .... Ms. Sharon MURRAY
76 Dean of Health Sciences .... Dr. Esther HASKVITZ
06 Registrar .... Ms. Andrea DEMAYO
07 Director of Admissions .... Mr. Andrew PALUMBO
88 Dean of School of Management .... Dr. Dan ROBESON
53 Dean School of Education .... Dr. Lori QUIGLEY
29 Director of Alumni Relations .... Ms. Alicia PEPE
29 Director Alumnae Relations .... Ms. Joan CLIFFORD
07 Director of Graduate & Adult Admiss .... Ms. Wendy DIEFENDORF
37 Assoc Director of Financial Aid .... Ms. Kelley ROBINSON
38 Director Student Counseling .... Vacant
15 Director of Human Resources .... Ms. Caryn KENT
09 Coord of Institutional Research .... Ms. Lori PIZER
18 Director Facilities Management .... Mr. John ZAJACESKOWSKI
28 Dir Cultural Enrichment/Diversity .... Ms. Sabrina MC GINTY
36 Director of Advising .... Ms. Karen SCHELL
36 Director of Advising .... Ms. Stacy GONZALEZ
26 Dir of Communications & Marketing .... Ms. Shannon BALLARD GORMAN
92 Director of Honors Programs .... Dr. Julie MCINTYRE
21 Senior Director of Finance .... Mr. Thomas GIAQUINTO
96 Dir of Purchasing/Accts Payable .... Ms. Paula SELMER

Saint Bernard's School of Theology & Ministry (B)

120 French Road, Rochester NY 14618-3822
County: Monroe
FICE Identification: 002815
Unit ID: 195155
Telephone: (585) 271-3657
Carnegie Class: Spec/Faith
FAX Number: (585) 271-2045
Calendar System: Semester
URL: www.stbernards.edu
Established: 1893
Annual Graduate Tuition & Fees: $3,220
Enrollment: 103
Coed
Affiliation or Control: Roman Catholic
IRS Status: 501(c)3
Highest Offering: Master's; No Undergraduates
Program: Professional
Accreditation: THEOL

01 President .... Sr. Patricia A. SCHOELLES, SSJ
05 Academic Dean .... Dr. Devadasan N. PREMNATH
06 Registrar .... Mrs. Ellen MORNINGSTAR
21 Accounting/Computer Operations .... Ms. Mary MUGGLETON
07 Admissions Director .... Ms. Laura SMITH
51 Director Continuing Education .... Rev. George HEYMAN
08 Librarian .... Ms. Sheila SMITH
30 Director of Advancement .... Ms. Laura HAMILTON

St. Bonaventure University (C)

St. Bonaventure NY 14778-9999
County: Cattaraugus
FICE Identification: 002817
Unit ID: 195164
Telephone: (716) 375-2000
Carnegie Class: Master's L
FAX Number: (716) 375-2005
Calendar System: Semester
URL: www.sbu.edu
Established: 1858
Annual Undergrad Tuition & Fees: $27,890
Enrollment: 2,519
Coed
Affiliation or Control: Roman Catholic
IRS Status: 501(c)3
Highest Offering: Master's
Program: Liberal Arts And General; Teacher Preparatory; Professional
Accreditation: M, BUS, CACREP, TED

01 President .... Dr. Margaret CARNEY, OSF
05 Provost and VP for Academic Affairs .... Dr. Michael J. FISCHER
32 Vice Provost for Student Life .... Mr. Richard C. TRIETLEY, JR.
10 Senior VP Finance & Administration .... Ms. Brenda MCGEE
26 Vice Pres University Relations .... Dr. Emily F. SINSABAUGH
42 Vice Pres University Ministries .... Mr. Robert M. DONIUS
88 Vice Pres for Franciscan Mission .... Bro. F. Edward COUGHLIN, OFM
30 Vice Pres for Advancement .... Mrs. Mary C. DRISCOLL
30 Assoc VP Development .... Mr. Matthew J. TORNAMBE
84 Associate VP for Enrollment .... Ms. Kate DILLON HOGAN
88 Assoc VP for Franciscan Mission .... Mr. Lawrence SOROKES
57 Assoc VP/Exec Dir of Q Arts Center .... Mr. Joseph LOSCHIAVO
04 Director of Operations Ofc of Pres .... Mr. Thomas BUTTAFARRO, JR.
15 Director Human Resources .... Mrs. Anne CIOLEK
07 Director of Admissions .... Ms. Monica EMERY
37 Director of Financial Aid .... Vacant
39 Exec Dir Res Living/Chief Judicial .... Ms. Nichole GONZALEZ
14 Director Technology Services .... Mr. Michael HOFFMAN
08 Director of Friedsam Mem Library .... Mr. Paul J. SPAETH
38 Director Counseling .... Dr. Roger E. KEENER
41 Director of Athletics .... Mr. Steve WATSON
06 Registrar & Dir of Inst Research .... Ms. Ann LEHMAN
29 Director of Alumni Services .... Mr. Joseph V. FLANAGAN
36 Director of Career Services .... Ms. Connie F. WHITCOMB
43 University Counsel .... Mr. J. Michael SHANE
23 Director of the Student Infirmary .... Vacant
18 Director Physical Plant .... Mr. Philip G. WINGER
21 Controller .... Mrs. Nancy K. TAYLOR
19 Director of Safety and Security .... Mr. Vito CZYZ
40 Manager Bookstore .... Ms. Annette MCGRAW
44 Director Annual Fund .... Vacant
92 Director of Honors Program .... Vacant
96 Dir of Budget & Purchasing .... Ms. Lorraine SMITH
88 Director Franciscan Institute .... Br. F. Edward COUGHLIN, OFM
49 Dean School of Arts & Sci .... Dr. Wolfgang NATTER
50 Dean School of Business .... Vacant
58 Dean School of Graduate Studies .... Dr. Peggy Y. BURKE
53 Dean School of Education .... Dr. Peggy Y. BURKE
60 Dean Jandoli Sch Journ/Mass Comm .... Vacant

St. Elizabeth College of Nursing (D)

2215 Genesee Street, Utica NY 13501-5998
County: Oneida
FICE Identification: 006461
Unit ID: 195687
Telephone: (315) 798-8144
Carnegie Class: Assoc/PrivNFP
FAX Number: (315) 798-8271
Calendar System: Semester
URL: www.secon.edu
Established: 1904
Annual Undergrad Tuition & Fees: $13,438
Enrollment: 245
Coed
Affiliation or Control: Independent Non-Profit
IRS Status: 501(c)3
Highest Offering: Associate Degree
Program: 2-Year Principally Bachelor's Creditable
Accreditation: M, ADNUR

01 President .... Mrs. Marian KOVATCHITCH

St. Francis College (E)

180 Remsen Street, Brooklyn NY 11201-4398
County: Kings
FICE Identification: 002820
Unit ID: 195173
Telephone: (718) 522-2300
Carnegie Class: Bac/Diverse
FAX Number: (718) 522-1274
Calendar System: Semester
URL: www.stfranciscollege.edu
Established: 1859
Annual Undergrad Tuition & Fees: $18,100
Enrollment: 2,526
Coed
Affiliation or Control: Independent Non-Profit
IRS Status: 501(c)3
Highest Offering: Master's
Program: Liberal Arts And General; Teacher Preparatory; Nursing Emphasis
Accreditation: M, NURSE, @TEAC

01 President .... Mr. Brendan J. DUGAN
05 Vice Pres Academic Affs/Acad Dean .... Dr. Timothy J. HOULIHAN
10 Vice Pres Finance & Administration .... Mrs. June MCGRISKEN
26 Vice Pres Govt/Community Relations .... Mrs. Linda WERBEL DASHEFSKY
30 Vice President of Development .... Mr. Thomas FLOOD
84 Asst Vice Pres Enrollment Mgmt .... Mr. Joseph CUMMINGS
15 Asst Vice Pres Human Resources .... Mr. Richard COLADARCI
20 Asst Academic Dean .... Dr. Michelle HIRSCH
35 Asst Dn Freshmen Stds/Acad Support .... Ms. Monica MICHALSKI
27 Chief Information Officer .... Mr. Guy F. CARLSEN
06 Registrar .... Ms. Roxanne PERSAUD
32 Dean of Students .... Dr. Cheryl A. HOWELL
07 Director of Admissions .... Mr. John MCAULIFFE
08 Director Library .... Dr. James SMITH
36 Director of Career Placement Center .... Ms. Naomi KINLEY
18 Director of Facilities Management .... Mr. Kevin O'ROURKE
29 Director of Alumni Relations .... Mr. Dennis MCDERMOTT
41 Director of Athletics .... Ms. Irma GARCIA
42 Director Campus Ministry .... Bro. Thomas GRADY, OSF
09 Director of Institutional Research .... Mr. Steven CATALANO
21 Controller .... Mr. John RAGNO

St. John Fisher College (F)

3690 East Avenue, Rochester NY 14618-3597
County: Monroe
FICE Identification: 002821
Unit ID: 195720
Telephone: (585) 385-8000
Carnegie Class: DRU
FAX Number: (585) 899-3870
Calendar System: Semester
URL: www.sjfc.edu
Established: 1948
Annual Undergrad Tuition & Fees: $26,260
Enrollment: 4,020
Coed
Affiliation or Control: Independent Non-Profit
IRS Status: 501(c)3
Highest Offering: Doctorate
Program: Liberal Arts And General; Teacher Preparatory; Business Emphasis
Accreditation: M, BUS, CACREP, NURSE, PHAR, TED

01 President .... Dr. Donald E. BAIN
04 Exec Asst to Pres/Secy to Board .... Ms. Joan R. BENULIS
05 Provost/Dean of College .... Dr. Ronald J. AMBROSETTI
84 Sr Vice Pres Enrollment Management .... Dr. Gerard J. ROONEY
10 Vice President for Finance/CFO .... Mr. Thomas E. O'NEIL
30 Vice Pres Institutional Advancement .... Dr. William J. O'CONNER
32 VP Student Affairs & Diversity .... Dr. Richard DEJESUS-RUEFF
49 Assoc VP Acad Affs/Dean Arts & Sci .... Dr. David S. PATE
50 Dean School of Business .... Dr. David G. MARTIN
53 Dean School of Education .... Dr. Wendy A. PATERSON
66 Dean School of Nursing .... Dr. Dianne C. COONEY MINER
67 Dean School of Pharmacy .... Dr. Scott A. SWIGART
28 Director Multicultural Affairs .... Mr. Yantee SLOBERT
06 Registrar .... Ms. Julia M. THOMAS
16 Director of Human Resources .... Ms. Karen J. GAGE
27 Director Marketing & Communications .... Ms. Anne R. GEER
06 Associate Registrar .... Ms. Cheryl O. EVANS
08 Director of the Library .... Ms. Melissa JADLOS
14 Chief Information/Computing Officer .... Mr. Stacy S. SLOCUM
15 Director of Payroll & Benefits .... Ms. Mary R. POWLEY
29 Director Alumni Relations .... Mr. Christopher B. SULLIVAN
37 Director Student Financial Aid .... Mrs. Angela B. MONNAT
42 Chaplain/Director Campus Ministry .... Rev. Joseph M. LANZALACO
19 Director of Safety & Security .... Mr. Michael E. MCCARTHY
41 Athletic Director .... Mr. Robert A. WARD
18 Director of Physical Plant .... Mr. Larry P. JACOBSON
21 Controller .... Ms. Linda M. STEINKIRCHNER
23 Director of Wellness Center .... Ms. Maureen A. NICHE
31 Director of Community Service .... Mrs. Sally J. VAUGHAN
07 Director of Freshman Admissions .... Ms. Stacy A. LEDERMANN
07 Dir of Transfer/Graduate Admissions .... Mr. Jose PERALES
09 Director of Institutional Research .... Ms. Elizabeth A. LACHANCE
35 Director Student Affairs .... Mr. Thomas C. RODGERS
36 Director Student Placement .... Ms. Betsy MCDERMOTT
105 Webmaster .... Ms. Jody C. BENEDICT

St. John's University (G)

8000 Utopia Parkway, Queens NY 11439-0001
County: Queens
FICE Identification: 002823
Unit ID: 195809
Telephone: (718) 990-6161
Carnegie Class: DRU
FAX Number: (718) 990-5723
Calendar System: Semester
URL: www.stjohns.edu
Established: 1870
Annual Undergrad Tuition & Fees: $33,875
Enrollment: 21,354
Coed
Affiliation or Control: Roman Catholic
IRS Status: 501(c)3
Highest Offering: Doctorate
Program: Liberal Arts And General; Teacher Preparatory; Professional
Accreditation: M, ARCPA, ART, AUD, BUS, BUSA, CACREP, CLPSY, EMT, LAW, LIB, MT, PHAR, RAD, SCPSY, SP, TEAC

01 President .... Rev. Donald J. HARRINGTON, CM
10 Sr VP Finance/Operations/Treaurer .... Ms. Martha HIRST
05 Provost .... Dr. Julia A. UPTON, RSM
03 Exec VP Mission & Student Services .... Rev. James J. MAHER, CM
16 Sr VP Human Res/Strategic Plan/IR .... Ms. Mary T. HARPER HAGAN
100 Sr VP/Chief of Staff to Pres .... Mr. Robert D. WILE
101 Vice Pres & Secretary of University .... Dr. Dorothy E. HABBEN
20 Vice Pres Academic Support Services .... Dr. Andre A. MCKENZIE
31 Vice President Community Relations .... Mr. Joseph A. SCIAME
09 VP Institutional Research/Acad Plng .... Dr. Clover W. HALL
84 Vice President Enrollment Mgmt .... Ms. Beth EVANS
18 VP Facilities/Branch Campus/Conf Sv .... Mr. Brij B. ANAND
19 Vice President Public Safety .... Mr. Thomas J. LAWRENCE
104 Vice President Global Programs .... Mr. Anthony R. PACHECO
13 Vice Pres of Info Technology/CIO .... Mr. Joseph J. TUFANO
21 VP for Business Affairs & CFO .... Ms. Jacqueline TRAVISANO
42 VP University Ministry and Events .... Dr. Pamela G. SHEA-BYRNES
32 VP Student Affairs .... Dr. Kathryn T. HUTCHINSON
37 Assoc VP Student Financial Svcs .... Mr. Jorge L. RODRIGUEZ
20 Vice Provost .... Dr. Derek V. OWENS
49 Dean St. John's College .... Dr. Jeffrey W. FAGEN
53 Dean Sch of Edu/Academic VP SI Camp .... Dr. Jerrold ROSS
50 Dean Tobin Col of Business .... Dr. Victoria L. SHOAF
67 Dean Pharmacy/Allied Health Prof .... Dr. Robert MANGIONE
107 Dean Col of Professional Studies .... Dr. Kathleen VOUTE MACDONALD
61 Dean School of Law .... Mr. Michael A. SIMONS
08 Interim Dean University Libraries .... Ms. Theresa M. MAYLONE
20 Assoc Provost Administration .... Ms. Linda A. SHANNON
20 Associate Provost Planning/Res Mgmt .... Dr. Diane S. HERGENROTHER
35 Assoc VP Student Affairs & Dean .... Dr. Jose R. RODRIGUEZ
35 Assoc VP Student Affairs .... Dr. Darren M. MORTON
104 Assoc VP Global Studies .... Mr. Matthew G. PUCCIARELLI
14 Asssoc VP Information Technology .... Ms. Maura A. WOODS
86 Asst VP Government Relations .... Mr. Brian BROWNE
26 Asst VP Media Relations .... Mr. Dominic SCIANNA
21 Asst VP and Exec Dir - SI Campus .... Mr. Gerard A. MCENERNEY
43 General Counsel .... Mr. Joseph E. OLIVA
21 Controller .... Mr. Anthony MACALUSO
06 University Registrar .... Ms. Joanne A. LLERANDI
90 Exec Director User Services .... Mr. Kenneth J. MAHLMEISTER
88 Exec Director Vincentian Center .... Sr. Margaret J. KELLY, DC
88 Exec Dir Aux & Conf Services .... Ms. Bernadette GROGAN LAVIN
36 Exec Director Career Center .... Ms. Denise C. HOPKINS
15 Director Human Resources Svcs .... Ms. Cynthia F. SIMPSON
29 Director Alumni Relations .... Mr. William G. SCHAEFFER
07 Director Admissions .... Ms. Karen A. VAHEY
38 Dir Ctr Counseling & Consultation .... Dr. Edward A. HATTAUER

37 Dir Financial Aid Staten Isl Campus .... Ms. Theresa C. CANTARELLA
39 Director Residence Life .... Mr. Eric M. FINKELSTEIN
44 Director Gift Planning .... Ms. Susan M. DAMIANI
23 Director Queens Health Services .... Mrs. Pauline TUMMINO, RN
23 Director SI Health Services .... Mrs. Margaret A. TIERNEY, RN
96 Director Purchasing .... Mr. Jeffery I. WEISS
41 Athletic Director .... Mr. Chris P. MONASCH
92 Director Honors Program .... Dr. Robert FORMAN
56 Director Special Programs .... Mrs. Cecilia M. RUSSO
88 Director Ctr for Teaching/Learning .... Dr. Maura C. FLANNERY
85 Dir Internatl Students/Scholar Svcs .... Ms. Krista L. GARD
21 Director Internal Audit .... Mr. Alex J. HOEHN
25 Director Grants & Research .... Mr. Jared E. LITTMAN
20 Acad Asst VP - SI Campus .... Dr. Christopher CUCCIA
36 Assoc Dir Career Ctr Staten Island .... Ms. Roseann T. SORENSEN
35 Assoc Dean Student Life - SI Campus .... Ms. Kimberly J. PALMIERI-MOUDED
40 Manager of Bookstore .... Mrs. Denise SERVIDIO

Saint Joseph's College, New York (A)

245 Clinton Avenue, Brooklyn NY 11205-3688
County: Kings FICE Identification: 002825
Unit ID: 195544
Telephone: (718) 940-5300 Carnegie Class: Master's M
FAX Number: (718) 636-7245 Calendar System: Semester
URL: www.sjcny.edu
Established: 1916 Annual Undergrad Tuition & Fees: $18,415
Enrollment: 1,260 Coed
Affiliation or Control: Independent Non-Profit IRS Status: 501(c)3
Highest Offering: Master's
Program: Liberal Arts And General; Teacher Preparatory; Professional; Fine Arts Emphasis
Accreditation: M, ADNUR, NUR, SP, @TEAC

01 President .... Sr. Elizabeth A. HILL
05 Provost .... Sr. Loretta A. MCGRANN
44 Vice Pres Institutional Advancement .... Ms. Nancy J. CONNORS
88 Vice Pres/Dean Adult & Profess Educ .... Dr. Thomas G. TRAVIS
84 VP Enrollment Mgmt/Dir Admissions .... Mrs. Theresa LAROCCA MEYER
20 Academic Dean Arts & Sciences .... Dr. Richard GREENWALD
32 Dean of Students .... Dr. Susan HUDEC
10 Chief Financial Officer .... Mr. John C. ROTH
13 Chief Information Officer .... Mr. Kenneth MCCOLLUM
08 Director of Library .... Dr. William MENG
06 Registrar .... Mr. Robert PERGOLIS
37 Director of Financial Aid .... Ms. Amy THOMPSON
38 Director Counseling/Career Services .... Mr. Frank LATERRA
35 Dir of Co-Curricular Activities .... Mrs. Sherrie VAN ARNAM
29 AVP Alumni Relations/Stewardship .... Ms. Mary Jo B. CHIARA
21 Controller .... Mr. Matthew BRELLIS
88 Director of Child Study Center .... Dr. Susan STRAUT COLLARD
18 Director Physical Plant .... Mr. Alvin DORTA
30 Director Development .... Ms. Clare KEHOE
15 Director of Human Resources .... Ms. D'adra CRUMP
09 Director of Institutional Research .... Ms. Lillian ZHU
28 Director of Diversity .... Mr. Rupert CAMPBELL
26 Public Affairs Manager .... Mr. Michael BANACH
13 Director of Core Technologies .... Mr. Kevin HUTCHINSON
14 Director of Enterprise Systems .... Ms. Michelle PAPAJOHN
90 Director of Academic Computing .... Ms. Lichele ABEAR
41 Director of Athletics .... Mr. Frank CARBONE

Saint Joseph's College, New York - Suffolk Campus (B)

155 W Roe Boulevard, Patchogue NY 11772-2399
County: Suffolk FICE Identification: 029081
Unit ID: 195562
Telephone: (631) 687-5100 Carnegie Class: Master's M
FAX Number: (631) 654-1782 Calendar System: Semester
URL: www.sjcny.edu
Established: 1916 Annual Undergrad Tuition & Fees: $18,425
Enrollment: 3,875 Coed
Affiliation or Control: Independent Non-Profit IRS Status: 501(c)3
Highest Offering: Master's
Program: Liberal Arts And General; Teacher Preparatory; Professional
Accreditation: &M, NRPA

01 President .... Sr. Elizabeth A. HILL
05 Provost .... Sr. Loretta A. MCGRANN
44 Vice Pres Institutional Advancement .... Ms. Nancy J. CONNORS
20 Vice Pres/Dean Adult & Profess Educ .... Dr. Thomas TRAVIS
84 Vice Pres for Enrollment Management .... Mrs. Theresa LAROCCA MEYER
07 Assoc VP Enrollment/Dir Admissions .... Ms. Georgia-Lynn LAMENS
30 Assoc VP for Grants & Major Gifts .... Ms. Clare KEHOE
49 Int Academic Dean Arts & Sciences .... Ms. Doris STRATMANN
10 Chief Financial Officer .... Mr. John C. ROTH
32 Dean of Students .... Dr. Susan HUDEC
06 Registrar .... Mr. Robert PERGOLIS
08 Director of Library .... Mrs. Terry CORBIN-HUTCHINSON
37 Director of Financial Aid .... Ms. Amy THOMPSON
35 Director Co-Curricular Activities .... Ms. Marian RUSSO
38 Director Counseling/Career Services .... Mr. Frank LATERRA
18 Director Physical Plant .... Ms. Linda VIGNATO
41 Athletic Director .... Mr. Donald LIZAK
27 Chief Information Officer .... Mr. Kenneth MCCOLLUM
15 Director of Human Resources .... Ms. D'adra CRUMP
21 Controller .... Mr. Matthew BRELLIS
29 Director of Alumni Relations .... Mr. Matthew COLSON
09 Director of Institutional Research .... Ms. Lillian ZHU
28 Director of Diversity .... Mr. Rupert CAMPBELL
26 Director of Public Relations .... Ms. Jessica MCALEER
13 Director of Core Technologies .... Mr. Kevin HUTCHINSON
14 Director of Enterprise Solutions .... Ms. Michelle PAPAJOHN
90 Director of Academic Computing .... Ms. Lichele ABEAR

† Regional accreditation is carried under the parent institution in Brooklyn, NY.

St. Joseph's College of Nursing (C)

206 Prospect Avenue, Syracuse NY 13203-1806
County: Onondaga Identification: 666397
Unit ID: 195191
Telephone: (315) 448-5040 Carnegie Class: Assoc/PrivNFP
FAX Number: (315) 448-5745 Calendar System: Semester
URL: www.sjhsyr.org/sjhhc/sjhcon
Established: 1898 Annual Undergrad Tuition & Fees: N/A
Enrollment: 276 Coed
Affiliation or Control: Independent Non-Profit IRS Status: 501(c)3
Highest Offering: Associate Degree
Program: Occupational; 2-Year Principally Bachelor's Creditable; Nursing Emphasis
Accreditation: @M

01 Dean .... Mrs. Marianne MARKOWITZ

Saint Joseph's Seminary (D)

Dunwoodie, #201 Seminary Avenue, Yonkers NY 10704-1852
County: Westchester FICE Identification: 002826
Unit ID: 195571
Telephone: (914) 968-6200 Carnegie Class: Spec/Faith
FAX Number: (914) 376-2019 Calendar System: Quarter
URL: www.dunwoodie.edu
Established: 1896 Annual Graduate Tuition & Fees: $12,900
Enrollment: 177 Male
Affiliation or Control: Roman Catholic IRS Status: 501(c)3
Highest Offering: Master's; No Undergraduates
Program: Professional
Accreditation: M, THEOL

01 Rector .... M.Rev. Gerald T. WALSH
05 Academic Dean .... Rev. Kevin P. O'REILLY
32 Dean of Students/Admissions .... Rev. Andrew R. KING
08 Director Library Services .... Sr. Monica WOOD, SC
10 Director Finance .... Mr. Stephen DIDIMAMOFF
30 Director of Development .... Mrs. Jeannie STAPLETON-SMITH
42 Director Campus Ministry .... Rev. Charles SZIVOS
42 Director Campus Ministry .... Rev. Donald F. HAGGERTY
06 Registrar .... Sr. Mary Frances MILLS
38 Director of Psychological Services .... Dr. Richard GALLAGHER
18 Director of Buildings & Grounds .... Mr. Robert SCULLY

St. Lawrence University (E)

23 Romoda Drive, Canton NY 13617-1423
County: St. Lawrence FICE Identification: 002829
Unit ID: 195216
Telephone: (315) 229-5011 Carnegie Class: Bac/A&S
FAX Number: (315) 229-5502 Calendar System: Other
URL: www.stlawu.edu
Established: 1856 Annual Undergrad Tuition & Fees: $42,735
Enrollment: 2,423 Coed
Affiliation or Control: Independent Non-Profit IRS Status: 501(c)3
Highest Offering: Master's
Program: Liberal Arts And General; Teacher Preparatory
Accreditation: M, TEAC

01 President .... Dr. William FOX
05 Vice Pres/Dean Academic Affairs .... Dr. Valerie D. LEHR
30 Vice Pres University Advancement .... Mr. Michael P. ARCHIBALD
10 Vice President Finance & Treasurer .... Ms. Kathryn L. MULLANEY
32 Vice Pres/Dean Student Life .... Dr. Joseph TOLLIVER
07 Vice Pres/Dean Admissions/Fin Aid .... Mr. Jeffrey RICKEY
26 VP for Employee/Community Relations .... Mrs. Lisa M. CANIA
21 Assoc Vice President for Finance .... Ms. Carol GABLE
89 Associate Dean of the First-Year .... Dr. Catherine A. CROSBY-CURRIE
35 Associate Dean of Student Life .... Mr. Rance DAVIS
06 Registrar .... Ms. Carolyn FILLIPPI
37 Director of Financial Aid .... Mrs. Patricia J B. FARMER
08 Librarian .... Vacant
36 Director of Career Planning .... Dr. Carol BATE
09 Director of Institutional Research .... Mrs. Christine ZIMMERMAN
18 Chief Facilities/Physical Plant .... Mr. Daniel B. SEAMAN
20 Asst Dean of Academic Affairs .... Ms. Lorie MACKENZIE
29 Director Alumni Relations .... Ms. Kimberly HISSONG
35 Director Student Affairs .... Dr. Matha E. THORNTON
23 Director of Health & Counseling .... Ms. Pat ELLIS
84 Director Enrollment Management .... Vacant
96 Director of Purchasing .... Ms. Ruta OZOLS

St. Paul's School of Nursing (F)

30-50 Whitestone Expressway, 4th Fl, Flushing NY 11354
County: Queens FICE Identification: 012364
Unit ID: 189811
Telephone: (718) 357-0500 Carnegie Class: Assoc/PrivFP
FAX Number: (718) 357-4683 Calendar System: Semester
URL: www.stpaulsschoolofnursing.com
Established: 1969 Annual Undergrad Tuition & Fees: $18,600
Enrollment: 165 Coed
Affiliation or Control: Proprietary IRS Status: Proprietary
Highest Offering: Associate Degree
Program: Occupational; 2-Year Principally Bachelor's Creditable; Nursing Emphasis
Accreditation: ABHES

01 President .... Lynn SALVAGE
66 Regional Dean of Nursing Schools .... Genevieve M. JENSEN
37 Financial Aid Director .... Vacant
07 Asst Director of Admissions .... Augie PEREIRA
08 Head Librarian .... Chris SCHNUPP
10 Chief Financial/Business Officer .... Eric SEDA
06 Registrar .... Suzanne SCHNEIDER

Saint Paul's School of Nursing-Staten Island (G)

2 Teleport Dr Ste 203, 2 Corp Comm, Staten Island NY 10311
County: Richmond FICE Identification: 009479
Unit ID: 195784
Telephone: (718) 818-6470 Carnegie Class: Not Classified
FAX Number: (718) 818-6020 Calendar System: Semester
URL: www.stpaulsschoolofnursing.com
Established: 1904 Annual Undergrad Tuition & Fees: $19,457
Enrollment: 297 Coed
Affiliation or Control: Proprietary IRS Status: Proprietary
Highest Offering: Associate Degree
Program: Occupational; 2-Year Principally Bachelor's Creditable; Nursing Emphasis
Accreditation: ABHES

01 School Director .... Mr. Oleg RABINOVICH
05 Director of Education .... Mr. Robert JANNICELLI
06 Registrar .... Ms. Sandra HETZEL
10 Bursar .... Ms. Olga FORINA
32 Director of Student Services .... Mr. Jordan ZOLTOWSKY
37 Director of Financial Aid .... Ms. Nayamka WARD

St. Thomas Aquinas College (H)

125 Route 340, Sparkill NY 10976-1050
County: Rockland FICE Identification: 002832
Unit ID: 195243
Telephone: (845) 398-4000 Carnegie Class: Master's S
FAX Number: (845) 359-8136 Calendar System: 4/1/4
URL: www.stac.edu
Established: 1952 Annual Undergrad Tuition & Fees: $23,220
Enrollment: 2,077 Coed
Affiliation or Control: Independent Non-Profit IRS Status: 501(c)3
Highest Offering: Master's
Program: Liberal Arts And General; Teacher Preparatory; Professional
Accreditation: M, IACBE, TED

01 President .... Dr. Margaret M. FITZPATRICK, SC
11 Vice Pres Administration & Finance .... Mr. Joseph DONINI
05 Provost/Vice Pres Academic Affairs .... Mr. L. John DURNEY
32 Vice Pres/Dean of Student Affairs .... Dr. Kirk MANNING
84 Vice Pres Enrollment Mgmt/ Marketing .... Mr. Vincent CRAPANZANO
30 Vice President of Development .... Mr. Kevin DUIGNAN
15 Sr Exec Director Human Resources .... Mrs. Patricia PACCHIANA
07 Director Admissions .... Ms. Danielle MACKAY
08 Librarian .... Vacant
06 Registrar .... Mrs. Mildred ALEXIOU
36 Director Placement Services .... Ms. Rachel JACKIEWICZ
37 Director Financial Aid .... Vacant
50 Director Business .... Mr. Michael MURPHY
53 Director Education .... Dr. Meenakshi GAJRIA
79 Director Humanities .... Dr. Robert MURRAY
81 Director Natural Science/Math .... Dr. Mary Ellen FERRARO
83 Director Social Sciences .... Dr. Stacy SEWELL
90 Director of Computing Services .... Ms. Sunny ANTHWAL
09 Director of Institutional Research .... Dr. Renee QUINTYNE
18 Chief Facilities/Physical Plant .... Mr. Patrick LAMBERT
21 Controller .... Mrs. Jennifer MAZZA
29 Director Alumni Relations .... Ms. Joanne FAVATA
35 Director Student Affairs .... Vacant
38 Director Student Counseling .... Dr. Louis MUGGEP
26 Associate Director Communications .... Ms. Bridget CLARK

Saint Vladimir's Orthodox Theological Seminary (I)

575 Scarsdale Road, Crestwood NY 10707-1699
County: Westchester FICE Identification: 002833
Unit ID: 195580
Telephone: (914) 961-8313 Carnegie Class: Spec/Faith
FAX Number: (914) 961-4507 Calendar System: Semester
URL: www.svots.edu
Established: 1938 Annual Graduate Tuition & Fees: $10,762
Enrollment: 60 Coed
Affiliation or Control: Independent Non-Profit IRS Status: 501(c)3
Highest Offering: Master's; No Undergraduates
Program: Religious Emphasis
Accreditation: THEOL

01 President .... M.Blsd. Metropolitan JONAH
00 Chancellor .... V.Rev. Chad HATFIELD
05 Dean .... Rev. John BEHR
10 Assoc Chanc for Finance .... Ms. Melanie RINGA
30 Assoc Chanc for Advancement .... Mr. Theodore BAZIL
20 Assoc Dean Academic Affairs .... Dr. John BARNET
32 Assoc Dean for Student Affairs .... Rev. David MEZYNSKI
08 Librarian/Circulation .... Ms. Eleana SILK
13 Director of Computer Systems .... Mr. Georgios KOKONAS
35 Student Affairs Administrator .... Mrs. Ann SANCHEZ
07 Director Recruitment/Outreach .... Pdn. Joseph MATUSIAK
21 Business Manager .... Mr. Ted BAZIL
40 Bookstore/Operations Manager .... Rev Dn. Gregory HATRAK

Salvation Army School for Officer Training (A)

201 Lafayette Avenue, Suffern NY 10901-4707
County: Rockland Identification: 666020
Telephone: (845) 368-7200 Carnegie Class: Not Classified
FAX Number: (845) 357-6644 Calendar System: Other
URL: www.use.salvationarmy.org
Established: N/A Annual Undergrad Tuition & Fees: $1,070
Enrollment: 77 Coed
Affiliation or Control: Independent Non-Profit IRS Status: 501(c)3
Highest Offering: Associate Degree
Program: Professional
Accreditation: NY

01 Principal .... Major Ronald R. FOREMAN
03 Associate Principal .... Major Dorine M. FOREMAN
11 Asst Principal for Administration .... Major James B. COCKER

Samaritan Hospital School of Nursing (B)

2215 Burdett Avenue, Troy NY 12065
County: Rensselaer FICE Identification: 009248
Unit ID: 196289
Telephone: (518) 271-3285 Carnegie Class: Not Classified
FAX Number: N/A Calendar System: Semester
URL: www.nehealth.com
Established: N/A Annual Undergrad Tuition & Fees: $8,599
Enrollment: 133 Coed
Affiliation or Control: Independent Non-Profit IRS Status: 501(c)3
Highest Offering: Associate Degree
Program: Nursing Emphasis
Accreditation: NY

01 Executive Director .... Ms. Linda D'ARCANGELIS

Sarah Lawrence College (C)

1 Meadway, Bronxville NY 10708-5999
County: Westchester FICE Identification: 002813
Unit ID: 195304
Telephone: (914) 337-0700 Carnegie Class: Bac/A&S
FAX Number: (914) 395-2668 Calendar System: Semester
URL: www.slc.edu
Established: 1926 Annual Undergrad Tuition & Fees: $44,220
Enrollment: 1,670 Coed
Affiliation or Control: Independent Non-Profit IRS Status: 501(c)3
Highest Offering: Master's
Program: Liberal Arts And General
Accreditation: M, @TEAC

01 President .... Dr. Karen R. LAWRENCE
05 Dean of the College .... Dr. Jerrilynn D. DODDS
10 Vice President Finance/Operations .... Mr. Joseph GIOVANNELLI
30 Vice President for Advancement .... Mr. Charles J. RASBERRY
26 Vice Pres Communication & Marketing .... Dr. Gerald A. SCHORIN
11 Vice President for Administration .... Thomas L. BLUM
15 VP Human Resources/Legal Affairs .... Julie AUSTER
88 Assoc VP for Advancement .... Ellen REYNOLDS
20 Associate Dean of the College .... Dr. Mary PORTER
32 Dean of Studies & Student Life .... Dr. Allen GREEN
35 Dean of Student Affairs .... Dr. Paige CRANDALL
07 Dean of Admission & Financial Aid .... Amy ABRAMS
58 Dean Graduate Studies .... Susan GUMA
06 Registrar .... Daniel LICHT
08 Librarian .... Charling FAGAN
13 Director Information Systems .... Sean JAMESON
29 Director of Alumni Relations .... Cheryl CIPRO
36 Director Career Counseling .... Angela CHERUBINI
44 Major Gifts Officer .... Adele CONNOR
28 Director of Diversity .... Natalie GROSS
18 Director of Facilities .... Maureen GALLAGHER
19 Director of Public Safety .... Larry HOFFMAN

SBI Campus-An Affiliate of Sanford-Brown (D)

320 S Service Road, Melville NY 11747-3201
County: Suffolk FICE Identification: 011647
Unit ID: 192156
Telephone: (631) 370-3300 Carnegie Class: Assoc/PrivFP
FAX Number: (631) 293-5872 Calendar System: Quarter
URL: www.sbmelville.com
Established: 2008 Annual Undergrad Tuition & Fees: $10,030
Enrollment: 500 Coed
Affiliation or Control: Proprietary IRS Status: Proprietary
Highest Offering: Associate Degree
Program: Occupational; 2-Year Principally Bachelor's Creditable
Accreditation: ACICS, MAAB

01 President .... Dr. Eric RICIOPPO
05 Director of Education .... Dr. Ajith CHERIYAN
06 Registrar .... Mr. Michael KLEIN
07 Director of Admissions .... Mr. Nicholas FERLISI

Schenectady County Community College (E)

78 Washington Avenue, Schenectady NY 12305
County: Schenectady FICE Identification: 006785
Unit ID: 195322
Telephone: (518) 381-1200 Carnegie Class: Assoc/Pub-U-SC
FAX Number: (518) 346-0379 Calendar System: Semester
URL: www.sunysccc.edu
Established: 1967 Annual Undergrad Tuition & Fees (In-District): $3,414
Enrollment: 5,225 Coed
Affiliation or Control: State/Local IRS Status: 501(c)3
Highest Offering: Associate Degree
Program: Occupational; 2-Year Principally Bachelor's Creditable
Accreditation: M, ACFEI, MUS

01 President .... Dr. Quintin B. BULLOCK
05 Vice President of Academic Affairs .... Dr. Penny A. HAYNES
10 Vice President of Administration .... Dr. William F. ANDERSON
32 Vice President of Student Affairs .... Ms. Martha J. ASSELIN
103 Actg Dean of Workforce Development .... Ms. Denise BRUCKER
37 Director of Financial Aid .... Mr. Brian F. MCGARVEY
20 Assistant Dean Academic Affairs .. Ms. Angela M. PRESTIACOMO
11 Asst Dean Administrative Services .... Mr. Michael P. D'ANNIBALE
88 Assistant Dean for Assessment & Int .... Dr. Leonard GAINES, JR.
45 Asst Dean for Planning/Acct/Effect .... Mr. Darren JOHNSON
30 Executive Director of Development .... Ms. Carmel PATRICK
06 Registrar .... Ms. Laurie A. HEMPSTEAD
07 Director of Admissions .... Mr. David G. SAMPSON
08 Director Library Services .... Ms. Lynne O. KING
90 Director of Academic Computing .... Mr. Nicholas G. LTAIF
18 Director of Campus Maintenance .... Mr. Alan J. YAUNEY
27 Chief Information Officer .... Mr. Dan NICOLAESCU
44 Dir Annual Giving/Scholarships/Alum .... Ms. Vladia BONIEWSKI
91 Manager of Administrative Computing .... Mr. Arthur PAOLELLI
26 Public Rels/Publications Specialist .... Ms. Heather L. MEANEY
36 Coordinator Career/Employment Svcs .... Mr. Robert FREDERICK
15 Coordinator Personnel Services/AAO .... Ms. Carolyn PINN
09 Coordinator Institutional Research .... Mr. Dale J. MILLER
28 Coord Multicult/Educ/Oppty Pgms .... Mr. Jason BENITEZ
21 Coordinator for Financial Services .... Ms. Aimee S. WARFIELD
04 Assistant to the President/BOT .... Ms. Paula OHLHOUS

School of Visual Arts (F)

209 E 23rd Street, New York NY 10010-3994
County: New York FICE Identification: 007468
Unit ID: 197151
Telephone: (212) 592-2000 Carnegie Class: Spec/Arts
FAX Number: (212) 725-3587 Calendar System: Semester
URL: www.sva.edu
Established: 1947 Annual Undergrad Tuition & Fees: $27,070
Enrollment: 4,051 Coed
Affiliation or Control: Proprietary IRS Status: Proprietary
Highest Offering: Master's
Program: Fine Arts Emphasis
Accreditation: M, ART, CIDA

00 Acting Chairman .... Milton GLASER
01 President .... David J. RHODES
03 Executive Vice President .... Anthony P. RHODES
05 Provost .... Jeffrey NESIN
10 Chief Financial Officer .... Gary SHILLET
32 Exec Dir of Student Affairs/Admiss .... Javier VEGA
26 Exec Director of External Relations .... Susan MODENSTEIN
13 Chief Information Officer .... Cosmin TOMESCU
06 Registrar .... Jon TODD
07 Director Admission .... Adam ROGERS
35 Director of Student Affairs .... Megan MANNATO
08 Director Visual Arts Library .... Robert LOBE
37 Director Financial Aid .... William BERRIOS
36 Director Career Development .... Jennifer PHILLIPS
30 Director Development/Alumni Affairs .... Carrie LINCOURT
19 Director Security .... Nick AGJMURATI
15 Director of Human Resources .... Frank AGOSTA
09 Director of Institutional Research .... Jerold DAVIS
27 Director of Communications .... Michael GRANT

Seminary of the Immaculate Conception (G)

440 W Neck Road, Huntington NY 11743-1696
County: Suffolk FICE Identification: 002683
Unit ID: 195429
Telephone: (631) 423-0483 Carnegie Class: Spec/Faith
FAX Number: (631) 423-2346 Calendar System: Semester
URL: www.icseminary.edu
Established: 1926 Annual Graduate Tuition & Fees: $20,300
Enrollment: 128 Coed
Affiliation or Control: Roman Catholic IRS Status: 501(c)3
Highest Offering: Doctorate; No Undergraduates
Program: Professional; Religious Emphasis
Accreditation: M, THEOL

01 Rector .... Msgr. Peter I. VACCARI
03 Vice Rector .... Msgr. Richard HENNING
05 Academic Dean .... Sr. Mary Louise BRINK, SC
32 Dean of Seminarians .... Rev. Nicholas ZIENTARSKI
38 Director of Spiritual Formation .... Rev. Charles R. FINK
08 Librarian .... Ms. Elyse BAUM-HAYES
10 Director Finance & Business .... Mr. Dennis J. SCHLOSSER
06 Registrar .... Ms. Kathryn L. ZAHNER

Sh'or Yoshuv Rabbinical College (H)

1 Cedar Lawn Avenue, Lawrence NY 11559-1714
County: Nassau FICE Identification: 025059
Unit ID: 195438
Telephone: (516) 239-9002 Carnegie Class: Spec/Faith
FAX Number: (516) 239-9003 Calendar System: Semester
URL: www.shoryoshuv.org
Established: 1963 Annual Undergrad Tuition & Fees: $9,460
Enrollment: 235 Male
Affiliation or Control: Independent Non-Profit IRS Status: 501(c)3
Highest Offering: Second Talmudic Degree
Program: Teacher Preparatory; Professional
Accreditation: RABN

01 Dean .... Rabbi Naftalie JAEGER
05 Director .... Rabbi Avrohom HALPERN
32 Director of Student Affairs .... Rabbi Moshe GREENE
06 Registrar .... Mrs. Sharon JACOBOWITZ
37 Director SFA .... Mr. Moshe RUBIN

Siena College (I)

515 Loudon Road, Loudonville NY 12211-1462
County: Albany FICE Identification: 002816
Unit ID: 195474
Telephone: (518) 783-2300 Carnegie Class: Bac/A&S
FAX Number: (518) 783-4293 Calendar System: Semester
URL: www.siena.edu
Established: 1937 Annual Undergrad Tuition & Fees: $27,430
Enrollment: 3,423 Coed
Affiliation or Control: Independent Non-Profit IRS Status: 501(c)3
Highest Offering: Master's
Program: Liberal Arts And General; Teacher Preparatory
Accreditation: M, BUS, SW, TED

01 President .... Fr. Kevin MULLEN, OFM
05 Vice President for Academic Affairs .... Dr. Linda L. RICHARDSON
32 Vice President for Student Affairs .... Dr. Maryellen GILROY
10 Vice President for Finance & Admin .... Mr. Paul T. STEC
84 VP for Enrollment Management .... Mr. Ned J. JONES
30 VP for Development & External Affs .... Mr. David B. SMITH
100 Chief of Staff .... Fr. Kenneth P. PAULLI, OFM
13 Chief Information Officer .... Mr. Thomas A. HULL
49 Dean of Liberal Arts .... Dr. Ralph J. BLASTING
50 Dean of Business .... Dr. Jeffrey A. MELLO
81 Dean of Science .... Dr. Karen S. QUAAL
20 Assoc VP Acad Affs/Student Success .... Dr. Peter C. ELLARD
45 Assoc VP Acad Affs/Inst Effectivns .... Dr. Penelope W. BRUNNER
15 Asst VP for Human Resources .... Ms. Cynthia B. KING-LEROY
07 Asst VP Admissions/Dir Admissions .... Ms. Heather M. RENAULT
21 Asst VP for Finance & Admin .... Ms. Mary C. STRUNK
18 Asst VP for Facilities Management .... Mr. Mark FROST
35 Asst VP Stdnt Affs/Dean of Students .... Ms. Jeanne M. OBERMAYER
19 Asst VP Stdnt Aff/Dir Public Safety .... Mr. Michael PAPADOPOULOS
86 Asst VP Acad Affs/Govt & Found Rels .. Mr. Alfredo MEDINA, JR.
06 Registrar .... Mr. James SERBALIK
37 Asst Vice Pres Financial Aid .... Ms. Mary K. LAWYER
08 Dir of Library/Audio Visual Svcs .... Mr. Gary B. THOMPSON
43 College Counsel .... Ms. Sandra M. CASEY
92 Director of Honors Program .... Dr. Lois K. DALY
88 Associate Dean of Students .... Mr. J. L. BEBB
88 Associate Dean of Students .... Mr. John R. FELIO
39 Director of Residence Life .... Ms. Kathleen BRANNOCK
41 Director of Athletics .... Mr. John D'ARGENIO
36 Director of Career Center .... Ms. Debra DELBELSO
88 Director of Project Management Ofc .... Mr. Rad W. TAYLOR
42 Chaplain of the College .... Fr. Gregory JAKUBOWICZ, OFM
88 Dir Franciscan Ctr/Svc & Advocacy .. Fr. Mathias F. DOYLE, OFM
26 Dir Strategic Comm/Integrated Mktg .... Ms. Delcy FOX
38 Director of Counseling Center .... Dr. Wally B. BZBELL
29 Director of Alumni Relations .... Ms. Mary Beth FINNERTY
09 Dir of Institutional Research .... Dr. Jon ENRIQUEZ
88 Dir of Risk Analysis/Project Mgmt .... Ms. Sandy SERBALIK
94 Dir Sr Thea Bowman Ctr for Women .... Dr. Shannon O'NEILL
23 Director of Health Services .... Ms. Carrie HOGAN
40 Bookstore Manager .... Mr. Richard IVES
88 Director of Development .... Mr. Bob P. KLEIN
44 Director of Planned Giving .... Mr. Jack R. SISE
28 Dir of Damietta Cross-Cultural Ctr .... Mr. Oscar J. MAYORGA
104 Director of Study Abroad/Intl Pgms .... Bro. Brian C. BELANGER, OFM
96 Dir of Auxiliary Svcs & Procurement .... Ms. Laura S. PARRY
09 Institutional Researcher .... Vacant

Simmons Institute of Funeral Service, Inc. (A)

1828 South Avenue at W Brighton,
Syracuse NY 13207-2098
County: Onondaga FICE Identification: 010837
Unit ID: 195492
Telephone: (315) 475-5142 Carnegie Class: Assoc/PrivFP
FAX Number: (315) 475-3817 Calendar System: Semester
URL: www.simmonsinstitute.com
Established: 1900 Annual Undergrad Tuition & Fees: $10,600
Enrollment: 32 Coed
Affiliation or Control: Proprietary IRS Status: Proprietary
Highest Offering: Associate Degree
Program: 2-Year Principally Bachelor's Creditable
Accreditation: FUSER

01 President/CEO ... Maurice C. WIGHTMAN

Skidmore College (B)

815 N Broadway, Saratoga Springs NY 12866-1632
County: Saratoga FICE Identification: 002814
Unit ID: 195526
Telephone: (518) 580-5000 Carnegie Class: Bac/A&S
FAX Number: (518) 580-5936 Calendar System: Semester
URL: www.skidmore.edu
Established: 1911 Annual Undergrad Tuition & Fees: $42,380
Enrollment: 2,752 Coed
Affiliation or Control: Independent Non-Profit IRS Status: 501(c)3
Highest Offering: Master's
Program: Liberal Arts And General; Teacher Preparatory; Professional
Accreditation: M, ART, SW, @TEAC

01 President ... Dr. Philip A. GLOTZBACH
05 Vice President Academic Affairs ... Dr. Susan A. KRESS
10 Vice President Finance/Treasurer ... Mr. Michael D. WEST
30 Vice President for Advancement ... Mr. Michael T. CASEY
16 Assoc VP Bus Aff/Dir Human Res ... Ms. Barbara E. BECK
20 Dean of Faculty ... Dr. Muriel POSTON
32 Dean of Student Affairs ... Ms. W. Rochelle CALHOUN
07 Dean of Admissions & Financial Aid ... Ms. Mary Lou W. BATES
71 Dean of Special Programs ... Dr. Jeffrey O. SEGRAVE
06 Registrar/Director Inst Research ... Ms. Ann L. HENDERSON
20 Associate Dean Academic Advising ... Dr. Corey FREEMAN-GALLANT
20 Associate Dean of Faculty ... Dr. Paty RUBIO
35 Int Assoc Dean Student Affairs ... Mr. David KARP
39 Asst Dean Stdnt Affs/Dir Resid Life ... Mr. Donald B. HASTINGS
89 Assoc Dean/Dir of First Year Exper ... Dr. Beau BRESLIN
45 Exec Dir Strategic Initiatives ... Ms. Barbara L. KRAUSE
26 Executive Director Communications ... Mr. Dan FORBUSH
102 Dir Foundations & Corporate Rels ... Mr. Barry PRITZKER
46 Director of Sponsored Research ... Mr. Bill TOMLINSON
13 Director Center Info Tech Services ... Mr. Justin D. SIPHER
105 Director of Web Development ... Mr. Andy CAMP
31 Director Community Education ... Ms. Sharon A. ARPEY
87 Dir Summer Sessions/Summer Pgms ... Dr. Auden THOMAS
41 Athletic Director ... Dr. Gail L. CUMMINGS-DANSON
28 Director for Intercultural Studies ... Vacant
22 Asst Dir EEO & Workforce Diversity ... Mr. Herb CROSSMAN
91 Director of MIS ... Mr. Jeffrey A. CLARK
104 Dir of Off-Campus Study & Exchanges ... Ms. Cori FILSON
26 Director of Community Relations ... Mr. Robert S. KIMMERLE
44 Director Donor Relations ... Ms. Mary L. SOLOMONS
30 Director of Development ... Ms. Lori EASTMAN
29 Director of Alumni Affairs/Events ... Mr. Michael SPOSILI
36 Director of Career Services ... Vacant
37 Director of Financial Aid ... Ms. Beth POST-LUNDQUIST
38 Director Counseling Center ... Dr. Julia C. ROUTBORT
21 Director of Business Services ... Ms. Christine KACZMAREK
88 Director of HEOP ... Vacant
23 Director of Health Services ... Ms. Pamela HOULE
18 Director of Facilities Services ... Mr. Daniel RODECKER
19 Director of Campus Safety ... Mr. Dennis S. CONWAY
08 College Librarian ... Ms. Ruth S. COPANS
28 Director Student Diversity Programs ... Ms. Mariel L. MARTIN
96 Director of Purchasing ... Mrs. Carol N. SCHNITZER
42 Dir of Religious & Spiritual Life ... Mr. Rick CHRISMAN
24 Director of Media Services ... Mr. T. Hunt CONARD
09 Director of Institutional Research ... Mr. Joseph STANKOVICH
40 Manager Skidmore Shop ... Mr. Jon NEIL
101 Coordinator of Trustee Affairs ... Ms. Jeanne M. SISSON
04 Special Asst to the President ... Ms. Elizabeth B. BOURQUE

Sotheby's Institute of Art (C)

570 Lexington Ave, 6th Floor, New York NY 10022
County: New York Identification: 667007
Telephone: (212) 517-3929 Carnegie Class: Not Classified
FAX Number: (212) 517-6568 Calendar System: Semester
URL: www.sothebysinstitute.com
Established: N/A Annual Graduate Tuition & Fees: $40,416
Enrollment: 117 Coed
Affiliation or Control: Proprietary IRS Status: Proprietary
Highest Offering: First Professional Degree; No Undergraduates
Program: Professional; Fine Arts Emphasis
Accreditation: ART

01 Director ... Ms. Lesley A. CADMAN

*State University of New York System Office (D)

State University Plaza, Albany NY 12246-0001
County: Albany FICE Identification: 008788
Unit ID: 195827
Telephone: (518) 320-1100 Carnegie Class: N/A
FAX Number: (518) 320-1561
URL: www.suny.edu

01 Chancellor ... Dr. Nancy L. ZIMPHER
05 Provost and Sr Vice Chancellor ... Dr. David LAVALLEE
88 Chanc's Dpty to Ed Pipeline of SUNY ... Ms. Johanna DUNCAN-POITIER
10 Interim Chief Financial Officer ... Mr. Brian HUTZLEY
102 Senior VP Research Foundation ... Vacant
101 V Chanc/Sec of Univ/Pres Rsch Fndtn ... Vacant
20 Vice Chanc Academic Programs ... Dr. Elizabeth BRINGSJORD
15 Vice Chancellor Human Resources ... Mr. Curtis LLOYD
20 Associate Vice Chancellor ... Ms. Aimee BERNSTEIN
20 Associate Provost ... Dr. Robert KRAUSHAAR
18 Vice Chanc for Capital Facilities ... Mr. Robert HAELEN
86 Vice Chanc Government Relations ... Vacant
85 Vice Chancellor for Global Affairs ... Dr. Mitchel LEVENTHAL
28 Vice Provost Diversity/Educ Equity ... Vacant
43 Vice Chancellor & General Counsel ... Mr. William F. HOWARD
88 VP/General Counsel Charter Sch Inst ... Mr. Ralph ROSSI
20 Deputy Provost ... Vacant
09 Assc Provost Inst Research/Analysis ... Dr. John PORTER
35 Assoc Provost Opportunity Programs ... Vacant
19 Asst VC for University Police ... Vacant
32 Assoc VC for Student Life ... Dr. Edward ENGELBRIDE
21 University Auditor ... Mr. Michael ABBOTT
26 Asst Vice Chanc/Communications ... Mr. Morgan HOOK
86 Asst Vice Chanc/Govt.Relations ... Ms. Stacey HENGSTERMAN

*State University of New York at Albany (E)

1400 Washington Avenue, Albany NY 12222-1000
County: Albany FICE Identification: 002835
Unit ID: 196060
Telephone: (518) 442-3300 Carnegie Class: RU/VH
FAX Number: N/A Calendar System: Semester
URL: www.albany.edu
Established: 1844 Annual Undergrad Tuition & Fees (In-State): $6,830
Enrollment: 17,615 Coed
Affiliation or Control: State IRS Status: 501(c)3
Highest Offering: Doctorate
Program: Liberal Arts And General; Teacher Preparatory; Professional
Accreditation: M, BUS, BUSA, CLPSY, COPSY, LIB, PH, PLNG, SCPSY, SPAA, SW, TEAC

02 President ... George M. PHILIP
05 Provost/Vice Pres for Academic Affs ... Susan D. PHILLIPS
46 Vice President for Research ... James DIAS
10 Int Vice Pres Finance & Business ... Stephen BEDITZ
32 Vice President Student Success ... Christine A. BOUCHARD
30 Vice Pres University Development ... Fardin SANAI
26 Vice Pres Communications/Marketing ... Catherine HERMAN
54 Sr VP/CEO Col of Nanoscale Sci/Eng ... Alain KALOYEROS
41 VP Athletic Adm/Dir Intercol Athl ... Lee MCELROY
21 Assoc Vice President & Controller ... Kevin WILCOX
35 Assoc Vice Pres for Student Success ... John MURPHY
45 Assoc Vice President for Research ... Robert O. WEBSTER
09 Asst VP Inst Rsrch/Plng/Efftvnss ... Bruce SZELEST
18 Assistant Vice President Facilities ... John GIARRUSSO
28 Asst VP Diversity/Affirm Action ... Tamra MINOR
84 Vice Provost Enrollment Management ... Wayne LOCUST
97 Vice Prov Undergraduate Education ... Sue S. FAERMAN
49 Dean of Arts & Sciences ... Edelgard WULFERT
53 Dean School of Education ... Robert BANGERT-DROWNS
50 Dean School of Business ... Donald S. SIEGEL
69 Dean School of Public Health ... Philip NASCA
61 Dean of Criminal Justice ... Alan J. LIZOTTE
80 Interim Dean Rockefeller College ... David ROUSSEAU
70 Dean of Social Welfare ... Katharine BRIAR-LAWSON
77 Dean Col of Computing & Information ... Peter BLONIARZ
58 Dean of Graduate Studies ... Kevin WILLIAMS
13 Chief Information Officer ... Christine E. HAILE
29 Exec Director Alumni Association ... Lee SERRAVILLO
13 Director Academic Computing ... Felix WU
100 Chief of Staff ... Vincent DELIO
38 Director Advisement Services Center ... Suzanne K. FREED
07 Director of Admissions ... Robert ANDREA
38 Director of Health/Counseling Svcs ... Estela RIVERO
36 Director Career Development ... Philippe J. ABRAHAM
96 Director of Purchasing ... Edward KANE, JR.

*State University of New York at Binghamton (F)

Vestal Parkway E, Box 6000, Binghamton NY 13902-6000
County: Broome FICE Identification: 002836
Unit ID: 196079
Telephone: (607) 777-2000 Carnegie Class: RU/H
FAX Number: (607) 777-4000 Calendar System: Semester
URL: www.binghamton.edu
Established: 1946 Annual Undergrad Tuition & Fees (In-State): $6,881
Enrollment: 14,895 Coed
Affiliation or Control: State IRS Status: 501(c)3
Highest Offering: Doctorate
Program: Liberal Arts And General; Professional
Accreditation: M, BUS, CLPSY, CS, ENG, MUS, NURSE, SPAA, SW, TEAC

02 President ... Dr. C. Peter MAGRATH
88 University Ombudsman ... Ms. Dawn OSBORNE-ADAMS
100 Chief of Staff ... Dr. Terrence DEAK
05 Vice Pres Academic Affs/Provost ... Dr. Jean-Pierre MILEUR
10 Vice President Administration ... Mr. James R. VANVOORST
32 Vice Pres Student Affairs ... Mr. Brian T. ROSE
26 Vice President External Affairs ... Ms. Marcia R. CRANER
09 Vice President for Research ... Dr. Bahgat SAMMAKIA
104 Vice Prov International Education ... Dr. Katharine KREBS
45 Vice Prov Strat/Fiscal Plng & UG Ed ... Dr. Michael F. MCGOFF
84 Vice Prov Enrollment Management ... Ms. Sandra STARKE
58 Vice Prov/Dean of Graduate School ... Dr. Nancy E. STAMP
18 Assoc VP Facilities Management ... Mr. Lawrence J. ROMA
35 Dean of Students ... Dr. Elizabeth DROZ
25 Assoc Vice President Research ... Mr. Stephen A. GILJE
29 Assoc VP for External Affairs ... Ms. Sheila DOYLE
26 Asst Vice Pres Univ Comm/Mktg ... Mr. Gregory DELVISCIO
21 Assoc VP Computing Services ... Mr. Mark V. REED
35 Asst Vice Pres Student Life ... Mr. Terry WEBB
04 Exec Assistant to the President ... Ms. Laura L. O'NEIL
11 Assoc Vice Pres Admin Services ... Ms. JoAnn NAVARRO
15 Asst Vice Pres for Human Resources ... Mr. Joseph P. SCHULTZ
30 Chief Development Officer ... Ms. Marcia R. CRANER
07 Int Dir Undergraduate Admissions ... Ms. Sandra STARKE
08 Dean of Libraries ... Mr. John M. MEADOR, JR.
85 Director Intl Students/Scholar Svcs ... Ms. Ellen H. BADGER
86 Director of State Relations ... Mr. Terrence KANE
37 Int Dir Stdnt Financial Aid/Employ ... Mr. Dennis J. CHAVEZ
06 University Registrar ... Vacant
38 Director Health & Counseling ... Ms. Johann FIORE CONTE
36 Director Career Development Center ... Ms. Nancy A. PAUL
19 Director Public Safety ... Mr. John R. SCHWARTZ
41 Interim Director Athletics ... Mr. James NORRIS
71 Director EOP/Spec Programs ... Mr. Randall EDOUARD
22 Director of Affirmative Action/EEO ... Ms. Valerie J. HAMPTON
28 Director Multi-Cultural Res Ctr ... Ms. Nicole SIRJU-JOHNSON
92 Director Binghamton Univ Scholars ... Mr. George CATALANO
94 Exec Director of Women's Studies ... Ms. Dara J. SILBERSTEIN
96 Director of Purchasing ... Mr. Kenneth G. WASKIE
09 Dir Inst Research & Assessment ... Mr. Sean MCKITRICK
49 Dean Arts & Science Harpur College ... Dr. Donald NIEMAN
53 Dean School of Education ... Dr. S. G GRANT
50 Dean School of Management ... Dr. Upinder S. DHILLON
54 Dn Watson Sch Engr/Applied Science ... Dr. Hari SRIHARI
66 Dean Decker School of Nursing ... Dr. Joyce A. FERRARIO
31 Dean Community and Public Affairs ... Dr. Patricia INGRAHAM
106 Director Continuing Educ/Outreach ... Mr. Thomas KOWALIK

*State University of New York at Buffalo (G)

3435 Main Street, Buffalo NY 14214
County: Erie FICE Identification: 002837
Unit ID: 196088
Telephone: (716) 645-2000 Carnegie Class: RU/VH
FAX Number: N/A Calendar System: Semester
URL: www.buffalo.edu
Established: 1846 Annual Undergrad Tuition & Fees (In-State): $7,136
Enrollment: 28,509 Coed
Affiliation or Control: State IRS Status: 501(c)3
Highest Offering: Doctorate
Program: Liberal Arts And General; Professional
Accreditation: M, ANEST, AUD, BUS, BUSA, CEA, CLPSY, CORE, DA, DENT, DIETI, ENG, IPSY, LAW, #LIB, MED, MT, NMT, NURSE, OT, PH, PHAR, PLNG, PSPSY, PTA, SP, SW, TEAC

02 President ... Dr. Satish K. TRIPATHI
05 Int Provost/Exec VP Academic Affs ... Dr. Harvey G. STENGER, JR.
10 Exec VP Univ Support Services ... Vacant
32 Vice President Student Affairs ... Mr. Dennis R. BLACK
17 Int Vice President Health Sciences ... Dr. Michael CAIN
30 Vice President External Affairs ... Ms. Marsha S. HENDERSON
46 Vice President for Research ... Dr. Alexander CARTWRIGHT
15 Sr VP Hum Resources/Chief of Staff ... Vacant
58 Vice Provost Graduate Education ... Mr. John T. HO
20 Vice Provost/Dean Undergraduate Ed ... Dr. Scott WEBER
20 Vice Provost for Faculty Affairs ... Ms. Lucinda M. FINLEY
104 Vice Provost for International Educ ... Dr. Stephen C. DUNNETT
45 Assoc VP Academic Planning & Budget ... Mr. Sean P. SULLIVAN
21 Assoc Vice President & Controller ... Mr. Michael F. LEVINE
18 Assoc Vice Pres Univ Facilities ... Mr. Michael F. DUPRE
08 Int Assoc VP for Univ Libraries ... Mr. Austin BOOTH
27 Int Assoc VP Information Technology ... Mr. Thomas FURLANI
37 Asst VP/Director Financial Aid ... Ms. Jennifer A. POLLARD
09 Sr Asst VP/Dir Inst Analysis ... Mr. Craig W. ABBEY
96 Asst Vice Pres Procurement Services ... Mr. Daniel VIVIAN
27 Assoc VP Univ Communications ... Mr. Joseph A. BRENNAN
22 Int Dir Equity/Diversity/AA Admin ... Ms. Sharon E. NOLAN-WEISS
41 Director of Athletics ... Mr. Warde J. MANUEL
20 Director Academic Services CIT ... Vacant
91 Director Enterprise Application Svc ... Ms. Susan A. HUSTON
07 Director of Admissions ... Ms. Patricia G. ARMSTRONG
19 Chief of Police ... Mr. Gerald W. SCHOENLE, JR.
39 Int Dir Campus Living ... Ms. Andrea COSTANTINO
38 Director of Counseling Services ... Dr. Sharon L. MITCHELL
23 Dir Hlth Svcs/Stdnt Wellness Coord ... Ms. Susan M. SNYDER
36 Director Career Services ... Ms. Arlene F. KAUKUS
85 Director Intl Students/Scholar Svc ... Ms. Ellen A. DUSSOURD
40 Director University Bookstores ... Mr. Gregory NEUMANN
92 Admin Dir Univ Honors College ... Ms. Krista L. HANYPSIAK

29 Sr Assoc Director Alumni Relations — Mr. Jay R. FRIEDMAN
48 Dean School Arch & Planning — Dr. Robert SHIBLEY
49 Dean College of Arts/Sciences — Dr. Bruce PITMAN
52 Dean School Dental Medicine — Dr. Michael L. GLICK
53 Dean Graduate Sch of Education — Dr. Mary H. GRESHAM
54 Act Dean School Engr/Applied Sci — Dr. Rajan BATTA
61 Dean School of Law — Prof. Makau W. MUTUA
50 Dean School of Management — Dr. Arjang A. ASSAD
63 Dean School Medicine/Biomed Sci — Dr. Michael E. CAIN
66 Dean School of Nursing — Dr. Jean K. BROWN
67 Dean School Pharmacy/Pharm Sciences — Dr. Wayne K. ANDERSON
76 Dean Sch Public Hlth/Hlth Prof — Dr. Lynn T. KOZLOWSKI
70 Dean School of Social Work — Dr. Nancy J. SMYTH

*State University of New York at Fredonia (A)

138 Fenton Hall, Fredonia NY 14063-1136

County: Chautauqua
FICE Identification: 002844
Unit ID: 196158
Telephone: (716) 673-3111
Carnegie Class: Master's M
FAX Number: N/A
Calendar System: Semester
URL: www.fredonia.edu
Established: 1826
Annual Undergrad Tuition & Fees (In-State): $6,333
Enrollment: 5,769
Coed
Affiliation or Control: State
IRS Status: 501(c)3
Highest Offering: Master's
Program: Liberal Arts And General; Teacher Preparatory; Professional
Accreditation: M, MUS, SP, SW, TED, THEA

02 President — Dr. Dennis L. HEFNER
05 Vice President for Academic Affairs — Dr. Virginia SCHAEFER HORVATH
11 Interim VP for Administration — Mrs. Karen R. PORPIGLIA
30 Vice Pres University Advancement — Dr. David M. TIFFANY
32 Vice President for Student Affairs — Dr. David E. HERMAN
35 Asst Vice Pres for Student Affairs — Ms. Monica J. WHITE
20 Assoc VP Curriculum & Acad Support — Dr. Melinda Ann KARNES
84 Assoc Vice Pres for Enrollment Mgmt — Mr. Daniel M. TRAMUTA
58 AVP Graduate Studies & Research — Dr. Kevin P. KEARNS
83 Dean Natural & Social Sciences — Vacant
79 Dean Arts & Humanities — Dr. John L. KIJINSKI
50 Dean School of Business — Dr. Russell P. BOISJOLY
53 Dean College of Education — Dr. Christine E. GIVNER
102 Director Corp/Univ Advancement — Dr. David M. TIFFANY
18 Director Facilities Services — Mr. Kevin P. CLOOS
06 Registrar — Mr. Scott D. SAUNDERS
07 Director of Admissions — Mr. John C. DEARTH
37 Director Financial Aid — Mr. Daniel M. TRAMUTA
08 Director Library Services — Mr. Randolph Lee GADIKIAN
09 Dir Institutional Research/Planning — Dr. Xiao Y. ZHANG
36 Director of Career Development — Ms. Tracy COLLINGWOD
19 Chief University Police — Ms. Ann K. MCCARRON-BURNS
25 Director of Sponsored Programs — Ms. Maggie BRYAN-PETERSON
39 Director Residence Life — Mr. Gary L. BICE, JR.
41 Athletic Director — Mr. Gregory D. PRECHTL
23 Director of Health Services — Ms. Patricia A. BORIS
38 Director Counseling — Dr. Sally J. TURNER
49 Coord of Acad Advising/Liberal Arts — Vacant
90 Academic Information Technology — Mr. John MCCUNE
15 Director of Human Resources — Mr. Michael D. DALEY
26 Director of Public Relations — Mr. Michael BARONE
85 Director of Multicultural Affairs — Ms. Averl R. OTIS
92 Director of Honors Program — Dr. David KINKELA
94 Director of Women's Studies — Dr. Adrienne L. MCCORMICK
96 Director of Purchasing — Mrs. Shari K. MILLER
28 Dir of Diversity/Affirmative Action — Mrs. Sandra A. LEWIS
29 Director Alumni Affairs — Ms. Patricia A. FERALDI

*State University of New York at New Paltz (B)

1 Hawk Drive, New Paltz NY 12561-2443

County: Ulster
FICE Identification: 002846
Unit ID: 196176
Telephone: (845) 257-7869
Carnegie Class: Master's L
FAX Number: (845) 257-3009
Calendar System: Semester
URL: www.newpaltz.edu
Established: 1823
Annual Undergrad Tuition & Fees (In-State): $6,158
Enrollment: 7,885
Coed
Affiliation or Control: State
IRS Status: 501(c)3
Highest Offering: Beyond Master's But Less Than Doctorate
Program: Liberal Arts And General; Teacher Preparatory; Professional
Accreditation: M, ART, ENG, MUS, NURSE, SP, TED, THEA

02 President — Dr. Donald P. CHRISTIAN
100 Chief of Staff/AVP Communication — Ms. Shelly A. WRIGHT
05 Provost — Vacant
11 Vice Pres Administration & Finance — Ms. Jacqueline DISTEFANO
32 Student Affairs Vice President — Dr. L. David ROONEY
84 Vice Pres Enrollment Management — Mr. L. David EATON
13 Asst Vice Pres Tech/Info Systems — Mr. Jonathan D. LEWIT
15 Asst Vice Pres Human Resources — Ms. Marda REID
21 Asst Vice President Administration — Ms. Michele HALSTEAD
09 Asst VP Inst Research/Planning — Dr. Jacqueline ANDREWS
18 Asst VP Facilities Management — Mr. John SHUPE
07 Dean of Admissions — Ms. Lisa JONES
07 Asst Dean/Dir Freshmen Admissions — Ms. Kimberly STRANO
30 Director of Development — Ms. Sally CROSS

08 Director College Library — Ms. Chui-Chun LEE
36 Director Career Resource Center — Ms. Tonda S. HIGHLEY
37 Director of Financial Aid — Mr. Daniel SISTARENIK
06 Registrar — Ms. Bernadette MORRIS
29 Director Alumni Affairs — Vacant
38 Director Student Counseling — Dr. Gweneth LLOYD
26 Dir Communication & Marketing — Ms. Suzanne GRADY
96 Director of Purchasing/Procurement — Mr. David FARBANIEC
19 Director Security/Safety — Mr. David DUGATKIN
53 Interim Dean of Education — Dr. Karen BELL
57 Dean Fine & Performing Arts — Dr. Mary HAFELI
49 Dean Liberal Arts & Sciences — Dr. James SCHIFFER
54 Int Dean Science and Engineering — Dr. Daniel FREEDMAN
50 Dean School of Business — Dr. Hadi SALAVITABAR
58 Int Asc Provost/Dean Graduate Sch — Dr. Laurel GARRICK DUHANEY

*State University of New York at Stony Brook (C)

310 Administration Building, Stony Brook NY 11794-0701

County: Suffolk
FICE Identification: 002838
Unit ID: 196097
Telephone: (631) 632-6265
Carnegie Class: RU/VH
FAX Number: (631) 632-6621
Calendar System: Semester
URL: www.stonybrook.edu
Established: 1957
Annual Undergrad Tuition & Fees (In-State): $6,820
Enrollment: 24,594
Coed
Affiliation or Control: State
IRS Status: 501(c)3
Highest Offering: Doctorate
Program: Liberal Arts And General; Teacher Preparatory; Professional
Accreditation: M, ARCPA, CLPSY, CS, DENT, DIETI, ENG, IPSY, MED, MIDWF, MT, NURSE, OT, PH, POLYT, PTA, SURGT, SW, TED

02 President — Dr. Samuel L. STANLEY
05 Interim Provost — Dr. Nancy SQUIRES
63 Sr VP HSC/Dean School of Medicine — Dr. Kenneth KAUSHANSKY
46 Vice President Research — Vacant
32 Vice President Student Affairs — Dr. Peter M. BAIGENT
11 Vice Pres Administration & Finance — Ms. Karol GRAY
30 Vice Pres University Advancement — Mr. Dexter BAILEY
88 VP Econ Devel/Dean Engr/Applied Sci — Dr. Yacov SHAMASH
100 Chief Deputy to President — Dr. Tonjanita JOHNSON
45 Asst VP for Budget — Mr. Mark MACIULAITIS
18 Vice President Facilities/Services — Ms. Barbara CHERNOW
26 Asst Vice Pres Communications — Ms. Yvette ST. JACQUES
39 Asst Vice Pres Campus Residences — Dr. Dallas BAUMAN
17 CEO University Hospital — Dr. Steven STRONGWATER
84 Assoc Prov Enrollment/Retent Mgmt — Dr. Peter BAIGENT
13 Chief Information Officer — Mr. Chris KIELT
43 Associate Counsel — Ms. Susan BLUM
49 Dean College Arts & Sciences — Dr. Nancy SQUIRES
54 Dean Col of Engr & Applied Science — Dr. Yacov SHAMASH
88 Dean School of Marine & Atmos Sci — Dr. Minghua ZHANG
52 Dean School of Dental Medicine — Dr. Ray WILLIAMS
68 Dean Div Physical Educ & Athletics — Mr. James FIORE
58 Dean Graduate School — Dr. Lawrence MARTIN
51 Dean Sch Profess Devel & Cont Educ — Dr. Paul EDELSON
07 Asst Provost Admission & Fin Aid — Mr. Matthew WHELAN
76 Dean School Health Technology Mgmt — Dr. Craig LEHMANN
35 Dean of Students — Dr. Jerrold STEIN
66 Dean School of Nursing — Dr. Lee XIPPOLITOS
70 Dean School of Social Welfare — Dr. Frances L. BRISBANE
08 Director & Dean of Libraries — Mr. Andrew WHITE
86 Vice President External Relations — Ms. Elaine CROSSON
88 Exec Dir LI State Vets Home — Mr. Fred SGANGA
19 Chief of Police — Mr. Robert LENAHAN
15 Asst VP Human Resource Svcs — Ms. Lynn JOHNSON
28 Dir Diversity/AA/Equal Employ Oppty — Ms. Christina LAW
09 Director Planning & Inst Research — Vacant
85 Dean International Programs — Dr. William ARENS
102 Exec Dir of Stony Brook Foundation — Ms. Karol GRAY
29 Director Alumni Relations — Vacant
23 Director University Health Services — Dr. Rachel BERGESON
38 Director Counseling Center — Dr. Jenny HWANG
36 Director Career Placement Center — Ms. Marianna SAVOCA
06 Interim Registrar — Ms. Diane BELLO
37 Financial Aid/Scholarships — Ms. Jacqueline PASCARIELLO
50 Dean College of Business — Dr. Manuel LONDON
08 Director Health Sciences Library — Mr. Spencer MARSH
27 University Media Relations Officer — Ms. Lauren SHEPROW
96 Director of Purchasing/Procurement — Mr. James FABIAN
60 Dean School of Journalism — Mr. Howard SCHNEIDER

*State University of New York Health Science Center at Brooklyn (D)

450 Clarkson Avenue, Brooklyn NY 11203-2098

County: Kings
FICE Identification: 002839
Unit ID: 196255
Telephone: (718) 270-1000
Carnegie Class: Spec/Med
FAX Number: (718) 270-4092
Calendar System: Semester
URL: www.downstate.edu
Established: 1860
Annual Undergrad Tuition & Fees (In-State): $4,970
Enrollment: 1,694
Coed
Affiliation or Control: State
IRS Status: 501(c)3
Highest Offering: Doctorate
Program: Occupational; Liberal Arts And General; Professional
Accreditation: M, ANEST, ARCPA, DMS, MED, MIDWF, NURSE, OT, PH, PTA, RAD, SURGT

02 President — Dr. John C. LAROSA
03 Chief Executive Officer — Ms. Debra CAREY
10 Interim Chief Financial Officer — Mr. Paul DAVIS
11 COO/Exec Vice Pres Administration — Mr. Ivan M. LISNITZER
63 Sr VP Biomed Research/Dean Col Med — Dr. Ian L. TAYLOR
18 Interim Vice President Facilities — Dr. Alvin BERK
17 SVP Inst Dev/Phylthrpy/VP Acad Affs — Dr. JoAnn BRADLEY
32 Assoc VP Student Aff/Dean of Stdnts — Dr. Lorraine TERRACINA
45 Asst Vice Pres for Planning — Ms. Dorothy R. FYFE
39 Asst Vice Pres Stdnt Life/Housing — Ms. Meg O'SULLIVAN
16 AVP Labor Relations — Mr. Leonzo CUIMAN
15 AVP for Personnel — Ms. Hendrina GOELOE-ALSTON
46 Asst Provost Scientific Affairs — Mr. John M. ALLEN
58 Dean School Graduate Studies — Dr. Mark STEWART
66 Dean College of Nursing — Dr. Daisy CRUZ-RICHMAN
20 Asst Dean Academic Development — Vacant
30 Director Institutional Advancement — Ms. Ellen WATSON
13 Interim Chief Information Officer — Mr. Ernest WEBER
17 Interim Medical Director — Dr. Michael LUCCHESI
08 Director of Libraries — Dr. Richard M. WINANT
90 Dir Scientific/Acad Computer Ctr — Dr. Mathew AVITABLE
07 Director of Admissions — Ms. Shushawana DEOLIVEIRA
06 Registrar — Ms. Anne SHONBRUN
37 Director Student Financial Aid — Mr. James NEWELL
21 Bursar — Mr. Charles CONWAY
51 Director of CME — Ms. Edeline MITTEN
23 Actg Director of Student Health Svc — Dr. Sigrid ULRICH
28 Director Ofc Opportunity/Diversity — Mr. Kevin ANTOINE
29 Exec Dir Alumni Assn Col Medicine — Ms. Jill DITCHIK
38 Director of Student Counseling — Dr. Christine V. SAUNDERS-FIELDS
19 Chief of Police — Mr. Thomas F. DUGAN
09 Director of Institutional Research — Ms. Barbara LAWRENCE
26 Chief Public Relations Officer — Ms. Ellen WATSON
96 Director of Purchasing — Mr. Carter LARD

*State University of New York Upstate Medical University (E)

750 E Adams Street, Syracuse NY 13210-2375

County: Onondaga
FICE Identification: 002840
Unit ID: 196307
Telephone: (315) 464-5540
Carnegie Class: Spec/Med
FAX Number: (315) 464-8823
Calendar System: Semester
URL: www.upstate.edu
Established: 1834
Annual Undergrad Tuition & Fees (In-State): $5,545
Enrollment: 1,547
Coed
Affiliation or Control: State
IRS Status: 501(c)3
Highest Offering: Doctorate
Program: Professional
Accreditation: M, #ARCPA, DENT, DMOLS, IPSY, MED, MT, NURSE, PERF, PTA, RAD, RTT

02 President — Dr. David R. SMITH
63 Dean College of Medicine — Dr. Steven J. SCHEINMAN
17 CEO University Hospital — Dr. John MCCABE
10 Vice President Finance & Management — Mr. Steven BRADY
05 Vice President Academic Affairs — Dr. Lynn CLEARY
46 VP Research/Dean Col Grad Studies — Dr. Steven GOODMAN
32 Dean Student Affairs — Dr. Julie R. WHITE
102 Exec Director HSC Foundation — Ms. Eileen PEZZI
26 Dir Marketing/Communic/Public Rels — Ms. Melanie M. RICH
66 Dean College of Nursing — Dr. Elvira SZIGETI
76 Dean College Health Profession — Dr. Hugh W. DONNER
06 Registrar/Dir Inst Research — Ms. Jennifer MARTIN TSE
25 Director Research Administration — Mr. David W. TEMPLE
29 Director of Medical Alumni Affairs — Mr. Vincent KUSS
15 Assoc VP Human Resources — Mr. Eric FROST
13 Chief Information Officer — Ms. Teresa J. WAGNER
08 Director of Libraries — Ms. Christina POPE
28 Dir Diversity & Affirmative Action — Ms. Maxine THOMPSON
07 Director of Admissions — Ms. Jennifer C. WELCH
18 Chief Facilities/Physical Plant — Mr. Gary KITTELL
21 Assistant Vice President Finance — Mr. Eric SMITH
37 Director Student Financial Aid — Mr. Michael PEDE

*State University of New York, The College at Brockport (F)

350 New Campus Drive, Brockport NY 14420-2914

County: Monroe
FICE Identification: 002841
Unit ID: 196121
Telephone: (585) 395-2211
Carnegie Class: Master's L
FAX Number: (585) 395-2401
Calendar System: Semester
URL: www.brockport.edu
Established: 1867
Annual Undergrad Tuition & Fees (In-State): $6,176
Enrollment: 8,589
Coed
Affiliation or Control: State
IRS Status: 501(c)3
Highest Offering: Master's
Program: Liberal Arts And General; Teacher Preparatory; Professional
Accreditation: M, BUS, CACREP, CS, DANCE, NRPA, NURSE, SPAA, SW, TED, THEA

02 President — Dr. John R. HALSTEAD
05 Provost & VP Academic Affairs — Dr. Anne E. HUOT
10 VP Administration & Finance — Mr. Louis M. SPIRO
32 VP Enrollment Mgmt/Student Affairs — Dr. Kathryn WILSON
30 VP Advancement — Ms. Roxanne JOHNSTON
20 Vice Provost — Dr. P. Michael FOX
58 Asst to Provost Grad Educ & Scholar — Dr. Susan SEEM
28 Asst Provost for Diversity — Dr. Joel FRATER

84 Asst VP Enroll Mgmt ... Mr. Jimmy JUNG
35 Asst VP Student Affairs ... Ms. Leah A. BARRETT
18 Asst VP Facilities & Planning ... Mr. Thomas F. DREYER
21 Asst VP Finance & Management ... Ms. Karen M. RIOTTO
13 Assoc Provost & CIO ... Mr. Frank WOJCIK
49 Dean Arts/Humanities & Social Sci ... Dr. Darwin PRIOLEAU
50 Dean Business ... Dr. Daniel PETREE
53 Dean Education & Human Services ... Dr. Douglas SCHEIDT
68 Dean Health & Human Performance ... Dr. Frank SHORT
81 Interim Dean Science & Mathematics ... Dr. Jose MALIEKAL
13 Director of Info Tech System ... Mr. David R. STRASENBURGH
07 Director of Undergrad Admissions ... Mr. Bernard VALENTO
44 Exec Dir of Advancement ... Mr. Michael ANDRIATCH
56 Exec Dir Brockport Metro Center ... Dr. Karen SCHUHLE-WILLIAMS
44 Exec Dir of Dev & Alumni Relations ... Mr. Bradley C. SCHREIBER
51 Exec Dir Continuing Professional Ed ... Ms. Kathleen H. GROVES
104 Exec Dir International Education ... Dr. Ralph R. TRECARTIN
26 Exec Dir Public Relations ... Mr. David MIHALYOV
37 Director of Financial Aid ... Mr. J. Scott ATKINSON
36 Director of Career Services ... Dr. Claire VANDENBERGHE
19 Chief of University Police ... Mr. Robert J. KEHOE
06 College Registrar ... Mr. Peter DOWE
16 Director of Human Resources ... Ms. Amy KAHN
22 Affirmative Action Officer ... Ms. Adrienne COLLIER
23 Director Student Health/Counselling ... Ms. Elizabeth S. CARUSO
39 Director of Residential Life ... Mr. David K. BAGLEY
41 Director of Athletics ... Mr. Noah D. LEFEVRE
25 Director of Grants Development ... Ms. Colleen DONALDSON
92 Director of Honors Program ... Dr. Donna M. KOWAL
09 Director of Inst Effectiveness ... Dr. Jeffrey T. LASHBROOK
96 Director of Procurement & Payment ... Mr. Mark W. STACY
94 Int Director of Women's Studies ... Dr. Barbara LESAVOY
86 Coordinator of Government Relations ... Mr. David MIHALYOV

*State University of New York College at Buffalo (A)

1300 Elmwood Avenue, Buffalo NY 14222-1091

County: Erie — FICE Identification: 002842 — Unit ID: 196130
Telephone: (716) 878-4000 — Carnegie Class: Master's L
FAX Number: (716) 878-3039 — Calendar System: Semester
URL: www.buffalostate.edu
Established: 1871 — Annual Undergrad Tuition & Fees (In-State): $6,053
Enrollment: 12,419 — Coed
Affiliation or Control: State — IRS Status: 501(c)3
Highest Offering: Master's
Program: Liberal Arts And General; Teacher Preparatory; Professional
Accreditation: M, ART, THEA, CIDA, DIETC, DIETD, ENGT, JOUR, MUS, NAIT, SP, SW, TED

02 President ... Dr. Aaron M. PODOLEFSKY
100 Asst Vice President/Chief of Staff ... Dr. Bonita R. DURAND
05 Provost ... Dr. Dennis K. PONTON
10 Vice President Finance & Management ... Dr. Stanley KARDONSKY
32 Vice President Student Affairs ... Dr. Hal D. PAYNE
30 Vice Pres Inst Advancement & Devel ... Dr. Susanne P. BAIR
28 Int Sr Advisor to Pres/Diversity ... Dr. Scott L. JOHNSON
20 Interim Assoc VP Teacher Education ... Dr. John F. SISKAR
21 Assoc VP Budget & Planning ... Vacant
84 Associate Vice Pres Enrollment Mgmt ... Mr. Mark J. PETRIE
21 Assoc Vice President & Comptroller ... Mr. James A. THOR
102 Director College & Foundation ... Mr. Robert L. BAUMET
35 Assoc Vice President Campus Life ... Dr. Timothy R. ECKLUND
35 Asc VP Student Affs/Dean Students ... Dr. Charles B. KENYON
18 Assoc VP Facilities Planning ... Mr. Slawko F. MEDINAC
14 Assoc Vice Pres Computing Services ... Ms. Judith B. BASINSKI
09 Assoc VP Curriculum/Assessment ... Dr. Rosalyn A. LINDNER
26 Assoc VP College Relations ... Mr. Timothy J. WALSH
08 Assoc VP Library/Instr Technology ... Ms. Maryruth F. GLOGOWSKI
44 Assoc VP Development ... Ms. Jane A. ARMBRUSTER
86 Assoc VP Government Relations ... Mr. William J. BENFANTI
51 Assoc VP Continuing Prof Studies ... Dr. Margaret A. SHAW-BURNETT
20 Dean Univ Col/AVP Undergrad Ed ... Dr. Scott L. JOHNSON
53 Interim Dean Education ... Dr. Paul G. THEOBALD
49 Dean Arts & Humanities ... Mr. Benjamin C. CHRISTY
83 Dean Natural & Social Science ... Dr. Mark W. SEVERSON
50 Interim Dean Professions ... Dr. Kevin F. MULCAHY
58 Dean Graduate School ... Dr. Kevin J. RAILEY
36 Director of Career Development ... Ms. Stephanie B. ZUCKERMAN-AVILES
07 Director Admissions ... Dr. Carmela THOMPSON
06 Registrar ... Mr. Mark T. BAUSILI
37 Director of Financial Aid ... Mr. Kent M. MCGOWAN
88 Director of Student Accounts ... Ms. Susan F. WRIGHT
38 Director Counseling Center ... Dr. Joan L. MCCOOL
41 Director Intercollegiate Athletics ... Mr. Jerry S. BOYES
39 Director of Residence Life ... Mr. Kris A. KAUFMAN
23 Director Student Health Center ... Dr. Theresa R. STEPHAN HAINS
85 Director Intl Student Affairs ... Dr. Jean F. GOUNARD
15 Assoc VP Human Resource Management ... Ms. Susan J. EARSHEN
26 Director Public Relations ... Ms. Phyllis A. CAMESANO
29 Director of Alumni Affairs ... Ms. Jennifer L. HEISEY
88 Director Research Admin/Svcs ... Mr. Ted TURKLE
88 Director Special Events & Protocol ... Ms. Pamela B. VOYER
88 Director Campus Services ... Mr. Terry M. HARDING
88 Director Events Management ... Mr. Thomas E. COATES
21 Director Budget & Internal Controls ... Ms. Rebecca J. SCHENK
09 Director Institutional Research ... Mr. Yves M. GACHETTE
19 Chief University Police ... Mr. Peter M. CAREY
88 Director Parking Services ... Ms. Jayme S. RITER

96 Director of Purchasing ... Ms. Therese M. LOCHER
40 Manager BSC Bookstore ... Ms. Lynn M. PUMA
88 Director Student Life ... Ms. Gail V. WELLS
88 Interim Director Disability Service ... Dr. Amy ROSEN-BRAND
43 Director Judicial Affairs ... Dr. Latonia D. GASTON-MARSH

*State University of New York College at Cortland (B)

PO Box 2000, Cortland NY 13045-0900

County: Cortland — FICE Identification: 002843 — Unit ID: 196149
Telephone: (607) 753-2011 — Carnegie Class: Master's L
FAX Number: (607) 753-5999 — Calendar System: Semester
URL: www.cortland.edu
Established: 1868 — Annual Undergrad Tuition & Fees (In-State): $6,339
Enrollment: 7,358 — Coed
Affiliation or Control: State — IRS Status: 501(c)3
Highest Offering: Master's
Program: Liberal Arts And General; Teacher Preparatory; Professional
Accreditation: M, NRPA, TED

02 President ... Dr. Erik J. BITTERBAUM
05 Provost ... Dr. Mark PRUS
32 Vice Pres Student Affairs ... Mr. C. Gregory SHARER
30 Vice Pres Institutional Advancement ... Dr. Raymond FRANCO
10 Vice President Business/Finance ... Dr. William SHAUT
21 VP/Assoc Finance & Management ... Ms. Mary K. MURPHY
27 Assoc Provost for Info Resources ... Ms. Amy BERG
18 Assoc VP Facilities Management ... Ms. Nasrin PARVIZI
20 Assoc Prov for Academic Affairs ... Dr. Carol VAN DER KARR
04 Exec Assistant to the President ... Dr. Virginia LEVINE
07 Director of Admissions ... Mr. Mark YACAVONE
09 Assoc Dir Inst Rsrch/Assessment ... Dr. Merle CANFIELD
08 Director of Libraries ... Ms. Gail WOOD
06 Registrar ... Vacant
36 Director of Career Services ... Mr. John SHIRLEY
15 Director of Human Resources ... Ms. Joanne BARRY
29 Director Alumni Affairs ... Ms. Stacey GOLDYN-MOLLER
38 Int Dir Counseling/Student Devel ... Ms. Billie Jean GOFF
37 Dir of Student Financial Aid ... Ms. Karen GALLAGHER
19 Chief of University Police ... Mr. Steven DANGLER
91 Director Admin Computing Svcs ... Mr. Daniel SIDEBOTTOM
90 Director Acad Computing Svcs ... Ms. Lisa KAHLE
107 Dean Professional Studies ... Dr. John COTTONE
49 Dean Arts & Sciences ... Dr. Bruce MATTINGLY
26 Chief Public Relations Officer ... Mr. Frederic PIERCE
53 Int Dean of Education ... Dr. Andrea LACHANCE
93 Director Educational Oppty Program ... Dr. Lewis ROSENGARTEN
92 Director of Honors Program ... Vacant
94 Director of Women's Studies ... Dr. Caroline KALTEFLEITER
96 Director of Purchasing ... Mr. Samuel COLOMBO
22 Affirmative Action Officer ... Ms. Wendy M. MCALLISTER
28 Director Multicultural Life ... Ms. Noelle PALEY
41 Athletic Director ... Mr. Mike URTZ

*State University of New York College at Geneseo (C)

1 College Circle, Geneseo NY 14454-1401

County: Livingston — FICE Identification: 002845 — Unit ID: 196167
Telephone: (585) 245-5000 — Carnegie Class: Master's S
FAX Number: (585) 245-5005 — Calendar System: Semester
URL: www.geneseo.edu
Established: 1871 — Annual Undergrad Tuition & Fees (In-State): $6,758
Enrollment: 5,694 — Coed
Affiliation or Control: State — IRS Status: 501(c)3
Highest Offering: Master's
Program: Liberal Arts And General; Teacher Preparatory; Professional
Accreditation: M, BUS, SP, TED

02 President ... Dr. Christopher C. DAHL
05 Provost ... Dr. Carol S. LONG
20 Associate Provost ... Dr. David F. GORDON
11 Vice President Administration ... Dr. James B. MILROY
32 Vice Pres for Student & Campus Life ... Dr. Robert A. BONFIGLIO
30 Vice President College Advancement ... Mr. Michael J. CATILLAZ
84 Assoc Vice Pres Enrollment Mgmt ... Dr. William L. CAREN
10 Assoc VP Administration/Controller ... Mr. Brice M. WEIGMAN
27 Asst Vice Pres Communications ... Mr. Anthony T. HOPPA
86 Asst Prov of International Affairs ... Dr. Rebecca LEWIS
15 Asst Vice Pres Human Resources ... Ms. Julie A. BRIGGS
26 Asst VP for College Advancement ... Ms. Deborah G. HILL
29 Asst VP for Alumni Relations ... Ms. Rose ANDERSON
58 Dean of College ... Vacant
35 Dean of Students ... Dr. Leonard SANCILIO
07 Director of Admissions ... Ms. Kristine M. SHAY
08 Interim Director College Libraries ... Mr. Cyril OBERLANDER
13 Director Computing/Info Technology ... Ms. Susan E. CHICHESTER
37 Director of Financial Aid ... Mr. Archie L. CURETON
25 Director of Sponsored Research ... Dr. Anne E. BALDWIN
09 Director of Institutional Research ... Dr. Julie M. RAO
06 Registrar ... Mr. Delbert W. BROWN
36 Interim Director Career Services ... Ms. Elizabeth M. SEAGER
22 Affirmative Action Officer ... Ms. Gloria LOPEZ
88 Director of Multicultural Affairs ... Ms. Fatima R. JOHNSON
19 Chief of University Police ... Mr. Salvatore J. SIMONETTI
17 Director Counseling & Health Svcs ... Ms. Melinda C. DUBOIS
18 Chief Facilities/Physical Plant ... Mr. George F. STOOKS
21 Director Budget/Financial Analysis ... Vacant

38 Clinical Dir Counseling Services ... Dr. Beth K. CHOLETTE
96 Director of Purchasing ... Ms. Rebecca E. ANCHOR

*State University of New York College at Old Westbury (D)

Box 210, 223 Store Hill Road, Old Westbury NY 11568-0210

County: Nassau — FICE Identification: 007109 — Unit ID: 196237
Telephone: (516) 876-3000 — Carnegie Class: Bac/A&S
FAX Number: (516) 876-3209 — Calendar System: Semester
URL: www.oldwestbury.edu
Established: 1965 — Annual Undergrad Tuition & Fees (In-State): $6,324
Enrollment: 4,027 — Coed
Affiliation or Control: State — IRS Status: 501(c)3
Highest Offering: Master's
Program: Liberal Arts And General; Teacher Preparatory; Professional
Accreditation: M, TED

02 President ... Dr. Calvin O. BUTTS, III
03 Executive Vice President ... Ms. Mona G. RANKIN
05 Provost/Vice Pres Academic Affairs ... Dr. Patrick O'SULLIVAN
84 Vice President Enrollment Services ... Ms. Mary MARQUEZ BELL
32 Vice President Student Affairs ... Dr. Mary L. LANGLIE
10 VP Div of Business & Finance/CFO ... Mr. Len L. DAVIS
16 Asst to Pres for Admin/Dir HR ... Mr. William P. KIMMINS
30 Asst to President for Advancement ... Mr. Michael G. KINANE
53 Dean School of Education ... Dr. Ruben L. GONZALEZ
21 Assoc Vice Pres/Business Affairs ... Ms. Deirdre M. DOWD
21 Assoc VP of Business Compliance ... Mr. Arthur H. ANGST, JR.
88 Asst Vice Pres Academic Affairs ... Mr. Ronald J. WELTON
88 Asst Vice Pres Academic Affairs ... Mr. Anthony BARBERA
35 Dean of Students ... Mr. Rollie O. BUCHANAN
50 Dean School of Business ... Dr. Nejdet DELENER
49 Interim Dean School of Arts & Sci ... Dr. Barbara HILLERY
19 Chief of Police ... Mr. Michael C. YANNIELLO
26 Director Public & Media Relations ... Mr. Michael G. KINANE
13 Chief Information Officer ... Mr. Marc P. SEYBOLD
06 Registrar ... Ms. Patricia A. SMITH
96 Director of Purchasing ... Mr. Patrick ADAMS
89 Director First-Year Experience ... Dr. Laura M. ANKER
31 Director of Community Relations ... Ms. Carolyn BENNETT
38 Dir Counseling/Psych Wellness Svcs ... Dr. Trisha BILLARD
29 Director of Alumni Affairs ... Ms. Penny J. CHIN
88 Environmental Health & Safety Ofcr ... Ms. Michelle GLOVER-BROWN
88 Coordinator of Scholarships ... Ms. Pritpal KAINTH
09 Director of Institutional Research ... Ms. Sandra KAUFMANN
08 Library Director ... Mr. Stephen KIRKPATRICK
88 Dir Educational Opportunity Program ... Mr. Alonzo L. MCCOLLUM
88 Director of Student Activities ... Ms. Suzanne MCLOUGHLIN
23 Director of Student Health Services ... Ms. Susan R. MUNDY
88 Director of Sponsored Programs ... Mr. Thomas MURPHY
37 Director Financial Aid ... Ms. Mildred O'KEEFE
39 Director of Residential Life ... Mr. Usama SHAIKH
18 Director of Facilities ... Mr. Paul THEISEN
102 Dir Corp & Foundation Relations ... Vacant
41 Director of Athletics ... Vacant

*State University of New York College at Oneonta (E)

108 Ravine Parkway, Oneonta NY 13820-4015

County: Otsego — FICE Identification: 002847 — Unit ID: 196185
Telephone: (607) 436-3500 — Carnegie Class: Master's S
FAX Number: N/A — Calendar System: Semester
URL: www.oneonta.edu
Established: 1889 — Annual Undergrad Tuition & Fees (In-State): $6,397
Enrollment: 5,987 — Coed
Affiliation or Control: State — IRS Status: 501(c)3
Highest Offering: Master's
Program: Liberal Arts And General; Teacher Preparatory; Professional
Accreditation: M, MUS, AAFCS, BUS, DIETD, DIETI, TED

02 President ... Dr. Nancy KLENIEWSKI
04 Senior Assistant to the President ... Ms. Colleen E. BRANNAN
05 Provost/Vice Pres Academic Affairs ... Dr. E. Maria THOMPSON
32 Vice President Student Development ... Dr. Steven R. PERRY
10 Vice Pres Finance/Administration ... Mr. Todd D. FOREMAN
30 Vice President College Advancement ... Mr. Paul J. ADAMO
09 Assoc Prov Inst Assessment & Eff ... Dr. Patricia L. FRANCIS
83 Int Dean Behavioral/Applied Science ... Dr. Alexander THOMAS
83 Int Dean Science/Social Science ... Dr. Julie FREEMAN
58 Director of Graduate Studies ... Mr. Patrick J. MENTE
50 Assoc Dean Economics/Business ... Dr. Wade L. THOMAS
53 Associate Dean Education ... Dr. Joanne M. CURRAN
84 Assoc Vice Pres Enrollment Mgmt ... Mr. Roger B. SULLIVAN
35 Assoc Vice President Student Life ... Dr. Jeanne C. MILLER
19 Assoc VP Stdt Dev/Chief of Police ... Dr. Barton R. INGERSOLL
15 Sr Exec Employee Services Officer ... Ms. Lisa M. WENCK
18 Assoc Vice Pres Facilities/Safety ... Mr. Thomas M. RATHBONE
90 Dir Academic Info Tech Services ... Mr. Steven J. MANISCALCO
07 Director of Admissions ... Ms. Karen A. BROWN
29 Director of Alumni Affairs ... Ms. Laura MADELONE
44 Director Annual Giving ... Mr. Mark A. PIEKARSKI
41 Athletic Director ... Ms. Tracey M. RANIERI
21 Budget Control Officer/Budget Dir ... Ms. Julie ROSEBOOM
25 Director Business Services ... Ms. Betty M. TIRADO
36 Dir Career Dev/Student Emp Svcs ... Vacant

14 Interim Director Computer Center ... Ms. Susan C. SMITH
38 Director Counseling Services ... Dr. Melissa A. FALLON
24 Director Creative Media Services ... Mr. David W. GEASEY
28 Dir Office of Equity & Inclusion ... Dr. B. Cecilia ZAPATA
37 Director Financial Aid ... Mr. Bill GOODHUE
09 Senior Staff Assoc Inst Research ... Dr. Steven D. JOHNSON
85 Director of International Education ... Ms. Carol I. MANDZIK
89 Director Orientation/First Year Exp ... Ms. Monica C. GRAU
96 Purchasing Manager ... Ms. Cynthia L. MERES
06 College Registrar ... Ms. Maureen P. ARTALE
39 Director Residential Community Life ... Ms. Michele LUETTGER
93 Director Special Programs/EOP ... Ms. Lynda D. BASSETTE
23 Director Student Health Services ... Ms. Ricky O' DONNELL
26 Director of Communications ... Mr. Hal S. LEGG

*State University of New York College at Oswego (A)

7060 State Route 104, Oswego NY 13126-3501
County: Oswego FICE Identification: 002848
Unit ID: 196194
Telephone: (315) 312-2500 Carnegie Class: Master's L
FAX Number: (315) 312-5799 Calendar System: Semester
URL: www.oswego.edu
Established: 1861 Annual Undergrad Tuition & Fees (In-State): $6,307
Enrollment: 8,297 Coed
Affiliation or Control: State IRS Status: 501(c)3
Highest Offering: Master's
Program: Liberal Arts And General; Teacher Preparatory; Professional
Accreditation: M, ART, BUS, MUS, TED, THEA

02 President ... Dr. Deborah F. STANLEY
05 Interim VP Academic Affairs/Provost ... Dr. Lorrie A. CLEMO
10 Vice President Admin/Finance ... Mr. Nicholas A. LYONS
84 Vice Pres Student Affs/Enroll Mgmt ... Dr. Joseph F. GRANT, JR.
30 Vice Pres Devel/Alumni Relations ... Ms. Kerry DORSEY
32 Assoc VP/Dean of Students Affs .. Dr. James SCHARFENBERGER
18 Asst VP for Facilities Services ... Mr. Thomas SIMMONDS
21 Asst Vice Pres for Finance & Budget ... Mr. Byron SMITH
20 Associate Provost ... Dr. Rameen MOHAMMADI
04 Ex Asst to Pres/Spec Ast Soc Equity ... Mr. Howard GORDON
26 Director of Public Affairs ... Ms. Julie H. BLISSERT
25 Dir Research/Sponsored Pgms ... Dr. Jack GELFAND
94 Director Women's Studies ... Dr. Tonia RAMALHA
06 Registrar ... Mr. Jerret LEMAY
08 Director of Libraries ... Vacant
91 Director Admin Computer Center ... Mr. Michael C. PISA
37 Director of Financial Aid ... Mr. Mark HUMBERT
09 Director Inst Research & Assessment ... Dr. Mehran NOJAN
36 Director Career Services ... Mr. Gary MORRIS
38 Director Counseling Services Center ... Dr. Bruce MEYER
15 Dir Human Resources/Affirm Act Ofcr ... Ms. Marta SANTIAGO
19 University Police Chief ... Ms. Cynthia ADAM
23 Director of Student Health Center ... Ms. Elizabeth BURNS
56 Asst Prov Distance Lrng/Info Resour ... Dr. Michael AMEIGH
28 Assoc Prov Multicltrl Pgms & Opps ... Ms. Catherine SANTOS
39 Dir Residence Life/Housing ... Dr. Richard KOLENDA
41 Athletic Director ... Mr. Timothy HALE
96 Director Purchasing ... Mr. Mark COLE
13 Chief Technology Officer ... Mr. Joseph MOREAU
29 Director Alumni Relations ... Vacant
07 Director of Admissions/Enroll Mgmt ... Dr. Joseph GRANT
40 College Store Manager ... Ms. Susan RABY
49 Dean Col Liberal Arts & Sciences ... Dr. Rhonda MANDEL
53 Interim Dean School of Education ... Dr. Pamela MICHAEL
58 Dean Graduate Studies/Research ... Dr. David KING
50 Dean School of Business ... Dr. Richard J. SKOLNIK
51 Dean of Extended Learning ... Ms. Yvonne PETRELLA
88 Dean of Comm/Media & the Arts ... Mr. Fritz MESSERE

*State University of New York College at Plattsburgh (B)

101 Broad Street, Plattsburgh NY 12901-2637
County: Clinton FICE Identification: 002849
Unit ID: 196246
Telephone: (518) 564-2000 Carnegie Class: Master's L
FAX Number: (518) 564-7827 Calendar System: Semester
URL: www.plattsburgh.edu
Established: 1889 Annual Undergrad Tuition & Fees (In-State): $6,144
Enrollment: 6,441 Coed
Affiliation or Control: State IRS Status: 501(c)3
Highest Offering: Master's
Program: Liberal Arts And General; Teacher Preparatory; Professional
Accreditation: M, BUS, CACREP, DIETD, NURSE, SP, SW, TEAC

02 President ... Dr. John ETTLING
04 Exec Assistant to the President ... Mr. Keith D. TYO
05 Provost/Vice Pres Academic Affairs ... Dr. James LISZKA
32 VP Student Affairs/Enrollment Mgmt ... Mr. William LAUNDRY
11 Vice President for Administration ... Mr. John R. HOMBURGER
30 Vice Pres Institutional Advancement ... Ms. Anne WHITMORE-HANSEN
20 Assistant to the Provost ... Ms. Diane MERKEL
26 Asc Vice Pres Institutional Advance ... Vacant
21 Asst Vice Pres Administration ... Ms. Diana M. LAPORTE
39 Asst Vice Pres/Dir Residence Life ... Mr. Bryan HARTMAN
12 Dean Branch Campus at ACC ... Dr. David HILL
08 Dean Library/Information Services ... Ms. Cerise OBERMAN
35 Dean of Students ... Mr. Stephen MATTHEWS
29 Director of Alumni Relations ... Ms. Joanne NELSON
30 Director of Development ... Ms. Faith OSBORNE-LONG
37 Director of Financial Aid ... Mr. Todd MORAVEC
18 Director of Facilities ... Mr. Kevin ROBERTS
36 Director Career Development ... Ms. Carolyn DELCORE
23 College Physician ... Dr. Kathleen CAMELO
19 Chief University Police ... Ms. Arlene SABO
41 Director of Athletics ... Mr. Bruce DELVENTHAL
07 Director of Admissions ... Mr. Richard J. HIGGINS
22 Director of Affirmative Action ... Dr. Lynda J. AMES
09 Director of Institutional Research ... Mr. Robert KARP
15 Director of Human Resources ... Ms. Susan WELCH
06 Registrar ... Mr. Michael J. WALSH
44 Director of Annual Giving ... Mr. Paul D. LEDUC
40 Director of College Store ... Mr. Jerry DECELLE
28 Director of Diversity ... Vacant
96 Director of Purchasing ... Mr. Joseph TESORIERE
46 Dir Sponsored Research/Programs ... Mr. Michael SIMPSON
91 Supervising Programmer-Analyst ... Mr. Thomas J. HIGGINS
49 Dean of Arts & Sciences ... Dr. Kathleen H. LAVOIE
50 Dean of Business/Economics ... Dr. Raymond GUYDOSH
53 Dean Educ/Health/Human Services ... Dr. Michael MORGAN

*State University of New York College at Potsdam (C)

44 Pierrepont Avenue, Potsdam NY 13676-2294
County: Saint Lawrence FICE Identification: 002850
Unit ID: 196200
Telephone: (315) 267-2000 Carnegie Class: Master's L
FAX Number: (315) 267-2496 Calendar System: Semester
URL: www.potsdam.edu
Established: 1816 Annual Undergrad Tuition & Fees (In-State): $6,506
Enrollment: 4,413 Coed
Affiliation or Control: State IRS Status: 501(c)3
Highest Offering: Master's
Program: Liberal Arts And General; Teacher Preparatory; Professional; Fine Arts Emphasis
Accreditation: M, IACBE, MUS, TED

02 President ... Dr. John F. SCHWALLER
05 Provost ... Dr. Margaret E. MADDEN
10 Vice President for Business Affairs ... Mr. Michael D. LEWIS
32 Vice President for Student Affairs ... Vacant
30 Vice President College Advancement ... Ms. Vicki L. TEMPLETON-CORNELL
09 VP Inst Effect/Enrollment Mgmt ... Dr. Enrico A. MILLER
04 Assistant to the President ... Ms. Carol M. ROURKE
90 Associate VP for Academic Affairs ... Dr. Gerald L. RATLIFF
20 Assistant Provost ... Dr. Jill R. PEARON
18 Asst Vice Pres for Facilities ... Mr. Tony DITULLIO
88 Director of Special Programs ... Mr. Shailindar SINGH
90 Asst Vice Pres for Information Tech ... Mr. Andy A. HARRADINE
53 Dean Education & Prof Studies ... Dr. Peter S. BROUWER
49 Dean of Arts and Sciences ... Dr. Steven J. MARQUSEE
64 Dean of Music ... Dr. Michael R. SITTON
35 Dean of Students ... Mr. William G. MORRIS
51 Director of Extended Education ... Dr. Thomas W. FUHR
15 Director for Human Resources ... Ms. Mary K. DOLAN
08 Director of Libraries ... Ms. Jenica P. ROGERS
06 Registrar ... Dr. Ramona M. RALSTON
07 Director of Admissions ... Mr. Thomas W. NESBITT
37 Director of Financial Aid ... Ms. Susan C. ALDRICH
36 Director of Career Planning ... Ms. Karen I. HAM
38 Director of Counseling Center ... Ms. Gena C. NELSON
19 Chief of University Police ... Mr. John A. KAPLAN
29 Director of Alumni Relations ... Ms. Mona O. VROMAN
31 Executive Dir of Auxiliary Corp ... Mr. Daniel J. HAYES
23 Director of Health Services ... Dr. Richard E. MOOSE
39 Director of Residence Life ... Mr. Eric D. DUCHSCHERER
40 Director of College Bookstore ... Ms. Constance V. ROBINSON
41 Athletic Director ... Mr. James A. ZALACCA
25 Director Research & Sponsored Pgms ... Dr. Nancy M. DODGE-REYOME
21 Assistant VP Business Affairs ... Mr. David E. KIRWAN
28 Director of Diversity Center ... Ms. Sheila M. MARSHALL
92 Director of Honors Program ... Dr. Thomas N. BAKER
94 Director of Women's Studies ... Dr. Jacqueline K. GOODMAN
26 Asst VP Marketing/Communications ... Ms. Deborah L. DUDLEY
86 Community and Gov Rel Associate ... Ms. Alexandra M. JACOBS

*Purchase College, State University of New York (D)

735 Anderson Hill Road, Purchase NY 10577-1402
County: Westchester FICE Identification: 006791
Unit ID: 196219
Telephone: (914) 251-6000 Carnegie Class: Bac/A&S
FAX Number: (914) 251-6014 Calendar System: Semester
URL: www.purchase.edu
Established: 1967 Annual Undergrad Tuition & Fees (In-State): $5,915
Enrollment: 4,175 Coed
Affiliation or Control: State IRS Status: 501(c)3
Highest Offering: Master's
Program: Liberal Arts And General; Professional
Accreditation: M, ART

02 President ... Mr. Thomas J. SCHWARZ
19 Chief of University Police ... Mr. Joseph OLENIK
10 CFO/VP Operations ... Ms. Judy NOLAN
05 Provost/Exec VP Academic Affairs ... Dr. Barbara DIXON
32 Vice President Student Affairs ... Dr. Robin KAUFMAN
84 VP Enroll Mgmt/Integrated Mktg ... Mr. Dennis CRAIG
57 Director Conservatory Theatre Arts ... Dr. Gregory TAYLOR
51 Exec Dir Liberal Stds/Cont Educ ... Ms. Danielle D'AGOSTO
81 Dean Sch Natural/Social Sciences ... Dr. Suzanne KESSLER
79 Chair School of Humanities ... Dr. Louise YELIN
20 Associate Provost ... Dr. William BASKIN
88 Artistic Dir Performing Arts Center ... Mr. Wiley HAUSAM
88 Interim Dir Neuberger Museum of Art ... Ms. Lea EMERY
08 Director of the Library ... Mr. Patrick F. CALLAHAN
64 Director Conservatory of Music ... Dr. Suzanne FARRIN
88 Director School of Art & Design ... Mr. Ravi RAJAN
13 Director Campus Technology Services ... Mr. Bill JUNOR
37 Director Student Financial Services ... Ms. Corey YORK
38 Director of Counseling Center ... Dr. Glenn POLLACK
36 Director Career Development ... Ms. Wendy MOROSOFF
15 Director of Human Resources ... Ms. Kathleen FARRELL
41 Inter Collegiate Athletic Director ... Mr. Ernie PALMIERI
39 Dir Residence & Camp Life/Stdnt Dev ... Mr. John DELATE
96 Director of Purchasing ... Mr. Nikolaus LENTNER
06 Exec Dir Enroll Svcs/Assoc Dean Ac ... Ms. Patricia BICE
09 Director of Institutional Research ... Ms. Barbara MOORE
18 Dir Capital Facilities Planning ... Mr. Christopher GAVLICK
29 Director Alumni Affairs ... Vacant
22 Acting Affirmative Action Officer ... Mr. Ricardo ESPINALES
88 Environmental Health/Safety Officer ... Mr. Edward MUSAL
44 Director Annual Giving ... Ms. Carla WEILAND-ZALEZNAK
27 Interim Dir Commun & Creative Svcs ... Ms. Sandy DYLAK

*State University of New York College of Agriculture and Technology at Cobleskill (E)

Route 7, Knapp Hall, Cobleskill NY 12043
County: Schoharie FICE Identification: 002856
Unit ID: 196033
Telephone: (518) 255-5011 Carnegie Class: Bac/Assoc
FAX Number: (518) 255-5333 Calendar System: Semester
URL: www.cobleskill.edu
Established: 1911 Annual Undergrad Tuition & Fees (In-State): $5,895
Enrollment: 2,566 Coed
Affiliation or Control: State IRS Status: 501(c)3
Highest Offering: Baccalaureate
Program: Occupational; 2-Year Principally Bachelor's Creditable; Liberal Arts And General; Technical Emphasis
Accreditation: M, ACFEI, EMT, HT

02 President ... Dr. Candace VANCKO
05 Provost & Vice Pres Academic Affs ... Dr. Deb THATCHER
04 Assistant to President ... Ms. Amy HEALY
32 VP for Student Develop/Student Life ... Mr. Steven M. ACKERKNECHT
11 Vice Pres Administration ... Mr. Patrick WIATER
30 VP for Institutional Advancement ... Ms. Regina LAGATTA
35 Asst VP for Student Devel/Col Life ... Mr. Edward ASSELIN
47 Dean Agriculture/Natural Res ... Dr. Timothy MOORE
50 Dean Business & Computer Tech ... Mr. Michael J. MCCASKEY
49 Dean Liberal Arts & Sciences ... Dr. Susan ZIMMERMAN
08 Dean Library/Information Svcs ... Ms. Elizabeth ORGERON
27 Director of Communications ... Mr. Scott SILVERSTEN
06 Registrar ... Ms. Tara WINTER
10 Chief Business Officer ... Ms. Carol VOSATKA
07 Director of Admissions ... Vacant
39 Director of Residential Life ... Mr. Edward E. ASSELIN
36 Int Director of Student Success Ctr ... Ms. Donna PESTA
30 Director Development/Alumni Affairs ... Mrs. Lois E. GOBLET
23 Director Wellness Center ... Ms. Mary RADLIFF
37 Director of Financial Aid ... Mr. Brian D. SMITH
35 Director Student Union ... Mr. Jeffrey C. FOOTE
41 Director of Athletics ... Mr. Kevin MCCARTHY
13 Director Information Tech Services ... Mr. James DUTCHER
19 Director University Police Dept ... Mr. Frank LAWRENCE
09 Dir of IR and Assessment ... Ms. Jennifer L. GRAY
15 Director Human Resources ... Mr. R. Erik SEASTEDT
18 Director Facilities/Physical Plant ... Mr. Philip M. ARNOLD
40 Manager Bookstore ... Mr. Darrin LYONS
21 Associate Business Officer ... Ms. Louise BIRON
38 Director Student Counseling ... Ms. Lynn ONTL
85 Director of International Programs ... Ms. Susan JAGENDORF
96 Director of Purchasing ... Ms. Laura GROSS
25 Dir of Grants and Sponsored Program ... Mr. Barry GELL
88 Director of EOP ... Mr. Derwin BENNETT
88 Dir of Student Accounts ... Ms. Margaret GRIPPIN

*State University of New York College of Agriculture and Technology at Morrisville (F)

PO Box 901, Morrisville NY 13408-0901
County: Madison FICE Identification: 002859
Unit ID: 196051
Telephone: (315) 684-6000 Carnegie Class: Bac/Assoc
FAX Number: (315) 684-6116 Calendar System: Semester
URL: www.morrisville.edu
Established: 1908 Annual Undergrad Tuition & Fees (In-State): $6,342
Enrollment: 3,454 Coed
Affiliation or Control: State IRS Status: 501(c)3
Highest Offering: Baccalaureate
Program: Occupational; 2-Year Principally Bachelor's Creditable; Technical Emphasis
Accreditation: M, ACBSP, ADNUR, DIETT, ENGT

02 President ..... Dr. Bjong W. YEIGH
05 Vice President Academic Affairs ..... Dr. David E. ROGERS
11 Vice Pres Admin Svcs & Info Tech ..... Ms. Jean L. BOLAND
32 Dean of Students ..... Mr. Geoffrey S. ISABELLE
47 Dean School Agric/Natural Resource .. Dr. Christopher L. NYBERG
50 Interim Dean School Business ..... Dr. Christopher L. NYBERG
81 Dean School Science/Technology ..... Ms. Christine A. CRING
49 Dean School of Liberal Arts ..... Dr. Paul F. GRIFFIN
97 Dean School of General Studies ..... Ms. Jeannette H. EVANS
30 Interim Exec Dir Inst Advancement ..... Mr. Nicholas J. GRIMMER
26 Dir Public Relations/Govt Affairs ..... Ms. Amy L. ROBERTS
06 Dir of Inst Research & Registrar ..... Ms. Marian D. WHITNEY
07 Interim Director of Admissions ..... Ms. Heather R. HAIGHT
37 Director of Financial Aid ..... Ms. Dacia L. BANKS
08 Director of Library ..... Ms. Christine A. RUDECOFF
18 Director Physical Plant ..... Mr. F. Michael NATALUK
38 Director Health Services ..... Mr. Benjamin J. DOMINGO
10 Director Business Affairs ..... Ms. Mary Ellen BURDICK
15 Dir Human Svcs/Affirmative Action ..... Ms. Armanda KING
29 Coordinator of Alumni Relations ..... Ms. Kelly E. GARDNER
96 Purchasing Assistant ..... Ms. Karen H. PITTS

State University of New York College of Environmental Science and Forestry (A)

1 Forestry Drive, Syracuse NY 13210-2778
County: Onondaga FICE Identification: 002851
Unit ID: 196103
Telephone: (315) 470-6500 Carnegie Class: Master's S
FAX Number: (315) 470-6779 Calendar System: Semester
URL: www.esf.edu
Established: 1911 Annual Undergrad Tuition & Fees (In-State): $5,946
Enrollment: 2,718 Coed
Affiliation or Control: State IRS Status: 501(c)3
Highest Offering: Doctorate
Program: Liberal Arts And General; Professional
Accreditation: M, ENG, FOR, LSAR

02 President ..... Dr. Cornelius B. MURPHY, JR.
05 Vice Pres Academic Affairs/Provost ..... Dr. Bruce C. BONGARTEN
11 Vice President for Administration ..... Mr. Joseph RUFO
84 Vice Pres Enrollment Mgmt/Marketing ..... Dr. Robert C. FRENCH
46 Vice Provost for Research ..... Dr. Neil H. RINGLER
20 Assoc Prov for Instruction ..... Mr. Scott S. SHANNON
32 Dean Student Life/Experiential Lrng ..... Dr. Anne E. LOMBARD
10 Director of Business Affairs ..... Mr. David R. DZWONKOWSKI
13 Director of Info Tech ..... Mr. Yuming TUNG
15 Director Human Resources ..... Ms. Marcia A. BARBER
27 Director of Communications ..... Mrs. Claire B. DUNN
30 Director of Development ..... Ms. Brenda T. GREENFIELD
19 Director of University Police ..... Mr. Scott M. BECKSTED
08 Director of College Libraries ..... Mr. Stephen WEITER
07 Director of Admissions ..... Mrs. Susan H. SANFORD
06 Registrar ..... Mr. Raymond W. BLASKIEWICZ
37 Director of Financial Aid ..... Mr. John E. VIEW
29 Director Alumni Affairs ..... Mr. Justin F. CULKOWSKI
09 Director of Institutional Planning ..... Dr. Maureen O. FELLOWS
28 Director of Multicultural Affairs ..... Dr. Raydora S. DRUMMER FRANCIS
18 Chief Facilities/Physical Plant ..... Ms. Amy K. RITTER
21 Associate Business Officer ..... Ms. Danette J. DESIMONE
36 Career Planning & Devel Officer ..... Mr. John TURBEVILLE
86 Director Government Relations ..... Dr. Maureen O. FELLOWS
35 Director Student Activities ..... Mrs. Laura CRANDALL

State University of New York College of Optometry (B)

33 W 42nd Street, New York NY 10036-8003
County: New York FICE Identification: 009929
Unit ID: 196228
Telephone: (212) 938-4000 Carnegie Class: Spec/Health
FAX Number: (212) 938-5696 Calendar System: Semester
URL: www.sunyopt.edu
Established: 1971 Annual Graduate Tuition & Fees: $18,600
Enrollment: 303 Coed
Affiliation or Control: State IRS Status: 501(c)3
Highest Offering: Doctorate; No Undergraduates
Program: Professional
Accreditation: M, OPT, OPTR

02 President ..... Dr. David A. HEATH
05 VP Academic Affs/Academic Dean ..... Dr. David TROILO
11 VP For Administration and Finance ..... Mr. David A. BOWERS
32 Vice President Student Affairs ..... Dr. Jeffrey L. PHILPOTT
17 Int Vice Pres for Clinical Affairs ..... Dr. Richard SODEN
30 Vice President Advance/Public Rels ..... Ms. Ann WARWICK
04 Assistant to the President ..... Ms. Karen DEGAZON
09 Director Policy/Planning/Evaluation ..... Dr. Steven SCHWARTZ
08 Librarian ..... Ms. Elaine WELLS
16 Director of Personnel Services ..... Mr. Douglas SCHADING
37 Financial Aid Officer ..... Mr. Vito CAVALLARO
06 Registrar ..... Mrs. Jacqueline ESTEVEZ MARTINEZ
20 Dir Inst Vision Research/Assoc Dean ..... Dr. Jerome FELDMAN

*Alfred State College (C)

10 Upper College Drive, Alfred NY 14802-1196
County: Allegany FICE Identification: 002854
Unit ID: 196006
Telephone: (607) 587-4010 Carnegie Class: Bac/Assoc
FAX Number: N/A Calendar System: Semester
URL: www.alfredstate.edu
Established: 1908 Annual Undergrad Tuition & Fees (In-State): $6,242
Enrollment: 3,717 Coed
Affiliation or Control: State IRS Status: 501(c)3
Highest Offering: Baccalaureate
Program: 2-Year Principally Bachelor's Creditable; Nursing Emphasis
Accreditation: M, ADNUR, CONST, ENGT

02 President ..... Dr. John M. ANDERSON
05 Vice Pres Academic Affairs ..... Dr. Stephen HAVLOVIC
32 Vice President Student Affairs ..... Dr. Steven J. TYRELL
11 VP Administration & Enrollment ..... Mrs. Valerie B. NIXON
84 Assoc VP Enrollment Management ..... Mrs. Deborah J. GOODRICH
20 Assoc Vice Pres Academic Affairs ..... Mr. Charles V. NEAL
35 Associate VP for Student Life ..... Mr. Neil F. BENEDICT
54 Dean School of Mgmt & Engr Tech ..... Dr. John WILLIAMS
30 Director Institutional Advancement ..... Dr. Derek M. WESLEY
13 Director Computer Services ..... Mr. Michael A. CASE
15 Director Human Res/Affirm Action ..... Ms. Wendy DRESSER-RECKTENWALD
37 Sr Dir Student Financial Services ..... Mrs. Jane A. GILLILAND
29 Director Alumni Relations ..... Ms. Colleen ARGENTIERI
18 Director of Physical Plant ..... Mr. Glenn R. BRUBAKER
14 Asst Director of Computing Services ..... Mr. Carl H. RAHR, JR.
23 Int Dir Student Health Services ..... Ms. Vanessa V. STACHOWSKI
38 Director Learning Center ..... Ms. Janette B. THOMAS
19 Chief University Police ..... Mr. Gregory S. SAMMONS
09 Director Institutional Research ..... Mrs. Nancy B. SHEARER
96 Director of Purchasing ..... Mr. Glen E. CLINE
10 Chief Business Officer ..... Ms. Lisa M. PORTER
26 Chief Public Relations Officer ..... Ms. Cynthia S. SANTORA
36 Director of Career Services ..... Ms. Elaine MORSMAN
04 Exec Assistant to the President ..... Ms. Hollie HALL
49 Dean School of Arts & Sciences ..... Dr. Terry W. TUCKER
75 Dean School of Applied Technology ..... Mr. Craig R. CLARK

*SUNY Canton-College of Technology (D)

Canton NY 13617-1098
County: Saint Lawrence FICE Identification: 002855
Unit ID: 196015
Telephone: (315) 386-7011 Carnegie Class: Bac/Assoc
FAX Number: (315) 386-7930 Calendar System: Semester
URL: www.canton.edu
Established: 1906 Annual Undergrad Tuition & Fees (In-State): $6,521
Enrollment: 3,649 Coed
Affiliation or Control: State IRS Status: 501(c)3
Highest Offering: Baccalaureate
Program: Occupational; 2-Year Principally Bachelor's Creditable; Technical Emphasis
Accreditation: M, ADNUR, DH, ENGT, PTAA

02 President ..... Dr. Joseph L. KENNEDY
05 Provost ..... Dr. Carli C. SCHIFFNER
11 Interim Vice Pres Administration ..... Ms. Christine D. GRAY
30 Vice President for Advancement ..... Mr. David M. GERLACH
32 Int Vice Pres of Student Affairs ..... Dr. Molly A. MOTT
35 Dean of Students ..... Mr. Daniel J. SWEENEY
72 Dean Canino Sch Engineer Technology ..... Dr. David J. WELLS
76 Int Dean Sch Sci/Hlth/Crim Justice ..... Dr. Kenneth M. ERICKSON
50 Dean School Business/Liberal Arts ..... Dr. Linda A. HEILMAN
30 Asst VP Advancement/Dir Athletics ..... Mr. Randy B. SIEMINSKI
100 Chief of Staff/Govt Relations Ofcr ..... Mr. Ryan P. DEUEL
101 Secretary to the College Council ..... Ms. Stacey L. BASFORD
04 Executive Asst to President ..... Ms. Stacey L. BASFORD
10 Chief Business Officer ..... Ms. Christine D. GRAY
35 Interim Director Student Activities ..... Mr. Michael J. PERRY
28 Director of Diversity & Orientation ..... Ms. Lashawanda T. INGRAM
96 Director of Purchasing ..... Ms. Bethany A. MARTIN
37 Director of Financial Aid ..... Ms. Kerrie L. COOPER
15 Director of Human Resources ..... Ms. Elizabeth A. CONNOLLY
36 Director of Career Services ..... Mr. David F. NORENBERG
06 Registrar ..... Ms. Pamela E. ENSER
08 Head Librarian ..... Ms. Mary L. BUCHER
18 Asst Director of Physical Plant ..... Mr. Gerald O. SAWYER
19 Chief of University Police ..... Mr. William F. MASON
23 Director of Health Services ..... Ms. Patricia A. TODD
26 Dir Public Rels/Asst VP Advancement ..... Mr. Randy B. SIEMINSKI
40 Manager Campus Store ..... Mr. Corey JORDAN
39 Director of Residence Life ..... Ms. Courtney D. BISH
09 Director of Institutional Research ..... Dr. Mary Lou A. D'ALLEGRO
13 Chief Information Officer ..... Dr. Molly A. MOTT
22 Director of Affirmative Action ..... Ms. Elizabeth A. CONNOLLY
29 Director of Alumni Affairs ..... Ms. Peggy S. LEVATO
38 Director of Counseling ..... Ms. Melinda A. MILLER
07 Director Admissions ..... Ms. Nicole CAMPBELL
18 Dir Facilities/Capital Improvement ..... Mr. Michael R. MCCORMICK
44 Director of Development ..... Ms. Peggy S. LEVATO
88 User Support Services Manager ..... Ms. Theresa C. CORBINE
104 Director International Programs ..... Ms. Marela FIACCO
105 Web Designer/Coordinator ..... Mr. Travis G. SMITH
25 Grants Coordinator ..... Ms. JoAnne M. FASSINGER

*State University of New York College of Technology at Delhi (E)

2 Main Street, Delhi NY 13753
County: Delaware FICE Identification: 002857
Unit ID: 196024
Telephone: (607) 746-4000 Carnegie Class: Bac/Assoc
FAX Number: (607) 746-4208 Calendar System: Semester
URL: www.delhi.edu
Established: 1913 Annual Undergrad Tuition & Fees (In-State): $6,880
Enrollment: 3,331 Coed
Affiliation or Control: State IRS Status: 501(c)3
Highest Offering: Baccalaureate
Program: Occupational; 2-Year Principally Bachelor's Creditable; Liberal Arts And General
Accreditation: M, ACFEI, ADNUR, CONST, NUR

02 President ..... Dr. Candace S. VANCKO
05 Provost ..... Dr. John S. NADER
32 Vice President for Student Life ..... Ms. Barbara E. JONES
10 Vice Pres for Business & Finance ..... Mr. Brian G. HUTZLEY
30 Director Development/Alumni Affairs ..... Mr. Joel M. SMITH
84 Dean Enrollment Services ..... Mr. Craig S. WESLEY
15 Dir of Human Resources/Admin Svcs ..... Ms. Bonnie G. MARTIN
36 Coordinator Career & Transfer Svcs ..... Ms. Kristin A. DEFOREST
08 Director of the Resnick Library ..... Ms. Pamela J. PETERS
26 Director Communications/Marketing ..... Mr. Joel M. SMITH
51 Director Business & Community Svcs ..... Ms. Glenda V. ROBERTS
19 Chief of University Police ..... Mr. Perri D. DEFREECE
20 Director of Resnick Learning Center ..... Ms. Michele T. DEFREECE
18 Director of Physical Plant ..... Mr. David A. LOVELAND
41 Director of Athletics ..... Mr. Robert H. BACKUS
06 Registrar/Dir of Inst Research ..... Ms. Nancy L. SMITH
29 Alumni/Annual Giving Coordinator ..... Ms. Lucinda C. BRYDON
37 Director of Financial Aid ..... Ms. Nancy B. HUGHES
38 Director Counseling & Health Svcs ..... Ms. Lori B. OSTERHOUDT
07 Director of Admissions ..... Mr. Robert W. MAZZEI
21 Director of Business Affairs ..... Ms. Carol M. BISHOP
39 Director of Residence Life ..... Mr. John J. PADOVANI
13 Chief Information Officer ..... Mr. Jonathan R. BRENNAN

*State University of New York Empire State College (F)

2 Union Avenue, Saratoga Springs NY 12866-4390
County: Saratoga FICE Identification: 010286
Unit ID: 196264
Telephone: (518) 587-2100 Carnegie Class: Master's M
FAX Number: (518) 587-2886 Calendar System: Other
URL: www.esc.edu
Established: 1971 Annual Undergrad Tuition & Fees (In-State): $5,245
Enrollment: 11,985 Coed
Affiliation or Control: State IRS Status: 501(c)3
Highest Offering: Master's
Program: Liberal Arts And General; Professional
Accreditation: M, NURSE, @TEAC

02 President ..... Dr. Alan R. DAVIS
100 Chief of Staff ..... Ms. Patrice DECOSTER
05 Provost/Vice Pres Academic Affairs ..... Dr. Meg BENKE
10 Vice President for Administration ..... Mr. Paul TUCCI
86 VP for Communications & Govt Rels ..... Ms. Mary Caroline VAN DER VEER
32 VP for Enroll Mgmt & Student Svcs ..... Dr. Hugh B. HAMMETT
30 VP for External Affairs ..... Vacant
13 VP for Integrated Technologies ..... Mr. David O'NEILL
09 VP for Plng & Inst Effectiveness ..... Dr. Mitchell S. NESLER
20 Vice Prov for Academic Development ..... Dr. Marjorie W. LAVIN
106 Vice Prov for Global/Online Lrng ..... Vacant
88 Vice Prov for Reg Ctrs & Ntd Lrng ..... Dr. Deborah AMORY
12 Dean Central New York Center ..... Dr. Nikki SHRIMPTON
12 Dean Genesee Valley Center ..... Dr. Jonathan R. FRANZ
88 Dean HVA Center for Labor Studies ..... Dr. Michael MERRILL
12 Dean Hudson Valley Center ..... Dr. Robert TRULLINGER
12 Dean Long Island Center ..... Dr. Michael SPITZER
12 Dean Metropolitan Center ..... Dr. Cynthia L. WARD
12 Dean Niagara Frontier Center ..... Dr. Nan M. DIBELLO
12 Dean Northeast Center ..... Dr. Gerald F. LORENTZ
106 Int Dean Center for Distance Lng ..... Dr. Thomas MACKEY
58 Dean Center for Graduate Programs ..... Dr. Robert J. CLOUGHERTY
20 Asst Vice Pres for Academic Pgms ..... Dr. Tai M. ARNOLD
21 Asst Vice Pres for Adminstration ..... Mr. Frederick BARTHELMAS
30 Asst Vice Pres for Development ..... Vacant
84 Interim Asst VP for Enrollment Mgmt ..... Ms. Jennifer D'AGOSTINO
14 Asst VP for Integrated Tech Infras ..... Mr. Curt KING
07 Asst Director Admissions ..... Ms. Tina MASSA
72 Director Academic Technology ..... Ms. Suzanne HAYES
91 Director Admin Applications ..... Mr. Mark CLAVERIE
88 Director Advancement Services ..... Ms. Vicki SCHAAKE
29 Dir Alumni and Student Relations ..... Ms. Maureen WINNEY
44 Director Annual Giving ..... Ms. Diane THOMPSON
21 Director Business Affairs ..... Ms. Becky PALMIERI
88 Director Capital Projects ..... Vacant
88 Dir Center for Mentoring & Learning ..... Dr. Katherine JELLY
20 Dir Col Acad Sppt/H V Arsdale Labor ..... Ms. Sophia MAVOGIANNIS
20 Dir Col Acad Sppt/Long Island Ctr ..... Ms. Mildred VAN BERGEN
20 Dir Collegewide Academic Review ..... Dr. Nan TRAVERS
35 Dir Collegewide Student Services ..... Ms. Patricia MYERS
27 Director of Communications ..... Mr. David HENAHAN
88 Dir Cmty College Partnerships ..... Mr. Brian GOODALE
88 Dir Corp & Community Partnerships ..... Ms. Lisa SAX
88 Dir Environmental Sustainability ..... Ms. Sadie ROSS
18 Director Facilities and Maintenance ..... Mr. Rick REIMANN
37 Director Financial Aid ..... Ms. Kristina DELBRIDGE
44 Director Gift Planning ..... Vacant
30 Director of Development ..... Mr. Toby TOBROCKE
86 Director Government Relations ..... Dr. John D'AGATI
25 Director Grants & Contracts ..... Ms. Lorraine ANTHONY
16 Interim Asst VP for Human Resource ..... Ms. Mary Ellen R. KEENEY

88 Director Marketing .... Ms. Renelle SHAMPENY
88 Director Outcomes Asessment .... Vacant
88 Director Project Management .... Mr. Walter LEWIS
96 Director Procurement .... Mr. Charley SUMMERSELL
88 Director Publications .... Mr. Kirk STARCZEWSKI
19 Director Campus Safety & Security .... Mr. Thomas VUMBACO
21 Director Student Accounts .... Ms. Pamela MALONE
88 Dir Veteran & Military Education .... Ms. Linda FRANK
26 Senior Director of Marketing .... Dr. John MCKENNA
22 Affirmative Action Officer .... Ms. Mary MORTON
06 Registrar .... Ms. Mary EDINBURGH

† The enrollment number declined as an artifact of the transition to a new system-imposed reporting scheme.

*Farmingdale State College (A)

2350 Broadhollow Road, Farmingdale NY 11735-1021
County: Suffolk FICE Identification: 002858
Unit ID: 196042
Telephone: (631) 420-2000 Carnegie Class: Bac/Diverse
FAX Number: N/A Calendar System: Semester
URL: www.farmingdale.edu
Established: 1912 Annual Undergrad Tuition & Fees (In-State): $6,030
Enrollment: 7,000 Coed
Affiliation or Control: State IRS Status: 501(c)3
Highest Offering: Baccalaureate
Program: Liberal Arts And General; Professional
Accreditation: M, ADNUR, DH, ENGT, MLTAD, NAIT, NUR, PNUR

02 President .... Dr. Hubert KEEN
05 Provost/Vice Pres for Academic Affs .... Dr. Lucia CEPRIANO
10 Senior Vice President & CFO .... Mr. George P. LAROSA
32 VP Student Affairs/Enrollment Mgmt .... Dr. Lucia CEPRIANO
26 Vice Pres Institutional Advancement .... Mr. Patrick CALABRIA
30 Chief Development Officer .... Dr. Henry SIKORSKI
20 Assistant Provost .... Vacant
11 Asst Vice President Admin Services .... Vacant
35 Asst Vice President Student Life .... Dr. Tom CORTI
35 Dean of Students .... Ms. Theresa ESNES-JOHNSON
07 Director of Admissions .... Mr. James HALL
19 Chief University Police .... Mr. Marvin FISCHER
18 Director of Physical Plant .... Mr. John S. DZINANKA
27 Director of Communications .... Ms. Kathryn S. COLEY
06 Registrar .... Ms. Cindy MCCUE
08 Head Librarian .... Mr. Michael KNAUTH
15 Director Human Resources .... Ms. Marybeth INCANDELA
36 Director Career Plng & Development .... Ms. Dolores CIACCIO
37 Director Financial Aid .... Ms. Diane KAZANECKI-KEMPTER
09 Institutional Research Associate .... Mr. Robert SIMINS
23 Director Student Health Services .... Ms. Audrey KRAPF
41 Director Athletics .... Mr. Michael HARRINGTON
39 Director Campus Housing .... Vacant
102 President Farmingdale Foundation .... Mr. Richard OVERTON
24 Director Media Resources .... Mr. Martin BRANDT
29 Director Alumni Affairs .... Ms. Eileen HASSON
28 Director of Diversity .... Ms. Veronica HENRY
38 Director Student Success Center .... Ms. Marguerite FAGELLA-D'ALOSIO
40 Manager Bookstore .... Ms. Roberta MIRRO
21 Controller .... Mr. Richard HUME
96 Purchasing Assistant .... Ms. Erika WACHTER
75 Dean Long Island Educ Oppty Center .... Mr. Brian MAHER
50 Dean School of Business .... Dr. Lorraine GREENWALD
76 Dean School Health Sciences .... Dr. Marie HAYDEN-MILES
49 Dean Sch of Arts & Sciences .... Dr. Eleanor FAPOHUNDA
54 Dean Sch Engineer Technology .... Dr. Kamal SHAHRABI

*State University of New York Institute of Technology at Utica-Rome (B)

100 Seymour Road, Utica NY 13502
County: Oneida FICE Identification: 011678
Unit ID: 196112
Telephone: (315) 792-7100 Carnegie Class: Master's M
FAX Number: (315) 792-7222 Calendar System: Semester
URL: www.sunyit.edu
Established: 1966 Annual Undergrad Tuition & Fees (In-State): $6,114
Enrollment: 2,826 Coed
Affiliation or Control: State IRS Status: 501(c)3
Highest Offering: Master's
Program: Liberal Arts And General; Professional; Technical Emphasis
Accreditation: M, BUS, ENGT, NURSE

02 President .... Dr. Bjong W. YEIGH
04 Assistant to the President .... Ms. Laurie HARTMAN
05 Provost/Vice Pres Academic Affairs .... Dr. William DURGIN
11 Vice President Administration .... Mr. Bruce E. REICHEL
13 Associate Provost ILR .... Mr. Kyle JOHNSON
15 Associate VP Human Resources .... Mr. Anthony F. PANEBIANCO
84 Assistant VP .... Ms. Marybeth LYONS
79 Director Communications/Humanities .... Dr. Mary PERRONE
83 Director Social & Behavioral Sci .... Dr. Paul SCHULMAN
77 Director Computer Info Sciences .... Dr. John MARSH
54 Director Engineering Technologies .... Dr. Daniel JONES
81 Director Engineering Science & Math .... Dr. Andrew WOLFE
66 Director Nursing & Health Profess .... Dr. Darlene DELPRATO
07 Director Admissions .... Ms. Jennifer PHELAN-NINH
41 Director Athletics .... Mr. Kevin M. GRIMMER
21 Director Business Affairs .... Ms. Annette AGNESS
35 Director Campus Life .... Mr. John BORNER
36 Director Career Services .... Vacant
38 Dir Counseling & Special Pgms .... Mr. David GARRETT
30 Director Development .... Mr. Peter PERKINS
18 Director Facilities .... Mr. Carson SORRELL
23 Director Health & Wellness Center .... Ms. Jo RUFFRAGE
09 Director Institutional Research .... Ms. Valerie FUSCO
26 Director Public Relations .... Mr. John SWANN
19 Director Public Safety .... Mr. Gary BEAN
39 Director Residential Life & Housing .... Mr. John BORNER
46 Director Spon Research/Cont Prof Ed .... Ms. Deborah TYKSINSKI
37 Director Student Financial Aid .... Vacant
06 Registrar .... Mr. John LASHER
58 Coordinator Graduate Center .... Ms. Maryrose RAAB
29 Alumni & Advancement Services .... Ms. Brenda DOW
96 Purchasing .... Mr. Michael DURR

*State University of New York Maritime College (C)

6 Pennyfield Avenue, Throggs Neck NY 10465-4198
County: Bronx FICE Identification: 002853
Unit ID: 196291
Telephone: (718) 409-7200 Carnegie Class: Bac/Diverse
FAX Number: (718) 409-7392 Calendar System: Semester
URL: www.sunymaritime.edu
Established: 1874 Annual Undergrad Tuition & Fees (In-State): $6,846
Enrollment: 1,891 Coed
Affiliation or Control: State IRS Status: 501(c)3
Highest Offering: Master's
Program: Liberal Arts And General; Professional
Accreditation: M, ENG

02 President .... VADM. John W. CRAINE
04 Executive Assistant to President .... Vacant
05 Vice Pres Academic Affairs/Provost .... Dr. Joseph C. HOFFMAN
11 Vice President Operations .... Ms. Elizabeth PRAETORIUS
32 Commandant of Cadets/Master TSES .... CAPT. Richard S. SMITH
10 Dir of Business Affairs/CBO .... Mr. Keith MURPHY
26 Vice President University Relations .... CAPT. Thomas W. GREENE
20 Associate Provost .... Dr. Gilbert TRAUB
07 Dean of Admissions .... Mr. Jonathan WHITE
32 Dean of Students .... Dr. Irene R. DELGADO
30 Director of Development/CDO .... Mr. John CONNOLLY
26 Exec Director of External Affairs .... Ms. Mary MUECKE
27 Director of Communications/PR .... Ms. Jane BARTNETT
15 Director Human Resources .... Ms. LuAnn AUGUSTINE-PLAISANCE
18 Exec Dir Phys Plant/Plant Superin .... Mr. William RUEGER
88 Company Security Officer/Maritime .... MajGen. Robert WOLF
19 Chief University Police/Facility SO .... Mr. John DILLON
84 Exec Dir Enroll Svcs/Financial Aid .... Mr. Paul BAMONTE
41 Director of Athletics .... Mr. Dick HACK
88 Director of the Waterfront .... Mr. Robert CRAFA
09 Dir of Institutional Rsrch/Asses .... Dr. Michael CAPPETO
88 Coord Institutional Effectiveness .... Ms. Iris VANKERCKHOVE
06 Registrar .... Ms. Sarah GRADY
08 Head of Library .... Ms. Constantia CONSTANTINOU
107 Chair of Prof Education/Training .... CAPT. Ernest FINK
07 Director of Graduate Admissions .... MajGen. Robert WOLF
88 Assistant Director of Admissions .... Mr. Matthew GAROFALOW
88 Director of Conference Services .... Ms. Nancy RUEGER
21 Director of Student Accounts .... Ms. Denise ALBERTELLI
36 Director Career Services .... Mr. Paul BAMONTE
13 Chief Information Tech Officer .... Mr. Daniel MASTROMARINO
22 Affirmative Action Officer .. Ms. Lu-Ann AUGUSTINE-PLAISANCE
96 Manager of Purchasing/Contracts .... Vacant
40 Director of Ship's Store .... Ms. Florence MANDRACHIA
38 EOP/University Counselor .... Ms. Cortney WORRELL
88 Construction/Capital Programs Mgr .... Mr. William HERRMANN
85 Coord Intl Student Svcs .... Ms. Devon SWITZER

*Suffolk County Community College Central Administration (D)

533 College Road, Selden NY 11784-2899
County: Suffolk Identification: 666658
Unit ID: 366395
Telephone: (631) 451-4000 Carnegie Class: N/A
FAX Number: (631) 451-4715
URL: www.sunysuffolk.edu

01 President .... Dr. Shaun L. MCKAY
04 Exec Assistant to the President .... Vacant
03 Executive Vice President .... Mr. George GATTA, JR.
43 College General Counsel .... Mr. Louis S. PETRIZZO
05 Vice Pres Academic/Student Affairs .... Vacant
10 VP Business/Financial Affairs .... Mr. James AMOROSO
30 Vice Pres Institutional Advancement .... Ms. Mary Lou ARANEO
45 VP Planning/Inst Effectiveness .... Dr. Nathaniel PUGH
20 Assoc VP Academic Affairs .... Vacant
32 Assoc VP of Student Affairs .... Dr. Marvin L. BRIGHT
31 Assoc VP Workforce/Econ Development .... Mr. John LOMBARDO
16 Assistant VP Employee Resources .... Mr. Jeffrey L. TEMPERA
07 College Dean Enroll/Mgt .... Vacant
06 College Registrar .... Ms. Anna FLACK
37 Director of Financial Aid .... Vacant
88 Director of Publications .... Ms. Mary FEDER

*Suffolk County Community College Ammerman Campus (E)

533 College Road, Selden NY 11784-2899
County: Suffolk FICE Identification: 002878
Unit ID: 195951
Telephone: (631) 451-4000 Carnegie Class: Not Classified
FAX Number: (631) 451-4015 Calendar System: Semester
URL: www.sunysuffolk.edu
Established: 1959 Annual Undergrad Tuition & Fees (In-District): $4,670
Enrollment: 26,719 Coed
Affiliation or Control: State/Local IRS Status: 501(c)3
Highest Offering: Associate Degree
Program: Occupational; 2-Year Principally Bachelor's Creditable
Accreditation: M, ADNUR, PNUR, PTAA

02 Executive Dean/Campus CEO .... Dr. James SHERWOOD
32 Assoc Dean of Student Services .... Mr. Charles BARTOLOTTA

*Suffolk County Community College Eastern Campus (F)

121 Speonk-Riverhead Road, Riverhead NY 11901-3499
County: Suffolk FICE Identification: 004816
Unit ID: 195942
Telephone: (631) 548-2500 Carnegie Class: Not Classified
FAX Number: (631) 369-2641 Calendar System: Semester
URL: www.sunysuffolk.edu
Established: 1977 Annual Undergrad Tuition & Fees (In-District): $4,670
Enrollment: 26,719 Coed
Affiliation or Control: State/Local IRS Status: 501(c)3
Highest Offering: Associate Degree
Program: Occupational; 2-Year Principally Bachelor's Creditable
Accreditation: &M, DIETT

02 Executive Dean & Campus CEO .... Dr. Evon W. WALTERS
32 Assoc Dean of Student Services .... Dr. Robert BEODEKER

*Suffolk County Community College Grant Campus (G)

1001 Crooked Hill Road, Brentwood NY 11717-1091
County: Suffolk FICE Identification: 013204
Unit ID: 195960
Telephone: (631) 851-6700 Carnegie Class: Not Classified
FAX Number: (631) 851-6509 Calendar System: Semester
URL: www.sunysuffolk.edu
Established: 1974 Annual Undergrad Tuition & Fees (In-District): $4,670
Enrollment: 26,719 Coed
Affiliation or Control: State/Local IRS Status: 501(c)3
Highest Offering: Associate Degree
Program: Occupational; 2-Year Principally Bachelor's Creditable
Accreditation: &M, ADNUR, OTA

02 Exec Dean & Campus CEO .... Dr. James KEANE
32 Assoc Dean of Student Services .... Dr. Meryl ROGERS

Sullivan County Community College (H)

112 College Road, Loch Sheldrake NY 12759-5721
County: Sullivan FICE Identification: 002879
Unit ID: 195988
Telephone: (845) 434-5750 Carnegie Class: Assoc/Pub-R-S
FAX Number: (845) 434-4806 Calendar System: Semester
URL: www.sullivan.suny.edu
Established: 1962 Annual Undergrad Tuition & Fees (In-District): $4,742
Enrollment: 1,755 Coed
Affiliation or Control: State/Local IRS Status: 501(c)3
Highest Offering: Associate Degree
Program: Occupational; 2-Year Principally Bachelor's Creditable
Accreditation: M, ACBSP, ADNUR

01 President .... Dr. Mamie HOWARD GOLLADAY
05 Vice Pres Academic & Student Affs .... Dr. Robert SCHULTZ
11 Vice Pres Administrative Affairs .... Mr. Jeffrey A. SHAPIRO
20 Asst VP Academic/Student Affairs .... Ms. Iman ELGINBEHI
32 Dean Student Services .... Vacant
51 Dean Workforce Devel/Cont Educ .... Dr. Stephen MITCHELL
39 Asst Dean Student Life & Housing .... Mr. James GOLDFARB
31 Dir Spec Events/Campus Activities .... Ms. Hillary EGELAND
10 Chief Business Officer .... Ms. Susan HORTON
18 Chief Facilities/Physical Plant .... Mr. Tracy HALL
07 Director Admissions/Registration .... Ms. Sari ROSENHECK
21 Controller .... Ms. Susan HORTON
30 Director Inst Development/Outreach .... Ms. Maria INGRASSIA
37 Director of Financial Aid .... Mr. James WINDERL
08 Director of Library Services .... Mr. Jon GRENNAN
35 Director Student Activities .... Ms. Adrianna MAYSON
88 Director Early Childhood .... Ms. Deborah BOGORAD
41 Director of Athletics .... Mr. Chris DEPEW
15 Director of Human Resources .... Ms. Sharon SAND
09 Director Institutional Research .... Dr. Ronald STEVENS
25 Grants Writer .... Vacant
38 Director Student Counseling .... Ms. Rose HANOFEE
96 Purchasing Agent .... Ms. Lorry IRWIN
13 Int Dir Campus Computer Services .... Ms. Cheryl WELSCH
06 Coord of Registration Services .... Dr. Laura SAMPSON
26 Coord of Public & Alumni Relations .... Vacant

50 Chair Business/Information Tech .... Ms. Mary SUDOL
79 Chair Liberal Arts & Humanities .... Dr. Paul REIFENHEISER
107 Chair Professional Studies .... Mr. Michael FISHER
83 Chair Health/Social/Behavioral Sci .... Dr. Beverly MOORE
81 Chair Mathematics/Natural Sciences ...... Ms. Debra LEWKIEWICZ

Swedish Institute College of Health Sciences (A)

226 W 26th Street, New York NY 10001-6700
County: New York FICE Identification: 021700
Unit ID: 196389
Telephone: (212) 924-5900 Carnegie Class: Spec/Health
FAX Number: (212) 924-7600 Calendar System: Semester
URL: www.swedishinstitute.edu
Established: 1916 Annual Undergrad Tuition & Fees: $11,375
Enrollment: 566 Coed
Affiliation or Control: Proprietary IRS Status: Proprietary
Highest Offering: Master's
Program: Occupational; Professional
Accreditation: ACCSC, ACUP

01 President .... Dr. William C. ECKARDT
03 Senior Vice President .... Ms. Paula J. ECKARDT
10 Chief Financial Officer .... Mr. John P. TONKINSON
11 Dean Administration/Operations .... Mr. Yick Pon HUEY
05 Dean Academic Affs/Acupuncture Pgm .... Dr. Sheila GEORGE
29 Dean of Alumni Services .... Ms. Meg DARNELL
86 Dean of Regulatory Affairs .... Ms. Gina MARTIN
05 Dean Academic Affs/Acupuncture Pgm .... Dr. Jeffrey YUEN
07 Director of Admissions .... Ms. Jennifer ACIPELLA
88 Dean for Massage Therapy .... Ms. Lucy LIBEN
13 Director of Information Technology .... Mr. Benn LI
32 Director of Student Services .... Ms. Jessica FERRANTE
26 Director of Public Relations .... Ms. Barbara GOLDSCHMIDT
37 Financial Aid Director .... Ms. Martha P. PADILLA
08 Director of Library Services .... Ms. Rimma PERELMAN
06 Registrar .... Mr. Trey GILBERT
21 Bursar .... Ms. Mary ALVAREZ
51 Manager of Continuing Education .... Ms. Daniella SANTORO
40 Bookstore Manager .... Mr. Dan YUEN

Syracuse University Main Campus (B)

Syracuse NY 13244-1100
County: Onondaga FICE Identification: 002882
Unit ID: 196413
Telephone: (315) 443-1870 Carnegie Class: RU/H
FAX Number: (315) 443-3503 Calendar System: Semester
URL: www.syr.edu
Established: 1870 Annual Undergrad Tuition & Fees: $37,667
Enrollment: 20,407 Coed
Affiliation or Control: Independent Non-Profit IRS Status: 501(c)3
Highest Offering: Doctorate
Program: Liberal Arts And General; Teacher Preparatory; Professional
Accreditation: M, ART, AUD, BUS, CACREP, CIDA, CLPSY, CS, DIETD, DIETI, ENG, JOUR, LAW, LIB, MFCD, MUS, SCPSY, SP, SPAA, SW, TED

01 Chancellor & President .... Dr. Nancy CANTOR
05 Vice Chanc/Prov Academic Affs .... Dr. Eric F. SPINA
03 Executive Vice President & CFO .... Dr. Louis G. MARCOCCIA
43 Sr Vice Pres General Counsel .... Mr. Thomas S. EVANS
30 ExecVP Advancement/External Affairs .... Mr. Thomas J. WALSH
32 Sr Vice Pres/Dean Student Affairs .... Rev. Thomas V. WOLFE
46 Vice Pres Research .... Dr. Gina LEE-GLAUSER
41 Athletic Director .... Dr. Daryl J. GROSS
26 Sr Vice Pres Public Affairs .... Mr. Kevin C. QUINN
84 Vice Pres Enrollment Management .... Mr. Donald A. SALEH
10 Vice President Business Operations .... Ms. Jena P. MCWHA
13 Vice Pres Information Tech/CIO .... Mr. Christopher M. SEDORE
08 Dean of University Libraries .... Dr. Suzanne E. THORIN
88 Senior Assc Provost .... Dr. Karen ALSTON
20 Assc Provost Academic Programs .... Ms. Sandra N. HURD
88 Assc Provost Entrep Innovation .... Dr. Bruce KINGMA
48 Dean School of Architecture .... Dr. Mark ROBBINS
49 Dean Col of Arts & Sciences .... Dr. George M. LANGFORD
53 Dean School of Education .... Dr. Douglas P. BIKLEN
76 Dean Col of Sport & Human Dynamics .... Dr. Diane Lyden MURPHY
54 Dean Col Engineering & Computer Sci .... Dr. Laura J. STEINBERG
62 Dean School of Information Studies .... Dr. Elizabeth D. LIDDY
61 Dean College of Law .... Dr. Hannah ARTERIAN
50 Dean Whitman School of Management .... Dr. Melvin T. STITH
80 Dean Maxwell Sch of Citizenship .... Dr. James B. STEINBERG
60 Dean Newhouse School of Public Comm .... Ms. Lorraine BRANHAM
57 Dean Col Visual & Performing Arts .... Ms. Ann CLARKE
58 Dean Graduate Studies .... Dr. Ben R. WARE
51 Dean University College .... Ms. Bethaida GONZALEZ
101 Secretary Board of Trustees .... Ms. Elizabeth B. O'ROURKE

Talmudical Institute of Upstate New York (C)

769 Park Avenue, Rochester NY 14607-3046
County: Monroe FICE Identification: 025506
Unit ID: 196440
Telephone: (585) 473-2810 Carnegie Class: Spec/Faith
FAX Number: (585) 442-0417 Calendar System: Semester
Established: 1974 Annual Undergrad Tuition & Fees: $5,500
Enrollment: 23 Male
Affiliation or Control: Independent Non-Profit IRS Status: 501(c)3
Highest Offering: Second Talmudic Degree
Program: Professional
Accreditation: RABN

01 Dean .... Rabbi Menachem DAVIDOWITZ
03 Executive Vice President .... Rabbi Shlomo NOBLE

Talmudical Seminary of Bobov (D)

4820 16th Avenue, Brooklyn NY 11204-1108
County: Kings FICE Identification: 041155
Unit ID: 451404
Telephone: (718) 436-2122 Carnegie Class: Spec/Faith
FAX Number: (718) 436-5341 Calendar System: Semester
Established: 2005 Annual Undergrad Tuition & Fees: $5,650
Enrollment: 197 Male
Affiliation or Control: Independent Non-Profit IRS Status: 501(c)3
Highest Offering: First Talmudic Degree
Program: Teacher Preparatory; Professional; Religious Emphasis
Accreditation: RABN

01 Dean .... Rabbi Joshua RUBIN

Talmudical Seminary Oholei Torah (E)

667 Eastern Parkway, Brooklyn NY 11213-3397
County: Kings FICE Identification: 012011
Unit ID: 196431
Telephone: (718) 774-5050 Carnegie Class: Spec/Faith
FAX Number: (718) 778-0784 Calendar System: Semester
Established: 1956 Annual Undergrad Tuition & Fees: $9,350
Enrollment: 334 Male
Affiliation or Control: Independent Non-Profit IRS Status: 501(c)3
Highest Offering: First Talmudic Degree
Program: Teacher Preparatory
Accreditation: RABN

01 Chief Executive Officer .... Mendel MARSOW
05 Dean .... Elchonon LESCHES
10 Business Officer .... Gary SUSSKIND
37 Financial Aid Officer .... Sholom ROSENFELD

Teachers College, Columbia University (F)

525 West 120th Street, New York NY 10027
County: New York FICE Identification: 003979
Unit ID: 196468
Telephone: (212) 678-3000 Carnegie Class: RU/H
FAX Number: (212) 678-4048 Calendar System: Semester
URL: www.tc.columbia.edu
Established: 1887 Annual Graduate Tuition & Fees: $36,930
Enrollment: 5,274 Coed
Affiliation or Control: Independent Non-Profit IRS Status: 501(c)3
Highest Offering: Doctorate; No Undergraduates
Program: Teacher Preparatory; Professional
Accreditation: M, CLPSY, COPSY, DIETI, SCPSY, SP, TED

01 President .... Dr. Susan H. FUHRMAN
05 Provost & VP for Academic Affairs .... Dr. Thomas JAMES
100 Ast to Pres/Sec to Col/Chf of Staff .... Mr. Scott FAHEY
10 Vice Pres Finance & Administration .... Mr. Harvey SPECTOR
30 Vice Pres Devel/External Affairs .... Ms. Suzanne MURPHY
22 Vice President/Dir Diversity/Cmty .... Ms. Janice S. ROBINSON
20 Vice Provost .... Dr. William BALDWIN
21 Assoc Vice Pres/Controller .... Mr. Henry PERKOWSKI
31 Assoc Vice Pres Auxiliary Services .... Mr. James MITCHELL
88 Asc VP/Spec Advisor to CU Provost .... Dr. Nancy STREIM
20 Associate Vice Provost .... Dr. Katie EMBREE
06 Registrar .... Ms. Diana MAUL
14 Director Computing/Information Svcs .... Ms. Ena HAINES
90 Manager Academic Computing .... Mr. George SCHUESSLER
08 Library Director .... Dr. Gary NATRIELLO
09 Director of Institutional Studies .... Mr. Scott SCHNACKENBERG
36 Director Career Services/Stdnt Life .... Ms. Marianne TRAMELLI
15 Director Human Resources .... Mr. Randy GLAZER
19 Chief of Campus Safety/Security .... Mr. John DE ANGELIS
43 General Counsel .... Ms. Lori FOX
25 Director Grants/Sponsored Programs .... Mr. Paul KRAN
25 Director Contracts & Grants .... Mr. John HERNANDEZ
26 Exec Director of External Affairs .... Mr. Joe LEVINE
29 Asst Director Alumni Relations .... Ms. Lindsey BRENAN
07 Director of Admissions .... Dr. Thomas ROCK
18 Director of Facilities .... Ms. Suzanne JABLONSKI
32 Dir Student Activities/Programs .... Ms. Maria HATAIER
84 Assoc Dean Enrollment/Student Svcs .... Dr. Thomas ROCK
21 Manager Administrative Services .... Ms. Patricia WALKER
37 Director Student Financial Aid .. Ms. Melanie WILLIAMS-BETHEA
39 Director of Resident Life .... Mr. Dewayne WHITE
85 Director of International Affairs .... Dr. Portia WILLIAMS

† Affiliated with Columbia University in the City of New York.

Technical Career Institutes (G)

320 W 31st Street, New York NY 10001-2789
County: New York FICE Identification: 011031
Unit ID: 196477
Telephone: (212) 594-4000 Carnegie Class: Assoc/PrivFP
FAX Number: (212) 330-0898 Calendar System: Semester
URL: www.tcicollege.edu
Established: 1909 Annual Undergrad Tuition & Fees: $11,850
Enrollment: 4,495 Coed
Affiliation or Control: Proprietary IRS Status: Proprietary
Highest Offering: Associate Degree
Program: Occupational; 2-Year Principally Bachelor's Creditable; Technical Emphasis
Accreditation: M, NY, ENGT, OPD

01 Chief Executive Officer .... Dr. John MCGRATH
01 President .... Mr. William TALBOT
05 Provost & VP for Academic Affairs .... Dr. Peter SLATER
07 Acting Vice Pres for Admissions .... Mr. Bernard PRICE
11 Exec Vice Pres Administration .... Mr. Felix PRETTO
37 Vice President Financial Aid .... Ms. Cynthia FEKARIS
09 Vice Pres for Research and Planning .... Ms. Susanna KUNG
10 Vice President/CFO .... Mr. Richard GOLDENBERG
20 Dean of Academic Administration .... Ms. Pansy JAMES
49 Dean of Arts & Sciences .... Dr. John LUUKKONEN
88 Dean of Environmental Control .... Ms. Regina CAHILL
50 Dean of Business and New Media Tech .... Ms. Clotilde DILLON
72 Dean of Technology .... Mr. Seyed AKHAVI
76 Dean of Health Sciences and Tech .... Dr. Michael MEIR

Tompkins Cortland Community College (H)

170 North Street, PO Box 139, Dryden NY 13053-8504
County: Tompkins FICE Identification: 006788
Unit ID: 196565
Telephone: (607) 844-8211 Carnegie Class: Assoc/Pub-R-M
FAX Number: (607) 844-9665 Calendar System: Semester
URL: www.tc3.edu
Established: 1968 Annual Undergrad Tuition & Fees (In-District): $4,450
Enrollment: 3,557 Coed
Affiliation or Control: State/Local IRS Status: 501(c)3
Highest Offering: Associate Degree
Program: Occupational; 2-Year Principally Bachelor's Creditable
Accreditation: M, ADNUR

01 President .... Dr. Carl E. HAYNES
03 Provost and VP of College .... Dr. John R. CONNERS
32 Dean of Student Life .... Mr. Jim HULL
05 Dean of Instruction .... Mr. Carl PENZIUL
08 Library Director .... Mr. Gregg KIEHL
84 Dean Operations & Enrollment Mgmt ...... Ms. Blixy K. TAETZSCH
20 Assoc Dean Curriculum & Acad Record . Ms. Jane F. HAMMOND
14 Director of Technology Support .... Mr. Brian ACKLEY
88 Dean Org Success & Learning .... Ms. Kathryn WUNDERLICH
09 Assoc Dean IR and Org Learning .... Dr. Kristine ALTUCHER
38 Director Counseling/Career Svc .... Ms. Amy TRUEMAN
37 Director of Financial Aid .... Ms. Sharon KARWOWSKI
26 Dean of External Relations .... Dr. Bruce RYAN
15 Human Resources Administrator .... Ms. Sharon DOVI
07 Director of Admissions .... Mr. Sandy DRUMLUK
21 Director of Budget & Finance .... Ms. Susan DEWEY
13 Dean of Campus Technology ... Mr. Martin G. CHRISTOFFERSON
19 Director of Safety & Security .... Mr. J. Beau SAUL
41 Athletic Director .... Mr. Mick R. MCDANIEL
39 Director Residence Life .... Ms. Darese DOSKAL-SCAFFIDO
36 Director Counseling/Career Services .... Ms. Amy TRUEMAN
91 Manager Academic Computer Services .... Mr. Dino LEOPARDI
18 Director of Facilities .... Mr. James TURNER
23 Director of Health Services .... Ms. Shari SHAPLEIGH
28 Director of Multicultural Services .... Mr. Seth THOMPSON

Torah Temimah Talmudical Seminary (I)

507 Ocean Parkway, Brooklyn NY 11218-5913
County: Kings FICE Identification: 021916
Unit ID: 196583
Telephone: (718) 853-8500 Carnegie Class: Spec/Faith
FAX Number: (718) 438-5779 Calendar System: Semester
Established: 1978 Annual Undergrad Tuition & Fees: $9,550
Enrollment: 201 Male
Affiliation or Control: Independent Non-Profit IRS Status: 501(c)3
Highest Offering: Second Talmudic Degree
Program: Teacher Preparatory; Professional
Accreditation: RABN

01 President & Dean .... Rabbi L. MARGULIES
03 Executive Director .... Rabbi Yaakov APPLEGRAD
05 Chief Academic Officer .... Rabbi Lipa GELDWORTH
37 Financial Aid Administrator .... Mr. Mendel ROCHLITZ
38 Director of Guidance .... Rabbi Yirmiya GUGENHEIMER
11 Administrator .... Rabbi Yisroel KLEINMAN

Touro College (J)

27 W 23rd Street, 5th Floor, New York NY 10010
County: New York FICE Identification: 010142
Unit ID: 196592
Telephone: (212) 463-0400 Carnegie Class: Master's L
FAX Number: (212) 627-9144 Calendar System: Semester
URL: www.touro.edu
Established: 1970 Annual Undergrad Tuition & Fees: $14,300
Enrollment: 17,417 Coordinate
Affiliation or Control: Independent Non-Profit IRS Status: 501(c)3
Highest Offering: Doctorate
Program: Liberal Arts And General; Professional
Accreditation: M, ARCPA, LAW, OSTEO, OT, #OTA, @PHAR, PTA, SP, SW, @TEAC

01 President ... Dr. Alan KADISH
05 Sr VP for Graduate/Professional Ed ... Dr. Shalom HIRSCHMAN
10 Senior Vice President & CFO ... Mr. Melvin M. NESS
11 Sr Vice Pres/Chief Admin Officer ... Mr. Alan SCHOOR
03 Senior VP for College Affairs ... Mr. Moshe KRUPKA
30 Vice Pres Institutional Advancement ... Dr. Eric LEVINE
20 Dean Faculty/VP Undergrad Acad Affs ... Dr. Stanley L. BOYLAN
58 Vice Pres of Graduate Division ... Dr. Anthony POLEMENI
88 Vice Pres for National Programs ... Dr. Jay SEXTER
56 Exec Vice President/Admin of NYSCAS ... Ms. Eva SPINELLI-SEXTER
32 Dean of Students/VP Planning ... Mr. Robert GOLDSCHMIDT
09 Dean Inst Rsrch/Review/Enroll Mgmt ... Mr. Ira TYSZLER
43 General Counsel ... Mr. Michael NEWMAN
61 Dean Jacob D Fuchsberg Law Center ... Dr. Lawrence RAFUL
63 Dean Col of Osteopathic Medicine ... Dr. Robert GOLDBERG
67 Dean College of Pharmacy ... Dr. Stuart FELDMAN
70 Dean School of Social Work ... Dr. Steven HUBERMAN
76 Dean of School of Health Sciences ... Dr. Louis H. PRIMAVERA
58 Dean Grad School Jewish Studies ... Dr. Michael A. SHMIDMAN
94 Dean Women's Division ... Dr. Marion STOLTZ-LOIKE
12 Dean Lander College for Men ... Dr. Moshe Z. SOKOL
50 Dean Graduate School of Business ... Dr. Michael WILLIAMS
84 Dean Enrollment Management ... Mr. Ira TYSZLER
38 Dean of Advising & Counseling ... Dr. Avery HOROWITZ
51 Asst Dean School Lifelong Education ... Dr. Charlotte HOLZER
06 Asst Dean Enroll Mgmt/Registrar ... Mr. Vladmir ROZIN
37 Exec Dir Financial Aid/Compliance ... Mrs. Carol ROSENBAUM
08 Director of Libraries ... Ms. Bashe SIMON
07 Director of Admissions ... Mr. Arthur WIGFALL
76 Director Physician Asst Program ... Dr. Joseph TOMMASINO
75 Director of Occupational Therapy ... Dr. Stephanie DAPICE-WONG
76 Act Director of Physical Therapy ... Ms. Jill HORBACEWICZ
90 Dir Acad Comp/On Grad Sch of Tech ... Dr. Issac HERSKOWITZ
13 Director of OIT ... Mr. Mark SHOR
13 Chief Info Security Officer ... Ms. Patricia CIUFFO
19 Director of Security ... Ms. Lydia PEREZ
19 Dir of Emergency Preparedness ... Ms. Shoshana YEHUDAH
15 Director of Human Resources ... Ms. Roberta JACKSON
96 Director of Purchasing ... Ms. Wanda HERNANDEZ
18 Dir of Facilities/Real Estate ... Mr. Robert VALENTINE
21 Controller ... Mr. Stuart LIPPMAN
26 Dir of Communication/External Rels ... Ms. Barbara FRANKLIN
29 Director Alumni Relations ... Ms. Esther INGBER
36 Director Student Placement ... Mr. Stuart ANSEL
09 Director of Assessment ... Dr. Eric LINDEN
88 Pgm Dir Speech Lang Path/Grad Pgm ... Ms. Hindy LUBINSKY

Tri-State College of Acupuncture (A)

80 Eighth Avenue, #400, New York NY 10011-0890
County: New York FICE Identification: 025460
Unit ID: 130581
Telephone: (212) 242-2255 Carnegie Class: Spec/Health
FAX Number: (212) 242-2920 Calendar System: Semester
URL: www.tsca.edu
Established: 1982 Annual Graduate Tuition & Fees: $19,750
Enrollment: 172 Coed
Affiliation or Control: Proprietary IRS Status: Proprietary
Highest Offering: Master's; No Undergraduates
Program: Professional
Accreditation: ACUP

01 Executive Director ... Dr. Mark D. SEEM
11 Director of Operations ... Barry NEWMAN
06 Registrar ... Sandra TURNER

Trocaire College (B)

360 Choate Avenue, Buffalo NY 14220-2094
County: Erie FICE Identification: 002812
Unit ID: 196653
Telephone: (716) 826-1200 Carnegie Class: Assoc/PrivNFP
FAX Number: (716) 828-6109 Calendar System: Semester
URL: www.trocaire.edu
Established: 1958 Annual Undergrad Tuition & Fees: $13,010
Enrollment: 1,184 Coed
Affiliation or Control: Independent Non-Profit IRS Status: 501(c)3
Highest Offering: Baccalaureate
Program: Occupational; 2-Year Principally Bachelor's Creditable
Accreditation: M, ADNUR, DIETT, MAC, PNUR, RAD, SURGT

01 President ... Dr. Paul B. HURLEY, JR.
05 Vice President of Academic Affairs ... Mr. Thomas J. MITCHELL
10 VP for Finance/Administration ... Mr. Richard BERNECKI
30 Vice Pres Institutional Advancement ... Mr. John VECCHIO
32 Dean Student Affairs ... Mr. Tony FUNIGIELLO
20 Academic Dean-Non Nursing Studies ... Rev. Robert M. MOCK
46 Dean Research/Planning/Assessment ... Dr. Richard T. LINN
84 Dean Program Devel/Enrollment Mgt ... Dr. Michael LAFEVER
66 Dean Acad Affs for Nursing Studies ... Dr. Marian MEYERS
15 Exec Dir Human Resources/Col Sppt ... Mrs. Rebecca BOYLE
35 Student Activities Coordinator ... Mr. Jon HUDACK
14 Sr InformationTechnology Specialist ... Ms. Robin LOOMIS
51 Director Life Long Learning ... Mrs. Mary Ann CHERNOWSKI
105 Director Data Administration ... Ms. Michele PETERS
37 Director of Financial Aid ... Ms. Janet MCGRATH
25 Director of Grants/Govt Relations ... Ms. Sandra MILLER
16 Payroll/Benefits/Human Res Coord ... Ms. Linda SANSONE
06 Registrar ... Mrs. Theresa HORNER
36 Director Career Center ... Mrs. Claire DARSTEIN
42 Campus Ministry ... Sr. Marie Andre MAIN

18 Facilities Director ... Mrs. Margaret ANDRZEJEWSKI
66 Director of Nursing ... Dr. Carol FANUTTI
30 Dir Development/Alumni Relations ... Mrs. Joan P. WILLIAMS
07 Director of Admissions ... Mrs. Maria POVLACK
105 Dir College Communications/Web Mgr ... Mrs. Kathy POPIELSKI
38 Director Student Counseling ... Ms. Joyce KAISER
40 Manager Bookstore ... Ms. Debbie CAMMARATA
88 Web Editor ... Ms. Jackie BRYANT

Ulster County Community College (C)

491 Cottekill Road, PO Box 557, Stone Ridge NY 12484
County: Ulster FICE Identification: 002880
Unit ID: 196699
Telephone: (845) 687-5000 Carnegie Class: Assoc/Pub-R-M
FAX Number: (845) 687-5083 Calendar System: Semester
URL: www.sunyulster.edu
Established: 1961 Annual Undergrad Tuition & Fees (In-District): $4,128
Enrollment: 3,694 Coed
Affiliation or Control: State/Local IRS Status: 501(c)3
Highest Offering: Associate Degree
Program: Occupational; 2-Year Principally Bachelor's Creditable
Accreditation: M, ADNUR

01 President ... Dr. Donald C. KATT
84 Vice Pres & Dean Enrollment Mgmt ... Ms. Ann MARROTT
05 Dean of Academic Affairs ... Dr. John GANIO
30 Dean of Advancement/Continuing Educ ... Ms. Marianne COLLINS
10 Dean of Admin/Chief Business Ofcr ... Mr. Mark KOMDAT
04 Executive Assistant to President ... Ms. Jean ROSE
20 Assoc Dean of Academic Affairs ... Ms. Cornelia DENVIR
32 Assoc Dean for Student Services ... Mr. John FRAMPTON
08 Director of Library Services ... Ms. Kari MACK
37 Director of Financial Aid ... Mr. Christopher CHANG
06 Registrar ... Ms. Marion GOSS
41 Athletic Director ... Vacant
19 Director of Safety & Security ... Mr. Wayne FREER
07 Director of Admissions ... Vacant
26 Chief Public Relations Officer ... Ms. Ann MARROTT
36 Int Dir Stdnt Plcmnt/Acad Sppt Svcs ... Ms. Jane KITHCART
35 Director Student Affairs ... Ms. Ann MARROTT
18 Director of Plant Operations ... Mr. Steven FREER
09 Director of Institutional Research ... Mr. Clarence (Hank) MILLER
103 Workforce Development ... Mr. Christopher MARX
15 Coordinator of Personnel Services ... Mrs. Debra DELANOY
21 Coordinator of Accounting ... Ms. Amy WINTERS
96 Coord Procurement/General Services ... Mr. Stephen GALLART

Unification Theological Seminary (D)

30 Seminary Drive, Barrytown NY 12507-5021
County: Dutchess FICE Identification: 032163
Unit ID: 246789
Telephone: (845) 752-3000 Carnegie Class: Spec/Faith
FAX Number: (845) 758-2156 Calendar System: Semester
URL: www.uts.edu
Established: 1975 Annual Graduate Tuition & Fees: $10,760
Enrollment: 100 Coed
Affiliation or Control: Unification Church IRS Status: 501(c)3
Highest Offering: Doctorate; No Undergraduates
Program: Professional
Accreditation: M

01 President ... Dr. Richard PANZER
05 Academic Dean ... Dr. Kathy WININGS
88 Director of Field Education ... Dr. Jacob DAVID
06 Registrar ... Mrs. Ute DELANEY
07 Admissions Officer ... Ms. Davetta Ann OGUNLOLA
08 Library Director ... Dr. Keisuke NODA
32 Dean of Students ... Vacant
11 COO ... Mr. Paul STUPPLE
18 Plant Director ... Mr. Carl VERDERBER
10 Controller ... Mrs. Miki FRANKLIN

Union College (E)

807 Union Street, Schenectady NY 12308-3181
County: Schenectady FICE Identification: 002889
Unit ID: 196866
Telephone: (518) 388-6000 Carnegie Class: Bac/A&S
FAX Number: (518) 388-6800 Calendar System: Trimester
URL: www.union.edu
Established: 1795 Annual Undergrad Tuition & Fees: $54,273
Enrollment: 2,150 Coed
Affiliation or Control: Independent Non-Profit IRS Status: 501(c)3
Highest Offering: Baccalaureate
Program: Liberal Arts And General; Professional
Accreditation: M, ENG

01 President ... Dr. Stephen C. AINLAY
05 Dean Faculty/VP Academic Affs ... Dr. Therese A. MCCARTY
30 Vice President College Relations ... Mr. Stephen A. DARE
10 Vice President for Finance & Admin ... Ms. Diane T. BLAKE
07 Vice President of Admissions/FA ... Mr. Matthew J. MALATESTA
04 Exec Assistant to the President ... Ms. Kathryn L. QUINN
32 Vice President of Student Affairs ... Dr. Stephen C. LEAVITT
54 Dean of Engineering ... Dr. Cherrice A. TRAVER
88 Dean of Academic Depts ... Dr. David M. HAYES
20 Dean of Interdisciplinary Studies ... Dr. J. Douglass KLEIN
20 Dean of Studies ... Dr. Kristin A. BIDOSHI
13 Chief Information Officer ... Ms. Ellen Y. BORKOWSKI

06 Registrar ... Ms. Penelope S. ADEY
29 Director Alumni Relations ... Mr. Dominick F. FAMULARE
08 Director of Library ... Mr. Thomas G. MCFADDEN
27 Sr Director Communications ... Ms. Jill C. HUNGSBERG
37 Director of Financial Aid ... Ms. Linda M. PARKER
38 Director of Student Counseling ... Mr. Marcus S. HOTALING
36 Director of Career Devel Center ... Mr. Robert C. SOULES
15 Director of Human Resources ... Mr. Eric NOLL
41 Director of Athletics ... Mr. James MCLAUGHLIN
22 Sr Director Campus Diversity/AA ... Dr. Gretchel L. HATHAWAY
19 Director Campus Safety ... Mr. Christopher HAYEN
39 Director Residence Life ... Ms. Molly MACELROY

† Tuition figure is a comprehensive fees figure.

Union Graduate College (F)

80 Nott Terrace, Schenectady NY 12308-3131
County: Schenectady FICE Identification: 038813
Unit ID: 446932
Telephone: (518) 631-9900 Carnegie Class: Master's M
FAX Number: (518) 631-9901 Calendar System: Trimester
URL: www.uniongraduatecollege.edu
Established: 2003 Annual Graduate Tuition & Fees: $2,585
Enrollment: 450 Coed
Affiliation or Control: Independent Non-Profit IRS Status: 501(c)3
Highest Offering: Master's; No Undergraduates
Program: Professional
Accreditation: M, NY, BUS, HSA, TEAC

01 President ... Dr. Laura SCHWEITZER
10 Vice President of Finance/Operation ... Joseph MCDONALD
84 VP Enrollment Mgmt/Student Svcs ... Joanne FITZGERALD
30 VP Institutional Advancement ... Dan CHRISTOPHER
06 Registrar/Director of Admissions ... Rhonda SHEEHAN
50 Dean School of Management ... Dr. Alan BOWMAN
54 Dean School of Engineering ... Bob KOZIK
53 Dean School of Education ... Dr. Patrick ALLEN
76 Director Center for Bioethics ... Dr. Robert BAKER
07 Director Student Recruitment ... Erin WHEELER
36 Coordinator of Career Services ... Jane FLEURY
09 Director Institutional Research ... Amy NEVIN
29 Coordinator of Alumni Relations ... Kim PERRONE
13 Director of Information Technology ... Robert KEENAN
37 Director Financial Aid ... Nikki GALLUCCI

Union Theological Seminary (G)

3041 Broadway, New York NY 10027-5792
County: New York FICE Identification: 002890
Unit ID: 196884
Telephone: (212) 662-7100 Carnegie Class: Spec/Faith
FAX Number: (212) 280-1416 Calendar System: Semester
URL: www.utsnyc.edu
Established: 1836 Annual Graduate Tuition & Fees: $21,890
Enrollment: 350 Coed
Affiliation or Control: Independent Non-Profit IRS Status: 501(c)3
Highest Offering: Doctorate; No Undergraduates
Program: Religious Emphasis
Accreditation: M, THEOL

01 President ... Dr. Serene JONES
10 VP Finance & Operations ... Mr. Richard A. MADONNA, JR.
30 VP for Institutional Advancement ... Vacant
05 Dean of Academic Affairs ... Dr. Daisy L. MACHADO
21 Controller ... Vacant
32 Associate Dean Student Life ... Ms. Yvette WILSON
08 Director Library ... Vacant
04 Special Assistant to the President ... Ms. Tania BRUNO
06 Registrar ... Ms. Edith T. HUNTER
18 Director Facilities/Physical Plant ... Mr. Michael MALONEY
39 Director Student Housing ... Mr. Michael ORZECHOWSKI
07 Admissions Director ... Ms. Jennifer THOMPSON

United Talmudical Seminary (H)

191 Rodney Street, Brooklyn NY 11211-7900
County: Kings FICE Identification: 011189
Unit ID: 197018
Telephone: (718) 963-9770 Carnegie Class: Spec/Faith
FAX Number: (718) 963-9775 Calendar System: Semester
Established: 1949 Annual Undergrad Tuition & Fees: $9,500
Enrollment: 1,637 Male
Affiliation or Control: Independent Non-Profit IRS Status: 501(c)3
Highest Offering: Second Talmudic Degree
Program: Teacher Preparatory; Professional
Accreditation: RABN

01 Dean ... Rabbi Zalman TEITLBAUM
05 Assoc Dean Scholastic Services ... Rabbi Yeruchem DEUTSCH
37 Financial Aid Administrator ... Mr. Bernard KATZ
11 Administrator ... Mr. Isaac BREUER
10 Business Officer ... Mr. Abraham KAHAN

University of Rochester (I)

Rochester NY 14627-0033
County: Monroe FICE Identification: 002894
Unit ID: 195030
Telephone: (585) 275-2121 Carnegie Class: RU/VH
FAX Number: (585) 275-0359 Calendar System: Semester
URL: www.rochester.edu
Established: 1850 Annual Undergrad Tuition & Fees: $41,802

Enrollment: 10,111 Coed
Affiliation or Control: Independent Non-Profit IRS Status: 501(c)3
Highest Offering: Doctorate
Program: Liberal Arts And General; Teacher Preparatory; Professional
Accreditation: M, BUS, CACREP, CLPSY, DENT, ENG, IPSY, MED, MFCD, MUS, NURSE, PDPSY, PH, TED

01 President .... Mr. Joel SELIGMAN
05 Provost/Executive Vice President .... Dr. Ralph W. KUNCL
10 Sr VP Administration & Fin/CFO .... Mr. Ronald J. PAPROCKI
03 VP/University Dean .... Mr. Paul J. BURGETT
49 Sr VP/Dean Faculty/Arts/Sci & Engr .... Mr. Peter LENNIE
17 Sr VP Health Sciences/Med Ctr CEO .... Dr. Bradford C. BERK
45 Sr VP for Institutional Resources .... Mr. Douglas PHILLIPS
30 Sr VP/Chief Advancement Officer .... Mr. Jim THOMPSON
43 Sr VP/General Counsel .... Ms. Sue STEWART
26 VP for Communications .... Mr. Bill MURPHY
13 Vice President/Chief Info Officer .... Mr. David E. LEWIS
15 Assoc VP Human Resources .... Mr. Charles J. MURPHY
58 Vice Provost/Univ Dean Grad Studies .... Dr. Margaret KEARNEY
100 General Sect/Pres Chief of Staff .... Ms. Lamar R. MURPHY
28 Vice Provost Fac Devel & Diversity .... Ms. Vivian LEWIS
08 Dean River Campus Libraries .... Vacant
88 Vice President/Laser Lab Director .... Mr. Robert L. MCCRORY
84 Dean AS&E Undergrad Admis & Fin Aid .... Mr. Jonathan BURDICK
21 Assoc VP for Budgets & Planning .... Ms. Holly CRAWFORD
32 Dean of Students Arts/Sci & Engr .... Mr. Matthew BURNS
63 Dean School of Medicine & Dent .... Dr. Mark B. TAUBMAN
64 Dean Eastman School of Music .... Mr. Douglas LOWRY
66 Dean School of Nursing .... Ms. Kathy P. PARKER
50 Dean Simon Grad Sch Business Admin .... Mr. Mark ZUPAN
53 Dean Warner Grad Sch Educ & Hum Dev .... Ms. Raffaella BORASI
89 Dean of Freshmen Arts/Sci & Engr .... Ms. Marcy KRAUS
88 Dean of Sophmores Arts/Sci & Engr .... Ms. Vicki ROTH
37 Assoc Dean Enroll & Fin Aid A/S&E .... Mr. Charles PULS
35 Assoc Dean Students Arts/Sci & Engr .... Ms. Anne-Marie ALGIER
23 Strong Health Chief Medical Officer .... Dr. Raymond MAYEWSKI
52 Director Eastman Dental Center .... Dr. Cyril MEYEROWITZ
25 Assoc VP Research & Project Admin .... Ms. Gunta LIDERS
18 Assoc VP Facilities & Services .... Mr. Richard PIFER
86 Executive Director Govt Relations .... Mr. Peter J. ROBINSON
96 Director Corporate Purchasing .... Mr. Philip S. PROFETA
04 Executive Asst to the President .... Ms. Susan NIGGLI
06 Registrar .... Ms. Nancy SPECK
19 Director of University Security .... Mr. Walter MAULDIN
57 Director Memorial Art Gallery .... Mr. Grant HOLCOMB
29 Exec Director Alumni Relations .... Mr. Kevin P. WESLEY
93 Director Minority Student Affairs .... Mr. Norman B. BURNETT
94 Director Gender & Women's Studies .... Ms. Honey MECONI
41 Director of Athletics & Recreation .... Mr. George VANDERZWAAG
39 Dir Res Life & Housing Services .... Ms. Laurel CONTOMANOLIS
36 Asst Dean/Director Career Center .... Mr. Burton NADLER
42 Director Religious & Spiritual Life .... Ms. Allison STOKES
101 Administrator to Board of Trustees .... Ms. Jackie E. KING

USC The Business College (A)

201 Bleecker Street, Utica NY 13501-2200
County: Oneida FICE Identification: 009077
Unit ID: 197081
Telephone: (315) 733-2300 Carnegie Class: Assoc/PrivFP
FAX Number: (315) 733-9281 Calendar System: Semester
URL: www.uscny.edu
Established: 1896 Annual Undergrad Tuition & Fees: $12,750
Enrollment: 453 Coed
Affiliation or Control: Proprietary IRS Status: Proprietary
Highest Offering: Associate Degree
Program: Occupational; 2-Year Principally Bachelor's Creditable; Business Emphasis
Accreditation: NY

01 President & Treasurer .... Mr. Philip M. WILLIAMS
03 Exec Vice Pres/Asst to President .... Mr. Scott K. WILLIAMS
11 Exec Vice President Administration .... Mr. John L. CROSSLEY
05 Exec Vice President for Academics .... Mr. Daniel MURPHY
103 VP Corp/Workforce Develop .... Mr. Don REESE
10 Vice President of Finance .... Mr. Richard H. HILTON
12 Director Canastota Branch .... Mrs. Wendy M. CARY
06 Registrar/Bursar .... Mrs. Marian J. NIELSON
18 Facilities Manager Physical Plant .... Mr. Joel B. NOLAN
30 Director of Development .... Mr. Jeffrey H. OWEN
08 Head Librarian .... Ms. Anne NASSAR
37 Director of Student Financial Aid .... Mr. Fred P. ZUCALLA
12 Int Dir Oneonta Campus/Dn Students .... Mr. Jeffrey HELD
07 Director of Admissions .... Mrs. Leslie V. CROSLEY
43 General Counsel .... Mr. John H. STORY, JR.
13 Director Information Technology .... Mr. James D. BUYEA
36 Director of Career Services .... Mrs. Susan SHEAFFER

U.T.A. Mesivta of Kiryas Joel (B)

PO Box 2009, Monroe NY 10949-8509
County: Orange FICE Identification: 038023
Unit ID: 446604
Telephone: (845) 783-9901 Carnegie Class: Spec/Faith
FAX Number: (845) 782-3620 Calendar System: Semester
Established: 1999 Annual Undergrad Tuition & Fees: $7,500
Enrollment: 1,310 Male
Affiliation or Control: Independent Non-Profit IRS Status: 501(c)3
Highest Offering: First Talmudic Degree
Program: Teacher Preparatory; Professional
Accreditation: RABN

01 President .... Elias HOROWITZ
05 Rosh Yeshiva .... Rabbi Aharon TEITELBAUM
37 Financial Aid Director .... David SCHWARTZ

Utica College (C)

1600 Burrstone Road, Utica NY 13502-4892
County: Oneida FICE Identification: 002883
Unit ID: 197045
Telephone: (315) 792-3111 Carnegie Class: Master's M
FAX Number: (315) 792-3292 Calendar System: Semester
URL: www.utica.edu
Established: 1946 Annual Undergrad Tuition & Fees: $29,996
Enrollment: 3,595 Coed
Affiliation or Control: Independent Non-Profit IRS Status: 501(c)3
Highest Offering: Doctorate
Program: Liberal Arts And General; Teacher Preparatory; Professional
Accreditation: M, NURSE, OT, PTA, TEAC

01 President .... Dr. Todd S. HUTTON
05 Provost & Vice Pres Academic Aff .... Dr. Judith A. KIRKPATRICK
10 Vice Pres Financial Affs/Treasurer .... Mr. R. Barry WHITE
32 Vice Pres Stdnt Affs/Dean of Stdnts .... Dr. Kenneth E. KELLY
04 Executive Assistant to President .... Ms. Kim D. LAMBERT
30 Senior VP & Chief Advanc Officer .... Ms. Laura CASAMENTO
09 Vice Pres for Planning & Analysis .... Ms. Carol MACKINTOSH
84 Vice President for Enrollment Mgmt .... Mr. Patrick A. QUINN
88 Vice President for Strategic Initiv .... Dr. James C. BROWN
20 Associate Provost .... Dr. Robert M. HALLIDAY
26 Asst VP Marketing/Communication .... Mr. Kelly L. ADAMS
76 Dean for Health Professions/Educ .... Dr. Dale SCALISE-SMITH
49 Dean for Arts & Sciences .... Dr. John H. JOHNSEN
50 Dean for Business & Justice Studies .... Ms. Patricia SWANN
35 Associate Dean of Students .... Ms. Alane P. VARGA
21 Director of Student Acct Operation .... Ms. Gail TUTTLE
29 Director Alumni & Parent Relations .... Mr. Mark C. KOVACS
08 Asst VP for Library & IITS .... Ms. Beverly J. MARCOLINE
36 Director Career Services .... Mr. Edward PULASKI
37 Exec Dir of Student Financial Svcs .... Ms. Laura BEDFORD
06 Registrar .... Mr. Dominic PASSALACQUA
44 Director of Development .... Mr. Athony VILLANTI
41 Director of Physical Educ/Athletics .... Mr. James A. SPARTANO
39 Director of Residence Life .... Ms. Uchenna BAKER
13 Infrastructure Manager .... Mr. John KAFTAN
16 Director of Human Resources .... Vacant
38 Dean Stdnt Success/Dir Stdnt Devel .... Mr. Stephen M. PATTARINI
14 Dir College Info & Application Svcs .... Mr. Scott HUMPHREY
24 Dir Multimedia & Computer User Svcs .... Ms. Kathleen RANDALL
31 Exec Dir Corp/Professional Pgms .... Ms. Joni L. PULLIAM
51 Director of Credit Programs .... Ms. Evelyn FAZEKAS
85 Dean of International Education .... Dr. Laurence W. ROBERTS, II
07 Director of Enrollment Management .... Ms. Lisa BRONK
18 Director Facilities Management .... Mr. Donald L. HARTER
19 Director of Campus Safety .... Mr. James SAPONARO
92 Director Honors Program .... Dr. Diane MATZA
28 Dir Office of Opportunity Programs .... Ms. Johnni F. MAHDI
96 Manager of Purchasing .... Ms. Bobbie H. SMOROL

† Utica College maintains an academic tie with Syracuse University that allows undergraduates to receive a Syracuse University degree.

Vassar College (D)

124 Raymond Avenue, Poughkeepsie NY 12604-0001
County: Dutchess FICE Identification: 002895
Unit ID: 197133
Telephone: (845) 437-7000 Carnegie Class: Bac/A&S
FAX Number: (845) 437-7187 Calendar System: Semester
URL: www.vassar.edu
Established: 1861 Annual Undergrad Tuition & Fees: $54,530
Enrollment: 2,400 Coed
Affiliation or Control: Independent Non-Profit IRS Status: 501(c)3
Highest Offering: Master's
Program: Liberal Arts And General
Accreditation: M, @TEAC

01 President .... Dr. Catharine B. HILL
05 Dean of the Faculty .... Dr. Jonathan CHENETTE
20 Dean of the College .... Dr. Christopher ROELLKE
10 Vice President for Finance & Admin .... Ms. Elizabeth A. EISMEIER
30 Vice President for Development .... Ms. Catherine E. BAER
26 Vice Pres for College Relations .... Ms. Susan DEKREY
90 Vice Pres for Computing/Info Svcs .... Mr. Bret INGERMAN
32 Dean of Students .... Dr. David H. BROWN
07 Dean Admission/Financial Aid .... Mr. David M. BORUS
49 Dean of Studies .... Dr. Joanne LONG
20 Associate Dean College .... Mr. Edward L. PITTMAN
35 Assoc Dean Col/Dir Campus Activit .... Ms. Teresa QUINN
06 Registrar .... Ms. Colleen MALLET
08 Director of the Libraries .... Ms. Sabrina PAPE
37 Director of Financial Aid .... Mr. Michael P. FRAHER
36 Director Career Development Center .... Ms. Mary P. RAYMOND
87 Director Conferences/Summer Pgms .... Ms. Katherine BUSH
39 Director Residential Life .... Mr. Luis INOA
09 Director of Institutional Research .... Mr. David DAVIS-VAN ATTA
15 Director Human Resources .... Ms. Ruth SPENCER
18 Exec Dir Buildings & Grounds .... Mr. Thomas ALLEN
38 Director of Psychological Services .... Dr. Sylvia BALDERRAMA
96 Director of Purchasing .... Ms. Rosaleen CARDILLO

Vaughn College of Aeronautics and Technology (E)

86-01 23rd Avenue, Flushing NY 11369
County: Queens FICE Identification: 002665
Unit ID: 188340
Telephone: (718) 429-6600 Carnegie Class: Bac/Assoc
FAX Number: (718) 429-0256 Calendar System: Semester
URL: www.vaughn.edu
Established: 1932 Annual Undergrad Tuition & Fees: $18,500
Enrollment: 1,552 Coed
Affiliation or Control: Independent Non-Profit IRS Status: 501(c)3
Highest Offering: Master's
Program: 2-Year Principally Bachelor's Creditable; Liberal Arts And General; Professional
Accreditation: M, ENGT, IACBE

01 President .... Dr. John C. FITZPATRICK
05 Sr Vice Pres Academic/Student Affs .... Dr. Sharon B. DEVIVO
10 Vice Pres for Business & Finance .... Mr. Robert G. WALDMANN
84 Vice President Enrollment Services .... Mr. Ernie SHEPELSKY
11 Asst VP College Services/Human Res .... Mr. Paul MIRANDA
20 Asst Vice Pres of Academic Affairs .... Vacant
45 Asst VP Academic Support Svcs .... Mr. Said LAMHAOUAR
35 Asst Vice Pres Student Affairs .... Mr. John AGNELLI
84 Asst Vice Pres Enrollment Mgmt .... Mr. Vincent PAPANDREA
37 Director of Financial Aid .... Ms. Dorothy MARTIN
06 Registrar .... Mrs. Beatriz CRUZ
08 Librarian .... Ms. Joanne JAYNE
102 Exec Dir Corp/Foundation Relations .... Ms. Kalli KOUTSOUTIS
26 Director of Public Affairs .... Mr. James SMITH
96 Director of Purchasing .... Vacant
09 Director of Institutional Research .... Vacant
13 Asst Director Computer Operations .... Mr. Hamwant (Neil) SINGH

Villa Maria College of Buffalo (F)

240 Pine Ridge Road, Buffalo NY 14225-3999
County: Erie FICE Identification: 002896
Unit ID: 197142
Telephone: (716) 896-0700 Carnegie Class: Assoc/PrivNFP4
FAX Number: (716) 896-0705 Calendar System: Semester
URL: www.villa.edu
Established: 1960 Annual Undergrad Tuition & Fees: $16,000
Enrollment: 507 Coed
Affiliation or Control: Independent Non-Profit IRS Status: 501(c)3
Highest Offering: Baccalaureate
Program: Occupational; 2-Year Principally Bachelor's Creditable; Fine Arts Emphasis
Accreditation: M, CIDA, PTAA

01 President .... Sr. Marcella Marie GARUS
05 Vice President for Academic Affairs .... Dr. Janet REOHR
10 Vice President for Business Affairs .... Mr. Vincent GRIZANTI
30 Vice President for Development .... Sr. Mary Marcine BOROWIAK
32 Vice President for Student Affairs .... Sr. Mary Louis RUSTOWICZ
44 Asst to Vice Pres for Development .... Ms. Kathy SEIBOLD
20 Asst to Vice Pres for Academic Affs .... Ms. Janice HERCHMER
06 Registrar .... Vacant
84 Director of Enrollment Management .... Mr. Kevin DONOVAN
08 Director of Library .... Sr. Mary Anna FALBO
37 Director of Financial Aid .... Ms. Laura FITZGERALD
09 Director of Institutional Research .... Sr. Mary Albertine STACHOWSKI
38 Director Student Counseling .... Ms. Palma M. ZANGHI
13 Director of Computer Services .... Ms. Christine E. PALCZEWSKI
88 Systems Analyst .... Mr. Robert STRUBLE
18 Plant & Grounds Manager .... Mr. David WISNER
23 Director of Health Services .... Mrs. Minerva MONTIJO
25 Director of Grants .... Mrs. Mary ROBINSON
51 Instructional Design & Program Dev .... Mr. Fredrick RODGERS
36 Director of Career Development .... Ms. Deborah HANDZLIK
42 Director of Campus Ministry .... Mr. Frank ANTONUCCI
85 Director of Foreign Students .... Ms. Palma ZANGHI
27 Cooridinator of Communications .... Ms. Barbara HOOVEN
35 Director of Student Life .... Ms. Ceceile PAWLOWSKI
88 Archivist .... Sr. Anita BENECKI
22 Affirmative Action Officer .... Ms. Diane M. HANDZLIK
29 Director of Alumni Relations .... Ms. Mary MERIGOLD
24 Coordinator of Educational Media .... Mrs. Barbara WETZEL
88 Coord Academic Success Center .... Dr. Aimee WOZNICK
76 Business/Educ/Health Science Dept .... Mr. Todd BAKER
77 Director of Computer Services .... Ms. Christine PALCZEWSKI
57 Art Department Chair .... Ms. Sandra REICIS
64 Music Department Chair .... Sr. Barbara AMROZOWICZ
49 Liberal Arts Department Chair .... Dr. Matthew GIORDANO

Wagner College (G)

1 Campus Road, Staten Island NY 10301-4479
County: Richmond FICE Identification: 002899
Unit ID: 197197
Telephone: (718) 390-3100 Carnegie Class: Master's M
FAX Number: (718) 390-3467 Calendar System: Semester
URL: www.wagner.edu
Established: 1883 Annual Undergrad Tuition & Fees: $35,620
Enrollment: 1,839 Coed
Affiliation or Control: Independent Non-Profit IRS Status: 501(c)3
Highest Offering: Master's
Program: Liberal Arts And General; Teacher Preparatory; Professional
Accreditation: M, ACBSP, ARCPA, NUR, TED

01 President .... Dr. Richard GUARASCI
11 Vice President for Administration .... Mr. David MARTIN
05 Provost/Vice Pres Academic Affairs .... Dr. Lily D. MCNAIR
10 Vice Pres Business & Finance .... Mr. William MEA
84 Vice Pres Enrollment Management .... Mr. Angelo ARAIMO
09 Int VP Instititutional Research .... Ms. Myra GARCIA
26 Chief of Staff/VP Communications .... Mr. Joseph ROMANO
04 Assistant to the President .... Ms. Pat FITZPATRICK
32 Vice Pres and Dean of Campus Life .... Ms. Ruta SHAH-GORDON
21 Asst Vice Pres/Controller .... Mr. John CARRESCIA
88 Dean of Assessment .... Dr. Anne LOVE
20 Associate Provost .... Dr. Jeffrey KRAUS
06 Registrar .... Mr. Jeffrey KRAUS
13 Director of Information Technology .... Mr. Dilawar GREWAL
42 Chaplain/Special Asst to the Pres .... Vacant
29 Director Alumni Relations .... Mr. Kenneth LAM
39 Director Housing .... Ms. Sarah KLEIN
30 Director of Development .... Ms. Kristen KOEHLER
18 Chief Facilities/Physical Plant .... Mr. Dominick FONTANO
41 Director of Athletics .... Mr. Walter HAMELINE
23 Director of Health Services .... Ms. Kathleen OBERFELDT
19 Director Security/Safety .... Mr. Anthony MARTINESI
15 Director Personnel Services .... Ms. Tania ROSSINI
37 Director Student Financial Aid .... Ms. Theresa WEIMER
58 Coordinator of Graduate Studies .... Dr. Jeffrey KRAUS

Webb Institute (A)

298 Crescent Beach Road, Glen Cove NY 11542-1398
County: Nassau FICE Identification: 002900
Unit ID: 197221
Telephone: (516) 671-2213 Carnegie Class: Spec/Engg
FAX Number: (516) 674-9838 Calendar System: Semester
URL: www.webb-institute.edu
Established: 1889 Annual Undergrad Tuition & Fees: N/A
Enrollment: 80 Coed
Affiliation or Control: Independent Non-Profit IRS Status: 501(c)3
Highest Offering: Baccalaureate
Program: Professional; Technical Emphasis
Accreditation: M, ENG

01 President .... RADM. Robert C. OLSEN, JR.
05 Dean .... Prof. Richard P. NEILSON
20 Assistant Dean .... Prof. Richard C. HARRIS
08 Librarian .... Ms. Patricia M. PRESCOTT
10 Director of Financial Affairs .... Mr. Andrew BERKO
32 Director of Student Affairs .... Ms. Cristen NAUD
18 Director of Facilities .... Mr. Geoffrey G. WHITELY
07 Director of Enrollment Management .... Mr. William G. MURRAY
29 Director of Alumni Relations .... Ms. Gailmarie SUJECKI
26 Chief Public Relations Officer .... Ms. Holly D. LEMOINE
90 Computer Systems Manager .... Ms. Erica L. HANSEN
06 Registrar .... Ms. Jocelyn M. WILSON

Weill Cornell Medical College (B)

1300 York Avenue, F113, New York NY 10065-4805
County: New York FICE Identification: 004762
Unit ID: 190424
Telephone: (212) 746-5454 Carnegie Class: Spec/Med
FAX Number: (212) 746-8424 Calendar System: Quarter
URL: www.med.cornell.edu
Established: 1898 Annual Graduate Tuition & Fees: $46,000
Enrollment: 395 Coed
Affiliation or Control: Independent Non-Profit IRS Status: 501(c)3
Highest Offering: Doctorate; No Undergraduates
Program: Professional
Accreditation: &M, ARCPA, DENT, IPSY, MED

01 Provost/Med Affs/Dean Medical Col ... Dr. Antonio M. GOTTO, JR.
100 Exec Administrator/Dean's Office .... Ms. Annette M. WILLIAMS
30 Vice Provost Development .... Mr. Larry SCHAFER
26 Vice Prov Public/Govt/Cmty Affairs .... Ms. Myrna MANNERS
03 Exec Vice Provost/Sr Exec Vice Dean .... Dr. David P. HAJJAR
11 Exec Vice Provost .... Mr. Stephen M. COHEN
09 Assistant Provost Research Admin .... Dr. Harry M. LANDER
43 Deputy Univ Counsel/Sec of Med Col .... Mr. James R. KAHN
05 Senior Assoc Dean Education .... Dr. Carol STOREY-JOHNSON
20 Sr Assoc Dean Clinical Affairs .... Dr. Michael G. STEWART
88 Chief Medical Officer Phys Org .... Dr. Daniel M. KNOWLES
17 Associate Dean Burke Hospital .... Dr. Mary Beth WALSH
20 Associate Dean Curricular Affairs .... Dr. Peter M. MARZUK
17 Associate Dean Affiliations .... Dr. Oliver T. FEIN
22 Assoc Dean Student Affs/EO Pgms .... Dr. Carlyle H. MILLER
07 Associate Dean Admissions .... Dr. Charles BARDES
51 Assoc Dean Continuing Medical Educ ... Dr. Scott J. GOLDSMITH
20 Associate Dean Academic Affairs .... Dr. Shari R. MIDONECK
53 Assistant Dean Departmental Assoc . Dr. Marcus M. REIDENBERG
10 Associate Dean Billing Compliance .... Dr. Stephen J. THOMAS
88 Associate Dean Clinical Research .... Dr. Ralph L. NACHMAN
58 Assoc Dean Grad School Med Sciences .... Dr. Randi B. SILVER
23 Associate Dean Healthcare System .... Dr. Eliot J. LAZAR
12 Associate Dean Intercampus Affairs .... Dr. Caren A. HELLER
58 Associate Dean MSK Cancer Center ..... Dr. Thomas J. FAHEY, JR.
53 Associate Dean Pre-Med Educ Qatar ..... Dr. Michael D. JOHNSON
07 Assistant Dean of Admissions .... Ms. Lori NICOLAYSEN
88 Assoc Dean Research Strategy Qatar .... Mr. Eelco A. SLAGTER
88 Assoc Dean Translational Research .... Dr. Julianne IMPERATO-MCGINLEY
53 Assistant Dean Education Admin .... Mr. Jason KORENKIEWICZ
20 Assistant Dean Faculty Affairs .... Dr. Mark A. ALBANO
58 Assistant Dean Graduate School .... Ms. Francoise FREYRE
32 Assistant Dean Student Affairs .... Dr. Elizabeth A. WILSON-ANSTEY
09 Assistant Dean Rsrch Dev Outreach .... Dr. Brian D. LAMON
08 Librarian of Medicine .... Ms. Colleen CUDDY

† Regional accreditation is carried under the parent institution Cornell University, Ithaca, NY.

Wells College (C)

170 Main Street, Aurora NY 13026-0500
County: Cayuga FICE Identification: 002901
Unit ID: 197230
Telephone: (315) 364-3266 Carnegie Class: Bac/A&S
FAX Number: (315) 364-3227 Calendar System: Semester
URL: www.wells.edu
Established: 1868 Annual Undergrad Tuition & Fees: $33,400
Enrollment: 553 Coed
Affiliation or Control: Independent Non-Profit IRS Status: 501(c)3
Highest Offering: Baccalaureate
Program: Liberal Arts And General; Teacher Preparatory
Accreditation: M, @TEAC

01 President .... Ms. Lisa Marsh RYERSON
05 Provost and Dean of the College .... Dr. Cindy SPEAKER
11 Chief Operating Officer .... Mr. Terry NEWCOMB
10 Treasurer and Controller .... Mr. John DENTES
30 Vice President for Advancement .... Mr. Michael MCGREEVEY
04 Assistant to the President .... Ms. Meredith COOK VANDUYNE
32 Dean of Students .... Mr. Joel MCCARTHY
07 Dir of Admissions/Financial Aid .... Ms. Susan SLOAN
06 Registrar .... Mr. Andre SIAMUNDELE
08 Library Director .... Ms. Muriel GODBOUT
37 Director Financial Aid .... Ms. Cathleen PATELLA
44 Director of Annual Giving .... Ms. Pamela SHERADIN
26 Dir of Communications/Marketing .... Ms. Ann ROLLO
19 Director of Security .... Mr. David GARDNER
15 Manager of Human Resources .... Ms. Kit VAN ORMAN
18 Chief Facilities/Physical Plant .... Mr. James CHASE

Westchester Community College (D)

75 Grasslands Road, Valhalla NY 10595-1636
County: Westchester FICE Identification: 002881
Unit ID: 197294
Telephone: (914) 606-6600 Carnegie Class: Assoc/Pub-S-SC
FAX Number: (914) 606-6780 Calendar System: Semester
URL: www.sunywcc.edu
Established: 1946 Annual Undergrad Tuition & Fees (In-District): $2,075
Enrollment: 13,893 Coed
Affiliation or Control: State/Local IRS Status: 501(c)3
Highest Offering: Associate Degree
Program: Occupational; 2-Year Principally Bachelor's Creditable
Accreditation: M, DIETT, RAD

01 President .... Dr. Joseph N. HANKIN
05 Vice President Academic Affairs .... Dr. Chet H. ROGALSKI
32 Vice Pres Student Personnel Svcs .... Ms. Juana REINA
11 Vice Pres Administrative Services .... Mr. Pat D'IMPERIO
102 VP Ext Affs/Exec Dir Found for WCC .. Mr. Robert SCHLESINGER
51 Dean Community/Adult/Cont Educ .... Dr. Marjorie GLUSKER
81 Assoc Dean Math/Phys Engr/Tech .... Mr. Ted NYGREEN
76 Assoc Dean Natural/Health Sciences .... Mr. Michael OLIVETTE
83 Assoc Dean Bus/Behav/Soc Sci Svcs .... Mr. Jeffrey A. CONTE
79 Assoc Dean Arts/Humanities/Lrng Res .... Dr. Jianping WANG
22 Associate Dean of EOC .... Ms. Renee GUY
35 Assoc Dean Student Personnel Svcs .... Mr. Kevin B. SLAVIN
08 Asc Dn Lrng Res/Dist Lrng/Inst Tech .... Ms. Pamela POLLARD
26 Director of College/Cmty Relations .... Mr. Patrick HENNESSEY
06 Registrar .... Ms. Susan S. STANTON
37 Dir of Student Financial Assistance .... Mrs. Eleanor A. HACKETT
13 Act Dir of Information Technology .... Mr. Anthony SCORDINO
07 Director of Admissions .... Ms. Gloria LEON
38 Director of Counseling .... Mr. Donald WEIGAND
16 Director Human Resources .... Ms. Sabrina J. CHANDLER
88 Director Faculty Student Assoc .... Mr. John BOYLE
09 Director Inst Research & Planning .... Ms. Nancy M. DERIGGI
19 Director of Security .... Mr. Brian P. DOLANSKY
24 Director Media Services .... Mr. Thomas GALA
41 Athletic Director .... Mr. Larry MASSARONI
21 Assoc Business Officer/Controller .... Mr. Mario CAVALLI
18 Director Physical Plant .... Mr. Kevin GARVEY
96 Deputy Purchasing Agent .... Mr. Richard CASHMAN
27 Publications Manager .... Mr. Craig FISCHER
23 Coordinator Student Health Services .... Ms. Janice GILROY
75 Coord of Transfer & Career Service ..... Dr. Gwen D. ROUNDTREE

Wood Tobé-Coburn School (E)

Eight E 40 Street, New York NY 10016-0190
County: New York FICE Identification: 007405
Unit ID: 197522
Telephone: (212) 686-9040 Carnegie Class: Assoc/PrivFP
FAX Number: (212) 686-9171 Calendar System: Semester
URL: www.woodtobecoburn.edu
Established: 1879 Annual Undergrad Tuition & Fees: $15,700
Enrollment: 575 Coed
Affiliation or Control: Proprietary IRS Status: Proprietary
Highest Offering: Associate Degree
Program: Occupational; 2-Year Principally Bachelor's Creditable
Accreditation: NY, MAC

01 President .... Ms. Sandra GRUNINGER
05 Director of Education .... Ms. Arlette BALRAM
07 Director of Admissions .... Ms. Sandra ANDUJAR-WENDLAND
32 Student Services Director .... Ms. Yessika GARCIA
37 Financial Aid Administrator .... Ms. Linda WALTERS
36 Placement Director .... Ms. Lisa RINI

Yeshiva Derech Chaim (F)

1573 39th Street, Brooklyn NY 11218-4413
County: Kings FICE Identification: 022651
Unit ID: 197647
Telephone: (718) 438-5476 Carnegie Class: Spec/Faith
FAX Number: (718) 435-9285 Calendar System: Semester
Established: 1975 Annual Undergrad Tuition & Fees: $9,400
Enrollment: 165 Male
Affiliation or Control: Independent Non-Profit IRS Status: 501(c)3
Highest Offering: Second Talmudic Degree
Program: Professional; Religious Emphasis
Accreditation: RABN

01 President .... Rabbi Mordechai RENNERT
01 President .... Rabbi Yisroel PLUTCHOK

Yeshiva D'Monsey Rabbinical College (G)

2 Roman Boulevard, Monsey NY 10952-3106
County: Rockland FICE Identification: 031473
Unit ID: 420325
Telephone: (845) 426-3276 Carnegie Class: Spec/Faith
FAX Number: (845) 352-1119 Calendar System: Semester
Established: 1984 Annual Undergrad Tuition & Fees: $4,350
Enrollment: 74 Male
Affiliation or Control: Independent Non-Profit IRS Status: 501(c)3
Highest Offering: Second Talmudic Degree
Program: Teacher Preparatory; Professional
Accreditation: RABN

01 Rosh Yeshiva .... Rabbi Moishe GREEN
05 Rosh Yeshiva .... Rabbi Ruvain GREEN
37 Financial Aid Director .... Rabbi Aron BERGER

Yeshiva of Far Rockaway (H)

802 Hicksville Road, Far Rockaway NY 11691-5219
County: Queens FICE Identification: 041196
Telephone: (718) 327-7600 Carnegie Class: Not Classified
FAX Number: (718) 327-1430 Calendar System: Semester
Established: 1969 Annual Undergrad Tuition & Fees: $9,500
Enrollment: 54 Male
Affiliation or Control: Independent Non-Profit IRS Status: 501(c)3
Highest Offering: First Talmudic Degree
Program: Professional; Religious Emphasis
Accreditation: RABN

01 President .... Rabbi Yechiel I. PERR
03 Executive Director .... Rabbi Shayeh KOHN
32 Dean of Students .... Rabbi Dovid KLEINKAUFMAN

Yeshiva Gedolah Imrei Yosef D'Spinka (I)

1466 56th Street, Brooklyn NY 11219-4696
County: Kings FICE Identification: 030001
Unit ID: 375230
Telephone: (718) 851-8721 Carnegie Class: Spec/Faith
FAX Number: (718) 686-8849 Calendar System: Semester
Established: 1987 Annual Undergrad Tuition & Fees: $7,000
Enrollment: 120 Male
Affiliation or Control: Independent Non-Profit IRS Status: 501(c)3
Highest Offering: First Talmudic Degree
Program: Teacher Preparatory
Accreditation: @RABN

01 President .... Mordechai MAJEROWITZ

Yeshiva Gedolah Ohr Yisrael (J)

2899 Nostrand Avenue, Brooklyn NY 11229
County: Kings Identification: 667077
Telephone: (718) 382-8702 Carnegie Class: Not Classified
FAX Number: (718) 382-8703 Calendar System: Semester
Established: 1999 Annual Undergrad Tuition & Fees: $6,500
Enrollment: 68 Male
Affiliation or Control: Independent Non-Profit IRS Status: 501(c)3
Highest Offering: First Talmudic Degree
Program: Professional
Accreditation: RABN

01 Rosh Yeshiva .... Avraham ZUCKER
10 Treasurer .... Avi KAHN

Yeshiva Karlin Stolin Beth Aaron V'Israel Rabbinical Institute (K)

1818 54th Street, Brooklyn NY 11204-1545
County: Kings FICE Identification: 025058
Unit ID: 197601
Telephone: (718) 232-7800 Carnegie Class: Spec/Faith
FAX Number: (718) 331-4833 Calendar System: Semester

Established: 1948 Annual Undergrad Tuition & Fees: $6,900
Enrollment: 83 Male
Affiliation or Control: Independent Non-Profit IRS Status: 501(c)3
Highest Offering: Second Talmudic Degree
Program: Teacher Preparatory; Professional
Accreditation: RABN

01 Chief Executive Officer .... Rabbi Yochanan PILCHICK
05 Dean Theology/Chief Acad Officer .... Rabbi Chaim WOLPIN
06 Registrar .... Rabbi Aryeh WOLPIN
08 Librarian .... Rabbi Yochanan GOLDHABER
10 Fiscal Officer .... Rabbi Irving PERRES
37 Financial Aid Director .... Rabbi Mayer PILCHICK
33 Dean of Men .... Rabbi Gedelyah MACHLIS

Yeshiva and Kolel Bais Medrash Elyon (A)

73 Main Street, Monsey NY 10952-3013
County: Rockland Identification: 666707
Unit ID: 245777
Telephone: (845) 356-7064 Carnegie Class: Spec/Faith
FAX Number: (845) 356-7065 Calendar System: Semester
Established: 1977 Annual Undergrad Tuition & Fees: $7,800
Enrollment: 33 Male
Affiliation or Control: Independent Non-Profit IRS Status: 501(c)3
Highest Offering: Second Talmudic Degree
Program: Professional
Accreditation: @RABN

01 President .... Rabbi Israel FALK
05 Dean .... Rabbi Don UNGARISCHER

Yeshiva and Kollel Harbotzas Torah (B)

1049 E 15th Street, Brooklyn NY 11230-4462
County: Kings FICE Identification: 023506
Unit ID: 245731
Telephone: (718) 692-0208 Carnegie Class: Spec/Faith
FAX Number: (718) 692-0363 Calendar System: Semester
Established: 1969 Annual Undergrad Tuition & Fees: $6,200
Enrollment: 38 Male
Affiliation or Control: Independent Non-Profit IRS Status: 501(c)3
Highest Offering: Second Talmudic Degree
Program: Professional
Accreditation: @RABN

01 President .... Rabbi Y. BITTERSFELD

Yeshiva of Machzikai Hadas (C)

1301 47th Street, Brooklyn NY 11219
County: Kings FICE Identification: 041381
Unit ID: 455257
Telephone: (718) 853-2442 Carnegie Class: Spec/Faith
FAX Number: (718) 853-2504 Calendar System: Semester
Established: 2001 Annual Undergrad Tuition & Fees: $5,700
Enrollment: 277 Male
Affiliation or Control: Independent Non-Profit IRS Status: 501(c)3
Highest Offering: First Talmudic Degree
Program: Professional
Accreditation: RABN

01 Rosh Yeshiva .... Rabbi Yidel MONHEIT

Yeshiva Mikdash Melech (D)

1326 Ocean Parkway, Brooklyn NY 11230-5655
County: Kings FICE Identification: 025068
Unit ID: 197610
Telephone: (718) 339-1090 Carnegie Class: Spec/Faith
FAX Number: (718) 998-9321 Calendar System: Semester
URL: www.mikdashmelech.org
Established: 1972 Annual Undergrad Tuition & Fees: $7,000
Enrollment: 120 Male
Affiliation or Control: Independent Non-Profit IRS Status: 501(c)3
Highest Offering: Second Talmudic Degree
Program: Teacher Preparatory; Professional; Religious Emphasis
Accreditation: RABN

01 Dean .... Rabbi Haim BENOLIEL
05 Dean of Faculty .... Rabbi David LOPIAN
06 Registrar .... Rabbi Josh SANANES
10 Chief Business Officer .... Rabbi Avraham BENOLIEL
11 Administrator .... Rabbi Amram SANANES

Yeshiva of Nitra Rabbinical College (E)

194 Division Avenue, Brooklyn NY 11211-7199
County: Kings FICE Identification: 011670
Unit ID: 197674
Telephone: (718) 387-0422 Carnegie Class: Spec/Faith
FAX Number: (718) 387-9400 Calendar System: Semester
Established: 1946 Annual Undergrad Tuition & Fees: $7,300
Enrollment: 226 Male
Affiliation or Control: Independent Non-Profit IRS Status: 501(c)3
Highest Offering: Second Talmudic Degree
Program: Professional
Accreditation: RABN

01 President .... Mr. Alexander FISCHER
03 Vice President .... Mr. Mendel KLEIN
05 Dean .... Rabbi Samuel D. UNGAR
11 Administrative Officer .... Mr. Ernest SCHWARTZ

Yeshiva Shaar HaTorah-Grodno (F)

83-96 117th Street, Kew Gardens NY 11415
County: Queens FICE Identification: 021520
Unit ID: 197692
Telephone: (718) 846-1940 Carnegie Class: Spec/Faith
FAX Number: (718) 850-7916 Calendar System: Semester
Established: 1976 Annual Undergrad Tuition & Fees: $15,400
Enrollment: 88 Male
Affiliation or Control: Independent Non-Profit IRS Status: 501(c)3
Highest Offering: Second Talmudic Degree
Program: Professional
Accreditation: RABN

01 Administrator .... Rabbi Yoel YANKELEWITZ

Yeshiva Shaarei Torah of Rockland (G)

91 W Carlton Road, Suffern NY 10901-4013
County: Rockland FICE Identification: 034963
Unit ID: 441609
Telephone: (845) 352-3431 Carnegie Class: Spec/Faith
FAX Number: (845) 352-3433 Calendar System: Semester
Established: 1977 Annual Undergrad Tuition & Fees: $12,000
Enrollment: 7 Male
Affiliation or Control: Independent Non-Profit IRS Status: 501(c)3
Highest Offering: First Talmudic Degree
Program: Professional
Accreditation: RABN

01 President .... Rabbi Mordechai WOLMARK
30 Chief Devel Officer/Financial Aid .... Mrs. Teri SCHILLER
06 Registrar .... Rabbi Neil RATNER

Yeshiva of the Telshe Alumni (H)

4904 Independence Avenue, Riverdale NY 10471
County: Bronx FICE Identification: 025463
Unit ID: 431983
Telephone: (718) 601-3523 Carnegie Class: Spec/Faith
FAX Number: (718) 601-2141 Calendar System: Semester
Established: 1981 Annual Undergrad Tuition & Fees: $7,900
Enrollment: 95 Male
Affiliation or Control: Independent Non-Profit IRS Status: 501(c)3
Highest Offering: First Talmudic Degree
Program: Teacher Preparatory; Professional
Accreditation: RABN

01 President .... Rabbi Avrohom AUSBAND
03 Executive Director .... Rabbi Noson JOSEPH
29 Director Alumni Relations .... Rabbi Yosef FREILICH

Yeshiva University (I)

500 W 185th Street, New York NY 10033-3201
County: New York FICE Identification: 002903
Unit ID: 197708
Telephone: (212) 960-5400 Carnegie Class: RU/VH
FAX Number: (212) 960-0055 Calendar System: Semester
URL: www.yu.edu
Established: 1886 Annual Undergrad Tuition & Fees: $32,550
Enrollment: 6,385 Coordinate
Affiliation or Control: Independent Non-Profit IRS Status: 501(c)3
Highest Offering: Doctorate
Program: Liberal Arts And General; Professional
Accreditation: M, CLPSY, DENT, IPSY, LAW, MED, PSPSY, SW, @TEAC

01 President .... Mr. Richard M. JOEL
05 Provost/Sr VP Academic Affairs .... Dr. Morton LOWENGRUB
17 Vice President Medical Affairs .... Dr. Allen M. SPIEGEL
10 Vice President Business Affairs/CFO .... Mr. J. Michael GOWER
30 Vice Pres Institutional Advancement .... Mr. Daniel T. FORMAN
11 Vice President University Affairs .... Dr. Herbert C. DOBRINSKY
13 VP Information Technology/CIO .... Mr. Marc MILSTEIN
43 VP Legal Affs/Secretary/Gen Counsel .... Mr. Andrew J. LAUER
32 Vice President University Life .... Dr. Hillel DAVIS
26 Vice Pres Communications/Pub Affs .... Mrs. Georgia B. POLLAK
18 Vice Pres Administrative Services .... Mr. Jeffrey ROSENGARTEN
100 Vice Pres/Chief of Staff .... Mr. Josh JOSEPH
04 Assistant to President .... Ms. Cynthia PHELPS
08 Dean of University Libraries .... Mrs. Pearl BERGER
35 Senior Univ Dean of Students .... Dr. Victor SCHWARTZ
88 Dean of Students .... Mr. David HIMBER
49 Dean Yeshiva College .... Dr. Barry EICHLER
49 Dean Undergrad Jewish Studies .... Rabbi Yona REISS
49 Dean Stern College for Women .... Dr. Karen BACON
50 Dean Sy Syms School of Business .... Dr. Michael J. GINZBERG
49 Dean Mazer School .... Rabbi Yona REISS
63 Dean Albert Einstein Col Medicine .... Dr. Allen M. SPIEGEL
58 Dean Ferkauf Graduate School .... Dr. Lawrence J. SIEGEL
58 Dean Bernard Revel Graduate School .... Dr. David BERGER
58 Dean Azrieli Graduate School .... Dr. David SCHNALL
58 Director Sue Golding Grad Program .... Dr. Victoria FREEDMAN
70 Dean Wurzweiler School Social Work .... Dr. Sheldon R. GELMAN
84 Director Enrollment Management .... Dr. John B. FISHER
06 Interim University Registrar .... Dr. John B. FISHER
37 Director of Student Finances .... Mr. Robert FRIEDMAN
07 Director Undergraduate Admissions .... Mr. Michael KRANZLER
29 Director University Alumni Affairs .... Ms. Barbara BIRCH
09 Director of Institutional Research .... Dr. Ariel FISHMAN
96 Director of Purchasing .... Mr. Jack ZENCHECK
15 Director Human Resources .... Ms. Yvonne RAMIREZ
38 Director Student Counseling .... Dr. Chaim NISSEL

Yeshivas Novominsk (J)

1690 60th Street, Brooklyn NY 11204-2138
County: Kings FICE Identification: 031271
Unit ID: 405058
Telephone: (718) 438-2727 Carnegie Class: Spec/Faith
FAX Number: (718) 438-2472 Calendar System: Semester
Established: 1988 Annual Undergrad Tuition & Fees: $9,000
Enrollment: 134 Male
Affiliation or Control: Independent Non-Profit IRS Status: 501(c)3
Highest Offering: First Talmudic Degree
Program: Teacher Preparatory; Professional
Accreditation: RABN

01 Administrative Director .... Rabbi Lipa BRENNAN
32 Dean of Students .... Rabbi Yaakov PERLOW

Yeshivath Viznitz (K)

PO Box 446, Monsey NY 10952-0446
County: Rockland FICE Identification: 013027
Unit ID: 197735
Telephone: (845) 731-3700 Carnegie Class: Spec/Faith
FAX Number: (845) 356-7359 Calendar System: Semester
Established: 1946 Annual Undergrad Tuition & Fees: $5,850
Enrollment: 540 Male
Affiliation or Control: Independent Non-Profit IRS Status: 501(c)3
Highest Offering: Second Talmudic Degree
Program: Teacher Preparatory; Professional
Accreditation: RABN

01 President .... Gershon NEIMAN
10 Chief Fiscal Officer .... Rabbi J. LURIA

Yeshivath Zichron Moshe (L)

PO Box 580, South Fallsburg NY 12779-0580
County: Sullivan FICE Identification: 011821
Unit ID: 197744
Telephone: (845) 434-5240 Carnegie Class: Spec/Faith
FAX Number: (845) 434-1009 Calendar System: Semester
Established: 1969 Annual Undergrad Tuition & Fees: $10,790
Enrollment: 199 Male
Affiliation or Control: Independent Non-Profit IRS Status: 501(c)3
Highest Offering: Second Talmudic Degree
Program: Professional
Accreditation: RABN

01 President .... Rabbi Ephraim Y. SHER
37 Director Student Financial Aid .... Rabbi Dov PERECMAN
06 Registrar .... Mrs. Miryom R. MILLER

NORTH CAROLINA

Apex School of Theology (M)

2945 S Miami Boulevard, Ste 114-115,
Durham NC 27703-8024
County: Durham FICE Identification: 035134
Unit ID: 441511
Telephone: (919) 572-1625 Carnegie Class: Spec/Faith
FAX Number: (919) 572-1762 Calendar System: Other
URL: www.apexsot.edu
Established: 1995 Annual Undergrad Tuition & Fees: $625
Enrollment: 550 Coed
Affiliation or Control: Independent Non-Profit IRS Status: 501(c)3
Highest Offering: Doctorate
Program: Religious Emphasis
Accreditation: TRACS

01 President .... Dr. Joseph E. PERKINS
03 Executive Vice President .... Vacant
05 Academic Dean/Graduate Dean .... Dr. Lafayette MAXWELL
06 Registrar .... Dr. Henry D. WELLS
08 Head Librarian .... Ms. Cynthia RUFFIN
106 Director of E-Learning .... Dr. John CHAPMAN
88 Director Doctor of Ministry Program .... Dr. Terry THOMAS
10 Director of Finance .... Mr. Dexter PERRY
20 Undergraduate Dean .... Dr. Herbert DAVIS
88 Dean Master of Arts Christian Couns .... Dr. John F. BRADSHAW
73 Dean Doctor of Ministry .... Dr. Sherman TRIBBLE
32 Director Student Affairs/Dist Lrng .... Dr. John CHAPMAN

The Art Institute of Charlotte (N)

2110 Water Ridge Parkway, Charlotte NC 28217-4536
County: Mecklenburg FICE Identification: 021105
Unit ID: 197832
Telephone: (704) 357-8020 Carnegie Class: Spec/Arts
FAX Number: (704) 357-1133 Calendar System: Quarter

URL: www.aich.artinstitutes.edu
Established: 1973 Annual Undergrad Tuition & Fees: $23,054
Enrollment: 1,060 Coed
Affiliation or Control: Proprietary IRS Status: Proprietary
Highest Offering: Baccalaureate
Program: Occupational
Accreditation: ACICS

01 President ... Mr. Maurice LEE
04 Exec Assistant to the President ... Mrs. Melanie BRANNON
05 Dean of Academic Affairs ... Mr. Doug L. HEAPS
32 Dean of Student Affairs ... Mrs. Janice SUMNER
07 Senior Director of Admissions ... Mrs. Michelle L. LAING-IDLE
10 Dir of Admin & Finance Services ... Mr. Richard L. WALKER
21 Accounting Supervisor ... Miss Lauren BROWN
06 Registrar ... Ms. Martha MILLER
08 Director of Library Services ... Mrs. Cheryl Ann COYLE
15 Director of Human Resources ... Mrs. Katherine CLARK
36 Director Career Services ... Ms. I. Darchele SMITH
91 Asst Director of Technology ... Mr. Lon CHANG
40 Supply Store Manager ... Ms. Debra SULLIVAN

Barton College (A)

704-A College Street, PO Box 5000,
Wilson NC 27893-7000
County: Wilson FICE Identification: 002908
Unit ID: 197911
Telephone: (252) 399-6300 Carnegie Class: Bac/Diverse
FAX Number: (252) 399-6571 Calendar System: Semester
URL: www.barton.edu
Established: 1902 Annual Undergrad Tuition & Fees: $30,618
Enrollment: 1,200 Coed
Affiliation or Control: Christian Church (Disciples Of Christ)
IRS Status: 501(c)3
Highest Offering: Master's
Program: Liberal Arts And General; Teacher Preparatory
Accreditation: SC, NUR, SW, TED

01 President ... Dr. Norval C. KNETEN
10 Vice Pres Finance & Aministration ... Mr. Kris LYNCH
05 Vice President Academic Affairs ... Dr. John MARSDEN
100 Senior Advisor to President ... Mrs. Carolyn H. BROWN
31 Vice President External Relations ... Dr. Kelly M. THOMPSON
32 Vice President Student Life ... Mr. George SOLAN
30 Asst VP Inst Advancement ... Vacant
35 Asst Vice Pres for Student Affairs ... Ms. Holly ZACHARIAS
21 Comptroller ... Vacant
06 Registrar ... Ms. Sheila MILNE
08 Librarian ... Mr. Rodney U. LIPPARD
42 Chaplain ... Rev. Hollie E. WOODRUFF
36 Director of Career Services ... Mr. Lance W. KAHN
23 Director of Health Services ... Mrs. Amy BRIDGERS
26 Director of Public Relations ... Mrs. Kathy DAUGHETY
29 Director of Alumni Affairs ... Ms. Summer BROCK
07 Director of Admissions ... Ms. Amanda METTS
15 Director Human Resources ... Mrs. Linda TYSON
37 Director Student Financial Aid ... Ms. Bridget ELLIS
87 Director Summer Sch/Cont Education ... Dr. Deborah KING
14 Director Computer Center ... Mr. Kent WHEELESS
40 Bookstore Manager ... Ms. Brenda DAVIDSON
41 Athletic Director ... Mr. Gary HALL
13 Director of Information Technology ... Ms. Callie BISSETTE
35 Director of Student Activities ... Mr. Jared TICE
18 Director of Physical Plant ... Mr. Phil BEHE
09 Director of Institutional Research ... Mr. Robert HUDSON
50 Interim Dean School of Business ... Ms. Patricia BURRUS
53 Dean School of Education ... Dr. Jackie ENNIS
66 Dean School of Nursing ... Dr. Sharon SARVEY
88 Dean School of Behavioral Sciences ... Dr. Barbara CONKLIN

Belmont Abbey College (B)

100 Belmont Mount Holly Road, Belmont NC 28012-1802
County: Gaston FICE Identification: 002910
Unit ID: 197984
Telephone: (704) 461-6700 Carnegie Class: Bac/Diverse
FAX Number: (704) 461-6670 Calendar System: Semester
URL: www.bac.edu
Established: 1876 Annual Undergrad Tuition & Fees: $26,182
Enrollment: 1,678 Coed
Affiliation or Control: Roman Catholic IRS Status: 501(c)3
Highest Offering: Baccalaureate
Program: Liberal Arts And General; Teacher Preparatory
Accreditation: SC

01 President ... Dr. William K. THIERFELDER
05 VP Academic Affs/Dean of Faculty ... Dr. Carson DALY
84 Vice Pres Enrollment & Student Affs ... Dr. Lucas LAMADRID
11 Vice Pres Administration & Finance ... Mr. Wayne SCROGGINS
26 Vice President College Relations ... Mr. Ken DAVISON
04 Assistant to the President ... Ms. Rita F. LEWIS
29 Director of Alumni Relations ... Ms. Chris Goff PEELER
08 Director of the Library ... Mr. Donald BEAGLE
06 Registrar ... Fr. David BROWN, OSB
09 Director of Institutional Research ... Dr. Sandra NICKS
36 Director Career Counseling/Placemnt ... Ms. Stephannie MILES
27 Director Marketing ... Mr. Edward JONES
37 Director of Student Financial Aid ... Mrs. Anne A. STEVENS
38 Director Counseling Services ... Vacant
41 Athletic Director ... Mr. Quin MONAHAN
21 Staff Accountant ... Ms. Patti PIZZANO
19 Chief of Campus Police ... Mr. Shane STARNES
42 Director of Campus Ministry ... Ms. Tricia STEVENSON
30 Dir Stewardship & Strategic Plng ... Mr. David TARGONSKI
15 Director of Human Resources ... Ms. Mary Beth MCAVOY
18 Chief Facilities/Physical Plant ... Mr. J. R. MARR
07 Director of Admissions ... Mr. Roger JONES

Bennett College for Women (C)

900 E Washington Street, Greensboro NC 27401-3239
County: Guilford FICE Identification: 002911
Unit ID: 197993
Telephone: (336) 273-4431 Carnegie Class: Bac/A&S
FAX Number: (336) 370-8688 Calendar System: Semester
URL: www.bennett.edu
Established: 1873 Annual Undergrad Tuition & Fees: $15,800
Enrollment: 766 Female
Affiliation or Control: United Methodist IRS Status: 501(c)3
Highest Offering: Baccalaureate
Program: Liberal Arts And General; Teacher Preparatory
Accreditation: #SC, SW, TED

01 President ... Dr. Julianne MALVEAUX
05 Provost/Academic Vice President ... Dr. Esther TERRY
100 Chief of Staff ... Dr. James DIXON
10 Vice President for Fiscal Affairs ... Ms. LaTonya FLAMER
39 Director of Residence Life ... Ms. Ruth DENNIS-PHILLIPS
04 Executive Assistant to President ... Ms. Dehavalyn BLACK
30 Vice Pres Inst Advancement ... Mr. W. Anthony NEAL
26 Dir Public Relations & Publication ... Ms. Wanda MOBLEY
09 Dir Institutional Effective/Rsrch ... Ms. Xiaowen QIN
20 Assoc Provost of Academic Affs ... Dr. Millicent RAINEY
84 Vice Pres Enrollment Mgmt ... Mr. Les FERRIER
06 Registrar ... Vacant
08 Director of Holgate Library ... Ms. Joan WILLIAMS
07 Director of Admissions ... Ms. Jocelyn BIGGS
37 Director of Financial Aid ... Ms. Keisha RAGSDALE
29 Director Alumnae Affairs ... Ms. Audrey FRANKLIN
36 Director Career Services ... Ms. Ilona MCGRIFF
38 Director of Counseling Services ... Vacant
23 Director of Health Services ... Ms. Shaina CRUDUP
15 Director of Human Resources ... Ms. Linda MACK
42 Chaplain/Director Campus Ministry ... Rev. Natalie MCLEAN
83 Chair Social Sciences/Educ Division ... Dr. Rhonda WHITE
79 Chair Humanities/Fine Arts Division ... Vacant
81 Chair Natural & Behavioral Sciences ... Dr. Susan CURTIS
97 Dean of Academic Support ... Dr. Audrey WARD

Brevard College (D)

One Brevard College Drive, Brevard NC 28712-3306
County: Transylvania FICE Identification: 002912
Unit ID: 198066
Telephone: (828) 883-8292 Carnegie Class: Bac/A&S
FAX Number: (828) 884-3790 Calendar System: Semester
URL: www.brevard.edu
Established: 1853 Annual Undergrad Tuition & Fees: $22,700
Enrollment: 668 Coed
Affiliation or Control: United Methodist IRS Status: 501(c)3
Highest Offering: Baccalaureate
Program: Liberal Arts And General
Accreditation: SC, MUS, TEAC

01 Interim President ... Dr. Charles TEAGUE
05 VP Academic Affairs/Dean of Faculty ... Dr. John S. HARDT
10 Vice President for Business/Finance ... Ms. Deborah P. HALL
30 Vice Pres Institutional Advancement ... Mrs. Susan L. COTHERN
07 Vice Pres Admissions/Financial Aid ... Mr. Matthew COX
04 Assistant to the President ... Ms. Cheryl K. TINSLEY
32 Dean of Students ... Dr. Christopher J. HOLLAND
44 Director of Development ... Ms. Huldah WARREN
13 Director of Information Technology ... Dr. Michael W. FUIKS
06 Registrar ... Mrs. Alyse W. HOLLINGSWORTH
37 Director of Financial Aid ... Mrs. Beth POCOCK
26 Dir of Marketing/Donor Relations ... Ms. Carole FUTRELLE
08 Director of Library ... Mr. Michael M. MCCABE
29 Director of Alumni Affairs ... Mrs. Lisa B. FORT
31 Director of Community Education ... Mrs. Carol PERSEK
19 Chief of Campus Police ... Mr. Dan WOOD
23 Director of Medical Services ... Mrs. Susan E. MARTIN, RN
41 Director of Athletics ... Mr. Juan MASCARO
18 Director of Facilities/Grounds ... Mr. Joseph BROWN
24 Director Academic Enrichment Ctr ... Ms. Shirley E. ARNOLD
36 Dir Ofc Career Exploration/Devel ... Vacant
92 Director of Honors Program ... Dr. Laura L. FRANKLIN
21 Controller ... Mr. Thomas Ove ANDERSEN
38 Coordinator of Counseling Services ... Ms. Deanne DASBURG
57 Interim Chair Division of Fine Arts ... Mrs. Jo PUMPHREY
79 Chair Division of Humanities ... Dr. Mary L. BRINGLE
83 Chair Div of Social Studies ... Dr. Helen C. GIFT
81 Chair Div Env Stds/Math/Nat Science ... Dr. Kenneth DUKE

Cabarrus College of Health Sciences (E)

401 Medical Park Drive, Concord NC 28025-3959
County: Cabarrus FICE Identification: 006477
Unit ID: 198109
Telephone: (704) 403-1555 Carnegie Class: Spec/Health
FAX Number: (704) 403-2077 Calendar System: Semester
URL: www.cabarruscollege.edu
Established: 1942 Annual Undergrad Tuition & Fees: $10,740
Enrollment: 432 Coed
Affiliation or Control: Independent Non-Profit IRS Status: 501(c)3
Highest Offering: Baccalaureate
Program: Occupational; 2-Year Principally Bachelor's Creditable; Nursing Emphasis
Accreditation: SC, ADNUR, MAC, NURSE, OTA, SURGT

01 Chancellor ... Dr. Dianne O. SNYDER
05 Provost ... Dr. Margaret B. PATCHETT
11 Dean for Admin & Financial Svcs ... Mr. Mark E. COLEMAN
09 Dean Inst Research/Plng/Assessment ... Mr. Timothy J. KENNEDY
66 ADN Program Chair ... Ms. Renee HYDE
66 BSN Program Chair ... Ms. Molly PATTON
76 Program Coord/Health Service Mgmt ... Mrs. Sandi J. LANE
07 Director of Admissions ... Mr. Mark A. ELLISON
32 Director of Student Services ... Mrs. Angela M. FERGUSON
37 Director of Financial Aid ... Ms. Valerie RICHARD
06 Registrar ... Mr. Michael P. SMITH

Campbell University (F)

PO Box 97, Buies Creek NC 27506-0097
County: Harnett FICE Identification: 002913
Unit ID: 198136
Telephone: (910) 893-1200 Carnegie Class: Master's L
FAX Number: (910) 893-1424 Calendar System: Semester
URL: www.campbell.edu
Established: 1887 Annual Undergrad Tuition & Fees: $23,720
Enrollment: 6,954 Coed
Affiliation or Control: Baptist IRS Status: 501(c)3
Highest Offering: Doctorate
Program: Liberal Arts And General; Teacher Preparatory; Professional
Accreditation: SC, #ARCPA, LAW, PHAR, SW, TED, THEOL

01 President ... Dr. Jerry M. WALLACE
05 Vice Pres Academic Affs & Provost ... Dr. M. Dwaine GREENE
10 Vice President Business/Treasurer ... Mr. Jim O. ROBERTS
30 Vice President for Advancement ... Mr. Britt DAVIS
32 Vice President for Student Life ... Dr. Dennis BAZEMORE
84 Vice Pres Enrollment Management ... Dr. John ROBERSON
07 Asst Vice Pres of Admissions ... Mr. Jason HALL
49 Dean of College of Arts & Science ... Dr. Mark L. HAMMOND
61 Dean of the Law School ... Dr. Melissa ESSARY
50 Dean Lundy-Fetterman Sch Business ... Dr. Ben HAWKINS
53 Dean School of Education ... Dr. Karen NERY
67 VP of Health Sciences and Dean ... Dr. Ronald W. MADDOX
63 Dean of Osteopathic Medical School ... Dr. John M. KAUFFMAN, JR.
35 Dean of Students ... Dr. Sherry L. HAEHL
51 Director Continuing Education ... Mr. Thomas G. HARRIS
06 Registrar ... Mr. David MCGIRT
21 Assistant Treasurer ... Mr. Win QUAKENBUSH
29 Director of Alumni Relations ... Rev. Doug JONES
89 Director of Freshman Experience ... Dr. Jennifer A. LATINO
08 Librarian ... Mrs. Borree KWOK
37 Director of Financial Aid ... Mrs. Michelle DAY
14 Director of Computing Services ... Mr. Chris BUCKLEY
26 Director of Public Information ... Ms. Haven HOTTEL
15 Human Resources Director ... Mr. Bob COGSWELL
18 Chief Facilities/Physical Plant ... Mr. David MARTIN
38 Director Student Counseling ... Mrs. Laura RICH
96 Director of Purchasing ... Mr. Douglas WILLIAMSON
92 Director of Honors Program ... Dr. Ann ORTIZ
09 Director of Institutional Research ... Dr. Timothy D. METZ

Carolina Bible College (G)

817 S. McPherson Church Road, Fayetteville NC 28303
County: Cumberland Identification: 667012
Telephone: (910) 323-5614 Carnegie Class: Not Classified
FAX Number: (910) 323-0425 Calendar System: Semester
URL: www.carolinabiblecollege.org
Established: 1973 Annual Undergrad Tuition & Fees: $4,850
Enrollment: 97 Coed
Affiliation or Control: Non-denominational IRS Status: 501(c)3
Highest Offering: Baccalaureate
Program: Religious Emphasis
Accreditation: @BI

01 President ... Mr. Bill KORVER
05 Academic Dean ... Dr. Harry GHEE
06 Registrar ... Ms. Kathy SCHULTINGKEMPER
07 Director of Admissions ... Ms. Pamela RECOD

Carolina Christian College (H)

PO Box 777, Winston-Salem NC 27102
County: Forsyth FICE Identification: 035703
Unit ID: 199971
Telephone: (336) 744-0900 Carnegie Class: Spec/Faith
FAX Number: (336) 744-0901 Calendar System: Semester
URL: www.carolina.edu
Established: 1945 Annual Undergrad Tuition & Fees: $3,385
Enrollment: 54 Coed
Affiliation or Control: Independent Non-Profit IRS Status: 501(c)3
Highest Offering: Baccalaureate
Program: Liberal Arts And General; Religious Emphasis
Accreditation: BI

01 President ... Dr. Donald R. YOUNG
05 Academic Dean ... Ms. LaTanya V. LUCAS
32 Dean of Students ... Mr. Rickey D. LAWS
08 Library Director ... Ms. Laura RHODEN
37 Financial Aid Director ... Vacant

Carolina Graduate School of Divinity (A)

2400 Old Chapman St., Greensboro NC 27403

County: Guilford FICE Identification: 039395
Telephone: (336) 315-8660 Carnegie Class: Not Classified
FAX Number: (336) 315-8660 Calendar System: Semester
URL: www.ceds.edu
Established: 2003 Annual Graduate Tuition & Fees: $10,000
Enrollment: 55 Coed
Affiliation or Control: Interdenominational IRS Status: 501(c)3
Highest Offering: Doctorate; No Undergraduates
Program: Professional; Religious Emphasis
Accreditation: THEOL

01 President .... Dr. Frank P. SCURRY
05 Vice President for Academics .... Dr. Terry W. EDDINGER
32 Director of Student Life .... Dr. Darryl A. BODIE
06 Director of Student Records .... Mrs. Cindy H. BODIE
37 Director of Financial Aid .... Ms. Shirley P. CARTER
10 Business Manager .... Mrs. Rosalie CARR

Carolinas College of Health Sciences (B)

PO Box 32861, 1200 Blythe Boulevard, Charlotte NC 28232-2861

County: Mecklenburg FICE Identification: 031042
Unit ID: 433174
Telephone: (704) 355-5043 Carnegie Class: Assoc/Pub-Spec
FAX Number: (704) 355-5967 Calendar System: Semester
URL: www.CarolinasCollege.edu
Established: 1990 Annual Undergrad Tuition & Fees (In-District): $11,475
Enrollment: 524 Coed
Affiliation or Control: Local IRS Status: 501(c)3
Highest Offering: Associate Degree
Program: 2-Year Principally Bachelor's Creditable
Accreditation: SC, ANEST, ADNUR, MT, RAD, SURGT

01 President .... Dr. Ellen SHEPPARD
05 Provost .... Dr. Janice TERRELL
10 Dean of Business/Finance/Technology .... Ms. Kim BRADSHAW
32 Dean Student Svcs/Enrollment Mgmt .... Dr. T. Hampton HOPKINS
66 Dean of Nursing .... Dr. Deborah BLACKWELL
97 Dean Assessment/Gen Ed/Pre-Nursing .... Dr. Lori LIEVING
76 Director Surgical Technology .... Ms. Rebecca F. CUTHBERTSON
76 Director Radiologic Technology .... Mr. Doug FRANKENBURG
76 Director Radiation Therapy .... Mr. Lee BRASWELL
76 Director Medical Technology .... Ms. Kelly SHIRLEY
06 Registrar .... Ms. Sue ROUX
07 Admissions Coordinator .... Ms. Rhoda RILLORTA
37 Financial Aid Coordinator .... Ms. Jill POWELL
29 Director Alumni Relations .... Dr. Ellen SHEPPARD
90 Instructional Tech Coordinator .... Mr. Larry TURNER
26 Chief Public Relations Officer .... Mr. Kevin MCCARTHY
36 Director Student Placement .... Ms. Nancy WATKINS
51 Director Continuing Education .... Ms. Susan THOMASSON

Catawba College (C)

2300 W Innes Street, Salisbury NC 28144-2488

County: Rowan FICE Identification: 002914
Unit ID: 198215
Telephone: (704) 637-4111 Carnegie Class: Bac/Diverse
FAX Number: (704) 637-4444 Calendar System: Semester
URL: www.catawba.edu
Established: 1851 Annual Undergrad Tuition & Fees: $25,160
Enrollment: 1,323 Coed
Affiliation or Control: United Church Of Christ IRS Status: 501(c)3
Highest Offering: Master's
Program: Liberal Arts And General; Teacher Preparatory
Accreditation: SC, TED

01 Interim President .... Dr. Joseph B. OXENDINE
03 Senior Vice President/Chaplain .... Dr. Kenneth W. CLAPP
30 Sr Vice Pres/Chief of Development .... Mr. Thomas C. CHILDRESS
05 Provost .... Dr. Richard STEPHENS
04 Admin Assistant to President .... Mrs. Linda G. HAMILTON
10 Chief Financial Officer .... Mr. Charles F. WILLIAMS
15 Chief Human Resources Officer .... Mr. Larry G. FARMER
26 Chief Public Relations Officer .... Mrs. Tonia BLACK-GOLD
32 Dean of Students .... Mr. G. Ben SMITH
08 Head Librarian .... Dr. Steve MCKINZIE
06 Registrar .... Ms. Carol GAMBLE
07 Director of Admissions .... Ms. Dawn SNOOK
09 Director Institutional Research .... Dr. Carla EASTIS
37 Director of Financial Assistance .... Ms. Melanie C. MCCULLOCH
36 Director of Placement .... Ms. Robin PERRY
88 Director Sports Info & Promotion .... Mr. Jim D. LEWIS
40 Director Bookstore .... Mrs. Stephanie TAYLOR
41 Athletic Director .... Mr. Dennis W. DAVIDSON
18 Chief Facilities/Physical Plant .... Mr. Eric NIANOURIS
29 Director Alumni Relations .... Ms. Margaret FAUST
38 Director Student Counseling .... Dr. Nancy ZIMMERMAN
39 Director of Residence Life .... Ms. Sarah ROSSINI

Charlotte School of Law (D)

2145 Suttle Avenue, Charlotte NC 28208

County: Mecklenburg FICE Identification: 041435
Unit ID: 455169
Telephone: (704) 971-8500 Carnegie Class: Not Classified
FAX Number: (704) 971-8599 Calendar System: Semester
URL: www.charlottelaw.org
Established: 2008 Annual Graduate Tuition & Fees: $17,850
Enrollment: 252 Coed
Affiliation or Control: Proprietary IRS Status: Proprietary
Highest Offering: First Professional Degree; No Undergraduates
Program: Professional
Accreditation: LAW

01 President .... Mr. Dennis STONE
05 Interim Dean .... Ms. Denise SPRIGGS
20 Associate Dean for Academics .... Ms. Phyliss CRAIG-TAYLOR
32 Associate Dean for Students .... Vacant
07 Associate Dean for Admissions .... Mr. Forrest STANFORD
08 Assoc Dean for Library/Info Svcs .... Vacant
10 Associate Dean for Business/Finance .... Mr. Frank TOLIVER
06 Dir of Academic Svcs/Registration .... Ms. Traci FLEURY
37 Director of Financial Aid .... Ms. Lauren MACK

Chowan University (E)

One University Place, Murfreesboro NC 27855-1844

County: Hertford FICE Identification: 002916
Unit ID: 198303
Telephone: (252) 398-6500 Carnegie Class: Bac/Diverse
FAX Number: (252) 398-1190 Calendar System: Semester
URL: www.chowan.edu
Established: 1848 Annual Undergrad Tuition & Fees: $20,700
Enrollment: 1,300 Coed
Affiliation or Control: Baptist IRS Status: 501(c)3
Highest Offering: Master's
Program: Liberal Arts And General
Accreditation: SC, MUS, TED

01 President .... Dr. M. Chrisopher WHITE
05 Vice President Academic Affairs .... Dr. Danny B. MOORE
10 Vice President Business Affairs .... Mr. Donnie O. CLARY
32 Vice President Student Affairs .... Mr. P. Randy HARRELL
30 Vice President Advancement .... Mr. John TAYLOE
15 Vice President Human Resources .... Mr. John A. HINTON
07 Vice President Admissions .... Mr. Chad HOLT
13 Exec Dir Info Tech/Network Svcs .... Mr. James R. HOWELL
06 Registrar .... Ms. Donna WOODARD
26 Director of Public Relations .... Mr. Joshua BARKER
08 Head Librarian .... Mrs. Georgia E. WILLIAMS
37 Director of Financial Aid .... Mrs. Sharon ROSE
42 Campus Minister .... Ms. Mari E. WILES
18 Director Physical Plant .... Mr. Bob ROWE
19 Chief of Security .... Mr. Derek A. BURKE
35 Director Student Life .... Ms. Laurica YANCEY
38 Director Counseling/Career Services .... Mrs. Frances E. COLE
39 Director Housing & Residence Life .... Mr. Brandon ZOCH
41 Athletics Director .... Mr. Dennis HELSEL
09 Director Institutional Research .... Mr. Daniel MCCAMISH
88 Director Upward Bound .... Mr. E. Frank STEPHENSON
21 Director Business Services .... Mrs. Julie W. EMORY
29 Director Alumni Services .... Mr. Michael P. TEMPLE
49 Dean Liberal Arts .... Dr. John DILUSTRO
50 Dean Business .... Dr. Linda MILES
53 Dean Education .... Dr. Brenda S. TINKHAM
40 Bookstore Manager .... Ms. Quiana MANN

Davidson College (F)

PO Box 5000, Davidson NC 28035-5000

County: Mecklenburg FICE Identification: 002918
Unit ID: 198385
Telephone: (704) 894-2000 Carnegie Class: Bac/A&S
FAX Number: (704) 894-2005 Calendar System: Semester
URL: www.davidson.edu
Established: 1837 Annual Undergrad Tuition & Fees: $38,866
Enrollment: 1,742 Coed
Affiliation or Control: Presbyterian Church (U.S.A.) IRS Status: 501(c)3
Highest Offering: Baccalaureate
Program: Liberal Arts And General
Accreditation: SC

01 President .... Dr. Carol E. QUILLEN
05 Vice Pres Acad Affs/Dean of Faculty .... Dr. Clark G. ROSS
26 Vice President College Relations .... Ms. Eileen M. KEELEY
10 Vice Pres Finance & Administration .... Mr. Edward A. KANIA
32 VP Student Life/Dean of Students .... Dr. Thomas C. SHANDLEY
07 VP & Dean Admissions/Financial Aid .... Mr. Christopher J. GRUBER
20 Assoc Dean Academic Administration .... Ms. Leslie M. MARSICANO
20 Assoc Dean for Curriculum .... Dr. Patrick J. SELLERS
20 Assoc Dean Teaching/Lrng/Rsrch .... Dr. Verna M. CASE
06 Registrar .... Dr. Hansford M. EPES, JR.
13 Exec Director Information Tecnology .... Mr. Mur K. MUCHANE
37 Director Financial Aid .... Mr. David GELINAS
15 Director of Human Resources .... Dr. Kim BALL
41 Director of Athletics .... Mr. James E. MURPHY, III
08 Director of the Library .... Ms. Gillian (Jill) S. GREMMELS
29 Director Alumni Relations .... Vacant
27 Director College Communications .... Ms. Stacey SCHMEIDEL
21 Controller/Director Business Svcs .... Ms. Lori GASTON
18 Director Facilities & Engineering .... Mr. David M. HOLTHOUSER
19 Director of Public Safety & Police .... Ms. Adrienne M. MURRAY
36 Director Career Services .... Mr. Nathan J. ELTON
35 Director of College Union .... Mr. William H. BROWN
39 Dir Resid Life/Assoc Dean Students .... Dr. Patty A. PERILLO
42 College Chaplain .... Dr. Robert C. SPACH
71 Dir Cntr for Interdisiplinary Stds .... Dr. Scott D. DENHAM
82 Assoc Dean Int'l Programs/Studies .... Dr. M. Christopher ALEXANDER
09 Director Institutional Research .... Ms. Linda M. LEFAUVE
25 Director of Grants & Contracts .... Dr. Mary W. MUCHANE
24 Director Instructional Support .... Ms. Diane S. STIRLING
38 Director Student Counseling Center .... Dr. Trish MURRAY
44 Director of Annual Fund .... Ms. Maria ALDRICH
96 Director of Purchasing .... Ms. Elizabeth S. CHRISTENBURY
40 Bookstore Manager .... Ms. Gwendolyn S. GARDNER

DeVry University - Charlotte Center (G)

2015 Ayrsley Town Blvd, Suite 109, Charlotte NC 28273-4068

County: Mecklenburg Identification: 666215
Unit ID: 442365
Telephone: (704) 362-2345 Carnegie Class: Spec/Bus
FAX Number: (704) 362-2668 Calendar System: Semester
URL: www.devry.edu
Established: 2001 Annual Undergrad Tuition & Fees: $15,294
Enrollment: 757 Coed
Affiliation or Control: Proprietary IRS Status: Proprietary
Highest Offering: Master's
Program: Occupational; Professional; Business Emphasis
Accreditation: &NH

01 Campus Director .... Ms. Regina CAMPBELL

† Regional accreditation is carried under the parent institution in Downers Grove, IL.

DeVry University - Raleigh/Durham (H)

1600 Perimeter Park Drive, Ste 100, Morrisville NC 27560-8421

County: Wake Identification: 666562
Telephone: (919) 463-1380 Carnegie Class: Not Classified
FAX Number: (919) 468-5688 Calendar System: Semester
URL: www.devry.edu
Established: 1931 Annual Undergrad Tuition & Fees: $15,294
Enrollment: 514 Coed
Affiliation or Control: Proprietary IRS Status: Proprietary
Highest Offering: Master's
Program: Professional; Business Emphasis
Accreditation: &NH

01 Campus Director .... Sandy GARETON

† Regional accreditation is carried under the parent institution in Downers Grove, IL.

Duke University (I)

Durham NC 27706-8001

County: Durham FICE Identification: 002920
Unit ID: 198419
Telephone: (919) 684-8111 Carnegie Class: RU/VH
FAX Number: (919) 684-3200 Calendar System: Semester
URL: www.duke.edu
Established: 1838 Annual Undergrad Tuition & Fees: $40,665
Enrollment: 14,983 Coed
Affiliation or Control: Independent Non-Profit IRS Status: 501(c)3
Highest Offering: Doctorate
Program: Liberal Arts And General; Teacher Preparatory; Professional
Accreditation: SC, ANEST, ARCPA, BUS, CLPSY, ENG, #FOR, IPSY, LAW, MED, NURSE, PA, PTA, TED, THEOL

01 President .... Richard H. BRODHEAD
05 Provost .... Peter LANGE
11 Exec Vice Pres for Administration .... Tallman TRASK, III
26 Vice President Public Affairs .... Michael J. SCHOENFELD
45 President/Duke Management Company .... Neal TRIPLETT
30 Vice Pres Alumni Affs/Development .... Robert S. SHEPARD
23 VP Admin Duke Univ Health Systems .... Monte BROWN
32 Vice President for Student Affairs .... Larry MONETA
22 Vice Pres for Institutional Equity .... Benjamin D. REESE
10 Vice President Financial Services .... Timothy WALSH
17 Chief Exec Officer Duke Univ Hosp .... William J. FULKERSON, JR.
88 Vice Pres - Chief Medical Officer .... Gary L. STILES
15 Vice President for Administration .... Kyle CAVANAUGH
41 Vice Pres & Director of Athletics .... Kevin WHITE
101 Vice Pres & University Secretary .... Richard RIDDELL
17 Chancellor for Health Affairs .... Victor DZAU
30 VP Duke Med Devel/Alumni Affairs .... Ellen MEDEARIS
72 Vice Chanc Science & Technology .... Peter AGRE
31 Assoc Vice Pres Campus Services .... Kemel DAWKINS
31 Assoc VP Community Affairs DUHS .... Maryann BLACK
35 Asst VP Student Affs/Dean Students .... Sue WASIOLEK
19 Assoc VP Campus Safety and Security .... Aaron GRAVES
07 Dean Undergraduate Admissions .... Christoph O. GUTTENTAG
21 Exec Vice Provost Finance & Admin .... James S. ROBERTS
13 Vice Prov Information Technology .... Tracy FUTHEY
88 Vice Provost Interdisciplin Studies .... Susan ROTH
20 Vice Provost for Academic Affairs .... John SIMON
88 Vice Provost Academic & Admin Svcs .... Vacant
88 Director Intl Area Studies .... Gilbert MERKX
88 Vice Prov Faculty Diversity & Dev .... Nancy ALLEN
88 Vice Provost for the Arts .... Scott A. LINDTORTH

46 Vice Provost for Research .... James N. SIEDOW
29 Executive Director Alumni Affairs .... Sterly WILDER
36 Executive Director Career Devel Ctr .... William WRIGHT-SWADEL
21 Exec Director of Internal Audits .... Michael L. SOMICH
23 Exec Dir Student Health Service .... William PURDY
38 Exec Director of Student Counseling .... Kathy R. HOLLINGSWORTH
06 Registrar .... Bruce W. CUNNINGHAM
08 Librarian/Vice Prov Library Affairs .... Deborah JAKUBS
43 University Counsel .... Pamela BERNARD
09 Director of Institutional Research .... David JAMIESON-DRAKE
37 Asst Vice Provost/Dir Financial Aid .... Alison RABIL
87 Director of Summer Session .... Paula E. GILBERT
61 Dean of Law School .... David F. LEVI
63 Dn Sch Med/Sr Vice Chanc Acad Affs .... Nancy ANDREWS
50 Dean Fuqua School of Business .... Blair H. SHEPPARD
65 Dean School of the Environment .... William L. CHAMEIDES
73 Dean of the Divinity School .... Richard HAYS
58 Dean Grad School/Vice Prov Grad Ed .... Jo Rae WRIGHT
49 Dean Faculty Arts/Science .... Laurie PATTON
88 Dean of the Natural Sciences .... Robert CALDERBANK
49 Dean Acad Affs Trinity Col Arts/Sci .... Lee D. BAKER
66 Dean School of Nursing .... Catherine GILLISS
54 Dean of Engineering .... Thomas KATSOULEAS
83 Dean of the Humanities .... Srinivas ARAVAMUDAN
83 Dean of the Social Sciences .... Angela M. O'RAND
53 Dean and Vice Provost Undergrad Ed .... Stephen NOWICKI
94 Director of Women's Studies .... Ranjana KHANNA
93 Director Ofc of Intercultural Affs .... Julian SANCHEZ
88 Director Duke University Press .... Stephen A. COHN
18 Vice President for Facilities .... John NOONAN
27 Chief Info Ofcr/Vice Pres Duke Med .... Art GLASGOW
88 Vice Chanc for Clinical Research .... Robert M. CALIFF
88 Vice Pres Ambul Svcs/Chief Med Ofcr .... Michael CUFFE
88 Exec Vice Dean Admin Sch Med .... Scott GIBSON
88 Vice Pres/Vice Prov Global Strategy .... Michael H. MERSON
88 Vice Chanc Corp and Venture Devel .... Robert L. TABER
45 VP Bus Devel & Chf Strat Plng Ofcr .... Mollie O'NEILL

Elon University (A)

2700 Campus Box, Elon NC 27244-2010
County: Alamance — FICE Identification: 002927
Unit ID: 198516
Telephone: (336) 278-2000 — Carnegie Class: Master's S
FAX Number: N/A — Calendar System: 4/1/4
URL: www.elon.edu
Established: 1889 — Annual Undergrad Tuition & Fees: $27,881
Enrollment: 5,709 — Coed
Affiliation or Control: Independent Non-Profit — IRS Status: 501(c)3
Highest Offering: Doctorate
Program: Liberal Arts And General; Teacher Preparatory; Professional
Accreditation: SC, BUS, JOUR, LAW, PTA, TED

01 President .... Dr. Leo M. LAMBERT
03 Executive Vice President .... Dr. Gerald L. FRANCIS
100 Chief of Staff .... Mrs. Lisa KEEGAN
101 Secretary to the Board of Trustees .... Mr. Jeff STEIN
05 Provost/Vice Pres Academic Affairs .... Dr. Steven D. HOUSE
07 VP of Admissions/Financial Planning .... Ms. Susan C. KLOPMAN
10 Vice Pres Business/Finance/Tech .... Mr. Gerald O. WHITTINGTON
30 Vice Pres Institutional Advancement .... Mr. James B. PIATT
32 Vice Pres/Dean of Student Life .... Dr. G. Smith JACKSON
26 Asst VP/Director of University Rels .... Mr. Daniel J. ANDERSON
20 Associate VP of Academic Affairs .... Dr. Mary B. WISE
20 Associate Provost for Academic Affs .... Dr. Connie BOOK
88 Associate Provost for Faculty Affs .... Dr. Tim PEEPLES
21 Asst VP for Business and Finance .... Vacant
49 Dean College of Arts & Sci .... Dr. Alison MORRISON-SHETLAR
50 Int Dean Love School of Business .... Dr. Scott BUECHLER
60 Dean of School of Communications .... Dr. Paul F. PARSONS
53 Dean of School of Education .... Dr. David H. COOPER
61 Dean of School of Law .... Mr. George JOHNSON
88 Associate Dean Physical Therapy .... Dr. Elizabeth A. ROGERS
85 Dean of International Programs .... Mr. Woody PELTON
35 Assistant VP of Student Life .... Mrs. Jana Lynn F. PATTERSON
08 Dean and University Librarian .... Ms. Kate D. HICKEY
41 Director of Athletics .... Mr. Dave L. BLANK
06 Registrar/Assistant to the Provost .... Mr. Mark R. ALBERTSON
88 Assoc Dean for Law Admissions .... Mr. Alan WOOLIEF
42 University Chaplain .... Dr. Janet FULLER
37 Director of Financial Planning .... Mr. M. Patrick MURPHY
29 Director Alumni Relations .... Ms. Sallie HUTTON
88 Assoc Dean of Academic Support .... Dr. Becky OLIVE-TAYLOR
36 Exec Director of Career Services .... Dr. Tom VECCHIONE
88 Director Construction Management .... Mr. Neil F. BROMILOW
18 Director of Physical Plant .... Mr. Robert BUCHHOLZ
15 Director of Human Resources .... Mr. Ronald A. KLEPCYK
31 Director of Auxiliary Services .... Ms. Vickie L. SOMERS
19 Director of Campus Safety & Police .... Mr. Charles J. GANTOS, JR.
23 Director of Health Services .... Vacant
38 Director Counseling Services .... Mr. Bruce F. NELSON
27 Assistant VP of Technology/CIO .... Mr. Christopher D. FULKERSON
09 Director Institutional Research .... Dr. Robert I. SPRINGER
13 Assistant CIO .... Mr. Christopher C. WATERS
25 Director of Sponsored Programs .... Ms. Bonnie BRUNO
93 Director of Multicultural Center .... Mr. Leon T. WILLIAMS
92 Director of Honors Program .... Dr. Maureen VANDERMAAS-PEELER
94 Director Women's Stds/Gender Stds .... Dr. Kirstin RINGELBERG
96 Director of Purchasing .... Mr. Jeff HENDRICKS
88 Sustainability Coordinator .... Ms. Elaine DURR

Gardner-Webb University (B)

PO Box 897 (110 South Main Street), Boiling Springs NC 28017-0897
County: Cleveland — FICE Identification: 002929
Unit ID: 198561
Telephone: (704) 406-2361 — Carnegie Class: Master's L
FAX Number: (704) 406-4329 — Calendar System: Semester
URL: www.gardner-webb.edu
Established: 1905 — Annual Undergrad Tuition & Fees: $23,120
Enrollment: 4,314 — Coed
Affiliation or Control: Baptist — IRS Status: 501(c)3
Highest Offering: Doctorate
Program: 2-Year Principally Bachelor's Creditable; Liberal Arts And General; Teacher Preparatory; Professional; Business Emphasis
Accreditation: SC, ACBSP, ADNUR, CACREP, MUS, NUR, TED, THEOL

01 President .... Dr. A. Frank BONNER
05 Provost & Senior Vice President .... Dr. Benjamin C. LESLIE
04 Sr Assistant to the President .... Mrs. Glenda S. CROTTS
10 Vice President for Business/Finance .... Mr. Mike W. HARDIN
26 Sr VP University Rels Marketing .... Mr. Ralph W. DIXON, JR.
30 Vice President for Advancement .... Mr. Monte WALKER
32 Vice Pres/Dean Student Development .... Dr. Delores HUNT
84 Vice Pres Enrollment Management .... Mrs. Debra HINTZ
41 Vice President for Athletics .... Mr. Chuck S. BURCH
09 Vice President Plng/Inst Research .... Dr. Jeffrey L. TUBBS
18 Assoc Vice Pres for Operations .... Mr. Wayne E. JOHNSON
91 Assoc VP for Technology Services .... Mr. Joey BRIDGES
20 Associate Provost for Schools .... Dr. Gayle B. PRICE
49 Assoc Provost for Arts & Sciences .... Dr. Earl LEININGER
21 Asst Vice President Business .... Mr. Jeff S. INGLE
51 Asst Provost for Distance Learning .... Dr. Bobbie COX
07 Dir of Undergraduate Admissions .... Ms. Kristen SETZER
37 Director of Financial Planning .... Mrs. Summer ROBERTSON
06 Registrar .... Mrs. LouAnn P. SCATES
35 Director of Academic Advising .... Dr. Doug BRYAN
19 Chief of University Police .... Mr. Barry JOHNSON
27 Dir of University & Media Relations .... Mr. Noel T. MANNING
08 Director of the Library .... Ms. Mary ROBY
38 Dir of Counseling & Career Svcs .... Ms. Cindy WALLACE
89 Director of Freshmen Programs .... Vacant
58 Dean of Graduate School .... Dr. Franki BURCH
73 Dean of Divinity School .... Dr. Robert W. CANOY
66 Dean of Nursing School .... Dr. Rebecca BECK-LITTLE
50 Director of School Management .... Dr. Sue C. CAMP
92 Director of Honors Program .... Dr. Thomas H. JONES
88 Director Program for Blind/Deaf .... Mrs. Cheryl J. POTTER
21 Comptroller .... Mrs. Robin G. HAMRICK
35 Director Student Activities .... Ms. Karissa L. WEIR
42 Minister to the University .... Dr. Tracy C. JESSUP
39 Director of Residence Life .... Ms. Sherry INGRAM
50 Dean of Business School .... Dr. Anthony I. NEGBENEBOR
15 Director Human Resources .... Mr. W. Scott WHITE
29 Director Alumni Relations .... Ms. Meghan DALTON
44 Director of Annual Campaign .... Mr. Greg POE
24 Asst Dir University Media Relations .... Ms. Kathy MARTIN
40 Bookstore Manager .... Mr. Wayne MERRITT
96 Director of Operations Support .... Vacant

Grace College of Divinity (C)

5117 Cliffdale Road, Fayetteville NC 28314
County: Cumberland — Identification: 667013
Telephone: (910) 221-2224 — Carnegie Class: Not Classified
FAX Number: (910) 221-2226 — Calendar System: Semester
URL: www.gcdivinity.org
Established: 2000 — Annual Undergrad Tuition & Fees: $2,435
Enrollment: 128 — Coed
Affiliation or Control: Independent Non-Profit — IRS Status: 501(c)3
Highest Offering: Baccalaureate
Program: Religious Emphasis
Accreditation: @BI

01 President .... Dr. Steven CROWTHER
05 Academic Dean .... Dr. Ron CREWS
84 Dean of Enrollment Management .... Mr. Bryan MCMILLAN
32 Dean of Students .... Ms. Kristen RIETKERK
11 Vice President of Administration .... Mr. Dick GAFFNEY
10 Chief Financial Officer .... Omayra COON
08 Librarian .... Mr. David ASPINALL

Greensboro College (D)

815 W Market Street, Greensboro NC 27401-1875
County: Guilford — FICE Identification: 002930
Unit ID: 198598
Telephone: (336) 272-7102 — Carnegie Class: Bac/Diverse
FAX Number: (336) 271-6634 — Calendar System: Semester
URL: www.greensborocollege.edu
Established: 1838 — Annual Undergrad Tuition & Fees: $25,000
Enrollment: 1,169 — Coed
Affiliation or Control: United Methodist — IRS Status: 501(c)3
Highest Offering: Master's
Program: Liberal Arts And General; Teacher Preparatory
Accreditation: SC, @ACBSP, MUS, TED

01 President .... Dr. Lawrence D. CZARDA
11 Vice President for Administration .... Ms. Marci H. PEACE
05 VP Academic Affairs/Dean of Faculty .... Dr. Paul L. LESLIE
32 Vice President for Student Affairs .... Dr. Robin DANIEL
84 Vice Pres Enrollment Mgmt & Mktg .... Ms. Colleen F. MURPHY
10 Vice President Facilities .... Ms. Susan SESSLER
58 Dean Graduate/Professional Studies .... Dr. Rebecca F. BLOMGREN
10 Vice President for Finance .... Vacant
13 Assoc Vice President for Technology .... Ms. Pamela R. MCKIRDY
88 Asst Vice President Academic Admin .... Mrs. Martha M. BUNCH
30 Exec Director Inst Advancement .... Mrs. Carolyn DEFRANCESCO
27 Dir of External Communications .... Mr. Lex ALEXANDER
37 Exec Director of Financial Aid .... Mr. Ron ELMORE
06 Registrar .... Ms. Carol WILLIAMS
07 Interim Director of Admissions .... Ms. Julianne SCHATZ
36 Director Career Exploration & Dev .... Mr. Brent ATWATER
09 Dir Institutional Assessment/Plng .... Dr. Nancy M. MCELVEEN
09 Director Institutional Rsrch & SIS .... Ms. Phyllis P. CHAMBERS
20 Director Academic Success Program .... Mr. Reginald L. WILSON
15 Director of Human Resources .... Mrs. Sharon P. HUNT
18 Director of the Physical Plant .... Mr. Doug B. MONTGOMERY
19 Director of Campus Security .... Mr. Calvin L. GILMORE
23 Director of Student Health Services .... Vacant
53 Director of Teacher Education .... Vacant
38 Dir Counseling/Disability Services .... Ms. Shahnaz KHAWAJA
92 Dir George Center for Honors Stds .... Dr. John WOELL
94 Director Women's Studies .... Dr. Rhonda BURNETTE-BLETSCH
44 Director of Annual Giving .... Ms. Kristen BROWN
29 Director of Alumni Relations .... Ms. Julie L. HAYES
42 Campus Minister .... Rev. Robert BREWER
21 Director of Finance & Controller .... Mr. Chris ELMORE
08 Director of Library Services .... Ms. Christine A. WHITTINGTON
35 Associate Dean of Students .... Ms. Ilona OWENS
40 Bookstore Manager .... Mr. Cliff BRALY, JR.
21 Budget Analyst .... Mr. Peter O. EVENSON

Guilford College (E)

5800 W Friendly Avenue, Greensboro NC 27410-4173
County: Guilford — FICE Identification: 002931
Unit ID: 198613
Telephone: (336) 316-2000 — Carnegie Class: Bac/A&S
FAX Number: (336) 316-2950 — Calendar System: Semester
URL: www.guilford.edu
Established: 1837 — Annual Undergrad Tuition & Fees: $30,430
Enrollment: 2,828 — Coed
Affiliation or Control: Friends — IRS Status: 501(c)3
Highest Offering: Baccalaureate
Program: Liberal Arts And General; Teacher Preparatory
Accreditation: SC

01 President .... Dr. Kent J. CHABOTAR
05 Vice President & Academic Dean .... Dr. Adrienne M. ISRAEL
04 Executive Asst to the President .... Mrs. Joyce A. EATON
45 Asst to President for Planning .... Mr. Jeff E. FAVOLISE
11 Vice President Administration .... Mr. Jonathan P. VARNELL
10 Vice President Finance .... Mr. Gregory F. BURSAVICH
30 Vice Pres Institutional Advancement .... Mr. Michael J. POSTON
84 Vice Pres for Enrollment Services .... Mr. B. Randy DOSS
32 Vice President Student Affairs .... Mr. Aaron L. FETROW
26 Assoc VP Communications & Marketing .... Mr. R. Ty BUCKNER
29 Assoc Vice Pres Alumni Relations .... Mr. Jerry W. HARRELSON
21 Associate Vice President Finance .... Mr. James WILSON
51 Assoc VP/Dean Continuing Education .... Dr. Rita S. SEROTKIN
31 Director Community Learning .... Mr. Alan C. MUELLER
20 Assistant Academic Dean .... Ms. Erin D. DELL
20 Assistant Academic Dean .... Dr. Barbara G. BOYETTE
37 Director Student Financial Svcs .... Mr. Paul COSCIA
06 Registrar .... Mrs. Norma L. MIDDLETON
18 Director Facilities Engineering .... Mr. Dan YOUNG
08 Director of the Library .... Mrs. Leah DUNN
41 Director of Athletics .... Mr. Tom J. PALOMBO
19 Director of Public Safety .... Mr. Ron M. STOWE
15 Director Human Resources .... Mr. Frederick R. DEVINE
09 Dir Institutional Research/Assess .... Dr. Owen Kent GRUMBLES
90 Director Info Technology & Services .... Mrs. Teresa SANFORD
42 Campus Ministry Coordinator .... Rev. Max L. CARTER
87 Director of Summer School .... Dr. Rita S. SEROTKIN
38 Director Student Counseling .... Ms. Gaither M. TERRELL
28 Director Multicultural Education .... Ms. Holly WILSON
92 Director Honors Program .... Dr. Donald A. SMITH
89 Director of First Year Program .... Mr. Clay E. HARSHAW
96 Director of Purchasing .... Ms. Tracy A. HALL
104 Director Study Abroad .... Dr. Jack ZERBE

Heritage Bible College (F)

PO Box 1628, Dunn NC 28335-1628
County: Harnett — FICE Identification: 030893
Unit ID: 198677
Telephone: (910) 892-3178 — Carnegie Class: Spec/Faith
FAX Number: (910) 891-1809 — Calendar System: Semester
URL: www.heritagebiblecollege.edu
Established: 1971 — Annual Undergrad Tuition & Fees: $8,820
Enrollment: 72 — Coed
Affiliation or Control: Other — IRS Status: 501(c)3
Highest Offering: Baccalaureate
Program: Occupational; 2-Year Principally Bachelor's Creditable; Religious Emphasis
Accreditation: TRACS

01 President .... Dr. Elvin BUTTS
05 Academic Dean .... Dr. Herbert CARTER
32 Dean Student Services .... Mr. Angel PADILLA
06 Registrar .... Ms. Traci NEWTON
07 Admissions .... Ms. Peggy PARKER

08 Librarian .... Ms. Janet PARKER
10 Business Administrator .... Ms. Sandra FRAZIER
37 Director Financial Aid .... Ms. LeAnne STRICKLAND
09 Director of Inst Effectiveness .... Ms. Hazel KING
20 Associate Academic Officer .... Mr. Stephen RZONCA
29 Director Alumni Relations .... Ms. Traci NEWTON
30 Director of Advancement .... Vacant

High Point University (A)

833 Montlieu Avenue, High Point NC 27262-3598
County: Guilford FICE Identification: 002933
Unit ID: 198695
Telephone: (336) 841-9000 Carnegie Class: Bac/Diverse
FAX Number: (336) 841-4599 Calendar System: Semester
URL: www.highpoint.edu
Established: 1924 Annual Undergrad Tuition & Fees: $37,800
Enrollment: 4,040 Coed
Affiliation or Control: United Methodist IRS Status: 501(c)3
Highest Offering: Master's
Program: Liberal Arts And General; Teacher Preparatory; Professional
Accreditation: SC, ACBSP, CIDA, TED

01 President .... Dr. Nido R. QUBEIN
05 Provost .... Dr. Dennis G. CARROLL
10 VP of Financial Affairs .... Mr. William H. DUNCAN
13 Vice President Information Services . Mr. Wellington O. DESOUZA
31 VP of Community Relations .... Dr. Donald A. SCARBOROUGH
100 Vice President and Chief of Staff .... Mr. Christopher H. DUDLEY
32 VP of Student Life .... Mrs. Gail C. TUTTLE
84 Vice President of Enrollment .... Mr. Andy BILLS
41 Director of Athletics .... Mr. Craig D. KEILITZ
88 Assoc VP of Inst Effectiveness .... Dr. Alberta H. HERRON
27 Asst VP of Communication & Culture .... Mr. Roger D. CLODFELTER, JR.
35 Dean of Students .... Dr. Kevin C. SNYDER
76 Dean of School of Health Sciences .... Dr. Daniel E. ERB
57 Dean of School of Art and Design .... Dr. John C. TURPIN
42 Dean of the Chapel .... Dr. Harold C. WARLICK, JR.
49 Dean of College of Arts & Science .... Dr. Carole B. STONEKING
50 Dean of School of Business .... Dr. James B. WEHRLEY
53 Dean of School of Education .... Dr. Marlann W. TILLERY
58 Assoc Dean of Graduate Studies .... Mrs. Tracy L. COLLUM
20 Assoc Dean Academic Development .... Dr. Allen GOEDEKE
88 Bishop in Residence .... Bishop Thomas B. STOCKTON
23 Medical Director .... Dr. Danielle MAHAFFEY
19 Chief of Security .... Mr. Jeff A. KARPOVICH
08 Director of Library Services .... Mr. David L. BRYDEN
06 Registrar .... Ms. Diana L. ESTEY
07 Director of Admissions .... Ms. Beth W. MCCARTHY
29 Director of Alumni Relations .... Ms. Jill THOMPSON
21 Director of Accounting Services .... Mr. James H. SPESSARD
15 Director of Human Resources .... Mrs. Kathy S. SMITH
37 Director of Student Accounts .... Mrs. Teresa L. KANE
38 Director of Student Counseling .... Ms. Lynda D. NOFFSINGER
88 Director of Experiental Learning .... Dr. Kelly A. NORTON
18 Dir of Construction and Renovation .... Mr. Ron GUERRA
18 Director of Facility Operations .... Mr. Stephen L. POTTER
88 Dir Stdnt Activities & Engagement .... Ms. Hillary C. KOKAJKO
88 Director of Judicial Affairs .... Ms. Heather P. BEATTY
88 Director of University Events .... Ms. Melissa L. ANDERSON
09 Coordinator of Inst Assessment .... Ms. Jillian P. PETTIT
44 Director of Special Gifts .... Mr. Gene R. KININMONTH
88 Director of WOW! .... Mr. Troy J. THOMMPSON
88 Dir Athletic Facilities/Operations .... Mr. Ryan TRESSEL
06 Associate Registrar .... Ms. Ann M. MILLER
39 Senior Director of Student Housing .... Ms. Sarah E. HAAK
40 Manager Bookstore .... Mr. William HOLSTON
36 Director of Career Services .... Mr. Eric J. MELNICZEK
44 Director of Annual Giving .... Mr. Chad M. HARTMAN
85 Director of International Education .... Ms. Judy DANLEY
18 Director Campus Enhancement .... Ms. Katherine MARTIN
27 Media Relations Coordinator .... Ms. Pamela J. HAYNES
04 Admin Assistant to President .... Ms. Judy K. RAY
88 Manager of University Mail Center .... Mr. Michael R. HALL

Hood Theological Seminary (B)

1810 Lutheran Synod Drive, Salisbury NC 28144-5768
County: Rowan FICE Identification: 036633
Unit ID: 443076
Telephone: (704) 636-7611 Carnegie Class: Spec/Faith
FAX Number: (704) 636-7699 Calendar System: Semester
URL: www.hoodseminary.edu
Established: 1904 Annual Undergrad Tuition & Fees: $6,450
Enrollment: 270 Coed
Affiliation or Control: African Methodist Episcopal Zion Church
IRS Status: 501(c)3
Highest Offering: Doctorate
Program: Professional; Religious Emphasis
Accreditation: THEOL

01 President .... Dr. Albert AYMER
05 Actg Academic Dean .... Dr. Albert AYMER
32 Dean of Students .... Dr. Dora R. MBUWAYESANGO
10 Fiscal Officer .... Dr. Regina M. DANCY
30 Development Officer .... Mrs. Margaret KLUTTZ
06 Registrar .... Ms. Nancy BAKER

ITT Technical Institute (C)

5520 Dillard Drive, Suite 100, Cary NC 27518
County: Wake Identification: 666704
Unit ID: 451936
Telephone: (919) 233-2520 Carnegie Class: Not Classified
FAX Number: (919) 463-5850 Calendar System: Quarter
URL: www.itt-tech.edu
Established: N/A Annual Undergrad Tuition & Fees: N/A
Enrollment: 435 Coed
Affiliation or Control: Proprietary IRS Status: Proprietary
Highest Offering: Baccalaureate
Program: Technical Emphasis
Accreditation: ACICS

† Branch campus of ITT Technical Institute, Spokane Valley, WA.

ITT Technical Institute (D)

4135 S Stream Boulevard, Suite 200, Charlotte NC 28217-4555
County: Mecklenburg Identification: 666161
Unit ID: 448442
Telephone: (704) 423-3100 Carnegie Class: Assoc/PrivFP4
FAX Number: N/A Calendar System: Quarter
URL: www.itt-tech.edu
Established: 2006 Annual Undergrad Tuition & Fees: N/A
Enrollment: 813 Coed
Affiliation or Control: Proprietary IRS Status: Proprietary
Highest Offering: Baccalaureate
Program: Technical Emphasis
Accreditation: ACICS

† Branch campus of ITT Technical Institute, Fort Wayne, IN.

ITT Technical Institute (E)

10926 David Taylor Drive, Suite 100, Charlotte NC 28262
County: Mecklenburg Identification: 666705
Unit ID: 456445
Telephone: (704) 548-2300 Carnegie Class: Not Classified
FAX Number: N/A Calendar System: Quarter
URL: www.itt-tech.edu
Established: N/A Annual Undergrad Tuition & Fees: N/A
Enrollment: 386 Coed
Affiliation or Control: Proprietary IRS Status: Proprietary
Highest Offering: Baccalaureate
Program: Technical Emphasis
Accreditation: ACICS

† Branch campus of ITT Technical Institute, Murray, UT.

ITT Technical Institute (F)

4050 Piedmont Parkway, Suite 110, High Point NC 27265
County: Guilford Identification: 666703
Unit ID: 451990
Telephone: (336) 819-5900 Carnegie Class: Not Classified
FAX Number: (336) 819-5950 Calendar System: Quarter
URL: www.itt-tech.edu
Established: N/A Annual Undergrad Tuition & Fees: N/A
Enrollment: 457 Coed
Affiliation or Control: Proprietary IRS Status: Proprietary
Highest Offering: Baccalaureate
Program: Technical Emphasis
Accreditation: ACICS

† Branch campus of ITT Technical Institute, San Diego, CA.

Johnson & Wales University-Charlotte (G)

801 W Trade Street, Charlotte NC 28202-1122
County: Mecklenburg Identification: 666375
Unit ID: 445708
Telephone: (980) 598-1000 Carnegie Class: Bac/Assoc
FAX Number: (980) 598-1111 Calendar System: Quarter
URL: www.jwu.edu
Established: 2004 Annual Undergrad Tuition & Fees: $25,107
Enrollment: 2,587 Coed
Affiliation or Control: Independent Non-Profit IRS Status: 501(c)3
Highest Offering: Baccalaureate
Program: Occupational; 2-Year Principally Bachelor's Creditable
Accreditation: &EH

01 President .... Mr. Arthur J. GALLAGHER
05 Vice President .... Mr. Tarun MALIK
20 Dean of Academic Affairs .... Mr. Peter LEHMULLER
07 Director of Admissions .... Mr. Joseph CAMPOS
11 Exec Director of Operations .... Mr. Mark NORMAN
08 Director of Library Services .... Dr. Richard MONIZ
19 Director Campus Safety & Security .... Mr. Robert ALLEN
23 Director of Health/Counseling Svcs .... Vacant
26 Director of Public Relations .... Ms. Melinda LAW
36 Dir Experiential Educ & Career Svcs .... Ms. Deborah LANGENSTEIN
30 Dir Development/Alumni Relations .... Ms. Nelia A. VAN GOOR
32 Dean of Students .... Ms. Tanaya WALTERS
06 Registrar .... Ms. Laurie HASLAM
18 Chief Facilities/Physical Plant .... Mr. Glenn HAMILTON
39 Director of Residential Life .... Vacant
96 Purchasing Director .... Mr. Evan NASH
85 International Student Advisor .... Ms. Karyn MONIZ
10 Campus Controller .... Ms. Allison DIAZ
13 Director of Campus Services .... Mr. Chesley BLACK
15 Human Resources Team Leader .... Ms. Tracy SMITH
88 Dean of Culinary Education .... Mr. Mark ALLISON
50 Dept Chair College of Business .... Dr. Roland SPARKS
88 Dept Chair Hospitality College .... Ms. Ann-Marie WELDON
49 Dept Chair School of Arts & Science .... Vacant
88 Dept Chair College of Culinary Arts .... Mr. Jerry LANUZZA

† Regional accreditation is carried under the parent institution in Providence, RI.

Johnson C. Smith University (H)

100 Beatties Ford Road, Charlotte NC 28216-5398
County: Mecklenburg FICE Identification: 002936
Unit ID: 198756
Telephone: (704) 378-1000 Carnegie Class: Bac/A&S
FAX Number: (704) 372-1242 Calendar System: Semester
URL: www.jcsu.edu
Established: 1867 Annual Undergrad Tuition & Fees: $17,368
Enrollment: 1,331 Coed
Affiliation or Control: Independent Non-Profit IRS Status: 501(c)3
Highest Offering: Baccalaureate
Program: Liberal Arts And General; Teacher Preparatory
Accreditation: SC, ACBSP, SW, TED

01 President .... Dr. Ronald L. CARTER
03 Exec Vice Pres/Chief Operating Ofcr .... Dr. Elfred A. PINKARD
10 Vice Pres for Finance .... Mr. Gerald HECTOR
30 Vice President for Inst Advancement .... Ms. Joy PAIGE
86 Asst VP Government Sponsored Pgms .... Dr. Diane BOWLES
11 Exec Asst to President for Admin .... Ms. Cathy HURD
84 Dean Enrollment Services .... Mr. George G. HARRIS
05 Council of Deans Chair/Dean of STEM .... Dr. Magdy ATTIA
49 Dean of Arts and Letters .... Dr. Donald N. MAGER
107 Dean of Professional Studies .... Dr. Helen CALDWELL
06 Dean Univ Records/Financial Aid .... Mr. George G. HARRIS
32 Dean of Student Development .... Ms. Cathy JONES
51 Dean of Metropolitan College .... Dr. Zenobia EDWARDS
08 Director of the Library .... Ms. Monika RHUE
07 Director of Admissions .... Mr. Dwight SANCHEZ
14 Director Information Technology .... Mr. John NORRIS
15 Director of Human Resources .... Ms. Latrelle P. MCALLISTER
09 Dir Plng/Assess/Effect/Rsrch .... Ms. Kelli RAINEY
26 Director Public Relations .... Vacant
29 Director Alumni Affairs .... Mr. Ron MATTHEWS
37 Int Director Financial Aid .... Ms. Keisha RAMEY
38 Director Counseling and Testing .... Ms. LaSonya BROWN
19 Director of Campus Police .... Mr. Gregory C. HARRIS
41 Athletic Director .... Mr. Stephen JOYNER, SR.
42 Director of Religious Life .... Ms. Cathy JONES
92 Director of Honors College .... Dr. Lakeshia LEGETTE
30 Director of Development .... Ms. Karen LAWLER
102 Director Foundations Rel/Priv Grant .... Mrs. Evelyn LEATHERS
102 Director of Corporate Relations .... Mr. Torrey FEIMSTER
36 Director Career Services .... Mrs. Barbara WILKS
39 Director Residence Life .... Mr. Terry MCPHERSON
40 Manager of Bookstore .... Ms. Robin SORENSEN
96 Purchasing Manager .... Mr. Joe MAJORS
16 Manager Risk Management .... Ms. Debra HOLLIS
18 Maintenance Supervisor .... Mr. Andrew BERRY
88 Coordinator of Retention .... Ms. Lisa DURHAM
23 Health Center Coordinator .... Ms. Marian JONES

King's College (I)

322 Lamar Avenue, Charlotte NC 28204-2493
County: Mecklenburg FICE Identification: 002937
Unit ID: 382504
Telephone: (704) 372-0266 Carnegie Class: Assoc/PrivFP
FAX Number: (704) 348-2029 Calendar System: Semester
URL: www.kingscollege.org
Established: 1901 Annual Undergrad Tuition & Fees: $13,700
Enrollment: 688 Coed
Affiliation or Control: Proprietary IRS Status: Proprietary
Highest Offering: Associate Degree
Program: Occupational; 2-Year Principally Bachelor's Creditable
Accreditation: ACICS, MAC

01 School Director .... Mrs. Diane RYON
05 School Director/Chief Academic Ofcr .... Ms. Barbara ROCKECHARLIE

Laurel University (J)

1215 Eastchester Drive, High Point NC 27265-3115
County: Guilford FICE Identification: 002935
Unit ID: 198747
Telephone: (336) 887-3000 Carnegie Class: Spec/Faith
FAX Number: (336) 889-2261 Calendar System: Semester
URL: www.laureluniversity.edu
Established: 1903 Annual Undergrad Tuition & Fees: $10,930
Enrollment: 151 Coed
Affiliation or Control: Independent Non-Profit IRS Status: 501(c)3
Highest Offering: Master's
Program: Professional; Religious Emphasis
Accreditation: BI

01 President .... Dr. Larry D. MCCULLOUGH
05 Undergraduate Academic Dean .... Dr. John LINDSEY
06 Registrar .... Mr. Greg WORKMAN
84 Director of Enrollment Management .... Mr. Jeremy REESE

37 Director of Financial Aid .... Mrs. Shirley CARTER
18 Director of Facilities and Grounds .... Mr. Eugene ALBERTSON
08 Librarian .... Mrs. April LINDSEY
10 Chief Financial Officer .... Mr. David WHITE
38 Director of Human Resources .... Mrs. Kathy CUTRELL
32 Director of Student Life .... Mr. Kevin DUNOVANT
03 Dean School of Mgt & Exec Vice Pres .... Dr. Owen ALLEN
51 Dean of Adult Profess & Grad Stds .... Mr. Gary LOUNSBERRY
106 Director of Distance Education .... Mr. Marty HILL
26 Public Relations Director .... Ms. Wanda CLARK
29 Alumni Coordinator .... Mrs. April LINDSEY

Lees-McRae College (A)

PO Box 128, 191 Main Street, Banner Elk NC 28604-0128
County: Avery FICE Identification: 002939
Unit ID: 198808
Telephone: (828) 898-5241 Carnegie Class: Bac/Diverse
FAX Number: (828) 898-8814 Calendar System: Semester
URL: www.lmc.edu
Established: 1900 Annual Undergrad Tuition & Fees: $23,175
Enrollment: 906 Coed
Affiliation or Control: Presbyterian Church (U.S.A.) IRS Status: 501(c)3
Highest Offering: Baccalaureate
Program: Liberal Arts And General; Teacher Preparatory
Accreditation: SC, NURSE, @TEAC, THEA

01 President .... Dr. Barry M. BUXTON
05 Provost/Dean Faculty .... Dr. Debra THATCHER
10 VP Finance & Business Affairs .... Mr. Ken BUCHANAN
30 Vice Pres Institutional Advancement .... Vacant
84 Int Vice Pres Enrollment Management .... Ms. Cathy SHELL
32 Dean of Students .... Mrs. Allison M. NORRIS
07 Assoc Director of Admissions . Ms. Rebekah GRAHAM SAYLORS
29 Director of Alumni Relations .... Ms. Sandy M. RAMSEY
09 Director of Institutional Research .... Dr. John KEENER
08 Director of Libraries .... Mr. Russell TAYLOR
88 Sports Information Director .... Mr. Jason LEVESQUE
06 Registrar .... Ms. Nan MCADEN
04 Secretary to the President .... Mrs. Patti J. MANNING
37 Financial Aid Director .... Ms. Cathy SHELL
18 Director of Physical Plant .... Mr. Jay TREADWAY
44 Director of Prospect Research .... Mrs. Frankie NEEDHAM
26 Assoc Director of Communications .... Ms. Meghan WRIGHT
15 Director Human Resources/Telecomm .... Mrs. Carolyn WARD
38 Director Student Counseling .... Ms. Susan SHUFORD
21 Assoc Business Ofcr/Dir Accounting .... Vacant
96 Dir Col Post Ofc/Purchasing Clerk ... Ms. Gwendolyn LOWRANCE
41 Athletic Director .... Mr. Craig MCPHAIL

Lenoir-Rhyne University (B)

625 7th Avenue NE, Hickory NC 28601-3984
County: Catawba FICE Identification: 002941
Unit ID: 198835
Telephone: (828) 328-1741 Carnegie Class: Bac/Diverse
FAX Number: (828) 328-7368 Calendar System: Semester
URL: www.lr.edu
Established: 1891 Annual Undergrad Tuition & Fees: $26,524
Enrollment: 1,837 Coed
Affiliation or Control: Evangelical Lutheran Church In America
IRS Status: 501(c)3
Highest Offering: Master's
Program: Liberal Arts And General; Teacher Preparatory; Professional
Accreditation: SC, ACBSP, @DIETI, NURSE, OT, TED

01 President .... Dr. Wayne POWELL
05 Provost .... Dr. Larry HALL
10 Vice President Finance/Admin .... Mr. Peter KENDALL
30 Vice Pres Institutional Advancement .... Mr. Scott SHRODE
32 Dean of Students .... Dr. Katie FISHER
84 Vice President for Enrollment Mgmt .... Ms. Rachel NICHOLS
104 Assoc Dean Global Learning .... Ms. Charlotte WILLIAMS
58 Dean Grad Studies/Lifelong Learning .... Dr. Amy WOOD
97 Assoc Dean Co-Curricular Programs .... Mr. Leonard GEDDES
06 Registrar .... Ms. Kathy HAHN
08 Librarian .... Ms. Rita JOHNSON
15 Director of Human Resources .... Mr. Rick NICHOLS
40 Director of Bookstore .... Ms. Leslie SKAFF
18 Director of Facilities/Plant .... Mr. Otis PITTS
41 Athletic Director .... Mr. Neill MCGEACHY
42 Campus Pastor .... Rev. Andrew WEISNER
19 Director of Security .... Mr. Norris YODER
92 Director of Honors Program .... Dr. Joshua RING
13 Chief Information Officer .... Ms. Melissa MULLINAX
26 Director of Marketing/Communication .... Mr. Mike LANGFORD
88 Director of Conferences & Events .... Ms. Janet MATTHEWS
29 Director of Alumni Relations .... Ms. Suzanne JACKSON
07 Director of Admissions .... Ms. Karen FEEZOR
09 Director of Institutional Research .... Dr. Ginger BISHOP
37 Director Student Financial Aid .... Mr. Eric BRANDON
38 Dir Student Counseling/Placement .... Ms. Jenny SMITH
88 Dir Liberal Arts/Visiting Writers .... Dr. Rand BRANDES
88 Dir of Deaf/Hard-of-Hearing Svcs .... Ms. Shawn FRANK
88 Institute on Obesity .... Ms. Michelle RIMER
65 Institute on Conservation .... Dr. John BRZORAD
85 Coord of International Programs .... Dr. Duane KIRKMAN
53 College of Education/Human Services .... Dr. Hank WEDDINGTON
76 College of Health Sciences .... Dr. Katherine PASOUR
49 College of Arts & Sciences .... Dr. Dan KISER
81 Col of Professional/Math Studies .... Mr. William MAUNEY

Living Arts College @ School of Communication Arts (C)

3000 Wakefield Crossing Drive, Raleigh NC 27614-7076
County: Wake FICE Identification: 031090
Unit ID: 421832
Telephone: (919) 488-8500 Carnegie Class: Assoc/PrivFP
FAX Number: (919) 488-8490 Calendar System: Quarter
URL: www.living-arts-college.edu
Established: 1992 Annual Undergrad Tuition & Fees: $25,680
Enrollment: 399 Coed
Affiliation or Control: Proprietary IRS Status: Proprietary
Highest Offering: Baccalaureate
Program: Occupational; Technical Emphasis
Accreditation: ACICS, MAC

01 Director .... Ms. Debra A. HOOPER

Livingstone College (D)

701 W Monroe Street, Salisbury NC 28144-5298
County: Rowan FICE Identification: 002942
Unit ID: 198862
Telephone: (704) 216-6000 Carnegie Class: Bac/Diverse
FAX Number: (704) 216-6217 Calendar System: Semester
URL: www.livingstone.edu
Established: 1879 Annual Undergrad Tuition & Fees: $15,708
Enrollment: 1,156 Coed
Affiliation or Control: African Methodist Episcopal Zion Church
IRS Status: 501(c)3
Highest Offering: Baccalaureate
Program: Liberal Arts And General; Teacher Preparatory; Professional
Accreditation: SC, SW, TED

01 President .... Dr. Jimmy R. JENKINS, SR.
04 Exec Asst to the President .... Mr. State ALEXANDER
05 Vice Pres Academic Affairs .... Dr. Leroy SIMMONS
10 VP Business & Finance/Operations .... Mr. William JAMES
32 Vice President Student Affairs .... Vacant
30 Vice Pres Inst Advance/College Rels .... Dr. Herman FELTON
35 Assoc Vice Pres of Student Affairs .... Vacant
20 Asst Vice Pres Academic Affairs .... Dr. Tom COAXUM
38 Dean of Counseling Services .Mrs. Elizabeth ALSTON-PINCKNEY
06 Registrar .... Mrs. Wendy JACKSON
08 Director Library Services .... Dr. Gwendolyn PEART
26 Director of Public Relations .... Mr. State W. ALEXANDER
37 Director of Financial Aid .... Ms. Sheri JEFFERSON
36 Dir Career Counseling/Placement ... Mrs. Vicki MCMOORE-GRAY
14 Director of Computer Info Systems .... Vacant
15 Director of Human Resources .... Ms. Sharon THOMPSON
29 Director Alumni Affairs .... Ms. Carmen C. WILDER
09 Director of Institutional Research .... Mr. Robert L. MCINNIS
84 Dir Enrollment Mgmt & Admissions .... Vacant
40 Bookstore Director .... Mr. Jerome FUNDERBURK
41 Athletic Director .... Vacant
96 Director of Purchasing .... Ms. Debra WOOD
18 Assoc Director of Physical Plant .... Mrs. Sherlyn EDWARDS
23 Health Services Manager .... Vacant
07 Director of Admissions .... Mr. Les FERRIER, JR.

Louisburg College (E)

501 N Main Street, Louisburg NC 27549-7705
County: Franklin FICE Identification: 002943
Unit ID: 198871
Telephone: (919) 496-2521 Carnegie Class: Assoc/PrivNFP
FAX Number: (919) 496-7141 Calendar System: Semester
URL: www.louisburg.edu
Established: 1787 Annual Undergrad Tuition & Fees: $14,722
Enrollment: 678 Coed
Affiliation or Control: United Methodist IRS Status: 501(c)3
Highest Offering: Associate Degree
Program: 2-Year Principally Bachelor's Creditable
Accreditation: SC

01 President .... Rev Dr. Mark D. LA BRANCHE
05 VP of Academic Life .... Dr. James C. ECK
11 VP of Administration/Inst Effect .... Vacant
30 Vice Pres Institutional Advancement .... Mr. Kurt CARLSON
32 Vice President of Student Life .... Mr. Jason E. MODLIN
10 Vice President of Finance .... Ms. Belinda FAULKNER
84 Vice Pres of Enrollment Management . Ms. Stephanie B. TOLBERT
29 Alumni Director .... Ms. Jamie PATRICK
06 Registrar .... Ms. Martha E. HEDGEPETH
08 Librarian .... Ms. Candace L. JONES
38 Director of Counseling Services .... Ms. Fonda PORTER
37 Director of Financial Aid .... Ms. Vickie FLEMING
09 Director of Institutional Research .... Mr. Charles B. SLOAN
26 Director of College Communications .... Ms. Amy MCMANUS
18 Chief Facilities/Physical Plant .... Mr. Steve SPARKS

Mars Hill College (F)

PO Box 370, Mars Hill NC 28754-0370
County: Madison FICE Identification: 002944
Unit ID: 199099
Telephone: (828) 689-1307 Carnegie Class: Bac/Diverse
FAX Number: (828) 689-1478 Calendar System: Semester
URL: www.mhc.edu
Established: 1856 Annual Undergrad Tuition & Fees: $23,318
Enrollment: 1,175 Coed
Affiliation or Control: Other Protestant IRS Status: 501(c)3
Highest Offering: Master's
Program: Liberal Arts And General; Teacher Preparatory
Accreditation: SC, MUS, SW, TED, THEA

01 President .... Dr. Dan G. LUNSFORD
30 Vice President for Inst Advancement .... Mr. Harold (Bud) G. CHRISTMAN
05 Exec Vice Pres Acad & Student Affs .... Dr. John W. WELLS
32 Asst Vice Pres for Student Life .... Dr. Craig GOFORTH
07 Dean of Admissions/Financial Aid .... Mr. Ed HOFFMEYER
06 Dean Academic Records/Resource .... Ms. Edith L. WHITT
08 Director of Library Services .... Ms. Beverly ROBERTSON
26 Director of Public Information .... Mr. Mike D. THORNHILL
10 Vice Pres for Finance .... Mr. Neil TILLEY
42 Campus Chaplain .... Rev. Stephanie MCLESKEY
41 Director of Athletics .... Mr. David W. RIGGINS
37 Director of Financial Aid .... Ms. Amanda RANDOLPH
29 Director of Alumni Relations .... Mrs. Ophelia H. DEGROOT
85 Director International Education .... Mr. Gordon HINNERS
09 Director Institutional Research .... Dr. Suzanne C. KLONIS
38 Director Student Counseling .... Ms. Cassandra PAVONE
15 Director of Human Resources .... Ms. Deana K. HOLLAND
13 Director Information Technology Svc .... Mr. Gerald D. BALL
18 Director of Facilities .... Mr. Donald EDWARDS
40 Director of Bookstore .... Mr. Darryl R. NORTON
51 Dean of Adult & Graduate Studies .... Ms. Marie NICHOLSON
97 Chair of General Studies .... Ms. Cathy L. ADKINS

Meredith College (G)

3800 Hillsborough Street, Raleigh NC 27607-5298
County: Wake FICE Identification: 002945
Unit ID: 198950
Telephone: (919) 760-8600 Carnegie Class: Bac/Diverse
FAX Number: (919) 760-2828 Calendar System: Semester
URL: www.meredith.edu
Established: 1891 Annual Undergrad Tuition & Fees: $27,770
Enrollment: 2,132 Female
Affiliation or Control: Independent Non-Profit IRS Status: 501(c)3
Highest Offering: Master's
Program: Liberal Arts And General; Teacher Preparatory; Professional
Accreditation: SC, BUS, CIDA, DIETD, DIETI, MUS, SW, TED

01 President .... Dr. Jo ALLEN
05 Sr Vice Pres Academic Admin .... Dr. Denise ROTONDO
20 VP for Academic Planning/Prgms .... Dr. Elizabeth WOLFINGER
30 Vice Pres Institutional Advancement .... Dr. Charles "Lennie" BARTON
10 Vice Pres for Business & Finance .... Mr. Craig BARFIELD
32 Vice President for College Programs .... Dr. Jean JACKSON
84 Assoc VP Enrollment Management .... Dr. Danny GREEN
35 Dean of Students .... Ms. Ann C. GLEASON
06 Registrar .... Ms. Amanda STEELE-MIDDLETON
09 Dir of Assessment & Inst Research .... Vacant
08 Director Library Info Services .... Ms. Laura DAVIDSON
07 Director of Admissions .... Ms. Jen MILLER-HOGG
37 Director of Financial Assistance .... Mr. Kevin MICHAELSEN
26 Director of Marketing/Col Commun .... Ms. Kristi EAVES-MCLENNAN
35 Dir Student Activ/Leadership Devel .... Ms. Cheryl S. JENKINS
28 Dir Commuter Life/Diversity Pgms .... Ms. Tomecca SLOANE
36 Director of Career Planning .... Dr. Marie B. SUMEREL
29 Dir of Alumnae & Parent Relations .... Ms. Hilary ALLEN
30 Director of Counseling Center .... Ms. Beth A. MEIER
58 Director of Graduate Studies .... Dr. Denise ROTONDO
39 Director Resident Life/Housing .... Ms. Heidi LECOUNT
55 Dir Undergrad Degree Pgm Women 23+ .... Dr. Susan ADAMS
20 Director of Academic Advising .... Ms. Amy HITLIN
31 Dir Cmty Outreach & Campus Events .... Mr. Bill BROWN
23 Director Health Services .... Ms. Sherri HENDERSON
42 Campus Minister .... Rev. Stacy PARDUE
13 Chief Information Officer .... Mr. Jeffrey HOWLETT
19 Chief Campus Police .... Mr. David KENNEDY
15 Director of Human Resources .... Ms. Pamela DAVIS
18 Int Chief Facilities/Physical Plant .... Mr. Harry CADMAN
21 Controller .... Ms. Lori DUKE

Methodist University (H)

5400 Ramsey Street, Fayetteville NC 28311-1498
County: Cumberland FICE Identification: 002946
Unit ID: 198969
Telephone: (910) 630-7000 Carnegie Class: Bac/Diverse
FAX Number: (910) 630-7317 Calendar System: Semester
URL: www.methodist.edu
Established: 1956 Annual Undergrad Tuition & Fees: $25,551
Enrollment: 2,416 Coed
Affiliation or Control: United Methodist IRS Status: 501(c)3
Highest Offering: Master's
Program: Liberal Arts And General; Teacher Preparatory
Accreditation: SC, ACBSP, ARCPA, SW, TED

01 President .... Dr. Ben E. HANCOCK, JR.
05 Vice Pres for Academic Affairs .... Dr. Delmas S. CRISP, JR.
10 Vice President for Business Affairs .... Mr. Gene T. CLAYTON
32 Vice President for Student Affairs .... Vacant
30 Vice President for Development .... Mrs. Robin DAVENPORT
09 VP of Institutional Research .... Dr. Donald L. LASSITER
20 Associate VP for Academic Affairs .... Ms. Jane W. GARDINER
84 Director Enrollment Management .... Mr. Rick D. LOWE
42 Chaplain/Director Campus Ministry .... Rev. Michael W. SAFLEY
26 Director of Public Relations .... Mrs. Pam MCEVOY
35 Assoc Dean Student Services .... Vacant

41 Director of Athletics .... Mr. Robert T. MCEVOY
29 Director of Alumni Affairs .... Ms. Lauren C. WIKE
07 Dean of Admissions .... Mr. Jamie W. LEGG
37 Director of Financial Aid .... Ms. Bonnie J. ADAMSON
06 Registrar .... Ms. Jasmin K. BROWN
08 Head Librarian .... Ms. Tracey PEARSON
85 Director Foreign Students .... Ms. Magda BAGGETT
19 Director Security/Safety .... Mr. James K. PHILLIPS
15 Director Personnel Services .... Mrs. Debra YEATTS
18 Chief Facilities/Physical Plant ... Mr. Thomas W. DAUGHTREY, III
21 Associate Business Officer .... Ms. Dawn AUSBORN
35 Assoc Dean Student Services .... Mr. William H. WALKER
36 Director Student Placement .... Ms. Antoinette P. BELLAMY
38 Director Student Counseling .... Ms. Darlene HOPKINS
96 Director of Purchasing .... Ms. Deborah DEMBOSKY
14 Director Institutional Computing .... Mr. Samuel J. CLARK, III

Mid-Atlantic Christian University (A)

715 N Poindexter, Elizabeth City NC 27909-4054
County: Pasquotank FICE Identification: 022809
Unit ID: 199458
Telephone: (252) 334-2000 Carnegie Class: Bac/Diverse
FAX Number: (252) 334-2071 Calendar System: Semester
URL: www.macuniversity.edu
Established: 1948 Annual Undergrad Tuition & Fees: $11,200
Enrollment: 169 Coed
Affiliation or Control: Churches Of Christ IRS Status: 501(c)3
Highest Offering: Baccalaureate
Program: Liberal Arts And General; Religious Emphasis
Accreditation: SC, BI

01 President .... Dr. D. Clay PERKINS
05 Vice President Academic Affairs .... Dr. Kevin W. LARSEN
10 Vice President Finance .... Mr. Kurtis L. KIGHT
84 Vice President Enrollment Services .... Dr. Ken S. GREENE
30 Vice President Development .... Mr. W. Keith WOOD
09 Director of Institutional Research .... Dr. Kevin W. LARSEN
06 Registrar .... Miss Joan U. SAWYER
08 Director of Library .... Vacant
38 Counselor .... Mr. Donald W. MCKINNEY
37 Financial Aid Administrator .... Mrs. Lisa W. PIPKIN
18 Superintendent Buildings & Grounds .....Mr. Phillip N. ALLIGOOD
21 Assistant Vice President Finance .... Mrs. Carol M. STUART
42 Campus Minister .... Mr. Chris STANLEY
49 Chair of Arts and Sciences .... Dr. Robert W. SMITH
73 Chair of Biblical Studies .... Dr. Lee M. FIELDS

Miller-Motte Technical College (B)

5000 Market Street, Wilmington NC 28405-3430
County: New Hanover FICE Identification: 030632
Unit ID: 198978
Telephone: (910) 392-4660 Carnegie Class: Spec/Health
FAX Number: (910) 799-6224 Calendar System: Quarter
URL: www.miller-motte.com
Established: 1916 Annual Undergrad Tuition & Fees: $14,508
Enrollment: 1,192 Coed
Affiliation or Control: Proprietary IRS Status: Proprietary
Highest Offering: Baccalaureate
Program: Occupational
Accreditation: ACICS, DA, MAC, SURGT

01 Campus Director .... Mr. David TIPPS
07 Director of Admissions .... Mr. Adam MERRITT

† Branch campus of Miller-Motte Technical College, TN.

Montreat College (C)

PO Box 1267, 310 Gaither Circle,
Montreat NC 28757-1267
County: Buncombe FICE Identification: 002948
Unit ID: 199032
Telephone: (828) 669-8011 Carnegie Class: Master's S
FAX Number: (828) 669-9554 Calendar System: Semester
URL: www.montreat.edu
Established: 1916 Annual Undergrad Tuition & Fees: $23,164
Enrollment: 1,066 Coed
Affiliation or Control: Non-denominational IRS Status: 501(c)3
Highest Offering: Master's
Program: Liberal Arts And General; Teacher Preparatory
Accreditation: SC, IACBE, TED

01 President .... Dr. Dan STRUBLE
04 Exec Assistant to the President .... Ms. Kim MCMURTRY
05 Senior Vice President and Provost .... Dr. Marshall FLOWERS
10 Vice President for Finance .... Mr. Geoff BREMER
88 Vice President for Adult Studies .... Mr. Jonathan SHORES
32 Vice President for Student Services .... Mr. Charles A. LANCE
30 Vice President for Advancement .... Mr. Joe KIRKLAND
13 Vice President for Technology .... Mr. Tom O. MCMURTRY
42 Chaplain .... Mr. Steve WOODWORTH
08 Library Director .... Ms. Elizabeth R. PEARSON
06 Registrar .... Ms. Merrill N. MCCARTHY
37 Director of Financial Aid .... Vacant
26 Director of Communications .... Ms. Annie CARLSON
38 Director of Counseling .... Ms. Jane CARTER
41 Athletic Director .... Mr. Craig JACKSON
35 Director of Student Activities .... Mr. Jim DAHLIN
40 Bookstore Manager .... Ms. Carly BRAENDEL
09 Assoc Dean of Academics & Inst Eff .... Ms. Becky FRAWLEY

19 Chief of Campus Police .... Mr. N. Scott ADAMS
07 Director of Admissions .... Mr. Joey HIGGINS

Mount Olive College (D)

634 Henderson Street, Mount Olive NC 28365-1263
County: Wayne FICE Identification: 002949
Unit ID: 199069
Telephone: (919) 658-2502 Carnegie Class: Bac/Diverse
FAX Number: (919) 658-7180 Calendar System: Semester
URL: www.moc.edu
Established: 1951 Annual Undergrad Tuition & Fees: $15,550
Enrollment: 3,855 Coed
Affiliation or Control: Original Free Will Baptist Church IRS Status: 501(c)3
Highest Offering: Baccalaureate
Program: Liberal Arts And General
Accreditation: SC, ACBSP

01 President .... Dr. Philip P. KERSTETTER
03 Executive Vice President .... Dr. Carol G. CARRERE
05 VP for Academic Affairs .... Dr. Ellen S. JORDAN
88 VP for Special Services .... Dr. Opey D. JEANES
10 Interim VP Finance & Treasurer .... Ms. Debra SMITH
84 VP for Enrollment .... Dr. Barbara R. KORNEGAY
32 VP for Student Affairs .... Dr. Dan SULLIVAN
30 VP for Institutional Advancement .... Mr. Kevin J. JEAN
50 Interim Dean School of Business .... Dr. Ellen JORDAN
49 Dean School of Arts and Sciences .... Dr. Kenneth D. HINES
08 Director of Library Services .... Ms. Pamela R. WOOD
12 Director of MOC New Bern .... Mr. Guy BRADBURY
12 Director of MOC Jacksonville .... Mr. Guy BRADBURY
12 Director of MOC Goldsboro .... Dr. Opey JEANES
12 Director of MOC Evening College .... Mr. Stanley J. ELLIOTT
12 Director of MOC Wilmington .... Dr. Marna R. MCMURRY
12 Director MOC Research Triangle Park .... Ms. Lisa NUESELL
07 Director of Admissions .... Mr. Timothy E. WOODARD
06 Registrar .... Mr. David L. BOURGEOIS
36 Director of Career Center .... Vacant
27 Director of Public Relations .... Ms. Rhonda E. JESSUP
102 Dir Foundations & Sponsored Program .... Vacant
102 Dir Young Alumni Relations .... Ms. Vickie S. ROBINSON
44 Director of Annual Fund .... Mr. Yeeka YAU
37 Director of Financial Aid .... Ms. Katrina K. LEE
29 Director of Alumni Relations .... Vacant
15 Director of Human Resources .... Mr. Stephen A. SWEET
23 Student Health Services .... Ms. Joanne L. MORGAN
42 Campus Chaplain .... Ms. Carla WILLIAMSON
04 Assistant to the President .... Ms. Katherine B. GARDNER
18 Superintendent Building & Grounds .... Mr. Jeff D. BROGDEN
40 Bookstore Manager .... Mr. Brian GRIFFIN
41 Athletics Director .... Mr. Jeffrey M. EISEN
13 Director Technology Support .... Mr. Robert R. PRUETT
88 Director Technology Services .... Mr. Kenneth M. DAVIS, JR.
92 Director Honors Program .... Dr. Ellen JORDAN
09 Director Inst Research & Planning .... Vacant

New Life Theological Seminary (E)

3117 Whting Avenue / PO Box 790106,
Charlotte NC 28206-4910
County: Mecklenburg FICE Identification: 038273
Unit ID: 444778
Telephone: (704) 334-6882 Carnegie Class: Spec/Faith
FAX Number: (704) 334-6885 Calendar System: Semester
URL: www.nlts.edu
Established: 1996 Annual Undergrad Tuition & Fees: $7,300
Enrollment: 100 Coed
Affiliation or Control: Independent Non-Profit IRS Status: 501(c)3
Highest Offering: Master's
Program: Religious Emphasis
Accreditation: TRACS

01 President .... Dr. Eddie G. GRIGG
04 Executive Asst to the President .... Mrs. Carolina CORDERO
05 Vice President of Academic Affairs .... Rev. Robert A. YOST
32 Vice President of Student Affairs .... Dr. Nathaniel PEARCE
30 Director of Advancement .... Mr. Michael ANDRUS
06 Registrar/Dir International Student .... Ms. Judith R. MAIN
08 Head Librarian .... Mr. Seth ALLEN
07 Director of Admissions .... Mrs. Paula EMRICH
10 Chief Finance Officer .... Mr. Al WITT, JR.

*North Carolina Community College System (F)

200 W Jones Street, 5001 MSC, Raleigh NC 27699-5001
County: Wake FICE Identification: 033445
Unit ID: 199166
Telephone: (919) 807-7100 Carnegie Class: N/A
FAX Number: (919) 807-7164
URL: www.nccommunitycolleges.edu

01 President .... Dr. R. Scott RALLS
03 Exec Vice President/Chief of Staff .... Mr. Kennon BRIGGS
103 Sr VP Tech & Workforce Development .... Dr. Saundra WILLIAMS
05 Vice Pres Academic & Student Svcs ..... Dr. Sharron MORRISSEY
10 Vice President Business & Finance .... Ms. Jennifer HAYGOOD
101 Dir State Brd Affs/Ex Asst to Pres .... Mr. Richard SULLINS
04 Special Assistant to the President .... Ms. Pia MCKENZIE
46 VP Engagement/Strategic Innovation .... Ms. Linda WEINER

*Alamance Community College (G)

1247 Jimmie Kerr Road/PO Box 8000,
Graham NC 27253-8000
County: Alamance FICE Identification: 005463
Unit ID: 199786
Telephone: (336) 578-2002 Carnegie Class: Assoc/Pub-S-MC
FAX Number: (336) 578-1987 Calendar System: Semester
URL: www.alamancecc.edu
Established: 1958 Annual Undergrad Tuition & Fees (In-District): $1,626
Enrollment: 5,524 Coed
Affiliation or Control: State/Local IRS Status: 501(c)3
Highest Offering: Associate Degree
Program: Occupational; 2-Year Principally Bachelor's Creditable
Accreditation: SC, ACFEI, DA, MAC, MLTAD

02 President .... Dr. Martin H. NADELMAN
05 Executive Vice President .... Dr. Gene C. COUCH, JR.
10 Vice Pres Admin & Fiscal Svcs .... Mr. Mark NEWSOME
30 VP Institutional Advancement .... Ms. Carolyn RHODE
20 Dean of Curriculum Programs .... Dr. William T. MCNEILL
51 Dean of Continuing Education ...... Ms. Karen HOLDING-JORDAN
32 Dean of Student Development .... Dr. Carol DISQUE
50 Assoc Dean Business Technologies .... Mr. Scott QUEEN
72 Assoc Dean Industrial/Graphics Tech .... Mr. Wally M. SHEARIN
49 Assoc Dean Arts & Sciences .... Ms. Catherine W. JOHNSON
69 Assoc Dean Health & Public Svcs .... Ms. Connie STACK
21 Controller .... Ms. Michelle CHEWNING
11 Director Administrative Services .... Mr. Erik CONTI
16 Director Human Resources .... Ms. Lorri ALLISON
08 Director Learning Resources Center .... Ms. Sheila STREET
26 Director Public Information/Mktg .... Mr. Edward WILLIAMS
56 Director Occupational Ext Program .... Mr. David PARKER
84 Director Enrollment Management .... Ms. Elizabeth BREHLER
37 Director Financial Aid .... Ms. Liz SOLAZZO
36 Director Counseling & Career Svcs .... Mr. Steven C. REINHARTSEN
38 Special Needs/Counseling Svcs Coord .... Ms. Monica ISBELL
35 Academic Support Specialist .... Mr. John EVANS
09 Institutional Researcher .... Ms. Teresa WALKER

*Asheville - Buncombe Technical Community College (H)

340 Victoria Road, Asheville NC 28801-4897
County: Buncombe FICE Identification: 004033
Unit ID: 197887
Telephone: (828) 254-1921 Carnegie Class: Assoc/Pub-R-L
FAX Number: (828) 251-6355 Calendar System: Semester
URL: www.abtech.edu
Established: 1959 Annual Undergrad Tuition & Fees (In-District): $1,998
Enrollment: 8,141 Coed
Affiliation or Control: State/Local IRS Status: 501(c)3
Highest Offering: Associate Degree
Program: Occupational; 2-Year Principally Bachelor's Creditable
Accreditation: SC, ACFEI, DA, DH, DMS, MAC, MLTAD, RAD, SURGT

02 President .... Dr. Hank DUNN
10 VP Business & Finance/CFO .... Mr. Scott MCKINNEY
11 Vice Pres Administrative Services .... Mr. C. Max QUEEN
13 Vice Pres Information Technology .... Mr. Brian WILLIS
05 Interim VP Instructional Services .... Ms. Melissa QUINLEY
20 Associate VP Instructional Services .... Mr. Ned H. FOWLER
32 Vice President Student Services .... Dr. Dennis KING
100 Special Asst to President .... Ms. Sara SMITH
103 Sr Exec Dir Econ Wrkfrc Dev/Cont Ed .... Ms. Shelley WHITE
04 Executive Administrative Assistant .... Ms. Martha SHANKS
49 Interim Dean Arts & Sciences .... Ms. Sue OLESIUK
30 Exec Director/College Advancement .... Ms. Sana EFIRD
50 Dean Business & Hospitality Educ .... Mr. Philip LEFTWICH
54 Dean Engineering & Applied Tech ..... Mr. Vernon D. DAUGHERTY
91 Director Info Systems Technology .... Mr. David C. MCKINNEY
38 Director Counseling .... Dr. Deborah L. HARMON
84 Dir Recruitment/Student Activities .... Ms. Michele HATHCOCK
61 Director Law Enforcement Academy .... Ms. Dianne L. DAVIS
21 Director Business Services .... Ms. Lisa EVANS
37 Director of Financial Aid .... Ms. Donna TURNER
06 Registrar .... Mr. Scott C. DOUGLAS
07 Director of Admissions .... Ms. Lisa F. BUSH
24 Director Library Services .... Ms. Carol FLEMING
12 Director Madison County Campus .... Dr. Connie S. BUCKNER
18 Director Plant Operations .... Mr. Benny R. SMITH
19 Director Security .... Ms. Kara KELLER
31 Director Community Services .... Ms. Brinda W. CALDWELL
08 Librarian .... Ms. Martha DICKENS
09 Director Research & Planning .... Mr. David B. WHITE
15 Vice President Human Resources & OD .... Ms. Kaye N. WAUGH
27 Director Communications & Marketing . Ms. Mona L. CORNWELL
28 Director of Diversity .... Vacant
40 Bookstore Manager .... Mr. Tom BENOIT
96 Coordinator of Purchasing .... Ms. Rebecca R. WATKINS
72 Coordinator Technology Services .... Mr. Cris HARSHMAN

*Beaufort County Community College (I)

Box 1069, Washington NC 27889-1069
County: Beaufort FICE Identification: 008558
Unit ID: 197966
Telephone: (252) 946-6194 Carnegie Class: Assoc/Pub-R-S
FAX Number: (252) 946-0271 Calendar System: Semester
URL: www.beaufortccc.edu
Established: 1967 Annual Undergrad Tuition & Fees (In-District): $2,192

Enrollment: 1,898 Coed
Affiliation or Control: State/Local IRS Status: 501(c)3
Highest Offering: Associate Degree
Program: Occupational; 2-Year Principally Bachelor's Creditable
Accreditation: SC, MLTAD

02	President	Dr. David MCLAWHORN
05	Dean of Instruction	Mr. Wesley BEDDARD
11	Dean of Administrative Services	Dr. Phillip PRICE
32	Dean of Student Services	Dr. Crystal ANGE
51	Dean of Continuing Education	Mr. Chet JARMAN
45	Dir of Planning/Inst Effectiveness	Mrs. Doreen RICHTER
26	Director of Public Relations	Mrs. Judy JENNETTE
55	Dir of Evening/Off Campus Svcs	Mr. Clay CARTER
76	Chairperson Allied Health	Mr. Wesley BEDDARD
49	Chairperson Arts & Sciences	Mr. Dixon BOYLES
50	Chairperson Business	Mrs. Donna DUNN
72	Chairperson Industrial Technology	Vacant
08	Dir Learning Resources Center	Mrs. Penny SERMONS
88	Network Administrator	Mr. Brown MCFADDEN
91	System Administrator	Mr. Chuck HAUSER
15	Director of Human Resources	Mrs. Pam CUMMINGS
19	Director of Campus Police	Mr. Hal SWINDELL
06	Registrar	Mrs. Camille RICHARDSON
37	Director of Financial Aid	Mr. Harold SMITH
07	Director of Admissions	Mr. Gary BURBAGE
38	Director of Counseling	Vacant
88	Director of Retention Services	Mrs. Sue BROOKSHIRE
36	Director of Career Center	Mrs. Sandy MCFADDEN
103	Dir of Business & Industry Svcs	Mr. Lentz STOWE

*Bladen Community College (A)

PO Box 266, Dublin NC 28332-0266
County: Bladen FICE Identification: 007987
Unit ID: 198011
Telephone: (910) 879-5500 Carnegie Class: Assoc/Pub-R-S
FAX Number: (910) 879-5564 Calendar System: Semester
URL: www.bladencc.edu
Established: 1967 Annual Undergrad Tuition & Fees (In-State): $2,198
Enrollment: 1,865 Coed
Affiliation or Control: State IRS Status: 501(c)3
Highest Offering: Associate Degree
Program: Occupational; 2-Year Principally Bachelor's Creditable; Technical Emphasis
Accreditation: SC

02	President	Dr. William FINDT
10	Vice President for Finance	Mr. Jay STANLEY
05	VP for Instruction & Student Svcs	Mr. Jeffrey KORNEGAY
32	Dean of Students	Ms. Marva DINKINS
08	Director Learning Resource Ctr	Ms. Sherwin RICE
55	Dean Distance & Evening Programs	Ms. Ann RUSSELL
84	Dean of Enrollment Management	Mr. Barry PRIEST
09	Dir Institutional Effect & Planning	Ms. Harriet HOBBS
18	Director of Facilities	Mr. Charles YOUNG
20	Assoc to VP Instruct & Student Svcs	Mr. Lynn KING
21	Controller	Ms. Sharon COE
37	Director of Financial Aid	Ms. Samantha BENSON
15	Human Resources Officer	Ms. Tiina MUNDY
26	Public Information Officer	Mr. Jack MCDUFFIE
30	Director of Resource Development	Mr. Stephen PRINCE

*Blue Ridge Community College (B)

180 W Campus Drive, Flat Rock NC 28731-4728
County: Henderson FICE Identification: 009684
Unit ID: 198039
Telephone: (828) 694-1700 Carnegie Class: Assoc/Pub-R-M
FAX Number: (828) 694-1690 Calendar System: Semester
URL: www.blueridge.edu
Established: 1969 Annual Undergrad Tuition & Fees (In-District): $1,860
Enrollment: 2,512 Coed
Affiliation or Control: State/Local IRS Status: 501(c)3
Highest Offering: Associate Degree
Program: Occupational; 2-Year Principally Bachelor's Creditable
Accreditation: SC, SURGT

05	VP for Instruction	Dr. Alan H. STEPHENSON
10	VP for Finance and Operations	Ms. Rhonda K. DEVAN
32	VP for Student Services	Ms. Marcia L. STONEMAN
13	VP for Technology	Mr. David N. HUTTO
51	VP for Continuing Education	Ms. Julie G. THOMPSON
30	Chief Inst Advancement Officer	Dr. Chad MERRILL
49	Dean for Arts and Sciences	Mr. David H. DAVIS
72	Dean for Applied Technology	Mr. Jim RHODES
76	Dean for Allied Health	Ms. Rita D. CONNER
97	Dean for Basic Skills	Mr. Rick MARSHALL
50	Dean for Business/Service Careers	Ms. Celeste P. OPREAN
102	Exec Dir Educational Foundation	Ms. Ann F. GREEN
45	Research Coordinator	Ms. Carol Ann LYDON
06	Registrar	Ms. Kirsten H. BUNCH
07	Director of Admissions	Ms. Marcia L. STONEMAN
08	Librarian	Ms. Susan D. WILLIAMS
21	Director Financial Services	Ms. Shannon BISHOP
37	Financial Aid Officer	Ms. Lisanne MASTERSON
38	Director for Counseling	Vacant
91	Director of Network Services	Mr. Steve YOUNG
18	Facilities Director	Mr. Peter HEMANS
26	Director of Public Relations	Ms. Lee Anna HANEY
35	Student Activities Coordinator	Ms. April KILLOUGH
84	Director Enrollment Management	Ms. Cathy STEPHENSON
96	Director of Purchasing	Ms. Carolyn ALLEY
15	Director Human Resources	Mr. Tommy OAKMAN

*Brunswick Community College (C)

PO Box 30, Supply NC 28462-0030
County: Brunswick FICE Identification: 021707
Unit ID: 198084
Telephone: (910) 755-7300 Carnegie Class: Assoc/Pub-R-S
FAX Number: (910) 754-7805 Calendar System: Semester
URL: www.brunswickcc.edu
Established: 1979 Annual Undergrad Tuition & Fees (In-State): $1,700
Enrollment: 1,540 Coed
Affiliation or Control: State IRS Status: 501(c)3
Highest Offering: Associate Degree
Program: Occupational; 2-Year Principally Bachelor's Creditable; Business Emphasis
Accreditation: SC

02	President	Dr. Susanne H. ADAMS
05	Vice Pres for Academic Services	Ms. Sharon THOMPSON
10	Vice President Budget and Finance	Dr. Benjamin A. DEBLOIS
32	VP Student Svcs/Academic Support	Dr. Edith LANG
11	Vice President Operations	Mr. Jerry L. THRIFT
09	Coordinator Inst Effectiveness	Ms. Pamela FEDERLINE
08	Director Library	Ms. Carmen BLANTON
06	Registrar	Mr. Lawrence PAKOWSKI
15	Director Human Resources	Vacant
19	Public Safety/Police Director	Mr. Lindsay WALTON
18	Physical Plant Director	Ms. Donna BAXTER
102	Executive Director Foundation	Mr. Mike CAPACCIO
26	Director of Marketing & Public Info	Vacant
37	Financial Aid/Veterans Affs Coord	Ms. Paula ALMOND
72	Dean Professional Technical Service	Ms. Gina ROBINSON
49	Dean Arts & Sciences	Ms. Jennifer WOODHEAD

*Caldwell Community College and Technical Institute (D)

2855 Hickory Boulevard, Hudson NC 28638-1399
County: Caldwell FICE Identification: 004835
Unit ID: 198118
Telephone: (828) 726-2200 Carnegie Class: Assoc/Pub-R-M
FAX Number: (828) 726-2216 Calendar System: Semester
URL: www.cccti.edu
Established: 1964 Annual Undergrad Tuition & Fees (In-District): $1,872
Enrollment: 4,965 Coed
Affiliation or Control: State/Local IRS Status: 501(c)3
Highest Offering: Associate Degree
Program: Occupational; 2-Year Principally Bachelor's Creditable
Accreditation: SC, DMS, NMT, PTAA, RAD

02	President	Dr. Kenneth A. BOHAM
03	Executive Vice President	Dr. David R. SHOCKLEY
18	Vice President Facility Services	Mr. Donnie BASSINGER
32	Vice President Student Services	Mr. Mark POARCH
51	VP Adult/Corp/Continuing Education	Mrs. Elaine LOCKHART
12	Executive Director Watauga Campus	Dr. Sandra PHILLIPS
84	Dir Enrollment Mgmt Services	Ms. Dena HOLMAN
08	Director Learning Resources Center	Mrs. Marischa B. COOKE
37	Director Financial Aid	Mrs. Eva HARMON
36	Dir Career Planning/Job Placement	Mr. Rick HEW
07	Director Admissions and Records	Ms. Dena HOLMAN
15	Director Human Resources	Mrs. Kathy SEITZ
26	Director Marketing & Communications	Mrs. Sherry WILSON
10	Controller	Mr. Scott ROGERS
09	Director Inst Effectiveness/Rsrch	Mrs. Carolyn EVERT
26	Public Relations Officer	Ms. Marla CHRISTIE
102	Director Foundation Office	Mrs. Marla CHRISTIE
28	Director of Diversity	Mrs. Alice LENTZ
35	Director Student Affairs	Mr. Mark POARCH
38	Director Student Counseling	Mr. Shannon BROWN
96	Director of Purchasing	Mrs. Pam ROUSE
40	Manager Bookstore	Mr. Michael PHILYAW

*Cape Fear Community College (E)

411 N Front Street, Wilmington NC 28401-3993
County: New Hanover FICE Identification: 005320
Unit ID: 198154
Telephone: (910) 362-7000 Carnegie Class: Assoc/Pub-R-L
FAX Number: (910) 763-2279 Calendar System: Semester
URL: www.cfcc.edu
Established: 1958 Annual Undergrad Tuition & Fees (In-District): $1,945
Enrollment: 9,065 Coed
Affiliation or Control: State/Local IRS Status: 501(c)3
Highest Offering: Associate Degree
Program: Occupational; 2-Year Principally Bachelor's Creditable
Accreditation: SC, ADNUR, DA, DH, DMS, OTA, RAD, SURGT

02	President	Dr. Eric B. MCKEITHAN
05	Vice President of Instruction	Dr. Amanda LEE
10	Vice President of Business Services	Ms. Camellia N. RICE
32	Vice President of Student Development	Ms. Carol J. CULLUM
09	Vice Pres of Inst Effectiveness	Ms. Kim LAWING
18	Director of Institutional Services	Mr. Kenneth D. PEARCE
06	Registrar	Mr. Phil FARINHOLT
102	Exec Director of the CFCC Found Inc	Ms. Margaret ROBISON
84	Director of Enrollment Management	Ms. Linda KASYAN
08	Director Learning Resources Center	Ms. Catherine LEE
37	Director of Financial Aid	Ms. Jo-Ann CRAIG
36	Director of Career & Testing	Mr. Patrick PITTMAN
26	Public Information Officer	Mr. David M. HARDIN
13	Director Info Technology Services	Mr. David CHAPPELL
15	Director Personnel	Mr. John UPTON
41	Dir Student Activities/Athletics	Mr. Robert MCGEE
96	Director of Purchasing & Inventory	Mr. Brooke MESEROLE
38	Director Student Counseling	Ms. Jacqueline FOSTER
21	Assoc Business Officer/Controller	Mr. Ravi VELAUTHAPILLAI
28	Director of Diversity	Mr. David HARDIN
07	Director of Admissions	Ms. Linda KASYAN
29	Director Alumni Relations	Ms. Dana MCKOY
30	Chief Development	Ms. Margaret ROBISON
51	Dean of Continuing Education	Mr. Clarence L. SMITH
75	Dean Vocational/Technical Education	Mr. Robert J. PHILPOTT
49	Dean Arts & Sciences	Ms. Orangel J. DANIELS
105	Webmaster	Ms. Christina HEIKKILA

*Carteret Community College (F)

3505 Arendell Street, Morehead City NC 28557-2989
County: Carteret FICE Identification: 008081
Unit ID: 198206
Telephone: (252) 222-6000 Carnegie Class: Assoc/Pub-R-S
FAX Number: (252) 222-2514 Calendar System: Semester
URL: www.carteret.edu
Established: 1963 Annual Undergrad Tuition & Fees (In-District): $2,191
Enrollment: 1,917 Coed
Affiliation or Control: State/Local IRS Status: 501(c)3
Highest Offering: Associate Degree
Program: Occupational; 2-Year Principally Bachelor's Creditable
Accreditation: SC, ADNUR, MAC, RAD

02	President	Dr. Kerry L. YOUNGBLOOD
05	VP for Instruction/Student Support	Dr. Fran EMORY
11	Vice Pres Administrative Services	Ms. Janet N. SPRIGGS
51	Vice Pres Corporate & Community	Mr. Perry L. HARKER
30	VP College Advance/Ex Dir CCC Found	Vacant
04	Executive Assistant to President	Ms. Brenda REASH
08	Director LRC	Ms. Elizabeth BAKER
32	Senior Director Student Services	Ms. Robie MCFARLAND
55	Director of Evening Programs	Vacant
13	Director Information Technology	Mr. Ken E. MARTIN
15	Director of Human Resources	Ms. Barbara I. COOPER
76	Div Director Health Sciences	Ms. Laurie A. FRESHWATER
75	Div Director Service Technology	Ms. Evanglene REELS
50	Div Director Business Technologies	Ms. Mary G. WALTON
61	Div Director Legal & Community Svcs	Ms. Susan H. MCINTYRE
37	Financial Aid Officer	Ms. Brenda J. LONG
06	Registrar	Ms. Tammi COBLE
07	Admissions Officer	Mr. Joseph A. CROOM
09	Dir of Institutional Effectiveness	Ms. Jennifer A. ULZ
18	Dir Operations/Auxiliary Services	Ms. Pam OLSSON
26	Director of Public Affairs	Mr. Morgan SMITH
57	Director Arts & Sciences	Ms. Sharon B. MILLS
40	Bookstore Manager	Vacant
96	Purchasing Officer	Ms. Donna L. CUMBIE
106	Director Distance Learning	Mr. Patrick J. KEOUGH

*Catawba Valley Community College (G)

2550 Highway 70, SE, Hickory NC 28602-9699
County: Catawba FICE Identification: 005318
Unit ID: 198233
Telephone: (828) 327-7000 Carnegie Class: Assoc/Pub-R-M
FAX Number: (828) 327-7276 Calendar System: Semester
URL: www.cvcc.edu
Established: 1960 Annual Undergrad Tuition & Fees (In-District): $1,560
Enrollment: 5,545 Coed
Affiliation or Control: State/Local IRS Status: 501(c)3
Highest Offering: Associate Degree
Program: Occupational; 2-Year Principally Bachelor's Creditable
Accreditation: SC, ADNUR, DH, EEG, EMT, POLYT, RAD, SURGT

02	President	Dr. Garrett D. HINSHAW
05	Vice President of Instruction	Dr. Keith MACKIE
11	Vice President of Administration	Vacant
10	Vice President of Fiscal Affairs	Mr. Wes BUNCH
103	Director of Economic Workforce Dev	Mr. Ron VALENTINI
32	Vice Pres Student Svcs/Technology	Mr. Bill DULIN
35	CEO of of Student Services	Mrs. Cindy COULTER
15	Director Human Resources	Mr. Mike KIDD
06	Director of Admissions/Records	Ms. Paula HOLLAR
21	Controller	Ms. Robyn F. CHAPMAN
37	Director Scholarships/Financial Aid	Ms. Debbie BARGER
09	Ofc Accountability/Efficienc/Effect	Mr. Kevin ROUSE
88	Director Industrial Training	Ms. Crystal GLENN
88	Director Small Business Center	Ms. Bonnie SWEETING
50	Director Business/Technolgy Ext	Ms. Susan KILLIAN
88	Director Hosiery Technology Center	Mr. Daniel C. ST. LOUIS
13	Director Information Technologies	Mr. Ken ELLIOTT
19	Director Campus Safety/Security	Mr. Skip ISENHOUR
27	Director Community Relations	Ms. Mary K. MILLER
31	Director Community Education	Ms. Louise GARRISON
36	Counselor/Job Placement Svcs Coord	Ms. Kathy CAREY
16	Coordinator Health/Human Services	Ms. Donna TRADO

*Central Carolina Community College (H)

1105 Kelly Drive, Sanford NC 27330-9000
County: Lee FICE Identification: 005449
Unit ID: 198251

Telephone: (919) 775-5401 Carnegie Class: Assoc/Pub-R-M
FAX Number: (919) 718-7380 Calendar System: Semester
URL: www.cccc.edu
Established: 1958 Annual Undergrad Tuition & Fees (In-District): $2,216
Enrollment: 5,267 Coed
Affiliation or Control: State/Local IRS Status: 501(c)3
Highest Offering: Associate Degree
Program: Occupational; 2-Year Principally Bachelor's Creditable
Accreditation: SC, DA, DH, MAC, POLYT

02 President .... Dr. T. Eston MARCHANT
05 Vice Pres/Chief Academic Officer .... Dr. Lisa M. CHAPMAN
11 Vice Pres for Administrative Svcs .... Mr. Wayne G. ROBINSON
32 Vice President Student Services .... Mr. Ken R. HOYLE
51 VP Economic & Community Development .... MS. Stelfanie P. WILLIAMS
30 VP of Institutional Advancement .... Mrs. Celia HURLEY
12 Provost Chatham Campus .... Dr. Karen H. ALLEN
12 Provost Harnett Campus .... Mr. William R. TYSON
08 Director of Library Services .... Ms. Tara GUTHRIE
15 Director Human Resources .... Ms. Stacey CARTER-COLEY
102 Foundation Executive Director .... Ms. Diane F. GLOVER
06 Registrar .... Ms. Michelle WHEELER
26 Director Marketing & Public Affairs .... Ms. Marcie DISHMAN
18 Physical Plant Manager .... Mr. Ronnie MEASAMER
37 Director Student Financial Aid .... Mr. David BOWMAN
96 Director of Purchasing .... Mrs. Starlene P. JACKSON
75 Dean Vocational/Technical Programs .... Dr. Stephan ATHANS
50 Dean Business/Media Tech/Publ Srvs .... Mrs. Joni P. PAVLIK
88 Dean College Transfer/Public Svc .... Vacant

*Central Piedmont Community College (A)

PO Box 35009, Charlotte NC 28235-5009
County: Mecklenburg FICE Identification: 002915
Unit ID: 198260
Telephone: (704) 330-2722 Carnegie Class: Assoc/Pub-U-MC
FAX Number: (704) 330-5045 Calendar System: Semester
URL: www.cpcc.edu
Established: 1963 Annual Undergrad Tuition & Fees (In-District): $2,264
Enrollment: 19,921 Coed
Affiliation or Control: State/Local IRS Status: 501(c)3
Highest Offering: Associate Degree
Program: Occupational; 2-Year Principally Bachelor's Creditable
Accreditation: SC, ACFEI, CVT, CYTO, DA, DH, ENGT, MAC, MLTAD, PTAA, SURGT

02 President .... Dr. P. Anthony ZEISS
03 Executive Vice President .... Dr. Kathy DRUMM
05 Vice President for Learning .... Mr. Richard ZOLLINGER
84 VP Enrollment & Student Services .... Dr. Marcia CONSTON
10 VP Finance/Administrative Services .... Mr. Michael MOSS
04 Exec Assistant to the President .... Ms. Susan OLESON-BRIGGS
30 Assoc VP for Inst Advancement .... Dr. Kevin MCCARTHY
13 Assoc VP for Technology .... Mr. David KIM
11 Assoc VP Financial Svcs .... Ms. Diep TONG
20 Assoc VP Learning .... Dr. Deborah BOUTON
32 Assoc VP Student Services .... Dr. Melvin L. GAY
18 Assoc VP Facilities & Construction .... Mr. Rich ROSENTHAL
09 Assoc VP Institutional Research .... Dr. Terri MANNING
88 Assoc VP Compliance and Audit .... Dr. Brenda LEONARD
15 Assoc VP of Human Resources .... Mr. Paul SANTOS
25 Assoc VP Government Rels & Grants .... Mr. Michael HORN
26 PIO & Asst to Pres Cmty Rels/Mktg .... Mr. Jeffrey LOWRANCE
12 Dean Levine Campus .... Dr. Edith MCELROY
12 Dean Merancas Campus .... Ms. Beverly DICKSON
12 Dean Central Campus .... Mr. Paul KOEHNKE
12 Interim Dean Cato Campus .... Ms. Janet MALKEMES
12 Dean Harris Campus .... Ms. Mary VICKERS-KOCH
12 Dean Harper Campus .... Mr. Jay POTTER
54 Dean STEM .... Mr. Chad RAY
88 Dean Retention Services .... Dr. Clint MCELROY
35 Dean Student Life/Service Learning .... Mr. Mark HELMS
38 Dean Student Success Services .... Ms. Rita DAWKINS
84 Dean Enrollment Management .... Mr. Daniel MCEACHERN
08 Dean Libraries .... Ms. Gloria KELLEY
88 Dean Community Development .... Ms. Kathi POLIS
07 Dean Enrollment Services .... Ms. April JONES

*Cleveland Community College (B)

137 S Post Road, Shelby NC 28152-6296
County: Cleveland FICE Identification: 008082
Unit ID: 198321
Telephone: (704) 484-4000 Carnegie Class: Assoc/Pub-R-M
FAX Number: (704) 484-4036 Calendar System: Semester
URL: www.clevelandcommunitycollege.edu
Established: 1965 Annual Undergrad Tuition & Fees (In-District): $1,661
Enrollment: 4,011 Coed
Affiliation or Control: State/Local IRS Status: 501(c)3
Highest Offering: Associate Degree
Program: Occupational; 2-Year Principally Bachelor's Creditable
Accreditation: SC, RAD

02 President .... Dr. L. Steve THORNBURG
05 Vice President of Academic Programs .... Dr. Becky SAIN
32 Vice President of Student Services .... Mr. Andy GARDNER
10 Senior VP Finance/Admin Svcs .... Mr. Tommy GREENE
51 Vice Pres of Continuing Education .... Dr. Barbara GREENE
26 Senior Dean Cmty Relations/Devel .... Mr. Eddie HOLBROOK
84 Dean of Enrollment Management .... Vacant
20 Executive VP of Instr & Student Dev .... Mrs. Shannon KENNEDY
102 Executive Director Foundation .... Mr. U. L. PATTERSON, III
09 Dir Planning/Inst Effectiveness .... Mrs. Laura BOWEN
40 Bookstore Manager .... Vacant
06 Registrar .... Vacant
07 Director of Enrollment Services .... Ms. Nedra MADDOX
37 Financial Aid Coordinator .... Vacant
08 Dean of Learning Resources .... Mrs. Barbara MCKIBBIN
96 Director of Purchasing .... Mrs. Kathy EVERETT
18 Director of Physical Plant .... Mr. Mark FOX
19 Director of Campus Security .... Mr. Bill NEAL
15 Human Resources & Safety Manager .... Vacant
24 Coord of Audiovisual Services .... Mr. Danny MORTON
14 Systems Administrator .... Mr. Mike FALLS
90 Computer Network Administrator .... Mr. Robin DYER
49 Dean Arts/Sciences/Public Service .... Mrs. Barbara ROMICH
50 Dean Business Technologies .... Dr. John LATTIMORE
75 Dean Vocation Engineering Tech .... Mr. Michael MCSWAIN
88 Dean Basic Skills .... Dr. Chris NANNEY

*Coastal Carolina Community College (C)

444 Western Boulevard, Jacksonville NC 28546-6816
County: Onslow FICE Identification: 005316
Unit ID: 198330
Telephone: (910) 455-1221 Carnegie Class: Assoc/Pub-R-M
FAX Number: (910) 455-7027 Calendar System: Semester
URL: www.coastalcarolina.edu
Established: 1963 Annual Undergrad Tuition & Fees (In-District): $1,838
Enrollment: 5,103 Coed
Affiliation or Control: State/Local IRS Status: 501(c)3
Highest Offering: Associate Degree
Program: Occupational; 2-Year Principally Bachelor's Creditable
Accreditation: SC, DA, DH, MLTAD, SURGT

02 President .... Dr. Ronald K. LINGLE
03 Executive Vice President .... Mr. David L. HEATHERLY
05 VP Instruction/Info Resources .... Mr. Dewey H. LEWIS
51 Vice Pres for Inst Effect & Cont Ed .... Ms. Sharon R. MCGINNIS
32 Division Chair for Student Services .... Dr. Donald R. HERRING
16 Personnel Officer .... Ms. Renita G. LOGAN
26 Pub Info Ofcr/Ex Dir Col Foundation .... Ms. Colette B. TEACHEY
06 Dir Admin/Data Mgmt Svc/Registrar .... Ms. Sue FLAHARTY
10 Dir Physical Plant & Aux Services .... Ms. Carol PHILLIPS
37 Director for Financial Aid Services .... Ms. Tammy LYON
88 Director for Veterans Services .... Mr. Christopher P. SABIN
88 Director Economic Development .... Ms. Anne C. SHAW

*College of the Albemarle (D)

1208 North Road Street, Elizabeth City NC 27906-2327
County: Pasquotank FICE Identification: 002917
Unit ID: 197814
Telephone: (252) 335-0821 Carnegie Class: Assoc/Pub-R-M
FAX Number: (252) 335-2011 Calendar System: Semester
URL: www.albemarle.edu
Established: 1960 Annual Undergrad Tuition & Fees (In-District): $1,877
Enrollment: 2,981 Coed
Affiliation or Control: State/Local IRS Status: 501(c)3
Highest Offering: Associate Degree
Program: Occupational; 2-Year Principally Bachelor's Creditable
Accreditation: SC, ADNUR, MAC, MLTAD, SURGT

02 President .... Dr. Kandi W. DEITEMEYER
10 VP Business & Admin Services .... Mr. James TURDICI
05 Vice President for Learning .... Ms. Althea A. RIDDICK
32 VP for Student Suc & Enr Mgnt .... Mr. Steven WOODBURN
51 VP Workforce Dev & Cont Edu .... Ms. Suzanne ROHRBAUGH
12 Dean Dare County Campus .... Mr. Joseph T. TURNER
35 Assistant Dean Student Services .... Vacant
26 Director Marketing & Communications .... Mrs. Lisa A. JOHNSON
07 Director Admissions & Testing .... Mr. Kenneth L. KRENTZ
37 Director Scholarship/Student Aid .... Ms. Angela R. GODFREY-DAWSON
88 Director Student Activities .... Mrs. Maenecia COLE
06 Registrar .... Ms. Andrea DANCE
88 Director Small Business Center .... Ms. Ginger H. O'NEAL
78 Director Coop Educ/Job Placement .... Mr. Charles K. CARTER
04 Exec Assistant to the President .... Ms. Sandra W. STRICKLAND
08 Director Learning Resources Center .... Mr. Robert B. SCHENCK
12 Dean Edenton-Chowan Campus .... Ms. B. Lynn HURDLE-WINSLOW
13 Director Mgmt Information Services .... Mr. Wayman WHITE
15 Director Human Resources .... Ms. Wendy W. BRICKHOUSE
18 Director Physical Facilities .... Mr. Richard R. SEYMOUR
21 Controller .... Ms. Theresa BERENS
40 Director Admin Support Services .... Ms. Deborah R. HOLLAND
08 Dir Learning Resources Ctr-Dare .... Mr. George STRAWLEY
36 Director Counseling & Career Devel .... Mr. John M. WELLS
09 Director of Inst Effectiveness .... Dr. Eric LOVIK
88 Coord Prison Education Programs .... Mr. Cecil PHILPOTT
24 Coord Learning Lab & Learning Ctr .... Dr. Ann PARKINSON
88 Director Secondary Education .... Ms. Rita O. JENNINGS
49 Division Chair Arts and Sciences .... Mr. Bobby ADAMS
50 Dept Chair Business and Office Tech .... Ms. Karen ALEXANDER
76 Divison Chair Health & Public Svc .... Mr. Joseph DESTEFANO
83 Department Chair Social Sciences .... Mr. Rodger ROSSMAN
76 Department Chair Health Sciences .... Ms. Martha P. JOHNSON
60 Dept Chair Language & Literature .... Mr. Dean ROUGHTON
75 Dept Chair Const & Industrial Tech .... Mr. Stanley NIXON
88 Interim Director Gateway to College .... Mr. Kelvin BROWN
88 Director Business & Economic Devel .... Ms. Amy GIBBONS
77 Dept Chair Computer Systems & Elect .... Mrs. Jane ROSSMAN
103 Dir Workforce & Cont Educ .... Ms. Lynda HESTER
57 Department Chair Fine Arts .... Mrs. Patricia STERRITT
50 Div Chair Business/Engr/Ind Tech .... Vacant
88 Dept Chair Developmental Studies .... Ms. Ruth WARREN
88 Department Chair Public Services .... Mrs. Robin O. ZINSMEISTER
88 Div Chair Foundational Studies .... Ms. Michelle WATERS
19 Director Public Safety & Preparedns .... Vacant
25 Director of Institutional Grants .... Vacant
88 Dir Basic Skills/Workforce Reading .... Mr. Timothy SWEENEY

*Craven Community College (E)

800 College Court, New Bern NC 28562-4984
County: Craven FICE Identification: 006799
Unit ID: 198367
Telephone: (252) 638-7200 Carnegie Class: Assoc/Pub-R-M
FAX Number: (252) 638-4232 Calendar System: Semester
URL: www.cravencc.edu
Established: 1965 Annual Undergrad Tuition & Fees (In-District): $1,122
Enrollment: 3,681 Coed
Affiliation or Control: State/Local IRS Status: 501(c)3
Highest Offering: Associate Degree
Program: Occupational; 2-Year Principally Bachelor's Creditable
Accreditation: SC, MAC, @PTAA

02 President .... Dr. Catherine CHEW
05 Exec Vice Pres Academic Affairs .... Dr. Maria FRASER-MOLINA
10 Vice Pres for Financial/Admin Svcs .... Ms. Kary PORTER
32 Vice Pres for Student Services .... Mr. Daryl MINUS
51 Dean of Continuing Education .... Mr. Layne HARPINE
12 Dean of the Havelock Campus .... Mr. Gerald M. BOUCHER, JR.
84 Dean of Enrollment/Registrar .... Mr. John A. FONVILLE
49 Dean of Liberal Arts .... Ms. Maria PHARR
76 Dean Health Programs .... Ms. Kathleen GALLMAN
36 Dean of Career Programs .... Mr. Mark FAITHFUL
30 Exec Director Development/Outreach .... Ms. Suzanne GIFFORD
62 Director of Library Services .... Mrs. Catherine C. CAMPBELL
13 Chief Information/Distance Ed Ofcr .... Dr. Paul (P.D.) SCOTT
21 Controller .... Mrs. Cynthia PATTERSON
15 Director of Human Resources .... Mrs. Vickie MOSELEY-JONES
07 Int Director Admissions .... Mr. Mit MCLEAN
37 Director of Financial Aid .... Ms. Kathryn M. BANKS
45 Director of Research & Planning .... Mrs. Jill FEGLEY
18 Director Facilities/Security .... Mr. Larry HENDERSON
91 Director Computer Services .... Ms. Deborah JOYNER
88 Director Customized Training .... Mr. David C. BAUER, JR.
19 Asst Dir Security/Night Operations .... Mr. H. Steven CARTER
40 Bookstore Manager .... Mr. Joseph WASHBURN
96 Purchasing Agent .... Mr. Hiram Todd MURPHREY
26 Public Information Officer .... Mr. Sandy W. WALL
90 Lead Computer Support Specialist .... Mr. Otis J. SWINT, JR.

*Davidson County Community College (F)

PO Box 1287, Lexington NC 27293-1287
County: Davidson FICE Identification: 002919
Unit ID: 198376
Telephone: (336) 249-8186 Carnegie Class: Assoc/Pub-S-SC
FAX Number: (336) 249-0379 Calendar System: Semester
URL: www.davidsonccc.edu
Established: 1958 Annual Undergrad Tuition & Fees (In-District): $1,725
Enrollment: 4,431 Coed
Affiliation or Control: State/Local IRS Status: 501(c)3
Highest Offering: Associate Degree
Program: Occupational; 2-Year Principally Bachelor's Creditable
Accreditation: SC, ADNUR, HT, MAC, MLTAD

02 President .... Dr. Mary E. RITTLING
05 VP Academic Programs & Services .... Ms. Jeannine WOODY
32 VP Student Affairs .... Ms. Kim W. SEPICH
10 VP Financial/Administrative Svcs .... Mr. Rusty HUNT
30 Exec Dir Ext Affairs & Foundation .... Ms. Jenny M. VARNER
09 Exec Dir Rsrch Planning Innovation .... Ms. Susan BURLESON
51 Dean Cmty Educ/Wrkfrce Dev/Entship .... Mr. Jim DONNELLY
76 Dean Health/Wellness/Pub Safety .... Vacant
49 Dean Arts/Sciences/Education .... Dr. Mark BRANSON
88 Dean Foundational Stdnt/Acad Supp .... Ms. Christy FORREST
50 Dean Business Engineering Technical .... Mr. Randy LEDFORD
12 Dean Davie Campus .... Ms. Teresa KINES
35 Dean Student Support & Campus Life .... Mr. Stephen CAMP
21 Dean Financial/Admin Svcs .... Ms. Laura L. YARBROUGH
06 Dir Student Records/Registration .... Ms. Sabra L. RICE
07 Director Admissions & Financial Aid .... Ms. Lori BLEVINS
36 Director Career Development .... Mr. Charles MAYER
18 Director Physical Plant Services .... Mr. Skip EDWARDS

*Durham Technical Community College (G)

1637 Lawson Street, Durham NC 27703-5023
County: Durham FICE Identification: 005448
Unit ID: 198455
Telephone: (919) 536-7200 Carnegie Class: Assoc/Pub-U-SC
FAX Number: (919) 686-3601 Calendar System: Semester
URL: www.durhamtech.edu
Established: 1961 Annual Undergrad Tuition & Fees (In-District): $1,664
Enrollment: 5,642 Coed
Affiliation or Control: State/Local IRS Status: 501(c)3

Highest Offering: Associate Degree
Program: Occupational; 2-Year Principally Bachelor's Creditable
Accreditation: SC, ADNUR, DT, MAC, OPD, OTA, PNUR, SURGT

02 President .... Dr. William G. INGRAM
03 Senior Vice President .... Ms. Wanda S. MAGGART
05 VP Student Learning/Devel & Support .... Dr. Valarie J. EVANS
10 VP Finance and Administration .... Mr. Robert KEENEY
51 VP Corporate & Continuing Education .... Ms. Jamie GLASS
88 Exec Dir Center for Global Learner .... Ms. Constanza GOMEZ-JOINS
04 Assistant to the President .... Vacant
04 Executive Secy to the President .... Ms. Angela G. PERRY
09 Director Institutional Research .... Dr. Teri L. KAASA
07 Director of Admissions .... Ms. Iesha M. CLEVELAND
30 Director Resource Development .... Ms. Gayle SIMS
14 Executive Director Info Tech Svcs .... Ms. Beverly S. MCCOMB
15 Director Human Resources .... Ms. Patricia A. HEMINGWAY SMITH
08 Director Library & Media Services .... Ms. Irene H. LAUBE
55 Coordinator Evening College .... Mr. Felix M. DRYE
18 Director Facility Services .... Mr. Richard A. MCKOWN
37 Director Financial Aid .... Mr. Everett M. JETER
96 Director Auxiliary Services .... Ms. Yolanda V. MOORE-JONES
20 Exec Dean Student Learning & Assess .... Dr. Peter W. WOOLDRIDGE
49 Dean Arts & Sciences .... Dr. Thomas E. GOULD
76 Dean Health Technologies .... Ms. Melissa OAKLEY OCKERT
50 Assoc Dean/Business & Public Svc .... Mr. Wayne E. DURKEE
38 Executive Dean Student Development ...... Mr. D. Thomas JAYNES
75 Dean Career and Technical Programs ...... Ms. Pamela G. SENEGAL
77 Assoc Dean Info Systems Technology .... Ms. Charlene C. WEST
06 Dean Student Services .... Vacant
19 Director Campus Police & Safety .... Ms. Sarah L. MINNIS

*Edgecombe Community College (A)

2009 W Wilson Street, Tarboro NC 27886-9399
County: Edgecombe FICE Identification: 008855
Unit ID: 198491
Telephone: (252) 823-5166 Carnegie Class: Assoc/Pub-R-M
FAX Number: (252) 823-6817 Calendar System: Semester
URL: www.edgecombe.edu
Established: 1967 Annual Undergrad Tuition & Fees (In-District): $2,128
Enrollment: 3,661 Coed
Affiliation or Control: State/Local IRS Status: 501(c)3
Highest Offering: Associate Degree
Program: Occupational; 2-Year Principally Bachelor's Creditable
Accreditation: SC, MAC, RAD, SURGT

02 President .... Dr. Deborah L. LAMM
05 Vice President of Instruction .... Dr. Kristi L. SNUGGS
11 Vice Pres Administrative Services .... Mr. Charlie R. HARRELL
32 Vice President Student Services .... Mr. Michael J. JORDAN
20 Asc VP Instruct/Curriculum/Cont Ed .... Mr. Lynn CALE
51 Dean Continuing Education .... Ms. Helen CLARK
84 Dean Enrollment Management .... Ms. Ginny MCLENDON
45 Director of Inst Effectiveness .... Ms. Sheila HOSKINS
26 Director of Public Information .... Ms. Mary T. BASS
08 Director of Library Services .... Ms. Rejeanor SCOTT
06 Registrar .... Ms. Cathy P. DUPREE
15 Director Personnel Services .... Ms. Janice TOLSON
18 Chief Facilities/Physical Plant .... Mr. Donald R. CAUDLE
37 Director Student Financial Aid .... Mr. Henry ANDERSON

*Fayetteville Technical Community College (B)

PO Box 35236, 2201 Hull Road,
Fayetteville NC 28303-0236
County: Cumberland FICE Identification: 007640
Unit ID: 198534
Telephone: (910) 678-8400 Carnegie Class: Assoc/Pub-R-L
FAX Number: (910) 678-8269 Calendar System: Semester
URL: www.faytechcc.edu
Established: 1961 Annual Undergrad Tuition & Fees (In-State): $1,890
Enrollment: 10,705 Coed
Affiliation or Control: State IRS Status: 501(c)3
Highest Offering: Associate Degree
Program: Occupational; 2-Year Principally Bachelor's Creditable
Accreditation: SC, ADNUR, DA, DH, FUSER, PTAA, RAD, SURGT

02 President .... Dr. Larry KEEN
11 Vice Pres for Administrative Svcs .. Mr. Joseph W. LEVISTER, JR.
05 Vice Pres for Academic/Student Svcs .... Dr. Barbara TANSEY
15 VP Human Res/Inst Effect/Assessment .... Mr. Carl MITCHELL
10 Vice Pres for Business and Finance .... Mrs. Betty J. SMITH
30 Vice Pres Institutional Advancement .... Mr. Brent MICHAELS
72 Vice Pres Learning Technologies .... Mr. Bob J. ERVIN
51 Assoc Vice Pres for Continuing Educ .... Dr. Joe W. MULLIS
32 Assoc Vice Pres Student Services .... Vacant
56 Assoc Vice Pres Off-Campus Programs .... Mr. Phillip JACKSON
84 Dean of Enrollment Management .... Mr. Harper SHACKELFORD
06 Registrar .... Ms. Melissa A. JONES
21 Controller .... Mrs. Robin DEAVER
07 Director of Admissions .... Vacant
13 Director Management Information Svc .... Mr. Roderick BROWER
38 Director of Counseling Services ..... Ms. DeSandra WASHINGTON
37 Int Financial Aid Director .... Ms. Christine PORCHIA
18 Director of Facility Services .... Mr. Sanford CAIN
96 Purchasing Agent .... Mr. Dustin TAYLOR
50 Dean of Business Programs .... Mr. William GRIFFIN
49 Dean College Transfer/Gen Educ Pgms .... Mr. Ray WALTERS
76 Dean of Health Programs .... Ms. Mary JOHNSON
54 Dean Engr/Pub Svs/Applied Tech Pgms .... Vacant

*Forsyth Technical Community College (C)

2100 Silas Creek Parkway,
Winston-Salem NC 27103-5197
County: Forsyth FICE Identification: 005317
Unit ID: 198552
Telephone: (336) 723-0371 Carnegie Class: Assoc/Pub-U-SC
FAX Number: (336) 761-2399 Calendar System: Semester
URL: www.forsythtech.edu
Established: 1960 Annual Undergrad Tuition & Fees (In-State): $1,885
Enrollment: 9,147 Coed
Affiliation or Control: State IRS Status: 501(c)3
Highest Offering: Associate Degree
Program: Occupational; 2-Year Principally Bachelor's Creditable
Accreditation: SC, DA, DH, DMS, ENGT, MAC, NMT, RAD, RTT

02 President .... Dr. Gary M. GREEN
05 Vice Pres Instructional Services .... Dr. Conley F. WINEBARGER
13 Vice Pres of Planning & Info Svcs .... Ms. Rachel M. DESMARAIS
32 Vice President Student Services .... Ms. Jewel B. CHERRY
30 VP Inst Advancement/Exec Dir Found .... Dr. Sharon B. COVITZ
10 Vice President Business Services .... Ms. Wendy R. EMERSON
103 Vice Pres Economic & Workforce Dev .... Vacant
04 Exec Assistant to the President .... Ms. Sherri W. BOWEN
50 Dean Business Info Tech Div .... Mr. G. Bernard YEVIN
79 Dean of Humanities/Social Sci Div .... Ms. Yolanda WILSON
81 Dean Math/Science & Technologies .... Mr. Michael V. AYERS
54 Dean of Engineering Tech Div .... Mr. Leonard R. KISER
17 Dean of Health Tech Div .... Ms. Jan G. OVERMAN
31 Dean Community/Economic Development .... Ms. Sharon D. ANDERSON
08 Dean Learning Resources .... Mr. J. Randel CANDELARIA
88 Dean Adult Literacy .... Mr. Michael E. HARRIS
66 Director Nursing .... Ms. Bonnie G. POPE
76 Director Imaging .... Ms. Deborah D. TAYLOR
76 Director Health Services .... Ms. Jean E. MIDDLESWARTH
84 Dean Enrollment & Student Svcs .... Vacant
21 Dean Financial Services .... Ms. Melanie NUCKOLS
38 Dir Student Success Ctr/Counseling .... Mr. Joe E. MCINTOSH
15 Director Human Resources .... Mr. Gregory M. CHASE
09 Director Institutional Effectivenes .... Ms. Dana DALTON
14 Director Information Systems .... Mr. Randall A. ROBERTSON
88 Dir Recruiting/Student Support Svcs .... Mr. Edwin B. WADDELL
37 Director Student Financial Services .... Mr. Ricky C. HODGES
06 Director Records/Registrar .... Ms. Gwen WHITAKER
07 Director of Admissions .... Ms. Jean M. GROOME
18 Director Physical Plant Services .... Mr. Scot R. QUESENBERRY
19 Director Campus Police .... Mr. Renarde D. EARL
88 Director Small Business Center .... Vacant
35 Director Student Activities .... Ms. Beverly N. LEWIS
96 Director Purchasing/Equipment .... Mr. Philip L. MCCLUNG
40 Director Auxiliary Svcs/Bookstore .... Mr. Brian A. HICKS
12 Director Grady Swisher Center .... Dr. B. J. SINEATH
12 Director Mazie Woodruff Center .... Ms. Verdel I. HAYES
12 Director Northwest Forsyth Center .... Ms. Kristie F. BAITY
12 Director Stokes County Operations .... Ms. Ann B. WATTS

*Gaston College (D)

201 Highway 321 S, Dallas NC 28034-1499
County: Gaston FICE Identification: 002973
Unit ID: 198570
Telephone: (704) 922-6200 Carnegie Class: Assoc/Pub-S-SC
FAX Number: (704) 922-2323 Calendar System: Semester
URL: www.gaston.edu
Established: 1964 Annual Undergrad Tuition & Fees (In-District): $2,480
Enrollment: 6,151 Coed
Affiliation or Control: State/Local IRS Status: 501(c)3
Highest Offering: Associate Degree
Program: Occupational; 2-Year Principally Bachelor's Creditable
Accreditation: SC, ACBSP, DIETT, ENGT, MAC

02 President .... Dr. Patricia A. SKINNER
10 Vice Pres Finance/Operations & Fac .... Vacant
05 Vice President of Academic Affairs .... Dr. Don AMMONS
20 Associate VP Academic Affairs .... Dr. Dewey DELLINGER
32 Vice President for Student Services .... Dr. Silvia Patricia RIOS-HUSAIN
35 Associate VP for Student Affairs .... Ms. Audrey SHERRILL
103 Vice Pres of Economic/Workforce Dev .... Dr. Linda L. GREER
04 Exec Assistant to the President .... Ms. Sylvia DIXON
09 Director Institutional Rsrch/Plng .... Dr. Rex J. CLAY
08 Dir Learning Resource Ctr/Library .... Dr. Harry COOKE
13 Chief Technology Services Officer .... Ms. Savonne MCNEILL
38 Director Counsel/Career Development .... Vacant
84 Director Enrollment Mgmt/Admission .... Dr. Terry BRASIER
06 Director of Registration/Records .... Ms. Alisa ROY
37 Director of Financial Aid .... Ms. Peggy OATES
19 Chief of Campus Police .... Mr. Billy LYTTON
15 Director Human Resources and Safety .... Mr. Todd BANEY
18 Director Facilities Management .... Mr. Orlando ANGELES
26 Director of Marketing/PR .... Ms. Stephanie MICHAEL-PICKETT
30 Chief Development Officer .... Ms. Sylvia BAJOREK
96 Director of Purchasing .... Mr. Chuck WRAY
21 Controller .... Mr. Bruce COLE
40 Director Bookstore .... Mr. Charles WILSON
49 Dean of Liberal Arts & Science .... Ms. Heather WOODSON
72 Dean Engr/Industrial Technologies .... Mr. Virgil COX
66 Dean Health Education .... Dr. Sharon STARR
50 Dean Business & Information Tech .... Dr. Betsy JONES
51 Dean Cont Educ and Public Safety .... Dr. Karen LESS

*Guilford Technical Community College (E)

PO Box 309, Jamestown NC 27282-0309
County: Guilford FICE Identification: 004838
Unit ID: 198622
Telephone: (336) 334-4822 Carnegie Class: Assoc/Pub-S-MC
FAX Number: (336) 819-2007 Calendar System: Semester
URL: www.gtcc.edu
Established: 1958 Annual Undergrad Tuition & Fees (In-State): $1,828
Enrollment: 14,937 Coed
Affiliation or Control: State IRS Status: 501(c)3
Highest Offering: Associate Degree
Program: Occupational; 2-Year Principally Bachelor's Creditable
Accreditation: SC, ACFEI, DA, DH, MAC, PTAA, SURGT

02 President .... Dr. G. Randy PARKER
03 Executive Vice President .... Mrs. Rae Marie SMITH
05 VP of Student Learning & Success .... Dr. Brenda KAYS
11 Vice Pres Administrative Services .... Vacant
10 Interim VP of Business & Finance .... Ms. Nancy B. SOLLOSI
20 Assoc VP Student Learning & Success .... Dr. Alison WIERS
51 VP Corporate & Continuing Educ .... Mr. Leroy STOKES
30 Exec Dir Institutional Advancement .... Mr. Alan PIKE
12 Dean Greensboro Campus .... Mr. Manuel DUDLEY
12 Dean High Point Campus .... Ms. Janette N. MCNEILL
20 Dean Student Support Services ...... Ms. Jacqueline L. PETTIFORD
88 Dean Student Success Services .... Dr. Beverley A. GASS
50 Dean Business & Industry .... Mr. Brian HADERLIE
102 Director of Development .... Mr. Neil BELENKY
15 Director of Human Resources .... Ms. Jean R. JACKSON
13 Chief Information Officer .... Ms. Sandie I. KIRKLAND
18 Director of Construction .... Mr. Dan J. SITKO
09 Director of Institutional Research .... Ms. Stephanie WRIGHT
07 Director of Admissions .... Mr. Jesse CROSS
35 Director of Student Life .... Ms. Berri V. CROSS
88 Director of Basic Skills-Greensboro .... Ms. Pat B. FREEMAN
88 Director of Basic Skills-High Point ...... Ms. Stephany C. COUSINS
37 Director Financial Aid .... Ms. Lisa A. KORETOFF
19 Chief of Campus Police .... Mr. Jerry W. CLARK
06 Registrar .... Mr. Brad E. BURCH
21 Assistant Director of Finance .... Ms. Angela M. CARTER
40 Bookstore Manager .... Mr. Shawn G. DEE
36 Coordinator Career Services .... Mr. Daniel J. GRIGG
38 Director Counseling & Assessment .... Ms. Angela LEAK
29 Coord Resource Dev/Alumni Affairs .... Ms. Margot L. HORNEY
08 Dir of Library Svcs/Lrng Resources .... Vacant

*Halifax Community College (F)

PO Drawer 809, Weldon NC 27890-0809
County: Halifax FICE Identification: 007986
Unit ID: 198640
Telephone: (252) 536-4221 Carnegie Class: Assoc/Pub-R-S
FAX Number: (252) 536-4144 Calendar System: Semester
URL: www.halifaxcc.edu
Established: 1967 Annual Undergrad Tuition & Fees (In-District): $2,117
Enrollment: 1,777 Coed
Affiliation or Control: State/Local IRS Status: 501(c)3
Highest Offering: Associate Degree
Program: Occupational; 2-Year Principally Bachelor's Creditable; Business Emphasis
Accreditation: SC, DH, MLTAD

02 President .... Dr. Ervin V. GRIFFIN
05 Vice Pres Academic Affairs .... Dr. Erica HOLMES
10 Vice President Admin Services .... Ms. Deborah ARMSTRONG
32 Dean Student Svcs & Enrollment Mgmt .... Mrs. Barbara BRADLEY-HASTY
20 Dean of Curriculum Programs .... Ms. B. T. BROWN
06 Registrar .... Ms. Veliky DAWN
07 Director of Admissions .... Mr. James Bernard WASHINGTON
08 Director Learning Resources .... Ms. Mary Gail COOPER
09 Dir of Institutional Effectiveness .... Dr. Edwin IMASUEN
30 Vice Pres Institutional Advancement .... Dr. Linnie CARTER
40 Bookstore Manager .... Mrs. Doris GARNER
38 Director Counseling Services .... Ms. Teresa MAYLER
18 Chief Facilities/Physical Plant .... Mr. Ray HESTER
84 Director Enrollment Management .... Mrs. Julia HORSLEY
37 Director of Financial Aid .... Mrs. Tara KEETER
96 Purchasing Agent .... Mrs. Tina CURRY
15 Personnel Officer .... Mrs. Delois BATTLE-MERCER
14 Computer Network Manager .... Mr. Jerry THOMPSON
49 Div Chair Arts & Sciences .... Mr. Calvin STANSBURY
50 Div Chair Business/Commercial Tech .... Mr. Lateef BALOGUN
76 Division Chair Health Sciences .... Mrs. Kelly HARVEY
88 Div Chair Public Service Technology .... Mrs. B. T. BROWN
75 Div Chair Vocation/Industrial Tech .... Mr. Hunter TAYLOR
04 Admin Assistant to the President .... Ms. Hilda J. HAWKINS

*Haywood Community College (G)

185 Freedlander Drive, Clyde NC 28721-9453
County: Haywood FICE Identification: 008083
Unit ID: 198668
Telephone: (828) 627-2821 Carnegie Class: Assoc/Pub-R-M
FAX Number: (828) 627-3606 Calendar System: Semester
URL: www.haywood.edu

Established: 1965 Annual Undergrad Tuition & Fees (In-State): $2,128
Enrollment: 2,522 Coed
Affiliation or Control: State IRS Status: 501(c)3
Highest Offering: Associate Degree
Program: Occupational; 2-Year Principally Bachelor's Creditable; Technical Emphasis
Accreditation: SC, MAC

02 President Dr. Rose JOHNSON
05 Interim Vice Pres of Academic Svcs Dr. Buddy TIGNOR
32 VP Student Success Svcs Dr. Laura LEATHERWOOD
11 Executive Director Admin Svcs Vacant
10 Exec Director Business Operations Mrs. Karen DENNEY
103 VP Workforce Development Dr. Laura LEATHERWOOD
13 Executive Director of Technology Dr. Annemarie TIMMERMAN
84 Director of Enrollment Management Mrs. Jennifer HERRERA
37 Director Student Financial Aid Ms. Misty GUGE
18 Chief Facilities/Physical Plant Mr. Scott PAGE
26 Director Marketing & Communications Ms. Debbie DAVIS
15 Director of Human Resources Mrs. Marsha STINES
36 Career Development Specialist Ms. Emma DECHANT
09 Data Manager Institutional Research Mr. Matt HOYLE

*Isothermal Community College (A)

PO Box 804, Spindale NC 28160-0804
County: Rutherford FICE Identification: 002934
Unit ID: 198710
Telephone: (828) 286-3636 Carnegie Class: Assoc/Pub-R-M
FAX Number: (828) 286-1120 Calendar System: Semester
URL: www.isothermal.edu
Established: 1964 Annual Undergrad Tuition & Fees (In-District): $2,166
Enrollment: 2,928 Coed
Affiliation or Control: State/Local IRS Status: 501(c)3
Highest Offering: Associate Degree
Program: Occupational; 2-Year Principally Bachelor's Creditable
Accreditation: SC

02 President Dr. Myra B. JOHNSON
11 Vice Pres Administrative Services Mr. Stephen MATHENY
05 VP Academic/Stdnt Svcs/Instl Assess Dr. Kim GOLD
103 VP Cmty/Workforce Educ/Inst Advance Mr. Thad HARRILL
32 Dean of Student Affairs Dr. Karen JONES
50 Dean of Business Sciences Ms. Kim ALEXANDER
49 Dean of Arts & Sciences Dr. Kathy ACKERMAN
75 Dean of Applied Science/Technology Ms. Amber THOMPSON
51 Dean of Continuing Education Ms. Donna HOOD
12 Director of Polk Campus Mrs. Kate BARKSCHAT
20 Director Academic Development Ms. Debbie PUETT
08 Director Library Services Mr. Charles WIGGINS
10 Controller Mrs. Amy M. PENSON
37 Financial Aid Officer Mr. Jeff BOYLE
26 Dir Marketing/Community Relations Mr. Mike GAVIN
18 Dir Plant Operations/Maintenance Mr. Rick EDWARDS
38 Director Student Counseling Testing Mr. Johnny SMITH
84 Director of Enrollment Management Ms. Alice MCCLUNEY
06 Registrar Ms. Kelly METCALF
96 Director of Purchasing Ms. Trish HUNTSINGER
13 Director of Information Technology Mr. Robby WALTERS
40 Bookstore Manager Mr. Mel K. MCCURRY

*James Sprunt Community College (B)

PO Box 398, Kenansville NC 28349-0398
County: Duplin FICE Identification: 007687
Unit ID: 198729
Telephone: (910) 296-2400 Carnegie Class: Assoc/Pub-R-S
FAX Number: (910) 296-1636 Calendar System: Semester
URL: www.jamessprunt.edu
Established: 1964 Annual Undergrad Tuition & Fees (In-State): $1,705
Enrollment: 1,558 Coed
Affiliation or Control: State IRS Status: 501(c)3
Highest Offering: Associate Degree
Program: Occupational; 2-Year Principally Bachelor's Creditable; Technical Emphasis
Accreditation: SC, MAC

02 Chief Executive Officer/President Dr. Lawrence L. ROUSE
05 VP of Curriculum Services Ms. June DAVIS
51 VP of Continuing Education Dr. Unita KNIGHT
10 VP of Admin & Fiscal Services Mr. John HARDISON
32 VP of Student Services Mr. Toney BOND
30 VP of College Advancement Mr. Robert TURNER
06 Registrar Ms. Patricia NORRIS
07 Admissions Specialist Ms. Lea W. GRADY
37 Director Financial Aid/Vet Affairs Vacant
38 Director of Student Counseling Mr. Joseph L. TILLMAN
08 Director Library Services Ms. Patricia KLIMSCHOT
15 Director Human Services Program Ms. Kristy BRINSON
51 Director Continuing Education Vacant
97 Director of General Education Mr. Andy CAVENAUGH
55 Director Evening Programs Mr. Will WRENN
09 Director of Institutional Research Mr. Andrew WALKER
18 Chief Facilities/Physical Plant Mr. Arthur KORNEGAY
96 Director of Purchasing Ms. Toni HENDERSON

*Johnston Community College (C)

PO Box 2350, 245 College Road,
Smithfield NC 27577-2350
County: Johnston FICE Identification: 009336
Unit ID: 198774
Telephone: (919) 934-3051 Carnegie Class: Assoc/Pub-S-SC
FAX Number: (919) 209-2142 Calendar System: Semester
URL: www.johnstoncc.edu
Established: 1969 Annual Undergrad Tuition & Fees (In-District): $1,685
Enrollment: 5,765 Coed
Affiliation or Control: State/Local IRS Status: 501(c)3
Highest Offering: Associate Degree
Program: Occupational; 2-Year Principally Bachelor's Creditable
Accreditation: SC, DMS, MAC, RAD

02 President Dr. David N. JOHNSON
10 VP Finance & Administrative Svcs Mr. Michael CROSS
05 Vice Pres Curriculum Programs Mrs. Dee Dee D. DAUGHTRY
51 Vice Pres of Continuing Education Mr. Talbert MYERS
32 Vice Pres of Student Services Dr. Pamela J. HARRELL
30 VP Institutional Effectiveness Mrs. Dale A. O'NEILL
102 Executive Director of Foundation Ms. Twyla C. WELLS
13 Executive Director Info Technology Mr. Hal MURY
08 Director Learning Resources Center Ms. Christine B. ROBERTS
09 Dir of Institutional Effectiveness Dr. Donna L. SHUMATE
105 Internet Info Systems Coordinator Ms. Lisa H. MCLAURIN
06 Registrar Ms. Deena H. HENRY
37 Financial Aid Officer Mrs. Betty C. WOODALL
88 Director of Auditorium Mr. Ken H. MITCHELL
07 Director of Admissions/Counseling Mrs. Joan S. MCLENDON
15 Director Human Resouces Mrs. Tonya P. JACKSON
103 Director Workforce Development Mrs. Joy T. CALLAHAN
26 Chief Public Relations Officer Mrs. Traci D. ASHLEY
18 Manager Facilities/Physical Plant Mr. Michael MASSEY
96 Coordinator of Purchasing Mr. Doug PATE

*Lenoir Community College (D)

231 Highway 58 South, Kinston NC 28502-0188
County: Lenoir FICE Identification: 002940
Unit ID: 198817
Telephone: (252) 527-6223 Carnegie Class: Assoc/Pub-R-M
FAX Number: (252) 233-6879 Calendar System: Semester
URL: www.lenoircc.edu
Established: 1958 Annual Undergrad Tuition & Fees (In-District): $2,146
Enrollment: 3,792 Coed
Affiliation or Control: State/Local IRS Status: 501(c)3
Highest Offering: Associate Degree
Program: Occupational; 2-Year Principally Bachelor's Creditable
Accreditation: SC, ACFEI, MAC, POLYT, RAD, SURGT

02 President Dr. Brantley BRILEY
51 VP Continuing Education Dr. Jay CARRAWAY
11 VP of Administrative Services Ms. Deborah SUTTON
05 VP Academic & Student Services Dr. Deborah GRIMES
10 Chief Financial Officer Ms. Deborah S. SUTTON
06 Registrar Mrs. Emily SMITH
84 Director Enrollment Mgmt/Admissions Ms. Pam MAZINGO
32 Dean of Student Services Mr. Levy BROWN
37 Director of Student Financial Aid Mrs. Reekitta DEAVER
27 Director of Information Services Mr. Lee WETHERINGTON
09 Dir Planning Rsch/Inst Effective Vacant
15 Director Human Resources Ms. Lisa BARROW
18 Director of Maintenance Mr. Reed LOVICK
41 Dir Student Center/Athletic Pgms Mr. Stony WINE
21 Director of Financial Services Ms. Jessica MCMAHON
96 Director of Purchasing Mrs. Rhonda REEDER
26 Director of Mktg/Recruiting/Comm Mrs. Richy HUNEYCUTT
30 Director Institutional Advancement Mrs. Jeanne KENNEDY
36 Director Coop Ed/Job Dev/Placement Mrs. Frances GASKINS
08 Coordinator of Learning Resources Mr. Carenado DAVIS
50 Dean of Business/Industrial Pgms Mr. Gary CLEMENTS
49 Dean of Arts & Sciences Dr. John Paul BLACK
76 Dean of Health Sciences Programs Dr. Alexis WELCH
89 Director of Freshman Studies Mrs. Evelyn KELLY
92 Dean/Director of Honors Program Dr. John Paul BLACK
93 Dean/Director of Minority Students Mr. Levy BROWN
94 Dean/Director of Women's Studies Dr. Deborah GRIMES
35 Director Student Activities Ms. Samara TAFT

*Martin Community College (E)

1161 Kehukee Park Road, Williamston NC 27892-9988
County: Martin FICE Identification: 007988
Unit ID: 198905
Telephone: (252) 792-1521 Carnegie Class: Assoc/Pub-R-S
FAX Number: (252) 792-0826 Calendar System: Semester
URL: www.martin.cc.nc.us
Established: 1967 Annual Undergrad Tuition & Fees (In-State): $1,596
Enrollment: 755 Coed
Affiliation or Control: State IRS Status: 501(c)3
Highest Offering: Associate Degree
Program: Occupational; 2-Year Principally Bachelor's Creditable
Accreditation: SC, DA, MAC, PTAA

02 President Dr. Ann R. BRITT
05 Dean Curriculum Pgm/Dean Stdnt Svcs Dr. Phyllis J. BROUGHTON
11 Dean of Administrative Services Ms. Cynthia MODLIN
04 Asst to Pres for Business/Industry Mr. Billy BARBER
37 Financial Aid Director Ms. Michelle LANE COBB
38 Counselor Dr. Thomas POWELL
06 Registrar & Admissions Officer Vacant
07 Admissions Counselor Mr. Jim BUSSELL
51 Int Exec Dir Continuing Education Mr. Walter V. WHITFIELD
75 Department Chair Technology Ms. Barbara M. DALY
50 Department Chair Business Ms. Bess L. PATTON
97 Department Chair General Studies Vacant

14 Systems Administrator Ms. Donna ROGERS
18 Director of Facilities Mr. Jackie F. HAISLIP
15 Human Resource Officer Ms. Rebecca P. WOOLARD
88 Telecommunication/Network Manager Mr. Elijah T. FREEMAN

*Mayland Community College (F)

PO Box 547, Spruce Pine NC 28777-0547
County: Avery FICE Identification: 011197
Unit ID: 198914
Telephone: (828) 765-7351 Carnegie Class: Assoc/Pub-R-S
FAX Number: (828) 765-0728 Calendar System: Semester
URL: www.mayland.edu
Established: 1971 Annual Undergrad Tuition & Fees (In-District): $1,817
Enrollment: 1,567 Coed
Affiliation or Control: State/Local IRS Status: 501(c)3
Highest Offering: Associate Degree
Program: Occupational; 2-Year Principally Bachelor's Creditable; Technical Emphasis
Accreditation: SC, MAC

02 President Dr. John C. BOYD
05 Vice Pres Instructional Services Mrs. Rhia CRAWFORD
10 Vice President Administrative Svcs Mr. Gerald HYDE
32 Vice Pres Student Services Dr. John GOSSETT
17 Dean of Nursing Program Ms. Sheryl YOUNG
49 Dean of Arts & Sciences Ms. Beth MITCHELL
08 Dean Learning Resources Center Mr. Jon WILMESHERR
09 Institutional Effectiveness Mrs. Liz SILVERS
06 Registrar Ms. Tracy E. WEBBER
88 Director of Basic Skills Programs Mr. Steve GUNTER
12 Director Avery County Programs Mrs. Melissa C. PHILLIPS
12 Director of Mitchell County Cont Ed Mr. Chris HELMS
12 Director Yancey County Programs Ms. Rita EARLEY
37 Director Student Financial Aid Ms. Pamela ELLIS
18 Director Facilities/Physical Plant Mr. Lee WHITTINGTON
13 Director Mgt Information Systems Mr. Tommy R. LEDFORD
07 Director of Admissions Dr. Monica BOYD
105 Webmaster Mr. David K. BIDDIX
15 Director Personnel Services Ms. Jennifer R. ISAACS
26 Chief Public Relations Officer Mrs. Beth MORRIS
96 Coordinator of Purchasing/Equipment Mr. Sam PRESNELL

*McDowell Technical Community College (G)

54 College Drive, Marion NC 28752-8728
County: McDowell FICE Identification: 008085
Unit ID: 198923
Telephone: (828) 652-6021 Carnegie Class: Assoc/Pub-R-S
FAX Number: (828) 652-1014 Calendar System: Semester
URL: www.mcdowelltech.edu
Established: 1964 Annual Undergrad Tuition & Fees (In-District): $1,416
Enrollment: 1,519 Coed
Affiliation or Control: State/Local IRS Status: 501(c)3
Highest Offering: Associate Degree
Program: Occupational; 2-Year Principally Bachelor's Creditable
Accreditation: SC

02 President Dr. Bryan W. WILSON
05 Vice President for Learning Mrs. Shirley F. BROWN
20 Dean Academic Programs Dr. James BENTON
09 Director of Inst Effectiveness Mr. Ladelle HARMON
26 Director of External Relations Mr. Michael K. LAVENDER
13 Director of Technology/Info Systems Mr. Elmer R. MACOPSON
08 Director of Library Services Ms. Sharon P. SMITH
88 Director of Correctional Programs Mr. Frank D. SILVER
88 Director of Industrial Training Mr. Eddie SHUFORD
88 Director of Health Sciences Mrs. Penny CROSS
06 Registrar Ms. Kelly HAMLIN
37 Dir Student Financial Aid/Counselor Ms. Kim M. LEDBETTER
36 Director of Student Enrichment Ctr Mrs. Donna SHORT
88 Director of Adult Basic Skills Mrs. Shelba M. MURRAY
88 Counselor/VA Director Mrs. Donna SHORT
55 Director Evening Programs Vacant
51 Director of Continuing Education Mr. William B. LEDBETTER
88 Director Basic Law Enforcement Trng Mr. Stacy BUFF
07 Director of Admissions Mr. Rick L. WILSON
30 Resource Development Vacant
106 Coordinator of Distance Education Mrs. Joan WEILER
16 Coord of Human Resources Devel Mrs. Jean H. EDWARDS
18 Coord Maintenance/Custodial Svcs Mr. Carl COSTNER
88 Coord of Small Business Center Mr. H. Dean KANIPE
04 Assistant to the President Mrs. Rhonda SILVER

*Mitchell Community College (H)

500 W Broad Street, Statesville NC 28677-5293
County: Iredell FICE Identification: 002947
Unit ID: 198987
Telephone: (704) 878-3200 Carnegie Class: Assoc/Pub-R-M
FAX Number: (704) 878-0872 Calendar System: Semester
URL: www.mitchellcc.edu
Established: 1852 Annual Undergrad Tuition & Fees (In-State): $1,878
Enrollment: 3,768 Coed
Affiliation or Control: State IRS Status: 501(c)3
Highest Offering: Associate Degree
Program: Occupational; 2-Year Principally Bachelor's Creditable
Accreditation: SC, ADNUR, MAC

02 President Dr. Douglas O. EASON

05 Vice President of Instruction — Dr. Tim BREWER
10 Vice Pres of Finance/Administration — Mr. Richard J. LEFEVRE
103 Vice Pres Workforce Development/CEC — Ms. Carol JOHNSON
32 Dean Student Services — Mr. Dan MANNING
09 Director Inst Effectiveness — Ms. Zaneta SUMMERS
08 Int Director of Learning Resources — Ms. Vicki CALDWELL
37 Director of Financial Aid — Ms. Candace COOPER
18 Exec Dir Facilities/Auxiliary Svcs — Mr. Gary JOHNSON
29 Director Alumni Relations — Vacant
26 Chief Public Relations Officer — Ms. Kathy HOLLAND
30 Director Development/Col Rels — Mr. Harry STILLERMAN

*Montgomery Community College (A)

1011 Page Street, Troy NC 27371-0787
County: Montgomery — FICE Identification: 008087
Unit ID: 199023
Telephone: (910) 576-6222 — Carnegie Class: Assoc/Pub-R-S
FAX Number: (910) 576-2176 — Calendar System: Semester
URL: www.montgomery.edu
Established: 1967 — Annual Undergrad Tuition & Fees (In-District): $1,695
Enrollment: 896 — Coed
Affiliation or Control: State/Local — IRS Status: 501(c)3
Highest Offering: Associate Degree
Program: Occupational; 2-Year Principally Bachelor's Creditable
Accreditation: SC, DA, MAC

02 President — Dr. Mary P. KIRK
05 VP of Instruction/Continuing Ed — Dr. Jeff HAMILTON
11 VP of Administrative Services — Roger REYNOLDS
32 VP of Student Services — Beth SMITH
97 Dean of Curriculum Programs — Randy GUNTER
51 Dean of Continuing Education — Gary SAUNDERS
102 Executive Director Foundation/Grant — Gay ROATCH
26 Public Information Officer — Michele HAYWOOD
106 Dir of Distance Learning/Prof Dev — Tom M. SARGENT
09 Dir Institutional Effectiveness — Carol L. SARGENT
13 Dir of Information Technology — Mitch WALKER
04 Assistant to the President — Korrie ERVIN
30 Director of Counseling Services — Margo H. GADDY
07 Admissions Officer — Karen FRYE
37 Director of Financial Aid — Doni S. CODY
15 Coordinator Of Human Resources — Susan MCLEOD
10 Accountant — Angela SEDBERRY
18 Director of Facilities — Kevin MCNEILL
35 Student Activities Coordinator — Riley BEAMAN

*Nash Community College (B)

522 N Old Carriage Road, Rocky Mount NC 27804-0488
County: Nash — FICE Identification: 008557
Unit ID: 199087
Telephone: (252) 443-4011 — Carnegie Class: Assoc/Pub-R-M
FAX Number: (252) 451-8201 — Calendar System: Semester
URL: www.nashcc.edu
Established: 1967 — Annual Undergrad Tuition & Fees (In-District): $1,728
Enrollment: 3,252 — Coed
Affiliation or Control: State/Local — IRS Status: 501(c)3
Highest Offering: Associate Degree
Program: Occupational; 2-Year Principally Bachelor's Creditable; Business Emphasis
Accreditation: SC, MAC, PTAA

02 President — Dr. William S. CARVER, II
05 Vice President for Instruction — Dr. Deborah H. GRIFFITHS
10 VP Finance/Administrative Services — Ms. Annette H. DISHNER
30 Assoc VP Institutional Advancement — Ms. Pat E. DANIELS
08 Dean Learning Resources — Ms. R. Lynette FINCH
88 Director Small Business Center — Mr. Fred BROOKS
86 Assoc VP Community & Govt Affairs — Dr. Keith SMITH
32 Assoc VP Student & Enrollment Svcs — Mr. Larry K. MITCHELL
21 Assoc VP Finance — Ms. Stephanie B. FISHER
14 Director Institutional Technology — Mr. Jonathan VESTER
07 Admissions Officer — Ms. Dorothy GARDNER
06 Registrar — Ms. Kathy S. ADCOX
37 Financial Aid Officer — Ms. Tammy LESTER
15 Director Human Resources — Ms. Susan L. BARKALOW
04 Executive Asst to the President — Ms. Susan H. NIPPER
31 Director Institutional Services — Mr. James M. QUIGLEY
18 Director of Facilities — Mr. C. Ted KENNEDY

*Pamlico Community College (C)

PO Box 185, Grantsboro NC 28529-0185
County: Pamlico — FICE Identification: 007031
Unit ID: 199263
Telephone: (252) 249-1851 — Carnegie Class: Assoc/Pub-R-S
FAX Number: (252) 249-2377 — Calendar System: Semester
URL: www.pamlicocc.edu
Established: 1962 — Annual Undergrad Tuition & Fees (In-District): $1,808
Enrollment: 543 — Coed
Affiliation or Control: State/Local — IRS Status: 501(c)3
Highest Offering: Associate Degree
Program: Occupational; 2-Year Principally Bachelor's Creditable; Technical Emphasis
Accreditation: SC, EEG, MAC

02 President — Dr. Cleve H. COX
11 Vice Pres Administrative Svcs — Mr. James CURRY
05 Vice Pres Instructional Svcs — Dr. Larry W. GRACIE
32 Vice Pres of Student Services — Mr. Jamie GIBBS

*Piedmont Community College (D)

PO Box 1197, 1715 College Drive, Roxboro NC 27573-1197
County: Person — FICE Identification: 009646
Unit ID: 199324
Telephone: (336) 599-1181 — Carnegie Class: Assoc/Pub-R-M
FAX Number: (336) 597-3817 — Calendar System: Semester
URL: www.piedmontcc.edu
Established: 1970 — Annual Undergrad Tuition & Fees (In-District): $2,221
Enrollment: 2,663 — Coed
Affiliation or Control: State/Local — IRS Status: 501(c)3
Highest Offering: Associate Degree
Program: Occupational; 2-Year Principally Bachelor's Creditable; Technical Emphasis
Accreditation: SC

02 President — Dr. Walter C. BARTLETT
05 Vice Pres Instruction/Student Devel — Mr. Michael S. DOSSETT
51 Vice President Continuing Education — Dr. Doris W. CARVER
11 Vice Pres Administrative Services — Mr. Robert E. SIMONS
12 Executive Director Caswell Campus — Vacant
20 Dean Caswell Curriculum Programs — Ms. Shelly T. STONE
32 Dean Student Development — Mr. R. Leland PROCTOR
08 Dean Learning Resources Center — Ms. Gretchen M. BELL
06 Coordinator Student Records — Vacant
13 Director Mgmt Information Services — Mr. William P. HILLE
09 Dir Research/Inst Effectiveness — Ms. Tina BRYANT-ALLEN
15 Director Personnel/Payroll — Ms. Pamelia C. HOBBS
102 Director PCC Foundation Inc — Ms. Elizabeth R. TOWNSEND
26 Director Public Information — Ms. Bonnie H. DAVIS
37 Dir Financial Aid/Veterans Affairs — Ms. Frances M. LUNSFORD
40 Manager Bookstore — Ms. Tammy H. MORRIS
25 Director Grants — Dr. Karen BOWEN
07 Coordinator Admissions — Ms. Sheila D. WILLIAMSON
18 Coordinator Buildings and Grounds — Mr. Bruce CHISHOLM
97 Dean General Educ/Devel Studies — Dr. Dawn LANGLEY
75 Dean Technical/Occupational Pgms — Ms. Judy S. BRADSHER
50 Dean Business Studies and Tech — Dr. Sherry L. STOUT-STEWART
66 Dean Health Sciences and Human Svcs — Ms. Kelly H. HOLDER

*Pitt Community College (E)

PO Drawer 7007, Greenville NC 27835-7007
County: Pitt — FICE Identification: 004062
Unit ID: 199333
Telephone: (252) 493-7200 — Carnegie Class: Assoc/Pub-R-L
FAX Number: (252) 321-4458 — Calendar System: Semester
URL: www.pittcc.edu
Established: 1961 — Annual Undergrad Tuition & Fees (In-State): $1,808
Enrollment: 8,498 — Coed
Affiliation or Control: State — IRS Status: 501(c)3
Highest Offering: Associate Degree
Program: Occupational; 2-Year Principally Bachelor's Creditable
Accreditation: SC, ADNUR, DMS, MAC, OTA, POLYT, RAD, RADDOS, RTT

02 President — Dr. Dennis MASSEY
05 Vice President Academic Affairs — Dr. Pamela HILBERT
11 Vice Pres Administrative Services — Ms. Susan EVERETT
32 Vice President Student Development — Dr. Donald R. SPELL
30 Vice Pres Institutional Advancement — Mrs. Susan Q. NOBLES
20 Asst Vice Pres Academic Affairs — Vacant
35 Asst Vice Pres Student Development — Mrs. Leslie D. ROGERS
13 AVP Information Technology/Services — Mr. Rick OWENS
04 Administrative Asst to President — Mrs. Kathy M. CARNES
31 Dean Economic & Cmty Development — Dr. David LUSK
08 Dean Learning Resources — Ms. Lisa C. DRIVER
09 Dean of Planning & Research — Dr. Larry C. DENDY
46 Resource Development Director — Vacant
15 Director of Human Resources — Ms. Debra P. MCGOWAN
91 Director of Admin Computing — Mrs. Janet MINTERN
06 Registrar — Ms. Joanne T. CERES
38 Director of Counseling — Ms. Kimberly WILLIAMSON
88 Director Basic Skills Program — Ms. Marilyn BEAUMONT
18 Director of Facilities — Mr. Walter Ashley DAIL
103 Director of JobLink Career Center — Vacant
84 Director of Admiss & Enroll Mgmt — Ms. Joanne T. CERES
41 Athletic Director — Mr. William BAILEY
29 Director of Alumni Relations — Mrs. Ashley SMITH
36 Director of Student Placement — Mrs. Amy FRASER
96 Director of Purchasing — Mr. Wade QUINN
19 Chief-Public Safety/Campus Police — Mr. Alan T. EDWARDS
88 Director Business & Industry Svcs — Mrs. Mary PARAMORE
104 Director Study Abroad — Mrs. Darlene SMITH-WORTHINGTON
09 Dir Institutional Effectiveness — Dr. Brian MILLER
37 Director Financial Aid — Mrs. Lisa M. REICHSTEIN
10 Business Manager — Mr. Ricky BROWN
40 Manager of College Store — Mrs. Judy HARRIS
106 Coord Instructional Tech/Dist Ed — Mr. Don HAZELWOOD
55 Coord/Counselor Evening Programs — Mr. Kendrick PRICE
50 Division Dean of Business — Mr. Donald E. LEE
76 Division Dean Health Sciences — Ms. Donna V. NEAL
49 Division Dean of Art & Sciences — Dr. Stephanie MANLEY-ROOK
75 Div Dean Construct/Indus Tech — Mr. Van MADRAY
61 Div Dean Legal Sci/Public Svc — Dr. Dan MAYO

*Randolph Community College (F)

PO Box 1009, Asheboro NC 27204-1009
County: Randolph — FICE Identification: 005447
Unit ID: 199421
Telephone: (336) 633-0200 — Carnegie Class: Assoc/Pub-S-SC
FAX Number: (336) 629-4695 — Calendar System: Semester
URL: www.randolph.edu
Established: 1962 — Annual Undergrad Tuition & Fees (In-District): $1,896
Enrollment: 3,082 — Coed
Affiliation or Control: State/Local — IRS Status: 501(c)3
Highest Offering: Associate Degree
Program: Occupational; 2-Year Principally Bachelor's Creditable
Accreditation: SC, ADNUR

02 President — Dr. Robert S. SHACKLEFORD, JR.
11 Vice Pres Administrative Services — Ms. Daffie H. MATTHEWS
05 Vice Pres Instructional Services — Ms. Anne B. HOCKETT
32 Vice President Student Services — Mr. James W. KELLEY
101 Exec Asst to Pres/Board of Trustees — Ms. Wanda C. BROWN
88 Dean of Basic Skills — Ms. Amanda P. BYRD
62 Dean Library Services — Ms. Deborah S. LUCK
106 Director Distance Education — Mr. Kelly KIRK
09 Director Planning & Assessment — Ms. Karen R. RITTER
30 Assoc VP Institutional Advancement — Ms. Susan V. MILNER
27 Director Communications — Ms. Cathy D. HEFFERIN
15 Director of Human Resources — Ms. Nancy BULLINS
37 Director Student Financial Aid — Mr. Chad WILLIAMS
06 Director Enrollment Mgmt/Registrar — Ms. Brandi F. HAGERMAN
18 Facilities Director — Ms. Cindi J. GOODWIN
96 Purchasing Agent — Ms. Sharon P. REYNOLDS
21 Controller — Ms. Susan I. RICE
51 Dean Corporate & Continuing Educ — Mr. Robert LESLIE
26 Senior Director Marketing — Ms. Shelley W. GREENE
12 Director Archdale Center — Ms. Lisa L. BOCK
88 Director ESTC/Coord Fire Services — Mr. Brian C. CAUSEY

*Richmond Community College (G)

Box 1189, Hamlet NC 28345-1189
County: Richmond — FICE Identification: 005464
Unit ID: 199449
Telephone: (910) 410-1700 — Carnegie Class: Assoc/Pub-R-S
FAX Number: (910) 582-7028 — Calendar System: Semester
URL: www.richmondcc.edu
Established: 1964 — Annual Undergrad Tuition & Fees (In-District): $2,186
Enrollment: 2,162 — Coed
Affiliation or Control: State/Local — IRS Status: 501(c)3
Highest Offering: Associate Degree
Program: Occupational; 2-Year Principally Bachelor's Creditable; Technical Emphasis
Accreditation: SC

02 President — Dr. W. Dale MCINNIS
32 Vice President Student Development — Ms. Saundra RICHARDSON
05 Vice President for Instruction — Ms. Johnnie SIMPSON
10 VP Admin Svcs/Chief Financial Ofcr — Mr. Brent BARBEE
51 Vice President for Continuing Educ — Mr. Steve SMITH
55 Dean of Evening Programs — Dr. Carl HOWALD
08 Dean of Learning Resources — Ms. Carolyn BITTLE
88 Director of Basic Skills — Ms. Sherry BYRD
30 Dean of Research & Instnl Effect — Mr. William COUNCIL
06 Registrar — Ms. Wanda B. WATTS
09 Director of Institutional Research — Ms. Lucinda COLE
15 Director Personnel Services — Ms. Gaye CLARK
26 Public Relations Officer — Ms. Anne MORRIS
21 Controller — Mr. Bobby RITTER
37 Director Student Financial Aid — Mr. Bruce BLACKMON
96 Purchasing Officer — Ms. Toni GOODWIN
18 Director of Facility Services — Mr. Glenn SIMS
38 Director Student Counseling — Ms. Sharon GOODMAN
07 Director of Admissions — Ms. Daphne STANCIL

*Roanoke-Chowan Community College (H)

109 Community College Road, Ahoskie NC 27910-9522
County: Hertford — FICE Identification: 008613
Unit ID: 199467
Telephone: (252) 862-1200 — Carnegie Class: Assoc/Pub-R-S
FAX Number: (252) 862-1358 — Calendar System: Semester
URL: www.roanokechowan.edu
Established: 1967 — Annual Undergrad Tuition & Fees (In-District): $1,200
Enrollment: 986 — Coed
Affiliation or Control: State/Local — IRS Status: 501(c)3
Highest Offering: Associate Degree
Program: Occupational; 2-Year Principally Bachelor's Creditable
Accreditation: SC

02 President — Dr. Ralph G. SONEY
05 Dean of Curriculum Programs — Dr. Pocahantas JONES
103 Dean Workforce Development — Mr. AJ TYSON
88 Dean Basic Skills — Mrs. Michelle MEISCHEID
32 Assoc Dean of Student Devel Svcs — Mrs. Wendy VANN
10 Dean of Finance & Administration — Ms. Carolyn LA DOW
08 Dean of Learning Resources/Dist Ed — Mrs. Monique MITCHELL
06 Registrar — Mrs. Belinda SMITH
18 Chief Facilities/Physical Plant — Mr. Ray BURKETT
38 Director Student Counseling — Ms. Sandra COPELAND
37 Director Financial Aid — Mrs. Trisha SAWYER
09 Compliance & Data Director — Mr. Juan E. VAUGHAN, II
15 Human Resources Coordinator — Mrs. Amy F. WIGGINS
13 Coord Info Svcs/Network Admin — Mr. Randolph HARRIS
36 Director Student Support — Ms. Lorraine C. MITCHELL
26 Marketing/Public Information — Mr. Justin MCKEITHAN

Robeson Community College (A)

PO Box 1420, Lumberton NC 28359-1420
County: Robeson FICE Identification: 008612
Unit ID: 199476
Telephone: (910) 272-3700 Carnegie Class: Assoc/Pub-R-M
FAX Number: (910) 272-3328 Calendar System: Semester
URL: www.robeson.edu
Established: 1965 Annual Undergrad Tuition & Fees (In-District): $2,086
Enrollment: 2,638 Coed
Affiliation or Control: State/Local IRS Status: 501(c)3
Highest Offering: Associate Degree
Program: Occupational; 2-Year Principally Bachelor's Creditable
Accreditation: SC, SURGT

02 President .... Dr. Charles V. CHRESTMAN
05 Vice Pres Instruction/Support Svcs .... Dr. Mark O. KINLAW
51 Vice Pres Adult & Continuing Educ .... Vacant
10 Vice President Business Services .... Mrs. Tami GEORGE
11 VP for Institutional Services .... Mr. Alphonzo MCRAE
55 Asst VP Public Svc/Appl Tech Pgms ... Mr. William L. LOCKLEAR
88 Asst VP Univ Transfer/Bus/Hlth Pgms .... Ms. Sheila A. REGAN
32 Asst Vice Pres Student Services .... Mr. Bill L. MAUNEY
07 Director of Admissions .... Ms. Judith A. REVELS
22 Director Affirm Action/Equal Oppty .... Mr. Alphonzo MCRAE
08 Director of Library .... Mrs. Marilyn L. HUNT
38 Director Counseling & Testing .... Mr. Danford GROVES
06 Registrar .... Mrs. Beth CARMICAL
37 Director Financial Aid .... Mr. Ronnie LOCKLEAR
09 Director of Institutional Research .... Mrs. Lisa O. HUNT
18 Chief Facilities/Physical Plant .... Mr. Stanley FREEMAN
102 Director College Foundation .... Ms. Lynda W. PARLETT
35 Director Student Affairs .... Mr. Billy MAUNEY
36 Director Student Placement .... Mr. Danford GROVES
29 Director Alumni Relations .... Ms. Lynda W. PARLETT
84 Director Enrollment Management .... Mrs. Beth CARMICAL
13 Systems Administrator .... Mr. James TAGLIARENI
15 Personnel Services Specialist .... Ms. Pam ROMANO
96 Purchasing Specialist .... Mr. Jason O. LEVISTER

*Rockingham Community College (B)

PO Box 38, Wentworth NC 27375-0038
County: Rockingham FICE Identification: 002958
Unit ID: 199485
Telephone: (336) 342-4261 Carnegie Class: Assoc/Pub-R-M
FAX Number: (336) 349-9986 Calendar System: Semester
URL: www.rockinghamcc.edu
Established: 1963 Annual Undergrad Tuition & Fees (In-District): $1,995
Enrollment: 2,631 Coed
Affiliation or Control: State/Local IRS Status: 501(c)3
Highest Offering: Associate Degree
Program: Occupational; 2-Year Principally Bachelor's Creditable
Accreditation: SC, SURGT

02 President .... Dr. Michael S. HELMICK
05 Vice President Instruction .... Dr. Shelia K. RUHLAND
11 VP of Administrative Services .... Mr. Steven W. WOODRUFF
32 Vice Pres for Student Development .. Dr. Robert S. LOWDERMILK
88 Assoc VP Administrative Services .... Dr. E. Anthony GUNN
51 Dean of Continuing Education .... Mr. William PIERSON
50 Dean of Business Technologies .... Ms. Sandra K. GANN
75 Dean Industrial Technologies .... Mr. C. M. FRAZIER
79 Dean of Humanities/Social Science .... Dr. Penne L. PRIGGE
81 Dean of Sciences & Math .... Ms. Celeste H. ALLIS
76 Dean of Health Sciences .... Mr. Thomas W. HARDING
08 Director of Library Services .... Ms. Kimberly SHIREMAN
09 Director Inst Research/Planning .... Mr. H. David SMATHERS
30 Director Development/Foundation .... Ms. Gaye B. CLIFTON
14 Dir Technology Support Services .... Ms. Gretchan PARRISH
37 Director of Financial Aid .... Ms. Coe Ann TRENT
84 Director of Enrollment Services .... Ms. Leigh T. HAWKINS
35 Director Student Life .... Mr. Dean MYRICK
40 Bookstore Manager .... Ms. Della J. GASTON
15 Director Human Resources .... Ms. Dana HUSKEY
27 Director Public Information .... Ms. Kim PRYOR
96 Director of Purchasing .... Mr. John PARRISH

*Rowan-Cabarrus Community College (C)

Box 1595, Salisbury NC 28145-1595
County: Rowan FICE Identification: 005754
Unit ID: 199494
Telephone: (704) 637-7222 Carnegie Class: Assoc/Pub-S-MC
FAX Number: (704) 637-3692 Calendar System: Semester
URL: www.rowancabarrus.edu
Established: 1961 Annual Undergrad Tuition & Fees (In-State): $2,260
Enrollment: 7,383 Coed
Affiliation or Control: State IRS Status: 501(c)3
Highest Offering: Associate Degree
Program: Occupational; 2-Year Principally Bachelor's Creditable
Accreditation: SC, ADNUR, DA, RAD

02 President .... Dr. Carol SPALDING
05 Academic Vice President .... Dr. Rod TOWNLEY
30 VP College Advancement .... Dr. Jarrett T. CHANDLER
10 Acting Chief Financial Officer .... Ms. Jennifer TONNESON
32 Vice President Student Services .... Ms. Gaye MCCONNELL
51 Vice Pres Corporate and Cont Educ .... Ms. Jeanie MOORE
21 Assoc Vice Pres Fin & Business Svcs .... Mr. Derrick ATKINS
14 Assoc Vice Pres Info Tech Svcs .... Mr. Jeremy CAMPBELL
18 Assoc VP Facilities/Environ Oprtns .... Mr. Tim FOLEY
55 Director Evening & Weekend Oper .... Mr. Mike HENSLEY
20 Assoc Academic Vice President .... Mr. Ron SCOZZARI
13 Assoc Dean Information Technology .... Mr. Ian STEVENS
50 Dean Science Bus Math & Info Tech .... Dr. Marcy CORJAY
49 Dean Liberal Arts & General Educ .... Dr. Carolyn HOLBERT
76 Dean Health & Public Svcs Tech .... Mr. Terry CHAPMAN
54 Dean Industrial & Engr Technologies .... Mr. Gary BIGELOW
88 Assoc VP Cont Educ Pre-College Stds .... Mrs. Cheryl MARSH
08 Director Learning Resource Center .... Mr. Rodney LIPPARD
103 Dean Corporate Programs .... Mrs. Ann MORRIS
31 Dean Community Devel Programs .... Mr. Larry YON
72 Dean Eductional Resource Services .... Ms. Debra NEESMITH
71 Dean Spec Pgm/Coord Cosmetology Ctr .... Mrs. Lou DORTON-SHUE
18 Director Facilities Services .... Mr. Gayle PHIPPS
06 Director Registration & Records .... Mrs. Joan CREEGER
07 Director Admissions & Enrollment .... Mr. Rob DUNNAM
15 Director Human Resources .... Mrs. Tina HAYNES
38 Director Counseling and Career Svs .... Ms. Misty MOLER
37 Director Fin Aid & VA Benefit .... Mrs. Lisa LEDBETTER
26 Dir College Relations Mktg & Comm .... Ms. Paula DIBLEY
35 Director Student Life & Leadership .... Ms. Natasha LIPSCOMB
37 Dir Scholarships & Job Placement .... Vacant
21 Controller .... Mrs. Debbie HOPKINS
46 Director Curriculum Development .... Vacant
102 Executive Director RCCC Foundation .... Mrs. Celeste A. GRUNER
25 Director Grants Development .... Mrs. Daphne LEWIS

*Sampson Community College (D)

PO Box 318, Clinton NC 28329-0318
County: Sampson FICE Identification: 007892
Unit ID: 199625
Telephone: (910) 592-8081 Carnegie Class: Assoc/Pub-R-S
FAX Number: (910) 592-8048 Calendar System: Semester
URL: www.sampsoncc.edu
Established: 1967 Annual Undergrad Tuition & Fees (In-District): $2,205
Enrollment: 1,695 Coed
Affiliation or Control: State/Local IRS Status: 501(c)3
Highest Offering: Associate Degree
Program: Occupational; 2-Year Principally Bachelor's Creditable
Accreditation: SC

02 President .... Dr. William C. AIKEN
05 Vice President of Academic Affairs .... Dr. Tim WRIGHT
10 Vice President of Finance .... Mrs. Virginia S. LUCAS
11 Vice President of Administration .... Dr. William J. STARLING
32 Dean of Student Services .... Ms. Amy NOEL
07 Director of Admissions .... Mr. Oscar RODRIGUEZ
06 Registrar .... Mrs. Denise Q. RACKLEY
27 Public Information Office .... Ms. Erica JONES
37 Director Financial Aid .... Ms. Judye TART
08 Director Library Services .... Mr. Mark RUSHING
30 Resource Development Officer .... Mrs. Lisa TURLINGTON
15 Personnel Officer .... Mrs. Frankie K. SUTTER
35 Director Student Support Services .... Ms. Lisa DOBSON
51 Dean of Continuing Education .... Mrs. Ann BUTLER

*Sandhills Community College (E)

3395 Airport Road, Pinehurst NC 28374-8283
County: Moore FICE Identification: 002961
Unit ID: 199634
Telephone: (910) 692-6185 Carnegie Class: Assoc/Pub-R-M
FAX Number: (910) 695-1823 Calendar System: Semester
URL: www.sandhills.edu
Established: 1963 Annual Undergrad Tuition & Fees (In-State): $1,687
Enrollment: 4,500 Coed
Affiliation or Control: State IRS Status: 501(c)3
Highest Offering: Associate Degree
Program: Occupational; 2-Year Principally Bachelor's Creditable
Accreditation: SC, MLTAD, POLYT, RAD, SURGT

02 President .... Dr. John R. DEMPSEY
05 Sr VP Instruction/Student Services .... Dr. John T. TURNER
10 VP Business/Administrative Svcs .... Dr. Richard GOUGH
09 Dean of Institutional Plng/Rsrch .... Mrs. Kristie SULLIVAN
32 Dean of Student Services .... Mrs. Kellie SHOEMAKE
35 Dean of Student Life .... Mr. David FARMER
04 Exec Assistant to the President .... Mrs. Wendy B. DODSON
10 Chief Business Officer .... Mrs. Cynthia BARTON
20 Dean of Instruction .... Dr. Rebecca ROUSH
51 Dean Continuing Education .... Ms. Andi KORTE
30 Dean of Institutional Advancement .... Mr. Rick H. SMITH
08 Director of Learning Resources .... Dr. John STACEY
06 Director of Records & Registration .... Ms. Phyllis DOWDY
37 Financial Aid Officer .... Ms. Heather WILLETT
106 Director of Distance Learning .... Ms. Wendy KAUFFMAN
14 Director of Computer Center .... Ms. Dorothy SAVIN
19 Director of Security/Safety .... Mr. David REECE
18 Physical Plant Manager .... Mr. Melvin RITTER
15 Director Human Resources .... Ms. Wendy B. DODSON
21 Assistant Business Officer .... Mr. Joseph BROWN
26 Director of Marketing and PR .... Mr. Karen MANNING
40 Bookstore Manager .... Ms. Jessica RUSSELL

*South Piedmont Community College (F)

PO Box 126, Polkton NC 28135-0126
County: Anson/Union FICE Identification: 007985
Unit ID: 197850
Telephone: (704) 272-5300 Carnegie Class: Assoc/Pub-R-M
FAX Number: (704) 272-5350 Calendar System: Semester
URL: www.spcc.edu
Established: 1999 Annual Undergrad Tuition & Fees (In-District): $2,237
Enrollment: 2,808 Coed
Affiliation or Control: State/Local IRS Status: 501(c)3
Highest Offering: Associate Degree
Program: Occupational; 2-Year Principally Bachelor's Creditable; Business Emphasis
Accreditation: SC, DMS, MAC, SURGT

02 President .... Dr. Stanley M. SIDOR
05 VP Student Learning .... Dr. Gene LOFLIN
10 VP of Finance & Administration Svcs .... Mr. John DEVITTO
32 VP Student Success .... Mrs. Elaine CLODFELTER
04 Exec Assistant to President .... Ms. Rita ADAMS
51 VP Corporate & Continuing Education ... Mr. Stuart WASILOWSKI
13 Exec Director Information Services .... Mr. Ernest SIMONS
08 Dean Learning Assessment & Resource .... Ms. Lynn GAMBON
06 Director of Records/Registrar .... Ms. Cathy HORNE
07 Director of Admissions/Enrollment .... Ms. Tracie BOONE
09 Director of Institutional Research .... Mr. Mark LUPTON
21 Director of Financial Services .... Ms. Michelle BROCK
26 Chief Public Information Officer .... Ms. Rosemary BRITT
15 Director Human Resources .... Ms. Susan R. FLAKE
18 Director Facility & Property Svcs .... Mr. William M. TRUETT
37 Director of Financial Aid .... Mr. John RATLIFF
84 Director Student Recruitment .... Mr. Scott COLLIER
96 Director of Purchasing .... Mr. Joe CAMERON
102 Exec Dir of Foundation & Cmty Rels .... Ms. Hayne WHITE
49 Chair Arts & Science .... Ms. Valerie JONES
76 Chair Allied Health .... Ms. Alice BRADLEY
88 Dean Learning Tech & Accountability .... Ms. Jill MILLARD
97 Dean Educational Programs .... Ms. Vicki HOLT
88 Chair Dev Educ & Academic Support .... Ms. Sharon CELLEMME
38 Director Counseling .... Ms. Serena JOHNSON
88 Director Adult Basic Skills Program .... Ms. Denise WILSON

*Southeastern Community College (G)

4564 Chadbourn Highway, PO Box 151,
Whiteville NC 28472-0151
County: Columbus FICE Identification: 002964
Unit ID: 199722
Telephone: (910) 642-7141 Carnegie Class: Assoc/Pub-R-M
FAX Number: (910) 642-5658 Calendar System: Semester
URL: www.sccnc.edu
Established: 1964 Annual Undergrad Tuition & Fees (In-State): $2,018
Enrollment: 2,074 Coed
Affiliation or Control: State IRS Status: 501(c)3
Highest Offering: Associate Degree
Program: Occupational; 2-Year Principally Bachelor's Creditable
Accreditation: SC, MLTAD

02 President .... Dr. Kathy MATLOCK
10 Vice President Operations/Finance .... Ms. Betty Jo RAMSEY
32 VP Student Development Services .... Ms. Matlynn B. YEOMAN
05 Vice Pres Curriculum Instruction .... Dr. Morgan PHILLIPS
51 VP Continuing Educ & Economic Dev .... Mrs. Beverlee S. NANCE
30 Exec Dean Institutional Advancement .... Mrs. Sue W. HAWKS
35 Dean of Student Services .... Mr. James F. FOWLER
06 Dir of Student Records/Registrar .... Mrs. Sylvia TART
08 Librarian .... Mrs. Kay HOUSER
07 Admissions/Records Assistant .... Ms. Shirley FLOYD
37 Director of Financial Aid .... Mr. Glenn HANSON
09 Director of Research & Assessment .... Ms. Susan HOUSEMAN
15 Director Personnel Services .... Ms. Betty Jo SANDERS
18 Chief Facilities/Physical Plant .... Ms. Betty Jo SANDERS
26 Director of Public Information .... Mrs. Karen A. VAUGHN
21 Controller/Operations/Finance .... Ms. Donna TURBEVILLE

*Southwestern Community College (H)

447 College Drive, Sylva NC 28779-8581
County: Jackson FICE Identification: 008466
Unit ID: 199731
Telephone: (828) 339-4000 Carnegie Class: Assoc/Pub-R-M
FAX Number: (828) 586-3129 Calendar System: Semester
URL: www.southwesterncc.edu
Established: 1964 Annual Undergrad Tuition & Fees (In-District): $2,224
Enrollment: 2,304 Coed
Affiliation or Control: State/Local IRS Status: 501(c)3
Highest Offering: Associate Degree
Program: Occupational; 2-Year Principally Bachelor's Creditable
Accreditation: SC, DMS, EMT, MLTAD, PTAA, RAD

02 Interim President/Exec VP/CFO .... Dr. Janet K. BURNETTE
05 Vice Pres Instructional Services .... Dr. Tom BROOKS
11 VP for Administrative Services .... Ms. Janet K. BURNETTE
51 VP Extension/Economic Development .... Ms. Susan MCCASKILL
12 VP Macon Campus/Inst Dev .... Dr. Connie M. HAIRE
13 VP Information Technology .... Mr. Ryan SCHWIEBERT
84 Dean of Enrollment Svcs/Stdnt Svcs .... Dr. Phil WEAST
06 Registrar .... Ms. Christy DEAVER
08 Director of Learning Resources .... Mrs. Dianne LINDGREM
09 Dean Research & Planning Officer .... Mr. Delos D. MONTEITH
27 Public Information Officer .... Ms. Rose GARRET
37 Coordinator of Financial Aid .... Ms. Melody L. LAWRENCE

*Stanly Community College (A)

141 College Drive, Albemarle NC 28001-7458
County: Stanly FICE Identification: 011194
Unit ID: 199740
Telephone: (704) 982-0121 Carnegie Class: Assoc/Pub-R-M
FAX Number: (704) 982-0819 Calendar System: Semester
URL: www.stanly.edu
Established: 1971 Annual Undergrad Tuition & Fees (In-District): $1,929
Enrollment: 3,149 Coed
Affiliation or Control: State/Local IRS Status: 501(c)3
Highest Offering: Associate Degree
Program: Occupational; 2-Year Principally Bachelor's Creditable
Accreditation: SC, MAC, MLTAD

02 President .... Dr. Mike TAYLOR
05 Exec VP Student/Academic Affairs .... Mrs. Robin MCCREE
10 Chief Financial Officer .... Mrs. Becky WALL
13 Chief Technology Officer .... Mr. Jim HILLIER
51 VP Cont Ed & Crutchfield Campus .... Dr. Tanya DAVIS
04 Exec Assistant to the President .... Mrs. Gaye WOOD
26 Asst to the President Marketing/PR .... Mrs. Michelle PEIFER
32 Interim Dean of Students .... Mr. Tony OETTINGER
51 Dean Continuing Education .... Mrs. Kathy GARDNER
76 Dean Health & Public Svcs .... Dr. Tammy CRUMP
72 Dean Business & Technology .... Mrs. Merlin AMIRTHARAJ
106 Dean Stanly Online .... Mr. Dennis SOUTHER
75 Dean of Technical & Vocational Pgms .... Mr. Ed THOMAS
06 Assoc Dean of Records/Registrar .... Mrs. Kristina EUDY
07 Assoc Dean of Admissions/Counseling .... Mrs. Denise ROSS
20 Assoc Dean of Academic Affairs .... Mrs. Tammy MCILWAINE
21 Controller .... Mrs. Debra HARWOOD
18 Director of Physical Plant .... Mr. David HINSON
88 Director of Learning Technologies .... Dr. Jana ULRICH
102 Foundation Director .... Mrs. Janet SISTARE
37 Dir Financial Aid/Veterans Affairs .... Ms. Petra FIELDS
15 Director Human Resources .... Miss Donna KIMREY
08 Director Library Services .... Mrs. Erin ALLEN
88 Director Basic Skills .... Ms. Dianne COOKER
24 Dir Testing/Media Specialist Svcs .... Mr. Mark SAMPLE
96 Purchasing Agent .... Mrs. Shelley OSBORNE

*Surry Community College (B)

630 S Main Street, Dobson NC 27017-0304
County: Surry FICE Identification: 002970
Unit ID: 199768
Telephone: (336) 386-8121 Carnegie Class: Assoc/Pub-R-M
FAX Number: (336) 386-8951 Calendar System: Semester
URL: www.surry.edu
Established: 1964 Annual Undergrad Tuition & Fees (In-State): $1,600
Enrollment: 3,503 Coed
Affiliation or Control: State IRS Status: 501(c)3
Highest Offering: Associate Degree
Program: Occupational; 2-Year Principally Bachelor's Creditable
Accreditation: SC, MAC, PTAA

02 Interim President .... Dr. James REEVES
05 Vice Pres Curriculum Programs .... Dr. Jami WOODS
10 Vice Pres Financial Services .... Mr. Tony L. MARTIN
32 Vice Pres Student Development .... Mrs. Jamie P. CHILDRESS
45 Vice President Planning .... Dr. Anne R. HENNIS
51 VP Corporate & Cont Education .... Dr. George O. SAPPENFIELD
11 Vice Pres of Administrative Svcs .... Mrs. Susan PENDERGRAFT
49 Dean of Arts & Sciences .... Ms. Connie WOLFE
50 Dean of Business/Computers/Engr .... Mr. Mike MILLER
55 Dean of Evening Studies .... Mr. Bob HEMMINGS
08 Assoc Dean of Learning Resources .... Dr. David WRIGHT
84 Assoc Dean Enrollment Mgmt .... Mr. Brian WEBB
37 Director Student Financial Aid .... Mrs. Andrea SIMPSON
14 Director Computer Center .... Ms. Rhonda HAZELWOOD
18 Chief Facilities & Physical Plant .... Mr. Randy ROGERS
40 Bookstore Manager .... Ms. Debbie WOLFE
41 Athletic Director .... Mr. Mark TUCKER
15 Human Resources Generalist .... Mrs. Melonie WEATHERS
96 Director of Purchasing .... Mrs. Cindy A. GALLIMORE
35 Coordinator Student Activities .... Mr. Tony V. SEARCY
07 Director of Admissions .... Mrs. Renita HAZELWOOD
19 Chief Campus Police .... Mr. Martin W. SHROPSHIRE

*Tri-County Community College (C)

21 Campus Circle, Murphy NC 28906-7919
County: Cherokee FICE Identification: 009430
Unit ID: 199795
Telephone: (828) 837-6810 Carnegie Class: Assoc/Pub-R-S
FAX Number: (828) 837-0028 Calendar System: Semester
URL: www.tricountycc.edu
Established: 1964 Annual Undergrad Tuition & Fees (In-State): $2,187
Enrollment: 1,474 Coed
Affiliation or Control: State IRS Status: 501(c)3
Highest Offering: Associate Degree
Program: Occupational; 2-Year Principally Bachelor's Creditable; Technical Emphasis
Accreditation: SC, MAC

02 President .... Dr. Donna TIPTON-ROGERS
11 Exec Vice Pres for Operations .... Ms. Jan WESTMORELAND
05 VP for Instructional Services .... Ms. Linda LOVINGOOD
09 VP for Institutional Effectiveness .... Dr. Steve WOOD
13 Dir of Computing & Information Mgt .... Mr. Jason OUTEN
30 Vice Pres for Resource Development .... Dr. Terrie KELLY
103 Dir of Economic & Workforce Develop .... Mr. Paul WORLEY
45 VP College & Community Initiatives .... Mr. Bo GRAY
12 Asst to Pres Graham Cty Operations .... Ms. Charlene WOOD
88 Dean Plng/Research Student Engage .... Mr. Jason CHAMBERS
04 Asst to Pres for Special Events .... Ms. Judy OWENBY
21 Comptroller/Chief Financial Officer .... Mr. Bill VESPASIAN
15 Director of Human Resources .... Ms. Sallie BAKER
91 Systems Administrator/Data Base Mgr .... Mr. Troy FORSYTH
08 Dean Learning Resources & Assessmt .... Ms. Linda KRESSAL
106 Distance Learning Coordinator .... Mr. Wes CHASTAIN
38 Coordinator Career/Counseling/Test .... Ms. Linda HOWELL
26 Communications Officer .... Ms. Carrie MCGAHA
06 Registrar - Curriculum .... Ms. Holly HYDE
37 Director of Financial Aid .... Ms. Diane OWL
96 Purchasing Agent .... Ms. Judy OWENBY
32 Director of Student Affairs .... Ms. Dotie STAFFORD-ORTEGA

*Vance-Granville Community College (D)

PO Box 917, Henderson NC 27536-0917
County: Vance FICE Identification: 009903
Unit ID: 199838
Telephone: (252) 492-2061 Carnegie Class: Assoc/Pub-R-M
FAX Number: (252) 430-0460 Calendar System: Semester
URL: www.vgcc.edu
Established: 1969 Annual Undergrad Tuition & Fees (In-State): $1,875
Enrollment: 4,352 Coed
Affiliation or Control: State Related IRS Status: 501(c)3
Highest Offering: Associate Degree
Program: Occupational; 2-Year Principally Bachelor's Creditable
Accreditation: SC, MAC, RAD

02 President .... Mr. Randy PARKER
05 Vice President of Instruction .... Dr. Angela BALLENTINE
10 Vice Pres for Finance & Operations .... Mr. Matt WILLIAMS
13 Vice Pres Information Technology .... Dr. Kenneth A. LEWIS, JR.
30 Vice President of Inst Advancement .... Ms. JoAnna JONES
32 Vice President of Student Affairs .... Mr. A. Gene PURVIS
31 Vice Pres Cmty/Economic Development .... Ms. Vanessa JONES
12 Dean South Campus .... Ms. Cecilia B. WHEELER
12 Dean Franklin County Campus .... Ms. Bobbie Jo C. MAY
12 Dean Warren County Campus .... Mr. George A. HENDERSON
08 Director Learning Resources Center .... Mr. Dave TRUDEAU
06 Registrar .... Ms. Kathy KTUL
15 Director of Human Resources .... Ms. Katherine WILLIAMSON
37 Director Financial Aid .... Mr. Frank A. CLARK
18 Director of Plant Operations .... Mr. Jack PUCKETT
27 Director of Marketing .... Ms. Elaine STEM
38 Director Student Counseling .... Mr. Daniel ALVARADO
07 Director of Admissions .... Ms. Tonya WADDLE
09 Director of Institutional Research .... Dr. Rodney FOTH
40 Bookstore Manager .... Ms. Sandra NEWTON

*Wake Technical Community College (E)

9101 Fayetteville Road, Raleigh NC 27603-5696
County: Wake FICE Identification: 004844
Unit ID: 199856
Telephone: (919) 866-5000 Carnegie Class: Assoc/Pub-U-MC
FAX Number: (919) 779-3360 Calendar System: Semester
URL: www.waketech.edu
Established: 1958 Annual Undergrad Tuition & Fees (In-District): $2,210
Enrollment: 17,864 Coed
Affiliation or Control: State/Local IRS Status: 501(c)3
Highest Offering: Associate Degree
Program: Occupational; 2-Year Principally Bachelor's Creditable
Accreditation: SC, ACFEI, DA, DH, MAC, MLTAD, RAD, SURGT

02 President .... Dr. Stephen C. SCOTT
03 Executive Vice President .... Mr. Gerald A. MITCHELL
11 Executive VP Administrative Affairs .... Vacant
10 Chief Business Officer .... Mrs. Debra S. WALLACE
43 General Counsel .... Ms. Clay T. HINES
05 Senior VP Curriculum Education Svcs .... Mr. Bryan K. RYAN
32 Senior VP Student Services .... Mrs. Rita H. JERMAN
51 Senior VP Continuing Education Svcs .... Mr. Samuel STRICKLAND
10 VP of Financial & Business Svcs .... Mr. Arthur W. ANDREWS
102 VP College Dev/Exec Dir Foundation .... Mr. O. Mort CONGLETON
12 Assoc VP Northern Wake Campus & HR .... Dr. D. Gayle GREENE
84 Assoc Vice Pres Enrollment Services .... Mr. John W. SAPARILAS
13 Chief Information Officer .... Dr. Darryl D. MCGRAW
18 Facility Engineering Officer .... Mr. Wendell B. GOODWIN
21 Chief Accounting Officer .... Ms. Marla L. TART
26 Director of Public Relations .... Mrs. Laurie C. CLOWERS
46 Director of IE/Research & Events .... Dr. John B. BOONE
30 Director of Development .... Mrs. Stephanie S. LAKE
25 Dean Sponsored Pgms & Fed Relations .... Mrs. Carol C. WHITE
84 Dean Enrollment/Records/Registrar .... Dr. Rosemary J. KELLY
06 Dean Records & Reg/Registrar CE .... Ms. Margaret R. ROBERTON
35 Dean of Students .... Dr. Paul A. NORMAN
72 Dean Educ Svcs & Technology .... Mr. Ray L. TIMS
37 Dean Student Support Svcs .... Mrs. Regina M. HUGGINS
35 Dean Student Svcs Northen Campus .... Mrs. Karen B. PHINAZEE
88 Sr Dir BioNetwork Learning Center .... Ms. Ana M. MCCLANAHAN
38 Associate Dean Advising/Retention .... Mr. Kevin A. BROWN
07 Dean Admissions/Outreach Services .... Ms. Susan R. BLOOMFIELD
08 Director Library Services .... Ms. Jackie L. CASE
27 Director Design & Publications .... Mrs. Francie W. SANDERSON
36 Director of Placement .... Mrs. Deborah L. HADLEY
15 Director of Human Resources .... Ms. Benita I. CLARK
19 Director of Security Svcs .... Mr. Robert S. GREGORY
76 Dean Health Sciences Campus .... Mrs. Dianne B. HINSON
81 Dean Mathematics/Sciences Div .... Ms. Tonya P. FORBES
79 Dean Arts/Humanities/Soc Sci Div .... Dr. Diane E. LODDER
50 Dean Business Technology .... Mrs. Sandra L. DIETRICH
75 Dean Applied Technologies .... Mr. Sammie C. THORNTON
12 Academic Dean Western Wake Campus .... Mr. James A. ROBERSON
55 Dean Evening Division .... Ms. Pamela M. LITTLE
51 Dean Community Projects/Educ Pgms .... Ms. Martha O. WILLIAMS
20 Dean Academic Support Division .... Vacant
77 Dean Computer & Engineering Tech .... Ms. Angela L. BEQUETTE
88 Dean Public Safety/Svc Occupations .... Mr. Anthony M. CAISON
88 Dean of Basic Skills .... Mrs. Susan B. PAYNE
50 Dean of Business & Industry .... Mr. Wayne A. LOOTS

*Wayne Community College (F)

3000 Wayne Memorial Drive Box 8002, Goldsboro NC 27533-8002
County: Wayne FICE Identification: 002980
Unit ID: 199892
Telephone: (919) 735-5151 Carnegie Class: Assoc/Pub-R-M
FAX Number: (919) 736-9425 Calendar System: Semester
URL: www.waynecc.edu
Established: 1957 Annual Undergrad Tuition & Fees (In-District): $2,220
Enrollment: 3,977 Coed
Affiliation or Control: State/Local IRS Status: 501(c)3
Highest Offering: Associate Degree
Program: Occupational; 2-Year Principally Bachelor's Creditable
Accreditation: SC, ADNUR, DA, DH, MAC, PNUR

02 President .... Dr. Kay H. ALBERTSON
05 Vice President Academic Services .... Dr. Peggy S. TEAGUE
32 Vice President Student Services .... Dr. Linda M. NELMS
51 VP Cont Educ/Workforce Preparedness .... Mr. Ray BURRELL
30 Assoc VP Institutional Advancement .... Mr. Bill T. THOMPSON
72 Division Head Applied Technologies .... Mr. Ernic WHITE
57 Division Head Arts & Sciences .... Mr. Gene SMITH
50 Div Head Business & Computer Tech .... Mrs. Beth HOOKS
76 Division Head Allied Health .... Mrs. Pattie PFEIFFER
88 Division Head Public Safety .... Ms. Beverly DEANS
62 Head Librarian .... Dr. Aletha ANDREW
12 Coordinator Seymour Johnson AFB .... Mrs. Dori FRASER
92 Honors Program Coordinator .... Mr. Brandon JENKINS
45 Chief Admin Support Services .... Mr. Bill THOMPSON
24 Director Media Production .... Mrs. Michelle TURNAGE
13 Director Information Systems .... Ms. Katherine JONES
18 Chief Facilities/Physical Plant .... Mr. Edward E. FARRIS
19 Chief Security .... Mr. Willie L. BRINSON
40 Director Bookstore .... Mrs. Trellie HERRING
51 Director Continuing Education .... Vacant
88 Director Business/Industry Center .... Mr. Joe MCMICHAEL
07 Director Admissions & Records .... Mrs. Susan M. SASSER
37 Director Student Financial Aid .... Mrs. Brenda D. MERCER
84 Dir Student Devel/Enrollment Mgmt .... Mrs. Joanna MORRISETTE
36 Coordinator Job Placement .... Mrs. Lorie WALLER
78 Director Cooperative Education .... Ms. Anne MILLINGTON
35 Student Activities Coordinator .... Mr. James BYNUM
10 Chief Financial Officer .... Mrs. Joy KORNEGAY
96 Accountant/Equipment Coordinator .... Mr. Mark R. JOHNSON
102 Executive Director of Foundation .... Mr. Jack KANNAN
26 Public Information Officer .... Ms. Tara HUMPHRIES
16 Personnel Coordinator .... Mrs. Ina R. RAWLINSON
55 Evening Div Curriculum/Cont Educ .... Mr. Richard HARRIS

*Western Piedmont Community College (G)

1001 Burkemont Avenue, Morganton NC 28655-4504
County: Burke FICE Identification: 002982
Unit ID: 199908
Telephone: (828) 438-6000 Carnegie Class: Assoc/Pub-R-M
FAX Number: (828) 438-6015 Calendar System: Semester
URL: www.wpcc.edu
Established: 1964 Annual Undergrad Tuition & Fees (In-State): $1,600
Enrollment: 3,117 Coed
Affiliation or Control: State IRS Status: 501(c)3
Highest Offering: Associate Degree
Program: Occupational; 2-Year Principally Bachelor's Creditable
Accreditation: SC, ADNUR, DA, MAC, MLTAD

02 President .... Dr. Jim W. BURNETT
10 Exec Vice Pres/Chief Financial Ofcr .... Mr. Malone C. MCNEELY
05 Vice President Academic Affairs .... Dr. Chad BLEDSOE
32 Vice President Student Development .... Ms. Emily L. WILLIAMSON
51 Dean of Continuing Education .... Mr. Lee KISER
35 Dean of Student Services .... Ms. Susan WILLIAMS
08 Dean Learning Resources/Technology .... Mr. Daniel R. SMITH
54 Dean Science/Engineering/Math .... Mr. Michael DANIELS
79 Dean Humanities/Social Sciences .... Mrs. Mary C. SAFFORD
76 Dean Health Sciences .... Dr. Linda S. SATEY
50 Dean Business Technologies .... Vacant
21 Controller .... Mrs. Sandra K. HOILMAN
06 Registrar .... Mrs. Joan P. HOGAN
15 Director Human Resources .... Ms. Lisa H. SESSIONS
07 Director of Admissions .... Mrs. Jennifer PROPST
37 Director Student Financial Aid .... Mr. Keith A. CONLEY
91 Director Management Info Systems .... Ms. Nancy E. NORRIS
09 Director of Planning & Research .... Mr. William L. LEFEVERS

96 Director of Purchasing ... Ms. Linda CARSWELL
18 Director of Maintenance ... Vacant

Wilkes Community College (A)

1328 S Collegiate Drive, Wilkesboro NC 28697-0120
County: Wilkes FICE Identification: 002983
Unit ID: 199926
Telephone: (336) 838-6100 Carnegie Class: Assoc/Pub-R-M
FAX Number: (336) 903-3219 Calendar System: Semester
URL: www.wilkescc.edu
Established: 1965 Annual Undergrad Tuition & Fees (In-State): $2,248
Enrollment: 2,721 Coed
Affiliation or Control: State IRS Status: 501(c)3
Highest Offering: Associate Degree
Program: Occupational; 2-Year Principally Bachelor's Creditable; Technical Emphasis
Accreditation: SC, DA, MAC

02 President ... Dr. Gordon G. BURNS
05 Sr VP of Instruction ... Dr. Dean E. SPRINKLE
32 VP of Instr Support/Student Svcs ... Ms. Kim E. FAW
10 Senior VP of Administration ... Mr. D. Morgan FRANCIS, JR.
18 Assoc VP Facilities Services ... Mr. Frank S. SHUFORD
30 Exec Director/Endowment ... Ms. Allison PHILLIPS
51 VP of Continuing Education ... Mr. Calvin R. DULL
13 Assoc VP Information Technology ... Mr. Mike WINGLER
12 Assoc VP Ashe Campus ... Mr. Christopher D. ROBINSON
12 Director Alleghany Center ... Ms. Jayne PHIPPS-BOGER
06 Registrar ... Ms. Melonie KILBY
07 Director of Admissions ... Mr. Scott JOHNSON
37 Director of Financial Aid ... Ms. Vickie G. CALL
35 Director Student Support Services ... Ms. Angela SCHEUERMANN
08 Interim Director Learning Resources ... Ms. Christy EARP
45 Inst Effectiveness Exec Director ... Mr. J. Kelly PIPES, III
15 Director of Human Resources ... Mr. Tracy D. MCENTIRE
38 Director Counseling & Career Svcs ... Dr. Lynda K. BLACK
84 Director Enrollment Mgmt/Stdnt Life ... Ms. Jane BOWMAN
26 PIO & Relations Officer ... Ms. Amber HERMAN
50 Dean Business/Public Svc Tech Div ... Mrs. Robin PHILLIPS-HAUSER
76 Dean Health Sciences Division ... Ms. Joyce MINTON
49 Dean Arts & Sciences Division ... Ms. Blair M. HANCOCK
72 VP Adv Industrial/Health Tech ... Mr. John HAUSER
106 Chair e-Learning & Prof Development ... Mrs. Deborah M. MCGUIRE

Wilson Community College (B)

902 Herring Avenue, Wilson NC 27893-3310
County: Wilson FICE Identification: 004845
Unit ID: 199953
Telephone: (252) 291-1195 Carnegie Class: Assoc/Pub-R-M
FAX Number: (252) 243-7148 Calendar System: Semester
URL: www.wilsoncc.edu
Established: 1958 Annual Undergrad Tuition & Fees (In-State): $1,913
Enrollment: 2,132 Coed
Affiliation or Control: State IRS Status: 501(c)3
Highest Offering: Associate Degree
Program: Occupational; 2-Year Principally Bachelor's Creditable
Accreditation: SC, SURGT

02 President ... Dr. Rusty STEPHENS
05 Vice Pres Instruction/Student Devel ... Dr. Denise L. SESSOMS
10 Vice Pres for Finance & Admin Svcs ... Mr. Hadie C. HORNE
51 Dean of Cont Educ/Sustainability ... Mr. Robert D. HOLSTEN
32 Dean of Student Development ... Mr. Don L. BOYETTE
76 Associate Dean of Allied Health ... Ms. Glenda P. BONDURANT
88 Assoc Dean Trades/Public Services ... Ms. Kelly KINGRY
49 Assoc Dean Arts & Sciences/ Dev Std ... Ms. Debra S. HOLLEY
50 Assoc Dean of Business/Comp Tech ... Ms. Lorraine RAPER
15 Dir of Human Resources/Marketing ... Ms. Denise M. HORNE
08 Head Librarian ... Mr. Gerry J. O'NEILL
45 Planning & Research Director ... Ms. Pat B. PERRY
21 Controller ... Ms. Jessica S. JONES
07 Director of Admissions/Registrar ... Mr. Leonard W. MANSFIELD
18 Director of Facilities ... Mr. Tim H. STRICKLAND
37 Dir of Financial Aid/Vet Affairs ... Mr. S. Rex BISSETTE
102 Director of Foundation ... Ms. Lynn WAGNER
13 Director of IT & Audit Services ... Ms. Linda MOORING
96 Purchasing Manager ... Ms. Donna A. TURNER
40 Bookstore Manager ... Ms. Kaschia SPELLS

North Carolina Wesleyan College (C)

3400 N Wesleyan Boulevard,
Rocky Mount NC 27804-8630
County: Nash FICE Identification: 002951
Unit ID: 199209
Telephone: (252) 985-5100 Carnegie Class: Bac/Diverse
FAX Number: (252) 985-5231 Calendar System: 4/1/4
URL: www.ncwc.edu
Established: 1956 Annual Undergrad Tuition & Fees: $24,890
Enrollment: 1,408 Coed
Affiliation or Control: United Methodist IRS Status: 501(c)3
Highest Offering: Baccalaureate
Program: Liberal Arts And General; Teacher Preparatory
Accreditation: SC, TED

01 President ... Mr. James A. GRAY, III
05 Vice President Academic Affairs ... Dr. Jay STUBBLEFIELD
10 Vice President of Finance ... Mrs. Loren W. LOOMIS-HUBBELL
30 Vice President of Development . Mr. Christopher NORMAN, CFRE
84 Vice President of Enrollment ... Mr. Bill ALLEN
32 VP Student Affairs/Dean of Students ... Mr. Randy WILLIAMS
09 Director of Institutional Research ... Mr. Larry KELLEY
06 Registrar ... Mr. Cliff SULLIVAN
08 Director of Library ... Mrs. Kathy WINSLOW
26 Director of Communications ... Vacant
23 Director Wellness Ctr/College Nurse ... Ms. Holly FAIRLEY
36 Director Internship & Career Center ... Ms. Tiffany ALEXANDER
19 Director of Campus Security ... Vacant
41 Director of Athletics ... Mr. John THOMPSON
29 Director Alumni Rels/Annual Fund ... Mr. Joshua CAIN
21 Controller ... Ms. Robin CHAMP
37 Director of Financial Aid ... Ms. Leah HILL
15 Director of Human Resources ... Mr. Darrell S. WHITLEY
18 Chief Facilities/Physical Plant ... Mr. Attila SZEKES
07 Interim Director of Admissions ... Ms. Lori MELTON
38 Director Student Counseling ... Ms. Leslie VEACH
40 Manager College Store ... Ms. Rachel T. DIX

Peace College (D)

15 E Peace Street, Raleigh NC 27604-1194
County: Wake FICE Identification: 002953
Unit ID: 199272
Telephone: (919) 508-2000 Carnegie Class: Bac/A&S
FAX Number: (919) 508-2326 Calendar System: Semester
URL: www.peace.edu
Established: 1857 Annual Undergrad Tuition & Fees: $25,686
Enrollment: 558 Female
Affiliation or Control: Presbyterian Church (U.S.A.) IRS Status: 501(c)3
Highest Offering: Baccalaureate
Program: Liberal Arts And General
Accreditation: SC

01 President ... Dr. Debra M. TOWNSLEY
04 Executive Secretary to President ... Ms. Patricia L. LUKASZEWSKI
05 Provost ... Dr. Debbie M. COTTRELL
30 Exec Dir of Development & Alumnae ... Ms. Julie E. RICCIARDI
10 Vice Pres Finance & Administration ... Mr. George A. YEARWOOD
107 Dean Wm Peace School of Prof Stds ... Ms. Laurie ALBERT
15 Director Human Resources ... Ms. Amber M. KIMBALL
84 Dean of Enrollment & Adult Educ ... Mr. Matthew T. GREEN
88 Dean of Student & Academic Services ... Mr. Jerry J. NUESELL
35 Assistant Dean of Students ... Vacant
06 Registrar ... Ms. Susan L. GREINER
08 Director of Library Services ... Mr. Nathan J. HELLMERS
27 Chief Information Officer ... Mr. Larry ESSARY
18 Director of Facilities ... Mr. John B. CRANHAM
19 Director Campus Safety & Security ... Mr. Michael A. JOHN
23 Director of Health Services ... Ms. Mari LIPPIG
35 Director of Student Engagement ... Vacant
36 Director of Career Services ... Ms. Barbara M. EFIRD
37 Director of Financial Aid ... Ms. Angela J. KIRKLEY
41 Director of Athletics ... Mr. P. Kelly JOHNSON, JR.
42 Chaplain ... Rev. R. Lee CARTER
21 Comptroller ... Ms. Susan T. CHILDS
84 Vice Pres Enrollment Mgmt/Admission . Ms. Amber L. STENBECK
07 Associate Director of Admissions ... Ms. Jenny L. PEACOCK
40 Bookstore Manager ... Ms. Brittany LITTLE
44 Director of Loyalty Fund ... Vacant
39 Assistant Dean for Campus Life ... Ms. Dawn M. DILLON

Pfeiffer University (E)

48380 US Highway 52 N / PO Box 960,
Misenheimer NC 28109-0960
County: Stanly FICE Identification: 002955
Unit ID: 199306
Telephone: (704) 463-1360 Carnegie Class: Master's L
FAX Number: (704) 463-1363 Calendar System: Semester
URL: www.pfeiffer.edu
Established: 1885 Annual Undergrad Tuition & Fees: $21,230
Enrollment: 1,961 Coed
Affiliation or Control: United Methodist IRS Status: 501(c)3
Highest Offering: Master's
Program: Liberal Arts And General; Teacher Preparatory; Professional
Accreditation: SC, MFCD, MUS, TED

01 President ... Mr. Michael C. MILLER
04 Executive Assistant to President ... Ms. Shari L. DUNN
11 Chief Operations Officer ... Vacant
10 Vice President for Finance ... Ms. Robin A. LESLIE
05 Provost/VP Academic Affairs ... Dr. Tracy Y. ESPY
84 VP for Enrollment Mgmt/Marketing ... Mr. Michael POLL
32 VP for Student Development ... Dr. Russell SHARPLES
30 VP for Advancement ... Vacant
07 Director of Undergrad Admissions .. Ms. Terry PARKER-JEFFRIES
20 Associate VP for Academic Affairs ... Dr. Alan BELCHER
06 Registrar ... Ms. Lourdes SILVA
15 Director of Human Resources ... Ms. Kathy ODELL
09 Director Institutional Rsrch/Plng ... Ms. Eva EISNAUGLE
26 Director Inst Communications ... Ms. Susan G. MESSINA
38 Director Counseling/Residence Educ ... Ms. Laura HERRICK
08 Acquisitions Librarian ... Mr. John MERCER, JR.
37 Director of Financial Aid ... Ms. Amy BROWN
13 Acting Director of IT ... Mr. Peter FREER
07 Associate Director of Admissions ... Ms. Diane MARTIN
20 Dir of Academic Support Services ... Dr. Jim E. GULLEDGE
19 Int Dir of Campus Safety & Security ... Mr. Erik MCGINNIS
23 Director of Health Services ... Vacant
18 Director of Facilities ... Ms. Sharon K. BARD
41 Athletic Director ... Ms. Mary Ann SUNBURY
42 Minister to the University ... Rev. Dana MCKIM
36 Director of Career Services ... Vacant
35 Dir Student Activ/Judicial Affairs ... Vacant
50 Dean Sch of Business/Dean MBA Pgm ... Vacant
53 Dean of School of Education ... Vacant
79 Dean of School of Humanities ... Dr. David HECKEL
81 Dean Sch of Natural & Health Sci ... Dr. Mark MCCALLUM
83 Dean Sch of Soc & Behav Sciences ... Dr. Donald POE, JR.
51 Exec Dir School of Adult Studies ... Vacant
88 Director of MBA/MHA Program ... Dr. Joel VICKERS
88 Exec Director Intl Business Studies ... Vacant
58 Director MS Org Leadership & Change ... Vacant
58 Director of MCE Program ... Rev. Kathleen KILBOURNE
102 Assoc VP Adv/Dir Corp & Found Rels ... Vacant
44 Director of Alumni & Annual Giving ... Mr. Paul CLARK
39 Director of Residence Life ... Ms. Rebecca MCQUEEN
40 Bookstore Manager ... Vacant
12 Director of Triangle Campus ... Mr. Bennie L. FELTS

Piedmont Baptist College and Graduate School (F)

420 S Broad Street, Winston-Salem NC 27101-5197
County: Forsyth FICE Identification: 002956
Unit ID: 199315
Telephone: (336) 725-8344 Carnegie Class: Spec/Faith
FAX Number: (336) 725-5522 Calendar System: Semester
URL: www.pbc.edu
Established: 1945 Annual Undergrad Tuition & Fees: $11,740
Enrollment: 411 Coed
Affiliation or Control: Independent Non-Profit IRS Status: 501(c)3
Highest Offering: Doctorate
Program: Liberal Arts And General; Teacher Preparatory; Religious Emphasis
Accreditation: TRACS

01 President ... Dr. Charles W. PETITT
00 Chancellor ... Dr. Howard L. WILBURN
05 Provost ... Dr. Beth D. ASHBURN
11 Vice President of Administration ... Mr. Barry GRIFFITH
20 Vice President of Academics ... Dr. Jeff MCCANN
30 Director of Advancement ... Dr. Jeffrey CRUM
06 Registrar ... Mrs. Darlene RICHTER
08 Librarian ... Mrs. Delores FULTON
32 Dean of Students ... Mr. Erich RICHTER
34 Dean of Women ... Mrs. Rebecca BOTTOMS

Queens University of Charlotte (G)

1900 Selwyn Avenue, Charlotte NC 28274-0001
County: Mecklenburg FICE Identification: 002957
Unit ID: 199412
Telephone: (704) 337-2200 Carnegie Class: Master's M
FAX Number: (704) 337-2517 Calendar System: Semester
URL: www.queens.edu
Established: 1857 Annual Undergrad Tuition & Fees: $25,356
Enrollment: 2,530 Coed
Affiliation or Control: Presbyterian Church (U.S.A.) IRS Status: 501(c)3
Highest Offering: Master's
Program: Liberal Arts And General; Teacher Preparatory; Professional; Business Emphasis
Accreditation: SC, ACBSP, ADNUR, BUS, MUS, NURSE, TED

01 President ... Dr. Pamela L. DAVIES
05 VP Academic Affairs & Provost ... Dr. Abiodun GOKE-PARIOLA
30 Vice Pres University Advancement ... Mr. James BULLOCK
84 Vice Pres Enrollment Management ... Dr. Brian RALPH
10 Vice Pres for Finance ... Mrs. Susan GARY
26 Vice Pres Marketing & Cmty Rels ... Mrs. Rebecca ANDERSON
45 VP Campus Planning and Services ... Mr. Bill NICHOLS
11 CFO & VP for Administration ... Mr. Matthew PACKEY
29 Exec Director Alumni Relations ... Ms. Sara BLAKENEY
32 Dean of Students ... Dr. John DOWNEY
06 Registrar ... Mr. Ed ADAMS
07 Dir Tradition Undergrad Admissions ... Mr. Will LEE
09 Director of Inst Research & Assess ... Dr. Jamie SLATER
39 Director Residence Life ... Mr. Thom SHEPARD
14 Director Information Technology ... Mr. Glenn LOOMER
15 Director of Human Resources ... Ms. Teri ORSINI, SPHR
08 University Librarian ... Dr. Carol W. JORDAN
36 Exec Dir Internships/Career Pgm ... Mr. Bill MEANS
42 Chaplain/Director Campus Ministry ... Rev. J. Diane MOWREY
19 Chief of Campus Police ... Mr. Johnnie RAVENELL
41 Director of Athletics ... Ms. Jeannie KING
88 Director of Belk Intl Programs ... Dr. Eric J. LIEN
18 Facilities Manager ... Mr. Tim ESTEP
50 Dean of McColl School of Business ... Mr. Terry BRODERICK
49 Int Dean Col of Arts & Sciences ... Dr. Lynn MORTON
53 Dean School of Education ... Dr. Darrel MILLER
66 Dean Blair College of Health ... Dr. William CODY
55 Dean of Hayworth College ... Mrs. Krista TILLMAN
60 Dean Knight School of Communication ... Mr. Van KING
04 Exec Director Pres Affairs ... Mrs. Tamara BURRELL
21 Treasurer ... Mrs. Christy MAJORS
19 AVP Campus Safety & Security ... Mr. Clarence BIRKHEAD

Reformed Theological Seminary (H)

2101 Carmel Road, Charlotte NC 28226-6399
County: Mecklenburg Identification: 666785
Unit ID: 405924

Telephone: (704) 366-5066 Carnegie Class: Not Classified
FAX Number: (704) 366-9295 Calendar System: 4/1/4
URL: www.rts.edu
Established: 1992 Annual Graduate Tuition & Fees: $14,655
Enrollment: 306 Coed
Affiliation or Control: Independent Non-Profit IRS Status: 501(c)3
Highest Offering: Doctorate; No Undergraduates
Program: Professional; Religious Emphasis
Accreditation: &SC, &THEOL

00 Chancellor & CEO ....Dr. Robert C. CANNADA, JR.
01 President ....Dr. Michael A. MILTON
05 Academic Dean ....Dr. Michael J. KRUGER
10 Vice Pres Business Administration ....Mr. Stephen J. HALVORSON
30 Vice President Development ....Mr. Charlie DUNN
32 Dean Student Development ....Dr. Rodney A. CULBERTSON, JR.
34 Dean of Women ....Mrs. Tari WILLIAMSON
07 Director of Admissions ....Mr. Stephane JEANRENAUD
08 Library Director ....Mr. Kenneth J. MCMULLEN
09 Director Institutional Assessment ....Mrs. Pauline M. STONE
06 Registrar ....Mrs. Angela P. QUEEN
13 Director Information Technology ....Mr. Todd WHITING

† Regional accreditation is carried under the parent institution in Jackson, MS.

St. Andrews Presbyterian College (A)

1700 Dogwood Mile, Laurinburg NC 28352-5598
County: Scotland FICE Identification: 002967
Unit ID: 199698
Telephone: (910) 277-5000 Carnegie Class: Bac/Diverse
FAX Number: (910) 277-5020 Calendar System: Semester
URL: www.sapc.edu
Established: 1896 Annual Undergrad Tuition & Fees: $30,552
Enrollment: 441 Coed
Affiliation or Control: Presbyterian Church (U.S.A.) IRS Status: 501(c)3
Highest Offering: Baccalaureate
Program: Liberal Arts And General
Accreditation: &SC, TED

01 President ....Mr. Paul BALDASARE
05 Vice Pres Acad Affs/Dean of College ....Dr. Robert J. HOPKINS
10 Vice Pres Business and Finance ....Ms. Terry LAUGHTER
11 Vice Pres Administration ....Mr. Glenn T. BATTEN
30 Vice Pres Institutional Advancement ....Vacant
84 Vice Pres Enrollment ....Ms. Cynthia R. ROBINSON
32 Dean of Students/Athletic Director ....Mr. Glenn T. BATTEN
06 Registrar ....Ms. Deborah A. SMITH
08 Interim Librarian ....Ms. Mary MCDONALD
14 Director of Computer Services ....Mr. Tony D. INSKEEP
56 Assoc Dean Adult & Extension Pgm ....Dr. William T. MCCONNELL
15 Director Personnel Services ....Ms. Millie ENGLISH
18 Chief Facilities/Physical Plant ....Mr. William S. JAMES
29 Director of Alumni Relations ....Vacant
36 Director Career Services ....Ms. Renee P. JONES
37 Director Student Financial Aid ....Ms. Kimberly A. DRIGGERS
09 Director of Institutional Research ....Ms. Deborah A. SMITH
26 Director of Communications ....Ms. Melissa HOPKINS
35 Sr Assoc Dean of Students/Security ....Mr. Lewis STROUD
40 Director Bookstore ....Ms. Janet SCHILLING
20 Associate Academic Officer ....Dr. Edna A. LOFTUS
96 Director of Purchasing ....Mr. William S. JAMES
07 Director of Admissions ....Ms. Kirsten SIMMONS

† Branch campus of Webber International University, FL.

Saint Augustine's College (B)

1315 Oakwood Avenue, Raleigh NC 27610-2298
County: Wake FICE Identification: 002968
Unit ID: 199582
Telephone: (919) 516-4000 Carnegie Class: Bac/Diverse
FAX Number: (919) 828-0817 Calendar System: Semester
URL: www.st-aug.edu
Established: 1867 Annual Undergrad Tuition & Fees: $17,160
Enrollment: 1,508 Coed
Affiliation or Control: Protestant Episcopal IRS Status: 501(c)3
Highest Offering: Baccalaureate
Program: Liberal Arts And General; Teacher Preparatory
Accreditation: SC, TED

01 President ....Dr. Dianne BOARDLEY SUBER
04 Exec Assistant to the President ....Mrs. Gloria T. ROWLAND
89 Special Asst to Pres/FYE Director ....Mr. Michael P. JACKSON
03 Executive Vice President ....Mr. Leon L. SCOTT
05 Provost ....Dr. B. Connie ALLEN
30 VP Institutional Advancement ....Mr. Marc A. NEWMAN
10 Vice Pres for Business & Finance ....Vacant
32 Vice Pres Enroll Mgmt/Student Svcs ....Vacant
88 VP Strategic Initiatives ....Dr. Ronald H. BROWN
21 Asst Vice Pres for Business/Finance ....Ms. Angela N. HAYNES
20 Asst VP Academic Affairs ....Dr. Orlando E. HANKINS
21 Asst Vice President/Comptroller ....Ms. Peta-Gaye SHAW
26 Assoc VP Marketing & Communication ....Mrs. Shelley M. WILLINGHAM-HINTON
09 Asst VP Institutional Research ....Dr. Tammalyn M. THOMAS-GOLDEN
35 Dean of Students & Residential Life ....Mrs. Doris J. BULLOCK
42 Chaplain ....Vacant
13 Chief Information Officer ....Dr. Stephen G. SCHOLZ
15 Director Human Resources ....Ms. Lottie R. FERRELL
41 Director Athletics ....Mr. George D. WILLIAMS
06 Registrar ....Ms. Crystal G. WILLIAMS
50 Dean Business & Computer Science ....Mr. Kent R. LUSK
83 Dean Social Sciences ....Dr. Paul K. BAKER
81 Dean Natural Sciences/Mathematics ....Dr. Mark A. MELTON
76 Dean Allied Health ....Dr. Hengameh G. ALLEN
49 Interim Dean Liberal Arts & Educ ....Dr. M. Iyailu MOSES
56 Dean Extended Studies ....Dr. Roland N. BULLARD
07 Director Admissions ....Mr. Jorge E. SOUSA
37 Director Financial Aid/Scholarships ....Ms. Nadine Y. FORD
08 Interim Director Library Services ....Mr. Clevell S. ROSEBORO
36 Director Career Services ....Ms. Nichole R. LEWIS
19 Acting Chief of Police ....Mr. George H. BOYKIN, III
18 Director Physical Plant ....Ms. Sonya Y. CANNADY
29 Director Alumni Affairs ....Ms. Sheryl H. XIMINES
90 Director Academic Computing ....Ms. Carlene J. MORGAN

Salem College (C)

601 South Church Street, Winston-Salem NC 27101
County: Forsyth FICE Identification: 002960
Unit ID: 199607
Telephone: (336) 721-2600 Carnegie Class: Bac/A&S
FAX Number: (336) 917-5339 Calendar System: 4/1/4
URL: www.salem.edu
Established: 1772 Annual Undergrad Tuition & Fees: $22,360
Enrollment: 1,039 Female
Affiliation or Control: Moravian Church IRS Status: 501(c)3
Highest Offering: Master's
Program: Liberal Arts And General; Teacher Preparatory; Professional
Accreditation: SC, MUS, TED

01 President ....Dr. Susan E. PAULY
05 VP Acad & Stdnt Affs/Dn of College ....Dr. Susan CALOUINI
30 VP for Institutional Advancement ....Ms. Vicki SHEPPARD
07 Dean Admissions & Financial Aid ....Ms. Katherine K. WATTS
32 Dean of Students ....Ms. Krispin W. BARR
58 Dean of Graduate Studies ....Dr. Susan GEBHARD
51 Dean of Continuing Studies ....Ms. Suzanne WILLIAMS
20 Int Dean Undergraduate Studies ....Dr. Gary LJUNGQUIST
11 Director of Administration ....Ms. Anna GALLIMORE
08 Librarian ....Dr. Rose A. SIMON
44 Director Annual Giving ....Ms. Laura SLAWTER
13 Director Information Technology ....Mr. Paul BENNINGER
15 Director of Payroll & Benefits ....Ms. Peggy BLACKBURN
10 Chief Financial Officer ....Mr. Derek BRYAN
38 Director Counseling Services ....Mr. Jack LOCICERO
37 Director Student Financial Aid ....Ms. Lori LEWIS
27 Director of Communications ....Ms. Jacqueline MCBRIDE
26 Assistant Director Public Relations ....Ms. Jennifer BRINGLE
36 Director Career Devel/Internships ....Ms. Esther GONZALEZ
06 Registrar/Dir Inst Research ....Mr. Mark ASHLEY
18 Chief Facilities/Physical Plant ....Mr. Rick DUGGINS
29 Director Alumnae Relations ....Ms. Karla GORT
21 Accounts Receivable Manager ....Ms. Nikki BROCK
21 Accounts Payable Manager ....Ms. Judy SIGMON
19 Coordinator Institutional Services ....Mr. Tommy WILLIAMSON

Shaw University (D)

118 E South Street, Raleigh NC 27601
County: Wake FICE Identification: 002962
Unit ID: 199643
Telephone: (919) 546-8200 Carnegie Class: Bac/Diverse
FAX Number: (919) 546-8301 Calendar System: Semester
URL: www.shawuniversity.edu
Established: 1865 Annual Undergrad Tuition & Fees: $13,226
Enrollment: 2,722 Coed
Affiliation or Control: Baptist IRS Status: 501(c)3
Highest Offering: Master's
Program: Liberal Arts And General
Accreditation: SC, KIN, SW, TED, THEOL

01 Interim President ....Dr. Dorothy COWSER YANCY
100 Chief of Staff ....Mr. Mack WARD
32 Vice Pres Student Affairs/Admin ....Dr. Jeffrey SMITH
05 Vice Pres Academic Affairs ....Dr. Marilyn SUTTON-HAYWOOD
10 Int VP for Fiscal Affairs ....Mr. Malcolm WEEKES
30 VP Institutional Advancement ....Ms. Anita BROWER
45 Dir of Stratetic Planning/Inst Res ....Dr. Cecil MCMANUS
84 Dean of Enrollment Management ....Ms. Rochelle KING
42 Assoc Dean of Chapel ....Ms. Donna BATTLE
15 Director of Human Resources ....Ms. Diane CRAWFORD
32 Dean of Students ....Ms. Doris BULLOCK
08 Dir of Library Services ....Ms. Carolyn PETERSON
21 Controller ....Mr. Malcolm WEEKES
06 Registrar ....Ms. Jody HAMILTON-DAVIS
27 Chief Information Officer ....Mr. Hooshang FOROUDASTAN
49 Dean Col of Arts and Sciences ....Dr. Renata DUSENBURY
58 Dean Col of Grad/Prof Studies ....Dr. Gaddis FAULCON
73 Dean Shaw Univ Divinity School ....Dr. Bruce GRADY
37 Director of Financial Aid ....Ms. Rochelle KING
29 Director Alumni Affairs ....Vacant
18 Facility Manager ....Mr. Darrell DANIELS
96 Director of Purchasing ....Mrs. Cynthia HILL
25 Int Dir Inst for HSC Research ....Dr. Moses GOLDMAN
25 Int Dir Title III/Sponsored Pgms ....Mr. Mack WARD
38 Director of Counseling Center ....Ms. Jerelene CARVER
88 Dir Judicial Affairs ....Ms. Agnes BAXTER
39 Dir Residence Life ....Ms. Shannon BENNETT
36 Dir Experiential Lrng/Career Devel ....Dr. Denise VAUGHN
21 Bursar ....Ms. Shirley FENNELL
50 Chair Dept Business/Public Admin ....Dr. Mma KALU
53 Chair Department Education ....Dr. Paula MOTEN-TOLSON
81 Chair Dept Natural Science/Math ....Dr. Renata DUSENBURY
76 Chair Dept Allied Health ....Dr. James MCCALLUM
79 Chair Department of Humanities ....Dr. Desire' BALOUBI
60 Chair Dept Mass Communication ....Dr. Kandace HARRIS
57 Chair Dept Visual/Performing Arts ....Mr. George HATCHER
83 Interim Chair Dept Social Sciences ....Dr. Lana RIGGINS
77 Chair Dept Computer/Information Sci ....Dr. Walter JOHNSON
88 Chair Dept Religion/Philosophy ....Dr. William THURSTON

Shepherds Theological Seminary (E)

6051 Tryon Road, Cary NC 27518-9316
County: Wake Identification: 666396
Telephone: (800) 672-3060 Carnegie Class: Not Classified
FAX Number: (919) 459-0022 Calendar System: Semester
URL: www.shepherds.edu
Established: 2003 Annual Graduate Tuition & Fees: $5,060
Enrollment: 80 Coed
Affiliation or Control: Independent Non-Profit IRS Status: 501(c)3
Highest Offering: Master's; No Undergraduates
Program: Professional; Religious Emphasis
Accreditation: TRACS

01 President ....Dr. Stephen DAVEY
05 Vice President & Dean ....Dr. Larry PETTEGREW
06 Registrar ....Dr. Randall L. MCKINION
07 Director of Recruitment ....Dr. Douglas BOOKMAN
18 Chief Facilities/Physical Plant ....Dr. Samuel WINCHESTER
30 Development ....Dr. William BARBER
37 Financial Aid Officer ....Mrs. Lucy BURGGRAFF

South College (F)

29 Turtle Creek Drive, Asheville NC 28803-3152
County: Buncombe FICE Identification: 010264
Unit ID: 198242
Telephone: (828) 277-5521 Carnegie Class: Assoc/PrivFP4
FAX Number: (828) 277-6151 Calendar System: Quarter
URL: www.southcollegenc.edu
Established: 1905 Annual Undergrad Tuition & Fees: $14,700
Enrollment: 270 Coed
Affiliation or Control: Proprietary IRS Status: Proprietary
Highest Offering: Baccalaureate
Program: Occupational; 2-Year Principally Bachelor's Creditable
Accreditation: ACICS, MAC, PTAA, RAD, SURGT

00 President/Owner ....Mr. Stephen A. SOUTH
01 Executive Director ....Ms. Trina VAZQUEZ
05 Dean of Academic Affairs ....Vacant
10 Business Manager ....Mr. Wayne WOODROW
07 Director of Admissions ....Vacant
37 Financial Aid Officer ....Ms. Ronda BLACKMAN
08 Head Librarian ....Ms. Jennifer FINLEY

Southeastern Baptist Theological Seminary (G)

Box 1889, Wake Forest NC 27588-1889
County: Wake FICE Identification: 002963
Unit ID: 199759
Telephone: (919) 761-2100 Carnegie Class: Not Classified
FAX Number: N/A Calendar System: Semester
URL: www.sebts.edu
Established: 1950 Annual Undergrad Tuition & Fees: $8,090
Enrollment: 2,281 Coed
Affiliation or Control: Southern Baptist IRS Status: 501(c)3
Highest Offering: Doctorate
Program: Professional
Accreditation: SC, THEOL

01 President ....Dr. Daniel L. AKIN
05 Academic Vice Pres/Dean of Faculty ....Dr. Kenneth KEATHLEY
10 Sr VP for Business Administration ....Mr. Ryan HUTCHINSON
20 Associate Academic Officer ....Dr. Travis E. WRIGHT
06 Registrar ....Mr. Sheldon ALEXANDER
07 Director of Admissions ....Mr. Shane BAKER
09 Institutional Effectiveness Coord ....Dr. Travis E. WRIGHT
29 Director of Alumni Development ....Mr. Albie BRICE
30 Vice Pres Institutional Advancement ....Mr. Dennis DARVILLE
37 Director of Financial Aid ....Dr. Don ALLARD

Southern Evangelical Seminary (H)

3000 Tilley Morris Road, Matthews NC 28105-8635
County: Union FICE Identification: 036115
Unit ID: 438522
Telephone: (704) 847-5600 Carnegie Class: Not Classified
FAX Number: (704) 845-1747 Calendar System: Semester
URL: www.ses.edu
Established: 1992 Annual Undergrad Tuition & Fees: $6,710
Enrollment: 622 Coed
Affiliation or Control: Independent Non-Profit IRS Status: 501(c)3
Highest Offering: Doctorate
Program: Religious Emphasis
Accreditation: TRACS

01 President & COO ....Mr. Robert C. WESTRA
07 Director of Admissions/Exec VP ....Mr. Duke HALE
05 Dean of the Seminary ....Dr. Wayne R. DETZLER

10 Business Manager ... Mrs. Joan C. SOLHEIM
08 Librarian ... Mr. Ronald I. JORDAHL
06 Registrar ... Dr. Douglas E. POTTER
29 Director Alumni Relations ... Mrs. Cheryl Y. MADDOX
30 Director of Development ... Mr. Eric T. GUSTAFSON
35 Director Student Services ... Mrs. Cheryl Y. MADDOX
04 Administrative Asst to President ... Mrs. Christina S. WOODSIDE
33 Dean of Men ... Mr. Duke HALE
34 Dean of Women ... Mrs. Nora M. HALE
40 Director Bookstore ... Mr. David S. ONUFER
88 Director Missions ... Mr. Simon BRACE
106 Dir Online Education/E-learning ... Dr. Daniel JANOSIK
13 Director Information Technology ... Mr. David BLACKARD

University of North Carolina General Administration (A)

Box 2688, 910 Raleigh Road, Chapel Hill NC 27515-2688
County: Orange
FICE Identification: 002971
Unit ID: 199175
Telephone: (919) 962-1000
Carnegie Class: N/A
FAX Number: (919) 962-2751
URL: www.northcarolina.edu

01 President ... Mr. Thomas W. ROSS
100 Chief of Staff ... Mr. Jeffrey DAVIES
05 Sr Vice Pres Academic Affairs ... Dr. Suzanne ORTEGA
10 Vice President for Finance ... Mr. Charles E. PERUSSE
45 Vice Pres for Academic Planning ... Vacant
13 Vice Pres Information Resources/CIO ... Mr. John LEYDON
43 VP Legal Affairs/General Counsel ... Ms. Laura B. LUGER
46 Vice Pres Research/Sponsored Pgms ... Dr. Steven LEATH
101 Secretary of the University ... Mr. Bart CORGNATI
86 Vice President for Govt Relations ... Ms. Anita WATKINS
86 Vice President for Federal Rels ... Ms. Kimrey RHINEHARDT
26 Vice President for Communications ... Ms. Joni WORTHINGTON
15 Vice Pres for Human Resources ... Mr. William FLEMING

*Appalachian State University (B)

Boone NC 28608-0001
County: Watauga
FICE Identification: 002906
Unit ID: 197869
Telephone: (828) 262-2000
Carnegie Class: Master's L
FAX Number: (828) 262-2347
Calendar System: Semester
URL: www.appstate.edu
Established: 1899
Annual Undergrad Tuition & Fees (In-State): $5,743
Enrollment: 17,222
Coed
Affiliation or Control: State
IRS Status: 501(c)3
Highest Offering: Doctorate
Program: Liberal Arts And General; Teacher Preparatory; Professional
Accreditation: SC, AAFCS, ART, BUS, CACREP, CIDA, CS, DIETD, DIETI, IPSY, MFCD, MUS, NRPA, NURSE, SP, SPAA, SW, TED, THEA

02 Chancellor ... Dr. Kenneth E. PEACOCK
05 Int Provost/Exec Vice Chancellor ... Dr. Lorin A. BAUMHOVER
10 Int Vice Chanc Business Affairs ... Mr. Greg M. LOVINS
32 Vice Chanc Student Development ... Ms. Cindy A. WALLACE
30 Vice Chanc Univ Advancement ... Ms. Susan H. PETTYJOHN
20 Int Vice Provost for Undergrad Educ ... Dr. Mike W. MAYFIELD
45 Assoc Vice Prov for Resource Mgmt ... Dr. Tim BURWELL
26 Assc VC Univ Comm/Cultural Affairs ... Mr. Hank T. FOREMAN
84 Assoc VC Enrollment Management ... Mrs. Susan DAVIES
22 Director Ofc Equity/Diversity/Compl ... Ms. Linda M. FOULSHAM
29 Exec Director of Alumni Affairs ... Mr. Patrick K. SETZER
43 General Counsel ... Mr. Dayton T. COLE
13 Chief Info Officer/ITS ... Vacant
06 Registrar ... Ms. Andrea C. WAWRZUSIN
38 Director Counsel/Psychological Svcs ... Dr. Dan L. JONES
37 Director Student Financial Aid ... Ms. Esther MANOGIN
15 Dir Human Resource Services ... Mr. Patrick J. MCCOY
36 Director Career Development Ctr ... Ms. Marjorie R. ELLIS
09 Dir Inst Research/Assessment Plng ... Dr. Bobby SHARP
51 Director Continuing Education ... Mr. Tom FISHER
41 Athletic Director ... Mr. Charles G. COBB
49 Dean College Arts & Sciences ... Dr. Anthony G. CALAMAI
50 Dean College of Business ... Dr. Randal K. EDWARDS
53 Dean College of Education ... Dr. Charles DUKE
57 Dean College Fine/Applied Arts ... Dr. Glenda TREADAWAY
64 Dean School of Music ... Dr. Bill L. PELTO
58 Dean Graduate Studies/Research ... Dr. Edelma D. HUNTLEY
08 University Librarian ... Dr. Mary L. REICHEL
18 Director of Physical Plant ... Mr. Michael J. O'CONNOR
21 Budget Director ... Ms. Betsy PAYNE
35 Dean of Students/Assoc VC Stdnt Dev ... Mr. J.J J. BROWN
07 Director of Admissions ... Mr. Lloyd SCOTT
96 Director of Purchasing ... Mr. Jeff TALBOT
28 Int Dir Multicultural Student Devel ... Mr. Augusto E. PENA

*East Carolina University (C)

1000 East Fifth Street, Greenville NC 27858-4353
County: Pitt
FICE Identification: 002923
Unit ID: 198464
Telephone: (252) 328-6212
Carnegie Class: DRU
FAX Number: (252) 328-4155
Calendar System: Semester
URL: www.ecu.edu
Established: 1907
Annual Undergrad Tuition & Fees (In-State): $5,364
Enrollment: 27,783
Coed
Affiliation or Control: State
IRS Status: 501(c)3
Highest Offering: Doctorate
Program: Liberal Arts And General; Teacher Preparatory; Professional
Accreditation: SC, ANEST, ARCPA, ART, AUD, BUS, CIDA, CONST, CORE, DENT, DIETD, DIETI, ENG, MED, MFCD, MIDWF, MT, MUS, NAIT, NRPA, NURSE, OT, PH, PLNG, PTA, SP, SPAA, SW, TED

02 Chancellor ... Dr. Steve BALLARD
100 Chief of Staff ... Mr. Philip ROGERS
05 Provost & Sr Vice Chanc Acad Affs ... Dr. Marilyn SHEERER
32 Vice Chancellor for Student Affairs ... Dr. Virginia HARDY
17 Vice Chanc Health Sciences ... Dr. Phyllis N. HORNS
10 Vice Chanc Administration & Finance ... Dr. Frederick NISWANDER
30 Vice Chanc Univ Advancement ... Dr. Mickey DOWDY
46 VC Research/Graduate Studies ... Dr. Deirdre MAGEEAN
29 Assoc VC for Alumni Relations ... Mr. Paul CLIFFORD
39 Assoc VC Camp Liv/Dining ... Mr. William L. MCCARTNEY, JR.
38 Assoc Vice Chanc & Dean of Stdnts ... Dr. Lynn M. ROEDER
35 Assoc Dean of Students ... Dr. Lathan E. TURNER
22 Assc Prov Equity/Diversity/Cmty Rel ... Dr. Taffye BENSON-CLAYTON
43 University Attorney ... Ms. Donna G. PAYNE
09 Associate Provost IPRE ... Dr. David WEISMILLER
41 Athletic Director ... Mr. Terry HOLLAND
13 CIO and Assoc Vice Chanc ITCS ... Dr. Joe NORRIS
15 Assoc Vice Chanc Human Resources ... Mr. John TOLLER
07 Director of Admissions ... Mr. Anthony BRITT
06 Registrar ... Ms. Angela R. ANDERSON
18 Assoc VC for Campus Opers ... Mr. William BAGNELL
21 Assoc VC for Business Services ... Mr. A. Scott BUCK
19 Assoc VC Environ Health & Safety ... Mr. Bill KOCH
08 Director Library Services ... Dr. Larry BOYER
88 Director Health Sciences Library ... Dr. Dorothy A. SPENCER
26 Exec Dir University Communications ... Mr. John DURHAM
37 Director of Financial Aid ... Ms. Julie POORMAN
19 Director/Chief of Police ... Mr. Scott SHELTON
51 Director of Continuing Studies ... Dr. F. Clayton SESSOMS
82 Assoc VC of International Affs ... Dr. Jim GEHLHAR
27 Director of Publications ... Mr. Jimmy ROSTAR
88 Director of Military Programs ... Dr. Steve DUNCAN
96 Director of Purchasing ... Mr. Kevin CARRAWAY
49 Dean College of Arts & Sciences ... Dr. Alan R. WHITE
76 Dean Sch Allied Health Sciences ... Dr. Stephen W. THOMAS
68 Dean Col Health/Human Performance ... Dr. Glen G. GILBERT
59 Dean College of Human Ecology ... Dr. Judy SIGUAW
66 Dean College of Nursing ... Dr. Sylvia BROWN
50 Interim Dean College of Business ... Dr. Stanley G. EAKINS
57 Interim Dean Col Fine Arts/Comm ... Dr. Michael DORSEY
53 Dean College of Education ... Dr. Linda PATRIARCA
72 Dean of Col Tech/Computer Sci ... Dr. David WHITE
58 Dean Graduate School ... Dr. Paul GEMPERLINE
36 Director Career Center ... Vacant
92 Interim Dean Honors College ... Dr. Richard R. EAKIN
26 Director of University Marketing ... Mr. Clint BAILEY
63 Dean Brody School of Medicine ... Dr. Paul R G. CUNNINGHAM
52 Dean School of Dental Medicine ... Vacant
88 Asst VC Recreational/Wellness Svcs ... Ms. Nancy MIZE
21 Director of Internal Audit ... Ms. Stacie TRONTO
88 Assoc VC for Academic Outreach ... Dr. Elmer POE
20 Assoc VC for Academic Programs ... Dr. Linner GRIFFIN
21 Director for Financial Services ... Ms. Anne JENKINS
84 Assoc Provost for Enrollment Svcs ... Dr. John FLETCHER

*Elizabeth City State University (D)

1704 Weeksville Road, Elizabeth City NC 27909-7806
County: Pasquotank
FICE Identification: 002926
Unit ID: 198507
Telephone: (252) 335-3400
Carnegie Class: Bac/Diverse
FAX Number: (252) 335-3731
Calendar System: Semester
URL: www.ecsu.edu
Established: 1891
Annual Undergrad Tuition & Fees (In-State): $4,691
Enrollment: 3,307
Coed
Affiliation or Control: State
IRS Status: 501(c)3
Highest Offering: Master's
Program: Liberal Arts And General; Teacher Preparatory; Fine Arts Emphasis
Accreditation: SC, BUS, MUS, NAIT, SW, TED

02 Chancellor ... Dr. Willie J. GILCHRIST
04 Exec Asst to the Chancellor ... Ms. Gwendolyn SANDERS
05 Provost/VC Academic Affairs ... Dr. Ali A. KHAN
10 VC for Business & Finance ... Mr. Benjamin DURANT
32 VC for Student Affairs ... Dr. Anthony BROWN
30 VC for Institutional Advancemnt ... Mr. William G. SMITH
43 Asst to Chanc for Legal Affairs ... Ms. Bernetta H. BROWN
35 Assoc VC for Student Affairs ... Mrs. Deborah G. BRANCH
35 Assoc VC for Student Affairs ... Ms. Barbaina M. HOUSTON-BLACK
20 Assoc VC Academic Affs/Acad Support ... Dr. W. E. THOMAS
13 Director of Information Systems ... Mr. Matthew SIMPSON
38 Dir Counsel/Test Student Affairs ... Ms. Felicia BROWN
27 Chief Information Officer ... Mr. Anthony K. ADADE
06 Registrar ... Mr. Vincent L. BEAMON
84 Director Enrollment Management ... Dr. Monette WILLIAMS
09 Dir Institutional Effectiveness/Res ... Dr. Damon R. WADE
08 Director of Library Services ... Dr. Juanita MIDGETTE
07 Director of Admissions ... Mr. Darius EURE
37 Director Student Financial Aid ... Mr. Kenneth B. WILSON
36 Director of Career Services ... Mr. Brutus N. JACKSON
15 Director Human Resources ... Mrs. Donna JAMES-WHIDBEE
29 Director of Alumni Relations ... Ms. Barbara B. SUTTON
18 Director Facilities/Physical Plant ... Vacant
26 Director of Marketing ... Ms. Rhonda M. HAYES
87 Int Director of Summer School ... Mr. Warren E. POOLE
41 Athletic Director ... Mr. Thurlis J. LITTLE

21 Director of Budgets ... Mrs. Sharnita L. WILSON-PARKER
92 Director of Honors Program ... Dr. Velma B. BLACKMON
96 Director of Purchasing ... Mr. Frankie M. BRINKLEY
53 Int Dean Sch Education & Psychology ... Dr. Charles D. CHERRY
49 Dean Sch of Arts & Humanities ... Dr. Murel M. JONES
50 Dean Sch of Business & Economics ... Dr. David BEJOU
81 Dean Sch of Math/Science/Technology ... Dr. Harry S. BASS

*Fayetteville State University (E)

1200 Murchison Road, Fayetteville NC 28301-4298
County: Cumberland
FICE Identification: 002928
Unit ID: 198543
Telephone: (910) 672-1111
Carnegie Class: Master's M
FAX Number: (910) 672-1769
Calendar System: Semester
URL: www.uncfsu.edu
Established: 1867
Annual Undergrad Tuition & Fees (In-State): $5,361
Enrollment: 5,781
Coed
Affiliation or Control: State
IRS Status: 501(c)3
Highest Offering: Doctorate
Program: Liberal Arts And General; Teacher Preparatory
Accreditation: SC, BUS, MUS, NURSE, SW, TED

02 Chancellor ... Dr. James A. ANDERSON
100 Vice Chancellor and Chief of Staff ... Dr. Thomas CONWAY
05 Provost & Vice Chanc Academic Affs ... Dr. Jon YOUNG
10 Vice Chancellor Business/Finance ... Mr. Robert L. BOTLEY
32 Vice Chancellor Student Affairs ... Dr. Janice HAYNIE
30 Vice Chancellor Inst Advancement ... Mr. Arthur G. AFFLECK
13 Vice Chanc Info Technology/CIO ... Mr. Arasu GANESAN
44 Asst Vice Chanc for Advancement ... Ms. Mary H. BAILEY
35 Assoc Vice Chanc Student Affairs ... Ms. Juanette COUNCIL
18 Assoc Vice Chanc Facilities Mgmt ... Mr. Rudolph CARDENAS
21 Asst VC Business/Financ/Comptroller ... Ms. Jolene ELKINS
20 Assoc Vice Chanc Academic Affs ... Dr. Curtis CHARLES
15 Assoc Vice Chanc Human Resources ... Ms. Denise BROWN-HART
88 AVC Inst Research/Testing/Title III ... Ms. Tendai JOHNSON
85 Asst VC Acad Affs/Interntl Studies ... Dr. Chen YUNKAI
88 Senior Assoc Vice Chancellor ... Dr. Perry A. MASSEY
45 Assoc VC Pgms/Plng/Assessment ... Vacant
84 Assoc VC for Enrollment Management ... Ms. Roxie SHABAZZ
36 Director Career Svcs & Bus Mgr SA ... Ms. Helene CAMERON
92 Program Director Honors ... Dr. Booker T. ANTHONY
06 Registrar ... Ms. Sarah BAKER
29 Director of Alumni Affairs ... Mrs. Michaela BROWN
26 Director Public Relations ... Mr. Jeff WOMBLE
08 Director of Library Services ... Mr. Bobby C. WYNN
07 Director of Admissions ... Ms. Ulisa BOWLES
90 Director of IT Operations ... Ms. Michelle WHITAKER
09 Director Institutional Research ... Mr. Ivan WALKER
39 Director of Residence Life ... Mr. Greg MOYD
37 Director Student Financial Aid ... Ms. Kamesia EWING
43 General Counsel ... Mrs. Wanda LESSANE JENKINS
41 Athletic Director ... Dr. Edward MCLEAN
96 Director of Purchasing ... Ms. Willie MCINTYRE
38 Dir Center Personal Development ... Mr. Fred SAPP
28 Director of Diversity ... Vacant
88 Dean University College ... Dr. John I. BROOKS
66 Department Chair Nursing ... Dr. Afua ARHIN
50 Dean School Business/Economics ... Dr. Assad TAVAKOLI
53 Dean School of Education ... Dr. Leontye LEWIS
58 Dean Graduate Stds/Sponsored Rsrch ... Dr. LaDelle OLION
49 Dean College of Arts and Sciences ... Dr. David BARLOW

*North Carolina Agricultural and Technical State University (F)

1601 E Market Street, Greensboro NC 27411-0001
County: Guilford
FICE Identification: 002905
Unit ID: 199102
Telephone: (336) 334-7500
Carnegie Class: DRU
FAX Number: (336) 334-7136
Calendar System: Semester
URL: www.ncat.edu
Established: 1891
Annual Undergrad Tuition & Fees (In-State): $5,570
Enrollment: 10,795
Coed
Affiliation or Control: State
IRS Status: 501(c)3
Highest Offering: Doctorate
Program: Liberal Arts And General; Teacher Preparatory; Professional
Accreditation: SC, AAFCS, BUS, BUSA, CACREP, CONST, @CORE, CS, DIETD, ENG, #JOUR, LSAR, MUS, NAIT, NUR, SW, TED, THEA

02 Chancellor ... Dr. Harold L. MARTIN
05 Provost/Vice Chanc Academic Affairs ... Dr. Linda T. ADAMS
10 Vice Chanc Business & Finance ... Mr. Robert POMPEY, JR.
30 Vice Chanc University Advancement ... Dr. Mark KIEL
46 Int VC for Research/Economic Dev ... Dr. Celestine NTUEN
32 Vice Chancellor of Student Affairs ... Dr. Melody C. PIERCE
15 Vice Chancellor for Human Resources ... Ms. Linda R. MCABEE
13 Vice Chanc Info Tech & Telecom/CIO ... Ms. Barbara J. ELLIS
43 General Counsel ... Dr. J. Charles WALDRUP
20 Assoc VC for Undergraduate Pgm ... Vacant
27 Assoc Vice Chanc for Univ Relations ... Ms. Nicole PRIDE
21 Asst Vice Chanc Budget & Planning ... Mrs. Akua J. MATHERSON
84 Assoc VC Acad Affs/ Enrollment Mgmt ... Dr. Lori HUNTER
87 Asst Vice Chanc of Summer School ... Dr. Eric A. CHEEK
18 Asst VC for Bus/Finance/Facilities ... Mr. Andrew M. PERKINS, JR.
19 Asst VC Police/Public Safety ... Mr. Glen C. NEWELL
08 Dean of Library Services ... Ms. Vicki COLEMAN
47 Int Dean Agric/Environmental Sci ... Dr. William M. RANDLE
49 Dean Arts & Sciences ... Dr. Goldie S. BYRD
53 Interim Dean School of Education ... Dr. Dorothy D. LEFLORE
54 Interim Dean of Engineering ... Dr. Robin N. COGER

58 Interim Dean of Graduate School ... Dr. Sanjiv SARIN
66 Dean of Nursing ... Dr. Inez TUCK
50 Dean of Business & Economics ... Dr. Quiester CRAIG
72 Dean School of Technology ... Dr. Benjamin O. UWAKWEH
88 Dean Joint Sch Nanoscience/Nanoengr ... Dr. James G. RYAN
09 Director Inst Research/Planning ... Dr. G. Scott JENKINS
06 University Registrar ... Mr. Lester LUGO
07 Director of Admissions ... Ms. Keyana SCALES
37 Director Financial Aid ... Mrs. Sherri M. AVENT
36 Director Career Services ... Ms. Joyce P. EDWARDS
91 Dir Info Systems/Data Center Ops ... Mr. Maurice TYLER
29 Director of Alumni Affairs ... Mrs. Leonora C. BRYANT
85 Dir International Student Affairs ... Ms. Loretha GRAVES
88 Dir Multicultural Student Center ... Dr. Maria T. PALMER
41 Director of Athletics ... Mr. Earl M. HILTON, III
39 Dir Student Housing/Residence Life ... Ms. Linda D. INMAN
23 Director Student Health Services ... Mrs. Linda WILSON
38 Director of Counseling Service ... Dr. Vivian D. BARNETTE
25 Director of Contracts/Grants ... Ms. Lavonne MATTHEWS
92 Director of Honors Program ... Dr. Michael CUNDALL, JR.
96 Director of Purchasing ... Mr. Ted A. LITTLE
26 Director of Media Relations ... Mrs. Nettie ROWLAND
40 Manager of Bookstore ... Mrs. Donna MORRIS-POWELL

*North Carolina Central University (A)

1801 Fayetteville Street, Durham NC 27707-3129

County: Durham FICE Identification: 002950
Unit ID: 199157
Telephone: (919) 530-6100 Carnegie Class: Master's L
FAX Number: (919) 530-5014 Calendar System: Semester
URL: www.nccu.edu
Established: 1910 Annual Undergrad Tuition & Fees (In-State): $5,688
Enrollment: 8,645 Coed
Affiliation or Control: State IRS Status: 501(c)3
Highest Offering: Doctorate
Program: Liberal Arts And General; Teacher Preparatory; Professional
Accreditation: SC, ACBSP, BUS, CACREP, DIETD, DIETI, LAW, LIB, NRPA, NUR, SP, SW, TED, THEA

02 Chancellor ... Dr. Charlie NELMS
05 Provost/Vice Chanc Academic Affairs ... Dr. Kwesi AGGREY
100 Vice Chanc/Chief of Staff ... Ms. Susan HESTER
43 General Counsel ... Ms. Melissa JACKSON HALLOWAY
11 Vice Chanc Admin & Finance ... Dr. Wendall M. DAVIS
32 Vice Chanc Student Affs/Enroll Mgt ... Dr. Kevin D. ROME
30 Vice Chanc Inst Advancement ... Ms. Lois DELOATCH
88 Asst VC for University Programs ... Dr. Janice A. HARPER
20 Asst VC for Academic Services ... Dr. Bernice D. JOHNSON
45 Asst VC for Strategic Planning ... Dr. Bijoy SAHOO
10 Asst Vice Chancellor/ Comptroller ... Ms. Yolanda E. BANKS-DEAVER
35 Asst VC Student Affs/Dean Stdnts ... Mr. Louis A. VELEZ
20 Assoc Vice Chanc Academic Affairs ... Dr. Franklin B. CARVER
15 Assoc Vice Chanc Human Resources ... Mr. James C. DOCKERY
13 Chief Information Officer ... Mr. John SMITH
88 Asst Dean Stdnts/Coord Greek Affs ... Mr. Andre D. VANN
07 Asst VC/Admissions Director ... Ms. Jocelyn L. FOY
31 Dir Govt & Community Relations ... Ms. Starla H. TANNER
44 Director Major Gifts ... Mr. Randal V. CHILDS
88 Director Biomanufacturing Institute ... Dr. Li-An YEH
44 Director Annual Giving ... Ms. Risha D. BAILEY
06 Registrar ... Dr. Jerome GOODWIN
91 Administrative Technology Services ... Mr. Donald R. NOLEN
29 Director of Alumni Affairs ... Ms. Anita WALTON
26 Director of Public Relations ... Ms. Miji BELL
37 Director of Student Financial Aid ... Ms. Sharon J. OLIVER
08 Director Library Services ... Ms. Theodosia T. SHIELDS
19 Chief of Campus Police & Security ... Ms. Glenda BEARD
88 Director Academic Advising ... Mrs. Sara BELL-LUCAS
88 Director Art Museum ... Mr. Kenneth G. RODGERS
18 Director Physical Plant ... Mr. Tuy TRAN
39 Director Residential Life ... Ms. Jennifer WILDER
41 Director Athletics ... Ms. Ingrid WICKER-MCCREE
09 Dir Research/Evaluation/Planning ... Mr. Shawn STEWART
96 Director of Purchasing ... Mr. Godfrey HERNDON
92 Director of Honors Program ... Dr. Timothy HOLLEY
38 Director of Counseling Center ... Dr. Carolyn D. MOORE-ASSEM
22 Dir Equal Opportunity/Affirm Act ... Ms. Anita KNIGHT
84 Director Enrollment Management ... Ms. Jocelyn L. FOY
40 Manager Bookstore ... Ms. Stephanie L. GETCHELL
58 Dean School Graduate Studies ... Dr. Chanta HAYWOOD
61 Dean of the Law School ... Dr. Raymond C. PIERCE
62 Dean School of Library/Info Science ... Dr. Irene OWENS
50 Dean School of Business ... Dr. Bijoy SAHOO
88 Dean of University College ... Dr. Bernice DUFFY JOHNSON
49 Dean College of Liberal Arts ... Dr. Carleton E. WILSON
53 Dean School of Education ... Dr. Cecelia STEPPE-JONES

*North Carolina State University (B)

Raleigh NC 27695-0001

County: Wake FICE Identification: 002972
Unit ID: 199193
Telephone: (919) 515-2011 Carnegie Class: RU/VH
FAX Number: N/A Calendar System: Semester
URL: www.ncsu.edu
Established: 1887 Annual Undergrad Tuition & Fees (In-State): $6,529
Enrollment: 34,376 Coed
Affiliation or Control: State IRS Status: 501(c)3
Highest Offering: Doctorate
Program: Occupational; Liberal Arts And General; Teacher Preparatory; Professional
Accreditation: SC, ART, BUS, BUSA, CACREP, CS, ENG, FOR, LSAR, NRPA, SCPSY, SPAA, SW, TED, VET

02 Chancellor ... Dr. William Randy WOODSON
05 Provost/Exec Vice Chancellor ... Dr. Warwick A. ARDEN
43 Vice Chanc & General Counsel ... Ms. Eileen GOLDGEIER
10 Vice Chanc Finance & Business ... Mr. Charles D. LEFFLER
46 Vice Chanc Research/Grad Studies ... Dr. Terri L. LOMAX
32 Vice Chancellor Student Affairs ... Dr. Thomas H. STAFFORD, JR.
30 Vice Chanc Univ Advancement ... Mr. Nevin E. KESSLER
27 Vice Chanc Information Technology ... Dr. Marc I. HOIT
100 Assistant to the Chancellor ... Ms. P. J. TEAL
26 Asst to Chanc External Affairs ... Mr. Kevin HOWELL
84 Vice Prov Enroll Mgmt/Services ... Dr. Louis D. HUNT
56 V Prov Dist Educ/Lrng Tech Apps ... Dr. Thomas K. MILLER
08 Vice Provost/Director of Libraries ... Ms. Susan K. NUTTER
22 Vice Prov Equal Opportunity/Equity ... Ms. Joanne G. WOODARD
91 Assoc Vice Chanc Res Mgt/Info Sys ... Mr. Stephen W. KETO
18 Assoc Vice Chanc Facilities ... Mr. Kevin J. MACNAUGHTON
39 Assoc Vice Chanc Student Housing ... Dr. Timothy R. LUCKADOO
29 Assoc Vice Chanc Alumni Relations ... Mr. Benny SUGGS
15 Assoc Vice Chanc Human Resources ... Ms. Barbara L. CARROLL
19 Director Public Safety ... Mr. Thomas C. YOUNCE
09 Director Univ Planning/Analysis ... Ms. Karen P. HELM
07 Director Undergrad Admissions ... Mr. Thomas H. GRIFFIN
06 Registrar ... Dr. Louis D. HUNT
25 Director Contracts & Grants ... Mr. Earl N. PULLIAM
27 Director News Services ... Mr. Keith P. NICHOLS
37 Director of Financial Aid ... Ms. Julia R. MALLETTE
38 Director of Counseling Center ... Dr. M. Lee SALTER
41 Director Athletics ... Ms. Deborah YOW
21 Treasurer ... Ms. Kathy S. HART
88 Director of Materials Management ... Mr. Robert D. WOOD
20 Dean Undergrad Academic Programs ... Dr. John T. AMBROSE
79 Dean Humanities/Social Sciences ... Dr. Jeffery P. BRADEN
48 Dean of Design ... Dr. Marvin J. MALECHA
54 Dean of Engineering ... Dr. Louis A. MARTIN-VEGA
47 Dean Agriculture/Life Sciences ... Dr. Johnny C. WYNNE
65 Dean of Natural Resources ... Dr. Robert D. BROWN
53 Dean of Education ... Dr. Jayne FLEENER
50 Dean of Management ... Dr. Ira R. WEISS
81 Dean Physical/Mathematical Sciences ... Dr. Daniel L. SOLOMON
88 Dean of Textiles ... Dr. Blanton GODFREY
74 Interim Dean of Veterinary Medicine ... Dr. David BRISTOL
58 Dean of Graduate School ... Dr. Duane K. LARICK

*University of North Carolina at Asheville (C)

1 University Heights, Asheville NC 28804-8503

County: Buncombe FICE Identification: 002907
Unit ID: 199111
Telephone: (828) 251-6600 Carnegie Class: Bac/A&S
FAX Number: (828) 251-6495 Calendar System: Semester
URL: www.unca.edu
Established: 1927 Annual Undergrad Tuition & Fees (In-State): $5,063
Enrollment: 3,765 Coed
Affiliation or Control: State IRS Status: 501(c)3
Highest Offering: Master's
Program: Liberal Arts And General; Teacher Preparatory
Accreditation: SC, BUS, TED

02 Chancellor ... Dr. Anne PONDER
100 Chief of Staff ... Ms. Christine RILEY
05 Provost/VC Academic Affairs ... Dr. Jane K. FERNANDES
10 Vice Chancellor Finance/Operations ... Mr. John PIERCE
30 Exec Director Foundation ... Vacant
32 Vice Chanc for Student Affairs ... Dr. Bill HAGGARD
41 Director of Athletics ... Ms. Janet R. CONE
43 University General Counsel ... Mr. Lucien CAPONE
15 Dir Human Resources/Affirmative Act ... Mrs. Elizabeth R. BAGWELL
09 Director of Institutional Research ... Dr. Archer R. GRAVELY
20 Asst Provost Academic Admin ... Ms. Patricia MCCLELLAN
81 Dean Natural Science ... Dr. Keith KRUMPE
79 Dean Humanities ... Dr. Gwen ASHBURN
83 Dean Social Science ... Dr. Jeff KONZ
88 Dean University Programs ... Dr. Edward J. KATZ
51 Asst Provost Grad/Cont Educ ... Vacant
08 University Librarian ... Mr. James R. KUHLMAN
13 Chief Information Officer ... Mr. Jeff WILLIAMS
07 Dean Admissions ... Ms. Patrice MITCHELL
25 Director Contracts & Grants ... Dr. Gerard VOOS
56 Director Extension/Distance Ed ... Vacant
06 Registrar ... Ms. Debbie RACE
18 Dir Facilities Mgmt & Planning ... Vacant
21 Assoc Vice Chancellor of Finance ... Ms. Suzanne BRYSON
21 Controller ... Ms. Karen SHAW
40 Director of Bookstore ... Mr. David PERKINS
19 Director of Public Safety ... Mr. Eric BOYCE
96 Director of Purchasing ... Ms. Betty J. PONDER
29 Dir Alumni Relations & Univ Events ... Dr. Kevan D. FRAZIER
26 Director Communication & Mktg ... Ms. Debbie GRIFFITH
27 Director of News Services ... Ms. Merianne MILLER
44 Director of Development ... Mrs. Julie C. HEINITSH
23 Dir Student Health/Counseling ... Mr. John CUTSPEC
39 Director Residential Education ... Ms. Melanie RHODARMER
39 Director Housing Operations ... Mr. Vollie BARNWELL
36 Director of Career Center ... Vacant
35 Dean of Students ... Ms. Jackie MCHARGUE
37 Assoc Director Financial Aid ... Ms. Beth BARTLETT
04 Exec Asst to Chancellor ... Ms. Lynn SPAIGHT

*University of North Carolina at Chapel Hill (D)

Chapel Hill NC 27599-0001

County: Orange FICE Identification: 002974
Unit ID: 199120
Telephone: (919) 962-2211 Carnegie Class: RU/VH
FAX Number: (919) 962-5604 Calendar System: Semester
URL: www.unc.edu
Established: 1789 Annual Undergrad Tuition & Fees (In-State): $7,009
Enrollment: 29,390 Coed
Affiliation or Control: State IRS Status: 501(c)3
Highest Offering: Doctorate
Program: Occupational; Liberal Arts And General; Teacher Preparatory; Professional
Accreditation: SC, AUD, BUS, CACREP, CLPSY, CORE, DA, DENT, DH, DIETC, DMOLS, HSA, IPSY, JOUR, LAW, LIB, MED, MT, NMT, NUR, NURSE, OT, PH, PHAR, PLNG, PTA, RAD, RADDOS, RTT, SCPSY, SP, SPAA, SW, TED

02 Chancellor ... Dr. Holden THORP
03 Provost/Exec Vice Chancellor ... Dr. Bruce CARNEY
43 Vice Chancellor/General Counsel ... Ms. Leslie C. STROHM
11 Vice Chanc Finance & Administration ... Dr. Richard L. MANN
32 Vice Chancellor Student Affairs ... Mr. Winston B. CRISP
30 Vice Chanc University Advancement ... Mr. Matthew G. KUPEC
16 Vice Chanc Human Resources ... Ms. Brenda R. MALONE
13 VC Info Technology/Chief Info Ofcr ... Mr. Larry D. CONRAD
04 Secretary of the University ... Ms. Brenda W. KIRBY
46 Vice Chancellor Research ... Dr. Barbara ENTWISLE
26 Assoc VC University Relations ... Ms. Nancy DAVIS
24 Asst Vice Chanc Teaching/Learning ... Dr. Charles GREEN
05 Executive Associate Provost ... Mr. Ronald STRAUSS
08 Assoc Prov/University Librarian ... Ms. Sarah MICHALAK
10 Assoc Prov Finance Acad Planning ... Dr. Dwayne PINKNEY
20 Assoc Provost Academic Initiatives ... Dr. Carol TRESOLINI
18 Assoc Vice Chanc Facilities Plng ... Mr. Bruce L. RUNBERG
31 Assoc Vice Chanc Campus Services ... Ms. Carolyn W. ELFLAND
93 Int Assoc Prov/Div Multicultural ... Ms. Terri HOUSTON
09 Asst Prov Inst Research/Assessment ... Dr. Lynn E. WILLIFORD
39 Dir Housing & Residential Education ... Dr. Larry HICKS
41 Director of Athletics ... Mr. Richard A. BADDOUR
06 Asst Prov/University Registrar ... Mr. Christopher DERICKSON
07 Asst Prov/Dir Undergrad Admissions ... Dr. Stephen M. FARMER
29 Director of Alumni Affairs ... Mr. Douglas S. DIBBERT
37 Assoc Prov/Dir Scholar/Student Aid ... Ms. Shirley A. ORT
36 Director University Career Services ... Mr. Ray ANGLE
38 Director Counseling & Wellnes Svc ... Dr. Allen H. O'BARR
44 Int Director of Annual Giving ... Ms. Rebecca BRAMLETT
22 Equal Opportunity/ADA Officer ... Ms. Ann E. PENN
19 Director of Public Safety ... Major Jeff B. MCCRACKEN
51 Director Division of Cont Education ... Mr. Rob BRUCE
27 Assoc VC University Relations ... Ms. Nancy DAVIS
96 Dir Procurement Services ... Ms. Margaret PENDERGRASS
35 Assoc VC Student Affairs ... Ms. Bettina SHUFORD
87 Dean of the Summer School ... Ms. Jan YOPP
49 Dean College Arts & Sciences ... Dr. Karen GIL
61 Dean School of Law ... Mr. John C. BOGER
63 Dean School of Medicine ... Dr. William L. ROPER
66 Dean School of Nursing ... Dr. Kristen M. SWANSON
52 Dean School of Dentistry ... Dr. Jane WEINTRAUB
58 Dean of Graduate School ... Dr. Steven W. MATSON
50 Dean Kenan-Flagler Business School ... Dr. James DEAN
70 Dean School of Social Work ... Dr. Jack M. RICHMAN
67 Dean School of Pharmacy ... Dr. Robert A. BLOUIN
60 Int Dean Sch Journalism/Mass Comm ... Dr. Dulcie STRAUGHAN
62 Dean School of Info/Library Science ... Dr. Gary MARCHIONINI
69 Dean School of Public Health ... Dr. Barbara K. RIMER
53 Dean School of Education ... Dr. Bill MCDIARMID
57 Dean School of Government ... Dr. Michael SMITH
23 Asst VC for Campus Health Services ... Dr. Mary COVINGTON
92 Associate Dean Honors Program ... Dr. James L. LELOUDIS

*University of North Carolina at Charlotte (E)

9201 University City Boulevard, Charlotte NC 28223-0001

County: Mecklenburg FICE Identification: 002975
Unit ID: 199139
Telephone: (704) 687-2000 Carnegie Class: DRU
FAX Number: (704) 687-2144 Calendar System: Semester
URL: www.uncc.edu
Established: 1946 Annual Undergrad Tuition & Fees (In-State): $5,440
Enrollment: 25,063 Coed
Affiliation or Control: State IRS Status: 501(c)3
Highest Offering: Doctorate
Program: Liberal Arts And General; Teacher Preparatory; Professional
Accreditation: SC, BUS, BUSA, CACREP, ENG, ENGT, EXSC, HSA, IPSY, NURSE, PH, SPAA, SW, TED

02 Chancellor ... Dr. Philip L. DUBOIS
101 Senior Asst to the Chancellor ... Ms. Donna C. BRADY
05 Vice Chanc Academic Affs/Provost ... Dr. Joan F. LORDEN
20 Senior Associate Provost ... Dr. Jay RAJA
88 Assoc Provost/Academic Services ... Dr. Cynthia WOLF JOHNSON
10 Vice Chancellor Business Affairs ... Ms. Elizabeth A. HARDIN
30 Vice Chancellor Univ Advancement ... Mr. Niles F. SORENSEN
86 Spec Asst for Constituent Relations ... Ms. Betty DOSTER
32 Vice Chancellor Student Affairs ... Dr. Arthur R. JACKSON
46 Vice Chanc Research/Federal Rels ... Dr. Stephen R. MOSIER
13 Vice Chanc for Info Tech Svcs/CIO ... Dr. James L. DOMINICK
18 Assoc Vice Chanc Facilities Mgmt ... Mr. Philip M. JONES, JR.

08 University Librarian .... Mr. Stanley J. WILDER
82 Asst Provost for Intl Programs .... Mr. Joel A. GALLEGOS
51 Exec Dir Extended Acad Programs .... Dr. Constance M. MARTIN
26 Director of Public Relations .... Mr. John D. BLAND
31 Director Community Affairs .... Ms. Ashley OSTER
39 Assoc Vice Chanc/Dir Residence Life .... Ms. Jacklyn A. SIMPSON
21 Assoc Vice Chancellor for Finance .... Ms. Susan H. BROOKS
58 Assoc Provost/Dean Graduate School .... Dr. Thomas L. REYNOLDS
84 Assoc Provost for Enrollment Mgmt .... Ms. Tina M. MCENTIRE
43 General Counsel .... Mr. David E. BROOME, JR.
07 Director Undergraduate Admissions .... Ms. Tina M. MCENTIRE
35 Dean of Students/Assoc VC Stdnt Aff .... Dr. Michele M. HOWARD
37 Director of Financial Aid .... Mr. Anthony D. CARTER
38 Assoc VC Health Programs & Services .... Dr. David B. SPANO
36 Director University Career Center .... Ms. Denise Dwight SMITH
40 Campus Bookstore Manager .... Mr. Jimmy E. GRINNELL
29 Director Alumni Affairs .... Mr. Gilbert A. ROSSI
88 Assoc VC Risk Mgmt/Safety/Security .... Mr. Henry D. JAMES
19 Chief/Dir Police & Public Safety .... Mr. Jeffrey A. BAKER
09 Asst Provost Institutional Reseach .... Mr. Stephen A. COPPOLA
88 Assoc Prov Strategic Bus Prtnrshps .... Dr. Robert G. WILHELM
41 Director of Athletics .... Ms. Judy W. ROSE
96 Director of Purchasing .... Mr. Randy DUNCAN
93 Dir Multicultural Academic Services .... Dr. Sam T. LOPEZ
23 Admin Director Student Health Svcs .... Mr. David ROUSMANIERE
15 Assoc Vice Chanc HumanRes/Aff Act .... Mr. Gary W. STINNETT
85 Director Intl Student/Scholar Svcs .... Ms. Marian E. BEANE
104 Director Study Abroad .... Mr. Brad SEKULICH
48 Dean College of Arts/Architecture .... Mr. Kenneth A. LAMBLA
50 Dean College of Business .... Dr. Steven H. OTT
54 Dean College of Engineering .... Dr. Robert E. JOHNSON
53 Dean College of Education .... Dr. Mary Lynne CALHOUN
49 Dean Col of Liberal Arts & Sciences .... Dr. Nancy A. GUTIERREZ
88 Dean College Health & Human Svcs .... Dr. Nancy FEY-YENSAN
72 Dean College Computing/Informatics .... Dr. Yi DENG
97 Dean University College .... Dr. John SMAIL
92 Assoc Dean of Honors College .... Dr. Albert A. MAISTO
06 University Registrar .... Mr. Christopher B. KNAUER
44 Director of Gift Planning .... Dr. Carl E. JOHNSON
102 Dir Corp and Foundation Relations .... Ms. Gayle SIMS
88 Assoc Provost Metro Studies/Ext Pgm .... Dr. Owen J. FURUSETH
88 Exec Dir Institute for Social Cap .... Dr. Sharon G. PORTWOOD

University of North Carolina at Greensboro (A)

PO Box 26170,1000 Spring Garden St,
Greensboro NC 27402-6170

County: Guilford FICE Identification: 002976
Unit ID: 199148
Telephone: (336) 334-5000 Carnegie Class: RU/H
FAX Number: (336) 256-0408 Calendar System: Semester
URL: www.uncg.edu
Established: 1891 Annual Undergrad Tuition & Fees (In-State): $5,504
Enrollment: 18,582 Coed
Affiliation or Control: State IRS Status: 501(c)3
Highest Offering: Doctorate
Program: Liberal Arts And General; Teacher Preparatory; Professional
Accreditation: SC, ANEST, BUS, BUSA, CACREP, CEA, CIDA, CLPSY, CS, DANCE, DIETD, DIETI, LIB, MUS, NRPA, NUR, NURSE, PH, SP, SPAA, SW, TED, THEA

02 Chancellor .... Dr. Linda P. BRADY
100 Chief of Staff .... Ms. Bonita J. BROWN
05 Provost and VC for Academic Affairs .... Dr. David H. PERRIN
10 Vice Chancellor Business Affairs .... Mr. Reade TAYLOR
11 Vice Chanc Info Tech Services .... Dr. James H. CLOTFELTER
32 Vice Chanc for Student Affairs .... Dr. Cheryl M. CALLAHAN
30 Vice Chanc University Advancement .... Dr. Patricia W. STEWART
43 University Counsel .... Mr. Steve SERCK
20 Vice Provost .... Dr. Alan J. BOYETTE
97 Dean of Undergraduate Studies .... Dr. Steve ROBERSON
46 Vice Chanc Research & Econ Devel .... Dr. Terri L. SHELTON
85 Assoc Provost Intl Programs .... Dr. Penelope J. PYNES
45 Assoc Prov Planning & Assessment .... Dr. Rebecca G. ADAMS
15 Assoc VC Human Resource Services .... Dr. Edna CHUN
21 Associate VC Financial Services .... Mr. Steven W. RHEW
18 Associate Vice Chanc for Facilities .... Mr. Jorge QUINTAL
88 Associate VC for Campus Enterprises .... Mr. Michael T. BYERS
09 Director of Institutional Research .... Dr. Sarah D. CARRIGAN
26 Associate VC University Relations .... Ms. Helen D. HEBERT
91 Associate VC for Administrative Sys .... Mr. Joel DUNN
35 Assistant VC for Student Affairs .... Dr. Vickie J. MCNEIL
88 Associate VC for Enterprise Admin Appl .... Ms. Laura R. YOUNG
44 Asst VC for Central Develop Pgms .... Ms. Lynn BRESKO
88 Asst VC for Foundation Finance .... Ms. Jill HILLYER
58 Dean of Graduate School .... Dr. William R. WIENER
49 Dean of Arts & Sciences .... Dr. Timothy D. JOHNSTON
50 Dean of Business & Economics .... Dr. McRae BANKS
53 Dean of Education .... Dr. Karen WIXSON
68 Dean of Health & Human Sciences .... Dr. Celia R. HOOPER
64 Dean of Music .... Dr. John J. DEAL
66 Dean of Nursing .... Dr. Lynne G. PEARCEY
08 Dean of University Libraries .... Ms. Rosann V. BAZIJIAN
06 University Registrar .... Dr. Kelly A. ROWETT-JAMES
07 Director of Admissions .... Ms. Lise K. KELLER
29 Director of Alumni Relations .... Ms. Linda CARTER
88 Director of Campus Recreation .... Ms. Cynthia HARDY
23 Director Student Health Services .... Dr. Tresa M. SAXTON
36 Director Career Services Center .... Ms. Donna J. SECKAR
51 Dean Division of Continual Lrng .... Dr. Robert M. BROWN
25 Director Contracts and Grants .... Ms. Lou HARRELL
38 Director Counseling/Testing Center .... Dr. Bruce G. LYNCH
37 Director of Financial Aid .... Ms. Deborah TOLLEFSON
39 Director Housing & Residence Life .... Mr. Timothy JOHNSON
41 Director Intercollegiate Athletics .... Ms. Kim RECORD
88 Director of Orientation .... Dr. Kim SOUSA-PEOPLES
19 Assoc VC for Safety and Emergency .... Mr. Rollin DONELSON
28 Director Multicultural Affairs .... Ms. Audrey O. LUCAS
96 Director of Purchasing .... Mrs. Elaine AYERS
40 University Bookstore Manager .... Mr. Brad LIGHT

*University of North Carolina at Pembroke (B)

One University Drive, PO Box 1510,
Pembroke NC 28372-1510

County: Robeson FICE Identification: 002954
Unit ID: 199281
Telephone: (910) 521-6000 Carnegie Class: Master's M
FAX Number: (910) 521-6176 Calendar System: Semester
URL: www.uncp.edu
Established: 1887 Annual Undergrad Tuition & Fees (In-State): $4,668
Enrollment: 6,944 Coed
Affiliation or Control: State IRS Status: 501(c)3
Highest Offering: Master's
Program: Liberal Arts And General; Teacher Preparatory; Business Emphasis
Accreditation: SC, MUS, NURSE, SW, TED

02 Chancellor .... Dr. Kyle R. CARTER
05 Provost/Vice Chanc Academic Affairs .... Dr. Kenneth D. KITTS
10 Vice Chancellor Business Affairs .... Mr. R. Neil HAWK
32 Vice Chancellor Student Affairs .... Dr. Diane O. JONES
30 Vice Chancellor for Advancement .... Vacant
84 Vice Chanc Enrollment Management .... Mrs. Jackie CLARK
26 Special Asst for Constituent Rels .... Dr. Glen G. BURNETTE, JR.
41 Athletic Director .... Mr. Dan KENNEY
20 Int Assoc Vice Chanc Acad Planning .... Dr. Elizabeth NORMANDY
35 Assoc Vice Chanc Student Affairs .... Dr. Lisa SCHAEFFER
13 Assoc VC Info Res/Chief Info Ofcr .... Mr. Robert L. ORR
85 Assoc Vice Chanc International Pgms .... Dr. James CALLAGHAN
43 General Counsel .... Mr. Joshua MALCOLM
39 Dir Housing and Resident Life .... Mr. R. Preston SWINEY
49 Interim Dean of Arts & Sciences .... Dr. Mark CANADA
08 Dean of Library Services .... Dr. Elinor FOSTER
58 Dean of Graduate Studies .... Dr. Sara SIMMONS
02 Dean of Honors College .... Dr. Jesse PETERS
53 Dean of School of Education .... Dr. Leah FIORENTINO
50 Dean of School of Business .... Dr. Cammie HUNT
29 Director Alumni Relations .... Ms. Renee STEELE
09 Dir Institutional Research/Planning .... Dr. Beverly KING
36 Director Career Services Center .... Dr. Denisha BONDS
38 Director Counseling/Testing Center .... Dr. Monica Z. OSBURN
06 Registrar .... Ms. Sharon KISSICK
37 Director Financial Aid .... Ms. Jenelle HANDCOX
96 Director of Business Services .... Ms. Denise CARROLL
15 Director of Human Resources .... Vacant
44 Director of Donor Relations .... Ms. Teresa OXENDINE
25 Dir for Center Sponsored Research .... Dr. Linda LITTLE
88 Director Public Administration Pgm .... Dr. Michael R. HAWTHORNE
24 Director of Media Center .... Vacant
27 Public Communications Specialist .... Mr. Scott BIGELOW
21 Asst VC Business Affs/Controller .... Mr. George GUTHRIE
40 Director of Bookstore .... Ms. Karen SWINEY
88 Sports Information Director .... Mr. Todd ANDERSON
07 Director of Admissions .... Ms. Lela CLARK
18 Director of Physical Plant .... Mr. Larry FREEMAN
28 Dir Multicultural/Minority Affairs .... Mr. Robert L. CANIDA, II
88 Dir Fac Plng/Construction/Univ Engr .... Mr. Michael CLARK
88 Dir Ctr for Academic Excellence .... Vacant

*University of North Carolina at Wilmington (C)

601 S College Road, Wilmington NC 28403-3297

County: New Hanover FICE Identification: 002984
Unit ID: 199218
Telephone: (910) 962-3000 Carnegie Class: Master's L
FAX Number: (910) 962-4050 Calendar System: Semester
URL: www.uncw.edu
Established: 1947 Annual Undergrad Tuition & Fees (In-State): $5,672
Enrollment: 13,071 Coed
Affiliation or Control: State IRS Status: 501(c)3
Highest Offering: Doctorate
Program: Liberal Arts And General; Teacher Preparatory; Professional
Accreditation: SC, BUS, MUS, NRPA, NUR, NURSE, SPAA, SW, TED

02 Chancellor .... Dr. Rosemary DEPAOLO
05 Provost/Vice Chanc Acad Affs .... Dr. Cathy BARLOW
10 Vice Chancellor Business Affairs .... Dr. Charles MAIMONE
32 Vice Chanc for Student Affairs .... Ms. Patricia L. LEONARD
30 Vice Chanc University Advancement .... Mrs. Mary M. GORNTO
13 Vice Chanc Inform Technology Sys .... Dr. Debra SAUNDERS-WHITE
31 Int VC Public Svc/Continuing Stds .... Mr. Tom BARTH
21 Sr Assoc Vice Chanc Bus Affairs .... Mrs. Kay M. WARD
20 Assoc Vice Chanc Academic Affairs .... Dr. Johnson O. AKINLEYE
44 Assoc Vice Chanc Univ Advancement .... Ms. Marla D. RICE-EVANS
20 Associate Provost .... Dr. Terrence M. CURRAN
21 Assoc Vice Chanc Business Services .... Ms. Sharon H. BOYD
21 Assoc VC Business Affs Facilities .... Mr. David C. GIRARDOT
28 Assoc Vice Chanc Campus Diversity .... Vacant
26 Asst to Chanc Mktg & Communications .... Ms. Cynthia J. LAWSON
09 Asst VC Institutional Rsrch/Assess .... Ms. Lisa CASTELLINO
35 Dean of Students .... Dr. Michael A. WALKER
07 Associate Provost for Admissions .... Dr. Terrence M. CURRAN
85 Asst Provost International Programs .... Dr. Denise DIPUCCIO
15 Director Human Resources .... Mr. William A. FLEMING
100 Chief of Staff .... Mr. Max ALLEN
22 Assistant to Chancellor for EEO/AA .... Mr. William A. FLEMING
06 Registrar .... Mr. Gilbert C. BOWEN
08 University Librarian .... Mr. Sherman L. HAYES
45 Director University Planning .... Dr. Kenneth W. SPACKMAN
37 Director Fin Aid/Veterans Svcs .... Ms. Emily J. BLISS
46 Director of Sponsored Programs .... Ms. Pamela B. WHITLOCK
18 Director of Physical Plant .... Mr. Thomas A. FRESHWATER
19 Director Envir Health & Safety .... Mr. Stanley H. HARTS
23 Dir Student Health/Wellness Center .... Ms. Katrin WESNER
31 Director of Auxiliary Services .... Mr. Richard A. FAUSON
41 Director of Athletics .... Mr. Jimmy BASS
36 Director Career Services .... Mr. Thomas D. RAKES
29 Director of Alumni Relations .... Mr. Rob MCINTURF
96 Director of Purchasing .... Ms. Mary E. FORSYTHE
38 Director Student Counseling Center .... Dr. Lynne REEDER
40 Manager Bookstore .... Mr. Chuck HUGHES
49 Dean College Arts & Sciences .... Dr. David P. CORDLE
50 Dean Cameron School of Business .... Dr. Lawrence S. CLARK
53 Int Dean Watson School of Education .... Dr. Karen WETHERILL
66 Dean School of Nursing .... Dr. James D. MCCANN
58 Dean of Graduate School .... Dr. Robert D. ROER
76 Int Dean Col Health & Human Svcs .... Dr. Johnson O. AKINLEYE

*University of North Carolina School of the Arts (D)

1533 S Main Street, Winston-Salem NC 27127-2738

County: Forsyth FICE Identification: 003981
Unit ID: 199184
Telephone: (336) 770-3399 Carnegie Class: Spec/Arts
FAX Number: (336) 770-3375 Calendar System: Semester
URL: www.uncsa.edu
Established: 1963 Annual Undergrad Tuition & Fees (In-State): $6,908
Enrollment: 865 Coed
Affiliation or Control: State IRS Status: 501(c)3
Highest Offering: Master's
Program: Fine Arts Emphasis
Accreditation: SC

02 Chancellor .... Mr. John MAUCERI
05 Chief Academic Officer .... Dr. David P. NELSON
10 Senior Director of Business Affairs .... Ms. Carin IOANNOU
11 Chief Operating Officer .... Mr. George BURNETTE
32 Vice Chancellor Student Life .... Vacant
30 Vice Chancellor Devel/Public Rels .... Vacant
18 Assoc VC Facilities/Services .... Mr. Chrispher BOYD
09 Director Institutional Research .... Dr. Geri COCHRAN
07 Director of Admissions .... Ms. Sheeler LAWSON
08 Librarian .... Ms. Vicki WEAVIL
26 Director of Public Relations .... Ms. Marla CARPENTER
06 Registrar .... Ms. Erin MORIN
15 Director Human Resources .... Ms. Gwen BURSTON
37 Director Financial Aid .... Mrs. Jane KAMIAB
49 Dean Grad/Undergrad Studies .... Vacant
64 Dean of Music .... Dr. Wade WEAST
57 Dean of Dance .... Mr. Ethan STIEFEL
88 Dean of Design Production .... Mr. Joseph TILFORD
88 Dean of Drama .... Mr. Gerald FREEDMAN
13 Director Information Systems .... Ms. Lisa SMITH
19 Director of Campus Police .... Ms. Dorothy CHEESEBRO
29 Director of Alumni Relations .... Vacant
38 Director of Student Counseling .... Mr. Thomas MURRAY

*Western Carolina University (E)

Cullowhee NC 28723-9646

County: Jackson FICE Identification: 002981
Unit ID: 200004
Telephone: (828) 227-7211 Carnegie Class: Master's L
FAX Number: (828) 227-7202 Calendar System: Semester
URL: www.wcu.edu
Established: 1889 Annual Undergrad Tuition & Fees (In-State): $6,367
Enrollment: 9,407 Coed
Affiliation or Control: State IRS Status: 501(c)3
Highest Offering: Doctorate
Program: Liberal Arts And General; Teacher Preparatory; Professional
Accreditation: SC, ANEST, ART, BUS, CACREP, CIDA, CONST, DIETD, DIETI, EMT, ENGT, MUS, NURSE, PTA, SP, SW, TED, THEA

02 Chancellor .... Dr. David O. BELCHER
05 Interim Provost .... Dr. Linda SEESTEDT-STANFORD
10 Interim Vice Chanc Admin & Finance .... Mr. Robert EDWARDS
30 Vice Chanc Advance/External Affairs .... Mr. Clifton METCALF
32 Vice Chancellor Student Affairs .... Dr. Samuel MILLER
20 Sr Assoc Vice Chanc Academic Affs .... Dr. Fred HINSON
21 Acting Assoc VC Financial Services .... Mr. Bobby JUSTICE
35 Asst Vice Chanc Student Affairs .... Mrs. Jane ADAMS-DUNFORD
30 Assoc Vice Chancellor Development .... Mr. Jim MILLER
20 Associate Provost .... Dr. Beth TYSON-LOFQUIST
18 Assoc VC for Facilities Management .... Mr. Joe WALKER
100 Chief of Staff .... Ms. Dianne LYNCH
04 Assistant to the Chancellor .... Ms. Terry WELCH
44 Sr Director of Development .... Vacant
43 Legal Counsel .... Ms. Mary Ann LOCHNER

88 Director Student Support Services .... Mrs. Suzanne BAKER
38 Director of Counseling Services .... Dr. John RITCHIE
06 Registrar .... Mr. Larry HAMMER
07 Director of Student Recruitment .... Mr. Phil CAULEY
09 Asst Vice Chancellor for OIPE .... Dr. Melissa WARGO
37 Director of Financial Aid .... Ms. Trina ORR
15 Director of Human Resources .... Ms. Kathy WONG
27 Chief Information Officer .... Mr. Craig FOWLER
29 Director of Alumni Affairs .... Mr. Marty RAMSEY
08 Dean of Library Services .... Dr. Dana SALLY
19 Director University Police .... Mr. Earnest HUDSON
88 Division Educational Outreach .... Dr. Regis GILMAN
46 Assoc Dean Graduate Sch & Research ...... Dr. Kathleen BRENNEN
31 Director Auxiliary Services .... Mr. Jeff BEWSEY
41 Athletic Director .... Mr. Chip SMITH
23 Director University Health Services .... Ms. Pamela BUCHANAN
28 Director of Intercultural Affairs .... Mr. James FELTON
96 Director of Purchasing .... Mr. Arthur STEPHENS
40 Director Book & Supply Store .... Ms. Pamela DEGRAFFENREID
26 Director Marketing/Promotions .... Ms. Katharine KOCH
88 Director of Orientation .... Ms. Tammy HASKETT
38 Director Advising & Student Success .... Mr. David GOSS
36 Director of Career Services .... Ms. Mardy ASHE
27 Sr Director Comm & Public Relations .... Mr. Bill STUDENC
57 Dean of Fine & Performing Arts .... Dr. Robert KEHRBERG
58 Dean Graduate School & Research .... Dr. Scott HIGGINS
49 Interim Dean Arts & Sciences .... Dr. H. Gibbs KNOTTS
72 Dean Kimmel Sch Constr Mgmt/Tech .... Dr. Robert MCMAHAN
50 Interim Dean of Business .... Dr. Louis E. BUCK, JR.
53 Dean Education/Allied Professions .... Dr. Perry SCHOON
76 Interim Dean Health/Human Sciences .... Dr. Marie HUFF
92 Dean of Honors College .... Dr. Brian RAILSBACK

*Winston-Salem State University (A)

601 MLK Jr. Drive, 200 Blair Hall,
Winston-Salem NC 27110-0001
County: Forsyth — FICE Identification: 002986
Unit ID: 199999
Telephone: (336) 750-2000 — Carnegie Class: Master's M
FAX Number: (336) 750-2049 — Calendar System: Semester
URL: www.wssu.edu
Established: 1892 — Annual Undergrad Tuition & Fees (In-State): $5,254
Enrollment: 6,345 — Coed
Affiliation or Control: State — IRS Status: 501(c)3
Highest Offering: Doctorate
Program: Liberal Arts And General; Teacher Preparatory; Professional
Accreditation: SC, BUS, @CORE, CS, MT, MUS, NRPA, NURSE, OT, PTA, @SW, TED

02 Chancellor .... Dr. Donald J. REAVES
05 Provost/VC Academic Affairs .... Dr. Brenda ALLEN
32 Vice Chancellor Student Affairs .... Dr. Trae COTTON
09 Asst Prov Plng/Assessmt/Research .... Dr. Carolynn BERRY
45 Int Asst Prov Administration/Plng .... Ms. Letitia CORNISH
20 Sr Assoc Provost Academic Affairs ...... Dr. Merdis J. MCCARTER
10 Vice Chanc Finance & Administration .... Mr. Gerald E. HUNTER
21 Assoc VC Financial Plng & Budget .... Dr. Randy W. MILLS
30 Vice Chanc University Advance .... Mrs. Michelle COOK
18 Assoc Vice Chanc Facilities Mgmt .... Mr. Owen J. COOKS
27 Assoc Provost Info Resources/CIO .... Mr. Justin D. MCKENZIE
51 Assoc Dir Cont Educ/Summer Sessions ... Mr. W. Kenneth BULLS
88 Director Internal Audit/Compliance .... Ms. Shannon B. HENRY
53 Dean Sch Educ/Human Performance .... Dr. Manuel VARGAS
19 Chief of Campus Police .... Mrs. Patricia D. NORRIS
08 Librarian .... Dr. Mae L. RODNEY
39 Int Director Hous/Residence Life .... Mr. Peter BLUTREICH
37 Director of Financial Aid .... Mr. Robert MUHAMMED
15 Asst Vice Chanc Human Resources .... Mr. Ivan V. FOSTER
36 Asst Director of Career Services .... Mrs. LaMonica SINGLETON
27 Director Public & Media Relations .... Ms. Nancy N. YOUNG
26 Director Marketing/Publications .... Ms. Sigrid HALL-PITTSLEY
88 Dir Enrollment Communications .... Ms. Cathy HOOTS
29 Director of Alumni Affairs .... Mr. Gregory G. HAIRSTON
44 Director Institutional Annual Fund .... Mrs. Kimberly REESE
35 Director of Student Activities .... Ms. Ebony RAMSEY
23 Director of Student Health Center .... Ms. Ether JOE
41 Athletic Director .... Mr. William HAYES
101 Asst to the Chancellor/Sec of Univ .... Mrs. RaVonda DALTON-RANN
07 Asst VC Enrollment Services .... Mrs. Tomikia LEGRANDE
43 General Legal Counsel .... Mrs. Camille KLUTTZ-LEACH
96 Director Purchasing .... Mr. Alan IRELAND
90 Director Academic Computer Center .... Mr. Cuthrell JOHNSON
50 Dean School Business/Economics .... Dr. Jessica M. BAILEY
88 Assoc Provost Life Long Learning .... Dr. Doria K. STITTS
49 Dean College Arts & Sciences .... Dr. Charles W. FORD, JR.
76 Dean School of Health Sciences .... Dr. Peggy VALENTINE
89 Dean of University College .... Dr. Michele RELEFORD
92 Int Director of Honors College .... Dr. Soncerey L. MONTGOMERY
88 Director of Title III .... Dr. Everette L. WITHERSPOON
88 Asst Provost Faculty Affairs .... Dr. Denise PEARSON

Wake Forest University (B)

1834 Wake Forest Road, Winston-Salem NC 27109-8758
County: Forsyth — FICE Identification: 002978
Unit ID: 199847
Telephone: (336) 758-5000 — Carnegie Class: RU/H
FAX Number: (336) 758-6074 — Calendar System: Semester
URL: www.wfu.edu
Established: 1834 — Annual Undergrad Tuition & Fees: $40,032
Enrollment: 7,162 — Coed
Affiliation or Control: Independent Non-Profit — IRS Status: 501(c)3
Highest Offering: Doctorate
Program: Liberal Arts And General; Teacher Preparatory; Professional
Accreditation: SC, ANEST, ARCPA, BUS, BUSA, CACREP, DENT, LAW, MED, MT, TED, THEOL

01 President .... Dr. Nathan O. HATCH
43 VP Gen Counsel/Sec Board of Trust .... Mr. J. Reid MORGAN
03 Sr Vice Pres/Chief Financial Ofcr .... Vacant
10 Exec VP Finance/Admin/Chf Oper Ofcr .... Mr. B. Hofler MILAM
17 Sr Vice Pres Health Affairs .... Vacant
11 Vice President for Administration .... Dr. Matthew S. CULLINAN
30 Vice Pres University Advancement .... Mr. Mark A. PETERSEN
32 Vice Pres Student Life .... Mr. Kenneth A. ZICK
88 Vice Pres/Chief Investment Officer .... Mr. James J. DUNN
05 Provost .... Vacant
20 Assoc Provost Academic Initiatives .... Ms. Jennifer COLLINS
04 Senior Advisor to the President .... Ms. Sandra C. BOYETTE
35 Assoc VP/Dean of Student Services .... Mr. Harold R. HOLMES
44 Ast VP/Dir Parent/Donor Relations .... Ms. Minta A. MCNALLY
30 Asst VP/Director of Development .... Mr. Robert T. BAKER
13 Assoc Prov for Information Systems .... Dr. Rick MATTHEWS
46 Vice Provost for Research .... Dr. Mark WELKER
49 Dean of the College .... Dr. Jacquelyn FETROW
63 Dean School Med/Int Health Sci Pres .... Dr. Edward ABRAHAM
58 Dean Graduate School Arts/Sciences .... Dr. Lorna G. MOORE
61 Dean School of Law .... Mr. Blake MORANT
50 Dean of Business .... Mr. Steven REINEMUND
73 Dean of Divinity .... Dr. Gail R. O'DAY
89 Assoc Dean & Dean of Freshmen .... Dr. Paul N. ORSER
09 Dir Inst Research/Academic Admin .... Mr. Ross A. GRIFFITH
08 Dir of the Z Smith Reynolds Library .... Dr. Lynn SUTTON
85 Director of International Studies .... Steven DUKE
07 Director of Admissions .... Ms. Martha B. ALLMAN
37 Director of Financial Aid .... Mr. William T. WELLS
36 VP/Office of Personal & Career Dev .... Mr. Andy CHAN
06 Registrar .... Mr. Harold PACE
41 Director of Athletics .... Mr. Ronald D. WELLMAN
15 Assoc Vice Pres of Human Resources .... Mr. Mike TESH
18 Director Facilities Management .... Mr. James ALTY
38 Dir University Counseling Center ...... Dr. Marianne A. SCHUBERT
84 Director Enrollment Management .... Vacant
23 Director Student Health Service .... Dr. Cecil D. PRICE
39 Exec Dir of Residential Services .... Vacant
40 Exec Director Business Services .... Mr. Donald J. MOSER
42 Chaplain .... Rev. Timothy L. AUMAN
19 Chief University Police .... Ms. Regina G. LAWSON
22 EEO Mgr/Diversity & Compliance Dir .... Ms. Doris A. MCLAUGHLIN
96 Director Purchasing .... Mr. Phillip E. HENDRIX
94 Director Women's & Gender Studies .... Dr. Wanda BALZANO

Warren Wilson College (C)

PO Box 9000, Asheville NC 28815-9000
County: Buncombe — FICE Identification: 002979
Unit ID: 199865
Telephone: (828) 298-3325 — Carnegie Class: Bac/A&S
FAX Number: (828) 771-7097 — Calendar System: Semester
URL: www.warren-wilson.edu
Established: 1894 — Annual Undergrad Tuition & Fees: $26,674
Enrollment: 992 — Coed
Affiliation or Control: Presbyterian Church (U.S.A.) — IRS Status: 501(c)3
Highest Offering: Master's
Program: Liberal Arts And General; Teacher Preparatory
Accreditation: SC, SW

01 President .... Dr. William S. PFEIFFER
05 VP Academic Affairs/Dean of College .... Dr. Paula K. GARRETT
11 VP for Administration/Finance .... Mr. Jonathan D. EHRLICH
30 Int Vice Pres Advancement .... Mr. Richard BLOMGREN
32 Dean of Students .... Ms. Deborah L. MYERS
88 Dean of Work .... Mr. Ian ROBERTSON
07 Dean of Admission/Dir Marketing .... Mr. Richard BLOMGREN
88 Dean of Service-Learning .... Ms. Cathy KRAMER
20 Assoc Dean for Faculty .... Ms. Carol HOWARD
06 Registrar .... Miss Christa L. BRIDGMAN
09 Dir Educ Assessment/Inst Research .... Dr. Donald W. RAY
08 Director Library .... Dr. Christine R. NUGENT
37 Director Financial Aid .... Ms. Kathy P. PACK
21 Controller .... Ms. Mary DAVIS
44 Director Annual Giving .... Ms. Miranda HIPPLE
29 Interim Director Alumni Relations .... Mr. Rodney LYTLE
26 Director of Media Relations .... Mr. Benjamin J. ANDERSON
88 Advance Communications/Project Dir .... Ms. Brooke SEUFERT
20 Director Academic Support Service .... Ms. Lyn O'HARE
88 Director of Service Leaning .... Ms. Brooke MILLSAPS
35 Director Student Services .... Mr. James LAUER
38 Director of Counseling .... Mr. Arthur SHUSTER
36 Director Career Services .... Mr. Bates CANON
42 Director of Spiritual Life .... Rev. Leah MCCULLOUGH
41 Director of Athletics .... Ms. Stacey ENOS
91 Dir Admin Data Processing .... Ms. Omega HODGES
40 Director Campus Store .... Ms. Stephanie COLEMAN
15 Director Human Resources .... Ms. Gail BAYLOR
18 Director Facilities Mgmt/Tech Svcs .... Mr. Paul BRAESE
19 Director Public Safety .... Mr. Terry PAYNE
88 Exec Dir Environment Leadership Ctr .... Dr. Margo FLOOD
88 Director Swannanoa Gathering .... Mr. Jim MAGILL
104 Director of International Programs .... Ms. Naomi OTTERNESS
42 College Chaplain .... Mr. Steve RUNHOLT
28 Director of Multicultural Affairs .... Vacant
96 Director of Purchasing .... Ms. Deborah ANSTROM
13 Manager Computing Services .... Mr. David HARPER

85 International Student Adviser .... Ms. Lorrie JAYNE
88 Conference Coordinator .... Ms. Liz BRACE

Wingate University (D)

220 N. Camden Street, Wingate NC 28174-0157
County: Union — FICE Identification: 002985
Unit ID: 199962
Telephone: (704) 233-8000 — Carnegie Class: Master's S
FAX Number: (704) 233-8192 — Calendar System: Semester
URL: www.wingate.edu
Established: 1896 — Annual Undergrad Tuition & Fees: $22,180
Enrollment: 2,373 — Coed
Affiliation or Control: Southern Baptist — IRS Status: 501(c)3
Highest Offering: Doctorate
Program: Liberal Arts And General; Teacher Preparatory; Professional; Business Emphasis
Accreditation: SC, ACBSP, ARCPA, MUS, PHAR, TED

01 President .... Dr. Jerry E. MCGEE
05 Senior VP Academic Affairs .... Dr. Martha S. ASTI
10 VP Business/Chief Financial Ofcr ..... Mr. Charles E. TAYLOR, JR.
30 Vice President Resource Development .... Mr. E. Vincent TILSON
41 Vice Pres & Director of Athletics .... Mr. R. Stephen POSTON
32 VP for Student Life/Enrollment Mgmt .... Mr. T. Rhett BROWN
21 Asst VP for Business Operations .... Mr. Scott E. HUNSUCKER
23 Asst VP for Health Sciences Div .... Mr. Roy Lee RAGSDALE, JR.
12 Asst VP Matthews Campus .... Dr. Greg CLEMMER
32 Dean of Student Affairs .... Mrs. Glenda H. BEBBER
49 Dean School Arts & Sciences .... Dr. H. Donald MERRILL
50 Dean School of Business .... Mr. Joe M. GRAHAM
67 Dean School of Pharmacy .... Dr. Robert B. SUPERNAW
53 Dean School of Education .... Dr. Sarah H. BURNS
08 Director of Library .... Mrs. Amee M. ODOM
12 Dean of the Metro College .... Mr. Greg R. CLEMMER
35 Director of Involvement .... Ms. Brandy SHOTT
30 Director of Development .... Dr. Wayne D. WIKE
09 Director Inst Research/Registrar .... Mrs. Nicci C. BROWN
37 Director Student Financial Planning ...... Ms. Teresa G. WILLIAMS
26 Dir of Marketing/Communications .... Ms. Jennifer GASKINS
91 Director Administrative Computing .... Mr. Timothy D. HERRIN
29 Director of Alumni Development .... Vacant
42 Minstr to Stdnts/Asst Dn Stdnt Affs .... Rev. A. Dane JORDAN
40 Manager of Campus Store .... Mr. Danny KEY
19 Director of Campus Safety .... Vacant
44 Director of Annual Giving .... Vacant
44 Dir of Major Gifts & Planned Giving ... Mr. J. Theodore JOHNSON
27 Asst Dir Marketing & Communications .... Vacant
38 Director of Counseling Services .... Ms. Jessica HYLTON
13 Director of Information Technology .... Ms. Jeanette K. BUJAK
36 Dir of Internships and Career Svcs .... Ms. Sharon ROBINSON
15 Human Resources Coordinator .... Mrs. Lisa B. RAGSDALE
39 Dir Resid Life/Asst Dn Stdnt Affs .... Mr. Patrick BIGGERSTAFF
35 Dir of Retention/Asst Dn Stdnt Affs .... Ms. Kristin WHARTON

NORTH DAKOTA

Cankdeska Cikana Community College (E)

PO Box 269, 214 First Avenue,
Fort Totten ND 58335-0269
County: Benson — FICE Identification: 022365
Unit ID: 200208
Telephone: (701) 766-4415 — Carnegie Class: Tribal
FAX Number: (701) 766-4077 — Calendar System: Semester
URL: www.littlehoop.edu
Established: 1974 — Annual Undergrad Tuition & Fees: $2,525
Enrollment: 252 — Coed
Affiliation or Control: Independent Non-Profit — IRS Status: 501(c)3
Highest Offering: Associate Degree
Program: Occupational; 2-Year Principally Bachelor's Creditable
Accreditation: NH

01 President .... Dr. Cynthia A. LINDQUIST
05 Vice President Academics .... Dr. Leander MCDONALD
10 Vice President for Finance .... Ms. Chelly MERKEL-VEER
32 Vice Pres Student Services .... Ms. Erica CAVANAUGH
06 Registrar .... Mr. Ermen BROWN, JR.

Ft. Berthold Community College (F)

PO Box 490, New Town ND 58763-0490
County: Mountrail — FICE Identification: 025537
Unit ID: 200086
Telephone: (701) 627-4738 — Carnegie Class: Tribal
FAX Number: (701) 627-3609 — Calendar System: Semester
URL: www.fbcc.bia.edu
Established: 1973 — Annual Undergrad Tuition & Fees: $2,100
Enrollment: 215 — Coed
Affiliation or Control: Independent Non-Profit — IRS Status: 501(c)3
Highest Offering: Associate Degree
Program: Occupational; 2-Year Principally Bachelor's Creditable
Accreditation: NH

01 President .... Mr. Russell D. MASON, JR.
05 Academic Dean .... Dr. Bob WOODLE
32 Dean of Students .... Ms. Rosalyn BAKER
10 Chief Finance Manager .... Mr. Kim CONNOLE
37 Financial Aid Administration .... Ms. Beverly MASON

06 Registrar ....Ms. Kathy KRAFT
08 Librarian ....Mrs. Quincee BAKER
38 Counselor ....Vacant
40 Bookstore Manager ....Ms. Iona LITTLE WHITEMAN

Jamestown College (A)

6000 College Lane, Jamestown ND 58405-0001
County: Stutsman FICE Identification: 002990
Unit ID: 200156
Telephone: (701) 252-3467 Carnegie Class: Bac/Diverse
FAX Number: (701) 253-4318 Calendar System: Semester
URL: www.jc.edu
Established: 1883 Annual Undergrad Tuition & Fees: $22,970
Enrollment: 967 Coed
Affiliation or Control: Presbyterian Church (U.S.A.) IRS Status: 501(c)3
Highest Offering: Master's
Program: Liberal Arts And General; Teacher Preparatory; Professional
Accreditation: NH, IACBE, NUR

01 President ....Dr. Robert S. BADAL
05 Vice Pres/Dean Academic Affairs ....Dr. Gary WATTS
32 Dean of Students ....Mr. Gary VAN ZINDEREN
10 Vice President for Business Affairs ....Mr. Thomas R. HECK
30 Vice President for Inst Advancement ....Ms. Polly J. PETERSON
84 Vice Pres Enrollment Management ....Ms. Tena LAWRENCE
04 Assistant to the President ....Ms. Liz SCHWARTZ
06 Registrar ....Mr. Michael P. WOODLEY
37 Student Financial Aid Officer ....Mrs. Marge M. MICHAEL
08 Librarian ....Mrs. Phyllis K. BRATTON
36 Director Experiential Education ....Ms. Pat J. RINDE
27 Director Information Office ....Ms. Donna SCHMITZ
41 Athletic Director ....Mr. Lawrie PAULSON
14 Director Computer Center ....Mr. Tim KACHEL
18 Chief Facilities/Physical Plant ....Mr. Mark KOEPKE
42 Chaplain ....Rev. Darin NAMMINGA
101 Secretary to the Board of Trustees ....Ms. Liz SCHWARTZ

Medcenter One College of Nursing (B)

512 N 7th Street, Bismarck ND 58501-4494
County: Burleigh FICE Identification: 009354
Unit ID: 200244
Telephone: (701) 323-6271 Carnegie Class: Spec/Health
FAX Number: (701) 323-6289 Calendar System: Semester
URL: www.medcenterone.com/collegeofnursing
Established: 1988 Annual Undergrad Tuition & Fees: $10,851
Enrollment: 90 Coed
Affiliation or Control: Independent Non-Profit IRS Status: 501(c)3
Highest Offering: Baccalaureate
Program: Nursing Emphasis
Accreditation: NH, NURSE, RAD

01 Provost/Dean ....Dr. Karen K. LATHAM
20 Associate Dean ....Dr. Wanda F. ROSE
32 Director Student Services ....Ms. Mary J. SMITH
37 Dir Student Financial Aid/Registrar ....Ms. Janell D. THOMAS
08 Head Librarian ....Mr. Travis SCHULTZ
10 Chief Business Officer ....Ms. Candy RIFFEY

*North Dakota University System Office (C)

600 E Boulevard Avenue, Dept 215,
Bismarck ND 58505-0230
County: Burleigh FICE Identification: 033434
Telephone: (701) 328-2960 Carnegie Class: N/A
FAX Number: (701) 328-2961
URL: www.ndus.edu

01 Chancellor ....William G. GOETZ
05 Vice Chanc Academic/Student Affairs ....Michel HILLMAN
10 Vice Chanc Administrative Affairs ....Laura GLATT
45 Vice Chancellor Strategic Planning ....Marsha KROTSENG
13 Chief Information Officer ....Randall THURSBY
24 Director Interactive Video Network ....Jerry ROSTAD
37 Director Financial Aid ....Peggy WIPF
16 Human Resources ....Laura GLATT
20 Academic Affairs Associate ....Aimee COPAS
37 Indn Schlrshp Pgm/Dir St Aprvd Agy ....Rhonda SCHAUER
21 Director of Finance ....Cathy MCDONALD
88 Dir Followup Info on ND Educ & Trng ....Michelle OLSEN
43 General Counsel/Executive Secretary ....H. P. SEAWORTH
26 Public Affairs Director ....Debra ANDERSON
88 Director Financial Reporting ....Robin PUTNAM
86 Federal Relations Coordinator ....Peggy WIPF
106 Distance Education Coordinator ....Robert LARSON
88 Articulation & Transfer ....Lisa JOHNSON
88 Dir Consortium for Subst Abuse Prev ....Jane VANGSNESS
88 Coord ND Col Access Challenge Pgm ....Tim MUELLER

*University of North Dakota Main Campus (D)

264 Centennial Drive, Grand Forks ND 58202
County: Grand Forks FICE Identification: 003005
Unit ID: 200280
Telephone: (701) 777-2011 Carnegie Class: RU/H
FAX Number: (701) 777-2696 Calendar System: Semester
URL: www.und.edu
Established: 1883 Annual Undergrad Tuition & Fees (In-State): $7,092
Enrollment: 14,194 Coed
Affiliation or Control: State IRS Status: 501(c)3
Highest Offering: Doctorate
Program: Liberal Arts And General; Teacher Preparatory; Professional
Accreditation: NH, AAB, ANEST, ARCPA, ART, BUS, CLPSY, COPSY, CS, CYTO, DIETC, ENG, HT, LAW, MED, MT, MUS, NAIT, NURSE, OT, PTA, SP, SPAA, SW, TED, THEA

02 President ....Dr. Robert O. KELLEY
29 Exec Vice Pres & CEO Alumni Assoc ....Mr. Tim O'KEEFE
05 Vice Pres Academic Affairs/Provost ....Dr. Paul LEBEL
10 Vice President Operations/Finance ....Ms. Alice BREKKE
32 Vice Pres Student Affairs ....Dr. Lori REESOR
17 Vice President Health Affairs ....Dr. Joshua WYNNE
46 Vice Pres Research/Economic Devel ....Dr. Phyllis E. JOHNSON
26 Exec Assoc VP University Rels ....Mr. Peter JOHNSON
88 Assoc VP Outreach Services ....Dr. Joshua RIEDY
35 Associate VP & Dean of Students ....Dr. Cara HALGREN
21 Assoc VP Finance/Operations ....Ms. Peggy LUCKE
21 Assoc VP Finance/Operations ....Ms. Margaret MYERS
45 Assoc Vice Pres Research/Econ Dev ....Dr. Barry MILAVETZ
45 Asst VP Research/Economic Devel ....Dr. Mark HOFFMANN
25 Asst VP Grants/Contracts Admin ....Mr. David O. SCHMIDT
25 AVP Intellectual Prop Comm/Econ Dev ....Mr. Michael MOORE
88 Assoc VP for Health & Wellness ....Dr. Laurie BETTING
08 Director of Libraries ....Mr. Wilbur STOLT
27 Chief Information Officer ....Dr. Joshua RIEDY
06 Registrar ....Dr. Suzanne ANDERSON
15 Dir Human Resources/Payroll Svcs ....Ms. Diane L. NELSON
19 Chief of University Police ....Mr. Duane J. CZAPIEWSKI
38 Director Counseling Center ....Dr. Myron VEENSTRA
84 Int Exec Dir Enrollment Services ....Ms. Lisa BURGER
07 Director of Admissions ....Dr. Deb MELBY
36 Director Career Services/Coop Educ ....Mr. Mark A. THOMPSON
87 Director Summer Sessions ....Ms. Diane HADDEN
20 Director Instructional Development ....Dr. Anne KELSCH
22 Affirmative Action Officer ....Ms. Sally J. PAGE
37 Director Student Financial Aid ....Ms. Robin HOLDEN
39 Director Residence Services ....Ms. Judy L. SARGENT
23 Director of Student Health ....Ms. Michelle D. ESLINGER
43 General Counsel ....Ms. Julie EVANS
41 Director Athletics ....Mr. Brian FAISON
18 Director of Facilities Management ....Mr. Larry L. ZITZOW
85 Director International Programs ....Mr. Ray LAGASSE
21 Controller ....Ms. Sharon LOILAND
88 Director Judicial Affs/Crisis Pgm ....Vacant
09 Director of Institutional Research ....Ms. Carmen WILLIAMS
94 Director Women's Center ....Ms. Kay MENDICK
96 Director Purchasing ....Mr. Scott SCHREINER
30 Chief Development Officer ....Mr. Tim O'KEEFE
92 Director Honors Program ....Dr. Sally PYLE
28 Dir Multicultural Student Services ....Vacant
19 Dir Emergency Mgmt & Public Safety ....Mr. Terry SANDO
13 Deputy CIO IT Systems & Services ....Mr. Rick ANDERSON
21 Budget Manager ....Ms. Cindy FETSCH
40 Manager University Bookstore ....Mr. Derek SCHUCKMAN
49 Int Dean of Arts & Sciences ....Dr. Kathleen TIEMANN
58 Int Dean of Graduate School ....Dr. Wayne SWISHER
61 Dean School of Law ....Ms. Kathryn RAND
66 Dean College of Nursing ....Dr. Denise KORNIEWICZ
50 Dean Business/Public Administration ....Dr. Dennis J. ELBERT
54 Dean School Engr/Mines ....Dr. Hesham EL-REWINI
53 Dean Col Education/Human Devel ....Dr. Dan RICE
88 Dean of Aerospace Sciences ....Dr. Bruce SMITH
63 Dean Sch Medicine/Health Science ....Dr. Joshua WYNNE

*Dickinson State University (E)

291 Campus Drive, Dickinson ND 58601-4896
County: Stark FICE Identification: 002989
Unit ID: 200059
Telephone: (701) 483-2507 Carnegie Class: Bac/Diverse
FAX Number: (701) 483-2006 Calendar System: Semester
URL: www.dickinsonstate.edu
Established: 1918 Annual Undergrad Tuition & Fees (In-State): $5,611
Enrollment: 2,668 Coed
Affiliation or Control: State IRS Status: 501(c)3
Highest Offering: Baccalaureate
Program: Liberal Arts And General; Teacher Preparatory
Accreditation: NH, IACBE, MUS, NUR, PNUR, TED

02 President ....Dr. Richard J. MCCALLUM
05 Vice President for Academic Affairs ....Dr. Jon L. BRUDVIG
10 Vice President for Business Affairs ....Mr. Alvin G. BINSTOCK
32 Vice Pres for Student Development ....Mr. Hal HAYNES
49 Dean of Arts & Sciences ....Dr. Kenneth HAUGHT
53 Dean of Educ/Business/Applied Sci ....Dr. Douglas A. LAPLANTE
102 Exec Dir Alumni Assoc/Foundation ....Mr. Kevin J. THOMPSON
26 Director of University Relations ....Ms. Constance WALTER
41 Director of Intercollege Athletics ....Mr. Tim DANIEL
88 Ex Dir Strom Ctr for Entrpshp & Ino ....Mr. Steve GLASSER
56 Director of Extended Learning ....Mr. John HURLIMANN
07 Director of Enrollment Services ....Mr. Norman COLEY
06 Director of Academic Records ....Mr. Marshall R. MELBYE
08 Director of Library Services ....Ms. Rita ENNEN
13 Director of Computer Services ....Mr. Todd HAUF
37 Director of Financial Aid ....Ms. Sandy L. KLEIN
88 Director Academic Success Center ....Dr. Stacie VARNSON
88 Director of Food Service ....Mr. Todd MATTHEWS
40 Manager University Store ....Ms. Loretta A. HEIDT
21 Controller ....Mr. Mark S. LOWE
36 Director of Career Services ....Ms. Bonnie G. BOHLMAN
09 Coordinator of Institutional Rsrch ....Mr. Scott STAUDINGER
28 Director of Multicultural Center ....Ms. Ronnie WALKER

39 Housing Coordinator ....Ms. Lydia DWORSHAK
15 Coordinator Personnel Services ....Ms. Gail EBELTOFT

*Mayville State University (F)

330 3rd Street, NE, Mayville ND 58257-1299
County: Traill FICE Identification: 002993
Unit ID: 200226
Telephone: (701) 788-2301 Carnegie Class: Bac/Diverse
FAX Number: (701) 788-4748 Calendar System: Semester
URL: www.mayvillestate.edu
Established: 1889 Annual Undergrad Tuition & Fees (In-State): $6,084
Enrollment: 982 Coed
Affiliation or Control: State IRS Status: 501(c)3
Highest Offering: Baccalaureate
Program: 2-Year Principally Bachelor's Creditable; Liberal Arts And General; Teacher Preparatory; Business Emphasis
Accreditation: NH, TED

02 President ....Dr. Gary D. HAGEN
04 Executive Administrative Assistant ....Mrs. Shirley K. RUX
05 Vice President for Academic Affairs ....Dr. Keith A. STENEHJEM
10 Vice President for Business Affairs ....Mr. Steven P. BENSEN
32 VP for Student Affairs/Inst Researc ....Dr. Raymond H. GERSZEWSKI
08 Director of Library Services ....Vacant
37 Director of Financial Aid ....Mrs. Shirley M. HANSON
06 Registrar ....Mrs. Pamela K. BRAATEN
84 Director of Enrollment Services ....Mr. James MOROWSKI
36 Dir Career Services & Internships ....Mr. Jay A. HENRICKSON
39 Director of Student Housing ....Mr. G. Scott BERRY
40 Director of Bookstore ....Mrs. Pam B. SOHOLT
41 Athletic Director ....Mr. Mike K. MOORE
18 Physical Plant Director ....Mr. Dennis N. SCHULTZ
26 Chief Public Relations Officer ....Ms. Beth I. SWENSON
18 Director of Facilities Services ....Mr. Bob J. KOZOJED
15 HR Administrator ....Mr. Steven P. BENSEN
13 Director of Information Technology ....Mr. Patrick W. STEELE
14 Director of Computer Center ....Mr. Shawn D. OGBURN
105 Director of Web Services ....Mr. James E. BURMEISTER
07 Director of Admissions & Ext Learn ....Ms. Misti L. WUORI
96 Business Office Accountant ....Mrs. Janice E. JORGENSEN
30 Chief Development ....Mrs. Susan S. OMDALEN

*Minot State University (G)

500 University Avenue W, Minot ND 58707-0001
County: Ward FICE Identification: 002994
Unit ID: 200253
Telephone: (701) 858-3000 Carnegie Class: Master's M
FAX Number: (701) 839-6933 Calendar System: Semester
URL: www.minotstateu.edu
Established: 1913 Annual Undergrad Tuition & Fees (In-State): $5,763
Enrollment: 3,866 Coed
Affiliation or Control: State IRS Status: 501(c)3
Highest Offering: Beyond Master's But Less Than Doctorate
Program: Liberal Arts And General; Teacher Preparatory; Professional; Business Emphasis
Accreditation: NH, IACBE, MUS, NUR, SP, SW, TED

02 President ....Dr. David FULLER
05 VP for Academic Affairs ....Dr. Lenore KOCZON
10 Vice President for Finance/Admin ....Mr. Brian FOISY
30 Vice President for Advancement ....Mr. Marv SEMRAU
32 Vice President for Student Affairs ....Dr. Richard J. JENKINS
21 Controller ....Ms. Jonelle WATSON
06 Registrar ....Ms. Rebecca PORTER
08 Director of the Library ....Mr. Stephen BANISTER
35 Director of Student Life ....Ms. Lisa ERIKSMOEN
37 Director of Financial Aid ....Mr. Dale GEHRING
58 Dean of Graduate School ....Dr. Linda CRESAP
50 Dean College of Business ....Dr. JoAnn LINRUD
49 Dean College Arts & Science ....Dr. Conrad DAVIDSON
53 Dean Col Education/Health Sci ....Dr. Neil NORDQUIST
51 Dean Continuing Education ....Dr. Kristin WARMOTH
29 Director Alumni Relations ....Ms. Tawnya BERNSDORF
14 Director Computer Services ....Ms. Cathy HORVATH
40 Director Bookstore ....Ms. Sandra FOLEY
41 Athletic Director ....Mr. Rick HEDBERG
27 Director of Public Information ....Ms. Susan NESS
18 Director of Plant Services ....Mr. Roger KLUCK
15 Director of Human Resources ....Mr. Wesley MATTHEWS
12 Dean of Dakota College at Bottineau ....Dr. Kenneth GROSZ
36 Director of Campus Career Services ....Ms. Lynda BERTSCH
38 Director of Student Services ....Ms. Evelyn KLIMPEL
25 Grants & Contracts Accountant ....Ms. Laurel HYATT
07 Dean of Admissions ....Mr. Kevin HARMON
09 Director of Institutional Research ....Ms. Cari OLSON

*North Dakota State University Main Campus (H)

P.O. Box 6050, Fargo ND 58108-6050
County: Cass FICE Identification: 002997
Unit ID: 200332
Telephone: (701) 231-8011 Carnegie Class: RU/VH
FAX Number: (701) 231-8722 Calendar System: Semester
URL: www.ndsu.edu
Established: 1890 Annual Undergrad Tuition & Fees (In-State): $7,270
Enrollment: 14,407 Coed
Affiliation or Control: State IRS Status: 501(c)3
Highest Offering: Doctorate
Program: Liberal Arts And General; Teacher Preparatory; Professional

Accreditation: NH, ART, BUS, CACREP, CIDA, CONST, DIETC, DIETD, ENG, EXSC, LSAR, MFCD, MUS, NURSE, PHAR, TED, THEA

02 President .... Dr. Dean BRESCIANI
05 Provost/Vice Pres Academic Affairs .... Dr. J. Bruce RAFERT
10 Vice President Business & Finance .... Mr. Bruce BOLLINGER
32 Vice President for Student Affairs .... Mr. Prakash C. MATHEW
46 Vice Pres Research Crea Act & Tech .... Dr. Philip BOUDJOUK
88 Vice President Ag/Univ Extension .... Dr. D. C. COSTON
14 Associate VP IT & CIO .... Vacant
30 Exec Dir NDSU Dev Found/Alumni Assn .... Mr. James C. MILLER
86 VP Information Technology .... Ms. Bonita NEAS
22 VP Equity/Diversity/Global Outreach .... Mrs. Eveadean MYERS
35 Associate Vice Pres Student Affairs . Dr. Catherine (Kate) HAUGEN
15 Assoc VP Business & Finance .... Vacant
88 Assoc VP Interdisciplinary Research .... Dr. Gregory J. MCCARTHY
88 Assoc VP Sponsored Programs Admin .... Ms. Valrey V. KETTNER
06 University Registrar .... Dr. Kristi D. WOLD-MCCORMICK
84 Coordinator Enrollment Management .... Mr. Viet DOAN
08 Dean of Libraries .... Dr. Michelle REID
35 Dean Student Life .... Ms. Janna M. STOSKOPF
51 Dir Distance/Continuing Education .... Ms. Lisa NORDICK
37 Director Student Financial Services .... Ms. Jeanette E. ENEBO
36 Director Career Center .... Ms. Jill J. WILKEY
27 Media Relations Director .... Vacant
88 Asst VP University Relations .... Ms. Laura MCDANIEL
47 Dean of Agriculture/Dir Exp Station .... Dr. Kenneth A. GRAFTON
50 Dean Business Administration .... Dr. Ronald D. JOHNSON
54 Dean Engineering/Architecture .... Dr. Gary R. SMITH
59 Dean Human Development & Education .... Dr. Virginia L. CLARK JOHNSON
49 Dean Arts/Humanities/Social Science .... Dr. Kent SANDSTROM
81 Dean of Science & Math .... Dr. Kevin D. MCCAUL
67 Dean of Pharmacy/Nursing/Allied Sci .... Dr. Charles D. PETERSON
58 Dean Col of Grad/Inter Studies .... Dr. David A. WITTROCK
56 Director NDSU Extension Service .... Mr. Duane D. HAUCK
89 Assoc Dean University Studies .... Dr. Carolyn A. SCHNELL
21 Director of Budget .... Ms. Cynthia ROTT
25 Manager Grant & Contract Acctng .... Ms. Karen HENDRICKSON
18 Director Facilities Management .... Mr. Mike ELLINGSON
19 Dir of Univ Police/Safety Officer .... Mr. Raymond E. BOYER
38 Director Counseling/Disability Svcs .... Dr. William BURNS
23 Director Wellness Center .... Mr. Gary T. FISHER
39 Director of Residence Life .... Mr. Michael D. HARWOOD
40 Director Bookstore .... Ms. Carol J. MILLER
41 Director of Athletics .... Mr. Gene F. TAYLOR
43 General Counsel .... Mr. Rick D. JOHNSON
57 Director Fine Arts .... Dr. E. John MILLER
09 Director Inst Research/Analysis .... Dr. William D. SLANGER
96 Director of Purchasing .... Ms. Stacey O. WINTER
07 Director of Admissions .... Mr. Jobey L. LICHTBLAU

*Valley City State University (A)

101 College Street, SW, Valley City ND 58072-4098
County: Barnes FICE Identification: 003008
Unit ID: 200572
Telephone: (701) 845-7990 Carnegie Class: Bac/Diverse
FAX Number: (701) 845-7253 Calendar System: Semester
URL: www.vcsu.edu
Established: 1889 Annual Undergrad Tuition & Fees (In-State): $6,196
Enrollment: 1,285 Coed
Affiliation or Control: State IRS Status: 501(c)3
Highest Offering: Master's
Program: Liberal Arts And General; Teacher Preparatory
Accreditation: NH, MUS, TED

02 President .... Dr. Steven W. SHIRLEY
05 Vice President Academic Affairs .... Dr. Margaret DAHLBERG
10 Vice President Business Affairs .... Ms. Trudy COLLINS
32 Vice President Student Affairs .... Mr. Glen J. SCHMALZ
53 Dean Sch of Educ/Graduate Stds .... Dr. Gary THOMPSON
08 Library Director .... Ms. Donna JAMES
20 Director Student Academic Services .... Ms. Janet M. DRAKE
37 Director Student Financial Aid .... Ms. Betty A. SCHUMACHER
36 Director Career Services .... Ms. Marcia J. FOSS
14 Chief Information Officer .... Mr. Joseph TYKWINSKI
41 Athletic Director .... Mr. Jack DENHOLM
84 Director of Enrollment Services .... Ms. Charlene STENSON
30 Director of University Advancement .... Mr. Larry J. ROBINSON
18 Director of Facilities Services .... Mr. Ron POMMERER
07 Director of Admissions & Records .... Ms. Charlene STENSON
15 Director of Human Resources .... Mr. Derek HUGHES
44 Asst Dir University Advancement .... Ms. Kim HESCH
38 Director of Student Counseling .... Ms. Erin KLINGENBERG
26 Director Marketing/Communications .... Mr. Doug ANDERSON
40 Director Bookstore .... Mr. Todd ROGELSTAD
06 Registrar .... Ms. Jody KLIER

*Bismarck State College (B)

PO Box 5587, Bismarck ND 58506-5587
County: Burleigh FICE Identification: 002988
Unit ID: 200022
Telephone: (701) 224-5400 Carnegie Class: Assoc/Pub4
FAX Number: (701) 224-5550 Calendar System: Semester
URL: www.bismarckstate.edu
Established: 1939 Annual Undergrad Tuition & Fees (In-State): $3,485
Enrollment: 4,177 Coed
Affiliation or Control: State IRS Status: 501(c)3
Highest Offering: Baccalaureate
Program: Occupational; 2-Year Principally Bachelor's Creditable; Liberal Arts And General
Accreditation: NH, EMT, ENGT, MLTAD, SURGT

02 President .... Dr. Larry C. SKOGEN
03 Executive Vice President .... Mr. David CLARK
05 Provost/VP Academic Affairs .... Dr. Drake CARTER
30 VP College Advance/Exec Dir Found .... Mr. Gordy BINEK
88 VP National Energy Ctr of Excellenc .... Ms. Kari KNUDSON
20 Associate VP for Academic Affairs .... Dr. Jane SCHULZ
32 Associate VP for Student Affairs .... Dr. Donna FISHBECK
10 Assoc VP for Finance & Operations .... Mrs. Tamara BARBER
88 Assoc VP Nat Energy Ctr of Excell .... Mr. Bruce EMMIL
51 Assoc VP Cont Educ/Training & Innov .... Mrs. Carla HIXSON
07 Dir Admissions/Enrollment Services .... Mr. Greg STURM
20 Dean of Faculty .... Dr. Janelle MASTERS
08 Director of Library Services .... Ms. Marlene ANDERSON
26 Director of College Relations .... Mrs. Mary FRIESZ
41 Director of Athletics .... Mr. Buster GILLISS
106 Chief Dist Learning/Military Affair .... Mr. Lane HUBER
37 Director of Financial Aid .... Mr. Jeff JACOBS
51 Dir of Cont Educ/Trng & Innovation .... Ms. Lori HEINSOHN
88 Project Manager NECE .... Mr. Zachery ALLEN
88 Dir Great Plains Energy Corridor .... Vacant
88 Program Manager NECE .... Mr. Kevin HOLMSTROM
88 Program Manager NECE .... Mr. Dan SCHMIDT
88 Program Manager NECE .... Mr. Wade VOGEL
46 Dir of Resource Development .... Ms. Julie ERICKSON
35 Director Student & Residence Life .... Ms. Heather SHEEHAN
18 Chief Buildings/Grounds Officer .... Mr. Robert KUNTZ
06 Director Academic Records/Registrar .... Mr. Tom LENO
16 Chief Human Resources Officer .... Mrs. Rita LINDGREN
13 Chief Information Services Officer .... Mr. Elmer WEIGEL
40 Bookstore Manager/Purchasing Coord .... Mrs. Tanya FUHER
36 Dir Couseling and Advising Services .... Mr. Jay MEIER
44 Development Manager .... Mrs. Gina BUCHHOLTZ
09 Institutional Research Analyst .... Mr. Mike KUBISIAK
29 Alumni Coordinator .... Mrs. Rita NODLAND
04 Executive Assistant to President .... Mrs. Debbie VAN BERKOM

*Dakota College at Bottineau (C)

105 Simrall Boulevard, Bottineau ND 58318-1198
County: Bottineau FICE Identification: 002995
Unit ID: 200314
Telephone: (701) 228-2277 Carnegie Class: Assoc/Pub2in4
FAX Number: (701) 228-5468 Calendar System: Semester
URL: www.dakotacollege.edu
Established: 1907 Annual Undergrad Tuition & Fees (In-State): $3,857
Enrollment: 863 Coed
Affiliation or Control: State IRS Status: 501(c)3
Highest Offering: Associate Degree
Program: Occupational; 2-Year Principally Bachelor's Creditable
Accreditation: NH

02 Campus Dean .... Dr. Ken GROSZ
10 Director of Financial Affairs .... Mr. James BORKOWSKI
32 Assoc Dean for Student Affairs .... Ms. Paula BERG
05 Assoc Dean for Academic Affairs .... Mr. Larry BROOKS
08 Librarian .... Dr. Debra SYVERTSON
07 Director of Admissions .... Ms. Leann WEBER
06 Registrar .... Ms. Paula BERG
37 Director Financial Aid .... Ms. Valerie HEILMAN
41 Athletic Director .... Mr. Scott JOHNSON
29 Director Alumni Relations .... Ms. Brandy SIMPSON
18 Chief Facilities/Physical Plant .... Mr. James BORKOWSKI
39 Housing Director .... Mr. Eric KESTER-MABON
28 Director of Diversity .... Ms. Colette SCHIMETZ
40 Bookstore Manager .... Ms. Janeen POLLMAN

*Lake Region State College (D)

1801 College Drive N, Devils Lake ND 58301-1598
County: Ramsey FICE Identification: 002991
Unit ID: 200192
Telephone: (701) 662-1600 Carnegie Class: Assoc/Pub-R-M
FAX Number: (701) 662-1570 Calendar System: Semester
URL: www.lrsc.edu
Established: 1941 Annual Undergrad Tuition & Fees (In-State): $3,908
Enrollment: 1,913 Coed
Affiliation or Control: State IRS Status: 501(c)3
Highest Offering: Associate Degree
Program: Occupational; 2-Year Principally Bachelor's Creditable
Accreditation: NH

02 President .... Dr. Mike BOWER
05 Vice Pres of Instruction Services .... Mr. Douglas D. DARLING
10 Vice Pres Administrative Services .... Mr. Corry G. KENNER
32 Assoc Vice Pres Student Services .... Mr. Randall FIXEN
12 Director of Branch Campus .... Mr. John COWGER
30 Chief of Devel/Dir Alumni Relations .... Ms. Laurel GOULDING
84 Director of Enrollment Management .... Ms. Stephanie SHOCK
37 Dir Student Finan Aid/Placemnt Svcs .... Ms. Katie NETTELL
88 Director Food Service .... Ms. Myrna UNGER
18 Superintendent Buildings/Grounds .... Mr. Donald JORGENSON
08 Librarian .... Ms. Celeste ERTELT
41 Director Athletics .... Mr. Duane SCHWAB
13 Chief Information Officer .... Ms. Toofawn SIMHAI
15 Chief of Personnel .... Mr. Corry G. KENNER
40 Director of Bookstore .... Ms. Melissa STOTTS
06 Registrar .... Mr. Daniel JOHNSON
26 Chief Public Relations Officer .... Ms. Erin WOOD
31 Director Community Services .... Mr. Dan DREISSEN
09 Director of Inst Research/Diversity .... Ms. Laurel GOULDING
29 Dir Alumni Relations/Stdnt Affs .... Ms. Laurel GOULDING
28 Director of Diversity .... Mrs. Nicole CLAUSSEN
38 Coordinator Counseling Services .... Dr. Randall FIXEN
07 Director of Admissions .... Ms. Stephanie SHOCK
21 Associate Business Officer .... Ms. Joann KITCHENS

*North Dakota State College of Science (E)

800 N Sixth Street, Wahpeton ND 58076-0002
County: Richland FICE Identification: 002996
Unit ID: 200305
Telephone: (800) 342-4325 Carnegie Class: Assoc/Pub-R-M
FAX Number: (701) 671-2145 Calendar System: Semester
URL: www.ndscs.edu
Established: 1903 Annual Undergrad Tuition & Fees (In-State): $4,181
Enrollment: 2,833 Coed
Affiliation or Control: State IRS Status: 501(c)3
Highest Offering: Associate Degree
Program: Occupational; 2-Year Principally Bachelor's Creditable
Accreditation: NH, DA, DH, OTA, PNUR

02 President .... Dr. John RICHMAN
05 VP Academic & Student Affairs .... Mr. Harvey LINK
11 Vice Pres Administrative Affairs .... Mr. Mike RENK
35 Dean Student Affairs .... Vacant
84 Dir Enroll Svcs/Finan Aid/Placement .... Mrs. Karen REILLY
08 Director Library .... Ms. Karen M. CHOBOT
26 Dir Marketing/Communications/PR .... Mrs. Barbara SPAETH-BAUM
29 Director of Alumni Foundation .... Mr. Brad BARTH
41 Athletic Director .... Mr. Scott SCHUMACHER
15 Human Resource Director .... Mr. David LINDBERG
09 Director of Institutional Research .... Mrs. Gloria DOHMAN
18 Director Facilities/Physical Plant .... Mr. Dallas FOSSUM
20 Academic Services Director .... Ms. Maria KADUC
39 Director of Residence Life .... Mrs. Melissa JOHNSON
06 Associate Registrar .... Mrs. Barb MUND
21 Business Manager .... Mr. Keith JOHNSON
24 Instructional Technology Coord .... Mr. Tom HICKMAN
07 Admissions Counselor .... Mr. Dale GROSZ
38 Counseling Center .... Mr. Vince PLUMMER
96 Director of Purchasing .... Mr. David MEYER
49 Dean Arts Sciences/Business .... Mr. Ken KOMPELIEN
72 Dean Technology/Services Division .... Mrs. Barbara BANG
64 Director of Music .... Ms. Laurie LEKANG
56 Dean of Extended Learning .... Mrs. Margaret WALL
88 Dean of College Outreach .... Mrs. Patricia KLINE

*Williston State College (F)

1410 University Avenue, Williston ND 58801-1326
County: Williams FICE Identification: 003007
Unit ID: 200341
Telephone: (701) 774-4200 Carnegie Class: Assoc/Pub-R-S
FAX Number: (701) 774-4275 Calendar System: Semester
URL: www.willistonstate.nodak.edu
Established: 1961 Annual Undergrad Tuition & Fees (In-State): $3902.08
Enrollment: 932 Coed
Affiliation or Control: State IRS Status: 501(c)3
Highest Offering: Associate Degree
Program: Occupational; 2-Year Principally Bachelor's Creditable
Accreditation: NH

02 President .... Raymond NADOLNY
05 Vice President for Instruction .... Wanda MEYER
103 CEO of Workforce Education Train .... Deanette PIESIK
32 VP for Student Services .... Jan SOLEM
10 Vice President for Business Affairs .... Justin MADDISON
26 VP College Advancement .... Terry OLSON

Rasmussen College - Bismarck (G)

1701 East Century Avenue, Bismarck ND 58503
County: Burleigh Identification: 666301
Unit ID: 20001301
Telephone: (701) 530-9600 Carnegie Class: Bac/Assoc
FAX Number: (701) 530-9604 Calendar System: Quarter
URL: www.rasmussen.edu
Established: 1902 Annual Undergrad Tuition & Fees: $16,340
Enrollment: 463 Coed
Affiliation or Control: Proprietary IRS Status: Proprietary
Highest Offering: Baccalaureate
Program: Occupational; 2-Year Principally Bachelor's Creditable
Accreditation: &NH, MLTAD

01 Campus Director .... Mr. Doug GARDNER

† Regional accreditation carried under the parent institution in Lake Elmo, MN.

Rasmussen College - Fargo/Moorhead (H)

4012 19th Avenue, SW, Fargo ND 58103-7196
County: Cass FICE Identification: 004846
Unit ID: 200013
Telephone: (701) 277-3889 Carnegie Class: Bac/Assoc
FAX Number: (701) 277-5604 Calendar System: Quarter
URL: www.rasmussen.edu
Established: 1902 Annual Undergrad Tuition & Fees: $16,340
Enrollment: 1,264 Coed
Affiliation or Control: Proprietary IRS Status: Proprietary
Highest Offering: Baccalaureate

Program: Occupational; 2-Year Principally Bachelor's Creditable
Accreditation: &NH, MAC

01 Campus Director ... Ms. Elizabeth LARGENT

† Regional acrreditation is carried under parent institution in Lake Elmo, MN.

Sitting Bull College (A)

9299 Highway 24, Fort Yates ND 58538-9706
County: Sioux — FICE Identification: 021882
Unit ID: 200466
Telephone: (701) 854-8000 — Carnegie Class: Tribal
FAX Number: (701) 854-8197 — Calendar System: Semester
URL: www.sittingbull.edu
Established: 1971 — Annual Undergrad Tuition & Fees: $4,410
Enrollment: 314 — Coed
Affiliation or Control: Tribal Control — IRS Status: 501(c)3
Highest Offering: Baccalaureate
Program: Occupational; 2-Year Principally Bachelor's Creditable
Accreditation: NH

01 President ... Dr. Laurel VERMILLION
05 Vice President of Academic Affairs ... Dr. Koreen RESSLER
10 Vice President of Business Affairs ... Ms. Leonica ALKIRE
32 Vice Pres of Student Services ... Ms. Julie DESJARLAIS
37 Director Financial Student Aid ... Ms. Donna SEABOY
06 Registrar ... Ms. Melody SILK
08 Head Librarian ... Mr. Mark HOLMAN
40 Director of Bookstore ... Mrs. Renee VERMILLION

Trinity Bible College (B)

50 S 6th Avenue, Ellendale ND 58436-7150
County: Dickey — FICE Identification: 012059
Unit ID: 200484
Telephone: (701) 349-3621 — Carnegie Class: Spec/Faith
FAX Number: (701) 349-5443 — Calendar System: Semester
URL: www.trinitybiblecollege.edu
Established: 1948 — Annual Undergrad Tuition & Fees: $13,090
Enrollment: 285 — Coed
Affiliation or Control: Assemblies Of God Church — IRS Status: 501(c)3
Highest Offering: Baccalaureate
Program: Liberal Arts And General
Accreditation: NH, BI

01 President ... Rev. G. L. (Jack) STROM
05 Vice President Academic Affairs ... Dr. Dayton KINGSRITER
10 Vice Pres of Business & Finance ... Rev. Tim GLASS
32 Director of Student Life ... Mr. Jeremy WEFLEN
06 Academic Registrar ... Ms. Rachelle SPRINGER
84 Director of Enrollment ... Ms. Stephanie DENBOW
08 Librarian ... Mrs. Diane OLSON
37 Director Student Financial Aid ... Ms. Stella PHOENIX
36 Student Placement ... Mr. Joseph DONNELL
13 Director of Computer Services ... Mr. Dirk COE

Turtle Mountain Community College (C)

Box 340, Belcourt ND 58316-0340
County: Rolette — FICE Identification: 023011
Unit ID: 200527
Telephone: (701) 477-7862 — Carnegie Class: Tribal
FAX Number: (701) 477-7807 — Calendar System: Semester
URL: www.tm.edu
Established: 1972 — Annual Undergrad Tuition & Fees: $2,000
Enrollment: 766 — Coed
Affiliation or Control: Independent Non-Profit — IRS Status: 501(c)3
Highest Offering: Baccalaureate
Program: Occupational; 2-Year Principally Bachelor's Creditable; Technical Emphasis
Accreditation: NH

01 President ... Jim L. DAVIS
05 Academic Dean ... Larry HENRY
32 Dean Student Affs/Dir Financial Aid ... Wanda LADUCER
08 Bookstore Director ... Kathe ZASTE
10 Comptroller ... Tracy AZURE
75 Director Vocational/Education ... Sheila TROTTIER
06 Registrar ... Angel GLADUE
36 Career Ladder Coordinator ... Vacant
31 Dir of Community/Adult Education ... Sandra LAROCQUE
07 Director of Admissions ... Joni LAFONTAINE
15 Director Personnel Services ... Bill GOURNEAU
37 Financial Aid Officer ... Sheila MORIN
40 Director of Bookstore ... Leonard DAUPHINAIS
18 Chief Facilities/Physical Plant ... Wesley DAVIS
30 Chief Development ... Dave RIPLEY
13 Chief Informational Officer ... Vacant
25 Sponsored Programs Officer ... Larretta HALL
35 Student Support Services Coord ... Steve DECOTEAU

United Tribes Technical College (D)

3315 University Drive, Bismarck ND 58504-7596
County: Burleigh — FICE Identification: 022429
Unit ID: 200554
Telephone: (701) 255-3285 — Carnegie Class: Tribal
FAX Number: (701) 530-0605 — Calendar System: Semester
URL: www.uttc.edu
Established: 1969 — Annual Undergrad Tuition & Fees: $3,350
Enrollment: 600 — Coed
Affiliation or Control: Independent Non-Profit — IRS Status: 501(c)3
Highest Offering: Associate Degree
Program: Occupational; 2-Year Principally Bachelor's Creditable
Accreditation: NH, PNUR

01 President ... Dr. David GIPP
05 Vice Pres Academic Career/Tech Educ ... Dr. Phil BAIRD
32 Vice Pres Student & Campus Services ... Dr. Russell SWAGGER
10 Dean Finance & Business Services ... Vacant
07 Director of Admissions ... Ms. Vivian GILLETTE
06 Registrar ... Ms. Joetta MCLEOD
46 Director Research ... Vacant
15 Director Human Resources ... Ms. Barbara LITTLE OWL
20 Director Academic Support Services ... Vacant
84 Director Enrollment Management ... Mr. Nathan STRATTON
19 Director Security & Safety ... Mr. James REDTOMAHAWK
37 Director Financial Aid ... Vacant
41 Athletic Director ... Mr. Daryl BEARS TAIL
13 Network Manager ... Mr. Brian DECOTEAU

University of Mary (E)

7500 University Drive, Bismarck ND 58504-9652
County: Burleigh — FICE Identification: 002992
Unit ID: 200217
Telephone: (701) 255-7500 — Carnegie Class: Master's L
FAX Number: (701) 255-7687 — Calendar System: Other
URL: www.umary.edu
Established: 1959 — Annual Undergrad Tuition & Fees: $13,600
Enrollment: 2,977 — Coed
Affiliation or Control: Roman Catholic — IRS Status: 501(c)3
Highest Offering: Doctorate
Program: Liberal Arts And General; Professional
Accreditation: NH, EXSC, IACBE, NURSE, OT, PTA, SW

01 President ... Fr. James P. SHEA
05 Vice President for Academic Affairs ... Dr. Diane FLADELAND
10 Vice President Financial Affairs ... Mr. Brent WINIGER
32 Vice President Student Development ... Dr. Timothy SEAWORTH
84 Vice President Enrollment Services ... Mrs. Brenda KASPARI
26 Vice President for Public Affairs ... Mr. Neal KALBERER
06 Registrar ... Mr. Rod SCHEETT
08 Librarian ... Mrs. Cheryl BAILEY
37 Director of Financial Aid ... Mrs. Brenda ZASTOUPIL

OHIO

Academy of Court Reporting (F)

2044 Euclid Avenue, Cleveland OH 44115
County: Cuyahoga — FICE Identification: 021521
Unit ID: 200633
Telephone: (216) 861-3222 — Carnegie Class: Assoc/PrivFP
FAX Number: (216) 861-4517 — Calendar System: Quarter
URL: www.acr.edu
Established: 1970 — Annual Undergrad Tuition & Fees: $22,765
Enrollment: 330 — Coed
Affiliation or Control: Proprietary — IRS Status: Proprietary
Highest Offering: Associate Degree
Program: Occupational
Accreditation: ACICS

01 School Director ... Mrs. Lynn M. MIZANIN

Akron Institute of Herzing University (G)

1600 S Arlington Street, Suite 100, Akron OH 44306-3958
County: Summit — FICE Identification: 020695
Unit ID: 200785
Telephone: (330) 724-1600 — Carnegie Class: Assoc/PrivFP
FAX Number: (330) 724-9688 — Calendar System: Semester
URL: www.akroninstitute.com
Established: 1970 — Annual Undergrad Tuition & Fees: $10,560
Enrollment: 841 — Coed
Affiliation or Control: Proprietary — IRS Status: Proprietary
Highest Offering: Associate Degree
Program: Occupational; 2-Year Principally Bachelor's Creditable; Technical Emphasis
Accreditation: &NH, ADNUR, MAC

01 President ... Mr. David LARUE

† Regional accreditation is carried under the parent institution in Madison, WI.

Allegheny Wesleyan College (H)

2161 Woodsdale Road, Salem OH 44460-8920
County: Columbiana — FICE Identification: 034573
Unit ID: 200873
Telephone: (330) 337-6403 — Carnegie Class: Spec/Faith
FAX Number: (330) 337-6255 — Calendar System: Semester
URL: www.awc.edu
Established: 1956 — Annual Undergrad Tuition & Fees: $7,740
Enrollment: 46 — Coed
Affiliation or Control: Wesleyan Church — IRS Status: 501(c)3
Highest Offering: Baccalaureate
Program: Liberal Arts And General; Religious Emphasis
Accreditation: BI

01 President ... Dr. Robert E. ENGLAND
05 Interim Academic Dean ... Dr. Robert E. ENGLAND
10 Business Manager ... Mr. Troy MUIR
32 Dean of Students ... Mrs. Eveline MCHUGH
26 Director of Public Relations ... Mr. Tom SANDERS
06 Registrar & Director Admissions ... Mrs. Jeanne ZVARITCH
08 Head Librarian ... Mrs. Alice WEINGARD
37 Financial Aid Administrator ... Mrs. Esther PHELPS
09 Dir of Institutional Effectiveness ... Miss Angela REYNOLDS
40 Bookstore Manager ... Dr. Robert E. ENGLAND
33 Dean of Men ... Mr. Stephen TROYER
34 Dean of Women ... Mrs. Eveline MCHUGH
07 Director of Admissions ... Mrs. Jeanne ZVARITCH
18 Chief Facilities/Physical Plant ... Mr. Darrin PATTERSON
21 Associate Business Officer ... Mr. Darrell MONTGOMERY
29 Director Alumni Relations ... Rev. John DYE
35 Director Student Affairs ... Mrs. Eveline MCHUGH
38 Director Student Counseling ... Mrs. Kimberly FORD

American Institute of Alternative Medicine (I)

6685 Doubletree Avenue, Columbus OH 43229-1113
County: Franklin — FICE Identification: 035344
Unit ID: 441636
Telephone: (614) 825-6255 — Carnegie Class: Not Classified
FAX Number: (614) 825-6279 — Calendar System: Other
URL: www.aiam.edu
Established: 1990 — Annual Undergrad Tuition & Fees: N/A
Enrollment: 230 — Coed
Affiliation or Control: Independent Non-Profit — IRS Status: 501(c)3
Highest Offering: Master's
Program: Professional
Accreditation: ACUP, ACCSC

01 President ... John W. ELAM

*Antioch University (J)

900 Dayton Street, Yellow Springs OH 45387-1635
County: Greene — FICE Identification: 003010
Unit ID: 442392
Telephone: (937) 769-1351 — Carnegie Class: N/A
FAX Number: (937) 769-1350
URL: www.antioch.edu

01 Chancellor ... Dr. Tullisse A. MURDOCK
10 Vice Chanc/Chief Financial Officer ... Ms. Pari SABETY
05 Vice Chanc Univ Academic Affairs ... Dr. Laurien ALEXANDRE
30 Vice Chanc Univ Advancement ... Mr. Grady JONES
13 Vice Chancellor CIO ... Mr. Michael BOEHM
15 Director HR Systems/Payroll Svcs ... Ms. Suzette CASTONGUAY
26 Director of Communications ... Ms. Lynda SIRK
91 Dir Administrative Info Systems ... Ms. Candice SANTELL
04 Executive Asst to the Chancellor ... Ms. Leslie BATES

† Parent institution of Antioch University Midwest in OH; Antioch University Seattle in WA; Antioch University New England in NH; and Antioch University Los Angeles and Antioch University Santa Barbara in CA.

*Antioch University Midwest (K)

900 Dayton Street, Yellow Springs OH 45387-1745
County: Greene — Identification: 666811
Unit ID: 245892
Telephone: (937) 769-1800 — Carnegie Class: Master's M
FAX Number: (937) 769-1805 — Calendar System: Quarter
URL: midwest.antioch.edu/
Established: 1988 — Annual Undergrad Tuition & Fees: $15,898
Enrollment: 695 — Coed
Affiliation or Control: Independent Non-Profit — IRS Status: 501(c)3
Highest Offering: Master's
Program: Liberal Arts And General; Teacher Preparatory; Professional
Accreditation: &NH, TED

02 President ... Dr. Michael FISHBEIN
32 Dean Student Services ... Ms. Darlene ROBERTSON
13 Director Information Systems ... Mr. Eric FOLKMAN
37 Director Student Financial Aid ... Ms. Kathy JOHN
15 Director Personnel Services ... Ms. Suzette CASTONGUAY
21 Associate Business Officer ... Ms. Deborah CARAWAY
84 Director Enrollment Services ... Mr. Oscar ROBINSON
100 Chief of Staff ... Ms. Deena KENT-HUMMEL
88 Chair Management Leadership & Chang ... Dr. Richard MCGUIGAN
53 Chair School of Education ... Dr. Marian GLANCY
49 Assoc Dean Liberal Studies ... Dr. Joseph CRONIN
88 Chair Analysis & Engagement ... Dr. Richard MCGUIGAN
18 Chief Facilities/Physical Plant ... Mr. Ray SIMONELLI
06 Registrar ... Dr. Maureen HEACOCK
29 Director Alumni Relations ... Ms. Kimberly HORTON
26 Director Marketing & Communications ... Mr. Walt ULBRICHT

† Regional accreditation is carried under the parent institution in Yellow Springs, OH.

Antonelli College (L)

124 E Seventh Street, Cincinnati OH 45202-2592
County: Hamilton — FICE Identification: 012891
Unit ID: 201016
Telephone: (800) 505-4338 — Carnegie Class: Assoc/PrivFP
FAX Number: (513) 241-9396 — Calendar System: Quarter

URL: www.antonellicollege.edu
Established: 1947 Annual Undergrad Tuition & Fees: $28,450
Enrollment: 402 Coed
Affiliation or Control: Proprietary IRS Status: Proprietary
Highest Offering: Associate Degree
Program: Occupational
Accreditation: ACCSC

01 Director ... Ms. Karen GAUTRIEAU
05 Director of Education ... Ms. Frances CARROLL
32 Director Student Services ... Ms. Leah ELKINS
06 Registrar ... Ms. Shawnya AMENDOLA
36 Career Services Coordinator ... Ms. Betty POLING-BOLLAS

Art Academy of Cincinnati (A)

1212 Jackson Street, Cincinnati OH 45202-7106
County: Hamilton FICE Identification: 003011
Unit ID: 201061
Telephone: (513) 562-6262 Carnegie Class: Spec/Arts
FAX Number: (513) 562-8778 Calendar System: Semester
URL: www.artacademy.edu
Established: 1869 Annual Undergrad Tuition & Fees: $23,540
Enrollment: 208 Coed
Affiliation or Control: Independent Non-Profit IRS Status: 501(c)3
Highest Offering: Master's
Program: Fine Arts Emphasis
Accreditation: NH, ART

01 Interim President ... David T. JOHNSON
10 Vice President Finance/Operations ... Nancy GLIER
84 Vice President of Enrollment Mgmt ... Vacant
05 Interim Academic Dean ... Diane K. SMITH
37 Director of Financial Aid ... Kristina OLBERDING
06 Registrar ... Sue HUTCHENS
31 Director of Community Education ... Troy BROWN
18 Director of Facilities ... Jack HENNEN
32 Student Life Coordinator ... Elizabeth NEAL

The Art Institute of Cincinnati (B)

1171 East Kemper Road, Cincinnati OH 45246-3322
County: Hamilton FICE Identification: 021286
Unit ID: 200624
Telephone: (513) 751-1206 Carnegie Class: Assoc/PrivFP
FAX Number: (513) 751-1209 Calendar System: Quarter
URL: www.aic-arts.edu
Established: 1976 Annual Undergrad Tuition & Fees: $17,066
Enrollment: 21 Coed
Affiliation or Control: Proprietary IRS Status: Proprietary
Highest Offering: Associate Degree
Program: Occupational
Accreditation: ACCSC

00 CEO ... Ms. Marion K. ALLMAN
01 President ... Mr. Sean M. MENDELL

The Art Institute of Ohio-Cincinnati (C)

8845 Governor's Hill Drive, Cincinnati OH 45249
County: Hamilton Identification: 666693
Unit ID: 446668
Telephone: (513) 833-2400 Carnegie Class: Not Classified
FAX Number: (513) 833-2411 Calendar System: Quarter
URL: www.artinstitutes.edu/cincinnati
Established: 2004 Annual Undergrad Tuition & Fees: $23,088
Enrollment: 754 Coed
Affiliation or Control: Proprietary IRS Status: Proprietary
Highest Offering: Baccalaureate
Program: Occupational; 2-Year Principally Bachelor's Creditable; Professional; Technical Emphasis
Accreditation: &NH, ACFEI

† Regional accreditation is carried under the parent institution The Illinois Institute of Art, Chicago, IL.

Ashland University (D)

401 College Avenue, Ashland OH 44805-3799
County: Ashland FICE Identification: 003012
Unit ID: 201104
Telephone: (419) 289-4142 Carnegie Class: DRU
FAX Number: (419) 289-5333 Calendar System: Semester
URL: www.ashland.edu
Established: 1878 Annual Undergrad Tuition & Fees: $28,582
Enrollment: 6,490 Coed
Affiliation or Control: Brethren Church IRS Status: 501(c)3
Highest Offering: Doctorate
Program: Liberal Arts And General; Teacher Preparatory; Professional
Accreditation: NH, ACBSP, @DIETD, MUS, NURSE, SW, TED, THEOL

01 President ... Dr. Frederick J. FINKS
73 President Theological Seminary ... Dr. John C. SHULTZ
05 Provost ... Dr. Frank E. PETTIGREW
32 VP Student Affairs/Dean of Students ... Mrs. B. Sue HEIMANN
84 Vice Pres Enroll Mgt & Marketing ... Dr. Scott D. VAN LOO
30 Assoc VP Inst Advance & Campaigns ... Ms. Margaret POMFRET
13 Vice Pres Information Technology ... Mr. Curtis WHITE
18 Vice Pres Facilities/Mgmt & Plng ... Mr. Rick M. EWING, II
21 Vice President Business Opers ... Mr. James L. KIRTLAND
44 Assoc Vice President Development ... Mr. Ralph V. TOMASSI, JR.
42 Dean of Religious Life ... Dr. Dan L. LAWSON
06 Registrar ... Ms. Kathleen HALL
08 Director of the Library ... Mr. Edward M. KRAKORA
37 Director Student Financial Aid ... Mr. Stephen C. HOWELL
29 Director Alumni/Parent Relations ... Mr. Jeff ALIX
15 Director of Human Resources ... Mr. John R. BRANDON
71 Director Gill Center Outreach ... Mr. John J. DOWDELL
31 Director Auxiliary Services ... Mr. Matthew D. PORTNER
36 Executive Director Career Services ... Ms. Karen HAGANS
19 Director of Safety Services ... Mr. David B. MCLAUGHLIN
26 Director of Public Relations ... Mr. Steven M. HANNAN
38 Dir Psychological & Counseling Svcs ... Dr. Oscar T. MCKNIGHT
39 Director Residence Life ... Ms. Catherine M. GELETKA
40 Director Bookstore ... Mrs. Terri C. HUDSON
41 Director of Athletics ... Mr. William J. GOLDRING
88 Exec Dir Ashbrook Ctr ... Dr. Peter W. SCHRAMM
23 Director Student Health Center ... Ms. Linda ROEDER
44 Director Legacy Estate Programs ... Mr. Matthew HARRIS
09 Director of Institutional Research ... Mrs. Karen A. LITTLE
35 Director Student Life ... Ms. Nicole L. DYER
07 Director of Admissions ... Vacant
49 Dean College of Arts & Sciences ... Dr. Dawn WEBER
73 Dean Theological Seminary ... Dr. Dale R. STOFFER
50 Dean College Business/Econ ... Dr. Jeffery RUSSELL
53 Dean College of Education ... Dr. James P. VANKEUREN
58 Dean Graduate School ... Dr. W. Greg GERRICK
66 Dean College of Nursing ... Ms. Faye GRUND
51 Dean School of Continuing Educ ... Mr. Dwight MCELFRESH
51 Dir Professional Development ... Dr. Marilyn TROYER
28 Director of Diversity ... Mr. Charles J. HARKNESS
105 Dir Web Services ... Mr. Terrance HENRY
88 Dir Student Success & Retention ... Mrs. Kathy STONE
28 Dir Multicultural Stdnt Svcs & Stds ... Mr. Jonathan E. LOCUST, JR.
104 Exec Dir International Programs ... Dr. Nathan D. MYERS

Athenaeum of Ohio (E)

6616 Beechmont Avenue, Cincinnati OH 45230-5900
County: Hamilton FICE Identification: 003013
Unit ID: 201140
Telephone: (513) 231-2223 Carnegie Class: Spec/Faith
FAX Number: (513) 231-3254 Calendar System: Quarter
URL: www.athenaeum.edu
Established: 1829 Annual Graduate Tuition & Fees: $19,500
Enrollment: 221 Coed
Affiliation or Control: Roman Catholic IRS Status: 501(c)3
Highest Offering: Master's; No Undergraduates
Program: Professional; Religious Emphasis
Accreditation: NH, THEOL

01 President & Rector ... Rev. Benedict O'CINNSEALAIGH
03 Vice President ... Mr. Dennis K. EAGAN
05 Dean of Athenaeum ... Rev. Earl K. FERNANDES
08 Librarian ... Mrs. Tracy KOENIG
30 Director of Development ... Mr. James JACKSON
06 Registrar ... Mr. Michael E. SWEENEY
88 Dir Lay Pastoral Ministry Program ... Dr. Susan MCGURGAN
71 Dean Special Studies Division ... Dr. Terrance D. CALLAN

ATS Institute of Technology (F)

325 Alpha Park, Highland Heights OH 44143-2216
County: Cuyahoga FICE Identification: 034685
Unit ID: 439455
Telephone: (440) 449-1700 Carnegie Class: Assoc/PrivFP
FAX Number: (440) 449-1389 Calendar System: Quarter
URL: www.atsinstitute.edu
Established: 1997 Annual Undergrad Tuition & Fees: $22,412
Enrollment: 250 Coed
Affiliation or Control: Proprietary IRS Status: Proprietary
Highest Offering: Associate Degree
Program: Occupational
Accreditation: ACICS

01 Director ... Ms. Yelena BYKOV
37 Director of Financial Aid ... Ms. Yelena KSENDZOVSKY
07 Co-Admissions Director ... Ms. Julia PROTSKY
07 Co-Admissions Director ... Ms. Debbie LINKOFF

Aultman College of Nursing and Health Sciences (G)

2600 6th Street SW, Canton OH 44710-1702
County: Stark FICE Identification: 006487
Unit ID: 201177
Telephone: (330) 363-6347 Carnegie Class: Assoc/PrivNFP
FAX Number: (330) 580-6654 Calendar System: Semester
URL: www.aultmancollege.edu
Established: 2004 Annual Undergrad Tuition & Fees: $16,740
Enrollment: 284 Coed
Affiliation or Control: Independent Non-Profit IRS Status: 501(c)3
Highest Offering: Associate Degree
Program: 2-Year Principally Bachelor's Creditable; Nursing Emphasis
Accreditation: NH, ADNUR

01 President ... Ms. Rebecca R. CROWL
11 Chief Internal Affairs Officer ... Ms. Jeannine SHAMBAUGH
26 Chief External Affairs Officer ... Ms. Vi LEGGETT
07 Director Administrative Services ... Ms. Susan B. SHEPHERD
45 Director Strategic Implementation ... Ms. Lyn SABINO
97 Asst Director of General Education ... Dr. Jean PADDOCK
66 Director Division of Nursing ... Dr. Melissa M. SMITH
76 Director Allied Health ... Ms. Sherri COLE

Baldwin-Wallace College (H)

275 Eastland Road, Berea OH 44017-2088
County: Cuyahoga FICE Identification: 003014
Unit ID: 201195
Telephone: (440) 826-2900 Carnegie Class: Master's L
FAX Number: (440) 826-2329 Calendar System: Semester
URL: www.bw.edu
Established: 1845 Annual Undergrad Tuition & Fees: $35,076
Enrollment: 4,263 Coed
Affiliation or Control: United Methodist IRS Status: 501(c)3
Highest Offering: Master's
Program: Liberal Arts And General; Teacher Preparatory; Professional
Accreditation: NH, MUS, TED

01 President ... Mr. Richard W. DURST
03 Senior Vice President ... Mr. Richard L. FLETCHER
05 Vice Pres Academic Affairs/Dean ... Dr. Mary Lou HIGGERSON
30 Vice President for Advancement ... Mr. William J. SPIKER
10 Vice President for Finance & Admin ... Mr. William M. RENIFF
32 VP Student Affairs/Dean of Students ... Dr. Trina DOBBERSTEIN
84 Vice Pres of Enrollment Management ... Ms. Susan DILENO
26 Asst VP/Director College Relations ... Mr. George RICHARD
20 Associate Academic Dean ... Dr. Guy FARISH
35 Director of Student Success Initiat ... Mr. Marcos RIVERA
51 Director of Adult Learning ... Mr. George ROGERS
08 Director of Ritter Library ... Dr. Patrick SCANLAN
13 Chief Information Officer ... Mr. Greg G. FLANIK
44 Director Annual Giving ... Mr. John N. TEMPLEMAN
29 Director Alumni Relations ... Mr. Terry J. KURTZ
44 Director Development Gift Plng ... Mr. Thomas H. KONKOLY
37 Director of Financial Aid ... Dr. George ROLLESTON
15 Asst VP for Human Resources ... Mr. Sam RAMIREZ
38 Director of Counseling Services ... Ms. Joy D. WYATT
36 Director of Academic Advising ... Ms. Margaret STINER
06 Registrar ... Ms. Linda L. YOUNG
07 Director of Undergraduate Admission ... Ms. Pattie SKRHA
88 Dir of Adult/Cont Educ Admission ... Ms. Winifred GERHARDT
18 Director of Buildings & Grounds ... Mr. William KERBUSCH
88 Director of Intercultural Education ... Dr. Judith B. KRUTKY
96 Director of Purchasing ... Ms. Karen STENGER
28 Director Campus Diversity Affairs ... Mr. Paul JAMES

Beckfield College (I)

225 Pictoria Drive Suite 200, Cincinnati OH 45246
Identification: 666673
Unit ID: 452373
Telephone: (513) 671-1920 Carnegie Class: Not Classified
FAX Number: (513) 671-1927 Calendar System: Other
URL: www.beckfield.edu
Established: 1984 Annual Undergrad Tuition & Fees: N/A
Enrollment: 365 Coed
Affiliation or Control: Proprietary IRS Status: Proprietary
Highest Offering: Associate Degree
Program: Occupational
Accreditation: ACICS

01 President ... Ms. Diane WOLFER
05 Campus Director ... Mr. Edward RITO

† Branch campus of Beckfield College, Florence, KY.

Belmont Technical College (J)

120 Fox Shannon Place, Saint Clairsville OH 43950-9766
County: Belmont FICE Identification: 009941
Unit ID: 201283
Telephone: (740) 695-9500 Carnegie Class: Assoc/Pub-R-M
FAX Number: (740) 695-2247 Calendar System: Quarter
URL: www.btc.edu
Established: 1969 Annual Undergrad Tuition & Fees (In-State): $3,784
Enrollment: 2,289 Coed
Affiliation or Control: State IRS Status: 501(c)3
Highest Offering: Associate Degree
Program: Occupational; 2-Year Principally Bachelor's Creditable
Accreditation: NH, MAC

01 President ... Dr. Joseph E. BUKOWSKI
05 VP of Learning & Student Services ... Dr. Rebecca KURTZ
11 Vice Pres of Administrative Affairs ... Mr. John S. KOUCOUMARIS
32 Dean of Student Services ... Mr. Peter LAW
20 Exec Dean of Academic Affairs ... Dr. Brenda LOHRI-POSEY
09 Dean Institutional Research/Plng ... Dr. Jane EVANS
08 Assoc Dean Lrng/Info Svcs/Tech ... Mrs. Cathy BENNETT
103 Dean Workforce Devel/Econ Devel ... Dr. Holly BENNETT
18 Director of Facilities ... Mr. Terry LOY
06 Registrar ... Mrs. Colleen SECKMAN
15 Exec Director of HR & Org Dev ... Ms. Marge HAWTHORNE
37 Assoc Dean of Financial Aid ... Mr. Jody PEELER
07 Director of Recruitment ... Mr. Michael STERLING
20 Director of Educational Services ... Mrs. Elayne STUPAK
24 Dir Library/Info/Lrng Commons Svcs ... Ms. Joyce BAKER
54 Faculty Admin Industrial Trades Pgm ... Mr. Dirk DECOY
26 Director of Marketing/Strat Comm ... Mrs. Laura DOTY
29 Director Alumni Relations ... Ms. Erin NEELY

36 Transfer/Articulat/Academic Advisor ..... Ms. Jane BLACK
27 Exec Dir of Information Services ..... Mr. Matthew TARBETT
30 Dir of Dev & External Affairs ..... Mr. RJ KONKOLESKI

Bexley Hall Seminary (A)

583 Sheridan Avenue, Columbus OH 43209
County: Franklin FICE Identification: 037473
Unit ID: 443702
Telephone: (614) 231-3095 Carnegie Class: Not Classified
FAX Number: (614) 231-3236 Calendar System: Semester
URL: www.bexley.edu
Established: N/A Annual Graduate Tuition & Fees: $14,672
Enrollment: 11 Coed
Affiliation or Control: Independent Non-Profit IRS Status: 501(c)3
Highest Offering: Master's; No Undergraduates
Program: Religious Emphasis
Accreditation: THEOL

01 Interim President ..... Dr. Robert BOTTOMS
05 Dean ..... Mr. Thomas FERGUSON

Bluffton University (B)

1 University Drive, Bluffton OH 45817-2104
County: Allen FICE Identification: 003016
Unit ID: 201371
Telephone: (419) 358-3000 Carnegie Class: Bac/Diverse
FAX Number: (419) 358-3323 Calendar System: Semester
URL: www.bluffton.edu
Established: 1899 Annual Undergrad Tuition & Fees: $26,154
Enrollment: 1,129 Coed
Affiliation or Control: Mennonite Church IRS Status: 501(c)3
Highest Offering: Master's
Program: Liberal Arts And General; Teacher Preparatory; Business Emphasis
Accreditation: NH, DIETD, MUS, SW, TED

01 President ..... Dr. James M. HARDER
10 Vice President for Fiscal Affairs ..... Mr. Kevin A. NICKEL
30 Vice President for Inst Advancement ..... Dr. Hans HOUSHOWER
05 Vice Pres & Dean Academic Affairs ..... Dr. Sally W. SOMMER
84 VP for Enrollment Mgt/Student Life ..... Dr. Eric W. FULCOMER
21 Chief Business Officer ..... Mr. Richard LICHTLE
08 Director of Libraries ..... Ms. Mary Jean JOHNSON
06 Registrar ..... Ms. Iris NEUFELD
26 Chief Public Relations Officer ..... Mrs. Robin BOWLUS
29 Dir of Alumni Relations/Annual Giv ..... Mrs. Julia SZABO
37 Director of Student Financial Aid ..... Mr. Lawrence MATTHEWS
07 Director of Admissions ..... Mr. Chris JEBSEN
18 Director Building/Grounds ..... Mr. Mustaq AHMED
15 Director Human Resources ..... Mrs. Julie KRUPP

Bowling Green State University (C)

220 McFall Center, Bowling Green OH 43403-0001
County: Wood FICE Identification: 003018
Unit ID: 201441
Telephone: (419) 372-2531 Carnegie Class: RU/H
FAX Number: (419) 372-8446 Calendar System: Semester
URL: www.bgsu.edu
Established: 1910 Annual Undergrad Tuition & Fees (In-State): $10,044
Enrollment: 20,222 Coed
Affiliation or Control: State IRS Status: 501(c)3
Highest Offering: Doctorate
Program: Liberal Arts And General; Teacher Preparatory; Professional
Accreditation: NH, ART, BUS, BUSA, CACREP, CLPSY, CONST, CORE, DIETD, DIETI, IPSY, JOUR, MT, MUS, NAIT, NRPA, NURSE, PH, SP, SW, TED, THEA

01 President ..... Dr. Mary Ellen MAZEY
05 Int Sr VP Academic Affairs/Provost ..... Dr. Rodney K. ROGERS
10 CFO/VP Finance & Admin ..... Ms. Sherideen S. STOLL
32 Vice President Student Affairs ..... Vacant
04 Asst to President/Administration ..... Ms. Anne M. TRACY
30 VP Univ Advancement/Pres BGSU Found ..... Mr. Thomas S. HILES
84 VP Enrollment Management ..... Mr. Albert N. COLOM
35 Asst VP Student Affs/Dean of Stdnts ..... Ms. Jill CARR
11 Assoc VP for Campus Operations ..... Mr. Bruce MEYER
27 Int Chief Communications Officer ..... Mr. David KIELMEYER
29 Director Alumni Affairs ..... Ms. Montique R. COTTON KELLY
46 Founding VP Research & Econ Dev ..... Dr. Michael Y. OGAWA
41 Asst VP Student Affs/Dir Rec Sports ..... Dr. Stephen KAMPF
41 Director of Athletics ..... Mr. Gregory A. CHRISTOPHER
16 Chief Human Resources Officer ..... Ms. Rebecca C. FERGUSON
39 Director of Residence Life ..... Ms. Sarah WATERS
35 Asst VP Student Affairs/Aux Svcs ..... Ms. Melissa A. HUDSON-NOWAK
46 Assoc VP Capital Planning & Design ..... Mr. Steve P. KRAKOFF
13 Interim Chief Information Officer ..... Mr. John M. ELLINGER
43 VP Legal Affairs & Govt Relations ..... Mr. Sean P. FITZGERALD
22 Director Equity & Diversity ..... Vacant
58 Interim Dean Graduate College ..... Vacant
49 Dean College Arts/Sciences ..... Dr. Simon N. MORGAN-RUSSELL
50 Interim Dean College Business Admin ..... Dr. B. Madhu RAO
51 Exec Director Cont & Extended Educ ..... Dr. Marcia SALAZAR-VALENTINE
53 Dean College Educ/Human Development ..... Dr. Brad COLWELL
12 Dean Firelands College ..... Dr. William BALZER
69 Dean College Health/Human Services ..... Dr. Linda PETROSINO
08 Dean University Libraries ..... Ms. Sara BUSHONG
64 Dean College of Musical Arts ..... Dr. Jeffrey A. SHOWELL
72 Dean College of Technology ..... Dr. Faris A. MALHAS
57 Director of School of Art ..... Dr. Katerina R. RAY
60 Dir Sch of Media & Communication ..... Dr. Terry RENTNER
88 Dir Sch Human Move/Sport/Leisure ..... Dr. Philip F. XIE
88 Dir Sch Family & Consumer Sciences ..... Dr. Deborah G. WOOLDRIDGE
88 Dir School of Intervention Services ..... Dr. Trinka MESSENHEIMER
53 Dir Sch Educ Fnds/Leadership/Policy ..... Dr. Rachel REINHART
53 Dir Sch of Teaching and Learning ..... Dr. Cindy HENDRICKS
92 Director Honors Program ..... Dr. Paul A. MOORE
106 Assc VP Acad Technology & eLearning ..... Dr. Bruce L. EDWARDS
85 Dir Ctr for International Programs ..... Mr. Paul HOFMANN
21 Exec Dir of Business Operations ..... Mr. Bradley K. LEIGH
07 Asst VP/Director Admissions ..... Mr. Gary D. SWEGAN
21 Dir Budgeting & Resource Planning ..... Mr. Geofrey L. TRACY
09 Director of Institutional Research ..... Dr. William E. KNIGHT
06 University Registrar ..... Mr. Christopher P. COX
40 Director Bookstore ..... Mr. Jeffrey D. NELSON
19 Director Public Safety ..... Ms. Monica M. MOLL
36 Dir Career Ctr/Student Employment ..... Ms. Annette BADIK
23 Exec Director Center for Health ..... Mr. Richard G. SIPP
38 Assoc Director Counseling Center ..... Dr. Garrett GILMER
37 Director Student Financial Aid ..... Ms. Laura EMCH
23 Assoc Dir Student Health Services ..... Ms. Barbara HOFFMAN
44 Director of Annual Giving ..... Ms. Shannon SPENCER
101 Secretary to the Board ..... Dr. Patrick PAUKEN
88 Co-Gen Manager WBGU Public Media ..... Mr. Anthony E. SHORT
88 Co-Gen Manager WBGU Public Media ..... Ms. Tina L. SIMON
35 Director TRIO Collegiate Services ..... Mr. Sidney CHILDS
21 Internal Auditing & Adv Svcs ..... Vacant
88 Director Women's Center ..... Dr. Mary M. KRUEGER
88 Assoc Director Disability Services ..... Ms. Peggy DENNIS
88 Dir President's Leadership Acad ..... Dr. Julie A. SNYDER
88 Director Dining Services ..... Mr. Michael L. PAULUS
96 Director of Business Operations ..... Mr. Andrew D. GRANT
88 Director Student Employment ..... Ms. Michelle SIMMONS
88 Director Learning Commons ..... Mr. Mark NELSON
88 Director Advising Services ..... Mr. Dermot M. FORDE
88 Asst VP Non-Trad & Transfer Svcs ..... Dr. Barbara L. HENRY
20 Vice Provost Strategic Initiatives ..... Dr. Joseph FRIZADO
65 Dir Sch Earth/Environ & Society ..... Dr. Charles ONASCH

Bowling Green State University Firelands College (D)

One University Drive, Huron OH 44839-9719
County: Erie FICE Identification: 007856
Unit ID: 201432
Telephone: (419) 433-5560 Carnegie Class: Assoc/Pub-R-S
FAX Number: (419) 433-9696 Calendar System: Semester
URL: www.firelands.bgsu.edu
Established: 1967 Annual Undergrad Tuition & Fees (In-State): $4,670
Enrollment: 2,507 Coed
Affiliation or Control: State IRS Status: 501(c)3
Highest Offering: Baccalaureate
Program: Occupational; 2-Year Principally Bachelor's Creditable
Accreditation: &NH

01 Dean ..... Dr. William K. BALZER
05 Int Assoc Dean Academic Pgms Svcs ..... Dr. Andrew J. KURTZ
09 Asst Dean Plng/Research/Effective ..... Vacant
10 Director Budget & Operations ..... Mr. Mark R. CHARVILLE
84 Dir Enroll Mgt/Stdnt Retention Svcs ..... Ms. Debralee DIVERS
06 Registrar ..... Ms. Vicki B. HILLIS
13 Director Technology Support Svcs ..... Ms. Julie A. HAMANN
30 Chief Development Officer ..... Ms. Stacey M. HARTLEY
26 Director Marketing & Communication ..... Mr. Dean D. SCHNURR
08 Head Librarian ..... Ms. Sharon R. BRITTON
51 Director for Educational Outreach ..... Ms. Kelly J. CUSACK
36 Career Services Coordinator ..... Mr. John L. CLARK
88 Dir Student Academic Enhancement ..... Ms. Penny L. NEMITZ
19 Campus Security ..... Mr. Edward E. WIMMER
105 Web Production Manager ..... Mr. James A. KIMBLE
40 Sales Manager Bookstore ..... Ms. Bonnie G. LINDSLEY
20 Manager Academic Advising ..... Ms. Amy L. MCKINLEY
35 Coord Student/Campus Activities ..... Ms. Sandra V. DICARLO
24 Audio Visual Specialist ..... Mr. Earl B. LISK, III

† Regional accreditation is carried under the parent institution in Bowling Green, OH.

Bradford School (E)

2469 Stelzer Road, Columbus OH 43219-3129
County: Franklin FICE Identification: 004853
Unit ID: 202161
Telephone: (614) 416-6200 Carnegie Class: Assoc/PrivFP
FAX Number: (614) 416-6210 Calendar System: Semester
URL: www.bradfordschoolcolumbus.edu
Established: 1985 Annual Undergrad Tuition & Fees: $12,600
Enrollment: 378 Coed
Affiliation or Control: Proprietary IRS Status: Proprietary
Highest Offering: Associate Degree
Program: Occupational
Accreditation: ACICS, MAC

01 President ..... Mr. Dennis BARTELS
05 Director of Education ..... Ms. Barbara ELLISON
07 Director of Admissions ..... Ms. Raeann LEE

Brown Mackie College-Akron (F)

755 White Pond Drive, Suite 101, Akron OH 44320-4221
County: Summit Identification: 666470
Unit ID: 205647
Telephone: (330) 869-3600 Carnegie Class: Assoc/PrivFP
FAX Number: (330) 869-3650 Calendar System: Other
URL: www.brownmackie.edu
Established: 1927 Annual Undergrad Tuition & Fees: $11,124
Enrollment: 1,063 Coed
Affiliation or Control: Proprietary IRS Status: Proprietary
Highest Offering: Associate Degree
Program: Occupational; 2-Year Principally Bachelor's Creditable; Business Emphasis
Accreditation: ACICS, MAC, OTA, SURGT

01 President ..... Ms. Kim AMES
05 Dean of Academic Affairs ..... Ms. Judith QUAYLE
06 Registrar ..... Ms. Ronnell NOVISKY
07 Senior Director of Admissions ..... Mr. Bill HORNSBERGER
36 Director of Career Services ..... Ms. Judith SPOONER

† Branch campus of Brown Mackie College-Cincinnati, Cincinnati, OH.

Brown Mackie College-Cincinnati (G)

1011 Glendale-Milford Road, Cincinnati OH 45215-1107
County: Hamilton FICE Identification: 005127
Unit ID: 205610
Telephone: (513) 771-2424 Carnegie Class: Assoc/PrivFP
FAX Number: (513) 771-3413 Calendar System: Other
URL: www.brownmackie.edu
Established: 1927 Annual Undergrad Tuition & Fees: $11,124
Enrollment: 1,574 Coed
Affiliation or Control: Proprietary IRS Status: Proprietary
Highest Offering: Associate Degree
Program: Occupational; 2-Year Principally Bachelor's Creditable; Business Emphasis
Accreditation: ACICS, MAC, SURGT

01 President ..... Mr. Ken RICHARDS
07 Senior Director of Admissions ..... Mr. Carmichael JAMES
06 Registrar ..... Ms. Courtney TENBOSCH
05 Dean of Academic Affairs ..... Ms. Tara DAILEY
36 Director of Career Services ..... Ms. Anita JONES

Brown Mackie College-Findlay (H)

1700 Fostoria Avenue, Suite 100, Findlay OH 45840-6857
County: Hancock FICE Identification: 026162
Unit ID: 375489
Telephone: (419) 423-2211 Carnegie Class: Assoc/PrivFP
FAX Number: (419) 423-0725 Calendar System: Other
URL: www.brownmackie.edu
Established: 1986 Annual Undergrad Tuition & Fees: $11,124
Enrollment: 834 Coed
Affiliation or Control: Proprietary IRS Status: Proprietary
Highest Offering: Associate Degree
Program: Occupational; 2-Year Principally Bachelor's Creditable; Business Emphasis
Accreditation: ACICS, OTA, SURGT

01 President ..... Mr. Wayne KORPICS
05 Dean of Academic Affairs ..... Ms. Lisa RUDASILL
07 Senior Director of Admissions ..... Vacant
06 Registrar ..... Ms. Heather ELLIOTT
36 Director of Career Services ..... Vacant

Brown Mackie College-North Canton (I)

4300 Munson Street, NW, Canton OH 44718-3674
County: Stark FICE Identification: 030778
Unit ID: 204316
Telephone: (330) 494-1214 Carnegie Class: Assoc/PrivFP
FAX Number: (330) 494-8112 Calendar System: Other
URL: www.brownmackie.edu
Established: 1985 Annual Undergrad Tuition & Fees: $11,124
Enrollment: 914 Coed
Affiliation or Control: Proprietary IRS Status: Proprietary
Highest Offering: Associate Degree
Program: Occupational; 2-Year Principally Bachelor's Creditable; Business Emphasis
Accreditation: ACICS, SURTEC

01 President ..... Mr. Peter PERKOWSKI
05 Dean of Academic Affairs ..... Ms. Marcy TREW
06 Registrar ..... Ms. Christine MONTINI
07 Senior Director of Admissions ..... Mr. Sanjay KETTY
36 Director of Career Services ..... Ms. Brenda RAYE

† Branch campus of Brown Mackie College-Tucson, Tucson, AZ.

Bryant & Stratton College (J)

1700 E 13th Street, Cleveland OH 44114-3203
County: Cuyahoga FICE Identification: 009343
Unit ID: 202684
Telephone: (216) 771-1700 Carnegie Class: Bac/Assoc
FAX Number: (216) 771-7787 Calendar System: Semester
URL: www.bryantstratton.edu
Established: 1854 Annual Undergrad Tuition & Fees: $21,750

Enrollment: 552 Coed
Affiliation or Control: Proprietary IRS Status: Proprietary
Highest Offering: Baccalaureate
Program: Occupational
Accreditation: &M

01 Campus Dir/Dir Cleveland Market .... Mr. John GIGARD
32 Dean of Student Services .... Dr. Clifford WALLACE

† Regional accreditation is carried under the parent institution (corporate office) in Buffalo, NY.

Bryant & Stratton College (A)

35350 Curtis Blvd, Eastlake OH 44095
County: Lake Identification: 666466
Unit ID: 369905
Telephone: (440) 510-1112 Carnegie Class: Bac/Assoc
FAX Number: (440) 306-2015 Calendar System: Semester
URL: www.bryantstratton.edu
Established: 1854 Annual Undergrad Tuition & Fees: $23,355
Enrollment: 974 Coed
Affiliation or Control: Proprietary IRS Status: Proprietary
Highest Offering: Associate Degree
Program: 2-Year Principally Bachelor's Creditable; Business Emphasis
Accreditation: &M, ADNUR

01 Campus Director .... Dr. Ted P. HANSEN
05 Dean of Instruction .... Dr. Florentine J. HOELKER
10 Business Office Manager .... Mr. Ian R. MARKS
36 Career Service Director .... Ms. Rhonda BUTLER

† Regional accreditation is carried under the parent institution (corporate office) in Buffalo, NY.

Bryant & Stratton College (B)

12955 Snow Road, Parma OH 44130-1013
County: Cuyahoga FICE Identification: 022744
Unit ID: 201469
Telephone: (216) 265-3151 Carnegie Class: Assoc/PrivFP4
FAX Number: (216) 265-0325 Calendar System: Semester
URL: www.bryantstratton.edu
Established: 1854 Annual Undergrad Tuition & Fees: $15,120
Enrollment: 672 Coed
Affiliation or Control: Proprietary IRS Status: Proprietary
Highest Offering: Baccalaureate
Program: 2-Year Principally Bachelor's Creditable
Accreditation: &M, MAC

01 Campus Director .... Mrs. Lisa MASON
05 Dean of Instruction .... Ms. Susan JELENIC
10 Business Manager .... Ms. Donna GOLDSTEIN
36 Director of Career Services .... Ms. Deborah JOHNS

† Regional accreditation is carried under the parent institution (corporate office) in Buffalo, NY.

Capital University (C)

1 College and Main Street, Columbus OH 43209-2394
County: Franklin FICE Identification: 003023
Unit ID: 201548
Telephone: (614) 236-6011 Carnegie Class: Master's M
FAX Number: (614) 236-6820 Calendar System: Semester
URL: www.capital.edu
Established: 1850 Annual Undergrad Tuition & Fees: $30,450
Enrollment: 3,629 Coed
Affiliation or Control: Evangelical Lutheran Church In America
IRS Status: 501(c)3
Highest Offering: First Professional Degree
Program: Liberal Arts And General; Teacher Preparatory; Professional
Accreditation: NH, ACBSP, LAW, MUS, NURSE, SW, TED

01 President .... Dr. Denvy A. BOWMAN
05 Vice Pres Academic/Student Affairs .... Dr. Richard M. ASHBROOK
10 Vice President Business & Finance .... Ms. Susan E. TATE
45 Exec VP Planning & Advancement .... Dr. Kevin W. SAYERS
32 Assoc VP for Student Affairs .... Dr. Betty M. LOVELACE
84 Assoc VP Enrollment Services .... Dr. Amy ADAMS
43 University Counsel .... Dr. Tanya J. POTEET
20 Associate Provost .... Dr. Terry D. LAHM
26 Asst Vice Pres External Relations .... Ms. Patricia CRAMER
21 Assistant VP Business & Finance .... Ms. Lori MCKIRNAN
44 Asst Vice President Major Gifts .... Ms. April NOVOTNY
100 Dir Pres Ofc/Liaison to Board Trust .... Ms. Nona S. MCGUIRE
27 Dir Communications/Media Relations .. Ms. D. Nichole JOHNSON
09 Director of Institutional Research .... Dr. Larry T. HUNTER
06 Registrar .... Mr. Brent KOERBER
37 Director of Financial Aid .... Ms. Susan E. KANNENWISCHER
07 Director of Admissions .... Ms. Amanda STEINER
29 Director Alumni/Parent Relations .... Ms. Diane LOESER
36 Director of Career Services .... Mr. Eric R. ANDERSON
08 University Librarian/Director IMC .... Ms. Belen FERNANDEZ
87 Director of Summer Programs .... Dr. Jerry P. THOMAS
88 Academic Service Coordinator .... Mr. Bruce EPPS
26 Director Public Relations .... Ms. Denise RUSSELL
41 Athletic Director .... Ms. Dawn STEWART
88 Director of Faith Relations .... Vacant
42 Campus Pastor .... Rev. Amy OEHLSCHLAEGER
13 Int Dir Information Technology .... Mr. Jeff GUILER
85 Director Intl Education & ESL Pgm .... Ms. Jennifer ADAMS
35 Director Student Activities .... Mr. Melvin ADAMS
18 Int Director Facilities Management .... Ms. Beth Anne CARMEN
15 Director of Human Resources .... Ms. Theresa FELDMEIER
38 Dir Univ Counseling/Health Svcs .... Dr. Shirley LANGE
28 Dir Diversity/Multiculturall Affs .... Vacant
92 Honors Program .... Dr. Stephen BAKER
40 Manager Bookstore .... Ms. Jackie WENNING
61 Dean of Law School .... Mr. Richard SIMPSON
64 Ast Dn Conservtry of Music/Sch Comm ...... Dr. Rocky J. REUTER
49 Dean Unified College .... Dr. Cedric ADDERLEY
50 Asst Dean Sch Management/Leadership .... Dr. Keirsten MOORE
66 Asst Dean Sch Nat Sci/Nursing/Hlth .... Dr. Jens HEMMINGSEN
83 Asst Dean Sch Social Sciences/Educ .... Dr. Jody FOURNIER
79 Assistant Dean School of Humanities .... Dr. David SUMMERS

Carnegie Career College (D)

1292 Waterloo Road, Mogadore OH 44260
County: Portage FICE Identification: 036933
Unit ID: 444477
Telephone: (330) 630-1132 Carnegie Class: Not Classified
FAX Number: (303) 628-3775 Calendar System: Other
URL: carnegieinstitute.net/
Established: N/A Annual Undergrad Tuition & Fees: N/A
Enrollment: 210 Coed
Affiliation or Control: Independent Non-Profit IRS Status: 501(c)3
Highest Offering: Associate Degree
Program: Occupational
Accreditation: ABHES

01 Director .... Ms. Marie CERONI

† Tuition varies by degree program.

Case Western Reserve University (E)

10900 Euclid Avenue, Cleveland OH 44106-7001
County: Cuyahoga FICE Identification: 003024
Unit ID: 201645
Telephone: (216) 368-2000 Carnegie Class: RU/VH
FAX Number: N/A Calendar System: Semester
URL: www.case.edu
Established: 1826 Annual Undergrad Tuition & Fees: $39,120
Enrollment: 9,837 Coed
Affiliation or Control: Independent Non-Profit IRS Status: 501(c)3
Highest Offering: Doctorate
Program: Liberal Arts And General; Professional
Accreditation: NH, AA, ANEST, BUS, BUSA, CLPSY, CS, DENT, DIETD, DIETI, ENG, LAW, MED, MIDWF, MUS, NUR, PH, SP, SW, TEAC

01 President .... Ms. Barbara R. SNYDER
05 Provost/Executive Vice President .... Dr. William A. BAESLACK, III
20 Deputy Provost/VP Academic Programs .... Dr. Lynn T. SINGER
10 Senior Vice Pres for Finance & CFO .... Mr. John F. SIDERAS
11 Senior Vice Pres for Administration .... Mr. John D. WHEELER
30 Sr VP for Univ Rels & Development .... Mr. Bruce A. LOESSIN
17 Vice President Medical Affairs .... Dr. Pamela B. DAVIS
46 Vice President for Research .... Vacant
13 Vice President Information Services .... Dr. Lov S. GONICK
32 Vice President for Student Affairs .... Mr. Glenn NICHOLLS
18 VP Campus Planning/Facilities Mgmt ..... Mr. Stephen CAMPBELL
16 Vice President for Human Resources .... Ms. Carolyn GREGORY
43 Int Vice President/General Counsel .... Ms. Colleen TREML
19 Vice President for Campus Services ..... Mr. Richard J. JAMIESON
26 Vice Pres for University Relations .... Ms. Lara A. KALAFATIS
86 Vice Pres for Government Relations .... Mr. David A. BELL
86 Exec Director Government Relations .... Ms. Jennifer RUGGLES
31 Dir Center for Cmty Partnerships .... Ms. Latisha JAMES
45 Vice Pres for University Planning .... Ms. Christine A. ASH
84 Vice Pres for Enrollment Management . Mr. Richard W. BISCHOFF
28 VP Inclusion/Diversity/Equal Opptny ...... Dr. Marilyn S. MOBLEY
26 Assoc VP Marketing/Communications .... Vacant
88 Treasurer .... Mr. Robert C. BROWN
88 Chief Investment Officer .... Ms. Sally STALEY
20 Vice Provost Undergrad Education .... Dr. Donald L. FEKE
88 Assoc Prov for International Affs .... Mr. David FLESHLER
100 Chief of Staff .... Ms. Chris SHERIDAN
88 Dean of Undergraduate Studies .... Mr. Jeffrey WOLCOWITZ
21 Controller .... Mr. Bradley W. FRALIC
06 Registrar .... Ms. Amy S. HAMMETT
29 Associate VP for Alumni Relations ..... Mr. Christopher J. VLAHOS
37 Director of Financial Aid .... Ms. Venus PULIAFICO
07 Director Undergraduate
Admissions .... Mr. Robert R. MCCULLOUGH
08 University Librarian .... Mr. Arnold HIRSHON
36 Director Career Center .... Dr. Thomas MATTHEWS
85 Dir International Student Svcs .... Ms. Elise LINDSAY
38 Director University Counseling Svcs .... Dr. James E. SELLERS
09 Director of Institutional Research .... Ms. Jean E. GUBBINS
96 Dir Procurement/Distribution Svcs .... Ms. Melinda BOYKIN
41 Athletic Director .... Dr. David DILES
61 Dean of Law .... Mr. Lawrence E. MITCHELL
49 Dean of Arts & Sciences .... Dr. Cyrus C. TAYLOR
63 Dean of Medicine .... Dr. Pamela B. DAVIS
66 Dean of Nursing .... Dr. Mary E. KERR
52 Dean of Dental Medicine .... Dr. Jerold S. GOLDBERG
50 Dean of Management .... Dr. N. Mohan REDDY
70 Dean Applied Social Science .... Dr. Grover C. GILMORE
54 Dean of Engineering .... Dr. Norman C. TIEN
58 Dean of Graduate Studies .... Dr. Charles E. ROZEK

Cedarville University (F)

251 N Main Street, Cedarville OH 45314-0601
County: Greene FICE Identification: 003025
Unit ID: 201654
Telephone: (937) 766-2211 Carnegie Class: Bac/Diverse
FAX Number: (937) 766-2760 Calendar System: Semester
URL: www.cedarville.edu
Established: 1887 Annual Undergrad Tuition & Fees: $24,840
Enrollment: 3,210 Coed
Affiliation or Control: Baptist IRS Status: 501(c)3
Highest Offering: Doctorate
Program: Liberal Arts And General; Teacher Preparatory; Professional
Accreditation: NH, ACBSP, CS, ENG, MUS, NURSE, SW, TED

01 President .... Dr. William E. BROWN
03 Provost .... Dr. John W. GREDY
05 Academic Vice President .... Dr. Thomas H. CORNMAN
10 Vice President for Business .... Mr. Phillip C. GRAFTON
30 Vice President for Advancement .... Mr. William L. BIGHAM
32 Vice President for Student Life .... Dr. Carl A. RUBY
42 Vice Pres for Christian Ministry .... Rev. Robert K. ROHM
84 Vice Pres Enrollment Management .... Mrs. Janice SUPPLEE
18 Vice President for Facilities .... Mr. Rodney JOHNSON
32 Dean of Students .... Miss Kirsten GIBBS
07 Director of Admissions .... Mr. Mark WEINSTEIN
06 Registrar .... Mrs. Frances CAMPBELL
34 Assoc Dean Women .... Miss Rebecca STOWERS
106 Sr Assoc Acad VP Col Extended Lrng .... Dr. Andy RUNYAN
16 Assoc VP of Human Resources .... Mrs. Lisa TODD
14 Assoc VP for Tech/Computer Services .... Dr. David L. ROTMAN
09 Associate VP for Strategic Planning .... Mr. David ORMSBEE
69 Assoc VP Col of Health Professions ...... Dr. Pamela D. JOHNSON
49 Assoc VP Col of Arts & Sciences .... Dr. Steven WINTEREGG
107 Assoc VP College of Professions .... Dr. Mark MCCLAIN
08 Dean of Library Services .... Mr. Lynn A. BROCK
37 Executive Director of Financial Aid .... Mr. Fred E. MERRITT
67 Dean School of Pharmacy .... Dr. Marc SWEENEY
38 Director of Counseling Services .... Mr. John M. POTTER
29 Director of Alumni Relations .... Mr. Jeff BESTE
36 Director Career Services .... Mr. Jeff REEP
87 Director Summer School/Cont Educ .... Vacant
92 Director Honors Program .... Dr. David MILLS
35 Associate Dean/Campus Life .... Mr. Brad D. SMITH
96 Director of Purchasing/Inventory .... Mr. Tim P. JOHNSON
04 Executive Asst to the President .... Mrs. Carol S. GEORGE
41 Athletic Director .... Dr. Alan GEIST
26 Director of Public Relations .... Mr. John DAVIS

Central Ohio Technical College (G)

1179 University Drive, Newark OH 43055-1767
County: Licking FICE Identification: 011046
Unit ID: 201672
Telephone: (740) 366-1351 Carnegie Class: Assoc/Pub-S-SC
FAX Number: (740) 366-5047 Calendar System: Quarter
URL: www.cotc.edu
Established: 1971 Annual Undergrad Tuition & Fees (In-State): $5,304
Enrollment: 4,515 Coed
Affiliation or Control: State IRS Status: 501(c)3
Highest Offering: Associate Degree
Program: Occupational; 2-Year Principally Bachelor's Creditable; Technical Emphasis
Accreditation: NH, ADNUR, DMS, RAD, SURGT

01 President .... Dr. Bonnie L. COE
10 Vice President Business & Finance .... Mr. David BRILLHART
05 Vice President for Academic Affairs .... Dr. Richard PRYSTOWSKY
84 VP for Enrollment Mgmt & Acad Affs .... Dr. John BERRY
15 VP for Instnl Planning & HR Develop .... Ms. Jacqueline PARRILL
08 Director of Library .... Ms. Susan SCOTT
06 Records Manager/Registrar .... Ms. Jacqueline STEWART
07 Director of Enrollment Management .... Ms. Tara HOUDESHELL
88 Director Child Development Center .... Vacant
27 Director Marketing/Public
Relations .... Ms. Alice HUTZEL-BATESON
37 Director Financial Aid/Veteran Affs .... Ms. Faith PHILLIPS
19 Director Public Safety .... Mr. Denny HOLLERN
29 Dir Alumni Rels/Development Officer .... Ms. Jennifer ROBERTS
35 Asst Director of Student Affairs .... Ms. Holly MASON
13 Chief Information Officer .... Mr. Howard IMHOF
38 Program Mgr Learn Asst Ctr Disabled .... Ms. Connie ZANG
11 Director of Operations .... Vacant
96 Manager of Purchasing .... Ms. Margaret CAMSTRA
18 Manager Facilities .... Dr. James R. WOOLARD
51 Coord of Community Svc/Learning .... Ms. Vorley TAYLOR
36 Dir Career Dev & Experiential Lrng .... Mr. Derek THATCHER
12 Coshocton Campus Administrator .... Ms. Melanie BOLENDER
12 Knox Campus Administrator .... Mr. Joel DANIELS
12 Pataskala Campus Administrator .... Ms. Julie MAURER
93 Minority Recruiter/Counselor .... Vacant
04 Assistant to the President .... Ms. Jan TOMLINSON

Central State University (H)

PO Box 1004, 1400 Brush Row Road,
Wilberforce OH 45384-1004
County: Greene FICE Identification: 003026
Unit ID: 201690
Telephone: (937) 376-6332 Carnegie Class: Bac/Diverse
FAX Number: (937) 376-6138 Calendar System: Semester
URL: www.centralstate.edu
Established: 1887 Annual Undergrad Tuition & Fees (In-State): $5,672

Enrollment: 2,288 Coed
Affiliation or Control: State IRS Status: 501(c)3
Highest Offering: Master's
Program: Liberal Arts And General; Teacher Preparatory; Business Emphasis
Accreditation: NH, ART, ENG, MUS, TED

01 President ... Mr. John W. GARLAND
04 Exec Asst to the President ... Mrs. Wendy HAYES
05 Provost/VP Academic Affairs ... Dr. Juliette B. BELL
10 Vice President Admin & Finance ... Mrs. Colette BURNETTE
30 Vice Pres Institutional Advancement ... Mr. Anthony FAIRBANKS
11 Asst VP Administration & Finance ... Vacant
32 Vice President for Student Affairs ... Mr. Jerryl BRIGGS
13 Vice Pres/Chief Information Officer ... Dr. Donald STEWARD
20 Assoc Vice Pres Academic Affairs ... Dr. Willie HOUSTON
06 Registrar ... Mrs. LaTonya BRANHAM
07 Director of Admissions ... Ms. Robin RUCKER
08 Director of Hallie Q Brown Library ... Mr. Johnny JACKSON
89 Int Dean Ctr Stdnt Academic Success ... Dr. LaKeysha CATRON
12 Dean CSU Dayton Campus ... Dr. Kaye JETER
09 Director Assessment/Inst Research ... Mr. Mohammad ALI
19 Chief of Police ... Chief Anthony PETTIFORD
26 Director Public Relations ... Ms. Francine ROBINSON
23 Medical Director ... Dr. Karen MATHEWS
29 Director Alumni Relations ... Mr. Keith PERKINS
88 Director Career Services ... Ms. Elizabeth BEEMER
37 Director Student Financial Aid ... Ms. Sonia SLOMBIA
39 Director Residence Life ... Mr. Raynaldo GILLUS
41 Athletic Director ... Mr. Kellen WINSLOW
42 Director Campus Ministry ... Rev. Nigel FELDER
46 Director Sponsored Research ... Mr. Morakinyo KUTI
49 Dean Coll of Humanities/Arts & Sci ... Dr. Lovette CHINWAH
50 Dean College Business & Industry ... Dr. Charles SHOWELL, JR.
53 Dean College of Education ... Dr. Reginald NNAZOR
15 Director of Human Resources ... Ms. Kimberly MANIGAULT
21 Director Business Svcs/Capital Dev ... Mr. Harlan HENDERSON
35 Dean of Students ... Vacant
25 Director Grants Accounting ... Vacant
92 Director Honors Program ... Vacant
21 Controller ... Ms. Beth ANDERSON
21 Budget Director ... Mr. Curtis PETTIS
38 Director Student Counseling ... Mr. Frank PORTER

Chancellor University (A)

3921 Chester Avenue, Cleveland OH 44114
County: Cuyahoga FICE Identification: 003043
Unit ID: 202611
Telephone: (216) 391-6937 Carnegie Class: Bac/Diverse
FAX Number: (216) 426-9296 Calendar System: Semester
URL: www.chancelloru.edu
Established: 1848 Annual Undergrad Tuition & Fees: $12,000
Enrollment: 733 Coed
Affiliation or Control: Proprietary IRS Status: Proprietary
Highest Offering: Master's
Program: Business Emphasis
Accreditation: NH, IACBE

01 Chancellor and Interim President ... Mr. Robert C. DAUGHERTY
84 Vice President Enrollment Services ... Ms. Leslie BRUGA
05 Provost/CAO ... Dr. Steven KERR
15 Vice President of Human Resources ... Dr. Theresa HUEFTLE
45 VP of Strategic Planning ... Dr. Trish GORMAN
06 Registrar ... Ms. Miria T. BATIG
08 Manager Student Knowledge Resource ... Mr. Richard D. BRHEL
37 Director Financial Aid ... Ms. Chris TUNEBURG
10 Chief Financial Officer ... Mr. Steve DEMKO
32 Senior Director Student Services ... Ms. Bethany BATEMAN
24 Assoc Dir of Learning & Acad Tech ... Mr. Daniel TAYLOR
04 Exec Asst to the President ... Ms. Kate HERRNSTEIN
09 Sr Dir of Institutional Research ... Dr. Dmitry SUSPITSIN
18 Director Facilities and IT ... Vacant
21 Controller ... Vacant
58 Exec VP Jack Welch Mgmt Institute ... Dr. Steve KERR
50 Dean College of Business ... Mr. Todd Allyn WILLIAMS
49 Dean College of Arts & Sciences ... Dr. Darius NAVRAN
107 Dean College Professional Studies ... Dr. Darius NAVRAN
88 Director of Assessment ... Ms. Kristina SMART
88 Director of Faculty T&D ... Ms. Janelle COUTURE
102 Sr Dir Corporate Dev Liason ... Mr. Kevan FORD
88 Director Student Info Systems ... Ms. Shauna YOUNG

Chatfield College (B)

20918 State Route 251, Saint Martin OH 45118-9059
County: Brown FICE Identification: 010880
Unit ID: 201751
Telephone: (513) 875-3344 Carnegie Class: Assoc/PrivNFP
FAX Number: (513) 875-3912 Calendar System: Semester
URL: www.chatfield.edu
Established: 1971 Annual Undergrad Tuition & Fees: $10,130
Enrollment: 328 Coed
Affiliation or Control: Independent Non-Profit IRS Status: 501(c)3
Highest Offering: Associate Degree
Program: 2-Year Principally Bachelor's Creditable; Fine Arts Emphasis
Accreditation: NH

01 President ... Mr. John P. TAFARO
10 Director of Finance ... Ms. Mary R. JACOBS
05 Academic Dean ... Dr. Roger COURTS
20 Site Director/Academic Coordinator ... Ms. Wanda HILL
37 Financial Aid Director ... Mrs. Zana SMITH
06 Registrar ... Mr. Frank CHAPIN

The Christ College of Nursing and Health Sciences (C)

2139 Auburn Avenue, Cincinnati OH 45219
County: Hamilton FICE Identification: 006489
Unit ID: 201821
Telephone: (513) 585-2401 Carnegie Class: Not Classified
FAX Number: (513) 585-3540 Calendar System: Semester
URL: www.thechristcollege.edu
Established: 2006 Annual Undergrad Tuition & Fees: $12,600
Enrollment: 314 Coed
Affiliation or Control: Independent Non-Profit IRS Status: 501(c)3
Highest Offering: Associate Degree
Program: 2-Year Principally Bachelor's Creditable; Nursing Emphasis
Accreditation: NH

01 President ... Dr. Nathan LONG
66 Academic Dean Nursing Education ... Ms. Kathleen CARISSIMI
05 Acad Dean Gen Educ/Instruct Support ... Mr. Michael SMITH
09 Dean Inst Assessment & Evaluation ... Ms. Carolyn HUNTER
30 Director of Development ... Ms. Danielle GENTRY-BARTH
32 Dean of Student Services ... Ms. Jill LOCH
10 College Bursar ... Ms. Cathy SILVERMAN
37 Director of Financial Aid ... Mr. Timothy RING
06 College Registrar ... Mr. Perry CARROLL
07 Admissions Counselor ... Mr. Bradley JACKSON
29 Counselor/Alumni Affairs Liaison ... Ms. Erica HAUKAP

Cincinnati Christian University (D)

2700 Glenway Avenue, Cincinnati OH 45204-3200
County: Hamilton FICE Identification: 003029
Unit ID: 201858
Telephone: (513) 244-8100 Carnegie Class: Spec/Faith
FAX Number: (513) 244-8140 Calendar System: Semester
URL: www.ccuniversity.edu
Established: 1924 Annual Undergrad Tuition & Fees: $14,604
Enrollment: 1,021 Coed
Affiliation or Control: Christian Churches And Churches of Christ
IRS Status: 501(c)3
Highest Offering: First Professional Degree
Program: Liberal Arts And General; Professional; Religious Emphasis
Accreditation: NH, BI, MUS, TEAC, THEOL

01 President ... Dr. David M. FAUST
05 Vice President Academic Affairs ... Dr. Jon A. WEATHERLY
32 Vice Pres Leadership Development ... Mr. Larry TRAVIS
30 Vice President for Advancement ... Mrs. Barbara RENDEL
10 Vice President Finance & Operations ... Mr. Chuck ABBOTT
20 Dean of Seminary ... Dr. Johnny PRESSLEY
20 Dean of College ... Dr. Jon A. WEATHERLY
51 Director College of Adult Learning ... Mr. Rick MCKENZIE
09 Dean of Dist Educ & Inst Research ... Dr. Paul PENNINGTON
06 Registrar ... Mr. Don A. THOMASON
08 Director of Libraries ... Mr. James H. LLOYD
35 Dean of Students ... Mrs. Kristin MERRILL
33 Dean of Men/Campus Minister ... Mr. Dan BURTON
37 Director of Financial Aid ... Vacant
07 Director Undergraduate Admissions ... Mr. David BRUNNER
29 Director of Alumni Ministries ... Mr. Mark KOERNER
21 Accounting Manager ... Mr. Randy KOEHLER
88 Dir Center for Church Advancement ... Mr. David ROADCUP
41 Director of Athletics ... Mr. Jason GILLESPIE
18 Director of Operations ... Mr. Michael NEAVILL
15 Human Resources Director ... Mrs. Nancy HARTMAN
14 Director of Computer Services ... Mr. James MCINTYRE
19 Director of Security ... Mrs. Karen LITTLE
40 Manager of Bookstore ... Miss Beth ROGERS
07 Director of Graduate Admissions ... Mr. Alex EDDY
38 Director Student Counseling ... Dr. Douglas SPEARS
28 Director of CUGO ... Mr. Steve SKAGGS
04 Assistant to the President ... Mrs. Wendy SPALDING

Cincinnati College of Mortuary Science (E)

645 W North Bend Road, Cincinnati OH 45224-1462
County: Hamilton FICE Identification: 010906
Unit ID: 201867
Telephone: (513) 761-2020 Carnegie Class: Spec/Other
FAX Number: (513) 761-3333 Calendar System: Quarter
URL: www.ccms.edu
Established: 1882 Annual Undergrad Tuition & Fees: $20,250
Enrollment: 70 Coed
Affiliation or Control: Independent Non-Profit IRS Status: 501(c)3
Highest Offering: Baccalaureate
Program: Occupational; Liberal Arts And General
Accreditation: NH, FUSER

01 President ... Ms. Karen GILES
84 Exec Director Enrollment Management ... Ms. Pat SULLIVAN

Cincinnati State Technical and Community College (F)

3520 Central Parkway, Cincinnati OH 45223-2690
County: Hamilton FICE Identification: 010345
Unit ID: 201928
Telephone: (513) 569-1500 Carnegie Class: Assoc/Pub-U-SC
FAX Number: (513) 569-1495 Calendar System: Other
URL: www.cincinnatistate.edu
Established: 1966 Annual Undergrad Tuition & Fees (In-State): $5,154
Enrollment: 11,000 Coed
Affiliation or Control: State IRS Status: 501(c)3
Highest Offering: Associate Degree
Program: Occupational; 2-Year Principally Bachelor's Creditable; Business Emphasis
Accreditation: NH, ACFEI, ADNUR, CONST, DIETT, DMS, ENGT, #MAC, MLTAD, OTA, SURGT

01 President ... Dr. O'dell OWENS
03 Executive Vice President ... Dr. Carolyn ANDERSON
05 Academic Vice President ... Dr. Monica POSEY
10 Vice President for Finance ... Mr. Michael GEOGHEGAN
30 Vice Pres Institutional Advancement ... Vacant
45 Vice Pres Strategic Initiatives ... Mr. Dan CAYSE
72 Dean of Engineering Technology ... Mr. Paul DENU
50 Dean of Business Technologies ... Mr. Nick NISSLEY
76 Dean Health Technologies ... Dr. Marianne KRISMER
81 Dean Humanities/Sciences ... Dr. Rayma SMITH
84 Dean Enrollment/Student Services ... Mr. Anthony CRUZ
06 Registrar ... Mr. Ryan HUNT
08 Director Library ... Ms. Kathryn O'GORMAN
26 Public Information Officer ... Ms. Jean MANNING
41 Dir Athletics/Student Activities ... Ms. Theresa CHECK
13 Chief Information Officer ... Mr. Frankie BAKER
18 Director of Facilities ... Mr. Ray MIRIZZI
51 Dean Corporate & Community Services ... Dr. Dennis ULRICH
09 Director of Institutional Research ... Ms. Anne FOSTER
07 Director of Admissions ... Ms. Gabriele BOECKERMANN
15 Director Human Resource ... Mr. Eugene BREYER
29 Director of Alumni Relations ... Ms. Carolmarie STOCK
32 Chief Student Life Officer ... Ms. Brenda MAPLES-STERRY
35 Director of Student Affairs ... Mrs. Sharon DAVIS
38 Director of Student Couseling ... Dr. Richard DANIELS
96 Director of Purchasing ... Mr. Jeff COOK
92 Coordinator Honors Program ... Ms. Marcha HUNLEY

Clark State Community College (G)

570 E Leffel Lane, PO Box 570,
Springfield OH 45501-0570
County: Clark FICE Identification: 004852
Unit ID: 201973
Telephone: (937) 325-0691 Carnegie Class: Assoc/Pub-U-SC
FAX Number: (937) 328-6142 Calendar System: Quarter
URL: www.clarkstate.edu
Established: 1966 Annual Undergrad Tuition & Fees (In-State): $6,156
Enrollment: 4,798 Coed
Affiliation or Control: State IRS Status: 501(c)3
Highest Offering: Associate Degree
Program: Occupational; 2-Year Principally Bachelor's Creditable
Accreditation: NH, ADNUR, MAC, MLTAD, PTAA

01 President ... Dr. Karen E. RAFINSKI
05 Vice Pres Academic/Student Affairs ... Dr. David H. DEVIER
10 Vice President Business Affairs ... Joseph R. JACKSON
30 Vice President of Advancement ... Kristin J. CULP
21 Controller ... Dixie A. DEPEW
12 Dean Greene Center ... Vacant
08 Dean Library/Educational Resources ... Mary Beth AUST-KEEFER
32 Dean of Stdnt Affs/Enrollment Mgmt ... Dr. Edward J. BUSHER
49 Dean Arts & Sciences/Public Svcs ... Martha CRAWMER
50 Dean Business/Applied Technologies ... Jane A. CAPE
76 Dean Health and Human Services ... Kathleen J. WILCOX
37 Financial Aid Director ... Kathy A. KLAY
06 Registrar ... Teresa A. MABRY
07 Director of Admissions ... Corey HOLLIDAY
13 Exec Dir Information Technology ... Barbara DESCHAPPELLES
102 Foundation/Executive Director ... Kristin J. CULP
45 Dir of Inst Plng/Research/Grants ... Vacant
15 Director of Human Resources ... Marvin NEPHEW
57 Director of Performing Arts Center ... Stuart A. SECTTOR
18 Dir Facilities/Oper/Maintenance ... Randall CONOVER
41 Dir Athletics/Act & Evening Svcs ... Ronald GORDON
51 Program Mgr Continuing Education ... Vacant
09 Institutional Research Technician ... Jennifer J. NICKELL

Cleveland Institute of Art (H)

11141 East Boulevard, Cleveland OH 44106-1710
County: Cuyahoga FICE Identification: 003982
Unit ID: 202046
Telephone: (216) 421-7000 Carnegie Class: Spec/Arts
FAX Number: (216) 421-7438 Calendar System: Semester
URL: www.cia.edu
Established: 1882 Annual Undergrad Tuition & Fees: $33,882
Enrollment: 534 Coed
Affiliation or Control: Independent Non-Profit IRS Status: 501(c)3
Highest Offering: Baccalaureate
Program: Professional; Fine Arts Emphasis
Accreditation: NH, ART

01 President ... Mr. Grafton J. NUNES
05 VP Academic & Faculty Affairs ... Mr. Chris WHITTEY
30 Sr Vice Pres Inst Advancement ... Mr. Michael COLE
10 Vice President Business Affairs/CFO ... Mrs. Almut ZVOSEC
26 Vice President Mktg & Communication ... Mr. Mark INGLIS
07 Exec Dir Enrollment & Financial Aid ... Mr. Robert BORDEN
37 Asst Director of Financial Aid ... Ms. Delores HALL
06 Registrar ... Mrs. Karen HUDY

08 Librarian ... Ms. Cristine ROM
07 Director of Admissions ... Vacant
13 Director Information Technology ... Mr. Michael KIMMEL
18 Director Safety & Facility Mgmt ... Mr. Howard D. WEINER
29 Director Annual Giving/Alumni Rels ... Mr. Michael KINSELLA
20 Director of Academic Services ... Vacant
44 Director Major Gifts/Planned Giving ... Ms. Margaret GUDBRANSON
15 Director Human Resources ... Mr. Raymond SCRAGG
32 Dean of Student Affairs ... Ms. Nancy NEVILLE
37 Director of Financial Aid ... Mr. Martin CARNEY
26 Director of Mktg & Communications ... Ms. Susan ILER
88 Marketing & Communications Writer ... Ms. Julie MASON
57 Art Director ... Mr. Richard SARIAN
88 Senior Writer ... Ms. Ann MCGUIRE

Cleveland Institute of Electronics (A)

1776 E 17th Street, Cleveland OH 44114-3679
County: Cuyahoga FICE Identification: 005210
Unit ID: 202064
Telephone: (216) 781-9400 Carnegie Class: Assoc/PrivFP
FAX Number: (216) 781-0331 Calendar System: Other
URL: www.cie-wc.edu
Established: 1934 Annual Undergrad Tuition & Fees: $3,770
Enrollment: 1,756 Coed
Affiliation or Control: Proprietary IRS Status: Proprietary
Highest Offering: Associate Degree
Program: Occupational
Accreditation: DETC

01 President ... Mr. J. Randall DRINKO
37 Director of Financial Aid ... Mr. Scott KATZENMEYER
88 Coordinator Veteran Affairs ... Mrs. Marites CAPISTRANO

Cleveland Institute of Music (B)

11021 East Boulevard, Cleveland OH 44106-1776
County: Cuyahoga FICE Identification: 003031
Unit ID: 202073
Telephone: (216) 791-5000 Carnegie Class: Spec/Arts
FAX Number: (216) 791-3063 Calendar System: Semester
URL: www.cim.edu
Established: 1920 Annual Undergrad Tuition & Fees: $41,260
Enrollment: 450 Coed
Affiliation or Control: Independent Non-Profit IRS Status: 501(c)3
Highest Offering: Doctorate
Program: Professional; Music Emphasis
Accreditation: NH, MUS

01 President ... Mr. Joel SMIRNOFF
03 Vice President/COO ... Mr. Eric BOWER
05 Dean ... Dr. Adrian DALY
51 Dean Prep/Continuing Education ... Ms. Sandra SHAPIRO
26 Director Marketing & Communications ... Ms. Lorraine SCHUCHART
30 Chief Development Officer ... Ms. Megan GRANSON
13 Director Systems Management ... Ms. Aimee BARTON
07 Director of Admission ... Mr. William FAY
32 Associate Dean of Student Affairs ... Mr. David GILSON
37 Director Financial Aid ... Ms. Kristine GRIPP
21 Chief Financial Office ... Ms. Kristen KOLLAR
06 Registrar ... Mr. Hallie MOORE
15 Director Human Resources ... Mrs. Megan SWERBINSKY
08 Director of the Library ... Ms. Jean TOOMBS
18 Director Buildings & Grounds ... Mr. Alan VALEK
88 Director of Concerts & Events ... Ms. Lori WRIGHT
40 Bookstore Manager ... Ms. Antoinette MILLER

Cleveland State University (C)

2121 Euclid Avenue, Cleveland OH 44115-2214
County: Cuyahoga FICE Identification: 003032
Unit ID: 202134
Telephone: (216) 687-2000 Carnegie Class: RU/H
FAX Number: (216) 687-9366 Calendar System: Semester
URL: www.csuohio.edu
Established: 1964 Annual Undergrad Tuition & Fees (In-State): $8,952
Enrollment: 17,386 Coed
Affiliation or Control: State IRS Status: 501(c)3
Highest Offering: Doctorate
Program: Liberal Arts And General; Teacher Preparatory; Professional
Accreditation: NH, ARCPA, BUS, BUSA, CACREP, COPSY, ENG, ENGT, LAW, MUS, NURSE, OT, PH, PLNG, PTA, SP, SPAA, SW, TED

01 President ... Dr. Ronald M. BERKMAN
100 Chief of Staff ... Mr. Michael ARTBAUER
05 Provost ... Mr. Geoffrey s. MEARNS
10 Vice President Finance ... Ms. Stephanie MCHENRY
84 VP Enrollment/Student Affairs ... Ms. Carmen ALVAREZ BROWN
09 VP of Research & Graduate Studies ... Dr. George E. WALKER
28 Vice Pres Institutional Diversity ... Dr. Njeri NURU-HOLM
30 Vice Pres Univ Advancement ... Ms. Berinthia LEVINE
45 Vice Provost for Academic Planning ... Dr. Teresa LAGRANGE
20 Vice Provost Academic Affairs ... Dr. Vijaya KONANGI
26 Asst VP University Mktg/Admissions ... Mr. Robert SPADEMAN
15 Asst Vice Pres Human Resources Dev ... Mr. Robert PIETRYKOWSKI
88 Asst VP Campus Support Services ... Ms. Clare RAHM
21 Controller/Assoc VP Finance ... Mr. Brian COOK
32 Dean of Student Life ... Dr. James DRNEK
49 Dean Coll Liberal Arts/Soc Sci ... Dr. Gregory M. SADLEK
81 Dean College of Science ... Dr. Meredith R. BOND
50 Dean College Business Admin ... Dr. Robert F. SCHERER
53 Dean College Education ... Dr. Sajit ZACHARIAH
54 Interim Dean College of Engineering ... Dr. Chin KUO
58 Int Dean College Graduate Studies ... Dr. Crystal WEYMAN
61 Dean of College of Law ... Mr. Craig BOISE
80 Dean of College of Urban Affairs ... Dr. Edward HILL
43 General Counsel ... Ms. Sonali B. WILSON
86 Sr Advisor to Pres Government Rels ... Dr. William NAPIER
08 Director of Libraries ... Dr. Glenda THORNTON
22 Affirmative Affairs Officer ... Ms. Maria J. CODINACH
07 Interim Director Admissions ... Mr. Heike HEINRICH
09 Director Inst Research/Analysis ... Vacant
85 Director International Programs ... Mr. George BURKE
36 Director Career Services ... Ms. Yolanda BURT
38 Director Counseling Services ... Dr. Janilee B. WHEATON
19 Executive Director of Campus Safety ... Mr. Bernard BUCKNER
37 Director Student Financial Aid ... Ms. Rachel SCHMIDT
06 Registrar ... Ms. Janet STIMPLE
41 Director of Athletics ... Mr. John PARRY
29 Director Alumni Affairs ... Ms. Carolyn CHAMPION-SLOAN
18 Chief Facilities/Physical Plant ... Mr. Christopher K. WILSON
96 Director of Purchasing ... Vacant
92 Director Honors Program ... Dr. Peter MEIKSINS
28 Director of Diversity ... Ms. Melodie YATES

College of Mount St. Joseph (D)

5701 Delhi Road, Cincinnati OH 45233-1670
County: Hamilton FICE Identification: 003033
Unit ID: 204200
Telephone: (513) 244-4200 Carnegie Class: Master's M
FAX Number: (513) 244-4654 Calendar System: Semester
URL: www.msj.edu
Established: 1920 Annual Undergrad Tuition & Fees: $23,500
Enrollment: 2,474 Coed
Affiliation or Control: Roman Catholic IRS Status: 501(c)3
Highest Offering: Doctorate
Program: Liberal Arts And General; Teacher Preparatory; Professional
Accreditation: NH, MUS, NURSE, PTA, SW, TEAC

01 President ... Dr. Anthony J. ARETZ
05 Chief Academic Officer/Dean Faculty ... Dr. Alan DECOURCY
30 Vice Pres Institutional Advancement ... Mr. Mark C. DISTASI
32 Dean of Students ... Dr. Douglas K. FRIZZELL
35 Assistant Dean of Students ... Mr. Daniel VAN VECHTEN
20 Associate Academic Dean ... Dr. Darla VALE
10 Chief Financial Officer ... Ms. Anne Marie WAGNER
06 Registrar ... Ms. Patsy KENNER
13 Chief Information Officer ... Mr. Keith A. WEBER
29 Director of Alumni Relations ... Ms. Nicki VELDHAUS
37 Director Student Admin Services ... Ms. Kathy KELLY
36 Director Career/Experiential Educ ... Ms. Margaret DAVIS
25 Dir Grants and Research ... Ms. Linda B. LIEBAU
18 Director Buildings & Grounds ... Mr. Dennis YOUNG
09 Director Institutional/Market Rsrch ... Mr. Joseph S. SPORTSMAN
07 Director of Admission ... Ms. Peggy MINNICH
88 Chief Compliance and Risk Officer ... Ms. Linda PANZECA
20 Assistant Academic Dean ... Ms. Judi HEILE
21 Controller Fiscal Operations ... Ms. Liane SZUCS
32 Director Wellness Center ... Ms. Patsy SCHWAIGER
08 Director Library ... Mr. Paul JENKINS
14 Director Instructional Technology ... Ms. Kim HUNTER
19 Director of Campus Police ... Mr. Tim CARNEY
41 Director of Athletics ... Mr. Steve RADCLIFFE
88 Director of Athletic Training ... Dr. Malissa MARTIN
88 Director Learning Center ... Ms. Susan BROGDEN
42 Director of Campus Ministry ... Ms. Andrea STILES
44 Director of Development ... Ms. Lisa ODENBECK
66 Dean of Health Sciences ... Dr. Susan JOHNSON
40 Manager of Bookstore ... Mr. Brad HOFFMAN
28 Coordinator Multicultural Affairs ... Ms. Larisa WRIGHT
50 Dean of Business ... Dr. Charles KRONCKE
53 Interim Dean of Education ... Mr. Paul SALLADA
81 Dean Behavioral/Natural Sciences ... Dr. Diana DAVIS
26 Director of Marketing ... Ms. Kathleen LUNDRIGAN
91 Director Administrative Computing ... Mr. Dan LUKAC
105 Webmaster ... Ms. Carolyn BOLAND
102 Director Donor Corporate Relations ... Ms. Jada MARCUM
44 Coordinator Annual Giving ... Ms. Stephanie HONEBRINK
89 Coordinator First Year Experience ... Dr. Patty MILLS
23 Coordinator Health Services ... Ms. Linda PRUSS

The College of Wooster (E)

1189 Beall Avenue, Wooster OH 44691-2363
County: Wayne FICE Identification: 003037
Unit ID: 206589
Telephone: (330) 263-2000 Carnegie Class: Bac/A&S
FAX Number: (330) 263-2427 Calendar System: Semester
URL: www.wooster.edu
Established: 1866 Annual Undergrad Tuition & Fees: $38,000
Enrollment: 1,855 Coed
Affiliation or Control: Independent Non-Profit IRS Status: 501(c)3
Highest Offering: Baccalaureate
Program: Liberal Arts And General; Teacher Preparatory
Accreditation: NH, MUS, TED

01 President ... Dr. Grant H. CORNWELL
05 Provost ... Dr. Carolyn NEWTON
10 Vice Pres Finance/Bus/Treasurer ... Ms. Laurie W. STICKELMAIER
30 Vice President for Development ... Vacant
84 Vice Pres Enrollment/College Rels ... Dr. Scott FRIEDHOFF
04 Exec Assistant to the President ... Ms. Bettye Jo MASTRINE
26 Assoc VP College Rels & Marketing ... Mr. John HOPKINS
18 Assc VP Facilities & Auxiliaries ... Ms. Jacqueline MIDDLETON
32 Dean of Students ... Mr. Kurt HOLMES
20 Dean Curriculum/Academic Engagement ... Dr. Henry B. KREUZMAN
20 Dean for Faculty Development ... Dr. Heather M. FITZGIBBON
38 Senior Associate Dean of Students ... Ms. Carolyn BUXTON
35 Assoc Dean of Students ... Dr. Anne GATES
35 Assoc Dean of Students ... Ms. Christie KRACKER
28 Ast Dn Students/Co-Dir Ctr for D&GE ... Ms. Susan LEE
85 Dir Office of Intl Student Affairs ... Ms. Ruth LOPEZ
09 Chief Information Planning Officer ... Dr. Ellen FALDUTO
06 Registrar ... Ms. Suzanne BATES
08 Director of Libraries ... Mr. Mark A. CHRISTEL
37 Director of Financial Aid ... Dr. David MILLER
27 Director Office Public Information ... Mr. John FINN
29 Dir of Alumni Rels & Wooster Fund ... Ms. Heidi A. MCCORMICK
36 Director Career Services ... Ms. Lisa KASTOR
35 Dir Student Center/Stdnt Activities ... Mr. Robert RODDA
41 Dir Phys Educ/Athletics/Recreat ... Dr. Keith BECKETT
18 Director Physical Plant Operations ... Mr. Doug LADITKA
19 Director Security/Protective Svcs ... Mr. Steven GLICK
16 Director of Human Resources ... Mr. Gary THOMPSON
39 Director of Residence Life ... Ms. Krista KRONSTEIN
42 Camp Chaplain/Dir Intfth Camp Mins ... Rev. Linda MORGAN-CLEMENT
101 Secretary of College/Chief Staff ... Ms. Angela JOHNSTON

Columbus College of Art & Design (F)

60 Cleveland Avenue, Columbus OH 43215-1758
County: Franklin FICE Identification: 003039
Unit ID: 202170
Telephone: (614) 224-9101 Carnegie Class: Spec/Arts
FAX Number: (614) 222-4040 Calendar System: Semester
URL: www.ccad.edu
Established: 1879 Annual Undergrad Tuition & Fees: $26,112
Enrollment: 1,359 Coed
Affiliation or Control: Independent Non-Profit IRS Status: 501(c)3
Highest Offering: Baccalaureate
Program: Professional; Fine Arts Emphasis
Accreditation: NH, ART, CIDA

01 President ... Mr. Dennison W. GRIFFITH
04 Exec Assistant to the President ... Ms. Sheri LUCAS
05 Provost ... Mr. Kevin J. CONLON
10 Senior Vice President/CFO ... Mr. Jeffrey A. FISHER
30 VP Institutional Advancement ... Ms. Stephanie HIGHTOWER
84 Vice Pres Enrollment Management ... Mr. Jonathan LINDSAY
32 Associate VP & Dean of Students ... Mr. Dwayne TODD
20 Associate Provost ... Ms. Char NORMAN
88 Dean Interior/Industrial Design ... Mr. Carl GARANT
49 Dean Liberal Arts ... Mr. Ed LATHY
88 Dean Visual Communication ... Mr. Richard ASCHENBRAND
60 Dean Media Studies ... Mr. Ron SAKS
57 Dean Foundation Studies & Fine Arts ... Ms. Julie TAGGART
58 Director Graduate Studies ... Mr. Ric PETRY
06 Registrar ... Ms. Michele KIBLER
13 Information Technology Director ... Mr. Tom FAIST
15 Director of Human Resources ... Ms. Barbara DAVIS
08 Head Librarian ... Ms. Gail STORER
19 Chief of Security ... Mr. Wallace TANKSLEY
18 Chief Facilities/Physical Plant ... Mr. Joseph SPYBEY
44 Director of Development ... Ms. Laurie Beth SWEENEY
27 Director Communications & Marketing ... Ms. Melissa RICKSECKER
38 Student Counseling Coordinator ... Ms. Amy SHEVRIN
37 Director Student Financial Aid ... Ms. Anna M. SCHOFIELD
36 Director Career Resources ... Ms. Cynthia GRAVINO

Columbus State Community College (G)

Box 1609, Columbus OH 43216-1609
County: Franklin FICE Identification: 006867
Unit ID: 202222
Telephone: (614) 287-5353 Carnegie Class: Assoc/Pub-U-SC
FAX Number: (614) 287-5113 Calendar System: Quarter
URL: www.cscc.edu
Established: 1963 Annual Undergrad Tuition & Fees (In-State): $2,916
Enrollment: 30,297 Coed
Affiliation or Control: State IRS Status: 501(c)3
Highest Offering: Associate Degree
Program: Occupational
Accreditation: NH, ACBSP, ACFEI, ADNUR, CONST, DH, DIETT, EMT, ENGT, HT, MAC, MLTAD, RAD, SURGT

01 President ... Dr. David T. HARRISON
05 Senior Vice Pres Academic Affairs ... Dr. John COOLEY
10 Sr Vice President & CFO ... Ms. Theresa GEHR
30 Vice Pres Institutional Advancement ... Mr. Will KOPP
13 Vice President Info Technology ... Mr. Hamid DANESH
45 Vice Pres for Knowledge Res/Plng ... Dr. Deborah D. COLEMAN
15 Vice President for Human Resources ... Mr. Timothy WAGNER
32 Vice Pres for Student Affairs ... Dr. Janet ROGERS
84 Dean of Enrollment Services ... Mr. Martin MALIWESKY
12 Interim Dean of Delaware Campus ... Mr. Angelo FROLE
49 Interim Dean of Arts & Sciences ... Ms. Karen MUIR
50 Dean of Technical/Career Programs ... Dr. Polly OWEN

35 Interim Dean Student Life .... Mr. Wayne COCCHI
44 Executive Director for Development .... Mr. Matt KELLY
14 Director of Data Center .... Mr. Etienne MARTIN
21 Director of Business Services .... Ms. Aletha SHIPLEY
06 Director of Records & Registration .... Dr. Regina A. PEAL
37 Dir Enroll/Fin Aid/Veterans Svcs .... Mr. David METZ
19 Director of Public Safety .... Dr. John NESTOR
18 Director of Facilities Services .... Mr. Paul GOGGIN
40 Director of Bookstore .... Vacant
28 Director of Diversity .... Ms. Renee HAMPTON
08 Director Educational Resources Ctr .... Mr. Bruce MASSIS
07 Director of Admissions .... Ms. Tari BLANEY

Cuyahoga Community College (A)

700 Carnegie Avenue, Cleveland OH 44115-2878

County: Cuyahoga FICE Identification: 003040
Unit ID: 202356
Telephone: (216) 987-4000 Carnegie Class: Assoc/Pub-U-MC
FAX Number: (216) 566-5977 Calendar System: Semester
URL: www.tri-c.edu
Established: 1963 Annual Undergrad Tuition & Fees (In-District): $2,537
Enrollment: 31,683 Coed
Affiliation or Control: State/Local IRS Status: 501(c)3
Highest Offering: Associate Degree
Program: Occupational; 2-Year Principally Bachelor's Creditable
Accreditation: NH, ACFEI, ADNUR, ARCPA, DH, DIETT, DMS, EEG, ENGT, MAC, MLTAD, NMT, OTA, POLYT, PTAA, RAD, SURGT

01 President .... Dr. Jerry Sue THORNTON
05 Exec Vice Pres Acadmic/Student Affs .... Dr. Jacquelyn JOSEPH-SILVERSTEIN
10 Exec Vice Pres Admin and Finance .... Dr. Craig FOLTIN
103 Exec Vice Pres Workforce & Econ Dev .... Ms. Susan MUHA
12 Campus President West Shore .... Dr. Michael J. THOMSON
12 Corporate College President .... Vacant
12 Campus President/VP West .... Dr. Patricia ROWELL
12 Campus President/VP Metro .... Dr. Michael SCHOOP
12 Campus President/VP East .... Dr. Belinda MILES
21 Vice Pres Finance/Business Services .... Mr. Mark POLATAJKO
76 Vice Pres Medical Educ Programs .... Dr. Patricia GRAY
15 Vice President Human Resources .... Ms. Judith MCMULLEN
31 Vice Pres Access & Col Pathways .... Mr. Terry BUTLER
30 Vice Pres Development Office .... Ms. Gloria MOOSMANN
13 Vice Pres/Chief Info Officer .... Mr. Gerard HOURIGAN
32 Vice Pres Student Sucess .... Vacant
09 VP Inst Planning/Effectiveness .... Dr. Jennifer SPIELVOGEL
86 Vice Pres Govt Affair/Comm Outreach .... Ms. Claire ROSACCO
18 Vice Pres Facilities Devel & Opers .... Mr. Peter MAC EWAN
84 Vice Pres Enrollment Management .... Mr. Pete ROSS
26 Vice Pres Marketing/Communications .... Mr. Alan MORAN
88 Vice President Sustainability .... Dr. Kevin SNAPE
43 Vice President Legal Services .... Ms. Rebecca MCMAHON
20 Vice Pres Academic Affairs .... Ms. Sandy ROBINSON
88 Vice Pres Business Development .... Mr. Harlan JACKSON
88 Associate VP Faculty Affairs & Prof .... Ms. Sandra MCKNIGHT
106 Associate VP eLearning/Innovation .... Ms. Christina ROYAL
19 Associate VP Public Safety .... Chief Clayton HARRIS
88 Exec Dir Business Continuity .... Mr. Tom SOMERVILLE
21 Exec Dir Acct/Finance Operation .... Mr. Michael ABOUSERHAL
88 Exec Director Media Engineering .... Mr. Robert BRYAN
88 Exec Dir Information Technology Svc .... Mr. Edward KLEINERT
84 Executive Director Enrollment Opers .... Ms. Angela JOHNSON
21 Exec Dir Plant Operations .... Mr. Blair BOSWORTH
88 Exec Dir Veteran Services/Programs .... Mr. Richard DE CHANT
26 Exec Dir Marketing .... Ms. Paula BAUGHN
21 Exec Dir Campus Svcs & Retail .... Mr. Chris MOIR
51 Executive Dirctor Cmty Cont Educ .... Ms. Sharon STYFFE
88 Exec Dir Access/College Pathways .... Mr. Kenneth HALE
96 Executive Dir Supplier Manage Svcs .... Ms. Cynthia LEITSON
50 Exec Dir Dev Corp Business .... Mr. Jeff HALL
44 Exec Dir Individual Giving .... Ms. Carol WOLF
103 Exec Dir Workforce Solutions .... Mr. Albert LEWIS
36 Exec Dir Career Dev & Trng Center .... Ms. Treacy CROWLEY
20 Dean Academic Affairs East .... Dr. John W. MARR, JR.
20 Dean Academic Affairs West .... Dr. Dennis SMITH
20 Dean Academic Affairs Metro .... Dr. Peggy BRADFORD
32 Dean Student Affairs West .... Ms. Diana DEL ROSARIO
32 Dean Student Affairs East .... Dr. Mel A. MAY
32 Dean Student Affairs Metro .... Ms. Karen MILLER
66 Dean Nursing Metro .... Dr. Marsha ATKINS
88 Dean Creative Arts .... Dr. Brian BETHUNE
88 Dean & GM Hospitality Mgmt .... Mr. Gregory FORTE
32 Dean Student Affairs West Shore .... Ms. Ann PROUDFIT
76 Assoc Dean Health & Science East .... Dr. Ross SANTELL
76 Assoc Dean Health & Science Metro .... Ms. Barbara MIKUSZEWSKI
76 Assoc Dean Health & Science West .... Dr. Donna MOORE-RAMSEY
81 Assoc Dean Math & Applied Tech West .... Dr. Guy HUTT
49 Assoc Dean Social Sciences West .... Dr. Carol FRANKLIN
49 Assoc Dean Liberal Arts East .... Mr. Vince DIMARIA
49 Assoc Dean Liberal Arts Metro .... Dr. Jocelyn LADNER-MATHIS
49 Assoc Dean Liberal Arts West .... Mr. Mark CURTIS-CHAVEZ
50 Assoc Dean Business/Math Tech Metro .... Dr. Pamela ELLISON
66 Assoc Dean Nursing .... Ms. Irene MEYER
88 Assoc Dean Academic Affairs .... Mr. Robert SEARSON
72 Assoc Dean Business & Technology .... Dr. Lorraine HARTLEY
54 Assoc Dean Engineering .... Mr. Dhirendra DAMJI
106 Assistant Dean eLearning .... Mr. Charles DULL
88 Asst Dean Honors & Exper Learning .... Mr. Herbert MAUSSER
35 Asst Dean Student Affairs .... Ms. Laura FINSON
35 Asst Dean Student Affairs .... Ms. Denise MCCORY
35 Asst Dean Student Affairs .... Ms. Julia RUANE
55 Asst Dean Academic Affairs .... Ms. Delia BOBER

Davis College (B)

4747 Monroe Street, Toledo OH 43623-4389

County: Lucas FICE Identification: 004855
Unit ID: 202435
Telephone: (419) 473-2700 Carnegie Class: Assoc/PrivFP
FAX Number: (419) 473-2472 Calendar System: Quarter
URL: www.daviscollege.edu
Established: 1858 Annual Undergrad Tuition & Fees: $15,450
Enrollment: 549 Coed
Affiliation or Control: Proprietary IRS Status: Proprietary
Highest Offering: Associate Degree
Program: Occupational; 2-Year Principally Bachelor's Creditable
Accreditation: NH, MAC

01 President .... Diane BRUNNER
05 Vice President Academic Affairs .... Vicky RYAN
32 Vice President of Student Services .... Mary RYAN
06 Registrar .... Marsha KLINGBEIL
37 Director Student Financial Aid .... Kelly PARKER
07 Director of Admissions .... Dana STERN
36 Director of Student Placement .... Nick NIGRO
04 Assistant to the President .... Jane MULLIKIN
13 Information Services Director .... Ann SHEIDLER
29 Director Alumni Relations .... Mary RYAN
31 Chief Community Relations Officer .... Tim BRUNNER
18 Chief Facilities/Physical Plant .... Greg RIPPKE
08 Librarian .... Peggy PETERSON-SENIUK
96 Purchasing .... Marilyn BOVIA

Daymar College-Chillicothe (C)

1410 Industrial Drive, Chillicothe OH 45601-3977

County: Ross FICE Identification: 020568
Unit ID: 205568
Telephone: (740) 774-6300 Carnegie Class: Assoc/PrivFP
FAX Number: (740) 774-6317 Calendar System: Quarter
URL: www.daymarcollege.edu
Established: 1962 Annual Undergrad Tuition & Fees: $16,610
Enrollment: 251 Coed
Affiliation or Control: Proprietary IRS Status: Proprietary
Highest Offering: Associate Degree
Program: Occupational; Technical Emphasis
Accreditation: ACICS

01 President .... Mr. Mark GABIS
12 Campus President .... Ms. Teresa BEESON
07 Senior Director of Admissions .... Ms. Robin RE
36 Dir of Career Svc & Cmty Relations .... Mr. Scott NEFF
37 Director Student Financial Services .... Ms. Lisa REED
06 Registrar .... Ms. Emily BOGGS
32 Director of Student Services .... Mr. Bob ARCHER

Daymar College-Jackson (D)

980 East Main, Jackson OH 45640

County: Jackson Identification: 666468
Unit ID: 205531
Telephone: (740) 286-1554 Carnegie Class: Assoc/PrivFP
FAX Number: (740) 286-4476 Calendar System: Quarter
URL: www.daymarcollege.edu
Established: 1976 Annual Undergrad Tuition & Fees: $16,610
Enrollment: 209 Coed
Affiliation or Control: Proprietary IRS Status: Proprietary
Highest Offering: Associate Degree
Program: Occupational
Accreditation: ACICS

01 Campus Director .... Dr. David SHELPMAN

† Branch campus of Daymar College, Chillicothe, OH.

Daymar College-Lancaster (E)

1522 Sheridan Drive, Lancaster OH 43130-1303

County: Fairfield Identification: 666469
Unit ID: 205559
Telephone: (740) 687-6126 Carnegie Class: Assoc/PrivFP
FAX Number: (740) 687-0431 Calendar System: Quarter
URL: www.daymarcollege.edu
Established: 1984 Annual Undergrad Tuition & Fees: $16,610
Enrollment: 145 Coed
Affiliation or Control: Proprietary IRS Status: Proprietary
Highest Offering: Associate Degree
Program: Occupational; Technical Emphasis
Accreditation: ACICS

07 Director of Admissions .... Ms. Robin RE

† Branch campus of Daymar College, Chillicothe, OH.

Daymar College-New Boston (F)

3879 Rhodes Avenue, Suite A,
New Boston OH 45662-4900

County: Scioto Identification: 667082
Unit ID: 205522
Telephone: (740) 456-4124 Carnegie Class: Not Classified
FAX Number: (740) 456-5163 Calendar System: Quarter
URL: www.daymarcollege.edu
Established: N/A Annual Undergrad Tuition & Fees: $15,600
Enrollment: 205 Coed
Affiliation or Control: Proprietary IRS Status: Proprietary
Highest Offering: Baccalaureate
Program: Technical Emphasis
Accreditation: ACICS

01 President .... Mark A. GABIS
12 Campus Director .... Rebecca MOWERY

† Branch campus of Daymar College, Chillicothe, TN.

The Defiance College (G)

701 N Clinton Street, Defiance OH 43512-1695

County: Defiance FICE Identification: 003041
Unit ID: 202514
Telephone: (419) 784-4010 Carnegie Class: Bac/Diverse
FAX Number: (419) 784-0426 Calendar System: Semester
URL: www.defiance.edu
Established: 1850 Annual Undergrad Tuition & Fees: $25,300
Enrollment: 1,083 Coed
Affiliation or Control: United Church Of Christ IRS Status: 501(c)3
Highest Offering: Master's
Program: Liberal Arts And General; Teacher Preparatory
Accreditation: NH, IACBE, SW, TED

01 President .... Mr. Mark C. GORDON
05 Provost/VP for Academic Affairs .... Dr. Barbara SCHIRMER
30 Vice Pres Institutional Advancement .... Mr. Richard A. PEJEAU
10 Vice Pres for Finance & Management .... Mrs. Lois N. MCCULLOUGH
32 VP Stdnt Engagement/Dean of Stdnts .... Dr. Kenneth A. WETSTEIN
84 Vice Pres for Enrollment Management .... Mr. Michael SUZO
88 Dean McMaster Sch Adv Hum .... Mrs. Mary Ann STUDER
20 Associate Academic Dean .... Dr. Donald S. KNUEVE
07 Director of Admissions .... Mr. Brad HARSHA
15 Director of Human Resources .... Ms. Mary E. BURKHOLDER
29 Director Alumni and Parent Relation .... Mr. David PLANT
08 Dir of Library and Instr Resource .... Mr. Andrew WHITIS
26 Director Public Relations/Marketing .... Mrs. Kathy M. PUNCHES
14 Director of Computer Services .... Mr. Todd R. HARPEST
06 Registrar .... Mrs. Mariah ORZOLEK
36 Director of Career Development .... Mrs. Lisa MARSALEK
37 Director of Financial Aid .... Mrs. Amy FRANCIS
41 Athletic Director .... Ms. Jenni MORRISON
42 Campus Minister/Church Relations .... Rev. Janice L. BECHTEL
28 Dir Intercultural Relations .... Ms. Mercedes CLAY
58 Dir Center for Adult/Graduate Pgms .... Ms. Sally B. BISSELL
39 Director of Residence Life .... Ms. Kim LAMMERS
18 Director of Physical Plant .... Mr. James CORESSEL
21 Director of Accounting .... Mrs. Kristine BOLAND

Denison University (H)

100 W College Street, Granville OH 43023-1359

County: Licking FICE Identification: 003042
Unit ID: 202523
Telephone: (740) 587-0810 Carnegie Class: Bac/A&S
FAX Number: (740) 587-6417 Calendar System: Semester
URL: www.denison.edu
Established: 1831 Annual Undergrad Tuition & Fees: $40,210
Enrollment: 2,142 Coed
Affiliation or Control: Independent Non-Profit IRS Status: 501(c)3
Highest Offering: Baccalaureate
Program: Liberal Arts And General
Accreditation: NH

01 President .... Dr. Dale T. KNOBEL
05 Provost .... Dr. Bradley W. BATEMAN
20 Associate Provost .... Dr. Susan P. GARCIA
20 Associate Provost .... Dr. Kimberly A. COPLIN
20 Associate Provost .... Dr. Toni C. KING
10 Vice President Finance & Management .... Mr. Seth H. PATTON
30 VP Institutional Advancement .... Ms. Julia BEYER HOUPT
32 Vice President Student Affairs .... Dr. Laurel B. KENNEDY
07 Vice Pres/Director of Admissions .... Mr. Perry H. ROBINSON
89 Dean of First-Year Students .... Dr. Matthew KRETCHMAR
35 Dean of Students .... Dr. Laura A. NEFF
06 Registrar .... Ms. Yadigar COLLINS
08 Interim Director of Libraries .... Ms. Mary Webb PROPHET
37 Dir of Financial Aid & Student Empl .... Ms. Nancy Z. HOOVER
14 Dir Information Technology Services .... Ms. Lisa BAZLEY
15 Director of Human Resources .... Mr. Jim ABLES
18 Director of Facilities Services .... Mr. Arthur J. CHONKO
19 Dir Security/Safety/Risk Mgmt .... Mr. Garret MOORE
26 Admin Dir of Univ Communications .... Mr. Jack HIRE
88 Creative Dir of Univ Communications .... Mr. Paul A. PEGHER
29 Director of Alumni Relations .... Mr. Steven R. CRAWFORD
36 Dir Career Exploration & Dev .... Ms. Kathleen I. POWELL
38 Director Health/Counseling Services .... Dr. Sonya M. TURNER-MURRAY
40 Manager of Bookstore/Business Svc .... Mr. Joseph E. WARMKE
42 Chaplain/Director of Religious Life .... Rev. Mark ORTEN
100 Special Asst to Pres/Chief of Staff .... Dr. Joyce MEREDITH
93 Dir Multicultural Stdnt Affs/Ast Dn .... Mr. Erik S. FARLEY
11 Director of Administrative Services .... Ms. Veronica HINTZ
09 Director of Institutional Research .... Dr. Todd M. JAMISON
41 Director of Athletics .... Ms. Nan CARNEY-DEBORD
88 Chief Investment Officer .... Ms. Adele N. GORRILLA

DevRy University - Cincinnati (A)

8800 Governors Hill Drive, Ste 100,
Cincinnati OH 45249-1367

County: Hamilton | Identification: 666563
Telephone: (513) 583-5000 | Carnegie Class: Not Classified
FAX Number: (513) 583-5035 | Calendar System: Semester
URL: www.devry.edu
Established: 1931 | Annual Undergrad Tuition & Fees: $15,294
Enrollment: 453 | Coed
Affiliation or Control: Proprietary | IRS Status: Proprietary
Highest Offering: Master's
Program: Professional; Business Emphasis
Accreditation: &NH

01 Campus Director .... Graham IRWIN

† Regional accreditation is carried under the parent institution in Downers Grove, IL.

DevRy University - Columbus Campus (B)

1350 Alum Creek Drive, Columbus OH 43209-2705

County: Franklin | FICE Identification: 003099
Unit ID: 202541
Telephone: (614) 253-7291 | Carnegie Class: Master's M
FAX Number: (614) 258-6773 | Calendar System: Semester
URL: www.devry.edu
Established: 1931 | Annual Undergrad Tuition & Fees: $15,294
Enrollment: 3,807 | Coed
Affiliation or Control: Proprietary | IRS Status: Proprietary
Highest Offering: Master's
Program: Occupational; Business Emphasis
Accreditation: &NH, ENGT

01 Metro President .... Ms. Scarlett HOWERY
32 Dean of Career and Student Services .... Ms. Kathy HOFF
08 Director of Library Services .... Mr. Bruce WEAVER
07 Director of Admissions .... Ms. Rachel DUNPHY
05 Dean of Academic Affairs .... Ms. Marilyn WIGGAM
72 Dean of Electronics .... Mr. Rasoul ESFAHANI
21 Director of Student Finance .... Ms. Jeanne K. FARNLACHER
06 Registrar .... Ms. Cynthia PRICE
15 HR Business Partner .... Mr. Wayne A. ANDERSON
36 Director of Career Services .... Ms. Amy RAAB

† Regional accreditation is carried under the parent institution in Downers Grove, IL.

DevRy University - Columbus North Center (C)

8800 Lyra Drive, Suite 120, Columbus OH 43240-2100

County: Franklin | Identification: 666217
Unit ID: 441140
Telephone: (614) 854-7500 | Carnegie Class: Not Classified
FAX Number: (614) 846-5780 | Calendar System: Semester
URL: www.devry.edu
Established: 2001 | Annual Undergrad Tuition & Fees: $15,294
Enrollment: 639 | Coed
Affiliation or Control: Proprietary | IRS Status: Proprietary
Highest Offering: Master's
Program: Occupational; Professional; Business Emphasis
Accreditation: &NH

01 Campus Dean .... Ms. Christine HOOVER

† Regional accreditation is carried under the parent institution in Downers Grove, IL.

DevRy University - Dayton (D)

3610 Pentagon Boulevard, Suite 100,
Dayton OH 45431-1708

County: Greene | Identification: 666564
Telephone: (937) 320-3200 | Carnegie Class: Not Classified
FAX Number: (937) 320-9380 | Calendar System: Semester
URL: www.devry.edu
Established: 1931 | Annual Undergrad Tuition & Fees: $15,294
Enrollment: 497 | Coed
Affiliation or Control: Proprietary | IRS Status: Proprietary
Highest Offering: Master's
Program: Professional; Business Emphasis
Accreditation: &NH

01 Center Dean .... Ken BAKER

† Regional accreditation is carried under the parent institution in Downers Grove, IL.

DevRy University - Seven Hills (E)

4141 Rockside Road, Suite 110, Seven Hills OH 44131

County: Cuyahoga | Identification: 666565
Telephone: (216) 328-8754 | Carnegie Class: Not Classified
FAX Number: (216) 328-8764 | Calendar System: Semester
URL: www.devry.edu
Established: 1931 | Annual Undergrad Tuition & Fees: $15,294
Enrollment: 691 | Coed
Affiliation or Control: Proprietary | IRS Status: Proprietary
Highest Offering: Master's
Program: Professional; Business Emphasis
Accreditation: &NH

01 Campus Director .... Joe ONORIO

† Regional accreditation is carried under the parent institution in Downers Grove, IL.

Eastern Gateway Community College - Jefferson County Campus (F)

4000 Sunset Boulevard, Steubenville OH 43952-3594

County: Jefferson | FICE Identification: 007275
Unit ID: 203331
Telephone: (740) 264-5591 | Carnegie Class: Assoc/Pub-R-M
FAX Number: (740) 264-1338 | Calendar System: Semester
URL: www.egcc.edu
Established: 1966 | Annual Undergrad Tuition & Fees (In-District): $2,790
Enrollment: 2,209 | Coed
Affiliation or Control: State/Local | IRS Status: 501(c)3
Highest Offering: Associate Degree
Program: Occupational; 2-Year Principally Bachelor's Creditable
Accreditation: NH, DA, MAC, MLTAD, RAD

01 President .... Dr. Laura M. MEEKS
05 Exec Vice Pres Academic/Stdnt Affs .... Dr. James BABER
10 Vice Pres Business Services/Treas .... Mr. James J. MCGRAIL, III
11 Vice Pres Administrative Services .... Mr. James E. MORGAN
46 Vice Pres Strategic Initiatives .... Mr. Thomas ROMACK
84 Dean Enrollment Management .... Ms. Patty Jo STURCH
76 Dean Health & Biological Sciences .... Mr. Jerrold SILVER
20 Int Dean/Library Services .... Mrs. Lois T. REKOWSKI
21 Controller .... Mr. C. Michael PAYNE
07 Director of Admissions .... Ms. Kristen TAYLOR
26 Dir Public Information/Web Coord .... Mrs. Ann M. KOON
37 Director Student Info/Financial Aid .... Ms. Kelly WILSON
103 Dir Workforce/Community Outreach .... Ms. Andrea BELL
14 Director Technology Services .... Mrs. Karen L. TUCCI
36 Director Career Services/Alumni .... Mrs. Judith MILLER
40 Director of Bookstore .... Mrs. Judith LUDE
21 Director Student Billing/Payroll .... Ms. Tonya LOGAN
18 Director Building & Grounds .... Mr. Julius J. DZIEWATKOSKI

Edison State Community College (G)

1973 Edison Drive, Piqua OH 45356-9239

County: Miami | FICE Identification: 012750
Unit ID: 202648
Telephone: (937) 778-8600 | Carnegie Class: Assoc/Pub-S-SC
FAX Number: (937) 778-1920 | Calendar System: Semester
URL: www.edisonohio.edu
Established: 1973 | Annual Undergrad Tuition & Fees (In-State): $3,819
Enrollment: 3,558 | Coed
Affiliation or Control: State | IRS Status: 501(c)3
Highest Offering: Associate Degree
Program: Occupational; 2-Year Principally Bachelor's Creditable
Accreditation: NH, ADNUR, MAC, MLTAD, PTAA

01 President .... Dr. Cristobal O. VALDEZ
04 Admin Asst to the President .... Ms. Heather LANHAM
05 Senior VP of Academic Affairs .... Ms. Sharon S. BROWN
11 VP of Administration & Finance .... Mr. Daniel R. REKE
90 VP of Information Technology .... Mr. David GANSZ
30 VP for Institutional Advancement .... Ms. Terri L. JACOMET
15 VP of Strategic Human Resources .... Mrs. Linda M. PELTIER
07 Director of Admissions .... Ms. Teresa ROTH
49 Dean of Arts and Science .... Mr. Richard S. BRITTEN
50 Dean of Business/Workforce Develop .... Ms. Shirley MOORE
69 Dean of Health/Public Services .... Ms. Gwendolyn A. STEVENSON
32 Dean of Student Affairs .... Mr. Scott M. BURNAM
09 Director of Institutional Research .... Ms. Rebecca P. TELFORD
38 Dean of Student Success .... Ms. Margaret D. SYKES
72 Dean of IT and Engineering .... Ms. Patricia A. ROSS
21 Controller .... Ms. Debbie A. HIRTZINGER
41 Coord of Recruiting & Athletics .... Mr. Chip J. HARE
37 Director of Financial Aid .... Ms. Kathi S. RICHARDS
26 Dir of Mktg/Community Relations .... Mr. Ryan C. HONEYMAN
07 Coord of Admissions/Activities .... Mr. Sean P. FORD

ETI Technical College of Niles (H)

2076-86 Youngstown-Warren Road, Niles OH 44446-4398

County: Trumbull | FICE Identification: 030790
Unit ID: 200590
Telephone: (330) 652-9919 | Carnegie Class: Assoc/PrivFP
FAX Number: (330) 652-4399 | Calendar System: Semester
URL: www.eticollege.edu
Established: 1989 | Annual Undergrad Tuition & Fees: $8,508
Enrollment: 276 | Coed
Affiliation or Control: Proprietary | IRS Status: Proprietary
Highest Offering: Associate Degree
Program: Occupational; 2-Year Principally Bachelor's Creditable
Accreditation: ACCSC

01 Director .... Mrs. Renee ZUZOLO
07 Director of Admissions .... Mrs. Diane MARSTELLER
37 Director Financial Aid .... Ms. Kay MADIGAN

Fortis College (I)

555 E Alex-Bell Road, Centerville OH 45459-6120

County: Montgomery | FICE Identification: 021907
Unit ID: 205179
Telephone: (937) 433-3410 | Carnegie Class: Assoc/PrivFP
FAX Number: (937) 435-6516 | Calendar System: Semester
URL: www.fortiscollege.edu
Established: 1970 | Annual Undergrad Tuition & Fees: $10,035
Enrollment: 1,107 | Coed
Affiliation or Control: Proprietary | IRS Status: Proprietary
Highest Offering: Associate Degree
Program: Occupational; 2-Year Principally Bachelor's Creditable
Accreditation: ACCSC, ADNUR, MAC

01 President .... Richard RUCKER
11 Director of Administration .... Terry FARRIS
05 Director Education .... Claude SMITH
07 Director Admissions .... Tony WALLACE
37 Director Financial Aid .... Tom BARKER

Fortis College (J)

2545 Bailey Road, Cuyahoga Falls OH 44221-2949

County: Summit | FICE Identification: 009412
Unit ID: 204307
Telephone: (330) 923-9959 | Carnegie Class: Assoc/PrivFP
FAX Number: (330) 923-0886 | Calendar System: Other
URL: www.fortis.edu
Established: 1922 | Annual Undergrad Tuition & Fees: $18,100
Enrollment: 340 | Coed
Affiliation or Control: Proprietary | IRS Status: Proprietary
Highest Offering: Associate Degree
Program: Occupational
Accreditation: ACCSC, DA

01 Director .... Ms. Carson BURKE

Fortis College (K)

653 Enterprise Parkway, Ravenna OH 44266-8058

County: Portage | FICE Identification: 023036
Unit ID: 201399
Telephone: (330) 297-7319 | Carnegie Class: Assoc/PrivFP
FAX Number: (330) 296-2159 | Calendar System: Quarter
URL: www.fortis.edu
Established: 1922 | Annual Undergrad Tuition & Fees: $11,950
Enrollment: 415 | Coed
Affiliation or Control: Proprietary | IRS Status: Proprietary
Highest Offering: Associate Degree
Program: Occupational; Business Emphasis
Accreditation: ACICS

01 Campus Director .... Ms. Sonya HARTBURG

Fortis College (L)

4151 Executive Parkway, Suite 120,
Westerville OH 43081-3860

County: Franklin | Identification: 666602
Unit ID: 450058
Telephone: (614) 882-2551 | Carnegie Class: Not Classified
FAX Number: (614) 882-2914 | Calendar System: Other
URL: www.fortis.edu
Established: 2010 | Annual Undergrad Tuition & Fees: $12,919
Enrollment: 598 | Coed
Affiliation or Control: Proprietary | IRS Status: Proprietary
Highest Offering: Associate Degree
Program: Occupational; 2-Year Principally Bachelor's Creditable
Accreditation: ABHES, RAD

01 President .... Mr. Marty EHRENBERG

Franciscan University of Steubenville (M)

1235 University Boulevard, Steubenville OH 43952-1763

County: Jefferson | FICE Identification: 003036
Unit ID: 205957
Telephone: (740) 283-3771 | Carnegie Class: Master's M
FAX Number: (740) 283-6472 | Calendar System: Semester
URL: www.franciscan.edu
Established: 1946 | Annual Undergrad Tuition & Fees: $20,800
Enrollment: 2,332 | Coed
Affiliation or Control: Roman Catholic | IRS Status: 501(c)3
Highest Offering: Master's
Program: Liberal Arts And General; Religious Emphasis
Accreditation: NH, NUR, SW, TED

01 President .... Rev. Terence HENRY, TOR
00 Chancellor .... Vacant
03 Executive Vice President .... Dr. Robert G. FILBY
05 Vice President for Academic Affairs .... Dr. Daniel KEMPTON
10 Vice President for Finance .... Mr. David M. SKIVIAT
30 Vice President for Advancement .... Mr. Michael HERNON
31 Vice Pres for Community Relations .... Rev. Richard DAVIS, TOR
46 Vice Pres for Mission Effectiveness .... Vacant
15 VP of Human Resources/Legal Counsel .... Mr. Adam SCURTI
32 Vice President of Student Life .... Mr. David A. SCHMIESING

84 Vice Pres of Enrollment Management ....Mr. Joel S. RECZNIK
88 Religious Administrator ....Rev. Richard DAVIS, TOR
42 University Chaplain ....Rev. Dominic SCOTTO, TOR
20 Asst Dean for Advising & Eve Div ....Mrs. Virginia L. ZORIC
13 Exec Dir of Information Technology ....Mr. Kevin G. SEBOLT
35 Asst Vice Pres of Student Life ....Ms. Catherine J. HECK
08 Director of Library ....Mr. William JAKUB
88 Exec Director Christian Outreach ....Mr. Mark H. NEHRBAS
44 Director of Planned Giving ....Dr. Mark E. RECZNIK
30 Director of Development ....Mr. Michael ANDREOLA
29 Director of Alumni Relations ....Mr. Timothy J. DELANEY
26 Director of Public Relations ....Miss Lisa M. FERGUSON
07 Director of Admissions ....Mrs. Margaret WEBER
07 Director of Graduate Enrollment ....Mr. Mark T. MCGUIRE
06 Registrar ....Mrs. Kathryn REEHL
37 Dir of Financial Aid/Student Accts ....Mr. John L. HERRMANN
09 Institutional Research Manager ....Mr. Mark A. ERSTE
21 Controller ....Mr. John A. STEITZ
96 Director of Business Services ....Ms. Marlene K. TERPENNING
40 Bookstore Manager ....Mr. John RECZNIK
91 Data Processing Manager ....Mr. Vince E. CARTLEDGE
16 Director of Human Resources ....Mr. Brenan PERGI
18 Director Physical Plant Services ....Mr. Joseph P. MCGURN
88 Director of Student Outreach ....Rev. Laurence UHLMAN, TOR
88 Director of Chapel Ministries ....Mr. Robert PALLADINO
88 Director of JCW Center/Planning ....Mrs. Kathy L. MUSCARI
104 Dir of Study Abroad/Internatl Pgms ....Miss Mary Beth COEN
38 Director of Counseling ....Mr. Joseph A. LOIZZO
41 Director of Athletics ....Mr. Christopher L. LEDYARD
36 Director Career Planning/Placement .....Mrs. Nancy S. RONEVICH
73 Director MA Theology Program ....Rev. Daniel J. PATTEE, TOR
50 Director MBA Program ....Mr. Joseph ZORIC
83 Director MA Counseling Program ....Dr. Milo C. MILBURN
53 Director MS Education Program ....Dr. Charles JOYCE
88 Director MA Philosophy Program ....Dr. Mark ROBERTS
90 Coord Academic Computer Services .Ms. Sandy M. RADVANSKY
28 Director of Diversity ....Vacant
66 Director MS Nursing ....Dr. Carolyn MILLER

Franklin University (A)

201 S Grant Avenue, Columbus OH 43215-5399
County: Franklin FICE Identification: 003046
Unit ID: 202806
Telephone: (614) 797-4700 Carnegie Class: Spec/Bus
FAX Number: N/A Calendar System: Trimester
URL: www.franklin.edu
Established: 1902 Annual Undergrad Tuition & Fees: $11,250
Enrollment: 8,018 Coed
Affiliation or Control: Independent Non-Profit IRS Status: 501(c)3
Highest Offering: Master's
Program: Professional; Business Emphasis
Accreditation: NH, IACBE

01 President ....Dr. David R. DECKER
11 Sr VP Adminstration/Chief of Staff ....Ms. Jane L. ROBINSON
05 Provost/Sr VP for Academic Affairs ....Dr. Christopher L. WASHINGTON
12 Director Indianapolis Location ....Ms. Marnie GLANNER
45 Sr Vice Pres Planning/Global Pgms ....Mr. Klaus HABERICH
27 VP Marketing/Domestic Expansions ....Ms. Linda M. STEELE
30 Vice Pres University Advancement ....Ms. Bonnie SMITH QUIST
15 Vice President for Human Resources .....Ms. Christi CABUNGCAL
09 VP Accred/Institutional Effective ....Dr. Pamela SHAY
22 VP for Institutional Compliance ....Ms. Evelyn LEVINO
04 Executive Assistant to President ....Ms. Bonnie MCCANN
32 Dean of Students ....Mr. Billy MOLASSO
20 Dean of Academic Affairs ....Vacant
20 Asst Dean Academic Affairs ....Mr. Wayne C. MILLER
88 Assoc Dean for Academic Projects ....Dr. Terry BOYD
88 Assoc Dean Cntr Professional Trng ....Dr. Garry MCDANIEL
10 Chief Financial Officer ....Mr. Marvin BRISKEY
13 Chief Information Officer ....Mr. Rick SUNDERMAN
20 Dir of Academic Support Services ....Ms. Susanne SMITH
06 Registrar ....Mr. Frank YANCHAK
08 Director of Library Services ....Mr. John CANTER
37 Director of Financial Aid ....Ms. Goldie LANGLEY
46 Director of Strategic Relations ....Ms. Jody NOREEN
35 Dir Undergradute Student Services ....Ms. Wendi ROBINSON
35 Dir Graduate Stdnt Svcs/Operations ....Ms. Leslie GIBBS
88 Executive Director Campus Services ....Mr. Patrick BENNETT
84 Exec Director of Enrollment Mgmt ....Mr. Scott BOOTH
12 Exec Dir Domestic Expan/Reg Cmps ....Mr. Bill CHAN
18 Director of Facilities ....Mr. Carl BROWN
26 Director of Public Relations ....Ms. Sherry MERCURIO
29 Director of Alumni Relations ....Ms. Julie BARRY
96 Director of Purchasing ....Mr. Bob DONAHUE
28 Director of Benefits ....Ms. Brenda LISTON
24 Director of Student Learning Center .... Mr. Christopher FIELDS
09 Dir of Institutional Effectiveness ....Ms. Jan LYDDON
88 Director of Teaching Effectiveness ....Vacant
104 Dir International Administration ....Mr. Michael STEPIEN
26 Director of Marketing ....Vacant
49 Dean Arts/Science & Technology ....Dr. Keith GROFF
50 Dean College of Business ....Dr. Ross WIRTH
72 Dean Acad Technology & Innovation ....Mr. Ron MORGAN

Gallipolis Career College (B)

1176 Jackson Pike, Suite 312, Gallipolis OH 45631-2600
County: Gallia FICE Identification: 030079
Unit ID: 205513
Telephone: (740) 446-4367 Carnegie Class: Assoc/PrivFP
FAX Number: (740) 446-4124 Calendar System: Quarter
URL: www.gallipoliscareercollege.edu
Established: 1962 Annual Undergrad Tuition & Fees: $22,800
Enrollment: 155 Coed
Affiliation or Control: Proprietary IRS Status: Proprietary
Highest Offering: Associate Degree
Program: 2-Year Principally Bachelor's Creditable; Business Emphasis
Accreditation: ACICS

01 President ....Mr. Robert L. SHIREY
05 Director ....Mr. Bo SHIREY
37 Director Student Financial Aid ....Mrs. Jeanette SHIREY
07 Director Admissions ....Mr. Mick CHILDS

God's Bible School and College (C)

1810 Young Street, Cincinnati OH 45202-6838
County: Hamilton FICE Identification: 022205
Unit ID: 202903
Telephone: (513) 721-7944 Carnegie Class: Spec/Faith
FAX Number: (513) 721-1357 Calendar System: Semester
URL: www.gbs.edu
Established: 1900 Annual Undergrad Tuition & Fees: $6,560
Enrollment: 310 Coed
Affiliation or Control: Interdenominational IRS Status: 501(c)3
Highest Offering: Baccalaureate
Program: Religious Emphasis
Accreditation: NH, BI

01 President ....Dr. Michael R. AVERY
05 Vice President Academic Affairs ....Dr. Ken R. FARMER
32 Vice President Student Development ....Mr. Richard MILES
30 Director Institutional Advancement ....Mrs. Faith AVERY
06 Registrar .... Mr. Christopher LAMBETH
08 Head Librarian ....Mr. Joshua AVERY
10 Director of Finance ....Mr. David FREDERICK
37 Director of Financial Aid ....Mr. Stephen BUCKLAND
18 Campus Administrator ....Mr. Tom BUTCHER
26 Director of Public Relations ....Mr. Don DAVISON
13 Coordinator Information Services ....Mr. Steve HARMS
07 Student Recruiter ....Mr. Adam PROFITT

Good Samaritan College of Nursing and Health Science (D)

375 Dixmyth Avenue, Cincinnati OH 45220-2489
County: Hamilton FICE Identification: 006494
Unit ID: 202912
Telephone: (513) 876-2743 Carnegie Class: Assoc/PrivNFP
FAX Number: (513) 862-3572 Calendar System: Semester
URL: www.gscollege.edu
Established: 2001 Annual Undergrad Tuition & Fees: $15,660
Enrollment: 316 Coed
Affiliation or Control: Independent Non-Profit IRS Status: 501(c)3
Highest Offering: Associate Degree
Program: 2-Year Principally Bachelor's Creditable; Nursing Emphasis
Accreditation: NH, ADNUR

01 President ....Mr. Morris COHEN
05 Dean of Academic Affairs .... Ms. Patricia MCMAHON
32 Dean of Students/Alumni ....Ms. Mary Jo KATHMAN
09 Dir of Inst Research/Assessment .... Ms. Sherry DOWNING

*Hebrew Union College-Jewish Institute of Religion Central Office (E)

3101 Clifton Avenue, Cincinnati OH 45220-2488
County: Hamilton FICE Identification: 008798
Unit ID: 203076
Telephone: (513) 221-1875 Carnegie Class: N/A
FAX Number: (513) 221-0321
URL: www.huc.edu

01 President ....Rabbi David ELLENSON
11 Chief Operating Officer/VP Admin .... Mr. Gary R. BOCKELMAN
30 Vice President for Inst Advancement .... Dr. Jane KARLIN
21 Director of Finance & Accounting ....Ms. Sandra M. MILLS
05 Vice President for Academic Affairs .... Rabbi Michael MARMUR
101 Admin Exec to Board of Governors .... Ms. Sylvia POSNER
26 National Dir Public Affs/Inst Plng .... Ms. Jean B. ROSENSAFT
44 Natl Dir of Institutional Giving ....Dr. Andrew GRANT
08 Director of Libraries ....Dr. David GILNER
79 Director American Jewish Archives ....Dr. Gary ZOLA
09 Coordinator of IR-Assessment ....Dr. David DIRLAM
29 Director of Alumni Relations ....Ms. Joy WASSERMAN
06 Interim National Registrar ....Mr. Adrian RICE
13 Director of Information Systems ....Mr. John H. BRUGGEMAN
106 Director of eLearning ....Mr. Gregg ALPERT
16 Director of Human Resources ....Ms. Colleen GILDAY
07 Director of Admissions ....Ms. Deborah SHAPIRO
37 Director of Financial Aid ....Ms. Roseanne ACKERLEY

† See branch campus listings in California and New York.

*Hebrew Union College-Jewish Institute of Religion (F)

3101 Clifton Avenue, Cincinnati OH 45220-2488
County: Hamilton FICE Identification: 003047
Unit ID: 203076
Telephone: (513) 221-1875 Carnegie Class: Spec/Faith
FAX Number: (513) 221-0321 Calendar System: Semester
URL: www.huc.edu
Established: 1875 Annual Graduate Tuition & Fees: $21,000
Enrollment: 95 Coed
Affiliation or Control: Jewish IRS Status: 501(c)3
Highest Offering: Doctorate; No Undergraduates
Program: Professional; Religious Emphasis
Accreditation: &M

05 Dean ....Rabbi Kenneth E. EHRLICH
73 Director Rabbinic School ....Rabbi Kenneth KANTER
58 Director Graduate Program ....Dr. Nili FOX
30 Director of Development Midwest ....Mrs. Judy LEVENSON
11 Director of Operations ....Mr. Ron REGULA
07 Regional Director of Admissions ....Rabbi Kenneth KANTER

† Regional accreditation is carried under the parent institution in New York, NY.

Heidelberg University (G)

310 E Market Street, Tiffin OH 44883-2462
County: Seneca FICE Identification: 003048
Unit ID: 203085
Telephone: (419) 448-2000 Carnegie Class: Master's S
FAX Number: (419) 448-2124 Calendar System: Semester
URL: www.heidelberg.edu
Established: 1850 Annual Undergrad Tuition & Fees: $23,670
Enrollment: 1,454 Coed
Affiliation or Control: United Church Of Christ IRS Status: 501(c)3
Highest Offering: Master's
Program: Liberal Arts And General; Teacher Preparatory
Accreditation: NH, CACREP, MUS, TED

01 President ....Dr. Robert HUNTINGTON
05 VP for Academic Affairs & Provost ....Dr. David WEININGER
10 Vice Pres for Admin & Business Affs ...... Mr. Richard RAYMOND
84 VP for Enrollment Mgmt ....Ms. Lindsay SOOY
30 VP Inst Advancement & Univ Rels ....Dr. James TROHA
20 Assoc VP Acad Affs/Dean Undergr Fac .... Dr. Vicki OHL
44 Assoc VP for Institutional Advance ....Dr. Kathryn VENEMA
13 Assoc VP for Information Resources .... Mr. Kurt HUENEMANN
18 Assoc VP for Facilities & Engrng .... Mr. Rodney MORRISON
06 Registrar ....Ms. Cindy SUTER
50 Dean of the School of Business ....Vacant
88 Director MA in Education Program ..... Dr. Diane ARMSTRONG
88 Director MA in Counseling Pgm ....Dr. Jo-Ann SANDERS
53 Director of School of Education ....Dr. Robert SWANSON
64 Director of School of Music ....Dr. John OWEN
92 Assoc Dean for Honors Program ....Dr. Doug COLLAR
104 Dir Intl & Multicult Academic Pgms ....Dr. Marc O'REILLY
36 Director Career Development ....Ms. Kristen LINDSAY
12 Director of Heidelberg at Arrowhead ....Mr. Allen UNDERWOOD
88 Dir Faculy Student Advise & Support ....Dr. Ellen NAGY
08 Director of Library ....Ms. Nancy RUBENSTEIN
41 Athletic Director ....Mr. Matt PALM
21 Business Officer ....Ms. Barb GABEL
37 Director Student Financial Aid ....Mrs. Juli WEININGER
30 Director of Development ....Mr. Lee MARTIN
29 Director of Alumni Relations ....Dr. Kathryn VENEMA
32 Dean of Student Affairs .... Mr. Dustin BRENTLINGER
39 Director of Residence Life ....Mr. Mark ZENO
88 Dir Student Activit/Leadership Dev ....Ms. Reetha PERANANAMGAM
15 Director of Human Resources .... Ms. Jeannine CURNS
21 Controller ....Mr. Mike FEHLEN
04 Assistant to the President ....Ms. Karen MILLER
40 Director of University Bookstore ....Ms. Gail ROBERTS
42 Director of Campus Ministry .... Rev. Paul STARK

Hiram College (H)

Box 67, Hiram OH 44234-0067
County: Portage FICE Identification: 003049
Unit ID: 203128
Telephone: (330) 569-3211 Carnegie Class: Bac/A&S
FAX Number: (330) 569-5494 Calendar System: Semester
URL: www.hiram.edu
Established: 1850 Annual Undergrad Tuition & Fees: $38,410
Enrollment: 1,363 Coed
Affiliation or Control: Independent Non-Profit IRS Status: 501(c)3
Highest Offering: Master's
Program: Liberal Arts And General; Teacher Preparatory
Accreditation: NH, MUS, NURSE, TED

01 President ....Mr. Thomas V. CHEMA
05 Interim Vice Pres & Dean of College ....Dr. Michael A. GRAJEK
10 Vice President Business & Finance .... Mr. Stephen W. JONES
30 Vice Pres Development & Alumni Rels ...Mr. Patrick S. ROBERTS
32 Vice President & Dean of Students ....Mr. Eric R. RIEDEL
07 Vice Pres Admission/Financial Aid ....Mr. James M. ABBUHL
87 Dean Weekend Col/Dir Summer Sess ....Ms. Cathy N. MANSOR
20 Associate Dean of the College .... Mr. Rodney J. HESSINGER
06 Registrar ....Ms. Virginia L. TAYLOR
08 Head Librarian ....Mr. David D. EVERETT
29 Director Alumni Relations ....Mr. John B. COYNE
37 Director Student Financial Services ....Ms. Andrea L. CAPUTO
36 Director of Career Services ....Ms. Kathryn M. CRAIG
14 Director of Computer Center ....Mr. Frank J. VENTURA
26 Director of College Relations ....Mr. Tom B. FORD
56 Dean of Extended Learning ....Mr. Paul E. BOWERS
09 Director of Institutional Research ....Dr. Michael A. GRAJEK
41 Director of Athletics ....Mr. Thomas E. MULLIGAN
42 Chaplain ....Mr. Jason A. BRICKER THOMPSON
15 Director of Human Resources ....Ms. Lynn M. KOSTRAB
18 Director of the Physical Plant ....Mr. Sam V. MORGANO

21 Controller/Director of Accounting ....Ms. Susan A. BOYLE
35 Director of Student Involvement ....Ms. Demetria B. ANDERSON
38 Director Student Counseling ....Ms. Lynn B. TAYLOR
28 Director Ethnic Diversity Affairs ....Ms. Detra E. WEST
96 Director of Purchasing ....Ms. Martha A. SCHETTLER

Hocking College (A)

3301 Hocking Parkway, Nelsonville OH 45764-9704
County: Athens FICE Identification: 007598
Unit ID: 203155
Telephone: (740) 753-3591 Carnegie Class: Assoc/Pub-R-L
FAX Number: (740) 753-7039 Calendar System: Quarter
URL: www.hocking.edu
Established: 1968 Annual Undergrad Tuition & Fees (In-State): $2,662
Enrollment: 6,533 Coed
Affiliation or Control: State IRS Status: 501(c)3
Highest Offering: Associate Degree
Program: Occupational; 2-Year Principally Bachelor's Creditable; Technical Emphasis
Accreditation: NH, ACBSP, ACFEI, ADNUR, MAC, PNUR, PTAA

01 President ....Dr. Ron J. ERICKSON
10 Senior Vice President & Treasurer ....Ms. Gina FETTY
05 Provost/VP Acad & Student Affairs ....Dr. Molly WEILAND
11 Int Vice President of Admin Svcs ....Dr. Myriah SHORT
37 Assoc VP Student Finance/Aux Svcs ....Dr. William ROTHMAN
24 Associate Vice President ....Dr. Rose Marie SMITH
88 Assistant to the Provost ....Mrs. Sally LOZADA
20 Dean of Reg Campuses/Industry Tech ....Dr. Josh LANCASTER
84 Dean of Enrollment Services ....Mrs. Lynn HULL
50 Dean School of Hospitality ....Mr. Tom LAMBRECHT
66 Dean Sch of Health & Nursing ....Dr. Molly WEILAND
36 Dean College & Career Success Ctr ....Dr. Stephen MILLER
13 Chief Technology Officer ....Mr. George HINKLE
19 Director Public Safety Services ....Mr. Calvin PRICE
08 Director Learning Resource Center ....Ms. Carrie ATOR-JAMES
15 Director Human Resources ....Mr. John SANDERS
26 Director Public Relations ....Ms. Judith SINNOTT
30 Director Marketing & Advancement ....Mr. J. R. BLACKBURN
19 Director Campus Safety ....Mr. David VALKINBURG
06 Registrar ....Mr. Alan MARKOVICH
18 Director Building/Grounds ....Mr. Ron MASH
29 Director Alumni Relations ....Mr. Paul HARPER
21 Controller/Assistant Treasurer ....Mrs. Anna JOHNSON
36 Coord Placement/Employee Relations ....Mr. Kraig CURRY
44 Advancement Coordinator ....Mr. Paul HARPER

Hondros College (B)

4140 Executive Parkway, Westerville OH 43081-3855
County: Franklin FICE Identification: 040743
Unit ID: 203386
Telephone: (614) 508-7277 Carnegie Class: Assoc/PrivFP
FAX Number: (614) 508-7280 Calendar System: Quarter
URL: www.nursing.hondros.edu
Established: 1981 Annual Undergrad Tuition & Fees: $20,622
Enrollment: 1,389 Coed
Affiliation or Control: Proprietary IRS Status: Proprietary
Highest Offering: Associate Degree
Program: Occupational; 2-Year Principally Bachelor's Creditable; Nursing Emphasis
Accreditation: ACICS

01 President ....Ms. Linda SCHWAN-HONDROS
05 President Degree Division ....Dr. Debbie ULRICH
07 Director of Admission ....Mr. Zachary SELBY
06 Registrar ....Ms. Sarah WILLIAMS

International College of Broadcasting (C)

6 S Smithville Road, Dayton OH 45431-1898
County: Montgomery FICE Identification: 013132
Unit ID: 203289
Telephone: (937) 258-8251 Carnegie Class: Assoc/PrivFP
FAX Number: (937) 258-8714 Calendar System: Semester
URL: www.icbcollege.com
Established: 1968 Annual Undergrad Tuition & Fees: $14,950
Enrollment: 105 Coed
Affiliation or Control: Proprietary IRS Status: Proprietary
Highest Offering: Associate Degree
Program: Occupational
Accreditation: ACCSC

01 President ....J. Michael LEMASTER
05 School Director ....Rhonda HORNE

ITT Technical Institute (D)

4717 Hilton Corporate Drive, Columbus OH 43232
Identification: 666706
Unit ID: 451963
Telephone: (614) 868-2000 Carnegie Class: Not Classified
FAX Number: (614) 868-2050 Calendar System: Quarter
URL: www.itt-tech.edu
Established: N/A Annual Undergrad Tuition & Fees: N/A
Enrollment: 411 Coed
Affiliation or Control: Proprietary IRS Status: Proprietary
Highest Offering: Baccalaureate
Program: Technical Emphasis
Accreditation: ACICS

† Branch campus of ITT Technical Institute, Spokane Valley, WA.

ITT Technical Institute (E)

3325 Stop Eight Road, Dayton OH 45414-3456
County: Montgomery FICE Identification: 009088
Unit ID: 203313
Telephone: (937) 264-7700 Carnegie Class: Assoc/PrivFP
FAX Number: N/A Calendar System: Quarter
URL: www.itt-tech.edu
Established: 1935 Annual Undergrad Tuition & Fees: N/A
Enrollment: 534 Coed
Affiliation or Control: Proprietary IRS Status: Proprietary
Highest Offering: Baccalaureate
Program: Technical Emphasis
Accreditation: ACICS

ITT Technical Institute (F)

3781 Park Mill Run Drive, Hilliard OH 43026-8110
County: Franklin Identification: 666318
Unit ID: 443535
Telephone: (614) 771-4888 Carnegie Class: Assoc/PrivFP
FAX Number: (614) 921-4179 Calendar System: Quarter
URL: www.itt-tech.edu
Established: 2003 Annual Undergrad Tuition & Fees: N/A
Enrollment: 543 Coed
Affiliation or Control: Proprietary IRS Status: Proprietary
Highest Offering: Baccalaureate
Program: Technical Emphasis
Accreditation: ACICS

† Branch campus of ITT Technical Institute, Spokane Valley, WA.

ITT Technical Institute (G)

1656 Henthorne Boulevard, Suite B,
Maumee OH 43537-3920
County: Lucas Identification: 666160
Unit ID: 448497
Telephone: (419) 861-6500 Carnegie Class: Assoc/PrivFP
FAX Number: N/A Calendar System: Quarter
URL: www.itt-tech.edu
Established: 2006 Annual Undergrad Tuition & Fees: N/A
Enrollment: 627 Coed
Affiliation or Control: Proprietary IRS Status: Proprietary
Highest Offering: Baccalaureate
Program: Technical Emphasis
Accreditation: ACICS

† Branch campus of ITT Technical Institute, Dayton, OH.

ITT Technical Institute (H)

4750 Wesley Avenue, Norwood OH 45212-2244
County: Hamilton Identification: 666546
Unit ID: 430379
Telephone: (513) 531-8300 Carnegie Class: Assoc/PrivFP
FAX Number: (513) 531-8368 Calendar System: Quarter
URL: www.itt-tech.edu
Established: 1995 Annual Undergrad Tuition & Fees: N/A
Enrollment: 699 Coed
Affiliation or Control: Proprietary IRS Status: Proprietary
Highest Offering: Baccalaureate
Program: Technical Emphasis
Accreditation: ACICS

† Branch campus of ITT Technical Institute, Nashville, TN.

ITT Technical Institute (I)

14955 Sprague Road, Strongsville OH 44136-1758
County: Cuyahoga Identification: 666547
Unit ID: 430388
Telephone: (440) 234-9091 Carnegie Class: Assoc/PrivFP
FAX Number: (440) 234-7568 Calendar System: Quarter
URL: www.itt-tech.edu
Established: 1994 Annual Undergrad Tuition & Fees: N/A
Enrollment: 513 Coed
Affiliation or Control: Proprietary IRS Status: Proprietary
Highest Offering: Baccalaureate
Program: Technical Emphasis
Accreditation: ACICS

† Branch campus of ITT Technical Institute, Dayton, OH.

ITT Technical Institute (J)

4700 Richmond Road,
Warrensville Heights OH 44128-5984
County: Cuyahoga Identification: 666379
Unit ID: 446923
Telephone: (216) 896-6500 Carnegie Class: Assoc/PrivFP
FAX Number: N/A Calendar System: Quarter
URL: www.itt-tech.edu
Established: N/A Annual Undergrad Tuition & Fees: N/A
Enrollment: 563 Coed
Affiliation or Control: Proprietary IRS Status: Proprietary
Highest Offering: Baccalaureate
Program: Technical Emphasis
Accreditation: ACICS

† Branch campus of ITT Technical Institute, Earth City, MO.

ITT Technical Institute (K)

1030 N Meridian Road, Youngstown OH 44509-4098
County: Mahoning FICE Identification: 009837
Unit ID: 206631
Telephone: (330) 270-1600 Carnegie Class: Assoc/PrivFP
FAX Number: (330) 270-8333 Calendar System: Quarter
URL: www.itt-tech.edu
Established: 1967 Annual Undergrad Tuition & Fees: N/A
Enrollment: 784 Coed
Affiliation or Control: Proprietary IRS Status: Proprietary
Highest Offering: Baccalaureate
Program: Technical Emphasis
Accreditation: ACICS

James A. Rhodes State College (L)

4240 Campus Drive, Lima OH 45804-3597
County: Allen FICE Identification: 010027
Unit ID: 203678
Telephone: (419) 995-8000 Carnegie Class: Assoc/Pub-R-M
FAX Number: (419) 221-0450 Calendar System: Quarter
URL: www.rhodesstate.edu
Established: 1971 Annual Undergrad Tuition & Fees (In-State): $4,413
Enrollment: 4,281 Coed
Affiliation or Control: State IRS Status: 501(c)3
Highest Offering: Associate Degree
Program: Occupational; 2-Year Principally Bachelor's Creditable
Accreditation: NH, ACBSP, ADNUR, DH, ENGT, MAC, OTA, PTAA, RAD

01 President ....Dr. Debra L. MCCURDY
05 Vice President for Academic Affairs ....Dr. Roberto GUTIERREZ
10 Vice President Business & Treasurer ....Mr. Chris R. SCHMIDT
32 Interim VP Student Affairs ....Ms. Judi MAZZARELLLI
30 Executitve Director of Development ....Mr. Henry "Tre" M. WALDREN
20 Int Asc VP Acad Affs/Dean Inst Svcs ....Mr. Will WELLS
07 Director of Admissions ....Ms. Traci R. COX
37 Director Student Financial Aid ....Ms. Cathy L. KOHLI
09 Director Institutional Research ....Mr. Steve S. MILLER
36 Director of Career Services ....Ms. Krista RICHARDSON
08 Head Librarian ....Ms. Tina SCHNEIDER
103 Exec Dir for Workforce & Econ Dev ....Dr. Matthew J. KINKLEY
15 Director Human Resources ....Mr. Jonathon HORN
50 Dean Div Business & Public Services ....Mr. Michael G. REX
54 InterimDean Div Info Tech/Engr Tech ....Mr. Roger NEWHOUSE
49 Dean Division of Arts & Sciences ....Mr. William C. WELLS
66 Dean Division of Nursing ....Ms. Carol SCHMIDT
76 Dean Div of Allied Health Sciences ....Mr. Richard N. WOODFIELD
45 Exec Dir Inst Effect/Planning ....Dr. Cynthia E. SPIERS
18 Chief Facilities/Physical Plant ....Mr. Chris R. SCHMIDT
21 Assoc Business Officer/Controller ....Mr. Mark RUSSELL
26 Coordinator Public Relations ....Ms. Paula J. SIEBENECK
06 Registrar ....Ms. Bonnie L. KING
35 Dean Student Development ....Mr. Martino HARMON

John Carroll University (M)

20700 N Park Boulevard, Cleveland OH 44118-4581
County: Cuyahoga FICE Identification: 003050
Unit ID: 203368
Telephone: (216) 397-1886 Carnegie Class: Master's L
FAX Number: (216) 397-4256 Calendar System: Semester
URL: www.jcu.edu
Established: 1886 Annual Undergrad Tuition & Fees: $31,710
Enrollment: 3,692 Coed
Affiliation or Control: Roman Catholic IRS Status: 501(c)3
Highest Offering: Master's
Program: Liberal Arts And General; Teacher Preparatory; Professional
Accreditation: NH, BUS, BUSA, CACREP, TED

01 President ....Rev. Robert L. NIEHOFF, SJ
43 General Counsel ....Ms. Maria ALFARO-LOPEZ
04 VP and Exec Asst to the President ....Dr. Jonathan E. SMITH
88 Asst to Pres for Mission & Identity ....Dr. Paul V. MURPHY
101 Asst to Pres/Sec to Board of Dir ....Ms. Laurie A. FRANTZ
05 Academic Vice President ....Dr. John T. DAY
32 Vice President for Student Affairs ....Dr. Mark D. MCCARTHY
84 Vice President for Enrollment ....Mr. Brian G. WILLIAMS
10 Vice President for Finance ....Mr. Richard F. MAUSSER
30 Vice President for Univ Advancement ....Ms. Doreen K. RILEY
20 Assoc Academic Vice President ....Dr. James H. KRUKONES
20 Assc Acad VP Acad Pgm/Fac Diversity ....Dr. Lauren L. BOWEN
45 Dir of Planning and Academic Budget ....Dr. Nicholas R. SANTILLI
49 Dean College of Arts & Sciences ....Dr. Jeanne COLLERAN
50 Dean Boler School of Business ....Dr. Karen SCHUELE
35 Dean of Students ....Dr. Sherri A. CRAHEN
39 Director of Residence Life ....Ms. Lisa M. BROWN
13 Chief Information Officer ....Mr. Michael BESTUL
26 Asst VP Intg Mktg & Communications ....Mr. John CARFAGNA
18 Assoc Vice Pres for Facilities ....Ms. Carol P. DIETZ
16 Director of Human Resources ....Mr. Charles STUPPY
08 Director of the Library ....Dr. Jeanne SOMERS
36 Director Center for Career Services ....Ms. Hilary FLANAGAN
28 Director Multicultural Affairs ....Ms. Danielle J. CARTER

85 Dir Center for Global Education .... Dr. Andreas SOBISCH
06 Registrar .... Mrs. Kathleen J. DIFRANCO
88 Bursar & Dir of Student Accounts .... Ms. Diane WARD
92 Director Honors Program .... Dr. Julia KAROLLE-BERG
07 Executive Director of Enrollment .... Mr. Steven P. VITATOE
37 Director of Financial Aid .... Ms. Claudia WENZEL
31 Dir Ctr for Service & Social Action .... Dr. Margaret FINUCANE
42 Director of Campus Ministry .... Mr. John SCARANO
38 Director Univ Counseling Center .... Dr. John M. ROPAR
24 Dir Instructional Tech Services .... Dr. Jay TARBY
23 Director Student Health Center .... Ms. Janet M. KREVH
41 Sr Director Athletics & Recreation .... Ms. Laurie MASSA
29 Director Alumni Relations .... Mr. David A. VITATOE
44 Director Planned Giving .... Mr. Peter R. BERNARDO
102 Dir Corp Relations and Major Gifts .... Ms. Christina BEG
88 Director Fdn Rels & Grant Writing .... Vacant
86 Dir Government & Community Rels .... Ms. Dora PRUCE
96 Director Purchasing & Aux Services .... Mr. Andrew F. FRONCZEK
19 Director Campus Safety Services .... Mr. Timothy PEPPARD
105 Dir Marketing Services (Web) .... Mr. Michael RICHWALSKY
88 Coordinator Institutional Effective .... Ms. Marilyn F. VALENCIA

Kaplan Career Institute (A)

8720 Brookpark Road, Brooklyn OH 44129

County: Cuyahoga | FICE Identification: 025829 | Unit ID: 206093

Telephone: (216) 485-0900 | Carnegie Class: Not Classified

FAX Number: (216) 661-6842 | Calendar System: Other

URL: cleveland.kaplancareerinstitute.com

Established: 1980 | Annual Undergrad Tuition & Fees: $15,522

Enrollment: 495 | Coed

Affiliation or Control: Proprietary | IRS Status: Proprietary

Highest Offering: Associate Degree

Program: Occupational; 2-Year Principally Bachelor's Creditable; Technical Emphasis

Accreditation: ACCSC

Kaplan College (B)

2745 Winchester Pike, Columbus OH 43232-4827

County: Franklin | FICE Identification: 011005 | Unit ID: 202189

Telephone: (614) 456-4600 | Carnegie Class: Assoc/PrivFP

FAX Number: (614) 456-4640 | Calendar System: Semester

URL: www.teccollege.com

Established: 1989 | Annual Undergrad Tuition & Fees: $10,600

Enrollment: 472 | Coed

Affiliation or Control: Proprietary | IRS Status: Proprietary

Highest Offering: Associate Degree

Program: Occupational

Accreditation: ACCSC

01 Director .... Mr. Jeffrey BODINER
07 Director of Admissions .... Mr. Nathan COLE
05 Director of Education .... Ms. Jennifer GLAZE
37 Director of Financial Aid .... Ms. Nicole MORGAN

Kaplan College (C)

2800 East River Road, Dayton OH 45439

County: Montgomery | FICE Identification: 020520 | Unit ID: 204626

Telephone: (937) 294-6155 | Carnegie Class: Assoc/PrivFP

FAX Number: (937) 294-2259 | Calendar System: Quarter

URL: dayton.kaplancollege.com

Established: 1971 | Annual Undergrad Tuition & Fees: $14,655

Enrollment: 757 | Coed

Affiliation or Control: Proprietary | IRS Status: Proprietary

Highest Offering: Associate Degree

Program: Occupational; Technical Emphasis

Accreditation: ACCSC

01 President .... Ms. Karen LARSEN-REUTER
05 Director of Education .... Ms. Carol JACOBS

Kent State University Main Campus (D)

PO Box 5190, Kent OH 44242-0001

County: Portage | FICE Identification: 003051 | Unit ID: 203517

Telephone: (330) 672-2121 | Carnegie Class: RU/H

FAX Number: (330) 672-2190 | Calendar System: Semester

URL: www.kent.edu

Established: 1910 | Annual Undergrad Tuition & Fees (In-State): $9,346

Enrollment: 19,918 | Coed

Affiliation or Control: State | IRS Status: 501(c)3

Highest Offering: Doctorate

Program: Liberal Arts And General; Teacher Preparatory; Professional

Accreditation: NH, AAB, ACBSP, ART, AUD, BUS, BUSA, CACREP, CIDA, CLPSY, CORE, DANCE, DIETD, DIETI, EXSC, JOUR, LIB, MUS, NAIT, NRPA, NURSE, SCPSY, SP, SPAA, TED, THEA

01 President .... Dr. Lester A. LEFTON
05 Provost/Sr VP Academic Affairs .... Dr. Robert G. FRANK
10 Vice Pres Finance & Administration .... Mr. Gregg S. FLOYD
16 Vice Pres Human Resources .... Mr. Willis WALKER
30 Vice Pres Institutional Advancement .... Mr. Eugene J. FINN
26 Vice Pres Univ Relations .... Ms. Iris E. HARVEY
32 VP Student Affairs/Enrollment Mgmt .... Mr. Greg I. JARVIE
46 Vice President Research .... Dr. W. Grant MCGIMPSEY
27 Vice Pres Information Services/CIO .... Mr. Edward G. MAHON
22 VP Diversity/Equity Inclusion .... Dr. Alfreda BROWN
20 Dean Undergraduate Studies .... Dr. Gary M. PADAK
35 Assoc Dean of Stdnts/Stdnt Ombuds .... Dr. Sheryl E. SMITH
45 Sr Assoc Provost .... Dr. Timothy J. CHANDLER
20 Assoc Provost Faculty Affairs .... Ms. Sue AVERILL
44 Assoc VP Univ Rels/Inst Advance .... Mr. Stephen G. SOKANY
84 Assoc Vice Pres Enrollment Managemt .... Mr. David GARCIA
29 Exec Director of Alumni Affairs .... Mrs. Lori RANDORF
07 Director of Admissions .... Ms. Nancy J. DELLAVECCHIA
06 Registrar .... Mr. Glenn DAVIS
43 University Counsel .... Mr. Willis WALKER
100 Sec Bd Trustees/Chief of Staff .... Ms. Charlene K. REED
41 Director Intercollegiate Athletics .... Mr. Joel NIELSON
22 Dir Equal Opportunity/Affirm Action .... Mr. James MCELROY
37 Director Student Financial Aid .... Mr. Mark EVANS
86 Director Government Relations .... Ms. Patricia A. MYERS
19 Director of Public Safety .... Mr. John PEACH
12 Dean Trumbull Campus .... Dr. Wanda THOMAS
09 Director of Institutional Research .... Dr. Sally A. KANDEL
96 Director of Procurement .... Mr. Timothy J. KONCZAL
49 Dean College of Arts & Sciences .... Dr. Timothy MOERLAND
50 Dean Business Administration .... Mr. Robert B. HEISLER, JR.
53 Dean of Education .... Dr. Daniel F. MAHONY
57 Dean of the Arts .... Dr. John CRAWFORD
66 Dean College of Nursing .... Dr. Laura DZUREC
51 Exec Director Continuing Studies .... Ms. Deborah C. HUNTSMAN
92 Dean Honors College .... Dr. Donald WILLIAMS
08 Dean Library & Media Services .... Dr. Mark WEBER
48 Dean Architect/Environ Design .... Mr. Douglas STEIDL
27 Dean Communication & Information ...... Dr. Stanley T. WEARDEN
72 Interim Dean College of Technology .... Dr. Jack R. GRAHAM
58 Dean of Graduate Studies .... Dr. Mary Ann STEPHENS

Kent State University Ashtabula Campus (E)

330 Lake Road W, Ashtabula OH 44004-2299

County: Ashtabula | FICE Identification: 003052 | Unit ID: 203447

Telephone: (440) 964-3322 | Carnegie Class: Assoc/Pub4

FAX Number: (440) 964-4269 | Calendar System: Semester

URL: www.ashtabula.kent.edu

Established: 1958 | Annual Undergrad Tuition & Fees (In-State): $5,288

Enrollment: 2,496 | Coed

Affiliation or Control: State | IRS Status: 501(c)3

Highest Offering: Associate Degree

Program: Occupational; 2-Year Principally Bachelor's Creditable

Accreditation: &NH, ACBSP, ADNUR, OTA, PTAA, RAD

01 Dean .... Dr. Susan J. STOCKER
05 Assistant Dean .... Mr. Kevin L. DEEMER
04 Senior Special Assistant .... Mr. John M. YESSO
08 Library Director .... Mr. Kevin L. DEEMER
20 Senior Academic Program Director .... Ms. Carol K. DRENNEN
10 Director Admin/Business Affairs .... Mr. W. David SCHULTZ
31 Corporate & Community Services .... Mr. John M. YESSO
21 Business Manager .... Ms. Amy S. THOMPSON
84 Dir Enrol Mgt/Registrar/Stdnt Svcs .... Ms. Kelly L. ANTHONY
13 Dir Computing/Info & Management .... Mr. Kevin K. ACIERNO
88 Director PT Asst/Tech Program .... Mr. R. Michael BLAKE
30 Senior Development Associate .... Ms. Pamela J. PALERMO
88 Director of Radiologic Technology .... Ms. Gail M. SCHROEDER
18 Chief Facilities/Physical Plant .... Mr. W. David SCHULTZ
26 Manager of Comm Marketing .... Ms. Cheryl A. GAMES
37 Coordinator Student Financial Aid .... Ms. Robyn M. GIFFORD
88 Dir of Respiratory Therapy Tech .... Mr. David A. GOSWICH
88 Director of Occupational Therapy .... Ms. Julie L. MIRABELL
66 Director of Nursing .... Ms. Connie A. BOWLER

† Regional accreditation is carried under the parent institution in Kent, OH.

Kent State University East Liverpool Campus (F)

400 E Fourth Street, East Liverpool OH 43920-3497

County: Columbiana | FICE Identification: 003056 | Unit ID: 203456

Telephone: (330) 385-3805 | Carnegie Class: Assoc/Pub2in4

FAX Number: (330) 382-7562 | Calendar System: Semester

URL: www.eliv.kent.edu

Established: 1965 | Annual Undergrad Tuition & Fees (In-State): $5,150

Enrollment: 1,372 | Coed

Affiliation or Control: State | IRS Status: 501(c)3

Highest Offering: Associate Degree

Program: Occupational; 2-Year Principally Bachelor's Creditable

Accreditation: &NH, ACBSP, ADNUR, OTA, PTAA

01 Dean .... Dr. Jeffrey NOLTE
05 Interim Assistant Dean .... Dr. Susan ROSSI
08 Library Director .... Ms. Susan M. WEAVER
88 Director Physical Therapy .... Dr. Mary Lynne FEDOR
66 Director of Nursing .... Dr. Frances Anne FREITAS
88 Director Occupational Therapy .... Ms. Harriett BYNUM
84 Director Enrollment Management .... Ms. Michelle LINGENFELTER
88 Director Justice Studies .... Ms. Lynnette RAWLINGS
13 Network Systems Manager .... Mr. Wallace AIKEN
21 Business Manager .... Mr. Henry TRENKELBACH
07 Admissions Coordinator .... Ms. Lisa FRANK
36 Coordinator Career Planning .... Ms. Deborah WOODS
88 Clin Coord Phys Therapy Asst Pgm .... Vacant
26 Marketing Assistant .... Ms. Bethany GADD

† Regional accreditation is carried under the parent institution in Kent, OH.

Kent State University Geauga Campus (G)

14111 Claridon-Troy Road, Burton Township OH 44021-9500

County: Geauga | FICE Identification: 003059 | Unit ID: 203526

Telephone: (440) 834-4187 | Carnegie Class: Assoc/Pub4

FAX Number: (440) 834-8846 | Calendar System: Semester

URL: www.geauga.kent.edu

Established: 1964 | Annual Undergrad Tuition & Fees (In-State): $4,586

Enrollment: 1,918 | Coed

Affiliation or Control: State | IRS Status: 501(c)3

Highest Offering: Master's

Program: Occupational; 2-Year Principally Bachelor's Creditable; Liberal Arts And General

Accreditation: &NH, ACBSP

01 Dean .... Dr. David MOHAN
05 Assistant Dean .... Dr. Donna M. RAMSEY
10 Chief Business Officer .... Mr. John GRANNY
84 Dir Enrollment Mgmt/Student Svcs .... Mr. Thomas HOILES
20 Dir of Academic Support Svcs .... Mr. Bennett MORRISON
37 Director Student Financial Aid .... Ms. Donna HOLCOMB
30 Director of Development .... Mr. Perry CLARK
35 Director Student Services .... Mr. Thomas HOILES
07 Admissions/Records .... Ms. Betty LANDRUS

† Regional accreditation is carried under the parent institution in Kent, OH.

Kent State University Salem Campus (H)

2491 State Road 45 South, Salem OH 44460-9412

County: Columbiana | FICE Identification: 003061 | Unit ID: 203492

Telephone: (330) 332-0361 | Carnegie Class: Bac/Assoc

FAX Number: (330) 337-4122 | Calendar System: Semester

URL: www.salem.kent.edu

Established: 1962 | Annual Undergrad Tuition & Fees (In-State): $9,346

Enrollment: 1,613 | Coed

Affiliation or Control: State | IRS Status: 501(c)3

Highest Offering: Baccalaureate

Program: Occupational; 2-Year Principally Bachelor's Creditable; Liberal Arts And General

Accreditation: &NH, ACBSP, NMT, RAD, RTT

01 Dean .... Dr. Jeffrey L. NOLTE
05 Assistant Dean .... Mr. Dave GUY
08 Director Library .... Ms. Lilith R. KUNKEL
84 Director of Enrollment Management ... Ms. Shelly LINGENFELTER
103 Director Workforce Development .... Ms. Diane KLOSS
30 Development Officer .... Mr. Matthew T. BUTTS
10 Business Manager .... Mr. Henry TRENKELBACH
36 Coordinator Career Planning .... Ms. Deborah WOODS
07 Admissions Counselor .... Ms. Kristin TOOTHMAN

† Regional accreditation is carried under the parent institution in Kent, OH.

Kent State University at Stark (I)

6000 Frank Avenue, NW, Canton OH 44720-9988

County: Stark | FICE Identification: 003054 | Unit ID: 203465

Telephone: (330) 499-9600 | Carnegie Class: Assoc/Pub4

FAX Number: (330) 494-6121 | Calendar System: Semester

URL: www.stark.kent.edu

Established: 1946 | Annual Undergrad Tuition & Fees (In-State): $5,288

Enrollment: 4,820 | Coed

Affiliation or Control: State | IRS Status: 501(c)3

Highest Offering: Baccalaureate

Program: Liberal Arts And General; Teacher Preparatory; Professional

Accreditation: &NH

01 Dean & Chief Administrative Officer .... Dr. Walter WAGOR
05 Associate Dean .... Dr. Ruth CAPASSO
10 Dir Business Affairs & Operations .... Vacant
84 Assistant Dean for Enrollment .... Ms. Mary S. SOUTHARDS
26 Dir External Affairs & Cmty Rels .... Ms. Tina BIASELLA
30 Development Officer .... Vacant
88 Outreach Program Director .... Ms. Kelli BAXTER
32 Director Student Services .... Ms. Diane WALKER
08 Library Director .... Mr. Rob KAIRIS
88 General Manager Conference Center .... Mr. Joseph FOLK
07 Director of Admissions .... Ms. Deb SPECK
37 Director Student Financial Aid .... Ms. Gail PUKYS
36 Director Student Placement .... Mr. Chris PAVELOI
15 Human Resource Generalist .... Ms. Michelle REID
38 Counseling Specialist .... Ms. Emily RIBNIK
13 Network Services Manager .... Ms. JoEllen KLCO
18 Senior Facilities Manager .... Mr. Brent WOOD
24 Manager Media Services .... Ms. Sue MARKOVICH
21 Business Manager .... Mr. Joseph POLACK
19 Security Supervisor .... Mr. Mark ELLIOTT
88 Special Events Coordinator .... Ms. Jenny HUTH

26 Marketing Coordinator .... Ms. Rachel FIGUEROA
20 Coordinator Academic Services .... Ms. Lisa HART

† Regional accreditation is carried under the parent institution in Kent, OH.

Kent State University Trumbull Campus (A)

4314 Mahoning Avenue, NW, Warren OH 44483-1998
County: Trumbull FICE Identification: 003064
Unit ID: 203474
Telephone: (330) 847-0571 Carnegie Class: Assoc/Pub4
FAX Number: (330) 675-8888 Calendar System: Semester
URL: www.trumbull.kent.edu
Established: 1954 Annual Undergrad Tuition & Fees (In-State): $5,110
Enrollment: 3,144 Coed
Affiliation or Control: State IRS Status: 501(c)3
Highest Offering: Associate Degree
Program: Occupational; 2-Year Principally Bachelor's Creditable
Accreditation: &NH, ACBSP

01 Dean .... Mr. Robert G. SINES
05 Assistant Dean .... Dr. Daniel E. PALMER
11 Director Admin/Business Services .... Ms. Elaine PETROSKY
06 Registrar .... Dr. James RITTER
08 Librarian .... Ms. Rose A. GUERRIERI
84 Assist Dir Enrollment Management .... Ms. Sarah HELMICK

† Regional accreditation is carried under the parent institution in Kent, OH.

Kent State University Tuscarawas Campus (B)

330 University Drive, NE,
New Philadelphia OH 44663-9403
County: Tuscarawas FICE Identification: 003062
Unit ID: 203483
Telephone: (330) 339-3391 Carnegie Class: Assoc/Pub2in4
FAX Number: (330) 339-3321 Calendar System: Semester
URL: www.tusc.kent.edu
Established: 1962 Annual Undergrad Tuition & Fees (In-State): $5,290
Enrollment: 2,802 Coed
Affiliation or Control: State IRS Status: 501(c)3
Highest Offering: Baccalaureate
Program: Occupational; 2-Year Principally Bachelor's Creditable
Accreditation: &NH, ACBSP, ADNUR, ENGT

01 Dean .... Dr. Gregg L. ANDREWS
05 Assistant Dean .... Dr. Fran HALDAR
84 Director Enroll Mgmt & Student Svcs .... Ms. Laurie DONLEY
51 Director Continuing Studies .... Ms. Patricia COMANITZ
10 Director Business & Admin Services .... Mr. Walt GRITZAN
66 Director Nursing .... Ms. Joan LAPPIN
08 Librarian .... Ms. Tollie BANKER
13 Network Systems Manager .... Mr. Shannon BAILEY
21 Business Manager .... Ms. Waliah POTO
26 Coordinator Public Relations .... Ms. Pam PATACCA
88 Coord Small Business Devel Ctr .... Mr. Stephen SCHILLIG
36 Coordinator Career Planning .... Mr. Rob BRINDLEY
37 Financial Aid Coordinator .... Ms. Dawn PLUG
88 Outreach Program Coordinator .... Mr. Joseph BELINSKY
88 Outreach Program Coordinator .... Ms. JoEllen SANDERS
88 Outreach Program Coordinator .... Mr. Terry THEIS
74 Acad Pgm Dir for Veterinary Tech ..... Dr. Ronald SOUTHERLAND
54 Acad Pgm Dir for Engineering Tech .... Dr. Kamal BICHARA
14 IT User Support Analyst .... Mr. Jeremy BAILEY
30 Director of Advancement .... Mr. Monte BALL

† Regional accreditation is carried under the parent institution in Kent, OH.

Kenyon College (C)

Gambier OH 43022-9623
County: Knox FICE Identification: 003065
Unit ID: 203535
Telephone: (740) 427-5000 Carnegie Class: Bac/A&S
FAX Number: (740) 427-3077 Calendar System: Semester
URL: www.kenyon.edu
Established: 1824 Annual Undergrad Tuition & Fees: $42,630
Enrollment: 1,632 Coed
Affiliation or Control: Independent Non-Profit IRS Status: 501(c)3
Highest Offering: Baccalaureate
Program: Liberal Arts And General
Accreditation: NH

01 President .... Dr. S. Georgia NUGENT
05 Provost .... Dr. Nayef SAMHAT
26 Vice President College Relations .... Ms. Sarah H. KAHRL
10 Vice President for Finance .... Mr. Joseph G. NELSON
13 Vice Pres Library & Info Svcs .... Mr. Ronald K. GRIGGS
100 Advisor to President .... Mr. Jesse E. MATZ
21 Assoc Vice President for Finance .... Ms. Teri L. BLANCHARD
32 Dean of Students .... Dr. Henry P. TOUTAIN
07 Dean of Admissions/Fin Aid .... Ms. Jennifer DELAHUNTY
20 Associate Provost .... Dr. Ric S. SHEFFIELD
08 Director of Information Resources .... Mr. Joseph M. MURPHY
06 Registrar/Dean Academic Support .... Ms. Ellen K. HARBOUT
44 Director Planned Giving .... Mr. Kyle W. HENDERSON
26 Director of Public Affairs .... Mr. Shawn PRESLEY
14 Director Systems Design/Consulting .... Mr. Ronald K. GRIGGS
29 Dir Alumni/Parent Rels/Annual Funds .... Ms. Lisa D. SCHOTT
37 Director of Financial Aid .... Mr. Craig A. DAUGHERTY
38 Director of Counseling Services .... Dr. Patrick K. GILLIGAN
15 Director of Human Resources .... Ms. Jennifer G. CABRAL
42 Director Board College Ministries .... Rev. Karl P B. STEVENS
21 Chief Business Officer .... Mr. Mark KOLMAN
22 Equal Opportunity Officer .... Mr. Jason E. TANENBAUM
19 Director of Campus Safety .... Mr. Robert D. HOOPER
09 Director of Institutional Research .... Mr. Ronald K. GRIGGS
21 Manager of Business Services .... Mr. Frederick S. LINGER
28 Director of Multicultural Affairs .... Mr. A. Chris KENNERLY

Kettering College of Medical Arts (D)

3737 Southern Boulevard, Kettering OH 45429-1299
County: Montgomery FICE Identification: 007035
Unit ID: 203544
Telephone: (937) 395-8601 Carnegie Class: Spec/Health
FAX Number: (937) 395-8106 Calendar System: Semester
URL: www.kcma.edu
Established: 1967 Annual Undergrad Tuition & Fees: $11,460
Enrollment: 917 Coed
Affiliation or Control: Seventh-day Adventist IRS Status: 501(c)3
Highest Offering: Master's
Program: Occupational; 2-Year Principally Bachelor's Creditable; Professional; Nursing Emphasis
Accreditation: NH, ADNUR, ARCPA, DMS, NUR, RAD

00 Chairman of the Board .... Mr. Fred M. MANCHUR
01 President .... Dr. Charles W. SCRIVEN
05 Dean for Academic Affairs .... Dr. William G. NELSON
08 Director of Library .... Mrs. Bev ERVIN
102 President Foundation .... Dr. Martin CLARK
15 Vice President Human Resources .... Mrs. Beverly MORRIS
84 Dean for Enrollment Services .... Mr. Victor BROWN
06 Director Academic Info & Records .... Mr. Jim NESBIT
32 Dean Assessment & Learning Support .... Dr. Beverly COBB
37 Director Student Financial Aid .... Mrs. Kim SNELL
40 Manager Bookstore .... Mrs. Stella FREEMAN
42 Chaplain Director Campus Ministry .... Mr. Clive WILSON
39 Residence Dean .... Mr. Jerry MAHN
26 Public Relations Officer .... Ms. Mindy CLAGGETT
29 Director Alumni Relations .... Mrs. Amy MORETTA
07 Director of Enrollment Services .... Mrs. Becky MCDONALD
10 Senior Finance Administrator .... Mr. Jack BURDICK
27 Senior Information Officer .... Mr. Jim NESBIT

Lake Erie College (E)

391 W Washington Street, Painesville OH 44077-3389
County: Lake FICE Identification: 003066
Unit ID: 203580
Telephone: (440) 375-7000 Carnegie Class: Master's S
FAX Number: (440) 375-7005 Calendar System: Semester
URL: www.lec.edu
Established: 1856 Annual Undergrad Tuition & Fees: $26,550
Enrollment: 1,143 Coed
Affiliation or Control: Independent Non-Profit IRS Status: 501(c)3
Highest Offering: Master's
Program: Liberal Arts And General; Teacher Preparatory; Professional; Business Emphasis
Accreditation: NH, IACBE, @TEAC

01 President .... Michael T. VICTOR
05 Interim Vice Pres Acad Affairs/CAO .... Jana HOLWICK
10 Vice Pres Administration & Finance .... Rick EPLAWY
30 Vice Pres Institutional Advancement .... Scott EVANS
84 VP Enroll Mgmt & Student Affairs .... Robin MCDERMOTT
53 Interim Dean of Education .... John MEEHL
50 Dean of Management Studies .... Prof. Robert TREBAR
88 Dean of Equine Studies .... Dr. Elisabeth GIEDT
06 Registrar .... Barbara ARILSON
88 Director Professional Development .... Kathleen HOMYOCK
37 Director of Financial Aid .... Patricia PANGONIS
15 Director of Human Resources .... Alexis HANNA
13 Director of Information Technology .... Jason SPOTZ
32 Dean of Students .... Billie DUNN
07 Director Admissions/Financial Aid .... Chris HARRIS
18 Director of Physical Plant .... Herb DILL
29 Dir of Alumni and Public Relations .... Susan LICATE
41 Director of Athletics .... Griz ZIMMERMANN
40 Bookstore Manager .... Michael NORRIS
08 Director of Lincoln Library .... Christopher BENNETT
21 Business Manager .... Andy MERRILL
39 Director of Residence Life .... Megan MCKENNA
18 Director Facilities/Event Planning .... Debra REMINGTON
09 Institutional Research Specialist .... Amanda ZINNI

Lakeland Community College (F)

7700 Clocktower Drive, Kirtland OH 44094-5198
County: Lake FICE Identification: 006804
Unit ID: 203599
Telephone: (440) 525-7000 Carnegie Class: Assoc/Pub-S-SC
FAX Number: (440) 525-7651 Calendar System: Semester
URL: www.lakelandcc.edu
Established: 1967 Annual Undergrad Tuition & Fees (In-District): $2,887
Enrollment: 9,866 Coed
Affiliation or Control: State/Local IRS Status: 501(c)3
Highest Offering: Associate Degree
Program: Occupational; 2-Year Principally Bachelor's Creditable
Accreditation: NH, ADNUR, DH, ENGT, HT, IFSAC, MAC, MLTAD, RAD, SURGT

01 President .... Dr. Morris W. BEVERAGE, JR.
05 Exec VP & Provost/Dean Faculty .... Dr. Frederick W. LAW
10 Sr Vice Pres Admin Svcs/Treasurer .... Mr. Michael E. MAYHER
100 Chief of Staff/Sr VP Inst Effectiv .... Ms. Mary Ann BLAKELEY
26 Chief Commun Ofcr/VP College Rels .... Ms. Dawn M. PLANTE
38 Assc Provst Teaching/Learning Effct .... Vacant
20 Assoc VP Student Development .... Mr. Richard J. NOVOTNY
83 Dean Social Science/Public Services .... Dr. Steven OLUIC
76 Dean Science/Health/Math .... Ms. Deborah L. HARDY
79 Dean Arts/Humanities .... Dr. Donald KILLEEN
50 Dean Business/Engineering .... Dr. Gary L. EITH
103 Dean Wrkfce Devel/Continuing Educ .... Mrs. Patricia J. HOYT
88 Dean of Learning Technologies .... Mr. William KNAPP
88 Senior Director Business Services .... Mr. Stefan MAGYARI
13 Dir Administrative Technologies .... Mr. Rick PENNY
31 Director Community Learning .... Dr. William BEISEL
21 Controller & Bursar .... Mr. Paul D. HENSCHEL
15 Director Hum Res/Organizational Dev .... Ms. Cathy BUSH
18 Director for Facilities Management .... Mr. Bert DIEHL
19 Chief of Police/Director of Safety .... Mr. Gerald JENKINS
07 Director for Admissions/Registrar .... Ms. Tracey L. COOPER
37 Dir Financial Aid/Enroll Support .... Ms. Melissa A. AMSPAUGH
35 Director of Student Activities .... Mr. Mario PETITTI
30 Dir Development/Alumni Relations .... Dr. Robert CAHEN
96 Director of Purchasing .... Mr. Tom A. KIRCHNER
09 Manager of Institutional Research .... Vacant

Lakewood College (G)

12900 Lake Avenue, Lakewood OH 44107-1558
County: Cuyahoga Identification: 666715
Telephone: (800) 517-0857 Carnegie Class: Not Classified
FAX Number: (216) 803-9899 Calendar System: Other
URL: www.lakewoodcollege.edu
Established: 1998 Annual Undergrad Tuition & Fees: $4,500
Enrollment: N/A Coed
Affiliation or Control: Independent Non-Profit IRS Status: 501(c)3
Highest Offering: Associate Degree
Program: Occupational
Accreditation: DETC

01 President .... Ms. Tanya HAGGINS

Laura and Alvin Siegal College of Judaic Studies (H)

26500 Shaker Boulevard, Beachwood OH 44122-7197
County: Cuyahoga FICE Identification: 012838
Unit ID: 202019
Telephone: (216) 464-4050 Carnegie Class: Not Classified
FAX Number: (216) 464-5827 Calendar System: Semester
URL: www.siegalcollege.edu
Established: 1963 Annual Undergrad Tuition & Fees: $17,990
Enrollment: 125 Coed
Affiliation or Control: Independent Non-Profit IRS Status: 501(c)3
Highest Offering: Master's
Program: Liberal Arts And General; Teacher Preparatory
Accreditation: NH

01 Interim President .... Dr. Seymour KOPELOWITZ
05 Provost .... Dr. Brian D. AMKRAUT
08 Chief Librarian .... Mrs. Jean LETTOFSKY
30 Director of Development .... Vacant
13 Director Information Technology .... Mr. Eli ASCHKENASY

Lincoln College (I)

149 Northland Boulevard, Cincinnati OH 45246-1116
County: Hamilton Identification: 666472
Unit ID: 205708
Telephone: (513) 874-0432 Carnegie Class: Assoc/PrivFP
FAX Number: (513) 874-0123 Calendar System: Quarter
URL: www.swcollege.net
Established: 1978 Annual Undergrad Tuition & Fees: $20,200
Enrollment: 605 Coed
Affiliation or Control: Proprietary IRS Status: Proprietary
Highest Offering: Associate Degree
Program: Occupational
Accreditation: ACICS, MAAB

01 Executive Director .... Mr. James D. VAAS

† Branch campus of Southwester College, Dayton, OH.

Lincoln College of Technology (J)

632 Vine Street, Suite 200, Cincinnati OH 45202-2421
County: Hamilton Identification: 666471
Unit ID: 205717
Telephone: (513) 421-3212 Carnegie Class: Assoc/PrivFP
FAX Number: (513) 421-8325 Calendar System: Quarter
URL: www.lincolncollegeoftechnology.com
Established: 1973 Annual Undergrad Tuition & Fees: $14,100
Enrollment: 517 Coed
Affiliation or Control: Proprietary IRS Status: Proprietary
Highest Offering: Associate Degree
Program: Occupational; 2-Year Principally Bachelor's Creditable; Business Emphasis
Accreditation: ACICS, MAAB

01 Executive Director ....Mr. Mark MANN

† Branch campus of Lincoln College of Technology, Dayton, OH.

Lincoln College of Technology (A)

111 W First Street, Suite 700, Dayton OH 45402-1105
County: Montgomery FICE Identification: 012128
Unit ID: 205726
Telephone: (937) 224-0061 Carnegie Class: Assoc/PrivFP
FAX Number: (937) 224-0065 Calendar System: Quarter
URL: www.lincolnedu.com
Established: 1978 Annual Undergrad Tuition & Fees: $14,550
Enrollment: 615 Coed
Affiliation or Control: Proprietary IRS Status: Proprietary
Highest Offering: Associate Degree
Program: Occupational
Accreditation: ACICS, MAAB

01 Director ....Mr. James A. SMOLINSKI
06 Registrar ....Ms. Goddess HARRIS
07 Director of Admissions ....Mr. Bill FURLONG
36 Director Student Placement ....Ms. Melanie JOHNSON
37 Director Student Financial Aid ....Ms. Abby WILKINS

Lincoln College of Technology (B)

201 E Second Street, Franklin OH 45005-2267
County: Warren Identification: 666473
Unit ID: 205692
Telephone: (937) 746-6633 Carnegie Class: Assoc/PrivFP
FAX Number: (937) 746-6754 Calendar System: Quarter
URL: www.lincolnedu.com
Established: 1978 Annual Undergrad Tuition & Fees: $19,000
Enrollment: 398 Coed
Affiliation or Control: Proprietary IRS Status: Proprietary
Highest Offering: Associate Degree
Program: Occupational; 2-Year Principally Bachelor's Creditable; Technical Emphasis
Accreditation: ACICS, MAAB

01 Director ....Ronald MILLS

† Branch campus of Southwester College, Dayton, OH.

Lorain County Community College (C)

1005 N Abbe Road, Elyria OH 44035-1691
County: Lorain FICE Identification: 003068
Unit ID: 203748
Telephone: (440) 365-5222 Carnegie Class: Assoc/Pub-U-SC
FAX Number: (440) 365-6519 Calendar System: Semester
URL: www.lorainccc.edu
Established: 1963 Annual Undergrad Tuition & Fees (In-District): $2,680
Enrollment: 13,929 Coed
Affiliation or Control: State/Local IRS Status: 501(c)3
Highest Offering: Associate Degree
Program: Occupational; 2-Year Principally Bachelor's Creditable
Accreditation: NH, ADNUR, ART, DH, DMS, ENGT, MAC, MLTAD, PNUR, PTAA, RAD, SURGT

01 President ....Dr. Roy A. CHURCH
46 VP Strategic & Institutional Devel ....Ms. Marcia J. BALLINGER
05 Provost/VP for Acad & Student Svcs ....Ms. Marcia BALLINGER
10 Vice President Admin Svcs/Treasurer ....Mr. David J. CUMMINS
88 Assoc Prov University Partnership ....Dr. John R. CROOKS
08 Dean Library-Instruction Media ....Mr. Keith E. WASHBURN
84 Dean Enroll Svcs/Fin Aid/Registrar ....Ms. Stephanie SUTTON
14 Int Director Information Systems ....Mr. Andrew DOVCI
15 Director Human Resources ....Mrs. Sydney LANCASTER
88 Dir Entrepreneurship Innov Inst ....Dr. James SHANAHAN
19 Director of Campus Security ....Mr. Keith BROWN
18 Director of Physical Plant ....Mr. Robert FLYER
51 Director Public Services ....Ms. Shara DAVIS
88 Dean Academic Foundations ....Dr. Generosa LOPEZ-MOLINA
57 Dir Stocker Humanit/Fine Arts Ctr ....Ms. Janet HERMAN-BARLOW
09 Director Institutional Effect/Plng ....Dr. Shara DAVIS
96 Dir Purchasing/Facilities Planning ....Ms. Laura K. CARISSIMI
50 Dean of Business ....Dr. Robert B. YOUNG
54 Dean Engineering Tech ....Ms. Kelly ZELESNIK
76 Dean Allied Health & Nursing ....Dr. Frank P. WARD
79 Dean Arts/Humanities ....Dr. Robert A. BECKSTROM
81 Dean Science/Math ....Dr. Palanivel MANOHARAN
83 Dean Social Science/Human Svc ....Dr. Sunil AHUJA
68 Dean Health/PE/Recreation ....Ms. Laurie J. CARLBERG

Lourdes University (D)

6832 Convent Boulevard, Sylvania OH 43560-2898
County: Lucas FICE Identification: 003069
Unit ID: 203757
Telephone: (419) 885-3211 Carnegie Class: Master's S
FAX Number: (419) 882-3987 Calendar System: Semester
URL: www.lourdes.edu
Established: 1958 Annual Undergrad Tuition & Fees: $13,176
Enrollment: 2,241 Coed
Affiliation or Control: Roman Catholic IRS Status: 501(c)3
Highest Offering: Master's
Program: Liberal Arts And General; Professional
Accreditation: NH, ANEST, IACBE, NURSE, SW, TEAC

01 President ....Dr. Robert C. HELMER
00 President Emerita ....Sr. Ann Francis KLIMKOWSKI
05 Provost ....Dr. Janet ROBINSON
32 Vice Pres for Student Life ....Ms. Roseanne GILL-JACOBSON
10 Vice Pres Finance & Administration ....Mr. Michael KILLIAN
42 Vice Pres for Mission & Ministry .Sr. Ann Carmen BARONE, OSF
30 Vice President for Inst Advancement ....Ms. Mary ARQUETTE
20 Associate Provost ....Dr. Keith SCHLENDER
49 Dean College of Arts & Sciences ....Dr. Geoffrey J. GRUBB
107 Dean Coll of Education & Human Svcs ....Dr. Michael J. SMITH
66 Dean College of Nursing ....Dr. Judy DIDION
50 Dean College Business & Leadership ....Dr. Dean LUDWIG
58 Dean of Graduate School ....Dr. Deborah SCHWARTZ
35 Dean of Students & Retention ....Dr. Kim GRIEVE
37 Director Financial Aid ....Ms. Denise MCCLUSKEY
26 Director of College Relations ....Ms. Helene SHEETS
08 Director of Library Services ....Sr. Sandra RUTKOWSKI
06 Registrar ....Ms. Michelle A. RABLE
13 Director of Information Technology ....Dr. LeRoy BUTLER
07 Director of Admissions ....Ms. Amy MERGEN
15 Director of Human Resources ....Mr. Scott SIMON
85 Director Foreign Students ....Vacant
36 Director of Career Counseling ....Ms. Janet DICKSON
11 Director of Administrative Systems ....Ms. Laurie ORZECHOWSKI
21 Director of Finance ....Ms. Brigette SADOWSKI
88 Director of Advising Center ....Ms. Mary DOUGLAS
29 Director Development/Alumni Affairs ....Ms. Aileen MEYER
18 Director of Facilities & Grounds ....Mr. Jim KALISZUK
09 Director of Institutional Research ....Ms. Pam CURAVO
40 Manager of Bookstore ....Ms. Jessica KLIMESH

Malone University (E)

2600 Cleveland Avenue NW, Canton OH 44709-3897
County: Stark FICE Identification: 003072
Unit ID: 203775
Telephone: (330) 471-8100 Carnegie Class: Master's M
FAX Number: (330) 471-8478 Calendar System: Semester
URL: www.malone.edu
Established: 1892 Annual Undergrad Tuition & Fees: $23,420
Enrollment: 2,511 Coed
Affiliation or Control: Friends IRS Status: 501(c)3
Highest Offering: Master's
Program: Liberal Arts And General; Teacher Preparatory; Professional
Accreditation: NH, ACBSP, IACBE, NURSE, SW, TED

01 Interim President ....Dr. Wilbert J. FRIESEN
10 Vice President for Finance/CFO ....Mrs. Joy E. BRATHWAITE
05 Interim Provost ....Dr. Donald L. TUCKER
30 Vice Pres for Univ Advancement ....Mr. Howard E. TAYLOR
84 Vice Pres for Enrollment Management ....Dr. Brock C. SCHROEDER
32 Vice Pres for Student Development ....Dr. Christopher T. ABRAMS
49 Dean Col of Theol/Arts & Sciences ....Dr. D. Nathan PHINNEY
51 Dean Sch of Business & Leadership ....Dr. Marjorie F. CARLSON HURST
53 Dean Sch of Education & Human Devel ....Dr. Rhoda C. SOMMERS
66 Dean Sch of Nursing & Health Sci ....Dr. Loretta M. REINHART
35 Assoc Dean Student Development ....Mr. Joshua L. PERKINS
21 Controller ....Mr. Ronald B. MESSNER
06 Registrar ....Mr. Gary L. PHELPS
07 Director of Admissions ....Mr. David L. KLEFFMAN
29 Dir of Alumni & Parent Relations ....Mrs. Deborah M. ROBINSON
44 Director of The Malone Fund ....Mr. F. Allen FRALEY
36 Director Career Development Center ....Mr. Douglas C. REICHENBERGER
27 Director of University Relations ....Mrs. Suzanne W. THOMAS
30 Director of Development ....Mr. John C. FEHLMAN
88 Director of Church Relations ....Mr. Timothy G. PITZER
105 Web Administrator ....Mr. Michael R. MILLER
37 Director of Financial Aid ....Mrs. Pamela S. PUSTAY
15 Director of Human Resources ....Mr. Michael J. FAIRLESS
13 Director of Info Technologies ....Mr. Clark D. HOOPES
41 Athletic Director ....Mr. Charles R. GRIMES
08 Director of Library Services ....Dr. Joseph A. MCDONALD
93 Director of Multicultural Services ....Mrs. Brenda D. STEVENS
18 Director of Physical Plant ....Mr. James E. PALONE
88 Director of Student Retention ....Mrs. Patricia L. LITTLE
91 Asst Dir of Info Technologies ....Mr. John D. RIVERS
90 Senior Systems Engineer ....Mr. Alexander YU
42 University Chaplain ....Rev. L. Randall HECKERT
40 Bookstore Manager ....Ms. Rebecca E. ABEL
09 Assistant to the Provost ....Ms. Karen R. WARNER
92 Director of Honors Programs ....Dr. Diane M. CHAMBERS
89 Dir of the College Experience Pgm ....Dr. Marcia K. EVERETT
38 Director of Counseling Center ....Mr. Timothy T. MORBER
23 Health Center Nurse ....Mrs. Janet A. PERKO
24 Technology Services Coordinator ....Mr. M. Adam KLEMANN

Marietta College (F)

215 Fifth Street, Marietta OH 45750-4033
County: Washington FICE Identification: 003073
Unit ID: 203845
Telephone: (740) 376-4000 Carnegie Class: Bac/Diverse
FAX Number: (740) 376-4896 Calendar System: Semester
URL: www.marietta.edu
Established: 1835 Annual Undergrad Tuition & Fees: $38,780
Enrollment: 1,604 Coed
Affiliation or Control: Independent Non-Profit IRS Status: 501(c)3
Highest Offering: Master's
Program: Liberal Arts And General; Teacher Preparatory; Professional
Accreditation: NH, ARCPA, ENG, TED

01 President ....Dr. Jean A. SCOTT
05 Interim Provost/Dean of Faculty ....Dr. Gamaliel (Gama) PERRUCI
10 Vice President for Admin & Finance ....Mr. Daniel C. BRYANT
30 Vice President College Advancement ....Ms. Lori A. LEWIS
84 Vice President for Enrollment ....Mr. David J. RHODES
32 Vice President for Student Life ....Dr. Robert A. PASTOOR
29 Assoc VP Alumni/College Relations ....Mr. Crompton (Hub) B. BURTON
44 Asst VP Advancement/Planned Giving ....Mr. Evan BOHNEN
88 Dean McDonough Ctr for Leadership ....Dr. Gamaliel (Gama) PERRUCI
101 Secretary Board of Trustees ....Mr. William H. DONNELLY
08 Director of Library ....Dr. N. Douglas ANDERSON
21 Interim Controller ....Ms. Traci PERRY
37 Director Student Financial Services ....Mr. Kevin D. LAMB
18 Director of Physical Plant ....Mr. Fred R. SMITH
38 Counseling Services ....Dr. J. Michael HARDING
06 Registrar ....Ms. Tina K. PERDUE
15 Director of Human Resources ....Ms. Victoria A. FORD
19 Chief of Campus Police ....Mr. Thomas M. SACCENTI
26 Director of College Relations ....Mr. Thomas D. PERRY
07 Director of Admissions ....Mr. Jason J. TURLEY
09 Director of Institutional Research ....Dr. Gregory J. DELEMEESTER
36 Career Center Director ....Ms. B. Hilles HUGHES
41 Director of Athletics ....Mr. Larry R. HISER
27 Chief Information Officer ....Mr. John R. DAVIS
63 Dir Physician Assistant Programs ....Dr. Gloria STEWART
85 Dir International Student Programs ....Ms. Christy BURKE
105 Webmaster ....Mr. Chris J. CRAIG
25 Grants Officer ....Ms. Elizabeth B. MCNALLY
51 Continuing Education ....Ms. Tina K. PERDUE
35 Dean of Students ....Mr. Bruce E. PETERSON
20 Assoc Provost for Academic Admin ....Dr. Mark A. MILLER

Marion Technical College (G)

1467 Mount Vernon Avenue, Marion OH 43302-5694
County: Marion FICE Identification: 010736
Unit ID: 203881
Telephone: (740) 389-4636 Carnegie Class: Assoc/Pub-R-M
FAX Number: (740) 389-6136 Calendar System: Quarter
URL: www.mtc.edu
Established: 1971 Annual Undergrad Tuition & Fees (In-State): $4,020
Enrollment: 2,763 Coed
Affiliation or Control: State IRS Status: 501(c)3
Highest Offering: Associate Degree
Program: Occupational; 2-Year Principally Bachelor's Creditable
Accreditation: NH, ADNUR, MAC, MLTAD, PTAA, RAD

01 President ....Dr. J. Richard BRYSON
10 Vice Pres Financial/Admin Services ....Mr. L. Douglas BOYER
05 Vice Pres Instructional Services ....Mr. Dennis BUDKOWSKI
32 VP of Student Svcs & Inst Advance ....Vacant
84 Dean of Enrollment Services ....Mr. Joel O. LILES
06 Registrar ....Mr. Jim LAVERY
13 Director Mgmt Information Systems ....Ms. Joy A. MOORE
26 Director of Public Relations ....Ms. Nikki WORKMAN
66 Dean of Nursing Technology ....Ms. Carol HOFFMAN
103 Director Ctr Workforce Development ....Vacant
15 Director Human Resources ....Ms. Brenda MCKINNON
88 Dir Physical Therapist Asst Pgm ....Ms. Susan COTTERMAN
88 Dir Occupational Therapy ....Mr. Chad SCHNEIDER
04 Assistant to Pres for Research/Plng ....Ms. Teresa PARKER
18 Coord Facil Improvements/Operations ....Ms. Leeann GRAU
37 Coordinator Student Financial Aid ....Ms. Deb LANGDON
54 Dean of Engineering Technology ....Vacant
50 Dean of Business/Information Tech ....Ms. Vicky WOOD
49 Dean of Arts and Sciences ....Mr. Scott POTTER
76 Dean of Allied Health ....Ms. Deborah BATES

Mercy College of Ohio (H)

2221 Madison Avenue, Toledo OH 43604
County: Lucas FICE Identification: 030970
Unit ID: 203960
Telephone: (419) 251-1313 Carnegie Class: Spec/Health
FAX Number: (419) 251-1570 Calendar System: Semester
URL: www.mercycollege.edu
Established: 1993 Annual Undergrad Tuition & Fees: $8,352
Enrollment: 1,197 Coed
Affiliation or Control: Roman Catholic IRS Status: 501(c)3
Highest Offering: Baccalaureate
Program: 2-Year Principally Bachelor's Creditable; Nursing Emphasis
Accreditation: NH, ADNUR, NUR, NURSE, POLYT, RAD

01 President ....Mr. John HAYWARD
05 VP Acad Affs/Dean of Faculty ....Dr. Anne LOOCHTAN
11 Vice Pres Administrative Services ....Mr. James L. HARTER
66 Associate Dean Nursing ....Dr. Maria NOWICKI
81 Associate Dean Science Division ....Dr. Barbara STOOS
97 Associate Dean General Studies ....Dr. Regan BROCK
76 Assoc Dean Allied Health/Dist Ed ....Dr. Kimberly WATSON
45 Director College Finances/Res Plng ..Ms. Joan M. RUTHERFORD
30 Director College Advancement ....Mr. Michael WHALEN
84 Dir Enroll Svcs/Chief Admiss Ofcr .Dr. Shelly MCCOY GRISSOM
08 Director Library/Resource Services ....Ms. Deborah JOHNSON
91 Manager College Admin Info Systems ....Mr. Gary BROCK
06 Registrar ....Ms. Heather HOPPE
37 Financial Aid Director ....Ms. Julie LESLIE
26 Director of Communications ....Ms. Denise HUDGIN
42 Dir Campus Ministry/Coord Ser Learn ....Sr. Sally BOHNETT

10 Business Officer .... Ms. Diane RAHN
88 Director Short Term Educ Programs .... Ms. Cheryl NUTTER
09 Director of Institutional Research .... Ms. Heather HOPPE
15 Director Personnel Services .... Ms. Janice BERNARD
18 Chief Facilities/Physical Plant .... Mr. James HARTER
29 Director Alumni Relations .... Sr. Barbara DAVIS
32 Chief Student Life Officer .... Ms. Lori EDGEWORTH
35 Assoc Dean Student Affs/Placement .... Ms. Jennifer PIZIO
38 Director Student Counseling .... Ms. Wendy NATHAN
88 Director Institutional Assessment .... Ms. Janell LANG
07 Director of Admissions .... Ms. Aimee BISHOP STUART
36 Director of Career & Prof Develop .... Ms. Lori EDGEWORTH

Methodist Theological School in Ohio (A)

3081 Columbus Pike, Delaware OH 43015-3211
County: Delaware — FICE Identification: 003075
Unit ID: 203997
Telephone: (740) 363-1146 — Carnegie Class: Spec/Faith
FAX Number: (740) 362-3135 — Calendar System: 4/1/4
URL: www.mtso.edu
Established: 1958 — Annual Graduate Tuition & Fees: $15,135
Enrollment: 214 — Coed
Affiliation or Control: United Methodist — IRS Status: 501(c)3
Highest Offering: Doctorate; No Undergraduates
Program: Professional; Religious Emphasis
Accreditation: NH, THEOL

01 President .... Rev. Jay A. RUNDELL
05 Academic Dean .... Dr. Randy I. LITCHFIELD
11 VP for Administrative Services .... Mr. Jonathan D. JUMP
04 Executive Asst to the President .... Ms. Linda J. OGDEN
27 Director of Communications .... Mr. Danny RUSSELL
29 Director Alumni & Church Relations .... Rev. Benita ROLLINS
26 Director of PR and Marketing .... Mr. Danny RUSSELL
07 Director of Admissions .... Mr. Jonathan D. JUMP
06 Registrar .... Ms. Sue LAMPHERE
08 Librarian .... Mr. Paul BURNAM
21 Controller .... Mrs. Carolyn ROTHERMEL
18 Director Buildings/Grounds .... Mr. James ROHLER
32 Director of Student Life .... Rev. Leslie TAYLOR
13 Director of Information Services .... Mr. Matthew REHM

Miami-Jacobs Career College (B)

150 E Gay Street, 1st Floor, Columbus OH 43215-3227
County: Franklin — Identification: 666465
Unit ID: 369862
Telephone: (614) 221-7770 — Carnegie Class: Assoc/PrivFP
FAX Number: N/A — Calendar System: Quarter
URL: www.ohio.academycourtreporting.com
Established: 1980 — Annual Undergrad Tuition & Fees: $13,450
Enrollment: 335 — Coed
Affiliation or Control: Proprietary — IRS Status: Proprietary
Highest Offering: Associate Degree
Program: Occupational
Accreditation: ACICS

01 President/Director .... Ms. Joanie KREIN
05 Director Education/Academic Affairs .... Ms. Erin DORMAN
37 Director Financial Aid .... Ms. Lori BEARD
36 Director of Career Plng/Placement .... Ms. Mary MCCARTNEY
06 Registrar .... Mr. Scott KENNEDY
07 Director of Admissions .... Ms. Carrie SCHEIZERER

Miami-Jacobs Career College (C)

110 N Patterson Boulevard, Dayton OH 45402-1771
County: Montgomery — FICE Identification: 003076
Unit ID: 204060
Telephone: (937) 222-7337 — Carnegie Class: Assoc/PrivFP
FAX Number: (937) 461-3384 — Calendar System: Quarter
URL: www.miamijacobs.edu
Established: 1860 — Annual Undergrad Tuition & Fees: $13,750
Enrollment: 690 — Coed
Affiliation or Control: Proprietary — IRS Status: Proprietary
Highest Offering: Associate Degree
Program: Occupational; 2-Year Principally Bachelor's Creditable
Accreditation: ACICS, COMTA, MAC, SURGT

01 Campus Director .... Mr. Ned SYNDER
11 Assoc Campus Director .... Ms. Angela MARTIN
05 Academic Dean .... Ms. Jennifer FRIEND
37 Director Student Financial Aid .... Ms. Marcia BYRD

Miami University (D)

501 E High Street, Oxford OH 45056-1846
County: Butler — FICE Identification: 003077
Unit ID: 204024
Telephone: (513) 529-1809 — Carnegie Class: RU/H
FAX Number: (513) 529-3841 — Calendar System: Semester
URL: www.muohio.edu
Established: 1809 — Annual Undergrad Tuition & Fees (In-State): $12,198
Enrollment: 23,426 — Coed
Affiliation or Control: State — IRS Status: 501(c)3
Highest Offering: Doctorate
Program: Liberal Arts And General; Teacher Preparatory; Professional
Accreditation: NH, ART, BUS, BUSA, CIDA, CLPSY, CS, DIETD, ENG, ENGT, IPSY, MUS, NUR, NURSE, SP, SW, TED, THEA

01 President .... Dr. David HODGE
05 Exec Vice Pres Academic Affs/Prov .... Dr. Bobby GEMPESAW
10 VP Finance & Bus Svcs/Treasurer .... Dr. David CREAMER
32 Vice President Student Affairs .... Dr. Barbara JONES
30 Vice Pres University Advancement .... Ms. Jayne E. WHITEHEAD
13 Int VP Information Technology .... Ms. Debra A. ALLISON
15 Ast Prov Personnel/Dir Acad Per Svc .... Dr. Janet L. COX
21 Assoc VP Finance/Business Svcs .... Dr. David A. ELLIS
20 Assoc Provost/VP Academic Affairs .... Dr. Michael E. DANTLEY
35 Assoc VP Student Affs/Dean Students .... Dr. Gerri S. MOSLEY-HOWARD
27 Assoc VP for Univ Communications .... Ms. Dionn M. TRON
18 Assoc VP Physical Facilities .... Vacant
84 Assoc VP Enrollment Mgmt .... Mr. Michael S. KABBAZ
28 Assoc VP Inst Diversity .... Dr. Ronald B. SCOTT
29 Asst Vice Pres Alumni Relations .... Mr. Raymond F. MOCK
26 Director Institutional Relations .... Mr. Randi Malcolm THOMAS
100 Secy Board/Exec Asst to President .... Mr. Stephen D. SNYDER
49 Int Dean College Arts & Science .... Dr. Phyllis CALLAHAN
76 Dean Kinesiology & Health .... Dr. Carine FEYTEN
50 Dean School of Business .... Dr. Roger L. JENKINS
57 Dean School of Fine Arts .... Dr. James P. LENTINI
72 Dean Sch Engineering/Applied Sci .... Dr. Marek DOLLAR
08 Dean & University Librarian .... Ms. Judith A. SESSIONS
58 Dean Graduate School .... Dr. Bruce J. COCHRANE
12 Dean Regional Campus .... Dr. G. Michael PRATT
88 Assoc Provost/Assoc Vice Pres .... Dr. Raymond F. GORMAN
07 Interim Director of Admission .... Ms. Ann LARSON
51 Director of Lifelong Learning .... Ms. Cheryl D. YOUNG
88 Univ Dir/Teach Effectiveness Pgm .... Dr. Cecilia M. SHORE
88 Univ Dir Liberal Educ/Assessment .... Dr. John P. TASSONI
92 Univ Dir Honors & Scholars Program .... Dr. Carolyn HAYNES
15 Sr Director Human Resources .... Ms. Carol HAUSER
88 Dir Center American/World Cultures .... Dr. Mary Jane BERMAN
23 Medical Director Student Health Svc .... Dr. Gregory CALKINS
104 Director Intl Education Services .... Dr. David KEITGES
06 University Registrar .... Mr. David M. SAUTER
36 Director Career Services .... Ms. Suzanne B. MARTIN
38 Director Student Counseling Service .... Dr. Kip C. ALISHIO
09 Director Institutional Research .... Ms. Denise A. KRALLMAN
27 Assoc Dir Univ Communications .... Ms. Claire M. WAGNER
19 Chief of Police/Dir Public Safety .... Mr. John MCCANDLESS
96 Sr Director Purchasing/Central Svcs .... Mr. William G. SHAWVER
43 University General Counsel .... Ms. Robin L. PARKER
22 Director Equity & Equal Opportunity .... Mr. Matthew L. BOAZ
41 Director Intercollegiate Athletics .... Mr. Brad J. BATES
23 Asst VP for Student Health & Well .... Ms. Gail A. WALENGA
04 Assistant to the President .... Ms. Deborah P. MASON

Miami University Hamilton Campus (E)

1601 University Boulevard, Hamilton OH 45011-3399
County: Butler — FICE Identification: 003079
Unit ID: 204006
Telephone: (513) 785-3000 — Carnegie Class: Assoc/Pub4
FAX Number: (513) 785-3145 — Calendar System: Semester
URL: www.ham.muohio.edu
Established: 1968 — Annual Undergrad Tuition & Fees (In-State): $4,632
Enrollment: 3,682 — Coed
Affiliation or Control: State — IRS Status: 501(c)3
Highest Offering: Baccalaureate
Program: Occupational; 2-Year Principally Bachelor's Creditable; Liberal Arts And General
Accreditation: &NH, ADNUR

01 Asc Provost/Dn of Regional Campuses .... Dr. G. Michael PRATT
05 Assoc Dean for Academic Affairs .... Dr. Michael CARRAFIELLO
32 Regional Assoc Dean of Students .... Dr. Robert H. RUSBOSIN
11 Sr Director of Administration .... Mr. Christopher CONNELL
06 Regional Dir Registration Records .... Ms. Joanna SHOFIELD
07 Director Recruitment/Admiss/Fin Aid .... Mr. Archie NELSON
08 Director Regional Campus Library .... Ms. Krista MCDONALD
27 Campus Communications Officer .... Mr. Perry RICHARDSON
30 Director of Advancement .... Ms. Mary BENNETT
22 Director of Multicultural Services .... Mr. Jimmie L. JONES
26 Director of Marketing .... Ms. Michele DIENNO
18 Director of Physical Facilities .... Mr. Scott BROWN
88 Director of Conference Services .... Mr. Brett COUCH
85 Director International Initiatives .... Ms. Chen FERGUSON
31 Director of Civic Engagement .... Ms. Annie MILLER

† Regional accreditation is carried under the parent institution in Oxford, OH.

Miami University Middletown (F)

4200 E University Boulevard, Middletown OH 45042-3497
County: Butler — FICE Identification: 003080
Unit ID: 204015
Telephone: (513) 727-3200 — Carnegie Class: Assoc/Pub4
FAX Number: (513) 727-3223 — Calendar System: Semester
URL: www.mid.muohio.edu
Established: 1963 — Annual Undergrad Tuition & Fees (In-State): $4,632
Enrollment: 2,272 — Coed
Affiliation or Control: State — IRS Status: 501(c)3
Highest Offering: Baccalaureate
Program: Occupational; 2-Year Principally Bachelor's Creditable; Liberal Arts And General
Accreditation: &NH, ADNUR

01 Associate Dean .... Dr. Cathy BISHOP-CLARK
07 Asst Director of Admissions .... Ms. Diane CANTONWINE
05 Assoc Dean Academic Affairs .... Dr. Rob SCHORMAN
32 Regional Sr Assoc Dean of Students .... Dr. Robert RUSBOSIN
08 Director of Regional Campus Library .... Mr. John BURKE
06 Regional Dir Records & Registration .... Ms. Joanna SHOFIELD
31 Dir Corporate Community Institute .... Ms. Pat MCNAB
10 Director Business Services .... Mr. Steve ULM
26 Director Public Affairs .... Mrs. Jan TOENNISSON
30 Director of Development .... Ms. Susan ARMACOST
18 Chief Facilities/Physical Plant .... Mr. Chuck MACK
35 Assistant Dean for Student Affairs .... Mrs. June FENING
37 Director Student Financial Aid .... Ms. Stacey ADAMS
38 Coord Counseling/Disability Svcs .... Ms. Nancy FERGUSON

† Regional accreditation is carried under the parent institution in Oxford, OH.

Mount Carmel College of Nursing (G)

127 S Davis Avenue, Columbus OH 43222-1504
County: Franklin — FICE Identification: 030719
Unit ID: 204176
Telephone: (614) 234-5800 — Carnegie Class: Spec/Health
FAX Number: (614) 234-2875 — Calendar System: Semester
URL: www.mccn.edu
Established: 1990 — Annual Undergrad Tuition & Fees: $16,604
Enrollment: 818 — Coed
Affiliation or Control: Roman Catholic — IRS Status: 501(c)3
Highest Offering: Master's
Program: Professional; Nursing Emphasis
Accreditation: NH, DIETI, NURSE

01 President .... Dr. Ann E. SCHIELE
05 Associate Dean Undergrad Nsg Pgm .... Dr. Barbara BARTA
05 Associate Dean Graduate Nursing Pgm .... Dr. Angela PHILLIPS-LOWE
06 Director of Records & Registration .... Ms. Karen L. GREENE
10 Director Business Affairs .... Ms. Kathy SMITH
07 Director Recruitment & Admissions .... Ms. Kim CAMPBELL
13 Systems Administrator .... Mr. Tim TABOL
37 Director Financial Aid .... Dr. Alyncia BOWEN
32 Director Student Life .... Ms. Colleen CIPRIANI
28 Director Diversity/Comm Initiative .... Ms. Kathlynne D. ESPY
04 Coord Administrative/Support Svcs .... Ms. Robin L. SHOCKLEY
29 Coordinator Alumni Affairs .... Ms. Phylis CROOK
26 Director College Relations .... Ms. Robin HUTCHINSON BELL
08 Director Library Services .... Mr. Stevo ROKSANDIC

Mount Vernon Nazarene University (H)

800 Martinsburg Road, Mount Vernon OH 43050-9500
County: Knox — FICE Identification: 007085
Unit ID: 204194
Telephone: (740) 392-6868 — Carnegie Class: Master's M
FAX Number: (740) 397-2769 — Calendar System: 4/1/4
URL: www.mvnu.edu
Established: 1968 — Annual Undergrad Tuition & Fees: $22,080
Enrollment: 2,609 — Coed
Affiliation or Control: Church Of The Nazarene — IRS Status: 501(c)3
Highest Offering: Master's
Program: Liberal Arts And General; Teacher Preparatory
Accreditation: NH, ACBSP, MUS, NURSE, SW, TED

01 President .... Dr. Daniel J. MARTIN
10 Vice President Finance/Treasurer .... Mr. Jeffrey B. SPEAR
05 Provost and CAO .... Dr. Henry W. SPAULDING, II
84 Vice President for Enrollment Dev .... Mr. Doug BANBURY
32 Vice President Student Life .... Dr. Lanette SESSINK
42 University Chaplain .... Rev. Scott PETERSON
20 Assoc VP for Academic Affairs .... Dr. Robert P. HAMILL
20 Associate VP for Academic Programs .... Dr. Michael VANZANT
30 Mgr Development Operations .... Mr. Ben BLAKE
21 Director of Business Services .... Mr. Alan D. SHAFFER
06 University Registrar .... Mr. Mel SEVERNS
24 Educational Resource Ctr Specialist .... Mrs. Vicki SNYDER
15 Director of Human Resources .... Mr. Patrick L. RHOTON
38 Director Counseling and Wellness .... Mr. Eric BROWNING
91 Director of Information Technology .... Mr. Stephen H. DOENGES
19 Coordinator of Campus Safety .... Mr. Rick JOHNSON
29 Director of Alumni Relations .... Mr. Thomas H. WEST
40 Director of the Bookstore .... Mrs. Gina A. BLANCHARD
41 Athletic Director .... Mr. Paul P. SWANSON
27 Director Communications .... Mr. Jeffrey SCOTT
53 Dir Teacher Education/Certification .... Dr. Debbie SHEPHERD-GREGG
37 Dir of Student Financial Services .... Mrs. Mary CANNON
18 Director of Facilities Management .... Mr. Dennis D. TAYLOR
21 Controller .... Mr. Steven JENKINS
35 Director of Student Involvement .... Mr. Travis KELLER
39 Director of Residence Life .... Vacant
28 Director Multicultural Affairs .... Mr. James M. SINGLETARY
09 Director Inst Research & Compliance .... Mrs. Kathy GRIFFITH

Muskingum University (I)

163 Stormont Street, New Concord OH 43762-1199
County: Muskingum — FICE Identification: 003084
Unit ID: 204264
Telephone: (740) 826-8211 — Carnegie Class: Master's M
FAX Number: (740) 826-8404 — Calendar System: Semester
URL: www.muskingum.edu
Established: 1837 — Annual Undergrad Tuition & Fees: $21,610
Enrollment: 2,290 — Coed
Affiliation or Control: Presbyterian Church (U.S.A.) — IRS Status: 501(c)3

Highest Offering: Master's
Program: Liberal Arts And General; Teacher Preparatory
Accreditation: NH, MUS, TED

01 President .... Dr. Anne C. STEELE
05 Vice President Academic Affairs .... Dr. James CALLAGHAN
10 Vice President Business & Finance .... Mr. James R. WILSON
30 Vice President of Inst Advancement .... Mr. Carson S. WALBURN
32 Dean of Student Life .... Mrs. Janet A. HEETER-BASS
84 Dean Enrollment/Dir Financial Aid .... Mr. Jeff W. ZELLERS
20 Associate Academic Dean .... Vacant
08 Director of Library .... Dr. Sheila J. ELLENBERGER
06 Registrar .... Mr. Daniel B. WILSON
36 Assistant Director Career Services .... Mrs. Jacquelyn L. VASCURA
13 Director of Computing Services .... Mr. Lewis M. DREBLOW
26 Director Public Relations .... Ms. Janice TUCKER-MCCLOUD
29 Director Alumni Relations .... Ms. Jennifer BRONNER
07 Director of Admissions .... Mrs. Beth DALONZO
19 Director of Public Safety .... Mr. Rex NEWBANKS
42 College Minister .... Rev. William MULLINS
18 Supt of Building & Grounds .... Mr. Kevin J. WAGNER
41 Director of Athletics .... Mr. Larry SHANK
21 Associate Business Officer .... Mr. Philip LAUBE
35 Director of Student Affairs .... Ms. Susan HOGLUND
37 Director of Student Financial Aid .... Mrs. Janet VEJSICKY
38 Director of Student Counseling .... Mrs. Tracy BUGGLIN
40 Manager of Bookstore .... Mr. Lee MILLER
15 Coordinator of Human Resources .... Ms. Kathy J. MOORE

National Institute of Massotherapy (A)

3681 Manchester Road, Suite 304, Akron OH 44319
County: Summit FICE Identification: 034684
Unit ID: 412003
Telephone: (330) 867-1996 Carnegie Class: Not Classified
FAX Number: (330) 867-6422 Calendar System: Other
URL: www.nim.edu
Established: N/A Annual Undergrad Tuition & Fees: $15,540
Enrollment: 58 Coed
Affiliation or Control: Proprietary IRS Status: Proprietary
Highest Offering: Associate Degree
Program: Occupational
Accreditation: CNCE

01 President .... Mr. Stephen PERKINSON

North Central State College (B)

2441 Kenwood Circle, Box 698, Mansfield OH 44901-0698
County: Richland FICE Identification: 005313
Unit ID: 204422
Telephone: (419) 755-4800 Carnegie Class: Assoc/Pub-R-M
FAX Number: (419) 755-4750 Calendar System: Quarter
URL: www.ncstatecollege.edu
Established: 1961 Annual Undergrad Tuition & Fees (In-State): $4,091
Enrollment: 3,637 Coed
Affiliation or Control: State IRS Status: 501(c)3
Highest Offering: Associate Degree
Program: Occupational; 2-Year Principally Bachelor's Creditable
Accreditation: NH, ACBSP, ADNUR, PTAA, RAD

01 President .... Mr. Donald L. PLOTTS
04 Exec Assistant to the President .... Mr. Stephen R. WILLIAMS
10 VP Business Svcs .... Mr. Koffi AKAKPO
05 Vice President for Academic Svcs .... Dr. Karen A. REED
26 Vice Pres Inst Advancement Team .... Ms. Betty E. WELLS
32 Vice Pres Lrng Support/Retention .... Ms. Margaret (Peg) A. MOIR
15 Director of Human Resources .... Mr. R. Douglas HANUSCIN
37 Director of Financial Aid .... Mr. James PHINNEY
07 Dir of Admissions/Enrollment Svcs .... Ms. Nikia FLETCHER
08 Director Library .... Ms. Beth BURNS
22 Counselor/Coord Disability Services .... Ms. Sandra LUCKIE
50 Dean of Business/Lib Arts/Public Sv .... Dr. Gregory BUSCH
103 Dean of Tech/Workforce Develop .... Dr. Gregory TIMBERLAKE
76 Dean Health & Public Services .... Mr. James L. HULL
13 Director Information Technology .... Mr. Bob MATNEY
06 Registrar .... Mr. Mark J. MONNES
18 Chief Facilities/Physical Plant .... Mr. Dean SCHAAD
96 Director of Purchasing .... Ms. Renee NUSSBAUM
102 Foundation Director .... Ms. Chriss HARRIS
09 Director of Institutional Research .... Mr. Thomas M. PRENDERGAST
88 Director of Retention Services .... Ms. Bev WALKER
88 Phi Theta Kappa Advisor .... Ms. Barb KEENER
66 Director of Nursing Programs .... Ms. Kelly GRAY
40 Campus Bookstore Manager .... Ms. Carla BUTDORFF
21 Controller .... Ms. Lori MCKEE
12 Executive Director of Kehoe Center .... Mr. Mark COLLINS
26 Director Marketing/Creative Design .... Mr. Keith STONER
105 Web Master .... Mr. Mark HUPP
88 Director of Tech Prep .... Mr. Tom KLUDING
51 Continuing Education Director .... Ms. Gina KAMWITHI
32 Coord Student Life Activities .... Ms. Elise RIGGLE
41 Int Coord Recreation/Intra Sports .... Ms. Jennifer RACER
29 Coord of Alumni/Employer Relations .... Ms. Mary J. RODRIGUEZ
36 Coordinator of Career Development .... Mr. Troy SHUTLER

Northeastern Ohio Universities Colleges of Medicine and Pharmacy (C)

PO Box 95, State Route 44, Rootstown OH 44272-0095
County: Portage FICE Identification: 024544
Unit ID: 204477
Telephone: (330) 325-2511 Carnegie Class: Spec/Med
FAX Number: (330) 325-7943 Calendar System: Other
URL: www.neoucom.edu
Established: 1973 Annual Graduate Tuition & Fees: $30,200
Enrollment: 767 Coed
Affiliation or Control: State IRS Status: 501(c)3
Highest Offering: First Professional Degree; No Undergraduates
Program: Professional
Accreditation: NH, IPSY, MED, PH, PHAR

01 President & Dean College of Med .... Dr. Jay Alan GERSHEN
05 Sr VP Acad Affs/Exec Assoc Dean .... Dr. Mark A. PENN
10 Interim VP Administration/Finance .... Ms. Debra K. STAATS
30 Vice Pres Institutional Advancement .... Mr. Lindsey H. LOFTUS
46 VP Research/Assoc Dean Grad Studies .... Dr. Walter E. HORTON, JR.
67 Dean College of Pharmacy .... Dr. David D. ALLEN
17 Assoc Dean Clinical Sciences .... Dr. Jay C. WILLIAMSON
69 Assoc Dean Cmty Health Science .... Dr. C. William KECK
43 General Counsel .... Mrs. Maria R. SCHIMER
32 Assistant Dean Student Affairs .... Mrs. Priscilla MOSS
17 Associate Dean Clinical/Akron .... Dr. Joseph ZARCONI
17 Asc Dean Clinical/Akron Child Hosp .... Dr. Michael HOLDER
17 Assoc Dean Clinical/Akron Gen Hosp .... Dr. James M. DOUGHERTY
17 Asc Dean Clinical/Barb Citiz Hosp .... Dr. J. Randall RICHARD
17 Asc Dean Clinical/Aultman Hospital .... Dr. Martha W. MAGOON
17 Assoc Dean Clinical/Mercymed Center .... Dr. J. Richard ZIEGLER
58 Associate Dean of Graduate Studies .... Dr. Walter E. HORTON, JR.
17 Assoc Dean Clinical/St Eliz Hosp .... Dr. Michael S. KAVIC
20 Assistant Dean of Curriculum .... Dr. Martha A. SILLING
17 Assistant Professor/Forum Hlth Sys .... Dr. Alan E. EDWARDS
100 Chief of Staff .... Ms. Kathleen C. RUFF
63 Assoc Dean Hlth Professions Ed .... Dr. Clint W. SNYDER
84 Exec Dir Enrollment Services .... Ms. Michelle CASSETTY
27 Chief Information Officer .... Mr. Arasu GANESAN
26 Director Public Relations .... Mr. Mark BOSKO
09 Director Inst Effectiveness .... Dr. Margarita D. KOKINOVA
15 Director Human Resources .... Ms. Marsha S. MILLS
86 Dir Government Relations/Sec BOT .... Mr. Richard LEWIS
44 Director Development .... Ms. Abbe TURNER
18 Director Physical Plant .... Mr. Blaine M. WYCKOFF
36 Dir Career Development & Advising .... Ms. Anita R. POKORNY
06 Director Student Services/Registrar .... Ms. Michelle L. CASSETTY
24 Dir Academic Technology Svcs .... Mr. Rey T. NOTARESCHI
13 Director Information Technology .... Vacant

Northwest State Community College (D)

22-600 State Route 34, Archbold OH 43502-9542
County: Henry FICE Identification: 008677
Unit ID: 204440
Telephone: (419) 267-5511 Carnegie Class: Assoc/Pub-R-M
FAX Number: (419) 267-3688 Calendar System: Semester
URL: www.northweststate.edu
Established: 1968 Annual Undergrad Tuition & Fees (In-State): $4,150
Enrollment: 3,510 Coed
Affiliation or Control: State IRS Status: 501(c)3
Highest Offering: Associate Degree
Program: Occupational; 2-Year Principally Bachelor's Creditable
Accreditation: NH, ACBSP, ADNUR, MAC

01 President .... Dr. Thomas L. STUCKEY
05 VP for Academics .... Ms. Cindy KRUEGER
30 VP for Institutional Advancement .... Ms. Mari YODER
103 VP Workforce Development .... Mr. Thomas WYLIE
50 Dean of Business Technologies .... Dr. Von R. PLESSNER
69 Dean of Allied Health & Public Svcs .... Mrs. Lori ROBISON
49 Dean of Arts & Science .... Ms. Lana EVANS
66 Dean of Nursing .... Mrs. Lori BIRD
06 Registrar .... Ms. Connie KLINGSHIRN
40 Bookstore Manager .... Mr. Larry ZUVERS
08 Director of Student Resources .... Ms. Kristi ROTROFF
18 Director of Plant Operations .... Mr. Timothy NELSON
90 Exec Director of Info Tech .... Mr. Matthew OSBORN
15 Director of Human Resources .... Mr. Denis CIACIUCH
21 Director of Business Services .... Ms. Lynn SPEISER
07 Director of Admissions .... Mr. Dennis GIACOMINO
10 Chief Fiscal Officer .... Ms. Kathy SOARDS
44 Chief Development .... Ms. Robbin WILCOX
37 Director Student Financial Aid .... Ms. Charlotte SORG
88 Dir Facil/Construction/Renovations .... Mrs. Lise' KONECNY
32 Coordinator Student Activities .... Mr. Keith F. VAN HORN

Notre Dame College (E)

4545 College Road, South Euclid OH 44121-4293
County: Cuyahoga FICE Identification: 003085
Unit ID: 204468
Telephone: (216) 381-1680 Carnegie Class: Bac/Diverse
FAX Number: (216) 381-3802 Calendar System: Semester
URL: www.notredamecollege.edu
Established: 1922 Annual Undergrad Tuition & Fees: $24,650
Enrollment: 2,137 Coed
Affiliation or Control: Roman Catholic IRS Status: 501(c)3
Highest Offering: Master's
Program: Liberal Arts And General; Teacher Preparatory
Accreditation: NH, NURSE, TED

01 President .... Dr. Andrew P. ROTH
05 Vice Pres Academic Affairs/Provost .... Dr. Mary B. BRECKENRIDGE
10 Sr Vice Pres Finance/Administration .... Mr. John C. PHILLIPS
45 Vice Pres for Assessment Planning .... Vacant
30 Vice Pres for Development .... Mr. David A. ARMSTRONG
31 Vice Pres for Board/Community Rels .... Ms. Karen L. POELKING
20 Assoc Dean of Academic Affairs .... Vacant
66 Nursing Division Chair .... Ms. Diane JEDLICKA
53 Education Division Chair .... Dr. John GALOVIC
81 Math & Science Division Chair .... Mr. David OROSZ
50 Business Division Chair .... Ms. Karen PENLER
57 Fine Arts Division Chair .... Ms. Rachel MORRIS
26 Director of Public Relations .... Vacant
07 Director of Traditional Admissions .... Ms. Beth FORD
07 Director of the Finn Center (Adult) .... Ms. Margaret OAKAR
32 Dean for Student Affairs .... Mr. Brian EMERSON
06 Registrar .... Ms. Jameka WINDHAM
37 Dir Student Financial Assistance .... Ms. Mary MCCRYSTAL
88 Director of Student Accounts .... Mr. Jason LAPINSKI
19 Director Security/Safety .... Mr. Michael DUGAN
18 Director Physical Plant .... Mr. Tom MEEKS
91 Director Information Technology .... Mr. Michael KIEC
15 Director Personnel Services .... Ms. Susan ANDERSON
08 Director of Library .... Ms. Karen ZOLLER
42 Director Ctr Campus Theol/Ministry .... Mr. Anthony CAMINO
78 Director Coop Educ & Career Devel .... Ms. Kimberly LANE
38 Director of Counseling Center .... Ms. Susan LIPIEC
39 Director of Residence Life .... Mr. Ronald WIAFE
29 Dir Alumni Rels/Asc Dir Development .... Mrs. Mary Elizabeth COTLEUR
04 Admin Assistant to the President .... Ms. April KENNEDY
27 Chief Information Officer .... Ms. Deborah SHEREN
26 Chief Communications Officer .... Mr. Brian JOHNSTON
106 Online Education/E-learning .... Mr. Rob DAVIS

Oberlin College (F)

173 West Lorain Street, Oberlin OH 44074-1057
County: Lorain FICE Identification: 003086
Unit ID: 204501
Telephone: (440) 775-8121 Carnegie Class: Bac/A&S
FAX Number: (440) 775-8886 Calendar System: 4/1/4
URL: www.oberlin.edu
Established: 1833 Annual Undergrad Tuition & Fees: $42,842
Enrollment: 2,948 Coed
Affiliation or Control: Independent Non-Profit IRS Status: 501(c)3
Highest Offering: Master's
Program: Liberal Arts And General; Teacher Preparatory; Professional
Accreditation: NH, MUS

01 President .... Mr. Marvin KRISLOV
10 Vice President for Finance .... Mr. Ronald R. WATTS
30 VP Development/Alumni Affair .... Mr. William BARLOW
26 Vice President College Relations .... Mr. Ben JONES
49 Dean College Arts & Sciences .... Dr. Sean DECATUR
64 Dean Conservatory Music .... Dr. David H. STULL
32 Dean of Student Life .... Dr. Eric ESTES
35 Dean of Studies/VP Strategic Init .... Dr. Kathryn STUART
07 Dean Admissions/Financial Aid .... Ms. Debra J. CHERMONTE
43 VP General Counsel and Secretary .... Sandhya SUBRAMANIAN
86 Spec Asst Community/Govt Relations .... Mrs. Sandra HODGE
21 Assoc Vice Pres Finance/Controller .... Mr. Mark R. BATES
29 Exec Director Alumni Assoc .... Ms. Danielle YOUNG
20 Assoc Dean of College Arts & Sci .... Ms. Joyce BABYAK
20 Assoc Dean of College Arts & Sci .... Dr. Heather HOGAN
14 Chief Tech Ofcr/Dir Computing Ctr .... Dr. John E. BUCHER
08 Director of Libraries .... Dr. Raymond A. ENGLISH
07 Director Admissions Conservatory .... Mr. Michael C. MANDEREN
38 Director of Counseling Center .... Vacant
57 Director of Allen Art Museums .... Dr. Stephanie WILES
06 Registrar .... Ms. Elizabeth CLERKIN
37 Director of Financial Aid .... Mr. Robert A. REDDY, JR.
09 Director of Institutional Research .... Mr. Ross PEACOCK
18 Asst VP for Facilities .... Mr. Tom PICCORELLI
36 Director Career Devel/Placement .... Vacant
42 Director Religious Life .... Gregory MCGONIGLE
39 Dir Residential/Dining Services .... Ms. Molly TYSON
41 Director of Physical Educ/Athletics .... Dr. William ROTH
19 Director of Safety & Security .... Ms. Marjorie BURTON
28 Director Multicultural Affairs .... Vacant
96 Director of Purchasing .... Mr. Gary W. KOEPP
15 Manager of Employee Relations .... Vacant

Ohio Business College (G)

1880 E Dublin-Granville Road, Columbus OH 43229
County: Franklin FICE Identification: 030658
Unit ID: 453747
Telephone: (614) 891-5030 Carnegie Class: Assoc/PrivFP
FAX Number: (614) 891-5130 Calendar System: Other
URL: www.ohiobusinesscollege.edu
Established: 1903 Annual Undergrad Tuition & Fees: $12,775
Enrollment: 156 Coed
Affiliation or Control: Proprietary IRS Status: Proprietary
Highest Offering: Associate Degree
Program: Occupational; 2-Year Principally Bachelor's Creditable
Accreditation: ACICS, MAC

01 President .... Mr. Dave GLEASON
12 Director .... Mr. Dennis HIRSH

Ohio Business College (A)

5202 Timber Commons Drive, Sandusky OH 44870-5894
County: Erie Identification: 666467
Unit ID: 203739
Telephone: (419) 627-8345 Carnegie Class: Assoc/PrivFP
FAX Number: (419) 627-1958 Calendar System: Quarter
URL: www.OhioBusinessCollege.Edu
Established: 1982 Annual Undergrad Tuition & Fees: $10,800
Enrollment: 475 Coed
Affiliation or Control: Proprietary IRS Status: Proprietary
Highest Offering: Associate Degree
Program: Occupational; Business Emphasis
Accreditation: ACICS

01 School Director .... Theresa M. FISHER
37 Lead Financial Aid Administrator .... Geri WILSON
36 Director of Career Services .... Tarina OGLESBY
06 Registrar .... Rohnda PICKERING
07 Director of Admissions .... Cecilia BLEVINS
05 Director of Education .... Greg SCHULTZ

† Branch campus of Ohio Business College, Sheffield Village, OH.

Ohio Business College, Lorain Branch (B)

5095 Waterford Drive, Sheffield Village OH 44035-0701
County: Lorain FICE Identification: 021585
Unit ID: 203720
Telephone: (440) 934-3101 Carnegie Class: Assoc/PrivFP
FAX Number: (440) 934-3105 Calendar System: Quarter
URL: www.ohiobusinesscollege.edu
Established: 1903 Annual Undergrad Tuition & Fees: $12,000
Enrollment: 400 Coed
Affiliation or Control: Proprietary IRS Status: Proprietary
Highest Offering: Associate Degree
Program: Occupational; 2-Year Principally Bachelor's Creditable
Accreditation: ACICS, MAC

01 Executive Director .... Mrs. Rosanne CATELLA
07 Admissions Director .... Mr. John TOBIN
37 Financial Manager .... Mrs. Christine TODD
36 Career Services .... Ms. Lisa DANEVICH

Ohio Christian University (C)

1476 Lancaster Pike, Circleville OH 43113-0458
County: Pickaway FICE Identification: 003030
Unit ID: 201964
Telephone: (740) 474-8896 Carnegie Class: Bac/Diverse
FAX Number: (740) 477-7755 Calendar System: Semester
URL: www.ohiochristian.edu
Established: 1948 Annual Undergrad Tuition & Fees: $16,750
Enrollment: 1,700 Coed
Affiliation or Control: Other Protestant IRS Status: 501(c)3
Highest Offering: Master's
Program: 2-Year Principally Bachelor's Creditable; Teacher Preparatory; Professional; Religious Emphasis
Accreditation: NH, BI, TEAC

01 President .... Dr. Mark A. SMITH
03 Executive Vice President .... Dr. Hank KELLY
05 Vice President of Academics .... Dr. Joe C. BROWN
10 Vice President of Finance .... Mr. Robert HARTMAN
30 Vice President for Advancement .... Mr. Mark TAYLOR
32 Vice President Student Development .... Rev. Rick CHRISTMAN
14 Vice President of IT/Operations .... Mr. Curtis CHRISTOPHER
09 Director of Institutional Research .... Ms. Heidi FREDERICK
06 Registrar .... Dr. Rodney SONES
84 Associate Vice Pres Enrollment .... Mr. Michael EGENREIDER
55 Associate Dean of Adult Programs .... Mr. Tim EADES
08 Director of Library Services .... Mrs. Barbara MEISTER
37 Director Student Financial Services .... Mr. Wes BROTHERS
41 Athletic Director .... Mr. Ben BELLMAN
29 Director Alumni Relations .... Ms. Julie SORLEY

Ohio College of Massotherapy (D)

225 Heritage Woods Drive, Akron OH 44321-1363
County: Summit FICE Identification: 031163
Unit ID: 204592
Telephone: (330) 665-1084 Carnegie Class: Assoc/PrivNFP
FAX Number: (330) 665-5021 Calendar System: Semester
URL: www.ocm.edu
Established: 1973 Annual Undergrad Tuition & Fees: $19,947
Enrollment: 70 Coed
Affiliation or Control: Proprietary IRS Status: Proprietary
Highest Offering: Associate Degree
Program: 2-Year Principally Bachelor's Creditable; Technical Emphasis
Accreditation: ACCSC

01 President .... Mr. Jeffrey S. MORROW
11 Director of Administration .... Mrs. Debra M. SMITH

Ohio College of Podiatric Medicine (E)

6000 Rockside Woods Boulevard, Independence OH 44131-2330
County: Cuyahoga FICE Identification: 003088
Unit ID: 204547
Telephone: (216) 231-3300 Carnegie Class: Spec/Health
FAX Number: (216) 231-0453 Calendar System: Semester
URL: www.ocpm.edu
Established: 1916 Annual Graduate Tuition & Fees: $32,333
Enrollment: 455 Coed
Affiliation or Control: Independent Non-Profit IRS Status: 501(c)3
Highest Offering: First Professional Degree; No Undergraduates
Program: Professional
Accreditation: NH, POD

01 President .... Dr. Thomas V. MELILLO
03 Executive Vice President .... Dr. David R. NICOLANTI
05 VP Clinical Educ/Dean Academic Affs .... Dr. Vincent J. HETHERINGTON
10 Vice President of Finance .... Mr. Jon C. CARLSON
08 Librarian .... Mrs. Donna M. PERZESKI
15 Director of Human Resources .... Mr. David DIXON
32 Dean of Student Affairs/Admissions .... Mrs. Lois LOTT
06 Director of Student Records .... Mr. David PUTMAN
09 Director Institutional Research .... Ms. Jill S. CARROLL
40 Manager Bookstore .... Vacant
29 Exec Director of Alumni Association .... Mr. Mark SYRONEY
36 Graduate Placement Coordinator .... Ms. Apryl KING
30 Institutional Advancement .... Mr. Mark SYRONEY
13 Manager Information Resources Mgmt .... Mr. Garrett GASTON
18 Facilities Manager .... Mr. Dan RIDGWAY
07 Recruiting Contact .... Mrs. Lois LOTT
96 Purchasing Agent .... Ms. Alice CUMMINGS

Ohio Dominican University (F)

1216 Sunbury Road, Columbus OH 43219-2099
County: Franklin FICE Identification: 003035
Unit ID: 204617
Telephone: (614) 253-2741 Carnegie Class: Master's L
FAX Number: (614) 252-0776 Calendar System: Semester
URL: www.ohiodominican.edu
Established: 1911 Annual Undergrad Tuition & Fees: $25,280
Enrollment: 3,210 Coed
Affiliation or Control: Roman Catholic IRS Status: 501(c)3
Highest Offering: Master's
Program: Liberal Arts And General; Teacher Preparatory; Professional
Accreditation: NH, @ACBSP, SW, TED

01 President .... Dr. Peter CIMBOLIC
05 Vice President Academic Affairs .... Dr. Alison BENDERS
32 Vice President Student Development .... Mr. James A. CARIDI
10 Vice Pres for University Resources .... Mr. Ronald J. SEIFFERT
51 VP Learning Enhanced Adult Degree .... Mr. David ARCHIBALD
30 Vice Pres University Relations .... Mr. Ronald J. SEIFFERT
21 Assoc Vice Pres Finance & Admin .... Mr. David KOSANOVIC
04 Executive Asst to the President .... Ms. Candie LESTER
35 Asst Vice Pres Student Development .... Ms. Sharon REED
20 Assoc Vice Pres Academic Affairs .... Dr. Linda SCHOEN
58 Dean Graduate/Professional Studies .... Dr. Jay YOUNG
06 Registrar .... Ms. Shirley MCBRAYER
07 Director of Admissions .... Ms. Nicole EVANS
08 Director of the Library .... Mr. James E. LAYDEN
37 Director of Financial Aid .... Ms. Laura MEEK
36 Director Career Services .... Mr. Gary SWISHER
38 Director of Counseling Services .... Mr. Michael LEWIS
85 Director of Intercultural Office .... Ms. Melissa OCHAL
26 Director of University Relations .... Ms. Beth KOWALSKI
42 Director of Campus Ministry .... Rev. John BOLL
91 Director of Computing Services .... Mr. Jim LIZOTTE
15 Director of Human Resources .... Ms. Debra R. GUILBERT
18 Director of Physical Facilities .... Mr. Sam WISE
29 Director of Alumni/AE Relations .... Ms. Ann SNIDER
39 Director of Resident Life .... Ms. Carry FLEMING
41 Interim Athletic Director .... Mr. Jeff BLAIR
24 Dir Center for Instruct Technology .... Dr. Renee AITKEN
96 Director of Purchasing .... Sr. Margaret WALSH
19 Director of Safety & Security .... Mr. John RACE
92 Director of Honors Program .... Mr. Matthew PONESSE
09 Director of Institutional Research .... Vacant

Ohio Northern University (G)

525 S Main Street, Ada OH 45810-1599
County: Hardin FICE Identification: 003089
Unit ID: 204635
Telephone: (419) 772-2000 Carnegie Class: Bac/Diverse
FAX Number: (419) 772-1932 Calendar System: Quarter
URL: www.onu.edu
Established: 1871 Annual Undergrad Tuition & Fees: $34,140
Enrollment: 3,570 Coed
Affiliation or Control: United Methodist IRS Status: 501(c)3
Highest Offering: First Professional Degree
Program: Liberal Arts And General; Teacher Preparatory; Professional; Business Emphasis
Accreditation: NH, BUS, CS, ENG, EXSC, LAW, MT, MUS, NAIT, NURSE, PHAR, TED

01 President .... Dr. Daniel A. DIBIASIO
05 Int Vice President Academic Affairs .... Dr. David C. CRAGO
10 Vice President Financial Affairs .... Dr. Robert W. RUBLE
30 Acting VP of University Advancement .... Mr. Ken W. BLOCK
84 Vice Pres/Dean of Enrollment .... Mrs. Karen P. CONDENI
32 VP Student Affairs/Dean of Students .... Dean Adriane THOMPSON-BRADSHAW
49 Dean of Arts & Sciences .... Dr. Catherine ALBRECHT
54 Dean of Engineering .... Dr. Eric T. BAUMGARTNER
67 Dean of Pharmacy .... Dr. Jon E. SPRAGUE
50 Dean Business Administration .... Dr. James W. FENTON
61 Dean of Law .... Dr. David C. CRAGO
35 Dean of Students .... Vacant
30 Exec Director of Development .... Mr. Kenneth BLOCK
06 Assistant Registrar .... Mrs. Andrea RICHARDSON
08 Librarian .... Mr. Paul M. LOGSDON
14 Director of Computer Center .... Mr. C. Lawrence BUSCH
36 Interim Director Career Services .... Mr. Justin COURTNEY
61 Dir Law Ext Affs/Career Strategies .... Mrs. Cheryl KITCHEN
38 Director of Counseling .... Dr. Michael SCHAFER
29 Director of Alumni Relations .... Ms. Ann DONNELLY HAMILTON
08 Law Librarian .... Dr. Nancy A. ARMSTRONG
42 University Chaplain .... Rev. Vernon LASALA
18 Director of Physical Plant .... Mr. Marc STALEY
13 Director of Technology .... Mr. George GULBIS
09 Director of Institutional Research .... Dr. Omer MINHAS
15 Director of Human Resources .... Ms. Tonya PAUL
20 Associate Academic Officer .... Dr. Juliet K. HURTIG
37 Director of Student Financial Aid .... Mrs. Melanie WEAVER
92 Director of Honors Program .... Dr. Patrick T. CROSKERY
21 Bursar .... Mrs. Amber L. CARPENTER
26 Dir of Communications & Marketing .... Ms. Carol FLAX
07 Director of Admissions .... Ms. Deborah MILLER
06 Registrar .... Ms. Tamela S. BASH
28 Director Multicultural Development .... Mr. Clyde W. PICKETT
41 Athletic Director .... Mr. Thomas SIMMONS
27 Assoc Director Public Information .... Ms. Mary WILKIN
44 Director of Annual Giving .... Ms. Kelly BRANT
96 Manager of Purchasing .... Ms. Vicki J. NIESE

The Ohio State University Main Campus (H)

154 W. 12th Avenue, Columbus OH 43210-1358
County: Franklin FICE Identification: 003090
Unit ID: 204796
Telephone: (614) 292-6446 Carnegie Class: RU/VH
FAX Number: (614) 292-9180 Calendar System: Quarter
URL: www.osu.edu
Established: 1870 Annual Undergrad Tuition & Fees (In-State): $9,420
Enrollment: 56,064 Coed
Affiliation or Control: State IRS Status: 501(c)3
Highest Offering: Doctorate
Program: Liberal Arts And General; Teacher Preparatory; Professional
Accreditation: NH, ART, AUD, BUS, BUSA, CEA, CIDA, CLPSY, CS, DANCE, DENT, DH, DIETC, DIETD, DIETI, ENG, FOR, HSA, IPSY, LAW, LSAR, MED, MFCD, MIDWF, MT, MUS, NMT, NURSE, OPT, OPTR, OT, PERF, PH, PHAR, PLNG, PTA, RTT, SP, SPAA, SW, TED, THEA, VET

01 President .... Dr. E. Gordon GEE
100 Spc Asst to Pres for Op & Strgc Com .... Ms. Melinda CHURCH
05 Executive Vice Pres/Provost .... Dr. Joseph A. ALUTTO
32 Vice President Ofc of Student Life . Dr. Javaune ADAMS-GASTON
10 Senior VP Business & Finance & CFO .... Mr. Geoffrey CHATAS
20 Vice Provost for Academic Planning .... Mr. Michael J. BOEHM
43 Sr VP & General Counsel .... Mr. Christopher M. CULLEY
15 VP & Chief Human Resources Officer .... Ms. Kathleen MCCUTCHEON
46 Vice Pres Research .... Dr. Caroline WHITACRE
86 Sr Vice Pres Ofc of Govt Affairs .... Mr. Curt STEINER
23 Sr Vice Pres Health Sci .... Dr. Steve G. GABBE
47 Vice Pres & Exec Dean FAES .... Dr. Bobby D. MOSER
30 Sr Vice President Development .... Dr. Jeff KAPLAN
28 Vice Prov Diversity & Inclusion .... Dr. Valerie LEE
58 Vice Provost/Dean Grad School .... Dr. Patrick S. OSMER
18 Assoc VP Facilities Op/Dev .... Ms. Mary L. READEY
84 Director of Enrollment Mgmt .... Ms. Gail C. STEPHENOFF
39 Asst VP Student Life/Housing .... Mr. Fred FOTIS
07 Asst VP UG Admissions/First-Yr Exp .... Ms. Mabel G. FREEMAN
21 Asst Vice Pres Business/Finance .... Vacant
13 Chief Information Officer .... Ms. Kathleen STARKOFF
08 Director of Libraries .... Ms. Carol P. DIEDRCHS
86 Assoc Vice Pres Govt Relations .... Mr. Richard S. STODDARD
101 Secretary Board of Trustees .... Dr. David O. FRANTZ
22 Employment Law/Compliance Mgr .... Ms. Olga ESQUIVEL-GONZALEZ
17 VP Health Svcs .... Dr. Peter E. GEIER
06 University Registrar .... Mr. Bradley A. MYERS
85 Vice Prov Global Strat/Intl Aff's .... Dr. William I. BRUSTEIN
40 General Manager OSU Bookstores .... Ms. Kathy SMITH
90 Int Exec Dir Ohio Supercomputr Ctr .... Mr. Steve GORDON
29 Pres/CEO OSU Alumni Association .... Mr. Archie GRIFFIN
41 Director Athletics .... Mr. Gene SMITH
12 Executive Dean of Reg Campuses .... Vacant
49 Exec Dean Arts & Sciences .... Dr. Joseph E. STEINMETZ
88 Int Dean Colleges of Bio Sci & MPS .... Vacant
50 Dean Fisher Col of Business .... Dr. Christine A. POON
52 Dean College of Dentistry .... Dr. Carole A. ANDERSON
53 Dean College of Educ & Hum Ecology .... Dr. Cheryl L. ACHTERBERG
54 Dean College of Engineering .... Dr. David B. WILLIAMS
57 Dean Colleges of the Arts & Hum .... Vacant
79 Dean College of Humanities .... Vacant
61 Dean College of Law .... Dr. Alan C. MICHAELS

63 VP & Exec Dean Health Sci ....Dr. Wiley W. SOUBA, JR.
88 Dean College of Optometry ....Dr. Melvin D. SHIPP
67 Dean College of Pharmacy ....Dr. Robert W. BRUEGGEMEIER
83 Dean College of Soc & Behav Sci ....Vacant
70 Dean College of Social Work ....Dr. Tom GREGOIRE
74 Dean Col Veterinary Medicine ....Dr. Lonnie KING
66 Dean College of Nursing ....Dr. Elizabeth R. LENZ
81 Dean College Math/Physical Science ....Vacant
63 Int Dean College of Medicine ....Dr. Catherine LUCEY
09 Director Inst Research/Planning ....Ms. Julie CARPENTER-HUBIN
37 Director Student Financial Aid ....Ms. Diane L. STEMPER
38 Asst VP & Dir Younkin Success Ctr ....Ms. Louise A. DOUCE
96 Assoc Director of Purchasing ....Ms. Cris PENN
11 Sr Vice Pres Admin & Planning ....Mr. Jack D. KASEY

The Ohio State University Agricultural Technical Institute (A)

1328 Dover Road, Wooster OH 44691-4000

County: Wayne FICE Identification: 010687
Unit ID: 204662
Telephone: (330) 264-3911 Carnegie Class: Assoc/Pub2in4
FAX Number: (330) 287-1333 Calendar System: Quarter
URL: www.ati.ohio-state.edu
Established: 1971 Annual Undergrad Tuition & Fees (In-State): $6,300
Enrollment: 700 Coed
Affiliation or Control: State IRS Status: 501(c)3
Highest Offering: Associate Degree
Program: Occupational; 2-Year Principally Bachelor's Creditable
Accreditation: NH

01 Director ....Dr. Stephen P. NAMETH
20 Associate Director ....Dr. Steven M. NEAL
26 Public Relations Coordinator ....Ms. Frances P. WHITED
37 Coordinator Student Financial Aid ....Ms. Barbara LAMOREAUX
07 Admissions Coordinator ....Vacant
21 Business Manager 2 ....Ms. Rita M. SMOLKO
32 Coordinator Student Programs ....Ms. Kathy E. MAKSYMICZ
40 Bookstore Manager ....Ms. Patricia A. PAXTON
08 Library Director ....Ms. Sharon HOLDERMAN
19 Assistant Chief Campus Police ....Mr. Gregory K. FERRELL
13 Systems Manager ....Mr. Rick L. MITCHELL
23 Staff Nurse ....Ms. Karen S. MYERS
50 Director Business Trng & Educ Svcs .....Ms. Kimberly J. SAYERS
30 Sr Director of Development ....Vacant
39 Housing Coordinator ....Ms. Ashley E. BRIGHTBILL
00 Coordinator Disability Services ....Ms. Silvia H. HENRISS
88 Program Director Program EXCEL ....Ms. Dee Dee SNYDER
06 Academic Records Manager ....Ms. Peggy E. LAMBERT
29 Assistant to Director ....Ms. Helen THOMPSON
38 SOAR Coordinator Stdnt Success Svcs ....Ms. Nancy BROOKER
18 Facilities Support Services ....Mr. Thomas N. GILT

The Ohio State University at Lima Campus (B)

4240 Campus Drive, Lima OH 45804-3597

County: Allen FICE Identification: 003092
Unit ID: 204671
Telephone: (419) 995-8600 Carnegie Class: Bac/Diverse
FAX Number: (419) 995-8483 Calendar System: Quarter
URL: lima.osu.edu/
Established: 1959 Annual Undergrad Tuition & Fees (In-State): $6,102
Enrollment: 1,530 Coed
Affiliation or Control: State IRS Status: 501(c)3
Highest Offering: Baccalaureate
Program: Liberal Arts And General
Accreditation: &NH

01 Dean & Director ....Dr. John R. SNYDER
05 Associate Dean ....Dr. Michael A. CUNNINGHAM
10 Assoc Director ....Mr. Devon N. PHELPS
101 Exec Asistant to Dean & Director ....Ms. Jeanne M. MOORMAN
20 Assistant Dean ....Dr. Roger L. NIMPS
37 Coordinator Student Financial Aid ....Mr. Josh LUKE
08 Head Librarian ....Dr. Tina SCHNEIDER
27 Director of Communications ....Ms. Pamela K. JOSEPH
15 Human Resources Generalist ....Ms. Whitney CLARK
13 Director of Technology Services ....Mr. James M. KERR
24 Program Mgr Educational/Media Tech ....Ms. Lynn A. TRINKO
88 Asst Dean/Admin Dir of Advising ....Mr. James M. MILLER
36 Coordinator of Career Services ....Ms. Donna G. LAMB
30 Director of Development ....Ms. Amanda L. MILLER
06 Coordinator Student Records ....Mr. Kevin SMITH
32 Director of Student Life ....Mr. John UPSHAW
07 Associate Dir of Enrollment Svcs ....Ms. Beth A. KEEHN
21 Business Services Officer ....Ms. Cheri L. WISE
35 Coordinator Student Programs ....Vacant
28 Coordinator Minority Affairs ....Ms. Temple PATTON

† Regional accreditation is carried under the parent institution in Columbus, OH.

The Ohio State University Mansfield Campus (C)

1760 University Drive, Mansfield OH 44906-1599

County: Richland FICE Identification: 003093
Unit ID: 204680
Telephone: (419) 755-4011 Carnegie Class: Bac/Assoc
FAX Number: (419) 755-4241 Calendar System: Quarter
URL: mansfield.osu.edu/
Established: 1958 Annual Undergrad Tuition & Fees (In-State): $6,102
Enrollment: 1,405 Coed
Affiliation or Control: State IRS Status: 501(c)3
Highest Offering: Baccalaureate
Program: Liberal Arts And General; Teacher Preparatory
Accreditation: &NH

01 Dean & Director ....Dr. Stephen M. GAVAZZI
05 Associate Dean ....Dr. David TOVEY
08 Int Director Broomfield Library ....Ms. Kathryn DUNLAP
07 Director Admissions & Financial Aid ....Mr. Kenneth SIGLER
15 Human Resources Officer ....Ms. Cathy STIMPERT
18 Supt Phys Fac Security & Custodial ....Mr. Brian WHITE
32 Chief Student Life & Retention Ofcr ....Dr. Donna HIGHT
10 Fiscal Officer ....Ms. Carol FREYTAG
26 Asst Director University Relations ....Mr. Rodger C. SMITH
13 Senior Systems Manager ....Mr. Major PRICE
06 Registrar ....Mr. Bradley A. MYERS
21 Office Assistant Business Office ....Ms. Heather ARMSTRONG
30 Development Officer ....Mr. Andronic OROSAN
88 Coord Min Affairs & Student Success ...Mr. Dametraus JAGGERS

† Regional accreditation is carried under the parent institution in Columbus, OH.

The Ohio State University at Marion (D)

1465 Mount Vernon Avenue, Marion OH 43302-5628

County: Marion FICE Identification: 003094
Unit ID: 204699
Telephone: (740) 389-6786 Carnegie Class: Bac/Assoc
FAX Number: (614) 292-5817 Calendar System: Quarter
URL: osumarion.osu.edu
Established: 1957 Annual Undergrad Tuition & Fees (In-State): $6,102
Enrollment: 1,816 Coed
Affiliation or Control: State IRS Status: 501(c)3
Highest Offering: Master's
Program: Liberal Arts And General
Accreditation: &NH

01 Dean & Director ....Dr. Gregory S. ROSE
05 Associate Dean ....Dr. Bishun PANDEY
20 Assistant Dean ....Dr. Leslie BEYER-HERMSEN
08 Head Librarian ....Ms. Betsy BLANKENSHIP
88 Director Alber Enteprise Center ....Ms. Eileen SMITH
06 Records Mgmt Officer/Registrar ....Ms. Karin LANIUS
15 Assistant Office/ Human Resources ....Ms. Cheri KING
07 Asst Dir Admissions/Financial Aid ....Mr. Matt MOREAU
32 Director Student Affairs ....Mr. Dave BECKEL
30 Dir Community Rels & Development ....Mr. Dave CLABORN
18 Dir Physical Facilities ....Mr. Ron TURNER
10 Business Office Manager ....Ms. Karen CARROLL
26 Manager Communications/Marketing ....Mr. Wayne ROWE
38 Asst Dir Advising & Retention ....Ms. Chris TRAPP
36 Coordinator Career Services ....Mr. Will SMITH
28 Coordinator Diversity Initiatives ....Mr. Shawn JACKSON
41 Director Athletics ....Mr. Mark SISLER

† Regional accreditation is carried under the parent institution in Columbus, OH.

The Ohio State University Newark Campus (E)

1179 University Drive, Newark OH 43055-9990

County: Licking FICE Identification: 003095
Unit ID: 204705
Telephone: (740) 366-3321 Carnegie Class: Bac/Assoc
FAX Number: (740) 366-5047 Calendar System: Quarter
URL: www.newark.osu.edu
Established: 1957 Annual Undergrad Tuition & Fees (In-State): $6,102
Enrollment: 2,652 Coed
Affiliation or Control: State IRS Status: 501(c)3
Highest Offering: Baccalaureate
Program: Liberal Arts And General
Accreditation: &NH

01 Dean/Director ....Dr. William L. MACDONALD
32 Director of Student Life ....Mr. John BERRY
10 Dir Business & Finance ....Mr. David BRILLHART
16 Asst Dir Human Resources ....Ms. Nicia CARY
08 Directory of Library ....Ms. Susan SCOTT
05 Associate Dean ....Dr. Paul SANDERS
07 Director of Enrollment ....Ms. Ann DONAHUE
37 Director of Financial Aid ....Ms. Faith PHILLIPS
88 Director Child Development Center ....Vacant
96 Purchasing/Auxiliary Services Mgr ....Ms. Margaret CAMSTRA
18 Supt Facilities & Support Svcs ....Dr. James WOOLARD
06 Registrar ....Vacant
21 Director of Business Affairs ....Mr. Douglas WARTHEN
28 Pgm Manager Multi-Cultural Affairs ....Ms. Vorley TAYLOR
38 Personal Counselor ....Ms. Susan ADAMS
41 Pgm Coord Athletics/Phys Ed & Rec ....Mr. Bret WHITAKER
30 Director of Development ....Ms. Jennifer ROBERTS
26 Marketing & Public Relations Dir ... Ms. Alice HUTZEL-BATESON

† Regional accreditation is carried under the parent institution in Columbus, OH.

Ohio Technical College (F)

1374 E 51st Street, Cleveland OH 44103-1269

County: Cuyahoga FICE Identification: 011745
Unit ID: 204608
Telephone: (216) 881-1700 Carnegie Class: Assoc/PrivFP
FAX Number: (216) 881-9145 Calendar System: Quarter
URL: www.ohiotechnicalcollege.com
Established: 1969 Annual Undergrad Tuition & Fees: $26,280
Enrollment: 1,212 Coed
Affiliation or Control: Proprietary IRS Status: Proprietary
Highest Offering: Associate Degree
Program: Occupational
Accreditation: ACCSC

01 Director ....Mr. Tom KING

Ohio University Main Campus (G)

Athens OH 45701-2979

County: Athens FICE Identification: 003100
Unit ID: 204857
Telephone: (740) 593-1000 Carnegie Class: RU/H
FAX Number: N/A Calendar System: Quarter
URL: www.ohiou.edu
Established: 1804 Annual Undergrad Tuition & Fees (In-State): $9,870
Enrollment: 35,324 Coed
Affiliation or Control: State IRS Status: 501(c)3
Highest Offering: Doctorate
Program: Liberal Arts And General; Teacher Preparatory; Professional
Accreditation: NH, AAFCS, ADNUR, ART, AUD, BUS, BUSA, CACREP, CIDA, CLPSY, CORE, CS, DANCE, DIETD, ENG, ENGR, JOUR, MUS, NAIT, NRPA, NURSE, OSTEO, PH, PTA, SP, SW, TED, THEA

01 President ....Dr. Roderick J. MCDAVIS
100 Chief of Staff ....Ms. Rebecca L. WATTS
05 Executive Vice President & Provost ....Dr. Pam BENOIT
10 VP for Finance & Administration ....Mr. Stephen T. GOLDING
32 Vice President for Student Affairs ....Dr. Kent SMITH
30 VP Univ Advance/Pres/CEO OU Fdn ....Mr. Bryan BENCHOFF
27 Chief Information Officer ....Mr. J. Brice BIBLE
46 Int VP Research & Dean Grad College ....Dr. Joseph SHIELDS
43 General Counsel ....Mr. John J. BIANCAMANO
27 Exec Dir Comm/Marketing ....Ms. Renea MORRIS
80 Director of Government Relations ....Mr. Eric BURCHARD
88 Exec V Provost /Dean Univ Col ....Dr. David N. DESCUTNER
49 Int Dean College of Arts & Sciences ....Dr. Howard DEWALD
50 Dean College of Business ....Dr. Hugh SHERMAN
60 Int Dean Scripps Col Communication ....Dr. Scott TITSWORTH
53 Dean College of Education ....Dr. Renee A. MIDDLETON
54 Dean Russ Col Engineering/Tech ....Dr. Dennis IRWIN
57 Dean College of Fine Arts ....Mr. Charles A. MCWEENY
69 Dean Col Health/Human Services ....Dr. Randy LEITE
92 Dean Honors Tutorial College ....Dr. Jeremy WEBSTER
63 Dean Col Osteopathic Medicine ....Dr. John A. BROSE
62 Dean University Libraries ....Mr. Scott H. SEAMAN
35 Dean of Students ....Mr. Ryan T. LOMBARDI
12 Exec Dean Regional Campuses ....Dr. Dan EVANS
12 Dean Eastern Campus ....Dr. Richard GREENLEE
12 Dean Southern Campus ....Dr. William WILLAN
12 Int Dean Chillicothe Campus ....Dr. Martin TUCK
12 Dean Lancaster Campus ....Dr. James SMITH
12 Dean Zanesville Campus ....Dr. James W. FONSECA
20 Associate Provost Academic Affairs ....Vacant
58 Director Graduate Student Services ....Dr. Katherine TADLOCK
88 Assoc Provost International Affairs ....Vacant
28 Vice Prov Diversity/Access/Equity ....Dr. Brian BRIDGES
09 Assoc Prov Inst Rsrch/Assessment .....Dr. A. Michael WILLIFORD
41 Director of Athletics ....Mr. Jim SCHAUS
06 University Registrar ....Mrs. Debra M. BENTON
18 Assoc VP Finance/Admin/Facilities ....Mr. Harry WYATT
15 Assoc VP for Human Resources ....Ms. Linda LONSINGER
22 Director Institutional Equity ....Dr. Laura MYERS
29 Exec Director Alumni Relations ....Mr. Graham STEWART
36 Director Career Services ....Dr. Thomas F. KORVAS
07 Int Director of Admissions ....Ms. Candice BOEHNINGER
38 Director Counseling Services ....Vacant
44 Exec Dir of Develop Planned Giving ....Ms. Kelli BELL
37 Director Student Financial Aid ....Ms. Sondra R. WILLIAMS
23 Director Student Health Svcs ....Dr. Jack BROSE
87 Director Summer Sessions ....Dr. Pamela J. BROWN
96 Director of Procurement Services ....Ms. Laura NOWICKI
19 Chief of Police/Dir Campus Safety ....Mr. Andrew POWERS
85 Assoc Dir Intl Students/Fac Svcs ....Ms. Krista M. BEATTY
39 Asst Vice Pres Auxiliary Services ....Ms. Christine SHEETS
88 Asst VP for Economic & Tech Devel ....Vacant
25 Asst VP Res & Sponsored Programs ....Mr. Shane L. GILKEY
24 Media Library Manager ....Ms. Robin KRIVESTI

Ohio University Chillicothe Campus (H)

PO Box 629, 101 University Drive, Chillicothe OH 45601-0629

County: Ross FICE Identification: 003102
Unit ID: 204820
Telephone: (740) 774-7200 Carnegie Class: Assoc/Pub4
FAX Number: (740) 774-7295 Calendar System: Quarter
URL: www.chillicothe.ohiou.edu
Established: 1946 Annual Undergrad Tuition & Fees (In-State): $5,034
Enrollment: 2,500 Coed
Affiliation or Control: State IRS Status: 501(c)3
Highest Offering: Baccalaureate
Program: Occupational; 2-Year Principally Bachelor's Creditable
Accreditation: &NH

01 Dean ... Dr. Martin TUCK
05 Associate Dean ... Dr. James MCKEAN
08 Head Librarian ... Mr. Allan POLLCHIK
13 Dir Information/Technology Services ... Ms. Patricia A. GRIFFITH
18 Director Facilities Management ... Mr. David SCOTT
15 Director Personnel Services ... Vacant
26 Chief Public Relations Officer ... Mr. Jack JEFFERY
30 Chief Development ... Ms. Joyce ATWOOD
41 Athletic Director ... Ms. Kim MCKIMMY-KELLY
36 Coordinator of Student Support ... Mrs. Martha TANEDO
32 Coord of Student Affs/Stdnt Fin Aid ... Mrs. Ashlee RAUCKHORST
07 Coordinator of Student Recruitment ... Vacant

† Regional accreditation is carried under the parent institution in Athens, OH.

Ohio University Eastern Campus (A)

45425 National Road, Saint Clairsville OH 43950-9724
County: Belmont FICE Identification: 003101
Unit ID: 204802
Telephone: (740) 695-1720 Carnegie Class: Assoc/Pub4
FAX Number: (740) 695-7077 Calendar System: Quarter
URL: www.eastern.ohiou.edu
Established: 1957 Annual Undergrad Tuition & Fees (In-State): $2,974
Enrollment: 985 Coed
Affiliation or Control: State IRS Status: 501(c)3
Highest Offering: Master's
Program: 2-Year Principally Bachelor's Creditable; Liberal Arts And General; Teacher Preparatory; Professional
Accreditation: &NH

01 Campus Dean ... Dr. Richard W. GREENLEE
05 Associate Dean ... Mr. Michael MCTEAGUE
30 Assistant Dean for Development ... Vacant
20 Faculty Chairperson ... Dr. David CASTLE
10 Chief Business Officer ... Ms. Rosanna LEMASTERS
08 Director of Library ... Ms. Donna CAPEZZUTO
24 Director of Media ... Mr. Jay MORRIS
26 Director of Marketing ... Mr. E.J SCHODZINSKI
14 Computer Resources Coordinator ... Mr. Trent DUFFY
18 Director of Physical Plant ... Mr. Steven MCGUFFIN
17 Director Health/Phys Educ Center ... Mr. E.J SCHODZINSKI
40 Director Bookstore ... Mrs. Tammy WARD
32 Director Student Services ... Mr. Kevin CHENOWETH
14 Computer/Technology Specialist ... Mr. Peter LIM

† Regional accreditation is carried under the parent institution in Athens, OH.

Ohio University Lancaster Campus (B)

1570 Granville Pike, Lancaster OH 43130-1097
County: Fairfield FICE Identification: 003104
Unit ID: 204848
Telephone: (740) 654-6711 Carnegie Class: Assoc/Pub4
FAX Number: (740) 687-9497 Calendar System: Quarter
URL: www.ohiou.edu/lancaster
Established: 1968 Annual Undergrad Tuition & Fees (In-State): $5,300
Enrollment: 2,491 Coed
Affiliation or Control: State IRS Status: 501(c)3
Highest Offering: Master's
Program: Occupational; 2-Year Principally Bachelor's Creditable; Liberal Arts And General
Accreditation: &NH, MAC

01 Dean ... Dr. James SMITH
05 Associate Dean ... Dr. Paul ABRAHAM
30 Coordinator for Development ... Ms. Mandi CUSTER
18 Director of Physical Plant ... Mr. Rob EVANS
41 Athletic Director ... Mr. Jeff WHITEHEAD
08 Librarian ... Vacant
84 Student Services Enrollment Manager ... Ms. Patricia FOX
36 Dir Stdnt Place/Dir Ctr Adult Lrng ... Vacant
49 Coord Arts/Communicatns/Humanities ... Dr. Candice THOMAS-MADDOX
72 Coord Science & Technology Division ... Dr. Franco GUERRIERO
83 Coord Social Sciences/Applied Stds ... Ms. Janet BECKER
14 Director Computer Svcs/Instr Tech ... Mr. Paul ALLEN
26 Coordinator of Public Relations ... Ms. Jennifer LARUE

† Regional accreditation is carried under the parent institution in Athens, OH.

Ohio University Southern Campus (C)

1804 Liberty Avenue, Ironton OH 45638-2279
County: Lawrence Identification: 666000
Unit ID: 204839
Telephone: (740) 533-4600 Carnegie Class: Assoc/Pub4
FAX Number: (740) 533-4632 Calendar System: Quarter
URL: www.southern.ohiou.edu
Established: 1953 Annual Undergrad Tuition & Fees (In-State): $4,500
Enrollment: 2,060 Coed
Affiliation or Control: State IRS Status: 501(c)3
Highest Offering: Associate Degree
Program: Occupational; 2-Year Principally Bachelor's Creditable
Accreditation: &NH

01 President ... Dr. Roderick J. MCDAVIS
05 Dean ... Dr. William WILLAN
32 Director of Student Services ... Mr. Robert PLEASANT

† Regional accreditation is carried under the parent institution in Athens, OH.

Ohio University Zanesville Branch (D)

1425 Newark Road, Zanesville OH 43701-2695
County: Muskingum FICE Identification: 003108
Unit ID: 204866
Telephone: (740) 453-0762 Carnegie Class: Assoc/Pub4
FAX Number: (740) 453-6161 Calendar System: Quarter
URL: www.zanesville.ohiou.edu
Established: 1946 Annual Undergrad Tuition & Fees (In-State): $4,728
Enrollment: 1,983 Coed
Affiliation or Control: State IRS Status: 501(c)3
Highest Offering: Master's
Program: Occupational; 2-Year Principally Bachelor's Creditable; Liberal Arts And General
Accreditation: &NH

01 Interim Dean ... Dr. Richard GREENLEE
05 Associate Dean ... Dr. Alan PUNCHES
30 Assistant Dean for Development ... Mrs. Cindy LINN
32 Director of Student Services ... Ms. Susan MONTGOMERY
08 Library Director ... Mr. Tony HOPKINS
66 Associate Director of Nursing ... Mrs. Pamela SEALOVER
18 Director of Operations ... Mr. Joe KEATING
11 Assistant Director Operations ... Mr. George DMITRENAK
35 Assistant Director Student Services ... Mr. Jason HOWARD
37 Financial Aid Coordinator ... Mrs. Vicki DELUCAS

† Regional accreditation is carried under the parent institution in Athens, OH.

Ohio Valley College of Technology (E)

15258 State Route 170, East Liverpool OH 43920
County: Columbiana FICE Identification: 023014
Unit ID: 204884
Telephone: (330) 385-1070 Carnegie Class: Assoc/PrivFP
FAX Number: (330) 385-4606 Calendar System: Semester
URL: www.ovct.edu
Established: 1886 Annual Undergrad Tuition & Fees: $10,290
Enrollment: 220 Coed
Affiliation or Control: Proprietary IRS Status: Proprietary
Highest Offering: Associate Degree
Program: Occupational; 2-Year Principally Bachelor's Creditable; Technical Emphasis
Accreditation: ACICS, MAC

01 President/Executive Director ... Mr. Scott S. ROGERS
05 Assistant Director ... Ms. Debra A. SANFORD

Ohio Wesleyan University (F)

61 S Sandusky Street, Delaware OH 43015-2398
County: Delaware FICE Identification: 003109
Unit ID: 204909
Telephone: (740) 368-2000 Carnegie Class: Bac/A&S
FAX Number: (740) 368-3299 Calendar System: Semester
URL: www.owu.edu
Established: 1842 Annual Undergrad Tuition & Fees: $37,580
Enrollment: 1,850 Coed
Affiliation or Control: United Methodist IRS Status: 501(c)3
Highest Offering: Baccalaureate
Program: Liberal Arts And General
Accreditation: NH, MUS, TED

01 President ... Dr. Rockwell F. JONES
05 Provost ... Dr. David O. ROBBINS
10 VP for Finance/Administration ... Mr. Eric S. ALGOE
26 Vice Pres for University Relations ... Ms. Colleen GARLAND
84 VP Strategic Comm/Univ Enrollment ... Ms. Rebecca R. ECKSTEIN
32 Vice President for Student Affairs ... Dr. Craig E. ULLOM
07 Asst VP Admissions/Financial Aid ... Mr. Lee HARRELL
37 Asst VP Admission & Financial Aid .. Ms. Carol J. DELPROPOST
20 Dean of Academic Affairs ... Dr. Charles L. STINEMETZ
09 Assoc Dean Inst Research ... Dr. Dale E. SWARTZENTRUBER
88 Assoc Dean Assessment/Accreditation . Dr. Barbara S. ANDERECK
36 Director of Career Services ... Ms. Leslie DELERME
06 Registrar ... Ms. Shelly A. MCMAHON
08 Chief Info Officer/Dir of Libraries ... Ms. Cathi CARDWELL
14 Director of Computer Center ... Mr. Harold D. WIEBE
13 Exec Director Information Tech ... Mr. Brian A. RELLINGER
19 Director of Public Safety ... Mr. Robert A. WOOD
29 Director Alumni Relations ... Ms. Brenda E. DEWITT
26 Director Marketing/Communications ... Mr. Mark E. COOPER
85 Director International Student Svcs ... Mr. Darrell J. ALBON
18 Director Physical Plant ... Mr. Christopher J. SETZER
15 Director Human Resources ... Ms. Debra A. GUILBERT
31 Director Community Svc Learning ... Vacant
11 Director of Administrative Services ... Ms. Susan COOPERIDER
04 Asst to President/Board Secy ... Ms. Lisa D. JACKSON
23 Director Wellness Center ... Ms. Marsha A. TILDEN
35 Dean of Students ... Dr. Kimberlie L. GOLDSBERRY
38 Coord Counseling/Career/Health Svcs ... Dr. Colleen M. COOK
39 Director Residential Life ... Ms. Wendy L. PIPER
40 Bookstore Manager ... Mr. Kevin U. STITH
41 Director of Athletics ... Mr. Roger D. INGLES
42 Chaplain ... Rev. Jon R. POWERS
30 Development Officer ... Ms. Jayn L. BAILEY
89 Dean First Year Students ... Dr. Martin A. HIPSKY
92 Honors Program Codirector ... Dr. Edward H. BURTT
92 Honors Program Codirector ... Dr. Amy MCCLURE
93 Dir Multicultural Student Affairs ... Ms. Terree L. STEVENSON
102 Dir Foundation/Corp/Govt Relations ... Ms. Karen CROSMAN
07 Associate Director of Admissions ... Ms. Alisha M. COUCH
88 Special Assistant to the President ... Mr. Mark H. SHIPPS

Otterbein University (G)

1 Otterbein College, Westerville OH 43081-2006
County: Franklin FICE Identification: 003110
Unit ID: 204936
Telephone: (614) 890-3000 Carnegie Class: Master's M
FAX Number: (614) 823-3114 Calendar System: Semester
URL: www.otterbein.edu
Established: 1847 Annual Undergrad Tuition & Fees: $29,550
Enrollment: 3,080 Coed
Affiliation or Control: United Methodist IRS Status: 501(c)3
Highest Offering: Doctorate
Program: Liberal Arts And General; Teacher Preparatory; Professional
Accreditation: NH, ANEST, MUS, NUR, NURSE, TED, THEA

01 President ... Dr. Kathy A. KRENDL
05 Vice President Academic Affairs ... Dr. Victoria MCGILLIN
32 Vice President Student Affairs ... Mr. Robert M. GATTI
10 Vice President for Business Affairs ... Mrs. Rebecca D. VAZQUEZ-SKILLINGS
30 VP Institutional Advancement ... Ms. Heidi L. TRACY
84 Vice President for Enrollment ... Dr. Cass H. JOHNSON
20 Assoc VP AA/Dean Academic Services ... Dr. Susan R. FAGAN
91 Exec Director of Information Tech ... Mr. Jeff KASSON
08 Director of the Library ... Mrs. Lois F. SZUDY
06 Registrar ... Mr. Donald W. FOSTER
26 Exec Dir Marketing/Communications ... Mrs. Jennifer PEARCE
36 Director Career Planning/Placement ... Mrs. Margarette C. BARKHYMER
37 Director of Financial Aid ... Mr. Thomas V. YARNELL
41 Athletic Director ... Mr. Richard E. REYNOLDS
42 Chaplain ... Rev. Monty E. BRADLEY
51 Assoc Dean Grad & Cont Studies ... Ms. Kate CAREY
58 Dean School of Prof Studies ... Dr. Harriet FAYNE
49 Dean School of Arts/Sciences ... Dr. Paul EISENSTEIN
85 Exec Director Intl Programs ... Mr. Chris MUSICK
07 Director of Admissions ... Mrs. Catherine M. JOHNSON
15 Director Human Resources ... Mrs. Kathie L. GIBB
18 Director/Physical Plant ... Mr. David D. BELL
29 Director Alumni Relations ... Ms. Rebecca F. SMITH
28 Director of Diversity ... Dr. Lisa PATTERSON
96 Director of Purchasing ... Mr. Steven H. ROSENBERGER
21 Inst Rsrch Spec/Financial Analyst ... Mr. Christopher A. HAYTER
09 Asst VP for Institutional Planning ... Dr. Barbara I. WHARTON
19 Director of Security ... Mr. Larry BANASZAK
04 Executive Assistant to President ... Vacant

Owens Community College (H)

30335 Oregon, PO Box 10000, Toledo OH 43699-1947
County: Wood FICE Identification: 005753
Unit ID: 204945
Telephone: (567) 661-7000 Carnegie Class: Assoc/Pub-U-MC
FAX Number: N/A Calendar System: Semester
URL: www.owens.edu
Established: 1965 Annual Undergrad Tuition & Fees (In-State): $3,674
Enrollment: 19,980 Coed
Affiliation or Control: State IRS Status: 501(c)3
Highest Offering: Associate Degree
Program: Occupational; 2-Year Principally Bachelor's Creditable
Accreditation: NH, ACBSP, DH, DIETT, DMS, MAC, NAIT, OTA, PTAA, RAD, SURGT

01 President ... Dr. Larry MCDOUGLE
101 Secretary to the Board of Trustees ... Ms. Patricia JEZAK
04 Executive Assistant to President ... Ms. Vicki HENERY
05 Exec Vice President/Provost ... Dr. Renay SCOTT
10 Executive VP Business Affairs/CFO ... Mr. John SATKOWSKI
11 Vice President Administration ... Mr. Brian PASKVAN
20 Associate Vice Provost ... Ms. Tamara WILLIAMS
30 Exec Director College Development ... Ms. Ann SAVAGE
103 VP Workforce/Community Services ... Dr. Michael BANKEY
16 Interim VP Human Resources ... Ms. Lisa DUBOSE
12 Vice President Findlay Campus ... Dr. Melissa GREEN
13 Chief Information Officer ... Ms. Connie SCHAFFER
19 Chief of Police ... Mr. John BETORI
37 Associate Director Financial Aid ... Ms. Susanne SCHWARCK
18 Assoc Vice President Operations ... Mr. Michael MCDONALD
09 Director Organizational Research ... Ms. Debra RATHKE
72 Co-Int Dean School of Technology ... Mr. Randy WHARTON
72 Co-Int Dean School of Technology ... Mr. Glenn RETTIG
76 Dean School of Health Sciences ... Vacant
66 Dean School of Nursing ... Ms. Dawn WETMORE
50 Interim Dean School of Business ... Dr. Gretchen CARROLL
49 Dean School of Arts & Sciences ... Dr. Laurie FATHE
62 Dean Library ... Mr. Tom SINK
106 Director eLearning ... Mr. Mark KARAMOL
43 In-House Legal Counsel ... Dr. Natalie JACKSON
22 Equal Opp/Inclusiveness Officer ... Ms. Lisa DUBOSE
06 Registrar ... Vacant
26 Director Marketing/Communications ... Dr. Gary CORRIGAN
29 Director Alumni Affairs ... Ms. Laura MOORE
35 Director Student Life ... Mr. Chris GIORDANO
07 Director Admissions/Career Service ... Mr. Joseph CARONE

36 Specialist Admiss/Career Services .... Ms. Gentry DIXON
40 Director Bookstore/Food Services .... Mr. David WAHR
85 Director International Programs .... Ms. Deborah GAVLIK
41 Athletics Director .... Vacant

Payne Theological Seminary (A)

PO Box 474, Wilberforce OH 45384-0474

County: Greene FICE Identification: 010017
Unit ID: 204990
Telephone: (937) 376-2946 Carnegie Class: Spec/Faith
FAX Number: (937) 376-3330 Calendar System: 4/1/4
URL: www.payne.edu
Established: 1844 Annual Graduate Tuition & Fees: $7,240
Enrollment: 127 Coed
Affiliation or Control: African Methodist Episcopal IRS Status: 501(c)3
Highest Offering: Master's; No Undergraduates
Program: Professional
Accreditation: THEOL

01 President .... Rev.Dr. Leah GASKIN-FITCHUE
05 Academic Dean .... Vacant
30 Director of Development .... Rev. Jules HOWIE
36 Director of Planning & Placement .... Vacant
08 Head Librarian .... Mr. George JOHNSON

Pontifical College Josephinum (B)

7625 N High Street, Columbus OH 43235-1498

County: Franklin FICE Identification: 003113
Unit ID: 205027
Telephone: (614) 885-5585 Carnegie Class: Spec/Faith
FAX Number: (614) 885-2307 Calendar System: Semester
URL: www.pcj.edu
Established: 1888 Annual Undergrad Tuition & Fees: $18,999
Enrollment: 132 Male
Affiliation or Control: Roman Catholic IRS Status: 501(c)3
Highest Offering: Master's
Program: Liberal Arts And General; Professional; Religious Emphasis
Accreditation: NH, THEOL

01 Rector/President .... V.Rev. James A. WEHNER
03 Vice President .... R.Msgr. CHristopher J. SCHRECK
03 Vice Rector School of Theology .... Rev. Walter R. OXLEY
30 Vice President Advancement ..... R.Msgr. Christopher J. SCHRECK
40 Vice Rector College Liberal Arts .... Rev. John F. HEISLER
05 Academic Dean .... Dr. Michael D. ROSS
20 Assistant Academic Dean .... Dr. David J. DE LEONARDIS
10 Treasurer .... Mr. John ERWIN
06 Registrar .... Mrs. Barbara COUTS
08 Librarian .... Mr. Peter G. VERACKA
33 Dean of Men In Theology .... R.Msgr. Micahel A. OSBORN
33 Dean of Men In College .... Rev. John ROZEMBAJGIER
07 Director of Admissions College .... Rev. John F. HEISLER
37 Financial Aid Director .... Mrs. Marky LEICHTNAM

Professional Skills Institute (C)

5115 Glendale Avenue, Toledo OH 43614-1801

County: Lucas FICE Identification: 023377
Unit ID: 205054
Telephone: (419) 720-6670 Carnegie Class: Assoc/PrivFP
FAX Number: (419) 720-6674 Calendar System: Quarter
URL: www.proskills.com
Established: 1984 Annual Undergrad Tuition & Fees: $10,171
Enrollment: 475 Coed
Affiliation or Control: Proprietary IRS Status: Proprietary
Highest Offering: Associate Degree
Program: Occupational; 2-Year Principally Bachelor's Creditable; Nursing Emphasis
Accreditation: ABHES, PTAA

01 CEO .... Mr. Daniel FINCH
07 Admissions Coordinator .... Mr. Tony DICKENS

Rabbinical College of Telshe (D)

28400 Euclid Avenue, Wickliffe OH 44092-2584

County: Lake FICE Identification: 003115
Unit ID: 205124
Telephone: (440) 943-5300 Carnegie Class: Spec/Faith
FAX Number: (440) 943-5303 Calendar System: Quarter
Established: 1941 Annual Undergrad Tuition & Fees: $8,000
Enrollment: 59 Male
Affiliation or Control: Independent Non-Profit IRS Status: 501(c)3
Highest Offering: Doctorate
Program: Teacher Preparatory; Professional
Accreditation: RABN

01 President .... Rabbi Shlomo EISENBERGER
06 Registrar .... Rabbi Abraham MATITIA

Remington College Cleveland Campus (E)

14445 Broadway Avenue, Cleveland OH 44125-1900

County: Cuyahoga FICE Identification: 007777
Unit ID: 375416
Telephone: (216) 475-7520 Carnegie Class: Assoc/PrivFP
FAX Number: (216) 475-6055 Calendar System: Other
URL: www.remingtoncollege.edu
Established: 1990 Annual Undergrad Tuition & Fees: $16,686
Enrollment: 696 Coed
Affiliation or Control: Proprietary IRS Status: Proprietary
Highest Offering: Associate Degree
Program: Occupational
Accreditation: ACCSC

01 President .... Mr. Patrick RESETAR

† Branch campus of Remington College, Little Rock, AR.

Rosedale Bible College (F)

2270 Rosedale Road, Irwin OH 43029-9517

County: Madison FICE Identification: 034253
Unit ID: 439899
Telephone: (740) 857-1311 Carnegie Class: Assoc/PrivNFP
FAX Number: (877) 857-1312 Calendar System: Semester
URL: www.rosedale.edu
Established: 1952 Annual Undergrad Tuition & Fees: $8,075
Enrollment: 82 Coed
Affiliation or Control: Mennonite Church IRS Status: 501(c)3
Highest Offering: Associate Degree
Program: 2-Year Principally Bachelor's Creditable; Religious Emphasis
Accreditation: BI

01 President .... Mr. Daniel ZIEGLER
05 Academic Dean .... Mr. Phil WEBER
32 Dean of Students .... Mr. Chris JONES
10 Business Manager .... Mr. Alfred YODER
84 Director of Enrollment Services .... Ms. Elizabeth DILLER
08 Director of Library Services .... Mr. Reuben SAIRS
06 Registrar .... Ms. Bethany GEIB
21 Associate Business Officer .... Mr. Lynford SCHROCK
26 Chief Public Relations Officer .... Mr. Kenneth MILLER

Saint Mary Seminary and Graduate School of Theology (G)

28700 Euclid Avenue, Wickliffe OH 44092-2585

County: Lake FICE Identification: 004061
Unit ID: 205319
Telephone: (440) 943-7600 Carnegie Class: Not Classified
FAX Number: (440) 943-7577 Calendar System: Semester
URL: www.stmarysem.edu
Established: 1848 Annual Graduate Tuition & Fees: $9,825
Enrollment: 130 Coed
Affiliation or Control: Roman Catholic IRS Status: 501(c)3
Highest Offering: Doctorate; No Undergraduates
Program: Professional; Religious Emphasis
Accreditation: NH, THEOL

01 President/Rector .... V.Rev. Thomas W. TIFFT
05 Academic Dean/Dean of Students .... Rev. Mark A. LATCOVICH
06 Registrar .... Sr. Brendon ZAJAC, SND
08 Librarian .... Mr. Alan K. ROME
42 Spiritual Director .... Rev. Mark HOLLIS
10 Treasurer .... Mr. Philip GUBAN

School of Advertising Art (H)

1725 E David Road, Dayton OH 45440-1612

County: Montgomery FICE Identification: 025530
Unit ID: 205391
Telephone: (877) 300-9866 Carnegie Class: Assoc/PrivFP
FAX Number: (937) 294-5869 Calendar System: Quarter
URL: www.saa.edu
Established: 1983 Annual Undergrad Tuition & Fees: $24,987
Enrollment: 100 Coed
Affiliation or Control: Proprietary IRS Status: Proprietary
Highest Offering: Associate Degree
Program: Occupational; 2-Year Principally Bachelor's Creditable; Technical Emphasis
Accreditation: ACCSC

00 Owner .... Mr. Tim POTTER
00 Owner .... Ms. Linda POTTER
01 President/Creative Director .... Ms. Jessica GRAVES
03 Vice President .... Mr. Matt FLICK
06 Vice President/HR/Registrar .... Mr. Nathan SUMMERS
05 Director of Education .... Ms. Jennifer LORENZETTI
36 Director of Career Services & PR .... Ms. Joanie SPAIN
37 Director of Financial Aid .... Ms. Tamara ARMENT

Shawnee State University (I)

940 Second Street, Portsmouth OH 45662-4344

County: Scioto FICE Identification: 009942
Unit ID: 205443
Telephone: (740) 351-3205 Carnegie Class: Bac/A&S
FAX Number: (740) 351-3470 Calendar System: Semester
URL: www.shawnee.edu
Established: 1975 Annual Undergrad Tuition & Fees (In-State): $6,546
Enrollment: 4,554 Coed
Affiliation or Control: State IRS Status: 501(c)3
Highest Offering: Master's
Program: Occupational; Liberal Arts And General; Teacher Preparatory
Accreditation: NH, ADNUR, DH, MLTAD, NUR, OT, OTA, PTAA, RAD, TED

01 President .... Dr. Rita R. MORRIS
05 Provost/VP Academic Affairs .... Dr. David TODT
10 Vice President for Finance & Admin .... Ms. Elinda C. BOYLES
32 Vice President for Student Affairs .... Dr. Mary OLING-SISAY
43 General Counsel/Asst to the Pres .... Ms. Cheryl HACKER
84 Assoc Vice Pres Enrollment Mgmt .... Mr. Robert J. TRUSZ
20 Interim Associate Provost .... Dr. Paul MADDEN
26 Director Communications .... Ms. Elizabeth BLEVINS
107 Dean Professional Studies .... Dr. Jim KADEL
49 Dean College Arts & Sciences .... Dr. Timothy E. SCHEURER
08 Director Library .... Ms. Connie SALYERS-STONER
13 Director Univ Information Systems .... Mr. Charles WARNER
30 Director of Development .... Mr. Eric BRAUN
07 Director of Admission & Retention .... Mr. Robert J. TRUSZ
06 Registrar .... Mr. Mark MOORE
15 Director of Human Resources/Payroll .... Mr. Bane SYLVIA
41 Athletic Director .... Mr. Jeff HAMILTON
37 Director of Financial Aid .... Dr. Nicole NEAL
36 Director Career Services .... Mr. Stephen GREGORY
38 Director of Counseling & Psych Svcs .... Dr. Michael J. HUGHES
21 Assoc VP for Finance & Admin .... Ms. Joanne CHARLES
88 Director Student Success Center .... Mr. Dale TAYLOR
85 Director for International Pgms .... Ms. Rita HAIDER
24 Director Instructional Technology .... Mr. Pete DUNCAN
96 Dir of Purchasing & Mail Services .... Ms. Pat CARSON
88 Director University Outreach Svcs .... Ms. Ginnie MOORE
18 Director of Facilities .... Mr. Butch KOTCAMP
97 Director General Education Program .... Dr. Phil BLAU
04 Assistant to the President .... Ms. Mistie SPICER
09 Dir of Institutional Effectiveness .... Mr. Christopher SHAFFER
21 Controller .... Mr. Greg A. BALLENGEE

Sinclair Community College (J)

444 W Third Street, Dayton OH 45402-1460

County: Montgomery FICE Identification: 003119
Unit ID: 205470
Telephone: (937) 512-2500 Carnegie Class: Assoc/Pub-U-SC
FAX Number: (937) 512-5192 Calendar System: Quarter
URL: www.sinclair.edu
Established: 1887 Annual Undergrad Tuition & Fees (In-District): $2,481
Enrollment: 22,553 Coed
Affiliation or Control: State/Local IRS Status: 501(c)3
Highest Offering: Associate Degree
Program: Occupational; 2-Year Principally Bachelor's Creditable
Accreditation: NH, ACBSP, ACFEI, ADNUR, ART, DH, DIETT, ENGT, MAC, MUS, OTA, PTAA, RAD, SURGT, THEA

00 President Emeritus .... Dr. Ned J. SIFFERLEN
01 President .... Dr. Steven L. JOHNSON
05 Senior Vice President/Provost .... Dr. Helen GROVE
10 Vice Pres/Chief Financial Officer .... Mr. Jeff BOUDOURIS
32 Sr Vice Pres Student Services .... Mr. Michael CARTER
13 Sr Vice Pres for Info Technology .... Mr. Kenneth MOORE
31 Vice President Corporate Services .... Ms. Deb NORRIS
103 Vice Pres Workforce Development .... Ms. Deb NORRIS
45 Vice Pres Organizational Dev .... Dr. Mary GAIER
30 Vice President Advancement .... Ms. Madeline ISELI
20 Associate Provost .... Dr. Gloria GOLDMAN
106 Dean Distance Learning/Inst Support .... Ms. Nancy THIBEAULT
81 Dean of Science/Math/Engineering .... Dr. Roger ABERNATHY
50 Dean Business & Public Services .... Dr. Sue MERRELL
57 Int Dean Liberal Arts/Comm/Soc Sci .... Dr. Lori ZAKEL
76 Dean Life & Health Sciences .... Dr. David L. COLLINS
26 Director of Media Relations .... Ms. Natasha BAKER
07 Int Director Outreach Services .... Ms. Rebecca BUTLER
84 Int Sr Dir Enrollment Management .... Ms. Melissa TOLLE
38 Director Counseling Services .... Dr. Bobby J. BEAVERS
37 Director Financial Aid/Scholarships .... Ms. Carlyn BOZEMAN
08 Int Dir Learning Resources Center .... Ms. Rebecca BUTLER
09 Dir Research/Analytics/Reporting .... Ms. Laura MERCER
15 Director Human Resources .... Ms. Janet JONES
13 Director Info Technology Services .... Mr. Scott MCCOLLUM
25 Director Grants Devel/Govt Info .... Mr. Neil HERBKERSMAN
18 Director Facilities Management .... Mr. Thomas MESSINGER
88 Senior Director of Marketing .... Ms. Rebecca BUTLER
19 Director of Public Safety .... Mr. Charles GIFT
28 Diversity Officer .... Ms. Gwen JONES
86 Director Government Relations .... Ms. Madeline ISELI
43 Legal Counsel/Legal Affairs .... Ms. Lauren ROSS
45 Director Curriculum & Assessment .... Mr. Jared CUTLER
90 Manager Info Processing/Tech Svcs .... Ms. Donna BLANKENSHIP
72 Mgr Adv Integrated Manufacture Ctr .... Mr. Mike DONOVAN
36 Manager Career Services .... Mr. Matt MASSIE
96 Manager of Purchasing .... Mr. Mark SCHMID
24 Manager Media Services .... Ms. Susanne SMITH
35 Manager Student Activities .... Ms. Gwendolyn JONES
84 Manager Enrollment Services .... Mr. Peter BOLMIDA
40 Manager Tartan Campus Store .... Mr. Ron BULTEMA
29 Coordinator Alumni Affairs .... Ms. Karen USREY

Southern State Community College (K)

100 Hobart Drive, Hillsboro OH 45133-9488

County: Highland FICE Identification: 012870
Unit ID: 205966
Telephone: (937) 393-3431 Carnegie Class: Assoc/Pub-R-M
FAX Number: (937) 393-9370 Calendar System: Quarter
URL: www.sscc.edu
Established: 1975 Annual Undergrad Tuition & Fees (In-State): $3,850
Enrollment: 3,723 Coed
Affiliation or Control: State IRS Status: 501(c)3
Highest Offering: Associate Degree
Program: Occupational; 2-Year Principally Bachelor's Creditable

Accreditation: **NH**, ADNUR, MAC

01 President ... Dr. Kevin S. BOYS
05 Vice President Academic Affairs ... Dr. Ryan MCCALL
10 Vice President Business & Finance ... Mr. James E. BUCK
32 Vice Pres Student Svcs/Enroll Mgmt ... Mr. James BLAND
30 Vice Pres Instl Advancement ... Ms. Nicole ROADES
12 Director of Fayette Campus ... Ms. Jessica WISE
12 Director of South Campus ... Dr. Peggy CHALKER
12 Director of North Campus ... Ms. Therese LIMBERT
20 Dean Instruction ... Ms. Karen S. DAVIS
103 Dean Workforce Dev/Community Svcs ... Mr. John JOY
15 Director of Human Resources ... Ms. Mindy MARKEY
88 Dean of Adult Opportunity Center ... Ms. Karyn EVANS
88 Dean of Course Studies ... Mr. JR ROUSH
102 Executive Director Foundation ... Vacant
91 Computer System/Communication Mgr ... Ms. Shirley A. CORNWELL
26 Director of Public Relations ... Ms. Kris CROSS
06 Registrar ... Ms. Sharon PURVIS
66 Director of Nursing ... Dr. Julianne KREBS
08 Librarian ... Mr. Louis E. MAYS
37 Director Financial Aid ... Ms. Janeen S. DEATLEY
07 Dir Admission/Student Activities ... Ms. Wendy JOHNSON
41 Athletic Director ... Mr. Adam HOLBROOK
40 Bookstore Manager ... Ms. Jessica STEADMAN
13 Director Information Tech ... Mr. Dennis R. GRIFFITH
36 Director of Recruitment ... Mr. Tom PAYTON
84 Coordinator Enrollment Management ... Ms. Lisa COPAS

Stark State College (A)

6200 Frank Avenue, NW, North Canton OH 44720-7299
County: Stark — FICE Identification: 010881
Unit ID: 205841
Telephone: (330) 494-6170 — Carnegie Class: Assoc/Pub-R-L
FAX Number: (330) 497-6313 — Calendar System: Semester
URL: www.starkstate.edu
Established: 1960 — Annual Undergrad Tuition & Fees (In-District): $4,215
Enrollment: 14,834 — Coed
Affiliation or Control: State/Local — IRS Status: 501(c)3
Highest Offering: Associate Degree
Program: 2-Year Principally Bachelor's Creditable; Technical Emphasis
Accreditation: **NH**, ACBSP, ADNUR, DH, ENGT, MAC, MLTAD, OTA, PTAA

01 Interim President ... Mr. Thomas CHIAPPINI
05 Provost ... Dr. Dorey DIAB
11 Chief Operating Officer ... Vacant
27 Chief Information Officer ... Mr. Michael DRONEY
30 VP for Development and Ex Dir Found ... Mr. Paul FEASER
84 VP Student Services/Enrollment Mgmt ... Mrs. Cheryl RICE
16 VP for Human Resources ... Ms. Celeste JONES
53 Dean Education and Human Services ... Ms. Carrilyn LONG
49 Dean Liberal Arts ... Dr. Lada GIBSON-SHREVE
54 Dean Engineering Technology ... Dr. Peter KROPP
50 Dean Business and Entrep Studies ... Dr. Glenda ZINK
76 Dean Health Technologies ... Mr. John THORNTON
07 Dean Admissions/Student Services ... Mr. Wallace C. HOFFER
51 Dean Corp Svcs and Cont Educ ... Mrs. Barbara MILLIKEN
21 Controller ... Mr. David A. JOHNSON
14 Director Computer Services ... Mr. Greg LANKA
88 Sr Dir Emerg Tech and Strat Grant ... Ms. Rebecca PRIEST
36 Director of Career Development ... Ms. Kristin HANNON
37 Dean Financial Aid and Registration ... Ms. Amy BAKER
51 Director Continuing Education ... Mr. Russ O'NEILL
18 Director of Physical Plant and Cons ... Mr. Steve SPRADLING
90 Director Academic Computing ... Mr. Jeff LASH
40 Bookstore Manager ... Ms. Kathryn FEICHTER
06 Registrar ... Ms. Lisa KASUNIC
26 Director Marketing & Communications ... Ms. Irene LEWIS-MOTTS
21 Director of Budget ... Mr. Bruce WYDER
09 Director of Institutional Research ... Mr. Peter TRUMPOWER
88 Dean Teaching and Learning ... Ms. Wendy FORD
88 Dean Eng/Indus and Emerg Tech ... Dr. Peter KROPP
13 Dean Information Technology Div ... Ms. Cindy CLOSE
38 Dean Advising & Student Engagement ... Ms. Renee LILLY

Stautzenberger College (B)

1796 Indian Wood Circle, Maumee OH 43537-4007
County: Lucas — FICE Identification: 004866
Unit ID: 205887
Telephone: (419) 866-0261 — Carnegie Class: Assoc/PrivFP
FAX Number: (419) 867-9821 — Calendar System: Quarter
URL: www.sctoday.edu
Established: 1926 — Annual Undergrad Tuition & Fees: $10,418
Enrollment: 1,038 — Coed
Affiliation or Control: Proprietary — IRS Status: Proprietary
Highest Offering: Associate Degree
Program: Occupational; 2-Year Principally Bachelor's Creditable; Technical Emphasis
Accreditation: **ACICS**, MAC

01 President/Director ... Mr. George A. SIMON
03 Executive Vice President ... Mr. Brian E. NIEDZWIECKI
07 Dir of Admissions and Marketing ... Ms. Karen L. FITZGERALD
05 Dean of Academics ... Ms. Sarah E. ZIMMERMAN
37 Financial Aid Director ... Mrs. Mari L. HUFFMAN
36 Career Services Director ... Mr. Chase R. CHAMBERS

Temple Baptist College (C)

11965 Kenn Road, Cincinnati OH 45240-1313
County: Hamilton — FICE Identification: 037263
Unit ID: 206002
Telephone: (513) 851-3800 — Carnegie Class: Spec/Faith
FAX Number: (513) 589-3052 — Calendar System: Quarter
URL: www.templebaptist.edu
Established: 1972 — Annual Undergrad Tuition & Fees: $8,704
Enrollment: 60 — Coed
Affiliation or Control: Baptist — IRS Status: 501(c)3
Highest Offering: Baccalaureate
Program: Religious Emphasis
Accreditation: **TRACS**

01 President ... Dr. Scott REEFE
11 Exec VP/Dean Administrative Affairs ... Dr. Ernest WARREN
05 VP/Dean of Academic Affairs ... Dr. Bill G. DYKES
32 Dean of Student Affairs ... Vacant
37 Director of Financial Aid ... Mr. Stephen KLEINER
08 Director of Library Services ... Ms. Wren SHAVER
06 Registrar ... Dr. Shalini KOLLIPARA
09 Dean of Institutional Effectiveness ... Vacant

Terra State Community College (D)

2830 Napoleon Road, Fremont OH 43420-9670
County: Sandusky — FICE Identification: 008278
Unit ID: 206011
Telephone: (419) 334-8400 — Carnegie Class: Assoc/Pub-R-M
FAX Number: (419) 334-3719 — Calendar System: Semester
URL: www.terra.edu
Established: 1968 — Annual Undergrad Tuition & Fees (In-State): $3,978
Enrollment: 3,514 — Coed
Affiliation or Control: State — IRS Status: 501(c)3
Highest Offering: Associate Degree
Program: Occupational; 2-Year Principally Bachelor's Creditable; Technical Emphasis
Accreditation: **NH**

01 President ... Dr. Marsha S. BORDNER
11 Vice Pres for Admin Affairs ... Dr. Jerry WEBSTER
05 Vice Pres for Academic Affairs ... Mrs. Lisa JOZWIAK
10 Treasurer ... Mr. Randy MCCULLOUGH
54 Dean Technology/Science/Comm Div ... Vacant
49 Dean Arts & Sciences & Business ... Dr. Nancy J. SATTLER
37 Director Financial Aid ... Mr. Joseph SPENCER
102 Exec Dir of Foundation/Resource Dev ... Dr. Sue P. BABIONE
09 Director Inst Research/Registrar ... Ms. Lynette D. SULLIVAN
13 Director Information Technology ... Mr. Tim KINCAID
21 Director of Finance ... Ms. Renee D. BROWN
18 Director Plant Operations ... Mr. Robert W. HASLINGER
08 Librarian ... Ms. Mary K. BROESTL
26 Dir Mktg Public Rels/Enroll Svcs ... Ms. Mary E. MCCUE
36 Coordinator Career Services ... Ms. Joan GAMBLE
19 Coord Campus Safety/Evening Svcs ... Mr. Jeffery HUFFMAN

Tiffin University (E)

155 Miami Street, Tiffin OH 44883-2161
County: Seneca — FICE Identification: 003121
Unit ID: 206048
Telephone: (419) 447-6442 — Carnegie Class: Master's L
FAX Number: (419) 443-5022 — Calendar System: Semester
URL: www.tiffin.edu
Established: 1888 — Annual Undergrad Tuition & Fees: $19,124
Enrollment: 4,940 — Coed
Affiliation or Control: Independent Non-Profit — IRS Status: 501(c)3
Highest Offering: Master's
Program: 2-Year Principally Bachelor's Creditable; Liberal Arts And General
Accreditation: **NH**, ACBSP

01 President ... Dr. Paul MARION
05 Vice President for Academic Affairs ... Dr. Charles CHRISTENSEN
30 Vice Pres Development/Pub Affairs ... Dr. Michael GRANDILLO
10 Vice Pres Finance/Administration ... Mr. James WHITE
84 Vice Pres Enrollment Management ... Mr. Ron SCHUMACHER
12 Dean TU at Toledo ... Dr. Jason SLONE
88 Dean of Academic Support Programs ... Dr. Gene CRUTSINGER
04 Assistant to the President ... Ms. Nancy GILBERT
32 Dean of Students ... Ms. Lisa KIRCHNER
13 Exec Dir Information/Tech Services ... Mr. Leonard REAVES
07 Exec Director Undergrad Admissions ... Mr. Jeremy MARINIS
84 Exec Director Enrollment Services ... Ms. Annette STAUNTON
26 Exec Dir Media Rels/Publications ... Ms. Lisa WILLIAMS
38 Director of Academic Advising ... Ms. Judith GARDNER
06 Registrar ... Ms. Alice NICHOLS
41 Director Athletics ... Mr. Lonny ALLEN
21 Controller ... Mr. Robert WATSON
08 Head Librarian ... Ms. Frances FLEET
09 Director of Institutional Research ... Mr. Michael HERDLICK
15 Director Human Resources ... Ms. Lori HALL
29 Director Alumni Relations ... Ms. Celinda SCHERGER
36 Director of Career Development ... Ms. Carol MCDANNELL
18 Director of Facilities ... Mr. Harold KINN
22 Equal Opportunity Officer ... Ms. Lori HALL
39 Director of Residence Life ... Ms. Jennifer COMBS
44 Director of Annual Fund ... Mr. Tyson PINION
28 Director of Institutional Diversity ... Dr. Sharon PERRY-NAUSE
37 Director Student Financial Aid ... Ms. Andrea FABER
40 Bookstore Manager ... Mr. Charles LUTZ
49 Dean of Arts & Sciences ... Dr. Gene CRUTSINGER
50 Dean of Business ... Dr. Lillian SCHUMACHER
88 Int Dean Criminal Justice/Soc Sci ... Dr. Mike LEWIS
88 Dean Degree Completion Programs ... Ms. Nancy SULLIVAN
58 Dean of Graduate Studies ... Dr. Bonnie TIELL
92 Chair of Freshman Honors Program ... Prof. Pat MCLEOD

Tri-State Bible College (F)

506 Margaret Street, PO Box 445,
South Point OH 45680-8402
County: Lawrence — FICE Identification: 034754
Unit ID: 206154
Telephone: (740) 377-2520 — Carnegie Class: Spec/Faith
FAX Number: (740) 377-0001 — Calendar System: Semester
URL: www.tsbc.edu
Established: 1970 — Annual Undergrad Tuition & Fees: $7,700
Enrollment: 70 — Coed
Affiliation or Control: Independent Non-Profit — IRS Status: 501(c)3
Highest Offering: Master's
Program: 2-Year Principally Bachelor's Creditable; Professional; Religious Emphasis
Accreditation: **BI**

00 Chancellor ... Dr. Clifford L. MARQUARDT
01 President ... Dr. Jack L. FINCH
05 Chief Academic Administrator ... Kenneth C. LAW
10 Chief Financial Administrator ... Ms. Clyda HESTER

Trinity Lutheran Seminary (G)

2199 E Main Street, Columbus OH 43209-2334
County: Franklin — FICE Identification: 003044
Unit ID: 206215
Telephone: (614) 235-4136 — Carnegie Class: Spec/Faith
FAX Number: (614) 238-0263 — Calendar System: Semester
URL: www.TLSohio.edu
Established: 1830 — Annual Graduate Tuition & Fees: $14,390
Enrollment: 155 — Coed
Affiliation or Control: Evangelical Lutheran Church In America
IRS Status: 501(c)3
Highest Offering: Doctorate; No Undergraduates
Program: Professional; Religious Emphasis
Accreditation: **NH**, THEOL

01 President ... Dr. Mark R. RAMSETH
05 Academic Dean ... Dr. Brad A. BINAU
20 Associate Academic Dean ... Dr. Diane J. HYMANS
42 Dir Mentoring Ministries/Pastor ... Rev. Ruth C. FORTIS
07 Director Admissions ... Rev. Shari L. AYERS
06 Registrar ... Mrs. Carol M. DIXON
08 Director Hamma Library ... Mr. Ray A. OLSON
26 Director Communications/Marketing ... Ms. Margaret L. FARNHAM
37 Director Financial Aid ... Mrs. Melissa CURTIS POWELL
88 Director Contextual Education ... Rev. Jane E. JENKINS
88 Director MA in Church Music Program ... Ms. May L. SCHWARZ
58 Director Graduate Studies ... Dr. Walter F. TAYLOR, JR.
88 Director MACE/MAYFM/MTS Programs ... Dr. Mary E. HUGHES
44 Director Devel/Gift Planning Mgmt ... Ms. Jane A. KIRCHHOFF
21 Controller ... Mrs. Patricia A. FORK
29 Director Development/Alumni ... Rev. Gary A. SANDBERG
18 Director Facilities Management ... Ms. Laura K. PETERSON

Trumbull Business College (H)

3200 Ridge Road, Warren OH 44484-3272
County: Trumbull — FICE Identification: 020543
Unit ID: 206224
Telephone: (330) 369-3200 — Carnegie Class: Assoc/PrivFP
FAX Number: (330) 369-6792 — Calendar System: Quarter
URL: www.tbc-trumbullbusiness.com
Established: 1972 — Annual Undergrad Tuition & Fees: $26,500
Enrollment: 425 — Coed
Affiliation or Control: Proprietary — IRS Status: Proprietary
Highest Offering: Associate Degree
Program: Occupational
Accreditation: **ACICS**

01 President ... Mr. Dennis J. GRIFFITH
37 Director of Financial Aid ... Ms. Florence HENNING
36 Director of Student Placement ... Ms. Kimberly STRANIAK
12 Director of Branch Campus ... Mr. Kenneth C. MILLER
06 Registrar ... Ms. Teresa SHAMBACH

Union Institute & University (I)

440 E McMillan Street, Cincinnati OH 45206-1947
County: Hamilton — FICE Identification: 010923
Unit ID: 206279
Telephone: (513) 861-6400 — Carnegie Class: DRU
FAX Number: (513) 861-0779 — Calendar System: Semester
URL: www.myunion.edu
Established: 1964 — Annual Undergrad Tuition & Fees: $11,468
Enrollment: 1,508 — Coed
Affiliation or Control: Independent Non-Profit — IRS Status: 501(c)3
Highest Offering: Doctorate
Program: Liberal Arts And General; Teacher Preparatory; Professional
Accreditation: **NH**

01 President ... Dr. Roger H. SUBLETT

05 Provost Dr. Richard HANSEN
04 Executive Assistant to President Ms. Carolyn KRAUSE
10 Chief Fiscal Officer Mr. Edward WALTON
15 Vice President Human Resources Ms. Deborah EAMOE
84 VP Enrollment Management Mr. Jon MAYS
20 Assoc Provost Academic Programs Dr. Patricia BREWER
46 Assoc Provost Inst Effectiveness Dr. Elizabeth PRUDEN
88 Assoc VP Special Projects Dr. James ROCHELEAU
20 Asst VP Academic Affairs Dr. Brian WEBB
58 Dean PhD Interdisc Studies Pgm Dr. Larry PRESTON
58 Dean Graduate Studies in Education Dr. Arlene SACKS
58 Dean Graduate Studies in Psychology Dr. William LAX
21 Controller Vacant
06 Registrar Ms. Lew Rita MOORE
09 Director Institutional Research Ms. Linda C. VAN VOLKENBURGH
13 Director Information Technology Mr. Greg THOMPSON
18 Director Building Management Ms. Janet DAY
26 Asst VP Communications Ms. Carolyn KRAUSE
96 Director of Purchasing Mrs. Ruth A. RIDGE
12 Dean Undergrad Studies Miami Center Dr. Beryl WATNICK
12 Dean Undergrad Studies LA Center Dr. Elizabeth PASTORRES-PALFFY
12 Dean Undergrad Studies Cincinnati Dr. Carolyn TURNER
12 Dean Vermont Centers Dr. Dan LERNER
62 Director Gary Library Mr. Matthew PAPPATHAN
37 Director Financial Aid Ms. Lisa PERDOMO
29 Director Alumni Relations & Vet Aff Dr. Neal MEIER
51 Director Lifelong Learning Ms. Dayle DEARDURFF

United Theological Seminary (A)

4501 Denlinger Road, Dayton OH 45426-2308
County: Montgomery FICE Identification: 003122
Unit ID: 206288
Telephone: (937) 529-2201 Carnegie Class: Spec/Faith
FAX Number: (866) 433-8235 Calendar System: Semester
URL: www.united.edu
Established: 1871 Annual Graduate Tuition & Fees: $15,092
Enrollment: 360 Coed
Affiliation or Control: United Methodist IRS Status: 501(c)3
Highest Offering: Doctorate; No Undergraduates
Program: Professional; Religious Emphasis
Accreditation: NH, THEOL

01 President & CEO Dr. Wendy J. DEICHMANN
05 Vice Pres Academic Affairs & Dean Dr. David WATSON
10 Vice Pres Finance/Treasurer Mr. Ronald KUKER
30 Vice Pres Development Rev. Timothy FORBESS
88 Director of Doctoral Studies Dr. Harold HUDSON
06 Registrar Ms. Martha M. ANDERSON
13 Director of Information Technology Vacant
106 Dir Distance Learning/Educ Tech Ms. Phyllis ENNIST
08 Librarian Ms. Sarah D. BROOKS BLAIR
88 Director of Contextual Ministries Rev. Gary EUBANK
26 Director of Communications Ms. JoAnn WAGNER
29 Assoc Dir Alumni/ae Services Rev. Brice THOMAS
37 Director of Financial Aid Ms. Sandra TAYLOR
18 Facility Manager Mr. Roger BOWYER

The University of Akron, Main Campus (B)

302 Buchtel Common, Akron OH 44325
County: Summit FICE Identification: 003123
Unit ID: 200800
Telephone: (330) 972-7111 Carnegie Class: RU/H
FAX Number: (330) 972-6990 Calendar System: Semester
URL: www.uakron.edu
Established: 1870 Annual Undergrad Tuition & Fees (In-State): $9,260
Enrollment: 29,300 Coed
Affiliation or Control: State IRS Status: 501(c)3
Highest Offering: Doctorate
Program: 2-Year Principally Bachelor's Creditable; Liberal Arts And General; Teacher Preparatory; Professional
Accreditation: NH, AAFCS, ACBSP, ANEST, ART, AUD, BUS, BUSA, CACREP, CIDA, COPSY, DANCE, DIETC, DIETD, ENG, ENGT, IFSAC, IPSY, LAW, MAC, MFCD, MUS, NURSE, PH, SP, SPAA, SURGT, SW, TED

01 President Dr. Luis M. PROENZA
05 Senior Vice President & Provost Dr. Mike SHERMAN
46 Vice Pres Research/Dean of Grad Sch Dr. George R. NEWKOME
32 Vice President for Student Affairs Dr. Charles J. FEY
10 VP Finance & Administration/CFO Mr. David J. CUMMINS
43 Vice President & General Counsel Mr. Ted A. MALLO
26 Vice Pres Public Affs/Development Mr. John A. LAGUARDIA
13 VP Information Technology/CIO Mr. James L. SAGE
18 Vice Pres Capital Plng/Facil Mgmt Mr. Ted CURTIS
88 Assistant Secretary of the BOT Mr. Paul A. HEROLD
100 Vice President/Chief of Staff Mrs. Candace CAMPBELL JACKSON
101 Secretary Board of Trustees Mr. Ted A. MALLO
32 Assoc VP & Dean of Student Life Ms. Denine M. ROCCO
30 Assoc Vice Pres Development Mr. Timothy R. DUFORE
44 Special Assistant to the President Mr. Paul A. HEROLD
31 Assoc VP Community Relations Mr. David NYPAVER
21 Assc VP Treasury/Financial Planning Mr. Brian E. DAVIS
46 Assoc Vice President for Research Mr. Kenneth G. PRESTON
46 Assoc Vice President for Research Mr. Wayne H. WATKINS
21 Assoc Vice President & Controller Mr. John E. KOVATCH
84 Assoc VP Strategic Enrollment Mr. William KRAUS
38 Associate Vice Pres for Campus Life Mrs. Oletha THOMPSON
88 Assoc VP Strategic Init & Engage Mrs. Holly HARRIS BANE
88 Assoc VP Inclusion & Equity Mr. Lee A. GILL
27 Assoc VP Comm & Chief Comm Ofcr Vacant
19 Ast VP Camp Safety/Chf Univ Police Mr. Paul J. CALLAHAN
43 Asst VP & Assoc General Counsel Mr. Sidney C. FOSTER, JR.
29 Exec Director Alumni Association Mrs. Kimberly M. MORGAN
15 VP Talent Dev & Human Resources Dr. Becky J. HOOVER
38 Director Academic Advising Center Mrs. Nancy L. ROADRUCK
06 Registrar Mrs. Debra L. HAYES
07 Director of Admissions Ms. Diane R. RAYBUCK
09 Director Institutional Research Ms. Sabrina L. ANDREWS
13 Director Technology Transfer Mr. Kenneth G. PRESTON
57 Dean of Creative and Prof Arts Dr. Chand MIDHA
08 Dean of University Libraries Ms. Cheryl KERN-SIMIRENKO
49 Dean Buchtel College of Arts & Sci Dr. Chand MIDHA
54 Dean College of Engineering Dr. George K. HARITOS
53 Dean College of Education Dr. Mark D. SHERMIS
50 Dean College of Business Admin Dr. Ravi KROVI
57 Int Dean College Hlth Sci Human Svc Dr. Roberta A. DEPOMPEI
66 Int Dean of College of Nursing Dr. Roberta DEPOMPEI
72 Dean Summit College Mr. Stanley B. SILVERMAN
61 Dean of the School of Law Mr. Martin H. BELSKY
20 Dean University College Mr. Stanley B. SILVERMAN
54 Dean of Polymer Science/Engineering Dr. Stephen Z D. CHENG
12 Dean Wayne College Dr. John P. KRISTOFCO
37 Director Student Financial Aid Mrs. Michelle ELLIS
96 Director of Purchasing Mr. Andrew W. ROTH
88 Director of Internal Communications Mr. Robert KROPFF
105 University Webmaster Mr. Eric W. KRIEDER
92 Dean Honors College Dr. Dale H. MUGLER
88 Director UA Adult Focus Mrs. Laura H. CONLEY
41 Director Athletics Mr. Tom WISTRCILL
36 Director Counseling/Test/Career Ctr Dr. Juanita K. MARTIN
39 Director Residence Life & Housing Mr. John A. MESSINA
25 Director Rsrch Svcs/Sponsored Pgms Ms. Katie WATKINS-WENDELL
85 Int Director International Programs Ms. Linda E. MARX
23 Director Health Services Ms. Diane J. FASHINPAUR
14 Dir Hardware Opers/Oper Sys Svcs Mr. Thomas R. BEITL
21 Spec Asst to VP/IT & Spec Proj Mgr Mr. David G. WASIK
28 Dir Multicultural Development Ms. Fedearia A. NICHOLSON
88 Exec Dir University Park Alliance Mr. Eric A. JOHNSON
88 Information Security Officer Mrs. Deborah WHITE
88 Mgr Editorial Svcs/Inst Marketing Ms. Joette DIGNAN WEIR

The University of Akron-Wayne College (C)

1901 Smucker Road, Orrville OH 44667-9758
County: Wayne FICE Identification: 010818
Unit ID: 200846
Telephone: (330) 683-2010 Carnegie Class: Assoc/Pub2in4
FAX Number: (330) 684-8989 Calendar System: Semester
URL: www.wayne.uakron.edu
Established: 1972 Annual Undergrad Tuition & Fees (In-State): $5909.76
Enrollment: 2,603 Coed
Affiliation or Control: State IRS Status: 501(c)3
Highest Offering: Associate Degree
Program: Occupational; 2-Year Principally Bachelor's Creditable
Accreditation: NH

01 Interim Dean Dr. Paulette M. POPOVICH
04 Senior Administrative Assistant Ms. Lindsie B. WEBB
05 Associate Dean of Instruction Vacant
10 Sr Dir Business Operations/Finance Mrs. Tamara A. LOWE
32 Sr Dir Student Life/Enroll Mgmt Mr. Gordon K. HOLLY
18 Chief Facilities/Physical Plant Mr. W. Russ PUGH
26 Chief Public Relations Officer Mrs. Regina L. SCHWARTZ
08 Manager Library Services Mrs. Maureen T. LERCH
06 Registrar Mrs. Charlene LANCE
07 Director of Admissions Mrs. Alicia BROADUS
09 Director of Institutional Research Mr. William CLARK
15 Director Personnel Services Ms. Cathy E. COOPER
20 Associate Academic Officer Mr. Garth D. SCHOFFMAN
88 Assistant to the Dean Mr. Kevin E. ENGLE
35 Student Activities Coordinator Ms. Jackie E. ASHBAUGH
36 Coord Career and Assessment Svcs Ms. Carol J. PLEUSS
37 Manager Student Svcs/Financial Aid Vacant
38 Coordinator of Academic Advising Mr. L. Russ WILSON
96 Accounting Clerk Sr Ms. Amy M. HAYNES
13 Manager Technical Support Services Ms. Cher DEEDS
19 University Police Sgt. Scott A. KERR
40 Director Bookstore Mr. Patrick DUFF
41 Athletic Director Mr. Patrick S. RUFENER
103 Dir Cont Ed & Workforce Development Ms. Amy H. MAST

University of Cincinnati Main Campus (D)

2624 Clifton Avenue, Cincinnati OH 45221-0001
County: Hamilton FICE Identification: 003125
Unit ID: 201885
Telephone: (513) 556-6000 Carnegie Class: RU/VH
FAX Number: (513) 556-3237 Calendar System: Quarter
URL: www.uc.edu
Established: 1819 Annual Undergrad Tuition & Fees (In-State): $10,419
Enrollment: 41,357 Coed
Affiliation or Control: State IRS Status: 501(c)3
Highest Offering: Doctorate
Program: Liberal Arts And General; Teacher Preparatory; Professional
Accreditation: NH, ANEST, ART, AUD, BBT, BUS, CACREP, CIDA, CLPSY, CONST, CS, DANCE, DENT, DIETC, DIETD, EMT, ENG, ENGR, ENGT, LAW, MED, MIDWF, MT, MUS, NMT, NURSE, PHAR, PLNG, PTA, PTAA, SP, SURGA, SW, TED, THEA

01 President Dr. Gregory H. WILLIAMS
05 Sr VP/Provost Academic Affairs Dr. Santa J. ONO
11 Sr VP for Administration & Finance Mr. Robert AMBACH
03 Executive VP Ms. Karen K. FAABORG
46 Interim Vice President for Research Dr. William S. BALL
63 Dean Medicine/VP for Health Affairs Dr. Thomas F. BOAT
30 VP Development & Alumni Relations Mr. Michael W. CARROLL
86 Vice Pres Govt Rels/University Comm Mr. Gregory J. VEHR
32 Vice Pres Student Affairs & Svcs Dr. Mitchel D. LIVINGSTON
10 Vice President for Finance Mr. James D. PLUMMER
13 VP & CIO for Information Technology Dr. Michael LIEBERMAN
43 General Counsel Mr. Mitchell D. MCCRATE
15 Acting Sr Assoc VP Human Resources Ms. Sharon E. BUTLER
84 Sr Assoc Vice President Enrollment Dr. Caroline B. MILLER
21 Assoc VP Community Development Mr. Gerald A. SIEGERT
27 Assoc VP PR/Univ Spokesperson Mr. Greg HAND
07 Assoc Vice Pres for Admissions Dr. Thomas CANEPA
76 Dean Allied Health Sciences Dr. Elizabeth C. KING
49 Dean Arts & Sciences Dr. Valerie HARDCASTLE
50 Dean Business Administration Dr. David M. SZYMANSKI
64 Dean College Conservatory of Music Peter LANDGREN
48 Dean Design/Architecture/Art & Plng Dr. Robert PROBST
53 Dean Education Dr. Lawrence J. JOHNSON
54 Dean Engineering & Applied Science Dr. Carlo D. MONTEMAGNO
61 Dean Law Mr. Louis D. BILIONIS
66 Interim Dean Nursing Cheryl L. HOYING
67 Dean Pharmacy Dr. Daniel ACOSTA
70 Interim Director School Social Work Dr. Gerald J. BOSTWICK
08 Dean Library Dr. Victoria A. MONTAVON
29 Executive Director Alumni Affairs Mr. Myron HUGHES
41 Director Athletics Mr. Michael THOMAS
40 Director Bookstore Ms. Linda K. GINDELE
36 Director Career Development Dr. Katrina JORDAN
38 Director Counseling Center Vacant
22 Director Equal Opportunity Mr. George WHARTON
39 Director Housing/Food Service Mr. Todd DUNCAN
37 Director Student Financial Aid Ms. Connie WILLIAMS
09 Director Institutional Research Mr. Lee E. MORTIMER
19 Director Public Safety Mr. Eugene R. FERRARA
06 Registrar Dr. Douglas BURGESS
96 Director of Purchasing Mr. Thomas B. GUERIN
45 CoDir Institute for Policy Research Dr. Eric RADEMACHER
45 CoDir Institute for Policy Research Dr. Kimberly DOWNING

University of Cincinnati-Clermont College (E)

4200 Clermont College Drive, Batavia OH 45103-1785
County: Clermont FICE Identification: 010805
Unit ID: 201946
Telephone: (513) 732-5200 Carnegie Class: Assoc/Pub2in4
FAX Number: (513) 732-5275 Calendar System: Quarter
URL: www.ucclermont.edu
Established: 1972 Annual Undergrad Tuition & Fees (In-State): $5,034
Enrollment: 3,990 Coed
Affiliation or Control: State IRS Status: 501(c)3
Highest Offering: Baccalaureate
Program: Occupational; 2-Year Principally Bachelor's Creditable; Technical Emphasis
Accreditation: NH, MAC, SURGT

01 Dean Dr. Gregory S. SOJKA
05 Assoc Dean Academic Affairs Vacant
20 Assistant Dean Academic Affairs Ms. Mary F. STEARNS
08 Senior Librarian Ms. Rosemary YOUNG
24 Dir Learning Center Ms. Pam MAVI
76 Director Allied Health Ms. Sharman WILLMORE
09 Director of Institutional Research Ms. Susan RILEY
10 Asst Dean Administrative Services Mr. John R. NELSON
32 Asst Dean Enroll & Student Svcs Ms. Ann APPLETON
84 Director Advising & Registration Mr. Ryan HALL
84 Director of Enrollment Services Ms. Martha GEIGER
06 Registrar Ms. Beth NEWMAN
88 Director Disability Services Ms. Jennifer RADT
35 Director of Student Life Ms. Kimberly ELLISON
41 Program Coord/Athletic Director Mr. Brian SULLIVAN
18 Asst Dean Facilities & Tech Svcs Mr. Stephen W. YOUNG
30 Director of Development Ms. Meredith DELANEY
26 Director Marketing & Development Ms. Mae HANNA

University of Cincinnati-Raymond Walters College (F)

9555 Plainfield Road, Blue Ash OH 45236-1096
County: Hamilton FICE Identification: 004868
Unit ID: 201955
Telephone: (513) 745-5600 Carnegie Class: Assoc/Pub2in4
FAX Number: (513) 745-5780 Calendar System: Quarter
URL: www.rwc.uc.edu
Established: 1967 Annual Undergrad Tuition & Fees (In-State): $5,232
Enrollment: 4,820 Coed
Affiliation or Control: State IRS Status: 501(c)3
Highest Offering: Baccalaureate
Program: Occupational; 2-Year Principally Bachelor's Creditable
Accreditation: NH, ADNUR, ART, DH, MAC, RAD, RADDOS, RTT

01	Dean	Dr. Cady SHORT-THOMPSON
05	Assoc Dean Academic Affairs	Dr. Marlene R. MINER
10	Asst Dean/Dir Administrative Svcs	Mr. Eugene KRAMER
32	Asst Dean Student Services	Ms. Pamela LINEBACK
103	Asst Dean Workforce Development	Ms. Cheryl BRUEGGEMAN
26	Director College/Alumni Relations	Ms. Ginny HIZER
90	Network Resources Systems Engr	Mr. John F. WELLER
84	Director Enrollment Services	Mr. Christopher POWER
09	Director Institutional Research	Ms. Sandra PARKER
06	Registration Officer	Ms. Deborah L. SMITH
36	Director Career Services	Ms. Pamela LINEBACH
08	Library Director	Ms. Stephena HARMONY
24	Director Media Services	Mr. H. Michael SANDERS
35	Student Life Coordinator	Ms. Shelia YATES-MATTINGLY

University of Dayton (A)

300 College Park, Dayton OH 45469-0001

County: Montgomery
FICE Identification: 003127
Unit ID: 202480
Telephone: (937) 229-1000
Carnegie Class: RU/H
FAX Number: (937) 229-4000
Calendar System: Semester
URL: www.udayton.edu
Established: 1850
Annual Undergrad Tuition & Fees: $31,640
Enrollment: 11,199
Coed
Affiliation or Control: Roman Catholic
IRS Status: 501(c)3
Highest Offering: Doctorate
Program: Liberal Arts And General; Teacher Preparatory; Professional
Accreditation: NH, ART, BUS, BUSA, CACREP, DIETD, ENG, ENGT, LAW, MUS, PTA, SPAA, TED

01	President	Dr. Daniel J. CURRAN
05	Provost	Dr. Joseph E. SALIBA
32	VP Student Devel	Mr. William M. FISCHER
10	Vice Pres Finance & Admin Services	Mr. Thomas E. BURKHARDT
30	Vice Pres University Advancement	Ms. Deborah A. READ
41	Vice Pres/Director of Athletics	Mr. Timothy J. WABLER
15	Vice President Human Resources	Ms. Joyce M. CARTER
84	Vice President for Enrollment Mgmt	Mr. Sundar KUMARASAMY
46	Vice President of Research	Dr. Michael V. MCCABE
26	Assoc VP University Communications	Ms. Teresa J. RIZVI
44	Assoc VP Development	Mr. James F. BROTHERS
42	Director Campus Ministry	Ms. Crystal C. SULLIVAN
88	VP for Mission and Rector	Rev. James F. FITZ, SM
88	Univ Prof Faith/Culture	Dr. David J. O'BRIEN
31	Dir Ctr for Leadership in Community	Mr. Richard T. FERGUSON
20	Assoc Provost Faculty & Admin Affs	Dr. Patrick G. DONNELLY
88	Asc Prov Lrng Spprt/Dir Rch Tch Ctr	Dr. Deborah J. BICKFORD
90	Assoc Prov/Chief Information Ofcr	Dr. Thomas D. SKILL
06	Registrar	Mr. Thomas J. WESTENDORF
07	Asst VP/ Dean of Admission	Mr. Robert F. DURKLE
19	Director Public Safety	Mr. Bruce E. BURT
09	Director Institutional Studies	Ms. Susan K. SEXTON
21	Comptroller	Ms. Angela K. BUECHELE
36	Director Career Services	Mr. Jason C. ECKERT
38	Asst VP Student Dev/Dir Counseling	Dr. Steven D. MUELLER
18	VP for Facilities Management	Ms. Beth H. KEYES
23	Medical Director Univ Health Ctr	Dr. Mary P. BUCHWALDER
62	Dean University Libraries	Ms. Kathleen M. WEBB
49	Dean College Arts & Sciences	Dr. Paul H. BENSON
61	Dean School of Law	Mr. Paul E. MCGREAL
50	Interim Dean Sch of Business Admin	Dr. Joseph CASTELLANO
58	Assoc Provost and Dean Grad Studies	Dr. Paul M. VANDERBURGH
53	Dean School of Educ & Allied Prof	Dr. Kevin R. KELLY
54	Dean School of Engineering	Dr. Tony E. SALIBA
29	Asst VP Principal Gifts	Mr. Todd W. IMWALLE
35	Dir Student Life & Kennedy Union	Ms. Amy L. LOPEZ-MATTHEWS
37	Director of Financial Aid	Ms. Kathy M. HARMON
39	Asst Dean Students & Dir Res Life	Mr. Steven T. HERNDON
40	Manager UD Bookstore	Ms. Julie M. BANKS
43	Director Legal Affairs/Univ Counsel	Mr. John E. HART
96	Director of Purchasing	Mr. Ken R. SOUCY
92	Dir University Honors/Scholars Pgm	Dr. David W. DARROW
94	Director of Women's Studies	Dr. Rebecca S. WHISNANT
22	Dir Affirmative Action & Compliance	Ms. Patricia BERNAL-OLSON
86	Government/Regional Relations Dir	Mr. S. Ted BUCARO
28	Director of Diversity	Dr. Jack T. LING

The University of Findlay (B)

1000 North Main Street, Findlay OH 45840-3653

County: Hancock
FICE Identification: 003045
Unit ID: 202763
Telephone: (419) 422-8313
Carnegie Class: Master's L
FAX Number: (419) 434-4822
Calendar System: Semester
URL: www.findlay.edu
Established: 1882
Annual Undergrad Tuition & Fees: $28,104
Enrollment: 5,434
Coed
Affiliation or Control: Church Of God
IRS Status: 501(c)3
Highest Offering: Doctorate
Program: Occupational; Liberal Arts And General; Teacher Preparatory; Professional
Accreditation: NH, #ARCPA, ENGR, NMT, OT, PHAR, PTA, SW, @TEAC, TED

01	President	Dr. Katherine R. FELL
05	Vice President for Academic Affairs	Dr. Daniel J. MAY
10	Vice President for Business Affairs	Mr. Martin L. TERRY
30	Vice President Development	Mr. David FERGUSON
32	Vice President for Student Affairs	Mr. David W. EMSWELLER
04	Assistant to the President	Ms. Meg FLEMION
46	Dean Undergraduate Education	Dr. Marie A. LOUDEN-HANES
81	Dean College of Sciences	Dr. Terry SCHWANER
50	Dean College of Business	Dr. Paul SEARS
49	Dean College of Liberal Art	Dr. Gary JOHNSON
76	Dean College of Health Sciences	Dr. Andrea KOEPKE
67	Dean College of Pharmacy	Dr. Donald STANSLOSKI
53	Dean College of Education	Dr. Julie MCINTOSH
58	Dean of Graduate/Professional Stds	Dr. Thomas DILLON
18	Director of Physical Plant	Mr. Myreon K. COBB
09	Director of Institutional Research	Mr. Tony G. GOEDDE
06	Registrar	Mr. Tony G. GOEDDE
07	Director of Admissions	Ms. Donna GRUBER
41	Athletic Director	Mr. Steven P. RACKLEY
08	Director of Shafer Library	Mr. Robert W. SCHIRMER
37	Director of Financial Aid	Mr. Arman J. HABEGGER
13	Director of Computer Services	Mr. Scott WALTHOUR
29	Director of Alumni Affairs	Ms. Deanna SPRAW
26	Dir Public Relations/Media Rels	Ms. Suzanne ENGLISH
44	Director of Development	Mr. Charles SHEPARD, II
36	Director of Career Services	Ms. Janet M. TAYLOR
15	Director of Human Resources	Mr. Robert LINK
23	Director of Health Services	Ms. Julie R. YINGLING
38	Director Counseling Services	Ms. Karyn J. WESTRICK
40	Manager of Bookstore	Mr. Jay CANTERBURY
42	Director Christian Ministries	Rev. William D. MILLER
19	Director of Security/Safety	Mr. Kenneth WALERIUS
93	Dir Intercultural Student Services	Mr. Almar WALTER
21	Business Manager	Mr. Robert LINK
28	Director of Diversity	Mr. Almar WALTER
35	Chief Student Life Officer	Mr. David W. EMSWELLER
85	Dir Intl Student Admissions & Svcs	Ms. Penny GERDEMAN
101	Secretary to the Board of Trustees	Ms. C. Sue PIRSCHEL
25	Dir of Grants and Contract Admin	Ms. Jill GEAR

University of Mount Union (C)

1972 Clark Avenue, Alliance OH 44601-3993

County: Stark
FICE Identification: 003083
Unit ID: 204185
Telephone: (330) 821-5320
Carnegie Class: Bac/Diverse
FAX Number: (330) 823-3457
Calendar System: Semester
URL: www.mountunion.edu
Established: 1846
Annual Undergrad Tuition & Fees: $25,700
Enrollment: 2,255
Coed
Affiliation or Control: United Methodist
IRS Status: 501(c)3
Highest Offering: Master's
Program: Liberal Arts And General; Teacher Preparatory
Accreditation: NH, #ARCPA, MUS, TED

01	President	Dr. Richard F. GIESE
05	Vice Pres Acad Affs/Dean of Univ	Dr. Patricia H. DRAVES
10	Vice Pres Business Affs/Treasurer	Mr. Patrick D. HEDDLESTON
30	Vice President Univ Advancement	Mr. Gregory KING
32	Vice Pres Student Affs/Dean Stdnts	Mr. John FRAZIER
84	Vice President for Enrollment Mgmt	Ms. Amy A. TOMKO
26	Exec Director of Marketing	Ms. Melissa GARDNER
08	Librarian	Mr. Robert R. GARLAND
06	Registrar	Ms. Karen MORIARTY
07	Director of Admissions	Ms. Grace CHALKER
44	Director Annual Fund	Ms. Kim RODSTROM
44	Director of Planned Giving	Mr. David WOLPERT
14	Director Computer Information Sys	Ms. Tina STUCHELL
30	Director of Advance for Major Gifts	Mr. Matt STINSON
09	Director Assesment/Program Develop	Dr. Fang DU
29	Director Alumni/College Activities	Ms. Anne GRAFFICE
85	Director Center for Global Educ	Mr. Scott SLABAUGH
18	Director of Physical Plant	Mr. Blaine D. LEWIS
16	Director of Human Resources	Ms. Pamela NEWBOLD
39	Director of Housing	Ms. Michelle GAFFNEY
42	Chaplain	Rev. Martha D. CASHBURLESS
36	Director of Career Services	Ms. Rebecca DOAK
37	Director of Student Financial Svcs	Ms. Emily SWAIN
40	Manager of College Bookstore	Ms. Mary J. FISHER
41	Athletic Director	Mr. Larry T. KEHRES
04	Exec Assistant to the President	Ms. Laura E. GOOD
21	Assoc VP for Business Affairs	Mr. Ronald CROWL
28	Director of Diversity	Dr. Ivory LYONS
20	Associate Academic Officer	Dr. James THOMA
35	Associate Dean of Students	Ms. Karen PETKO
96	Director of Purchasing	Mr. John GREGORY

University of Northwestern Ohio (D)

1441 N Cable Road, Lima OH 45805-1498

County: Allen
FICE Identification: 004861
Unit ID: 204486
Telephone: (419) 227-3141
Carnegie Class: Assoc/PrivNFP4
FAX Number: (419) 229-6926
Calendar System: Quarter
URL: www.unoh.edu
Established: 1920
Annual Undergrad Tuition & Fees: $8,230
Enrollment: 4,128
Coed
Affiliation or Control: Independent Non-Profit
IRS Status: 501(c)3
Highest Offering: Master's
Program: Occupational
Accreditation: NH, ACBSP, MAC

01	President	Dr. Jeffrey A. JARVIS
05	Vice Pres Academic Affairs/Provost	Dr. Cheryl MUELLER
35	Vice President Student Affairs	Mrs. Marcia EICKHOLT
39	Director of Housing	Mr. Pat FINNERTY
15	Director of Human Resources	Ms. Geri MORRIS
10	Controller	Mr. James S. BRONDER
06	Director of Registration & Advising	Mr. Loren KORZAN
37	Director of Financial Aid	Mr. Wendell SCHICK
18	Chief Facilities/Physical Plant	Mr. Don RICKER
38	Director Student Counseling	Mr. Michael CALLAHAN
20	Associate Academic Officer	Mrs. Jenell BRAMLAGE
26	Chief Public Relations Officer	Mrs. Cheryl STEINWEDEL
29	Director Alumni Relations	Mrs. Jessica SPIERS
30	Chief Development	Mr. Steve FARMER
32	Chief Student Life Officer	Mr. Bob FRICKE
36	Director Career Services	Mrs. Nicole NEIMEYER
04	Executive Assistant to President	Mrs. Jennifer BENDELE
50	Dean of Business Division	Mr. Dean HOBLER
72	Dean Technological Division	Mr. Tom GROTHOUS
72	Dean Technological Division	Mr. Andy O'NEAL

University of Rio Grande (E)

218 N College Avenue, Rio Grande OH 45674-3100

County: Gallia
FICE Identification: 003116
Unit ID: 205203
Telephone: (740) 245-5353
Carnegie Class: Master's M
FAX Number: (740) 245-5266
Calendar System: Semester
URL: www.rio.edu
Established: 1876
Annual Undergrad Tuition & Fees: $19,466
Enrollment: 1,821
Coed
Affiliation or Control: Independent Non-Profit
IRS Status: 501(c)3
Highest Offering: Master's
Program: 2-Year Principally Bachelor's Creditable; Liberal Arts And General; Teacher Preparatory; Professional
Accreditation: NH, ADNUR, DMS, IACBE, IACBE, NUR, RAD, SW, TED

01	President	Dr. Barbara GELLMAN-DANLEY
05	Provost/VP of Academic Affairs	Dr. Kenneth PORADA
12	VP Admin Affs/Rio Grande Cmty Col	Ms. Luanne BOWMAN
11	Vice Pres Administrative Svcs/COO	Mr. Paul D. HARRISON
10	Vice President for Finance/CFO	Dr. Nayyer HUSSAIN
30	Vice Pres Institutional Advancement	Mrs. Beverly CRABTREE
15	Vice Pres Human Resources	Ms. Phyllis MASON
35	Dean Student Affairs	Mr. Aaron QUINN
41	Director of Athletics	Mr. Jeff LANHAM
04	Admin Assistant to the President	Ms. Carolyn HARRISON
07	Director Admissions	Vacant
06	Registrar	Mr. Mark ABELL
08	Director of the Library	Mr. J. David MAUER
29	Director of Alumni Relations	Mrs. Annette WARD
36	Director of Career Services	Ms. Susan HAFT
84	Director Enrollment Management	Mr. Mark ABELL
107	Dean College Professional Studies	Dr. Zaki SHARIF
49	Dean College of Liberal Arts & Sci	Dr. David LAWRENCE

University of Toledo (F)

2801 W Bancroft, Toledo OH 43606-3390

County: Lucas
FICE Identification: 003131
Unit ID: 206084
Telephone: (419) 530-4636
Carnegie Class: RU/H
FAX Number: (419) 530-4984
Calendar System: Semester
URL: www.utoledo.edu
Established: 1872
Annual Undergrad Tuition & Fees (In-State): $8,747
Enrollment: 23,085
Coed
Affiliation or Control: State
IRS Status: 501(c)3
Highest Offering: Doctorate
Program: Liberal Arts And General; Teacher Preparatory; Professional; Business Emphasis
Accreditation: NH, ADNUR, ARCPA, ART, BUS, CACREP, CLPSY, CS, CVT, DENT, ENG, ENGR, ENGT, KIN, LAW, MED, MUS, NRPA, NURSE, OT, PH, PHAR, PTA, SP, SPAA, SW, TED

01	President	Dr. Lloyd A. JACOBS
17	Exec VP/Chancellor Health Affairs	Dr. Jeffrey P. GOLD
05	Exec VP/Provost Academic Affairs	Dr. William E. MCMILLEN
17	Sr VP and Exec Director of UTMC	Dr. Scott L. SCARBOROUGH
10	CFO and VP for Finance	Dr. David O. DABNEY
43	Vice President General Counsel	Mr. Peter J. PAPADIMOS
32	Vice President for Student Affairs	Dr. Kaye PATTEN WALLACE
30	Vice Pres Institutional Advancement	Mr. C. Vernon SNYDER
26	VP Ext Affairs/Equity & Diversity	Mr. Lawrence J. BURNS
88	Sr Dir Fac Labor Rel	Dr. Kevin D. WEST
86	VP Government Relations	Dr. Frank J. CALZONETTI
46	VP Research	Dr. James P. TREMPE
58	Dean College of Graduate Studies	Dr. Patricia R. KOMUNIECKI
29	Assoc Vice Pres Alumni Relations	Mr. Daniel J. SAEVIG
15	Assoc Vice Pres Human Resources	Ms. Connie RUBIN
11	Vice Pres Administration	Mr. Charles LEHNERT
35	Assoc Vice Pres/Dean of Students	Ms. Michele C. MARTINEZ
13	VP for Info Tech/CIO	Dr. Godfrey ORWIGHO
39	Director Residence Life	Ms. Jo CAMPBELL
20	Vice Provost Academic Enterprises	Dr. Geoffrey MARTIN
37	Director Student Financial Aid	Ms. Carolyn G. BAUMGARTNER
41	Exec Dir Intercollegiate Athletics	Mr. Michael E. O'BRIEN
61	Dean College of Law	Mr. Daniel STEINBOCK
54	Dean College of Engineering	Dr. Nagi NAGANATHAN
50	Dean Business & Innovation	Dr. Thomas GUTTERIDGE
66	Dean of Nursing	Dr. Timothy GASPAR
67	Dean of Pharmacy	Dr. Johnnie EARLY
53	Dean Educ/Hlth Science/Human Serv.	Dr. Beverly J. SCHMOLL
88	Dean Adult & Lifelong Learning	Dr. Dennis LETTMAN
19	Chief of Police	Mr. Jeff NEWTON
36	Director Career Development	Ms. Beth E. NICHOLSON
85	Director Immigration Services	Mr. Peter I. THOMAS

25 Contract Compliance Specialist HSC .... Ms. Colleen MILLER
40 General Manager Bookstore SU .... Ms. Colleen STRAYER
101 Secretary to Brd of Trustees .... Ms. Joan STASA
102 President Foundation .... Ms. Brenda LEE
21 Director of Internal Audit .... Mr. David CUTRI
06 University Registrar .... Ms. Sherri ARMSTRONG
92 Dean Honors College .... Dr. Thomas BARDEN
88 Dean Innovative Learning .... Dr. Benjamin PRYOR
81 Dean Natural Sciences & Mathematics .... Dr. Karen BJORKMAN
88 Dean Visual & Performing Arts .... Ms. Debra DAVIS
83 Dean Languages/Lit & Soc Sciences .... Dr. Alice SKEENS
63 Dean Medicine & Life Sciences .... Dr. Jeffrey GOLD

Urbana University (A)

579 College Way, Urbana OH 43078-2091
County: Champaign FICE Identification: 003133
Unit ID: 206330
Telephone: (937) 484-1400 Carnegie Class: Bac/Diverse
FAX Number: (937) 484-1322 Calendar System: Semester
URL: www.urbana.edu
Established: 1850 Annual Undergrad Tuition & Fees: $20,984
Enrollment: 1,355 Coed
Affiliation or Control: Independent Non-Profit IRS Status: 501(c)3
Highest Offering: Master's
Program: Liberal Arts And General; Teacher Preparatory
Accreditation: NH, IACBE, NURSE

01 President .... Dr. Stephen JONES
05 VP Academic Affairs/Dean of Faculty .... Dr. Kirk PETERSON
30 Vice Pres Institutional Advancement .... Mr. James THORNTON
32 Dean of Students/Exec Dir Admin .... Dr. James (Chip) WEISGERBER
06 Registrar .... Mrs. Kathleen YODER
37 Director of Financial Aid .... Vacant
09 Director of Institutional Research .... Vacant
08 University Librarian .... Ms. Julie MCDANIEL
39 Director of Residence Life .... Mr. Mitch JOSEPH
14 Director Computer Center .... Vacant
26 Director of University Relations .... Mrs. Christina BRUUN-HORRIGAN
29 Director Alumni Relations .... Vacant
15 Director of Human Resources/Payroll .... Mrs. Audrey STEVENS
19 Director of Security/Safety .... Mr. Larry GLEESON
10 CFO .... Vacant
41 Athletic Director .... Mr. Doug YOUNG
40 Bookstore Manager .... Mr. Joe AMBUSKE

Ursuline College (B)

2550 Lander Road, Cleveland OH 44124-4398
County: Cuyahoga FICE Identification: 003134
Unit ID: 206349
Telephone: (440) 449-4200 Carnegie Class: Master's S
FAX Number: (440) 646-8318 Calendar System: Semester
URL: www.ursuline.edu
Established: 1871 Annual Undergrad Tuition & Fees: $24,910
Enrollment: 1,485 Female
Affiliation or Control: Roman Catholic IRS Status: 501(c)3
Highest Offering: Doctorate
Program: Liberal Arts And General; Teacher Preparatory; Professional; Nursing Emphasis
Accreditation: NH, IACBE, NURSE, SW, TED

01 President .... Sr. Diana STANO
04 Assistant to President .... Sr. Anna Margaret GILBRIDE
05 Vice President Academic Affairs .... Dr. JoAnne PODIS
10 Vice Pres & Chief Financial Officer .... Mr. David STEINER
30 Vice Pres Institutional Advancement .... Mr. Kevin GLADSTONE
18 Vice Pres of Facility Management .... Ms. June GRACYK
32 Vice President of Student Affairs .... Ms. Deanne HURLEY
84 Vice Pres of Enrollment Management ..... Mr. Thandabantu MACEO
58 Dean of Graduate Studies .... Dr. Debra FLEMING
49 Dean of Arts & Sciences .... Dr. Elizabeth KAVRAN
66 Dean Division of Nursing .... Dr. Christine WYND
88 Exec Director Accelerated Program .... Ms. Anne LUKAS
08 Director of Library .... Ms. Betsey BELKIN
06 Registrar .... Ms. Leah SULLIVAN
21 Accounting Manager .... Mr. Timothy REARDON
44 Director of Development .... Dr. Patrick RILEY
07 Director of Admissions .... Mr. Matthew MCCAFFREY
37 Director of Financial Aid .... Ms. Mary Lynn PERRI
29 Director Alumnae .... Ms. Tiffany MUSHRUSH
26 Dir of Marketing/Communications .... Ms. Angela DELPRETE
38 Director Counseling & Career Svcs .. Ms. Geraldine M. SULLIVAN
15 Director of Personnel .... Ms. Kelli KNAUS
14 Director of Computer Services .... Vacant
09 Director of Institutional Research .... Ms. Diane PETRUCCIO
102 Dir of Corp & Foundation Relations .... Vacant
39 Director of Residence Life .... Ms. Amy LECHKO
42 Director Campus Ministry .... Ms. Joann PIOTRKOWSKI
28 Director of Multicultural Affairs .... Ms. Tina ROAN
93 Director of Wellness Program .... Vacant
24 Media Coordinator .... Vacant
40 Manager Bookstore .... Ms. Jennifer BRAZALOVICS
41 Athletic Director .... Ms. Cynthia MCKNIGHT

Vatterott College-Cleveland (C)

5025 E Royalton Road,
Broadview Heights OH 44147-3502
County: Cuyahoga Identification: 666156
Unit ID: 442408
Telephone: (440) 526-1660 Carnegie Class: Assoc/PrivFP
FAX Number: (440) 526-1933 Calendar System: Other
URL: www.vatterott-college.edu
Established: 2002 Annual Undergrad Tuition & Fees: $19,500
Enrollment: 282 Coed
Affiliation or Control: Proprietary IRS Status: Proprietary
Highest Offering: Associate Degree
Program: Occupational
Accreditation: ACCSC

01 CEO & President .... Ms. Pam BELL
10 Chief Financial Officer .... Mr. Dennis BEAVERS
05 Vice President Academic Affairs .... Dr. Brandon SHEDRON
45 VP Regulatory Affs/Strategic Devel .... Mr. Aaron LACEY
43 General Counsel/Chief Administrator .... Mr. Scott CASANOVER
11 Campus Director .... Mr. Erick ANDRYSZA

† Branch campus of Vatterott College-North Park, Berkeley, MO.

Virginia Marti College of Art & Design (D)

11724 Detroit Avenue, Lakewood OH 44107-3002
County: Cuyahoga FICE Identification: 012896
Unit ID: 206394
Telephone: (216) 221-8584 Carnegie Class: Assoc/PrivFP
FAX Number: (216) 221-2311 Calendar System: Quarter
URL: www.vmcad.edu
Established: 1966 Annual Undergrad Tuition & Fees: $16,560
Enrollment: 247 Coed
Affiliation or Control: Proprietary IRS Status: Proprietary
Highest Offering: Associate Degree
Program: Occupational
Accreditation: ACCSC

01 Director .... Mrs. Virginia MARTI-VEITH
03 Assistant Director .... Mr. Dennis N. MARTI
37 Financial Aid Administrator .... Mrs. Jennifer V. MINKIEWICZ
06 Registrar .... Mrs. Lisa ALESSANDRO
07 Director of Admissions .... Mr. Quinn E. MARTI
36 Director of Student Svcs/Placement .... Mrs. Lisa MARTI

Walsh University (E)

2020 East Maple Street, NW,
North Canton OH 44720-3396
County: Stark FICE Identification: 003135
Unit ID: 206437
Telephone: (330) 499-7090 Carnegie Class: Master's M
FAX Number: (330) 499-7165 Calendar System: Semester
URL: www.walsh.edu
Established: 1958 Annual Undergrad Tuition & Fees: $22,500
Enrollment: 2,963 Coed
Affiliation or Control: Roman Catholic IRS Status: 501(c)3
Highest Offering: Doctorate
Program: Liberal Arts And General; Teacher Preparatory; Professional
Accreditation: NH, CACREP, NUR, PTA, TED

01 President .... Mr. Richard JUSSEAUME
05 Provost/VP Academic Affairs .... Dr. Laurence BOVE
10 Vice Pres Business & Finance/CFO .... Mr. Philip DANIELS
32 VP Student Affairs/Dean of Students .... Mr. Dale S. HOWARD
30 Vice President of Advancement .... Ms. Bridgette NEISEL
84 Vice Pres of Enrollment Management .... Mr. Brett FRESHOUR
41 Vice Pres for Athletics .... Mr. Dale S. HOWARD
20 Asc VP Academic Affs/Dean Instruct .... Mr. David J. BAXTER
20 Dean for Academic Affairs .... Dr. Andrew GRANT
35 Dean of Students .... Ms. Amy K. MALASKA
18 Director of Facilities & Grounds .... Mr. John SCHISSLER
13 Director of Information Systems .... Mr. Timothy OBERSCHLAKE
91 Director Administrative Computing .... Ms. Hope STANCIU
22 Director of Compliance .... Mrs. Ellen M. KUTZ
36 Director of Career Services .... Mrs. Shaanette FOWLER
38 Dir Of Herttna Counseling Ctr .... Mr. William MAXON-KANN
42 Director of Campus Ministry .... Mr. Miguel CHAVEZ
06 University Registrar .... Mrs. Edna MCCULLOH
08 Librarian .... Mr. Daniel S. SUVAK
26 Director University Relations .... Ms. Andrea MCCAFFREY
31 Dir Campus & Community Programs .... Ms. Jacqueline M. MANSER
37 Director Financial Aid .... Mrs. Holly VAN GILDER
15 Director of Human Resources .... Mr. Frank MCKNIGHT
29 Director of Alumni Relations .... Mr. Daniel GRAVO
28 Director of Multicultural Affairs .... Ms. Tiffany KINNARD
43 Assoc Dean Stdt Life/Judicial Affs .... Ms. Amy MALASKA

Washington State Community College (F)

710 Colegate Drive, Marietta OH 45750-9225
County: Washington FICE Identification: 010453
Unit ID: 206446
Telephone: (740) 374-8716 Carnegie Class: Assoc/Pub-R-M
FAX Number: (740) 374-9562 Calendar System: Quarter
URL: www.wscc.edu
Established: 1971 Annual Undergrad Tuition & Fees (In-State): $3,957
Enrollment: 2,366 Coed
Affiliation or Control: State IRS Status: 501(c)3
Highest Offering: Associate Degree
Program: Occupational; 2-Year Principally Bachelor's Creditable; Technical Emphasis
Accreditation: NH, MLTAD, PTAA

01 Interim President .... Dr. Mark E. NUTTER
10 Chief Financial Officer & Treasurer .... Mr. Jess N. RAINES
84 Chief Enrollment Management Officer .... Ms. Amanda K. HERB
27 Chief Information Officer .... Vacant
05 Chief Academic Officer .... Dr. Mark E. NUTTER
103 Exec Dir of Workforce Development ..... Ms. Laurene K. HUFFMAN
76 Dean of Health Sciences .... Dr. Dixie L. VAUGHAN
49 Dean of Arts and Sciences .... Vacant
50 Dean of Bus/Engr/Industrial Tech .... Ms. Brenda L. KORNMILLER
30 Director of Development .... Ms. Gail REYNOLDS
36 Director of Advising & Transfer .... Vacant
06 Registrar .... Mr. Michael D. WHITNABLE
07 Senior Director of Admissions .... Mr. Paul S. WELLS
15 Director Human Resources .... Ms. Susan MURDOCK
26 Dir of Marketing & Communications .... Vacant
37 Director of Financial Aid .... Ms. Emily G. SCHUCK
18 Director Plant Opers & Maintenance .... Mr. Byron L. HOFFEE
38 Director of Student Development .... Vacant
08 Head Librarian .... Ms. Georgene T. JOHNSON
40 Bookstore Operations Director .... Ms. Jennifer L. DAVIS
91 Dir Management Information Systems .... Mr. Doug D. MORRIS
37 Assistant Director of Financial Aid .... Ms. Kathy PATTERSON
88 Business Intelligence Specialist .... Mr. Michael P. HOWERTON
25 Grant Writer .... Vacant

Wilberforce University (G)

PO Box 1001, Wilberforce OH 45384-1001
County: Greene FICE Identification: 003141
Unit ID: 206491
Telephone: (937) 376-2911 Carnegie Class: Bac/Diverse
FAX Number: (937) 376-2627 Calendar System: Semester
URL: www.wilberforce.edu
Established: 1856 Annual Undergrad Tuition & Fees: $18,170
Enrollment: 693 Coed
Affiliation or Control: African Methodist Episcopal IRS Status: 501(c)3
Highest Offering: Master's
Program: Liberal Arts And General
Accreditation: NH, @CORE

01 President .... Dr. Patricia L. HARDAWAY
05 Vice President Academic Affairs .... Dr. Lewis JONES
10 Vice Pres Financial/Admin Affairs .... Vacant
30 Vice President Devel/Univ Relations .... Mr. Eppechal T. SMALLS
51 Vice Pres Adult/Continuing Educ .... Dr. Emeka O. MORAH
84 VP Student Devel/Enrollment Mgmt .... Vacant
04 Executive Assistant to President .... Vacant
32 Dean of Students .... Mr. Parris CARTER
07 Director of Admissions .... Mr. Juan ALEXANDER
26 Director of Public Relations .... Vacant
06 Registrar .... Mrs. Gail D. LASH
08 Chief Librarian .... Ms. Willette STINSON
29 Dir Alumni Relations/Development .... Mr. Milton WIGGINS
36 Director Coop Education/Career Svcs .... Mrs. Hila WILLIAMS
14 Director Computer Services .... Mr. Jeff CHOI
19 Campus Police Chief .... Chief David FOX
37 Director of Financial Services .... Vacant
38 Director Counseling Services .... Vacant
41 Athletic Director .... Vacant
18 Chief Facilities/Physical Plant .... Mr. William CANADAY
15 Human Resources Manager .... Mr. Lyman MONTGOMERY
40 Bookstore Manager .... Vacant

Wilmington College (H)

1870 Quaker Way, Wilmington OH 45177-2499
County: Clinton FICE Identification: 003142
Unit ID: 206507
Telephone: (937) 382-6661 Carnegie Class: Bac/Diverse
FAX Number: (937) 383-8583 Calendar System: Semester
URL: www.wilmington.edu
Established: 1870 Annual Undergrad Tuition & Fees: $26,840
Enrollment: 1,417 Coed
Affiliation or Control: Friends IRS Status: 501(c)3
Highest Offering: Master's
Program: Liberal Arts And General; Teacher Preparatory
Accreditation: NH, @TEAC

01 Interim President .... Dr. James M. REYNOLDS
05 Interim Vice Pres Academic Affairs .... Dr. Erika A. GOODWIN
10 Vice Pres Business/Finance .... Mr. Bradley J. MITCHELL
30 Vice President College Advancement .... Mr. Robert C. HARROD
84 Vice Pres Enrollment Management .... Mr. Mark DENNISTON
12 Vice President External Programs .... Ms. Iris KELSEN
32 Vice President for Student Affairs .... Ms. Sigrid B. SOLOMON
20 Interim Assoc VP Academic Affairs ..... Dr. Martha S. HENDRICKS
35 Assoc Vice Pres Student Affairs .... Mr. Kenneth A. LYDY
26 Director of Public Relations .... Mr. Randall F. SARVIS
41 Vice President Athletic Admin .... Dr. Terry A. RUPERT
06 Registrar/Asst Dean Acad Affairs .... Ms. Karen M. GARMAN
08 Director of Watson Library .... Dr. Jean K. MULHERN
15 Director of Human Resources .... Mr. Scott M. FARKAS
36 Director of Career Services .... Ms. Barbara E. KAPLAN
18 Director of Physical Plant .... Mr. Terry L. JOHNSON
29 Dir Alumni and Parent Relations .... Ms. Kathy L. MILAM
37 Director Student One Stop Center .... Ms. Cheryl LOUALLEN
07 Director of Admission .... Ms. Tina M. GARLAND
09 Director of Institutional Research .... Dr. Nancy J. ROSZELL
28 Director of Multicultural Affairs .... Mr. Arthur L. BROOKS
96 Purchasing Manager .... Ms. Laura BAESSLER

Winebrenner Theological Seminary (A)

950 N Main Street, Findlay OH 45840-3652
County: Hancock FICE Identification: 004060
Unit ID: 206516
Telephone: (419) 434-4200 Carnegie Class: Spec/Faith
FAX Number: (419) 434-4267 Calendar System: Trimester
URL: www.winebrenner.edu
Established: 1942 Annual Graduate Tuition & Fees: $13,125
Enrollment: 135 Coed
Affiliation or Control: Independent Non-Profit IRS Status: 501(c)3
Highest Offering: Doctorate; No Undergraduates
Program: Professional; Religious Emphasis
Accreditation: NH, THEOL

01 President/CEO ... Dr. David E. DRAPER
30 VP of Institutional Advancement ... Mr. Jim SMARKEL
05 VP of Academic Advancement ... Rev. Joel COCKLIN
07 Regional Coordinator Admiss/Devel ... Mr. Jim WILDER
08 Director of Library Services ... Mrs. Margaret HIRSCHY
06 Registrar ... Mrs. Shari BRANDEBERRY
04 Assistant to the President ... Ms. Marilynn C. DUNN

Wittenberg University (B)

PO Box 720, Springfield OH 45501-0720
County: Clark FICE Identification: 003143
Unit ID: 206525
Telephone: (937) 327-6231 Carnegie Class: Bac/A&S
FAX Number: (937) 327-6340 Calendar System: Semester
URL: www.wittenberg.edu
Established: 1845 Annual Undergrad Tuition & Fees: $36,434
Enrollment: 1,942 Coed
Affiliation or Control: Evangelical Lutheran Church In America
IRS Status: 501(c)3
Highest Offering: Master's
Program: Liberal Arts And General; Teacher Preparatory
Accreditation: NH, MUS, TED

01 President ... Dr. Mark H. ERICKSON
05 Provost ... Dr. Chris DUNCAN
10 Vice President Business & Finance ... Mr. Darrell B. KITCHEN
32 Vice Pres Stdnt Devel/Dean Students ... Dr. Sarah M. KELLLY
30 Vice Pres University Advancement ... Mr. Jim GEIGER
20 Assistant Provost Academic Svcs ... Ms. Van RUTHERFORD
89 Int Director 1st Year Experience ... Dr. Ty BUCKMAN
87 Dean Cmty Educ & Dir Summer Sess ... Dr. Elma L. MOORE
85 Director International Education ... Ms. JoAnn BENNETT
42 Director of Church Relations ... Mr. Robert L. WHITE
42 Co-Pastor to the University ... Rev. Rachel SANDUM TUNE
42 Co-Pastor to the University ... Rev. Anders S. TUNE
08 Director of the Library ... Mr. Douglas K. LEHMAN
14 Chief Information Officer ... Mr. Richard MICKOOL
26 Chief Marketing & Communications Of ... Mr. Mark SULLIVAN
31 Director Community Service ... Ms. Kristen L. COLLIER
06 Registrar ... Mr. Jack M. CAMPBELL
36 Director Career Center ... Vacant
24 Director Audio-Visual Services ... Mr. Lyndon C. MCCURDY
41 Director Athletics/Recreation ... Mr. Garnett H. PURNELL
58 Director Graduate Studies in Educ ... Dr. Regina POST
92 Director of Honors Program ... Dr. J. Fitz SMITH
94 Director of Women's Studies ... Dr. Lori J. ASKELAND
09 Director Institutional Research ... Dr. Jeff A. ANKROM
44 Exec Dir Major & Planned Giving ... Mr. Richard W. STENBERG
102 Dir Govt/Corporate & Found Rels ... Mrs. Lin ERICKSON
29 Director of Alumni Relations ... Ms. Linda M. BEALS
26 Director of Univ Communications ... Ms. Karen L. GERBOTH
27 Dir of News Services/Sports Info ... Mr. Ryan S. MAURER
105 Int Director New Media/Webmaster ... Mr. Ben MCCOMBS
35 Senior Dean of Students ... Ms. Dawn H. WHITE
39 Associate Dean for Residence Life ... Mr. Mark B. DEVILBISS
38 Director Student Counseling ... Ms. Linda M. LAUFFENBURGER
88 Director of Greek Life ... Ms. Kasey STEVENS
88 Director Student Activities ... Mr. Jonathan DURAJ
28 Director Multicultural Stdnt Pgms ... Mr. John YOUNG
23 Physician/Dir Health Services ... Dr. Kathrine MCKEE
07 Director of Admission ... Ms. Karen HUNT
37 Director of Financial Aid ... Mr. Jonathan RANDY GREEN
21 Assistant Director Budget ... Ms. Deborah S. DEWITT
18 Director Plant/Safety & Environment ... Mr. John E. PAULSEN
96 Director of Business Services ... Mrs. Donna M. PICKLESIMER
15 Assoc VP Human Resources ... Mrs. Maureen SHEEHAN MASSARO
19 Chief of Police ... Mr. Carl E. LONEY
40 Manager of Bookstore ... Mr. Tim GOGNAT

Wright State University Main Campus (C)

3640 Colonel Glenn Highway, Dayton OH 45435-0001
County: Greene FICE Identification: 003078
Unit ID: 206604
Telephone: (937) 775-3333 Carnegie Class: RU/H
FAX Number: (937) 775-3301 Calendar System: Quarter
URL: www.wright.edu
Established: 1964 Annual Undergrad Tuition & Fees (In-State): $8,070
Enrollment: 19,793 Coed
Affiliation or Control: State IRS Status: 501(c)3
Highest Offering: Doctorate
Program: Liberal Arts And General; Teacher Preparatory; Professional
Accreditation: NH, BUS, BUSA, CACREP, CLPSY, CORE, CS, ENG, IPSY, MED, MT, MUS, NURSE, PH, SPAA, SW, TED

01 President ... Dr. David R. HOPKINS
05 Provost ... Dr. Steven R. ANGLE
10 Sr VP Business/Fiscal Affairs ... Dr. Matthew V. FILIPIC
32 Vice President Student Affairs ... Dr. Dan ABRAHAMOWICZ
46 Vice Pres Research/Graduate Studies ... Dr. John (Jack) A. BANTLE
30 Vice President Univ Advancement ... Ms. Rebecca S. COLE
84 Vice Pres Enrollment Management ... Dr. Jacqueline MCMILLAN
20 Assoc Provost Undergrad Studies ... Dr. Thomas A. SUDKAMP
58 Dean Sch Graduate Studies ... Dr. Andrew T. HSU
04 Exec Vice President for Planning ... Dr. Robert J. SWEENEY
08 University Librarian ... Dr. Stephen P. FOSTER
26 Assoc VP Mktg/Communications ... Mr. George HEDDLESTON
15 Asst Vice Pres for Human Resources ... Mr. Allan BOGGS
18 Assc VP Facilities Plng/Development ... Ms. Vicky L. DAVIDSON
32 Associate Vice Pres Student Affairs ... Ms. Katherine W. MORRIS
50 Dean Raj Soin College of Business ... Dr. Berkwood M. FARMER
53 Dean Education/Human Services ... Dr. Charlotte HARRIS
54 Dean Engineering/Computer Science ... Dr. S. NARAYANAN
12 Dean WSU Lake Campus ... Dr. Bonnie MATHIES
49 Dean Liberal Arts ... Dr. Charles S. TAYLOR
66 Dean College of Nursing & Health ... Dr. Patricia A. MARTIN
63 Dean Boonshaft School of Medicine ... Dr. Howard PART
83 Dean Sch of Professional Psychology ... Dr. Larry C. JAMES
81 Dean Science/Mathematics ... Dr. Yi LI
06 Registrar ... Ms. Marian HOGUE
07 Director Undergraduate Admissions ... Ms. Cathleen M. DAVIS
13 Director Computing/Telecomm Svcs ... Mr. Paul R. HERNANDEZ
46 Asst VP Research/Sponsored Pgms ... Ms. Ellen REINSCH FRIESE
36 Director Career Services ... Ms. Cheryl KRUEGER
37 Director of Financial Aid ... Ms. Amy BARNHART
38 Director Counsel/Wellness Svcs ... Dr. Robert A. RANDO
29 Exec Dir Alumni Relations ... Ms. Susan K. SMITH
22 Director Affirmative Action Program ... Dr. Juanita L. WEHRLE-EINHORN
31 Assoc Director Event Svcs ... Ms. Jane SHELB
88 Director Disability Services ... Mr. Jeffrey A. VERNOOY
27 Assoc VP Public Affairs ... Mr. Robert E. HICKEY, JR.
41 Director of Athletics ... Mr. Bob GRANT
43 General Counsel ... Ms. Gwen M. MATTISON
24 Director CTR Teaching/Learning ... Dr. Daniel E. DESTEPHEN
40 Store Manager ... Ms. Jennifer L. GEBHART
85 Director Intl Student/Scholar Svcs ... Mr. Steven J. LYONS
39 Director Residence Services ... Mr. Daniel BERTSOS
19 Chief Police Department ... Mr. Michael MARTINSEN
96 Director of Purchasing ... Mr. Jerry D. BLACK
92 Director Honors Program ... Dr. Susan CARRAFIELLO
94 Director Womens Studies Program ... Dr. Kelli ZAYTOUN
09 Director of Institutional Research ... Mrs. Barbara J. BULLOCK

Wright State University Lake Campus (D)

7600 Lake Campus Drive, Celina OH 45822-2952
County: Mercer FICE Identification: 009169
Unit ID: 206613
Telephone: (419) 586-0300 Carnegie Class: Assoc/Pub2in4
FAX Number: (419) 586-0358 Calendar System: Quarter
URL: www.wright.edu/lake
Established: 1969 Annual Undergrad Tuition & Fees (In-State): $7,797
Enrollment: 1,490 Coed
Affiliation or Control: State IRS Status: 501(c)3
Highest Offering: Master's
Program: Liberal Arts And General
Accreditation: &NH

01 Dean ... Dr. Bonnie MATHIES
05 Associate Dean ... Dr. Robert M. HISKEY
32 Dir Student Svcs/Public Relations ... Ms. Sandi HOLDHEIDE
06 Registrar ... Ms. Billie J. HOBLER
31 Director Community Relations ... Mr. Gregory F. SCHUMM
30 Development Officer ... Dr. Thomas A. KNAPKE
08 Librarian ... Mr. Alexander PITTMAN
13 Director Computing & Telecommun ... Mr. Ronald E. DORSTEN
38 Chief Academic Advising & Testing ... Mr. Vaughn R. SCHELLHAUSE
53 Director of Teacher Education ... Ms. Paula K. BRYAN
20 Dir Academic/Instructional Pgms/Svc ... Dr. John R. WOLFE
07 Dir of Admissions/Pub Rels Speclst ... Ms. Elizabeth STAUGLER
18 Supervisor Buildings & Grounds ... Ms. Elizabeth J. STAUGLER
40 Manager of the Bookstore ... Ms. Patricia G. HOWARD
10 Business Manager ... Ms. Cassandra L. DORSTEN
37 Student Financial Aid Coordinator ... Ms. Sandra GILBERT

† Regional accreditation is carried under the parent institution in Dayton, OH.

Xavier University (E)

3800 Victory Parkway, Cincinnati OH 45207-1096
County: Hamilton FICE Identification: 003144
Unit ID: 206622
Telephone: (513) 745-3000 Carnegie Class: Master's L
FAX Number: (513) 745-4223 Calendar System: Semester
URL: www.xavier.edu
Established: 1831 Annual Undergrad Tuition & Fees: $31,160
Enrollment: 7,019 Coed
Affiliation or Control: Roman Catholic IRS Status: 501(c)3
Highest Offering: Doctorate
Program: Liberal Arts And General; Teacher Preparatory; Professional
Accreditation: NH, BUS, CACREP, CEA, CLPSY, HSA, MACTE, MUS, NURSE, OT, RAD, SW, TEAC

01 President ... Rev. Michael J. GRAHAM, SJ
11 Administrative Vice President ... Dr. John F. KUCIA
05 Provost & Chief Academic Officer ... Dr. Scott CHADWICK
10 Vice Pres Financial Administration ... Ms. Maribeth AMYOT
26 Vice Pres for University Relations ... Mr. Gary R. MASSA
88 Asst to Pres for Mission & Identity ... Dr. Debra MOONEY
13 Vice Pres Information Resources/CIO ... Mr. David DODD
84 Vice Pres for Student Enrollment ... Mr. Terry RICHARDS
28 Asst to Pres Diversity/Inclusion ... Ms. Cheryl L. NUNEZ
26 Director for Public Relations ... Ms. Deb DEL VALLE
27 Sr Mrktng Strategist/Ofc Univ Comm ... Mr. Robert R. HILL
30 Assoc VP for University Relations ... Ms. Susan ABEL
20 Assoc Provost for Academic Affairs ... Dr. Kandi M. STINSON
32 Assoc Prov Student Life/Leadership ... Dr. Kathleen SIMONS
18 Asc VP Facility Mgt/Capital Project ... Mr. Robert M. SHEERAN
41 Assoc Vice Pres/Director Athletics ... Mr. Michael A. BOBINSKI
24 Assoc VP Info Res/Dir Discovery Svc ... Mr. Robert M. COTTER
15 Assoc Vice Pres for Human Resources ... Mrs. Shari MICKEY-BOGGS
07 Dean Undergraduate Admission ... Mr. Aaron MEIS
12 Director Cintas Center ... Mr. Michael DUNN
44 Exec Dir Gifts & Estate Planning ... Mr. Mark MCLAUGHLIN
42 Dir Center for Mission/Identity ... Mr. Joseph SHADLE
06 Registrar ... Ms. Mary Alyce ORAHOOD
88 Director of Scholarships ... Mr. Paul H. CALME
85 Director for Internatl Student Svcs ... Ms. Lea MINNITI
105 Exec Dir Ofc University Commun ... Mr. Doug RUSCHMAN
39 Director of Residence Life ... Ms. Lori A. LAMBERT
40 Director of Bookstore ... Ms. Susan GRIFFIN
86 Dir of Comm & Government Relations ... Dr. Eugene L. BEAUPRE'
96 Director of Administrative Services ... Mr. Daniel R. SCHLOEMER
83 Dean College Social Sci/Health/Educ ... Dr. Mark MEYERS
36 Ex Dir Ofc Stdnt Involvement/Ldrshp ... Ms. Leah BUSAM
23 Director for Medical Services ... Ms. Mary ROSENFELDT
49 Dean College Arts & Sciences ... Dr. Janice B. WALKER
19 Director of Campus Police/Security ... Mr. Michael COUCH
37 Director of Financial Aid ... Mr. Todd EVERETT
43 General Counsel ... Mr. Joseph H. FELDHAUS
29 Director for Alumni Engagement ... Mr. Matt TRIPEPI
09 Sr Policy/Plng Analyst/Ofc of SIR ... Dr. Tammy KAHRIG
50 Int Dean Williams College Business ... Dr. R. Stafford R. JOHNSON
51 Actg Dean Center Adults/PT Students ... Ms. Sheila DORAN
35 Dean of Students ... Dr. Luther G. SMITH

Youngstown State University (F)

One University Plaza, Youngstown OH 44555-0001
County: Mahoning FICE Identification: 003145
Unit ID: 206695
Telephone: (330) 941-3000 Carnegie Class: Master's L
FAX Number: (330) 941-7169 Calendar System: Semester
URL: www.ysu.edu
Established: 1908 Annual Undergrad Tuition & Fees (In-State): $7,451
Enrollment: 15,436 Coed
Affiliation or Control: State IRS Status: 501(c)3
Highest Offering: Doctorate
Program: Occupational; Liberal Arts And General; Teacher Preparatory; Professional
Accreditation: NH, AAFCS, ANEST, ART, BUS, CACREP, DH, DIETC, DIETD, DIETT, EMT, ENG, ENGT, HT, MAC, MLTAD, MUS, NUR, PTA, SW, TED, THEA

01 President ... Dr. Cynthia E. ANDERSON
05 Provost ... Dr. Ikram KHAWAJA
11 Vice President for Finance/Admin ... Mr. Eugene P. GRILLI
04 Executive Assoc to the President ... Ms. Shannon TIRONE
32 VP for Student Affairs ... Mr. Jack FAHEY
30 VP for University Advancement ... Vacant
43 Univ General Counsel/Asst to Pres ... Ms. Holly A. JACOBS
49 Dean of Liberal Arts/Social Science ... Dr. Shearle FURNISH
50 Dean of Business Administration ... Dr. Betty Jo LICATA
53 Interim Dean of Education ... Dr. Mary Lou DIPILLO
54 Dean of Science/Tech/Eng/Math ... Dr. Martin A. ABRAHAM
57 Dean Fine & Performing Arts ... Mr. Byran DEPOY
76 Dean Health & Human Services ... Dr. Joseph L. MOSCA
58 Dean of Graduate Studies/Research ... Dr. Peter J. KASVINSKY
45 Assoc Provost Acad Pgms/Planning ... Dr. Bege K. BOWERS
20 Int Assoc Prov Acad Admin/Info Svcs ... Dr. Charles SINGLER
15 Chief Human Resources Officer ... Mr. Kevin W. REYNOLDS
13 Interim Chief Technology Officer ... Mr. Richard J. MARSICO
10 Exec Director Financial Services ... Ms. Eileen GREAF
41 Exec Director of Athletics ... Mr. Ronald A. STROLLO
26 Exec Dir of Mktg/Communications ... Mr. Mark W. VANTILBURG
35 Exec Director of Student Services ... Mr. John P. FAHEY
35 Exec Director of Student Life ... Mr. Matthew NOVOTNY
84 Exec Dir Enrollment Mgmt ... Vacant
08 Executive Director Library ... Mr. Paul J. KOBULNICKY
29 Int Exec Dir of Alumni Relations ... Ms. Jacquelyn LEVISEUR
28 Director Equal Oppty/Diversity ... Ms. Yulanda MCCARTY-HARRIS
07 Director Undergrad Recruit/Admiss ... Ms. Sue E. DAVIS
06 Registrar ... Ms. Jeanne HERMAN
19 Chief of University Police ... Mr. John J. GOCALA
18 Director of University Facilities ... Mr. John P. HYDEN
21 Director-Student Accts/Receivables ... Ms. Beth A. YEATTS
23 Dir Environ/Occup Health & Safety ... Mr. Daniel SAHLI
37 Director Financial/Scholarships ... Ms. Elaine RUSE
21 Director General Accounting ... Ms. Katrena J. DAVIDSON
88 Director Budget Planning ... Mr. Neal P. MCNALLY
21 Cash Management Officer ... Ms. Akhande KHAN
25 Director Grants & Sponsored Pgms ... Mr. Edward ORONA
09 Exec Dir Institutional Research ... Vacant

39 Director Housing Services .... Ms. Danielle MEYER
85 Administrator International Studies .... Mr. Jef C. DAVIS
14 Director Computer Center .... Mr. Richard J. MARSICO
30 Chief Development Officer .... Mr. Paul J. MCFADDEN
28 Director Student Diversity Programs .... Mr. William J. BLAKE
88 Dir Assoc Degree/Tech Prep Pgms .... Ms. Arlene FLOYD
40 Director of Bookstore .... Mr. Charles A. SABATINO
88 Director Support Services .... Mr. Danny J. O'CONNELL
88 Dir Electronic Maintenance Svcs .... Mr. Michael REPETSKI
90 Director Media/Acad Computing .... Mr. Michael S. HRISHENKO
92 Director Univ Scholars/Honors Pgm .... Dr. Ronald SHAKLEE
36 Director of Career Services .... Ms. Marijean BENEDICK
96 Director Procurement Services .... Mr. William WHEELOCK
88 Director Degree Audit .... Ms. Marie D. CULLEN
91 Director Network Services .... Mr. Jason T. RAKERS
35 Director for Student Progress .... Ms. Jonelle BEATRICE
35 Dir Campus Rec/Intramural Sports .... Mr. Jack RIGNEY
88 Director WYSU-FM .... Mr. Gary SEXTON

Zane State College (A)

1555 Newark Road, Zanesville OH 43701-2626
County: Muskingum FICE Identification: 008133
Unit ID: 204255
Telephone: (740) 454-2501 Carnegie Class: Assoc/Pub-R-M
FAX Number: (740) 454-0035 Calendar System: Quarter
URL: www.zanestate.edu
Established: 1969 Annual Undergrad Tuition & Fees (In-State): $4,230
Enrollment: 2,857 Coed
Affiliation or Control: State IRS Status: 501(c)3
Highest Offering: Associate Degree
Program: 2-Year Principally Bachelor's Creditable; Technical Emphasis
Accreditation: NH, ACFEI, ENGT, MAC, MLTAD, OTA, PTAA, RAD

01 President .... Dr. Paul R. BROWN
102 Exec Dir Inst Advancemnt/Foundation .... Ms. Pamela A. JIRA
05 Vice Pres Acad Svcs & Workforce Dev .... Dr. Chad BROWN
10 Vice Pres for Business Services .... Mr. Albert F. BROWN
32 Vice Pres for Student Svcs/Registra .... Dr. Dotty WELCH
54 Acad Dean Business & Engineering .... Mr. George HICKS
103 Dean Cambridge Campus .... Mr. Mike WITSON
15 Director of Human Resources .... Ms. Julie L. STERLING
13 Exec Dir of Info Tech Svcs .... Mr. Jeffrey DEVLIN
08 Library Director .... Mr. Tony HOPKINS
09 Director of Institutional Research .... Dr. Beth FISCHER
25 Director of Grants & Contracts .... Mrs. Larisa HARPER
07 Director of Admissions .... Mr. Paul J. YOUNG
37 Director Student Financial Aid .... Ms. Amanda B. REISINGER
36 Director Career/Employment Services .... Ms. Jamie K. CLARK
27 Director Marketing & Communications .... Ms. Tamra PACE
20 Assoc Dean of Dev Ed & First Year .... Ms. Rebecca R. AMENT
38 Director of Student Success Center .... Ms. Stacie J. CLAPPER
21 Director of Accounting Services .... Ms. Tammy S. HUFFMAN
40 Director of Bookstore Operations .... Ms. Linda D. METZ
19 Director of Safety and Security .... Mr. Terry R. MOORE
49 Dean of Arts and Sciences .... Mrs. Susan HOLDREN
76 Dean of Educ Health & Human Svcs .... Dr. Barbara SHELBY

OKLAHOMA

Bacone College (B)

2299 Old Bacone Road, Muskogee OK 74403-1568
County: Muskogee FICE Identification: 003147
Unit ID: 206817
Telephone: (918) 683-4581 Carnegie Class: Bac/Assoc
FAX Number: (918) 781-7422 Calendar System: Semester
URL: www.bacone.edu
Established: 1880 Annual Undergrad Tuition & Fees: $12,900
Enrollment: 1,184 Coed
Affiliation or Control: American Baptist IRS Status: 501(c)3
Highest Offering: Baccalaureate
Program: 2-Year Principally Bachelor's Creditable; Liberal Arts And General; Teacher Preparatory
Accreditation: NH, ADNUR, IACBE, NUR, RAD

01 President .... Rev Dr. Robert J. DUNCAN, JR.
03 Exec Vice Pres & Dean of Faculty .... Dr. Robert K. BROWN
88 Asst VP Center for American Indians .... Dr. Pete COSER
30 Asst VP Institutional Advancement .... Mr. Eugene BLANKENSHIP
84 Asst VP of Enrollment Management .... Dr. Dusty DELSO
42 Asst VP Church Rels/Camp Chaplain .... Rev Dr. Leroy THOMPSON
10 Chief Financial Officer .... Mr. Randall MAYHALL
88 Asst VP Ctr for Christian Ministry .... Rev Dr. Stephen WILEY
32 Asst VP Student Life .... Ms. Shelli HOPKINS
06 Registrar .... Mrs. Virginia THOMPSON
40 Bookstore Manager .... Ms. Christin SWAGERS
41 Asst VP Athletics .... Mr. Alan FOSTER
39 Dir Residential Life & Hospitality .... Ms. Denise WILCOX
37 Dir Enrollment Mgt/Student Fin Aid .... Ms. Kathye WATSON
15 Director Human Resources .... Ms. Carol WRIGHT
18 Chief Facilities/Physical Plant .... Vacant
35 Director of Student Services .... Mr. Dustin HOPKINS
29 Asst Director Alumni Relations .... Ms. Mallory LARGENT
09 Coord Institutional Assessment Data .... Ms. Linda MILAM
26 Director of External Relations .... Ms. Susie CAGLE
21 Controller .... Mr. Joe SNOW
36 Director of Career Services .... Ms. Jo COLLIER
105 Dir Web/Video Design Studio .... Mr. Dwayne PARTON
08 Librarian .... Ms. Frances A. DONELSON
13 Director of Network Systems .... Mr. Chris EHLERS

Brown Mackie College-Tulsa (C)

4608 South Garnett Road, Ste. 110, Tulsa OK 74146
County: Tulsa Identification: 666783
Unit ID: 455619
Telephone: (918) 628-3700 Carnegie Class: Not Classified
FAX Number: (918) 828-9083 Calendar System: Other
URL: www.brownmackie.edu
Established: N/A Annual Undergrad Tuition & Fees: $11,124
Enrollment: 422 Coed
Affiliation or Control: Proprietary IRS Status: Proprietary
Highest Offering: Baccalaureate
Program: Occupational; 2-Year Principally Bachelor's Creditable; Business Emphasis
Accreditation: ACICS, OTA, SURTEC

01 President .... John PAPPAS
07 Senior Director of Admissions .... Jim LILLARD
05 Dean of Academic Affairs .... James FOUNTAIN

† Branch campus of Brown Mackie College, South Bend, IN.

Cameron University (D)

2800 W Gore Boulevard, Lawton OK 73505-6377
County: Comanche FICE Identification: 003150
Unit ID: 206914
Telephone: (580) 581-2200 Carnegie Class: Master's S
FAX Number: (580) 581-2867 Calendar System: Semester
URL: www.cameron.edu
Established: 1908 Annual Undergrad Tuition & Fees (In-State): $4,590
Enrollment: 6,330 Coed
Affiliation or Control: State IRS Status: 501(c)3
Highest Offering: Master's
Program: Liberal Arts And General; Teacher Preparatory
Accreditation: NH, ACBSP, MUS, TED

01 President .... Dr. Cynthia S. ROSS
05 Provost .... Dr. John M. MCARTHUR
10 Vice Pres for Business & Finance .... Mr. Glen P. PINKSTON
30 Vice Pres University Advancement .... Mr. Albert D. JOHNSON, JR.
32 Vice President for Student Services .... Ms. Jennifer L. HOLLAND
84 Assoc Vice Pres Enrollment Mgmt .... Mrs. Jamie L. GLOVER
50 Dean School of Business .... Dr. Oris ODOM, II
79 Dean School of Liberal Arts .... Dr. Von E. UNDERWOOD
53 Dean Sch of Educ/Behav Science .... Dr. Ronna J. VANDERSLICE
01 Dean School Science/Tech .... Dr. Reza KAMALI
31 Director of Public Affairs .... Mr. Josh LEHMAN
08 Librarian .... Dr. Sheridan YOUNG
29 Director Alumni Relations .... Ms. Jennifer BOWEN
41 Director Athletic Administration .... Mr. Jim C. JACKSON
07 Director of Admissions .... Ms. Zoe W. DURANT
06 Registrar .... Mrs. Linda PHILLIPS
45 Dir Inst Rsrch/Assess/Accountabity .... Dr. Karla OTY
37 Director of Financial Assistance .... Mr. Donald HALL
13 Director Information Tech Services .... Ms. Debbie GOODE
15 Director of Human Resources .... Mr. Chase MASSIE
38 Director Student Development .... Dr. Jennifer PRUCHNICKI
35 Director Student Activities .... Mr. Zeak NAIFEH
19 Director Public Safety .... Mr. John DEBOARD
18 Int Director Physical Facilities .... Mr. Robert HANEFIELD
96 Director of Purchasing .... Mr. Richard MCCOMAS

Carl Albert State College (E)

1507 S McKenna, Poteau OK 74953-5208
County: Le Flore FICE Identification: 003176
Unit ID: 206923
Telephone: (918) 647-1200 Carnegie Class: Assoc/Pub-R-M
FAX Number: (918) 647-1201 Calendar System: Semester
URL: www.carlalbert.edu
Established: 1933 Annual Undergrad Tuition & Fees (In-State): $2,520
Enrollment: 2,673 Coed
Affiliation or Control: State IRS Status: 501(c)3
Highest Offering: Associate Degree
Program: Occupational; 2-Year Principally Bachelor's Creditable
Accreditation: NH, ACBSP, ADNUR, PTAA, RAD

01 President .... Dr. Brandon R. WEBB
32 Vice President for Student Affairs .... Ms. Leah MCLAUGHLIN
05 Vice President of Academic Affairs .... Dr. James YATES
10 Vice Pres for Business Operations .... Ms. Ramona BUCKNER
13 Information Technology Director .... Mr. Michael MARTIN
04 Assistant to the President .... Mr. Garry IVEY
26 Public Relations Director .... Ms. Judi WHITE
06 Registrar/Director Admissions .... Ms. Dee Ann DICKERSON
37 Director of Financial Aid .... Ms. Robin BENSON
85 Director Federal Programs .... Ms. Michelle WHITE
18 Chief Facilities/Physical Plant .... Mr. Garry IVEY
15 Director Personnel Services .... Ms. Vicki HILL
21 Assistant Finance Officer .... Ms. Melinda PIERCE

Clary Sage College (F)

3131 South Sheridan Road, Tulsa OK 74145-1102
County: Tulsa Identification: 666368
Unit ID: 450401
Telephone: (918) 298-8200 Carnegie Class: Assoc/PrivFP
FAX Number: (918) 298-0099 Calendar System: Semester
URL: www.clarysagecollege.com
Established: 2005 Annual Undergrad Tuition & Fees: $12,810
Enrollment: 300 Coed
Affiliation or Control: Proprietary IRS Status: Proprietary
Highest Offering: Associate Degree
Program: Occupational; 2-Year Principally Bachelor's Creditable; Technical Emphasis
Accreditation: ACICS

00 Founder/Owner .... Ms. Teresa KNOX
01 President .... Mr. Kevin KIRK
01 CEO .... Mr. Robert BRESCIA
05 Campus Director .... Ms. Raye MAHLBERG

† Branch campus of Community Care College, Tulsa, OK.

Community Care College (G)

4242 S Sheridan Road, Tulsa OK 74145-1119
County: Tulsa FICE Identification: 033674
Unit ID: 439570
Telephone: (918) 610-0027 Carnegie Class: Assoc/PrivFP
FAX Number: (918) 610-0029 Calendar System: Other
URL: www.communitycarecollege.edu
Established: 1995 Annual Undergrad Tuition & Fees: $12,235
Enrollment: 728 Coed
Affiliation or Control: Proprietary IRS Status: Proprietary
Highest Offering: Associate Degree
Program: Occupational
Accreditation: ACICS, MAAB, SURGT

00 Founder/CEO .... Ms. Teresa L. KNOX
01 President .... Mr. Kevin L. KIRK

Connors State College (H)

Route 1, Box 1000, Warner OK 74469-9700
County: Muskogee FICE Identification: 003153
Unit ID: 206996
Telephone: (918) 463-2931 Carnegie Class: Assoc/Pub-R-M
FAX Number: (918) 463-2233 Calendar System: Semester
URL: www.connorsstate.edu
Established: 1908 Annual Undergrad Tuition & Fees (In-State): $2,997
Enrollment: 2,713 Coed
Affiliation or Control: State IRS Status: 501(c)3
Highest Offering: Associate Degree
Program: Occupational; 2-Year Principally Bachelor's Creditable
Accreditation: NH, ADNUR

01 President .... Dr. Timothy W. FALTYN
03 Executive Vice President .... Dr. Jo Lynn A. DIGRANES
05 Vice President Academic Services .... Vacant
51 Vice Pres Cont Educ/Dir Muskogee .... Vacant
10 Vice President of Fiscal Services .... Ms. Sharon OWEN
32 VP Student Svcs/Enrollment Mgmt .... Dr. Ron RAMMING
84 Dean of Enrollment Services .... Vacant
37 Director of Financial Aid .... Ms. Jennifer WATKINS
08 Director of Learning Center .... Mrs. Margaret RIGNEY
13 Director Information Technology .... Mr. Heath HODGES
06 Registrar .... Ms. Sonya BAKER
18 Director Physical Plant .... Vacant
26 Director of Public Information .... Mr. Wayne BUNCH
15 Director Human Resources .... Ms. Gwendolyn DERRICK
09 Director of Institutional Research .... Dr. Ramona PIEARCY
30 Exec Dir for Institutional Advance .... Vacant
12 Dirctor of Muskogee Campuses .... Ms. Rhoda STRODE

DeVry University - Oklahoma City (I)

4013 NW Expressway Street, Ste 100,
Oklahoma City OK 73116-1695
County: Oklahoma Identification: 666566
Unit ID: 447485
Telephone: (405) 767-9516 Carnegie Class: Spec/Bus
FAX Number: (405) 842-4573 Calendar System: Semester
URL: www.devry.edu
Established: 1931 Annual Undergrad Tuition & Fees: $15,294
Enrollment: 279 Coed
Affiliation or Control: Proprietary IRS Status: Proprietary
Highest Offering: Master's
Program: Professional; Business Emphasis
Accreditation: &NH

01 Campus Director .... Anthony SPANO

† Regional accreditation is carried under the parent institution in Downers Grove, IL.

East Central University (J)

1100 E 14th Street, Ada OK 74820-6899
County: Pontotoc FICE Identification: 003154
Unit ID: 207041
Telephone: (580) 332-8000 Carnegie Class: Master's L
FAX Number: (580) 332-1623 Calendar System: Semester
URL: www.ecok.edu
Established: 1909 Annual Undergrad Tuition & Fees (In-State): $4,608
Enrollment: 4,903 Coed
Affiliation or Control: State IRS Status: 501(c)3
Highest Offering: Master's
Program: Liberal Arts And General; Teacher Preparatory; Professional
Accreditation: NH, ACBSP, CORE, MUS, NUR, SW, TED

01 President .... Dr. John R. HARGRAVE
05 Provost/Vice Pres Academic Affairs .... Dr. Duane C. ANDERSON

32 Vice President Student Development ....Dr. Gerald FORBES
10 Vice President Fiscal Affairs ....Dr. Steven TURNER
25 Assoc VP Sponsored Programs & Rsrch ....Vacant
20 Asst VP Academic Affairs ....Dr. Katricia PIERSON
53 Dean of Education ....Dr. Brenda RAWLING
50 Dean of Business ....Mr. Wendell GODWIN
51 Director Continuing Education ....Dr. G. Richard WETHERILL
35 Dean of Students ....Mr. Bronson WARREN
37 Director of Financial Aid ....Ms. Becky ISAACS
09 Director of Institutional Research ....Dr. Sheilynda STEWART
08 Librarian ....Dr. Adrianna LANCASTER
06 Registrar ....Ms. Pamla ARMSTRONG
14 Director Computer Center ....Mr. Frank WILLIAMS
41 Athletic Director ....Mr. Brian DEANGELIS
15 Director of Human Resources ....Mr. Lynn LOFTIN
19 Chief of Police ....Mr. Henry MILLER
18 Director Physical Plant ....Mr. Robert CASTLEBERRY
26 Dir of Marketing & Communication ....Ms. Amy FORD
29 Director Alumni Relations ....Ms. Buffy LOVELIS
84 Director Enrollment Management ....Ms. Bonita BLACKBURN
96 Director of Purchasing ....Ms. Jo Ann JOHNSON

Eastern Oklahoma State College (A)

1301 W Main Street, Wilburton OK 74578-4999
County: Latimer FICE Identification: 003155
Unit ID: 207050
Telephone: (918) 465-2361 Carnegie Class: Assoc/Pub-R-S
FAX Number: (918) 465-2431 Calendar System: Semester
URL: www.eosc.edu
Established: 1909 Annual Undergrad Tuition & Fees (In-State): $3,006
Enrollment: 2,065 Coed
Affiliation or Control: State IRS Status: 501(c)3
Highest Offering: Associate Degree
Program: Occupational; 2-Year Principally Bachelor's Creditable
Accreditation: NH, ADNUR

01 President ....Dr. Stephen E. SMITH
05 Vice President of Academic Affairs ....Dr. Karen D. HARRISON
10 Vice Pres of Business Affairs ....Ms. La Donna HOWELL
32 Vice Pres for Student Affairs ....Mr. Victor WOODS
12 Director of McAlester Campus ....Ms. Nicole HEATH
35 Dean of Students ....Dr. Sally DAVIS
30 Director of Development ....Mrs. Ann OWENS
27 Director Public Information ....Mr. Hank MOONEY
84 Dir Enrollment Mgmt/Financial Aid ....Mrs. Victor WOODS
13 Chief Technical Officer ....Mr. Jeff WEEMS
08 Director Library & Media Services ....Ms. Maria MARTINEZ
15 Director Personnel Services ....Mrs. Joyce BILLS
06 Registrar ....Mrs. Donna RICE
18 Chief Facilities/Physical Plant ....Mr. Rudy O'DONLEY
09 Director of Institutional Research ....Mr. Philip HAWTHORNE
29 Director Alumni Relations ....Mrs. Ann OWENS
37 Financial Aid Officer ....Ms. Patricia RECTOR

Family of Faith College (B)

PO Box 1805, Shawnee OK 74802-1805
County: Pottawatomie FICE Identification: 036763
Unit ID: 443058
Telephone: (405) 273-5331 Carnegie Class: Spec/Faith
FAX Number: (405) 273-8535 Calendar System: Semester
URL: www.familyoffaithcollege.edu
Established: 1992 Annual Undergrad Tuition & Fees: $5,410
Enrollment: 46 Coed
Affiliation or Control: Independent Non-Profit IRS Status: 501(c)3
Highest Offering: Baccalaureate
Program: Professional; Religious Emphasis
Accreditation: BI

01 President ....Dr. Samuel W. MATTHEWS
05 Vice President Academic Affairs ....Mrs. Elaine W. PHILLIPS
10 Vice President Operations/Finance ....Mr. Vaughn NEWMAN
32 Vice Pres Student Affs/Dir Fin Aid ....Mrs. Rhonda GAINES
46 Director of Resource Development ....Vacant
42 Director of Spiritual Life ....Mr. Daniel J. MATTHEWS
09 Dir of Accreditation/Assessment ....Mrs. Elaine W. PHILLIPS

Heritage College (C)

7100 I-35 Services Road, Suite 7118,
Oklahoma City OK 73149-2740
County: Oklahoma FICE Identification: 031151
Unit ID: 410070
Telephone: (405) 631-3399 Carnegie Class: Assoc/PrivFP
FAX Number: (405) 631-6711 Calendar System: Quarter
URL: www.heritage-education.com
Established: 2002 Annual Undergrad Tuition & Fees: $22,633
Enrollment: 993 Coed
Affiliation or Control: Proprietary IRS Status: Proprietary
Highest Offering: Associate Degree
Program: Occupational
Accreditation: ABHES, SURGT, SURTEC

01 Director ....Ms. Cheryl MORRIS

Hillsdale Free Will Baptist College (D)

PO Box 7208, Moore OK 73153-1208
County: Cleveland FICE Identification: 010266
Unit ID: 207157
Telephone: (405) 912-9000 Carnegie Class: Spec/Faith
FAX Number: (405) 912-9050 Calendar System: Semester
URL: www.hc.edu
Established: 1959 Annual Undergrad Tuition & Fees: $13,400
Enrollment: 259 Coed
Affiliation or Control: Free Will Baptist Church IRS Status: 501(c)3
Highest Offering: Master's
Program: Liberal Arts And General; Religious Emphasis
Accreditation: TRACS

01 President ....Dr. Timothy W. EATON
05 Chief Academic Officer ....Dr. Thomas L. MARBERRY
03 Executive Vice President ....Dr. Mark H. BRAISHER
30 Director Institutional Advancement ....Mr. Bob THOMPSON
07 Dir of Admissions/Dean of Students ....Vacant
37 Financial Aid Coordinator ....Ms. Denise CONKLIN
08 LRC Director ....Ms. Nancy J. DRAPER
13 Director of MIS ....Mr. Quentin C. LOOP
06 Registrar ....Ms. Patti ASHBY
58 Dean of Graduate Studies ....Dr. Mark H. BRAISHER
33 Men's Resident Life Coordinator ....Mr. Sam CRILLY
34 Women's Resident Life Coordinator ....Ms. Sammi MCCRARY
41 Athletic Director ....Ms. Autumn DRAKE
42 Chaplain/Director Campus Ministries ....Rev. Jeff SLOAN
40 Bookstore Manager ....Ms. Taylor PAULK
51 Coordinator of Adult Studies ....Ms. Patti ASHBY

ITT Technical Institute (E)

50 Penn Place Ofc Tower, Ste 305R,
Oklahoma City OK 73118
County: Oklahoma Identification: 666159
Unit ID: 448503
Telephone: (405) 810-4100 Carnegie Class: Assoc/PrivFP4
FAX Number: N/A Calendar System: Quarter
URL: www.itt-tech.edu
Established: 2006 Annual Undergrad Tuition & Fees: N/A
Enrollment: 514 Coed
Affiliation or Control: Proprietary IRS Status: Proprietary
Highest Offering: Baccalaureate
Program: Technical Emphasis
Accreditation: ACICS

† Branch campus of ITT Technical Institute, Tempe, AZ.

ITT Technical Institute (F)

8421 East 61st Street, Suite U, Tulsa OK 74133
County: Tulsa Identification: 666147
Unit ID: 448512
Telephone: (918) 615-3900 Carnegie Class: Assoc/PrivFP4
FAX Number: N/A Calendar System: Quarter
URL: www.itt-tech.edu
Established: 2006 Annual Undergrad Tuition & Fees: N/A
Enrollment: 602 Coed
Affiliation or Control: Proprietary IRS Status: Proprietary
Highest Offering: Baccalaureate
Program: Technical Emphasis
Accreditation: ACICS

† Branch campus of ITT Technical Institute, Tempe, AZ.

Langston University (G)

PO Box 907, Langston OK 73050-0907
County: Logan FICE Identification: 003157
Unit ID: 207209
Telephone: (405) 466-2231 Carnegie Class: Master's S
FAX Number: (405) 466-3461 Calendar System: Semester
URL: www.lunet.edu
Established: 1897 Annual Undergrad Tuition & Fees (In-State): $3,500
Enrollment: 2,762 Coed
Affiliation or Control: State IRS Status: 501(c)3
Highest Offering: Doctorate
Program: Liberal Arts And General; Teacher Preparatory; Professional
Accreditation: NH, ACBSP, CORE, DIETD, NUR, PTA, TED

01 President ....Dr. JoAnn W. HAYSBERT
05 Vice President Academic Affairs ....Dr. Clyde MONTGOMERY
10 Vice President Fiscal/Admin Affairs ....Mrs. Angela R. WATSON
32 VP Student Affairs/Enrollment Mgmt ....Dr. Angelia JONES
30 Vice Pres Inst Development/Advance ....Vacant
100 Chief of Staff ....Mrs. Cynthia S. BUCKLEY
04 Special Assistant to the President ....Dr. Melvin R. TODD
04 Special Assistant to the President ....Ms. Vickie G. JACKSON
20 Assoc VP Academic Affairs LU/OKC ....Dr. Blayne E. HINDS
20 COO/Assoc VP Academic Affs LU/
Tulsa ....Dr. Bruce W. MCGOWAN
20 Asst VP of Academic Affairs ....Dr. Patrena N. BENTON
21 Asst VP of Fiscal Affairs ....Ms. Debra G. MASTERS
44 Asst VP Inst Advanc/Campaign Dir ...... Mr. James R. DUNAVANT
35 Assistant VP of Student Affairs ....Mr. Marc FLEMON
27 Chief Information Officer ....Mr. Pritchard MONCRIFFE
29 Director Alumni Affairs ....Mrs. Vonnie W. ROBERTS
36 Dir Assessment/Career Placement ....Mr. James A. WALLACE
26 Director Public Relations ....Ms. Ashley N. GIBSON
07 Director of Admissions ....Ms. Josita L. BAKER
37 Director Financial Aid ....Ms. Shelia MCGILL
15 Director of Human Resources ....Mrs. Beverly H. SMITH
22 Dir LCDC Affirm Action/EEO Ofc ....Vacant
18 Director Facilities/Physical Plant ....Mr. Ruben D. OLIVER
38 Dir Professional Counseling Ctr ....Dr. William PRICE CURTIS
09 Director Inst Research & Planning ...... Mr. Mark B. MCCLENDON
08 Director of Libraries ....Ms. Bettye R. BLACK
06 Registrar ....Mrs. Kathy SIMMONS
41 Athletic Director ....Mr. Patric D. SIMON
21 Comptroller ....Mr. J.I JOHNSON
49 Dean School of Arts & Sci ....Dr. Clarence A. HEDGE
50 Dean School of Business ....Dr. Solomon S. SMITH
46 Dean School Agric/Applied Science ....Dr. Marvin BURNS
66 Dean Sch Nursing/Health Professions . Dr. Carolyn T. KORNEGAY
53 Acting Dean Sch Educ/Behav Sci ....Dr. Joe N. HORNBEAK
92 Dean Honors Program ....Vacant
88 Dean Physical Therapy Program ....Dr. Milagros JORGE
88 Dean Entrepreneurial Studies ....Dr. Surya P. SINGH
58 Director of Graduate Programs ....Dr. Alex O. LEWIS
19 Chief of Police ....Mr. Michael D. STORR
96 Director of Purchasing ....Mrs. Deirdra M. STEVENSON

Mid-America Christian University (H)

3500 SW 119th Street, Oklahoma City OK 73170-4500
County: Cleveland FICE Identification: 006942
Unit ID: 245953
Telephone: (405) 691-3800 Carnegie Class: Bac/Diverse
FAX Number: (405) 692-3165 Calendar System: Semester
URL: www.macu.edu
Established: 1953 Annual Undergrad Tuition & Fees: $14,118
Enrollment: 1,233 Coed
Affiliation or Control: Church Of God IRS Status: 501(c)3
Highest Offering: Master's
Program: Liberal Arts And General; Teacher Preparatory; Religious Emphasis
Accreditation: NH

01 President ....Dr. John D. FOZARD
05 Vice President for Academic
Affairs ....Dr. Kathaleen REID-MARTINEZ
84 Vice President for Enrollment Mgmt .... Mr. Maurice (Buddy) SHOE
30 Assoc VP for University Advancement ....Mr. Chris BURTON
32 Dean of Students ....Mrs. Jessica RIMMER
10 Chief Financial Officer ....Ms. Mici SARTIN
88 Exec Dir of Church Relations ....Rev. Morgan ALSIP
06 Registrar ....Vacant
37 Director Student Financial Services ....Mr. Doug CLEARY
07 Director of Admissions ....Mr. Dustin ROWTON
18 Director Facilities/Physical Plant ....Mr. Clark BAREFOOT
29 Director Alumni Relations ....Vacant
15 Chief Administration Officer (HR) ....Dr. Owen SEVIER
58 Dean Col of Adult & Graduate Stds ....Dr. Shirley RODDY
49 Asc Dean College of Arts & Sciences ...... Mrs. Julia CARPENTER

Murray State College (I)

One Murray Campus, Tishomingo OK 73460-3130
County: Johnston FICE Identification: 003158
Unit ID: 207236
Telephone: (580) 371-2371 Carnegie Class: Assoc/Pub-R-M
FAX Number: (580) 371-9844 Calendar System: Semester
URL: www.mscok.edu
Established: 1908 Annual Undergrad Tuition & Fees (In-State): $2,800
Enrollment: 2,714 Coed
Affiliation or Control: State IRS Status: 501(c)3
Highest Offering: Associate Degree
Program: Occupational; 2-Year Principally Bachelor's Creditable
Accreditation: NH, ADNUR, OTA, PTAA

01 President ....Ms. Joy MCDANIEL
04 Exec Assistant to President/Board ....Mr. Michael BURRELL
10 VP for Administration and Finance ....Vacant
05 VP for Academic Affairs ....Dr. Roger STACY
32 VP of Student Affairs ....Ms. Michaelle GRAY
37 Assoc Financial Aid Director ....Ms. Machelle ELLIS
08 Director of Library ....Ms. Mary RIXEN
74 Veterinary Tech Program Director ....Dr. Carey FLOYD
66 Director of Nursing ....Ms. Joni JETER
30 Director of Development/External Rels ....Vacant
20 Director of Academic Advisement ....Ms. Amanda BALDRIDGE
07 Registrar/Director of Admissions ....Ms. Genna MARTEN
15 Director of Human Resources ....Mr. Joe Pat HUGHES
35 Director of Student Life ....Ms. Linda ROBINS
18 Assistant VP of Facilities ....Mr. Gary COOK
26 Public Information Officer ....Ms. Erin KNIGHT

Northeastern Oklahoma Agricultural and Mechanical College (J)

200 I Street, NE, Miami OK 74354-6434
County: Ottawa FICE Identification: 003160
Unit ID: 207290
Telephone: (918) 542-8441 Carnegie Class: Assoc/Pub-R-M
FAX Number: (918) 542-9759 Calendar System: Semester
URL: www.neo.edu
Established: 1919 Annual Undergrad Tuition & Fees (In-State): $2,995
Enrollment: 2,324 Coed
Affiliation or Control: State IRS Status: 501(c)3
Highest Offering: Associate Degree
Program: Occupational; 2-Year Principally Bachelor's Creditable
Accreditation: NH, ADNUR, MLTAD, PTAA

01 President ....Dr. Jeffery L. HALE
05 Vice President Academic Affairs ....Vacant

10 Vice President for Fiscal Affairs ....Mrs. Jessica A. BOLES
32 VP Student Affairs/Enrollment Svcs ....Mrs. Amy ISHMAEL
20 Asst VP for Academic Affairs ....Ms. Bethene FAHNESTOCK
37 Director of Financial Aid ....Mr. David FISHER
26 Chief Public Relations Officer ....Ms. Katie SWEETEN
15 Director Human Resources ....Mrs. Marcia ENYART
18 Director Facilities/Physical Plant ....Mr. Steve GRIMES
27 Dir Public Information/Relations ....Ms. Katie SWEETEN
14 Asst Director Technology Services ....Mr. Brian SPARKS
30 Director Devel/Alumni Relations ....Mrs. Edie INGRAM
38 Director Academic Advising Center ....Mrs. Rachel LLOYD
41 Interim Athletic Director ....Mr. Dale PATTERSON
88 Economic Development Coordinator ....Vacant
105 Webmaster ....Mr. Brad HENDERSON
06 Registrar ....Mrs. Michelle SHACKELFORD
21 Asst Vice Pres for Fiscal Affairs ....Mr. Mark RASOR
40 Bookstore Manager ....Mrs. Dianne HEADLEE
36 Dir Ctr for Academic Success & Adv ....Mrs. Rachel LLOYD
08 Coordinator Library Services ....Ms. Sloane BROWN
47 Department Chair Agriculture ....Mrs. Shannon CUNNINGHAM
83 Department Chair Social Science ....Dr. Jeff BIRDSONG
57 Dept Chair Commun/Performing Arts ....Mr. Steve MCCURLEY
66 Director Nursing ....Mrs. Deborah MORGAN
81 Dept Chair Mathematics/Science ....Dr. Mark GRIGSBY
66 Dept Chr Nursing/Allied Hlth/Phy Ed ....Mrs. Deborah MORGAN
50 Dept Chair Business and Technology ....Mrs. Pat CREECH

Northeastern State University (A)

601 N Grand Avenue, Tahlequah OK 74464-2399
County: Cherokee FICE Identification: 003161
Unit ID: 207263
Telephone: (918) 456-5511 Carnegie Class: Master's L
FAX Number: (918) 458-2193 Calendar System: Semester
URL: www.nsuok.edu
Established: 1851 Annual Undergrad Tuition & Fees (In-State): $4,590
Enrollment: 9,588 Coed
Affiliation or Control: State IRS Status: 501(c)3
Highest Offering: First Professional Degree
Program: Liberal Arts And General; Teacher Preparatory; Professional; Business Emphasis
Accreditation: NH, ACBSP, DIETD, MUS, NUR, OPT, OPTR, SP, SW, TED

01 President ....Dr. Don BETZ
05 Provost & Vice Pres Academic Affs ....Dr. Martin TADLOCK
11 Vice President for Administration ....Mr. David KOEHN
26 Vice President for Univ Relations ....Mr. Mark KINDERS
21 Vice Pres for Operations ....Mr. Tim FOUTCH
20 Assoc Vice Pres Academic Affairs ....Dr. Janet BAHR
58 Asst VP Acad Affs/Dean Grad College ....Dr. Tom JACKSON
88 Int Asst VP Ctr Teaching/Learning ....Dr. Chuck ZIEHR
12 Dean Broken Arrow Campus ....Dr. Christee JENLINK
12 Dean Muskogee Campus ....Dr. Tim MCELROY
49 Dean Liberal Arts ....Dr. Paul WESTBROOK
50 Int Dean Col Business/Technology ....Dr. Roger COLLIER
53 Dean College of Education ....Dr. Kay GRANT
81 Dean Science & Health Professions ....Dr. Martin VENNEMAN
88 Dean Optometry ....Dr. Douglas PENISTEN
13 Chief Information Officer ....Mr. Chuck MIZE
10 Director Business Affairs ....Ms. Sue CATRON
08 Interim Dean of NSU Libraries ....Ms. Paula SETTOON
21 Director of Budget ....Ms. Christy LANDSAW
30 Director of Development ....Ms. Peggy GLENN-SUMMITT
44 Director of Annual Giving ....Ms. Penny MOORE
15 Director of Human Resources ....Dr. Martha ALBIN
37 Director Student Financial Services ....Dr. Teri COCHRAN
06 Associate Registrar ....Ms. Paula PAGE
88 Director High School & College Rels ....Mr. Jason JESSIE
84 Dean Enrollment Mgmt/Registrar ....Mr. Bill NOWLIN
35 Dean of Student Affairs ....Ms. Laura BOREN
18 Director of Physical Plant ....Mr. Joe SPENCE
41 Director of Athletics ....Mr. Tony DUCKWORTH
27 Director of Communications ....Mr. Thomas SMITH
19 Director of Campus Police ....Ms. Patti BUHL
29 Director Alumni Services ....Mr. Daniel JOHNSON
07 Director of Admission ....Dr. Dawn CAIN
06 Registrar ....Dr. Julie SAWYER
88 Director of Auxiliary Services ....Mr. Randall SHELTON
39 Director of Housing ....Mr. E. Thayne KING
32 Chief Student Life Officer ....Ms. Laura BOREN
38 Director Student Counseling ....Ms. Sheila SELF
96 Director of Purchasing ....Mr. Jerry COZBY
09 Coordinator Institutional Research ....Vacant

Northern Oklahoma College (B)

1220 E Grand Avenue, PO Box 310,
Tonkawa OK 74653-0310
County: Kay FICE Identification: 003162
Unit ID: 207281
Telephone: (580) 628-6200 Carnegie Class: Assoc/Pub-R-M
FAX Number: (580) 628-6209 Calendar System: Semester
URL: www.north-ok.edu
Established: 1901 Annual Undergrad Tuition & Fees (In-State): $2,526
Enrollment: 5,386 Coed
Affiliation or Control: State IRS Status: 501(c)3
Highest Offering: Associate Degree
Program: Occupational; 2-Year Principally Bachelor's Creditable
Accreditation: NH, ACBSP, ADNUR

01 President ....Dr. Cheryl EVANS
05 Vice President for Academic Affairs ....Mrs. Judy COLWELL
10 Vice President Financial Affairs ....Mrs. Anita SIMPSON
12 Vice President for Enid Campus ....Dr. Ed VINEYARD
32 Vice President for Student Affairs ....Vacant
26 Vice Pres for Devel/Cmty Rels ....Mrs. Sheri SNYDER
14 Director Information Technology ....Mr. Michael MACHIA
15 Director Human Resources ....Ms. Shannon CRANFORD
20 Dean of Instruction ....Dr. Pamela STINSON
35 Dean of Students-Enid ....Mr. Boomer APPLEMAN
35 Dean of Students-Tonkawa ....Mr. Jason JOHNSON
12 Assoc Vice Pres Stillwater Campus ....Ms. Debbie QUIREY
06 Assoc Vice Pres Enroll Mgt/Registr ....Dr. Rick EDGINGTON
08 Director of Library Services ....Mr. Benjamin HAINLINE
18 Assoc Vice Pres of Physical Plant ....Mr. Larry DYE
41 Athletic Director ....Mr. Greg KRAUSE
29 Director Alumni Relations ....Ms. Kirby TICKEL
37 Director Student Financial Aid ....Ms. Linda BROWN
40 Manager Student Bookstore ....Mrs. Jimilea JANSSON
96 Purchasing Agent ....Ms. Becky SIMMONS

Northwestern Oklahoma State University (C)

709 Oklahoma Boulevard, Alva OK 73717-2799
County: Woods FICE Identification: 003163
Unit ID: 207306
Telephone: (580) 327-1700 Carnegie Class: Master's S
FAX Number: (580) 327-1881 Calendar System: Semester
URL: www.nwosu.edu
Established: 1897 Annual Undergrad Tuition & Fees (In-State): $4,590
Enrollment: 2,311 Coed
Affiliation or Control: State IRS Status: 501(c)3
Highest Offering: Master's
Program: Liberal Arts And General; Teacher Preparatory; Professional
Accreditation: NH, NUR, SW, TED

01 President ....Dr. Janet L. CUNNINGHAM
05 Exec Vice Pres/Chief Acad Affairs ....Dr. Steven L. LOHMANN
11 Vice President for Administration ....Mr. David M. PECHA
32 VP Student Affairs/Enrollment Mgmt ....Mr. Brad M. FRANZ
26 Assoc VP for University Relations ....Mr. Steven J. VALENCIA
58 Assoc Dean of Graduate Studies ....Dr. Shawn P. HOLLIDAY
08 Chief Librarian ....Mrs. Susan K. JEFFRIES
06 Registrar ....Mrs. Sheri K. LAHR
30 Director of Students/Housing ....Mr. Marcus L. WALLACE
41 Athletic Director ....Mr. Andrew V. CARTER
18 Chief Facilities/Physical Plant ....Mr. E. James DETGEN
29 Director Alumni Relations ....Mrs. Lizabeth R. RICHEY
37 Director Student Financial Aid ....Mr. Calleb N. MOSBURG
38 Director of Student Life/Counselor ....Mr. Jason D. HILLMAN
07 Director of Recruitment ....Mr. Wm. Matt ADAIR
15 Human Resource Director ....Mrs. Joyce A. GARVIE
09 Institutional Research Specialist ....Ms. Rita J. CASTLEBERRY

Oklahoma Baptist University (D)

500 W University, Shawnee OK 74804-2590
County: Pottawatomie FICE Identification: 003164
Unit ID: 207403
Telephone: (405) 275-2850 Carnegie Class: Bac/Diverse
FAX Number: (405) 878-2069 Calendar System: Semester
URL: www.okbu.edu
Established: 1910 Annual Undergrad Tuition & Fees: $19,756
Enrollment: 1,777 Coed
Affiliation or Control: Southern Baptist IRS Status: 501(c)3
Highest Offering: Master's
Program: Liberal Arts And General; Teacher Preparatory; Professional
Accreditation: NH, ACBSP, MUS, NUR, NURSE, TED

01 President ....Dr. David W. WHITLOCK
05 Provost/Exec Vice Pres Campus Life ....Dr. Robert S. NORMAN
10 Exec VP Business Affs/Admin Svcs ....Mr. Randy L. SMITH
30 Vice Pres University Advancement ....Mr. Will SMALLWOOD
81 Dean College of Math and Science ....Mrs. Debbie BLUE
42 Campus Minister ....Mr. Dale M. GRIFFIN
44 Assoc VP University Advancement ....Mr. Martin O'GWYNN
79 Assc Provost/Dn Humanities/Soc Sci ....Dr. Pam ROBINSON
13 Asst Vice Pres Info Sys/Services ....Mr. Gary NICKERSON
08 Dean Library Services ....Dr. Richard CHEEK
32 Dean of Students ....Mr. Bobby CANTY
29 Exec Director OBU Alumni Assn ....Mrs. Lori R. HAGANS
11 Director of Executive Offices ....Mrs. Tonia KELLOGG
37 Director Student Financial Services ....Mrs. Jonna G. RANEY
12 Director Geiger Center ....Ms. Cynthia K. GATES
06 Director Academic Records ....Ms. Marcia MCQUERRY
20 Academic Director/Asst Registrar ....Mrs. Teri F. WALKER
21 Controller ....Mrs. Lauri A. FLUKE
15 Director of Human Resources ....Mr. Mike JOHNSON
35 Director of Campus Services ....Mr. Larry A. WALKER
19 Chief of University Police ....Mr. David SHANNON
41 Athletic Director ....Mr. Robert DAVENPORT
18 Dir Facilities Mgt & Services ....Mr. Robert CASH
96 Director of Purchasing ....Mr. Larry WALKER
07 Director of Admissions ....Mr. Bruce PERKINS
58 Director OBU Graduate School ....Dr. Scott HARRIS
38 Career Planning Counselor ....Ms. Stephanie MILLER
38 Counselor ....Mrs. Rilda SMITH
57 Dean of Fine Arts ....Dr. Ken GABRIELSE
73 Dean School Christian Service ....Dr. Mack MCCLELLAN
50 Dean School of Business ....Dr. David C. HOUGHTON
66 Dean School of Nursing ....Dr. Lana BOLHOUSE

Oklahoma Christian University (E)

PO Box 11000, Oklahoma City OK 73136-1100
County: Oklahoma FICE Identification: 003165
Unit ID: 207324
Telephone: (405) 425-5000 Carnegie Class: Master's M
FAX Number: (405) 425-5090 Calendar System: Semester
URL: www.oc.edu
Established: 1950 Annual Undergrad Tuition & Fees: $18,456
Enrollment: 2,216 Coed
Affiliation or Control: Independent Non-Profit IRS Status: 501(c)3
Highest Offering: Master's
Program: Liberal Arts And General; Teacher Preparatory; Professional
Accreditation: NH, ACBSP, CIDA, ENG, MUS, NURSE, TED

01 President ....Dr. Mike E. O'NEAL
03 Executive Vice President ....Dr. William GOAD
30 Sr Vice Pres for Advancement ....Dr. John DESTEIGUER
05 Sr Vice Pres for Academic Affairs ....Dr. Allison GARRETT
11 Vice President for Operations ....Mr. James W. JONES
10 Vice President for Finance ....Mr. Jeff BINGHAM
27 VP for University Communication ....Mr. Ron FROST
29 Vice President for Alumni Relations ....Mr. Kent ALLEN
44 Vice President for Planned Giving ....Mr. Stephen ECK
32 Vice Pres and Dean of Student Life ....Mr. Neil ARTER
84 Vice President for Enrollment Mgmt ....Mrs. Risa FORRESTER
14 Vice President for Information Tech ....Mr. John HERMES
88 Dir Academy of Leadership/Liberty ....Dr. Brian BUSH
58 Dean of Graduate Programs ....Dr. Don DREW
107 Dean Col of Professional Studies ....Dr. Phil LEWIS
73 Dean College of Biblical Studies ....Dr. Alan MARTIN
49 Dean College Arts & Sciences ....Dr. David LOWRY
06 Registrar ....Dr. Mickey D. BANISTER
08 Library Director ....Mrs. Tamie L. WILLIS
19 Chief of Police Dept ....Mr. John MATLOCK
41 Athletic Director ....Dr. Curtis JANZ
18 Director of Building Maintenance ....Mr. Cary FALLING
26 Assoc Director Marketing Services ....Mr. Wes MCKINZIE
37 Dir Student Financial Services ....Mr. Clint LARUE
104 Director of International Programs ....Mr. John OSBORNE
15 Human Resources Director ....Mr. Lynn HOOPER
31 Director of Church Relations ....Mr. Bob ROWLEY
42 Assoc Dean for Spiritual Life ....Mr. Chance VANOVER
89 Director of Freshman Programs ....Mrs. Amy JANZEN
102 Dir Foundation & Corporate Rels ....Ms. Jo GRIFFIN
88 Director of Creative Services ....Mr. Judson COPELAND
40 Manager of Bookstore ....Mr. James MENCER
09 Director of Institutional Research ....Mr. Gary LYONS
21 Controller ....Mr. Chris BOWMAN
07 Director of Admissions ....Mrs. Darci THOMPSON
36 Director of Career Services ....Mr. Mark CHAN
85 International Student Adviser ....Mrs. Tamara J. NEWELL
23 Director of Health Services ....Mrs. Pam FERGUSON
38 Director of Counseling Services ....Dr. Sheldon ADKINS
88 Director of Retention ....Ms. Katy ROYBAL

Oklahoma City Community College (F)

7777 S May Avenue, Oklahoma City OK 73159-4444
County: Oklahoma FICE Identification: 010391
Unit ID: 207449
Telephone: (405) 682-1611 Carnegie Class: Assoc/Pub-U-SC
FAX Number: (405) 682-7585 Calendar System: Other
URL: www.occc.edu
Established: 1972 Annual Undergrad Tuition & Fees (In-District): $2,850
Enrollment: 22,481 Coed
Affiliation or Control: State/Local IRS Status: 501(c)3
Highest Offering: Associate Degree
Program: Occupational; 2-Year Principally Bachelor's Creditable
Accreditation: NH, ACBSP, ADNUR, EMT, ENGT, OTA, PTAA

01 President ....Dr. Paul W. SECHRIST
03 Executive Vice President ....Dr. Jerry STEWARD
43 Legal Counsel ....Dr. Nancy GERRITY
05 Vice President Academic Affairs ....Dr. Felix J. AQUINO
32 VP Enrollment/Student Services ....Dr. Marion PADEN
15 Vice Pres Human Resources ....Mr. Gary A. LOMBARD
10 Vice President Business & Finance ....Dr. John BOYD
31 Vice Pres Community Development ....Mr. Steven BLOOMBERG
20 Associate VP Academic Affairs ....Mr. Greg GARDNER
37 Dean Student Financial Support Svcs ....Mr. Harold CASE
38 Dean of Student Development ....Dr. Liz LARGENT
06 Registrar ....Mr. Alan STRINGFELLOW
30 Exec Director Inst Advancement ....Mr. Lealon TAYLOR
45 Executive Director of Planning ....Mr. Stu HARVEY
13 Dir Info Tech Infrastructure ....Mr. David ANDERSON
88 Director Recreation and Fitness ....Ms. Roxanna BUTLER
44 Director of Development ....Ms. Jennifer HARRISON
88 Director Students Support Svcs ....Ms. Patricia STOWE
07 Dir of Recruitment & Admissions ....Mr. Jon HORINEK
35 Director of Student Life ....Vacant
18 Director of Facilities Management ....Mr. J. B. MESSER
40 Director of Student Store ....Ms. Brenda REINKE
88 Director Corporate Learning ....Ms. Delores JACKSON
26 Dir of Marketing & Public Relations ....Ms. Paula GOWER
35 Director Student Relations ....Ms. Erin LOGAN
25 Director of Grants & Contracts ....Mr. Joe SWALWELL
12 Director OKC Downtown College ....Dr. Gus PEKARA
36 Director Career Transitions Program ....Ms. Nora PUGH-SEEMSTER
88 Dir Child Development/Lab School ....Dr. Mary MCCOY
21 Bursar ....Ms. Brandi HENSON

08 Director of Library Services ... Ms. Barbara KING
09 Dir Institutional Effectiveness ... Dr. Janet PERRY
88 Director Cooperative Alliances ... Ms. Alexa MASHLAN
22 EEO/AA Compliance Officer ... Vacant
31 Dir Community Outreach & Education ... Ms. Jessica MARTINEZ-BROOKS
88 Coord OCCC Capitol Hill Center ... Mr. Sergio GALLEGOS
96 Purchasing Manager ... Ms. Lori WALKER
19 Dir Emergency Planning/Risk Mgmt ... Ms. Lisa TEEL

Oklahoma City University (A)

2501 N Blackwelder, Oklahoma City OK 73106-1493
County: Oklahoma FICE Identification: 003166
Unit ID: 207458
Telephone: (405) 208-5000 Carnegie Class: Master's L
FAX Number: N/A Calendar System: Semester
URL: www.okcu.edu
Established: 1904 Annual Undergrad Tuition & Fees: $28,190
Enrollment: 3,770 Coed
Affiliation or Control: United Methodist IRS Status: 501(c)3
Highest Offering: First Professional Degree
Program: Liberal Arts And General; Teacher Preparatory; Professional
Accreditation: NH, ACBSP, LAW, MACTE, MUS, NUR

01 President ... Mr. Robert H. HENRY
05 Acting Vice Pres Academic Affairs ... Dr. Susan BARBER
30 Vice Pres University Advancement ... Mr. John R. HILLIS
26 Vice Pres Univ/Church Relations ... Rev. Margaret A. BALL
10 Chief Financial Officer ... Mr. Brian HOLLAND
32 Vice President for Student Affairs ... Dr. Richard HALL
84 Asst VP/Dean Enrollment Services ... Mr. Eduardo PRIETO
35 Dean of Students ... Mr. John RIGGS
06 Registrar ... Mr. Charles MONNOT
09 Director of Institutional Research ... Mr. Michael JACKSON
08 Director Dulaney Browne Library ... Dr. Victoria SWINNEY
37 Director of Financial Aid ... Ms. Denise FLIS
27 Director of Communications ... Ms. Chris EDDINGTON
15 Asst VP/Director of Admin Services ... Ms. Liz HEDRICK
92 Director of Honors Program ... Dr. Virginia MCCOMBS
07 Director of Admissions ... Ms. Michelle LOCKHART
18 Chief Facilities/Physical Plant ... Mr. Jeff CASTLEBERRY
29 Director Alumni Relations ... Vacant
36 Director Career Planning/Placement ... Mr. Josh WADDELL
49 Dean College of Arts & Sciences ... Dr. Mark Y. DAVIES
50 Interim Dean School of Business ... Dr. Steve AGEE
61 Dean School of Law ... Mr. Lawrence K. HELLMAN
64 Dean School of Music ... Mr. Mark PARKER
66 Dean of School of Nursing ... Dr. Marvel WILLIAMSON
73 Dean School of Religion ... Dr. Mark DAVIES
88 Dean School of Amer Dance/Arts Mgt ... Mr. John BEDFORD
100 Chief of Staff ... Mr. Craig KNUTSON

Oklahoma Panhandle State University (B)

Box 430, Goodwell OK 73939-0430
County: Texas FICE Identification: 003174
Unit ID: 207351
Telephone: (580) 349-2611 Carnegie Class: Bac/Diverse
FAX Number: (580) 349-2302 Calendar System: Semester
URL: www.opsu.edu
Established: 1909 Annual Undergrad Tuition & Fees (In-State): $5,055
Enrollment: 1,387 Coed
Affiliation or Control: State IRS Status: 501(c)3
Highest Offering: Baccalaureate
Program: Liberal Arts And General
Accreditation: NH, NUR, TED

01 President ... Dr. David A. BRYANT
05 Vice Pres Academic Affairs/Outreach ... Dr. Wayne MANNING
10 Vice Pres Business & Fiscal Affairs ... Mr. Larry PETERS
47 Dean Agriculture ... Dr. Peter CAMFIELD
50 Dean Business & Technology ... Ms. Diane MURPHEY
53 Dean Education ... Dr. R. Wayne STEWART
57 Dean Liberal Arts ... Dr. Sara RICHTER
66 Dean Science/Mathematics/Nursing ... Dr. Justin COLLINS
06 Registrar/Director of Admissions ... Mr. Bobby JENKINS
37 Director Student Financial Aid ... Ms. Lori FERGUSON
09 Director Institutional Research ... Vacant
13 Director of Technology ... Mr. Howard HENDERSON
15 Director Personnel Services ... Ms. Cheryl ASHPAUGH
08 Director of Library ... Ms. Alton (Tony) HARDMAN
32 Director of Student Services ... Ms. Jessica LOFLAND
21 Comptroller ... Mr. Benny DAIN
38 Director Counseling/Career Services ... Ms. Christi HALE
26 Campus Communications Director ... Ms. Laura HAYS
41 Athletic Officer ... Mr. Jerry OLSON
40 Bookstore Manager ... Ms. Mandy BATENHORST
18 Director Physical Plant ... Mr. Bob SCOTT
29 Director Alumni Relations ... Ms. Janet KRAVIG
96 Director of Purchasing ... Ms. Jena MARR

Oklahoma State University (C)

Stillwater OK 74078
County: Payne FICE Identification: 003170
Unit ID: 207388
Telephone: (405) 744-5000 Carnegie Class: RU/H
FAX Number: N/A Calendar System: Semester
URL: osu.okstate.edu/
Established: 1890 Annual Undergrad Tuition & Fees (In-State): $7,107
Enrollment: 23,522 Coed
Affiliation or Control: State IRS Status: 501(c)3
Highest Offering: Doctorate
Program: Liberal Arts And General; Teacher Preparatory; Professional
Accreditation: NH, AAB, BUS, BUSA, CACREP, CIDA, CLPSY, COPSY, DIETD, DIETI, ENG, ENGT, FOR, JOUR, LSAR, MFCD, MUS, NRPA, SCPSY, SP, TED, THEA, VET

01 President ... Dr. V. Burns HARGIS
04 Exec Assistant to the President ... Ms. Deborah LANE
05 Provost & Senior Vice President ... Dr. Robert STERNBURG
10 Vice Pres Administration & Finance ... Mr. Joseph B. WEAVER, JR.
03 Vice President for Univ Relations ... Mr. Gary C. CLARK
32 Vice President Student Affairs ... Dr. Lee E. BIRD
46 Vice Pres Research/Tech Transfer ... Dr. Stephen W. MCKEEVER
28 Interim Assoc VP Inst Diversity ... Mr. Jason KIRKSEY
47 VP Agri Programs & Dean CASNR ... Dr. Robert E. WHITSON
41 Vice President Athletic Programs ... Mr. Mike HOLDER
20 Assoc Provost ... Dr. Pamela FRY
11 Associate Vice Pres Admin & Finance ... Mr. Joseph B. WEAVER, JR.
21 Assoc Vice President & Controller ... Ms. Kathy ELLIOTT
15 Asst Vice Pres Human Resources ... Ms. Elizabeth A. MATOY
102 President & CEO OSU Foundation ... Mr. Kirk A. JEWELL
29 President & CEO/Alumni Association ... Mr. Larry SHELL
88 Pres Ctr for Innovation & Econ Dev ... Dr. Joseph W. ALEXANDER
54 Dean Engineering/Architecture/Tech ... Dr. Karl N. REID, JR.
49 Dean Arts & Sciences ... Dr. Peter M. SHERWOOD
50 Dean Spears School of Business ... Dr. Lawrence CROSBY
53 Interim Dean Education ... Dr. Robert DAVIS
59 Dean College of Human Sciences ... Dr. Stephan M. WILSON
74 Dean Veterinary Medicine ... Dr. Michael D. LORENZ
58 Dean Graduate College ... Dr. Mark PAYTON
08 Dean Library ... Ms. Sheila G. JOHNSON
23 Director University Health Services ... Mr. Stephen K. ROGERS
27 Director Communication Services ... Mr. Gary SHUTT
26 Assoc VP Enroll Mgmt/Univ Mktg ... Mr. Kyle WRAY
07 Director Undergraduate Admissions ... Ms. Christine CRENSHAW
13 Chief Information Officer ... Ms. Darlene HIGHTOWER
43 Board of Regents Legal Counsel ... Mr. Charles E. DRAKE
06 Registrar ... Dr. K. Celeste CAMPBELL
39 Director Residential Life ... Dr. Matthew S. BROWN
38 Director University Counseling Svcs ... Dr. Suzanne M. BURKS
37 Director Financial Aid ... Dr. Charles W. BRUCE
92 Director Honors College ... Dr. Robert L. SPURRIER
36 Director Career Services ... Ms. Pam EHLERS
19 Director & Chief of Public Safety ... Mr. Michael ROBINSON
25 Dir Grants/Contracts/Financial Admn ... Dr. Robert DIXON
22 Director Affirmative Action ... Ms. Mackenzie WILFONG
24 Dir Inst Teaching/Lrng Excellence ... Mr. Blayne MAYFIELD
09 Director Inst Research/Info Mgmt ... Dr. Christie HAWKINS
96 Director of Purchasing ... Ms. Sharon S. TOY
18 Chief Facilities Officer ... Mr. Richard KRYSIAK
88 Student Union Director ... Mr. Mitch KILCREASE
40 Asst Dir Student Union Bookstore ... Mr. Lance HINKLE
85 Coord Intl Student & Scholars ... Mr. Tim T. HUFF

Oklahoma State University Center for Health Sciences College of Osteopathic Medicine (D)

1111 W 17th Street, Tulsa OK 74107-1898
County: Tulsa FICE Identification: 011282
Unit ID: 207315
Telephone: (918) 582-1972 Carnegie Class: Spec/Med
FAX Number: (918) 561-8412 Calendar System: Semester
URL: www.healthsciences.okstate.edu
Established: 1972 Annual Undergrad Tuition & Fees (In-State): $22,423
Enrollment: 427 Coed
Affiliation or Control: State IRS Status: 501(c)3
Highest Offering: First Professional Degree
Program: Professional
Accreditation: &NH, OSTEO

01 President ... Dr. Howard BARNETT
05 Provost and Dean ... Dr. Kayse SHRUM
10 COO/Vice Pres for Healthcare Admin ... Dr. James D. HESS
46 Vice Pres Research/Inst Advancement ... Dr. Leigh GOODSON
30 Asst Vice President for Development ... Ms. Marlo DUFFY TURNER
20 Int Vice Provost/Asoc Dn Biomed Sci ... Dr. Bruce A. BENJAMIN
84 Assoc Dean for Enrollment Mgmt ... Dr. Vivian M. STEVENS
20 Assoc Dean for Clinical Services ... Dr. Jenny ALEXOPULOS
20 Assoc Dean for Clinical Education ... Dr. Joan E. STEWART
13 Dir Info Technology/Lrng Tech Svcs ... Mr. Randall POPP
29 Director Alumni Affairs ... Mr. Ryan MILLER
88 Chief Medical Informatics Officer ... Mr. Jason BRAY
26 Director of Mktg/Communication Svcs ... Dr. Mary Bea DRUMMOND
35 Director Student Affairs ... Ms. Dana A. LIVINGSTON
06 Registrar ... Ms. Amanda SUMNER
07 Asst Director of Admissions ... Ms. Lindsey KIRKPATRICK

† Regional accreditation is carried under the parent institution in Stillwater, OK.

Oklahoma State University Institute of Technology-Okmulgee (E)

1801 E Fourth Street, Okmulgee OK 74447-3901
County: Okmulgee FICE Identification: 003172
Unit ID: 207564
Telephone: (918) 293-4678 Carnegie Class: Assoc/Pub4
FAX Number: (918) 293-4644 Calendar System: Trimester
URL: www.osuit.edu
Established: 1946 Annual Undergrad Tuition & Fees (In-State): $135
Enrollment: 2,562 Coed
Affiliation or Control: State IRS Status: 501(c)3
Highest Offering: Baccalaureate
Program: Occupational; 2-Year Principally Bachelor's Creditable; Technical Emphasis
Accreditation: NH, ADNUR, CS

01 Interim President ... Dr. David BOSSERMAN
05 VP Academic Affairs ... Dr. Linda AVANT
10 VP Fiscal Services ... Ms. Deborah MCINTYRE
84 VP Enrollment Management ... Ms. Ina AGNEW
26 VP University & External Relations ... Ms. Anita GORDY-WATKINS
76 Allied Health Services ... Ms. Jana MARTIN
49 Arts & Sciences ... Dr. Mark ALLEN
72 Automotive Technologies ... Mr. Bill VOORHEES
72 Construction Technologies ... Mr. Steve OLMSTEAD
88 Culinary Arts ... Mr. Rene JUNGO
72 Engineering Technologies ... Mr. Mike TAYLOR
88 Heavy Equipment & Vehicle Institute ... Mr. Roy ACHEMIRE
77 Information Technologies ... Dr. Scott NEWMAN
88 Visual Communications ... Mr. James MCCULLOUGH
88 Automotive/HEVi ... Mr. Steve DOEDE
37 Dir Student Financial Services ... Ms. Mary Lou BLEDSOE
45 Dir Inst Assessment & Research ... Vacant
13 Dir Computer Information Systems ... Ms. Lori BRYANT
07 Dir Admissions & Records ... Ms. Genie TRAMMELL
15 Dir Human Resources ... Ms. Paula NORTH
18 Dir Physical Plant Services ... Mr. Bob SEEBECK
88 Dir Student Union & Auxiliary Svcs ... Mr. James BYRD
32 Dir Student Life ... Mr. Bruce FORCE
39 Dir Residential Life ... Mr. Devin DEBOCK
08 Dir Learning Resource Center ... Ms. Jenny DUNCAN
96 Dir Purchasing ... Mrs. Chandra MILLER
12 Dir MAIP-Pryor Campus ... Mr. Scott FRY
06 Registrar ... Mr. Adam DEATHERAGE
38 Counselor ... Ms. Kathy AVERY
40 Manager Bookstore ... Ms. Barbara WRIGHT
27 Public Relations Officer ... Mr. Rex DAUGHERTY
19 Campus Police Chief ... Mr. Steve RODRIQUEZ
04 Admin Asst to President ... Ms. Claudette BUTCHER

Oklahoma State University - Oklahoma City (F)

900 N Portland Ave, Oklahoma City OK 73107-6195
County: Oklahoma FICE Identification: 009647
Unit ID: 207397
Telephone: (405) 947-4421 Carnegie Class: Assoc/Pub4
FAX Number: (405) 945-3289 Calendar System: Semester
URL: www.osuokc.edu
Established: 1961 Annual Undergrad Tuition & Fees (In-State): $3,696
Enrollment: 7,647 Coed
Affiliation or Control: State IRS Status: 501(c)3
Highest Offering: Baccalaureate
Program: Occupational; 2-Year Principally Bachelor's Creditable; Technical Emphasis
Accreditation: NH, ADNUR, @DIETT, DMS

01 President ... Ms. Natalie SHIRLEY
05 Vice President Academic Affairs ... Dr. Larry G. EDWARDS
10 Vice President Finance & Operations ... Ms. Ronda REECE
32 Vice President Student Services ... Dr. Jay KINZER
50 Asst VP for Business and Industry ... Ms. Heather KAY
20 Associate VP Academic Affairs ... Ms. Kim PEARSALL
84 Director Enrollment Mgmt/Admissions ... Mr. Kyle WILLIAMS
30 Associate VP Development OKC Region ... Ms. Sue REEL
13 Senior Director Information Svcs ... Mr. Jonathan FOZARD
08 Librarian ... Mr. David ROBINSON
37 Director Financial Aid ... Ms. Dessie CARTER
15 Director Personnel Services ... Ms. Melissa HERREN
18 Chief Facilities/Physical Plant ... Mr. Wade REED
26 Chief Public Relations Officer ... Ms. Evelyn BOLLENBACH
07 Assistant Director of Admissions ... Ms. Melissa GARNER
72 Dir of Technology Education Center ... Ms. Adrainne COVINGTON-GRAHAM
29 Director Alumni Relations ... Dr. JoElla FIELDS
96 Director of Purchasing ... Ms. Sharon FITZPATRICK
06 Registrar ... Ms. Keila WHITACKER
09 Director Inst Grants & Research ... Ms. Anna ROYER

Oklahoma State University - Tulsa (G)

700 N Greenwood Avenue, Tulsa OK 74106-0702
County: Tulsa Identification: 666053
Telephone: (918) 594-8000 Carnegie Class: Not Classified
FAX Number: (918) 594-8009 Calendar System: Semester
URL: www.osu-tulsa.okstate.edu
Established: 1999 Annual Undergrad Tuition & Fees (In-State): $5,701
Enrollment: 3,118 Coed
Affiliation or Control: State IRS Status: 501(c)3
Highest Offering: Doctorate
Program: Liberal Arts And General; Professional; Business Emphasis
Accreditation: &NH

01 President ... Dr. Howard G. BARNETT, JR.
11 Vice Pres Administration/Finance ... Dr. Ronald BUSSERT
05 VP Academic Affs/Chief Acad Ofcr ... Dr. Raj BASU

† Regional accreditation is carried under the parent institution in Stillwater, OK.

Oklahoma Technical College (A)

4444 South Sheridan, Tulsa OK 74145-1122

County: Tulsa Identification: 666718
Telephone: (918) 895-7500 Carnegie Class: Not Classified
FAX Number: (918) 665-7335 Calendar System: Other
URL: www.oklahomatechnicalcollege.com
Established: 2009 Annual Undergrad Tuition & Fees: $17,535
Enrollment: 77 Coed
Affiliation or Control: Proprietary IRS Status: Proprietary
Highest Offering: Associate Degree
Program: Occupational; 2-Year Principally Bachelor's Creditable; Technical Emphasis
Accreditation: ACICS

00 Owner/Founder ... Ms. Teresa L. KNOX
01 Chief Executive Officer ... Mr. Robert BRESCIA

Oklahoma Wesleyan University (B)

2201 Silver Lake Road, Bartlesville OK 74006-6299

County: Washington FICE Identification: 003151
Unit ID: 206835
Telephone: (918) 333-6151 Carnegie Class: Bac/Diverse
FAX Number: (918) 335-6228 Calendar System: Semester
URL: www.okwu.edu
Established: 1910 Annual Undergrad Tuition & Fees: $20,160
Enrollment: 1,171 Coed
Affiliation or Control: Wesleyan Church IRS Status: 501(c)3
Highest Offering: Master's
Program: 2-Year Principally Bachelor's Creditable; Liberal Arts And General; Teacher Preparatory; Professional
Accreditation: NH, IACBE, NURSE, TED

01 President ... Dr. Everett G. PIPER
05 Exec Vice Pres for Academic Affairs ... Dr. Robert MYERS
10 Vice President for Business Affairs ... Mr. James GOINGS
30 Vice President for Development ... Dr. Randall THOMPSON
32 Vice President for Student Life ... Mr. Kyle WHITE
88 VP for Academic Program Development ... Dr. Brett ANDREWS
07 Vice President Admissions ... Mr. John MEANS
20 Assoc VP for Academic Affairs ... Dr. Mark WEETER
53 Dean of School of Education ... Dr. Sheldon BUXTON
73 Dean of School of Religion & Phil ... Dr. Mark WEETER
49 Dean of School of Arts & Sciences ... Mrs. Gail RICHARDSON
50 Dean of School of Business ... Dr. Brett ANDREWS
06 Registrar ... Mrs. Cindy RIFFE
37 Director of Financial Aid ... Mrs. Kandi MOLDER
21 Director of Business Affairs ... Mrs. Andrea ZEPEDA
15 Human Resources Administrator ... Ms. Jessica WELTY
08 Librarian ... Vacant
14 Director of Computer Services ... Mr. Eric GOINGS
41 Athletic Director ... Mr. Kirk KELLEY
04 Executive Assistant to President ... Mrs. Kathy LINDQUIST
29 Director of Alumni ... Mrs. Janet ODDEN
39 Director Student Housing ... Vacant
33 Men's Resident Director ... Mr. Michael WILSON
34 Women's Resident Director ... Ms. Lonna HUNTER
84 Asst Dir for Enrollment Services ... Vacant
23 Director Student Health ... Mrs. Debra COOK
18 Director of Buildings and Grounds ... Mr. Mark SPENCER
40 Bookstore Manager ... Mrs. Jessica JARRETT

Oral Roberts University (C)

7777 S Lewis, Tulsa OK 74171-0003

County: Tulsa FICE Identification: 003985
Unit ID: 207582
Telephone: (918) 495-6161 Carnegie Class: Master's S
FAX Number: (918) 495-6033 Calendar System: Semester
URL: www.oru.edu
Established: 1965 Annual Undergrad Tuition & Fees: $20,746
Enrollment: 3,212 Coed
Affiliation or Control: Independent Non-Profit IRS Status: 501(c)3
Highest Offering: Doctorate
Program: Liberal Arts And General; Teacher Preparatory; Professional
Accreditation: NH, ACBSP, ENG, MUS, NURSE, SW, TED, THEOL

01 President ... Dr. Mark RUTLAND
03 Provost ... Dr. Ralph FAGIN
10 EVP and Chief Financial Officer ... Ms. Michelle FINLEY
11 EVP and Chief Operations Officer ... Mr. Tim PHILLEY
05 VP Academic Affairs ... Dr. Debra SOWELL
26 Vice Pres for University Relations ... Vacant
84 VP for Enrollment Management ... Dr. Nancy BRAINARD
88 VP of Sponsored Pgm & Admn Affairs ... Ms. Kelly BAILEY
13 Chief Information Officer ... Mr. Mark BENDER
21 Controller ... Ms. Ann Marie ELFRINK
42 Dean of Spiritual Formation ... Dr. Clarence BOYD
32 Dean of Student Development ... Dr. Dan GUAJARDO
08 Dean Learning Resources ... Dr. William JERNIGAN
50 Dean Col of Science & Engineering ... Dr. Dominic HALSMER
49 Dean Col of Arts & Cultural Studies ... Dr. Wendy SHIRK
73 Dean College Theology/Ministry ... Dr. Thomson MATHEW
50 Dean College of Business ... Dr. Steven GREENE
66 Dean & Chairman College of Nursing ... Dr. Kenda JEZEK
53 Dean College of Education ... Dr. Kim BOYD
33 Dean of Men ... Mr. Matthew OLSEN
34 Dean of Women ... Ms. Lori SYLVESTER
09 Director of Institutional Research ... Dr. Cal EASTERLING
41 Director for Athletics ... Mr. Mike CARTER
25 Director of Sponsored Programs ... Ms. Kim FALCON
38 Director of Student Counseling ... Ms. Michelle TAYLOR
89 Director of Freshmen Studies ... Mr. Danny ZIRIAX
92 Director of Honors Program ... Dr. John KORSTAD
21 Director Student Accounts ... Mr. Steve THANNICKAL
96 Director of Purchasing ... Ms. Jeanine HORTON
06 Registrar ... Mr. David FULMER
07 Director Admission ... Mr. Chris BELCHER
37 Director of Financial Aid ... Mr. William WOMACK
29 Director of Alumni Relations ... Mr. Jesse PISORS
19 Director of Security/Safety ... Mr. Jerry ISAACS
15 Director of Human Resources ... Mr. Bill WEBB
36 Director of Student Placement ... Ms. Allison JONES

Phillips Theological Seminary (D)

901 N Mingo Road, Tulsa OK 74116-5612

County: Tulsa FICE Identification: 025602
Unit ID: 414966
Telephone: (918) 610-8303 Carnegie Class: Spec/Faith
FAX Number: (918) 610-8404 Calendar System: Semester
URL: www.ptstulsa.edu
Established: 1907 Annual Graduate Tuition & Fees: $12,430
Enrollment: 169 Coed
Affiliation or Control: Christian Church (Disciples Of Christ)
IRS Status: 501(c)3
Highest Offering: Doctorate; No Undergraduates
Program: Professional; Religious Emphasis
Accreditation: NH, THEOL

01 President ... Gary PELUSO-VERDEND
51 Special Assistant to the President ... John M. IMBLER
05 Vice Pres Academic Affairs & Dean ... Don A. PITTMAN
30 Vice Pres Stewardship ... Brandi SULLIVAN
20 Assoc Dean Assessment and Faculty ... Joseph BESSLER
07 Assoc Dean Admissions/Student Svcs ... Belva Brown JORDAN
20 Assoc Dn/Dir Supervised Ministries ... John THOMAS
10 Chief Financial Officer ... Lora CONGER
88 Director Doctor of Ministry Program ... Nancy PITTMAN
07 Director of Recruitment ... Linda FORD
37 Director Student Financial Aid ... Ann JORDAN
08 Director of Library ... Sandy SHAPOVAL
44 Director of Planned Giving ... Virginia WALKER
29 Director of Alumni Relations ... Geoffrey BREWSTER
04 Executive Assistant to President ... Melanie K. TIPTON

Platt College (E)

309 South Ann Arbor Avenue,
Oklahoma City OK 73128-1112

County: Oklahoma Identification: 666341
Unit ID: 445258
Telephone: (405) 946-7799 Carnegie Class: Assoc/PrivFP4
FAX Number: (405) 943-2150 Calendar System: Other
URL: www.plattcollege.org
Established: 1979 Annual Undergrad Tuition & Fees: $28,500
Enrollment: 418 Coed
Affiliation or Control: Proprietary IRS Status: Proprietary
Highest Offering: Associate Degree
Program: Occupational; Nursing Emphasis
Accreditation: ACCSC, ACFEI, SURGT

01 Director ... Ms. Jane R. NOWLIN

† Branch campus of Platt College, Tulsa, OK.

Platt College (F)

3801 S Sheridan, Tulsa OK 74145-1132

County: Tulsa FICE Identification: 023068
Unit ID: 245962
Telephone: (918) 663-9000 Carnegie Class: Assoc/PrivFP
FAX Number: (918) 622-1240 Calendar System: Other
URL: www.plattcollege.org
Established: 1979 Annual Undergrad Tuition & Fees: $28,500
Enrollment: 600 Coed
Affiliation or Control: Proprietary IRS Status: Proprietary
Highest Offering: Baccalaureate
Program: Occupational
Accreditation: ACCSC

01 President ... Mr. Mike A. PUGLIESE
05 Director of Campus ... Ms. Stephanie THRASHER
66 Director of Nursing LPN Program ... Ms. Gay L. PEARCE
07 Director of Admission & Marketing ... Mr. Richard DIXON

Redlands Community College (G)

1300 S Country Club Road, El Reno OK 73036-5304

County: Canadian FICE Identification: 003156
Unit ID: 207069
Telephone: (405) 262-2552 Carnegie Class: Assoc/Pub-S-SC
FAX Number: (405) 422-1200 Calendar System: Semester
URL: www.redlandscc.edu
Established: 1938 Annual Undergrad Tuition & Fees (In-District): $3,210
Enrollment: 2,576 Coed
Affiliation or Control: State/Local IRS Status: 501(c)3
Highest Offering: Associate Degree
Program: Occupational; 2-Year Principally Bachelor's Creditable
Accreditation: NH, ADNUR

01 President ... Dr. Larry F. DEVANE
05 Vice President Instruction ... Mr. Bill BAKER
103 VP Workforce/Economic Development ... Mr. Jack BRYANT
10 Vice Pres Finance/Campus Services ... Mrs. Karen BOUCHER
30 VP Inst Advancement/Student Svcs ... Mr. Joel DRURY
88 Vice Pres Undergraduate Research ... Dr. Amanda EVERT
18 Director Physical Plant ... Mr. Richard BUCHHOLZ
76 Director Nursing/Allied Health ... Mrs. Deborah BUTTTRUM
72 Dir Liberal Studies/Mgmt Science ... Dr. Juanita KRITTENBRINK
81 Dir Math/Science/Developmental Stds ... Ms. Barbara KNOP-COX
08 Director Learning Resource Center ... Mrs. Christine DETTLAFF
06 Registrar/Director Student Records ... Mr. Dennis HARRIS
37 Director Financial Aid ... Mrs. Karen JEFFERS
41 Athletic Director ... Mr. Matt NEWGENT
14 Director Administrative Computing ... Mr. Troy MILLIGAN
22 Director of Upward Bound ... Ms. Toni MAXWELL
09 Director of Institutional Research ... Mr. Troy MILLIGAN
84 Director Enrollment Management ... Mrs. Tricia HOBSON
21 Associate Business Officer ... Mrs. Maxine CALVERT
56 Coordinator Alternative Education ... Ms. Arlie SCHRODER
36 Coordinator Career Services ... Mrs. Terri BARGER
15 Coordinator Personnel/Payroll ... Mrs. Kim ANDRADE
26 Coordinator Public Information ... Ms. Deirdre STEINER
29 Coordinator Alumni Relations ... Mrs. Athena JARVIS
32 Coordinator of Resident Life ... Ms. Margie MOORE

Rogers State University (H)

1701 W Will Rogers Boulevard,
Claremore OK 74017-2099

County: Rogers FICE Identification: 003168
Unit ID: 207661
Telephone: (918) 343-7777 Carnegie Class: Bac/Assoc
FAX Number: (918) 343-7898 Calendar System: Semester
URL: www.rsu.edu
Established: 1909 Annual Undergrad Tuition & Fees (In-State): $4,513
Enrollment: 4,386 Coed
Affiliation or Control: State IRS Status: 501(c)3
Highest Offering: Baccalaureate
Program: 2-Year Principally Bachelor's Creditable; Liberal Arts And General; Business Emphasis
Accreditation: NH, ADNUR, NUR

01 President ... Dr. Larry D. RICE
05 Vice President for Academic Affairs ... Dr. Richard BECK
03 Exec VP for Admin & Finance ... Mr. Tom VOLTURO
30 Vice President for Development ... Vacant
32 Vice Pres for Student Affairs ... Dr. Tobie TITSWORTH
35 Director of Student Development ... Ms. Misty SMITH
31 Vice Pres Community/Economic Devel ... Dr. Ray BROWN
09 Asst VP Accountability & Academics ... Dr. Mary MILLIKIN
12 Director Pryor Campus ... Ms. Sherry ALEXANDER
12 Provost Bartlesville Campus ... Mr. Bill BEIERSCHMITT
50 Dean School of Business & Tech ... Dr. Bruce GARRISON
83 Dean School of Liberal Arts ... Dr. Frank ELWELL
81 Dean Sch of Math/Sci/Hlth Sci ... Dr. Keith MARTIN
04 Assistant to the President ... Ms. Sharon KERN
08 Director of the Library ... Mr. J. Alan LAWLESS
07 Director of Admissions ... Ms. Julie RAMPEY
06 Registrar ... Ms. Cheryl HASSELL
29 Director Alumni & Special Events ... Ms. Marisa LITTLEFIELD
21 Comptroller/Asst Vice Pres Bus Affs ... Mr. Mark MEADORS
04 Exec Assistant to the President ... Ms. Rhonda SPURLOCK
18 Director Physical Plant ... Mr. Leonard SZOPINSKI
19 Director Campus Public Safety ... Mr. Gary BOERGERMANN
27 Director Public Information ... Mr. Brent ORTOLANI
37 Director of Financial Aid ... Mr. David BARRON
91 Director Administrative Computing ... Ms. Cathy BURNS
90 Director Information Technology ... Mr. Brian REEVES
15 Employment & Benefits Coordinator ... Ms. Kristi MALLETT
41 Director of Athletics ... Mr. Ryan BRADLEY
39 Director Residential Life ... Ms. Kyla SHORT
23 Director Student Health Clinic ... Ms. Lisa MARTIN

Rose State College (I)

6420 SE 15th, Midwest City OK 73110-2799

County: Oklahoma FICE Identification: 009185
Unit ID: 207670
Telephone: (405) 733-7311 Carnegie Class: Assoc/Pub-S-SC
FAX Number: (405) 733-7399 Calendar System: Semester
URL: www.rose.edu
Established: 1970 Annual Undergrad Tuition & Fees (In-District): $2,849
Enrollment: 9,668 Coed
Affiliation or Control: State/Local IRS Status: 501(c)3
Highest Offering: Associate Degree
Program: Occupational; 2-Year Principally Bachelor's Creditable
Accreditation: NH, ADNUR, DA, DH, MLTAD, RAD

01 President ... Dr. Terry BRITTON
05 Vice President for Academic Affairs ... Dr. Frances HENDRIX
10 Vice President for Business Affairs ... Mr. Keith OGANS
32 Vice President for Student Affairs ... Dr. Jeanie WEBB
14 Vice President for Info Technology ... Mr. John PRIMO
103 Vice President for Workforce Devel ... Mr. Stan GREIL
84 Asoc Vice Pres Enrollment Mgmt ... Mr. Dean FISHER
20 Associate VP Academic Affairs ... Dr. Jeff CALDWELL
35 Assoc Vice Pres for Student Life ... Dr. Kent LASHLEY
30 Exec Dir Institutional Advancement ... Ms. Lisa PITSIRI
16 Exec Dir Human Res/Affirm Act Ofcr ... Dr. Jana LEGAKO
06 Registrar/Dir Admissions & Records ... Ms. Mechelle AITSON-ROESSLER

37 Director Financial Aid — Mr. Steve DAFFER
26 Director Marketing/Public Relations — Mr. John CAIN
31 Director Community Learning Center — Mr. Joey DAVAULT
18 Director Operations — Mr. Ardie RODGERS
41 Dir Health & Wellness Activities — Mr. Chris LELAND
09 Dir Information Sys/Inst Research — Ms. Isabelle BILLEN
21 Director of Finance — Mr. Raymond BLANKE
36 Director Spec Svcs/Student Outreach — Dr. Joanne STAFFORD
25 Dir Grants and Contracts — Dr. Alan NEITZEL
29 Director Alumni Relations — Ms. Lindsay LANCASTER
08 Dean Learning Resources Center — Ms. Sharon SAULMON
50 Dean Business & Info Tech Division — Mr. Art ZENNER
54 Dean Engineering & Science Division — Mr. Dawcett MIDDLETON
79 Dean Humanities Division — Dr. Betty EDWARDS
76 Dean Health Sciences Division — Mr. Dan POINTS
83 Dean Social Sciences Division — Dr. Bret WOOD

St. Gregory's University (A)

1900 W MacArthur, Shawnee OK 74804-2499

County: Pottawatomie — FICE Identification: 003183
Unit ID: 207689
Telephone: (405) 878-5100 — Carnegie Class: Bac/Diverse
FAX Number: (405) 878-5198 — Calendar System: Semester
URL: www.stgregorys.edu
Established: 1875 — Annual Undergrad Tuition & Fees: $17,790
Enrollment: 749 — Coed
Affiliation or Control: Roman Catholic — IRS Status: 501(c)3
Highest Offering: Master's
Program: Liberal Arts And General; Technical Emphasis
Accreditation: NH

01 President — Mr. Gregory MAIN
03 Executive Vice President — Vacant
05 Provost — Dr. Janet W. SHEERAN
30 Director of Institutional Advance — Ms. Faith DELEHANTY
10 Int VP Finance & Administration — Mr. Terry MCCULLAR
88 VP for Mission & Identity — Rev. Nicholas AST
55 Dean College for Working Adults — Dr. Jean THORNBRUGH
49 Dean College of Arts & Sciences — Dr. Ron H. FAULK
32 Dean of Student Life — Mr. Joshua CLARY
06 Registrar — Mrs. Kay K. STITH
08 Library Director — Mrs. Anita SEMTNER
26 Director of Public Relations — Mr. Brad M. COLLINS
38 Director Student Counseling — Mrs. Melody HARRINGTON
37 Director Student Financial Aid — Ms. Debra GAMBILL
84 Assoc VP for Enrollment — Mr. Ronald G. BROWN
41 Athletic Director — Mr. Don SUMNER
85 Director of International Office — Mr. Spencer RYAN
15 Director of Human Resources — Mrs. Natalie R. MONTOYA
18 Co-Dir Facilities/Physical Plant — Mr. Joe CRUZ
18 Co-Dir Facilities/Physical Plant — Mr. Mark SAUNDERS
13 Interim Dir of Information Sys — Mr. Max A. JENKINS

Seminole State College (B)

PO Box 351, Seminole OK 74818-0351

County: Seminole — FICE Identification: 003178
Unit ID: 207740
Telephone: (405) 382-9950 — Carnegie Class: Assoc/Pub-R-M
FAX Number: (405) 382-3122 — Calendar System: Semester
URL: www.sscok.edu
Established: 1931 — Annual Undergrad Tuition & Fees (In-District): $3,180
Enrollment: 2,346 — Coed
Affiliation or Control: State/Local — IRS Status: 501(c)3
Highest Offering: Associate Degree
Program: Occupational; 2-Year Principally Bachelor's Creditable
Accreditation: NH, ADNUR, MLTAD

01 President — Dr. Jim W. UTTERBACK
05 Vice President for Academic Affairs — Dr. Paul GASPARRO
32 Vice President for Student Affairs — Dr. Brad WALCK
10 Vice President Fiscal Affairs — Mrs. Katherine BENTON
30 Vice Pres Institutional Advancement — Ms. Lana REYNOLDS
84 Director of Enrollment Management — Dr. Mark AMES
13 Director Mgmt Information Systems — Mr. Jack WHISENNAND
08 Librarian/Director Education Media — Mrs. Marguerite HEAROD
66 Director of Nursing — Mrs. Donna CHAMBERS
06 Registrar — Mrs. Debbie ROBERTSON
15 Director Personnel Services — Mrs. Courtney JONES
18 Chief Facilities/Physical Plant — Mr. Braden BROWN
20 Associate Academic Officer — Ms. Pam KOENIG
26 Coordinator of Media Relations — Ms. Dustie BUTNER

Southeastern Oklahoma State University (C)

1405 N 4th Avenue, Durant OK 74701-3330

County: Bryan — FICE Identification: 003179
Unit ID: 207847
Telephone: (580) 745-2000 — Carnegie Class: Master's M
FAX Number: (580) 745-2515 — Calendar System: Semester
URL: www.se.edu
Established: 1909 — Annual Undergrad Tuition & Fees (In-State): $4,465
Enrollment: 4,181 — Coed
Affiliation or Control: State — IRS Status: 501(c)3
Highest Offering: Master's
Program: Liberal Arts And General; Teacher Preparatory; Professional
Accreditation: NH, AAB, ACBSP, BUS, MUS, TED

01 President — Dr. Larry MINKS
05 Int Exec Vice Pres Acad Affairs — Dr. Douglas MCMILLAN
10 Vice President Business Services — Mr. Ross WALKUP
32 Vice President Student Services — Ms. Sharon ROBINSON
88 Vice Pres Educ Outreach & Proj Dev — Dr. Douglas MCMILLAN
20 AVP Acad Aff/Supprt/Dn Grad Studies — Dr. William Jerry POLSON
20 Asst VP Academic Affs/Instruction — Dr. Bryon CLARK
04 Exec Asst to President — Ms. Michele CAMPBELL
35 Dean of Students — Dr. Camille PHELPS
49 Dean Arts & Sciences — Dr. Lucretia SCOUFOS
50 Dean School of Business — Dr. Buddy GASTER
53 Dean Sch Educ/Behavior Sciences — Dr. William MAWER
07 Assoc Dean Admissions/Registrar — Ms. Kristie LUKE
88 Assoc Dean Academic Services — Mr. Tim BOATMUN
13 Exec Dir of Information Technology — Dr. Dan MOORE
30 Exec Director of Univ Advancement — Mr. Kyle STAFFORD
37 Director Student Financial Aid — Mr. Tony LEHRLING
36 Director of Career Management Ctr — Mr. Scott HENSLEY
08 Library Director — Ms. Sharon MORRISON
51 Director Continuing Education — Mr. Scott HENSLEY
41 Director of Athletics — Mr. Keith BAXTER
26 Director University Communications — Mr. Alan BURTON
15 Director Human Resources — Mrs. Cathy CONWAY
21 Director Finance/Controller — Ms. Kay Lynn ROBERTS
38 Director Student Counseling — Ms. Jane MCMILLAN
18 Director Facilities/Physical Plant — Mr. Eddie HARBIN
28 Special Asst to the Pres/Diversity — Dr. Claire STUBBLEFIELD
96 Purchasing Agent — Mrs. Carol COATS
40 Book Store Manager — Ms. Jackie CODNER
29 Director Alumni Relations — Ms. Stephanie SHADE-DAVISON

Southern Nazarene University (D)

6729 NW 39 Expressway, Bethany OK 73008-2694

County: Oklahoma — FICE Identification: 003149
Unit ID: 206862
Telephone: (405) 789-6400 — Carnegie Class: Master's L
FAX Number: (405) 491-6381 — Calendar System: Semester
URL: www.snu.edu
Established: 1899 — Annual Undergrad Tuition & Fees: $19,170
Enrollment: 2,051 — Coed
Affiliation or Control: Church Of The Nazarene — IRS Status: 501(c)3
Highest Offering: Master's
Program: Liberal Arts And General; Teacher Preparatory; Professional; Business Emphasis
Accreditation: NH, @ACBSP, MUS, NURSE, TED

01 President — Dr. Loren P. GRESHAM
03 Provost — Dr. Mary JONES
05 Acting Vice Pres Academic Affairs — Dr. Mary JONES
10 Vice President Financial Affairs — Ms. Donna NANCE
30 VP of Univ Advance & Church Rels — Dr. Terry TOLER
32 Vice President Student Development — Dr. Scott STRAWN
42 Vice Pres Spiritual Development — Dr. Brad STRAWN
84 Vice Pres of Enrollment Management — Mr. Mike REDWINE
20 Dean College of Humanities — Dr. Melany KYZER
81 Interim Dean Col of Sci & Health — Dr. Dennis WILLIAMS
06 Registrar — Mr. Charles CHITWOOD
07 Director Admissions — Dr. Linda CANTWELL
37 Director Student Financial Aid — Ms. Diana LEE
35 Director Student Affairs — Mrs. Marian REDWINE
38 Director Student Counseling — Mrs. Kimberly CAMPBELL
36 Director Career Planning/Placement — Mr. Chris PETERSON
08 Director Learning Resources Center — Dr. Arlita HARRIS
29 Director Alumni Relations — Ms. Kendra THOMSON
14 Director Information Technology — Mrs. Laureen SPRINGER
88 Director Academic Services — Mr. Wes LEE
09 Director Institutional Research — Vacant
58 Dean Col of Grad & Prof Study — Dr. Davis BERRYMAN
66 Director of Nursing — Dr. Katie SIGLER
15 Director Human Resources — Mr. Rick POWELL
18 Director of Physical Plant — Mr. Ron LESTER
24 Director Network — Mrs. Chichi FREELANDER
26 Director Communications & Marketing — Ms. Kendra THOMSON
40 Bookstore Manager — Mr. Reggie COLEMAN
41 Athletic Director — Mr. Bobby MARTIN
88 Dean College of Teach & Learn — Dr. Dennis WILLIAMS
50 Dean Col of Bus/Educ & KSM — Dr. Sylvia GOODMAN

Southwestern Christian University (E)

PO Box 340, 7210 NW 39th Expressway, Bethany OK 73008-0340

County: Oklahoma — FICE Identification: 003180
Unit ID: 207856
Telephone: (405) 789-7661 — Carnegie Class: Bac/Diverse
FAX Number: (405) 495-0078 — Calendar System: Semester
URL: www.swcu.edu
Established: 1946 — Annual Undergrad Tuition & Fees: $11,850
Enrollment: 390 — Coed
Affiliation or Control: Pentecostal Holiness Church — IRS Status: 501(c)3
Highest Offering: Master's
Program: Liberal Arts And General; Religious Emphasis
Accreditation: NH

01 President — Dr. Ed HUCKEBY
05 Provost & VP Academic Affairs — Dr. Reggies WENYIKA
10 Vice President for Fiscal Affairs — Mr. Wallace O. HAMILTON
30 Vice President for Advance/Develop — Mr. Jon R. CHASTEEN
32 Vice President for Student Affairs — Mr. David H. CHISSOE
41 Athletic Director — Mr. Mark ARTHUR
37 Director of Financial Aid — Mrs. Billie STEWART
07 Director of Admissions & Enrollment — Mr. Chad PUGH
08 Director of Library Services — Mrs. Marilyn HUDSON
06 Registrar — Mrs. Jean PERDUE
58 Dean of Adult & Graduate Studies — Dr. Terry TRAMEL
107 Dean of Professional Studies — Mrs. Adrian HINKLE
49 Dean of Arts & Sciences — Dr. Donna MCCOY
18 Director of Plant/Property Mgmt — Mr. Jeff PATTERSON
26 Director of Sports Information/PR — Ms. Kasey GARDNER
13 Director of Information Technology — Mr. David WIGGINS

Southwestern Oklahoma State University (F)

100 Campus Drive, Weatherford OK 73096-3098

County: Custer — FICE Identification: 003181
Unit ID: 207865
Telephone: (580) 772-6611 — Carnegie Class: Master's M
FAX Number: (580) 774-3795 — Calendar System: Semester
URL: www.swosu.edu
Established: 1901 — Annual Undergrad Tuition & Fees (In-State): $4,590
Enrollment: 5,399 — Coed
Affiliation or Control: State — IRS Status: 501(c)3
Highest Offering: First Professional Degree
Program: Liberal Arts And General; Teacher Preparatory; Professional
Accreditation: NH, ENGT, IACBE, MLTAB, MUS, NAIT, NUR, OTA, PHAR, PTAA, RAD, SW, TED

01 President — Dr. Randy L. BEUTLER
05 Senior Vice President & Provost — Dr. Blake I. SONOBE
10 Vice Pres Administration & Finance — Mr. Thomas W. FAGAN
30 Asst to Pres for Inst Advancement — Ms. Lynne F. THURMAN
32 VP Student Affairs/Assoc Provost — Dr. Cynthia R. FOUST
26 Assoc VP Marketing/Public Relations — Mr. Brian D. ADLER
10 Dir Business Affairs/Comptroller — Ms. Brenda K. BURGESS
35 Dean of Students/Dir Student Act — Ms. Cynthia R. DOUGHERTY
13 Dir Information Technology Services — Mr. Mark D. ENGELMAN
06 Registrar — Mr. Daniel R. ARCHER
08 Library Director — Dr. Jonathan D. SPARKS
37 Director Student Financial Services — Mr. Jerome L. WICHERT
15 Dir Human Resources/Affirm Action — Mr. M. David MISAK
84 Dir Enrollment Mgmt/Career Svcs — Mr. Todd T. BOYD
57 Director Fine Arts Center — Mr. Kevin J. BARTEL
41 Athletic Director — Mr. Todd A. THURMAN
09 Director Institutional Research — Ms. Denisa A. ENGELMAN
06 Registrar Sayre Campus — Ms. G. Kim SEYMOUR
37 Dir Financial Svcs/Sayre Campus — Mr. Ron KISTLER
38 Director Counseling Services — Ms. Kim K. LIEBSCHER
18 Director Physical Plant — Mr. Rick SKINNER
36 Asst Director Career Services — Ms. Tiffany HAWKINS
58 Dean College of Prof/Grad Studies — Dr. Ken G. ROSE
49 Dean College of Arts & Sciences — Dr. Radwan A. AL-JARRAH
67 Interim Dean College of Pharmacy — Dr. Dennis F. THOMPSON
12 Dean College of Assoc/Applied Prog — Dr. Jim R. JAMES
76 Associate Dean Sch of Allied Health — Dr. Gary D. WOLGAMOTT
53 Assoc Dean Sch of Behavioral Sci — Dr. L. Chad KINDER
50 Assoc Dean School of Business/Tech — Dr. Leslie D. CRALL
66 Associate Dean School of Nursing — Dr. Barbara A. PATTERSON

† Campus at Sayre offers a two-year degree and is regionally accredited (NH) under parent institution. Other specialized accreditation: RAD, MLTAB.

Spartan College of Aeronautics and Technology (G)

8820 E Pine Street, Tulsa OK 74115

County: Tulsa — FICE Identification: 007678
Unit ID: 207254
Telephone: (918) 836-6886 — Carnegie Class: Spec/Tech
FAX Number: (918) 831-5287 — Calendar System: Other
URL: www.spartan.edu
Established: 1928 — Annual Undergrad Tuition & Fees: $15,000
Enrollment: 1,286 — Coed
Affiliation or Control: Proprietary — IRS Status: Proprietary
Highest Offering: Baccalaureate
Program: Occupational; 2-Year Principally Bachelor's Creditable; Technical Emphasis
Accreditation: ACCSC

01 CEO/President — Mr. Jeremy GIBSON
10 CFO/Vice President Finance — Mr. Blaine WALKER
05 Vice Pres Educ/Lic/Accreditation — Mr. Ryan GOERTZEN
11 Vice President Administration — Mr. Dean RILING

Tulsa Community College (H)

6111 E Skelly Drive, Tulsa OK 74135-6198

County: Tulsa — FICE Identification: 009763
Unit ID: 207935
Telephone: (918) 595-7000 — Carnegie Class: Assoc/Pub-U-MC
FAX Number: (918) 595-7910 — Calendar System: Semester
URL: www.tulsacc.edu
Established: 1968 — Annual Undergrad Tuition & Fees (In-State): $3,043
Enrollment: 26,815 — Coed
Affiliation or Control: State — IRS Status: 501(c)3
Highest Offering: Associate Degree
Program: Occupational; 2-Year Principally Bachelor's Creditable
Accreditation: NH, ADNUR, DH, MAC, MLTAD, OTA, PTAA, RAD

01 President — Dr. Thomas K. MCKEON
04 Assistant to the President — Ms. Norma L. RODGERS
10 Vice President & CFO — Mr. Jeff NEVINS
05 Vice President & CAO — Dr. Ric N. BASER

32 Assoc Vice Pres Student Affairs ... Ms. Jan L. CLAYTON
20 Assoc Vice Pres Academic Affairs ... Dr. Donna G. WOOD
15 Asst Vice Pres for Human Resources ... Ms. Patricia L. FISCHER
12 Provost Southeast Campus ... Dr. Brett S. CAMPBELL
12 Provost Northeast Campus ... Dr. John GIBSON
12 Provost Metro Campus ... Dr. Flo E. POTTS
12 Provost West Campus ... Dr. Peggy D. DYER
26 Vice President External Affairs ... Ms. Lauren F. BROOKEY
08 Dean Learning Res Ctr/Librarian ... Mr. Michael J. RUSK
28 Dean of Diversity/Civic Engagement ... Mr. Tony J. ALONSO
51 Dean of Continuing Education ... Dr. Cheryl J. MARRS
18 Director Physical Facilities ... Ms. Jemina C. LOTTI
13 Chief Technology Officer ... Mr. Sean A. WEINS
37 Dir Financial Aid/Scholarship Svcs ... Vacant
96 Dir Purch & Inventory Control ... Mr. Bill CREECH
07 Dir Admissions Records Registration ... Ms. Traci HECK
09 Dir Planning/Inst Research ... Dr. Mary A. MILLIKIN
19 Director Campus Police ... Mr. William M. HORTON
40 Director Campus Store Operations ... Mr. Ken A. JONES
27 Director Marketing Communications ... Ms. Sue A. BROWN
21 Director Administrative Services ... Dr. Frederick D. ARTIS
92 Director of Honors Program ... Ms. Susan ONEAL

Tulsa Welding School (A)

2545 E 11th Street, Tulsa OK 74104-3909

County: Tulsa — FICE Identification: 009618
Unit ID: 207962
Telephone: (918) 587-6789 — Carnegie Class: Assoc/PrivFP
FAX Number: (918) 587-8170 — Calendar System: Other
URL: www.weldingschool.com
Established: 1949 — Annual Undergrad Tuition & Fees: $16,977
Enrollment: 1,030 — Coed
Affiliation or Control: Proprietary — IRS Status: Proprietary
Highest Offering: Associate Degree
Program: Occupational
Accreditation: ACCSC

01 President ... Ms. Mary KELLY
03 Vice Pres/Executive Director ... Mrs. Debbie BURKE
05 Director of Training ... Mr. David GILLIAM
07 Director of Admissions ... Mr. Mike THURBER
37 Director of Financial Aid ... Mrs. Teresa FRANKLIN
36 Director of Employment ... Mr. Alan CURLER

University of Central Oklahoma (B)

100 N University Drive, Edmond OK 73034-5209

County: Oklahoma — FICE Identification: 003152
Unit ID: 206941
Telephone: (405) 974-2000 — Carnegie Class: Master's L
FAX Number: (405) 341-4964 — Calendar System: Semester
URL: www.uco.edu
Established: 1890 — Annual Undergrad Tuition & Fees (In-State): $4,995
Enrollment: 17,101 — Coed
Affiliation or Control: State — IRS Status: 501(c)3
Highest Offering: Master's
Program: Liberal Arts And General; Teacher Preparatory; Professional
Accreditation: NH, ACBSP, CIDA, CS, DIETD, DIETI, ENG, EXSC, FUSER, MUS, NUR, SP, TED

01 President ... Dr. W. Roger WEBB
03 Executive Vice President ... Mr. Steve KREIDLER
05 Provost/Vice Pres Academic Affairs ... Dr. William RADKE
32 Vice President Student Affairs ... Dr. Kathryn GAGE
13 Vice President Information Tech ... Dr. Cynthia ROLFE
84 Vice Pres Enrollment Management ... Dr. Myron POPE
26 Vice Pres University Relations ... Mr. Charlie JOHNSON
11 Assoc VP Administration ... Mr. Mark MOORE
20 Vice Prov/Assoc VP Academic Affairs ... Dr. Patricia LAGROW
20 Asst Vice Pres Academic Affairs ... Dr. Lori BEASLEY
10 Asst VP Admin Financial Services ... Ms. Lisa HARPER
18 Asst Vice Pres Admin/Facilities Mgt ... Mr. Mark RODOLF
35 Asst Vice Pres Student Affairs ... Mr. Cole STANLEY
04 Special Assistant to President ... Ms. Amy ROGALSKY
102 President UCO Foundation ... Mrs. Anne HOLZBERLEIN
41 Athletic Director ... Mr. Joe MULLER
04 Executive in Residence ... Dr. Douglas FOX
09 Director Institutional Research ... Ms. Cindy BOLING
31 Exec Director Auxiliary Enterprises ... Mr. Robert LINDLEY
08 Exec Director University Libraries ... Dr. Bonnie MCNEELY
37 Director Student Financial Aid ... Ms. Susan PRATER
29 Director Alumni Relations ... Mr. Al JONES
38 Dir Counsel/Test/Disabl Support Svc ... Dr. Bruce LOCHNER
85 Director International Student Svcs ... Dr. Dennis DUNHAM
39 Director Residential Life ... Mr. Josh OVEROCKER
19 Director Public Safety ... Mr. Jeff HARP
23 Director Wellness Center ... Mr. Mark HERRIN
14 Director Project Management ... Ms. Sandra THOMAS
15 Director Employee Services ... Ms. Jeanette PATTON
88 Exec Dir Leadership Central ... Dr. Cheryl STEELE
36 Career Counselor ... Ms. Carrol MCALLISTER
22 Equity/Affirmative Action Officer ... Dr. Brad MORELLI
50 Dean of Business Administration ... Dr. Mickey HEPNER
53 Dean College Education ... Dr. James MACHELL
49 Dean College of Liberal Arts ... Dr. Pamela WASHINGTON
81 Dean College Math/Science ... Dr. John BARTHELL
58 Dean Graduate Studies ... Dr. Richard BERNARD
57 Dean College Fine Arts & Design ... Dr. John CLINTON

University of Oklahoma Norman Campus (C)

660 Parrington Oval, Norman OK 73019-3070

County: Cleveland — FICE Identification: 003184
Unit ID: 207500
Telephone: (405) 325-0311 — Carnegie Class: RU/VH
FAX Number: (405) 325-7605 — Calendar System: Semester
URL: www.ou.edu
Established: 1890 — Annual Undergrad Tuition & Fees (In-State): $5,750
Enrollment: 26,478 — Coed
Affiliation or Control: State — IRS Status: 501(c)3
Highest Offering: Doctorate
Program: Liberal Arts And General; Teacher Preparatory; Professional
Accreditation: NH, AAB, BUS, BUSA, CIDA, CONST, COPSY, CS, ENG, JOUR, LAW, LIB, LSAR, MUS, PLNG, SW, TED, THEA

01 President ... Mr. David L. BOREN
03 Exec VP Administration & Finance ... Mr. Nick HATHAWAY
101 VP Univ Gov/Exec Secy Bd of Regents ... Dr. Chris PURCELL
05 Senior Vice President/Provost ... Dr. Nancy L. MERGLER
43 VP of Univ/General Counsel ... Mr. Anil GOLLAHALLI
11 Assoc VP Administration & Finance ... Mr. Byron MILLSAP
32 Vice President for Student Affairs ... Mr. Clarke STROUD
30 Vice Pres for University Devel ... Mr. Jim HALL, III
51 VP Univ Outreach Col/Dn Col Lib Std ... Dr. James P. PAPPAS
58 Dean Grad College ... Dr. T. H. Lee WILLIAMS
46 Vice President for Research ... Dr. Kelvin DROEGEMEIER
26 Vice President for Public Affairs ... Ms. Catherine BISHOP
13 Assoc VP/Interim Chief Info Ofcr ... Ms. Loretta EARLY
86 Vice Pres for Governmental Relation ... Mr. Danny C. HILLIARD
20 Associate Provost/Dir of Acad Integ ... Dr. Gregory M. HEISER
20 Assoc Provost for Academic Advising ... Dr. Joyce L. ALLMAN
09 Assoc Provost/Dir Inst Research ... Ms. Cheryl K. JORGENSON
06 Registrar/VP Enroll/Stdnt Fin Svcs ... Mr. Matt HAMILTON
35 Director Student Life ... Ms. Kristen PARTRIDGE
10 Chief Fin Ofcr/AVP Admin & Finance ... Mr. Chris KUWITZKY
29 Assoc VP/Exc Dir OU Assc/Alumni Aff ... Mr. Rennie COOK
18 Director Physical Plant ... Mr. Brian ELLIS
39 Director of Housing & Food Services ... Mr. David L. ANNIS
41 Director of Athletics ... Mr. Joe CASTIGLIONE
21 Controller ... Ms. Terri B. PINKSTON
21 Dir of Financial Support Services ... Ms. Karen CAGLEY
23 Director Goddard Health Center ... Dr. William WAYNE
36 Director Career Services ... Ms. Bette J. SCOTT
19 Chief of Police ... Ms. Liz WOOLLEN
15 Director of Human Resources ... Mr. Julius HILBURN
22 Equal Opportunity Office ... Dr. Shad B. SATTERTHWAITE
07 Director of Admissions ... Mr. Mark MCMASTERS
25 Assoc VP for Research Services ... Ms. Andrea D. DEATON
85 Director Internatl Student Services ... Ms. Monica A. SHARP
104 Interim Director Education Abroad ... Ms. Alice KLOKER
37 Director of Financial Aid ... Ms. Caryn L. PACHECO
48 Dean College of Architecture ... Dr. Charles W. GRAHAM
49 Dean College Arts & Sciences ... Dr. Paul BELL
53 Dean College of Education ... Dr. Gregg GARN
54 Dean College of Engineering ... Dr. Thomas L. LANDERS
57 Dean College of Fine Arts ... Mr. Rich TAYLOR
61 Dean College of Law ... Mr. Joseph HARROZ, JR.
62 Dean University Libraries ... Mr. Sul H. LEE
65 Dean Col Atmospheric/Geographic Sci ... Dr. Berrien MOORE, III
50 Dean Price College of Business ... Dr. Kenneth R. EVANS
92 Dean Honors College ... Dr. David H. RAY
60 Dn Gaylord Col Journ/Mass Comm ... Dr. Joe S. FOOTE
89 Dean University College ... Dr. Douglas D. GAFFIN
88 Dean Earth and Energy ... Dr. Larry R. GRILLOT
82 Vice Provost for Internatl Programs ... Dr. Zachariah P. MESSITTE

University of Oklahoma Health Sciences Center (D)

1000 Stanton L. Young Boulevard,
Oklahoma City OK 73117

County: Oklahoma — FICE Identification: 005889
Unit ID: 207342
Telephone: (405) 271-4000 — Carnegie Class: Spec/Med
FAX Number: N/A — Calendar System: Semester
URL: www.ouhsc.edu
Established: 1910 — Annual Undergrad Tuition & Fees (In-State): $8,908
Enrollment: 3,847 — Coed
Affiliation or Control: State — IRS Status: 501(c)3
Highest Offering: Doctorate
Program: Occupational; Professional
Accreditation: &NH, ARCPA, AUD, DENT, DH, DIETC, DIETD, DIETI, DMS, ENGR, HSA, IPSY, MED, NMT, NUR, OT, PDPSY, PH, PHAR, PTA, RAD, RADDOS, RTT, SP

01 Senior Vice President & Provost ... Dr. M. Dewayne ANDREWS
05 Vice Provost Academic Affairs ... Dr. Valerie WILLIAMS
23 Vice Provost for Health Sciences ... Dr. Marcia M. BENNETT
11 Vice Pres Administrative & Finance ... Mr. Kenneth D. ROWE
32 Vice President Student Affairs ... Mr. Clarke STROUD
46 Vice President for Research ... Dr. John J. IANDOLO
23 Vice President for Health Affairs ... Dr. Dewayne ANDREWS
27 Vice President for Public Affairs ... Ms. Catherine F. BISHOP
13 Int Vice Pres Info Technology/CIO ... Ms. Loretta M. EARLY
28 Asst Provost Diversity/Cmty Prtnshp ... Mr. Brian K. CORPENING
35 Exec Director HSC Student Affairs ... Ms. Kate STANTON
102 Dir Oklahoma Health Ctr Foundation ... Mr. Hershel LAMIRAND
30 Director Development ... Vacant
06 Registrar ... Ms. Lori KLIMKOWSKI
07 Director of Admissions ... Mr. Scott BOEH
09 Director of Instutional Research ... Ms. Carole CALL
29 Director Alumni & Annual Programs ... Ms. Carol MODISETTE
18 Director of Operations ... Mr. Don P. CAIL
43 Legal Counsel ... Ms. Peggy CLAY
22 Univ Equal Opportunity Officer ... Dr. Shad SATTERTHWAITE
37 Director Student Financial Aid ... Ms. Pamela JORDAN
08 Director Robert M Bird Library ... Dr. C. Marty THOMPSON
16 Director of Human Resources ... Mr. Julius HILBURN
96 Director of Purchasing ... Ms. Jean WILSON
63 Exec Dean College of Medicine ... Dr. Dewayne ANDREWS
76 Dean College Allied Health ... Dr. P. Kevin RUDEEN
52 Dean College of Dentistry ... Dr. Stephen K. YOUNG
66 Dean College of Nursing ... Dr. Lazelle BENEFIELD
67 Dean College of Pharmacy ... Dr. JoLaine DRAUGALIS
69 Dean College Public Health ... Dr. Gary E. RASKOB
63 Dean College of Medicine-Tulsa ... Dr. Daniel DUFFY
58 Dean Graduate College ... Dr. James J. TOMASEK

† Regional accreditation is carried under the parent institution in Norman, OK.

University of Science and Arts of Oklahoma (E)

1727 W Alabama, Chickasha OK 73018-5322

County: Grady — FICE Identification: 003167
Unit ID: 207722
Telephone: (405) 224-3140 — Carnegie Class: Bac/A&S
FAX Number: (405) 574-1220 — Calendar System: Trimester
URL: www.usao.edu
Established: 1908 — Annual Undergrad Tuition & Fees (In-State): $5,040
Enrollment: 1,050 — Coed
Affiliation or Control: State — IRS Status: 501(c)3
Highest Offering: Baccalaureate
Program: Liberal Arts And General; Teacher Preparatory
Accreditation: NH, MUS, TED

01 President ... Dr. John H. FEAVER
05 VP for Academic Affairs ... Dr. Dexter MARBLE
10 Vice Pres for Business & Finance ... Mr. Mike D. COPONITI
11 Vice Pres for Enrollment Management ... Ms. Monica TREVINO
30 Vice Pres University Advancement ... Dr. Michael NEALEIGH
13 VP for Information Services & Tech ... Ms. Lynn BOYCE
07 Registrar/Dir of Enrollment/Records ... Mr. Joe W. EVANS
44 Director Annual Giving & Grants ... Ms. Melissa HOWE
08 Director of Nash Library ... Ms. Kelly BROWN
37 Director of Financial Aid ... Ms. Nancy I. MOATS
32 Dean of Students/Dir Student Svcs ... Ms. Nancy HUGHES
26 Director Media/Community Relations ... Mr. Randy TALLEY
29 Director of Alumni Development ... Mr. Eric FEUERBORN
18 Director of Physical Plant ... Mr. Tim A. STIGER
14 Director of Data Processing ... Mr. Jim HOPKINS
09 Director of Institutional Research ... Ms. Lynn BOYCE
15 Director Personnel Services ... Mr. Mike COPONITI
49 Chair Div of Arts & Humanities ... Dr. Brenda BROWN
50 Chair Div of Business & Social Sci ... Dr. Christopher WALKER
53 Chair Division of Education ... Dr. Vicki FERGUSON
81 Chair Div of Science/Physical Educ ... Dr. Darryel REIGH
88 Chair Interdisciplinary Studies ... Dr. Jennifer LONG

University of Tulsa (F)

800 S Tucker, Tulsa OK 74104

County: Tulsa — FICE Identification: 003185
Unit ID: 207971
Telephone: (918) 631-2000 — Carnegie Class: DRU
FAX Number: (918) 631-2033 — Calendar System: Semester
URL: www.utulsa.edu
Established: 1894 — Annual Undergrad Tuition & Fees: $30,866
Enrollment: 4,185 — Coed
Affiliation or Control: Independent Non-Profit — IRS Status: 501(c)3
Highest Offering: Doctorate
Program: Liberal Arts And General; Teacher Preparatory; Professional
Accreditation: NH, BUS, CLPSY, CS, ENG, LAW, MUS, NUR, SP, TEAC

01 President ... Dr. Steadman UPHAM
05 Provost/Vice Pres Academic Affairs ... Dr. Roger N. BLAIS
45 Sr Vice Pres Planning & Outreach ... Dr. Janis I. ZINK
13 Vice President Info Services ... Dr. Dale A. SCHOENEFELD
10 Vice President Business & Finance ... Mr. Kevan C. BUCK
84 Vice Pres Enrollment/Student Svcs ... Dr. Roger W. SOROCHTY
88 VP Museum Affs/Exec Dir Gilcrease ... Dr. Duane KING
100 Chief of Staff ... Ms. Jacqueline H. CALDWELL
46 Vice President for Research ... Dr. Allen R. SOLTOW
09 Director Inst Research & Records ... Dr. Michael W. BARNES
41 Athletic Director ... Mr. Lawrence CUNNINGHAM
42 University Chaplain ... Dr. Jeffrey FRANCIS
20 Vice Provost ... Ms. Winona M. TANAKA
58 Dean Graduate School ... Dr. Janet A. HAGGERTY
49 Dean Arts & Sciences ... Dr. Dale T. BENEDIKTSON
54 Dean Engineering/Natural Sciences ... Dr. Steven J. BELLOVICH
50 Dean Business Administration ... Dr. A. Gale SULLENBERGER
61 Dean of Law ... Ms. Janet LEVIT
08 RM & Ida McFarlin Dean of Library ... Mr. Adrian W. ALEXANDER
84 Assoc VP Enrollment/Student Svcs ... Mr. Earl JOHNSON
32 Assoc VP Enrollment/Student Svcs ... Ms. Yolanda D. TAYLOR
30 Assoc VP Institutional Advancement ... Dr. Kayla K. ACEBO
06 Registrar ... Ms. Ginna V. LANGSTON
08 McFarlin Library Director ... Ms. Francine J. FISK
07 Dean of Admission ... Mr. Earl JOHNSON
23 Director Health Center ... Ms. Stephanie FELL

85 Dean International Students .... Ms. Pamela A. SMITH
15 Associate VP for Human Resources .... Mr. Wayne PAULISON
18 Assoc VP Operations/Physical Plant .... Mr. Robert SHIPLEY
51 Associate Dean Continuing Education ... Dr. J. Phillip APPLEGATE
104 Assoc Dean Global Education .... Dr. Cheryl MATHERLY
19 Director Campus Security .... Mr. Joseph F. TIMMONS
31 Assoc Dean of Students/Community Sv .... Mr. Michael MILLS
36 Director Career Services .... Ms. Shelly HOLLY
29 Director Alumni Relations .... Ms. Amy M. FREIBERGER
21 Director of Finance & Budget .... Mr. Michael D. THESENVITZ
37 Director Student Financial Svcs .... Ms. Vicki A. HENDRICKSON
38 Director of Student Counseling .... Dr. Thomas J. BRIAN
96 Director of Purchasing .... Mr. Jerry R. HOLLOWAY
26 Director University Relations .... Mr. David E. HAMBY
39 Assoc VP/Director Housing .... Ms. Melissa H. FRANCE
101 Secy of Board of Trustees .... Ms. June E. BROWN
35 Coordinator Student Activities .... Mr. Steven E. DENTON
04 Sr Admin Associate to President .... Ms. Tia CREAMER

Vatterott College-Oklahoma City (A)

4621 NW 23rd Street, Oklahoma City OK 73127-2103
County: Oklahoma Identification: 666061
Unit ID: 437060
Telephone: (405) 945-0088 Carnegie Class: Assoc/PrivFP
FAX Number: (405) 945-0788 Calendar System: Other
URL: www.vatterott-college.edu
Established: 1997 Annual Undergrad Tuition & Fees: $16,750
Enrollment: 457 Coed
Affiliation or Control: Proprietary IRS Status: Proprietary
Highest Offering: Associate Degree
Program: Occupational; Technical Emphasis
Accreditation: ACCSC

01 CEO & President .... Ms. Pam BELL
10 Chief Financial Officer .... Mr. Dennis BEAVERS
05 Chief Academic Officer .... Mr. Brandon SHEDRON
11 Chief Administrative Officer .... Mr. Scott CASANOVER
12 Campus Director .... Mr. David GORDON

† Branch campus of Vatterott College, Quincy, IL.

Vatterott College-Tulsa (B)

4343 S 118th E Avenue, Ste A, Tulsa OK 74146-4406
County: Tulsa Identification: 666102
Unit ID: 440882
Telephone: (918) 835-8288 Carnegie Class: Assoc/PrivFP
FAX Number: (918) 836-9698 Calendar System: Other
URL: www.vatterott-college.edu
Established: 1997 Annual Undergrad Tuition & Fees: $26,900
Enrollment: 394 Coed
Affiliation or Control: Proprietary IRS Status: Proprietary
Highest Offering: Associate Degree
Program: Occupational; Technical Emphasis
Accreditation: ACCSC

01 CEO & President .... Ms. Pam BELL
10 Chief Financial Officer .... Mr. Dennis BEAVERS
05 Vice President Academic Affairs .... Dr. Brandon SHEDRON
30 VP Regulatory Affs/Strategic Devel .... Mr. Aaron LACEY
43 General Counsel/Chief Administrator .... Mr. Scott CASANOVER
12 Campus Director .... Ms. Traci HORTON

† Branch campus of Vatterott College, St. Ann, MO.

Western Oklahoma State College (C)

2801 N Main Street, Altus OK 73521-1397
County: Jackson FICE Identification: 003146
Unit ID: 208035
Telephone: (580) 477-2000 Carnegie Class: Assoc/Pub-R-M
FAX Number: (580) 477-7777 Calendar System: Semester
URL: www.wosc.edu
Established: 1926 Annual Undergrad Tuition & Fees (In-State): $2,843
Enrollment: 4,661 Coed
Affiliation or Control: State IRS Status: 501(c)3
Highest Offering: Associate Degree
Program: Occupational; 2-Year Principally Bachelor's Creditable
Accreditation: NH, ADNUR, RAD

01 President .... Dr. Phil BIRDINE
04 Admin Secretary to the President .... Ms. Briar RINGGOLD
05 VP for Academic & Student Supp Svcs .... Ms. Lisa GREENLEE
10 Vice President for Business Affairs .... Ms. Tricia LATHAM
30 Vice Pres Development & Alumni Rels .... Mr. Larry K. DUFFY
49 Dean Arts & Sciences .... Dr. Jason MORRISON
20 Dean of Student Support Services .... Mr. Chad WIGINTON
72 Dean of Technical Programs .... Ms. Chrystal OVERTON
13 Dir Info Svcs/Distance Educ/CTO .... Mr. Kent BROOKS
27 Director Public Information .... Ms. Mallory NEWTON
07 Director of Admissions & Registrar .... Ms. Lana SCOTT
37 Director of Student Financial Aid .... Ms. Myrna J. CROSS
29 Director of Alumni Relations .... Vacant
40 Bookstore Manager .... Ms. Sheila LA FERNEY
41 Dir Physical Educ/Athletic Devel .... Mr. Bob PEARSON
62 Director of Learning Resources .... Mr. Tony HARDMAN
15 Director Personnel Services .... Ms. April NELSON
18 Director Physical Plant & Safety .... Mr. Doyle JENCKS
38 Counselor .... Ms. April DILL
96 Asst Director of Purchasing .... Ms. Vicki ELKINS
81 Science Instructor .... Dr. Toni COAKLEY
79 Art Instructor .... Mr. Jerry BRYAN
88 History Instructor .... Mr. Mickey GRAHAM

OREGON

American College of Healthcare Sciences (D)

5940 SW Hood Avenue, Portland OR 97239-3719
County: Multnomah Identification: 666365
Telephone: (503) 244-0726 Carnegie Class: Not Classified
FAX Number: (503) 244-0727 Calendar System: Semester
URL: www.achs.edu
Established: 1978 Annual Undergrad Tuition & Fees: $13,500
Enrollment: 500 Coed
Affiliation or Control: Proprietary IRS Status: Proprietary
Highest Offering: Master's
Program: Occupational; 2-Year Principally Bachelor's Creditable; Professional
Accreditation: DETC

01 President .... Dorene PETERSEN
11 Acting Director of Operations .... Tracey MILLER
03 Chief Institutional Officer .... Erika YIGZAW
06 Registrar .... Heather BALEY
26 Director of Marketing/Military Rels .... Kate HARMON

The Art Institute of Portland (E)

1122 NW Davis Street, Portland OR 97209-2911
County: Multnomah FICE Identification: 007819
Unit ID: 208239
Telephone: (503) 228-6528 Carnegie Class: Spec/Arts
FAX Number: (503) 228-4227 Calendar System: Quarter
URL: www.artinstitutes.edu/portland
Established: 1963 Annual Undergrad Tuition & Fees: $21,645
Enrollment: 1,880 Coed
Affiliation or Control: Proprietary IRS Status: Proprietary
Highest Offering: Baccalaureate
Program: Occupational, Liberal Arts And General
Accreditation: NW, CIDA

01 President .... Dr. Steven GOLDMAN
05 Dean of Academic Affairs .... Dr. Ronald ENGELDINGER
06 Registrar .... Ms. Kristin MCGILLIVRAY
07 Director of Admission .... Mr. Alan YANDA
08 Head Librarian .... Ms. Tricia JUETTEMEYER
37 Financial Aid Director .... Mr. Mickey JACOBSON

† Granted candidacy at the Master's level.

Birthingway College of Midwifery (F)

12113 SE Foster Road, Portland OR 97266-4042
County: Multnomah FICE Identification: 036683
Unit ID: 442949
Telephone: (503) 760-3131 Carnegie Class: Spec/Health
FAX Number: (503) 760-3332 Calendar System: Semester
URL: www.birthingway.edu
Established: 1993 Annual Undergrad Tuition & Fees: $16,600
Enrollment: 79 Coed
Affiliation or Control: Independent Non-Profit IRS Status: 501(c)3
Highest Offering: Baccalaureate
Program: Professional
Accreditation: MEAC

01 President .... Ms. Holly SCHOLLES
10 Finance Coordinator .... Ms. Nina THOMPSON
32 Student Affairs Coordinator .... Ms. Rhonda RAY
05 Faculty Coordinator .... Ms. Nancy LONGATAN
37 Financial Aid Coordinator .... Ms. Julia REID
06 Registrar .... Ms. Dawn BAKER

Blue Mountain Community College (G)

PO Box 100, Pendleton OR 97801-0100
County: Umatilla/Morrow/Baker FICE Identification: 003186
Unit ID: 208275
Telephone: (541) 276-1260 Carnegie Class: Assoc/Pub-R-M
FAX Number: (541) 278-5886 Calendar System: Quarter
URL: www.bluecc.edu
Established: 1962 Annual Undergrad Tuition & Fees (In-District): $4,080
Enrollment: 2,821 Coed
Affiliation or Control: State/Local IRS Status: 501(c)3
Highest Offering: Associate Degree
Program: Occupational; 2-Year Principally Bachelor's Creditable; Business Emphasis
Accreditation: NW, DA

01 President .... Mr. John H. TURNER
05 Vice President of Instruction .... Mr. Dan LANGE
10 Vice President of Operations .... Mr. Clark WILLIAMS
20 Vice Pres of Economic Development .... Mr. Art HILL
15 Director for Human Resources .... Mr. Arthur DOHERTY
08 Director of Library & Media Svcs .... Ms. Shannon VAN KIRK
07 Registrar/Dir of Admiss & Records .... Ms. Theresa BOSWORTH
18 Supervisor Facilities/Phy Plant .... Mr. Steve PLATT
102 Director Foundation .... Ms. Margaret GIANOTTI
29 Director Alumni Relations .... Ms. Bobbi KRISTOVICH
25 Director of Grants .... Ms. Susan PLASS
37 Director of Student Financial Aid .... Ms. Cristina SWEEK

Carrington College - Portland (H)

2004 Lloyd Center, 3rd Floor, Portland OR 97232-1309
County: Multnomah FICE Identification: 030425
Unit ID: 246035
Telephone: (503) 761-6100 Carnegie Class: Assoc/PrivFP
FAX Number: (503) 761-3351 Calendar System: Other
URL: www.carrington.edu
Established: N/A Annual Undergrad Tuition & Fees: $13,475
Enrollment: 943 Coed
Affiliation or Control: Proprietary IRS Status: Proprietary
Highest Offering: Associate Degree
Program: Occupational; 2-Year Principally Bachelor's Creditable
Accreditation: ACICS, DH, MAAB

01 Executive Campus Director .... Ms. Debra MARCUS

Central Oregon Community College (I)

2600 NW College Way, Bend OR 97701-5998
County: Deschutes FICE Identification: 003188
Unit ID: 208318
Telephone: (541) 383-7700 Carnegie Class: Assoc/Pub-R-M
FAX Number: (541) 383-7506 Calendar System: Quarter
URL: www.cocc.edu
Established: 1949 Annual Undergrad Tuition & Fees (In-District): $2,934
Enrollment: 7,002 Coed
Affiliation or Control: Local IRS Status: 501(c)3
Highest Offering: Associate Degree
Program: Occupational; 2-Year Principally Bachelor's Creditable
Accreditation: NW, ACFEI, DA, MAC

01 President .... Dr. James E. MIDDLETON
05 Vice President for Instruction .... Dr. Karin M. HILGERSOM
30 Vice Pres Institutional Advancement .... Mr. Matthew J. MCCOY
10 Vice Pres/Chief Financial Officer .... Mr. Kevin KIMBALL
12 Dean N Campus/Continuing Education .... Dr. Shirley METCALF
20 Instructional Dean .... Ms. Leslie MINOR
84 Dean of Student/Enrollment Svcs .... Ms. Alicia MOORE
07 Int Dir of Admissions & Records .... Ms. Aimee METCALF
08 Director Library Services .... Mr. David D. BILYEU
26 Director College Relations .... Mr. Ronald S. PARADIS
14 Director Information Technology .... Mr. Dan CECCHINI
18 Director Campus Services .... Mr. Joe VIOLA
15 Director Human Resources .... Mr. Eric BUCKLES
22 Affirmative Action Officer .... Mrs. Sharla ANDRESEN
37 Director Financial Aid .... Mr. Kevin MULTOP
28 Dir of Multicultural Activities .... Ms. Karen ROTH
32 Director of Student Life .... Mr. Gordon PRICE
40 Bookstore Manager .... Ms. Lori A. WILLIS
36 Coordinator of Career Services .... Ms. Vickery VILES

Chemeketa Community College (J)

PO Box 14007, Salem OR 97309-7070
County: Marion FICE Identification: 003218
Unit ID: 208390
Telephone: (503) 399-5000 Carnegie Class: Assoc/Pub-R-L
FAX Number: (503) 399-5214 Calendar System: Quarter
URL: www.chemek.cc.or.us
Established: 1962 Annual Undergrad Tuition & Fees (In-District): $3,132
Enrollment: 4,204 Coed
Affiliation or Control: Local IRS Status: 501(c)3
Highest Offering: Associate Degree
Program: Occupational; 2-Year Principally Bachelor's Creditable
Accreditation: NW, ADNUR, DA, EMT, IFSAC

01 President/Chief Executive Officer .... Dr. Cheryl ROBERTS
05 Vice Pres/Chief Academic Officer .... Dr. Patrick LANNING
10 Chief Financial Officer .... Ms. Julie A. HUCKESTEIN
20 Dean General Education/Trans Stds .... Dr. David HALLETT
16 Executive Dean .... Mr. Andrew BONE
32 Ex Dean Student Devel/Learning Res .... Mr. Jim EUSTROM
88 Exec Dean Regional Education Svcs .... Dr. Cheryl FALK
68 Dean Life Sci/Health/PE/Athletics .... Mr. Johnny MACK
79 Dean Humanities & Communications .... Mr. Don BRASE
66 Dean Dental Asst/Med Asst/Nursing .... Ms. Kay CARNEGIE
37 Dean Financial Aid/Enrollment Svcs .... Ms. Kathy CAMPBELL
38 Dean Counseling/Career Services .... Ms. Jill WARD
72 Dean Applied Technologies .... Mr. Glen MILLER
81 Dean Math/Science/Technologies .... Mr. Michael MILHAUSEN
83 Dean Early Chld/Hum Svc/Soc Sci/Ed .... Ms. Malia SATHRUM
84 Dean Marketing/Student Recruitment .... Mr. Greg HARRIS
45 Dean Curriculum Resource Center .... Dr. Maureen MCGLYNN
65 Dean Natural Resources .... Dr. D. Craig ANDERSON
102 Executive Director Foundation .... Mr. Andrew BONE
08 Director Learning Resource Center .... Ms. Natalie BEACH
88 Director Enterprise Services .... Mr. Mike DEROCHIER
21 Director Business Services .... Ms. Miriam ROZIN
18 Director Facilities & Operations .... Mr. Phil WRIGHT
15 Director Human Resources .... Ms. Peggy BORJESSON
19 Director Public Safety .... Mr. Bill KOHLMEYER
40 Manager Auxiliary Services .... Mr. Phil FREY
06 Registrar .... Ms. Minna GELDER
41 Athletic Director .... Ms. Cassie BELMODIS
50 Dir Chemeketa Ctr for Bus/Industry .... Ms. Diane MCLARAN
88 Director Reg Prof Tech Educ .... Ms. Trish HAKOLA

103 Workforce Integration .... Mr. Imara JABARI
28 Director of Diversity & Equity .... Vacant
35 Director Student Life/Retention .... Mr. Manuel GUERRA
07 Director of Admissions .... Ms. Melissa FREY
96 Director of Purchasing .... Ms. Eileen MILLER
30 Development .... Ms. Nancy DUNCAN
25 Grants Coordinator .... Ms. Diane SCHMITZ

Clackamas Community College (A)

19600 Molalla Avenue, Oregon City OR 97045-7998
County: Clackamas FICE Identification: 004878
Unit ID: 208406
Telephone: (503) 594-6000 Carnegie Class: Assoc/Pub-S-MC
FAX Number: N/A Calendar System: Quarter
URL: www.clackamas.edu
Established: 1966 Annual Undergrad Tuition & Fees (In-District): $3,563
Enrollment: 3,456 Coed
Affiliation or Control: Local IRS Status: 501(c)3
Highest Offering: Associate Degree
Program: Occupational; 2-Year Principally Bachelor's Creditable
Accreditation: NW, MAC

01 President .... Dr. Joanne TRUESDELL
05 VP Instruct & Stdnt Svcs/Provost .... Ms. Elizabeth LUNDY
11 Vice President of College Services .... Mr. Courtney WILTON
04 Executive Asst to the President .... Ms. Debbie JENKINS
30 Dn Col Advanc/Chf Govt/Cmty Rel Dir .... Ms. Shelly PARINI
102 Executive Director Foundation .... Ms. Karen MARTINI
27 Public Information Officer .... Ms. Janet PAULSON
88 Dean Acad Found/Connections Div .... Mr. Phillip KING
06 Registrar .... Ms. Tara SPREHE
32 Assoc Dean Acad Found/Connect Div .... Mr. Jim MARTINEAU
13 Dean/CIO Information Technology .... Ms. Kim CAREY
49 Dean Arts & Sciences .... Mr. Bill BRIARE
46 Dean Curriculum/Planning/Research .... Mr. Steffen MOLLER
88 Director Educational Partnerships .... Ms. Cyndi ANDREWS
72 Dean Tech/Hlth Occup/Workforce Div .... Mr. Scott GILTZ
12 Dean Regional Educational Services .... Ms. Theresa TUFFLI
15 Dean Human Resources .... Ms. Marsha EDWARDS
21 Director Business Services .... Ms. Chris ROBUCK
11 Dean Campus Services .... Mr. Bob COCHRAN
18 Director Plant Operations .... Mr. Kirk PEARSON
35 Director Student Activities .... Ms. Mindy BROWN
37 Director Student Financial Svcs .... Ms. Chippi BELLO
41 Director Athletics/Health/PE .... Mr. Jim MARTINEAU

Clatsop Community College (B)

1653 Jerome, Astoria OR 97103-3698
County: Clatsop FICE Identification: 003189
Unit ID: 208415
Telephone: (503) 325-0910 Carnegie Class: Assoc/Pub-R-M
FAX Number: (503) 325-5738 Calendar System: Quarter
URL: www.clatsopcc.edu
Established: 1958 Annual Undergrad Tuition & Fees (In-District): $4,308
Enrollment: 1,535 Coed
Affiliation or Control: State/Local IRS Status: 501(c)3
Highest Offering: Associate Degree
Program: Occupational; 2-Year Principally Bachelor's Creditable
Accreditation: NW

01 President .... Dr. Larry GALIZIO
05 Vice President Instruction .... Dr. Stephen SCHOONMAKER
10 Vice President College Services .... Dr. Lindi OVERTON
32 Dean Student Services .... Mr. Roger FRIESEN
06 Registrar .... Mr. Chris OUSLEY
26 Chief Public Rels Officer/Marketing .... Ms. Patricia WARREN
78 Dir Co-op Educ & Special Project .... Ms. Joanie WEATHERLY
51 Director Distance Education .... Mrs. Kirsten HORNING
15 Director Personnel Services .... Ms. Leslie LIPE
37 Director Student Financial Aid .... Vacant
09 Director of Institutional Research .... Vacant
18 Chief Facilities/Physical Plant .... Mr. Greg DORCHEUS
21 Associate Business Officer .... Ms. Margaret ANTILLA
29 Director of Alumni Relations/Devel .... Ms. Patricia WARREN
84 Assoc Dean Enrollment Management .... Mr. Chris OUSLEY

Columbia Gorge Community College (C)

400 East Scenic Drive, The Dalles OR 97058
County: Wasco Identification: 666639
Unit ID: 420556
Telephone: (541) 506-6000 Carnegie Class: Not Classified
FAX Number: N/A Calendar System: Quarter
URL: www.cgcc.cc.or.us/
Established: 1977 Annual Undergrad Tuition & Fees (In-District): $3,384
Enrollment: 1,290 Coed
Affiliation or Control: State/Local IRS Status: 501(c)3
Highest Offering: Associate Degree
Program: 2-Year Principally Bachelor's Creditable
Accreditation: @NW, MAC

01 President .... Dr. Frank TODA
05 Chief Academic Officer .... Dr. Susan WOLFF
10 Chief Financial Officer .... Saundra BUCHANAN
88 Chief Talent and Strategy Officer .... Robb VAN CLEAVE
32 Chief Student Services Officer .... Karen CARTER
30 Chief Inst Advancement Officer .... Dan SPATZ
13 Chief Technology Officer .... Bill BOHN

Concorde Career College (D)

1425 NE Irving Street, Suite 300, Portland OR 97232
County: Multnomah FICE Identification: 008887
Unit ID: 208479
Telephone: (503) 281-4181 Carnegie Class: Not Classified
FAX Number: (503) 281-6739 Calendar System: Other
URL: www.concorde.edu/campus/portland
Established: N/A Annual Undergrad Tuition & Fees: N/A
Enrollment: 707 Coed
Affiliation or Control: Proprietary IRS Status: Proprietary
Highest Offering: Associate Degree
Program: Occupational
Accreditation: ACCSC, DA

01 Campus President .... Kim IERIEN

Concordia University (E)

2811 NE Holman, Portland OR 97211-6099
County: Multnomah FICE Identification: 003191
Unit ID: 208488
Telephone: (503) 288-9371 Carnegie Class: Master's L
FAX Number: (503) 280-8518 Calendar System: Quarter
URL: www.cu-portland.edu
Established: 1905 Annual Undergrad Tuition & Fees: $24,900
Enrollment: 2,114 Coed
Affiliation or Control: Lutheran Church - Missouri Synod
IRS Status: 501(c)3
Highest Offering: Master's
Program: Liberal Arts And General; Teacher Preparatory
Accreditation: NW, SW

01 President .... Dr. Charles E. SCHLIMPERT
26 Exec Vice Pres External Affairs .... Dr. Gary WITHERS
102 Exec Vice Pres Strategic Planning .... Mr. Johnnie DRIESSNER
05 Provost/Chief Academic Officer .... Dr. Mark E. WAHLERS
10 Chief Financial Officer .... Mr. Dennis J. STOECKLIN
32 VP Student Svcs/Enrollment Mgmt .... Dr. Glenn C. SMITH
04 Assistant to the President .... Ms. Linda JAMES
30 Chief Development Officer .... Mr. Kevin MATHENY
06 Registrar .... Mr. Paul REVERE
07 Director Admissions & Enroll Mgmt .... Ms. Bobi SWAN
09 Director of Institutional Research .... Mr. Ron FONGER
15 Director of Human Resources .... Ms. Andrea OTEN
18 Chief Facilities/Physical Plant .... Mr. Doug MEYER
20 Associate Academic Officer .... Vacant
88 Chief Public Relations Officer .... Ms. Madeline TURNOCK
29 Director Alumni Relations .... Ms. Brooke KRYSTOSEK
35 Dean of Students .... Mr. Steve DEKLOTZ
08 Librarian .... Mr. Brent MAI
37 Director Student Financial Aid .... Ms. Rhoda RESEBURG
41 Athletic Director .... Dr. Matthew ENGLISH
38 Director Student Counseling .... Ms. Jaklin PEAKE
85 Director of International Studies .... Ms. Linda ROUNTREE
42 Campus Pastor .... Rev. Greg FAIROW
13 Chief Information Officer .... Vacant
50 Dean School of Management .... Dr. Steve BRAUN
53 Dean College of Education .... Dr. Joe MANNION
49 Dean Theol Studies/Arts/Sciences .... Dr. Charles KUNERT
88 Dean Col of Health/Human Service .... Dr. Mark JAGER
61 Dean School of Law .... Ms. Cathy SILAK

Corban University (F)

5000 Deer Park Drive, SE, Salem OR 97317
County: Marion FICE Identification: 001339
Unit ID: 210331
Telephone: (503) 581-8600 Carnegie Class: Bac/Diverse
FAX Number: (503) 585-4316 Calendar System: Semester
URL: www.corban.edu
Established: 1935 Annual Undergrad Tuition & Fees: $24,976
Enrollment: 1,159 Coed
Affiliation or Control: Independent Non-Profit IRS Status: 501(c)3
Highest Offering: Master's
Program: Liberal Arts And General; Teacher Preparatory; Professional
Accreditation: NW

01 President .... Dr. Reno R. HOFF
05 Provost/Executive Vice President .... Dr. Matthew LUCAS
10 Vice President For Business .... Mr. Kevin BRUBAKER
32 Vice President For Student Life .... Dr. Nancy HEDBERG
26 Vice President for Marketing .... Mr. J. Steven HUNT
30 Vice President for Advancement .... Mr. Mike BATES
84 Vice Pres for Enrollment Management .... Mr. Marty ZIESEMER
35 Dean of Students .... Miss Brenda ROTH
11 Campus Administrator .... Dr. Leroy GOERTZEN
53 Dean of Education .... Dr. Janine ALLEN
51 Dean of Adult Services .... Miss Nancy MARTYN
50 Dean of Business .... Vacant
91 Chief Information Systems Officer .... Mr. Brian SCHMIDT
18 Director of Campus Care .... Mr. Tom SAMEK
06 Registrar .... Dr. Chris VETTER
08 Librarian .... Mr. Floyd VOTAW
39 Director of Residential Life .... Mr. Jim D'ADOSTA
42 Director of Campus Ministries .... Dr. Dan HUBER
41 Athletic Director .... Mr. Dave JOHNSON
36 Director Academic & Career Services .... Mr. Daren MILIONIS
37 Director Student Financial Aid .... Mr. Nathan WARTHAN
29 Director Alumni Relations .... Mrs. Deleen WILLS
38 Director Student Counseling .... Mrs. Stephanie HUSK

21 Associate Business Officer .... Mr. Brian ELLIOTT
40 Bookstore Manager .... Ms. Heather ULBRIGHT

DeVry University - Portland (G)

9755 SW Barnes Road, Suite 150,
Portland OR 97225-6651
Identification: 666567
Unit ID: 444033
Telephone: (503) 296-7468 Carnegie Class: Spec/Bus
FAX Number: (503) 296-6114 Calendar System: Semester
URL: www.devry.edu
Established: 1931 Annual Undergrad Tuition & Fees: $15,294
Enrollment: 325 Coed
Affiliation or Control: Proprietary IRS Status: Proprietary
Highest Offering: Master's
Program: Professional; Business Emphasis
Accreditation: &NH

01 Campus Director .... Leslee HEINRICHS

† Regional accreditation is carried under the parent institution in Downers Grove, IL.

Everest College (H)

425 Southwest Washington, Portland OR 97204-2296
County: Multnomah FICE Identification: 009079
Unit ID: 210359
Telephone: (503) 222-3225 Carnegie Class: Assoc/PrivFP
FAX Number: (503) 228-6926 Calendar System: Quarter
URL: www.everest-college.com
Established: 1955 Annual Undergrad Tuition & Fees: $14,700
Enrollment: 783 Coed
Affiliation or Control: Proprietary IRS Status: Proprietary
Highest Offering: Associate Degree
Program: Occupational; 2-Year Principally Bachelor's Creditable
Accreditation: ACICS, MAC

01 President .... Mrs. Patti LOPRESTI
05 Chief Academic Officer .... Ms. Elaine SEYMAN
07 Director of Admissions .... Ms. Cindy SLUSHER
06 Registrar .... Mrs. Renee HATFIELD
37 Director Student Financial Aid .... Mrs. Nicole TONE
36 Director of Student Placement .... Mr. Martin RYAN
10 Business Manager .... Ms. Michelle MESMAN MICHAELIS

George Fox University (I)

414 N Meridian, Newberg OR 97132-2697
County: Yamhill FICE Identification: 003194
Unit ID: 208822
Telephone: (503) 538-8383 Carnegie Class: Master's L
FAX Number: (503) 554-3834 Calendar System: Semester
URL: www.georgefox.edu
Established: 1891 Annual Undergrad Tuition & Fees: $27,180
Enrollment: 3,388 Coed
Affiliation or Control: Friends IRS Status: 501(c)3
Highest Offering: Doctorate
Program: Liberal Arts And General; Teacher Preparatory; Business Emphasis
Accreditation: NW, CLPSY, ENG, MUS, NURSE, SW, TED, THEOL

01 President .... Dr. Robin E. BAKER
03 Vice President/Dean of Seminary .... Dr. Charles J. CONNIRY, JR.
05 Provost .... Dr. Patrick ALLEN
10 Exec VP Finance/Business Operations .... Mr. Ted ALLEN
30 Vice President Advancement .... Ms. Shari SCALES
32 Vice President Student Life .... Dr. Bradley A. LAU
84 Vice Pres Enrollment Services .... Mr. Dale E. SEIPP, JR.
26 Vice Pres Marketing/Communications .... Mr. Robert K. WESTERVELT
04 Executive Assistant to President .... Ms. Missy D. TERRY
21 Asst VP Financial Affairs .... Mr. Dave KELLEY
08 University Librarian .... Mr. Merrill L. JOHNSON
06 Registrar .... Ms. Melissa THOMAS
26 Asst Dir of University Relations .... Vacant
36 Director of Career Services .... Ms. Bonnie J. JERKE
18 Director of Plant Services .... Mr. Clyde G. THOMAS
37 Exec Dir Student Financial Svcs .... Mr. Robert A. CLARKE
96 Director Purchasing/Admin Services .... Mr. Andy DUNN
41 Director of Athletics .... Mr. Craig B. TAYLOR
105 Director of Web Development .... Mr. Peter CRACKENBERG
15 Director Human Resources .... Ms. Peggy L. KILBURG
42 University Pastor .... Ms. Sarah BALDWIN
27 Director Public Information .... Mr. Rob FELTON
13 Chief Information Officer .... Mr. Greg SMITH
19 Director Security Services .... Mr. Ed GIEROK
38 Dir Health and Counseling Services .... Dr. William C. BUHROW
29 Director of Alumni Relations .... Mr. Robby LARSON
45 Director of Strategic Planning .... Dr. MaryKate MORSE
49 Dean School of Arts & Sciences .... Mr. Hank HELSABECK
83 Dean Sch Behavioral/Health Sci .... Dr. James E. FOSTER
53 Dean School of Education .... Dr. Linda SAMEK
50 Dean School of Business .... Dr. Dirk BARRAM
88 Dean of Transitions & Inclusion .... Mr. Joel PEREZ

Gutenberg College (J)

1883 University Street, Eugene OR 97403-1368
County: Lane FICE Identification: 039324
Unit ID: 420510
Telephone: (541) 683-5141 Carnegie Class: Not Classified

FAX Number: (541) 683-6997 Calendar System: Quarter
URL: www.gutenberg.edu
Established: 1994 Annual Undergrad Tuition & Fees: $11,203
Enrollment: 39 Coed
Affiliation or Control: Independent Non-Profit IRS Status: 501(c)3
Highest Offering: Baccalaureate
Program: Liberal Arts And General; Religious Emphasis
Accreditation: TRACS

01 President ... David CRABTREE
03 Vice President ... Richard BOOSTER
05 Dean ... Thomas DEWBERRY
07 Admissions Director ... Tim MCINTOSH
06 Registrar ... Chris SWANSON

Heald College, Portland (A)

6035 NE 78th Court, Portland OR 97218
County: Multnomah FICE Identification: 037454
Unit ID: 430148
Telephone: (503) 229-0492 Carnegie Class: Assoc/PrivFP
FAX Number: (503) 229-0498 Calendar System: Quarter
URL: www.heald.edu
Established: 1863 Annual Undergrad Tuition & Fees: N/A
Enrollment: 1,148 Coed
Affiliation or Control: Independent Non-Profit IRS Status: 501(c)3
Highest Offering: Associate Degree
Program: Occupational
Accreditation: &WJ, MAC

01 Campus President ... Mr. Jason FERGUSON
36 Director of Career Services ... Ms. Taunji FALKENBERG
37 Director of Financial Aid ... Ms. Elizabeth VONAU

† Regional accreditation is carried under the parent institution Heald College, Central Office in San Francisco, CA.

ITT Technical Institute (B)

9500 NE Cascades Parkway, Portland OR 97220
County: Multnomah FICE Identification: 011852
Unit ID: 208965
Telephone: (503) 255-6500 Carnegie Class: Spec/Tech
FAX Number: (503) 255-8381 Calendar System: Quarter
URL: www.itt-tech.edu
Established: 1971 Annual Undergrad Tuition & Fees: N/A
Enrollment: 953 Coed
Affiliation or Control: Proprietary IRS Status: Proprietary
Highest Offering: Baccalaureate
Program: Technical Emphasis
Accreditation: ACICS

Klamath Community College (C)

7390 S 6th Street, Klamath Falls OR 97603-7121
County: Klamath FICE Identification: 034283
Unit ID: 428392
Telephone: (541) 882-3521 Carnegie Class: Assoc/Pub-R-S
FAX Number: (541) 885-7758 Calendar System: Quarter
URL: www.klamathcc.edu
Established: 1996 Annual Undergrad Tuition & Fees (In-District): $1,776
Enrollment: 1,422 Coed
Affiliation or Control: State/Local IRS Status: 501(c)3
Highest Offering: Associate Degree
Program: Occupational; 2-Year Principally Bachelor's Creditable
Accreditation: NW

01 President ... Mr. Gerald HAMILTON
11 Vice Pres Administrative Services ... Ms. Renee FERGUSON
05 Dean for Learning Services ... Dr. Galyn CARLILE
32 Dean for Student Services ... Ms. Julie MURRAY-JENSEN
10 Chief Business Officer ... Mr. Jack NOWAK
13 Director Information Services ... Mr. Paul BREEDLOVE
15 Exec Director Human Resources ... Ms. Karren ANDREWS
18 Chief Facilities/Physical Plant ... Mr. Mike GRIFFITH
37 Financial Aid Specialist ... Ms. Donna FULTON

Lane Community College (D)

4000 E 30th Avenue, Eugene OR 97405-0640
County: Lane FICE Identification: 003196
Unit ID: 209038
Telephone: (541) 463-3000 Carnegie Class: Assoc/Pub-R-L
FAX Number: (541) 463-5201 Calendar System: Quarter
URL: www.lanecc.edu
Established: 1964 Annual Undergrad Tuition & Fees (In-District): $4,500
Enrollment: 12,157 Coed
Affiliation or Control: Local IRS Status: 501(c)3
Highest Offering: Associate Degree
Program: Occupational; 2-Year Principally Bachelor's Creditable
Accreditation: NW, ACFEI, DA, DH, MAC, @PTAA

01 President ... Dr. Mary SPILDE
05 Vice Pres Instruction/Student Svcs ... Dr. Sonya CHRISTIAN
11 Vice President College Operations ... Vacant
32 Exec Dean/Stdt Svc/Career Tech ... Ms. Andrea NEWTON
20 Executive Dean/Transfer ... Mr. Don MCNAIR
28 Chief Diversity Officer ... Dr. Donna KOECHIG
13 Chief Information Officer ... Mr. Bill SCHUETZ
10 Chief Financial Officer ... Mr. Greg MORGAN
35 Executive Dean/Student Affairs ... Ms. Helen GARRETT
15 Director Human Resources ... Mr. Dennis CARR
09 Dir Inst Research/Assess/Planning ... Dr. Craig TAYLOR
84 Int Director Enrollment Services ... Mr. John HAMBLIN
18 Director Facilities Mgmt/Planning ... Mr. Dave WILLIS
35 Director Student Life & Leadership ... Dr. Barbara DELANSKY
19 Director Public Safety ... Mr. Jace SMITH
08 Library Director ... Ms. Marika PINEDA
38 Dir Counseling/Student Placement ... Mr. Jerry DELEON
37 Director of Financial Aid ... Vacant
41 Int Dir Athletic/Health/Phys Educ ... Mr. Rodger BATES
96 Director of Finance/Purchasing ... Mr. Stan BARKER
26 Chief Public Relations Officer ... Ms. Tracy SIMMS
102 Foundation Director ... Ms. Janet ANDERSON

Le Cordon Bleu College of Culinary Arts in Portland (E)

600 SW 10th Avenue, Suite 500, Portland OR 97205-2793
County: Multnomah FICE Identification: 030226
Unit ID: 375841
Telephone: (503) 223-2245 Carnegie Class: Assoc/PrivFP
FAX Number: (503) 223-0126 Calendar System: Other
URL: www.chefs.edu/portland
Established: 1983 Annual Undergrad Tuition & Fees: $17,550
Enrollment: 956 Coed
Affiliation or Control: Proprietary IRS Status: Proprietary
Highest Offering: Associate Degree
Program: Occupational
Accreditation: ACICS, ACFEI

01 Campus President ... Julia BROOKS
05 Vice President Academic Affairs ... Wendy BENNETT
07 Vice Pres of Admissions & Marketing ... Kimberly VELASQUEZ
10 Vice Pres of Finance/Accounting ... Don GILL
32 Vice President Student Services ... Marsha PARMER
13 Director of IT & Facilities ... Bryan LEVINE
06 Registrar ... Linda M. SCHOEN
37 Director Student Finances ... Katie STONE
21 Controller ... David COFFMAN

Lewis and Clark College (F)

0615 SW Palatine Hill, Portland OR 97219-7899
County: Multnomah FICE Identification: 003197
Unit ID: 209056
Telephone: (503) 768-7000 Carnegie Class: Bac/A&S
FAX Number: (503) 768-7055 Calendar System: Semester
URL: www.lclark.edu
Established: 1867 Annual Undergrad Tuition & Fees: $38,500
Enrollment: 3,584 Coed
Affiliation or Control: Independent Non-Profit IRS Status: 501(c)3
Highest Offering: Doctorate
Program: Liberal Arts And General; Teacher Preparatory; Professional
Accreditation: NW, CACREP, LAW, MFCD, TED

01 President ... Dr. Barry GLASSNER
03 Vice President & Provost ... Dr. Jane M. ATKINSON
05 Dean of College of Arts & Sciences ... Dr. Tuajuanda C. JORDAN
10 Vice Pres Business/Finance/Treas ... Mr. Carl VANCE
30 Vice Pres Institutional Advancement ... Mr. Gregory A. VOLK
43 VP General Counsel/Secy of College ... Mr. David ELLIS
88 Assoc Vice President Campus Life ... Dr. Michael B. FORD
44 Director of Annual Giving & Develop ... Mr. Aaron WHITEFORD
18 Assoc Vice Pres Facilities ... Vacant
26 Assoc VP Public Affs/ Communications ... Mr. Tom KRATTENMAKER
15 Assoc VP/Director Human Resources ... Mr. Isaac DIXON
29 Director Alumni/Parent Pgms ... Mr. Andrew MCPHEETERS
21 Associate Vice Pres for Finance/Con ... Mr. George BATTISTEL
53 Dean Grad Sch Education/Counseling ... Dr. Scott FLETCHER
61 Dean of the Law School ... Mr. Robert KLONOFF
49 Assoc Dean College of Arts/Science ... Dr. Jane HUNTER
32 Dean of Students ... Vacant
28 Asc Dn Stdnts/Dir Multicultural Aff ... Ms. Latricia BRAND
85 Assoc Dean Intl Stdnts & Scholars ... Mr. Brian WHITE
08 Interim Director of Library ... Mr. Mark DAHL
13 Interim Chief Technology Officer ... Ms. Keiko PITTER
06 Registrar College of Arts/Sciences ... Vacant
06 Registrar Law School ... Ms. Susan GALYEN
06 Registrar Graduate School ... Mr. Curt LUTTRELL
07 Dean of Admissions & Financial Aid ... Ms. Lisa MEYER
37 Interim Director of Financial Aid ... Ms. Anastacia DILLON
27 Senior Communications Officer ... Vacant
19 Director of Campus Safety ... Mr. Timothy O'DWYER
42 Dean of the Chapel ... Dr. Mark DUNTLEY
41 Director of Phys Educ & Athletics ... Mr. Clark YEAGER
39 Director of Residential Services ... Ms. Sandi BOTTEMILLER
24 Dir of Instructional Media Svcs ... Mr. Patrick RYALL
39 Assoc Dean of Students ... Mr. Jeffrey FELD-GORE
17 Asc Dean Stdnts/Wellness Svcs/Psych ... Dr. John HANCOCK

Linfield College (G)

900 SE Baker Street, McMinnville OR 97128-6894
County: Yamhill FICE Identification: 003198
Unit ID: 209065
Telephone: (503) 883-2200 Carnegie Class: Bac/A&S
FAX Number: (503) 883-2472 Calendar System: 4/1/4
URL: www.linfield.edu
Established: 1858 Annual Undergrad Tuition & Fees: $32,416
Enrollment: 2,652 Coed
Affiliation or Control: American Baptist IRS Status: 501(c)3
Highest Offering: Master's
Program: Liberal Arts And General; Teacher Preparatory; Professional
Accreditation: NW, MUS, NURSE

01 President ... Dr. Thomas HELLIE
05 Vice Pres Acad Affs/Dean of Faculty ... Ms. Susan AGRE-KIPPENHAN
10 Vice Pres Finance/Administration ... Mr. W. Glenn FORD
26 Vice Pres for College Relations ... Mr. Bruce WYATT
84 Vice Pres for Enrollment Management ... Mr. Daniel PRESTON
32 VP Student Svcs/Dean of Students ... Ms. Susan HOPP
43 Advisor to the Pres & General Couns ... Mr. John MCKEEGAN
66 Dean of Nursing ... Dr. Bonnie SAUCIER
20 Associate Dean of Faculty ... Dr. Nancy DRICKEY
20 Associate Dean of Faculty ... Dr. Martha VAN CLEAVE
35 Associate Dean of Students ... Mr. Jeff MACKAY
15 Senior Director of Human Resources ... Ms. Linda POWELL
18 Director Facilities & Auxiliary Svc ... Mr. Brad SINN
28 Director Multicultural Programs ... Mr. Barry TUCKER
06 Registrar ... Dr. Eileen BOURASSA
07 Director of Admission ... Ms. Lisa KNODLE-BRAGIEL
08 Library Director ... Ms. Susan BARNES WHYTE
09 Director of Institutional Research ... Ms. Jennifer BALLARD
37 Director of Financial Aid ... Ms. Keri BURKE
13 Chief Technology Officer ... Mr. Irv WISWALL
91 Assoc Director Integrated Tech Svcs ... Mr. Phil SETH
105 Webmaster ... Mr. Jonathan PIERCE
85 Director of International Programs ... Dr. Shaik ISMAIL
51 Dean of Continuing Education ... Dr. Kathleen BEMIS
19 Director of Security ... Mr. Robert CEPEDA
38 Director of Counseling Services ... Dr. John F. KERRIGAN, JR.
26 Director of Public Relations ... Ms. Mardi MILEHAM
44 Director of Annual Giving ... Ms. Christina DISS
44 Director of Planned Giving ... Mr. Craig HAISCH
102 Dir Corp & Foundation Relations ... Ms. Catherine JARMIN MILLER
29 Director of Alumni Relations ... Ms. Debbie HARMON
36 Director Career & Community Svcs ... Mr. Michael HAMPTON
42 Chaplain ... Dr. David MASSEY
41 Athletic Director ... Mr. Scott CARNAHAN
40 Bookstore Manager ... Ms. Amber SIMMONS

Linn-Benton Community College (H)

6500 SW Pacific Boulevard, Albany OR 97321-3774
County: Linn FICE Identification: 006938
Unit ID: 209074
Telephone: (541) 917-4999 Carnegie Class: Assoc/Pub-R-L
FAX Number: (541) 917-4445 Calendar System: Quarter
URL: www.linnbenton.edu
Established: 1966 Annual Undergrad Tuition & Fees (In-District): $3,780
Enrollment: 8,250 Coed
Affiliation or Control: State/Local IRS Status: 501(c)3
Highest Offering: Associate Degree
Program: Occupational; 2-Year Principally Bachelor's Creditable
Accreditation: NW, DA, MAC

01 President ... Dr. Gregory J. HAMANN
05 Vice President Academic Affairs ... Ms. Carol SCHAAFSMA
10 Vice Pres Finance & Operations ... Mr. Jim HUCKESTEIN
32 Vice President Student Services ... Dr. Bruce CLEMETSEN
15 Director Human Resources ... Mr. Scott ROLEN
37 Director of Student Financial Aid ... Ms. Bev GERIG
12 Director Albany Community Education ... Mr. Joel WHITE
12 Director East Linn Centers ... Ms. Dawn MCNANNAY
12 Director Benton Center ... Mr. Jeff DAVIS
84 Director Enrollment Services ... Mr. Danny AYNES
88 Dean Instructional Facilities Plng ... Mr. Fred HAYNES
68 Dean Athletics and Emergency Plng ... Vacant
81 Dean Science/Engr & Tech ... Mr. Dan LARA
49 Dean Liberal Arts/Soc Sys & HP ... Ms. Beth HOGELAND
20 Dean Instruction ... Vacant
30 Director Institutional Advancement ... Ms. B.J NICOLETTI
21 Budget Officer ... Ms. Betty NIELSEN
35 Director Student Life & Leadership ... Vacant
36 Dir Career Svcs/Stdnt Counseling ... Mr. Mark WEISS
13 Director Information Services ... Ms. Ann ADAMS
26 Director College Advancement ... Ms. Marlene PROPST
20 Dean of Instruction ... Vacant
50 Dean Business/Health Care & Work ... Ms. Ann MALOSH
06 Registrar ... Vacant
18 Chief Facilities/Physical Plant ... Mr. Scott KRAMBUHL
44 Chief Development Officer ... Mr. John MCARDLE
08 Dean Academic Devel/Library Svcs ... Vacant
88 Assoc Dean Student Development ... Ms. Lynne COX

Marylhurst University (I)

PO Box 261, 17600 Pacific Highway,
Marylhurst OR 97036-0261
County: Clackamas FICE Identification: 003199
Unit ID: 209108
Telephone: (503) 636-8141 Carnegie Class: Master's L
FAX Number: (503) 636-9526 Calendar System: Quarter
URL: www.marylhurst.edu
Established: 1893 Annual Undergrad Tuition & Fees: $18,405
Enrollment: 1,917 Coed
Affiliation or Control: Independent Non-Profit IRS Status: 501(c)3
Highest Offering: Master's
Program: Liberal Arts And General
Accreditation: NW, CIDA, IACBE, MUS

01 President .... Dr. Judith JOHANSEN
05 Vice President Academic Affairs .... Dr. David PLOTKIN
10 Vice President Finance & Facilities .... Mr. Michael LAMMERS
30 Vice Pres Institutional Advancement .... Ms. Lynn MAWE
15 Vice President for Human Resources .... Ms. Celina RATLIFFE
27 Vice President Info Tech/CIO .... Dr. Ethan BENATAN
84 Associate VP Enrollment Mgmt .... Ms. Beth WOODWARD
04 Assistant to the President .... Ms. Judy MILLENBACH
32 Dean of Students .... Mr. Bill ZUELKE
07 Director of Admissions .... Mr. Chris SWEET
88 Dean of Assessment .... Dr. Melanie BOOTH
06 Registrar .... Ms. Gwen HYATT
08 University Librarian .... Ms. Nancy HOOVER
26 Director Marketing & Communications .... Ms. Shirley SKIDMORE
44 Manager Annual Giving .... Ms. Sandra MARRON
25 Director of University Events .... Ms. Cheryl HANSEN
37 Director of Financial Aid .... Ms. Tracy REISINGER
88 Director Art Therapy Graduate Pgm .... Ms. Christine TURNER
72 Director Center for Learning Tech .... Vacant
13 Director of Information Systems .... Mr. Rick CAMPBELL
18 Director of Facilities .... Mr. Mark STRULOEFF
88 Director Music Therapy .... Ms. Christine KORB
64 Chairperson Music Department .... Dr. John PAUL
57 Co-Chairperson & Dir Art Department .... Mr. Paul SUTINEN
57 Co-Chrpn Art Dpt/Dir Int Design Dpt .... Ms. Nancy HISS
73 Chrpsn Religious Studies & Phil .... Dr. Jeroid ROUSSELL
88 Chrpsn Grad Interdisciplinary Stds .... Dr. Debrah BOKOWSKI
88 Chrpsn Interdisciplinary Studies .... Mr. Simeon DREYFUSS
79 Chrpsn Cultural & Historal Studies .... Dr. David DENNY
81 Dean of Faculty/Chair Science&Math .... Dr. Jan DABROWSKI
83 Chairperson Human Sciences .... Dr. Jennifer SASSER
50 Director Business & Real Estate .... Mr. Bob HANKS
88 Chairperson Real Estate Studies .... Vacant
88 Chrpsn English Literature/Writing .... Dr. Meg ROLAND
60 Chairperson Communication Studies .... Mr. Jeff SWEENEY

Mount Angel Seminary (A)

1 Abbey Drive, Saint Benedict OR 97373-0505

County: Marion | FICE Identification: 003203 | Unit ID: 209241

Telephone: (503) 845-3951 | Carnegie Class: Spec/Faith
FAX Number: (503) 845-3128 | Calendar System: Semester
URL: www.mountangelabbey.org
Established: 1887 | Annual Undergrad Tuition & Fees: $34,750
Enrollment: 207 | Coed
Affiliation or Control: Roman Catholic | IRS Status: 501(c)3
Highest Offering: Master's
Program: Liberal Arts And General; Professional
Accreditation: NW, THEOL

01 President/Rector .... Msgr. Richard PAPERINI
05 Vice President/Academic Dean .... Dr. Elaine PARK
08 Librarian .... Ms. Victoria ERTELT
10 Business Manager .... Fr. Martin GRASSEL, OSB
06 Registrar & Student Financial Aid .... Ms. Marina KEYS
32 Dean of Students College .... Rev. Paschal CHELINE, OSB
32 Dean of Students Theology .... Abbot Peter EBERLE, OSB
20 Academic Dean College .... Dr. Creighton LINDSAY
85 Director of Foreign Students .... Ms. Tamara SWANSON-ORR
07 Director of Admissions .... Fr. Ralph RECKER, OSB
04 Admin Assistant to the President .... Mrs. Marge O. DOLEAC
13 Director of Information Technology .... Br. Samuel BERNING, OSB
40 Director of Bookstore .... Mrs. Beth WELLS
20 Academic Dean Theology .... Dr. Seymour HOUSE

Mt. Hood Community College (B)

26000 SE Stark, Gresham OR 97030-3300

County: Multnomah | FICE Identification: 003204 | Unit ID: 209250

Telephone: (503) 491-6422 | Carnegie Class: Assoc/Pub-S-SC
FAX Number: (503) 491-7389 | Calendar System: Quarter
URL: www.mhcc.edu
Established: 1965 | Annual Undergrad Tuition & Fees (In-District): $5,505
Enrollment: 7,406 | Coed
Affiliation or Control: Local | IRS Status: 501(c)3
Highest Offering: Associate Degree
Program: Occupational; 2-Year Principally Bachelor's Creditable
Accreditation: NW, DH, FUSER, MAC, PTAA, SURGT

01 Interim President .... Dr. Michael D. HAY
11 Int VP of Administrative Services .... Mr. Bill FARVER
05 Int Vice President of Instruction .... Ms. Christie PLINSKI
32 Vice Pres Student Svcs & Enrollment .... Dr. David MINGER
30 Vice Pres of College Advancement .... Ms. Cassie MCVEETY
46 VP Research/Planning/Inst Effect .... Dr. Nancy SZOFRAN
38 Dean Student Success Services .... Mr. Robert COX
15 Director Human Resources .... Ms. Mara KERSHAW
88 Dir Child Dev/Family Support Pgms .... Ms. Jean WAGNER
18 Director Facilities Management .... Mr. Richard BYERS
21 Dir Budget Office & Auxiliary Svcs .... Ms. JoAnn ZAHN
10 Director Fiscal & Business Services .... Ms. Jamie SIMMS
06 Registrar .... Ms. Peggy MAAS
37 Director Student Financial Aid .... Vacant
36 Director Student Placement .... Ms. Christi HART
13 Chief Information Officer .... Mr. Jay CROWTHERS
08 Dean Information Resources .... Vacant
76 Dean Allied Health .... Dr. Donna LARSON
81 Dean Soc Science/Math & Eng .... Ms. Christie PLINSKI
50 Dean Business/CAS/HPE .... Vacant
72 Dean Science & Technology .... Dr. Clyde JENSEN

79 Dean Humanities .... Dr. Ursula IRWIN
93 Dean Adult/HS Comm Learning .... Mr. Marc GOLDBERG

Multnomah University (C)

8435 NE Glisan Street, Portland OR 97220-5898

County: Multnomah | FICE Identification: 003206 | Unit ID: 209287

Telephone: (503) 255-0332 | Carnegie Class: Spec/Faith
FAX Number: (503) 254-1268 | Calendar System: Semester
URL: www.multnomah.edu
Established: 1936 | Annual Undergrad Tuition & Fees: $19,990
Enrollment: 915 | Coed
Affiliation or Control: Independent Non-Profit | IRS Status: 501(c)3
Highest Offering: First Professional Degree
Program: Teacher Preparatory; Religious Emphasis
Accreditation: NW, BI, THEOL

01 President .... Dr. Daniel R. LOCKWOOD
05 Chief Academic Officer/Provost .... Dr. Wayne G. STRICKLAND
11 Chief Administrative Officer .... Ms. Gina BERQUIST
10 Chief Financial Officer .... Mr. Russell LACY
30 Sr Vice President of Advancement .... Mr. Paul A. GRIFFIN
73 VP/Academic Dean Biblical Seminary .... Dr. Robert R. REDMAN
32 Director/Dean of Students .... Mr. Jon MATHIS
39 Dean of Resident & Commuter Life .... Mr. David GROOM
35 Dean of Students .... Miss Karen J. FANCHER
09 Dir of Institutional Effectiveness .... Dr. David FUNK
20 Associate Academic Dean .... Mr. David W. JONGEWARD
06 Registrar .... Miss Amy M. STEPHENS
21 Controller .... Mr. Brian YAW
18 Executive Director of Facilities .... Mr. Lloyd L. HELM
08 Librarian .... Dr. Philip M. JOHNSON
37 Director Student Financial Aid .... Mrs. Mary MCGLOTHLAN
42 Director of Student Ministries .... Mr. Jim N. SAEMENES
36 Seminary Director of Placement .... Dr. Roger TRAUTMANN
13 Director Information Technology .... Mrs. Brenda GIBSON
15 Director of Human Resources .... Miss Tracy L. MORESCHI
23 Director Health Services .... Mrs. Jana POLING
41 Athletic Director .... Miss Lois VOS
26 Dir of Promotions & Communication .... Mr. Robert LEARY
07 Director of Admissions .... Mr. Palmer MUNTZ
29 Director Alumni Relations .... Miss Michelle PEEL
30 Director of Development .... Vacant
04 Assistant to the President .... Mrs. Denise STONE

National College of Natural Medicine (D)

049 SW Porter Street, Portland OR 97201-4878

County: Multnomah | FICE Identification: 025340 | Unit ID: 209296

Telephone: (503) 552-1555 | Carnegie Class: Spec/Health
FAX Number: (503) 499-0022 | Calendar System: Quarter
URL: www.ncnm.edu
Established: 1956 | Annual Graduate Tuition & Fees: $21,060
Enrollment: 528 | Coed
Affiliation or Control: Independent Non-Profit | IRS Status: 501(c)3
Highest Offering: Doctorate; No Undergraduates
Program: Professional
Accreditation: NW, ACUP, NATUR

01 President .... Dr. David J. SCHLEICH
05 Interim Provost/VP Academic .... Dr. Andrea SMITH
10 Chief Financial Officer/VP Finances .... Mr. Gerald BORES
30 VP of Advancement .... Ms. Susan HUNTER
26 VP Marketing .... Ms. Sandra SNYDER
09 Dean of Inst Research & Compliance .... Ms. Laurie MCGRATH
17 Dean of Naturopathic Medicine .... Dr. Margot LONGENECKER
88 Dean Classical Chinese Medicine .... Dr. Laurie REGAN
32 Dean of Student Affairs .... Ms. Cheryl MILLER
46 Dean Helfgott Research Inst .... Dr. Heather ZWICKEY
23 Dean of Clinical Operations .... Dr. Jill SANDERS
15 Director of Human Resources .... Mr. Steve JOHNSON
07 Director of Admissions .... Mr. Rigo NUNEZ
37 Director of Financial Aid .... Ms. Laurie RADFORD
06 Registrar .... Ms. Kelly GAREY
04 Executive Asst to the President .... Ms. Gail HOUGHTON
40 Dir Retail Operations .... Ms. Nora SANDE
88 Director of Professional Formation .... Dr. Marnie LOOMIS
08 Director of Library .... Dr. Rick SEVERSON

New Hope Christian College (E)

2155 Bailey Hill Road, Eugene OR 97405-1194

County: Lane | FICE Identification: 021597 | Unit ID: 208725

Telephone: (541) 485-1780 | Carnegie Class: Spec/Faith
FAX Number: (541) 343-5801 | Calendar System: Semester
URL: www.newhope.edu
Established: 1925 | Annual Undergrad Tuition & Fees: $12,535
Enrollment: 119 | Coed
Affiliation or Control: Other | IRS Status: 501(c)3
Highest Offering: Baccalaureate
Program: Religious Emphasis
Accreditation: BI

00 Chancellor .... Mr. Wayne CORDEIRO
01 President .... Mr. Wayne CORDEIRO
11 Chief of Operations .... Mr. Gary MATSDORF
04 Assistant to the President .... Mrs. Mary WAIALEALE
04 Executive Assistant .... Mrs. Freida P. ARNS
05 Academic Dean .... Dr. Larry R. BURKE
30 Director of College Advancement .... Mr. Wayne CORDEIRO
29 Director of Alumni Relations .... Vacant
32 Director of Student Life .... Mr. Steven POETZL
10 Business Administrator .... Mr. Paul SHERIDON
06 Registrar .... Ms. Sarah SLATER
07 Enrollment Management .... Mr. Sean MCCARTIN
37 Director of Financial Aid .... Mr. Nathan ICENHOWER
08 Head Librarian .... Ms. Jan KELLEY
38 Director of Christian Counseling .... Mr. David F. ORTEGA

Northwest Christian University (F)

828 E 11th Avenue, Eugene OR 97401-3745

County: Lane | FICE Identification: 003208 | Unit ID: 209409

Telephone: (541) 343-1641 | Carnegie Class: Bac/Diverse
FAX Number: (541) 343-9159 | Calendar System: Semester
URL: www.nwcu.edu
Established: 1895 | Annual Undergrad Tuition & Fees: $23,600
Enrollment: 623 | Coed
Affiliation or Control: Christian Church (Disciples Of Christ) | IRS Status: 501(c)3
Highest Offering: Master's
Program: Liberal Arts And General; Teacher Preparatory
Accreditation: #NW, IACBE

01 President .... Dr. Joe WOMACK
05 VP Academic Affairs/Dean of Faculty .... Dr. Dennis LINDSAY
10 Vice Pres Finance/Administration .... Ms. Lisa CASTLEBURY
30 Vice President Advancement .... Dr. Greg STRAUSBAUGH
32 VP Student Development/Enrollment .... Mr. Michael FULLER
49 Dean Arts & Sciences .... Dr. Mick BOLLENBAUGH
50 Dean Business & Management .... Dr. Michael KENNEDY
53 Dean School of Education .... Dr. Jim HOWARD
09 Director Institutional Research .... Dr. Xuemei YANG
39 Dir of Residence Life/Student Svcs .... Ms. Jocelyn HUBBS
08 Director Kellenberger Library .... Mr. Steve SILVER
06 Registrar .... Mr. Aaron PRUITT
42 Campus Pastor .... Mr. Troy DEAN
37 Director Financial Aid .... Mr. David HAGGARD
07 Director Undergraduate Admissions .... Ms. Jennifer SAMPLES
35 Director Student Programs .... Ms. Kirsten MADSEN
18 Plant Manager .... Mr. Oskar BUCHER
40 Bookstore Manager .... Vacant
41 Athletic Director .... Mr. Corey R. ANDERSON
36 Dir Svc Learning/Career Placement .... Ms. Angela DOTY
24 Media/Computer Lab Supervisor .... Mr. Doug VERMILYEA
04 Administrative Assistant .... Ms. Carla AYDELOTT
29 Director Alumni & Donor Relations .... Ms. Jennine JONES
44 Director Annual Fund .... Ms. Beth WALSH

Oregon College of Art and Craft (G)

8245 SW Barnes Road, Portland OR 97225-6349

County: Multnomah | FICE Identification: 030073 | Unit ID: 209533

Telephone: (503) 297-5554 | Carnegie Class: Spec/Arts
FAX Number: (503) 297-3155 | Calendar System: Semester
URL: www.ocac.edu
Established: 1907 | Annual Undergrad Tuition & Fees: $23,306
Enrollment: 145 | Coed
Affiliation or Control: Independent Non-Profit | IRS Status: 501(c)3
Highest Offering: Baccalaureate
Program: Fine Arts Emphasis
Accreditation: NW, ART

01 President .... Ms. Denise MULLEN
10 Chief Financial Officer .... Mr. Lee MILLIGAN
05 Academic Dean .... Ms. Kate BODIN
30 Director of Development .... Ms. MaryAnn DEFFENBAUGH
07 Chief Enroll Officer/Dir of Admiss .... Ms. Anne BOERNER
06 Registrar .... Ms. Devon SIMPSON
08 Head of Library Services .... Ms. Lori JOHNSON
56 Extension Program Director .... Vacant
32 Director of Student Services .... Mr. Peter LARSON
37 Director of Financial Aid .... Ms. Linda ANDERSON
04 Exec Assistant to the President .... Ms. Kris KEBISEK

Oregon College of Oriental Medicine (H)

10525 SE Cherry Blossom Drive, Portland OR 97216-2859

County: Multnomah | FICE Identification: 026037 | Unit ID: 369659

Telephone: (503) 253-3443 | Carnegie Class: Spec/Health
FAX Number: (503) 253-2701 | Calendar System: Quarter
URL: www.ocom.edu
Established: 1983 | Annual Graduate Tuition & Fees: $23,548
Enrollment: 284 | Coed
Affiliation or Control: Independent Non-Profit | IRS Status: 501(c)3
Highest Offering: Doctorate; No Undergraduates
Program: Professional
Accreditation: @NW, ACUP

01 President .... Dr. Michael GAETA
05 Vice President for Academic Affairs .... Dr. Tim CHAPMAN
10 Vice President for Finance .... Susan SLOAN
32 Dean of Academic & Student Affairs .... Carol TAUB
09 Planning & Inst Assessment Officer .... Shelley STUMP

88 Dean of Doctoral Studies ... Dr. Beth BURCH
46 Associate Dean of Research ... Dr. Deborah ACKERMAN
30 Development Officer ... Glenn FEE
15 Director of Human Resources ... Michelle VALINTIS
26 Director of Community Relations ... Gretchen HORTON
23 Assoc Dean of Clinical Education ... Dr. Debra MULROONEY
06 Registrar ... Carol ACHESON
13 Director of Operations & Technology ... Chris CHIACCHIERINI

Oregon Culinary Institute (A)

1701 SW Jefferson Street, Portland OR 97201-2571

County: Multnomah | Identification: 666177
Telephone: (503) 961-6200 | Carnegie Class: Not Classified
FAX Number: (503) 961-6240 | Calendar System: Other
URL: www.oregonculinaryinstitute.com
Established: 2006 | Annual Undergrad Tuition & Fees: $16,735
Enrollment: 235 | Coed
Affiliation or Control: Proprietary | IRS Status: Proprietary
Highest Offering: Associate Degree
Program: Occupational; Fine Arts Emphasis
Accreditation: ACICS

01 President ... Mr. Eric STROMQUIST
05 Director of Education ... Mr. Brian WILKE
07 Location Director/Admissions ... Mr. Ray COLVIN
36 Career Services Director ... Ms. Nina TUTHILL-RANGER
37 Financial Aid Director ... Ms. Sarah PETERS
31 Community Relations Director ... Mr. Kevin RICHARDS
06 Education Coordinator ... Mr. Ryan GAGE

† Branch campus of Pioneer Pacific College, Wilsonville, OR.

*Oregon University System (B)

PO Box 3175, Eugene OR 97403-0175

County: Lane | FICE Identification: 009190
Unit ID: 209445
Telephone: (541) 346-1000 | Carnegie Class: N/A
FAX Number: (541) 346-5764
URL: www.ous.edu

01 Chancellor ... Mr. George P. PERNSTEINER
10 VC Finance & Administration ... Dr. Jay KENTON
05 Vice Chanc for Academic Strategies ... Dr. Sona ANDREWS
21 Asst VC Budget/Operations ... Ms. Jan LEWIS
15 Director Labor & Employee Relations ... Vacant
43 Director Legal Services ... Dr. Ryan HAGEMANN
86 Director Government Relations ... Vacant
09 Director Institutional Research ... Mr. Robert KIERAN

*Eastern Oregon University (C)

One University Boulevard, La Grande OR 97850-2807

County: Union | FICE Identification: 003193
Unit ID: 208646
Telephone: (541) 962-3672 | Carnegie Class: Master's S
FAX Number: (541) 962-3493 | Calendar System: Quarter
URL: www.eou.edu
Established: 1929 | Annual Undergrad Tuition & Fees (In-State): $7,046
Enrollment: 4,137 | Coed
Affiliation or Control: State | IRS Status: 501(c)3
Highest Offering: Master's
Program: Liberal Arts And General; Teacher Preparatory; Professional
Accreditation: NW, IACBE

02 President ... Dr. Robert DAVIES
05 Provost/Vice Pres Academic Affairs ... Dr. Steven ADKISON
32 Vice President for Student Affairs ... Dr. Camille CONSOLVO
10 Vice President for Finance & Admin ... Mr. Lon WHITAKER
30 Vice Pres University Advancement ... Mr. Tim SEYDEL
20 Associate VP for Academic Affairs ... Dr. Sarah WITTE
49 Acting Dean College Arts & Science ... Dr. Sarah WITTE
50 Dean College of Business & Educ ... Dr. Michael JAEGER
37 Director of Financial Aid ... Vacant
08 Director of Pierce Library ... Ms. Karen CLAY
07 Director of Admissions ... Vacant
06 Registrar ... Ms. Carolyn BLOYED
15 Director of Human Resources ... Mr. Dennis HOPWOOD
29 Dir of Annual Giving and Alumni Rel ... Mr. Jon LARKIN
41 Director of Athletics ... Mr. Robert CASHELL
39 Director of Residence Life ... Mr. Stephen JENKINS
18 Director of Facilities & Planning ... Mr. David LAGESON
38 Director Counseling Center ... Dr. Thacher CARTER
04 Exec Assistant to the President ... Ms. Kristen BINGAMAN
21 Director of Business Affairs ... Ms. Lara MOORE
36 Director of Acad & Career Advising ... Ms. Liz BURTON
88 Director of Learning Center ... Ms. Anna Maria DILL
35 Director of Student Relations ... Ms. Colleen DUNNE-CASCIO
19 Campus Security/Public Safety Ofcr ... Mr. Scott DEPRIEST

*Oregon Health & Science University (D)

3181 SW Sam Jackson, Portland OR 97201-3098

County: Multnomah | FICE Identification: 004882
Unit ID: 209490
Telephone: (503) 494-8311 | Carnegie Class: Spec/Med
FAX Number: (503) 494-5738 | Calendar System: Quarter
URL: www.ohsu.edu
Established: 1974 | Annual Undergrad Tuition & Fees (In-State): $15,940
Enrollment: 2,721 | Coed
Affiliation or Control: State | IRS Status: 501(c)3
Highest Offering: Doctorate
Program: Professional
Accreditation: NW, ANEST, ARCPA, DENT, DIETI, EMT, IPSY, MED, MIDWF, MT, NURSE, PH, RTT

02 President ... Dr. Joseph E. ROBERTSON
05 Vice Provost Academic/Student Affs ... Dr. Robert VIEIRA
53 Interim Provost ... Mr. David ROBINSON
18 Assoc VP Facilities/Physical Plant ... Mr. Scott PAGE
06 Registrar/Director of Financial Aid ... Ms. Cherie HONNELL
63 Dean School of Medicine ... Dr. Mark RICHARDSON
52 Dean School of Dentistry ... Dr. Jack CLINTON
66 Dean School of Nursing ... Dr. Michael BLEICH
17 Director University Hospital ... Mr. Peter RAPP
88 Director Vollum Inst Adv Biomed Res ... Dr. Richard H. GOODMAN
15 Director of Human Resources ... Vacant
08 Director Health Sciences Libraries ... Mr. Chris SHAFFER
46 Director of Research Services ... Dr. Daniel DORSA
27 Director Corporate Communications ... Ms. Lora L. CUYKENDALL
88 Director Child Devel/Rehab Center ... Dr. Brian ROGERS
37 Director Student Financial Aid ... Ms. Cherie HONNELL
28 Director of Diversity ... Ms. Leslie GARCIA
35 Director Student Affairs ... Ms. Karen SERESUN

*Oregon Institute of Technology (E)

3201 Campus Drive, Klamath Falls OR 97601-8801

County: Klamath | FICE Identification: 003211
Unit ID: 209506
Telephone: (541) 885-1000 | Carnegie Class: Bac/Diverse
FAX Number: (541) 885-1101 | Calendar System: Quarter
URL: www.oit.edu
Established: 1947 | Annual Undergrad Tuition & Fees (In-State): $7,404
Enrollment: 3,783 | Coed
Affiliation or Control: State | IRS Status: 501(c)3
Highest Offering: Master's
Program: Liberal Arts And General; Technical Emphasis
Accreditation: NW, DH, ENG, ENGR, ENGT, IACBE, MT, POLYT

02 President ... Dr. Christopher MAPLES
05 Provost/Vice Pres Academic Affairs ... Mr. Bradley BURDA
10 Int VP Finance/Administration ... Ms. Mary Ann ZEMKE
32 VP Student Affairs/Enrollment Mgmt ... Dr. Erin FOLEY
30 Int Vice Pres of Development ... Mrs. Robin THOMPSON
35 Dean of Students ... Dr. Erin FOLEY
12 Director Portland Operations ... Mr. Richard K. SWANSON
37 Director of Financial Aid ... Ms. Tracey A. LEHMAN
15 Director of Human Resources ... Mr. Ron MCCUTCHEON
07 Director of Admissions ... Vacant
06 Registrar ... Ms. Wendy PEDERSEN
38 Director of Counseling ... Vacant
21 Int Director of Business Affairs ... Ms. Sara REUTER
13 Chief Information Officer ... Mr. Andy ABBOTT
23 Director Student Health Services ... Vacant
18 Director Facilities Services ... Mr. David W. EBSEN
41 Athletic Director ... Mr. Michael J. SCHELL
35 Director Campus Life ... Ms. Jane RIDER
36 Director of Career Services ... Vacant
09 Director of Institutional Research ... Vacant
29 Director Alumni Relations ... Mrs. Robin THOMPSON

*Oregon State University (F)

Corvallis OR 97331-8507

County: Benton | FICE Identification: 003210
Unit ID: 209542
Telephone: (541) 737-0123 | Carnegie Class: RU/VH
FAX Number: (541) 737-3033 | Calendar System: Quarter
URL: www.oregonstate.edu
Established: 1868 | Annual Undergrad Tuition & Fees (In-State): $7,744
Enrollment: 24,900 | Coed
Affiliation or Control: State | IRS Status: 501(c)3
Highest Offering: Doctorate
Program: Liberal Arts And General; Teacher Preparatory; Professional
Accreditation: NW, BUS, BUSA, CONST, CS, DIETD, DIETI, ENG, ENGR, FOR, IPSY, PH, PHAR, TED, VET

02 President ... Dr. Edward J. RAY
05 Provost/Executive Vice President ... Dr. Sabah U. RANDHAWA
10 Vice Pres Finance/Administration ... Mr. Mark E. MCCAMBRIDGE
30 Vice Pres University Advancement ... Vacant
46 Vice President for Research ... Mr. Rick SPINRAD
20 Vice Prov Academic Affs/Intl Pgms ... Dr. Rebecca WARNER
13 Vice Prov for Information Svcs/CIO ... Ms. Lois BROOKS
32 Vice Prov for Student Affairs ... Dr. Larry D. ROPER
56 Vice Prov Univ Outreach/Engagement ... Dr. Scott REED
12 V Prov/Campus Ex Ofcr OSU-Cascades ... Dr. Rebecca JOHNSON
84 Asst Provost Enrollment Management ... Ms. Kate M. PETERSON
102 President & CEO OSU Foundation ... Mr. Mike GOODWIN
47 Dean of Agricultural Sciences ... Dr. Sonny RAMASWAMY
50 Dean of Business ... Dr. Ilene K. KLEINSORGE
54 Dean of Engineering ... Dr. Ronald L. ADAMS
65 Dean of Forestry ... Dr. Hal J. SALWASSER
68 Dean of Health & Human Sciences ... Dr. Tammy BRAY
49 Interim Dean of Liberal Arts ... Dr. Larry D. ROPER
88 Dean of Oceanic & Atmos Science ... Dr. Mark R. ABBOTT
67 Dean of Pharmacy ... Dr. Mark ZABRISKIE
81 Dean of Science ... Dr. Sherman H. BLOOMER
74 Dean of Veterinary Medicine ... Dr. Cyril CLARKE
51 Assoc Provost Extended Campus ... Dr. David A. KING
58 Dean of Graduate School ... Dr. Sally K. FRANCIS
35 Dean of Student Life ... Dr. Mamta ACCAPADI
92 Dean University Honors College ... Dr. Daniel J. ARP
53 Dean of Education ... Dr. Sam STERN
08 University Librarian ... Ms. Faye CHADWELL
22 Dir Affirmative Action/Equal Oppty ... Mr. Angelo GOMEZ
43 General Counsel ... Ms. Meg REEVES
41 Director Intercollegiate Athletics ... Mr. Robert J. DE CAROLIS
88 Director Intl Education & Outreach ... Dr. Sunil KHANNA
36 Director of Career Services ... Mr. Douglas COCHRAN
37 Dir of Financial Aid/Scholarship ... Mr. Doug SEVERS
31 Director Memorial Union ... Mr. Michael HENTHORNE
23 Director Student Health Services ... Dr. Phillip C. HISTAND
38 Dir Univ Counseling/Psych Svcs ... Dr. Mariette BROUWERS
39 Director Univ Housing/Dining Svcs ... Mr. Thomas A. SCHEUERMANN
06 Registrar ... Mr. Thomas K. KUO
07 Director of Admissions ... Vacant
24 Director Media & Outreach Services ... Mr. John GREYDANUS
14 Dir of Enterprise Computing Service ... Ms. Catherine M. WILLIAMS
21 Director of Business Affairs ... Mr. Aaron D. HOWELL
88 Director Business Services ... Mr. Brian K. THORSNESS
15 Director of Human Resources ... Ms. Jacquelyn T. RUDOLPH
18 Director Facility Services ... Mr. Vincent MARTORELLO
19 Director Public Safety ... Mr. Jack T. ROGERS
29 Exec Dir of Alumni Association ... Mr. Scott GREENWOOD
86 Director Government Relations ... Mr. Jock S. MILLS
44 Director of Annual Giving ... Ms. Lacie LA RUE
27 Dir News/Comm Svcs/Asst Vice Pres ... Mr. Todd H. SIMMONS
26 Director of University Marketing ... Ms. Melody K. OLDFIELD
105 Asst Director Web Communications ... Mr. David A. BAKER
20 Dir Academic Planning/Assessment ... Vacant
28 Director of Community & Diversity ... Dr. Terryl J. ROSS
09 Director of Institutional Research ... Mr. Salvador CASTILLO
40 General Mgr & CEO OSU Bookstores ... Mr. Steve E. ECKRICH
96 Manager Procurement/Contract Svcs ... Ms. Kelly L. KOZISEK

*Portland State University (G)

PO Box 751, Portland OR 97207-0751

County: Multnomah | FICE Identification: 003216
Unit ID: 209807
Telephone: (503) 725-3000 | Carnegie Class: RU/H
FAX Number: (503) 725-4882 | Calendar System: Quarter
URL: www.pdx.edu
Established: 1946 | Annual Undergrad Tuition & Fees (In-State): $6,686
Enrollment: 25,636 | Coed
Affiliation or Control: State | IRS Status: 501(c)3
Highest Offering: Doctorate
Program: Liberal Arts And General; Teacher Preparatory; Professional
Accreditation: NW, BUS, BUSA, CACREP, CORE, CS, ENG, MUS, PH, PLNG, SP, SPAA, SW, TED, THEA

02 President ... Dr. Wim WIEWEL
43 General Counsel ... Mr. David REESE
05 Provost ... Dr. Roy KOCH
10 Vice President Finance/Admin ... Dr. Monica RIMAI
30 VP for University Advancement ... Ms. Francoise AYLMER
100 Chief of Staff ... Ms. Lois DAVIS
84 VP Enroll Mgmt & Student Affairs ... Dr. Jackie BALZER
46 VP Rsrch & Strategic Partnerships ... Dr. Jonathon FINK
51 Vice Provost of Extended Studies ... Vacant
20 Vice Prov Acad Personnel ... Dr. Carol MACK
88 Vice Provost International Affairs ... Dr. Gil LATZ
21 Assoc VP Finance & Planning ... Ms. Dee WENDLER
15 Assc Vice President Human Resources ... Ms. Cathy LATOURETTE
20 Assoc Vice Prov Academic Services ... Mr. Dan FORTMILLER
39 Director Housing & Transportation ... Mr. John ECKMAN
32 Asoc V Prov Stdnt Affs/Enroll Mgmt ... Mrs. Agnes HOFFMAN
22 Chief Diversity Officer ... Dr. Jilma MENSES
26 Asst Vice Pres Communications ... Mr. Christopher BRODERICK
09 Director Inst Research/Planning ... Dr. Kathi A. KETCHESON
19 Director Public Safety ... Vacant
96 Purchasing Mgr/Contractor Admin ... Ms. Karen PRESTON
13 AVP Strategic Plng/Prtnrshps/Tech ... Mr. Mark GREGORY
91 Director of Information Services ... Ms. Ann HARRIS
90 Director User Support Services ... Mr. Jahed SUKHUN
31 Dir Cmty Univ Prtnrshp/Ctr Acad Exc ... Dr. Kevin KECSKES
23 Med Dir Student Health/Counseling ... Dr. Mark BAJOREK
08 University Librarian ... Vacant
36 Associate Vice Provost Career Services ... Mr. Dan FORTMILLER
85 Director International Affairs ... Ms. Judy VAN DYCK
18 Director Facilities & Planning ... Ms. Robyn PIERCE
41 Athletics Director ... Mr. Michael T. CHISHOLM
06 Director of Registration & Records ... Ms. Cindy BACCAR
89 Director University Studies ... Mr. Sukhwant S. JHAJ
92 Director University Honors Program ... Dr. Lawrence WHEELER
29 Asst Vice President Alumni Affairs ... Ms. Patricia E. SQUIRE
38 Dir Couns/Psychological Svcs ... Dr. Dana TASSON
44 Director for Annual Giving ... Ms. Melinda PETERSEN
49 Dean Col of Liberal Arts/Sciences ... Vacant
50 Dean School Business Administration ... Dr. Scott DAWSON
53 Dean Graduate Sch of Education ... Dr. Randy HITZ
54 Dean Col Engr/Computer Science ... Dr. Renjeng SU
57 Dean School Fine/Performing Arts ... Ms. Barbara SESTAK
70 Dean Graduate School Social Work ... Vacant
80 Dean College Urban/Public Affairs ... Dr. Lawrence WALLACK
37 Director Student Financial Aid ... Mr. Phillip RODGERS
21 Vice Provost Fiscal Strategies ... Mr. Kevin REYNOLDS
20 Vice Prov Academic Pgm/Instruction ... Ms. Melody ROSE
35 Assoc Vice Provost Student Affairs ... Ms. Michele TOPPE
88 Interim Director ... Mr. Greg FLORES
27 Chief Information Officer ... Ms. Sharon BLANTON

*Southern Oregon University (A)

1250 Siskiyou Boulevard, Ashland OR 97520-5001
County: Jackson FICE Identification: 003219
Unit ID: 210146
Telephone: (541) 552-7672 Carnegie Class: Master's L
FAX Number: (541) 552-6329 Calendar System: Quarter
URL: www.sou.edu
Established: 1872 Annual Undergrad Tuition & Fees (In-State): $6,090
Enrollment: 6,444 Coed
Affiliation or Control: State IRS Status: 501(c)3
Highest Offering: Master's
Program: Liberal Arts And General; Professional
Accreditation: NW, CACREP, MUS

02 President .... Dr. Mary CULLINAN
05 Provost and VP for Academic Affairs .... Dr. James KLEIN
11 VP for Administration & Finance .... Mr. Craig MORRIS
32 Vice President for Student Affairs .... Mr. Jon ELDRIDGE
30 VP Dev/Exec Dir SOU Foundation .... Ms. Sylvia KELLEY
15 Assoc VP for Human Resource Svcs .... Vacant
26 Dir Interactive Mktg & Media Rels .... Mr. James BEAVER
18 Dir for Facilities Mgmt & Planning .... Mr. Drew GILLELAND
20 Assoc Provost Academic Affairs .... Dr. Susan WALSH
84 Asst VP of Enrollment .... Mr. Rick WEEMS
21 Director of Business Services .... Mr. Steve LARVICK
08 Dean of Library .... Mr. Paul ADALIAN
35 Executive Director for Student Life .... Vacant
51 Exec Dir Division of Continuing Edu .... Ms. Jeanne STALLMAN
35 Dean of Students .... Dr. Laura O'BRYON
49 Dean College of Arts & Sciences .... Dr. Alissa ARP
19 Co-Director of Campus Public Safety .... Mr. Stephen ROSS
19 Co-Director of Campus Public Safety .... Mr. Richard WALSH
14 Director of Information Technology .... Ms. Teri O'ROURKE
29 Director of Alumni Affairs .... Ms. Doreen O'SKEA
21 Assoc Director of Business Services .... Vacant
106 Director of Distance Education .... Dr. Jennifer MCVAY-DYCHE
88 Exec Dir of Schneider Museum of Art .... Vacant
88 Dir of Accelerated Baccalaureate Pgm .... Mr. Curt BACON
28 Director of Diversity .... Mr. Jonathan ELDRIDGE
44 Annual Fund Coordinator .... Ms. Chava FLORENDO
88 Donor Relations Coordinator .... Ms. Sarah KASSEL
88 Director of Performing Arts .... Mr. Noel KORAN

*University of Oregon (B)

Eugene OR 97403-1226
County: Lane FICE Identification: 003223
Unit ID: 209551
Telephone: (541) 346-1000 Carnegie Class: RU/VH
FAX Number: (541) 346-3017 Calendar System: Quarter
URL: www.uoregon.edu
Established: 1876 Annual Undergrad Tuition & Fees (In-State): $8,789
Enrollment: 23,342 Coed
Affiliation or Control: State IRS Status: 501(c)3
Highest Offering: Doctorate
Program: Liberal Arts And General; Professional
Accreditation: NW, ART, BUS, BUSA, CEA, CIDA, CLPSY, COPSY, IPSY, JOUR, LAW, LSAR, MFCD, MUS, PLNG, SCPSY, SP, SPAA

02 President .... Dr. Richard W. LARIVIERE
04 Senior Assistant to the President .... Dr. David R. HUBIN
04 Assistant Vice President .... Mr. Timothy R. BLACK
05 Senior Vice President & Provost .... Dr. James C. BEAN
10 Vice Pres Finance & Admin .... Ms. Frances L. DYKE
32 Vice President for Student Affairs .... Dr. Robin H. HOLMES
30 Vice Pres University Relations .... Dr. Michael W. REDDING
46 Vice Pres Research/Graduate Stds .... Dr. Kimberly A. ESPY
20 Vice Provost Undergraduate Studies .... Dr. Karen U. SPRAGUE
28 Vice Pres Inst Equity/Diversity .... Dr. Charles MARTINEZ
13 Vice Prov Information Services/CIO .... Dr. Don HARRIS
85 Vice Provost International Affairs .... Dr. D. Fred SIMON
30 Asst VP Campaign Initiatives .... Mr. Shane G. GIESE
21 Assoc Vice Pres Budget & Finance .... Ms. Laura E. HUBBARD
86 Assoc Vice Pres Public/Govt Affairs .... Ms. Betsy A. BOYD
29 AVP Alumni Affairs/Exec Dir UOAA .. Mr. Timothy R. CLEVENGER
43 General Counsel .... Mr. L. Randy GELLER
102 Chief Investment Officer Foundation .... Mr. Jay NAMYET
06 University Registrar .... Ms. Susan M. EVELAND
07 Director of Admissions .... Mr. Brian L. HENLEY
08 Philip H Knight Dean of Libraries .... Ms. Deborah A. CARVER
21 Dir Business Affairs and Controller .... Mr. Kelly B. WOLF
37 Director Student Financial Aid .... Mr. James J. BROOKS
36 Director of Career Center .... Ms. Deborah T. CHERECK
15 Assoc VP Human Resources .... Ms. Linda L. KING
18 Assoc VP Campus Operations .... Mr. George E. HECHT
22 Director Affirmative Action .... Ms. Penny J. DAUGHERTY
41 Director Intercollegiate Athletics .... Mr. Rob A. MULLENS
56 Senior Dir UO Academic Extension .... Mr. Curt D. LIND
49 Dean College Arts & Sciences .... Dr. Scott L. COLTRANE
48 Dean Architecture & Allied Arts .... Ms. Frances BRONET
50 Dean College of Business .... Dr. Cornelis A. DE KLUYVER
53 Dean College of Education .... Dr. Michael D. BULLIS
60 Dean School of Journalism & Comm ... Dr. Timothy W. GLEASON
58 Vice Prov Grad Studies & Assoc Dean .... Dr. Sandra MORGEN
61 Dean School of Law .... Ms. Margaret L. PARIS
64 Dean School of Music & Dance .... Dr. C. Brad FOLEY
92 Dean Clark Honors College .... Dr. David FRANK
09 Director of Institutional Research .... Dr. JP MONROE
35 Associate VP for Student Affairs .... Mr. Mike EYSTER
38 Dir Counseling & Testing Center .... Dr. Shelly K. KERR
84 Vice Provost Enrollment Management ... Mr. Roger J. THOMPSON
96 Dir Purchasing & Contracting Svcs .... Ms. Cathey D. SUSMAN

*Western Oregon University (C)

345 N Monmouth Avenue, Monmouth OR 97361-1394
County: Polk FICE Identification: 003209
Unit ID: 210429
Telephone: (503) 838-8000 Carnegie Class: Master's M
FAX Number: (503) 838-8474 Calendar System: Quarter
URL: www.wou.edu
Established: 1856 Annual Undergrad Tuition & Fees (In-State): $7,428
Enrollment: 6,233 Coed
Affiliation or Control: State IRS Status: 501(c)3
Highest Offering: Beyond Master's But Less Than Doctorate
Program: Liberal Arts And General; Teacher Preparatory
Accreditation: NW, CORE, MUS, TED

02 President .... Dr. John P. MINAHAN
05 Provost/VP Academic Affairs .... Dr. Monty K. NEELY
32 Vice President Student Affairs .... Dr. Gary DUKES
10 Vice President Business & Finance .... Mr. Mark WEISS
35 Dean of Students .... Ms. Tina M. FUCHS
49 Dean Col Liberal Arts & Sciences .... Dr. Stephen SCHECK
53 Dean College of Education .... Dr. Hilda ROSSELLI
07 Asc Prov Admiss Retent/Enroll Mgmt .... Mr. David MCDONALD
56 Exec Dir Division Extended Pgms .... Ms. JoNan LEROY
06 Registrar .... Ms. Nancy FRANCE
30 Director of Development .... Mr. Tommy LOVE
08 Director Hamersly Library .... Dr. Allen MCKIEL
13 Director University Computing Svcs .... Mr. William KERNAN
15 Director Human Resources .... Ms. Judy J. VANDERBURG
18 Director Physical Plant .... Mr. Tom NEAL
19 Director University Public Safety .... Mr. Jay CAREY
23 Dir Student Health/Counseling Ctr .... Mr. Luis ROSA
26 Dir Public Relations/Communications .... Ms. Denise VISUANO
32 Director Student Life .... Mr. Jon TUCKER
37 Director Financial Aid .... Ms. Donna FOSSUM
41 Athletic Director .... Mr. Daniel HARE
46 Dir of Teaching Research Institute .... Dr. Ella TAYLOR
85 Dir Intl Students/Scholars Affairs .... Mr. Neng YANG
88 Dir Multicultural Student Svcs/Pgms .... Ms. Anna HERNANDEZ-HUNTER
22 Director AAEO .... Ms. Judy J. VANDERBURG
29 Director Alumni Relations .... Ms. Adrienne HARE
25 Project & Contract Officer .... Mr. Stan HAGEN

Pacific Northwest College of Art (D)

1241 NW Johnson Street, Portland OR 97209-3023
County: Multnomah FICE Identification: 003207
Unit ID: 209603
Telephone: (503) 226-4391 Carnegie Class: Spec/Arts
FAX Number: (503) 226-3587 Calendar System: Semester
URL: www.pnca.edu
Established: 1909 Annual Undergrad Tuition & Fees: $27,926
Enrollment: 639 Coed
Affiliation or Control: Independent Non-Profit IRS Status: 501(c)3
Highest Offering: Master's
Program: Fine Arts Emphasis
Accreditation: NW, ART

01 President .... Dr. Thomas MANLEY
05 Vice Pres/Dean of Academic Affairs .... Mr. Greg WARE
10 Vice Pres Finance/Administration .... Mrs. Nancy BARROWS
04 Assistant to the President .... Ms. Caitlin BERGEON
20 Dean of BFA .... Ms. Melissa MCCLURE
51 Director of Continuing Education .... Mr. Patrick FORSTER
37 Director Financial Aid .... Ms. Heidi LOCKE
26 Director of Communications .... Mrs. Becca BIGGS
06 Registrar .... Ms. Jenifer DEKALB
08 Director of Library Services .... Mr. Dan MCCLURE
07 Director of Admissions .... Mr. Chris SWEET

Pacific University (E)

2043 College Way, Forest Grove OR 97116-1797
County: Washington FICE Identification: 003212
Unit ID: 209612
Telephone: (503) 357-6151 Carnegie Class: Master's L
FAX Number: (503) 352-2242 Calendar System: Semester
URL: www.pacificu.edu
Established: 1849 Annual Undergrad Tuition & Fees: $33,612
Enrollment: 3,363 Coed
Affiliation or Control: Independent Non-Profit IRS Status: 501(c)3
Highest Offering: Doctorate
Program: Liberal Arts And General; Teacher Preparatory; Professional
Accreditation: NW, ARCPA, CLPSY, DH, IPSY, MUS, OPT, OPTR, OT, PHAR, PTA, @SW, TED

01 President .... Dr. Lesley M. HALLICK
05 Vice Pres Academic Affairs/Provost .... Dr. John MILLER
10 Vice Pres Finance & Administration .... Mr. Mike MALLERY
26 Vice President University Relations .... Mr. Phil AKERS
32 Vice President of Student Life .... Ms. Eva KREBS
20 Vice Provost for Research .... Dr. Chris WILKES
21 Assistant Vice Pres for Finance .... Mr. William RAY
26 Assoc VP for University Relations .... Ms. Jan STRICKLIN
18 Dir of Facilities/Safety Management .... Mr. Harold ROARK
07 Executive Director of Admissions .... Ms. Karen DUNSTON
84 Registrar .... Ms. Anne HERMAN
37 Director Financial Aid .... Mr. Mike JOHNSON
27 Chief Information Officer .... Mr. James FLEMING
88 Director of Conference Services .... Ms. Lois HORNBERGER
88 Director University Events .... Ms. Paula THATCHER
76 Exec Dean Col of Health Professions .... Dr. Ann BARR
49 Dean of Arts & Sciences .... Dr. John W. HAYES
63 Dean of Optometry .... Dr. Jennifer SMYTHE
67 Dean of Pharmacy .... Dr. Sue STEIN
53 Dean College of Education .... Dr. Mark ANKENY
83 Dean Sch Professional Psychology .... Dr. Michel HERSEN
41 Athletic Director .... Mr. Kenneth SCHUMANN
76 Director School Physical Therapy .... Dr. Richard RUTT
76 Dir School Occupational Therapy .... Dr. John WHITE
15 Director of Human Resources .... Mr. Troy STRASS
23 Director of Health Services .... Ms. Kathryn L. EISENBARTH
88 Acad Coord/English Language Inst .... Ms. Monique GRINDELL
44 Director of Annual Giving .... Ms. Kristin STORFA
07 Exec Director of Grad/Prof Admiss .... Mr. Jon-Erik LARSEN
76 Director Physician Asst Studies .... Ms. Judy ORTIZ
29 Director Alumni Relations .... Ms. Martha CALUS-MCLAIN
88 Dir External Relations Optometry .... Ms. Jeanne OLIVER
08 Library Director .... Ms. Marita KUNKEL
88 Senior Editor/Writer .... Mr. Steve DODGE
32 Dir Univ Center/Student Activities .... Mr. Steve KLEIN
36 Director Career Development .... Mr. Brian O'DRISCOLL
52 Program Director-Dental .... Ms. Lisa ROWLEY
40 Manager Bookstore .... Ms. Stacie BLANKENHORN
38 Director Counseling Center .... Ms. Robin KEILLOR
09 Director of Institutional Research .... Mr. William O'SHEA

Pioneer Pacific College (F)

27501 SW Parkway Avenue, Wilsonville OR 97070-9296
County: Clackamas FICE Identification: 023301
Unit ID: 210076
Telephone: (503) 682-3903 Carnegie Class: Assoc/PrivFP4
FAX Number: (503) 682-1514 Calendar System: Other
URL: www.pioneerpacific.edu
Established: 1981 Annual Undergrad Tuition & Fees: $11,900
Enrollment: 746 Coed
Affiliation or Control: Proprietary IRS Status: Proprietary
Highest Offering: Baccalaureate
Program: Occupational
Accreditation: ACICS

01 President .... Mr. Don MOUTOS
00 Board Chairman .... Mr. Raymond C. GAUTHIER
12 Portland Metro Campus President .... Mr. Don MOUTOS
12 OCI Campus President .... Mr. Eric STROMQUIST
12 Springfield Campus President .... Mr. Eric ARMSTRONG
10 Chief Financial Officer .... Mr. Mark MORELAND
05 Vice President of Academic Affairs .... Ms. Sandra WIGGINS
07 Vice President of Admissions .... Ms. Vicki CHURCH
37 Executive Director of Financial Aid .... Mr. Michael HARGRAVE
22 Compliance Officer .... Mr. Andrew BERNHARD
21 Controller .... Mr. Don ECK
26 Director of Marketing .... Ms. Basia PETRI
06 Lead Registrar .... Ms. Etta SCHWAB
50 Program Director Business-WLS .... Ms. Carin DYKZEUL
50 Program Director Business-CLK .... Mr. David WILHOYTE
50 Program Director Business-SPR .... Ms. Linda FARMER
61 Program Director Legal-WLS .... Ms. Vanesa PANCIC-MEIER
61 Program Director Legal-CLK .... Mr. Warren MOE
76 Program Director Medical-HCI .... Ms. Jennifer SCHILLING
76 Program Director Health-WLS & HCI .... Ms. Roxanne STEVENS
76 Program Director Massage-HCI .... Dr. Kim SCHMALTZ
76 Program Director Limited Xray .... Ms. Monica QUINTERO-DEVLAEMINCK
76 Program Director Limited X-Ray-SPR .... Ms. Katheryn MADISON
76 Program Director Medical-SPR .... Ms. Jody WEARIN
77 Program Director IT-WLS .... Mr. Rob MORRISON
77 Program Director IT-SPR .... Mr. Ed MCLAUGHLIN
66 Program Director Nursing .... Ms. Kim VOGEL
80 Program Director Criminal Just-WLS .... Mr. James FORD
80 Program Director Criminal Just-SPR .... Ms. Pamela MOORE
67 Program Director Pharmacy-HCI .... Dr. Kim SCHMALTZ
67 Program Director Pharmacy- SPR .... Ms. Lisa RUSSELL
08 Librarian .... Ms. Jill SLED

Portland Community College (G)

PO Box 19000, Portland OR 97280-0990
County: Multnomah FICE Identification: 003213
Unit ID: 209746
Telephone: (503) 244-6111 Carnegie Class: Assoc/Pub-U-MC
FAX Number: (503) 977-4960 Calendar System: Quarter
URL: www.pcc.edu
Established: 1961 Annual Undergrad Tuition & Fees (In-District): $2,990
Enrollment: 26,383 Coed
Affiliation or Control: Local IRS Status: 501(c)3
Highest Offering: Associate Degree
Program: Occupational; 2-Year Principally Bachelor's Creditable
Accreditation: NW, ADNUR, DA, DH, DT, MAC, MLTAD, RAD

01 District President .... Dr. Preston PULLIAMS
03 District Vice President .... Mr. Randy MCEWEN
05 VP Academic & Student Affairs .... Dr. Christine CHAIRSELL
11 Vice Pres Administrative Services .... Mr. Wing-Kit CHUNG
10 Assoc VP Financial Services .... Ms. Cherie CHEVALIER
91 Assoc VP Information Tech Svcs .... Ms. Leslie RIESTER
12 Campus President Sylvania .... Dr. Linda GERBER
12 Campus President Cascade .... Dr. Algie GATEWOOD
12 Campus President Rock Creek .... Dr. David RULE
12 Int Campus President Extended Lrng .... Dr. Craig KOLINS
20 Dean Instruction Sylvania Campus .... Mr. Jeff TRIPLET

20	Dean Instruction Cascade Campus	Mr. Scott HUFF
20	Dean Instr Rock Creek Campus	Ms. Birgitte RYSLINGE
50	Dean Instr/Stdnt Dev/Ext Lrng Camp	Dr. Craig KOLINS
32	Dean Student Dev Sylvania Campus	Dr. Diane MULLIGAN
32	Dean Stdnt Dev Rock Creek Campus	Ms. Narce RODRIGUEZ
32	Dean Student Dev Cascade Campus	Dr. Linda REISSER
32	Dean Student Affairs	Ms. Veronica GARCIA
15	Director Human Resources	Mr. Jerry DONNELLY
18	Director Facilities Management	Mr. Tim DONAHUE
08	Director Libraries	Ms. Donna REED
26	Director Institutional Advancement	Ms. Kristin WATKINS
09	Dir Institutional Effectiveness	Ms. Laura MASSEY
19	Director Public Safety	Mr. Ken GOODWIN
37	Director Financial Aid	Dr. Corbett GOTTFRIED
22	Director Affirmative Action	Ms. Sylvia WELCH
30	Chief Development Officer	Mr. Rick ZUROW

Reed College (A)

3203 SE Woodstock Boulevard, Portland OR 97202-8199
County: Multnomah FICE Identification: 003217
Unit ID: 209922
Telephone: (503) 771-1112 Carnegie Class: Bac/A&S
FAX Number: (503) 777-7769 Calendar System: Semester
URL: www.reed.edu
Established: 1908 Annual Undergrad Tuition & Fees: $42,540
Enrollment: 1,477 Coed
Affiliation or Control: Independent Non-Profit IRS Status: 501(c)3
Highest Offering: Master's
Program: Liberal Arts And General
Accreditation: NW

01	President	Mr. Colin S. DIVER
05	Dean of the Faculty	Dr. Ellen Keck STAUDER
26	Vice President College Relations	Dr. Hugh PORTER
10	Vice President & Treasurer	Mr. Edwin O. MCFARLANE
32	Vice Pres/Dean Student Services	Dr. Michael BRODY
04	Exec Asst to the President	Ms. Dawn THOMPSON
28	Dean Institutional Diversity	Ms. Crystal WILLIAMS
35	Assoc Dean of Stdnts for Acad Supp	Ms. Lily COPENAGLE
39	Assoc Dean Student & Campus Life	Mr. Peter MEAGHER
23	Director Health & Counseling	Ms. Kathryn SMITH
07	Dean of Admission	Mr. Keith TODD
06	Registrar	Ms. Nora MCLAUGHLIN
08	College Librarian	Ms. Victoria L. HANAWALT
30	Director of Development	Ms. Jan KURTZ
37	Director of Financial Aid	Ms. Leslie LIMPER
09	Director of Institutional Research	Dr. Jon W. RIVENBURG
26	Director of Public Affairs	Ms. Jennifer BATES
29	Director of Alumni Relations	Mr. Michael TESKEY
13	Chief Technology Officer	Dr. Martin D. RINGLE
90	Director of Academic Computing	Mr. Gary G. SCHLICKEISER
91	Director Administrative Computing	Mr. Gary D. NORBRATEN
21	Controller	Ms. Tracy L. FRANTEL
15	Director of Human Resources	Ms. Connie HELLESON
44	Director Annual Funds	Mr. David RUBIN
102	Dir Corporate/Foundation Support	Ms. Diane GUMZ
104	Director International Programs	Dr. Paul DEYOUNG
36	Director of Career Services	Mr. Ron ALBERTSON
88	Director of Special Programs	Ms. Barbara A. AMEN
18	Director Facilities Operations	Mr. Townsend ANGELL
19	Director Community Safety	Mr. Gary GRANGER
40	Manager of the Bookstore	Mr. Ueli STADLER
68	Director of Physical Education	Mr. Michael LOMBARDO

Rogue Community College (B)

3345 Redwood Highway, Grants Pass OR 97527-9298
County: Josephine FICE Identification: 010182
Unit ID: 209940
Telephone: (541) 956-7500 Carnegie Class: Assoc/Pub-R-L
FAX Number: (541) 471-3591 Calendar System: Quarter
URL: www.roguecc.edu
Established: 1970 Annual Undergrad Tuition & Fees (In-District): $3,609
Enrollment: 9,260 Coed
Affiliation or Control: Local IRS Status: 501(c)3
Highest Offering: Associate Degree
Program: Occupational; 2-Year Principally Bachelor's Creditable
Accreditation: NW

01	President	Dr. Peter ANGSTADT
05	VP of Instrution/CAO	Ms. Cheryl MARKWELL
10	VP of College Services/CFO/AA	Ms. Lynda WARREN
20	Dean Instruction & College Prep	Ms. Linda RENFRO
20	Dean Instruction & Career/Technical	Ms. Rena B. DUNHAM
20	Dean Instruction & Transfer Ed	Mr. Kirk GIBSON
103	Director SBDC	Mr. Rick LEIBOWITZ
103	Dean Instruction & Workforce	Ms. Jeanne HOWELL
13	Chief Infomation Office/CIO	Mr. Curtis SOMMERFELD
08	Head Librarian	Mr. Thomas MILLER
18	Facilities and Project Manager	Mr. Pat HUEBSCH
32	VP of Student Services/CSSO	Ms. Kori BIEBER
102	Executive Director Foundation	Ms. Jennifer WHEATLEY
15	Director HR & Risk Management	Ms. Jenny ROSSKNECHT
84	Director Enrollment Services	Ms. Claudia SULLIVAN
24	Director Instructional Media	Mr. Rich KIRK
21	Dir Budget & Financial Services	Ms. Lisa STANTON
40	Director Auxiliary Services	Ms. Pat GUNTER
26	Dir Marketing & Community Relations	Ms. Margaret BRADFORD
37	Director Student Financial Aid	Ms. Anna MANLEY
13	Director I/T Network & User Support	Mr. Mike MCCLURE
105	Director Internet & Telecommunic	Ms. Susie ASHBRIDGE
71	Director TRiO-EOC	Mr. Jason FIANO
71	Director TRiO-SSS	Ms. Rene MCKENZIE
51	Apprenticeship Coordinator	Ms. Cathy PIERSON
96	Contract and Procurment Manager	Ms. Jodie FULTON
25	Grants and Planning Coordinator	Ms. Mary O'KIEF
91	Coordinator of IT Programming Svcs	Mr. Jeff MILLER
91	Applications Programmer/Analyst II	Mr. Grant HUBLER

Southwestern Oregon Community College (C)

1988 Newmark Avenue, Coos Bay OR 97420-2911
County: Coos FICE Identification: 003220
Unit ID: 210155
Telephone: (541) 888-2525 Carnegie Class: Assoc/Pub-R-M
FAX Number: (541) 888-7285 Calendar System: Quarter
URL: www.socc.edu
Established: 1961 Annual Undergrad Tuition & Fees (In-District): $4,500
Enrollment: 5,019 Coed
Affiliation or Control: Local IRS Status: 501(c)3
Highest Offering: Associate Degree
Program: Occupational; 2-Year Principally Bachelor's Creditable
Accreditation: NW, ACFEI

01	President	Dr. Patty SCOTT
11	VP Administrative Services	Ms. Linda KRIDELBAUGH
05	VP Instructional Services	Vacant
12	Dean Curry County	Ms. Janet PRETTI
32	Dean Student Services	Vacant
84	Exec Director Enrollment Management	Mr. Tom NICHOLLS
102	Exec Director Foundation	Ms. Karen PRINGLE
13	Exec Director Integrated Technology	Ms. Kat FLORES
88	Exec Director OCCI (Culinary)	Mr. Shawn HANLIN
20	Associate Dean Learning	Ms. Kris CRUSOE
20	Associate Dean Learning	Ms. Diana SCHAB
41	Director Athletics	Mr. Mike HERBERT
07	Director of Admissions/Registrar	Mr. Tom NICHOLLS
19	Director Campus Safety	Mr. Joe THOMAS
30	Director College Advancement	Vacant
103	Director Community & Workforce Dev	Ms. Karen HELLAND
18	Director Facilities Services	Mr. David MCKINEY
29	Director of Alumni Relations	Ms. Karen PRINGLE
37	Director Financial Aid	Ms. Avena SINGH
15	Exec Director Human Resources	Ms. Rachele SUMMERVILLE
08	Director Learning Resources	Vacant
66	Director Nursing	Ms. Susan WALKER
39	Director Residence Life	Mr. Jeff WHITEY
88	Director SOCC Business Dev Center	Ms. Arlene SOTO
38	Director Student Support Srvcs	Mr. Tim DAILEY
40	Manager Bookstore	Ms. Dede CLEMENTS
09	Institutional Researcher	Ms. Robin BUNNELL
35	Coordinator Student Life and Events	Ms. Karina SMITH
04	Exec Asst to the Pres/Board of Educ	Ms. Deb NICHOLLS

Tillamook Bay Community College (D)

4301 3rd Street, Tillamook OR 97141
County: Tillamook Identification: 666647
Unit ID: 420723
Telephone: (503) 842-8222 Carnegie Class: Not Classified
FAX Number: (503) 842-8336 Calendar System: Semester
URL: www.tillamookbay.cc
Established: 1981 Annual Undergrad Tuition & Fees (In-District): $4,624
Enrollment: 467 Coed
Affiliation or Control: State/Local IRS Status: 501(c)3
Highest Offering: Associate Degree
Program: 2-Year Principally Bachelor's Creditable
Accreditation: @NW

01	President	Dr. Constance C. GREEN
05	Dean of Instructional Services	Dr. Lori GATES
11	Dean of Administrative Services	Mr. Ron ELLISON

Treasure Valley Community College (E)

650 College Boulevard, Ontario OR 97914-3423
County: Malheur FICE Identification: 003221
Unit ID: 210234
Telephone: (541) 881-8822 Carnegie Class: Assoc/Pub-R-M
FAX Number: (541) 881-2717 Calendar System: Quarter
URL: www.tvcc.cc
Established: 1961 Annual Undergrad Tuition & Fees (In-District): $4,320
Enrollment: 2,754 Coed
Affiliation or Control: Local IRS Status: 501(c)3
Highest Offering: Associate Degree
Program: Occupational; 2-Year Principally Bachelor's Creditable
Accreditation: NW

01	President	Ms. Dana YOUNG
05	Dean of Instruction	Mr. Albert BUYOK
11	Dean of Administrative Services	Mr. Randy R. GRIFFIN
08	Librarian	Mr. Dennis GILL
32	Dean Student Services	Mr. Eric ELLIS
37	Financial Aid Advisor	Mr. Keith RAAB
14	Director Data Processing	Mr. Scott CARPENTER
07	Director of Admissions	Ms. Stephanie OESTER
15	Director of Human Resources	Ms. Shawn SMITH
51	Director of Continuing Education	Ms. Linda SIMMONS
18	Dir of Housing/Building & Grounds	Mr. Bernie BABCOCK
10	Comptroller	Mr. Jonathan GILLEN
35	Director of Student Activities	Mr. Justin CORE
41	Athletic Director	Mr. Ed ARONSON
88	Corrections Education Director	Mr. Edward ALVES
06	Registrar	Ms. Debbie KRIEGH
09	Director of Institutional Research	Vacant
28	Director of Diversity	Mr. Eric ELLIS
30	Chief Development	Ms. Cathy YASUDA
40	Bookstore Manager	Mr. Kjetil ROM
38	Vocational Counselor	Ms. Lori EYLER

Umpqua Community College (F)

PO Box 967, Roseburg OR 97470-0226
County: Douglas FICE Identification: 003222
Unit ID: 210270
Telephone: (541) 440-4600 Carnegie Class: Assoc/Pub-R-M
FAX Number: (541) 440-4637 Calendar System: Quarter
URL: www.umpqua.edu
Established: 1964 Annual Undergrad Tuition & Fees (In-District): $4,176
Enrollment: 4,946 Coed
Affiliation or Control: Local IRS Status: 501(c)3
Highest Offering: Associate Degree
Program: Occupational; 2-Year Principally Bachelor's Creditable
Accreditation: NW, ADNUR

01	President	Dr. Joe OLSON
05	Vice President Instruction Services	Dr. Javier AYALA
11	Vice President Administrative Svcs	Mr. Tom ECKERD
32	Vice President Student Development	Dr. Lynn MOORE
84	Director Enrollment Management	Mr. David FARRINGTON
38	Director Counseling Services	Ms. Mandie PRITCHARD
37	Director of Financial Aid	Ms. Laurie SPANGENBERG
14	Director Instructional Technology	Mr. Jared SHEFFIELD
08	Director of Library Services	Mr. David HUTCHISON
18	Director of Facilities	Mr. Jess MILLER
31	Director of Community Education	Ms. Robynne VAN WINKLE
09	Director Inst Research/Assess/Plng	Mr. Dan YODER
15	Director Personnel Services	Ms. Joanne HAYES
26	Chief Public Rel/Dir Community Rel	Mr. Bentley GILBERT
96	Director of Purchasing	Ms. Cathy VAUGHN

University of Portland (G)

5000 N Willamette Boulevard, Portland OR 97203-5798
County: Multnomah FICE Identification: 003224
Unit ID: 209825
Telephone: (503) 943-8000 Carnegie Class: Master's L
FAX Number: (503) 943-7491 Calendar System: Semester
URL: www.up.edu
Established: 1901 Annual Undergrad Tuition & Fees: $32,330
Enrollment: 3,706 Coed
Affiliation or Control: Independent Non-Profit IRS Status: 501(c)3
Highest Offering: Master's
Program: Liberal Arts And General; Teacher Preparatory; Professional
Accreditation: NW, BUS, CS, ENG, MUS, NURSE, SW, TED, THEA

01	President	Rev. E. William BEAUCHAMP, CSC
05	Provost	Bro. Donald J. STABROWSKI, CSC
03	Executive Vice President	Rev. Mark L. POORMAN, CSC
26	Vice Pres for University Relations	Mr. James LYONS
11	Vice Pres for Univeristy Operations	Mr. James B. RAVELLI
10	Vice Pres for Financial Affairs	Vacant
100	Executive Asst to the Pres	Rev. Gerard J. OLINGER, CSC
32	Assoc Vice Pres Student Life	Rev. John J. DONATO, CSC
07	Dean of Admissions	Mr. Jason MCDONALD
21	Controller	Mr. Eric BARGER
06	Registrar	Ms. Roberta LINDAHL
30	Assoc Vice Pres Student Development	Mr. Bryce STRANG
36	Director Career Services	Ms. Amy CAVANAUGH
15	Director for Human Resources	Ms. Bryn SOPKO
37	Director Student Financial Aid	Ms. Janet TURNER
27	Director Public Information Office	Ms. Laurie KELLEY
49	Dean Arts & Sciences	Rev. Stephen C. ROWAN
50	Dean of the Business School	Dr. Robin ANDERSON
66	Dean of Nursing	Dr. Joanne WARNER
54	Dean of Engineering	Dr. Sharon JONES
53	Dean of Education	Dr. John WATZKE
23	Director University Health Services	Dr. Paul MYERS
19	Director of Public Safety	Mr. Harold BURKE-SIVERS
29	Director Alumni Relations	Ms. Carmen GASTON
39	Director Residence Life	Mr. Michael WALSH
41	Athletic Director	Mr. Larry WILLIAMS
42	Director Campus Ministry	Rev. Gary S. CHAMBERLAND, CSC
102	Director Foundation Development	Ms. Kathy A. KENDALL-JOHNSTON
18	Director Facilities Planning Constr	Mr. Paul J. LUTY
18	Director Physical Plant	Mr. Thomas BLUME
40	Director Bookstore	Ms. Erin SCHUMACHER-BRIGHT
88	Director University Events	Mr. William O. REED
09	Director of Institutional Research	Ms. Karen NELSON
35	Director Student Activities	Mr. Jeromy KOFFLER

University of Western States (H)

2900 NE 132nd Avenue, Portland OR 97230-3099
County: Multnomah FICE Identification: 012309
Unit ID: 210438
Telephone: (503) 256-3180 Carnegie Class: Spec/Health
FAX Number: (503) 251-5723 Calendar System: Quarter
URL: www.uws.edu
Established: 1904 Annual Undergrad Tuition & Fees: $8,865
Enrollment: 514 Coed
Affiliation or Control: Independent Non-Profit IRS Status: 501(c)3

Highest Offering: Doctorate
Program: Professional
Accreditation: NW, CHIRO

01 President ....Dr. Joseph BRIMHALL
05 Exec Vice President & Provost ....Dr. David WICKES
10 Vice President Financial Affairs ....Ms. Nancy MITZEN
20 Vice President Academic Affairs ....Dr. Gary SCHULTZ
84 VP Enrollment & Student Affairs ....Dr. Patrick BROWNE
23 Vice President of Clinics ....Dr. Joseph PFEIFER
46 Dean of Research ....Dr. Mitch HAAS
13 Chief Information Officer ....Mr. Kris ROSENBERG
04 Executive Coordinator ....Ms. Bonnie FLATT
27 Director of Communications ....Mr. Todd LOGGAN
15 Director Human Resources ....Ms. Carrie LOEWEN
37 Financial Aid Officer ....Ms. Helen FAITH
06 Registrar ....Ms. Michelle DODGE
08 University Librarian ....Ms. Janet TAPPER

Warner Pacific College (A)

2219 SE 68th Avenue, Portland OR 97215
County: Multnomah FICE Identification: 003225
Unit ID: 210304
Telephone: (503) 517-1000 Carnegie Class: Bac/Diverse
FAX Number: (503) 517-1350 Calendar System: Semester
URL: www.warnerpacific.edu
Established: 1937 Annual Undergrad Tuition & Fees: $18,290
Enrollment: 1,511 Coed
Affiliation or Control: Church Of God IRS Status: 501(c)3
Highest Offering: Master's
Program: Liberal Arts And General; Teacher Preparatory
Accreditation: NW

01 President ....Dr. Andrea P. COOK
03 Executive Vice President ....Vacant
05 Vice Pres Acad Affs/Dean of Faculty ....Dr. Cole DAWSON
10 Vice Pres of Operations ....Mr. Steve STENBERG
30 Vice President for Inst Advancement ....Mr. Kevin BRYANT
32 Dean of Students ....Vacant
20 Assoc VP for Acad Affairs/Dean ADP ....Dr. Toni PAULS
84 Exec Dir of Enrollment Management ....Mrs. Shannon MACKEY
37 Dir of Student Financial Services ....Vacant
41 Director of Athletics ....Mr. Ryan KAISER
08 Director of Library Services ....Ms. Sue KOPP
06 Registrar ....Ms. Victoria CUMINGS
13 Director of Information Services ....Vacant
29 Director of Alumni/Church Relations ....Mrs. Cindy POLLARD
27 Director of College Communications ....Mr. Scott THOMPSON
42 Dir of Contextualized Ministries ....Mr. Jess BIELMAN
39 Dir of Res Life & Judicial Affairs ....Mr. Jared VALENTINE
18 Director of Plant Services ....Vacant
15 Dir of Human Resources/Prof Devel ....Mrs. Bev FITTS
09 Director of Institutional Research ....Mr. Gale ROID
40 Director Bookstore ....Mrs. Mimi FONSECA
26 Dir of Marketing/College Relations ....Ms. Lani FAITH
38 Director Student Counseling ....Dr. Denise LOPEZ HAUGEN
21 Associate Business Officer ....Mr. Nathan DUNBAR
35 Dir Leadership Dev and Stdnt Pgm ....Ms. Traci VOGT
36 Director of Academic Support ....Mr. Rod JOHANSON
28 Dir of Multicultural Recruit/Retent ....Ms. Rachel DIXON

Western Seminary (B)

5511 SE Hawthorne Boulevard, Portland OR 97215-3399
County: Multnomah FICE Identification: 007178
Unit ID: 210368
Telephone: (503) 517-1800 Carnegie Class: Spec/Faith
FAX Number: (503) 517-1801 Calendar System: Semester
URL: www.westernseminary.edu
Established: 1927 Annual Graduate Tuition & Fees: $10,680
Enrollment: 679 Coed
Affiliation or Control: Independent Non-Profit IRS Status: 501(c)3
Highest Offering: Doctorate; No Undergraduates
Program: Professional; Religious Emphasis
Accreditation: NW, THEOL

01 President ....Dr. Randal R. ROBERTS
05 Academic Dean ....Dr. Marc CORTEZ
30 Vice President for Advancement ....Mr. Greg MOON
20 Associate Academic Dean ....Vacant
06 Dean Student Devel/Registrar ....Dr. Robert W. WIGGINS
10 Controller/Business/Finance ....Ms. Patricia A. PRICHARD
32 Dean of Students ....Dr. Ken EPP
36 Director of Student Placement ....Dr. Larry MCCRACKEN
13 Director of Information Services ....Mrs. Valerie MAINRIDGE
37 Financial Aid Director ....Miss Brooke MITTS
56 Asst Director of Distance Education ....Mr. Jon RAIBLEY
21 Associate Business Officer ....Mrs. Christina BOTTIGLIA
15 Human Resources Dir/Dir Communic ....Miss Julia SEAL
08 Library Director ....Dr. Robert A. KRUPP
84 Director Enrollment Services/Mktg ....Mr. P.J OSWALD
29 Director Alumni Relations ....Dr. Larry MCCRACKEN
18 Chief Facilities/Physical Plant ....Mr. Cliff STEIN
106 Director of Distance Education ....Mr. James STEWART

Willamette University (C)

900 State Street, Salem OR 97301-3930
County: Marion FICE Identification: 003227
Unit ID: 210401
Telephone: (503) 370-6300 Carnegie Class: Bac/A&S
FAX Number: (503) 370-6148 Calendar System: Semester
URL: www.williamette.edu
Established: 1842 Annual Undergrad Tuition & Fees: $39,012
Enrollment: 2,694 Coed
Affiliation or Control: Independent Non-Profit IRS Status: 501(c)3
Highest Offering: Master's
Program: Liberal Arts And General; Teacher Preparatory; Professional
Accreditation: NW, BUS, LAW, MUS, SPAA, TED

01 President ....Dr. Stephen THORSETT
10 Vice President Financial Affs ....Mr. W. Arnold YASINSKI
30 Interim Vice President Development ....Ms. Denise CALLAHAN
07 Vice President Enrollment ....Ms. Madeleine RHYNEER
13 Vice President Integrated Tech ....Dr. John D. BALLING
11 Vice President Administrative Svcs ....Mr. James R. BAUER
04 Exec/Admin Assistant to President ....Ms. Kristen GRAINGER
32 Dean of Campus Life ....Dr. David A. DOUGLASS
49 Dean of Liberal Arts ....Dr. Marlene MOORE
61 Dean of Law ....Mr. Peter LETSOU
50 Dean Graduate School Management ....Ms. Debra RINGOLD
42 Chaplain ....Dr. Charles I. WALLACE, JR.
23 Director of Bishop Wellness Center ....Ms. Margaret TROUT
88 Director Center Dispute Resolution ....Dr. Richard BIRKE
91 Director Administrative Computing ..Mr. Harvey J. PRUDHOMME
37 Director Student Financial Aid ....Ms. Patricia K. HOBAN
09 Director of Institutional Research ....Dr. Michael J. MOON
06 University Registrar ....Ms. Annie RUSSELL
08 University Librarian ....Ms. Deborah B. DANCIK
21 Controller ....Mr. Robert N. OLSON
40 Bookstore Director ....Mr. Donald C. BECKMAN
104 Director of International Education ....Mr. Kris LOU
41 Interim Athletic Director ....Mr. Dave RIGSBY
29 Senior Director Alumni Relations ....Vacant
44 Director of Planned Giving ....Mr. Stephen F. BRIER
15 Director of Human Resources ....Mr. Keith GRIMM
35 Director of Student Activities ....Ms. Lisa C. HOLLIDAY
36 Director Career Services ....Dr. Gerald B. HOUSER
28 Director of Multicultural Affairs ....Mr. Gordon K. TOYAMA
18 Manager Operations/Energy ....Mr. Gary GRIMM
96 Purchasing Coordinator ....Mr. Micheal K. SERAPHIN
26 Director of Marketing Communication ....Ms. Karen KLIMCZAK

PENNSYLVANIA

Albright College (D)

13th & Bern Streets, PO Box 15234,
Reading PA 19612-5234
County: Berks FICE Identification: 003229
Unit ID: 210571
Telephone: (610) 921-2381 Carnegie Class: Bac/A&S
FAX Number: (610) 921-7530 Calendar System: 4/1/4
URL: www.albright.edu
Established: 1856 Annual Undergrad Tuition & Fees: $33,990
Enrollment: 2,401 Coed
Affiliation or Control: United Methodist IRS Status: 501(c)3
Highest Offering: Master's
Program: Liberal Arts And General; Teacher Preparatory; Professional
Accreditation: M

01 President ....Dr. Lex O. MCMILLAN, III
05 Provost/Vice Pres Academic Affairs .Dr. Andrea E. CHAPDELAINE
10 Vice President Finance & Admin ....Mr. William W. WOOD
30 Vice President Advancement ....Dr. Timothy A. MCELWEE
84 VP Enrollment Mgt/Dean Admission ...Mr. Gregory E. EICHHORN
32 VP Student Affairs/Dean of Students ....Dr. Gina-Lyn CRANCE
26 Assoc Vice Pres Col Rels/Marketing ..Ms. Barbara J. MARSHALL
04 Executive Assistant to President ....Mrs. Kathy L. CAFONCELLI
20 Dean of Undergraduate Studies ....Dr. Joseph M. THOMAS
08 Library Director ....Ms. Rosemary L. DEEGAN
44 Dir Major Gifts/Programs/Services ....Mr. Brian PINTO
13 Network & Computer Support Mgr ....Mr. Hoerr U. JASON
13 Applications Support Manager ....Ms. Gena HOWARD
21 Controller ....Mr. Rick W. MELCHER
37 Director of Financial Aid ....Ms. Mary Ellen DUFFY
58 Dean of Graduate & Professional Div ....Dr. Sarel P. FUCHS
35 Assistant Dean of Students ....Ms. Amanda HANINCIK
06 Registrar ....Mr. David C. BALLABAN
36 Director Career Development Center ....Ms. Karen V. EVANS
39 Int Director of Residential Life ....Ms. Rebecca PEAL MORROW
38 Director of Counseling
Center ....Dr. Brenda J. INGRAM-WALLACE
29 Dir of Alumni Relations ....Mrs. Megan BERMUDEZ
18 Director Facilities/Operations/Svcs ....Mr. Kevin GAFFNEY
41 Co-Athletic Director ....Mr. Richard E. FERRY
41 Co-Athletic Director ....Ms. Janice J. LUCK
19 Director of Safety & Security ....Mr. Thomas MCDANIEL
40 Book Store Manager ....Ms. Coreen MCCAFFERTY
23 Director of Gable Health Center ....Ms. Samantha WESNER
42 Chaplain ....Rev. Paul E. CLARK
22 Affirmative Action Coord/Dir HR ....Mr. Timothy J. STEINROCK
85 Director Multi-Ethnic Student Affs ....Mr. Jason H. HARTSFIELD
88 Int Dir of Accelerated Degree Pgm ....Mr. Kevin EZZELL
09 Asst Dir of Institutional Research ....Mr. Jack LAFAYETTE
35 Director of Student Activities ....Mr. Bradley A. SMITH
25 Director of Grants ....Ms. Darlene ROTH
92 Director Honors Program ....Dr. Julia F. HEBERLE
07 Director of Admission ....Mr. Christopher H. BOEHM
107 Dean of Adult & Prof Studies ....Dr. Andra M. BASU
88 Director of Conferences ....Ms. Lois A. KUBINAK

Allegheny College (E)

520 N Main, Meadville PA 16335-3902
County: Crawford FICE Identification: 003230
Unit ID: 210669
Telephone: (814) 332-3100 Carnegie Class: Bac/A&S
FAX Number: (814) 724-6032 Calendar System: Semester
URL: www.allegheny.edu
Established: 1815 Annual Undergrad Tuition & Fees: $36,190
Enrollment: 2,153 Coed
Affiliation or Control: Independent Non-Profit IRS Status: 501(c)3
Highest Offering: Baccalaureate
Program: Liberal Arts And General
Accreditation: M

01 President ....Dr. James H. MULLEN
03 Exec Vice President & Treasurer ....Dr. David W. MCINALLY
30 Vice Pres Devel & Alumni Affairs ....Ms. Marjorie S. KLEIN
84 Dean Enrollment & Financial Aid ....Ms. Jennifer D. WINGE
04 Assistant to the President ....Ms. Pamela S. HIGHAM
28 Chief Diversity Ofce/Asc Dn of Col ....Dr. Lawrence T. POTTER
21 Senior Associate Vice President ....Mr. Larry K. LEE
45 Assoc Vice Pres for Advancement ....Mr. Bruce WHITEHAIR
05 Dean of the College ....Dr. Linda C. DEMERITT
32 Dean of Students ....Mr. Joseph J. DICHRISTINA
20 Associate Dean of the College ....Dr. Ben L. SLOTE
37 Assoc Dean Enrollment/Financial Aid ....Ms. Sheryle A. PROPER
88 Ex Dir Learning Info/Tech Svcs ....Dr. Richard A. HOLMGREN
06 Registrar ....Dr. Ann D. SHEFFIELD
08 Library Director ....Ms. Linda G. BILLS
15 Director of Human Resources ....Ms. Patricia A. FERREY
19 Director Campus Safety & Security ....Dr. Jeffrey A. SCHNEIDER
44 Director of Annual Giving ....Mrs. Sally B. HANLEY
18 Director Physical Plant ....Mr. Cliff K. WILLIS
91 Director Administrative Computing ....Mr. Richard A. METZGER
29 Director Alumni Affairs ....Mr. Philip R. FOXMAN
41 Director of Athletics ....Vacant
31 Director Community Service ....Dr. David RONCOLATO
14 Dir Tech Computer & Networking Svcs ....Mr. Tim W. HUNTER
101 Asst to Pres for Board Relations ....Ms. Gillian F. FORD
38 Director of Counseling Center ....Ms. Yvonne M. EATON-STULL
102 Director of Found/Corporate Rels ....Dr. Ann H. ARESON
28 Director of Diversity Affairs ....Ms. Cherjanet LENZY
09 Director of Institutional Research ....Ms. Marian D. SHERWOOD
36 Director Career Services ....Ms. Michaeline M. SHUMAN
35 Director Student Involvement ....Ms. Gretchen A. SYMONS
21 Associate Vice President of Finance ....Ms. Linda S. WETSELL
42 Chaplain ....Dr. Jane Ellen NICKELL
88 Dir Center Political Participation ....Dr. Daniel M. SHEA
88 Assoc Director Learning Commons ....Mr. John J. MANGINE
84 Assoc Dir Enrollment/Communication ....Ms. Penny M. FRANK
40 Manager of Bookstore ....Mr. Peter M. LEBAR
96 Purchasing Coordinator ....Ms. Kathleen M. CONAWAY

Alvernia University (F)

400 Saint Bernardine Street, Reading PA 19607-1799
County: Berks FICE Identification: 003233
Unit ID: 210775
Telephone: (610) 796-8200 Carnegie Class: Master's M
FAX Number: (610) 777-6632 Calendar System: Semester
URL: www.alvernia.edu
Established: 1958 Annual Undergrad Tuition & Fees: $26,830
Enrollment: 2,906 Coed
Affiliation or Control: Roman Catholic IRS Status: 501(c)3
Highest Offering: Doctorate
Program: Liberal Arts And General; Teacher Preparatory; Professional
Accreditation: M, ACBSP, NURSE, OT, SW

01 President ....Dr. Thomas F. FLYNN
05 Provost ....Dr. Shirley J. WILLIAMS
10 VP for Finance & Administration ....Mr. Douglas F. SMITH
30 Vice Pres for Advancement ....Mr. J. Michael PRESSIMONE
32 Vice Pres Univ Life/Dean of Stdnts ..Dr. Joseph J. CICALA, RSM
84 Vice Pres for Enrollment
Management ....Mr. John R. MCCLOSKEY, JR.
42 Vice President For Mission ....Sr. Rosemary STETS, OSF
26 Assoc VP Marketing & Communication ....Mr. Brad DREXLER
35 Dean of Students ....Ms. Kristel KEMMERER
35 Director of Student Activities ....Ms. Abby SWATCHICK
39 Director Residence Life ....Ms. Karolina DREHER
06 Registrar ....Ms. Beki STEIN
21 Controller ....Ms. Jada D. CAMPBELL
29 Director Alumni Donor Relations ....Ms. Susan MARTZ
08 Grad Program Librarian/Archivist ....Dr. Eugene S. MITCHELL
92 Director Honors Program ....Dr. Victoria WILLIAMS
41 Int Director Athletics & Recreation ....Ms. Laura GINGRICH
07 Director of Admissions ....Mr. Jeffrey DITTMAN
09 Director of Institutional Research ....Dr. Evelina PANAYOTOVA
15 Director Personnel Services ....Ms. Stacy YERGER
18 Chief Facilities/Physical Plant ....Mr. David REPPERT
26 Chief Public Relations Officer ....Ms. Gale MARTIN
36 Director of Career Services ....Ms. Jennifer GITTINGS-DALTON
37 Int Dir Student Financial Planning ....Ms. Christine SAADL
96 Director of Purchasing ....Ms. Cynthia URICK
28 Director of Diversity ....Ms. Mary LOZADA
21 Associate Business Officer ....Ms. Gwynne KOLODZIEJSKI
31 Dir Ctr for Community Engagement ....Ms. Ginny HAND
58 Dean of Graduate & Cont Studies ....Mrs. Joan B. LEWIS
49 Dean of Arts & Sciences ....Dr. Kevin GODFREY
76 Dean Professional Programs ....Ms. Karen S. THACKER

The American College (G)

270 S Bryn Mawr Avenue, Bryn Mawr PA 19010-2196
County: Delaware FICE Identification: 033173
Unit ID: 210809
Telephone: (610) 526-1000 Carnegie Class: Spec/Bus
FAX Number: (610) 526-1310 Calendar System: Quarter

URL: www.theamericancollege.edu
Established: 1927 Annual Graduate Tuition & Fees: $5,040
Enrollment: 533 Coed
Affiliation or Control: Independent Non-Profit IRS Status: 501(c)3
Highest Offering: Master's; No Undergraduates
Program: Professional
Accreditation: M

01	President & CEO	Dr. Laurence BARTON
03	Senior Vice President	Mr. Steven TARR
05	Vice Pres Academic Affs & Dean	Dr. Walter J. WOERHEIDE
11	Chief Operating Officer	Mr. Neal R. FEGELY
26	Chief Marketing Officer	Mr. Jack HONDROS
13	Vice President Information Systems	Mr. Ed M. MCEVOY
30	Sr Vice President Advancement	Mr. Charles CRONIN
107	Vice Pres Professional Education	Mr. Russell J. FIGUEIRA
09	Assoc VP Assessment & Examinations	Mr. William T. MULROY
04	Admin Assistant to the President	Ms. Mary C. VARNER
15	Exec Director Human Resources	Ms. Amy DEWEY
06	Registrar	Mr. Damon KEY
08	Librarian/Mgr Knowledge Center	Ms. Virginia E. WEBB
88	Managing Director Exam Systems	Ms. Diane M. HAMMONDS

Antonelli Institute of Art and Photography (A)

300 Montgomery Avenue, Erdenheim PA 19038-8242
County: Montgomery FICE Identification: 007430
Unit ID: 210890
Telephone: (215) 836-2222 Carnegie Class: Assoc/PrivFP
FAX Number: (215) 836-2794 Calendar System: Semester
URL: www.antonelli.edu
Established: 1938 Annual Undergrad Tuition & Fees: $19,590
Enrollment: 203 Coed
Affiliation or Control: Proprietary IRS Status: Proprietary
Highest Offering: Associate Degree
Program: Occupational
Accreditation: ACCSC

01	President	Dr. John D. HAYDEN
05	Director of Education	Ms. Trish FLEMING
37	Financial Aid Officer	Ms. Stephanie SHOWALTER
32	Director of Student Services	Mr. John CALLAN
07	Director of Admissions/Marketing	Mr. Anthony DETORE

Arcadia University (B)

450 S Easton Road, Glenside PA 19038-3295
County: Montgomery FICE Identification: 003235
Unit ID: 211088
Telephone: (215) 572-2900 Carnegie Class: Master's L
FAX Number: (215) 572-0240 Calendar System: Semester
URL: www.arcadia.edu
Established: 1853 Annual Undergrad Tuition & Fees: $33,490
Enrollment: 3,963 Coed
Affiliation or Control: Independent Non-Profit IRS Status: 501(c)3
Highest Offering: Doctorate
Program: Liberal Arts And General; Teacher Preparatory; Professional
Accreditation: M, ACBSP, ARCPA, ART, PTA

01	President	Mr. Carl OXHOLM, III
05	Provost & VP Academic Affairs	Dr. Steve O. MICHAEL
10	Vice President Finance & Treasurer	Mr. Michael J. COVENEY
30	Vice Pres University Advancement	Mr. Nick COSTA
30	Vice President Development	Dr. Janet E. WALBERT
84	Vice Pres Enrollment Management	Vacant
104	VP Exec Dir College of Global Stds	Dr. Nicolette D. CHRISTENSEN
32	Assoc VP Student Affairs/Dean	Mr. Joshua STERN
27	CIO	Mr. Jose DIEUDONNE
26	Chief Mktg & Communications Officer	Ms. Lori STAHL-BAUER
49	Dean College of Arts and Sciences	Vacant
18	Assoc VP Facilities/Capital Plng	Mr. Thomas J. MACCHI
21	Assoc Vice President for Finance	Ms. Colleen BURKE
07	Assoc VP Enrollment Management	Mr. Mark LAPREZIOSA
100	Assoc VP/Exec Dir Office of Pres	Dr. Mark P. CURCHACK
15	Asst VP for Human Resources/AAO	Ms. Lynette ALLEN-COLLINS
44	Asst VP University Advancement	Ms. Diana FRAZIER
76	Dean College of Health Sciences	Dr. Archie J. VOMACHKA
51	Dean Continuing Studies	Mr. Erik NELSON
88	Dean College of Global Studies	Dr. Dennis DUTSCHKE
35	Assoc Dean of Students	Ms. Dian TAYLOR-ALLEYNE
88	Dean International Affairs	Dr. Warren HAFFAR
39	Director Residence Life	Ms. Catherine MATTINGLY
50	Dean School of Business	Vacant
28	Assoc Dean Multicultural Affairs	Ms. Judith DALTON
20	Asst Dean Undergraduate Studies	Mr. Bruce KELLER
107	Asst Dean Grad & Prof Studies	Ms. Mary Kate MCNULTY
06	Registrar	Mr. William ELNICK
08	Exec Dir Library & Info Technology	Mr. Eric MCCLOY
36	Director of Career Development	Mr. Michael HERTEL
41	Director Athletics & Recreation	Ms. Shirley LIDDLE
29	Director Alumni Relations	Ms. Georgene PILLING
09	Director Institutional Research	Mr. Will PADDOCK
19	Director of Public Safety	Mr. James BONNER
38	Director Wellness Services	Ms. Cynthia RUTHERFORD
21	Controller	Ms. Julie A. ROSNER
96	Payroll and Purchasing Manager	Ms. Sharon ANTHONY
25	Director Sponsored Research Pgms	Ms. Barbara SHEEHAN
27	Director Communications	Dr. Shekhar DESHPANDE
88	Director Theatre Arts	Mr. Mark WADE
37	Exec Dir Financial Aid Systems	Ms. Elizabeth RIHL-LEWINSKY
88	Director Campus Visits and EM	Ms. Kathleen BEARDSLEY
88	Dir Instruct Tech/Library Research	Ms. Jeanne BUCKLEY
88	Dir Network & Info Security Systems	Mr. Marc ROCQUE
91	Director Systems Integration	Mr. Scott GRABUS
69	Director Public Health/Health Educ	Dr. Andrea COVELLI-KOVACH
88	Director Administrative Services	Ms. Mimi BASSETTI
88	Gallery Director	Mr. Richard TORCHIA
79	Director MA in English/Humanities	Dr. Richard WERTIME
88	Director EdD in Special Educ	Dr. Christina AGER
88	Dir Institutional Relations CGS	Ms. Lorna STERN
79	Director Liberal Studies	Dr. Jonathan CHURCH
44	Director Annual Fund	Ms. Judith MCNAMARA
88	Director EM & Financial Aid	Ms. Holly R. KIRKPATRICK

Art Institute of Philadelphia (C)

1622 Chestnut Street, Philadelphia PA 19103-5198
County: Philadelphia FICE Identification: 008350
Unit ID: 210942
Telephone: (215) 567-7080 Carnegie Class: Spec/Arts
FAX Number: (215) 405-6398 Calendar System: Quarter
URL: www.aiph.aii.edu
Established: 1966 Annual Undergrad Tuition & Fees: $222,275
Enrollment: 3,556 Coed
Affiliation or Control: Proprietary IRS Status: Proprietary
Highest Offering: Baccalaureate
Program: Occupational
Accreditation: @M, ACICS, ACFEI, CIDA

01	President	Mr. Michael DEPRISCO
05	Dean of Academic Affairs	Dr. Raymond BECKER
10	Director Admin & Financial Services	Mr. James MORETTI
07	Director of Admissions	Mr. Larry MCHUGH
36	Director of Career Services	Mr. Edward HUNTER
04	Exec Assistant to the President	Ms. Sheila HALL
09	Dir of Institutional Effectiveness	Ms. Heather RAMSEY
20	Assoc Dean of Academic Affairs	Mr. Harry COSTIGAN
32	Associate Dean of Students	Ms. Ashley FORSYTH
37	Director Student Financial Services	Ms. Freddi-beth ROCKENBACH
06	Registrar	Mr. James KEANE
08	Library Director	Ms. Ruth SCHACHTER
38	Counselor	Ms. Eileen MCMULLEN
40	Manager-Supply Store	Ms. Sharon MASULLO
85	Regional Internatl Student Advisor	Mr. Glenn GROVES

Art Institute of Pittsburgh (D)

420 Boulevard of the Allies, Pittsburgh PA 15219-1301
County: Allegheny FICE Identification: 007470
Unit ID: 210960
Telephone: (412) 263-6600 Carnegie Class: Spec/Arts
FAX Number: (412) 263-3715 Calendar System: Quarter
URL: www.artinstitutes.edu/pittsburgh
Established: 1921 Annual Undergrad Tuition & Fees: $21,915
Enrollment: 14,392 Coed
Affiliation or Control: Proprietary IRS Status: Proprietary
Highest Offering: Baccalaureate
Program: Occupational
Accreditation: M, ACFEI, CIDA

01	President	Mr. George W. SEBOLT
10	Vice Pres/Dir Admin/Financial Svcs	Ms. Janice M. VUCIC
05	VP/Dean Academic Affairs	Mr. Daniel GARLAND
32	Vice Pres/Director Student Affairs	Ms. Nadine W. JOSEPHS
36	VP/Director Career Services	Vacant
07	Director of Admissions	Mr. Lee COLKER
37	Director Student Financial Aid	Ms. Gayle J. KNIGHT
15	Director Human Resources	Ms. Malinda A. HALLETT
97	Director General Education	Ms. Maria BOADA
88	Dir Graphic/Dig Design/Advertising	Ms. Shirley W. YEE
72	Director of Technology	Mr. George ALBERT
88	Director Interactive Media Design	Dr. Warren K. WAKE
88	Dir Indust Dsgn Tech/Entertnmt Dsgn	Mr. Greg L. BUTLER
88	Director Media Arts & Animation	Mr. Hans WESTMAN
88	Director of Photography	Mr. Andrew ENGLISH
88	Dir Interior Design/Residential Pln	Ms. Kelly J K. SPEWOCK
06	Registrar	Ms. Diane E. CARNEY
84	Enrollment Management Supervisor	Ms. Lara SEBOLT
88	Director Culinary	Mr. Michael ZAPPONE
88	Dir Fashion/Retail Mktng/Fashn Dsgn	Ms. Stephanie TAYLOR
88	Dir Video Production/Visual Effects	Mr. Andres TAPIA URZUA
88	College Affiliate/HS Articulation	Ms. Karen SOLTIS

The Art Institute of York - Pennsylvania (E)

1409 Williams Road, York PA 17402-9012
County: York FICE Identification: 025578
Unit ID: 210906
Telephone: (717) 755-2300 Carnegie Class: Assoc/PrivFP
FAX Number: (717) 840-1951 Calendar System: Other
URL: www.artinstitutes.edu/york
Established: 1952 Annual Undergrad Tuition & Fees: $31,200
Enrollment: 653 Coed
Affiliation or Control: Proprietary IRS Status: Proprietary
Highest Offering: Baccalaureate
Program: Liberal Arts And General; Professional
Accreditation: ACICS

01	President	Mr. Tim HOWARD
05	Dean of Academic Affairs	Ms. Marla PRICE
07	Senior Director of Admissions	Mr. Scott VUKODER
32	Dean of Student Affairs	Ms. Laura RYDER

Baptist Bible College and Seminary (F)

538 Venard Road, Clarks Summit PA 18411-1297
County: Lackawanna FICE Identification: 002670
Unit ID: 211024
Telephone: (570) 586-2400 Carnegie Class: Spec/Faith
FAX Number: (570) 586-1753 Calendar System: Semester
URL: www.bbc.edu
Established: 1932 Annual Undergrad Tuition & Fees: $17,040
Enrollment: 995 Coed
Affiliation or Control: Baptist IRS Status: 501(c)3
Highest Offering: Doctorate
Program: Teacher Preparatory; Religious Emphasis
Accreditation: M, BI

01	President	Mr. James E. JEFFERY
05	Provost	Dr. James R. LYTLE
10	Vice President Business/Finance	Mr. Hal G. CROSS
30	Vice Pres Inst Advancement	Mr. Don PATTEN
84	Vice Pres Enrollment Management	Mr. Ken SHEPARD
20	Seminary Dean	Dr. Michael STALLARD
32	Dean of Students	Mr. Matthew POLLOCK
33	Associate Dean	Mr. Ted BOYKIN
34	Associate Dean	Mrs. Carol S. KING
04	President's Assistant	Mrs. Kathy M. COMPTON
06	Registrar	Mr. Allen R. DREYER
08	Librarian	Mr. Joshua B. MICHAEL
09	Director of Institutional Research	Dr. Barry C. SMITH
37	Director of Financial Aid	Mr. Steve BROWN
26	Exec Dir Communications/Marketing	Mr. Ken KNELLY
19	Director Safety/Security	Mr. Tom MORRIS
84	Director of Enrollment	Mr. Sean MCPHERSON
18	Chief Facilities/Physical Plant	Mr. Wayne STEVENS
13	Manager of Information/Technology	Mr. Timothy COREY
73	Dean School of Bible and Theology	Dr. David LACKEY
53	Dean of School of Education	Dr. Ritch KELLEY
49	Dean of School of Arts & Sciences	Dr. Steve SHUMAKER
88	Dean of School of Global Ministries	Dr. Dennis WILHITE
07	Director of Admissions	Vacant
15	Director Personnel Services	Mr. Manning BROWN
29	Director Alumni Relations	Mr. Mark STECKIEL
36	Director Student Placement	Mr. Roddy HANNAH

Berks Technical Institute (G)

2205 Ridgewood Road, Wyomissing PA 19610-1168
County: Berks FICE Identification: 022539
Unit ID: 213534
Telephone: (610) 372-1722 Carnegie Class: Assoc/PrivFP
FAX Number: (610) 376-4684 Calendar System: Other
URL: www.berks.edu
Established: 1974 Annual Undergrad Tuition & Fees: $14,400
Enrollment: 1,105 Coed
Affiliation or Control: Proprietary IRS Status: Proprietary
Highest Offering: Associate Degree
Program: Occupational; Technical Emphasis
Accreditation: ACCSC, MAC

01	President	Mr. Joseph F. REICHARD
05	Dean	Ms. Cheryl GARMAN

Biblical Theological Seminary (H)

200 N Main Street, Hatfield PA 19440-2499
County: Montgomery FICE Identification: 023230
Unit ID: 211130
Telephone: (215) 368-5000 Carnegie Class: Spec/Faith
FAX Number: (215) 368-2301 Calendar System: Semester
URL: www.biblical.edu
Established: 1971 Annual Graduate Tuition & Fees: $13,667
Enrollment: 268 Coed
Affiliation or Control: Independent Non-Profit IRS Status: 501(c)3
Highest Offering: Doctorate; No Undergraduates
Program: Professional; Religious Emphasis
Accreditation: M, THEOL

01	President	Dr. David G. DUNBAR
32	VP for Student Advancement	Mrs. Pamela J. SMITH
05	Academic Dean	Dr. R. Todd MANGUM
10	Controller	Mr. Wayne A. DAVIDSON
20	Director of Academic Services	Mr. Eric T. HOUSEKNECHT
08	Director of Library Services	Mr. Daniel N. LAVALLA
13	Director of Information Technology	Mr. Kelly PFLEIGER
18	Director of Physical Plant	Mr. Anthony W. PLETSCHER
42	Director DMin Program	Vacant
30	Director of Development	Mr. William G. MEINEL

Bidwell Training Center (I)

1815 Metropolitan Street, Pittsburgh PA 15233-2200
County: Allegheny FICE Identification: 031015
Unit ID: 211149
Telephone: (412) 323-4000 Carnegie Class: Assoc/PrivNFP
FAX Number: (412) 325-7378 Calendar System: Semester
URL: www.bidwell-training.org
Established: 1968 Annual Undergrad Tuition & Fees: $8,200

Enrollment: 175 Coed
Affiliation or Control: Independent Non-Profit IRS Status: 501(c)3
Highest Offering: Associate Degree
Program: Occupational
Accreditation: ACCSC

01 Exec Director/Sr Vice President .... Ms. Valerie NJIE
07 Director of Admissions .... Mr. Ken HUSELTON

Bradford School (A)

125 W Station Square Dr, Ste 129,
Pittsburgh PA 15219-2602
County: Allegheny FICE Identification: 009721
Unit ID: 211200
Telephone: (412) 391-6710 Carnegie Class: Assoc/PrivFP
FAX Number: (412) 471-6714 Calendar System: Semester
URL: www.bradfordpittsburgh.edu
Established: 1968 Annual Undergrad Tuition & Fees: $11,730
Enrollment: 520 Coed
Affiliation or Control: Proprietary IRS Status: Proprietary
Highest Offering: Associate Degree
Program: Occupational
Accreditation: ACICS, DA, MAC

01 President .... Mr. Vincent S. GRAZIANO

Bryn Athyn College of the New Church (B)

PO Box 717, Bryn Athyn PA 19009-0717
County: Montgomery FICE Identification: 003228
Unit ID: 210492
Telephone: (267) 502-2400 Carnegie Class: Bac/A&S
FAX Number: (215) 938-2658 Calendar System: Trimester
URL: www.brynathyn.edu
Established: 1876 Annual Undergrad Tuition & Fees: $24,081
Enrollment: 181 Coed
Affiliation or Control: Church of New Jerusalem IRS Status: 501(c)3
Highest Offering: Master's
Program: Liberal Arts And General; Teacher Preparatory; Professional
Accreditation: M

01 President .... Dr. Kristin KING
10 Vice President & Treasurer .... Mr. Daniel T. ALLEN
84 Vice Pres Enrollment Management .... Ms. Stephanie NILES
03 Dean .... Dr. Charles W. LINDSAY
73 Dean of Theological School .... Rev. Andrew M T. DIBB
05 Dean of Academic Affairs .... Dr. Allen BEDFORD
32 Dean of Student Affairs .... Dr. Brian HENDERSON
89 Director First Year Experience .... Ms. Hilary BRYNTESSON
30 Director of Development .... Mr. Wayne M. PARKER
21 Business Manager .... Mr. W. Lesley ALDEN
18 Dir Consolidated Plant Operations .... Mr. Tim M. BARBAGALLO
08 Director of Swedenborg Library .... Mrs. Carroll C. ODHNER
36 Career Counselor .... Dr. Sonia S. WERNER
41 Director of Athletics .... Mr. Matthew KENNEDY
40 Bookstore Manager .... Mrs. Mary L. ODHNER
13 Director of Information Technology .... Ms. Lelia HOWARD
15 Director of Human Resources .... Mr. Joseph H. WEISS
19 Director of Security & Safety .... Mr. R. Scott COOPER
42 Chaplain .... Rev. Ray J. SILVERMAN

Bryn Mawr College (C)

101 N Merion Avenue, Bryn Mawr PA 19010-2899
County: Montgomery FICE Identification: 003237
Unit ID: 211273
Telephone: (610) 526-5000 Carnegie Class: Bac/A&S
FAX Number: (610) 526-7450 Calendar System: Semester
URL: www.brynmawr.edu
Established: 1885 Annual Undergrad Tuition & Fees: $54,044
Enrollment: 1,755 Female
Affiliation or Control: Independent Non-Profit IRS Status: 501(c)3
Highest Offering: Doctorate
Program: Liberal Arts And General
Accreditation: M, SW

01 President .... Jane D. MCAULIFFE
05 Provost .... Kimberly E. CASSIDY
49 Dean of Undergraduate College .... Michele A. RASMUSSEN
11 Chief Administrative Officer .... Jerry A. BERENSON
10 Chief Financial Officer & Treasurer .... John GRIFFITH
30 Chief Development Officer .... Ms. Donna FRITHSEN
07 Chief Enrollmnt/Communications Ofcr .... Jennifer J. RICKARD
08 Director Libraries/Chief Info Ofcr .... Elliott SHORE
58 Dean of Graduate Studies .... Mary OSIRIM
28 Asst Dean/Dir Intercultural Affairs .... Vanessa CHRISTMAN
06 Registrar .... Kirsten O'BEIRNE
37 Director of Financial Aid .... Ethel M. DESMARAIS
19 Director of Public Safety .... Tom KING
29 Exec Director Alumnae Association .... Wendy M. GREENFIELD
68 Director of Athletics & Physical Ed .... Kathleen TIERNEY
21 Controller .... Ms. Betsy STEWART
09 Director of Institutional Research .... Mark A. FREEMAN
18 Chief Facilities/Physical Plant .... Glenn R. SMITH

Bucknell University (D)

701 Moore Avenue, Lewisburg PA 17837
County: Union FICE Identification: 003238
Unit ID: 211291
Telephone: (570) 577-2000 Carnegie Class: Bac/A&S
FAX Number: (570) 577-3760 Calendar System: Semester
URL: www.bucknell.edu
Established: 1846 Annual Undergrad Tuition & Fees: $43,628
Enrollment: 3,615 Coed
Affiliation or Control: Independent Non-Profit IRS Status: 501(c)3
Highest Offering: Master's
Program: Liberal Arts And General; Teacher Preparatory; Professional
Accreditation: M, CS, ENG, MUS

01 President .... Dr. John C. BRAVMAN
05 Provost .... Dr. Michael A. SMYER
10 VP for Finance & Administration .... Mr. David J. SURGALA
30 VP Development & Alumni Rels .... Dr. Scott G. ROSEVEAR
43 General Counsel .... Mr. Wayne A. BROMFIELD
27 VP for Communications .... Dr. Peter F. MACKEY
20 Assoc Provost/Dean of Grad Studies .... Dr. James P. RICE
20 Assoc Provost/Dean Summer School .... Dr. Robert M. MIDKIFF, JR.
49 Dean of Arts & Sciences .... Dr. George C. SHIELDS
54 Dean of Engineering .... Dr. Keith W. BUFFINTON
13 Chief Information Officer .... Mr. Param S. BEDI
21 Associate VP for Finance .... Mr. Dennis W. SWANK
29 Assoc VP Development & Alumni Rels .... Ms. Kathleen GRAHAM
41 Director of Athletics & Recreation .... Mr. John P. HARDT
88 Chief Investment Officer .... Mr. Christopher D. BROWN
88 Treasurer and Controller .... Mr. Michael S. COVER
32 Dean of Students .... Ms. Susan LANTZ
28 Chief Officer for Diversity/ Equity .... Mr. Rolando A. ARROYO-SUCRE
18 Associate VP for Facilities .... Mr. Dennis W. HAWLEY
16 Executive Director Human Resources .... Ms. Marcia K. HOFFMAN
23 Director Student Health Services .... Dr. Donald W. STECHSCHULTE
88 Int Executive Dir Leadership Gifts .... Mr. Robert D. RATHBUN
88 Exec Dir of Campaign Administration .... Ms. Shelby K. RADCLIFFE
09 Asst VP Planning & Inst Research .... Dr. Jerome S. RACKOFF
45 Director of Strategy Implementation .... Mr. Edward J. LOFTUS
08 Director of Library Services .... Ms. Carrie E. RAMPP
14 Dir Tech Infrastructure & User Svcs .... Mr. J. Christopher WEBER
91 Dir of Enterprise Systems .... Mr. Mark YERGER
19 Chief of Public Safety .... Mr. Jason D. FRIEDBERG
88 Director of Business Services .... Ms. Lori J. WILSON
88 Dir Parents Fund & Family Programs .... Ms. Ann L. DISTEFANO
44 Director of Gift Planning .... Ms. Melissa M. DIEHL
07 Dean of Admissions .... Mr. Robert G. SPRINGALL
44 Director of the Annual Fund .... Mr. Joshua L. GRILL
88 Director of Principal Gifts .... Mr. Kenneth C. HALL
102 Dir Corporate & Foundation Rels .... Mr. David M. FOREMAN
88 Dir Donor & Volunteer Recognition .... Ms. Cynthia J. GARRETT
88 Dir Business Operations for Provost .... Ms. Pamela A. BENFER
15 Dir Compensation & Employment Svcs .... Ms. Gene L. CRAWFORD
15 Director of Benefits & HRIS .... Ms. Cindy L. BILGER
07 Asst VP for Enrollment Management .... Mr. Mark D. DAVIES
88 Exec Director of Events Mgmt Office .... Ms. Judith L. MICKANIS
37 Director of Financial Aid .... Ms. Andrea C. LEITHNER STAUFFER
38 Director of Psychological Services .... Dr. Linda L. LOCHER
36 Exec Director of Career Services .... Ms. Pamela G. KEISER
06 Associate Registrar .... Ms. Melissa A. WEBER
06 Associate Registrar .... Mr. Dennis M. HOPPLE
35 Associate Dean of Students .... Ms. Amy A. BADAL
35 Associate Dean of Students .... Mr. Daniel C. REMLEY
42 University Chaplain .... Ms. Thomasina A. YUILLE
104 Director of International Education .... Mr. Stephen K. APPIAH-PADI
88 Sr Dir of News & Media Relations .... Vacant
105 Dir Digital Communications .... Ms. Roberta L. SIMS
88 Dir of Publications/Print & Mail .... Ms. Lisa D. HOOVER
88 Exec Dir Weis Center Perform Arts .... Ms. Kathryn L. MAGUET
88 Dir of Samek Art Gallery .... Mr. Richard J. RINEHART
96 Director of Procurement Services .... Mr. Donald A. KRECH
22 Affirmative Action Officer .... Ms. Linda L. BENNETT
88 Dir Civic Engagement & Service Lrng .... Ms. Janice R. BUTLER
93 Director Multicultural Student Svcs .... Vacant
92 Honors Council Chair .... Dr. Erin L. JABLONSKI
88 Director of Writing Center .... Ms. Deirdre M. O'CONNOR
94 Dir Women's & Gender Studies Pgm .... Dr. Coralynn V. DAVIS

Bucks County Community College (E)

275 Swamp Road, Newtown PA 18940-4106
County: Bucks FICE Identification: 003239
Unit ID: 211307
Telephone: (215) 968-8000 Carnegie Class: Assoc/Pub-S-MC
FAX Number: (215) 968-8129 Calendar System: Semester
URL: www.bucks.edu
Established: 1964 Annual Undergrad Tuition & Fees (In-District): $3,458
Enrollment: 11,273 Coed
Affiliation or Control: Local IRS Status: 501(c)3
Highest Offering: Associate Degree
Program: Occupational; 2-Year Principally Bachelor's Creditable
Accreditation: M, ACBSP, ADNUR, ART, MUS, RAD

05 Provost/Dean of Academic Affairs .... Dr. Annette L. CONN
10 VP for Administrative Affairs & CFO .... Mr. Dennis W. MATTHEWS
32 VP Student Affairs/Dean of Students .... Ms. Barbara H. YETMAN
51 Vice Pres Cont Educ/Workforce Devel .... Ms. Barbara A. MILLER
27 Vice Pres/Chief Info Tech Officer .... Ms. Deborah NOBLE
21 Exec Dir Budget & Internal Audit .... Ms. Nancy PRUSKOWSKI
20 Dean Academic & Curricular Svcs .... Ms. Catherine C. MCELROY
88 Dean Learning Resources .... Dr. Maureen MCCREADIE
84 Asst Dean for Enrollment Services .... Ms. Liz M. KULICK
38 Asst Dean Advising & Stdnt Planning .... Ms. Christine HAGEDORN
102 Exec Director of the Foundation .... Mr. Tobias BRUHN
18 Exec Director Physical Plant .... Mr. Mark P. GRISI
26 Exec Dir Marketing/Public Relations .... Ms. Marta KAUFMANN
12 Exec Director Upper County Campus .... Dr. Rodney E. ALTEMOSE
04 Exec Assistant to President .... Ms. Kathleen C. FEDORKO
15 Exec Director Human Resources .... Ms. Tracey DONALDSON
96 Director of Purchasing .... Mr. James F. LOUGHERY
106 Director Online Learning .... Ms. Georglyn L. DAVIDSON
37 Director Financial Aid .... Ms. Donna M. WILKOSKI
36 Director Career Services .... Ms. Sharon STEPHENS
35 Director of Student Life Programs .... Mr. Matt J. CIPRIANO
09 Director of Institutional Research .... Ms. Christine BOYLE
103 Asst VP Cont Educ/Workforce Devel .... Ms. Christine GILLESPIE
19 Director of Security/Safety .... Mr. Dennis MCCAULEY
08 Director Library Services .... Ms. Linda MCCANN
41 Athletic Director .... Dr. Priscilla RICE
20 Executive Assistant to Provost .... Dr. William FORD
07 Director of Admissions .... Ms. Marlene T. BARLOW
12 Exec Dir Lower Bucks Campus .... Mr. James H. SELL
88 Exec Dir Public Safety Training .... Mr. Fred HUNSINGER
06 Registrar .... Mr. Robert MALEY
29 Director Alumni Relations .... Ms. Adrienne CLARKE

Butler County Community College (F)

107 College Drive, Butler PA 16002
County: Butler FICE Identification: 003240
Unit ID: 211343
Telephone: (724) 287-8711 Carnegie Class: Assoc/Pub-S-SC
FAX Number: (724) 285-6047 Calendar System: Semester
URL: www.bc3.edu
Established: 1965 Annual Undergrad Tuition & Fees (In-District): $3,168
Enrollment: 4,429 Coed
Affiliation or Control: Local IRS Status: 501(c)3
Highest Offering: Associate Degree
Program: Occupational; 2-Year Principally Bachelor's Creditable
Accreditation: M, ACBSP, ADNUR, MAC, PTAA

01 President .... Dr. Nicholas C. NEUPAUER
05 Vice President for Academic Affairs .... Dr. Francie P. SPIGELMYER
11 VP for Administration & Finance .... Mr. James A. HRABOSKY
32 Vice President for Student Services .... Vacant
51 VP Continuing Ed Off-Campus Centers .... Mr. William T. O'BRIEN
10 Chief Business Officer .... Mr. Wm. Jake FRIEL
50 Dean of Business .... Ms. Rosemary C. KEASEY
83 Dean of Social Science/Humanities .... Mr. William L. MILLER
66 Dean of Nursing/Allied Health .... Dr. Patricia MIHALCIN
72 Interim Dean of Nat Science/Tech .... Mr. Matt KOVAC
106 Dean of Education Technology .... Ms. Ann MCCANDLESS
08 Dean of Library Services .... Mr. Stephen M. JOSEPH
35 Dean of Students .... Vacant
103 Exec Dir Workforce Dev Training .... Dr. Stephen R. CATT
16 Director Human Resources .... Ms. Linda M. DODD
26 Director of Public Relations .... Ms. Susan J. CHANGNON
51 Director Adult/Continuing Education .... Mr. Paul M. LUCAS
06 Director of Records & Registration .... Ms. Ruth A. SCOTT
13 Director Telecommunications & MIS .... Mr. Rick H. MICHELINI
32 Director of Student Life .... Mr. Rob A. SNYDER
09 Dir Instl Research/Strategic Plng .... Ms. Sharla M. ANKE
18 Director of Facilities .... Mr. Brian R. OPITZ
07 Director of Admissions .... Ms. Pattie A. BAJUSZIK
12 Director of Lawrence County Center .... Ms. Diane M. DECARBO
12 Director Cranberry Center .... Mr. Alex J. GLADIS
12 Director of LindenPointe-Mercer Co .... Mr. John P. SUESSER
12 Director of Upper Allegheny Region .... Ms. Jill MARTIN-REND
37 Financial Aid Director .... Ms. Julianne E. LOUTTIT
41 Athletic Director .... Mr. Rob A. SNYDER
21 Director of College Services .... Ms. Cathy L. HILL
50 Director of Business/Industry Trng .... Ms. Lisa M. CAMPBELL
38 Director Student Counseling .... Vacant
29 Director Alumni Relations .... Ms. Michelle E. JAMIESON
45 Director of Advancement .... Ms. Ruth PURCELL
19 Director of Campus Police/Security .... Mr. Patrick W. MASSARO
88 Director of Cultural Center .... Mr. Lawrence E. STOCK
88 Director of Children's Center .... Ms. Judith A. ZUZACK
88 Associate Director Admissions .... Mr. Sean M. CARROLL
40 Bookstore Manager .... Mrs. Donna L. PALLONE

Byzantine Catholic Seminary of SS. Cyril and Methodius (G)

3605 Perrysville Avenue, Pittsburgh PA 15214-2229
County: Allegheny FICE Identification: 041180
Unit ID: 444103
Telephone: (412) 321-8383 Carnegie Class: Spec/Faith
FAX Number: (412) 321-9936 Calendar System: Semester
URL: www.byzcathsem.edu
Established: 1950 Annual Graduate Tuition & Fees: $19,200
Enrollment: 18 Coed
Affiliation or Control: Other IRS Status: 501(c)3
Highest Offering: Master's; No Undergraduates
Program: Liberal Arts And General; Religious Emphasis
Accreditation: THEOL

01 Rector .... Rev. John G. PETRO
04 Administrative Assistant .... Sr. Margaret A. ANDRAKO
05 Academic Dean .... Rev. Joseph RAPTOSH

Cabrini College (H)

610 King of Prussia Road, Radnor PA 19087-3698
County: Delaware FICE Identification: 003241
Unit ID: 211352
Telephone: (610) 902-8100 Carnegie Class: Master's L

FAX Number: (610) 902-8309 Calendar System: Semester
URL: www.cabrini.edu
Established: 1957 Annual Undergrad Tuition & Fees: $32,266
Enrollment: 3,440 Coed
Affiliation or Control: Roman Catholic IRS Status: 501(c)3
Highest Offering: Master's
Program: Liberal Arts And General
Accreditation: M, SW

01 President ... Dr. Marie A. GEORGE
05 Provost/Vice Pres Academic Affairs ... Dr. Anne SKLEDER
45 VP for Institutional Planning ... Ms. Joan NEAL
10 Interim CFO/VP Admin ... Dr. Robert ALLISON
30 VP Institutional Advancement ... Mrs. Sharon Kerrigan LOMAN
32 Vice Pres for Student Development ... Dr. Christine LYSIONEK
84 Vice Pres of Enrollment Management ... Mr. Dennis M. KELLY
26 Vice Pres Marketing/Communications ... Mr. Gene CASTELLANO
20 Dean for Academic Affairs ... Dr. Jeffrey GINGERICH
35 Dean of Students ... Mr. George STROUD
58 Dean of Grad Studies ... Dr. Martha COMBS
04 Exec Assistant to the President ... Ms. Betsy STILES
06 Registrar ... Ms. Phyllis BEAN
08 Library Director ... Dr. Roberta JACQUET
14 Director of Info Tech & Resources ... Ms. Marlayne DUNOVICH
19 Director of Public Safety ... Ms. Lillian BURROUGHS
18 Dir Construction/Plng/Facilities ... Mr. Howard HOLDEN
29 Dir of Alumni Programs and Giving ... Ms. Rachel MCCARTER
37 Director of Financial Aid ... Mr. Mike COLAHAN
36 Dir of Cooperative Educ/Career Svcs ... Ms. Nancy HUTCHISON
41 Director of Athletics ... Mr. Joseph GIUNTA
15 Director of Human Resources ... Vacant
21 Controller ... Ms. Diane SCUTTI
24 Coord of Education Resources Center ... Ms. Mary BUDZILOWICZ
40 Bookstore Manager ... Ms. Michele CONROY
105 Web Master ... Mr. Matt HOLMES
09 Director of Institutional Research ... Ms. Lisa PLUMMER
35 Director of Student Activities ... Mrs. Anne FILIPPONE
11 Dir of Admin Services/Purchasing ... Ms. Heather CARDAMONE
92 Co-Director of the Honors Program ... Dr. Paul WRIGHT
92 Co-Director of the Honors Program ... Dr. Leonard PRIMIANO
28 Dir Student Diversity Initiatives ... Vacant
38 Director Student Counseling ... Ms. Sara MAGGITTI
39 Director of Residence Life ... Ms. Sue KRAMER

Calvary Baptist Theological Seminary (A)

1380 S Valley Forge Road, Lansdale PA 19446-4797
County: Montgomery FICE Identification: 038993
Unit ID: 211370
Telephone: (215) 368-7538 Carnegie Class: Spec/Faith
FAX Number: (215) 368-1003 Calendar System: Semester
URL: www.cbs.edu
Established: 1976 Annual Graduate Tuition & Fees: $6,300
Enrollment: 106 Coed
Affiliation or Control: Independent Non-Profit IRS Status: 501(c)3
Highest Offering: Doctorate; No Undergraduates
Program: Professional; Religious Emphasis
Accreditation: M

01 President ... Dr. Samuel L. HARBIN
05 Seminary Dean ... Dr. Jeffrey P. TUTTLE
06 Registrar ... Mr. Clint J. BANZ
08 Director of Library Services ... Mr. David C. EVANS
10 Business Manager ... Mr. Nicholas Y. YZZI

Cambria-Rowe Business College (B)

422 S 13th Street, Indiana PA 15701-2804
County: Indiana Identification: 666476
Unit ID: 428329
Telephone: (724) 463-0222 Carnegie Class: Assoc/PrivFP
FAX Number: (724) 463-7246 Calendar System: Quarter
URL: www.crbc.net
Established: 1891 Annual Undergrad Tuition & Fees: $10,890
Enrollment: 130 Coed
Affiliation or Control: Proprietary IRS Status: Proprietary
Highest Offering: Associate Degree
Program: Occupational; 2-Year Principally Bachelor's Creditable; Business Emphasis
Accreditation: ACICS

01 President ... Mr. William COWARD
03 Executive Director ... Mr. Michael ARTIM
12 Director ... Mr. Jeffrey ALLEN
05 Director of Education ... Mrs. Angela SEIDEL
20 Assistant Director of Education ... Mrs. Amy BEITEL
84 Director of Enrollment Services ... Mrs. Linda WESS
37 Financial Aid Officer ... Mrs. Kathy CHRISTY
36 Director of Career Services ... Mrs. Missy HILL
07 Director of Admissions ... Mrs. Amanda ARTIM

† Branch campus of Cambria-Rowe Business College, Johnstown, PA.

Cambria-Rowe Business College (C)

221 Central Avenue, Johnstown PA 15902-2494
County: Cambria FICE Identification: 004889
Unit ID: 211398
Telephone: (814) 536-5168 Carnegie Class: Assoc/PrivFP
FAX Number: (814) 536-5160 Calendar System: Quarter
URL: www.crbc.net
Established: 1891 Annual Undergrad Tuition & Fees: $10,890
Enrollment: 175 Coed
Affiliation or Control: Proprietary IRS Status: Proprietary
Highest Offering: Associate Degree
Program: Occupational; 2-Year Principally Bachelor's Creditable; Business Emphasis
Accreditation: ACICS

01 President ... Mr. William COWARD
03 Executive Director ... Mr. Michael ARTIM
88 Director ... Mr. Jeffrey ALLEN
05 Director of Education ... Mrs. Angela SEIDEL
36 Director of Career Services ... Mrs. Gretchen RUMMEL
84 Director of Enrollment Services ... Mrs. Linda WESS
07 Director of Admission ... Mrs. Amanda ARTIM
37 Financial Aid Officer ... Mrs. Judy MILLER
10 Business Manager ... Mrs. LeAnna BRKOVICH
07 Admissions Representative ... Mrs. Christi VALKO

Career Training Academy (D)

4314 Old William Penn Hwy, Ste 103, Monroeville PA 15146-1455
County: Allegheny Identification: 666051
Unit ID: 408312
Telephone: (412) 372-3900 Carnegie Class: Assoc/PrivFP
FAX Number: (412) 373-4262 Calendar System: Other
URL: www.careerta.edu
Established: 1992 Annual Undergrad Tuition & Fees: $19,559
Enrollment: 72 Coed
Affiliation or Control: Proprietary IRS Status: Proprietary
Highest Offering: Associate Degree
Program: Occupational; 2-Year Principally Bachelor's Creditable; Technical Emphasis
Accreditation: ACCSC, MAC

01 Director ... Mrs. Lisa SHUMAKER

† Branch campus of Career Training Academy, New Kensington, PA.

Career Training Academy (E)

950 Fifth Avenue, New Kensington PA 15068-6308
County: Westmoreland FICE Identification: 026095
Unit ID: 210951
Telephone: (724) 337-1000 Carnegie Class: Assoc/PrivFP
FAX Number: (724) 335-7140 Calendar System: Other
URL: www.careerta.edu
Established: 1986 Annual Undergrad Tuition & Fees: $19,559
Enrollment: 104 Coed
Affiliation or Control: Proprietary IRS Status: Proprietary
Highest Offering: Associate Degree
Program: Occupational; 2-Year Principally Bachelor's Creditable; Technical Emphasis
Accreditation: ACCSC

01 President ... Mr. John M. REDDY

Career Training Academy (F)

1500 Shoppes at Northwayjavascript:, Pittsburgh PA 15237-3015
County: Allegheny Identification: 666100
Unit ID: 440174
Telephone: (412) 367-4000 Carnegie Class: Assoc/PrivFP
FAX Number: (412) 369-7223 Calendar System: Other
URL: www.careerta.edu
Established: 1986 Annual Undergrad Tuition & Fees: $19,529
Enrollment: 84 Coed
Affiliation or Control: Proprietary IRS Status: Proprietary
Highest Offering: Associate Degree
Program: Occupational; 2-Year Principally Bachelor's Creditable; Technical Emphasis
Accreditation: ACCSC

01 Director ... Carla RYBA

† Branch campus of Career Training Academy, New Kensington, PA.

Carlow University (G)

3333 Fifth Avenue, Pittsburgh PA 15213-3165
County: Allegheny FICE Identification: 003303
Unit ID: 211431
Telephone: (412) 578-6000 Carnegie Class: Master's M
FAX Number: (412) 578-6668 Calendar System: Semester
URL: www.carlow.edu
Established: 1929 Annual Undergrad Tuition & Fees: $23,504
Enrollment: 2,267 Coed
Affiliation or Control: Roman Catholic IRS Status: 501(c)3
Highest Offering: Doctorate
Program: Liberal Arts And General; Teacher Preparatory; Professional
Accreditation: M, NURSE, SW

01 President ... Dr. Mary E. HINES
05 Provost/VP Academic Affairs ... Dr. Margaret K. MCLAUGHLIN
10 CFO/VP Finance and Operations ... Mr. Tyler A. KELSCH
30 VP Advancement ... Ms. Karen E. GALENTINE
26 VP Communications & External Rels ... Ms. Louise C. SCIANNAMEO
88 Special Asst to Pres/Mercy Heritage ... Sr. Sheila A. CARNEY
32 Dean Student Affairs ... Ms. Jennifer CARLO
04 Asst to the President ... Ms. Barbara L. GILLES
15 Director Human Resources ... Ms. Andra M. TOKARSKY
42 Campus Minister ... Ms. Siobhan K. DEWITT
58 Interim Dean Graduate School ... Dr. Robert A. REED
49 Dean Arts and Sciences ... Dr. Karyn Z. SPROLES
06 Registrar ... Mr. Jason KRALL
20 Assoc Provost Enrollment Management ... Ms. Judith A. BOLSINGER
88 Principal Campus School ... Ms. Patricia D. COOPER
58 Sr Dir Adult & Graduate Admissions ... Ms. Susan S. SHUTTER
07 Director Admissions ... Ms. Susan M. WINSTEL
12 Dir Cranberry Education Center ... Mr. James V. SHANKEL
12 Dir Greensburg Education Center ... Ms. Wendy S. PHILLIPS
36 Director Career Center ... Ms. Cynthia S. SMITH
08 Director Library Services ... Ms. Elaine J. MISKO
85 Coordinator Center for Global Lrng ... Mr. Garrett D. MARGLIOTTI
09 Director Instnl Rsrch & Effective ... Ms. Anne M. CANDREVA
35 Director Student Activities ... Mr. Christopher M. MEANER
39 Director Residence Life ... Ms. Mary Beth HALFERTY
38 Director Counseling Services ... Dr. Lisa A. OSACHY
23 Director Health Services ... Ms. Mary Frances REIDELL
41 Director Athletics ... Mr. George S. SLIMAN
88 Director Wellness & Fitness Svcs ... Ms. Julie M. GAUL
28 Director Diversity Initiative ... Ms. Barbara G. JOHNSON
21 Controller ... Ms. Dorothy M. ANTONUCCI
27 CIO ... Mr. John HALLIS
18 Director Facilities ... Mr. Taylor G. BLICE
19 Chief of Police ... Ms. Tami L. ALLIAS
37 Director Financial Aid ... Ms. Natalie L. WILSON
88 Director Student Accounts ... Ms. Linda C. ROOT
40 Manager Bookstore ... Ms. Tracy HILL
44 Exec Director Advancement ... Ms. Anita S. DACAL
29 Director Alumnae/i Relations ... Ms. Rose M. WOOLLEY
44 Director of Carlow Fund ... Ms. Linda R. MADDEN-BRENHOLTS
27 Asst Dir Media & Public Rels ... Mr. Andrew G. WILSON
105 Manager Web Communications ... Ms. Kristin A. RAUP

Carnegie Mellon University (H)

5000 Forbes Avenue, Pittsburgh PA 15213-3890
County: Allegheny FICE Identification: 003242
Unit ID: 211440
Telephone: (412) 268-2000 Carnegie Class: RU/VH
FAX Number: (412) 268-2330 Calendar System: Semester
URL: www.cmu.edu
Established: 1900 Annual Undergrad Tuition & Fees: $43,812
Enrollment: 11,818 Coed
Affiliation or Control: Independent Non-Profit IRS Status: 501(c)3
Highest Offering: Doctorate
Program: Liberal Arts And General; Teacher Preparatory; Professional
Accreditation: M, ART, BUS, ENG, MUS, SPAA

01 President ... Dr. Jared L. COHON
05 Provost/Executive Vice President ... Dr. Mark S. KAMLET
10 Vice President and CFO ... Ms. Deborah J. MOON
30 Vice President for Univ Advancement ... Mrs. Robbee KOSAK
46 Vice President for Research ... Dr. Richard D. MCCULLOUGH
43 Vice President/General Counsel ... Ms. Mary Jo DIVELY
101 Secretary Board of Trustees ... Ms. Cheryl M. HAYS
04 Exec Asst to Pres & Office Mgr ... Ms. Cathy A. LIGHT
20 Vice Provost for Education ... Dr. Amy L. BURKERT
11 Vice President for Campus Services ... Dr. Michael C. MURPHY
13 Vice Provost for Comp Svcs/CIO ... Mr. Joel M. SMITH
15 Assoc VP Chief Human Resources Ofcr ... Ms. Dianne KENNEY
29 Assoc Vice Pres Alumni Relations ... Mr. Andrew SHAINDLIN
102 Asst VP Corporate/Fdn Relations ... Ms. Kathy R. LACHENAUER
18 Asc VP Campus Design/Facility Devel ... Mr. Ralph R. HORGAN
22 Asst Vice Pres for Diversity & EOS ... Mr. Everett L. TADEMY
26 Asst Vice Pres For Media Relations ... Ms. Teresa THOMAS
28 Asst Vice Pres for Diversity & EOS ... Mr. Everett L. TADAMY
45 Director University Planning ... Mr. Russell D. O'LARE
41 Director Athletics & Physical Educ ... Ms. Susan BASSETT
19 Director Security/Chief Univ Police ... Mr. Thomas A. OGDEN
84 Co-Director of Enrollment Services ... Mr. John R. PAPINCHAK
84 Co-Director of Enrollment Services ... Mrs. Linda M. ANDERSON
14 Director Software Engr Inst ... Dr. Paul D. NIELSEN
07 Director of Admission ... Mr. Michael STEIDEL
08 Dean of University Libraries ... Dr. Gloriana ST. CLAIR
96 Director of Procurement ... Vacant
06 Registrar ... Mr. John R. PAPINCHAK
09 Director of Institutional Research ... Ms. Janel SUTKUS
36 Director of Career Center ... Mr. Farouk DEY
38 Dir Counseling & Psychological Svcs ... Dr. Cynthia K. VALLEY
32 Dean Student Affairs ... Ms. Gina CASALEGNO
54 Dean Carnegie Inst of Technology ... Dr. Pradeep K. KHOSLA
57 Interim Dean College Fine Arts ... Dr. Dan J. MARTIN
49 Dean Human & Social Science ... Dr. John P. LEHOCZKY
50 Dean Tepper School of Business ... Dr. Robert DAMMON
81 Dean Mellon College of Science ... Dr. Frederick J. GILMAN
80 Dean Heinz Sch Publ Policy/Mgmt ... Dr. Ramayya KRISHNAN
77 Dean School of Computer Science ... Dr. Randal E. BRYANT
35 Asst Dean of Student Affairs ... Ms. Anne WITCHNER

Cedar Crest College (I)

100 College Drive, Allentown PA 18104-6196
County: Lehigh FICE Identification: 003243
Unit ID: 211468
Telephone: (610) 437-4471 Carnegie Class: Bac/Diverse
FAX Number: (610) 437-5955 Calendar System: Semester
URL: www.cedarcrest.edu
Established: 1867 Annual Undergrad Tuition & Fees: $29,710
Enrollment: 1,666 Female

Affiliation or Control: United Church Of Christ IRS Status: 501(c)3
Highest Offering: Master's
Program: Liberal Arts And General; Teacher Preparatory; Professional
Accreditation: M, ACBSP, DIETD, @DIETI, NMT, NUR, SW

Code	Title	Name
01	President	Ms. Carmen T. AMBAR
05	Provost	Dr. Betty POWELL
10	Chief Financial Officer	Ms. Audra KAHR
84	Interim VP for Enrollment Mgmt	Ms. Mariea NOBLITT
30	Vice Pres Institutional Advancement	Ms. Patricia MORAN
32	Vice President of Student Affairs	Dr. Kimberly OWENS
35	Acting Dean of Students	Ms. Denise O'NEILL
06	Registrar	Ms. Janet BAKER
20	Associate Provost	Dr. Elizabeth MEADE
29	Exec Director for Alumnae Affairs	Mrs. Susan S. COX
19	Chief of Campus Safety and Security	Mr. Mark VITALOS
18	Director of Facilities	Mr. Joseph HARTNER
08	Library Director	Ms. Mary Beth FREEH
91	Director Administrative Technology	Mrs. Kathleen CUNNINGHAM
09	Dir of Institutional Research	Ms. Marie WILDE
04	Exec Assistant to the President	Ms. Cheryl WENNER
26	Director Marketing/Cmty Outreach	Ms. Kerri PUSKAR
15	Director Personnel Services	Ms. Margie GRANDINETTI
37	Actg Dir Student Financial Services	Ms. Valerie KREISER
22	Director Health/Counseling Services	Ms. Nancy ROBERTS
27	Media Relations Associate	Mr. David JWANIER
96	Purchasing Coordinator	Ms. Karen KHATTARI
40	Manager Bookstore	Ms. Maureen YOACHIM

Central Pennsylvania College (A)

College Hill Road, Summerdale PA 17093-0309
County: Cumberland FICE Identification: 004890
Unit ID: 211477
Telephone: (800) 759-2727 Carnegie Class: Bac/Diverse
FAX Number: (717) 732-5254 Calendar System: Quarter
URL: www.centralpenn.edu
Established: 1881 Annual Undergrad Tuition & Fees: $19,988
Enrollment: 1,482 Coed
Affiliation or Control: Proprietary IRS Status: Proprietary
Highest Offering: Baccalaureate
Program: Occupational; 2-Year Principally Bachelor's Creditable; Professional; Business Emphasis
Accreditation: M, MAC, PTAA

Code	Title	Name
01	President	Mr. Todd A. MILANO
05	Vice Pres/Chief Academic Officer	Ms. Melissa M. VAYDA
06	Director Records & Registration	Mr. Jen CORRELL
03	Provost	Ms. Janice MOORE
20	Academic Dean	Ms. Kathy ANDERSEN
26	Marketing Services Manager	Mrs. Mary E. WETZEL
07	Admissions Director	Ms. Stacey SCOT
51	Dir Continuing Education Admissions	Ms. Michelle MEISER
18	Facilities Director	Mr. Rodney GROFF
37	Financial Aid Director	Ms. Kathy J. SHEPARD
35	Student Affairs Director	Mr. Ed LIESCH
09	Institutional Research Director	Col. Wilbur E. GRAY
36	Career Services Coordinator	Mr. Steven HASSINGER

Chatham University (B)

Woodland Road, Pittsburgh PA 15232-2826
County: Allegheny FICE Identification: 003244
Unit ID: 211556
Telephone: (412) 365-1100 Carnegie Class: Master's L
FAX Number: (412) 365-1505 Calendar System: Other
URL: www.chatham.edu
Established: 1869 Annual Undergrad Tuition & Fees: $30,355
Enrollment: 2,288 Female
Affiliation or Control: Independent Non-Profit IRS Status: 501(c)3
Highest Offering: Doctorate
Program: Liberal Arts And General; Teacher Preparatory; Professional
Accreditation: M, ARCPA, CIDA, LSAR, NURSE, OT, PTA, SW

Code	Title	Name
01	President	Dr. Esther L. BARAZZONE
05	Vice President Academic Affairs	Dr. Laura S. ARMESTO
10	Vice Pres Finance/Administration	Mr. Walter B. FOWLER
84	Vice Pres Enrollment Management	Ms. Wendy BECKEMEYER
32	Vice President Student Affairs	Dr. Zauyah WAITE
30	Vice Pres University Advancement	Vacant
51	Dean Continuing/Prof Studies	Dr. Sharon FROSS
88	Dean Sch Sustainability/Environment	Dr. David HASSENZAHL
21	Asst Vice Pres Finance	Ms. Jennifer LUNDY
04	Executive Assistant to President	Mr. Sean COLEMAN
20	Asst VP of Academic Affairs	Dr. Michele COLVARD
27	Chief Communications Officer	Mr. Paul KOVACH
58	Dean College of Graduate Studies	Dr. Sharon FROSS
09	Director of Institutional Research	Dr. Robert ZHANG
06	Registrar	Ms. Jennifer BRONSON
37	Director of Financial Aid	Ms. Jennifer A. BURNS
08	Director of Library	Ms. Jill AUSEL
29	Director Alumnae Affairs	Ms. Tina TUMINELLA
44	Director of Annual Giving	Ms. Erin BRYER
102	Director of Foundation/Corp Support	Ms. Kate FREED
15	Director of Human Resources	Mr. Frank M. GRECO
18	Director of Facilities Management	Mr. Robert R. DUBRAY
19	Director of Safety & Security	Mr. Bernard D. MERRICK
41	Director of Athletics	Vacant
36	Director Career Development	Ms. Monica RITTER
38	Director of Student Counseling	Ms. Elsa M. ARCE
35	Director Student Activities	Ms. Heather BLACK

Chestnut Hill College (C)

9601 Germantown Avenue, Philadelphia PA 19118-2693
County: Philadelphia FICE Identification: 003245
Unit ID: 211583
Telephone: (215) 248-7000 Carnegie Class: Master's L
FAX Number: (215) 248-7155 Calendar System: Semester
URL: www.chc.edu
Established: 1924 Annual Undergrad Tuition & Fees: $29,100
Enrollment: 2,369 Coed
Affiliation or Control: Roman Catholic IRS Status: 501(c)3
Highest Offering: Doctorate
Program: Liberal Arts And General; Teacher Preparatory
Accreditation: M, CLPSY, MACTE

Code	Title	Name
01	President	Sr. Carol Jean VALE, SSJ
05	Vice Pres for Academic Affairs	Dr. Kenneth SOPRANO
09	Vice Pres Admin Instl Svcs & Events	Vacant
10	Sr Vice Pres for Financial Affairs	Ms. Lauri STRIMKOVSKY
30	Vice President for Inst Advancement	Mr. Kenneth HICKS
32	Vice President for Student Life	Dr. Lynn ORTALE
90	VP for Information Technology & CIO	Dr. George MCKENNA
11	Asst to Pres for Administration	Sr. Kathryn MILLER, SSJ
42	Asst to Pres for Mission & Ministry	Sr. Mary DARRAH, SSJ
58	Dean School of Graduate Studies	Dr. Steven GUERRIERO
34	Dean School of Undergrad Studies	Sr. Cecelia J. CAVANAUGH, SSJ
51	Dean of Continuing Studies	Dr. Elaine GREEN
08	Dean Library/Information Resources	Sr. Mary Josephine LARKIN, SSJ
07	Vice President for Admissions	Ms. Jodie KING
20	Director for Academic Advising	Ms. Gale CARLIN
06	Registrar	Ms. Deborah EBBERT
35	Director of Student Activities	Ms. Emily SCHADEMAN
38	Director Counseling Center	Sr. Sheila KENNEDY, SSJ
85	Foreign Student Advisor	Mr. James MCLAUGHLIN
28	Dir Cultural Diversity Initiatives	Vacant
92	Director of Honors Programs	Vacant
23	Director Health Services	Ms. Shannon ROBERTS
36	Director of Career Services	Ms. Nancy DACHILLE
07	Dir Admission/Sch Graduate Studies	Ms. Jayne MASHETT
07	Director Accelerated Admissions	Sr. Mary Esther LEE, SSJ
21	Controller	Mr. Michael GAVANUS
37	Director Financial Aid	Mr. Nicholas FLOCCO
44	Director of Development	Ms. Catherine QUINN
09	Director of Institutional Research	Sr. Patricia O'DONNELL, SSJ
102	Dir Corporate/Found/Govt Relations	Vacant
29	Director of Alumnae/i Affairs	Ms. Patricia CANNING
41	Director of Athletics	Ms. Lynn TUBMAN
15	Director Human Resources	Ms. Michelle MOCARSKY
19	Dir Security/Safety/Bldgs/Grounds	Mr. Raymond HALLMAN
18	Director of Physical Plant	Mr. Mark MCGRATH
91	Administrative Software Manager	Ms. Darlene BROWN
24	Audio Visual Manager	Sr. Florence E. SULLIVAN, SSJ
26	Public Relations Director	Ms. Kathleen SPIGELMYER
40	Manager of Campus Store	Vacant

CHI Institute (D)

177 Franklin Mills Boulevard, Philadelphia PA 19154-3140
County: Bucks FICE Identification: 022898
Unit ID: 211617
Telephone: (215) 612-6600 Carnegie Class: Assoc/PrivFP
FAX Number: (215) 612-6695 Calendar System: Quarter
URL: www.chitraining.com
Established: 1982 Annual Undergrad Tuition & Fees: $13,140
Enrollment: 698 Coed
Affiliation or Control: Proprietary IRS Status: Proprietary
Highest Offering: Associate Degree
Program: Occupational
Accreditation: ACCSC

Code	Title	Name
01	President	Ms. Jamie PEAK
07	Director of Admissions	Mr. Dan WATKINS
05	Education Department Head	Mrs. Dorothy MCCADEN
36	Director of Placement	Ms. Cheryl BRAIDES
37	Director Financial Aid	Ms. Nina BALAGOUR

CHI Institute/Broomall Campus (E)

1991 Sproul Road, Suite 42, Broomall PA 19008-3516
County: Delaware FICE Identification: 007781
Unit ID: 215646
Telephone: (610) 353-7630 Carnegie Class: Assoc/PrivFP
FAX Number: (610) 359-1370 Calendar System: Quarter
URL: www.chitraining.com
Established: 1958 Annual Undergrad Tuition & Fees: $21,000
Enrollment: 783 Coed
Affiliation or Control: Proprietary IRS Status: Proprietary
Highest Offering: Associate Degree
Program: Occupational; 2-Year Principally Bachelor's Creditable; Technical Emphasis
Accreditation: ACCSC

Code	Title	Name
01	President	Mrs. Adrienne SCOTT
05	Director of Education	Mr. Warren HOWELL
36	Placement Director	Mr. James LINCKE
07	Director of Admissions	Mr. Bill SCHNELL

The Commonwealth Medical College (F)

525 Pine Street, Scranton PA 18509
County: Lackawanna Identification: 667004
Unit ID: 456542
Telephone: (570) 504-7000 Carnegie Class: Not Classified
FAX Number: (570) 504-7289 Calendar System: Semester
URL: www.thecommonwealthmedical.com
Established: 2009 Annual Graduate Tuition & Fees: $37,650
Enrollment: 169 Coed
Affiliation or Control: Independent Non-Profit IRS Status: 501(c)3
Highest Offering: Doctorate; No Undergraduates
Program: Professional
Accreditation: @M, #MED

Code	Title	Name
00	President Emeritus & Founding Dean	Dr. Robert D'ALESSANDRI
01	Interim President and Dean	Dr. Lois Margaret NORA
45	Vice Pres & Assoc Dean for Planning	Ms. Virginia HUNT
28	Vice Pres Social Justice/Diversity	Ms. Ida L. CASTRO
05	Senior Assoc Dean Academic Affairs	Dr. Maurice CLIFTON
32	Associate Dean for Student Affairs	Dr. David AXLER
30	Chief Development Officer	Mr. Brian CAMPBELL
13	Dir of Technology Infrastructure	Mr. Douglas CARROLL, JR.
15	Director of Human Resources	Mr. Joseph CORTESE
10	Interim Chief Financial Officer	Mr. Richard CRATER
21	Dir Budgeting & Financial Services	Mr. Sam DIAZ
58	Dir Fac Affairs/Grad Medical Educ	Ms. Andrea DIMATTIA
105	Director of Web Services	Mr. Jay FORTIN
35	Director of Student Affairs	Ms. Julia KOLCHARNO
06	Registrar	Mr. Edward LAHART
37	Director of Financial Aid	Ms. Ellen MCGUIRE
91	Director of Administrative Systems	Mr. John KEARNEY
08	Director of Library	Ms. Joanne MUELLENBACH
18	Chief Facility & Public Safety Ofcr	Mr. James RYAN
07	Director of Admissions	Ms. Debra STALK
27	CIO/Assoc Dean for Technology	Mr. Wayne THOMPSON
44	Dir Annual Giving/Special Events	Mr. Michael WALSH

Commonwealth Technical Institute (G)

727 Goucher Street, Johnstown PA 15905-3092
County: Cambria FICE Identification: 025366
Unit ID: 212975
Telephone: (814) 255-8200 Carnegie Class: Assoc/PrivNFP
FAX Number: (814) 255-5709 Calendar System: Semester
URL: www.hgac.org
Established: 1959 Annual Undergrad Tuition & Fees: $15,128
Enrollment: 237 Coed
Affiliation or Control: Proprietary IRS Status: Proprietary
Highest Offering: Associate Degree
Program: Occupational
Accreditation: ACCSC, DA

Code	Title	Name
01	President	Donald RULLMAN
03	Executive Vice President	Carol MACKEL
05	Chief Academic Officer	Barbara PETERSEN
07	Director Admissions	Jason GIES
32	Chief Student Life Officer	Jill MORICONI
37	Director Student Financial Aid	Sylvia SABO
38	Director Student Counseling	Keith RAGER

Community College of Allegheny County (H)

800 Allegheny Avenue, Pittsburgh PA 15233-1895
County: Allegheny FICE Identification: 003231
Unit ID: 210605
Telephone: (412) 323-2323 Carnegie Class: Assoc/Pub-U-MC
FAX Number: (412) 237-3037 Calendar System: Semester
URL: www.ccac.edu
Established: 1966 Annual Undergrad Tuition & Fees (In-District): $2,338
Enrollment: 61,614 Coed
Affiliation or Control: State/Local IRS Status: 501(c)3
Highest Offering: Associate Degree
Program: Occupational; 2-Year Principally Bachelor's Creditable
Accreditation: M, ADNUR, DIETT, DMS, MAC, MLTAD, NMT, OTA, PTAA, RAD, RTT, SURGT

Code	Title	Name
01	President	Dr. Alex JOHNSON
05	VP Academic/Student Affairs	Dr. Mary Frances ARCHEY
10	Vice Pres Business & Admin/CFO	Ms. Joyce BRECKENRIDGE
12	Campus President Allegheny	Dr. Elmer HAYMON, JR.
12	Campus President Boyce	Hon. Charles MARTONI
12	Campus President North	Dr. Donna IMHOFF
12	Campus President South	Ms. Charlene NEWKIRK
30	Vice Pres Inst Advance/Ext Affairs	Ms. Nancilee BURZACHECHI
102	Exec Director of Foundation	Ms. Rose Ann DICOLA
13	Exec Dir Information Tech Svcs	Mr. Ibrahim GARBIOGLU
20	Assistant Dean Academic Management	Ms. Frances DICE
06	Registrar	Ms. Frances DICE
15	Exec Director of Human Resources	Vacant
26	Exec Dir Communications & Marketing	Ms. Tanya SANDERS-MARKS
51	Exec Dir Center Professional Dev	Mr. Reginald OVERTON
09	Exec Dir of Strategic Planning	Mr. Kevin SMAY
18	Director of Facilities Management	Mr. Bob HAMILTON
21	Controller	Mr. Paul SWEARENGIN
25	Director Contracts & Grants	Dr. Carol YOANNONE
96	Director Purchasing/Contracts Admin	Mr. James CAIRNS

28	Special Asst to Pres for Diversity	Vacant
04	Assistant to the President	Ms. Bonita L. RICHARDSON
88	Director of Field Operations	Mr. Mike O'BRIEN
22	Personnel Generalist	Mr. Paul SCHWARTZMILLER
103	Exec Dir CCAC/County Wkforce Allian	Dr. Charles BLOCKSIDGE
04	Exec Assistant to the President	Mr. David HOOVLER

Community College of Beaver County (A)

1 Campus Drive, Monaca PA 15061-2588

County: Beaver — FICE Identification: 006807 — Unit ID: 211079
Telephone: (724) 480-2222 — Carnegie Class: Assoc/Pub-S-SC
FAX Number: (724) 480-3573 — Calendar System: Semester
URL: www.ccbc.edu
Established: 1966 — Annual Undergrad Tuition & Fees (In-District): $3,660
Enrollment: 3,013 — Coed
Affiliation or Control: State/Local — IRS Status: 501(c)3
Highest Offering: Associate Degree
Program: Occupational; 2-Year Principally Bachelor's Creditable
Accreditation: M, ADNUR

01	President	Dr. Joe D. FORRESTER
05	VP Learning and Student Success	Mrs. Melissa D. DENARDO
03	Vice President Finance & Operations	Mr. Stephen R. DANIK
16	Vice Pres Human Resource Dev	Vacant
26	VP Community Relations/Development	Ms. Nancy DICKSON
13	Vice Pres Information Technology	Mr. Walter LUKHAUP
38	Dean Academic Support Services	Ms. Janice M. KAMINSKI
103	Assoc VP Career & Workforce Dev	Ms. Karen DEICHERT
09	Director Institutional Research	Mr. Brian HAYDEN
06	Dean of Enrollment Services	Mr. Scott F. ENSWORTH
18	Director Physical Plant Ops	Mr. Robert MOLLENKOPF
37	Director Student Financial Svcs	Ms. Janet DAVIDSON
04	Assistant to President	Ms. Jo Ann COATES
76	Division Dir Health Sciences	Mrs. Linda A. GALLAGHER
50	Division Dir Business/Technologies	Ms. Deborah MICHEALS
49	Division Dir Liberal Arts & Science	Dr. John GALL
88	Division Dir Aviation	Mr. Carmen ROMEO

Community College of Philadelphia (B)

1700 Spring Garden Street, Philadelphia PA 19130-3991

County: Philadelphia — FICE Identification: 003249 — Unit ID: 215239
Telephone: (215) 751-8000 — Carnegie Class: Assoc/Pub-U-SC
FAX Number: (215) 751-8762 — Calendar System: Semester
URL: www.ccp.edu
Established: 1965 — Annual Undergrad Tuition & Fees (In-District): $4,080
Enrollment: 19,503 — Coed
Affiliation or Control: State/Local — IRS Status: 501(c)3
Highest Offering: Associate Degree
Program: Occupational; 2-Year Principally Bachelor's Creditable
Accreditation: M, ADNUR, DH, MAC, MLTAD, RAD

01	President	Dr. Stephen M. CURTIS
10	Vice President Finance/Planning	Dr. Thomas R. HAWK
05	Vice President Academic Affairs	Dr. Judith R. GAY
30	Vice Pres Institutional Advancement	Ms. Marsha M. RAY
32	Vice President Student Affairs	Dr. Samuel HIRSCH
86	Vice Pres Marketing/Government Rels	Ms. Lynette BROWN-SOW
43	General Counsel/VP Human Resources	Ms. Jill GARFINKLE-WEITZ
13	Chief Information Officer	Ms. Jody BAUER
35	Dean of Students	Mr. Ronald C. JACKSON
88	Dean of Student Systems	Dr. Beatrice JONES
49	Dean Liberal Studies	Dr. Sharon THOMPSON
51	Dean Div Adult/Community Education	Dr. David E. THOMAS
72	Div Dean of Business/Technology	Vacant
09	Director Institutional Research	Dr. Jane M. GROSSET
06	Director Stdnt Records/Registration	Ms. Bonnie HARRINGTON
18	Chief Facilities/Physical Plant	Mr. Harry MOORE
28	Affirmative Action Director	Mr. Simon BROWN
07	Director of Recruitment/Admissions	Mr. Luke KASIM
37	Director Financial Aid	Mr. Gim LIM
96	Director of Purchasing	Ms. Marsia HENLEY
38	Dept Head Student Counseling	Mr. Todd JONES
36	Coord Career Info/Placement Svcs	Ms. Tarsha SCOVENS
29	Coord Alumni Rels/Annual Giving	Ms. Lyvette BROOKS
25	Coord Grants/Prospect Research	Ms. Anne GRECO

Consolidated School of Business (C)

2124 Ambassador Circle, Lancaster PA 17603-2389

County: Lancaster — FICE Identification: 030299 — Unit ID: 260354
Telephone: (717) 394-6211 — Carnegie Class: Assoc/PrivFP
FAX Number: (717) 394-6213 — Calendar System: Other
URL: www.csb.edu
Established: 1981 — Annual Undergrad Tuition & Fees: $25,700
Enrollment: 165 — Coed
Affiliation or Control: Proprietary — IRS Status: Proprietary
Highest Offering: Associate Degree
Program: Occupational
Accreditation: ACICS

01	CEO/President	Mr. Robert L. SAFRAN
03	Vice President	Mr. William HOYT
10	Controller	Mr. Craig D. ELLIS
37	Financial Aid Director	Mr. William H. HOYT
36	Placement Director	Ms. Diane GRANT
13	Data Systems Director	Mr. Gholamereza SALARI
32	Student Services Director	Ms. Linda KRUSHINSKY
21	Bursar	Mrs. Gail I. DOUGHERTY
23	Medical Coordinator	Mrs. Cynthia L. DESTAFANO

Consolidated School of Business (D)

1605 Clugston Road, York PA 17404-1798

County: York — FICE Identification: 022896 — Unit ID: 211820
Telephone: (717) 764-9550 — Carnegie Class: Assoc/PrivFP
FAX Number: (717) 764-9469 — Calendar System: Other
URL: www.csb.edu
Established: 1981 — Annual Undergrad Tuition & Fees: $25,250
Enrollment: 173 — Coed
Affiliation or Control: Proprietary — IRS Status: Proprietary
Highest Offering: Associate Degree
Program: Occupational
Accreditation: ACICS

01	CEO/President	Mr. Robert L. SAFRAN
03	Vice President	Mr. Craig D. ELLIS
36	Placement Director	Mr. Paul CULBERTSON
10	Controller	Mr. Craig D. ELLIS
07	Director of Admissions	Ms. Derena CEDENO
21	Bursar	Mrs. Gail E. DOUGHERTY
13	Data Systems Director	Ms. Linda L. HOFFMASTER
32	Director Student Services	Ms. Jennifer HATCH
37	Financial Aid Director	Mr. Bill HOYT
23	Medical Coordinator	Mrs. Cynthia L. DESTAFANO

Curtis Institute of Music (E)

1726 Locust Street, Philadelphia PA 19103-6187

County: Philadelphia — FICE Identification: 003251 — Unit ID: 211893
Telephone: (215) 893-5252 — Carnegie Class: Spec/Arts
FAX Number: (215) 893-9065 — Calendar System: Semester
URL: www.curtis.edu
Established: 1924 — Annual Undergrad Tuition & Fees: $1,300
Enrollment: 163 — Coed
Affiliation or Control: Independent Non-Profit — IRS Status: 501(c)3
Highest Offering: Master's
Program: Professional; Music Emphasis
Accreditation: M, MUS

01	President & Director	Mr. Roberto DIAZ
03	Executive Vice President	Ms. Elizabeth WARSHAWER
05	Dean	Mr. John MANGAN
30	Vice President for Development	Ms. Elizabeth A. WRIGHT
26	Vice President for Communications	Ms. Melinda WHITING
06	Registrar	Mr. Paul BRYAN
07	Admissions Officer	Mr. Christopher HODGES
08	Librarian	Ms. Elizabeth WALKER
29	Director Alumni/Parent Relations	Ms. Anne O'DONNELL

Dean Institute of Technology (F)

1501 W Liberty Avenue, Pittsburgh PA 15226-1197

County: Allegheny — FICE Identification: 009186 — Unit ID: 211909
Telephone: (412) 531-4433 — Carnegie Class: Assoc/PrivFP
FAX Number: (412) 531-4435 — Calendar System: Quarter
URL: www.deantech.edu
Established: 1947 — Annual Undergrad Tuition & Fees: $12,800
Enrollment: 225 — Coed
Affiliation or Control: Proprietary — IRS Status: Proprietary
Highest Offering: Associate Degree
Program: Occupational; Technical Emphasis
Accreditation: ACCSC

01	President	Mr. James S. DEAN
05	Director of Education	Mr. Richard D. ALI
07	Director of Admissions	Mr. Steven J. FALAVOLITO
37	Director Student Financial Aid	Ms. Nancy S. GROM
36	Placement Director	Ms. Valerie A. HAGEDORN
27	Director Information Office	Mr. Nicholas D. ALI

Delaware County Community College (G)

901 S Media Line Road, Media PA 19063-1094

County: Delaware — FICE Identification: 007110 — Unit ID: 211927
Telephone: (610) 359-5000 — Carnegie Class: Assoc/Pub-S-SC
FAX Number: (610) 359-5343 — Calendar System: Semester
URL: www.dccc.edu
Established: 1967 — Annual Undergrad Tuition & Fees (In-District): $5,848
Enrollment: 12,705 — Coed
Affiliation or Control: State/Local — IRS Status: 501(c)3
Highest Offering: Associate Degree
Program: Occupational; 2-Year Principally Bachelor's Creditable
Accreditation: M, ADNUR, MAC, SURGT

01	President	Dr. Jerome S. PARKER
10	Vice Pres Administration/Treasurer	Mr. John A. GLAVIN, JR.
05	Provost	Dr. Virginia M. CARTER
30	Vice President for Advancement	Ms. Kathleen A. BRESLIN
12	Vice Provost & Vice Pres Chester Co	Dr. Mary Jo BOYER
15	Vice President of Human Resources	Ms. Connie L. MCCALLA
84	Vice President of Enrollment Mgmt	Ms. Frances M. CUBBERLEY
13	VP & CIO Information Technology	Mr. George J. SULLIVAN
32	Vice Provost Student/Instr Support	Dr. Grant S. SNYDER
96	Assoc VP Admin & Facilities Plng	Mr. Jeffrey S. BAUN
88	Director Learning Centers	Ms. Dawn M. MOSCARIELLO
88	Director Municipal Police Academy	Mr. William DAVIS
106	Director Distance Learning Services	Mr. Alexander PLUCHUTA
37	Director of Financial Aid	Mr. Raymond L. TOOLE
08	Director of Library Services	Dr. Karen M. REGE
07	Dir Admissions/Enrollment Services	Ms. Hope L. DIEHL
36	Director Career/Counseling Center	Ms. Christine M. DOYLE
06	Registrar	Mr. Thomas W. LUGG
09	Assoc Vice Prov Inst Effectiveness	Dr. Christopher TOKPAH
21	Associate VP Finance	Mr. William J. MARKLE
103	Director Workforce Entry Center	Ms. Susan E. BOND
85	Director International Student Svs	Ms. Lydia J. DELL'OSA
15	Director Human Resources	Mr. Christopher M. DICKERMAN
14	Director OIT/Technical Services	Ms. Bianca VALENTE
91	Director Admin Computing	Mr. Bob HARDCASTLE
29	Director Alumni Programs	Mr. Douglas J. FERGUSON
25	Director Grants Management	Ms. Susan M. SHISLER-RAPP
31	Director Community Education	Ms. Nan L. SMITH
35	Director Campus Life	Ms. Amy WILLIAMS-GAUDIOSO
19	Director Safety & Security	Mr. Raymond VISCUSI
12	Director Pennocks Bridge Campus	Ms. Jane SCHURMAN
88	Director Southeast Center	Ms. Shantelle K. JENKINS
89	Director, First Year Experiences	Dr. Kendrick MICKENS
88	Director Assessment Center	Ms. Carol MULLIN
96	Director Purchasing	Ms. Jenny M. RARIG
18	Dir Plant Oper/Construction Svcs	Mr. Tony DELUCA
103	Dean Workforce Dev & Cmty Educ	Ms. Karen KOZACHYN
80	Dean Public Services & Soc Svcs	Ms. Linda J. COLLIER
72	Dean Tech/Engineering & Math	Dr. John R. AGAR
88	Acting Dean Learning Support Svcs	Ms. Dolores E. MARTINO
50	Dean Business & Computer Info Sys	Dr. Eric R. WELLINGTON
12	Acting Dean Branch Campuses	Mr. John CRAIG
79	Dean Comm/Arts & Humanities	Dr. Clayton A. RAILEY III
40	Manager Bookstore	Mr. Kris STACHOWIAK

Delaware Valley College (H)

700 E Butler Avenue, Doylestown PA 18901-2697

County: Bucks — FICE Identification: 003252 — Unit ID: 211981
Telephone: (215) 345-1500 — Carnegie Class: Bac/Diverse
FAX Number: (215) 345-5277 — Calendar System: Semester
URL: www.delval.edu
Established: 1896 — Annual Undergrad Tuition & Fees: $30,646
Enrollment: 1,703 — Coed
Affiliation or Control: Independent Non-Profit — IRS Status: 501(c)3
Highest Offering: Master's
Program: Liberal Arts And General
Accreditation: M

01	President	Dr. Joseph S. BROSNAN
04	Exec Assistant to the President	Ms. Angela T. RECKNER
05	VP Acad Affairs/Dean of the Faculty	Dr. Bashar W. HANNA
32	VP Student Affairs/Dean of Students	Mr. John BROWN
10	VP for Finance & Administration	Mr. Arthur GLASS
30	Vice President for Inst Advancement	Mr. Joseph ERCKERT
84	Vice Pres for Enrollment Management	Mr. Norman JONES
49	Dean Bus/Educ/Arts & Sciences	Dr. Benjamin RUSILOSKI
47	Interim Dean Agriculture/Environ	Mr. Russell REDDING
06	Registrar	Mr. Adam T. WICHRYK
41	Athletic Director	Mr. Frank F. WOLFGANG
26	Director of College Communications	Mr. Lanny MORGNANESI
07	Director of Admissions	Mr. Steven W. ZENKO
36	Director Career Services	Ms. Tracy DEPEDRO
08	Librarian	Mr. Peter A. KUPERSMITH
37	Director Student Financial Aid	Mrs. Joan HOCK
51	Director Continuing Education	Mr. Robert J. MCNEILL, JR.
38	Director Counseling/Learn Support	Mrs. Karen KRZYZKOWSKI
23	Director Health Services	Ms. Judy WOOD-LEVIEN
14	Director of Client Services	Mr. James LINDEN
39	Director of Residence Life	Mr. Derek SMITH
19	Director Security/Public Safety	Mr. Steven JOHNSON
09	Director Institutional Research	Ms. Elisabeth ERVIN-BLANKENHEIM
15	Director Human Resources	Ms. Elaine SPIRO
18	Director Physical Plant	Mr. Theodore STANIEWICZ
44	Director Annual Fund	Ms. Jennifer ROCK
96	Director of Purchasing	Mr. William LYLE
04	Special Assistant to President	Mr. Donald FELDSCHER

DeSales University (I)

2755 Station Avenue, Center Valley PA 18034-9568

County: Lehigh — FICE Identification: 003986 — Unit ID: 210739
Telephone: (610) 282-1100 — Carnegie Class: Master's L
FAX Number: (610) 282-2254 — Calendar System: Semester
URL: www.desales.edu
Established: 1965 — Annual Undergrad Tuition & Fees: $28,000
Enrollment: 3,199 — Coed
Affiliation or Control: Roman Catholic — IRS Status: 501(c)3
Highest Offering: Master's
Program: Liberal Arts And General; Teacher Preparatory; Professional
Accreditation: M, ACBSP, ARCPA, NUR

01 President ....Dr. Bernard F. O'CONNOR, OSFS
04 Admin Assistant to the President ....Ms. Mary A. GOTZON
05 Provost/Vice Pres Academic Affairs ....Dr. Karen WALTON
06 Registrar ....Mr. Thomas MANTONI
08 Librarian ....Ms. Deborah MALONE
51 Dean of Lifelong Learning ....Ms. Deborah BOOROS
88 Dean of Undergraduate Education ....Dr. Robert BLUMENSTEIN
36 Director Career Svcs & Internships ....Ms. Kristen EICHOLTZ
30 Vice Pres Institutional Advancement ....Mr. Thomas L. CAMPBELL
86 Director of Government Relations ....Fr. Bernard F. O'CONNOR, OSFS
102 Director Foundation/Corp Relations ....Mrs. Judith BARBERICH
26 Executive Director of Communication ....Mr. Thomas MCNAMARA
44 Executive Dir of Annual Giving ....Ms. Lina BARBIERI
29 Director of Alumni Relations ....Mr. Dug SALLEY
10 VP for Admin/Finance & Campus Env ....Mr. Robert J. SNYDER
45 Assoc VP for Admin & Planning ....Mr. Peter RAUTZHAN
21 Director of Finance/Treasurer ....Mr. Michael SWEETANA
19 Director of Security ....Chief Stuart BEDICS
09 Director of Institutional Research ....Deacon George KELLY
96 Exec Dir of Campus Environment ....Mr. Marc ALBANESE
18 Director of Facilities ....Mr. Ed REBORATTI
40 Campus Store Manager ....Ms. Laura ANTONSON
16 Director of Human Resources ....Mr. Joseph TRELLA
15 Employment Benefits Coordinator ....Ms. Elizabeth GARCIA
13 Director of Information Technology ....Mr. James MAHACHEK
32 Vice President Student Life ....Dr. Gerard JOYCE
84 Dean of Enrollment Mgmt ....Mrs. Mary BIRKHEAD
35 Dean of Students ....Mrs. Linda ZERBE
39 Director of Residence Life ....Ms. Leah BREISCH
07 Director of Admissions ....Mr. Derrick WETZEL
37 Director of Student Financial Aid ....Mrs. Joyce FARMER
42 Chaplain ....Rev. John HANLEY, OSFS
38 Director of Counseling Center ....Dr. Gregg S. AMORE
41 Athletic Director ....Mr. Scott COVAL
28 Director Multicultural/Intl Affairs ....Vacant
58 Dean of Graduate Education ....Dr. Peter LEONARD, OSFS

DeVry University - Fort Washington Campus (A)

1140 Virginia Drive, Fort Washington PA 19034-3204
County: Philadelphia Identification: 666218
Unit ID: 442824
Telephone: (215) 591-5700 Carnegie Class: Master's S
FAX Number: (215) 591-5863 Calendar System: Semester
URL: www.devry.edu
Established: 1931 Annual Undergrad Tuition & Fees: $15,294
Enrollment: 1,300 Coed
Affiliation or Control: Proprietary IRS Status: Proprietary
Highest Offering: Master's
Program: Occupational; Professional; Business Emphasis
Accreditation: &NH, ENGT

01 Metro President ....Adena JOHNSTON
03 Group Vice President ....Darryl FIELD
05 Manager Academic Operations ....Lynn COPPOLA
32 Student Services Manager ....Abby GODFREY
06 Registrar ....Olivia MARTINEZ
07 Senior Director of Admissions ....Steve COHEN
37 Director of Student Finance ....Fatisha STRICKLAND
08 Director of Library Services ....Nana OWUSU
15 HR Business Partner ....Alexander PATANO
36 Director of Career Services ....Jeffrey GREENBERG
31 Director of Community Outreach ....Emily HEFFNER

† Regional accreditation is carried under the parent institution in Downers Grove, IL.

DeVry University - King of Prussia (B)

150 Allendale Road, Suite 3201,
King of Prussia PA 19406-2926
County: Montgomery Identification: 666570
Telephone: (610) 205-3130 Carnegie Class: Not Classified
FAX Number: (610) 205-3170 Calendar System: Semester
URL: www.devry.edu
Established: 1931 Annual Undergrad Tuition & Fees: $15,294
Enrollment: 277 Coed
Affiliation or Control: Proprietary IRS Status: Proprietary
Highest Offering: Master's
Program: Professional; Business Emphasis
Accreditation: &NH

01 Center Dean ....Christal JENNINGS

† Regional accreditation is carried under the parent institution in Downers Grove, IL.

DeVry University - Philadelphia (C)

1800 JFK Boulevard, Suite 200,
Philadelphia PA 19103-7410
County: Philadelphia Identification: 666568
Telephone: (215) 568-2911 Carnegie Class: Not Classified
FAX Number: (215) 568-1255 Calendar System: Semester
URL: www.devry.edu
Established: 1931 Annual Undergrad Tuition & Fees: $15,294
Enrollment: 1,139 Coed
Affiliation or Control: Proprietary IRS Status: Proprietary
Highest Offering: Master's
Program: Professional; Business Emphasis
Accreditation: &NH

01 Metro President ....Adena JOHNSTON

† Regional accreditation is carried under the parent institution in Downers Grove, IL.

DeVry University - Pittsburgh (D)

210 Sixth Avenue, Suite 200, Pittsburgh PA 15222-2606
County: Allegheny Identification: 666569
Telephone: (412) 642-9072 Carnegie Class: Not Classified
FAX Number: (412) 642-9201 Calendar System: Semester
URL: www.devry.edu
Established: 1931 Annual Undergrad Tuition & Fees: $15,294
Enrollment: 516 Coed
Affiliation or Control: Proprietary IRS Status: Proprietary
Highest Offering: Master's
Program: Professional; Business Emphasis
Accreditation: &NH

01 Campus Director ....Al MCLAUGHLIN

† Regional accreditation is carried under the parent institution in Downers Grove, IL.

Dickinson College (E)

Box 1773, College & Louther Street,
Carlisle PA 17013-2896
County: Cumberland FICE Identification: 003253
Unit ID: 212009
Telephone: (717) 243-5121 Carnegie Class: Bac/A&S
FAX Number: N/A Calendar System: Semester
URL: www.dickinson.edu
Established: 1783 Annual Undergrad Tuition & Fees: $43,060
Enrollment: 2,414 Coed
Affiliation or Control: Independent Non-Profit IRS Status: 501(c)3
Highest Offering: Baccalaureate
Program: Liberal Arts And General; Teacher Preparatory
Accreditation: M

01 President ....Dr. William G. DURDEN
05 Provost and Dean of the College ....Dr. Neil B. WEISSMAN
84 VP Enroll/Comm & Dean Admissions ....Ms. Stephanie BALMER
32 VP for Student Development ....Dr. April L. VARI
10 VP Finance & Administration ....Mr. Thomas A K. QUEENAN
30 VP College Advancement ....Dr. Donald A. HASSELTINE
27 VP & Chief Information Officer ....Mr. Robert E. RENAUD
15 Vice Pres Human Resource Services ....Mr. John A. WEIS
43 General Counsel ....Ms. Dana E. SCADUTO
100 Chief of Staff/Secretary of College ....Ms. Karen N. FARYNIAK
18 Assoc VP Campus Operations ....Mr. Kenneth E. SHULTES
20 Associate Provost ....Dr. Robert P. WINSTON
30 Assoc VP Advancement/Assoc Provost ....Ms. Christina P. VAN BUSKIRK
88 Associate Provost for Curriculum ....Ms. Brenda K. BRETZ
28 Spcl Asst Pres Inst & Divrsty Init ....Ms. Joyce A. BYLANDER
21 Assoc VP President/Assoc Treasurer ....Mr. David S. WALKER
26 Associate VP Enroll/Communications ....Vacant
06 Registrar/Summer School ....Ms. Karen A. WEIKEL
09 Director Institutional Research ....Dr. Michael J. JOHNSON
88 Assoc VP Advancement/Dir Lead Givg ....Ms. Carolyn G. YEAGER
37 Director of Financial Aid ....Mr. Richard A. HECKMAN
104 Exec Dir of Global Ed/Assoc Provost ....Mr. Stephen C. DEPAUL
94 Asst Prof Women's & Gender Studies ....Dr. Stephanie GILMORE
38 Director of Counseling Center ....Dr. Alecia D. SUNDSMO
36 Exec Dir Career /Asst VP Stdnt Dev ....Mr. Patrick D. MULLANE
35 Dean of Students ....Mr. Leonard E. BROWN, JR.
24 Director Instruct & Media Services ....Ms. Patricia A. PEHLMAN
27 Director of Media Relations ....Ms. Christine M. DUGAN
44 Executive Director of Annual Giving ....Ms. Kathleen A. MARCELLO
41 Dir Physical Education & Athletics ....Dr. Leslie J. POOLMAN
23 Director Student Health Services ....Ms. Mary E. POLSON
40 Dir College Bookstore/Central Svcs ....Mr. David A. NELSON
19 Director of Public Safety ....Ms. Dolores A. DANSER
91 Director Enterprise Systems ....Ms. Jill M. FORRESTER
29 Director Alumni & Parent Relations ....Mr. Daniel R. DELGIORNO
42 Director Religious Life/Cmty Svcs ....Ms. Mira A. HEWLETT
28 Director of Diversity Initiatives ....Ms. Paula M. LIMA

Douglas Education Center (F)

130 Seventh Street, Monessen PA 15062-1097
County: Westmoreland FICE Identification: 020683
Unit ID: 212045
Telephone: (724) 684-3684 Carnegie Class: Assoc/PrivFP
FAX Number: (724) 684-7463 Calendar System: Semester
URL: www.dec.edu
Established: 1904 Annual Undergrad Tuition & Fees: $20,735
Enrollment: 341 Coed
Affiliation or Control: Proprietary IRS Status: Proprietary
Highest Offering: Associate Degree
Program: Occupational; 2-Year Principally Bachelor's Creditable; Fine Arts Emphasis
Accreditation: ACICS

01 President ....Mr. Jeffrey D. IMBRESCIA
05 Vice President of Academic Affairs ....Ms. Patricia A. DECONCILIS
20 Director of Academic Progress ....Ms. Susan F. WEAVER
20 Academic Affairs Coordinator ....Ms. N. Renee MCDOWELL
84 Director of Enrollment Services ....Ms. Sherry L. WALTERS

07 Admissions Representative ....Ms. Loretta CASTANA
07 Admissions Representative/Instructo ....Mr. Tony BAEZ MILAN
07 Admissions Representative/Recruiter ....Ms. Victoria COCHRAN
10 Director of Financial Svcs/Bursar ....Ms. Donna M. SHIPLEY
37 Director of Financial Aid ....Ms. Alison PFENDER
36 Director of Career Services ....Mr. John MATECHEN
26 Director of Marketing ....Mr. Kevin G. FEAR
27 Public Relations Coordinator ....Ms. Katharine E. KELLAR
88 Director of Cosmetology ....Ms. Karen S. NELSON
13 Information Technology Coordinator ....Mr. Wayne NAGLE

Drexel University (G)

3141 Chestnut Street, Philadelphia PA 19104-2875
County: Philadelphia FICE Identification: 003256
Unit ID: 212054
Telephone: (215) 895-2000 Carnegie Class: RU/H
FAX Number: (215) 895-1414 Calendar System: Quarter
URL: www.drexel.edu
Established: 1891 Annual Undergrad Tuition & Fees: $34,500
Enrollment: 23,637 Coed
Affiliation or Control: Independent Non-Profit IRS Status: 501(c)3
Highest Offering: Doctorate
Program: Liberal Arts And General; Professional
Accreditation: M, ANEST, ARCPA, ART, BUS, CEA, CIDA, CLPSY, CONST, CS, DENT, DIETD, ENG, ENGT, HT, LAW, LIB, MED, MFCD, NUR, NURSE, PA, PH, PTA, RAD

01 President ....Mr. John A. FRY
05 Provost/Sr Vice Pres Acad Affairs ....Dr. Mark L. GREENBERG
17 Dean/Senior VP Health Sciences ....Dr. Richard V. HOMAN
30 Sr VP Institutional Advancement ....Dr. Elizabeth DALE
10 Sr Vice Pres Finance/Treasurer/CFO ....Mrs. Helen Y. BOWMAN
32 Sr VP Admin Services/Student Life ....Mr. James R. TUCKER
84 Senior VP Enrollment Management ....Ms. Joan T. MCDONALD
26 Sr VP University Communications ....Ms. Lori DOYLE
13 Vice Pres Info Resources/Technology ....Dr. John BIELEC
43 Sr VP & General Counsel ....Mr. Michael J. EXLER
03 Sr VP & Executive Director ....Mr. Brian KEECH
88 Vice President Internal Audit ....Mr. James SEAMAN
21 Vice Pres & Assoc Treasurer ....Mr. Eric OLSON
20 Vice Provost Academic Affairs ....Dr. N. John DINARDO
46 Vice Provost of Research ....Dr. Deborah CRAWFORD
09 Vice Provost Institutional Research ....Dr. Bernard F. LENTZ
88 Vice Provost Partnerships ....Dr. Lucy E. KERMAN
18 Vice Pres Univ Facilities ....Dr. Robert FRANCIS
16 Vice President Human Resources ....Ms. Deborah GLENN
88 Vice President & Comptroller ....Ms. Susan WILMER
49 Dean College Arts & Sciences ....Dr. Donna MURASKO
50 Dean LeBow College of Business ....Dr. George TSETSEKOS
54 Dean College of Engineering ....Dr. Bruce EISENSTEIN
107 Dean Goodwin Col Professional Stds ....Dr. William F. LYNCH
72 Dean Col Info Science & Technology ....Dr. David E. FENSKE
92 Dean of Pennoni Honors College ....Dr. D.B JONES
62 Dean of Libraries ....Dr. Danuta NITECKI
58 Dean/CEO Center for Grad Studies ....Dr. Frank LINNEHAN
61 Dean Earle Mack School of Law ....Mr. Roger J. DENNIS
66 Dean College of Nursing/Health Prof ....Dr. Gloria DONNELLY
69 Dean School of Public Health ....Dr. Marla J. GOLD
19 Sr Assoc VP Public Safety ....Mr. Domenic CECCANECCHIO
88 Senior Assoc Vice President ....Ms. Rita LARUE
25 Sr Assoc Vice Provost for Research ....Mr. Michael EDWARDS
41 Athletic Director ....Dr. Eric A. ZILLMER
45 Assoc VP Financial Planning ....Ms. Amy BOSIO
14 Assoc VP Info Resources & Tech ....Mr. Kenneth BLACKNEY
90 Assoc VP Info Resources & Tech ....Dr. Michael SCHEUERMANN
29 Associate VP Alumni Relations ....Ms. Cristina A. GESO
102 Assoc Vice Pres Corp & Found Rels ....Ms. Patricia DAVIS AUSTIN
32 Assoc Vice Pres/Dean of Students ....Mr. David A. RUTH
96 Assoc Vice Pres Procurement ....Dr. Joseph A. CAMPBELL
44 Assoc VP Planned Giving ....Mr. Stephen MILLER
78 Assoc Vice Prov Career Dev Center ....Mr. Peter FRANKS
93 Assoc Vice Provost AARD ....Ms. Antoinette TORRES
22 Asst Vice Pres Equality & Diversity ....Ms. Michele ROVINSKY
88 Asst Vice Pres Recruitment ....Dr. Lois "Casey" TURNER
07 Asst Vice Pres Admissions ....Ms. Erin FINN
35 Assoc Dean of Students ....Dr. Rebecca L. WEIDENSAUL
23 Asst Dean Counseling & Health Svc ....Dr. Annette MOLYNEUX
85 Asst Dean Intl Stdnts Scholars Svc ....Ms. Adrienne KEKEC
06 Registrar ....Mr. Joseph J. SALOMONE
24 Director Instructional Media Svcs ....Mr. Christopher GIBSON
37 Asst VP EM Planning/Financial Aid ....Ms. Melissa M. ENGLUND
38 Assoc Director of Counseling ....Dr. Amy HENNING
39 Director University Housing ....Mr. Joseph RUSSO
104 Asst Vice Provost Study Abroad ....Ms. Daniela ASCARELLI
105 Director of Web Development ....Mr. James MERGENTHAL
04 Executive Asst President's Office ....Ms. Anita MCEVOY
36 Sr Asst Director Career Services ....Mr. Andrew DUFFY
40 Manager Bookstore ....Mr. John RORER
106 President/CEO Drexel e-Learning ....Mr. Arthur ZAMKOFF

DuBois Business College (H)

One Beaver Drive, DuBois PA 15801-2401
County: Clearfield FICE Identification: 004893
Unit ID: 212072
Telephone: (814) 371-6920 Carnegie Class: Assoc/PrivFP
FAX Number: (814) 371-3974 Calendar System: Quarter
URL: www.dbcollege.com
Established: 1885 Annual Undergrad Tuition & Fees: $12,250
Enrollment: 255 Coed
Affiliation or Control: Proprietary IRS Status: Proprietary
Highest Offering: Associate Degree

Program: Occupational
Accreditation: ACICS

01 President and Director ... Ms. Jackie D. SYKTICH
05 Academic Dean ... Ms. Mary O. JONES
37 Financial Aid Director ... Ms. Karen S. ALDERTON
07 Director of Admissions ... Ms. Terry KHOURY
36 Career Services ... Ms. Barbara M. MARTINI
12 Director Huntingdon Campus ... Mr. Howard DIVINS
12 Director Oil City Campus ... Mrs. Kathie BROWN

DuBois Business College (A)

1001 Moore Street, Huntingdon PA 16652-1800
County: Huntingdon | Identification: 666479
Unit ID: 439303
Telephone: (814) 641-0440 | Carnegie Class: Assoc/PrivFP
FAX Number: (814) 641-0205 | Calendar System: Quarter
URL: www.dbcollege.com
Established: 1885 | Annual Undergrad Tuition & Fees: $9,930
Enrollment: 61 | Coed
Affiliation or Control: Proprietary | IRS Status: Proprietary
Highest Offering: Associate Degree
Program: Occupational
Accreditation: ACICS

01 Director ... Mr. Howard DIVINS

† Branch campus of DuBois Business College, DuBois, PA.

DuBois Business College (B)

701 E Third Street, Oil City PA 16301-2407
County: Venango | Identification: 666480
Unit ID: 439312
Telephone: (814) 677-1322 | Carnegie Class: Assoc/PrivFP
FAX Number: (814) 677-8237 | Calendar System: Quarter
URL: www.dbcollege.com
Established: 1996 | Annual Undergrad Tuition & Fees: $13,600
Enrollment: 75 | Coed
Affiliation or Control: Proprietary | IRS Status: Proprietary
Highest Offering: Associate Degree
Program: Occupational
Accreditation: ACICS

01 Director ... Ms. Kathryn A. BROWN

† Branch campus of DuBois Business College, DuBois, PA.

Duquesne University (C)

600 Forbes Avenue, Pittsburgh PA 15282-0001
County: Allegheny | FICE Identification: 003258
Unit ID: 212106
Telephone: (412) 396-6000 | Carnegie Class: RU/H
FAX Number: (412) 396-4186 | Calendar System: Semester
URL: www.duq.edu
Established: 1878 | Annual Undergrad Tuition & Fees: $26,413
Enrollment: 10,230 | Coed
Affiliation or Control: Roman Catholic | IRS Status: 501(c)3
Highest Offering: Doctorate
Program: Liberal Arts And General; Teacher Preparatory; Professional
Accreditation: M, ARCPA, BUS, CACREP, CEA, CLPSY, LAW, MUS, NURSE, OT, PHAR, PTA, SCPSY, SP, TED

01 President ... Dr. Charles J. DOUGHERTY
04 Assistant to President ... Ms. Mary F. MCINTYRE
05 Provost/Academic Vice President ... Dr. Ralph L. PEARSON
10 Vice President Management Business ... Mr. Stephen A. SCHILLO
32 Exec Vice Pres for Student Life ... Rev. Sean HOGAN, CSSP
30 VP for University Advancement ... Mr. John J. PLANTE
88 Vice President Mission & Identity ... Rev. James MCCLOSKEY
43 VP Legal Affairs & General Counsel ... Ms. Linda S. DRAGO
20 Assoc Academic Vice Pres Research ... Dr. Alan W. SEADLER
20 Assoc Academic Vice President ... Dr. Daniel K. DONNELLY
21 Assoc Vice Pres Financial Affairs ... Mr. David P. GROUSOSKY
88 AVP Interdiscp Schlrshp/Spec Projs ... Vacant
13 Executive Director CTS ... Dr. John H. ZIEGLER
18 Exec Director Facilities Management ... Mr. George FECIK
31 Exec Director Auxiliary Services ... Mr. David DIPETRO
85 Exec Director Intl Programs ... Dr. Roberta C. ARONSON
84 Assoc Vice Pres Enrollment Mgmt ... Mr. Paul-James CUKANNA
06 Registrar ... Ms. Kim HOERITZ
08 Librarian ... Dr. Laverna M. SAUNDERS
29 Director Alumni Relations ... Ms. Julie SHEPARD
35 Director Student Affairs ... Rev. Sean HOGAN, CSSP
09 Director of Institutional Research ... Mr. James L. RITCHIE
37 Director Financial Aid ... Mr. Richard C. ESPOSITO
15 Director of Human Resource Mgmt ... Ms. Mary Ellen BANEY
19 Director of Security ... Mr. James J. CAPUTO
88 Dir Environmental Health/Safety ... Ms. Madelyn REILLY
18 Director of Facilities Management ... Mr. Rodney W. DOBISH
36 Director of Career Services ... Ms. Nicole FELDHUES
41 Director of Athletics ... Mr. Greg J. AMODIO
26 Director Public Affairs ... Ms. Bridget M. FARE
86 Director of Government Relations ... Ms. Michelle A. CASTRO
22 Director Affirmative Action ... Dr. Judith R. GRIGGS
23 Director Health Service ... Ms. Barbara E. GALDERISE
38 Director Univ Counseling Center ... Dr. Ian C. EDWARDS
39 Director Residence Life ... Mrs. Sharon G. OELSCHLAGER
42 Director Campus Ministry ... Rev. Raymond FRENCH, CSSP
28 Director of Multicultural Affairs ... Dr. Rahmon HART
96 Director of Purchasing/Support Svcs ... Ms. Cynthia A. VINARSKI
50 Dean Business & Administration ... Dr. Alan R. MICIAK
66 Dean of Nursing ... Dr. Eileen H. ZUNGOLO
67 Dean of Pharmacy ... Dr. J. Douglas BRICKER
64 Dean of Music ... Dr. Edward W. KOCHER
53 Dean of Education ... Dr. Olga M. WELCH
76 Dean of Health Sciences ... Dr. Gregory H. FRAZER
61 Dean of Law ... Mr. Ken GORMLEY
49 Dean of Liberal Arts/Graduate ... Dr. Christopher DUNCAN
65 Dean of Natural/Environment Sci ... Dr. David W. SEYBERT
88 Dean Leadership & Profess Advanc ... Dr. Dorothy E. BASSETT
40 Bookstore Manager ... Mr. John KACHUR
88 Internal Auditor ... Mr. Aaron MITCHAM

Eastern University (D)

1300 Eagle Road, Saint Davids PA 19087-3696
County: Delaware | FICE Identification: 003259
Unit ID: 212133
Telephone: (610) 341-5800 | Carnegie Class: Master's L
FAX Number: (610) 341-1377 | Calendar System: Semester
URL: www.eastern.edu
Established: 1925 | Annual Undergrad Tuition & Fees: $25,800
Enrollment: 4,476 | Coed
Affiliation or Control: American Baptist | IRS Status: 501(c)3
Highest Offering: Doctorate
Program: 2-Year Principally Bachelor's Creditable; Liberal Arts And General; Teacher Preparatory; Professional
Accreditation: M, EXSC, NURSE, SW

01 President ... Dr. David R. BLACK
73 Chancellor/Dean of the Seminary ... Dr. Christopher A. HALL
10 Vice Pres for Finance/Operations ... Mr. J. Pernell JONES
03 Senior Vice President/Chief Mkt Ofc . Dr. M. Thomas RIDINGTON
05 Provost ... Dr. David A. KING
32 Vice Pres for Student Development ... Ms. Bettie Ann BRIGHAM
30 Vice President Development ... Mr. Derek RITCHIE
84 Exec Director CAS Enrollment ... Mr. Michael DZIEDZIAK
84 Exec Director of Enrollment(CCGPS) ... Mr. David GEIGER
84 Dir of Seminary Admissions ... Dr. Stephen HUTCHISON
15 Director of Human Resources ... Mrs. Kacey BERNARD
06 Registrar/VP Administration ... Mrs. Diana S. BACCI
04 Exec Asst to the President ... Mrs. Heather NORCINI
35 Dean of Students ... Mr. Daryl HAWKINS
12 Dean Esperanza College ... Dr. Elizabeth CONDE-FRAZIER
49 Dean Arts and Sciences ... Dr. Beth M. DORIANI
58 Dean Grad/Professional Studies ... Dr. Debra HEATH-THORNTON
53 Assoc Dean Education ... Mr. Harry GUTELIUS
66 Chair Department of Nursing ... Dr. MaryAnne PETERS
18 Exec Director Campus Services ... Mr. Carl ALTOMARE
91 Director Administrative Computing ... Mr. Dwight FOWLER
105 Webmaster ... Mr. Valdimir GORDYNSKIY
09 Director Institutional Research ... Mr. Thomas A. DAHLSTROM
09 Assoc Provost Inst Effectiveness ... Dr. Christine P. MAHAN
27 Exec Director of Communications ... Mrs. Linda OLSON
88 Director Student Accounts ... Ms. Lisa HOLLAND
08 Library Director ... Mr. James L. SAUER
08 Director Seminary Library ... Ms. Melody MAZUK
42 University Chaplain ... Rev Dr. Joseph B. MODICA
42 Seminary Chaplain ... Rev. Willette BURGIE-BRYANT
37 Director of Student Aid ... Ms. Lauren PIZZO
90 Director of Academic Computing ... Mr. Philip MUGRIDGE
36 Director of Careers and Calling ... Ms. Tess BRADLEY
29 Director Alumni Relations ... Mrs. Mary GARDNER
41 Director of Athletics ... Mr. Brad FIELDS
19 Director of Campus Security ... Mr. Jim MAGEE
88 Director of Conferences ... Ms. Meggin CAPERS
38 Dir Counseling/Academic Support ... Dr. Lisa M. HEMLICK
23 Director College Health Center ... Mrs. Janet TOPPER
96 Manager of Purchasing ... Ms. Patricia G. ROOT
85 International Student Advisor ... Rev. Kathy KAUTZ DE ARANGO
39 Coordinator of Housing ... Mr. Chris K. YODER
40 Bookstore Manager ... Mr. Frank MARTINEZ, JR.
88 Chair Urban Studies ... Dr. K-Lee JOHNSON
28 Dir Multicultural Stdnt Initiatives ... Ms. Jackie IRVING
89 Director Interdisciplinary Studies ... Mrs. Julie ELLIOTT
92 Dean Honors College ... Dr. Jonathan YONAN

† Parent institution of Palmer Theological Seminary.

Elizabethtown College (E)

1 Alpha Drive, Elizabethtown PA 17022-2298
County: Lancaster | FICE Identification: 003262
Unit ID: 212197
Telephone: (717) 361-1000 | Carnegie Class: Bac/Diverse
FAX Number: (717) 361-1207 | Calendar System: Semester
URL: www.etown.edu
Established: 1899 | Annual Undergrad Tuition & Fees: $34,830
Enrollment: 2,415 | Coed
Affiliation or Control: Church Of The Brethren | IRS Status: 501(c)3
Highest Offering: Master's
Program: Liberal Arts And General; Teacher Preparatory; Professional
Accreditation: M, ACBSP, ENG, MUS, OT, SW

01 President ... Dr. Carl J. STRIKWERDA
05 Provost & Sr Vice President ... Dr. Susan TRAVERSO
10 Vice President for Finance ... Mr. Richard L. BAILEY
30 Vice President for Advancement ... Mr. David C. BEIDLEMAN
11 Vice President for Administration ... Mr. David B. DENTLER
84 VP Admissions/Enrollment Mgmt ... Mr. Paul CRAMER
15 Associate VP for Human Resources ... Ms. Nancy E. FLOREY
32 Dean of Students ... Dr. Marianne CALENDA
20 Dean of Faculty ... Dr. Fletcher MCCLELLAN
51 Dean Ctr Continuing Educ/Dist Lrng ... Mr. John KOKOLUS
06 Associate Academic Dean/Registrar ... Dr. Elizabeth A. RIDER
07 Assoc Dean Admissions/Enroll Mgmt ... Ms. Debra H. MURRAY
35 Asst Dean of Students & Dir of CSS ... Ms. Stephanie A. RANKIN
26 Exec Dir Marketing/ Communications ... Ms. Elizabeth A. BRAUNGARD
13 Exec Director Information/Tech Svcs ... Mr. Ronald P. HEASLEY
102 Exec Dir Foundation/Govt Relations ... Ms. Lesley M. FINNEY
09 Director Institutional Research ... Dr. Richard BASOM
27 Director of Communications ... Ms. Lori BURKE
37 Director of Financial Aid ... Ms. Elizabeth K. MCCLOUD
08 College Librarian & Dir of Library ... Ms. BethAnn ZAMBELLA
45 Director of Research & Planning ... Mr. Richard E. BASOM
29 Director Alumni Devel & Programs ... Mr. Mark A. CLAPPER
19 Director of Campus Security ... Mr. Jack R. LONGENECKER
41 Director of Athletics ... Ms. Nancy J. LATIMORE
23 Dir Health & Counseling Services ... Ms. Alexandra SPAYD
40 Director of Business Services ... Vacant
88 Director of Food Services ... Mr. Eric C. TURZAI
42 Chaplain of the College ... Dr. Tracy SADD
92 Director Honor Program ... Dr. Dana G. MEAD
18 Dir of Facilities Mgmt/Construction ... Mr. Joseph METRO
28 Director of Diversity ... Ms. Diane ELLIOTT
21 Busines Office Support ... Ms. Jonina DUPLER

Erie Business Center, Main (F)

246 W Ninth Street, Erie PA 16501-1392
County: Erie | FICE Identification: 004894
Unit ID: 212425
Telephone: (814) 456-7504 | Carnegie Class: Assoc/PrivFP
FAX Number: (814) 456-6015 | Calendar System: Trimester
URL: www.eriebc.edu
Established: 1884 | Annual Undergrad Tuition & Fees: $11,800
Enrollment: 300 | Coed
Affiliation or Control: Proprietary | IRS Status: Proprietary
Highest Offering: Associate Degree
Program: Occupational
Accreditation: ACICS

01 President ... Mr. Charles P. MCGEARY
03 Chief Executive Officer ... Mr. Samuel L. MCCAUGHTRY
12 Director-Erie Campus ... Ms. Donna B. PERINO

Erie Business Center South (G)

170 Cascade Galleria, New Castle PA 16101-3900
County: Lawrence | FICE Identification: 003305
Unit ID: 213686
Telephone: (724) 658-9066 | Carnegie Class: Assoc/PrivFP
FAX Number: (724) 658-3083 | Calendar System: Trimester
URL: www.eriebc.edu/newcastle
Established: 1884 | Annual Undergrad Tuition & Fees: $7,164
Enrollment: 62 | Coed
Affiliation or Control: Proprietary | IRS Status: Proprietary
Highest Offering: Associate Degree
Program: Occupational; 2-Year Principally Bachelor's Creditable; Business Emphasis
Accreditation: ACICS

01 Director ... Mr. Steven R. OROURKE

† Branch campus of Erie Business Center Main, Erie, PA.

Erie Institute of Technology (H)

490 Millcreek Mall, Erie PA 16565-1002
County: Erie | FICE Identification: 022039
Unit ID: 212434
Telephone: (814) 868-9000 | Carnegie Class: Assoc/PrivFP
FAX Number: (814) 868-9977 | Calendar System: Semester
URL: www.erieit.edu
Established: 1958 | Annual Undergrad Tuition & Fees: $18,000
Enrollment: 300 | Coed
Affiliation or Control: Proprietary | IRS Status: Proprietary
Highest Offering: Associate Degree
Program: Occupational; Technical Emphasis
Accreditation: ACCSC

01 Director ... Mr. Paul FITZGERALD
05 Director of Education ... Ms. Kate HUSHON
37 Financial Aid Officer ... Ms. Kim CLARK
07 Admissions Director ... Ms. Barb BOLT
36 Placement Director ... Mr. Bill BURCHFIELD

Evangelical Theological Seminary (I)

121 S College Street, Myerstown PA 17067-1222
County: Lebanon | FICE Identification: 003263
Unit ID: 212443
Telephone: (717) 866-5775 | Carnegie Class: Spec/Faith
FAX Number: (717) 866-4667 | Calendar System: 4/1/4
URL: www.evangelical.edu
Established: 1953 | Annual Graduate Tuition & Fees: $11,160
Enrollment: 153 | Coed
Affiliation or Control: Evangelical Congregational Church
IRS Status: 501(c)3
Highest Offering: Master's; No Undergraduates
Program: Professional; Religious Emphasis
Accreditation: M, THEOL

01 President ..... Dr. Anothony L. BLAIR
30 Vice Pres Institutional Advancement ..... Rev. Ann E. STEEL
10 Vice President Finance & Operations ..... Mr. Kevin C. HENRY
05 Dean of Academic Programs ..... Dr. Laurie A. MELLINGER
07 Dean of Admissions ..... Mr. Thomas M. MAIELLO
08 Head Librarian ..... Dr. Terry M. HEISEY
18 Director of Buildings & Grounds ..... Mr. William J. ROBERTSON
88 Database Manager ..... Mrs. Marsha A. CONLEY
06 Registrar/Financial Aid Admin ..... Mr. Ellis I. KIRK

Everest Institute (A)

100 Forbes Avenue, Suite 1200,
Pittsburgh PA 15222-3618
County: Allegheny FICE Identification: 007091
Unit ID: 212090
Telephone: (412) 261-4520 Carnegie Class: Assoc/PrivFP
FAX Number: (412) 261-4546 Calendar System: Quarter
URL: www.everest.edu
Established: 1840 Annual Undergrad Tuition & Fees: $17,056
Enrollment: 589 Coed
Affiliation or Control: Proprietary IRS Status: Proprietary
Highest Offering: Associate Degree
Program: Occupational; 2-Year Principally Bachelor's Creditable; Business Emphasis
Accreditation: ACICS, MAC

01 President/Director ..... Mr. Scott BEHMER
05 Dean ..... Mrs. Michele ZOLLNER
07 Director of Admissions ..... Ms. Lynn FISCHER
04 Assistant to the President ..... Mrs. Michele JANEDA
36 Director of Career Services ..... Ms. Dana MELVIN
37 Director of Student Finance ..... Mrs. Annette VOSE
20 Associate Director of Education ..... Mr. John GOLOFSKI
10 Director of Student Accounts ..... Mrs. Amy FERREE

Fortis Institute (B)

5757 West Ridge Road, Erie PA 16506-1013
County: Erie FICE Identification: 030108
Unit ID: 216418
Telephone: (814) 838-7673 Carnegie Class: Assoc/PrivFP
FAX Number: (814) 838-8642 Calendar System: Quarter
URL: www.tsbi.org
Established: 1984 Annual Undergrad Tuition & Fees: $10,900
Enrollment: 859 Coed
Affiliation or Control: Proprietary IRS Status: Proprietary
Highest Offering: Associate Degree
Program: Occupational
Accreditation: ACICS, DH, MAAB, MAC, MLTAD, RAD

01 President ..... Mr. Guy EULIANO
05 Academic Dean ..... Mr. Doug ALLEN
10 Business Officer ..... Ms. Elizabeth GEANOUS
07 Admissions ..... Ms. Karen LAPAGLIA
37 Financial Aid ..... Mrs. Renee WRIGHT
36 Placement ..... Mrs. Wendy FUGATE

Fortis Institute (C)

166 Slocum Street, Forty Fort PA 18704-2347
County: Luzerne FICE Identification: 030115
Unit ID: 249609
Telephone: (570) 288-8400 Carnegie Class: Assoc/PrivFP
FAX Number: (570) 287-7936 Calendar System: Other
URL: www.fortis.edu
Established: 1984 Annual Undergrad Tuition & Fees: $21,150
Enrollment: 434 Coed
Affiliation or Control: Proprietary IRS Status: Proprietary
Highest Offering: Associate Degree
Program: Occupational
Accreditation: ACCSC

01 Campus President ..... Ruth BRUMAGIN
05 Director of Education ..... Joanne GIOVANNINI
07 Director of Admissions ..... Heather CONTARDI

Fortis Institute (D)

517 Ash Street, Scranton PA 18509
County: Lackawanna FICE Identification: 030116
Unit ID: 385503
Telephone: (570) 558-1818 Carnegie Class: Not Classified
FAX Number: (570) 342-4537 Calendar System: Other
URL: www.fortis.edu/scranton-pennsylvania.php
Established: 1922 Annual Undergrad Tuition & Fees: N/A
Enrollment: 259 Coed
Affiliation or Control: Proprietary IRS Status: Proprietary
Highest Offering: Associate Degree
Program: Occupational
Accreditation: ACCSC, DH

01 Campus President ..... Ms. Madeline LEVY CRUZ

† Tuition varies by degree program.

Franklin & Marshall College (E)

PO Box 3003, Lancaster PA 17604-3003
County: Lancaster FICE Identification: 003265
Unit ID: 212577
Telephone: (717) 291-3911 Carnegie Class: Bac/A&S
FAX Number: (717) 291-4183 Calendar System: Semester
URL: www.fandm.edu
Established: 1787 Annual Undergrad Tuition & Fees: $42,510
Enrollment: 2,335 Coed
Affiliation or Control: Independent Non-Profit IRS Status: 501(c)3
Highest Offering: Baccalaureate
Program: Liberal Arts And General
Accreditation: M

01 President ..... Dr. Daniel R. PORTERFIELD
10 Vice Pres for Finance and Treasurer ..... Vacant
30 Vice Pres for College Advancement ..... Mr. Lewis THAYNE
84 VP Enroll Mgmt & Dean of Admission ..... Mr. Daniel G. LUGO
26 VP Admin Svcs & External Affairs ..... Mr. Keith ORRIS
27 Vice Pres for College Communication ..... Vacant
05 Provost/Dean of Faculty ..... Dr. Ann STEINER
20 Dean of the College ..... Dr. Kent C. TRACHTE
88 Assoc Dean of Col & Dir Klehr Ctr ..... Dr. Ralph TABER
21 Assoc Vice President for Finance ..... Mr. Gregory L. FULMER
11 Associate VP for Administration ..... Mr. Barry BOSLEY
88 Associate VP of Development ..... Ms. Mary D. WOOLSON
45 Sr Asc Dean Fac/VP Plng & Inst Res ..... Dr. Alan S. CANIGLIA
20 Associate Dean of Faculty ..... Dr. Carol DEWET
100 Chief of Staff ..... Dr. Samuel HOUSER
08 College Librarian ..... Ms. Pamela SNELSON
44 Major Gifts Officer ..... Ms. Catherine T. FERRY
85 Assoc Dean International Programs ..... Vacant
36 Associate Dean/House Prefect ..... Dr. Roger A. GODIN
46 Associate Dean of Faculty ..... Dr. Michael BILLIG
46 Associate Dean of Faculty ..... Dr. Carmen TISNADO
32 Associate Dean of Students ..... Dr. Marion A. COLEMAN
88 Associate Dean/House Prefect ..... Ms. Katharine J. SNIDER
88 Associate Dean/House Prefect ..... Dr. Suzanna L. RICHTER
88 Senior Assoc Dean of the College ..... Dr. Steven P. O'DAY
88 Associate Dean/House Prefect ..... Dr. David M. STAMESHKIN
88 Associate Dean/House Prefect ..... Dr. Amy R. MORENO
88 Associate Dean/Senior Prefect ..... Dr. Todd DEKAY
21 Assistant Controller ..... Ms. Kathryn ELLIEHAUSEN-SLOBOZIEN
15 Director Human Resources ..... Ms. Nancy ESHLEMAN
18 Director Facilities & Operations ..... Ms. Maria T. CIMILLUCA
19 Director Public Safety ..... Mr. Mike ROSSANO
23 Director Health Services ..... Dr. Amy A. MYERS
13 Assoc Provost & Chief Info Officer ..... Dr. Jonathan C. ENOS
37 Director Financial Aid ..... Mr. Clarke C. PAINE
38 Clinical Dir Counseling Services ..... Dr. Christine G. CONWAY
90 Dir Instructional & Emerg Technol ..... Dr. Oscar RETTERER
09 Director of Institutional Research ..... Dr. Alan CANIGLIA
06 Registrar & Assoc Director Inst Res ..... Ms. Christine D. ALEXANDER
29 Director of Alumni Programs ..... Ms. Cathy ROMAN
07 Director of Admission ..... MS. Julie A. KERICH

Gannon University (F)

University Square, Erie PA 16541-0001
County: Erie FICE Identification: 003266
Unit ID: 212601
Telephone: (814) 871-7000 Carnegie Class: Master's L
FAX Number: (814) 871-7338 Calendar System: Other
URL: www.gannon.edu
Established: 1925 Annual Undergrad Tuition & Fees: $25,522
Enrollment: 4,219 Coed
Affiliation or Control: Roman Catholic IRS Status: 501(c)3
Highest Offering: Doctorate
Program: Liberal Arts And General; Teacher Preparatory; Professional
Accreditation: M, ACBSP, ANEST, ARCPA, CACREP, CS, ENG, NURSE, OT, PTA, RAD, SW

01 Interim President ..... Dr. Phil KELLY
05 Provost/VP Academic Affairs ..... Dr. Keith TAYLOR
10 Vice President Finance/Admin ..... Mrs. Linda L. WAGNER
30 Vice Pres University Advancement ..... Mr. Jack SIMS
88 Vice President for Mission ..... Rev. George STROHMEYER
84 Vice President for Enrollment ..... Mr. William EDMONDSON
04 Assistant to the President ..... Mrs. Darlene A. THEISEN
50 Dean Col Humanities/Business/Educ ..... Dr. Timothy M. DOWNS
76 Dean Col Science/Engr/Health Sci ..... Dr. Carolyn B. MASTERS
58 Dean of Graduate Studies ..... Mr. Michael J. O'NEILL
32 Dean of Student Development ..... Mr. Ward H. MCCRACKEN
84 Int Dean of Enrollment Services ..... Mr. Richard E. SUKITSCH
49 Director of Liberal Studies ..... Dr. Penny L. SMITH
08 Director Nash Library ..... Mr. Ken BRUNDAGE
46 Director Univ Planning & Research ..... Vacant
37 Director of Financial Aid ..... Ms. Sharon A. KRAHE
06 Registrar ..... Ms. Marilyn A. MOORE
36 Director Coop Education/Career Svcs ..... Mr. James M. FINEGAN
35 Director of Student Living ..... Mr. Doug R. ZIMMERMAN
23 Head Nurse ..... Ms. Ali SCHNEIDER
35 Dir Student Organiz/Leadership Dev ..... Ms. Beth Ann SCHICK
29 Director Development & Alumni Rels ..... Ms. Cathy FRESCH
27 Dir Pub Rels & Communications ..... Mrs. Karla M. WLUDYGA
44 Dir of Research/Foundation Rels ..... Ms. Anita L. MILLER
21 Controller ..... Mr. Jeffrey S. TAYLOR
45 Director of Budgeting ..... Ms. Mary Kathleen DRAGHI
16 Director of Human Resources ..... Mr. Robert J. CLINE
41 Director of Athletics ..... Mr. Mark RICHARD
19 Director Campus Police & Safety ..... Mr. James G. WALDON
14 Director of Computing/Telecomm ..... Mr. Mark JORDANO
42 University Chaplain ..... Rev. George STROHMEYER
07 Director of Admissions ..... Mr. Terrence R. KIZINA
09 Director of Institutional Research ..... Mr. Eric SPONSELLER
15 Director Human Resources ..... Mr. Robert J. CLINE
18 Chief Facilities/Physical Plant ..... Mr. Gary G. GARNIC
26 Chief Media Relations Officer ..... Mr. Nick G. PRONKO
38 Director Student Counseling ..... Mr. James M. FINEGAN
96 Director of Purchasing ..... Mr. Andrew TEETS
40 Bookstore Manager ..... Mr. Tony MARCHEWKA

Geneva College (G)

3200 College Avenue, Beaver Falls PA 15010-3599
County: Beaver FICE Identification: 003267
Unit ID: 212656
Telephone: (724) 846-5100 Carnegie Class: Bac/Diverse
FAX Number: (724) 847-6687 Calendar System: Semester
URL: www.geneva.edu
Established: 1848 Annual Undergrad Tuition & Fees: $23,330
Enrollment: 2,071 Coed
Affiliation or Control: Reformed Presbyterian Church IRS Status: 501(c)3
Highest Offering: Master's
Program: Liberal Arts And General; Teacher Preparatory; Professional
Accreditation: M, ACBSP, CACREP, CVT, ENG

01 President ..... Dr. Kenneth A. SMITH
03 Executive Vice President ..... Mr. Larry K. GRIFFITH
05 Provost ..... Dr. Kenneth P. CARSON
30 Vice Pres of Advancement ..... Dr. Jeffrey A. JONES
10 Assoc Vice Pres & Controller ..... Mr. Stephen C. ROSS
15 Assoc Vice Pres & Director of HR ..... Mr. Timothy R. BAIRD
32 Dean of Students ..... Mr. Michael J. LOOMIS
20 Dean of Faculty and Administration ..... Dr. Terri B. WILLIAMS
84 Dean of Enrollment Management ..... Mr. David B. LAYTON
35 Associate Dean of Students ..... Vacant
51 Director of Adult Education ..... Dr. Ralph N. PHILLIPS
06 Registrar ..... Mrs. Andrea L. KORCAN-BUZZA
37 Director of Financial Aid ..... Mr. Steven K. BELL
08 Librarian ..... Dr. John G. DONCEVIC
26 Director Public Relations ..... Mrs. Cheryl L. JOHNSTON
29 Director of Alumni Relations ..... Mr. Thomas J. STEIN
88 Assoc Dir Parent & Church Relations ..... Mrs. Rebecca J. PHILLIPS
14 Director of Computer Services ..... Mr. Larry R. WINGARD
41 Director of Athletics ..... Dr. Kimerly R. GALL
18 Director of Physical Plant ..... Mr. R. Jeffrey LYDIC
36 Director of Career Development ..... Mr. Robert L. ROSTONI
85 International Admissions Counselor ..... Vacant
88 Director International Student Svcs ..... Ms. Ann E. BURKHEAD
40 Campus Store Manager ..... Ms. Rachael VAN DERVEER
19 Director of Security ..... Mr. Dennis E. DAMAZO
44 Director of Planned Giving ..... Mrs. Wendy B. SMITH
93 Dir Multiethnic Student Services ..... Vacant
92 Director Honors Program ..... Dr. David F. KUHNS
39 Director of Residence Life ..... Mr. Neil A. BEST
23 Health Services Director ..... Mrs. Connie I. ERWIN
96 Director of Purchasing ..... Mrs. Nancy GRAHAM
21 Accounting and Payroll Manager ..... Ms. Ruth Ann HARTZEL
38 ACCESS Director ..... Mrs. Nancy I. SMITH

Gettysburg College (H)

300 N Washington Street, Gettysburg PA 17325-1486
County: Adams FICE Identification: 003268
Unit ID: 212674
Telephone: (717) 337-6000 Carnegie Class: Bac/A&S
FAX Number: (717) 337-6008 Calendar System: Semester
URL: www.gettysburg.edu
Established: 1832 Annual Undergrad Tuition & Fees: $42,610
Enrollment: 2,660 Coed
Affiliation or Control: Evangelical Lutheran Church In America
IRS Status: 501(c)3
Highest Offering: Baccalaureate
Program: Liberal Arts And General
Accreditation: M

01 President ..... Dr. Janet MORGAN RIGGS
03 Executive Vice President ..... Ms. Jane D. NORTH
05 Provost ..... Dr. Christopher ZAPPE
30 Vice Pres Dev & Alumni/Parent Rels ..... Mr. Robert KALLIN
10 Vice President Finance/Treasurer ..... Mr. Daniel T. KONSTALID
32 Vice President for College Life ..... Dr. Julie L. RAMSEY
84 Vice Pres Enrollment/Education Svcs ..... Ms. Barbara B. FRITZE
13 Vice President Information Tech ..... Dr. Rod TOSTEN
45 Assoc Provost for Planning ..... Mrs. Rhonda GOOD
20 Assoc Provost for Faculty ..... Ms. Elizabeth VITI
21 Associate Vice President/Treasurer ..... Mr. Christopher DELANEY
26 Exec Dir of Comm & Marketing ..... Mr. Paul W. REDFERN
35 Associate Dean of College Life ..... Mr. Thomas J. MOTTOLA
44 Assistant Vice Pres for Development ..... Ms. Susan PYRON
93 Dean Intercultural Advancement ..... Mr. H. Pete CURRY, JR.
06 Registrar ..... Mr. James DUFFY
37 Director of Financial Aid ..... Ms. Christina L. GORMLEY
07 Director Admissions ..... Ms. Gail M. SWEEZEY
42 Chaplain ..... Rev. Joseph A. DONNELLA, II
09 Director for Institutional Analysis ..... Dr. Salvatore CIOLINO
38 Exec Dir of Health & Counseling ..... Ms. Kathy BRADLEY
36 Director of Career Services ..... Ms. Kathleen L. WILLIAMS
08 Head Librarian ..... Ms. Robin WAGNER
44 Director of Annual Giving ..... Mr. Christopher HARMON
29 Director of Alumni Relations ..... Mr. Joe LYNCH
41 Athletic Director ..... Mr. David W. WRIGHT
19 Director of Campus Safety/Security ..... Mr. William J. LAFFERTY
18 Director Facilities Planning & Mgmt ..... Mr. James BIESECKER
21 Controller ..... Ms. Christine M. HARTMAN
80 Director Center for Public Service ..... Ms. Gretchen NATTER
39 Director Residence Life ..... Mr. Victor ARCELUS
20 Director of Academic Advising ..... Ms. Gail Ann RICKERT

23 Director Health Services .... Mr. Frederick W. KINSELLA
35 Director Student Activities .... Ms. Keira KANT
40 Director of College Bookstore .... Mr. Michael J. KOTLINSKI
94 Coord Women/Gender/Sexuality Stds .... Dr. Temma BERG
96 Director of Procurement .... Ms. Patricia K. VERDEROSA
15 Co-Director Human Resources .... Ms. Jennifer R. LUCAS
15 Co-Director Human Resources .... Ms. Regina Z. CAMPO

Gratz College (A)

7605 Old York Road, Melrose Park PA 19027-3010
County: Montgomery FICE Identification: 004058
Unit ID: 212771
Telephone: (215) 635-7300 Carnegie Class: Master's L
FAX Number: (215) 635-1046 Calendar System: Semester
URL: www.gratz.edu
Established: 1895 Annual Undergrad Tuition & Fees: $13,000
Enrollment: 430 Coed
Affiliation or Control: Independent Non-Profit IRS Status: 501(c)3
Highest Offering: Doctorate
Program: Liberal Arts And General; Teacher Preparatory; Professional
Accreditation: M

01 Chief Operating Officer/Acting CEO .... Ms. Joy W. GOLDSTEIN
05 Dean Academic Affairs/Dir Cont Educ .... Dr. Jerry M. KUTNICK
32 Dean of Students .... Dr. Ruth SANDBERG
04 Executive Asst to President .... Ms. Linda FISHER
26 Chief Public Relations Officer .... Ms. Lisa BEN-SHOSHAN
08 Director of Tuttleman Library .... Mr. Eliezer WISE
10 Director of Finance .... Ms. Eileen O'DONNELL
07 Director of Student Life/Admissions .... Mr. Ross M. LEVY
06 Director of Student Records .... Ms. Anne SCHWANHOLT
15 Director Personnel Services .... Ms. Linda FISHER
30 Dir of Institutional Advancement .... Mr. Michael BALABAN
20 Director of Academic Affairs .... Ms. Ruth SCHAPIRA
37 Student Financial Services Advisor .... Ms. Karen WEST

Grove City College (B)

100 Campus Drive, Grove City PA 16127-2104
County: Mercer FICE Identification: 003269
Unit ID: 212805
Telephone: (724) 458-2000 Carnegie Class: Bac/A&S
FAX Number: (724) 458-2190 Calendar System: Semester
URL: www.gcc.edu
Established: 1876 Annual Undergrad Tuition & Fees: $13,598
Enrollment: 2,499 Coed
Affiliation or Control: Presbyterian Church (U.S.A.) IRS Status: 501(c)3
Highest Offering: Baccalaureate
Program: Liberal Arts And General; Teacher Preparatory; Professional
Accreditation: M, ENG

01 President .... Dr. Richard G. JEWELL
05 Provost & VP for Academic Affairs .... Dr. William P. ANDERSON, JR.
10 Vice Pres for Financial Affairs .... Mr. Roger K. TOWLE
32 Vice Pres For Student Life/Learning .... Mr. Larry E. HARDESTY
30 Vice President for Inst Advancement .. Mr. Jeffrey D. PROKOVICH
11 Vice President for Operations .... Mr. Thomas W. GREGG
13 Vice Pres/Chief Information Officer .... Dr. Vincent F. DISTASI
04 Assistant to the President .... Ms. Betty L. TALLERICO
49 Dean of School of Arts/Letters .... Dr. John A. SPARKS
81 Dean School of Engr/Science .... Dr. Stacy G. BIRMINGHAM
84 Dean Enrollment Svcs/Registrar .... Dr. John G. INMAN
35 Dean of Students .... Mrs. S. Ann STRANAHAN
15 Dir of HR & Business Operations .... Mrs. Marci K. WAGNER
07 Director of Admissions .... Mr. Jeffrey C. MINCEY
88 Admn Dir For Ctr For Vision/Values .... Mr. Lee S. WISHING, III
36 Director of Career Services .... Mr. James T. THRASHER
08 Librarian .... Ms. Diane H. GRUNDY
37 Director of Financial Aid .... Mr. Thomas G. BALL
88 Dir Std Rec/Club Sports/Frat Life .... Mr. Andrew A. TONCIC, JR.
35 Director Stdnt Activities/Programs .... Mr. T. Scott GORDON
19 Director of Campus Safety .... Mr. Seth J. VAN TIL
23 Director of Health & Wellness Ctr .... Mrs. Amy E. PAGANO
40 Bookstore Manager .... Mrs. Carrie J. GAULT
41 Athletic Director .... Dr. Donald L. LYLE
42 Dean of the Chapel .... Rev. F. Stanley KEEHLWETTER
29 Sr Dir Alumni & College Relations .... Ms. Melissa A. MACLEOD
38 Director of College Counseling .... Dr. Suzanne N. HOUK
39 Director of Residence Life .... Ms. Jamie R. SWANK

Gwynedd-Mercy College (C)

1325 Sumneytown Pike, PO Box 901,
Gwynedd Valley PA 19437-0901
County: Montgomery FICE Identification: 003270
Unit ID: 212832
Telephone: (215) 646-7300 Carnegie Class: Master's M
FAX Number: (215) 641-5596 Calendar System: Semester
URL: www.gmc.edu
Established: 1948 Annual Undergrad Tuition & Fees: $27,120
Enrollment: 2,653 Coed
Affiliation or Control: Roman Catholic IRS Status: 501(c)3
Highest Offering: Master's
Program: Occupational; Liberal Arts And General; Teacher Preparatory; Nursing Emphasis
Accreditation: M, ADNUR, CVT, IACBE, NUR, RTT

01 President .... Dr. Kathleen C. OWENS
05 Interim VP Academic Affairs .... Dr. Robert FUNK
10 Vice President Finance .... Mr. Kevin O'FLAHERTY
30 Vice Pres Institutional Advancement .... Mr. Gerald (Jerry) MCLAUGHLIN
84 Vice Pres for Enrollment & SS .... Dr. Cheryl HORSEY
101 Secretary of the Institution/Board .... Ms. Barbara MCHALE
06 Registrar .... Ms. Therese ANDERSON
08 Director of Library .... Mr. Daniel SCHABERT
37 Director of Student Financial Aid .. Sr. Barbara KAUFMANN, RSM
29 Director Alumni Relations .... Ms. Shannon BLACKER-BRUNO
35 Director Student Activities .... Mr. Thomas FRIEL
09 Director of Institutional Research .... Mr. Monty YOUNG
15 Director Human Resources .... Ms. Donna HAWKINS
18 Chief Facilities/Physical Plant .... Mr. Joseph GUCKAVAN
21 Controller .... Ms. Mary GILBERT
26 Director of Marketing .... Ms. Charlene DI SARLO
38 Director Counseling .... Ms. Jeanne MCGOWAN
07 Director of Undergrad Admissions .... Ms. Michele DIEHL
07 Director of Graduate Admissions .... Ms. Andrea PORTER
96 Manager of Purchasing .... Ms. Joyce SCHARLE

Harcum College (D)

750 Montgomery Avenue, Bryn Mawr PA 19010-3476
County: Montgomery FICE Identification: 003272
Unit ID: 212869
Telephone: (610) 525-4100 Carnegie Class: Assoc/PrivNFP
FAX Number: (610) 526-6009 Calendar System: Semester
URL: www.harcum.edu
Established: 1915 Annual Undergrad Tuition & Fees: $19,500
Enrollment: 1,453 Coed
Affiliation or Control: Independent Non-Profit IRS Status: 501(c)3
Highest Offering: Associate Degree
Program: Occupational; 2-Year Principally Bachelor's Creditable; Technical Emphasis
Accreditation: M, ADNUR, DA, DH, EEG, HT, MLTAD, OTA, PTAA, RAD

01 President .... Dr. Jon Jay DETEMPLE
05 VP of Academic & Legal Affairs .... Ms. Julia INGERSOLL
10 Vice Pres of Finance & Operations .... Mr. Barry COHEN
32 Dean of Student Affairs .... Dr. George THORNTON
07 Dean of Admissions .... Ms. Nicola C. DIFRONZO-HEITZER
30 VP of College Advancement .... Ms. Sachi MALLACH
51 Exec Director of Contining Studies .... Dr. Denise BEAUCHAMP
18 Facilities Director .... Mr. Nikolay KARPALO
15 Director of Human Resources .... Ms. Claudine VITA
06 Registrar .... Ms. Madeleine V. WRIGHTSON
08 Director of Library Services .... Ms. Ann E. RANIERI
85 Director International Student Pgms .... Ms. Debra L. YOUNG-YASSINE
26 Chief Public Relations Officer .... Mr. Andy BACK
29 Director of Alumni Relations .... Ms. Melissa SAMANGO
38 Director of Student Counseling .... Ms. Kathy ANTHONY
36 Dir of Career & Transfer Services .... Mr. Graham BOTTREL
37 Director of Student Financial Aid .... Mr. Eli MOINESTER
39 Director of Residence Life .... Mr. Urick LEWIS
35 Director of Student Activities .... Ms. Janelle WILLIAMS
09 Coordinator Institutional Research .... Ms. Donna PARKER
106 Asst VP for Distance Learning .... Mr. Tim ELY

Harrisburg Area Community College (E)

1 HACC Drive, Harrisburg PA 17110-2999
County: Dauphin FICE Identification: 003273
Unit ID: 212878
Telephone: (717) 780-2300 Carnegie Class: Assoc/Pub-U-MC
FAX Number: (717) 780-2551 Calendar System: Semester
URL: www.hacc.edu
Established: 1964 Annual Undergrad Tuition & Fees (In-District): $4,950
Enrollment: 23,210 Coed
Affiliation or Control: State/Local IRS Status: 501(c)3
Highest Offering: Associate Degree
Program: Occupational; 2-Year Principally Bachelor's Creditable
Accreditation: M, ACBSP, ACFEI, ADNUR, CVT, DA, DH, DMS, EMT, MAC, MLTAD, PNUR, RAD, SURGT

01 President/CEO .... Dr. John J. SYGIELSKI
05 Provost/VP Academic Affairs .... Dr. Ronald R. YOUNG
32 VP Student Affairs/Enrollment Mgmt .... Dr. Rob R. STEINMETZ
10 Vice Pres Finance/College Resources .... Mr. George A. FRANKLIN
31 Vice Pres College & Community Devel .... Ms. Nancy M. ROCKEY
16 VP Human Res/Organizational Devel .... Ms. Meredith E. TULLI
26 Vice President of Public Relations .... Mr. Patrick M. EARLY
12 Campus VP Lancaster .... Dr. L. Marshall WASHINGTON
12 Campus VP Lebanon .... Dr. Kathleen R. KRAMER
12 Campus VP Gettysburg .... Ms. Jennifer L. WEAVER
12 Campus VP York .... Ms. Jean M. TREUTHART
106 Campus VP Virtual .... Dr. Larry J. ADAMS
49 Dean Comm/Humanities & the Arts .... Mr. Thaddeus SAMPSON
20 Dean Academic Affairs/Technology .... Dr. Virgil C. GANESCU
81 Dean Mathematics/Science .... Ms. Jennifer N. BAAR
51 Dean Transitional Studies .... Dr. Lori A. FAIR
08 Campus Director Library Harrisburg .... Mr. David PAPPAS
20 Dean Academic Affairs Admin .... Dr. Cynthia A. DOHERTY
88 Dean Retention Services .... Ms. Dory S. LEAHEY
84 Dean Enrollment Services/Registrar .... Ms. Roz E. OGDEN
35 Associate Dean Student Life .... Vacant
04 Asst to Pres/Dir Affirmative Action .... Mr. David J. MORRISON
91 Exec Dir Information Tech Svcs .... Mr. Andrew B. MORROW
30 Exec Dir Inst Advance/HACC Fndtn .... Mrs. Jayne B. ABRAMS
96 Exec Director Business/Aux Svcs .... Mr. Thomas J. FOGARTY
88 Director Performing Artist Series .... Ms. Theresa L. GUERRISI
19 Director Safety & Security .... Mr. Charles A. ANDERSON
29 Director Alumni Affairs .... Ms. Maureen G. HOEPFER
40 Director College Bookstores .... Mr. Kyle J. DIBRITO
21 Controller .... Ms. Barbara L. HUTCHINSON
18 Director of Facilities Management .... Mr. George A. FRANKLIN
88 Dir Global Education .... Mr. Michael B. SANDY
90 Campus Director Technical Services ... Mr. Christopher T. FULLER
09 Director Institutional Research .... Dr. Glen D. LUM
37 Director Financial Aid .... Mr. James J. CARIDEO
07 Dir Enrollment Services .... Ms. Tisa R. RILEY
36 Dir Office for Academic Success .... Ms. Marguerite M. MACDONALD
38 Campus Assoc Dir Counseling Svcs . Mr. Matthew D. BRASWELL
102 Board Manager HACC Foundation .... Ms. Bonny R. ELLIS

Harrisburg University of Science and Technology (F)

326 Market Street, Harrisburg PA 17101-2116
County: Dauphin FICE Identification: 039483
Unit ID: 446640
Telephone: (717) 901-5100 Carnegie Class: Bac/A&S
FAX Number: (717) 901-3152 Calendar System: Trimester
URL: www.harrisburgu.edu
Established: 2001 Annual Undergrad Tuition & Fees: $22,500
Enrollment: 355 Coed
Affiliation or Control: Independent Non-Profit IRS Status: 501(c)3
Highest Offering: Master's
Program: Professional; Technical Emphasis
Accreditation: M

01 President .... Dr. Melvyn D. SCHIAVELLI
05 Provost & Executive Vice President .... Dr. Eric D. DARR
20 Associate Provost .... Ms. Bili MATTES
10 Controller & VP Finance .... Mr. Duane MAUN
30 Assoc VP Devel & Alumni Relations .... Mr. Ryan T. RILEY
32 Director of Student Services .... Ms. Laura DIMINO
13 Director of Technology Services .... Mr. Alex PITZNER
26 Associate VP Comm & Marketing .... Mr. Steven M. INFANTI
15 Associate VP Human Resources .... Ms. Linda WRIGHT
09 Director Compliance & Research .... Mr. Keith A. GREEN
37 Director Financial Aid Services .... Mr. Vincent P. FRANK
06 Director Records & Registration .... Ms. Jeanne WAGNER
84 Director Enrollment Management .... Mr. Timothy DAWSON

Haverford College (G)

370 Lancaster Avenue, Haverford PA 19041-1392
County: Delaware & Montgomery FICE Identification: 003274
Unit ID: 212911
Telephone: (610) 896-1000 Carnegie Class: Bac/A&S
FAX Number: (610) 896-4202 Calendar System: Semester
URL: www.haverford.edu
Established: 1833 Annual Undergrad Tuition & Fees: $42,208
Enrollment: 1,177 Coed
Affiliation or Control: Independent Non-Profit IRS Status: 501(c)3
Highest Offering: Master's
Program: Liberal Arts And General
Accreditation: M

01 President .... Stephen G. EMERSON
05 Provost .... Linda BELL
10 Vice Pres Finance & Administration .... G. Richard WYNN
30 VP of Advancement .... Michael KIEFER
20 Dean of the College .... Martha DENNEY
07 Dean of Admission .... Jess LORD
85 Dean of Intl Academic Programs .... Donna MANCINI
89 Dean of Freshmen Students .... Raisa WILLIAMS
21 Asst VP for Budgeting and Finance .... Michael CASEL
88 Assistant VP of Inst Advancement .... Diane WILDER
11 Senior Executive Administrator .... Violet BROWN
41 Director of Athletics .... Wendall SMITH
26 Exec Dir Marketing & Communication .... Chris MILLS
09 Director of Institutional Research .... Catherine FENNELL
08 Librarian .... Terry SNYDER
15 Director of Human Resources .... Christopher CHANDLER
21 Controller & Assistant Treasurer .... Kathi RUFFIN
96 Director of Purchasing .... Samuel WILLIAMS
18 Director of Physical Plant .... Ron TOLA
19 Director of Safety & Security .... Thomas KING
88 Director Conferences/Dir Campus Ctr .... Dorothy LABE
88 Director of Dining Services .... Bernie CHUNG
40 Bookstore Manager .... Julie SUMMERFIELD
39 Director of Student Housing .... Marianne SMITH
34 Director of Women's Center .... Mary Louise ALLEN
23 Director of Health Services .... Catherine SHARBAUGH
38 Director Counseling/Disability Svcs .... Richard E. WEBB
36 Director of Career Development .... Liza BERNARD
06 Registrar .... Lee WATKINS
37 Director of Financial Aid .... David HOY
88 Director Leadership Gifts .... Ann WEST FIGUEREDO
44 Director of Annual Giving .... Deborah STRECKER
88 Director of Gift Planning .... Steven KAVANAUGH
102 Dir Foundation/Corporate Relations .... John MOSTELLER
28 Director of Diversity/Assoc Dean .... Vacant
29 Director of Alumni Relations .... Deborah STRECKER
32 Coordinator of Student Activities .... Jason MCGRAW
27 Chief Information Officer .... Joseph SPADARO

Holy Family University (H)

9801 Frankford Avenue, Philadelphia PA 19114-2009
County: Philadelphia FICE Identification: 003275
Unit ID: 212984

Telephone: (215) 637-7700　Carnegie Class: Master's L
FAX Number: (215) 637-3787　Calendar System: Semester
URL: www.holyfamily.edu
Established: 1954　Annual Undergrad Tuition & Fees: $25,290
Enrollment: 3,270　Coed
Affiliation or Control: Roman Catholic　IRS Status: 501(c)3
Highest Offering: Doctorate
Program: Liberal Arts And General; Teacher Preparatory; Professional
Accreditation: M, ACBSP, NURSE, RAD, @TEAC

01 President .... Sr. Francesca ONLEY
05 Vice President Academic Affairs .... Sr. Maureen MCGARRITY
10 Vice Pres Finance & Administration .... Mr. John JASZCZAK
30 Vice Pres Institutional Advancement .... Ms. Margaret S. KELLY
13 Vice Pres Information Technology .... Mr. Robert LAFOND
32 Vice President for Student Services .... Sr. Marcella BINKOWSKI
21 AVP Finance/Budget/Inst Rsrch .... Mr. Michael E. VAN THUYNE
84 Assoc VP for Enrollment Services .... Mr. Robert REESE
06 Assoc VP Academic Svcs/Registrar .... Ms. Ann Marie VICKERY
12 Exec Director of Newtown Campus .... Ms. Karen GALARDI
37 Director of Student Financial Aid .... Mrs. Janice HETRICK
21 Treasurer .... Sr. M. Paul ROZANSKA
15 Asst Vice Pres Human Resources .... Ms. Renee ROSENFELD
08 Director of Library Services .... Ms. Lori SCHWABENBAUER
36 Director of the Career Center .... Mr. Donald BROM
26 Dir Marketing & Public Relations .... Mr. Thomas DURSO
38 Director Counseling Center .... Dr. Diana PIPERATA
42 Chaplain/Campus Minister .... Rev. James MACNEW
07 Director of Undergraduate Admission .... Ms. Lauren CAMPBELL
41 Athletic Director .... Mrs. Sandra MICHAEL
58 Dean of the School of Education .... Dr. Leonard G. SOROKA
66 Dean Sch Nursing/Allied Hlth Profns .... Dr. Christine ROSNER
49 Dean of School of Arts & Sciences .... Dr. Michael MARKOWITZ
50 Dean of School of Business Admin .... Dr. Jan DUGGAR
51 Assoc Vice Pres Extended Learning .... Mrs. Honour MOORE
58 Assoc Dean School of Education .... Dr. Antoinette SCHIAVO
29 Director Alumni & Parent Giving .... Ms. Marie ZECCA
09 Dir of Inst Research & Assessment .... Mr. Chad L. MAY
18 Chief Facilities/Physical Plant .... Mr. John JASZCZAK
96 Director of Purchasing .... Mrs. Marie MELNICK
28 Coordinator Diversity .... Dr. Gloria KERSEY-MATUSIAK
39 Director of Residence Life .... Mr. Brett BUCKRIDGE

Hussian School of Art (A)

111 S Independence Mall East, #300,
Philadelphia PA 19100-2521
County: Philadelphia　FICE Identification: 007469
Unit ID: 212993
Telephone: (215) 574-9600　Carnegie Class: Assoc/PrivFP
FAX Number: (215) 574-9800　Calendar System: Semester
URL: www.hussianart.edu
Established: 1946　Annual Undergrad Tuition & Fees: $14,550
Enrollment: 145　Coed
Affiliation or Control: Proprietary　IRS Status: Proprietary
Highest Offering: Associate Degree
Program: Occupational
Accreditation: ACCSC

01 President .... Mr. Bruce WARTMAN
05 Vice President/Director Education .... Mr. Wilbur O. CRAWFORD
32 Administrator/Student Services .... Ms. Maureen P. FLANAGAN
37 Director Student Financial Aid .... Ms. Susan J. COHEN
07 Admissions Director .... Ms. Lynne WARTMAN
10 Bookkeeper/Accounting .... Ms. Stephanie HAYS
101 Executive Secretary .... Ms. Jodi BRABAZON

Immaculata University (B)

1145 King Road, Immaculata PA 19345-0654
County: Chester　FICE Identification: 003276
Unit ID: 213011
Telephone: (610) 647-4400　Carnegie Class: DRU
FAX Number: (610) 251-1668　Calendar System: Semester
URL: www.immaculata.edu
Established: 1920　Annual Undergrad Tuition & Fees: $28,850
Enrollment: 4,456　Coed
Affiliation or Control: Roman Catholic　IRS Status: 501(c)3
Highest Offering: Doctorate
Program: 2-Year Principally Bachelor's Creditable; Liberal Arts And General; Teacher Preparatory; Professional
Accreditation: M, CLPSY, DIETD, DIETI, MUS, NURSE

01 President .... Sr. R. Patricia FADDEN
05 Vice President Academic Affairs .... Sr. Ann HEATH
10 Vice Pres Finance/Administration .... Ms. Jenni SAUER
30 Vice Pres University Advancement .... Ms. Theresa GRENTZ
32 Vice President Student Development .... Dr. Stephen PUGLIESE
27 VP of University Communications .... Mr. Robert COLE
20 Associate VP of Academic Affairs .... Mr. Phillip HUBBARD
06 Registrar .... Ms. Janice BATES
09 Director Inst Research/Assessment .... Ms. Erin R. EBERSOLE
08 Director of Library .... Mr. Jeffrey D. ROLLISON
37 Director Student Financial Aid .... Mr. Robert FOREST
44 Senior Director of Gift Planning .... Sr. Rita O'LEARY
91 Director Administrative Computing .... Dr. Thomas EGAN
26 Director Public Relations .... Ms. Marie MOUGHAN
29 Alumni Director .... Ms. Cathy DERNONCOURT
36 Director Career Advisement .... Ms. Diane MASSEY
41 Athletic Director .... Ms. Patricia CANTERINO
85 International Student Advisor .... Sr. Catarin CONJAR
90 Director Academic Technology .... Ms. Sharon AINSLEY
42 Chaplain .... Fr. Chris ROGERS
58 Dean Graduate Division .... Dr. Janet KANE
34 Dean College of Undergrad Studies .... Sr. Elaine GLANZ
51 Dean College of Lifelong Learning .... Dr. Sam WRIGHTSON
19 Director Campus Safety .... Mr. Eugene BIAGIOTTI
15 Director of Personnel Services .... Mrs. Cathey PASSIN
18 Director of Physical Plant .... Mr. Dennis SHORES
44 Director of the Annual Fund .... Ms. Karen D. MATWEYCHUK
42 Director of Campus Ministry .... Sr. Cathy NALLY
07 Director of Admissions .... Ms. Rebecca BOWLBY
20 Associate Dean of Academic Affairs .... Ms. Mary Kate BOLAND

International Institute for Restorative Practices (C)

P.O. Box 229, Bethlehem PA 18016-0229
County: Northampton　Identification: 666688
Unit ID: 448691
Telephone: (610) 807-9221　Carnegie Class: Not Classified
FAX Number: (610) 807-0423　Calendar System: Semester
URL: www.iirp.org
Established: N/A　Annual Graduate Tuition & Fees: $19,800
Enrollment: 91　Coed
Affiliation or Control: Independent Non-Profit　IRS Status: 501(c)3
Highest Offering: Master's; No Undergraduates
Program: Professional
Accreditation: M

01 President .... Mr. Theodore WACHTEL
05 Vice President for Academic Affairs .... Dr. Patrick MCDONOUGH

ITT Technical Institute (D)

3330 Tillman Drive, Bensalem PA 19020-2030
County: Bucks　Identification: 666320
Unit ID: 440642
Telephone: (215) 244-8871　Carnegie Class: Assoc/PrivFP
FAX Number: (215) 244-8872　Calendar System: Quarter
URL: www.itt-tech.edu
Established: 2003　Annual Undergrad Tuition & Fees: N/A
Enrollment: 766　Coed
Affiliation or Control: Proprietary　IRS Status: Proprietary
Highest Offering: Associate Degree
Program: Technical Emphasis
Accreditation: ACICS

† Branch campus of ITT Technical Institute, Lake Mary, FL.

ITT Technical Institute (E)

1000 Meade Street, Dunmore PA 18512-3195
County: Lackawanna　Identification: 666150
Unit ID: 448460
Telephone: (570) 330-0600　Carnegie Class: Assoc/PrivFP
FAX Number: N/A　Calendar System: Quarter
URL: www.itt-tech.edu
Established: 2006　Annual Undergrad Tuition & Fees: N/A
Enrollment: 323　Coed
Affiliation or Control: Proprietary　IRS Status: Proprietary
Highest Offering: Associate Degree
Program: Technical Emphasis
Accreditation: ACICS

† Branch campus of ITT Technical Institute, Lake Mary, FL.

ITT Technical Institute (F)

449 Eisenhower Blvd., Suite 100,
Harrisburg PA 17111-2302
County: Cumberland　Identification: 666548
Unit ID: 430351
Telephone: (717) 565-1700　Carnegie Class: Assoc/PrivFP
FAX Number: (717) 691-9273　Calendar System: Quarter
URL: www.itt-tech.edu
Established: 1994　Annual Undergrad Tuition & Fees: N/A
Enrollment: 505　Coed
Affiliation or Control: Proprietary　IRS Status: Proprietary
Highest Offering: Associate Degree
Program: Technical Emphasis
Accreditation: ACICS

† Branch campus of ITT Technical Institute, Indianapolis, IN.

ITT Technical Institute (G)

760 Moore Road, King of Prussia PA 19406-1212
County: Montgomery　Identification: 666322
Unit ID: 442347
Telephone: (610) 491-8004　Carnegie Class: Assoc/PrivFP
FAX Number: (610) 491-9047　Calendar System: Quarter
URL: www.itt-tech.edu
Established: 2002　Annual Undergrad Tuition & Fees: N/A
Enrollment: 572　Coed
Affiliation or Control: Proprietary　IRS Status: Proprietary
Highest Offering: Associate Degree
Program: Technical Emphasis
Accreditation: ACICS

† Branch campus of ITT Technical Institute, Murray, UT.

ITT Technical Institute (H)

10 Parkway Center, Pittsburgh PA 15220-3801
County: Allegheny　Identification: 666483
Unit ID: 414841
Telephone: (412) 937-9150　Carnegie Class: Assoc/PrivFP
FAX Number: (412) 937-9425　Calendar System: Quarter
URL: www.itt-tech.edu
Established: 1992　Annual Undergrad Tuition & Fees: N/A
Enrollment: 389　Coed
Affiliation or Control: Proprietary　IRS Status: Proprietary
Highest Offering: Associate Degree
Program: Technical Emphasis
Accreditation: ACICS

† Branch campus of ITT Technical Institute, Youngstown, IN.

ITT Technical Institute (I)

100 Pittsburgh Mills Cir, Ste 100, Tarentum PA 15084
County: Allegheny　Identification: 666482
Unit ID: 430360
Telephone: (724) 274-1400　Carnegie Class: Assoc/PrivFP
FAX Number: (412) 856-4501　Calendar System: Quarter
URL: www.itt-tech.edu
Established: 1996　Annual Undergrad Tuition & Fees: N/A
Enrollment: 304　Coed
Affiliation or Control: Proprietary　IRS Status: Proprietary
Highest Offering: Associate Degree
Program: Technical Emphasis
Accreditation: ACICS

† Branch campus of ITT Technical Institute, Youngstown, IN.

JNA Institute of Culinary Arts (J)

1212 S Broad Street, Philadelphia PA 19146-3119
County: Philadelphia　FICE Identification: 031033
Unit ID: 419341
Telephone: (215) 468-8800　Carnegie Class: Assoc/PrivFP
FAX Number: (215) 468-8838　Calendar System: Quarter
URL: www.culinaryarts.edu
Established: 1988　Annual Undergrad Tuition & Fees: $20,075
Enrollment: 86　Coed
Affiliation or Control: Proprietary　IRS Status: Proprietary
Highest Offering: Associate Degree
Program: Occupational; 2-Year Principally Bachelor's Creditable; Technical Emphasis
Accreditation: ACCSC

01 Director .... Mr. Joseph DIGIRONIMO
07 Director of Admission .... Mr. Robert FOX

Johnson College (K)

3427 N Main Avenue, Scranton PA 18508-1495
County: Lackawanna　FICE Identification: 021142
Unit ID: 213233
Telephone: (570) 342-6404　Carnegie Class: Assoc/PrivNFP
FAX Number: (570) 348-2181　Calendar System: Semester
URL: www.johnson.edu
Established: 1916　Annual Undergrad Tuition & Fees: $16,362
Enrollment: 472　Coed
Affiliation or Control: Independent Non-Profit　IRS Status: 501(c)3
Highest Offering: Associate Degree
Program: 2-Year Principally Bachelor's Creditable; Technical Emphasis
Accreditation: ACCSC, RAD

01 President & CEO .... Dr. Ann L. PIPINSKI
05 Vice President Academic Affairs .... Mr. Dominick A. CARACHILO
13 Director of Information Services .... Ms. Sue PHILLIPS
37 Financial Aid Director .... Mr. Matthew PETERS
84 Vice Pres of Enrollment Services .... Ms. Melissa IDE
32 Student Support Coordinator .... Ms. Lynn KRUSHINSKI
10 Chief Financial Officer .... Mr. Jeffrey NOVAK
08 Head Librarian .... Mrs. Michele M. SREBRO
04 Assistant to the President .... Ms. Lisa TOOLE
06 Associate Registrar .... Mrs. Cathy BECKAGE
38 Asst Dir Student Support Services .... Ms. Linda LEARN
51 Director of Continuing Education .... Mrs. Marie ALLISON
39 Residence/Student Life Coordinator .... Vacant
30 VP of Institutional Advancement .... Ms. Katie LEONARD
15 Human Resources Assistant .... Ms. Diane DOLINSKY
36 Assoc Dir of Career Services .... Ms. Roseann MARTINETTI
11 Director of Operations .... Mr. Don RYAN
32 Director of Student Life .... Ms. Devon FAWCETT
29 Assoc Dir of Development .... Mrs. Tami PEASE
07 Assoc Director of Admissions .... Ms. Ann NEALON
18 Facilities Manager .... Mr. Bill KELLY
09 Dir of Program & Research .... Mrs. Shirley HELBING

Juniata College (L)

1700 Moore Street, Huntingdon PA 16652-2119
County: Huntingdon　FICE Identification: 003279
Unit ID: 213251
Telephone: (814) 641-3000　Carnegie Class: Bac/A&S
FAX Number: (814) 641-3199　Calendar System: Semester
URL: www.juniata.edu
Established: 1876　Annual Undergrad Tuition & Fees: $34,090
Enrollment: 1,593　Coed
Affiliation or Control: Independent Non-Profit　IRS Status: 501(c)3

Highest Offering: Baccalaureate
Program: Liberal Arts And General; Teacher Preparatory
Accreditation: M, SW

01 President ... Dr. Thomas R. KEPPLE, JR.
05 Provost/Exec Vice Pres Student Dev ... Dr. James J. LAKSO
84 Exec VP Enrollment and Retention ... Mr. John S. HILLE
10 Vice President Finance/Operations ... Mr. Robert E. YELNOSKY
26 Vice President Advancement/Mkt ... Mr. Gabriel WELSCH
14 Assoc Vice President & CIO ... Mr. David J. FUSCO
30 Exec Director of Development ... Ms. Kimberly KITCHEN
88 Exec Director of Marketing ... Ms. Rosann BROWN
84 Dean of Enrollment ... Ms. Michelle M. BARTOL
85 Dean International Programs ... Ms. Jenifer S. CUSHMAN
06 Registrar ... Ms. Athena D. FREDERICK
36 Director Career Services ... Dr. Darwin V. KYSOR
37 Enrollment Mgr/Dir Student Fin Plng ... Ms. Valerie D. RENNELL
08 Library Director ... Mr. John W. MUMFORD
91 Director Admin Information Svcs ... Ms. Barbara J. HUGHES
15 Director of Human Resources ... Ms. Gail LEIBY-ULRICH
32 Dean of Students ... Mr. Kris R. CLARKSON
09 Dir Institutional Planning/Research ... Ms. Carlee K. RANALLI
18 Director of Facilities Services ... Mr. Tristan S. DEL GIUDICE
39 Director Public Safety/Res Life ... Vacant
41 Athletic Director ... Mr. Greg M. CURLEY
90 Dir Technology Solutions Center ... Mr. Joel C. PHEASANT
21 Budget Director & Bursar ... Ms. Susan F. SHONTZ
21 Director of Acct and Business Oper ... Mr. Jeffrey L. SAVINO
44 Exec Dir Constituent Relations ... Mrs. Linda M. CARPENTER
35 Assistant Dean of Students ... Mr. Daniel J. COOK-HUFFMAN
42 College Chaplain ... Mr. L. David WITKOVSKY
20 Director of Academic Support Svcs ... Ms. Sarah M. CLARKSON
88 Director of Student Activities ... Ms. Jessica JACKSON
88 Assoc Dir Conferences & Events ... Ms. Lorri P. SHIDELER
07 Director of Enrollment Operations ... Ms. Terri L. BOLLMAN-DALANSKY
38 Director of Student Counseling ... Ms. M. Beth WILLIAMS
28 Int Dir of Diversity and Inclusion ... Dr. Grace M. FALA
29 Director Alumni Relations ... Mr. James R. WATT

Kaplan Career Institute (A)

5650 Derry Street, Harrisburg PA 17111-4112
County: Dauphin FICE Identification: 004910
Unit ID: 251075
Telephone: (717) 564-4112 Carnegie Class: Assoc/PrivFP
FAX Number: (717) 564-3779 Calendar System: Quarter
URL: www.kci-harrisburg.com
Established: 1918 Annual Undergrad Tuition & Fees: N/A
Enrollment: 650 Coed
Affiliation or Control: Proprietary IRS Status: Proprietary
Highest Offering: Associate Degree
Program: Occupational
Accreditation: ACICS, MAC

01 Executive Director ... Sherry ROSENBERG
07 Director Admissions ... Mark HALE
36 Director Student Placement ... Jennifer RIORDAN
05 Actg Director of Education ... Sherry ROSENBERG
37 Director Student Financial Aid ... Sarah BROOKER

Kaplan Career Institute - ICM Campus (B)

10 Wood Street, Pittsburgh PA 15222-1977
County: Allegheny FICE Identification: 007436
Unit ID: 213002
Telephone: (412) 261-2647 Carnegie Class: Assoc/PrivFP
FAX Number: (412) 261-6491 Calendar System: Quarter
URL: www.kcipittsburgh.com
Established: 1963 Annual Undergrad Tuition & Fees: $17,310
Enrollment: 1,186 Coed
Affiliation or Control: Proprietary IRS Status: Proprietary
Highest Offering: Associate Degree
Program: Occupational; 2-Year Principally Bachelor's Creditable; Technical Emphasis
Accreditation: ACICS, MAC, OTA

01 President ... Mr. Hunter H. HOPKINS
05 Director of Education ... Mr. Thomas E. ROCKS, JR.
37 Director of Financial Aid ... Mr. Chris FOX
07 Director of Admissions HS ... Ms. Rebekah SABO
07 Director of Admissions ... Ms. Lori MILLER
10 Director of Finance ... Ms. Denise RINGER-FISHER
36 Director of Career Services ... Ms. Jennifer KELLY

Keystone College (C)

One College Green, P.O. Box 50,
La Plume PA 18440-0200
County: Lackawanna FICE Identification: 003280
Unit ID: 213303
Telephone: (570) 945-8000 Carnegie Class: Bac/Diverse
FAX Number: (570) 945-8962 Calendar System: Semester
URL: www.keystone.edu
Established: 1868 Annual Undergrad Tuition & Fees: $19,620
Enrollment: 1,761 Coed
Affiliation or Control: Independent Non-Profit IRS Status: 501(c)3
Highest Offering: Baccalaureate
Program: Liberal Arts And General
Accreditation: M

01 President ... Dr. Edward G. BOEHM, JR.
05 VP Academic Affairs/Dean of College ... Dr. Thea HARRINGTON
32 VP Student Affairs/Dean Students ... Dr. Robert J. PERKINS
84 Vice Pres Enrollment ... Ms. Sarah KEATING
10 Vice Pres Finance & Administration ... Mr. Kevin WILSON
30 Exec Dir Institutional Advancement ... Ms. Sharon BURKE
91 Director Information Technology ... Mr. Charles L. PROTHERO
06 Registrar ... Ms. Kate OWENS
26 Senior Director College Relations ... Mr. Fran CALPIN
37 Dir Financial Assistance & Planning ... Ms. Ginger B. KLINE
29 Director of Alumni Outreach ... Ms. Christina FENTON-MACE
36 Director Career Development ... Ms. Rhea V. ELLIS DUKE
08 Director Miller Library ... Ms. Mari FLYNN
15 Director of Human Resources ... Ms. Alberta GRUSHINSKI
35 Director Student Activities ... Ms. Lucilia MCCONKEY
09 Institutional Researcher ... Ms. Linda WOZNIAK

Keystone Technical Institute (D)

2301 Academy Drive, Harrisburg PA 17112-1012
County: Dauphin FICE Identification: 022342
Unit ID: 210483
Telephone: (717) 545-4747 Carnegie Class: Assoc/PrivFP
FAX Number: (717) 901-9090 Calendar System: Semester
URL: www.kti.edu
Established: 1980 Annual Undergrad Tuition & Fees: $15,000
Enrollment: 379 Coed
Affiliation or Control: Proprietary IRS Status: Proprietary
Highest Offering: Associate Degree
Program: Occupational; 2-Year Principally Bachelor's Creditable; Technical Emphasis
Accreditation: ACCSC

01 President ... Mr. David W. SNYDER
03 Vice President ... Ms. Andrea SNYDER
05 Dean of Education ... Dr. Delmar HART
06 Registrar/Dir Stdnt Financial Aid ... Ms. Tracy STEWART
10 Chief Business Officer ... Mr. Dennis FIELDS
07 Admissions Officer ... Mr. Mark DYKEMA

King's College (E)

133 N River Street, Wilkes-Barre PA 18711-0801
County: Luzerne FICE Identification: 003282
Unit ID: 213321
Telephone: (570) 208-5900 Carnegie Class: Master's S
FAX Number: (570) 825-9049 Calendar System: Semester
URL: www.kings.edu
Established: 1946 Annual Undergrad Tuition & Fees: $27,680
Enrollment: 2,725 Coed
Affiliation or Control: Roman Catholic IRS Status: 501(c)3
Highest Offering: Master's
Program: Liberal Arts And General; Teacher Preparatory; Professional; Business Emphasis
Accreditation: M, ARCPA, BUS, TED

01 President ... Rev. John RYAN, CSC
05 Vice President for Academic Affairs ... Dr. Nicholas A. HOLODICK
10 Vice Pres Business Affs/Treasurer ... Dr. Lisa M. MCCAULEY
30 Interim Vice President Development ... Mr. William LYNN
32 Vice President for Student Affairs .. Ms. Janet E. MERCINCAVAGE
04 Assistant to the President ... Vacant
20 Assoc VP for Academic Affairs ... Dr. Joseph EVAN
13 Exec Dir Info & Tech Svc Div ... Mr. Paul J. MORAN
08 Director of Library ... Dr. Terrence F. MECH
84 Assoc VP Enroll/Academic Svcs ... Ms. Teresa M. PECK
35 Assoc Vice Pres Student Affairs ... Mr. Robert B. MCGONIGLE
07 Director of Admissions ... Mr. James ANDERSON
50 Dean Wm G McGowan Sch Business ... Dr. Barry WILLIAMS
06 Registrar ... Mr. Daniel T. CEBRICK
37 Director of Financial Aid ... Ms. Donna CERZA
42 Chaplain/Director Campus Ministry ... Rev. Richard C. HOCKMAN, CSC
36 Director Career Planning & Placemnt ... Mr. Christopher SUTZKO
14 Computer Operations Manager ... Ms. Patricia L. KELLAR
16 Director of Human Resources ... Ms. Erin A. SAVITSKI
26 Director of Public Relations ... Mr. John MCANDREW
29 Director of Alumni Relations ... Ms. Laura HADEN
18 Director Facilities & Grounds ... Mr. Patrick MULLARKEY
19 Director of Security/Safety ... Mr. Robert SENA
41 Dir of Intercollegiate Athletics ... Ms. Cheryl J. ISH
21 Comptroller ... Mr. Thomas GRABER
39 Director of Residence Life ... Ms. Megan SELLICK
44 Director of Annual Giving Programs ... Ms. Kimberly K. CARDONE
58 Dean of Graduate Programs ... Dr. Elizabeth S. LOTT
55 Director Evening/Weekend Programs .. Ms. Maureen E. SHERIDAN
09 Director of Institutional Research ... Ms. Marian K. PALMERI
28 Director of College Diversity ... Mr. Nathan WARD
96 Director of Purchasing ... Mr. Herbert G. GODFREY
92 Director of the Honors Program ... Dr. William IRWIN
90 Managing Dir of User Services ... Mr. Raymond G. PRYOR
91 Managing Director for MIS ... Mr. William M. CORCORAN
15 Director of Human Resources ... Ms. Erin A. SAVITSKI

La Roche College (F)

9000 Babcock Boulevard, Pittsburgh PA 15237-5898
County: Allegheny FICE Identification: 003987
Unit ID: 213358
Telephone: (412) 367-9300 Carnegie Class: Bac/Diverse
FAX Number: (412) 536-1062 Calendar System: Semester
URL: www.laroche.edu
Established: 1963 Annual Undergrad Tuition & Fees: $23,160
Enrollment: 1,416 Coed
Affiliation or Control: Roman Catholic IRS Status: 501(c)3
Highest Offering: Master's
Program: Liberal Arts And General; Professional
Accreditation: M, ACBSP, ADNUR, ANEST, ART, CIDA, NUR

01 President ... Sr. Candace INTROCASO, CDP
04 Admin Asst to the President ... Ms. Karen P. WILLOUGHBY
05 Vice President Academic Affairs ... Dr. Howard J. ISHIYAMA
26 VP for Enrollment Mgmt & Mktg ... Mr. William FIRMAN
10 Vice President for Finance ... Mr. Robert VOGEL
32 Vice Pres Student Life/Dean Stdnts ... Ms. Colleen RUEFLE
11 Vice Pres Administrative Services ... Mr. George T. ZAFFUTO
30 Assoc VP for Development ... Ms. Janet DENNIS
43 General Counsel ... Ms. Mary Beth FETCHKO
20 Assoc VP Academic Affairs ... Dr. Rosemary MCCARTHY
20 Assoc Vice Pres Academic Affairs ... Dr. Thomas G. SCHAEFER
36 Asst Dean Academic/Career Advising ... Ms. Marie DEEM
35 Director of Student Development ... Mr. David DAY
83 Div Chair Natural & Behavioral Sci ... Ms. Jane ARNOLD
79 Div Chair Humanities ... Sr. Michele BISBEY, CDP
50 Div Chair Business ... Ms. Lee WHITEMAN
57 Div Chair Design ... Ms. Maria RIPEPI
53 Div Chair Education & Nursing ... Dr. Kathleen A. SULLIVAN
06 Registrar ... Ms. Joan CUTONE
08 Director Library/Learning Center ... Ms. Laverne COLLINS
07 Director of Admissions ... Vacant
26 Director of Mktg & Media Relations ... Ms. Mary Gray DELBUONO
37 Director of Financial Aid ... Ms. Sharon PLATT
41 Director of Athletics ... Mr. Jim TINKEY
42 Director of Campus Ministry ... Fr. Peter HORTON
07 Director Grad Studies/Adult Ed ... Ms. Hope SCHIFFGENS
39 Director Residence Life ... Mr. Christopher WILLIS
14 Director Information Technology ... Ms. Terri BALLARD
85 Director International Student Svcs ... Ms. Natasha GARRETT
29 Director Alumni Relations ... Ms. Gina MILLER
44 Director of Major Gifts ... Mr. John SMITH
21 Director Budget & Finance ... Mr. John PETRUS
09 Director of Institutional Research ... Ms. Patricia A. CONNOLLY
18 Director of Facilities Management ... Mr. J.R YOUNG
38 Director Counseling Services ... Ms. Lori AREND
19 Director Public Safety ... Mr. David HILKE
15 Director Human Resources ... Vacant
40 Bookstore Manager ... Mr. Tim JONES

La Salle University (G)

1900 W Olney Avenue, Philadelphia PA 19141-1199
County: Philadelphia FICE Identification: 003287
Unit ID: 213367
Telephone: (215) 951-1000 Carnegie Class: Master's L
FAX Number: (215) 951-1488 Calendar System: Semester
URL: www.lasalle.edu
Established: 1863 Annual Undergrad Tuition & Fees: $34,840
Enrollment: 6,636 Coed
Affiliation or Control: Roman Catholic IRS Status: 501(c)3
Highest Offering: Doctorate
Program: Liberal Arts And General; Teacher Preparatory; Professional
Accreditation: M, ANEST, BUS, CLPSY, DIETC, DIETD, MFCD, NURSE, SP, SW

01 President ... Bro. Michael J. MCGINNISS
05 Vice Pres Academic Affairs/Provost ... Dr. Joseph R. MARBACH
04 Exec Assistant to the President ... Dr. Alice L. HOERSCH
04 Exec Assistant to the President ... Bro. Joseph WILLARD
30 Vice Pres University Advancement ... Mr. R. Brian ELDERTON
84 Vice President Enrollment Services ... Mr. John F. DOLAN
10 VP Finance and Admin and Treasurer ... Mr. Matthew MCMANNESS
32 VP Student Affairs/Dean of Students ... Dr. James E. MOORE
20 Assistant Provost ... Bro. John MCGOLDRICK
49 Dean School of Arts & Sciences ... Dr. Thomas A. KEAGY
50 Dean Sch of Business Administration ... Mr. Paul R. BRAZINA
51 Dean Col of Professional/Cont Stds ... Dr. Joseph Y. UGRAS
66 Dean Sch of Nursing/Health Sciences ... Dr. Zane R. WOLF
22 Asst VP Admin/Plng/Affirm Action ... Ms. Rose Lee PAULINE
26 Asst VP Mktg & Communications ... Mr. Joseph W. DONOVAN
29 Asst Vice Pres of Alumni Relations ... Mr. James K. GULICK
86 Asst Vice Pres Government Affairs ... Mr. Edward A. TURZANSKI
44 Asst Vice President Development ... Ms. Terry K. TRAVIS
21 Asst Vice Pres Business Systems ... Ms. Robinette RAMSEY-BARNES
21 Asst VP Finance & Asst Treasurer ... Ms. Rebecca L. HORVATH
88 Asst Vice Pres Enrollment Services ... Ms. Kathryn E. PAYNE
88 Asst Vice Pres Enrollment Services ... Mr. Michael J. PAYNE
88 Asst Vice Pres Enrollment Services ... Mr. Paul J. REILLY
88 Director Advancement Services ... Ms. Elizabeth LOCHNER
88 Director Economic Development ... Mr. William J. DEVITO
88 Director Graduate Bilingual Studies ... Dr. Luis GOMEZ
82 Director Grad Ctr/East Europe Stds ... Dr. Bernard G. BLUMENTHAL
77 Director Grad Computer Info Science ... Ms. Margaret MCCOEY
53 Director Graduate Education Program ... Dr. Harris LEWIN
83 Director Grad Clinic-Counsel Psych ... Dr. Donna A. TONREY
73 Director Grad Theol & Ministry ... Fr. Francis J. BERNA
60 Director Grad Prof Communication ... Dr. Marianne DAINTON
66 Director Undergraduate Nursing ... Dr. Barbara HOERST
66 Director Graduate Nursing ... Dr. Kathleen CZEKANSKI
102 Director Corporate Relations ... Ms. Gloria PUGLIESE
25 Director Grants/Research ... Dr. Fred J. FOLEY
35 Senior Assoc Dean of Students ... Mr. Alan B. WENDALL
35 Associate Dean of Students ... Dr. Lane B. NEUBAUER
35 Assistant Dean of Students ... Ms. Anna M. ALLEN
51 Asst Dean Prof/Continuing Studies ... Ms. Elizabeth A. HEENAN

42 Director Univ Ministry & Service ....Bro. Robert J. KINZLER
92 Director University Honors Program ....Dr. Richard A. NIGRO
13 Chief Information Officer ....Mr. Edward NICKERSON
08 Director of the Library ....Mr. John S. BAKY
18 Director Physical Facilities ....Mr. Robert C. KROH, JR.
19 Director Safety & Security ....Mr. Arthur GROVER
16 Director Human Resources ....Dr. Margurete WALSH
41 Athletic Director ....Dr. Thomas BRENNAN
88 Director of Major Gifts ....Bro. Charles E. GRESH
30 Director of Development ....Bro. John MCDONNELL
44 Director of The La Salle Fund ....Mr. Trey ULRICH
30 Director of Prospect Development ....Ms. Sarah PARNUM CADBURY
36 Director of Career Services ....Mr. Louis A. LAMORTE, JR.
36 Exec Dir Career & Employ Svcs ....Mr. Steve MCGONIGLE
07 Executive Director of Admission ....Mr. James C. PLUNKETT
37 Director Student Financial Services ......Mr. Michael WISNIEWSKI
06 Registrar ....Mr. Dominic J. GALANTE
09 Director Institutional Research ....Dr. Michael J. ROSZKOWSKI
96 Director of Procurement ....Vacant
88 Dir Doctoral Clinical Psychology ....Dr. Kelly MCCLURE
88 Director Graduate English Studies ....Dr. Stephen P. SMITH
88 Grad Director Instr Technology Mgt ....Dr. Bobbe G. BAGGIO
88 Director Part-time MBA Program ....Ms. Denise SAURENNANN
88 Director Full-time MBA Program ....Ms. Elizabeth A. SCOFIELD
40 Manager Campus Store ....Mr. Mark ALLAN
28 Multicultural Education Coordinator ....Ms. Cherlyn L. RUSH

Lackawanna College (A)

501 Vine Street, Scranton PA 18509-3206
County: Lackawanna — FICE Identification: 003283
Unit ID: 213376
Telephone: (570) 961-7810 — Carnegie Class: Assoc/PrivNFP
FAX Number: (570) 961-7858 — Calendar System: 4/1/4
URL: www.lackawanna.edu
Established: 1894 — Annual Undergrad Tuition & Fees: $12,010
Enrollment: 1,561 — Coed
Affiliation or Control: Independent Non-Profit — IRS Status: 501(c)3
Highest Offering: Associate Degree
Program: Occupational; 2-Year Principally Bachelor's Creditable; Business Emphasis
Accreditation: M, DMS, @PTAA, SURGT

01 President ....Mr. Raymond ANGELI
03 Executive Vice President ....Mr. Mark VOLK
10 Vice President Financial Affairs ....Mr. Dan MRYKALO
11 Vice President Administration ....Dr. Gail SCARAMUZZO
05 Vice President Academic Affairs ....Dr. Jill MURRAY
30 Assoc VP for Inst Advancement ....Mrs. Bridget FITZPATRICK
32 Dean of Student Affairs ....Mrs. Suellen MUSEWICZ
35 Dean of Students ....Mr. Mark DUDA
84 Dean of Enrollment Management ....Mr. Brian COSTANZO
20 Associate Dean of Curriculum ....Mrs. Erica BARONE-PRICCI
20 Associate Dean of Faculty ....Vacant
26 Exec Dir Communications & Marketing ....Mr. Chris KUCHARSKI
29 Director Alumni Relations ....Ms. Ashley FETTERMAN
09 Director Institutional Research ....Mrs. Laura DUDA
88 Dir Programming & Special Events ....Mr. Jim CULLEN
88 Director Community Concerts ....Ms. Wendy EVANS
51 Director of Adult Education ....Mrs. Anita COLA
41 Director of Athletics ....Mrs. Kim MECCA
88 Director of Advising & Transfer Svc .Mrs. Barbara NOWOGORSKI
88 Director Community Outreach & Pgms ....Ms. Jo-Ann ORCUTT
06 Registrar ....Mrs. Theresa SCOPELLITI
19 Direcrtor of Public Safety ....Mr. Gary SHOENER
12 Director of Hazelton Center ....Ms. Marianne PINDAR
12 Director of Lake Region Center ....Ms. Kim VANGARELLI
12 Director New Milford Center ....Vacant
91 Director Admin Computing Svcs ....Mr. Edward WARGO
08 Library Director ....Mrs. Mary Beth ROCHE
102 Director of Grant Support Services ....Ms. Michelle WILLIAMS
39 Director Housing & Residence Life ....Mr. Stephen DUDA
15 Director of Human Resources ....Mrs. Sharon EBERT
18 Director of Facilities ....Mr. Joseph ERRICO
37 Director of Financial Aid ....Mrs. Barbara HAPEMAN
12 Director Towanda Center ....Ms. Joyce KERRICK
13 Director of MIS ....Mrs. Melanie KOWALSKI
35 Director of Student Activities ....Ms. Karen LEGGE
88 Director of Health Club Facilities ....Mr. Joseph LUCIANO
07 Asst Director of Admissions ....Ms. Stacey MUCHAL

Lafayette College (B)

Easton PA 18042-1798
County: Northampton — FICE Identification: 003284
Unit ID: 213385
Telephone: (610) 330-5000 — Carnegie Class: Bac/A&S
FAX Number: (610) 330-5127 — Calendar System: Semester
URL: www.lafayette.edu
Established: 1826 — Annual Undergrad Tuition & Fees: $40,340
Enrollment: 2,379 — Coed
Affiliation or Control: Independent Non-Profit — IRS Status: 501(c)3
Highest Offering: Baccalaureate
Program: Liberal Arts And General; Professional
Accreditation: M, CS, ENG

01 President ....Mr. Daniel H. WEISS
05 Provost ....Dr. Wendy L. HILL
30 Vice Pres Devel/College Relations ....Mr. James W. DICKER
10 Vice Pres Business Affairs/Treas ....Mr. Mitchell L. WEIN
32 VP Campus Life/Sr Diversity Officer ......Dr. Celestino Jose LIMAS
16 Vice President Human Resources .....Ms. Leslie F. MUHLFELDER
27 Vice President for Communications ....Mr. Robert J. MASSA
13 Sp Ast to Pres/Info Tech Strategies ....Mr. Matthew HYDE
21 Assoc VP Bus Affairs/Controller ....Mr. Paul H. ZIMMERMAN
54 Director of Engineering ....Vacant
04 Executive Assistant ....Dr. James F. KRIVOSKI
84 Dean Admissions & Financial Aid ....Mr. Gregory MACDONALD
20 Dean of the College ....Dr. Hannah W. STEWART-GAMBINO
08 Dean of Libraries/Info Tech Svcs ....Mr. Neil J. MCELROY
07 Director of Admissions ....Mr. Matthew HYDE
37 Director Student Financial Aid ....Ms. Arlina B. DENARDO
09 Director of Institutional Research ....Dr. James P. SCHAFFER
06 Registrar ....Mr. Francis A. BENGINIA
41 Director of Athletics ....Dr. Bruce E. MCCUTCHEON
36 Director Career Services ....Ms. Linda N. ARRA
23 Director Health Services ....Dr. Jeffrey E. GOLDSTEIN
38 Director Counseling Center ....Dr. Karen J. FORBES
19 Director of Public Safety ....Mr. Hugh W. HARRIS
18 Dir Physical Planning & Plant Oper ....Mr. Bruce S. FERRETTI
29 Director Alumni Affairs ....Vacant
15 Director Employment ....Ms. Lisa Youngkin REX
96 Manager of Procurement ....Ms. Linda L. JROSKI

Lake Erie College of Osteopathic Medicine (C)

1858 W Grandview Boulevard, Erie PA 16509-1025
County: Erie — FICE Identification: 030908
Unit ID: 407629
Telephone: (814) 866-6641 — Carnegie Class: Spec/Med
FAX Number: (814) 866-8123 — Calendar System: Semester
URL: www.lecom.edu
Established: 1993 — Annual Graduate Tuition & Fees: $29,235
Enrollment: 2,788 — Coed
Affiliation or Control: Independent Non-Profit — IRS Status: 501(c)3
Highest Offering: First Professional Degree; No Undergraduates
Program: Professional
Accreditation: M, DENT, OSTEO, PHAR

01 President/CEO ....Dr. John M. FERRETTI
05 Provost/Sr Vice Pres/Dean Acad Affs ....Dr. Silvia M. FERRETTI
10 Vice Pres of Fiscal Affairs/CFO ....Mr. Richard P. OLINGER
67 VP Acad Affs/Dn LECOM Sch Pharmacy ....Dr. Hershey BELL
12 Vice Pres for LECOM at Seton Hill ....Dr. Irving FREEMAN
52 Dean School of Dental Medicine ....Dr. Robert HIRSCH
05 Assoc Dean Acad Affairs Bradenton ....Dr. Robert GEORGE
12 Assc Dn Ops/Dist Ed Pharm Bradenton ....Dr. Sunil JAMBHEKAR
88 Assoc Dean of Clinical Education ....Dr. Dennis E. AGOSTINI
88 Assoc Dean of Preclinical Educ ....Dr. Christine KELL
88 Asst Dean Clinical Educ Bradenton ....Dr. Anthony J. FERRETTI
88 Asst Dean Preclinical Ed Bradenton ....Dr. Mark COTY
20 Asst Dean Acad Affairs Bradenton ....Dr. Ronald BEREZNIAK
63 VP Med Educ & Program Development ....Dr. Chet EVANS
20 Assoc Dean of Faculty ....Dr. Rachel OGDEN
20 Assoc Dean of Curriculum ....Dr. Julie WILKINSON
88 Assistant Dean for Assessment ....Dr. Theresa SCHWEIGER
09 Director of Institutional Research ....Mr. Matt CETIN
32 Dir Stdnt Affs/Fin Aid/Enrol Mgmt ....Ms. Susan LAZZARO
26 Director Communications/Marketing ....Mr. Pierre A. BELLICINI
08 Dir of Learning Resources/Educ Tech .....Mr. Robert M. SCHNICK
72 Director of Information Technology ....Mr. Michael E. LEE
46 Director of Research ....Dr. Bertalan DUDAS
15 Director of Human Resources ....Ms. JoAnn I. JEWELL
38 Director Behavioral Health ....Dr. Paul KOVACS
20 Director of Faculty Development ....Dr. Mark TERRELL
27 Asst Dir Communications/Marketing ....Mr. Michael POLIN
18 Building Operations Supervisor ....Mr. Carl F. MULLINAX
37 Associate Director of Financial Aid ....Ms. Bonnie CRILLEY
06 Registrar ....Mr. Jeremy SIVILLO
07 Admissions Coordinator ....Ms. Amy W. ROWE
40 Bookstore Manager ....Ms. Alice PUZAROWSKI

Lancaster Bible College (D)

901 Eden Road, Lancaster PA 17601-5036
County: Lancaster — FICE Identification: 003285
Unit ID: 213400
Telephone: (717) 569-7071 — Carnegie Class: Spec/Faith
FAX Number: (717) 560-8260 — Calendar System: Semester
URL: www.lbc.edu
Established: 1933 — Annual Undergrad Tuition & Fees: $17,160
Enrollment: 923 — Coed
Affiliation or Control: Independent Non-Profit — IRS Status: 501(c)3
Highest Offering: Doctorate
Program: Religious Emphasis
Accreditation: M, BI

01 President ....Dr. Peter W. TEAGUE
04 Assistant to the President ....Mrs. Judith M. HECKAMAN
05 Vice President for Academic Affairs ....Dr. Philip E. DEARBORN
84 VP for Enrollment Management ....Mr. Josh BEERS
30 VP of Advancement ....Mr. Tim HEITZ
10 Director of Finance ....Mr. Matthew MASON
09 Director of Institutional Research ....Dr. Dale MORT
20 Associate VP of Academic Affairs ....Dr. Gary BREDFELDT
06 Associate VP & Registrar ....Mr. Jeffrey HOOVER
32 Associate VP for Student Services ....Mr. Robert MCMICHAEL
26 Director of Marketing ....Mr. Peter CASTOR
07 Director of Enrollment Services ....Mr. Scott BOYER
38 Director of Student Care ....Ms. Annette HERNANDEZ
38 Director of Leadership Development ....Mr. Bernt KING
08 Librarian ....Mr. Gerald E. LINCOLN
37 Director of Financial Aid ....Mrs. Karen L. FOX
21 Controller ....Mr. Matthew MASON
18 Director of Plant Operations ....Mr. Steve MUSSER
23 Director of Health Services ....Mrs. Mary Lou JOLINE
29 Dir of Alumni/Ministry Relations ....Mr. Cameron MARTIN
41 Athletic Director ....Mr. Peter BEERS
15 Director of Human Resources ....Mrs. Paula POOLE

Lancaster General College of Nursing and Health Sciences (E)

410 N Lime Street, Lancaster PA 17602-2337
County: Lancaster — FICE Identification: 009863
Unit ID: 442356
Telephone: (717) 544-4912 — Carnegie Class: Assoc/PrivNFP
FAX Number: (717) 544-5970 — Calendar System: Semester
URL: www.lancastergeneralcollege.edu
Established: 1903 — Annual Undergrad Tuition & Fees: $18,000
Enrollment: 1,143 — Coed
Affiliation or Control: Independent Non-Profit — IRS Status: 501(c)3
Highest Offering: Baccalaureate
Program: 2-Year Principally Bachelor's Creditable; Nursing Emphasis
Accreditation: M, ADNUR, CVT, DMS, MT, NMT, NURSE, RAD, SURGT

01 President ....Dr. Mary Grace SIMCOX
05 Vice President of Academic Affairs ......Ms. Penni LONGENECKER
10 Vice President of Finance & Admin ....Mr. Thomas HULSTINE
20 Vice President Learning Development .. Ms. Donna WILLIAMSON
06 Registrar ....Mr. James DONOHUE
07 Director of Admissions ....Mr. Lyn LONGENECKER
84 Dean of Enrollment Management ....Dr. Sandra ZERBY

Lancaster Theological Seminary (F)

555 W James Street, Lancaster PA 17603-2812
County: Lancaster — FICE Identification: 003286
Unit ID: 213446
Telephone: (717) 393-0654 — Carnegie Class: Spec/Faith
FAX Number: (717) 393-4254 — Calendar System: Semester
URL: www.lancasterseminary.edu
Established: 1825 — Annual Graduate Tuition & Fees: $13,900
Enrollment: 157 — Coed
Affiliation or Control: United Church Of Christ — IRS Status: 501(c)3
Highest Offering: Doctorate; No Undergraduates
Program: Professional; Religious Emphasis
Accreditation: M, THEOL

01 President ....Dr. Carol E. LYTCH
10 Vice President Business & Finance ....Ms. Valerie A. CALHOUN
05 Vice Pres Academic Affairs & Dean ....Dr. David M. MELLOTT
07 Director of Admissions ....Rev. Kendal N. BROWN
08 Director Library Services ....Rev. Richard R. BERG
06 Registrar ....Mrs. Judith G. HUMMER
29 Director Alumni Relations ....Rev. Paul EYER
13 Director Computing/Information Mgmt ....Rev. Chris BELDAN
30 Exec Director of Advancement ....Ms. Kelly Lyons SCHOBER
04 Assistant to the President ....Ms. Peggy H. STAUFFER

Lansdale School of Business (G)

290 Wissahickon Ave, North Wales PA 19454-4114
County: Montgomery — FICE Identification: 007779
Unit ID: 213473
Telephone: (215) 699-5700 — Carnegie Class: Assoc/PrivFP
FAX Number: (215) 699-8770 — Calendar System: Semester
URL: www.LSB.edu
Established: 1918 — Annual Undergrad Tuition & Fees: $9,975
Enrollment: 480 — Coed
Affiliation or Control: Proprietary — IRS Status: Proprietary
Highest Offering: Associate Degree
Program: Occupational; 2-Year Principally Bachelor's Creditable; Business Emphasis
Accreditation: ACICS

01 President ....Mr. Marlon D. KELLER
03 Executive Director ....Mrs. Marianne H. JOHNSON
05 Academic Dean ....Mr. David P. HEFFLEY
20 Dean of Faculty ....Mrs. Laura V. O'REILLY
32 Student Services Coordinator ....Ms. Debora GAHMAN
08 Librarian ....Mrs. Marie B. WALCROFT
10 Director of Student Finance ....Mr. Robert RUSSO
36 Career Services Coordinator ....Ms. Jodi L. TASHMAN

Laurel Business Institute (H)

11 East Penn Street, Uniontown PA 15401-3453
County: Fayette — FICE Identification: 025462
Unit ID: 250027
Telephone: (724) 439-4900 — Carnegie Class: Assoc/PrivFP
FAX Number: (724) 439-3607 — Calendar System: Semester
URL: www.laurel.edu
Established: 1985 — Annual Undergrad Tuition & Fees: $11,985
Enrollment: 299 — Coed
Affiliation or Control: Proprietary — IRS Status: Proprietary
Highest Offering: Associate Degree
Program: Occupational; Technical Emphasis
Accreditation: ACICS

01 President ....Mrs. Nancy M. DECKER
05 Vice President of Education .... Mrs. Valerie S. BACHARACH

20 Dir Academic Affairs & Compliance ...... Mrs. Bonnie Jean MARSH
13 Network Administrator ...... Mrs. JoAnna MEESE
15 Vice President of Human Resources ...... Mr. Chuck SANTORE, JR.
37 Director of Financial Aid ...... Ms. Stephanie M. MIGYANKO
10 Vice President of Finance ...... Ms. Vicki M. JOLLIFFE
07 Director of Admission/Marketing ...... Mr. Douglas S. DECKER

Laurel Technical Institute (A)

200 Sterling Avenue, Sharon PA 16146

County: Mercer FICE Identification: 020925
Unit ID: 215992
Telephone: (724) 983-0700 Carnegie Class: Assoc/PrivFP
FAX Number: (724) 983-8355 Calendar System: Quarter
URL: www.laurel.edu
Established: 1925 Annual Undergrad Tuition & Fees: $11,985
Enrollment: 294 Coed
Affiliation or Control: Proprietary IRS Status: Proprietary
Highest Offering: Associate Degree
Program: Occupational; 2-Year Principally Bachelor's Creditable
Accreditation: ACICS

01 President ...... Ms. Nancy DECKER
05 Director ...... Mr. Douglas DECKER

Le Cordon Bleu Institute of Culinary Arts in Pittsburgh (B)

717 Liberty Avenue, Pittsburgh PA 15222-3500

County: Allegheny FICE Identification: 030068
Unit ID: 367413
Telephone: (412) 566-2433 Carnegie Class: Assoc/PrivFP
FAX Number: (412) 566-2434 Calendar System: Semester
URL: www.chefs.edu/pittsburgh
Established: 1986 Annual Undergrad Tuition & Fees: $17,550
Enrollment: 2,011 Coed
Affiliation or Control: Proprietary IRS Status: Proprietary
Highest Offering: Associate Degree
Program: Occupational
Accreditation: ACCSC

01 President ...... Mr. Pearce MILLER
05 Director Education ...... Mr. Michael RAINSFORTH
10 Controller ...... Ms. Elizabeth MCKEE
37 Director Student Finance ...... Mr. Paul STEELE
06 Registrar ...... Ms. Tina PENNO
22 Compliance Director ...... Mrs. Jessica SANDERS
04 Executive Assistant ...... Ms. Penny LEWIS
88 Dean Hotel/Restaurant Management ...... Mr. Jeff SANTICOLA
88 Dean of Culinary Arts ...... Mr. William M. HUNT
88 Dean of Pastry Arts ...... Mr. Jeff WARD
08 Dean of Library Services ...... Mrs. Tabitha DILLON
32 Assoc Dean of Students ...... Mr. Terry MORAN

† In teachout mode until June 2012.

Lebanon Valley College (C)

101 N College Avenue, Annville PA 17003-1400

County: Lebanon FICE Identification: 003288
Unit ID: 213507
Telephone: (717) 867-6161 Carnegie Class: Bac/Diverse
FAX Number: (717) 867-6124 Calendar System: Semester
URL: www.lvc.edu
Established: 1866 Annual Undergrad Tuition & Fees: $33,200
Enrollment: 2,065 Coed
Affiliation or Control: United Methodist IRS Status: 501(c)3
Highest Offering: Doctorate
Program: Liberal Arts And General; Teacher Preparatory; Professional
Accreditation: M, ACBSP, MUS, PTA

01 President ...... Dr. Stephen C. MACDONALD
05 Vice Pres Acad Affs/Dean of Faculty ...... Dr. Michael R. GREEN
30 Vice President for Advancement ...... Ms. Anne M. BERRY
11 Vice President Administration/IT ...... Mr. Robert A. RILEY
10 Vice President for Finance ...... Mrs. Deborah R. FULLAM
84 Vice President Enrollment ...... Mr. William J. BROWN
32 Vice President for Student Affairs ...... Mr. Gregory H. KRIKORIAN
04 Exec Assistant to the President ...... Ms. Beth DOUGLAS
20 Associate Dean of the Faculty ...... Dr. Ann E. DAMIANO
06 Registrar ...... Mr. Jeremy A. MAISTO
08 Librarian ...... Mr. Frank MOLS
42 Chaplain ...... Rev. Paul FULLMER
51 Director of Grad Studies/Cont Educ ...... Ms. Hope I. WITMER
32 Dean Student Services ...... Ms. Rosemary YUHAS
37 Director Financial Aid ...... Mrs. Kendra M. FEIGERT
36 Director of Career Services ...... Ms. Sharon M. GIVLER
41 Director of Athletics ...... Mr. Richard L. BEARD
29 Director of Alumni ...... Ms. Jayanne HAYWARD
44 Director of Development ...... Ms. Jamie N. CECIL
26 Director of College Relations ...... Dr. Thomas M. HANRAHAN
27 Assoc Director of College Relations ...... Ms. Kelly A. ALSEDEK
21 Controller ...... Ms. Eleanor LEWIS
18 Sr Director of Facilities Services ...... Mr. Donald SANTOSTEFANO
19 Director of Public Safety ...... Mr. Brent OBERHOLTZER
15 Director Human Resources ...... Mrs. Ann C. HAYES
28 Director of Multicultural Affairs ...... Ms. Venus RICKS
35 Director Student Activities ...... Mrs. Jennifer M. EVANS
104 Director of Study Abroad ...... Ms. Jill T. RUSSELL
90 Director of Client Services ...... Mr. Michael C. ZEIGLER
91 Director of Info Mgt Services ...... Mr. Robert J. DILLANE
39 Director of Residential Life ...... Mr. Jason A. KUNTZ
38 Director of Counseling ...... Dr. Stephanie A. FALK
38 Director of Disability Services ...... Ms. Yvonne FOSTER
09 Director of Institutional Research ...... Mrs. Jennifer S. LIEDTKA
40 Manager of the College Store ...... Mr. Chad M. SCHREIER
50 Director of the MBA Program ...... Ms. Jennifer K. EASTER
96 Director of Business Services ...... Mr. Todd M. LATSHAW

Lehigh Carbon Community College (D)

4525 Education Park Drive, Schnecksville PA 18078-2598

County: Lehigh FICE Identification: 006810
Unit ID: 213525
Telephone: (610) 799-2121 Carnegie Class: Assoc/Pub-S-SC
FAX Number: (610) 799-1527 Calendar System: Semester
URL: www.lccc.edu
Established: 1966 Annual Undergrad Tuition & Fees (In-District): $3,240
Enrollment: 8,101 Coed
Affiliation or Control: Local IRS Status: 501(c)3
Highest Offering: Associate Degree
Program: Occupational; 2-Year Principally Bachelor's Creditable
Accreditation: M, ACBSP, ADNUR, MAC, OTA, PNUR, PTAA

01 President ...... Dr. Donald W. SNYDER
05 VP Academic/Student Dev ...... Dr. Thomas C. LEAMER
11 VP Admin Svc & Workforce/Cmty Dev ...... Ms. Ann D. BIEBER
10 VP Finance & Facilities ...... Mr. Larry W. ROSS
04 Admin Secy to President and Board ...... Mrs. Cindy L. BROOKS
32 Dean of Students ...... Ms. Peggy M. HEIM
62 Dean Library and Info Tech ...... Mr. David S. VOROS
88 Dean of Academic Services ...... Dr. Barry L. SPRIGGS
13 Interim Chief Information Officer ...... Mr. Anwar KARIM
106 Assoc Dean Distance Education ...... Mr. Dominic CHRISTISON
20 Associate Academic Dean ...... Dr. Michael L. TORRENCE
20 Associate Academic Dean ...... Ms. Larissa M. VERTA
103 Assoc Dean Wrkfrce/Community Svc ...... Ms. Marsha E. FELSTEN
88 Assoc Dean Educational Support Svcs ...... Ms. Michelle A. CARLINO
30 Assoc Dean Inst Advancement ...... Ms. Heather L. KUHNS
09 Assoc Dean Inst Research/Planning ...... Ms. Glynis DANIELS
45 Assoc Dean Planning & Assessment ...... Ms. Cecelia A. CONNELLY-WEIDA
21 Assistant Controller-Accounting ...... Ms. Shannon HELMER
21 Assistant Controller-Services ...... Ms. Marybeth CAVOSI-O'DEA
102 Executive Director of Foundation ...... Mr. Timothy J. HERRLINGER
38 Director Advising and Counseling ...... Ms. Susan J. FREAD
07 Director of Admissions ...... Vacant
88 Dir of Application Support Services ...... Ms. Shirley DELONG
36 Director Career Services ...... Ms. Christina L. MOYER
88 Accreditation and Curriculum ...... Mr. Scott W. AQUILA
88 Director of High School Connections ...... Ms. Jennifer K. NEEB
15 Director of Human Resources ...... Ms. Donna M. WILLIAMS
88 Dir Infrastructure Svcs ...... Mr. Ervin J. MEASE
88 Dir Learning Communities & Fac Dev ...... Dr. Alison JAMESON
103 Director Workforce Training ...... Ms. Lois M. YEAKEL
66 Director Nursing ...... Ms. Juanita G. KANESS
35 Director of Student Life ...... Ms. Gene F. EDEN
14 Director IT Services ...... Mr. Patrick J. CLARKE
18 Director of Facilities Management ...... Mr. Carl S. PECKITT, JR.
37 Director of Financial Aid ...... Ms. Marian L. SNYDER
25 Director of Academic Grants ...... Ms. Linda L. MESICS
106 Dir of Distance Lrng/Instruct Tech ...... Ms. Beverly J. BENFER
41 Director of Athletics ...... Ms. Jocelyn M. BECK
88 Director of Early Learning Center ...... Ms. Kathy MOSLEY
96 Director of Purchasing ...... Ms. Susan E. LINDENMUTH
12 Dir Carbon/Schuylkill Cty Ed Svcs ...... Ms. Jeanne Y. MILLER
88 Dir of Literacy and Job Training ...... Ms. Suzy L. WELLIVER
31 Director of Community Services ...... Ms. Terri K. KEEFE
88 Controller ...... Ms. Connie BURNS
88 ESC Lab Supervisor ...... Ms. Debra A. CONDON
25 Dir Institutional Advancement Grant ...... Mr. Thomas J. MULDERICK
74 Acting Dir Veterinary Tech Program ...... Ms. Samantha FRIEDENBERG
27 Director Marketing and Publications ...... Ms. Paula HANNAM
21 Bursar ...... Ms. Diane M. TRAINER
06 Registrar ...... Ms. Sandra L. MOSSER
19 Supervisor of Security & Safety ...... Mr. Kevin J. MILES
40 Bookstore Manager ...... Ms. Jennifer ERB

Lehigh University (E)

27 Memorial Drive W, Bethlehem PA 18015-3094

County: Northampton FICE Identification: 003289
Unit ID: 213543
Telephone: (610) 758-3000 Carnegie Class: RU/H
FAX Number: (610) 691-5420 Calendar System: Semester
URL: www.lehigh.edu
Established: 1865 Annual Undergrad Tuition & Fees: $51,800
Enrollment: 7,051 Coed
Affiliation or Control: Independent Non-Profit IRS Status: 501(c)3
Highest Offering: Doctorate
Program: Liberal Arts And General; Teacher Preparatory; Professional
Accreditation: M, BUS, BUSA, COPSY, CS, ENG, SCPSY, THEA

01 President ...... Dr. Alice P. GAST
05 Provost & VP for Academic Affairs ...... Dr. Patrick V. FARRELL
10 Vice Pres Finance & Administration ...... Ms. Margaret F. PLYMPTON
88 VP for International Affairs ...... Dr. Mohamed S. EL-AASSER
30 Vice President Advancement ...... Mr. Joseph P. KENDER, JR.
46 VP & Assoc Prov Research/Graduate ...... Dr. Alan J. SNYDER
26 VP Communications & Public Affairs ...... Mr. Frederick J. MCGRAIL
88 Chief Investment Officer ...... Mr. Peter M. GILBERT
09 Vice Provost Institutional Research ...... Dr. J. Gary LUTZ
32 Vice Provost Student Affairs ...... Dr. John W. SMEATON
13 Vice Provost Library & Tech Svcs ...... Dr. Bruce M. TAGGART
86 Assoc VP for Govt Relations ...... Mr. William D. MICHALERYA
21 Assoc VP Finance/Asst Secy Board ...... Ms. Denise M. BLEW
15 Assoc Vice Pres for Human Resources ...... Ms. Jacqueline MATTHEWS
18 Assoc Vice Pres Facilities Services ...... Mr. Anthony L. CORALLO
20 Deputy Provost Academic Affairs ...... Mr. Gerald P. LENNON
35 Assoc Vice Provost Dean of Students ...... Ms. Sharon K. BASSO
29 Asst Vice Pres of Alumni Relations ...... Mr. Robert W. WOLFENDEN
31 Asst VP Community & Regional Affs ...... Mr. Dale A. KOCHARD
54 Dean Engineering & Applied Science ...... Dr. S. David WU
49 Dean Arts & Sciences ...... Dr. Anne S. MELTZER
50 Dean of Business & Economics ...... Dr. Paul R. BROWN
53 Dean of Education ...... Dr. Gary M. SASSO
07 Dean of Admissions/Financial Aid ...... Mr. J. Leon WASHINGTON
41 Murray H Goodman Dean of Athletics ...... Mr. Joseph D. STERRETT
06 Registrar ...... Mr. Emil A. GNASSO
37 Director Financial Aid ...... Ms. Linda F. BELL
106 Director Distance Education ...... Ms. Margaret A. PORTZ
36 Director Career Services ...... Ms. Donna L. GOLDFEDER
23 Director Health Center ...... Dr. Susan C. KITEI
39 Director Residential Services ...... Mr. Ozzie BREINER
40 Director Bookstore ...... Mr. Steve A. SCHATTEN
19 Chief University Police ...... Mr. Edward K. SHUPP
38 Director of Counseling Services ...... Dr. Ian T. BIRKY
42 Chaplain ...... Rev. Lloyd H. STEFFEN
43 General Counsel ...... Mr. Frank A. ROTH
21 Director of Budget ...... Mr. Stephen J. GUTTMAN
28 Director of Diversity ...... Mr. Henry U. ODI
96 Manager Strategic Sourcing ...... Ms. Jane ALTEMOSE

Lincoln Technical Institute (F)

5151 Tilghman Street, Allentown PA 18104-3298

County: Lehigh FICE Identification: 007759
Unit ID: 213570
Telephone: (610) 398-5300 Carnegie Class: Assoc/PrivFP
FAX Number: (610) 395-2706 Calendar System: Semester
URL: www.lincolntech.com
Established: 1946 Annual Undergrad Tuition & Fees: N/A
Enrollment: 894 Coed
Affiliation or Control: Proprietary IRS Status: Proprietary
Highest Offering: Associate Degree
Program: Occupational
Accreditation: ACCSC

01 Executive Director ...... Mrs. Lisa M. KUNTZ
05 Director of Education ...... Ms. Anne CONNELY
11 Director of Administrative Services ...... Mrs. Jennie I. HUNSICKER
37 Director of Financial Aid ...... Mrs. Angela REPPERT
07 Director of Admissions ...... Mr. Mark GARNER
36 Director of Career Services ...... Mrs. Charmain BRODY

Lincoln Technical Institute (G)

9191 Torresdale Avenue, Philadelphia PA 19136-1595

County: Philadelphia FICE Identification: 007832
Unit ID: 213589
Telephone: (215) 335-0800 Carnegie Class: Assoc/PrivFP
FAX Number: (215) 335-1443 Calendar System: Other
URL: www.lincolntech.com
Established: 1946 Annual Undergrad Tuition & Fees: $28,872
Enrollment: 658 Coed
Affiliation or Control: Proprietary IRS Status: Proprietary
Highest Offering: Associate Degree
Program: Occupational
Accreditation: ACCSC

01 Executive Director ...... Mr. Mark BOHEN
07 Dir Admiss High School/Adult Educ ...... Mr. Pat FITTIPALDI
32 Director of Student Services ...... Mr. Jaime ANTEL
05 Director of Education ...... Mr. Mitchell YOURMAN
11 Director Administrative Services ...... Ms. Gina ALTSHULER
36 Director of Career Services ...... Mrs. Sharon BARRETT

Lincoln University (H)

PO Box 179, 1570 Baltimore Pike, Lincoln University PA 19352-0999

County: Chester FICE Identification: 003290
Unit ID: 213598
Telephone: (484) 365-8000 Carnegie Class: Master's L
FAX Number: (484) 365-7316 Calendar System: Semester
URL: www.lincoln.edu
Established: 1854 Annual Undergrad Tuition & Fees (In-State): $9,984
Enrollment: 2,361 Coed
Affiliation or Control: State Related IRS Status: 501(c)3
Highest Offering: Master's
Program: Liberal Arts And General
Accreditation: M

01 President ...... Dr. Ivory V. NELSON
100 Asst to Pres/Mgr Board of Trustees ...... Ms. Diane M. BROWN
05 Provost/Sr VP Acad & Student Affs ...... Vacant
10 Vice Pres Fiscal Affairs/Treasurer ...... Mr. Howard E. MERLIN
84 VP Student Affs/Enroll Mgmt ...... Vacant
30 Executive Vice President ...... Mr. Michael B. HILL
07 Director Admissions ...... Ms. Germel EATON-CLARKE
08 Director of Library ...... Mr. Tracey HUNTER HAYES

26 Director of Communications ... Vacant
29 Director of Alumni Relations ... Ms. Theresa BRASWELL
06 Registrar ... Ms. Catherine RUTLEDGE
13 Director of Information Technology ... Mr. Steven CAROL
09 Asst VP Institutional Effectiveness ... Dr. Renford A B. BREVETT
44 Dir Development & Major Gifts ... Vacant
15 Chief Human Resources Officer ... Dr. Debbie BULLOCK
19 Director of Public Safety/Security ... Mr. Larry WOODS
102 Dir Foundation/Corporate Relations ... Mr. Andre DIXON
36 Director Counseling/Career Svcs Ctr ... Mr. Ralph SIMPSON
41 Director of Athletics ... Ms. Dianthia FORD-KEE
42 Chaplain ... Mr. Frederick FAISON
21 Controller ... Ms. Danielle JONES
18 Chief Facilities/Physical Plant ... Mr. John THOMPSON
39 Int Dean Students and Campus Life ... Ms. Thelma ROSS
85 Director International Services ... Ms. Constance L. LUNDY
23 Director Health Services ... Ms. Velva GREENE-RAINEY
58 Dir Graduate Student Svcs/Admission ... Ms. Jernice LEA
37 Director Financial Aid ... Ms. Thelma L. ROSS
96 Director of Purchasing ... Ms. Lynnette F. SCOTT
81 Dean Sch of Natural Sciences & Math ... Dr. John O. CHIKWEM
83 Dean Sch Social Sci/Behavioral Stds ... Dr. Judith A W. THOMAS
79 Dean School of Humanities/Grad Stds ... Vacant

Lutheran Theological Seminary at Gettysburg (A)

61 Seminary Ridge, Gettysburg PA 17325-1795
County: Adams FICE Identification: 003291
Unit ID: 213631
Telephone: (717) 334-6286 Carnegie Class: Spec/Faith
FAX Number: (717) 334-3469 Calendar System: 4/1/4
URL: www.ltsg.edu
Established: 1826 Annual Graduate Tuition & Fees: $13,050
Enrollment: 168 Coed
Affiliation or Control: Evangelical Lutheran Church In America
IRS Status: 501(c)3
Highest Offering: Doctorate; No Undergraduates
Program: Professional; Religious Emphasis
Accreditation: M, THEOL

01 President ... Rev. Michael L. COOPER-WHITE
30 Chief Advancement Officer ... Rev. Kathleen O. REED
10 Chief Financial Officer ... Dr. Marty STEVENS
05 Dean of the Seminary ... Dr. Robin J. STEINKE
08 Library Director and Archivist ... Dr. Briant BOHLEKE
06 Registrar ... Dr. Marty STEVENS
26 Exec Asst to Pres for Comm/Plng ... Rev. John R. SPANGLER
91 Director of Info Systems/Ed Tech ... Mr. Donald L. REDMAN
15 Asst to the Pres/Personnel Officer ... Mrs. Carol A. TROYER
07 Director of Admissions ... Rev. Virginia PRICE
21 Financial Services Manager ... Ms. Debra ECK

Lutheran Theological Seminary at Philadelphia (B)

7301 Germantown Avenue, Philadelphia PA 19119-1794
County: Philadelphia FICE Identification: 003292
Unit ID: 213640
Telephone: (215) 248-4616 Carnegie Class: Spec/Faith
FAX Number: (215) 248-4577 Calendar System: Other
URL: www.ltsp.edu
Established: 1864 Annual Graduate Tuition & Fees: $14,990
Enrollment: 355 Coed
Affiliation or Control: Evangelical Lutheran Church In America
IRS Status: 501(c)3
Highest Offering: Doctorate; No Undergraduates
Program: Professional; Religious Emphasis
Accreditation: M, THEOL

01 President ... Dr. Philip D. KREY
05 Dean ... Dr. J. Paul RAJASHEKAR
10 Vice President Finance & Operation ... Mr. Curtis A. HAYNES
30 Vice President LTSP Foundation ... Rev. John V. PUOTINEN
08 Director of the Library ... Dr. Karl KRUEGER
07 Director of Admissions ... Rev. Louise N. JOHNSON
32 Director of Student Services ... Dr. John BERNTSEN
06 Registrar ... Ms. Rene DIEMER
19 Director of Security/Safety ... Mr. Vincent FERGUSON
13 Director Information Technology ... Mr. Kyle BARGER
27 Director of Communications ... Mr. John KAHLER
40 Manager LTSP Bookstore ... Rev. Heidi RODRICK SCHNAATH
42 Chaplain ... Dr. Jayakiran SEBASTIAN

Luzerne County Community College (C)

1333 S Prospect Street, Nanticoke PA 18634-3899
County: Luzerne FICE Identification: 006811
Unit ID: 213659
Telephone: (570) 740-0200 Carnegie Class: Assoc/Pub-S-SC
FAX Number: (570) 740-0386 Calendar System: Semester
URL: www.luzerne.edu
Established: 1966 Annual Undergrad Tuition & Fees (In-District): $3,090
Enrollment: 7,249 Coed
Affiliation or Control: Local IRS Status: 501(c)3
Highest Offering: Associate Degree
Program: Occupational; 2-Year Principally Bachelor's Creditable
Accreditation: #M, ADNUR, DA, DH, SURGT

01 President ... Mr. Thomas P. LEARY
04 Spec Ast to Pres Policy/Staff Devel ... Ms. Laura KATRENICZ
05 Vice Pres Academic Affairs/Provost ... Dr. Dana CLARK
32 Vice President Student Development ... Mr. Thomas P. LEARY
103 VP Workforce/Community Development ... Ms. Susan SPRY
45 VP Training Inst Ext Affairs Plng ... Dr. Joseph GRILLI
16 Dean Human Resources ... Mr. John SEDLAK
66 Dean of Nursing/Health Sciences ... Vacant
50 Dean of Business/Technologies ... Mr. Gary MROZINSKI
49 Dean of Arts & Sciences ... Vacant
10 Dean Finance ... Mr. Joseph GASPER
13 Chief Technology Office ... Mr. Don NELSON
07 Director Admissions & Recruiting ... Mr. James DOMZALSKI
37 Director of Student Financial Aid ... Ms. Mary KOSIN
08 Director of Library Services ... Mrs. Mia W. BASSHAM
38 Dir Counseling/Academic Advising ... Mr. Randy LIGHT
35 Dir Student Activities/Athletics ... Ms. Mary SULLIVAN
09 Director Inst Research/Planning ... Ms. Graceann PLATUKUS
36 Director Career Services ... Ms. Mary GHILANI
18 Director of Physical Plant ... Mr. Keith GRAHAM
30 Exec Dir of Resource Development ... Ms. Sandra NICHOLAS
84 Director Enrollment Management ... Mr. Jim DOMZALSKI
26 Chief Public Relations Officer ... Mrs. Lisa NELSON
29 Director Alumni Relations ... Ms. Bonnie LAUER
96 Director of Purchasing ... Mr. Len OLZINSKI

Lycoming College (D)

700 College Place, Williamsport PA 17701-5192
County: Lycoming FICE Identification: 003293
Unit ID: 213668
Telephone: (570) 321-4000 Carnegie Class: Bac/A&S
FAX Number: (570) 321-4337 Calendar System: Semester
URL: www.lycoming.edu
Established: 1812 Annual Undergrad Tuition & Fees: $31,168
Enrollment: 1,321 Coed
Affiliation or Control: United Methodist IRS Status: 501(c)3
Highest Offering: Baccalaureate
Program: Liberal Arts And General
Accreditation: M

01 President ... Dr. James E. DOUTHAT
05 Provost and Dean of the College ... Dr. Philip W. SPRUNGER
10 Vice Pres Administration/Planning ... Dr. Sue S. GAYLOR
30 Vice President for Advancement ... Mr. Charles W. EDMONDS
07 Vice Pres Admissions/Financial Aid ... Mr. James D. SPENCER
21 Controller/Chf Financial Ofcr/Treas ... Ms. Michelle M. JONES
32 Dean Student Affairs ... Dr. Daniel P. MILLER
89 Assistant Dean for Freshmen ... Ms. Regina M. COLLINS
08 Director of Snowden Library ... Ms. Janet M. HURLBERT
06 Registrar ... Vacant
26 Director of College Relations ... Mr. Jerry T. RASHID
37 Director of Financial Aid ... Mr. James LAKIS
14 Assoc Dean/Chief Information Ofcr ... Mr. David B. HEFFNER
36 Director of Career Services ... Ms. MaryJo CAMPANA
29 Director Alumni Relations ... Ms. Amy S. DOWLING
44 Planned Giving Officer ... Ms. Karen M. SHEAFFER
19 Director of Safety & Security ... Mr. Donald TROUTMAN
35 Director of Student Programs ... Mr. Lawrence P. MANNOLINI, III
39 Director Residence Life ... Mr. Andrew W. KILPATRICK
41 Director of Athletics ... Vacant
30 Senior Major Gift Officer ... Mr. Gregory J. BELL
44 Director of Annual Giving ... Ms. Meghan E. HEPLER
42 Campus Minister ... Rev. Jeffrey L. LECRONE
16 Director of Human Resources ... Ms. Jackie BILGER
18 Chief Facilities/Physical Plant ... Mr. F. Douglas KUNTZ
23 Director of Health Services ... Ms. Sondra L. STIPCAK
38 Director Student Counseling ... Mr. Townsend VELKOFF
40 Campus Store Manager ... Ms. Patricia E. BAUSINGER
92 Lycoming Scholars ... Dr. Michelle A. BRIGGS
94 Women's Studies ... Dr. N. J. STANLEY
15 Human Resources Coordinator ... Mrs. Cathleen A. LUTZ

Manor College (E)

700 Fox Chase Road, Jenkintown PA 19046-3399
County: Montgomery FICE Identification: 003294
Unit ID: 213774
Telephone: (215) 885-2360 Carnegie Class: Assoc/PrivNFP
FAX Number: (215) 576-6564 Calendar System: Semester
URL: www.manor.edu
Established: 1947 Annual Undergrad Tuition & Fees: $90,478
Enrollment: 900 Coed
Affiliation or Control: Independent Non-Profit IRS Status: 501(c)3
Highest Offering: Associate Degree
Program: Occupational; 2-Year Principally Bachelor's Creditable
Accreditation: M, ACBSP, DA, DH

01 President ... Sr. M. Cecilia JURASINSKI, OSBM
05 Dean Academic Affs/Exec Vice Pres ... Mrs. Sally P. MYDLOWEC
84 VP of Enrollment Management ... Vacant
10 Director of Finance ... Mr. Thomas J. HILL
08 Library Director ... Ms. Beth LANDER
32 Dean of Students ... Sr. Marie Francis WALCHONSKY, OSBM
30 Director of Development ... Ms. Marialice STANZESKI
38 Director Counseling Office ... Ms. Linda PETERSON
07 Director of Admissions ... Mr. Jeffrey P. LEVINE
26 Director of Public Relations ... Mr. Steve GREENBAUM
06 Registrar ... Mr. Richard E. KUKOWSKI
29 Director Alumni Relations ... Ms. Marialice STANZESKI
41 Director of Athletics ... Mr. Robert REEVES
37 Director of Financial Aid ... Mr. Peter LYSIONEK
18 Maintenance Supervisor ... Mr. Petro DOLINAY
09 Director of Institutional Research ... Sr. Monica LESNICK, OSBM
15 Human Resources Generalist ... Ms. Brittney RICHARDSON
40 Bookstore Manager ... Ms. Mary ZAKRZEWSKI
20 Assistant Dean Academic Affairs ... Ms. Jane R. ZEGESTOWSKY

Marywood University (F)

2300 Adams Avenue, Scranton PA 18509-1598
County: Lackawanna FICE Identification: 003296
Unit ID: 213826
Telephone: (570) 348-6211 Carnegie Class: Master's L
FAX Number: (570) 961-4769 Calendar System: Semester
URL: www.marywood.edu
Established: 1915 Annual Undergrad Tuition & Fees: $28,175
Enrollment: 3,479 Coed
Affiliation or Control: Roman Catholic IRS Status: 501(c)3
Highest Offering: Doctorate
Program: Liberal Arts And General; Teacher Preparatory; Professional
Accreditation: M, ACBSP, ARCPA, ART, CACREP, CLPSY, DIETC, DIETD, DIETI, MUS, NUR, SP, SW, TED

01 President ... Sr. Anne MUNLEY
05 Vice Pres Academic Affairs ... Dr. Alan LEVINE
10 VP Business Affairs/Treasurer ... Mr. Joseph X. GARVEY, JR.
30 Vice Pres University Advancement ... Dr. Clayton N. PHEASANT
32 Vice President Student Life ... Dr. Raymond P. HEATH
84 Vice Pres Enrollment Management ... Ms. Ann BOLAND-CHASE
101 Secretary Univ & General Counsel ... Ms. Mary T. GARDIER PATERSON
15 Asst Vice Pres for Human Resources ... Dr. Patricia E. DUNLEAVY
26 Asst VP for Marketing and Comm ... Mr. Peter KILCULLEN
18 Asst VP for Buildings & Grounds ... Mrs. Wendy YANKELITIS
44 Asst Vice Pres for Development ... Vacant
35 Dean of Students ... Dr. Amy PACIEJ-WOODRUFF
49 Dean College Liberal Arts/Sciences ... Dr. Michael FOLEY
53 Dean Reap College Educ/Human Dev ... Dr. Mary Anne FEDRICK
76 Dean Col of Health/Human Svcs ... Vacant
88 Dn Col of Creative Performing Arts ... Mr. Collier B. PARKER
48 Dean School of Architecture ... Mr. Gregory K. HUNT
90 Director User Support Services ... Dr. Michael MIRABITO
70 Director School of Social Work ... Dr. Lloyd L. LYTER
08 Director of Library Services ... Mrs. Catherine H. SCHAPPERT
06 Registrar ... Ms. Rosemary BURGER
07 Dir of University Admissions ... Mr. Christian DIGREGORIO
21 Controller/Asst Treasurer ... Mr. Kevin J. MAY
21 Dir Fiscal Affairs/Asst Controller ... Ms. Melissa A. SADDLEMIRE
13 Dir of ERP Migration ... Mr. Michael P. GIBBONS
88 Asst Director Buildings & Grounds ... Mr. Myron MARCINEK
37 Director of Financial Aid ... Mr. Stanley F. SKRUTSKI
102 Dir Corp/Found/Govt Relations ... Ms. Renee GREGORI ZEHEL
44 Director of Planned Giving ... Ms. Elizabeth A. CONNERY
26 Communications Director ... Ms. Juneann GRECO
44 Director of Capital Resources ... Mr. Paul J. STRUNK
29 Director of Alumni Development ... Mr. Leon JOHN, JR.
42 Chaplain/Asst Dir Campus Ministry ... Rev. Brian F. VAN FOSSEN
39 Director Housing/Residence Life ... Ms. Elizabeth J. SECHLER
41 Director Athletics/Recreation ... Dr. Mary Jo GUNNING
36 Director of Career Services ... Dr. Carole R. GUSTITUS
42 Director of Campus Ministry ... Sr. Catherine LUXNER
88 Director of Dining Services ... Mr. Thomas K. NOTCHICK
27 Chief Information Officer ... Mr. Anthony SPINILLO
27 Telecommunications Manager ... Mr. Martin O'CONNOR
19 Sr Dir Sec/Safety/Environ Complnce ... Mr. David R. ELLIOTT
23 Director of Student Health Services ... Ms. Linda MCDADE
38 Director Counseling & Student Devel ... Dr. Robert S. SHAW
40 Bookstore Manager ... Ms. Erin B. OSTROSKI
104 Assoc Dir International Affairs ... Mr. David A. CRISCI
14 Director of Operations ... Mr. John B. PORTER
30 Director Advancement Services ... Ms. Gretchen FRITZ
30 Dir Constituent Rels/Marywood Fund ... Ms. Michele ZABRISKI
35 Dir of Student Act/Leadership Devel ... Mr. Carl OLIVERI
28 Director of Diversity Services ... Dr. Lia Richards PALMITER
88 Director Human Physiology Lab ... Dr. Gerald S. ZAVORSKY
09 Director Inst Rsrch/Assessment ... Dr. Ellen M. BOYLAN
45 Chief Planning Officer ... Vacant
90 Manager of Academic Computing ... Ms. Katherine P. LEWIS

McCann School of Business & Technology (G)

370 Maplewood Drive, Humbolt Ind Pk,
Hazleton PA 18202-9790
County: Luzerne Identification: 666484
Unit ID: 213871
Telephone: (570) 454-6172 Carnegie Class: Not Classified
FAX Number: (570) 454-6286 Calendar System: Quarter
URL: www.mccann.edu
Established: 1897 Annual Undergrad Tuition & Fees: $11,520
Enrollment: 690 Coed
Affiliation or Control: Proprietary IRS Status: Proprietary
Highest Offering: Associate Degree
Program: Occupational
Accreditation: ACICS, MAC, SURGT

01 Director ... Ms. Barbara J. REESE
05 Director of Education ... Mr. Frank BERLETH
36 Career Services Director ... Mr. William BURKE
07 Director of Admissions ... Mr. Jason BLOZOWSKY

† Branch campus of McCann School of Business & Technology, Pottsville, PA.

McCann School of Business & Technology (A)

2650 Woodglen Road, Pottsville PA 17901-1335
County: Schuylkill FICE Identification: 004898
Unit ID: 438212
Telephone: (570) 622-7622 Carnegie Class: Assoc/PrivFP
FAX Number: (570) 622-7770 Calendar System: Quarter
URL: www.mccannschool.edu
Established: 1897 Annual Undergrad Tuition & Fees: $11,500
Enrollment: 562 Coed
Affiliation or Control: Proprietary IRS Status: Proprietary
Highest Offering: Associate Degree
Program: Occupational
Accreditation: ACICS, MAC

01 Director Pottsville Campus .... Ms. Shannon BRENNAN
05 Director of Education .... Ms. MaryLou ORAM
36 Director of Career Services .... Ms. Michelle SCRIBBICK

McCann School of Business & Technology (B)

1147 N Fourth Street, Sunbury PA 17801-3413
County: Northumberland Identification: 666485
Unit ID: 438221
Telephone: (570) 286-3058 Carnegie Class: Not Classified
FAX Number: (570) 286-4723 Calendar System: Quarter
URL: www.mccannschool.com
Established: 1897 Annual Undergrad Tuition & Fees: $12,400
Enrollment: 1,230 Coed
Affiliation or Control: Proprietary IRS Status: Proprietary
Highest Offering: Associate Degree
Program: Occupational
Accreditation: ACICS, MAC, SURGT

01 Campus Director .... Ms. Susan M. LYNCH
07 Admissions Representative .... Ms. Lisa DAVIS
36 Career Services Representative .... Ms. Carol SHAFER

† Branch campus of McCann School of Business & Technology, Pottsville, PA.

Mercyhurst College (C)

501 E 38th Street, Erie PA 16546-0001
County: Erie FICE Identification: 003297
Unit ID: 213987
Telephone: (814) 824-2000 Carnegie Class: Master's S
FAX Number: (814) 824-2438 Calendar System: Trimester
URL: www.mercyhurst.edu
Established: 1926 Annual Undergrad Tuition & Fees: $27,657
Enrollment: 4,388 Coed
Affiliation or Control: Roman Catholic IRS Status: 501(c)3
Highest Offering: Master's
Program: Occupational; 2-Year Principally Bachelor's Creditable; Liberal Arts And General; Teacher Preparatory; Professional
Accreditation: M, ADNUR, DANCE, #IACBE, MLTAD, MUS, OTA, PTAA, SW

01 President .... Dr. Thomas J. GAMBLE
03 Provost/Sr Counselor to President .... Dr. James M. ADOVASIO
05 Vice Pres Acad Affs/Dean of College .... Dr. Phil J. BELFIORE
84 VP Enrollment & Adult/Grad Pgm .... Dr. Michael P. LYDEN
10 Vice Pres of Finance & Treasurer .... Ms. Jane M. KELSEY
12 Exec Vice Pres Mercyhurst - NE/West .... Dr. Gary M. BROWN
30 Vice Pres Development/Alumni Rels .... Dr. David J. LIVINGSTON
32 Vice Pres of Student Development .... Dr. Gerry A. TOBIN
21 Associate Business Officer .... Mr. James F. LIEB
14 Director Computing Services .... Mrs. Patricia H. BENEKOS
18 Director Facilities/Physical Plant .... Mr. Kenneth STEPHERSON
38 Director Student Counseling Service .... Ms. Judy SMITH
07 Director of Undergrad Admissions .... Mr. Christopher COONS
06 Registrar .... Sr. Patricia WHALEN
08 Director of Libraries .... Ms. Darcy JONES
39 Dir Residential Life/Stdnt Conduct .... Ms. Alice AGNEW
19 Director of Public Safety Programs .... Mr. Robert KUHN
29 Director of Alumni Services .... Mr. Ryan PALM
42 Director of Campus Ministry .... Fr. James PISZKER
37 Director of Student Financial Svcs .... Ms. Carrie NEWMAN
41 Director of Athletics .... Mr. Joseph KIMBALL
09 Director of Institutional Research .... Mrs. Sheila W. RICHTER
15 Director Human Resources .... Mr. Jim TOMETSKO
28 Director Multicultural Affairs .... Ms. Petrina WILLIAMS

Messiah College (D)

One College Avenue, Grantham PA 17027-0800
County: Cumberland FICE Identification: 003298
Unit ID: 213996
Telephone: (717) 766-2511 Carnegie Class: Bac/Diverse
FAX Number: (717) 691-6025 Calendar System: Semester
URL: www.messiah.edu
Established: 1909 Annual Undergrad Tuition & Fees: $28,356
Enrollment: 2,808 Coed
Affiliation or Control: Interdenominational IRS Status: 501(c)3
Highest Offering: Master's
Program: Liberal Arts And General; Teacher Preparatory; Professional
Accreditation: M, THEA, ACBSP, ART, DIETD, ENG, MUS, NURSE, SW

01 President .... Dr. Kim S. PHIPPS
05 Provost .... Dr. Randall G. BASINGER
10 Vice President for Finance .... Vacant
30 Vice President for Advancement .... Mr. Barry G. GOODLING
11 Vice President of Operations .... Mrs. Kathrynne G. SHAFER
84 Vice Pres for Enrollment Management .... Mr. John A. CHOPKA
32 Vice Provost & Dean of Students .... Dr. Kristin M. HANSEN-KIEFFER
27 Assoc Provost/Chief Info Officer .. Dr. William G. STRAUSBAUGH
28 Spec Asst Prov & Pres Div Affairs .... Dr. Bernardo A. MICHAEL
42 College Pastor .... Rev. Eldon E. FRY
57 Dean School of the Arts .... Dr. Richard E. ROBERSON
53 Dean Sch Business/Educ/Social Sci .... Dr. Susan S. HASSELER
79 Dean School of Humanities .... Dr. Peter K. POWERS
81 Dean School of Sci/Engr/Health .... Dr. W. Ray NORMAN
104 Director Intl Programs & EpiCenter .... Mrs. Wendy S. LIPPERT
93 Director of Multicultural Programs .... Ms. Tatiana DIAZ
85 Director Intl Student Programs .... Ms. Dorca KISARE-RESSLER
35 Associate Dean of Students .... Mr. Douglas M. WOOD
07 Director of Admissions .... Mrs. Dana J. BRITTON
37 Director of Financial Aid .... Mr. Gregory L. GEARHART
39 Director of Housing .... Ms. Rhonda L. GOOD
15 Director Human Resources .... Ms. Amanda A. COFFEY
21 Controller/Dir Financial Operations .... Mrs. Wendy S. STARNER
96 Director of Procurement .... Mrs. Danelle L. WATSON
06 Registrar .... Mr. James J. SOTHERDEN
08 Director of the Murray Library .... Mr. Jonathan D. LAUER
91 Director Information Services .... Mr. John P. LUFT
90 Dir Academic Technology Services .... Mrs. Berte THOMPSON
09 Assoc Dir Institutional Research .... Ms. Laura MILLER
30 Director of Development .... Dr. Jon C. STUCKEY
26 Dir of Marketing & Public Relations .... Mrs. Carla E. GROSS
29 Director Alumni & Parent Relations .... Mr. Jay MCCLYMONT
44 Director of Annual Giving .... Mrs. Rachel L. PEASE
38 Director Counseling/Health Services .... Dr. Philip J. LAWLIS
12 Program Dir Philadelphia Campus .... Mr. Ryan R. GLADWIN
41 Interim Director of Athletics .... Mr. Jack COLE
92 Dir of the College Honors Program .... Dr. Dean C. CURRY
18 Director of Facility Services .... Mr. Bradley A. MARKLEY
36 Director of Career Development .... Mrs. Christina R. HANSON
40 Director of Campus Store .... Ms. Mindy W. LANGE
19 Director Safety/Dispatch Services .... Mrs. Cindy L. BURGER
23 Coordinator of Health Services .... Mrs. Judith M. GROOP

Metropolitan Career Center Computer Technology Institute (E)

100 S Broad Street, Suite 830, Philadelphia PA 19110-1018
County: Philadelphia FICE Identification: 031091
Unit ID: 214023
Telephone: (215) 568-9215 Carnegie Class: Assoc/PrivNFP
FAX Number: (215) 568-3511 Calendar System: Semester
URL: www.CareersInIT.org
Established: 1974 Annual Undergrad Tuition & Fees: $23,994
Enrollment: 189 Coed
Affiliation or Control: Independent Non-Profit IRS Status: 501(c)3
Highest Offering: Associate Degree
Program: Occupational; Technical Emphasis
Accreditation: ACCSC

01 President .... Dr. Richard COHEN
03 School Director .... Ms. Amy MILLER
10 Vice President of Finance .... Ms. Deborah OLIVIER
88 Executive Director .... Ms. Linda HAHN
05 Director of Education .... Ms. Josanne FORD
37 Financial Aid Director .... Ms. Madeline SARGENT
13 Director of Information Technology .... Mr. George ECHENHOFER
07 Admissions Representative .... Mr. Samuel JOHNSON
36 Relationship Manager .... Ms. Christina HARRIS

Misericordia University (F)

301 Lake Street, Dallas PA 18612-1098
County: Luzerne FICE Identification: 003247
Unit ID: 214069
Telephone: (570) 674-6400 Carnegie Class: Master's M
FAX Number: (570) 675-2441 Calendar System: Semester
URL: www.misericordia.edu
Established: 1924 Annual Undergrad Tuition & Fees: $12,995
Enrollment: 1,936 Coed
Affiliation or Control: Roman Catholic IRS Status: 501(c)3
Highest Offering: Doctorate
Program: Liberal Arts And General; Teacher Preparatory; Professional
Accreditation: M, DMS, IACBE, NMT, NURSE, OT, PTA, RAD, SP, SW

01 President .... Dr. Michael A. MACDOWELL
10 Vice Pres Finance & Administration .... Mr. John RISBOSKIN
05 Vice President Academic Affairs .... Dr. Mari P. KING
30 VP of Institutional Advancement .... Ms. Susan M. HELWIG
32 Vice President of Student Affairs .... Sr. Jean MESSAROS
45 VP of Planning/Assessment & Rsrch .... Dr. Barbara SAMUEL LOFTUS
45 Chief Information/Planning Officer .... Vacant
21 Controller .... Mr. Ronald S. HROMISIN
06 Registrar .... Mr. Joseph REDINGTON
84 Director Enrollment Management .... Ms. Jane F. DESSOYE
29 Director Alumni Relations .... Ms. Denise MISCAVAGE
08 Librarian .... Ms. Martha STEVENSON
04 Admin Assistant to the President .... Ms. Carol FAHNESTOCK
96 Director of Purchasing .... Mr. Thomas F. KANE
38 Exec Dir Learning Resource Ctr .... Ms. Amy LAHART
42 Co-Director Campus Ministry .... Ms. Christine SOMERS
42 Chaplain/Co-Dir Campus Ministry .... Fr. Donald WILLIAMS
41 Director of Athletics .... Mr. David MARTIN
39 Director of Residents .... Ms. Donna ELLIS
13 Director of Management Info Systems .... Mr. Joseph J. MACK
14 Director of Information Technology .... Mr. Val APANOVICH
35 Director of Student Activities .... Ms. Darcy BRODMERKEL
36 Dir Insalaco Ctr Career Development ... Ms. Bernadette RUSHMER
102 Dir Foundation/Government Relations .... Mr. Larry PELLEGRINI
51 Director of Adult Education .... Vacant
16 Director of Human Resources .... Ms. Pamela PARSNIK
07 Director of Admissions .... Mr. Glenn BOZINSKI
26 Dir of Public Relations/Marketing .... Mr. James ROBERTS
37 Director of Financial Aid .... Ms. Susan FRONZONI
28 Director of Diversity .... Dr. Linda TROMPETTER
19 Director Security/Safety .... Mr. Robert CRAGLE
18 Director of Facilities .... Mr. Paul MURPHY
09 Director of Institutional Research .... Vacant
90 Manager of User Services .... Mr. David A. JOHNDROW

Montgomery County Community College (G)

340 Dekalb Pike, Blue Bell PA 19422-1400
County: Montgomery FICE Identification: 004452
Unit ID: 214111
Telephone: (215) 641-6300 Carnegie Class: Assoc/Pub-S-MC
FAX Number: (215) 641-6647 Calendar System: Semester
URL: www.mc3.edu
Established: 1964 Annual Undergrad Tuition & Fees (In-District): $3,276
Enrollment: 14,796 Coed
Affiliation or Control: State/Local IRS Status: 501(c)3
Highest Offering: Associate Degree
Program: Occupational; 2-Year Principally Bachelor's Creditable
Accreditation: M, ADNUR, DH, IFSAC, MAC, MLTAD, RAD, SURGT

01 President .... Dr. Karen A. STOUT
32 VP Student Affairs .... Dr. Steady MOONO
27 VP for Information Technology .... Ms. Celeste M. SCHWARTZ
10 VP for Finance & Administration .... Mr. Thomas FREITAG
26 Vice Pres of Devel & External Affs .... Ms. Sharon BEALES
84 VP Inst Effective & Enrollment Mgmt .... Dr. Kathrine SWANSON
05 VP for Academic Affairs & Provost .... Dr. Victoria BASTECKI-PEREZ
06 Registrar .... Ms. Cynthia MCCABE
30 Exec Dir of Major & Planned Gifts .... Ms. Debra KHATEEB
15 Executive Director Human Resources .... Ms. Diane O'CONNOR
21 Exec Director of Accounting .... Mr. Michael MANDRACHIA
07 Director of Admissions .... Ms. Penelope SAWYER
08 Director of Library Services .... Ms. Diane LOVELACE
37 Director of Financial Aid .... Ms. Tracey RICHARDS
09 Director of Institutional Research .... Mr. Leon HILL
28 Dir Equity & Diversity Initiatives .... Ms. Rose MAKOFSKE
29 Coordinator of Alumni Relations .... Ms. Lisa ALTOMARE
27 Director Media/Public Relations .... Ms. Alana MAUGER
103 Dean Workforce Development & CE .... Ms. Suzanne HOLLOMAN
100 Chief of Staff .... Ms. Margaret LEE-CLARK

Moore College of Art and Design (H)

20th and The Parkway, Philadelphia PA 19103-1179
County: Philadelphia FICE Identification: 003300
Unit ID: 214148
Telephone: (215) 568-4515 Carnegie Class: Spec/Arts
FAX Number: (215) 568-8017 Calendar System: Semester
URL: www.moore.edu
Established: 1848 Annual Undergrad Tuition & Fees: $31,478
Enrollment: 556 Female
Affiliation or Control: Independent Non-Profit IRS Status: 501(c)3
Highest Offering: Master's
Program: Fine Arts Emphasis
Accreditation: M, ART, CIDA

01 President .... Dr. Happy C. FERNANDEZ
10 Vice Pres Finance & Administration .... Mr. William L. HILL, II
05 Academic Dean .... Ms. Dona LANTZ
32 Dean of Students .... Ms. Ruth ROBBINS
20 Assoc Dean Educational Support Svcs .... Mrs. Claudine R. THOMAS
39 Asst Dean Res Life/Events Mkt Mgr .... Ms. Carienne MYSLINSKI
88 Executive Director of Galleries .... Ms. Kaytie JOHNSON
51 Co-Director of Continuing Education .... Ms. Judith WOODWORTH
51 Co-Director of Continuing Education .... Mrs. Natalie PAYNE
26 Director of Communications .... Ms. Amanda MOTT
30 Director of Development .... Ms. Linda PORCH
29 Director Alumnae Affairs .... Ms. Doris CHORNEY
08 Library Director .... Ms. Sharon WATSON-MAURO
07 Director of Admissions .... Ms. Hesseung LEE
37 Director of Financial Aid .... Ms. Melissa WALSH
06 Registrar .... Ms. Dianne SARIDAKIS
18 Director Facilities/Physical Plant .... Mr. Kenneth FERRETTI
15 Director Human Resources .... Ms. Rachel PHILLIPS
36 Director Career Services .... Ms. Belena CHAPP
58 Director of Graduate Programs .... Mr. Ian VERSTEGEN
90 Academic Computing Manager .... Mr. Dennis DAWTON

Moravian College (I)

1200 Main Street, Bethlehem PA 18018-6650
County: Northampton FICE Identification: 003301
Unit ID: 214157
Telephone: (610) 861-1300 Carnegie Class: Bac/A&S
FAX Number: (610) 625-7918 Calendar System: Semester
URL: www.moravian.edu

Established: 1742　Annual Undergrad Tuition & Fees: $33,446
Enrollment: 2,057　Coed
Affiliation or Control: Moravian Church　IRS Status: 501(c)3
Highest Offering: Master's
Program: Liberal Arts And General; Teacher Preparatory; Professional; Nursing Emphasis
Accreditation: **M**, MUS, NURSE, THEOL

01 President ... Dr. Christopher M. THOMFORDE
04 Assistant to the President ... Ms. Julie DEL GIORNO
05 Vice President Academic Affairs ... Dr. Gordon WEIL
10 Vice President Finance & Admin ... Mr. Dennis A. DOMCHEK
21 Treasurer ... Ms. Anne M. REID
30 Vice Pres Institutional Advancement ... Mr. Gary CARNEY
32 Vice President Student Affairs ... Ms. Beverly KOCHARD
73 Vice Pres/Dean of the Seminary ... Dr. Frank CROUCH
84 Vice President for Enrollment ... Mr. Bernard J. STORY
35 Dean of Students ... Dr. Nicole LOYD
88 Director of Leadership Development ... Ms. Catherine DANTSIN
20 Assoc Dean for Academic Affairs ... Dr. Carol TRAUPMAN-CARR
24 Director of Learning Services ... Ms. Laurie ROTH
88 Director of Event Management ... Mrs. Ann E. CLAUSSEN
21 Dir Business/Financial Operations ... Mr. Mark REED
21 Bursar ... Ms. Susan O'HARE
96 Assoc Director of Business Affairs ... Mr. Brian G. BLENIS
15 Chief Human Resources Officer ... Mr. Jon B. CONRAD
44 Director of Leadership Giving ... Ms. Bertie KNISELY
18 Dir Facilities Mgt Plng/Construct ... Mr. Douglas J. PLOTTS
19 Director of Campus Safety ... Mr. George BOKSAN
26 Director of Public Relations ... Mr. Michael P. WILSON
08 Library Director ... Mr. David SCHAPPERT
06 Registrar ... Mrs. Mary Margaret GROSS
88 Director of Sports Information ... Mr. Mark J. FLEMING
27 Director of Publications ... Mrs. Susan O. WOOLLEY
29 Director of Alumni Relations ... Ms. Marsha STILES
37 Director of Financial Aid ... Ms. Colby MCCARTHY
36 Director Career Development Svcs ... Ms. Amy SAUL
38 Director of Counseling ... Dr. Ronald J. KLINE
58 Dean Continuing/Graduate Studies ... Dr. Donna SMITH
13 Director Information Technology ... Mr. Stephen MCKINNEY
40 Director of Bookstore ... Mrs. Sandra M. GIORDANO
41 Director of Athletics ... Mr. Paul R. MOYER
42 College Chaplain ... Rev. Hopeton C. CLENNON
88 Director of the Payne Gallery ... Dr. Diane C. RADYCKI
88 Director of Constituent Relations ... Ms. Deborah L. EVANS
23 Health Services Coordinator ... Mrs. Mary S. SEK
88 Director of International Studies ... Mr. Kerry SETHI
28 Dir Instl Diversity/Multicul Affs ... Ms. Sharon A. BROWN
24 Media Center Manager ... Mr. Craig UNDERWOOD
09 Director Institutional Research ... Ms. Carole A. REESE

Mount Aloysius College (A)

7373 Admiral Peary Highway, Cresson PA 16630-1999
County: Cambria　FICE Identification: 003302
Unit ID: 214166
Telephone: (814) 886-4131　Carnegie Class: Bac/Assoc
FAX Number: (814) 886-2978　Calendar System: Semester
URL: www.mtaloy.edu
Established: 1853　Annual Undergrad Tuition & Fees: $18,750
Enrollment: 1,611　Coed
Affiliation or Control: Independent Non-Profit　IRS Status: 501(c)3
Highest Offering: Master's
Program: Occupational; 2-Year Principally Bachelor's Creditable; Liberal Arts And General
Accreditation: **M**, ADNUR, DMS, MAC, MLTAD, NUR, PTAA, SURGT

01 President ... Dr. Thomas P. FOLEY, J.D.
05 Sr VP Academic Affs/Dean of Faculty ... Dr. Timothy FULOP
11 Sr VP Administrative Services ... Ms. Suzanne P. CAMPBELL
32 VP Student Affs/Dean Students ... Dr. Jane M. GRASSADONIA
84 VP Enrollment Mgmt/Dean Admissions ... Mr. Francis C. CROUSE, JR.
30 VP Institutional Advancement ... Mr. John H. ANDERSON
10 Controller/CFO ... Ms. Donna K. YODER
06 Registrar ... Mr. Christopher M. LOVETT
08 Director of Library Services ... Ms. Brandi K. PORTER
37 Director of Financial Aid ... Ms. Stacy L. SCHENK
15 Director of Human Resources ... Ms. Tonia J. GORDON
26 Director of Communications ... Vacant
44 Major Gifts Officer ... Mr. Michael A. GREER
13 Director of Information Technology ... Mr. Rich J. SHEA
23 Director of Health Services ... Ms. Shannon D. GROVE
40 Director of Bookstore ... Ms. Christine M. CLINTON
41 Director of Athletics ... Mr. Ryan M. SMITH
19 Director of Safety & Security ... Mr. William H. TREXLER
18 Director of Physical Plant ... Mr. Gerald RUBRITZ
09 Institutional Researcher ... Mr. Bryan J. PEARSON
36 Director Career Services ... Mr. Larry W. BRUGH
38 Dir Student Counseling/Disabilities ... Ms. Marisa L. EVANS
39 Director of Residence Life ... Vacant
42 Director Campus Ministry ... Sr. Nancy E. DONOVAN, RSM
44 Director Annual Giving ... Ms. Cynthia M. HENDERSON

Muhlenberg College (B)

2400 West Chew Street, Allentown PA 18104-5586
County: Lehigh　FICE Identification: 003304
Unit ID: 214175
Telephone: (484) 664-3100　Carnegie Class: Bac/A&S
FAX Number: (484) 664-3234　Calendar System: Semester
URL: www.muhlenberg.edu
Established: 1848　Annual Undergrad Tuition & Fees: $39,915
Enrollment: 2,209　Coed
Affiliation or Control: Evangelical Lutheran Church In America　IRS Status: 501(c)3
Highest Offering: Baccalaureate
Program: Liberal Arts And General; Teacher Preparatory
Accreditation: **M**

01 President ... Dr. Peyton R. HELM
05 Provost ... Dr. John G. RAMSAY
10 Treasurer & Vice Pres for Finance ... Mr. Kent DYER
26 Vice President of Public Relations ... Mr. Michael S. BRUCKNER
30 VP Development & Alumni Relations ... Ms. Rebekkah L. BROWN
15 Vice President of Human Resources ... Ms. Anne SPECK
04 Exec Assistant to the President ... Mr. Ken BUTLER
102 Asst VP Corporate/Found & Govt Rels ... Ms. Deborah J. KIPP
32 Dean of Students ... Ms. Karen GREEN
88 Dean of College for Academic Life ... Dr. Carol SHINER WILSON
20 Assoc Dean Institutional Assessment ... Dr. Kathleen E. HARRING
86 Assoc Dean International Programs ... Dr. Donna M. KISH-GOODLING
37 Associate Dean Financial Aid ... Mr. Gregory S. MITTON
88 Assistant Dean of Academic Life ... Ms. Wendy P. COLE
29 Alumni Relations Director ... Ms. Jenny MCLARIN
55 Dean Wescoe Sch Muhlenberg College ... Ms. Jane E. HUDAK
07 Dean Admissions/Financial Aid ... Mr. Christopher HOOKER-HARING
08 Director of Trexler Library ... Vacant
06 Registrar ... Ms. Deborah TAMTE-HORAN
13 Director Information Technology ... Mr. Harry E. MILLER
19 Director of Campus Safety/Security ... Mr. Tom P. DOUGHERTY
39 Director of Residence Life ... Ms. Janette SCHUMACHER
36 Director of the Career Center ... Ms. Cailin M. PACHTER
21 Assistant Treasurer ... Mr. Jason FEIERTAG
23 Director of Student Health Services ... Ms. Brynnmarie DORSEY
38 Director Counseling Services ... Ms. Anita KELLY
42 Chaplain ... Rev. Peter S. BREDLAU
09 Director of Institutional Research ... Ms. Nicole HAMMEL
18 Chief Facilities/Physical Plant ... Mr. Michael H. BREWER
96 Director of Purchasing ... Ms. Elizabeth M. LEES
40 Bookstore Manager ... Ms. Karen R. DELARCO

Neumann University (C)

One Neumann Drive, Aston PA 19014-1298
County: Delaware　FICE Identification: 003988
Unit ID: 214272
Telephone: (610) 459-0905　Carnegie Class: Master's M
FAX Number: (610) 459-1370　Calendar System: Semester
URL: www.neumann.edu
Established: 1965　Annual Undergrad Tuition & Fees: $23,350
Enrollment: 3,073　Coed
Affiliation or Control: Roman Catholic　IRS Status: 501(c)3
Highest Offering: Doctorate
Program: Liberal Arts And General; Teacher Preparatory; Professional
Accreditation: **M**, ACBSP, CACREP, MT, NUR, PTA

01 President ... Dr. Rosalie M. MIRENDA
05 Vice President Academic Affairs ... Dr. Gerard P. O'SULLIVAN
43 Vice President and General Counsel ... Mr. Jonathan PERI
10 Vice Pres Finance/Administration ... Mr. Joseph GORMAN
42 Vice President Mission/Ministry ... Sr. Marguerite O'BEIRNE, OSF
30 Vice Pres Inst Advance/Univ Rels ... Mr. Henry A. SUMNER
84 Vice Pres Enrollment/Student Affs ... Mr. Dennis J. MURPHY
15 Vice President Human Resources ... Mr. David W. BROWNLEE
49 Dean Division of Arts & Science ... Dr. Mac GIVEN
50 Dean Div of Business & Info Mgmt ... Ms. Janet MASSEY
53 Dean Div of Education/Human Svcs ... Dr. Joseph E. GILLESPIE
51 Dean Div Cont Adult/Prof Studies ... Dr. Patricia SZYMURSKI
66 Dean Div Nursing/Health Sciences ... Dr. Kathleen HOOVER
04 Assistant to President ... Ms. Danielle WAGNER
06 Registrar ... Mr. Larry S. FRIEDMAN
18 Facilities Director ... Mr. Earl WORSHAM
19 Director Safety & Security ... Mr. Leon FRANCIS
08 Director Library ... Mr. John Michael POWELL
26 Exec Director Mktg/Communications ... Mr. Stephen BELL
09 Director Inst Research/Planning ... Dr. Ayshe ERGIN
88 Coord Graduate Pastoral Counseling ... Mr. Len DI PAUL
42 Chaplain ... Rev. Jude Michael KRILL, OFM
44 Director Annual Giving/Prospect Mgt ... Ms. Christina FARRELL
29 Dir Alumni Rels/Special Programs ... Ms. Judith STANAITIS
88 Director Inst Gifts/Donor Rels ... Ms. Josephina E. BANNER
38 Director Counseling ... Mr. Michael D'ANGELO
39 Director Residence Life ... Mr. Michael WEBSTER
13 Director University Computing ... Mr. David O'LEARY
24 Director Academic Resource Center ... Ms. Theresa HUKE
41 Director Athletics ... Mr. Chuck SACK
36 Director Career Services ... Mrs. Carol A. DOUGHERTY
32 Director of Academic Advising ... Mr. Michael MULLEN
88 Director Child Development Center ... Ms. Mary Ann MELISI
21 Controller ... Mr. John YOUHOUSE
37 Director Financial Assistance ... Ms. Deborah CRAWLEY
23 Director Health Services ... Ms. Janet GEDDIS
96 Director of Purchasing ... Ms. Elena BARRAR
88 Director Physical Therapy Program ... Dr. Robert POST
88 Coord Sport Management Program ... Dr. Sandra SLABIK
07 Director of Admissions ... Ms. Christina CERENZIA
88 Dir Cntr for Sport/Spir/Char Devel ... Dr. Edward T. HASTINGS

New Castle School of Trades (D)

4164 US 422, Pulaski PA 16143-2522
County: Lawrence　FICE Identification: 007780
Unit ID: 214290
Telephone: (724) 964-8811　Carnegie Class: Assoc/PrivFP
FAX Number: (724) 964-8177　Calendar System: Other
URL: www.ncstrades.com
Established: 1945　Annual Undergrad Tuition & Fees: $15,595
Enrollment: 672　Coed
Affiliation or Control: Proprietary　IRS Status: Proprietary
Highest Offering: Associate Degree
Program: Occupational; 2-Year Principally Bachelor's Creditable; Technical Emphasis
Accreditation: ACCSC

01 Director ... Mr. Jim W. BUTTERMORE
05 Director of Education ... Mr. Tony GIOVANNELLI
07 Director Admiss/Veterans Affs Ofcr ... Mr. Jim CATHELINE
10 Fiscal Director ... Mrs. JoAnn MELNIK
36 Director Student Placement ... Ms. Carrie KRAYNAK
37 Director Student Financial Aid ... Miss Trudy SOTTER

Newport Business Institute (E)

945 Greensburg Road, Lower Burrell PA 15068-3929
County: Westmoreland　FICE Identification: 004901
Unit ID: 214315
Telephone: (724) 339-7542　Carnegie Class: Assoc/PrivFP
FAX Number: (724) 339-2950　Calendar System: Quarter
URL: www.nbi.edu
Established: 1895　Annual Undergrad Tuition & Fees: $10,600
Enrollment: 80　Coed
Affiliation or Control: Proprietary　IRS Status: Proprietary
Highest Offering: Associate Degree
Program: Occupational
Accreditation: ACICS

01 Director ... Mr. Ray WROBLEWSKI
05 Dean of Academic Affairs ... Mr. Michael CHOMA
58 Director of Graduate Services ... Mrs. Nancy DONATUCCI
37 Director of Financial Aid ... Mrs. Rosemary LEIPERTZ
07 Admissions Coordinator ... Mr. Don ACKER

Newport Business Institute (F)

941 W Third Street, Williamsport PA 17701-5855
County: Lycoming　FICE Identification: 004914
Unit ID: 216986
Telephone: (570) 326-2869　Carnegie Class: Assoc/PrivFP
FAX Number: (570) 326-2136　Calendar System: Quarter
URL: www.nbi.edu
Established: 1955　Annual Undergrad Tuition & Fees: $12,075
Enrollment: 111　Coed
Affiliation or Control: Proprietary　IRS Status: Proprietary
Highest Offering: Associate Degree
Program: Occupational
Accreditation: ACICS

01 Director ... Ms. Mary O. WEAVER

Northampton Community College (G)

3835 Green Pond Road, Bethlehem PA 18020-7599
County: Northampton　FICE Identification: 007191
Unit ID: 214379
Telephone: (610) 861-5300　Carnegie Class: Assoc/Pub-S-MC
FAX Number: (610) 861-5070　Calendar System: Semester
URL: www.northampton.edu
Established: 1966　Annual Undergrad Tuition & Fees (In-District): $3,420
Enrollment: 11,328　Coed
Affiliation or Control: State/Local　IRS Status: 170(c)1
Highest Offering: Associate Degree
Program: Occupational; 2-Year Principally Bachelor's Creditable
Accreditation: **M**, ACBSP, ADNUR, DH, DMS, FUSER, PNUR, RAD, SURGT

01 President ... Dr. Arthur L. SCOTT
05 Vice President Academic Affairs ... Dr. Jeffrey W. FOCHT
11 Vice Pres Administrative Affairs ... Ms. Helene M. WHITAKER
10 Vice President Finance & Operations ... Mr. James F. DUNLEAVY
30 Vice Pres Institutional Advancement ... Ms. Susan K. KUBIK
32 Vice President Student Affairs ... Ms. Margaret MCGUIRE-CLOSSON
31 Vice President Community Education ... Dr. Paul E. PIERPOINT
12 Dean Monroe Campus ... Dr. Matthew J. CONNELL
79 Dean Humanities & Social Sciences ... Dr. Christine PENSE
53 Dean Education/Academic Success ... Dr. Elizabeth BUGAIGHIS
50 Interim Dean Business & Technology ... Ms. Denise FRANCOIS-SEENY
76 Dean Allied Health & Sciences ... Ms. Carolyn BORTZ
13 Chief Technology Ofcr/Computer Svcs ... Ms. Donna POSIVAK
27 Director Public Info/Community Rels ... Ms. Heidi BUTLER
06 Registrar ... Ms. Carolyn H. MOYER
07 Director Admissions ... Mr. James MCCARTHY
37 Director Financial Aid ... Ms. Cynthia L. KING
45 Dir Plng/Assessment/Instl Effective ... Dr. E. Jill HIRT
15 Director of Human Resources ... Ms. Kathy SIEGFRIED
09 Director of Institutional Research ... Ms. Kathy KAPCSOS
18 Director Buildings & Grounds ... Mr. Mark K. CULP
29 Director Alumni Relations ... Ms. Melissa STARACE
36 Director Career Services ... Ms. Karen VERES
38 Director Counseling & Support Svcs ... Ms. Carolyn M. BRADY
96 Director of Purchasing ... Vacant

Oakbridge Academy of Arts (H)

1250 Greensburg Road, Lower Burrell PA 15068-3843
County: Westmoreland　FICE Identification: 021535
Unit ID: 376039
Telephone: (724) 335-5336　Carnegie Class: Assoc/PrivFP
FAX Number: (724) 335-3367　Calendar System: Quarter

URL: www.oaa.edu
Established: 1972 Annual Undergrad Tuition & Fees: $15,300
Enrollment: 55 Coed
Affiliation or Control: Proprietary IRS Status: Proprietary
Highest Offering: Associate Degree
Program: 2-Year Principally Bachelor's Creditable; Fine Arts Emphasis
Accreditation: ACCSC

01 Director ... Ms. Janie GATTY
07 Admissions Coordinator ... Mr. Matthew BELFERMAN
06 Registrar ... Ms. Debra WELLS

Orleans Technical Institute (A)

2770 Red Lion Road, Philadelphia PA 19114-1014
County: Philadelphia FICE Identification: 021830
Unit ID: 214528
Telephone: (215) 728-4700 Carnegie Class: Assoc/PrivNFP
FAX Number: (215) 854-1880 Calendar System: Semester
URL: www.orleanstech.edu
Established: 1986 Annual Undergrad Tuition & Fees: $10,180
Enrollment: 677 Coed
Affiliation or Control: Independent Non-Profit IRS Status: Exempt
Highest Offering: Associate Degree
Program: Occupational
Accreditation: ACCSC

01 Campus Director ... Ms. Jayne SINIARI
88 Director Court Reporting Program ... Ms. Carol CRAWFORD

Pace Institute (B)

606 Court Street, Reading PA 19601-3542
County: Berks FICE Identification: 022895
Unit ID: 214838
Telephone: (610) 375-1212 Carnegie Class: Assoc/PrivFP
FAX Number: (610) 375-1924 Calendar System: Semester
URL: www.paceinstitute.com
Established: 1980 Annual Undergrad Tuition & Fees: $7,008
Enrollment: 259 Coed
Affiliation or Control: Proprietary IRS Status: Proprietary
Highest Offering: Associate Degree
Program: Occupational
Accreditation: ACICS

01 President ... Ms. Rhoda E. DERSH
05 School Director ... Ms. Christine WULLERT

Palmer Theological Seminary of Eastern University (C)

6 Lancaster Avenue, Wynnewood PA 19096-3430
County: Montgomery FICE Identification: 003260
Unit ID: 212124
Telephone: (610) 896-5000 Carnegie Class: Not Classified
FAX Number: (610) 649-3834 Calendar System: 4/1/4
URL: www.palmerseminary.edu
Established: 1925 Annual Graduate Tuition & Fees: $24,015
Enrollment: 438 Coed
Affiliation or Control: American Baptist IRS Status: 501(c)3
Highest Offering: Doctorate; No Undergraduates
Program: Professional
Accreditation: THEOL

01 President ... Rev Dr. Wallace Charles SMITH
05 Vice Pres Academic Affairs & Dean ... Dr. Elouise RENICH FRASER
10 Vice President and COO ... Mr. Anup KAPUR
04 President's Assistant ... Ms. Ruth E. MCFARLAND
20 Associate Dean ... Dr. Colleen DIRADDO
15 Director of Human Resources ... Ms. Kacey BERNARD
30 Director of Development ... Ms. Mary GARDNER
42 Dir Stdnt Form/Seminary Chaplain ... Rev. Willette A. BURGIE-BRYANT
88 Director D Min Marriage & Family ... Dr. Peter SCHRECK
08 Library Director ... Ms. Melody MAZUK
09 Director of Institutional Research ... Dr. Thomas DAHLSTROM
06 Associate Registrar ... Mr. Craig MILLER
07 Director Admissions ... Dr. Stephen S. HUTCHISON
26 Exec Dir Marketing & Communications ... Mr. Randall L. FRAME
18 Manager Plant Operations ... Mr. Carmen ANUZZI
24 Educational Technologist ... Ms. Masego KEBAETSE

† Affiliated with Eastern University, Saint Davids, PA.

Peirce College (D)

1420 Pine Street, Philadelphia PA 19102-4699
County: Philadelphia FICE Identification: 003309
Unit ID: 214883
Telephone: (215) 545-6400 Carnegie Class: Bac/Diverse
FAX Number: (215) 670-9366 Calendar System: Semester
URL: www.peirce.edu
Established: 1865 Annual Undergrad Tuition & Fees: $15,900
Enrollment: 2,139 Coed
Affiliation or Control: Independent Non-Profit IRS Status: 501(c)3
Highest Offering: Baccalaureate
Program: Occupational; Business Emphasis
Accreditation: M, ACBSP

01 President & CEO ... Mr. James J. MERGIOTTI
05 Senior VP Acad Advancement/Provost ... Dr. Patricia A. RUCKER
10 Senior VP Finance & Administration ... Mr. James M. VITALE
13 Chief Information Officer ... Mr. Christopher L. DUFFY
32 Dean of Students ... Dr. Rita J. TOLIVER-ROBERTS
26 Asst VP Marketing/Communication ... Ms. Lisa PARIS
18 Chief Auxiliary Services Officer ... Mr. Vito R. CHIMENTI
16 Asst VP Human Resources ... Ms. Harriet S. GOLEN
20 Associate Dean Academic Operations ... Mr. Jon LENROW
84 Dean Enrollment Management ... Ms. Nadine M. MAHER
37 Chief Business & Financial Svc Ofcr ... Mr. Brad K. HODGE
09 Dean Academic Programs & Research ... Ms. Debra S. SCHRAMMEL
21 Controller ... Ms. Karen M. BRIGGS
88 Program Manager Inst Support ... Ms. Amy A. CALIENDO

Penn Commercial Business/ Technical School (E)

242 Oak Spring Road, Washington PA 15301-6822
County: Washington FICE Identification: 004902
Unit ID: 214892
Telephone: (724) 222-5330 Carnegie Class: Assoc/PrivFP
FAX Number: (724) 222-4722 Calendar System: Quarter
URL: www.penncommercial.edu
Established: 1929 Annual Undergrad Tuition & Fees: $19,000
Enrollment: 450 Coed
Affiliation or Control: Proprietary IRS Status: Proprietary
Highest Offering: Associate Degree
Program: Occupational; Technical Emphasis
Accreditation: ACICS, MAC

01 Director ... Mr. Robert S. BAZANT
11 Vice President of Operations ... Ms. Marianne ALBERT
04 Assistant to the President ... Ms. Jennifer POLAND
84 VP of Marketing & Enrollment ... Mr. Michael JOYCE
32 Director of Student Affairs ... Ms. Betty SHINGLE
37 Director of Financial Aid ... Ms. Jenny SLESH
88 Director of Education ... Ms. Nicole LANE
05 Director of Academic Affairs ... Ms. Sandy PHILLIPS
09 Dir of Reports & Statistics ... Mrs. Melissa PAPSON
88 Dir of Student Support Services ... Mr. Larry BEVAN
36 Dir of Career Services ... Mrs. Kristin WISSINGER

Penn State University Park (F)

201 Old Main, University Park PA 16802-1503
County: Centre FICE Identification: 003329
Unit ID: 214777
Telephone: (814) 865-4700 Carnegie Class: RU/VH
FAX Number: N/A Calendar System: Semester
URL: www.psu.edu
Established: 1855 Annual Undergrad Tuition & Fees (In-State): $15,984
Enrollment: 43,998 Coed
Affiliation or Control: State Related IRS Status: 501(c)3
Highest Offering: Doctorate
Program: 2-Year Principally Bachelor's Creditable; Liberal Arts And General; Teacher Preparatory; Professional
Accreditation: M, ADNUR, ART, BUS, BUSA, CACREP, CEA, CLPSY, COPSY, CORE, DIETD, DIETI, DIETT, ENG, FOR, HSA, IPSY, JOUR, LSAR, MUS, NUR, NURSE, SCPSY, SP, TED, THEA

01 President ... Dr. Graham B. SPANIER
46 Vice Pres Research/Dean Grad School ... Dr. Henry FOLEY
32 Vice President Student Affairs ... Dr. Damon SIMS
26 Vice President University Relations ... Mr. William M. MAHON, III
30 Sr Vice Pres Devel/Alumni Relations ... Mr. Rodney P. KIRSCH
10 Sr VP Finance & Business/Treas ... Mr. Albert G. HORVATH
31 Vice President Outreach ... Dr. Craig D. WEIDEMANN
11 VP for Administration ... Dr. Thomas G. POOLE
104 Vice Provost for Global Programs ... Dr. Michael A. ADEWUMI
43 Vice President & General Counsel ... Ms. Cynthia A. BALDWIN
05 University Provost ... Dr. Rodney A. ERICKSON
49 Vice Pres & Dean Undergrad Educ ... Dr. Robert N. PANGBORN
20 Vice Provost Academic Affairs ... Dr. Blannie E. BOWEN
28 Vice Provost Educational Equity ... Dr. W. Terrell JONES
12 Vice Pres Commonwealth Campuses ... Dr. Madlyn HANES
03 Executive Vice President ... Dr. Rodney A. ERICKSON
13 Vice Provost Information Tech ... Mr. Kevin M. MOROONEY
09 Exec Dir Ofc Plng/Inst Assessment ... Ms. Louise E. SANDMEYER
22 Vice Provost for Affirmative Action ... Dr. Kenneth F. LEHRMAN, III
45 University Budget Officer ... Mr. Stephen R. CURLEY
21 Corporate Controller ... Mr. Joseph J. DONCSECZ
21 Assoc VP Finance/Business Comm Oper ... Mr. Daniel W. SIEMINSKI
16 Assoc Vice Pres Human Resources ... Dr. Susan BASSO
18 Assoc Vice Pres Physical Plant ... Mr. H. Ford STRYKER
21 Assoc Vice Pres Aux & Business Svcs ... Ms. Gail A. HURLEY
51 Associate Vice President Outreach ... Mr. Wayne D. SMUTZ
27 Director of Public Information ... Ms. Lisa M. POWERS
39 Asst Vice President HFS & Res Life ... Dr. Stanley LATTA
37 Exec Director for Student Aid ... Ms. Anna M. GRISWOLD
29 Exec Director Alumni Association ... Mr. Roger L. WILLIAMS
21 Exec Director Investment Management ... Mr. David BRANIGAN
07 Exec Dir of Undergrad Admissions ... Ms. Anne L. ROHRBACH
38 Sr Director Counseling/Psych Svcs ... Dr. Dennis E. HEITZMANN
41 Director Intercollegiate Athletics ... Mr. Timothy M. CURLEY
86 Special Asst for Government Affairs ... Dr. Richard D. DIEUGENIO
06 University Registrar ... Ms. Karen L. SCHULTZ
36 Sr Director Career Services ... Dr. Jack R. RAYMAN
17 Sr VP for Health Affairs & Dean ... Dr. Harold L. PAZ
08 Dean of Univ Libraries/Scholar Comm ... Ms. Barbara I. DEWEY
47 Dean of Agricultural Sciences ... Dr. Bruce A. MCPHERON
48 Dean Arts & Architecture ... Dr. Barbara O. KORNER
50 Dean Business ... Dr. James B. THOMAS
60 Dean of Communications ... Dr. Douglas A. ANDERSON
65 Dean Earth & Mineral Sciences .. Dr. William E. EASTERLING, III
53 Dean of Education ... Dr. David H. MONK
54 Dean of Engineering ... Dr. David N. WORMLEY
58 Dean of the Graduate School ... Dr. Henry FOLEY
76 Dean Health & Human Development ... Dr. Ann C. CROUTER
66 Director School of Nursing ... Dr. Paula F. MILONE-NUZZO
56 Assoc Dean Cooperative Extension ... Dr. Dennis D. CALVIN
83 Dean of Liberal Arts ... Dr. Susan WELCH
81 Dean of Science ... Dr. Daniel J. LARSON
72 Dean Info Sciences/Technology ... Dr. David L. HALL
92 Dean of Honors College ... Dr. Christian BRADY
61 Dean School of Law ... Mr. Philip MCCONNAUGHAY
63 Dean College of Medicine ... Dr. Harold L. PAZ
75 Chief College of Technology ... Dr. Davie J. GILMOUR
44 Director of Annual Giving ... Mr. Howard HEEVNER
25 Sr Assoc Dir Sponsored Programs ... Dr. John W. HANOLD
19 Director University Police ... Mr. Stephen G. SHELOW
23 Dir University Health Services ... Dr. Margaret E. SPEAR
96 Director of Procurement Services ... Ms. Joyce A. HANEY
31 Director Campus & Comm Affairs ... Ms. Barbara ETTARO
102 Director Corporate/Foundation Rels ... Ms. Shelley BIRDSONG-MADDEX
04 Exec Admin Asst to President ... Mrs. Carmella MULROY-DEGENHART
40 General Manager Bookstore ... Mr. Steve J. FALKE
25 Contract Coordinator ... Mr. Richel PERRETTI
15 Director Human Resources ... Mr. Robert L. MANEY
21 Director of Internal Audit ... Mr. Daniel P. HEIST

† The legal name of Penn State and all its campuses is The Pennsylvania State University. For communication purposes, the name is shortened to Penn State followed by the name of the campus.

Penn State Abington (G)

1600 Woodland Road, Abington PA 19001-3900
County: Montgomery FICE Identification: 003342
Unit ID: 214801
Telephone: (215) 881-7300 Carnegie Class: Bac/A&S
FAX Number: (215) 881-7412 Calendar System: Semester
URL: www.abington.psu.edu
Established: 1950 Annual Undergrad Tuition & Fees (In-State): $13,102
Enrollment: 3,476 Coed
Affiliation or Control: State Related IRS Status: 501(c)3
Highest Offering: Baccalaureate
Program: Occupational; 2-Year Principally Bachelor's Creditable; Liberal Arts And General; Teacher Preparatory
Accreditation: &M

01 Chancellor ... Dr. Karen WILEY SANDLER
05 Academic Affairs ... Dr. Samir OUZOMGI
32 Student Affairs ... Ms. Gale J. SIEGEL
06 Registrar ... Ms. Joan M. RAUDENBUSH
30 Development/Alumni Relations ... Ms. Victoria BLEVINS

† Regional accreditation is carried under the parent institution in University Park, PA.

Penn State Altoona (H)

3000 Ivyside Park, Altoona PA 16601-3777
County: Blair FICE Identification: 003331
Unit ID: 214689
Telephone: (814) 949-5000 Carnegie Class: Bac/Diverse
FAX Number: (814) 949-5011 Calendar System: Semester
URL: www.aa.psu.edu
Established: 1929 Annual Undergrad Tuition & Fees (In-State): $13,636
Enrollment: 4,147 Coed
Affiliation or Control: State Related IRS Status: 501(c)3
Highest Offering: Baccalaureate
Program: Occupational; 2-Year Principally Bachelor's Creditable; Liberal Arts And General; Teacher Preparatory
Accreditation: &M, ENGT

01 Chancellor ... Dr. Lori J. BECHTEL-WHERRY
05 Academic Affairs ... Dr. Kenneth A. WOMACK
32 Student Affairs ... Mr. Sean C. KELLY
06 Registrar ... Ms. Margaret B. MC NULTY
30 Development/Alumni Relations ... Ms. N. Susan WOODRING

† Regional accreditation is carried under the parent institution in University Park, PA.

Penn State Beaver (I)

100 University Drive, Monaca PA 15061-2799
County: Beaver FICE Identification: 003332
Unit ID: 214698
Telephone: (724) 773-3800 Carnegie Class: Bac/A&S
FAX Number: (724) 773-3557 Calendar System: Semester
URL: www.br.psu.edu
Established: 1964 Annual Undergrad Tuition & Fees (In-State): $13,102
Enrollment: 906 Coed
Affiliation or Control: State Related IRS Status: 501(c)3
Highest Offering: Baccalaureate
Program: Occupational; 2-Year Principally Bachelor's Creditable; Liberal Arts And General
Accreditation: &M

01 Chancellor ... Dr. Gary B. KEEFER
05 Academic Affairs ... Dr. Donna J. KUGA
32 Student Affairs ... Dr. Christopher RIZZO
06 Registrar ... Ms. Gloria S. DESCHLER
30 Development/Allumni Relations ... Ms. Diana L. PATTERSON

† Regional accreditation is carried under the parent institution in University Park, PA.

Penn State Berks (A)

Tulpehocken Road, PO Box 7009, Reading PA 19610-6009
County: Berks FICE Identification: 003334
Unit ID: 214704
Telephone: (610) 396-6000 Carnegie Class: Bac/Diverse
FAX Number: (610) 396-6024 Calendar System: Semester
URL: www.bk.psu.edu
Established: 1924 Annual Undergrad Tuition & Fees (In-State): $13,636
Enrollment: 2,771 Coed
Affiliation or Control: State Related IRS Status: 501(c)3
Highest Offering: Baccalaureate
Program: Occupational; 2-Year Principally Bachelor's Creditable; Liberal Arts And General; Teacher Preparatory
Accreditation: &M, ENGT, OTA

01 Chancellor ... Dr. Susan P. SPEECE
05 Academic Affairs ... Dr. Paul ESQUEDA
32 Student Affairs ... Dr. Blaine E. STEENSLAND
06 Registrar ... Dr. David BENDER
30 Director of Development/Alumni ... Mr. David DELOZIER

† Regional accreditation is carried under the parent institution in University Park, PA.

Penn State Brandywine (B)

25 Yearsley Mill Road, Media PA 19063-5596
County: Delaware FICE Identification: 006922
Unit ID: 214731
Telephone: (610) 892-1350 Carnegie Class: Bac/Diverse
FAX Number: (610) 892-1357 Calendar System: Semester
URL: www.de.psu.edu
Established: 1966 Annual Undergrad Tuition & Fees (In-State): $13,102
Enrollment: 1,613 Coed
Affiliation or Control: State Related IRS Status: 501(c)3
Highest Offering: Baccalaureate
Program: Occupational; 2-Year Principally Bachelor's Creditable; Liberal Arts And General; Teacher Preparatory
Accreditation: &M

01 Chancellor ... Dr. Sophia T. WISNIEWSKA
05 Academic Affairs ... Dr. Paul J. DEGATEGNO
32 Student Affairs ... Mr. Matthew R. SHUPP
06 Registrar ... Ms. Joanna MCGOWAN
30 Development/Alumni Relations ... Ms. Michelle C. JOHNSON

† Regional accreditation is carried under the parent institution in University Park, PA.

The Penn State Dickinson School of Law (C)

150 S College Street, Carlisle PA 17013-2861
County: Cumberland FICE Identification: 003254
Unit ID: 212018
Telephone: (717) 240-5000 Carnegie Class: Spec/Law
FAX Number: (717) 243-4443 Calendar System: Semester
URL: www.dsl.psu.edu
Established: 1834 Annual Graduate Tuition & Fees: $38,234
Enrollment: 630 Coed
Affiliation or Control: State Related IRS Status: 501(c)3
Highest Offering: First Professional Degree; No Undergraduates
Program: Professional
Accreditation: &M, LAW

01 Dean ... Mr. Philip J. MCCONNAUGHAY
05 Academic Affairs ... Ms. Marie T. REILLY
06 Registrar ... Ms. Shari L. WELCH
32 Student Affairs ... Ms. Holly A. PARRISH
30 Development/Alumni Relations ... Ms. Kelly R. RIMMER

† Regional accreditation is carried under the parent institution in University Park, PA.

Penn State DuBois (D)

One College Place, DuBois PA 15801-3199
County: Clearfield FICE Identification: 003335
Unit ID: 214740
Telephone: (814) 375-4700 Carnegie Class: Bac/Assoc
FAX Number: (814) 375-4784 Calendar System: Semester
URL: www.ds.psu.edu
Established: 1935 Annual Undergrad Tuition & Fees (In-State): $12,994
Enrollment: 919 Coed
Affiliation or Control: State Related IRS Status: 501(c)3
Highest Offering: Baccalaureate
Program: Occupational; 2-Year Principally Bachelor's Creditable; Liberal Arts And General
Accreditation: &M, ENGT, OTA, #PTAA

01 Chancellor ... Dr. Anita D. MCDONALD
05 Academic Affairs ... Dr. Debra L. STRAUSSFOGEL
32 Student Affairs ... Ms. Rebecca A. PENNINGTON
06 Registrar ... Ms. Jeanne HUNTER
30 Development/Alumni Relations ... Ms. Jean A. WOLF

† Regional accreditation is carried under the parent institution in University Park, PA.

Penn State Erie, The Behrend College (E)

5091 Station Road, Erie PA 16563-0001
County: Erie FICE Identification: 003333
Unit ID: 214591
Telephone: (814) 898-6000 Carnegie Class: Master's S
FAX Number: (814) 898-6461 Calendar System: Semester
URL: www.pserie.psu.edu
Established: 1926 Annual Undergrad Tuition & Fees (In-State): $13,636
Enrollment: 4,359 Coed
Affiliation or Control: State Related IRS Status: 501(c)3
Highest Offering: Master's
Program: Occupational; 2-Year Principally Bachelor's Creditable; Liberal Arts And General
Accreditation: &M, BUS, ENG, ENGT

01 Chancellor ... Dr. Donald L. BIRX
05 Academic Affairs ... Dr. David J. CHRISTIANSEN
32 Student Affairs ... Dr. Kenneth P. MILLER
06 Registrar ... Dr. Mary Ellen BAYUK
30 Development/Alumni Relations ... Ms. Margaret TAYLOR

† Regional accreditation is carried under the parent institution in University Park, PA.

Penn State Fayette, The Eberly Campus (F)

PO BOX 519, Rt 119 N, One Univ Dr, Uniontown PA 15401-0519
County: Fayette FICE Identification: 003336
Unit ID: 214759
Telephone: (724) 430-4100 Carnegie Class: Bac/Assoc
FAX Number: (724) 430-4184 Calendar System: Semester
URL: www.fe.psu.edu
Established: 1934 Annual Undergrad Tuition & Fees (In-State): $13,040
Enrollment: 1,037 Coed
Affiliation or Control: State Related IRS Status: 501(c)3
Highest Offering: Baccalaureate
Program: Occupational; 2-Year Principally Bachelor's Creditable; Liberal Arts And General
Accreditation: &M, ENGT, @PTAA

01 Chancellor ... Dr. Francis K. ACHAMPONG
05 Academic Affairs ... Dr. Delia B. CONTI
32 Student Affairs ... Mr. Brian D. FERNANDES
06 Registrar ... Ms. Germaine M. FOTTA
30 Development/Alumni Relations ... Ms. Lori A. OMATICK

† Regional accreditation is carried under the parent institution in University Park, PA.

Penn State Great Valley School of Graduate Professional Studies (G)

30 E Swedesford Road, Malvern PA 19355-1488
County: Chester FICE Identification: 003348
Unit ID: 214607
Telephone: (610) 648-3200 Carnegie Class: Master's L
FAX Number: (610) 889-1334 Calendar System: Semester
URL: www.gv.psu.edu
Established: 1963 Annual Graduate Tuition & Fees: $21,522
Enrollment: 795 Coed
Affiliation or Control: State Related IRS Status: 501(c)3
Highest Offering: Master's; No Undergraduates
Program: Professional
Accreditation: &M, BUS

01 Chancellor ... Dr. Craig S. EDELBROCK
05 Academic Affairs ... Vacant
32 Student Affairs ... Vacant
29 Development/Alumni Relations ... Ms. Suzanne CRUIT
06 Registrar ... Ms. Carla A. HOLWAY

† Regional accreditation is carried under the parent institution in University Park, PA.

Penn State Greater Allegheny (H)

4000 University Drive, McKeesport PA 15132-7698
County: Allegheny FICE Identification: 003339
Unit ID: 214786
Telephone: (412) 675-9000 Carnegie Class: Bac/A&S
FAX Number: (412) 675-9043 Calendar System: Semester
URL: www.mk.psu.edu
Established: 1947 Annual Undergrad Tuition & Fees (In-State): $13,102
Enrollment: 768 Coed
Affiliation or Control: State Related IRS Status: 501(c)3
Highest Offering: Baccalaureate
Program: Occupational; 2-Year Principally Bachelor's Creditable; Liberal Arts And General
Accreditation: &M

01 Chancellor ... Dr. Curtiss E. PORTER
05 Academic Affairs ... Dr. Kurt C. TORELL
06 Registrar ... Ms. Victoria GARWOOD
30 Development/Alumni Relations ... Mr. Anthony B. HOLTZ
32 Student Affairs ... Mr. Glenn J. BEECH

† Regional accreditation is carried under the parent institution in University Park, PA.

Penn State Harrisburg (I)

777 W Harrisburg Pike, Middletown PA 17057-4898
County: Dauphin FICE Identification: 006814
Unit ID: 214713
Telephone: (717) 948-6452 Carnegie Class: Master's L
FAX Number: (717) 948-6008 Calendar System: Semester
URL: www.hbg.psu.edu
Established: 1966 Annual Undergrad Tuition & Fees (In-State): $13,628
Enrollment: 4,224 Coed
Affiliation or Control: State Related IRS Status: 501(c)3
Highest Offering: Doctorate
Program: Occupational; 2-Year Principally Bachelor's Creditable; Liberal Arts And General; Teacher Preparatory
Accreditation: &M, BUS, ENG, ENGT, SPAA, TED

01 Chancellor ... Dr. Mukund S. KULKARNI
05 Academic Affairs ... Dr. Omid ANSARY
32 Student Affairs ... Ms. Felicia L. BROWN-HAYWOOD
30 Development/Alumni Relations ... Ms. Marissa HOOVER
06 Registrar ... Dr. Margaret BOMAN

† Regional accreditation is carried under the parent institution in University Park, PA.

Penn State Hazleton (J)

76 University Drive, Hazleton PA 18202-1291
County: Luzerne FICE Identification: 003338
Unit ID: 214768
Telephone: (570) 450-3000 Carnegie Class: Bac/A&S
FAX Number: (570) 450-3182 Calendar System: Semester
URL: www.hn.psu.edu
Established: 1934 Annual Undergrad Tuition & Fees (In-State): $13,048
Enrollment: 1,303 Coed
Affiliation or Control: State Related IRS Status: 501(c)3
Highest Offering: Baccalaureate
Program: Occupational; 2-Year Principally Bachelor's Creditable; Liberal Arts And General
Accreditation: &M, ENGT, MLTAD, PTAA

01 Chancellor ... Dr. Gary M. LAWLER
05 Academic Affairs ... Dr. Elizabeth J. WRIGHT
32 Student Affairs ... Mr. Marquis L. BENNETT
30 Development/Alumni Relations ... Mr. Kevin J. SALAWAY
06 Registrar ... Ms. Michele JAIS

† Regional accreditation is carried under the parent institution in University Park, PA.

Penn State Lehigh Valley (K)

8380 Mohr Lane, Fogelsville PA 18051-9999
County: Lehigh FICE Identification: 003330
Unit ID: 214670
Telephone: (610) 285-5000 Carnegie Class: Bac/Diverse
FAX Number: (610) 285-5220 Calendar System: Semester
URL: www.lv.psu.edu
Established: 1912 Annual Undergrad Tuition & Fees (In-State): $13,094
Enrollment: 920 Coed
Affiliation or Control: State Related IRS Status: 501(c)3
Highest Offering: Baccalaureate
Program: Occupational; 2-Year Principally Bachelor's Creditable; Liberal Arts And General; Teacher Preparatory
Accreditation: &M

01 Chancellor ... Dr. Ann M. WILLIAMS
05 Academic Affairs ... Dr. Kenneth A. THIGPEN
06 Registrar ... Ms. Katherine D. ECK
30 Development/Alumni Relations ... Ms. Lynn STAPLES
32 Student Affairs ... Ms. Tiffany CRESSWELL-YEAGER

† Regional accreditation is carried under the parent institution in University Park, PA.

Penn State Milton S. Hershey Medical Center College of Medicine (L)

500 University Drive, Box 850, Hershey PA 17033-2360
County: Dauphin FICE Identification: 006813
Unit ID: 214616
Telephone: (717) 531-8521 Carnegie Class: Spec/Med
FAX Number: N/A Calendar System: Semester
URL: www.hmc.psu.edu
Established: 1964 Annual Graduate Tuition & Fees: $40,052
Enrollment: 800 Coed
Affiliation or Control: State Related IRS Status: 501(c)3
Highest Offering: Doctorate; No Undergraduates
Program: Professional
Accreditation: &M, MED

01 Chancellor ... Dr. Harold L. PAZ
05 Academic Affairs ... Dr. Richard J. SIMONS
30 Development/Alumni Relations ... Ms. Kristen B. ROZANSKY
32 Student Affairs ... Ms. Susan KELLEY
06 Registrar ... Ms. Diane E. GILL

† Regional accreditation is carried under the parent institution in University Park, PA.

Penn State Mont Alto (A)

One Campus Drive, Mont Alto PA 17237-9703
County: Franklin FICE Identification: 003340
Unit ID: 214795
Telephone: (717) 749-6000 Carnegie Class: Bac/Assoc
FAX Number: (717) 749-6069 Calendar System: Semester
URL: www.ma.psu.edu
Established: 1929 Annual Undergrad Tuition & Fees (In-State): $13,102
Enrollment: 1,252 Coed
Affiliation or Control: State Related IRS Status: 501(c)3
Highest Offering: Baccalaureate
Program: Occupational; 2-Year Principally Bachelor's Creditable; Liberal Arts And General
Accreditation: &M, OTA, PTAA

01 Chancellor ... Dr. David C. GNAGE
05 Academic Affairs ... Dr. Francis K. ACHAMPONG
32 Student Affairs ... Ms. Andrea D. CHRISTOPHER
06 Registrar ... Ms. Linda S. MONN
30 Development/Alumni Relations ... Mr. Randall R. ACKERMAN

† Regional accreditation is carried under the parent institution in University Park, PA.

Penn State New Kensington (B)

3550 Seventh Street Road, Route 780, Upper Burrell PA 15068-1798
County: Westmoreland FICE Identification: 003341
Unit ID: 214625
Telephone: (724) 334-5466 Carnegie Class: Bac/Diverse
FAX Number: (724) 334-6052 Calendar System: Semester
URL: www.nk.psu.edu
Established: 1958 Annual Undergrad Tuition & Fees (In-State): $13,048
Enrollment: 873 Coed
Affiliation or Control: State Related IRS Status: 501(c)3
Highest Offering: Baccalaureate
Program: Occupational; 2-Year Principally Bachelor's Creditable; Liberal Arts And General
Accreditation: &M, ENGT, RAD

01 Chancellor ... Dr. Kevin J. SNIDER
05 Academic Affairs ... Dr. Arlene E. HALL
32 Student Affairs ... Ms. Theresa A. BONK
06 Registrar ... Ms. Mary T. DUBBINK
30 Development/Alumni Relations ... Ms. Donna M. SPEER

† Regional accreditation is carried under the parent institution in University Park, PA.

Penn State Schuylkill (C)

200 University Drive, Schuylkill Haven PA 17972-2208
County: Schuylkill FICE Identification: 003343
Unit ID: 214810
Telephone: (570) 385-6000 Carnegie Class: Bac/Diverse
FAX Number: (570) 385-3672 Calendar System: Semester
URL: www.sl.psu.edu
Established: 1934 Annual Undergrad Tuition & Fees (In-State): $12,994
Enrollment: 1,031 Coed
Affiliation or Control: State Related IRS Status: 501(c)3
Highest Offering: Master's
Program: Occupational; 2-Year Principally Bachelor's Creditable; Liberal Arts And General
Accreditation: &M, RAD

01 Chancellor ... Dr. R. Keith HILLKIRK
05 Academic Affairs ... Dr. Stephen R. COUCH
32 Student Affairs ... Mr. Matthew J. SWATCHICK
06 Registrar ... Ms. Elyce M. LYKINS
30 Development/Alumni Relations ... Ms. Jane ZINTAK

† Regional accreditation is carried under the parent institution in University Park, PA.

Penn State Shenango (D)

147 Shenango Avenue, Sharon PA 16146-1597
County: Mercer FICE Identification: 003345
Unit ID: 214634
Telephone: (724) 983-2803 Carnegie Class: Bac/Diverse
FAX Number: (724) 983-2820 Calendar System: Semester
URL: www.shenango.psu.edu
Established: 1965 Annual Undergrad Tuition & Fees (In-State): $12,994
Enrollment: 714 Coed
Affiliation or Control: State Related IRS Status: 501(c)3
Highest Offering: Baccalaureate
Program: Occupational; 2-Year Principally Bachelor's Creditable; Liberal Arts And General
Accreditation: &M, ENGT, PTAA

01 Chancellor ... Dr. Fredric M. LEEDS
05 Academic Affairs ... Dr. Ira S. SALTZ
32 Student Affairs ... Dr. Jane A. WILLIAMS
30 Development/Alumni Relations ... Mr. Steven L. HESSMANN
06 Registrar ... Mr. Matthew E. GORAL

† Regional accreditation is carried under the parent institution in University Park, PA.

Penn State Wilkes-Barre (E)

PO Box PSU, Old Route 115, Lehman PA 18627-0217
County: Luzerne FICE Identification: 003346
Unit ID: 214643
Telephone: (570) 675-2171 Carnegie Class: Bac/Diverse
FAX Number: (570) 675-8308 Calendar System: Semester
URL: www.wb.psu.edu
Established: 1916 Annual Undergrad Tuition & Fees (In-State): $12,994
Enrollment: 766 Coed
Affiliation or Control: State Related IRS Status: 501(c)3
Highest Offering: Baccalaureate
Program: Occupational; 2-Year Principally Bachelor's Creditable; Liberal Arts And General
Accreditation: &M, ENG, ENGT

01 Chancellor ... Dr. Charles H. DAVIS
05 Academic Affairs ... Dr. Theodora A. JANKOWSKI
32 Student Affairs ... Ms. Katherine M. FLANAGAN-HERSTEK
06 Registrar ... Ms. Margaret B. ESOPI
30 Development/Alumni Relations ... Mr. Anthony J. SHIPULA

† Regional accreditation is carried under the parent institution in University Park, PA.

Penn State Worthington-Scranton (F)

120 Ridge View Drive, Dunmore PA 18512-1602
County: Lackawanna FICE Identification: 003344
Unit ID: 214652
Telephone: (570) 963-2500 Carnegie Class: Bac/Diverse
FAX Number: (570) 963-2543 Calendar System: Semester
URL: www.sn.psu.edu
Established: 1923 Annual Undergrad Tuition & Fees (In-State): $12,966
Enrollment: 1,386 Coed
Affiliation or Control: State Related IRS Status: 501(c)3
Highest Offering: Baccalaureate
Program: Occupational; 2-Year Principally Bachelor's Creditable; Liberal Arts And General
Accreditation: &M, ENGT

01 Chancellor ... Dr. Mary-Beth KROGH-JESPERSEN
05 Academic Affairs ... Dr. Molly WERTHEIMER
06 Registrar ... Ms. Allison L. BURNS
30 Development/Alumni Relations ... Ms. Maria J. RUSSONIELLO
35 Director Student Affairs ... Mr. William V. BRYAN

† Regional accreditation is carried under the parent institution in University Park, PA.

Penn State York (G)

1031 Edgecomb Avenue, York PA 17403-3398
County: York FICE Identification: 003347
Unit ID: 214829
Telephone: (717) 771-4000 Carnegie Class: Bac/Diverse
FAX Number: (717) 771-4062 Calendar System: Other
URL: www.yk.psu.edu
Established: 1926 Annual Undergrad Tuition & Fees (In-State): $12,966
Enrollment: 1,509 Coed
Affiliation or Control: State Related IRS Status: 501(c)3
Highest Offering: Baccalaureate
Program: Occupational; 2-Year Principally Bachelor's Creditable; Liberal Arts And General
Accreditation: &M, ENGT

01 Chancellor ... Dr. Joel M. RODNEY
05 Academic Affairs ... Dr. Joseph P. MCCORMICK
32 Student Affairs ... Dr. Sharon CHRIST
06 Registrar ... Mr. Frank P. MILLER, JR.
30 Development/Alumni Relations ... Ms. Diane K. HERSHEY

† Regional accreditation is carried under the parent institution in University Park, PA.

Pennco Tech (H)

3815 Otter Street, Bristol PA 19007-3696
County: Bucks FICE Identification: 009449
Unit ID: 214944
Telephone: (215) 785-0111 Carnegie Class: Assoc/PrivFP
FAX Number: (215) 785-1945 Calendar System: Other
URL: www.penncotech.com
Established: 1973 Annual Undergrad Tuition & Fees: $17,200
Enrollment: 500 Coed
Affiliation or Control: Proprietary IRS Status: Proprietary
Highest Offering: Associate Degree
Program: Occupational
Accreditation: ACCSC

01 CEO ... Michael S. HOBYAK
03 School Director ... Fred PARCELLS
05 Director of Education ... Gordon ERNEST
07 Director of Admissions ... Glenn SLATER
06 Registrar ... Sondra KOOB
35 Director Student Services ... Lee COBEIGH
37 Admin Mgr/Dir Student Financial Aid ... Fran GRANDVILLE
36 Director Student Placement ... Teresa SCHEERER

Pennsylvania Academy of the Fine Arts (I)

128 N Broad Street, Philadelphia PA 19102-1424
County: Philadelphia FICE Identification: 021073
Unit ID: 214971
Telephone: (215) 972-7600 Carnegie Class: Spec/Arts
FAX Number: (215) 569-0153 Calendar System: Semester
URL: www.pafa.edu
Established: 1805 Annual Undergrad Tuition & Fees: $27,270
Enrollment: 353 Coed
Affiliation or Control: Independent Non-Profit IRS Status: 501(c)3
Highest Offering: Master's
Program: Liberal Arts And General; Professional; Fine Arts Emphasis
Accreditation: @M, ART

01 President & CEO ... Dr. David R. BRIGHAM
30 Senior Vice President Development ... Ms. Melissa DERUITER
26 Senior Vice President of Marketing ... Ms. Marsha BRAVERMAN
05 Dean School of Fine Arts/Sr VP ... Mr. Jeffrey CARR
10 Vice Pres of Finance & Operations ... Mr. John BERG
07 VP of Admissions & Financial Aid ... Mr. Stan GREIDUS
32 Dean of Student Affairs ... Ms. Anne K. STASSEN
18 Director of Operations and Safety ... Mr. Ed POLETTI
19 Director of Security ... Mr. Jimmie GREENO
37 Director of Financial Aid ... Ms. Denise COULTER
06 Registrar ... Mr. Peter MEDWICK
08 Head Librarian ... Mr. Brian DUFFY

Pennsylvania College of Art & Design (J)

204 N Prince Street, Box 59, Lancaster PA 17608-0059
County: Lancaster FICE Identification: 022699
Unit ID: 215053
Telephone: (717) 396-7833 Carnegie Class: Spec/Arts
FAX Number: (717) 396-1339 Calendar System: Semester
URL: www.pcad.edu
Established: 1982 Annual Undergrad Tuition & Fees: $18,980
Enrollment: 282 Coed
Affiliation or Control: Independent Non-Profit IRS Status: 501(c)3
Highest Offering: Baccalaureate
Program: Professional; Fine Arts Emphasis
Accreditation: M, ART

01 President ... Ms. Mary Colleen HEIL
05 Academic Dean ... Mr. Marc TORICK
32 Dean of Students ... Ms. Pamela RICHARDSON
26 Director of Public Relations ... Mrs. Mary STADDEN
10 Director of Finance ... Mrs. Patricia ERNST
84 Dir of Admiss/Mktg & Recruitment ... Ms. Natalie LASCEK-SPEAKMAN
37 Director Financial Aid ... Mr. J. David HERSHEY
08 Library Director ... Ms. Karen HUTCHISON
30 Director of Development ... Ms. Angela SPICKLER
51 Director of Continuing Education ... Mrs. Tracy BEYL
18 Director of Physical Plant ... Mr. Dan FREILER
06 Registrar ... Ms. Faith GADDIE

Pennsylvania College of Technology (K)

One College Avenue, Williamsport PA 17701-5799
County: Lycoming FICE Identification: 003395
Unit ID: 366252
Telephone: (570) 326-3761 Carnegie Class: Bac/Assoc
FAX Number: (570) 327-4503 Calendar System: Semester
URL: www.pct.edu
Established: 1965 Annual Undergrad Tuition & Fees (In-State): $13,590
Enrollment: 6,290 Coed
Affiliation or Control: State IRS Status: 501(c)3
Highest Offering: Baccalaureate
Program: Occupational; 2-Year Principally Bachelor's Creditable; Technical Emphasis
Accreditation: M, ACBSP, ACFEI, ADNUR, ARCPA, CONST, DH, EMT, ENGT, IACBE, NAIT, NUR, OTA, PNUR, RAD, SURGT

01 President ... Dr. Davie Jane GILMOUR
03 Senior Vice President ... Dr. William J. MARTIN
05 VP Assessment/Research/Planning ... Dr. Nasrin FATIMA
10 VP for Finance/CFO ... Ms. Suzanne T. STOPPER
30 Vice Pres Institutional Advancement ... Mr. Barry R. STIGER
32 Special Asst to Pres/Student Affrs ... Mr. Ward W. CALDWELL
20 Assistant VP for Academic Services ... Mrs. Carolyn R. STRICKLAND
20 Associate VP for Instruction ... Mr. Tom F. GREGORY
04 Administrative Asst to President ... Mrs. Valerie A. BAIER
88 VP for Info Tech and Business ... Mr. James E. CUNNINGHAM
103 Exec Dir Workforce/Economic Devel ... Mr. Larry L. MICHAEL
50 Dean Business & Computer Technology ... Dr. Edward A. HENNINGER
88 Dean Construction & Design Tech ... Mr. Marc E. BRIDGENS
76 Dean Health Sciences ... Mrs. Sharon WATERS
54 Dean Indust & Engineer Tech ... Mr. Donald O. PRASTER

49 Dean Integrated Studies ....Dr. Clifford P. COPPERSMITH
65 Dean Natural Resource Management ....Dr. Mary A. SULLIVAN
88 Dean Transportation Technology ....Mr. Colin W. WILLIAMSON
88 Dean for Hospitality ....Mr. Frederick W. BECKER
102 Exec Dir of Penn College Foundation ....Mr. Robert C. DIETRICH
13 Chief Information Officer ....Mr. Michael M. CUNNINGHAM
08 Director of the Madigan Library ....Ms. Lisette N. ORMSBEE
56 Director Instruc Tech/Distance Lrng ....Mr. Walter J. SHULTZ
37 Assoc Dean of Admissions & Fin Aid ....Mr. Dennis L. CORRELL
18 Director of General Services ....Mr. Walter D. NYMAN
09 Director Institutional Research ....Mr. Brian CYGAN
22 VP Human Resources/Employees/EEO ....Mrs. Linda M. MORRIS
15 VP for College Services ....Mr. R. David KAY
06 Registrar ....Mr. Dennis L. DUNKLEBERGER
38 Director of Advisement Center ....Mr. Stephen R. HAEFNER
36 Dir Counsel/Career & Disability Svc ....Dr. Jennifer MCLEAN
39 Director Residence Life ....Mr. Brian M. JOHNSON
19 Chief of Police ....Mr. Chris E. MILLER
27 Director College Info/Cmty Rels ....Mrs. Elaine J. LAMBERT
88 Director Academic Support Services ....Dr. Kimberly L. BOLIG
35 Director Student Activities ....Mrs. Kimberly R. CASSEL
29 Director Alumni Relations ....Ms. Valerie L. FESSLER
26 Director of Corporate Relations ....Ms. Debra M. MILLER
88 Director Children Learning Center ....Ms. Karen W. PAYNE
40 Director of College Store ....Mr. Matthew P. BRANCA
41 Director of Athletics ....Mr. Scott E. KENNELL
90 Manager Academic Computing ....Ms. Constance M. VITOLINS
91 Director Administrative Info Sys ....Mr. Randall L. MONROE
23 Student Health Center Director ....Mr. Carl L. SHANER
88 Coordinator of Disability Services ....Ms. Kay E. DUNKLEBERGER
85 International Programs Specialist ....Ms. Shanin L. DOUGHERTY
25 Director of Grants & Contracts ....Ms. Alice M. SCHUSTER
96 Director/Procurement Services ....Ms. Karen P. FESSLER

† Affiliate of Pennsylvania State University.

Pennsylvania Highlands Community College (A)

101 Community College Way, Johnstown PA 15904-2949
County: Cambria
FICE Identification: 031804
Unit ID: 414911
Telephone: (814) 262-6400
Carnegie Class: Assoc/Pub-R-M
FAX Number: (814) 262-6410
Calendar System: Semester
URL: www.pennhighlands.edu
Established: 1994
Annual Undergrad Tuition & Fees (In-District): $4,160
Enrollment: 1,942
Coed
Affiliation or Control: State/Local
IRS Status: 501(c)3
Highest Offering: Associate Degree
Program: Occupational; 2-Year Principally Bachelor's Creditable
Accreditation: M

01 President ....Dr. Walter J. ASONEVICH
05 Vice Pres/Dean Academic Affairs ....Dr. Edward NICHOLS
10 Vice Pres Finance & Admin Services ....Lorraine SYLVIA
32 Vice Pres Student Svcs ....David VOLPE
20 Assoc Dean of Instruction ....Erica REIGHARD
20 Assoc Dean of Instruction ....Michele RICE
06 Registrar ....Michelle STUMPS
07 Director of Admissions ....Jeffrey MAUL
15 Exec Dir of Human Resources ....Ginny ALTEMUS
21 Director of Finance/Admin Services ....Christopher PRIBULSKY
37 Director Student Financial Aid ....Brenda COUGHENOUR
26 Director of Marketing ....Raymond WEIBLE, JR.
35 Director of Student Activities ....Suzanne BRUGH
18 Director of Facilities Operation ....Reb BROWNLEE

Pennsylvania Institute of Health and Technology (B)

PO Box 278, Mount Braddock PA 15465-0278
County: Fayette
Identification: 666035
Unit ID: 261861
Telephone: (724) 437-4600
Carnegie Class: Assoc/PrivFP
FAX Number: (724) 437-6053
Calendar System: Quarter
URL: www.piht.edu
Established: 1987
Annual Undergrad Tuition & Fees: $11,985
Enrollment: 155
Coed
Affiliation or Control: Proprietary
IRS Status: Proprietary
Highest Offering: Associate Degree
Program: Occupational
Accreditation: ACICS

01 Director ....Ms. Robin ADDIS
05 Director of Student Services ....Mrs. Mary Jo BARNHART
37 Exec Director Financial Aid ....Ms. Patricia A. CALLEN
36 Career Services Director ....Ms. Sue Ann PRIEMER

† Branch campus of West Virginia Junior College, Morgantown, WV.

Pennsylvania Institute of Technology (C)

800 Manchester Avenue, Media PA 19063-4098
County: Delaware
FICE Identification: 010998
Unit ID: 214582
Telephone: (610) 892-1500
Carnegie Class: Assoc/PrivNFP
FAX Number: (610) 892-1510
Calendar System: Semester
URL: www.pit.edu
Established: 1953
Annual Undergrad Tuition & Fees: $10,800
Enrollment: 915
Coed
Affiliation or Control: Independent Non-Profit
IRS Status: 501(c)3
Highest Offering: Associate Degree
Program: Occupational; 2-Year Principally Bachelor's Creditable, Technical Emphasis
Accreditation: M

01 President ....Mr. John C. STRAYER
05 Dean of Academic Affairs ....Dr. Robert E. HANCOX
32 Dean Student Services ....Dr. Dona M. FABRIZIO
20 Assoc Dean of Academic Affairs ....Dr. Eileen MCGOVERN
13 Chief Information Officer ....Mr. Jack BACON
10 Chief Financial Officer ....Ms. Annamarie CASSIDY
06 Registrar ....Mr. Craig M. JACOBS
08 Director of the Library ....Ms. Lynea ANDERMAN
18 Director of Facilities ....Mr. Frederick FIVECOAT
36 Director Career Placement/Transfer ....Ms. Valerie RICCARDI
36 Dir Career Plct/Extrn Sch Prof Pgms ....Ms. Kamira EVANS
37 Financial Aid Director ....Ms. Crystal DONNELLY
07 Director of Admissions ....Mr. John DETURRIS

Pennsylvania School of Business (D)

406 W Hamilton Street, Allentown PA 18101-1604
County: Lehigh
FICE Identification: 022552
Unit ID: 213057
Telephone: (610) 841-3333
Carnegie Class: Assoc/PrivFP
FAX Number: (610) 841-3334
Calendar System: Semester
URL: www.psb.edu
Established: 1980
Annual Undergrad Tuition & Fees: $23,300
Enrollment: 432
Coed
Affiliation or Control: Proprietary
IRS Status: Proprietary
Highest Offering: Associate Degree
Program: Occupational
Accreditation: ACCSC

01 President ....Mr. Michael J. O'BRIEN
10 Controller ....Ms. Michele TAYLOR
05 Dean of Education ....Ms. Dani J. PHELPS
07 Director of Admissions ....Mr. Sam JARVIS
37 Director of Financial Aid ....Ms. Stephanie A. AZUR
36 Director of Career Services ....Ms. Cynthia PHILLIPS

*Pennsylvania State System of Higher Education, Office of the Chancellor (E)

Dixon University Ctr, 2986 N 2nd St, Harrisburg PA 17110-1201
County: Dauphin
FICE Identification: 029371
Unit ID: 214661
Telephone: (717) 720-4010
Carnegie Class: N/A
FAX Number: (717) 720-4011
URL: www.passhe.edu

01 Chancellor ....Dr. John C. CAVANAUGH
03 Executive Vice Chancellor ....Dr. Peter H. GARLAND
10 Vice Chancellor Admin/Finance ....Mr. James S. DILLON
21 Assoc Vice Chancellor Admin/Finance ....Ms. Lois M. JOHNSON
18 Asst Vice Chancellor Facilities ....Mr. Steven DUPES
05 Vice Chanc Academic/Student Affairs ....Vacant
20 Sr Assoc Vice Chanc A/S Affairs ....Dr. Kathleen HOWLEY
16 Vice Chancellor HR/LR ....Mr. Gary K. DENT
15 Asst Vice Chancellor LR ....Mr. Michael A. MOTTOLA
86 Vice Chancellor External Relations ....Ms. Karen BALL
43 Chief Legal Counsel ....Mr. Leo PANDELADIS

*Bloomsburg University of Pennsylvania (F)

400 E Second Street, Bloomsburg PA 17815-1399
County: Columbia
FICE Identification: 003315
Unit ID: 211158
Telephone: (570) 389-4000
Carnegie Class: Master's L
FAX Number: (570) 389-3700
Calendar System: Semester
URL: www.bloomu.edu
Established: 1839
Annual Undergrad Tuition & Fees (In-State): $8,082
Enrollment: 10,091
Coed
Affiliation or Control: State
IRS Status: 501(c)3
Highest Offering: Doctorate
Program: Liberal Arts And General; Teacher Preparatory; Professional
Accreditation: M, ANEST, ART, AUD, BUS, CS, ENGR, ENGT, EXSC, MUS, NURSE, SP, SW, TED, THEA

02 President ....Dr. David L. SOLTZ
05 Sr VP/Provost Academic Affairs ....Dr. Ira BLAKE
10 Vice Pres Finance/Administration ....Dr. Richard RUGEN
32 Vice Pres Student Affairs ....Dr. Dionne D. SOMERVILLE
30 Vice Pres University Advancement ....Mr. Erik EVANS
22 Deputy to Pres for Equity ....Dr. Robert WISLOCK
04 Exec Asst to the President ....Ms. Brenda CROMLEY
20 Asst Vice Pres Academic Affairs ....Dr. Jonathan LINCOLN
58 Asst VP/Dean Grad Stds/Research ....Dr. Lawrence FRITZ
13 Asst Vice Pres Tech & Lib Services ....Mr. Wayne C. MOHR
18 Asst VP for Facilities Management ....Mr. Eric NESS
21 Asst VP Finance/Budget & Bus Svcs ....Ms. Claudia THRUSH
35 Asst Vice Pres Student Affairs ....Dr. Jeff C. LONG
26 Asst Vice Pres External Relations ....Mr. Jim HOLLISTER
49 Dean College of Liberal Arts ....Dr. James BROWN
50 Dean College of Business ....Dr. Michael TIDWELL
72 Dean College of Science/Technology ....Dr. Robert P. MARANDE
53 Interim Dean College of Education ....Dr. Elizabeth MAUCH
15 Director Human Resources/Labor Rel ....Mr. Jerry REED
46 Director of Research/Sponsored Pgms ....Dr. Jerrold R. HARRIS
06 Registrar ....Mr. Joseph KISSELL
07 Director of Admissions ....Mr. Christopher J. KELLER
36 Interim Director Career Development ....Ms. Jeanne R. FITZGERALD
38 Director of Counsel & Human Devel ....Dr. William R. HARRAR
37 Int Director Student Financial Aid ....Mr. John BIERYLA
90 Manager Technology Support Services ....Mr. David S. CELLI
29 Director of Alumni Affairs ....Ms. Lynda MICHAELS
40 Manager University Store ....Ms. Beth CHRISTIAN
39 Director of Residence Life ....Mr. Thomas KRESCH
41 Director of Athletics ....Mr. Michael S. MCFARLAND
85 Director International Education ....Dr. Madhav P. SHARMA
42 Director Protestant Campus Ministry ....Rev. Maggie GILLESPIE
42 Director Catholic Campus Ministry ....Rev. Timothy MARCOE
19 Dir Univ Safety & Police ....Mr. Tom PHILLIPS
92 Director University Honors Program ....Dr. Stephen KOKOSKA
96 Director of Purchasing & Operations ....Mr. Jeffrey MANDEL
08 Interim Director Library Services ....Mr. David MAGOLIS
91 Dir Applications Develop/Operations ....Mr. James C. GESSNER
09 Director of Institutional Research ....Ms. Karen L. SLUSSER
28 Asst to Provost for Diversity ....Dr. Irvin WRIGHT
44 Director of Annual Giving ....Ms. Eileen M. EVERT
27 Director of Communications ....Ms. Rosalee RUSH
45 Interim Dir Planning & Assessment ....Dr. Sheila JONES
103 Dir Corporate & Continuing Educ ....Mr. Thomas FLETCHER
30 Director Development ....Ms. Susan TRIMMER

*California University of Pennsylvania (G)

250 University Avenue, California PA 15419-1394
County: Washington
FICE Identification: 003316
Unit ID: 211361
Telephone: (724) 938-4000
Carnegie Class: Master's L
FAX Number: (724) 938-4138
Calendar System: Semester
URL: www.calu.edu
Established: 1852
Annual Undergrad Tuition & Fees (In-State): $9,034
Enrollment: 9,400
Coed
Affiliation or Control: State
IRS Status: 501(c)3
Highest Offering: Master's
Program: 2-Year Principally Bachelor's Creditable; Liberal Arts And General; Teacher Preparatory; Professional
Accreditation: M, ART, CACREP, CS, ENGT, NAIT, NRPA, NURSE, PTAA, SP, SW, TED, THEA

02 President ....Dr. Angelo ARMENTI, JR.
05 Provost/Vice Pres Academic Affairs ....Ms. Geraldine JONES
10 Interim VP Administration & Finance ....Mr. Robert THORN
32 VP Student Development & Services ....Dr. Lenora ANGELONE
30 VP for University Development ....Mr. Ron HUIATT
13 VP Information Technology ....Dr. Charles MANCE
04 Special Assistant to the President ....Mr. Norman G. HASBROUCK
09 Director Institutional Research ....Mr. Richard L. KLINE
88 Executive Dir Special Initiatives ....Mr. Timothy M. BUCHANAN
58 Interim Dean of Graduate Studies ....Dr. John CENCICH
20 Associate Provost ....Dr. Bruce BARNHART
20 Interim Associate Provost ....Dr. Stanley KOMACEK
20 Assoc Provost/Student Retent Ofcr ....Dr. Harry M. LANGLEY
30 Assoc Vice Pres for Development ....Mr. Howard GOLDSTEIN
30 Assoc Vice Pres for Development ....Mr. Mitch KOZIKOWSKI
56 Exec Director Southpointe Center ....Ms. Ellen NESSER
72 Dean of Science/Technology ....Dr. Leonard A. COLELLI
49 Interim Dean of Liberal Arts ....Dr. Mohamed YAMBA
53 Act Dean Col Education/Human Svcs ....Dr. Kevin A. KOURY
62 Dean of Library Services ....Mr. Douglas HOOVER
07 Dean of Admissions ....Dr. William A. EDMONDS
37 Director of Financial Aid ....Mrs. Jill FERNANDES
37 Sr Assoc Director of Financial Aid ....Mr. Jeff DERUBBO
06 Registrar ....Ms. Heidi WILLIAMS
36 Director of Career Services ....Ms. Rhonda GIFFORD
92 Director Honors Program ....Dr. Donald S. LAWSON
29 Director of Alumni Relations ....Ms. Amy LOMBARD
88 Director of University Exhibitions ....Mr. Walter P. CZEKAJ
44 Director of Planned Giving ....Mr. Gordon CORE
38 Assoc VP Student Development & Svcs ....Dr. Timothy SUSICK
14 Computer Systems Manager ....Ms. Rebecca NICHOLS
39 Director of Housing ....Mr. Shawn URBINE
94 Director Women's Studies ....Dr. Marta MCCLINTOCK
85 International Student Advisor ....Mr. John WATKINS
41 Athletic Director ....Dr. Tom PUCCI
88 Assoc VP of Athletic Development ....Mr. Frank BAUER
15 Interim Director of Personnel ....Ms. Pamela MURPHY
22 Special Assistant to President EEEO ....Dr. Lisa MCBRIDE
19 Chief of Police ....Mr. Robert F. DOWNEY
18 Director of Physical Plant ....Mr. Michael PEPLINSKI
26 Director of Communications & PR ....Mrs. Christine KINDL
27 Director of Publications ....Mr. Greg SOFRANKO
40 Book Store Manager ....Mr. David ALBERTS
96 Director of Purchasing ....Ms. Judith LAUGHLIN
26 Interim Vice Pres Marketing ....Mr. Craig S. BUTZINE

*Cheyney University of Pennsylvania (H)

Cheyney and Creek Roads, Cheyney PA 19319-0200
County: Delaware
FICE Identification: 003317
Unit ID: 211608
Telephone: (610) 399-2000
Carnegie Class: Master's S
FAX Number: (610) 399-2415
Calendar System: Semester
URL: www.cheyney.edu
Established: 1837
Annual Undergrad Tuition & Fees (In-State): $7,718
Enrollment: 1,586
Coed
Affiliation or Control: State
IRS Status: 501(c)3

Highest Offering: Master's
Program: Liberal Arts And General; Teacher Preparatory
Accreditation: M, TED

02 President ... Dr. Michelle R. HOWARD-VITAL
05 Provost/VP Academic Affairs ... Dr. Ivan BANKS
10 Vice Pres Finance & Administration ... Mr. Gerald COLEMAN
30 Int Vice President Inst Advancement ... Mr. Lawrence GREEN
32 VP Student Affairs/Student Life ... Dr. Susanne D. PHILLIPS
08 Dean Library Services ... Dr. Lut NERO
53 Dean School Education ... Dr. Cathine GILCHRIST
49 Dean School Arts & Sciences ... Dr. Bernadette CARTER
38 Actg Chairperson Guidance & Counsel ... Ms. Elaine CARTER
06 Registrar ... Ms. Brenda SHIELDS
37 Director Financial Aid ... Mr. James V. BROWN
13 Director of Information Technology ... Mr. Howard HUDSON
07 Director Admissions ... Ms. Gemma STEMLEY
09 Director Institutional Research ... Mr. Harding FAULK, JR.
15 Director Human Resources ... Ms. Jo-Anne HARRIS
26 Director Public Relations/Marketing ... Ms. Antoinette COLON
18 Deputy Dir Facilities Management ... Mr. Carl M. WILLIAMS
19 Director Public Safety ... Mr. Lawrence RICHARDS
36 Director Career Services ... Ms. Marcia ROBINSON
41 Interim Director Athletics ... Dr. Gregory SMITH
17 College Physician ... Dr. Constance MCKELVEY
43 University Legal Counsel ... Ms. Jacqualine BARNETT
35 Director Student Affairs ... Ms. Sharon THORN
21 Dir Business Support Service ... Ms. Monique BAYLOR
25 Contract Compliance Officer ... Mr. Michael FLANAGAN
22 Social Equity ... Ms. Barbara SIMMONS
29 Director Alumni Relations ... Mr. Gregory BENJAMIN
39 Director Student Housing ... Mr. Donzelle TILLER
103 Dir Economic/Workforce Devel ... Ms. Sharon CANNON
24 Director Telecommunications ... Mr. Phil PAGLIARO

*Clarion University of Pennsylvania (A)

840 Wood Street, Clarion PA 16214-1232
County: Clarion FICE Identification: 003318
Unit ID: 211644
Telephone: (814) 393-2000 Carnegie Class: Master's L
FAX Number: (814) 393-1826 Calendar System: Semester
URL: www.clarion.edu
Established: 1867 Annual Undergrad Tuition & Fees (In-State): $8,540
Enrollment: 7,315 Coed
Affiliation or Control: State IRS Status: 501(c)3
Highest Offering: Master's
Program: 2-Year Principally Bachelor's Creditable; Liberal Arts And General; Teacher Preparatory; Professional
Accreditation: M, ART, BUS, LIB, MUS, NUR, SP, TED

02 President ... Dr. Karen M. WHITNEY
05 Provost/Academic Vice President ... Dr. Ronald NOWACZYK
32 Vice Pres Student & University Affs ... Mr. Harry E. TRIPP
10 Vice Pres Finance/Administration ... Mr. Paul BYLASKA
20 Associate Provost ... Dr. Susan C. TURELL
30 Director of Development ... Vacant
21 Assoc VP for Finance/Administration ... Mr. Timothy P. FOGARTY
22 Asst to President for Social Equity ... Dr. Jocelind E. GANT
12 Executive Dean Venango Campus ... Dr. Christopher M. REBER
84 Dean of Enrollment Management ... Mr. William D. BAILEY
08 Dean of Libraries ... Dr. Terry S. LATOUR
49 Dean of Arts & Sciences ... Dr. Rachelle P. PRIOLEAU
50 Dean of Business Administration ... Dr. James G. PESEK
66 Director Nursing & Allied Health ... Dr. Sharon FALKENSTERN
58 Associate VP for Graduate Studies ... Dr. Arthur J. ACTON
09 Int Director Institutional Research ... Ms. Rose M. LOGUE
06 Registrar ... Ms. Lisa L. HEPLER
21 Director of Budgets ... Vacant
14 Assoc VP for Information Technology ... Mr. Samuel T. PULEIO
46 Director Faculty Research ... Dr. Brenda S. DEDE
26 Dir of Marketing & Communications ... Mr. David LOVE
37 Director of Financial Aid ... Mr. Kenneth E. GRUGEL
18 Int Director of Facilities Mgmt ... Mr. Dan A. FLEMING
88 Exec Dir Programming & Devel Ctr ... Ms. Carol A. ROTH
29 Director of Alumni Relations ... Ms. Brooke MURRAY
36 Int Director Career Services ... Ms. Diana BRUSH
39 Director of Residence Life ... Ms. Michelle L. KEALEY
19 Director of Public Safety ... Ms. Glen L. REID
41 Athletic Director ... Mr. David J. KATIS
96 Director of Purchasing ... Mr. Rein A. POLD

*Clarion University-Venango Campus (B)

1801 W First Street, Oil City PA 16301-3297
County: Venango FICE Identification: 003319
Unit ID: 211662
Telephone: (814) 676-6591 Carnegie Class: Not Classified
FAX Number: (814) 676-1348 Calendar System: Semester
URL: www.clarion.edu/venango
Established: 1961 Annual Undergrad Tuition & Fees (In-State): $7,650
Enrollment: 1,078 Coed
Affiliation or Control: State IRS Status: 501(c)3
Highest Offering: Master's
Program: Liberal Arts And General
Accreditation: &M, ADNUR, NAIT, NUR

02 Executive Dean ... Dr. Christopher M. REBER
32 Director of Student Affairs ... Ms. Emily AUBELE
26 Dir of Marketing & Univ Relations ... Ms. Jerri GENT
10 Director of Finance/Administration ... Ms. Debra SOBINA
07 Coord Admissions/Financial Aid ... Mr. LaTrobe BARNITZ
04 Assistant to the Executive Dean ... Ms. Kay E. ENSLE

*East Stroudsburg University of Pennsylvania (C)

200 Prospect Street, East Stroudsburg PA 18301-2999
County: Monroe FICE Identification: 003320
Unit ID: 212115
Telephone: (570) 422-3211 Carnegie Class: Master's L
FAX Number: (570) 422-3777 Calendar System: Semester
URL: www.esu.edu
Established: 1893 Annual Undergrad Tuition & Fees (In-State): N/A
Enrollment: 7,387 Coed
Affiliation or Control: State IRS Status: 501(c)3
Highest Offering: Master's
Program: Liberal Arts And General; Teacher Preparatory; Professional
Accreditation: M, EXSC, NRPA, NUR, PH, SP, TED

02 President ... Dr. Robert J. DILLMAN
05 Provost ... Dr. Van A. REIDHEAD
32 Vice President Student Affairs ... Dr. Doreen TOBIN
10 Vice Pres Finance & Administration ... Mr. Richard A. STANESKI
46 Vice Pres Econ Dev & Research Supp ... Ms. Mary Frances POSTUPACK
102 President & CEO ESU Foundation ... Mr. Frank FALSO
84 Interim Vice Pres Enrollment Mgmt ... Dr. Victoria SANDERS
58 Vice Provost & Graduate Dean ... Dr. Marilyn WELLS
49 Dean of Arts & Sciences ... Dr. Peter HAWKES
68 Dean of Health Sciences ... Dr. Mark KILKER
53 Dean of Education ... Dr. Pamela KRAMER-ERTEL
50 Dean of Business and Management ... Dr. Alla WILSON
08 Dean of Library & Univ Collections . Dr. Edward OWUSU-ANSAH
20 Assoc Provost for Acad & Inst Effec ... Dr. Yun KIM
35 Asst Vice President Student Affairs ... Mr. Warren ANDERSON
100 Interim Chief of Staff ... Mr. Miguel BARBOSA
88 Asst Vice Pres Instruct Supp & Outr ... Mr. Michael SOUTHWELL
07 Director of Admissions ... Mr. Jeffrey JONES
06 Registrar/Dir Enrollment Services ... Ms. Kizzy MORRIS
37 Assoc Dir Enroll Svcs/Financial Aid ... Ms. Phyllis SWINSON
36 Director of Career Services ... Dr. Dennis B. STEIGERWALT
38 Director Counseling Center ... Dr. John A. ABBRUZZESE
41 Director Intercollegiate Athletics ... Dr. Thomas GIOGLIO
39 Director of Residence Life ... Mr. Robert M. MOSES
88 Dir of Student Activity Association ... Mr. Fredric A. MOSES
21 Controller ... Ms. Donna R. BULZONI
14 Director of Computing Services ... Mr. Robert D'AVERSA
15 Director of Human Resources ... Ms. Teresa FRITSCHE
18 Director Facilities Management ... Mr. Syed S. ZAIDI
96 Director of Procurement/Contracting ... Mr. Michael CRAPP
29 Director of Alumni Relations ... Mr. Mike SARAKA
26 Director University Relations ... Mr. Douglas SMITH

*Edinboro University of Pennsylvania (D)

219 Meadville Street, Edinboro PA 16444-0001
County: Erie FICE Identification: 003321
Unit ID: 212160
Telephone: (814) 732-2000 Carnegie Class: Master's L
FAX Number: (814) 732-2880 Calendar System: Semester
URL: www.edinboro.edu
Established: 1857 Annual Undergrad Tuition & Fees (In-State): $8,359
Enrollment: 8,642 Coed
Affiliation or Control: State IRS Status: 501(c)3
Highest Offering: Beyond Master's But Less Than Doctorate
Program: Occupational; 2-Year Principally Bachelor's Creditable; Liberal Arts And General; Teacher Preparatory; Professional
Accreditation: M, ART, ACBSP, CACREP, CORE, MUS, NUR, NURSE, SP, SW, TED

02 Interim President ... Dr. Jim MORAN
05 Provost/VP Academic Affairs ... Dr. Philip E. GINNETTI
10 Vice Pres Finance & Administration ... Mr. Gordon J. HERBST
32 Vice President for Student Affairs ... Dr. Kahan SABLO
30 Vice Pres University Advancement ... Vacant
100 Exec Assistant to the President ... Vacant
20 Sr Exec Associate to the Provost ... Ms. Judy KUBEJA
14 Assoc VP Tech & Communications ... Dr. Andrew C. LAWLOR
15 Assoc VP Human Res/Fac Rels ... Mr. Sid BOOKER
88 Assoc VP for Partnerships & Develop ... Mr. Terrence C. CARLIN
08 Assoc Vice President Univ Libraries ... Dr. Donald H. DILMORE
18 Director of Facilities Management ... Mr. James MILLER
27 Assistant VP Comm and Marketing ... Vacant
37 Asst VP Student Financial Aid ... Ms. Dorothy H. BODY
07 Director of Undergrad Admissions ... Mr. Craig GROOMS
22 Dir of Social Equity/Ombudsperson ... Ms. Valerie O. HAYES
49 Dean College of Arts and Sciences ... Dr. Terry L. SMITH
58 Dean of Graduate Studies/Research ... Dr. Alan BIEL
53 Dean School of Education ... Dr. Nomsa GELETA
06 Registrar ... Mr. Tim W. PILEWSKI
36 Director of Ctr for Career Develop ... Dr. Jody GALLAGHER
29 Director Alumni Relations ... Mr. Jon PULICE
41 Athletic Director ... Mr. Bruce BAUMGARTNER
38 Dir Counseling/Psychological Svcs ... Dr. Michael BUCELL
19 Chief University Police ... Mr. Clark PETERS
39 Dir Residence Life & Orientation ... Ms. Kim KENNEDY
12 Dir & Outreach Coord EUP in Erie ... Ms. Janet L. BOWKER
12 Coordinator EUP in Meadville ... Vacant
23 Medical Dir Student Health Services ... Dr. Ronald C. MARTIN
106 Director of Online Programs ... Mr. Rick WAGONSELLER

40 Director Auxiliary Operations ... Mr. Paul B. KIGHTLINGER
85 Director Intl Student Svcs ... Ms. Linda KIGHTLINGER
25 Director Sponsored Programs ... Ms. Rene HEARNS
88 Dir Networks & Telecommunications ... Ms. Karen MURDZAK
90 Dir Desktop Systems/Learning Tech ... Mr. Dennis J. BRADLEY
13 Director Enterprise Systems ... Ms. Sallie A. TERPACK
96 Asst Director Purchasing & Contract ... Ms. Darla SPAID
102 Director of Major Gifts ... Ms. Julie A. CHACONA
44 Dir of Annual Fund & Stewardship ... Ms. Marilyn GOELLNER
88 Director of Budget and Payroll ... Mr. Sean BLILEY
21 Controller ... Mr. Wayne T. OCHS
35 Director of Campus Life ... Ms. Michelle BARBICH
17 Nurse Supervisor ... Ms. Darla ELDER
24 Learning Technology Svcs Manager ... Mr. Randall MCCASLIN

*Indiana University of Pennsylvania (E)

Indiana PA 15705-0001
County: Indiana FICE Identification: 003277
Unit ID: 213020
Telephone: (724) 357-2100 Carnegie Class: DRU
FAX Number: (724) 357-6213 Calendar System: Semester
URL: www.iup.edu
Established: 1875 Annual Undergrad Tuition & Fees (In-State): $8,362
Enrollment: 15,126 Coed
Affiliation or Control: State IRS Status: 501(c)3
Highest Offering: Doctorate
Program: Liberal Arts And General; Teacher Preparatory; Professional
Accreditation: M, ACFEI, ART, BUS, CACREP, CLPSY, DIETD, DIETI, ENGR, EXSC, MUS, NURSE, SP, TED, THEA

02 Interim President ... Dr. David J. WERNER
05 Provost & VP Academic Affairs ... Dr. Gerald W. INTEMANN
11 Vice Pres Administration/Finance ... Dr. Cornelius WOOTEN
32 Vice President Student Affairs ... Dr. Rhonda H. LUCKEY
30 Vice Pres University Relations ... Vacant
20 Assoc VP Academic Administration ... Dr. John N. KILMARX
58 Dean Grad School and Research ... Dr. Timothy P. MACK
16 Associate VP Human Resources ... Ms. Helen KENNEDY
79 Dean College Human Social Science ... Dr. Yaw A. ASAMOAH
50 Dean Eberly Col Bus/Inform Tech ... Dr. Robert C. CAMP
20 Assoc Provost for Acad Pgms & Plng ... Dr. Inno ONWUEME
53 Interim Dean College Educ/Educ Tech ... Dr. Keith DILS
81 Dean Col Natural Science & Math ... Dr. Deanne SNAVELY
57 Dean College of Fine Arts ... Mr. Michael J. HOOD
66 Int Dean Col Health & Human Svcs ... Dr. Mary SWINKLER
84 Assoc VP Enrollment Management ... Mr. James BEGANY
08 Interim Dean of Libraries ... Dr. Luis GONZALEZ
35 Dean of Students ... Vacant
06 Registrar ... Mr. Robert SIMON
38 Counseling Center ... Dr. Patti SHAFFER
27 Chief Information Officer ... Mr. Bill BALINT
04 Inst Research Planning & Assessment ... Mrs. Barbe MOORE
14 Exec Dir of Technology Services Ctr ... Mr. Todd CUNNINGHAM
37 Asst VP Enrollment/Dir of Fin Aid ... Ms. Patricia MCCARTHY
28 Dir Social Equity/Civic Engagement ... Vacant
19 Int Dir University Safety/Police ... Mr. Sam CLUTTER
36 Director of Career Services ... Mr. Mark E. ANTHONY
29 Exec Director Alumni Association ... Mrs. Mary Jo LYTTLE
44 Director Annual Giving ... Ms. Emily SMELTZ
85 Director International Affairs ... Ms. Michele PETRUCCI
46 Assistant Dean for Research ... Dr. Hilliary CREELY
39 Director Housing/Residence Life ... Mr. Michael LEMASTERS
40 Bookstore Director ... Mr. Tim SHARBAUGH
41 Director Athletics ... Dr. Francis CONDINO
23 Director Health Services ... Mr. Scott GIBSON
12 Dean Northpointe Campus ... Ms. Patricia D. SCOTT
12 Dean Punxsutawney Campus ... Dr. Terry APPOLONIA
43 Staff Attorney ... Ms. Jacqueline R. MORROW
26 Director of Public Relations ... Ms. Michelle SHAFFER FRYLING
96 Director of Purchasing ... Mr. Robert BOWSER
10 Assoc Vice President for Finance ... Mrs. Susanna C. SINK
04 Exec Assistant to the President ... Ms. Robin GORMAN

*Kutztown University of Pennsylvania (F)

15200 Kutztown Road, Kutztown PA 19530-0730
County: Berks FICE Identification: 003322
Unit ID: 213349
Telephone: (610) 683-4000 Carnegie Class: Master's L
FAX Number: (610) 683-4693 Calendar System: Semester
URL: www.kutztown.edu
Established: 1866 Annual Undergrad Tuition & Fees (In-State): $8,359
Enrollment: 10,107 Coed
Affiliation or Control: State IRS Status: 501(c)3
Highest Offering: Master's
Program: Liberal Arts And General; Teacher Preparatory; Professional
Accreditation: M, ART, MUS, NUR, SW, TED

02 President ... Dr. F. Javier CEVALLOS
05 Vice Pres Academic & Stdnt Affairs ... Dr. Carlos VARGAS-ABURTO
10 VP Administration & Finance ... Mr. Gerald L. SILBERMAN
102 Executive Director KU Foundation ... Mr. Jason KETTER
30 Assoc Vice Pres Univ Advancement ... Mr. John C. GREEN
22 Assoc Vice Pres Equity & Compliance ... Mr. Jesus PENA
20 Vice Provost Academic Affairs ... Dr. Carole WELLS
21 Asst Vice Pres Admin & Finance ... Mr. Kenneth LONG
32 Assoc Vice Provost & Dean Students ... Mr. Robert WATROUS
27 Asst Vice Provost/Info Technology ... Mr. Mitchell FREED
15 Executive Director Human Resources ... Ms. Sharon M. PICUS

18 Asst Vice President for Facilities ... Mr. Robert J. GRIMM
34 Assistant Provost Enrollment Svcs ... Vacant
38 Dean College Visual/Performing Arts ... Dr. William J. MOWDER
49 Actg Dean College Liberal Arts/Sci ... Dr. Anne E. ZAYAITZ
50 Dean College of Business ... Dr. William DEMPSEY
53 Dean College Education ... Dr. Darrell GARBER
52 Dean Library Services ... Dr. Barbara DARDEN
88 Dean for Students/Campus Life ... Mr. Robert T. WATROUS
26 Director of University Relations ... Mr. Matthew SANTOS
09 Institutional Research Manager ... Ms. Natalie SNOW
06 Registrar ... Ms. Michelle HUGHES
37 Director of Financial Aid ... Mr. Bernard L. MCCREE
39 Director Housing/Residential Svcs ... Mr. Kent R. DAHLQUIST
41 Director of Athletics ... Mr. Gregory BAMBERGER
38 Director Counseling & Psych Svcs ... Dr. Deborah BARLIEB
96 Director of Purchasing ... Mr. Joseph COCO
07 Interim Director of Admissions ... Ms. Valerie REIDOUT
19 Acting Chief of Police ... Mr. John DILLON
36 Director Career/Community Services ... Ms. Kerri GARDI
29 Director Alumni Engagement ... Mr. Alex OGEKA

Lock Haven University of Pennsylvania (A)

401 N Fairview Street, Lock Haven PA 17745-2390
County: Clinton — FICE Identification: 003323
Unit ID: 213613
Telephone: (570) 484-2011 — Carnegie Class: Master's S
FAX Number: (570) 484-2432 — Calendar System: Semester
URL: www.lhup.edu
Established: 1870 — Annual Undergrad Tuition & Fees (In-State): $8,238
Enrollment: 5,450 — Coed
Affiliation or Control: State — IRS Status: 170(c)1
Highest Offering: Master's
Program: Liberal Arts And General; Teacher Preparatory
Accreditation: M, ADNUR, ARCPA, NRPA, SW, TED

02 President ... Dr. Michael FIORENTINO, JR.
05 Vice Pres Academic Affs/Provost ... Vacant
10 Vice Pres Finance/Admin/Technology ... Mr. William HANELLY
32 Vice President for Student Affairs ... Dr. Linda D. KOCH
45 Asst to Pres for Planning Assess ... Vacant
49 Dean Arts & Sciences ... Dr. David WHITE
53 Dean Education & Human Services ... Vacant
12 Int Dean Clearfield Branch Campus ... Dr. Marianne HAZEL
85 Dean of International Studies ... Vacant
09 Director Institutional Research ... Mr. Mike ABPLANALP
15 Director of Human Resources ... Ms. Deana HILL
07 Director of Admissions ... Mr. Stephen LEE
06 Registrar ... Mrs. Jill MITCHLEY
28 Director of Diversity ... Mr. Albert W. JONES
37 Director of Financial Aid ... Dr. James THEEUWES
36 Director of Career Services ... Ms. Joan C. WELKER
26 Director Marketing & Communications ... Ms. Mary WHITE
19 Director of Public Safety ... Mr. Paul ALTIERI
18 Director of Facilities ... Mr. David B. PROCTOR
41 Director of Athletics ... Ms. Sharon E. TAYLOR
66 Director of Nursing Program ... Ms. Kimberly OWENS
38 Director of Counseling ... Dr. Dan E. TESS
90 Dir Computing/Instructional Tech ... Mr. Donald W. PATTERSON
17 Director of Physician Asst Program ... Mr. Walt EISENHAUER
92 Director Honors Program ... Dr. Jacqueline WHITLING
94 Director Women's Studies ... Dr. Kimberly ALEXANDER
93 Director Minority Students ... Mr. Kenneth L. HALL
40 Manager University Bookstore ... Mr. James KOWNACKI
29 Director Alumni Relations ... Ms. Tammy RICH

*Mansfield University of Pennsylvania (B)

Academy Street, Mansfield PA 16933-1697
County: Tioga — FICE Identification: 003324
Unit ID: 213783
Telephone: (570) 662-4000 — Carnegie Class: Master's M
FAX Number: (570) 662-4995 — Calendar System: Semester
URL: www.mansfield.edu
Established: 1857 — Annual Undergrad Tuition & Fees (In-State): $7,434
Enrollment: 3,500 — Coed
Affiliation or Control: State — IRS Status: 501(c)3
Highest Offering: Master's
Program: Liberal Arts And General; Teacher Preparatory
Accreditation: M, DIETD, MUS, NUR, RAD, SW, TED

02 President ... Dr. Maravene LOESCHKE
05 Provost/Vice Pres Academic Affairs ... Dr. Peter KELLER
11 Vice Pres Administration/Finance ... Mr. Allan J. GOLDEN
30 Vice Pres for Univ Advancement ... Vacant
39 Assoc Vice Pres Residence Life ... Mr. Chuck COLBY
49 Dean of Arts & Sciences ... Mr. James BROWN
53 Dean of Education ... Ms. Joy BURKE
15 Exec Dir Org Dev & Employee Rels ... Ms. Dia CARLETON
08 Director Library/Info Resource Svcs ... Dr. Scott L. DIMARCO
13 Director of Information Technology ... Ms. Connie L. BECKMAN
84 Exec Director Enrollment Management ... Mr. Brian D. BARDEN
26 Director Public Rels/Publications ... Mr. Dennis R. MILLER
37 Director of Financial Aid ... Ms. Barbara SCHMITT
88 Dir Center for Lifelong Learning ... Ms. Susan W. SWEET
19 Director University Police & Safety ... Ms. Christine SHEGAN
41 Director of Athletics ... Mr. Roger N. MAISNER
85 Director of Multicultural Affairs ... Ms. Annie L. COOPER
25 Director of Grants Development ... Ms. Anne LOUDENSLAGER

09 Dir Institutional Rsrch/Assess Data ... Dr. John COSGROVE
29 Director of Alumni Relations ... Ms. Denise BERG
96 Director of Purchasing ... Mr. Tekeste B. ABRAHAM
18 Director of Facilities ... Mr. Benjamin JONES
06 Registrar ... Ms. Lori CASS
38 Director of Counseling Center ... Mr. William S. CHABALA
90 Coord Academic Computing Support ... Ms. Tamela BASTION

*Millersville University of Pennsylvania (C)

PO Box 1002, Millersville PA 17551-0302
County: Lancaster — FICE Identification: 003325
Unit ID: 214041
Telephone: (717) 872-3024 — Carnegie Class: Master's L
FAX Number: (717) 872-3968 — Calendar System: 4/1/4
URL: www.millersville.edu
Established: 1855 — Annual Undergrad Tuition & Fees (In-State): $6,240
Enrollment: 8,729 — Coed
Affiliation or Control: State — IRS Status: 501(c)3
Highest Offering: Master's
Program: Liberal Arts And General; Teacher Preparatory; Professional
Accreditation: M, ACBSP, ART, CS, ENGR, MUS, NAIT, NUR, SW, TED

02 President ... Dr. Francine G. MCNAIRY
05 Vice Pres Academic Affs/Provost ... Dr. Vilas A. PRABHU
10 Vice Pres Finance & Administration ... Mr. Roger BRUSZEWSKI
32 Vice President for Student Affairs ... Dr. Aminta H. BREAUX
30 Vice Pres University Advancement ... Mr. Gerald C. ECKERT
13 Vice Pres Information Resources ... Mr. Robert (Chip) GERMAN, JR.
22 Interim Asst to Pres Soc Equity/Div ... Mr. Hiram G. MARTINEZ
20 Associate Provost Academic Admin ... Dr. Jeffrey R. ADAMS
20 Asst Vice President Academic Svc ... Dr. Minor (Will) REDMOND
45 Asst VP Plng Assessment/Analysis ... Dr. Lisa R. SHIBLEY
21 Assoc Vice Pres Finance/ Admin ... Mr. Kenneth E. DEARSTYNE, JR.
15 Associate Vice Pres Human Resources ... Mr. Louis P. DESOL
26 Asst Vice Pres for Advancement ... Ms. Amy H. DMITZAK
37 Asst VP Stdnt Affs/Dir Fin Aid ... Mr. Dwight G. HORSEY
39 Asst VP Stdnt Affs/Dir Housing ... Mr. Thomas J. RICHARDSON
25 Asst Vice President Development ... Ms. Jan L. EDWARDS
53 Dean of Education ... Dr. Jane S. BRAY
79 Int Dean Humanities/Social Sciences ... Dr. Diane UMBLE
81 Dean of Science & Mathematics ... Dr. Robert T. SMITH
58 Dean Graduate Studies ... Dr. Victor DESANTIS
84 Assoc Provost Enrollment Management ... Dr. Douglas ZANDER
06 Registrar ... Ms. Candace DEEN
36 Director Career Services ... Ms. Margo J. SASSAMAN
18 Dir Capital Const/Contract/Design ... Mr. Arthur DICKINSON
38 Director Counseling/Human Devel ... Dr. Kelsey K. BACKELS
19 Chief of University Police ... Mr. Peter J. ANDERS
23 Director of Univ Health Service ... Dr. Susan F. NORTHWALL
41 Dir of Intercollegiate Athletics ... Ms. Peg KAUFFMAN
40 Manager University Bookstore ... Ms. Audrey HERR
42 Minister-Campus ... Rev. Darrell WOOMER
42 Minister-Catholic ... Fr. Pang TCHEOU
44 Director of Planned Giving ... Mr. Francis SCHODOWSKI
29 Exec Dir for Alumni/Cmty Rels ... Mr. Steven A. DIGUISEPPE
44 Asst Dir Advancement Services ... Mr. Derek M. HOFFMAN
44 Asst Director Annual Fund ... Vacant
09 Director Institutional Research ... Mr. Joseph E. REVELT
30 Director of Development ... Ms. Martha P. MACADAM
30 Asst Dir of Major Gifts ... Ms. Linda ROUSH
102 Dir of Foundation & Govt Support ... Mr. Rene MUNOZ
44 Director Campaigns/Special Giving ... Vacant
96 Director of Purchasing ... Mr. David C. ERRICKSON
19 Interim Dir of Maint Operations ... Mr. Frederick G. EDDINGER
100 Executive Deputy/Chief of Staff ... Dr. James MCCOLLUM
12 Dir Millersville Univ-Lancaster ... Mr. Harvey OWEN
04 Assistant to the President ... Vacant

*Shippensburg University of Pennsylvania (D)

1871 Old Main Drive, Shippensburg PA 17257-2200
County: Cumberland — FICE Identification: 003326
Unit ID: 216010
Telephone: (717) 477-7447 — Carnegie Class: Master's L
FAX Number: (717) 477-1273 — Calendar System: Semester
URL: www.ship.edu
Established: 1871 — Annual Undergrad Tuition & Fees (In-State): $6,239
Enrollment: 8,326 — Coed
Affiliation or Control: State — IRS Status: 501(c)3
Highest Offering: Master's
Program: Liberal Arts And General; Teacher Preparatory; Professional
Accreditation: M, BUS, CACREP, CS, #JOUR, SW, TED

02 President ... Dr. William N. RUUD
03 Exec VP Ext & University Relations ... Dr. G. F. (Jody) HARPSTER
05 Provost & Sr VP Academic Affairs ... Dr. Barbara G. LYMAN
10 Vice Pres Administration/Finance ... Dr. Jan (Denny) TERRELL
102 Pres Shippensburg Univ Foundation ... Mr. John CLINTON
32 Vice Pres for Student Affairs ... Dr. Roger L. SERR
13 Vice Pres Information Tech/Services ... Dr. Rick RUTH
20 Associate Provost ... Dr. Tracy A. SCHOOLCRAFT
20 Assoc Provost/Dean of Acad Outreach ... Dr. Christine SAX
84 Dean of Admiss/Dir of Enroll Mgmt ... Dr. Thomas SPEAKMAN
35 Dean of Students ... Dr. David L. LOVETT
06 Registrar ... Ms. Cathy J. SPRENGER
36 Director Career Development ... Vacant

37 Director Financial Aid ... Dr. Sandra TARBOX
29 Exec Dir University/AlumniRelations ... Mr. Tim EBERSOLE
27 Director Publications & Advertising ... Ms. Laura LUDLAM
88 Exec Dir Univ Communications/Mrktg ... Dr. Peter GIGLIOTTI
08 Dean Library & Multi-Media Services ... Dr. Marian SCHULTZ
22 Director Social Equity ... Dr. Melodye WEHRUNG
88 Director Womens Center ... Ms. Stephanie ERDICE
09 Director Inst Research & Planning ... Mr. Mark PILGRIM
25 Dir Spons Pgm/Inst Public Svc ... Mr. Christopher WONDERS
15 Director Human Resources ... Dr. David TOPPER
38 Director Counseling Services ... Dr. Philip W. HENRY
88 Director of Conferences ... Mr. Randy HAMMOND
53 Dean College Education & Human Svcs ... Dr. James R. JOHNSON
49 Dean College Arts & Science ... Dr. James MIKE
50 Dean College of Business ... Dr. John KOOTI
88 Dean Special Academic Programs ... Dr. Marian SCHULTZ
18 Chief Facilities/Physical Plant ... Mr. Lance BRYSON
96 Director of Purchasing/Contracting ... Ms. Deborah MARTIN
19 Director Public Safety ... Ms. Cytha D. GRISSOM
41 Athletic Director ... Mr. Jeff A. MICHAELS
04 Exec Asst to the President ... Ms. Robin MAUN

*Slippery Rock University of Pennsylvania (E)

1 Morrow Way, Slippery Rock PA 16057-1326
County: Butler — FICE Identification: 003327
Unit ID: 216038
Telephone: (724) 738-9000 — Carnegie Class: Master's L
FAX Number: (724) 738-2169 — Calendar System: Semester
URL: www.sru.edu
Established: 1889 — Annual Undergrad Tuition & Fees (In-State): $8,800
Enrollment: 8,852 — Coed
Affiliation or Control: State — IRS Status: 501(c)3
Highest Offering: Doctorate
Program: Liberal Arts And General; Teacher Preparatory; Professional
Accreditation: M, ART, CACREP, CS, DANCE, EXSC, MUS, NRPA, NUR, PTA, SW, TED, THEA

02 President ... Dr. Robert M. SMITH
05 Provost/Vice Pres Academic Affairs ... Dr. William F. WILLIAMS
10 Vice Pres Finance/Administration ... Dr. Charles T. CURRY
32 Vice President Student Life ... Dr. Constance L. FOLEY
30 Vice President for Univ Advancement ... Ms. Barbara A. ENDER
21 Asst Vice Pres for Finance ... Vacant
18 Asst Vice Pres for Facilities ... Mr. Herbert F. CARLSON
35 Asst Vice Pres for Student Services ... Dr. John S. BONANDO
38 Asst Vice Pres for Student Devel ... Dr. Paula OLIVERO
15 Asst Vice Pres Human Resources ... Ms. Lynne M. MOTYL
28 Asst VP Diversity & Equal Oppty ... Ms. Holly M. MCCOY
04 Assistant to the President ... Ms. Tina L. MOSER
24 Assoc Provost Info & Admin Tech ... Mr. Simeon ANANOU
84 Assoc Provost Enrollment Services ... Dr. Amanda A. YALE
30 Exec Director Univ Advancement ... Dr. Edward R. BUCHA
26 Exec Director Public Relations ... Ms. Rita E. ABENT
37 Director Student Financial Aid ... Ms. Patricia A. HLADIO
19 Director Public Safety ... Mr. William J. RUDLOFF
19 Director University Police ... Mr. Michael SIMMONS
09 Director Institutional Research ... Ms. Carrie J. BIRCKBICHLER
08 Director of Library Services ... Mr. Philip J. TRAMDACK
14 Director Computer Services ... Vacant
06 Director Acad Records/Summer School ... Mr. Eliott G. BAKER
07 Director Undergraduate Admissions ... Vacant
23 Director Health Services ... Ms. Kristina B. CHIPREAN
36 Associate Director Career Services ... Mr. John F. SNYDER
29 Director Alumni Affairs ... Vacant
76 Dean Col Health Environment/Sci ... Dr. Susan E. HANNAM
07 Director Graduate Admissions ... Ms. Angela PIVEROTTO
41 Athletic Director ... Mr. Paul A. LUEKEN
39 Director Housing/Residence Life ... Mr. Kevin D. CURRIE
85 Director International Services ... Ms. Pamela J. FRIGOT
25 Director Grants & Sponsored Rsrch ... Ms. Nancy L. CRUIKSHANK
38 Director of Student Counseling ... Dr. Carol L. HOLLAND
93 Director of Minority Students ... Ms. Corinne J. GIBSON
96 Director of Purchasing ... Mr. Mark S. COMBINE
92 Director of Honors Program ... Dr. Bradley WILSON
57 Dean Col of Hum/Fine/Perf Arts ... Dr. Eva TSUQUIASHI-DADDESIO
50 Dean Col Business/Info/Social Scs ... Dr. Kurt SHIMMEL
53 Dean College of Education ... Dr. Kathleen M. STRICKLAND

*West Chester University of Pennsylvania (F)

University & High Street, West Chester PA 19383-0001
County: Chester — FICE Identification: 003328
Unit ID: 216764
Telephone: (610) 436-1000 — Carnegie Class: Master's L
FAX Number: (610) 436-3115 — Calendar System: Semester
URL: www.wcupa.edu
Established: 1871 — Annual Undergrad Tuition & Fees (In-State): $6,588
Enrollment: 14,492 — Coed
Affiliation or Control: State — IRS Status: 501(c)3
Highest Offering: Master's
Program: Liberal Arts And General; Teacher Preparatory; Professional
Accreditation: M, BUS, CACREP, CS, DIETD, EXSC, MUS, NURSE, PH, SP, SW, TED, THEA

02 President ... Dr. Greg R. WEISENSTEIN
04 Executive Deputy to President ... Mr. Lawrence A. DOWDY
05 Vice Pres Academic Affairs/Provost ... Dr. Linda L. LAMWERS

11 Vice President Admin/Finance ... Mr. Mark P. MIXNER
32 VP Student Affs/Dean of Students ... Dr. Matthew M. BRICKETTO
30 Vice President Advancement ... Dr. Mark G. PAVLOVICH
13 Vice Pres Information Services ... Mr. Adel BARIMANI
88 Assoc VP Sponsored Research ... Dr. Michael AYEWOH
15 Assoc Vice Pres Human Resources ... Mr. Michael T. MALOY
58 Assoc Provost/Dean Grad Studies ... Dr. Darla S. COFFEY
64 Dean College Visual/Performing Arts ... Dr. Timothy V. BLAIR
76 Dean College Health Science ... Dr. Donald E. BARR
53 Dean College Education ... Dr. Kenneth D. WITMER
50 Dean College Business/Public Affs ... Dr. Christopher M. FIORENTINO
49 Dean College Arts/Sciences ... Dr. Lori A. VERMEULEN
20 Dean Undergrad Stds/Stdt Suppt Svcs ... Dr. Idna M. CORBETT
35 Asst Vice Pres Student Affairs ... Dr. Thomas J. PURCE
35 Asst Vice Pres Student Affairs ... Ms. Diane DEVESTERN
102 Exec Director WCU Foundation ... Mr. Richard T. PRZYWARA
10 Asst VP Finance/Business Svcs ... Ms. Bernadette HINKLE
104 Asst VP International Programs ... Dr. David A. WRIGHT
106 Exec Director Distance Education ... Dr. Rui LI
23 Asst Dean Stdnts/Dir Health Center ... Ms. Mary Ann HAMMOND
88 Director Graduate Enrollment ... Dr. Lawrence WALSH
22 Director Social Equity ... Ms. Barbara SCHNELLER
09 Director Institutional Research ... Ms. Lisa YANNICK
21 Dir Accounting/Financial Reporting ... Mr. Kevin MCCADDEN
88 Interim Director Budget ... Ms. Denise MOUNT
26 Director Public Relations/Marketing ... Ms. Pamela SHERIDAN
88 Director Publications/Printing Svcs ... Ms. Cynthia BEDNAR
88 Director Cultural/Community Affairs ... Mr. John RHEIN
90 Spec Asst to VP Information Svcs ... Dr. James FABREY
06 Registrar ... Mr. Joeseph SANTIVASCI
21 Bursar/Director Student Finan Svcs ... Mr. Daniel PAULETTI
07 Director Admissions ... Ms. Marsha L. HAUG
08 Director Library Services ... Mr. Richard SWAIN
88 Director Teacher Education Center ... Dr. James B. PRICE
36 Director Career Devel Center ... Ms. Rebecca ROSS
88 Int Dir Academic Development Pgm ... Dr. Allan HILL
88 Interim Dir Learning Asst/Resource ... Ms. Gerardina KENNEY
37 Director Financial Aid ... Mr. Dana C. PARKER
38 Director Counseling Center ... Dr. Julie PERONE
29 Director Alumni Relations ... Ms. Megan CANTALUPO
41 Director Athletics ... Dr. Edward M. MATEJKOVIC
88 Director Sports Information ... Mr. James ZUHLKE
28 Director Multicultural Affairs ... Mr. Jeromo HUTSON
94 Director Women's Center ... Dr. Adale SHOLOCK
18 Exec Director Facilities Management ... Mr. Greg CUPRAK
18 Exec Direct Facilities Design/Const ... Ms. Dolores GIARDINA
19 Director Public Safety ... Mr. Michael D. BICKING
96 Director Purchasing/Contract Svcs ... Ms. Marianne PEFFALL
91 Dir Administrative Computing Systms ... Mr. Patrick LENZI
88 Dir Admin Computing Application Dev ... Ms. Chaw-ye CHANG
88 Director Network/Telecommunications ... Mr. Joseph SINCAVAGE
39 Director Housing Services ... Mr. Peter GALLOWAY
39 Director Residence Life ... Ms. Marion MCKINNEY
88 Dir Judicial Affairs/Student Assist ... Ms. Lynn KLINGENSMITH
88 Director Sykes Student Union ... Mr. David TIMMANN
40 Student Svcs Inc Bookstore Manager ... Mr. Stephen MANNELLA

Philadelphia Biblical University (A)

200 Manor Avenue, Langhorne Manor PA 19047-2990

County: Bucks | FICE Identification: 003351 | Unit ID: 215114
Telephone: (215) 752-5800 | Carnegie Class: Master's S
FAX Number: (215) 702-4341 | Calendar System: Semester
URL: www.pbu.edu
Established: 1913 | Annual Undergrad Tuition & Fees: $20,888
Enrollment: 1,241 | Coed
Affiliation or Control: Independent Non-Profit | IRS Status: 501(c)3
Highest Offering: First Professional Degree
Program: Liberal Arts And General; Teacher Preparatory; Professional; Religious Emphasis
Accreditation: M, BI, IACBE, MUS, SW

01 President ... Dr. Todd J. WILLIAMS
05 Provost ... Dr. Brian G. TOEWS
11 Sr Vice Pres Finance & Admin ... Mr. Jan M. HAAS
30 Sr Vice Pres Univ Advancement ... Mr. Scott A. KEATING
15 Vice Pres Human Resources ... Ms. Mary BOYER
20 Vice Pres Educational Resources ... Dr. Timothy K. HUI
32 Vice Pres Student Life ... Mr. J. Scott CAWOOD
26 Vice Pres Marketing/Communications ... Ms. Lisa WEIDMAN
06 Registrar ... Dr. Steven SCHLENKER
07 Director of Admissions ... Mr. Jamie GLEASON
10 Controller ... Mr. Jeff EUBANK
18 Director Campus Services ... Mr. Robert WATSON
12 Director Wisconsin Campus ... Mr. Mark A. JALOVICK
04 Assistant to President ... Ms. Jodi L. TODD
13 Director Information Technology ... Mr. Curt D. WINTERS
37 Director Financial Aid ... Vacant
09 Director Institutional Research ... Dr. Lynn H. WALLACE
42 Director University Ministries ... Ms. Michele MCALACK
39 Director Resident Life ... Mr. Stephen HAUSER
29 Director Alumni Relations ... Vacant
19 Chief of Security ... Mr. Chris LLOYD
23 Director Health Services ... Ms. Alison KIKENDALL
40 Manager of Bookstore ... Mr. Charles GLOVER
38 Director Student Counseling ... Mr. Baron KING
36 Director Career Center ... Ms. Teri T. CANTANIO
21 Asst Director Business Services ... Dr. Andrew HUI
96 Purchasing Agent ... Ms. Wendy HULME

Philadelphia College of Osteopathic Medicine (B)

4170 City Avenue, Philadelphia PA 19131-1694

County: Philadelphia | FICE Identification: 003352 | Unit ID: 215123
Telephone: (215) 871-6100 | Carnegie Class: Spec/Med
FAX Number: (215) 871-6719 | Calendar System: Semester
URL: www.pcom.edu
Established: 1899 | Annual Graduate Tuition & Fees: $41,537
Enrollment: 2,287 | Coed
Affiliation or Control: Independent Non-Profit | IRS Status: 501(c)3
Highest Offering: Doctorate; No Undergraduates
Program: Professional
Accreditation: M, ARCPA, CLPSY, OSTEO, @PHAR

01 President & CEO ... Dr. Matthew SCHURE
05 Provost/Senior VP Acad Affairs/Dean ... Dr. Kenneth J. VEIT
10 Vice Pres Finance/Treasurer/CFO ... Mr. Peter DOULIS
30 Vice Pres Alumni Rels/Development ... Ms. Florence D. ZELLER
58 Vice Pres Grad Pgms/Academic Plng ... Dr. Robert G. CUZZOLINO
84 Assoc Vice Pres Enrollment Mgmt ... Vacant
88 Vice Dean Clinical Education ... Dr. Richard A. PASCUCCI
76 Sr Assoc Dean Preclinical Ed/Rsrch ... Dr. Richard M. KRIEBEL
51 Assoc Dean Primary Care/Cont Educ ... Dr. Eugene MOCHAN
32 Assistant Dean of Student Affairs ... Dr. Tina WOODRUFF
88 Dir of Ungraduate Educ Clinical ... Dr. Allan MCLEOD
26 Director Marketing/Communications ... Ms. Wendy ROMANO
37 Director Student Financial Aid ... Ms. Nancy MARTORANO
15 Director Human Resources ... Ms. Rita C. FORDE
08 Chair of Library/Exec Director ... Ms. Etheldra TEMPLETON
06 Registrar ... Ms. Deborah CASTELLANO
20 Interim Chief Academic Officer ... Ms. Deborah A. BENVENGER
18 Chief Facilities/Plant Operations ... Mr. Frank H. WINDLE
29 Dir Alumni Relations/Development ... Ms. Pamela J. RUOFF
96 Director of Purchasing ... Ms. Natalie COOPER

Philadelphia University (C)

School House Ln & Henry Avenue, Philadelphia PA 19144-5497

County: Philadelphia | FICE Identification: 003354 | Unit ID: 215099
Telephone: (215) 951-2700 | Carnegie Class: Master's L
FAX Number: (215) 951-2615 | Calendar System: Semester
URL: www.philau.edu
Established: 1884 | Annual Undergrad Tuition & Fees: $30,356
Enrollment: 3,619 | Coed
Affiliation or Control: Independent Non-Profit | IRS Status: 501(c)3
Highest Offering: Doctorate
Program: Professional
Accreditation: M, ARCPA, ART, CIDA, LSAR, MIDWF, OT

01 President ... Dr. Stephen SPINELLI, JR.
11 VP for Administration/COO ... Dr. Geoffrey CROMARTY
10 Chief Financial Officer ... Mr. James P. HARTMAN
05 Provost ... Dr. Randy SWEARER
30 VP Development & Alumni Relations ... Mr. Jesse SHAFER
26 Vice Pres Marketing/Public Rels ... Ms. Patricia M. BALDRIDGE
13 Vice President Campus Info Res ... Mr. Jeff CEPULL
84 Dean of Enrollment Management ... Ms. Christine GREB
32 Dean of Students ... Dr. Mark GOVONI
18 Asst Vice Pres for Operations ... Mr. J. Thomas BECKER
15 Asst Vice Pres Human Resources ... Ms. Katherine FLANNERY
48 Dean College of Architecture ... Vacant
81 Dean Col of Science & Health ... Dr. Matt BAKER
88 Dean College of Design Engineering ... Dr. Ron KANDER
50 Dean School of Business Admin ... Dr. Sue LEHRMAN
58 Director Sch Grad Continuing Stds ... Mr. Frank CONGDON
08 Director of Library Services ... Ms. Karen ALBERT
38 Director Advising/Counseling ... Dr. Patricia THATCHER
41 Athletic Director ... Mr. Thomas R. SHIRLEY, JR.
29 Director Alumni Relations ... Ms. Linda J. HOLLENBACK
36 Director of Career Placement ... Ms. Patricia SHAFER
40 Director College Store ... Ms. Shirley A. LANDIS
37 Director Financial Aid ... Ms. Lisa J. COOPER
23 Director Health Services ... Ms. Karen DAHLQUIST
06 Registrar ... Ms. Julia AGGREH
39 Director of Residence Life Educ ... Vacant
19 Director Safety & Security ... Mr. Jeffrey BAIRD
35 Director Student Activities ... Mr. Timothy J. BUTLER
09 Director of Institutional Research ... Mr. Mark PALLADINO

Pittsburgh Institute of Aeronautics (D)

5 Allegheny County Airport, West Mifflin PA 15122-2674

County: Allegheny | FICE Identification: 005310 | Unit ID: 215381
Telephone: (412) 346-2100 | Carnegie Class: Assoc/PrivNFP
FAX Number: (412) 466-0513 | Calendar System: Quarter
URL: www.pia.edu
Established: 1929 | Annual Undergrad Tuition & Fees: $19,770
Enrollment: 200 | Coed
Affiliation or Control: Independent Non-Profit | IRS Status: 501(c)3
Highest Offering: Associate Degree
Program: Occupational
Accreditation: ACCSC

01 President/CFO ... Mr. John GRAHAM, III
53 Director ... Dr. James MADER
03 Executive Vice President ... Ms. Sue MARKLE
29 Director of Alumni Services ... Mr. Greg NULL

Pittsburgh Institute of Mortuary Science (E)

5808 Baum Boulevard, Pittsburgh PA 15206-3706

County: Allegheny | FICE Identification: 010814 | Unit ID: 215390
Telephone: (412) 362-8500 | Carnegie Class: Assoc/PrivNFP
FAX Number: (412) 362-1684 | Calendar System: Trimester
URL: www.pims.edu
Established: 1939 | Annual Undergrad Tuition & Fees: $15,000
Enrollment: 209 | Coed
Affiliation or Control: Independent Non-Profit | IRS Status: 501(c)3
Highest Offering: Associate Degree
Program: Occupational; 2-Year Principally Bachelor's Creditable
Accreditation: FUSER

01 President & CEO ... Eugene C. OGRODNIK
06 Registrar ... Karen S. ROCCO

Pittsburgh Technical Institute (F)

1111 McKee Road, Oakdale PA 15071-3205

County: Allegheny | FICE Identification: 007437 | Unit ID: 215415
Telephone: (412) 809-5100 | Carnegie Class: Assoc/PrivFP
FAX Number: (412) 809-5320 | Calendar System: Quarter
URL: www.pti.edu
Established: 1946 | Annual Undergrad Tuition & Fees: N/A
Enrollment: 2,078 | Coed
Affiliation or Control: Proprietary | IRS Status: Proprietary
Highest Offering: Associate Degree
Program: Occupational; 2-Year Principally Bachelor's Creditable; Technical Emphasis
Accreditation: M, MAC, SURGT

01 President ... Mr. Gregory DEFEO
03 Executive Vice President ... Mr. George PRY
05 Sr Vice Pres Academic Affairs ... Mr. Mark SCOTT
10 Sr Vice Pres Financial Affairs ... Mr. Terry FARRELL
07 Vice Pres Admissions ... Mr. Jeffrey ABRAHAM
10 Vice President of Business Affairs ... Mr. Chuck CUBELIC
21 Vice President Financial Services ... Mrs. Connie FRIEDBERG
32 Vice President Student Services ... Mr. Keith MERLINO
20 Vice President Education ... Ms. Eileen RILEY
30 Vice President of Inst Advancement ... Mrs. Ruth DELACH
36 Vice President Graduate Services ... Vacant
09 Vice Pres of Strategic Initiatives ... Mr. Jeff BELSKY
43 General Counsel ... Mr. Jack MCGINTY
06 Registrar ... Mrs. Patricia TARVIN
08 Library Director ... Mrs. Ruth WALTER
26 Chief Public Relations Officer ... Mrs. Linda ALLAN
16 Director of Human Resources ... Ms. Nancy SHEPPARD
13 IS Department Director ... Mr. John KOVAC
39 Housing Director ... Ms. Gloria RITCHIE
40 Bookstore Manager ... Mrs. Cynthia KLEIN
29 Alumni Coordinator ... Mrs. Christine IOLI

Pittsburgh Theological Seminary (G)

616 N. Highland Avenue, Pittsburgh PA 15206-2596

County: Allegheny | FICE Identification: 003356 | Unit ID: 215424
Telephone: (412) 362-5610 | Carnegie Class: Spec/Faith
FAX Number: (412) 363-3260 | Calendar System: Quarter
URL: www.pts.edu
Established: 1794 | Annual Graduate Tuition & Fees: $10,449
Enrollment: 305 | Coed
Affiliation or Control: Presbyterian Church (U.S.A.) | IRS Status: 501(c)3
Highest Offering: Doctorate; No Undergraduates
Program: Professional; Religious Emphasis
Accreditation: M, THEOL

01 President ... Dr. William J. CARL, III
05 Vice Pres Acad Affs/Dean of Faculty ... Dr. Byron H. JACKSON
30 Vice Pres Strategic Advance/Mktg ... Mr. Thomas J. PAPPALARDO
32 Vice Pres Stdnt Svcs/Dean of Stdnts ... Mr. John WELCH
07 Associate Dean Admissions/Vocations ... Ms. Sherry SPARKS
06 Registrar ... Ms. Anne B. MALONE
08 Director of the Library ... Dr. Sharon TAYLOR
88 Director of Field Education ... Dr. Carolyn J. JONES
29 Director of Alumni/ae Services ... Ms. Carolyn CRANSTON
88 Director Doctor of Ministry Program ... Dr. Susan KENDALL
51 Director Cont Educ/Special Events ... Dr. James DAVISON
37 Dir Financial Aid/Admissions Ofcr ... Ms. Cheryl DEPAOLIS

Point Park University (H)

201 Wood Street, Pittsburgh PA 15222-1984

County: Allegheny | FICE Identification: 003357 | Unit ID: 215442
Telephone: (412) 391-4100 | Carnegie Class: Master's L
FAX Number: (412) 392-3998 | Calendar System: Semester
URL: www.pointpark.edu
Established: 1960 | Annual Undergrad Tuition & Fees: $23,720
Enrollment: 4,077 | Coed
Affiliation or Control: Independent Non-Profit | IRS Status: 501(c)3
Highest Offering: Master's
Program: Liberal Arts And General; Teacher Preparatory; Professional
Accreditation: M, DANCE, ENGT, IACBE

01 President .... Dr. Paul HENNIGAN
05 Sr VP Academic and Student Affairs .... Dr. Karen MCINTYRE
10 Sr VP Finance and Operations .... Ms. Bridget MANCOSH
26 VP of External Affairs .... Ms. Mariann GEYER
18 Vice Pres for Operations .... Mr. William D. CAMERON
30 Vice Pres Development/AlumniAffairs .... Mr. Richard HASKINS
84 Asst VP Strategic Plng/Enrollment .... Ms. Trudy WILLIAMS
96 Asst VP Procurement/Business Svcs .... Ms. Ruth RAULUK
32 Dean of Student Affairs .... Mr. Keith PAYLO
53 Chair Education .... Dr. Darlene MARNICH
79 Actg Chair Humanities/Human Science .... Ms. Kim BELL
88 Chair of Faculty .... Dr. Heather STARR FIEDLER
54 Act Chair Natural Science/Engr Tech .... Dr. John KUDLAC
88 Chair Criminal Justice/Intell Stds .... Mr. Greg ROGERS
88 Chair Management .... Ms. Margaret GILFILLAN
88 Chair Theatre .... Ms. Sheila MCKENNA
88 Chair Dance .... Ms. Susan STOWE
88 Chair Cinema .... Mr. Nelson CHIPMAN
57 Dean Conservatory of Perform Arts .... Mr. Frederick JOHNSON
49 Actg Dean School Arts and Sciences .... Dr. Robert FESSLER
60 Acting Dean School of Communication .... Mr. Ronald ALLAN-LINDBLOM
50 Dean School of Business .... Dr. Angela ISAAC
04 Exec Assistant to the President .... Ms. Nina CAMPBELL
06 Registrar .... Ms. Jennifer FEDELE
15 Director Human Resources .... Mr. Guy CATANIA
21 Director of Finance/Controller .... Mr. Jim HARDT
44 Senior Dir Development/Stewardship .... Ms. Lynn CUMMINGS
08 Director/Librarian/Academic Svcs .... Ms. Liz EVANS
37 Sr Assoc Director of Financial Aid .... Ms. Sandra CRONIN
26 Sr Dir Marketing & Communications .. Ms. Mary Ellen SOLOMON
39 Director of Campus Life .... Ms. Janet D. EVANS
07 Director of Admissions .... Ms. Joell MINFORD
36 Director of Career Services .... Mr. Jan-Mitchell SHERRILL
41 Director of Athletics .... Mr. Dan SWALGA
09 Director Institutional Research .... Mr. Christopher CHONCEK
54 Dir of Sciences/Engineering Mgmt .... Dr. John KUDLAC
88 Dir Conference & Event Services .... Ms. Terri SNOE
29 Manager of Alumni Relations .... Mr. John PINE
38 Student Counseling .... Ms. Patti SCHWARTZ

Prism Career Institute-Upper Darby Campus (A)

6800 Market Street, Upper Darby PA 19082-1926

County: Delaware | FICE Identification: 023013 | Unit ID: 215433
Telephone: (610) 789-6700 | Carnegie Class: Assoc/PrivFP
FAX Number: (610) 789-5208 | Calendar System: Semester
URL: www.prismcareerinstitute.edu
Established: 1981 | Annual Undergrad Tuition & Fees: $10,897
Enrollment: 406 | Coed
Affiliation or Control: Proprietary | IRS Status: Proprietary
Highest Offering: Associate Degree
Program: Occupational
Accreditation: ACCSC

01 Campus President .... Mr. Jeremiah STAROTOLI
05 Acting Director of Education .... Ms. Amy BERRIOS
07 Director of Admissions .... Ms. Dina M. GENTILE

Reading Area Community College (B)

PO Box 1706, Reading PA 19603-1706

County: Berks | FICE Identification: 010388 | Unit ID: 215585
Telephone: (610) 372-4721 | Carnegie Class: Assoc/Pub-R-M
FAX Number: (610) 372-4264 | Calendar System: Semester
URL: www.racc.edu
Established: 1971 | Annual Undergrad Tuition & Fees (In-District): $4,100
Enrollment: 5,417 | Coed
Affiliation or Control: State/Local | IRS Status: 501(c)3
Highest Offering: Associate Degree
Program: Occupational; 2-Year Principally Bachelor's Creditable
Accreditation: M, ADNUR, MLTAD, PNUR

01 President .... Dr. Anna D. WEITZ
05 Sr VP of Academic Affairs/Provost .... Dr. A. Wade DAVENPORT
10 Sr VP Business Svcs/Treasurer .... Mr. Theodore BASSANO
32 VP/Student Development .... Ms. Diane MARABELLA
103 VP of Workforce Development .... Dr. Robert VAUGHN
30 VP of Institutional Advancement .... Mr. Michael NAGEL
84 VP Enrollment Management .... Ms. Maria MITCHELL
08 Assistant Dean Library Services .... Ms. Mary Ellen HECKMAN
37 Director Financial Aid/Registrar .... Mr. Benjamin ROSENBERGER
15 Director Human Resources .... Mr. Scott HEFFELFINGER
26 Director of Public Relations .... Ms. Melissa KUSHNER
13 Director Information Technology .... Mr. Chet WINTERS
21 Controller .... Ms. Dolores PETERSON
96 Purchasing Manager .... Mr. Michael HODOWANEC
09 Dir of Asessment/Research/Planning .... Ms. Mary FLAGG
35 Coordinator of Student Activities .... Ms. Sue GELSINGER
88 Dir of Miller Center for the Arts .... Ms. Cathleen STEPHEN
07 Dir of Enrollment Services .... Ms. Calley STEVENS-TAYLOR

Reconstructionist Rabbinical College (C)

1299 Church Road, Wyncote PA 19095-1898

County: Montgomery | FICE Identification: 022734 | Unit ID: 215619
Telephone: (215) 576-0800 | Carnegie Class: Spec/Faith
FAX Number: (215) 576-6143 | Calendar System: Semester
URL: www.rrc.edu
Established: 1968 | Annual Graduate Tuition & Fees: $19,000
Enrollment: 57 | Coed
Affiliation or Control: Jewish | IRS Status: 501(c)3
Highest Offering: Doctorate; No Undergraduates
Program: Professional
Accreditation: M

01 President .... Rabbi Dan EHRENKRANTZ
05 Chief Academic Officer/Dean .... Dr. Tamar KAMIONKOWSKI
11 Vice President Administration .... Mrs. Jennifer S. ABRAHAM
10 Controller .... Ms. Lisa COHEN
20 Dean Academic Administration .... Ms. Barbara HIRSH
07 Asst VP Rabbinic Formation/Admiss .... Rabbi Amber POWERS
08 Director of the Library .... Ms. Deborah STERN

Reformed Episcopal Seminary (D)

826 Second Avenue, Blue Bell PA 19422-1257

County: Montgomery | Identification: 667050
Telephone: (610) 292-9852 | Carnegie Class: Not Classified
FAX Number: (610) 292-9853 | Calendar System: Quarter
URL: www.reseminary.edu
Established: 1887 | Annual Graduate Tuition & Fees: $5,940
Enrollment: 14 | Coed
Affiliation or Control: Reformed Episcopal Church | IRS Status: 501(c)3
Highest Offering: Master's; No Undergraduates
Program: Religious Emphasis
Accreditation: @THEOL

01 Chancellor and President .... RtRev. David L. HICKS
05 Provost and Dean .... VenDr. Jon W. ABBOUD
20 Asistant Academic Dean .... RevDr. Jonathan S. RICHES
105 Director Web Services .... Mr. Gregory R. WRIGHT

Reformed Presbyterian Theological Seminary (E)

7418 Penn Avenue, Pittsburgh PA 15208-2594

County: Allegheny | FICE Identification: 003358 | Unit ID: 215628
Telephone: (412) 731-8690 | Carnegie Class: Spec/Faith
FAX Number: (412) 731-4834 | Calendar System: Quarter
URL: www.rpts.edu
Established: 1810 | Annual Graduate Tuition & Fees: $9,540
Enrollment: 100 | Coed
Affiliation or Control: Reformed Presbyterian Church | IRS Status: 501(c)3
Highest Offering: Master's; No Undergraduates
Program: Professional
Accreditation: THEOL

01 President .... Dr. Jerry F. O'NEILL
05 Dean of the Faculty .... Dr. Dennis J. PRUTOW
06 Registrar/Head Librarian .... Mr. Thomas G. REID, JR.
40 Bookstore Manager .... Ms. Sharon SAMPSON
10 Treasurer .... Mr. James MCFARLAND
07 Dir of Admissions & Financial Aid .... Mr. John MCCOMBS

The Restaurant School at Walnut Hill College (F)

4207 Walnut Street, Philadelphia PA 19104-3518

County: Philadelphia | FICE Identification: 021928 | Unit ID: 215637
Telephone: (215) 222-4200 | Carnegie Class: Spec/Other
FAX Number: (215) 222-4219 | Calendar System: Other
URL: www.walnuthillcollege.edu
Established: 1974 | Annual Undergrad Tuition & Fees: $22,400
Enrollment: 471 | Coed
Affiliation or Control: Proprietary | IRS Status: Proprietary
Highest Offering: Baccalaureate
Program: 2-Year Principally Bachelor's Creditable
Accreditation: ACCSC

01 President .... Mr. Daniel LIBERATOSCIOLI
30 Vice President College Advancement .... Mr. Karl D. BECKER
11 Vice President Administrative Svcs .. Ms. Peggy LIBERATOSCIOLI
07 Director of Admissions .... Vacant
05 Dean of Academic Affairs .... Ms. Lenore BOCCIA
10 Chief Business Officer .... Mr. Chris MOLZ
32 Chf Student Life Ofcr/Stdnt Plcmnt .... Ms. Sabrina JORDAN
51 Director Continuing Education .... Ms. Jocelyn WOOD
88 Director of Culinary Arts .... Chef Tom DELCAMP
88 Director School of Management .... Mr. David MORROW

Robert Morris University (G)

6001 University Boulevard, Moon Township PA 15108-1189

County: Allegheny | FICE Identification: 003359 | Unit ID: 215655
Telephone: (412) 397-3000 | Carnegie Class: Master's L
FAX Number: (412) 397-5958 | Calendar System: Semester
URL: www.rmu.edu
Established: 1921 | Annual Undergrad Tuition & Fees: $22,405
Enrollment: 4,967 | Coed
Affiliation or Control: Independent Non-Profit | IRS Status: 501(c)3
Highest Offering: Doctorate
Program: Teacher Preparatory; Professional
Accreditation: M, BUS, CS, ENG, NMT, NURSE, TEAC

01 President .... Dr. Gregory G. DELL'OMO
10 Sr Vice Pres for Business Affairs .... Mr. Dan W. KIENER
05 Provost/Sr VP Academic Affairs .... Mr. David L. JAMISON
30 Sr VP Institutional Advancement .... Mr. Jay T. CARSON
43 Vice President & General Counsel .... Mr. Sidney ZONN
21 Vice President Financial Operations .... Mr. Jeffrey A. LISTWAK
15 Vice President of Human Resources .... Mr. Peter K. FAIX
106 VP Online and Off-Campus Programs .... Dr. Darcy B. TANNEHILL
84 VP Enrollment Management .... Mr. Michael FRANTZ
88 Exec Dir Bayer Ctr Nonprofit Mgmt .... Ms. Peggy M. OUTON
60 Dean School Comm/Info Systems .... Dr. Barbara J. LEVINE
50 Dean School of Business .... Dr. Derya A. JACOBS
54 Dean Sch Engr/Math/Science .... Dr. Maria V. KALEVITCH
53 Dean Sch Education/Social Sciences .... Dr. Mary Ann RAFORTH
66 Dean School Nursing/Health Sciences .... Dr. Lynda J. DAVIDSON
32 Chief Stdt Life Ofcr/Dean Students .... Mr. John MICHALENKO
26 Assoc VP Institutional Advancement .... Ms. Nina MARGIOTTA
88 Assoc VP/Dir Sponsorships .... Mr. Donald K. SMITH
07 Dean of Admissions .... Ms. Kellie L. LAURENZI
13 VP & Chief Information Officer .... Ms. Ellen G. WIECKOWSKI
18 VP & Chief Facilities Officer .... Mr. Perry F. ROOFNER
26 VP & Chief Marketing Officer .... Ms. Kyle FISHER
41 Director of Athletics .... Dr. Craig S. COLEMAN
08 Dean University Libraries .... Dr. Frances J. CAPLAN
20 Associate Provost .... Dr. Lawrence A. TOMEI
20 Associate Provost .... Dr. Frederick G. KOHUN
21 Controller .... Ms. Melissa A. MICCO
06 Registrar .... Mr. Frank E. PERRY
18 Director Public Safety .... Mr. Randy L. MINK
36 Director Career Center .... Ms. Kishma DECASTRO-SALLIS
39 Director Residence Life .... Mr. Ronald C. SHIDEMANTLE
38 Director Center for Student Success .... Ms. Cassandra L. ODEN
27 Senior Director Public Relations .... Mr. Jonathan POTTS
09 Director Institutional Research .... Mr. David R. MAJKA
96 Director Business Operations .... Mr. Neal F. BINSTOCK
37 Director Student Financial Aid ... Ms. Stephanie N. HENDERSHOT
29 Director Devel/Alumni Relations .... Mr. Warner O. JOHNSON
88 Dean Engaged Learning .... Dr. Shari L. PAYNE

Rosedale Technical Institute (H)

215 Beecham Drive, Suite 2, Pittsburgh PA 15205-9791

County: Allegheny | FICE Identification: 012050 | Unit ID: 215682
Telephone: (412) 521-6200 | Carnegie Class: Assoc/PrivNFP
FAX Number: (412) 521-2520 | Calendar System: Semester
URL: www.rosedaletech.org
Established: 1949 | Annual Undergrad Tuition & Fees: $12,480
Enrollment: 367 | Coed
Affiliation or Control: Independent Non-Profit | IRS Status: 501(c)3
Highest Offering: Associate Degree
Program: Occupational; 2-Year Principally Bachelor's Creditable; Technical Emphasis
Accreditation: ACCSC

01 President .... Dennis F. WILKE
05 Director of Education .... Jim SHORE
07 Director of Admissions .... Debbie BIER

Rosemont College (I)

1400 Montgomery Avenue, Rosemont PA 19010-1699

County: Montgomery | FICE Identification: 003360 | Unit ID: 215691
Telephone: (610) 527-0200 | Carnegie Class: Master's M
FAX Number: (610) 527-0341 | Calendar System: Semester
URL: www.rosemont.edu
Established: 1921 | Annual Undergrad Tuition & Fees: $29,050
Enrollment: 863 | Coed
Affiliation or Control: Roman Catholic | IRS Status: 501(c)3
Highest Offering: Master's
Program: Liberal Arts And General; Teacher Preparatory
Accreditation: M

01 President .... Dr. Sharon LATCHAW HIRSH
05 Provost/VP Academic/Student Affairs .... Dr. B. Christopher DOUGHERTY
10 VP for Finance & Administration .... Mrs. Mary Beth TSIKALAS
27 Director of Financial Aid .... Ms. Sarah FEVIG
30 Vice Pres College Relations .... Ms. Christyn MORAN
32 Dean of Students .... Mr. David A. SURRATT
84 Vice President for Enrollment Mgmt .... Mr. Kevin M. MCINTYRE
88 Vice President for Mission .... Sr. Jeanne Marie HATCH, SHCJ
08 Exec Director of Library Services .... Mrs. Catherine FENNELL
58 Int Dean Schs Grad/Prof Stds .... Mrs. Paulette HUTCHINSON
20 Int Academic Dean Undergrad College .... Mrs. Paulette HUTCHINSON
29 Director of Alumni Relations .... Vacant
26 Director of Public Relations .... Ms. Roberta PERRY
06 Registrar/Dir of Inst Research .... Mr. Joseph T. ROGERS
41 Director of Athletics .... Ms. Lynn S. ROTHENHOEFER
15 Director of Human Resources .... Ms. Jane FEDEROWICZ
42 Director of Campus Ministry .... Ms. Elizabeth SMALL
40 Store Manager Campus Bookstore ..... Ms. Wioletta M. MARTINEZ
18 Chief Facil/Phys Plant/Pub Safety .... Mr. Raymond A. BROWN
38 Director Student Counseling .... Ms. Olga GUERRA
39 Director of Res Life/Asst Dean .... Mr. Lee PLENN
19 Director of Public Safety .... Mr. Chuck LORENZ
21 Controller .... Mr. Ronald LAHER

Saint Charles Borromeo Seminary (A)

100 E Wynnewood Road, Wynnewood PA 19096-3099
County: Montgomery FICE Identification: 003364
Unit ID: 216047
Telephone: (610) 667-3394 Carnegie Class: Spec/Faith
FAX Number: (610) 667-7635 Calendar System: Semester
URL: www.scs.edu
Established: 1832 Annual Undergrad Tuition & Fees: $18,775
Enrollment: 244 Male
Affiliation or Control: Roman Catholic IRS Status: 501(c)3
Highest Offering: Master's
Program: Liberal Arts And General; Professional
Accreditation: M, THEOL

Code	Title	Name
01	Rector & President	Rev. Shaun L. MAHONEY
03	Vice Rector	Rev. Joseph W. BONGARD
10	Vice Pres of Finance & Operations	Mrs. Elaine K. RICE
73	Academic Dean Theology Division	Rev. Robert A. PESARCHICK
49	Academic Dean College Division	Mr. James F. GROWDON
73	Acad Dean Religious Studies Div	Vacant
33	Dean of Men College	Rev. Robert B. MCDERMOTT
33	Dean of Men Theol/Dir of Liturgy	Rev. Patrick J. WELSH
06	Registrar	Mr. Lawrence A. HEYMAN
30	Director of Development	Mr. David L. OSBORNE
08	Director of Library Services	Mrs. Cait KOKOLUS
42	Director Spiritual Formation Col	Rev. Anthony J. COSTA
42	Director Spiritual Formation Theol	Rev. Joseph F. GLEASON
88	Director Pastoral/Apostolic Form	Rev. Michael H. SPITZER
64	Director of Music	Dr. Theodore E. KIEFER
21	Director of Financial Services	Ms. Mary D. D'URSO
37	Director Student Financial Aid	Ms. Nora DOWNEY
13	Director of Information Technology	Mr. Stephen D. SANKEY
19	Director of Safety and Security	Mr. Nicholas MANCINI

Saint Francis University (B)

PO Box 600, Loretto PA 15940-0600
County: Cambria FICE Identification: 003366
Unit ID: 215743
Telephone: (814) 472-3000 Carnegie Class: Master's L
FAX Number: (814) 472-3003 Calendar System: Semester
URL: www.francis.edu
Established: 1847 Annual Undergrad Tuition & Fees: $27,808
Enrollment: 2,364 Coed
Affiliation or Control: Roman Catholic IRS Status: 501(c)3
Highest Offering: Doctorate
Program: Liberal Arts And General; Teacher Preparatory; Professional
Accreditation: M, ARCPA, IACBE, NURSE, OT, PTA, SW, @TEAC

Code	Title	Name
01	President	Rev. Gabriel ZEIS, TOR
05	Provost	Dr. Wayne POWEL
10	Vice President for Finance	Mr. Robert G. DATSKO
32	Vice Pres for Student Development	Dr. Frank MONTECALVO
42	VP Mission Effective & Integration	Rev. Daniel F. SINISI
45	Vice Pres for Strategic Initiatives	Ms. Patricia SEROTKIN
30	Vice President for Advancement	Mr. Robert CRUSCIEL
84	Vice Pres for Enrollment Management	Ms. Erin E. MCCLOSKEY
08	Dean of Library Services	Ms. Sandra A. BALOUGH
97	Assoc Dean of General Education	Vacant
84	Assoc Dean of Enrollment Management	Mr. Robert R. BEENER
06	Registrar	Dr. Stephen R. ROMBOUTS
09	Director of Institutional Research	Mr. Daniel KOSHUTE
37	Financial Aid Director	Mr. Jamie KOSH
26	Director Marketing & Public Affairs	Ms. Marie YOUNG
44	Director of Development	Ms. Marie B. MELUSKY
38	Director of Counseling Center	Mr. David P. WILSON
14	Director Computer Services	Mr. George F. PYO
29	Director of Alumni Relations	Ms. Anita M. BAUMANN
51	Director Continuing Education	Ms. Julie BARRIS
18	Director of Physical Plant	Mr. Doug EPPLEY
21	Controller	Mr. Thomas R. FRITZ
41	Director of Athletics	Mr. Bob S. KRIMMEL
88	Dir Small Business Devel Center	Mr. Edward R. HUTTENHOWER
19	Director Security & Safety	Mr. Donald MILES
39	Director of Residence Life	Mr. T. J BRECCIAROLI
42	Director of Campus Ministry	Rev. Chris DOBSON
24	Dir Academic Center for Enrichment	Vacant
35	Assoc Dean of Student Life	Mr. Dominick F. PERUSO
15	Director of Human Resources	Ms. Heather J. MECK
28	Director of Multicultural Affairs	Ms. Lynne BANKS
96	Director of Purchasing	Mr. William AGOSTA
20	Associate Provost	Dr. Peter R. SKONER
40	Manager of Bookstore	Vacant

Saint Joseph's University (C)

5600 City Avenue, Philadelphia PA 19131-1376
County: Philadelphia FICE Identification: 003367
Unit ID: 215770
Telephone: (610) 660-1000 Carnegie Class: Master's L
FAX Number: (610) 660-3300 Calendar System: Semester
URL: www.sju.edu
Established: 1851 Annual Undergrad Tuition & Fees: $36,480
Enrollment: 8,916 Coed
Affiliation or Control: Roman Catholic IRS Status: 501(c)3
Highest Offering: Doctorate
Program: Liberal Arts And General; Teacher Preparatory; Professional
Accreditation: M, ANEST, BUS, BUSA

Code	Title	Name
01	Interim President	Mr. John W. SMITHSON
05	Provost	Dr. Brice R. WACHTERHAUSER
03	Senior Vice President	Vacant
88	Vice President Mission & Identity	Dr. E. Springs STEELE
32	VP Student Life/Assoc Provost	Dr. Cary M. ANDERSON
11	Vice Pres Administrative Services	Mr. Kevin W. ROBINSON
30	Interim VP Dev/Alumni Relations	Ms. Katie SHIELDS
26	Vice President External Affairs	Ms. Joan F. CHRESTAY
10	Vice President Financial Affairs	Dr. Louis J. MAYER
45	Vice President Planning	Dr. Kathleen D. GAVAL
43	General Counsel	Ms. Marianne SCHIMELFINIG
04	Assistant Vice President	Ms. Sarah F. QUINN
20	Vice Provost	Dr. Paul L. DEVITO
49	Dean College Arts & Sciences	Dr. William MADGES
50	Dean Haub School of Business	Dr. Joseph A. DIANGELO, JR.
41	Assoc VP/Director Athletics	Mr. Dominick J. DIJULIA
51	Assoc Dean College Prof & Lib Stds	Vacant
58	Assoc Dean & Exec Dir Grad A&S	Dr. Sabrina DETURK
84	Assoc Provost Enrollment Mgmt	Mr. John G. HALLER
06	Registrar	Mr. Gerard J. DONAHUE
08	University Librarian Drexel Library	Ms. Evelyn MINICK
21	Asst VP Financial Affs & Treasury	Mr. James B. QUERY
21	Asst VP & Controller	Mr. Joseph CASSIDY
86	Asst VP Govt & Community Rels	Mr. Wadell RIDLEY, JR.
15	Assistant VP Human Resources	Ms. Sharon O'GRADY EISENMANN
13	Asst VP Information Technology	Mr. Joseph F. PETRAGNANI
13	Chief Information Officer	Mr. Francis J. DISANTI
27	Asst VP Marketing Communications	Mr. Joseph M. LUNARDI
88	Asst VP Planning & Assessment	Ms. Dawn M. BURDSALL
88	Asst VP Student Development	Dr. Mary Elaine PERRY
88	Asst VP Student Ed Support Services	Ms. Jacqueline M. STARKS
26	Asst VP Univ Communications	Ms. Harriet K. GOODHEART
29	Exec Dir Annual/Regional Campaign	Vacant
24	Exec Dir Inst Tech/Dist Learning	Dr. David LEES
07	Exec Director UG Admissions	Ms. Maureen MATHIS
105	Exec Dir Web & Support Services	Mr. Jeffery J. BACHOVCHIN
22	Director Benefits and Wellness	Ms. Anne MUNLEY
42	Director Campus Ministry	Mr. Thomas J. SHEIBLEY
36	Director Career Development Center	Mr. Brett WOODARD
38	Director Counseling/Pers Dev Ctr	Dr. Gregory NICHOLLS
18	Director Facilities Management	Mr. Kevin M. KANE
37	Director Financial Assistance	Ms. Eileen TUCKER
92	Director Honors Program	Dr. Maria S. MARSILIO
28	Director Institutional Diversity	Dr. Valerie DUDLEY
88	Director Multicultural Life	Dr. Shoshanna EDWARDS-ALEXANDER
19	Director Public Safety & Security	Mr. John M. HENFEY
96	Director Purchasing	Mr. William O. ANDERSON
39	Director Residence Life	Mr. John A. JEFFERY
23	Director Student Health Center	Ms. Laura HURST
35	Dir Student Leadership/Activities	Dr. Beth HAGOVSKY
09	Assoc Dir Institutional Research	Ms. Annemarie M. BARTLETT

St. Tikhon's Orthodox Theological Seminary (D)

PO Box 130, South Canaan PA 18459-0130
County: Wayne FICE Identification: 039193
Unit ID: 216180
Telephone: (570) 561-1818 Carnegie Class: Not Classified
FAX Number: (570) 937-3100 Calendar System: Semester
URL: www.stots.edu
Established: 1938 Annual Undergrad Tuition & Fees: $4,950
Enrollment: 106 Male
Affiliation or Control: Other IRS Status: 501(c)3
Highest Offering: First Professional Degree
Program: Religious Emphasis
Accreditation: THEOL

Code	Title	Name
01	President	M.Blsd. Metropolitan JONAH
03	Rector	Rt Rev. Bishop TIKHON
05	Dean	V.Rev. Alexander ATTY

Saint Vincent College (E)

300 Fraser Purchase Road, Latrobe PA 15650-2690
County: Westmoreland FICE Identification: 003368
Unit ID: 215798
Telephone: (724) 805-2500 Carnegie Class: Bac/A&S
FAX Number: (724) 805-2019 Calendar System: Semester
URL: www.stvincent.edu
Established: 1846 Annual Undergrad Tuition & Fees: $31,844
Enrollment: 1,937 Coed
Affiliation or Control: Roman Catholic IRS Status: 501(c)3
Highest Offering: Doctorate
Program: Liberal Arts And General; Professional
Accreditation: M, ACBSP, ANEST

Code	Title	Name
01	President	Br. Norman W. HIPPS, OSB
05	VP Academic Affairs	Dr. John SMETANKA
10	VP/Chief Finance/Admin Officer	Mr. Dennis THIMONS
30	Vice Pres Institutional Advancement	Ms. Tracy BRANSON
32	VP Student Affairs	Ms. Mary COLLINS
07	Asst Vice Pres Admission	Mr. David A. COLLINS
13	Chief Information Officer	Vacant
20	Dean of Studies	Ms. Alice J. KAYLOR
50	Dean McKenna Sch Bus/Econ/Govt	Dr. Gary QUINLIVAN
60	Dean Sch Soc Sci/Communication/Educ	Dr. MaryBeth SPORE
79	Dean Humanities & Fine Arts	Rev. Rene KOLLAR, OSB
81	Dean Science/Math & Computing	Dr. Stephen M. JODIS
06	Registrar	Ms. Celine R. BRUDNOK
08	Librarian	Bro. David KELLY, OSB
29	Director of Alumni Affairs	Mr. Michael GERDICH
26	Director of Public Relations	Mr. Donald A. ORLANDO
36	Director Career Services	Ms. Courtney BAUM
15	Director of Human Resources	Ms. Judith MAHER
42	Director of Campus Ministry	Rev. Vincent ZIDEK, OSB
23	Director Wellness Center	Ms. Mary Alice ARMOUR
19	Director Public Safety	Mr. Steve BROWN
41	Athletic Director	Rev. Myron KIRSCH, OSB
39	Director Resident Life	Mr. Robert BAUM
96	Dir of Purchasing/Chief Fire Dept	Mr. Terry NOEL
09	Director of Institutional Research	Ms. Maren HESS
18	Director of Facility Management	Mr. Larry HENDRICK
40	Manager Book Center	Rev. Anthony GROSSI, OSB
88	Exec Dir Fred Rogers Center	Ms. Rita CATALANO
88	Coord of Grad Admission & Cont Educ	Ms. Lisa GLESSNER

Saint Vincent Seminary (F)

300 Fraser Purchase Road, Latrobe PA 15650-2690
County: Westmoreland Identification: 666018
Unit ID: 215813
Telephone: (724) 805-2592 Carnegie Class: Spec/Faith
FAX Number: (724) 532-5052 Calendar System: Semester
URL: www.saintvincentseminary.edu
Established: 1846 Annual Undergrad Tuition & Fees: $32,482
Enrollment: 71 Coed
Affiliation or Control: Roman Catholic IRS Status: 501(c)3
Highest Offering: Master's
Program: Religious Emphasis
Accreditation: THEOL

Code	Title	Name
01	Rector	V.Rev. Justin MATRO, OSB
88	Director of Spiritual Formation	Rev. Aaron N. BUZZELLI, OSB
05	Academic Dean	Dr. Michel THERRIEN
03	Vice-Rector	Rev. John-Mary TOMPKINS, OSB

Salus University (G)

8360 Old York Road, Elkins Park PA 19027-1516
County: Philadelphia FICE Identification: 003311
Unit ID: 214564
Telephone: (215) 780-1400 Carnegie Class: Spec/Health
FAX Number: (215) 780-1325 Calendar System: Quarter
URL: www.salus.edu
Established: 1919 Annual Undergrad Tuition & Fees: $32,810
Enrollment: 767 Coed
Affiliation or Control: Independent Non-Profit IRS Status: 501(c)3
Highest Offering: Doctorate
Program: Professional
Accreditation: M, ARCPA, AUD, OPT, OPTR

Code	Title	Name
01	President	Dr. Thomas L. LEWIS
05	Vice Pres/Dean Academic Advancement	Dr. Anthony F. DISTEFANO
10	Vice Pres Finance/Business Affairs	Mr. Donald KATES
17	VP/Exec Director The Eye Institute	Dr. Susan OLESZEWSKI
45	Vice President for Inst Planning	Ms. Lynne CORBOY
32	Dean Student Affairs	Mr. Robert E. HORNE
20	Exec Assistant to the Dean	Ms. Karen BOYKIN
09	Asst Dir Research Admin	Ms. Lydia PARKE
06	Registrar	Ms. Shannon BOSS
07	Director of Admissions	Dr. James CALDWELL
13	Director Management Info Services	Mr. Alex ANDERSON
38	Director Personal/Prof Development	Ms. Natalie LECKERMAN
37	Assoc Dean Student Financial Affs	Dr. H. Lawrence MCCLURE
18	Director Physical Plant	Mr. Rick ECHEVARRI
30	Chief Development	Ms. Lynne CORBOY
26	Chief Public Relations Officer	Ms. Peggy SHELLY
27	Director Publications/Communication	Ms. Peggy SHELLY
29	Director Alumni Relations/Giving	Ms. Heather GIAMPAPA
51	Coord Continuing/Post-Graduate Educ	Mrs. Melissa PADILLA
58	Chairperson Graduate Studies	Dr. Kathleen HUEBNER
40	Bookstore Manager	Mr. Joe NOCE
12	Director Bennett Center	Ms. Janice MIGNOGNA
24	Director Instructional Media	Mr. Glenn ROEDEL
36	Director Student Placement	Ms. Janice MIGNOGNA
84	Director Enrollment Management	Dr. Larry MCCLURE
88	Exec Dir Inst Visually Impaired	Dr. Audrey SMITH
08	Head Librarian	Mr. Keith LAMMERS
19	Director of Security	Mr. Joe KELLENBENZ
15	Dir Human Resources/Affirm Action	Ms. Maura ALEXANDER
96	Director of Purchasing	Mr. Steve SCHEPS

Sanford-Brown Institute-Pittsburgh (H)

421 Seventh Avenue, Pittsburgh PA 15219-1907
County: Allegheny FICE Identification: 022023
Unit ID: 216782
Telephone: (412) 281-2600 Carnegie Class: Assoc/PrivFP
FAX Number: (412) 281-0319 Calendar System: Other
URL: www.sanfordbrown.edu/Pittsburgh
Established: 1979 Annual Undergrad Tuition & Fees: N/A
Enrollment: 788 Coed
Affiliation or Control: Proprietary IRS Status: Proprietary
Highest Offering: Associate Degree
Program: Occupational
Accreditation: ACCSC, DMS, MAAB, RAD

Code	Title	Name
01	President-Pittsburgh	Patti L. YAKSHE
12	President-Monroeville	R. Thomas CONTRELLA

37 Dir Student Financial Aid/Finance .... George SANTUCCI
05 Director of Education .... Melissa RUSSO
15 Dir of Compliance/Human Resources .... Christa STYNES
07 Director of Admissions .... Jose DELPIEAGO
06 Registrar .... Amy ROBERTS
13 Director of Information Technology .... Mark MARCI
36 Director of Career Services .... Ernie JUNSTRON

Sanford-Brown Institute-Wilkins Township (A)

777 Penn Center Boulevard, Bldg 7, Pittsburgh PA 15235
County: Allegheny Identification: 666526
Unit ID: 376136
Telephone: (412) 373-6400 Carnegie Class: Assoc/PrivFP
FAX Number: (412) 373-2544 Calendar System: Semester
URL: www.sanfordbrown.edu/Wilkins-Township
Established: 1987 Annual Undergrad Tuition & Fees: $13,990
Enrollment: 562 Coed
Affiliation or Control: Proprietary IRS Status: Proprietary
Highest Offering: Associate Degree
Program: Occupational; 2-Year Principally Bachelor's Creditable
Accreditation: ACCSC, MAAB, SURGT

01 President .... Mr. R. Thomas CONTRELLA

† Branch campus of Sanford-Brown Institute-Pittsburgh, Pittsburgh, PA.

Seton Hill University (B)

Seton Hill Drive, Greensburg PA 15601-1599
County: Westmoreland FICE Identification: 003362
Unit ID: 215947
Telephone: (724) 834-2200 Carnegie Class: Bac/Diverse
FAX Number: (724) 830-4611 Calendar System: Semester
URL: www.setonhill.edu
Established: 1883 Annual Undergrad Tuition & Fees: $28,754
Enrollment: 2,231 Coed
Affiliation or Control: Roman Catholic IRS Status: 501(c)3
Highest Offering: Master's
Program: Liberal Arts And General; Teacher Preparatory; Professional
Accreditation: M, ARCPA, DENT, DIETC, IACBE, MFCD, MUS, SW, TEAC

01 President .... Dr. JoAnne W. BOYLE
32 Vice President Mission/Student Life .... Dr. Lois SCULCO, SC
05 Provost & Dean of the Faculty .... Dr. Mary Ann GAWELEK
10 Vice Pres Finance & Administration .... Mr. Paul ROMAN
84 Vice Pres Enrollment Svcs/Registrar .... Mrs. Barbara C. HINKLE
44 Vice Pres Institutional Advancement .... Ms. Christine MUESELER
13 Vice Pres Computers & Technology .... Mr. Phil KOMARNY
21 Controller .... Mr. Paul EDSALL
35 Dean of Student Services .... Dr. Charmaine R. STRONG
07 Director Admissions .... Mrs. Sheri BETT
08 Director of Library .... Mr. David STANLEY
30 Director Development .... Ms. Molly ROBB SHIMKO
29 Director of Alumni Relations .... Ms. Mary COX
37 Director of Financial Aid .... Ms. Maryann DUDAS
36 Director of Career Development .... Mrs. Rebecca R. CAMPBELL
15 Director Personnel Services .... Mrs. Darlene SAUERS
18 Director Facilities .... Mr. Bill VOKES
41 Executive Athletic Director .... Mr. Chris SNYDER
42 Director Campus Ministry .... Sr. Maureen O'BRIEN
88 Dir Natl Educ Ctr Women in Business .... Mrs. Jayne HUSTON
04 Assistant to the President .... Mrs. Carol ZOLA
06 Registrar .... Ms. Barbara HINKLE
38 Director Student Counseling .... Ms. Teresa BASSI-COOK

South Hills School of Business and Technology (C)

480 Waupelani Drive, State College PA 16801-4516
County: Centre FICE Identification: 013263
Unit ID: 216083
Telephone: (814) 234-7755 Carnegie Class: Assoc/PrivFP
FAX Number: (814) 234-0926 Calendar System: Quarter
URL: www.southhills.edu
Established: 1970 Annual Undergrad Tuition & Fees: $14,358
Enrollment: 801 Coed
Affiliation or Control: Proprietary IRS Status: Proprietary
Highest Offering: Associate Degree
Program: Occupational
Accreditation: ACICS, DMS

01 President & Owner .... Mr. S. Paul MAZZA
05 Director .... Mr. Mark MAGGS

Susquehanna University (D)

514 University Avenue, Selinsgrove PA 17870-1025
County: Snyder FICE Identification: 003369
Unit ID: 216278
Telephone: (570) 372-4395 Carnegie Class: Bac/A&S
FAX Number: (570) 372-4040 Calendar System: Semester
URL: www.susqu.edu
Established: 1858 Annual Undergrad Tuition & Fees: $35,860
Enrollment: 2,305 Coed
Affiliation or Control: Evangelical Lutheran Church In America
IRS Status: 501(c)3
Highest Offering: Baccalaureate
Program: Liberal Arts And General; Teacher Preparatory
Accreditation: M, BUS, MUS

01 President .... Dr. L. Jay LEMONS
03 Exec VP for Admin & Planning .... Ms. Sara G. KIRKLAND
05 Provost .... Dr. Carl O. MOSES
10 Vice Pres for Finance .... Mr. Michael COYNE
26 Vice President for Univ Relations .... Mr. Ronald A. COHEN
84 Vice Pres Enrollment Management .... Ms. Deborah STIEFFEL
32 Vice Pres of Student Life & Dean .... Dr. Philip E. WINGER
27 Assoc VP for Communications .... Ms. Angie BURROWS
30 Asst Vice President Gift Planning .... Mr. Doug SEABERG
28 Chief Diversity Officer .... Ms. Lisa M. SCOTT
04 Exec Assistant to the President .... Vacant
04 Senior Admin Asst to the President .... Ms. Sharon POPE
49 Dean School Natural/Social Sciences .... Dr. Lucien T. WINEGAR
57 Dean Sch Arts/Humanities/Comm .... Dr. Valerie G. MARTIN
50 Dean Weis School of Business .... Dr. Alicia JACKSON
38 Assoc Dean & Director of Counseling .... Ms. Anna Beth PAYNE
89 Asst Dean/First Year Programs .... Ms. Caroline MERCADO
28 Director of Multicultural Affairs .... Ms. Dena SALERNO
07 Director of Admissions .... Mr. Chris A. MARKLE
08 Director of the Library .... Ms. Kathleen GUNNING
37 Director of Financial Aid .... Ms. Helen S. NUNN
06 Registrar .... Mr. Alex G H. SMITH
42 University Chaplain .... Rev. Mark Wm RADECKE
13 Chief Information Officer .... Mr. Mark D. HUBER
41 Director of Athletics .... Ms. Pamela SAMUELSON
18 Director of Facilities Management .... Mr. Chris C. BAILEY
36 Director of Career Services .... Ms. Brenda FABIAN
88 Director Conference and Event Mgt .... Ms. Christine D. JAEGERS
29 Director of Alumni Relations .... Ms. Becky DEITRICK
09 Dir of Institutional Research .... Dr. Colleen FLEWELLING
102 Dir of Corp/Foundation Support .... Mr. Ed CLARKE
104 Dir Cross Cultural Off-Campus Pgm .... Dr. Scott MANNING
15 Director Human Resources/Risk Mgmt .... Ms. Maureen N. PUGH
19 Director of Public Safety .... Mr. Tom RAMBO
44 Director of the Annual Fund .... Mr. Jason MCCAHAN
92 Director of Honors Program .... Dr. James POMYKALSKI
20 Dir of Inst Research & Asst Provost .... Dr. Colleen FLEWELLING

Swarthmore College (E)

500 College Avenue, Swarthmore PA 19081-1390
County: Delaware FICE Identification: 003370
Unit ID: 216287
Telephone: (610) 328-8000 Carnegie Class: Bac/A&S
FAX Number: (610) 328-8673 Calendar System: Semester
URL: www.swarthmore.edu
Established: 1864 Annual Undergrad Tuition & Fees: $41,150
Enrollment: 1,524 Coed
Affiliation or Control: Independent Non-Profit IRS Status: 501(c)3
Highest Offering: Baccalaureate
Program: Liberal Arts And General
Accreditation: M, ENG

01 President .... Rebecca S. CHOPP
05 Provost .... Thomas STEPHENSON
10 Vice President Finance/Treasurer .... Suzanne P. WELSH
30 Vice President Alumni/Development .... Stephen D. BAYER
04 VP Col/Cmty Rels/Exec Asst to Pres .... Maurice G. ELDRIDGE
18 Vice Pres Facilities & Services .... C. Stuart HAIN
16 Vice Pres for Human Resources .... Melanie YOUNG
26 Vice President for Communications .... Nancy NICELY
21 Asst Vice Pres Finance & Controller .... Eileen E. PETULA
45 Associate Vice Pres for Planning .... Garikai CAMPBELL
32 Dean of Students .... Elizabeth BRAUN
07 Dean of Admissions & Financial Aid .... Jim BOCK
28 Assoc Dean Multicultural Affairs .... Vacant
06 Registrar .... Martin O. WARNER
08 College Librarian .... Peggy SEIDEN
09 Director Institutional Research .... Robin H. SHORES
29 Director of Alumni Relations .... Lisa LEE
37 Director of Financial Aid .... Laura TALBOT
36 Director Career Services .... Nancy BURKETT
19 Director Security/Safety Services .... Vacant
22 Director Equal Opportunity Office .... Sharmaine LAMAR
23 Director Worth Health Center .... Beth KOTARSKI
38 Director Psychological Services .... David RAMIREZ
41 Director Physical Educ/Athletics .... Adam HERTZ
44 Director Annual Giving .... Mary Beth MILLS
13 Chief Information Technology Ofcr .... Gayle R. BARTON
35 Student Activities Coordinator .... Paury FLOWERS

Talmudical Yeshiva of Philadelphia (F)

6063 Drexel Road, Philadelphia PA 19131-1296
County: Philadelphia FICE Identification: 012523
Unit ID: 216311
Telephone: (215) 473-1212 Carnegie Class: Spec/Faith
FAX Number: (215) 477-5065 Calendar System: Semester
Established: 1953 Annual Undergrad Tuition & Fees: $8,100
Enrollment: 220 Male
Affiliation or Control: Independent Non-Profit IRS Status: 501(c)3
Highest Offering: Second Talmudic Degree
Program: Teacher Preparatory; Professional; Religious Emphasis
Accreditation: RABN

01 President .... Mr. Erwin WEINBERG
05 Dean .... Rabbi Shmuel KAMENETSKY
05 Dean .... Rabbi Yehuda SVEI
05 Dean .... Rabbi Sholom KAMENETSKY

Temple University (G)

1801 N. Broad Street, Philadelphia PA 19122-6072
County: Philadelphia FICE Identification: 003371
Unit ID: 216339
Telephone: (215) 204-7000 Carnegie Class: RU/H
FAX Number: (215) 204-5694 Calendar System: Semester
URL: www.temple.edu
Established: 1884 Annual Undergrad Tuition & Fees (In-State): $13,006
Enrollment: 37,367 Coed
Affiliation or Control: State Related IRS Status: 501(c)3
Highest Offering: Doctorate
Program: 2-Year Principally Bachelor's Creditable; Liberal Arts And General; Teacher Preparatory; Professional
Accreditation: M, ART, BUS, CLPSY, DANCE, DENT, ENG, ENGT, HSA, IPSY, JOUR, LAW, LSAR, MED, MUS, NRPA, NURSE, OT, PH, PHAR, POD, PTA, SCPSY, SP, SW, TEAC, THEA

01 President .... Dr. Ann WEAVER HART
100 Vice President/Chief of Staff .... Mr. William T. BERGMAN, JR.
43 Univ Counsel/Univ Secretary/Sr VP .... Mr. George E. MOORE
05 Provost/Sr VP Academic Affairs .... Dr. Richard M. ENGLERT
17 Sr EVP Health Sci/CEO Health System .... Dr. Larry R. KAISER
03 Sr Vice Provost Strategic Init/ Comm .... Dr. Elizabeth LEEBRON TUTELMAN
10 Sr VP/CFO & Treasurer .... Mr. Anthony E. WAGNER
11 Asst VP Administration/Planning .... Ms. Kathryn P. D'ANGELO
21 Assoc VP Finance .... Mr. William J. WILKINSON
26 Sr VP Govt/Community & Public Affs .... Mr. Kenneth LAWERENCE, JR.
32 VP for Student Affairs .... Dr. Theresa A. POWELL
35 Assoc VP Student Affairs .... Dr. Stephanie IVES
39 Assoc VP Stdnt Affairs/Housing .... Mr. Michael SCALES
27 VP Computer/Financial Svcs/CIO .... Mr. Timothy C. O'ROURKE
30 Sr VP Institutional Advancement .... Mr. David UNRUH
46 Sr VP Research/Graduate Education .... Mr. Kenneth J. BLANK
16 Sr Assoc VP Finance/HR .... Mr. Kenneth H. KAISER
15 Assoc VP HR .... Mr. Harry A. YOUNG
88 Sr Vice Provost Faculty Dev/Affairs .... Dr. Diane C. MAELSON
88 Assoc Vice Provost Faculty Affairs .... Ms. Nelia VIVEIROS
20 Vice Provost Undergraduate Programs .... Dr. Peter JONES
20 Vice Prov Acad Affairs/ Assessment .... Dr. Jodi LEVINE LAUFGRABEN
08 Dean for University Libraries .... Mr. Larry ALFORD
21 Assoc VP/ Controller .... Mr. Frank ANNUNZIATO
18 Assoc VP Facilities Management .... Mr. Andy RICCARDI
88 Assoc VP Business Services .... Mr. Richard RUMER
22 Assoc VP Multicultural Affairs .... Ms. Rhonda L. BROWN
84 Senior Vice Provost Enrollment .... Mr. William N. BLACK
29 Asst Vice Pres Alumni Relations .... Ms. Audrey SCHNEIDER
06 Registrar .... Ms. Wendy KUTCHNER
41 Director Intercollegiate Athletics .... Mr. William BRADSHAW
38 Director Tuttleman Counseling Svcs .... Dr. John L. DIMINO
36 Sr Director Student Svcs .... Ms. Rachel BROWN
09 Director Institutional Research .... Mr. John V. MOORE, III
85 Sr Vice Provost Intl Affairs .... Dr. Hai-Lung DAI
88 Sr Dir International Student Svcs .... Dr. Martyn J. MILLER
88 Asst VP International Affairs .... Ms. Denise A. CONNERTY
23 Assoc Director Health Services .... Dr. Mark DENYS
40 Bookstore Manager .... Mr. Jim HANLEY
37 Director Student Financial Services .... Dr. John F. MORRIS
96 Director of Purchasing .... Ms. Theresa E. BURT
49 Dean Liberal Arts .... Dr. Teresa SCOTT SOUFAS
53 Interim Dean of Education .... Dr. James Earl DAVIS
58 Dean of University College .... Dr. Richard ENGLERT
57 Acting Dean Tyler School of Art .... Dr. Robert STROKER
61 Dean Law School .... Dr. Joanne A. EPPS
64 Dean of Music .... Dr. Robert STROKER
50 Dean Business/Management .... Dr. Moshe PORAT
52 Dean of Dentistry .... Dr. Amid ISMAIL
63 Dean of Medicine .... Dr. Larry R. KAISER
67 Dean of Pharmacy .... Dr. Peter H. DOUKAS
54 Dean Engineering .... Dr. Keya SADEGHIPOUR
88 Dean Podiatric Medicine .... Dr. John A. MATTIACCI
72 Dean Science & Technology .... Dr. Hai-Lung DAI
60 Interim Dean Communications/Theater .... Dr. Thomas JACOBSON
76 Dean Health Professions & Social Wk .... Dr. Michael SITLER
88 Dean of Tourism/Hospitality Mgmt .... Dr. Moshe PORAT
12 Dean Environmental Design .... Dr. Teresa SCOTT SOUFAS
88 Bursar .... Mr. David R. GLEZERMAN
97 Director General Education .... Mr. Istvan L. VARKONYI
88 Exec Dir Ambler/Ctr City Campuses .... Mr. William PARSHALL
88 Dean Temple Japan .... Dr. Bruce STRONACH
88 Dean Temple Rome .... Mr. Kim STROMMEN

Thaddeus Stevens College of Technology (H)

750 E King Street, Lancaster PA 17602-3198
County: Lancaster FICE Identification: 007912
Unit ID: 216296
Telephone: (717) 299-7730 Carnegie Class: Assoc/Pub-R-S
FAX Number: (717) 299-7748 Calendar System: Semester
URL: www.stevenscollege.edu
Established: 1905 Annual Undergrad Tuition & Fees (In-State): $6,530
Enrollment: 906 Coed
Affiliation or Control: State IRS Status: 501(c)3
Highest Offering: Associate Degree
Program: Occupational; 2-Year Principally Bachelor's Creditable
Accreditation: M

01 President .... Dr. William E. GRISCOM

32 Vice President for Student Services ....Mr. Paul E. CAMERON
10 Vice President Finance and Admin ....Mrs. Betty TOMPOS
05 Int Vice President Academic Affairs .... Dr. William R. THOMPSON
84 Director of Enrollment Services ....Ms. Erin NELSEN
08 Learning Resources Center Director .... Ms. Diane AMBRUSO
09 Director of Research & Planning ....Mrs. Maria L. QUERRY
51 Director Cont Educ/Workforce Devel ....Mr. Mark BORGER
06 Registrar ....Mr. Bernard MCCREE
07 Director of Admissions ....Ms. Erin NELSEN
15 Director of Personnel Services ....Vacant
26 Dir of Marketing/Public Information ....Mr. Chad BAKER
38 Director of Student Counseling ....Ms. Debra SCHUCH
28 Director Multicultural Affairs ....Mr. Paul CULBRETH
29 Alumni Foundation Exec Director ....Mr. Alex MUNRO
37 Director Financial Aid/Registrar ....Mr. Michael DEGROFT
41 Athletic Director ....Ms. Deb CARTER
96 Director of Purchasing ....Ms. Nancy FROESCHLE
30 Director of Development ....Mr. Allen TATE
35 Int Director Student Services ....Mr. Chris METZLER
36 Career Services Director ....Ms. Laurie GROVE
18 Facilities Maintenance Manager ....Mr. Gene DUNCAN, JR.

† Qualified individuals are eligible for full scholarships based on family/financial status.

Thiel College (A)

75 College Avenue, Greenville PA 16125-2181
County: Mercer FICE Identification: 003376
Unit ID: 216357
Telephone: (724) 589-2000 Carnegie Class: Bac/Diverse
FAX Number: (724) 589-2850 Calendar System: Semester
URL: www.thiel.edu
Established: 1866 Annual Undergrad Tuition & Fees: $25,156
Enrollment: 1,096 Coed
Affiliation or Control: Evangelical Lutheran Church In America
IRS Status: 501(c)3
Highest Offering: Baccalaureate
Program: Liberal Arts And General; Teacher Preparatory
Accreditation: M

01 President ....Dr. Troy D. VAN AKEN
05 Vice Pres Academic Affairs ....Dr. Lynn FRANKEN
30 Vice President College Advancement ....Mr. David J. GROBER
10 Vice President for Finance & CFO ....Mr. Greg GARBER
21 Vice President Auxil Enterprise/CTO ....Mr. William BEIL
04 Special Assistant to the President ....Ms. Nancy HOLCOMB
32 Dean of Students ....Mr. Michael MCKINNEY
84 Dean of Enrollment ....Mrs. Amy BECHER
51 Dean of Educational Outreach ....Vacant
44 Dir of Special & Planned Giving ....Mr. Mario MARINI
08 Library Director ....Mr. Allen MORRILL
27 Director Information Office ....Ms. Joyce CARR
15 Director Human Resources ....Mrs. Susan SWARTZBECK
36 Career Service Director ....Mrs. Heather BALAS
19 Chief of Public Safety .... Mr. Donald AUBRECHT
41 Director of Athletics .... Mr. John LEIPHEIMER
06 Registrar ....Ms. Denise UREY
29 Director of Alumni .... Ms. Lauren OMAN
42 Campus Pastor ....Rev. Harold BIXBY
37 Financial Aid Director ....Ms. Cynthia H. FARRELL
09 Director Institutional Research ....Mrs. Susan C. RICHARDS
23 Coordinator Health Services ....Mrs. Pamela M. DESPO

Thomas Jefferson University (B)

11th and Walnut Streets, Philadelphia PA 19107-5083
County: Philadelphia FICE Identification: 012393
Unit ID: 216366
Telephone: (215) 955-6000 Carnegie Class: Spec/Med
FAX Number: (215) 955-5587 Calendar System: Quarter
URL: www.jefferson.edu
Established: 1824 Annual Undergrad Tuition & Fees: $32,159
Enrollment: 3,509 Coed
Affiliation or Control: Independent Non-Profit IRS Status: 501(c)3
Highest Offering: Doctorate
Program: Liberal Arts And General; Professional
Accreditation: M, ANEST, CYTO, DENT, DMS, MED, MT, NMT, NURSE, OT, PH, @PHAR, PTA, RAD, RADDOS, RADMAG, RTT

01 President ....Dr. Robert L. BARCHI
63 Dean Jefferson Medical College .... Dr. Mark L. TYKOCINSKI
05 Sr VP Academic Affairs ....Dr. Michael J. VERGARE
26 Senior VP Univ Marketing/Relations ....Ms. Carmhiel J. BROWN
10 Vice President for Finance & CFO ....Mr. Richard J. SCHMID
30 Sr VP for Development ....Mr. Frederick E. RUCCIUS
43 Sr VP & University Counsel .... Ms. Cristina G. CAVALIERI
46 Vice President for Research ....Dr. Steven E. MCKENZIE
18 Vice Pres for Facilities Mgmt ....Mr. Ronald E. BOWLAN
15 Interim VP Human Resources ....Mr. Alfred C. SALVATO
100 Chief of Staff ....Ms. Janice K. MARINI
58 Dean Jeff Col Grad Studies .... Dr. Gerald GRUNWALD
20 Assoc Sr VP Academic Affairs .... Dr. James ERDMANN
66 Dean Jefferson School of Nursing ....Dr. Mary SCHAAL
67 Dean Jefferson School of Pharmacy ....Dr. Rebecca FINLEY
76 Dean Jefferson Sch Hlth Professions ....Dr. Janice P. BURKE
69 Dean Jefferson Sch of Pop Health .... Dr. David NASH
32 Dean of Student & Admissions JMC ....Dr. Clara A. CALLAHAN
07 Asst Dean of Admissions ....Dr. Karen JACOBS ASTLE
06 University Registrar ....Dr. Raelynn COOTER
29 Exec Director of Alumni Assoc JMC ....Dr. Phillip J. MARONE
08 University Librarian ....Mr. Edward W. TAWYEA
22 Univ Affirmative Action Officer ....Dr. Karen GLASER
23 Medical Director Univ Health Svcs ....Dr. Ellen M. O'CONNOR
24 Director Medical Media Services ....Mr. Pejman MAKARECHI
35 Assoc VP Student Affairs .... Mr. William THYGESON
39 Manager Housing/Residence Life ....Ms. Patricia CRISTIANO KELLY
37 Univ Director Student Financial Aid .... Ms. Susan BATCHELOR
40 Director Bookstore .... Ms. Patricia HAAS
91 Chief Information Officer ....Mr. P. Douglas HERRICK
19 Director of Security ....Mr. Robert B. HENDRICK
85 Dir International Exchange Services ....Ms. Janice M. BOGEN
07 Dir Admission/Recruitment/Grad Stds .... Mr. Marc STEARNS
28 Asst Dean Diversity/Minority Affs ....Ms. Luz M. ORTIZ
96 Director of Purchasing ....Mr. Robert C. BURKHOLDER
35 Associate Dean Student Affairs ....Dr. Charles A. POHL

Triangle Tech, Dubois (C)

PO Box 551, Dubois PA 15801-0551
County: Clearfield FICE Identification: 021744
Unit ID: 216454
Telephone: (814) 371-2090 Carnegie Class: Assoc/PrivFP
FAX Number: (814) 371-9227 Calendar System: Semester
URL: www.triangle-tech.edu
Established: 1982 Annual Undergrad Tuition & Fees: $14,558
Enrollment: 325 Coed
Affiliation or Control: Proprietary IRS Status: Proprietary
Highest Offering: Associate Degree
Program: Occupational; 2-Year Principally Bachelor's Creditable; Technical Emphasis
Accreditation: ACCSC

01 Director ....Mrs. Stephanie A. CRAIG
03 Assistant Director ....Mr. Steve CURLL
05 Academic Affairs Advisor .... Mrs. Joan HOCKMAN
07 Admiss/Recruiting/Training Coord ....Vacant
07 Admiss/Recruiting/Training Coord ....Ms. Janie A. DEJESUS
36 Career Advisor ....Mrs. Dori FORDOSKI
37 Financial Aid Administrator ....Ms. Michelle L. JASHINSKI

Triangle Tech, Erie (D)

2000 Liberty Street, Erie PA 16502-2594
County: Erie FICE Identification: 020902
Unit ID: 216427
Telephone: (814) 453-6016 Carnegie Class: Assoc/PrivFP
FAX Number: (814) 454-2818 Calendar System: Semester
URL: www.triangle-tech.edu
Established: 1976 Annual Undergrad Tuition & Fees: $12,200
Enrollment: 156 Coed
Affiliation or Control: Proprietary IRS Status: Proprietary
Highest Offering: Associate Degree
Program: Occupational
Accreditation: ACCSC

00 CEO ....Mr. James R. AGRAS
01 Campus Director ....Mr. Ken ADAMS
03 Executive Vice President ....Mr. Rudy K. AGRAS
07 Vice President of Admissions ....Mr. John A. MAZZARESE

Triangle Tech, Greensburg (E)

222 E Pittsburgh Street, Suite A,
Greensburg PA 15601-3304
County: Westmoreland FICE Identification: 021290
Unit ID: 216445
Telephone: (724) 832-1050 Carnegie Class: Assoc/PrivFP
FAX Number: (724) 834-0325 Calendar System: Semester
URL: www.triangle-tech.edu
Established: 1944 Annual Undergrad Tuition & Fees: $12,976
Enrollment: 262 Coed
Affiliation or Control: Proprietary IRS Status: Proprietary
Highest Offering: Associate Degree
Program: Occupational; 2-Year Principally Bachelor's Creditable; Technical Emphasis
Accreditation: ACCSC

00 Chairman/CEO ....James R. AGRAS
01 President ....Timothy J. MCMAHON
07 Director of Admissions ....John A. MAZZARESE
05 Senior Director .... Deborah G. HEPBURN
12 Actg Director of Branch Campus/CEO .... Deborah HEPBURN

Triangle Tech, Pittsburgh (F)

1940 Perrysville Avenue, Pittsburgh PA 15214-3897
County: Allegheny FICE Identification: 007839
Unit ID: 216436
Telephone: (412) 359-1000 Carnegie Class: Assoc/PrivFP
FAX Number: (412) 359-1012 Calendar System: Semester
URL: www.triangle-tech.edu
Established: 1944 Annual Undergrad Tuition & Fees: $14,600
Enrollment: 300 Coed
Affiliation or Control: Proprietary IRS Status: Proprietary
Highest Offering: Associate Degree
Program: Occupational; 2-Year Principally Bachelor's Creditable; Technical Emphasis
Accreditation: ACCSC

00 Chairman/CEO ....James R. AGRAS
01 President ....Timothy J. MCMAHON
07 Director of Admissions ....Jason VALLOZZI
05 Senior Director .... Deborah G. HEPBURN
12 School Director ....Paul T. BEADLE

Trinity Episcopal School for Ministry (G)

311 11th Street, Ambridge PA 15003-2397
County: Beaver FICE Identification: 022993
Unit ID: 216463
Telephone: (724) 266-3838 Carnegie Class: Spec/Faith
FAX Number: (724) 266-4617 Calendar System: Semester
URL: www.tsm.edu
Established: 1976 Annual Graduate Tuition & Fees: $10,170
Enrollment: 155 Coed
Affiliation or Control: Protestant Episcopal IRS Status: 501(c)3
Highest Offering: Doctorate; No Undergraduates
Program: Professional
Accreditation: THEOL

01 Dean/President ....V.Rev. Justyn TERRY
05 Academic Dean ....Rev Dr. Mark STEVENSON
11 Dean Administration/Dir DMin Degree ....Rev Dr. H. Lawrence THOMPSON, III
32 Dean of Students ....Rev. Tina LOCKETT
37 Financial Aid Director ....Ms. Stacey WILLIARD
06 Dir Academic Support Tech/Registrar ....Rev. William STARKE
07 Director of Admissions ....Rev. Tina LOCKETT
08 Library Director ....Ms. Susanah HANSON
21 Director of Accounting ....Mrs. Karen GETZ
30 Director of Development ....Mrs. Leslie DEILY

The University of the Arts (H)

320 S Broad Street, Philadelphia PA 19102-4944
County: Philadelphia FICE Identification: 003350
Unit ID: 215105
Telephone: (215) 717-6000 Carnegie Class: Spec/Arts
FAX Number: (215) 717-6045 Calendar System: Semester
URL: www.uarts.edu
Established: 1876 Annual Undergrad Tuition & Fees: $33,500
Enrollment: 2,355 Coed
Affiliation or Control: Independent Non-Profit IRS Status: 501(c)3
Highest Offering: Master's
Program: Liberal Arts And General; Teacher Preparatory; Professional; Fine Arts Emphasis
Accreditation: M, ART, MUS

01 President ....Mr. Sean T. BUFFINGTON
05 Provost ....Dr. Kirk E. PILLOW
26 Vice Pres University Communications .... Mr. Paul F. HEALY
32 Vice President of Student Affairs ....Dr. Alan LEFFERS
20 Assistant Provost ....Mr. James SAVOIE
30 Vice Pres Advancement ....Ms. Lucille HUGHES
04 Exec Assistant to the President ....Ms. Jennifer KANZLER
10 Vice Pres Finance/Administration .... Mr. Stephen LIGHTCAP
15 Director of Personnel Services ....Ms. Jennifer EDWARDS
08 Assoc Provost/Director of Libraries .... Ms. Carol GRANEY
19 Director of Public Safety ....Mr. Randolph MERCED
27 Vice Pres Technology & Info Svcs ....Mr. Thomas CARNWATH
90 Director Academic Computing ....Vacant
91 Director of Information Systems ....Mr. Jack POST
91 Director Network Services ....Mr. Kevin BRENNAN
07 VP Enroll Mgmt/Dean of Admissions .... Ms. Sue GANDY
06 Registrar ....Ms. Margaret KIP
37 VP Enroll Mgmt/Dean of Fin Aid .... Ms. Chris PESOTSKI
57 Dean College Art/Media & Design ... Mr. Christopher SHARROCK
79 Dean of Liberal Arts ....Dr. Peter STAMBLER
51 Director of Continuing Studies ....Ms. Erin ELMAN
35 Director of Student Life .... Ms. Kathleen EMBLETON
36 Director of Career Services .... Ms. Elisa SEEHERMAN
38 Director Student Counseling ....Mr. Brian HAINSTOCK
09 Director of Institutional Research ....Ms. Beth E. FREDERICK
85 Dir International Student Services ....Ms. Mara FLAMM
29 Director Alumni & Parent Relations .... Ms. Lauren VILLANUEVE

University of Pennsylvania (I)

3401 Walnut Street, Room 352B,
Philadelphia PA 19104-6228
County: Philadelphia FICE Identification: 003378
Unit ID: 215062
Telephone: (215) 898-5000 Carnegie Class: RU/VH
FAX Number: (215) 898-5756 Calendar System: Semester
URL: www.upenn.edu
Established: 1740 Annual Undergrad Tuition & Fees: $42,098
Enrollment: 25,007 Coed
Affiliation or Control: Independent Non-Profit IRS Status: 501(c)3
Highest Offering: Doctorate
Program: Liberal Arts And General; Teacher Preparatory; Professional
Accreditation: M, ANEST, BUS, CEA, CS, DENT, ENG, HSA, IPSY, LAW, LSAR, MED, MIDWF, NURSE, PH, SW, VET

01 President .... Dr. Amy GUTMANN
03 Executive Vice President .... Mr. Craig CARNAROLI
05 Provost ....Dr. Vincent PRICE
06 Registrar ....Vacant
07 Dean of Admissions ....Mr. Eric J. FURDA
32 Vice Provost University Life .... Dr. Valarie S. MCCOULLUM
10 Vice Pres Finance & Treasurer ....Mr. Stephen D. GOLDING
18 Vice Pres Facil/Real Est Svcs ....Ms. Anne PAPAGEORGE

17 CEO Univ of PA Health System ... Dr. Ralph W. MULLER
08 Vice Provost/Dir of Libraries ... Mr. Harry C. ROGERS
13 Vice Pres Info Systems/Computing ... Ms. Robin H. BECK
100 Vice Pres & Chief of Staff ... Mr. Gregory S. ROST
38 Vice Pres Institutional Affairs ... Ms. Joann MITCHELL
30 Vice Pres Dev/Alumni Relations ... Mr. John H. ZELLER
16 Vice Pres Human Resources ... Dr. John J. HEUER
36 Vice Pres Govt & Community Affairs ... Mr. Jeffrey COOPER
19 Vice President Public Safety ... Ms. Maureen RUSH
26 Vice Pres for Univ Communications ... Mr. Stephen J. MACCARTHY
88 Vice Pres Business Services ... Ms. Marie D. WITT
45 Vice Pres Budget Mgmt Analysis ... Ms. Bonnie C. GIBSON
43 Senior Vice Pres/General Counsel ... Ms. Wendy S. WHITE
101 Secretary of the University ... Ms. Leslie L. KRUHLY
20 Vice Provost for Education ... Dr. Andrew N. BINNS
20 Assoc Provost Faculty Affairs ... Dr. Lynn H. LEES
29 Asst Vice Pres Alumni Relations ... Mr. Fredrick H. WAMPLER
88 Vice Provost for Research ... Dr. Steven J. FLUHARTY
88 Assoc Vice Provost Rsrch Svcs ... Ms. Pamela S. CAUDILL
14 Assoc Vice Pres Networking/ Telecom ... Mr. Michael A. PALLADINO
88 Assoc VP Audit Compl & Privacy ... Ms. Mary Lee BROWN
31 Assoc VP/Dir Ctr Cmty Partnerships ... Dr. Ira HARKAVY
28 Assoc Vice Prov Equity & Access ... Rev. William GIPSON
21 Comptroller ... Mr. John F. HORN
63 Exec Vice Pres/Dean Sch of Medicine ... Dr. J. L. JAMESON
70 Dean School Social Policy/Practice ... Dr. Richard J. GELLES
49 Dean School Arts & Sciences ... Dr. Rebecca W. BUSHNELL
50 Dean Wharton School ... Dr. Thomas S. ROBERTSON
60 Dean Annenberg Sch Communications ... Dr. Michael X. DELLI CARPINI
53 Dean Graduate School Education ... Dr. Andrew C. PORTER
57 Dean PennDesign ... Ms. Marilyn J. TAYLOR
61 Dean School of Law ... Mr. Michael A. FITTS
66 Dean School of Nursing ... Dr. Afaf I. MELEIS
52 Dean School of Dental Medicine ... Dr. Denis F. KINANE
74 Dean School of Veterinary Medicine ... Dr. Joan C. HENDRICKS
54 Dean School of Engr/Applied Science ... Dr. Eduardo D. GLANDT
35 Assoc VP Student Services ... Ms. Michelle H. BROWN
85 Dir Intl Student & Scholar Svcs ... Dr. Rodolfo R. ALTAMIRANO
36 Dir of Career Services ... Ms. Patricia L. ROSE
37 Dir Student Financial Aid ... Mr. William M. SCHILLING
35 Executive Director Student Affairs ... Mr. Hikaru KOZUMA
38 Int Dir Counseling/Psych Services ... Dr. William B. ALEXANDER
97 Int Exec Dir Sch Lib Prof Studies ... Ms. Nora E. LEWIS
102 Exec Director Corporate Relations ... Dr. Don BONE
102 Exec Director Foundation Relations ... Ms. Eleanor C. HING FAY
22 Exec Dir Affirm Action & Equal Op ... Mr. Sam B. STARKS
23 Dir Student Health Services ... Dr. Evelyn WIENER
88 Mgng Dir Annenberg Cr/Penn Presents ... Dr. Michael J. ROSE
88 Dir Morris Arboretum ... Mr. Paul W. MEYER
88 Dir Institute of Contempory Art ... Ms. Claudia GOULD
88 Dir Museum of Archlgy/Anthrplgy ... Dr. Richard A. HODGES
88 Director Research Services ... Ms. Deborah M. FISHER
41 Dir Intercollegiate Athletics ... Mr. Steven BILSKY
24 IT Director ... Mr. James F. JOHNSON
91 IT Exec Dir Admin Info Tech ... Ms. Jeanne F. CURTIS
39 Dir College Houses & Academic Svcs ... Dr. Leslie J. DELAUTER
96 Chief Procurement Officer ... Vacant
42 Associate University Chaplain ... Rev. Charles L. HOWARD
09 Asst VP Inst Research & Analysis ... Ms. Stacey J. LOPEZ

University of Pittsburgh (A)

4200 Fifth Avenue, Pittsburgh PA 15260-3583
County: Allegheny FICE Identification: 003379
Unit ID: 215293
Telephone: (412) 624-4141 Carnegie Class: RU/VH
FAX Number: N/A Calendar System: Semester
URL: www.pitt.edu
Established: 1787 Annual Undergrad Tuition & Fees (In-State): $14,936
Enrollment: 28,823 Coed
Affiliation or Control: State Related IRS Status: 501(c)3
Highest Offering: Doctorate
Program: Liberal Arts And General; Teacher Preparatory; Professional
Accreditation: M, ANEST, #ARCPA, AUD, BUS, CEA, CLPSY, CORE, DENT, DH, DIETC, DIETD, ENG, HSA, HT, IPSY, LAW, LIB, MED, NURSE, OPE, OT, PERF, PH, PHAR, PTA, SP, SPAA, SW, @TEAC, THEA

01 Chancellor ... Mr. Mark A. NORDENBERG
05 Sr Vice Chancellor & Provost ... Dr. Patricia E. BEESON
63 Sr VC Health Sci/Dean Sch of Med ... Dr. Arthur S. LEVINE
03 Exec Vice Chanc/General Counsel ... Mr. Jerome COCHRAN
101 Secy of Brd of Trustees/Asst Chanc ... Dr. B. Jean FERKETISH
88 Associate Chancellor ... Dr. Vijai P. SINGH
10 Chief Financial Officer ... Mr. Arthur G. RAMICONE
30 Vice Chancellor Inst Advancement ... Mr. Albert J. NOVAK, JR.
43 Exec Vice Chanc & General Counsel ... Mr. Jerome COCHRAN
22 Dir Aff Action/Diversity & Inclus ... Ms. Carol W. MOHAMED
26 Vice Chancellor Public Affairs ... Mr. Robert HILL
100 Vice Chanc Cmty Init/Chief of Staff ... Mr. G. Reynolds CLARK
86 Vice Chanc Governmental Relations ... Mr. Paul A. SUPOWITZ
18 Assoc Vice Chanc Facilities Mgmt ... Mr. Joseph W. FINK
15 Assoc Vice Chanc Human Resources ... Mr. Ronald W. FRISCH
88 Assoc Vice Chanc Mgmt Info & Analy ... Ms. Jane W. THOMPSON
27 Sr Assoc Vice Chanc Univ News/Mag ... Mr. John HARVITH
20 Vice Provost Undergraduate Studies ... Dr. Juan J. MAFREDI
58 Vice Provost Graduate Studies ... Dr. Alberta M. SBRAGIA
88 Asst Provost Strategic/Program Dev ... Ms. Sheila W. RATHKE
45 Vice Prov Acad Plng/Resource Mgmt ... Dr. David N. DEJONG
46 Vice Provost for Research ... Dr. George E. KLINZING
20 Vice Provost for Faculty Affairs ... Dr. Andrew R. BLAIR
29 Assoc Vice Chanc Alumni Relations ... Mr. Jeffrey GLEIM
21 Associate Vice Chancellor Business ... Mr. James V. EARLE
06 Interim University Registrar ... Mr. Ralph E. HERTEL
41 Athletic Director ... Mr. Steve C. PEDERSON
07 Director Admissions & Financial Aid ... Dr. Betsy A. PORTER
32 Vice Provost and Dean of Students ... Dr. Kathy W. HUMPHREY
49 Dean Sch Arts & Sci/Col Gen Studies ... Dr. N. John COOPER
92 Dean University Honors College ... Dr. Edward M. STRICKER
50 Dean Jos M Katz Gr Sch Bus ... Dr. John T. DELANEY
53 Dean of School of Education ... Dr. Alan M. LESGOLD
54 Dean Swanson School of Engineering ... Dr. Gerald D. HOLDER
61 Dean of School of Law ... Ms. Mary A. CROSSLEY
80 Dean Grad Sch Public/Intl Affs ... Dr. John T. KEELER
70 Dean School of Social Work ... Dr. Larry E. DAVIS
62 Dean School Information Sciences ... Dr. Ronald L. LARSEN
52 Dean School of Dental Medicine ... Dr. Thomas W. BRAUN
66 Dean of School of Nursing ... Dr. Jaqueline DUNBAR-JACOB
67 Dean School of Pharmacy ... Dr. Patricia D. KROBOTH
69 Dean Grad School Public Health ... Dr. Donald S. BURKE
76 Dean School Health & Rehab Science ... Dr. Clifford E. BRUBAKER
40 Interim Director Book Centers ... Ms. Debra R. FYOCK
24 Dir Ctr Instruct Dev/Distance Educ ... Ms. Cynthia GOLDEN
13 Dir Computer Svcs/Systems Devel ... Ms. Jinx P. WALTON
104 Interim Dir International Services ... Dr. Charles L. NIEMAN
09 Director Institutional Research ... Ms. Cynthia A. ROBERTS
21 Director Internal Audit ... Mr. John P. ELLIOTT
36 Interim Director Career Development ... Ms. Karin M. ASHER
25 Director Research ... Mr. Allen A. DIPALMA
38 Director of Counseling Center ... Mr. James A. COX, JR.
08 Director Univ Library System ... Mr. Rush G. MILLER
19 Chief University Police ... Mr. Timothy R. DELANEY
23 Director Student Health Svcs ... Dr. Elizabeth WETTICK
96 Manager Purchasing Services ... Mr. Thomas E. YOUNGS, JR.
44 Sr Exec Director Planned Giving ... Mr. Walter E. BROWN
102 Exec Dir Corp & Found Relations ... Mr. Andrew B. KOVALCIK
04 Exec Asst to the Chancellor ... Ms. Mary Jo RACE

University of Pittsburgh at Bradford (B)

300 Campus Drive, Bradford PA 16701-2812
County: McKean FICE Identification: 003380
Unit ID: 215266
Telephone: (814) 362-7500 Carnegie Class: Bac/Diverse
FAX Number: (814) 362-7578 Calendar System: Semester
URL: www.upb.pitt.edu
Established: 1963 Annual Undergrad Tuition & Fees (In-State): $22,500
Enrollment: 1,698 Coed
Affiliation or Control: State Related IRS Status: 501(c)3
Highest Offering: Baccalaureate
Program: Liberal Arts And General; Teacher Preparatory; Professional
Accreditation: &M, ADNUR, NUR

01 President ... Dr. Livingston ALEXANDER
05 Vice President Academic Affairs ... Dr. Steven E. HARDIN
32 Vice Pres/Dean Student Affairs ... Dr. K. James EVANS
10 Vice President for Business Affairs ... Mr. Richard T. ESCH
20 Associate Dean of Academic Affairs ... Dr. Lauren E. YAICH
35 Assoc Dn Stdnt Affs/Dir Career Svcs ... Dr. Holly J. SPITTLER
39 Assoc Dean Student Affs/Dir Housing ... Dr. Ronald S. BINDER
30 Exec Dir Institutional Advancement ... Mrs. Jill M. BALLARD
26 Director Communications & Marketing ... Mrs. Patricia FRANTZ CERCONE
07 Director of Admissions ... Mr. Alex P. NAZEMETZ
06 Registrar/Asst Dean Academic Affs ... Mr. James L. BALDWIN
37 Director Financial Aid ... Ms. Melissa IBANEZ
88 Director Academic Sucess Center ... Vacant
66 Director of Nursing ... Dr. Lisa FIORENTINO
08 Director of Library Services ... Ms. Trisha A. MORRIS
51 Director Adult Continuing Education ... Mr. Raymond R. GEARY, JR.
41 Director Athletics/Recreat Sports ... Ms. Lorraine R. MAZZA
21 Director Budget & Fiscal Reporting ... Mr. Steve WILLIAMS
18 Director Facilities Management ... Mr. Peter J. BUCHHEIT
19 Director of Campus Police & Safety ... Mr. Dan SONGER
13 Dir Computing/Telecom/Media Svcs ... Mr. Donald C. LEWICKI
88 Coordinator of Community Engagement ... Mrs. Tonya J. ACKLEY
29 Director Alumni Relations ... Ms. Lindsay RETCHLESS
88 Director Student Activities ... Ms. Christina L. GRAHAM
23 Director of Student Health Services ... Ms. Bonnie K. MCMILLEN
38 Director Counseling Services ... Dr. Leslie L. RHINEHART
31 Director of Auxiliary Services ... Mr. Rhett KENNEDY
88 Director of Arts Programming ... Mr. Randy L. MAYES
15 Manager Human Resources ... Ms. Laurel E. PHILLIPS
40 Manager Book Center ... Ms. Leasa A. MALEY
96 Manager of Purchasing ... Ms. Heidi A. ANDERSON
83 Chair Div Behavioral/Social Sci ... Dr. Stephen ROBAR
76 Chair Div Biological/Health Sci ... Dr. Mary MULCAHY
79 Chair Div Communications/Arts ... Mr. Jeff GUTERMAN
50 Chair Div of Management/Education ... Dr. Betsy MATZ
81 Chair Div Phys/Computational Sci ... Dr. Yong-Zhuo CHEN
09 Director of Institutional Research ... Mr. James L. BALDWIN
28 Director of Diversity ... Mrs. Liza J. GREVILLE
36 Director Student Placement ... Dr. Holly J. SPITTLER

† Regional accreditation is carried under the parent institution in Pittsburgh, PA.

University of Pittsburgh at Greensburg (C)

150 Finoli Drive, Greensburg PA 15601-5898
County: Westmoreland FICE Identification: 003381
Unit ID: 215275
Telephone: (724) 837-7040 Carnegie Class: Bac/A&S
FAX Number: (724) 836-9901 Calendar System: Semester
URL: www.upg.pitt.edu
Established: 1963 Annual Undergrad Tuition & Fees (In-State): $12,176
Enrollment: 1,883 Coed
Affiliation or Control: State Related IRS Status: 501(c)3
Highest Offering: Baccalaureate
Program: Liberal Arts And General; Business Emphasis
Accreditation: &M

01 President ... Dr. Sharon P. SMITH
05 Vice Pres of Academic Affairs ... Dr. J. Wesley JAMISON
11 Vice President Administration ... Mr. Carl A. ROSSMAN
20 Assistant VP for Academic Affairs ... Dr. Dean E. NELSON
32 Dean of Student Services ... Mr. Rick A. FOGLE
07 Director of Admissions ... Ms. Heather KABALA
08 Director Millstein Library ... Dr. Patricia M. DUCK
14 Dir Computer Svcs & Info Systems ... Mr. William E. MARTIN
06 Registrar ... Ms. Linda SMITH
15 Director Human Resources ... Ms. Joyce BUCCHI
37 Director of Financial Aid ... Ms. Brandi DARR
41 Director of Athletics/Recreation ... Mr. Anthony BERICH
18 Director Plant Maintenance ... Mr. Joe A. OLCZAK
21 Director Business Affairs ... Mrs. Ronna COLLAND
30 Dir Univ Rels/Instl Advancement ... Ms. Jodi KRAISINGER
36 Director Career Services ... Ms. Elizabeth TIEDEMANN
38 Director of Counseling ... Ms. Gayle PAMERLEAU
26 Director Media Relations ... Ms. Susan ISOLA
96 Purchasing Administrator ... Mr. Allen TEDROW
29 Coordinator Alumni Affairs ... Ms. Julie L. DLUGOS

† Regional accreditation is carried under the parent institution in Pittsburgh, PA.

University of Pittsburgh at Johnstown (D)

450 Schoolhouse Road, Johnstown PA 15904-2990
County: Cambria FICE Identification: 003382
Unit ID: 215284
Telephone: (814) 269-7000 Carnegie Class: Bac/Diverse
FAX Number: (814) 269-2096 Calendar System: Semester
URL: www.pitt-johnstown.pitt.edu
Established: 1927 Annual Undergrad Tuition & Fees (In-State): $12,158
Enrollment: 2,965 Coed
Affiliation or Control: State Related IRS Status: 501(c)3
Highest Offering: Baccalaureate
Program: Liberal Arts And General; Teacher Preparatory
Accreditation: &M, ENGT, SURGT

01 President ... Dr. Jem SPECTAR
88 Assoc VP Aux Svcs/Special Project ... Mr. Christian J. STUMPF
10 Vice Pres Finance & Administration ... Dr. Kelly M. AUSTIN
05 Vice Pres for Academic Affairs ... Dr. Janet L. GRADY
32 Vice Pres of Student Affairs ... Mr. Jon WESCOTT
04 Secretary to the President ... Mrs. Susan K. PALOV
84 Vice Pres of Enroll Svcs & Planning ... Dr. James F. GYURE
29 Assoc VP Alumni/Community Relations ... Mr. Robert W. KNIPPLE
30 Chief Advancement Officer ... Mrs. Lynn I. BARGER
11 Dir of Facilities Admin & Contracts ... Mr. Robert BLASCHAK
08 Director Library ... Ms. Deborah RINDERKNECHT
13 Associate Vice Pres for Info Tech ... Mr. J. Jeffrey SERNELL
06 Registrar ... Mrs. Marilyn A. ALBERTER
22 Sr Officer for Equity & Inclusion ... Ms. Laura PERRY-THOMPSON
26 Director Marketing ... Mrs. Kimberly M. MILLER
15 Campus Director Of Human Resources ... Mrs. Pamela J. SABOL
18 Director of Facilities Operations ... Mr. Andrew M. CSIKOS
35 Director of Student Activities ... Mr. Bryan VALENTINE
38 Director Wellness Center ... Ms. Katrin A. WOLFE
37 Director Financial Aid ... Mrs. Jeanine M. LAWN
19 Director of Campus Police ... Mr. Kevin GRADY
23 Exec Dir of Health & Wellness Svcs ... Mrs. Theresa M. HORNER
39 Director Housing & Residence Life ... Mr. Mark A. DOUGHERTY
40 Dir Bookstore/Convenience Store ... Mr. John ZIATS
41 Athletics Director ... Mr. Patrick PECORA
96 Coordinator of Purchasing ... Mr. Nathan TENEROWICZ
21 Coordinator of Business Office Opers ... Mrs. Janet E. VALINE
85 Director of International Services ... Mrs. Jennifer S. KIST
88 Dir Conference & Auxiliary Services ... Mrs. Joyce A. RADOVANIC
07 Director of Admissions ... Mr. Bernard J. SARNESO
51 Dir of Advanced & Continuing Educ ... Mrs. Stephanie KORBER
88 Director of Academic Success Center ... Mrs. Katherine KINSINGER
88 Director of Operations ... Mrs. Dolores BERKEY
36 Director Career Services ... Ms. Angie BOYD

† Regional accreditation is carried under the parent institution in Pittsburgh, PA.

University of Pittsburgh at Titusville (E)

504 E Main, Titusville PA 16354-2097
County: Crawford FICE Identification: 003383
Unit ID: 215309
Telephone: (814) 827-4400 Carnegie Class: Assoc/Pub2in4
FAX Number: (814) 827-4448 Calendar System: Semester
URL: www.upt.pitt.edu
Established: 1963 Annual Undergrad Tuition & Fees (In-State): $11,118
Enrollment: 514 Coed
Affiliation or Control: State Related IRS Status: 501(c)3
Highest Offering: Associate Degree
Program: 2-Year Principally Bachelor's Creditable

Accreditation: &M, ADNUR, PTAA

01 President ..... Dr. William A. SHIELDS
05 Vice Pres for Academic Affairs ..... Dr. David FITZ
10 Vice President for Business Affairs ..... Ms. Denise MCCLOSKEY
32 Vice Pres for Student Affairs ..... Dr. Checka LEINWALL
84 Exec Director Enrollment Management ..... Mr. John MUMFORD
13 Director of Computing and Telecomm ..... Ms. Lori BROWN
08 Library Director ..... Mr. Patrick HALL
06 Registrar ..... Mr. Christopher COAT
21 Assoc Business Ofcr/Dir Stdnt Accts ..... Ms. Nicole NEELY
15 Director Human Resources ..... Ms. Debra BIGGERSTAFF
18 Director of Facilities Management ..... Mr. Jon N. EDWARDS
26 Director Public Relations ..... Ms. Tammy KNAPP
40 Director of Bookstore ..... Ms. Margaret J. MCMAHON
29 Director Alumni Relations ..... Ms. Tammy KNAPP
37 Director Student Financial Aid ..... Ms. Sue Ann BLOOM
96 Director of Purchasing ..... Ms. Pamela KREPPS
41 Athletic Director ..... Mr. Tim SNEERINGER

† Regional accreditation is carried under the parent institution in Pittsburgh, PA.

University of the Sciences in Philadelphia (A)

600 S 43rd Street, Philadelphia PA 19104-4495
County: Philadelphia FICE Identification: 003353
Unit ID: 215132
Telephone: (215) 596-8800 Carnegie Class: Spec/Health
FAX Number: (215) 895-1100 Calendar System: Semester
URL: www.usciences.edu
Established: 1821 Annual Undergrad Tuition & Fees: $30,580
Enrollment: 2,868 Coed
Affiliation or Control: Independent Non-Profit IRS Status: 501(c)3
Highest Offering: Doctorate
Program: Professional
Accreditation: M, OT, PHAR, PTA

01 President ..... Dr. Philip P. GERBINO
05 Provost ..... Dr. Russell DI GATE
10 Senior VP for Finance & CFO ..... Mr. Joseph G. TRAINOR
11 Senior VP of Operations and COO ..... Ms. Sara CAMPBELL
88 Senior VP for Div External Affairs ..... Mr. William ASHTON
30 VP for Institutional Advancement ..... Ms. Ann SATTERTHWAITE
31 Vice Pres Community Partnerships ..... Ms. Elizabeth BRESSI-STOPPE
26 Vice President of Marketing ..... Ms. Maria BUEHER
102 VP Corporate Relatons ..... Dr. Susan BARRETT
100 Chief of Staff ..... Dr. Peter MILLER
13 Exec Dir Information Technology ..... Mr. John MASCIANTONIO
20 Assoc Provost Academic Affairs ..... Vacant
84 Assoc Provost for Enrollment Mgmt ..... Ms. Barbara ELLIOTT
27 Associate Provost/CIO ..... Dr. Mark NESTOR
37 Director of Financial Aid ..... Ms. Paula LEHRBERGER
06 Registrar ..... Mr. Alan SIMS
07 Executive Director of Admissions ..... Ms. Diana COLLINS
29 Director of Alumni Relations ..... Ms. Nancy SHILS
08 Director of Library Services ..... Mr. Charles MYERS
58 Dean Graduate Studies ..... Dr. Rodney WIGENT
32 Dean of Students ..... Dr. William J. CUNNINGHAM
67 Dean of Pharmacy ..... Dr. Lisa LAWSON
49 Dean Misher College Arts & Sci ..... Dr. Suzanne K. MURPHY
76 Dean Samson College of Health Sci ..... Dr. Laurie SHERWEN
88 Dean of Mayes College ..... Dr. Andrew PETERSON
15 Dir Human Resources/Affirm Act Ofcr ..... Ms. Rosalie I. JONES
19 Chief Security Officer ..... Mr. Bernard GOLLOTTI
41 Athletic Director ..... Mr. Robert C. MORGAN
35 Director of Student Life ..... Ms. Susanne E. FERRIN
39 Residence Life Administrator ..... Mr. Ryan CROCETTO
85 Director of Multicultural Affairs ..... Mr. Walter PERRY
09 Director of Institutional Research ..... Ms. Anne B. HOROWITZ
21 Controller/Asst VP Finance ..... Ms. Brigid K. ISACKMAN
36 Director Career Services ..... Ms. Kimberly BRYANT
38 Director Student Counseling ..... Dr. Paul FURTAW
96 Manager University Purchasing ..... Mr. Thomas MOIANI
88 Executive Director Business Support ..... Mr. Bernard GOLLOTTI
88 Assistant Provost Spec Projects ..... Dr. John CONNORS
88 Director Academic Advising ..... Mr. Joseph CANADAY
18 Executive Director Facilities ..... Mr. John MCCAFFREY

The University of Scranton (B)

Scranton PA 18510-4622
County: Lackawanna FICE Identification: 003384
Unit ID: 215929
Telephone: (570) 941-7400 Carnegie Class: Master's L
FAX Number: (570) 941-6369 Calendar System: Semester
URL: www.scranton.edu
Established: 1888 Annual Undergrad Tuition & Fees: $35,692
Enrollment: 6,070 Coed
Affiliation or Control: Roman Catholic IRS Status: 501(c)3
Highest Offering: Doctorate
Program: Liberal Arts And General; Teacher Preparatory; Professional
Accreditation: M, ANEST, BUS, CACREP, CORE, CS, HSA, NURSE, OT, PTA, @TEAC, TED

01 President ..... Rev. Kevin P. QUINN, SJ
03 Executive Vice President ..... Dr. Patrick F. LEAHY
05 Provost/Academic VP ..... Dr. Harold BAILLIE
10 Vice President Finance/Treasurer ..... Mr. Edward J. STEINMETZ
32 Vice President Student Affairs ..... Dr. Vincent CARILLI
45 VP Plng/Chief Information Officer ..... Dr. Jerome P. DESANTO
26 VP for Alumni & Public Relations ..... Mr. Gerald ZABOSKI
16 VP Human Resources ..... Ms. Patricia A. DAY
42 VP for University Ministries ..... Rev. Richard MALLOY, SJ
43 General Counsel ..... Mr. Robert FARRELL
49 Dean Arts & Sciences ..... Dr. Brian P. CONNIFF
50 Dean Kania School Management ..... Dr. Michael O. MENSAH
58 Dean Grad School/Continuing Educ ..... Dr. William J. WELSH
88 Dean Panuska Col of Prof Studies ..... Dr. Debra A. PELLEGRINO
35 Dean of Students ..... Ms. Anitra M. MCSHEA
08 Dean of the Library/Info Fluency ..... Mr. Charles E. KRATZ, JR.
51 Asst Dean of OL/Off Campus Program ..... Ms. Regina B. BENNETT
21 Assistant Vice President Finance ..... Mr. Robert J. THOMAS
11 Assoc Vice Pres Admin Services ..... Vacant
88 Assoc Provost for Civic Engagement ..... Dr. Steven G. JONES
20 Assoc Provost for Academic Affairs ..... Dr. Joseph H. DREISBACH
07 Assoc VP Admiss & Undergrad Enroll ..... Mr. Joseph ROBACK
84 Asst Provost of Student Enrollment ..... Ms. Mary Kay ASTON
21 Assistant Provost of Operations ..... Ms. Anne Marie STAMFORD
06 Registrar ..... Ms. Helen STAGER
37 Director of Financial Aid ..... Mr. William R. BURKE
36 Director of Career Services ..... Mrs. Constance F. MCDONNELL
29 Director of Alumni Relations ..... Ms. Maryjane S. ROONEY
28 Director of Equity/Diversity Office ..... Ms. Rosette B. ADERA
09 Dir Inst Research/Assessment ..... Ms. Valerie A. TAYLOR
38 Director of Counseling Center ..... Mr. Thomas P. SMITH
96 Director of Purchasing ..... Mr. Gary ZAMPANO

Ursinus College (C)

PO Box 1000, 601 E Main Street, Collegeville PA 19426-1000
County: Montgomery FICE Identification: 003385
Unit ID: 216524
Telephone: (610) 409-3000 Carnegie Class: Bac/A&S
FAX Number: (610) 489-0627 Calendar System: Semester
URL: www.ursinus.edu
Established: 1869 Annual Undergrad Tuition & Fees: $41,650
Enrollment: 1,780 Coed
Affiliation or Control: Independent Non-Profit IRS Status: 501(c)3
Highest Offering: Baccalaureate
Program: Liberal Arts And General; Teacher Preparatory
Accreditation: M

01 President ..... Dr. Bobby FONG
05 Vice Pres Acad Affs/Dean of College ..... Dr. Judith T. LEVY
10 Vice Pres Finance & Administration ..... Mr. Winfield L. GUILMETTE
30 Senior Vice Pres for Advancement ..... Ms. Jill A. MARSTELLER
84 Vice President for Enrollment ..... Mr. Richard G. DIFELICIANTONIO
32 Vice Pres of Student Affairs/Dean ..... Ms. Deborah O. NOLAN
21 Associate Vice Pres/Controller ..... Mr. James COOPER
07 Dean of Admissions ..... Mr. Richard FLOYD
51 Director Continuing Education ..... Ms. Ellen MATTHEWS
08 Library Director ..... Mr. Charles JAMISON
36 Director of Placement Services ..... Mrs. Carla M. RINDE
18 Director of Physical Facilities ..... Mr. Andrew FEICK
41 Director of Athletics ..... Mrs. Laura MOLIKEN
27 Director College Communications ..... Vacant
37 Director Student Financial Services ..... Mrs. Suzanne SPARROW
06 Registrar ..... Ms. Barbara A. BORIS
29 Director of Alumni Relations ..... Vacant
20 Associate Academic Officer ..... Dr. Annette V. LUCAS
15 Director Personnel Services ..... Ms. Kelly WILLIAMS

Valley Forge Christian College (D)

1401 Charlestown Road, Phoenixville PA 19460-2399
County: Chester FICE Identification: 003306
Unit ID: 216542
Telephone: (610) 935-0450 Carnegie Class: Bac/Diverse
FAX Number: (610) 935-9353 Calendar System: Semester
URL: www.vfcc.edu
Established: 1939 Annual Undergrad Tuition & Fees: $15,652
Enrollment: 1,147 Coed
Affiliation or Control: Assemblies Of God Church IRS Status: 501(c)3
Highest Offering: Master's
Program: Liberal Arts And General; Teacher Preparatory; Professional; Religious Emphasis
Accreditation: M, @SW

01 President ..... Dr. Donald G. MEYER
05 Provost & VP of Academic Affairs ..... Dr. Philip D. MCLEOD
10 VP of Finance and Development ..... Dr. Daniel W. MORTENSEN
32 VP of Student Life ..... Rev. Jennifer D. GALE
06 Registrar ..... Mr. Russ CAMBRIA
37 Director of Financial Aid ..... Mrs. Linda STEIN
08 Librarian/Dir Storms Research Ctr ..... Mr. Paul MATHIAS
36 Director Career Services ..... Ms. Beverly ASHFORTH
14 Director of Information Technology ..... Mr. Brian SWOMLEY
18 Director of Operations ..... Mr. William WERKHEISER
41 Director of Athletics ..... Mr. Jon MACK
07 Director of Admissions ..... Rev. William CHENCO
39 Residence Director ..... Mr. Glen BURRIDGE
39 Residence Director ..... Ms. Gamey KIM
39 Residence Director ..... Ms. Theresa LITTLE
39 Residence Director ..... Mr. Reginald CHAPPLE
15 Director Human Resources ..... Mrs. Veronica BIRD
40 Director of Bookstore ..... Vacant
29 Director Alumni Relations ..... Mrs. Kristie OVERLY
84 Exec Director Enrollment Management ..... Mrs. Evie MEYER
21 Comptroller ..... Mr. Jonathan CAPECI
88 Director of Accounting ..... Mrs. Betty SMITH
09 Director of Institutional Research ..... Dr. Judy DUNHAM
26 Chief Public Relations Officer ..... Mrs. Michelle MALONEY

Valley Forge Military College (E)

1001 Eagle Road, Wayne PA 19087-3695
County: Delaware FICE Identification: 003386
Unit ID: 216551
Telephone: (610) 989-1200 Carnegie Class: Not Classified
FAX Number: (610) 975-9642 Calendar System: Semester
URL: www.vfmac.edu
Established: 1935 Annual Undergrad Tuition & Fees: $34,875
Enrollment: 227 Coed
Affiliation or Control: Independent Non-Profit IRS Status: 501(c)3
Highest Offering: Associate Degree
Program: 2-Year Principally Bachelor's Creditable
Accreditation: M

01 President ..... Col. David R. GRAY
05 VP Academic Affs/Int College Dean ..... Col. John CHURCH
32 Commandant of Cadets ..... Maj. Robert WOOD
30 Vice President for Development ..... Mr. Dennis SPIZUOCO
10 Chief Financial Officer ..... Mr. Vincent VUONO
18 Director of Facilities ..... Mr. Bryan K. GEILING
20 Assistant Dean ..... Col. Nan S. HOOD
84 Dean of Enrollment Management ..... Mr. Mark OSBORNE
08 Director of Library Services ..... LTC. Jean L. SMITH
37 Director of Financial Aid ..... Vacant
102 Director Corporate/Foundation Rels ..... Mrs. Ann SINATRA
15 Director of Human Resources ..... Ms. Marianne MEADE
13 Director Information Technology ..... Mr. Michael BROCK
41 Director of Athletics ..... Col. Dominick P. LORUSSO

Vet Tech Institute (F)

125 Seventh Street, Pittsburgh PA 15222-3400
County: Allegheny FICE Identification: 008568
Unit ID: 213914
Telephone: (412) 391-7021 Carnegie Class: Assoc/PrivFP
FAX Number: (412) 232-4348 Calendar System: Semester
URL: www.vettechinstitute.edu
Established: 1958 Annual Undergrad Tuition & Fees: $13,880
Enrollment: 348 Coed
Affiliation or Control: Proprietary IRS Status: Proprietary
Highest Offering: Associate Degree
Program: Occupational; Technical Emphasis
Accreditation: ACCSC

01 Director ..... Jackie FLYNN

Villanova University (G)

800 Lancaster Avenue, Villanova PA 19085-1699
County: Delaware FICE Identification: 003388
Unit ID: 216597
Telephone: (610) 519-4500 Carnegie Class: Master's L
FAX Number: (610) 519-5000 Calendar System: Semester
URL: www.villanova.edu
Established: 1842 Annual Undergrad Tuition & Fees: $41,110
Enrollment: 10,428 Coed
Affiliation or Control: Roman Catholic IRS Status: 501(c)3
Highest Offering: Doctorate
Program: Liberal Arts And General; Teacher Preparatory; Professional
Accreditation: M, ANEST, BUS, BUSA, CS, ENG, LAW, NURSE, SPAA

01 President ..... Rev. Peter M. DONOHUE, OSA
43 Vice President & General Counsel ..... Ms. Dorothy A. MALLOY
05 Vice President for Academic Affairs ..... Rev. Kail C. ELLIS, OSA
30 Vice Pres University Advancement ..... Mr. Michael O'NEILL
11 Vice Pres Administration/Finance ..... Mr. Kenneth G. VALOSKY
13 Vice Pres/Chief Information Officer ..... Mr. Stephen FUGALE
32 Vice President for Student Life ..... Rev. John P. STACK, OSA
27 Vice Pres University Communication ..... Ms. Ann DIEBOLD
20 Assoc Vice Pres Academic Affairs ..... Dr. Craig WHEELAND
15 AVP Human Res/Affirm Action Ofcr ..... Dr. Ellen LACORTE
45 Assoc Vice Pres for Auxiliary Svcs ..... Mr. Frederick C. SIEBER
29 Asst Vice Pres for Alumni Affairs ..... Mr. Gary R. OLSEN
46 Asst Vice Pres for Research ..... Dr. Milton T. COLE
51 Asst Vice Pres for Academic Affairs ..... Dr. Robert D. STOKES
28 Asst VP Multicultural Affairs ..... Dr. Teresa A. NANCE
84 Dean Enrollment Management ..... Mr. Stephen R. MERRITT
09 Exec Dir Planning/Inst Research ..... Dr. James F. TRAINER
18 Exec Director Facilities Management ..... Mr. Robert MORRO
42 Executive Director Campus Ministry ..... Rev. Joseph L. FARRELL, OSA
88 Asoc Dean Enrol Mgt For Stdnt Info ..... Ms. Catherine H. CONNOR
84 Asc Dn Enr Mgt Univ Admiss/Fin Asst ..... Mr. George J. WALTER
07 Director University Admission ..... Mr. Michael GAYNOR
08 Librarian/Dir of Falvey Library ..... Mr. Joseph LUCIA
35 Dean of Students ..... Mr. Paul F. PUGH
49 Dean Liberal Arts & Sciences ..... Dr. Jean A. LINNEY
50 Actg Dean Villanova Sch of Business ..... Dr. Kevin D. CLARK
58 Dean Graduate Studies LA&S ..... Dr. Adele LINDENMEYR
61 Dean School of Law ..... Mr. John GOTANDA
66 Dean of Nursing ..... Dr. M. Louise FITZPATRICK
54 Dean of Engineering ..... Dr. Gary A. GABRIELE
55 Director Part Time Studies ..... Mr. James R. JOHNSON
85 Director Intl/Human Services ..... Mr. Stephen T. MCWILLIAMS
37 Director Financial Assistance ..... Ms. Bonnie Lee BEHM
19 Director of Public Safety ..... Mr. David TEDJESKE
36 Director Career Services ..... Ms. Nancy J. DUDAK

92 Director of the Honors Program .... Dr. Thomas W. SMITH
38 Director of Univ Counseling Center ....Dr. Joan G. WHITNEY
94 Dir Women's Studies Programming .... Dr. Lisa SEWELL
94 Dir Women's Studies Academics ....Dr. Jean LUTES
39 Director Office of Residence Life .... Mr. Thomas DE MARCO
96 Director of Procurement ....Mr. John R. DURHAM
26 Director of Media Relations ....Mr. Jonathan GUST
40 Director of University Shop ....Mr. Frank L. HENNINGER
41 Director of Athletics .... Mr. Vincent P. NICASTRO
23 Medical Director Student Health Ctr ....Dr. Brian BULLOCK
23 Director Health Center ....Dr. Mary MCGONIGLE
06 Associate Registrar ....Ms. Melissa D. GERDING
24 Assoc Director Media Technologies ....Mr. Michael C. HOFFBERG
22 Asc Dir Center Multicultural Affs .... Ms. Linda COLEMAN
04 Special Asst to President/Ext Rels ....Rev. George F. RILEY

Washington & Jefferson College (A)

60 S Lincoln Street, Washington PA 15301-4801
County: Washington FICE Identification: 003389
Unit ID: 216667
Telephone: (724) 222-4400 Carnegie Class: Bac/A&S
FAX Number: (724) 223-6534 Calendar System: 4/1/4
URL: www.washjeff.edu
Established: 1781 Annual Undergrad Tuition & Fees: $35,960
Enrollment: 1,460 Coed
Affiliation or Control: Independent Non-Profit IRS Status: 501(c)3
Highest Offering: Baccalaureate
Program: Liberal Arts And General; Teacher Preparatory
Accreditation: M

01 President ....Dr. Tori HARING-SMITH
04 Special Assistant to the President ....Vacant
05 VP Academic Affairs/Dean of Faculty .... Dr. James C. WHITE, II
10 CFO/VP Business/Finance .... Mr. Dennis MCMASTER
30 VP Development/Alumni Relations ....Mr. Michael P. GRZESIAK
84 Vice President for Enrollment ....Mr. Alton E. NEWELL
21 Assoc VP for Business & Finance .... Mr. Thomas SZEJKO
32 VP and Dean of Student Life .... Mr. Byron MCCRAE
44 Exec Dir Campaigns/Advancement Oper ...Ms. Karen CRENSHAW
20 Associate Dean of the Faculty .... Dr. Charles HANNON
28 Asst Dean Stdnt Life/Dir Diver Pgm ....Ms. Teanca SHEPHERD
18 Director of Facilities and Planning ....Mr. Troy BONTE
26 Dir Comm/Special Asst to President .... Ms. Karen OOSTERHOUS
06 Registrar ....Ms. Leslie MAXIN
29 Exec Dir Alumni Relations & Dev ....Ms. Michele HUFNAGEL
07 Director of Admission .... Mr. Robert ADKINS
37 Director Financial Aid ....Ms. Michelle ANDERSON
13 Dir of Information/Technology Svcs ....Mr. Daniel FAULK
15 Director Human Resources ....Ms. Susan MEHALIK
19 Director Protection Services ....Mr. Edward E. COCHRAN
36 Director Career Services .... Ms. Roberta CROSS
40 Bookstore Manager ....Ms. Cynthia BRICELAND
41 Director of Athletics ....Mr. William DUKETT
08 Director of Library Services ....Ms. Alexis RITTENBERGER
102 Foundation & Corp Relations Officer ....Ms. Julie THROCKMORTON
39 Assoc Dean Stdnt Life/Dir Res Life .... Mr. Steven ANDERSON
91 Assoc Director for Admin Computing .... Mr. Michael A. TIMKO
104 Dir of Global Education ....Ms. Tracie SEBASTIAN-FRUEHAUF
88 Associate Dean for Assessment ....Mr. James SLOAT
88 Asst Dean for Academic Advising .... Ms. Catherine SHERMAN
88 Director Conferences and Events .... Ms. Maureen VALENTINE
38 Director of Counseling Services .... Ms. Lisa HAMILTON

Waynesburg University (B)

51 W College Street, Waynesburg PA 15370-1222
County: Greene FICE Identification: 003391
Unit ID: 216694
Telephone: (724) 627-8191 Carnegie Class: Master's L
FAX Number: (724) 627-6416 Calendar System: Semester
URL: www.waynesburg.edu
Established: 1849 Annual Undergrad Tuition & Fees: $19,090
Enrollment: 2,516 Coed
Affiliation or Control: Presbyterian Church (U.S.A.) IRS Status: 501(c)3
Highest Offering: Doctorate
Program: Liberal Arts And General; Teacher Preparatory; Professional
Accreditation: M, NURSE

01 President ....Dr. Timothy R. THYREEN
45 Sr Vice Pres Inst Planning/Research ....Mr. Richard L. NOFTZGER
05 Provost ....Dr. Robert J. GRAHAM
30 Exec VP Institutional Advancement ....Mr. Doug LEE
10 Sr VP Business & Finance ....Mr. Roy R. BARNHART
07 Sr VP Enrollment & Univ Relations ....Ms. Robin L. KING
41 Athletic Director .... Mr. Rick SHEPAS
06 Registrar ....Mrs. Vicki WILSON
13 Exec Dir Information Technology ....Mr. Peter MAHONEY
08 Int Library Director .... Ms. Rea REDD
18 Director of Facilites Management ....Mr. John BURKE
26 Director of College Relations ....Mrs. Bethany DOYLE
36 Director of Placement ....Mrs. Marie E. COFFMAN
38 Student Counselor ....Mrs. Jane S. OWEN
21 Business Ofc Supervisor/Controller .... Mr. Dave MARTIN
23 Director of Health Services .... Mrs. Carol YOUNG
42 Chaplain .... Mr. Tom RIBAR
15 Director Human Resources ....Mr. Tom HELMICK
37 Director Student Financial Aid .... Mr. Matthew STOKAN

Westminster College (C)

319 South Market Street, New Wilmington PA 16172-0001
County: Lawrence FICE Identification: 003392
Unit ID: 216807
Telephone: (724) 946-8761 Carnegie Class: Bac/A&S
FAX Number: (724) 946-7132 Calendar System: Semester
URL: www.westminster.edu
Established: 1852 Annual Undergrad Tuition & Fees: $30,310
Enrollment: 1,588 Coed
Affiliation or Control: Presbyterian Church (U.S.A.) IRS Status: 501(c)3
Highest Offering: Master's
Program: Liberal Arts And General; Teacher Preparatory
Accreditation: M, MUS

01 President ....Dr. Richard H. DORMAN
05 Vice Pres Academic Affs/Dean of Col ....Dr. Jesse T. MANN
30 VP Inst Advancement/Chief Dev Ofcr .... Ms. Gloria C. CAGIGAS
10 Vice Pres Finance/Mgmt Services .... Mr. Kenneth J. ROMIG
06 Registrar ....Ms. June PIERCE
07 Vice President for Enrollment ....Mr. Bradley P. TOKAR
42 Dean of the Chapel .... Rev. James R. MOHR
32 VP Student Affairs/Dean of Students .... Dr. Neal A. EDMAN
35 Assoc Dean of Student Affairs ....Ms. Camille HAWTHORNE
37 Director Student Financial Aid ....Ms. Cheryl GERBER
08 Head Librarian .... Ms. Molly P. SPINNEY
36 Director of Career Center ....Ms. Linda B. MEADE
29 Director of Alumni Relations ....Ms. Mary C. JAMES
27 Sr Dir Marketing/Communications ....Mr. Mark A. MEIGHEN
13 Director of Information Systems ....Mr. Paul N. WALLACE
51 Dir Cont Educ/Lifelong Learning ....Ms. Elizabeth HINES
58 Director Graduate Programs ....Vacant
41 Athletic Director ....Mr. James E. DAFLER
18 Director of Physical Plant ....Mr. Owen W. WAGNER
21 Business Manager .... Mr. Donald E. SHELENBERGER
24 Director of Audio-Visual Aids ....Mr. Gary L. SWANSON
19 Director of Public Safety ....Mr. William A. BRANDT
09 Director of Institutional Research ....Dr. Gary D. LILLY
23 Director Health Services ....Ms. Melissa M. BARON
40 Bookstore Manager ....Ms. Sandra L. SHEARER
21 Controller ....Ms. Christine A. MILLER
15 Director of Human Resources ....Ms. Kimberlee K. CHRISTOFFERSON
38 Counselor ....Ms. Barbara I. QUINCY
28 Director of Diversity Services ....Ms. Jeannette HUBBARD

Westminster Theological Seminary (D)

Chestnut Hill, PO Box 27009, Philadelphia PA 19118-0009
County: Montgomery FICE Identification: 003393
Unit ID: 216816
Telephone: (215) 887-5511 Carnegie Class: Spec/Faith
FAX Number: (215) 887-5404 Calendar System: 4/1/4
URL: www.wts.edu
Established: 1929 Annual Graduate Tuition & Fees: $13,330
Enrollment: 628 Coed
Affiliation or Control: Independent Non-Profit IRS Status: 501(c)3
Highest Offering: Doctorate; No Undergraduates
Program: Liberal Arts And General; Professional; Religious Emphasis
Accreditation: M, THEOL

01 President ....Dr. Peter A. LILLBACK
30 Vice Pres Development .... Mr. William B. VINCENT
05 Vice President Academic Affairs .... Dr. Carl TRUEMAN
45 Vice Pres Institutional Projects ....Dr. Daivd GARNER
32 Associate Dean of Students .... Ms. Jayne V. CLARK
88 Dean Student/Ministerial Formation .... Rev. Greg HOBAUGH
11 Chief Operating Officer ....Mr. A. D. DABNEY
06 Registrar & Director Financial Aid ....Ms. Melinda E. DUGAN
07 Director of Admissions ....Mr. Jonathan BRACK
08 Director of Library Services .... Mr. Alexander FINLAYSON
73 Director D.Min/Supervised Ministry .... Mr. Timothy Z. WITMER
40 Director Bookstore ....Mr. Chun LAI
21 Comptroller ....Mr. Erik V. DAVIS
15 Director Human Resources ....Ms. Karin DEUSSING
13 Director Information Technology ....Mr. Joe MYSHKO
18 Chief Facilities/Physical Plant .... Mr. Robert M. SEXTON
29 Director Alumni Relations ....Mr. John CURRIE

Westmoreland County Community College (E)

145 Pavilion Lane, Youngwood PA 15697-1895
County: Westmoreland FICE Identification: 010176
Unit ID: 216825
Telephone: (724) 925-4000 Carnegie Class: Assoc/Pub-S-SC
FAX Number: (724) 925-1150 Calendar System: Semester
URL: www.wccc.edu
Established: 1970 Annual Undergrad Tuition & Fees (In-District): $2,910
Enrollment: 7,410 Coed
Affiliation or Control: Local IRS Status: 501(c)3
Highest Offering: Associate Degree
Program: Occupational; 2-Year Principally Bachelor's Creditable
Accreditation: M, ACFEI, ADNUR, DA, DH, MAC

01 President ....Dr. Daniel J. OBARA
05 Vice Pres Academic Affs/Stdnt Svcs ....Dr. Carol A. RUSH
11 Vice Pres Administrative Services ....Mr. Ronald E. EBERHARDT
51 VP Cont Educ/Workforce & Cmty Devel ....Dr. Patrick E. GERITY
20 Assoc VP Academic Affairs ....Dr. Nicole REAVES
25 Director of Grants ....Ms. Debra J. WILLIAMS

15 Director Human Resources ....Ms. Lauren M. FARRELL
08 Director Learning Res & Sp Projects ....Ms. Kathleen A. KEEFE
77 Dean Computer Tech/Business ....Mr. Edwin C. NELSON
76 Dean Health Profess/Biology ....Dr. Kathleen A. MALLOY
72 Dean Mathematics/Sciences ....Vacant
79 Dean Public Svc/Human/Soc Science .... Dr. Andrew BARNETTE
32 Dean of Students .... Ms. Diane D. HIGHTOWER
84 Director Enrollment Management ....Vacant
37 Director Financial Aid ....Mr. Gary A. MEANS
18 Director Facilities ....Mr. John C. DETISCH
21 Controller ....Mr. Timothy W. STAHL
14 Director Information Technology ....Mr. Patrick R. MCKULA
88 Director College Services ....Mr. Ronald A. KRIVDA
26 Director Public Relations ....Ms. Anna Marie PALATELLA
07 Director Admissions ....Ms. Janice T. GRABOWSKI
41 Coordinator Student Life/Athletics ....Mr. Richard G. HOLLER
96 Coordinator of Purchasing ....Ms. Kim A. HIMLER
36 Coord Student Placement/Coop Ed ....Ms. Cheryl A. NOEL
10 Chief Business Officer ....Mr. Ronald E. EBERHARDT
102 Exec Director Education Foundation ....Ms. Debra D. WOODS
103 Dean Workforce Development ....Mr. Douglas J. JENSEN
09 Director of Institutional Research .... Mr. Randal M. FINFROCK

Widener University (F)

One University Place, Chester PA 19013-5792
County: Delaware FICE Identification: 003313
Unit ID: 216852
Telephone: (610) 499-4000 Carnegie Class: DRU
FAX Number: (610) 876-9751 Calendar System: Semester
URL: www.widener.edu
Established: 1821 Annual Undergrad Tuition & Fees: $34,762
Enrollment: 6,630 Coed
Affiliation or Control: Independent Non-Profit IRS Status: 501(c)3
Highest Offering: Doctorate
Program: Liberal Arts And General; Teacher Preparatory; Professional
Accreditation: M, BUS, CLPSY, ENG, HSA, IPSY, LAW, NURSE, PTA, SW, TED

01 President .... Dr. James T. HARRIS, III
05 Interim Sr Vice President & Provost .... Dr. Stephen C. WILHITE
10 Sr Vice Pres Administration/Finance .... Mr. Joseph J. BAKER
30 Vice Pres University Advancement .... Ms. Linda S. DURANT
13 Chief Information Officer .... Mr. Peter D. SHOUDY
21 Associate VP & Controller .... Ms. Catherine MCGEEHAN
11 Associate VP of Administration ....Mr. George E. HASSEL
84 Assoc Vice Pres Enrollment Mgmt .... Dr. Lawrence T. LESICK
26 Asst Vice Pres University Relations ....Ms. Lou Anne BULIK
18 Director of Operations .... Mr. Carl G. PIERCE
58 Interim Assoc Provost Grad Studies .... Dr. Michael W. LEDOUX
20 Associate Provost Undergraduate ..... Dr. Geraldine A. BLOEMKER
32 Assoc Provost/Dean of Students ....Dr. Denise D. GIFFORD
54 Dean School of Engineering ....Dr. Fred A. AKL
49 Dean College Arts & Sciences ....Dr. Matthew POSLUSNY
50 Dean School of Business Admin ....Dr. Savas OZATALAY
66 Dean School of Nursing ....Dr. Deborah R. GARRISON
51 Dean University College ....Dr. Emily C. RICHARDSON
88 Dean Sch of Hospitality Management ....Mr. Nicholas J. HADGIS
88 Dean Sch Human Svc Professions .... Dr. Stephen C. WILHITE
21 Bursar ....Ms. Diana BARRACLOUGH
08 Librarian ....Dr. Robert E. DANFORD
37 Director of Financial Aid ....Mr. Thomas K. MALLOY
06 Director of Records/Registration ....Dr. Steven H. FOXMAN
29 Director of Alumni Engagement ....Ms. Tina A. PHILLIPS
09 Director of Institutional Research ....Dr. Stephen W. THORPE
36 Placement Director ....Ms. Barbara M. BUCKLEY
78 Director of Cooperative Education ....Mr. Craig A. SINGLE
41 Director of Athletics ....Mr. Jack L. SHAFER
85 Director International Student Svcs .... Ms. Lois J. FULLER
19 Director of Campus Safety .... Mr. Patrick SULLIVAN
23 Director of Health Services .... Ms. Lynn A. NELSON-RUSSOM
24 Head of Multimedia/Classroom Spprt ....Mr. Eric WOEBKENBERG
40 Manager Campus Bookstore .... Mr. Chester HENSEL
91 Director Information Systems ....Mrs. Linda TAYLOR
88 Director Technical Resources ....Mr. Perry M. DRAYFAHL
15 Director of Human Resources .... Mr. Marty J. CORMICAN
96 Director of Purchasing ....Mr. Clayton D. SHELDON
07 Director of Admissions ....Mr. Edwin R. WRIGHT
89 Dir Student Success/Retention ....Mr. Timothy J. CAIRY
97 Dir Honors Program in General Educ .... Dr. Ilene LIEBERMAN
94 Director of Women's Studies .... Dr. Annalisa CASTALDO

† See Delaware listing of Widener University School of Law - Delaware Campus.

Wilkes University (G)

84 W South Street, Wilkes-Barre PA 18766-0001
County: Luzerne FICE Identification: 003394
Unit ID: 216931
Telephone: (570) 408-5000 Carnegie Class: Master's L
FAX Number: (570) 408-2934 Calendar System: Semester
URL: www.wilkes.edu
Established: 1933 Annual Undergrad Tuition & Fees: $28,210
Enrollment: 5,926 Coed
Affiliation or Control: Independent Non-Profit IRS Status: 501(c)3
Highest Offering: Doctorate
Program: Liberal Arts And General; Teacher Preparatory; Professional
Accreditation: M, ACBSP, CEA, ENG, NURSE, PHAR

01 President .... Dr. Joseph E. GILMOUR
05 Provost .... Dr. C. Reynold VERRET
30 Vice Pres University Advancement ....Mr. Michael WOOD
10 Vice President & General Counsel .... Mr. Loren D. PRESCOTT

21 Controller .... Ms. Janet KOBYLSKI
84 Vice President Enrollment Services ...... Ms. Melanie MICKENSON
32 Vice President Student Affairs .... Dr. Paul S. ADAMS
16 Vice President Human Resources Dev .... Vacant
20 Associate Provost .... Dr. Vernon HARPER
35 Dean of Students .... Mr. Mark R. ALLEN
35 Associate Dean Student Affairs .... Ms. Barbara E. KING
54 Dean Col of Science & Engineering .... Dr. Dale BRUNS
49 Dean College of Arts & Humanities .... Dr. Linda WINKLER
67 Dean Nesbitt Col Pharm/Nursing .... Dr. Bernard GRAHAM
58 Dean Grad/Prof Studies/Sch of Educ .... Dr. Michael SPEZIALE
50 Int Dean Sidh School of Business .... Dr. Jeffrey ALVES
62 Dean Library .... Mr. John STACHACZ
09 Director Information/Analysis/Plng .... Mr. Brian BOGERT
29 Executive Director Alumni Relations .... Ms. Sandra CARROLL
41 Director of Athletics .... Ms. Addy MALATESTA
23 Director Health Services .... Ms. Diane E. O'BRIEN
36 Director Career Services .... Mrs. Carol A. BOSACK-KOSEK
39 Director Residence Life .... Ms. Elizabeth ROVEDA
58 Director Graduate Teach Education .... Ms. Kristine PRUETT
06 Registrar .... Mrs. Susan A. HRITZAK
37 Dir of Financial Aid/Stdnt Services .... Mr. Joseph ALAIMO
26 Dir Mktg&Com/Sp Ast to Pres Gov Rel .... Mr. Jack A. CHIELLI
18 Director Facilities Services .... Mr. John PESTA
14 Chief Information Officer .... Ms. Gloria BARLOW
07 Director of Admissions .... Ms. Amy PATTON
28 Spec Asst to Pres for Multicul Affs .... Vacant
96 Director Procurement & Finan Svcs .... Mr. Justin KRAYNACK
15 Director Human Resource Services .... Mr. Joseph HOUSENICK
38 Campus Counselor .... Ms. Melissa GAUDIO
38 Campus Counselor .... Ms. Susan BISKUP
102 Director of Corp/Found/Govt Rels .... Mrs. Anne PELAK
35 Dir Student Svc Ctr/Student Svcs .... Ms. Janine BECKER
04 Admin Asst to the President .... Ms. Susan DIBONIFAZIO

Williamson Free School of Mechanical Trades (A)

106 S New Middletown Road, Media PA 19063-5299
County: Delaware FICE Identification: 041238
Unit ID: 216940
Telephone: (610) 566-1776 Carnegie Class: Not Classified
FAX Number: (610) 566-6502 Calendar System: Semester
URL: www.williamson.edu
Established: 1888 Annual Undergrad Tuition & Fees: N/A
Enrollment: 250 Male
Affiliation or Control: Independent Non-Profit IRS Status: 501(c)3
Highest Offering: Associate Degree
Program: Occupational
Accreditation: ACCSC

01 President .... Mr. Guy S. GARDNER
05 Vice President of Education & CAO .... Mr. Thomas E. WISNESKI
10 Vice President of Finance & CFO .... Mr. Gregory L. LINDEMUTH
30 Vice President of Inst Advancement .... Mr. Peter D'ORAZIO
11 Vice Pres of Plans & Operations .... Mr. Jim HANNIGAN
32 Dean of Students .... Mr. Thomas J. MOFFITT
84 Director of Enrollments .... Mr. Jason C. MERILLAT
41 Director of Athletics .... Mr. Dale H. PLUMMER
42 Chaplain/Counselor .... Rev. Mark A. SPECHT
06 Registrar .... Ms. Anne M. HAYES
36 Director of Placement .... Ms. Margaret T. KINGHAM
26 Director of Public Relations .... Mr. Carl A. VAIRO

Wilson College (B)

1015 Philadelphia Avenue, Chambersburg PA 17201-1285
County: Franklin FICE Identification: 003396
Unit ID: 217013
Telephone: (717) 262-4141 Carnegie Class: Bac/Diverse
FAX Number: (717) 264-1578 Calendar System: 4/1/4
URL: www.wilson.edu
Established: 1869 Annual Undergrad Tuition & Fees: $29,340
Enrollment: 800 Female
Affiliation or Control: Presbyterian Church (U.S.A.) IRS Status: 501(c)3
Highest Offering: Master's
Program: Liberal Arts And General; Teacher Preparatory
Accreditation: M

01 President .... Dr. Barbara K. MISTICK
05 VP for Academic Affairs/Dean of Fac .... Dr. Mary HENDRICKSON
30 Vice President College Advancement .... Mr. Jeffrey A. ZUFELT
10 Vice President for Finance & Admin .... Vacant
84 Vice President/Dean of Enrollment .... Ms. Mary Ann NASO
32 Vice President for Student Dev/Dean .... Ms. Carolyn PERKINS
06 Registrar .... Ms. Jean B. HOOVER
37 Dean of Financial Aid .... Ms. Linda D. BRITTAIN
09 Asst Dean IR and Assesment .... Dr. Elizabeth ANDERSON
08 Director of Library .... Ms. Kathleen MURPHY
18 Director of Physical Plant .... Mr. Jack KELLY
27 Communications Associate .... Ms. Cathy MENTZER
40 Director of Bookstore .... Ms. Deborah GAYNOR
41 Athletic Director .... Ms. Lori FREY
51 Director of Conferences .... Ms. Kathy LEHMAN
29 Director of Alumnae Programs .... Vacant
44 Director of Annual Fund .... Ms. Denise MCDOWELL
15 Director Human Resources .... Mr. Don KIME
20 Assoc Dean of Academic Advising .... Dr. Deborah AUSTIN
21 Assoc VP for Finance/Admin .... Ms. Lori TOSTEN
26 Chief Public Relations Officer .... Ms. Debra COLLINS
36 Director of Career Development .... Mr. Jay PFEIFFER
38 Director of Student Counseling .... Ms. Cindy SHOEMAKER

88 Director of Women With Children Pgm .... Ms. Katherine KOUGH
37 Coordinator of Financial Aid .... Ms. Christine KNOUSE
28 Coordinator of Diversity .... Vacant
42 Chaplain .... Rev. Rosie MAGEE
39 Director of Residence Life .... Ms. Sherri SADOWSKI

Won Institute of Graduate Studies (C)

137 S Easton Road, Glenside PA 19038
County: Montgomery FICE Identification: 039493
Unit ID: 442064
Telephone: (215) 884-8942 Carnegie Class: Spec/Health
FAX Number: (215) 884-9002 Calendar System: Trimester
URL: www.woninstitute.edu
Established: 2002 Annual Graduate Tuition & Fees: $16,900
Enrollment: 72 Coed
Affiliation or Control: Independent Non-Profit IRS Status: 501(c)3
Highest Offering: Master's; No Undergraduates
Program: Professional; Religious Emphasis
Accreditation: M, ACUP

01 President .... Dr. Bokin KIM
11 Chief Administrative Officer .... Ms. Colleen O'CONNELL
10 Chief Financial Officer .... Ms. Maria PERRY
05 Chief Academic Officer .... Dr. Linda LELII
06 Registrar .... Rev. Sangwon HWANG
08 Librarian .... Mrs. Pat KING
07 Admissions Officer .... Rev. Hojin PARK

WyoTech-Blairsville (D)

500 Innovation Drive, Blairsville PA 15717-8060
County: Indiana Identification: 666305
Unit ID: 441089
Telephone: (724) 459-9500 Carnegie Class: Assoc/PrivFP
FAX Number: (724) 459-6499 Calendar System: Quarter
URL: www.wyotech.edu
Established: 1966 Annual Undergrad Tuition & Fees: $29,250
Enrollment: 1,600 Coed
Affiliation or Control: Proprietary IRS Status: Proprietary
Highest Offering: Associate Degree
Program: Occupational; Technical Emphasis
Accreditation: ACCSC

01 President .... Mr. Arthur HERMAN

† Branch campus of Wyoming Technical Institute, Laramie, WY.

Yeshiva Beth Moshe (E)

930 Hickory Street, Scranton PA 18505-2196
County: Lackawanna FICE Identification: 013134
Unit ID: 217040
Telephone: (570) 346-1747 Carnegie Class: Spec/Faith
FAX Number: (570) 346-2251 Calendar System: Semester
Established: 1965 Annual Undergrad Tuition & Fees: $8,300
Enrollment: 72 Male
Affiliation or Control: Independent Non-Profit IRS Status: 501(c)3
Highest Offering: Second Talmudic Degree
Program: Teacher Preparatory; Professional; Religious Emphasis
Accreditation: RABN

01 Chief Executive Officer .... Rabbi Yaakov SCHNAIDMAN
03 Executive Director .... Rabbi Avraham PRESSMAN

York College of Pennsylvania (F)

Country Club Road, York PA 17405-7199
County: York FICE Identification: 003399
Unit ID: 217059
Telephone: (717) 846-7788 Carnegie Class: Master's S
FAX Number: (717) 849-1607 Calendar System: Semester
URL: www.ycp.edu
Established: 1787 Annual Undergrad Tuition & Fees: $15,880
Enrollment: 4,638 Coed
Affiliation or Control: Independent Non-Profit IRS Status: 501(c)3
Highest Offering: Doctorate
Program: Liberal Arts And General; Teacher Preparatory; Professional
Accreditation: M, ACBSP, ANEST, CS, ENG, MUS, NRPA, NURSE

01 President .... Dr. George W. WALDNER
05 Dean of Academic Affairs .... Dr. Dominic DELLICARPINI
11 Dean of Administrative Service .... Dr. Frank P. MUSSANO
10 Chief Financial Officer .... Mr. Matthew SMITH
20 Dean of Academic Services .... Dr. Deborah D. RICKER
32 Dean of Student Affairs .... Mr. Joseph F. MERKLE
18 Dean of Campus Operations .... Dr. Kenneth M. MARTIN
30 Director Development .... Ms. Camilla B. RAWLEIGH
44 Dean of College Advancement .... Mr. Daniel S. HELWIG
41 Asst Dean Athletics & Recreation .... Mr. Paul SAIKIA
84 Asst Dean Enrollment Management .... Mr. Stephen NEITZ
07 Director of Admissions .... Mrs. Nancy C. SPATARO
06 Registrar .... Ms. Rebecca C. LINK
08 Librarian .... Ms. Susan M. CAMPBELL
37 Director of Financial Aid .... Mr. Calvin H. WILLIAMS
13 Director of Information Technology .... Mr. Robert L. ROBINSON
29 Director Alumni Relations .... Mr. Bruce WALL
36 Director of Career Services .... Ms. Beverly A. EVANS
06 Director of Records .... Mrs. Debra L. SHIMMEL
19 Director of Public Safety .... Mr. Edward C. BRUDER
39 Director of Residence Life .... Mr. Kevin D. FEIL

26 Asst Dean Institutional Advancement .... Mrs. Mary E. DOLHEIMER
31 Director Community Education .... Mr. Leroy M. KEENEY
15 Director Human Resources .... Mrs. Vicki L. STEWART
38 Director Counseling Services .... Mrs. Karen JONES
91 Dir Administrative Computer Center .... Mr. Brian K. SMELTZER
23 Director Health Services .... Mrs. Rita CLAYTON
40 Director Bookstore .... Mrs. Lynn P. FERRO
88 Director College & Special Events .... Ms. Sherry HEFLIN
102 Dir Corporate/Foundation/Govt Rels .... Mr. Chad LINDER
27 College Editor .... Mrs. Alicia BRUMBACH
42 Director of Religious Activities .... Mrs. Louise WORLEY
31 Dir Center for Community Engagement .... Mrs. Jan HERROLD
09 Director of Institutional Research .... Ms. Elizabeth CARROLL
28 Director of Multicultural Affairs .... Mr. Darrien DAVENPORT
24 Learning Center Coordinator .... Mrs. Cindy CRIMMINS
44 Sr Dir Principal & Planned Gifts .... Mr. Mark RANK

Yorktowne Business Institute (G)

West Seventh Avenue, York PA 17404-9946
County: York FICE Identification: 021208
Unit ID: 217086
Telephone: (717) 846-5000 Carnegie Class: Assoc/PrivFP
FAX Number: (717) 848-4584 Calendar System: Other
URL: www.ybi.edu
Established: 1977 Annual Undergrad Tuition & Fees: $8,950
Enrollment: 817 Coed
Affiliation or Control: Proprietary IRS Status: Proprietary
Highest Offering: Associate Degree
Program: Occupational
Accreditation: ACICS

01 President .... Dr. James P. MURPHY
03 Executive Director .... Ms. Elizabeth M. DREIBELBIS
50 Business Department Chair .... Ms. Lynda R. MEYERS
06 Registrar .... Ms. Lisa MCGOWAN
37 Director Student Financial Aid .... Ms. Deborah BOSTIC
08 Director Library Services .... Ms. Lynda MEYERS
36 Director Student Placement .... Mr. Jeff REGNERER
18 Chief Facilities/Physical Plant .... Mr. Frederick WEIBLE
88 Acting Director Culinary Arts .... Mr. Robert GENET
10 Business Officer .... Vacant
55 Evening Administrator .... Mr. Dean FRIEND
26 Marketing Director .... Mr. John A. DREIBELBIS
88 Teaching Kitchen Manager .... Ms. Kim CRIM

YTI Career Institute (H)

2900 Fairway Drive, Altoona PA 16602
County: Blair FICE Identification: 030819
Unit ID: 375939
Telephone: (814) 944-5643 Carnegie Class: Not Classified
FAX Number: (814) 944-5309 Calendar System: Quarter
URL: www.yti.edu
Established: 2006 Annual Undergrad Tuition & Fees: $12,980
Enrollment: 353 Coed
Affiliation or Control: Proprietary IRS Status: Proprietary
Highest Offering: Associate Degree
Program: Occupational
Accreditation: ACCSC

01 Director of Education .... Mr. Ken LOENDOWSKI

YTI Career Institute (I)

1405 Williams Road, York PA 17402-9017
County: York FICE Identification: 021274
Unit ID: 217077
Telephone: (717) 757-1100 Carnegie Class: Assoc/PrivFP
FAX Number: (717) 757-4964 Calendar System: Quarter
URL: www.yti.edu
Established: 1967 Annual Undergrad Tuition & Fees: $20,000
Enrollment: 1,373 Coed
Affiliation or Control: Proprietary IRS Status: Proprietary
Highest Offering: Associate Degree
Program: Occupational
Accreditation: ACCSC, ACFEI, DA, MAC

01 Chairman and CEO .... Mr. Timothy FOSTER
12 President - York .... Mr. Mark MILLEN
12 President - Capital Region .... Mr. Erin CARLIN
12 President - Lancaster .... Mr. Michael MARINO
12 President - Altoona .... Mr. Kenneth LEWANDOWSKI
12 President - MTC .... Mr. Mark MILLEN
03 Executive Vice President .... Mr. Mike WRIGHT
05 Sr VP Education & Regulatory .... Mrs. Sherry BOMBERGER
16 VP Human Resources .... Mrs. Carla HORN
10 CFO .... Mr. Andrew EMMERLING
14 Director of Technology .... Mr. Andrew HIPPLE

RHODE ISLAND

Brown University (J)

1 Prospect Street, Providence RI 02912-9127
County: Providence FICE Identification: 003401
Unit ID: 217156
Telephone: (401) 863-1000 Carnegie Class: RU/VH
FAX Number: (401) 863-3700 Calendar System: Semester
URL: www.brown.edu
Established: 1764 Annual Undergrad Tuition & Fees: $42,230
Enrollment: 8,695 Coed

Affiliation or Control: Independent Non-Profit IRS Status: 501(c)3
Highest Offering: Doctorate
Program: Liberal Arts And General; Professional
Accreditation: EH, ENG, IPSY, MED, PDPSY, PH

01	President	Ruth J. SIMMONS
05	Provost	Mark S. SCHLISSEL
30	Sr Vice Pres for Advancement	Steven A. KING
102	Sr VP Corporation Affs/Governance	Russell C. CAREY
10	Exec VP Finance/Administration	Elizabeth HUIDEKOPER
45	Exec VP for Plng/Sr Advisor to Pres	Richard R. SPIES
26	VP Public Affairs/Univ Relations	Marisa A. QUINN
43	Vice President/General Counsel	Beverly E. LEDBETTER
13	Vice Pres Computing/Info Services	Michael P. PICKETT
44	VP of Development/Campaign Director	Vacant
29	Vice President Alumni Affairs	Todd G. ANDREWS
18	Vice Pres for Facilities Management	Stephen M. MAIORISI
46	Vice President for Research	Clyde L. BRIANT
15	Vice Pres for Human Resources	Karen DAVIS
20	Deputy Provost	Joseph S. MEISEL
35	Vice Pres Campus Life/Student Svcs	Margaret M. KLAWUNN
88	Associate Provost	Nancy R. DUNBAR
31	Director State/Community Relations	Albert A. DAHLBERG
63	Dean Medicine & Biological Sciences	Edward WING
58	Dean of Graduate School	Peter M. WEBER
20	Dean of the Faculty	Kevin MCLAUGHLIN
20	Dean of the College	Katherine BERGERON
07	Dean of Admission	James S. MILLER
08	University Librarian	Harriette HEMMASI
21	University Controller/Assistant VP	Donald S. SCHANCK
11	Sr Business Analyst/Project Manager	Vacant
41	Director of Athletics	Michael GOLDBERGER
06	Registrar	Robert F. FITZGERALD
37	Director of Financial Aid	James TILTON
19	Dir Public Safety/Chief of Police	Mark J. PORTER
38	Director Student Counseling	Belinda JOHNSON
28	Dir of Institutional Diversity	Valerie PETIT WILSON
96	Purchasing Manager	Raymond STEWART
09	Coord for Institutional Research	Katharine T. BARNES

Bryant University (A)

1150 Douglas Pike, Smithfield RI 02917-1291
County: Providence FICE Identification: 003402
Unit ID: 217165
Telephone: (401) 232-6000 Carnegie Class: Spec/Bus
FAX Number: (401) 232-6319 Calendar System: Semester
URL: www.bryant.edu
Established: 1863 Annual Undergrad Tuition & Fees: $33,357
Enrollment: 3,606 Coed
Affiliation or Control: Independent Non-Profit IRS Status: 501(c)3
Highest Offering: Beyond Master's But Less Than Doctorate
Program: Liberal Arts And General; Business Emphasis
Accreditation: EH, BUS

00	Chairman Board of Trustees	Mr. Thomas A. TAYLOR
01	President	Mr. Ronald K. MACHTLEY
04	Exec Asst & Corp Secretary	Dr. Roger L. ANDERSON
05	VP Academic Affairs	Dr. Jose-Marie GRIFFITHS
32	VP & Dean Student Affairs	Dr. J. Thomas EAKIN
84	VP Enrollment Management	Ms. Lorna J. HUNTER
10	VP Business Affairs	Mr. Barry F. MORRISON
30	VP University Advancement	Mr. James DAMRON
13	VP Information Services	Dr. Arthur GLOSTER, II
16	Assoc VP Human Resources	Ms. Linda S. LULLI
18	Asst VP Campus Management	Mr. Brian J. BRITTON
21	Asst VP Business & Controller	Mr. Farokh BHADA
49	Dean College of Arts & Sciences	Dr. David LUX
50	Interim Dean College of Business	Ms. Carol DEMORANVILLE
58	Asst Dean Graduate School	Mr. Kristopher T. SULLIVAN
51	Dir Exec Development Center	Ms. Annette CERILLI
50	Dir Chafee Ctr for Intl Business	Mr. James SEGOVIS
88	Exec Dir Inst for Family Enterprise	Dr. William T. O'HARA
88	Dir RI Export Assistance Center	Mr. Raymond FOGARTY
89	Dir Academic Center for Excellence	Dr. Laurie L. HAZARD
20	Asst to VP Academic & Dir Advising	Ms. Lori JOHNSON
06	Registrar	Ms. Susan MCLACKEN
20	Asst to VP Academic Affairs	Ms. Elizabeth A. POWERS
35	Assoc Dean of Students	Mr. Robert E. SLOSS
39	Assoc Dean Residence Life	Mr. John DENIO
35	Assoc Dean Student Life	Ms. Judy KAWAMOTO
88	Dir Bryant Center Operations	Mr. Richard DANKEL
36	Dir Career Services	Ms. Judith CLARE
42	Chaplain Campus Ministry	Rev. Philip DEVENS
38	Dir Counseling Services	Mr. William PHILLIPS
23	Dir Health Services	Ms. Susan CURRAN
28	Dir Intercultural Center	Ms. Shontay DELALUE-KING
19	Dir Public Safety	Mr. George S. CORONADO
31	Dir Student Involvement Center	Mr. John LINDSAY
88	Dir Women's Center	Ms. Toby SIMON
07	Dir Admission	Ms. Michelle BEAUREGARD
07	Dir Transfer Admission	Ms. Brenda DORAN
07	Sr Assoc Dir Mulitcult Admission	Ms. Priscilla ALICEA
07	Assoc Dir International Admission	Mr. John ERIKSEN
37	Dir Financial Aid	Mr. John B. CANNING
88	Dir Conferences & Special Events	Ms. Sheila GUAY
96	Dir Purchasing & Support Services	Ms. Paulette RATTIGAN
44	Exec Dir Development	Ms. Robin MAREK
29	Dir Alumni Relations	Ms. Robin T. WARDE
90	Dir Acad Computing & Media Svcs	Mr. Phillip LOMBARDI
91	Dir Admin Systems	Ms. Janice FAGAN
14	Dir Computer & Telecomm Svcs	Mr. Richard SIEDZIK
08	Dir Library Services	Ms. Mary F. MORONEY
15	Assoc Dir Human Resources	Ms. Catherine CURRIE
41	Dir Athletics	Mr. Bill SMITH
09	Dir Planning & Inst Research	Dr. Thomas J. DIMIERI
82	Exec Dir US-China Institute	Dr. Hong YANG
40	Manager Bookstore	Mr. Stanley STOWIK

Community College of Rhode Island (B)

400 East Avenue, Warwick RI 02886-1807
County: Kent FICE Identification: 003408
Unit ID: 217475
Telephone: (401) 825-1000 Carnegie Class: Assoc/Pub-U-MC
FAX Number: (401) 825-2365 Calendar System: Semester
URL: www.ccri.edu
Established: 1964 Annual Undergrad Tuition & Fees (In-State): $3,653
Enrollment: 17,775 Coed
Affiliation or Control: State IRS Status: 501(c)3
Highest Offering: Associate Degree
Program: Occupational; 2-Year Principally Bachelor's Creditable
Accreditation: EH, ACBSP, ADNUR, COMTA, DA, DH, DMS, HT, MLTAD, OTA, PNUR, PTAA, RAD

01	President	Mr. Ray DI PASQUALE
05	Vice President for Academic Affairs	Ms. Lela M. MORGAN
10	Vice President for Business Affairs	Mr. Robert SHEA, JR.
32	Assoc VP for Student Services	Dr. Ronald L. SCHERTZ
84	Int Dean of Enrollment Services	Ms. Deborah J. AIKEN
11	Director of Administration	Mr. William R. FERLAND
49	Dean Arts/Humanities/Soc Sciences	Vacant
66	Dean of Nursing/Allied Health	Dr. Maureen MCGARRY
50	Dean Business/Science/Technology	Dr. Peter N. WOODBERRY
51	Dean of CWCE	Ms. Robin Ann SMITH
08	Dean Library	Ms. Ruth D. SULLIVAN
07	Asst Dean of Enrollment Services	Mr. John PANZICA
21	Controller	Mr. Carl TOFT
35	Associate Dean of Students	Dr. Rebecca H. YOUNT
15	Director of Human Resources	Ms. Sheri L. NORTON
12	Dir Ctr Advanced Tech & Careers	Mr. Vincent BALASCO
13	Chief Information Officer	Mr. Stephen A. VIEIRA
19	Director of Security	Mr. Richard A. ROBINSON
26	Director Marketing & Communications	Mr. Richard H. COREN
30	Director of Inst Advancement	Vacant
41	Director of Athletics	Mr. Joseph PAVONE
09	Director Inst Research/Planning	Dr. William LEBLANC
21	Bursar	Mr. Dennis J. GRASSINI
88	Director Access to Opportunity	Ms. Tracy KARASINSKI
40	Director Bookstore Operations	Mr. Donald B. BAKER
29	Director of Alumni Affairs	Ms. Marisa ALBINI
18	Chief Facilities/Physical Plant	Mr. Kenneth MCCABE
96	Director of Purchasing	Mr. Raymond DEANGELIS
21	Business Manager	Ms. Ruth A. BARRINGTON
36	Coordinator Career Services	Ms. Camille NUMRICH
37	Director of Financial Aid	Mr. Joel FRIEDMAN

Johnson & Wales University (C)

8 Abbott Park Place, Providence RI 02903-3703
County: Providence FICE Identification: 003404
Unit ID: 217235
Telephone: (401) 598-1000 Carnegie Class: DRU
FAX Number: (401) 598-2880 Calendar System: Quarter
URL: www.jwu.edu
Established: 1914 Annual Undergrad Tuition & Fees: $25,107
Enrollment: 10,974 Coed
Affiliation or Control: Independent Non-Profit IRS Status: 501(c)3
Highest Offering: Doctorate
Program: Occupational; 2-Year Principally Bachelor's Creditable; Teacher Preparatory; Professional
Accreditation: EH, DIETD

00	Chairman of the Board	Mr. John A. YENA
01	Chancellor	Mr. John J. BOWEN
12	Providence Campus President/COO	Ms. Mim L. RUNEY
32	Vice President of Student Affairs	Mr. Ronald MARTEL
05	University Provost	Ms. Veera GAUL
30	Sr Vice Pres Institutional Advance	Ms. Patricia A. MCLAUGHLIN
85	Senior VP of Special Projects	Mr. Kenneth R. LEVY
10	Treasurer and CFO	Mr. William F. MCARDLE
18	Sr Vice Pres Facilities Management	Mr. Merlin A. DECONTI
43	Sr VP and General Counsel	Mr. Wayne M. KEZIRIAN
20	Associate Provost	Mr. James GRIFFIN
10	Vice Chancellor & Executive VP	Mr. Thomas L. DWYER, JR.
36	VP of Experiential Ed & Career Svc	Ms. Maureen DUMAS
11	Sr VP of Compliance/Int Audit/Risk	Ms. Robin KRAKOWSKY
84	Sr VP of Enrollment Management	Mr. Kenneth F. DISAIA
20	Vice President of Academic Affairs	Mr. Jeffrey SENESE
15	Vice President of Human Resources	Ms. Diane D'AMBRA
21	Asst Treasurer & VP of Finance	Mr. Joseph J. GREENE
58	Dean of Graduate School	Mr. Frank SARGENT
88	Dean of the College of Culinary Art	Mr. Kevin DUFFY
88	Dean of The Hospitality College	Mr. Richard BRUSH
50	Dean of the College of Business	Mr. David MITCHELL
49	Dean of A&S	Ms. Angela RENAUD
72	Dean of the School of Technology	Mr. Frank TWEEDIE
88	Vice President of Auxiliary Service	Mr. Michael DOWNING
18	Vice President of Facilities Mgmt	Mr. Christopher PLACCO
13	VP of IT and CIO	Mr. John A. SMITHERS
32	VP of Student Services	Ms. Marie BERNARDO-SOUSA
43	Sr VP of Law & Policy & Corp Secret	Ms. Barbara L. BENNETT
96	Director of Procurement	Mr. Michael GILLARDI
36	Director of Ext Educ & Career Svcs	Ms. Sheri ISPIR
09	Director of Institutional Research	Mr. Christopher HOURIGAN
19	Exec Dir of Campus Safety/Security	Major Michael P. QUINN
21	University Budget Director	Ms. Eileen T. HASKINS
88	University Dean of Culinary Educ	Mr. Karl J. GUGGENMOS
88	Director of Student Communications	Ms. Kristine E. MCNAMARA
88	Dean of Culinary Academics	Mr. Paul J. MCVETY
88	Dir of Acad Accountability & Init	Ms. Cynthia L. PARKER

Mater Ecclesiae College (D)

60 Austin Avenue, Greenville RI 02828-1440
County: Providence FICE Identification: 041449
Telephone: (401) 949-2820 Carnegie Class: Not Classified
FAX Number: (401) 949-0291 Calendar System: Semester
URL: www.mecollege.org
Established: 1991 Annual Undergrad Tuition & Fees: N/A
Enrollment: 70 Female
Affiliation or Control: Independent Non-Profit IRS Status: 501(c)3
Highest Offering: Baccalaureate
Program: Liberal Arts And General; Religious Emphasis
Accreditation: EH

01	President	Ms. Lourdes FERNANDEZ
05	Dean of Academic Affairs	Dr. Patricia CAMARERO
07	Director of Admissions	Vacant
10	Director of Financial/Admin Affairs	Vacant
21	Business Manager	Ms. Maritza SILVA

New England Institute of Technology (E)

2500 Post Road, Warwick RI 02886-2266
County: Kent FICE Identification: 007845
Unit ID: 217305
Telephone: (401) 467-7744 Carnegie Class: Bac/Assoc
FAX Number: (401) 738-5122 Calendar System: Quarter
URL: www.neit.edu
Established: 1940 Annual Undergrad Tuition & Fees: $18,525
Enrollment: 3,298 Coed
Affiliation or Control: Independent Non-Profit IRS Status: 501(c)3
Highest Offering: Master's
Program: Occupational; 2-Year Principally Bachelor's Creditable; Liberal Arts And General; Technical Emphasis
Accreditation: EH, ADNUR, ENGT, OTA, PTAA, SURGT

01	President	Dr. Richard I. GOUSE
03	Executive Vice President	Mr. Seth A. KURN
05	Senior Vice President and Provost	Dr. Thomas F. WYLIE
10	Senior Vice Pres for Finance	Ms. Cheryl C. CONNORS
32	Vice Pres Student Support Services	Ms. Catherine B. KENNEDY
21	Vice President for Finance	Mr. Robert R. THEROUX
20	Associate Provost	Dr. William FERRANTE
07	Director of Admissions	Mr. Mark BLONDIN
37	Director Financial Aid	Ms. Anna KELLY
04	Assoc Provost & Spec Asst to Pres	Mr. Douglas SHERMAN, JR.
08	Director Library	Ms. Sharon CHARETTE
36	Director of Career Services	Ms. Patricia BLAKEMORE
31	Director Auxiliary Services	Mr. Patrick TRACEY
06	Registrar	Ms. Doreen LASIEWSKI
35	Director Student Affairs	Ms. Lee PEEBLES
29	Dir Alumni Relations/Chief Deveop	Mr. Allan LANGER

Providence College (F)

1 Cunningham Square, Providence RI 02918-0001
County: Providence FICE Identification: 003406
Unit ID: 217402
Telephone: (401) 865-1000 Carnegie Class: Master's L
FAX Number: (401) 865-2057 Calendar System: Semester
URL: www.providence.edu
Established: 1917 Annual Undergrad Tuition & Fees: $40,150
Enrollment: 5,065 Coed
Affiliation or Control: Roman Catholic IRS Status: 501(c)3
Highest Offering: Master's
Program: Liberal Arts And General; Teacher Preparatory
Accreditation: EH, MT, SW

01	President	Rev. Brian J. SHANLEY, OP
03	Asst to Pres & Exec Vice President	Ms. Ann MANCHESTER-MOLAK
03	Executive Vice President	Rev. Kenneth R. SICARD, OP
05	Sr Vice President Academic Affairs	Dr. Hugh F. LENA
10	Sr VP for Finance & Business/CFO	Mr. John M. SWEENEY
30	Sr VP for Institutional Advancement	Mr. David C. WEGRZYN
32	Int Vice Pres Student Affairs Admin	Dr. Steven A. SEARS
43	Vice President/General Counsel	Ms. Marifrances MCGINN
42	Vice Pres for Mission & Ministry	Rev. Joseph J. GUIDO, OP
04	Special Asst to Pres for Devel Proj	Mr. Joseph P. BRUM
21	Assoc VP for Finance/Asst Treasurer	Ms. Jacqueline M. WHITE
35	Assoc VP for Student Affairs Admin	Dr. Steven A. SEARS
20	Associate VP for Academic Affairs	Dr. Brian J. BARTOLINI
44	Assoc VP Institutional Advancement	Ms. Lisa M. BOUSQUET
41	Assoc Vice Pres for Athletics	Mr. Robert G. DRISCOLL, JR.
07	Assoc VP Admissions/Enrollment Plng	Mr. Christopher P. LYDON
26	Assoc VP for College Rels/Planning	Ms. Patricia S. VIEIRA
15	Assoc Vice Pres for Human Resources	Ms. Kathleen M. ALVINO
20	Asst Vice Pres for Academic Affairs	Mr. Charles J. HABERLE
21	Asst Vice Pres for Business Svcs	Mr. Warren S. GRAY
29	Asst Vice Pres for Alumni Relations	Mr. Robert FERREIRA, JR.

13 Asst VP for Information Technology ... Ms. Rebecca RAMOS
46 Asst VP Capital Projects & Fac Plng ... Mr. Mark F. RAPOZA
43 Asst VP/Assoc General Counsel ... Ms. Gail A. DYER
58 Dean of Undergrad & Grad Studies ... Rev. Mark D. NOWEL, OP
49 Dean School of Arts & Sciences ... Dr. Sheila M. ADAMUS LIOTTA
107 Dean School of Professional Studies ... Dr. Brian M. MCCADDEN
50 Interim Dean School of Business ... Dr. Mary Jane LENON
51 Dean School of Continuing Education ... Dr. Janet L. CASTLEMAN
39 Interim Dean of Residence Life ... Ms. Emily A. GHIORSE
84 Dean of Enrollment Services ... Ms. Yvonne D. ARRUDA
104 Dean of International Studies ... Mr. Adrian G. BEAULIEU
51 Assoc Dean Sch of Continuing Educ ... Ms. Madeleine A. METZLER
37 Exec Director of Financial Aid ... Ms. Sandra J. OLIVEIRA
19 Exec Director Safety & Security ... Mr. John J. LEYDEN
36 Executive Director of Career Servic ... Mr. John B. NONNAMAKER
18 Exec Director of Physical Plant ... Mr. William J. HARTIGAN
08 Director Library ... Dr. Donald Russell BAILEY
21 Treasurer ... Rev. Kenneth R. SICARD, OP
09 Director of Institutional Research ... Mr. Thomas E. FRANK
88 Director of Advancement Services ... Vacant
88 Director of Telecommunications ... Mr. Carmine R. PISCOPO
92 Program Dir Liberal Arts Honors ... Dr. Stephen J. LYNCH
96 Director Cntrl Purchasing/Receiving ... Mr. Mark S. MCGOVERN
88 Director of Academic Services ... Mr. Bryan D. MARINELLI
88 Dean of Student Programming ... Ms. Sharon L. HAY
38 Director Personal Counseling ... Dr. John T. HOGAN
28 Chief Diversity Officer ... Vacant
36 Assoc Director Career Planning ... Ms. Patricia A. GOFF

Rhode Island College (A)

600 Mount Pleasant Avenue, Providence RI 02908-1991

County: Providence FICE Identification: 003407

Unit ID: 217420

Telephone: (401) 456-8000 Carnegie Class: Master's L

FAX Number: (401) 456-8379 Calendar System: Semester

URL: www.ric.edu

Established: 1854 Annual Undergrad Tuition & Fees (In-State): $7,268

Enrollment: 9,155 Coed

Affiliation or Control: State IRS Status: 501(c)3

Highest Offering: Doctorate

Program: Liberal Arts And General; Teacher Preparatory; Professional

Accreditation: EH, ART, MUS, NURSE, SW, TED

01 President ... Dr. Nancy CARRIUOLO
05 Vice President Academic Affairs ... Dr. Ronald E. PITT
10 Vice Pres Administration & Finance ... Mr. William H. GEARHART
32 Vice President Student Affairs ... Dr. Gary M. PENFIELD
30 Vice President College Advancement ... Mr. James G. SALMO
107 Assoc VP Prof Studies & Cont Ed ... Ms. Renee VACHON DANHO
20 Int Asst Vice Pres Academic Affairs ... Dr. Holly L. SHADOIAN
21 Asst Vice Pres Finance/Controller ... Mr. Paul D. FORTE
14 Asst Vice Pres Information Services ... Dr. Richard W. PRULL
15 Asst Vice President Human Resources ... Mr. Robert G. TETREAULT
49 Dean Faculty Arts & Sciences ... Dr. Earl L. SIMSON
53 Dean School Education & Human Dev ... Dr. Alexander SIDORKIN
66 Dean School of Nursing ... Dr. Jane WILLIAMS
50 Dean School of Management ... Dr. David M. BLANCHETTE
70 Dean School of Social Work ... Dr. Roberta S. PEARLMUTTER
58 Int Dean of Graduate Studies ... Dr. Leslie SCHUSTER
08 Director of the Library ... Mr. Hedi BENAICHA
35 Dean of Students ... Dr. Scott D. KANE
100 Assistant to the President ... Mr. Michael E. SMITH
26 Director of News & Public Relations ... Ms. Jane E. FUSCO
105 Director Web Services ... Ms. Karen M. RUBINO
07 Int Director of Admissions ... Ms. Lucille RIOS SAUNDERS
06 Director of Records ... Mr. James C. DORIAN
37 Director Student Financial Aid ... Mr. James T. HANBURY
25 Director of Research & Grants ... Ms. Lisa SMOLSKI
18 Director Facilities & Operations ... Vacant
90 Director User Support Services ... Ms. Patricia H. HAYS
91 Director MIS ... Dr. Bin YU
13 Director Network/Telecommunications ... Mr. Henk E. SONDER
19 Int Director of Security ... Mr. Frederick W. GHIO
09 Asst Dir Inst Research/Planning ... Mrs. Jennifer A. ELLIS
96 Director of Purchasing ... Ms. Jessica L. SILVA
41 Director of Athletics ... Mr. Donald E. TENCHER
39 Director Residential Life/Housing ... Ms. Teresa L. BROWN
36 Director Career Development Center ... Ms. Linda S. KENT-DAVIS
23 Director College Health Services ... Ms. Lynn A. WACHTEL
38 Director Counseling Center ... Dr. Thomas J. LAVIN
29 Director Alumni Affairs ... Vacant
04 Admin Assistant to the President ... Ms. Donna NARODOWY

Rhode Island School of Design (B)

2 College Street, Providence RI 02903-2784

County: Providence FICE Identification: 003409

Unit ID: 217493

Telephone: (401) 454-6100 Carnegie Class: Spec/Arts

FAX Number: (401) 454-6320 Calendar System: 4/1/4

URL: www.risd.edu

Established: 1877 Annual Undergrad Tuition & Fees: $39,777

Enrollment: 2,406 Coed

Affiliation or Control: Independent Non-Profit IRS Status: 501(c)3

Highest Offering: Master's

Program: Liberal Arts And General; Professional; Fine Arts Emphasis

Accreditation: EH, ART, LSAR

01 President ... Dr. John MAEDA
100 Chief of Staff ... Ms. Mara HERMANO
101 Trustees Relations Officer ... Ms. Molly GARRISON
04 Executive Assistant to President ... Ms. Marina MIHALAKIS
05 Interim Provost ... Ms. Rosanne SOMERSON
32 Senior VP for Students & Enrollment ... Ms. Jean EDDY
26 VP Media + Partners ... Ms. Rebecca BERMONT
30 Vice Pres Institutional Engagement ... Mr. Eric GRAAGE
10 Exec Vice Pres Admin/Finance ... Mr. William DECATUR
16 Vice Pres Human Resource ... Ms. Candace BAER
88 Director of Museum of Art ... Mr. John W. STRYKER
20 Interim Assoc Prov Acad Affairs ... Ms. Patricia PHILLIPS
48 Interim Dean Architecture & Design ... Mr. William NEWKIRK
57 Interim Dean of Fine Arts ... Ms. Anais MISSAKIAN
58 Dean of Graduate Studies ... Vacant
49 Dean of Liberal Arts ... Dr. Barbara VON ECKARDT
88 Dean of Foundation Studies ... Ms. Joanne STRYKER
20 Director of Academic Affairs ... Ms. Sheila D'AMMASSA
08 Director of Library ... Ms. Carol S. TERRY
51 Dean Continuing Education ... Dr. Brian K. SMITH
85 Director International Programs ... Ms. Claudia FORD
35 Assoc Provost for Student Affairs ... Dr. Raj BELLANI
07 Director of Admissions ... Mr. Edward NEWHALL, JR.
105 Assistant VP Communications ... Mr. Brian CLARK
31 Director of Media Relations ... Ms. Jaime MARLAND
88 Dir Strat Alliances in RISD Media ... Ms. Junko CARTER
102 Dir Corp & Foundation Relations ... Ms. Pamela HARRINGTON
88 Director Advancement Services ... Ms. Suzanne CULLION
29 Director of Alumni Relations ... Ms. Christina HARTLEY
44 Director of Leadership Giving ... Ms. Louise OLSON
44 Director Annual Giving ... Mr. James WOLKEN
21 Assoc VP Finance & Business Svcs ... Vacant
13 Assoc VP Information Technology ... Mr. Ralph FASANO
18 Assoc VP Facilities & Safety ... Mr. Jack SILVA
19 Director Public Safety ... Mr. Ken BILODEAU
45 Director Budget ... Ms. Linda MURPHY CHURCH
09 Director Institutional Research ... Ms. Jennifer DUNSEATH
43 General Counsel ... Mr. Steven MCDONALD
86 Director Government Relations ... Ms. Babette ALLINA
15 Director of Employment Relations ... Ms. Elizabeth RAINONE
06 Registrar ... Mr. Steven BERENBACK
38 Dir Student Development/Counseling ... Mr. Wayne ASSING
37 Director Financial Aid ... Mr. Anthony GALLONIO
28 Director of Multicultural Affairs ... Mr. Tony JOHNSON
29 Director of Career Center ... Mr. Gregory J. VICTORY
21 Controller ... Ms. Susan ROTHSTEIN
88 Director of Risk & Prop Management ... Mr. Edward RENZI
40 Director of Retail & Dining ... Ms. Virginia DUNLEAVY

Roger Williams University (C)

One Old Ferry Road, Bristol RI 02809-2921

County: Bristol FICE Identification: 003410

Unit ID: 217518

Telephone: (401) 253-1040 Carnegie Class: Master's S

FAX Number: N/A Calendar System: Semester

URL: www.rwu.edu

Established: 1956 Annual Undergrad Tuition & Fees: $29,718

Enrollment: 4,680 Coed

Affiliation or Control: Independent Non-Profit IRS Status: 501(c)3

Highest Offering: Doctorate

Program: Liberal Arts And General; Teacher Preparatory; Professional

Accreditation: EH, BUS, CONST, ENG, LAW

01 President ... Dr. Donald J. FARISH
05 Provost/Sr VP for Academic Affairs ... Dr. Laura DEABRUNA
11 Sr Vice Pres Finance/Administration ... Mr. Jerome WILLIAMS
43 Sr VP Legal Affs/General Counsel ... Mr. Robert H. AVERY
84 Sr VP Enrollment/Mgmt/Communication ... Ms. Lynn M. FAWTHROP
04 Executive Assistant to President ... Ms. Brenda L. LITTLEFIELD
10 Vice President for Finance ... Mr. James C. NOONAN
32 Vice President for Student Affairs ... Mr. John J. KING
30 Vice Pres University Advancement ... Mr. Robert WEST
13 VP & Chief Information Officer ... Mr. Joseph F. PANGBORN
45 Assoc VP Strategic Plng/Cmty Rels ... Vacant
08 Int Dn Univ Lib Svcs/Dir Honors Pgm ... Ms. Betsy P. LEARNED
32 Dean of Students ... Dr. Kathleen N. MCMAHON
84 Dean of Enrollment Management ... Mr. Jason PINA
88 Asst VP Enrollment Mgmt/Retenton ... Ms. Tracy M. DACOSTA
28 Assoc Dean/Dir Intercultural Center ... Ms. Andrea DIAZ
35 Ast Dn Stdnts/Dir Stdnt Pgm/Ldrshp ... Ms. Tamara VON GEORGE
61 Dean School of Law ... Mr. David A. LOGAN
48 Dean Sch Arch/Art & Hist Preserv ... Mr. Stephen E. WHITE
50 Dean Gabelli School of Business ... Dr. Jerry DAUTERIVE
54 Dean Sch Engrng/Comput/Constr Mgmt ... Dr. Robert A. POTTER
61 Dean School of Justice Studies ... Dr. Stephanie PICOLO MANZI
53 Dean School of Education ... Dr. Mieko KAMII
51 Assc Dir Cont Studies/Grad Admiss ... Ms. Jamie GRENON
49 Dean Feinstein Col Arts & Sciences ... Dr. Robert COLE
55 Dean Instruct Sys Dev/Spec Projects ... Mr. Kenneth T. OSBORNE
96 Exec Dir of Contracts/Purchasing ... Mr. Thomas A. DIDARIO
29 Exec Dir Alumni Rels/Events Mgmt ... Ms. Allison CHASE PADULA
06 Registrar ... Mr. Daniel P. VILENSKI
07 Exec Dir Undergraduate Admissions ... Mr. Didier BOUVET
45 Director of Planning/Project Mgmt ... Mr. Peter WILBUR
19 Director of Public Safety ... Mr. John BLESSING
102 Ex Dir Grnts Corp/Found/Stratg Init ... Ms. Michele M. ALLAUX
41 Dir Athletics/Intramurals/Recreat ... Vacant
18 Director of Facilities Management ... Mr. John TAMEO
36 Director of Career Services ... Ms. Robin L. BEAUCHAMP
38 Director Counseling & Student Devel ... Dr. James A. AZAR
23 Director Health Services ... Ms. Anne M. ANDRADE
39 Director of Housing ... Mr. Anthony MONTEFUSCO
46 Director Research & Campaigns ... Ms. Nancy L. HARRIS
39 Director Residence Life/Women's Ctr ... Ms. Jennifer STANLEY
09 Director Institutional Research ... Mr. Gregory ROGERS
37 Int Director Student Financial Aid ... Ms. Tracy M. DACOSTA
40 Manager Bookstore ... Vacant

Salve Regina University (D)

100 Ochre Point Avenue, Newport RI 02840-4192

County: Newport FICE Identification: 003411

Unit ID: 217536

Telephone: (401) 847-6650 Carnegie Class: Master's M

FAX Number: (401) 341-2925 Calendar System: Semester

URL: www.salve.edu

Established: 1934 Annual Undergrad Tuition & Fees: $32,800

Enrollment: 2,618 Coed

Affiliation or Control: Roman Catholic IRS Status: 501(c)3

Highest Offering: Doctorate

Program: Liberal Arts And General; Teacher Preparatory; Professional

Accreditation: EH, ART, CORE, IACBE, NUR, SW

01 President ... Dr. Jane GERETY, RSM
05 Vice President Academic Affairs ... Dr. Dean DE LA MOTTE
32 Vice President Student Affairs ... Dr. Margaret HIGGINS
30 VP University Rels/Advancement ... Mr. Michael L. SEMENZA
10 Vice President Administration & CFO ... Mr. William B. HALL
84 Vice President Enrollment Services ... Ms. Laura E. MCPHIE-OLIVEIRA
45 Vice Pres Mission Integration/Plang ... Sr. Leona MISTO, RSM
27 Assoc Vice Pres Univ Rels/CCO ... Ms. Kristine HENDRICKSON
21 Assoc Vice Pres Finance/Controller ... Mr. Michael N. GRANDCHAMP
13 Assoc Vice Pres Info Technology/CIO ... Mr. Thomas H. BRENNAN
15 Assoc Vice Pres Human Resources/AAO ... Mrs. Diane F. BLANCHETTE
20 Asst Vice Pres Academic Affairs ... Dr. Donna M. COOK
07 Dean of Undergraduate Admissions ... Ms. Colleen EMERSON
35 Dean of Students ... Mr. John F. QUINN, JR.
49 Dean of Art & Sciences ... Dr. Laura L. O'TOOLE
20 Dean of Professional Studies ... Dr. Traci WARRINGTON
06 Registrar ... Dr. James H. TERRY
37 Director of Financial Aid ... Ms. Aida MIRANTE
29 Assoc Director Alumni & Parent Pgms ... Ms. Katherine S. BREZINA
41 Athletic Director ... Mr. Colin SULLIVAN
09 Director Institutional Research ... Mr. Frederick C. PROMADES
08 Director of Library Services ... Ms. Kathleen BOYD
39 Director of Residence ... Mr. Dennis J. DEL GIZZO
90 Director Academic Computing ... Mr. Brian A. MCDONNELL
18 Director of Facilities ... Mr. Eric MILNER
19 Director of Security/Safety ... Mr. John MIXTER
40 Director of Bookstore ... Mr. Michael LEDDY
44 Assoc Director of Annual Giving ... Ms. Victoria DUCLOS-BARRETT
23 Director of Health Services ... Mrs. Mary Kay CONNELL
35 Director of Student Activities ... Ms. Heather BARBOUR
36 Director of Career Development ... Mr. Michael WISNEWSKI
96 Director of Purchasing ... Ms. Francine MONFETTE
104 Director of International Programs ... Vacant
38 Dir of Student Counseling Services ... Ms. Elizabeth MINIFIE

University of Rhode Island (E)

Kingston RI 02881-0806

County: Washington FICE Identification: 003414

Unit ID: 217484

Telephone: (401) 874-1000 Carnegie Class: RU/H

FAX Number: (401) 874-7149 Calendar System: Semester

URL: www.uri.edu

Established: 1892 Annual Undergrad Tuition & Fees (In-State): $11,366

Enrollment: 16,294 Coed

Affiliation or Control: State IRS Status: 501(c)3

Highest Offering: Doctorate

Program: Liberal Arts And General; Teacher Preparatory; Professional

Accreditation: EH, BUS, BUSA, CLPSY, CYTO, DIETD, DIETI, ENG, LIB, LSAR, MFCD, MUS, NURSE, PHAR, PTA, SCPSY, SP, TED

01 President ... Dr. David M. DOOLEY
04 Assistant to the President ... Ms. Michelle S. CURRERI
05 Provost/Vice Pres Academic Affairs ... Dr. Donald H. DEHAYES
46 Vice Pres Research/Economic Devel ... Dr. Peter ALFONSO
30 Vice Pres University Advancement ... Mr. Robert M. BEAGLE
32 Vice President Student Affairs ... Dr. Thomas R. DOUGAN
10 Vice President for Administration ... Mr. Robert A. WEYGAND
20 Vice Provost Ac Fn & Ac Prsnl ... Dr. Clifford H. KATZ
84 Vice Provost Enrollment Management ... Mr. Dean LIBUTTI
27 Chief Information Officer ... Mr. Garrett A. BOZYLINSKY
51 V Prov Urban Pgms/Dn Col Cont Educ ... Dr. John H. MCCRAY, JR.
20 Int Vice Provost Faculty Affairs ... Dr. Laura BEAUVAIS
28 Assoc VP Community/Equity/Diversity ... Ms. Kathryn A. FRIEDMAN
49 Dean of Arts & Sciences ... Dr. Winifred E. BROWNELL
50 Dean Business Administration ... Dr. Mark M. HIGGINS
54 Dean of Engineering ... Dr. Raymond M. WRIGHT
88 Dean Graduate School Oceanography ... Dr. David M. FARMER
69 Dean Human Sciences & Services ... Dr. Wm. Lynn MCKINNEY
66 Dean of Nursing ... Dr. Dayle F. JOSEPH
67 Dean of Pharmacy ... Mr. Ronald P. JORDAN
07 Dean of Admissions ... Ms. Cynthia L. BONN
08 Dean of Library ... Mr. Dave MASLYN

88 Dean University College Dr. Jayne E. RICHMOND
58 Dean of Graduate School Dr. Nasser H. ZAWIA
44 Assoc Vice President Development Mr. Paul H. WITHAM
43 General Counsel Mr. Louis J. SACCOCCIO
26 Asst Vice Pres Public Affairs Ms. Andrea M. HOPKINS
16 Asst Vice Pres Human Resource Admin Ms. Anne Marie COLEMAN
88 Asst Vice Pres Research Admin Dr. S. Bradley MORAN
88 Asst VP Intell Property Mgmt/Comm Mr. David SADOWSKI
35 Asst VP Stdnt Affs & Dean of Stdnts Dr. Jason B. PINA
18 Asst Vice Pres Business Services Mr. J. Vernon WYMAN
39 Asst VP Student Affairs & Dir HRL Mr. Lester K. YENSAN
53 Director School of Education Dr. David BYRD
92 Director Honors Program Dr. Richard MCINTYRE
21 Dir Budget & Financial Planning Ms. Linda BARRETT
21 Controller Ms. Sharon B. BELL
100 Exec Asst to Pres & Dir PSPD Mr. Abu BAKR
37 Sr Assoc Dir Enrol Svcs/Fin Aid Ms. Bonnie A. SACCUCCI
22 Director Affirm Act/Equal Oppty/Div Ms. Roxanne GOMES
27 Director of Communications Ms. Linda A. ACCIARDO
23 Director Health Services Mr. Charles M. HENDERSON, III
38 Director Counseling Center Dr. Robert SAMUELS
41 Director of Athletics Mr. Thorr D. BJORN
15 Director Personnel Services Ms. Laura KENERSON
90 Dir Media & Technology Services Mr. David S. PORTER
91 Dir University Computing Systems Mr. Charlie SCHIFINO
104 Dir Intl Educ & Natl Student Exchg Dr. Dania C. BRANDFORD-CALVO
19 Director Security Dr. Robert F. DRAPEAU
96 Director Purchasing & Univ Stores Ms. Elizabeth A. GIL
36 Director Career Services Dr. Roberta K. KOPPEL
29 Exec Dir Alumni Relations/Secy Assn Ms. Michele NOTA
40 Administrator Bookstore Mr. Paul WHITNEY
88 Spec Asst to the Prov for Acad Plng Ms. Ann M. MORRISSEY

SOUTH CAROLINA

Aiken Technical College (A)

PO Drawer 696, Aiken SC 29802-0696
County: Aiken FICE Identification: 010056
Unit ID: 217615
Telephone: (803) 593-9231 Carnegie Class: Assoc/Pub-R-M
FAX Number: (803) 593-6641 Calendar System: Semester
URL: www.atc.edu
Established: 1972 Annual Undergrad Tuition & Fees (In-District): $1,861
Enrollment: 3,128 Coed
Affiliation or Control: State/Local IRS Status: 501(c)3
Highest Offering: Associate Degree
Program: Occupational; 2-Year Principally Bachelor's Creditable; Technical Emphasis
Accreditation: SC, ACBSP, ADNUR, DA, MAC, RAD, SURGT

01 President Dr. Susan A. WINSOR
05 Vice President Academic Affairs Dr. Gemma FROCK
11 Vice Pres Administrative Services Mr. Andy JORDAN
103 VP Workforce & Business Devel Dr. Gemma FROCK
84 Dean of Enrollment Management Vacant
09 Director Inst Planning/Research Mr. Donald MILES
102 Int Director Foundation & Grants Ms. Mary COMMONS
38 Director Counseling/Stdnt Placement Mr. Rich WELDON
37 Director of Financial Aid Ms. Amanda CHITTUM
27 Director of Information Services Mr. Tom SLIZEWSKI
13 Director of Computer Center/MIS Mr. Ray TIMMONS
16 Personnel Officer Ms. Sylvia BYRD
18 Chief of Maintenance Mr. Mike DUNCAN
10 Chief Business Officer Mr. Don TRUE
96 Director of Purchasing Ms. Toni MARSHALL

Allen University (B)

1530 Harden Street, Columbia SC 29204-1085
County: Richland FICE Identification: 003417
Unit ID: 217624
Telephone: (803) 376-5700 Carnegie Class: Bac/A&S
FAX Number: N/A Calendar System: Semester
URL: www.allenuniversity.edu
Established: 1870 Annual Undergrad Tuition & Fees: $10,884
Enrollment: 848 Coed
Affiliation or Control: African Methodist Episcopal IRS Status: 501(c)3
Highest Offering: Baccalaureate
Program: Liberal Arts And General; Teacher Preparatory
Accreditation: SC

01 President Dr. Pamela M. WILSON
03 Executive Vice President Dr. Willie L. PARSON
51 Sr Vice Pres College Prof Adults Dr. Walter C. HOWARD
05 Vice President Academic Affairs Dr. Lady June HUBBARD-COLE
10 Vice President Fiscal Affairs Mr. Thomas POITIER
13 Vice Pres Information Technology Dr. Willie PARSON
30 Vice Pres Institutional Advancement Ms. Melanie JONES
32 Vice Pres Student Life Dr. Eric JACKSON
45 VP Planning/Research/Sponsored Pgms Mr. Marcus V. BELL
35 Assoc Vice Pres Student Affairs Dr. Lynnette L. RICHARDSON
43 General Counsel Mr. Renardo L. HICKS
06 Registrar Ms. Marilyn YOUNG
07 Director of Admissions Ms. Terri PARKER
15 Director of Human Resources Mrs. Paige MOORE
18 Facilities/Physical Plant Director Mr. Timothy TAYLOR
23 Director Health Services Mrs. Aprella HENSON
26 Director of Public Relations Vacant
09 Director of Institutional Research Ms. Marilyn C. YOUNG
29 Director of Alumni Relations Vacant
37 Director of Student Financial Aid Ms. Yolanda GEIGER
36 Director Student Placement Vacant
38 Director Counseling Services Mr. N. INNOCENT

Anderson University (C)

316 Boulevard, Anderson SC 29621-4035
County: Anderson FICE Identification: 003418
Unit ID: 217633
Telephone: (864) 231-2000 Carnegie Class: Bac/Diverse
FAX Number: (864) 231-2004 Calendar System: Semester
URL: www.andersonuniversity.edu
Established: 1911 Annual Undergrad Tuition & Fees: $20,910
Enrollment: 2,512 Coed
Affiliation or Control: Other IRS Status: 501(c)3
Highest Offering: Doctorate
Program: Liberal Arts And General; Teacher Preparatory
Accreditation: SC, ACBSP, ART, MUS, TED

01 President Dr. Evans P. WHITAKER
05 Provost Dr. Danny M. PARKER
10 VP for Finance and Administration Mr. John M. KUNST
30 VP for Institutional Advancement Mr. R. Dean WOODS
84 VP for Enrollment Management Mr. D. Omar RASHED
42 Vice President for Christian Life Dr. J. Robert CLINE
32 Vice Pres of Student Development Dr. Bob L. HANLEY
14 Chief Information Officer Mr. Peter B. HARVIN
41 Director of Athletics Mrs. Nancy P. SIMPSON
09 Dir of Enrollment Mgt Sys & Ext Rpt Mr. Daryl A. IVERSON
20 Associate Provost Mrs. Susan B. WOOTEN
28 Assoc VP for Student Development Dr. Beverly RICE MCADAMS
06 University Registrar Mrs. Kendra B. WOODSON
08 Director of Library Services Mr. Kent A. MILLWOOD
26 Director Marketing & Communications Mr. Barry D. RAY
07 Director of Admissions Ms. Pam ROSS
37 Dir Financial Aid Planning Mrs. Rebekah BURDICK
15 Director of Human Resources Mrs. Darlene M. FISHER
18 Chief Facilities/Physical Plant Mr. Dennis H. MCKEE
38 Director of Counseling Services Vacant
29 Director of Alumni Relations Mr. Chad NELMS
36 Director Career Services Ms. Kelly A. BELL
39 Assoc Director of Residence Life Mr. Tim JARED
23 Director Health Services Mrs. Deb A. TAYLOR
21 Controller Ms. Kristie C. COLE
32 Dean of Student Life Mr. Jonathan GROPP
88 Director for Student Success Ms. L. Dianne KING
35 Director of Student Activities Ms. Sara MUDD

Benedict College (D)

Harden and Bland Streets, Columbia SC 29204-1086
County: Richland FICE Identification: 003420
Unit ID: 217721
Telephone: (803) 253-5000 Carnegie Class: Bac/Diverse
FAX Number: (803) 253-5059 Calendar System: Semester
URL: www.benedict.edu
Established: 1870 Annual Undergrad Tuition & Fees: $17,190
Enrollment: 3,147 Coed
Affiliation or Control: Independent Non-Profit IRS Status: 501(c)3
Highest Offering: Baccalaureate
Program: Liberal Arts And General; Teacher Preparatory
Accreditation: SC, ACBSP, ART, NRPA, SW, TED

01 President Dr. David H. SWINTON
05 Senior Vice Pres Academic Affairs Dr. Janeen WITTY
03 Executive Vice President Dr. Ruby W. WATTS
10 Vice President Business/Finance Mrs. Brenda S. WALKER
32 Vice President Student Affairs Mr. Gary E. KNIGHT
44 Vice Pres Institutional Advancement Mrs. Barbara C. MOORE
35 Dean of Students Mr. Rufus C. WATTS
20 Assoc Vice Pres Academic Affairs Dr. George A. DEVLIN
21 Asst VP for Business & Finance Ms. Kathryn JONES
26 Director of Public Relations Ms. Kymm HUNTER
07 Director of Admissions/Student Mktg Mrs. Phyllis THOMPSON
29 Assistant VP for Alumni Relations Mrs. Ada A. BELTON
13 Dir Management Information Systems Mr. Robert SQUIREWELL
15 Director of Human Resources Mrs. Betty A. JENKINS
06 Registrar/Director Student Records Mrs. Wanda A. SCOTT-KINNEY
41 Athletics Director Mr. Willie WASHINGTON
38 Director Service Learning & Leaders Ms. Tondaleya JACKSON
39 Director Community Life Mr. Michael REBIMBUS
42 Dir Campus Ministry/Dean of Chapel Mr. Thomas DAVIS
19 Director Campus Safety Mr. Haywood M. BAZEMORE
36 Director Career Services Ms. Karen W. RUTHERFORD
37 Director Financial Aid Ms. Sul BLACK
19 Director Physical Plant Mr. Abu AHMED
08 Director of Library Mrs. Darlene ZINNERMAN-BETHEA
25 Coordinator Title III Mrs. Doris W. JOHNSON
49 Dean Sch Human/Arts/Soc Sci Mr. Charles AUSTIN
50 Dean School of Business/Econ Mr. Gerald SMALLS
53 Dean School of Education Dr. Allen COLES
72 Dean Sch Science/Tech/Engrng/Math Dr. Samir S. RAYCHOUDHURY
92 Dean School of Honors Dr. Warren ROBINSON
57 Chair Fine Arts Mr. Charles BROOKS
50 Int Chair Business Admin/Mgmt/Mktg Dr. Ebuta EKURE
57 Int Chair Education and Family Stds Dr. Mona THORNTON
70 Chair Social Work Dr. Dorothy OSGOOD
88 Chair English/Foreign Language Dept Dr. Carolyn DRAKEFORD
88 Chair Bio/Chem/Enviroment Hlth Sci Dr. Helene TAMBOUE
81 Chair Math/Computer Science Ms. Fereshtah ZAHED
54 Int Chair Physics/Engineering Dr. Fouzi H. ARAMMASH
88 Int Chair Economics/Finance/Acctg Dr. Syed MAHDI

Bob Jones University (E)

1700 Wade Hampton Boulevard, Greenville SC 29614-0001
County: Greenville FICE Identification: 003421
Unit ID: 217749
Telephone: (864) 242-5100 Carnegie Class: Spec/Faith
FAX Number: (864) 235-6661 Calendar System: Semester
URL: www.bju.edu
Established: 1927 Annual Undergrad Tuition & Fees: $12,730
Enrollment: 3,794 Coed
Affiliation or Control: Independent Non-Profit IRS Status: 501(c)3
Highest Offering: Doctorate
Program: Liberal Arts And General; Religious Emphasis
Accreditation: TRACS

00 Chancellor Dr. Bob JONES, III
01 President Dr. Stephen JONES
05 Exec Vice Pres for Academic Affairs Dr. Gary M. WEIER
11 Executive Vice Pres for Operations Mr. Marshall E. FRANKLIN
10 Vice President for Finance Mr. John D. MATTHEWS
05 Provost Dr. David A. FISHER
32 Dean of Students Dr. Eric D. NEWTON
20 Director of Educational Services Dr. N. Daniel SMITH
18 Chief Facilities Management Officer Mr. Mark W. KOPP
26 Chief Publications Officer Mr. Bill APELIAN
27 Chief Communication Officer Ms. Carol A. KEIRSTEAD
13 Chief Information Officer Mr. Marvin P. REEM
84 Director of Enrollment Planning Dr. Jeffrey D. HEATH
09 Dir of Institutional Effectiveness Rev. Phillip R. GERARD
06 Registrar Dr. N. Daniel SMITH
07 Director of Admissions Mr. Gary A. DEEDRICK
08 Director of Libraries Mr. Joseph L. ALLEN
88 Director of Ministerial Training Dr. M. Bruce MCALLISTER
30 Director of Advancement Mr. Thomas H. HALL
37 Director of Financial Aid Mr. Chris BAKER
37 Asst Director of Financial Aid Mr. Kevin DELP
33 Dean of Men Mr. Jonathan G. DAULTON
34 Dean of Women Ms. Deneen LAWSON
49 Dean College of Arts and Science Dr. Robert R. TAYLOR
50 Dean School of Business Dr. Aaron C. GOLDSMITH
53 Dean School of Education Dr. Brian A. CARRUTHERS
57 Dean Sch Fine Arts & Communication Dr. Darren P. LAWSON
73 Dean School of Religion Dr. Royce B. SHORT
73 Dean Seminary/Grad Sch of Religion Dr. Stephen J. HANKINS

Brown Mackie College-Greenville (F)

75 Beattie Place, Ste. 100, Greenville SC 29601-2155
County: Greenville Identification: 666781
Unit ID: 456791
Telephone: (864) 239-5301 Carnegie Class: Not Classified
FAX Number: (864) 232-4094 Calendar System: Other
URL: www.brownmackie.edu
Established: 2009 Annual Undergrad Tuition & Fees: $11,124
Enrollment: 742 Coed
Affiliation or Control: Proprietary IRS Status: Proprietary
Highest Offering: Baccalaureate
Program: Occupational; 2-Year Principally Bachelor's Creditable; Business Emphasis
Accreditation: ACICS

01 President Karen BURGESS
07 Senior Director of Admissions Laura WALKER
05 Dean of Academic Affairs Brian WYSKO

† Branch campus of Brown Mackie College, Tucson, AZ.

Central Carolina Technical College (G)

506 N Guignard Drive, Sumter SC 29150-2499
County: Sumter FICE Identification: 003995
Unit ID: 218858
Telephone: (803) 778-1961 Carnegie Class: Assoc/Pub-R-M
FAX Number: (803) 778-7880 Calendar System: Semester
URL: www.cctech.edu
Established: 1962 Annual Undergrad Tuition & Fees (In-State): $3,476
Enrollment: 4,282 Coed
Affiliation or Control: State IRS Status: 501(c)3
Highest Offering: Associate Degree
Program: Occupational; 2-Year Principally Bachelor's Creditable; Technical Emphasis
Accreditation: SC, ADNUR, MAC, PNUR, SURGT

01 President Dr. Tim HARDEE
05 Vice President for Academics Ms. Susan MCMASTER
11 VP for Administration & Planning Mrs. Ann A. COOPER
10 Vice President for Business Affairs Ms. Terry L. BOOTH
32 Vice President for Student Affairs Ms. Lisa BRACKEN
04 Assistant to the President Ms. Emma Lee RICKARD
51 Director Cont Educ/Workforce Devel Ms. Elizabeth WILLIAMS
08 Dean of Learning Resources Ms. Nancy BISHOP
102 Director Foundation Ms. Meree MCALISTER
26 Director Public Relations Mr. Neal CROTTS
15 Director of Personnel Mrs. Ronalda S. STOVER
13 Director Information Systems Dr. Vicky G. MALONEY

06 Registrar ..... Ms. Henrietta SCOTT
37 Director Student Financial Aid ..... Ms. Sarah DOWD
09 Dir Research/Institutional Effect ..... Mr. Bryan MAY
07 Director of Admissions & Counseling ..... Mrs. Barbara WRIGHT
54 Dean of Industrial and Engineering ..... Mr. Ernest NEAL
76 Dean of Health Sciences ..... Ms. Miriam LANEY
50 Dean of Business/Public Service ..... Mr. David WATSON
53 Dean of General Education ..... Mr. Myles WILLIAMS

Charleston School of Law (A)

81 Mary Street, PO Box 535, Charleston SC 29402
County: Charleston FICE Identification: 040963
Unit ID: 451510
Telephone: (843) 329-1000 Carnegie Class: Not Classified
FAX Number: N/A Calendar System: Semester
URL: www.charlestonlaw.edu
Established: 2003 Annual Graduate Tuition & Fees: $36,774
Enrollment: 702 Coed
Affiliation or Control: Proprietary IRS Status: Proprietary
Highest Offering: First Professional Degree; No Undergraduates
Program: Professional
Accreditation: LAW

01 Dean ..... Mr. Andrew L. ABRAMS
05 Associate Dean Academic Affairs ..... Ms. Margaret M. LAWSON
07 Associate Dean Admissions ..... Mr. John S. BENFIELD
32 Associate Dean of Students ..... Ms. Abby EDWARDS SAUNDERS
08 Assoc Dean of Library/Tech Svcs ..... Ms. Lisa SMITH-BUTLER
10 Chief Financial Officer ..... Ms. Wende WOOD

Charleston Southern University (B)

PO Box 118087, Charleston SC 29423-8087
County: Charleston FICE Identification: 003419
Unit ID: 217688
Telephone: (843) 863-7000 Carnegie Class: Master's M
FAX Number: (843) 863-8074 Calendar System: Semester
URL: www.csuniv.edu
Established: 1964 Annual Undergrad Tuition & Fees: $20,600
Enrollment: 3,231 Coed
Affiliation or Control: Southern Baptist IRS Status: 501(c)3
Highest Offering: Master's
Program: Liberal Arts And General; Teacher Preparatory; Professional
Accreditation: SC, IACBE, MUS, NUR, TED

01 President ..... Dr. Jairy C. HUNTER, JR.
05 Vice President Academic Affairs ..... Dr. Donald MARTIN
10 Vice President for Business Affairs ..... Mr. Luke BLACKMON
04 Assistant to the President ..... Mrs. Katie DEPOPPE
84 Vice Pres Enrollment Management ..... Mrs. Debbie WILLIAMSON
45 Vice Pres Planning/Athletics ..... Dr. Rick BREWER
26 Vice Pres Advancement & Marketing ..... Mr. David BAGGS
30 Executive Director of Development ..... Mr. Bill WARD
32 Dean of Students ..... Mr. Clark CARTER
91 Director of Administrative Services ..... Mr. Shannon PHILLIPS
08 Director of the Library ..... Mrs. Sandra HUGHES
06 Registrar ..... Mrs. Amanda SISSION
29 Director of BUC Club ..... Ms. Cathryn BRODERHAUSEN
88 Asst to the VP for Retention ..... Mr. Rex NESTOR
21 Associate Business Officer ..... Mrs. Janet MIMS
26 Director of Integrated Marketing ..... Mr. John STRUBEL
09 Dir of Institutional Effectiveness ..... Mr. Jeffrey BABETZ
50 Dean of Business ..... Dr. John B. DUNCAN
58 Director MBA Program ..... Dr. Darin GERDES
58 Dean Education ..... Dr. Norma HARPER
83 Dean Humanities/Social Sciences ..... Dr. David NAYLOR
81 Dean Science & Mathematics ..... Dr. Jeryl JOHNSON
66 Dean of Nursing ..... Dr. Tara HULSEY
51 College of Adult Professional Stds ..... Dr. James JONES
41 Athletic Director ..... Mr. Hank SMALL
42 Director Campus Ministry ..... Vacant
19 Director Security ..... Mr. Donald LITTLE
90 Director Computing & Info Science ..... Mr. James ROBERTS
18 Director Physical & Auxiliary Svcs ..... Mr. Nick CIMORELLI
29 Director of Alumni Relations ..... Miss Beth BOYLE
07 Director of Admission ..... Mr. James M. RHOTON
15 Director of Personnel Services ..... Mrs. Lindsey WALKE
36 Director Career Planning ..... Mrs. Hester YOUNG
38 Director Student Counseling ..... Mr. Rufus WOFFORD
96 Director of Purchasing ..... Mrs. Linda PARKER
37 Director Student Financial Aid ..... Mrs. Teri KARGES
39 Director Residence Life ..... Mr. Corey HUMPHRIES

The Citadel, The Military College of South Carolina (C)

171 Moultrie Street, Charleston SC 29409-0001
County: Charleston FICE Identification: 003423
Unit ID: 217864
Telephone: (843) 953-5012 Carnegie Class: Master's L
FAX Number: (843) 953-5287 Calendar System: Semester
URL: www.citadel.edu
Established: 1842 Annual Undergrad Tuition & Fees (In-State): $10,216
Enrollment: 3,402 Coed
Affiliation or Control: State IRS Status: 501(c)3
Highest Offering: Beyond Master's But Less Than Doctorate
Program: Liberal Arts And General; Teacher Preparatory; Professional
Accreditation: SC, BUS, CACREP, CS, ENG, TED

01 President ..... LtGen. John W. ROSA
05 Provost/Dean of College ..... BGen. Samuel M. HINES, JR.
18 Vice Pres Facilities/Engineering ..... Col. George D. YEATTS
10 Exec VP Finance Admin & Operations ..... BGen. Thomas J. ELZEY
26 Vice President for External Affairs ..... Col. L. Jeffrey PEREZ
04 Executive Assistant to President ..... Col. Thomas G. PHILIPKOSKY
32 Commandant of Cadets ..... Col. Leo A. MERCADO
43 General Counsel ..... Mr. Mark C. BRANDENBURG
20 Assoc Provost Academic Affairs ..... Col. Mark A. BEBENSEE
20 Assoc Prov Plng/Assess/Evaluation ..... LtCol. Tara F. MCNEALY
58 Assoc Provost/Citadel Graduate Col ..... Col. Steve A. NIDA
07 Director of Admissions ..... LtCol. John W. POWELL, JR.
06 Registrar ..... Maj. Sylvia L. NESMITH
41 Director Intercollegiate Athletics ..... Mr. Larry W. LECKONBY
35 Director of Cadet Activities ..... Col. Robert A. SBERNA
29 Director Alumni Affairs/Placement ..... Mr. Michael F. ROGERS
08 Interim Director of Library ..... Maj. Elizabeth CONNOR
13 Director Info Technology Services ..... Mr. Richard NELSON
37 Director Financial Aid/ Scholarships ..... LtCol. Henry M. FULLER, JR.
15 Director of Human Resources ..... Col. Dennis D. CARPENTER
36 Director of Student Placement ..... Mr. Brent A. STEWART
38 Director of Student Counseling ..... Dr. Suzanne BUFANO
11 Director of The Citadel Staff ..... Col. Joseph W. TREZ
09 Institutional Research Coordinator ..... Mrs. Lisa L. PACE
19 Director Security/Safety ..... Maj. William A. FLETCHER
23 College Physician ..... Dr. Carey M. CAPELL
40 Director of the Cadet Store ..... Mr. Kenneth A. WOODRUFF
42 Chaplain/Dir Religious Activities ..... Col. Joel C. HARRIS
92 Director Honors Program ..... Col. Jack W. RHODES
86 Director Govt & Community Affairs ..... Col. Cardon B. CRAWFORD
96 Director of Purchasing ..... Mr. John L. WALKER
30 Chief Development ..... Mr. Dennis P. BERGVALL
28 Chief Diversity Officer ..... Vacant
50 Dean of the School of Bus Admin ..... Col. Ronald F. GREEN
53 Dean of the School of Education ..... Col. Tony W. JOHNSON
54 Dean of the School of Engineering ..... Col. Ronald W. WELCH
81 Dean of the School of Science/Math ..... Col. Isaac S. METTS
79 Dean Sch Humanities/Social Sciences ..... Col. Winifred B. MOORE

Claflin University (D)

400 Magnolia Street, Orangeburg SC 29115-4477
County: Orangeburg FICE Identification: 003424
Unit ID: 217873
Telephone: (803) 535-5000 Carnegie Class: Bac/A&S
FAX Number: (803) 531-2860 Calendar System: Semester
URL: www.claflin.edu
Established: 1869 Annual Undergrad Tuition & Fees: $13,370
Enrollment: 1,920 Coed
Affiliation or Control: United Methodist IRS Status: 501(c)3
Highest Offering: Master's
Program: Liberal Arts And General
Accreditation: SC, MUS, ACBSP, TED

01 President ..... Dr. Henry N. TISDALE
03 Executive Vice President ..... Mr. Drexel B. BALL
05 Vice President for Academic Affairs ..... Vacant
10 Vice President for Fiscal Affairs ..... Vacant
30 Vice Pres Institutional Advancement ..... Rev. Whittaker V. MIDDLETON
32 Vice Pres Student Devel & Services ..... Dr. Leroy A. DURANT
45 VP Plng/Assessment/Information Svcs ..... Dr. Zia HASAN
20 Associate VP for Academic Affairs ..... Vacant
21 Associate VP for Fiscal Affairs ..... Mrs. Tijuana R. HUDSON
26 Asst VP Communications & Marketing ..... Ms. Sonja BENNETT
35 Asst VP Student Devel & Services ..... Mr. James R. PAYNE
07 Director of Admissions ..... Mr. Michael ZEIGLER
79 Dean Sch Humanities & Soc Science ..... Dr. Peggy STEVENSON-RATLIFF
50 Dean School of Business ..... Dr. Harpal S. GREWAL
53 Interim Dean School of Education ..... Dr. Courtney A. HOWARD
81 Dean Sch Natural Sciences & Math ..... Dr. Verlie A. TISDALE
13 Asst VP Information Tech Svcs ..... Mr. James E. BRENN
51 Interim Dir of Prof & Cont Studies ..... Dr. Gloria SEABROOK
88 Director of Special Events ..... Ms. Franette BOYD
08 Library Director ..... Ms. Marilyn Y. GIBBS
37 Director of Financial Aid ..... Ms. Terria C. WILLIAMS
36 Director of Career Development ..... Mrs. Carolyn R. SNELL
18 Director Plant Operations ..... Mr. Mike DUNNAVANT
41 Athletic Director ..... Dr. Timothy J. AUTRY
15 Director of Human Resources ..... Ms. Shirley A. BIGGS
06 Registrar ..... Mrs. Roe B. HUNT
29 Director Alumni Relations ..... Mr. Marcus BURGESS
19 Chief of Campus Public Safety ..... Mr. Steven A. PEARSON
96 Director of Auxiliary Services ..... Mr. Rodeny B. HUDSON
88 Director of Sponsored Programs ..... Ms. Veronica GOODMAN
04 Executive Admin Asst to President ..... Ms. Melvenia WILLIAMS

Clemson University (E)

201 Sikes Hall, Clemson SC 29634-0001
County: Pickens FICE Identification: 003425
Unit ID: 217882
Telephone: (864) 656-3311 Carnegie Class: RU/H
FAX Number: (864) 656-4040 Calendar System: Semester
URL: www.clemson.edu
Established: 1889 Annual Undergrad Tuition & Fees (In-State): $12,668
Enrollment: 19,453 Coed
Affiliation or Control: State IRS Status: 501(c)3
Highest Offering: Doctorate
Program: Liberal Arts And General; Teacher Preparatory; Professional
Accreditation: SC, ART, BUS, BUSA, CACREP, CONST, CS, DIETD, ENG, ENGR, FOR, IPSY, LSAR, NRPA, NURSE, PLNG, TED

01 President ..... Mr. James F. BARKER
43 General Counsel ..... Vacant
05 Vice President Acad Affairs/Provost ..... Dr. Doris R. HELMS
10 Chief Financial Officer ..... Mr. Brett A. DALTON
32 Vice President Student Affairs ..... Ms. Gail DISABATINO
101 Executive Secretary to the Board ..... Ms. Angie LEIDINGER
30 Vice President for Advancement ..... Mr. A. Neill CAMERON, JR.
88 Vice Pres Public Svc/Agriculture ..... Dr. John W. KELLY, JR.
46 Vice President for Research ..... Dr. Gerald SONNENFELD
27 Vice Prov Computer/Info Technology ..... Mr. James R. BOTTUM
20 Vice Prov/Dean Undergrad Studies ..... Dr. Janice W. MURDOCH
29 Chief Alumni Officer ..... Mr. Brian J. O'ROURKE
18 Chief Facilities Officer ..... Mr. Robert J. WELLS, JR.
35 Associate VP/Dean of Students ..... Dr. Joy S. SMITH
26 Chief Public Affairs Officer ..... Ms. Catherine T. SAMS
08 Dean of Libraries ..... Ms. Kay WALL
07 Director of Admissions ..... Mr. Robert S. BARKLEY
06 Registrar ..... Mr. Stanley B. SMITH
37 Director of Financial Aid ..... Mr. Chuck KNEPFLE
36 Director of Career Center ..... Vacant
38 Director Counseling/Psych Services ..... Dr. Raquel J. CONTRERAS
47 Dean Col Agric/Forestry/Life Sci ..... Dr. Thomas R. SCOTT
58 Dean Grad School/Assoc Vice Provost ..... Vacant
48 Dean Col Arch/Arts/Humanities ..... Dr. Richard E. GOODSTEIN
54 Dean Col Engineering/Sciences ..... Dr. Esin GULARI
50 Dean Col Business/Behavioral Sci ..... Dr. Claude C. LILLY
53 Dean Col Health/Educ/Human Dev ..... Dr. Lawrence R. ALLEN
09 Director Institutional Research ..... Dr. S. Wickes WESTCOTT, III
39 Executive Director of Housing ..... Ms. Verna G. HOWELL
41 Director of Athletics ..... Dr. Terry Don PHILLIPS
44 Director of Estate & Planned Giving ..... Ms. Jovanna J. KING
22 Director Access & Equity ..... Mr. Byron A. WILEY
23 Director Student Health Services ..... Mr. George W. CLAY
15 Chief Human Resources ..... Vacant
91 Executive Director Enterprise Appl ..... Ms. Deborah WHITTEN
25 Director Sponsored Programs ..... Dr. Vincent S. GALLICCHIO
19 Director Law Enforcement & Safety ..... Chief Johnson LINK
96 Director of Purchasing ..... Mr. Michael NEBESKY

Clinton Junior College (F)

1029 Crawford Road, Rock Hill SC 29730-5152
County: York FICE Identification: 004923
Unit ID: 217891
Telephone: (803) 327-7402 Carnegie Class: Assoc/PrivNFP
FAX Number: (803) 327-3261 Calendar System: Semester
URL: www.clintonjuniorcollege.edu
Established: 1894 Annual Undergrad Tuition & Fees: $4,735
Enrollment: 148 Coed
Affiliation or Control: African Methodist Episcopal Zion Church
IRS Status: 501(c)3
Highest Offering: Associate Degree
Program: Liberal Arts And General
Accreditation: TRACS

01 President ..... Dr. Elaine J. COPELAND
04 Assistant to the President ..... Ms. Cheryl A. WEBB
05 VP/Dean for Academic Affairs ..... Ms. Janis S. PENDLETON
30 Vice President Development ..... Mr. William TABOR
32 Vice President for Student Affairs ..... Dr. Robert M. COPELAND, JR.
10 Director of Business & Finance ..... Ms. Archinya INGRAM
06 Registrar ..... Mrs. Altavese HUNT
37 Financial Aid ..... Ms. Sadie PYE-JUMPER
08 Librarian ..... Ms. Minora HICKS
41 Athletic Dir/Womens Basketbl Coach ..... Mr. Roderick WOODS
18 Director Facilities/Bldgs/Grounds ..... Rev. Lloyd SNIPES
07 Admissions Director ..... Dr. Robert COPELAND
35 Coord Student Support Services ..... Ms. Omega HONEYWOOD
88 Mens Basketball Coach ..... Mr. Lester SMITH

Coastal Carolina University (G)

PO Box 261954, Conway SC 29528-6054
County: Horry FICE Identification: 003451
Unit ID: 218724
Telephone: (843) 347-3161 Carnegie Class: Master's S
FAX Number: (843) 349-2990 Calendar System: Semester
URL: www.coastal.edu
Established: 1954 Annual Undergrad Tuition & Fees (In-State): $9,760
Enrollment: 8,706 Coed
Affiliation or Control: State IRS Status: 501(c)3
Highest Offering: Master's
Program: Liberal Arts And General
Accreditation: SC, ART, BUS, CS, MUS, TED, THEA

01 President ..... Dr. David A. DECENZO
05 Provost/Sr VP Acad & Student Affs ..... Dr. Robert J. SHEEHAN
03 Executive Vice President ..... Dr. Edgar L. DYER
10 Vice Pres Finance/Administration ..... Ms. Staci A. BOWIE
84 Vice Pres for Enrollment Services ..... Dr. Judy W. VOGT
30 Interim Vice Pres Philanthropy ..... Mr. Lawson HOLLAND
27 Vice Pres University Communications ..... Vacant
50 Dean Business Administration ..... Dr. J. Ralph BYINGTON
53 Interim Dean of Education ..... Dr. Edward JADALLAH
79 Int Dean of Humanities & Fine Arts ..... Dr. Daniel ENNIS
81 Dean of Science ..... Dr. Michael H. ROBERTS
08 Dean Library Services ..... Dr. Barbara BURD
32 VP Stdnt Affs/Dean of Stdnts ..... Ms. Haven HART
16 Exec Dir HR & Organizational Dev ..... Ms. Pat WEST
13 Exec Director Info Technology Svcs ..... Mr. Abdallah HADDAD
20 Assoc Provost Admin/Academic ..... Ms. Sallie CLARKSON
20 Assoc Prov Assessment/Accreditation ..... Dr. John P. BEARD

58 Assoc Provost/Dir Graduate Studies .... Dr. James O. LUKEN
25 Int Assoc Prov Grants/Spons Rsrch ....Dr. Robert F. YOUNG
09 Director of Inst Rsrch/Assessment ....Ms. Christine L. MEE
27 Assoc VP University Relations .... Dr. Deborah K. CONNER
06 University Registrar .... Mr. Daniel M. LAWLESS
19 Director Public Safety .... Mr. David ROPER
21 Controller .... Ms. Lori CHURCH
28 Dir Multicultural Student Services .... Ms. Patricia SINGLETON-YOUNG
41 Director of Athletics .... Mr. Hunter R. YURACHEK
38 Director of Counseling Services .... Dr. Jennie M. CASSIDY
85 Director of International Programs .... Mr. Geoffrey J. PARSONS
39 Director of Housing/Residence Life .... Mr. Steve HARRISON
37 Director of Financial Aid .... Mr. Greg THORNBURG
92 Director Honors Program .... Dr. Philip E. WHALEN
36 Director Career Services .... Dr. Tom WOODLE
96 Dir Procurement/Business Services .... Mr. Dean P. HUDSON
18 Dir University Projects & Planning .... Mr. T. Rein MUNGO
26 Chief Public Relations Officer .... Ms. Martha S. HUNN
29 Director Alumni Relations .... Ms. Jean Ann BRAKEFIELD
104 Exec Dir Global Initiatives .... Dr. Darla J. DOMKE-DAMONTE
07 Dir Enrollment/Assoc Dir Admissions .... Ms. Meredith KAHL

Coker College (A)

300 E College Avenue, Hartsville SC 29550-3797
County: Darlington FICE Identification: 003427
Unit ID: 217907
Telephone: (843) 383-8000 Carnegie Class: Bac/Diverse
FAX Number: (843) 383-8048 Calendar System: Semester
URL: www.coker.edu
Established: 1908 Annual Undergrad Tuition & Fees: $20,548
Enrollment: 1,106 Coed
Affiliation or Control: Independent Non-Profit IRS Status: 501(c)3
Highest Offering: Baccalaureate
Program: Liberal Arts And General; Teacher Preparatory
Accreditation: SC, MUS, SW

01 President .... Dr. Robert L. WYATT
04 Exec Assistant to the President .... Ms. Bonnie WILCOX
05 Provost & Dean of the Faculty .... Dr. Patricia G. LINCOLN
30 VP Institutional Advancement .... Mr. Thomas W. GIFFIN
10 Vice President Business Operations .... Mr. Gerald D. SILVER
84 VP Enrollment/Student Services .... Dr. Stephen B. TERRY
32 Dean of Students .... Dr. Jason UMFRESS
55 Assoc Dean Adult Learner Pgm .... Dr. Barbara JACKOWSKI
78 Asst Dean/Dir CTR Engaged Learning .... Mrs. Darlene SMALL
26 Exec Dir Marketing/Communication .... Mr. R. Kyle SAVERANCE
39 Director of Residence Life .... Ms. April A. PALMER
41 Director of Athletics .... Ms. Lynn GRIFFIN
07 Director of Admissions .... Mr. Adam CONNOLLY
06 Registrar .... Ms. Stacy R. ATKINSON
18 Director of the Physical Plant .... Mr. Russell CROFT
21 Controller .... Mrs. Robin A. PERDUE
37 Director of Financial Aid .... Mrs. Betty B. WILLIAMS
44 Director of Annual Giving .... Mr. Wesley J. DANIELS
29 Director of Alumni Affairs .... Ms. Lyn BLACKMON
38 Director Counseling Services .... Dr. Katherine KELLY
35 Dir Student Activities/Leadership .... Ms. Lisa POTOKA
88 Director of Advancement Services .... Mrs. Patricia H. DAMPIER
15 Director of Human Resources .... Mrs. Janice B. BULLARD
38 Director of Career Services .... Ms. Deanne FRYE
44 Director Planned Giving/Cmty Rels .... Mr. Frank BUSH
08 Director of Library .... Ms. Alexa BARTEL

College of Charleston (B)

66 George Street, Charleston SC 29424-0100
County: Charleston FICE Identification: 003428
Unit ID: 217819
Telephone: (843) 953-5507 Carnegie Class: Master's M
FAX Number: (843) 953-5811 Calendar System: Semester
URL: www.cofc.edu
Established: 1770 Annual Undergrad Tuition & Fees (In-State): $9,616
Enrollment: 11,532 Coed
Affiliation or Control: State IRS Status: 501(c)3
Highest Offering: Master's
Program: Liberal Arts And General
Accreditation: SC, BUS, BUSA, CS, MUS, SPAA, TED, THEA

01 President .... Dr. George BENSON
05 VP Acad Affairs/Provost .... Dr. George W. HYND
10 Exec VP Business Affairs .... Mr. Steven C. OSBORNE
32 Exec VP Student Affairs .... Dr. Victor K. WILSON
30 Exec VP Institutional Advancement .... Mr. George P. WATT, JR.
84 Assoc Vice Pres Enrollment Planning .... Mr. Donald C. BURKARD
26 VP Marketing & Communications .... Mr. Mike HASKINS
31 Assoc Dean Community Relations .... Ms. Evelyn H. NADEL
43 Senior VP Legal Affairs .... Mr. Thomas A. TRIMBOLI
100 Chief of Staff .... Dr. Brian MCGEE
12 Int Director Lowcountry Grad Ctr .... Dr. Sue SOMMER-KRESSE
20 Int Assoc VP Academic Experience .... Dr. Lynne E. FORD
20 Assoc VP Accountability & Accred .... Vacant
22 Director Human Rels/Minority Affs .... Ms. Jo Ann DIAZ
08 Dean Libraries/Acad Info Svcs .... Dr. David J. COHEN
58 Dean Grad School/Asc Prov Research .... Dr. Amy T. MCCANDLESS
20 Senior Vice Provost Academic Affair .... Dr. Beverly E. DIAMOND
20 Assoc Provost for Faculty Affairs .... Dr. Deanna M. CAVENY
35 Dean of Students .... Dr. Jeri O. CABOT
57 Dean School of the Arts .... Ms. Valerie B. MORRIS
50 Dean School of Business .... Dr. Alan T. SHAO
53 Dean School of Education .... Dr. Frances C. WELCH
79 Dean Humanities/Social Science .... Dr. Cynthia J. LOWENTHAL
81 Dean School of Science & Math .... Dr. Michael AUERBACH
79 Dean Languages/Culture & World Affs .... Dr. David J. COHEN
92 Dean Honors College .... Dr. John H. NEWELL, JR.
36 Director of Career Services .... Mr. Denny D. CIGANOVIC
06 Registrar .... Ms. Catherine C. BOYD
15 Director of Human Resources .... Mr. Tom R. CASEY
21 Director of Budgets .... Mr. Samuel B. JONES
51 Director Adult Student Services .... Ms. Dorinda Q. HARMON
29 Dir Institutional Advancement Comm .... Ms. Karen B. JONES
37 Director Financial Asst/Veteran Aff .... Mr. Donald R. GRIGGS
91 Director IT Network & Program Svcs .... Ms. Marcia K. MOORE
27 Chief Information Officer .... Dr. Robert E. CAPE
19 Chief Public Safety .... Chief Paul VERRECCHIA
41 Athletic Director .... Mr. Joe HULL, JR.
23 Director Health Services .... Ms. Jane RENO-MUNRO
39 Dean Residence Life & Housing .... Mr. John T. CAMPBELL
38 Dir Counseling/Substance Abuse Svcs .... Dr. Frank C. BUDD
09 Director of Institutional Research .... Vacant
25 Director of Research/Grants Admin .... Ms. Susan A. RIVALEAU
40 Bookstore Manager .... Ms. Rebecca GRAY
18 Director of Physical Plant .... Mr. John A. CORDRAY, JR.
12 Interim Dir Col of Charleston North .... Dr. Sue SOMMER-KRESSE
104 Director Intl Education & Programs .... Dr. Andrew SOBIESUO
26 Dir College Publications .... Mr. Mark E. BERRY
87 Director Summer Programs .... Mr. Michael C. PHILLIPS
96 Director of Procurement .... Ms. Wendy E. WILLIAMS

Columbia College (C)

1301 Columbia College Drive, Columbia SC 29203-5998
County: Richland FICE Identification: 003430
Unit ID: 217934
Telephone: (803) 786-3012 Carnegie Class: Master's M
FAX Number: (803) 754-3178 Calendar System: Semester
URL: www.columbiasc.edu
Established: 1854 Annual Undergrad Tuition & Fees: $25,050
Enrollment: 1,369 Female
Affiliation or Control: United Methodist IRS Status: 501(c)3
Highest Offering: Master's
Program: Liberal Arts And General; Teacher Preparatory
Accreditation: SC, ART, DANCE, MUS, SW, TED

01 President .... Dr. Caroline B. WHITSON
05 Provost/VP for Academic Affairs .... Dr. Laurie B. HOPKINS
10 Vice President for Finance .... Mr. John D. JONES
84 Vice Pres for Enrollment Management .... Dr. Ronald G. WHITE
46 Exec Director Leadership Institute .... Dr. Linda B. SALANE
30 Vice President for Advancement .... Ms. Barbara E. PARKS
32 Dean Student Affairs .... Ms. LaNae R. BRIGGS
29 Exec Director of Alumnae Relations .... Ms. Sara SNELL
11 Director of Administrative Services .... Ms. Virginia A. RICKER
06 Registrar/Dir Institutional Rsrch .... Dr. Scott A. SMITH
08 Dir of Library & Info Tech Services .... Mr. Dan MURPHY
19 Chief of Police .... Chief Howard M. COOK
25 Director of Grants .... Vacant
37 Director of Financial Aid .... Ms. Donna QUICK
36 Director of the Career Center .... Ms. Fiona LOFTON
14 Director of Info Technology .... Mr. Dave MEDEIROS
18 Director of Facilities Management .... Mr. Lowell CUPPS
23 Director of Student Health Services .... Vacant
26 Executive Director Public Relations .... Ms. Rebecca B. MUNNERLYN
41 Director of Athletics .... Ms. Kelly COX
40 Director Bookstore .... Mr. Chris FREEMAN
38 Director Counseling Services .... Ms. Birma GAINOR
04 Executive Assistant to President .... Ms. Donna S. TURNER
07 Director of Admissions .... Ms. Julie A. KING
92 Director Honors Program/Faculty Dev .... Dr. John ZUBIZARRETA

Columbia International University (D)

PO Box 3122, Columbia SC 29230-3122
County: Richland FICE Identification: 003429
Unit ID: 217925
Telephone: (803) 754-4100 Carnegie Class: Master's S
FAX Number: (803) 786-4209 Calendar System: Semester
URL: www.ciu.edu
Established: 1923 Annual Undergrad Tuition & Fees: $17,520
Enrollment: 1,029 Coed
Affiliation or Control: Independent Non-Profit IRS Status: 501(c)3
Highest Offering: Doctorate
Program: Liberal Arts And General; Professional
Accreditation: SC, BI, THEOL

01 President .... Dr. William H. JONES
00 Chancellor .... Dr. George W. MURRAY
05 Senior Vice President/Provost .... Dr. Jim LANPHER
30 Sr Vice Pres Development/Operations .... Mr. D. Keith MARION
84 VP Enrollment Mgmt/Communications .... Mr. Michael BLACKWELL
73 Dean Columbia Biblical Seminary .... Dr. John HARVEY
49 Dean College of Arts and Sciences .... Dr. Bryan BEYER
53 Dean College of Education .... Dr. Milton V. UECKER
88 Dean College of Counselling .... Dr. Harvey PAYNE
104 Dean College Intercultural Studies .... Dr. Michael BARNETT
09 Dir Institutional Research/Assess .... Mr. Jeff MILLER
56 Director of Distance Education .... Mr. Rob MCDOLE
08 Information/Resource Services .... Mrs. Michele BRANCH-FRAPPIER
06 University Registrar .... Mrs. Tammy TURKETT
16 Chief of Personnel .... Mr. Donald E. JONES
29 Director of Alumni .... Dr. Roy KING
32 Dean of Students .... Mr. Rick SWIFT
07 Director University Admissions .... Ms. Sandra RHYNE
14 Director Computer Services .... Mrs. Michele BRANCH-FRAPPIER
18 Director Physical Plant .... Mr. Robert REGISTER
40 Director of Business Services .... Mr. Roger L. TILTON
21 Controller .... Mr. Larry F. HUSS
30 Director Development .... Mr. Frank BEDELL
37 Director Financial Aid .... Ms. Sandra RHYNE
26 Chief Public Relations Officer .... Mrs. Polly SHOEMAKER
88 General Mgr WMHK/WRCM Radio .... Mr. Joseph PAULO
36 Director Student Placement .... Mrs. Stephanie BRYANT

Converse College (E)

580 E Main, Spartanburg SC 29302-0006
County: Spartanburg FICE Identification: 003431
Unit ID: 217961
Telephone: (864) 596-9000 Carnegie Class: Master's M
FAX Number: (864) 596-9158 Calendar System: 4/1/4
URL: www.converse.edu
Established: 1889 Annual Undergrad Tuition & Fees: $27,320
Enrollment: 1,263 Female
Affiliation or Control: Independent Non-Profit IRS Status: 501(c)3
Highest Offering: Beyond Master's But Less Than Doctorate
Program: Liberal Arts And General; Teacher Preparatory; Professional; Business Emphasis
Accreditation: SC, ART, MFCD, MUS, TED

01 President .... Dr. Elizabeth A. FLEMING
05 VP Academic Affs/Dean Sch Human/Sci .... Dr. Jeffrey H. BARKER
10 Vice Pres Finance/Administration .... Mrs. Susan A. STEVENSON
84 Vice Pres Enrollment Management .... Ms. Sally J. HAMMOND
30 Vice President Inst Advancement .... Dr. Robert STEWART
32 Dean of Students .... Dr. Molly DUESTERHAUS
58 Dean Graduate Educ/Special Programs .... Dr. Kathy GOOD
64 Dean School of the Arts .... Mr. Richard HIGGS
08 Librarian .... Mr. Wade WOODWARD
37 Director of Financial Aid .... Mrs. Peggy P. COLLINS
06 Registrar .... Mrs. Mary L. BROWN
15 Human Resources Director .... Mrs. Sandy GORDIN
29 Director of Alumnae .... Ms. Ginger CHURCH
13 Chief Technology Officer .... Mr. John JAMES
36 Director of Career Services .... Ms. Witney FISHER
26 Director of Communications .... Mrs. Beth LANCASTER
04 Admin Assistant to the President .... Mrs. Stacey BREWER
38 Director Student Counseling .... Dr. Carol EPPS
09 Director Institutional Research .... Mrs. Ann M. PLETCHER
07 Director of Admissions .... Ms. April LEWIS
18 Chief Facilities/Physical Plant .... Mr. Hayden HUTCHINGS
35 Director Student Affairs .... Ms. Rhonda MINGO
18 Facilities Planner .... Mr. Mark L. OSINGA

Denmark Technical College (F)

PO Box 327, Denmark SC 29042-0327
County: Bamberg FICE Identification: 005363
Unit ID: 217989
Telephone: (803) 793-5176 Carnegie Class: Assoc/Pub-R-S
FAX Number: (803) 793-5942 Calendar System: Semester
URL: www.denmarktech.edu
Established: 1948 Annual Undergrad Tuition & Fees (In-State): $2,594
Enrollment: 1,033 Coed
Affiliation or Control: State IRS Status: 501(c)3
Highest Offering: Associate Degree
Program: Occupational; 2-Year Principally Bachelor's Creditable
Accreditation: SC, ACBSP, ENGT

01 President .... Dr. Michael M. TOWNSEND, SR.
05 VP Academic Affairs/Student Svcs .... Vacant
09 Vice Pres Inst Research/Plng/Dev .... Dr. Ashok KABISATPATHY
103 Associate VP Economic & Workforce .... Mr. Robert BROWN
16 Human Resources Director .... Ms. Tanika BRYANT
32 Dean of Student Services .... Ms. Avis GATHERS
10 Business Manager .... Mr. Andreas CORLEY
08 Dean of Learning Resources Center .... Ms. Bobbi JONES
13 Information Technology Director .... Mr. Derrick STEWARD
19 Chief of Public Safety .... Mr. Wilbur WALLACE
84 Director of Enrollment Management .... Vacant
25 Director of Grants & Contracts .... Mrs. Teresa MACK
36 Director Career Plng/Placement .... Mr. Jay FIELDS
37 Financial Aid Director .... Mrs. Connie WILLIAMS
20 Dean of Instruction .... Mrs. Shannon WILLIAMS
49 Dean of Arts & Sciences .... Vacant
54 Dean Industrial/Related Technology .... Dr. Ambrish LAVANIA
50 Dean Business/Computer/Related Tech .... Ms. Antonia ROBERTS
26 Director of Mktg & Media Relations .... Mr. Timothy HICKS
07 Director of Advisement .... Ms. Margaree BONNETTE

Erskine College (G)

PO Box 338, 2 Washington Street,
Due West SC 29639-0338
County: Abbeville FICE Identification: 003432
Unit ID: 217998
Telephone: (864) 379-2131 Carnegie Class: Bac/A&S
FAX Number: (864) 379-2167 Calendar System: 4/1/4
URL: www.erskine.edu
Established: 1837 Annual Undergrad Tuition & Fees: $26,475
Enrollment: 811 Coed
Affiliation or Control: Other IRS Status: 501(c)3
Highest Offering: Doctorate
Program: Liberal Arts And General; Professional

Accreditation: SC, TED, THEOL

01 President ... Dr. David A. NORMAN
05 Interim Vice President & Dean ... Dr. N. Bradley CHRISTIE
10 Vice President Finance & Operations . Mr. Gregory W. HASELDEN
32 Vice President Student Services ... Dr. Robyn R. AGNEW
73 Interim VP Theological Seminary ... Dr. Steve D. LOWE
30 Director of Development ... Mr. Wes MCALLISTER
06 Registrar ... Mrs. Charlene M. HAYNES
37 Director of Student Financial Aid ... Mrs. Becky PRESSLEY
08 Librarian ... Mr. John F. KENNERLY
13 Director of Information Technology ... Mr. Robert S. CLARKE, III
09 Director of Institutional Research ... Mrs. Tracy M. SPIRES
41 Athletic Director ... Mr. Mark L. PEELER
42 Chaplain ... Mr. Paul G. PATRICK
21 Controller ... Mr. Christian M. HABEGER
15 Director Human Resources ... Ms. Hope S. HARRISON
19 Director of Public Safety ... Mr. Charles R. ESTEP
40 Interim Manager of Bookstore ... Mr. Christian M. HABEGER
35 Dean of Students ... Dr. S. Bryan RUSH
36 Director Career Services ... Mr. Dustin NEW
26 Chief Communications Officer ... Mr. Cliff L. SMITH
29 Director of Alumni Affairs ... Mr. William L. FERGUSON
44 Interim Director of Sem Development ... Ms. Jane D. GREENE
73 Dean Theological Seminary ... Dr. Robert W. BELL

Florence - Darlington Technical College (A)

PO Box 100548, Florence SC 29501-0548

County: Florence FICE Identification: 003990
Unit ID: 218025
Telephone: (843) 661-8324 Carnegie Class: Assoc/Pub-R-M
FAX Number: (843) 661-8011 Calendar System: Semester
URL: www.fdtc.edu
Established: 1964 Annual Undergrad Tuition & Fees (In-District): $3,456
Enrollment: 5,855 Coed
Affiliation or Control: State/Local IRS Status: 501(c)3
Highest Offering: Associate Degree
Program: Occupational; 2-Year Principally Bachelor's Creditable
Accreditation: SC, ACBSP, ADNUR, DA, DH, MLTAD, RAD, SURGT

01 President ... Dr. Charles W. GOULD
05 Vice President Academic Affairs ... Dr. Dale DOTY
10 Vice President Business & Finance ... Mr. Tim O'DELL
32 Vice President Student Services ... Dr. Shelley FORTIN
30 Vice Pres Institutional Advancement ... Ms. Jill HEIDEN
72 Assoc VP Technical & General Educ ... Ms. Suzanne JENNINGS
76 Assoc VP Health & Sciences ... Dr. Vivian LILLY
13 Assoc Vice Pres Information Tech ... Mr. Bill GRIFFENBERG
15 Director Internal Relations ... Ms. Terry DINGLE
09 Director Institutional Research ... Ms. Melissa MILLER
26 Director Public Relations ... Mr. Edward BETHEA
72 Director Manufacturing/Technology ... Mr. Jack ROACH
06 Registrar ... Ms. Abby VILLAR
37 Director Financial Aid ... Mr. Joseph DURANT
18 Chief Facilities/Physical Plant ... Mr. Harrison FORD, III
40 Director Bookstore ... Mr. Bob GARAND
96 Director of Purchasing ... Ms. Lorena MCLEOD
07 Director of Admissions ... Ms. Elaine HODGES

Forrest Junior College (B)

601 E River Street, Anderson SC 29624-2498

County: Anderson FICE Identification: 004924
Unit ID: 218043
Telephone: (864) 225-7653 Carnegie Class: Assoc/PrivFP
FAX Number: (864) 261-7471 Calendar System: 4/1/4
URL: www.forrestcollege.edu
Established: 1946 Annual Undergrad Tuition & Fees: $9,420
Enrollment: 108 Coed
Affiliation or Control: Proprietary IRS Status: Proprietary
Highest Offering: Associate Degree
Program: Occupational; 2-Year Principally Bachelor's Creditable
Accreditation: ACICS, MAC

00 Chairman Board of Directors ... Dr. John RE
01 President ... Rebecca STOVALL
101 Secy/Treasurer Board of Directors ... Charles PALMER
06 Fin Records Coordinator/Registrar ... Elizabeth FLOYD
32 Admissions/Student Svcs Coord ... Jean T. HOLLOWAY
08 Information Resource Coordinator ... Marian SMARR
76 Allied Health Programs Coordinator ... Sandra CARTER
07 Admissions Rep ... Derrick OWENS

Francis Marion University (C)

PO Box 100547, Florence SC 29501-0547

County: Florence FICE Identification: 009226
Unit ID: 218061
Telephone: (843) 661-1362 Carnegie Class: Master's S
FAX Number: (843) 661-1202 Calendar System: Semester
URL: www.fmarion.edu
Established: 1970 Annual Undergrad Tuition & Fees (In-State): $8,455
Enrollment: 4,032 Coed
Affiliation or Control: State IRS Status: 501(c)3
Highest Offering: Master's
Program: Liberal Arts And General; Teacher Preparatory; Professional
Accreditation: SC, ART, BUS, NUR, TED, THEA

01 President ... Dr. Luther F. CARTER
05 Provost/Dean Col of Liberal Arts ... Dr. Richard N. CHAPMAN
11 Vice President Business Affairs ... Mr. John J. KISPERT
10 Vice President Administration ... Dr. Charlene WAGES
30 Vice President Devel/Exec Dir ... Mr. John P. DOWD
26 VP Public & Community Affairs ... Mr. Darryl L. BRIDGES
84 Assoc Provost For Academic Affiars ... Dr. Peter KING
32 Vice President for Student Affairs ... Mrs. Teresa RAMEY
21 Asst Vice Pres for Accounting ... Mr. M. Augustus MCDILL
88 Asst Vice Pres Financial Services ... Mrs. Brinda A. JONES
08 Dean of the Library ... Mrs. Joyce M. DURANT
20 Asst Provost/Dir Graduate Programs ... Dr. Jeannette MYERS
37 Financial Assistance Director ... Ms. Kimberly M. ELLISOR
41 Athletic Director ... Mr. Murray G. HARTZLER
06 Registrar ... Mrs. H. Elizabeth MCLEAN
38 Director Counseling and Testing ... Dr. Rebecca L. LAWSON
18 Director of Facilities Management ... Mr. Ralph U. DAVIS
36 Director Career Development ... Ms. Dollie J. NEWHOUSE
07 Director of Admissions ... Mrs. Perry T. WILSON
35 Asst Dean of Students ... Ms. R. Daphne CARTER
29 Director of Alumni Affairs ... Mr. Julian M. YOUNG
96 Director of Purchasing ... Mr. Eric L. GARRIS
92 Director of Honors Program ... Dr. Pamela A. ROOKS
27 Chief Information Officer ... Mr. John DIXON

Furman University (D)

3300 Poinsett Highway, Greenville SC 29613-0001

County: Greenville FICE Identification: 003434
Unit ID: 218070
Telephone: (864) 294-2000 Carnegie Class: Bac/A&S
FAX Number: (864) 294-3001 Calendar System: Semester
URL: www.furman.edu
Established: 1826 Annual Undergrad Tuition & Fees: $39,560
Enrollment: 2,944 Coed
Affiliation or Control: Independent Non-Profit IRS Status: 501(c)3
Highest Offering: Master's
Program: Liberal Arts And General; Teacher Preparatory; Professional
Accreditation: SC, MUS, TED

01 President ... Mr. Rodney A. SMOLLA
05 VP Academic Affairs & Dean ... Dr. John S. BECKFORD
10 VP for Finance & Administration ... Ms. Mary Lou MERKT
32 Vice President for Student Life ... Ms. Connie L. CARSON
30 Vice President for Development ... Mr. Michael D. GATCHELL
26 VP Marketing/Public Relations ... Mr. Mark L. KELLY
20 Associate Academic Dean ... Dr. Paula S. GABBERT
06 University Registrar ... Mr. Brad E. BARRON
87 Director Graduate Studies ... Dr. Troy M. TERRY
08 Director Libraries ... Dr. Janis M. BANDELIN
19 Director of Public Safety ... Mr. Robert M. MILLER
45 Director Planning & Inst Research ... Mr. Donald E. PIERCE
37 Assoc Vice Pres of Financial Aid ... Mr. Forrest M. STUART
29 Director of Alumni Association ... Mr. Tom A. TRIPLITT
07 Assoc Vice President of Admissions ... Mr. Brad POCHARD
44 Director of Annual Giving ... Mr. John KEMP
44 Director of Planned Giving ... Mr. Steve PERRY
25 Grants Administrator ... Ms. Judith J. ROMANO
28 Director of Multicultural Affairs ... Ms. Idella G. GLENN
94 Director of Women's Studies ... Dr. Nicholas F. RADEL
15 Asst VP Human Resources/AAO ... Ms. Pamela BARKETT
27 Chief Information Officer ... Mr. Fred MILLER
85 Asst Dean Intl Educ/Study Away ... Dr. Kailash KHANDKE
36 Director Career Services ... Mr. John D. BARKER
11 Asst VP Admin Services ... Dr. Boyd YARBROUGH
18 Asst VP for Facilities Services ... Mr. Jeff P. REDDERSON
51 Director Continuing Education ... Mr. Brad BECHTOLD
41 VP & Director of Athletics ... Dr. Gary E. CLARK
88 Director UG Research & Internships ... Dr. Tim G. FEHLER
88 Director CTEL ... Dr. Jane LOVE
17 Director Student Health Services ... Dr. Paul V. CATALANA
38 Director Counseling Center ... Dr. Stephen DAWES
39 Director University Housing ... Mr. Ronald C. THOMPSON
88 Director Disability Services ... Ms. Gina PARRIS
42 Chaplain ... Dr. Vaughn CROWETIPTON
40 Director Bookstore ... Ms. Jessica ELLIS
04 Assistant to President ... Ms. Cindy ALEXANDER
21 Budget Director ... Ms. Amy BLACKWELL
96 Director of Purchasing ... Ms. Lishan YAU
35 Director Student Activities ... Mr. Scott DERRICK

Golf Academy of America (E)

3268 Waccamaw Boulevard, Myrtle Beach SC 29579-9451

County: Horry Identification: 666490
Unit ID: 434690
Telephone: (800) 342-7342 Carnegie Class: Assoc/PrivFP
FAX Number: (843) 236-4448 Calendar System: Semester
URL: www.golfacademy.edu
Established: 1998 Annual Undergrad Tuition & Fees: $33,824
Enrollment: 366 Coed
Affiliation or Control: Proprietary IRS Status: Proprietary
Highest Offering: Associate Degree
Program: Occupational; Business Emphasis
Accreditation: ACICS

01 President ... Mr. Chris HUNKLER
12 Campus Director ... Mr. James HART, JR.

† Branch campus of Virginia College, Birmingham, AL.

Greenville Technical College (F)

PO Box 5616, Greenville SC 29606-5616

County: Greenville FICE Identification: 003991
Unit ID: 218113
Telephone: (864) 250-8000 Carnegie Class: Assoc/Pub-U-MC
FAX Number: (864) 250-8507 Calendar System: Semester
URL: www.gvltec.edu
Established: 1962 Annual Undergrad Tuition & Fees (In-State): $1,874
Enrollment: 14,886 Coed
Affiliation or Control: State IRS Status: 501(c)3
Highest Offering: Associate Degree
Program: Occupational; 2-Year Principally Bachelor's Creditable; Technical Emphasis
Accreditation: SC, ACBSP, ACFEI, ADNUR, DA, DH, DMS, EMT, ENGT, MAC, MLTAD, OTA, PNUR, PTAA, RAD, SURGT

01 President ... Dr. Keith MILLER
05 Vice President for Education ... Mr. Steven B. VALAND
10 Vice President for Finance ... Mrs. Jacqueline R. DIMAGGIO
32 VP Student/Diversity & Student Affs ... Mr. J. Curtis HARKNESS
88 Vice Pres Corporate and Economic ... Mrs. Cynthia G. EASON
45 VP Institutional Effectiveness ... Mrs. Lauren SIMER

Horry-Georgetown Technical College (G)

2050 Highway 501 E, Conway SC 29526-9521

County: Horry FICE Identification: 004925
Unit ID: 218140
Telephone: (843) 347-3186 Carnegie Class: Assoc/Pub-R-M
FAX Number: (843) 347-4207 Calendar System: Semester
URL: www.hgtc.edu
Established: 1966 Annual Undergrad Tuition & Fees (In-District): $1,765
Enrollment: 7,780 Coed
Affiliation or Control: State/Local IRS Status: 501(c)3
Highest Offering: Associate Degree
Program: Occupational; 2-Year Principally Bachelor's Creditable
Accreditation: SC, ACBSP, ACFEI, ADNUR, DA, DH, DMS, EMT, ENGT, PNUR, PTAA, RAD, SURGT

01 President ... Mr. Neyle WILSON
05 Senior VP for Academic Affairs ... Dr. Marilyn FORE
10 Vice President for Business Affairs ... Mr. Harold HAWLEY
13 VP for Tech/Institutional Planning ... Mr. Ralph SELANDER
103 VP Workforce Devel & Continuing Ed ... Mr. Gregory MITCHELL
84 Asc VP Enrollment Dev/Registration ... Mr. George SWINDOLL
32 Asc VP Student Affs/Campus Life ... Mr. Greg THOMPSON
20 AVP Acad Affs/Dean Academic Support ... Ms. Rene SMITH
49 AVP Acad Affs/Dean Arts & Sciences ... Dr. Shirley BUTLER
15 Assoc VP Human Res/Employee Rel ... Ms. Judy HARDEE
08 AVP/Dean Library/Educ Technology ... Ms. Peggy SMITH
20 AVP Academic Affs/Dean General Inst ... Dr. Philip RENDER
21 AVP Controller/Finance Office ... Ms. Ellen BLACK
12 Provost Georgetown Campus ... Mr. Murray VERNON
26 Chief Public Relations Officer ... Mr. Gregory THOMPSON
18 Superintendent Bulidings & Grounds ... Mr. Kevin BROWN
37 Dir of Financial Aid/Veterans Affs ... Ms. Susan THOMPSON
06 Registrar ... Mr. George SWINDELL
07 Director of Admissions ... Ms. Thyssene FREDERICK
36 Director Career Resource Center ... Ms. April GARNER
38 Director Student Success & Support ... Ms. Melissa BATTEN
09 Dir Institutional Rsrch/Assessment ... Ms. Lori HEAFNER
96 Procurement Manager ... Ms. Diana CECALA

ITT Technical Institute (H)

1628 Browning Road, Suite 180, Columbia SC 29210

County: Greenville Identification: 666162
Unit ID: 450225
Telephone: (803) 216-6000 Carnegie Class: Assoc/PrivFP4
FAX Number: N/A Calendar System: Quarter
URL: www.itt-tech.edu
Established: 2006 Annual Undergrad Tuition & Fees: N/A
Enrollment: 611 Coed
Affiliation or Control: Proprietary IRS Status: Proprietary
Highest Offering: Baccalaureate
Program: Technical Emphasis
Accreditation: ACICS

† Branch campus of ITT Technical Institute, Nashville, TN.

ITT Technical Institute (I)

6 Independence Pointe, Greenville SC 29615-4506

County: Greenville Identification: 666549
Unit ID: 413866
Telephone: (864) 288-0777 Carnegie Class: Spec/Tech
FAX Number: (864) 297-0930 Calendar System: Quarter
URL: www.itt-tech.edu
Established: 1992 Annual Undergrad Tuition & Fees: N/A
Enrollment: 690 Coed
Affiliation or Control: Proprietary IRS Status: Proprietary
Highest Offering: Baccalaureate
Program: Technical Emphasis
Accreditation: ACICS

† Branch campus of ITT Technical Institute, Nashville, TN.

Lander University (J)

320 Stanley Avenue, Greenwood SC 29649-2099

County: Greenwood FICE Identification: 003435
Unit ID: 218229
Telephone: (864) 388-8000 Carnegie Class: Bac/Diverse
FAX Number: (864) 388-8890 Calendar System: Semester
URL: www.lander.edu

Established: 1872 Annual Undergrad Tuition & Fees (In-State): $9,504
Enrollment: 3,060 Coed
Affiliation or Control: State IRS Status: 501(c)3
Highest Offering: Master's
Program: Liberal Arts And General; Teacher Preparatory; Professional; Business Emphasis
Accreditation: SC, ART, BUS, MACTE, MUS, NUR, NURSE, TED

01 President .... Dr. Daniel W. BALL
05 Provost/Vice Pres Academic Affairs .... Dr. Danny L. MCKENZIE
10 Vice Pres Business/Administration .... Mrs. Glenda RIDGELY
32 Vice President for Student Affairs .... Mr. H. Randall BOUKNIGHT
30 Vice President for Univ Advancement .... Mr. Ralph PATTERSON
84 Dean of Enrollment Services .... Vacant
07 Director of Admissions .... Mrs. Jennifer M. MATHIS
08 Librarian .... Mr. David S. MASH
38 Director Counseling .... Ms. Debra J. FRANKS
41 Athletic Director .... Mr. Jefferson J. MAY
15 Director Human Resources .... Ms. Jeannie MCCALLUM
19 Director University Police .... Mr. Ray O. MANLEY
26 Director of Public Information .... Mrs. Megan PRICE
37 Director of Financial Aid .... Mr. Fred HARDIN
36 Director of Career Services .... Vacant
21 Controller .... Mr. Tom COVAR
40 Dir Bookstore/Procurement/Print Svc .... Mrs. Mary W. MCDANIEL
13 Dir Office Inform Tech Services .... Ms. Robin P. LAWRENCE
18 Director Physical Plant/Engr Svcs .... Mr. Jeff S. BEAVER
09 Dir Institutional Rsrch/Registrar .... Mr. Mac KIRKPATRICK
29 Director Alumni Relations .... Ms. Myra SHAFFER

Limestone College (A)

1115 College Drive, Gaffney SC 29340-3799
County: Cherokee FICE Identification: 003436
Unit ID: 218238
Telephone: (864) 489-7151 Carnegie Class: Bac/Diverse
FAX Number: (864) 487-8706 Calendar System: Semester
URL: www.limestone.edu
Established: 1845 Annual Undergrad Tuition & Fees: $20,000
Enrollment: 3,419 Coed
Affiliation or Control: Independent Non-Profit IRS Status: 501(c)3
Highest Offering: Baccalaureate
Program: Liberal Arts And General; Teacher Preparatory; Professional
Accreditation: SC, MUS, SW, TED

01 President .... Dr. Walt R. GRIFFIN
03 Exec Vice Pres/VP Academic Affairs .... Dr. Karen W. GAINEY
10 Vice President Financial Affairs .... Mr. David S. RILLING
30 Vice Pres Institutional Advancement .... Dr. William H. BAKER
84 Vice President Enrollment Services . Mr. Christopher N. PHENICIE
32 Vice President Student Services .... Mr. Robert A. OVERTON
13 Vice Pres Information Technology .... Mr. C. R. HORTON
41 Vice Pres Intercollegiate Athletics .... Mr. Michael H. CERINO
30 Assoc Vice Pres for Development .... Ms. Kelly T. CURTIS
14 Assoc VP Information Technology .... Mr. C. Adam LONG
20 Assoc Vice Pres Academic Affairs .... Dr. Mark A. REGER
45 Assoc Vice Pres Planning/Assessment .... Dr. Bonnie M. WRIGHT
88 Dean of Retention Services .... Dr. Charles J. CUNNING
04 Administrative Asst to President .... Mrs. Nani Lou S. COOPER
106 Dir Extended Campus Internet Pgm .... Mr. C. R. HORTON
56 Dir Extended Campus Classroom Pgm .... Mrs. Patricia L. SOKOLS
06 Registrar .... Ms. Brenda F. WATKINS
37 Director Financial Aid .... Mr. Bobby T. GREER
44 Director of Development .... Ms. Tisha L. THOMPSON
08 Director Library .... Mrs. Lori J. HETRICK
26 Director Communications .... Mr. Eric LAWSON
35 Director Student Services .... Ms. Jessica D. GOINS
36 Director Career Services .... Ms. Ileka L. LEAKS
90 Director Network Services .... Dr. Scott D. BERRY
18 Director Physical Plant .... Mr. R. Lynn LAWHON
09 Director Institutional Research .... Mr. Franklin L. MITCHELL
92 Director Academic Honors Program .... Dr. Thomas J. THOMSON
83 Assoc Dean/Director Social Work .... Mr. Jackie A. PUCKETT
19 Chief of Public Safety .... Mr. Richard E. SIMMONS
21 Controller .... Mr. L. Wayde DAWSON
23 Campus Nurse .... Mrs. Sandy B. GREEN
44 Director Advancement Services .... Mrs. Brandi P. HARTMAN
20 Director of Academic Advising .... Ms. Brenda F. WATKINS
29 Director Alumni/Parent Programs .... Mr. Kristopher C. BARNHILL
88 Dir Christian Ed/Leadership Program .... Rev. J. Ron SINGLETON
88 Director of Food Services .... Mr. Geoffrey W. ELKINS
88 Director of Sports Information .... Mr. Joshua J. DARLING
88 Assoc Business Manager .... Mr. Franklin L. MITCHELL
42 College Chaplain .... Rev. J. Ron SINGLETON
88 Dir Pgm for Alternative Lrng Styles .... Ms. Karen W. KEARSE
53 Director Teacher Education .... Dr. Shelly A. MEYERS
15 Dir Human Resources/AAEEO Officer .... Ms. Sharon D. HAMMONDS
88 Assoc Dir Extended Internet Pgm .... Ms. Diana L. BEDENBAUGH
40 Campus Store Manager .... Mrs. Patti H. MCCRAW
38 College Counselor .... Mrs. Mary B. CAMPBELL
107 Chair Div of Professional Studies .... Dr. Paul R. LEFRANCOIS
88 Chair Div of Natural Sciences .... Mr. Brian F. AMELING
49 Chair Div of Arts & Letters .... Dr. Gena E. POOVEY
83 Chair Div Social & Behav Sciences .... Dr. Betsy A. WITT

Lutheran Theological Southern Seminary (B)

4201 N Main Street, Columbia SC 29203-5898
County: Richland FICE Identification: 003437
Unit ID: 218265
Telephone: (803) 786-5150 Carnegie Class: Spec/Faith
FAX Number: (803) 786-6499 Calendar System: Semester
URL: www.ltss.edu
Established: 1830 Annual Graduate Tuition & Fees: $14,760
Enrollment: 152 Coed
Affiliation or Control: Evangelical Lutheran Church In America
IRS Status: 501(c)3
Highest Offering: Master's; No Undergraduates
Program: Professional; Religious Emphasis
Accreditation: THEOL

01 President .... Rev Dr. Marcus J. MILLER
05 Vice Pres Academic Affairs/Dean .... Rev Dr. Virginia C. BARFIELD
10 Dir of Administration and Finance .... Mr. Andrew D. SMITH
30 Vice President Seminary Development .... Mr. Ron WALRATH
08 Librarian .... Dr. Lynn A. FEIDER
06 Registrar/Financial Aid Director .... Dr. Virginia C. BARFIELD
27 Director Communications .... Mr. Andrew BOOZER
07 Director Admissions .... Ms. Jenny TOMALKA
44 Director Seminary Advancement .... Vacant

Medical University of South Carolina (C)

179 Ashley Avenue, Charleston SC 29425
County: Charleston FICE Identification: 003438
Unit ID: 218335
Telephone: (843) 792-2300 Carnegie Class: Spec/Med
FAX Number: N/A Calendar System: Semester
URL: www.musc.edu
Established: 1824 Annual Undergrad Tuition & Fees (In-State): $14,500
Enrollment: 2,556 Coed
Affiliation or Control: State IRS Status: Exempt
Highest Offering: Doctorate
Program: Professional
Accreditation: SC, ANEST, ARCPA, DENT, DIETI, HSA, HT, IPSY, MED, NURSE, OT, PERF, PHAR, PTA

01 President .... Dr. Raymond S. GREENBERG
100 Chief of Staff .... Dr. Sabra C. SLAUGHTER
05 VP Acad Affairs & Provost .... Dr. Mark S. SOTHMANN
17 VP Med Affairs & Dean Col of Med .... Dr. Etta D. PISANO
10 Vice President Finance & Admin .... Ms. Lisa P. MONTGOMERY
30 Vice President Development .... Mr. William J. FISHER
20 Assoc Prov Education/Student Life .... Dr. Darlene L. SHAW
46 Associate Provost Research .... Dr. Stephen M. LANIER
52 Dean of Dental Medicine .... Dr. John J. SANDERS
76 Interim Dean of Health Professions .... Dr. Lisa SALADIN
58 Dean of Graduate Studies .... Dr. Perry V. HALUSHKA
66 Dean of Nursing .... Dr. Gail W. STUART
67 Exec Dean SC College of Pharmacy .... Dr. Joseph T. DIPIRO
67 Int Campus Dean SC Col of Pharmacy .... Dr. Philip D. HALL
88 Exec Dir SC Area Hlth Ed Consortium .... Dr. David R. GARR
17 Exec Director Medical Center .... Mr. W. Stuart SMITH
08 Director of Libraries .... Dr. Thomas G. BASLER
84 Director Enrollment Management .... Mr. George W. OHLANDT
28 Exec Director Student Programs .... Dr. Willette S. BURNHAM
43 General Counsel .... Mr. Joseph C. GOOD
26 Director Public Relations .... Dr. Sarah KING
13 Chief Information Officer .... Dr. Frank C. CLARK
22 Dir Affirm Act/Equal Opportunity .... Mr. Wallace T. BONAPARTE
07 Director of Admissions .... Ms. Lyla HUDSON
18 Chief Facilities/Physical Plant .... Mr. John MALMROSE
06 Registrar .... Ms. Sandra L. MORRIS
15 Director Personnel Services .... Ms. Susan H. CARULLO
38 Director Student Counseling .... Dr. Alice Q. LIBET
29 Director Alumni Affairs .... Ms. Jean M. GROOMS
37 Director Student Financial Aid .... Dr. Cecile E. KAMATH
96 Director of Purchasing .... Ms. Betty SANDIFER

Midlands Technical College (D)

PO Box 2408, Columbia SC 29202-2408
County: Richland FICE Identification: 003993
Unit ID: 218353
Telephone: (803) 738-8324 Carnegie Class: Assoc/Pub-U-MC
FAX Number: (803) 738-7784 Calendar System: Semester
URL: www.midlandstech.edu
Established: 1974 Annual Undergrad Tuition & Fees (In-District): $3,906
Enrollment: 12,078 Coed
Affiliation or Control: State/Local IRS Status: 501(c)3
Highest Offering: Associate Degree
Program: Occupational; 2-Year Principally Bachelor's Creditable
Accreditation: SC, ACBSP, ADNUR, DA, DH, ENGT, MAC, MLTAD, NMT, PNUR, PTAA, RAD, SURGT

01 President .... Dr. Marshall Sonny WHITE
04 Exec Assistant to the President .... Ms. Nancy PEDERSEN
05 Vice President Academic Affairs .... Dr. Ronald DRAYTON
10 Sr Vice Pres of Business Affairs .... Dr. Ronald RHAMES
49 Assoc Vice Pres Arts & Sciences .... Dr. Diane CARR
32 Vice Pres Student Development Svcs .... Ms. Sandi OLIVER
30 Vice President for Advancement .... Ms. Starnell BATES
51 VP Economic Devel & Continuing Educ .... Dr. Barrie KIRK
21 Assoc Vice Pres for Business Affs .... Ms. Debbie WALKER
88 AVP SDS: Trio Cmty Support Pgms .... Ms. Mary HOLLOWAY
15 Director of Human Resources .... Ms. Crystal ROOKARD
06 Registrar .... Ms. Susan HOUCK
13 Director Information Resource Mgmt .... Mr. Tony HOUGH
25 Director of Resource Development .... Ms. Alice APPLEBY
37 Director of Student Financial Aid .... Mrs. Angela WILLIAMS
08 Interim Director of Library .... Ms. Florence MAYES
09 Dir Assessment/Research/Planning .... Ms. Dorcas A. KITCHINGS
18 Director of Operations .... Mr. Craig E. HESS
35 Director of Campus Life .... Mr. Hart HAYDEN
31 Director of Auxiliary Services .... Mr. Stanley BOLTON
38 Director of Counseling .... Mr. Phil MORRIS
50 Dept Chair of Business Department .... Mr. Melvin HAWKINS, JR.
54 Director of Engineering Tech .... Dr. Clint CHANDLER
76 Director of Health Science Dept .... Ms. Martha HANKS
07 Director of Admissions .... Ms. Sylvia LITTLEJOHN
27 Director of Public Information .... Mr. Todd GAVIN
96 Director of Purchasing .... Ms. Rochelle DANIELS
36 Director Student Employment Service .... Ms. Sarah TRICE
14 Coordinator of Programming Services .... Mr. Carl CARRAWAY
44 Director of Development .... Mr. Tom SCHLICTMAN

Miller-Motte Technical College (E)

8085 Rivers Avenue, Suite E, North Charleston SC 29406
County: Charleston Identification: 666256
Unit ID: 441025
Telephone: (843) 574-0101 Carnegie Class: Assoc/PrivFP
FAX Number: (843) 266-3424 Calendar System: Semester
URL: www.miller-motte.edu
Established: 1916 Annual Undergrad Tuition & Fees: $14,800
Enrollment: 871 Coed
Affiliation or Control: Proprietary IRS Status: Proprietary
Highest Offering: Associate Degree
Program: Occupational
Accreditation: ACICS, MAC, SURGT

01 Director of Branch Campus .... Mr. David SESSOMS

† Branch campus of Miller-Motte Technical College, Clarksville, TN.

Morris College (F)

100 W College Street, Sumter SC 29150-3599
County: Sumter FICE Identification: 003439
Unit ID: 218399
Telephone: (803) 934-3200 Carnegie Class: Bac/Diverse
FAX Number: (803) 773-3687 Calendar System: Semester
URL: www.morris.edu
Established: 1908 Annual Undergrad Tuition & Fees: $10,530
Enrollment: 1,048 Coed
Affiliation or Control: Baptist IRS Status: 501(c)3
Highest Offering: Baccalaureate
Program: Liberal Arts And General; Teacher Preparatory
Accreditation: SC, ACBSP, TED

01 President .... Dr. Luns C. RICHARDSON
05 Academic Dean .... Dr. Leroy STAGGERS
10 Director of Business Affairs .... Mr. Robert EAVES
86 Director Planning/Govt Relations .... Mrs. Dorothy S. CHEAGLE
32 Interim Dean Student Affairs .... Rev. Eliza E. BLACK
15 Personnel Officer .... Mr. Roy GRAHAM
42 College Minister .... Rev. Charles M. PEE
07 Director Admissions & Records .... Ms. Deborah C. CALHOUN
08 Director Learning Resources Ctr .... Mrs. Janet S. CLAYTON
37 Director of Financial Aid .... Mrs. Sandra S. GIBSON
13 Director MIS/Computer Center .... Mr. Rodney JOHNSON
36 Director Career Services Center .... Ms. Margaret A. BAILEY
09 Director of Assessment .... Vacant
29 Alumni Affairs Officer .... Mrs. Altoya A. FELDER-DEAS
38 Director Counseling & Testing Ctr .... Dr. Lula J. GARY
39 Director Residential Life .... Mr. Jerome SMITH
23 Director of Health Services .... Mrs. Johnell ROGERS
41 Director of Athletics .... Mr. Clarence M. HOUCK
26 Director Public Relations .... Ms. Nicole WILLIAMS
30 Director Inst Advanc/Church Rels .... Rev. Melvin MACK
96 Director of Purchasing .... Mr. Robert EAVES
97 Director of Freshmen Studies .... Dr. Reginald A. BESS
92 Director of Honors Program .... Dr. Joseph K. POPOOLA
06 Registrar .... Ms. Deborah C. CALHOUN
18 Chief Facilities/Physical Plant .... Mr. Roy GRAHAM
20 Associate Academic Officer .... Ms. Kay M. RHOADS
21 Associate Business Officer .... Vacant
40 Bookstore Manager .... Ms. Jeanette MOSES-HOLMES
35 Coordinator Student Activities .... Mr. Alston FREEMAN
19 Coordinator Security Services .... Ms. Lucille W. WILLIAMS

Newberry College (G)

2100 College, Newberry SC 29108-2126
County: Newberry FICE Identification: 003440
Unit ID: 218414
Telephone: (800) 845-4955 Carnegie Class: Bac/Diverse
FAX Number: (803) 321-5627 Calendar System: Semester
URL: www.newberry.edu
Established: 1856 Annual Undergrad Tuition & Fees: $22,925
Enrollment: 1,112 Coed
Affiliation or Control: Evangelical Lutheran Church In America
IRS Status: 501(c)3
Highest Offering: Baccalaureate
Program: Liberal Arts And General; Teacher Preparatory
Accreditation: SC, MUS, NURSE, TED

01 President .... Dr. Venard S. KOERWER
05 Interim VP for Academic Affairs .... Dr. Timothy G. ELSTON
10 CFO & Executive VP for Admin Affs .... Dr. Steven FELD
11 Sr VP for Operations & Campus Plng .... Mr. Dexter ODOM
84 Acting Dir of Enroll Management .... Ms. Sheila WENDELN
32 Dean of Students .... Ms. Kay BANKS
30 Sr VP for Inst Advance & Athletics .... Mr. Brad EDWARDS

41 Director of Athletics ... Ms. Robin MULLER
15 Director of Human Resources ... Mrs. Debbie L. PEAKE
09 Exec Dir of Inst Effectiveness ... Dr. Don W. JOHNSON-TAYLOR
06 Registrar ... Mrs. Carol A. BICKLEY
04 Exec Assistant to the President ... Ms. Joanne BOST
29 Director of Alumni Relations ... Rev. John D. DERRICK
08 Librarian ... Mr. Larry E. ELLIS
18 Director of Facilities ... Mr. Fred ERRIGO
26 Director of Public Relations ... Ms. Sharon LACKEY
42 Chaplain ... Rev. Ernie WORMAN
21 Director of Accounting ... Mrs. Landee BUZHARDT
38 Director of Wellness Services ... Mrs. Martha DORRELL
37 Director Student Financial Aid ... Ms. Missy LUTZ

North Greenville University (A)

PO Box 1892, Tigerville SC 29688-1892
County: Greenville FICE Identification: 003441
Unit ID: 218441
Telephone: (864) 977-7000 Carnegie Class: Bac/Diverse
FAX Number: (864) 977-7021 Calendar System: Semester
URL: www.ngu.edu
Established: 1892 Annual Undergrad Tuition & Fees: $131,396
Enrollment: 2,318 Coed
Affiliation or Control: Southern Baptist IRS Status: 501(c)3
Highest Offering: Doctorate
Program: Liberal Arts And General; Religious Emphasis
Accreditation: SC, MUS, TED

01 President/CEO ... Dr. James B. EPTING
04 Admin Assistant for President ... Ms. Elise STYLES
05 Vice President Academics ... Dr. Randall PANNELL
32 Vice President Student Services ... Dr. Tony BEAM
58 Vice Pres/Dean Graduate Studies ... Dr. J. Samuel ISGETT
10 Vice President Business Affairs ... Ms. Michelle L. SABOU
07 VP Admissions/Financial Planning ... Ms. Keli SEWELL
30 Vice President Advancement ... Mr. Alex MILLER
88 Vice Pres Denominational Relations ... Rev. Mayson EASTERLING
42 Vice President Campus Ministries ... Dr. Steve CROUSE
44 VP Crusader Club/Corp Found Giving ... Mr. J. Wayne LANDRITH
45 Director Academic Plng & Assessment ... Mr. Paul GARRETT
35 Director Student Services ... Mr. Billy WATSON
09 Director of Institutional Research ... Dr. George A. HOPSON
06 Registrar ... Ms. Pam FARMER
18 Director of College Properties ... Mr. Larry BARNWELL
41 Athletic Director ... Ms. Jan MCDONALD
34 Director Residential Living Women ... Ms. Lorry GREEN
33 Director Residential Living Men ... Mr. Donald LILLY
08 Director Learning Center ... Ms. Carla MCMAHAN
19 Director Public Safety ... Mr. Rick MORRIS
88 Dean of Graduate Enrollment ... Mrs. Tawana SCOTT
26 Director Public Rels/Stewardship ... Mr. LaVerne B. HOWELL
29 Director Alumni Affairs/Annual Fund ... Mr. Jason ROSS
15 Human Resource Manager ... Mrs. Lindi FOWLER
40 Bookstore Manager ... Mrs. Cindy COWAN
38 Personal Counselor ... Dr. Bill MCMANUS
36 Career Services Coordinator ... Ms. Lisa SNYDER
23 Director Health Services ... Ms. Kathy BAILEY
30 Executive Director Development ... Rev. Joe F. HAYES
14 Director Computer Services ... Mr. Paul GARRETT
37 Financial Aid Director ... Mr. Michael JORDAN
53 Dean Education ... Dr. Robin JOHNSON
79 Dean Humanities ... Dr. Cathy SEPKO
57 Dean Fine Arts ... Dr. Jacquelyn H. GRIFFIN
81 Dean Sciences ... Dr. Tom ALLEN
73 Dean Christian Studies ... Dr. Walter JOHNSON
50 Dean Business ... Dr. Ralph JOHNSON

Northeastern Technical College (B)

1201 Chesterfield Hwy, Cheraw SC 29520
County: Chesterfield FICE Identification: 007602
Unit ID: 217837
Telephone: (843) 921-6900 Carnegie Class: Assoc/Pub-R-S
FAX Number: (843) 537-6148 Calendar System: Semester
URL: www.netc.edu
Established: 1969 Annual Undergrad Tuition & Fees (In-State): $4,968
Enrollment: 1,221 Coed
Affiliation or Control: State IRS Status: 501(c)3
Highest Offering: Associate Degree
Program: Occupational; 2-Year Principally Bachelor's Creditable
Accreditation: SC

01 President ... Dr. Ron BARTLEY
05 Vice Pres Instruction/Student Svcs ... Dr. Forest MAHAN
10 Vice Pres Administration & Finance ... Mrs. Debbie Q. CHEEK
30 Director for Inst Advancement ... Mr. Atticus SIMPSON
15 Director for Human Resources ... Mrs. Donna CHAVIS

Orangeburg-Calhoun Technical College (C)

3250 Saint Matthews Road, Orangeburg SC 29118-8299
County: Orangeburg FICE Identification: 006815
Unit ID: 218487
Telephone: (803) 536-0311 Carnegie Class: Assoc/Pub-R-M
FAX Number: (803) 535-1388 Calendar System: Semester
URL: www.octech.edu
Established: 1966 Annual Undergrad Tuition & Fees (In-State): $3,554
Enrollment: 2,773 Coed
Affiliation or Control: State IRS Status: 501(c)3
Highest Offering: Associate Degree
Program: Occupational; 2-Year Principally Bachelor's Creditable
Accreditation: SC, ACBSP, ADNUR, ENGT, MAC, PNUR, RAD

01 President ... Dr. Walt TOBIN, JR.
10 Vice President Business Affairs ... Mrs. Henrietta C. GUTHRIE
32 Vice President of Student Services ... Mrs. Barbara M. FELDER
20 Associate Vice President ... Mrs. Donna ELMORE
11 Dean of Administration ... Mr. Mike HAMMOND
46 Dean Planning/Research/Development ... Ms. Faith MCCURRY
36 Dean Career Training/Development ... Mrs. Rebecca BATTLE-BRYANT
13 Director Information Technology ... Mr. Gary A. FOLEY
62 Dean Learning Resource Center ... Mrs. Harris MURRAY
18 Chief Facilities/Physical Plant ... Mr. James S. BRYANT, III
38 Student Counseling/Placement ... Vacant
37 Director Student Financial Aid ... Mr. Chris DOOLEY
08 Director Library Services ... Mrs. Harris MURRAY
06 Registrar ... Vacant
07 Director of Recruiting ... Ms. Semetta QUICK
19 Chief of Safety/Security ... Mr. Douglas STOKES
09 Dir Acad Spprt/Institutional Effect ... Mr. Cleveland WILSON
21 Business Manager ... Mr. Kim R. HUFF
15 Human Resource Manager ... Ms. Rose BOZARD
96 Procurement Manager ... Mrs. Scarlet GEDDINGS

Piedmont Technical College (D)

620 N. Emerald Road, PO Box 1467,
Greenwood SC 29648-1467
County: Greenwood FICE Identification: 003992
Unit ID: 218520
Telephone: (864) 941-8324 Carnegie Class: Assoc/Pub-R-M
FAX Number: (864) 941-8555 Calendar System: Semester
URL: www.ptc.edu
Established: 1966 Annual Undergrad Tuition & Fees (In-District): $3,423
Enrollment: 5,703 Coed
Affiliation or Control: State/Local IRS Status: 501(c)3
Highest Offering: Associate Degree
Program: Occupational; 2-Year Principally Bachelor's Creditable
Accreditation: SC, ACBSP, ADNUR, ENGT, FUSER, MAC, RAD, SURGT

01 President ... Dr. L. Rayburn BROOKS
10 Vice Pres Business & Finance ... Ms. Paige CHILDS
05 Vice President Educational Affairs ... Dr. Susan TIMMONS
32 Vice Pres Student Devel/Mrktng Div ... Ms. Becky R. MCINTOSH
51 Assoc Vice Pres Cont Educ/Econ Dev ... Mr. Rusty DENNING
24 Assoc VP Instructional Technology ... Dr. Joel GRIFFIN
12 Dean County Centers ... Dr. Jennifer WILBANKS
76 Dean Health Sciences ... Mr. Jerry ALEWINE
54 Dean Engr/Industrial Technologies ... Mr. Keith LASURE
49 Dean Arts & Sciences/Trans Studies ... Ms. Donna FOSTER
66 Dean Nursing Education ... Ms. Rosalie STEVENSON
35 Dean Student Services ... Mr. J. Andrew OMUNDSON
09 Director of Inst Effectiveness ... Ms. Zeolean F. KINARD
26 Director Marketing/Public Relations ... Mr. Joshua BLACK
88 Director College Outreach ... Mr. Steve B. COLEMAN
18 Director Facilities/Management ... Mr. S. Dale WILSON
102 Foundation Exec Dir/Alumni Affairs ... Ms. Fran K. WILEY
08 Librarian ... Mr. Daniel MEREDITH
19 Director Public Safety ... Mr. Terry LEDFORD
36 Assoc Dean Student Services ... Mr. David R. ROSENBAUM
37 Director of Financial Aid ... Ms. Deborah H. WILLIAMS
06 Registrar ... Ms. Tanisha LATIMER
21 Controller ... Ms. Paige CHILDS
15 Human Resource Manager ... Ms. Debbie THARPE
21 Manager Business Office ... Ms. Crystal PITTMAN

Presbyterian College (E)

503 S Broad Street, Clinton SC 29325-2865
County: Laurens FICE Identification: 003445
Unit ID: 218539
Telephone: (864) 833-2820 Carnegie Class: Bac/A&S
FAX Number: (864) 833-8481 Calendar System: Semester
URL: www.presby.edu
Established: 1880 Annual Undergrad Tuition & Fees: $31,280
Enrollment: 1,235 Coed
Affiliation or Control: Presbyterian Church (U.S.A.) IRS Status: 501(c)3
Highest Offering: Doctorate
Program: Liberal Arts And General; Teacher Preparatory
Accreditation: SC, MUS, @PHAR, TED

01 President ... Dr. John V. GRIFFITH
100 Chief of Staff ... Mr. Robert E. STATON, JR.
04 Assistant to the President ... Ms. Rosanne R. BRASWELL
05 Provost ... Dr. Anita O. GUSTAFSON
10 Exec VP Finance/Administration ... Mr. Morris M. GALLOWAY, JR.
30 Vice President for Advancement ... Mr. Raymond CARNLEY
84 VP of Enrollment/Communications ... Ms. Deborah THOMPSON
67 Dean School of Pharmacy ... Dr. Richard E. STULL
13 Dean Information Technology ... Vacant
35 Dean of Student Life ... Vacant
20 Dean Academic Programs ... Dr. Michael A. NELSON
42 Dean of Religious Life ... Dr. Jeri Parris PERKINS
32 Interim Dean of Campus Life ... Ms. Linda C. JAMEISON
30 Exec Dir Foundation/Corporate Dev ... Ms. M. Genevra KELLY
27 Exec Director of Communications ... Vacant
41 Exec Director of Athletics ... Mr. Brian P. REESE
29 Director Alumni Assn/Parents Pgm ... Mr. Comer H. RANDALL
08 Librarian ... Mr. David W. CHATHAM
38 Director Counseling Services ... Mrs. Susan C. GENTRY-WRIGHT
37 Director of Financial Aid ... Mr. Jeffery S. HOLLIDAY
21 Controller ... Mrs. Karen R. MATTISON
19 Director of Campus Police ... Mr. Lawrence P. MULHALL
06 Registrar ... Mr. W. Keith KARRIKER
16 Director Human Resources ... Ms. Barbara H. FAYAD
09 Director of Institutional Research ... Dr. Norman B. BRYAN, JR.
18 Exec Director Business Operations ... Mr. L. David WALKER

Sherman College of Chiropractic (F)

PO Box 1452, Spartanburg SC 29304-1452
County: Spartanburg FICE Identification: 020637
Unit ID: 218751
Telephone: (864) 578-8770 Carnegie Class: Spec/Health
FAX Number: (864) 599-7145 Calendar System: Quarter
URL: www.sherman.edu
Established: 1973 Annual Graduate Tuition & Fees: $25,780
Enrollment: 184 Coed
Affiliation or Control: Independent Non-Profit IRS Status: 501(c)3
Highest Offering: Doctorate; No Undergraduates
Program: Professional
Accreditation: SC, CHIRO

01 President ... Dr. Jon C. SCHWARTZBAUER
05 Vice Pres for Academic Affairs ... Dr. Robert IRWIN
84 Vice Pres for Enrollment Services ... Mrs. Kelley ASHCRAFT
10 Vice Pres for Business & Finance ... Mr. Tim D. REVELS
32 Dean of Student Services ... Mrs. LaShanda HUTTO-HARRIS
29 Dir Alumni Rels/Instl Advancement ... Ms. Marggi ROLDAN
06 Registrar ... Ms. Melody SABIN
08 Librarian ... Mrs. Crissy LEWIS
37 Financial Aid Director ... Mrs. Kathy WILSON
45 Director of Planning Assessment ... Vacant

South Carolina State University (G)

300 College Street, NE, Orangeburg SC 29117-0001
County: Orangeburg FICE Identification: 003446
Unit ID: 218733
Telephone: (803) 536-7000 Carnegie Class: DRU
FAX Number: (803) 533-3622 Calendar System: Semester
URL: www.scsu.edu
Established: 1896 Annual Undergrad Tuition & Fees (In-State): $9,198
Enrollment: 4,362 Coed
Affiliation or Control: State IRS Status: 501(c)3
Highest Offering: Doctorate
Program: Liberal Arts And General; Teacher Preparatory; Professional; Business Emphasis
Accreditation: SC, AAFCS, ART, BUS, CACREP, CORE, CS, DIETD, ENG, ENGT, MUS, NURSE, SP, SW, TED

01 President ... Dr. George E. COOPER
04 Exec Asst to the President ... Ms. Shondra N. ABRAHAM
05 Vice President Academic Affairs ... Dr. Joyce A. BLACKWELL
10 Vice Pres Fiscal Affs/Mgt Info Sys ... Vacant
32 Vice President Student Affairs ... Dr. Charles SMITH
30 Vice Pres Inst Advancement ... Mr. Anthony HOLLOMAN
46 VP Research/EconDevel/Pub Svc ... Dr. G Dale WESSON
100 Chief of Staff & Gen Counsel ... Mr. Edwin D. GIVENS
20 Assoc Vice Pres Academic Affs ... Dr. John JONES
20 Int Assoc Vice Pres Academic Affs ... Dr. Christine R. BOONE
44 Asst Vice President Development ... Dr. John BERRY
21 Asst Vice Pres Fiscal Affs/Mgt Info ... Mr. Joe PEARMAN
35 Asst Vice Pres Student Affairs ... Dr. Valarie FIELDS
84 Asst VP Enrollment Management ... Mr. Antonio BOYLE
29 Asst Vice Pres Alumni Relations ... Vacant
46 Int Asst VP Sponsored Programs ... Mr. Elbert R. MALONE
72 Dean Col Sci/Math/Engineering Tech ... Dr. Kenneth D. LEWIS
53 Dean Col Educ/Humanities/Soc Sci ... Dr. Leonard A. MCINTYRE
58 Dean School of Graduate Studies ... Dr. Thomas E. THOMPSON
50 Dean Col Business/Applied Prof Sci ... Dr. Robert T. BARRETT
08 Dean Library & Information Services ... Ms. Mary L. SMALLS
11 Exec Dir Admin & Cont Improvement ... Vacant
88 Exec Dir Student Success Retention ... Dr. Carl E. JONES
09 Exec Dir Institutional Effectivenes ... Dr. Rita J. TEAL
45 Exec Director of Planning ... Ms. Joyce GREEN
88 Asst Exec Dir Stdnt Success Retent ... Mr. Terrence M. CUMMINGS
06 Registrar ... Mrs. Annie R. BELTON
07 Director Admissions/Recruitment ... Mr. Antonio BOYLE
13 Dir Univ Computing/Info Tech Svcs ... Dr. James L. MYERS
37 Director Financial Aid to Students ... Mrs. Sandra DAVIS
38 Director Counsel/Hlth/Psycmtrc Svcs ... Dr. Cherilyn Y. TAYLOR
21 Controller ... Mr. Ernie M. TORRES
09 Director Institutional Research ... Ms. Betty R. BOATWRIGHT
26 Director Univ Relations & Mktg ... Ms. Erica PRIOLEAU-TAYLOR
36 Int Director of Career Placement ... Mr. Joseph THOMAS
15 Director Human Resource Mgmt ... Ms. Anna D. HAIGLER
41 Director Athletics ... Mrs. Charlene M. JOHNSON
18 Director of Facilities Mgmt ... Mr. Charles ALEXANDER
96 Director Procurement Services ... Mrs. Mary L. SIMS
39 Asst Director of Residential Life ... Ms. Jennifer TOWNSEND-GAMBLE
19 Chief of Campus Police ... Mr. Gregory HARRIS
92 Dir Honors Exchange/Intl Program ... Dr. Harriet A. ROLAND
88 Director Sports Information ... Mr. William P. HAMILTON
35 Director of Student Life ... Mr. Terrance ALDRIDGE
88 Int Director of Internal Audit ... Mr. Kelvin WASHINGTON
25 Dir Grants & Contract Accounting ... Ms. Mildred L. DANIELS
88 Director of Title III ... Ms. Gloria D. PYLES
88 Director of Staff Development ... Ms. Patricia GIBSON-HAIGLER
28 Director of Multicultural Affairs ... Ms. Carolyn G. FREE
88 Asst Dir Educational Technology Svc ... Dr. Frederick M. EVANS
88 Station Manager WSSB-FM ... Mr. Milton E. MCKISSICK
88 Athletics Compliance Coordinator ... Mr. Robert CHATMAN

South University Columbia Campus (A)

9 Science Court, Columbia SC 29203-6400
County: Richland FICE Identification: 004922
Unit ID: 251312
Telephone: (803) 799-9082 Carnegie Class: Master's S
FAX Number: (803) 935-4382 Calendar System: Quarter
URL: www.southuniversity.edu
Established: 1899 Annual Undergrad Tuition & Fees: $20,380
Enrollment: 1,342 Coed
Affiliation or Control: Proprietary IRS Status: Proprietary
Highest Offering: Master's
Program: Professional; Business Emphasis
Accreditation: &SC, MAC, NURSE

01 President .... Mr. Gregory J. SHIELDS
04 Exec Assistant to the President .... Ms. Missy THOMPSON
05 Dean of Academic Affairs .... Mr. David SHOOP
32 Dean of Student Affairs .... Mr. Jon DRIGGERS
10 Business Officer .... Ms. Tiffany ETHEREDGE
06 Registrar .... Ms. Melinda WILLIAMS
07 Director of Admissions .... Ms. Trisha WADE
08 Librarian .... Mrs. Amanda DIFETERICI
37 Director Student Financial Aid .... Mr. Walt HAVERSAT
40 Director Bookstore .... Mr. Todd POWELL

† Regional accreditation is carried under the parent institution in Savannah, GA.

Southern Wesleyan University (B)

907 Wesleyan Drive, PO Box 1020,
Central SC 29630-1020
County: Pickens FICE Identification: 003422
Unit ID: 217776
Telephone: (864) 644-5000 Carnegie Class: Master's L
FAX Number: (864) 644-5900 Calendar System: Semester
URL: www.swu.edu
Established: 1906 Annual Undergrad Tuition & Fees: $20,550
Enrollment: 1,872 Coed
Affiliation or Control: Wesleyan Church IRS Status: 501(c)3
Highest Offering: Master's
Program: Liberal Arts And General; Teacher Preparatory; Professional
Accreditation: SC, MUS, TED

01 President .... Dr. Todd S. VOSS
04 Assistant to the President .... Vacant
10 Sr VP for Finance & Treasurer .... Mr. Marshall L. ATCHESON
05 Provost .... Dr. Keith IDDINGS
11 VP for Admin & Program Operations .... Dr. Gary CARR
30 Vice President for Development .... Rev. James E. WIGGINS
32 Vice President for Student Life .... Dr. W. Joseph BROCKINTON
49 Dean College of Arts & Sciences .... Dr. Walt SINNAMON
50 Dean School of Business .... Dr. Royce CAINES
53 Dean of School of Education .... Dr. Paul SHOTSBERGER
37 Assoc VP of Student Financial Svcs .... Mr. Jeff DENNIS
37 Director of Financial Aid .... Mr. Kim JENERETTE
13 Director Information Technology .... Mr. Mike PREUSZ
18 Director of Physical Plant .... Mr. Jonathan CATRON
09 Assoc VP for Planning & Assessment .... Dr. Daryl D. COUCH
57 Chair Fine Arts .... Mrs. Jane P. DILL
73 Chair Religion .... Dr. Christina ACCORNERO
79 Chair Humanities .... Dr. Betty MEALY
83 Chair Social Sciences .... Dr. Steven HAYDUK
35 Associate VP for Student Life .... Ms. Mia HORACE
38 Director of Counseling & Health Svc .... Mrs. Carol SINNAMON
29 Exec Dir of Alumni/Constituent Rels .... Mrs. Joy L. BRYANT
07 Dir of Admissions & Enrollment Mgmt .... Mrs. Amanda YOUNG
08 Director of Library Services .... Mr. Robert E. SEARS
41 Athletic Director .... Mr. Chris WILLIAMS
06 Registrar .... Mr. Rock MCCASKILL
26 Director of Communications .... Ms. Janelle E. BEAMER

Spartanburg Community College (C)

I-85 Business, PO Box 4386, Spartanburg SC 29305-4386
County: Spartanburg FICE Identification: 003994
Unit ID: 218830
Telephone: (864) 592-4600 Carnegie Class: Assoc/Pub-U-SC
FAX Number: (864) 592-4642 Calendar System: Semester
URL: www.sccsc.edu
Established: 1963 Annual Undergrad Tuition & Fees (In-State): $3,640
Enrollment: 5,871 Coed
Affiliation or Control: State IRS Status: 501(c)3
Highest Offering: Associate Degree
Program: Occupational; 2-Year Principally Bachelor's Creditable
Accreditation: SC, ACBSP, ACFEI, ADNUR, DA, ENGT, MAC, MLTAD, RAD, SURGT

01 President .... Dr. Para JONES
03 Executive Vice President .... Mr. Henry C. GILES, JR.
05 Vice President Academic Affairs .... Dr. Cheryl COX
45 Vice President for Planning & Info .... Dr. Patricia P. ABELL
32 Vice President for Student Affairs .... Mr. Ron JACKSON
51 Vice Pres Corporate & Community Ed .... Dr. David A. JUST
12 Exec Director Tyger River Campus .... Mrs. Lynn F. DALE
12 Executive Director Cherokee Campus .... Mr. Daryl SMITH
102 Exec Director SCC Foundation .... Mr. Sam HOOK
20 Dean of Instruction .... Dr. Pam HAGAN
08 Dean of Learning Resources .... Mr. Mark ROSEVEARE
46 Dean of Assessment/Cont Improvement .... Ms. Sandy WINKLER
76 Dean Health & Human Services .... Dr. Rita A. MELTON
15 Director of Human Resources .... Mr. Rick TEAL
13 Director Information Technologies .... Mr. Peter C. GALLEN
18 Director of Physical Plant .... Mr. Ron SWITZER
84 Director Enrollment Services .... Mrs. Kathy F. MCKINZIE
09 Director of Institutional Research .... Mr. Jack R. BOURGEOIS
26 Chief Public Relations Officer .... Mrs. Cheri A. HUCKS
29 Director Alumni Relations .... Vacant
38 Director Student Counseling .... Mrs. Phyllis ROGERS
14 Director Computer Center .... Mrs. Tina S. REID
19 Director Security/Safety .... Mr. Andre KERR
96 Director of Procurement .... Mr. Wade SMITH
06 Registrar .... Ms. Celia N. BAUSS
21 Business Manager .... Mr. Cecil L. HUTCHERSON
37 Director of Financial Aid .... Mrs. Nancy T. GARMROTH

Spartanburg Methodist College (D)

1000 Powell Mill Road, Spartanburg SC 29301-5899
County: Spartanburg FICE Identification: 003447
Unit ID: 218821
Telephone: (864) 587-4000 Carnegie Class: Assoc/PrivNFP
FAX Number: (864) 587-4355 Calendar System: Semester
URL: www.smcsc.edu
Established: 1911 Annual Undergrad Tuition & Fees: $13,893
Enrollment: 790 Coed
Affiliation or Control: United Methodist IRS Status: 501(c)3
Highest Offering: Associate Degree
Program: 2-Year Principally Bachelor's Creditable
Accreditation: SC

01 President .... Dr. Colleen P. KEITH
05 Vice President for Academic Affairs .... Dr. Anita K. BOWLES
10 Vice President for Business Affairs .... Mr. Eric MCDONALD
84 Vice Pres for Enrollment Management .... Mr. Daniel L. PHILBECK
30 Vice President for Inst Advancement .... Mr. Bob FUZY
06 Registrar .... Ms. Jill R. JOHNSON
08 Librarian .... Mr. James P. HALLER
04 Admin Assistant to the President .... Ms. Vicki D. KENNEDY
32 Dean of Students .... Mr. Ron LAFFITTE
20 Exec Dir of Academic Services .... Vacant
14 Exec Dir Info Tech/Campus Svcs .... Mr. Bill ROACH
27 Dir Public Information/Webmaster .... Vacant
44 Director of Development .... Mr. Don TATE
37 Director of Financial Aid .... Mrs. Emily STAGGS
38 Director of Student Counseling .... Mr. Pete AYLOR
42 Chaplain/Director of Church Rels .... Rev. Candice Y. SLOAN
41 Athletic Director .... Mr. Tim WALLACE
18 Director Facilities Mgmt/Purchasing .... Mr. Rick JOLLEY
29 Director Alumni Relations .... Mrs. Leah L. PRUITT
15 Dir of Human Resources/College Acct .... Mrs. Jeanette R. DUNN
35 Director of Student Support Svcs .... Ms. Sharon PORTER
44 Director Gift Planning .... Rev. Michael E. BOWERS
19 Chief of Campus Safety .... Ms. Teresa D. FERGUSON
07 Director of Admissions .... Mr. Michael QUEEN
09 Director of Assessment Activities .... Mr. Robert W. ISENHOWER

Technical College of the Lowcountry (E)

921 S Ribaut Road, PO Box 1288,
Beaufort SC 29901-1288
County: Beaufort FICE Identification: 009910
Unit ID: 217712
Telephone: (843) 525-8211 Carnegie Class: Assoc/Pub-R-M
FAX Number: (843) 525-8330 Calendar System: Semester
URL: www.tcl.edu
Established: 1972 Annual Undergrad Tuition & Fees (In-State): $3,540
Enrollment: 2,990 Coed
Affiliation or Control: State IRS Status: 501(c)3
Highest Offering: Associate Degree
Program: Occupational; 2-Year Principally Bachelor's Creditable
Accreditation: SC, ACBSP, ADNUR, COMTA, PNUR, PTAA, RAD, SURGT

01 President .... Dr. Thomas C. LEITZEL
10 Vice President for Finance .... Mr. Hayes WISER
05 Vice President for Academic Affairs .... Dr. Gina MOUNFIELD
30 Vice Pres for Cont Ed/Inst Advance .... Ms. Nancy WEBER
32 Vice President for Student Affairs .... Dr. Matteel JONES
09 Director Research/Planning .... Ms. Camille MYERS
15 Director of Personnel .... Ms. Sonya LYTTLE
20 Interim Dean Instruct Support Svcs .... Ms. Cindy HALSEY
50 Div Dean Business Technologies .... Dr. Kenneth FLICK
49 Div Dean Arts & Sciences .... Dr. Wesla FLETCHER
66 Division Dean Health Sciences .... Ms. Marge SAPP
35 Director of Student Support .... Mr. Rodney ADAMS
14 Director of Computer Center .... Mr. Floyd HENDERSON
84 Director of Enrollment Mgmt .... Ms. Cleo MARTIN
37 Director Financial Aid .... Ms. Cleo MARTIN
45 Director of Inst Effectiveness .... Mr. Floyd WASHBURN
26 Public Relations Director .... Ms. Leigh COPELAND
21 Associate Business Officer .... Ms. Irina GREER
40 Bookstore Director .... Ms. Louise RENNIX
18 Director of Physical Plant .... Mr. Albert BLACKWELL
36 Job Placement Coordinator .... Ms. Melanie GALLION
38 Director Student Activities .... Ms. Ashley FAUBION
96 Director of Purchasing .... Ms. Carol MACK
06 Registrar .... Mr. Brad THOMAS

Tri-County Technical College (F)

PO Box 587, Pendleton SC 29670-0587
County: Anderson FICE Identification: 004926
Unit ID: 218885
Telephone: (864) 646-8361 Carnegie Class: Assoc/Pub-S-SC
FAX Number: (864) 646-1895 Calendar System: Semester
URL: www.tctc.edu
Established: 1962 Annual Undergrad Tuition & Fees (In-District): $3,570
Enrollment: 6,941 Coed
Affiliation or Control: State/Local IRS Status: 501(c)3
Highest Offering: Associate Degree
Program: Occupational; 2-Year Principally Bachelor's Creditable
Accreditation: SC, ACBSP, ADNUR, DA, MAC, MLTAD, PNUR, SURGT

01 President .... Dr. Ronnie L. BOOTH
05 Vice President Academic Affairs .... Dr. Phil J. BUCKHIESTER
10 Vice Pres Administration & Finance .... Mr. Gregg STAPLETON
30 VP Economic & Institutional Advance .... Mr. John LUMMUS
32 Vice President for Student Affairs .... Mr. Dan A. HOLLAND
51 Dean of Continuing Education .... Mr. Rick COTHRAN
84 Dean of Enrollment Management .... Mrs. Amanda BLANTON
88 Dean of Student Development .... Vacant
49 Dean Arts & Sciences Division .... Dr. Gwen OWENS
72 Dean Engineering Technology Div .... Mr. Eugene GRANT
50 Dean Business/Human Services Div .... Mrs. Jackie BLAKLEY
76 Dean Health Education Division .... Dr. Lynn LEWIS
20 Associate VP of Academic Affairs .... Ms. Susan ALLEN
08 Head Librarian .... Ms. Marla ROBERSON
37 Student Financial Aid Director .... Mr. Bill WHITLOCK
13 Director Computer Operations .... Mr. Lee TENNENT
26 Dir Public Relations/Communication .... Mrs. Rebecca W. EIDSON
44 Director of Development .... Mrs. Elisabeth GADD
29 Manager of Donor Relations & Alumni .... Mrs. Courtney WHITE
15 Director of Personnel Services .... Mrs. Sharon COLCOLOUGH
07 Director of Admissions .... Ms. Renae FRAZIER
06 Registrar .... Mr. Scott HARVEY
09 Director of Institutional Research .... Mr. Chris MARINO
18 Chief Facilities/Physical Plant .... Mr. Ken KOPERA
21 Associate Business Officer .... Mrs. Faye ALLEN
96 Director of Purchasing .... Ms. Kristal DOHERTY
41 Athletic Director .... Ms. Angie ABRAHAM
38 Director of Student Life/Counseling .... Ms. Croslena JOHNSON

Trident Technical College (G)

PO Box 118067, Charleston SC 29423-8067
County: Charleston FICE Identification: 004920
Unit ID: 218894
Telephone: (843) 574-6111 Carnegie Class: Assoc/Pub-U-MC
FAX Number: (843) 574-6541 Calendar System: Semester
URL: www.tridenttech.edu
Established: 1964 Annual Undergrad Tuition & Fees (In-District): $3,600
Enrollment: 15,790 Coed
Affiliation or Control: State/Local IRS Status: 501(c)3
Highest Offering: Associate Degree
Program: Occupational; 2-Year Principally Bachelor's Creditable
Accreditation: SC, ACBSP, ACFEI, ADNUR, DA, DH, EMT, MAC, MLTAD, OTA, PNUR, PTAA, RAD

01 President .... Dr. Mary THORNLEY
10 Vice Pres Finance & Administration .... Mr. Scott POELKER
05 Vice President Academic Affairs .... Dr. Patricia ROBERTSON
32 Vice President Student Services .... Dr. Elise DAVIS-MCFARLAND
30 Vice President Advancement .... Ms. Meg HOWLE
51 Vice Pres Continuing Educ/Econ Dev .... Mr. Rew GODOW, JR.
13 Vice Pres Information Technology .... Mr. Bernie STRAUB
45 Assoc VP Planning/Accreditation .... Ms. Suzy BARR
20 Asst Vice Pres Academic Programs .... Ms. Susan NORTON
35 Asst Vice Pres for Student Svcs .... Ms. Lynne ANKERSEN
20 Asst Vice President Instruction .... Mr. Eddie SIMMONS
09 Director Institutional Research .... Ms. Catharine ALMQUIST
16 Director Human Resources .... Ms. DeVetta HUGHES
96 Dir Procurement/Risk Management .... Ms. Carol BELCHER
40 Dir Auxiliary Enterprises/Bookstore .... Ms. Jloundia PINCKNEY
27 Director Marketing .... Ms. Tina AHLEMANN
27 Director Public Info .... Mr. David HANSEN
30 Assistant VP for Advancement .... Ms. Kimberley STURGEON
29 Director Alumni/Donor Relations .... Ms. Dana HALL
44 Dir Planned Giving/Resource Dev .... Mr. Keith RUMRILL
102 Executive Director Foundation .... Ms. Kathleen FORBES
06 Registrar .... Ms. Pamela DROSTE
14 Dir Information Technology Training .... Mr. Joseph GIBSON
36 Director Career Employment Services .... Mr. Brian ALMQUIST
35 Director Student Activities .... Ms. Ann WELTY
07 Director Admissions .... Ms. Clara MARTIN
37 Director Financial Aid .... Ms. Ellen GREEN
81 Dean Science & Mathematics .... Mr. Bill LANDRY
79 Dean Humanities & Social Sciences .... Dr. Tim BROWN
88 Dean The Learning Center .... Ms. Pamela LEONARD-RAY
50 Dean Business Technology .... Ms. Connie JOLLY
76 Dean Allied Health .... Dr. Richard HERNANDEZ
54 Dean Engineering/Industrial Tech .... Ms. Christine LANG
88 Dean Culinary Inst of Charleston .... Mr. Mike SABOE
61 Dean Law-Related Studies .... Mr. John UNGARO
08 Dean Learning Resources .... Ms. Charnette SINGLETON
66 Dean Nursing .... Ms. Muriel HORTON
38 Asst Vice Pres Student Development .... Ms. Pamela BROWN
88 Dean Comm/Family/Child Studies .... Ms. Stephany HEWITT
88 Dean Dis Learn/Broadcast Services .... Dr. Roscoe THORNTHWAITE
84 Dean Enrollment Management .... Mr. John JAMROGOWICZ
75 Dean Aeronautical Studies .... Dr. Barry FRANCO

38 Dir Counseling & Disability Svcs ... Ms. Pam MIDDLETON
12 Director Berkeley Campus ... Mr. Bob WALKER
12 Director Palmer Campus ... Dr. Louester ROBINSON
78 Director Cooperative Education ... Dr. Edna BOROSKI
19 Director Public Safety ... Mr. Lawrence SAVIDGE

University of South Carolina Columbia (A)

Columbia SC 29208-0001
County: Richland FICE Identification: 003448
Unit ID: 218663
Telephone: (803) 777-7000 Carnegie Class: RU/VH
FAX Number: (803) 777-0101 Calendar System: Semester
URL: www.sc.edu
Established: 1801 Annual Undergrad Tuition & Fees (In-State): $4,893
Enrollment: 29,597 Coed
Affiliation or Control: State IRS Status: 501(c)3
Highest Offering: Doctorate
Program: Liberal Arts And General; Teacher Preparatory; Professional
Accreditation: SC, ANEST, ART, BUS, BUSA, CACREP, CEA, CLPSY, CORE, CS, ENG, HSA, IPSY, JOUR, LAW, LIB, MED, MUS, NURSE, PH, PTA, SCPSY, SP, SPAA, SW, TED, THEA

01 President ... Dr. Harris PASTIDES
03 Vice President & CIO ... Dr. William F. HOGUE
05 Exec VP Academic Affs/Provost ... Dr. Michael AMIRIDIS
10 Vice President Finance & Planning ... Mr. Ed WALTON
32 VP Student Affairs/VProv Acad Suppt ... Dr. Dennis A. PRUITT
16 Vice President Human Resources ... Mr. Christopher D. BYRD
30 VP Development & Alumni Relations . Mrs. Michelle DODENHOFF
12 VP/Exec Dean Regional Campuses ... Dr. Chris P. PLYLER
46 VP Research & Grad Education ... Vacant
26 Vice President Communications ... Ms. Luanne M. LAWRENCE
101 Secretary to Board of Trustees ... Mr. Thomas L. STEPP
20 Vice Provost & Dean Undergrad Stds ... Dr. Helen I. DOERPINGHAUS
58 Int Dean Graduate School ... Dr. Timothy MOUSSEAU
84 Asst Vice Provost Enrollment Mgmt ... Mr. Scott VERZYL
08 Dean of Libraries ... Dr. Tom MCNALLY
43 General Counsel ... Mr. Walter H. PARHAM
09 Dir Inst Assessment & Compliance ... Dr. Philip S. MOORE
18 Assoc VP for Facilities ... Mr. Thomas D. QUASNEY
27 Director Publications/Printing ... Mr. Laurence W. PEARCE
19 Director Law Enforcement & Safety ... Mr. Christopher L. WUCHENICH
37 Dir Stdnt Financial Aid/Scholarshp ... Dr. Edgar MILLER
36 Director Career Center ... Mr. Thomas HALASZ
06 University Registrar ... Ms. Barbara R. BLANEY
22 Exec Asst to Pres Equal Oppty Pgm ... Mr. Bobby D. GIST
21 Budget Director ... Mrs. Leslie G. BRUNELLI
07 Director of Admissions ... Dr. Mary WAGNER
39 Director Housing & Residential Svcs ... Dr. Gene LUNA
38 Dir Counseling/Human Devel Center ... Dr. Deborah C. BECK
41 Director of Athletics ... Mr. Eric HYMAN
35 Assoc VP for Student Life ... Mr. Jerry T. BREWER
23 Director of Student Health Services ... Ms. Deborah BECK
27 Director Media Relations ... Ms. Margaret M. LAMB
96 Director of Purchasing ... Mrs. Venis MANIGO
29 Director Alumni Association ... Ms. Marsha A. COLE
49 Dean College Arts & Sciences ... Dr. Mary Anne FITZPATRICK
88 Int Dn Hospitality/Retail/Sport Mgt ... Mr. Brian MIHALIK
50 Dean Darla Moore Sch Business ... Dr. Hildy TEEGEN, III
53 Dean College of Education ... Dr. Les STERNBERG
54 Dean Col Engineering & Computing ... Dr. Anthony P. AMBLER
69 Int Dean College of Public Health ... Dr. G. Thomas CHANDLER
60 Dn College of Mass Comm/Infor Stdys . Mr. Charles BIERBAUER
61 Dean School of Law ... Dr. Walter F. PRATT, JR.
63 Dean School of Medicine ... Dr. Richard A. HOPPMANN
64 Dean School of Music ... Dr. Tayloe HARDING
66 Dean College of Nursing ... Dr. Peggy HEWLETT
67 Dean College of Pharmacy ... Dr. Joseph T. DIPIRO
70 Dean College of Social Work ... Dr. Dennis L. POOLE

University of South Carolina Aiken (B)

471 University Parkway, Aiken SC 29801-6399
County: Aiken FICE Identification: 003449
Unit ID: 218645
Telephone: (803) 648-6851 Carnegie Class: Bac/Diverse
FAX Number: (803) 641-3362 Calendar System: Semester
URL: www.usca.edu
Established: 1961 Annual Undergrad Tuition & Fees (In-State): $8,374
Enrollment: 3,254 Coed
Affiliation or Control: State IRS Status: 501(c)3
Highest Offering: Master's
Program: Liberal Arts And General; Teacher Preparatory
Accreditation: SC, BUS, MUS, NUR, TED

01 Chancellor ... Dr. Thomas L. HALLMAN
05 Exec Vice Chanc Academic Affairs ... Dr. Suzanne OZMENT
79 College Coordinator Hum & Soc Sci ... Dr. Tom MACK
83 College Coordinator Sciences ... Dr. Edward CALLEN
50 Int Dean of the School of Business ... Dr. David HARRISON
53 Dean of the School of Education ... Dr. Jeffrey M. PRIEST
66 Dean of the School of Nursing ... Dr. Maggie DORSEY
88 Dir Academic Success Center ... Dr. Stephanie FOOTE
09 Dir Institutional Effectiveness ... Dr. Lloyd A. DAWE
08 Dir of Library ... Ms. Jane TUTEN
88 Dir Ruth Patrick Sci Ed Center ... Dr. Gary SENN
25 Dir Sponsored Research ... Dr. Bill PIRKLE
24 Dir Center for Teaching Excellence ... Mr. Keith PIERCE
10 Vice Chanc Business & Finance ... Ms. Virginia S. HUDOCK
40 Dir Bookstore ... Ms. Heidi DIFRANCO
88 Dir Campus Support Services ... Mr. Jeff JENIK
88 Dir Children's Center ... Ms. Lynn WILLIAMS
88 Dir Convocation Center ... Mr. Matt HERPICH
88 Dir Food Services ... Mr. Jon MANEY
12 Dir of Etherredge Center ... Ms. Jane SCHUMACHER
21 Dir of Business Services ... Ms. Gwen ASHLEY
15 Dir Human Resources & Affirm Action ... Ms. Maria CHANDLER
17 Dir Wellness Center ... Ms. Mila PADGETT
18 Asst Chanc Facilities Management ... Mr. Mike JARA
84 Vice Chancellor Enrollment Services ... Mr. Randy R. DUCKETT
07 Dir of Admissions ... Mr. Andrew HENDRIX
58 Coordinator Grad Studies/Residency ... Ms. Karen MORRIS
36 Dir of Career Services ... Mr. Corey FERALDI
37 Dir Financial Aid ... Mr. Glenn SHUMPERT
06 Registrar ... Ms. Vivian D. GRICE
27 Vice Chancellor Information Tech ... Mr. Mike LEMONS
14 Interim Dir Client Services ... Mr. Chris SPIRES
90 Dir Communications & Hardware ... Mr. Bob WIESNER
13 Dir Network System & Infrastructure ... Ms. Joann WILLIAMSON
32 Vice Chancellor Student Services ... Dr. Deborah KLADIVKO
41 Dir of Athletics ... Mr. Douglas R. WARRICK, JR.
38 Dir Counseling & Disablilities ... Ms. Cynthia B. GELINAS
17 Interim Dir Student Health Center ... Ms. Cynthia B. GELINAS
39 Dir Housing & Univ Police ... Mr. Deri WILLS
28 Dir Intercultural Programs ... Ms. Stacie WILLIAMS
35 Dir of Student Involvement ... Mr. Ahmed SAMAHA
19 Chief of Police ... Lt. Elijah PRICE, III
30 Vice Chancellor Advancement ... Dr. Deidre MARTIN
29 Dir of Alumni Relations/Annual Fund ... Ms. Jamie RAYNOR
51 Dir Conferences & Continuing Ed .. Ms. Mary Anne CAVANAUGH
44 Dir Major Gifts ... Ms. Linda EVANS
26 Dir Marketing & Community Relations ... Mr. Preston SPARKS
105 Dir Visual Comm & Web Development ... Mr. Jeff MASTROMONICO

University of South Carolina Beaufort (C)

1 University Boulevard, Bluffton SC 29909-6085
County: Beaufort FICE Identification: 003450
Unit ID: 218654
Telephone: (843) 208-8000 Carnegie Class: Bac/Diverse
FAX Number: (843) 208-8299 Calendar System: Semester
URL: www.uscb.edu
Established: 1959 Annual Undergrad Tuition & Fees (In-State): $7,756
Enrollment: 1,754 Coed
Affiliation or Control: State IRS Status: 501(c)3
Highest Offering: Baccalaureate
Program: Liberal Arts And General; Teacher Preparatory; Professional
Accreditation: SC, NURSE, TED

01 Chancellor ... Dr. Jane UPSHAW
05 Exec Vice Chanc Academic Affairs ... Dr. Harvey VARNET
32 Vice Chanc for Student Development ... Dr. Douglas OBLANDER
10 Vice Chancellor Finance/Operations ... Mr. Earle HOLLEY
26 Vice Chanc University Advancement ... Dr. Lynn MCGEE
31 Assoc Chanc Community Outreach ... Dr. C. Leary BELL
18 Director of Facilities ... Mr. Mike PARROTT
20 Assoc Vice Chanc Acad Affairs ... Dr. Harvey VARNET
13 Chief Information Officer ... Mr. Eddie KING
08 Director of Library ... Dr. Harvey VARNET
06 Registrar ... Ms. Andrea WAWRZUSIN
07 Director of Admissions ... Mr. Joffery BLAIR
37 Director of Financial Aid ... Ms. Patricia GREENE
30 Director of Development ... Ms. Colleen CALLAHAN
09 Dir Inst Effectiveness/Research ... Ms. Jodi HERRIN
19 Director of Security ... Mr. Henry GARBADE
35 Director of Student Life ... Ms. Kate TORBORG-VERMILYEA
15 Manager of Human Resources ... Dr. Sue GOLABEK

University of South Carolina Lancaster (D)

PO Box 889, Lancaster SC 29721-0889
County: Lancaster FICE Identification: 003453
Unit ID: 218672
Telephone: (803) 313-7000 Carnegie Class: Assoc/Pub2in4
FAX Number: (803) 313-7106 Calendar System: Semester
URL: usclancaster.sc.edu
Established: 1959 Annual Undergrad Tuition & Fees (In-State): $5,888
Enrollment: 1,588 Coed
Affiliation or Control: State IRS Status: 501(c)3
Highest Offering: Associate Degree
Program: Occupational; 2-Year Principally Bachelor's Creditable
Accreditation: &SC, ACBSP, ADNUR, PNUR

01 Dean ... Dr. John CATALANO
05 Assoc Dean for Acad & Student Affs ... Dr. M. Ron COX
84 Director of Enrollment Management ... Mrs. Karen FAILE
08 Head Librarian ... Ms. Shari ELIADES
10 Business Manager/Dir of Planning ... Mr. Paul JOHNSON
37 Director Financial Aid ... Mr. Ken COLE
32 Director of Student Life ... Ms. Laura HUMPHREY
16 Human Resources Officer ... Ms. Tracey A. MOBLEY
51 Director Trio Programs ... Ms. Thelathia B. BAILEY
30 Director of Development ... Mr. Ralph GARRIS
26 Director of Public Information ... Ms. Shana DRY
14 Director of Computer Services ... Mr. Blake FAULKENBERRY
41 Athletics Director ... Mr. Rick WALTERS
18 Dir Custodial Svcs Groundskeeping ... Mr. Butch LUCAS
23 Director of Health Services ... Dr. William F. RINER
19 Dir Law Enforcement & Safety ... Dr. John E. RUTLEDGE

† Regional accreditation is carried under University of South Carolina - Columbia.

University of South Carolina Salkehatchie (E)

PO Box 617, Allendale SC 29810-0617
County: Allendale FICE Identification: 003454
Unit ID: 218681
Telephone: (803) 584-3446 Carnegie Class: Assoc/Pub2in4
FAX Number: (803) 584-5038 Calendar System: Semester
URL: uscsalkehatchie.sc.edu
Established: 1965 Annual Undergrad Tuition & Fees (In-State): $5,888
Enrollment: 1,150 Coed
Affiliation or Control: State IRS Status: 501(c)3
Highest Offering: Associate Degree
Program: 2-Year Principally Bachelor's Creditable
Accreditation: &SC

01 Dean ... Dr. Ann C. CARMICHAEL
05 Assoc Dean Academic Affairs ... Dr. Roberto REFINETTI
32 Asc Dean Student Svcs/Dir Athletics ... Ms. Jane T. BREWER
10 Director of Finance ... Mr. Mark J. CRAIG
08 Head Librarian ... Mr. Daniel JOHNSON
37 Director Financial Aid ... Ms. Julie HADWIN
18 Director Facilities/Safety ... Dr. William A. SANDIFER
40 Bookstore Manager ... Mr. Lamar HEWETT
35 Assoc Dean Student Services ... Ms. Jane T. BREWER
15 Director of Human Resources ... Dr. William A. SANDIFER
07 Admissions Coordinator ... Ms. Carmen BROWN
30 Chief Development ... Dr. Ann C. CARMICHAEL
84 Director Enrollment Mgmt & Grants ... Ms. Christin E. HOLLIDAY
88 Director Leadership Center ... Ms. Ann RICE

† Regional accreditation is carried under University of South Carolina - Columbia.

University of South Carolina Sumter (F)

200 Miller Road, Sumter SC 29150-2498
County: Sumter FICE Identification: 003426
Unit ID: 218690
Telephone: (803) 775-8727 Carnegie Class: Assoc/Pub2in4
FAX Number: (803) 775-2180 Calendar System: Semester
URL: www.uscsumter.edu
Established: 1966 Annual Undergrad Tuition & Fees (In-State): $5,888
Enrollment: 1,192 Coed
Affiliation or Control: State IRS Status: 501(c)3
Highest Offering: Associate Degree
Program: 2-Year Principally Bachelor's Creditable
Accreditation: &SC

01 Dean of the University ... Dr. C. Leslie CARPENTER
05 Assoc Dean Academic Affairs ... Dr. Anthony M. COYNE
30 Asst Dean University Advancement ... Mr. Carl R. MCINTOSH
32 Assoc Dean for Student Affairs ... Mr. Lynwood WATTS
10 Assoc Dean for Admin/Financial Svcs ... Mr. Bruce K. BLUMBERG
79 Chr Div of Hum/Social Science/Educ ... Dr. Richard S. BELL
49 Chair Division of Arts & Letters ... Dr. Hayes D. HAMPTON
81 Chr Div of Science/Math & Engr ... Dr. James E. PRIVETT
50 Chr Div of Business/Admin/ Economics ... Dr. Kay OLDHOUSER DAVIS
88 Faculty Organization Chair ... Dr. Andrew J. KUNKA
09 Director of Institutional Research ... Mr. Charles W. WRIGHT
08 Head Librarian ... Ms. Sharon H. CHAPMAN
07 Director of Admissions ... Mr. Keith E. BRITTON
38 Director Advisement/Counseling ... Ms. C. Gail PACK
56 Director of Distance Education ... Ms. Jean B. CARRANO
51 Director of Continuing Education ... Ms. Susan S. BRABHAM
35 Director Student Life ... Vacant
14 Director of Computer Services ... Mr. George R. THOMPSON, III
26 Dir of Public Relations/Marketing ... Ms. Misty F. HATFIELD
40 Bookstore Manager ... Ms. Julie MCCOY
15 Human Resources Officer ... Ms. Marchetta L. WILLIAMS
21 Budget/Planning/Grants Director ... Ms. Joann V. GROOVER
88 Dir SC Center for Oral Narration ... Dr. Michele N. REESE
29 Director of Alumni Relations ... Ms. Erica G. CHRISTMAS
37 Coord Fin Aid/Scholarships/Vet Affs ... Ms. Sue A. SIMS

† Regional accreditation is carried under University of South Carolina - Columbia.

University of South Carolina Union (G)

PO Drawer 729, Union SC 29379-0729
County: Union FICE Identification: 004927
Unit ID: 218706
Telephone: (864) 429-8728 Carnegie Class: Assoc/Pub2in4
FAX Number: (864) 427-3682 Calendar System: Semester
URL: uscunion.sc.edu
Established: 1965 Annual Undergrad Tuition & Fees (In-State): N/A
Enrollment: 530 Coed
Affiliation or Control: State IRS Status: 501(c)3
Highest Offering: Associate Degree
Program: Occupational; 2-Year Principally Bachelor's Creditable
Accreditation: &SC

01 Interim Dean .... Dr. Stephen H. LOWE
84 Director Enrollment Services .... Mr. Terry E. YOUNG
37 Director Financial Aid .... Mr. Robert HOLCOMBE
15 Human Resources .... Ms. Susan P. JETT
10 Business Manager .... Ms. Michele S. LEE
40 Bookstore Manager .... Ms. Tanja BLACK
14 Director of Information Technology .... Mr. Wesley C. BELK

† Regional accreditation is carried under University of South Carolina - Columbia.

University of South Carolina Upstate (A)

800 University Way, Spartanburg SC 29303-4996
County: Spartanburg FICE Identification: 006951
Unit ID: 218742
Telephone: (864) 503-5000 Carnegie Class: Bac/Diverse
FAX Number: (864) 503-5375 Calendar System: Semester
URL: www.uscupstate.edu
Established: 1967 Annual Undergrad Tuition & Fees (In-State): $9,072
Enrollment: 5,439 Coed
Affiliation or Control: State IRS Status: 501(c)3
Highest Offering: Master's
Program: Liberal Arts And General; Teacher Preparatory
Accreditation: SC, ART, BUS, CS, ENGT, NURSE, TED

01 Chancellor .... Dr. John C. STOCKWELL
05 Sr Vice Chanc for Acad Affair .... Dr. Marsha DOWELL
13 Vice Chanc Information Technology .... Ms. Jeanne SKUL
10 Vice Chancellor Business Affairs .... Mr. Robert A. CONNELLY
11 Vice Chanc Admin & Business Affs .... Ms. Sheryl TURNER-WATTS
30 Vice Chanc University Advancement .... Mr. Michael E. IRVIN
32 Dean of Students .... Mrs. Laura PUCKETT-BOLER
06 Registrar .... Vacant
84 Asst Vice Chanc Enrollment Services .... Ms. Donette STEWART
35 Asst Vice Chanc Student Affairs .... Ms. Frances L. JARRETT-HORTIS
27 Telecommunications Manager .... Mr. Robbie COTHRAN
08 Dean of the Library .... Ms. Frieda M. DAVISON
37 Director Financial Aid .... Ms. Allison SULLIVAN
49 Dean of Arts & Sciences .... Dr. Dirk SCHLINGMANN
50 Dean Business Administration .... Dr. Darrell F. PARKER
53 Dean of Education .... Dr. Charles LOVE
66 Dean of Nursing .... Dr. Lynette HAMLIN
58 Chair Graduate Education .... Dr. Rebecca L. STEVENS
102 Director Dev & Found Scholarships .... Mrs. Bea W. SMITH
40 Bookstore Manager .... Mr. Jerry CARROLL
41 Athletic Director .... Mr. H. Michael HALL
18 Director of Facilities Management .... Mr. Frederick D. PUNCKE
09 Dir of Inst Assessment & Planning .... Mr. C. Sam BINGHAM
96 Director of Purchasing .... Mr. Janice DELLINGER
26 Director University Communications .... Ms. Tammey E. WHALEY
19 Chief of Police .... Mr. Klay PETERSON
35 Director of Student Life .... Ms. Khrystal SMITH
39 Director of Housing .... Mr. Ron DALTON
23 Director of Health Services .... Ms. Lou Anne WEBER
88 Exec Dir Univ Boards & Public Affs .... Mr. John F. PERRY

Voorhees College (B)

PO Box 678, Denmark SC 29042-0678
County: Bamberg FICE Identification: 003455
Unit ID: 218919
Telephone: (803) 780-1010 Carnegie Class: Bac/Diverse
FAX Number: (803) 780-1015 Calendar System: Semester
URL: www.voorhees.edu
Established: 1897 Annual Undergrad Tuition & Fees: $10,780
Enrollment: 701 Coed
Affiliation or Control: Protestant Episcopal IRS Status: 501(c)3
Highest Offering: Baccalaureate
Program: Liberal Arts And General
Accreditation: SC, ACBSP

01 President .... Dr. Cleveland L. SELLERS, JR.
05 Exec Vice Pres Academic Affairs .... Dr. Carl A. CARPENTER
32 Vice President Student Affairs .... Dr. Perna CARTER
10 Int VP Fiscal/Admin Affairs/CFO .... Mrs. V. Diane O'BERRY
30 Vice Pres Institutional Advancement .... Mr. Courtney DAVENPORT
09 VP Planning & Information Mgmt .... Mr. Samuel BLACKWELL
84 Int Dean Enrollment Management .... Mr. Willie JEFFERSON
35 Director of Student Life/Counseling .... Mrs. Sarah SIMPSON
08 Administrative Librarian .... Dr. Marie MARTIN
37 Director of Financial Aid .... Mr. Augusta KITCHEN
18 Director of Physical Plant .... Mr. Eddie PATTERSON
29 Director Alumni Affairs .... Ms. Dorothy PATTERSON
36 Director Career Planning & Outreach .... Mr. Gerald DEVAUGHN
42 Chaplain .... Rev. Ira JOHNSON
41 Director of Athletics .... Mr. Willie JEFFERSON
19 Director of Security .... Mr. James WELDON
23 Director of Health Services .... Ms. Helen SHERMAN
06 Registrar .... Ms. Melika JACKSON
07 Director of Admissions .... Mr. Joseph MONTGOMERY
15 Director of Human Resources .... Ms. Andraea HERRIN
13 Chief Technology Officer .... Mr. Timothy KENTOPP
21 Internal Auditor .... Vacant
40 Bookstore Manager .... Mrs. Shanda RUFFIN
26 Coordinator Media Rels/Marketing .... Mrs. Teesa BRUNSON
04 Exec Assistant to the President .... Ms. Sandra GLOSTER
50 Chrpn Business & Professional Stds .... Dr. Bernard MOSES
49 Chairperson of Arts & Sciences .... Dr. Doris WARD

Williamsburg Technical College (C)

601 Martin Luther King, Jr. Avenue, Kingstree SC 29556-4103
County: Williamsburg FICE Identification: 009322
Unit ID: 218955
Telephone: (843) 355-4110 Carnegie Class: Assoc/Pub-R-S
FAX Number: (843) 355-4296 Calendar System: Semester
URL: www.wiltech.edu
Established: 1969 Annual Undergrad Tuition & Fees (In-District): $5,178
Enrollment: 729 Coed
Affiliation or Control: State/Local IRS Status: 501(c)3
Highest Offering: Associate Degree
Program: Occupational; 2-Year Principally Bachelor's Creditable
Accreditation: SC, ACBSP

01 President .... Dr. Kim M. MCGINNIS
10 Chief Business Officer .... Ms. Melissa A. COKER
05 Dean of Instruction .... Mr. Clifton R. ELLIOTT
32 Dean of Student Svs/Financial Aid .... Dr. Eric A. BROWN
51 Director Continuing & Tech Educ Pgm .... Vacant
08 Library Director .... Ms. Demetra WALKER
07 Admissions Counselor .... Ms. Cheryl DUBOSE
30 Chief Devel Officer & Grants Coord .... Mrs. Mona DUKES
37 Financial Aid Officer .... Mrs. Jean BOOS
09 Research/Systems Analyst .... Mr. T. Kent COKER
06 Director Enrollment and Record Svcs .... Ms. Alexis WRIGHT
18 Director of Physical Plant .... Mr. Tyrone THOMAS
15 Director Human Resources .... Mr. Will M. BROWN
26 Chief Public Relations Officer .... Mrs. Mona B. DUKES

Winthrop University (D)

Oakland Avenue, Rock Hill SC 29733-0001
County: York FICE Identification: 003456
Unit ID: 218964
Telephone: (803) 323-2211 Carnegie Class: Master's L
FAX Number: (803) 323-3001 Calendar System: Semester
URL: www.winthrop.edu
Established: 1886 Annual Undergrad Tuition & Fees (In-State): $12,698
Enrollment: 5,998 Coed
Affiliation or Control: State IRS Status: 501(c)3
Highest Offering: Beyond Master's But Less Than Doctorate
Program: Liberal Arts And General; Teacher Preparatory; Professional
Accreditation: SC, ART, BUS, CACREP, CIDA, CS, DANCE, DIETD, DIETI, JOUR, MUS, SW, TED, THEA

01 President .... Dr. Anthony J. DIGIORGIO
05 Acting VP Academic Affairs .... Dr. Debra BOYD
10 Vice President Finance & Business .... Mr. J. P. MCKEE
30 Vice Pres University Advancement .... Dr. Kathryn HOLTEN
32 Vice President of Student Life .... Dr. Frank P. ARDAIOLO
29 Vice Pres Development and Alumni .... Mr. Brien LEWIS
21 Associate VP Finance/Business .... Ms. Amanda F. MAGHSOUD
18 Assoc VP Facilities Management .... Mr. Walter A. HARDIN
15 Associate VP Human Resource .... Ms. Lisa COWART
100 Exec Assistant to President .... Dr. Kimberly A. FAUST
26 Asst to President Public Affairs .... Ms. Rebecca MASTERS
04 Asst to Pres University Events .... Ms. DeeAnna BROOKS
13 Assoc VP Information Technology .... Mr. James HAMMOND
58 Dean of Graduate School .... Dr. Yvonne MURNANE
20 Asst Vice Pres Academic Affairs .... Mr. Tim DRUEKE
49 Interim Dean College Arts & Science .... Dr. Peter JUDGE
50 Dean Col of Business Administration .... Dr. Roger D. WEIKLE
53 Dean College of Education .... Dr. Jennie RAKESTRAW
64 Dean College of Visual/Perf .... Dr. David WOHL
08 Dean Library Services .... Dr. Mark Y. HERRING
89 Dean University College .... Dr. Gloria JONES
35 Dean of Students .... Ms. Bethany MARLOWE
26 Director University Relations .... Ms. Ellen M. WILDER-BYRD
41 Athletic Director .... Mr. Thomas N. HICKMAN
25 Director Sponsored Pgms/Research .... Ms. Teresa R. JUSTICE
90 Director Academic Computing .... Mr. Patrice BRUNEAU
91 Director Admin System/Programming .... Mr. Larry W. FERGUSON
29 Director of Alumni Relations .... Ms. Debbie GARRICK
06 Registrar .... Ms. Gina JONES
07 Director of Admissions .... Ms. Deborah G. BARBER
37 Director of Financial Aid .... Ms. Leah STURGIS
19 Director of Campus Police .... Mr. Frank J. ZEBEDIS
38 Interim Director Health/Counseling .... Ms. Mary Jo BARRETO
39 Director of Residence Life .... Ms. Cynthia A. CASSENS
36 Director Career Development /Svcs .... Ms. Amy SULLIVAN
96 Director Procurement/Risk Mgmt .... Mr. Bob REID
53 Director Teaching/Learning Ctr .... Dr. John BRYD

W.L. Bonner College (E)

4430 Argent Court, Columbia SC 29203-5901
County: Richland FICE Identification: 038564
Unit ID: 446613
Telephone: (803) 754-3950 Carnegie Class: Spec/Faith
FAX Number: (803) 754-9700 Calendar System: Semester
URL: www.wlbc.edu
Established: 1995 Annual Undergrad Tuition & Fees: $6,800
Enrollment: 148 Coed
Affiliation or Control: Independent Non-Profit IRS Status: 501(c)3
Highest Offering: Baccalaureate
Program: Liberal Arts And General; Religious Emphasis
Accreditation: BI

01 President and Founder .... Bishop William L. BONNER
05 Chief Academic Officer .... Ms. Elaine MCQUEEN
10 Chief Fiscal Officer .... Vacant

Wofford College (F)

429 N Church Street, Spartanburg SC 29303-3663
County: Spartanburg FICE Identification: 003457
Unit ID: 218973
Telephone: (864) 597-4000 Carnegie Class: Bac/A&S
FAX Number: (864) 597-4018 Calendar System: 4/1/4
URL: www.wofford.edu
Established: 1854 Annual Undergrad Tuition & Fees: $33,190
Enrollment: 1,541 Coed
Affiliation or Control: United Methodist IRS Status: 501(c)3
Highest Offering: Baccalaureate
Program: Liberal Arts And General; Teacher Preparatory
Accreditation: SC

01 President .... Dr. Benjamin B. DUNLAP
10 Senior Vice Pres Operations/Finance .... Mr. Robert L. KEASLER
05 Sr VP Academic Affs/Dean of College .... Dr. David S. WOOD
30 Sr VP Development/College Relations .... Mr. Marion B. PEAVEY
11 Vice President Administration .... Mr. David M. BEACHAM
32 Vice President Student Affairs .... Ms. Roberta H. BIGGER
46 Vice Pres Education Technology .... Dr. David M. WHISNANT
84 Vice President for Enrollment .... Mr. Brand R. STILLE
09 Vice Pres Academic Admin & Planning .... Dr. Boyce M. LAWTON, III
27 Assoc VP Communications/Marketing .... Dr. Doyle W. BOGGS
18 Assoc VP Facilities/Cap Projects .... Mr. Jason H. BURR
36 Dean Ctr for Professional Excellnce .... Mr. Scott COCHRAN
08 Dean of Library/Dir Cultural Events .... Mr. Oakley H. COBURN
23 Assoc Dean Students/Dir Health Svcs .... Ms. Beth D. WALLACE
04 Exec Assistant to the President .... Ms. Mary A. GILMAN
88 Dean of International Programs .... Dr. Ana Maria WISEMAN
41 Director of Athletics .... Mr. Richard A. JOHNSON
06 College Registrar .... Ms. Jennifer R. ALLISON
42 Chaplain .... Dr. Ronald R. ROBINSON
29 Dir of Alumni Affairs/Parent Assn .... Mrs. Debbi N. THOMPSON
19 Campus Safety Director .... Mr. Randy HALL
15 Human Resources Director .... Ms. Carole B. LISTER

York Technical College (G)

452 S Anderson Road, Rock Hill SC 29730-3395
County: York FICE Identification: 003996
Unit ID: 218991
Telephone: (803) 327-8000 Carnegie Class: Assoc/Pub-S-SC
FAX Number: (803) 327-8059 Calendar System: Semester
URL: www.yorktech.edu
Established: 1964 Annual Undergrad Tuition & Fees (In-State): $3,628
Enrollment: 6,000 Coed
Affiliation or Control: State IRS Status: 501(c)3
Highest Offering: Associate Degree
Program: Occupational; 2-Year Principally Bachelor's Creditable
Accreditation: SC, ACBSP, ADNUR, DA, DH, ENGT, MLTAD, PNUR, RAD, SURGT

01 President .... Dr. Greg F. RUTHERFORD
05 Exec Vice Pres Acad/Student Affs .... Dr. Carolyn G. STEWART
10 VP Business & Support Svcs .... Dr. Marc TARPLEE
32 Assoc VP Academic/Student Affairs .... Vacant
30 Vice President for Advancement .... Vacant
50 Assoc VP Business/Computer/AA/AS .... Mr. Jack BAGWELL
76 Assoc VP Health & Human Services .... Ms. Linda WEAVER-GRIGGS
54 Assoc VP Industry/Engineering Tech .... Mr. Sidney VALENTINE
103 Assoc VP Economic/Workforce Devel .... Dr. Joanne ZUKOWSKI
08 Librarian .... Ms. Kristine JONES
35 Dean of Students .... Ms. Kelly T. DAWKINS
88 Dean Center for Teaching/Learning .... Ms. Kathy L. HOELLEN
71 ReadySC Program Manager .... Ms. Marianne BORDERS
26 Public Relations Officer .... Vacant
09 Director of Institutional Research .... Ms. Mary Beth SCHWARTZ
15 Director of Human Resources . Ms. Edwina ROSEBORO-BARNES
37 Director Student Financial Aid .... Mrs. Angela FOWLER
13 Information Services Director .... Mr. Ronald G. SCOTT
18 Facilities Management Director .... Mr. Robert L. BROWN
45 Director of Planning .... Mrs. Jacquelyn H. NESBITT
06 Registrar .... Mrs. Brandy PINER
07 Director of Admissions .... Mr. Kenny ALDRIDGE

SOUTH DAKOTA

Augustana College (H)

2001 S Summit, Sioux Falls SD 57197-0001
County: Minnehaha FICE Identification: 003458
Unit ID: 219000
Telephone: (605) 274-0770 Carnegie Class: Bac/Diverse
FAX Number: (605) 274-5299 Calendar System: 4/1/4
URL: www.augie.edu
Established: 1860 Annual Undergrad Tuition & Fees: $26,590
Enrollment: 1,794 Coed
Affiliation or Control: Evangelical Lutheran Church In America
IRS Status: 501(c)3
Highest Offering: Master's
Program: Liberal Arts And General; Teacher Preparatory; Professional
Accreditation: NH, MUS, NURSE, TED

01 President Mr. Robert C. OLIVER
05 Interim Vice Pres Academic Affairs Dr. Murray HAAR
32 Vice President Student Services Dr. James B. BIES
10 Vice Pres Finance/Administration Mr. Thomas MEYER
30 Vice President for Advancement Mr. Jonathan M. HENKES
07 Vice President for Admission Ms. Nancy DAVIDSON
15 Vice President of Human Resources Ms. Jane T. KUPER
11 Assoc VP Admin/Chief Info Officer Mr. Daniel D. DRENKOW
21 Assoc Vice President for Finance Ms. Carol SPILLUM
20 Associate Academic Dean Dr. Mike WANOUS
32 Associate Dean of Students Ms. Tracy L. RIDDLE
37 Director of Financial Aid Ms. Brenda MURTHA
08 Director of Library Ms. Ronelle THOMPSON
36 Director Career Center Ms. Sandi VIETOR
13 Director Mgmt Information Systems Ms. Debra FREDERICK
18 Chief Facilities/Physical Plant Mr. Frank HUGHES
29 Director of Alumni Relations Ms. Mary TOSO
41 Athletic Director Mr. Bill GROSS
06 Registrar Ms. Joni KRUEGER

Colorado Technical University (A)

3901 W 59th Street, Sioux Falls SD 57108-2272
County: Lincoln Identification: 666731
Unit ID: 402615
Telephone: (605) 361-0200 Carnegie Class: Master's S
FAX Number: (605) 361-5954 Calendar System: Quarter
URL: www.coloradotech.edu
Established: 1965 Annual Undergrad Tuition & Fees: $12,700
Enrollment: 1,060 Coed
Affiliation or Control: Proprietary IRS Status: Proprietary
Highest Offering: Master's
Program: 2-Year Principally Bachelor's Creditable; Professional
Accreditation: &NH, MAC

01 President Dr. David HEFLIN
10 Controller Mr. Daniel RAAK
07 Vice President of Admissions Ms. Catherine ALLEN
05 Director of Education Dr. Tim MAIFELD
32 Director of Student Services Ms. Anna HECKENLAIBLE
37 Assistant Director of Financial Aid Ms. Alissa HEADRICK

† Regional accreditation is carried under the parent institution in Colorado Springs, CO.

Dakota Wesleyan University (B)

1200 W University, Mitchell SD 57301-4398
County: Davison FICE Identification: 003461
Unit ID: 219091
Telephone: (605) 995-2600 Carnegie Class: Bac/Diverse
FAX Number: N/A Calendar System: Semester
URL: www.dwu.edu
Established: 1885 Annual Undergrad Tuition & Fees: $20,810
Enrollment: 744 Coed
Affiliation or Control: United Methodist IRS Status: 501(c)3
Highest Offering: Master's
Program: Liberal Arts And General; Teacher Preparatory
Accreditation: NH, ADNUR

01 President Dr. Robert G. DUFFETT
03 Provost & Executive Vice President Ms. Amy NOVAK
10 Vice Pres for Business & Finance Ms. Theresa KRIESE
30 Vice President for Inst Advancement Rev. Neil BLAIR
26 Vice Pres of University Relations Ms. Lori ESSIG
06 Registrar Ms. Karen KNOELL
08 Chief Info Ofcr/Dir Lrng Resources Mr. Kevin KENKEL
88 Dir Kelley Ctr for Entrepreneurship Ms. Rhonda POLE
88 Dn Col Ldrshp/Pub Svc/Dir McGov Ctr Dr. Donald SIMMONS
81 Dean Col Health/Fitness & Science Dr. Rochelle VON EYE
79 Dean College Arts & Humanities Dr. Vince REDDER
88 Director Development Mr. Allen LEPKE
29 Director of Alumni Relations Ms. Jackie WENTWORTH
37 Director of Financial Aid Ms. Kristy O'KIEF
13 Director of Information Technology Mr. Matt MOORE
15 Director of Human Resources Mr. Corey MELLEGAARD
42 Campus Pastor Rev. Brandon VETTER
66 Administrative Chair Nursing Dept Dr. Adele JACOBSON
41 Athletic Director Mr. Curt HART
18 Director of Physical Plant Mr. Louis SCHOENFELDER
32 Director of Student Life Ms. Diana GOLDAMMER
35 Director Student Support Services Ms. Kate MILLER
07 Director of Recruitment Ms. Melissa HERR-VALBURG
38 Student Support Services Counselor Ms. Sara THOMPSON
40 Director of University Services Ms. Lori SOLBERG
88 Day Care Director/Teacher Ms. Linda HOFER

Kilian Community College (C)

300 E 6th Street, Sioux Falls SD 57103-7020
County: Minnehaha FICE Identification: 021446
Unit ID: 219055
Telephone: (605) 221-3100 Carnegie Class: Assoc/PrivNFP
FAX Number: (605) 336-2606 Calendar System: Semester
URL: www.kilian.edu
Established: 1976 Annual Undergrad Tuition & Fees: $8,300
Enrollment: 390 Coed
Affiliation or Control: Independent Non-Profit IRS Status: 501(c)3
Highest Offering: Associate Degree
Program: Occupational; 2-Year Principally Bachelor's Creditable
Accreditation: NH

01 President Mr. Mark MILLAGE
11 Dean of Institutional Services Mr. Craig JUCHT
37 Financial Aid Director Ms. Carolyn HELGERSON
06 Registrar/Dir of Inst Research Ms. Janet K. GARCIA
26 Director of Marketing Vacant
88 Director Student Success Center Ms. Rose TOERING
07 Director of Admissions Ms. Mary KLOCKMAN
30 Director of Development Ms. Wendy MCDONNEL
04 Assistant to the President Ms. Joyce HUBREGTSE
08 Librarian Vacant
10 Manager Business Office Vacant
18 Chief Facilities/Physical Plant Mr. Herb ROE
49 Instruction Liberal Arts Division Ms. Cheryl J. HARTMAN
50 Instruction Business Division Ms. Wendy JANSEN

Lake Area Technical Institute (D)

230 11th Street NE, PO Box 730,
Watertown SD 57201-2869
County: Codington FICE Identification: 005309
Unit ID: 219143
Telephone: (605) 882-5284 Carnegie Class: Assoc/Pub-R-S
FAX Number: (605) 882-6299 Calendar System: Semester
URL: www.lakeareatech.edu
Established: 1965 Annual Undergrad Tuition & Fees (In-District): $5,546
Enrollment: 1,436 Coed
Affiliation or Control: Local IRS Status: 501(c)3
Highest Offering: Associate Degree
Program: Occupational; Technical Emphasis
Accreditation: NH, DA, MAC, MLTAD, OTA, PNUR, PTAA

01 President Ms. Debra SHEPHARD
03 Executive Vice President Mr. Michael CARTNEY
84 Director of Enrollment Mr. Lee QUALE
05 Dean of Instruction Ms. Kim BELLUM
26 Chief Public Relations Officer Ms. LuAnn STRAIT
31 Business/Industry Coordinator Mr. Steven HAUCK
32 Student Services Coordinator Mr. Shane ORTMEIER
37 Financial Aid Coordinator Ms. Marlene SEEKLANDER
38 Academic Counselor Ms. Jeanette TRUE

Mitchell Technical Institute (E)

1800 E Spruce, Mitchell SD 57301-2002
County: Davison FICE Identification: 008284
Unit ID: 219189
Telephone: (605) 995-3025 Carnegie Class: Assoc/Pub-R-S
FAX Number: (605) 995-3083 Calendar System: Semester
URL: www.mitchelltech.edu
Established: 1968 Annual Undergrad Tuition & Fees (In-District): $6,335
Enrollment: 1,109 Coed
Affiliation or Control: Local IRS Status: 501(c)3
Highest Offering: Associate Degree
Program: Occupational; 2-Year Principally Bachelor's Creditable; Technical Emphasis
Accreditation: NH, MAC, MLTAD, RAD

01 President Mr. Greg VON WALD
05 Vice President for Academic Affairs Ms. Vicki WIESE
11 Vice Pres for Admin Svcs/CFO Mr. Michael HOFFMAN
13 Vice President for Technology Mr. Dan MUCK
88 Vice Pres for Industrial Relations Mr. Mark GERHARDT
84 Dean of Enrollment Mr. Scott FOSSUM
06 Registrar Ms. Janet GREENWAY
37 Director Student Financial Aid Mr. Grant UECKER
07 Admissions Coordinator Mr. Clayton DEUTER
38 Learning Services Coordinator Ms. Julie HART-SCHUTTE
09 Director of Institutional Research Ms. Marla SMITH
20 Associate Academic Officer Ms. Carol GRODE-HANKS
26 Director of Marketing Ms. Julie BROOKBANK
30 Foundation Director Ms. Heather LENTZ

Mount Marty College (F)

1105 W 8th, Yankton SD 57078-3724
County: Yankton FICE Identification: 003465
Unit ID: 219198
Telephone: (605) 668-1011 Carnegie Class: Bac/Diverse
FAX Number: (605) 668-1607 Calendar System: Semester
URL: www.mtmc.edu
Established: 1936 Annual Undergrad Tuition & Fees: $20,656
Enrollment: 1,185 Coed
Affiliation or Control: Roman Catholic IRS Status: 501(c)3
Highest Offering: Master's
Program: Liberal Arts And General; Teacher Preparatory; Professional; Nursing Emphasis
Accreditation: NH, ANEST, NURSE

01 President Dr. Joseph N. BENOIT
04 Asst to the Pres/Asst Sec to Board Ms. Carla ENG
05 Interim VP for Academic Affairs Mr. Robert TERESHINSKI
10 Vice Pres Finance/Administration Ms. Daisy HALVORSON
32 Vice President of Student Affairs Ms. Sarah CARDA
42 Director of Campus Ministry Br. David MCGINNIS
30 Interim VP Insitutional Advancement Ms. Chris TUDOR
84 Director of Admission Ms. Paula TACKE
09 Director of Institutional Research Dr. Alan FERRIS
58 Director of Nurse Anesthesia Dr. Alfred LUPIEN
88 Director of Pastoral Ministries Vacant
12 Director of Watertown Campus Dr. Linda SCHURMANN
44 Director of Development Vacant

29 Director of Alumni Relations Ms. Jen MOSER
26 Director College Relations & Mktg Ms. Sheila KUCHTA
37 Director Student Financial Aid Mr. Ken KOCER
06 Registrar Ms. Jonna SUPURGECI
13 Director Information Support Servic Mr. Paul LAMMERS
08 Director of Library Ms. Sandra BROWN
40 Dir Bookstore/Central Scheduling Ms. Mary ABBOTT
38 Dir Student Counseling Vacant
41 Athletic Director Mr. Chuck IVERSON
36 Director Student Placement Ms. Estelle JOHNSON
18 Chief Facilities/Physical Plant Mr. Steve HERMANSON
15 Human Resources Specialist Ms. Julie DATHER

National American University (G)

5301 S Highway 16, Suite 200, Rapid City SD 57701-8932
County: Pennington FICE Identification: 004057
Unit ID: 219204
Telephone: (605) 721-5200 Carnegie Class: Master's S
FAX Number: (605) 721-5241 Calendar System: Quarter
URL: www.national.edu
Established: 1941 Annual Undergrad Tuition & Fees: $27,140
Enrollment: 9,643 Coed
Affiliation or Control: Proprietary IRS Status: Proprietary
Highest Offering: Master's
Program: Occupational; Liberal Arts And General; Professional
Accreditation: NH, IACBE, MAC

01 University President Dr. Jerry L. GALLENTINE
05 Provost/General Counsel Dr. Samuel KERR
58 System VP Grad Stds/Dean Grad Sch Dr. Phyllis OKREPKIE
12 Regional President-West/Southwest Ms. Lisa KNIGGE
12 Regional President-E/SE/Midwest Ms. Michaelle HOLLAND
20 Assoc Provost/Sys VP Curricul/Instr Ms. Marilyn HOLMGREN
10 Chief Executive Officer Dr. Ronald SHAPE
06 Registrar Mr. Tom MAHON
37 Director of Financial Aid Ms. Cheryl BULLINGER
29 Director Alumni Relations Mr. Guy TILLETT
21 Director of Student Accounts Ms. Linda POTTORFF
08 System Librarian Ms. Pat HAMILTON
12 Campus Exec Ofcr-Ellsworth AFB Mr. John TERRY
12 Campus Exec Ofcr-Rapid City Dr. John QUINN
12 Camp Ex Ofcr-Albuque/Dir Rio Rancho Ms. Brenda GRAVES
12 Campus Exec Ofcr-Bloomington Mr. Roger SAGE
12 Campus Exec Ofcr-Brooklyn Center Mr. Travis JENSEN
12 Campus Exec Ofcr-Colorado Springs Ms. Audrey DERUBIS
12 Campus Exec Ofcr-Overland Park KS Mr. Doug STICHLER
12 Campus Exec Ofcr-Roseville Mr. Gene MUILENBURG
12 Campus Exec Ofcr-Sioux Falls Ms. Lisa HOUTSMA
12 Campus Exec Ofcr-Independence Dr. Sue DARBY
12 Campus Exec Ofcr-Zona Rosa Mr. Tim DZUBAY
12 Campus Exec Ofcr-Austin Ms. Karina ELLIOTT-LONG
12 Campus Exec Ofcr-Denver Ms. Charlene FIELDS
12 Director-Watertown Education Center Ms. Heidi SCHOOLEY
12 Campus Exec Ofcr-Wichita Ms. Ruth COOK

Oglala Lakota College (H)

Box 490, Kyle SD 57752-0490
County: Shannon FICE Identification: 014659
Unit ID: 219277
Telephone: (605) 455-6000 Carnegie Class: Tribal
FAX Number: (605) 455-2787 Calendar System: Semester
URL: www.olc.edu
Established: 1971 Annual Undergrad Tuition & Fees: $2,825
Enrollment: 1,831 Coed
Affiliation or Control: Tribal Control IRS Status: 501(c)3
Highest Offering: Master's
Program: Liberal Arts And General
Accreditation: NH, SW

01 President Mr. Thomas H. SHORTBULL
05 Vice President for Instruction Mr. Gerald GIRAUD
10 Vice President for Business Ms. Arlene QUIST
06 Registrar Ms. Leslie MESTETH
08 Director Learning Resources Ms. Lavera ROSE
15 Personnel Director Ms. Christina JANIS
37 Financial Aid Director Ms. Billi HORNBECK
84 Director Enrollment Management Ms. Leslie MESTETH
07 Director of Admissions Ms. Leslie MESTETH
09 Director of Institutional Research Mr. Andrew THOMPSON
21 Assoc Business Ofcr/Dir Purchasing Ms. Mla FERGUSON
29 Director Alumni Relations Ms. Marilyn POURIER
89 Director of Freshman Studies Mr. Tom RAYMOND
13 MIS Director Mr. Cliff DELONG
30 Inst Development Coordinator Ms. Marilyn POURIER
51 Community/Cont Education Coord Ms. Susan HEATHERSHAW
88 Applied Science Department Chair Mr. Doug NOYES
81 Math & Science Department Chair Mr. Jason TINANT
49 Art & History Department Chair Mr. Anthony FRESQUEZ
53 Education Department Chair Mr. Thomas RAYMOND
66 Nursing Department Chair Ms. Joan NELSON
83 Human Services Department Chair Dr. Jeffrey OLSON
88 LAKOTA Studies Department Chair Ms. Karen LONE HILL

Presentation College (I)

1500 N Main Street, Aberdeen SD 57401-1280
County: Brown FICE Identification: 003467
Unit ID: 219295
Telephone: (605) 225-1634 Carnegie Class: Bac/Diverse
FAX Number: (605) 229-8330 Calendar System: Semester
URL: www.presentation.edu
Established: 1951 Annual Undergrad Tuition & Fees: $15,260

Enrollment: 718 Coed
Affiliation or Control: Roman Catholic IRS Status: 501(c)3
Highest Offering: Baccalaureate
Program: Liberal Arts And General
Accreditation: NH, ADNUR, IACBE, MAC, NUR, RAD, SURGT, SW

01 Interim President ... Ms. Virginia TOBIN
05 Vice Pres for Academics ... Dr. James JOHNSON
10 Vice Pres for Finance ... Ms. Cathy HALL
84 Vice Pres for Enrollment ... Ms. JoEllen LINDNER
32 Vice Pres for Student Services ... Mr. Bob SCHUCHARDT
30 Vice President for Advancement ... Ms. Lori HARMEL
06 Registrar ... Ms. Maureen SCHUCHARDT
08 Librarian ... Ms. Lea BRIGGS
37 Director Student Financial Aid ... Ms. Janel WAGNER
09 Assessment Coordinator ... Ms. Nancy VANDER HOEK
15 Director of Human Resources ... Mr. Jason PETTIGREW
29 Alumni Coord/Major Gifts Officer ... Mr. Joddy MEIDINGER
26 Coord Marketing/Graphic Design ... Mr. Mark ZOELLNER

Sinte Gleska University (A)

Antelope Lake Circle, PO Box 105,
Mission SD 57555-0105
County: Todd FICE Identification: 021437
Unit ID: 219374
Telephone: (605) 856-5880 Carnegie Class: Tribal
FAX Number: (605) 856-5401 Calendar System: Semester
URL: www.sintegleska.edu
Established: 1970 Annual Undergrad Tuition & Fees: $2,175
Enrollment: 2,473 Coed
Affiliation or Control: Independent Non-Profit IRS Status: 501(c)3
Highest Offering: Master's
Program: Liberal Arts And General; Teacher Preparatory; Professional
Accreditation: NH

01 President ... Mr. Lionel BORDEAUX
11 Vice Pres Admin/Dean Stdnt Svcs ... Mr. Michael BENGE
06 Registrar ... Mr. Harvey HERMAN
08 Librarian ... Ms. Diana DILLION
10 Act Dir Business Ofc/Financial Ofcr ... Ms. Alisa BARLETT
37 Director Financial Aid ... Mr. William HAY
55 Director Adult Education ... Mr. James SHERMAN, III

Sioux Falls Seminary (B)

2100 S Summit Ave, Sioux Falls SD 57105-2729
County: Minnehaha FICE Identification: 004056
Unit ID: 219240
Telephone: (605) 336-6588 Carnegie Class: Spec/Faith
FAX Number: (605) 335-9090 Calendar System: 4/1/4
URL: www.sfseminary.edu
Established: 1858 Annual Graduate Tuition & Fees: $15,530
Enrollment: 138 Coed
Affiliation or Control: North American Baptist IRS Status: 501(c)3
Highest Offering: Doctorate; No Undergraduates
Program: Professional; Religious Emphasis
Accreditation: NH, THEOL

01 President ... Dr. G. Michael HAGAN
05 Academic Vice President & Dean ... Dr. Ronald D. SISK
10 Chief Financial Officer ... Mr. Jason D. KLEIN
30 Executive Dir/Leadership Foundation ... Mr. Benjamin G. LEE
58 Director of Doctoral Studies ... Dr. Gary E. STRICKLAND
06 Registrar ... Ms. Brenda L. MEDALEN
26 Director Public Relations/Marketing ... Ms. Shanda L. STRICHERZ
84 Director of Enrollment & Fin Aid ... Mr. Nathan M. HELLING

Sisseton-Wahpeton College (C)

PO Box 689, Sisseton SD 57262-0689
County: Roberts FICE Identification: 022773
Unit ID: 219408
Telephone: (605) 698-3966 Carnegie Class: Tribal
FAX Number: (605) 698-3132 Calendar System: Semester
URL: www.swc.tc
Established: 1979 Annual Undergrad Tuition & Fees (In-District): $3,960
Enrollment: 261 Coed
Affiliation or Control: Local IRS Status: 501(c)3
Highest Offering: Associate Degree
Program: Occupational; 2-Year Principally Bachelor's Creditable
Accreditation: NH

01 President ... Dr. Steven HEYD
10 Chief Financial Officer ... Mr. Dennis STUGELMEYER
08 Director Resource Center ... Vacant
37 Financial Aid Officer ... Ms. Janel MANY LIGHTNINGS
07 Director of Admissions ... Mrs. Darlene REDDAY
45 Planner/Developer ... Ms. Pam WYNIA
66 Director Nursing ... Dr. Barb DAHLEN

*South Dakota State Board of Regents System Office (D)

306 E Capitol Avenue, Suite 200, Pierre SD 57501-2545
County: Hughes FICE Identification: 033438
Telephone: (605) 773-3455 Carnegie Class: N/A
FAX Number: (605) 773-5320
URL: www.sdbor.edu

01 Executive Director ... Dr. Jack R. WARNER
11 System VP Administrative Services ... Dr. Monte KRAMER
05 System Vice Pres Academic Affairs ... Dr. Samuel GINGERICH
46 System Vice President for Research ... Dr. Gary JOHNSON
43 General Counsel ... Dr. James F. SHEKLETON
21 Internal Auditor ... Ms. Shelly ANDERSON
15 Director of Human Resources ... Dr. Janice MINDER
09 Information/Research Officer ... Dr. Janelle TOMAN
45 Director of Policy & Planning ... Dr. Paul GOUGH
13 Int Director Information Systems ... Mr. David HANSEN
46 Information Research Analyst ... Ms. Tracy MERCER

*The University of South Dakota (E)

414 E Clark, Vermillion SD 57069-2390
County: Clay FICE Identification: 003474
Unit ID: 219471
Telephone: (605) 677-5011 Carnegie Class: RU/H
FAX Number: (605) 677-5073 Calendar System: Semester
URL: www.usd.edu
Established: 1862 Annual Undergrad Tuition & Fees (In-State): $7,689
Enrollment: 10,151 Coed
Affiliation or Control: State IRS Status: 501(c)3
Highest Offering: Doctorate
Program: Liberal Arts And General; Teacher Preparatory; Professional
Accreditation: NH, ADNUR, ARCPA, ART, AUD, BUS, CACREP, CLPSY, DH, DIETI, JOUR, LAW, MED, MUS, OT, PTA, SP, SPAA, SW, TED, THEA

02 President ... Mr. James W. ABBOTT
05 Provost/Vice Pres Academic Affairs ... Dr. Charles A. STABEN
17 Vice President Health Affairs ... Dr. Rodney R. PARRY
10 Vice Pres Finance - CFO ... Ms. Sheila GESTRING
46 Vice President for Research ... Dr. Laura J. JENSKI
26 VP of Marketing/Enrollment Svcs ... Mr. Jeffrey S. BAYLOR
11 Vice Pres Administration & ITS ... Ms. Roberta S. AMBUR
20 Assoc Vice Pres Academic Affairs ... Ms. Lynn B. ROGNSTAD
08 Dean of Libraries ... Dr. Anne C. MOORE
32 Dean of Students ... Dr. James PARKER
29 Exec Dir Alumni Association ... Ms. Kersten JOHNSON
96 Director of Purchasing ... Mr. Darby GANSCHOW
15 Director Human Resources ... Ms. Diane S. ZAK
22 Affirmative Action Officer ... Ms. Roberta H. HAKL
18 Acting Dir Facilities Management ... Mr. John DAVIS
37 Director of Financial Aid ... Ms. Julie H. PIER
09 Director of Institutional Research ... Dr. Biao ZHANG
36 Dir Ctr for Academic & Career Plng ... Mr. Steve WARD
28 Chief Diversity Officer ... Vacant
06 Acting Registrar ... Dr. Kurt HACKEMER
41 Athletic Director ... Mr. David SAYLER
38 Director Student Counseling ... Vacant
19 Director Public Safety ... Mr. Peter E. JENSEN
84 Dean of Enrollment ... Mr. Scott POHLSON
49 Dean College Arts & Sciences ... Dr. Matthew C. MOEN
50 Dean School of Business ... Mr. Michael J. KELLER
51 Dean Continuing Education ... Dr. Laurie J. BECVAR
53 Dean School of Education ... Dr. Rick MELMER
57 Dean College Fine Arts ... Dr. Larry SCHOU
58 Dean of Graduate Education ... Dr. Laurie J. BECVAR
61 Interim Dean School of Law ... Mr. Thomas GEU

*Black Hills State University (F)

1200 University Street, Spearfish SD 57799-9500
County: Lawrence FICE Identification: 003459
Unit ID: 219046
Telephone: (605) 642-6011 Carnegie Class: Master's S
FAX Number: (605) 642-6214 Calendar System: Semester
URL: www.bhsu.edu
Established: 1883 Annual Undergrad Tuition & Fees (In-State): $7,424
Enrollment: 4,722 Coed
Affiliation or Control: State IRS Status: 501(c)3
Highest Offering: Master's
Program: 2-Year Principally Bachelor's Creditable; Liberal Arts And General; Teacher Preparatory
Accreditation: NH, MUS, TED

02 President ... Dr. Kay SCHALLENKAMP
05 Provost/Vice Pres Academic Affairs ... Dr. Rodney CUSTER
10 Vice President Finance/Admin ... Ms. Kathy J. JOHNSON
30 Vice Pres University Advancement ... Mr. Steve L. MEEKER
32 Vice President for Student Life ... Dr. Lois FLAGSTAD
20 Assoc Vice Pres Academic Affairs ... Dr. Kristi PEARCE
26 Director Marketing & Communications ... Ms. Corinne HANSEN
27 Chief Information Officer ... Dr. Warren WILSON
37 Director Student Financial Aid ... Ms. Deb HENRIKSEN
38 Director Counseling Center ... Dr. James FLEMING
39 Director Residence Life ... Mr. Michael L. ISAACSON
35 Director Student Services ... Ms. Jane KLUG
15 Director of Human Resources ... Ms. Nancy GRASSEL
06 Registrar ... Ms. April M. MEEKER
07 Director of Admissions ... Ms. Beth OAKS
21 Director of Business Services ... Mr. Rob HOUDEK
18 Director Facilities/Physical Plant ... Mr. Art JONES
29 Director Alumni Relations ... Mr. Tom WHEATON
09 Director of Institutional Research ... Ms. Erin HOLMES
08 Director Library Operations ... Mr. Scott AHOLA
36 Director of Career Center ... Ms. Arlene HOLMES
104 Director International Studies ... Dr. James FLEMING
30 Director of Development ... Mr. Dwight HANSEN
19 Director Security/Safety ... Mr. Myron SULLIVAN
40 Director University Bookstore ... Mr. Michael JASTORFF
41 Director of Athletics ... Mr. Jhett ALBERS
13 Director Network & Computer Svcs ... Mr. Fred NELSON
49 Int Dean College of Arts & Sciences ... Dr. Curtis CARD
50 Dean College of Business ... Dr. Priscilla ROMKEMA
53 Interim Dean College of Education ... Dr. Patricia SIMPSON
106 Dean Educational Outreach ... Mr. Rajeev BUKRALIA
92 Director of Honors Program ... Dr. Amy FUQUA

*Dakota State University (G)

820 N Washington Avenue, Madison SD 57042-1799
County: Lake FICE Identification: 003463
Unit ID: 219082
Telephone: (605) 256-5111 Carnegie Class: Master's S
FAX Number: (605) 256-5316 Calendar System: Semester
URL: www.dsu.edu
Established: 1881 Annual Undergrad Tuition & Fees (In-State): $6,897
Enrollment: 3,101 Coed
Affiliation or Control: State IRS Status: 501(c)3
Highest Offering: Doctorate
Program: 2-Year Principally Bachelor's Creditable; Liberal Arts And General; Teacher Preparatory; Technical Emphasis
Accreditation: NH, ACBSP, TED

02 President ... Dr. Douglas D. KNOWLTON
05 Vice President for Academic Affairs .. Dr. Cecelia M. WITTMAYER
10 Vice Pres for Business & Admin Svcs ... Mr. Stacy L. KRUSEMARK
32 Vice Pres/Dean Student Affairs ... Mr. Jesse WISE, III
30 Vice Pres for Univ Advancement ... Ms. Judith PAYNE
50 Dean College Business/Info Systems ... Dr. Tom L. HALVERSON
53 Dean College of Education ... Dr. Judith L. DITTMAN
49 Dean College of Arts and Sciences ... Dr. Kari L. FORBES-BOYTE
58 Dean of Graduate Studies/Research ... Dr. Omar F. EL-GAYAR
41 Director of Athletics ... Mr. Gene R. WOCKENFUSS
36 Director of Career Services ... Dr. Marie A. LOHSANDT
08 Director of Library ... Ms. Ethelle S. BEAN
13 Director of Computing Services ... Mr. W. David ZOLNOWSKY
29 Director Alumni/Public Relations ... Ms. Jona M. SCHMIDT
18 Director of Physical Plant ... Mr. Patrick C. KEATING
06 Registrar ... Ms. Sandra E. ANDERSON
37 Director Financial Aid ... Ms. Denise R. GRAYSON
38 Director Student Development ... Mr. O. Keith BUNDY
39 Dir of Student Union/Residence Life ... Mr. Steven J. BARTEL
35 Director of Student Activities ... Ms. Amanda L. PARPART
04 Admin Assistant to the President ... Ms. Linda J. BROZIK
16 Director Human Resources ... Ms. Maria D. HARDER
88 Director Extended Programs ... Dr. Margaret A. O'DRIEN
07 Director of Admission ... Ms. Amy S. CRISSINGER
92 Dir Ctr Excell Computer Info Sys ... Dr. Wayne E. PAULI
09 Director of Assessment ... Ms. Carrie A. AHERN
21 Comptroller ... Ms. Amy L. DOCKENDORF
25 Dir of Ctr for Adv of HIT ... Mr. Dan FRIEDRICH
85 International Programs Coordinator ... Ms. Jacy FRY
40 Director of Bookstore ... Mr. Dale P. DAVIS
88 Director Center of Info Assurance ... Dr. Kevin F. STREFF
25 Director of Budget & Grants Admin ... Ms. Sara HARE
25 Director of Sponsored Programs ... Dr. Mickie L. KREIDLER
28 Diversity Coordinator ... Ms. Jennifer ARANDA

*Northern State University (H)

1200 S Jay Street, Aberdeen SD 57401-7198
County: Brown FICE Identification: 003466
Unit ID: 219259
Telephone: (605) 626-3011 Carnegie Class: Bac/Diverse
FAX Number: (605) 626-3022 Calendar System: Semester
URL: www.northern.edu
Established: 1901 Annual Undergrad Tuition & Fees (In-State): $6,951
Enrollment: 3,296 Coed
Affiliation or Control: State IRS Status: 501(c)3
Highest Offering: Master's
Program: Liberal Arts And General; Teacher Preparatory; Business Emphasis
Accreditation: NH, MUS, TED

02 President ... Dr. James M. SMITH
05 Vice Pres Academic Affs/Provost ... Dr. Thomas HAWLEY
10 Vice Pres Finance/Administration ... Mr. Don ERLENBUSCH
32 Vice President for Student Affairs ... Ms. Rhoda SMITH
29 Vice Pres Alumni Relations ... Mr. Mike BIRGEN
102 President/CEO of Foundation ... Mr. Todd JORDRE
06 Registrar ... Ms. Peggy HALLSTROM
07 Director of Admissions ... Mr. Allan VOGEL
08 Director of Library ... Mr. Robert RUSSELL
36 Director Counsel/Service Learning ... Ms. Deb THORSTENSON
09 Institutional Research Officer ... Mr. Ross NORMAN
25 Director Grants Sponsored Research ... Ms. Karen MARCHANT
13 Director of Computer Services ... Ms. Joann POMPLUN
37 Dir Student Financial Assistance ... Ms. Sharon KIENOW
39 Director Student Devel/Residence ... Mr. Todd TUCKER
21 Comptroller ... Ms. Veronica PAULSON
15 Director of Human Resources ... Ms. Susan BOSTIAN
26 Director of University Relations ... Ms. Brenda DREYER
43 General Counsel ... Mr. John MEYER
18 Director of Facilities Management ... Mr. Monte MEHLHOFF
49 Dean College of Arts & Science ... Dr. Celestino MENDEZ
50 Dean School of Business ... Dr. Willard BROUCEK
53 Dean School of Education ... Dr. Connie GEIER
57 Dean School of Fine Arts ... Dr. Alan LAFAVE
56 Director of Extended Studies ... Mr. Ronald BROWNIE
41 Director of Athletics ... Mr. Robert OLSON
40 Director of Bookstore ... Ms. Beth RASMUSSON
38 Director Student Counseling ... Ms. Deb THORSTENSON

96 Director of Purchasing .... Mr. Earl WEISENBURGER
92 Director Honors Program .... Dr. Erin FOUBERG
28 Multicultural Advisor .... Mr. Peni MOUNGA
35 Director Student Affairs .... Mr. Bart CARITHERS

*South Dakota School of Mines and Technology (A)

501 E Saint Joseph, Rapid City SD 57701-3995

County: Pennington FICE Identification: 003470
Unit ID: 219347
Telephone: (605) 394-2511 Carnegie Class: Spec/Engg
FAX Number: (605) 394-6131 Calendar System: Semester
URL: www.sdsmt.edu
Established: 1885 Annual Undergrad Tuition & Fees (In-State): $14,700
Enrollment: 2,354 Coed
Affiliation or Control: State IRS Status: 501(c)3
Highest Offering: Doctorate
Program: Professional; Technical Emphasis
Accreditation: NH, CS, ENG

02 President .... Dr. Robert A. WHARTON
05 Provost/Vice Pres Academic Affs .... Dr. Duane HRNCIR
10 Vice Pres Business/Administration ..Mr. Timothy G. HENDERSON
46 Vice President of Research .... Dr. Ronald J. WHITE
32 VP Student Affs/Dean of Students ....Dr. Patricia G. MAHON
30 VP for University Advancement ....Vacant
20 Associate Provost Academic Affairs ....Dr. Kathryn E. ALLEY
84 Assoc Provost for Enrollment Mgmt .... Dr. Michael C. GUNN
21 Director of Business Services ....Mrs. Sandra R. FISCHER
07 Int Director of Admissions ....Ms. Molly FRANKL
29 Director of Alumni Association ....Mr. Timothy J. VOTTERO
90 Director Information Tech Svcs ....Mr. Bryan J. SCHUMACHER
08 Director Devereaux Library ....Ms. Patricia M. ANDERSEN
36 Director Career Services .... Dr. Darrell R. SAWYER
37 Director of Financial Aid .... Mr. David W. MARTIN
88 Int Dir Inst Atmospheric Sciences .... Dr. Paul L. SMITH
41 Director of Athletics .... Dr. Dick KAISER
102 President SDSM&T Foundation ....Vacant
15 Dir Human Resources/ Affirm Action .... Mrs. Deborah L. SLOAT
18 Director of Facility Services .... Mr. David BRIDGE
11 Director of Administrative Services ....Ms. Terry H. GRANT
39 Dir Residence Life & Judicial Affs ....Ms. Maureen C. WILSON
85 Director Ivanhoe International Ctr .... Ms. Susan R. AADLAND
58 Int Dean Graduate Education .... Dr. Antonette M. LOGAR
38 Director Student Counseling Svcs ....Ms. Jolie A. MCCOY
84 Registrar and Dir Academic Services .... Ms. Barbara DOLAN
94 Dir Women in Science/Engrng Pgm ....Vacant
09 Director of Retention & Testing .... Dr. Pat BEU
26 Director of Communications ....Vacant
06 Registration Officer .... Mrs. Kathryn CRAWFORD
40 Manager College Bookstore ....Mr. Marlin L. KINZER
35 Student Activities Coordinator .... Mr. Michael KEEGAN

*South Dakota State University (B)

Brookings SD 57007-2298

County: Brookings FICE Identification: 003471
Unit ID: 219356
Telephone: (605) 688-4151 Carnegie Class: RU/H
FAX Number: (605) 688-5822 Calendar System: Semester
URL: www.sdstate.edu
Established: 1881 Annual Undergrad Tuition & Fees (In-State): $6,887
Enrollment: 12,816 Coed
Affiliation or Control: State IRS Status: 501(c)3
Highest Offering: Doctorate
Program: Liberal Arts And General; Teacher Preparatory; Professional
Accreditation: NH, AAFCS, CACREP, CIDA, CONST, CORE, CS, DIETD, ENG, ENGT, JOUR, MT, MUS, NURSE, PHAR, TED

02 President .... Dr. David L. CHICOINE
05 Provost/Vice Pres Academic Affairs .... Dr. Laurie NICHOLS
32 Vice President Student Affairs .... Dr. Marysz RAMES
45 Vice President of Research .... Dr. Kevin KEPHART
13 VP for Information Technology ....Dr. Michael ADELAINE
10 Vice Pres Finance & Budget ....Mr. Wesley G. TSCHETTER
20 Assoc Vice Pres for Academic Affs .... Dr. Mary Kay HELLING
18 Asst Vice Pres Facilities Services .... Mr. Dean KATTELMANN
88 Asst VP AA Intl Affairs/Outreach ....Vacant
04 Executive Asst to the President .... Mr. Robert OTTERSON
08 Dean of the Library .... Dr. Kristi TORNQUIST
97 Dean of General Studies .... Dr. Keith CORBETT
51 Dean Continuing & Extended Educ .... Dr. Gail TIDEMANN
07 Director of Admissions ....Ms. Tracy WELSH
06 Registrar .... Dr. Aaron AURE
38 Acting Director Wellness ....Mr. Mark EKELAND
37 Financial Aid Officer .... Mr. Jay A. LARSEN
15 Director Human Resources ....Mr. Wesley TSCHETTER
102 President & CEO of Foundation ....Mr. Steve ERPENBACH
29 Director of Alumni Affairs .... Mr. Matt FUKS
14 Director Admin & Research Computing .Mr. Delmar R. JOHNSON
19 Chief Security/Safety ....Mr. Tim HEATON
39 Director of Residential Life ....Ms. Connie CRANDALL
40 Director of Bookstore ....Mr. Derek PETERSON
41 Director of Athletics .... Mr. Justin SELL
28 Dir of Diversity/Equal Opportunity ......Dr. Jennifer (Jalme) NOLAN
56 Interim Director of Extension ....Dr. Barry DUNN
26 Dir Marketing/Image/Communications ....Mr. Michael LOCKREM
24 Mgr Instructional Design Services ....Dr. Shouhong ZHANG
85 International Students Advisor ....Ms. Stephanie DESOUSA
47 Dean Agriculture/Biological Sci ....Dr. Barry DUNN
49 Acting Dean of Arts & Sciences .... Dr. David HILDERBRAND
54 Dean of Engineering .... Dr. Lewis BROWN
53 Dean Education & Human Science .... Dr. Jill THORNGREN
66 Dean of Nursing .... Dr. Roberta K. OLSON
67 Dean of Pharmacy .... Dr. Dennis HEDGE
58 Acting Dean of Graduate School .... Dr. Mary Kay HELLING
92 Dean Honors College .... Dr. Timothy NICHOLS

Southeast Technical Institute (C)

2320 N Career Avenue, Sioux Falls SD 57107-1302

County: Minnehaha FICE Identification: 007764
Unit ID: 219426
Telephone: (605) 367-7624 Carnegie Class: Assoc/Pub-R-M
FAX Number: (605) 367-8305 Calendar System: Semester
URL: www.southeasttech.edu
Established: 1968 Annual Undergrad Tuition & Fees (In-District): $5,100
Enrollment: 3,069 Coed
Affiliation or Control: Local IRS Status: 501(c)3
Highest Offering: Associate Degree
Program: Occupational
Accreditation: NH, CVT, DMS, EEG, NMT, SURGT

01 President .... Mr. Jeffrey R. HOLCOMB
05 Vice President of Academics .... Mr. Jim JACOBSEN
10 Vice President Finance & Operations ....Mr. Rich KLUIN
32 Vice Pres Student Affs/Inst Rsrch .... Mr. Tracy NOLDNER
35 Director of Students .... Mr. Jim ROKUSEK
50 Training Solutions Institute ....Mr. Lon HIRD
06 Registrar .... Ms. Kristie VORTHERMS
15 Human Resources Specialist .... Ms. Kathy STRUCK
20 Director of Academic Support ....Dr. Craig PETERS
26 Marketing Coordinator .... Ms. Margaret PENNOCK
88 Non-traditional Student/SGA Coord .... Ms. DiAnn KOTHE
102 Foundation Director ....Ms. Michelle LOUNSBERY
37 Financial Aid Officer ....Ms. Lynette GRABOWSKA
21 Business Manager .... Mr. James WESTCOTT
38 Personal Counselor .... Ms. Nicole MCMILLIN

University of Sioux Falls (D)

1101 W 22nd Street, Sioux Falls SD 57105-1699

County: Minnehaha FICE Identification: 003469
Unit ID: 219383
Telephone: (605) 331-5000 Carnegie Class: Bac/Diverse
FAX Number: (605) 331-6615 Calendar System: 4/1/4
URL: www.usiouxfalls.edu
Established: 1883 Annual Undergrad Tuition & Fees: $22,850
Enrollment: 1,267 Coed
Affiliation or Control: American Baptist IRS Status: 501(c)3
Highest Offering: Master's
Program: Liberal Arts And General; Teacher Preparatory; Professional
Accreditation: NH, IACBE, NURSE, SW, TED

01 President .... Dr. Mark BENEDETTO
04 Exec Assistant to the President .... Ms. Karen BANGASSER
10 VP for Business and Finance ....Ms. Marsha DENNISTON
05 Provost/Vice Pres Academic Affairs .... Dr. Brett BRADFIELD
30 VP Institutional Advancement .... Mr. Jon HIATT
15 VP of Human Resources .... Ms. Julie GEDNALSKE
13 AVP Information Tech .... Mr. William BARTELL
32 AVP Student Dev/Dean of Students .... Rev. Karen SUMNER
42 Dean of the Chapel .... Rev. Dennis L. THUM
06 Registrar ....Vacant
21 Controller .... Ms. Susan THIE
37 Director of Financial Aid .... Ms. Laura A. OLSON
08 Director of Library Services .... Ms. Judy CLAUSON
84 Dir of Enrollment Management ....Ms. Billie STREUFERT
18 Director Buildings/Grounds .... Mr. Rod VOELLER
40 Bookstore Manager .... Ms. Lesley GORBY
41 Athletic Director .... Mr. William SANCHEZ
88 Dir of Degree Completion Program .... Ms. LuAnn GROSSMAN
58 Chair Business/Dir of MBA/Asst Prof ...... Ms. Rebecca MURDOCK
53 Chair Fredrikson School Education ....Ms. Julie MCAREAVEY
57 Chair Fine Arts/Associate Professor ....Ms. Nancy OLIVE
81 Chair Natural Sciences/Assoc Prof .... Dr. William SOEFFING
79 Chair Humanities/Asst Professor ....Ms. Nicholle SCHUELKE
66 Founding Director School of Nursing .... Dr. Barbara VELLENGA
83 Chair Social Sciences .... Dr. Sharon COOL

Western Dakota Technical Institute (E)

800 Mickelson Drive, Rapid City SD 57703-4018

County: Pennington FICE Identification: 010170
Unit ID: 219480
Telephone: (605) 394-4034 Carnegie Class: Assoc/Pub-R-S
FAX Number: (605) 394-1789 Calendar System: Semester
URL: www.wdt.edu
Established: 1968 Annual Undergrad Tuition & Fees (In-District): $4,032
Enrollment: 1,152 Coed
Affiliation or Control: Local IRS Status: 501(c)3
Highest Offering: Associate Degree
Program: Occupational
Accreditation: NH, SURGT

01 President .... Dr. Craig BAILEY
03 Vice President .... Dr. Cathy ANDERSON
32 Dean Student Services ....Ms. Janell OBERLANDER
26 Director of Marketing/Admissions ....Mr. Stephen BUCHHOLZ
37 Financial Aid Coordinator .... Ms. Starla RUSSELL
36 Student Placement Coordinator .... Mr. Curt LAUINGER
38 Student Services Counselor .... Ms. Rae GETZ

TENNESSEE

All Saints Bible College (F)

930 Mason Street, Memphis TN 38126

County: Shelby Identification: 667014
Telephone: (901) 322-0120 Carnegie Class: Not Classified
FAX Number: (901) 947-3504 Calendar System: Semester
URL: www.allsaintsonline.info
Established: 2002 Annual Undergrad Tuition & Fees: N/A
Enrollment: 70 Coed
Affiliation or Control: Church of God in Christ IRS Status: 501(c)3
Highest Offering: Baccalaureate
Program: Religious Emphasis
Accreditation: @BI

01 Chancellor .... Bishop Charles E. BLAKE
11 Interim Administrator .... Dr. Granville SCRUGGS

American Baptist College (G)

1800 Baptist World Center Drive, Nashville TN 37207-4952

County: Davidson FICE Identification: 010460
Unit ID: 219505
Telephone: (615) 256-1463 Carnegie Class: Spec/Faith
FAX Number: (615) 226-7855 Calendar System: Semester
URL: www.abcnash.edu
Established: 1924 Annual Undergrad Tuition & Fees: $8,385
Enrollment: 103 Coed
Affiliation or Control: Baptist IRS Status: 501(c)3
Highest Offering: Baccalaureate
Program: Liberal Arts And General
Accreditation: BI

01 President ....Dr. Forrest E. HARRIS, SR.
05 Vice President Academic Affairs ....Dr. Renita WEEMS
84 Director of Enrollment Management .. Ms. Marcella F. LOCKHART
10 Chief Financial Officer .... Ms. Clara A. WILLIAMS
11 Chief of Campus Operations ....Ms. Joyce ACKLEN
08 Interim Director Library Services .... Ms. Cherisna JEAN-MARIE
04 Asst to Pres for Faculty Support ....Mr. Marcus TUBBS
32 Dir Student Svcs/Extention Pgms ....Mr. James SANFORD

Aquinas College (H)

4210 Harding Road, Nashville TN 37205-2005

County: Davidson FICE Identification: 003477
Unit ID: 219578
Telephone: (615) 297-7545 Carnegie Class: Bac/Assoc
FAX Number: (615) 279-3892 Calendar System: Semester
URL: www.aquinascollege.edu
Established: 1961 Annual Undergrad Tuition & Fees: $19,050
Enrollment: 747 Coed
Affiliation or Control: Roman Catholic IRS Status: 501(c)3
Highest Offering: Baccalaureate
Program: 2-Year Principally Bachelor's Creditable; Liberal Arts And General; Teacher Preparatory
Accreditation: SC, ADNUR, NUR

01 President .... Sr. Mary Sarah GALBRAITH, OP
11 Vice Pres Administrative Affairs .Sr. Mary Cecilia GOODRUM, OP
05 Vice President for Academic Affairs ....Sr. Elizabeth Anne ALLEN, OP
88 Director of Communications ....Ms. Lauri BROWN
26 Vice Pres Institutional Advancement ....Mr. Timothy STRANSKY
07 Director of Admissions .... Mrs. Connie HANSOM
06 Registrar ....Ms. Etta MASON
08 Librarian .... Mr. Mark HALL
30 Director of Development .... Ms. Jeanne SCHULLER
40 Bookstore Manager .... Mr. Alan BRADLEY
66 Director of RN-BSN Nursing Program ....Bro. Ignatius PERKINS, OP
66 Director of ASN Nursing Program .... Mrs. Margaret DANIEL
20 Director of Education .... Sr. Mary Anne ZUBERBUELER, OP
37 Director of Financial Aid ....Ms. Kylie PRUITT
10 Business Manager .... Mr. Roger MUEHE
35 Director of Student Affairs ....Mrs. Suzette TELLI
09 Director of Institutional Research ....Sr. Mary BENDYNA, OP
29 Director of Alumni Relations ....Vacant
18 Chief of Facilities/Physical Plant ....Mr. John WALL
15 Director Personnel Services ....Mrs. Loretta CLARK
88 Director of Student Learning Svcs ..Mrs. Lindsey HINDS-BROWN
88 Director of Catechetics ....Sr. Mary Michael FOX, OP

Argosy University, Nashville (I)

100 Centerview Drive, Suite 225, Nashville TN 37214-3438

County: Davidson Identification: 666668
Unit ID: 450535
Telephone: (615) 525-2800 Carnegie Class: Not Classified
FAX Number: (615) 525-2900 Calendar System: Semester
URL: www.argosy.edu
Established: 2001 Annual Undergrad Tuition & Fees: $14,580
Enrollment: 537 Coed
Affiliation or Control: Proprietary IRS Status: Proprietary
Highest Offering: Doctorate
Program: Professional
Accreditation: &NH

01 Campus President ... Dr. Sandra L. WISE
07 Director of Admissions ... Ms. Erica BLIGEN
32 Director of Student Services ... Ms. Stacy A. WADDELL
06 Registrar ... Ms. Christine DYBATA
21 Student Finance Coordinator ... Mr. Josh YARBOROUGH
15 Human Resources Director ... Ms. Faith GLASPIE-ELLIS

† Regional accreditation is carried under the parent institution in Chicago, IL.

Baptist Memorial College of Health Sciences (A)

1003 Monroe Avenue, Memphis TN 38104-3199
County: Shelby FICE Identification: 034403
Unit ID: 219639
Telephone: (901) 575-2247 Carnegie Class: Spec/Health
FAX Number: (901) 572-2461 Calendar System: Trimester
URL: www.bchs.edu
Established: 1994 Annual Undergrad Tuition & Fees: $9,810
Enrollment: 1,022 Coed
Affiliation or Control: Independent Non-Profit IRS Status: 501(c)3
Highest Offering: Baccalaureate
Program: Occupational; Professional
Accreditation: SC, DMS, NMT, NURSE, RAD, RTT

01 President ... Dr. Betty S. MCGARVEY
10 Vice President Business/Admin Svcs ... Ms. Leanne SMITH
05 Chief Academic Officer/Provost ... Dr. William J. SOBOTOR
97 Dean General Studies ... Dr. Barry SCHULTZ
66 Dean Nursing ... Dr. Anne M. PLUMB
76 Dean Allied Health ... Dr. Linda REED
32 Dean Student Services ... Ms. Nancy REED
16 Exec Director Admin Support Svcs ... Ms. Adonna CALDWELL
06 Registrar ... Ms. Jana D. TURNER
07 Director of Admissions ... Ms. Lissa MORGAN
09 Dir of Institutional Effectiveness ... Ms. Pam MOSS
29 Director Alumni Relations ... Mrs. Bamby COUNCE
35 Manager Student Affairs ... Mr. Jeremy WILKES
37 Supervisor Student Financial Aid ... Ms. Janet BONNEY-BAKER

Belmont University (B)

1900 Belmont Boulevard, Nashville TN 37212-3757
County: Davidson FICE Identification: 003479
Unit ID: 219709
Telephone: (615) 460-6000 Carnegie Class: Master's L
FAX Number: (615) 460-6446 Calendar System: Semester
URL: www.belmont.edu
Established: N/A Annual Undergrad Tuition & Fees: $24,960
Enrollment: 5,896 Coed
Affiliation or Control: Non-denominational IRS Status: 501(c)3
Highest Offering: Doctorate
Program: Liberal Arts And General; Teacher Preparatory; Professional
Accreditation: SC, ART, BUS, BUSA, MACTE, MUS, NURSE, OT, @PHAR, PTA, SW, TED

01 President ... Dr. Robert C. FISHER
05 Provost ... Dr. Thomas D. BURNS
11 Vice Pres for Admin & Univ Counsel ... Dr. Jason ROGERS
30 Vice Pres University Advancement ... Dr. Bethel THOMAS
10 Vice President Finance & Operations ... Mr. Steven T. LASLEY
04 Vice Pres for Presidential Affairs ... Dr. Susan H. WEST
42 Vice Pres Spiritual Development ... Dr. Todd LAKE
50 Dean College of Business ... Dr. Patrick RAINES
64 Dean College Visual/Performing Arts ... Dr. Cynthia A. CURTIS
49 Dean College Arts & Sciences ... Dr. Bryce SULLIVAN
76 Dean College Health Sciences ... Vacant
73 Dean School of Religion ... Dr. Darrell GWALTNEY
61 Dean College of Law ... Mr. Jeffrey S. KINSLER
32 Dean of Students ... Mr. Andrew J. JOHNSTON
84 Dean Enrollment Services ... Dr. David MEE
81 Assoc Dean School of Science ... Dr. Robert GRAMMER
85 Director of International Education ... Ms. Katherine SKINNER
15 Director of Human Resources ... Mrs. Sally MCKAY
37 Director of Financial Aid ... Mrs. Patricia SMEDLEY
29 Director of Alumni Relations ... Ms. Debbie COPPINGER
18 Director of Facilities Management ... Mr. Fred THOMPSON
19 Director of Safety & Security ... Mr. Terry A. WHITE
90 Director Technology Services ... Mr. Randall REYNOLDS
06 University Registrar ... Mr. Steven REED
08 Director of Library Services ... Dr. Ernest W. HEARD, JR.
41 Athletic Director ... Mr. Michael D. STRICKLAND
40 Manager Bookstore ... Mrs. Catherine MURPHY
36 Dir Career Svcs/Cooperative Educ ... Mrs. Patricia JACOBS
27 Director of Communications ... Mr. Greg S. PILLON
09 Director of Institutional Research ... Dr. Roy (Ike) IKENBERRY
20 Assistant Provost ... Vacant

Bethel University (C)

325 Cherry Avenue, McKenzie TN 38201-1705
County: Carroll FICE Identification: 003480
Unit ID: 219718
Telephone: (731) 352-4000 Carnegie Class: Master's M
FAX Number: (731) 352-4069 Calendar System: Semester
URL: www.bethelu.edu
Established: 1842 Annual Undergrad Tuition & Fees: $13,552
Enrollment: 4,395 Coed
Affiliation or Control: Cumberland Presbyterian IRS Status: 501(c)3
Highest Offering: Master's
Program: Liberal Arts And General; Teacher Preparatory
Accreditation: SC, #ARCPA, NURSE

01 President ... Dr. Robert D. PROSSER
05 Chief Academic Officer ... Dr. Phyllis CAMPBELL
49 VP College of Liberal Arts ... Dr. Ronald DEMING
107 VP College of Prof Studies ... Ms. Kelly SANDERS-KELLEY
06 University Registrar ... Ms. Becky HAMES
10 Asst to Pres of Financial Affairs ... Mr. Keith PRIESTLEY
07 Director of Admissions, CLA ... Mrs. Tina HODGES
30 Director of Development ... Mr. Mike PARKER
32 Dean of Student Development ... Mr. James STEWART
37 Director of Financial Aid ... Vacant
26 Director of Public Relations ... Ms. Jennifer GLASS
38 Director Student Counseling ... Mrs. Sandy LOUDEN
18 Director of Physical Facilities ... Mr. Steve PROSSER
42 Chaplain ... Rev. Anne HAMES
08 Library Director ... Ms. Jill WHITFILL
15 Int Human Resource Director ... Dr. Phyllis CAMPBELL
41 Athletic Director ... Mr. Glenn HAYES
09 Director of Institutional Research ... Dr. Mary Jane HAWTHORNE
29 Director Alumni Relations ... Mrs. Myra CARLOCK
88 Dir College of Criminal Justice ... Mr. Jimmy Ray FARRIS
53 Dir College of Education ... Dr. J. Randolph CROMWELL
58 Dean College of Graduate Studies ... Dr. Dorothy BLACK

Bryan College (D)

PO Box 7000, Dayton TN 37321-7000
County: Rhea FICE Identification: 003536
Unit ID: 219790
Telephone: (423) 775-2041 Carnegie Class: Bac/Diverse
FAX Number: (423) 775-7330 Calendar System: Semester
URL: www.bryan.edu
Established: 1930 Annual Undergrad Tuition & Fees: $19,550
Enrollment: 1,149 Coed
Affiliation or Control: Independent Non-Profit IRS Status: 501(c)3
Highest Offering: Master's
Program: Liberal Arts And General; Teacher Preparatory
Accreditation: SC, IACBE

01 President ... Dr. Stephen D. LIVESAY
04 Exec Assistant to the President ... Ms. Margaret A. LEGG
05 Academic Vice President ... Dr. Bradford W. SAMPLE
10 Vice President for Finance ... Mr. Vance J. BERGER
30 Vice Pres for College Advancement ... Mr. Blake W. HUDSON
11 Vice President of Operations ... Mr. Timothy J. HOSTETLER
84 Vice Pres for Enrollment Management ... Dr. Michael C. SAPIENZA
42 Vice Pres for Spiritual Formation ... Dr. Matt A. BENSON
58 Dean Sch of Adult & Graduate Stds ... Dr. Michael K. CHASE
32 Dean of Students ... Mr. Bruce MORGAN
37 Director of Financial Aid ... Mr. Rick J. TAPHORN
13 Director of Information Systems ... Mr. Stephen M. PAULSON
06 Registrar ... Ms. Janet M. PIATT
08 Director of Library Sciences ... Dr. Gary N. FITSIMMONS
26 Director of Public Information ... Mr. Thomas A. DAVIS
15 Director Personnel Services ... Mrs. Barbara J. FAVORITE
41 Athletic Director ... Dr. Sanford ZENSEN
18 Director of Physical Plant ... Mr. Doug W. SCHOTT
29 Director of Alumni Affairs ... Mr. David C. TROMANHAUSER
07 Director of Admissions ... Mr. Aaron K. PORTER
88 Accreditation Liaison ... Dr. Kenneth M. FROEMKE

Carson-Newman College (E)

1646 Russell Avenue, PO Box 557,
Jefferson City TN 37760-2204
County: Jefferson FICE Identification: 003481
Unit ID: 219806
Telephone: (865) 471-2000 Carnegie Class: Bac/Diverse
FAX Number: (865) 471-3502 Calendar System: Semester
URL: www.cn.edu
Established: 1851 Annual Undergrad Tuition & Fees: $22,274
Enrollment: 2,065 Coed
Affiliation or Control: Southern Baptist IRS Status: 501(c)3
Highest Offering: Master's
Program: Liberal Arts And General; Teacher Preparatory; Professional
Accreditation: SC, AAFCS, ART, DIETD, MUS, NURSE, TED

01 President ... Dr. J. Randall O'BRIEN
05 Provost ... Dr. Kina S. MALLARD
30 Vice President for Advancement ... Dr. Danny NICHOLSON
32 Vice President Student Affairs ... Mr. Rodney DYER
35 Dean of Student Affairs ... Ms. Shelley BALL
08 Director of Library Services ... Mr. Bruce KOCOUR
27 Vice President for Communications ... Mr. Parker LEAKE
29 Director of Alumni Affairs ... Mr. David BUCHANAN
36 Director Student Success ... Mrs. Amy HUMPHREY
37 Director Financial Aid ... Ms. Danette SEALE
38 Director Counseling Services ... Mrs. Jennifer CATLETT
07 Director of Admissions ... Ms. Melanie REDDING
44 Dir Charitable Gift Plan/Annual Fnd ... Mr. Chris CATES
90 Director of Campus Computing ... Mr. Mark SEAGROVES
09 Director of Institutional Research ... Ms. Gail GREENE
18 Chief Facilities/Physical Plant ... Mr. Ondes WEBSTER
06 Registrar ... Mrs. Sheryl GRAY
92 Director of Honors Program ... Dr. Brian AUSTIN
79 Dean Division of Humanities ... Dr. Mary BALDRIDGE
50 Dean Division Business & Economics ... Dr. Clyde HERRING
53 Dean Division of Education ... Dr. Sharon TEETS
59 Dean Div Family & Consumer Sciences ... Dr. Kitty R. COFFEY
57 Dean Division of Fine Arts ... Dr. D. Clark MEASELS
83 Dean Division Social Sciences ... Dr. Laura WADLINGTON
81 Dean Division Natural Science/Math ... Dr. Steve KARR
66 Dean of Nursing ... Dr. Gregory CASALENUOVO
15 Director Personnel Services ... Mr. Jimmy WYATT

Chattanooga College (F)

3805 Brainerd Road, Chattanooga TN 37411-3798
County: Hamilton FICE Identification: 022042
Unit ID: 220118
Telephone: (423) 624-0077 Carnegie Class: Assoc/PrivFP
FAX Number: (423) 624-1575 Calendar System: Quarter
URL: www.chattanoogacollege.edu
Established: 1968 Annual Undergrad Tuition & Fees: $9,825
Enrollment: 379 Coed
Affiliation or Control: Proprietary IRS Status: Proprietary
Highest Offering: Associate Degree
Program: Occupational
Accreditation: ACCSC

01 Director ... Mr. William G. FAOUR
37 Director Financial Aid ... Mrs. Evelyn DAVIS
07 Director Admissions ... Mr. Toney C. MCFADDEN

Christian Brothers University (G)

650 East Parkway S, Memphis TN 38104-5581
County: Shelby FICE Identification: 003482
Unit ID: 219833
Telephone: (901) 321-3000 Carnegie Class: Master's M
FAX Number: (901) 321-3494 Calendar System: Semester
URL: www.cbu.edu
Established: 1871 Annual Undergrad Tuition & Fees: $25,520
Enrollment: 1,731 Coed
Affiliation or Control: Roman Catholic IRS Status: 501(c)3
Highest Offering: Master's
Program: Liberal Arts And General; Teacher Preparatory; Professional
Accreditation: SC, ENG, TED

01 President ... Dr. John SMARRELLI, JR.
05 Vice President Academic Affairs ... Dr. Frank BUSCHER
11 Vice Pres Administration & Finance ... Mr. Dan WORTHAM
30 Vice Pres Institutional Advancement ... Mr. Andrew PRISLOVSKY
84 VP for Enrollment Management ... Mr. Jim SCHLIMMER
32 Vice Pres Mission and Identity ... Dr. Evelyn MCDONALD
35 Dean of Students ... Ms. Karen CONWAY
13 Dean Information Technology ... Mr. David A. PIERCE
26 Exec Dir Communications/Marketing ... Ms. Elisa MARUS
06 Registrar ... Mrs. Melody L. NABORS
36 Director Career Center ... Ms. Betty E. MCWILLIE
08 Director of Plough Library ... Ms. Kay CUNNINGHAM
07 Director of Admissions ... Dr. Anne H. KENWORTHY
38 Director of Counseling ... Mrs. Sadie LISENBY
37 Director Financial Resources ... Mr. Jim SHANNON
09 Dir Inst Research/Effectiveness ... Vacant
39 Director Residence Life ... Vacant
35 Director Student Life ... Mr. Mario BROWN
42 Director of Ministry and Mission ... Vacant
92 Director Honors Program ... Dr. Tracie L. BURKE
41 Athletic Director ... Mr. Joseph P. NADICKSBERND
44 Director Development ... Ms. Brenda PEARSON
29 Director Alumni ... Ms. Karen VIOTTI
21 Controller ... Mr. Thomas COCHRAN
15 Director of Personnel ... Mr. Kenneth MASSA
18 Chief Facility/Physical Plant ... Mr. Philip R. YELVINGTON
19 Director of Security ... Mr. John D. LOTRIONTE
40 Director Bookstore ... Vacant
50 Dean School of Business ... Dr. Jack HARGETT
54 Dean School of Engineering ... Dr. Eric WELCH
49 Dean School of Arts ... Dr. Paul A. HAUGHT
81 Dean School of Science ... Dr. Johnny B. HOLMES
53 Dir Graduate/Professional Stds Pgms ... Vacant
58 Director Graduate Education Program ... Dr. Talana VOGEL
58 Director MBA Program ... Dr. Scott LAWYER
58 Director Engineering Management Pgm ... Dr. Neal JACKSON

Concorde Career College (H)

5100 Poplar Avenue, Suite 132, Memphis TN 38137-0132
County: Shelby FICE Identification: 021571
Unit ID: 219903
Telephone: (901) 761-9494 Carnegie Class: Assoc/PrivFP
FAX Number: (901) 761-3293 Calendar System: Semester
URL: www.concorde.edu
Established: 1967 Annual Undergrad Tuition & Fees: $8,045
Enrollment: 750 Coed
Affiliation or Control: Proprietary IRS Status: Proprietary
Highest Offering: Associate Degree
Program: Occupational
Accreditation: COE, DA, DH, MAC, @PTAA, SURGT

01 Executive Campus Director ... Mr. Tommy STEWART

Cumberland University (I)

One Cumberland Square, Lebanon TN 37087-3554
County: Wilson FICE Identification: 003485
Unit ID: 219949
Telephone: (615) 444-2562 Carnegie Class: Master's M
FAX Number: (615) 444-2569 Calendar System: Semester
URL: www.cumberland.edu
Established: 1842 Annual Undergrad Tuition & Fees: $19,200
Enrollment: 1,375 Coed
Affiliation or Control: Independent Non-Profit IRS Status: 501(c)3

Highest Offering: Master's
Program: Liberal Arts And General; Teacher Preparatory; Professional
Accreditation: SC, ACBSP, NUR

01 President .... Dr. Harvill C. EATON
03 Executive Vice President .... Mr. Eddie PAWLAWSKI
05 Vice President for Academic Affairs . Dr. Wilbur (Pete) PETERSON
11 Vice President for Administration .... Dr. Joe GRAY
10 Vice President of Finance .... Ms. Judy G. JORDAN
32 Dean of Students .... Mrs. Lisa MACKE
53 Dean Education .... Dr. Charles COLLIER
49 Dean Liberal Arts & Sciences .... Dr. Laurie DISHMAN
50 Dean Labry School/Technology .... Dr. Judy BEAVERS
66 Dean Nursing .... Dr. Carol Anne BACH
57 Dean Music & the Arts .... Dr. Ted ROSE
101 Sec to President/Board of Trustees .... Ms. Leslie STEELE
30 Exec Dir Development/Alumni Rels .... Mr. Jonathan HAWKINS
08 Director Library Services .... Ms. Eloise HITCHCOCK
07 Director of Enrollment/Fin Services .... Ms. Beatrice LACHANCE
41 Athletic Director .... Mr. Dewayne ALEXANDER
06 Registrar .... Ms. Regena B. POSS
15 Human Resources Director .... Ms. Vickie RICKARD
38 Director Student Counseling .... Vacant
13 Chief Information Officer .... Mr. Tony DEDMAN
09 Director of Institutional Research .... Mr. Larry F. VAUGHAN
26 Chief Public Relations Officer .... Mr. Phillip CARTER
40 Manager Bookstore .... Ms. Stephani DE ROUEN
36 Dir of Career Services/Internships .... Mrs. Ronie MCPEAK

Daymar Institute (A)

1860 Wilma Rudolph Boulevard,
Clarksville TN 37040-6718
County: Montgomery Identification: 666492
Unit ID: 368443
Telephone: (931) 552-7600 Carnegie Class: Assoc/PrivFP
FAX Number: (931) 552-3624 Calendar System: Quarter
URL: www.daymarinstitute.edu
Established: 1954 Annual Undergrad Tuition & Fees: $16,610
Enrollment: 712 Coed
Affiliation or Control: Proprietary IRS Status: Proprietary
Highest Offering: Associate Degree
Program: Technical Emphasis
Accreditation: ACICS, @PTAA

01 President .... Mr. Mark GABIS
12 Campus President .... Ms. Katharine PURNELL
05 Director of Education .... Ms. Elizabeth ASHY
07 Director of Admissions .... Mr. Alphonse PRATHER

† Branch campus of Daymart Institute, Nashville, TN.

Daymar Institute (B)

415 Golden Bear Court, Murfreesboro TN 37128-5508
County: Rutherford Identification: 666392
Unit ID: 444255
Telephone: (615) 217-9347 Carnegie Class: Assoc/PrivFP
FAX Number: (615) 217-9348 Calendar System: Quarter
URL: www.daymarinstitute.edu
Established: 2003 Annual Undergrad Tuition & Fees: $16,610
Enrollment: 599 Coed
Affiliation or Control: Proprietary IRS Status: Proprietary
Highest Offering: Associate Degree
Program: Technical Emphasis
Accreditation: ACICS

01 President .... Mark A. GABIS
12 Campus President .... Deborah BROWN
05 Director of Education .... Jackie RODDY
07 Director of Admissions .... Jennifer VIOLA
32 Director of Student Services .... Kandy BRASHEAR
37 Director of Financial Services .... Julia FRIEDNER
06 Senior Registrar .... Julie ROHALY

† Branch campus of Daymar Institute, Nashville, TN.

Daymar Institute (C)

340 Plus Park Boulevard, Nashville TN 37217-1056
County: Davidson FICE Identification: 004934
Unit ID: 220002
Telephone: (615) 361-7555 Carnegie Class: Assoc/PrivFP
FAX Number: (615) 367-2736 Calendar System: Quarter
URL: www.daymarinstitute.edu
Established: 1884 Annual Undergrad Tuition & Fees: $16,610
Enrollment: 577 Coed
Affiliation or Control: Proprietary IRS Status: Proprietary
Highest Offering: Associate Degree
Program: Technical Emphasis
Accreditation: ACICS

01 President .... Mr. Mark A. GABIS
12 Campus Director .... Mr. Kevin SUHR
07 Director of Admissions .... Ms. Elizabeth COLLIER
10 Director of Financial Services .... Ms. Janie RAGER
36 Director of Career Services .... Mr. Barry HOWARD
06 Registrar .... Mr. Michael GILLIAM
36 Director of Career Services .... Ms. Sara COLLIVER

DeVry University - Memphis (D)

6401 Poplar Avenue, Suite 600, Memphis TN 38119-4808
County: Shelby Identification: 666571
Unit ID: 450517
Telephone: (901) 537-2560 Carnegie Class: Spec/Bus
FAX Number: (901) 682-1326 Calendar System: Semester
URL: www.devry.edu
Established: 1931 Annual Undergrad Tuition & Fees: $15,294
Enrollment: 269 Coed
Affiliation or Control: Proprietary IRS Status: Proprietary
Highest Offering: Master's
Program: Professional; Business Emphasis
Accreditation: &NH

01 Campus Director .... Mr. William WEST

† Regional accreditation is carried under the parent institution in Downers Grove, IL.

DeVry University - Nashville (E)

3343 Perimeter Hill Drive, Ste 200,
Nashville TN 37211-4157
County: Davidson Identification: 666589
Telephone: (615) 445-3456 Carnegie Class: Not Classified
FAX Number: (615) 331-1635 Calendar System: Semester
URL: www.devry.edu
Established: 1931 Annual Undergrad Tuition & Fees: $15,294
Enrollment: 305 Coed
Affiliation or Control: Proprietary IRS Status: Proprietary
Highest Offering: Master's
Program: Professional; Business Emphasis
Accreditation: &NH

01 Campus Director .... Peter POWELL

† Regional accreditation is carried under the parent institution in Downers Grove, IL.

Emmanuel Christian Seminary (F)

1 Walker Drive, Johnson City TN 37601-9989
County: Carter FICE Identification: 012547
Unit ID: 220136
Telephone: (423) 926-1186 Carnegie Class: Spec/Faith
FAX Number: (423) 926-6198 Calendar System: Semester
URL: www.esr.edu
Established: 1961 Annual Graduate Tuition & Fees: $10,400
Enrollment: 150 Coed
Affiliation or Control: Christian Churches And Churches of Christ
IRS Status: 501(c)3
Highest Offering: Doctorate; No Undergraduates
Program: Professional
Accreditation: SC, THEOL

01 President .... Dr. Michael L. SWEENEY
05 Dean .... Dr. Jack HOLLAND
10 Director of Finance .... Mr. David B. MARSHALL
30 Executive Director of Development .... Mr. Dan R. LAWSON
08 Librarian .... Mr. John M. WADE
07 Director of Admissions & Recruitmen .... Ms. Erin C. LAYTON
42 Chaplain .... Mrs. Heather E. HOLLAND
26 Director of Ministry Enhancement .... Mr. John E. WASEM

Fisk University (G)

1000 17th Avenue N, Nashville TN 37208-3051
County: Davidson FICE Identification: 003490
Unit ID: 220181
Telephone: (615) 329-8500 Carnegie Class: Bac/A&S
FAX Number: N/A Calendar System: Semester
URL: www.fisk.edu
Established: 1866 Annual Undergrad Tuition & Fees: $19,362
Enrollment: 580 Coed
Affiliation or Control: Independent Non-Profit IRS Status: 501(c)3
Highest Offering: Master's
Program: Liberal Arts And General; Teacher Preparatory
Accreditation: SC, MUS

01 President .... Dr. Hazel R. O'LEARY
05 Executive Vice President & Provost .... Dr. Princilla E. MORRIS
10 Vice President for Finance and CFO .... Mr. Clancy ROBERTS
04 Exec Assistant to the President .... Mrs. Sherri B. RUCKER
30 Vice President of Inst Advancement .... Mrs. Shirley RANGE
26 Public Relations Specialist .... Mr. Greg BRYANT
09 VP of Inst Assessment & Research .... Dr. Michael SELF
32 VP of Student Engagement & Enroll .... Mr. Jason MERIWETHER
13 Acting Dir Info Technology Svcs .... Mr. Joseph CURTIS
29 Exec Director of Alumni Affairs .... Mrs. Adrienne LATHAM
20 Vice Provost for Acad Initiatives .... Mr. Arnold BURGER
07 Dean of Admission .... Mr. Keith CHANDLER
37 Director of Financial Aid .... Mrs. Russelle KEESE
06 Registrar .... Ms. Stephanie CAGE
08 University Librarian .... Dr. Jessie C. SMITH
58 Interim Dean of Graduate Studies .... Dr. Lee LIMBIRD
41 Dir of Athletics & Intramural Pgms .... Mr. Anthony OWENS
42 Dean of the Chapel .... Rev. Jason CURRY
25 Director of Sponsored Programs .... Ms. Beverly ROBINSON
44 Director of Planned Giving .... Vacant
18 Director of Facilities .... Mr. Norman RAPP
19 Director of Public Safety .... Mr. Mickey WEST
96 Director of Purchasing .... Vacant
36 Director Career Development .... Ms. Natara GARVIN
38 Coordinator of Student Counseling .... Ms. Sheila PETERS
15 Director of Human Resources .... Ms. JaCenda DAVIDSON
21 Comptroller .... Mrs. Debra MICHAEL

Fortis Institute (H)

1025 Highway 111, Cookeville TN 38501-4305
County: Putnam FICE Identification: 023263
Unit ID: 418870
Telephone: (931) 526-3660 Carnegie Class: Assoc/PrivFP
FAX Number: (931) 372-2603 Calendar System: Quarter
URL: www.fortis.edu/cookeville-tennessee.php
Established: 1970 Annual Undergrad Tuition & Fees: $11,500
Enrollment: 215 Coed
Affiliation or Control: Proprietary IRS Status: Proprietary
Highest Offering: Associate Degree
Program: Occupational
Accreditation: COE, MLTAD, RAD, SURGT

01 Campus Director .... Mr. Bill STRADLEY
05 Dean of Education .... Ms. Rebecca BLALOCK

Fountainhead College of Technology (I)

3203 Tazewell Pike, Knoxville TN 37918-2530
County: Knox FICE Identification: 007439
Unit ID: 221795
Telephone: (865) 688-9422 Carnegie Class: Spec/Tech
FAX Number: (865) 688-2419 Calendar System: Semester
URL: www.fountainheadcollege.edu
Established: 1947 Annual Undergrad Tuition & Fees: $14,550
Enrollment: 250 Coed
Affiliation or Control: Proprietary IRS Status: Proprietary
Highest Offering: Baccalaureate
Program: Occupational
Accreditation: ACCSC

01 President .... Mr. Richard W. RACKLEY

Free Will Baptist Bible College (J)

3606 West End Avenue, Nashville TN 37205-2498
County: Davidson FICE Identification: 030018
Unit ID: 220206
Telephone: (615) 383-1340 Carnegie Class: Bac/Diverse
FAX Number: (615) 269-6028 Calendar System: Semester
URL: www.fwbbc.edu
Established: 1942 Annual Undergrad Tuition & Fees: $11,646
Enrollment: 282 Coed
Affiliation or Control: Free Will Baptist Church IRS Status: 501(c)3
Highest Offering: Baccalaureate
Program: Liberal Arts And General; Teacher Preparatory; Religious Emphasis
Accreditation: SC, BI

01 President .... Dr. J. Matthew PINSON
05 Provost .... Dr. Greg KETTEMAN
10 Vice President Financial Affairs .... Mr. Thomas A. SASS
45 VP Institutional Planning/Registrar .... Vacant
30 Vice Pres Institutional Advancement .... Mr. David WILLIFORD
32 VP Student Svcs/Dean of Students .... Dr. Jon FORLINES
34 Dean of Women .... Mrs. Susan FORLINES
21 Comptroller .... Mr. Craig MAHLER
08 Librarian .... Mrs. Carol REID
18 Director of Plant Operations .... Mr. Sandy GOODFELLOW
26 Director of Public Relations .... Dr. Jack WILLIAMS
84 Dir of Enrollment Svcs/Fin Aid .... Mr. Jeff CAUDILL
106 Dir of Online and Adult Studies .... Mr. Rusty CAMPBELL
51 Director of Adult Degree Program .... Ms. Tina TOLBERT
09 Director of Institutional Research .... Mr. Wayne SPRUILL
41 Athletic Director .... Mr. Gary TURNER

Freed-Hardeman University (K)

158 E Main, Henderson TN 38340-2398
County: Chester FICE Identification: 003492
Unit ID: 220215
Telephone: (731) 989-6000 Carnegie Class: Master's M
FAX Number: (731) 989-6065 Calendar System: Semester
URL: www.fhu.edu
Established: 1869 Annual Undergrad Tuition & Fees: $17,204
Enrollment: 1,992 Coed
Affiliation or Control: Churches Of Christ IRS Status: 501(c)3
Highest Offering: Beyond Master's But Less Than Doctorate
Program: 2-Year Principally Bachelor's Creditable; Liberal Arts And General; Teacher Preparatory
Accreditation: SC, ACBSP, SW, TED

01 President .... Dr. Joe A. WILEY
04 Executive Assistant to President .... Mrs. Donna M. STEELE
10 Exec VP and CFO .... Dr. Dwayne H. WILSON
30 Vice President for Univ Advancement .... Mr. Dave CLOUSE
05 Vice Pres Academics/Enrollment Mgmt .... Dr. Charles VIRES
88 VP for Spiritual Development .... Dr. Samuel T. JONES
32 Vice Pres Student Services .... Dr. Wayne SCOTT
13 VP for Innovation and Technology .... Mr. Mark SCOTT

20 Associate Vice President Academics ....Dr. Vicki M. JOHNSON
41 Director of Athletics ....Mr. Michael F. MCCUTCHEN
29 Asst VP for Alumni Relations ....Mrs. Betsy HESSELRODE
07 Interim Director of Admissions ....Mr. Joseph ASKEW
35 Dean of Students ....Dr. Wayne SCOTT
35 Dean of Student Life ....Mr. Tony M. ALLEN
06 Registrar ....Mr. Larry R. OLDHAM
37 Director of Financial Aid ....Mr. Jay SATTERFIELD
40 University Book Store Manager ....Mr. Dan LUSSIER
08 Head Librarian ....Mrs. A. Hope SHULL
70 Director of Social Work Program ....Mrs. Nadine G. MCNEAL
24 A-V Supervisor ....Mrs. Gail B. NASH
21 Controller ....Mr. Barry V. SMITH
45 Asst VP for Instnl Effectiveness ....Dr. James Q. EDMONDS
09 Director of Institutional Research ....Mr. Micah SMITH
15 Director HR/Purchasing ....Mr. Russell EPPERSON
18 Director Facilities ....Mr. Jeff BARKMAN
26 Director Marketing & Univ Relations ....Mr. Judson B. DAVIS
73 Dean of School Biblical Studies ....Dr. Billy R. SMITH
50 Dean School of Business ....Dr. Keith SMITH
53 Dean School of Education ....Dr. Sharen CYPRESS
49 Dean School of Arts & Humanities ......Dr. W. Stephen JOHNSON
81 Dean School of Science & Math ....Dr. LeAnn SELF-DAVIS
92 Dean of Honors College ....Dr. Jenny JOHNSON
23 Campus Physician ....Dr. Kenneth R. CARGILE
84 Dir of Enrollment Management ....Vacant
104 Dir of International Studies ....Dr. Jenny JOHNSON
38 Director of Counseling ....Mrs. Nicole YOUNG

Harding School of Theology (A)

1000 Cherry Road, Memphis TN 38117-5499
County: Shelby FICE Identification: 004081
Unit ID: 107035
Telephone: (901) 761-1350 Carnegie Class: Not Classified
FAX Number: (901) 761-1358 Calendar System: Semester
URL: www.hst.edu
Established: 1958 Annual Graduate Tuition & Fees: $14,016
Enrollment: 189 Coed
Affiliation or Control: Churches Of Christ IRS Status: 501(c)3
Highest Offering: Doctorate; No Undergraduates
Program: Professional; Religious Emphasis
Accreditation: &NH, THEOL

01 President ....Dr. David B. BURKS
05 Vice President/Dean ....Dr. Evertt W. HUFFARD
07 Director of Admissions ....Mr. Mark PARKER
08 Librarian ....Mr. Don L. MEREDITH
10 Business Office Manager ....Ms. Brenda M. DAVID
30 Director of Advancement ....Mr. Larry J. ARICK
20 Associate Dean ....Dr. Steve MCLEOD

† Regional accreditation is carried under Harding University, Searcy, AR.

Hiwassee College (B)

225 Hiwassee College Drive, Madisonville TN 37354
County: Monroe Identification: 666777
Unit ID: 220312
Telephone: (423) 442-2001 Carnegie Class: Not Classified
FAX Number: (423) 420-1929 Calendar System: Semester
URL: www.hiwassee.edu
Established: 1850 Annual Undergrad Tuition & Fees: $15,300
Enrollment: 153 Coed
Affiliation or Control: United Methodist IRS Status: 501(c)3
Highest Offering: Baccalaureate
Program: Liberal Arts And General
Accreditation: @TRACS, DH

01 President ....Dr. Robin J. TRICOLI
05 Vice President/Academic Dean ....Dr. Beth R. SCRUGGS
10 VP Business Affairs & Treasurer ....Richard BARTREM
07 Associate VP Financial Aid ....Ron HEMPHILL

Huntington College of Health Sciences (C)

1204 Kenesaw Avenue, Suite D, Knoxville TN 37919-7700
County: Knox Identification: 666971
Unit ID: 371274
Telephone: (800) 290-4226 Carnegie Class: Not Classified
FAX Number: (865) 524-8339 Calendar System: Semester
URL: www.hchs.edu
Established: 1985 Annual Undergrad Tuition & Fees: $4,950
Enrollment: 430 Coed
Affiliation or Control: Proprietary IRS Status: Proprietary
Highest Offering: Master's
Program: Occupational
Accreditation: DETC

01 Chief Executive Officer ....Dr. Art PRESSER
05 Dean of Academics ....Mr. Gene BRUNO
10 Director of Finance ....Mr. Robert SCHMAEF
11 Director of Administration ....Ms. Christy MARTIN

International Academy of Design and Technology (D)

1 Bridgestone Park, Nashville TN 37214-2428
County: Davidson Identification: 666347
Unit ID: 446817
Telephone: (615) 232-7384 Carnegie Class: Spec/Arts
FAX Number: (615) 883-5285 Calendar System: Quarter
URL: www.iadtnashville.com
Established: 2004 Annual Undergrad Tuition & Fees: $18,687
Enrollment: 564 Coed
Affiliation or Control: Proprietary IRS Status: Proprietary
Highest Offering: Baccalaureate
Program: Occupational; Liberal Arts And General
Accreditation: ACICS

01 President ....Mr. Richard WECHNER
37 Director of Financial Aid ....Ms. Lisa KENNICOTT

† Branch campus of International Academy of Design and Technology, Pittsburgh, PA.

ITT Technical Institute (E)

5600 Brainerd Road, Suite G-1, Chattanooga TN 37411
County: Hamilton Identification: 666708
Unit ID: 450261
Telephone: (423) 510-6800 Carnegie Class: Not Classified
FAX Number: (423) 510-6850 Calendar System: Quarter
URL: www.itt-tech.edu
Established: N/A Annual Undergrad Tuition & Fees: N/A
Enrollment: 333 Coed
Affiliation or Control: Proprietary IRS Status: Proprietary
Highest Offering: Baccalaureate
Program: Technical Emphasis
Accreditation: ACICS

† Branch campus of ITT Technical Institute, Knoxville, TN.

ITT Technical Institute (F)

7260 Goodlett Farms Parkway, Cordova TN 38016-4908
County: Shelby Identification: 666550
Unit ID: 413884
Telephone: (901) 381-0200 Carnegie Class: Spec/Tech
FAX Number: (901) 381-0299 Calendar System: Quarter
URL: www.itt-tech.edu
Established: 1994 Annual Undergrad Tuition & Fees: N/A
Enrollment: 912 Coed
Affiliation or Control: Proprietary IRS Status: Proprietary
Highest Offering: Baccalaureate
Program: Technical Emphasis
Accreditation: ACICS

† Branch campus of ITT Technical Institute, Earth City, MO.

ITT Technical Institute (G)

10208 Technology Drive, Knoxville TN 37932-3343
County: Knox FICE Identification: 030734
Unit ID: 366650
Telephone: (865) 671-2800 Carnegie Class: Spec/Tech
FAX Number: (865) 671-2811 Calendar System: Quarter
URL: www.itt-tech.edu
Established: 1988 Annual Undergrad Tuition & Fees: N/A
Enrollment: 943 Coed
Affiliation or Control: Proprietary IRS Status: Proprietary
Highest Offering: Baccalaureate
Program: Technical Emphasis
Accreditation: ACICS

ITT Technical Institute (H)

2845 Elm Hill Pike, Nashville TN 37214-3717
County: Davidson FICE Identification: 023598
Unit ID: 151494
Telephone: (615) 889-8700 Carnegie Class: Spec/Tech
FAX Number: (615) 872-7209 Calendar System: Quarter
URL: www.itt-tech.edu
Established: 1984 Annual Undergrad Tuition & Fees: N/A
Enrollment: 1,010 Coed
Affiliation or Control: Proprietary IRS Status: Proprietary
Highest Offering: Baccalaureate
Program: Technical Emphasis
Accreditation: ACICS

John A. Gupton College (I)

1616 Church Street, Nashville TN 37203-2920
County: Davidson FICE Identification: 008859
Unit ID: 220464
Telephone: (615) 327-3927 Carnegie Class: Assoc/PrivNFP
FAX Number: (615) 321-4518 Calendar System: Semester
URL: www.guptoncollege.com
Established: 1946 Annual Undergrad Tuition & Fees: $9,120
Enrollment: 125 Coed
Affiliation or Control: Independent Non-Profit IRS Status: 501(c)3
Highest Offering: Associate Degree
Program: Occupational; 2-Year Principally Bachelor's Creditable
Accreditation: SC, FUSER

01 President ....Mr. B. Steven SPANN
08 Library Director ....Mr. William P. BRUCE
06 Registrar ....Mrs. Lisa BOLIN

Johnson University (J)

7900 Johnson Drive, Knoxville TN 37998-0001
County: Knox FICE Identification: 003495
Unit ID: 220473
Telephone: (865) 573-4517 Carnegie Class: Spec/Faith
FAX Number: (865) 251-2337 Calendar System: Semester
URL: www.johnsonu.edu
Established: 1893 Annual Undergrad Tuition & Fees: $9,430
Enrollment: 816 Coed
Affiliation or Control: Christian Churches And Churches of Christ
IRS Status: 501(c)3
Highest Offering: Doctorate
Program: Liberal Arts And General; Teacher Preparatory
Accreditation: SC, BI

01 President ....Dr. Gary E. WEEDMAN
00 President Emeritus ....Dr. David L. EUBANKS
05 Vice President for Academics ....Dr. Richard K. BEAM
10 Vice Pres for Business and Finance ....Mr. Chris ROLPH
32 Vice President for Student Services ....Mr. David LEGG
30 Vice President for Advancement ....Mr. Philip A. EUBANKS
08 Librarian ....Miss Carrie B. LOWE
06 Registrar ....Mrs. Sandra J. BLEVINS
07 Deanof Enrollment Services ....Dr. Tim WINGFIELD
37 Financial Aid Director ....Mr. Larry RECTOR
45 Dir Institutional Effectiveness ....Dr. Mark PIERCE
41 Athletic Director ....Mrs. Anyssa BLACKBURN
18 Director of Plant Services ....Mr. John LINSENBIGLER
92 Director of Honors Program ....Dr. Gerald L. MATTINGLY
15 Director Human Resources ....Mrs. Ruthanne BEAM
26 Director of Public Relations ....Mr. Kevin O'BRIEN
38 Director Student Counseling ....Dr. Sean RIDGE
96 Director of Purchasing ....Vacant

Kaplan Career Institute (K)

750 Envious Lane, Nashville TN 37217-1342
County: Davidson FICE Identification: 023262
Unit ID: 246202
Telephone: (615) 279-8300 Carnegie Class: Assoc/PrivFP
FAX Number: (615) 297-6678 Calendar System: Other
URL: www.kci-nashville.com
Established: 1981 Annual Undergrad Tuition & Fees: $14,799
Enrollment: 732 Coed
Affiliation or Control: Proprietary IRS Status: Proprietary
Highest Offering: Associate Degree
Program: Occupational
Accreditation: COE, DA

01 Executive Director ....Mr. Adam BUTLER

King College (L)

1350 King College Road, Bristol TN 37620-2699
County: Sullivan FICE Identification: 003496
Unit ID: 220516
Telephone: (423) 968-1187 Carnegie Class: Master's M
FAX Number: (423) 968-4456 Calendar System: Other
URL: www.king.edu
Established: 1867 Annual Undergrad Tuition & Fees: $24,052
Enrollment: 1,949 Coed
Affiliation or Control: Presbyterian Church (U.S.A.) IRS Status: 501(c)3
Highest Offering: Master's
Program: Liberal Arts And General; Teacher Preparatory; Professional; Nursing Emphasis
Accreditation: SC, NURSE

01 President ....Dr. Gregory D. JORDAN
10 Vice President Finance/Operations ....Mr. James P. DONAHUE
32 Vice President for Student Affairs ....Dr. Robert A. LITTLETON
84 Vice President of Enrollment Mgmt ....Mr. Micah R. CREWS
05 Dean of the Faculty ....Vacant
05 Provost ....Dr. Paul M. PERCY
30 Assoc Vice Pres Marketing & Devel ....Mrs. A. LeAnn HUGHES
08 Dean of Library Services ....Ms. Julie A. ROBERSON
06 Registrar/Dir Regist & Records ....Mrs. Sarah L. DILLOW
44 Chief Development Officer ....Mr. John W. KING
09 Director of Institutional Research ....Dr. J. Kevin DEFORD
29 Director of Alumni Relations ....Mrs. Finley L. GREEN
42 Chaplain ....Dr. Fred F. STRANG
21 Director of Business Operations ....Mr. Thomas R. LARSON
36 Director of Career Development ....Ms. Donna H. FELTY
41 Athletic Director ....Mr. James D. HICKS
38 Director of Counseling ....Mr. Charles S. THOMPSON
88 Sports Information Director ....Mr. Glen G. RENFRO
40 Bookstore Manager ....Ms. Susan D. MARSHALL
37 Director Student Financial Aid ....Ms. Nancy M. BEVERLY
84 Director of Recruitment ....Mr. Charles G. KING
18 Chief Facilities/Physical Plant ....Mr. Todd THOMAS
35 Assoc Dean Student Development ....Mr. Matthew S. PELTIER
92 Director of Honors Program ....Dr. Mark E. DOLLAR
26 Director Marketing & Communications .Mrs. Miranda D. COOPER
27 Assoc Director of Communication ....Mrs. Laura K. BOGGAN

Lane College (M)

545 Lane Avenue, Jackson TN 38301-4598
County: Madison FICE Identification: 003499
Unit ID: 220598
Telephone: (731) 426-7500 Carnegie Class: Bac/A&S
FAX Number: (731) 427-3987 Calendar System: Semester
URL: www.lanecollege.edu

Established: 1882 Annual Undergrad Tuition & Fees: $8,220
Enrollment: 2,222 Coed
Affiliation or Control: Christian Methodist Episcopal IRS Status: 501(c)3
Highest Offering: Baccalaureate
Program: Liberal Arts And General; Teacher Preparatory
Accreditation: SC

01 President .... Dr. Wesley C. MCCLURE
03 Executive Vice President .... Ms. Sharron T. BURNETT
05 Vice President Academic Affairs .... Dr. Lora B. BAILEY
10 Vice President Business & Finance .... Mr. Melvin R. HAMLETT
32 Vice President Student Affairs .... Ms. Sherrill B. SCOTT
30 Vice Pres Inst Advance/Dir Alum Aff .... Mr. Richard H. DONNELL
04 Exec Assistant to the President .... Ms. Darlette C. SAMUELS
18 Chief Facilities/Physical Plant .... Mr. Michael BATES
26 Chief Public Relations Officer .... Ms. Darlette C. SAMUELS
09 Director Institutional Research .... Dr. Fred OKANDA
08 Librarian .... Ms. Lan WANG
07 Director of Admissions .... Ms. Evelyn BROWN
06 Registrar .... Mr. Terry W. BLACKMON
37 Director of Financial Aid .... Mr. Tony CALHOUN
20 Director Academic Assessment .... Dr. Joy MORDICA
84 Director Enrollment Management .... Ms. Kelly R. BOYD
89 Director of Freshman Studies .... Dr. Monique J. JONES
96 Director of Purchasing .... Ms. Tammy MCDOUGAL
36 Director Placement Services .... Ms. Virginia S. CRUMP
13 Director Information Technology .... Mr. Earnest L. MITCHELL, III
15 Director of Personnel .... Ms. Juanita MARSHALL
19 Director Security .... Mr. Ernest BOYD
40 Director Bookstore .... Mr. Carter B. MCCLURE
19 Director of Safety .... Ms. Aleshia COX
20 Associate Academic Officer .... Dr. Virginia S. CRUMP
21 Associate Business Officer .... Mr. Duan ROBINSON
41 Director of Athletics .... Mr. Derrick BURROUGHS
29 Director Alumni Relations .... Ms. Charlise ANDERSON
35 Director Student Affairs .... Ms. Erika MCCLAIN
27 Chief Information Officer .... Ms. Tori L. HALIBURTON

Lee University (A)

1120 N Ocoee Street, Cleveland TN 37320-3450
County: Bradley FICE Identification: 003500
Unit ID: 220613
Telephone: (423) 614-8100 Carnegie Class: Master's M
FAX Number: (423) 614-8083 Calendar System: Semester
URL: www.leeuniversity.edu
Established: 1918 Annual Undergrad Tuition & Fees: $12,680
Enrollment: 4,377 Coed
Affiliation or Control: Church Of God IRS Status: 501(c)3
Highest Offering: Beyond Master's But Less Than Doctorate
Program: Liberal Arts And General; Teacher Preparatory
Accreditation: SC, ACBSP, MUS, TED

01 President .... Dr. C. Paul CONN
04 Executive Assistant to President .... Mrs. Stephanie TAYLOR
10 Vice President Business & Finance .... Mr. Chris CONINE
05 Vice President for Academic Affairs .... Dr. Carolyn DIRKSEN
11 Vice President for Administration .... Dr. Walter MAULDIN
84 Vice President for Enrollment .... Mr. Phil COOK
26 VP for University Relations .... Dr. Jerome HAMMOND
32 VP for Student Development .... Mr. Mike HAYES
27 VP for Information Services .... Dr. Jayson VAN HOOK
21 Comptroller .... Mr. Duane PACE
37 Director of Student Aid .... Mr. Mike ELLIS
35 Dean of Students .... Mr. Alan MCCLUNG
15 Director of Human Resources .... Mrs. Ann MCELRATH
13 Interim Director of IT .... Mr. Chris GOLDEN
13 Interim Director of IT Systems .... Mr. Nate TUCKER
29 Director of Alumni Relations .... Mrs. Mitzi MEW
39 Director of Residential Life .... Ms. Tracey CARLSON
06 Registrar .... Ms. Cathy THOMPSOM
21 Bursar .... Ms. Kristy HARNER
08 Librarian .... Ms. Barbara MCCULLOUGH
42 Director of Campus Ministries .... Rev. Jimmy HARPER
25 Director of Grants .... Mrs. Vanessa HAMMOND
19 Director of Campus Safety .... Mr. Ashley MEW
23 Director of Health Services .... Mr. Mickey MOORE
27 Director of Public Information .... Mr. Brian CONN
73 Dean School of Religion .... Dr. Terry CROSS
49 Dean College of Arts & Sciences .... Dr. Matthew MELTON
53 Dean College of Education .... Dr. Deborah MURRAY
64 Dean School of Music .... Dr. William GREEN
51 Director of External Studies .... Mr. Ben PEREZ
07 Director of Graduate Enrollment .... Ms. Vicki GLASSCOCK
38 Director Counseling & Testing .... Ms. Christin LOGUE
18 Director of Physical Plant .... Mr. Larry BERRY
41 Athletic Director .... Mr. Larry CARPENTER
104 Director of Global Perspectives .... Ms. Beth THOMPSON

LeMoyne-Owen College (B)

807 Walker Avenue, Memphis TN 38126-6595
County: Shelby FICE Identification: 003501
Unit ID: 220604
Telephone: (901) 435-1000 Carnegie Class: Bac/Diverse
FAX Number: (901) 435-1699 Calendar System: Semester
URL: www.loc.edu
Established: 1862 Annual Undergrad Tuition & Fees: $10,318
Enrollment: 987 Coed
Affiliation or Control: Multiple Protestant Denominations
IRS Status: 501(c)3
Highest Offering: Baccalaureate
Program: Liberal Arts And General; Teacher Preparatory; Business Emphasis
Accreditation: SC, TED

01 President .... Mr. Johnnie B. WATSON
05 Dean of Academic Affairs .... Dr. Barbara FRANKLE
10 Chief Financial Officer .... Mr. Jim DUGGER
11 Exec Asst to Pres Admin Services .... Ms. Shirley HILL
32 Dean of Students .... Ms. Edythe COBB
30 Chief Advancement Officer .... Mr. Roger BROWN
16 Director of Human Resources .... Mr. Michael WASHINGTON
08 Librarian .... Ms. Annette BERHE
37 Director Student Financial Services .... Ms. Phyllis TORRY
06 Registrar .... Mr. Addie HARVEY
36 Director Career Services/Placement .... Dr. Denita HEDGEMAN
29 Director of Alumni Relations .... Ms. Frankie JEFFRIES
14 Director Information Technology .... Mr. Angus SMALL
07 Director Admissions & Recruitment .... Mrs. June CHINN-JOINTER
21 Controller .... Ms. Colleen GIBSON
09 Dir Instl Research/Assess/ Effective .... Mr. Reoungeneria MCFARLAND
92 Head of Dubois Honors Program .... Dr. Imani FRYAR
50 Int Chair Div Business & Econ Devel .... Dr. Katherine CAUSEY
53 Chair Education Division .... Dr. Ralph CALHOUN
57 Chair Div Fine Arts & Humanities .... Dr. Linda WHITE
65 Chair Div Natural & Math Science .... Dr. Delphia HARRIS
83 Chair Div Social & Behavioral Sci .... Dr. Cheryl GOLDEN
38 Director Student Counseling .... Mr. Tony WHITSON
41 Director of Athletics .... Mr. William ANDERSON
18 Chief Facilities/Physical Plant .... Mr. Anthony COWAN

Lincoln Memorial University (C)

6965 Cumberland Gap Parkway,
Harrogate TN 37752-1901
County: Claiborne FICE Identification: 003502
Unit ID: 220631
Telephone: (423) 869-3611 Carnegie Class: Master's L
FAX Number: (423) 869-6250 Calendar System: Semester
URL: www.lmunet.edu
Established: 1897 Annual Undergrad Tuition & Fees: $17,750
Enrollment: 4,445 Coed
Affiliation or Control: Independent Non-Profit IRS Status: 501(c)3
Highest Offering: Doctorate
Program: Liberal Arts And General; Teacher Preparatory; Professional
Accreditation: SC, ADNUR, ANEST, #ARCPA, MT, NUR, OSTEO, SW

01 President .... Dr. B. James DAWSON
11 Vice President for Administration .... Vacant
30 Vice Pres University Advancement .... Ms. Cynthia L. WHITT
05 Vice Pres Academic Affairs/Provost .... Dr. Clayton HESS
10 Vice President of Finance .... Ms. Kimberlee BONTRAGER
84 Dean of Enrollment Management .... Vacant
53 Dean of School of Education .... Dr. Michael CLYBURN
49 Dean of Arts and Sciences .... Dr. Amiel JARSTFER
32 Dean of Students .... Mr. Frank E. SMITH
04 Exec Assistant to the President .... Mrs. Janet SMITH
37 Executive Director of Financial Aid .... Mr. Bryan ERSLAN
09 Director of Institutional Research .... Vacant
41 Athletic Director .... Mr. Roger VANNOY
18 Director of Physical Plant .... Vacant
15 Director of Human Resources .... Ms. Libby KING
96 Director Purchasing/Accts Payable .... Ms. Pat TENNYSON
06 Registrar .... Ms. Helen BAILEY
90 Director of Acad Computing Support .... Vacant
42 University Chaplain .... Dr. Ray PENN
43 Legal Counsel .... Mr. J. Thomas BAUGH
13 Chief Information Officer .... Vacant
26 Director of Public Relations .... Mrs. Kate M. REAGAN
29 Director Alumni Services .... Mr. Donnie LIPSCOMB
40 Bookstore Manager .... Mr. Rick CROWDER

Lipscomb University (D)

One University Park Dr., Nashville TN 37204-3951
County: Davidson FICE Identification: 003486
Unit ID: 219976
Telephone: (615) 966-1000 Carnegie Class: Master's L
FAX Number: (615) 966-1798 Calendar System: Semester
URL: www.lipscomb.edu
Established: 1891 Annual Undergrad Tuition & Fees: $23,494
Enrollment: 3,742 Coed
Affiliation or Control: Churches Of Christ IRS Status: 501(c)3
Highest Offering: Doctorate
Program: Liberal Arts And General; Teacher Preparatory; Professional
Accreditation: SC, ACBSP, DIETD, DIETI, ENG, MUS, NUR, @PHAR, SW, TED, THEOL

01 President .... Dr. L. Randolph LOWRY, III
05 Provost .... Dr. W. Craig BLEDSOE
45 Senior VP Strategic Initiatives .... Dr. Nancy MAGNUSSON DURHAM
10 Senior VP Finance & Administration .... Mr. Danny TAYLOR
30 Senior VP Advancement .... Vacant
26 VP University Relations .... Mr. Walt LEAVER
29 VP Development & Alumni Relations .... Dr. Bennie L. HARRIS
32 VP Student Develop/Dean Campus Life .... Dr. Scott MCDOWELL
26 VP Communications & Marketing .... Ms. Deby K. SAMUELS
20 Assoc Prov Acad Admin & Strat Init .... Dr. Susan C. GALBREATH
43 General Counsel .... Dr. Phillip ELLENBURG
41 Director of Athletics .... Mr. Philip HUTCHESON
20 Associate Provost Academic Support .... Mr. Steve PREWITT
20 Assoc Provost for Grad Studies .... Dr. Randy BOULDIN
88 Assoc Prov for Inst Effectiveness .... Dr. Elaine GRIFFIN
79 Dean College of Arts & Sciences .... Dr. Norma BURGESS
73 Dean College of Bible & Ministry .... Dr. Terry BRILEY
50 Dean College of Business .... Mr. Turney STEVENS
53 Dean College of Education .... Dr. Candice MCQUEEN
81 Dean College of Engineering .... Dr. Fred GILLIAM
67 Dean College of Pharmacy .... Dr. Roger DAVIS
39 Associate Dean & Dir Residence Life .... Dr. Sam SMITH
35 Associate Dean of Campus Life .... Ms. Sarah GAMBLE
21 Associate VP Finance .... Mr. Darrell DUNCAN
102 Associate VP Advancement .... Mr. David ENGLAND
13 Assoc VP Information Technology/CIO .... Mr. Mike GREEN
44 Senior Director of Development .... Mr. Mark MEADOR
07 Senior Director of Admissions .... Mr. Rick HOLAWAY
06 Registrar .... Mrs. Janet CATES
37 Director of Financial Aid .... Mrs. Karita WATERS
08 Director of Library Services .... Mrs. Carolyn WILSON
19 Director of Campus Safety .... Mr. Brad WYATT
36 Director of Career Development Ctr .... Mrs. Monica WENTWORTH
88 Director of Student Advocacy .... Ms. Teresa WILLIAMS
55 Director Adult Learning Pgm .... Dr. Teresa CLARK
73 Dir of Hazelip School of Theology .... Dr. Mark BLACK
88 Dir of Grad Exercise & Nutrition .... Dr. Karen ROBICHAUD
58 Director of Graduate Education .... Dr. Deborah BOYD
83 Dir of Grad Stds in Psych & Counsel .... Dr. Jake MORRIS
58 Associate Dean of Graduate Business .... Dr. Mike KENDRICK
88 Asst Dean of Executive Education .... Dr. John LOWRY
88 Exec Dir Inst for Conflict Mgmt .... Dr. Larry BRIDGESMITH
88 Exec Dir Inst for Chrn Spirituality .... Dr. Earl LAVENDER
88 Exec Dir Inst for Law Justice & Soc .... Dr. Charla LONG
88 Exec Dir Inst for Civic Leadership .... Dr. Linda SCHACHT
88 Exec Dir Inst for Sustain Practice .... Mr. Dodd GALBREATH
38 Director Counseling Center .... Dr. Paul CATES
23 Director of Health Services .... Mrs. Bethany MASSEY
88 Director of Spiritual Outreach .... Mr. Steve DAVIDSON
28 Asst Dean Intercultural Development .... Mrs. Tenielle BUCHANAN
28 Asst Dean Intercultural Engagement .... Mrs. Jessica GARCIA VAN DE GRIEK
09 Director of Institutional Research .... Mr. Matt REHBEIN
15 Director Human Resources .... Mr. Matt TILLER
88 Director of Campus Enhancement .... Mr. Tom WOOD
18 Director of Campus & Retail Ops .... Mr. Jeff WILSON
91 Director of Admin Computing .... Mr. Joe TRIMBLE
105 Director of Information Security .... Mr. Dave WAGNER
96 Director of Purchasing .... Vacant

Martin Methodist College (E)

433 W Madison Street, Pulaski TN 38478-2799
County: Giles FICE Identification: 003504
Unit ID: 220701
Telephone: (931) 363-9804 Carnegie Class: Bac/Diverse
FAX Number: (931) 363-9818 Calendar System: Semester
URL: www.martinmethodist.edu
Established: 1870 Annual Undergrad Tuition & Fees: $19,997
Enrollment: 1,071 Coed
Affiliation or Control: United Methodist IRS Status: 501(c)3
Highest Offering: Baccalaureate
Program: Liberal Arts And General
Accreditation: SC, NURSE

01 President .... Dr. Ted R. BROWN
05 Vice President of Academic Affairs .... Dr. James T. MURRELL
10 VP for Finance & Administration .... Mr. David J. STEPHENS
32 VP Campus Life/Enrollment Mgmt .... Mr. Robby C. SHELTON
30 Vice Pres for College Advancement .... Dr. Jack L. GREGORY
06 Registrar/Dir Institutional Rsrch .... Dr. Dennis E. HASKINS
41 Athletic Director .... Mr. Jeff N. BAIN
42 Chaplain .... Rev. Laura KIRKPATRICK
08 Librarian .... Mr. Richard MADDEN
40 Director of Bookstore .... Mrs. Margaret W. JACKSON
29 Alumni Affairs Director .... Mrs. Edna LUNA
04 Assistant to the President .... Mrs. Kim W. HARRISON
07 Director of Admissions .... Mrs. Lisa SMITH
15 Director Personnel Services .... Mr. James R. HLUBB
21 Controller .... Ms. Rhonda CLINARD
37 Director Student Financial Aid .... Mrs. Emma HLUBB
18 Chief Facilities/Physical Plant .... Mr. Fred HYDE
26 Director of Public Relations .... Mr. Grant VOSBURGH
38 Dir Student Counseling/Career/Svcs .... Ms. Doris F. WOSSUM
85 Director Foreign Students .... Ms. Georgia UDE
13 Director of Technology .... Mr. Edward MARTIN

Maryville College (F)

502 E Lamar Alexander Parkway,
Maryville TN 37804-5907
County: Blount FICE Identification: 003505
Unit ID: 220710
Telephone: (865) 981-8000 Carnegie Class: Bac/A&S
FAX Number: (865) 981-8010 Calendar System: Semester
URL: www.maryvillecollege.edu
Established: 1819 Annual Undergrad Tuition & Fees: $29,230
Enrollment: 1,080 Coed
Affiliation or Control: Presbyterian Church (U.S.A.) IRS Status: 501(c)3
Highest Offering: Baccalaureate
Program: Liberal Arts And General; Teacher Preparatory; Professional
Accreditation: SC, MUS

01 President .... Dr. William T. BOGART
05 Interim VP & Dean of College .... Dr. Barbara WELLS
10 Vice President & Treasurer .... Mr. Dana SMITH
32 Vice President & Dean of Students .... Ms. Vandy KEMP

84 VP for Enrollment .... Dr. Dolph HENRY
30 VP of Advancement & Cmty Rels .... Ms. Holly SULLIVAN
21 Asst Vice Pres for Finance .... Ms. Nancy PYANOE
26 Director of Communications .... Ms. Karen ELDRIDGE
20 Associate Dean .... Dr. Martha P. CRAIG
35 Assoc Dean of Students/Campus Life .... Ms. Michelle BALLEW-SAFEWRIGHT
35 Assoc Dean of Students/Student Dev .... Dr. Andy LEWTER
06 Registrar .... Ms. Kathy WILSON
90 Dir of Instructional Technology .... Dr. Steven JAMES
24 Director of Learning Center .... Ms. Lori HUNTER
36 Director of Career Resources .... Ms. Thema MCCOWAN
37 Director of Financial Aid .... Mr. Richard BRAND
41 Athletic Director .... Ms. Kandis SCHRAM
08 Director of the Library .... Ms. Angela QUICK
18 Director of Physical Plant .... Mr. Andy K. MCCALL
42 Campus Minister .... Rev. Anne MCKEE
04 Assistant to President .... Ms. Laura M. CASE
13 Director of Information Technology .... Mr. Mark FUGATE
15 Director of Human Resources .... Ms. Keni LANAGAN
09 Director Inst Research .... Dr. Martha P. CRAIG
38 Director of Counseling .... Mr. Bruce HOLT
44 Director of Annual Giving .... Mr. Eric BELLAH
29 Dir of Stewardship & Alumni Bd Rels .... Ms. Diana CANACARIS
22 Director of Minority Services .... Mr. Larry ERVIN

Meharry Medical College (A)

1005 Dr. D. B. Todd Jr. Boulevard, Nashville TN 37208-3501

County: Davidson FICE Identification: 003506
Unit ID: 220792
Telephone: (615) 327-6111 Carnegie Class: Spec/Med
FAX Number: (615) 327-6540 Calendar System: Semester
URL: www.mmc.edu
Established: 1876 Annual Graduate Tuition & Fees: $45,872
Enrollment: 781 Coed
Affiliation or Control: Independent Non-Profit IRS Status: 501(c)3
Highest Offering: Doctorate; No Undergraduates
Program: Professional
Accreditation: SC, DENT, MED, PH

01 President & Chief Executive Officer .... Dr. Wayne J. RILEY
03 Executive Vice President & Provost .... Vacant
32 Sr Vice Pres Student/Academic Affs .... Dr. Pamela WILLIAMS
17 Sr Vice President Health Affairs .... Dr. Charles P. MOUTON
30 Sr VP Advancement/College Relations .... Mr. Robert S. POOLE
10 Senior Vice President & CFO .... Mrs. LaMel BANDY-NEAL
45 Vice President for Research .... Dr. Russell POLAND
35 Assoc VP Student Svcs/Enroll Mgmt .... Mrs. Karen LEWIS
91 Vice Pres Information Technology .... Mr. Andrew JACKSON
11 Assoc Vice President Administration .... Dr. Bernard RAY
16 Assoc Vice Pres Human Resources .... Ms. Leslie CARROLL
26 Assoc VP Marketing/Communications .... Ms. Janet CALDWELL
31 Sr Assoc Vice Pres External Affairs .... Mr. Osei MEVS
43 General Counsel/VP & Sr Vice Pres .... Mr. Benjamin RAWLINS
58 Dean Graduate Studies .... Dr. Maria DE FATIMA LIMA
51 Director Lifelong Learning .... Dr. Allyson FLEMING
63 Dean School of Medicine .... Dr. Charles P. MOUTON
76 Dean Allied Health Professions .... Vacant
52 Dean School of Dentistry .... Dr. Janet H. SOUTHERLAND
29 Int Exec Director Alumni Affairs .... Dr. Henry MOSES
07 Director Admissions & Recruitment .... Mr. Allen MOSLEY
08 Director of Library .... Ms. Fatima MNCUBE-BARNES
19 Director Campus Safety & Security .... Mr. Richard BRIGGANCE
25 Director Grants & Contracts .... Mr. George WILLIAMS
46 Assoc VP for Research-Grants Mgmt .... Vacant
37 Director Student Financial Aid .... Ms. Barbara THARPE
09 Director Institutional Research .... Dr. Chau-Kuang CHEN
100 Special Assistant & Chief of Staff .... Mrs. Lisa JOHNSON
18 Director Campus Operations .... Mr. George N. KELLY
38 Director Counseling Center .... Ms. Sharda D. MISHRA
06 Registrar .... Ms. Shanita BROWN
96 Director of Procurement .... Mr. Larry HOLDEN

Memphis College of Art (B)

1930 Poplar Avenue, Overton Park, Memphis TN 38104-2764

County: Shelby FICE Identification: 003507
Unit ID: 220808
Telephone: (901) 272-5100 Carnegie Class: Spec/Arts
FAX Number: (901) 272-5104 Calendar System: Semester
URL: www.mca.edu
Established: 1936 Annual Undergrad Tuition & Fees: $24,400
Enrollment: 444 Coed
Affiliation or Control: Independent Non-Profit IRS Status: 501(c)3
Highest Offering: Master's
Program: Professional
Accreditation: SC, ART

01 President .... Dr. Ronald L. JONES
05 Dean of Academic Affairs .... Mr. Ken STRICKLAND
10 Vice Pres Finance & Administration .... Ms. Sherry YELVINGTON
30 Vice President College Advancement .... Ms. Kim WILLIAMS
84 Vice Pres Enrollment/Student Svcs .... Ms. Susan S. MILLER
08 Head Librarian .... Ms. Leslie HOLLAND
04 Assistant to President .... Vacant
07 Director Admissions .... Ms. Annette JAMES-MOORE
32 Director Student Life .... Ms. Carla RUFFER
37 Director Financial Aid .... Mr. Aaron WHITE
06 Registrar .... Ms. Elesha NEWBERRY
13 Director Computing Services .... Mr. Gordon DOVER
19 Director Safety & Security .... Mr. Donald KELLY
26 Director Public Relations .... Ms. Michelle BYRD
29 Director Alumni & Donor Relations .... Ms. LeeAnn WARNER
31 Coordinator Community Education .... Ms. Cecelia PALAZOLA
21 Assoc Business Officer/Staff Acct .... Ms. Heather RAGLAND
36 Director Career Services .... Ms. Gadsby CRESON

Memphis Theological Seminary (C)

168 East Parkway S at Union, Memphis TN 38104-4395

County: Shelby FICE Identification: 010529
Unit ID: 220871
Telephone: (901) 458-8232 Carnegie Class: Spec/Faith
FAX Number: (901) 452-4051 Calendar System: Semester
URL: www.memphisseminary.edu
Established: 1852 Annual Graduate Tuition & Fees: $12,540
Enrollment: 313 Coed
Affiliation or Control: Cumberland Presbyterian IRS Status: 501(c)3
Highest Offering: Doctorate; No Undergraduates
Program: Professional; Religious Emphasis
Accreditation: SC, THEOL

01 President .... Dr. Daniel J. EARHEART-BROWN
05 Vice President Academic Affs & Dean .... Dr. Robert S. WOOD
30 Vice President of Advancement .... Mrs. Cathi JOHNSON
08 Librarian .... Mr. Steven R. EDSCORN
51 Assoc Dean Continuing Education .... Mr. Pete GATHJE
10 Vice President of Operations/CFO .... Mrs. Cassandra F. PRICE-PERRY
32 Director of Student Services .... Dr. Barry L. ANDERSON
06 Dir Acad Rec/Regist & Accreditation .... Dr. Gail D. ROBINSON

Mid-America Baptist Theological Seminary (D)

2095 Appling Road, Cordova TN 38016-4911

County: Shelby FICE Identification: 029172
Unit ID: 220914
Telephone: (901) 751-8453 Carnegie Class: Not Classified
FAX Number: (901) 751-8454 Calendar System: Semester
URL: www.mabts.edu
Established: 1972 Annual Undergrad Tuition & Fees: $4,150
Enrollment: 415 Coed
Affiliation or Control: Independent Non Profit IRS Status: 501(c)3
Highest Offering: Doctorate
Program: 2-Year Principally Bachelor's Creditable; Teacher Preparatory; Professional
Accreditation: SC

01 President .... Dr. Michael R. SPRADLIN
03 Executive Vice President .... Dr. Bradley THOMPSON
05 Academic Vice President .... Dr. Tim SEAL
30 Vice Pres Institutional Advancement .... Mr. Duffy GUYTON
10 Chief Financial Officer .... Mr. Randy REDD
20 Director of Masters & Associate Pgm .... Dr. Kirk KILPATRICK
12 Director NE Branch .... Dr. Shawn BUICE
06 Registrar .... Mr. Harry DUFFEL
08 Director of Library Services .... Mr. Terrence BROWN
42 Director of Practical Missions .... Dr. Jeff BRAWNER
07 Director of Admissions .... Dr. Andy HYNES
04 Admin Assistant to the President .... Mrs. Maria WOOTEN
18 Supt of Buildings & Grounds .... Mr. Gene APPLEBURY
40 Manager Bookstore .... Mr. Brad JOHNSON

Mid-South Christian College (E)

PO Box 181056, Memphis TN 38181

County: Shelby Identification: 667046
Telephone: (901) 375-4400 Carnegie Class: Not Classified
FAX Number: (901) 375-4085 Calendar System: Semester
URL: www.midsouthcc.org
Established: 1959 Annual Undergrad Tuition & Fees: $4,414
Enrollment: 19 Coed
Affiliation or Control: Independent Non-Profit IRS Status: 501(c)3
Highest Offering: Baccalaureate
Program: Religious Emphasis
Accreditation: @BI

01 President .... Mr. Larry GRIFFIN
05 Academic Dean .... Mr. Wray GRAHAM
32 Director of Student Services .... Mr. Brent LINN
30 Chief Development Officer .... Mr. John BLIFFEN
88 Director Institutional Improvement .... Mr. Greg WADDELL

Middle Tennessee School of Anesthesia (F)

PO Box 417, 315 Hospital Drive, Madison TN 37116-6414

County: Davidson FICE Identification: 007783
Unit ID: 220996
Telephone: (615) 868-6503 Carnegie Class: Spec/Health
FAX Number: (615) 868-9885 Calendar System: Quarter
URL: www.mtsa.edu
Established: 1950 Annual Graduate Tuition & Fees: $28,859
Enrollment: 210 Coed
Affiliation or Control: Independent Non-Profit IRS Status: 501(c)3
Highest Offering: Master's; No Undergraduates
Program: Professional
Accreditation: SC, ANEST

01 President .... Dr. Kenneth L. SCHWAB
05 Vice President/Dean .... Dr. Mary E. DEVASHER

Miller-Motte Technical College (G)

1820 Business Park Drive, Clarksville TN 37040-6023

County: Montgomery FICE Identification: 026142
Unit ID: 382771
Telephone: (931) 553-0071 Carnegie Class: Assoc/PrivFP
FAX Number: (931) 552-2916 Calendar System: Quarter
URL: www.miller-motte.com
Established: 1916 Annual Undergrad Tuition & Fees: $10,900
Enrollment: 557 Coed
Affiliation or Control: Proprietary IRS Status: Proprietary
Highest Offering: Associate Degree
Program: Occupational
Accreditation: ACICS, MAC, POLYT, SURGT

01 Director .... Ms. Gina CASTLEBERRY
05 Director of Education .... Ms. Kala MATHIS
37 Financial Aid Director .... Ms. Debbie STRATMAN
06 Registrar .... Ms. Patricia CLINE
36 Director of Career Development .... Mr. John MCCASLIN
07 Director of Admissions .... Ms. Gayle KILGORE
72 CIS/Technology Division .... Mr. Bruce LIVESAY

Milligan College (H)

1 Milligan College, Milligan College TN 37682-4000

County: Carter FICE Identification: 003511
Unit ID: 221014
Telephone: (423) 461-8700 Carnegie Class: Bac/Diverse
FAX Number: (423) 461-8755 Calendar System: Semester
URL: www.milligan.edu
Established: 1866 Annual Undergrad Tuition & Fees: $25,260
Enrollment: 1,140 Coed
Affiliation or Control: Independent Non-Profit IRS Status: 501(c)3
Highest Offering: Master's
Program: Liberal Arts And General; Teacher Preparatory; Professional
Accreditation: SC, NURSE, OT, TED

01 President .... Dr. William B. GREER
05 Vice Pres Academic Affairs/Dean .... Dr. Mark A. MATSON
32 Vice President Student Affairs .... Mr. Mark FOX
30 Vice Pres Institutional Advancement .... Mr. Jack SIMPSON
84 Vice Pres Enrollment Management .... Ms. Lee FIERBAUGH
21 Vice Pres Business & Finance .... Mrs. Jacqui STEADMAN
06 Registrar/Institutional Research .... Mrs. Sue SKIDMORE
07 Director of Admissions .... Ms. Tracy BRINN
08 Director of Library Services .... Mr. Gary DAUGHT
35 Director of Student Activities .... Mrs. Katy MOSBY
29 Director of Alumni Relations .... Ms. Theresa GARBE
15 Director Personnel Services .... Ms. Linda LAWSON
37 Coordinator of Financial Aid .... Ms. Diane KEASLING
26 Coordinator of Church Relations .... Mrs. Phyllis FOX
36 Director Student Placement .... Ms. Beth ANDERSON
18 Service Manager Facilities .... Mr. Ken BROYLES
28 Director of Diversity .... Mr. Ernesto VILLARREAL

Nashville Auto-Diesel College (I)

1524 Gallatin Road, Nashville TN 37206-3298

County: Davidson FICE Identification: 007440
Unit ID: 221148
Telephone: (615) 226-3990 Carnegie Class: Assoc/PrivFP
FAX Number: (615) 262-8466 Calendar System: Other
URL: www.nadcedu.com
Established: 1919 Annual Undergrad Tuition & Fees: $24,600
Enrollment: 2,200 Coed
Affiliation or Control: Proprietary IRS Status: Proprietary
Highest Offering: Associate Degree
Program: Occupational
Accreditation: ACCSC

01 President .... Mr. Jim COAKLEY
03 Vice President .... Mr. Doug FOX
05 Vice President Education .... Mr. Scott REYNOLDS
26 Vice President Marketing .... Mr. Cary OLIVER
37 Director of Financial Aid .... Mr. Chris BIDDLE
84 Director of Enrollment .... Vacant
06 Registrar .... Mr. Gary WHITE

National College of Business and Technology (J)

1328 Highway 11 W, Bristol TN 37620-8530

County: Sullivan Identification: 666500
Telephone: (423) 878-4440 Carnegie Class: Not Classified
FAX Number: (923) 793-1060 Calendar System: Quarter
URL: www.ncbt.edu
Established: 1886 Annual Undergrad Tuition & Fees: $9,500
Enrollment: 492 Coed
Affiliation or Control: Proprietary IRS Status: Proprietary
Highest Offering: Baccalaureate
Program: Occupational; Technical Emphasis
Accreditation: ACICS, MAC

01 Director .... Ms. Doris COMBS

National College of Business and Technology (A)

1638 Bell Road, Nashville TN 37211
County: Davidson FICE Identification: 004617
Unit ID: 388043
Telephone: (615) 333-3344 Carnegie Class: Assoc/PrivFP
FAX Number: (615) 333-3429 Calendar System: Quarter
URL: www.ncbt.edu
Established: 1991 Annual Undergrad Tuition & Fees: $9,049
Enrollment: 1,590 Coed
Affiliation or Control: Proprietary IRS Status: Proprietary
Highest Offering: Baccalaureate
Program: Occupational
Accreditation: ACICS, MAC

01 Director .... Mr. Patrick PATTERSON

North Central Institute (B)

168 Jack Miller Boulevard Suite A,
Clarksville TN 37042-4810
County: Montgomery FICE Identification: 030791
Unit ID: 418889
Telephone: (931) 431-9700 Carnegie Class: Assoc/PrivFP
FAX Number: (931) 431-9771 Calendar System: Semester
URL: www.nci.edu
Established: 1988 Annual Undergrad Tuition & Fees: $13,755
Enrollment: 282 Coed
Affiliation or Control: Proprietary IRS Status: Proprietary
Highest Offering: Associate Degree
Program: Occupational; 2-Year Principally Bachelor's Creditable; Technical Emphasis
Accreditation: COE

01 President .... Dr. John D. MCCURDY

Nossi College of Art (C)

590 Cheron Road, Nashville TN 37115
County: Davidson FICE Identification: 025782
Unit ID: 368452
Telephone: (615) 514-2787 Carnegie Class: Spec/Arts
FAX Number: (615) 514-2788 Calendar System: Trimester
URL: www.nossi.edu
Established: 1973 Annual Undergrad Tuition & Fees: $14,100
Enrollment: 372 Coed
Affiliation or Control: Proprietary IRS Status: Proprietary
Highest Offering: Baccalaureate
Program: Occupational; 2-Year Principally Bachelor's Creditable
Accreditation: ACCSC

01 President .... Ms. Nossi VATANDOOST
07 Admissions Director .... Ms. Mary ALEXANDER
37 Financial Aid Director .... Ms. Mary KIDD

O'More College of Design (D)

423 S Margin Street, Franklin TN 37064
County: Williamson FICE Identification: 021064
Unit ID: 221254
Telephone: (615) 794-4254 Carnegie Class: Spec/Arts
FAX Number: (615) 790-1662 Calendar System: Semester
URL: www.omorecollege.edu
Established: 1970 Annual Undergrad Tuition & Fees: $23,880
Enrollment: 205 Coed
Affiliation or Control: Independent Non-Profit IRS Status: 501(c)3
Highest Offering: Baccalaureate
Program: Occupational; Liberal Arts And General; Fine Arts Emphasis
Accreditation: ACCSC, CIDA

01 President and CEO .... Dr. Mark HILLIARD
05 Executive VP and Provost .... Mr. Lance WESTBROOKS
06 Registrar .... Ms. Amy SHELTON
10 Director of Business Affairs .... Ms. Teresa CORLEY
08 Librarian and Bookstore Manager .... Ms. Allison CRAWFORD
84 Vice President of Enrollment .... Mr. Chris LEE
88 Chair Visual Communications .... Mr. Jeff FUQUA
88 Chair Fashion Design/Merch .... Ms. Jamie ATLAS
88 Chair Interior Design .... Mr. David KOELLEIN
49 Academic Dean/Chair Liberal Arts .... Ms. Shari FOX
57 Chair Fine Arts .... Ms. Janet CRUZ
19 Director of Security .... Mr. DeWayne PULLIAM

Oxford Graduate School (E)

500 Oxford Drive, Dayton TN 37321-6736
County: Rhea FICE Identification: 038403
Telephone: (423) 775-6596 Carnegie Class: Not Classified
FAX Number: (423) 775-6599 Calendar System: Trimester
URL: www.ogs.edu
Established: 1981 Annual Graduate Tuition & Fees: $31,500
Enrollment: 98 Coed
Affiliation or Control: Independent Non-Profit IRS Status: 501(c)3
Highest Offering: Doctorate; No Undergraduates
Program: Professional
Accreditation: TRACS

01 Interim President .... Dr. Kimberly GEIGER
00 Chancellor .... Dr. Rebecca F. TUCKER
05 Vice President Acadmic Affairs .... Dr. Joshua REICHARD
07 Vice President of Recruitment .... Dr. Richard M. SHARP
08 Head Librarian .... Dr. Sara LAMBERT
09 EVP Director Institutional Research .... Vacant
10 Chief Business Officer .... Ms. Sharlene DANIEL
29 Director Alumni Relations .... Dr. Robert PAGE
35 Director Student Services .... Ms. Joanne PHILLIPS
37 Director Financial Aid .... Dr. Richard ROBERTS
42 Chaplain .... Vacant
44 Director Planned Gifts .... Vacant
06 Registrar .... Mrs. Joanne PHILLIPS
84 Director Enrollment Management .... Mr. Rick SHARP

Pentecostal Theological Seminary (F)

900 Walker Street, NE, Cleveland TN 37311
County: Bradley FICE Identification: 021883
Unit ID: 219842
Telephone: (423) 478-1131 Carnegie Class: Spec/Faith
FAX Number: (423) 478-7711 Calendar System: 4/1/4
URL: www.ptseminary.edu
Established: 1975 Annual Graduate Tuition & Fees: $14,603
Enrollment: 199 Coed
Affiliation or Control: Church Of God IRS Status: 501(c)3
Highest Offering: Doctorate; No Undergraduates
Program: Professional
Accreditation: SC, THEOL

01 President .... Dr. Steven J. LAND
05 Int Vice President for Academics .... Dr. Sang Ehil HAN
42 VP for Ministry Formation .... Dr. Oliver L. MCMAHAN
10 Vice President for Finance .... Mr. Robert E. BUXTON
30 Vice Pres Institutional Advancement .... Rev. Ken R. DAVIS
04 Exec Assistant to the President .... Mrs. Teresa GILBERT
27 Director Recruitment/Communications ... Dr. J. Anthony LOMBARD
07 Director of Admissions/Registrar .... Ms. Anita F. BLEVINS
15 Director of Administrative Services .... Mrs. Alanna L. HENRY
18 Dir of Facilities/Support Services .... Mr. Welton WRISTON
29 Dir Donor Services/Alumni Relations .... Mrs. Joylita TERPSTRA
35 Director of Student Services .... Dr. Jimmy DUPREE
37 Director of Financial Aid .... Mrs. Robin SLUDER
38 Director of Counseling/Testing .... Dr. Douglas SLOCUMB

Remington College (G)

2710 Nonconnah Boulevard, Memphis TN 38132-2110
County: Shelby Identification: 666062
Unit ID: 412599
Telephone: (901) 345-1000 Carnegie Class: Assoc/PrivFP4
FAX Number: (901) 396-8310 Calendar System: Quarter
URL: www.remingtoncollege.edu
Established: 1987 Annual Undergrad Tuition & Fees: $14,745
Enrollment: 1,030 Coed
Affiliation or Control: Proprietary IRS Status: Proprietary
Highest Offering: Baccalaureate
Program: Occupational; 2-Year Principally Bachelor's Creditable
Accreditation: ACCSC

01 President .... Dr. Lori K. MAY

† Branch campus of Remington College, Mobile, AL.

Remington College (H)

441 Donelson Pike, Suite 150, Nashville TN 37214-3558
County: Davidson Identification: 666307
Unit ID: 445249
Telephone: (615) 889-5520 Carnegie Class: Assoc/PrivFP
FAX Number: (615) 493-9385 Calendar System: Other
URL: www.remingtoncollege.edu
Established: 2003 Annual Undergrad Tuition & Fees: $14,745
Enrollment: 440 Coed
Affiliation or Control: Proprietary IRS Status: Proprietary
Highest Offering: Associate Degree
Program: Occupational
Accreditation: ACCSC, DH

01 Campus President .... Mr. Larry COLLINS

† Branch campus of Remington College, Mobile, AL.

Rhodes College (I)

2000 North Parkway, Memphis TN 38112-1690
County: Shelby FICE Identification: 003519
Unit ID: 221351
Telephone: (901) 843-3000 Carnegie Class: Bac/A&S
FAX Number: N/A Calendar System: Semester
URL: www.rhodes.edu
Established: 1848 Annual Undergrad Tuition & Fees: $36,464
Enrollment: 1,721 Coed
Affiliation or Control: Presbyterian Church (U.S.A.) IRS Status: 501(c)3
Highest Offering: Master's
Program: Liberal Arts And General
Accreditation: SC

01 President .... Dr. William E. TROUTT
05 Provost .... Dr. Michael R. DROMPP
10 VP for Finance & Business Affairs .... Mr. J. Allen BOONE
13 Vice Pres for Information Services . Dr. Robert M. JOHNSON, JR.
30 Vice President for Development .... Ms. Jennifer G. WADE
84 Vice Pres Enrollment/Communications .... Ms. Carey THOMPSON
32 Dean of Students .... Ms. Carol E. CASEY
35 Associate Dean of Students .... Ms. Kathleen LAAKSO
20 Assoc Dean of Academic Affairs .... Dr. Brian W. SHAFFER
20 Assoc Dean of Academic Affairs .... Dr. John S. OLSEN
20 Assoc Dean of Academic Affairs .... Dr. Robert J. STRANDBURG
06 Registrar .... Ms. DeAnna ADAMS
37 Director of Financial Aid .... Ms. Ashley BIANCHI
08 Librarian .... Ms. Darlene D. BROOKS
21 Comptroller .... Mr. Kyle WEBB
29 Director of Alumni Relations .... Mr. Warren A. RICHEY
15 Director of Human Resources .... Ms. Claire R. SHAPIRO
14 Director of Info Tech Services .... Dr. Charles LEMOND
19 Director of Campus Safety .... Mr. Ike SLOAS
41 Director of Athletics .... Mr. Michael T. CLARY
36 Director of Career Services .... Ms. Sandra G. TRACY
38 Director of Counseling Services .... Mr. Robert B. DOVE
18 Director of Physical Plant .... Mr. Brian E. FOSHEE
44 Director of Planned Giving .... Mr. Jim DUNCAN
27 Director of Communications .... Mr. Ken WOODMANSEE
09 Director of Information Services .... Dr. James E. ECKLES
04 Exec Assistant to the President .... Ms. Melody H. RICHEY
96 Physical Plant Business Manager .... Ms. Amy J. RADFORD

Sewanee: The University of the South (J)

735 University Avenue, Sewanee TN 37383-1000
County: Franklin FICE Identification: 003534
Unit ID: 221519
Telephone: (931) 598-1000 Carnegie Class: Bac/A&S
FAX Number: (931) 598-1145 Calendar System: Semester
URL: www.sewanee.edu
Established: 1857 Annual Undergrad Tuition & Fees: $32,092
Enrollment: 1,536 Coed
Affiliation or Control: Protestant Episcopal IRS Status: 501(c)3
Highest Offering: Doctorate
Program: Liberal Arts And General; Professional
Accreditation: SC, THEOL

01 Vice Chancellor & President .... Dr. John M. MCCARDELL, JR.
05 Provost .... Dr. Linda B. LANKEWICZ
30 Vice President University Relations .... Mr. Jay FISHER
13 Assoc Provost Info Tech/Librarian .... Dr. Vicki G. SELLS
49 Dean College of Arts & Sciences .... Dr. John J. GATTA
73 Dean School of Theology .... Rev Dr. William S. STAFFORD
32 Dean of Students .... Mr. Eric G. HARTMAN
20 Assoc Dean Arts & Sciences .... Dr. Larry H. JONES
20 Assoc Dean Arts and Sciences .... Dr. Richard G. SUMMERS
10 Treasurer .... Dr. Jerry FORSTER
09 Director of Institutional Research .... Dr. Robert A. LESTER, III
06 Registrar .... Mr. Paul G. WILEY
07 Dean of Admission & Financial Aid .... Ms. Lee Ann M. AFTON
26 Exec Dir Marketing/Communications .... Mr. Mark L. KELLY
15 Director of Human Resources .... Ms. Donna L. PIERCE
41 Director of Athletics .... Mr. Mark F. WEBB
29 Director of Alumni Relations .... Ms. Susan S. ASKEW
36 Director of Career Services .... Ms. Kim D. HEITZENRATER
38 Director of University Counseling .... Dr. David L. SPAULDING
93 Director of Minority Affairs .... Mr. Eric V. BENJAMIN
04 Exec Asst to Vice Chanc & President .... Ms. Sarah STAPLETON
18 Director of Physical Plant Services .... Mr. John P. VINEYARD
43 University Legal Counsel .... Ms. Donna L. PIERCE
35 Associate Dean of Students .... Dr. Alex M. BRUCE
19 Chief of Police .... Mr. Robert W. WHITE
21 Assistant Treasurer .... Ms. Sarah R. SUTHERLAND
23 Director of Univ Health Services .... Ms. Anne M. SITZ
24 Director of Media Services .... Mr. Larry E. WOOD
42 University Chaplain .... Rev. Thomas E. MACFIE
96 Director of Purchasing .... Mr. Randall K. TAYLOR

South College (K)

3904 Lonas Drive, Knoxville TN 37909-3323
County: Knox FICE Identification: 004938
Unit ID: 220552
Telephone: (865) 251-1800 Carnegie Class: Bac/Assoc
FAX Number: (865) 584-7335 Calendar System: Quarter
URL: www.southcollegetn.edu
Established: 1882 Annual Undergrad Tuition & Fees: $16,650
Enrollment: 1,045 Coed
Affiliation or Control: Proprietary IRS Status: Proprietary
Highest Offering: Doctorate
Program: Occupational; Teacher Preparatory; Professional
Accreditation: SC, ARCPA, MAC, NMT, NUR, PTAA, RAD

01 President .... Mr. Stephen A. SOUTH
05 Executive VP .... Dr. Kim B. HALL
11 Vice Pres Administrative Services .... Mr. Steve WOODFORD
13 VP Information Tech/Facilities .... Mr. Ron HALL
09 VP Inst Effective/Student Svcs .... Ms. Barbara BRIMI
10 Chief Financial Officer .... Mr. Mark HAUB
21 Controller .... Mr. Kevin SPARKS
07 Director of Admissions .... Mr. Walter HOSEA
26 Public Relations Coordinator .... Mr. Norman HAMMITT
36 Job Placement Coordinator .... Mr. Gary TAYLOR
06 Registrar .... Ms. Kim WOOD
37 Director of Financial Aid .... Mr. Larry BROADWATER
08 Librarian .... Ms. Mary MCHUGH
72 Director Instructional Technology .... Dr. Jamie NELSON

Southern Adventist University (A)

Box 370, 4881 Taylor Circle, Collegedale TN 37315-0370
County: Hamilton
FICE Identification: 003518
Unit ID: 221661
Telephone: (423) 236-2000
Carnegie Class: Bac/Diverse
FAX Number: (423) 236-1000
Calendar System: Semester
URL: www.southern.edu
Established: 1892
Annual Undergrad Tuition & Fees: $18,324
Enrollment: 3,053
Coed
Affiliation or Control: Seventh-day Adventist
IRS Status: 501(c)3
Highest Offering: Master's
Program: Liberal Arts And General; Teacher Preparatory
Accreditation: SC, ADNUR, CS, IACBE, MUS, NUR, SW, TED

01 President ... Dr. Gordon BIETZ
05 Vice Pres Academic Administration ... Dr. Robert YOUNG
10 Vice President Finance ... Mr. Tom VERRILL
32 Vice President Student Services ... Dr. William R. WOHLERS
45 Vice Pres Strategic Initiatives ... Mrs. Vinita R. SAUDER
30 Vice President Advancement ... Mr. Chris CAREY
07 Vice Pres Enrollment Services ... Mr. Marc A. GRUNDY
20 Associate VP Academic Admin ... Dr. Volker HENNING
21 Associate VP Financial Admin ... Mr. Marty HAMILTON
09 Director Inst Research/Planning ... Dr. Hollis JAMES
08 Director of Libraries ... Mr. Josip MOCNIK
06 Director Records & Advisement ... Mrs. Joni I. ZIER
13 Director of Computer Center ... Mr. Henry L. HICKS
15 Director Personnel Services ... Mrs. Pat COVERDALE
26 Chief Public Relations Officer ... Ms. Ingrid SKANTZ
29 Director Alumni Relations ... Ms. Evonne CROOK
38 Director Student Counseling ... Mr. Jim WAMPLER
33 Dean of Men ... Mr. Dwight E. MAGERS
34 Dean of Women ... Ms. Kassy KRAUSE
50 Dean School of Business/Mgmt ... Dr. Donald C. VAN ORNAM
53 Dean School of Education/Psych ... Dr. John MCCOY
57 Dean School of Visual Art/Design ... Mr. Randy CRAVEN
60 Dean School of Journalism/Comm ... Dr. Greg RUMSEY
64 Dean School of Music ... Dr. Scott BALL
66 Dean School of Nursing ... Dr. Barbara JAMES
68 Dean Sch of Phys Ed/Health/Wellness ... Dr. Phil GARVER
73 Dean School of Religion ... Dr. Greg KING
77 Dean School of Computing ... Dr. Rick HALTERMAN
70 Chair Social Work/Family Studies ... Dr. Rene' DRUMM
72 Chair Technology ... Mr. Dale WALTERS
81 Chair Mathematics ... Dr. Kevin BROWN
76 Chair Biology/Allied Health ... Dr. Keith SNYDER
88 Chair Chemistry ... Dr. Rhonda J. SCOTT
88 Chair English ... Dr. Jan HALUSKA
88 Chair History ... Dr. Dennis PETTIBONE
88 Chair Modern Languages ... Dr. Carlos P. PARRA
88 Chair Physics ... Dr. Chris HANSEN
18 Chief Facilities/Physical Plant ... Mr. Clair KITSON
35 Director Student Affairs ... Ms. Kari SHULTZ
37 Director Student Financial Aid ... Mr. Jason MERRYMAN
96 Director of Purchasing ... Mr. Russell ORRISON

Southern College of Optometry (B)

1245 Madison Avenue, Memphis TN 38104-2222
County: Shelby
FICE Identification: 003517
Unit ID: 221670
Telephone: (901) 722-3200
Carnegie Class: Spec/Health
FAX Number: (901) 722-3279
Calendar System: Trimester
URL: www.sco.edu
Established: 1932
Annual Graduate Tuition & Fees: $26,178
Enrollment: 486
Coed
Affiliation or Control: Independent Non-Profit
IRS Status: 501(c)3
Highest Offering: Doctorate; No Undergraduates
Program: Professional
Accreditation: SC, OPT, OPTR

01 President ... Dr. Richard W. PHILLIPS
04 Executive Admin Assistant to Pres ... Ms. Sandra S. STEPHENS
05 Vice President for Academic Affairs ... Dr. Lewis REICH
30 Vice President for Inst Advancement ... Dr. Kristin K. ANDERSON
44 Director of Development ... Mr. George MILLER
29 Alumni Relations ... Ms. Carla O'BRIEN
10 Vice President for Finance & Admin ... Mr. David L. WEST
13 Director of Information Services ... Mr. Dean SWICK
18 Director of Physical Plant ... Mr. Danny ANDERSON
17 Vice Pres for Clinical Programs ... Dr. James E. VENABLE
23 Director of Clinic Operations ... Mr. Gary SNUFFIN
06 Vice President for Student Services ... Mr. Joseph H. HAUSER
07 Dir of Admissions/Enrollment Svcs ... Mr. Michael ROBERTSON
07 Director of Student Recruitment ... Ms. Sunnie EWING
08 Director of Library ... Dr. Sharon TABACHNICK
27 Dir of Communications/Media Svcs ... Mr. Jim HOLLIFIELD
16 Vice President for Human Resources ... Ms. Ann Z. FIELDS
37 Director of Financial Aid ... Ms. Cindy GARNER

*Tennessee Board of Regents Office (C)

1415 Murfreesboro Road, Nashville TN 37217-2833
County: Davidson
FICE Identification: 029031
Unit ID: 409379
Telephone: (615) 366-4400
Carnegie Class: N/A
FAX Number: (615) 366-3922
URL: www.tbr.edu

01 Chancellor ... Mr. John G. MORGAN
05 Vice Chancellor Academic Affairs ... Dr. Paula MYRICK SHORT
10 Vice Chanc Business & Finance ... Mr. Dale SIMS
11 Vice Chanc Admin & Fac Mgmt ... Mr. David B. GREGORY
12 Vice Chanc TN Technology Centers ... Mr. James KING
13 Vice Chanc Information Systems ... Mr. Tom DANFORD
43 General Counsel ... Ms. Christine A. MODISHER
09 Asst Vice Chanc Research/Assess ... Mr. Greg SCHUTZ
20 Assoc Vice Chanc Academic Affairs ... Dr. Treva G. BERRYMAN
20 Assoc Vice Chanc Academic Affairs ... Dr. S. Kay CLARK
20 Assoc Vice Chance Academic Affairs ... Dr. Pamela KNOX
21 Assistant Vice Chancellor Business ... Vacant
16 Asst Vice Chanc for HR ... Ms. April PRESTON
21 Assistant Vice Chancellor Business ... Ms. Renee STEWART
88 Exec Dir of Operations for ROCC ... Dr. Raylean HENRY
26 Director of Communications ... Ms. Monica GREPPIN

*Austin Peay State University (D)

601 College Street, Clarksville TN 37044-0002
County: Montgomery
FICE Identification: 003478
Unit ID: 219602
Telephone: (931) 221-7011
Carnegie Class: Master's L
FAX Number: (931) 221-7475
Calendar System: Semester
URL: www.apsu.edu
Established: 1927
Annual Undergrad Tuition & Fees (In-State): $6,432
Enrollment: 10,723
Coed
Affiliation or Control: State
IRS Status: 501(c)3
Highest Offering: Beyond Master's But Less Than Doctorate
Program: Liberal Arts And General; Teacher Preparatory; Professional; Fine Arts Emphasis
Accreditation: SC, ART, ENGT, MT, MUS, NUR, RAD, SW, TED

02 President ... Mr. Timothy L. HALL
04 Exec Asst to the President ... Ms. Carol D. CLARK
05 Provost/VP Acad Affairs ... Dr. Tristan M. JOSEPH DENLEY
10 Vice President for Finance & Admin ... Mr. Mitch ROBINSON
43 University Attorney ... Vacant
20 Assistant VP Academic Affairs ... Mr. Brian JOHNSON
32 VP for Student Affairs ... Dr. Sherryl BYRD
21 Asst Vice Pres for Finance ... Mr. Timothy HURST
84 Assoc Provost for Enrollment Mgmt ... Dr. Beverly BOGGS
30 Exec Director Univ Advancement ... Mr. J. Roy GREGORY
31 Dir Community/Business Rels ... Ms. Carol CLARK
26 Exec Dir Marketing/Public Rels ... Mr. Bill PERSINGER
12 Exec Dir APSU Fort Campbell ... Dr. William COX
29 Dir Alumni and Annual Giving ... Ms. Nicole PETERSON
21 Director Budgets ... Ms. Sonja STEWART
08 Director Library ... Mr. Joe WEBER
13 Director of Information Technology ... Mr. Charles B. WALL
09 Dir Inst Research & Effectiveness ... Vacant
07 Director of Admissions ... Vacant
06 Registrar ... Ms. Telaina WRIGLEY
18 Director of Plant Administration ... Mr. Thomas HUTCHINS
45 Dir Facilities Planning & Projects ... Mr. Al WESTERMAN
41 Athletics Director ... Mr. David H. LOOS
27 Director of Athletic Information ... Mr. Brad J. KIRTLEY
37 Director of Student Financial Aid ... Ms. Donna PRICE
36 Director Academic Advisement ... Ms. Barbara BLACKSTON
38 Dir of Student Counseling Services ... Dr. Lowell RODDY
35 Dean of Students ... Mr. Gregory SINGLETON
88 Dir African Amer Cultural Ctr ... Mr. Henderson HILL
15 Director Human Resources ... Mr. Michael HAMLET
19 Director Public Safety ... Mr. Lantz BILES
39 Director Housing/Resident Life ... Mr. F. Joe MILLS
21 Director Internal Audit ... Ms. Jacqueline STRUCKMEYER
25 Director of Grants ... Mr. Andrew SHEPARD-SMITH
96 Director of Purchasing ... Ms. Judy BLAIN
22 Dir Affirmative Action ... Ms. Sheila M. BRYANT
49 Dean College Arts & Letters ... Dr. Dixie WEBB
81 Dean Col Science & Math ... Dr. Jaime TAYLOR
53 Dean Col Behav Health Science ... Dr. David DENTON
58 Dean College Graduate Studies ... Dr. Dixie DENNIS
51 Exec Dir Extended & Distance Educ ... Mr. Dana WILLETT

*East Tennessee State University (E)

807 University Parkway, Johnson City TN 37614-6500
County: Washington
FICE Identification: 003487
Unit ID: 220075
Telephone: (423) 439-1000
Carnegie Class: DRU
FAX Number: (423) 439-5770
Calendar System: Semester
URL: www.etsu.edu
Established: 1911
Annual Undergrad Tuition & Fees (In-State): $6,271
Enrollment: 14,382
Coed
Affiliation or Control: State
IRS Status: 501(c)3
Highest Offering: Doctorate
Program: Occupational; Liberal Arts And General; Teacher Preparatory; Professional; Business Emphasis
Accreditation: SC, AAFCS, ART, AUD, BUS, BUSA, CACREP, CS, DH, DIETD, DIETI, ENGR, ENGT, JOUR, MED, MUS, NURSE, PH, PHAR, POLYT, PTA, RAD, SP, SW, TED

02 President ... Dr. Paul E. STANTON, JR.
100 Chief of Staff/Assoc VP ... Dr. Jane M. JONES
05 Provost/Vice Pres Academic Affairs ... Dr. Bert C. BACH
10 Vice Pres Finance & Administration ... Dr. David D. COLLINS
17 Vice President Health Affairs/COO ... Dr. Wilsie S. BISHOP
30 Vice Pres University Advancement ... Dr. Richard A. MANAHAN
41 Athletic Director ... Mr. C. David MULLINS, JR.
28 Special Asst to Pres Cultural Div ... Ms. Mary V. JORDAN
88 Director of Internal Audit ... Ms. Rebecca B. LEWIS
43 University Counsel ... Mr. Edward J. KELLY
26 Exec Director of Univ Relations ... Mr. Fred W. SAUCEMAN
84 Vice Provost Enrollment Services ... Dr. Ramona A. WILLIAMS
51 Dean Cont Studies & Acad Outreach ... Dr. Richard E. OSBORN
46 Vice Prov Research/Sponsored Pgms ... Dr. William R. DUNCAN
32 VProv Student Aff/Dean of Students ... Dr. Joe H. SHERLIN
20 Vice Provost Academic Affairs ... Dr. M. Marshall GRUBE
20 VProv Ugrad Ed/Dir Plan & Analysis ... Dr. William G. KIRKWOOD
18 Assoc VP for Facilities Management ... Mr. William B. RASNICK, JR.
35 Associate Vice Pres Student Affairs ... Dr. Sally LEE
13 Assoc VP/Chief Information Officer ... Mr. Mark S. BRAGG
96 Assoc VP Procurement/Contract Svcs ... Ms. Katherine M. KELLEY
21 Assoc VP Financial Services ... Dr. B. J. KING
44 Assoc VP Univ Adv/Planned Giving ... Mr. Jeffrey W. ANDERSON
29 Assoc VP Univ Adv/Exec Dir Alumni ... Mr. Robert M. PLUMMER
106 AVP/Ex Dir E-Learning & Online Ed ... Dr. Karen D. KING
09 Asst VP Institutional Research ... Dr. Jack A. SANDERS
86 Asst VP for Governmental Relations ... Dr. Robert V. ACUFF
49 Dean College Arts & Science ... Dr. Gordon K. ANDERSON
50 Dean College of Business/Technology ... Dr. Linda R. GARCEAU
76 Dean College of Clin & Rehab Sci ... Dr. Nancy J. SCHERER
53 Dean College of Education ... Dr. W. Hal KNIGHT
92 Dean Honors College ... Dr. Rebecca A. PYLES
63 Dean College of Medicine ... Dr. Philip C. BAGNELL
67 Dean College of Pharmacy ... Dr. Larry D. CALHOUN
66 Dean College of Nursing ... Dr. Wendy M. NEHRING
69 Dean College of Public Health ... Dr. Randolph F. WYKOFF
58 Dean School of Graduate Studies ... Dr. Cecilia A. MCINTOSH
08 Interim Dean of Libraries ... Dr. Jean C. FLANIGAN
06 University Registrar ... Ms. Sheryl L. BURNETTE
07 Director of Admissions ... Mr. T. Michael PITTS
36 Dir Career & Internship Services ... Dr. David E. MAGEE, JR.
38 Director Counseling Center ... Dr. Steve D. BROWN
12 Director of ETSU at Kingsport ... Ms. Patricia L. STAFFORD
37 Director of Financial Aid ... Ms. Margaret L. MILLER
92 Director University Honors Program ... Dr. Michael A. CODY
39 Director Student Housing ... Dr. Bonnie L. BURCHETT
85 Dir International Programs/Services ... Ms. Maria D. COSTA
93 Multicultural Director ... Ms. Laura C. TERRY
19 Director Public Safety ... Chief Jack R. COTREL
25 Director of Sponsored Programs ... Dr. Louise C. NUTTLE
87 Director of Summer School ... Ms. Sarah E. BRADFORD
94 Director of Women's Studies ... Dr. Karen L. CAJKA
105 Web Manager ... Ms. Michaele D. LAWS
15 Dir Empl Relations/Compensation/Dev ... Ms. Diana D. MCCLAY
15 Director Benefits/Retirement/HRIS ... Ms. Tammy S. HAMM

*Middle Tennessee State University (F)

1301 E Main Street, Murfreesboro TN 37132-0001
County: Rutherford
FICE Identification: 003510
Unit ID: 220978
Telephone: (615) 898-2300
Carnegie Class: DRU
FAX Number: (615) 898-5538
Calendar System: Semester
URL: www.mtsu.edu
Established: 1911
Annual Undergrad Tuition & Fees (In-State): $6,753
Enrollment: 26,430
Coed
Affiliation or Control: State
IRS Status: 501(c)3
Highest Offering: Doctorate
Program: Liberal Arts And General; Teacher Preparatory
Accreditation: SC, AAB, AAFCS, ART, BUS, BUSA, CACREP, CIDA, CS, DIETD, ENGT, JOUR, MUS, NAIT, NRPA, NUR, NURSE, SW, TED

02 President ... Dr. Sidney A. MCPHEE
03 University Provost ... Dr. Brad BARTEL
30 Vice President Devel/Univ Relations ... Mr. William J. BALES
31 Community Engagement/Asst to Pres ... Dr. Gloria L. BONNER
04 Exec Assistant to the President ... Ms. Kimberly S. EDGAR
10 Senior Vice Pres Business & Finance ... Dr. John W. COTHERN
32 VP Stdnt Affs/V Prov Enroll Mgmt ... Dr. Debra K. SELLS
14 VP Info Tech/Chief Info Officer ... Mr. Bruce PETRYSHAK
58 Vice Provost Rsrch/Dean Grad Stds ... Dr. Michael ALLEN
35 Assoc Vice Pres/Dean Student Life ... Ms. Sarah SUDAK
27 Assoc Vice Pres Mktg/Communications ... Mr. Andrew OPPMAN
07 Assoc Vice Prov Admis & Enroll Svcs ... Dr. David CICOTELLO
13 Assoc Vice Pres Info Technology ... Mr. Tom WALLACE
21 Assoc Vice Pres Business Office ... Mr. Michael E. GOWER
05 Vice Prov for Academic Affairs ... Dr. John OMACHONU
15 Asst Vice Pres Human Resource Svcs ... Ms. Kathy I. MUSSELMAN
18 Asst Vice Pres Facilities Services ... Mr. David W. GRAY
11 Asst Vice Pres Admin/Business Svcs ... Ms. Kathryn CRISP
49 Dean College of Liberal Arts ... Dr. Mark BYRNES
81 Dean Col Basic/Applied Science ... Dr. Thomas J. CHEATHAM
53 Dean College of Education ... Dr. Lana SEIVERS
83 Dean College Behavioral & Hlth Sci ... Dr. Harold WHITESIDE
50 Dean College of Business ... Dr. E. James BURTON
60 Dean College Mass Communication ... Dr. Roy MOORE
51 Dean University College ... Dr. Mike A. BOYLE
43 Univ Counsel & Asst to the Pres ... Ms. Heidi ZIMMERMAN
08 Interim Dean University Library ... Mr. Donald CRAIG
26 Director News & Public Affairs ... Mr. Thomas J. TOZER
44 Director Development Office ... Mr. Nick PERLICK
09 Exec Dir Inst Effect/Plng/Research ... Ms. Fay PARHAM
29 Director Alumni Relations ... Ms. Ginger C. FREEMAN
37 Dir of Financial Aid & Scholarship ... Mr. Stephen WHITE
38 Director Counseling Services ... Dr. Jane TIPPS
36 Dir Career & Employment Center ... Mr. Bill FLETCHER
19 Chief of Police/Dir Public Safety ... Mr. Carl S. PEASTER
23 Director of Health Services ... Mr. Richard L. CHAPMAN
40 Director Bookstore ... Mr. Jeff WHITWELL
41 Athletic Director ... Mr. Chris John MASSARO
06 Director Technical Services ... Ms. Teresa THOMAS

06	Registrar	Ms. Cathy KIRCHNER
24	Director Instructional Tech Center	Dr. Constance R. SCHMIDT
90	Asst Vice Pres Acad & Instruct Tech	Ms. Barbara J. DRAUDE
45	Asst Vice Pres Entrprse Rsrce Plng	Mrs. Lisa C. ROGERS
25	Dir Research & Sponsored Programs	Dr. Myra K. NORMAN
92	Dean University Honors College	Dr. John R. VILE
93	Dir Intercultural/Diversity Affairs	Mr. Vincent WINDROW
94	Director Women's Studies	Dr. Tina JOHNSON

*Tennessee State University (A)

3500 John A Merritt Boulevard, Nashville TN 37209-1561

County: Davidson FICE Identification: 003522
Unit ID: 221838
Telephone: (615) 963-5000 Carnegie Class: DRU
FAX Number: (615) 963-7412 Calendar System: Semester
URL: www.tnstate.edu
Established: 1912 Annual Undergrad Tuition & Fees (In-State): $6,088
Enrollment: 8,930 Coed
Affiliation or Control: State IRS Status: 501(c)3
Highest Offering: Doctorate
Program: Occupational; Liberal Arts And General; Teacher Preparatory; Professional
Accreditation: SC, AAFCS, ADNUR, ART, BUS, COPSY, CS, DH, DIETD, ENG, MUS, NAIT, NUR, OT, PTA, SP, SPAA, SW, TED

02	President	Dr. Portia H. SHIELDS
05	Provost	Dr. Dennis GENDRON
04	Executive Asst to President	Dr. Jewel WINN
10	VP Business & Finance	Mrs. Cynthia BROOKS
32	VP Student Affairs	Dr. A. Dexter SAMUELS
30	VP Univ Relations & Development	Vacant
41	Athletic Director	Mrs. Teresa LAWRENCE-PHILLIPS
43	University Legal Counsel	Mr. Laurence PENDLETON
84	Assoc Provost Enrollment Mgmt	Dr. John CADE
20	Assoc VP Academic Affairs	Dr. Patricia CROOK
20	Assoc VP Academic Affairs Ext Ed	Dr. Evelyn NETTLES
20	Assoc VP Academic Affairs	Dr. Ken LOONEY
20	Assoc VP Academic Aff Planning	Dr. Peter NWOSU
15	Assoc VP/Dir Human Resources	Ms. Linda C. SPEARS
46	Assoc VP Research & Sponsored Pgm	Dr. Michael BUSBY
21	Assoc VP Finance/Accounting	Mr. Robert HUGHES
18	Assoc VP Facilities/Physical Plant	Mr. Ronnie BROOKS
13	Assoc VP Computer Info Technology	Mr. Khalid M. CHAUDHARY
29	Asst VP Alumni Affairs	Ms. Michelle VIERA
88	Asst VP Budget/Travel	Mr. Bradley WHITE
09	Dir Inst Effectiveness & Research	Dr. G. Pamela BURCH-SIMS
28	Dir Equity Diversity & Compliance	Vacant
37	Director Financial Aid	Ms. Amy B. WOOD
06	Registrar	Mrs. Thelria HARDAWAY
27	Director Media Relations	Mr. Richard DELAHAYA
19	Chief TSU Police Department	Mr. James KIZER
08	Dean Libraries & Media Centers	Dr. Yildiz B. BINKLEY
49	Dean College of Liberal Arts	Dr. Gloria JOHNSON
50	Dean College of Business	Dr. Tilden J. CURRY
53	Dean College of Education	Dr. Peter MILLET
54	Dean College of Engr/Tech/Comp Sci	Dr. S. Keith HARGROVE
47	Dean Agriculture/Human & Nat Sci	Dr. Chandra REDDY
58	Dean School of Graduate Studies	Dr. Alex SEKWAT
88	Dean College Public Svcs/Urban Aff	Dr. Bruce ROGERS
76	Dean College of Health Sciences	Dr. Kathleen MCENERNEY
66	Assoc Dean/Dir of Nursing	Dr. Kathy MARTIN

*Tennessee Technological University (B)

1000 N Dixie Avenue, Cookeville TN 38505-0001

County: Putnam FICE Identification: 003523
Unit ID: 221847
Telephone: (931) 372-3101 Carnegie Class: Master's L
FAX Number: (931) 372-3898 Calendar System: Semester
URL: www.tntech.edu
Established: 1915 Annual Undergrad Tuition & Fees (In-State): $6,438
Enrollment: 11,538 Coed
Affiliation or Control: State IRS Status: 501(c)3
Highest Offering: Doctorate
Program: Liberal Arts And General; Teacher Preparatory; Professional
Accreditation: SC, AAFCS, ART, BUS, BUSA, CS, DIETD, EMT, ENG, MUS, NAIT, NURSE, TED

02	President	Dr. Robert R. BELL
05	Provost/Vice President Acad Affairs	Dr. Mark STEPHENS
10	Vice Pres Planning & Finance	Dr. Claire STINSON
32	Vice President Student Affairs	Mr. Marc BURNETT
56	VP Extended Pgms/Regional Devel	Dr. Susan ELKINS
30	Vice President Univ Advancement	Mr. Mark HUTCHINS
20	Assoc Provost/Vice Pres Acad Affs	Dr. Xiaoming (Sharon) HUO
58	Assoc VP for Research/Grad Studies	Dr. Francis O. OTUONYE
13	Assoc VP for Info Tech Svcs	Mr. Danny R. REESE
32	Dean of Students	Mr. Ed BOUCHER
37	Director Financial Aid	Mr. Lester MCKENZIE
08	Director Library & Learning Assist	Dr. Doug BATES
09	Director Institutional Research	Dr. Glenn W. JAMES
45	Director of Institutional Planning	Vacant
15	Director of Human Resources	Mr. Michael COWAN
19	Director of University Police	Ms. Gay SHEPHERD
39	Director of Housing	Mr. Charles MACKE
41	Director of Athletics	Mr. Mark WILSON
18	Director of Physical Plant	Mr. Jack BUTLER
38	Director Counseling Center	Vacant
36	Director Career Services	Ms. Alice CAMUTI
27	Assoc VP Communications & Mkting	Ms. Karen LYKINS
85	Director Intl Student Affairs	Mr. Charles WILKERSON
06	Director Records & Registrar	Ms. Elizabeth ROGERS
92	Director Honors Program	Dr. Rita BARNES
93	Director Minority Affairs	Vacant
96	Director of Purchasing	Ms. Judy M. HULL
21	Associate Business Officer	Mr. Jeff YOUNG
26	Chief Public Relations Officer	Ms. Karen LYKINS
29	Director Alumni Relations	Ms. Tracey DUNCAN
28	Director of Diversity/Legal Affairs	Ms. Rachel RADER
07	Director of Admissions	Ms. Vanessa PALMER
19	Dir Campus Safety & Environment	Mr. James COBB
84	Director Enrollment Management	Dr. Robert HODUM
49	Dean of Arts & Sciences	Dr. Paul SEMMES
54	Dean of Engineering	Dr. Joseph RENCIS
47	Dean of Agricultural/Human Sciences	Dr. Pat BAGLEY
50	Dean of Business Administration	Dr. James JORDAN WAGNER
53	Dean College of Education	Dr. Matt SMITH

*The University of Memphis (C)

Memphis TN 38152

County: Shelby FICE Identification: 003509
Unit ID: 220862
Telephone: (901) 678-2000 Carnegie Class: RU/H
FAX Number: N/A Calendar System: Semester
URL: www.memphis.edu
Established: 1912 Annual Undergrad Tuition & Fees (In-State): $7,212
Enrollment: 22,421 Coed
Affiliation or Control: State IRS Status: 501(c)3
Highest Offering: Doctorate
Program: Liberal Arts And General; Teacher Preparatory; Professional
Accreditation: SC, AAFCS, ART, AUD, BUS, BUSA, CACREP, CIDA, CLPSY, COPSY, CORE, CS, DIETD, DIETI, ENG, ENGT, HSA, IPSY, JOUR, LAW, MUS, NURSE, PLNG, SP, SPAA, SW, TED, THEA

02	President	Dr. Shirley C. RAINES
05	Provost	Dr. Ralph J. FAUDREE
04	Exec Assistant to the President	Dr. David N. COX
10	Vice President Business & Finance	Mr. David G. ZETTERGREN
13	Vice Pres Information Systems/CIO	Dr. Douglas E. HURLEY
86	Exec Asst Pres Govt Relations	Mr. Kevin F. ROPER
30	Vice President Advancement	Mrs. Julie A. JOHNSON
32	Vice President Student Affairs	Dr. Rosie P. BINGHAM
26	Vice Pres Marketing/Communication	Mr. Robert H. EOFF
41	Director of Athletics	Mr. R. C. JOHNSON
43	University Counsel	Ms. Sheryl H. LIPMAN
46	Vice Provost for Research	Dr. Andrew W. MEYERS
45	VP Assessment/Inst Rsrch/Reporting	Dr. Thomas J. NENON
84	Asst Vice Provost Enrollment Svcs	Ms. Betty HUFF
58	Vice Prov Graduate Studies	Dr. Karen D. WEDDLE-WEST
88	VP Undergrad Programs	Dr. Shannon BLANTON
35	Asst VP Student Affs/Stdnt Dev	Dr. Stephen H. PETERSEN
18	Asst Vice Pres Physical Plant	Mr. Michael L. ALLEN
21	Assistant Vice President Finance	Ms. Jeannie SMITH
15	Asst Vice Pres Human Resources	Ms. Maria ALAM
44	Assoc Vice Pres Development	Mr. Bobby A. PRINCE
102	Director Donor Relations	Dr. Dan S. BEASLEY
27	Assoc Vice Pres Marketing/Comm	Ms. Linda H. BONNIN
08	Dean U of M Libraries	Dr. Sylverna V. FORD
09	Director Institutional Research	Dr. Gary L. DONHARDT
36	Director Career & Employment Svcs	Ms. Alisha R. HENDERSON
06	Registrar	Ms. Donna S. VAN CANNEYT
37	Director of Student Aid	Mr. Richard RITZMAN
96	Director of Purchasing	Ms. Canty ROBBINS
29	Dir Alumni & Constituent Relations	Ms. Tammy L. HEDGES
92	Director University Honors Program	Dr. Melinda L. JONES
07	Director of Admissions	Dr. Brian MEREDITH
22	Equal Oppty/Affirm Action Comp Ofcr	Ms. Michelle R. BANKS
88	Dn Sch Audio/Speech-Lang Pathology	Dr. Maurice I. MENDEL
49	Dean of Arts & Science	Dr. Henry A. KURTZ
50	Dean Business & Economics	Dr. Rajiv GROVER
53	Dean of Education	Dr. Donald I. WAGNER
54	Dean of Engineering	Dr. Richard C. WARDER, JR.
55	Dean of University College	Dr. Dan L. LATTIMORE
57	Dean Communication & Fine Arts	Dr. Richard R. RANTA
61	Dean School of Law	Mr. Kevin H. SMITH
66	Dean School of Nursing	Dr. Lin ZHAN
69	Dean School of Public Health	Dr. Lisa M. KLESGES
94	Director Women's Studies	Dr. Wanda RUSHING

*Chattanooga State Community College (D)

4501 Amnicola Highway, Chattanooga TN 37406-1097

County: Hamilton FICE Identification: 003998
Unit ID: 219824
Telephone: (423) 697-4400 Carnegie Class: Assoc/Pub-R-L
FAX Number: N/A Calendar System: Semester
URL: www.chattanoogastate.edu
Established: 1963 Annual Undergrad Tuition & Fees (In-State): $3,567
Enrollment: 11,841 Coed
Affiliation or Control: State IRS Status: 501(c)3
Highest Offering: Associate Degree
Program: Occupational; 2-Year Principally Bachelor's Creditable
Accreditation: SC, @ACBSP, ADNUR, DA, DH, DMS, EMT, ENGT, MAC, NMT, PTAA, RAD, RTT, SURGT

02	President	Dr. James L. CATANZARO
04	Special Assistant to the President	Mr. Joe HELSETH
09	Asc VP Institutional Effectiveness	Ms. Eva LEWIS
05	Provost/Vice Pres Academic Affairs	Dr. Fannie HEWLETT
10	Exec Vice Pres Business & Finance	Ms. Tammy SWENSON
32	Vice President Student Services	Dr. Elaine SWAFFORD
31	Vice President Economic & Comm Dev	Mr. Jeff OLINGY
72	Vice President for Technology	Dr. Jim BARROTT
44	Assoc Vice Pres Fund Development	Ms. Holly REEVE
20	Assoc Vice Pres Academic Affairs	Ms. Kimberly MCCORMICK
21	Assistant VP Business & Finance	Ms. Susan JOSEPH
35	Asst Vice Pres Student Affairs	Ms. Debbie ADAMS
18	Asst VP Plant Operations/Facil Plng	Mr. Steve HUSKINS
56	Asst VP Distributed Education	Ms. Judy LOWE
25	Asst VP Grants/Contracts/Stdnt Acct	Ms. Debbie MAILEN
51	Director Continuing Education	Ms. Ju-Hsin LUSK
09	Director of Institutional Research	Vacant
26	Director of Marketing	Ms. Patty BROWN
15	Director Human Resources	Mr. Tom CRUM
06	Registrar	Ms. Norma LEE
36	Director Student Placement	Ms. Sheila ALBRITTON
37	Director Student Financial Aid	Ms. Jeanne HINCHEE
28	Director of Diversity	Ms. Mary KNAFF
41	Athletic Director	Mr. Steve JAECKS
08	Dean Library Services	Mrs. Vickie LEATHER
76	Dean Allied Health & Nursing	Dr. Howard YARBROUGH
79	Dean Humanities & Fine Arts	Dr. Don ANDREWS
83	Dean Social/Behavioral Sciences	Ms. Anne CARROLL
81	Dean Math & Sciences	Dr. Mosunmola GEORGE-TAYLOR
50	Dean Business/Info Tech	Vacant
32	Dean Student Life/Judicial Affairs	Ms. Sandy KLUTTZ
75	Dean Tennessee Technology Center	Dr. Mike RICKETTS
54	Dean Engineering Technology	Mr. Tim MCGHEE

*Cleveland State Community College (E)

PO Box 3570, Cleveland TN 37320-3570

County: Bradley FICE Identification: 003999
Unit ID: 219879
Telephone: (423) 472-7141 Carnegie Class: Assoc/Pub-R-M
FAX Number: (423) 478-6255 Calendar System: Semester
URL: www.clevelandstatecc.edu
Established: 1967 Annual Undergrad Tuition & Fees (In-State): $3,417
Enrollment: 3,753 Coed
Affiliation or Control: State IRS Status: 501(c)3
Highest Offering: Associate Degree
Program: Occupational; 2-Year Principally Bachelor's Creditable
Accreditation: SC, ADNUR, MAC, NAIT

02	President	Dr. Carl HITE
05	Vice President for Academic Affairs	Dr. Jerry FAULKNER
32	Vice President for Student Services	Dr. Michael STOKES
11	Vice President Admin & Finance	Dr. Thomas WRIGHT
09	Director of Institutional Research	Ms. Marcia OWENS
37	Director of Financial Aid	Mrs. Brenda DISORBO
30	Director of Inst Advancement	Ms. Beirne BEATY
26	Director Marketing & Promotions	Mr. Tony BARTOLO
06	Director Admissions & Records	Ms. Midge BURNETTE
15	Director of Human Resources	Mrs. Joan BATES
08	Director of the Library	Ms. Mary Evelyn LYNN
14	Director of College Computing	Mr. Rick CUMBY
19	Coordinator Campus Security	Mr. John WITTMAIER
50	Dean of Business & Technology	Ms. Sherra WITT
66	Dean of Health & Wellness	Mrs. Nancy LABINE
79	Int Dean Humanities/Social Sciences	Mr. Fred WOOD
81	Dean of Math/Science	Dr. Mitchell RHEA
38	Director Student Development	Mr. Mark WILSON
31	Dir Training & Continuing Education	Mr. Lloyd LONGNION
18	Director of Plant Operations	Mr. Kim PARKER
21	Director of Budget & Accounting	Mrs. Shirley ELDREDGE
84	Director of Student Relations	Mr. Jason SEWELL

*Columbia State Community College (F)

1665 Hampshire Pike, Columbia TN 38401-5653

County: Maury FICE Identification: 003483
Unit ID: 219888
Telephone: (931) 540-2722 Carnegie Class: Assoc/Pub-R-M
FAX Number: (931) 540-2535 Calendar System: Semester
URL: www.columbiastate.edu
Established: 1966 Annual Undergrad Tuition & Fees (In-State): $3,357
Enrollment: 5,592 Coed
Affiliation or Control: State IRS Status: 501(c)3
Highest Offering: Associate Degree
Program: Occupational; 2-Year Principally Bachelor's Creditable
Accreditation: SC, ADNUR, EMT, RAD

02	President	Dr. Janet F. SMITH
03	Executive Vice President/Provost	Dr. Margaret SMITH
10	Vice Pres Financial/Admin Services	Mr. Kenneth R. HORNER
20	Assoc VP Faculty/Curric & Programs	Ms. Joni L. LENIG
32	Assoc VP Student Services	Ms. Cecelia JOHNSON
13	Assoc VP Info Technology	Ms. Emily SICIENSKY
21	Assoc VP Business Services	Ms. Elaine CURTIS
27	Director Marketing & Public Rels	Mr. Paul J. HICKEY
28	Asst to Pres for Access & Diversity	Ms. Christa S. MARTIN
07	Director Recruitment & Admissions	Mr. David OGDEN
06	Director Records	Ms. Sharon G. BOWEN
15	Director Human Resources	Mr. Randy L. ELSTON
08	Director Library	Ms. Kathy BREEDEN
38	Coord Counseling & Orientation	Dr. Paula J. PETTY-WARD
09	Director Inst Effect and Planning	Ms. Nancy RAMSEY
37	Director Financial Aid	Ms. Brenda D. BURNEY

102 Devel Officer/Foundation Secretary ... Vacant
41 Director Athletics ... Mr. Louis M. CONNER
18 Director Facility Services ... Mr. David HALL
56 Dean Extended Svcs & Will Campus ... Dr. Shanna JACKSON
29 Dev Officer/Alumni Rel & Comm Evnts ... Ms. Beth DUFFIELD
35 Director Student Success ... Vacant
96 Coordinator Purchasing ... Ms. Jerri H. GROOMS

Dyersburg State Community College (A)

1510 Lake Road, Dyersburg TN 38024-2450
County: Dyer FICE Identification: 006835
Unit ID: 220057
Telephone: (731) 286-3200 Carnegie Class: Assoc/Pub-R-M
FAX Number: (731) 286-3333 Calendar System: Semester
URL: www.dscc.edu
Established: 1967 Annual Undergrad Tuition & Fees (In-State): $3,367
Enrollment: 3,749 Coed
Affiliation or Control: State IRS Status: 501(c)3
Highest Offering: Associate Degree
Program: Occupational; 2-Year Principally Bachelor's Creditable
Accreditation: SC, ACBSP, ADNUR, SURGT

02 President ... Dr. Karen A. BOWYER
05 Vice President for the College ... Dr. Mary Ann SELLARS
10 Vice President Finance/Admin Svcs ... Mr. Lowell HOFFMANN
30 Vice Pres Institutional Advancement ... Ms. Tina MORRIS
13 Vice President Technology ... Ms. Diane CAMPER
32 Asst VP for Acad & Student Affairs ... Mr. J. Dan GULLETT
20 Assistant VP for Learning ... Dr. Kay PATTERSON
35 Dean of Student Services ... Ms. Larenda FULTZ
08 Dean Learning Resources Center ... Ms. Teresa JOHNSON
37 Director of Financial Aid ... Mrs. Sandra ROCKETT
09 Director of Institutional Research ... Ms. Tina MORRIS
15 Director Personnel Services ... Ms. Sheilah GILLAHAN
103 Director of Workforce Development ... Ms. Margaret PRATER
29 Dir Alumni Relations/Public Info ... Ms. Jane PATE
38 Director Student Counseling ... Dr. Karen RUTLEDGE
41 Director of Athletics ... Mr. Alan BARNETT
18 Director of Physical Plant ... Mr. Kent JETTON
07 Director of Admissions ... Mr. J. Dan GULLETT
96 Director of Purchasing ... Ms. Amy WATTS
45 Manager of Assessment ... Mr. Doug HODGE
21 Business & Student Fin Svcs Manager ... Ms. Donna MEALER
72 Coord Business/Technology Div ... Ms. Rene STANLEY
66 Dean of Nursing & Allied Health Div ... Vacant
51 Dean of Continuing Education ... Ms. Tina MORRIS

*Jackson State Community College (B)

2046 North Parkway, Jackson TN 38301-3797
County: Madison FICE Identification: 004937
Unit ID: 220400
Telephone: (731) 424-3520 Carnegie Class: Assoc/Pub-R-M
FAX Number: (731) 425-2647 Calendar System: Semester
URL: www.jscc.edu
Established: 1965 Annual Undergrad Tuition & Fees (In-State): $3,364
Enrollment: 5,361 Coed
Affiliation or Control: State IRS Status: 501(c)3
Highest Offering: Associate Degree
Program: Occupational; 2-Year Principally Bachelor's Creditable
Accreditation: SC, ACBSP, ADNUR, EMT, MLTAD, NAIT, PTAA, RAD

02 President ... Dr. Bruce BLANDING
05 Interim VP of Academic Affairs ... Mr. Bobby SMITH
10 Vice Pres of Finance & Admin Affs ... Mr. Horace W. CHASE
30 Exec Dir Institutional Advancement ... Ms. Dee HENDERSON
49 Dean of Arts & Sciences ... Ms. Diana FORDHAM
107 Dean of Professional & Tech Studies ... Mr. Barry JENNISON
32 Dean of Student Services ... Mr. Bobby SMITH
88 Internal Auditor ... Mrs. Angela P. BROWN
15 Dir Human Resources/Affirm Action ... Mrs. Amy WEST
09 Dir Institutional Effectiveness ... Dr. Beth STEWART
51 Dean of Continuing Education ... Ms. Leah GRAY
13 Director of Information Technology ... Ms. Dana NAILS
21 Director of Business Services ... Mr. Tim DELLINGER
18 Director of Physical Plant ... Mr. Gerald BATCHELOR
96 Director of Purchasing ... Mr. Robert D. HEMRICK
12 Director Lexington Campus ... Ms. Sandy STANFILL
12 Director Savannah Campus ... Mrs. Meda FALLS
12 Director Humboldt Campus ... Mr. Matthew MCLEAN
07 Director Admissions ... Mrs. Andrea WINCHESTER
26 Director Public Relations ... Vacant
37 Director Student Financial Aid ... Ms. Dewana LATIMER
06 Registrar ... Ms. Frances EDMONSON

*Motlow State Community College (C)

PO Box 8500, Lynchburg TN 37352-8500
County: Moore FICE Identification: 006836
Unit ID: 221096
Telephone: (931) 393-1500 Carnegie Class: Assoc/Pub-R-M
FAX Number: (931) 393-1681 Calendar System: Semester
URL: www.mscc.edu
Established: 1969 Annual Undergrad Tuition & Fees (In-State): $3,372
Enrollment: 5,256 Coed
Affiliation or Control: State IRS Status: 501(c)3
Highest Offering: Associate Degree
Program: Occupational; 2-Year Principally Bachelor's Creditable
Accreditation: SC, ACBSP, ADNUR

02 President ... Dr. MaryLou APPLE
05 Provost & VP for Student Affairs ... Dr. Bonny COPENHAVER
10 Vice Pres for Business & Management ... Ms. Hilda TUNSTILL
32 Asst Vice President Student Affairs ... Ms. Regina BURDEN
13 VP Info Technology & Admin Services ... Dr. Eddie STONE
20 Asst Vice Pres for Academic Affair ... Dr. Jay MAY
18 Director of Facilities ... Mr. Billy GARNER
14 Director of Technical Operations ... Mr. Ron GAULT
31 Director Student & Campus Relations ... Ms. Brenda CANNON
08 Director of Libraries ... Mr. Stuart GAETJENS
37 Executive Director of Financial Aid ... Mr. Joe MYERS
38 Director Counseling & Testing ... Ms. Toni ADKINS
07 Director of Admissions & Records ... Ms. Greer ALSUP
66 Interim Director of Nursing ... Ms. Amy HUFF
41 Director of Athletics ... Mr. Gary BARFIELD
09 Dir of Research/Planning & Comm ... Ms. Sylvia COLLINS
90 Director Center for Academic Tech ... Dr. Shelly MCCOY
12 Director McMinnville Center ... Ms. Melody EDMONDS
12 Director Fayetteville Center ... Ms. Laura MONKS
12 Director Smyrna Site ... Ms. Cheryl HYLAND
36 Dir of Career Placement & Extended ... Mr. Tom DILLINGHAM
04 Admin Assistant to the President ... Ms. Christy GLENN
15 Director of Human Resources ... Ms. Laura JENT
96 Director of Purchasing ... Ms. Sandy SCHAFFER

*Nashville State Community College (D)

120 White Bridge Road, Nashville TN 37209-4515
County: Davidson FICE Identification: 008145
Unit ID: 221184
Telephone: (615) 353-3333 Carnegie Class: Assoc/Pub-U-MC
FAX Number: (615) 353-3713 Calendar System: Semester
URL: www.nscc.edu
Established: 1969 Annual Undergrad Tuition & Fees (In-State): $3,208
Enrollment: 9,853 Coed
Affiliation or Control: State IRS Status: 501(c)3
Highest Offering: Associate Degree
Program: Occupational; 2-Year Principally Bachelor's Creditable; Business Emphasis
Accreditation: SC, ACBSP, ACFEI, NAIT, OTA, SURGT

02 President ... Dr. George H. VAN ALLEN
05 Vice President of Academic Affairs ... Dr. Kimberly K. ESTEP
10 Vice Pres Finance & Administration ... Mrs. Mary M. CROSS
88 Exec Assistant to the President ... Ms. Eileen C. CRANE
45 Assoc VP Planning/Assessment ... Mr. Ted M. WASHINGTON
09 Assoc VP Institutional Research ... Mr. Ted M. WASHINGTON
30 Exec Dir of Devel/Dir Public Affs ... Mr. Keith D. FERGUSON
32 Dean of Students ... Dr. Carol J. MARTIN-OSORIO
21 Internal Auditor ... Mr. Robert HANKINS
06 Registrar ... Mr. Lance L. WOODARD
07 Director of Admissions ... Ms. Laura L. POTTER
14 Director of Computer Services ... Mr. Carl G. DURY
19 Director of Safety and Security ... Mr. Derrek G. SHEUCRAFT
37 Director of Financial Aid ... Mr. James J. MORAN
15 Dir Human Res/Affirm Act/Diversity ... Ms. Lori B. MADDOX
18 Director of Operations/Maintenance ... Mr. Jim T. DAWSON
103 Dir Workforce and Community Dev ... Ms. Gail G. PHILLIPS
27 Manager of Publications ... Ms. Ellen L. ZINK
106 Director of Online Learning ... Ms. Kathy S. EMERY
51 Coord Special Interest/CEUs ... Ms. Betty P. BROZ
83 Dean of Health & Social Sciences ... Dr. Pamela C. MUNZ
72 Dean of Info/Eng Technologies ... Ms. Karen L. STEVENSON
81 Dean Math & Natural Sciences ... Dr. Jennifer A. KNAPP
79 Dean English/Humanities & Arts ... Ms. Valerie S. BELEW
62 Dean Lrng Resources & Distance Educ ... Dr. Faye JONES
50 Dean Bus Technology & Applied Arts ... Ms. Karen L. STEVENSON
96 Director of Purchasing ... Ms. Jo SMITH
29 Director Alumni Relations ... Mr. Keith D. FERGUSON
66 Director of Nursing ... Ms. Cynthia G. WALLER

*Northeast State Technical Community College (E)

PO Box 246, 2425 Highway 75, Blountville TN 37617-0246
County: Sullivan FICE Identification: 005378
Unit ID: 221908
Telephone: (423) 323-3191 Carnegie Class: Assoc/Pub-R-M
FAX Number: (423) 279-7636 Calendar System: Semester
URL: www.northeaststate.edu
Established: 1965 Annual Undergrad Tuition & Fees (In-State): $2,945
Enrollment: 6,775 Coed
Affiliation or Control: State IRS Status: 501(c)3
Highest Offering: Associate Degree
Program: Occupational; 2-Year Principally Bachelor's Creditable
Accreditation: SC, ACBSP, ADNUR, CVT, DA, EMT, MLTAD, NAIT, SURGT

02 President ... Dr. Janice H. GILLIAM
04 Exec Assistant to the President ... Ms. Megan NEELEY
05 Vice Pres Academic Affairs ... Ms. Allana R. HAMILTON
10 Vice President Business Affairs ... Dr. Steven CAMPBELL
32 Vice President for Student Affairs ... Dr. Jon P. HARR
13 Vice Pres Info Tech/Computer Svcs ... Mr. Fred LEWIS
09 VP of Institutional Effectiveness ... Dr. Susan E. GRAYBEAL
30 Vice Pres Institutional Advancement ... Vacant
28 Asst Vice Pres Multicultural Affs ... Vacant
56 Asst VP Evening/Distance Educ ... Dr. James C. LEFLER
15 Director Human Resources ... Ms. Gerri S. BROCKWELL
26 Dir Community Relations/Marketing ... Mr. Robert CARPENTER
08 Director of the Learning Resources ... Mr. Duncan A. PARSONS

79 Dean Humanities ... Mr. William WILSON
81 Dean Math ... Ms. Nancy FORRESTER
76 Dean Health Related Profession ... Mr. Don COLEMAN
72 Dean Technology/Education ... Mr. Michael H. BLEDSOE
83 Dean Behavior/Social Services ... Dr. Xiaoping WANG
81 Dean Science ... Ms. Alana R. HAMILTON

*Pellissippi State Community College (F)

PO Box 22990, Knoxville TN 37933-0990
County: Knox FICE Identification: 012693
Unit ID: 221643
Telephone: (865) 694-6400 Carnegie Class: Assoc/Pub-U-MC
FAX Number: (865) 694-6435 Calendar System: Semester
URL: www.pstcc.edu
Established: 1974 Annual Undergrad Tuition & Fees (In-State): $3,414
Enrollment: 11,049 Coed
Affiliation or Control: State IRS Status: 501(c)3
Highest Offering: Associate Degree
Program: Occupational; 2-Year Principally Bachelor's Creditable
Accreditation: SC, ACBSP

02 President ... Dr. L. Anthony WISE
05 Interim Vice Pres Learning ... Ms. Lois G. REYNOLDS
13 Vice President Information Services ... Mr. Robert G. BRYAN
10 Vice President Business & Finance ... Mr. Ronald L. KESTERSON
30 VP College Advancement/Exec Dir Fdn ... Ms. Peggy M. WILSON
31 Exec Dir Business/Community Svcs ... Ms. Teri T. BRAHAMS
32 VP Stdnt Success & Enroll Mgmt ... Dr. Rebecca L. ASHFORD
20 Dean Instructional Programs ... Dr. Dennis R. ADAMS
12 Asst Dean Blount County Programs ... Ms. Holly L. BURKETT
12 Asst Dean Magnolia Ave Programs ... Ms. Rosalyn P. TILLMAN
12 Asst Dean Division Street Programs ... Dr. Mike NORTH
35 Asst VP Student Success ... Ms. Mary C. BLEDSOE
20 Asst VP of Learning ... Ms. Lois REYNOLDS
84 Asst VP Enrollment Services ... Ms. Leigh A. TOUZEAU
36 Director of Placement ... Ms. Carolyn N. CARSON
88 Dir Svc for Students w/Disabilities ... Ms. Ann E. SATKOWIAK
38 Director Counseling Department ... Vacant
26 Director Marketing & Communications ... Ms. Julia H. WOOD
06 Registrar ... Ms. Melanie PARADISE
08 Director of Library Services ... Mr. J. Peter NERZAK
24 Dir Educ Technology Svcs ... Ms. Audrey WILLIAMS
37 Director of Financial Aid ... Mr. Paul MCKINNEY
09 Dir Inst Effectiveness/Res/Plan ... Dr. Sharon L. YARBROUGH
18 Director Facilities/Safety/Security ... Mr. David G. WALTON
96 Director of Purchasing ... Mr. John S. CLARK
15 Dir Human Resources/Affirm Action ... Ms. Karen D. QUEENER
21 Asst VP Business Services ... Ms. Renee R. MOORE
44 Director Major Gift Development ... Mr. Leslie G. FOUT
29 Dir Alumni Rel & Foundation Events ... Ms. Patricia T. MYERS
91 Dir Applications Programming Sup ... Mr. James "Dean" COPPLE
90 Dir Network & Technical Services ... Ms. Linda C. PETERSON
07 Director of Admissions & Comm Ctr ... Ms. Heather HATFIELD
28 Director of Access & Diversity ... Ms. Gayle E. WOOD

*Roane State Community College (G)

276 Patton Lane, Harriman TN 37748-5011
County: Roane FICE Identification: 009914
Unit ID: 221397
Telephone: (865) 354-3000 Carnegie Class: Assoc/Pub-R-M
FAX Number: (865) 882-4585 Calendar System: Semester
URL: www.roanestate.edu
Established: 1971 Annual Undergrad Tuition & Fees (In-State): $3,381
Enrollment: 6,938 Coed
Affiliation or Control: State IRS Status: 501(c)3
Highest Offering: Associate Degree
Program: Occupational; 2-Year Principally Bachelor's Creditable
Accreditation: SC, ACBSP, ADNUR, COMTA, DH, EMT, OPD, OTA, POLYT, PTAA

02 President ... Dr. Gary GOFF
05 Vice Pres for Student Learning ... Dr. Chris WHALEY
10 Vice Pres for Business & Finance ... Mr. Danny C. GIBBS
32 VP Student Services/Enrollment Mgmt ... Ms. Teresa S. DUNCAN
12 VP ORBC & Ctrs/Exec Dir RSCC Found ... Ms. Melinda HILLMAN
21 Asst VP Fiscal/Auxiliary Services ... Ms. Jamie WILMOTH
35 Asst VP Student Services ... Ms. Beverly J. BONNER
84 Asst Vice President Enrollment Svcs ... Ms. Joy GOLDBERG
72 Asst Vice Pres of Info Technology ... Mr. Timothy D. CARROLL
09 Asst VP Institutional Research ... Ms. Karen L. BRUNNER
15 Director of Human Resources ... Mr. Odell FEARN
08 Director of Library Services ... Mr. Robert M. BENSON
11 Director of Administrative Systems ... Mr. Chris PANKRATZ
06 Director of Records & Registration ... Ms. Brenda RECTOR
07 Director of Admissions/Recruitment ... Ms. Maria GONZALES
18 Director Physical Plant & Expo Ctr ... Mr. Stan R. STARKEY
29 Director Alumni Relations ... Ms. Tamsin MILLER
96 Director of Purchasing ... Mr. Jack WALKER
36 Placement Coordinator ... Ms. Kim HARRIS

*Southwest Tennessee Community College (H)

PO Box 780, Memphis TN 38101-0780
County: Shelby FICE Identification: 010439
Unit ID: 221485
Telephone: (901) 333-5000 Carnegie Class: Assoc/Pub-U-MC
FAX Number: (901) 333-5270 Calendar System: Semester
URL: www.southwest.tn.edu
Established: 2000 Annual Undergrad Tuition & Fees (In-State): $3,381

Enrollment: 13,362 Coed
Affiliation or Control: State IRS Status: 501(c)3
Highest Offering: Associate Degree
Program: Occupational; 2-Year Principally Bachelor's Creditable
Accreditation: SC, ACBSP, ADNUR, DIETT, EMT, ENGT, MLTAD, PTAA, RAD

02 President ... Dr. Nathan L. ESSEX
04 Assistant to the President ... Ms. Carol BROWN
05 Provost/Executive Vice President ... Dr. Joanne BASSETT
41 Athletic Director ... Mr. Verties SAILS, JR.
30 Vice Pres Institutional Advancement ... Ms. Karen F. NIPPERT
10 Vice Pres Finance & Admin Services ... Mr. Ronald G. PARR
32 Vice Pres Student Svcs/Enroll Mgmt ... Dr. Carol TOSH
84 Exec Director Enrollment Management ... Ms. Kathryn JOHNSON
26 Exec Director of Comm & Marketing ... Mr. Robert G. MILLER
15 Exec Director Hum Res/Affirm Action ... Mr. Paul THOMAS
06 Registrar ... Ms. Barbara WELLS
18 Director Physical Plant ... Vacant
96 Director of Purchasing ... Ms. Michelle NEWMAN
37 Dir Student Financial Aid-Macon ... Ms. Chateeka FARRIS
37 Dir Student Financial Aid-Union ... Ms. Tina STUDAWAY
09 Institutional Research Analyst ... Mr. Donald C. MYERS

*Volunteer State Community College (A)

1480 Nashville Pike, Gallatin TN 37066-3188
County: Sumner FICE Identification: 009912
Unit ID: 222053
Telephone: (615) 452-8600 Carnegie Class: Assoc/Pub-S-SC
FAX Number: (615) 230-3577 Calendar System: Semester
URL: www.volstate.edu
Established: 1970 Annual Undergrad Tuition & Fees (In-State): $3,367
Enrollment: 8,989 Coed
Affiliation or Control: State IRS Status: 501(c)3
Highest Offering: Associate Degree
Program: Occupational; 2-Year Principally Bachelor's Creditable
Accreditation: SC, ACBSP, DA, DMS, EMT, MLTAD, POLYT, PTAA, RAD

02 President ... Dr. Warren R. NICHOLS
04 Exec Assistant to the President ... Mr. Kenyatta LOVETT
05 Vice President Academic Affairs ... Dr. Bruce SCISM
10 Vice President Business & Finance ... Ms. Beth COOKSEY
32 Vice President Student Services ... Mrs. Patty T. POWELL
30 Vice Pres for Resource Development ... Ms. Karen MITCHELL
45 Vice Pres Inst Planning/Research ... Ms. Jane MCGUIRE
20 Asst Academic Vice President ... Mr. Jim HIETT
21 Asst Vice Pres Business & Finance ... Ms. Kathy Y. JOHNSON
35 Asst Vice Pres Student Services ... Ms. Emily SHORT
51 Asst VP/Dean Continuing Education ... Mrs. Hilary B. MARABETI
76 Assoc Vice Pres/Dean Allied Health ... Mr. Elvis BRANDON
79 Dean Humanities ... Dr. Alycia EHLERT
53 Dean Social Science/Education ... Ms. Phyllis FOLEY
81 Dean Math & Science ... Ms. Nancy MORRIS
50 Dean Business ... Dr. John ESPEY
88 Director of Development Studies Pgm ... Ms. Kay DAYTON
15 Dir Personnel/Affirm Act/Human Res ... Ms. Lori CUTRELL
08 Director Library Services ... Ms. Louise KELLY
07 Director Admissions & Records ... Mr. Tim AMYX
13 Director Information Technology ... Mr. Brian KRAUS
37 Director Student Financial Aid ... Mrs. Sue H. PEDIGO
26 Director Public Relations ... Mrs. Tami WALLACE
18 Senior Director Physical Plant ... Mr. Gary HUME
19 Chief Security & Safety ... Mr. William D. ROGAN
41 Director of Athletics ... Mr. Bobby HUDSON
56 Director Distance Learning ... Mr. Seth SPARKMAN
88 Special Adult Programs/ADA Director ... Ms. Kathy SOWELL
55 Dir Student Activ/Eve Student Svcs ... Dr. Monique ROBINSON-WRIGHT
09 Director of Institutional Research ... Mrs. Ann Marie CALDERON
96 Director Purchasing ... Mr. Terry MCGOVERN
24 Director Media Services ... Mr. Terry HEINEN
88 Director Retention Support Services ... Ms. Emily SHORT
36 Director Student Placement ... Dr. Rick PARRENT
38 Director Counseling & Testing ... Ms. Teresa BROWN
28 Director of Diversity ... Dr. Monique ROBINSON-WRIGHT
45 Coordinator Resource Development ... Ms. Lori JOHNSON
88 Director Center of Emphasis ... Ms. Kyla WEBB
06 Registrar ... Mr. Tim AMYX
29 Director Alumni Relations ... Ms. Lori JOHNSON
84 Director Enrollment Management ... Ms. Patty POWELL

*Walters State Community College (B)

500 S Davy Crockett Parkway, Morristown TN 37813-6899
County: Hamblen FICE Identification: 008863
Unit ID: 222062
Telephone: (423) 585-2600 Carnegie Class: Assoc/Pub-R-L
FAX Number: (423) 585-6853 Calendar System: Semester
URL: www.ws.edu
Established: 1969 Annual Undergrad Tuition & Fees (In-State): $3,375
Enrollment: 6,959 Coed
Affiliation or Control: State IRS Status: 501(c)3
Highest Offering: Associate Degree
Program: Occupational; 2-Year Principally Bachelor's Creditable
Accreditation: SC, ACBSP, ACFEI, ADNUR, EMT, NAIT, PTAA

02 President ... Dr. Wade R. MCCAMEY
04 Exec Director to the President ... Ms. Brenda L. SMALL
05 Vice President Academic Affairs ... Dr. Lori CAMPBELL
10 Vice President Business Affairs ... Dr. Rosemary JACKSON
32 Vice President Student Affairs ... Dr. Foster CHASON
30 Vice Pres for College Advancement ... Mr. Henry DRINNON
45 VP for Planning/Research/Assessment ... Dr. Debbie L. MCCARTER
20 Asst Vice Pres for Academic Affairs ... Dr. James E. CRAWFORD
35 Asst Vice Pres Student Affairs ... Mr. Michael A. CAMPBELL
18 Ast Vice Pres Facilities Management ... Mr. Max E. WILLIAMS
21 Asst Vice Pres Business Affairs ... Mr. Roger D. BEVERLY
28 Spec Asst to Pres for Diversity ... Ms. W. Ann BOWEN
08 Dean of Library ... Dr. Douglas D. CROSS
31 Dean/Dir Cmty & Economic Devel ... Mr. Joseph L. COMBS
19 Dean of Public Safety Division ... Mr. Thomas STRANGE
17 Dean Health Programs ... Ms. Marty K. RUCKER
12 Dean Greenville/Greene Co Center ... Ms. Drucilla W. MILLER
12 Dean Sevier County Campus ... Ms. Sue FRAZIER
83 Dean of Behavioral/Social Sciences ... Dr. Marilyn R. BOWERS
50 Dean of Business ... Dr. Evelyn J. HONAKER
79 Dean of Humanities ... Dr. James E. CRAWFORD, JR.
81 Dean of Mathematics ... Dr. John P. LAPRISE
49 Dean of Natural Science ... Dr. Jeffrey T. HORNER
75 Dean of Technical Education ... Mr. Thomas R. SEWELL
06 Dean Student Info System/Records ... Mr. James D. WILDER
103 Dean Ctr for Workforce Development ... Dr. Nancy B. BROWN
37 Dean of Financial Aid ... Ms. Linda J. MASON
38 Exec Director Counseling/Testing ... Mr. Andy HALL
15 Exec Dir of Human Resources ... Ms. Tammy GOODE
26 Exec Director of Public Information ... Mr. James B. PECTOL
13 Exec Director for Information ... Mr. Joey E. SARGENT
41 Director of Athletics ... Dr. Foster CHASON
07 Director of Admissions ... Ms. Mary A. RUSH
19 Chief of Campus Police ... Ms. Sarah ROSE
89 Director Freshmen Studies ... Dr. Marilyn R. BOWERS
92 Director Honors Program ... Ms. Janice M. DONAHUE
96 Director of Purchasing ... Mr. Shawn A. WILLIAMS
27 Int Dir of Communication Services ... Mr. Bill R. MOREFIELD
29 Coordinator of Alumni Relations ... Ms. Wanda HARRELL
84 Coordinator Enrollment Development ... Mr. Marlin R. CURNUTT
93 Coord Minority Student Recruit ... Ms. Sheila D. MORRIS

Tennessee Temple University (C)

1815 Union Avenue, Chattanooga TN 37404-3587
County: Hamilton FICE Identification: 003524
Unit ID: 221856
Telephone: (423) 493-4100 Carnegie Class: Spec/Faith
FAX Number: (423) 493-4497 Calendar System: Semester
URL: www.tntemple.edu
Established: 1946 Annual Undergrad Tuition & Fees: $11,760
Enrollment: 947 Coed
Affiliation or Control: Baptist IRS Status: 501(c)3
Highest Offering: Doctorate
Program: Liberal Arts And General; Teacher Preparatory; Professional; Business Emphasis
Accreditation: TRACS

01 Interim President ... Dr. Jim O'NEILL
00 Chancellor ... Dr. David E. BOULER
03 Dean of Seminary ... Dr. Jim O'NEILL
05 Vice President of Academic Services ... Dr. Susan B. LOVETT
11 Chief Operations Officer ... Dr. Jeff RECTOR
106 Director of Online Learning ... Mr. Byron EDENS
06 Registrar ... Mr. Richard D. VAUPEL
08 Librarian ... Mr. Kevin WOODRUFF
32 Director of Student Services ... Mrs. Pam FREJOSKY
41 Interim Athletic Director ... Dr. Jeff RECTOR
19 Director of Security ... Mr. Aaron PARCEL
13 Director of Information Technology ... Mr. Wes THOMPSON
20 Director of Academic Support ... Mrs. Trudy OWENS
35 Director Student Development ... Mr. Joe FREJOSKY
37 Director Student Financial Aid ... Mrs. Jennifer BUCKLES
26 Dir of Mktg/Strategic Initiatives ... Mr. Eric LOVETT

Tennessee Wesleyan College (D)

204 East College St., Athens TN 37303
County: McMinn FICE Identification: 003525
Unit ID: 221731
Telephone: (423) 745-7504 Carnegie Class: Bac/Diverse
FAX Number: (423) 744-9968 Calendar System: Semester
URL: www.twcnet.edu
Established: 1857 Annual Undergrad Tuition & Fees: $19,000
Enrollment: 1,103 Coed
Affiliation or Control: United Methodist IRS Status: 501(c)3
Highest Offering: Baccalaureate
Program: Liberal Arts And General; Teacher Preparatory
Accreditation: SC, NURSE

01 President ... Dr. Harley KNOWLES
05 Vice President for Academic Affairs ... Dr. Suzanne A. HINE
11 Vice Pres Administration ... Mr. Larry WALLACE
10 Vice Pres Financial/Business Affs ... Mrs. Gail HARRIS
32 Vice President for Student Life ... Dr. Scott MASHBURN
84 Vice President for Enrollment ... Mr. Stan HARRISON
09 Asst VP Inst Research & Retention ... Mrs. Traci N. WILLIAMS
04 Admin Assistant to President ... Mrs. Gail ROGERS
08 Assoc Dean of Library Svcs ... Mrs. Sandra CLARIDAY
06 Registrar ... Mrs. Julie MCCASLIN
37 Director of Financial Aid ... Mr. Robert K. PERRY
29 Director of Alumni Relations ... Ms. Jessica EDWARDS
41 Athletic Director ... Mr. Donny MAYFIELD
15 Human Resources Director ... Mrs. Pam DAVIS
18 Chief of Facilities/Physical Plant ... Mr. Mike INGRAM
26 Director Public Relations ... Mr. Blake MCCASLIN
35 Director of Student Activities ... Ms. Ginger GIVENS
13 Director of Information Technoloy ... Mr. Joe PASSMORE

Trevecca Nazarene University (E)

333 Murfreesboro Road, Nashville TN 37210-2877
County: Davidson FICE Identification: 003526
Unit ID: 221892
Telephone: (615) 248-1200 Carnegie Class: DRU
FAX Number: (615) 248-7728 Calendar System: Semester
URL: www.trevecca.edu
Established: 1901 Annual Undergrad Tuition & Fees: $19,990
Enrollment: 2,345 Coed
Affiliation or Control: Church Of The Nazarene IRS Status: 501(c)3
Highest Offering: Doctorate
Program: Liberal Arts And General; Teacher Preparatory; Professional
Accreditation: SC, ARCPA, MUS, NURSE, TED

01 President ... Dr. Dan BOONE
05 University Provost ... Dr. Stephen M. PUSEY
10 Exec Vice Pres Finance & Admin ... Mr. David CALDWELL
26 Vice President External Relations ... Mrs. Peggy J. COONING
20 Assoc Provost/Dean Academic Affairs ... Dr. Carole MAXSON
32 Assoc Provost/Dean of Student Dev ... Mr. Stephen A. HARRIS
84 Assoc Provost/Dean of Enroll Mgmt ... Dr. Kathy BAUGHER
73 Dean of School of Religion/Chaplain ... Dr. Timothy M. GREEN
50 Dean of Business and Management ... Dr. Jim HIATT
51 Dean of College Lifelong Learning ... Dr. Dave PHILLIPS
53 Dean of the School of Education ... Dr. Esther SWINK
49 Dean of School of Arts & Science ... Dr. Lena WELCH
08 Director Library Services ... Mrs. Ruth KINNERSLEY
09 Director Institutional Research ... Ms. Donna K. TUDOR
06 Registrar ... Mrs. Becky NIECE
35 Assoc Dean Community Life ... Mr. Matt SPRAKER
39 Assoc Dean Residential Life ... Mrs. Ronda LILIENTHAL
19 Director of Security ... Mr. Norm ROBINSON
07 Director of Undergrad Admissions ... Ms. Holly WHITBY
41 Athletic Director ... Vacant
36 Director Counseling Services ... Dr. Sara HOPKINS
88 Coordinator of Sophomore Year Pgm ... Ms. Jennifer NEELY
88 Coordinator of Senior Year Programs ... Mrs. Nicole RABALAIS
106 Director Online Learning ... Ms. Angela WETMORE
21 Director of Financial Services ... Mr. Chuck SEAMAN
15 Director Personnel Services ... Mr. Steve SEXTON
13 Director of Information Tech Svcs ... Mr. Scott CREEL
37 Financial Aid Director ... Mr. Eddie WHITE
23 Director Health Services ... Dr. Gerald M. MOREDOCK
18 Chief Facilities/Physical Plant ... Mr. Glen LINTHICUM
44 Senior Stewardship Officer ... Mr. Richard UNDERWOOD
29 Director of Alumni Services ... Mrs. Nancy DUNLAP
26 Dir of Communications/Marketing ... Mrs. Jan GREATHOUSE

Tusculum College (F)

60 Shiloh Road, Greeneville TN 37743-9997
County: Greene FICE Identification: 003527
Unit ID: 221953
Telephone: (423) 636-7300 Carnegie Class: Master's S
FAX Number: (423) 638-7166 Calendar System: Other
URL: www.tusculum.edu
Established: 1794 Annual Undergrad Tuition & Fees: $20,910
Enrollment: 2,249 Coed
Affiliation or Control: Presbyterian Church (U.S.A.) IRS Status: 501(c)3
Highest Offering: Master's
Program: Liberal Arts And General; Teacher Preparatory
Accreditation: SC

01 President ... Dr. Nancy B. MOODY
05 Provost & Academic Vice President ... Dr. Kimberly ESTEP
30 Int VP Institutional Advancement ... Ms. Heather PATCHETT
10 Vice Pres/Chief Financial Officer ... Mr. Steve GEHRET
84 VP for Enrollment Management ... Dr. Tom STEIN
20 Associate VP for Academic Affairs ... Dr. Melinda DUKES
32 Dean of Students ... Dr. David MCMAHAN
35 Associate Dean of Students ... Ms. Jonita ASHLEY-PAULEY
29 Assoc Dir Alumni/Parent Relations ... Vacant
06 Registrar ... Ms. Nancy J. THOMPSON
21 Controller ... Ms. Tracey JULIAN
07 Director of Operations/Admissions ... Ms. Melissa RIPLEY
20 Asst VP for Academic Affairs ... Dr. H. Gregory HAWKINS
15 Director Human Resources ... Ms. Mary SONNER
36 Director Career Counseling ... Ms. Amanda WADDELL
08 Librarian ... Mr. Myron J. SMITH, JR.
42 College Minister ... Mr. Mark STOKES
37 Director of Financial Aid ... Ms. Melena VERITY
41 Athletic Director ... Mr. Frankie DEBUSK
27 Director of Communications ... Ms. Suzanne RICHEY
13 Director of Information Systems ... Dr. Blair HENLEY
18 Director Facilities Management ... Mr. Mark STOKES
92 Director of Honors Program ... Dr. Angela KEATON
40 Bookstore Manager ... Mr. Cliff HOY

Union University (G)

1050 Union University Drive, Jackson TN 38305-3697
County: Madison FICE Identification: 003528
Unit ID: 221971
Telephone: (731) 668-1818 Carnegie Class: Master's L
FAX Number: (731) 661-5175 Calendar System: 4/1/4
URL: www.uu.edu
Established: 1823 Annual Undergrad Tuition & Fees: $24,100
Enrollment: 4,186 Coed
Affiliation or Control: Southern Baptist IRS Status: 501(c)3
Highest Offering: Doctorate
Program: Liberal Arts And General

Accreditation: SC, ANEST, ART, ENG, MUS, NURSE, @PHAR, SW, TED

01 President ... Dr. David S. DOCKERY
05 Provost/Executive Vice Pres ... Dr. Carla D. SANDERSON
10 Sr Vice Pres Business Svcs ... Mr. Gary L. CARTER
30 Sr Vice Pres University Relations ... Dr. Jerry TIDWELL
26 Vice Pres for Church Relations ... Dr. Richard WELLS
84 Sr Vice Pres Enrollment Services ... Mr. Rich GRIMM
12 Vice Pres for Regional Campuses ... Dr. Jimmy H. DAVIS
32 VP Student Svcs/Dean of Students ... Dr. Kimberly THORNBURY
49 VP Acad Admin/Dean Col Arts & Sci ... Dr. Gene FANT
42 Vice President for Spiritual Life ... Dr. Gregory THORNBURY
21 Assoc Vice Pres Business Svcs ... Mr. Robert SIMPSON
08 Assoc VP Academic Res/Dir Library ... Ms. Anna B. MORGAN
29 Assoc VP Univ Relations/Alumni Svcs ... Vacant
27 Assoc VP University Communications ... Mr. Mark KAHLER
90 Assoc VP Information Technology ... Mr. James AVERY
15 Assoc VP Business Svcs/Human Res ... Mr. John CARBONELL
07 Asst VP for Undergraduate Admiss ... Mr. Robbie GRAVES
37 Assistant VP for Financial Planning ... Mr. John BRANDT
50 Dean School of Business ... Dr. Keith ABSHER
66 Dean School of Nursing ... Dr. Timothy SMITH
53 Exec Dean Col Educ/Human Studies ... Dr. Tom ROSEBROUGH
88 Dean School of Theology Missions ... Dr. Gregory THORNBURY
67 Dean School of Pharmacy ... Dr. Sheila MITCHELL
91 Assoc Dir Information Technology ... Miss Karen MCWHERTER
36 Asst Dean Students/Dir Career Svcs ... Mrs. Jackie TAYLOR
13 Director of Data Management ... Mr. David PORTER
46 Director of Development Services ... Mrs. Katrina BRADFIELD
06 Registrar ... Mrs. Jane BETTS
19 Director of Security/Safety ... Mr. Carson HAWKINS
18 Chief Facilities/Physical Plant ... Mr. David MCBRIDE
20 Associate Academic Officer ... Dr. Barbara MCMILLIN

*University of Tennessee System Office (A)

800 Andy Holt Tower, Knoxville TN 37996-0180
County: Knox FICE Identification: 008051
Unit ID: 221722
Telephone: (865) 974-1000 Carnegie Class: N/A
FAX Number: (865) 974-3753
URL: www.tennessee.edu

01 President ... Dr. Joe DIPIETRO
03 Executive Vice President ... Dr. David E. MILLHORN
05 Interim VP Acad Affs/Stdnt Success ... Dr. Katherine N. HIGH
30 Int VP Development/Alumni Affairs ... Mr. Scott RABENOLD
26 VP for Public & Govt Relations ... Mr. Hank C. DYE
45 Vice President for Research ... Dr. David E. MILLHORN
10 Treasurer & CIO/Acting CFO ... Mr. Charles (Butch) M. PECCOLO, JR.
43 VP/General Counsel/Secretary ... Ms. Catherine S. MIZELL
16 Chief Human Resources Officer ... Ms. Linda HENDRICKS
86 Vice President of Public Service ... Dr. Mary JINKS
47 Vice President for Agriculture ... Dr. Joseph A. DIPIETRO
28 VP for Equity and Diversity ... Mr. Theotis ROBINSON
04 Exec Assistant to the President ... Mr. Keith CARVER
21 Exec Dir Auditing/Consulting Svcs ... Ms. Judy BURNS
29 Exec Dir UT Natl Alumni Assn ... Mr. Lofton K. STUART

*University of Tennessee, Knoxville (B)

1331 Circle Park, Andy Holt Tower, Knoxville TN 37996-0184
County: Knox FICE Identification: 003530
Unit ID: 221759
Telephone: (865) 974-1000 Carnegie Class: RU/VH
FAX Number: (865) 974-1182 Calendar System: Semester
URL: www.utk.edu
Established: 1794 Annual Undergrad Tuition & Fees (In-State): $8,396
Enrollment: 30,312 Coed
Affiliation or Control: State IRS Status: 501(c)3
Highest Offering: Doctorate
Program: Liberal Arts And General; Teacher Preparatory; Professional
Accreditation: SC, AAFCS, ANEST, ART, BUS, BUSA, CACREP, CIDA, CLPSY, COPSY, CORE, DENT, DIETD, DIETI, ENG, FOR, IPSY, JOUR, LAW, LIB, MT, MUS, NMT, NRPA, NURSE, PH, RAD, SCPSY, SP, SW, TED, VET

02 Chancellor ... Dr. Jimmy G. CHEEK
100 Chancellor's Chief of Staff ... Vacant
05 Provost/Senior VC for Acad Affairs ... Dr. Susan D. MARTIN
32 Vice Chancellor for Student Affairs ... Mr. W. Timothy ROGERS
46 Int Vice Chanc Research/Engagement ... Dr. Wes HINES
10 Vice Chanc Finance & Administration ... Mr. Chris CIMINO
27 Vice Chanc for Communications ... Ms. Margie NICHOLS
30 Vice Chanc Development/Alumni Affs ... Ms. Linda S. DAVIDSON
20 Vice Provost for Faculty Affairs ... Dr. Sarah GARDIAL
20 Vice Provost Academic Operations ... Vacant
58 Vice Provost/Dean Graduate School ... Dr. Carolyn R. HODGES
39 Asst VC/Exec Dir Univ Housing ... Mr. Ken STONER
51 Asst Provost Univ Outrch/Cont Educ ... Dr. Norvel BURKETT
07 Asst Provost Enrollment Svcs ... Mr. Richard L. BAYER
18 Exec Director Facilities Services ... Mr. J. Michael SHERRELL
41 Men's Athletic Director ... Mr. Michael E. HAMILTON
41 Women's Athletic Director ... Ms. Joan CRONAN
28 Director Equity/Diversity Office ... Dr. Marva RUDOLPH
37 Director of Financial Aid ... Mr. Jeffrey G. GERKIN
09 Interim Dir Inst Research/Assessmt ... Mr. Donald CUNNINGHAM
38 Director of Student Counseling ... Dr. Victor BARR
06 Registrar ... Ms. Monique W. ANDERSON
47 Dean Ag Sciences/Natural Resources ... Dr. Caula BEYL
48 Dean of Architecture and Design ... Dr. John MCRAE
50 Dean Business Administration ... Dr. Jan R. WILLIAMS
60 Dean Communication/Information ... Dr. Michael WIRTH
53 Dean Educ/Health/Human Sciences ... Dr. Robert RIDER
54 Dean of Engineering ... Dr. Wayne DAVIS
61 Dean of Law ... Prof. Douglas BLAZE
49 Dean of Arts & Sciences ... Dr. Theresa LEE
66 Dean of Nursing ... Dr. Joan L. CREASIA
70 Dean of Social Work ... Dr. Karen SOWERS
74 Dean of Veterinary Medicine ... Dr. James P. THOMPSON
47 Dean of Agricultural Extension Svc ... Dr. Tim L. CROSS
08 Dean of Libraries ... Dr. Steve SMITH

*University of Tennessee Health Science Center (C)

800 Madison Avenue, Memphis TN 38163-0002
County: Shelby FICE Identification: 006725
Unit ID: 221704
Telephone: (901) 448-5500 Carnegie Class: Not Classified
FAX Number: (901) 448-7750 Calendar System: Semester
URL: www.uthsc.edu
Established: 1911 Annual Undergrad Tuition & Fees (In-State): $6,106
Enrollment: 2,837 Coed
Affiliation or Control: State IRS Status: 501(c)3
Highest Offering: Doctorate
Program: Professional
Accreditation: &SC, ANEST, CYTO, DENT, DH, IPSY, MED, MT, NURSE, OT, PHAR, PTA

02 Chancellor ... Dr. Steve J. SCHWAB
03 Executive Vice Chancellor ... Dr. Kennard D. BROWN
76 Dean of Allied Health Sci ... Dr. Noma B. ANDERSON
52 Dean of Dentistry ... Dr. Timothy L. HOTTEL
58 Dean of Graduate Health Sciences ... Dr. Cheryl R. SCHEID
63 Dean of Medicine ... Dr. David STERN
63 Dean Medicine Chattanooga ... Dr. David C. SEABERG
63 Dean Medicine Knoxville ... Dr. James J. NEUTENS
66 Interim Dean of Nursing ... Dr. Susan R. JACOB
67 Dean of Pharmacy ... Dr. Dick R. GOURLEY
05 VC Academic/Faculty/Student Affs ... Dr. Cheryl R. SCHEID
13 Chief Information Officer ... Dr. Kennard D. BROWN
30 Int VC Development/Alumni Affairs ... Ms. Bethany GOOLSBY
10 Vice Chancellor Finance/Operations ... Mr. Anthony A. FERRARA
46 Vice Chancellor for Research ... Dr. Leonard R. JOHNSON
09 Asst VC of Inst Research/Educ Tech ... Dr. Chanchai MCDONALD
32 Asst VC for Student Affairs ... Ms. Sonya SMITH
07 Director of Admissions ... Mr. Ron K. PATTERSON
19 Director of Campus Police ... Chief L. Ida WALLS-UPCHURCH
35 Dir of Campus Rec/Student Life ... Mr. Frank HARRISON
27 Director of Communications/Mktg ... Ms. Sheila CHAMPLIN
31 Dir of Community Affairs ... Ms. Pam HOUSTON
28 Director of Equity & Diversity ... Dr. Michael L. ALSTON
18 Director of Facilities ... Mr. J. Bruce STILES
37 Director of Financial Aid ... Mr. John H. LEWIS
15 Director of Human Resources ... Mr. Jerry S. HALL
62 Director of Lib/Biocomm Ctr ... Dr. Thomas A. SINGARELLA
96 Director of Purchasing Svcs ... Mr. Victor CRUTCHFIELD
38 Dir of Student Acad Support Svcs ... Ms. Kathy L. GIBBS
06 Registrar ... Dr. Glenda K. ALEXANDER
40 Director of Bookstore ... Ms. Bobbie BALDWIN
48 Director of Architecture and Plng ... Mr. Kenny BRADSHAW
88 VC Clinical Affairs ... Dr. David STERN
88 Asst VC Faculty Administration ... Dr. Cynthia RUSSELL

*University of Tennessee at Chattanooga (D)

615 McCallie Avenue, Chattanooga TN 37403-2504
County: Hamilton FICE Identification: 003529
Unit ID: 221740
Telephone: (423) 425-4111 Carnegie Class: Master's L
FAX Number: (423) 425-2200 Calendar System: Semester
URL: www.utc.edu
Established: 1886 Annual Undergrad Tuition & Fees (In-State): $6,718
Enrollment: 10,781 Coed
Affiliation or Control: State IRS Status: 501(c)3
Highest Offering: Doctorate
Program: Liberal Arts And General; Teacher Preparatory; Professional
Accreditation: SC, ANEST, ART, BUS, BUSA, CACREP, CIDA, CS, DIETD, ENG, JOUR, MUS, NURSE, OT, PTA, SPAA, SW, TED, THEA

02 Chancellor ... Dr. Roger G. BROWN
05 Provost/Vice Chanc Academic Affs ... Dr. Phillip OLDHAM
30 Vice Chanc University Advancement ... Mr. Bob LYON
10 Vice Chanc Finance/Operations ... Dr. Richard BROWN
32 Vice Chanc Student Development ... Dr. John DELANEY
20 Assoc Provost for Academic Affairs ... Dr. Jocelyn SANDERS
21 Assoc Vice Chanc Business/Fin Affs ... Ms. Deborah PARKER
26 Asst VC University Relations ... Mr. Chuck CANTRELL
18 Asst VC Operations/Fac Plng & Mgt ... Mr. Tom M. ELLIS
91 Asst Vice Chancellor for Info Tech ... Mr. Monty WILSON
21 Asst VC Business Activities/Bursar ... Ms. Vanasia Conley PARKS
35 Asst VC Student Development ... Dr. Dee Dee ANDERSON
100 Chief of Staff ... Ms. Terry DENNISTON
08 Dean of Lupton Library ... Ms. Theresa LIEDTKA
88 Assoc Dean of Student Life ... Mr. Jim HICKS
07 Asst VC Enrollment Services ... Mr. Yancy FREEMAN
06 Director of Records and Registrar ... Ms. Linda ORTH
13 Director of Information Systems ... Mr. Richard GAMBRELL
09 Dir of Planning/Eval/Inst Research ... Dr. Richard R. GRUETZEMACHER
36 Dir of Placement/Student Employment ... Mrs. Jean DAKE
15 Director of Human Resources ... Mr. Dan WEBB
38 Director of Counseling ... Dr. Nancy BADGER
37 Director of Financial Aid ... Ms. Dianne COX
41 Director of Athletics ... Mr. Rick HART
49 Dean of Arts & Sciences ... Dr. Herbert BURHENN
50 Dean of Business Administration ... Dr. Robert DOOLEY
53 Dean of Health/Educ/Prof Studies ... Dr. Mary TANNER
54 Dean of Engineering/Comp Science ... Dr. William SUTTON
58 Dean of Graduate School ... Dr. Jerlad AINSWORTH
66 Director of Nursing ... Dr. Katherine S. LINDGREN
22 Director of Equity & Diversity ... Dr. Bryan SAMUEL
78 Director of Cooperative Education ... Mr. Hugh L. PREVOST, JR.
46 Director of Grants/Research ... Ms. Meredith PERRY
29 Director of Alumni Affairs ... Ms. Jayne HOLDER
14 Director of Admin Computing ... Ms. Glenda F. SULLIVAN
96 Mgr of Business Svcs (Purchasing) ... Mr. Charles SCOTT

*University of Tennessee at Martin (E)

544 University Street, Martin TN 38238-0001
County: Weakley FICE Identification: 003531
Unit ID: 221768
Telephone: (731) 881-7000 Carnegie Class: Master's M
FAX Number: (731) 881-7019 Calendar System: Semester
URL: www.utm.edu
Established: 1900 Annual Undergrad Tuition & Fees (In-State): $6,718
Enrollment: 8,467 Coed
Affiliation or Control: State IRS Status: 501(c)3
Highest Offering: Master's
Program: Liberal Arts And General; Teacher Preparatory; Professional
Accreditation: SC, AAFCS, BUS, DIETD, DIETI, ENG, JOUR, MUS, NUR, SW, TED

02 Chancellor ... Dr. Thomas A. RAKES
05 Vice Chancellor for Academic Affs ... Dr. E. Jerald OGG
10 Int Vice Chanc for Finance & Admin ... Ms. Nancy J. YARBROUGH
32 Vice Chancellor for Student Affairs ... Dr. Margaret Y. TOSTON
30 Vice Chancellor for Univ Advancemnt ... Ms. Len P. SOLOMONS
20 Assoc Vice Chanc for Academic Affr ... Dr. Victoria S. SENG
21 Asst Vice Chanc for Finance & Admin ... Ms. Nancy J. YARBROUGH
35 Asst Vice Chanc for Student Affairs ... Mr. David J. BELOTE
44 Asst VChanc Devel & Planned Giving ... Ms. Jeanna C. SWAFFORD
04 Exec Assistant to the Chancellor ... Ms. Edie B. GIBSON
29 Asst Vice Chanc for Alumni Rels ... Mr. Charley T. DEAL
06 Dir of Acad Recorda & Registrar ... Ms. Brandy D. CARTMELL
07 Director of Admissions ... Ms. Judy M. RAYBURN
28 Equity and Diversity Officer ... Dr. Rosemary GRAY
15 Director of Human Resources ... Mr. James (Phillip) BRIGHT
09 Int Dir Institutional Research ... Dr. Desiree A. MCCULLOUGH
41 Director Intercollegiate Athletics ... Mr. Phil W. DANE
08 Director of Library ... Ms. Mary V. CARPENTER
18 Director of Physical Plant Opers ... Mr. Tim J. NIPP
19 Director of Public Safety ... Mr. Scott D. ROBBINS
96 Purchasing Agent ... Ms. Lori A. HUTCHERSON
37 Int Director Student Financial Asst ... Ms. Sheryl FRAZIER
38 Dir Student Health & Counseling Svc ... Ms. Shannon DEAL
39 Director of Student Housing ... Mr. Earl WRIGHT
26 Director of University Relations ... Mr. Robert (Bud) D. GRIMES
85 Int Dir Tenn Intensive English Pgm ... Mr. Charles (Gary) WILSON
47 Int Dean Col Agri & App Sciences ... Dr. Jerry GRESHAM
50 Dean Col Business & Global Affairs ... Dr. Ernest R. MOSER
53 Dean Col Educ/Health & Behav Sci ... Dr. Mary Lee HALL
79 Dean Col Humanities/Fine Arts ... Dr. Lynn M. ALEXANDER
54 Interim Dean Col Engr & Natural Sci ... Dr. Richard J. HELGESON

Vanderbilt University (F)

2201 West End Avenue, Nashville TN 37240-0002
County: Davidson FICE Identification: 003535
Unit ID: 221999
Telephone: (615) 322-7311 Carnegie Class: RU/VH
FAX Number: (615) 343-5555 Calendar System: Semester
URL: www.vanderbilt.edu
Established: 1873 Annual Undergrad Tuition & Fees: $41,578
Enrollment: 12,714 Coed
Affiliation or Control: Independent Non-Profit IRS Status: 501(c)3
Highest Offering: Doctorate
Program: Liberal Arts And General; Teacher Preparatory; Professional
Accreditation: SC, AUD, BUS, CACREP, CLPSY, DENT, DIETI, DMS, ENG, IPSY, LAW, MED, MIDWF, MT, MUS, NMT, NUR, PERF, PH, RTT, SP, TED, THEOL

01 Chancellor ... Dr. Nicholas ZEPPOS
05 Provost/Vice Chancellor ... Dr. Richard C. MCCARTY
17 Vice Chancellor Health Affairs ... Dr. Jeffrey BALSER
10 Vice Chanc/Chief Financial Officer ... Mr. Brett SWEET
11 Vice Chanc Administration ... Mr. Jerry FIFE
30 Vice Chanc Dev & Alumni Relations ... Ms. Susie STALCUP
15 Chief Human Resouce Ofcr ... Ms. Traci NORDBERG
26 VC Univ Affs/Gen Counsel/Stdnt Life ... Dr. David WILLIAMS
29 Exec Asc VC Development/Alumni Rels ... Mr. Robert EARLY
20 Assoc Vice Chanc Academic Affairs ... Mr. John MCDANIEL
18 Deputy VC Facilities & Environment ... Mr. Judson NEWBERN
27 Vice Chancellor for Public Affairs ... Ms. Beth FORTUNE
09 Director Institutional Rsrch ... Dr. Roberta BELL
21 Vice Chancellor for Investments ... Mr. Matthew WRIGHT
20 Assoc Provost Undergrad Education ... Ms. Cynthia CYRUS
58 Vice Prov Research/Dn Graduate Sch ... Dr. Dennis G. HALL

84 Vice Provost Enrollment .... Dr. Douglas CHRISTIANSEN
13 Dean Student Info Tech Support .... Mr. F. Clark WILLIAMS
21 Deputy VC Finance/Controller .... Ms. Betty L. PRICE
06 Registrar .... Mr. Cheng KHOO
07 Dean of Admissions .... Dr. Douglas CHRISTIANSEN
07 Dir Undergraduate Admissions .... Mr. John GAINES
37 Exec Director of Financial Aid .... Dr. David D. MOHNING
38 Director Counseling Center .... Dr. Rhonda VENABLE
36 Director of Career Center .... Ms. Cynthia FUNK
46 Director Sponsored Research .... Dr. John CHILDRESS
14 Assoc Vice Chancellor ITS .... Mr. Matthew HALL
32 Dean of Students .... Mr. Mark BANDAS
49 Dean College Arts & Science .... Dr. Carolyn DEVER
63 Dean School of Medicine .... Dr. Jeffrey R. BALSER
54 Dean School of Engineering .... Dr. Kenneth F. GALLOWAY
66 Dean School of Nursing .... Dr. Colleen CONWAY-WELCH
53 Dean of Peabody College .... Dr. Camilla P. BENBOW
64 Dean Blair School of Music .... Dr. Mark WAIT
73 Dean of the Divinity School .... Dr. James HUDNUT-BEUMLER
61 Dean of the School of Law .... Dr. Chris GUTHRIE
50 Dean Owen Grad School of Mgmt .... Dr. James BRADFORD
88 Dean of the Commons .... Dr. Frank WCISLO
42 University Chaplain .... Rev. Gary WHITE
19 Director Police & Security .... Mr. Alan GUYET
22 Dir Opportunity Dev Center .... Ms. Anita JENIOUS
23 Assoc Dean Health & Wellness .... Dr. John W. GREENE
41 Director of Sport Operations .... Mr. Brockton WILLIAMS

Vatterott College-Memphis (A)

2655 Dividend Drive, Memphis TN 38132-1713

County: Shelby Identification: 666308
Unit ID: 440873
Telephone: (901) 761-5730 Carnegie Class: Assoc/PrivFP
FAX Number: (901) 763-2897 Calendar System: Other
URL: www.vatterott-college.edu
Established: 1969 Annual Undergrad Tuition & Fees: $10,930
Enrollment: 727 Coed
Affiliation or Control: Proprietary IRS Status: Proprietary
Highest Offering: Associate Degree
Program: Occupational
Accreditation: ACCSC

01 CEO & President .... Ms. Pam BELL
10 Chief Financial Officer .... Mr. Dennis BEAVERS
05 Chief Academic Officer .... Dr. John TUCKER
11 Chief Administrative Officer .... Mr. Erio COMICI
12 Campus Director .... Mr. Christopher COLEMAN

† Branch campus of Vatterott College-North Park, Berkeley, MO.

Victory University (formerly Crichton College) (B)

255 N Highland Street, Memphis TN 38111-1375

County: Shelby FICE Identification: 009982
Unit ID: 220941
Telephone: (901) 320-9700 Carnegie Class: Bac/Diverse
FAX Number: (901) 320-9709 Calendar System: Semester
URL: www.victory.edu
Established: 1941 Annual Undergrad Tuition & Fees: $10,050
Enrollment: 725 Coed
Affiliation or Control: Proprietary IRS Status: Proprietary
Highest Offering: Master's
Program: Occupational; 2-Year Principally Bachelor's Creditable; Liberal Arts And General; Teacher Preparatory; Professional; Business Emphasis
Accreditation: SC

01 President .... Dr. John M. BOREK, JR.
03 Provost .... Dr. Jim JEREMIAH
11 Dir Operations & Public Safety .... Mr. Troy GRAHAM
13 Director IT & Telecommunications .... Mr. Todd WILLIAMS
09 Dir Inst Effectiveness & Research .... Dr. Suzan SMITH
84 Exec Dir Enrollment Management .... Mrs. Carolyn CATES
07 Director of Admissions .... Ms. Shelley DUNN
05 Vice President Academic Affairs .... Dr. William CHANEY
06 Registrar .... Ms. Erica TAYLOR
73 Chair Bible & Theology .... Dr. Troy MILLER
83 Chair Behavioral Studies .... Dr. William CHANEY
50 Chair Business .... Dr. Brodie I. JOHNSON
53 Interim Chair Education .... Dr. William CHANEY
79 Chair Arts and Science .... Dr. Yolanda HARPER
08 Director Library .... Ms. Pamela B. WALKER
37 Director Student Finance Center .... Mr. Todd WILLIAMS
32 Director Student Development .... Mr. Brian DUFFY
10 Chief Financial Officer .... Mr. Troy GRAHAM
15 Director Human Resources .... Mrs. Julie TYLER
41 Athletic Director .... Mr. Scott ROBINSON

Virginia College School of Business and Health (C)

721 Eastgate Loop, Chattanooga TN 37411-5600

County: Hamilton Identification: 666136
Unit ID: 450289
Telephone: (423) 893-2000 Carnegie Class: Assoc/PrivFP4
FAX Number: (423) 893-2010 Calendar System: Quarter
URL: www.vc.edu
Established: 2006 Annual Undergrad Tuition & Fees: $15,616
Enrollment: 501 Coed
Affiliation or Control: Proprietary IRS Status: Proprietary
Highest Offering: Baccalaureate
Program: 2-Year Principally Bachelor's Creditable; Liberal Arts And General
Accreditation: ACICS

01 Campus President .... Mr. Michael OERTLE
37 Director of Financial Planning .... Mr. Travis W. CAPEHART
36 Director of Career Services .... Mr. Michael E. JOHNSON
07 Director of Admissions .... Mr. Keith CANTRELL
10 Controller .... Ms. Karen BAIRAKTARIS

Visible Music College (D)

1015 South Cooper Street, Memphis TN 38104

County: Shelby FICE Identification: 039823
Unit ID: 449764
Telephone: (901) 381-3939 Carnegie Class: Spec/Arts
FAX Number: (901) 377-0544 Calendar System: Semester
URL: www.visible.edu
Established: 2000 Annual Undergrad Tuition & Fees: $22,700
Enrollment: 107 Coed
Affiliation or Control: Independent Non-Profit IRS Status: 501(c)3
Highest Offering: Baccalaureate
Program: Professional; Music Emphasis
Accreditation: TRACS

01 President .... Ken STEORTS
05 Vice President of Academics .... Shannon KROPF
32 Vice President Student Development .... Peet STRYDOM
07 Admissions Coordinator .... Marisa BAKER
10 Vice President Business Strategies .... Sam GARRETT
08 Librarian .... Vacant
26 Communications Coordinator .... Sue STRYDOM
37 Director of Financial Aid .... LaKeisha MURRY
06 Registrar .... Mary Ann GARDNER

Watkins College of Art, Design & Film (E)

2298 Rosa L. Parks Boulevard, Nashville TN 37228-1306

County: Davidson FICE Identification: 030888
Unit ID: 392840
Telephone: (615) 383-4848 Carnegie Class: Spec/Arts
FAX Number: (615) 383-4849 Calendar System: Semester
URL: www.watkins.edu
Established: 1885 Annual Undergrad Tuition & Fees: $18,900
Enrollment: 396 Coed
Affiliation or Control: Independent Non-Profit IRS Status: 501(c)3
Highest Offering: Baccalaureate
Program: Fine Arts Emphasis
Accreditation: SC, ART, CIDA

01 President .... Ms. Ellen MEYER
30 Vice Pres Institutional Advancement .... Ms. Hilrie BROWN
05 Vice Pres Academic Affairs .... Mr. John SULLIVAN
10 Vice Pres Finance and Operations ..... Ms. Mary Ellen LOTHAMER
07 Dir Admissions .... Ms. Linda SCHWAB
26 Dir External Relations .... Ms. Caroline DAVIS
06 Registrar .... Ms. Tracie JOHNSON
37 Dir Financial Aid .... Ms. Regina GILBERT
08 Library Dir .... Ms. Lisa WILLIAMS
13 Dir Information Technology .... Mr. Chris MCQUISTION
18 Interim Dir Facilities .... Mr. Hank HYMEL
88 Chair Film School .... Mr. Steve WOMACK
57 Chair Fine Art Department .... Mr. Terry THACKER
88 Coord Graphic Design Department .... Mr. Dan BRAWNER
88 Chair Interior Design Department .... Ms. Jennifer OVERSTREET
88 Chair Photography Department .... Ms. Robin PARIS
97 Dir General Education .... Ms. Cary Beth MILLER
51 Dir Community Education .... Ms. Rebecca BERRIOS
32 Dir Student Life .... Ms. Samantha BRZOZOWSKI

West Tennessee Business College (F)

1186 Highway 45 Bypass, Jackson TN 38301

County: Madison FICE Identification: 004947
Unit ID: 222099
Telephone: (731) 668-7240 Carnegie Class: Not Classified
FAX Number: (731) 668-3824 Calendar System: Other
URL: www.wtbc.edu
Established: 1888 Annual Undergrad Tuition & Fees: $15,200
Enrollment: 610 Coed
Affiliation or Control: Proprietary IRS Status: Proprietary
Highest Offering: Associate Degree
Program: Occupational
Accreditation: ACICS

01 Executive Director .... C. Vicki BURCH
05 Academic Dean .... LaVerne ADAMS
10 Chief Fiscal Officer .... Kim JONES
06 Registrar .... Sheila JOHNSON
07 Admissions Director .... Ann RECORD

† Tuition for each program includes books.

Williamson Christian College (G)

200 Seaboard Lane, Franklin TN 37067-8237

County: Williamson FICE Identification: 035135
Unit ID: 443340
Telephone: (615) 771-7821 Carnegie Class: Spec/Faith
FAX Number: (615) 771-7810 Calendar System: Semester
URL: www.williamsoncc.edu
Established: 1996 Annual Undergrad Tuition & Fees: $9,450
Enrollment: 80 Coed
Affiliation or Control: Non-denominational IRS Status: 501(c)3
Highest Offering: Baccalaureate
Program: Professional; Religious Emphasis
Accreditation: BI

01 President .... Pastor Stephen HIGGINS
30 Vice President Advancement .... Dr. Ed SMITH
05 Exec Vice Pres Academic Affairs .... Dr. Sharon LANDERS
32 Vice President for Student Develop .... Ms. Karen HUDSON
11 Vice President for Operations .... Mr. Don SCHMIDT
09 Director Institutional Effectivess .... Dr. Tony BUCHANAN
08 Librarian .... Vacant
06 Registrar/Dir of Admissions .... Ms. Robyn WOLLAS
37 Manager of Financial Aid .... Ms. Becky WILLINGHAM
84 Director Enrollment Management .... Vacant

TEXAS

Abilene Christian University (H)

ACU Box 29100, Abilene TX 79699-9100

County: Taylor FICE Identification: 003537
Unit ID: 222178
Telephone: (325) 674-2000 Carnegie Class: Master's L
FAX Number: (325) 674-2202 Calendar System: Semester
URL: www.acu.edu
Established: 1906 Annual Undergrad Tuition & Fees: $25,270
Enrollment: 4,728 Coed
Affiliation or Control: Churches Of Christ IRS Status: 501(c)3
Highest Offering: Doctorate
Program: Liberal Arts And General; Teacher Preparatory; Professional
Accreditation: SC, BUS, CIDA, DIETD, JOUR, MFCD, MUS, NURSE, SP, SW, @TEAC, THEOL

01 President .... Dr. Phil SCHUBERT
100 Senior Advisor to the President .... Ms. Suzanne ALLMON
05 Provost .... Dr. Jeanine B. VARNER
03 Vice President of the University .... Dr. Gary D. MCCALEB
30 Vice President for Advancement .... Mr. Phil BOONE
32 VP for Student Life/Dean Students ...... Dr. Jean-Noel THOMPSON
88 Chief Investment Ofcr/Pres ACIMCO .... Mr. Jack W. RICH
43 General Counsel .... Mr. Slade SULLIVAN
00 Chancellor .... Dr. Royce MONEY
88 Exec Assistant to the Chancellor .... Mr. Jim HOLMANS
102 Vice Chancellor/Pres ACU Foundation .... Mr. Dan T. GARRETT
88 Senior Vice President Emeritus .... Dr. Robert D. HUNTER
20 Vice Provost .... Dr. Ken CUKROWSKI
97 Asst Provost for General Educ .... Dr. Gregory STRAUGHN
49 Dean College of Arts & Sciences .... Dr. Charles MATTIS
73 Dean College Biblical Studies/GST .... Dr. Jack R. REESE
50 Dean College of Business Admin .... Dr. Rick S. LYTLE
53 Dean College of Educ/Human Svcs .... Dr. MaLesa BREEDING
92 Dean Honors College .... Dr. Stephen JOHNSON
58 Dean Graduate School .... Dr. Carley DODD
66 Dean School of Nursing .... Dr. Susan KEHL
89 Director of First-Year Program .... Dr. Eric GUMM
08 Dean Library/Information Resources .... Dr. John WEAVER
104 Exec Dir Ctr International Educ .... Dr. Kevin KEHL
106 Assoc Provost for Online Programs .... Dr. Carol WILLIAMS
106 Director of Online Education .... Mr. Corey PATTERSON
42 Assistant Dean for Spiritual Life .... Mr. Mark LEWIS
36 Director Career Center .... Ms. MaryEllen OLSON
06 Registrar .... Mr. Bart HERRIDGE
37 Director Student Financial Services .... Mr. Ed KERESTLY
84 Acting Chief Enrollment Officer .... Mr. Kevin CAMPBELL
26 Chief Marketing Officer .... Mr. Jason GROVES
35 Associate VP for Student Life .... Dr. Jeff ARRINGTON
23 Director of Medical Clinic .... Dr. Ellen B. LITTLE
39 Director Residence Life .... Mr. John DELONY
28 Director Multicultural Enrichment .... Mr. Russell KIRBY
38 Director Univ Counseling Center .... Mr. Steve ROWLANDS
31 Director Ctr Service-Lrng/Volunteer .... Ms. Nancy A. COBURN
45 Chief Info & Planning Officer .... Mr. Kevin J. ROBERTS
18 Exec Dir Facilities/Campus Develop .... Mr. Zane DENNIS
10 Chief Financial Officer .... Mr. Kelly YOUNG
13 Exec Dir of Information Technology .... Mrs. Kay REEVES
24 Exec Dir Adams Ctr Teaching/Lrng .... Mr. George SALTSMAN
105 Director Web Integration/Prgmng .... Dr. James D. LANGFORD
29 Dir of Alumni Rels & Annual Project .... Mr. Craig FISHER
19 Chief of ACU Police .... Mr. Jimmy ELLISON
44 Director of Major Gifts .... Mr. Don GARRETT
41 Director of Athletics .... Mr. Jared MOSLEY
15 Director of Human Resources .... Ms. Wendy JONES
88 Director Instruction/Faculty Devel .... Dr. Dwayne HARAPNUIK
09 Director Inst Research/Assessment .... Dr. Tom A. MILHOLLAND
96 University Purchasing Manager .... Ms. Sandy HALL
40 Chief Business Services Officer .... Mr. Anthony T. WILLIAMS
101 Secretary to the Board of Trustees .... Mr. Slade SULLIVAN
04 Exec Assistant Office of President .... Ms. Stephanie WOODLEE

The Academy of Health Care Professions (I)

6505 Airport Blvd, Suite 102, Austin TX 78752

County: Travis FICE Identification: 034263
Unit ID: 437635
Telephone: (512) 892-2835 Carnegie Class: Not Classified
FAX Number: (512) 892-6643 Calendar System: Other
URL: www.ahcp.edu
Established: N/A Annual Undergrad Tuition & Fees: $20,500
Enrollment: 244 Coed
Affiliation or Control: Proprietary IRS Status: Proprietary
Highest Offering: Associate Degree
Program: Occupational

Accreditation: ABHES

01 Director .... Ms. Lori BJORGO

The Academy of Health Care Professions (A)

240 Northwest Mall, Houston TX 77092
County: Harris　FICE Identification: 031281
Unit ID: 392257
Telephone: (713) 425-3100　Carnegie Class: Not Classified
FAX Number: (713) 425-3192　Calendar System: Other
URL: www.ahcp.edu
Established: 1988　Annual Undergrad Tuition & Fees: N/A
Enrollment: 353　Coed
Affiliation or Control: Proprietary　IRS Status: Proprietary
Highest Offering: Associate Degree
Program: Occupational; 2-Year Principally Bachelor's Creditable
Accreditation: ABHES, SURGT, SURTEC

Alamo Community College District Central Office (B)

201 W Sheridan, San Antonio TX 78204-1429
County: Bexar　FICE Identification: 003607
Unit ID: 222497
Telephone: (210) 485-0020　Carnegie Class: N/A
FAX Number: (210) 486-9166
URL: www.alamo.edu

01 Chancellor .... Dr. Bruce LESLIE
05 Vice Chanc for Academic Success .... Dr. Robert AGUERO
11 Vice Chanc for Finance & Admin .... Ms. Diane E. SNYDER
32 Vice Chancellor for Student Success .... Dr. Adelina SILVA
103 Vice Chanc Economic/Workforce Devel ... Dr. Federico ZARAGOZA
44 VC Plng/Performance/Inform/Systems .... Dr. Thomas CLEARY
15 Assoc Vice Chanc Employee Services .... Ms. Linda BOYER-OWENS
27 Assoc Vice Chanc Communications .... Mr. Leo ZUNIGA
18 Assoc Vice Chanc Facilities .... Mr. John STRYBOS
20 Assoc VC Acad Partnershp/Initatives .... Dr. Jo-Carol FABIANKE
10 Assoc VC Finance & Fiscal Services .... Ms. Pamela ANSBOURY
04 Deputy to the Chancellor .... Dr. Adriana CONTRERAS
30 Exec Director Inst Advancement .... Mr. Jim ESKIN
21 Director of Internal Audit .... Ms. Patricia MAJOR
96 Director Acquisitions & Admin Svcs .... Mr. Gary O'BAR
41 Athletic Director .... Vacant
19 Chief Department of Public Safety .... Mr. Don ADAMS
21 Controller .... Ms. Angelia DEBARROS
12 President Northwest Vista College .... Dr. Jacqueline CLAUNCH
12 President San Antonio College .... Dr. Robert ZEIGLER
12 President St Philip's College .... Dr. Adena WILLIAMS LOSTON
12 President Palo Alto College .... Dr. Ana (Cha) GUZMAN
12 President Northeast College .... Dr. Eric RENO

*Northwest Vista College (C)

3535 N Ellison Drive, San Antonio TX 78251-4217
County: Bexar　FICE Identification: 033723
Unit ID: 420398
Telephone: (210) 486-4000　Carnegie Class: Assoc/Pub-U-MC
FAX Number: (210) 486-9105　Calendar System: Semester
URL: www.alamo.edu/nvc
Established: 1995　Annual Undergrad Tuition & Fees (In-District): $1,614
Enrollment: 15,921　Coed
Affiliation or Control: Local　IRS Status: 501(c)3
Highest Offering: Associate Degree
Program: 2-Year Principally Bachelor's Creditable
Accreditation: SC

02 President .... Dr. Jacqueline CLAUNCH
03 Vice President for College Services .... Mrs. Julie PACE
05 Vice President of Academics .... Dr. Jimmie BRUCE
32 Vice President of Student Success .... Dr. Diana MUNIZ
30 Director Institutional Advancement .... Mrs. Lynne DEAN
08 Dean of Learning Resources .... Ms. Christine CROWLEY
07 Associate Director of Admissions .... Ms. Beautrice BUTLER
36 Dean of Student Success .... Mrs. Deborah GAITAN
26 Dir of Public Relations & Marketing .... Mrs. Renata SERAFIN
27 Director Info/Communications Tech .... Mr. Bryant BONNER
56 Dean of Instructional and Extended .... Dr. John CARNES
37 Director of Financial Aid .... Mr. Noe ORTIZ
21 Assistant Bursar .... Mrs. Norma GONZALEZ
39 Assoc Director of Residency/Reports .... Ms. Briget TORRES
15 Sr Human Resources Generalist .... Mr. Manuel CERDA
45 Director of Resources & College Dev .... Mr. Carlos AGUIRRE
18 Superintendent NVC .... Mr. Bernie ZERTUCHE
103 Dean of Workforce Development .... Mr. Patrick FONTENOT
88 Dean of Interdisciplinary Programs .... Dr. Mary DIXSON
09 Director of Institutional Research .... Dr. Eliza HERNANDEZ
88 Coordinator Scholarship & Alumni .... Mrs. Lucy GAUNA
84 Director of Enrollment Management .... Mrs. Robin CARRILLO

*Palo Alto College (D)

1400 W Villaret, San Antonio TX 78224-2499
County: Bexar　FICE Identification: 023413
Unit ID: 246354
Telephone: (210) 486-3000　Carnegie Class: Assoc/Pub-U-MC
FAX Number: (210) 921-5005　Calendar System: Semester
URL: www.alamo.edu
Established: 1985　Annual Undergrad Tuition & Fees (In-District): $1,889
Enrollment: 8,300　Coed
Affiliation or Control: Local　IRS Status: 501(c)3
Highest Offering: Associate Degree
Program: Occupational; 2-Year Principally Bachelor's Creditable
Accreditation: SC

02 President .... Dr. Ana M. GUZMAN
05 Vice President Academic Affairs .... Dr. Stacey JOHNSON
11 Vice Pres College Services .... Dr. Beatriz JOSEPH
32 Vice President of Student Affairs .... Dr. Mike FLORES
49 Dean Arts & Sciences .... Ms. Elizabeth TANNER
10 Chief Business Officer .... Dr. Beatriz JOSEPH
49 Dean Science/Advanced/Applied Tech .... Mr. Gary SHELMAN
08 Dean of Learning Resources .... Ms. Tina MESA
26 Int Director of Public Relations .... Ms. Ginger HALL CARNES
21 Bursar .... Mr. Daniel ROCHA
84 Director of Enrollment Management .... Ms. Elizabeth VILLARUAL
37 Director Student Financial Services .... Mr. Lamar DUARTE
41 Athletic Director .... Mr. John LIBBY
32 Dean of Student Affairs .... Dr. Robert GARZA
18 Chief Facilities/Physical Plant .... Mr. Sergio RIVERA
38 Director Student Counseling .... Ms. Yolanda REYNA
29 Director Alumni Relations .... Ms. Danielle ESPINOZA
09 Dir Inst Rsrch/Plng/Effectiveness .... Ms. Catherine CHAPA
30 Chief Development .... Ms. Sherry BOYLES

*St. Philip's College (E)

1801 Martin Luther King, San Antonio TX 78203-2098
County: Bexar　FICE Identification: 003608
Unit ID: 227854
Telephone: (210) 486-2000　Carnegie Class: Assoc/Pub-U-MC
FAX Number: N/A　Calendar System: Semester
URL: www.alamo.edu/spc/
Established: 1898　Annual Undergrad Tuition & Fees (In-District): $1,710
Enrollment: 10,828　Coed
Affiliation or Control: Local　IRS Status: 501(c)3
Highest Offering: Associate Degree
Program: Occupational; 2-Year Principally Bachelor's Creditable
Accreditation: SC, ACFEI, HT, MLTAD, OTA, PTAA, RAD, SURGT

02 President .... Dr. Adena WILLIAMS LOSTON
05 Vice Pres for Academic Affairs .... Ms. Ruth DALRYMPLE
32 Vice Pres of Student Success .... Dr. Sherrie LANG
11 Vice President for College Svcs .... Ms. Lacy HAMPTON
12 Vice Pres Admin Southwest Campus .... Vacant
35 Dean Student Success .... Mr. Paul MACHEN
08 Dean Interdisciplinary Programs .... Dr. Karen SIDES
75 Dean Applied Science & Tech .... Ms. Maureen CARTLEDGE
49 Dean Arts & Science .... Ms. Mary COTTIER
76 Dean of Health Sciences .... Ms. Rose SPRUILL
51 Director Continuing Ed/Extend Svcs .... Mr. Erick AKINS
37 Director of Financial Aid .... Mr. Diego BERNAL
45 Director Planning & Research .... Ms. Mecca SALAHUDDIN
10 Bursar .... Ms. Sophia GONZALEZ
26 Int Dir Community & Public Rels .... Mr. Jorge RAMIREZ
30 Director Institutional Advancement .... Mr. Jorge TREVINO
72 Director Instructional Technology .... Dr. Julia BRIGGS
18 Chief Facilities/Physical Plant .... Ms. Sherry TOLIVER
29 Director Alumni Relations .... Dr. Sharon CROCKETT-BELL
96 Chief Budget Manager .... Mr. Paul BORREGO
07 Int Director Enrollment Management .... Ms. Ana Lisa GARZA

*San Antonio College (F)

1300 San Pedro Avenue, San Antonio TX 78212-4299
County: Bexar　FICE Identification: 009163
Unit ID: 227924
Telephone: (210) 486-0000　Carnegie Class: Assoc/Pub-U-MC
FAX Number: N/A　Calendar System: Semester
URL: www.alamo.edu/sac
Established: 1925　Annual Undergrad Tuition & Fees (In-District): $2,568
Enrollment: 24,949　Coed
Affiliation or Control: Local　IRS Status: 501(c)3
Highest Offering: Associate Degree
Program: Occupational; 2-Year Principally Bachelor's Creditable
Accreditation: SC, ADNUR, DA, DT, FUSER, IFSAC, MAC

02 President .... Dr. Robert E. ZEIGLER
05 Vice President of Academic Affairs .... Dr. Jessica HOWARD
32 Vice President of Student Affairs .... Dr. Robert H. VELA
11 Vice President of College Services .... Mr. David E. MRIZEK
72 Dean Professional & Tech Educ .... Ms. Vernell E. WALKER
49 Dean of Arts & Sciences .... Dr. Conrad KRUEGER
51 Dean Cont Educ/Training Network .... Mr. Tim ROCKEY
56 Dean Evening/Weekend/Distance Educ .... Mr. Ruben FLORES
08 Dean of Learning Resources .... Dr. Alice JOHNSON
84 Director of Enrollment Services .... Ms. Helen TORRES
37 Coordinator of Financial Aid .... Mr. Tom CAMPOS
35 Director of Student Activities .... Mr. Jorge POSADAS
85 Coordinator International Students .... Vacant
26 Director Public Relations .... Ms. Deborah M. MARTIN
45 Director Resource & College Devel .... Ms. Susan B. ESPINOZA
23 Director Health Services .... Ms. Paula DAGGETT
29 Coordinator of Alumni and Friends .... Vacant
18 Chief Facilities/Physical Plant .... Mr. David ORTEGA
38 Interim Dean of Student Affairs .... Ms. Emma MENDIOLA
88 Directo of P-16 Initiatives Gateway .... Dr. Maryellen MILLS

Alvin Community College (G)

3110 Mustang Road, Alvin TX 77511-4898
County: Brazoria　FICE Identification: 003539
Unit ID: 222567
Telephone: (281) 756-3500　Carnegie Class: Assoc/Pub-R-L
FAX Number: (281) 756-3854　Calendar System: Semester
URL: www.alvincollege.edu
Established: 1948　Annual Undergrad Tuition & Fees (In-District): $1,432
Enrollment: 5,721　Coed
Affiliation or Control: Local　IRS Status: 501(c)3
Highest Offering: Associate Degree
Program: Occupational; 2-Year Principally Bachelor's Creditable
Accreditation: SC, ADNUR, DMS, POLYT

01 President .... Dr. A. Rodney ALLBRIGHT
05 Dean Instruction/Provost .... Dr. John BETHSCHEIDER
11 Dean Financial/Admin Services .... Dr. Darryl STEVENS
06 Registrar .... Ms. Irene M. ROBINSON
08 Director Library Services .... Mr. Tom BATES
10 Director Fiscal Affairs/Controller .... Mr. Karl STAGER
14 Director Computer Services .... Vacant
37 Dir Student Financial Aid Placement .... Ms. Dora SIMS
45 Dir Institutional Effectiveness .... Mr. Patrick SANGER
15 Director Human Resources .... Ms. Lang WINDSOR
18 Director Physical Plant .... Mr. Bill NIELSON
29 Director Alumni Relations .... Ms. Wendy DEL BELLO
07 Director Admissions/Acad Advising ... Ms. Stephanie STOCKSTILL
09 Director of Inst Effective/Research .... Mr. Patrick SANGER
51 Dean Cont Educ/Pearland Center ..... Dr. Patricia HERTENBERGER
32 Dean of Students .... Ms. JoAn ANDERSON
75 Dean Technical Programs .... Dr. John BETHSCHEIDER
26 Chief Public Relations Officer .... Ms. Wendy DEL BELLO

Amarillo College (H)

PO Box 447, Amarillo TX 79178-0001
County: Potter　FICE Identification: 003540
Unit ID: 222576
Telephone: (806) 371-5000　Carnegie Class: Assoc/Pub-R-L
FAX Number: (806) 371-5370　Calendar System: Semester
URL: www.actx.edu
Established: 1929　Annual Undergrad Tuition & Fees (In-District): $2,092
Enrollment: 11,675　Coed
Affiliation or Control: State/Local　IRS Status: 501(c)3
Highest Offering: Associate Degree
Program: Occupational; 2-Year Principally Bachelor's Creditable
Accreditation: SC, ADNUR, DH, FUSER, MLTAD, MUS, NMT, OTA, PTAA, RAD, RTT, SURGT

01 President .... Dr. Paul MATNEY
05 VP of Academic Affairs .... Dr. Russell LOWERY-HART
10 VP of Business Affairs .... Mr. Terry BERG
51 Dean of Continuing Education .... Mrs. Kim D. DAVIS
32 VP of Student Affairs .... Mr. Robert C. AUSTIN
13 Chief Information Officer .... Mr. Lee M. COLAW
46 Chief of Planning/Advancement .... Ms. Danita L. MCANALLY
102 Dir AC Foundation/Development .... Mrs. Kathleen B. DOWDY
76 Director Ctr Cont Health Care Educ .. Mrs. Kimberly A. COWLEY
18 Director Physical Plant .... Mr. Bruce COTGREAVE
37 Director Financial Aid .... Mrs. Mary K. MOONEY
08 Director AC Library Network .... Mr. Mark HANNA
06 Registrar .... Mrs. Diane BRICE
27 Chief of Communication/Mktg .... Mrs. Ellen R. GREEN
15 Director of Admin Svcs/Human Res .... Mr. Lynn L. THORNTON
19 Director of Police .... Mr. Michael W. DUVAL
26 Director Found Mktg/Special Events .. Mrs. Tracy D. DOUGHERTY
35 Assoc VP of Student Affairs .... Mrs. April L. SESSLER
38 Director Advising & Counseling .... Mr. Jason A. NORMAN
88 Director Amarillo Museum of Art .... Vacant
88 Director Criminal Justice Program .... Ms. Toni GRAY
96 Director of Purchasing .... Mrs. Vickie SHELTON
88 Dean of Academic Transfer Pgms .... Mr. Jerry E. MOLLER
76 Dean of Health Sciences .... Mr. Bill E. CRAWFORD
75 Dean of Career/Tech Education .... Dr. Shawn M. FOUTS
88 Dean of Academic Success .... Dr. Tamara T. CLUNIS

Amberton University (I)

1700 Eastgate Drive, Garland TX 75041
County: Dallas　FICE Identification: 022594
Unit ID: 222628
Telephone: (972) 279-6511　Carnegie Class: Master's L
FAX Number: (972) 279-9773　Calendar System: Quarter
URL: www.amberton.edu
Established: 1971　Annual Undergrad Tuition & Fees: $5,600
Enrollment: 1,474　Coed
Affiliation or Control: Independent Non-Profit　IRS Status: 501(c)3
Highest Offering: Master's
Program: Professional; Business Emphasis
Accreditation: SC

01 President .... Dr. Melinda REAGAN
05 Academic Dean .... Dr. Don HEBBARD
30 Dean Univ Advance/VP Strategic Svcs .... Dr. Jo Lynn LOYD
10 Chief Business Officer .... Mr. Brent BRADSHAW
06 Registrar .... Ms. Marge MASSEY
32 Director Student Services .... Mr. Bill GILBREATH
84 Director for Recruiting .... Mr. Glenn SORRELLS
08 Head Librarian .... Ms. Judy GIBSON
29 Dir Alumni Relations & Inst Rsch .... Dr. Jo Lynn LOYD
07 Director of Admissions .... Dr. Don HEBBARD
40 Director Bookstore .... Mr. Dwayne BLACK

American College of Acupuncture and Oriental Medicine (A)

9100 Park West Drive, Houston TX 77063-4104

County: Harris FICE Identification: 031533
Unit ID: 429085
Telephone: (713) 780-9777 Carnegie Class: Spec/Health
FAX Number: (713) 781-5781 Calendar System: Trimester
URL: www.acaom.edu
Established: 1991 Annual Graduate Tuition & Fees: $11,638
Enrollment: 130 Coed
Affiliation or Control: Proprietary IRS Status: Proprietary
Highest Offering: Master's; No Undergraduates
Program: Professional
Accreditation: @SC, ACUP

01 President .... Dr. John Paul LIANG
03 Vice President .... Mr. Sam RAIA
05 Dean of Academic Affairs .... Dr. Wen HUANG
20 Dean of Clinical Training .... Dr. Baisong ZHONG

American InterContinental University-Houston Campus (B)

9999 Richmond Avenue, Houston TX 77042-4516

County: Harris Identification: 666335
Unit ID: 445133
Telephone: (832) 201-3600 Carnegie Class: Spec/Bus
FAX Number: (832) 201-3637 Calendar System: Quarter
URL: www.houston.aiuniv.edu
Established: 2003 Annual Undergrad Tuition & Fees: N/A
Enrollment: 557 Coed
Affiliation or Control: Proprietary IRS Status: Proprietary
Highest Offering: Master's
Program: Professional; Business Emphasis
Accreditation: &NH, ACBSP

01 Campus President .... Mr. Steve MALUTICH

† Regional accreditation is carried under the parent institution in Hoffman Estates, IL.

Anamarc College (C)

3210 Dyer, El Paso TX 79930

County: El Paso FICE Identification: 037563
Unit ID: 444389
Telephone: (915) 351-8100 Carnegie Class: Not Classified
FAX Number: (915) 351-8300 Calendar System: Other
URL: www.anamarc.edu
Established: N/A Annual Undergrad Tuition & Fees: $11,813
Enrollment: 710 Coed
Affiliation or Control: Proprietary IRS Status: Proprietary
Highest Offering: Associate Degree
Program: Occupational
Accreditation: ACICS

01 President .... Mr. Pablo FUENTES
03 Chief Executive Officer .... Dr. Ana Maria PINA HOUDE
10 Vice President of Finance .... Mr. Jaime LOWENBERG
15 Vice President of Human Resources .... Ms. Elena LIGGINGS
46 VP of Educ Research & Technology .... Mr. Sergio ZAPATA
06 Registrar .... Ms. Elsa PINA
37 Financial Aid Director .... Mr. Rick AMBRIZ

Angelina College (D)

PO Box 1768, Lufkin TX 75902-1768

County: Angelina Identification: 006661
Unit ID: 222822
Telephone: (936) 639-1301 Carnegie Class: Assoc/Pub-R-M
FAX Number: (936) 639-4299 Calendar System: Semester
URL: www.angelina.edu
Established: 1966 Annual Undergrad Tuition & Fees (In-District): $1,710
Enrollment: 5,927 Coed
Affiliation or Control: State/Local IRS Status: 501(c)3
Highest Offering: Associate Degree
Program: Occupational; 2-Year Principally Bachelor's Creditable
Accreditation: SC, DMS, RAD, SURGT

01 President .... Dr. Larry M. PHILLIPS
05 Vice President/Dean of Instruction .... Dr. Patricia M. MCKENZIE
10 Vice President Business Services .... Mr. Joe MADDEN
31 Vice Pres of Community Services .... Dr. Frederick W. KANKE
32 Dean of Student Services .... Mr. James TWOHIG
13 Dir Management Information Systems .... Mr. Kenneth STREET
37 Director Student Financial Aid .... Mrs. Sue JONES
18 Chief Facilities/Physical Plant .... Mr. Steve CAPPS
84 Director Enrollment Services .... Mr. Jeremy THOMAS
09 Coord Instnl Effectiveness & Q.E.P. .... Dr. Monica PETERS
27 Coordinator Marketing/Development .... Mr. Gary STALLARD
15 Coord of Human Resources .... Mrs. Tifini WHIDDON
06 Registrar & Records Coordinator .... Mrs. Sandra COX

Angelo State University (E)

2601 West Avenue N, San Angelo TX 76909-0001

County: Tom Green FICE Identification: 003541
Unit ID: 222831
Telephone: (325) 942-2555 Carnegie Class: Master's M
FAX Number: (325) 942-2038 Calendar System: Semester
URL: www.angelo.edu
Established: 1928 Annual Undergrad Tuition & Fees (In-State): $6,211
Enrollment: 6,155 Coed
Affiliation or Control: State IRS Status: 501(c)3
Highest Offering: Doctorate
Program: 2-Year Principally Bachelor's Creditable; Liberal Arts And General; Teacher Preparatory; Professional; Business Emphasis
Accreditation: SC, ACBSP, ADNUR, MUS, NUR, PTA, @SW, TED

01 President .... Dr. Joseph C. RALLO
05 Interim Provost/VP Academic Affs .... Dr. Brian J. MAY
30 Vice President for Development .... Dr. Jason C. PENRY
10 VP for Finance and Administration .... Mr. Michael REID
45 VP Strategy/Planning & Policy .... Dr. James M. LIMBAUGH
32 VP for Student Affs & Enroll Mgmt .... Dr. Vance R. VALERIO
20 Vice Provost .... Dr. Nancy ALLEN
58 Dean College of Graduate Studies .... Dr. Brian MAY
49 Dean of College of Arts & Sciences .... Dr. Paul SWETS
50 Dean College Business .... Dr. Corbett F. GAULDEN, JR.
53 Dean College of Education .... Dr. John MIAZGA
66 Dean College Health & Human Service .... Dr. Leslie MAYRAND
84 Assoc VP for Enrollment Mgmt .... Mr. Steven KLEIN
06 Director of Registrar Services .... Ms. Cindy WEEAKS
09 Asst VP Inst Res & Effectiveness .... Dr. Sarah LOGAN
08 Exec Director of Library .... Dr. Maurice G. FORTIN
36 Director Career Development .... Ms. Julie J. RUTHENBECK
15 Director of Human Resources .... Mr. Kurtis R. NEAL
14 Director Process/Integ Tech Archite .... Mr. Jeff SEFCIK
37 Director Student Financial Aid .... Ms. Michelle BENNETT
27 Director Communications & Mktg .... Mr. Preston LEWIS
29 Executive Director Alumni Assoc .... Vacant
35 Exec Dir Student Life & Services .... Mr. Philip N. MEARS
88 Director for Stdnt Involvement .... Mr. Rick E. GREIG
18 Director of Facilities Management .... Mr. Jay HALBERT
39 Director of Residential Programs .... Ms. Connie H. FRAZIER
40 Manager Bookstore .... Ms. Margaret BOX
51 Director Extended Studies .... Dr. Michael PEREZ
41 Athletic Director .... Ms. Kathleen L. BRASFIELD
19 Chief of University Police .... Mr. James E. ADAMS
13 Assoc VP Information Technology/CIO .... Mr. Douglas FOX
21 Exec Director of Business Services .... Mr. Greg PECINA
96 Director Purchasing and Operations .... Ms. Margaret MATA
92 Director of Honors Program .... Dr. Shirley EOFF
04 Executive Asst to the President .... Ms. Adelina C. MORALES
104 Director Center International Stds .... Dr. Sharynn TOMLIN

† Affiliated with Texas Tech University in Lubbock, TX

AOMA Graduate School of Integrative Medicine (F)

4701 West Gate Boulevard, Austin TX 78745

County: Travis FICE Identification: 031564
Unit ID: 429094
Telephone: (512) 454-1188 Carnegie Class: Spec/Health
FAX Number: (512) 454-7001 Calendar System: Quarter
URL: www.aoma.edu
Established: 1993 Annual Graduate Tuition & Fees: $11,767
Enrollment: 213 Coed
Affiliation or Control: Proprietary IRS Status: Proprietary
Highest Offering: Master's; No Undergraduates
Program: Professional
Accreditation: SC, ACUP

01 President .... Dr. William R. MORRIS
11 VP Student Svcs/Operations .... Ms. Anne PROVINCE
05 Vice President of Faculty .... Dr. Qianzhi WU
32 Dean of Students .... Mr. Robert LAGUNA
20 Program Director .... Ms. Lesley HAMILTON
08 Head Librarian .... Mr. David YORK
07 Dir Admissions & Student Services .... Ms. Hannah THORNTON
06 Registrar .... Ms. Kristen BORTHWICK
58 Dean of Academics .... Dr. Yuxin HE
88 Director of Herbal Studies .... Dr. Dongxin MA
88 Director of Biomedical Sciences .... Dr. Raja MANDYAM
45 Director of Research .... Dr. Yuxing LIU
88 Director Acupuncture .... Dr. Zheng ZENG
23 Clinic Business Director .... Ms. Laura COFFEY
18 Facilities Manager .... Mr. Stuart A. BAILEY
20 Academic Advisor .... Mr. Robert LAGUNA
31 Community Services Coordinator .... Ms. Sarah BENTLEY

Argosy University, Dallas (G)

5001 Lyndon B. Johnson Freeway, Farmers Branch TX 75244

County: Dallas Identification: 666181
Unit ID: 442222
Telephone: (214) 890-9900 Carnegie Class: Spec/Health
FAX Number: (214) 696-3900 Calendar System: Semester
URL: www.argosy.edu/dallas
Established: 2002 Annual Undergrad Tuition & Fees: $14,580
Enrollment: 629 Coed
Affiliation or Control: Proprietary IRS Status: Proprietary
Highest Offering: Doctorate
Program: Professional
Accreditation: &NH

01 Campus President .... Dr. Ronald HYSON
05 Vice President of Academic Affairs .... Dr. Nannette GLENN
32 Director of Student Services .... Brigit MATTIX
08 Director of Library Services .... Lee A. DETZEL
07 Director of Admissions .... Emily PECK
10 Business Manager .... Joy BIBB
06 Registrar .... Karl BARNETT
21 Assoc Dir of Student Account Svcs .... Karen WILKERSON
18 Director of Facilites and IT .... Rod CASKEY

† Regional accreditation is carried under the parent institution in Chicago, IL.

Arlington Baptist College (H)

3001 W Division, Arlington TX 76012-3497

County: Tarrant FICE Identification: 020814
Unit ID: 222877
Telephone: (817) 461-8741 Carnegie Class: Spec/Faith
FAX Number: (817) 274-1138 Calendar System: Semester
URL: www.abconline.edu
Established: 1939 Annual Undergrad Tuition & Fees: $7,000
Enrollment: 219 Coed
Affiliation or Control: Baptist IRS Status: 501(c)3
Highest Offering: Master's
Program: Teacher Preparatory; Professional; Religious Emphasis
Accreditation: BI

01 President .... Dr. D. L MOODY
05 Academic Dean .... Dr. Helen SULLIVAN
32 Dean of Students .... Rev. Emil BALLIET
10 Business Manager/Dir Financial Aid .... Mr. Gerald SMITH
06 Registrar/Director Admissions .... Ms. Janie TAYLOR
08 Head Librarian .... Ms. Jill BOTTICELLI
18 Director Physical Plant .... Mr. Mike JAMISON
21 Office Manager .... Mrs. Jill BOTTICELLI
40 Director Bookstore .... Mrs. Vickie BRYANT
30 Director Institutional Advancement .... Rev. Michael EVANS
41 Athletic Director .... Mr. Cliff MCDANIEL

Art Institute of Dallas (I)

8080 Park Lane, Suite 100, Dallas TX 75231-5900

County: Dallas FICE Identification: 025396
Unit ID: 224776
Telephone: (214) 692-8080 Carnegie Class: Spec/Arts
FAX Number: (214) 696-4898 Calendar System: Quarter
URL: www.aid.edu
Established: 1964 Annual Undergrad Tuition & Fees: $23,424
Enrollment: 2,084 Coed
Affiliation or Control: Proprietary IRS Status: Proprietary
Highest Offering: Baccalaureate
Program: Occupational; Fine Arts Emphasis
Accreditation: SC, ACFEI, CIDA

01 President .... Dr. Thomas W. NEWSOM
05 Vice President of Academic Affairs .... Dr. Leslie C. BAUGHMAN
07 Sr Director of Admissions .... Mrs. Dawn POLK-BRIDGES
11 Director Admin & Financial Svcs .... Mrs. Cecilia COLBERT
32 Dean of Student Affairs .... Mrs. April CHATHAM
36 Director Career Services .... Ms. Miriam K. JOHNSTON
15 Director Human Resources .... Ms. Shannon FULMER

The Art Institute of Houston (J)

4140 Southwest Freeway, Houston TX 77027

County: Harris FICE Identification: 021171
Unit ID: 222938
Telephone: (713) 623-2040 Carnegie Class: Spec/Arts
FAX Number: (713) 966-2700 Calendar System: Quarter
URL: www.aih.aii.edu
Established: 1978 Annual Undergrad Tuition & Fees: $29,280
Enrollment: 2,278 Coed
Affiliation or Control: Proprietary IRS Status: Proprietary
Highest Offering: Baccalaureate
Program: Occupational
Accreditation: SC, ACFEI, CIDA

01 President .... Larry HORN
05 Dean of Academic Advising .... Dr. Kenneth C. PASCAL
32 Dean of Student Affairs .... Michael MCKENNA
11 Dir Administrative/Financial Svcs .... Tom KUPER
07 Senior Director of Admissions .... Jane CHASTANT
15 Director of Human Resources .... Paige SHELTON
36 Director of Career Services .... Mary Kate ROBINSON

ATI Career Training Center (K)

10003 Technology Boulevard W, Dallas TX 75220-4316

County: Dallas FICE Identification: 025966
Unit ID: 249247
Telephone: (214) 902-8191 Carnegie Class: Assoc/PrivFP
FAX Number: (214) 358-7500 Calendar System: Semester
URL: www.aticareertraining.edu
Established: 1986 Annual Undergrad Tuition & Fees: $19,875
Enrollment: 1,367 Coed
Affiliation or Control: Proprietary IRS Status: Proprietary
Highest Offering: Associate Degree
Program: Occupational
Accreditation: #ACCSC

01 Executive Director of the School .... Ms. Sandra RASKA
37 Director Student Financial Aid .... Ms. Lyn CROSS
07 Director of Admissions .... Ms. Shermie HARGROVE

Austin College (A)

900 N Grand Avenue, Sherman TX 75090-4400
County: Grayson FICE Identification: 003543
Unit ID: 222983
Telephone: (903) 813-2000 Carnegie Class: Bac/A&S
FAX Number: (903) 813-3199 Calendar System: 4/1/4
URL: www.austincollege.edu
Established: 1849 Annual Undergrad Tuition & Fees: $31,270
Enrollment: 1,309 Coed
Affiliation or Control: Presbyterian Church (U.S.A.) IRS Status: 501(c)3
Highest Offering: Master's
Program: Liberal Arts And General; Teacher Preparatory
Accreditation: SC

01 President .... Dr. Marjorie HASS
05 Vice President Academic Affairs .... Dr. Michael A. IMHOFF
32 Vice Pres Student Affairs/Athletics .... Mr. Timothy P. MILLERICK
30 Vice Pres Institutional Advancement .... Mr. Brooks A. HULL
10 Vice President for Business Affairs .... Ms. Heidi B. ELLIS
84 Vice President for Inst Enrollment .... Ms. Nan M. DAVIS
20 Associate VP for Inst Effectiveness .... Dr. Karen H. NELSON
07 Asst VP Institutional Enrollment .... Ms. Laurie COULTER
88 Assistant VP for Inst Advancement .... Ms. Cary E. WACKER
09 Director Inst Planning/Research .... Vacant
88 Exec Dir Transfer/Intrntl Admission .... Mr. David DILLMAN
42 Chaplain/Dir of Church Relations .... Dr. John D. WILLIAMS
35 Director of Student Life .... Mr. Michael DEEN
06 Registrar .... Mr. Texas RUEGG
08 College Librarian/Library Director .... Mr. John R. WEST
21 Director of Finance .... Ms. Sheryl BRADSHAW
79 Dean of Humanities .... Dr. Patrick DUFFEY
81 Dean of Sciences .... Dr. Steve GOLDSMITH
83 Dean of Social Sciences .... Dr. Jerry B. JOHNSON
15 Director of Human Resources .... Mr. Keith L. LAREY
38 Dean of Student Services .... Dr. Rosemarie ROTHMEIER
36 Director Career Services .... Ms. Margie A. NORMAN
13 Exec Director Information Tech .... Mr. Bill EDGETTE
58 Director of Graduate Program .... Dr. Barbara N. SYLVESTER
104 Director Study Abroad .... Dr. Truett CATES
51 Coordinator of Continuing Education .... Ms. Carolyn CRANFORD
26 Director of Public Affairs .... Dr. Lynn Z. WOMBLE
29 Director Alumni & Parent Relations .... Ms. Cindy BEAN
25 Director of Stewardship .... Ms. Jill J. ROBERTS
44 Director of Leadership Giving Pgms .... Ms. Paula JONSE
19 Chief of Police .... Mr. James PERRY
40 Manager of Campus Store .... Ms. Linda FRANZEO
44 Senior Director of Development .... Ms. Ingrid HEALY
27 Sr Dir Editorial Communications .... Ms. Vickie S. KIRBY
18 Director of Physical Plant .... Mr. John L. JENNINGS
96 Purchasing Representative .... Ms. Jeannean SMITH

Austin Community College District (B)

5930 Middle Fiskville Road, Austin TX 78752-4390
County: Travis FICE Identification: 012015
Unit ID: 222992
Telephone: (512) 223-7000 Carnegie Class: Assoc/Pub-U-MC
FAX Number: (512) 223-7185 Calendar System: Semester
URL: www.austincc.edu
Established: 1972 Annual Undergrad Tuition & Fees (In-District): $1,740
Enrollment: 44,100 Coed
Affiliation or Control: State/Local IRS Status: 501(c)3
Highest Offering: Associate Degree
Program: Occupational; 2-Year Principally Bachelor's Creditable
Accreditation: SC, ACBSP, ACFEI, ADNUR, DH, DMS, EMT, MLTAD, OTA, PNUR, PTAA, RAD, SURGT

01 President/CEO .... Dr. Stephen B. KINSLOW
03 Exec Vice Pres College Operations .... Dr. Mary HENSLEY
10 Exec VP Finance & Administration .... Mr. Ben B. FERRELL
05 VP Instruction .... Mr. Michael T. MIDGLEY
32 VP Student Support/Success Systems .... Dr. Kathleen E. CHRISTENSEN
16 VP Human Resources .... Ms. Geraldine TUCKER
20 AVP College Access Programs .... Ms. Stephanie HAWLEY
24 AVP Instructional Resources/Tech .... Dr. Richard L. SMITH
13 AVP Information Technology .... Mr. Stanley T. GUNN
21 AVP Finance & Budget .... Mr. Neil W. VICKERS
09 VP Effectiveness & Accountability .... Ms. Soon O. MERZ
88 AVP Student Success .... Dr. Richard R. ARMENTA
17 Executive Dean Health Sciences .... Dr. Eileen KLEIN
51 Executive Dean Continuing Education .... Mr. Hector AGUILAR
88 Dean Appl Tech/Multimedia/Pub Svc .... Dr. Gary W. HAMPTON
50 Dean Business Studies .... Mr. Charles C. QUINN
72 Dean Computer Studies/Adv Tech .... Ms. Linda S. SMARZIK
57 Dean Arts & Humanities .... Mr. Lyman W. GRANT
60 Dean Communications .... Dr. Hazel WARD
81 Dean Math & Science .... Dr. David FONKEN
83 Dean Social & Behavioral Sciences .... Ms. Gaye Lynn SCOTT
62 Dean Library Services .... Dr. Julie B. TODARO
35 Dean Student Svcs-South Austin Camp .... Ms. Yolanda M. CHAPA
35 Dean Student Svcs-Riverside Campus .... Dr. Virginia M. FRAIRE
35 Dean Student Svcs-Cypress Creek Cam .... Ms. Amber L. KELLEY
35 Dean Student Svcs-Eastview Campus .... Mr. Dorado M. KINNEY
35 Dean Student Services-Northridge .... Mr. Clint R. RODENFELS
35 Dean Student Services-Pinnacle .... Mr. George R. REYES
35 Dean Student Services-Round Rock .... Dr. Louella H. TATE
35 Dean Student Services-Rio Grande .... Dr. Voncille T. WRIGHT
88 Executive Director Adult Education .... Mr. David S. BORDEN
88 Exec Dir Customized Trng/Bus Assmt .... Ms. Kathy M. WALTON
88 Exec Director School Relations .... Ms. Luanne E. PRESTON
88 Exec Dir Early College HS .... Ms. Sharon H. FREDERICK
25 Exec Dir Grant Development .... Ms. Mary E. HARRIS
88 Exec Dir Tech Prep Consortium .... Mr. Patrick W. ABBOTT
88 Exec Dir College & Career Prep Pgm .... Ms. Annette K. GREGORY
18 Exec Dir Facilities & Construction .... Mr. William S. MULLANE
27 Exec Dir Public Info & College Mktg .... Ms. Brette E. LEA
102 Executive Director ACC Foundation .... Ms. Stephanie C. DIINA-DEMPSEY
88 Executive Director .... Ms. Susan P. DAWSON
07 Director Admissions/Records .... Ms. Linda A. KLUCK
80 Dir Ctr for Pub Policy & Pol Stds .... Mr. William R. YOUNG
88 Director Internal Audit .... Mr. Imad A. MOUCHAYLEH
37 Director Student Asst/Veterans .... Ms. Teresita BAZAN
88 Director P-16 Initiatives .... Mr. Gary L. MADSEN
88 Director Analysis & Policy .... Mr. Jim VANOVERSCHELDE
04 Spec Asst to Pres External Affairs .... Ms. Linda K. YOUNG
04 Special Asst to the President/CEO .... Mr. Joe M. LOSTRACCO

Austin Graduate School of Theology (C)

7640 Guadalupe Street, Austin TX 78752
County: Travis FICE Identification: 023628
Unit ID: 247825
Telephone: (512) 476-2772 Carnegie Class: Spec/Faith
FAX Number: (512) 476-3919 Calendar System: Semester
URL: www.austingrad.edu
Established: 1976 Annual Undergrad Tuition & Fees: $9,300
Enrollment: 100 Coed
Affiliation or Control: Independent Non-Profit IRS Status: 501(c)3
Highest Offering: Master's
Program: Liberal Arts And General; Professional; Religious Emphasis
Accreditation: SC

01 President .... Dr. Stanley G. REID
07 Admissions Director/Registrar .... Mrs. Celeste SCARBAROUGH
37 Financial Aid Administrator .... Mr. Dave ARTHUR

Austin Presbyterian Theological Seminary (D)

100 E 27th Street, Austin TX 78705-5797
County: Travis FICE Identification: 003544
Unit ID: 223001
Telephone: (512) 472-6736 Carnegie Class: Spec/Faith
FAX Number: (512) 479-0738 Calendar System: Semester
URL: www.austinseminary.edu
Established: 1902 Annual Graduate Tuition & Fees: $11,945
Enrollment: 127 Coed
Affiliation or Control: Presbyterian Church (U.S.A.) IRS Status: 501(c)3
Highest Offering: Doctorate; No Undergraduates
Program: Professional
Accreditation: SC, THEOL

01 President .... Rev. Theodore J. WARDLAW
05 Academic Dean .... Dr. Michael JINKINS
10 Vice President for Business Affairs .... Mr. Kurt A. GABBARD
26 Vice Pres Institutional Advancement .... Ms. Donna SCOTT
32 Vice Pres Student Affairs/Vocation .... Rev. Jackie SAXON
07 Vice President for Admissions .... Rev. John H. BARDEN
88 Director of Seminary Relations .... Rev. David EVANS
30 Director of Development .... Ms. Elizabeth SHUMAKER
51 Dir Christian Leadership Education .... Rev. Janet MAYKUS
08 Director of the Library .... Rev. Timothy LINCOLN
06 Registrar .... Ms. Jacqueline D. HEFLEY

Baptist Health System School of Health Professions (E)

8400 Datapoint Drive, San Antonio TX 78229
County: Bexar Identification: 006606
Unit ID: 223083
Telephone: (210) 297-9630 Carnegie Class: Not Classified
FAX Number: (210) 297-0075 Calendar System: Semester
URL: www.bshp.edu
Established: 1903 Annual Undergrad Tuition & Fees: N/A
Enrollment: 495 Coed
Affiliation or Control: Proprietary IRS Status: Proprietary
Highest Offering: Associate Degree
Program: Occupational
Accreditation: ABHES, ADNUR, RAD, SURGT, SURTEC

01 Dean .... Dr. Karen A. STIEFEL

† Tuition varies by degree program.

Baptist Missionary Association Theological Seminary (F)

P.O. Box 670/1530 E Pine Street,
Jacksonville TX 75766-5407
County: Cherokee FICE Identification: 023312
Unit ID: 223117
Telephone: (903) 586-2501 Carnegie Class: Spec/Faith
FAX Number: (903) 586-0378 Calendar System: Semester
URL: www.bmats.edu
Established: 1957 Annual Undergrad Tuition & Fees: $4,850
Enrollment: 132 Coed
Affiliation or Control: Baptist IRS Status: 501(c)3
Highest Offering: Master's
Program: Professional
Accreditation: SC, THEOL

01 President .... Dr. Charley HOLMES
06 Registrar .... Dr. Philip ATTEBERY

Baptist University of the Americas (G)

8019 S Pan Am Expressway, San Antonio TX 78224-1336
County: Bexar FICE Identification: 037333
Unit ID: 444398
Telephone: (210) 924-4338 Carnegie Class: Spec/Faith
FAX Number: (210) 924-2701 Calendar System: Semester
URL: www.bua.edu
Established: 1947 Annual Undergrad Tuition & Fees: $6,600
Enrollment: 233 Coed
Affiliation or Control: Baptist IRS Status: 501(c)3
Highest Offering: Baccalaureate
Program: 2-Year Principally Bachelor's Creditable; Liberal Arts And General; Religious Emphasis
Accreditation: BI

01 President .... Mr. Rene MACIEL
10 Chief Financial Officer .... Mr. Mike MCCARTHY
30 Vice President for Advancement .... Rev. Teo CISNEROS
03 Executive Vice President & Provost .... Dr. Javier ELIZONDO
05 Dean of Curriculum & Faculty Devel .... Dr. F. Marconi MONTEIRO
04 Special Assistant to the President .... Mr. Craig BIRD
84 Director of Enrollment Management .... Ms. Mary RANJEL
37 Financial Aid Administrator .... Mrs. Araceli ACOSTA
88 Dean of the Bible Baptist Institute .... Dr. Moises RODRIGUEZ

Baylor College of Medicine (H)

One Baylor Plaza, Houston TX 77030-3411
County: Harris FICE Identification: 004949
Unit ID: 223223
Telephone: (713) 798-4951 Carnegie Class: Spec/Med
FAX Number: (713) 798-3692 Calendar System: Quarter
URL: www.bcm.edu
Established: 1900 Annual Graduate Tuition & Fees: $19,868
Enrollment: 1,489 Coed
Affiliation or Control: Independent Non-Profit IRS Status: 501(c)3
Highest Offering: Doctorate; No Undergraduates
Program: Professional
Accreditation: SC, ANEST, ARCPA, DIETI, IPSY, MED

00 Chancellor .... Dr. Bobby R. ALFORD
01 President and CEO .... Dr. Paul KLOTMAN
17 Sr VP and Dean Clinical Affairs .... Dr. Stephen J. SPANN
10 Sr VP Finance & Admin/CFO .... Mrs. Kim DAVID
30 VP Development/Advancement .... Ms. Lisa KENNEDY
43 Vice Pres/General Counsel/Corp Sec .... Mr. Robert F. CORRIGAN, JR.
27 VP Communications/Govt Rels .... Ms. Claire M. BASSETT
63 Sr VP/Dean of Medical Education .... Dr. Stephen B. GREENBERG
58 Sr VP/Dean Grad Sch Biomed Science .... Dr. William R. BRINKLEY
76 Sr VP & Dean Allied Health Programs .... Dr. J. David HOLCOMB
15 Vice President Human Resources .... Dr. Rachel CAILLOUET
46 Vice President for Research .... Dr. Adam KUSPA
93 Senior Associate Dean .... Dr. James L. PHILLIPS
07 Senior Associate Dean Admissions .... Dr. Lloyd H. MICHAEL
51 Sr Assoc Dean Continuing Education .... Dr. C. Michael FORDIS, JR.
32 Sr Associate Dean Student Affairs .... Dr. Donald T. DONOVAN
58 Sr Assoc Dean Graduate School .... Dr. Hiram F. GILBERT
88 Associate Dean Graduate School .... Dr. Scott F. BASINGER
63 Sr Assoc Dean Grad Medical Educ .... Dr. Linda ANDREWS
88 Associate Dean Res Assurances .... Dr. Stacey L. BERG
88 Associate Dean Medical Education .... Dr. Elizabeth A. NELSON
88 Asst Dean Graduate Education .... Dr. Gayle R. SLAUGHTER
88 Asst Dean Graduate Medical Educ .... Dr. Jacqueline LEVESQUE
88 Associate Dean for Admissions .... Dr. Graciela B. VILLARREAL
35 Assoc Dean Student Affairs & Admin .... Dr. Florence F. EDDINS-FOLENSBEE
09 Associate Dean for Research .... Dr. Placido GRINO
88 Associate Dean Clinical Affairs .... Dr. John W. BURRUSS
88 Assoc Dean Undergrad Med Education .... Dr. Jerry C. GOODMAN
13 Int Chief Info Technology Officer .... Ms. Jenifer JARRIEL
21 Controller .... Mr. Douglas R. SPADE
88 Chief Performance Improvement Ofcr .... Mr. Navneet KATHURIA
37 Director Student Financial Planning .... Ms. Hilda DELEON
06 Registrar/Dir of Student Affairs .... Mr. John RAPP
88 Director Environmental Safety .... Mr. Paul MURACA
23 Director Occupational Medicine .... Dr. James E. KELAHER
29 Sr Director Alumni Affairs .... Ms. Barbara WALKER
25 Sr Director of Grants & Contracts .... Mr. Peter J. MARABELLA
19 Director of Security .... Vacant
85 Director International Services .... Ms. Bonnie WEISMAN
22 Sr Director Employee Relations .... Mr. Dane K. FRIEND
96 Director Supply Chain Management .... Mr. Bud BOCCHINO
28 Co-Chair Diversity Council .... Dr. Gayle R. SLAUGHTER

Baylor University (I)

One Bear Place #97096, Waco TX 76798
County: McLennan FICE Identification: 003545
Unit ID: 223232
Telephone: (254) 710-1011 Carnegie Class: RU/H
FAX Number: (254) 710-3557 Calendar System: Semester
URL: www.baylor.edu
Established: 1845 Annual Undergrad Tuition & Fees: $32,088
Enrollment: 14,900 Coed
Affiliation or Control: Baptist IRS Status: 501(c)3
Highest Offering: Doctorate

Program: Liberal Arts And General; Teacher Preparatory; Professional
Accreditation: SC, AAFCS, BUS, BUSA, CIDA, CLPSY, CS, DIETD, ENG, HSA, JOUR, LAW, MIDWF, MUS, NMT, NURSE, PTA, RAD, SP, SW, TED, THEA, THEOL

01 President & CEO .... Judge Kenneth W. STARR
05 Executive Vice President & Provost .... Dr. Elizabeth DAVIS
29 Exec Vice President of Alumni Assoc .... Mr. Jeffrey L. KILGORE
32 Vice President Student Life .... Dr. Kevin JACKSON
30 Vice President Univ Development .... Dr. Jerry T. HAAG
10 Vice Pres Finance & Administration .... Dr. Reagan RAMSOWER
26 Vice President Marketing & Comm .... Mr. John BARRY
13 VP for IT & Dean of Libraries .... Ms. Pattie ORR
84 Asst Vice Pres Enrollment Mgmt .... Mrs. Diana M. RAMEY
07 Asst Vice President of Admissions .... Ms. Jennifer CARRON
21 Treasurer .... Mr. Bob C. SPENCE
21 Asc VP Operational Plng/Budget Dir ... Mr. Wilson E. MCGREGOR
09 Director Inst Research/Testing .... Dr. Kathleen MORLEY
37 Asst Vice Pres Student Fin Services .... Mrs. Jackie DIAZ
15 Associate VP for Human Resources .... Mr. John WHELAN
91 Associate VP Information Sys/Svcs .... Mrs. Becky L. KING
08 Associate Dean of Libraries .... Mr. Bill HAIR
93 Advisor for Minority Affairs .... Mrs. Pearle BEVERLY
04 Assistant to the President .... Vacant
49 Dean College of Arts/Sciences .... Dr. Lee C. NORDT
50 Dean School of Business .... Dr. Terry S. MANESS
53 Dean School of Education .... Dr. Jon ENGELHARDT
61 Dean School of Law .... Mr. Bradley J B. TOBEN
64 Dean School of Music .... Dr. William V. MAY
66 Interim Dean School of Nursing .... Dr. Martha M. BRADSHAW
58 Dean Graduate School .... Dr. Larry LYON
73 Dean Truett Theological Sem .... Dr. David GARLAND
54 Dean Engineering & Computer Science .. Dr. Benjamin S. KELLEY
92 Dean Honors College .... Dr. Thomas S. HIBBS
43 General Counsel .... Mr. Charles D. BECKENHAUER
85 Int Dir Ctr for International Educ .... Mr. Naymond KEATHLEY
35 Dean for Campus Life .... Dr. Martha Lou SCOTT
39 Dean Student Learning & Engagement .... Mr. Jeff DOYLE
42 University Chaplain .... Dr. Burt BURLESON
88 Assoc Dn Judicial/Legal Stdnt Svcs ...... Ms. Bethany J. MCCRAW
41 Director of Athletics .... Mr. Ian J. MCCAW
20 Director Academic Support Programs .... Ms. Sally E. FIRMIN
06 Director of Registration .... Ms. Anna Kay HOLLON-HARRIS
23 Medical Director Health Center .... Dr. Sharon STERN
36 Int Director Career Services Center .... Mr. Brandon MILLER
18 Director of Facilities Management .... Mr. Don BAGBY
19 Director of Public Safety .... Mr. James W. DOAK
25 Director of Sponsored Programs .... Ms. Lisa MCKETHAN
38 Dir Counseling Svcs/Integrated Life .... Dr. Jim MARSH
40 General Manager Bookstore .... Mr. Paul LITTLE
27 Director Univ Oper/Host Services .... Mr. Chris KRAUSE
100 Chief of Staff .... Dr. Karla LEEPER
86 Director of Governmental Relations .... Ms. Rochonda FARMER-NEAL
90 Director of Academic Technology Ctr .... Mr. Timothy M. LOGAN
96 Dir of Purchasing/Campus Services .... Mr. Tom HOFFMEYER

Blinn College (A)

902 College Avenue, Brenham TX 77833-4098
County: Washington FICE Identification: 003549
Unit ID: 223427
Telephone: (979) 830-4000 Carnegie Class: Assoc/Pub-R-L
FAX Number: (979) 830-4030 Calendar System: Semester
URL: www.blinn.edu
Established: 1883 Annual Undergrad Tuition & Fees (In-District): $1,728
Enrollment: 17,755 Coed
Affiliation or Control: State/Local IRS Status: 501(c)3
Highest Offering: Associate Degree
Program: Occupational; 2-Year Principally Bachelor's Creditable
Accreditation: SC, ADNUR, DH, EMT, IFSAC, PTAA, RAD

01 President/CEO .... Dr. Harold NOLTE, JR.
05 Vice President Academic Affairs .... Dr. Debra R. LACOUR
32 Int Vice Pres Student Services .... Dr. Kathleen ANZIVINO
10 Vice Pres Administrative Services .... Dr. Van MILLER
12 Provost of Brazos County Campuses .... Dr. Ted RASPILLER
103 VP Applied Science/Workforce Educ .... Dr. Robert BRICK
35 Dean of Students .... Dr. John D. HARRIS
32 Dean of Student Services .... Dr. Michel ZUCH
20 Dean Academic Affairs .... Dr. John BEAVER
09 Dean Inst Effectiveness/Accred .... Dr. Rosemary SUNDET
35 Associate Dean Student Affairs .... Mr. Robert J. HABERMANN
35 Associate Dean Student Affairs .... Mrs. Ann E. WEIR
27 Exec Admin of External Affairs .... Ms. Cathy BOEKER
11 Exec Dir Operations Brazos County .... Mr. Ted HAJOVSKY
102 Executive Director Foundation .... Mr. Joe Al PICONE
18 Exec Dir Facilities/Planning/Constr .... Mr. Richard O'MALLEY
12 Director Schulenburg Campus .... Ms. Rebecca GARLICK
12 Director Sealy Campus .... Ms. Jeri DULANEY
06 Registrar .... Ms. Julie MAASS
21 Director Accounting .... Mr. Thomas BRAZZEL
08 Director Library Services .... Ms. Linda FLYNN
38 Director of Counseling .... Mr. Robert LOVELIDGE
13 Dir Administrative Computing Svcs .... Ms. Christine WIED
37 Director Financial Aid .... Mr. Casey ACKER
15 Director Human Resources .... Ms. Karla ROPER
41 Athletic Director .... Mr. Dick SPEAS
18 Dir Facilities Maint/Transportation .... Mr. Dennis KOCICH
19 Chief College Police Department .... Mr. Claude FREE
96 Director Purchasing .... Mr. Ross SCHROEDER
07 Director Admissions & Records .... Ms. Sonia PATEL
27 Director of School Relations .... Ms. Jennifer BYNUM
26 Dir Marketing/Media Relations .... Mr. Jeff TILLEY
27 Asst Dir Marketing/Media Relations .... Mr. Brandon WEBB
29 Coord Campus Events/Alumni Affairs .... Mr. Glen VIERUS

Brazosport College (B)

500 College Drive, Lake Jackson TX 77566-3199
County: Brazoria FICE Identification: 007287
Unit ID: 223506
Telephone: (979) 230-3000 Carnegie Class: Assoc/Pub4
FAX Number: (979) 230-3443 Calendar System: Semester
URL: www.brazosport.edu
Established: 1948 Annual Undergrad Tuition & Fees (In-District): $1,692
Enrollment: 5,000 Coed
Affiliation or Control: Local IRS Status: 501(c)3
Highest Offering: Baccalaureate
Program: Occupational; 2-Year Principally Bachelor's Creditable
Accreditation: SC, EMT

01 President .... Dr. Millicent M. VALEK
05 Dean Educational Programs/Service .... Dr. Ken TASA
26 Dean for Information/Community Res .... Dr. John C. RAY
32 Dean for Student Services .... Dr. Pamela DAVENPORT
10 Dean for Business & Admin Services .... Mr. Fred SCOTT
15 Dean Human Resources & Payroll .... Dr. Herb E. MILES
08 Director Library Services .... Ms. Tami WISOFSKY
09 Director Institutional Research .... Dr. David PRESTON
07 Director Admissions/Registrar .... Mr. Wade WILSON
31 Director Community Education .... Ms. Catherine HANSON
21 Internal Auditor .... Mr. Christopher BAHR
27 Director/Public Info & Comm .... Dr. Patty SAYES
13 Director/Information Technology .... Mr. Ron PARKER
37 Director of Financial Aid .... Ms. Kay WRIGHT

Brite Divinity School (C)

2855 S University Drive, Fort Worth TX 76129-0001
County: Tarrant Identification: 666228
Unit ID: 450304
Telephone: (817) 257-7575 Carnegie Class: Spec/Faith
FAX Number: (817) 257-7305 Calendar System: Semester
URL: www.brite.tcu.edu
Established: 1873 Annual Graduate Tuition & Fees: $18,000
Enrollment: 224 Coed
Affiliation or Control: Independent Non-Profit IRS Status: 501(c)3
Highest Offering: Doctorate; No Undergraduates
Program: Professional; Religious Emphasis
Accreditation: SC, THEOL

01 President & Chief Executive Officer .... Dr. D. Newell WILLIAMS
10 Vice President Business/Finance .... Alisa CODY
07 Director of Admission .... Valerie FROSTMAN

Career Point College (D)

599 Spencer Lane, San Antonio TX 78201
County: Bexar FICE Identification: 025911
Unit ID: 224439
Telephone: (210) 732-3000 Carnegie Class: Not Classified
FAX Number: (210) 734-9225 Calendar System: Other
URL: www.careerpointcollege.edu
Established: 1921 Annual Undergrad Tuition & Fees: $16,480
Enrollment: 1,844 Coed
Affiliation or Control: Proprietary IRS Status: Proprietary
Highest Offering: Baccalaureate
Program: Occupational; 2-Year Principally Bachelor's Creditable
Accreditation: ACICS

01 Director .... Ms. Kim MURGUIA

Center for Advanced Legal Studies (E)

3910 Kirby Drive, Suite 200, Houston TX 77098-4151
County: Harris FICE Identification: 026047
Unit ID: 379782
Telephone: (713) 529-2778 Carnegie Class: Assoc/PrivFP4
FAX Number: (713) 523-2715 Calendar System: Other
URL: www.paralegal.edu
Established: 1987 Annual Undergrad Tuition & Fees: $11,550
Enrollment: 250 Coed
Affiliation or Control: Proprietary IRS Status: Proprietary
Highest Offering: Associate Degree
Program: Occupational; Technical Emphasis
Accreditation: COE

01 President/CEO .... Mr. Doyle HAPPE

Central Texas College (F)

PO Box 1800, Killeen TX 76540-9990
County: Bell FICE Identification: 004003
Unit ID: 223816
Telephone: (254) 526-7161 Carnegie Class: Assoc/Pub-Spec
FAX Number: (254) 526-0817 Calendar System: Semester
URL: www.ctcd.edu
Established: 1965 Annual Undergrad Tuition & Fees (In-District): $1,416
Enrollment: 33,891 Coed
Affiliation or Control: Local IRS Status: 501(c)3
Highest Offering: Associate Degree
Program: Occupational; 2-Year Principally Bachelor's Creditable
Accreditation: SC, ADNUR, EMT, MLTAD

01 Chancellor .... Dr. James R. ANDERSON
03 Deputy Chanc Resource Mgmt .... Mr. Robert C. FARRELL
03 Deputy Chanc International/Navy Op .... Mr. Jim YEONOPOLUS
03 Deputy Chanc DL/TX Campus Op .... Mr. Bill ALEXANDER
05 Deputy Chanc Educ Pgm/Supp Svcs .... Dr. Dana WATSON
12 Dean Ft Hood/Service Area Campus .... Dr. Tina ADY
12 Dean Central Campus .... Mr. John HUNT
32 Dean Student Services .... Dr. Johnelle WELSH
08 Dean Library Services .... Ms. Deba SWAN
38 Associate Dean Guidance/Counseling .... Mr. David MCCLURE
06 Systems Registrar .... Ms. Lillian KROEGER
10 Comptroller .... Mr. Bob LIBERTY
16 Director Human Resource Mgmt .... Ms. Holly JORDAN
88 Director Risk Management .... Ms. Deborah SHIBLEY
106 Director Distance Education/Ed Tech .... Ms. Sharon DAVIS
18 Director Facilities Management .... Mr. Jim O'BRIEN
21 Director Business Services .... Ms. Michele CARTER
30 Director College Development .... Ms. Judy HEARTFIELD
09 Director Institutional Effectivenes .... Vacant
13 Director Information Technology .... Mr. Bruce KENDALL
07 Director Admissions/Recruitment .... Mr. Stephen O'DONOVAN
88 Director Testing .... Mr. George ERSKINE
85 Director International Student Svcs .... Mr. Byron EAKIN
88 Director Student Support Services .... Ms. Denise PERGL
88 Director Substance Abuse Resource . Dr. Gerald MAHONE-LEIWS
36 Director Career Planning/Placement .... Ms. Elaine RILEY
27 Dir Community Relations/Marketing .... Ms. Barbara MERLO
88 Liaison Military Programs .... Ms. Diana CASTILLO
19 Chief Police/Security Services .... Ms. Mary WHEELER
40 Manager Bookstore .... Mr. Gary FUDA

Cisco Junior College (G)

101 College Heights, Cisco TX 76437-1900
County: Eastland FICE Identification: 003553
Unit ID: 223898
Telephone: (254) 442-5000 Carnegie Class: Assoc/Pub-R-M
FAX Number: (254) 442-5100 Calendar System: Semester
URL: www.cisco.edu
Established: 1940 Annual Undergrad Tuition & Fees (In-State): $2,280
Enrollment: 4,215 Coed
Affiliation or Control: State IRS Status: 501(c)3
Highest Offering: Associate Degree
Program: Occupational; 2-Year Principally Bachelor's Creditable
Accreditation: SC, MAC, PNUR, SURGT

01 President .... Mr. Bobby SMITH
03 Executive Vice President .... Vacant
05 Vice Pres of LearningServices .... Ms. Dani DAY
32 Vice President for Student Services .... Dr. Jerry DODSON
12 Provost Abilene Education Center .... Dr. Carol DUPREE
84 Dean of Enrollment Management .... Mr. Olin O. ODOM, III
38 Dean of Counseling .... Mr. Randy LEATH
30 Director of Development .... Ms. Martha MONTGOMERY
37 Director of Financial Aid .... Ms. Dianne PHARR
15 Director Human Resources .... Ms. Pamela PAGE
35 Director New Student Services .... Ms. Paula CARPENTER
08 Director of Libraries .... Ms. Heather WILLIAMSON

Clarendon College (H)

PO Box 968, Clarendon TX 79226-0968
County: Donley FICE Identification: 003554
Unit ID: 223922
Telephone: (806) 874-3571 Carnegie Class: Assoc/Pub-R-S
FAX Number: (806) 874-3201 Calendar System: Semester
URL: www.clarendoncollege.edu
Established: 1898 Annual Undergrad Tuition & Fees (In-District): $2,592
Enrollment: 1,583 Coed
Affiliation or Control: State/Local IRS Status: 501(c)3
Highest Offering: Associate Degree
Program: Occupational; 2-Year Principally Bachelor's Creditable
Accreditation: SC

01 President .... Dr. Phil E. SHIRLEY
05 Dean of Instruction .... Mr. Tex BUCKHAULTS
12 Vice Pres of Campus Affairs .... Mr. Ray JARAMILLO
32 Dean of Student Services .... Mr. Tex BUCKHAULTS
08 Librarian .... Ms. Reagan SILVA
11 Dean of Admission Services .... Ms. Annette FERGUSON
37 Director of Financial Aid .... Ms. Michele COPELIN
06 Registrar .... Ms. Brandi HAVENS
81 Div Chr Science/Health/Liberal Arts .... Mrs. Scarlet ESTLACK

Coastal Bend College (I)

3800 Charco Road, Beeville TX 78102-2197
County: Bee FICE Identification: 003546
Unit ID: 223320
Telephone: (361) 358-2838 Carnegie Class: Assoc/Pub-R-M
FAX Number: (361) 358-3971 Calendar System: Semester
URL: www.coastalbend.edu
Established: 1965 Annual Undergrad Tuition & Fees (In-District): $2,400
Enrollment: 4,348 Coed
Affiliation or Control: State/Local IRS Status: 501(c)3
Highest Offering: Associate Degree
Program: Occupational; 2-Year Principally Bachelor's Creditable
Accreditation: SC, DH, RAD

01 President .... Dr. Thomas B. BAYNUM

32 Dean of Student Services ....Ms. Velma ELIZALDE
11 Dean of Administrative Services ....Ms. Ruth CUDE
07 Director of Admissions/Registrar ....Ms. Alicia ULLOA
30 Dir Institutional Advancement/PR ....Ms. Susan SMEDLEY
05 Director of Academic Programs ....Mrs. Alma ADAMEZ
25 Director of Grants/Special Projects ....Mrs. Velma ELIZALDE
37 Director of Financial Aid ....Ms. Nora MORALES
12 Director of Alice Campus ....Dr. Patricia CANDIA
12 Director of Kingsville Campus ....Mrs. Ann HARRELL
12 Coordinator Pleasanton Campus ....Ms. Teresa VILLANUEVA
09 Institutional Research Director ....Mr. Randy LINDEMAN
08 Director Library Services ....Ms. Sarah MILNARICH
15 Personnel Director ....Ms. Kathlyn PATTON
18 Chief Facilities/Physical Plant ....Mr. David ROME
26 Chief Public Relations Officer ....Mr. Adrian JACKSON

College of Biblical Studies-Houston (A)

7000 Regency Square, Houston TX 77036-3211
County: Harris FICE Identification: 034224
Unit ID: 388520
Telephone: (713) 785-5995 Carnegie Class: Spec/Faith
FAX Number: (713) 785-5998 Calendar System: Trimester
URL: www.cbshouston.edu
Established: 1976 Annual Undergrad Tuition & Fees: $9,036
Enrollment: 447 Coed
Affiliation or Control: Independent Non-Profit IRS Status: 501(c)3
Highest Offering: Baccalaureate
Program: Religious Emphasis
Accreditation: BI

01 President ....Dr. Jay A. QUINE
00 Chancellor ....Dr. William D. BOYD
04 Exec Administrative Assistant ....Mrs. Vicki PATTERSON
05 VP Academic Affairs/Acad Dean ....Mr. Joseph D. PARLE
10 VP Finance & Business Affairs ....Mr. Terence D. JUNG
30 Vice President Development ....Vacant
32 VP Enrollment Services ....Mr. Paul D. KEITH
08 Director of Library Services ....Mr. Artis LOVELADY, III
09 Assoc VP Institutionl Effectiveness ....Dr. Beverly R. LUCAS
13 Director Information Technology ....Mr. M. Shane BOOTHE
06 Registrar ....Ms. Laura Y. HAMILTON
88 Dir Christian Service Program ....Dr. Andre MORGAN
21 Controller ....Mrs. Betty-Ann W. MCNAIR
15 Director Human Resources ....Mrs. Patricia ARBUCKLE
26 Director of Communications ....Mr. T. Lee BOULDIN
37 Director Student Financial Aid ....Ms. Roshanna HARDISON
40 Director Bookstore ....Mr. Terry BRYAN
84 Director of Marketing and PR ....Ms. Meliinda MERILAT

College of the Mainland (B)

1200 Amburn Road, Texas City TX 77591-2499
County: Galveston FICE Identification: 007096
Unit ID: 226408
Telephone: (409) 938-1211 Carnegie Class: Assoc/Pub-R-M
FAX Number: (409) 938-1306 Calendar System: Semester
URL: www.com.edu
Established: 1966 Annual Undergrad Tuition & Fees (In-District): $1,623
Enrollment: 4,352 Coed
Affiliation or Control: Local IRS Status: 501(c)3
Highest Offering: Associate Degree
Program: Occupational; 2-Year Principally Bachelor's Creditable
Accreditation: SC, ADNUR, EMT, MAC

01 President ....Dr. Michael ELAM
05 Vice President Instruction ....Dr. Amy LOCKLEAR
10 VP College & Financial Services ....Ms. Lisa TEMPLER
32 VP for Enrollment/Student Success ....Dr. Rod FLUKER
15 Associate VP Human Resources ....Ms. Teresa HUDSON
20 Dean General Education Programs ....Dr. Amy LOCKLEAR
35 Assoc VP Student Success & Conduct ....Ms. Kris KIMBARK
06 Assoc VP for Enrollment/Registrar ....Mrs. Kelly MUSICK
18 Assoc VP Facility Services ....Mr. Peter EARLY
08 Director Library Services ....Ms. Kathryn PARK
27 Chief Information Officer ....Mr. David DIVINE
26 Director Marketing & Communications ....Ms. Lana PIGAO
37 Director of Student Financial Svcs ....Mr. Carl GORDON
102 Director of Foundation ....Ms. Monica O'NEAL
28 Director of Diversity & Equity ....Ms. Lonica BUSH
96 Director of Purchasing ....Mr. Nunzio ARCIDIACONO
09 Director of Inst Research & Effec ....Dr. Katherine FRIEDRICH
21 Controller ....Ms. Helen DUVALL

The College of Saint Thomas More (C)

3020 Lubbock Avenue, Fort Worth TX 76109-2323
County: Tarrant FICE Identification: 031894
Unit ID: 420352
Telephone: (817) 923-8459 Carnegie Class: Bac/A&S
FAX Number: (817) 924-3206 Calendar System: Semester
URL: www.cstm.edu
Established: 1981 Annual Undergrad Tuition & Fees: $12,850
Enrollment: 73 Coed
Affiliation or Control: Roman Catholic IRS Status: 501(c)3
Highest Offering: Baccalaureate
Program: Liberal Arts And General
Accreditation: SC

00 Chancellor Emeritus ....Dr. James A. PATRICK
01 President ....Mr. Michael KING
05 Dean ....Dr. Ryan D. MADISON
06 Registrar/Dir Stdnt Financial Aid ....Mr. John HEITZENRATER
08 Head Librarian ....Vacant
10 Bursar ....Vacant
88 Office Manager ....Mrs. Sharon KIRK

Collin County Community College District (D)

3452 Spur 399, McKinney TX 75069
County: Collin FICE Identification: 023614
Unit ID: 247834
Telephone: (972) 758-3800 Carnegie Class: Assoc/Pub-S-MC
FAX Number: (972) 758-5468 Calendar System: Semester
URL: www.collin.edu
Established: 1985 Annual Undergrad Tuition & Fees (In-District): $1,434
Enrollment: 27,069 Coed
Affiliation or Control: State/Local IRS Status: 501(c)3
Highest Offering: Associate Degree
Program: Occupational; 2-Year Principally Bachelor's Creditable
Accreditation: SC, ADNUR, DH, SURGT

01 President ....Dr. Cary A. ISRAEL
05 Sr VP Acad Affairs/Student Dev ....Dr. Colleen SMITH
12 VP/Provost Spring Creek Campus ....Dr. Mary MCRAE
12 VP/Provost Preston Ridge Campus ....Dr. Brenda K. KIHL
12 VP/Provost Central Park Campus ....Dr. Sherry SCHUMANN
32 Vice President Student Development ....Dr. Barbara MONEY
10 Vice President Admin Svcs & CFO ....Mr. Ralph G. HALL
16 Vice Pres Org Effectiveness & HR ....Ms. Kim K. DAVISON
26 Executive Director College & PR ....Ms. Lisa R. VASQUEZ
09 Assoc VP Rsrch & Inst Effectiveness ....Dr. Thomas K. MARTIN
20 Int AVP Teach/Learning ....Dr. Kimberly HARRIS
20 Dean Acad Affs-STEM Preston Ridge ....Mr. Jon HARDESTY
20 Dean Acad Aff Preston Ridge Campus ....Dr. Michael MCCONACHIE
20 Dean Acad Affs Central Park Campus ....Ms. Brenda C. CARTER
57 Dean Fine Arts ....Ms. Gaye M. COOKSEY
50 Dean Business/Computer Systems ....Mr. William J. BLITT
79 Dean Communications/Humanities ....Ms. Marianne LAYER
83 Dean Social/Behavioral Sciences ....Mr. Gary B. HODGE
81 Dean Mathematics/Natural Science ....Dr. L. Cameron NEAL, JR.
76 Dean Health Sciences/Emergency Svcs ....Mr. Abe JOHNSON
88 Dean Developmental Education ....Dr. Donald WEASENFORTH
51 Assoc VP Cont Educ/Workforce Dev ....Mr. Stephen R. HARDY
102 Executive Director of Foundation ....Ms. Bonni BROPHY
35 Dean of Students ....Mr. Terrence BRENNAN
88 Dean Acad Advising/Student Success ....Ms. Stephanie MEINHARDT
06 Registrar/Director Admissions ....Mr. Todd E. FIELDS
84 Dean Enroll/Acad Success Momentum ....Ms. Alicia L. HUPPE
38 Assoc Dean Counseling/Career Svcs ....Dr. Linda R. QUALIA
37 Director Financial Aid/Vets Affairs ....Ms. Debra WILKISON
85 International Student Coordinator ....Ms. Rebecca C. CROWELL
13 Chief Information Systems Officer ....Mr. David R. HOYT
21 Assoc VP/Controller ....Vacant
21 Assoc VP Financial Svcs & Reporting ....Ms. Barbara JINDRA
19 Dist Dir Safety/Sec/Fac/Construct ....Mr. Ed C. LEATHERS
96 Director Purchasing ....Ms. Cynthia L. WHITE
40 Director Auxiliary Services ....Mr. David S. HUSTED
15 AVP Human Resources/Org Dev ....Ms. Norma SMITH
88 Assoc Dean Collin Higher Ed Center ....Dr. Eric YEAGER
08 Exec Dir Library Preston Ridge Cam ....Mr. John MULLIN
08 Exec Dir Library Central Park Cam ....Ms. Bobbie LONG
08 Exec Dir Library Spring Creek Cam ....Ms. Linda KYPRIOS

Commonwealth Institute of Funeral Service (E)

415 Barren Springs, Houston TX 77090-5913
County: Harris FICE Identification: 003556
Unit ID: 366261
Telephone: (281) 873-0262 Carnegie Class: Assoc/PrivNFP
FAX Number: (281) 873-5232 Calendar System: Quarter
URL: www.commonwealth.edu
Established: 1936 Annual Undergrad Tuition & Fees: $14,456
Enrollment: 177 Coed
Affiliation or Control: Independent Non-Profit IRS Status: 501(c)3
Highest Offering: Associate Degree
Program: Occupational
Accreditation: FUSER

01 President ....Mr. Jason C. ALTIERI
05 Chief Academic Officer ....Mr. Stuart MOEN
20 Associate Academic Officer ....Mr. Christopher LAYTON
37 Director Student Financial Aid ....Ms. Jessika JENKINS
06 Registrar ....Ms. Patricia MORENO
08 Head Librarian ....Ms. Therisa MASSEY

Computer Career Center (F)

6101 Montana Avenue, El Paso TX 79925-2021
County: El Paso FICE Identification: 025720
Unit ID: 365204
Telephone: (915) 779-8031 Carnegie Class: Assoc/PrivFP
FAX Number: (915) 779-8097 Calendar System: Semester
URL: www.computercareercenter.com
Established: 1987 Annual Undergrad Tuition & Fees: $12,750
Enrollment: 394 Coed
Affiliation or Control: Proprietary IRS Status: Proprietary
Highest Offering: Associate Degree
Program: Occupational
Accreditation: COE, MAAB, MAC

01 Campus Director ....Mr. Antonio RICO
01 Campus Director ....Ms. Rebecca CANCHOLA
06 Registrar ....Ms. Valerie PARKS
07 Director of Admissions ....Ms. Andre ROYOS
36 Director Career Services ....Ms. Patricia STEPHENS
37 Director Student Financial Aid ....Ms. Mary VELARDE
63 Director Medical ....Ms. Juana CERVANTES

Concordia University Texas (G)

11400 Concordia University Drive, Austin TX 78726
County: Travis FICE Identification: 003557
Unit ID: 224004
Telephone: (512) 313-3000 Carnegie Class: Master's L
FAX Number: (512) 313-3339 Calendar System: Semester
URL: www.concordia.edu
Established: 1926 Annual Undergrad Tuition & Fees: $22,920
Enrollment: 2,573 Coed
Affiliation or Control: Lutheran Church - Missouri Synod
IRS Status: 501(c)3
Highest Offering: Master's
Program: Liberal Arts And General; Teacher Preparatory; Professional
Accreditation: SC, IACBE

01 President & CEO ....Dr. Thomas CEDEL
05 Provost ....Dr. Alan RUNGE
20 Asst Provost Quality Enhancement ....Dr. Trey BUCHANAN
10 Vice President Business Services ....Ms. Pamela LEE
30 Vice President External Relations ....Mr. Don ADAM
11 Vice President University Services ....Rev. David KLUTH
45 VP Strategic Planning & Assessment ....Mr. C. Gary BELCHER
84 Vice Prov Enrollmnt/Student Support ....Ms. Kristi KIRK
55 Vice Provost for Remote Operations ....Ms. Tammy STEWART
42 Campus Pastor ....Rev. Bruce PEFFER
50 Dean College of Business ....Dr. Donald CHRISTIAN
53 Dean College of Education ....Dr. James MCCONNELL
49 Dean College of Liberal Arts ....Dr. Ken SCHMIDT
81 Dean College of Science ....Dr. Michael MOYER
55 Center Dean Austin ....Dr. DeEadra ALBERT-GREEN
55 Center Dean Ft Worth ....Dr. Mary MAY
55 Center Dean Houston ....Mr. Christopher LESLIE
55 Center Dean San Antonio ....Dr. Mary DARDEN
06 Registrar ....Ms. Connie BERAN
41 Athletic Director ....Mr. Daniel HUNTLEY
32 Director of Student Services ....Mr. Richard POWERS
08 Director of Library Services ....Ms. Mikail MCINTOSH-DOTY
66 Director Nursing Program ....Dr. Joy PENTICUFF
58 Director MED Graduate Program ....Dr. Chris WINKLER
58 Director MBA Graduate Program ....Dr. Elise BRAZIER
37 Director Student Financial Services ....Mr. Russell JEFFREY
07 Director of Admissions ....Ms. Kristin COULTER
13 Director of Information Systems ....Mr. DeWayne MANGAN
19 Chief of Police ....Vacant
15 Director Human Resources ....Ms. Colleen CRAWFORD
40 Director Bookstore ....Vacant
09 Director of Institutional Research ....Vacant
29 Director Alumni Relations ....Ms. Amy HUTH
18 Director Facilities Management ....Mr. Eric BOOTH
21 Director of Finance ....Ms. Cynthia GOODWIN
38 Director Student Success Center ....Ms. Ruth COOPER
36 Director Career Center ....Ms. Joyce SINCLAIR
26 Associate VP Communications ....Ms. Melinda BRASHER
35 Assistant Director Student Services ....Mr. John ADAMS
39 Director of Residential Life ....Ms. Sarah EBERLE

Court Reporting Institute of Dallas (H)

1341 W Mockingbird Lane, Suite 200E,
Dallas TX 75247-4968
County: Dallas FICE Identification: 021192
Unit ID: 224183
Telephone: (214) 350-9722 Carnegie Class: Assoc/PrivFP
FAX Number: (214) 631-0143 Calendar System: Quarter
URL: www.crid.com
Established: 1978 Annual Undergrad Tuition & Fees: $13,800
Enrollment: 548 Coed
Affiliation or Control: Proprietary IRS Status: Proprietary
Highest Offering: Associate Degree
Program: Occupational; 2-Year Principally Bachelor's Creditable; Technical Emphasis
Accreditation: ACICS

01 Campus Director ....Mr. Larry P. PAIZ
05 Academic Dean ....Mr. William HOLLER

Court Reporting Institute of Houston (I)

13101 Northwest Freeway, Suite 100, Houston TX 77040
County: Harris Identification: 666730
Telephone: (713) 996-8300 Carnegie Class: Not Classified
FAX Number: (713) 996-8360 Calendar System: Quarter
URL: www.crid.com
Established: 1978 Annual Undergrad Tuition & Fees: $9,320
Enrollment: 800 Coed
Affiliation or Control: Proprietary IRS Status: Proprietary
Highest Offering: Associate Degree
Program: Occupational
Accreditation: ACICS

01	Campus Director	Mr. DeShunta WOODS

† Branch campus of Court Reporting Institute of Dallas, Dallas, TX.

Criswell College (A)

4010 Gaston Avenue, Dallas TX 75246-1537

County: Dallas — FICE Identification: 041218 — Unit ID: 224208
Telephone: (214) 821-5433 — Carnegie Class: Not Classified
FAX Number: (214) 818-1310 — Calendar System: Semester
URL: www.criswell.edu
Established: 1970 — Annual Undergrad Tuition & Fees: $8,500
Enrollment: 361 — Coed
Affiliation or Control: Independent Non-Profit — IRS Status: 501(c)3
Highest Offering: Master's
Program: Religious Emphasis
Accreditation: SC

01	President	Jerry JOHNSON
05	Executive Vice Pres & Provost	Lamar E. COOPER, SR.
30	Vice President for Development	Vacant
10	Vice President Business & Finance	Mike RODGERS
84	Director Enrollment/Academic Svcs	Joe THOMAS

Culinary Institute LeNotre (B)

7070 Allensby, Houston TX 77022-4322

County: Harris — FICE Identification: 037233 — Unit ID: 444565
Telephone: (713) 692-0077 — Carnegie Class: Not Classified
FAX Number: (713) 692-7399 — Calendar System: Other
URL: www.culinaryinstitute.edu
Established: 1998 — Annual Undergrad Tuition & Fees: N/A
Enrollment: 370 — Coed
Affiliation or Control: Proprietary — IRS Status: Proprietary
Highest Offering: Associate Degree
Program: Occupational
Accreditation: ACCSC, ACFEI

01	School Director	Mark STROEH

Dallas Baptist University (C)

3000 Mountain Creek Parkway, Dallas TX 75211-9299

County: Dallas — FICE Identification: 003560 — Unit ID: 224226
Telephone: (214) 333-7100 — Carnegie Class: Master's L
FAX Number: (214) 333-6863 — Calendar System: 4/1/4
URL: www.dbu.edu
Established: 1898 — Annual Undergrad Tuition & Fees: $5,470
Enrollment: 19,800 — Coed
Affiliation or Control: Baptist — IRS Status: 501(c)3
Highest Offering: Doctorate
Program: Liberal Arts And General; Teacher Preparatory; Professional
Accreditation: SC, ACBSP, MUS

01	President	Dr. Gary R. COOK
04	Assistant to the President	Mr. Mitchell BENNETT
03	Executive Vice President	Dr. J. Blair BLACKBURN
05	Provost	Dr. Gail G. LINAM
10	Vice President Financial Affairs	Mr. Eric BRUNTMYER
20	VP Graduate/Corp Affs/Sr Asc Prov	Dr. Dennis C. DOWD
26	VP External Affs/Dir Stdnt Ctr	Mr. Dennis B. LINAM
30	Vice Pres University Advancement	Mr. Adam WRIGHT
32	Dean of Students and Spiritual Life	Mr. Jay HARLEY
13	Vice Pres for Technology	Mr. Matt MURRAH
27	Vice Pres for Communications	Mr. Blake KILLINGSWORTH
11	Assoc Vice Pres for Admin Affairs	Dr. Ozzie INGRAM
20	Associate Provost	Mrs. Deemie J. NAUGLE
50	Dean College of Business	Dr. Charlene CONNER
81	Dean Col of Natural Science & Math	Dr. Beverly S. GILTNER
53	Dean College of Education	Dr. Charles CARONA
57	Dean College of Fine Arts	Dr. Ronald BOWLES
73	Dean College Christian Faith	Dr. Steven K. MULLEN
79	Dean Col Humanity/Social Science	Dr. Mike WILLIAMS
107	Dean College Professional Studies	Dr. Donovan FREDRICKSEN
06	Registrar	Mrs. Linda M. RONEY
07	Director Undergrad Admissions	Mr. Bobby SOTO
08	Director of Library	Ms. Debra COLLINS
37	Director of Financial Aid	Mr. Lee FERGUSON
15	Director of Human Resources	Mrs. Tamy ROGERS
56	Director Weekend College	Ms. Joyce WALLACE
23	Director Health Services	Mrs. Linda J. BANNICK
41	Director of Athletics	Mr. Ryan ERWIN
19	Director of Security	Mr. Donald KABETZKE
85	Director of International Students	Mrs. Rebecca BROWN
38	Director Student Counseling Center	Mrs. Joan DAVIS
18	Asst Vice Pres for Admin Affairs	Mr. Jonathan TEAT
36	Director of Career Services	Ms. Marion A. HILL
35	Associate Dean of Students	Ms. Heather HADLOCK
29	Director Alumni Relations and Commu	Mr. Cory HINES
96	Director of Purchasing	Mrs. Dorothy PARKER
42	Dir Intercessory Prayer Ministry	Ms. Cyndi PETTIT
88	Academic Projects Administrator	Ms. Lou ESPARZA
58	Director of Graduate Studies	Mrs. Kit P. MONTGOMERY
43	General Counsel	Mr. Dan MALONE
21	Controller	Mrs. Mendi M. MCMAHAN
40	Manager Bookstore	Mrs. Kristy ERWIN
09	Coordinator Institutional Reporting	Mrs. K. Annette ARMEY
24	Coordinator Media Services	Mr. Jonathan HOOVER

Dallas Christian College (D)

2700 Christian Parkway, Dallas TX 75234-7299

County: Dallas — FICE Identification: 006941 — Unit ID: 224244
Telephone: (972) 241-3371 — Carnegie Class: Spec/Faith
FAX Number: (972) 241-8021 — Calendar System: 4/1/4
URL: www.dallas.edu
Established: 1950 — Annual Undergrad Tuition & Fees: $10,890
Enrollment: 310 — Coed
Affiliation or Control: Christian Churches And Churches of Christ — IRS Status: 501(c)3
Highest Offering: Baccalaureate
Program: Teacher Preparatory; Professional; Religious Emphasis
Accreditation: BI

01	President	Mr. Dustin D. RUBECK
05	Vice President of Academic Affairs	Dr. Paul KISSLING
30	Vice President Institutional Advanc	Vacant
31	Vice President of Community	Mr. Mark WORLEY
06	Registrar	Mrs. Crystal LAIDACKER
37	Director Financial Aid	Ms. Pamela JONES
07	Director Admissions	Mr. Matthew MEEKS
18	Director of Physical Plant	Mr. Gary ADAMS

*Dallas County Community College District Office (E)

1601 South Lamar, Dallas TX 75215

County: Dallas — FICE Identification: 009331 — Unit ID: 224253
Telephone: (214) 378-1601 — Carnegie Class: N/A
FAX Number: (214) 378-1810
URL: www.dcccd.edu

01	Chancellor	Dr. Wright L. LASSITER, JR.
05	Exec Vice Chanc Educational Affs	Dr. Andrew C. JONES
10	Exec Vice Chanc Business Affairs	Mr. Ed DESPLAS
15	Exec Vice Chanc Human & Org Devel	Mr. Denys S. BLELL
20	Exec Dist Dir WF Educ & Compliance	Mr. Don PERRY
18	Asc Vice Chanc Facil Mgmt/Architect	Mr. Clyde PORTER
43	District Legal Counsel	Mr. Robert J. YOUNG
26	Vice Chanc Public & Govt Affairs	Mr. Justin H. LONON
102	Assoc Vice Chanc Foundation	Mrs. Betheny REID
09	Assoc Vice Chanc Planning/Research	Mrs. Susan H. HALL
101	Executive Director Board Relations	Mrs. Kathryn B. TUCKER
30	Assoc Vice Chanc Resource Develop	Mrs. Betheny REID
96	Director of Purchasing	Mr. Philip TODD
62	Director of Technical Services	Mr. Paul E. DUMONT

*Brookhaven College (F)

3939 Valley View, Dallas TX 75244-4997

County: Dallas — FICE Identification: 021002 — Unit ID: 223524
Telephone: (972) 860-4700 — Carnegie Class: Assoc/Pub-U-MC
FAX Number: (972) 860-4897 — Calendar System: Semester
URL: www.brookhavencollege.edu
Established: 1978 — Annual Undergrad Tuition & Fees (In-District): $1,984
Enrollment: 12,784 — Coed
Affiliation or Control: State/Local — IRS Status: 501(c)3
Highest Offering: Associate Degree
Program: Occupational; 2-Year Principally Bachelor's Creditable
Accreditation: SC, ADNUR, EMT, RAD

02	President	Dr. Thom D. CHESNEY
05	Vice President of Academic Affairs	Mr. Rodger BENNETT
10	Vice President of Business Services	Mr. George HERRING
32	Vice Pres of Student Services	Mr. Oscar LOPEZ
50	Exec Dean Business Studies	Mr. Sandy WYCHE
36	Assoc VP Career & Program Resources	Ms. Marilyn K. KOLESAR-LYNCH
103	Assoc VP Workforce/Continuing Educ	Mr. Vernon L. HAWKINS
45	Exec Dean Educational Resources	Ms. Sarah FERGUSON
57	Interim Exec Dean Fine Arts/Phys Ed	Mr. Rick MAXWELL
81	Executive Dean Science/Math	Ms. Doris ROUSEY
23	Exec Dean of Health/Human Svcs	Dr. Juanita FLINT
09	AVP Plng/Rsrch/Inst Effectiveness	Dr. Michael DENNEHY
90	Director of Info Tech	Mr. Michael DEASON
83	Exec Dean Social Sci/Distance Lrng	Mr. Sam GOVEA
27	Executive Dean Communications	Ms. Kendra VAGLIENTI
88	Dean of Student Success	Ms. Brenda DALTON
26	Asst Dir Marketing & Public Info	Ms. Meridith DANFORTH
07	Director of Admissions/Registrar	Ms. Thoa Hoang VO
41	Director of Athletics	Ms. Lynne LEVESQUE
21	Director of Business Operations	Vacant
36	Director Career Development Center	Ms. Annette WILSON
88	Dir Ellison Miles Geotech Institute	Vacant
18	Director of Facilities Services	Mr. Tommy GALLEGOS
15	Exec Dir of Human Resources	Ms. Terri EDRICH
85	Director of Multicultural Center	Vacant
35	Dir Office of Student Life	Mr. Brian BORSKI
19	Captain of College Police	Mr. John KLINGENSMITH
23	Nurse Health Services	Ms. Mildred KELLEY
04	Assistant to President	Ms. Carrie SCHWEITZER

*Cedar Valley College (G)

3030 N Dallas Avenue, Lancaster TX 75134-3799

County: Dallas — FICE Identification: 003561 — Unit ID: 223773
Telephone: (972) 860-8201 — Carnegie Class: Assoc/Pub-U-MC
FAX Number: (972) 860-8207 — Calendar System: Semester
URL: www.cedarvalleycollege.edu
Established: 1974 — Annual Undergrad Tuition & Fees (In-District): $1,350
Enrollment: 6,221 — Coed
Affiliation or Control: State/Local — IRS Status: 501(c)3
Highest Offering: Associate Degree
Program: Occupational; 2-Year Principally Bachelor's Creditable
Accreditation: SC

02	President	Dr. Jennifer L. WIMBISH
05	Vice President of Instruction	Dr. David EVANS
32	Vice Pres Student Svcs/Enroll Mgmt	Ms. Anna MAYS
10	Vice President Business Services	Mr. Huan LUONG
81	Director Dean Math/Science/Health	Dr. Jennie POLLARD
09	Dir Inst Research/Effectiveness	Mr. Marlon MOTE
49	Division Dean Liberal Arts	Dr. Pam GIST
50	Div Dean Bus/Science/Technology	Dr. Ruben JOHNSON
20	Dean Instructional SupportDist Ed	Mrs. Lisa NIGHTINGALE
51	Dean Continuing Education	Mrs. Rose BLAIR
08	Assoc Dean Education Resources	Ms. Edna M. WHITE
26	Assoc Dean External Relations	Dr. Jerry D. COTTON
07	Director of Admissions/Registrar	Ms. Carolyn D. WARD
18	Director Facilities Management	Mrs. Cindy A. ROGERS
26	Dir Marketing & Public Relations	Mrs. Sonya SPENCER
15	Director Human Resources	Mrs. Debbie SPECK
37	Director of Financial Aid	Ms. Decha REID
88	Director of Upward Bound	Ms. Olivia GUERRA
88	Director of Independent Study	Vacant
35	Coordinator Office Student Life	Ms. Myioshi U. HOLMES
36	Senior Placement Coordinator	Mr. Mike J. ALFORD

*Eastfield College (H)

3737 Motley Drive, Mesquite TX 75150-2033

County: Dallas — FICE Identification: 008510 — Unit ID: 224572
Telephone: (972) 860-7100 — Carnegie Class: Assoc/Pub-U-MC
FAX Number: (972) 860-8373 — Calendar System: Semester
URL: www.eastfieldcollege.edu
Established: 1970 — Annual Undergrad Tuition & Fees (In-District): $1,230
Enrollment: 13,307 — Coed
Affiliation or Control: State/Local — IRS Status: 170(c)1
Highest Offering: Associate Degree
Program: Occupational; 2-Year Principally Bachelor's Creditable
Accreditation: SC

02	President	Dr. Jean L. CONWAY
05	VP Teaching and Learning	Mr. Michael J. GUTIERREZ
10	VP Business Services	Vacant
45	VP Organizational Development	Dr. Thomas J. GRACA
32	Executive Dean Student Services	Ms. Linda C. RICHARDSON
35	Dean Outreach & Student Development	Ms. Dina M. SOSA-HEGARTY
26	Director Communications & Outreach	Ms. Sharon L. COOK
15	Executive Director Human Resources	Vacant
12	Exec Dir Pleasant Grove Campus	Mr. Javier E. OLGUIN
45	Associate Vice President	Mr. Donald BAYNHAM
04	Admin Assistant to the President	Vacant
20	Dean Academic Enrichment	Ms. Elizabeth NICHOLS
57	Executive Dean Arts & Literature	Ms. Rachel B. WOLF
72	Executive Dean Career Technologies	Mr. Gerald F. KOZLOWSKI
81	Executive Dean College Readiness	Mr. Ricardo RODRIGUEZ
81	Executive Dean Science	Dr. Gretchen K. RIEHL
83	Executive Dean Social Sciences	Dr. Richard J. CINCLAIR
103	Executive Dean Workforce Devel	Dr. Lindle D. GRIGSBY
51	Dean Continuing Education	Vacant
08	Dean Educational Resources	Ms. Karla J. GREER
20	Associate Dean Teaching & Learning	Ms. Lucinda A. GONZALES
07	Director Admissions & Registration	Ms. Glynis K. MILLER
88	Director Advising	Vacant
37	Director Financial Aid	Ms. Carrie A. WAGER
35	Interim Director Student Life	Ms. Judy A. SCHWARTZ
41	Director Intercollegiate Athletics	Mr. Anthony S. FLETCHER
23	Director Health Center	Ms. Cynthia S. TAYLOR
38	Professional Counselor	Mr. Jeff QUAN
88	Director Disability Services	Ms. Barbara L. WHITE
21	Director Business Operations	Ms. Esther BUENO
21	Financial Manager	Ms. Heidi M. BASSETT
21	Asst Director Business Operatation	Ms. Linda S. ZABOJNIK
13	Dean Information Technology	Mr. John M. CRISWELL
18	Director Facilities Management	Mr. Arthur SYKES
90	Manager Educational Computing	Mr. Jack O. THIEHOFF
91	Manager Administrative Computing	Ms. Dana R. HASKINS
09	Dean Planning/Research and IE	Ms. Constance L. HOWELLS
46	Dean Resource Development	Ms. Whitney C. HOUSTON
19	Director College Police	Chief Tyler J. MOORE
88	Director College Effectiveness	Vacant

*El Centro College (I)

801 Main Street, Dallas TX 75202-3604

County: Dallas — FICE Identification: 004453 — Unit ID: 224615
Telephone: (214) 860-2037 — Carnegie Class: Assoc/Pub-U-MC
FAX Number: (214) 860-2335 — Calendar System: Semester
URL: www.elcentrocollege.edu
Established: 1966 — Annual Undergrad Tuition & Fees (In-District): $1,572
Enrollment: 9,761 — Coed
Affiliation or Control: State/Local — IRS Status: 501(c)3
Highest Offering: Associate Degree
Program: Occupational; 2-Year Principally Bachelor's Creditable
Accreditation: SC, ACFEI, ADNUR, CVT, DMS, MAC, MLTAD, PNUR, RAD, SURGT

02 President .... Dr. Paul J. MCCARTHY
05 Exec VP Acad Affairs/Stdnt Success .... Dr. Micheal B. JACKSON
17 VP Health/Economic Development .... Ms. Sondra G. FLEMMING
10 VP Business Services .... Mr. David A. BROWNING
50 Exec Dean Bus/Pub Svc/Info Tech .... Mr. Howard H. FINNEY
60 Exec Dean Communications/Math .... Ms. Lisa M. THERIOT
49 Assoc Instruct Dean Arts & Sciences .... Mr. Eddy RAWLINSON
76 Exec Dean Health Occupations .... Dr. Mary L. MCPHERSON
84 Exec Dean Student/Enrollment Svcs .... Ms. Fela ALFARO
32 Exec Dean Student Dev/Support Svcs .... Mr. James L. HANDY
12 Executive Dean BJP Campus .... Ms. Pyeper L. WILKINS
12 Executive Director West Campus .... Ms. Ana-Maria RODRIGUEZ
88 Ombudsman .... Dr. Bettie L. TULLY
09 Dean Institutional Effectiveness .... Dr. Karen C. LALJIANI
08 Asst Dean Educational Resources .... Dr. Norman HOWDEN
25 Exec Dean Resource Development .... Ms. Pyeper L. WILKINS
06 Director Admissions/Registrar .... Ms. Rebecca J. GARZA
37 Dir Student Financial Support/Svcs .... Ms. Pam A. LUCAS
88 Dist Dir Health Career Res Ctr .... Dr. Molly H. BOYD
36 Director Career Svcs .... Vacant
19 College Director College Police .... Mr. Calvin R. RICHARDS
26 Director Marketing/Communications .... Ms. Priscilla A. STALEY
15 Exec Director Human Resources .... Mr. Robert P. GARCIA
38 Director Testing Center .... Mr. Monty E. FRANCIS
18 Director Facilities Services .... Mr. William E. BUTLER
21 College Director Business Operation .... Ms. Susan G. PIERCE
85 Coordinator International Center .... Mr. Robert G. REYES
35 Director Ofc of Student Life ..... Ms. Shanee' S. HOLMES-MOORE
23 College Nurse .... Mr. Ken L. JOHNSON
91 Director Information Technology .... Mr. Michael C. JOHNSON
88 Chief Sustainable Devolopment Ofcr .... Dr. Bryan A. REECE
40 Manager Bookstore .... Ms. Patricia WILLIAMS

*Mountain View College (A)

4849 W Illinois, Dallas TX 75211-6599

County: Dallas | FICE Identification: 008503 | Unit ID: 226930
Telephone: (214) 860-8680 | Carnegie Class: Assoc/Pub-U-MC
FAX Number: (214) 860-8521 | Calendar System: Semester
URL: www.mountainviewcollege.edu
Established: 1970 | Annual Undergrad Tuition & Fees (In-District): $540
Enrollment: 8,463 | Coed
Affiliation or Control: State/Local | IRS Status: 501(c)3
Highest Offering: Associate Degree
Program: Occupational; 2 Year Principally Bachelor's Creditable
Accreditation: SC

02 President .... Mr. Felix A. ZAMORA
05 Int Vice President of Instruction .... Dr. Gene GIBBONS
32 VP Student Svcs/Enrollment Mgmt .... Dr. Leonard GARRETT
10 Vice President Business Services .... Ms. Sharon DAVIS
84 Dean Enrollment Management .... Dr. John PRUIT
90 Dean Educational Resources .... Mr. Jim CORVEY
45 Dean Education Center .... Mr. Moises ALMENDARIZ
06 Registrar .... Ms. Glenda HALL
18 Director Facilities Services .... Mr. Allan KNOTT
09 Dir of Planning/Research & IE .... Mr. Jerry SCHEERER
37 Interim Director Financial Aid .... Mr. James HUBENER
35 Director of Student Life .... Ms. Cathy EDWARDS
88 Director Contract Training .... Ms. Vonice CHAMP
26 Director Public Info/Marketing .... Ms. Marci GARROTT
21 Director of Business Office .... Mr. Tim SOYARS
07 Asst Director of Admissions .... Ms. Linda OSAGIE
38 Director of Advising .... Ms. Antonia KILPATRICK
15 Director Human Resources .... Mr. Willie NEAL
36 Career Placement Specialist .... Ms. Regina GARNER

*North Lake College (B)

5001 N MacArthur Boulevard, Irving TX 75038-3899

County: Dallas | FICE Identification: 020774 | Unit ID: 227191
Telephone: (972) 273-3000 | Carnegie Class: Assoc/Pub-U-MC
FAX Number: (972) 273-3014 | Calendar System: Semester
URL: www.dcccd.edu
Established: 1977 | Annual Undergrad Tuition & Fees (In-District): $1,080
Enrollment: 12,018 | Coed
Affiliation or Control: State/Local | IRS Status: 501(c)3
Highest Offering: Associate Degree
Program: Occupational; 2-Year Principally Bachelor's Creditable; Technical Emphasis
Accreditation: SC, CONST

02 Interim President .... Ms. Christa SLEJKO
05 Vice President Academic Affairs .... Dr. Martha HUGHES
31 VP Community and Economic Develop .... Dr. Paul KELEMEN
10 Interim Vice Pres Business Services .... Ms. Shannon WEAVER
45 Vice Pres Planning & Development .... Ms. Candace CASTILLO
84 VP Stdnt Svcs/Enrollment Mgmt .... Ms. Mary CIMINELLI
88 Director of Learning Resources .... Mr. Kent SEAVER
07 Director Admissions & Registration .... Ms. Francyenne MAYNARD
26 Director Marketing & Public Info .... Ms. Gina FEDERER
12 Ex Director North and South Campus .... Mr. Arthur JAMES
08 Head Librarian .... Dr. Enrique CHAMBERLAIN
18 Director Facilities Services .... Mr. John WATSON
19 Director Campus Police .... Mr. Chris DRAKE
09 Director of Institutional Research .... Ms. Teresa ISBELL
15 Director Human Resources .... Ms. Ella BARBER
21 Associate Business Officer .... Ms. Susan KLUTTS
32 Dir Stdnt Prog/Resources/Hlth Svcs .... Ms. Virginia JONES
103 Interim Director Workforce Dev/CE .... Ms. Lynn SMITH-BRUSH

38 Dir Acad Advising Career Edu Pl .... Ms. DeAira KENNEMER
83 Executive Dean Liberal Arts .... Mrs. Zena JACKSON
81 Exec Dean Math/Science .... Dr. Marilyn MAYS
50 Exe Dean Arts/Bus/Sports Sci Tech .... Dr. David EVANS
12 Exec Dean West Campus .... Mr. Mike COOLEY

*Richland College (C)

12800 Abrams Road, Dallas TX 75243-2199

County: Dallas | FICE Identification: 008504 | Unit ID: 227766
Telephone: (972) 238-6194 | Carnegie Class: Assoc/Pub-U-MC
FAX Number: (972) 238-6978 | Calendar System: Semester
URL: www.rlc.dcccd.edu
Established: 1972 | Annual Undergrad Tuition & Fees (In-District): $1,080
Enrollment: 19,690 | Coed
Affiliation or Control: State/Local | IRS Status: 501(c)3
Highest Offering: Associate Degree
Program: Occupational; 2-Year Principally Bachelor's Creditable
Accreditation: SC, MAC

02 Interim President .... Dr. Kathryn K. EGGLESTON
04 Dean/Exec Assistant to President .... Ms. Janet C. JAMES
05 Interim VP Teaching & Learning .... Dr. Zarina BLANKENBAKER
32 VP for Student Development .... Mr. Tony E. SUMMERS
10 VP for Business Services .... Mr. Ron M. CLARK
50 Exec Dean Sch of Engr/Business/Tech .... Ms. Martha A. HOGAN
79 Exec Dean Human/Fine & Perf Arts .... Dr. Sherry L. DEAN
81 Exec Dean of Math/Science/Hlth Prof .... Dr. Raymond P. CANHAM
09 Exec Dean Plng/Rsrch/Inst Effect .... Ms. Fonda L. VERA
60 Exec Dean World Lang/Cultures/Comm ... Ms. Susan E. BARKLEY
88 Exec Dean Lrng Enrich & Acad Dev .... Ms. Mary K. DARIN
41 Director Athletic Programs .... Mr. Tony E. SUMMERS
76 Assoc Dean of Health Professions .... Ms. Shannon YDOYAGA
35 Director of Student Life .... Ms. Bobbie J. HARRISON
08 Director of Library Services .... Ms. Lennijo HENDERSON
26 Dir College Comm and Marketing .... Ms. Whitney ROSENBALM
18 Director of Facilities Services .... Mr. Eddie C. HUESTON
15 Executive Director Human Resources .... Vacant
19 Chief of College Police .... Mr. Robert D. BAKER
12 Principal Richland Collegiate HS .... Dr. Kristyn EDNEY
84 Assoc VP Enrollment/Supt RCHS .... Ms. Donna WALKER

Dallas Institute of Funeral Service (D)

3909 S Buckner Boulevard, Dallas TX 75227-4314

County: Dallas | FICE Identification: 010761 | Unit ID: 224271
Telephone: (214) 388-5466 | Carnegie Class: Assoc/PrivNFP
FAX Number: (214) 388-0316 | Calendar System: Quarter
URL: www.dallasinstitute.edu
Established: 1945 | Annual Undergrad Tuition & Fees: $15,000
Enrollment: 141 | Coed
Affiliation or Control: Independent Non-Profit | IRS Status: 501(c)3
Highest Offering: Associate Degree
Program: Occupational; 2-Year Principally Bachelor's Creditable; Technical Emphasis
Accreditation: FUSER

01 President .... Mr. James M. SHOEMAKE

Dallas Theological Seminary (E)

3909 Swiss Avenue, Dallas TX 75204-6493

County: Dallas | FICE Identification: 003562 | Unit ID: 224305
Telephone: (214) 824-3094 | Carnegie Class: Spec/Faith
FAX Number: (214) 841-3625 | Calendar System: Semester
URL: www.dts.edu
Established: 1924 | Annual Graduate Tuition & Fees: $12,830
Enrollment: 2,001 | Coordinate
Affiliation or Control: Independent Non-Profit | IRS Status: 501(c)3
Highest Offering: Doctorate; No Undergraduates
Program: Professional; Religious Emphasis
Accreditation: SC, THEOL

01 President .... Dr. Mark L. BAILEY
05 Vice Pres Academic Affs/Acad Dean .... Dr. John D. GRASSMICK
32 Vice Pres/Dean Student Services .... Dr. Robert J. GARIPPA
10 Vice President Business & Finance .... Mr. Dale C. LARSON
30 Vice President for Advancement .... Ms. Kimberly B. TILL
26 Vice President for Communications .... Mr. Mark M. YARBROUGH
11 Vice President Campus Operations .... Mr. Robert F. RIGGS
100 Exec Assistant to the President .... Mr. Robert F. RIGGS
102 Int Exec Dir Dallas Seminary Fdn .... Ms. Kimberly B. TILL
84 Assoc Acad Dean Enrollment Services .... Dr. Eugene W. POND
20 Assoc Acad Dean Academic Admin .... Dr. James H. THAMES
56 Assoc Acad Dean External Education .. Dr. Mark M. YARBROUGH
37 Director of Financial Aid & HR .... Ms. Karen G. HOLDER
58 Director of Ph.D. Studies .... Dr. Richard A. TAYLOR
58 Director of D.Min. Studies .... Dr. D. Scott BARFOOT
09 Director of Inst Research/Effective .... Dr. Eugene W. POND
06 Registrar .... Mr. Benjamin I. SIMPSON
88 Exec Dir of Leadership Center .... Dr. Andrew B. SEIDEL
07 Director of Admissions .... Mr. Joshua J. BLEEKER
08 Library Director .... Mr. Marvin T. HUNN, II
29 Director of Alumni .... Mr. Gregory A. HATTEBERG
36 Director of Placement .... Mr. Robert KAUMEYER
24 Director of Media Support .... Mr. James W. HOOVER
105 Director of Web Development .... Mr. John C. DYER
42 Chaplain .... Rev. G. William BRYAN

34 Adviser to Women Students .... Ms. Lynn Etta G. MANNING
93 Adviser to African-American Studnts ... Dr. Terrance S. WOODSON
85 International Student Adviser .... Ms. Jenny MCGILL
18 Dir Facilities & Plant Operations .... Mr. B. Kevin FOLSOM
40 Bookstore Manager .... Mr. Kevin D. STERN
13 Director of Information Technology .... Mr. Richard D. BLAKE
19 Director of Campus Police .... Mr. John S. BLOOM
39 Director of Housing & Food Services ...... Mr. Drew H. WILLIAMS
12 Exec Director of Houston Extension .... Dr. David R. KLINGLER
106 Dir Online and External Studies .... Mr. Robert M. ABEGG
88 Director of Online Chinese Studies .... Dr. Samuel CHIA
38 Director of Counseling Services .... Dr. J. Lee JAGERS
15 Director Personnel Services .... Ms. Karen G. HOLDER
21 Associate Business Officer .... Ms. Patricia MAYABB
35 Director Student Affairs .... Dr. Robert J. GARIPPA

Del Mar College (F)

101 Baldwin, Corpus Christi TX 78404-3897

County: Nueces | FICE Identification: 003563 | Unit ID: 224350
Telephone: (361) 698-1200 | Carnegie Class: Assoc/Pub-R-L
FAX Number: (361) 698-1559 | Calendar System: Semester
URL: www.delmar.edu
Established: 1935 | Annual Undergrad Tuition & Fees (In-District): $2,700
Enrollment: 12,236 | Coed
Affiliation or Control: Local | IRS Status: 501(c)3
Highest Offering: Associate Degree
Program: Occupational; 2-Year Principally Bachelor's Creditable
Accreditation: SC, ADNUR, ART, DA, DH, DMS, MLTAD, MUS, NMT, OTA, PTAA, RAD, SURGT, THEA

01 President .... Dr. Mark ESCAMILLA
05 VP of Instruction & Provost .... Dr. Fernando FIGUEROA
10 VP Administration/Finance/Stdnt Svc .... Dr. Lee SLOAN
45 Exec Dir Strategic Planning .... Mr. Lenora KEAS
26 Exec Director Comm and Leg Affs .... Ms. Claudia JACKSON
30 Director Development .... Ms. Mary MCQUEEN
88 Int Dean Student Outreach/Reg .... Dr. Leonard RIVERA
35 Int Dean Student Eng & Retention .... Ms. Sandra VALERIO
49 Dean Division Arts & Sciences .... Dr. Jonda HALCOMB
50 Dean Div Business/Prof/Tech Ed .... Dr. Larry LEE
15 Interim Director of Human Resources .... Mr. Warner COLLIER
22 Interim Director EEO/AA Compliance .... Mr. Warner COLLIER
21 Comptroller .... Mr. John J. JOHNSON
96 Director of Purchasing/Business Svc .... Mr. Charles TINES
13 Chief Information/Technology Ofcr .... Mr. August ALFONSO
19 Director Risk Mgmt/Safety .... Mr. Kelly L. WHITE
18 Director Physical Facilities .... Mr. Willie KELLER, JR.
37 Director Financial Aid .... Mr. Enrique GARCIA, JR.
06 Registrar .... Vacant
32 Dir Stdnt Leadership/Campus Life .... Ms. Beverly CAGE
88 Director Cash Management .... Ms. Cathy WEST
88 Director Testing .... Ms. Criselda LEAL
08 Director of Learning Resources .... Ms. Chris M. TETZLAFF-BELHASEN
09 Dir Inst Research/Effectiveness .... Mr. David ANDRUS

DeVry University - Austin (G)

11044 Research Boulevard, Ste B100, Austin TX 78759-5292

County: Travis | Identification: 666573
Telephone: (512) 231-2500 | Carnegie Class: Not Classified
FAX Number: (512) 342-1716 | Calendar System: Semester
URL: www.devry.edu
Established: 1931 | Annual Undergrad Tuition & Fees: $15,294
Enrollment: 389 | Coed
Affiliation or Control: Proprietary | IRS Status: Proprietary
Highest Offering: Master's
Program: Professional; Business Emphasis
Accreditation: &NH

01 Campus Director .... Lorraine BEACH

† Regional accreditation is carried under the parent institution in Downers Grove, IL.

DeVry University - Fort Worth (H)

301 Commerce Street, Suite 2000, Fort Worth TX 76102-4120

County: Tarrant | Identification: 666574
Telephone: (817) 810-9114 | Carnegie Class: Not Classified
FAX Number: (817) 810-9112 | Calendar System: Semester
URL: www.devry.edu
Established: 1931 | Annual Undergrad Tuition & Fees: $15,294
Enrollment: 318 | Coed
Affiliation or Control: Proprietary | IRS Status: Proprietary
Highest Offering: Master's
Program: Professional; Business Emphasis
Accreditation: &NH

01 Center Dean .... John STUART

† Regional accreditation is carried under the parent institution in Downers Grove, IL.

DeVry University - Houston Campus (A)

11125 Equity Drive, Houston TX 77041-8217

County: Fort Bend Identification: 666219
Telephone: (713) 973-3100 Carnegie Class: Not Classified
FAX Number: (713) 896-0293 Calendar System: Semester
URL: www.devry.edu
Established: 1931 Annual Undergrad Tuition & Fees: $15,294
Enrollment: 2,348 Coed
Affiliation or Control: Proprietary IRS Status: Proprietary
Highest Offering: Master's
Program: Occupational; Professional; Business Emphasis
Accreditation: &NH, ENGT

01 Metro President .... Kim NUGENT
58 Senior Graduate Center Dean .... Annette OLLSEN
37 Director of Student Finance .... Dong SUH
36 Assoc Director of Career Services .... Jerel SHOWERS
15 HR Business Partner .... Sandra NEWMAN
08 Director of Library Services .... Lloyd WEDES
07 Vice President of Admissions .... David WOOD
97 Dean of General Education .... Adrian SHAPIRO
54 Dean of Electronics & ET .... Teddy IVANITZKI
06 Registrar .... Valerie ACFALLE

† Regional accreditation is carried under the parent institution in Downers Grove, IL.

DeVry University - Irving Campus (B)

4800 Regent Boulevard, Irving TX 75063-2439

County: Dallas FICE Identification: 010139
Unit ID: 224402
Telephone: (972) 929-6777 Carnegie Class: Master's M
FAX Number: (972) 929-2802 Calendar System: Semester
URL: www.devry.edu
Established: 1931 Annual Undergrad Tuition & Fees: $15,294
Enrollment: 2,292 Coed
Affiliation or Control: Proprietary IRS Status: Proprietary
Highest Offering: Master's
Program: Occupational; Professional; Business Emphasis
Accreditation: &NH, ENGT

01 Metro President .... Ms. Dawn OWENS
06 Registrar .... Ms. Kalyani (Sandhya) SEWNUNDUN
07 Director of Admissions .... Mr. Justin POND
36 Dean of Career & Student Services .... Ms. Rhonda GAINES
05 Dean of Academic Affairs .... Ms. Emily SMITH
15 HR Business Partner .... Ms. Shingai CHIGWEDERE
54 Dean of Electronics .... Mr. Christian PENCIU
50 Dean of Business & Technology .... Mr. Craig LASSEIGNE
77 Dean of CIS .... Mr. William MCCLURE

† Regional accreditation is carried under the parent institution in Downers Grove, IL.

DeVry University - Richardson (C)

2201 North Central Expressway,
Richardson TX 75080-2754

County: Dallas Identification: 666575
Telephone: (972) 792-7450 Carnegie Class: Not Classified
FAX Number: (972) 437-6892 Calendar System: Semester
URL: www.devry.edu
Established: 1931 Annual Undergrad Tuition & Fees: $15,294
Enrollment: 371 Coed
Affiliation or Control: Proprietary IRS Status: Proprietary
Highest Offering: Master's
Program: Professional; Business Emphasis
Accreditation: &NH

01 Center Dean .... Renee DOYAL

† Regional accreditation is carried under the parent institution in Downers Grove, IL.

East Texas Baptist University (D)

One Tiger Drive, Marshall TX 75670-1498

County: Harrison FICE Identification: 003564
Unit ID: 224527
Telephone: (903) 935-7963 Carnegie Class: Bac/Diverse
FAX Number: (903) 938-1705 Calendar System: Semester
URL: www.etbu.edu
Established: 1912 Annual Undergrad Tuition & Fees: $19,200
Enrollment: 1,197 Coed
Affiliation or Control: Southern Baptist IRS Status: 501(c)3
Highest Offering: Master's
Program: Liberal Arts And General
Accreditation: SC, MUS, NURSE

01 President .... Dr. Samuel W. "Dub" OLIVER
05 Provost/Vice Pres Academic Affairs .... Dr. Sherilyn EMBERTON
30 Vice Pres University Advancement ..... Mrs. Catherine CRAWFORD
42 Vice Pres Spiritual Development .... Dr. Scott BRYANT
10 Vice Pres Administration & Finance .... Mr. Ned CALVERT
32 Vice President for Student Affairs .... Dr. Dennis ROBERTSON
84 Vice Pres for Enrollment Mgmt/Mktg .... Mr. Vince BLANKENSHIP
35 Dean of Students .... Ms. Magen BUNYARD
09 Dir Inst Research/Effectiveness .... Mrs. Karen WILEY
07 Director of Admissions .... Mr. Jason SOLES
13 Director of Inst Technology .... Mr. Barry HALE
06 University Registrar .... Mr. Chris WOOD
29 Director of Alumni Relations .... Ms. Lindsay CULBERTSON
66 Dean School of Nursing .... Dr. Ellen FINEOUT-OVERHOLT
08 Director of Library .... Ms. Cynthia PETERSON
26 Director of Public Relations .... Mr. Mike MIDKIFF
37 Director of Financial Aid .... Mr. Tommy YOUNG
41 Director of Athletics .... Mr. Kent REEVES
38 Director Academic Advising .... Mr. Bob FLANNERY
88 Director Baptist Student Ministry .... Mr. Mark YATES
40 Director of Bookstore .... Mr. Bill WARDEN
44 Director of Alumni Development .... Mr. Paul TAPP
18 Director of Physical Facilities .... Mr. Eric WILBURN
88 Director Rec & Athletic Facilities .... Mr. Randy PRINGLE
35 Director of Student Activities .... Mr. Blair PREVOST
88 Director Great Commission Center .... Mr. Allan THOMPSON
53 Dean School of Education .... Dr. Donna LUBCKER
88 Dean School of Christian Studies .... Dr. John HARRIS
83 Dean School of Nat/Soc Sciences .... Dr. Lynn NEW
50 Dean School of Business .... Dr. Scott RAY
79 Dean School of Humanities .... Dr. Jerry SUMMERS
85 Director of International Education .... Mr. Alan HUESING
21 Director of Financial Services .... Mr. Richard HUTSELL
88 Director of Student Success .... Mrs. Bonnie JONES
57 Dean School of Fine Arts .... Dr. Tom WEBSTER
102 Director of Major Gifts .... Dr. Dane FOWLKES

El Paso Community College (E)

PO Box 20500, El Paso TX 79998-0500

County: El Paso FICE Identification: 010387
Unit ID: 224642
Telephone: (915) 831-2000 Carnegie Class: Assoc/Pub-U-MC
FAX Number: (915) 831-6507 Calendar System: Semester
URL: www.epcc.edu
Established: 1969 Annual Undergrad Tuition & Fees (In-District): $2,310
Enrollment: 29,909 Coed
Affiliation or Control: Local IRS Status: 501(c)3
Highest Offering: Associate Degree
Program: Occupational; 2-Year Principally Bachelor's Creditable
Accreditation: SC, ADNUR, DA, DH, DMS, MAC, MLTAD, PTAA, RAD, SURGT

01 Interim President .... Dr. Ernst E. ROBERTS, II
05 Vice President Instruction .... Dr. Dennis BROWN
13 Vice Pres Information Tech/CIO .... Dr. Jenny GIRON
103 Vice Pres Wrkfc/Economic Dev & CE .... Ms. Yolanda AHNER
32 Vice President Student Services .... Ms. Linda GONZALEZ
46 Vice President of Research .... Mr. Saul C. CANDELAS
20 Assoc VP Instruct Res/Technology .... Dr. Jenny GIRON
10 Assoc VP Budget & Financial Svcs .. Ms. Josette SHAUGHNESSY
15 Assoc VP Employee Relations .... Ms. Nancy N. NELSON
26 Dir Marketing & Community Rels .... Ms. Joyce CORDELL
35 Dean of Students .... Vacant
88 Dean Instruct Programs-MDP Campus .... Vacant
76 Dean Health Occupations/Math/Sci .... Dr. Paula MITCHELL
50 Dean Arts/Bask/Comp/Oc Educ/Soc Sci .... Dr. Eileen CONKLIN
57 Dean Arts/Bask/Comm & Soc Sci .... Ms. Joyce RITCHEY
79 Dean ESL Reading Social Science .... Ms. Susana RODARTE
81 Dean Arch/Arts/Math/Science .... Vacant
88 Dean American Lang/BS/Comm/PA .... Mr. Claude MATHIS
53 Dean Education & Occ Programs .... Dr. Jaime D. FARIAS
66 Dean Nursing .... Ms. Paula G. MEAGHER
12 Dean Instructional Pgms-NW Campus .... Dr. Lydia TENA
45 Director Inst Effectiveness .... Dr. Ron STROUD
08 Director Library Technical Services .... Mr. Luis CHAPARRO
21 Comptroller .... Mr. Fernando FLORES
36 Director Career Services .... Ms. Carla CARDOZA
18 Director Physical Plant .... Mr. Richard L. LOBATO
19 Chief of Police .... Chief Jose L. RAMIREZ
24 Director Center Instr Telecommunic .... Vacant
15 Director Personnel Services .... Ms. Elizabeth OLGUIN-RYAN
07 Exec Director Admissions/Registrar .... Mr. Daryle HENDRY
96 Dir Purchasing & Contract Mgmt .... Mr. Ruben C. GALLARDO
09 Director Institutional Research .... Dr. Carol KAY
16 Director Human Resources Devel .... Mr. Alex HERNANDEZ
31 Director Inst & Community Planning .... Ms. Dolores GROSS
21 Director Budget .... Mr. Jerry FULTON
88 Manager Literacy Programs .... Mrs. Sara MARTINEZ
85 Director International Education .... Dr. Miguel A. MARTINEZ-LASSO
102 Exec Dir Foundation/Development .... Dr. Christy PONCE
88 Dir Ctr for Students w/Disabilities .... Ms. Janet M. LOCKHART
88 Director Recruitment/School Rels .... Ms. Nita CORRAL-NAVA
88 Director Testing Service .... Mrs. Carolyn BUNTYN
25 Director Grants Management .... Mr. Alfred C. LAWRENCE
103 Director Workforce Development .... Ms. Luz E. TABOADA
56 Director Distance Learning .... Mr. Robert P. JONES
88 Director Student Success .... Ms. Irma G. CAMACHO
88 Dir Law Enforcement Trng Academy .... Mr. Barry J. BOGLE
28 Director of Diversity Programs .... Mrs. Olga CHAVEZ

Everest College (F)

6080 N Central Expressway, Dallas TX 75206-5202

County: Dallas Identification: 666254
Unit ID: 442790
Telephone: (214) 234-4850 Carnegie Class: Assoc/PrivFP
FAX Number: (214) 696-6208 Calendar System: Quarter
URL: www.everest-college.com
Established: 2003 Annual Undergrad Tuition & Fees: $13,599
Enrollment: 1,453 Coed
Affiliation or Control: Proprietary IRS Status: Proprietary
Highest Offering: Associate Degree
Program: Occupational; Business Emphasis
Accreditation: ACICS

01 President .... Christopher PETERS
05 Academic Dean .... Glenn THAXTON
07 Director of Admissions .... Jahmil JONES
37 Director of Financial Aid .... Kevin HODGE

† Branch campus of Everest College, Portland, OR.

Frank Phillips College (G)

PO Box 5118, Borger TX 79008-5118

County: Hutchinson FICE Identification: 003568
Unit ID: 224891
Telephone: (806) 457-4200 Carnegie Class: Assoc/Pub-R-S
FAX Number: (806) 457-4224 Calendar System: Semester
URL: www.fpctx.edu
Established: 1948 Annual Undergrad Tuition & Fees (In-District): $1,023
Enrollment: 1,227 Coed
Affiliation or Control: Local IRS Status: 501(c)3
Highest Offering: Associate Degree
Program: Occupational; 2-Year Principally Bachelor's Creditable
Accreditation: SC

01 President .... Dr. Jud HICKS
11 Vice Pres Administrative Services .... Dr. Jud HICKS
05 Vice President of Academic Affairs .... Ms. Shannon CARROLL
12 Dean of FPC Allen Campus .... Dr. Lew HUNNICUTT
08 Director of the Library .... Mr. Jason PRICE
06 Registrar .... Vacant
09 Director of Institutional Research .... Vacant
18 Chief Facilities/Physical Plant .... Ms. Regina HANEY
26 Col Advancement/Community Rels Ofcr .... Ms. Jerri AYLOR
103 Dean of Career & Technical Educ .... Mr. Jack STANLEY
103 Associate Dean of Workforce .... Vacant
37 Co-Dir Student Financial Services .... Ms. Beverly FIELDS
37 Co-Dir Student Financial Services .... Ms. Dianne ENSEY
38 Director Student Counseling .... Ms. Marilee COOPER
84 Director Enrollment Management .... Ms. Michele STEVENS
56 Coordinator of Extended Education .... Ms. Kim PIEDRA
10 Director of Accounting .... Ms. Bridey MCCORMACK

Galveston College (H)

4015 Avenue Q, Galveston TX 77550-7496

County: Galveston FICE Identification: 004972
Unit ID: 224961
Telephone: (409) 944-4242 Carnegie Class: Assoc/Pub-R-M
FAX Number: (409) 944-1500 Calendar System: Semester
URL: www.gc.edu
Established: 1966 Annual Undergrad Tuition & Fees (In-District): $1,558
Enrollment: 2,319 Coed
Affiliation or Control: State/Local IRS Status: 501(c)3
Highest Offering: Associate Degree
Program: Occupational; 2-Year Principally Bachelor's Creditable; Business Emphasis
Accreditation: SC, ADNUR, EMT, NMT, RAD, RTT, SURGT

01 President .... Dr. Myles SHELTON
05 Vice President of Instruction .... Dr. Debra KUHL
11 Vice President for Administration .... Dr. Gaynelle H. HAYES
32 Vice President of Student Services .... Dr. Phyllis A. PEPIN
75 Dean of Tech & Prof Education .... Ms. Vera LEWIS-JASPER
10 Director of Business Services .... Mr. M. Jeff ENGBROCK
14 Dir of Information Technology .... Mr. George CROSSLAND
30 Dir of Inst Advancement/Foundation .... Mr. Joseph E. HUFF, III
15 Dir Human Resources/Risk Management .... Ms. Mary Jan LANTZ
41 Athletic Director/Head Coach .... Mr. Ken DELCAMBRE
07 Director Admissions/Registrar .... Dr. Kimberly ELLIS
66 Director of Nursing .... Ms. Elaine RENOLA
09 Director Inst Effectiveness/Rsrch .... Dr. Deeanna L. ANTOSH
18 Director of Facilities/Security .... Mr. Tim W. SETZER
37 Director of Financial Aid .... Mr. Ron C. CRUMEDY
62 Dir of Library/Learning Resources .... Dr. Alan M. UYEHARA
04 Executive Assistant .... Ms. Carla D. BIGGERS

Graduate Institute of Applied Linguistics (I)

7500 W Camp Wisdom Road, Dallas TX 75236-5629

County: Dallas FICE Identification: 038513
Telephone: (972) 708-7340 Carnegie Class: Not Classified
FAX Number: (972) 708-7396 Calendar System: Other
URL: www.gial.edu
Established: 1999 Annual Graduate Tuition & Fees: $13,360
Enrollment: 85 Coed
Affiliation or Control: Independent Non-Profit IRS Status: 501(c)3
Highest Offering: Master's; No Undergraduates
Program: Professional; Religious Emphasis
Accreditation: SC

01 President .... Dr. David A. ROSS
05 Chief Academic Officer .... Dr. Doug TIFFIN
10 Chief Financial Officer .... Mr. Rod JENKINS
30 Vice President for Advancement .... Mr. James W. WALTON
32 Dean of Students .... Ms. Ruth E. SCHILBERG
06 Registrar .... Mr. Sean M. SCOTT
07 Director of Admissions .... Mrs. Kelly D. WALTER
08 Librarian .... Ms. Ferne L. WEIMER
44 Director of Development .... Dr. Douglas R. TIFFIN
09 Director of Inst Research/Svcs .... Mr. Richard E. LYNCH

13 Director of Computing Services .... Mr. Chuck WALEK
26 Chief Public Relations Officer .... Mr. Richard M. SMITH
21 Business Manager .... Mr. Paul W. SETTER

Grayson County College (A)

6101 Grayson Drive, Denison TX 75020-8299
County: Grayson FICE Identification: 003570
Unit ID: 225070
Telephone: (903) 465-6030 Carnegie Class: Assoc/Pub-R-M
FAX Number: (903) 463-5284 Calendar System: Semester
URL: www.grayson.edu
Established: 1963 Annual Undergrad Tuition & Fees (In-District): $1,840
Enrollment: 5,289 Coed
Affiliation or Control: State/Local IRS Status: 501(c)3
Highest Offering: Associate Degree
Program: Occupational; 2-Year Principally Bachelor's Creditable
Accreditation: SC, ADNUR, DA, MLTAD

01 President .... Dr. Alan SCHEIBMEIR
05 Vice President of Instruction .... Dr. Jeanie HARDIN
10 Vice President of Business Services .... Mr. Giles BROWN
13 Vice Pres of Information Technology .... Mr. Gary PAIKOWSKI
32 Vice President Student Services .... Vacant
31 Vice Pres Resource/Community Devel .... Dr. Roy E. RENFRO
07 Director of Admissions/Records .... Mrs. Kimberly FARIS
37 Director of Financial Aid .... Ms. Donna KING
14 Director of Computer Center .... Mr. Mike BROWN
19 Director Campus Police .... Vacant
26 Dir of Public Information/Marketing .... Mrs. Shelle R. CASSELL
21 Director of Fiscal Services .... Mr. Danny HYATT
40 Bookstore Manager .... Ms. Brenda FOX
41 Athletic Director .... Ms. Theresa BARNETT

Hallmark College of Aeronautics (B)

10401 W IH 10, San Antonio TX 78230
County: Bexar Identification: 666623
Unit ID: 225201
Telephone: (210) 690-9000 Carnegie Class: Assoc/PrivFP
FAX Number: (210) 690-8225 Calendar System: Other
URL: www.hallmarkcollege.edu
Established: 1969 Annual Undergrad Tuition & Fees: $29,872
Enrollment: 857 Coed
Affiliation or Control: Proprietary IRS Status: Proprietary
Highest Offering: Associate Degree
Program: Occupational
Accreditation: ACCSC

01 President .... Mr. Joseph B. FISHER
07 Vice President of Admissions .... Ms. Sonia ROSS
05 Campus Director .... Mr. Brett JOHNSON

Hallmark College of Technology (C)

10401 IH-10 W, San Antonio TX 78230-1737
County: Bexar FICE Identification: 010509
Unit ID: 225201
Telephone: (210) 690-9000 Carnegie Class: Assoc/PrivFP
FAX Number: (210) 697-8225 Calendar System: Other
URL: www.hallmarkcollege.edu
Established: 1969 Annual Undergrad Tuition & Fees: $23,925
Enrollment: 523 Coed
Affiliation or Control: Proprietary IRS Status: Proprietary
Highest Offering: Baccalaureate
Program: Occupational; 2-Year Principally Bachelor's Creditable; Technical Emphasis
Accreditation: ACCSC, MAC

00 College Systems President .... Mr. Joseph B. FISHER
01 Campus President .... Vacant
07 Director of Admissions .... Mr. Joe LONG
26 Vice President of Marketing .... Ms. Sonia ROSS
06 Dean of Academics .... Dr. Eric SMITH

Hardin-Simmons University (D)

2200 Hickory, Abilene TX 79698-0001
County: Taylor FICE Identification: 003571
Unit ID: 225247
Telephone: (325) 670-1000 Carnegie Class: Master's M
FAX Number: (325) 670-1267 Calendar System: Semester
URL: www.hsutx.edu
Established: 1891 Annual Undergrad Tuition & Fees: $22,460
Enrollment: 2,312 Coed
Affiliation or Control: Baptist IRS Status: 501(c)3
Highest Offering: Doctorate
Program: Liberal Arts And General; Teacher Preparatory; Professional
Accreditation: SC, ACBSP, MUS, NURSE, PTA, SW, THEOL

01 President .... Dr. Lanny HALL
05 Provost & Chief Academic Officer .... Dr. Thomas V. BRISCO
10 Sr VP Finance & Chief Oper Ofcr .... Mr. Harold R. PRESTON
30 VP for Advancement .... Mr. Mike HAMMACK
32 Sr Vice Pres Student Development ... Dr. Michael A. WHITEHORN
84 Vice Pres for Enrollment Management .... Dr. J. Shane DAVIDSON
07 Assoc VP for Enrollment Svcs .... Mr. Jim JONES
04 Exec Assistant to the President .... Ms. Vicki D. HOUSE
53 Dean Irvin School of Education .... Dr. Pamela K. WILLIFORD
49 Dean College of Liberal Arts .... Dr. Alan STAFFORD
50 Dean School of Business .... Mr. Michael MONHOLLON
64 Dean School of Music/Fine Arts .... Mr. Bob BROOKS
73 Dean Logsdon School of Theology .... Dr. Don WILLIFORD
58 Dean of Graduate School .... Dr. Nancy KUCINSKI
66 Dean School of Nursing .... Dr. Nina OUIMETTE
81 Dean School Sciences/Mathematics .... Dr. Christopher L. MCNAIR
14 Assoc Vice Pres Technical Services .... Mr. Travis P. SEEKINS
21 Assoc VP/Controller for Finance/Mgt .... Mr. Don P. ASHMORE
38 Assoc VP Academic Advising/Retent .... Mrs. Gracie CARROLL
08 Dean/Dir of University Libraries .... Mrs. Alice W. SPECHT
09 Director of Institutional Research .... Mrs. Lori BLAKE
06 Registrar .... Mrs. Kacey HIGGINS
35 Dean of Students .... Mr. Forrest MCMILLAN
29 Director of Alumni Relations .... Mrs. Britt E. JONES
19 Chief of Police .... Mr. Frank LOZA
23 University Nurse .... Mrs. Sue A. BIGGS
42 Chaplain .... Dr. Kelly PIGOTT
39 Associate Dean of Students .... Mr. Ben JOHNSON
36 Director of Career Services .... Mrs. Kelley WOOD
15 Director of Human Resources .... Mr. John SNAPP
27 Dir of University Communications .... Mrs. Brenda HARRIS
37 Dir Student Fin Aid & Scholarships .... Mrs. Bridget MOORE
18 Facilities Services Director .... Mr. Tim MCCARRY
41 Athletic Director .... Mr. John M. NEESE
85 Director of International Studies .... Dr. Allan J. LANDWER
26 Public Relations Director .... Mrs. Janlyn THAXTON
93 Coordinator of Minority Programs .... Dr. Joe H. ALCORTA
28 Coord of Student Diversity .... Dr. Kelvin J. KELLEY

Hill College (E)

112 Lamar Drive, Hillsboro TX 76645-2711
County: Hill FICE Identification: 003573
Unit ID: 225371
Telephone: (254) 659-7500 Carnegie Class: Assoc/Pub-R-M
FAX Number: (254) 582-7591 Calendar System: Semester
URL: www.hillcollege.edu
Established: 1923 Annual Undergrad Tuition & Fees (In-District): $1,480
Enrollment: 4,439 Coed
Affiliation or Control: Local IRS Status: 501(c)3
Highest Offering: Associate Degree
Program: Occupational; 2-Year Principally Bachelor's Creditable
Accreditation: SC

01 President .... Dr. Sheryl S. KAPPUS
04 Executive Asst to the President .... Ms. Sharon MIDDLEBROOK
05 Int Vice President Instruction .... Mr. Roger SCHUSTEREIT
11 Vice Pres Administrative Services .... Mr. Billy D. CURBO
32 Vice President Student Services .... Dr. Robert RIZA
16 VP Human Resources/Org Devel .... Mrs. Debra HARGROVE
13 Assoc VP Information Technology .... Mrs. Jessie WHITE
21 Assoc Dean Financial Services .... Mrs. Debbie GERIK
08 Dean of Education Support Svcs ...... Mr. Joseph SHAUGHNESSY
09 Assoc Dean Inst Plng Research .... Mrs. Jessyca BROWN
12 Exec Dir JCC/Dean of Students .... Mr. Bill GILKER
41 Athletic Director .... Mr. Paul BROWN
26 Director of Marketing & Public Rels .... Ms. Nikki WILMOTH
38 Director of Counseling .... Mrs. Salley SCHMID
06 Dir Stdnt Records & Registration .... Ms. Sherry DAVIS
37 Director of Financial Aid .... Ms. Susan RUSSELL
07 Dir Dual Credit/Early Enrollment .... Ms. Denise STEWART
07 Dir School Relations & Recruiting .... Mr. Scott WARREN
88 Special Asst to the President .... Ms. Wendie HERNANDEZ

Houston Baptist University (F)

7502 Fondren Road, Houston TX 77074-3298
County: Harris FICE Identification: 003576
Unit ID: 225399
Telephone: (281) 649-3000 Carnegie Class: Master's M
FAX Number: (281) 649-3012 Calendar System: Semester
URL: www.hbu.edu
Established: 1960 Annual Undergrad Tuition & Fees: $25,445
Enrollment: 2,597 Coed
Affiliation or Control: Southern Baptist IRS Status: 501(c)3
Highest Offering: Master's
Program: Liberal Arts And General; Teacher Preparatory; Professional
Accreditation: SC, ACBSP, ADNUR, NUR

01 President .... Dr. Robert B. SLOAN
05 Interim Provost .... Dr. Robert STACEY
10 Vice President Financial Operations .... Ms. Sandra N. MOONEY
26 Vice Pres University Communication .... Mr. Kimberly GAYNOR
30 Vice President for Advancement .... Mr. Charles BACARISSE
26 Vice Pres University Relations .... Mrs. Sharon E. SAUNDERS
84 Vice Pres Enrollment Management .... Mr. James STEEN
20 Associate Provost .... Ms. Ritamarie TAUER
20 Associate Provost .... Dr. Robert D. STACEY
21 Asst VP for Treasury Operations .... Mr. Hugh MCCLUNG
79 Dean College of Arts & Humanities .... Dr. Chris HAMMONS
50 Dean School of Business .... Dr. Mohan KURUVILLA
81 Dean College of Science & Math .... Dr. Doris C. WARREN
92 Dean Honors College .... Dr. Robert STACEY
53 Interim Dean School of Education .... Dr. Randy WILSON
66 Dean School Nursing & Allied Health .... Dr. Margaret UGALDE
41 Athletic Director .... Mr. Steve C. MONIACI
06 University Registrar .... Ms. Erinn HUGHES
40 Director of Bookstore .... Mr. Anthony MARTIN
07 Director of Admissions .... Mr. Eduardo BORGES
08 Director of Libraries .... Ms. Ann NOBLE
42 Director Spiritual Life .... Ms. Colette CROSS
21 Sr Director Financial Services .... Ms. Jene GABBARD
88 Assoc Director Scholarships .... Ms. Janet FENG
29 Director of Alumni Relations .... Ms. Vivian CAMACHO
39 Director Housing Operations .... Mr. Mark ENDRASKE
13 Int Dir of Information Technology .... Mr. Trent CARROLL
19 Director Police .... Mr. Charles MILLER
09 Sr Director Institutional Research .... Dr. Phil RHODES
32 Chief Student Life Officer .... Mr. Whittington GOODWIN
88 SACS Liaison .... Ms. Ritamarie TAUER
04 Admin Asst to the President .... Ms. Judy FERGUSON

Houston Community College (G)

3100 Main Street, Houston TX 77002
County: Harris FICE Identification: 010633
Unit ID: 225423
Telephone: (713) 718-2000 Carnegie Class: Assoc/Pub-U-MC
FAX Number: N/A Calendar System: Semester
URL: www.hccs.edu
Established: 1971 Annual Undergrad Tuition & Fees (In-State): $1,616
Enrollment: 61,867 Coed
Affiliation or Control: State IRS Status: 501(c)3
Highest Offering: Associate Degree
Program: Occupational; 2-Year Principally Bachelor's Creditable
Accreditation: SC, DA, DH, EMT, ENGT, HT, MAC, MLTAD, NMT, OTA, PTAA, RAD, SURGT

01 Chancellor .... Dr. Mary S. SPANGLER
04 Executive Asst to Chancellor .... Dr. Doretha EASON
03 COO/Deputy Chancellor .... Dr. Arthur Q. TYLER
43 General Counsel .... Ms. Renee BYAS
05 Vice Chancellor Instruction .... Dr. Charles M. COOK
32 Vice Chancellor Student Success .... Dr. Diana PINO
14 Vice Chancellor Information Tech .... Mr. William E. CARTER
45 VC Planning and Inst Effectiveness .... Dr. Daniel SEYMOUR
11 Chief Administative Svcs Officer .... Mr. Winston DAHSE
15 Chief Human Resource Officer .... Mr. Willie WILLIAMS
22 Director EEO/Compliance .... Mr. David CROSS
10 Controller/Chief Financial Officer .... Mr. Ron E. DEFALCO
26 Chief Communications Officer .... Mr. Daniel ARGUIJO, JR.
76 Dean Health Science Programs .... Dr. Michael EDWARDS
66 Department Chair Vocational Nursing .... Ms. Deborah SIMMONS-JOHNSON
07 Director of Admissions & Registrar .... Ms. Mary LEMBURG
09 Exec Dir of Inst Research & Innov .... Dr. Martha OBURN
46 Director Resource Development .... Ms. Georgia CARMICHAEL
102 Executive Director Foundation .... Dr. Kelly ZUNIGA
19 Environmental Safety Manager .... Mr. Oscar GONZALES
12 President-Northeast College .... Dr. Margaret FORD FISHER
12 President-Southwest College .... Dr. Fena GARZA
12 President-Central College .... Dr. William HARMON
12 President-Southeast College .... Dr. Irene PORCARELLO
12 President-Northwest College .... Dr. Zachary HODGES
12 President-Coleman College .... Dr. Betty K. YOUNG
85 Ex Dir International Initiatives .... Ms. Gigi Diemuyen DO-NGUYEN
18 Dir Bldg Operations/Property Mgmt ...... Ms. Jackquline SWINDLE
29 Alumni Relations Officer .... Ms. Lauren STROMAN
96 Ex Dir Purchasing/Procurement Oper ... Mr. Rogelio ANASAGASTI
35 Director Student/Financial Services ... Mr. Hernando BALDONADO
37 Director Student Financial Aid .... Mr. Scott MOORE
88 Assoc VC of Academic Instruction .... Dr. Steve LEVEY
21 Ex Dir Financial & Budget Control .... Ms. Karla BENDER

Houston Graduate School of Theology (H)

2501 Central Parkway, Suite A19,
Houston TX 77092-7726
County: Harris FICE Identification: 023202
Unit ID: 246345
Telephone: (713) 942-9505 Carnegie Class: Spec/Faith
FAX Number: (713) 942-9506 Calendar System: Semester
URL: www.hgst.edu
Established: 1983 Annual Graduate Tuition & Fees: $10,600
Enrollment: 202 Coed
Affiliation or Control: Independent Non-Profit IRS Status: 501(c)3
Highest Offering: Doctorate; No Undergraduates
Program: Professional; Religious Emphasis
Accreditation: THEOL

01 President .... Dr. James FERR
05 Assoc Dean-Curriculum & Instruction .... Dr. Chuck PITTS
73 Dir of D.Min Program .... Dr. Becky L. TOWNE
10 Chief Financial Officer .... Ms. Janell RAY
06 Registrar .... Ms. Kristin DOMERACKI
08 Director of Library Services .... Ms. Janet KENNARD

Howard College (I)

1001 Birdwell Lane, Big Spring TX 79720-3799
County: Howard FICE Identification: 003574
Unit ID: 225520
Telephone: (432) 264-5000 Carnegie Class: Assoc/Pub-R-M
FAX Number: (432) 264-5082 Calendar System: Semester
URL: www.howardcollege.edu
Established: 1945 Annual Undergrad Tuition & Fees (In-District): $2,012
Enrollment: 4,760 Coed
Affiliation or Control: State/Local IRS Status: 501(c)3
Highest Offering: Associate Degree
Program: Occupational; 2-Year Principally Bachelor's Creditable
Accreditation: SC, ADNUR, DH, RAD, SURGT

01 President ... Dr. Cheryl T. SPARKS
03 Executive Vice President ... Mr. Terry HANSEN
05 Vice President Academic Affairs ... Dr. Amy BURCHETT
12 Provost SW Col Inst for the Deaf ... Dr. Mark MYERS
12 Provost San Angelo ... Ms. LeAnne BYRD
12 Provost Big Spring ... Dr. Javier FLORES
103 Campus Dean for Workforce Devel ... Ms. Kinsey HANSEN
04 Executive Asst to the President ... Ms. Julie BAILEY
06 Registrar ... Ms. Donna MERRICK
08 Dean of Libararies ... Mr. Luis KINCADE
14 Director of Computer Services ... Mr. Ed ROBERTS
09 Dir of Institutional Effectiveness ... Ms. Barbara WALKER
56 Distance Learning Coordinator ... Ms. Kym CLARK
18 Director of Physical Plant ... Mr. Robert WILLIAMS
27 Director Information/Marketing ... Ms. Cindy SMITH
41 Athletic Director ... Mr. Britt SMITH
10 Controller ... Ms. Brenda CLAXTON
15 Director Human Resources/Payroll ... Ms. Rhonda KERNICK
96 Director of Purchasing ... Mr. Jason MIMS
37 Director of Financial Aid ... Ms. Rebecca VILLANUEVA
35 Director Student Affairs ... Ms. Lorinda HERROD
21 Assistant Controller-Student Acct ... Ms. Margaret CERVANTES
21 Assistant Controller-Fiscal Acct ... Mrs. Cherry FURQUERON
30 Director Institutional Advancement ... Mrs. Jan FORESYTH

Howard Payne University (A)

1000 Fisk Street, Brownwood TX 76801-2794
County: Brown FICE Identification: 003575
Unit ID: 225548
Telephone: (325) 646-2502 Carnegie Class: Bac/Diverse
FAX Number: (325) 649-8975 Calendar System: Semester
URL: www.hputx.edu
Established: 1889 Annual Undergrad Tuition & Fees: $19,950
Enrollment: 1,290 Coed
Affiliation or Control: Baptist IRS Status: 501(c)3
Highest Offering: Master's
Program: Liberal Arts And General; Teacher Preparatory
Accreditation: SC, IACBE, MUS, SW

01 President ... Dr. William N. ELLIS
05 Provost/Chief Academic Officer ... Dr. Mark TEW
10 Sr Vice Pres Finance/Administration ... Mrs. Brenda MCLENDON
30 Sr VP Institutional Advancement ... Dr. Brad JOHNSON
32 Vice Pres Stdnt Life/Dean Stdnts ... Mr. Brent A. MARSH
26 Assoc VP Mktng/Comm/Sp Asst to Pres ... Ms. Louise SHARP
44 Vice President Development ... Mr. Paul A. DUNNE
15 Asst VP for Bus & Hum Resources ... Mr. Bill FISHBACK
06 Registrar ... Mrs. Lana WAGNER
37 Director Financial Aid ... Mrs. Glenda HUFF
07 Director of Admission ... Mrs. Trudy MOHRE
36 Dir Academic Testing/Career Svcs ... Mr. Sam MCCUTCHEN
40 Director Bookstore ... Ms. Teresa BAIRD
29 Coordinator of Alumni Relations ... Mrs. Kristy MITCHELL
27 Director of Publications ... Mr. Kyle C. MIZE
88 Alumni and Media Relations Asst ... Ms. Kalie LOWRIE
41 Athletic Director ... Mr. Mike JONES
91 Director Administrative Computing ... Mr. Randy WEEHUNT
18 Director Facilities & Planning ... Mr. Stan PENA
90 Computer Network Administrator ... Mr. Clarence FOTHERGILL
09 Director Institutional Research ... Ms. Angie HESTON
45 Director Institutional Effectivenes ... Dr. Brent MARSH
04 Executive Assistant to President ... Mrs. Betty BROOME
38 University Counselor ... Dr. Athena BEAN
56 Dean Extended Education ... Dr. Robert TUCKER
08 Dean of Libraries ... Mrs. Nancy K. ANDERSON
81 Dean School of Science & Math ... Dr. Lynn LITTLE
50 Dean School of Business ... Dr. Leslie F. PLAGENS
53 Dean School of Ecucation ... Dr. Mike ROSATO
64 Dean Sch Music/Fine Arts/Extend Ed ... Dr. Robert TUCKER
73 Dean School of Christian Studies ... Dr. Donnie AUVENSHINE
79 Dean School of Humanities ... Dr. Justin MURPHY

Huston-Tillotson University (B)

900 Chicon Street, Austin TX 78702-2795
County: Travis FICE Identification: 003577
Unit ID: 225575
Telephone: (512) 505-3000 Carnegie Class: Bac/A&S
FAX Number: (512) 505-3190 Calendar System: Semester
URL: www.htu.edu
Established: 1875 Annual Undergrad Tuition & Fees: $12,430
Enrollment: 901 Coed
Affiliation or Control: Multiple Protestant Denominations
IRS Status: 501(c)3
Highest Offering: Baccalaureate
Program: Liberal Arts And General
Accreditation: SC

01 President & CEO ... Dr. Larry L. EARVIN
04 Executive Assistant to President ... Mr. Terry S. SMITH
05 Provost/VP Academic & Student Affs ... Dr. Vicki V. LOTT
32 Dean of Student Affairs ... Ms. Yvonne ORTIZ-PRINCE
30 VP for Institutional Advancement ... Dr. Roderick L. SMOTHERA
10 VP for Administration & Finance ... Mrs. Valerie D. HILL
20 Associate Provost ... Vacant
08 Director Library & Media Services ... Ms. Patricia A. WILKINS
36 Director Career & Grad Development ... Mr. Paul LEVERINGTON
41 Director of Athletics ... Mr. Alvin L. MOORE
84 Dean Enrollment Management ... Mr. J. Robert SHINDELL
06 Registrar ... Mrs. Earnestine J. STRICKLAND
25 Dir Sponsored PRGs/Title III Coord ... Mr. Hillary A. WILLIAMS
09 Director Inst Research & Assessment ... Dr. Thereisa COLEMAN
13 Director Information Technology ... Mr. Raymond JACOBS
26 Dir Communication & Marketing ... Mrs. Linda Y. JACKSON
18 Director of Facilities ... Mr. William S. GRIMES
30 Director of Development/Major Gifts ... Mr. Maurice MCCLONEY
29 Director of Alumni Affairs ... Ms. LaJuana R. NAPIER
35 Interim Dir Campus Life & FYE ... Ms. Destiny S. THOMPSON
88 Dir of Ctr for Academic Excellence ... Ms. Ericka D. JONES
15 Director of Human Resources ... Ms. Joy S. KING
37 Director Student Financial Aid ... Mr. Antonio HOLLOWAY
38 Dir Counseling & Consultation Ctr ... Ms. Erica J. WILKINS
42 University Chaplain ... Rev. Donald E. BREWINGTON
07 Director of Admissions ... Mrs. Shakitha STINSON
49 Interim Dean of Arts & Sciences ... Dr. Michael L. HIRSCH
50 Dean of Business & Technology ... Dr. Steven EDMOND
88 Director of Disability Services ... Mr. James E. TYSON
23 University Nurse ... Ms. Dianna G. DEAN

International Academy of Design and Technology (C)

4511 Horizon Hill Boulevard, San Antonio TX 78229
Identification: 666733
Unit ID: 450465
Telephone: (210) 530-9449 Carnegie Class: Not Classified
FAX Number: (210) 530-9463 Calendar System: Semester
URL: www.iadtsanantonio.com
Established: N/A Annual Undergrad Tuition & Fees: $11,900
Enrollment: 725 Coed
Affiliation or Control: Proprietary IRS Status: Proprietary
Highest Offering: Associate Degree
Program: 2-Year Principally Bachelor's Creditable; Fine Arts Emphasis
Accreditation: ACICS

01 Campus Director ... Mr. Gilbert DELEON

† Branch campus of International Academy of Design and Technology, Tampa, FL.

International Business College (D)

5700 Cromo Drive, El Paso TX 79912
County: El Paso FICE Identification: 009082
Unit ID: 225779
Telephone: (915) 842-0422 Carnegie Class: Not Classified
FAX Number: (915) 562-3371 Calendar System: Other
URL: www.ibcelpaso.com
Established: N/A Annual Undergrad Tuition & Fees: $11,900
Enrollment: 251 Coed
Affiliation or Control: Proprietary IRS Status: Proprietary
Highest Offering: Associate Degree
Program: Occupational
Accreditation: ACICS

01 President ... Margie AGUILAR

ITT Technical Institute (E)

551 Ryan Plaza Drive, Arlington TX 76011-3919
County: Tarrant FICE Identification: 023286
Unit ID: 225849
Telephone: (817) 794-5100 Carnegie Class: Assoc/PrivFP
FAX Number: (817) 275-8446 Calendar System: Quarter
URL: www.itt-tech.edu
Established: 1982 Annual Undergrad Tuition & Fees: N/A
Enrollment: 855 Coed
Affiliation or Control: Proprietary IRS Status: Proprietary
Highest Offering: Baccalaureate
Program: Technical Emphasis
Accreditation: ACICS

ITT Technical Institute (F)

6330 Highway 290 E, Suite 150, Austin TX 78723-1035
County: Travis Identification: 666551
Unit ID: 366678
Telephone: (512) 467-6800 Carnegie Class: Assoc/PrivFP
FAX Number: (512) 467-6677 Calendar System: Quarter
URL: www.itt-tech.edu
Established: 1985 Annual Undergrad Tuition & Fees: N/A
Enrollment: 798 Coed
Affiliation or Control: Proprietary IRS Status: Proprietary
Highest Offering: Baccalaureate
Program: Technical Emphasis
Accreditation: ACICS

† Branch campus of ITT Technical Institute, Indianapolis, IN.

ITT Technical Institute (G)

2950 South Gessner, Houston TX 77063-3751
County: Harris FICE Identification: 023287
Unit ID: 225858
Telephone: (713) 952-2294 Carnegie Class: Assoc/PrivFP
FAX Number: (713) 952-2393 Calendar System: Quarter
URL: www.itt-tech.edu
Established: 1983 Annual Undergrad Tuition & Fees: N/A
Enrollment: 688 Coed
Affiliation or Control: Proprietary IRS Status: Proprietary
Highest Offering: Baccalaureate
Program: Technical Emphasis
Accreditation: ACICS

† Branch campus of ITT Technical Institute, Indianapolis, IN.

ITT Technical Institute (H)

15651 North Freeway, Houston TX 77090-5903
County: Harris Identification: 666554
Unit ID: 366696
Telephone: (281) 873-0512 Carnegie Class: Assoc/PrivFP
FAX Number: (281) 873-0518 Calendar System: Quarter
URL: www.itt-tech.edu
Established: 1985 Annual Undergrad Tuition & Fees: N/A
Enrollment: 1,007 Coed
Affiliation or Control: Proprietary IRS Status: Proprietary
Highest Offering: Baccalaureate
Program: Technical Emphasis
Accreditation: ACICS

† Branch campus of ITT Technical Institute, Indianapolis, IN.

ITT Technical Institute (I)

2101 Waterview Parkway, Richardson TX 75080-2208
County: Dallas Identification: 666327
Unit ID: 434052
Telephone: (972) 690-9100 Carnegie Class: Assoc/PrivFP
FAX Number: (972) 690-0853 Calendar System: Quarter
URL: www.itt-tech.edu
Established: 2003 Annual Undergrad Tuition & Fees: N/A
Enrollment: 706 Coed
Affiliation or Control: Proprietary IRS Status: Proprietary
Highest Offering: Baccalaureate
Program: Technical Emphasis
Accreditation: ACICS

ITT Technical Institute (J)

5700 Northwest Parkway, San Antonio TX 78249-3303
County: Bexar FICE Identification: 030714
Unit ID: 377069
Telephone: (210) 694-4612 Carnegie Class: Assoc/PrivFP
FAX Number: (210) 694-4651 Calendar System: Quarter
URL: www.itt-tech.edu
Established: 1988 Annual Undergrad Tuition & Fees: N/A
Enrollment: 767 Coed
Affiliation or Control: Proprietary IRS Status: Proprietary
Highest Offering: Baccalaureate
Program: Technical Emphasis
Accreditation: ACICS

ITT Technical Institute (K)

1001 Magnolia Avenue, Webster TX 77598-5418
County: Harris Identification: 666552
Unit ID: 427663
Telephone: (281) 316-4700 Carnegie Class: Assoc/PrivFP
FAX Number: N/A Calendar System: Quarter
URL: www.itt-tech.edu
Established: 1995 Annual Undergrad Tuition & Fees: N/A
Enrollment: 469 Coed
Affiliation or Control: Proprietary IRS Status: Proprietary
Highest Offering: Baccalaureate
Program: Technical Emphasis
Accreditation: ACICS

† Branch campus of ITT Technical Institute, Arlington, TX.

Jacksonville College (L)

105 B. J. Albritton Drive, Jacksonville TX 75766-4759
County: Cherokee FICE Identification: 003579
Unit ID: 225876
Telephone: (903) 586-2518 Carnegie Class: Assoc/PrivNFP
FAX Number: (903) 586-0743 Calendar System: Semester
URL: www.jacksonville-college.edu
Established: 1899 Annual Undergrad Tuition & Fees: $7,516
Enrollment: 402 Coed
Affiliation or Control: Baptist IRS Status: 501(c)3
Highest Offering: Associate Degree
Program: 2-Year Principally Bachelor's Creditable
Accreditation: SC

01 President ... Dr. Edwin CRANK
05 Academic Dean/Registrar ... Ms. Tampa J. CLARK
32 Dean of Students ... Mr. David W. HUBBARD
08 Director of the Library ... Ms. Alice A. DILLON

Jarvis Christian College (M)

Highway 80 E, PR 7631, Hawkins TX 75765-1470
County: Wood FICE Identification: 003637
Unit ID: 225885
Telephone: (903) 769-5700 Carnegie Class: Bac/Diverse
FAX Number: (903) 769-4842 Calendar System: Semester
URL: www.jarvis.edu
Established: 1912 Annual Undergrad Tuition & Fees: $13,467
Enrollment: 522 Coed
Affiliation or Control: Christian Church (Disciples Of Christ)
IRS Status: 501(c)3

Highest Offering: Baccalaureate
Program: Liberal Arts And General; Teacher Preparatory
Accreditation: **SC**, ACBSP

01 President ... Dr. Cornell THOMAS
05 Vice President Academic Affairs ... Dr. Ivan FIGUEROA
11 Vice Pres Administration & Finance ... Mr. Reginald DICKENS
32 Vice President Student Affairs ... Dr. Christopher TOOTE
30 Vice Pres Institutional Advancement ... Dr. William SMIALEK
37 Asst Vice Pres of Financial Aid ... Ms. MaEsther FRANCIS
35 Assoc Vice Pres Student Affairs ... Dr. Robert HARPER
13 Director Information Technology ... Mr. Timothy ARMSTRONG
06 Registrar/Dir Inst Research ... Mr. Autry ACREY
08 Director Media Services ... Mr. William HAMPTON
29 Director of Alumni Affairs ... Mr. Gary WHITAKER
07 Director Admissions/Recruitment ... Mrs. Felecia TYISKA
26 Director Public Relations/Publicity ... Mr. Larry EVERETT
19 Chief of Security ... Mr. Christopher TOOTE
04 Assistant to the President ... Mrs. Delilah HALL
36 Placement Specialist ... Dr. Lorene HOLMES
38 Director Student Development ... Vacant
41 Athletic Director ... Mrs. Elissia BURWELL
42 College Pastor ... Mr. Olin FREGIA
18 Physical Plant Director ... Vacant
15 Director Human Resources ... Dr. Dorothy LANGLEY
20 Associate Academic Officer ... Dr. Mary MCKINNEY-JONES
96 Director of Purchasing ... Mrs. Winifred WASHINGTON

Kaplan College (A)

12005 Ford Road, Suite 100, Dallas TX 75234
County: Dallas — FICE Identification: 032723
Unit ID: 382896
Telephone: (972) 385-0641 — Carnegie Class: Not Classified
FAX Number: (972) 385-0641 — Calendar System: Other
URL: dallas.kaplancollege.com
Established: N/A — Annual Undergrad Tuition & Fees: $13,500
Enrollment: 250 — Coed
Affiliation or Control: Proprietary — IRS Status: Proprietary
Highest Offering: Associate Degree
Program: Occupational; Technical Emphasis
Accreditation: **COE**

Kaplan College (B)

8360 Burnham Road, Ste 100, El Paso TX 79907
County: El Paso — FICE Identification: 025919
Telephone: (915) 595-1935 — Carnegie Class: Not Classified
FAX Number: N/A — Calendar System: Other
URL: www.kaplan.edu
Established: N/A — Annual Undergrad Tuition & Fees: $15,200
Enrollment: 892 — Coed
Affiliation or Control: Proprietary — IRS Status: Proprietary
Highest Offering: Associate Degree
Program: Occupational
Accreditation: **ACCSC**, MAC

01 Director of Education ... Ms. Nova PENA

Kaplan College (C)

7142 San Pedro Avenue, Suite 100,
San Antonio TX 78216
County: Bexar — FICE Identification: 009466
Unit ID: 364955
Telephone: (210) 733-0777 — Carnegie Class: Not Classified
FAX Number: (210) 340-6603 — Calendar System: Other
URL: nsan-antonio.kaplancollege.com
Established: N/A — Annual Undergrad Tuition & Fees: $1,082
Enrollment: 1,175 — Coed
Affiliation or Control: Proprietary — IRS Status: Proprietary
Highest Offering: Associate Degree
Program: Occupational; 2-Year Principally Bachelor's Creditable; Technical Emphasis
Accreditation: **ACCSC**, MAC

Kaplan College (D)

6441 NW Loop 410, San Antonio TX 78238
County: Bexar — FICE Identification: 031158
Telephone: (210) 308-8584 — Carnegie Class: Not Classified
FAX Number: (210) 308-8985 — Calendar System: Other
URL: www.kaplancollege.com
Established: N/A — Annual Undergrad Tuition & Fees: $27,400
Enrollment: 1,058 — Coed
Affiliation or Control: Proprietary — IRS Status: Proprietary
Highest Offering: Associate Degree
Program: Occupational
Accreditation: **COE**, MAC

01 President ... Ms. Becky ANDERSON

KD Studio-Actors Conservatory (E)

2600 N Stemmons Fwy, Suite 117, Dallas TX 75207-2111
County: Dallas — FICE Identification: 023182
Unit ID: 225991
Telephone: (214) 638-0484 — Carnegie Class: Assoc/PrivFP
FAX Number: (214) 630-5140 — Calendar System: Semester
URL: www.kdstudio.com
Established: 1979 — Annual Undergrad Tuition & Fees: $12,850
Enrollment: 183 — Coed
Affiliation or Control: Proprietary — IRS Status: Proprietary
Highest Offering: Associate Degree
Program: Occupational
Accreditation: **THEA**

01 Chief Executive Officer ... Ms. Kathy TYNER

Kilgore College (F)

1100 Broadway, Kilgore TX 75662-3299
County: Gregg — FICE Identification: 003580
Unit ID: 226019
Telephone: (903) 984-8531 — Carnegie Class: Assoc/Pub-R-M
FAX Number: (903) 983-8600 — Calendar System: Semester
URL: www.kilgore.edu
Established: 1935 — Annual Undergrad Tuition & Fees (In-District): $1,272
Enrollment: 6,691 — Coed
Affiliation or Control: Local — IRS Status: 501(c)3
Highest Offering: Associate Degree
Program: Occupational; 2-Year Principally Bachelor's Creditable
Accreditation: **SC**, ADNUR, PTAA, SURGT

01 President ... Dr. William M. HOLDA
05 Vice President of Instruction ... Dr. Gerald M. STANGLIN
11 Vice Pres Administrative Services ... Mr. Duane MCNANEY
32 Vice President Student Development ... Dr. Mike JENKINS
57 Div Dean Liberal & Fine Arts ... Dr. Richard HARRISON
81 Div Dean Science/Math/Health Sci ... Mrs. Louise WILEY
50 Div Dean Business/Tech/Lang Devel ... Mr. Randy LEWELLEN
72 Div Dean Adult Voc Educ/Public Svcs ... Mr. Mike EARLEY
12 Div Dean of Longview Center ... Dr. Julie H. FOWLER
06 Registrar ... Mrs. Staci MARTIN
15 Director of Human Resources ... Mr. Tony JOHNSON
13 Director of Information Technology ... Mr. John COLVILLE
08 Director Library ... Ms. Kathy FAIR
40 Manager of Bookstore ... Ms. Carolyn WILLIAMS
18 Director Physical Plant ... Mr. Dalton SMITH
19 Chief of Police ... Chief Martin PESSINK
84 Dir of Marketing & Enrollment Mgmt ... Mr. Trey HATTAWAY
04 Assistant to the President ... Mrs. Karol PRUETT
30 Director of Development ... Mr. David E. WYLIE
37 Financial Aid Officer ... Mrs. Annette MORGAN
85 International Student Advisor ... Vacant
88 Supervisor Risk Management ... Mr. Perry MYERS
27 Coordinator of Public & Sports Info ... Mr. Chris CRADDOCK
09 Coord of Institutional Research ... Ms. Robin HUSKEY
36 Coordinator of Career Services ... Ms. Patty BELL
29 Coordinator of Alumni Relations ... Mrs. Paula JAMERSON
38 Coordinator of Counseling ... Mrs. Pam GATTON
96 Purchasing Agent ... Ms. Tammie PASCOE

Laredo Community College (G)

West End Washington Street, Laredo TX 78040-4395
County: Webb — FICE Identification: 003582
Unit ID: 226134
Telephone: (956) 722-0521 — Carnegie Class: Assoc/Pub-R-L
FAX Number: (956) 721-5381 — Calendar System: Semester
URL: www.laredo.edu
Established: 1946 — Annual Undergrad Tuition & Fees (In-District): $3,430
Enrollment: 9,994 — Coed
Affiliation or Control: Local — IRS Status: 501(c)3
Highest Offering: Associate Degree
Program: Occupational; 2-Year Principally Bachelor's Creditable; Technical Emphasis
Accreditation: **SC**, ADNUR, MLTAD, OTA, PTAA, RAD

01 President ... Dr. Juan L. MALDONADO
05 Vice President for Instruction ... Dr. Dianna L. MILLER
32 Vice President for Student Services ... Dr. Vincent R. SOLIS
25 Vice President for Resource Develop ... Dr. Nora R. GARZA
10 Chief Admin & Financial Officer ... Mr. Eleazar GONZALEZ
86 Chief Ext Affairs/Econ Dev Officer ... Mr. Blas CASTANEDA
88 Institutional Effectiveness Officer ... Dr. Federico SOLIS, JR.
49 Dean Arts & Humanities ... Mr. Phil W. WORLEY
12 Dean - LCC South ... Mr. Luciano RAMON
103 Dean of Workforce Education ... Ms. Roxanne VEDIA
81 Dean of Sciences ... Mr. J. Alfredo INIGUEZ-JIMENEZ
35 Dean of Students ... Mr. Robert L. OCHOA
84 Dean of Enrollment Management ... Mr. J. Felix GAMEZ
09 Dir Institutional Research & Plng ... Mrs. Maria Luisa RAMIREZ
08 Director of Library ... Mr. Thomas W. LAFLEUR
13 Director Information Technology ... Mr. Jose A. PENA, JR.
21 Comptroller ... Mr. Cesar E. VELA, JR.
18 Director Physical Plant ... Mr. Jacob C. FLORES
27 Dir Marketing/Public Relations ... Mrs. Deirdre REYNA
88 Internal Auditor ... Vacant
37 Director Student Financial Aid ... Dr. Romeo R. MORENO
07 Director Enrollment & Registration ... Ms. Martha S. TREVINO
51 Director of Continuing Education ... Ms. Sandra L. CORTEZ
41 Athletic Director ... Mr. Troy G. VAN BRUNT
06 Registrar ... Ms. Olga D. RUBIO
15 Director of Human Resources ... Mr. Lee SPAIN
31 Dir Donor Relations & Spec Proj ... Ms. Millicent SLAUGHTER
38 Director of Student Success Ctr ... Mr. Carmelino CASTILLO, JR.
96 Director of Purchasing ... Mr. Ramiro V. MARTINEZ
19 Chief of Campus Police ... Mr. Ray CORTEZ
23 Director of Health Services ... Ms. Melissa GARCIA
24 Associate Director of Media Center ... Mr. Ceferino IZAGUIRRE

Le Cordon Bleu College of Culinary Arts in Austin (H)

3110 Esperanza Crossing Suite 100, Austin TX 78758
County: Travis — FICE Identification: 025693
Unit ID: 364973
Telephone: (512) 837-2665 — Carnegie Class: Assoc/PrivFP
FAX Number: (512) 977-9753 — Calendar System: Other
URL: www.chefs.edu/austin
Established: 1981 — Annual Undergrad Tuition & Fees: $45,200
Enrollment: 1,032 — Coed
Affiliation or Control: Proprietary — IRS Status: Proprietary
Highest Offering: Associate Degree
Program: Occupational; Technical Emphasis
Accreditation: **ACICS**, ACFEI

01 President ... Steve SMITH

Le Cordon Bleu College of Culinary Arts in Dallas (I)

11830 Webb Chapel Road, Suite 1200, Dallas TX 75234
Identification: 666728
Unit ID: 452063
Telephone: (214) 647-8505 — Carnegie Class: Not Classified
FAX Number: (972) 406-9935 — Calendar System: Semester
URL: www.chefs.edu/dallas
Established: N/A — Annual Undergrad Tuition & Fees: $34,500
Enrollment: 1,046 — Coed
Affiliation or Control: Proprietary — IRS Status: Proprietary
Highest Offering: Associate Degree
Program: Occupational; 2-Year Principally Bachelor's Creditable
Accreditation: **ACICS**

01 President ... Ms. Maureen K. CLEMENTS

† Branch campus of Le Cordon Bleu College of Culinary Arts, Austin, TX.

Lee College (J)

511 S Whiting, PO Box 818, Baytown TX 77522-0818
County: Harris — FICE Identification: 003583
Unit ID: 226204
Telephone: (281) 427-5611 — Carnegie Class: Assoc/Pub-S-MC
FAX Number: (281) 425-6555 — Calendar System: Semester
URL: www.lee.edu
Established: 1934 — Annual Undergrad Tuition & Fees (In-District): $1,470
Enrollment: 6,719 — Coed
Affiliation or Control: State/Local — IRS Status: 501(c)3
Highest Offering: Associate Degree
Program: Occupational; 2-Year Principally Bachelor's Creditable
Accreditation: **SC**, ADNUR

01 President ... Dr. Michael T. MURPHY
101 Admin Asst Pres/Secy to Board ... Vacant
05 VP Instruction ... Dr. Cathy KEMPER
32 VP Student Affairs ... Dr. Donnetta SUCHON
38 Assoc Dean/Dir Counseling Services ... Dr. Rosemary COFFMAN
10 VP Finance & Administration ... Mr. Steve EVANS
21 Executive Dir Accounting ... Mr. Keith SCHEFFLER
12 Dean of Huntsville Center at TDCJ ... Ms. Donna P. ZUNIGA
30 Exec Dir Institutional Advancement ... Ms. Mary Ann AMELANG
14 Exec Dir Tech/Research/Planning ... Dr. Carolyn A. LIGHTFOOT
18 Executive Director Physical Plant ... Mr. Alvin SCHNEIDER
06 Registrar ... Ms. Becki S. GRIFFITH
07 Director College Relations ... Mr. Steve LESTARJETTE
96 Director Purchasing ... Mr. Mike SPARKES
103 Director Continuing Education ... Ms. Jonna CAGLE-PAGE
15 Director Human Resources ... Mrs. Amanda SUMMERS
37 Director Financial Aid ... Mrs. Sharon MULLINS
40 Director Auxiliary Services ... Ms. Suzanne MACHALA
41 Director Athletics ... Mr. Roy CHAMPAGNE
08 Dir Library/Instructional Support ... Mr. Paul ARRIGO
25 Grants Development Officer ... Ms. Pam WARFORD
26 Public Relations Manager ... Mrs. Anikka AYALA-ROGERS
36 Stdnt Career/Employment Specialist ... Ms. Cindy PEREZA

LeTourneau University (K)

PO Box 7001, 2100 S Mobberly Ave,
Longview TX 75607-7001
County: Gregg — FICE Identification: 003584
Unit ID: 226231
Telephone: (903) 233-3000 — Carnegie Class: Master's M
FAX Number: (903) 233-3101 — Calendar System: Semester
URL: www.letu.edu
Established: 1946 — Annual Undergrad Tuition & Fees: $24,120
Enrollment: 3,304 — Coed
Affiliation or Control: Independent Non-Profit — IRS Status: 501(c)3
Highest Offering: Master's
Program: Liberal Arts And General; Teacher Preparatory; Professional
Accreditation: **SC**, ENG, ENGT, IACBE

01 President ... Dr. Dale A. LUNSFORD
05 Provost & Executive Vice President ... Dr. Philip COYLE
30 VP University Development ... Mr. Ben MARCH
10 VP Finance/Administration ... Mr. Mike HOOD
32 Dean of Students ... Mr. Corey ROSS
84 VP Enrollment Services ... Mrs. Linda H. FITZHUGH
45 VP Accreditation & Quality Assuranc ... Mrs. Marila D. PALMER

58 VP Grad/Professional Studies ... Dr. Carol GREEN
20 Assoc VP Academic Affairs ... Dr. Steven D. MASON
84 Asst VP Enroll Mgmt/Mkt Research ... Mr. Christopher W. FONTAINE
18 Asst VP of Facilities Services ... Mr. Daniel FIEDLER
53 Dean School of Education ... Dr. Wayne JACOBS
50 Dean School of Business ... Dr. Bob WHARTON
54 Dean Sch Engineering & Engr Tech ... Dr. Ronald DELAP
49 Dean School of Arts & Sciences ... Dr. Larry FRAZIER
88 Dean School of Aeronautical Science ... Mr. Fred L. RITCHEY
35 Assoc Dean Student Life ... Mr. Chad MELTON
30 Assoc VP University Development ... Mr. Scott FOSSEY
08 Director Learning Resource Center ... Vacant
41 Director of Athletics ... Ms. Terri DEIKE
46 Director Office of Sponsored Pgms ... Mr. Paul R. BOGGS
56 Director Distance Lrng ... Vacant
13 Chief Information Officer ... Mr. Matthew HENRY
15 Director of Human Resources ... Mrs. Natalie THOMAS
23 Director Health Services ... Ms. Shela B. DAWSON
42 University Chaplain ... Dr. Harold F. CARL
19 Chief of Police ... Mr. Terrance A. TURNER
36 Director of Career Development ... Mr. Steven J. GATTON
06 University Registrar ... Mrs. Ginger MOORE
07 Director of Admissions ... Mr. James R. TOWNSEND
29 Director of Alumni & Parent Rels ... Mrs. Martha STEED
26 Director of Univ Relations ... Ms. Janet RAGLAND
102 Dir of Corp/Foundation Relations ... Mr. Randall YEAKLEY
44 Dir of Gift Planning and Endowed ... Mr. Bryan E. BENSON
12 Director Austin Educational Ctr ... Dr. R. Murlene WATWOOD
12 Director Dallas Educational Center ... Dr. Bonita VINSON
12 Director Houston Education Center ... Dr. R. Murlene WATWOOD
71 Dir Curriculum/Academic Resources ... Mr. Julian R. COWART
21 Controller ... Ms. Vikki KEILERS
09 Sr Dir Inst Effectiv & Retention ... Dr. Pamela JOHNSON
88 Asst to the President for Outreach ... Dr. Tim WATSON
96 Purchasing Agent ... Mrs. Jana CAMPBELL
88 Executive Dir Ctr for Faith & Work ... Mr. Bill PEEL

Lincoln College of Technology (A)

2915 Alouette Drive, Grand Praire TX 75052
County: Tarrant FICE Identification: 008353
Unit ID: 226277
Telephone: (972) 660-5701 Carnegie Class: Not Classified
FAX Number: (972) 660-6148 Calendar System: Other
URL: www.lincolntech.com
Established: N/A Annual Undergrad Tuition & Fees: $19,341
Enrollment: 1,839 Coed
Affiliation or Control: Proprietary IRS Status: Proprietary
Highest Offering: Associate Degree
Program: Occupational
Accreditation: ACCSC

01 Executive Director ... Mr. Paul MCGURIK

Lon Morris College (B)

800 College Avenue, Jacksonville TX 75766-2900
County: Cherokee FICE Identification: 003585
Unit ID: 226329
Telephone: (903) 589-4000 Carnegie Class: Assoc/PrivNFP
FAX Number: (903) 586-8562 Calendar System: Semester
URL: www.lonmorris.edu
Established: 1873 Annual Undergrad Tuition & Fees: $14,200
Enrollment: 815 Coed
Affiliation or Control: United Methodist IRS Status: 501(c)3
Highest Offering: Associate Degree
Program: 2-Year Principally Bachelor's Creditable; Business Emphasis
Accreditation: SC

01 President ... Dr. Miles L. MCCALL
10 Vice Pres Business Admin Affairs ... Mr. Tommy FERGUSON
05 Provost ... Dr. Loretta GALLEGOS
06 Academic Dean/Registrar ... Dr. John ROSS
32 Interim Dean of Students ... Mr. Kent WILLIS
37 Director Financial Aid ... Ms. Kayla CHRISTIANSEN
07 Director Admissions ... Ms. Jessica N. CHILES
08 Librarian ... Ms. Linda GRAY
35 Director of Campus Life ... Mr. David GEHRELS
09 Director of Institutional Research ... Dr. Danny POTTER
15 Director Human Resources ... Ms. Carolyn NANNI
41 Athletic Director ... Mr. Dale DOTSON
42 Chaplain ... Rev. Rhett ANSLEY

Lone Star College System (C)

5000 Research Forest Drive,
The Woodlands TX 77381-4399
County: Harris FICE Identification: 011145
Unit ID: 227182
Telephone: (832) 813-6500 Carnegie Class: Assoc/Pub-S-MC
FAX Number: N/A Calendar System: Semester
URL: www.lonestar.edu
Established: 1972 Annual Undergrad Tuition & Fees (In-District): $1,408
Enrollment: 69,339 Coed
Affiliation or Control: State/Local IRS Status: 501(c)3
Highest Offering: Associate Degree
Program: Occupational; 2-Year Principally Bachelor's Creditable
Accreditation: SC, ADNUR, CEA, DH, DMS, EMT, MAC, OTA, PTAA, RAD, SURGT

01 Chancellor ... Dr. Richard CARPENTER
03 Senior Executive Vice Chancellor ... Dr. Rand KEY
05 Vice Chanc Acad Affs/Stdnt Success ... Dr. Donetta GOODALL
10 Vice Chanc for Admin & Finance ... Ms. Cynthia GILLIAM
27 Vice Chanc Information Technology ... Mr. Shah ARDALAN
26 Vice Chancellor External Affairs ... Mr. Ray LAUGHTER
43 General Counsel ... Mr. Brian NELSON
101 Special Asst to Chancellor/Board ... Ms. Helen CLOUGHERTY
12 President of LSC-Kingwood ... Dr. Katherine PERSSON
12 President of LSC-Tomball ... Dr. Susan KARR
12 President of LSC-North Harris ... Dr. Steve HEAD
12 President of LSC-Montgomery ... Dr. Austin LANE
12 President of LSC-CyFair ... Dr. Audre LEVY
27 Assoc Vice Chanc Marketing & Comm ... Ms. Laura MORRIS
18 AVC Construction/Facilities ... Mr. Jimmy MARTIN
28 Exec Dir Employmnt Svcs & Diversity ... Vacant
15 Sys Dir Compensatn/Records/Benefits ... Ms. Lisa COWART
105 Executive Director Web Development ... Ms. Jennifer MURILLO
21 Assoc Vice Chanc Business Services ... Ms. Carin HUTCHINS
21 Assoc Vice Chanc Accounting ... Ms. Diane NOVAK
16 Assoc Gen Counsel Human Resources ... Ms. Anne ZEMEK
20 Assoc VC Curriculum & Instr ... Dr. Linda LUEHRS-WOLFE
106 Assoc Vice Chanc Lonestar On-line ... Vacant
35 Assoc VC for Student Success ... Vacant
103 Assoc VC Workforce & Econ Dev ... Ms. Linda HEAD
86 AVC Govt Affairs & Inst Adv ... Mr. Jonathan DURFIELD
09 AVC Ofc Research/Inst Effectiveness ... Dr. Siobhan FLEMING
08 Director Library/LSC-North Harris ... Ms. Pradeep LELE
13 Assoc VC Office Tech Services ... Mr. Link ALANDER
20 Assoc VC Educ Partnerships/P-16 Init ... Dr. Ronald BROWN
08 Dean Ed Support Svcs/LSC-Kingwood ... Ms. Peggy WHITLEY
08 Director Library/LSC-Montgomery ... Dr. Janice PEYTON
08 Director Library/LSC-Cy Fair ... Mr. Michael STAFFORD
08 Director Library/Tomball ... Ms. Pamela SHAFER
37 Director Student Financial Aid ... Mr. Reggie BRAZZLE
21 Director Internal Audit ... Vacant
19 Chief of Police/Dir Pub Safety ... Mr. Richard GREGORY
96 Director of Purchasing ... Ms. Laura RIVERA

Lubbock Christian University (D)

5601 19th Street, Lubbock TX 79407-2099
County: Lubbock FICE Identification: 003586
Unit ID: 226383
Telephone: (806) 796-8800 Carnegie Class: Master's S
FAX Number: (806) 720-7255 Calendar System: Semester
URL: www.lcu.edu
Established: 1957 Annual Undergrad Tuition & Fees: $16,870
Enrollment: 2,028 Coed
Affiliation or Control: Churches Of Christ IRS Status: 501(c)3
Highest Offering: Master's
Program: Liberal Arts And General; Teacher Preparatory
Accreditation: SC, NUR, SW

01 Chancellor ... Dr. L. Ken JONES
03 Executive Vice President ... Dr. Brian STARR
05 Provost & Chief Academic Officer ... Dr. Rodney B. BLACKWOOD
43 General Counsel ... Mrs. Monica BARNARD
26 Vice President University Relations ... Mr. John C. KING
10 Vice Pres for Financial Services ... Mrs. Tia CLARY
13 Vice President for Technology ... Dr. Karl MAHAN
107 Dean Col of Professional Studies ... Dr. Steve GERMAN
49 Dean College Liberal Arts/Education ... Dr. Susan BLASSINGAME
73 Dean Col Biblical Stds/Behavior Sci ... Dr. Jesse LONG
09 Asst VP for Instl Effectiveness ... Dr. Randy SELLERS
32 Asst VP for Student Success ... Mr. Mondy R. BREWER
41 Athletic Director ... Mr. Paul HISE
06 Registrar ... Mrs. Janice STONE
37 Director of Financial Assistance ... Mrs. Amy HARDESTY
35 Dean of Students ... Mr. Josh STEPHENS
08 Director of Library Services ... Ms. Rebecca J. VICKERS
18 Director of Campus Facilities ... Mr. Mike SELLECK
38 Director Student Counseling ... Ms. Janelle M. BUCHANAN
92 Director of Honors Program ... Dr. Stacy PATTY
23 Director of Medical Clinic ... Dr. Jeff SMITH
13 Director of Technology Services ... Mr. Robert SMITH
88 Director of Disability Services ... Mr. Alisha WALLACE
39 Director of Residental Life ... Mrs. Sunny PARK
07 Director of Admissions ... Mr. Charlie WEBB
15 Human Resources Director ... Mrs. Brenda LOWE
29 Director Alumni Relations ... Mr. Matt PADEN
19 Director of Security ... Mr. Michael SMITH
40 Bookstore Manager ... Mrs. Denise MCNEILL

McLennan Community College (E)

1400 College Drive, Waco TX 76708-1498
County: McLennan FICE Identification: 003590
Unit ID: 226578
Telephone: (254) 299-8000 Carnegie Class: Assoc/Pub-R-L
FAX Number: (254) 299-8654 Calendar System: Semester
URL: www.mclennan.edu
Established: 1965 Annual Undergrad Tuition & Fees (In-District): $2,568
Enrollment: 9,500 Coed
Affiliation or Control: State/Local IRS Status: 501(c)3
Highest Offering: Associate Degree
Program: Occupational; 2-Year Principally Bachelor's Creditable; Nursing Emphasis
Accreditation: SC, ADNUR, EEG, MLTAD, PTAA, RAD, SURGT

01 President ... Dr. Johnette MCKOWN
10 Vice Pres Finance & Administration ... Mr. Gene GOOCH
05 Vice President Instruction ... Dr. Donald BALMOS
46 Vice President Program Development ... Mr. Al POLLARD
32 Vice President Student Services ... Dr. Santos MARTINEZ
09 Vice Pres Research/Plng & Info Tech ... Dr. Paul ILLICH
102 Exec Director McLennan CC Found ... Mr. Harry HARELIK
11 Director of Administrative Services ... Ms. Lori SOUTHERN
37 Director of Financial Aid ... Mr. James KUBACAK
26 Director Community Relations ... Ms. Lisa WILHELMI
41 Director Athletics ... Mrs. Shawn TROCHIM
06 Director Records & Registration ... Mr. Herman V. TUCKER
07 Director Admissions & Recruitment ... Mrs. Karen CLARK
08 Director Library Services ... Mr. Daniel MARTINSEN
15 Director Human Resources ... Mrs. Phyllis BLACKWOOD
18 Director Physical Plant ... Mrs. Dianne E. FEYERHERM
21 Director Financial Services ... Mrs. Terry LECHLER
103 Dean of Workforce Education ... Dr. Ronald EPPS
49 Dean of Arts & Sciences ... Vacant
51 Dean of Continuing Education ... Mr. Frank GRAVES

McMurry University (F)

1400 Sayles Boulevard, Abilene TX 79697-0002
County: Taylor FICE Identification: 003591
Unit ID: 226587
Telephone: (325) 793-3800 Carnegie Class: Bac/Diverse
FAX Number: (325) 793-6800 Calendar System: Semester
URL: www.mcm.edu
Established: 1923 Annual Undergrad Tuition & Fees: $21,870
Enrollment: 1,414 Coed
Affiliation or Control: United Methodist IRS Status: 501(c)3
Highest Offering: Master's
Program: Liberal Arts And General; Teacher Preparatory
Accreditation: SC, NURSE

01 President ... Dr. John H. RUSSELL
05 Vice President for Academic Affairs ... Dr. Paul FABRIZIO
10 Vice Pres for Financial Affairs ... Mrs. Lisa L. WILLIAMS
84 Vice Pres Enroll Mgmt/Student Rels ... Vacant
30 Vice President for Inst Advancement ... Mr. Steve CRISMAN
13 Vice Pres for Info & Support Svcs ... Mr. Brad POORMAN
105 Webmaster ... Mr. Jim QUINNETT
90 Customer Service Director ... Mr. Freddie FAMBLE, JR.
11 Director of Administrative Systems ... Ms. Kathy DENSLOW
06 Registrar ... Mrs. Carolyn A. CALVERT
08 Director Jay-Rollins Library ... Ms. Terry YOUNG
24 Director of Media Center ... Mr. David WILLIAMS
32 Dean of Students ... Ms. Vanessa ROBERTS
81 Dean Sch Natural/Computational Sci ... Dr. Alicia WYATT
83 Dean Sch Social Sciences/Religion ... Dr. Phil LEMASTERS
57 Dean School of Arts & Letters ... Dr. Christina WILSON
50 Dean School of Business ... Dr. K. O. LONG
53 Dean School of Education ... Dr. Perry Kay HALEY-BROWN
66 Dean School of Nursing ... Dr. Nina OUIMETTE
07 Interim Director of Admission ... Ms. Kimberly POLIGALA
35 Dir Student Activities/Orientation ... Mr. Peter ANZOLLITTO
37 Director of Financial Aid ... Mrs. Rachel ATKINS
12 Dyess Air Force Base Pgm Director ... Dr. Rosemary K. WALLACE
18 Director Physical Plant ... Mr. John HARVEY
21 Controller ... Mrs. Carole RICKETTS
15 Director of Human Resources ... Ms. Lecia HUGHES
26 Director Univ/External Relations ... Ms. Nancy SMITH
27 Assoc Dir of University Relations ... Mr. Gary ELLISON
09 Dir of Institutional Effectiveness ... Dr. Thomas BENOIT
46 Director of Institutional Research ... Ms. Terry NIXON
29 Director Alumni/Church Relations ... Mr. Greeley MYERS
36 Director of Counseling/Career Svcs ... Mr. James GREER
38 Asst Dir Counseling & Career Svcs ... Ms. Karen DOUGLAS
41 Athletic Director ... Mr. Ron HOLMES
42 University Chaplain ... Rev. Tim KENNEDY
19 Director of Security/Safety ... Mr. Mark R. ODOM
23 University Nurse ... Ms. Ronda HOELSCHER
92 Director Honors Program ... Dr. Philip LE MASTERS
106 Online Ed Design Support Specialist ... Ms. Vicki DUNNAM

Midland College (G)

3600 N Garfield, Midland TX 79705-6397
County: Midland FICE Identification: 009797
Unit ID: 226806
Telephone: (432) 685-4500 Carnegie Class: Assoc/Pub4
FAX Number: (432) 685-4714 Calendar System: Semester
URL: www.midland.edu
Established: 1969 Annual Undergrad Tuition & Fees (In-District): $864
Enrollment: 6,344 Coed
Affiliation or Control: Local IRS Status: 501(c)3
Highest Offering: Baccalaureate
Program: Occupational; 2-Year Principally Bachelor's Creditable
Accreditation: SC, ADNUR, DMS

01 President ... Dr. Steve THOMAS
03 Executive Vice President ... Dr. Richard C. JOLLY
05 Vice President of Instruction ... Dr. Rex PEEBLES
10 Vice Pres Administrative Services ... Mr. Rick BENDER
32 Vice President Student Services ... Ms. Rita Nell DIFFIE
30 Vice President of Inst Advancement ... Dr. Eileen PIWETZ
13 Vice Pres Information Techonology ... Mr. Dennis SEVER
20 Assoc Vice Pres of Instruction ... Dr. Deana M. SAVAGE
20 Assoc Vice Pres of Instruction ... Dr. Stan G. JACOBS
04 Assistant to the President ... Mrs. Bahola EDWARDS
32 Dean Stdnt Svcs/Spec Populations ... Vacant
106 Dean of Distance Learning ... Mr. Dale BEIKIRCH
50 Dean of Business Studies ... Mr. Gavin FRANTZ

57 Dean of Fine Arts ... Mr. Billy FEELER
72 Dean of Technical Studies ... Mr. Curt PERVIER
76 Dean of Health Sciences ... Dr. Becky HAMMACK
81 Dean of Math & Sciences ... Dr. Margaret WADE
83 Dean Social & Behavioral Sciences ... Dr. Will MORRIS
06 Registrar ... Mrs. Angela BALCH
08 Head Librarian ... Mr. John DEATS
15 Exec Director of Human Services ... Ms. Zaira VALERIANO
18 Chief of Facilities/Physical Plant ... Mr. Ken RILEY
19 Director Security ... Mr. Martin GARCIA
27 Dean of Public Information ... Ms. Rebecca BELL
35 Director Student Affairs ... Vacant
40 Director Bookstore ... Ms. Barbara UNDERWOOD
41 Athletic Director ... Mr. Forrest ALLEN
09 Director of Institutional Research ... Mr. Thomas CORLL
36 Director Student Placement ... Vacant
37 Director Student Financial Aid ... Ms. Latisha WILLIAMS
96 Purchasing Agent ... Ms. Barbara FENNELL
84 Dean of Enrollment ... Dr. Michael CHAVEZ
07 Director of Admissions/Recruitment ... Dr. Ryan GIBBS

Midwestern State University (A)

3410 Taft Boulevard, Wichita Falls TX 76308-2095
County: Wichita FICE Identification: 003592
Unit ID: 226833
Telephone: (940) 397-4000 Carnegie Class: Master's M
FAX Number: (940) 397-4042 Calendar System: Semester
URL: www.mwsu.edu
Established: 1922 Annual Undergrad Tuition & Fees (In-State): $6,910
Enrollment: 6,426 Coed
Affiliation or Control: State IRS Status: 501(c)3
Highest Offering: Master's
Program: Liberal Arts And General; Teacher Preparatory; Professional
Accreditation: SC, BUS, DH, ENG, ENGT, MUS, NURSE, RAD, SW

01 President ... Dr. Jesse W. ROGERS
05 Provost ... Dr. Alisa WHTE
58 Dean of Graduate School ... Dr. Pattie HAMILTON
46 VP Inst Effectiveness ... Dr. Robert E. CLARK
10 VP Administration & Finance ... Mr. Juan SANDOVAL
30 VP Univ Advncmnt & Stdnt Affairs ... Dr. Howard M. FARRELL
32 Assoc VP Student Affairs ... Dr. Keith LAMB
18 Assoc VP Facilities Services ... Mr. Kyle OWEN
14 Director Information Systems ... Mr. Michael DYE
06 Registrar ... Ms. Darla INGLISH
08 University Librarian ... Dr. Clara LATHAM
35 Dean of Students ... Mr. Dail NEELY
37 Director of Student Financial Aid ... Ms. Kathy PENNARTZ
38 Director of Counseling Center ... Dr. Pam MIDGETT
51 Director of Extended Education ... Dr. Pamela MORGAN
07 Director of Admissions ... Ms. Barbara MERKLE
19 Chief of Police ... Mr. Dan WILLIAMS
27 Int Dir Public Info/Marketing ... Ms. Julie GAYNOR
30 Dir Donor Services and Scholarships ... Ms. Laura PETERSON
36 Director Career Management Center ... Mr. Dirk WELCH
41 Director of Athletics ... Mr. Charles CARR
15 Director of Human Resources ... Ms. Dianne WEAKLEY
09 Dir of Inst Research & Plng ... Vacant
21 Controller ... Ms. Gail FERGUSON
23 Director Vinson Health Center ... Ms. Peggy A. BOOMER
50 Interim Dean College Business Admin ... Dr. Barbara NEMECEK
53 Dean College of Education ... Dr. Matthew CAPPS
57 Dean College of Fine Arts ... Dr. Ron FISCHLI
76 Dean College Health Sci/Human Svcs ... Dr. Susan SPORTSMAN
79 Dean College Humanities/Social Sci ... Dr. Samuel E. WATSON, III
81 Int Dean College of Science & Math ... Dr. Rodney CATE
86 Director Board & Govt Relations ... Ms. Deborah L. BARROW
29 Director of Alumni Relations ... Ms. Leslee PONDER
88 Director of Academic Success Center ... Ms. Naoma CLARK
105 Webmaster ... Mr. Robert STEFLIK
96 Director of Purchasing ... Mr. Stephen SHELLEY
88 Dir Disability Support Services ... Ms. Debra HIGGINBOTHAM
88 Dir Student Development/Orientation ... Mr. Matthew PARK
39 Director Housing & Residence Life ... Mr. Michael MILLS
44 Director Annual Fund ... Vacant
85 Director of International Education ... Dr. Larry WILLIAMS
92 Director Honors Program ... Dr. Mark FARRIS
88 Director Testing Center ... Ms. Lynn DUCIOAME
88 Director International Services ... Dr. Randy GLEAN
88 Director Budget & Management ... Ms. Valarie MAXWELL
88 Director Museum ... Vacant
88 Director Student Support Services ... Ms. Lisa ESTRADA-HAMBY
88 Campus Postal Supervisor ... Ms. Cindy LOVELESS

Navarro College (B)

3200 W Seventh Avenue, Corsicana TX 75110-4899
County: Navarro FICE Identification: 003593
Unit ID: 227146
Telephone: (903) 874-6501 Carnegie Class: Assoc/Pub-R-L
FAX Number: (903) 874-4636 Calendar System: Semester
URL: www.navarrocollege.edu
Established: 1946 Annual Undergrad Tuition & Fees (In-District): $1,362
Enrollment: 10,166 Coed
Affiliation or Control: Local IRS Status: 501(c)3
Highest Offering: Associate Degree
Program: Occupational; 2-Year Principally Bachelor's Creditable
Accreditation: SC, ADNUR, MLTAD, OTA

01 District President ... Dr. Richard M. SANCHEZ
12 President Ellis Co Campuses ... Dr. Harold NOLTE
05 Vice President Academic Affairs ... Dr. Kenneth MARTIN
10 Vice President Finance & Admin ... Ms. Gertrud MORENO
30 Vice Pres Institutional Advancement ... Dr. Tommy STRINGER
32 Vice President Student Services ... Ms. Maryann HAILEY
84 Vice Pres Enrollment Mgmt/Inst Stds ... Mr. T. Dewayne GRAGG
15 Director Human Resources ... Ms. Marcy BALLEW
26 Director Marketing Relations ... Ms. Donna PARISH
41 Athletic Director ... Mr. Roark MONTGOMERY
49 Dean of Arts/Sciences/Humanities ... Dr. Larry WEAVER
72 Dean Career & Technical Education ... Dr. Harold HOUSLEY
12 Dean of Midlothian Campus ... Dr. Cubie WARD
12 Dean of NC South ... Mr. Guy FEATHERSTON
21 Comptroller ... Ms. Aaron YORK
51 Director Continuing Education ... Ms. Kristin WALKER
08 Director of Libraries ... Mr. Tim KEVIL
06 Registrar ... Mr. David EDWARDS
18 Chief Facilities/Physical Plant ... Mr. Karl HUMPHRIES
14 Director of Computer Center ... Ms. Dana HOLLAND
37 Director Student Financial Aid ... Mr. Edward C. EPHLIN
35 Director Student Affairs ... Mr. Phil W. SIMS
40 College Store Coordinator ... Ms. Nancy JOHNSON

North Central Texas College (C)

1525 W California Street, Gainesville TX 76240-4699
County: Cooke FICE Identification: 003558
Unit ID: 224110
Telephone: (940) 668-7731 Carnegie Class: Assoc/Pub-R-L
FAX Number: (940) 668-6049 Calendar System: Semester
URL: www.nctc.edu
Established: 1924 Annual Undergrad Tuition & Fees (In-District): $1,470
Enrollment: 9,462 Coed
Affiliation or Control: State/Local IRS Status: 501(c)3
Highest Offering: Associate Degree
Program: Occupational; 2-Year Principally Bachelor's Creditable
Accreditation: SC, ADNUR, SURGT

01 President ... Dr. Eddie L. HADLOCK
05 Vice President of Instruction ... Vacant
32 Vice President of Student Services ... Dr. Billy ROESSLER
11 Dean of Administrative Services ... Dr. Stephen BROYLES
10 Vice President Financial Services ... Dr. Janie NEIGHBORS
30 Vice Pres Institutional Advancement ... Ms. Debbie SHARP
12 Dean of Denton County Campuses ... Mr. Roy CULBERSON
18 Sr Dir of Campus Operations ... Mr. Robbie BAUGH
12 Dean of Bowie & Graham Campuses ... Mrs. Emily KLEMENT
09 Dir Inst Research & Effectiveness ... Mr. David BROWN
06 Registrar/Director of Admission ... Ms. Kari FORD
08 Librarian ... Ms. Diane ROETHER
37 Financial Aid Director ... Ms. Ashley TATUM
38 Director of Advisement ... Mrs. Tracey FLENIKEN
26 Asst to Pres Marketing/Cmty Rels ... Mr. Rodger BOYCE
41 Athletic Director ... Mr. Van HEDRICK
66 Dean of Nursing Program ... Mrs. Gie ARCHER
32 Director of Student Life ... Ms. Kim BROWN
72 Dean of Applied Sciences ... Vacant
49 Dean of Arts & Sciences ... Dr. Larry GILBERT

Northeast Texas Community College (D)

PO Box 1307, Mount Pleasant TX 75456-1307
County: Titus FICE Identification: 023154
Unit ID: 227225
Telephone: (903) 434-8100 Carnegie Class: Assoc/Pub-R-M
FAX Number: (903) 572-6712 Calendar System: Semester
URL: www.ntcc.edu
Established: 1984 Annual Undergrad Tuition & Fees (In-District): $1,668
Enrollment: 3,226 Coed
Affiliation or Control: Local IRS Status: 501(c)3
Highest Offering: Associate Degree
Program: Occupational; 2-Year Principally Bachelor's Creditable; Teacher Preparatory
Accreditation: SC, DH, MAC, MLTAD, PTAA, RAD

01 President ... Dr. Brad W. JOHNSON
04 Executive Asst to the President ... Ms. Pat L. TALLANT
05 Executive Vice Pres for Instruction ... Dr. Ron CLINTON
11 Vice Pres Administrative Services ... Ms. Beth THOMPSON
30 Vice Pres Institutional Advancement ... Dr. Jonathan W. MCCULLOUGH
32 VP for Student & Outreach Services ... Dr. Judy G. TRAYLOR
37 Dean Enroll/Dir Student Fin Assist ... Ms. Kim LAWRENCE
76 Dean of Allied Health Professions ... Dr. Jena HAMRA
50 Dean of Bus/Tech/Continuing Educ ... Mr. Kevin ROSE
84 Associate Dean of Outreach Services ... Ms. Melody HENRY
18 Director of Plant Services ... Mr. Tim JOHNSTON
51 Director of Continuing Education ... Ms. Teresa WOOTEN
08 Director Learning Resource Center ... Mr. Lonnie P. BEENE
91 Director of Computer Services ... Mr. Kenneth GOODSON
26 Director Marketing/Public Relations ... Ms. Jodi WEBER
06 Registrar ... Ms. Betsy GOODING
15 Director Human Resources ... Ms. Diana HALL
10 Controller ... Ms. Jaci M. MERRITT
09 Dir Institutional Effectiveness ... Ms. Toni LABEFF
88 Advisor/Retention Specialist ... Mr. Miles YOUNG
36 Career Development/Advisor ... Ms. Lynda WATSON

Oblate School of Theology (E)

285 Oblate Drive, San Antonio TX 78216-6693
County: Bexar FICE Identification: 003595
Unit ID: 227289
Telephone: (210) 341-1366 Carnegie Class: Spec/Faith
FAX Number: (210) 341-4519 Calendar System: Semester
URL: www.ost.edu
Established: 1903 Annual Graduate Tuition & Fees: $13,265
Enrollment: 176 Coed
Affiliation or Control: Roman Catholic IRS Status: 501(c)3
Highest Offering: Doctorate; No Undergraduates
Program: Professional; Religious Emphasis
Accreditation: SC, THEOL

01 President ... Rev. Ronald ROLHEISER
03 Executive Vice President ... Rev. Warren BROWN
11 Vice Pres Administrative Affairs ... Rev. David KALERT
30 Director for Development ... Mrs. Lea KOCHANEK
05 Academic Dean ... Dr. Scott WOODWARD
20 Associate Dean ... Sr. Linda GIBLER
88 Director Oblate Renewal Center ... Rev. Rocky GRIMARD
10 Director of Finance ... Mr. Rene ESPINOSA
18 Director of Operations ... Mr. Morris LIM
08 Director of the Library ... Ms. Maria GARCÍA
06 Registrar & Admissions ... Mr. James OBERHAUSEN
51 Assoc Dean of Continuing Educ ... Mrs. Rose MARDEN
88 Director Lay Ministry Institute ... Mrs. Bonnie ABADIE
88 Director Ministry to Ministers Pgm ... Rev. Vincent LOUWAGIE
45 Director Long Term Planning ... Rev. David KALERT
88 Director DMin Program ... Rev. John MARKEY
15 Director Personnel Services ... Mr. Rene ESPINOSA

Odessa College (F)

201 W University Boulevard, Odessa TX 79764-7127
County: Ector FICE Identification: 003596
Unit ID: 227304
Telephone: (432) 335-6400 Carnegie Class: Assoc/Pub-R-M
FAX Number: (432) 335-6860 Calendar System: Semester
URL: www.odessa.edu
Established: 1946 Annual Undergrad Tuition & Fees (In-District): $2,280
Enrollment: 5,211 Coed
Affiliation or Control: Local IRS Status: 501(c)3
Highest Offering: Associate Degree
Program: Occupational; 2-Year Principally Bachelor's Creditable
Accreditation: SC, ADNUR, MUS, PTAA, RAD

01 President ... Dr. Gregory D. WILLIAMS
05 Vice President for Instruction ... Dr. Ken TUNSTALL
10 Vice President Business Affairs ... Ms. Virginia E. CHISUM
32 Vice President for Student Services ... Dr. David BAUSKE
100 Chief of Staff ... Dr. Tanya G. HUGHES
30 Exec Dir of Resource Development ... Vacant
11 Exec Dir of Administration & HR ... Ms. Amy W. HENDRICK
106 Exec Dir OC Global Instr Svcs ... Mr. Corey DAVIS
75 Dean of Career/Tech & Wrkforce Educ ... Mr. Ian ROARK
49 Dean of Arts & Sciences ... Ms. Kathryn KEEN
84 Exec Director of Enrollment Mgmt ... Mr. Trey WETENDORF
06 Registrar ... Ms. Rebecca BEARD
41 Director Intercollegiate Athletics ... Mr. Wayne BAKER
37 Director Student Financial Svcs ... Ms. Dee NESMITH
18 Interim Director Physical Plant ... Mr. Bryan HEIFNER
26 Dir Media Relations/Publications ... Ms. Cheri DALTON
38 Director Counseling/Recruiting ... Mr. Trey WETENDORF
96 Dir of Purchasing/Business Services ... Ms. Cindy CURNUTT

Our Lady of the Lake University (G)

411 SW 24th Street, San Antonio TX 78207-4689
County: Bexar FICE Identification: 003598
Unit ID: 227331
Telephone: (210) 434-6711 Carnegie Class: DRU
FAX Number: (210) 431-3928 Calendar System: Semester
URL: www.ollusa.edu
Established: 1895 Annual Undergrad Tuition & Fees: $22,756
Enrollment: 2,765 Coed
Affiliation or Control: Roman Catholic IRS Status: 501(c)3
Highest Offering: Doctorate
Program: Liberal Arts And General; Teacher Preparatory
Accreditation: SC, ACBSP, COPSY, SP, SW

01 President ... Dr. Tessa M. POLLACK
03 Executive Vice President ... Dr. David C. ESTES
05 Vice President for Academic Affairs ... Dr. Helen J. STREUBERT
32 Vice President of Student Life ... Mr. Jack L. HANK
10 Vice President Finance & Facilities ... Mr. Allen R. KLAUS
30 Vice Pres Institutional Advancement ... Mr. Daniel YOXALL
84 Vice Pres of Enrollment Management ... Mr. Michael E. ACOSTA
26 Vice Pres Communications/Marketing ... Mr. Daniel YOXALL
42 Vice President of Mission/Ministry ... Ms. Gloria URRABAZO
88 Exec Asst to VP Inst Advancement ... Ms. Alexandra GARCIA
35 Asst Vice Pres Student Life ... Ms. Mary F. SCOTKA
04 Exec Asst to President/Govt Rels ... Mrs. Susan A. SCHLEICHER
13 Chief Technology Officer ... Mr. Joseph G. DECK
18 Director Physical Plant ... Mr. Darrell R. GLASSCOCK
15 Director Human Resources ... Mr. Phillip VARGAS
06 Registrar ... Mrs. Norma J. ANDERSON
14 Director Network & Telecomm ... Mr. David LYTLE
45 Dir Institutional/Effectiveness ... Dr. Lei WANG
19 Interim Police Chief ... Mr. David JUAREZ
39 Director Residence Life ... Mr. Mark R. CENTER
36 Director Career Counsel/Placement ... Ms. Rhonda J. BOYLES
38 Director of Counseling Services ... Dr. Rosa ESPINOSA
23 Director Student Health Services ... Ms. Julie STUCKEY
40 Director Bookstore ... Mr. Edward CROCE
102 Corporate Relations Officer ... Ms. Roxanne SANCHEZ

46 Director of Advancement Services .... Mr. John SANCHEZ
30 Dir of Stewardship/Constituent Rels .... Ms. Asia CIARAVINO
37 Asst Director of Financial Aid .... Ms. Esmerelda M. FLORES
29 Asst Dir Stewrdshp/Constituent Rels .... Ms. Alexandra GARCIA
88 Asst Dir of Advancement Services .... Ms. Cyndi CAVAZOS

Panola College (A)

1109 West Panola Street, Carthage TX 75633-2397
County: Panola FICE Identification: 003600
Unit ID: 227386
Telephone: (903) 693-2000 Carnegie Class: Assoc/Pub-R-M
FAX Number: (903) 693-5588 Calendar System: Semester
URL: www.panola.edu
Established: 1947 Annual Undergrad Tuition & Fees (In-District): $1,900
Enrollment: 2,324 Coed
Affiliation or Control: Local IRS Status: 501(c)3
Highest Offering: Associate Degree
Program: Occupational; 2-Year Principally Bachelor's Creditable
Accreditation: SC, ADNUR, OTA

01 President .... Dr. Gregory S. POWELL
05 Vice President of Instruction .... Dr. Joe SHANNON
32 Vice President of Student Services .... Mr. Don CLINTON
10 Vice President of Fiscal Services .... Mr. Steve WILLIAMS
08 Director of Library .... Ms. Zeny JETT
07 Director of Admissions/Registrar .... Mr. Jeremy DORMAN
26 Director Recruiting/College Rels .... Mr. Van PATTERSON
103 Dir of Workforce & Economic Devel .... Mrs. Linda BARLOW
30 Exec Dir Institutional Advancement .... Mr. Van PATTERSON
09 Director of Institutional Research .... Mrs. Christine BLAIR
106 Dean Distance Education/Webmaster .... Mrs. Ann MORRIS
12 Director of Shelby County Operation .... Mrs. Natalie OSWALT
12 Director of Marshall Operations .... Mrs. Laura WOOD
76 Dean of Health Sciences .... Dr. Barbara CORDELL
14 Computer Services Director .... Mr. Allen WEST
11 Director of Administrative Services .... Mr. Mike EDENS
19 Campus Police Chief .... Mr. Ernie DAVIS
37 Director Student Financial Aid .... Mrs. Denise WELCH

Paris Junior College (B)

2400 Clarksville Street, Paris TX 75460-6298
County: Lamar FICE Identification: 003601
Unit ID: 227401
Telephone: (903) 785-7661 Carnegie Class: Assoc/Pub-R-M
FAX Number: (903) 782-0370 Calendar System: Semester
URL: www.parisjc.edu
Established: 1924 Annual Undergrad Tuition & Fees (In-District): $1,560
Enrollment: 6,214 Coed
Affiliation or Control: State/Local IRS Status: 501(c)3
Highest Offering: Associate Degree
Program: Occupational; 2-Year Principally Bachelor's Creditable
Accreditation: SC, ADNUR, RAD, SURGT

01 President .... Dr. Pamela D. ANGLIN
32 Vice President for Student Services .... Vacant
10 Vice President Business Services .... Mr. John EASTMAN
05 Vice President Academic Studies .... Mr. L. D. CHANEY
103 Vice President Workforce Education .... Mr. John SPRADLING
07 Director of Admissions .... Mrs. Sheila REECE
06 Registrar .... Mrs. Rita TAPP
37 Director Student Financial Aid .... Mrs. Linda SLAWSON
08 Director Library Services .... Mr. Carl COVERT
38 Director Student Development .... Mrs. Barbara THOMAS
09 Director Institutional Research .... Mrs. Beverly MATTHEWS
30 Director Institutional Advancement .... Mr. Derald BULLS
35 Director Student Affairs .... Mr. Kenneth WEBB
84 Director Enrollment Management .... Mrs. Sheila REECE
14 Director Computer Center .... Mrs. Mary HOLBROOK MIMS
26 Chief Public Relations Officer .... Ms. Margaret RUFF
18 Manager Plant Operations .... Mr. Randall COX

Parker University (C)

2540 Walnut Hill Lane, Dallas TX 75229-5609
County: Dallas FICE Identification: 023053
Unit ID: 243823
Telephone: (972) 438-6932 Carnegie Class: Spec/Health
FAX Number: (214) 902-2496 Calendar System: Trimester
URL: www.parker.edu
Established: 1982 Annual Undergrad Tuition & Fees: $26,300
Enrollment: 891 Coed
Affiliation or Control: Independent Non-Profit IRS Status: 501(c)3
Highest Offering: Doctorate
Program: Professional
Accreditation: SC, CHIRO, COMTA

01 President .... Dr. Fabrizio MANCINI
05 Provost .... Dr. Gery HOCHANADEL
20 Vice President of Academic Affairs .... Dr. Kenneth THOMAS
10 Chief Financial Officer .... Mr. David GARAFOLA
20 Academic Dean .... Dr. Gene GIGGLEMAN
84 Dean of Enrollment .... Ms. Lynn NASATO
32 Dean of Students .... Mr. Victor BALLESTEROS
51 Director Continuing Education .... Ms. Michelle YUNGBLUT
06 Registrar .... Ms. Renee CARRILLO
37 Director Financial Aid .... Ms. Jackie STEVENS
08 Head Librarian .... Mrs. Becky SULLIVAN
38 Student Counseling Director .... Dr. Jacqueline ELBEL
16 Chief Human Resources Officer .... Ms. Sandra MCLEAN

19 Director Safety/Security .... Mr. Scott CHRISTENSEN
41 Athletic Director .... Mr. Steve WELLER
46 Dean of Research Institute .... Dr. Ronald RUPPERT
29 Director Alumni Relations .... Mr. Tim GUNN
26 Chief Marketing Officer .... Mr. Matt EISERLOH
91 Director of Information Services .... Vacant
18 Chief Facilities/Physical Plant .... Mr. Frank TILLERY
35 Director Student Activities .... Mrs. Wendy NULPH
96 Director of Purchasing .... Mr. Philip CERVANTES
17 Asst Dean of Clinic .... Dr. Larry STOLAR

Paul Quinn College (D)

3837 Simpson Stuart Road, Dallas TX 75241-4398
County: Dallas FICE Identification: 003602
Unit ID: 227429
Telephone: (214) 376-1000 Carnegie Class: Bac/Diverse
FAX Number: (214) 379-5559 Calendar System: Semester
URL: www.pqc.edu
Established: 1872 Annual Undergrad Tuition & Fees: $15,340
Enrollment: 207 Coed
Affiliation or Control: African Methodist Episcopal IRS Status: 501(c)3
Highest Offering: Baccalaureate
Program: Liberal Arts And General; Teacher Preparatory
Accreditation: #SC, TRACS

01 President .... Mr. Michael J. SORRELL
05 Vice Pres Academic Affairs .... Dr. Kizuwanda GRANT
10 COO & Vice President Fiscal .... Mr. Antwane OWENS
84 Director of Enrollment Management .... Vacant
32 Dean of Students .... Ms. Kelsel THOMPSON
06 Registrar .... Ms. Beverly SMITH
08 Librarian/Director LRC .... Ms. Clarice MEDLEY-WEEKS
13 Director IT .... Vacant
41 Dir Athletics/Intramural Sports .... Mr. James SUMMERS
37 Director of Financial Aid .... Vacant
35 Director Student Support Svcs .... Dr. Marguerite MCCLINTON
19 Director of Facilities .... Mrs. Marieta OGLESBY
09 Director of Institutional Research .... Vacant
29 Director of Alumni Relations .... Vacant
23 Nurse .... Ms. Glenda DAVIS
107 Div Chair Professional Studies .... Mr. Reginald GRAY
53 Division Chair Education .... Dr. Kizuwanda GRANT
100 Chief of Staff .... Ms. Lori PRICE
88 Director of Service Learning .... Ms. Elizabeth WATTLEY

Ranger College (E)

1100 College Circle, Ranger TX 76470-3298
County: Eastland FICE Identification: 003603
Unit ID: 227687
Telephone: (254) 647-3234 Carnegie Class: Assoc/Pub-R-S
FAX Number: (254) 647-1656 Calendar System: Semester
URL: www.rangercollege.edu
Established: 1926 Annual Undergrad Tuition & Fees (In-District): $2,140
Enrollment: 1,616 Coed
Affiliation or Control: Local IRS Status: 501(c)3
Highest Offering: Associate Degree
Program: Occupational; 2-Year Principally Bachelor's Creditable
Accreditation: SC

01 President .... Dr. William J. CAMPION
03 Executive VP Brownwood .... Dr. Don BOSTIC
10 Dean of Finance .... Mr. Warren RAPPLEYE
84 Dean of Enrollment Management .... Mr. John SLAUGHTER
32 Dean of Students .... Mr. Johnny GANN
05 Dean of Student Learning .... Mr. Billy ADAMS
06 Registrar .... Vacant
08 Director of Learning Resources .... Mr. Michael CUNNINGHAM
18 Director of Maintenance & Grounds .... Mr. Charles LEMASTER
37 Director of Financial Aid .... Mr. Don HILTON
41 Athletic Director .... Mr. Jack ALLEN
15 Director of Personnel .... Miss Laura YECK
36 Director Student Placement .... Ms. Vicki LOWRANCE
38 Dir Academic Counseling & Testing .... Ms. Vicki LOWRANCE
21 Bursar .... Ms. Evonne CHERRY
40 Director Bookstore .... Miss Cindy STRINGER

Redeemer Theological Seminary (F)

3838 Oak Lawn Avenue, Ste 200, Dallas TX 75219
County: Dallas Identification: 667055
Telephone: (214) 528-8600 Carnegie Class: Not Classified
FAX Number: N/A Calendar System: Semester
URL: www.redeemerseminary.org
Established: 1999 Annual Graduate Tuition & Fees: $12,000
Enrollment: 136 Coed
Affiliation or Control: Independent Non-Profit IRS Status: 501(c)3
Highest Offering: Master's; No Undergraduates
Program: Professional; Religious Emphasis
Accreditation: @THEOL

01 President .... Steven T. VANDERHILL
05 Academic Dean .... Douglas M. GROPP

Remington College (G)

3110 Hayes Road, Suite 380, Houston TX 77082-2782
County: Harris FICE Identification: 030265
Unit ID: 380094
Telephone: (281) 899-1240 Carnegie Class: Assoc/PrivFP
FAX Number: (281) 597-8466 Calendar System: Quarter
URL: www.remingtoncollege.edu
Established: 1981 Annual Undergrad Tuition & Fees: $14,745
Enrollment: 526 Coed
Affiliation or Control: Proprietary IRS Status: Proprietary
Highest Offering: Baccalaureate
Program: Occupational
Accreditation: ACCSC

01 President .... Ms. LaShundia BROOKS
05 Director of Education .... Vacant
07 Director of Admissions .... Mr. Mark DONAHUE
37 Director of Financial Aid .... Mrs. Rhoda HAMILTON

Remington College-Dallas Campus (H)

1800 Eastgate Drive, Garland TX 75041-5513
County: Dallas Identification: 666037
Unit ID: 223463
Telephone: (972) 686-7878 Carnegie Class: Assoc/PrivFP
FAX Number: (972) 686-5116 Calendar System: Quarter
URL: www.remingtoncollege.edu
Established: 1987 Annual Undergrad Tuition & Fees: $27,500
Enrollment: 692 Coed
Affiliation or Control: Proprietary IRS Status: Proprietary
Highest Offering: Baccalaureate
Program: 2-Year Principally Bachelor's Creditable
Accreditation: ACCSC

01 Campus President .... Mr. Skip WALLS
05 Academic Dean .... Mr. Billy FERRELL

† Branch campus of Remington College, Lafayette, LA.

Remington College-Fort Worth Campus (I)

300 E Loop 820, Fort Worth TX 76112-1225
County: Tarrant Identification: 666063
Unit ID: 377111
Telephone: (817) 451-0017 Carnegie Class: Assoc/PrivFP
FAX Number: (817) 496-1257 Calendar System: Quarter
URL: www.remingtoncollege.edu
Established: 1988 Annual Undergrad Tuition & Fees: N/A
Enrollment: 754 Coed
Affiliation or Control: Proprietary IRS Status: Proprietary
Highest Offering: Baccalaureate
Program: Occupational
Accreditation: ACCSC

01 President .... Mr. Greg FALCON

† Branch campus of Remington College, Tampa, FL.

Rice University (J)

PO Box 1892, Houston TX 77251-1892
County: Harris FICE Identification: 003604
Unit ID: 227757
Telephone: (713) 348-0000 Carnegie Class: RU/VH
FAX Number: N/A Calendar System: Semester
URL: www.rice.edu
Established: 1891 Annual Undergrad Tuition & Fees: $35,551
Enrollment: 5,879 Coed
Affiliation or Control: Independent Non-Profit IRS Status: 501(c)3
Highest Offering: Doctorate
Program: Liberal Arts And General; Professional
Accreditation: SC, BUS, ENG, @TEAC

01 President .... Mr. David W. LEEBRON
101 Deputy Sec to Board of Trustees .... Ms. Cynthia L. WILSON
05 Provost .... Dr. George L. MCLENDON
11 Vice President Administration .... Dr. Kevin KIRBY
10 Vice President Finance .... Ms. Kathy COLLINS
30 Vice President Resource Development .. Mr. Darrow ZEIDENSTEIN
88 Vice Pres Investments/Treasurer .... Mr. Scott W. WISE
84 Vice President for Enrollment .... Mr. Chris MUNOZ
26 Vice President for Public Affairs .... Ms. Linda THRANE
13 Vice Provost Information Technology .... Dr. Kamran KHAN
46 Vice Provost Research .... Dr. James COLEMAN
20 Vice Provost for Academic Affairs .... Dr. Carol QUILLEN
15 Associate Vice Pres Human Resources .... Ms. Mary A. CRONIN
91 Assoc Vice Pres for Admin Systems ...... Mr. Randy CASTIGLIONI
18 Assoc VP Facil Engr & Planning .... Ms. Barbara BRYSON
20 Associate Vice Provost .... Dr. David K. VASSAR
43 General Counsel .... Mr. Richard A. ZANSITIS
06 Registrar .... Mr. David TENNEY
07 Dean for Undergraduate Enrollment .... Ms. Julie BROWNING
29 Director Alumni Affairs/Univ Events .... Ms. Ann PETERSON
88 Director International Opportunity .... Ms. Barbara HARRISON
37 Director Student Financial Services .... Ms. Anne E. WALKER
13 Director Enterprise Application .... Ms. Andrea MARTIN
25 Director of Sponsored Research .... Ms. Nancy NISBETT
41 Director of Athletics .... Mr. Chris DEL CONTE
85 Director Intl Students/Scholars .... Dr. Adria BAKER
31 Dir of Community Involvement Ctr .... Mr. Mac GRISWOLD
39 Director of Housing & Dining .... Mr. Mark DITMAN
23 Director Student Health Services .... Dr. Mark JENKINS
09 Director of Institutional Research .... Dr. Leona URBISH
21 University Controller .... Ms. Evelyn STEWART
21 Director of Internal Audit .... Ms. Janet COVINGTON
19 Chief of Campus Police .... Mr. Bill TAYLOR
22 Director of Affirmative Action .... Mr. Russell BARNES
27 Director of News & Media Relations .... Mr. B.J ALMOND

21 Director Administrative Services ... Mr. Eugen RADULESCU
40 Manager Bookstore ... Ms. Evelyn MORTON
79 Dean of School of Humanities ... Dr. Nicolas SHUMWAY
58 Dean Graduate/Postdoctoral Stds ... Dr. Paula SANDERS
20 Dean of Undergraduate Education ... Dr. John S. HUTCHINSON
48 Dean of Architecture ... Dr. Sarah M. WHITING
64 Dean of Shepherd School of Music ... Dr. Robert YEKOVICH
54 Dean GR Brown School Engineering ... Dr. Sallie KELLER-MCNULTY
50 Dean J H Jones Graduate Sch of Mgt ... Dr. William H. GLICK
83 Dean of Social Sciences ... Dr. Lyn RAGSDALE
81 Dean of Wiess Sch Natural Science ... Dr. Daniel CARSON
51 Dean Glasscock Sch Continuing Stds ... Dr. Mary MCINTIRE
88 Asst Dean Student Judicial Pgms ... Dr. Donald OSTDIEK
38 Asst Dean Student Counseling ... Dr. Lindley DORAN

Rio Grande Bible Institute (A)

4300 South Business 281, Edinburg TX 78539-9650
County: Hidalgo — Identification: 666395
Telephone: (956) 380-8100 — Carnegie Class: Not Classified
FAX Number: (956) 380-8256 — Calendar System: Semester
URL: www.riogrande.edu
Established: 1946 — Annual Undergrad Tuition & Fees: $6,550
Enrollment: 95 — Coed
Affiliation or Control: Independent Non-Profit — IRS Status: 501(c)3
Highest Offering: Baccalaureate
Program: Professional; Religious Emphasis
Accreditation: BI

01 Chief Executive Officer ... Dr. Lawrence B. WINDLE
04 Administrative Assistant to CEO ... Ms. Evelyn WORTHINGTON
05 Chief Academic Administrator ... Dr. Manuel GUTIERREZ
32 Chief Student Development Officer ... Mr. David LOYOLA
10 Chief Financial Officer ... Mr. Keith HEPPNER
08 Chief Librarian ... Ms. Mary CANO
06 Registrar ... Mr. Julio VARELA
15 Director of Personnel ... Mr. Larry DICK
18 Director of Campus Services ... Mr. Gary WILLIAMS
26 Director of Ministerial Advancement ... Dr. Robert CRANE

St. Edward's University (B)

3001 S Congress Avenue, Austin TX 78704-6489
County: Travis — FICE Identification: 003621
Unit ID: 227845
Telephone: (512) 448-8400 — Carnegie Class: Master's L
FAX Number: (512) 448-8492 — Calendar System: Semester
URL: www.stedwards.edu
Established: 1885 — Annual Undergrad Tuition & Fees: $28,700
Enrollment: 5,454 — Coed
Affiliation or Control: Independent Non-Profit — IRS Status: 501(c)3
Highest Offering: Master's
Program: Liberal Arts And General; Teacher Preparatory; Professional; Business Emphasis
Accreditation: SC, SW

01 President ... Dr. George E. MARTIN
05 Executive Vice President/Provost ... Sr. Donna M. JURICK
10 Vice President Financial Affairs ... Ms. Rhonda D. CARTWRIGHT
30 Vice President for Advancement ... Mr. Michael F. LARKIN
26 Vice Pres Marketing/Enrollment Mgmt ... Ms. Paige BOOTH
32 Vice President for Student Affairs ... Dr. Sandra L. PACHECO
13 Vice President Information Tech ... Dr. David E. WALDRON
42 Director of Campus Ministry ... Fr. Richard S. WILKINSON
09 Assoc VP Inst Effectiveness/Rsrch ... Mr. Bhuban R. PANDEY
21 Assoc Vice Pres Financial Affairs ... Mr. Barton G. GLASER
107 AVP Prof Educ & Global Initiatives ... Dr. Thomas M. EVANS
20 Assoc VP for Academic Affairs ... Dr. Molly E. MINUS
07 Assoc VP/Dean Undergrad Admission ... Ms. Tracy L. MANIER
37 Assoc VP Student Financial Services ... Ms. Doris F. CONSTANTINE
32 Assoc VP/Dean of Students ... Ms. Lisa L. KIRKPATRICK
29 Assoc VP Alumni/Parent Programs ... Ms. Kippi R. GRIFFITH
100 Asst to Pres Strategic Planning ... Ms. Josie L. BARRETT
101 Asst to Pres Institutional Rels ... Ms. Cristina L. BORDIN
04 Executive Assistant to President ... Ms. Alice J. HIGGINS
83 Dean Behavioral Social Science ... Dr. Brenda J. VALLANCE
50 Dean Management & Business ... Ms. Marsha C. KELLIHER
53 Dean School of Education ... Dr. Grant W. SIMPSON, JR.
79 Dean School of Humanities ... Fr. Louis T. BRUSATTI
81 Dean School of Natural Sciences ... Dr. Thomas M. MITZEL
88 Interim Dean of New College ... Dr. Helene L. CAUDILL
88 Dean University Programs ... Dr. Marianne F. HOPPER
08 Director of Library ... Mr. Pongracz SENNYEY
06 Registrar ... Dr. Lance R. HAYES
36 Director Career Planning ... Ms. Barbara J. HENDERSON
44 Associate VP Development ... Mr. Joe DEMEDEIROS
104 Director Ofc of International Educ ... Mr. Stephen J. KAZAR
90 Director Instructional Technology ... Ms. Mary T. HOWERTON
18 Physical Plant Director ... Mr. Michael W. PETERSON
91 Director Administrative Computing ... Mr. Raymond J. SPINHIRNE
88 Director Digital Infrastructure ... Mr. Benjamin R. HOCKENHULL
88 Director Info Technology Resources ... Mr. Gaston HEBERT
19 Chief of Police ... Mr. Rudolph L. RENDON
27 Director of Communications ... Ms. Mischelle R. DIAZ
15 Acting Director Human Resources ... Ms. Deborah B. ZIMMERMAN
38 Director Health & Counseling Center ... Dr. Claudia C. CAROL
41 Athletic Director ... Ms. Debora W. TAYLOR
35 Director of Student Life ... Mr. Thomas B. SULLIVAN
39 Director Residence Life ... Mr. Dave ROZEBOOM
31 Director Auxiliary Services ... Mr. Michael C. STONE

88 Risk Manager ... Ms. Rebekah M. NAGY
21 Comptroller ... Mr. Paul R. SINTEF
102 Director Foundation Relations ... Ms. Carol A. JANUSZESKI
105 Manager Web Services ... Ms. Ellen R. SULLIVAN
89 Director Freshman Studies ... Dr. Lynn RUDLOFF
92 Director Honors Program ... Dr. Barbara FILIPPIDIS
88 Director Capstone Course ... Ms. Cory LOCK
40 Bookstore Director ... Ms. Melanie FOSTER

St. Mary's University (C)

One Camino Santa Maria, San Antonio TX 78228-8572
County: Bexar — FICE Identification: 003623
Unit ID: 228149
Telephone: (210) 436-3011 — Carnegie Class: Master's L
FAX Number: (210) 436-3500 — Calendar System: Semester
URL: www.stmarytx.edu
Established: 1852 — Annual Undergrad Tuition & Fees: $23,386
Enrollment: 4,105 — Coed
Affiliation or Control: Roman Catholic — IRS Status: 501(c)3
Highest Offering: Doctorate
Program: Liberal Arts And General; Teacher Preparatory; Professional
Accreditation: SC, BUS, CACREP, ENG, LAW, MFCD, MUS

01 President ... Dr. Charles L. COTRELL
05 Provost/Vice Pres Academic Affairs ... Mr. Andre HAMPTON
10 Vice Pres Administration & Finance ... Ms. Rebeckah J. DAY
84 Vice Pres Enrollment Management ... Ms. Suzanne M. PETRUSCH
32 Vice President Student Development ... Ms. Katherine SISOIAN
30 Vice Pres University Advancement ... Mr. Rocky KETTERING, III
88 Vice President Mission & Identity ... Rev. Rudy VELA, SM
50 Dean/Prof Bill Greehey Sch Business ... Dr. Tanuja SINGH
79 Dean/Assoc Prof Hum & Social Sci ... Dr. Janet B. DIZINNO
54 Dean/Prof Science/Engrng/Technology ... Dr. Winston EREVELLES
58 Dean & Professor Graduate School ... Dr. Henry FLORES
61 Dean of Law ... Mr. Charles CANTU
39 Director Residence Life ... Mr. James VILLARREAL
09 Director of Institutional Research ... Mr. Christopher M. ANTONS
100 Chief of Staff/Office of President ... Ms. Dianne L. PIPES
06 Registrar ... Ms. Christina VILLANUEVA
07 Director of Admissions ... Mr. Chadd J. BRIDWELL
08 Director Louis J Blume Library ... Dr. Palmer H. HALL
37 Director Financial Assistance ... Mr. David R. KRAUSE
30 Director Student Counseling ... Dr. Barbara HARDIN
36 Director of Career Services ... Ms. Amy DIEPENBROCK
90 Exec Director Academic Technology ... Mr. Daxing (Michael) CHEN
15 Director Human Resources ... Ms. Elsa YBANEZ
72 Int Exec Dir Tech Opers/Info Tech ... Mr. Todd YATES
91 Ex Dir Resource Mgt/Plng/Info/Tech ... Ms. Louisa A. MARTIN
13 Dir Network Tech Services/Info Tech ... Mr. Robert STOOKSBERRY
88 Director Tech User Support ... Vacant
42 Director University Ministry ... Mr. Wayne ROMO
30 Exec Director Univ Advancement ... Mr. Peter HANSEN
21 Director of Finance ... Ms. Mei-Lin LEE
21 Director of Accounting Operations ... Ms. Sheila NIX
26 Dir Media Relations/Communications ... Mrs. Gina FARRELL
18 Facilities Administrator ... Mr. William M. TAM

*San Jacinto College District (D)

4624 Fairmont Parkway, Pasadena TX 77504-3323
County: Harris — FICE Identification: 029137
Unit ID: 227988
Telephone: (281) 998-6150 — Carnegie Class: N/A
FAX Number: (281) 479-8127
URL: www.sanjac.edu

01 Chancellor ... Dr. Brenda HELLYER
05 Vice Chanc Instruct & Student Svcs ... Dr. Laurel WILLIAMSON
10 Vice Chanc of Fiscal Affairs ... Mr. Ken LYNN
16 Vice Chanc of Human Resources ... Mr. Stephen TRNCAK
27 Interim CIO ... Mr. Rob STANICIC
26 Assoc Vice Chancellor of Marketing ... Ms. Teri FOWLE
84 Vice Pres of Enrollment Svcs ... Dr. William RAFFETTO
32 Vice Pres of Student Development ... Dr. Brook ZEMEL
51 Vice Pres Cont & Prof Development ... Ms. Sarah JANES
88 Vice Pres Educational Tech Svcs ... Ms. Niki WHITESIDE
30 Vice Pres Organizational Develop ... Ms. Susan TEMPLE
88 Assoc VC of Educ Partnerships ... Ms. Pamela CAMPBELL
30 Interim Exec Dir of Development ... Ms. Ruth KEENAN
06 Dean Enroll Mgmt/College Registrar ... Dr. Wanda MUNSON
20 Dean of Teaching and Learning ... Dr. Catherine O'BRIEN
88 Dean of College Preparatory ... Dr. Rebecca GOOSEN
09 Director Rsrch/Inst Effectiveness ... Mr. George GONZALEZ
21 Director Acct & Financial Services ... Mr. Bill DICKERSON
96 Director of Contracts Purchasing ... Ms. Ann KOKX-TEMPLET
37 Director of Financial Aid ... Mr. Robert MERINO
88 Director Small Business Develop ... Mr. Richard PRETS

*San Jacinto College Central (E)

8060 Spencer Highway, Pasadena TX 77505-5903
County: Harris — FICE Identification: 003609
Unit ID: 227979
Telephone: (281) 476-1501 — Carnegie Class: Assoc/Pub-S-MC
FAX Number: (281) 476-1892 — Calendar System: Semester
URL: www.sanjac.edu
Established: 1960 — Annual Undergrad Tuition & Fees (In-District): $1,923
Enrollment: 15,035 — Coed
Affiliation or Control: Local — IRS Status: 501(c)3
Highest Offering: Associate Degree
Program: Occupational; 2-Year Principally Bachelor's Creditable
Accreditation: &SC, ADNUR, EMT, MLTAD, RAD, SURGT

02 President ... Dr. Neil MATKIN
05 Vice President of Learning ... Dr. Barbara HANSON
56 Dean Evening Div/Weekend College ... Dr. Timothy ELLIOTT
49 Dean of Liberal Arts ... Dr. Van WIGGINTON
75 Dean of Industrial and Applied Tech ... Dr. Steven HORTON
76 Dean of Health Sciences ... Ms. Edna ROBINSON
50 Dean of Business and Technology ... Mr. Michael KANE
11 Dean of Administration ... Dr. James BRASWELL
84 Dean of Enrollment Management ... Mr. Kevin MCKISSON
32 Dean of Student Development ... Ms. Kathy KNAPP
62 Director of Library ... Ms. Karen BLANKENSHIP
41 Director of Athletics ... Mr. Scott HORSTMAN
88 Dir of Educ Planning and Counseling ... Mr. Daniel NEULS
88 Dir of Educ Planning and Counseling ... Ms. Deborah MYLES
88 Director of Dual Credit ... Ms. Jaynie MITCHELL
07 Coordinator Enrollment Management ... Ms. Joan RONDOT
35 Coordinator Student Life ... Ms. Amanda ROSE
37 Coordinator of Financial Aid ... Ms. Vicki KANE
88 Coordinator of Testing ... Ms. Carita WEBSTER
36 Coordinator Career/Employment Ctr ... Mr. Ed VANDENBERG

† Regional accreditation is carried under the parent institution (district office) in Pasadena, TX.

*San Jacinto College North (F)

5800 Uvalde Road, Houston TX 77049-4599
County: Harris — Identification: 666747
Unit ID: 227997
Telephone: (281) 458-4050 — Carnegie Class: Not Classified
FAX Number: (281) 459-7125 — Calendar System: Semester
URL: www.sanjac.edu
Established: 1974 — Annual Undergrad Tuition & Fees (In-District): $1,923
Enrollment: 6,573 — Coed
Affiliation or Control: Local — IRS Status: 501(c)3
Highest Offering: Associate Degree
Program: Occupational; 2-Year Principally Bachelor's Creditable
Accreditation: &SC, ACFEI, EMT, MAC

02 President ... Dr. Allatia HARRIS
05 Vice President of Learning ... Dr. Richard BAILEY
76 Dean of Allied Health ... Ms. Serita DICKEY
90 Dean Educational Technology ... Dr. Gary FRIERY
55 Dean Evening/Weekend College ... Mr. James HALL
84 Dean of Enrollment Services ... Ms. Amy AMMERMAN
32 Dean of Student Development ... Ms. Clare IANNELLI
62 Director of Library ... Dr. Jan CRENSHAW
00 Interim Dir Educ Planning Counsel ... Ms. Christine TORRES
88 Director of Dual Credit ... Ms. Jennifer MOWDY
49 Dean of Liberal Arts ... Mr. Shawn SILMAN
07 Coordinator Enrollment Services ... Ms. Faye ALLEN
35 Coordinator of Student Life ... Mr. Lamar MCWAINE
37 Coordinator of Financial Aid ... Mr. Art ESCOBAR
88 Coordinator of Testing ... Mr. Ronald HOPKINS
36 Coordinator Career/Employment Ctr ... Ms. Natiesha WALKER
88 Coordinator Wellness Program ... Mr. Kory KOEHLER

† Regional accreditation is carried under the parent institution (district office) in Pasadena, TX.

*San Jacinto College South (G)

13735 Beamer Road, Houston TX 77089-6099
County: Harris — Identification: 666748
Unit ID: 228006
Telephone: (281) 484-1900 — Carnegie Class: Not Classified
FAX Number: (281) 922-3401 — Calendar System: Semester
URL: www.sanjac.edu
Established: 1979 — Annual Undergrad Tuition & Fees (In-District): $1,923
Enrollment: 10,497 — Coed
Affiliation or Control: Local — IRS Status: 501(c)3
Highest Offering: Associate Degree
Program: Occupational; 2-Year Principally Bachelor's Creditable
Accreditation: &SC, ADNUR, PTAA

02 President ... Dr. Maureen MURPHY
05 Vice President of Learning ... Dr. Toni PENDERGRASS
49 Dean of Liberal Arts ... Ms. Kathryn ROOSA
50 Dean Business & Technology ... Dr. Brenda JONES
11 Dean of Administration ... Mr. Joseph HEBERT
84 Interim Dean of Enrollment Mgmt ... Dr. Kerry MIX
32 Dean of Student Development ... Ms. Joanna ZIMMERMANN
55 Director of Evening Division ... Mr. John BOGGS
62 Director of Library ... Mr. Richard MCKAY
88 Dir of Educ Planning and Counseling ... Ms. Shelley RINEHART
88 Director of Dual Credit ... Ms. Judy HARRISON
92 Dean Honors Program ... Mr. Scott FURTWENGLER
07 Coordinator Enrollment Management ... Ms. Tami KELLY
35 Coordinator of Student Life ... Ms. Ellie MEYER
37 Coordinator of Financial Aid ... Ms. Sonia TOWNSEND
88 Coordinator of Testing ... Mr. Jeff WYLIN
36 Coordinator Career/Employment Ctr ... Ms. Deborah SMITH

† Regional accreditation is carried under the parent institution (district office) in Pasadena, TX.

Sanford-Brown College-Houston (H)

9999 Richmond Avenue, Houston TX 77042
County: Harris — Identification: 666382
Unit ID: 404499
Telephone: (713) 779-1110 — Carnegie Class: Assoc/PrivFP
FAX Number: (713) 779-2408 — Calendar System: Other
URL: www.sanfordbrown.edu/Houston
Established: 1992 — Annual Undergrad Tuition & Fees: $13,800

Enrollment: 2,400 Coed
Affiliation or Control: Proprietary IRS Status: Proprietary
Highest Offering: Associate Degree
Program: Occupational; 2-Year Principally Bachelor's Creditable; Nursing Emphasis
Accreditation: ACICS, DMS, MAAB, MLTAD, SURGT, SURTEC

01 President .... Mr. James C. GARRETT
07 Director of Admissions .... Ms. Vanessa SMITH

† Branch campus of Sanford-Brown College, Atlanta, GA.

Schreiner University (A)

2100 Memorial Boulevard, Kerrville TX 78028-5697
County: Kerr FICE Identification: 003610
Unit ID: 228042
Telephone: (830) 896-5411 Carnegie Class: Bac/Diverse
FAX Number: (830) 896-3232 Calendar System: Semester
URL: www.schreiner.edu
Established: 1923 Annual Undergrad Tuition & Fees: $19,755
Enrollment: 1,117 Coed
Affiliation or Control: Presbyterian Church (U.S.A.) IRS Status: 501(c)3
Highest Offering: Master's
Program: Liberal Arts And General; Teacher Preparatory; Professional
Accreditation: SC

01 President .... Dr. Timothy SUMMERLIN
05 Provost/Vice Pres Acad Affairs .... Dr. Charlie T. MCCORMICK
10 Vice Pres Administration & Finance .... Vacant
30 Vice Pres Advancement/Public Rels .... Mr. Mark TUSCHAK
32 Vice Pres Enrollment/Student Svcs .... Ms. Peg A. LAYTON
20 Assistant Provost .... Ms. Darlene BANNISTER
13 Chief Information Ofcr/Library/IT .... Dr. Candice SCOTT
27 Assistant Vice President Marketing .... Ms. Lane H. TAIT
07 Dean Admission/Financial Aid .... Vacant
42 Campus Minister .... Rev. Virginia NORRIS-LANE
37 Director Student Financial Aid .... Ms. Toni BRYANT
06 Registrar .... Ms. Darlene A. BANNISTER
26 Director of University Relations .... Ms. Amy ARMSTRONG
41 Athletic Director .... Mr. Ron MACOSKO
16 Director of Human Resources .... Ms. Mary WOODS
18 Chief Facilities/Physical Plant .... Mr. Dale MYERS
29 Director Alumni Relations .... Mr. Paul CAMFIELD
38 Director Student Counseling .... Ms. Carolyn S. OSBORN
21 University Comptroller .... Ms. Barbara SIEMERS
36 Director Student Placement .... Ms. Cristina MARTINEZ
09 Director of Institutional Research .... Dr. Gloria STEWART

Seminary of the Southwest (B)

Box 2247, Austin TX 78768-2247
County: Travis FICE Identification: 003566
Unit ID: 224712
Telephone: (512) 472-4133 Carnegie Class: Spec/Faith
FAX Number: (512) 472-3098 Calendar System: 4/1/4
URL: www.ssw.edu
Established: 1952 Annual Graduate Tuition & Fees: $13,227
Enrollment: 111 Coed
Affiliation or Control: Protestant Episcopal IRS Status: 501(c)3
Highest Offering: Master's; No Undergraduates
Program: Professional
Accreditation: SC, THEOL

01 Dean & President .... V.Rev. Douglas B. TRAVIS
05 Academic Dean .... Rev Dr. Cynthia BRIGGS KITTREDGE
11 Exec VP Administration & Finance .... Mr. John B. WATERS
27 Exec Director of Communications .... Ms. Nancy SPRINGER-BALDWIN
21 Accounting Director .... Mrs. Joan CALMAN
06 Registrar .... Mrs. Madelyn SNODGRASS
07 Director of Recruiting & Admissions .... Ms. Jennielle STROTHER
08 Director of the Booher Library .... Dr. Donald KEENEY
18 Maintenance Supervisor .... Mr. Marty ROBBINS
13 Director Instructional Technology .... Mr. Fito KAHN
44 Dir Annual Giving/Alumni Relations .... Ms. Adrian MATTHYS

South Plains College (C)

1401 College Avenue, Levelland TX 79336-6595
County: Hockley FICE Identification: 003611
Unit ID: 228158
Telephone: (806) 894-9611 Carnegie Class: Assoc/Pub-R-L
FAX Number: (806) 894-5274 Calendar System: Semester
URL: www.southplainscollege.edu
Established: 1957 Annual Undergrad Tuition & Fees (In-State): $2,654
Enrollment: 9,296 Coed
Affiliation or Control: State IRS Status: 501(c)3
Highest Offering: Associate Degree
Program: Occupational; 2-Year Principally Bachelor's Creditable
Accreditation: SC, ADNUR, EMT, @PTAA, SURGT

01 President .... Dr. Kelvin W. SHARP
05 Vice President Academic Affairs .... Mr. Darrell GRIMES
10 Vice Pres Finance & Administration .... Mr. Anthony G. RILEY
32 Vice President of Student Affairs .... Mr. David JONES
30 Vice Pres Institutional Advancement .... Mr. Stephen S. JOHN
76 Dean of Health Occupations .... Ms. Sue Ann LOPEZ
49 Dean of Arts & Sciences .... Mr. Yancy NUNEZ
75 Dean of Technical Education .... Mr. Rob M. BLAIR
51 Dean Continuing & Distance Educ .... Mr. Jim WALKER
07 Dean of Admissions & Records .... Mrs. Andrea RANGEL
35 Dean of Students .... Mr. David CONNER
12 Dean of Reefe Center .... Mrs. Cathy MITCHELL
09 Assoc Dean of Research & Reports .... Mr. Jack WARDLOW
26 Assoc Dean of College Relations .... Mr. Dane DEWBRE
13 Assoc Dean Information Technology .... Mr. Tim WINDERS
88 Assoc Dean Dual Credit .... Mr. Ron SPEARS
103 Assoc Dean Workforce Development .... Mr. Rafael AGUILERA
38 Director of Counseling & Guidance .... Mrs. Christi ANDERSON
37 Director of Financial Aid .... Ms. Jim Ann BATENHORST
08 Director of Libraries .... Ms. Fran COTTON
44 Director of Development .... Mr. Russell HALL
15 Director of Human Resources .... Mrs. Jeri Ann DEWBRE
41 Director of Athletics .... Mr. Joe TUBB
06 Registrar .... Mr. Andrew RUIZ
18 Director of Physical Plant .... Mr. Cary MARROW
84 Director of Enrollment Management .... Mrs. Kimbra QUINN
96 Director of Purchasing .... Mr. Dennis CHURCHWELL
40 Bookstore Manager .... Mr. Roger SHULL
28 Diversity Coord/Career Counselor .... Ms. Maria LOPEZ-STRONG

South Texas College (D)

3201 W Pecan, McAllen TX 78501-6699
County: Hidalgo FICE Identification: 031034
Unit ID: 409315
Telephone: (956) 872-5051 Carnegie Class: Assoc/Pub4
FAX Number: (956) 971-3739 Calendar System: Semester
URL: www.southtexascollege.edu
Established: 1993 Annual Undergrad Tuition & Fees (In-District): $2,460
Enrollment: 29,054 Coed
Affiliation or Control: State/Local IRS Status: 501(c)3
Highest Offering: Baccalaureate
Program: 2-Year Principally Bachelor's Creditable
Accreditation: SC, ACBSP, OTA, PTAA

01 President .... Dr. Shirley A. REED
05 Vice Pres Academic Affairs .... Mr. Juan E. MEJIA
10 Vice Pres Finance/Admin Services .... Ms. Diana A. PENA
32 Vice Pres Stdnt Affairs/Enroll Mgmt .... Dr. William SERRATA
13 Vice Pres Info Services/Planning .... Mr. Jose CRUZ
30 Vice Pres Institutional Advancement .... Vacant
88 Exec Officer for NAAMRE .... Ms. Wanda GARZA
83 Div Dean Liberal Arts/Soc Sci .... Dr. Margaretha BISCHOFF
50 Div Dean Business/Technology .... Mr. Mario REYNA
76 Int Div Dean Nursing/Allied Health .... Ms. Melba TREVINO
81 Interim Div Dean Math/Science .... Dr. Ali ESMAEILI
88 Dean Bach Deg Prog/Univ Rels .... Dr. Ali ESMAEILI
84 Interim Dean Enrollment Svcs .... Ms. Kimberly MCKAY
24 Dir Instructional Technologies .... Mr. Cody GREGG
37 Assoc Dean Student Financial Svcs .... Mr. Mike CARRANZA
21 Comptroller .... Ms. Maria ELIZONDO
16 Director Human Resources .... Ms. Shirley M. INGRAM
51 Dir Continuing/Prof & Workforce Ed .... Mr. Juan Carlos AGUIRRE
96 Director Purchasing .... Ms. Rebecca CAVAZOS
09 Dir Research/Analytical Svcs .... Dr. Brenda COLE
38 Dean Student Support Svcs .... Mr. Paul HERNANDEZ, JR.
18 Director Operations .... Mr. George MCCALEB
18 Director Facilities Plan/Construct .... Mr. Gerardo RODRIGUEZ, JR.
25 Dir Gr Dev/Accountability/Mgmt Svcs .... Dr. Luzelma CANALES
12 Campus Administrator Starr Cty .... Mr. Ruben SAENZ
12 Campus Administrator Mid-Valley .... Mr. Monte CHURCHILL
88 Employee Relations Officer .... Mr. Frank D. GOMEZ
106 Interim Director Distance Education .... Dr. Brett MILLAN
26 Director Public Rels/Marketing .... Ms. Jenny CUMMINGS
88 Dir Outreach/Orient/Wel Centers .... Ms. Kimberly MCKAY
07 Director Admissions/Registrar .... Mr. Matthew HEBBARD
88 Dir of Professional Development .... Ms. Lee GRIMES
20 Asst to VP Instructional Svcs .... Dr. Anahid PETROSIAN
19 Director Security .... Mr. Paul VARVILLE
09 Dir Inst Effectiv/Assessment .... Dr. Jinhao WANG
62 Interim Dean Lib Svcs/Instr Tech .... Mr. Cody GREGG
103 Int Assc Dean Cmty Engage/Wkfrc Dev .... Dr. Luzelma CANALES
14 Director for IT Services .... Mr. Daniel DE LEON
08 Director Library Technical Services .... Mr. Jesus CAMPOS
08 Director Library Public Services .... Ms. Noemi GARZA
88 Dir Student Lrg Outcomes/Assess .... Mr. Oscar HERNANDEZ
88 Int Dir Centers for Lrg Excellence .... Ms. Jennifer KNECHT
88 Director High School Programs .... Mr. Guadalupe CHAVEZ
90 Dir Info Commons Open Labs .... Dr. Lelia SALINAS
35 Int Assoc Dean Stdnt Life/Wellness .... Mr. Mike SHANNON

South Texas College of Law (E)

1303 San Jacinto Street, Houston TX 77002-7000
County: Harris FICE Identification: 004977
Unit ID: 228194
Telephone: (713) 659-8040 Carnegie Class: Spec/Law
FAX Number: (713) 646-2909 Calendar System: Semester
URL: www.stcl.edu
Established: 1923 Annual Graduate Tuition & Fees: $26,850
Enrollment: 1,305 Coed
Affiliation or Control: Independent Non-Profit IRS Status: 501(c)3
Highest Offering: First Professional Degree; No Undergraduates
Program: Professional
Accreditation: LAW

01 President & Dean .... Mr. Donald J. GUTER
03 Executive Vice President .... Ms. Helen JENKINS
101 Sr Exec Assistant to President/Dean .... Ms. Jennifer M. HUDSON
10 Senior Vice President & CFO .... Mr. Gregory A. BROTHERS
09 Vice Pres Strategic Plng/Inst Rsrch .... Mr. Jeffrey L. RENSBERGER
30 VP Development/Alumni Relations .... Ms. Kim PARKER
08 Vice Pres & Director Library Svcs .... Mr. David G. COWAN
20 Vice President & Associate Dean .... Mr. Bruce MCGOVERN
20 Vice President & Associate Dean .... Mr. T. Gerald TREECE
20 Vice President & Associate Dean .... Ms. Catherine G. BURNETT
13 VP Technology/Dir Info Systems .... Mr. Randy MARAK
15 Vice President Human Resources .... Mr. Steve ALDERMAN
38 Asst Dean for Academic Assistance .... Ms. Gena L. SINGLETON
06 Registrar .... Ms. Mandi GIBSON
51 Assoc Director of Cont Legal Educ .... Vacant
36 Director of Career Resources .... Ms. Ginna GALBRAITH
07 Assistant Dean for Admissions .... Ms. Alicia CRAMER
21 Controller .... Ms. Nancy N. JOHNSON
37 Director of Financial Aid .... Vacant
26 Dir Marketing/Communications .... Ms. Cheryl MCENTIRE
35 Assistant Dean .... Ms. Wanda MORROW
19 Director Security & Office Services .... Ms. Debbie GIBBINS
51 Director of Cont Legal Education .... Ms. Lisa DAHM
09 Exec Dir of Institutional Research .... Ms. Julie SAUNDERS
24 Dir Institutional Technology Svcs .... Mr. Terry SMITH
43 General Counsel .... Mr. Harry REED
30 Director Development/Relations .... Ms. Jackie LAMINACK
26 Manager of Public Relations .... Ms. Sheila HANSEL
44 Asst Director of Development .... Ms. Alice H. MORRIS
44 Manager of Gift Administration .... Mr. Anthony DAVIS

Southern Methodist University (F)

6425 Boaz Lane, Dallas TX 75205-0100
County: Dallas FICE Identification: 003613
Unit ID: 228246
Telephone: (214) 768-2000 Carnegie Class: RU/H
FAX Number: (214) 768-1001 Calendar System: Semester
URL: www.smu.edu
Established: 1911 Annual Undergrad Tuition & Fees: $39,430
Enrollment: 10,938 Coed
Affiliation or Control: United Methodist IRS Status: 501(c)3
Highest Offering: Doctorate
Program: Liberal Arts And General; Professional
Accreditation: SC, ART, BUS, CLPSY, CS, DANCE, ENG, IPSY, LAW, MUS, THEA, THEOL

01 President .... Dr. R. Gerald TURNER
05 Provost/Vice Pres Academic Affairs .... Dr. Paul W. LUDDEN
10 Vice President Business & Finance .... Ms. Christine CASEY
32 Vice President for Student Affairs .... Dr. Lori S. WHITE
30 Vice Pres Devel & External Affairs .... Mr. Brad E. CHEVES
43 Gen Counsel/VP Leg Affs/Govt Rels .... Mr. Paul J. WARD
11 Vice President Executive Affairs .... Dr. Thomas E. BARRY
49 Dean Dedman College .... Dr. William M. TSUTSUI
35 Assoc VP/Dean Student Life .... Dr. Lisa WEBB
21 Associate Vice President/Controller .... Mr. John O'CONNOR
45 Associate Vice President/Budgets .... Mr. Ernie BARRY
26 Assoc Vice President/Public Affairs .... Ms. Patti LASALLE
44 Asst Vice Pres Univ Development .... Ms. Pam CONLIN
15 Assoc VP Human Res & Business Svcs .... Dr. William DETWILER
88 Exec Dir Lecture Programs .... Ms. Dana WILCOX
57 Dean Meadows School of the Arts .... Dr. Jose A. BOWEN
61 Dean Dedman School of Law .... Mr. John B. ATTANASIO
54 Dean School of Engineering .... Dr. Geoffrey C. ORSAK
73 Dean Perkins School of Theology .... Dr. William B. LAWRENCE
50 Dean Cox School of Business .... Dr. Albert W. NIEMI, JR.
58 Assoc VP Research & Grad Studies .... Dr. James E. QUICK
53 Dean Sch of Educ/Human Devel .... Dr. David J. CHARD
08 Dean/Dir Central Univ Libraries .... Ms. Gillian M. MCCOMBS
20 Assoc Provost .... Dr. Harold W. STANLEY
20 Assoc Provost .... Ms. Linda S. EADS
84 Assoc VP for Enroll Management .... Dr. Stephanie DUPAUL
25 Asst VP for Research Administration .... Ms. Alicia BROSSETTE
41 Director of Athletics .... Mr. Steve ORSINI
06 Registrar .... Mr. John A. HALL
07 Exec Dir Admissions/Enrollment Mgmt .... Vacant
37 Director Financial Aid .... Mr. Marc PETERSON
36 Asst VP/ Exec Dir Career Center .... Dr. Troy T. BEHRENS
27 Chief Information Officer .... Mr. Joe GARGIULO
27 Exec Dir News & Media Relations .... Mr. Kent BEST
38 Director Counseling & Testing .... Dr. Karen SETTLE
23 Exec Director Health Services .... Mr. Patrick HITE
39 Dir Residence Life/Student Housing .... Mr. Steve LOGAN
04 Ex Ast to Pres/Dir Inst Access/Eqty .... Ms. Beth WILSON
09 Director of Institutional Research .... Dr. John M. KALB
21 Treasurer/Chief Investment Officer .... Mr. Michael A. CONDON
96 Director of Procurement .... Mr. Terrence CONNOR
42 University Chaplain .... Mr. Stephen RANKIN
24 Dir Ctr for Media/Instr Technology .... Dr. Bill DWORACZYK
29 Dir Alumni Relations/Programming .... Ms. Stacey PADDOCK

Southwest Career College (G)

1414 Geronimo Drive, El Paso TX 79925
County: El Paso FICE Identification: 041317
Unit ID: 451556
Telephone: (915) 778-4001 Carnegie Class: Not Classified
FAX Number: (915) 778-1575 Calendar System: Other
URL: www.swci-ep.com
Established: 2001 Annual Undergrad Tuition & Fees: N/A
Enrollment: 662 Coed
Affiliation or Control: Proprietary IRS Status: Proprietary
Highest Offering: Associate Degree
Program: Occupational
Accreditation: ABHES

01 School Director .... Mr. Benjamin ARRIOLA

Southwest Institute of Technology (A)

5424 Highway 290 W, Suite 200, Austin TX 78735-8890
County: Travis FICE Identification: 020936
Unit ID: 228291
Telephone: (512) 892-2640 Carnegie Class: Assoc/PrivFP
FAX Number: (512) 892-1045 Calendar System: Quarter
URL: www.swse.net
Established: 1958 Annual Undergrad Tuition & Fees: $40,200
Enrollment: 102 Coed
Affiliation or Control: Proprietary IRS Status: Proprietary
Highest Offering: Associate Degree
Program: Occupational; Technical Emphasis
Accreditation: ACCSC

01 Director ... Ms. Frances DAVIS
32 Director of Student Services ... Ms. Lori GARZA

Southwest Texas Junior College (B)

2401 Garner Field Road, Uvalde TX 78801-6221
County: Uvalde FICE Identification: 003614
Unit ID: 228316
Telephone: (830) 278-4401 Carnegie Class: Assoc/Pub-R-M
FAX Number: (830) 591-7354 Calendar System: Semester
URL: www.swtjc.net
Established: 1946 Annual Undergrad Tuition & Fees (In-District): $2,468
Enrollment: 6,235 Coed
Affiliation or Control: Local IRS Status: 501(c)3
Highest Offering: Associate Degree
Program: Occupational; 2-Year Principally Bachelor's Creditable; Teacher Preparatory
Accreditation: SC

01 President ... Dr. Ismael SOSA
05 Dean Instructional Services/CFO ... Mr. Hector GONZALES
30 Dean of Inst Advancement/Technology ... Dr. Blaine BENNETT
06 Registrar ... Dr. David DODGE
07 Dean of Admissions & Student Svc ... Mr. Joe BARKER
09 Director of Institutional Research ... Dr. Julie THOMAS
15 Director Human Resources ... Ms. Ana DRAGOO
18 Chief Facilities/Physical Plant ... Mr. Oscar GARCIA
26 Chief Public Relations Officer ... Mr. Willie EDWARDS
32 Chief Student Life Officer ... Mr. Joe BARKER
35 Director Student Affairs ... Ms. Jessica NUNEZ
37 Director Student Financial Aid ... Ms. Ann ALMARAZ
38 Director Student Counseling ... Ms. Lois KONE
84 Director Enrollment Management ... Mr. Joe BARKER
96 Director of Purchasing ... Mr. Jesse MARTINEZ

Southwestern Adventist University (C)

PO Box 567, 100 W Hillcrest St, Keene TX 76059-0567
County: Johnson FICE Identification: 003619
Unit ID: 228468
Telephone: (817) 645-3921 Carnegie Class: Bac/Diverse
FAX Number: (817) 202-6744 Calendar System: Semester
URL: www.swau.edu
Established: 1893 Annual Undergrad Tuition & Fees: $17,080
Enrollment: 790 Coed
Affiliation or Control: Seventh-day Adventist IRS Status: 501(c)3
Highest Offering: Master's
Program: Liberal Arts And General; Teacher Preparatory; Professional
Accreditation: SC, IACBE, NURSE

01 President ... Dr. Eric D. ANDERSON
05 VP for Academic Administration ... Dr. Benjamin MCARTHUR
10 VP for Financial Administration ... Mr. Larry W. GARRETT
30 VP for University Advancement ... Mr. Gary M. TEMPLE
84 VP for Enrollment ... Ms. Enga ALMEIDA
32 VP for Student Services ... Mr. James THE
42 VP for Spiritual Development ... Dr. William KILGORE
45 Director of Planning ... Dr. Thomas G. BUNCH
37 Asst VP for Student Finance ... Ms. Patricia A. NORWOOD
21 Asst VP Financial Administration ... Mr. Greg A. WICKLUND
06 Registrar ... Dr. Robert GARDNER
08 Librarian ... Ms. Cristina M. THOMSEN
34 Dean of Women ... Mrs. Janelle D. WILLIAMS
33 Assistant Dean of Men ... Mr. William IVERSON
13 Dir Information Technology Svcs ... Mr. E. Charles LEWIS
18 Plant Engineer ... Mr. Dale E. HAINEY
26 Director of Marketing ... Ms. Darcy FORCE
29 Director of Alumni Relations ... Ms. Beverly A. MENDENHALL
38 Director of Counseling & Testing ... Dr. R. Mark ALDRIDGE

Southwestern Assemblies of God University (D)

1200 Sycamore, Waxahachie TX 75165-2397
County: Ellis FICE Identification: 003616
Unit ID: 228325
Telephone: (972) 937-4010 Carnegie Class: Master's S
FAX Number: (972) 923-0488 Calendar System: Semester
URL: www.sagu.edu
Established: 1927 Annual Undergrad Tuition & Fees: $15,730
Enrollment: 2,064 Coed
Affiliation or Control: Assemblies Of God Church IRS Status: 501(c)3
Highest Offering: Master's
Program: Liberal Arts And General; Teacher Preparatory; Religious Emphasis
Accreditation: SC

01 President ... Dr. Kermit S. BRIDGES
05 Vice President for Academics ... Dr. Paul BROOKS
32 Vice President for Student Services ... Rev. Terry PHIPPS
10 Vice Pres for Business & Finance ... Rev. Jay TREWERN
30 Vice President for Univ Advancement ... Rev. Irby MCKNIGHT
84 Vice Pres Enrollment & Retention ... Rev. Eddie DAVIS
20 Dean of Academic Services ... Rev. Donny LUTRICK
58 Dean of Graduate Studies ... Dr. Robert HARDEN
73 Dean Col Bible & Church Ministries ... Dr. LeRoy BARTEL
79 Dean College of Arts & Professions ... Dr. Larry GOODRICH
09 Assoc Dean for Inst Effectiveness ... Dr. Terry MINTER
51 Asst Dean for Distance Education ... Rev. Joseph HARTMAN
06 Registrar ... Ms. Heather FRANCIS
35 Dean of Students ... Rev. Lance MECHE
89 Asst Dean for Student Success ... Rev. Rob BLAKNEY
88 Director of Achievement Center ... Ms. Valerie FITZWATER
14 Sr Dir Information Technology ... Rev. David BUSH
29 Director Alumni Relations ... Mr. Devin FERGUSON
08 Director of Learning Resources ... Mr. Eugene HOLDER
13 Director Campus Software ... Mr. Mark WALKER
21 Sr Dir of Business Services ... Mr. Jimmie LAMB
88 Senior Director of Accounting ... Ms. Candee LUTRICK
37 Sr Director of Financial Aid ... Mr. Jeff FRANCIS
19 Director of Security ... Mr. Michael MINTER
07 Director of Admissions ... Rev. Bryan BROOKS
24 Director of Media Services ... Mr. John COOKMAN
88 Director of Accounts Receivable ... Ms. Joan BUTLER
44 Sr Dir of Dev & Planned Giving ... Mr. Craig RINAS
36 Director of Career Services ... Ms. Beverly ROBINSON
41 Athletic Director ... Mr. Jesse GODDING
26 Director of University Marketing ... Mr. Ryan MCELHANY
15 Director Human Resources ... Mrs. Ruth ROBERTS
88 Director Educator Cert ... Ms. Janice WHITAKER
18 Projects Manager ... Mr. James DAVIS
38 Counselor ... Dr. Tim MYERS
88 Admissions Counselor ... Ms. Pat THOMPSON

Southwestern Baptist Theological Seminary (E)

PO Box 22607, Fort Worth TX 76122-0150
County: Tarrant FICE Identification: 003617
Unit ID: 228477
Telephone: (817) 923-1921 Carnegie Class: Spec/Faith
FAX Number: (817) 921-8766 Calendar System: Semester
URL: www.swbts.edu
Established: 1908 Annual Undergrad Tuition & Fees: $6,846
Enrollment: 2,791 Coed
Affiliation or Control: Southern Baptist IRS Status: 501(c)3
Highest Offering: Doctorate
Program: Professional; Religious Emphasis
Accreditation: SC, MUS, THEOL

01 President ... Dr. Paige PATTERSON
05 Executive Vice President/Provost ... Dr. Craig A. BLAISING
10 Vice Pres Business Administration ... Mr. Kevin ENSLEY
30 Vice Pres Institutional Advancement ... Mr. Mike C. HUGHES
32 Vice Pres for Student Services/Comm ... Dr. Thomas WHITE
88 Vice Pres of Strategic Initiatives ... Dr. Jason G. DUESING
20 Vice Provost for Academic Programs ... Dr. Edward PAULEY
06 Registrar & Assoc VP Inst Assessmnt ... Dr. Mark LEEDS
08 Dean of Libraries ... Dr. C. Berry DRIVER
73 Dean of the School of Theology ... Dr. David ALLEN
88 Dean Marshall Center for Theol Stds ... Dr. Rudy GONZALEZ
53 Dean Sch of Church & Fam Ministries ... Dr. Waylan OWENS
64 Dean School of Church Music ... Dr. Stephen JOHNSON
12 Dean Havard Sch for Theol Studies ... Dr. Denny AUTREY
73 Dean Sch of Evangelism & Missions ... Dr. Keith EITEL
49 Dean College at Southwestern ... Dr. Steven SMITH
94 Dean of Women's Programs ... Dr. Terri STOVALL
56 Dean Center for Extension Education ... Dr. Deron BILES
07 Director of Admissions ... Mr. Kyle WALKER

Southwestern Christian College (F)

Box 10, Terrell TX 75160-9002
County: Kaufman FICE Identification: 003618
Unit ID: 228486
Telephone: (972) 524-3341 Carnegie Class: Bac/Assoc
FAX Number: (972) 563-7133 Calendar System: Semester
URL: www.swcc.edu
Established: 1949 Annual Undergrad Tuition & Fees: $6,656
Enrollment: 224 Coed
Affiliation or Control: Churches Of Christ IRS Status: 501(c)3
Highest Offering: Baccalaureate
Program: Liberal Arts And General
Accreditation: SC

01 President ... Dr. Jack EVANS
30 Vice President for Instl Expansion ... Dr. James MAXWELL
05 Vice President Academic Affairs ... Mrs. Zoa Ann TURNER
10 Vice President Fiscal Affairs ... Mr. Douglas HOWIE
32 Vice President Student Affairs ... Mr. Ben FOSTER
08 Librarian ... Mrs. Doris JOHNSON
07 Director of Admissions ... Mr. Walter PRICE
37 Director of Financial Aid ... Ms. Tanya DEAN
44 Director of Development ... Mr. Jack EVANS, JR.

Southwestern University (G)

1001 E University Avenue, Georgetown TX 78626-6144
County: Williamson FICE Identification: 003620
Unit ID: 228343
Telephone: (512) 863-6511 Carnegie Class: Bac/A&S
FAX Number: (512) 863-5788 Calendar System: Semester
URL: www.southwestern.edu
Established: 1840 Annual Undergrad Tuition & Fees: $33,440
Enrollment: 1,372 Coed
Affiliation or Control: United Methodist IRS Status: 501(c)3
Highest Offering: Baccalaureate
Program: Liberal Arts And General; Teacher Preparatory
Accreditation: SC, MUS

01 President ... Dr. Jake B. SCHRUM
42 University Chaplain ... Ms. Beverly JONES
04 Executive Asst to the President ... Ms. Francie SCHROEDER
04 Sr Advisor Strategic Plng/Assess ... Dr. Ronald L. SWAIN
05 Provost/Dean of Faculty ... Dr. James W. HUNT
84 Vice Pres for Enrollment Services ... Vacant
30 Vice Pres Institutional Advancement ... Mr. C. Richard MCKELVEY
10 Vice President for Fiscal Affairs ... Mr. Richard L. ANDERSON
32 Vice President for Student Life ... Mr. Gerald D. BRODY
57 Dean of Sarofim School of Fine Arts ... Dr. Paul J. GAFFNEY
08 Dean of Library Services ... Ms. Lynne BRODY
20 Assoc VP Academic Administration ... Ms. Julie A. COWLEY
26 Assoc VP for University Relations ... Ms. Cindy LOCKE
21 Assoc Vice President for Finance ... Mr. Gary L. LOGAN
88 Assoc VP for Facility/Campus Svcs ... Mr. Bob D. MATHIS
13 Assoc VP for Information Tech Svcs ... Mr. Bob C. PAVER
15 Assoc VP for Human Resources ... Ms. Elma F. BENAVIDES
39 Assoc VP and Dean of Students ... Dr. Mike LEESE
07 Assoc VP for Enrollment Services ... Mr. Monty L. CURTIS
29 Assoc VP for Alumni Relations ... Ms. Georgianne HEWETT
44 Associate Vice Pres for Development ... Mr. Kent HUNTSMAN
41 Assoc VP/Dir Intercollegiate Athl ... Dr. Glada C. MUNT
35 Associate Dean for Student Life ... Ms. Jaime WOODY
88 Asst Dean Faculty Dev & Spons Pgms ... Dr. John MCCANN
06 Registrar ... Mr. David H. STONES
21 Controller ... Ms. Brenda THOMPSON
19 Chief of Police ... Ms. Deborah BROWN
37 Director of Financial Aid ... Mr. James GAETA
36 Director Career Services ... Mr. Roger YOUNG
20 Dir Academic Success ... Ms. Kimberly MURPHY
20 Dir Paideia Program/Assoc Professor ... Dr. David J. GAINES
85 Director Intercultural Learning ... Ms. Susan MENNICKE
27 Director of Communications ... Ms. Ellen DAVIS
38 Director Counseling/Health Services ... Dr. Judith SONNENBERG
18 Director Physical Plant ... Mr. Joe LEPAGE
09 Director Institutional Research ... Dr. Michelle ACHACOSO
28 Asst Director of Diversity Educ ... Vacant
31 Coordinator of Civic Engagement ... Ms. Suzanna PUKYS

Stephen F. Austin State University (H)

2008 Alumni Drive, Rusk 206,
Nacogdoches TX 75961-3940
County: Nacogdoches FICE Identification: 003624
Unit ID: 228431
Telephone: (936) 468-2011 Carnegie Class: Master's L
FAX Number: (936) 468-2202 Calendar System: Semester
URL: www.sfasu.edu
Established: 1921 Annual Undergrad Tuition & Fees (In-State): $6,586
Enrollment: 12,954 Coed
Affiliation or Control: State IRS Status: 501(c)3
Highest Offering: Doctorate
Program: Liberal Arts And General; Teacher Preparatory; Professional
Accreditation: SC, AAFCS, ART, BUS, CACREP, CIDA, CORE, CS, DIETD, DIETI, FOR, MUS, NUR, SP, SW, TED, THEA

01 President ... Dr. Baker PATTILLO
05 Provost/Vice Pres Academic Affairs ... Dr. Richard A. BERRY
10 Vice Pres Finance/Administration ... Mr. Danny R. GALLANT
32 Vice Pres for University Affairs ... Dr. Steve WESTBROOK
30 Vice President of Development ... Mr. Sid WALKER
29 Exec Director SFA Alumni Affairs ... Mr. Jeff DAVIS
20 Assoc Provost/VP Academic Affairs ... Dr. Mary Nelle BRUNSON
84 Exec Dir of Enrollment Management ... Ms. Monique COSSICH
26 Exec Dir Public Affairs/Marketing ... Mr. Robert E. WRIGHT
43 General Counsel ... Mr. Damon DERRICK
06 Registrar ... Ms. Lynda LANGHAM
09 Director Institutional Research ... Ms. Karyn HALL
08 Library Director ... Ms. Shirley DICKERSON
39 Director of Residence Life ... Mr. Winston BAKER
18 Director of Physical Plant ... Mr. Lee BRITTAIN
37 Director of Financial Aid ... Mr. Michael C. O'REAR
22 Director Affirmative Action ... Ms. Glenda HERRINGTON
14 Dir Computer/Communication Svcs ... Mr. Paul DAVIS
15 Personnel Director ... Ms. Glenda HERRINGTON
19 Chief of University Police ... Mr. Marc COSSICH
23 Director Health Clinic ... Dr. John H. MILLER
41 Director of Intercol Athletics ... Mr. Robert W. HILL
35 Dean Student Affairs ... Dr. Adam PECK
36 Director Counsel/Career Services ... Mr. Ralph BUSBY
96 Director of Procurement ... Ms. Diana BOUBEL
45 Dir Research/Sponsored Programs ... Dr. Carrie BROWN
28 Director Multicultural Affairs ... Dr. Terrence FRAZIER
58 Dean Graduate School ... Dr. James D. STANDLEY
49 Dean College Liberal/Applied Arts ... Dr. Brian MURPHY
47 Dean College Forestry/Agriculture ... Dr. Steven BULLARD
53 Dean of College of Education ... Dr. Judy A. ABBOTT
57 Dean College Fine Arts ... Dr. A.C. (Buddy) HIMES
50 Dean College of Business ... Dr. Danny R. ARNOLD
81 Int Dean College Sciences & Math ... Dr. Kimberly M. CHILDS

Tarrant County College District (A)

1500 Houston Street, Fort Worth TX 76102-6599
County: Tarrant FICE Identification: 003626
Unit ID: 228547
Telephone: (817) 515-5100 Carnegie Class: Assoc/Pub-U-MC
FAX Number: (817) 515-5295 Calendar System: Semester
URL: www.tccd.edu
Established: 1965 Annual Undergrad Tuition & Fees (In-District): $1,200
Enrollment: 44,355 Coed
Affiliation or Control: State/Local IRS Status: 501(c)3
Highest Offering: Associate Degree
Program: Occupational; 2-Year Principally Bachelor's Creditable
Accreditation: SC, ADNUR, DH, DIETT, EMT, PTAA, RAD, SURGT

01 Chancellor ... Dr. Erma C. JOHNSON HADLEY
05 Vice Chanc Ops/Acad Affs/Plng Svcs ... Dr. David A. WELLS
11 Vice Chanc Administration ... Dr. William W. LACE
10 Vice Chancellor for Finance ... Mr. Mark MCCLENDON
13 Vice Chanc Info/Technical Services ... Mrs. Maria T. SHELTON
27 VC Communications/External Affairs ... Mr. Reginald GATES
20 VP Teaching/Learning Svcs/SO Campus ... Dr. Jo K. BAGLEY
20 VP Teaching/Learning Svcs/NE Campus ... Dr. Jane HARPER
20 VP Teaching/Learning Svcs/NW Campus ... Dr. Leann ELLIS
20 Vice Pres Teaching/Learning Svcs/SE ... Ms. Barbara COHEN
20 Vice Pres Teaching/Learning Svcs/TR ... Dr. Gregory STEWART
32 VP Stdnt Dev/Educ Svcs/NE Campus . Ms. Magdalena DELA TEJA
32 VP Stdnt Dev/Educ Svcs/SE Campus ... Mr. Rusty FOX
32 VP Student Devel Svcs So Campus ... Mr. Juan GARCIA
32 VP Student Devel/Educational Svcs ... Dr. Joe RODE
12 Int President South Campus ... Dr. Joy GATES BLACK
12 President Northwest Campus ... Dr. Elva C. LEBLANC
12 President Northeast Campus ... Dr. Larry J. DARLAGE
12 President Southeast Campus ... Dr. Judith J. CARRIER
20 Assc Vice Chanc Teaching/Lrnng Svcs ... Dr. Tahita M. FULKERSON
45 Assoc Vice Chanc/Planning Budgeting ... Dr. Lily F. TERCERO
15 Assoc Vice Chanc Human Resources ... Dr. Ricardo CORONADO
35 Assoc VC Student Development Svcs ... Dr. Cathie W. JACKSON
21 Assoc Vice Chancellor Finance ... Mrs. Nancy H. CHANG
13 Assc Vice Chanc Information Systems ... Dr. Mary A. ROBBINS
51 Assoc Vice Chanc Cont Ed Svcs ... Dr. Kathleen A. NOBLE
30 Executive Director of Development ... Dr. Joe MCINTOSH
26 Director Public Rels/Marketing ... Mrs. Donna DAROVICH
18 Dir of Physical Plant Operations ... Mr. Gary PREATHER
19 Chief of Police ... Mr. Frank L. BUCHANAN
09 Director of Institutional Research ... Dr. Linda K. HINES
56 Director Distance Learning ... Dr. Kevin EASON
08 Dir Library Svcs Northeast Campus ... Dr. Steven W. HAGSTROM
08 Director Library Svcs South Campus ... Ms. Linda JENSON
08 Dir Library Svcs Northwest Campus ... Ms. Anna R. HOLZER
08 Dir Library Svcs Southeast Campus ... Mr. Mark DOLIVE
06 Registrar South Campus ... Mr. John D. SPENCER
06 Registrar Northeast Campus ... Mr. Brian D. BARRETT
06 Registrar Northwest Campus ... Ms. Aubra J. GANTT
06 Registrar Southeast Campus ... Mr. Juan C. TORRES
38 Director Counseling South Campus ... Mr. Clifton DOBBINS
38 Dir Counseling Northeast Campus ... Mr. Eddie SANDOVAL
38 Dir Counseling Southeast Campus ... Dr. Curtis HILL
37 Director Financial Aid District ... Mr. David XIMENEZ
37 Director Financial Aid South Campus ... Ms. JoLynn F. SPROLE
37 Dir Financial Aid Northeast Campus ... Ms. Dawn K. BROWN
37 Dir Financial Aid Northwest Campus ... Ms. Trina SMITH-PATTERSON
37 Dir Financial Aid Southeast Campus ... Ms. Erika T. WILLIAMS
23 Dir Student Devel Svcs NE Campus ... Dr. Paula VASTINE-NORMAN
23 Dir Health Services Nthwest Campus ... Ms. Evette C. BRAZZILE
24 Dir Instruction Media South Campus ... Ms. Sue E. SANDERS
24 Dir Instruction Media NE Campus ... Mr. David B. MEAD
24 Dir Learning Resources NW Campus ... Dr. John R. MARTIN, JR.
35 Dir Student Activities So Campus ... Mr. Zebedee D. STRONG
35 Dir Student Activities NW Campus ... Ms. Vesta M. WHEATLEY
35 Dir Student Devel Svcs SE Campus ... Mr. Douglas C. PEAK
84 Director Enrollment Services ... Mr. Fidel CASTILLO
96 Director of Business Svcs ... Mr. Richard INMAN
38 Dir Counseling Northwest Campus ... Dr. Ricks EDMONDSON
96 Director of Purchasing ... Mr. Mark A. MCMILLAN
36 Coord Student Career/Employmnt Svcs ... Ms. Sandra L. WALKER

Temple College (B)

2600 S First Street, Temple TX 76504-7435
County: Bell FICE Identification: 003627
Unit ID: 228608
Telephone: (254) 298-8282 Carnegie Class: Assoc/Pub-R-M
FAX Number: (254) 298-8277 Calendar System: Semester
URL: www.templejc.edu
Established: 1926 Annual Undergrad Tuition & Fees (In-District): $2,252
Enrollment: 5,966 Coed
Affiliation or Control: Local IRS Status: 501(c)3
Highest Offering: Associate Degree
Program: Occupational; 2-Year Principally Bachelor's Creditable
Accreditation: SC, ADNUR, DH, DMS, EMT, SURGT

01 President ... Dr. Glenda O. BARRON
11 AVP Finance/Info Tech Svcs ... Mr. Gary JACKSON
05 Vice Pres of Educational Services ... Dr. Mark A. SMITH
31 AVP Acad Outreach & Ext Programs ... Dr. Dan SPENCER
13 Senior Dir IT Services ... Mr. Donnie CARPENTER
15 Director Div of Resource Management ... Dr. Randy BACA
84 Div Dir Stdnt & Enroll Srvcs ... Mrs. Carey ROSE
08 Div Director of Learning Resources ... Mrs. Kathy FULTON
102 Exec Dir Temple College Foundation ... Mrs. Jennifer GRAHAM
09 AVP Comm Init & Spec Programs ... Dr. Jimmy ROBERTS
38 Director Student Advising ... Ms. Amy FLINN
04 Assistant to the President & Board ... Mrs. Judith DOHNALIK
37 Director of Financial Aid ... Mr. Fred PENA
27 Director College Communications ... Ms. Erin SPENCER
18 Dir Facilities/Physical Plant ... Mr. Skeet POWELL
96 Director of Purchasing ... Mrs. Deborah SVAJDA
32 Chief Student Life Officer ... Mrs. Ruth BRIDGES
07 Assoc Dir Admission & Records ... Mrs. Toni CUELLAR
41 Athletic Director ... Mr. Danny SCOTT
19 Chief of Police ... Mr. David BLANKEMEIER

Texarkana College (C)

2500 N Robison Road, Texarkana TX 75501-3099
County: Bowie FICE Identification: 003628
Unit ID: 228699
Telephone: (903) 838-4541 Carnegie Class: Assoc/Pub-R-M
FAX Number: (903) 832-5030 Calendar System: Semester
URL: www.texarkanacollege.edu
Established: 1927 Annual Undergrad Tuition & Fees (In-District): $1,546
Enrollment: 4,610 Coed
Affiliation or Control: Local IRS Status: 501(c)3
Highest Offering: Associate Degree
Program: Occupational; 2-Year Principally Bachelor's Creditable
Accreditation: SC, ADNUR

01 President ... Mr. James H. RUSSELL
10 Vice President for Admin & Finance ... Mr. Dan DOBELL
27 Chief Information Officer ... Dr. Art LEIBLE
45 Dir of Institutional Effectiveness ... Mrs. Jamie ASHBY
07 Director of Admissions ... Mr. Tom ELDER
38 Director of Counseling ... Vacant
51 Assoc Dean Evening & Cont Education ... Mr. Scotty HAYES
18 Chief Facilities/Physical Plant ... Mr. Rick BOYETTE
26 Inst Advancement & Public Rels ... Mrs. Suzy IRWIN
84 Recruitment Coordinator ... Ms. Shanetta CANNON

*The Texas A & M University System Office (D)

A&M System Bldg, 200 Technology Way,
College Station TX 77845-3424
County: Brazos FICE Identification: 003629
Unit ID: 228732
Telephone: (979) 458-6000 Carnegie Class: N/A
FAX Number: (979) 458-6044
URL: www.tamus.edu

01 Chancellor ... Mr. John SHARP
05 Vice Chancellor Academic Affairs ... Dr. Frank ASHLEY
86 Vice Chanc for Governmental Rels ... Dr. Stanton CALVERT
09 Vice Chanc for Strategic Initiative ... Dr. Brett GIROIR
21 Chief Business Officer ... Ms. B. J. CRAIN
18 Chief Facilities/Plng/Construc Ofcr ... Mr. Vergel L. GAY
10 Chief Investment Officer/Treasurer ... Mr. Greg ANDERSON
21 Chief Auditor ... Ms. Cathy SMOCK
100 Chief of Staff ... Ms. Janet SMALLEY
43 General Counsel ... Vacant
27 Chief Communications Officer ... Mr. Jason COOK
46 Chief Research Officer ... Dr. Jeffrey R. SEEMANN
19 Chief Safety Officer ... Mr. Chris MEYER
13 Chief Information Officer ... Mr. Pierce CANTRELL

*Prairie View A & M University (E)

L. W. Minor Street, Prairie View TX 77446-0519
County: Waller FICE Identification: 003630
Unit ID: 227526
Telephone: (936) 261-3311 Carnegie Class: Master's L
FAX Number: (936) 261-2115 Calendar System: Semester
URL: www.pvamu.edu
Established: 1876 Annual Undergrad Tuition & Fees (In-State): $6,855
Enrollment: 8,781 Coed
Affiliation or Control: State IRS Status: 501(c)3
Highest Offering: Doctorate
Program: Liberal Arts And General; Teacher Preparatory; Professional
Accreditation: SC, BUS, CS, DIETD, DIETI, ENG, ENGT, MUS, NUR, NURSE, SW, TED

02 President ... Dr. George C. WRIGHT
05 Provost/SR VP Academic Affairs ... Dr. E. Joahanne THOMAS-SMITH
20 Assoc Prov & Assoc VP Acad Afairs ... Dr. James J. WILSON, JR.
20 Assoc Prov & Assoc VP Acad Affairs ... Dr. Felicia M. NAVE
92 Director of Honors Program ... Dr. James J. WILSON, JR.
10 Sr Vice President Business Affairs ... Dr. Corey S. BRADFORD, SR.
32 VP for Student Affs/Inst Relations ... Dr. Lauretta F. BYARS
46 Vice President Research/Development ... Dr. Willie F. TROTTY
35 Vice Pres Student/Enrollment Svcs ... Vacant
10 Vice Pres Administration/Aux Svcs ... Mr. Fred E. WASHINGTON
20 Vice Provost & Dean of NWHC ... Dr. Michael L. MCFRAZIER
84 Assoc Provost Enrollment Mgmt ... Mr. Don BYARS
21 Asst VP for Financial Accounting ... Mr. Rod MIRELES
21 Asst VP for Financial Services ... Ms. Patricia BAUGHMAN
30 Director of Development ... Mr. Nelson E. BOWMAN
09 Director Institutional Research ... Mr. Dean WILLIAMSON
07 Dir of Undergraduate Admissions ... Ms. Mary E. GOOCH
18 Assistant VP of Physical Plant ... Mr. Larry J. WATSON
08 Director of Library ... Dr. Rosie L. ALBRITTON
15 Asst VP for Human Resources ... Mr. Albert R. GEE
37 Director of Financial Aid ... Mr. K. Michael FRANCOIS
36 Program Coord Residence Life ... Mr. Charles E. CROCKETT
63 Director Undergrad Med Acad ... Dr. Dennis E. DANIELS
41 Director of Athletics ... Mr. Fred E. WASHINGTON
14 Chief Information Officer ... Mr. Luis-Pablo GRIJALVA
58 Dean of the Graduate School ... Dr. Willie F. TROTTY
50 Dean College of Business ... Dr. Munir QUDDUS
53 Dean College of Education ... Dr. Lucian YATES
54 Dean College of Engineering ... Dr. Kendall T. HARRIS
47 Dean Col Agriculture/Human Sci ... Dr. Freddie L. RICHARDS
66 Dean College of Nursing ... Dr. Betty ADAMS
49 Dean College of Arts & Sciences ... Dr. Danny R. KELLEY
48 Dean School of Architecture ... Dr. Ikhlas SABOUNI
88 Int Dean Col of Juv Just/Psychology ... Dr. Dennis E. DANIELS
21 Manager of Treasury Services ... Ms. Equilla JACKSON
23 Director Health Center ... Ms. Thelma J. PIERRE
56 Administrator Coop Extension ... Dr. Freddie L. RICHARDS
19 Director Security/Safety ... Mr. Algray L. PETTUS
31 Asst VP Auxiliary Enterprises ... Ms. Tressey D. WILSON
29 Director Alumni Affairs ... Vacant
06 Registrar/Records ... Ms. Deborah J. DUNGEY
12 Exec Dir University College ... Ms. Lettie M. RAAB
28 Director of Diversity ... Ms. Elma D. GONZALEZ
85 Immigration Services Coord ... Mrs. Evelyn J. MCGINTY
26 Executive Dir for Communications ... Mrs. Sheleah D. REED
96 Procurement Sup/HUB Coordinator ... Mr. Jim A. NELMS
88 Director Budget & Reconciliation ... Mrs. Diane T. EVANS

*Tarleton State University (F)

1333 W Washington, Box T-0001,
Stephenville TX 76402-0001
County: Erath FICE Identification: 003631
Unit ID: 228529
Telephone: (254) 968-9000 Carnegie Class: Master's L
FAX Number: (254) 968-9920 Calendar System: Semester
URL: www.tarleton.edu
Established: 1899 Annual Undergrad Tuition & Fees (In-State): $6,450
Enrollment: 9,341 Coed
Affiliation or Control: State IRS Status: 501(c)3
Highest Offering: Doctorate
Program: Liberal Arts And General; Teacher Preparatory
Accreditation: SC, ACBSP, ENG, HT, MLTAD, MT, MUS, NURSE, SW

02 President ... Dr. F. Dominic DOTTAVIO
04 Executive Asst to the President ... Ms. Vickie E. SWAM
05 Provost/VPAA ... Dr. Karen MURRAY
30 Vice Pres Inst Advancement ... Dr. Rick RICHARDSON
10 Vice Pres Finance/Administration ... Mr. Jerry W. GRAHAM
32 Vice President Student Life ... Mr. Rusty JERGINS
84 VP Enrollment/Information Mgmt ... Dr. Brad CHILTON
20 Assoc VP for Academic Affairs ... Dr. Dwayne SNIDER
38 Asst VP Wellness/Career Devel ... Vacant
46 Assoc VP Academic Research/Grants ... Dr. Bert LITTLE
18 Assoc Vice Pres Physical Facilities ... Mr. Joe STANDRIDGE
21 Asst VP Finance/Administration ... Ms. Cynthia CARTER
35 Assoc Vice Pres Student Life ... Dr. Gilbert HINGA
26 Assoc VP Marketing/Communications ... Mr. Rod DAVIS
35 Asst VP Student Life Studies ... Mr. Robert (Mike) HAYNES
21 Asst VP Business Svcs/Controller ... Mr. Mike TATE
49 Dean College Science & Technology ... Dr. James PIERCE
50 Dean Col of Business Administration ... Dr. Adolfo BENAVIDES
47 Dean Col Agricul & Environ Sciences ... Dr. Donald L. CAWTHON
53 Dean College of Education ... Dr. Jill BURK
57 Dean College of Liberal & Fine Arts ... Dr. Dean MINIX
58 Dean College of Graduate Studies ... Dr. Linda M. JONES
88 Dean Student Success ... Dr. Dennis JONES
07 Director Undergraduate Admissions ... Ms. Cynthia HESS
28 Dir Student Disability Services ... Ms. Trina GEYE
08 University Librarian ... Mrs. Donna SAVAGE
31 Director of External Relations ... Ms. Janice HORAK
37 Director Student Financial Aid ... Ms. Betty MURRAY
09 Director Institutional Research ... Dr. Wayne ATCHLEY
13 Exec Director Information Resources ... Ms. Rebecca GRAY
15 Director Human Resources ... Ms. Angela C. BROWN
36 Director Career Services ... Ms. Darla DOTY
41 Athletic Director ... Mr. Lonn REISMAN
23 Director Student Health Center ... Ms. Bridgette BEDNARZ
19 Director University Police ... Mr. Justin WILLIAMS
39 Director Housing & Residence Life ... Ms. Elizabeth WALLACE
28 Int Dir Ofc Diversity/Inclusion ... Dr. Moumin QUAZI
24 Dir Instruct Tech/Distribut Educ ... Dr. Credence BAKER
44 Director of Development ... Ms. Sabra GUERRA
104 Dir International Academic Programs ... Dr. Marilyn ROBITAILLE
06 Registrar ... Ms. Denise GROVES
96 Director of Purchasing/HUB ... Ms. Beth CHANDLER
25 Grants/Contracts Administrator ... Ms. DeAnna POWELL
40 Manager Campus Store ... Ms. Christina STRADLEY
105 Web Administrator ... Ms. Daphne HUNT

*Texas A & M University System Health Science Center (G)

301 Tarrow Street, 7th Floor,
College Station TX 77840-7896
County: Brazos FICE Identification: 004948
Unit ID: 223214
Telephone: (979) 458-7200 Carnegie Class: Spec/Med
FAX Number: (979) 458-7202 Calendar System: Semester
URL: www.tamhsc.edu
Established: 1999 Annual Undergrad Tuition & Fees (In-State): $9,878

Enrollment: 1,958 Coed
Affiliation or Control: State IRS Status: 501(c)3
Highest Offering: Doctorate
Program: Professional
Accreditation: SC

02	President	Dr. Nancy W. DICKEY
05	Vice President for Academic Affairs	Dr. Roderick W. MCCALLUM
10	Vice Pres Finance & Administration	Dr. Barry C. NELSON
26	Vice Pres Pgm Devel & Cmty Outreach	Vacant
86	Vice President Governmental Affairs	Ms. Jenny E. JONES
46	Vice Pres Research/Graduate Studies	Dr. David S. CARLSON
30	VP for Institutional Advancement	Dr. Russell A. GIBBS
13	Interim Executive Director/CIO	Mr. Scott HONEA
52	Dean Baylor College of Dentistry	Dr. Lawrence E. WOLINSKY
63	Dean Col of Medicine/VP Clin Affs	Dr. Thomas S. SHOMAKER
66	Dean College of Nursing	Dr. Sharon A. WILKERSON
67	Dean College of Pharmacy	Dr. Indra K. REDDY
69	Dean School of Rural Public Health	Dr. Craig H. BLAKELY
88	Dir Inst for Biosciences & Tech	Vacant
100	Chief of Staff	Dr. Lee Ann RAY

† Tuition varies by program.

*Texas A & M Health Science Center Baylor College of Dentistry (A)

3302 Gaston Avenue, Dallas TX 75246-2098
County: Dallas Identification: 666240
Telephone: (214) 828-8100 Carnegie Class: Not Classified
FAX Number: (214) 874-4536 Calendar System: Semester
URL: www.bcd.tamhsc.edu
Established: 1905 Annual Undergrad Tuition & Fees (In-State): $6,386
Enrollment: 580 Coed
Affiliation or Control: State IRS Status: 501(c)3
Highest Offering: Doctorate
Program: Professional
Accreditation: &SC, DENT, DH

02	Dean	Dr. Lawrence E. WOLINSKY
10	Asc Dean for Finance/Administration	Ms. Juanna S. MOORE
05	Assoc Dean Academic Affairs	Dr. Charles W. BERRY
46	Assoc Dn Research/Graduate Studies	Dr. Larry L. BELLINGER
88	Associate Dean Clinical Affairs	Dr. Dean A. HUDSON
26	Exec Dir of Communications & Dev	Ms. Susan MITCHELL JACKSON
07	Exec Dir of Recruitment/Admissions	Dr. Barbara H. MILLER
51	Ex Dir Continuing Educ/Alumni Affs	Dr. Charles J. ARCORIA
09	Exec Dir of Institutional Research	Dr. Eric S. SOLOMON
18	Exec Dir of Facilities Services	Mr. Dale A. CHRISTENSEN
32	Associate Dean Student Affairs	Dr. Jack L. LONG
76	Director Dental Hygiene	Dr. Janice P. DEWALD
90	Director of Academic Computing	Ms. Regina L. COURTNEY
15	Regional Director Human Resources	Ms. Pat LOPEZ
37	Director Student Financial Aid	Ms. Kay EGBERT
08	Director Library	Ms. Cindy SCROGGINS
17	Director of Hospital Affairs	Dr. R. Gilbert TRIPLETT
83	Director of Social Services	Mrs. Leeanna BARTLETT
96	Assistant Manager Purchasing	Ms. Debbie RUFF
35	Director Student Affairs	Ms. Moira ALLEN

*Texas A & M International University (B)

5201 University Boulevard, Laredo TX 78041-1900
County: Webb FICE Identification: 009651
Unit ID: 226152
Telephone: (956) 326-2001 Carnegie Class: Master's L
FAX Number: (956) 326-2348 Calendar System: Semester
URL: www.tamiu.edu
Established: 1969 Annual Undergrad Tuition & Fees (In-State): $5,909
Enrollment: 6,419 Coed
Affiliation or Control: State IRS Status: 501(c)3
Highest Offering: Doctorate
Program: Liberal Arts And General; Teacher Preparatory
Accreditation: SC, BUS, NUR

02	President	Dr. Ray M. KECK, III
05	Provost/Vice Pres Academic Affs	Dr. Pablo ARENAZ
10	Vice Pres Finance & Administration	Mr. Juan J. CASTILLO, JR.
30	Vice Pres Institutional Advancement	Ms. Candy HEIN
32	Vice Pres for Student Success	Ms. Minita RAMIREZ
20	Assoc Vice Pres Academic Affairs	Mrs. Mary TREVINO
11	Assoc Vice Pres for Administration	Ms. Elizabeth N. MARTINEZ
13	Assoc VP Information Technology/CIO	Mr. Leebrian GASKINS
85	Asst VP for International Programs	Dr. Jamie S. ORTIZ
49	Dean College Arts & Sciences	Dr. Thomas R. MITCHELL
50	Dean College Business Admin	Dr. Stephen R. SEARS
53	Dean College of Education	Dr. Juan LIRA
66	Dean Canseco School of Nursing	Dr. Regina C. AUNE
08	Director Library	Mr. Douglas FERRIER
07	Director Admissions	Ms. Rosa A. DICKINSON
06	University Registrar	Mr. Oscar E. REYNA
15	Director of Human Resources	Ms. Sandra V. PENA
26	Director Public Rels Mktg/Info Svcs	Mr. Steve K. HARMON
37	Director Financial Aid	Ms. Laura M. ELIZONDO
41	Athletic Director	Dr. Leonard NARDONE
18	Chief Facilities/Physical Plant	Mr. Richard E. GENTRY
29	Director Alumni Relations	Ms. Yelitza Marie HOWARD
36	Director Career Services	Ms. Cassandra L. WHEELER
23	Assoc Director Student Health	Ms. Elizabeth DODIER
39	Director of Residence Life/Housing	Mr. Trevor C. LIDDLE
38	Dir of Student Couns/Hlth Svcs	Mr. Gilberto SALINAS
96	Director of Purchasing	Ms. Laura C. REA
92	Director of Honors Program	Dr. Carlos E. CUELLAR
21	Comptroller	Ms. Elena M. MARTINEZ
32	Director Student Affairs	Mr. Gerardo ALVA
35	Assoc Director Student Affairs	Mr. Miguel A. TREVINO
09	Director of Institutional Research	Ms. Elizabeth MARTINEZ

*Texas A & M University (C)

1248 TAMU, College Station TX 77843-1244
County: Brazos FICE Identification: 003632
Unit ID: 228723
Telephone: (979) 845-3211 Carnegie Class: RU/VH
FAX Number: N/A Calendar System: Semester
URL: www.tamu.edu
Established: 1876 Annual Undergrad Tuition & Fees (In-State): $8,480
Enrollment: 49,129 Coed
Affiliation or Control: State IRS Status: 501(c)3
Highest Offering: Doctorate
Program: Liberal Arts And General; Teacher Preparatory; Professional
Accreditation: SC, BUS, BUSA, CEA, CLPSY, CONST, COPSY, CS, DIETD, DIETI, ENG, ENGT, FOR, HSA, IPSY, LSAR, MED, NRPA, NURSE, PH, PLNG, SCPSY, SPAA, VET

02	President	Dr. R. Bowen LOFTIN
05	Provost/Exec VP Academic Affairs	Dr. Karan L. WATSON
11	Vice Pres Administration	Dr. Rodney P. MCCLENDON
10	Vice Pres Finance & CFO	Ms. B. J. CRAIN
32	Vice Pres Student Affairs	LtGen. Joseph F. WEBER
46	Vice Pres Research	Dr. Jeffrey R. SEEMANN
27	Vice Pres Marketing/Communications	Mr. Jason D. COOK
86	Vice Pres Governmental Relations	Mr. Michael O'QUINN
12	Vice Pres/CEO Texas A&M Galveston	RADM. Robert SMITH, III
13	Vice Pres/Assoc Prov IT	Dr. Pierce E. CANTRELL, JR.
28	Vice Pres/Assoc Prov Diversity	Dr. Christine STANLEY
20	Vice Provost for Academic Affairs	Dr. Pamela R. MATTHEWS
43	Deputy General Counsel	Mr. Scott A. KELLY
47	Dean Agriculture & Life Science	Dr. Mark A. HUSSEY
48	Dean Architecture	Dr. Jorge VANEGAS
50	Dean Business	Dr. Jerry STRAWSER
53	Dean Educ & Human Dev	Dr. Douglas J. PALMER
54	Dean Engineering	Dr. G. Kemble BENNETT
65	Dean Geosciences	Dr. Kate C. MILLER
80	Dean Govt & Public Policy	Amb. Ryan CROCKER
49	Dean Liberal Arts	Dr. Jose Luis BERMUDEZ
01	Dean Science	Dr. H. Joseph NEWTON
74	Dean Vet Med & Biomed Sciences	Dr. Eleanor M. GREEN
08	Int Dean/Director Libraries	Mr. Charles GILREATH
12	Dean & CEO Texas A&M at Qatar	Dr. Mark H. WEICHOLD
20	Dean of Faculties/Associate Provost	Dr. Antonio CEPEDA-BENITO
20	Int Assoc Prov Undergrad Studies	Dr. Christine A. STANLEY
20	Assoc Prov Graduate Studies	Dr. Karen L. BUTLER-PURRY
07	Asst VP Acad Services/Admissions	Mr. Scott MCDONALD
37	Exec Dir Student Financial Aid	Ms. Delisa F. FALKS
06	Registrar	Mr. Donald D. CARTER
41	Athletic Director	Mr. Bill BYRNE
26	Assoc VP Mktg & Comm/News	Ms. Sherylon CARROLL
15	Chief Human Resources Officer	Ms. Kathryn B. SYMANK
14	Exec Dir Computing & Info Svcs	Mr. Pete MARCHBANKS
19	Chief University Police	Mr. Elmer E. SCHNEIDER, JR.
18	Exec Dir Facilities	Mr. Rodney E. WEIS
36	Exec Dir Career Center	Dr. J. Leigh TURNER
23	Director Student Health Center	Dr. Martha C. DANNENBAUM
38	Exec Dir Student Counseling Svcs	Dr. Maggie GARTNER
39	Director Residence Life/Housing	Ms. Chareny L. RYDL
92	Exec Dir Honors Programs	Dr. Sumana DATTA
104	Dir Study Abroad	Dr. Jane FLAHERTY
96	Exec Dir Strategic Sourcing	Mr. Rex JANNE
09	Int Asst VP Inst Research	Mr. Dennis A. IGNATENKO
30	Sr Executive Development	Dr. Robert L. WALKER
102	Pres Texas A&M Foundation	Dr. Eddie J. DAVIS
29	Pres Assoc of Former Students	Mr. Porter GARNER
100	Chief of Staff to President	Mr. Matt FRY

*Texas A & M University at Galveston (D)

PO Box 1675, Galveston TX 77553-1675
County: Galveston FICE Identification: 010298
Unit ID: 228714
Telephone: (409) 740-4400 Carnegie Class: Bac/Diverse
FAX Number: (409) 740-4407 Calendar System: Semester
URL: www.tamug.edu
Established: 1962 Annual Undergrad Tuition & Fees (In-State): $7,834
Enrollment: 1,867 Coed
Affiliation or Control: State IRS Status: 501(c)3
Highest Offering: Master's
Program: Professional
Accreditation: &SC, ENG, ENGT

02	President & CEO	RADM. Robert SMITH, III
05	Int AVP Acad Affs/Chief Acad Ofcr	Dr. William A. SEITZ
58	Assoc VP Research/Graduate Studies	Dr. William SEITZ
12	Supt Texas State Maritime Acad	RADM. William W. PICKAVANCE, JR.
84	Assoc VP Enrollment Mgt/Ed Outreach	Dr. Donna LANG
10	Assoc Vice President Finance	Ms. Susan HERNANDEZ LEE
11	Asst Vice Pres for Administration	Dr. W. Brad MCGONAGLE
32	Asst VP Student Affs/Auxiliary Svcs	Mr. Grant W. SHALLENBERGER
09	Asst VP Research/Graduate Studies	Dr. Tammy L. HOLLIDAY
30	Director Development	Mr. Jack O'BRIEN
15	Director Personnel Services	Mr. Jeff BOYER
35	Director Student Affairs	Mr. Todd SUTHERLAND
37	Director Student Financial Aid	Mr. Dennis CARLTON
07	Exec Dir Admissions/Enrollment Mgmt	Ms. Cheryl GREFFENSTEET-MOON
18	Chief Facilities/Physical Plant	Ms. Tammy LOBAUGH
26	Dir Media Relations/Communications	Ms. Karen BIGLEY
36	Director Student Placement	Mr. Ken BAILEY
38	Director Student Counseling	Mr. Bob SINDYLEK
14	Dir Computing/Information Svcs	Mr. Steven CONWAY
88	Int Head Dept of Marine Biology	Dr. John SCHWARZ
97	Head Dept of General Academics	Dr. Joseph SZUCS
88	Head Dept Maritime Sys Engineering	Dr. Vijay PANCHANG
88	Hd Dept Marine Sci/Ocean/Coast Rec	Dr. Patrick LOUCHOUARN
88	Hd Dept Marine Transp/Maritime Admn	Dr. William T. MCMULLEN

*Texas A & M University - Commerce (E)

PO Box 3011, Commerce TX 75429-3011
County: Hunt FICE Identification: 003565
Unit ID: 224554
Telephone: (903) 886-5102 Carnegie Class: DRU
FAX Number: (903) 886-5888 Calendar System: Semester
URL: www.tamu-commerce.edu
Established: 1889 Annual Undergrad Tuition & Fees (In-State): $5,230
Enrollment: 10,218 Coed
Affiliation or Control: State IRS Status: 501(c)3
Highest Offering: Doctorate
Program: Liberal Arts And General; Teacher Preparatory; Professional
Accreditation: SC, BUS, CACREP, ENG, MUS, SW

02	President	Dr. Dan JONES
05	Provost/VP Academic Affairs	Dr. Larry LEMANSKI
10	Vice Pres Business & Administration	Mr. Bob BROWN
30	Vice Pres Institutional Advancement	Mr. Randy VAN DEVEN
26	Asst VP for Mktg Communications	Mr. Randy JOLLY
20	Int Assoc VP for Academic Affairs	Dr. Sandy WEEKS
20	Assoc VP for Student Access and Suc	Dr. Sharon JOHNSON
84	Dean of Enrollment Management	Mrs. Stephanie HOLLEY
21	Assoc VP & Dir of Financial Svcs	Ms. Alicia CURRIN
18	Exec Dir Facil Mgmt & Support Svcs	Mr. David MCKENNA
06	Registrar	Ms. Paige BUSSELL
21	Asst VP Business & Dir Employee Svc	Mr. Rex GIDDENS
88	Comptroller/Director of Accounting	Ms. Kim LAIRD
08	Library Director	Dr. Gregory MITCHELL
37	Director of Financial Aid	Ms. Maria RAMOS
14	Director Technology Services	Mr. Michael R. CAGLE
36	Director of Career Development	Mrs. Tina BOITNOTT
58	Dean Graduate Studies/Research	Dr. Allan HEADLEY
53	Dean Education & Human Services	Dr. Brent MANGUS
49	In. Dean Humanities/Soc Sci & Art	Dr. Salvatore ATTARDO
49	Int. Dean Science/Engr & Agric	Dr. Jerry PARISH
50	Dean of Business	Dr. Harold (Hal) P. LANGFORD
88	Dean of University College	Dr. Ricky DOBBS
07	Director of Undergraduate Admiss	Mr. Jody TODHUNTER
38	Director of Student Assessment	Ms. Wendy GRUVER
32	Dean of Campus Life & Student Dev	Mr. Brian NICHOLS
29	Director of Alumni Relations	Mr. Derryle PEACE
19	University Police Chief	Mrs. Donna SPINATO
12	Director Metroplex Center	Mrs. SuzAnne KEIFER
38	Director Counseling Center	Dr. Linda T. CLINTON
39	Residential Living & Learning	Mr. Dennis KOCH
41	Athletic Director	Mr. Carlton COOPER
88	Dir of Risk Management	Mr. Jeffrey MCMURRAY
23	Director Student Health Services	Ms. Maxine MENDOZA-WELCH
15	Asst VP for Business/Dir Empl Svcs	Mr. Rex GIDDENS
85	Dir International Student Services	Mr. John MARK JONES
96	Director of Purchasing/HUB Coord	Mr. Travis BALL
09	Director of Institutional Research	Mr. Jack HARRED
28	Dir of Diversity & Cultural Affair	Mr. Robert DOTSON
88	Safety Manager	Mr. Derek PREAS

*Texas A & M University - Corpus Christi (F)

6300 Ocean Drive, Unit 5756,
Corpus Christi TX 78412-5756
County: Nueces FICE Identification: 011161
Unit ID: 224147
Telephone: (361) 825-5700 Carnegie Class: DRU
FAX Number: (361) 825-5887 Calendar System: Semester
URL: www.tamucc.edu
Established: 1947 Annual Undergrad Tuition & Fees (In-State): $6,714
Enrollment: 9,976 Coed
Affiliation or Control: State IRS Status: 501(c)3
Highest Offering: Doctorate
Program: Liberal Arts And General; Teacher Preparatory; Professional
Accreditation: SC, BUS, BUSA, CACREP, CS, ENGR, ENGT, MT, MUS, NURSE

02	President	Dr. Flavius C. KILLEBREW
05	Provost/VP for Academic Affairs	Dr. Christopher L. MARKWOOD
10	Exec VP for Finance/Administration	Ms. Kathryn FUNK-BAXTER
30	Vice Pres Institutional Advancement	Dr. S. Trent HILL
32	Vice President Student Affairs	Dr. H. Eliot CHENAUX
20	Vice Provost Academic Affairs	Dr. Paul MEYER
21	Senior Assoc VP for Finance/Admin	Ms. Kathryn FUNK-BAXTER

100 Chief of Staff .... Dr. Mary SHERWOOD
13 Assoc Vice Pres Info Technology/CIO .... Mr. Terry TATUM
45 Assoc VP Planning/Inst Effectiv .... Dr. Paul E. ORSER
20 Assoc VP for Academic Affairs .... Dr. David BILLEAUX
84 Assoc VP Enrollment Management .... Ms. Margaret DECHANT
26 Asst VP Marketing/Communications .... Mr. Marshall COLLINS
44 Asst Vice Pres for Development .... Ms. Karen SELIM
35 Assoc Vice Pres/Dean of Students .... Ms. Ann DEGAISH
06 University Registrar .... Mr. Michael RENDON
08 Director of Bell Library .... Ms. Christine SHUPALA
07 Director of Admissions .... Dr. J. Christopher FLEMING
37 Director of Financial Assistance .... Ms. Jeannie GAGE
31 Director Community Outreach .... Dr. James NEEDHAM
15 Director Human Resources .... Ms. Debra CORTINAS
18 Director Physical Plant .... Mr. Mark NASH
29 Director Alumni Relations .... Ms. Evon ENGLISH
36 Director Career Services .... Ms. Joanna BENAVIDES-FRANKE
38 Dir Student Counseling/Development .... Dr. Carla BERKICH
28 Dir Equal Opportunity/Employee Rels .... Mr. Sam RAMIREZ
96 Director of Purchasing .... Ms. Judy HARRAL
21 Bursar .... Ms. Christina HOLZHEUSER
58 Dean Grad Ed/Asc VP Rsch/Schlo Act .... Vacant
49 Dean College Liberal Arts .... Dr. Kelly QUINTANILLA
50 Dean College of Business .... Dr. Moustafa H. ABDELSAMAD
53 Dean College of Education .... Dr. Arthur HERNANDEZ
54 Dean of Col Science & Engrng .... Dr. Frank PEZOLD
66 Dean College Nursing & Health Sci .... Dr. Mary Jane HAMILTON

*Texas A & M University - Kingsville (A)

700 University Boulevard, Kingsville TX 78363-8202
County: Kleberg — FICE Identification: 003639
Unit ID: 228705
Telephone: (361) 593-2111 — Carnegie Class: DRU
FAX Number: (361) 593-3107 — Calendar System: Semester
URL: www.tamuk.edu
Established: 1925 — Annual Undergrad Tuition & Fees (In-State): $6,640
Enrollment: 6,610 — Coed
Affiliation or Control: State — IRS Status: 501(c)3
Highest Offering: Doctorate
Program: Liberal Arts And General; Teacher Preparatory
Accreditation: SC, ACBSP, DIETD, DIETI, ENG, MUS, NAIT, PHAR, SP, SW

02 President .... Dr. Steven H. TALLANT
05 Provost & Vice Pres Acad Affs .... Dr. Rex F. GANDY
10 Vice Pres Finance & Administration .... Dr. Marilyn FOWLE
30 Vice Pres Institutional Advancement .... Mr. Scott GINES
32 Vice President Student Affairs .... Dr. Terisa C. REMELIUS
84 VP Enrollment Management .... Mr. Manuel LUJAN
27 Chief Information Officer .... Mr. Robert PAULSON
32 Dean of Students .... Ms. Kristin COMPARY
20 Associate VP Academic Affairs .... Dr. Duane GARDINER
58 Assoc VP Research and Grad Studies .... Dr. Ambrose ANORUO
88 Asst Vice Pres Special Programs .... Ms. Mary GONZALEZ
47 Dean Agriculture/Nat Res/Human Sci .... Dr. George A. RASMUSSEN
49 Dean Arts & Sciences .... Dr. Scott S. HUGHES
50 Dean Business Administration .... Dr. Tom DOCK
53 Dean Education .... Dr. Alberto RUIZ
54 Dean Engineering .... Dr. Stephan NIX
92 Dean Honors Program .... Dr. Dolores GUERRERO
89 Dean University College .... Dr. Daniel A. BROWN
26 Exec Dir Mktg & Comm .... Ms. Cheryl CAIN
08 Librarian .... Dr. Carol TIPTON
09 Director Planning and Assessment .... Ms. Vivian H. GOLIGHTLY
88 Director Citrus Center .... Dr. John DA GRACA
88 Director King Ranch Mgmt Institute .... Dr. Clay P. MATHIS
88 Director Wildlife Research Inst .... Dr. Fred BRYANT
88 Director Nat Toxins Res Ctr .... Dr. John C. PEREZ
88 Director Inst Sust Energy & Env .... Dr. Kim JONES
06 Registrar .... Mr. George WEIR
07 Director of Admission .... Mr. William H. CARTER
29 Director Development and Alumni Rel .... Ms. Yvonne TRACHTA
41 Director Athletics .... Mr. Kenneth OLIVER
40 Director Bookstore .... Ms. Mary GUTIERREZ
106 Director Distance Learning .... Vacant
44 Exec Dir Development & Alumni .... Ms. Heather ELSIK
88 Director Health and Wellness .... Dr. Alice BROWN
09 Director Institutional Research .... Dr. Alan TIPTON
88 Director John E. Conner Museum .... Mr. Hal HAM
16 Director Personnel Services .... Vacant
18 Director Physical Plant .... Mr. David STANDISH
26 Coordinator Public Relations .... Mr. Jason MARTON
88 Coordinator Publications .... Mr. Robert PENA
96 Executive Director Strategic Sourc .... Mr. Ralph STEPHENS
39 Director Residence Life .... Mr. Tom MARTIN
46 Director Sponsored Research .... Ms. Sandra L. GARCIA
35 Director Student Activities .... Mr. Seferino (Nino) MENDIETTA
19 Director of University Police .... Mr. Felipe GARZA
37 Director Student Financial Aid .... Mr. Ralph PERRI
38 Director Student Counseling .... Dr. Dianne BROWN
21 Supervisor Business Services .... Ms. Janet L. POLLARD
88 Advisor Pre-profession Programs .... Ms. Amanda MUNIZ
88 Bible Chair Baptist .... Mr. Mike CERVANTES
88 Bible Chair Catholic .... Vacant

*Texas A & M University-San Antonio (B)

1450 Gillette Boulevard, San Antonio TX 78224
County: Bexar — Identification: 666689
Telephone: (210) 932-6299 — Carnegie Class: Not Classified
FAX Number: (210) 932-6219 — Calendar System: Semester
URL: www.tamusa.tamus.edu
Established: 2009 — Annual Undergrad Tuition & Fees (In-District): $3,072
Enrollment: 3,057 — Coed
Affiliation or Control: State/Local — IRS Status: 501(c)3
Highest Offering: Master's
Program: Liberal Arts And General
Accreditation: &SC

02 President .... Dr. Maria Hernandez FERRIER
05 Chief Academic Officer/Provost .... Dr. Brent SNOW
10 Chief Financial Officer .... Kenneth MITTS
20 Associate Academic Officer .... Dr. Mary Ann GRAMS
50 Int AVP Acad Affs/Sch Head Business .... Dr. Tracy HURLEY
30 Chief of Development .... Dr. Charles RODRIGUEZ
09 Director of Institutional Research .... Dr. Raymond S. BOTELLO
26 Chief Public Relations Officer .... Marilu A. REYNA
53 Int Sch Head Kinesiology/Education .... Mr. Jose GARCIA

† Regional accreditation is carried under the parent institution, Texas A&M University-Kingsville in Kingsville, TX.

*Texas A & M University - Texarkana (C)

7101 University Avenue, Texarkana TX 75503
County: Bowie — FICE Identification: 031703
Unit ID: 224545
Telephone: (903) 223-3000 — Carnegie Class: Master's L
FAX Number: (903) 832-8890 — Calendar System: Semester
URL: www.tamut.edu
Established: 1971 — Annual Undergrad Tuition & Fees (In-State): $5,167
Enrollment: 1,803 — Coed
Affiliation or Control: State — IRS Status: 501(c)3
Highest Offering: Doctorate
Program: Liberal Arts And General; Professional
Accreditation: SC, NURSE

02 President .... Dr. Carlisle B. RATHBURN, III
05 Provost/Vice Pres Academic Affairs .... Dr. Rosanne STRIPLING
10 Vice Pres Finance & Administration .... Mr. Randy RIKEL
32 VP Student Engagement & Success .... Dr. Kent KELSO
88 Dean College of STEM .... Dr. Arthur LINKINS
53 Dean College Education/Liberal Art .... Dr. Glenda BALLARD
50 Dean College of Business .... Dr. Larry DAVIS
21 Controller .... Mr. James SCOGIN
07 Exec Dir Enrollment Services .... Mr. Richard BOLLINGER
37 Director Fin Aid & Veteran Svcs .... Ms. Alyssa MCCLURE
15 Director Human Resources & EEO .... Mr. Jerry HENRY
30 Director Institutional Advancement .... Mrs. LeAnne WRIGHT
09 AVP Institutional Effectiveness .... Ms. Carla SNYDER
08 Director Library .... Mrs. Teri STOVER
18 Director Physical Plant .... Mr. John MILLS
18 Director of Security .... Mr. John GANN
96 Director Purchasing .... Mrs. Cynthia HENDERSON
13 Int AVP of Information Technology .... Mr. Scott LENT
88 Director Payroll .... Mrs. Ramona GREEN
35 Director Student & Career Services .... Mr. Carl GREIG
84 Director Enrollment Management .... Mr. Toney FAVORS
27 Mgr Communications/Alumni Relation .... Mr. Bob BRUGGEMAN

*West Texas A & M University (D)

2403 Russell C. Long Blvd., Canyon TX 79015
County: Randall — FICE Identification: 003665
Unit ID: 229814
Telephone: (806) 651-0000 — Carnegie Class: Master's L
FAX Number: (806) 651-2126 — Calendar System: Semester
URL: www.wtamu.edu
Established: 1910 — Annual Undergrad Tuition & Fees (In-State): $6,482
Enrollment: 7,843 — Coed
Affiliation or Control: State — IRS Status: 501(c)3
Highest Offering: Doctorate
Program: Liberal Arts And General; Teacher Preparatory; Professional
Accreditation: SC, ENG, MUS, NURSE, SP, SW

02 President .... Dr. J. Patrick O'BRIEN
05 Provost/Vice Pres Acad Affairs .... Dr. James HALLMARK
10 Vice Pres for Business & Finance .... Mr. Gary W. BARNES
32 Vice President for Student Affairs .... Dr. Don D. ALBRECHT
26 Vice Pres Institutional Advancement .... Dr. Neal WEAVER
84 Vice Pres of Enrollment Management .... Mr. Dan D. GARCIA
30 Executive Director of Development .... Ms. Teresa CLEMONS
06 Registrar .... Ms. Tana J. MILLER
07 Director of Admissions .... Mr. Shawn O. THOMAS
08 Dir Information/Library Resources .... Ms. Shawna J. KENNEDY-WITTHAR
36 Dir Career Planning & Placement .... Ms. C. Denese SKINNER
37 Director Student Financial Aid .... Mr. James D. REED
51 Interim Dir Continuing Education .... Ms. Roxie PRANGLIN
23 Director Medical Service .... Dr. Jim GIBBS
18 Director Physical Plant .... Mr. Dan K. SMITH
19 Police Chief .... Chief Shawn G. BURNS
27 Director Communication Services .... Ms. Ann UNDERWOOD
29 Director of Alumni Relations .... Ms. Becky STOGNER
38 Director Counseling Services .... Ms. C. Denese SKINNER
41 Director of Athletics .... Mr. Michael MCBROOM
09 Director Institutional Research .... Dr. Gary D. KELLEY
13 Chief Information Officer .... Mr. James D. WEBB
96 Director of Purchasing .... Mr. Brian GLENN
40 Manager Bookstore .... Mr. Terry S. NEPPER
15 Director Personnel Services .... Mr. Harvey L. HUDSPETH
47 Dean Col Agr/Science/Engineering .... Dr. James R. CLARK
50 Dean College of Business .... Dr. Neil W. TERRY
53 Dean Col Education & Social Science .... Dr. Eddie W. HENDERSON
57 Dean College Fine Arts/Humanities .... Dr. James A. RENNIER
58 Dean Graduate School & Research .... Dr. Angela SPAULDING
66 Dean College of Nursing/Health Sci .... Dr. Dirk NELSON
21 Controller .... Mr. Rick JOHNSON

Texas Chiropractic College (E)

5912 Spencer Highway, Pasadena TX 77505-1699
County: Harris — FICE Identification: 003635
Unit ID: 228866
Telephone: (281) 487-1170 — Carnegie Class: Spec/Health
FAX Number: (281) 487-2009 — Calendar System: Trimester
URL: www.txchiro.edu
Established: 1908 — Annual Undergrad Tuition & Fees: N/A
Enrollment: 283 — Coed
Affiliation or Control: Independent Non-Profit — IRS Status: 501(c)3
Highest Offering: Doctorate
Program: Professional
Accreditation: SC, CHIRO

01 President/CEO .... Dr. Richard G. BRASSARD
05 Vice President/Provost .... Dr. Clay MCDONALD
10 Chief Financial Officer .... Mr. Bill QUINN
20 VP Academics & Program Development .... Dr. Al ADAMS
32 Vice President Student Affairs .... Dr. Steve HASLUND
20 Dean of Academic Affairs .... Dr. John MROZEK
84 Dean of Enrollment Management .... Dr. Fred ZUKER
23 Dean of Clinics .... Dr. Barry WIESE
06 Registrar .... Dr. Karlene DENBY
46 Director Research .... Dr. Will EVANS
15 Director of Human Resources .... Mrs. Sue ARNOLD
26 Director of Communications .... Ms. Patty BARNES
09 Director Institutional Research .... Dr. Kuan YANG
51 Director of Postgraduate .... Dr. Jason FLANAGAN
08 Director of Library Services .... Ms. Carol WEBB
37 Director Financial Aid .... Mr. Arthur GOUDEAU
96 Director of Purchasing .... Ms. Joanna LITTLE
29 Director of Alumni Relations .... Ms. Gabrielle GREENWADE
35 Director of Student Services .... Ms. Mary SUTTLE
07 Associate Director of Admissions .... Ms. Kristina HANSON
04 Admin Asst to President .... Ms. Glenda RAMIREZ
18 Physical Plant Supervisor .... Mr. Perry LATIOLAIS

Texas Christian University (F)

2800 S University Drive, Fort Worth TX 76129-2800
County: Tarrant — FICE Identification: 003636
Unit ID: 228875
Telephone: (817) 257-7000 — Carnegie Class: DRU
FAX Number: (817) 257-7333 — Calendar System: Semester
URL: www.tcu.edu
Established: 1873 — Annual Undergrad Tuition & Fees: $32,490
Enrollment: 9,142 — Coed
Affiliation or Control: Christian Church (Disciples Of Christ)
IRS Status: 501(c)3
Highest Offering: Doctorate
Program: Liberal Arts And General; Teacher Preparatory; Professional
Accreditation: SC, DANCE, ANEST, ART, BUS, BUSA, CIDA, CS, DIETC, DIETD, ENG, JOUR, MUS, NURSE, SP, SW

01 Chancellor .... Dr. Victor J. BOSCHINI, JR.
05 Provost/Vice Chanc Academic Affairs .... Dr. R. Nowell DONOVAN
10 Vice Chanc Finance & Administration .... Mr. Brian G. GUTIERREZ
30 Vice Chanc University Advancement .... Mr. Donald J. WHELAN, JR.
32 Vice Chancellor Student Affairs .... Dr. Kathryn CAVINS-TULL
26 Vice Chanc Mktg & Communication .... Ms. Tracy SYLER-JONES
86 Vice Chanc Government Affairs .... Mr. Larry D. LAUER
35 Assoc Vice Chanc Student Affairs .... Dr. Barbara B. HERMAN
35 Assoc Vice Chanc/Dean Campus Life .... Ms. Susan W. ADAMS
88 Assoc Vice Chanc Advancement Ops .... Dr. Roby V. KEY
29 Assoc Vice Chanc Alumni Relations .... Ms. Kristi M. HOBAN
16 Assoc Vice Chanc HR/Risk Mgmt .... Ms. Jill L. LASTER
21 Assoc Vice Chanc & Controller .... Ms. Cheryl L. WILSON
18 Assoc Vice Chanc for Facilities .... Mr. Willett R. STALLWORTH
44 Asst Vice Chanc Regional Devel .... Mr. Daniel G. GRIGG
28 Asst VC of Student Services .... Mr. Darron TURNER
88 Chief Investment Officer .... Mr. Jim HILLE
41 Director Athletics .... Mr. Christopher DEL CONTE
100 Chief of Staff .... Ms. Karen M. BAKER
20 Assoc Provost Academic Affairs .... Dr. Bonnie MELHART
20 Assoc Provost Academic Support .... Dr. Leo W. MUNSON
20 Assoc Provost Academic Plan/Budget .... Dr. Ann C. SEWELL
20 Assoc Provost Technology Support .... Mr. Ruben D. CHANLATTE
20 Asst Provost Inst Effectiveness .... Dr. Catherine WEHLBURG
49 Dean Addran College of Liberal Arts .... Dr. Andrew SCHOOLMASTER
50 Dean Neeley School of Business .... Dr. Homer EREKSON
60 Dean College of Communication .... Dr. David WHILLOCK
53 Dean College of Education .... Dr. Mary PATTON
57 Dean College of Fine Arts .... Dr. Scott SULLIVAN
66 Dean Harris Col Nurs/Hlth Science .... Dr. Paulette BURNS
54 Dean Col of Science & Engineering .... Dr. Demitris KOURIS
92 Dean John V Roach Honors College .... Dr. Peggy WATSON
08 Dean of the Library .... Dr. June KOELKER
07 Dean of Admission .... Mr. Raymond A. BROWN
13 Director Technology Resources .... Mr. Bryan LUCAS
88 Exec Dir Acad Resource Mgmt & Compl .... Ms. Susan G. CAMPBELL
22 Affirmative Action Officer .... Mr. Darron TURNER

06 Registrar/Dir Enrollment Management ....Mr. Patrick MILLER
19 Chief TCU Police ....Mr. Steve G. MCGEE
42 Minister to the University ....Rev. Angela KAUFMAN
21 Dir Budget & Financial Planning ....Mr. Kenneth JANAK
85 Director Center for Intl Studies ....Dr. Jane KUCKO
15 Director Compensation ....Ms. Dindy ROBINSON
25 Director Contract Administration ....Mr. Matthew WALLIS
15 Director Employee Relations ....Ms. Sharon E. BARNES
51 Director Extended Education ....Mr. David A. GREBEL
88 Director Freshman Admission ....Mr. Wes WAGGONER
23 Director Health Center ....Dr. Jane TORGERSON
09 Director Institutional Research ....Dr. Cathy COGHLAN
24 Director Instructional Services ....Mr. Larry E. KITCHENS
85 Director International Student Svcs ....Mr. John L. SINGLETON
38 Director Mental Health Services ....Dr. Linda WOLSZON
96 Director Purchasing ....Mr. Roger D. FULLER
39 Director Residential Services ....Mr. Craig ALLEN
37 Director Student Aid ....Mr. Michael H. SCOTT
88 Assoc Dean Student Development Svc ....Ms. Cynthia WALSH
25 Coord Research & Sponsored Projects ....Dr. Janis MOREY
36 Exec Director Univ Career Svcs ....Dr. John THOMPSON

Texas College (A)

2404 N Grand Avenue, Tyler TX 75702-1962
County: Smith FICE Identification: 003638
Unit ID: 228884
Telephone: (903) 593-8311 Carnegie Class: Bac/Diverse
FAX Number: (903) 593-0588 Calendar System: Semester
URL: www.texascollege.edu
Established: 1894 Annual Undergrad Tuition & Fees: $16,682
Enrollment: 927 Coed
Affiliation or Control: Christian Methodist Episcopal IRS Status: 501(c)3
Highest Offering: Baccalaureate
Program: 2-Year Principally Bachelor's Creditable; Liberal Arts And General; Teacher Preparatory
Accreditation: **SC**

01 President ....Dr. Dwight FENNELL
05 Vice President Academic Affairs ....Dr. Johnnye JONES
10 Vice Pres Business & Finance ....Mr. James HARRIS
32 Vice Pres Student Affairs ....Ms. Cynthia MARSHALL-BIGGINS
30 Vice President Development ....Vacant
07 Vice President of Admissions ....Mr. Anthony MEYERS
35 Dean of Students ....Mr. Calvin GREEN
06 Registrar ....Mr. John ROBERTS
09 Dir Inst Research/ Effectiveness ....Mrs. Cynthia MARSHALL-BIGGINS
08 Director of Library Services ....Ms. Joyce ARPS
13 Director of Information Technology ....Mr. Ocie FISHER
15 Director Human Resources ....Ms. Lois BOWIE
21 Comptroller ....Mr. Walter MOSLEY
36 Dir Counseling & Career Services ....Mr. Calvin GREEN
41 Athletic Director ....Ms. Devon N. THOMPSON
37 Director Financial Aid ....Ms. Cecelia K. JONES
18 Director Physical Plant ....Mr. James HARGRAVE
26 Director Public Relations ....Ms. Christie HOWARD
29 Coordinator Alumni Affairs ....Ms. Loretta DEWBERRY
88 Director of Special Projects ....Mrs. Angelia FENNELL

Texas College of Traditional Chinese Medicine (B)

4005 Manchaca Road, Austin TX 78704-6737
County: Travis FICE Identification: 031795
Unit ID: 430704
Telephone: (512) 444-8082 Carnegie Class: Spec/Health
FAX Number: (512) 444-6345 Calendar System: Trimester
URL: www.texastcm.edu
Established: 1990 Annual Undergrad Tuition & Fees: $14,000
Enrollment: 142 Coordinate
Affiliation or Control: Proprietary IRS Status: Proprietary
Highest Offering: Master's; No Lower Division
Program: Professional
Accreditation: **ACUP**

01 President ....Ms. Lisa LIN
05 Academic Dean ....Dr. Maoyi CAI
10 Vice President of Academics/Asessme ....Dr. Joseph MCMILLAN
11 Administrator ....Ms. Wai-Lan KUO
37 Financial Aid Officer ....Ms. Waiyan WONG
07 Director of Admission ....Dr. Steve RENAUD
17 Clinic Director ....Mr. Dragon CHU
88 Director Herbal Department ....Dr. Guili ZHENG
88 Director of Acupuncture Department ....Dr. Shao LI
88 Director Bio-Med Dept/Dean Students ....Dr. Maoyi CAI
08 Director of Library ....Ms. Sandra STEELE
46 Director of Research Department ....Dr. Haitao CAO
21 Operations Mgr Budget/Human Res ....Mr. Paul LIN

Texas Lutheran University (C)

1000 W Court Street, Seguin TX 78155-5999
County: Guadalupe FICE Identification: 003641
Unit ID: 228981
Telephone: (830) 372-8000 Carnegie Class: Bac/Diverse
FAX Number: (830) 372-8096 Calendar System: Semester
URL: www.tlu.edu
Established: 1891 Annual Undergrad Tuition & Fees: $23,800
Enrollment: 1,344 Coed
Affiliation or Control: Evangelical Lutheran Church In America
IRS Status: 501(c)3
Highest Offering: Baccalaureate
Program: Liberal Arts And General; Teacher Preparatory
Accreditation: **SC**, ACBSP, TEAC

01 President ....Dr. Stuart B. DORSEY
05 Interim Provost ....Dr. John MCCLUSKY
11 Asst to Pres Admin/Public Affairs ....Mr. Stephen P. ANDERSON
10 Vice President Finance ....Mr. Andrew NELSON
84 Vice President Enrollment Services ....Mr. Thomas OLIVER
30 VP for Development/Alumni Relations ....Ms. Nancy HERSHFIELD
44 Vice President for Principal Gifts ....Vacant
32 VP/Dean of Student Life & Learning ....Ms. Kristi QUIROS
06 Director of Records & Registration ....Mr. Glenn YOCKEY
08 Library Director ....Ms. Martha RINN
37 Director of Financial Aid ....Ms. Cathleen WRIGHT
42 Campus Pastor ....Rev. Greg RONNING
36 Director Career Services ....Ms. Kimberly WATTS
38 Director Counseling Services ....Ms. Terry WEERS
07 Director of Admissions ....Ms. Mandy OWEN
15 Director Personnel Services ....Mr. Andrew VASQUEZ
41 Director of Athletics ....Mr. Bill MILLER
09 Director of Institutional Research ....Ms. Jean CONSTABLE
04 Exec Assistant to the President ....Ms. Sharon CRAIG

Texas School of Business (D)

711 Airtex Drive, Houston TX 77073
County: Harris FICE Identification: 023122
Unit ID: 229036
Telephone: (281) 443-8900 Carnegie Class: Not Classified
FAX Number: (281) 443-0777 Calendar System: Other
URL: www.tsb.edu
Established: 1983 Annual Undergrad Tuition & Fees: $15,506
Enrollment: 585 Coed
Affiliation or Control: Proprietary IRS Status: Proprietary
Highest Offering: Associate Degree
Program: Occupational
Accreditation: **ACICS**

01 Campus Director ....Mr. J. D. KING

Texas School of Business-Friendswood (E)

3208 FM 528, Friendswood TX 77546
County: Harris Identification: 667051
Unit ID: 430127
Telephone: (281) 648-0880 Carnegie Class: Not Classified
FAX Number: (281) 648-0821 Calendar System: Other
URL: www.tsb.edu
Established: N/A Annual Undergrad Tuition & Fees: $15,506
Enrollment: 390 Coed
Affiliation or Control: Proprietary IRS Status: Proprietary
Highest Offering: Associate Degree
Program: Occupational
Accreditation: **ACICS**

01 Executive Director ....Ms. Kim ITO

† Branch campus of Texas School of Business, Houston, TX.

Texas School of Business-Southwest (F)

6363 Richmond Avenue, Suite 300, Houston TX 77057
Identification: 666729
Unit ID: 382054
Telephone: (713) 975-7527 Carnegie Class: Not Classified
FAX Number: (713) 974-2535 Calendar System: Other
URL: www.tsb.edu
Established: 1988 Annual Undergrad Tuition & Fees: $15,506
Enrollment: 378 Coed
Affiliation or Control: Proprietary IRS Status: Proprietary
Highest Offering: Associate Degree
Program: Occupational
Accreditation: **ACICS**

01 Executive Director ....Mr. Billy LEONARD

† Branch campus of Texas School of Business, Houston, TX.

Texas Southern University (G)

3100 Cleburne Street, Houston TX 77004-4584
County: Harris FICE Identification: 003642
Unit ID: 229063
Telephone: (713) 313-7011 Carnegie Class: DRU
FAX Number: (713) 313-1092 Calendar System: Semester
URL: www.tsu.edu
Established: 1947 Annual Undergrad Tuition & Fees (In-State): $7,462
Enrollment: 9,557 Coed
Affiliation or Control: State IRS Status: 170(c)1
Highest Offering: Doctorate
Program: Liberal Arts And General; Teacher Preparatory; Professional
Accreditation: **SC**, BUS, DIETD, ENGT, LAW, MT, NAIT, PHAR, PLNG, SW

01 President ....Dr. John M. RUDLEY
05 Provost/VP Academic Affs & Research ....Dr. Sunny E. OHIA
03 Executive Vice President ....Dr. James M. DOUGLAS
10 Vice President for Finance/CFO ....Mr. Jim C. MCSHAN
30 Vice Pres University Advancement ....Ms. Wendy H. ADAIR
100 Chief of Staff ....Ms. Janis J. NEWMAN
43 General Counsel ....Dr. Andrew C. HUGHEY
41 Athletic Director ....Dr. Charles F. MCCLELLAND
32 VP Student Svcs/Dean of Students ....Dr. William T. SAUNDERS
09 Int Assoc Provost/Assoc VP Research ....Dr. Adebayo O. OYEKAN
88 Dir Title III & Ofc of Sponsored Pr ....Ms. Demetria JOHNSON-WEEKS
15 Exec Director of Human Resources ....Mr. Brian K. DICKENS
31 Director of Communications ....Ms. Eva K. PICKENS
37 Special Assistant Financial Aid ....Mr. Hasan JAMIL
06 University Registrar ....Ms. Marilyn C. SQUARE
08 Int Exec Dir Libraries/Museums ....Ms. Norma P. BEAN
50 Interim Dean School of Business ....Dr. Ladelle M. HYMAN
51 Dean Col of Cont Educ/Asst Provost ....Dr. Kingston NYAMAPFENE
53 Interim Dean College of Education ....Dr. Lillian B. POATS
80 Int Dean School of Public Affairs ....Dr. Helen TAYLOR-GREENE
61 Dean School of Law ....Dr. Dannye HOLLEY
67 Dean Col of Pharmacy & Health Sci ....Dr. Barbara E. HAYES
88 Int Assoc Prov/VP Stdt Acad Enh Svc ....Dr. Betty B. COX
72 Dean College of Science/Technology ....Dr. Lei YU
60 Dean School of Communications ....Dr. James W. WARD
19 Chief of Police ....Chief Roger D. BYARS
35 Associate Dean of Students ....Dr. William A. THOMAS
86 Dir of Government Relations ....Mr. Broderick F. BUTLER
21 Exec Dir of Business Affairs ....Ms. Beverly W. RUFFIN
92 Thos F Freeman Honors College ....Dr. Humphrey A. REGIS
96 Exec Dir Procurement Services ....Mr. Gregory G. WILLIAMS
102 Director of Development ....Ms. Carolyne B. OLIVER
18 Asst VP Facilities & Construction ....Mr. Dilip M. ANKETELL
13 CIO/Information Technology ....Mr. Billy C. RECTOR
20 Assoc Provost/Assoc VP Acad Affairs ....Dr. Elizabeth BROWN-GUILLORY
58 Dean Graduate School ....Dr. Gregory H. MADDOX
21 Exec Dir Provost of Business Svcs ....Mr. Charles E. HENRY
88 Dir Acad Ret Svcs Spcl Asst/Provost ....Ms. Lori A. LABRIE
35 Associate Dean of Students ....Ms. Najla F. NAJIEB
39 Exec Director Campus Services & Ops ....Mr. Mark LAMBERT
88 Exec Director of Compliance ....Ms. Yolanda E. NIMMER-WILLIAMS
88 Dir of Special Events/Projects ....Ms. LaChanda J. JENKINS
88 Exec Director Budget ....Mr. Elias HAILU
88 Treasurer ....Mr. Louis W. EDWARDS
45 Director of Marketing ....Mr. Gregory K. HOLLAND
09 Asst Provost Inst Assess/Plng/Effec ....Dr. Claude R. SUPERVILLE
04 Exec Admin Asst to President ....Ms. Faith AGUIRRE
29 Director of Alumni Relations ....Ms. Connie L. COCHRAN
84 Exec Dir Enrollment Management ....Mr. Brian J. ARMSTRONG
88 Coordinator Academic Services ....Ms. Michaia N. MAYES
88 Director of Scholarships ....Ms. Jeanette J. OLIVER

Texas Southmost College (H)

80 Fort Brown, Brownsville TX 78520-4993
County: Cameron FICE Identification: 003643
Unit ID: 229072
Telephone: (956) 882-8200 Carnegie Class: Assoc/Pub-R-M
FAX Number: (956) 548-0020 Calendar System: Semester
URL: www.utb.edu
Established: 1926 Annual Undergrad Tuition & Fees (In-District): $5,994
Enrollment: 17,151 Coed
Affiliation or Control: State/Local IRS Status: 501(c)3
Highest Offering: Master's
Program: Occupational; 2-Year Principally Bachelor's Creditable
Accreditation: **SC**, ADNUR, CS, DMS, EMT, ENG, MLTAD, MUS, NUR, POLYT, RAD

01 UTB/TSC President ....Dr. Juliet V. GARCIA
10 Vice Pres Business Affairs ....Ms. Rosemary MARTINEZ
05 Vice President Academic Affairs ....Dr. Alan ARTIBISE
06 Registrar ....Mr. Albert BARREDA
66 Dean College of Nursing ....Dr. Nelda MARTINEZ

† In partnership with the University of Texas at Brownsville.

*Texas State Technical College System (I)

3801 Campus Drive, Waco TX 76705-1607
County: McLennan FICE Identification: 009642
Unit ID: 228671
Telephone: (254) 867-4891 Carnegie Class: N/A
FAX Number: (254) 867-3973
URL: www.tstc.edu

01 Chancellor ....Mr. Michael L. REESER
100 Vice Chancellor & Chief of Staff ....Mr. Jonathan HOEKSTRA
10 VC Financial Svcs & CFO ....Dr. J. Gary HENDRICKS
09 VC of IR & Commercialization ....Dr. Cesar MALDONADO
26 VC of Business Development ....Mr. Randall WOOTEN
05 VC of Instructional Services ....Dr. Elton E. STUCKLY, JR.
16 VC of Human Organizational Dev ....Mrs. Gail LAWERENCE
13 VC & Chief Technology Officer ....Mr. Rick HERRERA
09 Assoc Vice Chanc Educ Effectiveness ....Dr. D. Francette CARNAHAN
102 Assoc VC Resource Development ....Dr. Tara L. ODOM

*Texas State Technical College Harlingen (J)

1902 North Loop 499, Harlingen TX 78550-3697
County: Cameron FICE Identification: 009225
Unit ID: 229319
Telephone: (956) 364-4001 Carnegie Class: Assoc/Pub-R-M
FAX Number: (965) 364-5100 Calendar System: Trimester

URL: www.harlingen.tstc.edu
Established: 1969 Annual Undergrad Tuition & Fees (In-State): $5,148
Enrollment: 5,799 Coed
Affiliation or Control: State IRS Status: 501(c)3
Highest Offering: Associate Degree
Program: Occupational; 2-Year Principally Bachelor's Creditable; Technical Emphasis
Accreditation: SC, DA, DH, MAC, SURGT

02 President .... Dr. Cesar MALDONADO
100 Chief of Staff .... Mr. Adam HUTCHISON
32 Vice President for Student Devel .... Mrs. Cathy MAPLES
05 Associate VP of Academic Affairs .... Mrs. Barbara BENNETT
10 Vice Pres Financial/Admin Services .... Ms. Teri ZAMORA
20 Vice President for Student Learning .... Mr. Alfonso GUILLEN
88 Assoc VP Col Readiness & Advancmnt .... Mr. Javier DELEON
13 Chief Technology Officer .... Mr. Rick HERRERA
31 Assoc VP External Relations .... Ms. Angie GONZALEZ
26 Director of Marketing .... Mrs. Keri GUTIERREZ
09 Director Inst Effectivenes Research .... Dr. Richard K. PLOTT
15 Director Human/Organizational Dev .... Mrs. Mary PREPEJCHAL
19 Chief of Public Safety .... Mr. Aurelio TORRES
18 Director of Physical Plant .... Mr. Juan LOPEZ
55 Director of Evening School & ACE .... Mr. Juan LEAL
38 Director Student Counseling .... Ms. Liz SILVA
37 Director of Financial Aid .... Ms. Mary ADAMS
35 Director of Student Life .... Mrs. Adele CLINTON
41 Supervisor of Intramurals .... Mr. Armando DOMINGUEZ
08 Director of the Library .... Ms. Nancy HENDRICKS
96 Director of Purchasing .... Ms. Linda RODRIGUEZ-GUILLEN
36 Director of Placement/Coop Service .... Ms. Susan HOLMES
40 Supervisor Bookstore .... Ms. Susan FLORES
39 Supervisor Housing/Dormitories .... Mr. Carlos PEREZ
18 Director Physical Plant/Engineering .... Mr. Chuck SMITH
88 Director Staff Professional Dev .... Mrs. Cindy MATA
106 Director Distance Learning Educ .... Mr. Ram DELA ROSA
27 Director College Information .... Ms. Dora OLIVARES
22 Director Support Services .... Ms. Edda URREA
88 Director Instructional Support Svcs .... Mr. Steve SZYMONIAK
88 Director of Curriculum .... Mr. Juan GARCIA

*Texas State Technical College Marshall (A)

2650 East End Boulevard S, Marshall TX 75672-7402
County: Harrison FICE Identification: 033965
Unit ID: 408394
Telephone: (903) 935-1010 Carnegie Class: Assoc/Pub-R-S
FAX Number: (903) 935-9554 Calendar System: Semester
URL: www.marshall.tstc.edu
Established: 1993 Annual Undergrad Tuition & Fees (In-District): $2,886
Enrollment: 944 Coed
Affiliation or Control: State/Local IRS Status: 501(c)3
Highest Offering: Associate Degree
Program: Occupational; 2-Year Principally Bachelor's Creditable; Technical Emphasis
Accreditation: SC

02 President .... Mr. Randall E. WOOTEN
05 Vice Pres of Student Learning .... Dr. Irene CRAVEY
10 Vice Pres of Financial Services .... Mrs. Deborah L. SANDERS
84 Dean of Enrollment Management .... Vacant
32 Vice Pres of Student Services .... Mr. Brett O. BRIGHT
102 Assoc Vice Pres Corporate College .... Vacant
20 Associate Dean Learning Community .... Ms. Annette M. ELLIS
04 Exec Assistant to the President .... Mr. Marshal V. JOSLIN
06 Registrar .... Ms. Patricia A. ROBBINS
09 Dir of Inst Effect/Rsrch & Planning .... Mrs. Mittie D. HUTCHINS
15 Human & Organ Develop Executive .... Mr. Jeff W. BELL
36 Coordinator of Placement .... Mr. Benjamin CANTU
37 Financial Aid Specialist .... Mrs. Susan F. WINGATE
103 Assoc VP Workforce & Economic Dev .... Dr. Colleen HALUPA
13 Dir Network/Telecommunications Svcs .... Mr. Dennis J. BURRER
26 Chief Public Relations Officer .... Mr. Marshal V. JOSLIN
96 Director of Purchasing .... Mrs. Eloise REED

*Texas State Technical College Waco (B)

3801 Campus Drive, Waco TX 76705-1695
County: McLennan FICE Identification: 003634
Unit ID: 228680
Telephone: (254) 799-3611 Carnegie Class: Assoc/Pub-R-M
FAX Number: (254) 867-2006 Calendar System: Semester
URL: www.tstc.edu
Established: 1965 Annual Undergrad Tuition & Fees (In-State): $4,068
Enrollment: 4,975 Coed
Affiliation or Control: State IRS Status: 501(c)3
Highest Offering: Associate Degree
Program: Occupational; 2-Year Principally Bachelor's Creditable; Technical Emphasis
Accreditation: SC, DA

00 Chancellor .... Dr. Bill SEGURA
02 President .... Mr. Elton E. STUCKLY, JR.
03 Executive Vice President .... Mr. Rob WOLAVER
05 Vice Pres for Student Learning .... Mr. Ron SANDERS
10 Vice President Financial Services .... Mr. Paul WOODFIN
84 Assoc Vice Pres of Enrollment Svcs .... Mr. Marcus BALCH
103 Assoc VP for Workforce Development .... Mr. David DAY
20 Associate VP Student Learning .... Dr. Terry CONROY
20 Assoc VP for Student Development .... Ms. Sarah PATTERSON
08 Director of the Library .... Ms. Linda K. KOEPF
26 Director of Marketing/Comm .... Ms. Jan OSBURN
37 Director of Financial Aid .... Ms. Jackie ADLER
06 Registrar/Dir of Admissions .... Ms. Brenda MONTEMAYOR
09 Dir Inst Effectiveness Rsrch/Plng .... Dr. Ben COX
18 Director Physical Plant .... Mr. Selby HOLDER
29 Director Alumni Relations .... Ms. Autum OUTLAW
96 Dir Purchas/Acct Payable/Inventory .... Ms. Melissa WARREN
40 Supervisor of Bookstore .... Mr. Greg GUERCIO
23 Director Student Health Services .... Ms. Amanda SPENCER
19 Chief of Police .... Mr. Henry GUDENAU
14 Director of Net/Telcomm Svcs .... Ms. Shelli SCHERWIEZ
38 Director of Testing .... Ms. Pam HUNTER
15 Director Professional Development .... Mr. Louis MAZE
45 Director Ext Resource Development .... Ms. Carliss HYDE
88 Director Recruiting Services .... Mr. Marcus BALCH

*Texas State Technical College West Texas (C)

300 Homer K. Taylor Drive, Sweetwater TX 79556-4108
County: Nolan FICE Identification: 009932
Unit ID: 229328
Telephone: (325) 235-7300 Carnegie Class: Assoc/Pub-R-S
FAX Number: (325) 235-7320 Calendar System: Semester
URL: www.westtexas.tstc.edu
Established: 1970 Annual Undergrad Tuition & Fees (In-State): $7,722
Enrollment: 1,410 Coed
Affiliation or Control: State IRS Status: 501(c)3
Highest Offering: Associate Degree
Program: Occupational; 2-Year Principally Bachelor's Creditable; Technical Emphasis
Accreditation: SC

02 Interim President .... Ms. Gail LAWRENCE
04 Executive Assistant to President .... Ms. Gail LAWRENCE
05 Vice President Student Learning .... Mr. William THOMPSON
32 Vice President Student Development .... Mrs. Kathleen P. BUTLER
88 Vice Pres Corporate College .... Mr. Dixon BAILEY
10 Vice President Financial Services .... Vacant
11 Vice President Admin Svcs .... Mr. Ray FRIED
35 Assoc VP Student Development .... Mr. Jeff HOWARD
20 Associate VP Student Learning .... Mrs. Debbie KARL
20 Associate VP Student Learning .... Mrs. Annette SMITH
21 Assistant CFO .... Mr. Kevin SHIPP
19 Chief of Police .... Mr. Mike KELLER
06 Director Registrar & Records .... Mrs. Maria AGUIRRE-ACUNA
15 Interim Director Human Resources .... Mrs. Gail LAWRENCE
37 Director of Financial Aid .... Mrs. Connie CHANCE
08 Director Library .... Mr. Steven PERRY
96 Director of Purchasing .... Ms. Jessica CHAVIRA
45 Staff Development Officer .... Vacant
46 Manager Inst Planning & Research .... Mr. John ARNOLD
38 Coordinator Counseling & Testing .... Mr. Donald J. ARMSTRONG, JR.
36 Coord Career Planning & Placement .... Mr. Nick ALVARADO
35 Coordinator Student Activities .... Mr. Tod RYDEN
84 Director of Retention .... Mr. Jeff HOWARD
26 Chief Public Relations Officer .... Mrs. Julie CROMEENS
39 Housing Supervisor .... Mr. Lupe NAVARRETTE
40 Bookstore Manager .... Ms. Sherrie PARKS
13 Dir Network & Telecommunications .... Mrs. Shelli SCHERWITZ
84 Associate VP Enrollment Management .... Mr. Brian KIGHT
84 Associate VP Enrollment Management .... Mrs. Sherry STRICKLAND

*The Texas State University System (D)

200 E 10th Street, Suite 600, Austin TX 78701-2407
County: Travis FICE Identification: 033442
Telephone: (512) 463-1808 Carnegie Class: N/A
FAX Number: (512) 463-1816
URL: www.tsus.edu

01 Chancellor .... Brian MCCALL
43 Vice Chanc & General Counsel .... Fernando C. GOMEZ
10 Vice Chancellor for Finance .... Roland K. SMITH
86 VC Governmental Rels/Educ Policy .... Sean CUNNINGHAM
25 Vice Chanc Contract Administration .... Peter E. GRAVES
88 Assoc VC Legist/Systems Operation .... Diane CORLEY
18 Assoc Vice Chanc Facilities .... Rob Roy PARNELL
21 Director of Audits & Analysis .... Carole M. FOX
04 Exec Assistant to the Chancellor .... Kelly WYLIE

*Lamar Institute of Technology (E)

PO Box 10043, Beaumont TX 77710-0043
County: Jefferson FICE Identification: 036273
Unit ID: 441760
Telephone: (409) 880-8321 Carnegie Class: Assoc/Pub-S-SC
FAX Number: (409) 880-1711 Calendar System: Semester
URL: www.lit.edu
Established: 1995 Annual Undergrad Tuition & Fees (In-State): $3,578
Enrollment: 3,243 Coed
Affiliation or Control: State IRS Status: 501(c)3
Highest Offering: Associate Degree
Program: Occupational; 2-Year Principally Bachelor's Creditable; Technical Emphasis
Accreditation: SC, DH, DMS, RAD

02 President .... Dr. Paul SZUCH
05 Vice President for Academic Affairs .... Dr. Betty REYNARD
103 Vice Pres for Workforce Development .... Mr. Sam WILLIAMS
10 Vice President Finance & Operations .... Mr. Jonathan WOLFE
32 Vice President of Student Services .... Dr. Vivian JEFFERSON
15 Vice President for Human Resources .... Ms. Bertha FREGIA
37 Director of Student Financial Aid .... Ms. Lisa SCHROEDER
13 Director of Technology Services .... Mr. Isaac BARBOSA
30 Director of Development .... Ms. Joanne BROWN
26 Director of Marketing/Public Info .... Ms. Beth MILLER
29 Director Alumni Relations .... Ms. JoAnn BROWN
18 Facilities Coordinator .... Mr. Jack WIGGINS
36 Job Plcmnt/Student Activities Coord .... Vacant
09 Coord Inst Effectiveness and Grants .... Mr. David MOSLEY

*Lamar University (F)

PO Box 10009, Beaumont TX 77710-0009
County: Jefferson FICE Identification: 003581
Unit ID: 226091
Telephone: (409) 880-7011 Carnegie Class: DRU
FAX Number: (409) 880-8404 Calendar System: Semester
URL: www.lamar.edu
Established: 1923 Annual Undergrad Tuition & Fees (In-State): $7,650
Enrollment: 14,389 Coed
Affiliation or Control: State IRS Status: 501(c)3
Highest Offering: Doctorate
Program: Liberal Arts And General; Teacher Preparatory; Professional
Accreditation: SC, ACFEI, ADNUR, AUD, BUS, CS, DIETD, DIETI, ENG, MUS, NUR, SP, SW, TED

02 President .... Dr. James M. SIMMONS
05 Provost/Vice Pres Academic Affairs .... Dr. Stephen A. DOBLIN
10 Vice President Finance/Operations .... Dr. Gregg LASSEN
32 Vice President Student Affairs .... Dr. Barry W. JOHNSON
30 Vice President for Inst Advancement .... Ms. Camille MOUTON
58 Interim Dean of Graduate Studies .... Dr. Victor ZALOOM
20 Sr Assoc Provost for Academic Affs .... Dr. Kevin B. SMITH
16 Assoc Vice Pres Human Resources .... Ms. Bertha FREGIA
18 Int Assoc VP Facilities/Maint .... Mr. Leonardo CABALLERO
21 Associate Vice President Finance/Co .... Ms. Vicki WARD
14 Assoc Vice Pres for Information Sys .... Ms. Priscilla PARSONS
49 Dean College Arts & Sciences .... Dr. Brenda NICHOLS
50 Dean College of Business .... Dr. Henry VENTA
53 Dean College of Education .... Dr. Hollis LOWERY-MOORE
54 Dean College of Engineering .... Dr. Jack HOPPER
57 Dean Col Fine Arts & Communication .... Dr. Russ SCHULTZ
08 Director Library Services .... Mr. David J. CARROLL
06 Registrar .... Ms. Sherry WELLS
51 Exec Dir Div Continuing Education .... Dr. Richard BOTHEL
106 Director Division of Distance Learn .... Dr. Paula NICHOLS
35 Director of Academic Services .... Mr. James C. RUSH
44 Director of Development .... Ms. Janice TRAMMELL
09 Director Institutional Research .... Dr. Don PRICE
36 Dir Career Development/Placement .... Ms. Teresa SIMPSON
23 Director Health Services .... Ms. Janet WARNER
19 Chief University Police .... Mr. Dale FONTENOT
26 Public Relations Director .... Mr. Brian SATTLER
29 Director Alumni Relations .... Mr. Juan ZABALA
37 Director Student Financial Aid .... Ms. Jill ROWLEY
96 Director of Purchasing .... Mr. Jack D. TENNER

*Lamar State College-Orange (G)

410 Front Street, Orange TX 77630-5802
County: Orange FICE Identification: 023582
Unit ID: 226107
Telephone: (409) 883-7750 Carnegie Class: Assoc/Pub-R-M
FAX Number: (409) 882-3374 Calendar System: Semester
URL: www.lsco.edu
Established: 1969 Annual Undergrad Tuition & Fees (In-State): $3,880
Enrollment: 2,649 Coed
Affiliation or Control: State IRS Status: 501(c)3
Highest Offering: Associate Degree
Program: Occupational; 2-Year Principally Bachelor's Creditable
Accreditation: SC, MLTAD

02 President .... Dr. J. Michael SHAHAN
05 Vice President Academic Affairs .... Dr. Joseph KIRKLAND
10 Vice President Finance & Operations .... Mrs. Dana ROGERS
32 Vice Pres Student Svcs & Aux Ent .... Mrs. Barbara BURGESS
08 Director of Library Services .... Ms. Mary MCCOY
06 Registrar .... Mrs. Rebecca J. CAMPBELL
37 Director Student Financial Aid .... Mr. Kerry J. OLSON
15 Human Resources Director .... Mrs. Alicia GRAY
18 Director of Physical Plant .... Mr. David GOINS
26 Dir Marketing & Public Information .... Ms. Amanda ROWELL
13 Coord Information Resources .... Ms. Linda G. BURNETT
09 Coordinator Institutional Research .... Mr. Bishar M. SETHNA
25 Contracts/Grants Administrator .... Mrs. Dana N. ROGERS
76 Director of Allied Health .... Ms. Gina A. SIMAR
72 Director of Business/Technology .... Ms. Jacqueline A. SPEARS
49 Division Chair Arts & Science .... Mr. Mike MCNAIR
96 Director of Purchasing .... Mr. Raymond SMITH

*Lamar State College-Port Arthur (H)

1500 Procter Street, Port Arthur TX 77640-6604
County: Jefferson FICE Identification: 023485
Unit ID: 226116
Telephone: (409) 983-4921 Carnegie Class: Assoc/Pub-R-M
FAX Number: (409) 984-6032 Calendar System: Semester
URL: www.lamarpa.edu
Established: 1909 Annual Undergrad Tuition & Fees (In-State): $4,500
Enrollment: 2,374 Coed

Affiliation or Control: State IRS Status: 501(c)3
Highest Offering: Associate Degree
Program: Occupational; 2-Year Principally Bachelor's Creditable
Accreditation: SC, SURGT

02 President .... Dr. W. Sam MONROE
05 Vice President Academic Affairs .... Dr. Gary D. STRETCHER
10 Vice President for Finance .... Ms. Gwen RECK
32 Vice President Student Services .... Mr. Thomas G. NEAL
04 Admin Assistant to the President .... Mrs. Donna SCHION
08 Dean Library Services .... Mr. Peter B. KAATRUDE
06 Registrar .... Ms. Connie NICHOLAS
37 Director Financial Aid .... Ms. Diane HARGETT
45 Director Inst Effectiveness .... Dr. Nancy CAMMACK
18 Director of Physical Plant .... Mr. Stephen ARNOLD
27 Public Information Officer .... Mr. Gerry DICKERT
36 Career Placement Counselor .... Vacant
56 Dir Inmate Instructional Program .... Dr. Barbara HUVAL
13 Dir Information Technology Services .... Mr. Samir GHORAYEB
15 Director Human Resources .... Ms. Linda MCGEE
07 Director of Admissions .... Ms. Connie NICHOLAS
09 Director of Institutional Research .... Mrs. Petra UZORUO
51 Dean Academic/Continuing Educ Pgms .... Dr. Charles GONGRE
72 Dean Technical Programs .... Dr. Janis HUTCHINS
81 Department Head Science & Math .... Ms. Glenda DUPUIS
50 Dept Head Business/CIS Technology .... Mr. Michael TRAHAN
83 Department Head Liberal Arts .... Dr. Barbara HUVAL
76 Department Head Allied Health .... Ms. Janet HAMILTON

*Sam Houston State University (A)

1806 Avenue J, Suite 303, Huntsville TX 77341-0001
County: Walker FICE Identification: 003606
Unit ID: 227881
Telephone: (936) 294-1111 Carnegie Class: DRU
FAX Number: (936) 294-1465 Calendar System: Semester
URL: www.shsu.edu
Established: 1879 Annual Undergrad Tuition & Fees (In-State): $7,328
Enrollment: 17,236 Coed
Affiliation or Control: State IRS Status: 501(c)3
Highest Offering: Doctorate
Program: Liberal Arts And General; Teacher Preparatory; Professional
Accreditation: SC, BUS, CACREP, CLPSY, CS, DIETD, DIETI, MUS, TED

02 President .... Dr. Dana L. GIBSON
05 Provost/Vice Pres Academic Affairs .... Dr. Jaimie HEBERT
10 Vice President Finance & Operations .... Mr. Al HOOTEN
84 Vice Pres Enrollment Management .... Dr. Heather THIELEMANN
32 Vice President Student Services .... Mr. Frank PARKER
30 Vice President of Univ Advancement .... Mr. Frank R. HOLMES
13 Interim VP for IT .... Mr. Tom GRAF
41 Athletic Director .... Mr. Bobby WILLIAMS
20 Assoc Provost Academic Affairs .... Dr. Richard EGLSAER
20 Assoc VP Academic Affairs .... Dr. Kandi TAYEBI
21 Assoc VP Budget & Operations .... Dr. Randall POWELL
18 Assoc VP Facilities Management .... Mr. Doug J. GREENING
16 Assoc VP for HR & Risk Mgmt .... Mr. Dave HAMMONDS
14 Assoc VP for Information Resources .... Mr. Mark ADAMS
26 Assoc VP Marketing & Comm .... Ms. Kris RUIZ
04 Assistant to the President .... Ms. Kathy J. GILCREASE
06 Registrar .... Ms. Teresa T. RINGO
07 Director of Undergrad Admissions .... Mr. Trevor THORN
08 Director of Libraries .... Ms. Ann H. HOLDER
29 Director of Alumni Relations .... Mr. Charlie VIENNE
09 Director Institutional Research .... Dr. Rita CASO
37 Director Student Financial Aid .... Ms. Lisa TATOM
26 Director Communications .... Vacant
38 Director Counseling Services .... Dr. Drew MILLER
39 Director Residence Life .... Ms. Joellen N. TIPTON
19 Director Public Safety Services .... Mr. Kevin MORRIS
96 Director Procurement/Business Svcs .... Mr. John HITZEMAN
92 Director of Honors College .... Dr. Gene YOUNG
21 Controller .... Ms. Paige SMITH
50 Dean of Business Administration .... Dr. Mitchell MUEHSAM
81 Dean of Sciences .... Vacant
57 Dean of Fine Arts & Mass Comm .... Dr. Roberta SLOAN
61 Dean of Criminal Justice .... Dr. Vincent WEBB
53 Dean Education .... Dr. Genevieve BROWN
58 Dean of Graduate Studies .... Dr. Kandi TAYEBI
83 Dean Humanities/Social Sciences .... Dr. John DECASTRO

*Sul Ross State University (B)

PO Box C-114, Alpine TX 79832-0001
County: Brewster FICE Identification: 003625
Unit ID: 228501
Telephone: (432) 837-8032 Carnegie Class: Master's L
FAX Number: (432) 837-8334 Calendar System: Semester
URL: www.sulross.edu
Established: 1917 Annual Undergrad Tuition & Fees (In-State): $4,764
Enrollment: 3,129 Coed
Affiliation or Control: State IRS Status: 501(c)3
Highest Offering: Master's
Program: Occupational; Liberal Arts And General; Teacher Preparatory; Professional
Accreditation: #SC

02 President .... Dr. Ricardo MAESTAS
05 Int Provst/VP Acad & Student Affs .... Dr. Don COERS
10 Vice Pres for Finance & Operations .... Mr. Cesario E. VALENZUELA
12 Vice President Rio Grande College .... Vacant
11 Assoc VP Fac/Plng/Construct/Ops .... Mr. Jim W. CLOUSE
84 Assoc Vice Pres for Enrollment Mgmt .... Mr. Gregory SCHWAB
30 Assoc Vice President Advancement .... Mr. Leo G. DOMINGUEZ
12 Associate Provost & Dean RGC .... Dr. Paul SORRELS
04 Special Assistant to President .... Vacant
04 Assistant to the President .... Ms. Yvonne REALIVASQUEZ
06 Registrar .... Mr. Robert C. CULLINS
08 Dean Library & Info Technology .... Mr. Don DOWDEY
32 Dean of Student Life .... Mr. Leo DOMINGUEZ
92 Dir Honors Prog/Acad Ctr Excellence .... Dr. Kathy STEIN
27 Director News & Publications .... Mr. Stephen W. LANG
37 Dir Financial Assistance .... Mr. Mickey CORBETT
49 Dean Arts & Science .... Dr. Jimmy CASE
107 Dean Professional Studies .... Dr. Melanie CROY
47 Dean Agricult/Natural Resource Sci .... Dr. Robert J. KINUCAN
15 Director of Human Resources .... Mrs. Judy A. PERRY
18 Asst Director of Physical Plant .... Mr. Edmundo NATERA
19 Director Dept of Public Safety .... Mr. Johnnie L. HOLBROOKS
21 Controller .... Mr. Oscar JIMENEZ
39 Director Residential Living .... Ms. Brandy SNYDER
41 Athletic Director .... Ms. Kay E. WHITLEY
38 Interim Director Counseling Ctr .... Mr. Gregory SCHWAB
13 Chief Information Officer .... Mr. Jon ROE
96 Director of Purchasing .... Mr. Noe HERNANDEZ
88 Dir Center for Big Bend Studies .... Mr. Andy CLOUD
29 Director Alumni Affairs .... Mr. Saul GARZA
66 Director of Vocational Nursing .... Ms. Donna KUENSTLER
88 Director Museum of the Big Bend .... Ms. Elizabeth JACKSON
88 Director of Upward Bound .... Ms. Barbara VEGA
88 Director of University Archives .... Ms. Melleta BELL
88 Director Small Business Devel Ctr .... Mr. David WILSON
88 Director Law Enforcement Academy .... Ms. Kellie POWELL
88 Dir Publication Services Coord .... Ms. Lauren MENDIAS
07 Director Admissions & Records .... Ms. Claudia WRIGHT
88 Mail Service Supervisor .... Ms. Angela BERMUDEZ
88 Internal Auditor .... Ms. Stephanie NELSON
36 Coord Career Services & Testing .... Ms. Susan FOX-FORRESTER

*Texas State University-San Marcos (C)

601 University Drive, San Marcos TX 78666-4615
County: Hays FICE Identification: 003615
Unit ID: 228459
Telephone: (512) 245-2111 Carnegie Class: Master's L
FAX Number: (512) 245-3040 Calendar System: Semester
URL: www.txstate.edu
Established: 1899 Annual Undergrad Tuition & Fees (In-State): $8,232
Enrollment: 32,572 Coed
Affiliation or Control: State IRS Status: 501(c)3
Highest Offering: Doctorate
Program: Liberal Arts And General; Teacher Preparatory; Professional
Accreditation: SC, BUS, CACREP, CIDA, CS, DIETD, DIETI, ENG, HSA, IPSY, JOUR, MT, MUS, NRPA, PTA, RTT, SP, SPAA, SW, @TEAC

02 President .... Dr. Denise M. TRAUTH
05 Provost/Vice Pres Academic Affairs .... Dr. Gene BOURGEOIS
100 Special Assistant to the President .... Dr. Robert D. GRATZ
32 Vice President Student Affairs .... Dr. Joanne H. SMITH
10 Vice Pres Finance/Support Services .... Mr. William A. NANCE
30 Interim Vice Pres Univ Advancement .... Mr. Ted M. MCKINNON
13 Vice Pres Information Technology .... Dr. Carl V. WYATT
41 Director of Athletics .... Dr. Lawrence B. TEIS
83 Dean College of Applied Arts .... Dr. T. Jaime CHAHIN
50 Dean McCoy Col of Business Admin .... Dr. Denise T. SMART
57 Dean Col Fine Arts & Communication .... Dr. Timothy MOTTET
53 Dean College of Education .... Dr. Stan CARPENTER
76 Dean College Health Professions .... Dr. Ruth B. WELBORN
83 Dean College Liberal Arts .... Dr. Michael HENNESSY
81 Dean College of Science .... Dr. Stephen B. SEIDMAN
58 Dean The Graduate College .... Dr. J. Michael WILLOUGHBY
97 Dean University College .... Dr. Daniel BROWN
20 Assoc Vice Pres Academic Affairs .... Dr. Debbie M. THORNE
20 Associate Provost .... Vacant
18 Associate VP of Facilities .... Mr. Juan M. GUERRA
86 Assoc VP Research & Dir of Fed Rels .... Dr. Bill C. COVINGTON
35 Assoc VP Stdnt Affs/Dean of Stdnt .... Dr. Margarita M. ARELLANO
20 Assoc Vice Pres for Inst Effective .... Dr. Cathy A. FLEURIET
21 Assoc VP Financial Services .... Mr. Terry ONDREYKA
84 Assoc VP Enrollment Mgmt/Marketing .... Dr. Michael R. HEINTZE
08 Associate VP University Library .... Ms. Joan L. HEATH
20 Assistant VP for Academic Services .... Dr. Ronald C. BROWN
38 Asst VP/Director Counseling Center .... Dr. Gregory SNODGRASS
88 Assoc VP Finance/Support Svcs Plng .... Ms. Nancy NUSBAUM
14 Assoc VP for Technology Resources .... Mr. Mark HUGHES
90 Assoc VP Instructional Tech Support .... Dr. Milton C. NIELSEN
106 Interim Dir Disatnce/Extended Lrng .... Dr. Debbie M. THORNE
06 Registrar .... Ms. Lloydean M. ECKLEY
07 Asst VP Enroll Mgmt/Dir Ug Admiss .... Ms. Stephanie ANDERSON
91 Director Enterprise Systems .... Mr. Bill RAMPY
37 Director of Fin Aid & Scholarships .... Dr. Christopher MURR
36 Director Career Services .... Mr. Curtis P. SCHAFER
29 Director of Alumni Affairs .... Ms. Kim GANNON
27 Director News Services .... Mr. Mark S. HENDRICKS
31 Chief Community Relations .... Ms. Kim PORTERFIELD
15 Director of Human Resources .... Mr. John E. MCBRIDE
12 Director Round Rock Higher Educ Ctr .... Dr. Edna REHBEIN
25 Director of Sponsored Programs .... Mr. W. Scott ERWIN
19 Director University Police .... Mr. Ralph MEYER
23 Director Student Health Center .... Dr. Emilio CARRANCO
39 Director Housing & Residential Life .... Dr. Rosanne PROITE
85 Director International Office .... Dr. Robert M. SEESE
40 Manager University Bookstore .... Ms. Jacqueline SLAUGHTER
24 Director Education Technology Ctr .... Mr. Michael W. FARRIS
09 Director of Institutional Research .... Mr. Joseph M. MEYER
22 Chief Divsty Offc/Dir Equity & Acce .... Mr. Herman HORN
92 Director University Honors Program .... Dr. Heather C. GALLOWAY
93 Dir Center for Multicul/Gender Stds .... Dr. Sandra MAYO
96 Director Purchasing .... Ms. Jacque ALLBRIGHT
26 Director of University Marketing .... Ms. Diana HARRELL
88 Director of Audit & Compliance .... Vacant
89 Asst Dean of University College .... Dr. Pam J. WUESTENBERG
88 Asst VP/Dir of Multicul Stdnt Affs .... Dr. Sherri BENN
44 Director Annual Giving .... Ms. Celeste NORED
88 Asst VP for Development .... Mr. Ted M. MCKINNON
88 Director Campus Recreation .... Dr. Glenn HANLEY
88 Director LBJ Student Center .... Mr. Andy RHOADES
88 Director Retention Mgmt & Planning .... Dr. Jen BECK
88 Director Disability Services .... Ms. Tina SCHULTZ

Texas Tech University (D)

Lubbock TX 79409-2005
County: Lubbock FICE Identification: 003644
Unit ID: 229115
Telephone: (806) 742-2121 Carnegie Class: RU/H
FAX Number: (806) 742-2138 Calendar System: Semester
URL: www.ttu.edu
Established: 1923 Annual Undergrad Tuition & Fees (In-State): $4,532
Enrollment: 31,637 Coed
Affiliation or Control: State IRS Status: 170(c)1
Highest Offering: Doctorate
Program: Liberal Arts And General; Teacher Preparatory; Professional
Accreditation: SC, AAFCS, ARCPA, ART, BUS, BUSA, CACREP, CIDA, CLPSY, COPSY, DIETD, DIETI, ENG, ENGT, HSA, IPSY, LAW, LSAR, MED, MFCD, @MIDWF, MUS, SPAA, SW, TED, THEA

00 Chancellor .... Mr. Kent HANCE
01 President .... Dr. Guy BAILEY
101 Sec Board Regents/Ex Asst to Chanc .... Mr. Ben W. LOCK
05 Provost and Sr VP .... Dr. Bob SMITH
10 Chief Operating Ofcr/SVP Admin/Fin .... Mr. Kyle CLARK
30 Vice Chancellor Inst Advancement .... Dr. Kelly OVERLEY
86 Vice Chancellor Govt Relations .... Mr. J. Michael SANDERS
43 Vice Chanc & General Counsel .... Mr. Pat CAMPBELL
18 VC Facilities Planning Construction .... Mr. Michael MOLINA
20 Vice Provost & SVP Academic Affairs .... Dr. Valerie PATON
100 President's Chief of Staff .... Ms. Grace HERNANDEZ
29 EVP & CEO Texas Tech Alumni Assoc .... Dr. Bill DEAN
46 Vice President for Research .... Dr. Taylor EIGHMY
28 VP Inst Diversity & Vice Provost .... Dr. Juan S. MUNOZ
84 Sr Assoc VP Enrollment Management .... Dr. James BURKHALTER
20 Assoc Vice Provost Academic Affairs .... Dr. Gary ELBOW
20 Sr Vice Provost .... Dr. Rob STEWART
88 Assoc VP External Relations & Strat .... Ms. Mary LARSON DIAZ
21 Interim Asst Vice Pres & Controller .... Ms. Sharon WILLIAMSON
16 AVP Human Resources .... Mr. Doug BUCHANAN
106 Vice Chancellor .... Dr. Tim HUDSON
82 Assoc Vice Prov International Affs .... Mr. Tibor P. NAGY
13 Assoc VP Information Technology .... Mr. Sam SEGRAN
88 Asst VP & Dir Hospitality Services .... Dr. Samuel BENNETT
08 Dean of Libraries .... Dr. Donald DYAL
60 Dean Mass Communications .... Dr. Jerry HUDSON
35 Int Dean Stdnts/Dir Campus Life .... Ms. Amy L. MURPHY
37 Managing Dir Financial Aid .... Ms. Becky WILSON
27 Chief Information Officer .... Ms. Kay RHODES
06 Registrar .... Ms. Bobbie BROWN
07 Managing Director of Admissions .... Dr. Ethan LOGAN
26 Managing Dir Comms & Marketing .... Mr. Chris COOK
104 Director Study Abroad .... Ms. Sandy CROSIER
04 Administrative Asst to President .... Ms. Jessica CARRILLO
31 Assoc Dir Community Engagment .... Dr. Heather MARTINEZ
44 Senior Dir Annual Giving Programs .... Ms. Deborah FINLAYSON
23 Director Student Health Services .... Ms. Evelyn MCPHERSON
39 Managing Dir Student Housing .... Mr. Sean DUGGAN
36 Managing Director Career Center .... Mr. Jay KILLOUGH
15 Managing Director of HR Management .... Mr. Justin CLARK
22 Asst Vice Chanc Admin/Dir EEO .... Ms. Charlotte BINGHAM
38 Managing Dir Student Counseling .... Dr. Eileen NATHAN
41 Director of Athletics .... Mr. Kirby HOCUTT
47 Interim Dean Agricult Sci/Nat Res .... Dr. Michael GALYEAN
49 Dean of Arts & Sciences .... Dr. Lawrence SCHOVANEC
48 Dean of Architecture .... Mr. Andrew VERNOOY
50 Dean Business Administration .... Dr. Allen MCINNES
53 Dean of Education .... Dr. Scott RIDLEY
54 Dean of Engineering .... Dr. Albert SACCO
88 Dean of Human Sciences .... Dr. Linda HOOVER
61 Dean School of Law .... Ms. Darby DICKERSON
58 Interim Dean of Graduate School .... Dr. Peggy MILLER
92 Interim Dean Honors College .... Dr. Stephen FRITZ
57 Dean Visual & Performing Arts .... Dr. Carol EDWARDS
19 Chief of Police .... Mr. Ronald SEACRIST
09 Managing Dir Institutional Research .... Ms. Vicki WEST
96 Dir Purchasing & Contracting .... Ms. Jennifer ADLING

Texas Tech University Health Sciences Center (E)

3601 4th Street, Lubbock TX 79430-0001
County: Lubbock FICE Identification: 010674
Unit ID: 229337
Telephone: (806) 743-1000 Carnegie Class: Spec/Med
FAX Number: (806) 743-2118 Calendar System: Semester
URL: www.ttuhsc.edu
Established: 1969 Annual Undergrad Tuition & Fees (In-State): $7,223
Enrollment: 3,710 Coed
Affiliation or Control: State IRS Status: 501(c)3
Highest Offering: Doctorate

Program: Professional
Accreditation: SC, AUD, CORE, DMOLS, MED, MT, NURSE, OT, PHAR, PTA, SP

01 President .... Dr. Tedd MITCHELL
10 Exec Vice Pres for Finance Admin .... Mr. Elmo M. CAVIN, JR.
05 Sr Vice Pres Academic Affairs .... Dr. Rial D. ROLFE
26 Dir Communications & Marketing .... Ms. Mary CROYLE
17 Vice Pres Rural/Community Hlth .... Dr. Billy U. PHILIPS, JR.
13 Vice Pres Info Tech/Chief Info Ofcr .... Dr. Chip SHAW
100 Chief of Staff .... Ms. Didit MARTINEZ
43 Senior Assoc General Counsel .... Ms. Glenda HELFRICH
21 Assoc Vice Pres Business Affairs .... Mr. Mike CROWDER
46 Exec Vice President for Research .... Dr. Douglas M. STOCCO
14 Assoc VP Technology Services .... Mr. Joe GREEN
15 Asst Vice Pres of Human Resources .... Dr. Gena JONES
18 Asst Vice Pres of Physical Plant .... Mr. George MORALES
63 Dean of Medical School .... Dr. Steven L. BERK
58 Dean Grad Sch Biomed Sciences .... Dr. Douglas M. STOCCO
66 Dean of Nursing School .... Dr. Michael L. EVANS
76 Dean of Allied Health Sciences Sch .... Dr. Paul P. BROOKE, JR.
67 Dean of Pharmacy School .... Dr. Arthur NELSON, JR.
12 Reg Dean Medicine Amarillo Campus .... Dr. Richard JORDAN
12 Found Dean Medicine El Paso Campus .... Dr. J. Manuel DE LA ROSA
12 Reg Dean Medicine Odessa Campus .... Dr. John C. JENNINGS
66 Reg Dean Nursing Odessa Campus .... Dr. Sharon CANNON
76 Reg Dean Allied Health Amarillo .... Dr. Michael HOOTEN
76 Reg Dean Allied Health Odessa .... Dr. Manuel DOMENECH
06 Registrar .... Mr. David CARTER
08 Exec Director of HSC Libraries .... Mr. Richard C. WOOD
21 Director of Accounting Services .... Ms. Melody MILLER
22 Director of Equal Employment .... Ms. Charlotte BINGHAM
25 Director of Sponsored Programs .... Ms. Victoria RIVERA
37 Director of Financial Aid .... Mr. Marcus WILSON
27 Assoc Dir of Comm & Marketing .... Ms. Suzanna CISNEROS
25 Sr Director of Contracting .... Mr. Jim LEWIS
96 Senior Director of Purchasing .... Mr. John G. HAYNES
09 Lead Analyst Inst Research .... Mr. Kevin MCINTYRE
35 Managing Director Student Services .... Ms. Margret DURAN
29 Director of Alumni Relations .... Mr. Nathan RICE

Texas Wesleyan University (A)

1201 Wesleyan, Fort Worth TX 76105-1536
County: Tarrant FICE Identification: 003645
Unit ID: 229160
Telephone: (817) 531-4444 Carnegie Class: Master's L
FAX Number: (817) 531-4425 Calendar System: Semester
URL: www.txwes.edu
Established: 1890 Annual Undergrad Tuition & Fees: $19,780
Enrollment: 3,378 Coed
Affiliation or Control: United Methodist IRS Status: 501(c)3
Highest Offering: Doctorate
Program: Liberal Arts And General; Teacher Preparatory; Professional
Accreditation: SC, ACBSP, ANEST, LAW, MUS

01 President .... Mr. Frederick G. SLABACH
05 Provost .... Dr. Allen HENDERSON
10 Sr VP Finance & Administration .... Mr. William BLEIBDREY
30 VP University Advancement .... Ms. Joan CANTY
84 VP for Enrollment & Student Svcs .... Ms. Pati ALEXANDER
11 Assoc VP Admin Svcs/Human Resources .... Mr. Steve ROBERTS
26 Assistant Vice President for Mktg .... Mr. Chuck BURTON
20 Associate Provost .... Dr. Helena BUSSELL
41 Athletic Director .... Mr. Kevin MILLIKAN
53 Dean School of Education .... Dr. Carlos MARTINEZ
50 Dean of School of Business .... Dr. Hector QUINTANILLA
49 Dean School Arts & Letters .... Dr. Steven DANIELL
61 Dean School of Law .... Mr. Fred WHITE
83 Dean School of Natural & Social Sci .... Dr. Trevor MORRIS
35 Dean of Students .... Mr. Cary POOLE
39 Director of Residence Life .... Ms. Sharon MANSON
06 Registrar .... Ms. Kay VANTOORN
08 Library Science Assoc Professor .... Ms. Cindy POTTER
21 Controller .... Ms. Lori LOGAN
27 Communications Director .... Ms. Laura HANNA
07 Director of Admissions .... Ms. Holly KISER
37 Director Financial Aid .... Ms. Shanna HOLLIS
42 Chaplain .... Dr. Robert FLOWERS
38 Director of Counseling .... Dr. Michael ELLISON
29 Director Alumni Relations .... Ms. Gina PHILLIPS
15 Human Resources Director .... Ms. Kristi TAYLOR
96 Director of Purchasing .... Ms. Deborah CAVITT
36 Director of Career Services .... Ms. Sherri MATA
18 Director of Facilities/Security .... Mr. Ken DUNSON
45 Director Institutional Research .... Ms. Sherri CARABALLO
25 Director of Grants & Research .... Ms. Deborah ROARK
91 CIO/Inform & Communications Tech .... Mr. Marcus KERR

Texas Woman's University (B)

Box 425589, Denton TX 76204-5587
County: Denton FICE Identification: 003646
Unit ID: 229179
Telephone: (940) 898-2000 Carnegie Class: DRU
FAX Number: (940) 898-3198 Calendar System: Semester
URL: www.twu.edu
Established: 1901 Annual Undergrad Tuition & Fees (In-State): $5,046
Enrollment: 14,180 Coed
Affiliation or Control: State IRS Status: 501(c)3
Highest Offering: Doctorate
Program: Liberal Arts And General; Teacher Preparatory; Professional
Accreditation: SC, CACREP, COPSY, DANCE, DH, DIETD, DIETI, HSA, IPSY, LIB, MUS, NURSE, OT, PTA, SP, SW

01 President .... Dr. Ann STUART
05 Actg Provost & VP Academic Affairs .... Dr. Robert NEELY
10 Vice Pres Finance/Administration .... Dr. Brenda L. FLOYD
32 Vice President Student Life .... Dr. Richard A. NICHOLAS
13 Vice President Information Svcs .... Mr. Bill PALMERTREE
20 Assoc Vice Pres Academic Affairs .... Dr. Michael STANKEY
58 Assoc Provost/Dean Graduate School .... Dr. Jennifer MARTIN
26 Assoc Vice Pres Mkt/Communications .... Ms. Carolyn BARNES
84 Assoc Vice Pres Enrollment Services .... Mr. Gary RAY
21 Associate Vice President Finance .... Mr. Robert L. TUGGLE
18 Assoc Vice Pres Facilities .... Mr. Harold JOHNSON
15 Assoc Vice Pres Human Resources .... Mr. Lewis BENAVIDES
49 Dean College Arts & Sciences .... Dr. Ann STATON
69 Dean College Health Sciences .... Dr. Jimmy ISHEE
62 Dean College Professional Education .... Dr. Nan RESTINE
66 Dean College of Nursing .... Dr. Patricia HOLDEN-HUCHTON
07 Director of Admissions .... Ms. Erma M. NIETO
58 Assoc Dean for Graduate Studies .... Dr. JoAnn ENGLEBRECHT
09 Dir Inst Effectiveness & Research .... Dr. Carol KOMINSKI
43 General Counsel .... Mr. John LAWHON
08 Director of Libraries .... Ms. Sherilyn BYRD
37 Director Student Financial Aid .... Mr. Governor E. JACKSON
36 Director Career & Employment Svcs .... Ms. Deidre Lynn LESLIE
38 Director Counseling Center .... Dr. Denise LUCERO-MILLER
27 Director News & Information .... Ms. Amanda SIMPSON
19 Director of Public Safety .... Mr. John W. ERWIN
06 Registrar .... Ms. Jennifer BLALOCK
41 Athletic Director .... Ms. Chalese CONNORS
23 Director Student Health Services .... Dr. Connie MENARD
39 Director University Housing .... Dr. Joe BERTHIAUME
28 Director of Diversity .... Mr. Lewis BENAVIDES
29 Director Alumni Relations .... Ms. Anne SCOTT
30 Director Development .... Ms. Sharon VENABLE
40 Bookstore Manager .... Ms. Jennifer MADISON
96 Purchasing Manager .... Ms. Maybelle DEMORE

Trinity University (C)

One Trinity Place, San Antonio TX 78212-7200
County: Bexar FICE Identification: 003647
Unit ID: 229267
Telephone: (210) 999-7011 Carnegie Class: Master's M
FAX Number: (210) 999-7696 Calendar System: Semester
URL: www.trinity.edu
Established: 1869 Annual Undergrad Tuition & Fees: $32,166
Enrollment: 2,619 Coed
Affiliation or Control: Independent Non-Profit IRS Status: 501(c)3
Highest Offering: Master's
Program: Liberal Arts And General; Teacher Preparatory; Professional
Accreditation: SC, BUS, ENG, HSA, TED

01 President .... Dr. Dennis A. AHLBURG
05 VP Faculty and Student Affairs .... Dr. Michael R. FISCHER
10 VP Finance and Administration .... Mr. Mark DETTERICK
30 VP External Affairs .... Ms. Tracy CHRISTESON
27 VP Information Resources .... Dr. Charles B. WHITE
20 AVP Faculty and Student Affairs .... Dr. Sheryl R. TYNES
20 AVP Faculty and Student Affairs .... Dr. Duane COLTHARP
20 AVP Faculty and Student Affairs .... Dr. Diane SMITH
21 AVP Finance and Administration .... Ms. Ana M. WINDHAM
07 AVP Enrollment & Student Retention .... Mr. Christopher J. ELLERTSON
08 University Librarian .... Ms. Diane J. GRAVES
06 Registrar .... Mr. Alfred RODRIGUEZ
37 Director of Financial Aid .... Ms. Glendi GADDIS
38 Director Counseling/Health Svcs .... Dr. Gary W. NEAL
32 AVP Student Affairs & Dean of Stdnt .... Mr. David M. TUTTLE
31 Dir Campus/Community Involvement .... Dr. Raphael MOFFETT
36 Director of Career Services .... Mr. Brian HIRSCH
15 Assistant VP Human Resources .... Ms. Pamela JOHNSTON
13 Director of Information Technology .... Mr. Fred ZAPATA
26 AVP University Communications .... Ms. Sharon JONES SCHWEITZER
30 Director of Development .... Ms. Kathy MCNEILL
44 Director of Planned Giving .... Mr. Gaylon GREGER
29 Director of Alumni Relations .... Dr. MaryKay COOPER
51 Director Conferences/Special Pgms .... Ms. Ann G. KNOEBEL
04 Assistant to the President .... Ms. Claire SMITH
19 Chief of Police .... Mr. Paul CHAPA
18 Acting Director Buildings & Grounds .... Mr. Mike SCHWEITZER
40 Director of Bookstore .... Ms. Dora AMADOR
42 Chaplain .... Rev. Stephen R. NICKLE
09 Director Institutional Research .... Dr. Diane G. SAPHIRE
96 Director of Purchasing .... Ms. Cynthia LARA

Trinity Valley Community College (D)

100 Cardinal Road, Athens TX 75751-2734
County: Henderson FICE Identification: 003572
Unit ID: 225308
Telephone: (903) 677-8822 Carnegie Class: Assoc/Pub-S-MC
FAX Number: (903) 675-6316 Calendar System: Semester
URL: www.tvcc.edu
Established: 1946 Annual Undergrad Tuition & Fees (In-District): $3,360
Enrollment: 7,615 Coed
Affiliation or Control: State/Local IRS Status: 501(c)3
Highest Offering: Associate Degree
Program: Occupational; 2-Year Principally Bachelor's Creditable
Accreditation: SC, ADNUR, SURGT

01 President .... Dr. Glendon S. FORGEY
05 Vice President for Instruction .... Dr. Jerry KING
32 Vice President Student Services .... Dr. W. P. DRUMGOOLE
10 Vice Pres Administrative Services .... Mrs. Jean MCSPADDEN
20 Assoc VP Instruction Academic Educ .... Dr. Jeremy MCMILLEN
76 Provost Health Occupations .... Dr. Helen REID
12 Provost Kaufman County Campus .... Dr. Algia ALLEN
12 Provost Anderson County Campus .... Mr. Charles AKIN
09 Director of Institutional Planning .... Ms. Tina RUMMEL
08 Director Learning Resource Center .... Ms. Janice SUTTON
38 Director Guidance Center .... Ms. Linda DANIEL
91 Assoc VP of Information Technology .... Mr. Brett DANIEL
27 Public Information Officer .... Mrs. Jennifer HANNIGAN
07 Director School Relations .... Ms. Audrey HAWKINS
37 Dir Student Finan Aid/Veteran's Svc .... Ms. Julie LIVELY
41 Athletic Director .... Mr. Pat SMITH
103 Dean Workforce Education .... Mr. David MCANALLY
06 Registrar/Dean Enrollment Mgmt .... Dr. Colette HILLIARD
19 Campus Police Chief .... Ms. Dorothy HOUSTON
36 Placement Officer .... Mr. Dennis NOLLEY
40 Bookstore Manager .... Mr. James QUATTLEBAUM
35 Director Student Activities .... Mr. Harold JONES
31 Director Community Services .... Ms. Gayla ROBERTS
15 Director of Human Resources .... Ms. Jennifer ROBERTSON
18 Asst VP of Facilities Management .... Mr. David GRAEM

Tyler Junior College (E)

PO Box 9020, Tyler TX 75711-9020
County: Smith FICE Identification: 003648
Unit ID: 229355
Telephone: (903) 510-2200 Carnegie Class: Assoc/Pub-R-L
FAX Number: (903) 510-2632 Calendar System: Semester
URL: www.tjc.edu
Established: 1926 Annual Undergrad Tuition & Fees (In-District): $1,856
Enrollment: 11,736 Coed
Affiliation or Control: State/Local IRS Status: 501(c)3
Highest Offering: Associate Degree
Program: Occupational; 2-Year Principally Bachelor's Creditable; Business Emphasis
Accreditation: SC, DH, DMS, MLTAD, OPD, RAD, SURGT

01 President .... Dr. L. Michael METKE
10 Vice President Business Affairs .... Ms. Sarah E. VAN CLEEF
30 VP Advancement/External Affairs .... Dr. Kimberly A. RUSSELL
32 Vice President Student Affairs .... Dr. Johnny M. MOORE
05 Provost .... Dr. Homer M. HAYES
49 Int Dean Liberal Arts & Sciences .... Mrs. Shelley G. CARAWAY
76 Dean Nursing & Health Professions .... Mr. Paul R. MONAGAN
50 Dean Prof & Tech Programs .... Dr. W. Clayton ALLEN
07 Exec Dir Enrollment Mgmt Svcs .... Mrs. Janna L. CHANCEY
09 Exec Dir Inst Effect/Plng & Rsrch .... Dr. Cheryl L. ROGERS
62 Director Library Services .... Ms. Marian D. JACKSON
51 Dean Continuing Studies .... Dr. Aubrey D. SHARPE
21 Controller .... Ms. Carol A. HUTSON
06 Registrar .... Mrs. Andrea H. LINER
37 Director Financial Aid .... Ms. Devon WIGGINS
26 Dir Marketing/Public Information .... Mr. Fred M. PETERS
35 Director Student Life & Involvement .... Mr. Vincent NGUYEN
29 Director Alumni Relations .... Ms. Betty S. BRIGGS
36 Coordinator Career Services .... Ms. Annie A. LAN
84 Director Admissions & Dual Credit .... Mrs. Nidia HASSAN
16 Exec Dir Human Resources .... Mr. S. Kevin FOWLER
41 Director Intercol Athletics .... Dr. Timothy S. DRAIN
09 Dir Institutional Research .... Dr. Lee R. ALLARD
18 Exec Dir Facilities & Construction .... Mr. William L. KING
96 Director Purchasing & Contracts .... Mr. Michael CARUSO
19 Director Campus Safety .... Mr. Randal M. MELTON
13 Chief Information Officer .... Mr. Larry MENDEZ
39 Director Auxiliary Svcs .... Ms. Diana KAROL
44 Director Principal Gifts .... Mr. Mitch ANDREWS
36 Director Testing/Career Services .... Mr. Paul GOERTEMILLER
88 Director Academic Advising .... Mrs. Jan ADAMS
88 Dean Academic Foundations .... Ms. Lisa M. HARPER
88 Director SBDC .... Mr. Donald W. PROUDFOOT

University of Dallas (F)

1845 E Northgate Drive, Irving TX 75062-4736
County: Dallas FICE Identification: 003651
Unit ID: 224323
Telephone: (972) 721-5000 Carnegie Class: Master's L
FAX Number: (972) 721-5017 Calendar System: Semester
URL: www.udallas.edu
Established: 1956 Annual Undergrad Tuition & Fees: $29,325
Enrollment: 2,843 Coed
Affiliation or Control: Roman Catholic IRS Status: 501(c)3
Highest Offering: Doctorate
Program: Liberal Arts And General; Teacher Preparatory
Accreditation: SC, ACBSP

01 President .... Mr. Thomas W. KEEFE
04 Exec Admin Asst to the President .... Ms. Cathy MCCALEB
05 Executive VP & Provost .... Dr. J. William BERRY
20 Assistant Provost .... Vacant
10 Executive VP for Fince/Admin .... Mr. Robert M. GALECKE
11 Assoc VP for Administration .... Mr. Patrick DALY
30 Vice Pres for Advancement .... Ms. Amanda RAINEY
50 Dean College of Business .... Vacant
20 Dean of Undergraduate College .... Dr. C. W. EAKER
58 Dean Grad School of Liberal Arts .... Dr. David SWEET
72 Dean School of Ministry .... Dr. Brian SCHMISEK

32 Dean of Student Life — Mr. Joseph CASSIDY
84 Assoc Provost & Dean of Enroll Mgmt — Dr. John PLOTTS
38 Assoc Dean for Retention & Advising — Dr. Kathleen BURK
07 Assistant Dean of Admissions — Ms. Brooke DAILEY
06 Registrar — Mrs. Jan BURK
19 Campus Safety Supervisor — Mr. Charles STEADMAN
90 Director of Academic Computing — Mr. Malik DULANEY
91 Director Administrative Computing — Mr. Richard HAYTER
44 Director of Annual Giving — Mr. Jim LIVERNOIS
41 Director of Athletics — Mr. Richard STROCKBINE
42 Director of Campus Ministry — Mrs. Denise PHILLIPS
18 Director of Facilities — Mr. Jerry HABA
21 Director of Finance — Mr. Leonard A. ROBERTSON
15 Director of Human Resources — Mrs. Janis TOWNSEND
09 Director of Institutional Research — Dr. Leslie R. ODOM
08 Director of Library — Dr. Robert S. DUPREE
27 Director of Marketing & Comm — Mrs. Rebecca JACKSON
96 Director of Purchasing — Mr. Alan STERLING
104 Director for Rome/Summer Programs — Mrs. Becky DAVIES
23 Director of Student Health — Dr. Laurie KUGELMANN DEKAT
36 Director of Career Services — Ms. Julie JANIK

*University of Houston System (A)

212 Ezekiel Cullen Building, Houston TX 77204-2018

County: Harris — FICE Identification: 011721
Unit ID: 229407
Telephone: (713) 743-1000 — Carnegie Class: N/A
FAX Number: (713) 743-8837
URL: www.uhsa.uh.edu

01 Chancellor — Dr. Renu KHATOR
05 Sr VC for Academic Affairs/Provost — Dr. John J. ANTEL
43 Vice Chancellor/General Counsel — Ms. Dona G. CORNELL
10 Exec VC Administration/Finance — Dr. Carl P. CARLUCCI
32 Int Vice Chancellor Student Affairs — Dr. Michael J. LAWRENCE
86 VC Governmental Relations — Mr. Grover S. CAMPBELL
46 Vice Chancellor Research IPM — Dr. Rathindra N. BOSE
30 VC University Advancement — Vacant
26 AVC University Relations — Ms. Karen CLARKE
13 Assoc VC CIO/Information Technology — Dr. Dennis FOUTY
44 Assoc Vice Chancellor Development — Vacant
20 Assoc VC Academic Affairs — Dr. Elaine M. CHARLSON
21 Associate Vice Chancellor Finance — Mr. Thomas EHARDT
18 Assoc VC Plant Operations — Mr. Dave IRVIN
45 Associate Vice Chancellor Planning — Mr. Edward T. HUGETZ
20 Asst Vice Chanc Academic Affairs — Vacant
86 Asst Vice Chanc Govt Relations — Ms. Laura CALFEE
88 Asst Vice Chanc Development — Mr. Eli CIPRIANO
15 Exec Director Human Resources — Ms. Joan M. NELSON
04 Executive Associate to Chancellor — Dr. James E. ANDERSON
21 Director Internal Auditing — Mr. Don GUYTON
88 Treasurer — Mr. Raymond BARTLETT

*University of Houston (B)

212 Ezekiel Cullen Building, Houston TX 77204-2018

County: Harris — FICE Identification: 003652
Unit ID: 225511
Telephone: (713) 743-1000 — Carnegie Class: RU/VH
FAX Number: (713) 743-8837 — Calendar System: Semester
URL: www.uh.edu
Established: 1927 — Annual Undergrad Tuition & Fees (In-State): $9,211
Enrollment: 39,000 — Coed
Affiliation or Control: State — IRS Status: Exempt
Highest Offering: Doctorate
Program: Liberal Arts And General; Teacher Preparatory; Professional
Accreditation: SC, AAFCS, BUS, BUSA, CEA, CLPSY, CONST, COPSY, CS, DIETD, DIETI, ENG, ENGT, IPSY, LAW, MUS, OPT, OPTR, PHAR, SCPSY, SP, SW, TED

02 President — Dr. Renu KHATOR
05 Sr Vice Chanc/VP Acad Affs/Prov — Dr. John ANTEL
10 Exec VP Administration/Finance — Dr. Carl CARLUCCI
30 Vice Pres University Advancement — Vacant
32 Int Vice President Student Affairs — Dr. Michael J. LAWRENCE
86 Vice Pres Governmental Relations — Mr. Grover S. CAMPBELL
43 Vice President & General Counsel — Ms. Dona G. CORNELL
46 Vice President for Research — Dr. Rathindra N. BOSE
31 VP for Community Rels & Inst Access — Dr. Elwyn C. LEE
04 Executive Assoc to the President — Dr. James E. ANDERSON
29 President/CEO Alumni Affairs — Mr. Mike PEDE
13 Assoc VP Information Tech/CIO — Dr. Dennis FOUTY
26 Assoc VP University Relations — Ms. Karen B. CLARKE
30 Assoc Vice Pres for Development — Vacant
20 Exec Asc VP Academic & Faculty Affs — Dr. Elaine M. CHARLSON
84 Assoc VP for Enrollment Management — Mr. Stephen C. SOUTULLO
35 Asst Vice Pres Student Services — Dr. David B. SMALL
88 Assoc VP Student Dev/Dean of Stdnts — Dr. William MUNSON
91 Assoc Vice Pres Enterprise Sys — Dr. Arun JAIN
45 Assoc Vice Pres Planning/Outreach — Mr. Edward HUGETZ
21 Associate Vice President Finance — Mr. Tom EHARDT
88 Asst VP Undergraduate Studies — Dr. Agnes L. DEFRANCO
22 Exec Director Affirmative Action — Dr. Richard A. BAKER
09 Exec Dir Academic/Inst Information — Dr. Elizabeth A. BARLOW
41 Director of Athletics — Mr. Mack B. RHOADES, IV
37 Int Director Student Financial Aid — Mr. Sal LORIA
16 Exec Director Human Resources — Ms. Joan NELSON
18 Assoc Vice Pres Plant Operations — Mr. Dave IRVIN
51 Director Continuing Education — Ms. Mercedes SURATY-CLARKE
06 Registrar — Dr. Debbie HERMAN
07 Executive Director of Admissions — Ms. Djuana YOUNG
19 Chief of Police — Mr. Malcolm DAVIS
96 Int Director of Purchasing — Ms. Carla WEST
79 Dean Col Liberal Arts/Soc Sci — Dr. John ROBERTS
81 Dean Col Natural Sciences & Math — Dr. Mark A. SMITH
88 Dean College of Optometry — Dr. Earl SMITH, III
72 Dean College of Technology — Dr. William FITZGIBBON
54 Dean Cullen College of Engineering — Dr. Joseph W. TEDESCO
48 Dean College of Architecture — Ms. Patricia Belton OLIVER
70 Dean Graduate Coll of Social Work — Dr. Ira COLBY
67 Dean College of Pharmacy — Dr. Lamar PRITCHARD
53 Dean College of Education — Dr. Robert MCPHERSON
50 Int Dean Bauer Col Business Admin — Dr. Latha RAMCHAND
88 Dean Hilton Col Htl/Restaurant Mgt — Dr. John BOWEN
92 Dean Honors College — Dr. William MONROE
61 Dean UH Law Center — Dr. Raymond NIMMER
08 Dean University Libraries — Ms. Dana C. ROOKS

*University of Houston - Clear Lake (C)

Houston TX 77058-1098

County: Harris — FICE Identification: 011711
Unit ID: 225414
Telephone: (281) 283-7600 — Carnegie Class: Master's L
FAX Number: (281) 283-2219 — Calendar System: Semester
URL: www.uhcl.edu
Established: 1971 — Annual Undergrad Tuition & Fees (In-State): $5,160
Enrollment: 8,099 — Coed
Affiliation or Control: State — IRS Status: 501(c)3
Highest Offering: Doctorate
Program: Liberal Arts And General; Teacher Preparatory; Professional
Accreditation: SC, BUS, BUSA, CS, ENG, ENGR, HSA, MFCD, SW, TED

02 President — Dr. William A. STAPLES
05 Sr Vice Pres for Academic Affairs — Dr. Carl A. STOCKTON
10 Vice Pres Administration & Finance — Ms. Michelle DOTTER
04 Executive Assoc to the President — Ms. Mary Ann H. SHALLBERG
13 Assoc VP Information Resources — Dr. A. Glen HOUSTON
20 Assoc Vice Pres Academic Affairs — Dr. Mrinal MUGDH
30 Assoc VP University Advancement — Mr. Dion MCINNIS
32 Assoc Vice Pres Student Services — Dr. Darlene BIGGERS
21 Associate Vice President Finance — Mr. John CORDARY
84 Assoc Vice Pres Enrollment Mgmt — Dr. Yvette BENDECK
18 Assoc VP Facilities Mgmt/Construct — Mr. Ward MARTAINDALE
50 Dean School Business — Dr. Wm. Theodore CUMMINGS
81 Dean School Science/Computer Engr — Dr. Zbigniew CZAJKIEWICZ
79 Dean Sch Human Sci/Humanities — Dr. Bruce PALMER
53 Dean School Education — Dr. Dennis W. SPUCK
35 Interim Dean of Students — Mr. David A. RACHITA
28 Asst Dean Student Diversity — Ms. Linda C. BULLOCK
08 Exec Director Neumann Library — Ms. Karen WIELHORSKI
85 Exec Director Intl Initiatives — Dr. Sameer PANDE
45 Exec Director Planning & Assessment — Mr. Kevin BARLOW
15 Executive Director Human Resources — Ms. Katherine JUSTICE
14 Exec Director University Computing — Mr. Rodger CARR
21 Exec Dir of Procurement & Payables — Ms. Debra CARPENTER
25 Exec Dir Sponsored Programs — Mr. Paul MEYERS
37 Executive Director Financial Aid — Mr. Billy SATTERFIELD
88 Exec Dir Environment Inst Houston — Dr. George GUILLEN
06 Registrar/Director Academic Records — Vacant
56 Director Distance/Off-Campus Educ — Ms. Lisa GABRIEL
27 Director Communications — Ms. Theresa PRESSWOOD
29 Director Alumni & Cmty Relations — Ms. Charity ELLIS
19 Director Police — Mr. Paul WILLINGHAM
36 Director Career/Counseling Services — Dr. Alfred KAHN
09 Assoc Dir Institutional Research — Ms. Peggy JOHNSON
12 Dir Camp Operat/UHCL Pearland Camp — Ms. Kathy DUPREE
23 Dir Health & Disability Services — Ms. Susan L. PRIHODA
07 Exec Director of Admissions — Ms. Rauchelle JONES
40 Manager Bookstore — Mr. Brent WELLS

*University of Houston - Downtown (D)

1 Main Street, Houston TX 77002-1014

County: Harris — FICE Identification: 003612
Unit ID: 225432
Telephone: (713) 221-8001 — Carnegie Class: Bac/Diverse
FAX Number: (713) 221-8075 — Calendar System: Semester
URL: www.uhd.edu
Established: 1974 — Annual Undergrad Tuition & Fees (In-State): $4,786
Enrollment: 12,900 — Coed
Affiliation or Control: State — IRS Status: Exempt
Highest Offering: Master's
Program: Liberal Arts And General
Accreditation: SC, BUS, ENGT, @SW

02 President — Dr. William V. FLORES
04 Executive Assistant to President — Ms. Mary RODRIGUEZ
05 Provost/Sr Vice Pres Acad Affairs — Dr. Brian R. CHAPMAN
20 Assoc VPAA/Vice Prov/Dean Grad Std — Dr. Michael R. DRESSMAN
45 Assoc VP Inst Effectiveness — Dr. Patrick S. WILLIAMS
50 Dean College of Business — Dr. Donald BATES
79 Dean Col Humanities/Social Sci — Dr. Susan K. AHERN
88 Dean College of Public Service — Dr. Beth PELZ
81 Interim Dean Col Sciences & Tech — Dr. Akif UZMAN
97 Dean University College — Dr. Chris BIRCHAK
08 Executive Director WI Dykes Library — Ms. Pat ENSOR
106 Exec Dir Distance Education — Mr. Louis D. EVANS, III
09 Director of Institutional Research — Ms. Carol M. TUCKER
88 Director Sponsored Programs — Ms. Carolyn IVEY
88 Director of Academic Assessment — Dr. Lea CAMPBELL
88 Director Creative Services — Mr. Joe WYNNE
88 Director of Community Engagement — Dr. Jean DEWITT
92 Director of Scholars Academy — Dr. Mary Jo PARKER
88 Director Advising — Ms. Jemma CAESAR
88 Director Advising Services — Ms. Reyna ROMERO
88 Director Academic Support Center — Dr. Isidro GRAU
88 Director Academic Services — Mr. David MORALES
88 Exec Director Talent Search — Ms. Jennifer HIGHTOWER
88 Director Disability Services — Ms. Duraese HALL
88 Director Upward Bound — Ms. Dawanna LEWIS
72 Dir Applied Business/Technology Ctr — Mr. G. V. KRISHNAN
88 Director English Language Institute — Dr. Gail KELLERSBERGER
88 Director Criminal Justice Center — Mr. Rex WHITE
88 Dir Inst for Financial Literacy — Dr. James KANE
10 VP Administration & Finance — Mr. David M. BRADLEY
13 Assoc VP Information Technology — Mr. Hossein SHAHROKHI
24 Asst Dir Tech Learning Services — Mr. Lloyd MATZNER
91 Director Enterprise Systems — Mr. Kong YIN
88 Dir Technology Learning Services — Dr. Deborah CARRUTHERS
88 Dir User Support Services — Mr. Said FATTOUH
88 Director Technical Services — Ms. Grace DAVILA
88 Dir Comp/Telecom & Video Networks — Mr. Joe LONGORIA
21 Asst VP Business Affairs — Mr. George W. ANDERSON
25 Director Risk Mgmt & Compliance — Ms. Mary COOK
96 Coordinator Purchasing — Mr. Cory ODSTRCIL
18 Asst VP Facilities Management — Mr. Chris MCCALL
19 Chief of Police — Mr. Richard BOYLE
16 VP Employment Svcs & Operations — Ms. Ivonne MONTALBANO
15 Asst VP Employee Svcs/Records Mgmt — Ms. Betty POWELL
22 Asst VP Empl Trng/Camp Rels/AA Ofcr — Dr. Doug TEDUITS
84 VP Student Success & Enrollment Mgt — Vacant
35 Asst Vice Pres for Student Services — Mr. Tommy N. THOMASON
06 Registrar — Ms. Cynthia SANTOS
07 Director Admissions & Recruitment — Mr. Jose CANTU
37 Director of Scholarships & Fin Aid — Ms. LaTasha GOUDEAU
41 Director Sports & Fitness — Mr. Richard SEBASTIANI
36 Director Career Services — Mr. Stephen MARKERT
88 Director Testing Services — Ms. Po-Chu A. LEUNG
35 Assoc Dir Community Involvement — Ms. Liza ALONZO
88 Director International Programs — Mr. Spencer LIGHTSY
31 Director Community Relations — Ms. Janet HEITMILLER
30 VP Advancement & External Rels — Ms. Johanna WOLFE
26 Executive Director Public Affairs — Ms. Sue DAVIS

*University of Houston - Victoria (E)

3007 N Ben Wilson, Victoria TX 77901-4450

County: Victoria — FICE Identification: 013231
Unit ID: 225502
Telephone: (361) 570-4848 — Carnegie Class: Master's L
FAX Number: (361) 580-5534 — Calendar System: Semester
URL: www.uhv.edu
Established: 1973 — Annual Undergrad Tuition & Fees (In-State): $4,728
Enrollment: 4,095 — Coed
Affiliation or Control: State — IRS Status: 501(c)3
Highest Offering: Master's
Program: Liberal Arts And General; Teacher Preparatory; Professional
Accreditation: SC, BUS, CACREP, NURSE, @TEAC

02 President — Dr. Philip CASTILLE
11 Vice Pres Administration & Finance — Mr. Wayne B. BERAN
05 Provost/Vice Pres Academic Affs — Vacant
100 Chief of Staff — Dr. Margaret H. RICE
32 Associate Vice Pres Student Affairs — Ms. Chari NORGARD
49 Dean Arts & Sciences — Dr. Jeffrey DILEO
50 Dean Business Administration — Dr. Farhang NIROOMAND
53 Dean Education & Human Development — Dr. Lawrence ROSSOW
66 Dean Nursing — Dr. Kathryn TART
30 Sr Director University Advancement — Vacant
08 Senior Director of Library — Dr. Joe F. DAHLSTROM
14 Sr Director Information Technology — Mr. Joseph S. FERGUSON
15 Dir Human Resource/Affirmative Act — Ms. Laura L. SMITH
84 Sr Director of Enrollment Mgmt — Dr. Denee THOMAS
88 Dir Small Business Development Ctr — Mr. Paul J. HARPER
06 Registrar — Ms. Trudy WORTHAM
37 Director Financial Aid — Ms. Carolyn R. MALLORY
18 Director Facilities — Mr. Kevin MYERS
10 Director Business Services — Mr. Greg FANELLI
21 Comptroller — Ms. Valerie WALDEN
41 Director Athletics — Mr. Ashley WALYUCHOW
44 Director Stewardship/Planned Giving — Ms. Robin CADLE
102 Director Corp & Foundation Relation — Ms. Amy MUNDY
26 Interim Director Marketing — Ms. Paula COBLER
38 Director of Counseling Center — Dr. Jesus AROS
35 Director of Student Life & Services — Ms. Lindsey KOCH
09 Director Institutional Research — Dr. Tong-Ai ZHANG
88 Director Retention & Student Succ — Ms. Sandra HEINOLD

University of the Incarnate Word (F)

4301 Broadway, San Antonio TX 78209-6397

County: Bexar — FICE Identification: 003578
Unit ID: 225627
Telephone: (210) 829-6000 — Carnegie Class: Master's L
FAX Number: (210) 829-1220 — Calendar System: Semester
URL: www.uiw.edu
Established: 1881 — Annual Undergrad Tuition & Fees: $21,900
Enrollment: 7,708 — Coed
Affiliation or Control: Roman Catholic — IRS Status: 501(c)3
Highest Offering: Doctorate
Program: Liberal Arts And General; Teacher Preparatory; Professional
Accreditation: SC, ACBSP, CIDA, DIETD, DIETI, NMT, NURSE, @OPT, PHAR, THEA

01 President .... Dr. Louis J. AGNESE, JR.
00 Chancellor .... Sr. Helena MONAHAN
88 Mission Effectiveness .... Sr. Walter MAHER
04 Executive Assistant to President .... Ms. Damita FEDOR
26 Asst to the President/Communication .... Mr. Vincent RODRIQUEZ
43 General Counsel .... Ms. Cindy ESCAMILLA
05 Provost .... Dr. Denise DOYLE
84 Vice Pres Enrollment Mgt/Stdnt Svcs .Dr. David M. JURENOVICH
30 Vice Pres Institutional Advancement .... Sr. Kathleen COUGHLIN
10 Vice Pres for Finance & Technology .... Mr. Douglas ENDSLEY
104 Vice Pres International Programs .... Mr. Marcos FRAGOSO
56 Vice Pres of Ext Academic Programs .... Dr. Cyndi WILSON-PORTER
13 Chief Information Officer .... Mr. Marshall EIDSON
21 Comptroller .... Ms. Edith COGDELL
50 Dean H-E-B Sch Business & Admin .... Dr. Shawn DALY
57 Dean Humanities Arts & Social Sci .... Dr. Robert CONNELLY
66 Dean Nursing & Health Professions .... Dr. Kathleen LIGHT
53 Dean Dreeben School of Education .... Dr. Denise STAUDT
54 Dean Math Science Engineering .... Dr. Glenn JAMES
08 Dean Interactve Media & Design .... Dr. Sharon WELKEY
67 Dean Feik School of Pharmacy .... Dr. Arcelia JOHNSON-FANNIN
88 Acting Dean School of Optometry .... Dr. Andrew BUZZELLI
58 Dean of Grad Studies/Research .... Dr. Kevin VICHCALES
62 Dean of Library Services .... Dr. Cheryl ANDERSON
88 Asst to Provost/Dir of Assessment .... Vacant
55 Dean Sch of Extended Studies .... Mr. Vincent PORTER
106 Dean of Virtual University .... Ms. Rita RUSS
88 Dean Univ Preparatory Programs .... Mr. Daniel OCHOA
29 Director of Alumni Relations .... Ms. Lisa SCHULTZ
26 Director of Public Relations .... Ms. Debra DEL TORO
84 Dean of Enrollment .... Ms. Andrea CYTERSKI-ACOSTA
32 Dean of Student Success .... Ms. Sandy MCMAKIN
38 Dean of Counseling .... Dr. Keith TUCKER
20 Director of Academic Advising .... Mr. Moises TORRESCANO
88 Director Learning Assistance Center .... Ms. Cristina ARIZA
06 Registrar .... Dr. Bobbye G. FRY
37 Director of Financial Aid .... Ms. Amy CARCANAGUES
32 Dean of Campus Life .... Dr. Renee MOORE
39 Director of Residence Life .... Ms. Diane SANCHEZ
35 Dir University Events/Student Pgms .... Mr. Paul AYALA
23 Director of Health Services .... Ms. Marveen MAHON
42 Chaplain .... Fr. Tom DYMOWSKI
42 Director of Campus Ministry .... Ms. Elisabeth VILLARREAL
15 Director of Human Resources .... Ms. Annette THOMPSON
96 Director of Purchasing .... Mr. Sam WAGES
18 Director Facilities Mgmt & Services .... Mr. Steve HEYING
41 Director of Athletics .... Mr. Mark PAPICH
88 Director of Infrastructure Support .... Mr. Carl HAYWOOD
88 Director of Enterprise Systems .... Ms. Sandy GIVENS
88 Director Instructional Technology .... Ms. Ana GONZALES
72 Director of Technology Support .... Mr. Anthony RAMOS
09 Director of Institutional Research .... Ms. Robin LOGAN
07 Director of Admissions .... Ms. Heather RODRIGUEZ
36 Coordinator of Career Services .... Mr. Juan ALMENDAREZ

University of Mary Hardin-Baylor (A)

900 College Street, Belton TX 76513-2578
County: Bell FICE Identification: 003588
Unit ID: 226471
Telephone: (254) 295-8642 Carnegie Class: Master's S
FAX Number: (254) 295-4535 Calendar System: Semester
URL: www.umhb.edu
Established: 1845 Annual Undergrad Tuition & Fees: $21,520
Enrollment: 2,956 Coed
Affiliation or Control: Southern Baptist IRS Status: 501(c)3
Highest Offering: Doctorate
Program: Liberal Arts And General; Teacher Preparatory; Professional
Accreditation: SC, CACREP, MUS, NURSE, SW

01 President/CEO .... Dr. Randy G. O'REAR
03 Sr Vice Pres Admin/COO .... Dr. Steve THEODORE
05 Provost/Sr Vice Pres Academics .... Dr. Steve OLDHAM
45 Sr Vice Pres Campus Planning .... Mr. Edd MARTIN
00 Chancellor .... Dr. Jerry G. BAWCOM
30 Vice Pres for Development .... Mr. Brent DAVISON
102 Vice Pres Communication/Spec Proj .... Dr. Paula TANNER
32 Vice Pres for Student Life .... Dr. Byron WEATHERSBEE
41 Vice Pres Athletics .... Mr. Ben SHIPP
10 Vice Pres Business/Finance/CFO .... Mrs. Jennifer RAMM
15 Assoc Vice Pres Human Resources .... Mrs. Susan OWENS
13 Assoc Vice Pres Information Tech .... Mr. Brent HARRIS
84 Assoc Vice Pres Enrollment Mgmt .... Mr. Gary LAMM
18 Assoc Vice Pres for Facilities .... Mr. Bob PATTEE
20 Asst Provost .... Dr. Tammi COOPER
21 Controller .... Ms. Charla KAHLIG
49 Dean of Sciences .... Vacant
66 Dean of Nursing .... Dr. Sharon SOUTER
53 Dean of Education .... Dr. Marlene ZIPPERLEN
50 Dean of Business/Study Abroad Dir .... Dr. Jim KING
58 Interim Dean Graduate School .... Dr. Colin WILBORN
88 Dean of Christian Studies .... Dr. Tim CRAWFORD
57 Dean Visual/Performing Arts .... Mr. Ted BARNES
35 Dean of Students .... Mr. Ray MARTIN
39 Assoc Dean Students/Dir Residence .... Ms. Donna PLANK
04 Admin Assistant to the President .... Mrs. Phyllis ROGERS
06 Registrar .... Mrs. Amy MCGILVRAY
07 Director of Admissions & Recruiting .... Mr. Brent BURKS
08 Director Learning Resources .... Ms. Denise KARIMKHANI
26 Director Marketing/Public Relations .... Mr. James STAFFORD
09 Dir Inst Effectiveness & Research .... Ms. Bethany CHAPMAN
37 Director Financial Aid .... Mr. Ron BROWN

92 Director Honors Program .... Dr. David HOLCOMB
19 Director Campus Police .... Mr. Gary SARGENT
96 Director of Purchasing .... Mr. Mike FRAZIER
29 Director Alumni Relations .... Ms. Rebecca O'BANION
42 University Chaplain .... Dr. George LOUTHERBACK
36 Director Career Services .... Mr. Don OWENS
38 Director Couns Testing & Health .... Mr. Nate WILLIAMS
85 Dir International Student Services .... Mrs. Elizabeth TANAKA
44 Director Planned Giving .... Dr. Gene KIMES
40 Bookstore Manager .... Mrs. Debbie COTTRELL

University of North Texas (B)

1155 Union Circle #311277, Denton TX 76203-5013
County: Denton FICE Identification: 003594
Unit ID: 227216
Telephone: (940) 565-2000 Carnegie Class: RU/H
FAX Number: (940) 565-7600 Calendar System: Semester
URL: www.unt.edu
Established: 1890 Annual Undergrad Tuition & Fees (In-State): $7,900
Enrollment: 36,067 Coed
Affiliation or Control: State IRS Status: 501(c)3
Highest Offering: Doctorate
Program: Liberal Arts And General; Teacher Preparatory; Professional
Accreditation: SC, ART, AUD, BUS, BUSA, CACREP, CEA, CIDA, CLPSY, COPSY, CORE, CS, ENG, ENGT, JOUR, LIB, MUS, NRPA, SP, SPAA, SW, TED

00 Chancellor .... Mr. Lee F. JACKSON
01 President .... Dr. V. Lane RAWLINS
05 Provost/Vice Pres Academic Affairs .... Dr. Warrewn BURGGREN
10 Vice Pres Finance/Administration .... Mr. Andrew M. HARRIS
46 VP Research/Economic Development .... Dr. Vishwanath PRASAD
32 Vice President Student Affairs .... Dr. Elizabeth WITH
43 Vice Chancellor/General Counsel .... Ms. Nancy FOOTER
26 Vice President University Relations .... Ms. Deborah S. LELIAERT
30 VP for Advancement/Dir of Develop .... Ms. Lisa Birley BARONIO
09 Director Institutional Research .... Dr. Allen CLARK
41 Athletic Director .... Mr. Rick VILLARREAL
35 Dean Students .... Dr. Maureen MCGUINNESS
13 Vice President for Information Tech .... Mr. John HOOPER
21 Assoc VP Finance/Admin/Cont .... Vacant
28 VP Institutional Equity & Diversity .... Dr. Gilda GARCIA
20 Vice Provost for Educ Innovation .... Dr. Celia WILLIAMSON
18 Executive Director Facilities .... Mr. Charles JACKSON
84 Assoc VP Enrollment Management .... Dr. Troy JOHNSON
08 Dean of Libraries .... Dr. Martin HALBERT
37 Director Financial Aid .... Ms. Zelma DELEON
49 Dean College of Arts/Sciences .... Dr. Michael MONTICINO
50 Dean College Business Admin .... Dr. Finley GRAVES
53 Dean College of Education .... Dr. Jerry R. THOMAS
57 Dean School of Visual Arts .... Dr. Robert W. MILNES
88 Dean Col Public Affs/Community Svc .... Dr. Thomas L. EVENSON
64 Dean College of Music .... Dr. James C. SCOTT
59 Dean School of Merch & Hosp Mgmt .... Dr. Judith FORNEY
62 Dean College of Information .... Dr. Herman L. TOTTEN
88 Dean Toulouse Sch Grad Studies .... Dr. James MEERNIK
54 Dean College of Engineering .... Dr. Costas TSATSOULIS
90 Director Acad Computing/User Svcs .... Dr. Philip C. BACZEWSKI
91 Exec Dir Admin Information System .... Vacant
07 Director of Admissions .... Ms. Rebecca LOTHRINGER
51 Director Continuing Educ/Conf Mgmt .... Ms. Marilyn D. WAGNER
06 Registrar .... Ms. Lynn MCCREARY
15 Asst Vice Pres Human Resources .... Ms. Donna L. KEENER
36 Dir Stdnt Employment/Career Svcs .... Mr. Dan NAEGELI
38 Director of Counseling & Testing .... Dr. Judy A. MCCONNELL
19 Director/Chief of Police .... Mr. Richard S. DETER
39 Director Housing .... Dr. Elisabeth B. WARREN
85 Vice Provost/Assoc VP Intl Educ .... Dr. Richard NADER
40 Director UNT Bookstore .... Mr. Rodney DAVISON
23 Dir Stdnt Health Ctr/Wellness Svcs .... Vacant
29 Exec Dir Alum Rels/N Texas Exes .... Mr. Derrick MORGAN
96 Director of Purchasing/Payment Svcs .... Mr. Joey SAXON
92 Dean Honors College .... Dr. Gloria COX

University of North Texas Health Science Center at Fort Worth (C)

3500 Camp Bowie Boulevard, Fort Worth TX 76107-2699
County: Tarrant FICE Identification: 009768
Unit ID: 228909
Telephone: (817) 735-2000 Carnegie Class: Spec/Med
FAX Number: (817) 735-2486 Calendar System: Semester
URL: www.hsc.unt.edu
Established: 1966 Annual Graduate Tuition & Fees: $15,107
Enrollment: 1,579 Coed
Affiliation or Control: State IRS Status: 501(c)3
Highest Offering: Doctorate; No Undergraduates
Program: Professional
Accreditation: SC, ARCPA, OSTEO, PH, @PTA

01 President .... Dr. Scott B. RANSOM
10 Exec VP Finance/Administration .... Mr. Steve R. RUSSELL
86 Vice President Governmental Affairs .... Mr. Dan JENSEN
30 Sr VP Community Engagement .... Mr. Greg UPP
43 Vice Chanc & General Counsel .... Ms. Nancy FOOTER
63 Dean Texas Col of Osteopathic Med .... Dr. Bruce DUBIN
20 Assoc Dean Educational Programs .... Mr. Don PESKA
32 Vice Pres Student Affairs .... Dr. Thomas D. MOORMAN
08 VP Information Resources & Technolo .... Dr. Renee DRABIER
15 Vice Pres Human Resource Svcs .... Mr. Rand HORSMAN
81 VP Research & Biotechnology .... Dr. Glenn DILLON
51 Assoc VP for Professional/Cont Edu .... Ms. Pam MCFADDEN

58 Dean Grad Sch Biomedical Sciences .... Dr. J. K. VISHWANATHA
76 Dean School of Health Professions .... Dr. Warren ANDERSON
69 Dean of School of Public Health .... Dr. Richard KURZ
37 Director Student Financial Aid .... Mr. Michael HAYNES
06 Registrar .... Ms. Betty BELTON
19 Chief of Police .... Mr. Gary GAILLIARD
29 Asst Dev Dir/Donor Relations .... Ms. Amy BAKER
09 VP Strategy & Measurement .... Dr. Thomas FAIRCHILD
21 Asst VP Institutional Budgets .... Mr. Michael MUELLER
07 Asst Dean of Admissions & Outreach .... Mr. Joel DABOUB
18 Assoc VP Facilities Management .... Mr. Stephen BARRETT
26 VP Marketing & Communications .... Ms. Jean TIPS
96 Director of Purchasing .... Mrs. Lane NESTMAN

University of St. Thomas (D)

3800 Montrose Boulevard, Houston TX 77006-4696
County: Harris FICE Identification: 003654
Unit ID: 227863
Telephone: (713) 522-7911 Carnegie Class: Master's L
FAX Number: (713) 525-2125 Calendar System: Semester
URL: www.stthom.edu
Established: 1947 Annual Undergrad Tuition & Fees: $25,440
Enrollment: 3,437 Coed
Affiliation or Control: Roman Catholic IRS Status: 501(c)3
Highest Offering: Doctorate
Program: Liberal Arts And General; Teacher Preparatory; Professional
Accreditation: SC, ACBSP, BUS, @TEAC, THEOL

01 President .... Dr. Robert IVANY
04 Exec Assistant to the President .... Ms. Sandra CACKOWSKI
04 Admin Assistant to the President .... Ms. Shawna WALLSTEIN
11 Assoc VP of Administrative Svcs .... Mr. John MEUSER
05 Vice President Academic Affairs .... Dr. Dominic AQUILA
20 Associate VP Academic Affairs .... Dr. John PALASOTA
49 Dean Arts & Sciences .... Fr. Joseph PILSNER
73 Dean School of Theology .... Dr. Sandra C. MAGIE, CM
50 Dean Cameron School of Business .... Dr. Bahman MIRSHAB
53 Dean School of Education .... Dr. Robert LEBLANC
08 Director Doherty Library .... Mr. James PICCININNI
58 Dir Center for Thomistic Studies .... Dr. Mary C. SOMMERS
88 Director Center for Business Ethics .... Vacant
82 Director Center for Intl Studies .... Dr. Linda PETT-CONKLIN
88 Director Center for Irish Studies .... Ms. Lori GALLAGHER
88 Director Center for Faith & Culture .... Fr. Donald NESTI, CSSP
06 Registrar .... Ms. Kimberly SANDERS
13 Vice Pres Information Technology .... Mr. Gary MCCORMACK
90 Dir of Network & Campus Computing .... Mr. Tony REYNA
90 Director Technology Support Svcs .... Mr. Mark HENDERSON
91 Dir Administrative Computing Svcs .... Ms. Joanna E. PALASOTA
88 Director Central Computing Services .... Ms. Christine BARRY
32 Vice Pres Student Affairs .... Ms. Patricia MCKINLEY
35 Dean of Students .... Ms. Lindsey MCPHERSON
38 Exec Dir Counseling & Disability .... Dr. Rose SIGNORELLO
35 Assistant VP of Campus Life .... Mr. Matthew PRASIFKA
42 Dir of Campus Ministry/Chaplain .... Fr. Michael BUENTELLO
39 Director Residence Life .... Ms. Yolanda NORMAN
88 Director of Student Activities .... Ms. Angie MONTELONGO
88 Director of Recreational Sports .... Ms. Jessica DOMANN
10 Vice President for Finance .... Mr. James M. BOOTH
18 Asst VP Facilities Operations .... Mr. Howard A. ROSE
21 Controller .... Ms. Karen S. BURNS
88 Treasurer .... Ms. Susan ROSE
30 Vice President for Inst Advancement .... Mr. Ken DEDOMINICIS
44 Exec Dir Institutional Advancement .... Ms. Susan E. BRADFORD
44 Director of Development/Major Gifts .... Ms. Deborah CROFOOT-MORLEY
29 Director of Major Constitutents .... Ms. Kia KRITICOS
84 Vice Pres Marketing & Enroll Mgmt .... Ms. Vickie ALLEMAN
07 Director Admissions .... Mr. Lee HOLM
37 Dean of Scholarships/Financial Aid .... Ms. Lynda MCKENDREE
26 Dir of Marketing Communications .... Ms. Sandra SOLIZ
27 Director Publications .... Ms. Marionette MITCHELL

*University of Texas System Administration (E)

601 Colorado Street, Austin TX 78701-2982
County: Travis FICE Identification: 003655
Unit ID: 229090
Telephone: (512) 499-4201 Carnegie Class: N/A
FAX Number: (512) 499-4215
URL: www.utsystem.edu

01 Chancellor .... Dr. Francisco G. CIGARROA
05 Exec Vice Chanc Academic Affairs .... Dr. David B. PRIOR
17 Exec Vice Chanc Health Affairs .... Dr. Kenneth I. SHINE
10 Exec Vice Chanc Business Affairs .... Dr. Scott C. KELLEY
43 Vice Chanc & General Counsel .... Mr. Barry D. BURGDORF
86 Vice Chanc for Govt Relations .... Mr. Barry MCBEE
26 Vice Chanc for External Relations .... Dr. Randa S. SAFADY
86 Vice Chanc Federal Relations .... Mr. William SHUTE
45 Vice Chanc Strategic Initiatives .... Ms. Sandra K. WOODLEY
18 Assoc VC Facil Plng/Construction .... Mr. Michael O'DONNELL
13 Assoc VC & Chief Info Officer .... Mrs. Marg KNOX
21 Asst VC/Controller/Chief Budget Ofc .... Mr. Randy WALLACE
15 Assist Vice Chanc Employee Services .... Mr. Dan STEWART
27 Director Public Affairs .... Mr. Anthony P. DE BRUYN
88 Executive Director Real Estate .... Ms. Florence P. MAYNE
30 Dir Development/Gift Planning Svcs .... Ms. Julie LYNCH
19 Director of Police .... Mr. Michael J. HEIDINGSFIELD

The University of Texas at Arlington (A)

701 S Nedderman Drive, Arlington TX 76013

County: Tarrant FICE Identification: 003656
Unit ID: 228769
Telephone: (817) 272-2101 Carnegie Class: RU/H
FAX Number: (817) 272-5656 Calendar System: Semester
URL: www.uta.edu
Established: 1895 Annual Undergrad Tuition & Fees (In-State): $8,500
Enrollment: 32,975 Coed
Affiliation or Control: State IRS Status: 170(c)1
Highest Offering: Doctorate
Program: Liberal Arts And General; Teacher Preparatory; Business Emphasis
Accreditation: SC, ART, BUS, BUSA, CIDA, CS, ENG, LSAR, MUS, NURSE, PLNG, SPAA, SW, TED

02 President .... Mr. James D. SPANIOLO
03 Provost & Vice Pres Acad Affairs .... Dr. Donald R. BOBBITT
10 Vice Pres Business Affs/Controller .... Ms. Kelly DAVIS
32 Vice President Student Affairs .... Dr. Frank LAMAS
30 Vice President Development .... Mr. Jim LEWIS
46 Vice President Research & Fed Rels .... Dr. Ron ELSENBAUMER
13 Vice Pres Information Technology .... Dr. Maurice LEATHERBURY
11 Vice Pres Admin & Campus Operations .... Mr. John D. HALL
27 Vice President of Communications .... Mr. Jerry LEWIS
16 Vice President for Human Resources .... Ms. Jean HOOD
84 Sr Assoc VP Student Enrollment Svcs .... Dr. Dale WASSON
45 Assoc VP & Dir Inst Research/Plng .... Dr. Pamela M. HAWS
15 Asst Vice Pres Human Resources .... Ms. Eunice M. CURRIE
26 Asst Vice President Media Services .... Ms. Kristin SULLIVAN
18 Asst VP Campus Operation/Facilities .... Mr. Bill POOLE
88 Executive Dir University College .... Dr. Dawn REMMERS
04 Exec Associate to the President .... Ms. Marcy SANDERS
58 Dean of Graduate Studies .... Dr. Phil COHEN
48 Dean of Architecture .... Mr. Donald GATZKE
50 Dean Business Administration .... Dr. Daniel HIMARIOS
54 Dean of Engineering .... Dr. Bill CARROLL
49 Dean of Liberal Arts .... Dr. Beth WRIGHT
66 Dean of Nursing .... Dr. Elizabeth C. POSTER
81 Dean of Science .... Dr. Pamela JANSMA
70 Dean School of Social Work .... Dr. Scott RYAN
71 Dean Urban & Public Affairs .... Dr. Barbara BECKER
53 Dean College of Education .... Dr. Jeanne M. GERLACH
92 Dean Honors College .... Dr. Karl PETRUSO
08 Dean of Libraries .... Dr. Gerald D. SAXON
07 Exec Director Admissions & Records .... Dr. Hans GATTERDAM
29 Exec Director Alumni Association .... Ms. Lora MALONE
12 Exec Dir of UTA Ft Worth Center .... Mr. Mike WEST
37 Director of Financial Aid .... Dr. Karen KRAUSE
23 Director Student Health Center .... Mr. Robert BLUM
22 Director Equal Opportunity Services .... Mr. Eddie FREEMAN
24 Director Video Services .... Ms. Lisa EVANS-REAGAN
41 Athletic Director .... Mr. Peter D. CARLON
19 Dir Environmental Health Safety .... Ms. Leah HOY
85 Interim Exec Dir Intl Education .... Mr. Jay HORN
88 Director Multicultural Outreach .... Mr. Casey GONZALES
88 Director Multicultural Affairs .... Ms. Leticia MARTINEZ

*University of Texas at Austin (B)

Austin TX 78712-1026

County: Travis FICE Identification: 003658
Unit ID: 228778
Telephone: (512) 471-3434 Carnegie Class: RU/VH
FAX Number: (512) 471-8102 Calendar System: Semester
URL: www.utexas.edu
Established: 1883 Annual Undergrad Tuition & Fees (In-State): $9,794
Enrollment: 51,195 Coed
Affiliation or Control: State IRS Status: 170(c)1
Highest Offering: Doctorate
Program: Liberal Arts And General; Teacher Preparatory; Professional
Accreditation: SC, ART, AUD, BUS, BUSA, CIDA, CLPSY, COPSY, CORE, DANCE, DIETC, DIETD, ENG, IPSY, JOUR, LAW, LIB, LSAR, MUS, NURSE, PHAR, PLNG, SCPSY, SP, SPAA, SW

02 President .... Mr. William C. POWERS, JR.
05 Executive Vice Pres & Provost .... Dr. Steven W. LESLIE
10 Vice Pres & Chief Financial Officer .... Mr. Kevin P. HEGARTY
28 VP Diversity & Community Engagement .... Dr. Gregory J. VINCENT
11 Vice Pres for University Operations .... Dr. Patricia L. CLUBB
43 Vice President Legal Affairs .... Ms. Patricia A. OHLENDORF
26 Vice President Public Affairs .... Mr. Donald A. HALE
46 Vice President Research .... Dr. Juan M. SANCHEZ
32 Vice President Student Affairs .... Dr. Juan C. GONZALEZ
04 Deputy to the President .... Dr. Charles A. ROECKLE
04 Deputy to the President .... Ms. Nancy A. BRAZZIL
04 Executive Assistant to President .... Ms. Kathy R. BARTSCH
88 Vice Prov for Resource Management .... Dr. Daniel A. SLESNICK
07 Vice Prov & Dir Admissions .... Dr. Kedra B. ISHOP
20 Vice Provost for Faculty Affairs .... Dr. Neal E. ARMSTRONG
58 Vice Prov/Dean Graduate Studies .... Dr. Victoria RODRIGUEZ
88 Vice Provost for Health Affairs .... Dr. William M. SAGE
08 Vice Provost/Dir General Libraries .... Dr. Fred M. HEATH
45 V Prov Forecasting/Inst Res/Modelng .... Dr. John D. DOLLARD
20 Vice Provost International Programs .... Dr. Janet L. ELLZEY
20 Vice Provost .... Dr. Judith H. LANGLOIS
20 V Prov UG Educ & Faculty Governance .... Dr. Gretchen RITTER
20 Vice Provost for Special Projects .... Dr. N. Bruce WALKER
88 Vice Provost for Higher Ed Policy .... Dr. Harrison KELLER
21 Associate Vice Pres Budget Director .... Ms. Mary E. KNIGHT
21 Associate Vice President/ Controller .... Mr. Glenn (Fred) E. FRIEDRICH
09 Assoc V Prov/Dir Info Mgmt/Analysis .... Ms. Kristi D. FISHER
88 Associate Vice Provost .... Dr. R. Michael KERKER
88 Associate Vice President .... Ms. Renee L. WALLACE
30 Associate Vice Pres Development .... Mr. John H. MCCALL
30 Sr Associate Vice Pres Development .... Mr. David S. ONION
19 Assoc VP Campus Safety/Security .... Dr. Gerald R. HARKINS
18 Sr Assoc VP Facilities Management .... Dr. Steven A. KRAAL
15 Associate Vice Pres Human Resources .... Mr. Julien C. CARTER
22 Assoc VP Inst Equity/Workforce Div .... Ms. Linda H. MILLSTONE
38 Assoc VP Univ Health/Counsel Svcs .... Ms. Jeanne D. CARPENTER
46 Assoc VP Rsrch/Dir Spnsrd Projects .... Dr. Susan W. SEDWICK
06 Assoc VP Registrar .... Mr. Vincent (Shelby) STANFIELD
29 Assoc VP Off Rel Mgmt/Univ Events .... Ms. Susan W. CLAGETT
37 Director Student Financial Svcs .... Dr. Thomas G. MELECKI
35 Dean of Students/Sr Assoc Vice Pres .... Dr. Soncia R. REAGINS-LILLY
39 Director Housing & Food Service .... Dr. Floyd B. HOELTING
41 Men's Athletics Director .... Mr. DeLoss DODDS
41 Women's Athletics Director .... Ms. Christine A. PLONSKY
29 CEO/Exec Director Ex-Students Assn .... Ms. Leslie CEDAR
19 Chief University Police .... Mr. Robert E. DAHLSTROM
48 Dean of Architecture .... Dr. Frederick R. STEINER
50 Dean McCombs School of Business .... Dr. Thomas W. GILLIGAN
60 Dean of Communication .... Dr. Roderick P. HART
53 Dean of Education .... Dr. Manuel J. JUSTIZ
54 Dean of Engineering .... Dr. Gregory L. FENVES
57 Dean of Fine Arts .... Dr. Douglas J. DEMPSTER
62 Dean School of Information .... Dr. Andrew P. DILLON
65 Dean Jackson School of Geosciences .... Dr. Sharon MOSHER
61 Dean School of Law .... Mr. Lawrence SAGER
49 Dean of Liberal Arts .... Dr. Randy L. DIEHL
81 Dean of Natural Sciences .... Dr. Mary Ann RANKIN
66 Dean of Nursing .... Dr. Alexa M. STUIFBERGEN
67 Dean of Pharmacy .... Dr. M. Lynn CRISMON
80 Dean LBJ School Public Affs .... Mr. Robert L. HUTCHINGS
70 Dean Social Work .... Dr. Barbara W. WHITE
97 Dean of Undergraduate Studies .... Dr. Paul B. WOODRUFF
51 Dean Continuing/Innovat Education .... Dr. Judy C. ASHCROFT
88 Director Internal Audits .... Mr. Michael W. VANDERVORT
18 Director Facilities Services .... Mr. Michael A. MILLER
88 Executive Director Texas Union .... Mr. W. Andrew (Andy) SMITH
27 Interim Dir Univ of Texas Press .... Mr. David S. HAMRICK
88 Assoc Athl Dir/Dir Spec Events Ctr .... Mr. John M. GRAHAM
96 Assistant VP/Dir of Procurement .... Mr. Jerry A. FULLER

*The University of Texas at Brownsville (C)

80 Fort Brown, Brownsville TX 78520-4993

County: Cameron FICE Identification: 030646
Unit ID: 227377
Telephone: (956) 882-8200 Carnegie Class: Master's M
FAX Number: (956) 548-0020 Calendar System: Semester
URL: www.utb.edu
Established: 1973 Annual Undergrad Tuition & Fees (In-State): $4,872
Enrollment: 17,151 Coed
Affiliation or Control: State IRS Status: 501(c)3
Highest Offering: Doctorate
Program: Liberal Arts And General
Accreditation: SC, ADNUR, CACREP, CS, DMS, EMT, ENG, MLTAD, MUS, NUR, POLYT, RAD

02 President .... Dr. Juliet V. GARCIA
05 Provost .... Dr. Alan ARTIBISE
10 Vice President of Business Affairs .... Ms. Rosemary MARTINEZ
32 Vice President Student Affairs .... Dr. Hilda SILVA
13 Vice Pres Information Tech/CIO .... Ms. Clair GOLDSMITH
26 Vice Pres Economic Dev/Cmty Svcs .... Dr. Irvine DOWNING
30 Vice Pres Institutional Advancement .... Dr. Ruth A. RAGLAND
20 Vice President Academic Affairs .... Dr. Charles DAMERON
88 Sp Ast to Prov Partnership Affairs .... Dr. Wayne MOORE
84 Assoc Vice Pres Enrollment Mgmt .... Mr. Rene VILLARREAL
04 Exec Assistant to the President .... Dr. Marilyn J. WOODS
35 Dean of Students .... Dr. Mari FUENTES-MARTIN
97 Dean Col Applied Tech/General Stds .... Dr. Peter GAWENDA
58 Dean Graduate Studies .... Dr. Charles LACKEY
50 Dean School of Business .... Dr. Rafael OTERO
76 Dean School of Health Sciences .... Dr. Eldon NELSON
81 Dean College Science/Math/Tech .... Dr. Mikhail BOUNIAEV
53 Dean School of Education .... Dr. Miguel ESCOTET
49 Dean College Liberal Arts .... Mr. Daniel HEIMMERMANN
103 Dean Workforce Trng/Cont Education .... Mr. Jim HOLT
06 Registrar .... Mr. Albert BARREDA
07 Director of Admissions .... Ms. Rene VILLARREAL
09 Director of Institutional Research .... Ms. Blanca TREVINO BAUER
18 Director Physical Plant .... Mr. Abraham HERNANDEZ
37 Director Student Financial Aid .... Ms. Mari F. CHAPA
38 Director of Student Success .... Ms. Beatriz BECERRA-BARCKHOLTZ
15 Director Human Resources .... Mr. Rene CORONADO
21 Director Business Office .... Ms. Yolanda DE LA RIVA
96 Director of Purchasing .... Mr. William M. DODD
36 Director Program Student Placement .... Mr. Juan Andres RODRIGUEZ
29 Coordinator of Alumni Relations .... Ms. Veronica GARCIA

† In partnership with Texas Southmost College. Grants a Doctorate degree in cooperation with the University of Houston.

*The University of Texas at Dallas (D)

800 West Campbell Road, Richardson TX 75080

County: Collin FICE Identification: 009741
Unit ID: 228787
Telephone: (972) 883-2111 Carnegie Class: RU/H
FAX Number: (972) 883-2237 Calendar System: Semester
URL: www.utdallas.edu
Established: 1969 Annual Undergrad Tuition & Fees (In-State): $11,168
Enrollment: 17,128 Coed
Affiliation or Control: State IRS Status: 501(c)3
Highest Offering: Doctorate
Program: Liberal Arts And General; Professional
Accreditation: SC, AUD, BUS, BUSA, CS, ENG, IPSY, SP, SPAA

02 President .... Dr. David E. DANIEL
03 Provost/Exec VP Academic Affairs .... Dr. B. Hobson WILDENTHAL
10 Vice President for Business Affairs .... Dr. Calvin D. JAMISON
32 Vice President Student Affairs .... Dr. Darrelene RACHAVONG
30 VP Development/Alumni Relations .... Dr. Aaron CONLEY
46 VP Research/Economic Development .... Dr. Bruce GNADE
20 Vice Provost .... Dr. John WIORKOWSKI
26 Vice President for Communications .... Ms. Susan ROGERS
13 Vice President/Chief Info Officer .... Dr. James B. GARY
28 Vice President of Diversity .... Dr. Magaly SPECTOR
21 Asst Dir Budget/Resource Plng .... Mr. David K. GAARDER
84 Vice Provost Enrollment Mgmt .... Mr. Curt ELEY
21 Assoc VP Finance & Controller .... Ms. Wanda MIZUTOWICZ
09 Exec Director Strategic Planning .... Dr. Lawrence J. REDLINGER
35 Dean of Students .... Dr. Gene FITCH
58 Dean Graduate Studies .... Dr. Austin J. CUNNINGHAM
53 Dean Undergraduate Education .... Dr. Sheila AMIN GUTIERREZ DE PINERES
79 Dean School Arts & Humanities .... Dr. Dennis KRATZ
50 Dean School of Management .... Dr. Hasan PIRKUL
81 Dean Sch of Natural Science/Math .... Dr. Myron B. SALAMON
83 Dean School of Econ/Pol/Policy Sci .... Dr. James W. MARQUART
76 Dean Sch Behavioral/Brain Science .... Dr. Bert S. MOORE
97 Dean School General Studies .... Dr. George W. FAIR
54 Dean EJ Sch of Engr/Computer Sci .... Dr. Mark W. SPONG
08 Director of Libraries .... Dr. Ellen SAFLEY
37 Asst Provost/Acad Records .... Dr. Karen JARRELL
83 Director Bruton Center .... Vacant
12 Exec Director of Callier Center .... Dr. Thomas F. CAMPBELL
25 Assoc VP Research Administration .... Mr. Rafael MARTIN
18 Assoc VP Facilities Management .... Mr. Richard DEMPSEY
16 Asst VP Human Resource Management .... Mr. Larry L. WILSON
96 Asst VP Procurement Management .... Mr. Peter BOND
91 Asst VP Information Resources .... Dr. Sue TAYLOR
19 Chief of Police .... Mr. Larry ZACHARIAS
36 Director Career Services .... Mr. Michael DOTY
38 Director Student Counseling .... Mr. James P. CANNICI
88 Director of Audit and Compliance .... Ms. Toni MESSER
88 Director of Network/Telecomm .... Vacant
88 Director Teacher Education .... Dr. Scherry F. JOHNSON
41 Athletics Director .... Mr. Chris GAGE
78 Director Co-operative Education .... Mr. Michael J. CHOATE
90 Director Tech Customer Services .... Mr. Donald L. DAVIS
29 Director of Alumni Relations .... Ms. Erin DOUGHERTY

*University of Texas at El Paso (E)

500 W University Avenue, El Paso TX 79968-8900

County: El Paso FICE Identification: 003661
Unit ID: 228796
Telephone: (915) 747-5000 Carnegie Class: RU/H
FAX Number: (915) 747-5111 Calendar System: Semester
URL: www.utep.edu
Established: 1914 Annual Undergrad Tuition & Fees (In-State): $34,074
Enrollment: 22,106 Coed
Affiliation or Control: State IRS Status: 501(c)3
Highest Offering: Doctorate
Program: Liberal Arts And General; Teacher Preparatory; Professional
Accreditation: SC, BUS, BUSA, CORE, CS, ENG, MT, MUS, NURSE, OT, PTA, SP, SPAA, SW

02 President .... Dr. Diana S. NATALICIO
03 Sr Executive Vice President .... Dr. Howard DAUDISTEL
03 Executive Vice President .... Mr. Ricardo ADAUTO, III
04 Assistant to the President .... Ms. Estrella ESCOBAR
05 Provost/Vice Pres Academic Affairs .... Dr. Junius GONZALES
10 Vice President for Business Affairs .... Ms. Cindy VILLA
32 Vice President for Student Affairs .... Dr. Richard PADILLA
46 Vice President for Research .... Dr. Roberto OSEGUEDA
09 Vice Pres Info Resources & Planning .... Dr. Steve RITER
58 Acting Dean of Graduate School .... Dr. Ben FLORES
50 Dean of Business Administration .... Dr. Robert NACHTMANN
53 Dean of Education .... Dr. Josefina V. TINAJERO
54 Dean of Engineering .... Dr. Richard T. SCHOEPHOERSTER
49 Dean of Liberal Arts .... Dr. Patricia WITHERSPOON
66 Dean of Health Sciences .... Dr. Kathleen A. CURTIS
81 Dean of Science .... Dr. Anny MORROBEL-SOSA
66 Dean of School of Nursing .... Dr. Elias PROVENCIO-VASQUEZ
35 Associate VP/Dean of Students .... Dr. Gary EDENS
18 Assoc VP Business Affs/Facilities .... Mr. Greg L. MCNICOL
08 Assoc Vice President/Library .... Mr. Robert L. STAKES
26 Asst Vice Pres University Relations .... Mr. Beto LOPEZ
27 Assoc VP University Communication .... Mr. Chester JACINTO
22 Asst Vice Pres EO/AA Dept .... Ms. Sandy VASQUEZ
29 Asst VP Development/Alumni Rels .... Dr. Richard DANIEL
46 Assoc Provost for Resource Mgmt .... Ms. Elizabeth FLORES
84 Assoc Provost Enrollment Services .... Dr. Craig E. WESTMAN

06 Registrar .... Mr. Miguel SIFUENTES
15 Director of Human Resources Svcs .... Mr. Andrew PENA
19 Chief Campus Police .... Mr. Clifton WALSH
37 Interim Dir of Student Fin Aid .... Mr. Roy WILLIAMS
23 Interim CoDir of Student Health Ctr ..... Ms. Valerie FARRINGTON
36 Director of Career Services .... Mr. George BARTON
35 Asst VP Student Affairs .. Ms. Catherine M. MCCORRY-ANDALIS
46 Assoc VP Inst Eval/Rsrch & Planning .... Dr. Roy MATHEW
39 Director of Housing Services .... Mr. Charlie E. GIBBENS
40 Director of University Bookstore .... Mr. Fernando PADULA
41 Athletics Director .... Mr. Robert W. STULL
38 Director Counseling Services .... Ms. Sherri I. TERRELL
96 Dir Purchasing/General Services .... Ms. Diane N. DEHOYOS
07 Exec Dir Admissions/Recruitment .... Ms. Luisa M. HAVENS

*University of Texas - Pan American (A)

1201 W University Drive, Edinburg TX 78539-2970
County: Hidalgo FICE Identification: 003599
Unit ID: 227368
Telephone: (956) 665-2011 Carnegie Class: Master's L
FAX Number: (956) 665-2150 Calendar System: Semester
URL: www.utpa.edu
Established: 1927 Annual Undergrad Tuition & Fees (In-State): $7,212
Enrollment: 18,744 Coed
Affiliation or Control: State IRS Status: 501(c)3
Highest Offering: Doctorate
Program: Liberal Arts And General; Teacher Preparatory; Professional
Accreditation: SC, ARCPA, BUS, CORE, CS, DIETC, ENG, MT, MUS, NURSE, OT, SP, SW, THEA

02 President .... Dr. Robert S. NELSEN
04 Chief of Staff .... Ms. Lisa PRIETO
05 Provost/VP Academic Affairs .... Dr. Havidan RODRIGUEZ
10 Vice President for Business Affairs .... Mr. Martin BAYLOR
30 VP for University Advancement .... Ms. Janice ODOM
84 Vice President for Student Affairs .... Dr. Martha CANTU
13 CIO for Information Technology .... Dr. Jeffrey GRAHAM
20 Sr Vice Prov for Undergraduate Stds . Dr. Ana Maria RODRIGUEZ
21 Assoc Vice Pres BA & Comptroller .... Mr. Esequiel GRANADO
31 Exec Dir Ofc Ctr Oper/Community Svc .... Ms. Jessica SALINAS
08 Dean of the University Library .... Dr. Farzaneh RAZZAGHI
06 Director Records & Registration .... Vacant
14 Director of Computer Center .... Ms. Leota V. HULL
15 Director of Human Resources .... Ms. Francis RIOS
19 Chief University Police .... Mr. Roger STEARNS
26 Director University Relations .... Ms. Sandra Q. GUZMAN
36 Director Career Placement Services ...... Ms. Lourdes SERVANTES
37 Director Student Financial Services .... Mrs. Elaine RIVERA
29 Director Alumni Rels/Special Events .... Mrs. Debby GRANT
41 Director Intercollegiate Athletics .... Mr. Christopher KING
09 Exec Dir Inst Rsrch Effectiveness .... Dr. Susan GRIFFITH
53 Dean College of Education .... Dr. Salvador H. OCHOA
35 Dean of Students .... Dr. Calvin PHILLIPS
50 Dean Col Business Admin .... Dr. Teofilo OZUNA
38 Director of Couseling/Advisement .... Ms. Lise BLANKENSHIP
81 Dean College of Science and Math .... Dr. John M. TRANT
81 Dean College Science/Engineering .... Dr. David ALLEN
84 Director of Recruitment .... Ms. Debbie GILCHRIST
76 Dean Col Health Sci/Human Svcs .... Dr. Bruce REED
49 Dean College Arts & Humanities .... Dr. Dahlia GUERRA
83 Dean Social/Behavioral Sciences .... Dr. Walter DIAZ
18 Dir for Facilities & Physical Plant .... Mr. Oscar VILLARREAL
07 Assoc VP for Enrollment Services .... Dr. Maggie HINOJOSA
96 Director Materials Management .... Ms. Norma DRYER
25 Supervisor for Grants & Contracts .... Ms. Paula ZEPEDA
28 Director of Diversity .... Ms. Esmeralda GUERRA

*University of Texas at San Antonio (B)

One UTSA Circle, San Antonio TX 78249-0169
County: Bexar FICE Identification: 010115
Unit ID: 229027
Telephone: (210) 458-4011 Carnegie Class: RU/H
FAX Number: (210) 458-4187 Calendar System: Semester
URL: www.utsa.edu
Established: 1969 Annual Undergrad Tuition & Fees (In-State): $8,800
Enrollment: 30,258 Coed
Affiliation or Control: State IRS Status: 501(c)3
Highest Offering: Doctorate
Program: Liberal Arts And General; Teacher Preparatory; Professional
Accreditation: SC, ART, BUS, BUSA, CACREP, CIDA, ENG, MUS, SPAA, SW

02 President .... Dr. Ricardo ROMO
05 Provost/Vice Pres Academic Affairs .... Dr. John FREDERICK
10 Vice President for Business Affairs .... Mr. Kerry L. KENNEDY
32 Vice President Student Affairs .... Dr. Gage E. PAINE
31 Vice President Community Services .... Dr. Jude VALDEZ
30 Vice Pres Univ Advancement .... Ms. Marjie M. FRENCH
46 Vice President for Research .... Dr. Robert W. GRACY
11 Assoc Vice Pres for Administration .... Ms. Pamela BACON
20 Executive Vice Provost .... Mr. Julius M. GRIBOU
09 V Prov Acad Compliance/Inst Effect .... Dr. Sandra T. WELCH
12 Vice Provost for Downtown Campus .... Dr. Jesse T. ZAPATA
14 Vice Provost Information Officer .... Mr. Kenneth PIERCE
20 V Prov Acad Supt/Dean UGrad Studies .... Dr. Lawrence R. WILLIAMS
21 Assoc Vice Pres Financial Affairs .... Ms. Janet PARKER
15 Assoc VP Human Resources/ Developmt .... Ms. Barbara J. BARAN-CENTENO
27 Assoc VP University Communications .... Mr. David L. GABLER
37 Asst VP Student Fin Aid/Enroll Svcs .... Ms. Lisa G. BLAZER
07 Asst Vice President Admissions .... Mr. George E. NORTON
06 Asst Vice President & Registrar .... Dr. Joe R. DECRISTOFORO
35 Asst VP Student Svcs/Admin/Plng .... Mr. Samuel M. GONZALES
35 Assoc Vice Pres/Dean of Students .... Mr. Kevin PRICE
18 Assoc Vice President for Facilities .... Mr. Dave RIKER
09 Assoc V Prov Institutional Research .... Dr. Steven WILKERSON
106 Asst V Prov Dist Lrng Online/Enhanc .... Dr. Robert ROBINSON
88 Int Exec Dir Inst of Tex Cultures .... Dr. John DAVIS
08 Dean of Libraries .... Ms. Krisellen MALONEY
92 Dean Honors College .... Dr. Richard A. DIEM
58 Dean Graduate School .... Dr. Dorothy A. FLANNAGAN
50 Dean College of Business .... Dr. Lynda Y. DE LA VINA
57 Dean College of Liberal & Fine Arts .... Dr. Daniel J. GELO
54 Dean College of Engineering .... Dr. C. Mauli AGRAWAL
83 Dean College of Sciences .... Dr. George PERRY
48 Dean School of Architecture .... Prof. John MURPHY
53 Dean College Educ/Human Development .... Dr. Betty MERCHANT
80 Dean College of Public Policy .... Dr. Rogelio SAENZ
35 Associate Dean of Students .... Mr. John KAULFUS
19 Asst Chief of Police .... Mr. Daniel PENA
88 Director Studnt Disability Services .... Dr. Dianne P. HENGST
38 Director Counseling Services .... Dr. Thomas BAEZ
36 Director of Career Services .... Ms. Audrey MAGNUSON
41 Director Intercol Athletics .... Ms. Lynn HICKEY
25 Director Grants & Contracts .... Ms. Carol A. HOLLINGSWORTH
46 Director Rrsch Adv & Enhance .... Mr. Noe V. SALDANA
23 Director Student Health Services .... Dr. Beth WICHMAN
29 ASCT VP Alumni Program Mkt .... Mr. James C. MICKEY
43 Chief Legal Officer .... Ms. Elizabeth T. MITCHELL
26 Chief Communications Officer .... Mr. David L. GABLER
96 Director Purchasing & Dist Svcs .... Mr. Robert DICKENS
86 Director External Affairs .... Mr. Albert A. CARRISALEZ
85 Director International Programs .... Mr. Charles F. CRANE
22 Sr Equal Opportunity Investigator .... Mr. Leonard FLAUM, JR.

*University of Texas at Tyler (C)

3900 University Boulevard, Tyler TX 75799-6699
County: Smith FICE Identification: 011163
Unit ID: 228802
Telephone: (903) 566-7000 Carnegie Class: Master's L
FAX Number: (903) 566-7068 Calendar System: Semester
URL: www.uttyler.edu
Established: 1971 Annual Undergrad Tuition & Fees (In-State): $6,592
Enrollment: 6,476 Coed
Affiliation or Control: State IRS Status: 501(c)3
Highest Offering: Doctorate
Program: Liberal Arts And General; Teacher Preparatory; Professional
Accreditation: SC, BUS, ENG, NAIT, NURSE, TEAC

02 President .... Dr. Rodney H. MABRY
05 Interim Provost/VP Academic Affairs .... Dr. Donna DICKERSON
10 Vice President of Business Affairs .... Vacant
30 Vice President Univ Advancement .... Mr. Jerre IVERSEN
41 Vice Pres Auxilary Svcs & Athletics .... Dr. Howard PATTERSON
13 Vice President & CIO IT .... Dr. Sherri WHATLEY
20 Vice Provost AA/Grad Studies .... Dr. Donna DICKERSON
20 Associate Provost UG Programs .... Vacant
46 Assoc Vice President for Research .... Vacant
21 Associate VP for Business Affairs .... Ms. Sheryl DENNIS
11 Associate VP for Adminstration .... Mr. Jesse ACOSTA
15 Assoc VP/Director Human Resources .... Mr. Joe VORSAS
84 Interim Asst VP Enroll Mgmt & Mktg .... Ms. Candice LINDSEY
88 Asst Vice Pres for Assessment/IE .... Dr. Lou Ann BERMAN
32 Asst VP Student Affs/Dean Students .... Ms. Ona TOLLIVER
49 Dean College of Arts & Sciences .... Dr. Martin SLANN
50 Dean College Business & Technology .... Dr. Harold DOTY
53 Dean College Education & Psychology .... Dr. William GEIGER
54 Dean College Engineering & Comp Sci .... Dr. James NELSON
66 Dean College Nursing & Health Sci .... Dr. Linda KLOTZ
08 Director of the Library .... Ms. Jeanne PYLE
21 Director of Financial Services .... Ms. Carrie CLAYTON
18 Dir Facility/Plng/Construct/Oper .... Mr. Chip CLARK
29 Coordinator of Alumni Relations .... Vacant
100 Chief of Staff .... Vacant
27 Director Mktg & Communiation .... Ms. Beverley GOLDEN
38 Dir Stdnt Svc/Stdnt Couns/Test Ctr .... Ms. Ida MACDONALD
39 Director of Residence Life .... Mr. David R. HILL
96 Asst Dir Financial Services .... Mrs. Cindy TROYER
06 Registrar .... Ms. Sonja MORALE
09 Director of Institutional Analysis .... Dr. Sherri WHATLEY
19 Chief University Police .... Mr. Mike W. MEDDERS

*The University of Texas Health Science Center at Houston (UTHealth) (D)

PO Box 20036, Houston TX 77225-0036
County: Harris FICE Identification: 004951
Unit ID: 229300
Telephone: (713) 500-4472 Carnegie Class: Spec/Med
FAX Number: (713) 500-3026 Calendar System: Semester
URL: www.uthouston.edu
Established: 1972 Annual Undergrad Tuition & Fees (In-State): $7,475
Enrollment: 2,734 Coed
Affiliation or Control: State IRS Status: 501(c)3
Highest Offering: Doctorate
Program: Professional
Accreditation: SC, ANEST, DENT, DH, DIETI, ENGR, MED, NURSE, PH

02 Interim President .... Dr. Giuseppe N. COLASURDO
03 CFO/COO & Exec VP for Admin .... Mr. T. Kevin DILLON
45 Senior VP for Strategic Planning .... Dr. Osama I. MIKHAIL
05 Provost & Exec VP Academic Affs .... Vacant
46 Vice Dn Rsrch/Int Dir Molecular Med .... Dr. John HANCOCK
26 Vice Pres Institutional Advancement .... Vacant
15 VP/Chief Human Resources Officer .... Mr. Eric FERNETTE
43 VP/Chief Legal & Compliance Officer .... Ms. Arlene D. STALLER
86 VP/Chief Govt Relations Officer .... Ms. Sabrina MIDKIFF
104 VP International Programs .... Dr. Bryant BOUTWELL
31 VP Auxiliary Enterprises .... Mr. Charles A. FIGARI
13 VP/Chief Information Officer .... Mr. Richard L. MILLER
18 VP Facilities Planning & Engr .... Mr. Richard L. MCDERMOTT
10 Sr VP Finance & Budget .... Mr. Michael TRAMONTE
88 VP Finance and Legislative Affairs .... Ms. Laura D. SMITH
30 Asst VP Fundraising & Advancemnt .... Ms. Betsy C. FRANTZ
90 Asst VP Academic Technology .... Dr. William A. WEEMS
91 Director Administrative Technology .... Vacant
21 Director Internal Audit .... Ms. Lois K. PIERSON
08 Executive Director Library .... Vacant
06 Registrar .... Mr. Robert JENKINS
19 Chief of Police .... Mr. William ADCOX
41 Director Recreation/Intramural Pgms .... Ms. Pauline M. HABETZ
85 Director International Affairs ... Ms. Maria C. AREVALO-SANCHEZ
39 Director University Housing .... Mr. Billy C. HINTON
27 Dir Univ Communications/Pubs .... Ms. Karen K. KAPLAN
88 Director of Media Relations .... Ms. Meredith RAINE
37 Director Student Financial Svcs .... Ms. Wanda K. WILLIAMS
88 Director Employee Assistance Pgm ...... Mr. Thomas MASCHHOFF
28 Chief Academic Diversity Officer .... Dr. Ronald JOHNSON
52 Dean School of Dentistry .... Dr. John A. VALENZA
63 Dean Medical School .... Dr. Giuseppe N. COLASURDO
17 Exec Vice Dean Clinical Affairs .... Dr. Brent KING
66 Dean School of Nursing .... Dr. Patricia L. STARCK
69 Dean School of Public Health .... Dr. Roberta B. NESS
88 Dean School of Biomedical Inform .... Dr. Jack W. SMITH
58 Dean Grad Sch Biomed Science .... Dr. George M. STANCEL
25 Exec Director Sponsored Projects .... Ms. Johnna K. KINCAID
23 Executive Director Clinical-MS .... Dr. Thomas A. MACKEY
14 Director Data Center Operations .... Mr. Kevin B. GRANHOLD
22 EEO Advisor .... Mr. John RAYBURN
24 Director Educational Media-SPH .... Mr. Henry Y. FUNG
24 Director Educational & Tech-DB .... Dr. David TAYLOR
24 Director Ctr Education & Info-SON .... Ms. Linda L. CRAYS
72 Director Biomedical Info Tech-MS .... Dr. Stephen J. FATH
07 Associate Dean Admissions-MS .... Dr. Margaret MCNEESE
29 Assoc Dean Student & Alumni-SOD .... Dr. Hugh P. PIERPONT
07 Asst Dean Admissions-GSBS .... Dr. Victoria P. KNUTSON
07 Director of Admissions-SHIS .... Ms. Deborah A. TODD
35 Director Student Affairs-SON .... Ms. Laurie G. RUTHERFORD
35 Director of Student Affairs-SPH .... Dr. Mary A. SMITH

*University of Texas Health Science Center at San Antonio (E)

7703 Floyd Curl Drive, San Antonio TX 78229-3900
County: Bexar FICE Identification: 003659
Unit ID: 228644
Telephone: (210) 567-7000 Carnegie Class: Spec/Med
FAX Number: (210) 567-2025 Calendar System: Other
URL: www.uthscsa.edu
Established: 1959 Annual Undergrad Tuition & Fees (In-State): $7,490
Enrollment: 3,310 Coed
Affiliation or Control: State IRS Status: 501(c)3
Highest Offering: Doctorate
Program: Professional
Accreditation: SC, ARCPA, BBT, DENT, DH, EMT, HT, IPSY, MED, MT, NURSE, OT, PTA, RADDOS

02 President .... Dr. William L. HENRICH
03 Sr Exec Vice President & COO .... Mr. Michael E. BLACK
11 Exec VP for Facility Planning/Admin .... Mr. James D. KAZEN
10 Vice President & CFO .... Ms. Andrea M. MARKS
05 Vice Pres Academic Administration .... Dr. Theresa Y. CHIANG
13 Vice Pres & Chief Information Ofcr .... Mr. A. Jerome YORK
46 Vice President for Research .... Dr. Brian A. HERMAN
86 VP for Governmental Relations .... Mr. Armando DIAZ
30 Vice President for Development .... Ms. Deborah H. MORRILL
15 Vice Pres of Human Resources .... Mr. J. Michael TESH
100 Chief of Staff & Communications .... Ms. Mary E. DELAY
21 Asst Vice Pres for Business Affairs .... Mr. Gerard E. LONG
25 Asst VP Research/Sponsored Programs .. Ms. Jane A. YOUNGERS
18 Asst VP for Strategic Initiatives .... Mr. Darrell MAATSCH
63 Dean School of Medicine .... Dr. Francisco GONZALEZ-SCARANO
52 Dean Dental School .... Dr. Kenneth L. KALKWARF
58 Dean Graduate Biomed Science .... Dr. David WEISS
76 Int Dean School Health Professions .... Dr. Juanita WALLACE
66 Dean School of Nursing .... Dr. Eileen T. BRESLIN
32 Exec Dir for Student Services .... Dr. Theresa Y. CHIANG
06 Registrar .... Ms. Blanca GUERRA
08 Exec Director of Libraries .... Ms. Rajia C. TOBIA
19 Chief of Police .... Mr. Michael PARKS
22 Executive Director of EEO/AA Office .... Dr. Bonnie L. BLANKMEYER
37 Director of Financial Aid .... Mr. Robert T. LAWSON, JR.
38 Director of Counseling .... Dr. Kozue SHIBAZAKI
43 Senior Legal Officer .... Mr. Jack C. PARK
96 Director of Purchasing .... Ms. Vikki F. ROSS

*The University of Texas M.D. Anderson Cancer Center (A)

1515 Holcombe Boulevard, Houston TX 77030-4000
County: Harris FICE Identification: 025554
Unit ID: 416801
Telephone: (713) 792-6161 Carnegie Class: Spec/Health
FAX Number: N/A Calendar System: Semester
URL: www.mdanderson.org
Established: 1941 Annual Undergrad Tuition & Fees (In-District): N/A
Enrollment: 248 Coed
Affiliation or Control: State/Local IRS Status: 501(c)3
Highest Offering: Doctorate
Program: Professional
Accreditation: SC, CYTO, DENT, DMOLS, HT, MT, RAD, RADDOS, RTT

02 President .... Dr. John MENDELSOHN
05 Provost/Executive Vice President .... Dr. Raymond DUBOIS
10 Vice President Business Affairs .... Dr. Christopher FORREST
58 Asst Vice Pres Grad Stds/Research .... Dr. Karen SMITH
13 Asst Vice Pres/Dir Info Resources .... Mr. J. Keith YARBROUGH
49 Dean College of Arts & Science .... Dr. Mylan REDFERN
50 Dean School of Business .... Mr. Jack LADD
53 Dean School of Education .... Dr. Robert RISTOW
30 Director Institutional Advancement .... Vacant
07 Director Admissions .... Mr. Scott SMILEY
06 Registrar .... Mr. Hector GOVEA
37 Director Financial Aid .... Mr. Joe SANDERS
08 Director of Library Services .... Ms. Charlene SHULTS
15 Director Human Resources .... Ms. Linda ISHAM
51 Director Continuing Education .... Mr. Rey LASCANO
26 Interim Public Information Officer .... Ms. Iris FOSTER
41 Director Athletics .... Dr. Steve AICINENA
19 Chief of Police .... Chief Tom HAIN
18 Chief Facilities/Physical Plant .... Mr. Michael RULAND
29 Director Alumni Relations .... Mr. Stacy FUQUA
35 Director Student Affairs .... Dr. Susan LARA
36 Dir Student Placement/Counseling .... Mr. Tony LOVE
96 Interim Director of Purchasing .... Ms. Ynez ALDERSON

*The University of Texas Medical Branch (B)

301 University Boulevard, Galveston TX 77555-0100
County: Galveston FICE Identification: 004952
Unit ID: 228653
Telephone: (409) 772-1011 Carnegie Class: Spec/Med
FAX Number: N/A Calendar System: Semester
URL: www.utmb.edu
Established: 1891 Annual Undergrad Tuition & Fees (In-State): $6,712
Enrollment: 2,660 Coed
Affiliation or Control: State IRS Status: 170(c)1
Highest Offering: Doctorate
Program: Professional
Accreditation: SC, ARCPA, BBT, DENT, MED, MT, NURSE, OT, PH, PTA

02 President .... Dr. David L. CALLENDER
04 Exec Asst to the President .... Ms. Jandee ALARID
05 Exec VP/Prov & Dean Sch of Medicine .... Dr. Garland D. ANDERSON
17 Exec VP & CEO Health System .. Ms. Donna K. SOLLENBERGER
10 Exec VP & Chief Business/Fin Ofcr .... Mr. William R. ELGER
86 Sr VP Health Policy & Legis Affairs .... Dr. Ben G. RAIMER
88 VP & Chief Physician .... Dr. Rex M. MCCALLUM
17 Interim Chief Medical Officer .... Dr. Steve Q. QUACH
20 VP Education & Dean Sch of Nursing .... Dr. Pamela G. WATSON
76 VP & Dean Sch of Health Professions .... Dr. Elizabeth J. PROTAS
58 VP & Dean Grad Sch of Biomed Sci .... Dr. Cary W. COOPER
16 VP HR & Employee Services .... Dr. Ronald B. MCKINLEY
13 VP Information Services & CIO .... Mr. Ralph E. FARR
18 VP Facilities & Campus Services .... Mr. Michael B. SHRINER
21 VP Finance Academic Enterprise .... Mr. Cameron W. SLOCUM
21 VP Finance Clinical Enterprise .... Mr. David M. CONNAUGHTON
45 VP for Strategic Mgmt .... Dr. Rebecca SAAVEDRA
43 VP & Chief Legal Officer .... Ms. Carolee KING
26 VP Public Affairs .... Ms. Christine F. COMER
12 Dean Austin Programs .... Dr. T. S. SHOMAKER
35 Sr Assoc Dean Grad Sch Biomed Sci .... Dr. Dorian H. COPPENHAVER
35 Assoc Dean School of Medicine .... Dr. Lauree THOMAS
07 Assoc Dean Admiss School of Nursing .... Dr. Tina CUELLAR
35 Assoc Dean Health Professions .... Mr. Henry CAVAZOS
46 Assoc Dean Research Admin .... Mr. William G. NEW
08 Assoc VP Academic Res/Dir Library .... Mr. Brett A. KIRKPATRICK
09 Assoc VP Inst Effectiveness .... Dr. John C. MCKEE
26 Assoc VP Marketing .... Vacant
21 Assoc VP Fin Plng & Perf Mgmt .... Mr. Matthew FURLONG
21 Assoc VP Finance .... Ms. Celia BAILEY-OCHOA
88 Assoc VP Audit Services .... Ms. Kimberly HAGARA
30 Assoc VP Chief Develop Officer .... Ms. Betsy B. CLARDY
32 Assoc VP for Univ Student Services .... Mr. James MARTIN
29 Asst VP Alumni Relations .... Ms. Dixie MULLINS
28 Interim Inst Compliance Officer .... Ms. Carolee KING
84 Dir Enrollment Svcs/Univ Registrar .... Mr. Shawn DEVEAU
19 Chief of University Police .... Mr. Thomas ENGELLS
22 Dir Equal Opportunity/Diversity .... Mr. Joe A. GALVAN
23 Director Student Wellness .... Ms. Cynthia A. DESANTO
96 Int ED Supply Chain/Chf Purchasing .... Mr. Kyle BARTON
39 Dir Aux Enterprises-Housing/Bkstore .... Mr. Bruno P. CRISTELLI
38 Director Student Counseling .... Ms. Cynthia DESANTOS

*University of Texas of the Permian Basin (C)

4901 E University Boulevard, Odessa TX 79762-8122
County: Ector FICE Identification: 009930
Unit ID: 229018
Telephone: (432) 552-2020 Carnegie Class: Master's M
FAX Number: (432) 552-2374 Calendar System: Semester
URL: www.utpb.edu
Established: 1969 Annual Undergrad Tuition & Fees (In-State): $6,300
Enrollment: 4,063 Coed
Affiliation or Control: State IRS Status: 501(c)3
Highest Offering: Master's
Program: Liberal Arts And General; Teacher Preparatory; Professional
Accreditation: SC, ART, BUS, SW, TED

02 President .... Dr. W. David WATTS
04 Assistant to the President .... Ms. Carla P. NELSON
05 Provost/Vice Pres Academic Affairs .... Dr. William R. FANNIN
32 Provost & VP Student Services .... Dr. Susan LARA

*University of Texas Southwestern Medical Center at Dallas (D)

5323 Harry Hines Boulevard, Dallas TX 75390-9002
County: Dallas FICE Identification: 010019
Unit ID: 228635
Telephone: (214) 648-3111 Carnegie Class: Spec/Med
FAX Number: N/A Calendar System: Other
URL: www.utsouthwestern.edu
Established: 1943 Annual Undergrad Tuition & Fees (In-State): $7,980
Enrollment: 2,499 Coed
Affiliation or Control: State IRS Status: 501(c)3
Highest Offering: Doctorate
Program: Professional
Accreditation: SC, ARCPA, BBT, CLPSY, CORE, DIETC, EMT, IPSY, MED, MIL, MT, OPE, PTA, RTT

02 President .... Dr. Daniel K. PODOLSKY
100 Vice President & Chief of Staff .... Dr. Robin M. JACOBY
05 Exec VP Acad Aff/Provost/Dean SMS .... Dr. Gregory FITZ
03 Exec VP Health System Affairs .... Dr. Bruce A. MEYER
10 Exec Vice Pres Business Affairs .... Mr. John A. ROAN
46 Vice Provost/Dean of Basic Research .... Dr. David W. RUSSELL
88 Vice President Medical Affairs .... Dr. Peter J. PLANTES
88 Vice Pres Health System Fin Affairs .... Mr. Bruce M. FAIRBANKS
23 Vice President Clinical Operations .... Dr. John D. RUTHERFORD
88 Vice President University Hospitals .... Dr. Bruce A. MEYER
88 Chief Quality Officer .... Dr. Gary REED
86 Vice Pres Govt Affairs & Policy .... Dr. MaryEllen WEBER
27 Vice Pres Comm Mktg & Public Affs .... Mr. Tim DOKE
31 Vice President External Relations .... Mrs. Cynthia B. BASSEL
16 Vice President Human Resource .... Dr. William M. BEHRENDT
43 Vice President Legal Affairs .... Ms. Leah A. HURLEY
72 Vice Pres Technology Development .... Dr. Dennis K. STONE
30 Vice President Development .... Dr. Randy L. FARMER
102 Vice Pres Community and Corp Rels .... Mr. Ruben E. ESQUIVEL
13 Vice Pres Information Resources .... Mr. Kirk A. KIRKSEY
18 Vice President Facilities Mgmt .... Mr. Kirby L. VAHLE
29 Vice Pres Stdnt/Alumni Affs/Admiss .... Mr. J. W. NORRED
88 Vice President Research Admin .... Ms. Angela WISHON
88 Asst Vice President Practice Plan .... Mr. Iain BURCHELL
88 Asst Vice Pres HS Planning & Data M .... Ms. Marcia SCHNEIDER
96 Asst Vice Pres Materials Mgmt .... Mr. Paul D. BELEW
88 Asst Vice Pres Clinical Operations .... Ms. Stacey CLARK
88 Asst Vice Pres Marketing .... Ms. Dorothea BONDS
21 Asst Vice President Accounting .... Mr. George S. KOKORUDA
08 Asst Vice Pres Library Services .... Mrs. Laurie L. THOMPSON
20 Sr Assoc Dean Academic Admin .... Dr. Charles M. GINSBURG
45 Sr Assoc Dean Strategic Development .... Dr. Dwain L. THIELE
28 Assoc Dean Faculty Diversity & Dev .... Dr. Byron L. CRYER
88 Assoc Dean Global Health .... Dr. Fiemu E. NWARIAKU
51 Assoc Dean Medical Education .... Dr. Susan M. COX
63 Assoc Dean Undergrad Medical Educ .... Dr. Steve CANNON
32 Assoc Dean Student Affairs .... Dr. Angela MIHALIC
32 Assoc Dean Student Affairs .... Dr. James M. WAGNER
93 Assoc Dean Minority Student Affairs .... Dr. Shawna NESBITT
88 Associate Dean .... Dr. Perrie M. ADAMS
58 Dean Grad School Biomedical Science .... Dr. Michael G. ROTH
76 Dean School of Health Professions .... Dr. Raul CAETANO
06 Registrar/Financial Aid .... Mr. Charles L. KETTLEWELL
07 Assoc Director of Admissions .... Ms. Anne P. MCLANE

Vernon College (E)

4400 College Drive, Vernon TX 76384-4092
County: Wilbarger FICE Identification: 010060
Unit ID: 229504
Telephone: (940) 552-6291 Carnegie Class: Assoc/Pub-R-M
FAX Number: (940) 553-3902 Calendar System: Semester
URL: www.vernoncollege.edu
Established: 1970 Annual Undergrad Tuition & Fees (In-District): $1,944
Enrollment: 3,167 Coed
Affiliation or Control: State/Local IRS Status: 501(c)3
Highest Offering: Associate Degree
Program: Occupational; 2-Year Principally Bachelor's Creditable
Accreditation: SC, SURGT

01 President .... Dr. Dusty R. JOHNSTON
04 Admin Secretary to the President .... Ms. Mary KING
05 Dean of Instructional Services .... Dr. Gary Don HARKEY
11 Dean of Administrative Services .... Mr. Garry DAVID
32 Dean of Student Svs/Athletic Dir .... Mr. John B. HARDIN, III
07 Dean Admiss/Registr/Financial Aid .... Mr. Joe HITE
103 Assoc Dean of Workforce Ed & Trng .... Mrs. Shana MUNSON
21 Assoc Dean Administrative Svcs .... Vacant
30 Director of Inst Advancement .... Ms. Michelle ALEXANDER
09 Director of Institutional Research .... Mrs. Betsy HARKEY
37 Director Financial Aid .... Mrs. Melissa J. ELLIOTT
13 Director of Information Technology .... Mr. Jim BINION
08 Director of Library Services .... Ms. Marion GRONA
18 Director Physical Plant .... Mr. John MAHONEY
15 Director of Human Resources .... Mrs. Haven DAVID
39 Director of Housing .... Mr. Tony PEREZ
35 Assoc Dean of Student Services .... Mrs. Kristin HARRIS
06 Assistant Registrar .... Mrs. Sarah DAVENPORT
66 Dir Associate Degree in Nursing .... Ms. Cathy BOLTON
66 Dir Licensed Vocational Nursing .... Mr. Lynn KALSKI
88 Director of Student Relations .... Ms. Brandi BALLARD
35 Director of Student Activities .... Mr. Sjohonton FANNER
19 Director of Campus Police .... Mr. Chris BELL
51 Coordinator Continuing Education .... Mrs. Anne PATTERSON
88 Coordinator of Testing .... Mrs. Sharron SHELTON
56 Coordinator of Distance Learning .... Vacant
24 Media Specialist .... Mr. Gene FROMMELT

Vet Tech Institute of Houston (F)

4669 Southwest Freeway, Suite 100, Houston TX 77027
County: Harris FICE Identification: 021448
Unit ID: 223472
Telephone: (713) 629-8940 Carnegie Class: Not Classified
FAX Number: (713) 629-0059 Calendar System: Semester
URL: www.vettechinstitute.edu/houston
Established: 2007 Annual Undergrad Tuition & Fees: $13,530
Enrollment: 348 Coed
Affiliation or Control: Proprietary IRS Status: Proprietary
Highest Offering: Associate Degree
Program: Occupational
Accreditation: ACICS

01 Director/Chief Academic Officer .... Mr. Elbert HAMILTON, JR.

Victoria College (G)

2200 E Red River, Victoria TX 77901-4494
County: Victoria FICE Identification: 003662
Unit ID: 229540
Telephone: (361) 573-3291 Carnegie Class: Assoc/Pub-R-M
FAX Number: (361) 572-3850 Calendar System: Semester
URL: www.victoriacollege.edu
Established: 1925 Annual Undergrad Tuition & Fees (In-District): $1,920
Enrollment: 4,323 Coed
Affiliation or Control: Local IRS Status: 501(c)3
Highest Offering: Associate Degree
Program: Occupational; 2-Year Principally Bachelor's Creditable
Accreditation: SC, ADNUR, MLTAD, @PTAA

01 President .... Dr. Thomas E. BUTLER
05 Vice President of Instruction .... Dr. Patricia A. VANDERVOORT
10 VP Administrative Svcs .... Mr. Keith BLUNDELL
32 Vice President of Student Services .... Dr. Florinda CORREA
30 VP College Advance/External Affairs .... Ms. Jennifer L. YANCEY
45 Exec Director Planning/Special Proj .... Dr. Larry GARRETT
08 Director of Libraries .... Dr. Joe F. DAHLSTROM
06 Registrar Admissions & Records .... Ms. Michelle KLIMITCHEK
18 Director Physical Plant .... Mr. Robert DUFFIE
37 Director Financial Aid .... Ms. Kim OBSTA
15 Director Human Resources .... Ms. Terri KURTZ
26 Dir Marketing & Communications .... Mr. Darin KAZMIR
38 Director Advising/Counseling .... Ms. Ann BROGGER
96 Director of Purchasing .... Ms. Lydia HUBER
21 Director of Finance .... Ms. Tracey BERGSTROM
35 Student Center/Activities Director .... Ms. Elaine EVERETT-HENSLEY
38 Director of Testing & Assessment .... Ms. Sharon VACLAVIK
13 Director Technology Services .... Mr. Andy FARRIOR
04 Admin Asst to President .... Ms. Debbie RAINS

Virginia College at Austin (H)

6301 E Highway 290, Austin TX 78723-1027
County: Travis Identification: 666074
Unit ID: 441928
Telephone: (512) 371-3500 Carnegie Class: Assoc/PrivFP
FAX Number: (512) 371-3502 Calendar System: Quarter
URL: www.vc.edu
Established: 2002 Annual Undergrad Tuition & Fees: $14,782
Enrollment: 900 Coed
Affiliation or Control: Proprietary IRS Status: Proprietary
Highest Offering: Associate Degree
Program: Occupational
Accreditation: ACICS, MAAB, SURGT

01 Campus President .... Mr. Harvey M. GIBLIN
05 Academic Dean .... Ms. Virginia ESCOBEDO
07 Director of Admissions .... Mr. Jim BRANHAM
36 Director of Career Services .... Ms. Stacie ROYER
37 Director of Financial Planning .... Mr. Steve STRAMLER
06 Registrar .... Mr. Jeremy B. SAPP

† Branch campus of Virginia College, Birmingham, AL.

Wade College Infomart (A)

1950 Stemmons Fwy, Ste 4080, LB 562, Dallas TX 75207
County: Dallas FICE Identification: 010130
Unit ID: 226879
Telephone: (214) 637-3530 Carnegie Class: Assoc/PrivFP
FAX Number: (214) 637-0827 Calendar System: Trimester
URL: www.wadecollege.edu
Established: 1962 Annual Undergrad Tuition & Fees: $11,162
Enrollment: 264 Coed
Affiliation or Control: Proprietary IRS Status: Proprietary
Highest Offering: Baccalaureate
Program: Fine Arts Emphasis
Accreditation: SC

01 President Dr. Harry DAVROS
03 Vice President Mr. John CONTE
05 Director of Academic Affairs Ms. Mitzi MORRIS
11 Director of Institutional Support Ms. Kim PARKER
08 Head Librarian Mrs. Bobbie BAUMGARTEN
36 Director of Career Services Mrs. Valda MACREADY
07 Director of Admissions Ms. Julia ANDALMAN
37 Director Student Financial Aid Ms. Lisa HOOVER

Wayland Baptist University (B)

1900 West Seventh, Plainview TX 79072-6998
County: Hale FICE Identification: 003663
Unit ID: 229780
Telephone: (806) 291-1000 Carnegie Class: Master's L
FAX Number: (806) 291-1960 Calendar System: Semester
URL: www.wbu.edu
Established: 1908 Annual Undergrad Tuition & Fees: $11,320
Enrollment: 6,385 Coed
Affiliation or Control: Southern Baptist IRS Status: 501(c)3
Highest Offering: Master's
Program: 2-Year Principally Bachelor's Creditable; Liberal Arts And General; Teacher Preparatory
Accreditation: SC, MUS, NUR

01 President Dr. Paul W. ARMES
05 Executive Vice President/Provost Dr. Bobby L. HALL
84 Vice Pres Enrollment Management Dr. D. Claude LUSK
20 Vice Pres of External Campuses Dr. Elane SEEBO
30 Vice Pres Inst Advancement Vacant
10 Chief Financial Officer Mr. Jim SMITH
20 Assistant Academic Officer Mr. Stan DEMERRITT
12 Exec Dir/Campus Dean Albuquerque Dr. John B. COPELAND
12 Exec Dir/Campus DeanAltus Dr. J. M. GIVENS, JR.
12 Exec Dir/Campus Dean Amarillo Dr. J. B BOREN
12 Exec Dir/Campus Dean Anchorage Dr. Eric ASH
12 Exec Dir/Campus Dean Clovis Dr. Gary MITCHELL
12 Exec Dir/Campus Dean Fairbanks Vacant
12 Exec Dir/Campus Dean Hawaii Vacant
12 Exec Dir/Campus Dean Lubbock Dr. David BISHOP
12 Exec Dir/Campus Dean Phoenix Dr. D. Glenn SIMMONS
12 Exec Dir/Campus Dean San Antonio Dr. James ANTENEN
12 Exec Dir/Campus Dean Sierra Vista Dr. Robert MORRIS, III
12 Exec Dir/Campus Dean Wichita Falls Dr. Dean DANIEL
83 Acad Dean School Behav & Soc Sci Dr. Estelle OWENS
50 Academic Dean School of Business Dr. Otto B. SCHACHT
53 Academic Dean School of Education Dr. Jimmie L. TODD
57 Academic Dean School of Fine Arts Dr. Marti R. RUNNELS
79 Academic Dean School of Lang & Lit Dr. Cindy M. MCCLENAGAN
81 Academic Dean School Math/Sciences Dr. Herbert GROVER
64 Academic Dean School of Music Dr. Ann B. STUTES
66 Academic Dean School of Nursing Dr. Diane FRAZOR
73 Academic Dean Religion & Philosophy Dr. Paul L. SADLER
06 Registrar Mrs. Julie BOWEN
32 Exec Dir Student Development Mr. Tom HALL
21 Controller Mrs. Lezlie HUKILL
41 Athletic Director Dr. Greg FERIS
07 Director Admissions Mrs. Debbie STENNETT
29 Director Alumni Development Mr. Danny ANDREWS
88 Director Church Services Mr. Micheal SUMMERS
102 Director Corp Development Mr. Mike MELCHER
30 Director Development Ms. Hope ENGLISH
37 Director Financial Aid Mrs. Karen LAQUEY
58 Director of Graduate Services Miss Amanda STANTON
15 Director Human Resources Mr. Ron APPLING
13 Director Information Technology Mrs. Katrina SMITH
09 Dir Inst Research/Effectiveness Mrs. Penny POOLE
12 Director Kenya Campus Dr. Richard SHAW
08 Director Library Dr. Polly R. LACKEY
88 Director Property Management Mr. Danny W. MURPHREE
26 Director Public Relations Mrs. Teresa YOUNG
39 Director Student Housing Mrs. Nancy KEITH
32 Director of Student Ldrship & Activ Mrs. Teresa MOORE
42 Director Student Ministries Mr. Donnie BROWN
40 Director University Services Mr. Eddie C. TURNER
106 Director Virtual Campus Mr. Jay SAMPLE
105 Director Web Services Mrs. Charlotte SCHUMACHER
56 Coordinator External Records Ms. Brenda GONZALEZ
38 Coord Stdnt Counseling/Career Plng Mr. Michael COX
19 Chief of Police/WBU Mr. Lonnie BURTON
18 Chief Facilities/Physical Plant Mr. David MURPHREE
04 Exec Admin Asst to President Mrs. Carolyn ANDREWS

Weatherford College (C)

225 College Park Drive, Weatherford TX 76086-5699
County: Parker FICE Identification: 003664
Unit ID: 229799
Telephone: (817) 594-5471 Carnegie Class: Assoc/Pub-S-SC
FAX Number: (817) 598-6210 Calendar System: Semester
URL: www.wc.edu
Established: 1869 Annual Undergrad Tuition & Fees (In-District): $1,704
Enrollment: 5,676 Coed
Affiliation or Control: Local IRS Status: 501(c)3
Highest Offering: Associate Degree
Program: Occupational; 2-Year Principally Bachelor's Creditable
Accreditation: SC, ADNUR, IFSAC, RAD

01 President Dr. Kevin EATON
04 Exec Asst to the President Ms. Lisa SMITH
05 Interim VP of Inst & Stdnt Services Dr. Richard BOWERS
10 Vice Pres Financial/Admin Affairs Mrs. Andra R. CANTRELL
30 Vice Pres Institutional Advancement Mr. Brent BAKER
76 Dean of Health & Human Sciences Ms. Kathrine BOSWELL
05 Interim Dean of Academics Mr. Michael ENDY
53 Dean Educational/Instructional Sppt Ms. Rhonda TORRES
35 Dean of Student Services Ms. Kathy BASSHAM
103 Dean Workforce & Economic Devel Ms. Kay YOUNG
27 Dir Communications/Public Relations Mrs. Linda BAGWELL
56 Dean of Extended Campuses Mr. Duane DURRETT
88 Director Truck Driving Mr. Bubba SWEARINGIN
09 Dir Institutional Research Mr. Dewayne BERRY
35 Exec Director Student Development Mr. Doug JEFFERSON
88 Academic Advisor/Transf Specialist Ms. Teresa BROCK
88 Director Food Services Ms. Erin DAVIDSON
37 Director Student Financial Aid Mr. Donnie PURVIS
21 Controller Mrs. Ruth CAMPFIELD
15 Director Human Resources Mrs. Ralinda STONE
07 Director of Admissions Mr. Ralph WILLINGHAM
13 Director Technology Services Mr. Steven SANDIDGE
08 Director Library Services Mrs. Martha A. TANDY
18 Director of Facilities Mr. Joe HERNDON
96 Director of Purchasing Mrs. Jeanie HOBBS
45 Director of Resource Development Dr. Shirley CHENAULT
19 Chief of Campus Police Mr. Paul STONE
38 Director Student Counseling Ms. Peggy ARMSTRONG
88 Director Upward Bound Mr. Jeff KHALDEN
29 Director Alumni Relations Mr. Brent BAKER
22 Director of Workforce Education Ms. Janella KRUSE
53 Director of Instructional Support Ms. Sue COODY
53 Director of Education Dr. Joyce MELTON PAGES
06 Registrar Mrs. Vicki TRAWEEK
88 Exec Dir of Student Engagement Mr. Adam FINLEY
88 Director of Testing Ms. Lela MORRIS
88 Dir of Outreach/Student Success Ms. Kay LANDRUM
88 Director Special Populations Ms. Bernadean CONNELL
36 Dir Career & Transfer Center Dr. Leon ABBOTT

Western Technical College (D)

9451 Diana Drive, El Paso TX 79924-6936
County: El Paso Identification: 666103
Unit ID: 224660
Telephone: (915) 566-9621 Carnegie Class: Assoc/PrivFP
FAX Number: (915) 565-9903 Calendar System: Other
URL: www.westerntech.edu
Established: 1969 Annual Undergrad Tuition & Fees: $32,000
Enrollment: 594 Coed
Affiliation or Control: Proprietary IRS Status: Proprietary
Highest Offering: Associate Degree
Program: Occupational; 2-Year Principally Bachelor's Creditable
Accreditation: ACCSC

01 Director Ms. Mary CANO

Western Technical College (E)

9624 Plaza Circle, El Paso TX 79927-2105
County: El Paso FICE Identification: 020983
Unit ID: 224679
Telephone: (915) 532-3737 Carnegie Class: Assoc/PrivFP
FAX Number: (915) 532-6946 Calendar System: Other
URL: www.westerntech.edu
Established: 1969 Annual Undergrad Tuition & Fees: $31,000
Enrollment: 1,030 Coed
Affiliation or Control: Proprietary IRS Status: Proprietary
Highest Offering: Associate Degree
Program: Occupational; Technical Emphasis
Accreditation: ACCSC, PTAA

01 President Mr. Allan SHARPE
00 Chief Executive Officer Mr. Randy KUYKENDALL
11 Chief Administrative Officer Mr. Bill TERRELL
03 Excecutive VP/Director Branch Ms. Mary CANO
05 Dean of Academics Mr. Charles BROWN
10 Accountant Ms. Celi AVILA
37 Director Student Financial Services Ms. Danielle PICCHI
36 Director Career Services Ms. Helen GARCIA
07 Director Admission Ms. Laura PENA

Western Texas College (F)

6200 College Avenue, Snyder TX 79549-6189
County: Scurry FICE Identification: 009549
Unit ID: 229832
Telephone: (325) 573-8511 Carnegie Class: Assoc/Pub-R-M
FAX Number: (325) 573-9321 Calendar System: Semester
URL: www.wtc.edu
Established: 1969 Annual Undergrad Tuition & Fees (In-District): $1,728
Enrollment: 3,164 Coed
Affiliation or Control: State/Local IRS Status: 501(c)3
Highest Offering: Associate Degree
Program: Occupational; 2-Year Principally Bachelor's Creditable
Accreditation: SC

01 President Dr. Michael L. DREITH
05 Vice President/Chief Academic Ofcr Dr. John GIBSON
04 Assistant to the President Ms. Melanie SCHWERTNER
10 Chief Financial Officer Ms. Patricia CLAXTON
11 Chief Operation Officer Mr. Mike THORTON
09 Dean Inst Research & Effectiveness Mr. Britt CANADA
20 Dean of Academic Instruction Mr. Kyle SMITH
32 Dean of Student Services Mr. Ralph RAMON
72 Dean of Technology Mr. Roy BARTELS
30 Exec Director of Development Mr. Jeremiah BOATRIGHT
44 Dean of College Advancement Mr. Mike THORNTON
41 Athletic Director Ms. Tammy DAVIS
06 Registrar Ms. Ann GALYEAN
37 Director Student Financial Aid Ms. Kathy HALL
26 Director of College Relations Vacant
21 Controller Ms. Marjann MORROW
16 Director of Human Resources Ms. Kelly MCGINNIS
18 Director of Physical Plant Mr. Tommy WATTS
85 Dir International Student Services Ms. Julie SENTELL
41 Coordinator of Athletic Services Ms. Debra BURKE

Westwood College-Dallas (G)

8390 LBJ Freeway, Ex Ctr 1, Ste 100,
Dallas TX 75243-1215
County: Dallas Identification: 666427
Unit ID: 442505
Telephone: (214) 570-0100 Carnegie Class: Assoc/PrivFP
FAX Number: (214) 570-8502 Calendar System: Other
URL: www.westwood.edu
Established: 2002 Annual Undergrad Tuition & Fees: $13,058
Enrollment: 546 Coed
Affiliation or Control: Proprietary IRS Status: Proprietary
Highest Offering: Baccalaureate
Program: Professional; Technical Emphasis
Accreditation: ACICS, MAC

01 Campus President Paul KEPIC

† Branch campus of Westwood College-O'Hare Airport, Chicago, IL.

Westwood College-Fort Worth (H)

4232 North Freeway, Fort Worth TX 76137-5021
County: Tarrant Identification: 666434
Unit ID: 442499
Telephone: (817) 547-9600 Carnegie Class: Assoc/PrivFP
FAX Number: (817) 547-9602 Calendar System: Other
URL: www.westwood.edu
Established: 2002 Annual Undergrad Tuition & Fees: $14,655
Enrollment: 317 Coed
Affiliation or Control: Proprietary IRS Status: Proprietary
Highest Offering: Baccalaureate
Program: Occupational
Accreditation: ACICS, MAC

01 Executive Director Paul KEPIC

† Branch campus of Westwood College-DuPage, Woodbridge, IL.

Westwood College-Houston South (I)

7322 Southwest Freeway, #110, Houston TX 77074-2082
County: Harris Identification: 666309
Unit ID: 444060
Telephone: (713) 777-4433 Carnegie Class: Assoc/PrivFP
FAX Number: (713) 219-2088 Calendar System: Other
URL: www.westwood.edu
Established: 2003 Annual Undergrad Tuition & Fees: $13,825
Enrollment: 450 Coed
Affiliation or Control: Proprietary IRS Status: Proprietary
Highest Offering: Baccalaureate
Program: Occupational; 2-Year Principally Bachelor's Creditable; Technical Emphasis
Accreditation: ACCSC, ACICS, MAC

01 Campus President Dr. Kim NUGENT
05 Academic Dean Dr. Wendy JOHNSON
07 Director of Campus Admissions Mr. David EAKER
32 Director of Student Services Ms. Ashley RHODES
13 Campus Systems Administrator Mr. Eric OROZCO

† Branch campus of Westwood College-Denver North, Denver, CO.

Wharton County Junior College (J)

911 Boling Highway, Wharton TX 77488-3298
County: Wharton FICE Identification: 003668
Unit ID: 229841
Telephone: (979) 532-4560 Carnegie Class: Assoc/Pub-R-L
FAX Number: (979) 532-6545 Calendar System: Semester
URL: www.wcjc.edu
Established: 1946 Annual Undergrad Tuition & Fees (In-District): $2,520
Enrollment: 6,922 Coed
Affiliation or Control: Local IRS Status: 501(c)3
Highest Offering: Associate Degree
Program: Occupational; 2-Year Principally Bachelor's Creditable
Accreditation: SC, DH, EMT, PTAA, RAD, SURGT

01 President ... Ms. Betty A. MCCROHAN
05 Vice President of Instruction ... Ms. Leigh Ann COLLINS
10 Vice President Administrative Svcs ... Mr. Bryce KOCIAN
13 Vice President of Technology & IR ... Ms. Pamela YOUNGBLOOD
32 Vice President of Student Services ... Mr. David LEENHOUTS
21 Dean of Financial & Business Svcs ... Mr. Gus WESSELS
26 Director of Marketing & Comm ... Ms. Zina CARTER
07 Director Admissions & Registration ... Ms. Karen PREISLER
37 Director of Financial Aid ... Mr. Richard D. HYDE
08 Director Library Info/Tech Services ... Ms. Kwei HSU
18 Director of Facilities Management ... Mr. Mike FEYEN
15 Director of Human Resources ... Ms. Judy JONES
09 Director of Inst Effectiveness ... Dr. Danson JONES
96 Director of Purchasing ... Mr. Philip WUTHRICH

Wiley College (A)

711 Wiley Avenue, Marshall TX 75670-5199
County: Harrison FICE Identification: 003669
Unit ID: 229887
Telephone: (903) 927-3300 Carnegie Class: Bac/Diverse
FAX Number: (903) 938-8100 Calendar System: Semester
URL: www.wileyc.edu
Established: 1873 Annual Undergrad Tuition & Fees: $11,050
Enrollment: 1,351 Coed
Affiliation or Control: United Methodist IRS Status: 501(c)3
Highest Offering: Baccalaureate
Program: Liberal Arts And General; Teacher Preparatory
Accreditation: SC

01 President and CEO ... Dr. Haywood L. STRICKLAND
03 Executive Vice President & Provost ... Dr. Glenda F. CARTER
10 Vice Pres for Business & Finance ... Mrs. Willie M. HUGHEY
05 Vice President Academic Affairs ... Dr. Ernest J. PLATA
32 Vice President Student Affairs ... Dr. Joseph L. MORALE
30 Vice Pres Institutional Advancement ... Dr. Evelyn LEATHERS
13 Vice Pres Information Technology ... Mr. Nathaniel HEWITT
21 Assoc VP Business/Fiscal Affairs ... Ms. Pamela PRESSLEY
53 Asst Vice Pres/Dean of Education ... Dr. Robert L. WATKINS
42 College Chaplain ... Rev. Michelle HALL
04 Assistant to the President ... Mrs. Karen HELTON
50 Dean of Business & Technology ... Dr. Abdalla F. HAGAN
49 Dean of Sciences ... Dr. Kiflu BERHANE
97 Dean General Studies ... Dr. Sonya BURNETT-ANDRUS
79 Dean Social Sciences & Humanities ... Dr. Sherlynn H. BYRD
26 Director of Public Relations ... Ms. Tammy TAYLOR
08 Director of Library Services ... Mrs. Alma RAVENELL
06 Registrar ... Dr. Lalita W. ESTES
07 Director of Admissions ... Ms. Ashley BENNETT
15 Director Personnel Services ... Ms. Merdis F. BUCKLEY
18 Chief Facilities/Physical Plant ... Mr. Percy MURRAY
20 Assistant Academic Officer ... Dr. Sherlynn BYRD
37 Director of Financial Aid ... Mr. Eric B. KING
29 Director of Alumni Relations ... Ms. Alvena JONES
09 Director of Institutional Research ... Dr. Warren H. HAWKINS
11 Director Administrative Svcs ... Mr. O. Ivan WHITE
23 College Nurse ... Ms. Shonte EPPERSON
36 Dir Student Placement/Counseling ... Vacant
41 Director of Athletics ... Ms. Janet EATON
96 Director of Purchasing ... Mr. Darius Z. KIMBLE
35 Director of Student Development ... Vacant
84 Director Enrollment Management ... Ms. Ashley BENNETT

UTAH

Argosy University, Salt Lake City (B)

121 Election Road Suite 300, Draper UT 84020-7724
County: Salt Lake Identification: 666655
Unit ID: 452090
Telephone: (801) 601-5000 Carnegie Class: Not Classified
FAX Number: (801) 601-4990 Calendar System: Other
URL: www.argosy.edu/saltlakecity
Established: 2006 Annual Undergrad Tuition & Fees: $14,580
Enrollment: 294 Coed
Affiliation or Control: Proprietary IRS Status: Proprietary
Highest Offering: Doctorate
Program: Professional
Accreditation: &NH

01 Campus President ... David TIETJEN
05 Vice President of Academic Affairs ... Ms. Vana NESPOR
07 Director of Admissions ... Mr. Todd HARRISON
32 Director of Student Services ... Steve MERRILL
10 Director of Financial Services ... Mr. Jared CRANDALL
15 Human Resources Coordinator ... Mr. Jon BAY

† Regional accreditation is carried under the parent institution, Argosy University in Chicago, IL.

The Art Institute of Salt Lake City (C)

121 West Election Road, Draper UT 84020
County: Salt Lake Identification: 666694
Unit ID: 450049
Telephone: (801) 601-4700 Carnegie Class: Not Classified
FAX Number: (801) 601-4724 Calendar System: Semester
URL: www.artinstitutes.edu/saltlakecity
Established: 2007 Annual Undergrad Tuition & Fees: $17,488
Enrollment: 728 Coed
Affiliation or Control: Proprietary IRS Status: Proprietary
Highest Offering: Baccalaureate
Program: Liberal Arts And General; Fine Arts Emphasis
Accreditation: ACICS

01 President ... Dr. Ron MOSS

† Branch campus of The Art Institute of Las Vegas, Henderson, NV.

Brigham Young University (D)

Provo UT 84602-0002
County: Utah FICE Identification: 003670
Unit ID: 230038
Telephone: (801) 422-1211 Carnegie Class: DRU
FAX Number: (801) 422-0586 Calendar System: Semester
URL: www.byu.edu
Established: 1875 Annual Undergrad Tuition & Fees: $4,560
Enrollment: 32,947 Coed
Affiliation or Control: Latter-day Saints IRS Status: 501(c)3
Highest Offering: Doctorate
Program: Liberal Arts And General; Teacher Preparatory; Professional
Accreditation: NW, ART, BUS, BUSA, CLPSY, CONST, COPSY, CS, DANCE, DIETD, DIETI, ENG, ENGT, IPSY, JOUR, LAW, MFCD, MT, MUS, NRPA, NURSE, PH, SP, SPAA, SW, TEAC, THEA

01 President ... Dr. Cecil O. SAMUELSON
05 Academic Vice President ... Dr. Brent W. WEBB
11 Administrative Vice President ... Mr. Brian K. EVANS
44 Advancement Vice President ... Dr. Kevin J. WORTHEN
13 Vice Pres Info Tech/Chief Info Ofcr ... Dr. J. Kelly FLANAGAN
88 International Vice President ... Dr. Sandra ROGERS
32 Student Life Vice President ... Dr. Janet S. SCHARMAN
43 Asst to President/General Counsel ... Mr. Michael R. ORME
45 Asst to Pres Planning/Assessment ... Dr. James D. GORDON
27 Asst to Pres Univ Communications ... Mrs. Carri P. JENKINS
20 Assoc Acad Vice President Faculty ... Dr. Craig H. HART
20 Assoc Acad VP Undergraduate Stds ... Dr. Jeffrey D. KEITH
46 Assoc Acad VP Research/Grad Stds ... Dr. Alan R. HARKER
32 Assoc Student Life Vice Pres ... Dr. Ronald K. CHAPMAN
10 Chief Financial Officer ... Mr. Brian K. EVANS
18 Asst Admin VP Physical Facilities ... Mr. Ole M. SMITH
15 Asst Admin VP Human Resource Svcs ... Mr. Forrest FLAKE
35 Asst Admin VP/Stdnt Auxil Svc ... Mr. David A. HUNT
26 Assoc Advance VP Univ Relations ... Mr. John C. LEWIS
30 Executive Director Development ... Mr. Bruce M. SNOW
36 Exec Dir Stdnt Acad/Advisement Svcs ... Mr. Norm FINLINSON
35 Dean Student Life ... Mr. Vernon L. HEPERI
37 Director Financial Aid/Scholarships ... Mr. Steve HILL
88 Dean Undergraduate Education ... Dr. John D. BELL
08 University Librarian ... Mr. Randy J. OLSEN
58 Dean Graduate Studies ... Dr. Wynn C. STIRLING
51 Dean Continuing Education ... Dr. Wayne LOTT
47 Dean Life Sciences ... Dr. Rodney J. BROWN
54 Dean Engineering & Technology ... Dr. Alan R. PARKINSON
83 Dean Family Home & Social Science ... Dr. Benjamin M. OGLES
57 Dean Fine Arts & Communications ... Dr. Stephen M. JONES
68 Dean Health/Human Performance ... Vacant
79 Dean Humanities ... Dr. John ROSENBERG
61 Dean Law School ... Dr. James R. RASBAND
50 Dean Marriott School Management ... Dr. Gary C. CORNIA
53 Dean McKay School of Education ... Dr. K. Richard YOUNG
81 Dean Physical & Math Science ... Dr. Scott D. SOMMERFELDT
66 Dean Nursing ... Dr. Beth V. COLE
73 Dean Religious Education ... Dr. Terry BALL
09 Director Office of Assessment ... Dr. Danny R. OLSEN
06 Registrar ... Mr. Jeffery N. BUNKER
07 Director of Admissions ... Mr. Kirk STRONG
29 Managing Director Alumni Relations ... Ms. Linda PALMER
96 Director of Purchasing ... Mr. Tim HILL

Broadview University (E)

1902 W 7800 S, West Jordan UT 84088-4021
County: Salt Lake FICE Identification: 011166
Unit ID: 230056
Telephone: (801) 304-4224 Carnegie Class: Spec/Health
FAX Number: (801) 304-4229 Calendar System: Quarter
URL: www.broadviewuniversity.edu
Established: 1971 Annual Undergrad Tuition & Fees: $20,700
Enrollment: 710 Coed
Affiliation or Control: Proprietary IRS Status: Proprietary
Highest Offering: Master's
Program: Occupational; Technical Emphasis
Accreditation: ACICS, ADNUR, MAC

01 President ... Mr. Terry MYHRE
05 Director ... Mr. Mark STAATS

Careers Unlimited (F)

1176 S 1480 W, Orem UT 84058-4905
County: Utah FICE Identification: 034633
Unit ID: 448239
Telephone: (801) 426-8234 Carnegie Class: Spec/Health
FAX Number: (801) 224-5437 Calendar System: Other
URL: www.ucdh.edu
Established: 2006 Annual Undergrad Tuition & Fees: $22,700
Enrollment: 119 Coed
Affiliation or Control: Proprietary IRS Status: Proprietary
Highest Offering: Baccalaureate
Program: Occupational; 2-Year Principally Bachelor's Creditable
Accreditation: ACCSC, DH

01 College President ... Mr. Brent MOLEN
05 Director of Education ... Mr. Kenneth MOLEN

DeVry University - Sandy (G)

9350 South 150 East, Suite 420, Sandy UT 84070-2704
County: Salt Lake Identification: 666576
Unit ID: 448877
Telephone: (801) 565-5110 Carnegie Class: Spec/Bus
FAX Number: (801) 561-1710 Calendar System: Semester
URL: www.devry.edu
Established: 1931 Annual Undergrad Tuition & Fees: $15,294
Enrollment: 272 Coed
Affiliation or Control: Proprietary IRS Status: Proprietary
Highest Offering: Master's
Program: Professional; Business Emphasis
Accreditation: &NH

01 Campus Director ... Michael TOWNSLEY

† Regional accreditation is carried under the parent institution in Downers Grove, IL.

Eagle Gate College (H)

5588 S Green Street, Murray UT 84123-6965
County: Salt Lake FICE Identification: 021785
Unit ID: 230366
Telephone: (801) 333-8100 Carnegie Class: Assoc/PrivFP4
FAX Number: (801) 263-6520 Calendar System: Other
URL: www.eaglegatecollege.edu
Established: 1979 Annual Undergrad Tuition & Fees: $13,609
Enrollment: 461 Coed
Affiliation or Control: Proprietary IRS Status: Proprietary
Highest Offering: Baccalaureate
Program: Occupational
Accreditation: ACICS

01 President ... Mr. Marty SPURLOCK
07 Director of Admissions ... Mr. Aaron JOHNSON

Everest College (I)

3280 W 3500 South, West Valley City UT 84119
County: Salt Lake FICE Identification: 022985
Unit ID: 230472
Telephone: (801) 840-4800 Carnegie Class: Assoc/PrivFP4
FAX Number: (801) 969-0828 Calendar System: Quarter
URL: www.everest.edu
Established: 1982 Annual Undergrad Tuition & Fees: $16,289
Enrollment: 528 Coed
Affiliation or Control: Proprietary IRS Status: Proprietary
Highest Offering: Baccalaureate
Program: Occupational; 2-Year Principally Bachelor's Creditable; Business Emphasis
Accreditation: ACICS, MAC, SURGT

01 President ... Ms. Stephanie BYRD
05 Academic Dean ... Mrs. Krystal KAREH
10 Business Manager ... Mr. Scott LOIVOS
07 Director of Admissions ... Mr. Jim EGGERS
36 Director Career Services ... Mr. Robert PETERSON

Fortis College (J)

3949 South 700 East, Suite 150, Salt Lake City UT 84107
County: Salt Lake Identification: 666762
Unit ID: 456454
Telephone: (801) 713-0915 Carnegie Class: Not Classified
FAX Number: (801) 281-9620 Calendar System: Semester
URL: www.fortis.edu
Established: N/A Annual Undergrad Tuition & Fees: $16,160
Enrollment: 249 Coed
Affiliation or Control: Proprietary IRS Status: Proprietary
Highest Offering: Associate Degree
Program: Occupational
Accreditation: ACCSC, DH

01 Campus Director ... Kendall DEAN

† Tuition varies by degree program.

Independence University (K)

5295 S Commerce Drive, Suite G50,
Salt Lake City UT 84107
County: Salt Lake FICE Identification: 022061
Telephone: (800) 972-5149 Carnegie Class: Not Classified
FAX Number: (801) 263-0345 Calendar System: Other
URL: www.independence.edu
Established: 1978 Annual Undergrad Tuition & Fees: $12,100
Enrollment: 3,626 Coed
Affiliation or Control: Proprietary IRS Status: Proprietary
Highest Offering: Master's
Program: Professional
Accreditation: ACCSC

01 Executive Director ... Mr. Carl BARNEY

ITT Technical Institute (L)

920 West LeVoy Drive, Murray UT 84123-2500
County: Salt Lake FICE Identification: 023610
Unit ID: 230384
Telephone: (801) 263-3313 Carnegie Class: Spec/Tech

FAX Number: (801) 263-3497 Calendar System: Quarter
URL: www.itt-tech.edu
Established: 1984 Annual Undergrad Tuition & Fees: N/A
Enrollment: 868 Coed
Affiliation or Control: Proprietary IRS Status: Proprietary
Highest Offering: Baccalaureate
Program: Technical Emphasis
Accreditation: ACICS

Latter-Day Saints Business College (A)

95 N 300 W, Salt Lake City UT 84101-3500
County: Salt Lake FICE Identification: 003672
Unit ID: 230418
Telephone: (801) 524-8100 Carnegie Class: Assoc/PrivNFP
FAX Number: (801) 524-1900 Calendar System: Semester
URL: www.ldsbc.edu
Established: 1886 Annual Undergrad Tuition & Fees: $2,980
Enrollment: 1,809 Coed
Affiliation or Control: Latter-day Saints IRS Status: 501(c)3
Highest Offering: Associate Degree
Program: Occupational; 2-Year Principally Bachelor's Creditable; Business Emphasis
Accreditation: NW, MAC

01 President .... Mr. Larry J. RICHARDS
04 Admin Assistant to the President .... Ms. Cathy A. SMITH
05 Vice President for Academic Affairs .... Dr. Carolyn S. BROWN
11 Vice President Administration .... Mr. Jerold M. BRYAN
10 Vice President Finance/Controller .... Mr. Bob H. WISER
26 VP Public Affairs & Advancement .... Mr. Craig V. NELSON
20 Dean of Instuctional Support .... Mr. Tyler S. MORGAN
32 Acting Dean of Students .... Mr. Matthew D. TITTLE
13 Chief Information Officer .... Mr. R. Brent CHERRINGTON
36 Director of Career Services .... Mr. Steven L. ASAY
84 Director of Enrollment Management .... Ms. Renae L. RICHARDS
06 Registrar .... Ms. Tamra TAYLOR
08 Dir of Library/Inform Resources .... Ms. Karen A. HALES
88 Accounting Program Director .... Mr. D. Paul GARDINER
50 Business Department Chair .... Mr. Keith A. POELMAN
23 Medical Careers Department Chair .... Mr. Brett MERKLEY
77 Information Tech Department Chair .... Ms. Lynda D. HENRIE
83 Assoc of Science Department Chair .... Mr. Paul RICHARDS
88 Interior Design Department Chair .... Mr. Miles HUNSAKER
72 Business Info Systems Program Dir .... Mr. Kevin MCREYNOLDS
73 Institute of Religion Director .... Mr. Thomas MUMFORD
21 Assistant Controller .... Mr. Glenn MCGETTIGAN
37 Financial Aid Administrator .... Mr. J. Douglas HORNE
40 Bookstore Manager .... Ms. Rachel BINGHAM

Midwives College of Utah (B)

1174 E 2700 S, Suite 2, Salt Lake City UT 84106-2671
County: Utah Identification: 666281
Telephone: (866) 680-2756 Carnegie Class: Not Classified
FAX Number: (866) 207-2024 Calendar System: Semester
URL: www.midwifery.edu
Established: 1980 Annual Undergrad Tuition & Fees: $7,545
Enrollment: 126 Coed
Affiliation or Control: Independent Non-Profit IRS Status: 501(c)3
Highest Offering: Master's
Program: Occupational
Accreditation: MEAC

01 President .... Ms. Kristi RIDD-YOUNG
05 Academic Dean .... Ms. Nicole CROFT
04 Administrative Assistant .... Ms. Cindy WINWARD

Neumont University (C)

10701 S River Front Parkway Ste 300,
South Jordan UT 84095-3524
County: Salt Lake Identification: 666125
Unit ID: 445692
Telephone: (801) 302-2800 Carnegie Class: Spec/Tech
FAX Number: (801) 302-2811 Calendar System: Quarter
URL: www.neumont.edu
Established: 2003 Annual Undergrad Tuition & Fees: $23,100
Enrollment: 273 Coed
Affiliation or Control: Proprietary IRS Status: Proprietary
Highest Offering: Master's
Program: Professional; Technical Emphasis
Accreditation: ACICS

01 President/Campus Dir Utah .... Ned LEVINE
05 Provost .... Sam PUICH
32 Director of Student Services .... Erin MCCORMACK
06 Registrar/Dir Academic Programs .... Larry CRANDALL

Ogden-Weber Applied Technology College (D)

200 North Washington Boulevard, Ogden UT 84404-4089
County: Weber FICE Identification: 023465
Unit ID: 230490
Telephone: (801) 627-8300 Carnegie Class: Assoc/Pub-U-MC
FAX Number: (801) 395-3727 Calendar System: Other
URL: www.owatc.edu
Established: 1971 Annual Undergrad Tuition & Fees (In-District): $2,813
Enrollment: 2,504 Coed
Affiliation or Control: State/Local IRS Status: 501(c)3
Highest Offering: Associate Degree
Program: Occupational; Technical Emphasis
Accreditation: COE, MAC, PNUR

01 President & Chief Executive Officer .... Collette R. MERCIER
05 Vice Pres Instructional Services .... James TAGGART
32 Vice Pres for Student Services .... Rhonda LAURITZEN
10 Vice Pres for Campus Svcs/CFO .... Tyler CALL

† Campus of Utah College of Applied Technology, Salt Lake City, UT.

Provo College (E)

1450 W 820 N, Provo UT 84601-1305
County: Utah FICE Identification: 023608
Unit ID: 380438
Telephone: (801) 818-8900 Carnegie Class: Assoc/PrivFP
FAX Number: (801) 375-9728 Calendar System: Other
URL: www.provocollege.edu
Established: 1984 Annual Undergrad Tuition & Fees: $20,000
Enrollment: 410 Coed
Affiliation or Control: Proprietary IRS Status: Proprietary
Highest Offering: Associate Degree
Program: Occupational; Nursing Emphasis
Accreditation: ACCSC, ADNUR, PTAA

01 Campus President .... Mr. Gordon C. PETERS
05 Academic Dean .... Mrs. Kristy THOMPSON
10 Business Manager .... Mr. Darrin BARTUNEK
07 Director of Admissions .... Mr. Stewart HAGBERG
37 Financial Services Assoc Director .... Mr. Nick JOHNSON
06 Registrar .... Mrs. Marrybell MONTANO
32 Director of Student Services .... Ms. Traci CLARIDA
36 Director of Career Services .... Mrs. Diann DECKER

Rocky Mountain University of Health Professions (F)

561 East 1860 South, Provo UT 84606-7312
County: Utah Identification: 666019
Telephone: (801) 375-5125 Carnegie Class: Not Classified
FAX Number: (801) 375-2125 Calendar System: Trimester
URL: www.rmuohp.edu
Established: 1998 Annual Graduate Tuition & Fees: $15,000
Enrollment: 400 Coed
Affiliation or Control: Proprietary IRS Status: Proprietary
Highest Offering: Doctorate; No Undergraduates
Program: Professional
Accreditation: NW, @PTA

01 President .... Dr. Richard P. NIELSEN
03 Executive Vice President of Admin .... Dr. Michael SKURJA, JR.
05 Exec VP Academic Affs/Provost .... Dr. Larry BANKS
10 Vice President Finance .... Mr. Jeff BATE
30 Vice Pres of Advancement .... Dr. Les SMITH
20 Academic Dean .... Dr. Sandra PENNINGTON
09 Director of Research .... Dr. Mitchell J. RAUH
09 Dir of Institutional Effectiveness .... Ms. Jessica D. EGBERT

Stevens-Henager College (G)

PO Box 9428, Ogden UT 84409-0428
County: Weber FICE Identification: 003674
Unit ID: 230621
Telephone: (801) 394-7791 Carnegie Class: Bac/Assoc
FAX Number: (801) 621-0853 Calendar System: Quarter
URL: www.stevenshenager.edu
Established: 1891 Annual Undergrad Tuition & Fees: $18,300
Enrollment: 900 Coed
Affiliation or Control: Proprietary IRS Status: Proprietary
Highest Offering: Master's
Program: Occupational; 2-Year Principally Bachelor's Creditable
Accreditation: ACCSC, ADNUR, MAC, SURGT

01 Pres of Ogden Campus/Regional Dir .... Ms. Vicky DEWSNUP
07 Director of Admissions .... Mr. Brandon WRIGHT
32 Director of Student Services .... Mr. Doug BURCH

Stevens-Henager College (H)

1476 S Sandhill Road, Orem UT 84058-7310
County: Utah FICE Identification: 030030
Unit ID: 230630
Telephone: (801) 375-5455 Carnegie Class: Bac/Diverse
FAX Number: (801) 375-9836 Calendar System: Semester
URL: www.stevenshenager.edu
Established: 1962 Annual Undergrad Tuition & Fees: $14,867
Enrollment: 478 Coed
Affiliation or Control: Proprietary IRS Status: Proprietary
Highest Offering: Master's
Program: Business Emphasis
Accreditation: ACCSC, MAC

01 President .... Mr. Ken PLANT

Stevens-Henager College (I)

383 W Vine Street, Salt Lake City UT 84123
County: Salt Lake Identification: 666038
Unit ID: 438151
Telephone: (801) 281-7600 Carnegie Class: Bac/Diverse
FAX Number: (801) 281-7660 Calendar System: Quarter
URL: www.stevenshenager.edu
Established: 1891 Annual Undergrad Tuition & Fees: $38,500
Enrollment: 880 Coed
Affiliation or Control: Proprietary IRS Status: Proprietary
Highest Offering: Master's
Program: Occupational
Accreditation: ACCSC

01 President .... Ms. Vicky L. DEWSNUP
06 Registrar .... Ms. Carrie BARNETT
07 Director of Admissions .... Ms. Stephanie WILLIAMSON
08 Head Librarian .... Mr. David LEWIS
37 Director of Financial Aid .... Ms. Gina SEITZ

† Branch campus of Stevens-Henager College, Ogden, UT.

Uintah Basin Applied Technology College (J)

1100 East Lagoon Street, Roosevelt UT 84066
FICE Identification: 011165
Unit ID: 230676
Telephone: (435) 722-6900 Carnegie Class: Not Classified
FAX Number: (435) 722-6999 Calendar System: Semester
URL: www.ubatc.edu
Established: 1968 Annual Undergrad Tuition & Fees (In-State): $1,395
Enrollment: 1,683 Coed
Affiliation or Control: State IRS Status: 501(c)3
Highest Offering: Associate Degree
Program: Occupational; Technical Emphasis
Accreditation: COE, PNUR

01 Chief Executive Officer .... Mark D. WALKER
30 Vice Pres Economic Development .... Jean MOLD
32 Vice Pres of Student Services .... Bob NAYLOR
10 Vice Pres of Finance .... Keith SPROUSE
05 Vice Pres of Instruction .... John WAHL
04 Exec Assistant to the President .... Trenna BALLOU
06 Registrar .... Julene OLSEN
37 Financial Aid Coordinator .... Mark ANDERTON

† Campus of Utah College of Applied Technology, Salt Lake City, UT.

*Utah System of Higher Education (K)

The Gateway, 60 S 400 W, Salt Lake City UT 84101-1284
County: Salt Lake FICE Identification: 009339
Telephone: (801) 321-7101 Carnegie Class: N/A
FAX Number: (801) 321-7199
URL: www.higheredutah.org

01 Exec Ofcr/Commissioner of Higher Ed .... Dr. William A. SEDERBURG
05 Assoc Commissioner Academic Affairs .... Dr. Elizabeth J. HITCH
10 Assoc Commissioner Finance/Facilit .... Dr. Gregory STAUFFER
37 Exec Director Student Financial Aid .... Mr. David A. FEITZ
26 Assoc Commissioner Public Affairs .... Mr. David L. BUHLER
45 Asc Commissioner Economic Dev/Plng .... Dr. Cameron K. MARTIN
88 UESP Executive Director .... Ms. Lynne WARD

*The University of Utah (L)

201 South 1460 East, Salt Lake City UT 84112-1107
County: Salt Lake FICE Identification: 003675
Unit ID: 230764
Telephone: (801) 581-7200 Carnegie Class: RU/VH
FAX Number: (801) 581-3007 Calendar System: Semester
URL: www.utah.edu
Established: 1850 Annual Undergrad Tuition & Fees (In-State): $6,763
Enrollment: 30,819 Coed
Affiliation or Control: State IRS Status: 501(c)3
Highest Offering: Doctorate
Program: Liberal Arts And General; Teacher Preparatory; Professional
Accreditation: NW, ARCPA, AUD, BUS, BUSA, CEA, CLPSY, COPSY, CYTO, DANCE, DENT, DIETC, EMT, ENG, ENGR, IPSY, JOUR, LAW, MED, MIDWF, MT, MUS, NMT, NRPA, NURSE, OT, PH, PHAR, PLNG, PTA, SCPSY, SP, SPAA, SW, @TEAC

02 Interim President .... Dr. A. Lorris BETZ
05 Sr Vice Pres Academic Affairs .... Dr. David W. PERSHING
17 Sr VP Hlth Sci/CEO Univ Ut Hlth Ctr .... Dr. Vivan S. LEE
43 Vice President & General Counsel .... Mr. John K. MORRIS
11 Vice Pres Administrative Services .... Mr. Arnold B. COMBE
32 Vice President Student Affairs .... Dr. Barbara H. SNYDER
30 Vice Pres Institutional Advancement .... Mr. Fred C. ESPLIN
86 Vice President Government Relations .... Mr. Jason PERRY
16 Vice President for Human Resources .... Dr. Loretta F. HARPER
46 Vice President Research .... Dr. Thomas N. PARKS
88 Vice Pres Technology Venture Devel .... Dr. Jack W. BRITTAIN
27 Chief Information Officer .... Dr. Eric DENNA
101 Special Ast to Pres/Sec to the Univ .... Ms. Laura SNOW
04 Exec Asst to the President .... Ms. Elizabeth W. MCCOY
20 Assoc VP AA & Dean Undergrad Stds .... Dr. Martha S. BRADLEY
84 Sr Asc VP Student Affs/ Enroll Mgmt .... Mr. L. Kay HARWARD
45 Assoc VP Acad Affs/Budget/Planning .... Ms. Cathy ANDERSON
18 Assoc VP Admin Services/Facilities .... Mr. Michael G. PEREZ
10 Assoc VP Admin/Finance & Bus Svcs .... Mr. Jeffrey J. WEST
20 Assoc VP Acad Affs/Equity/Diversity .... Dr. Octavio VILLALPANDO
76 Associate Vice Pres Health Sciences .... Dr. Richard J. SPERRY
88 Associate Vice President Research .... Dr. Cynthia M. FURSE
15 Associate Vice Pres Human Resources .... Ms. Joan E. GINES

5 Associate Vice Pres Human Resources ... Mr. Thomas J. LOVERIDGE
38 Assoc VP Acad Affs/Faculty ... Dr. Amy WILDERMUTH
35 Assoc VP Stdnt Affs/Bus/Auxil Svcs ... Dr. Jerry L. BASFORD
26 Chief Mktg & Commun Officer ... Mr. William J. WARREN
21 Asst Vice Pres Admin Svc/Aux Svc ... Mr. Gordon N. WILSON
58 Dean Graduate School ... Dr. Chuck WIGHT
48 Dean Architecture & Planning ... Ms. Brenda C. SCHEER
50 Dean David Eccles Sch of Business ... Dr. Taylor RANDALL
53 Dean College of Education ... Dr. Michael L. HARDMAN
54 Dean College of Engineering ... Dr. Richard B. BROWN
57 Dean Col of Fine Arts/AVP the Arts ... Dr. Raymond TYMAS-JONES
68 Dean College of Health ... Dr. James E. GRAVES
92 Interim Dean Honors College ... Dr. Thomas G. RICHMOND
79 Dn Col Hum/AVP Acad Affs/Indply Std ... Dr. Robert D. NEWMAN
61 Dean S J Quinney College of Law ... Mr. Hiram CHODOSH
65 Dean Coll of Mines & Earth Science ... Dr. Francis H. BROWN
63 Dean School of Medicine ... Dr. David J. BJORKMAN
66 Dean College of Nursing ... Dr. Maureen R. KEEFE
67 Dean College of Pharmacy ... Dr. Chris M. IRELAND
81 Dean College of Science ... Dr. Pierre V. SOKOLSKY
83 Dean Col Social/Behavioral Science ... Dr. M. David RUDD
70 Dean College of Social Work ... Dr. Jannah H. MATHER
88 Dean of Students ... Ms. Annie NEBEKER-CHRISTENSEN
06 University Registrar ... Mr. Timothy J. EBNER
23 CEO University Hospitals & Clinics ... Mr. David E. ENTWISTLE
91 Ex Dir Proj/Applctns/Univ Info Tech ... Mr. Joseph R. TAYLOR
88 Director Institutional Review Board ... Mr. John P. STILLMAN
96 Director Purchasing ... Mr. James T. PARKER
94 Director Gender Studies ... Dr. Susie PORTER
77 Department Chair Sch of Computing ... Dr. Martin BERZINS
52 Dir Dental Clinic/Gen Prac Resideny ... Dr. Craige J. OLSON
07 Director Admissions ... Ms. Barbara FORTIN
29 Exec Director Alumni Association ... Mr. M. John ASHTON
44 Director Planned Giving ... Ms. Karin S. HARDY
37 Dir Financial Aid & Scholarships ... Mr. John CURL
08 Executive Director Marriott Library ... Ms. Joyce OGBURN
62 Dir Eccles Health Sciences Library ... Ms. Jean P. SHIPMAN
62 Dir S J Quinney Col of Law/Lib ... Ms. Rita T. REUSCH
36 Director of Career Services ... Mr. Stan D. INMAN
38 Director Counseling Center ... Dr. Lauren WEITZMAN
22 Dir Center Ethnic Student Affairs ... Ms. S. Mikiko KUMASAKA
39 Director Housing & Res Education ... Ms. Barbara REMSBURG
39 Director Univ Student Apartments ... Mr. Richard L. JAMES
88 Director UT Museum Natural History ... Dr. Sarah B. GEORGE
19 Director Public Safety ... Mr. Scott D. FOLSOM
40 Director Campus Bookstore ... Mr. Earl L. CLEGG
85 Director International Center ... Dr. Sabine KLAHR
41 Director Athletics ... Dr. Chris HILL
25 Dir Office of Sponsored Projects ... Mr. Brent K. BROWN
31 Director Univ-Neighborhood Partners ... Dr. Rosemarie HUNTER
09 Director Institutional Analysis ... Dr. Paul A. GORE

Southern Utah University (A)

351 W Center Blvd, Cedar City UT 84720-2470
County: Iron FICE Identification: 003678
Unit ID: 230603
Telephone: (435) 586-7700 Carnegie Class: Master's L
FAX Number: (435) 586-5475 Calendar System: Semester
URL: www.suu.edu
Established: 1897 Annual Undergrad Tuition & Fees (In-State): $5,198
Enrollment: 8,024 Coed
Affiliation or Control: State IRS Status: 501(c)3
Highest Offering: Master's
Program: Occupational; Liberal Arts And General; Teacher Preparatory
Accreditation: NW, ART, ACBSP, BUS, CS, DANCE, ENG, MUS, NURSE, TEAC

02 President ... Dr. Michael T. BENSON
05 Provost ... Dr. Bradley COOK
10 Vice Pres of Finance & Govt Rels ... Mr. Dorian PAGE
32 Vice President Student Services ... Dr. Donna M. EDDLEMAN
26 Vice Pres for University Relations ... Mr. Dean O'DRISCOLL
30 Vice Pres Advancement ... Mr. Stuart JONES
58 Assoc Provost/Dean of Graduate Stds ... Mr. William J. BYRNES
13 Assoc VP for Information Tech ... Mr. Glen E. PRYOR
84 Assoc VP for Enrollment Management ... Dr. Stephen ALLEN
18 VP Facilities Management & Planning ... Mr. David F. TANNER
08 Dean/Director Library/Univ Studies ... Mr. John EYE
51 Exec Dir Continuing/Profess Studies ... Dr. Kevin ROBINSON
21 Director Budget ... Mr. Bryant FLAKE
75 Director CTE ... Mr. David A. WARD
06 Registrar ... Mr. John ALLRED
15 Dir Personnel/Affirm Action Ofcr ... Mr. David T. MCGUIRE
88 Dean of University College ... Dr. Patrick CLARKE
27 Director of Communications ... Mrs. Jennifer A. BURT
37 Director of Financial Aid ... Ms. Jan CAREY-MCDONALD
29 Director of Alumni Relations ... Ms. Mindy BENSON
41 Athletic Director ... Mr. Ken BEAZER
43 Legal Counsel ... Mr. D. Michael CARTER
79 Dean Col Humanities/Soc Sci ... Dr. James MCDONALD
50 Dean School of Business ... Dr. Carl R. TEMPLIN
53 Dean College of Education ... Dr. Deborah HILL
81 Dean College of Science ... Dr. Robert EVES
57 Dean College Performing/Visual Arts ... Mrs. Shauna MENDINI
96 Director of Purchasing ... Mr. Peter J. HEILGEIST

*Utah State University (B)

Logan UT 84322-0001
County: Cache FICE Identification: 003677
Unit ID: 230728
Telephone: (435) 797-1000 Carnegie Class: RU/H
FAX Number: (435) 797-3880 Calendar System: Semester
URL: www.usu.edu
Established: 1888 Annual Undergrad Tuition & Fees (In-State): $5,563
Enrollment: 25,767 Coed
Affiliation or Control: State IRS Status: 501(c)3
Highest Offering: Doctorate
Program: Liberal Arts And General; Teacher Preparatory; Professional
Accreditation: NW, AUD, BUS, BUSA, CEA, CIDA, CORE, CS, DIETC, DIETD, DIETI, ENG, ENGR, FOR, IPSY, LSAR, MFCD, MUS, NRPA, PSPSY, SP, SW, @TEAC

02 President ... Dr. Stan L. ALBRECHT
05 Provost ... Dr. Raymond T. COWARD
43 General Counsel ... Mr. Craig J. SIMPER
10 Vice President Business & Finance ... Mr. Dave COWLEY
30 Vice Pres University Advancement ... Dr. Ross PETERSON
32 Vice President Student Services ... Mr. James MORALES
56 Vice Pres Extension & Agriculture ... Dr. Noelle E. COCKETT
46 VP Research/Dn Sch Graduate Stds ... Dr. Mark R. MCLELLAN
13 CIO/Assoc VP Information Technology ... Dr. Eric HAWLEY
18 Associate VP for Facilities ... Mr. Darrell E. HART
20 Vice Provost ... Dr. Laurens H. SMITH
08 Dean Libraries ... Mr. Richard CLEMENT
51 Vice Prov Regional Camp/Dist Educ ... Dr. Ronda R. MENLOVE
29 Exec Director Alumni Relations ... Mrs. Patty HALAUFIA
26 Exec Dir Public Relations/Marketing ... Mr. John W. DEVILBISS
09 Dir Analysis Assess/Accreditation ... Mr. Michael TORRENS
22 Director Affirmative Action/EEO ... Mr. David OTTLEY
41 Athletic Director ... Mr. Scott BARNES
25 Director Sponsored Programs ... Mr. Jeff COLEMAN
86 Director Government Relations ... Mr. Neil N. ABERCROMBIE
15 Director of Human Resources ... Ms. BrandE FAUPELL
19 Director University Police Dept ... Mr. Steven J. MECHAM
06 Registrar ... Mr. John D. MORTENSEN
44 Associate VP University Advancement ... Ms. Joan SCHEFFKE
36 Director Career Services/Coop Educ ... Ms. Donna E. CROW
37 Director of Financial Aid ... Mr. Steven SHARP
38 Director Counseling Center ... Dr. David BUSH
07 Dir Recruitment/Enrollment Svcs ... Mrs. Jenn TWISS
40 Director of Bookstore ... Mr. David PARKINSON
92 Director of Honors ... Dr. Christie L. FOX
96 Director of Purchasing ... Mr. Eugene HIGHAM
47 Dean of Agriculture ... Dr. Noelle E. COCKETT
57 Dean of Arts ... Dr. Craig JESSOP
50 Dean of Business ... Mr. Douglas D. ANDERSON
53 Dean of Education ... Dr. Beth FOLEY
54 Dean of Engineering ... Mr. H. Scott HINTON
79 Dean Humanities/Social Science ... Dr. John C. ALLEN
65 Dean of Natural Resources ... Dr. Nat FRAZER
81 Dean of Science ... Dr. James MACMAHON

*Utah Valley University (C)

800 W University Parkway, Orem UT 84058-5999
County: Utah FICE Identification: 004027
Unit ID: 230737
Telephone: (801) 863-8000 Carnegie Class: Bac/Diverse
FAX Number: (801) 226-5207 Calendar System: Semester
URL: www.uvu.edu
Established: 1941 Annual Undergrad Tuition & Fees (In-State): $2,285
Enrollment: 32,670 Coed
Affiliation or Control: State IRS Status: 501(c)3
Highest Offering: Master's
Program: Occupational; 2-Year Principally Bachelor's Creditable; Liberal Arts And General; Teacher Preparatory; Professional
Accreditation: NW, ADNUR, BUS, CS, DH, EMT, IFSAC, NUR, TEAC

02 President ... Dr. Matthew S. HOLLAND
05 Vice Pres Academic Affairs ... Dr. Ian WILSON
03 Vice Pres Finance & Administration ... Dr. Val L. PETERSON
32 Vice President Student Affairs ... Dr. Cory L. DUCKWORTH
30 Vice Pres Deveopment/Alumni ... Mr. Marc ARCHAMBAULT
26 Vice Pres University Relations ... Mr. Q. Val HALE
86 Special Assistant to the President ... Dr. Elaine E. ENGLEHARDT
10 Assoc Vice Pres Finance ... Mr. Michael R. FRANCIS
20 Assoc Vice Pres Engaged Learning ... Dr. Brian BIRCH
18 Assoc Vice Pres Facilities Planning ... Mr. Jim MICHAELIS
20 Assoc VP Undergrad Res/Intl Pgm ... Ms. Kathie DEBENHAM
84 Assc VP/Dean Stdnt Svcs/Enroll Mgmt ... Dr. Michelle TAYLOR
26 Assoc VP College Mktg/Communication ... Mr. Chris TAYLOR
44 Assoc Vice Pres Development ... Mrs. Carla BEECHER
88 Assoc VP Donor Engagement ... Ms. Jane URBASKA
35 Asst VP Stdnt Life/Dean of Stdnts ... Mr. Bob RASMUSSEN
21 Asst VP/Controller Business Svcs ... Mr. Kedric BLACK
88 Senior Dir Center Engaged Learning ... Mrs. Cary BOONE JONES
07 Sr Director Admissions/One Stop ... Ms. Liz CHILDS
32 Asc Vice Pres Stdnt Adv/Sppt Svcs ... Dr. Shad SORENSON
72 Dean Computing/Technology ... Mr. Ernie CAREY
57 Dean School of the Arts ... Dr. Newell DAYLEY
81 Dean Science & Health ... Dr. Samuel RUSHFORTH
50 Dean School of Business ... Dr. Norman WRIGHT
97 Interim Dean University College ... Dr. K.D TAYLOR
53 Dean School of Education ... Dr. Briant J. FARNSWORTH
15 Assoc Dire Human Res/Equity Officer ... Mr. Ron PRICE, JR.
37 Director Financial Aid/Scholarship ... Ms. Joanna MCCORMICK
19 Dir Public Safety/Chief of Police ... Mr. John BREWER
44 Director of Planned Giving ... Ms. Cristina PIANEZZOLA
09 Director Institutional Research ... Mr. Robert LOVERIDGE
41 Director Athletics ... Mr. Michael V. JACOBSEN
24 Director Studios & Engineering ... Mr. Will MCKINNON
40 Director Bookstore ... Ms. Louise BRIDGE
06 Registrar ... Ms. LuAnn SMITH
45 Exec Director Planning & Budgets ... Ms. Linda MAKIN
28 Director Multicultural Center ... Ms. Gwen ANDERSON
29 Director Alumni Relations ... Ms. Jeri L. ALLPHIN
38 Dir Career & Academic Counseling ... Mr. Adam BLACK
96 Director of Purchasing ... Mr. Ryan LINDSTROM

*Weber State University (D)

1001 University Circle, Ogden UT 84408-1001
County: Weber FICE Identification: 003680
Unit ID: 230782
Telephone: (801) 626-6000 Carnegie Class: Master's M
FAX Number: (801) 626-7922 Calendar System: Semester
URL: www.weber.edu
Established: 1889 Annual Undergrad Tuition & Fees (In-State): $4,548
Enrollment: 24,048 Coed
Affiliation or Control: State IRS Status: 501(c)3
Highest Offering: Master's
Program: Occupational; 2-Year Principally Bachelor's Creditable; Liberal Arts And General; Teacher Preparatory; Professional; Fine Arts Emphasis
Accreditation: NW, ADNUR, ART, BUS, BUSA, CIDA, CONST, DH, EMT, ENGT, MLTAD, MT, MUS, NUR, PNUR, SW, @TEAC, TED

02 President ... Dr. F. Ann MILLNER
05 Provost ... Dr. Michael B. VAUGHAN
20 Associate Provost ... Dr. Bruce BOWEN
20 Associate Provost ... Dr. Ryan THOMAS
10 Vice Pres Administrative Services ... Dr. Norm TARBOX
30 Vice Pres for Univ Advancement ... Dr. Brad MORTENSEN
32 Vice President Student Affairs ... Dr. Janet WINNIFORD
13 VP for Information Technology ... Dr. Bret R. ELLIS
35 Assoc VP for Student Affairs ... Dr. Brett PEROZZI
21 Asst VP for Financial Services ... Mr. Steven E. NABOR
15 Asst Vice Pres for Human Resources ... Ms. Cherrie NELSON
88 Vice Provost Innovation & Econo Dev ... Mr. Curt ROBERTS
11 Asst VP for Administrative Services ... Mr. Jerry G. GRAYBEAL
18 Assoc VP for Facilities Management ... Mr. Kevin HANSEN
06 Registrar ... Mr. Mark SIMPSON
19 Director Public Safety ... Vacant
29 Exec Director Alumni Association ... Ms. Lynell GARDNER
38 Dir Counseling & Psycholog Services ... Dr. Dianna K. ABEL
36 Director of Career Services ... Dr. Winn STANGER
37 Director of Financial Aid ... Mr. Jed SPENCER
51 Vice Prov & Dean Continuing Educ ... Dr. Bruce DAVIS
76 Dean Health Professions ... Dr. Yasmen SIMONIAN
50 Dean Business/Economics ... Dr. Jeffrey STEAGALL
53 Dean of Education ... Dr. Jack L. RASMUSSEN
83 Dean Social Behavioral Science ... Dr. Frank HARROLD
79 Dean of Arts & Humanities ... Dr. Madonne MINER
81 Dean of Science ... Dr. David MATTY
72 Dean of Applied Science & Tech ... Dr. David FERRO
27 Director of Media Relations ... Mr. John L. KOWALEWSKI
35 Dean of Students ... Dr. Jeffrey J. HURST
07 Director of Admissions ... Mr. Scott TEICHERT
08 University Librarian ... Ms. Joan HUBBARD
22 Dir Equal Opportunity/Affirm Action ... Dr. Barry G. GOMBERG
41 Dir of Intercollegiate Athletics ... Mr. Jerry BOVEE
40 Bookstore Director ... Mr. Tim ECK
25 Director Sponsored Projects ... Ms. Chris MILLARD
85 Director Services Intl Students ... Mr. Morteza EMAMI
23 Director Student Health Center ... Ms. Juliana P. LARSEN
26 Director Public Relations ... Ms. Allison B. HESS
91 Director Administrative Computing ... Vacant
43 University Counsel ... Dr. G. Richard HILL
39 Director Housing & Residence Life ... Mr. Daniel KILCREASE
96 Director of Purchasing ... Ms. Nancy E. EMENGER
28 Asst to President for Diversity ... Dr. Forrest C. CRAWFORD
92 Director of Honors Program ... Dr. Judy ELSLEY
88 Director Budget & Investments ... Mr. Brian L. SHUPPY
09 Director of Institutional Research ... Mr. Steve KERR
94 Coordinator of Women's Studies ... Dr. Parrilla DE KOKAL

*Utah State University-College of Eastern Utah (E)

451 E 400 N, Price UT 84501-2699
County: Carbon FICE Identification: 003676
Unit ID: 230092
Telephone: (435) 637-2120 Carnegie Class: Assoc/Pub-R-M
FAX Number: (435) 613-5422 Calendar System: Semester
URL: www.ceu.edu
Established: 1937 Annual Undergrad Tuition & Fees (In-State): $2,922
Enrollment: 2,172 Coed
Affiliation or Control: State IRS Status: 501(c)3
Highest Offering: Associate Degree
Program: Occupational; 2-Year Principally Bachelor's Creditable
Accreditation: &NW, ADNUR, PNUR

02 Chancellor ... Dr. Joe PETERSON
05 VC Academic Affairs/Student Svcs ... Dr. Greg BENSON
30 Vice Chanc Admin/Advancement ... Mr. Brad KING
12 Vice Chanc San Juan Campus ... Dr. Guy DENTON
10 Assoc Vice Chanc Finance/Controller ... Vacant
13 Assoc Vice Chanc Info Tech/CIO ... Mr. Eric MANTZ
88 AVC Prehistoric Museum ... Mr. Kenneth CARPENTER
32 Assoc Vice Chanc Student Services ... Dr. Alex HERZOG
37 Director of Financial Aid ... Mr. Kim BOOTH
06 Academic Records/Registrar ... Ms. Jan YOUNG
07 Director Admissions & Scholarships ... Mr. Todd OLSEN
08 Director of Library ... Ms. Lori BRASSAW
14 Computer Center Director ... Ms. Juanita MCEVOY
41 Athletic Director ... Mr. Dave PAUR
40 Bookstore Manager ... Ms. Susan LEONARD
19 Director of Public Safety ... Mr. James PRETTYMAN

96 Director of Purchasing .... Ms. Robyn SHERIFF
15 Dir Human Resources/Affirm Act .... Mr. Jay STEPHENS

† Regional accreditation is carried under the parent institution in Logan, UT.

*Dixie State College of Utah (A)

225 S 700 E, Saint George UT 84770-3876
County: Washington FICE Identification: 003671
Unit ID: 230171
Telephone: (435) 652-7500 Carnegie Class: Bac/Assoc
FAX Number: (435) 656-4001 Calendar System: Semester
URL: www.dixie.edu
Established: 1911 Annual Undergrad Tuition & Fees (In-State): $3,489
Enrollment: 8,553 Coed
Affiliation or Control: State IRS Status: 501(c)3
Highest Offering: Baccalaureate
Program: Occupational; 2-Year Principally Bachelor's Creditable; Liberal Arts And General; Teacher Preparatory; Professional
Accreditation: NW, ADNUR, DH, EMT, NUR, PNUR, @PTAA, RAD, SURGT, TEAC

02 President ....Dr. Stephen D. NADAULD
11 Vice Pres of College Services .... Mr. Stanley J. PLEWE
05 Exec Vice Pres Academic Services .... Dr. Donna DILLINGHAM-EVANS
32 Vice Pres Student Services .... Mr. Frank LOJKO
30 Vice Pres Institutional Advancement .... Ms. Christina SCHULTZ
49 Dean Sch Educ/Humanit/Arts/Soc Sci ....Dr. Don HINTON
50 Dean School Business .... Dr. William CHRISTENSEN
81 Dean Science & Allied Health .... Dr. Victor HASFURTHER
51 Dean Continuing Education .... Mr. Steve BRINGHURST
35 Dean of Students .... Mr. Del BEATTY
13 Dean of Information Services ....Mr. Gary J. KOEVEN
10 Exec Director Business Services ....Mr. A. Scott TALBOT
15 Exec Director of Human Resources ...... Ms. Pamela MONTRALLO
18 Executive Director Campus Services ....Ms. Sherry RUESCH
08 Director Library .... Ms. Vicki BLACK
40 Executive Director Auxiliaries ....Mr. T. Randy JUDD
37 Director Student Financial Aid ....Vacant
84 Exec Dir Enrollment Services .... Mr. David ROOS
06 Registrar ....Ms. Julie STENDER
38 Director Student Counseling .... Mr. J. D ROBERTSON
26 Director Public Relations .... Mr. Steve JOHNSON
18 Director Facilities Operation .... Mr. Doug WHITEHEAD
19 Director Security/Safety ....Mr. Don C. REID
41 Athletic Director ....Mr. Jason BOOTHE
39 Director Student Housing .... Mr. Dallin YOUNG
09 Director of Institutional Research .... Mr. Frank LOJKO
04 Exec Assistant to the President .... Mrs. Marilyn LAMOREAUX
35 Director of Student Activities .... Mrs. Donna STAFFORD
96 Director of Purchasing ....Ms. Jackie FREEMAN
29 Director of Alumni Relations .... Ms. Kalynn LARSON

*Snow College (B)

150 E College Avenue, Ephraim UT 84627-1299
County: Sanpete FICE Identification: 003679
Unit ID: 230597
Telephone: (435) 283-7000 Carnegie Class: Assoc/Pub-R-M
FAX Number: (435) 283-6879 Calendar System: Semester
URL: www.snow.edu
Established: 1888 Annual Undergrad Tuition & Fees (In-State): $2,910
Enrollment: 4,386 Coed
Affiliation or Control: State IRS Status: 501(c)3
Highest Offering: Associate Degree
Program: Occupational; 2-Year Principally Bachelor's Creditable
Accreditation: NW, @ACBSP, MUS, PNUR, THEA

02 President ....Dr. Scott L. WYATT
32 Vice President Student Affairs .... Mr. Craig MATHIE
05 Vice President for Academic Affairs .... Dr. Gary SMITH
10 VP Administrative Services ....Mr. Marvin DODGE
35 Dean of Student Life ....Vacant
75 Dean Career Technology Education ....Mr. Mike MEDLEY
36 Director of Student Success ....Ms. Susan LARSEN
08 Director Library/Information Svcs ....Mr. Jon OSTLER
09 Director Institutional Research .... Ms. Beckie HERMANSEN
15 Director Human Resource Development ....Mr. David DYCHES
18 Director Physical Plant Operations .... Mr. Bob OLIVER
24 Director TTC .... Mr. Chase MITCHELL
39 Director Student Housing .... Mr. Tim DOLAN
41 Athletic Director .... Mr. Robert NIELSON
06 Registrar ....Ms. Margie ANDERSON
07 Director Admissions/Communications .... Mr. Greg DART
21 Associate Business Officer .... Mr. John RUELL
26 Chief Public Relations Officer ....Vacant
35 Director Student Affairs ....Ms. Lindsey FIELD
37 Director Student Financial Aid .... Mr. Jack DALENE
38 Director Student Counseling .... Mr. Allen RIGGS
96 Director of Purchasing ....Mr. Michael JORGENSEN
30 Chief Development ....Ms. Rosie CONNOR

*Salt Lake Community College (C)

4600 S Redwood Road, Salt Lake City UT 84123-3197
County: Salt Lake FICE Identification: 005220
Unit ID: 230746
Telephone: (801) 957-4111 Carnegie Class: Assoc/Pub-U-MC
FAX Number: (801) 957-4444 Calendar System: Semester
URL: www.slcc.edu
Established: 1948 Annual Undergrad Tuition & Fees (In-State): $3,052
Enrollment: 34,654 Coed
Affiliation or Control: State IRS Status: 501(c)3
Highest Offering: Associate Degree
Program: Occupational; 2-Year Principally Bachelor's Creditable
Accreditation: NW, ACBSP, ACFEI, ADNUR, DH, MAC, OTA, PTAA, RAD, SURGT

02 President ....Dr. Cynthia A. BIOTEAU
05 Provost .... Dr. Chris PICARD
10 Business Services Vice Pres .... Mr. Dennis KLAUS
32 Student Services Vice President ....Dr. Deneece HUFTALIN
30 Vice Pres Institutional Advancement .... Mr. Tim SHEEHAN
20 Asst VP/Dean Professnl & Econ Devel ....Ms. Karen GUNN
20 Asst VP Institutional Effectiveness ....Ms. Barbara GROVER
20 Assistant VP of Budget Services .... Ms. Kimberly HENRIE
15 Assistant VP of Human Resources .... Mr. Craig GARDNER
18 Assistant VP of Facilities ....Mr. Robert ASKERLUND
35 Dean of Students/Assistant VP ....Dr. Marlin CLARK
45 Asst VP Student Planning & Support ....Dr. Nancy SINGER
84 Asst VP Student Enrollment Services ....Mr. Eric WEBER
26 Asst VP Institutional Mktg/Communic .... Ms. Alison MCFARLANE
75 Int Dean Apprent/Aviation/Tech Spec .... Mr. Rick BOUILLON
49 Dean Arts/Communication/New Media .... Dr. Anna SZABADOS
50 Dean School of Business .... Mr. Dennis BROMLEY
53 Dean General & Developmental Educ .... Dr. David HUBERT
76 Dean School of Health Sciences .... Dr. Loredana HAEGER
79 Dean Humanities & Social Sciences .... Dr. John MCCORMICK
81 Dean Science/Math & Engineering .... Dr. Clifton SANDERS
08 Dean Learning Resources ....Dr. Tiffany EVANS
41 Athletic Director .... Ms. Norma CARR
88 Director Student Ctr/Auxiliary Svc .... Mr. Jason BEAL
88 Executive Director Grand Theatre ....Mr. Richard SCOTT
38 Director Academic Advising .... Ms. Sonia PARKER
78 Director of Co-operative Education ....Mr. Jack HESLEPH
36 Dir Student Assessment/Placement .... Ms. Diana HARVEY
06 Registrar .... Ms. MaryEtta CHASE
37 Director Financial Aid ....Ms. Cristi MILLARD
19 Director Parking & Security .... Mr. Shane CRABTREE
88 Director of Risk Management .... Ms. Nancy SANCHEZ
27 Chief Information Officer .... Mr. Jim PULLIAM
21 Controller/Business Manager .... Mr. Douglas HANSEN
22 EEO Director ....Ms. Mozelle ORTON
96 Director of Purchasing .... Ms. Lois WIESEMANN
25 Director of Grants & Contracts ....Ms. Susan SALEM
30 Director of Development .... Ms. Nancy BROWN
09 Director of Institutional Research ....Mr. Ray EMETT
29 Alumni Coordinator ....Mr. Matt BUNKER

Vista College (D)

775 South 2000 East, Clearfield UT 84015
County: Davis FICE Identification: 025728
Unit ID: 377342
Telephone: (801) 774-9900 Carnegie Class: Not Classified
FAX Number: (801) 774-0111 Calendar System: Other
URL: www.vistacollege.edu
Established: N/A Annual Undergrad Tuition & Fees: $20,613
Enrollment: 101 Coed
Affiliation or Control: Proprietary IRS Status: Proprietary
Highest Offering: Associate Degree
Program: Occupational
Accreditation: ACCSC

01 Director .... Mr. Scott TOMLIN

Western Governors University (E)

4001 S 700 E, Suite 700, Salt Lake City UT 84107-2533
County: Salt Lake FICE Identification: 033394
Unit ID: 433387
Telephone: (801) 274-3280 Carnegie Class: Master's L
FAX Number: (801) 274-3305 Calendar System: Other
URL: www.wgu.edu
Established: 1996 Annual Undergrad Tuition & Fees: $5,780
Enrollment: 25,000 Coed
Affiliation or Control: Independent Non-Profit IRS Status: 501(c)3
Highest Offering: Master's
Program: Teacher Preparatory; Professional
Accreditation: NW, DETC, NURSE, TED

01 President ....Dr. Robert W. MENDENHALL
10 Vice Pres Finance/Administration .... David GROW
26 Vice President of Marketing .... Patrick PARTRIDGE
09 Vice Pres Quality/Inst Research ....Dr. James E. SCHNITZ
88 Vice Pres of Strategic Relations .... Ken SORBER
15 Vice President of Human Resources ....Nanette BLACK
20 Associate Provost Student Mentoring .... Chris MALLET
20 Assoc Provost Program Management ......Dr. Gregory W. FOWLER
20 Associate Provost Academic Services .... Dr. Stacey LUDWIG-JOHNSON
20 Assoc Provost Teachers Col/Accred .... Dr. Phil SCHMIDT
20 Associate Provost Assessment ....Dr. Janet W. SCHNITZ
76 Dean College of Health Professions .... Jan JONES-SCHENK
27 Director of Public Relations .... Joan MITCHELL
84 Director of Enrollment .... Eddie RIOS
88 Director of Marketing ....Mara FINESHRIBER
37 Director of Financial Aid ....Jenny ALLEN RYAN
29 Director Alumni Service ....Dr. Gregory W. FOWLER

Westminster College (F)

1840 S 1300 E, Salt Lake City UT 84105-3697
County: Salt Lake FICE Identification: 003681
Unit ID: 230807
Telephone: (801) 484-7651 Carnegie Class: Master's M
FAX Number: (801) 466-6916 Calendar System: Semester
URL: www.westminstercollege.edu
Established: 1875 Annual Undergrad Tuition & Fees: $27,182
Enrollment: 3,163 Coed
Affiliation or Control: Independent Non-Profit IRS Status: 501(c)3
Highest Offering: Master's
Program: Liberal Arts And General; Teacher Preparatory; Professional
Accreditation: NW, ACBSP, ANEST, NURSE, TEAC

01 President ....Dr. Michael S. BASSIS
05 Provost & VP Academic Affairs .... Dr. James E. SEIDELMAN
30 Vice Pres Institutional Advancement ....Mr. Stephen R. MORGAN
10 Vice Pres Finance & Administration .... Mr. Curtis W. RYAN
84 Interim VP Enrollment Services .... Dr. Gary DAYNES
26 Executive Director of Communication .... Ms. Laura A. MURPHY
32 Assoc Provost Student Development ....Dr. Susan D. HEATH
49 Dean School of Arts & Sciences ....Dr. Mary Jane CHASE
66 Dean School of Nursing/Hlth Science ....Dr. Sheryl STEADMAN
50 Dean School of Business .... Dr. Jin WANG
53 Dean School of Education .... Dr. Robert A. SHAW
106 Dean Division of New Learning ....Dr. Aric KRAUSE
35 Dean of Students .... Mr. Mark FERNE
100 Director of Government Relations ....Dr. Bob SELTZER
29 Dir Alumni/Community & Board Rels ....Ms. Annalisa A. HOLCOMBE
09 Assoc Provost Inst Research/Assess ....Dr. Paul PRESSON
88 Assoc Provost Integrative Learning .... Dr. Gary DAYNES
28 Assoc Provost Diversity/Global Lrng .... Dr. Bridget NEWELL
14 Chief Information Officer ....Mr. Robert ALLRED
88 Director of New Ventures ....Mr. Rex FALKENRATH
43 General Counsel/Risk Management .... Ms. Kelly D. HILL
21 Director of Accounting Services ....Ms. Jennifer MEDRANO
15 Director of Human Resources .... Mr. Darin JONES
06 Registrar .... Ms. Mindy WENNERGREN
37 Director of Financial Aid ....Mr. Sean VIEW
07 Director of Admissions .... Ms. Elizabeth KEY
18 Director Plant/Facilities .... Mr. Richard A. BROCKMYER
36 Director of Career Resource Center ....Mr. Mike CALDWELL
08 Director of Library .... Ms. Diane VANDERPOL
44 Asst VP Institutional Advancement .... Ms. Lisa ACTOR
96 Director of Purchasing ....Mr. Alfred W. JOHANSEN
35 Dir of Stdnt Involvement & Ldrship .... Ms. Trisha TEIG
39 Director of Residential Life .... Mr. Cullen GREEN
88 Director Start Center ....Ms. Deborah VICKERY
88 Director of Conferences .... Mr. Jeff BROWN
19 Director of Campus Patrol/Safety ....Mr. Saeed REZAI
41 Director of Athletics .... Mr. Shay WYATT
91 Admin Database Support Coordinator .... Mr. Kyle RIMA
42 Director of Spiritual Life ....Ms. Jan SAAED
38 Director of Campus Counseling ....Ms. Lisa JONES
92 Director of Honors Program .... Dr. Richard BADENHAUSEN

VERMONT

Bennington College (G)

One College Drive, Bennington VT 05201-6003
County: Bennington FICE Identification: 003682
Unit ID: 230816
Telephone: (802) 442-5401 Carnegie Class: Bac/A&S
FAX Number: (802) 447-4269 Calendar System: Semester
URL: www.bennington.edu
Established: 1932 Annual Undergrad Tuition & Fees: $42,800
Enrollment: 811 Coed
Affiliation or Control: Independent Non-Profit IRS Status: 501(c)3
Highest Offering: Master's
Program: Liberal Arts And General; Teacher Preparatory
Accreditation: EH

01 President .... Dr. Elizabeth COLEMAN
05 Dean of the College .... Ms. Isabel ROCHE
10 VP and Chief Financial Officer .... Ms. Laura KRAUSE
30 VP for External Relations ....Ms. Paige BARTELS
45 VP for Planning & Special Programs ....Ms. Joan GOODRICH
07 Dean of Admissions & Financial Aid ....Mr. Ken HIMMELMAN
32 Dean of Students .... Ms. Eva CHATTERJEE-SUTTON
11 VP for Planning and Administration .... Mr. David G. REES
26 Director of Communications ....Ms. Janet L. MARSDEN
88 Associate Provost .... Dr. Wendy HIRSCH
20 Associate Dean of the College .... Mr. Duncan DOBBELMANN
37 Director of Financial Aid ....Ms. Meg WOOLMINGTON
08 Director of Library & Info Services ....Ms. Oceana WILSON
36 Director of Field Work Term .... Ms. Tammy FRASER
15 Director of Human Resources ....Ms. Heather FALEY
18 Director of Facilities Management ....Mr. William TRONSEN

Burlington College (H)

351 North Avenue, Burlington VT 05401-8477
County: Chittenden FICE Identification: 012183
Unit ID: 230825
Telephone: (802) 862-9616 Carnegie Class: Bac/A&S
FAX Number: (802) 660-4331 Calendar System: Semester
URL: www.burlington.edu
Established: 1972 Annual Undergrad Tuition & Fees: $22,410
Enrollment: 192 Coed
Affiliation or Control: Independent Non-Profit IRS Status: 501(c)3
Highest Offering: Master's
Program: Liberal Arts And General
Accreditation: EH

01 President .... Vacant
05 Vice Pres Academic/Student Affairs .... Dr. Arthur C. HESSLER
10 VP of Administration/Finance .... Ms. Christine PLUNKETT
30 Vice Pres Instit Advancement .... Dr. Michael F. LUCK
32 Director of Students .... Mr. Greg LITCHFIELD
18 Director of Physical Plant .... Mr. Michael O'MALLEY
07 Director of Admissions .... Ms. Gillian HOMSTED
13 Director Information Technology .... Mr. Jordan M. YOUNG
78 Director Independent Study .... Ms. Emily SCHMIDT
06 Registrar .... Ms. Melissa LONG
08 Dir Library/Information Services .... Ms. Jessica ALLARD
37 Director of Financial Aid .... Ms. Lindy WALSH

Champlain College (A)

163 S Willard Street, Burlington VT 05402-0670
County: Chittenden FICE Identification: 003684
Unit ID: 230852
Telephone: (802) 860-2700 Carnegie Class: Bac/Diverse
FAX Number: (802) 860-2750 Calendar System: Semester
URL: www.champlain.edu
Established: 1956 Annual Undergrad Tuition & Fees: $28,350
Enrollment: 3,055 Coed
Affiliation or Control: Independent Non-Profit IRS Status: 501(c)3
Highest Offering: Master's
Program: Liberal Arts And General; Teacher Preparatory; Professional
Accreditation: **EH**, RAD, @SW

01 President .... Dr. David F. FINNEY
05 Provost .... Dr. Robin ABRAMSON
10 Vice President Finances .... David J. PROVOST
84 Vice Pres Enrollment/Student Life .... Dr. Mary Kay KENNEDY
30 Vice President Advancement .... Michele RICHARDSON
13 Asst Vice Pres Information Systems .... Paul DUSINI
32 Assoc Vice President Student Life .... Leslie AVERILL
20 Associate Provost .... Dr. Michelle MILLER
104 Associate Provost-Education Abroad .... Dr. James CROSS
53 Dean Education/Human Stds Div .... Dr. Susan ROWLEY
88 Dean Comm/Creative Media Division .... Dr. Jeffrey RUTENBECK
50 Dean Business Division .... Dr. Lynne BALLARD
77 Dean Information Tech/Science .... Dr. Ali RAFIEYMEHR
51 Dean Continuing/Online Education .... Vacant
09 Institutional Effectiveness Dir .... Ms. Diane HOWE
07 Director of Admissions .... Ian MORTIMER
06 Registrar .... Rebecca PETERSON
37 Director of Financial Aid .... Kristi JOVELL
38 Director of Counseling .... Carol MORAN-BROWN
18 Director of Physical Plant .... Thomas BONNETTE
19 Director of Security & Safety .... Richard LONG
23 Director Health Services .... Cissy MCCLELLAN
22 Director of Affirmative Action .... Sarah POTTER
39 Director of Residential Life .... Ashley MIKELL
85 Foreign Students Advisor .... Kathy LYNN
21 Comptroller .... Shelley NAVARI
27 Public Information & News Director .... Stephen MEASE
29 Director of Alumni Relations .... Alison JOHNSON
36 Director Career Services .... Dolly SHAW
15 Director Human Resources .... Sarah POTTER
08 Director Library .... Janet COTTRELL
28 Dir Student Diversity/Inclusion .... Ame LAMBERT
103 Director Workforce Development .... Melissa HERSH
04 Executive Assistant .... Diana AGUSTA
40 Bookstore Manager .... Susan BROWN

College of St. Joseph (B)

71 Clement Road, Rutland VT 05701-3899
County: Rutland FICE Identification: 003685
Unit ID: 231077
Telephone: (802) 773-5900 Carnegie Class: Master's S
FAX Number: (802) 776-5258 Calendar System: Semester
URL: www.csj.edu
Established: 1956 Annual Undergrad Tuition & Fees: $19,465
Enrollment: 418 Coed
Affiliation or Control: Roman Catholic IRS Status: 501(c)3
Highest Offering: Master's
Program: Liberal Arts And General; Teacher Preparatory; Professional
Accreditation: **EH**

01 President .... Dr. Frank G. MIGLORIE, JR.
05 Academic Dean .... Dr. Nancy J. KLINE
07 Dean of Admissions .... Mr. Alan E. YOUNG
32 Dean of Student Services .... Mr. Robert P. LUKASKIEWICZ
37 Director of Financial Aid .... Mrs. Julie ROSMUS
30 Dir Development/Alumni Relations .... Mrs. Deborah DOENGES
41 Director of Athletics .... Mr. Raymond FISH
06 Registrar .... Mrs. Patricia MIGLORIE
14 CIS Administrator .... Mr. Raymond GIBBS
35 Director of Student Support Svcs .... Ms. Linda JOHNSON
21 Controller .... Mrs. Karen REYNOLDS
18 Chief Facilities/Physical Plant .... Mr. Thomas BELAND
10 Business Manager .... Mrs. Kristie JOHNSON
49 Chair Arts & Sciences .... Dr. David BALFOUR
50 Chair Business .... Dr. Robert FOLEY
53 Chair Education .... Dr. Maria BOVE
15 Chair Psychology/Human Services .... Dr. Michael KESLER
08 Librarian .... Ms. Doreen MCCULLOUGH

Goddard College (C)

123 Pitkin Road, Plainfield VT 05667-9432
County: Washington FICE Identification: 003686
Unit ID: 230889
Telephone: (800) 468-4888 Carnegie Class: Master's M
FAX Number: (802) 454-1029 Calendar System: Semester
URL: www.goddard.edu
Established: 1863 Annual Undergrad Tuition & Fees: $14,982
Enrollment: 804 Coed
Affiliation or Control: Independent Non-Profit IRS Status: 501(c)3
Highest Offering: Master's
Program: Liberal Arts And General; Teacher Preparatory
Accreditation: **EH**

01 President .... Dr. Barbara VACARR
05 Interim Academic Vice President .... Dr. Marianne REIFF
10 Vice President Finance and Admin .... Ms. Faith BROWN
88 Exec Asst to Academic VP .... Mr. George HALLSMITH
30 Dean of Institutional Advancement .... Ms. Julie MARTIN
32 Associate Dean of Community Life .... Ms. Susan A. WILSON
06 Associate Academic Dean & Registrar .... Mr. Josh CASTLE
90 Associate Dean Library & IT Service .... Mr. Chris RIDDELL
37 Director of Financial Aid .... Ms. Beverly JENE
88 Director of Campus Services .... Mr. Paul SHPER
08 Director of Information Access .... Ms. Clara BRUNS
18 Director of Facilities Operations .... Mr. Scott BLANCHARD
12 Director of Port Townsend Campus .... Ms. Erin FRISTAD
21 Director of Business Office .... Ms. Sherri MOLLEUR
04 Exec Asst to President .... Ms. Caro THOMPSON
88 Manager of WGDR/WGDH Radio .... Mr. Kris GRUEN

Green Mountain College (D)

1 Brennan Circle, Poultney VT 05764-1199
County: Rutland FICE Identification: 003687
Unit ID: 230898
Telephone: (802) 287-8000 Carnegie Class: Bac/A&S
FAX Number: (802) 287-8099 Calendar System: Semester
URL: www.greenmtn.edu
Established: 1834 Annual Undergrad Tuition & Fees: $29,316
Enrollment: 790 Coed
Affiliation or Control: Independent Non-Profit IRS Status: 501(c)3
Highest Offering: Master's
Program: Liberal Arts And General; Teacher Preparatory
Accreditation: **EH**

01 President .... Dr. Paul J. FONTEYN
05 Vice President Academic Affairs .... Dr. William M. THROOP
10 Vice Pres Finance/Administration .... Mr. Joseph A. MANNING, III
32 Vice President Student Affairs .... Dr. Joseph PETRICK
04 Executive Assistant to President .... Ms. Jeanne V. ROOT
20 Dean of Faculty .... Dr. Thomas J. MAUHS-PUGH
84 Dean of Enrollment Management .... Mr. Robert J. GOULD
30 Director of Development .... Ms. Mary Lou WILLITS
06 Registrar .... Ms. Sharon L. HOFFMAN
18 Director of Facilities .... Mr. Glenn LAPLANTE
19 Director of Public Safety .... Mr. Steven BROWN
26 Director of Public Relations .... Mr. Kevin COBURN
40 Manager of Book Store .... Ms. Heather LYNG
41 Athletic Director .... Ms. Marybeth LENNOX
08 Director Library & Information Svcs .... Mr. Paul MILLETTE
85 Director of International Pgms .... Ms. Anne COLPITTS
13 Director Computing & Info Mgmt .... Mr. Jeffrey WRIGHT
42 Chaplain .... Ms. Shirley OSKAMP
29 Dir Alumni Relations/Annual Giving .... Vacant
36 Director of Career Counseling .... Ms. Renee BEAUPRE WHITE
92 Director of College Honors Program .... Dr. Jennifer SELLERS
37 Director Student Financial Aid .... Ms. Wendy ELLIS
15 Director Human Resources .... Ms. Janie EVANS
38 Director Student Counseling .... Ms. Jessica LEY

Landmark College (E)

River Road South, Putney VT 05346
County: Windham FICE Identification: 025326
Unit ID: 247649
Telephone: (802) 387-4767 Carnegie Class: Assoc/PrivNFP
FAX Number: (802) 387-6868 Calendar System: Semester
URL: www.landmark.edu
Established: 1985 Annual Undergrad Tuition & Fees: $49,000
Enrollment: 487 Coed
Affiliation or Control: Independent Non-Profit IRS Status: 501(c)3
Highest Offering: Associate Degree
Program: 2-Year Principally Bachelor's Creditable
Accreditation: **EH**

01 President .... Dr. Peter A. EDEN
03 Senior Vice President .... Dr. Brent BETIT
05 Academic Dean .... Dr. Adrienne MAJOR
10 Vice President Administration/Finan .... Mr. Alan RUSSELL
26 VP Public Relations & Marketing .... Mr. Steve MULLER
84 Vice Pres Enrollment Management .... Ms. Dale HEROLD
04 Assistant to the President .... Vacant
88 Dean Short-Term Pgms/Transfer Svcs .... Dr. John NISSEN
35 Dean of Students .... Mr. Michael LUCIANI
18 Director of Physical Plant .... Mr. James LOVERING
08 Head Librarian .... Ms. Jennifer LANN
06 Registrar .... Ms. Karen DAMIAN
41 Director Activities/Athletics .... Mr. James AUSTIN
37 Director Student Financial Aid .... Ms. Catherine MULLINS
38 Director of Student Counseling .... Mrs. Julie OSHERSON
23 Director of Health Services .... Ms. Simone HOLTON
40 Bookstore Manager .... Ms. Kimberly JUDD

Marlboro College (F)

PO Box A, Marlboro VT 05344-9999
County: Windham FICE Identification: 003690
Unit ID: 230940
Telephone: (802) 257-4333 Carnegie Class: Bac/A&S
FAX Number: (802) 257-4154 Calendar System: Semester
URL: www.marlboro.edu
Established: 1946 Annual Undergrad Tuition & Fees: $35,560
Enrollment: 279 Coed
Affiliation or Control: Independent Non-Profit IRS Status: 501(c)3
Highest Offering: Master's
Program: Liberal Arts And General
Accreditation: **EH**

01 President .... Ms. Ellen M. LOVELL
10 Senior Financial Mgmt Officer .... Ms. Anne PRATT
05 Dean of Faculty/Graduate Educ .... Mr. Richard GLEJZER
07 Dean of Admissions .... Ms. Nicole CURVIN
32 Dean of Students .... Mr. Ken SCHNECK
58 Associate Dean Graduate School .... Mr. Sean CONLEY
84 Dir Enrollment Stdt Svc at Grad Ctr .... Mr. Joseph HESLIN
46 Chief Planning & Budget Officer .... Mr. Bryant MORGAN
08 Librarian .... Ms. Emily ALLING
06 Registrar .... Ms. Virginia NELLIS
29 Director Alumni & Annual Programs .... Vacant
30 Director Development/ Communications .... Ms. Lisa M. CHRISTENSEN
18 Director of Plant Operations .... Mr. Dan J. COTTER
80 World Studies Director .... Vacant
40 Bookstore Manager .... Ms. Rebecca BARTLETT

Middlebury College (G)

Old Chapel, Middlebury VT 05753-6200
County: Addison FICE Identification: 003691
Unit ID: 230959
Telephone: (802) 443-5000 Carnegie Class: Bac/A&S
FAX Number: (802) 443-2071 Calendar System: 4/1/4
URL: www.middlebury.edu
Established: 1800 Annual Undergrad Tuition & Fees: $53,800
Enrollment: 2,532 Coed
Affiliation or Control: Independent Non-Profit IRS Status: 501(c)3
Highest Offering: Doctorate
Program: Liberal Arts And General
Accreditation: **EH**

01 President .... Dr. Ronald D. LIEBOWITZ
05 Provost/Chief Academic Officer .... Ms. Alison BYERLY
10 Vice Pres for Finance/Treasurer .... Mr. Patrick J. NORTON
11 Vice President for Administration .... Dr. Tim SPEARS
30 Sr Vice Pres/Philanthropic Advisor .... Mr. Michael SCHOENFELD
58 VP Language Sch/Sch Abroad/Grad Pgm .... Dr. Michael GEISLER
20 Dean of Curriculum .... Dr. Bob CLUSS
20 Dean of the Faculty .... Dr. Jim RALPH
28 Dean of College/Chf Diversity Ofcr .... Dr. Shirley COLLADO
20 Dn Plng/Assess/Dir Col Self Study .... Dr. Susan CAMPBELL
38 Exec Dir Health & Counseling Svcs .... Dr. Augustus JORDAN
08 Dean of Library & Information Svcs .... Mr. Michael D. ROY
07 Dean of Admissions .... Mr. Gregory B. BUCKLES
37 Assoc VP Student Financial Services .... Ms. Kim DOWNS
06 College Registrar .... Mr. LeRoy GRAHAM
21 Assoc VP Budget/Financial Planning .... Ms. Kristen C. ANDERSON
21 Asst Treasurer/Dir of Business Svcs .... Mr. Thomas CORBIN
15 Assoc VP for HR/Organiz Development .... Ms. Drew MACAN
19 Dir Public Safety/Assoc Dn Sdt Affs .... Ms. Elizabeth B. BURCHARD
29 Assoc VP for Alumni Relations .... Ms. Margaret STOREY GROVES
26 Executive Director Communications .... Mr. Timothy ETCHELLS
42 Chaplain .... Ms. Laurel JORDAN
41 Director of Athletics .... Mr. Erin QUINN
26 Director of Public Affairs .... Ms. Sarah RAY
88 President MIIS .... Dr. Sunder RAMASWAMY
40 Bookstore Manager .... Ms. Georgia BEST

† Tuition figure is a comprehensive fees figure.

New England Culinary Institute (H)

56 College Street, Montpelier VT 05602-9720
County: Washington FICE Identification: 022540
Unit ID: 230977
Telephone: (802) 223-6324 Carnegie Class: Spec/Other
FAX Number: (802) 225-3280 Calendar System: Semester
URL: www.neci.edu
Established: 1980 Annual Undergrad Tuition & Fees: $27,725
Enrollment: 615 Coed
Affiliation or Control: Proprietary IRS Status: Proprietary
Highest Offering: Baccalaureate
Program: Occupational; Technical Emphasis
Accreditation: **ACCSC**

01 CEO .... Mr. Francis VOIGT
01 President .... Mr. Bill MECKERT
84 Vice President Enrollment Managemnt .... Ms. Elena JENSEN
11 Vice President Admin & Finance .... Mr. Rob HOFMANN
05 Vice President Education .... Ms. Kathy FINCK
88 Vice President Food & Bev Ops .... Mr. Kevin O'DONNELL
88 Chair Baking & Pastry Programs .... Chef Michael RHOADS
88 Chair School of HRM .... Ms. Michelle FORD
45 Dirr Compliance Academic Services .... Ms. Laureen GAUTHIER
106 Director of Online Programs .... Chef Curtiss HEMM
32 Director of Student Services .... Dr. Eric KECK
06 Registrar .... Ms. Liz FITZGERALD
07 Director of Admissions .... Vacant
08 Head Librarian .... Ms. Jessica JOYAL
13 Director Information Technology .... Mr. Nik ZNAMENSKIS

15 Director Human Resources .... Ms. Jennifer ZETARSKI
18 Director of Facilities .... Mr. William COLGAN
36 Manager Career Services .... Ms. Ketlyn OLSON
06 Assistant Registrar .... Ms. Elizabeth SMITH

Norwich University (A)

158 Harmon Drive, Northfield VT 05663-1000
County: Washington FICE Identification: 003692
Unit ID: 230995
Telephone: (802) 485-2000 Carnegie Class: Master's L
FAX Number: (802) 485-2032 Calendar System: Semester
URL: www.norwich.edu
Established: 1819 Annual Undergrad Tuition & Fees: $29,704
Enrollment: 2,368 Coed
Affiliation or Control: Independent Non-Profit IRS Status: 501(c)3
Highest Offering: Master's
Program: Liberal Arts And General; Teacher Preparatory; Professional
Accreditation: EH, ACBSP, ENG, NUR, NURSE

01 President .... Dr. Richard W. SCHNEIDER
05 VP Academic Affairs/Dean of Faculty .... Dr. Guiyou HUANG
48 Dean School of Architecture .... Mr. Aron TEMPKIN
50 Dean School of Business .... Dr. Frank VANECEK
83 Dean School of Social Sciences .... Dr. Thomas TAYLOR
54 Dean School of Engineering .... Dr. Saeed MOAVENI
79 Dean School of Humanities .... Dr. Jonathan WALTERS
81 Dean School of Math/Science .... Ms. Cathy FREY
88 Dean School of National Services .... Col. Patrick BELATTE
30 Vice Pres Institutional Advancement .... Mr. David J. WHALEY
13 VP Strategic Partnership .... Mr. Phillip SUSMANN
84 VP of Enrollment & Communications .... Ms. Karen MCGRATH
29 Asst VP for Alumni and Vol Progrms .... Mr. Paul BOVA
20 Associate VP Academic Affairs .... Dr. Joseph BYRNE
32 Commandant/VP Student Affairs .... Dr. Michael KELLEY
04 Assistant to President .... Ms. Judith A. BAILEY
10 Chief Financial Officer .... Ms. Lauren WOBBY
11 Chief Administrative Officer .... Mr. David MAGIDA
88 Director of Retention & Enrollment .... Ms. Shelby WALLACE
88 Coord Office of Communications .... Mr. Mark ALBURY
35 Dean of Students .... Ms. Martha MATHIS
09 Dir Instnl Research/Effectiveness .... Ms. Ellalou ZIRBLIS
15 Director of Human Resources .... Mr. Jay WISNER
08 Head Librarian .... Ms. Ellen HALL
41 Athletic Director .... Mr. Anthony A. MARIANO
18 Director Facilities/Operations .... Mr. Bizhan YAHYAZADEH
37 Director Student Financial Aid .... Ms. Tracy STEINE
38 Director Student Counseling .... Dr. Melvin MILLER
07 Director of Admissions .... Ms. Sherri GILMORE

Saint Michael's College (B)

One Winooski Park, Colchester VT 05439-0001
County: Chittenden FICE Identification: 003694
Unit ID: 231059
Telephone: (802) 654-2000 Carnegie Class: Bac/A&S
FAX Number: (802) 654-2297 Calendar System: Semester
URL: www.smcvt.edu
Established: 1904 Annual Undergrad Tuition & Fees: $35,940
Enrollment: 2,457 Coed
Affiliation or Control: Roman Catholic IRS Status: 501(c)3
Highest Offering: Master's
Program: Liberal Arts And General; Teacher Preparatory
Accreditation: EH, CEA

01 President .... Dr. John J. NEUHAUSER
04 Assistant to the President .... Ms. Lisa B. POWLISON
05 Vice Pres Academic Affairs .... Dr. Karen A. TALENTINO
10 Vice President for Finance .... Mr. Neal ROBINSON
32 Vice President for Student Affairs .... Mr. Michael D. SAMARA
84 Vice President for Enrollment .... Mr. Jerry E. FLANAGAN
16 Vice President for Human Resources .... Mr. Michael J. NEW
30 VP for Institutional Advancement .... Mr. Patrick J. GALLIVAN
20 Dean of the College .... Dr. Jeffrey A. TRUMBOWER
42 Director Edmundite Campus Ministry .... Rev. Brian J. CUMMINGS, SSE
07 Director of Admission .... Ms. Jacqueline MURPHY
37 Director Student Financial Services .... Mr. Daniel R. COUTURE
06 Registrar .... Mr. John D. SHEEHEY
09 Director of Institutional Research .... Mr. John P. KULHOWVICK
29 Director of Alumni/Parent Relations .... Ms. Angela ARMOUR
35 Director Student Activities .... Ms. Grace A. KELLY
93 Dir Intercultural Student Affairs .... Mr. Moise ST. LOUIS
39 Director of Residence Life .... Mr. Louis DIMASI
88 Associate Dean of the College .... Dr. Joan R. WRY
104 Director of Study Abroad .... Ms. Peggy H. IMAI
92 Honors Program Faculty Coordinator .... Dr. Nicholas CLARY
94 Coord of Gender/Women's Studies .... Dr. Carey KAPLAN
08 Dir Library & Information Services .... Mr. John K. PAYNE
13 Chief Information Officer .... Mr. William O. ANDERSON
14 Director of Information Tech .... Ms. Billie MILES
26 Dir of Marketing/Communications .... Dr. Buff L. LINDAU
86 Dir Government/Community Relations ... Ms. Marilyn E. CORMIER
19 Director of Public Safety .... Mr. Peter D. SOONS
18 Director of Facilities .... Mr. David A. CUTLER
38 Director of Personal Counseling .... Ms. Linda HOLLINGDALE
36 Director of Career Development .... Ms. Christine CLARY
23 Director of Health Services .... Ms. Mary MASSON
41 Director of Athletics .... Dr. Geraldine KNORTZ
44 Director of Advancement Services .... Ms. Linda V. DONAHUE
102 Director of Foundation Relations .... Ms. Angela IRVINE

88 Financial Accounting Manager .... Ms. Shirley J. GOODELL-LACKEY
21 Director of Finance .... Ms. Mary Jane RUSSELL
96 Director of Business Services .... Mr. Robert ROBINSON
40 Bookstore Manager .... Mr. Stephen MCMAHON
31 Community Service Coordinator .... Ms. Heidi ST. PETER
105 Dir of Web Site Development .... Mr. Brian MACDONALD
44 Director of Individual Giving .... Ms. Terri P. SELBY

School for International Training (C)

Kipling Road, Brattleboro VT 05302-0676
County: Windham FICE Identification: 008860
Unit ID: 231068
Telephone: (802) 257-7751 Carnegie Class: Master's L
FAX Number: (802) 258-3248 Calendar System: Other
URL: www.worldlearning.org
Established: 1964 Annual Undergrad Tuition & Fees: $20,187
Enrollment: 843 Coed
Affiliation or Control: Independent Non-Profit IRS Status: 501(c)3
Highest Offering: Master's
Program: Teacher Preparatory; Professional
Accreditation: EH

01 President .... Dr. Adam WEINBERG
05 Provost & VP of Academic Affairs .... Dr. Lynne ROSANSKY
10 CFO .... Ms. Nancy R. BROCK
13 Vice Pres & Chief Information Ofcr .... Mr. Michael KEARNEY
43 General Counsel .... Ms. Lisa RAE
83 Dean SIT Graduate/Professional Stds .... Vacant
84 Dean External Rels/Strtgc Enrol Mgt .... Ms. Laurie BLACK
16 Director of Human Resources .... Mrs. Rachel HENRY
30 Director of Advancement .... Mr. Tom NAVIN
26 Director of Communications .... Ms. Laura INGALLS
28 Director Ctr for Intercultural Pgms .... Ms. Beatriz FANTINI
06 Registrar .... Ms. Jennifer CANNIZZARO
37 Director Financial Aid .... Ms. Michelle KRAJNIK
32 Director Student Services .... Mr. Tony DRAPELICK
18 Director Facilities Management .... Mr. Andrew MARTYN, SR.

Southern Vermont College (D)

982 Mansion Drive, Bennington VT 05201-6002
County: Bennington FICE Identification: 003693
Unit ID: 231086
Telephone: (802) 442-5427 Carnegie Class: Bac/Diverse
FAX Number: (802) 447-4695 Calendar System: Semester
URL: www.svc.edu
Established: 1926 Annual Undergrad Tuition & Fees: $19,800
Enrollment: 500 Coed
Affiliation or Control: Independent Non-Profit IRS Status: 501(c)3
Highest Offering: Baccalaureate
Program: Occupational; Liberal Arts And General
Accreditation: EH, ADNUR, NUR, RAD

01 President .... Dr. Karen GROSS
10 Chief Financial Officer/COO .... Mr. James BECKWITH
04 Executive Assistant .... Ms. Colleen LITTLE
41 Director of Athletics .... Vacant
05 Provost .... Dr. Albert C. DECICCIO
20 Associate Academic Dean .... Ms. Sylvia JIMISON
20 Associate Academic Dean .... Dr. Daniel C. YALOWITZ
50 Chair Business .... Mr. Eric DROUART
66 Chair Nursing .... Dr. Karen CLEMENT O'BRIEN
79 Chair of Humanities .... Dr. Scott O'CALLAGHAN
81 Chair of Science and Technology .... Dr. Barry FLANARY
83 Chair of Social Sciences .... Mr. Scott STEIN
08 Director Learning Resources .... Ms. Sarah SANFILIPPO
06 Registrar .... Mr. James FREDERICK
36 Director of Career Services .... Ms. Denise SPENCER
18 Director of Facilities .... Mr. Mark J. KLAUDER
32 Dean of Students .... Ms. Anne M. HOPKINS GROSS
38 Director of Counseling .... Mr. Michael GOODWIN
39 Director of Residence Life .... Ms. Sara PATCH
19 Director of Security .... Mr. George MARSHALL
07 Director of Admissions .... Vacant
37 Director of Financial Aid .... Ms. Joel PHELPS
30 Dean of Development .... Vacant
27 Director of Communications .... Ms. Susan BIGGS
29 Dir Alumni Relations/Annual Fund .... Ms. Daryl KENNY
16 Director of Human Resources .... Ms. Sue METZNER
88 Coord Learning Disabilities .... Mr. David A. LINDENBERG

Sterling College (E)

PO Box 72, Craftsbury Common VT 05827-0072
County: Orleans FICE Identification: 021435
Unit ID: 231095
Telephone: (802) 586-7711 Carnegie Class: Bac/A&S
FAX Number: (802) 586-2596 Calendar System: Semester
URL: www.sterlingcollege.edu
Established: 1958 Annual Undergrad Tuition & Fees: $26,034
Enrollment: 105 Coed
Affiliation or Control: Independent Non-Profit IRS Status: 501(c)3
Highest Offering: Baccalaureate
Program: Liberal Arts And General
Accreditation: EH

01 President .... Mr. William R. WOOTTON
03 Exec VP & Director of Financial Aid .... Mr. Ned R. HOUSTON
05 Dean of Academics .... Dr. Pavel CENKL
07 Director of Admissions .... Ms. Lynne BIRDSALL
04 Administrative Asst to President .... Ms. Michele MARTIN
21 Comptroller/Dir Student Accounts .... Ms. Deborah CLARK
08 Librarian .... Ms. Petra VOGEL
18 Director of Facilities .... Mr. Steve SMITH
38 Director Student Counseling .... Mr. Leland PETERSON
32 Dean of Students .... Ms. Jill FINEIS
30 Director Development/Alumni Rels .... Ms. Barbara MORROW
06 Registrar .... Ms. Laurie LAGGNER
36 Director Career Resource Center .... Ms. Jennifer PAYNE
24 Director of Media Relations .... Mr. Tim PATTERSON

University of Vermont (F)

South Prospect Street, Burlington VT 05405-0160
County: Chittenden FICE Identification: 003696
Unit ID: 231174
Telephone: (802) 656-3131 Carnegie Class: RU/H
FAX Number: N/A Calendar System: Semester
URL: www.uvm.edu
Established: 1791 Annual Undergrad Tuition & Fees (In-State): $14,784
Enrollment: 13,554 Coed
Affiliation or Control: State IRS Status: 501(c)3
Highest Offering: Doctorate
Program: Liberal Arts And General; Teacher Preparatory; Professional
Accreditation: EH, BUS, CACREP, CLPSY, DIETC, DIETD, ENG, MED, MT, NMT, NURSE, PTA, SP, SW, TED

01 Interim President .... Dr. A. John BRAMLEY
05 Senior Vice President & Provost .... Dr. Jane E. KNODELL
10 VP for Finance & Administration .... Mr. Richard H. CATE
32 Vice Pres for Student & Campus Life .... Dr. Thomas J. GUSTAFSON
46 VP Research & Dean Graduate Studies .... Dr. Domenico GRASSO
30 VP Development/Alumni Relations .... Mr. O. Richard BUNDY, III
43 VP Legal Affairs & General Counsel .... Ms. Francine T. BAZLUKE
86 VP Federal/State/Cmty Relations .... Ms. Karen N. MEYER
84 Vice Pres Enrollment Management .... Mr. Christopher H. LUCIER
20 Assoc Provost Faculty & Intl .... Dr. Gayle R. NUNLEY
20 Assoc Provost Curricular Affairs .... Dr. Brian V. REED
28 Chief Diversity Officer .... Dr. Wanda R. HEADING-GRANT
100 Chief of Staff .... Dr. Gary L. DERR
18 Assoc VP Admin & Facility Services .... Mr. William P. BALLARD
15 Assoc VP for Human Resources .... Ms. Barbara L. JOHNSON
35 AVP Campus Life & Dean of Students .... Dr. David A. NESTOR
29 Alumni & Parent Programs Director .... Mr. Alan E. RYEA
63 Dean College of Medicine .... Dr. Frederick C. MORIN, III
66 Dean Nursing & Health Sciences .... Dr. Patricia A. PRELOCK
49 Int Dean Arts & Sciences .... Dr. Joel M. GOLDBERG
47 Dean Agriculture & Life Sciences .... Dr. Thomas C. VOGELMANN
54 Int Dean Engineering & Math Sci .... Dr. Bernard F. COLE
53 Dean Education & Social Services .... Dr. Fayneese S. MILLER
50 Dean Business Administration .... Dr. Sanjay SHARMA
92 Dean Honors College .... Dr. S. Abu RIZVI
65 Dean Environment & Natural Resource .... Dr. Mary C. WATZIN
56 Dean Extension .... Dr. Douglas O. LANTAGNE
51 Dean Continuing Education .... Ms. Cynthia L. BELLIVEAU
08 Dean Libraries & Learning Resources .... Ms. Mara R. SAULE
06 Registrar .... Mr. Keith P. WILLIAMS
09 Director Institutional Research .... Dr. John F. RYAN
27 Director University Communications .... Mr. Enrique CORREDERA
13 Director Computing & Info Tech .... Dr. David TODD
25 Assoc VP Research Administration .... Ms. Ruth A. FARRELL
21 Assoc VP for Budget & Resource Mgmt .... Mr. Ted WINFIELD
19 Chief of Police Services .... Ms. Lianne M. TUOMEY
41 Director of Athletics .... Dr. Robert CORRAN
36 Director Career Services .... Ms. Pamela K. GARDNER
23 Director Ctr for Health & Wellbeing .... Dr. Jon K. PORTER
38 Counsel/Psych Services Program Dir .... Dr. Todd N. WEINMAN
39 Director Residential Life .... Ms. Stacey A. MILLER
40 Director University Bookstore .... Mr. Jay E. MENNINGER
85 Director Intl Education Services .... Ms. Kimberly A. HOWARD
102 Senior Corp & Foundations Officer .... Ms. Chrysanne N. CHOTAS
44 Senior Planned Giving Officer .... Ms. Becky P. ARNOLD
07 Director Graduate Admissions .... Mr. Ralph M. SWENSON, III
07 Director Undergraduate Admissions .... Dr. Elizabeth A. WISER
37 Director Student Financial Services .... Ms. Marie D. JOHNSON
96 Director Procurement Services .... Ms. Natalie L. GUILLETTE
94 Director Women's Center .... Ms. LuAnn K. ROLLEY
24 Access/Media Services Librarian .... Mr. Aaron F. NICHOLS
101 Board of Trustees Coordinator .... Ms. Corinne B. THOMPSON

Vermont College of Fine Arts (G)

36 College Street, Montpelier VT 05602-3145
County: Washington FICE Identification: 003697
Unit ID: 455992
Telephone: (802) 828-8600 Carnegie Class: Not Classified
FAX Number: (802) 828-8649 Calendar System: Semester
URL: www.vermontcollege.edu
Established: 2008 Annual Graduate Tuition & Fees: $18,917
Enrollment: 267 Coed
Affiliation or Control: Independent Non-Profit IRS Status: 501(c)3
Highest Offering: Master's; No Undergraduates
Program: Liberal Arts And General
Accreditation: EH

01 President .... Mr. Thomas Christopher GREENE
05 Academic Dean .... Mr. Gary MOORE
30 Exec Dir Institutional Advancement .... Mr. Peter NIELSEN

Vermont Law School (A)

164 Chelsea Street, PO Box 96,
South Royalton VT 05068-0096
County: Windsor FICE Identification: 011934
Unit ID: 231147
Telephone: (802) 831-1000 Carnegie Class: Spec/Law
FAX Number: (802) 831-1163 Calendar System: Semester
URL: www.vermontlaw.edu
Established: 1972 Annual Graduate Tuition & Fees: $43,468
Enrollment: 694 Coed
Affiliation or Control: Independent Non-Profit IRS Status: 501(c)3
Highest Offering: Doctorate; No Undergraduates
Program: Professional
Accreditation: EH, LAW

01 President & Dean ... Mr. Geoffrey B. SHIELDS
05 Vice Dean for Academic Affairs ... Mr. Gil KUJOVICH
36 Vice President of Operations ... Mr. Dennis STERN
20 Dep Vice Dean for Academic Affairs ... Mr. Mark LATHAM
10 Vice President for Finance & Admin ... Ms. Lorraine ATWOOD
88 Asoc Dn Env Law Pgm/Dir Env Law Ctr ... Mr. Marc MIHALY
32 Assoc Dean Student Affs & Diversity ... Ms. Shirley JEFFERSON
84 Assoc Dean for Enrollment Mgmt ... Ms. Kathy HARTMAN
30 Exec Director Inst Advancement ... Mr. Matt RIZZO
20 Asst Dean for Academic Affairs ... Ms. Clara GIMENEZ
101 Secretary of the Institution/Board ... Ms. Helen MCCARTHY
15 Director Human Resources ... Ms. Diane HAYES
08 Dir Cornell Library & Professor ... Mr. Carl A. YIRKA
21 Comptroller ... Ms. Andrea SYMONDS
06 Dir of Academic Proc & Registrar ... Ms. Kathy MAIELI
37 Associate Director of Financial Aid ... Ms. Patricia BRIGGS
18 Physical Plant Director ... Mr. Jim MCGRATH
26 Director of Communications ... Ms. Carol WESTBERG
91 Director of Information Technology ... Ms. Jeanne EICKS
04 Exec Asst to the President/Dean ... Ms. Rachel SAUERWEIN
40 Manager Barrister's Bookstore ... Ms. Amy MCDOWELL

*Vermont State Colleges System Office (B)

PO Box 359, Waterbury VT 05676-0359
County: Washington FICE Identification: 029162
Unit ID: 231156
Telephone: (802) 241-2520 Carnegie Class: N/A
FAX Number: (802) 241-3369
URL: www.vsc.edu

01 Chancellor ... Mr. Timothy J. DONOVAN
04 Exec Assistant to the Chancellor ... Ms. Julie MASSUCCO
43 Vice President/General Counsel ... Mr. William REEDY
10 Vice Pres/Chief Financial Officer ... Mr. Thomas ROBBINS
86 Director Cmty Rels & Public Policy ... Mr. Daniel SMITH
27 Chief Information Officer ... Ms. Linda HILTON
18 Director of Facilities ... Mr. Richard ETHIER
91 Director Admin Information Systems ... Ms. Dianne POLLACK
13 Director of System Info Tech ... Mr. Rick BLOOD
15 Director of Human Resources ... Ms. Nancy SHAW
09 Director of Institutional Research ... Ms. Hope SWANSON
88 Director of Payroll/Benefits ... Ms. Tracy SWEET

*Castleton State College (C)

86 Seminary Street, Castleton VT 05735-4453
County: Rutland FICE Identification: 003683
Unit ID: 230834
Telephone: (802) 468-5611 Carnegie Class: Bac/A&S
FAX Number: (802) 468-6470 Calendar System: Semester
URL: www.castleton.edu
Established: 1787 Annual Undergrad Tuition & Fees (In-State): $9,668
Enrollment: 2,017 Coed
Affiliation or Control: State IRS Status: 501(c)3
Highest Offering: Master's
Program: Liberal Arts And General; Teacher Preparatory
Accreditation: EH, ADNUR, SW

02 President ... Mr. David S. WOLK
04 Exec Assistant to the President ... Ms. Rita B. GENO
05 Academic Dean ... Dr. Joseph T. MARK
10 Dean of Administration ... Mr. Scott DIKEMAN
32 Dean of Students ... Mr. Dennis PROULX
20 Dean of Education ... Dr. Honoree FLEMING
35 Assistant Dean for Campus Life ... Ms. Victoria ANGIS
06 Registrar ... Ms. Lori PATTEN
08 Director Calvin Coolidge Library ... Ms. Sandra DULING
84 Dean of Enrollment ... Mr. Maurice OUIMET
37 Director Student Financial Aid ... Ms. Kathy O'MEARA
53 Director of Student Teaching ... Mr. Tim CLEARY
15 Director of Human Resources ... Ms. Lyn SAWYER
18 Director of Physical Plant ... Mr. Chuck LAVOIE
21 Controller ... Ms. Heidi WHITNEY
26 Director of Communications ... Mr. Ennis DULING
29 Alumni Affairs/Development Officer ... Mr. George MCGURL
36 Dir of Career Planning/Placement ... Ms. Judith CARRUTHERS
23 Wellness Center Director ... Ms. Martha COULTER
38 Director Student Counseling ... Vacant

*Community College of Vermont (D)

PO Box 489, Montpelier VT 05601
County: Washington FICE Identification: 011167
Unit ID: 230861
Telephone: (802) 828-2800 Carnegie Class: Assoc/Pub-R-L
FAX Number: (802) 828-2805 Calendar System: Semester
URL: www.ccv.edu
Established: 1970 Annual Undergrad Tuition & Fees (In-State): $6,520
Enrollment: 7,303 Coed
Affiliation or Control: State IRS Status: 501(c)3
Highest Offering: Associate Degree
Program: Occupational; 2-Year Principally Bachelor's Creditable
Accreditation: EH

02 President ... Ms. Joyce M. JUDY
84 Executive Dean ... Ms. Susan P. HENRY
11 Dean of Administration ... Dr. Barbara MARTIN
05 Dean of Academic Services ... Ms. Linda GABRIELSON
32 Dean of Student Services ... Ms. Deborah STEWART
12 Northeastern Regional Director ... Ms. Penne CIARALDI
12 NW Regional Operations Director ... Mr. Elmer KIMBALL
12 NW Regional Academic Director ... Ms. Dee STEFFAN
12 Southern Regional Director ... Ms. Tapp BARNHILL
24 Dean of Learning Technologies ... Mr. Eric SAKAI
15 Director Personnel Services ... Mrs. Lisa YAEGER
06 Registrar ... Mr. Thomas ARNER
07 Director of Admissions ... Mr. Adam WARRINGTON
09 Director of Institutional Research ... Mr. David BUCHDAHL
37 Director of Financial Aid ... Ms. Pam CHISHOLM
88 Director Student Support Services ... Ms. Heather WEINSTEIN
29 Director Alumni Relations/Develop ... Vacant
26 Chief Public Relations Officer ... Ms. Robin DUTCHER
10 Chief Business Officer ... Ms. Lorei DAWSON
18 Chief Facilities/Physical Plant ... Mr. Larry ELLIOTT

*Johnson State College (E)

337 College Hill, Johnson VT 05656-9898
County: Lamoille FICE Identification: 003688
Unit ID: 230913
Telephone: (802) 635-2356 Carnegie Class: Master's S
FAX Number: (802) 635-1230 Calendar System: Semester
URL: www.jsc.edu
Established: 1828 Annual Undergrad Tuition & Fees (In-State): $8,989
Enrollment: 1,925 Coed
Affiliation or Control: State IRS Status: 501(c)3
Highest Offering: Master's
Program: 2-Year Principally Bachelor's Creditable; Liberal Arts And General; Teacher Preparatory; Professional
Accreditation: EH

02 President ... Ms. Barbara E. MURPHY
05 Academic Dean ... Dr. Dan REGAN
11 Dean Administration/Chief Tech Ofcr ... Ms. Sharron R. SCOTT
32 Dean of Students ... Mr. David BERGH
84 Dean of Enrollment Services ... Ms. Penny HOWRIGAN
39 Asst Dean of Campus Life ... Ms. Michele WHITMORE
06 Registrar ... Mr. Douglas EASTMAN
51 Co-Director External Degree Program ... Mr. David CAVANAGH
51 Co-Director of External Degree Prgm ... Ms. Valerie EDWARDS
18 Director of Physical Plant ... Mr. Woody DIONNE
41 Director of Athletics & Recreation ... Ms. Barbara LOUGEE
38 Director of Counseling Services ... Ms. Cynthia HENNARD
30 Director Development/Alumni Rels ... Ms. Sally LAUGHLIN
36 Director Advising/Career Svcs ... Ms. Sara KINERSON
89 Director of First-Year Experience ... Ms. Margo WARDEN
19 Director Safety & Security ... Mr. Michael PALAGONIA
26 Dir College Communications ... Ms. Deborah BOUTON
37 Director Student Financial Aid ... Ms. Lisa CUMMINGS
15 Director Human Resources ... Ms. Sharon SCOTT
08 Librarian ... Mr. Joseph FARARA
79 Chair Humanities ... Dr. Frederick WISEMAN
53 Chair Education ... Dr. David MCGOUGH
65 Chair Environmental/Health Sciences ... Dr. Elizabeth DOLCI
57 Co-Chair Fine & Performing Arts ... Mr. Stephen BLAIR
57 Co-Chair Fine & Performing Arts ... Mr. Ken LESLIE
50 Co-Chair Business/Economics ... Mr. Reed FISHER
50 Co-Chair Business/Economics ... Mr. Todd COMEN
60 Co-Chair Writing/Literature ... Dr. Andrea PERHAM
60 Co-Chair Writing/Literature ... Mr. Daniel TOWNER
81 Chair Mathematics ... Dr. Julie THEORET
83 Co-Chair Behavioral Sciences ... Dr. Susan GREEN
83 Co-Chair Behavioral Sciences ... Dr. Eleanor WEBBER

*Lyndon State College (F)

1001 College Road, PO Box 919,
Lyndonville VT 05851-0919
County: Caledonia FICE Identification: 003689
Unit ID: 230931
Telephone: (802) 626-6200 Carnegie Class: Bac/Diverse
FAX Number: (802) 626-9770 Calendar System: Semester
URL: www.lyndonstate.edu
Established: 1911 Annual Undergrad Tuition & Fees (In-State): $9,468
Enrollment: 1,323 Coed
Affiliation or Control: State IRS Status: 501(c)3
Highest Offering: Master's
Program: Liberal Arts And General; Teacher Preparatory; Professional
Accreditation: EH, EXSC

02 Interim President ... Mr. Steve M. GOLD
05 Dean Academic & Student Affairs ... Dr. Donna DALTON
11 Dean of Administration ... Mr. Wayne T. HAMILTON
20 Associate Academic Dean ... Dr. John R. KASCENSKA
30 Dean of Institutional Advancement ... Mr. Robert E. WHITTAKER
07 Dean of Admissions & Marketing ... Vacant
32 Associate Dean for Student Affairs ... Mr. Jonathan M. DAVIS
18 Director of Physical Plant ... Mr. Thomas R. ARCHER
91 Chief Technology Officer ... Mr. Michael A. DENTE
29 Director of Development & Alumni ... Ms. Hannah J. MANLEY
21 Controller ... Ms. Sheilah M. LADD
08 Library Director ... Mr. Garet B. NELSON
20 Assistant Academic Dean ... Ms. Debra A. HALE
41 Director of Athletics ... Mr. Christopher T. UMMER
37 Director of Financial Aid ... Ms. Tanya W. BRADLEY
36 Director of Career Services ... Ms. Linda A. WACHOLDER
19 Director Public Safety ... Mr. George B. HACKING
88 Director Student Academic Support ... Mr. Robert G. MCCABE
88 Director of Broadcast Operations ... Ms. Darlene R. BOLDUC
88 Dir of Student Academic Development ... Ms. Debra M. BAILIN
27 Director Communications & Marketing ... Mr. Keith B. CHAMBERLIN
15 Director Human Resources ... Ms. Sandra L. FRANZ

*Vermont Technical College (G)

PO Box 500, Randolph Center VT 05061-0500
County: Orange FICE Identification: 003698
Unit ID: 231165
Telephone: (802) 728-1000 Carnegie Class: Bac/Assoc
FAX Number: (802) 728-1390 Calendar System: Semester
URL: www.vtc.edu
Established: 1866 Annual Undergrad Tuition & Fees (In-State): $11,770
Enrollment: 1,665 Coed
Affiliation or Control: State IRS Status: 501(c)3
Highest Offering: Baccalaureate
Program: Occupational; 2-Year Principally Bachelor's Creditable; Professional; Technical Emphasis
Accreditation: EH, ADNUR, DH, ENGT, PNUR

02 President ... Dr. Philip CONROY, JR.
05 Dean Academic Affairs ... Ms. Patricia MENCHINI
11 Dean of Administration ... Mr. John C. DANIELS
20 Dean of the College ... Mr. Michael J. VAN DYKE
13 Chief Technology Officer ... Mr. Michael WOODEN
84 Associate Dean of Enrollment ... Mr. Dwight CROSS
06 Registrar ... Mr. Mike DEMPSEY
37 Director Financial Aid ... Ms. Catherine MCCULLOUGH
29 Director Alumni Relations ... Ms. Carrie CLEMENT
23 Coordinator Health Services ... Vacant
19 Director Security/Safety ... Mr. Emile FREDETTE
18 Director Physical Plant ... Mr. Theodore MANAZIR
36 Career Counseling/Placement ... Ms. Lauri SYBEL
32 Director Student Life ... Ms. Mary Kathryn JUSKIEWICZ
66 Director Nursing Education ... Ms. Anna GERAC
15 Director of Human Resources ... Ms. Pamela ANKUDA
26 Director of Marketing ... Mr. Ben MERRILL
40 Manager Bookstore ... Mr. Joe HIRAK

VIRGINIA

ACT College (H)

1400 Key Blvd, Suite 100, Arlington VA 22209
County: Arlington FICE Identification: 030911
Unit ID: 419022
Telephone: (703) 527-6660 Carnegie Class: Assoc/PrivFP
FAX Number: (703) 527-6688 Calendar System: Quarter
URL: www.actcollege.edu
Established: 1983 Annual Undergrad Tuition & Fees: $13,470
Enrollment: 401 Coed
Affiliation or Control: Proprietary IRS Status: Proprietary
Highest Offering: Associate Degree
Program: Occupational
Accreditation: ABHES

01 President ... Mr. Jeff MOORE

Advanced Technology Institute (I)

5700 Southern Boulevard, Virginia Beach VA 23462-2409
County: City of Virginia Beach FICE Identification: 031275
Unit ID: 231411
Telephone: (757) 490-1241 Carnegie Class: Assoc/PrivFP
FAX Number: (757) 499-5929 Calendar System: Semester
URL: www.auto.edu
Established: 1993 Annual Undergrad Tuition & Fees: $22,950
Enrollment: 725 Coed
Affiliation or Control: Proprietary IRS Status: Proprietary
Highest Offering: Associate Degree
Program: Occupational; Technical Emphasis
Accreditation: ACCSC

01 Campus President ... Mr. Dick DAIGLE
05 Chief Academic Officer ... Mr. Chenek PICKA
07 Director of Admissions ... Mr. Joe ARELLANO
32 Director of Student Services ... Mr. Kirk CLAYTON
37 Director Student Financial Aid ... Mr. Chad MARTS

Appalachian College of Pharmacy (J)

1060 Dragon Road, Oakwood VA 24631
County: Buchanan Identification: 667019
Unit ID: 449922
Telephone: (276) 498-4190 Carnegie Class: Not Classified
FAX Number: (276) 498-4193 Calendar System: Semester
URL: www.acpharm.org
Established: 2003 Annual Graduate Tuition & Fees: $35,800
Enrollment: 208 Coed

Affiliation or Control: Independent Non-Profit IRS Status: 501(c)3
Highest Offering: Doctorate; No Undergraduates
Program: Professional
Accreditation: @SC, PHAR

01 President Mr. Michael G. MCGLOTHLIN
05 Dean Dr. Susan L. MAYHEW

Appalachian School of Law (A)

PO Box 2825, Grundy VA 24614-2825
County: Buchanan FICE Identification: 035593
Unit ID: 432348
Telephone: (800) 895-7411 Carnegie Class: Spec/Law
FAX Number: (276) 935-8261 Calendar System: Semester
URL: www.asl.edu
Established: 1995 Annual Undergrad Tuition & Fees: $30,025
Enrollment: 326 Coed
Affiliation or Control: Independent Non-Profit IRS Status: 501(c)3
Highest Offering: First Professional Degree
Program: Professional
Accreditation: LAW

01 Dean & Chief Operating Officer Mr. Clinton W. SHINN
08 Director of Library Mr. Charlie CONDON
36 Director of Career Services Mr. Brandon CURTIS
13 Director of Information Services Mr. Brian L. RATLIFF
31 Director of Community Services Ms. Jina M. SAULS
32 Director of Student Services Ms. Nancy J. PRUITT

Argosy University, Washington DC (B)

1550 Wilson Boulevard, Suite 600,
Arlington VA 22209-2435
County: Arlington Identification: 666788
Unit ID: 419457
Telephone: (703) 526-5800 Carnegie Class: Spec/Health
FAX Number: (703) 243-8973 Calendar System: Semester
URL: www.argosy.edu/washingtondc
Established: 1994 Annual Undergrad Tuition & Fees: $14,580
Enrollment: 1,327 Coed
Affiliation or Control: Proprietary IRS Status: Proprietary
Highest Offering: Doctorate
Program: Professional
Accreditation: &NH, CACREP, CLPSY

01 Campus President David EREKSON
05 Vice President of Academic Affairs Cynthia WORTHEN
07 Sr Director of Admissions William MARX
08 Director of Library Services Walter RUF
32 Director of Student Services Erik HUNTER
10 Dir Admin & Financial Services Elizabeth GREANEY
16 Human Resources Generalist Lan NGUYEN
06 Registrar Allison SANDERS
37 Dir of Student Financial Services Gretchen EITT

† Regional accreditation is carried under the parent institution, Argosy University in Chicago, IL.

Atlantic University (C)

215 67th Street, Virginia Beach VA 23451-8101
County: Virginia Beach Identification: 666653
Unit ID: 231402
Telephone: (757) 631-8101 Carnegie Class: Not Classified
FAX Number: (757) 631-8096 Calendar System: Trimester
URL: www.atlanticuniv.edu
Established: 1930 Annual Graduate Tuition & Fees: $13,000
Enrollment: 11,635 Coed
Affiliation or Control: Independent Non-Profit IRS Status: 501(c)3
Highest Offering: Master's; No Undergraduates
Program: Professional
Accreditation: DETC

01 CEO Kevin TODESCHI
05 Director of Academic Affairs Dr. Nancy L. ZINGRONE
32 Dean Student Services & Admissions Candis COLLINS
10 Educational Business Manager James VAN AUKEN

Averett University (D)

420 W Main Street, Danville VA 24541-3692
County: Independent City FICE Identification: 003702
Unit ID: 231420
Telephone: (434) 791-5600 Carnegie Class: Bac/Diverse
FAX Number: (434) 791-5637 Calendar System: Semester
URL: www.averett.edu
Established: 1859 Annual Undergrad Tuition & Fees: $24,480
Enrollment: 2,643 Coed
Affiliation or Control: Independent Non-Profit IRS Status: 501(c)3
Highest Offering: Master's
Program: Liberal Arts And General; Teacher Preparatory
Accreditation: SC

01 President Dr. Tiffany M. FRANKS
32 Executive Vice President Mr. Charles S. HARRIS
05 Vice Pres for Academic Affairs Dr. Janet LAUGHLIN
10 Vice President Business & Finance Mr. Thomas DAVIS
30 Vice Pres Institutional Advancement Mr. Albert RAWLEY
15 Vice President for Human Resources Mrs. Kathie TUNE
37 Director Student Financial Services Mr. Carl BRADSHER
84 Vice Pres Enrollment Management Dr. Stuart JONES
21 Controller Mr. Andy FITCH
08 Director of Library Ms. Elaine DAY
36 Director of Career Services Ms. Petrina CARTER
06 Registrar Mrs. Janet ROBERSON
26 Dir of Marketing/Communications Mr. Randy KING
29 Director Alumni Relations Mr. Dan HAYES
09 Dir Institutional Research/Effect Dr. Metta ALSOBROOK

Aviation Institute of Maintenance (E)

2211 S Military Highway, Chesapeake VA 23320
County: Chesapeake City FICE Identification: 031263
Unit ID: 427973
Telephone: (757) 363-2121 Carnegie Class: Assoc/PrivFP
FAX Number: (757) 363-2044 Calendar System: Other
URL: www.aviationmaintenance.edu
Established: 1993 Annual Undergrad Tuition & Fees: $34,990
Enrollment: 283 Coed
Affiliation or Control: Proprietary IRS Status: Proprietary
Highest Offering: Associate Degree
Program: Occupational
Accreditation: ACCSC

01 President Mr. Greg SMITH

Aviation Institute of Maintenance (F)

10640 Davidson Place, Manassas VA 20109
County: Prince William FICE Identification: 038834
Telephone: (703) 257-5515 Carnegie Class: Not Classified
FAX Number: (703) 257-5523 Calendar System: Other
URL: www.aviationmaintenance.edu
Established: N/A Annual Undergrad Tuition & Fees: $39,150
Enrollment: 190 Coed
Affiliation or Control: Proprietary IRS Status: Proprietary
Highest Offering: Associate Degree
Program: Occupational
Accreditation: ACCSC

01 Director of Education Mr. Michael CAROTHERS

Baptist Theological Seminary at Richmond (G)

3400 Brook Road, Richmond VA 23227-4536
County: Independent City FICE Identification: 031169
Unit ID: 366793
Telephone: (804) 355-8135 Carnegie Class: Spec/Faith
FAX Number: (804) 355-8182 Calendar System: Semester
URL: www.btsr.edu
Established: 1991 Annual Graduate Tuition & Fees: $10,395
Enrollment: 115 Coed
Affiliation or Control: Independent Non-Profit IRS Status: 501(c)3
Highest Offering: Doctorate; No Undergraduates
Program: Professional; Religious Emphasis
Accreditation: THEOL

01 President Dr. Ronald W. CRAWFORD
06 Registrar/Director of Financial Aid Ms. Ida Mae HAYS
05 Dean Dr. Israel GALINDO
10 Director of Business Affairs Dr. James F. PEAK, JR.
30 Assoc VP Advancement/Community Life Mrs. Ka'thy G. CHAPPELL

Bethel College (H)

1705 Todds Lane, Hampton VA 23666
County: Hampton City Identification: 667015
Unit ID: 458113
Telephone: (757) 826-1883 Carnegie Class: Not Classified
FAX Number: (757) 826-0458 Calendar System: Semester
URL: www.bethel-college.com
Established: 2004 Annual Undergrad Tuition & Fees: $5,660
Enrollment: 79 Coed
Affiliation or Control: Assemblies Of God Church IRS Status: 501(c)3
Highest Offering: Baccalaureate
Program: Religious Emphasis
Accreditation: @BI

01 President Mr. Glenn REYNOLDS
05 Academic Dean Dr. Ron DEBERRY
32 Dean of Students Dr. Jerry GOULD
06 Registrar Ms. Nanette BARTHOLOMEW
08 Library Director Ms. Janell SANFORD

Bluefield College (I)

3000 College Drive, Bluefield VA 24605-1799
County: Tazewell FICE Identification: 003703
Unit ID: 231554
Telephone: (276) 326-3682 Carnegie Class: Bac/Diverse
FAX Number: (276) 326-4288 Calendar System: Semester
URL: www.bluefield.edu
Established: 1922 Annual Undergrad Tuition & Fees: $19,980
Enrollment: 690 Coed
Affiliation or Control: Baptist IRS Status: 501(c)3
Highest Offering: Baccalaureate
Program: Liberal Arts And General; Teacher Preparatory
Accreditation: SC, TEAC

01 President Dr. David W. OLIVE
04 Assistant to the President Mrs. Diane T. SHOTT
05 VP for Academic Affairs Dr. Robert C. SHIPPEY, JR.
30 VP for Advancement Mrs. Mary R. BLANKENSHIP
10 VP for Finance & Admin Mrs. Sarah BEAMER
32 VP for Student Development Rev. David TAYLOR
84 VP for Enrollment Management Dr. Robert C. SHIPPEY, JR.
07 Interim Dir of Trad Admissions Mr. Mark HIPES
07 Director of Adult Admissions Mrs. Cathy PAYNE
06 Registrar Mrs. Cathy MATHERLY
08 Director of Library Services Ms. Nora LOCKETT
26 Director of Public Relations Mr. Chris SHOEMAKER
29 Director of Alumni Relations Mr. Joshua CLINE
09 Director of Institutional Research Mrs. Amanda JORDAN
37 Director of Financial Aid Mrs. Debbie CHECCHIO
42 Campus Minister Rev. David TAYLOR
41 Athletic Director Mr. Peter DRYER
40 Bookstore Manager Mrs. Judy VANNOY
18 Director of Maintenance Mr. Blair TAYLOR
19 Director of Campus Safety Dr. Kelly WALLS
15 Human Resources Coordinator Mrs. Karen THURMER

Bon Secours Memorial College of Nursing (J)

8550 Magellan Pkwy, Ste 1100, Richmond VA 23227
County: Henrico FICE Identification: 010043
Telephone: (804) 627-5300 Carnegie Class: Not Classified
FAX Number: (804) 627-5330 Calendar System: Semester
URL: www.bsmcon.edu
Established: 1998 Annual Undergrad Tuition & Fees: $7,200
Enrollment: 340 Coed
Affiliation or Control: Independent Non-Profit IRS Status: 501(c)3
Highest Offering: Baccalaureate
Program: Occupational; Nursing Emphasis
Accreditation: ACICS, DNUR

01 Dean of the College Dr. Susan BODIN
05 Vice Pres Academic Affairs/Provost Dr. Melanie H. GREEN
20 Asst Dean of Curriculum/Instruction Vacant
11 Asst Dean of Administration Ms. Carol GRECO
32 Asst Dean of Student Services Dr. Regina WELCH

Bridgewater College (K)

402 E College Street, Bridgewater VA 22812-1599
County: Rockingham FICE Identification: 003704
Unit ID: 231581
Telephone: (540) 828-8000 Carnegie Class: Bac/A&S
FAX Number: (540) 828-5479 Calendar System: 4/1/4
URL: www.bridgewater.edu
Established: 1880 Annual Undergrad Tuition & Fees: $26,750
Enrollment: 1,688 Coed
Affiliation or Control: Church Of The Brethren IRS Status: 501(c)3
Highest Offering: Baccalaureate
Program: Liberal Arts And General; Teacher Preparatory
Accreditation: SC

01 President Mr. George E. CORNELIUS
03 Executive Vice President Mr. Roy W. FERGUSON, JR.
05 Vice Pres/Dean of Academic Affairs Dr. Carol A. SCHEPPARD
10 Vice Pres for Finance & Treasurer Ms. Anne B. KEELER
30 Vice President for Inst Advancement Ms. Beverly S. BUTTERFIELD
26 Dir of Marketing & Communications Ms. Abbie PARKHURST
84 Vice President for Enrollment Mgmt Mr. Reggie WEBB
44 Director of Major Gifts Vacant
18 Exec Dir of Fac Support & Aux Svcs Mr. Teshome H. MOLALENGE
40 Bookstore Manager Mr. John OVERACKER
20 Associate Dean of Academic Affairs Dr. Edward W. HUFFSTETLER
32 Dean of Students Dr. William D. MIRACLE
36 Director of Career Services Ms. Sherry TALBOTT
88 Director of Academic Support Svcs Dr. Raymond W. STUDWELL, II
42 Chaplain Rev. Robert R. MILLER
07 Director of Admissions Mr. Jarret L. SMITH
37 Director of Financial Aid Mr. Scott D. MORRISON
21 Director of Budget & Analysis Mr. Jeffrey FIKE
13 Chief Info Officer/Dir of Info Tech Mr. Terry E. HOUFF
41 Director of Athletics Mr. Curtis L. KENDALL
38 Director of Counseling Services Mr. Randall HOOK
29 Director of Alumni Relations Ms. Ellen B. MILLER
09 Director of Institutional Research Ms. Dawn S. DALBOW
15 Director of Human Resources Ms. Victoria L. INGRAM
08 Library Director Mr. Andrew L. PEARSON
06 Registrar Ms. Cynthia K. HOWDYSHELL
21 Controller Ms. Mary S. SCHWAB
27 Editor/Dir of Media Relations Mr. Charles R. CULBERTSON
18 Director of Plant Operations Mr. David R. VANDEVANDER
19 Campus Police Chief Mr. Nicholas P. PICERNO
28 Minority Mentor Mr. James E. RAEFORD
23 Director of Student Health Services Ms. Paige FRENCH
35 Associate Dean of Students Ms. Crystal LYNN
28 Director of Multicultural Services Ms. Stephanie WILSON
88 Director of Dining Services Mr. J. A. YOUNG

Bryant & Stratton College (L)

8141 Hull Street Road, North Chesterfield VA 23235-6411
County: Chesterfield Identification: 666496
Unit ID: 231828
Telephone: (804) 745-2444 Carnegie Class: Bac/Assoc

FAX Number: (804) 745-6884 Calendar System: Trimester
URL: www.bryantstratton.edu
Established: 1854 Annual Undergrad Tuition & Fees: $15,570
Enrollment: 924 Coed
Affiliation or Control: Proprietary IRS Status: Proprietary
Highest Offering: Baccalaureate
Program: Occupational; Business Emphasis
Accreditation: &M, MAC

01 Campus Director .... Ms. Beth M. MURPHY
05 Dean of Instruction .... Ms. Darlene M. LACHUT
32 Dean of Student Services .... Ms. Deborah J. MERRITT
36 Career Service Director .... Ms. Brenda SANDS HINES
07 Director of Admissions .... Mr. David K. MAYLE
10 Business Office Director .... Ms. Ditamichelle TERRY

† Regional accreditation is carried under the parent institution (corporate office) in Buffalo, NY.

Bryant & Stratton College (A)

301 Centre Pointe Drive, Virginia Beach VA 23462-4417
County: Independent City FICE Identification: 010061
Unit ID: 231785
Telephone: (757) 499-7900 Carnegie Class: Bac/Assoc
FAX Number: (757) 499-9977 Calendar System: Semester
URL: www.bryantstratton.edu
Established: 1854 Annual Undergrad Tuition & Fees: $15,120
Enrollment: 838 Coed
Affiliation or Control: Proprietary IRS Status: Proprietary
Highest Offering: Baccalaureate
Program: 2-Year Principally Bachelor's Creditable; Business Emphasis
Accreditation: &M, MAC

01 Campus Director .... Mr. Lee E. HICKLIN
10 Business Office Director .... Mr. Erik BLACKWELL
05 Dean of Instruction .... Ms. Vivian D. ROGERS
32 Dean of Student Services .... Ms. Anita WYCHE
07 Director of Admissions .... Ms. Deana SUTHERLAND
36 Career Services Director .... Ms. Ronda TOLL
88 Director of Military Programs .... Mr. Arch WALPOLE

† Regional accreditation is carried under the parent institution (corporate office) in Buffalo, NY.

California University of Management and Sciences Virginia (B)

400 North Washington Street, Falls Church VA 22046
County: Fairfax Identification: 666734
Unit ID: 460075
Telephone: (703) 663-8088 Carnegie Class: Not Classified
FAX Number: (703) 663-8090 Calendar System: Quarter
URL: www.calums.edu/index_va.htm
Established: 2007 Annual Undergrad Tuition & Fees: N/A
Enrollment: N/A Coed
Affiliation or Control: Independent Non-Profit IRS Status: 501(c)3
Highest Offering: Master's
Program: Professional; Business Emphasis
Accreditation: ACICS

01 Branch Director .... Mr. Young KIM

† Branch campus of California University of Management and Sciences, Anaheim, CA.

Career Training Solutions (C)

100 Riverside Parkway, Suite 123, Fredericksburg VA 22406-1016
County: Stafford FICE Identification: 036543
Unit ID: 441858
Telephone: (540) 373-2200 Carnegie Class: Not Classified
FAX Number: (540) 373-4465 Calendar System: Other
URL: www.careertrainingsolutions.com
Established: 2000 Annual Undergrad Tuition & Fees: N/A
Enrollment: 358 Coed
Affiliation or Control: Proprietary IRS Status: Proprietary
Highest Offering: Associate Degree
Program: Occupational
Accreditation: COE

01 Chief Executive Officer .... Ms. A. Christine CARROLL

The Catholic Distance University (D)

120 E Colonial Highway, Hamilton VA 20158-9012
County: Loudoun FICE Identification: 041242
Unit ID: 377430
Telephone: (540) 338-2700 Carnegie Class: Not Classified
FAX Number: (540) 338-4788 Calendar System: Trimester
URL: www.cdu.edu
Established: 1983 Annual Undergrad Tuition & Fees: $2,935
Enrollment: 800 Coed
Affiliation or Control: Independent Non-Profit IRS Status: 501(c)3
Highest Offering: Master's
Program: Religious Emphasis
Accreditation: DETC

01 President .... Dr. Marianne E. MOUNT
58 Dean Graduate Programs .... Dr. Robert ROYAL
05 Undergraduate Dean .... Fr. Bevil BRAMWELL
88 Dean of Catechetical Programs .... Sr. Mary Margaret SCHLATHER
06 Graduate Registrar .... Ms. Judith WELSH
06 Undergraduate Registrar .... Mrs. Kathleen WOODDELL
08 Head Librarian .... Vacant
10 Director of Finance .... Mr. Charles COLVILLE
30 Director of Development .... Vacant
26 Director of Communications .... Ms. Therese CASHEN
35 Director Student Affairs .... Dr. Carolann CIRBEE
07 Director of Admissions .... Ms. Carol CIULLO
29 Director Alumni Relations .... Vacant
32 Chief Student Life Officer .... Dr. Carolann CIRBEE
37 Director Student Financial Aid .... Vacant
13 Director Computing Information Mgmt .... Mrs. Carol DALEY

Central Baptist Theological Seminary (E)

2221 Centerville Turnpike, Virginia Beach VA 23464-6847
County: Virginia Beach FICE Identification: 039663
Telephone: (757) 479-3706 Carnegie Class: Not Classified
FAX Number: (757) 479-4232 Calendar System: Semester
URL: www.baptistseminary.edu
Established: 1995 Annual Undergrad Tuition & Fees: $4,320
Enrollment: 85 Coed
Affiliation or Control: Baptist IRS Status: 501(c)3
Highest Offering: Master's
Program: Professional; Religious Emphasis
Accreditation: TRACS

01 Director of Operations .... Mr. Richard ERICKSON
05 Chief Academic Office .... Mr. Eric LEHNER
06 Registrar/Director of Admissions .... Ms. Valerie GAST
10 Chief Business Officer .... Dr. Thomas KEISER
09 Dir Institutional Effectiveness .... Dr. Robert TOMENENDAL
30 Director of Advancement .... Mr. Matt KLIEWER

Centura College (F)

7914 Midlothian Turnpike, Richmond VA 23235
County: Chesterfield FICE Identification: 031264
Unit ID: 427982
Telephone: (804) 330-0111 Carnegie Class: Not Classified
FAX Number: (804) 330-3800 Calendar System: Other
URL: www.centuracollege.edu/college-campus/richmond-va-college.as
Established: 1992 Annual Undergrad Tuition & Fees: $13,500
Enrollment: 290 Coed
Affiliation or Control: Proprietary IRS Status: Proprietary
Highest Offering: Associate Degree
Program: Occupational
Accreditation: ACCSC

Centura College (G)

2697 Dean Drive, Suite 100, Virginia Beach VA 23452-7431
County: City of Virginia Beach FICE Identification: 023344
Unit ID: 232016
Telephone: (757) 340-2121 Carnegie Class: Assoc/PrivFP4
FAX Number: (757) 340-9704 Calendar System: Other
URL: www.centura.edu
Established: 1969 Annual Undergrad Tuition & Fees: $13,500
Enrollment: 1,046 Coed
Affiliation or Control: Proprietary IRS Status: Proprietary
Highest Offering: Baccalaureate
Program: Occupational
Accreditation: ACCSC

01 Director .... Ms. Beth HALL

Christendom College (H)

134 Christendom Drive, Front Royal VA 22630-6534
County: Warren FICE Identification: 036653
Unit ID: 231703
Telephone: (540) 636-2900 Carnegie Class: Not Classified
FAX Number: (540) 636-1655 Calendar System: Semester
URL: www.christendom.edu
Established: 1977 Annual Undergrad Tuition & Fees: $19,884
Enrollment: 420 Coed
Affiliation or Control: Roman Catholic IRS Status: 501(c)3
Highest Offering: Master's
Program: Liberal Arts And General
Accreditation: SC

01 President .... Dr. Timothy T. O'DONNELL
10 Exec Vice President Finance & Admin .... Mr. Mark C. MCSHURLEY
05 Vice President Academic Affairs .... Dr. Steven C. SNYDER
30 Vice President for Advancement .... Mr. John F. CISKANIK
18 Vice Pres Operations/Facility Plng .... Mr. Michael S. FOECKLER
32 Dean of Student Life .... Mr. Jesse DORMAN
20 Academic Dean .... Dr. Patrick KEATS
07 Director of Admissions & Marketing .... Mr. Thomas MCFADDEN
06 Registrar .... Mr. Walter A. JANARO
08 Director of Christendom Library .... Mr. Andrew V. ARMSTRONG
37 Financial Aid Officer .... Mrs. Alisa L. POLK
29 Director Alumni & Career Devel .... Ms. Marie ANTUNES
13 Director of Computer Services .... Mr. Douglas S. BRIGGS
88 Registrar/Business Officer NDGS .... Miss Heidi KALIAN
41 Athletic Director .... Mr. Chris VANDERWOUDE
04 Assistant to the President .... Miss Melanie BAKER
58 Dean of the Graduate School .... Dr. Kristen BURNS

Christopher Newport University (I)

1 University Place, Newport News VA 23606-2998
County: Independent City FICE Identification: 003706
Unit ID: 231712
Telephone: (757) 594-7000 Carnegie Class: Master's S
FAX Number: (757) 594-7713 Calendar System: Semester
URL: www.cnu.edu
Established: 1960 Annual Undergrad Tuition & Fees (In-State): $10,084
Enrollment: 4,894 Coed
Affiliation or Control: State IRS Status: 501(c)3
Highest Offering: Master's
Program: Liberal Arts And General
Accreditation: SC, BUS, ENG, MUS, SW, THEA

01 President .... Sen. Paul S. TRIBLE
100 Chief of Staff .... Mrs. Cynthia R. PERRY
05 Provost .... Dr. Mark W. PADILLA
03 Executive Vice President .... Mr. William L. BRAUER
43 University Counsel .... Mr. William E. THRO
30 Vice Pres of University Advancement .... Mrs. Adelia P. THOMPSON
32 Vice President for Student Services .... Mr. Maurice J. O'CONNELL
15 Director of Human Resources .... Mrs. Lorraine M. WESTPHAL
41 Director of Athletics .... Mr. C. J. WOOLLUM
04 Exec Assistant to the President .... Mrs. Beverley D. MUELLER
10 University Comptroller .... Mrs. Diane REED
49 Dean College of Arts & Humanities .... Mr. Steven BREESE
83 Dean College of Social Sciences .... Dr. Robert E. COLVIN
88 Dean College Natural/Behav Sciences .... Dr. David C. DOUGHTY, JR.
07 Dean of Admissions .... Mr. Bob LANGE
06 Registrar .... Ms. Lisa D. RAINES
37 Director of Financial Aid .... Mrs. Mary L. WIGGINGTON
36 Director Center of Career Planning .... Ms. Elizabeth K. WESTLEY
35 Dean of Students .... Dr. Kevin M. HUGHES
39 Director of Housing .... Dr. Andy W. SHESTON
09 Director of Institutional Research .... Ms. Donna A. VARNER
13 Chief Information Officer .... Mr. Stephen S. CAMPBELL
08 University Librarian .... Ms. Mary SELLEN
19 Chief of University Police .... Mr. Jeffrey S. BROWN, SR.
21 Director of Internal Audit .... Ms. Christine LEDFORD
18 Director of Plant Operations .... Mr. Lennie I. ALGER
44 Director Planned Giving/Scholarship .... Ms. Lucy L. LATCHUM
96 Director of Materiel Management .... Mr. Ryan A. FEREBEE
29 Director Alumni Rels/Univ Events .... Ms. Amie E. GRAHAM
26 Director of Public Relations .... Ms. Lori A. JACOBS
28 Director of Equal Opportunity .... Ms. Michelle L. MOODY
38 Director of Counseling Services .... Mr. William V. RITCHEY

College of William & Mary (J)

PO Box 8795, Williamsburg VA 23187-8795
County: Independent City FICE Identification: 003705
Unit ID: 231624
Telephone: (757) 221-4000 Carnegie Class: RU/H
FAX Number: (757) 221-1259 Calendar System: Semester
URL: www.wm.edu
Established: 1693 Annual Undergrad Tuition & Fees (In-State): $13,132
Enrollment: 8,000 Coed
Affiliation or Control: State IRS Status: 501(c)3
Highest Offering: Doctorate
Program: Liberal Arts And General; Teacher Preparatory; Professional
Accreditation: SC, BUS, BUSA, CACREP, IPSY, LAW, TED

01 President .... Mr. W. Taylor REVELEY, III
05 Provost .... Dr. Michael HALLERAN
10 Vice President for Finance .... Mr. Samuel E. JONES
11 Vice President for Administration .... Mrs. Anna B. MARTIN
32 Vice President for Student Affairs .... Dr. Virginia M. AMBLER
30 Vice President for Development .... Mr. Sean M. PIERI
45 VP for Strategic Initiatives .... Dr. James R. GOLDEN
29 Executive VP Alumni Association .... Ms. Karen R. COTTRELL
86 Associate VP Government Relations .... Ms. Frances C. BRADFORD
20 Vice Provost for Academic Affairs .... Dr. Kathleen F. SLEVIN
20 Vice Provost Rsch & Grad Prof Stds .... Dr. Dennis M. MANOS
13 Assoc Prov Information Technology .... Mr. Courtney M. CARPENTER
84 Associate Provost for Enrollment .... Mr. Henry R. BROADDUS
09 Assoc Prov Inst Analysis and Effect .... Dr. Susan L. BOSWORTH
26 Director of University Relations .... Mr. Brian WHITSON
44 Assoc VP Development/Operations .... Ms. Teresa L. MUNFORD
18 Assoc VP Facilities Mgmt .... Mr. Dave SHEPARD
49 Int Dean Faculty of Arts & Sciences .... Dr. Gene TRACY
44 Assoc VP for Development .... Mr. Earl T. GRANGER
50 Dean School of Business Admin .... Dr. Lawrence B. PULLEY
53 Dean School of Education .... Dr. Virginia L. MCLAUGHLIN
58 Dean Graduate Studies & Research .... Dr. Laurie SANDERSON
61 Dean School of Law .... Mr. Davison M. DOUGLAS
88 Dean/Dir School of Marine Science .... Dr. John T. WELLS
49 Dean of Undergraduate Studies .... Dr. Kelly JOYCE
35 Dean of Students .... Ms. Patricia M. VOLP
41 Director of Athletics .... Mr. Terry DRISCOLL
07 Dean of Admission .... Mr. Henry R. BROADDUS
92 Dean Honors/Interdisciplinary Stds .... Dr. Joel D. SCHWARTZ
82 Int Dir Reves Ctr for Intl Studies .... Dr. Ronald ST. ONGE
25 Director of Sponsored Programs .... Ms. Jane LOPEZ

22 Director of Equal Opportunity ....Ms. Tammy H. CURRIE
37 Director Student Financial Aid ....Mr. Edward P. IRISH
08 Interim Dean University Libraries ....Ms. Beatriz HARDY
06 University Registrar ....Ms. Sara L. MARCHELLO
15 Assoc VP Human Resources ....Ms. Earleen H. O'ROARK
38 Director Counseling Center ....Dr. Warrenetta C. MANN
36 Director Career Center ....Ms. Mary E. SCHILLING
19 Chief W&M Police Department ....Mr. Donald R. CHALLIS
21 Director Financial Operations ....Mr. Bert BRUMMER
23 Director Student Health Center ....Dr. Virginia D. WELLS
28 Dir of Ctr for Student Diversity ....Dr. Vernon HURTE
39 Asst VP Stdnt Affs/Dir of Res Life ....Ms. Deb BOYKIN
96 Director of Procurement ....Ms. Linda N. ORR
40 Manager W&M Bookstore ....Ms. Kathy PACHECO
100 Asst to President/Chief of Staff ....Mr. Michael J. FOX
04 Executive Asst to President ....Ms. Cynthia A. BRAUER
102 Director Corporate & Found Rels ....Ms. Suzanne ARMSTRONG
104 Director of Global Education ....Ms. Sylvia MITTERNDORFER
88 Director of Creative Services ....Ms. Susan T. EVANS
88 Dean for Educational Policy ....Dr. Teresa LONGO

Columbia College (A)

8300 Merrifield Avenue, Fairfax VA 22031
County: Fairfax | FICE Identification: 041273
Unit ID: 455983
Telephone: (703) 206-0508 | Carnegie Class: Not Classified
FAX Number: (703) 206-0488 | Calendar System: Quarter
URL: www.ccdc.edu
Established: 1999 | Annual Undergrad Tuition & Fees: $6,500
Enrollment: 378 | Coed
Affiliation or Control: Proprietary | IRS Status: Proprietary
Highest Offering: Associate Degree
Program: Occupational
Accreditation: COE

01 President ....Dr. Richard KWANGSOO KIM

DeVry University - Arlington Campus (B)

2450 Crystal Drive, Arlington VA 22202-3843
County: Arlington | Identification: 666220
Unit ID: 440536
Telephone: (703) 414-4000 | Carnegie Class: Master's S
FAX Number: (703) 414-4023 | Calendar System: Semester
URL: www.devry.edu
Established: 1931 | Annual Undergrad Tuition & Fees: $15,294
Enrollment: 1,026 | Coed
Affiliation or Control: Proprietary | IRS Status: Proprietary
Highest Offering: Master's
Program: Occupational; Professional; Business Emphasis
Accreditation: &NH, ENGT

01 Metro President ....Ms. Loretta FRANKLIN
15 HR Business Partner ....Ms. Jennifer CAMDEN-CHAU
32 Dean Student Central ....Mr. Cary WHITCUP
37 Director of Student Finance ....Ms. Lisa BRANSON
07 Senior Director of Admissions ....Oronde BAYLOR
08 Director of Library Services ....Ms. Jane CARVAJAL
06 Registrar ....Ms. Cheri MAEA
05 Dean Academic Affairs ....Mr. Keith WRIGHT
36 Director of Career Services ....Ms. Michelle MERCURIO
54 Dean of the College of Engineering ....Mr. John GIANCOLA

† Regional accreditation is carried under the parent institution in Downers Grove, IL.

DeVry University - Chesapeake (C)

1317 Executive Boulevard, Suite 100,
Chesapeake VA 23320-3671
County: Chesapeake City | Identification: 666577
Telephone: (757) 382-5680 | Carnegie Class: Not Classified
FAX Number: (757) 549-5215 | Calendar System: Semester
URL: www.devry.edu
Established: 1931 | Annual Undergrad Tuition & Fees: $15,294
Enrollment: 532 | Coed
Affiliation or Control: Proprietary | IRS Status: Proprietary
Highest Offering: Master's
Program: Professional; Business Emphasis
Accreditation: &NH

01 Campus Director ....Joyce WHEATLEY

† Regional accreditation is carried under the parent institution in Downers Grove, IL.

DeVry University - Manassas (D)

10432 Balls Ford Rd, Suite 130,
Manassas VA 20109-2515
County: Prince William | Identification: 666222
Unit ID: 430333
Telephone: (703) 396-6608 | Carnegie Class: Not Classified
FAX Number: (703) 367-7242 | Calendar System: Semester
URL: www.devry.edu
Established: 1995 | Annual Undergrad Tuition & Fees: $15,294
Enrollment: 310 | Coed
Affiliation or Control: Proprietary | IRS Status: Proprietary
Highest Offering: Master's
Program: Occupational; Professional; Business Emphasis
Accreditation: &NH

01 Center Dean ....Lisa MULLALY

† Regional accreditation is carried under the parent institution in Downers Grove, IL.

Eastern Mennonite University (E)

1200 Park Road, Harrisonburg VA 22802-2462
County: Independent City | FICE Identification: 003708
Unit ID: 232043
Telephone: (540) 432-4000 | Carnegie Class: Bac/A&S
FAX Number: (540) 432-4444 | Calendar System: Semester
URL: www.emu.edu
Established: 1917 | Annual Undergrad Tuition & Fees: $26,400
Enrollment: 1,589 | Coed
Affiliation or Control: Mennonite Church | IRS Status: 501(c)3
Highest Offering: Master's
Program: Liberal Arts And General; Teacher Preparatory; Professional
Accreditation: SC, CACREP, NURSE, SW, TED, THEOL

01 President ....Dr. Loren E. SWARTZENDRUBER
05 Provost ....Dr. Fred L. KNISS
30 Vice President for Advancement ....Mr. Kirk L. SHISLER
10 Vice President for Finance ....Mr. Daryl W. BERT
84 Vice Pres Enrollment & Marketing ....Mr. Luke HARTMAN
32 Vice President for Student Life ....Dr. Kenneth L. NAFZIGER
20 Vice Pres & Undergrad Academic Dean .... Dr. Nancy HEISEY
73 Seminary Dean ....Dr. Michael A. KING
06 University Registrar ....Mr. David A. DETROW
27 Director of Marketing Services ....Ms. Andrea S. WENGER
07 Director Undergraduate Admissions .....Ms. Stephanie C. SHAFER
08 Director of Libraries ....Dr. Beryl H. BRUBAKER
37 Director of Financial Assistance ....Ms. Michele R. HENSLEY
36 Director Career Services/Testing ....Ms. Jennifer L. LITWILLER
29 Director of Alumni/Parent Relations ....Mr. Douglas J. NYCE
09 Director Institutional Research ....Dr. BJ MILLER
04 Assistant to the President ....Ms. Twila K. YODER
41 Athletic Director ....Mr. David A. KING
42 Campus Pastor ....Mr. Brian M. BURKHOLDER
13 Director of Information Systems ....Mr. Jack H. RUTT
18 Director of Physical Plant ....Mr. Eldon KURTZ
15 Director Human Resources ....Ms. Marcia J. ENGLE
21 Controller ....Mr. Timothy STUTZMAN
26 Chief Public Information Officer ....Mr. Michael J. ZUCCONI
35 Director Student Affairs ....Mr. Lawrence W. MILLER
38 Director Student Counseling ....Ms. Pamela D. COMER

Eastern Virginia Medical School (F)

Box 1980, Norfolk VA 23501-1980
County: Independent City | FICE Identification: 010338
Unit ID: 231970
Telephone: (757) 446-5600 | Carnegie Class: Spec/Med
FAX Number: (757) 446-5135 | Calendar System: Other
URL: www.evms.edu
Established: 1973 | Annual Graduate Tuition & Fees: $31,853
Enrollment: 897 | Coed
Affiliation or Control: Independent Non-Profit | IRS Status: 501(c)3
Highest Offering: Doctorate; No Undergraduates
Program: Professional
Accreditation: SC, ARCPA, CLPSY, IPSY, MED, PH, SURGA

01 President ....Mr. Harry T. LESTER
05 Dean & Provost ....Dr. Gerald J. PEPE
10 Vice Pres Administration/Finance .....Mr. Mark R. BABASHANIAN
11 Vice President External Affairs ....Ms. Claudia KEENAN
88 Vice Provost Planning/Health Prof ....Dr. Charles D. COMBS
07 Assoc Dean Med Admissions/Students ..Dr. Michael J. SOLHAUG
20 Associate Dean Education ....Dr. Thomas R. PELLEGRINO
88 Assoc Dean Clinical Affairs ....Dr. Alfred Z. ABUHAMAD
58 Assoc Dean Grad Medical Education ....Dr. Linda R. ARCHER
88 Assoc Dean Hum Sub Protection/IRB ......Dr. Robert F. WILLIAMS
09 Assoc Dean for Research ....Dr. William J. WASILENKO
50 Associate Dean Business Management ....Mr. David E. HUBAND
08 Assoc Dean Library/Lrng Resource ....Ms. Judith G. ROBINSON
20 Assoc Dean for Academic Affairs ....Dr. Ann E. CAMPBELL
43 General Counsel ....Ms. Stacy R. PURCELL
06 Registrar ....Ms. Jennifer H. GRAY
07 Director of Admissions ....Ms. Susan L. CASTORA
15 Director Human Resources ....Mr. Matthew R. SCHENK
18 Chief Facilities/Physical Plant ....Mr. Jack D. BEASLEY
37 Director Student Financial Aid ....Ms. Michelle D. BYERS
93 Asst Dean Student/Minority Affairs ....Ms. Gail C. WILLIAMS
96 Director of Materials Management ....Mr. Steven LEE
21 Director for Business Management ....Ms. Tammy A. POSTON
26 Director of Mktg & Communications ....Mr. Vincent A. RHODES
29 Director Alumni Affairs ....Ms. Melissa W. LANG
30 Director of Development ....Ms. Connie L. MCKENZIE
51 Director for Continuing Med Educ ....Ms. Drucie A. PAPAFIL

† Member of Virginia Consortium for Professional Psychology. No tuition given due to varying costs.

ECPI College of Technology (G)

5555 Greenwich Road, Virginia Beach VA 23462-6554
County: Independent City | FICE Identification: 010198
Unit ID: 248934
Telephone: (757) 671-7171 | Carnegie Class: Assoc/PrivFP4
FAX Number: (757) 671-8661 | Calendar System: Semester
URL: www.ecpi.edu
Established: 1966 | Annual Undergrad Tuition & Fees: $13,550
Enrollment: 12,764 | Coed
Affiliation or Control: Proprietary | IRS Status: Proprietary
Highest Offering: Master's
Program: Occupational
Accreditation: SC, ACFEI, MAAB, NUR

01 President ....Mr. Mark B. DREYFUS
12 Campus President ....Mr. Kevin PAVEGLIO
03 Vice President ....Mr. Ronald J. BALLANCE
13 VP Info Systems/Financial Aid ....Mr. Jeff ARTHUR

Edward Via College of Osteopathic Medicine (H)

2265 Kraft Drive, Blacksburg VA 24060
County: Montgomery | FICE Identification: 037093
Unit ID: 442806
Telephone: (540) 231-4000 | Carnegie Class: Not Classified
FAX Number: (540) 231-5252 | Calendar System: Semester
URL: www.vcom.vt.edu
Established: 2002 | Annual Graduate Tuition & Fees: $37,910
Enrollment: 757 | Coed
Affiliation or Control: Independent Non-Profit | IRS Status: 501(c)3
Highest Offering: Doctorate; No Undergraduates
Program: Professional
Accreditation: OSTEO

01 President ....Dr. James F. WOLFE
05 Executive Vice President & Dean ....Dr. Dixie TOOKE-RAWLINS
10 Associate Vice Pres Finance/CFO ....Mr. Mark HAMRIC
32 Assoc Vice Pres Student Services ....Mr. William KING
46 Assoc Vice Pres Research/Grad Stds ....Dr. Hara P. MISRA
11 Assoc Vice President Operations ....Mr. Bill PRICE
12 Vice Dean Carolinas Campus ....Dr. Timothy J. KOWALSKI
12 Vice Dean Virginia Campus ....Dr. Jan M. WILLCOX
58 Assoc Dean Post-Bac/Pre-med Program ....Dr. Francine ANDERSON
63 Assoc Dean Medical Education ....Dr. Brian W. HILL

Emory & Henry College (I)

PO Box 947, 30461 Garnand Drive,
Emory VA 24327-0947
County: Washington | FICE Identification: 003709
Unit ID: 232025
Telephone: (276) 944-4121 | Carnegie Class: Bac/A&S
FAX Number: (276) 944-6934 | Calendar System: Semester
URL: www.ehc.edu
Established: 1836 | Annual Undergrad Tuition & Fees: $27,040
Enrollment: 956 | Coed
Affiliation or Control: United Methodist | IRS Status: 501(c)3
Highest Offering: Master's
Program: Liberal Arts And General; Teacher Preparatory
Accreditation: SC, TEAC

01 President ....Dr. Rosalind REICHARD
04 Executive Assistant to President ....Mr. Mark R. GRAHAM
05 Interim VP Academic Affairs/Dean ....Dr. Linda H. DOBKINS
10 Vice Pres for Business and Finance .... Dr. Dirk E. WILMOTH
32 VP Student Life/Dean of Students ....Ms. Pamela L. GOURLEY
30 Int VP Institutional Advancement ....Mr. A. P. PERKINSON
84 Vice Pres for Enrollment Management ....Mr. David S. HAWSEY
09 Director of Institutional Research ....Mr. Kevork T. HORISSIAN
29 Director of Alumni Affairs ....Ms. Monica S. HOEL
37 Director Student Financial Planning ....Ms. Margaret MURPHY
06 Registrar ....Ms. Karla LEYBOLD-TAYLOR
36 Director of Career Planning ....Ms. Amanda GARDNER
38 Director Student Counseling ....Ms. Jill M. SMELTZER
26 Director Public Relations ....Mr. Dirk S. MOORE
08 Chief Information Officer/Librarian ...... Ms. Lorraine N. ABRAHAM
18 Director of Facilities Managment ....Mr. Mark PITCHER
40 Bookstore Manager ....Mr. Terry RICHARDSON
42 Chaplain ....Rev. Mary K. BRIGGS
15 Human Resources Manager ....Ms. Angie S. EDMONDSON
20 Associate Academic Officer ....Dr. Michael J. PUGLISI
35 Assistant Dean of Students ....Mr. Todd CLARK
21 Business Affairs Manager ....Ms. Benita BARE
07 Director of Admissions ....Mr. Joshua FLOYD

Ferrum College (J)

PO Box 1000, 215 Ferrum Mtn Road,
Ferrum VA 24088-9001
County: Franklin | FICE Identification: 003711
Unit ID: 232089
Telephone: (540) 365-2121 | Carnegie Class: Bac/Diverse
FAX Number: (540) 365-4269 | Calendar System: Semester
URL: www.ferrum.edu
Established: 1913 | Annual Undergrad Tuition & Fees: $26,260
Enrollment: 1,484 | Coed
Affiliation or Control: United Methodist | IRS Status: 501(c)3
Highest Offering: Baccalaureate
Program: Liberal Arts And General
Accreditation: SC, SW

01 President ....Dr. Jennifer L. BRAATEN
10 Senior Vice Pres for Business Affs ......Mr. Bobby W. THOMPSON
05 Provost & Executive Vice President ....Dr. Leslie T. LAMBERT
30 Vice Pres Institutional Advancement .... Mrs. Kimberly P. BLAIR
84 Vice Pres Enrollment Management ....Mr. Douglas E. CLARK
32 Vice President of Student Affairs ....Dr. Andrea P. ZUSCHIN
42 Dean of Chapel/Religious Life ....Rev. C. Wesley ASTIN, JR.

20 Dean Academic Pgms/Faculty Devel .... Dr. Gail SUMMER
04 Special Assistant to the President ....Mrs. Theresa M. POTTER
27 Dean of Info & Learning Mgmt & CIO ..Dr. Christine H. STINSON
06 Registrar ....Mrs. Yvonne S. WALKER
07 Director Admissions ....Mrs. Gilda Q. WOODS
09 Dir of Assessment & Inst Research .... Dr. Jolene D. HAMM
08 Exec Dir Stanley Library & Acad Ctr ....Mr. George LOVELAND
37 Director of Financial Aid ....Ms. Heather HOLLANDSWORTH
29 Director Alumni & Family Services ..Ms. Donna S. WILLIAMSON
26 Director of Public Relations .... Mr. John CARLIN
41 Director of Athletics ....Mr. J. Abraham NAFF
44 Director of Ferrum Fund .... Ms. Beth STEWART
18 Assoc Director of Physical Plant .... Mr. Sam E. MORAN
88 Dir Student Leadership & Engagement . Mr. David A. NEWCOMBE
13 Director of Computer Services ....Mr. Daniel K. HODGES
15 Director of Personnel Services .... Mrs. Mary Alice WHISENANT
40 Bookstore Manager .... Ms. Patty SIGMON
19 Director Ferrum College Police Dept ....Ms. Elizabeth LEGG
36 Dir Career Svcs/Student Employment ....Mr. Roland WALTERS
88 Disability Services Coordinator ....Ms. Nancy S. BEACH
91 Coord of Administrative Computing ....Mr. Tim BELCHER
28 Coordinator Multicultural Programs ....Mr. Justin MUSE
79 Dean School Arts & Humanities ....Dr. John W. BRUTON
81 Dean School Natural Science & Math ......Dr. David M. JOHNSON
83 Dean School Social Sciences ....Dr. Frederic B. TORIMIRO

George Mason University (A)

4400 University Drive, Fairfax VA 22030-4444
County: Fairfax FICE Identification: 003749
Unit ID: 232186
Telephone: (703) 993-1000 Carnegie Class: RU/H
FAX Number: (703) 993-1009 Calendar System: Semester
URL: www.gmu.edu
Established: 1957 Annual Undergrad Tuition & Fees (In-State): $9,266
Enrollment: 32,562 Coed
Affiliation or Control: State IRS Status: 501(c)3
Highest Offering: Doctorate
Program: Liberal Arts And General; Teacher Preparatory; Professional
Accreditation: SC, ART, BUS, BUSA, CEA, CLPSY, CS, ENG, HSA, IPSY, LAW, MUS, NRPA, NURSE, SPAA, SW, TED

01 President ....Dr. Alan G. MERTEN
100 Chief of Staff .... Dr. Thomas HENNESSEY, JR.
03 Vice Pres for Administration ....Vacant
05 Provost .... Dr. Peter N. STEARNS
10 Senior Vice President .... Dr. Maurice W. SCHERRENS
18 Vice President for Facilities .... Mr. Thomas G. CALHOUN
26 Vice President University Relations ....Ms. Christine M. LAPAILLE
30 VP University Devel/Alumni Affairs ....Mr. Marc BRODERICK
13 VP Info Technology/Chief Info Ofcr ....Dr. Joy R. HUGHES
32 Vice President for University Life .... Dr. Sandra J. SCHERRENS
46 VP Research/Economic Development ....Dr. Roger R. STOUGH
22 Director Equity & Diversity Svcs .... Mr. Corey D. JACKSON
16 Assoc Vice Pres for HR/Payroll .... Ms. Linda HARBER
43 University Counsel ....Mr. Thomas M. MONCURE
45 Chief Budget Officer ....Mr. Guilbert L. BROWN
20 Vice Provost Academic Affairs .....Dr. Linda A. SCHWARTZSTEIN
20 Assoc Prov for Undergrad Education .... Dr. Rick DAVIS
84 Assoc Prov for Enroll Plng & Admin ....Ms. Renate H. GUILFORD
58 Assoc Prov for Graduate Education .... Dr. Michelle MARKS
07 Dean of Admissions .... Dr. Andrew FLAGEL
35 Director Ofc of Student Involvement .... Ms. Lauren LONG
35 Assistant Vice Pres University Life ....Ms. Patricia J. CARRETTA
06 Registrar ....Ms. Susan H. JONES
37 Director Student Financial Aid ....Ms. Jevita ROGERS
36 Director University Career Services ....Dr. Janice SUTERA
08 University Librarian ....Mr. John G. ZENELIS
23 Exec Director Student Health Svcs ....Dr. Wagida A. ABDALLA
29 Assoc VP Alumni Affairs .... Ms. Christine CLARK-TALLEY
41 Dir of Intercollegiate Athletics .... Mr. Thomas J. O'CONNOR
19 Dir & Chief of University Police .... Mr. Michael F. LYNCH
49 Dean Col of Humanities/Social Sci ....Dr. Jack R. CENSER
61 Dean School of Law ....Dr. Daniel D. POLSBY
80 Dean School of Public Policy .... Dr. Edward RHODES
50 Dean School of Management .... Dr. Jorge HADDOCK
53 Dean College of Educ & Human Devel .....Dr. Mark R. GINSBERG
54 Dean Volgenau School of Engineering ..... Dr. Lloyd J. GRIFFITHS
66 Dean College of Health/Human Svcs ....Dr. Shirley TRAVIS
81 Dean College of Science ....Dr. Vikas CHANDHOKE
88 Dean Sch Conflict Analysis & Resol .... Dr. Andrea BARTOLI
88 Dean Col of Visual/Performing Arts ....Mr. William F. REEDER
38 Director Counseling Center ....Dr. Jeffrey W. POLLARD
09 Assoc Prov Institutional Research .... Ms. Kris M. SMITH
35 Associate Dean University Life ....Dr. Todd S. ROSE
96 Director of Purchasing and AP ....Mr. William R. HARDIMAN

Hampden-Sydney College (B)

College Road, PO Box 128,
Hampden-Sydney VA 23943-0667
County: Prince Edward FICE Identification: 003713
Unit ID: 232256
Telephone: (434) 223-6000 Carnegie Class: Bac/A&S
FAX Number: (434) 223-6350 Calendar System: Semester
URL: www.hsc.edu
Established: 1775 Annual Undergrad Tuition & Fees: $33,715
Enrollment: 1,058 Male
Affiliation or Control: Presbyterian Church (U.S.A.) IRS Status: 501(c)3
Highest Offering: Baccalaureate
Program: Liberal Arts And General
Accreditation: SC

01 President .... Dr. Christopher B. HOWARD
05 Provost/Dean of Faculty .... Dr. Robert T. HERDEGEN, III
10 Vice President Business Affairs ....Mr. C. Norman KRUEGER
30 Vice President Development ....Mr. C. Beeler BRUSH
11 Vice President for Administration ....Dr. V. Dale JONES
07 Dean of Admissions .... Ms. Anita H. GARLAND
20 Dean of the Faculty ....Dr. Elizabeth DEIS
32 Dean of Students ....Dr. David A. KLEIN
20 Associate Dean Academic Support ....Ms. Christa D. FYE
41 Athletic Director ....Mr. Richard P. EPPERSON, II
08 Librarian ....Dr. Cyrus I. DILLON, III
42 Chaplain ....Dr. David A. KECK
06 Registrar .... Ms. Dawn L. CONGLETON
37 Director of Financial Aid ....Ms. Zita BARREE
29 Director Alumni Relations ....Mr. Mark MEITZ
18 Director Physical Facilities ....Mr. Thomas L. GREGORY
27 Director of Publications .... Dr. Richard C. MCCLINTOCK
14 Director of Computing ....Mr. Robert C. MURRAY
36 Director Career Services ....Mr. L. Rucker SNEAD
23 Director Student Health Service ....Ms. Margaret P. GRAHAM
38 Director of Counseling ....Dr. Glen D. BOWMAN
15 Director of Human Resources ....Ms. Barbara ARMENTROUT
44 Director of Annual Fund ....Ms. Amy HUNT LAWSON
19 Director Security ....Mr. Jeffrey GEE
40 Bookstore Manager ....Mrs. Hazel N. BALDWIN
09 Director of Assessment ....Ms. Christine C. ROSS
26 Director of Public Relations ....Mr. Thomas H. SHOMO
21 Controller ....Mr. W. Glenn CULLEY, JR.
96 Director of Purchasing ....Ms. Janice D. BURKHART
35 Dir Student Activities & Orgs ....Mr. John RAMSAY
39 Director of Student Housing ....Mr. Wes LAWSON
102 Dir Corporate/Foundation Relations .... Mrs. Eunice CARWILE
104 Dir Office of International Studies ....Mrs. Mary COOPER

Hampton University (C)

Hampton VA 23668-0199
County: Independent City FICE Identification: 003714
Unit ID: 232265
Telephone: (757) 727-5000 Carnegie Class: Master's M
FAX Number: (757) 727-5085 Calendar System: Semester
URL: www.hamptonu.edu
Established: 1868 Annual Undergrad Tuition & Fees: $18,798
Enrollment: 5,253 Coed
Affiliation or Control: Independent Non-Profit IRS Status: 501(c)3
Highest Offering: Doctorate
Program: Liberal Arts And General; Teacher Preparatory; Professional
Accreditation: SC, AAB, CS, ENG, IACBE, JOUR, MUS, NUR, NURSE, PHAR, PTA, SP, TED

01 President ....Dr. William R. HARVEY
05 Provost ....Dr. Pamela V. HAMMOND
10 Vice Pres Business Affs/Treasurer ....Mrs. Doretha J. SPELLS
32 Vice Pres for Student Affairs ....Dr. Barbara L. INMAN
43 Vice President/General Counsel ....Atty. Faye HARDY-LUCAS
30 Vice President for Development .... Mr. Laron J. CLARK
04 Executive Assistant to President .... Dr. Charrita D. DANLEY
46 Special Asst to President/Research ....Dr. Elnora DANIEL
44 Asc VP Devel/Dir Capital Campaign ....Mrs. Harriet A. DAVIS
35 Assoc Vice Pres for Student Affairs ....Vacant
21 Asst VP Business Affs/Comptroller ....Ms. Nellie CRAWFORD
25 Asst Vice Pres Grants Management ....Mrs. Lillie F. GREEN
20 Asst Provost Academic Affairs ....Dr. Pollie MURPHY
72 Assistant Provost Technology ....Mr. Keith PERKINS
33 Dean of Men ....Mr. Woodson H. HOPEWELL, JR.
34 Dean of Women ....Miss Jewel B. LONG
07 Director of Admissions ....Mrs. Angela BOYD
06 Registrar ....Mrs. Jorsene COOPER
36 Dir Career Counsel/Planning Ctr ....Mrs. Vivian DAVID
38 Interim Director the Counseling Ctr ....Dr. Linda KIRKLAND-HARRIS
08 Administrator University Libraries ....Ms. Faye WATKINS
29 Director of Alumni Affairs ....Mrs. Mildred SWANN
15 Director of Human Resources ....Ms. Rikki THOMAS
14 Interim Director Computer Center ....Mr. Christopher VERNON
37 Financial Aid Officer ....Mr. Martin MILES
26 Director of University Relations ....Mrs. Yuri Rodgers MILLIGAN
09 Director Institutional Research ....Ms. Regina GIBBONS
85 Director International Programs ....Mrs. Marcia JACKSON
41 Director of Athletics ....Ms. Keshia CAMPBELL
23 Director Student Health Services .... Dr. Hannibal E. HOWELL
40 University Bookstore Manager ....Ms. Michelle R. MILLER
42 University Chaplain ....Rev. Debra L. HAGGINS
18 Director Buildings & Grounds ....Mr. Lowell MIDDLETON
87 Director of Summer Sessions ....Dr. Pollie MURPHY
19 Chief of Campus Police ....Mr. David GLOVER
86 Director Government Relations ....Mr. Wilbert L. THOMAS
96 Director of Purchasing ....Mr. Malcolm HAINES
53 Dean Sch Liberal Arts ....Dr. Mamie E. LOCKE
66 Dean School of Nursing ....Dr. Deborah JONES
81 Assistant Dean School of Science .... Dr. Michelle CLAVILLE
51 Dean Col Educ & Continuing Studies .....Dr. Cassandra HERRING
50 Dean School of Business ....Dr. Sid H. CREDLE
54 Dean Sch of Engineering/Technology ....Dr. Eric J. SHEPPARD
67 Dean School of Pharmacy ....Dr. Wayne HARRIS
58 Interim Dean the Graduate College ....Dr. William YOUNG
60 Dean Scripps Howard Sch Journ/Comm .... Mrs. Rosalynne WHITAKER-HECK

Heritage Institute-Manassas (D)

8255 Shoppers Square, Manassas VA 20111-2176
County: Prince William FICE Identification: 023045
Unit ID: 377421
Telephone: (703) 361-7775 Carnegie Class: Not Classified
FAX Number: (703) 335-9987 Calendar System: Other
URL: www.heritage-education.com
Established: 2002 Annual Undergrad Tuition & Fees: $22,144
Enrollment: 343 Coed
Affiliation or Control: Proprietary IRS Status: Proprietary
Highest Offering: Associate Degree
Program: Occupational
Accreditation: ABHES

01 Director ....Ms. Tess ANDERSON

Hollins University (E)

PO Box 9688, Roanoke VA 24020-1688
County: Roanoke FICE Identification: 003715
Unit ID: 232308
Telephone: (540) 362-6000 Carnegie Class: Bac/A&S
FAX Number: (540) 362-6642 Calendar System: 4/1/4
URL: www.hollins.edu
Established: 1842 Annual Undergrad Tuition & Fees: $30,220
Enrollment: 1,024 Female
Affiliation or Control: Independent Non-Profit IRS Status: 501(c)3
Highest Offering: Master's
Program: Liberal Arts and General; Teacher Preparatory
Accreditation: SC, TEAC

01 President ....Ms. Nancy O. GRAY
10 Vice Pres Finance/Administration ....Ms. Kerry EDMONDS
05 Chair of the Faculty ....Mr. Joe LEEDOM
32 Dean of Students ....Ms. Patty O'TOOLE
07 Associate Dean of Admissions ...Ms. Nikki JOHNSON WILLIAMS
20 Dean Academic Services ....Dr. Patricia HAMMER
28 Associate Dean Intercultural Pgms ....Ms. Jeri L. SUAREZ
04 Executive Assistant to President ....Ms. Brook E. DICKSON
88 Exec Dir Alumnae & Donor Relations ....Ms. Brenda MCDANIEL
06 Registrar ....Ms. Anna GOODWIN
08 Director of the Library ....Ms. Joan RUELLE
30 Director of Development ....Vacant
15 Director of Human Resources ....Ms. Alicia GODZWA
26 Director of Public Relations ....Mr. Jeff HODGES
29 Director of Alumnae Relations ....Ms. Ann CASSELL
36 Director Career Development Center .... Ms. Ashley GLENN
37 Director Financial Aid ....Ms. Mary Jean CORRISS
41 Director of Athletics ....Mr. David ZINN
09 Director of Institutional Research ....Ms. Anna GOODWIN
18 Director Plant Operations/Services ....Ms. May THOMAS

Institute for the Psychological Sciences (F)

2001 Jefferson Davis Hwy, Ste 511,
Arlington VA 22202-3609
County: Arlington FICE Identification: 038724
Unit ID: 445869
Telephone: (703) 416-1441 Carnegie Class: Spec/Health
FAX Number: (703) 416-8588 Calendar System: Semester
URL: www.ipsciences.edu
Established: 1998 Annual Graduate Tuition & Fees: $19,406
Enrollment: 72 Coed
Affiliation or Control: Independent Non-Profit IRS Status: 501(c)3
Highest Offering: Doctorate; No Undergraduates
Program: Professional
Accreditation: SC

01 President ....Rev. Charles SIKORSKY, LC
00 President Emeritus ....Rev. John HOPKINS, LC
05 Academic Dean ....Dr. Gladys A. SWEENEY
10 Vice President of Finance .... Mr. Roberto PARTARRIEU
84 Director Enrollment Svcs/Registrar ....Ms. Jennifer E. KARNS
30 Director Institutional Advancement .... Dr. Mary Ann LA FOEUR
07 Director of Admissions .... Ms. Anne-Marie DARDIS
08 Library Director .... Mr. Jeffrey ELLIOTT

ITT Technical Institute (G)

14420 Albemarle Point Pl, Suite 100,
Chantilly VA 20151-1750
County: Fairfax Identification: 666324
Unit ID: 441964
Telephone: (703) 263-2541 Carnegie Class: Spec/Tech
FAX Number: (703) 263-0846 Calendar System: Quarter
URL: www.itt-tech.edu
Established: 2003 Annual Undergrad Tuition & Fees: N/A
Enrollment: 715 Coed
Affiliation or Control: Proprietary IRS Status: Proprietary
Highest Offering: Baccalaureate
Program: Technical Emphasis
Accreditation: ACICS

† Branch campus of ITT Technical Institute, Knoxville, TN.

ITT Technical Institute (H)

863 Glenrock Road, Suite 100, Norfolk VA 23502-3701
County: Norfolk City Identification: 666555
Unit ID: 368601
Telephone: (757) 466-1260 Carnegie Class: Bac/Assoc
FAX Number: (757) 466-7630 Calendar System: Quarter
URL: www.itt-tech.edu
Established: 1988 Annual Undergrad Tuition & Fees: N/A
Enrollment: 1,235 Coed

Affiliation or Control: Proprietary IRS Status: Proprietary
Highest Offering: Baccalaureate
Program: Technical Emphasis
Accreditation: ACICS

† Branch campus of ITT Technical Institute, Newburgh, IN.

ITT Technical Institute (A)

300 Gateway Centre Parkway, Richmond VA 23235-5139
County: Chesterfield Identification: 666040
Unit ID: 437051
Telephone: (804) 330-4992 Carnegie Class: Spec/Tech
FAX Number: (804) 330-4993 Calendar System: Quarter
URL: www.itt-tech.edu
Established: 1998 Annual Undergrad Tuition & Fees: N/A
Enrollment: 866 Coed
Affiliation or Control: Proprietary IRS Status: Proprietary
Highest Offering: Baccalaureate
Program: Occupational; Technical Emphasis
Accreditation: ACICS

† Branch campus of ITT Technical Institute, Tampa, FL.

ITT Technical Institute (B)

7300 Boston Boulevard, Springfield VA 22153-2804
County: Fairfax Identification: 666321
Unit ID: 441955
Telephone: (703) 440-9535 Carnegie Class: Spec/Tech
FAX Number: (703) 440-9561 Calendar System: Quarter
URL: www.itt-tech.edu
Established: 2003 Annual Undergrad Tuition & Fees: N/A
Enrollment: 976 Coed
Affiliation or Control: Proprietary IRS Status: Proprietary
Highest Offering: Baccalaureate
Program: Technical Emphasis
Accreditation: ACICS

† Branch campus of ITT Technical Institute, Tampa, FL.

James Madison University (C)

800 S Main Street, Harrisonburg VA 22807-0001
County: Independent City FICE Identification: 003721
Unit ID: 232423
Telephone: (540) 568-6211 Carnegie Class: Master's L
FAX Number: N/A Calendar System: Semester
URL: www.jmu.edu
Established: 1908 Annual Undergrad Tuition & Fees (In-State): $8,448
Enrollment: 19,434 Coed
Affiliation or Control: State IRS Status: 501(c)3
Highest Offering: Doctorate
Program: Liberal Arts And General; Teacher Preparatory; Professional
Accreditation: SC, ARCPA, ART, AUD, BUS, BUSA, CACREP, CIDA, CS, DANCE, DIETD, ENGR, IPSY, MUS, NURSE, OT, PSPSY, SP, SW, TED, THEA

01 President .... Dr. Linwood H. ROSE
05 Provost/Vice Pres Academic Affairs .... Dr. Jerry BENSON
11 Sr Vice Pres Administration/Finance .... Mr. Charles W. KING
32 Sr VP Student Affairs/Univ Planning .... Dr. Mark J. WARNER
30 Sr Vice Pres University Advancement .... Dr. Joanne CARR
04 Exec Assistant to the President .... Mrs. Donna L. HARPER
81 Dean College Science/Math .... Dr. David F. BRAKKE
49 Dean College Arts/Letters .... Dr. David K. JEFFREY
72 Dean Col Integrat Science/Tech .... Dr. Sharon LOVELL
50 Dean College of Business .... Dr. Robert D. REID
57 Dean College Visual Performing Arts .... Dr. George E. SPARKS
53 Dean College of Education .... Dr. Phillip M. WISHON
58 Dean Graduate School .... Dr. Reid J. LINN
97 Dean University Studies .... Dr. Linda C. HALPERN
08 Dean of Libraries/Educ Technologies .... Mr. Ralph A. ALBERICO
43 University Counsel .... Ms. Susan L. WHEELER
45 Asst Vice Pres Budget Management .... Ms. Diane L. STAMP
07 Director of Admissions .... Mr. Michael D. WALSH
37 Dir Financial Aid & Scholarships .... Ms. Lisa L. TUMER
15 Director Human Resources .... Ms. Yohna CHAMBERS
09 Director Institutional Research .... Dr. Frank J. DOHERTY
41 Director of Athletics .... Mr. Jeffrey T. BOURNE
26 Dir Public Affairs & Univ Spokesman .... Mr. Donald K. EGLE
06 University Registrar .... Ms. Michele M. WHITE
19 Chief of Police .... Mr. Lee A. SHIFFLETT

Jefferson College of Health Sciences (Formerly Community Hospital) (D)

PO Box 13186, Roanoke VA 24031-3186
County: Independent City Identification: 006622
Unit ID: 231837
Telephone: (540) 985-8483 Carnegie Class: Spec/Health
FAX Number: (540) 985-9773 Calendar System: Semester
URL: www.jchs.edu
Established: 1982 Annual Undergrad Tuition & Fees: $19,750
Enrollment: 1,032 Coed
Affiliation or Control: Independent Non-Profit IRS Status: 501(c)3
Highest Offering: Master's
Program: Nursing Emphasis
Accreditation: SC, ARCPA, EMT, MT, NURSE, OT, OTA, PTAA

01 President .... Dr. Nathaniel L. BISHOP
05 Dean Academic Affairs .... Dr. Lisa ALLISON-JONES
10 Dean Administrative Services .... Ms. Anna S. MILLIRONS
84 Dean Enrollment Management/Planning .... Vacant
32 Dean Student Affairs .... Mr. Scott HILL
20 Assoc Dean for Academic Affairs .... Dr. Glen MAYHEW
17 Chair Communitty Health Sciences .... Ms. Sharon L. HATFIELD
88 Director Healthcare Management .... Ms. Janet PHILLIPS
63 Clinical Coordinator .... Dr. Wilton C. KENNEDY
63 Program Director Emergency Service .... Mr. John C. COOK
17 Dept Chr Arts & Sci/Dir Hlth Psych .... Mr. Francis DANE
83 Director Humanities and Soc Sci .... Mr. Darrell SHOMAKER
81 Director of Science/Math .... Dr. William B. MCVAUGH
66 Dept Chair Nursing .... Dr. Ava PORTER
66 Program Director BSN .... Dr. Rebecca GREER
66 Program Director BSN .... Dr. Melody SHARP
88 Dept Chr Rehab/Wellness/Dir PT Asst .... Dr. Michael S. KRACKOW
88 Director Occupation Therapy Masters .... Dr. David A. HAYNES
27 Coord Communications/Col Relations .... Mr. Mark A. LAMBERT
29 Coordinator Dev/Alumni Relations .... Vacant
25 Sponsored Projects Coordinator .... Ms. Amanda ELLINGER
07 Director of Admissions .... Ms. Judith O. MCKEON
37 Director of Financial Aid .... Ms. Debra J. JOHNSON
06 Registrar .... Ms. Linda C. WILLIAMS
08 Director Library .... Ms. Ramona THISS
35 Coordinator Student Affairs .... Mr. Zachary WIDNER
40 Manager Bookstore .... Ms. Janey W. HIGHTOWER
21 Bursar .... Ms. Vicki R. BROWN
09 Institutional Research Manager .... Vacant
18 Safety/Physical Plant Officer .... Ms. Susan L. BOOTH
38 Director Counseling and Wellness .... Dr. Jennifer SLUSHER
21 Senior Staff Accountant .... Ms. Vicki D. COLE
04 Administrative Secretary to Pres .... Ms. Priscilla DUBOIS
88 Program Director Health and Exc Sci .... Mrs. Ally BOWERSOCK
88 Director Occupational Therapy Asst .... Ms. Ave M. MITTA
88 Program Dir Physician Asst Program .... Ms. Patricia AIREY

The John Leland Center for Theological Studies (E)

405 N. Washington Street, Suite 200, Falls Church VA 22046
County: City of Falls Church Identification: 666340
Telephone: (703) 812-4757 Carnegie Class: Not Classified
FAX Number: (703) 812-4764 Calendar System: Other
URL: www.leland.edu
Established: 1998 Annual Graduate Tuition & Fees: $11,620
Enrollment: 75 Coed
Affiliation or Control: Baptist IRS Status: 501(c)3
Highest Offering: Master's; No Undergraduates
Program: Religious Emphasis
Accreditation: THEOL

01 President .... Dr. Mark J. OLSON
05 Academic Dean/Vice President .... Dr. Jeffrey G. WILLETTS
04 Exec Assistant to the President .... Ms. Andrea BAKKE
08 Librarian .... Ms. Jennifer M. FOUCHER
06 Registrar .... Ms. Andrea BAKKE
07 Director Recruiting/Admissions .... Ms. Taryn DEATON
10 Chief Business Officer .... Mrs. Ellen TEAGUE
21 Associate Business Officer .... Mrs. Joanne HENDRICKS
26 Chief Public Relations Officer .... Ms. Taryn DEATON

Liberty University (F)

1971 University Boulevard, Lynchburg VA 24502-2269
County: Independent City FICE Identification: 020530
Unit ID: 232557
Telephone: (434) 582-2000 Carnegie Class: Master's L
FAX Number: (434) 582-2304 Calendar System: Semester
URL: www.liberty.edu
Established: 1971 Annual Undergrad Tuition & Fees: $19,154
Enrollment: 55,223 Coed
Affiliation or Control: Baptist IRS Status: 501(c)3
Highest Offering: Doctorate
Program: Liberal Arts And General; Teacher Preparatory; Professional
Accreditation: SC, EXSC, LAW, NURSE, TED

01 Chancellor/President .... Mr. Jerry FALWELL, JR.
88 Vice Chancellor Spiritual Affairs .... Rev. Jonathan FALWELL
05 Vice Chancellor/Acting Provost .... Dr. Ronald S. GODWIN
10 Chief Financial Officer .... Mr. Don MOON
32 Vice President Student Affairs .... Dr. Mark L. HINE
11 Vice President Administration .... Mrs. Sharon HARTLESS
15 Vice President Human Resources .... Mrs. Laura J. WALLACE
88 Vice President for Spiritual Devel .... Dr. Dwayne CARSON
26 Vice Pres Exec Projects/Media Rels .... Mr. Johnnie MOORE
20 Vice Prov Grad Sch/Online Programs .... Dr. Ronald E. HAWKINS
20 Vice Prov Academic Administration .... Dr. Garth E. RUNION
21 Vice President Finance .... Mr. Anthony BECKLES
09 Vice Pres for Admin Info Management .... Mr. Larry SHACKLETON
45 AVP for Institutional Effectiveness .... Dr. H. William WHEELER
13 Chief Information Officer .... Mr. Matthew J. ZEALAND
06 Registrar .... Mr. Larry SHACKLETON
84 Vice Pres Enrollment Management .... Mr. Chris JOHNSON
07 Director of Admissions .... Mr. Terry ELAM
29 Manager of Alumni Affairs .... Mrs. Melissa SMALL
08 Dean of Library Services .... Dr. David BARNETT
33 Dir Student Care/Conduct Offices .... Mr. Keith ANDERSON
34 Senior Student Conduct Officer .... Ms. Andrea ADAMS
42 Academic Dean of the Seminary .... Dr. Dan MITCHELL
86 Dean Helms School of Government .... Mr. Shawn D. AKERS
37 Executive Director Financial Aid .... Dr. Robert L. RITZ
41 Director of Athletics .... Mr. Jeff BARBER
49 Dean College of Arts & Sciences .... Dr. Roger D. SCHULTZ
50 Dean School of Business .... Dr. Bruce K. BELL
60 Dean School of Communication .... Dr. William G. GRIBBIN
97 Exec Dir Ctr Acad Support/Adv Svcs .... Dr. Brian YATES
73 Dean School of Religion .... Dr. Elmer L. TOWNS
53 Dean School of Education .... Dr. Karen L. PARKER
35 Director of Student Activities .... Mr. Chris MISIANO
18 Vice Pres of Field Operations .... Mr. Scott STARNES
19 Chief of Police LUPD .... Col. Richard HINKLEY
72 Dean School of Engineering and CSCI .... Dr. Ronald SONES
28 Dir Ctr for Multicltrl Enrichment .... Ms. Melany PEARL
36 Director of Career Center .... Mrs. Carrie BARHNOUSE
106 Exec Director Online Programs .... Mr. John DONGES
58 Dean Academic Admin Graduate School .... Dr. Fred MILACCI
61 Dean School of Law .... Mr. Mathew D. STAVER
88 Dean School of Aeronautics .... Mr. David L. YOUNG

Longwood University (G)

201 High Street, Farmville VA 23909-1801
County: Prince Edward FICE Identification: 003719
Unit ID: 232566
Telephone: (434) 395-2000 Carnegie Class: Master's M
FAX Number: (434) 395-2635 Calendar System: Semester
URL: www.longwood.edu
Established: 1839 Annual Undergrad Tuition & Fees (In-State): $10,530
Enrollment: 4,831 Coed
Affiliation or Control: State IRS Status: 501(c)3
Highest Offering: Master's
Program: Liberal Arts And General; Teacher Preparatory; Professional
Accreditation: SC, BUS, MUS, NRPA, SP, SW, TED, THEA

01 President .... BGen. Patrick FINNEGAN
05 Provost/Vice Pres Academic Affairs .... Dr. Kenneth B. PERKINS
10 Vice Pres Administration & Finance .... Mrs. Kathy A. WORSTER
32 Vice President for Student Affairs .... Dr. Tim J. PIERSON
30 Vice Pres University Advancement .... Dr. Bryan K. ROWLAND
18 VP Facilities Mgmt/Real Property .... Mr. Richard W. BRATCHER
13 VP Inform/Instructional Tech Svcs .... Dr. Francis X. MOORE
26 Assoc VP Marketing/Communications .... Vacant
84 Int Dean of Enrollment Management .... Ms. Sallie D. MCMULLIN
09 Director Assessment & Inst Research .... Dr. Ling Y. WHITWORTH
06 Registrar .... Vacant
08 Dean of Library .... Mrs. Suzy SZASZ-PALMER
29 Director Alumni Relations .... Mrs. Nancy B. SHELTON
36 Director of Acad & Career Adv Ctr .... Ms. Mary M. SAUNDERS
38 Director Student Counseling .... Dr. Wayne R. O'BRIEN
37 Director Student Financial Aid .... Ms. Karen M. SCHINABECK
96 Director of Materiel Management .... Mr. James E. SIMPSON
15 Chief Human Resources Officer .... Ms. Della H. WICKIZER
18 Director Physical Plant .... Mr. Alvin B. MYERS
28 Director for Diversity & Inclusion .... Dr. Jamie R. RILEY

Lynchburg College (H)

1501 Lakeside Drive, Lynchburg VA 24501-3199
County: Independent City FICE Identification: 003720
Unit ID: 232609
Telephone: (434) 544-8100 Carnegie Class: Master's S
FAX Number: (434) 544-8499 Calendar System: Semester
URL: www.lynchburg.edu
Established: 1903 Annual Undergrad Tuition & Fees: $30,805
Enrollment: 2,643 Coed
Affiliation or Control: Christian Church (Disciples Of Christ)
IRS Status: 501(c)3
Highest Offering: Doctorate
Program: Liberal Arts And General; Teacher Preparatory; Professional
Accreditation: SC, @ACBSP, CACREP, EXSC, NURSE, @PTA

01 President .... Dr. Kenneth R. GARREN
05 Vice Pres & Dean for Academic Affs .... Dr. Julius A. SIGLER
10 Vice President Business & Finance .... Mr. Steve BRIGHT
30 Vice Pres Advancement .... Ms. Denise MCDONALD
84 Vice Pres Enrollment Management .... Mrs. Rita DETWILER
32 Vice Pres & Dean of Student Develop .... Mr. John G. ECCLES
50 Dean School Business & Economics .... Dr. Joseph TUREK
53 Dean School Education/Human Devel .... Dr. Jan STENNETTE
60 Dean Sch Communications & The Arts .... Dr. Oeida HATCHER
79 Dean Sch Humanities/Social Science .... Dr. Kim MCCABE
81 Dean School of Sciences .... Dr. Barry LOBB
76 Dean Sch Health Science/Human Perf .... Dr. Linda ANDREWS
06 Registrar/Asst Dean Acad/Stndt Info .... Mr. Jay K. WEBB
08 Director of the Library .. Mr. Christopher A. MILLSON-MARTULA
37 Coordinator of Financial Aid .... Ms. Michelle DAVIS

Mary Baldwin College (I)

Staunton VA 24401
County: Independent City FICE Identification: 003723
Unit ID: 232672
Telephone: (540) 887-7000 Carnegie Class: Master's S
FAX Number: (540) 886-5561 Calendar System: Other
URL: www.mbc.edu
Established: 1842 Annual Undergrad Tuition & Fees: $26,655
Enrollment: 2,326 Coed
Affiliation or Control: Presbyterian Church (U.S.A.) IRS Status: 501(c)3
Highest Offering: Master's
Program: Liberal Arts And General; Teacher Preparatory
Accreditation: SC, @SW, TEAC

01 President .... Dr. Pamela FOX
05 VP Academic Affairs/Dean .... Dr. Catharine O'CONNELL
10 Sr Vice President Business/Finance .... Mr. David MOWEN
84 Sr VP Enrollment Mgmt/Dean Stdnts .... Dr. Brenda BRYANT
30 Vice Pres Institutional Advancement .... Mr. David ATCHLEY
26 Vice President for Public Relations .... Ms. Crista CABE
88 Assoc VP for Inclusive Excellence .... Rev. Andrea CORNELL-SCOTT
58 Dean of Adult & Graduate Studies .... Vacant
09 Dean Inst Research/Registrar .... Dr. Lewis D. ASKEGAARD
27 Chief Information Officer .... Mr. Angus MCQUEEN
07 Executive Director Enrollment Mgmt .... Mr. Andrew MODLIN
08 Director of Library .... Ms. Carol CREAGER
58 Int Director of MAT .... Dr. James HARRINGTON
57 Director ML/MFA .... Dr. Paul MENZER
88 Director Program for Excep Gifted .... Dr. Stephanie FERGUSON
15 Director of Human Resources .... Ms. Shelly IRVINE
32 Exec Dir Stdnt Life/Asc Dean Stdnts .... Ms. Lisa WELLS
18 Chief Facilities/Physical Plant .... Mr. Brent DOUGLASS
21 Dir of Budgets/Business Operation .... Mr. Rick CZERWINSKI
29 Director of Alumni Relations .... Ms. Jennifer KIBLER
36 Director Career Development Svcs .... Ms. Julie CHAPPELL
37 Director of Financial Aid .... Ms. Robin DIETRICH

Marymount University (A)

2807 N Glebe Road, Arlington VA 22207-4299

County: Arlington FICE Identification: 003724
Unit ID: 232706
Telephone: (703) 522-5600 Carnegie Class: Master's L
FAX Number: (703) 284-1637 Calendar System: Semester
URL: www.marymount.edu
Established: 1950 Annual Undergrad Tuition & Fees: $23,972
Enrollment: 3,572 Coed
Affiliation or Control: Roman Catholic IRS Status: 501(c)3
Highest Offering: Doctorate
Program: Liberal Arts And General; Teacher Preparatory; Professional
Accreditation: SC, ACBSP, CACREP, CIDA, HSA, NURSE, PTA, TED

01 President .... Dr. Matthew D. SHANK
05 Provost and Vice Pres Acad Affairs .... Dr. Sherri L. HUGHES
10 Vice Pres for Financial Affairs .... Dr. Ralph KIDDER
84 Vice Pres Stdnt Devel & Enrollment .... Dr. Chris E. DOMES
30 Vice President for Development .... Ms. Emily MAHONY
26 Vice Pres Communications/Marketing .... Ms. Shelley A. DUTTON
20 Assoc Vice President Acad Affairs .... Dr. Robert OTTEN
20 Assoc Vice President Acad Affairs .... Dr. Liane SUMMERFIELD
49 Dean Arts & Sciences .... Dr. George CHEATHAM
50 Dean Business Administration .... Dr. James RYERSON
53 Dean Education & Human Services .... Dr. Wayne LESKO
76 Dean Health Professions .... Dr. Tess CAPPELLO
08 Dean Library & Learning Services .... Dr. Zary MOSTASHARI
06 University Registrar .... Mr. Scott SPENCER
13 Exec Director IT Services .... Ms. Claudia O'CONNOR
09 Exec Director Inst Effectiveness .... Mr. Michael SCHUCHERT
32 Assoc Vice President Student Dev .... Mr. Frank RIZZO
07 Director of Admissions Undergrad .... Mr. Michael CANFIELD
07 Director of Graduate Admissions .... Ms. Francesca REED
37 Director Financial Aid .... Ms. Deborah RAINES
42 Director Campus Ministry .... Rev. David SHARLAND
41 Director Athletics .... Mrs. Debbie WARREN
19 Dir of Campus Safety/Transportation .... Mr. Eric HOLS
91 Dir of Admin Information Services .... Vacant
39 Director of Residence Life .... Mr. Paul LYNCH
35 Director of Student Activities .... Mr. Vincent STOVALL
23 Director of Student Health Service .... Ms. Diane WHITE
38 Director Student Counseling .... Mr. Silvestro MENZANO
21 Asst Vice Pres and Controller .... Mr. Ronald SOMERVELL
15 Exec Dir Human Resource Svcs .... Mr. James HOBSON
18 Int Director of Physical Plant .... Mr. Robert RUSH
96 Coordinator of Purchasing .... Vacant
29 Exec Dir Development/Alumni Rels .... Mrs. Kathleen ZEIFANG
26 Director of Public Relations .... Ms. Laurie F. CALLAHAN

Medical Careers Institute (B)

1001 Omni Boulevard Suite 200,
Newport News VA 23606-4388

County: Newport News FICE Identification: 022472
Unit ID: 231642
Telephone: (757) 873-2423 Carnegie Class: Assoc/PrivFP
FAX Number: (757) 873-2472 Calendar System: Other
URL: www.medical.edu
Established: N/A Annual Undergrad Tuition & Fees: N/A
Enrollment: 19 Coed
Affiliation or Control: Proprietary IRS Status: Proprietary
Highest Offering: Associate Degree
Program: Occupational
Accreditation: &SC, MAAB, PTAA, RAD

01 President .... Ms. Alicia COLES
05 Vice President of Operations .... Ms. Barbara LARAR

† Regional accreditation is carried under the parent institution, ECPI College of Technology, in Virginia Beach, VA.

Medical Careers Institute (C)

2809 Emerywood Parkway, Suite 400,
Richmond VA 23294

County: Henrico Identification: 667038
Telephone: (804) 521-5999 Carnegie Class: Not Classified
FAX Number: (804) 521-5998 Calendar System: Other
URL: www.medical.edu
Established: N/A Annual Undergrad Tuition & Fees: N/A
Enrollment: N/A Coed
Affiliation or Control: Proprietary IRS Status: Proprietary
Highest Offering: Associate Degree
Program: Occupational
Accreditation: &SC, MAAB

01 Campus President .... Mr. Joseph DALTO

† Regional accreditation is carried under the parent institution ECPI College of Technology, Virginia Beach, VA.

Miller-Motte Technical College (D)

1011 Creekside Lane, Lynchburg VA 24502-4353

County: Lynchburg FICE Identification: 004992
Unit ID: 233091
Telephone: (434) 239-5222 Carnegie Class: Assoc/PrivFP
FAX Number: (434) 239-1069 Calendar System: Quarter
URL: www.miller-motte.com
Established: 1997 Annual Undergrad Tuition & Fees: $7,770
Enrollment: 398 Coed
Affiliation or Control: Proprietary IRS Status: Proprietary
Highest Offering: Associate Degree
Program: Occupational; Technical Emphasis
Accreditation: ACICS, SURGT

01 Director .... Mr. Kevin TIGHE

National College (E)

1819 Emmet Street, Charlottesville VA 22901-2812

County: Charlottesville City Identification: 666501
Telephone: (434) 295-0136 Carnegie Class: Not Classified
FAX Number: (434) 979-8061 Calendar System: Quarter
URL: www.ncbt.edu
Established: 1865 Annual Undergrad Tuition & Fees: N/A
Enrollment: 215 Coed
Affiliation or Control: Proprietary IRS Status: Proprietary
Highest Offering: Associate Degree
Program: Occupational; Business Emphasis
Accreditation: ACICS, MAC

01 President .... Mr. Frank LONGAKER
05 Director .... Dr. Kimberly MOORE
03 Executive Vice President .... Ms. Lenora DOWNING

† Branch campus of National College, Salem, VA.

National College (F)

336 Old Riverside Drive, Danville VA 24541-1819

County: Independent City Identification: 666502
Telephone: (434) 793-6822 Carnegie Class: Not Classified
FAX Number: (434) 793-3634 Calendar System: Quarter
URL: www.ncbt.edu
Established: N/A Annual Undergrad Tuition & Fees: $9,052
Enrollment: 365 Coed
Affiliation or Control: Proprietary IRS Status: Proprietary
Highest Offering: Baccalaureate
Program: Occupational; Business Emphasis
Accreditation: ACICS, MAC, SURGT

01 Campus Director .... Mr. Mark EVANS
03 Executive Vice President .... Ms. Lenora S. DOWNING

† Branch campus of National College, Salem, VA.

National College (G)

1515 Country Club Road, Harrisonburg VA 22801-9709

County: Rockingham Identification: 666503
Telephone: (540) 432-0943 Carnegie Class: Not Classified
FAX Number: (540) 432-1133 Calendar System: Quarter
URL: www.ncbt.edu
Established: 1986 Annual Undergrad Tuition & Fees: $12,900
Enrollment: 340 Coed
Affiliation or Control: Proprietary IRS Status: Proprietary
Highest Offering: Baccalaureate
Program: Occupational; Technical Emphasis
Accreditation: ACICS, MAC, SURGT

01 Director .... Mr. David ZIMMERMAN

† Branch campus of National College, Salem, VA.

National College (H)

104 Candlewood Court, Lynchburg VA 24502-2653

County: Lynchburg City Identification: 666504
Telephone: (434) 239-3500 Carnegie Class: Not Classified
FAX Number: (434) 239-3948 Calendar System: Quarter
URL: www.ncbt.edu
Established: 1886 Annual Undergrad Tuition & Fees: $8,900
Enrollment: 432 Coed
Affiliation or Control: Proprietary IRS Status: Proprietary
Highest Offering: Baccalaureate
Program: Occupational; Business Emphasis
Accreditation: ACICS, MAC

01 Director .... Mr. Bill BAKER

† Branch campus of National College, Salem, VA.

National College (I)

905 N. Memorial Boulevard, Martinsville VA 24112-2420

County: Martinsville City Identification: 666505
Telephone: (276) 632-5621 Carnegie Class: Not Classified
FAX Number: (276) 632-7915 Calendar System: Quarter
URL: www.ncbt.edu
Established: 1886 Annual Undergrad Tuition & Fees: $11,964
Enrollment: 475 Coed
Affiliation or Control: Proprietary IRS Status: Proprietary
Highest Offering: Associate Degree
Program: Occupational; Technical Emphasis
Accreditation: ACICS, MAC

01 Director .... Mr. John H. SCOTT

† Branch campus of National College, Salem, VA.

National College (J)

1813 E Main Street, Salem VA 24153-4598

County: Independent City FICE Identification: 003726
Unit ID: 232797
Telephone: (540) 986-1800 Carnegie Class: Assoc/PrivFP4
FAX Number: (540) 986-1344 Calendar System: Quarter
URL: www.ncbt.edu
Established: 1886 Annual Undergrad Tuition & Fees: $8,846
Enrollment: 450 Coed
Affiliation or Control: Proprietary IRS Status: Proprietary
Highest Offering: Master's
Program: Business Emphasis
Accreditation: ACICS, EMT, MAC

01 President .... Mr. Frank E. LONGAKER
03 Executive Vice President .... Ms. Lenora S. DOWNING
05 Campus Director .... Mr. Lewis BISHOP
07 Vice President Admissions .... Mr. Larry W. STEELE

Norfolk State University (K)

700 Park Avenue, Norfolk VA 23504-8000

County: Independent City FICE Identification: 003765
Unit ID: 232937
Telephone: (757) 823-8600 Carnegie Class: Master's L
FAX Number: (757) 823-2067 Calendar System: Semester
URL: www.nsu.edu
Established: 1935 Annual Undergrad Tuition & Fees (In-State): $6,700
Enrollment: 6,964 Coed
Affiliation or Control: State IRS Status: 501(c)3
Highest Offering: Doctorate
Program: Liberal Arts And General; Teacher Preparatory; Professional
Accreditation: SC, ADNUR, BUS, CLPSY, CS, DIETD, ENG, #JOUR, KIN, MT, MUS, NAIT, NUR, SW, TED

01 President .... Dr. Tony ATWATER
05 Provost .... Vacant
10 Acting Vice Pres Finance/Admin .... Mrs. Regina WILLIAMS
30 Vice Pres Univ Advancement .... Mr. Phillip D. ADAMS
32 Vice Pres Student Affairs .... Mrs. Sharon B. LOWE
46 Vice Pres for Research .... Dr. Joseph HALL
20 Interim Vice Provost for Undergrad .... Dr. Mildred K. FULLER
20 Vice Provost .... Dr. Clarence D. COLEMAN
84 Interim Exec Dir Enrollment Mgmt .... Mrs. Terricita E. SASS
35 Asst Vice Pres Student Affairs .... Vacant
43 University Counsel .... Ms. Pamela F. BOSTON
07 Dir of Recuirtment & Admissions .... Vacant
19 Chief of Campus Police .... Mr. Anthony H. WALKER
38 Director of Counseling .... Dr. Curtis K. GREAVES
06 Registrar .... Mrs. Regina BYNUM
08 Acting Library Director .... Dr. Tommy BOGGER
37 Director of Financial Aid .... Mr. Kevin J. BURNS
36 Director of Career Services .... Mr. Nash D. MONTOGMERY
15 Human Resources Director .... Mrs. Francie H. JOHNSON
14 Director Enterprise Information Sys .... Mrs. Alison D. DAVIS-TARIQ
29 Director of Alumni Relations .... Ms. Michelle D. HILL
49 Interim Dean of Liberal Arts .... Dr. Nuria CUEVAS
50 Dean of Business .... Dr. Steven D. PAPMARCOS
53 Dean of Education .... Dr. Jean P. BRAXTON
76 Dean of Science & Technology .... Dr. Sandra J. DELOATCH
70 Dean of Social Work .... Dr. Dorothy C. BROWNE
58 Acting Dean of Graduate Studies .... Dr. Mildred K. FULLER
86 Legislative and Community Liason .... Ms. Paula C. THOMPSON
26 Dir of Comm & Marketing .... Vacant
09 Dir Inst Research .... Vacant
39 Director of Residential Life .... Mrs. Faith M. FITZGERALD
40 Bookstore Manager .... Ms. Pamela WILLIAMSON
41 Athletic Director .... Mr. Marty L. MILLER
88 Univ Ombudsmen .... Vacant
18 Director of Facilities Management .... Ms. Karen D. BARRETT
85 Dir of Intl Student & Scholar Svcs .... Dr. William ALEXANDER
96 Director of Procurement .... Mr. Anthony E. CANNION
21 Controller .... Mrs. Michelle D. MARTIN

† Member of Virginia Consortium for Professional Psychology.

Old Dominion University (L)

5115 Hampton Boulevard, Norfolk VA 23529-0001

County: Independent City FICE Identification: 003728
Unit ID: 232982
Telephone: (757) 683-3000 Carnegie Class: RU/H
FAX Number: (757) 683-4505 Calendar System: Semester
URL: www.odu.edu
Established: 1930 Annual Undergrad Tuition & Fees (In-State): $8,144

Enrollment: 24,466 Coed
Affiliation or Control: State IRS Status: 501(c)3
Highest Offering: Doctorate
Program: Liberal Arts And General; Teacher Preparatory; Professional
Accreditation: SC, ANEST, ART, BUS, BUSA, CACREP, CLPSY, CYTO, DH, ENG, ENGT, EXSC, HT, MT, MUS, NMT, NRPA, NURSE, PH, PTA, SP, SPAA, TED, THEA

01 President ... Mr. John R. BRODERICK
05 Provost/VP Academic Affairs ... Dr. Carol SIMPSON
10 Vice President Admin & Finance ... Mr. Robert L. FENNING
20 Int Vice Provost/Dean Univ College ... Dr. David D. METZGER
46 Vice President for Research ... Dr. Mohammad A. KARIM
15 Act Vice Pres for Human Resources ... Ms. September C. SANDERLIN
30 Vice Pres University Advancement ... Mr. Alonzo C. BRANDON
32 VP Student Engagement & Enroll Svcs ... Dr. Ellen NEUFELDT
20 Assoc Vice Pres Academic Services ... Mr. James P. DUFFY
21 Asc VP Admn & Fin/Univ Budget Ofcr ... Ms. Deborah L. SWIECINSKI
09 Vice Prov Plng & Inst Effectiveness ... Dr. Martha S. SHARPE
56 Assoc VP Distance Learning ... Mr. Andrew R. CASIELLO
88 Asst Vice Pres Auxiliary Services ... Mr. Todd JOHNSON
13 Asst Vice Pres Comp & Comm Services ... Mr. James R. WATERFIELD
31 Asst Vice Pres Community Engagement ... Ms. Karen MEIER
84 Assoc Vice Pres Enrollment Mgmt ... Vacant
20 Asst VP Undergraduate Studies ... Ms. Judith M. BOWMAN
30 Asst Vice Pres for Development ... Dr. Anita S. FRIEDMAN
29 Asst Vice Pres of Alumni Relations ... Ms. Dana G. ALLEN
26 Asst VP Marketing & Communications ... Ms. Jennifer MULLEN
22 Asst VP Inst Equity & Diversity ... Ms. ReNee S. DUNMAN
49 Int Dean College Arts & Letters ... Dr. Charles E. WILSON, JR.
81 Dean College of Sciences ... Dr. Christopher PLATSOUCAS
76 Dean College Health Sciences ... Dr. Shelley MISHOE
50 Dean Col Business/Public Admin ... Dr. Gilbert R. YOCHUM
53 Dean College of Education ... Dr. Linda IRWIN-DEVITIS
54 Dean Col Engineering & Tech ... Dr. Oktay BAYSAL
92 Dean Honors College ... Dr. David D. METZGER
36 Asst Dean Career Management Center ... Mr. Tom WUNDERLICH
93 Asst Dean Multicultural Stdnt Svcs ... Ms. Lesa C. CLARK
35 Dean of Students ... Mr. Donald M. STANSBURY
43 General Counsel ... Mr. Patrick B. KELLY
85 Int Exec Dir International Programs ... Mr. Steven D. BELL
88 Exec Dir Cmty Development Corp ... Ms. E. Ann GRANDY
08 University Librarian ... Ms. Virginia O'HERRON
06 University Registrar ... Ms. Mary K. SWARTZ
07 Director of Admissions ... Ms. Nechell T. BONDS
41 Director of Athletics ... Dr. C. Wood SELIG
37 Director Student Financial Aid ... Ms. Veronica M. FINCH
31 Director Community Relations ... Ms. Cecelia T. TUCKER
88 Director Military Affairs ... Capt. F. Richard WHALEN
38 Director Counseling & Advising Svcs ... Dr. Lenora THOMPSON
23 Director Student Health Center ... Ms. Jennifer J. FOSS
85 Director Intl Students & Faculty ... Ms. Robbin FULMORE
91 Director Computing Information Svcs ... Mr. Michael S. LITTLE
39 Director of Student Housing ... Ms. Carole HENRY
18 Director Facilities Management ... Mr. R. Dillard GEORGE
88 University Controller ... Vacant
19 Acting Chief of Police ... Mr. George E. VOTAVA
27 Director of Public Relations ... Mr. Stephen P. DANIEL
28 Director of Diversity and EO/AA ... Ms. Pamela E. JACKSON
96 Director of Materiel Management ... Mr. Rick BERRY
94 Director Women's Studies ... Dr. Jennifer N. FISH
16 Director of Human Resources ... Ms. September C. SANDERLIN
35 Director of Student Life ... Ms. Nicole C. KIGER
40 Manager Bookstore ... Mr. Darryl ATKINSON
04 Assistant to the President ... Ms. Velvet L. GRANT
86 Asst to Pres for Govt Relations ... Ms. Elizabeth A. KERSEY

† Member of Virginia Consortium for Professional Psychology.

Patrick Henry College (A)

One Patrick Henry Circle, Purcellville VA 20132-3197
County: Loudoun FICE Identification: 039513
Unit ID: 233019
Telephone: (540) 338-1776 Carnegie Class: Bac/A&S
FAX Number: (540) 441-8119 Calendar System: Semester
URL: www.phc.edu
Established: 2000 Annual Undergrad Tuition & Fees: $22,758
Enrollment: 461 Coed
Affiliation or Control: Independent Non-Profit IRS Status: 501(c)3
Highest Offering: Baccalaureate
Program: Liberal Arts And General
Accreditation: TRACS

01 President ... Dr. Graham WALKER
00 Chancellor ... Dr. Michael P. FARRIS
05 Provost ... Dr. Gene E. VEITH
03 Exec Vice President & Treasurer ... Mr. Carl W. SCHREIBER
09 VP Instl Effective/Strat Initiative ... Dr. Laura E. MCCOLLUM
84 VP for Enrollment Management ... Mr. William KELLARIS
30 Vice President for Advancement ... Mr. Blake HUDSON
11 Vice Pres for Campus Services ... Mr. Earl W. HALL
49 Chairman Classical Liberal Arts Dep ... Dr. Stephen R. HAKE
80 Chairman Government Department ... Dr. Leslie D. SILLARS
06 Registrar ... Mr. Rodney J. SHOWALTER
56 Director of Distance Learning ... Dr. Robert G. SPINNEY
08 Director of the Library ... Ms. Charlessa E. MCCONNELL
32 Dean of Student Affairs ... Ms. Sandra K. CORBITT
07 Director of Admissions ... Ms. Rebekah A. KNABLE
26 Director of Communications ... Mr. David W. HALBROOK
10 Chief Financial Officer ... Mr. Daryl WOLKING
15 Director of Human Resources ... Ms. Barbara A. FINLAY
13 Chief Information Officer ... Mr. Jeff R. BURTNER

Potomac College (B)

1029 Herndon Parkway, Herndon VA 20170-5524
County: Fairfax Identification: 666178
Unit ID: 442639
Telephone: (703) 709-5875 Carnegie Class: Bac/Diverse
FAX Number: (703) 709-8976 Calendar System: Semester
URL: www.potomac.edu
Established: 1991 Annual Undergrad Tuition & Fees: $10,780
Enrollment: 145 Coed
Affiliation or Control: Proprietary IRS Status: Proprietary
Highest Offering: Baccalaureate
Program: 2-Year Principally Bachelor's Creditable; Professional; Business Emphasis
Accreditation: &M

01 President ... Dr. C. Cathleen RAFFAELI
05 Vice Pres Academic Affairs ... Dr. Cathy EBERHART
20 Academic Dean ... Mr. James MOSES
06 Director of Operations/Registrar ... Ms. Karen MORRIS
37 Financial Aid Director ... Ms. Phyllis CREWS
08 Librarian ... Vacant
32 Director of Student Services ... Mr. Marcus PALMORE
35 Assistant Director Student Services ... Mr. Ervan PEARSON

† Regional accreditation is carried under the parent institution in Washington, DC.

Protestant Episcopal Theological Seminary in Virginia (C)

3737 Seminary Road, Alexandria VA 22304-5201
County: Independent City FICE Identification: 003731
Unit ID: 233259
Telephone: (703) 370-6600 Carnegie Class: Not Classified
FAX Number: (703) 370-6234 Calendar System: Semester
URL: www.vts.edu
Established: 1823 Annual Graduate Tuition & Fees: $12,200
Enrollment: 187 Coed
Affiliation or Control: Protestant Episcopal IRS Status: 501(c)3
Highest Offering: Doctorate; No Undergraduates
Program: Professional; Religious Emphasis
Accreditation: THEOL

01 President/Dean ... Rev. Ian S. MARKHAM
05 Vice Pres/Assoc Dean Academic Affs ... Dr. Timothy F. SEDGWICK
11 VP for Administration/Finance ... Mrs. Heather ZDANCEWICZ
32 Assoc Dean of Students ... Dr. Amelia G. DYER
06 Registrar ... Mrs. Tamara A. SHEPHERD
08 Director of the Library ... Dr. Mitzi J. BUDDE

Radford University (D)

810 E Main Street, Radford VA 24142-0002
County: Independent City FICE Identification: 003732
Unit ID: 233277
Telephone: (540) 831-5000 Carnegie Class: Master's L
FAX Number: (540) 831-5142 Calendar System: Semester
URL: www.radford.edu
Established: 1910 Annual Undergrad Tuition & Fees (In-State): $8,320
Enrollment: 9,007 Coed
Affiliation or Control: State IRS Status: 501(c)3
Highest Offering: Doctorate
Program: Liberal Arts And General; Teacher Preparatory; Professional
Accreditation: SC, BUS, CACREP, CIDA, CS, DIETD, MUS, NRPA, NURSE, OT, @PTA, SP, SW, TED, THEA

01 President ... Ms. Penelope W. KYLE
04 Special Assistant to the President ... Ms. JoAnn KIERNAN
05 Provost & VP Academic Affairs ... Dr. Sam H. MINNER
10 Vice President for Finance & Admin ... Mr. Richard S. ALVAREZ
32 Vice President for Student Affairs ... Dr. Mark G. SHANLEY
30 VP Univ Advancement ... Vacant
84 Vice Provost for Enroll Plng & Mgmt ... Dr. Steven W. NAPE
20 Vice Prov for Academic Affairs ... Dr. William R. KENNAN
49 Dean Col Hum/Behav Sci ... Dr. Katherine HAWKINS
50 Dean of Business & Economics ... Dr. Faye W. GILBERT
53 Dean Education & Human Development ... Dr. Patricia B. SHOEMAKER
66 Dean Health & Human Services ... Dr. Raymond N. LINVILLE
57 Dean Visual/Performing Arts ... Dr. Joseph P. SCARTELLI
58 Dean College of Grad & Prof Studies ... Dr. Dennis O. GRADY
72 Dean Col of Sci & Technology ... Dr. J. Orion ROGERS
35 Assoc Vice Pres & Dean of Students ... Vacant
90 Associate VP Info Technology ... Mr. Edward OAKES
76 Assoc Dean Health & Human Services ... Dr. Ken M. COX
07 Dean of Admissions ... Mr. James PENNIX
06 Registrar ... Mr. Matthew S. BRUNNER
37 Director of Financial Aid ... Mrs. Barbara A. PORTER
39 Director of Residential Life ... Ms. Katherine W. LAVINDER
18 Director Facilities Operations ... Mr. Jorge W. COARTNEY
29 Assoc Dir of Alumni Relations ... Ms. Sandra BOND
29 Assoc Dir of Alumni Relations ... Ms. Melissa VIDMAR
41 Director Intercollegiate Athletics ... Mr. Robert LINEBURG
08 Interim University Librarian ... Mr. Steve HELM
13 Vice President Info Technology/CIO ... Mr. Danny M. KEMP
15 Director of Human Resources ... Ms. Joey C. SWORD
19 Director of University Police ... Chief Colleen T. ROBERTS
88 Int Dir Acad Engage/Career Svc/Comm ... Ms. Ellen TAYLOR
23 Director Student Health Services ... Ms. Jeanie SEAY
85 Director of International Programs ... Vacant
24 Director TV/Radio/Comm Svcs ... Ms. Ashlee B. CLAUD
25 Dir Sponsored Pgms/Grant Mgmt ... Mr. Thomas CRUISE
40 Manager University Bookstore ... Mr. Benjie SAUNDERS
96 Director of Material Management ... Ms. Pamela P. SIMPKINS
09 Asst Vice Provost/Dir Inst Research ... Dr. Debra R. TEMPLETON
38 Director Student Counseling ... Ms. Erin SULLIVAN
41 Director Univ Adv for Athletics ... Mr. Kelly R. UNDERWOOD
102 Exec Dir Univ Adv Corp & Foundation ... Ms. Robyn J. PORTERFIELD
88 University Controller ... Mr. William H. SHORTER
44 Director Annual Giving ... Vacant
88 Director Planning & Construction ... Mr. Roy E. SAVILLE
88 Dir Leadership/Professional Dev ... Vacant
86 Dir Govt/Non-Profit Assistance Ctr ... Dr. Bruce W. CHASE
88 Asst VP & Dir of Co-Curricular Act ... Mr. Kenneth J. BONK
39 Director of Housing Operations ... Mr. Jeffrey P. ORZOLEK
51 Int Dir Cntr Innovative Teach/Learn ... Mr. Charley COSMATO
28 Dir Ctr for Diversity & Inclusion ... Mr. Adrien DELOACH

Randolph College (E)

2500 Rivermont Avenue, Lynchburg VA 24503-1555
County: Independent City FICE Identification: 003734
Unit ID: 233301
Telephone: (434) 947-8000 Carnegie Class: Bac/A&S
FAX Number: (434) 947-8139 Calendar System: Semester
URL: www.randolphcollege.edu
Established: 1891 Annual Undergrad Tuition & Fees: $29,866
Enrollment: 550 Coed
Affiliation or Control: United Methodist IRS Status: 501(c)3
Highest Offering: Master's
Program: Liberal Arts And General; Teacher Preparatory
Accreditation: SC, TEAC

01 President ... Mr. John E. KLEIN
30 Vice Pres Institutional Advancement ... Ms. Jan MERIWETHER
10 Vice Pres Finance & Administration ... Mr. Christopher L. BURNLEY
32 VP Student Affs & Dean of Students ... Dr. Sarah L. SWAGER
05 VP Academic Affs & Dean of College ... Dr. Dennis G. STEVENS
84 VP Enrollment & Dean of Admissions ... Mr. John W. WHITE
20 Associate Dean of the College ... Ms. Paula J. WALLACE
29 Alumnae Director ... Ms. Heather A. GARNETT
09 Director of Institutional Research ... Dr. John F. KEENER
15 Director Human Resources ... Ms. Sharon SAUNDERS
18 Chief Facilities/Physical Plant ... Mr. Bobby BENNETT
21 Controller ... Mr. Jonathan TYREE
38 Director Student Counseling ... Dr. Anne HERSHBELL
08 Librarian ... Mr. Theodore J. HOSTETLER
06 Registrar ... Ms. Barbara S. THRASHER
37 Dir Student Financial Services ... Ms. Kay MATTOX
36 Director of Career Development ... Ms. Connie HAYES
13 Director of Information Technology ... Mr. Victor GOSNELL
26 Director of College Relations ... Vacant

Randolph-Macon College (F)

204 Henry Street, PO Box 5005, Ashland VA 23005-5505
County: Hanover FICE Identification: 003733
Unit ID: 233295
Telephone: (804) 752-7200 Carnegie Class: Bac/A&S
FAX Number: (804) 752-7231 Calendar System: Other
URL: www.rmc.edu
Established: 1830 Annual Undergrad Tuition & Fees: $32,265
Enrollment: 1,223 Coed
Affiliation or Control: United Methodist IRS Status: 501(c)3
Highest Offering: Baccalaureate
Program: Liberal Arts And General; Teacher Preparatory
Accreditation: SC, TEAC

01 President ... Mr. Robert R. LINDGREN
05 Provost/VP for Academic Affairs ... Dr. William T. FRANZ
10 Treasurer ... Mr. Paul DAVIES
30 Vice Pres for College Advancement ... Ms. Diane M. LOWDER
07 Dean of Admissions/Financial Aid ... Dr. David L. LESESNE
32 Dean of Students ... Dr. Grant L. AZDELL
29 Exec Dir Col Advancement for Alumni ... Mrs. Susan H. DONAVANT
08 Director of Library ... Dr. Virginia E. YOUNG
26 Dir of Marketing & Communications ... Mrs. Anne Marie LAURANZON
07 Director of Admissions ... Mr. Anthony F. AMBROGI
37 Director of Financial Aid ... Mrs. Mary Y. NEAL
14 Director of Information & Tech Svcs ... Mr. Thomas H. COPLER
06 Registrar ... Mrs. Alana DAVIS
36 Dir Counseling/Career Services ... Dr. D. Craig ANDERSON
09 Director of Institutional Research ... Dr. Timothy W. MERRILL
18 Director of Operations & Physical Plant ... Mr. Thomas P. DWYER
42 Chaplain ... Rev. Darrell L. HEADRICK
19 Director of Campus Safety ... Mr. Maurice J. KIELY
41 Athletic Director ... Mr. Jeffrey S. BURNS
15 Director Human Resources ... Mrs. Sharon S. JACKSON
21 Controller ... Mrs. Caroline C. BUSCH
20 Associate Dean of the College ... Dr. Lauren C. BELL
36 Director of Career Services ... Ms. Catherine A. ROLLMAN
35 Asst Dean of Students ... Mr. James D. MCGHEE, JR.
40 Bookstore Manager ... Mrs. Barclay F. DUPRIEST

Reformed Theological Seminary (A)

028 Balls Hill Road, McLean VA 22101
ounty: Fairfax Identification: 666079
elephone: (703) 448-3393 Carnegie Class: Not Classified
AX Number: (703) 738-7389 Calendar System: 4/1/4
RL: www.rts.edu
stablished: 1997 Annual Graduate Tuition & Fees: $14,655
nrollment: 139 Coed
ffiliation or Control: Independent Non-Profit IRS Status: 501(c)3
ighest Offering: Master's; No Undergraduates
rogram: Religious Emphasis
ccreditation: &SC, &THEOL

1 President .... Dr. Robert C. CANNADA, JR.
3 Executive Director .... Mr. Hugh WHELCHEL
7 Dir Admiss/Student Svcs/Registrar .... Mr. Geoffrey M. SACKETT

† Regional accreditation is carried under the parent institution in Jackson, MS.

Regent University (B)

000 Regent University Drive,
Virginia Beach VA 23464-9800
County: Independent City FICE Identification: 030913
Unit ID: 231651
Telephone: (757) 352-4127 Carnegie Class: DRU
AX Number: (757) 352-4381 Calendar System: Semester
URL: www.regent.edu
Established: 1977 Annual Undergrad Tuition & Fees: $15,308
Enrollment: 5,555 Coed
Affiliation or Control: Independent Non-Profit IRS Status: 501(c)3
Highest Offering: Doctorate
Program: Professional
Accreditation: SC, CACREP, CLPSY, LAW, TEAC, THEOL

01 President .... Dr. Carlos CAMPO
05 Exec Vice Pres for Academic Affairs .... Dr. Paul BONICELLI
32 Interim VP for Student Services .... Mr. Ryan BROWN
30 Vice President for Advancement .... Mrs. Ann LEBLANC
14 Vice President for Info Technology .... Mrs. Tracy R. STEWART
10 VP of Finance .... Mr. Dean A. WOOTEN
15 Vice President for Human Resources .... Mrs. Martha J. SMITH
26 VP for Marketing & Public Relations .... Ms. Sherri STOCKS
106 Assistant VP of Online Learning .... Mrs. Ginger ZILLGES
50 Dean Communication & the Arts .... Dr. Mitch LAND
38 Dean School of Global Leadership .... Dr. Bruce E. WINSTON
38 Dean Psychology & Counseling .... Dr. William HATHAWAY
73 Dean School of Divinity .... Dr. Michael D. PALMER
53 Dean School of Education .... Dr. Alan A. ARROYO
80 Dean School of Government .... Dr. Charles W. DUNN
61 Dean School of Law .... Mr. Jeffrey A. BRAUCH
97 Dean School of Undergrad Studies .... Dr. Gerson MORENO-RIANO
08 Dean of Libraries .... Dr. Sara BARON
43 General Counsel .... Mr. Louis A. ISAKOFF
06 Registrar .... Ms. Althea BISHARD
37 Director of Financial Aid .... Mr. Joseph DOBROTA
09 Director of Institutional Research .... Dr. Amanda WYNN
84 Director of Enrollment Management .... Mr. Matthew CHADWICK
18 Dir of Facilities & Engineering .... Mr. Richard JEMIOLA
29 Director of Alumni Relations .... Ms. Melissa FUQUAY
35 Director of Student Life .... Mr. Roger CHEEKS
96 Manager of Purchasing .... Mrs. Pauline CARRAWAY
42 Director of Campus Ministries .... Dr. Richard KIDD
84 Exec Dir Enrollment Marketing .... Mr. David PROFFITT
45 Exec Director Inst Effectiveness .... Dr. Jim DOWNEY
31 Director of Church Relations .... Mr. Brett COATES
88 Director of Military Affairs .... Mr. Dave BOISSELLE

Richard Bland College (C)

11301 Johnson Road, Petersburg VA 23805-7100
County: Independent City FICE Identification: 003707
Unit ID: 233338
Telephone: (804) 862-6100 Carnegie Class: Assoc/Pub2in4
FAX Number: (804) 862-6207 Calendar System: Semester
URL: www.rbc.edu
Established: 1960 Annual Undergrad Tuition & Fees (In-State): $3,472
Enrollment: 1,587 Coed
Affiliation or Control: State IRS Status: 501(c)3
Highest Offering: Associate Degree
Program: 2-Year Principally Bachelor's Creditable
Accreditation: SC

01 President .... Dr. James B. MCNEER
05 Provost .... Dr. LeAnn S. BINGER
10 Vice Pres Administration & Finance .... Dr. Russell E. WHITAKER, JR.
19 Director Security/Safety .... Mr. C. Scott DAVIS
30 Director Institutional Advancement .... Dr. LeAnn M. BINGER
09 Dir of Institutional Effectiveness .... Ms. Patricia A. HARVEY
06 Registrar .... Ms. Lois WRAY
08 Director of Library .... Dr. Virginia R. CHERRY
32 Director of Student Affairs .... Mr. Randy DEAN
13 Director of Info Tech Services .... Ms. Dorothy P. EDWARDS
37 Director of Financial Aid .... Mr. J. Tyler T. HART
07 Assoc Dir of Enrollment Services .... Mrs. Whitney GERSHOWITZ
15 Director of Human Resources .... Ms. Frances SCARBROUGH
18 Facilities/Physical Plant Manager .... Mrs. Michaele SHRIVER
96 Director of Purchasing .... Ms. Nichole COLLINS
35 Assoc Dir of Student Services .... Ms. Evanda WATTS-MARTINEZ
39 Assoc Dir of Residence Life .... Mr. Casey BLANKENSHIP

Roanoke College (D)

221 College Lane, Salem VA 24153-3747
County: Independent City FICE Identification: 003736
Unit ID: 233426
Telephone: (540) 375-2500 Carnegie Class: Bac/A&S
FAX Number: (540) 375-2205 Calendar System: Semester
URL: www.roanoke.edu
Established: 1842 Annual Undergrad Tuition & Fees: $32,900
Enrollment: 2,103 Coed
Affiliation or Control: Evangelical Lutheran Church In America
IRS Status: 501(c)3
Highest Offering: Baccalaureate
Program: Liberal Arts And General; Teacher Preparatory
Accreditation: SC, ACBSP, TEAC

01 President .... Mr. Michael C. MAXEY
05 Vice President/Dean of the College .... Dr. Richard A. SMITH
84 VP of Enrollment Services .... Ms. Brenda P. POGGENDORF
32 Vice President Student Affairs .... Dr. Eugene L. ZDZIARSKI, II
10 Vice President Business Affairs .... Mr. Mark P. NOFTSINGER
30 Vice President Resource Development .... Ms. Connie K. CARMACK
13 VP Info Technology/Public Relations .... Dr. James R. DALTON
09 Exec Dir Institutional Research .... Dr. Jack K. STEEHLER
20 Assoc Dean Academic Affairs/Admin .... Dr. Jennifer K. BERENSON
06 Assoc Dean Acad Affairs/Registrar .... Ms. Leah R. RUSSELL
35 Associate Dean of Student Life .... Mr. Robert M. HINES
39 Assistant Dean Residence Life .... Ms. Teresa P. BLETHYN
88 Asst Dn Stdt Activty/Dir Campus Ctr .... Mr. Mark T. PETERSEN
92 Director of Honors Programs .... Dr. Michael A. HAKKENBERG
08 Director of the Library .... Mr. Stanley F. UMBERGER
36 Director of Career Services .... Ms. Toni D. MCLAWHORN
24 Director Institutional Technology .... Mr. David H. MULFORD
31 Director Cmty Pgms/Special Events .... Ms. Stephanie P. GARST
26 Director of Public Relations .... Ms. Teresa T. GEREAUX
44 Director of Major & Planned Gifts .... Vacant
29 Director of Development/Alumni .... Mr. Jonathan E. LEE
37 Director of Financial Aid .... Mr. Thomas S. BLAIR
21 Director of Finance & Budget .... Ms. Kathryn A. VANNESS
91 Director Admin Information Services .... Ms. Mitzi B. STEELE
18 Manager Planning and Projects .... Mr. Larry S. WALKER
15 Director Human Resources .... Ms. Cathy S. DICKERSON
40 Bookstore Manager .... Mr. Philip C. ATKINS
19 Director Campus Safety .... Mr. Thomas H. TURNER
23 Director Student Health Services .... Ms. Sandra W. MCGHEE
41 Athletic Director .... Mr. M. Scott ALLISON
42 Chaplain .... Rev. R. Paul HENRICKSON
104 Director International Education .... Ms. Lorraine FLECK
38 Director Counseling Center .... Dr. J. P. Hap COX
28 Director of Multicultural Affairs .... Ms. Juliet J. LOWERY
04 Executive Assistant to President .... Ms. Joyce A. SINK
04 Senior Advisor to President .... Mr. McMillan H. JOHNSON

RSHT (E)

751 West Hundred Road, Chester VA 23836-2516
County: Chesterfield Identification: 666481
Telephone: (804) 751-9191 Carnegie Class: Not Classified
FAX Number: (804) 751-2599 Calendar System: Semester
URL: www.rsht.edu
Established: 1997 Annual Undergrad Tuition & Fees: N/A
Enrollment: N/A Coed
Affiliation or Control: Proprietary IRS Status: Proprietary
Highest Offering: Associate Degree
Program: Occupational
Accreditation: COE, RAD

01 Campus Director .... Debbie HARRIS
05 Academic Dean .... Sandra KERRICK

† Branch campus of RSHT, Richmond, VA.

RSHT (F)

1601 Willow Lawn Drive, Suite 320,
Richmond VA 23230-3423
County: Henrico FICE Identification: 034095
Unit ID: 437769
Telephone: (804) 288-1000 Carnegie Class: Not Classified
FAX Number: (804) 288-1006 Calendar System: Semester
URL: www.rsht.edu
Established: 1997 Annual Undergrad Tuition & Fees: N/A
Enrollment: 559 Coed
Affiliation or Control: Proprietary IRS Status: Proprietary
Highest Offering: Associate Degree
Program: Occupational
Accreditation: COE

01 Acting Campus Director .... Maxine STINE

Saint Paul's College (G)

115 College Drive, Lawrenceville VA 23868-1200
County: Brunswick FICE Identification: 003739
Unit ID: 233499
Telephone: (434) 848-3111 Carnegie Class: Bac/Diverse
FAX Number: (434) 848-6407 Calendar System: Semester
URL: www.saintpauls.edu
Established: 1888 Annual Undergrad Tuition & Fees: $13,210
Enrollment: 596 Coed
Affiliation or Control: Protestant Episcopal IRS Status: 501(c)3
Highest Offering: Baccalaureate
Program: Liberal Arts And General; Teacher Preparatory
Accreditation: #SC

01 President .... Dr. Robert L. SATCHER, SR.
10 Vice President Financial Affairs .... Mrs. Geraldine JONES
32 Vice President for Student Affairs .... Dr. Willie J. HARRIS
05 Provost/Vice Pres Academic Affairs .... Dr. Raymond HOLMES
30 Vice President for Inst Advancement .... Ms. Kimberly CETLOW
84 Director Enrollment Management .... Mr. William HERRINGTON
06 Int Dir Registration & Records .... Ms. Helen JACKSON
08 Librarian .... Mr. Marc FINNEY
37 Director of Financial Aid .... Mrs. Antionette HOUSE
26 Director of Public Relations .... Miss Germeka AKRIE
35 Director of Student Activities .... Mrs. Kimberly JACKSON
09 Director Institutional Research .... Dr. Barbara WYCHE
36 Director Career Planning/Placement .... Ms. Denise RICE
42 Chaplain .... Rev. Harry V. NEVELS, JR.
29 Director Alumni Relations .... Dr. Dianne BARNES-RHOADES
41 Athletic Director .... Mr. Le Roy H. BACOTE
15 Director of Human Resources .... Mrs. Alta M. THOMAS
35 Director of Student Support Svcs .... Ms. Audrey NELSON
18 Chief Facilities/Physical Plant .... Mr. LeRoy BACOTE
20 Associate Academic Officer .... Ms. Lunette ELLIS

Sanford-Brown College (H)

1980 Gallows Road, Vienna VA 22182
County: Fairfax FICE Identification: 009420
Unit ID: 234216
Telephone: (703) 556-8888 Carnegie Class: Bac/Assoc
FAX Number: (703) 556-0953 Calendar System: Quarter
URL: www.wbscareer.com
Established: 1950 Annual Undergrad Tuition & Fees: $16,328
Enrollment: 776 Coed
Affiliation or Control: Proprietary IRS Status: Proprietary
Highest Offering: Baccalaureate
Program: Occupational; 2-Year Principally Bachelor's Creditable; Liberal Arts And General
Accreditation: ACICS

01 President .... Dr. Raul GARZA

Sanz School (I)

6182 Arlington Blvd, Falls Church VA 22044
County: Fairfax FICE Identification: 025889
Unit ID: 131742
Telephone: (703) 237-6200 Carnegie Class: Not Classified
FAX Number: (703) 533-3750 Calendar System: Semester
URL: www.sanz.edu
Established: 1939 Annual Undergrad Tuition & Fees: $5,937
Enrollment: 1,672 Coed
Affiliation or Control: Proprietary IRS Status: Proprietary
Highest Offering: Associate Degree
Program: Occupational
Accreditation: COE

01 Executive Director .... Janet BARONE

Sentara College of Health Sciences (J)

1441 Crossways Blvd, Ste 105, Chesapeake VA 23320
County: Chesapeake City FICE Identification: 031065
Telephone: (757) 388-2900 Carnegie Class: Not Classified
FAX Number: (757) 388-2905 Calendar System: Semester
URL: www.sentara.edu
Established: 1992 Annual Undergrad Tuition & Fees: $17,315
Enrollment: 485 Coed
Affiliation or Control: Independent Non-Profit IRS Status: 501(c)3
Highest Offering: Baccalaureate
Program: Occupational
Accreditation: ACICS, CVT, DNUR

01 Dean Sentara Col of Health Sciences .... Ms. Shelly COHEN
66 Dean of Nursing .... Dr. Linda ALEKSA
05 Asst Dean Curriculum/Instruction .... Ms. Sue CARROLL
76 Asst Dean Dept of Allied Health .... Ms. Nora LEONARD
88 Program Dir Cardiovascular Ed/Tech .... Mr. Christopher NELSON
20 Program Education Director .... Ms. Sue STALLINGS
32 Asst Dean Dept of Student Svcs .... Ms. Lori TOWNSEND
08 Librarian .... Ms. Suzanne DUNCAN
37 Financial Aid Representative .... Ms. Mary Ann RIVERA
26 Marketing/Public Relations Rep .... Ms. Lisa WATERFIELD
07 Allied Health Admissions Recruiter .... Ms. Anesia DEAN
18 Building Maintenance .... Mr. Len SANDLOOP

Shenandoah University (K)

1460 University Drive, Winchester VA 22601-5195
County: Independent City FICE Identification: 003737
Unit ID: 233541
Telephone: (540) 665-4500 Carnegie Class: Master's L
FAX Number: N/A Calendar System: Semester
URL: www.su.edu
Established: 1875 Annual Undergrad Tuition & Fees: $27,940
Enrollment: 3,679 Coed
Affiliation or Control: United Methodist IRS Status: 501(c)3
Highest Offering: Doctorate
Program: Liberal Arts And General; Teacher Preparatory; Professional
Accreditation: SC, ARCPA, BUS, MIDWF, MUS, NURSE, OT, PHAR, PTA, TEAC

01 President .... Dr. Tracy FITZSIMMONS

05 Senior VP & VP Academic Affairs ....Dr. Bryon L. GRIGSBY
10 Vice Pres Administration/Finance ....Mr. Richard C. SHICKLE
32 Vice President for Student Life ......Dr. Rhonda VANDYKE COLBY
30 Vice Pres for Advancement ....Mr. Mitchell L. MOORE
84 VP for Enrol Mgmt & Student Success ....Dr. Clarresa MORTON
39 Assoc VP Student Life/Dir Rs Life ....Mr. Donald B. APPIARIUS
29 Assoc Vice Pres for Alumni Affairs ....Ms. Jane D. PITTMAN
44 Assoc Vice Pres for Advancement ....Ms. Vicky MEDLOCK
26 Assoc VP Marketing & Communications ....Mr. John HACHTEL
49 Dean of College of Arts & Sciences ......Dr. Calvin H. ALLEN, JR.
50 Dean of Byrd School of Business ....Dr. W. Randy BOXX
64 Dean of Shenandoah Conservatory ....Dr. Michael J. STEPNIAK
67 Dean of Dunn School of Pharmacy ....Dr. Alan B. MCKAY
07 Dean of Admissions ....Mr. David D. ANTHONY
35 Dir of Student Union/Activities ....Vacant
08 Director of Library Services ....Mr. Christopher A. BEAN
06 Registrar ....Ms. Melanie WINTER
26 Director of Marketing ....Ms. Cathy J. LORANGER
21 Comptroller ....Ms. Marcene GRAVES
37 Director of Financial Aid ....Ms. Nancy S. BRAGG
36 Director of Career Services ...Ms. Jennifer A. SPATARO-WILSON
18 Director of Physical Plant ....Mr. Gene E. FISHER
23 Director of Wellness Center ....Mr. Ronald G. STICKLEY
15 Director of Human Resources ....Ms. Marie C. LANDES
41 Athletic Director ....Dr. Wayne EDWARDS
91 Database & System Administrator ....Mr. David HOFFMAN
13 Director of Institutional Computing ....Mr. Quaiser ABSAR
66 Director Division of Nursing ....Dr. Kathryn M. GANSKE
88 Director Div of Athletic Training ....Dr. Rose A. SCHMIEG
88 Dir Div of Occupational Therapy ....Dr. Deborah A. MARR
88 Director Div of Physical Therapy ....Dr. Karen E. ABRAHAM
88 Sr Dir Advancement - Conservatory .....Mr. Bradley C. SNOWDEN
19 Director of Public Safety ....Mr. Wayne SEALOCK
102 Director Foundation Relations ....Ms. Jennifer BOUSQUET
31 Director Auxiliary Services ....Mr. John V. STEVENS
88 Director Div of Physician Asst Stds ....Mr. Anthony A. MILLER
20 Director of Academic Services ....Mrs. Deborah E. WYNE
42 Director of Church Relations ....Vacant
88 Dir Program in Respiratory Care ....Ms. Beverly RECNY
09 Director Institutional Research ....Ms. Melanie WINTER
40 Bookstore Manager ....Ms. Mary Ellen WELCH
96 Purchasing & Accts Pay Manager ....Ms. Ginny L. NORMAN
24 Coordinator Media Services ....Mr. David E. CHAVEZ
38 Director Student Counseling ....Ms. Nancy SCHULTE

Skyline College (A)

5234 Airport Road, Roanoke VA 24012-1603
County: Roanoke FICE Identification: 030927
Unit ID: 261931
Telephone: (540) 563-8080 Carnegie Class: Bac/Assoc
FAX Number: (540) 362-5400 Calendar System: Semester
URL: www.skyline.edu
Established: 1966 Annual Undergrad Tuition & Fees: $10,100
Enrollment: 500 Coed
Affiliation or Control: Proprietary IRS Status: Proprietary
Highest Offering: Baccalaureate
Program: Occupational; 2-Year Principally Bachelor's Creditable; Technical Emphasis
Accreditation: ACCSC, MAAB

01 Campus President .... Dr. Walter G. MERCHANT

Southeast Culinary and Hospitality College (B)

100 Piedmont Avenue, Bristol VA 24201-5699
County: Bristol FICE Identification: 041338
Unit ID: 451608
Telephone: (276) 591-5699 Carnegie Class: Assoc/PrivFP
FAX Number: (276) 591-5677 Calendar System: Semester
URL: www.southeastculinary.edu
Established: 2004 Annual Undergrad Tuition & Fees: $13,000
Enrollment: 115 Coed
Affiliation or Control: Proprietary IRS Status: Proprietary
Highest Offering: Associate Degree
Program: Occupational
Accreditation: COE

01 Chief Executive Officer ....Richard K. ERSKINE
05 Dean ....Everett HONAKER

Southern Virginia University (C)

One University Hill Drive, Buena Vista VA 24416-3097
County: Rockbridge FICE Identification: 003738
Unit ID: 233611
Telephone: (540) 261-8400 Carnegie Class: Bac/A&S
FAX Number: (540) 261-8451 Calendar System: Semester
URL: www.svu.edu
Established: 1867 Annual Undergrad Tuition & Fees: $18,300
Enrollment: 746 Coed
Affiliation or Control: Independent Non-Profit IRS Status: 501(c)3
Highest Offering: Baccalaureate
Program: Liberal Arts And General
Accreditation: @SC

01 President ....Dr. Rodney K. SMITH
05 Provost ....Dr. Madison U. SOWELL
10 Vice President Finance ....Mr. Robert E. HUCH
30 VP Institutional Advancement .... Mr. Richard WHITEHEAD
26 VP Communications & Marketing ....Mr. Burke OLSEN
07 VP Enrollment Services ....Mr. Brett GARCIA
13 VP Operations/Student Services ....Mr. Scott Y. DOXEY
20 Associate Provost ....Vacant
44 Director of Annual Giving ....Mr. Jeff ROBISON
35 Associate Dean of Students .... Mr. Joseph BOUCHELLE
10 Controller ....Mr. Jesse SEEGMILLER
08 Director of Library Services ....Mr. Duane WILSON
36 Director of Student Support ....Mr. Michael GIBBONS
41 Athletic Director ....Mr. Rick WINTERS
06 Registrar ....Ms. Whitney LARSEN
37 Director of Financial Aid ....Mr. John BRANDT
29 Director of Alumni Relations ....Mr. John FEINAUER
09 Director of Institutional Research .... Dr. John ARMSTRONG
15 Human Resources Assistant ....Ms. Kara CRAWFORD

Stratford University (D)

7777 Leesburg Pike, Falls Church VA 22043-2403
County: Fairfax FICE Identification: 025412
Unit ID: 438498
Telephone: (703) 821-8570 Carnegie Class: Master's L
FAX Number: (703) 734-5335 Calendar System: Quarter
URL: www.stratford.edu
Established: 1976 Annual Undergrad Tuition & Fees: $14,800
Enrollment: 1,600 Coed
Affiliation or Control: Proprietary IRS Status: Proprietary
Highest Offering: Master's
Program: Professional; Business Emphasis
Accreditation: ACICS, ACFEI

01 President ....Dr. Richard R. SHURTZ, II
03 Executive Director Falls Church ....Mary Ann SHURTZ
11 Chief Operating Officer ....Dr. James FLAGGERT
10 Chief Financial Officer ....John DOVI
50 Dean School of Business ....Dr. Lloyd GIBSON
12 Campus Director ....Christi HAYS
88 Dean School of Hospitality/Culinary ....Jordan LICHMAN
76 Dean of Allied Health ....Dr. Bennett SOLBERG
77 Dean Sch of Information Technology ....Naren KODALI
06 Registrar ....Heather RICHARDS
07 Director of Admissions ....Carl SIEBECKER
37 Director Business/Financial Aid ....Brian FORD
36 Director Career Services ....Lenie TIONGSON
21 Assistant Business Officer A/R ....Mila SKLYAR

Sweet Briar College (E)

Sweet Briar VA 24595-9998
County: Amherst FICE Identification: 003742
Unit ID: 233718
Telephone: (434) 381-6100 Carnegie Class: Bac/A&S
FAX Number: (434) 381-6173 Calendar System: 4/1/4
URL: www.sbc.edu
Established: 1901 Annual Undergrad Tuition & Fees: $31,095
Enrollment: 760 Female
Affiliation or Control: Independent Non-Profit IRS Status: 501(c)3
Highest Offering: Master's
Program: Liberal Arts And General
Accreditation: SC

01 President ....Dr. Jo Ellen PARKER
100 Vice President and Chief of Staff ....Mrs. Louise S. ZINGARO
04 Exec Asst Office of the President ....Mrs. Karen L. SUMMERS
09 Director Institutional Research ....Ms. Christy C. COLE
88 Director of the Tusculum Institute ....Dr. Lynn RAINVILLE
42 Chaplain ....Rev. Adam J. WHITE
05 Dean of the FacultyVP Acad Affs ...Dr. Amy JESSEN-MARSHALL
20 Assoc Dean Academic Affairs ....Dr. Jill GRANGER
08 Dir Integrated Information Systems ....Dr. John G. JAFFE
06 Registrar ....Ms. Deborah L. POWELL
25 Faculty Grants Officer ....Ms. Kathleen PLACIDI
85 Director International Studies ....Dr. Tiffany N. CUMMINGS
41 Director of Athletics ....Ms. Kelly S. MORRISON
104 Director Junior Year in Spain ....Ms. M. Celeste DELGADO-LIBRERO
104 Director Junior Year in France ....Dr. Margaret A. SCOUTEN
88 Director of Academic Advising ....Mrs. Kelly KRAFT-MEYER
07 Dean of Admissions ....Mr. Kenneth T. HUUS
10 Vice Pres Finance/Administration ....Mr. Scott SHANK
21 Assoc VP Finance/Administration ....Ms. Gail D. PAYNE
15 Director of Human Resources ....Ms. Caroyn BURTON
18 Director Physical Plant ....Mr. Steve BAILEY
19 Chief of Campus Police ....Mr. Willie H. NEAL
37 Director Financial Aid .... Mrs. Bobbi CARPENTER
40 Book Shop Manager ....Ms. Lynn LEWIS
96 Director Purchasing ....Ms. Cynthia L. PONTON
88 Coordinator Benefits ....Mrs. Judy SPROUSE
31 Director of Auxiliary Services ....Vacant
30 Vice Pres for Alumni/Development ....Ms. Heidi MCCRORY
29 Director of Alumnae Relations ....Mrs. Melissa COFFEY-GAY
44 Director of Development .... Ms. Connor FORREN
88 Dir Donor Relations & Operations ....Vacant
44 Director Major & Planned Gifts ....Mr. Garry BUTTNER
32 VP/Dean of Co-Curricular Life ....Ms. Cheryl L. STEELE
38 Mental Health Counselor/Health Svcs ....Vacant
36 Director Career Services ....Mr. Wayne F. STARK
39 Director Residence Life & Housing ....Ms. Chimene BOONE
23 Nurse Practioner/Dir Health Svcs ....Vacant
27 Director of Media/Marketing & Comm ....Mr. Zach O. KINCAID

Union Presbyterian Seminary (F)

3401 Brook Road, Richmond VA 23227-4597
County: Independent City FICE Identification: 003743
Unit ID: 233842
Telephone: (804) 355-0671 Carnegie Class: Spec/Faith
FAX Number: (804) 355-3919 Calendar System: Semester
URL: www.upsem.edu
Established: 1812 Annual Graduate Tuition & Fees: $12,320
Enrollment: 273 Coed
Affiliation or Control: Presbyterian Church (U.S.A.) IRS Status: 501(c)3
Highest Offering: Doctorate; No Undergraduates
Program: Professional; Religious Emphasis
Accreditation: SC, THEOL

01 President ....Dr. Brian K. BLOUNT
11 Vice President for Administration ....Mr. Michael B. CASHWELL
30 Vice Pres Institutional Advancement ....Mr. Richard WONG
05 Dn Union Presbyterian Sem(Richmond) .....Dr. Stanley SKRESLET
42 Chaplain & Dean of Students ....Rev. Edna J. BANES
12 Dean Union Presby Sem (Charlotte) ....Dr. Thomas W. CURRIE
20 Associate Dean Academic Programs ....Dr. E. Carson BRISSON
10 Controller ....Mr. Patrick K. COATS
07 Director of Admissions ....Ms. Kate Fiedler BOSWELL
06 Registrar ....Mr. Stanley HARGRAVES
08 Librarian ....Dr. Milton J. COALTER
13 Director Technology Services ....Mr. John R. WILSON
36 Director Student Placement ....Dr. Susan E. FOX

University of Management & Technology (G)

1901 Fort Myer Drive, Suite 700, Arlington VA 22209-1609
County: Arlington FICE Identification: 041103
Unit ID: 437097
Telephone: (703) 516-0035 Carnegie Class: Not Classified
FAX Number: (703) 516-0985 Calendar System: Semester
URL: www.umtweb.edu
Established: 1998 Annual Undergrad Tuition & Fees: $11,700
Enrollment: 8,500 Coed
Affiliation or Control: Proprietary IRS Status: Proprietary
Highest Offering: Doctorate
Program: Professional; Business Emphasis
Accreditation: DETC

01 President ....Dr. Yanping CHEN
05 Academic Dean ....Dr. J. Davidson FRAME

University of Mary Washington (H)

1301 College Avenue, Fredericksburg VA 22401-5300
County: Independent City FICE Identification: 003746
Unit ID: 232681
Telephone: (540) 654-1000 Carnegie Class: Master's L
FAX Number: (540) 654-1073 Calendar System: Semester
URL: www.umw.edu
Established: 1908 Annual Undergrad Tuition & Fees (In-State): $8,900
Enrollment: 5,203 Coed
Affiliation or Control: State IRS Status: 501(c)3
Highest Offering: Master's
Program: Liberal Arts And General; Teacher Preparatory
Accreditation: SC, MUS

01 President ....Mr. Richard V. HURLEY
03 Provost ....Dr. Jay A. HARPER
100 Chief of Staff ....Dr. Martin A. WILDER
10 Acting VP for Admin & Finance ....Mr. Richard R. PEARCE
32 Vice President Student Affairs ....Mr. Douglas N. SEARCY
30 Vice Pres for Advanc & Univ Rels ....Mr. Salvatore M. MERINGOLO
102 CEO of UMW Foundation ....Mr. Jeffrey W. ROUNTREE
13 VP Info Tech & CIO ....Ms. Dana GERMAN
88 VP Econ Dev & Regional Engagement ....Dr. Meta R. BRAYMER
15 Asst Vice Pres/Human Res/AAEEO .... Ms. Sabrina C. JOHNSON
40 Asst Vice Pres Business Services ....Ms. Erma A. BAKER
20 Assocate Provost ....Dr. John T. MORELLO
18 Assoc Vice Pres Facilities Services ....Mr. John P. WILTENMUTH, III
09 Asst Prov Inst Analy & Effect ....Mr. Taiwo A. ANDE
07 Dean of Admissions ....Ms. Kimberly JOHNSTON
53 Dean of College of Education ....Dr. Mary L. GENDERNALIK-COOPER
50 Dean College of Business ....Dr. Lynne D. RICHARDSON
20 Dean College of Arts & Sciences ....Dr. Richard FINKELSTEIN
20 Assoc Dean Academic Services ....Dr. JoAnn M. SCHRASS
35 Dean of Student Life ....Mr. Cedric B. RUCKER
37 Director of Financial Aid ....Ms. Debra J. HARBER
09 Director of Institutional Research ......Mr. Mathew C. WILKERSON
21 Internal Audit Director ....Ms. Tera D. KOVANES
39 Director of Residence Life ....Ms. Christine M. PORTER
06 Registrar ....Ms. Rita DUNSTON
41 Director of Athletics ....Dr. Edward H. HEGMANN
08 University Librarian ....Ms. Rosemary ARNESON
27 Director of Publications & Design ...... Ms. Anna B. BILLINGSLEY
24 Director of Dodd Auditorium ....Mr. Doug NOBLE
36 Director Career Services ....Mr. Gary F. JOHNSON
88 Assoc Dean of Advising Services ....Ms. Sallie W. BRAXTON
19 Chief of University Police ....Mr. Eddie L. PERRY
29 Director Alumni Relations ....Ms. Cynthia L. SNYDER
38 Director of Counseling/Psych Svcs ....Dr. Tevya M. ZUKOR
88 Director of Disability Services ....Ms. Sally SCOTT

23 University Physician ....Dr. P. Thomas RILEY
88 Director of University Galleries ....Ms. Anne TIMPANO
96 Director of Purchasing ....Mr. Kenneth C. MCCULLOUGH
27 Director News & Public Information ......Ms. Marty G. MORRISON
26 Director of Marketing ....Ms. Sabrina BROWN
28 Spec Asst Diversity & Inclusion ....Dr. Leah COX
105 University Webmaster ....Ms. Cathy DERECKI

University of Richmond (A)

28 Westhampton Way, Richmond VA 23173-1903
County: Independent City FICE Identification: 003744
Unit ID: 233374
Telephone: (804) 289-8000 Carnegie Class: Bac/A&S
FAX Number: (804) 287-6540 Calendar System: Semester
URL: www.richmond.edu
Established: 1830 Annual Undergrad Tuition & Fees: $43,170
Enrollment: 4,405 Coordinate
Affiliation or Control: Independent Non-Profit IRS Status: 501(c)3
Highest Offering: Doctorate
Program: Liberal Arts And General; Professional
Accreditation: SC, BUS, BUSA, LAW, TEAC

01 President ....Dr. Edward L. AYERS
05 Provost ....Dr. Stephen ALLRED
10 Vice President Business & Finance ....Mr. Hossein SADID
32 Vice President Student Affairs ....Dr. Stephen D. BISESE
30 Vice President Advancement .... Mr. Thomas C. GUTENBERGER
13 Vice Pres for Information Services ....Ms. Kathryn J. MONDAY
84 Vice Pres Enrollment Management ....Ms. Nanci TESSIER
100 Chief of Staff ....Dr. Lori G. SCHUYLER
101 Secretary Board of Trustees ....Ms. Ann Lloyd BREEDEN
04 Executive Assistant to President ....Ms. Carolyn R. MARTIN
88 President Spider Mgmt Company ....Mr. Srinivas PULAVARTI
16 Assoc Vice Pres Human Resources .... Mr. Carl K. SORENSEN
18 Interim Assoc Vice Pres Facilities .... Mr. Andrew S. MCBRIDE
29 Asst VP Alumni & Career Services ....Ms. Kristin J. WOODS
102 Asst VP Foundation/Corp/Govt Rels ... Ms. Michelle E. WAMSLEY
42 University Chaplain ....Rev. Craig T. KOCHER
07 Asst VP and Dean of Admissions ....Mr. Gil VILLANUEVA
08 Interim University Librarian ....Mr. Kevin BUTTERFIELD
09 Dir Institutional Effectiveness ....Dr. Patricia B. MURPHY
06 University Registrar ....Ms. Susan D. BREEDEN
37 Director of Financial Aid ....Ms. Cynthia B. DEFFENBAUGH
36 Director Career Development Center .. Ms. Leslie W. STEVENSON
38 Director of CAPS ....Dr. Peter O. LEVINESS
96 Director of Procurement ....Ms. Jean C. HINES
35 Assoc VP Student Development ....Dr. Tinina Q. CADE
41 Director of Athletics ....Mr. James D. MILLER
104 Director Study Abroad ....Ms. Michele D. COX
105 Director Web Services ....Mr. Eric F. PALMER
33 Dean of Richmond College ....Dr. Joseph R. BOEHMAN
34 Dean Westhampton College ....Dr. Juliette L. LANDPHAIR
49 Dean School of Arts & Sciences ....Dr. Kahtleen R. SKERRETT
50 Dean School of Business ....Dr. Nancy A. BAGRANOFF
61 Dean TC Williams Law School ....Dr. Wendy C. PERDUE
51 Dean School Continuing Studies ....Dr. James L. NARDUZZI
88 Dean Jepson School Leader Stds ....Dr. Sandra J. PEART
19 Assoc VP Publc Sfty/Chief of Police ....Mr. David M. MCCOY
23 Director Health Center ....Dr. Lynne P. DEANE
26 Asst VP for Communications ....Ms. Lisa VAN RIPER
40 Manager University Bookstore ....Mr. Roger L. BROOKS

University of Virginia (B)

Charlottesville VA 22903
County: Independent City FICE Identification: 003745
Unit ID: 234076
Telephone: (434) 924-0311 Carnegie Class: RU/VH
FAX Number: (434) 924-0938 Calendar System: Semester
URL: www.virginia.edu
Established: 1819 Annual Undergrad Tuition & Fees (In-State): $11,786
Enrollment: 24,391 Coed
Affiliation or Control: State IRS Status: 501(c)3
Highest Offering: Doctorate
Program: Liberal Arts And General; Teacher Preparatory; Professional
Accreditation: SC, BUS, BUSA, CACREP, CLPSY, CS, DENT, DIETI, ENG, IPSY, LAW, LSAR, MED, NURSE, PH, PLNG, RTT, SP, TEAC

01 President ....Dr. Teresa A. SULLIVAN
03 Exec Vice Pres/Chief Operating Ofcr ....Mr. Michael STRINE
101 Secretary Board of Visitors ....Ms. Susan G. HARRIS
05 Int Exec Vice President & Provost ....Mr. J. Milton ADAMS
30 Sr Vice Pres Devel/Public Affairs ....Mr. Robert D. SWEENEY
46 Vice President for Research ....Mr. Thomas C. SKALAK
10 Vice Pres/Chief Financial Officer ..... Ms. Yoke San L. REYNOLDS
21 Vice President Management/Budget .... Ms. Colette SHEEHY
17 Vice President & CEO Medical Center .....Mr. R. Edward HOWELL
32 Vice Pres/Chief Student Affs Ofcr ....Ms. Patricia M. LAMPKIN
13 Vice Pres/Chief Info Officer ....Mr. James L. HILTON
63 VP & Dean School of Medicine ....Dr. Steven T. DEKOSKY
28 Int VP/Chief Ofcr Diversity/Equity ....Mr. Marcus L. MARTIN
100 Chief of Staff/Assoc VP for Admin ....Ms. Nancy A. RIVERS
44 Sr Asc VP Dev/Principal Relship Dev ....Mr. Charles B. FITZGERALD
105 Dir of Web Services & Interac Media ....Mr. Zach WHEAT
88 Vice Prov for Academic Programs ....Mr. J. Milton ADAMS
88 Vice Prov Faculty Recruitmt/Retent ....Ms. Gertrude J. FRASER
20 Asc Prov Acad Spprt/Classroom Mgmt ....Ms. Martha Wynne STUART
88 Assoc VP Business Operations ....Mr. Richard A. KOVATCH
15 VP/Chief Human Resource Officer .... Ms. Susan CARKEEK
21 Asst Vice Pres Finance/Comptroller ....Mr. Stephen A. KIMATA
88 Interim Asst VP Research Admin ....Mr. Gerald J. KANE
26 Asst Vice Pres for Public Affairs ....Ms. Carol S. WOOD
88 Managing Dir UVA Investment Mgt Co ....Mr. Michael A. AKED
18 Chief Facilities Officer ....Mr. Donald E. SUNDGREN
06 Registrar ....Ms. Carol A J. STANLEY
07 Dean Undergraduate Admission ....Mr. Gregory W. ROBERTS
49 Dean School of Arts & Sciences ....Ms. Meredith J. WOO
61 Dean School of Law ....Mr. Paul G. MAHONEY
66 Dean School of Nursing ....Ms. Dorrie K. FONTAINE
54 Dean Schl Engr/Applied Science ....Mr. James H. AYLOR
48 Dean School of Architecture ....Ms. Kim TANZER
50 Dean Grad School Business Admin ....Mr. Robert F. BRUNER
50 Dean School of Commerce ....Mr. Carl P. ZEITHAML
53 Dean School of Education ....Mr. Robert C. PIANTA
80 Dean Sch Leadership/Public Policy ....Mr. Harry HARDING
51 Dean Cont & Prof Studies ....Mr. Billy K. CANNADAY
35 Associate VP/Dean of Students ....Mr. Allen W. GROVES
23 Director Student Health ....Dr. James C. TURNER
41 Dir Intercollegiate Athletic Pgms .... Mr. Craig K. LITTLEPAGE
43 Gen Counsel & Corporate Secretary ....Mr. Paul J. FORCH
31 Director Community Relations ....Ms. Ida Lee WOOTTEN
22 Director Equal Opportunity Pgms ...Ms. Darlene SCOTT-SCURRY
08 University Librarian ....Ms. Karin WITTENBORG
09 Dir Institutional Assess & Studies ....Mr. George A. STOVALL
88 Exec Director The Jefferson Trust ....Mr. Wayne COZART
37 Director Student Financial Svcs ....Ms. Yvonne B. HUBBARD
36 Exec Dir Univ Career Services ....Mr. James L. MCBRIDE, JR.
87 Dir Summer & Special Academic Pgms ....Mr. Dudley J. DOANE
104 Dir International Studies Office ....Mr. Dudley J. DOANE
19 Chief of Police ....Mr. Michael A. GIBSON
39 Interim Chief Housing Officer ....Ms. Patricia ROMER
40 Executive Director of UVa Bookstore ....Mr. Jonathan A. KATES
38 Director Counseling/Psych Services ....Mr. Russell FEDERMAN
93 Dean African-American Affairs ....Mr. Maurice APPREY
94 Dir Studies in Women & Gender ....Ms. Kath WESTON
96 Director of Procurement Services ....Mr. Eric N. DENBY

The University of Virginia's College at Wise (C)

One College Avenue, Wise VA 24293-4412
County: Wise FICE Identification: 003747
Unit ID: 233897
Telephone: (276) 328-0100 Carnegie Class: Bac/A&S
FAX Number: (270) 370-1012 Calendar System: Semester
URL: www.uvawise.edu
Established: 1954 Annual Undergrad Tuition & Fees (In-State): $7,721
Enrollment: 1,990 Coed
Affiliation or Control: State IRS Status: 501(c)3
Highest Offering: Baccalaureate
Program: Liberal Arts And General; Teacher Preparatory
Accreditation: SC, CS, ENG, NURSE, TEAC

01 Chancellor ....Dr. David J. PRIOR
46 Ex Asst to Chanc/Dir Strategic Plng ....Ms. Marcia K. QUESENBERRY
05 Provost/Vice Chan for Acad Affairs ....Dr. Sanders HUGUENIN
30 Vice Chanc Devel/College Relations ....Ms. Tami ELY
10 Vice Chanc Finance/ Administration ....Mr. Sim E. EWING
84 Vice Chancellor Enrollment Mgmt .....Mr. Russell D. NECESSARY
13 Vice Chanc for Info Technology ....Mr. Keith FOWLKES
41 Ast Vice Chanc Athletic Development ....Mr. Carroll W. DALE
20 Academic Dean ....Dr. Amelia J. HARRIS
32 Dean of Students ....Mrs. Jewell B. WORLEY
21 Comptroller ....Mrs. Kristy KISER
06 Registrar/Asst Academic Dean ....Ms. Narda PORTER
08 Director of the Library ....Mr. Robin P. BENKE
15 Director of Human Resources .... Ms. Stephanie D. PERRY
88 Director of College Services ....Mr. Joseph B. KISER
26 Director of News & Media Relations ....Ms. Kathy STILL
44 Director of Development ....Ms. Valerie LAWSON
29 Director of Alumni Relations ....Ms. Pamela J. COLLIE
37 Director of Financial Aid ....Mr. William D. WENDLE
35 Asst Dir of Student Activities ....Mr. Joshua JUSTICE
36 Director of Career Development ....Ms. Breanne SALYER
38 Personal Counselor/Health Services ....Ms. Rachel ROSE
19 Campus Police Chief ....Mr. Stephen L. MCCOY
12 Site Director UVA-Wise Programs ....Ms. Courtney L. CONNER
18 Director Facilities Planning/Mgmt ....Mr. Chad NODINE
09 Director of Institutional Research ....Mr. P. Scott BEVINS
24 Director of Media Services ....Mr. Randy G. GILMER
40 Bookstore Manager ....Mr. Scott LAWSON
39 Director of Residence Life ....Ms. Angela LEMKE

Virginia Baptist College (D)

4105 Plank Road, Fredericksburg VA 22407-4803
County: Spotsylvania FICE Identification: 038626
Telephone: (540) 785-5440 Carnegie Class: Not Classified
FAX Number: (540) 785-5441 Calendar System: Semester
URL: www.vbc.edu
Established: 1984 Annual Undergrad Tuition & Fees: $4,500
Enrollment: 84 Coed
Affiliation or Control: Baptist IRS Status: 501(c)3
Highest Offering: Master's
Program: Religious Emphasis
Accreditation: @TRACS

01 President ....Dr. Don FORRESTER

Virginia Commonwealth University (E)

901 W Franklin Street, Box 842527,
Richmond VA 23284-2527
County: Independent City FICE Identification: 003735
Unit ID: 234030
Telephone: (804) 828-0100 Carnegie Class: RU/VH
FAX Number: N/A Calendar System: Semester
URL: www.vcu.edu
Established: 1838 Annual Undergrad Tuition & Fees (In-State): $9,517
Enrollment: 32,303 Coed
Affiliation or Control: State IRS Status: 501(c)3
Highest Offering: Doctorate
Program: Liberal Arts And General; Teacher Preparatory; Professional
Accreditation: SC, ANEST, ART, BUS, BUSA, CACREP, CIDA, CLPSY, COPSY, CORE, CS, DANCE, DENT, DH, DIETI, EMT, ENG, HSA, IPSY, JOUR, MED, MT, MUS, NMT, NUR, OT, PDPSY, PH, PHAR, PLNG, PTA, RAD, RTT, SPAA, SW, TED, THEA

01 President VCU & VCU Health System ....Dr. Michael RAO
05 Provost & Vice Pres Academic Affs ....Dr. Beverly J. WARREN
10 Sr VP Finance & Administration ....Vacant
17 Vice Pres Health Science ....Dr. Sheldon M. RETCHIN
46 Vice President for Research ....Dr. Francis L. MACRINA
30 Vice Pres Development & Alumni Rel ....Mr. John I. BLOHM
86 Executive Dir of Government Relsi ....Mr. Mark E. RUBIN
32 VProv Student Affairs & Enrollment ....Dr. Henry G. RHONE
88 Vice Provost for Life Sciences ....Dr. Thomas F. HUFF
09 Asst Vice Provost Ctr Inst Effectiv ....Ms. Kelli A. PARMLEY
91 Chief Information Officer Tech Svcs ....Mr. Mark D. WILLIS
18 Assoc Vice Pres Facilities Mgmt ....Mr. Brian J. OHLINGER
88 Assoc Vice Pres Advancement ....Ms. Anne D. JACOBSON
21 Assoc Vice Pres Business Svcs/Treas ....Mr. Paul P. JEZ
21 Acting Vice Pres Finance & Admin ....Ms. Pamela A. CURREY
84 Assoc VProvost Student Affairs ....Ms. Delores T. TAYLOR
22 Assoc VProv Inst Equity/Dir EEO Svc .... Ms. Velma J. WILLIAMS
16 Exec Director Human Resources .... Ms. Cynthia H. ANDREWS
08 University Librarian ....Mr. John E. ULMSCHNEIDER
43 General Counsel ....Mr. David L. ROSS
41 Director of Athletics ....Mr. Norwood T. TEAGUE
88 Director of Business Services ....Ms. Diane L. REYNOLDS
39 Interim Dir Res Life & Housing ....Dr. Reuban B. RODRIGUEZ
06 Univ Registrar & Dir Records/Regis ....Ms. Anjour B. HARRIS
07 Dir of Undergraduate Admissions ....Ms. Sybil C. HALLORAN
37 Interim Director of Financial Aid ....Ms. Brenda L. BURKE
38 Dir of Counseling Services ....Dr. Jihad N. AZIZ
30 Dir of University Career Center ....Ms. Susan STORY
35 Assoc VProv/Dean Student Affs ....Dr. Reuban B. RODRIGUEZ
29 Asst VP University Alumni Relations ....Mr. Gordon A. MCDOUGALL
88 Exec Dir Global Eduation ....Dr. R. McKenna BROWN
88 Dir Ctr for Environmental Studies .... Dr. Gregory C. GARMAN
25 Asst Vice Pres Research Admin ....Ms. Susan E. ROBB
19 Chief of Police ....Mr. John A. VENUTI
31 VProv/Div Community Engagement .....Dr. Catherine W. HOWARD
94 Director Women's Studies ....Dr. Diana H. SCULLY
92 Dean Honors College ....Dr. Timothy L. HULSEY
67 Dean of Pharmacy ....Dr. Victor A. YANCHICK
66 Dean of Nursing ....Dr. Nancy F. LANGSTON
63 Dean of Medicine ....Dr. Jerome F. STRAUSS
53 Interim Dean School of Education ....Dr. Michael D. DAVIS
52 Dean of Dentistry ....Dr. David C. SARRETT
50 Dean School of Business ....Mr. Ed A. GRIER
49 Interim Dean Humanities & Sciences ....Dr. Fred M. HAWKRIDGE
57 Dean School of Arts ....Mr. Joseph H. SEIPEL
70 Dean School of Social Work ....Dr. James E. HINTERLONG
76 Dean Allied Health Professions ....Dr. Cecil B. DRAIN
58 Dean Graduate School ....Dr. F. Douglas BOUDINOT
54 Dean School of Engineering ....Dr. Russell D. JAMISON
35 Asst V Prov Stdnt Affs/Enrollment ....Dr. Charles J. KLINK
88 Assoc Dir for Special Projects ....Dr. Judy V. TURK
88 Assoc Director for Operations ....Dr. Deborah M. BROCK
88 Assoc Director of DIE ....Mr. Osama ALAMI
96 Director Procurement Payment Svcs .....Mr. C. Edward GIBBS
26 Executive Dir University Relations ....Ms. Pamela D. LEPLEY

*Virginia Community College System Office (F)

101 N 14th Street, Richmond VA 23219-3658
County: Independent City FICE Identification: 008904
Unit ID: 234146
Telephone: (804) 819-4901 Carnegie Class: N/A
FAX Number: (804) 819-4760
URL: www.vccs.edu

01 Chancellor ....Dr. Glenn DUBOIS
11 Vice Chanc Administrative Services .... Ms. Donna VANCLEAVE
05 Vice Chancellor Academic Services ....Dr. Susan WOOD
103 Vice Chanc Workforce Development ....Mr. Peter BLAKE
13 Vice Chancellor Information Tech ....Dr. Joy A. HATCH
30 Vice Chanc Institutional Advance .....Dr. Jennifer SAGER GENTRY
15 Assoc Vice Chanc Human Resource Svc ....Dr. Christopher LEE
18 Assoc Vice Chanc/Facility Mgmt ....Mr. Ed WATSON
43 General Counsel ....Ms. Rita WOLTZ
88 Director of Internal Audit ....Ms. Helen VANDERLAND
21 Controller ....Mr. Dave MAIR
04 Exec Assistant to the Chancellor ....Ms. Marlene MONDZIEL

*Blue Ridge Community College (G)

PO Box 80, Weyers Cave VA 24486-0080
County: Augusta FICE Identification: 006819
Unit ID: 231536

Telephone: (540) 234-9261 Carnegie Class: Assoc/Pub-R-M
FAX Number: (540) 234-8189 Calendar System: Semester
URL: www.brcc.edu
Established: 1965 Annual Undergrad Tuition & Fees (In-State): $4,098
Enrollment: 4,983 Coed
Affiliation or Control: State IRS Status: 501(c)3
Highest Offering: Associate Degree
Program: Occupational; 2-Year Principally Bachelor's Creditable
Accreditation: SC, ADNUR

02 President ....Dr. John A. DOWNEY
05 Vice Pres Instruction/Student Svcs ....Vacant
10 VP Finance/Administrative Svcs ....Dr. Robert BALDYGO
19 Security & Compliance Coordinator ....Mr. Wayne MARTIN
09 Coordinator Institutional Research ....Dr. Susan E. CROSBY
21 Associate Vice President of Finance ....Ms. Franki HAMPTON
15 Director of Human Resources ....Mr. Tim NICELY
30 Director Development ....Ms. Amy LASER KIGER
81 Dean Math/Science/Engineering ....Ms. Kim BLOSSER
79 Dean Humanities/SoclSci/Workforce ....Dr. Kevin RATLIFF
76 Dean Health & Human Services ....Dr. Hara CHARLIER
20 Dean Academic Support Services ....Ms. Annette WILLIAMS
08 Dean Learning Resources ....Mr. Francis J. MORAN
37 Financial Aid Officer ....Mr. Robert CLEMMER
26 Chief Public Relations Officer ....Ms. Bridget BAYLOR
36 Coord Career Services/Recruitment ....Mrs. Elizabeth HALL

*Central Virginia Community College (A)

3506 Wards Road, Lynchburg VA 24502-2498
County: Independent City FICE Identification: 004988
Unit ID: 231697
Telephone: (434) 832-7600 Carnegie Class: Assoc/Pub-R-M
FAX Number: (434) 386-4700 Calendar System: Semester
URL: www.cvcc.vccs.edu
Established: 1966 Annual Undergrad Tuition & Fees (In-State): $3,720
Enrollment: 5,479 Coed
Affiliation or Control: State IRS Status: 501(c)3
Highest Offering: Associate Degree
Program: Occupational; 2-Year Principally Bachelor's Creditable
Accreditation: SC, EMT, RAD

02 President ....Dr. John S. CAPPS
05 Vice Pres Academic Affs/Stdnt Svcs ....Dr. M. Geoffrey HICKS
10 Vice President Finance & Admin Svcs ....Mr. John K. POOLE
103 Int VP Ctr Workforce Dev/Cont Educ ....Mr. George SHERMAN
30 Vice Pres Institutional Advancement ....Mr. Donald M. SUTTON
13 Vice Pres of Information Technology ....Mr. James D. LIGHTFOOT
45 Dean Instnl Effectiveness/Planning ....Mr. Joey FRONHEISER
21 Chief Business Officer ....Ms. Cathryn MOBLEY
29 Director Alumni/Public Relations ....Mr. Donald M. SUTTON
96 Director of Purchasing ....Ms. Kimely DAVIS
37 Financial Aid Officer ....Ms. Deborah A. MARSHALL
15 Human Resource Manager ....Mr. Harold G. GILBERT
18 Capital Outlay Project Engineer ....Vacant
56 Distance Education Supervisor ....Ms. Susan S. BEASLEY
07 Coordinator of Admissions/Records ....Ms. Julie LOVING
08 Coordinator of Library Services ....Mr. Michael T. FEIN
78 Coord Apprenticeship/Coop Education ....Vacant
79 Dean Humanities/Social Science ....Dr. Muriel B. MICKLES
50 Dean of Business & Allied Health ....Dr. James LEMONS
81 Dean of Science/Math/Engineering ....Dr. Jeffrey W. LAUB

*Dabney S. Lancaster Community College (B)

PO Box 1000, Clifton Forge VA 24422-1000
County: Independent City FICE Identification: 004996
Unit ID: 231873
Telephone: (540) 863-2800 Carnegie Class: Assoc/Pub-R-S
FAX Number: (540) 863-2915 Calendar System: Semester
URL: www.dslcc.edu
Established: 1967 Annual Undergrad Tuition & Fees (In-State): $3,960
Enrollment: 1,522 Coed
Affiliation or Control: State IRS Status: 501(c)3
Highest Offering: Associate Degree
Program: Occupational; 2-Year Principally Bachelor's Creditable
Accreditation: SC, ACFEI, ADNUR

02 President ....Dr. Richard R. TEAFF
10 Vice President Finance/Admin Svcs ....Dr. Joyce A. EDWARDS
51 VP Continuing Educ/Workforce Svcs ....Mr. Gary S. KEENER
49 Dean Arts & Sciences ....Dr. Michael R. SCOTT
32 Director of Student Services ....Mr. Matt MCGRAW
35 Acting Director of Student Services ....Dr. Michael SCOTT
08 Director of Learning Resources ....Ms. Nova WRIGHT
09 Assessment Officer ....Dr. Michael SCOTT
06 Registrar ....Ms. Lorrie FERGUSON
21 Business Officer ....Ms. Angela GRAHAM
18 Buildings & Grounds Supervisor ....Mr. Ed N. KENNY
13 Coord of Computer Info Systems ....Ms. Tamra COTTRILL
37 Coord of Student Financial Aid ....Mrs. Sandra J. HAVERLACK
45 Planning & Funding Specialist ....Ms. Lynda N. THOMPSON

*Danville Community College (C)

1008 S Main Street, Danville VA 24541-4088
County: Independent City FICE Identification: 003758
Unit ID: 231882
Telephone: (434) 797-2222 Carnegie Class: Assoc/Pub-R-M
FAX Number: (434) 797-8514 Calendar System: Semester
URL: www.dcc.vccs.edu
Established: 1967 Annual Undergrad Tuition & Fees (In-State): $3,600
Enrollment: 4,534 Coed
Affiliation or Control: State IRS Status: 501(c)3
Highest Offering: Associate Degree
Program: Occupational; 2-Year Principally Bachelor's Creditable
Accreditation: SC

02 President ....Dr. Berkley C. RAMSEY
05 Vice Pres Academic/Student Services ....Dr. Christopher C. EZELL
10 Vice Pres Financial/Admin Services ....Mr. Scott BARNES
09 Director of Institutional Research ....Dr. Sherri H. HUFFMAN
30 Director of Development ....Mr. Shannon HAIR
26 Chief Public Relations Officer ....Ms. Andrea BURNEY

*Eastern Shore Community College (D)

29300 Lankford Highway, Melfa VA 23410-9755
County: Accomack FICE Identification: 003748
Unit ID: 232052
Telephone: (757) 789-1789 Carnegie Class: Assoc/Pub-R-S
FAX Number: (757) 789-1737 Calendar System: Semester
URL: www.es.vccs.edu
Established: 1971 Annual Undergrad Tuition & Fees (In-State): $3,332
Enrollment: 1,047 Coed
Affiliation or Control: State IRS Status: 501(c)3
Highest Offering: Associate Degree
Program: Occupational; 2-Year Principally Bachelor's Creditable
Accreditation: SC

02 President ....Dr. Linda THOMAS-GLOVER
05 Dean of Instruction ....Vacant
10 Vice Pres Finance & Administration ....Miss Cynthia A. ALLEN
32 Dean of Student Services ....Mr. Bryan SMITH
08 Director Learning Resources ....Mrs. Patricia L. PHILLIPS
06 Registrar ....Mrs. Connie FENTRESS
09 Director of Institutional Research ....Ms. Judith M. GRIER
26 Chief Public Relations Officer ....Ms. Laurie SWAIN
37 Director of Student Financial Aid ....Mr. Bryan SMITH
15 Director Personnel Services ....Ms. Diane WHEATLEY
18 Chief Facilities/Physical Plant ....Mr. Bobby MEARS
29 Director Alumni Relations/Devel ....Ms. Eve BELOTE
20 Associate Academic Officer ....Mrs. Robin RICH-COATES

*Germanna Community College (E)

2130 Germanna Highway, Locust Grove VA 22508-2102
County: Orange FICE Identification: 008660
Unit ID: 232195
Telephone: (540) 423-9030 Carnegie Class: Assoc/Pub-R-M
FAX Number: (540) 727-3207 Calendar System: Semester
URL: www.germanna.edu
Established: 1970 Annual Undergrad Tuition & Fees (In-State): $3,054
Enrollment: 7,139 Coed
Affiliation or Control: State IRS Status: 501(c)3
Highest Offering: Associate Degree
Program: Occupational; 2-Year Principally Bachelor's Creditable; Fine Arts Emphasis
Accreditation: SC, ADNUR, DA

02 President ....Dr. David A. SAM
04 Exec Assistant to the President ....Ms. Pamela D. SHIFFLETT
05 VP Academic & Student Services ....Dr. Ann WOOLFORD
11 VP Finance & Administrative Svcs ....Mr. Richard BREHM
103 VP Workforce & Community Educ ....Dr. Jeanne WESLEY
32 Dean of Student Services ....Ms. Pam FREDERICK
30 Director of Foundation & Alumni Rel ....Mr. Mike CATELL
09 Director of Planning & Assessment ....Dr. John DAVIS
08 Head Librarian ....Ms. Marcy PRIDE
72 Dean Professional & Technical Study ....Mr. William FIEGE
88 Dean Business Workforce Services ....Mr. Russell JAMES
55 Dean Distance Educ & Lrng Resources ....Dr. Yan Yan YONG
66 Dean of Nursing & Health Technology ....Ms. Mary GILKEY
16 Human Resources Officer ....Mr. Reginald RYALS
18 Building & Ground Supervisor ....Mr. Garland FENWICK
06 Registrar ....Mr. Michael DONLAN
13 Manager Technology Services ....Ms. Jacque LARSEN
37 Financial Aid Officer ....Mr. Michael FARRIS
26 Director of Marketing ....Ms. Barbara TAYLOR
21 Financial Services Coordinator ....Mr. Bill HEISEY
49 Dean of Arts & Sciences ....Dr. Deborah BROCK
103 Dean of Workforce Prof Development ....Ms. Martha O'KEEFE

*J. Sargeant Reynolds Community College (F)

PO Box 85622, Richmond VA 23285-5622
County: Henrico FICE Identification: 003759
Unit ID: 232414
Telephone: (804) 371-3000 Carnegie Class: Assoc/Pub-U-MC
FAX Number: (804) 371-3650 Calendar System: Semester
URL: www.reynolds.edu
Established: 1972 Annual Undergrad Tuition & Fees (In-State): $3,528
Enrollment: 12,629 Coed
Affiliation or Control: State IRS Status: 501(c)3
Highest Offering: Associate Degree
Program: Occupational; 2-Year Principally Bachelor's Creditable
Accreditation: SC, ACFEI, ADNUR, DA, DT, EMT, MLTAD, OPD, POLYT

02 President ....Dr. Gary L. RHODES
03 Executive Vice President ....Dr. Genene LEROSEN
30 Vice President Advancement ....Mrs. Elizabeth S. LITTLEFIELD
103 Vice Pres Comm Coll Workforce All ....Mr. Louis MCGINTY
10 VP of Finance & Admin ....Ms. Amelia M. BRADSHAW
05 Assoc Vice Pres Academic Affairs ....Dr. David LOOPE
45 Assoc VP Policy/Inst Effectiveness ....Mrs. Diane F. BRASINGTON
32 Assoc Vice Pres of Student Affairs ....Dr. Thomas HOLLINS, JR.
13 Assoc Vice President of Technology ....Mr. John N. AMBROSE
79 Dean Sch Arts/Human/Social Science ....Dr. Barbara M. GLENN
50 Interim Dean School Business ....Dr. Robert A. HEINZ
76 Int Dean School Nursing/Allied Hlth ....Mr. Joel ADLER
54 Dean Sch Engr/Manufacturing ....Dr. Robert A. HEINZ
81 Dean School Mathematics & Science ....Mr. Raymond BURTON
88 Dir Sch Culnry Arts/Tourism/Hosp ....Mr. David J. BARRISH
09 Dir Office of Inst Effectiveness ....Dr. Jackie R. BOURQUE
15 Director of Human Resources ....Ms. Corliss B. WOODSON
37 Director Financial Aid ....Mrs. Kiesha L. POPE
07 Director of Admissions & Records ....Mrs. Karen M. PETTIS-WALDEN
88 Assistant VP Workforce Development ....Ms. Cara DILLARD
88 Director Outreach & Recruitment ....Ms. Tracy GREEN
26 Dir of Marketing & Public Relations ....Mr. Malcolm T. HOLMES
08 Director Learning Resources Center ....Dr. Abdul J. MIAH
18 Director Facilities Mgmt/Plng ....Mr. Mark PROBST
88 Dir/Inst At-Risk Youth Middle Coll ....Ms. Mary Jo WASHKO
06 Registrar ....Ms. Denise S. TUNSTALL
88 Director Learning Communities ....Mr. Charles PETERSON, JR.
96 Purchasing Manager ....Mr. Christopher L. COLE
19 Chief of Police & Security Services ....Mr. Paul L. RONCA
20 Coordinator Instructional Services ....Mr. Ty CORBIN

*John Tyler Community College (G)

13101 Jefferson Davis Highway, Chester VA 23831-5316
County: Chesterfield FICE Identification: 004004
Unit ID: 232450
Telephone: (804) 796-4000 Carnegie Class: Assoc/Pub-S-MC
FAX Number: (804) 796-4163 Calendar System: Semester
URL: www.jtcc.edu
Established: 1965 Annual Undergrad Tuition & Fees (In-State): $3,570
Enrollment: 10,518 Coed
Affiliation or Control: State IRS Status: 501(c)3
Highest Offering: Associate Degree
Program: Occupational; 2-Year Principally Bachelor's Creditable
Accreditation: SC, ADNUR, FUSER

02 President ....Dr. Marshall W. SMITH
04 Executive Assistant to President ....Ms. Mara M. HILLIAR
05 VP for Academic/Student Affairs ....Dr. L. Ray DRINKWATER
10 VP for Finance & Admin Services ....Mr. William F. TAYLOR
103 Vice Pres for CC Workforce Alliance ....Mr. Mac L. MCGINTY
32 Dean of Student Services ....Dr. Chris PFAUTZ
54 Dean Engr/Business/Public Svcs ....Dr. Melody L. MOORE
49 Dean Arts/Humanities/Soc Sciences ....Dr. Mikell BROWN
81 Dean Math/Natural & Behavorial Sci ....Dr. Donna ALEXANDER
102 Interim Exec Director Foundation ....Ms. Beverley DEW
09 Dir Institutional Effectiveness ....Ms. Cynthia GRIFFITH
08 Librarian Chester Campus ....Ms. Linda LUEBKE
15 Director Human Resources ....Ms. Susan GRINNAN
13 Director Information Services ....Mr. Larry RUBES
37 Director Financial Aid ....Mr. Tony JONES
07 Dir Admission/Records/Registration ....Mrs. Joy L. JAMES
21 Business Manager ....Mr. Leon R. BROWN
19 Security Manager ....Mr. Frank MEDAGLIA
35 Coordinator Student Activities ....Ms. Amanda CARPENTER
36 Director Counseling Chester Campus ....Ms. Michelle TINDALL
36 Dir Counseling Midlothian Campus ....Dr. Ruth VARNEY
18 Director Facilities Operations ....Mr. Greg A. DUNAWAY
26 Director College Relations ....Ms. Joanne M. HORTON
66 Dean of Health Sciences ....Dr. Deborah ULMER
08 Librarian Midlothian Campus ....Ms. Helen MCKANN
06 Registrar ....Ms. Joy L. JAMES
96 Director of Purchasing ....Ms. Nancy M. JIMISON

*Lord Fairfax Community College (H)

173 Skirmisher Lane, Middletown VA 22645-1745
County: Frederick FICE Identification: 008659
Unit ID: 232575
Telephone: (540) 868-7000 Carnegie Class: Assoc/Pub-R-L
FAX Number: (540) 868-7100 Calendar System: Semester
URL: www.lfcc.edu
Established: 1970 Annual Undergrad Tuition & Fees (In-State): $2,936
Enrollment: 7,005 Coed
Affiliation or Control: State IRS Status: 501(c)3
Highest Offering: Associate Degree
Program: Occupational; 2-Year Principally Bachelor's Creditable; Business Emphasis
Accreditation: SC

02 President ....Dr. Cheryl THOMPSON-STACY
05 VP of Academic and Student Affairs ....Dr. Chris COUTTS
10 VP of Financial & Admin Services ....Mr. Chris BOIES
32 Vice President of Student Success ....Vacant
103 Asst Vice Pres Workforce Solutions ....Ms. Jeanian CLARK
20 Assoc VP of Instruction Middletown ....Dr. Morgan S. PHENIX
20 Assoc VP of Instruction Fauquier ....Dr. Judy BATSON
76 Assoc Dean Health Prof & Science ....Ms. Claudia J. MAZURKIEWICZ
88 Assoc Dean Bus/Tech/Dir HS Outreach ....Ms. Brenda K. BYARD
81 Assoc Dean Hum/Math/Social Sciences ....Dr. Richard L. ELAM
15 Human Resource Manager ....Ms. Karen N. FOREMAN
30 Director of Development ....Mr. David J. URSO

2 Manager Luray-Page County Center .... Ms. Judith J. SUDDITH
8 Director Learning Resources Center .... Mr. David R. GRAY
9 Dir Planning/Inst Effectiveness .... Dr. John H. MILAM
3 Coordinator Network Security .... Mr. Douglas M. SHRIER
5 Dean of Students - Middletown .... Dr. Karen H. BUCHER
4 Dir of Enrollment Mgt & Reg Service .... Vacant
8 Dir Stdnt Learning Svcs/Counseling .... Ms. Tammy LADREW
7 Coordinator Student Financial Aid .... Mr. Aaron WHITACRE
6 Procurement Officer .... Mr. Richard FARROW
1 Budget and Finance Director .... Ms. Margaret J. BARNETT
9 Law Enforecement Manager .... Mr. James ROY
6 Public Relations Marketing Manager .... Vacant
7 Coord Student Success .... Vacant
5 Coord Student Life & Info Services .... Ms. Brandy BOIES
36 Counselor Middle College .... Mr. Doug CUMBIA
08 Librarian .... Mr. Gregory MACDONALD
38 Coord of Dual Enrollment .... Ms. Heather BURTON
38 Coord Student Learning & TRIO SS .... Ms. Susan M. MARTIN
38 Coord/Dir LF Small Bus Dev Center .... Mr. William A. SIRBAUGH
38 Coord Business & Industry Trng .... Mr. Bill PENCE
35 Dean of Students - Fauquier .... Mr. Craig BENNETT
38 Director of Transition Programs .... Dr. Judith JAMES
27 Public Info/Grant & Sponsored Pgm .... Ms. Lyda C. KISER

Mountain Empire Community College (A)

3441 Mountain Empire Road,
Big Stone Gap VA 24219-4634

County: Wise — FICE Identification: 009629
Unit ID: 232788
Telephone: (276) 523-2400 — Carnegie Class: Assoc/Pub-R-M
FAX Number: (276) 523-8297 — Calendar System: Semester
URL: www.mecc.edu
Established: 1972 — Annual Undergrad Tuition & Fees (In-State): $2,928
Enrollment: 3,404 — Coed
Affiliation or Control: State — IRS Status: 501(c)3
Highest Offering: Associate Degree
Program: Occupational; 2-Year Principally Bachelor's Creditable
Accreditation: SC, ADNUR

02 President .... Dr. Scott HAMILTON
05 Vice Pres Academic & Student Svcs .... Dr. Richard PHILLIPS
10 Vice Pres Finance & Admin Services .... Ms. Patti W. CANTRELL
30 Vice Pres Institutional Advancement .... Ms. Donna G. STANLEY
07 Director of Enrollment Services .... Ms. Kristy HALL
32 Director of Student Services .... Ms. Lisa BUTCHER
08 Director of Library Services .... Mr. Michael GILLEY
51 Dir Continuing & Distance Education .... Ms. Sue Ella BOATRIGHT-WELLS
37 Director Financial Aid/Registrar .... Ms. Kristy HALL
09 Dir Inst Research/Chief PR Ofcr .... Dr. Sharon K. FISHER
14 Dir Ctr Computing & Info Technology .... Mr. Rickie N. CAMPBELL
15 Director Personnel Services .... Ms. Pam GILES
18 Chief Facilities/Physical Plant .... Mr. Gary NICKLES
49 Dean Arts & Sciences .... Ms. Carolyn H. REYNOLDS
72 Dean of Industrial Tech/Health Sci .... Mr. Tommy CLEMENTS
50 Dean of Business & Information Tech .... Ms. Vickie RATLIFF

New River Community College (B)

PO Box 1127, Dublin VA 24084-1127

County: Pulaski — FICE Identification: 005223
Unit ID: 232867
Telephone: (540) 674-3600 — Carnegie Class: Assoc/Pub-R-M
FAX Number: (540) 674-3642 — Calendar System: Semester
URL: www.nr.edu
Established: 1969 — Annual Undergrad Tuition & Fees (In-State): $3,632
Enrollment: 5,178 — Coed
Affiliation or Control: State — IRS Status: 501(c)3
Highest Offering: Associate Degree
Program: Occupational; 2-Year Principally Bachelor's Creditable
Accreditation: SC

02 President .... Dr. Jack M. LEWIS
04 Assistant to the President .... Mrs. Amy J. HALL
05 VP for Instruction/Student Svcs .... Dr. Patricia B. HUBER
10 Vice Pres for Finance & Technology .... Mr. John L. VAN HEMERT
30 VP for WD and External Relations .... Dr. Mark C. ROWH
20 Assoc VP/Assessment Coordinator .... Mrs. Teri D. MOORE
49 Dean of Arts & Sciences .... Mrs. Carol P. HURST
72 Dean Business & Technologies .... Mr. Dan A. LOOKADOO
09 Dir Inst Effectiveness/Research .... Dr. Frederick M. STREFF
06 Registrar .... Ms. Margaret G. TAYLOR
15 Human Resource Officer .... Mrs. Lois A. QUESENBERRY
102 Executive Director of Foundation .... Mrs. Angie E. COVEY
32 Counselor/Student Life Coordinator .... Mr. Benjamin KRAMER
35 Director of Student Affairs .... Ms. Margaret G. TAYLOR
37 Director of Student Financial Aid .... Mrs. Lori NUNN
38 Director of Student Counseling .... Ms. Margaret G. TAYLOR
18 Chief Facilities/Physical Plant .... Mr. Anthony J. NICOLO
21 Associate Vice President of Finance .... Ms. Bridget M. SAYLES
96 Purchasing Officer .... Mrs. Melissa P. ANDERSON
56 Dir Dist Educ/Offsite Campus Svcs .... Mrs. Linda C. CLAUSSEN
51 Director Transitional Programs .... Mrs. Jenny L. BOLTE
08 Coordinator of Library Services .... Mrs. Sandra B. SMITH
07 Coord Admissions/Records/Stdnt Svcs .... Ms. Margaret G. TAYLOR
88 Coordinator of WorkKeys Center .... Mrs. Patricia RYAN
88 Coordinator Center Hearing Impaired .... Ms. Lucy J. HOWLETT
88 Coordinator of Learning Disabled .... Ms. Jeananne F. DIXON
84 Enrollment Manager Coordinator .... Mrs. Deborah D. KENNEDY

*Northern Virginia Community College (C)

4001 Wakefield Chapel Road, Annandale VA 22003-3796

County: Fairfax — FICE Identification: 003727
Unit ID: 232946
Telephone: (703) 323-3000 — Carnegie Class: Assoc/Pub-S-MC
FAX Number: (703) 323-3767 — Calendar System: Semester
URL: www.nvcc.edu
Established: 1965 — Annual Undergrad Tuition & Fees (In-State): $3,306
Enrollment: 48,996 — Coed
Affiliation or Control: State — IRS Status: 501(c)3
Highest Offering: Associate Degree
Program: Occupational; 2-Year Principally Bachelor's Creditable
Accreditation: SC, ADNUR, DH, EMT, MLTAD, PTAA

02 President .... Dr. Robert G. TEMPLIN, JR.
05 Exec VP/Chief Academic Officer .... Dr. John T. DEVER
10 Actg Vice Pres Finance & Admin Svcs .... Ms. Dimitrina DIMKOVA
13 Vice Pres of Information Technology .... Dr. Steven G. SACHS
103 Vice Pres of Workforce Development .... Mr. William H. GARY, SR.
09 VP Inst Research & Planning .... Dr. George E. GABRIEL
20 Assoc VP Academic Services .... Dr. Sharon N. ROBERTSON
104 Assoc Vice Pres Global Studies .... Dr. Paul J. MCVEIGH
84 Assoc VP Stdnt Svcs & Enroll Mgmt .... Dr. Elizabeth HARPER
12 Provost Alexandria Campus .... Dr. Peter MAPHUMULO
12 Provost Annandale Campus .... Dr. Barbara L. SAPERSTONE
12 Provost Loudoun Campus .... Dr. Julie LEIDIG
12 Provost Manassas Campus .... Dr. Hortense B. HINTON
12 Provost Medical Education Campus .... Mr. Brian P. FOLEY
12 Provost Woodbridge Campus .... Dr. Sam HILL
102 Exec Dir NVCC Education Foundation .... Mr. John J. RUFFINO
22 Dir Affirm Act/Minority/Legal Affs .... Mr. Everett V. EBERHARDT
29 Director Alumni Relations .... Ms. Bonnie L. IDLE
25 Director of Grants Development .... Ms. Deborah E. MOTTSMAN-ROSEN
15 Director of Human Resources .... Ms. Shelli W. JARVIS
96 Director of Purchasing .... Mr. Edward J. MELLON
37 Dir Stdnt Financial Aid/Support Svc .... Ms. Joan A. ZANDERS
21 Business Manager .... Mr. Frederick R. TITTMANN
18 Chief Facilities/Physical Plant .... Mr. Derek M. HODGE
27 Public Information Officer .... Ms. Jessica M. BAXTER
19 Director Security/Safety .... Mr. William FLAGLER
86 Director Government Relations .... Mr. Dana KAUFFMAN

*Patrick Henry Community College (D)

645 Patriot Avenue, Martinsville VA 24112

County: Henry — FICE Identification: 003751
Unit ID: 233019
Telephone: (276) 638-8777 — Carnegie Class: Assoc/Pub-R-M
FAX Number: (276) 656-0320 — Calendar System: Semester
URL: www.ph.vccs.edu
Established: 1962 — Annual Undergrad Tuition & Fees (In-State): $3,625
Enrollment: 3,289 — Coed
Affiliation or Control: State — IRS Status: 501(c)3
Highest Offering: Associate Degree
Program: Occupational; 2-Year Principally Bachelor's Creditable
Accreditation: SC, ADNUR

02 President .... Dr. Max F. WINGETT
05 Vice Pres Student Development Svcs .... Dr. Kristin BISHOP
10 Vice Pres Finance & Admin Services .... Dr. Ronald EPPERLY
30 Vice Pres Institutional Advancement .... Ms. Natalie HARDER
56 Dean Extended Learning Services .... Mrs. Rhonda HODGES
20 Dean Institutional Support Svcs .... Vacant
72 Dean Div Occupational Tech Program .... Mr. Jeff FIELDS
49 Dean Div Arts & Science Programs .... Mr. Robert CLARY
38 Dean Student Development Svcs .... Mr. Jeff PORTER
22 Affirmative Action Coordinator .... Ms. Delores EANES
37 Financial Aid/Veterans Admin .... Mrs. Cindy KELLER
09 Coord Inst Research/Plng/Evaluation .... Mr. Kevin SHROPSHIRE
07 Coord of Admissions & Records .... Mr. Travis TISDALE
06 Registrar .... Ms. Jessica CARTER
15 Director of Personnel Services .... Ms. Delores EANES
18 Chief Facilities/Physical Plant .... Dr. Ronald EPPERLY
26 Chief Public Relations/Dir Alumni .... Mrs. Kristin LANDRUM
32 Director of Student Affairs .... Mr. Jeff PORTER
96 Director of Purchasing .... Ms. Carline DEAL

*Paul D. Camp Community College (E)

100 N College Drive, Franklin VA 23851-0737

County: Independent City — FICE Identification: 009159
Unit ID: 233037
Telephone: (757) 569-6700 — Carnegie Class: Assoc/Pub-R-S
FAX Number: (757) 569-6795 — Calendar System: Semester
URL: www.pdc.edu
Established: 1970 — Annual Undergrad Tuition & Fees (In-State): $3,255
Enrollment: 1,656 — Coed
Affiliation or Control: State — IRS Status: 501(c)3
Highest Offering: Associate Degree
Program: Occupational; 2-Year Principally Bachelor's Creditable
Accreditation: SC

02 President .... Dr. Paul W. CONCO
05 Vice Pres Inst/Student Development .... Dr. Maxine B. SINGLETON
10 Vice President Finance/Admin Svcs .... Dr. Joe EDENFIELD
30 Vice Pres Institutional Advancement .... Dr. Patsy R. JOYNER
20 Dean Franklin Academic Programs .... Dr. Joe EDENFIELD
20 Dean of Suffolk Academic Programs .... Dr. Harriette ARRINGTON
08 Director of Learning Resources .... Ms. Linza M. WEAVER
12 Academic Director-Smithfield .... Vacant
103 Director of Workforce Development .... Mr. Randy BETZ
09 Director of Institutional Research .... Dr. Jerry J. STANDAHL
18 Chief Facilities/Physical Plant .... Mr. James C. GORHAM
15 Human Resources Manager .... Ms. Annette E. EDWARDS
21 Business Office Manager .... Ms. Mary SPEIGHT
88 Development Studies Program Head .... Dr. Maxine B. SINGLETON
26 Public Relations Specialist .... Ms. Wendy HARRISON
96 Buyer Specialist .... Ms. J. Lynn PHILLIPS
37 Financial Aid Coordinator .... Ms. Teresa HARRISON
04 Assistant to the President .... Ms. JoAnne RUSSELL

*Piedmont Virginia Community College (F)

501 College Drive, Charlottesville VA 22902-7589

County: Independent City — FICE Identification: 009928
Unit ID: 233116
Telephone: (434) 977-3900 — Carnegie Class: Assoc/Pub-R-M
FAX Number: (434) 971-8232 — Calendar System: Semester
URL: www.pvcc.edu
Established: 1972 — Annual Undergrad Tuition & Fees (In-State): $3,665
Enrollment: 5,551 — Coed
Affiliation or Control: State — IRS Status: 501(c)3
Highest Offering: Associate Degree
Program: Occupational; 2-Year Principally Bachelor's Creditable; Liberal Arts And General
Accreditation: SC, ADNUR, EMT, RAD, SURGT

02 President .... Dr. Frank FRIEDMAN
05 VP Instruction/Student Svcs .... Dr. John DONNELLY
10 Vice President Finance/Admin Svcs .... Dr. William P. JACKAMEIT
79 Dean Humanities/Fine Arts/Soc Sci .... Dr. Clifford W. HAURY
50 Dean Business/Math/Technologies .... Dr. Chuck BOHLEKE
17 Dean Health & Life Sciences .... Dr. Kathy HUDSON
103 Dean Workforce Services .... Ms. Valerie PALAMOUNTAIN
32 Director of Student Svcs/Admissions .... Ms. Mary Lee WALSH
13 Chief Information Officer .... Mr. Shivaji SAMANTA
09 Dir Instl Research/Planning/Effect .... Dr. Tara ATKINS-BRADY
30 Dir Inst Advancement & Development .... Ms. Mary Jane KING
06 Registrar .... Ms. Lorraine CONCA
96 Director of Purchasing .... Ms. Marie C. MELTON
18 Superintendant Facilities .... Mr. David THOMPSON
15 Human Resources Manager .... Ms. Yvonne CAREY
26 Manager Marketing/Media Relations .... Ms. Anita SHOWERS
84 Outreach/Enrollment Services Mgr .... Ms. Heather LUTZ
08 Coordinator Library Services .... Ms. Linda CAHILL
37 Coordinator Financial Aid .... Ms. Carol LARSON
88 Coord Ctr Excellence in Instruction .... Vacant
88 Coordinator Advising & Transfer .... Mr. Kemper STEELE

*Rappahannock Community College (G)

12745 College Drive, Glenns VA 23149-0287

County: Gloucester — FICE Identification: 009160
Unit ID: 233310
Telephone: (804) 758-6700 — Carnegie Class: Assoc/Pub-S-MC
FAX Number: (804) 758-3852 — Calendar System: Semester
URL: www.rappahannock.edu
Established: 1970 — Annual Undergrad Tuition & Fees (In-State): $2,842
Enrollment: 3,757 — Coed
Affiliation or Control: State — IRS Status: 501(c)3
Highest Offering: Associate Degree
Program: Occupational; 2-Year Principally Bachelor's Creditable
Accreditation: SC

02 President .... Dr. Elizabeth H. CROWTHER
10 Vice Pres Finance & Admin Services .... Mr. D. Kim MCMANUS
05 VP Instruction/Student Development .... Dr. Tresia B. SAMANI
32 Dean Student Development .... Mr. Robert S. GRIFFIN
08 Dean of Learning Resources .... Ms. Cherie CARL
30 Dean of College Advancement .... Mr. Victor W. CLOUGH, JR.
09 Dir Institutional Effectiveness .... Dr. Karen C. NEWTZIE
06 College Registrar .... Ms. Felicia B. PACKETT
37 Financial Aid/Veteran Affairs Ofcr .... Ms. Carolyn A. WARD
15 Human Resources Manager .... Mrs. Caroline W. STELTER
18 Facilities/Physical Plant Manager .... Mr. Mark P. BEAVER

*Southside Virginia Community College (H)

109 Campus Drive, Alberta VA 23821-2930

County: Brunswick — FICE Identification: 008661
Unit ID: 233639
Telephone: (434) 949-1000 — Carnegie Class: Assoc/Pub-R-L
FAX Number: (434) 949-7863 — Calendar System: Semester
URL: www.southside.edu
Established: 1970 — Annual Undergrad Tuition & Fees (In-State): $2,916
Enrollment: 5,946 — Coed
Affiliation or Control: State — IRS Status: 501(c)3
Highest Offering: Associate Degree
Program: Occupational; 2-Year Principally Bachelor's Creditable
Accreditation: SC

02 President .... Dr. John J. CAVAN
12 Provost John H Daniel Campus .... Dr. Al ROBERTS
12 Provost Christanna Campus .... Dr. John D. SYKES, JR.
10 Vice Pres Finance & Administration .... Mr. Peter G. HUNT

25 VP Adult Education & Grants ..... Ms. Linda SHEFFIELD
13 Dean Information Services ..... Mr. Jack ANCELL
84 Dean Enrollment Mgt & Assoc Prof ..... Mr. Brent RICHEY
20 Dean of Instruction Daniel ..... Ms. Paula M. GASTENVELD
20 Dean of Instruction Christanna ..... Mr. Tom WISBEY
09 Dean Planning & Inst Effectiveness ..... Mr. Chad PATTON
66 Dean of Nursing/Health Technology ... Ms. Michelle K. EDMONDS
102 Exec Director SVCC Foundation ..... Mrs. Mary Jane ELKINS
08 Library Supervisor ..... Ms. Earnestine LEWIS
08 College Librarian ..... Ms. Libby BLANTON
26 Public Relations & Mktg Specialist ..... Ms. Christie C. HALES
37 Director of Financial Aid ..... Ms. Sally THARRINGTON
15 Human Resources Manager ..... Ms. Bethany W. HARRIS
18 Buildings/Grounds Supt Christanna ..... Mr. Roger WRAY
38 Dir Student Counseling Christanna ..... Ms. Judy SHEPHERD
38 Director Student Counseling Daniel ..... Mrs. Dorethea SIZEMORE
21 Business Manager ..... Mrs. Diane B. DANIEL
29 Alumni Relations SVCC ..... Mrs. Mary Jane ELKINS

*Southwest Virginia Community College (A)

Box SVCC, Richlands VA 24641-1101
County: Tazewell FICE Identification: 007260
Unit ID: 233648
Telephone: (276) 964-2555 Carnegie Class: Assoc/Pub-R-M
FAX Number: (276) 964-9307 Calendar System: Semester
URL: www.sw.edu
Established: 1967 Annual Undergrad Tuition & Fees (In-State): $2,892
Enrollment: 3,755 Coed
Affiliation or Control: State IRS Status: 501(c)3
Highest Offering: Associate Degree
Program: Occupational; 2-Year Principally Bachelor's Creditable
Accreditation: SC, ADNUR, EMT, OTA, RAD

02 President ..... Dr. J. Mark ESTEPP
05 Vice President of Instruction ..... Dr. Barbara J. FULLER
10 Vice Pres Finance & Admin Services ..... Dr. Leonard V. KOGUT
30 Vice Pres Institutional Advancement ..... Ms. Phyllis A. ROBERTS
51 Dean Continuing Education ..... Ms. Peggy BARBER
24 Dean Learning Resources ..... Vacant
32 Assoc Vice Pres Student Services ..... Mr. Roderick B. MOORE
44 Institutional Advancement Officer ..... Ms. Mary W. LAWSON
09 Institutional Research Officer ..... Dr. Edmond C. SMITH
18 Physical Plant Superintendent ..... Mr. Charles BANDY
19 Campus Police Chief ..... Mr. Ronnie KISER
15 Human Resources Manager ..... Ms. Martha L. RASNAKE
21 Financial Services Manager ..... Mr. Michael BALES
26 Public Relations Coordinator ..... Ms. Patsy G. BUSSARD
07 Coord Admissions/Counseling ..... Mr. James E. FARRIS
11 General Admin Coordinator ..... Ms. Rhonda L. VANDYKE
08 Coordinator of Library Services ..... Ms. Teresa A. ALLEY
56 Coord Distributed/Distance Learning ..... Vacant

*Thomas Nelson Community College (B)

99 Thomas Nelson Drive, Hampton VA 23666
County: Independent City FICE Identification: 006871
Unit ID: 233754
Telephone: (757) 825-2700 Carnegie Class: Assoc/Pub-S-SC
FAX Number: (757) 825-2763 Calendar System: Semester
URL: www.tncc.edu
Established: 1967 Annual Undergrad Tuition & Fees (In-State): $3,607
Enrollment: 9,233 Coed
Affiliation or Control: State IRS Status: 501(c)3
Highest Offering: Associate Degree
Program: Occupational; 2-Year Principally Bachelor's Creditable
Accreditation: SC, ADNUR, DH

02 President ..... Dr. Alvin J. SCHEXNIDER
05 Int Vice Pres for Academic Affairs ..... Mr. Norman P. HAHN
11 Vice President for Admin/Finance ..... Mr. Charles NURNBERGER
103 Vice Pres for Workforce Development ..... Dr. Deborah G. WRIGHT
44 Vice Pres Institutional Advancement ..... Mrs. Cynthia CALLAWAY
13 Director of Information Tech ..... Mr. Wayne DAVIS
32 Vice President for Student Affairs . Dr. Beverly WALKER-GRIFFEA
35 Assoc VP for Student Affairs ..... Dr. Vicki RICHMOND
10 Assoc VP for Financial Services ..... Ms. Teresa BAILEY
103 Assoc VP for Workforce Training/CE ..... Dr. Carmen BURROWS
79 Dean Communications/Humanities ..... Mr. Mitchell SMITH
81 Dean Math/Engr Tech ..... Ms. Patricia TAYLOR
50 Int Dean Public Services/Business ..... Mr. Raymond MUZIA
38 Dean of Student Development ..... Ms. Joyce JOHNSON
37 Dir Financial Aid/Veteran Affairs ..... Ms. Kathryn ANDERSON
18 Physical Plant Manager ..... Mr. Mark KRAMER
26 Director Public Relations/Marketing ..... Ms. Cecilia RAMIREZ
08 Director of Learning Resources ..... Ms. Aileen E. SCHWEITZER
09 Dir Inst Research and Effectiveness ..... Dr. James T. WALKE
21 Business Office Manager ..... Ms. Wan HU
15 Human Resources Manager ..... Ms. Lisa JOHNSON
21 Budget Office Manager ..... Mr. Lisle WILKE

*Tidewater Community College (C)

121 College Place, Norfolk VA 23510
County: Independent City FICE Identification: 003712
Unit ID: 233772
Telephone: (757) 822-1122 Carnegie Class: Assoc/Pub-S-SC
FAX Number: (757) 822-1060 Calendar System: Semester
URL: www.tcc.edu
Established: 1968 Annual Undergrad Tuition & Fees (In-State): $3,500
Enrollment: 31,308 Coed
Affiliation or Control: State IRS Status: 501(c)3
Highest Offering: Associate Degree
Program: Occupational; 2-Year Principally Bachelor's Creditable
Accreditation: SC, FUSER, ACFEI, ADNUR, DMS, EMT, MAC, OTA, PTAA

02 President ..... Dr. Deborah M. DICROCE
11 Exec Vice President Administration ..... Mr. Franklin T. DUNN
05 VP Student Learning/Chief Acad Ofcr ..... Dr. Daniel DEMARTE
10 Vice President Finance ..... Ms. Phyllis MILLOY
13 Vice President Info Systems ..... Mr. Richard ANDERSEN
103 Vice Pres Workforce Development ..... Dr. Theresa BRYANT
84 VP Student Success/Enrollment Mgmt ..... Dr. Alice R. MCADORY
44 Vice Pres Institutional Advancement ..... Mr. James P. TOSCANO
20 Assoc VP Academic Effectiveness ..... Dr. Lonnie J. SCHAFFER
20 AVP Faculty Dev/Curriculum Innovat ..... Dr. Diann HOLT
106 AVP eLrng/Technology Application ..... Vacant
12 Provost Chesapeake Campus ..... Dr. Linda RICE
12 Provost Portsmouth Campus ..... Dr. Terry L. JONES
12 Provost Virginia Beach Campus ..... Dr. Michael SUMMERS
12 Interim Provost Norfolk Campus ..... Dr. Lonnie SCHAFFER
09 Dir Institutional Effectiveness ..... Mr. Curtis K. AASEN
32 Dean of Student Svcs Chesapeake ..... Dr. Judy MCMILLAN
81 Dean Lang/Math/Science Chesapeake ..... Dr. Cynthia CADIEUX
50 Dean Bus/Pub Svc/Tech Chesapeake ..... Mr. James PERKINSON
32 Dean of Student Svcs Portsmouth ..... Mr. Randy SHANNON
50 Dean Bus/Pub Svcs/Tech Portsmouth ..... Ms. Ann AMBROSE
81 Dean Lang/Math/Science Portsmouth ..... Ms. Kimberly BEATTY
57 Director Visual Arts Center ..... Ms. Christina RUPSCH
32 Dean of Student Svcs Va Beach ..... Dr. Marilyn HODGE
50 Dean IT & Business Va Beach ..... Ms. Carolyn MCLELLAN
54 Int Dean Eng & Ind Tech Va Beach ..... Ms. Carolyn MCLELLAN
76 Dean Health Professions ..... Mr. Thomas CALOGRIDES, JR.
88 Int Dean Language & Speech Va Beach ..... Ms. Sandra HARRIS
81 Dean Math & Science Va Beach ..... Mr. Greg FRANK
83 Dean Social Sci & Pub Svc Va Beach ..... Dr. Michelle WOODHOUSE
32 Dean of Student Svcs Norfolk ..... Dr. Waldon HAGAN
50 Int Dean Bus/Pub Svcs/Tech Norfolk ..... Ms. Caroline RIVERA
81 Dean Lang/Math/Science Norfolk ..... Dr. Susan NICKENS
30 Interim Director of Development ..... Mr. Jackson SASSER
06 Registrar ..... Dr. Kellie SOREY
26 Chief Communications Officer ..... Ms. Laurie WHITE
96 Director of Materiel Management ..... Ms. Robin MOORE
18 Director Facilities Management ..... Mr. David GUGLIELMO
15 Director Human Resources ..... Ms. Gretna SMITH
37 Director Student Financial Aid ..... Ms. Jennifer HARPHAM

*Virginia Highlands Community College (D)

PO Box 828, Abingdon VA 24212-0828
County: Washington FICE Identification: 007099
Unit ID: 233903
Telephone: (276) 739-2400 Carnegie Class: Assoc/Pub-R-M
FAX Number: (276) 739-2590 Calendar System: Semester
URL: www.vhcc.edu
Established: 1967 Annual Undergrad Tuition & Fees (In-State): $3,630
Enrollment: 2,948 Coed
Affiliation or Control: State IRS Status: 501(c)3
Highest Offering: Associate Degree
Program: Occupational; 2-Year Principally Bachelor's Creditable
Accreditation: SC, ADNUR, OTA

02 President ..... Dr. Ron PROFFITT
05 VP Instruction & Student Services ..... Dr. Deborah C. CLEAR
10 VP Financial/Administrative Svcs ..... Vacant
30 Vice Pres Institutional Advancement ..... Mr. David N. MATLOCK
49 Dean Business/Human/Soc Sci ..... Ms. Alma Z. ROWLAND
72 Dean of Science & Engr Technologies ..... Mr. Robert E. MAY
66 Dean of Nursing and Allied Health ..... Ms. Kathy J. MITCHELL
103 Dean Workforce Training & Cont Educ ..... Ms. Melinda T. LELAND
08 Director Library/Instructional Svcs ..... Mr. Charles BOLING
37 Director of Financial Aid ..... Ms. Karen T. CHEERS
07 Director Admission/Records ..... Ms. Karen T. CHEERS
06 Registrar ..... Ms. Charlene EASTRIDGE
15 Director Personnel Services ..... Ms. Deborah S. HALE
32 Director Student Affs/Alumni Rels ..... Vacant
88 Director of Talent Search ..... Ms. Beth M. PAGE
88 Director Project EXCEL ..... Ms. Jackie T. CRAFT
38 Director Student Counseling ..... Vacant
21 Business Manager ..... Mr. Roger W. SPENCER
96 Director of Purchasing ..... Ms. Chelsa TAYLOR
88 Institutional Effectiveness ..... Ms. Jennifer D. ADDISON
90 Coord Academic Computing/Technology ..... Mr. Glen JOHNSON
26 Public Relations Officer ..... Ms. Anne M. DUNHAM
09 Institutional Research Officer ..... Mr. Jeff D. RUSSELL
18 Chief Facilities/Physical Plant ..... Mr. Ernest L. NUNLEY
19 Director of Security/Safety ..... Mr. David NECESSARY
36 Career Plng/Placement Spclst ..... Mr. Tony FULLER

*Virginia Western Community College (E)

PO Box 14007, Roanoke VA 24038-4007
County: Independent City FICE Identification: 003760
Unit ID: 233949
Telephone: (540) 857-8922 Carnegie Class: Assoc/Pub-R-L
FAX Number: (540) 857-6526 Calendar System: Semester
URL: www.virginiawestern.edu
Established: 1966 Annual Undergrad Tuition & Fees (In-State): $3,870
Enrollment: 8,800 Coed
Affiliation or Control: State IRS Status: 501(c)3
Highest Offering: Associate Degree
Program: Occupational; 2-Year Principally Bachelor's Creditable
Accreditation: SC, ACBSP, DH, RAD, RTT

02 President ..... Dr. Robert H. SANDEL
10 Vice Pres of Finance/Admin Services ..... Ms. Cheryl MILLER
05 Vice Pres Academic/Student Affairs ..... Dr. Tresia SAMAN
45 Dean Institutional Effectiveness .. Ms. Rachelle KOUDELIK-JONES
49 Dean Liberal Arts/Social Sciences ..... Dr. Elizabeth WILMER
81 Dean Nat Sci/Math/Health Tech Div ..... Dr. Bryan SCHAUBACH
50 Dean Bus/Sciences/Engineering/WFD ..... Mr. James W. POYTHRESS
09 Director Institutional Research ..... Ms. Carol ROWLETT
32 Dean of Student Services ..... Ms. Lori BAKER
06 Registrar ..... Ms. Meg A. PATTERSON
19 Campus Police Chief ..... Mr. Craig HARRIS
102 Foundation Executive Director ..... Ms. Katherine F. STRICKLAND
13 Information Technology Manager ..... Mr. David W. HARRISON
15 Human Resources Manager ..... Mr. Garry M. SHELTON
21 Business Manager ..... Mrs. Fredona AARON
37 Financial Aid Officer ..... Vacant
22 Workforce Development Officer ..... Ms. Leah COFFMAN
35 Coordinator Advising/Retention Svc ..... Dr. Gloria A. LINDSAY
08 Coordinator of the Library ..... Ms. Lynn HURT
18 Director of Facilities Mgmt Svcs ..... Mr. Kevin G. WITTER
36 Counselor Career Services ..... Dr. Ruth HENDRICK
24 Coordinator Learning Tech Center ..... Ms. Nancy COOK
25 Coord Grants Dev & Special Projects ..... Ms. Marilyn J. HERBERT-ASHTON
29 Alumni/Annual Giving Coord/Communic .. Mr. Erik W. WILLIAMS

*Wytheville Community College (F)

1000 E Main Street, Wytheville VA 24382-3308
County: Wythe FICE Identification: 003761
Unit ID: 234377
Telephone: (276) 223-4700 Carnegie Class: Assoc/Pub-R-M
FAX Number: (276) 223-4778 Calendar System: Semester
URL: www.wcc.vccs.edu
Established: 1963 Annual Undergrad Tuition & Fees (In-State): $3,630
Enrollment: 4,045 Coed
Affiliation or Control: State IRS Status: 501(c)3
Highest Offering: Associate Degree
Program: Occupational; 2-Year Principally Bachelor's Creditable
Accreditation: SC, ADNUR, DH, MLTAD, PTAA

02 President ..... Dr. Charlie WHITE
05 Vice Pres Instruction/Student Devel ..... Dr. William H. HIGHTOWER, JR.
10 Vice Pres Finance & Admin Services ..... Ms. Crystal Y. CREGGER
09 Director of Institutional Research ..... Dr. Kent E. GLINDEMANN
30 Vice Pres of College Development ..... Dr. Rhonda K. CATRON-WOOD
75 Vice Pres Cont Ed & Tech/Occ Pgms ..... Ms. Angela Y. LAWSON
50 Dean of Humanities & Business ..... Dr. Bruce E. BROWN
76 Dean of Science & Health ..... Dr. Lorri M. HUFFARD
32 Interim Dean of Student Services ..... Mr. Michael L. MCHONE
13 Director Acad/Admin Computing ..... Mr. Shawn MCREYNOLDS
06 Interim Registrar ..... Ms. Sabrina D. TERRY
15 Human Resources Manager ..... Ms. Linda R. NYE
26 Public Relations Coordinator ..... Mr. William A. VESELIK
08 Int Coordinator Library Services ..... Mr. George E. MATTIS, JR.
96 Procurement Officer ..... Vacant
106 Dir of Distance & Distrib Learning ..... Mr. Kenneth E. FAIRBANKS

Virginia Intermont College (G)

1013 Moore Street, Bristol VA 24201-4298
County: Independent City FICE Identification: 003752
Unit ID: 233912
Telephone: (276) 669-6101 Carnegie Class: Bac/A&S
FAX Number: (276) 669-5763 Calendar System: Semester
URL: www.vic.edu
Established: 1884 Annual Undergrad Tuition & Fees: $25,542
Enrollment: 586 Coed
Affiliation or Control: Baptist IRS Status: 501(c)3
Highest Offering: Baccalaureate
Program: Liberal Arts And General; Teacher Preparatory; Business Emphasis
Accreditation: SC, SW

01 President ..... Dr. E. Clorisa PHILLIPS
05 Provost ..... Ms. Anne SHUMAKER
32 Dean of Student Development ..... Ms. Kelli APPLEBY
04 Executive Coordinator for the Pres ..... Mrs. Pamela KUYKENDALL
07 Dean of Admissions ..... Mr. Tony ENGLAND
37 Director of Financial Aid ..... Ms. Denise POSEY
10 Chief Financial Officer ..... Mr. William KING
08 Librarian ..... Mr. Jonathan TALLMAN
36 Dir Placement & Career Planning ..... Ms. Bobbie STURGILL
06 Registrar ..... Ms. Pamela HAMMOND
09 Director of Institutional Research ..... Ms. Anne W. SHUMAKER
21 Associate Business Officer ..... Ms. Becky COVEY
29 Director of Alumni Relations ..... Ms. Deborah WHITAKER
38 Director of Student Counseling ..... Ms. Deborah PATTERSON
92 Director of Honors Program ..... Dr. Robert RAINWATER
15 Director Personnel Services ..... Ms. Linda MORGAN
26 Dir of Marketing/Communications ..... Ms. Lisa MITCHELL
18 Chief Facilities/Physical Plant ..... Mr. Con SAULS

Virginia International University (H)

11200 Waples Mill Road, Suite 360, Fairfax VA 22030
County: Fairfax FICE Identification: 041440
Telephone: (703) 591-7042 Carnegie Class: Not Classified

FAX Number: (703) 591-7046 Calendar System: Other
URL: www.viu.edu
Established: 1998 Annual Undergrad Tuition & Fees: N/A
Enrollment: N/A Coed
Affiliation or Control: Proprietary IRS Status: Proprietary
Highest Offering: Master's
Program: Professional; Business Emphasis
Accreditation: ACICS

01 President .... Dr. Isa SARAC
03 Vice President University Affairs .... Mr. Hasan K. BURK

Virginia Military Institute (A)

201 Smith Hall, Lexington VA 24450-0304
County: Independent City FICE Identification: 003753
Unit ID: 234085
Telephone: (540) 464-7230 Carnegie Class: Bac/A&S
FAX Number: (540) 464-7583 Calendar System: Semester
URL: www.vmi.edu
Established: 1839 Annual Undergrad Tuition & Fees (In-State): $20,630
Enrollment: 1,569 Coed
Affiliation or Control: State IRS Status: 501(c)3
Highest Offering: Baccalaureate
Program: Liberal Arts And General; Professional
Accreditation: SC, BUS, CS, ENG

01 Superintendent .... Gen. J. H. Benford PEAY
05 Dean of the Faculty .... BGen. R. Wane SCHNEITER
10 Deputy Superintendent Finance/Admin .... BGen. Robert L. GREEN
32 Commandant of Cadets .... Col. Thomas H. TRUMPS
100 Chief of Staff .... Col. Jeffrey H. CURTIS
04 Assistant to the Superintendent .... Col. Michael M. STRICKLER
21 Assoc Business Exec/Treasurer .... Col. Gary R. KNICK
07 Director of Admissions .... Col. Vernon L. BEITZEL
88 Exec Director Museum Programs .... Col. Keith E. GIBSON
37 Director of Financial Aid .... Col. Timothy P. GOLDEN
35 Deputy Commandant Cadet Life .... Col. L. E. HURLBUT
36 Director of Career Services .... Col. R. Samuel RATCLIFFE
41 Director Intercollegiate Athletics .... Mr. Donald T. WHITE
26 Director Communications & Marketing .... Col. Stewart D. MACINNIS
29 Executive VP Alumni Association .... LTC. Adam C. VOLANT
30 Exec VP VMI Foundation/Fund Raising ... Mr. Brian S. CROCKETT
88 Exec VP Keydet Club/Athletic Fund . Mr. Gregory M. CAVALLARO
06 Registrar .... LtCol. Janet M. BATTAGLIA
15 Director Human Resources .... Col. Robert B. SPORE
18 Director Physical Plant .... LTC. James L. WILLIAMS, JR.
09 Director Institutional Research .... Col. Elizabeth S. SECHLER
88 Director Auxiliary Services .... Col. James N. JOYNER
40 Manager Bookstore .... Ms. Patricia T. RULEY
42 Institute Chaplain .... Col. James S. PARK
17 Institute Physician .... Dr. David L. COPELAND
88 Director of Sports Information .... Mr. Wade H. BRANNER
08 Head Librarian .... Col. Donald H. SAMDAHL, JR.
38 Director of Cadet Counseling .... LtCol. Sarah L. JONES
14 Director Information Technology .... Col. Thomas F. HOPKINS
96 Director of Purchasing .... Maj. Kathy H. TOMLIN

† Tuition includes required room and board and quartermaster charges.

Virginia Polytechnic Institute and State University (B)

Blacksburg VA 24061-0202
County: Montgomery FICE Identification: 003754
Unit ID: 233921
Telephone: (540) 231-6000 Carnegie Class: RU/VH
FAX Number: (540) 231-9263 Calendar System: Semester
URL: www.vt.edu
Established: 1872 Annual Undergrad Tuition & Fees (In-State): $10,509
Enrollment: 31,006 Coed
Affiliation or Control: State IRS Status: 501(c)3
Highest Offering: Doctorate
Program: Liberal Arts And General; Teacher Preparatory; Professional
Accreditation: SC, ART, BUS, BUSA, CACREP, CEA, CIDA, CLPSY, CONST, CS, DIETD, DIETI, ENG, FOR, IPSY, LSAR, #MED, MFCD, MUS, PLNG, SPAA, TED, THEA, VET

01 President .... Charles W. STEGER
05 Senior Vice President & Provost .... Mark G. MCNAMEE
11 Vice President for Admin Services .... Sherwood G. WILSON
13 Vice Pres for Information Tech .... Earving L. BLYTHE
32 Vice President Student Affairs .... Edward SPENCER
30 Vice Pres Devel & University Rels .... Elizabeth A. FLANAGAN
29 Vice President Alumni Relations .... Thomas C. TILLAR, JR.
28 VP Diversity and Inclusion .... William T. LEWIS, SR.
46 Vice President for Research .... Robert WALTERS
20 Vice President and Dean UG Educ .... Daniel A. WUBAH
58 Vice President and Dean Grad Educ .... Karen P. DEPAUW
56 Vice President for Outreach .... John E. DOOLEY
10 Vice President for Finance and CFO .... M. Dwight SHELTON
07 Director of Undergrad Admissions .... Mildred JOHNSON
35 Dean of Students .... Thomas BROWN
16 Assoc Vice Pres for Human Resources .... Hal IRVIN
09 Director Institutional Research .... Kristen BUSH
43 General Counsel .... Kay K. HEIDBREDER
84 Asst VP Enrollment Mgmt & Registrar .... Wanda H. DEAN
45 Dir for Planning & Administration .... Jeb STEWART
37 Dir of Scholarships/Financial Aid .... Barry W. SIMMONS
23 Director Schiffert Health Center .... Kanitta CHAROENSIRI
18 Assoc Vice President for Facilities .... Michael J. COLEMAN
39 Int Dir of Housing & Dining Svcs .... Robert COFFEY
39 Int Dir of Housing & Dining Svcs .... Ken BELCHER
41 Athletic Director .... James WEAVER
26 Assoc Vice Pres Univ Relations .... Larry HINCKER
38 Director Student Counseling .... Chris FLYNN
30 Executive Director Bookstore .... Donald J. WILLIAMS
62 Dean of Libraries .... Tyler WALTERS
47 Dean of Agriculture/Life Sciences .... Alan GRANT
48 Dean of Architecture/Urban Studies .... Jack DAVIS
49 Dean College of Science .... Lay N. CHANG
50 Dean of Business .... Richard E. SORENSEN
54 Dean of Engineering .... Richard BENSON
79 Dean Liberal Arts & Human Sciences .... Sue OTT ROWLANDS
74 Dean of Veterinary Medicine .... Gerhardt SCHURIG
65 Dean of Natural Resources & Environ .... Paul M. WINISTORFER
96 Director of Purchasing .... W. Thomas KALOUPEK
90 Director Educational Technology .... John F. MOORE
91 Assoc Vice Pres for Enterprise Sys .... Deborah M. FULTON
12 Exec Dir National Capital Region .... James BOHLAND

Virginia State University (C)

One Hayden Street, Petersburg VA 23806-0001
County: Chesterfield FICE Identification: 003764
Unit ID: 234155
Telephone: (804) 524-5000 Carnegie Class: Master's S
FAX Number: (804) 524-6506 Calendar System: Semester
URL: www.vsu.edu
Established: 1882 Annual Undergrad Tuition & Fees (In-State): $15,970
Enrollment: 5,634 Coed
Affiliation or Control: State IRS Status: 501(c)3
Highest Offering: Doctorate
Program: Liberal Arts And General; Teacher Preparatory
Accreditation: SC, ART, BUS, CS, DIETD, DIETI, ENG, ENGT, MUS, @SW, TED

01 President .... Dr. Keith T. MILLER
100 Chief of Staff .... Mr. Cortez K. DIAL
10 Vice Pres Finance & Administration .... Mr. David J. MEADOWS
30 Vice President Development .... Dr. Robert L. TURNER, JR.
05 Provost/VP for Academic Affairs .... Dr. W. Weldon HILL
32 VP of Student Affairs & Enroll Mgmt .... Dr. Michael SHACKLEFORD
20 Vice Provost .... Dr. James E. HUNTER
15 Assoc VP for Human Resource .... Dr. Elliot WHEELAN
84 Asst VP/Student Enrollment Services .... Mr. Henry DEBOSE
21 Associate Business Officer .... Ms. Sheila MCNAIR
50 Dean School Business .... Dr. Mirta M. MARTIN
54 Dean Sch of Engineering Sci & Tech .... Dr. Pamela LEIGH-MACK
79 Dean Sch Liberal Arts & Education .... Dr. Andrew KANU
47 Dean Sch of Agriculture .... Dr. Jewel E. HAIRSTON
58 Dean Graduate Studies/Res/Outreach .... Dr. James E. HUNTER
62 Dean Library & Media Services ... Dr. Elsie S. WEATHERINGTON
44 Director of Development .... Ms. Nancy L. JONES
06 Registrar .... Ms. Debera BONNER
09 Director Inst Planning/Assessment .... Dr. Emmett L. RIDLEY
37 Interim Director of Financial Aid .... Mrs. Myra PHILLIPS
19 Director Police/Public Safety .... Mr. Michael WALLACE
04 Special Assistant to the President .... Mr. Jesse VAUGHAN
18 Director of Facilities .... Mr. Robert SUTHARD
07 Director Admissions & Recruitment .... Ms. Irene F. LOGAN
26 Director University Relations .... Mr. Thomas REED
22 Human Resources Manager .... Ms. Gayle ONEAL
14 Assoc VP & Chief Information .... Mr. Hubert B. HARRIS
39 Director Residence Facilities .... Dr. LaVerne BRIGGS
36 Director Career Plng & Placement .... Vacant
40 Bookstore Manager .... Mr. Kevin POWELL
92 Director Honors Program .... Dr. Gladys NUNNALLY
41 Athletic Director .... Mrs. Peggy DAVIS
42 Minister .... Rev. Delano DOUGLAS
44 Planned Giving Officer .... Mr. Jonathan YOUNG
29 Coordinator of Alumni Relations .... Ms. Andrea COLLINS
27 Deputy Chief Information Officer .... Ms. Stephanie A. HAYES
23 Director Student Health Services .... Mrs. Rebecca BRANCH-GRIFFIN
25 Contract Manager .... Ms. Linda SCOTT
87 Director Summer School Session .... Dr. Vykuntapathi THOTA
96 Director of Purchasing .... Mrs. Yolanda BUCK
38 Director Student Counseling .... Ms. LaKesha RONEY

Virginia Union University (D)

1500 N Lombardy Street, Richmond VA 23220-1784
County: Independent City FICE Identification: 003766
Unit ID: 234164
Telephone: (804) 257-5600 Carnegie Class: Bac/Diverse
FAX Number: (804) 257-5818 Calendar System: Semester
URL: www.vuu.edu
Established: 1865 Annual Undergrad Tuition & Fees: $14,630
Enrollment: 1,701 Coed
Affiliation or Control: Baptist IRS Status: 501(c)3
Highest Offering: Doctorate
Program: Liberal Arts And General; Teacher Preparatory; Professional
Accreditation: SC, ACBSP, SW, TED, THEOL

01 President .... Dr. Claude G. PERKINS
03 Senior Vice President .... Dr. Joseph F. JOHNSON
05 Vice President for Academic Affairs .... Dr. W. F. EVANS
32 VP Enrollmnt Mgmt & Stdnt Affs .... Vacant
10 Int VP Financial Affairs .... Mr. Louis ZAMMETT
30 Vice Pres Institutional Advancement .... Dr. Anthony THOMPSON
09 VP Research/Planning & Spec Prog .... Dr. Joy P. GOODRICH
26 Asst to Pres/Dir Public Relations ...... Ms. Shena L. CRITTENDON
53 Dean Evelyn R Syphax Sch Ed/Psy .... Vacant
81 Dean Math/Science & Technology .... Dr. Phillip W. ARCHER
50 Dean Sydney Lewis Sch of Business ..... Dr. Adelaja O. ODUTOLA
79 Dean School of Humanities & Soc Sci .... Dr. Linda G. SCHLICHTING
73 Dean School of Theology .... Dr. John W. KINNEY
25 Asst to President Title III Pgms .... Mr. Samuel T. RHOADES
15 Director Human Resources .... Ms. Hollace J. ENOCH
06 Interim Registrar .... Ms. Marilyn A. BROOKS
38 Director Counseling .... Vacant
29 Director of Alumni Affairs .... Ms. Kristie L. WHITE
08 Library Director .... Dr. Delores Z. PRETLOW
37 Director Financial Aid .... Mrs. Donna R. MACK-TATUM
27 Director Information Technology .... Mr. Robert R. GRAY
88 Lan Administrator .... Mr. Bryan K. ROYAL
36 Director Career Services .... Mrs. Penni SWEETENBURG-LEE
84 Director of Enrollment Management .... Dr. James S. EDWARDS
42 University Pastor .... Rev. Angelo V. CHATMON
41 Athletic Director .... Mr. Michael L. BAILEY
19 Chief University Police .... Col. Carlton G. EDWARDS
24 Audio Visual Coordinator .... Mr. JaPrince L. CARTER
21 Comptroller .... Ms. Stephanie M. WHITE
40 Bookstore Manager .... Ms. Angel POPE
39 Director of Residence Life .... Ms. Maro L. MITCHELL
23 University Physician .... Dr. Walton M. BELLE
31 Dir of Community & Student Rels .... Ms. Claudia E. WALL
18 Director Facilities .... Mr. David E. GORDON
96 Director of Purchasing .... Mr. Michael T. ADKINS

Virginia University of Lynchburg (E)

2058 Garfield Avenue, Lynchburg VA 24501-6417
County: Independent City FICE Identification: 003762
Unit ID: 234137
Telephone: (434) 528-5276 Carnegie Class: Spec/Faith
FAX Number: (434) 528-4257 Calendar System: Semester
URL: www.vul.edu
Established: 1886 Annual Undergrad Tuition & Fees: $16,400
Enrollment: 540 Coed
Affiliation or Control: Independent Non-Profit IRS Status: 501(c)3
Highest Offering: Doctorate
Program: Liberal Arts And General; Business Emphasis
Accreditation: TRACS

01 President .... Dr. Ralph REAVIS
05 Vice President of Academic Affairs .... Dr. Kathy C. FRANKLIN
20 Dean of the College .... Dr. Kathy C. FRANKLIN
30 VP for Institutional Advancement .... Dr. Doris S. CRAWFORD

Virginia Wesleyan College (F)

1584 Wesleyan Drive, Norfolk VA 23502-5599
County: Independent City FICE Identification: 003767
Unit ID: 234173
Telephone: (757) 455-3200 Carnegie Class: Bac/A&S
FAX Number: (757) 461-4944 Calendar System: 4/1/4
URL: www.vwc.edu
Established: 1961 Annual Undergrad Tuition & Fees: $29,180
Enrollment: 1,279 Coed
Affiliation or Control: United Methodist IRS Status: 501(c)3
Highest Offering: Baccalaureate
Program: Liberal Arts And General; Teacher Preparatory
Accreditation: SC, NRPA

01 President .... Dr. William T. GREER, JR.
05 VP Academic Affs/Dean of College .... Dr. Timothy G. O'ROURKE
32 VP Student Affs/Dean of Enrollment .. Mr. David E. BUCKINGHAM
10 Vice President of Finance .... Mr. Cary A. SAWYER
30 VP for College Advancement .... Ms. Mita K. VAIL
11 Vice President of Operations .... Mr. Bruce F. VAUGHAN
45 AVP Inst Rsrch/Effec/Dir Strat Plng .... Mr. Bryan PRICE
26 Director of College Communications .... Mrs. Laynee H. TIMLIN
35 Dean of Students .... Dr. Keith E. MOORE
88 Assoc VP for College Advancement .... Ms. Suzanne SAVAGE
07 Dean of Admissions .... Ms. Patricia C. PATTEN
20 Assoc Dean Special Acad Projects .... Ms. Debbie L. HICKS
20 Assoc Dean of the College .... Dr. Lisa P. CARSTENS
13 Chief Technology Officer .... Mr. Jack L. DMOCH
41 Director of Athletics .... Ms. Joanne M. RENN
09 Asst Director for Instnl Research .... Mr. Donald C. STAUFFER
55 Director of Adult Studies Program .... Mr. Thomas R. FARLEY
08 Library Director .... Ms. Jan S. PACE
15 Director of Human Resources .... Ms. Karla R. RASMUSSEN
06 Registrar .... Ms. Barbara S. ADAMS
37 Director of Financial Aid .... Ms. Teresa L. RHYNE
96 Director of Purchasing .... Ms. Midge ZIMMERMAN
31 Director of Community Service .... Ms. Diane E. HOTALING
36 Director of Career Services .... Ms. Lisa I. FENTRESS
19 Director of Security .... Mr. Jerry MANCE
39 Asst Dean Students/Dir Res Life .... Ms. McCarren CAPUTA
29 Director of Alumni Relations .... Ms. Kathleen M. JUDGE
91 Manager of Admin Computer Systems ..... Mr. Bruce T. ELDRIDGE
18 Director of Physical Plant .... Mr. David R. HOPPER
42 Chaplain .... Rev. Greg WEST
38 Director of Counseling .... Mr. James W. BROWN
44 Director of Special Gifts .... Ms. Lori MCCAREL
44 Director of Annual Giving .... Ms. Megan T. SPENCER
44 Dir Leadership & Planned Giving .... Dr. Mary Kate ANDRIS
40 Bookstore Manager .... Ms. Kim S. BROWN
92 Director Honors and Scholars .... Dr. Joyce B. EASTER
28 Director of International Programs .... Ms. Lena H. JOHNSON
88 Director of Student Activities .... Ms. Jennifer E. MITCHELL
23 Director of Health Services .... Ms. Valerie L. COVINGTON

Washington and Lee University (A)

204 W Washington Street, Lexington VA 24450-2116
County: Independent City FICE Identification: 003768
Unit ID: 234207
Telephone: (540) 458-8400 Carnegie Class: Bac/A&S
FAX Number: (540) 458-8945 Calendar System: Other
URL: www.wlu.edu
Established: 1749 Annual Undergrad Tuition & Fees: $41,927
Enrollment: 2,173 Coed
Affiliation or Control: Independent Non-Profit IRS Status: 501(c)3
Highest Offering: Doctorate
Program: Liberal Arts And General; Professional
Accreditation: SC, BUS, JOUR, LAW, @TEAC

01 President .... Dr. Kenneth P. RUSCIO
05 Interim Provost .... Dr. Robert A. STRONG
20 Associate Provost .... Dr. Elizabeth KNAPP
10 Vice Pres for Finance and Admin .... Mr. Steven G. MCALLISTER
30 Vice Pres University Advancement .... Mr. Dennis W. CROSS
32 VP for Stdnt Affs & Dean of Stdnts .... Ms. Sidney S. EVANS
04 Senior Asst to the President .... Dr. Valerie J. CUSHMAN
101 Sr Asst to Pres/Sec of University .... Mr. James D. FARRAR
43 General Counsel .... Ms. Leanne M. SHANK
22 Assoc Gen Counsel Compliance Spprt .... Ms. Jennifer E. KIRKLAND
49 Dean of the College .... Dr. Hank DOBIN
50 Dean of Commerce/Economics/Politics .... Dr. Larry C. PEPPERS
61 Interim Dean of Law School .... Mr. Mark A. GRUNEWALD
26 Exec Dir of Comm/Public Affairs .... Mr. Jeffery G. HANNA
89 Assoc Dean of Students/Dn Freshmen .... Mr. David M. LEONARD
35 Assoc Dean of Students .... Ms. Tamara Y. FUTRELL
30 Exec Dir of University Development .... Mr. Tres MULLIS
41 Director of Athletics .... Ms. Janine M. HATHORN
35 Dir Univ Commons/Campus Activities .... Mr. Jason L. RODOCKER
07 Dean of Admissions/Financial Aid .... Mr. William M. HARTOG
09 Asst Provost/Instit Effectiveness .... Dr. Debbie DAILEY
06 Associate University Registrar .... Ms. Barbara L. ROWE
08 Interim University Librarian .... Mr. John TOMBARGE
85 Director International Education .... Dr. Larry BOETSCH
29 Exec Director of Alumni Affairs .... Mr. Walter T. DUDLEY
15 Exec Director of Human Resources .... Ms. Amy BARNES
37 Director of Financial Aid .... Mr. James D. KASTER
18 Exec Dir Facilities/Capital Plng .... Mr. John HOOGAKKER
21 Associate Treasurer & Controller .... Mrs. Deborah Z. CAYLOR
13 Chief Technology Officer .... Mr. David SAACKE
24 Senior Academic Technologist .... Mr. John A. BLACKBURN
36 Director Undergrad Career Services .... Ms. Beverly T. LORIG
23 Director Student Health/Counseling .... Dr. Jane T. HORTON
96 Director of Auxiliary Services .... Mr. Paul F. RENZI
40 Director of Univ Bookstore .... Ms. Maureen BECKER

Washington Baptist University (B)

4300 Evergreen Lane, Annandale VA 22003
County: Fairfax Identification: 666234
Telephone: (703) 333-5904 Carnegie Class: Not Classified
FAX Number: (703) 333-5906 Calendar System: Semester
URL: www.wbcs.edu
Established: N/A Annual Undergrad Tuition & Fees: $4,590
Enrollment: N/A Coed
Affiliation or Control: Baptist IRS Status: 501(c)3
Highest Offering: Doctorate
Program: Religious Emphasis
Accreditation: @BI, @THEOL

01 President .... Dr. Peter M. CHANG
03 Executive Vice President .... Dr. Davis S. KIM
32 Dean of Students .... Mr. Sungchul HWANG

Westwood College-Annandale (C)

7619 Little River Turnpike 5th Fl, Annandale VA 22003
County: Fairfax Identification: 666599
Unit ID: 448628
Telephone: (877) 305-0049 Carnegie Class: Bac/Assoc
FAX Number: (703) 642-3772 Calendar System: Quarter
URL: www.westwood.edu
Established: 1953 Annual Undergrad Tuition & Fees: $14,500
Enrollment: 14,315 Coed
Affiliation or Control: Proprietary IRS Status: Proprietary
Highest Offering: Baccalaureate
Program: Occupational; Liberal Arts And General
Accreditation: ACICS

00 Regional Director .... Lauck WALTON
01 Campus President .... Mary Kay SVEDBERG

† Satellite campus of Westwood College-Arlington Ballston, Arlington, VA.

Westwood College-Arlington Ballston (D)

4300 Wilson Boulevard, Suite 200, Arlington VA 22203-4167
County: Arlington Identification: 666660
Unit ID: 447069
Telephone: (877) 268-5278 Carnegie Class: Bac/Assoc
FAX Number: (703) 243-3992 Calendar System: Quarter
URL: www.westwood.edu
Established: N/A Annual Undergrad Tuition & Fees: $14,500
Enrollment: 477 Coed
Affiliation or Control: Proprietary IRS Status: Proprietary
Highest Offering: Baccalaureate
Program: Occupational; Liberal Arts And General
Accreditation: ACICS

01 Campus President .... Valarie TRIMARCHI

† Branch campus of Westwood College-South Bay, Torrance, CA.

World College (E)

5193 Lake Shore Drive, Suite 105, Virginia Beach VA 23455-2500
County: Henrico FICE Identification: 041361
Unit ID: 419448
Telephone: (757) 464-4600 Carnegie Class: Not Classified
FAX Number: (757) 464-3687 Calendar System: Other
URL: www.cie-wc.edu
Established: 1992 Annual Undergrad Tuition & Fees: $3,770
Enrollment: 527 Coed
Affiliation or Control: Proprietary IRS Status: Proprietary
Highest Offering: Baccalaureate
Program: Technical Emphasis
Accreditation: DETC

01 President .... Mr. Randy DRINKO
05 Dean of Instruction .... Mr. Keith CONN
07 Admissions Counselor .... Mr. Scott KATZENMEYER

WASHINGTON

Antioch University Seattle (F)

2326 Sixth Avenue, Seattle WA 98121-1814
County: King Identification: 666812
Unit ID: 245883
Telephone: (206) 441-5352 Carnegie Class: Master's M
FAX Number: (206) 441-3307 Calendar System: Quarter
URL: www.antiochseattle.edu
Established: 1975 Annual Undergrad Tuition & Fees: $18,000
Enrollment: 1,000 Coed
Affiliation or Control: Independent Non-Profit IRS Status: 501(c)3
Highest Offering: Doctorate
Program: Liberal Arts And General; Teacher Preparatory; Professional; Business Emphasis
Accreditation: &NH, MFCD

01 President .... Dr. Cassandra MANUELITO-KERKVLIET
04 Exec Assistant to the President .... Ms. Wendy DAHL
05 VP Acad Affs & Dean of Faculty .... Dr. Peter M. ROJCEWICZ
30 Int VP Institutional Advancement .... Mr. John SIEGEL
11 Vice Pres Administration/Finance .... Ms. Betsy RALEIGH
88 Interim Dean of Psychology .... Dr. Jane HARMON JACOBS
32 Associate Dean & Dean of Students .... Ms. Shana HORMANN
06 Registrar .... Ms. Barbara TALMADGE
84 Dean of Enrollment Svcs/Admissions .... Dr. Doug ARNOLD
10 Chief Business Officer .... Ms. Betsy RALEIGH
08 Interim Library Director .... Ms. Beverly STUART
88 Administrative Services Director .... Ms. Lynn NAKAMURA
21 Budget Analyst .... Mr. Greg SCHULER
26 Director of Integrated Marketing .... Vacant
44 Director of Development .... Ms. Michelle WILKINSON
37 Financial Aid Director .... Ms. Katy STAHL
29 Director of Alumni Relations .... Mr. Eric WARN
18 Facilities Director .... Mr. Michael JOHNSON
51 Director of Continuing Education .... Ms. Debra ALDERMAN
97 Dir of BA Liberal Studies Program .... Dr. Bryan TOMASOVICH
53 Interim Dean School of Education .... Dr. Ed MIKEL
88 Interim Dir Ctr for Creative Chg .... Dr. Betsy GEIST
15 Sr HR Business Partner .... Ms. Pamela PETITT

† Regional accreditation is carried under the parent institution in Yellow Springs, Ohio.

Argosy University, Seattle (G)

2601 A Elliott Avenue, Seattle WA 98121-1318
County: King Identification: 666080
Unit ID: 439057
Telephone: (206) 283-4500 Carnegie Class: Master's S
FAX Number: (206) 283-5777 Calendar System: Semester
URL: www.argosy.edu/seattle
Established: 1999 Annual Undergrad Tuition & Fees: $14,580
Enrollment: 543 Coed
Affiliation or Control: Proprietary IRS Status: Proprietary
Highest Offering: Doctorate
Program: Professional
Accreditation: &NH

01 Campus President .... Dr. Tom DYER
05 Vice President of Academic Affairs .... Dr. Russell WRIGHT
07 Director of Admissions .... Tina JACOBS
32 Director of Student Services .... Deann KETCHUM
15 Human Resources Generalist .... Mark BRUNKE
21 Business Manager .... Brian GARDNER
08 Director of Library Services .... Andrew HARBISON
37 Director of Student Financial Svcs .... Sara DEWITT

† Regional accreditation is carried under the parent institution in Chicago, IL.

The Art Institute of Seattle (H)

2323 Elliott Avenue, Seattle WA 98121-1622
County: King FICE Identification: 022913
Unit ID: 234492
Telephone: (206) 448-0900 Carnegie Class: Spec/Arts
FAX Number: (206) 448-2501 Calendar System: Quarter
URL: www.ais.edu
Established: 1946 Annual Undergrad Tuition & Fees: $23,088
Enrollment: 2,439 Coed
Affiliation or Control: Proprietary IRS Status: Proprietary
Highest Offering: Baccalaureate
Program: Occupational
Accreditation: NW, ACFEI, CIDA

01 President .... Elden R. MONDAY, JR.
05 Vice Pres/Dean of Academic Affairs .... Dr. Scott CARNZ
15 Director of Human Resources .... Natasha J. OILAR
32 Dean of Student Affairs .... Megan KIJEWSKI
07 Senior Director of Admissions .... Liane SOOHOO
11 Director Admin/Financial Svcs .... Greg WOODARD
36 Director Career Services .... Jim MCGUIRE

Bainbridge Graduate Institute (I)

284 Madrona Way NE, Suite 124, Bainbridge Island WA 98110
FICE Identification: 041612
Unit ID: 458159
Telephone: (206) 855-9559 Carnegie Class: Not Classified
FAX Number: (206) 855-9045 Calendar System: Semester
URL: www.bgi.edu
Established: 2002 Annual Undergrad Tuition & Fees: $31,160
Enrollment: 197 Coed
Affiliation or Control: Independent Non-Profit IRS Status: 501(c)3
Highest Offering: Master's
Program: Professional; Business Emphasis
Accreditation: ACICS

01 President/Chief Executive Officer .... Mr. Gifford PINCHOT, III
05 Provost/Exec Vice President .... Ms. Jill BAMBURG
06 Registrar .... Ms. Lynn BRAUN
11 Director of Operations .... Mr. Jim MCRAE

Bakke Graduate University (J)

1013 8th Avenue, Suite 401, Seattle WA 98104-1222
County: King FICE Identification: 031108
Unit ID: 420705
Telephone: (206) 264-9100 Carnegie Class: Not Classified
FAX Number: (206) 264-8828 Calendar System: Semester
URL: www.bgu.edu
Established: 1990 Annual Graduate Tuition & Fees: N/A
Enrollment: 206 Coed
Affiliation or Control: Independent Non-Profit IRS Status: 501(c)3
Highest Offering: Doctorate; No Undergraduates
Program: Professional; Religious Emphasis
Accreditation: TRACS

00 Chancellor .... Dr. Ray BAKKE
01 President .... Dr. Brad SMITH
05 Academic Dean .... Dr. Gwen DEWEY
30 Vice President Advancement .... Mr. Robert STEINHAGEN
10 Chief Operations/Financial Ofcr .... Mr. Art ZYLSTRA
06 Registrar .... Dr. Judi MELTON
07 Director of Admissions Services .... Ms. Julie GUSTAVSON

Bastyr University (K)

14500 Juanita Drive NE, Kenmore WA 98028-4966
County: King FICE Identification: 022425
Unit ID: 235547
Telephone: (425) 602-3000 Carnegie Class: Spec/Health
FAX Number: (425) 823-6222 Calendar System: Quarter
URL: www.bastyr.edu
Established: 1978 Annual Undergrad Tuition & Fees: $20,625
Enrollment: 996 Coed
Affiliation or Control: Independent Non-Profit IRS Status: 501(c)3
Highest Offering: Doctorate
Program: Professional
Accreditation: NW, ACUP, DIETD, DIETI, MEAC, NATUR

01 President .... Dr. Daniel K. CHURCH
05 Senior Vice President/Provost .... Dr. Timothy C. CALLAHAN
10 Vice President for Finance & Admin .... Mr. Sheldon R. HABER
100 Chief of Staff .... Mr. Greg J. GOODE
30 Chief Development Officer .... Ms. Sheryl STIEFEL
32 Vice President of Student Affairs .... Ms. Susan WEIDER
06 Registrar .... Ms. Christine MASTERSON
08 Director of Library Services .... Ms. Jane SAXTON
29 Dir Alumni Relations/Career Svcs .... Mr. Thomas BULL
23 Dir Bastyr Ctr for Natural Health .... Dr. Jamey WALLACE
15 Director of Human Resources .... Mr. Keith WOODY
13 Director of Information Technology .... Ms. Marsha MCGOUGH
09 Director of Research Development .... Dr. Mark MARTZEN
26 Chief Public Relations Officer .... Mr. Derek WING
46 Senior Research Scientist .... Dr. Leanna STANDISH
40 Bookstore Manager .... Mr. Marty PETERSEN
07 Director of Admissions .... Mr. Ted OLSEN
37 Director Financial Aid .... Ms. Carol DUKE

18 Director Facilities and Safety .... Mr. Daniel CLARK
21 Controller .... Ms. Norma BUSH
38 Director Counseling and Wellness .... Ms. Cherlyn STOVER

Bates Technical College (A)

1101 S Yakima Avenue, Tacoma WA 98405-4895
County: Pierce FICE Identification: 005306
Unit ID: 235671
Telephone: (253) 680-7000 Carnegie Class: Assoc/Pub-U-MC
FAX Number: (253) 680-7101 Calendar System: Quarter
URL: www.bates.ctc.edu
Established: 1940 Annual Undergrad Tuition & Fees (In-State): $5,600
Enrollment: 3,328 Coed
Affiliation or Control: State IRS Status: 501(c)3
Highest Offering: Associate Degree
Program: Occupational; 2-Year Principally Bachelor's Creditable; Technical Emphasis
Accreditation: NW, DA, DT

01 President .... Mr. Lyle QUASIM
04 Exec Asst to the President .... Mr. Geof KAUFMAN
05 Vice President of Instruction .... Ms. Cheri LOILAND
32 Vice President of Student Services .... Mr. Ivan GORNE
10 Vice Pres Administrative Services .... Vacant
15 Vice President of Human Resources .... Ms. Vickie LACKMAN
12 Executive Dean Mohler Campus .... Mr. David HINMAN
12 Executive Dean South Campus .... Vacant
88 Dean of Educational Systems .... Vacant
09 Dean of Inst Rsrch/Plng/Assessment .... Ms. Summer KENESSON
20 Dean of Academic Programs .... Mr. Mike BRANDSTETTER
30 Director of Development .... Ms. Kimberly PLEGER
10 Director of Fiscal Services .... Ms. Janet LUXTRUM
18 Director Facilities & Operations .... Mr. Marty MATTES
06 Registrar .... Mr. Patrick BROWN
96 General Services Manager .... Mr. Spiro MANTHOU
37 Financial Aid Officer .... Ms. Susan NEESE
35 Director of Student Services .... Mr. Dion TEAGUE
28 College Diversity Coordinator .... Ms. Kathy FLORES

Bellevue College (B)

3000 Landerholm Circle, SE, Bellevue WA 98007-6484
County: King FICE Identification: 003769
Unit ID: 234669
Telephone: (425) 564-1000 Carnegie Class: Assoc/Pub4
FAX Number: (425) 564-4065 Calendar System: Quarter
URL: www.bellevuecollege.edu
Established: 1965 Annual Undergrad Tuition & Fees (In-State): $3,542
Enrollment: 16,019 Coed
Affiliation or Control: State IRS Status: 501(c)3
Highest Offering: Baccalaureate
Program: Occupational; 2-Year Principally Bachelor's Creditable; Professional
Accreditation: NW, ADNUR, CIDA, DMS, NMT, RADDOS, RTT

01 Interim President .... Mrs. Laura SAUNDERS
11 Vice Pres Administrative Services .... Ms. Rachel SOLEMSAAS
05 Vice President of Instruction .... Mr. Tom NIELSEN
15 Vice President Human Resources .... Mr. Cesar PORTILLO
30 Vice Pres Institutional Advancement .... Ms. Gaynor HILLS
32 Vice President of Student Services .... Dr. Tom PRITCHARD
103 Vice Pres of Workforce Development .... Dr. Paula BOYUM
13 Vice Pres of Information Resources .... Mr. Russell BEARD
51 Dean Continuing Education .... Mr. Bruce RIVELAND
79 Dean of Arts and Humanities .... Ms. Margaret HARADA
76 Dean of HSEWI .... Mr. Kevin MCCARTHY
83 Interim Dean of Social Science .... Ms. Virginia BRIDWELL
88 Associate Dean of Student Programs .... Mr. Faisal JASWAL
35 Associate Dean of Student Services .... Mr. Matt GROSHONG
85 Asst Dean Internatl Student Pgms .... Mr. Cris SAMIA
10 Exec Dir of Finance & Auxiliary Svc .... Ms. Jennifer STROTHER
08 Director Library/Media .... Ms. Myra VAN VACTOR
26 Director College & Community Rels .... Mr. Bart BECKER
37 Director Financial Aid .... Ms. Sherri BALLANTYNE
19 Director of Public Safety .... Mr. Ken CONDER
13 Director Computing Services .. Ms. Agnes FIGUEROA-MARTINEZ
91 Director IT Services .... Mr. Gary MAHN
41 Director of Athletics .... Mr. Bill O'CONNOR
09 Dir Institutional Effective/Rsrch .... Ms. Patricia JAMES
38 Student Counseling .... Mr. Harlan LEE
40 Manager Bellevue College Bookstore .... Ms. Kristen CONNELY
96 Manager of Purchasing .... Mr. Dexter JOHNSON

Bellingham Technical College (C)

3028 Lindebergh Avenue, Bellingham WA 98225-1599
County: Whatcom FICE Identification: 004999
Unit ID: 234696
Telephone: (360) 752-7000 Carnegie Class: Assoc/Pub-R-M
FAX Number: (360) 676-2798 Calendar System: Quarter
URL: www.btc.ctc.edu
Established: 1957 Annual Undergrad Tuition & Fees (In-District): $4,255
Enrollment: 3,900 Coed
Affiliation or Control: State/Local IRS Status: 501(c)3
Highest Offering: Associate Degree
Program: Occupational
Accreditation: NW, ACFEI, DA, DH, SURGT

01 President .... Dr. Patricia MCKEOWN
04 Exec Assistant to the President .... Ms. Ronda LAUGHLIN
05 Int Vice President of Instruction .... Ms. Carol LAGER
32 Vice President of Student Services .... Dr. Richard MEIER
11 VP of Administrative Services .... Ms. Debra JONES
72 Dean of Professional Technical Educ .... Mr. Rob COSTELLO
30 Exec Director College Advancement .... Ms. Mary HUMPHRIES
15 Director Human Resources .... Vacant
37 Director Financial Aid .... Mr. Mike FENTRESS
06 Director Registration/Enrollment .... Ms. Joan KAMMERZELL
13 Dir Computer/Inform Support Svcs .... Mr. Curtis PERERA
08 Director Library .... Ms. Jane BLUME
18 Chief Facilities/Physical Plant .... Mr. David JUNGKUNTZ
26 Director of Communications .... Ms. Marni Saling MAYER

Big Bend Community College (D)

7662 Chanute Street NE, Moses Lake WA 98837-3299
County: Grant FICE Identification: 003770
Unit ID: 234711
Telephone: (509) 793-2222 Carnegie Class: Assoc/Pub-R-M
FAX Number: (509) 762-6329 Calendar System: Quarter
URL: www.bigbend.edu
Established: 1962 Annual Undergrad Tuition & Fees (In-State): $3,500
Enrollment: 2,743 Coed
Affiliation or Control: State IRS Status: 501(c)3
Highest Offering: Associate Degree
Program: Occupational; 2-Year Principally Bachelor's Creditable
Accreditation: NW, ADNUR

01 President .... Dr. William C. BONAUDI
10 Vice Pres Administrative Services .... Ms. Gail HAMBURG
05 Vice Pres Instruction/Student Svcs .... Mr. Bob MOHRBACHER
15 VP of Human Resources & Labor .... Mrs. Holly MOOS
75 Dean Prof Technical Education .... Mr. Clyde RASMUSSEN
49 Dean of Arts & Sciences .... Ms. Kara GARRETT
53 Dean Educ/Health/Language Skills .... Vacant
32 Assoc VP of Student Services .... Ms. Candis LACHER
35 Director of Student Programs .... Ms. Kim JACKSON
37 Director of Financial Aid .... Mr. Andre GUZMAN
08 Dean of Library Resources .... Mr. Tim FUHRMAN
41 Director of Athletics .... Mr. Preston WILKS
06 Registrar .... Ms. Candis LACHER
102 Dir Inst Advancement/Exec Dir Found .... Mr. Douglas P. SLY
27 Publication & Information Director .... Ms. Autumn DIETRICH
21 Director of Business Services .... Ms. Charlene RIOS
40 Director of Bookstore .... Mrs. Caren COURTWRIGHT
18 Chief Facilities/Physical Plant .... Ms. Gail HAMBURG
96 Director of Purchasing .... Ms. Kathy ARITA
39 Residence Hall Coordinator .... Mr. Hugh SCHULTE
09 Dean of Institutional Research .... Ms. Valerie KIRKWOOD

Carrington College - Spokane (E)

10102 E Knox Ave., Suite 200, Spokane WA 99206-4187
County: Spokane Identification: 666385
Unit ID: 439118
Telephone: (509) 532-8888 Carnegie Class: Not Classified
FAX Number: (509) 533-5983 Calendar System: Other
URL: www.carrington.edu
Established: 1976 Annual Undergrad Tuition & Fees: $13,295
Enrollment: 820 Coed
Affiliation or Control: Proprietary IRS Status: Proprietary
Highest Offering: Associate Degree
Program: Occupational; 2-Year Principally Bachelor's Creditable
Accreditation: ACICS, MAAB, RAD

01 Executive Campus Director .... Mr. Peter TENNEY

Cascadia Community College (F)

18345 Campus Way, NE, Bothell WA 98011-8205
County: King FICE Identification: 034835
Unit ID: 439190
Telephone: (425) 352-8000 Carnegie Class: Assoc/Pub-S-SC
FAX Number: (425) 352-8313 Calendar System: Quarter
URL: www.cascadia.edu
Established: 2000 Annual Undergrad Tuition & Fees (In-District): $3,543
Enrollment: 3,590 Coed
Affiliation or Control: State/Local IRS Status: Exempt
Highest Offering: Associate Degree
Program: 2-Year Principally Bachelor's Creditable
Accreditation: NW

01 President .... Dr. Eric MURRAY
05 Vice President Academic Affs .... Vacant
20 Dean for Academic Affairs .... Mr. Walter HUDSICK
06 Registrar .... Ms. Bonnie ELLIS
09 Dir Institutional Research .... Ms. Susan HAMILTON
10 Chief Business Officer .... Mr. Terrence HSIAO
15 Director Personnel Services .... Ms. Gina LORENZ
18 Chief Facilities/Physical Plant .... Ms. Dee SLINEY
21 Associate Business Officer .... Mr. Larry CLARK
27 Chief Information Officer .... Ms. Meagan WALKER
32 Interim Chief Student Life Officer .... Mr. Brian NOVAK
37 Director Student Financial Aid .... Ms. Sybil SMITH
30 Chief Development .... Ms. Rebecca HASTINGS
38 Director Student Counseling .... Ms. Ana BLACKSTAD
84 Director Enrollment Management .... Ms. Erin BLAKENEY

Central Washington University (G)

400 E University Way, Ellensburg WA 98926-7501
County: Kittitas FICE Identification: 003771
Unit ID: 234827
Telephone: (509) 963-1111 Carnegie Class: Master's M
FAX Number: (509) 963-3206 Calendar System: Quarter
URL: www.cwu.edu
Established: 1890 Annual Undergrad Tuition & Fees (In-State): $7,959
Enrollment: 11,063 Coed
Affiliation or Control: State IRS Status: 501(c)3
Highest Offering: Master's
Program: Liberal Arts And General; Teacher Preparatory; Professional
Accreditation: NW, BUS, CACREP, CONST, DIETD, DIETI, EMT, ENGT, IPSY, MUS

01 President .... Dr. James L. GAUDINO
05 Provost/VP Academic & Student Life .... Dr. Marilyn LEVINE
10 CFO/VP Business & Financial Affairs .... Mr. George CLARK
100 Chief of Staff .... Ms. Sherer HOLTER
20 Assoc VP Undergraduate Studies .... Mr. Tracy PELLETT
21 Int Dir Organizational Effectivenes .... Mr. Edward DAY
84 Assoc VP Enrollment Management .... Mr. John SWINEY
32 Dean of Students .... Dr. Ethan BERGMAN
35 Assoc Dean Student Life .... Mr. Keith M. CHAMPAGNE
88 Assoc Dean Student Achievement .... Mr. Jesse NELSON
18 Asst VP for Facilities Management .... Mr. Bill VERTREES
15 Asst VP HR/Faculty Relations .... Mr. Dennis DEFA
14 Asst Vice Pres for Technology Svcs .... Mr. Carmen RAHM
58 Dean Graduate Studies .... Dr. Wayne QUIRK
49 Dean College of Arts/Humanities .... Dr. Marji MORGAN
50 Dean College of Business .... Dr. Roy SAVOIAN
53 Interim Dean Col Educ/Prof Studies .... Ms. Connie LAMBERT
83 Interim Dean Col of the Sciences .... Dr. Kirk JOHNSON
08 Dean of Library Services .... Dr. Patricia CUTRIGHT
30 Exec Dir/University Advancement .... Mr. Forrest RODGERS
85 Exec Dir Intl Stds & Programs .... Dr. Michael LAUNIUS
06 Registrar .... Ms. Tracy TERRELL
22 Director Equal Opportunity .... Ms. Staci SLEIGH-LAYMAN
41 Director Athletics .... Mr. Jack BISHOP
51 Director Continuing Education .... Mr. Kevin NEMETH
12 Asst VP University Centers .... Ms. Margaret BADGLEY
07 Director of Admissions .... Ms. Kathy GAER-CARLTON
37 Director of Financial Aid .... Ms. Agnes F. CANEDO
39 Assc Dean Univ Housing/Stdnt Living .... Mr. Richard DESHIELDS
19 Director Public Safety .... Mr. Michael LUVERA
26 Director Public Affairs .... Ms. Linda SCHACTLER

Centralia College (H)

600 Centralia College Boulevard,
Centralia WA 98531-4035
County: Lewis FICE Identification: 003772
Unit ID: 234845
Telephone: (360) 736-9391 Carnegie Class: Assoc/Pub-R-M
FAX Number: (360) 330-7573 Calendar System: Quarter
URL: www.centralia.edu
Established: 1925 Annual Undergrad Tuition & Fees (In-State): $3,542
Enrollment: 2,363 Coed
Affiliation or Control: State IRS Status: 501(c)3
Highest Offering: Associate Degree
Program: Occupational; 2-Year Principally Bachelor's Creditable
Accreditation: NW

01 President .... Dr. James M. WALTON
05 Vice President Instruction .... Mr. John MARTENS
32 Vice President of Students .... Dr. Michael GRUBIAK
10 Vice Pres Finance/Administration .... Mr. Steve WARD
15 VP Human Resources/Legal Affs .... Mr. Chris BAILEY
20 Dean Workforce Education .... Ms. Durrelle SULLIVAN
08 Dean of Library Services/E-Learning .... Ms. Sue GALLAWAY
88 Dean of Academic Transfer Programs .... T. R. GRATZ
09 Director of Institutional Research .... Ms. Mary Ann MEDLIN
103 Dir WorkFirst & Worker Retraining .... Ms. Beverley GESTRINE
84 Director of Enrollment Services .... Ms. Qy-Ana MANNING
37 Director of Financial Aid .... Ms. Tracy DAHL
13 Director Information Technology .... Mr. Patrick ALLISON
41 Director of Sports Programs .... Mr. Bob PETERS
29 Director Alumni Relations .... Ms. Julie JOHNSON
96 Director of Purchasing .... Ms. Bonnie MYER
26 Dir College Relations & Events Plng .... Mr. Don FREY
40 Bookstore Manager .... Ms. Tammy STRODEMIER
97 Program Coordinator .... Ms. Joanie ROGERSON

City University of Seattle (I)

11900 NE First Street, Bellevue WA 98005-3030
County: King FICE Identification: 013022
Unit ID: 234915
Telephone: (425) 637-1010 Carnegie Class: Master's L
FAX Number: (425) 709-7699 Calendar System: Quarter
URL: www.cityu.edu
Established: 1973 Annual Undergrad Tuition & Fees: $17,190
Enrollment: 2,644 Coed
Affiliation or Control: Independent Non-Profit IRS Status: 501(c)3
Highest Offering: Master's
Program: Liberal Arts And General; Teacher Preparatory; Professional; Business Emphasis
Accreditation: NW

01 President .... Mr. E. Lee GORSUCH, II
03 Vice President .... Ms. Melissa E. MECHAM
05 Provost .... Dr. Steven OLSWANG
10 CFO/VP Finance & Administration .... Mr. Bruce K. BRYANT
30 Vice President for Univ Advancement .... Mr. Christopher ROSS
88 Vice President European Operations .... Dr. Jan REBRO

50 Dean School of Management .... Dr. Kurt KIRSTEIN
53 Dean School of Education .... Ms. Judy HINRICHS
20 Dean Academic Affs-Europe .... Mr. David GRIFFIN
09 Director of Inst Effectiveness .... Dr. Elizabeth FOUNTAIN
101 Exec Asst Ofc of the President .... Ms. Lisa D. CORCORAN
06 Registrar .... Ms. Mary R. BELKNAP
21 Director of Finance .... Ms. Maria KREY
15 Director of Human Resources .... Mr. Timothy SPRAKE
08 Director Library Services .... Ms. Mary MARA
37 Director Student Financial Svcs .... Ms. Jean L. ROBERTS
29 Alumni Relations Manager .... Mr. Alex WEBSTER
90 Director of Information Technology .... Mr. Kevin H. BROWN
88 Veterans Affairs Officer .... Ms. Ry-Yon SAO
84 Recruitment Director .... Ms. Alyssa BORELLI
18 Facilities Manager .... Mr. Troy CRABREE

† Granted candidacy at the Doctorate level.

Clark College (A)

1933 Fort Vancouver Way, Vancouver WA 98663-3598
County: Clark FICE Identification: 003773
Unit ID: 234933
Telephone: (360) 992-2000 Carnegie Class: Assoc/Pub-U-SC
FAX Number: (360) 992-2871 Calendar System: Quarter
URL: www.clark.edu
Established: 1933 Annual Undergrad Tuition & Fees (In-State): $3,377
Enrollment: 16,054 Coed
Affiliation or Control: State IRS Status: 501(c)3
Highest Offering: Associate Degree
Program: Occupational; 2-Year Principally Bachelor's Creditable
Accreditation: NW, ADNUR, DH, EMT, MAC

01 President .... Mr. Robert KNIGHT
05 Int Vice President of Instruction .... Dr. Tim COOK
32 Vice President of Student Affairs .... Mr. William BELDON
11 Vice President of Admin Services .... Mr. Bob WILLIAMSON
16 Assoc Vice Pres of Human Resources .... Ms. Darcy ROURK
45 Assoc VP Planning/Instnl Effective .... Ms. Shanda DIEHL
51 Assoc VP Corp & Continuing Educ .... Vacant
84 Dean of Enrollment Services .... Mr. Alex MONTOYA
50 Dean Business/Technology .... Mr. Ted KOTSAKIS
79 Dean English/Comm/Hum/Basic Educ .... Dr. Ray KORPI
76 Dean Life Sci/Health & Phys Ed .... Mr. Blake BOWERS
83 Dean Social Sciences/Fine Arts .... Mr. Miles JACKSON
66 Assoc Dean of Nursing .... Ms. Jean DONOVAN
52 Director of Dental Hygiene .... Ms. Donna WITTMAYER
04 Exec Assistant to the President .... Ms. Leigh KENT
06 Registrar .... Ms. Kimberly MARSHEL
41 Interim Director of Athletics .... Mr. Denny HUSTON
15 Associate Director Human Resources .... Ms. Sue WILLIAMS
08 Dir of Library Services .... Ms. Michelle BAGLEY
13 Director of Computing Services .... Mr. Phil SHEEHAN
18 Director of Plant Services .... Mr. Jim GREEN
26 Exec Director of Communications .... Ms. Barbara KERR
36 Director Career/Employment Services .... Ms. Edie BLAKELY
37 Director of Financial Aid .... Ms. Karen DRISCOLL
07 Director of Admissions .... Ms. Sheryl ANDERSON
10 Director of Business Services .... Ms. Karen WYNKOOP
35 Dir Stdnt Life/Multicult Stdnt Affs .... Ms. Sarah GRUHLER
38 Director Advising & Counseling .... Mr. Andrew LONG
25 Director of Grant Development .... Ms. Shelley DAS
28 Director of Equity & Diversity .... Vacant
19 Director of Security & Safety .... Mr. Ken PACHECO
85 International Recruitment Manager .... Ms. Jody SHULNAK
40 Bookstore Manager .... Ms. Monica KNOWLES
88 Mature Learning & Travel Stds Mgr .... Ms. Tracy REILLY-KELLY
96 Purchasing Manager .... Ms. Lisa NELSON

Clover Park Technical College (B)

4500 Steilacoom Boulevard, SW,
Lakewood WA 98499-4004
County: Pierce FICE Identification: 005752
Unit ID: 234951
Telephone: (253) 589-5800 Carnegie Class: Assoc/Pub-S-MC
FAX Number: (253) 589-5601 Calendar System: Quarter
URL: www.cptc.edu
Established: 1942 Annual Undergrad Tuition & Fees (In-State): $6,307
Enrollment: 7,356 Coed
Affiliation or Control: State IRS Status: 501(c)3
Highest Offering: Associate Degree
Program: Occupational; 2-Year Principally Bachelor's Creditable; Technical Emphasis
Accreditation: NW, DA, HT, MAC, MLTAD, SURGT

01 President .... Dr. John W. WALSTRUM
04 Executive Assistant .... Cherie STEELE
05 Vice President Instruction .... Lori BANASZAK
10 Int Vice President Finance & Budget .... Kathy YOST
32 Vice President Student Services .... June STACEY-CLEMONS
26 VP Operations & College Relations .... Amy GOINGS
20 Associate Vice Pres Instruction .... Joyce LOVEDAY
16 Chief Human Res/Legal Affairs Off .... James TUTTLE
103 Dean of Workforce Development .... Mabel EDMONDS
13 Dir Information Technology .... Michael TAYLOR
37 Interim Director Financial Aid .... Wendy JOSEPH
19 Director Plant Services & Security .... Mike ANDERSON
12 Dir Northwest Career/Technical HS .... Loren DAVIS
56 Director Extended Learning .... Vacant
84 Director of Enrollment Services .... Judy MACDOUGALL
21 Controller .... Vacant

96 Purchasing Coord/Capital Projects .... Kate PURATICH
26 Marketing/Outreach Coordinator .... Janet HOLM
36 WorkFirst Special Projects Coord .... Christeen CROUCHET
09 Institutional Researcher .... Cynthia REQUA
40 Bookstore Coordinator .... Donna KOEHLER
18 Custodial Maintenance Coordinator .... Morris MILLER
06 Registrar .... Judy MACDOUGALL

Columbia Basin College (C)

2600 N 20th Avenue, Pasco WA 99301-3397
County: Franklin FICE Identification: 003774
Unit ID: 234979
Telephone: (509) 547-0511 Carnegie Class: Assoc/Pub-R-L
FAX Number: (509) 546-0401 Calendar System: Quarter
URL: www.columbiabasin.edu
Established: 1955 Annual Undergrad Tuition & Fees (In-State): $3,920
Enrollment: 7,232 Coed
Affiliation or Control: State IRS Status: 170(c)1
Highest Offering: Baccalaureate
Program: Occupational; 2-Year Principally Bachelor's Creditable
Accreditation: NW, ADNUR, DH, EMT, SURGT

01 President .... Dr. Richard CUMMINS
05 Vice President Instruction .... Mr. Curt FREED
11 Vice President of Administration .... Mr. William SARACENO
28 Vice Pres of Diversity/Outreach .... Mr. Martin VALADEZ
32 Vice President of Student Services .... Dr. Madeline JEFFS
15 VP Human Resources/Legal Affairs .... Ms. Camilla GLATT
21 Assist VP Fiscal Operations .... Mr. Mike GRINNELL
09 Dean for Institutional Effectivenes .... Dr. Joe MONTGOMERY
49 Dean Arts & Humanities .... Mr. Bill MCKAY
62 Dean Library Services .... Vacant
102 Executive Director Foundation .... Mr. Robert ROSSELLI
36 Dean Career Development .... Mr. Derek BRANDES
84 Registrar/Assoc Dean Enroll Svcs .... Ms. Patricia CAMPBELL
13 Director of Technology Services .... Mr. Brian DEXTER
40 Bookstore Director .... Ms. Debra BRUCE
18 Director of Plant Operations .... Mr. Chuck SCHMIDT
41 Athletic Director .... Mr. Scott ROGERS
26 Director of Communications .... Mr. Frank MURRAY
35 Director of Student Programs .... Ms. Alice SCHLEGEL
37 Director Student Financial Aid .... Ms. Ceci RATLIFF
96 Director of Purchasing .... Mr. Paul PAPIESE
06 Associate Registrar .... Ms. Donna KORSTAD

*Community Colleges of Spokane District 17 (D)

501 N Riverpoint Boulevard, Ste 126,
Spokane WA 99217-6000
County: Spokane FICE Identification: 010784
Telephone: (509) 434-5107 Carnegie Class: N/A
FAX Number: (509) 434-5120
URL: www.ccs.spokane.edu

01 Chancellor .... Dr. Christine JOHNSON
12 Pres Spokane Community College .... Dr. Joe DUNLAP
12 Int Pres Spokane Falls Comm College .... Ms. Pam PRAEGER
03 Chief Exec Ofcr Inst Extnd Lrng .... Mr. Scott MORGAN
05 Vice President of Learning SCC .... Dr. Carol RIESENBERG
05 Int Vice President of Learning SFCC .... Dr. Jim MINKLER
32 Vice Pres of Student Services SCC .... Dr. Terri M. MCKENZIE
32 VP of Student Services SFCC .... Mr. Alex ROBERTS
10 Chief Financial Officer .... Mr. Keith FOSTER
11 Chief Administration Officer .... Mr. Greg L. STEVENS
20 Int District Dir of Academic Svcs .... Dr. Janet GULLICKSON
26 Public Information Officer .... Ms. Anne M. TUCKER
41 Dist Director of Athletics PE/Rec .... Mr. Ken BURRUS
13 District Director Info Systems .... Mr. Dick HOL
102 Executive Director CCS Foundation .... Mr. Tony D. HIGLEY
07 District Director of Outreach .... Vacant
40 Director College Bookstores .... Ms. Catherine R. SCOTT
18 District Director of Facilities .... Mr. Dennis DUNHAM
96 Purchasing Manager .... Mr. Rod RAMER

*Spokane Community College (E)

North 1810 Greene Street, Spokane WA 99217-5499
County: Spokane FICE Identification: 003793
Unit ID: 236692
Telephone: (509) 533-7000 Carnegie Class: Assoc/Pub-R-L
FAX Number: (509) 533-8839 Calendar System: Quarter
URL: www.scc.spokane.edu
Established: 1963 Annual Undergrad Tuition & Fees (In-State): $3,601
Enrollment: 7,100 Coed
Affiliation or Control: State IRS Status: 501(c)3
Highest Offering: Associate Degree
Program: Occupational; 2-Year Principally Bachelor's Creditable; Technical Emphasis
Accreditation: NW, ACFEI, CVT, DA, DMS, EMT, MAC, RAD, SURGT

00 District Chancellor .... Dr. Christine JOHNSON
02 President .... Dr. Joe DUNLAP
05 Vice President Learning .... Ms. Carol RIESENBERG
32 VP Student/Instructional Services .... Dr. Terri MCKENZIE
84 Interim Dean of Enrollment Services .... Mr. Michael LENKER
49 Dean Arts & Sciences .... Dr. Virginia TOMLINSON
50 Dean Business/Hospitality/Info Tech .... Ms. Kathleen SILVAS
75 Dean for Technical Education .... Mr. Dave COX
76 Dean Health & Environmental Science .... Vacant

88 Dean Instructional Services .... Ms. Mary CARR
85 Dean of International Programs .... Mr. Thomas PATTERSON
35 Assoc Dean Student Development .... Vacant
41 Director Athletics/PE/Recreation .... Mr. Ken BURRUS
10 Chief Financial Officer .... Mr. Keith FOSTER
06 Registrar .... Ms. Robin YOUNG
37 Director Financial Aid .... Ms. Tammy ZIBELL
40 Director of College Bookstores .... Ms. Cathy SCOTT
15 Chief Human Resources Ofcr .... Mr. Greg STEVENS
26 Chief Public Relations Officer .... Ms. Anne TUCKER
30 District Development Officer .... Mr. Tony HIGLEY
20 District Academic Services Officer .... Dr. Janet GULLICKSON
28 Multicultural Director .... Ms. Kitara MCCLURE
29 Director Alumni Relations .... Ms. Janice EATHERTON
38 Director Student Counseling .... Vacant
96 Director of Purchasing .... Mr. Rodney RAMER
09 Manager Institutional Effectiveness .... Vacant
90 Computer Svcs Consult Supervisor .... Ms. Jo Lynne SHERMAN

*Spokane Falls Community College (F)

3410 W Fort George Wright Drive,
Spokane WA 99224-5288
County: Spokane FICE Identification: 009544
Unit ID: 236708
Telephone: (509) 533-3500 Carnegie Class: Assoc/Pub-R-L
FAX Number: (509) 533-3237 Calendar System: Quarter
URL: www.spokanefalls.edu
Established: 1967 Annual Undergrad Tuition & Fees (In-State): $3,495
Enrollment: 6,153 Coed
Affiliation or Control: State IRS Status: 501(c)3
Highest Offering: Associate Degree
Program: Occupational; 2-Year Principally Bachelor's Creditable
Accreditation: NW, PTAA

02 President .... Ms. Pamela TAJIMA PRAEGER
04 Exec Asst to the Pres .... Ms. Ann KIENHOLZ JURCEVICH
05 Vice President of Learning .... Dr. James MINKLER
32 Dean Student Life & Admin Services .... Mr. Alex ROBERTS
81 Dean Computing/Math & Science .... Mr. James BRADY
22 Dn Equity/Diversity/Spec Initiative .... Vacant
83 Dean Soc Science/Acad Initiatives .... Dr. Lisa AVERY
79 Dn Humanities/Acad Initiatives .... Mr. Glen COSBY
08 Dean Library/Instruct Support Svcs .... Ms. Mary Ann GOODWIN
103 Dean Bus/Prof Stds/Workforce .... Dr. Frank POWERS
68 Dean Physical Education .... Mr. Ken BURRUS
85 Dean of International Programs .... Dr. Tom PATTERSON
79 Dean Visual & Performing Arts .... Mr. Daniel O. WENGER
84 Assoc Dean Enrollment Services .... Mr. Steven BAYS
14 IT Manager .... Mr. Rod LARSE
38 Chair of Student Counseling .... Mr. Loren PEMBERTON
35 College Director Student Life .... Mr. Gregory ROBERTS
19 Security & Safety Supervisor .... Mr. Kenneth DEMELLO
37 Assoc Dean Fin Aid/Student Employ .... Ms. Jille SHANKAR
36 Assoc Dn Stdnt Success/Counsel/Adv .... Ms. Chrissy JONES
88 Dir Recruit/New Stdnt Entry Center .... Ms. Penny BUTTERS
30 Exec Director CCS Foundation .... Mr. Tony HIGLEY
51 Director Marketing/Outreach .... Ms. Penny BUTTERS
15 Chief Human Resources Officer .... Mr. Greg STEVENS
18 Director of Facilities .... Mr. Dennis DUNHAM
26 Public Information Officer .... Ms. Anne TUCKER
96 Director of Purchasing .... Mr. Rod RAMER
09 Mgr of Institutional Effectiveness .... Vacant

Cornish College of the Arts (G)

1000 Lenora Street, Seattle WA 98121-2707
County: King FICE Identification: 012315
Unit ID: 235024
Telephone: (206) 726-5151 Carnegie Class: Spec/Arts
FAX Number: (206) 720-1011 Calendar System: Semester
URL: www.cornish.edu
Established: 1914 Annual Undergrad Tuition & Fees: $30,880
Enrollment: 836 Coed
Affiliation or Control: Independent Non-Profit IRS Status: 501(c)3
Highest Offering: Baccalaureate
Program: Liberal Arts And General; Fine Arts Emphasis
Accreditation: NW, ART

01 President .... Dr. Nancy J. USCHER
05 Provost .... Dr. Lois A. HARRIS
30 Vice Pres Institutional Advancement .... Ms. Jane C. EWING
10 Chief Finance Officer .... Mr. Jeffrey R. RIDDELL
11 Chief Operations Officer .... Ms. Vicki CLAYTON
84 Dean of Enrollment Management .... Mr. Gary CRAIG
57 Interim Art Department Chairperson .... Ms. Bonnie BIGGS
57 Dance Department Chairperson .... Ms. Kathryn DANIELS
57 Design Department Chairperson .... Mr. Grant DONESKY
64 Music Department Chairperson .... Mr. Kent DEVEREAUX
57 Performance Production Dept Chair .... Mr. Dave TOSTI-LANE
57 Theater Department Chairperson .... Mr. Richard E T. WHITE
79 Humanities & Sciences Dept Chair .... Ms. Chris KELLETT
20 Associate Provost .... Ms. Jenifer WARD
32 Dean of Student Affairs .... Mr. Jerry HEKKEL
06 Registrar .... Ms. Adrienne M. BOLYARD
26 Director of Communications .... Ms. Karen BYSTROM
38 Director of Counseling Services .... Ms. Lori KOSHORK
15 Director of Human Resources .... Ms. Beverly PAGE
13 Director of Information Technology .... Mr. Mark LEDESMA
21 Controller .... Ms. Tina CHAMBERLAIN
08 Director of Library Services .... Ms. Hollis NEAR
30 Dir of Development/Alumni Relations .... Ms. Chris STOLLERY

7 Director of Admissions .... Ms. Sharron STARLING
8 Facilities Director .... Ms. Jenny FRAZIER
8 Business & Student Accounts Manager .... Mr. Jeff WYBORNY
9 Dir of Campus Safety & Security .... Mr. Brandon BIRD
7 Director of Financial Aid .... Ms. Monique THERIAULT

DeVry University - Bellevue Center (A)

600 108th Avenue NE, Suite 230,
Bellevue WA 98004-5110

County: King Identification: 666223
Unit ID: 440703
Telephone: (425) 455-2242 Carnegie Class: Not Classified
FAX Number: (425) 455-2322 Calendar System: Semester
URL: www.devry.edu
Established: 1999 Annual Undergrad Tuition & Fees: $15,294
Enrollment: 270 Coed
Affiliation or Control: Proprietary IRS Status: Proprietary
Highest Offering: Master's
Program: Occupational; Professional; Business Emphasis
Accreditation: &NH

01 Center Dean .... Yana TASKAR

† Regional accreditation is carried under the parent institution in Downers Grove, IL.

DeVry University - Federal Way Campus (B)

3600 S 344th Way, Federal Way WA 98001-9558

County: King Identification: 666224
Unit ID: 440545
Telephone: (253) 943-2800 Carnegie Class: Master's S
FAX Number: (253) 943-3295 Calendar System: Semester
URL: www.devry.edu
Established: 1931 Annual Undergrad Tuition & Fees: $15,294
Enrollment: 1,008 Coed
Affiliation or Control: Proprietary IRS Status: Proprietary
Highest Offering: Master's
Program: Occupational; Professional; Business Emphasis
Accreditation: &NH, ENGT

01 Metro President .... Ms. Maria DEZENBERG
05 Dean of Academic Affairs .... Mr. Bob DANIELLE
07 Senior Director of Admissions .... Ms. Michelle VANDERBILT
37 Director of Student Finance .... Ms. Jill PETRONE
97 Dean of General Education .... Ms. Julie BARBADILLO
06 Registrar .... Ms. Katrina ORCHARD
15 HR Business Partner .... Vacant
32 Dean of Career & Student Services .... Ms. Annette UNCANGCO
08 Director of Library Services .... Mr. Daniel LIESTMAN
77 Dean of Technology Programs .... Mr. Richard THOMAS
54 Dean of Electronics .... Mr. Jimmie RUSSELL

† Regional accreditation is carried under the parent institution in Downers Grove, IL.

DigiPen Institute of Technology (C)

9931 Willows Road, NE, Redmond WA 98052

FICE Identification: 037243
Unit ID: 443410
Telephone: (425) 558-0299 Carnegie Class: Bac/Diverse
FAX Number: (425) 558-0378 Calendar System: Semester
URL: www.digipen.edu
Established: 1988 Annual Undergrad Tuition & Fees: $15,450
Enrollment: 892 Coed
Affiliation or Control: Proprietary IRS Status: Proprietary
Highest Offering: Master's
Program: Professional; Technical Emphasis
Accreditation: ACCSC

01 President .... Mr. Claude COMAIR
03 Chief Operating Officer .... Mr. Jason Y. CHU
11 Sr Vice President of Administration ..... Ms. Meighan SHOESMITH
10 Sr Vice President of Operations .... Mr. Raymond YAN
37 Director of Financial Aid .... Ms. Kimberly KING
32 Director of Student Services .... Mr. Gordon DUTRISAC
07 Director of Admissions .... Ms. Angela KUGLER

Eastern Washington University (D)

526 5th Street, Cheney WA 99004-1619

County: Spokane FICE Identification: 003775
Unit ID: 235097
Telephone: (509) 359-6200 Carnegie Class: Master's L
FAX Number: (509) 359-6927 Calendar System: Quarter
URL: www.ewu.edu
Established: 1882 Annual Undergrad Tuition & Fees (In-State): $6,729
Enrollment: 11,534 Coed
Affiliation or Control: State IRS Status: 501(c)3
Highest Offering: Doctorate
Program: Liberal Arts And General; Teacher Preparatory; Professional
Accreditation: NW, BUS, CACREP, CEA, CS, DH, ENG, ENGT, MUS, NRPA, NURSE, OT, PLNG, PTA, SP, SW

01 President .... Dr. Rodolfo AREVALO
05 Vice Pres/Prov Academic Affs .... Dr. Rex FULLER
10 Vice President for Business/Finance .... Ms. Mary VOVES
32 Vice President for Student Affairs . Ms. Stacey MORGAN FOSTER
30 Vice President of Advancement .... Mr. Michael WESTFALL
20 Vice Prov Academic Res/Admin/Plng .... Dr. Linda KIEFFER
58 Vice Prov/Dean Grad/Undergrad Std .... Dr. Ronald DALLA
08 Dean of Libraries .... Mr. Richard WILSON
84 Assoc VP Enrollment Services .... Dr. Lawrence BRIGGS
41 Director Intercollegiate Athletics .... Mr. William CHAVES
21 Assoc VP Finance/Chief Fin Officer .... Ms. Toni HABEGGER
18 Assoc Vice Pres for Facilities .... Mr. Shawn KING
04 Exec Assistant to the President/BOT .... Ms. Catherine GOFF
100 Assoc to the President .... Ms. Laurie CONNELLY
86 Director of Government Relations .... Mr. David BURI
36 Assoc Dir Career Services Center .... Ms. Virginia HINCH
92 Director of University Honors .... Dr. Dana ELDER
07 Director of Admissions .... Ms. Shannon CARR
37 Director of Fin Aid & Scholarships .... Mr. Bruce DEFRATES
40 Dir of Bookstore/Pence Union Bldg .... Mr. Robert ANDERSON
85 Int Prog Dir Div of Educ Outreach . Ms. Sara SEXTON-JOHNSON
06 Director of Registration & Records .... Ms. Debra FOCKLER
09 Director of Institutional Research .... Dr. Colin ORMSBY
15 Director of Human Resources .... Ms. Jolynn ROGERS
29 Director of Alumni Advancement .... Ms. Lisa POPLAWSKI
96 Director Purchasing .... Ms. Susan BROWN
39 Director Housing/Residential Life .... Ms. Toni TAYLOR
38 Director Counseling & Psych Svcs .... Dr. Robert QUACKENBUSH
19 Director Public Safety/Chief Police ..... Chief Timothy L. WALTERS
44 Assoc Director of Annual Giving .... Ms. Pat SPANJER
27 Media Relations Specialist .... Mr. David MEANY
22 Dir Equal Opp/Affirm Action Coord .... Mrs. Gayla WRIGHT
50 Int Dean College of Business Admin .... Dr. Niel ZIMMERMAN
49 Dean College Arts/Letters/Education .... Dr. Lynn BRIGGS
83 Dean Col Social/Behav Sci/Soc Work .... Dr. Vickie SHIELDS
81 Dean Col Science Math & Technology .... Dr. Judd CASE
66 Dean Intercol Center Nursing Educ ...... Dr. Patricia BUTTERFIELD
35 Dean of Student Life .... Dr. Al THOMPSON

Edmonds Community College (E)

20000 68th Avenue W, Lynnwood WA 98036-5999

County: Snohomish FICE Identification: 005001
Unit ID: 235103
Telephone: (425) 640-1459 Carnegie Class: Assoc/Pub-S-MC
FAX Number: (425) 771-3366 Calendar System: Quarter
URL: www.edcc.edu
Established: 1967 Annual Undergrad Tuition & Fees (In-State): $3,572
Enrollment: 13,399 Coed
Affiliation or Control: State IRS Status: 501(c)3
Highest Offering: Associate Degree
Program: Occupational; 2-Year Principally Bachelor's Creditable
Accreditation: NW, CONST

01 President .... Dr. Jean HERNANDEZ
05 Vice President Instruction .... Dr. Marty R. CAVALLUZZI
10 Vice Pres/Chief Financial Ofcr .... Mr. Kevin MCKAY
30 Vice Pres Col Relations/Advancement ..... Mr. John MICHAELSON
16 Vice Pres Human Resources .... Mr. Mark CASSIDY
32 Vice President Student Services .... Mr. George SMITH
103 Int VP Workforce Devel/Training .... Ms. Susan LOREEN
85 Vice Pres International Education .... Mr. David J. CORDELL
08 Dean Learning Resources .... Ms. Lauri KRAM
84 Sr Asc Dean Stdnt Enroll/Fin Svcs .... Ms. Rae-Ellen REAS
35 Sr Assoc Dean Student Life/Devel .... Ms. Nicola SMITH
36 Int Assoc Dean Stdnt Success/Reten .... Ms. Stephanie BARON
04 Executive Asst to the President .... Ms. Patty MICHAJLA
102 Exec Director College Foundation .... Ms. Chris MARX
25 Exec Dir Grants Research/Effective .... Ms. Beth NICHOLS
26 Director Communications/Marketing .... Ms. Stephanie WIEGAND
13 Int Director Information Technology .... Ms. Eva SMITH
18 Chief Facilities/Physical Plant .... Mr. Paul DOHERTY
28 Director of Equity & Diversity .... Ms. Shirley SUTTON
96 Director of Purchasing .... Ms. Marian PAANANEN
27 Public Information Officer .... Ms. Michele GRAVES
19 Director Safety & Security .... Mr. Paul DOHERTY
41 Interim Athletics Director .... Mr. Clay BLACKWOOD
85 Dir International Student Services .... Ms. Lisa THOMPSON
09 Institutional Researcher .... Ms. Pat HUFFMAN

Everest College (F)

155 Washington Ave, Ste 200, Bremerton WA 98337

County: Kitsap FICE Identification: 023001
Unit ID: 234739
Telephone: (360) 473-1120 Carnegie Class: Not Classified
FAX Number: (360) 792-2404 Calendar System: Quarter
URL: www.everest.edu
Established: 1960 Annual Undergrad Tuition & Fees: $16,649
Enrollment: 410 Coed
Affiliation or Control: Proprietary IRS Status: Proprietary
Highest Offering: Associate Degree
Program: Occupational
Accreditation: ACICS

01 President .... Ms. Janet O'CONNELL

Everest College (G)

120 NE 136th Avenue, Suite 130, Vancouver WA 98684

County: Clark Identification: 666737
Unit ID: 236993
Telephone: (360) 254-3282 Carnegie Class: Not Classified
FAX Number: (360) 254-3035 Calendar System: Other
URL: www.everest.edu/campus/vancouver
Established: 1976 Annual Undergrad Tuition & Fees: $15,771
Enrollment: 453 Coed
Affiliation or Control: Proprietary IRS Status: Proprietary
Highest Offering: Associate Degree
Program: Occupational; 2-Year Principally Bachelor's Creditable
Accreditation: ACICS

01 President .... Mr. Brad KUCHENREUTHER

† Branch campus of Everest College, Portland, OR. Tuition varies by degree program.

Everett Community College (H)

2000 Tower Street, Everett WA 98201-1390

County: Snohomish FICE Identification: 003776
Unit ID: 235149
Telephone: (425) 388-9100 Carnegie Class: Assoc/Pub-U-SC
FAX Number: (425) 388-9129 Calendar System: Quarter
URL: www.everettcc.edu
Established: 1941 Annual Undergrad Tuition & Fees (In-State): $2,876
Enrollment: 11,792 Coed
Affiliation or Control: State IRS Status: 501(c)3
Highest Offering: Associate Degree
Program: Occupational; 2-Year Principally Bachelor's Creditable
Accreditation: NW, ADNUR, MAC

01 President .... Dr. David BEYER
04 Executive Assistant to President .... Ms. Cheryl BLACKBURN
05 Vice Pres Instruction/Student Svcs .... Dr. Sandra FOWLER-HILL
30 Vice Pres of College Advancement .... Dr. John OLSON
11 Vice Pres of Administrative Svcs .... Ms. Jennifer L. HOWARD
26 Vice Pres of College Services .... Mr. Patrick SISNEROS
12 Exec Dir Univ Ctr North Puget Sound .... Dr. Christine KERLIN
83 Dean Communication/Social Sciences .... Mr. Craig LEWIS
81 Dean of Math & Science .... Mr. Al FRIEDMAN
62 Dean of Arts & Learning Resources .... Ms. Jeanne LEADER
76 Dean Health Sciences/Public Safety .... Mr. Stu C. BARGER
53 Dean of Basic & Adult Education .... Mr. Darrell MIHARA
28 Dean Student Dev/Diversity Advocacy .... Ms. Christina CASTORENA
51 Director Continuing Education .... Ms. Karen LANDRY
35 Director Student Support Services .... Ms. Jessica CAIN
84 Dean Enrollment/Student Finan Svcs .... Ms. Laurie FRANKLIN
19 Dir of Campus Safety & Security .... Mr. Bob WRIGHT
12 Exec Director of Corporate Training .... Mr. John B. BONNER
09 Director Institutional Research .... Dr. Darryl DIETER
41 Director of Athletics .... Mr. Larry WALKER
40 Director of Bookstore .... Ms. Kerri KIRK
88 Dir Center for Disability Services .... Ms. Kathy COOK
88 Program Manager A .... Ms. Joy FITZPATRICK

The Evergreen State College (I)

2700 Evergreen Parkway, NW, Olympia WA 98505-0005

County: Thurston FICE Identification: 008155
Unit ID: 235167
Telephone: (360) 867-6000 Carnegie Class: Master's S
FAX Number: (360) 867-6577 Calendar System: Quarter
URL: www.evergreen.edu
Established: 1967 Annual Undergrad Tuition & Fees (In-State): $6,903
Enrollment: 4,833 Coed
Affiliation or Control: State IRS Status: 501(c)3
Highest Offering: Master's
Program: Liberal Arts And General
Accreditation: NW

01 President .... Dr. Thomas L. PURCE
05 Vice President/Provost .... Dr. Michael ZIMMERMAN
32 Vice President Student Affairs .... Dr. Arthur COSTANTINO
10 Vice President Finance/Admin .... Mr. John HURLEY
30 Vice President College Advancement .... Ms. D. Lee HOEMANN
84 Assoc Vice Pres for Enrollmt Mgmt .... Mr. Steve HUNTER
15 Assoc Vice Pres for Human Resources ...... Ms. Laurel UZNANSKI
08 Interim Dean of Library Services .... Ms. Sarah PEDERSEN
35 Dean Student/Academic Support Svcs .... Dr. Phyllis LANE
04 Exec Assistant to the President .... Mr. John CARMICHAEL
45 Exec Dir Operational Plng/Budget .... Mr. Steve TROTTER
22 Spec Asst to Pres/Equal Opportunity .... Mr. Paul GALLEGOS
22 Civil Rights Officer .... Ms. Nicole ACK
20 Academic Dean .... Dr. Ken TABBUTT
86 Director of Government Relations .... Dr. Julie GARVER
14 Director Computing & Communications .... Mr. Aaron POWELL
26 Director of College Relations .... Mr. Todd SPRAGUE
37 Director of Financial Aid .... Ms. Tracy HALL
06 Registrar .... Ms. Andrea COKER-ANDERSON
09 Director of Institutional Research .... Ms. Laura COGHLAN
18 Director of Facilities .... Mr. Paul SMITH
21 Director of Business Services .... Mr. Collin ORR
29 Director Alumni Relations .... Ms. R.J BURT
36 Director Career Development Center .... Mr. Mychael HEUER
38 Dir Counseling & Health Services .... Ms. Elizabeth MCHUGH
96 Director of Purchasing .... Vacant
07 Director of Admissions .... Mr. Bryan GOULD
88 Sustainability Coordinator .... Mr. Scott MORGAN

Faith Evangelical College & Seminary (J)

3504 N Pearl Street, Tacoma WA 98407-2607

County: Pierce FICE Identification: 036894
Unit ID: 443049
Telephone: (253) 752-2020 Carnegie Class: Spec/Faith
FAX Number: (253) 759-1790 Calendar System: Quarter
URL: www.faithseminary.edu
Established: 1969 Annual Undergrad Tuition & Fees: $8,800
Enrollment: 250 Coed

Affiliation or Control: Interdenominational IRS Status: 501(c)3
Highest Offering: Doctorate
Program: Professional; Religious Emphasis
Accreditation: TRACS

01 President ... Dr. Michael J. ADAMS
05 Executive Dean ... Dr. James D. GIBSON
09 Dir of Institutional Effectiveness ... Dr. Eric L. RICE
07 Admissions Officer ... Mrs. Lorrie WHATELY
08 Director Information/Library Svcs ... Vacant
88 Director of Korean Studies ... Dr. Kyu H. LEE
37 Financial Aid Officer ... Ms. Debi RICE
10 Chief Financial Officer ... Mr. Donald BELL
06 Registrar ... Dr. Bruce L. BRONOSKE
27 Communications Officer ... Ms. Alison B. ADAMS

Gonzaga University (A)

502 E Boone Avenue, Spokane WA 99258-0001
County: Spokane FICE Identification: 003778
Unit ID: 235316
Telephone: (509) 313-4220 Carnegie Class: Master's L
FAX Number: (509) 313-5718 Calendar System: Semester
URL: www.gonzaga.edu
Established: 1887 Annual Undergrad Tuition & Fees: $32,430
Enrollment: 7,837 Coed
Affiliation or Control: Roman Catholic IRS Status: 501(c)3
Highest Offering: Doctorate
Program: Liberal Arts And General; Teacher Preparatory; Professional; Fine Arts Emphasis
Accreditation: NW, ANEST, BUS, BUSA, CACREP, CEA, ENG, LAW, NURSE, TED

01 President ... Dr. Thayne M. MCCULLOH
05 Academic Vice President ... Dr. Patricia OCONNELL KILLEN
03 Executive Vice President ... Mr. Earl F. MARTIN
10 Vice President for Finance ... Mr. Charles J. MURPHY
88 Vice President for Mission ... Rev. Frank CASE
32 Vice President for Student Life ... Dr. Sue D. WEITZ
30 Vice President University Relations ... Ms. Margot J. STANFIELD
20 Assoc Academic Vice President ... Dr. Raymond REYES
06 Asst Academic Vice Pres/Registrar ... Ms. Jolanta A. WEBER
15 Asst Vice President Human Resources ... Mr. Dan C. BERRYMAN
88 Assistant VP for Marketing/Comm ... Mr. Dave SONNTAG
07 Dean of Admission ... Ms. Julie A. MCCULLOH
35 Dean of Students/Judicial Affairs ... Ms. Kassi KAIN
08 Dean of Libraries ... Dr. Eileen K. BELL-GARRISON
37 Dean of Student Finance Services ... Mr. James WHITE
13 Chief Information Officer ... Mr. Chris G. GILL
26 Director Cmty/Public Relations ... Ms. Mary Joan HAHN
29 Director Alumni & Parent Programs ... Mr. Bob D. FINN
36 Director Career Center ... Dr. Mary HEITKEMPER
38 Dir Counseling/Career Assessment ... Dr. Fernando ORITZ
49 Dean Arts & Sciences ... Dr. Marc J. MANGANARO
50 Dean School of Business ... Dr. Clarence D. BARNES
88 Dean School of Prof Studies ... Vacant
53 Dean of Education ... Dr. Jon D. SUNDERLAND
54 Dean of Engineering ... Dr. Dennis R. HORN
61 Dean of Law ... Ms. Jane KORN
09 Director of Institutional Research ... Ms. Jolanta A. WEBER
40 Director Bookstore ... Mr. Scott FRANZ
41 Director of Athletics ... Mr. Michael L. ROTH
42 Director of University Ministry ... Fr. Rick H. GANZ
43 Corporation Counsel ... Mr. Michael J. CASEY
18 Director Plant Services ... Mr. Kenneth R. SAMMONS
86 Director Government Relations ... Vacant
92 Director Honors Program ... Rev. Tim R. CLANCY, SJ
96 Manager of Purchasing ... Mr. Steve M. LUNDEN
104 Director Study Abroad ... Ms. Wanda L. REYNOLDS
25 Director Sponsored Research & Pgm ... Ms. Joann WAITE
88 Coordinator of Outcomes Assessment ... Mr. Daniel K. BUBB

Grays Harbor College (B)

1620 Edward P. Smith Drive, Aberdeen WA 98520-7500
County: Grays Harbor FICE Identification: 003779
Unit ID: 235334
Telephone: (360) 532-9020 Carnegie Class: Assoc/Pub-R-M
FAX Number: (360) 538-4299 Calendar System: Quarter
URL: www.ghc.edu
Established: 1930 Annual Undergrad Tuition & Fees (In-District): $3,511
Enrollment: 3,478 Coed
Affiliation or Control: State/Local IRS Status: 501(c)3
Highest Offering: Associate Degree
Program: Occupational; 2-Year Principally Bachelor's Creditable
Accreditation: NW, ADNUR

01 President ... Dr. Edward BREWSTER
05 Vice President for Instruction ... Ms. Laurie CLARY
10 Chief Financial Officer ... Ms. Barbara MCCULLOUGH
32 Vice President for Student Services ... Dr. Arlene TORGERSEN
75 Dean of Vocational Instruction ... Mr. Mike KELLY
56 Dean Transitions Pgms/Extended Lrng ... Ms. Cindy WILSON
35 Assoc Dean for Student Services ... Ms. Nancy DEVERSE
08 Assoc Dean Library/Media Services ... Mr. Stanley W. HORTON
07 Assoc Dean of Admissions ... Ms. Nancy DE VERSE
15 Chief Human Resources Officer ... Mr. David HALVERSTADT
37 Director Student Financial Aid ... Mr. Ben BEUSS
18 Dir Campus Operations/Sfty/Security ... Mr. Tony SIMONE
38 Director of Counseling ... Ms. Melissa BARNES
30 Chief Development Officer ... Mr. Wes PETERSON
26 Director Public Relations ... Ms. Jane F. GOLDBERG
09 Director Institutional Research ... Ms. Debbie REYNVAAN

Green River Community College (C)

12401 SE 320th Street, Auburn WA 98092-3699
County: King FICE Identification: 003780
Unit ID: 235343
Telephone: (253) 833-9111 Carnegie Class: Assoc/Pub-S-MC
FAX Number: (253) 288-3470 Calendar System: Quarter
URL: www.greenriver.edu
Established: 1965 Annual Undergrad Tuition & Fees (In-State): $3,228
Enrollment: 11,136 Coed
Affiliation or Control: State IRS Status: 501(c)3
Highest Offering: Associate Degree
Program: Occupational; 2-Year Principally Bachelor's Creditable
Accreditation: NW, OTA, PTAA

01 President ... Dr. Eileen E. ELY
05 Interim VP of Instruction ... Ms. Edith BANNISTER
13 Exec Dir of Information Technology ... Ms. Camella MORGAN
10 Vice President Business Affairs ... Mr. Rick BRUMFIELD
15 Vice President for Human Resources ... Ms. Lesley HOGAN
30 Exec Director of Development/Found ... Mr. George FRASIER
32 Vice President of Student Services ... Dr. Deborah CASEY
56 Vice Pres Extended Learning ... Ms. Edith BANNISTER
85 Assoc VP of International Programs ... Mr. Ross JENNINGS
75 Exec Dn Prof/Tech Ed/Trade Tech/Bus ... Dr. Leslie HEIZER NEWQUIST
49 Dean Instr/Math/Soc Sci/Fine Arts ... Ms. Christie GILLILAND
79 Assoc Dean Instr/English/Humanities ... Ms. Joyce HAMMER
81 Assoc Dean Instr/Science ... Ms. Cathy WELLS
76 Dean of Instr/Health/Family Studies ... Dr. Lelise HEIZER NEWQUIST
88 Dean of Instr/Capital Project ... Mr. Sam BALL
88 Ast Dn Inst Lang/Acad Skill/Wellnes ... Ms. Laura GRIEP
06 Registrar ... Ms. Denise BENNATTS
37 Director of Financial Aid ... Ms. Mary EDINGTON
21 Director of Business Services ... Ms. Debbie KNIPSCHIELD
21 Controller ... Ms. Teresa COLLINS
18 Director of Facilities ... Mr. Tom WEISWEAVER
27 Exec Director of Public Information ... Mr. John RAMSEY
51 Exec Dir Cont Educ/Off-Campus Sites ... Ms. Leslie MOORE
09 Director of Research & Planning ... Ms. Fia ELIASSON-CREEK
28 Director of Diversity Services ... Mr. Jhon VALENCIA
96 Purchasing Manager ... Ms. Patty SIKORA
31 Community Relations Coordinator ... Mr. Josh GERTSMAN
19 Director of Campus Safety ... Mr. Fred A. CREEK
41 Director Athletics ... Mr. Robert KICKNER

Heritage University (D)

3240 Fort Road, Toppenish WA 98948-9599
County: Yakima FICE Identification: 003777
Unit ID: 235422
Telephone: (509) 865-8500 Carnegie Class: Master's M
FAX Number: (509) 865-4469 Calendar System: Semester
URL: www.heritage.edu
Established: 1982 Annual Undergrad Tuition & Fees: $15,480
Enrollment: 1,276 Coed
Affiliation or Control: Independent Non-Profit IRS Status: 501(c)3
Highest Offering: Master's
Program: 2-Year Principally Bachelor's Creditable; Liberal Arts And General; Teacher Preparatory; Professional
Accreditation: NW, MT, SW

01 President ... Dr. John E. BASSETT
05 Vice President Academic Affairs ... Dr. Sneh B. VEENA
20 Asst VP Academic Affs/Support Pgm ... Ms. Bertha P. ORTEGA
30 Vice President Advancement ... Mr. Michael P. MOORE
21 Controller ... Ms. Siri J. STROM
06 Registrar ... Mr. Michael BUTTREY
53 Dean of Education/Psych Division ... Mr. James BORST
18 Director Physical Plant ... Mr. Rob CARROLL
37 Director of Financial Aid ... Ms. Dianne FERNANDEZ
08 Library Director ... Mr. Bill MCCAY
13 Director Information Services ... Mr. Jim BUSH
07 Dir of Admissions & Recruitment ... Mr. Miguel PUENTE
26 Communications Officer ... Ms. Bonnie HUGHES
04 Manager Executive Offices ... Ms. Betty J. SAMPSON
09 Director of Institutional Research ... Ms. Kay BASSETT
10 Chief Business Officer ... Mr. Rick R. GAGNIER
15 Director Personnel Services ... Ms. Veronica NARANJO
49 Assoc Academic Off/Dean Arts & Sci ... Dr. Kazuhiro SONODA
44 Annual Giving Officer ... Ms. Marie CONNOLLY
32 Chief Stdnt Life Ofcr/Dir Diversity ... Ms. Melissa FILOWSKI
35 Dir Stdnt Affs/Plcmnt/Counseling ... Ms. Idalia AGUILLON
29 Director Alumni Relations ... Mr. Nathan BRITT
36 Director Student Placement ... Ms. Irma DEPRIETO
84 Director Enrollment Management ... Mr. Miguel PUENTE
96 Director of Purchasing ... Ms. Geneva SAPP
38 Counselor for Student Life ... Ms. Rose PIMOMO

Highline Community College (E)

PO Box 98000, 2400 S 240th Street,
Des Moines WA 98198-9800
County: King FICE Identification: 003781
Unit ID: 235431
Telephone: (206) 878-3710 Carnegie Class: Assoc/Pub-S-MC
FAX Number: (206) 870-3754 Calendar System: Quarter
URL: www.highline.edu
Established: 1961 Annual Undergrad Tuition & Fees (In-State): $3,542
Enrollment: 7,538 Coed
Affiliation or Control: State IRS Status: 501(c)3
Highest Offering: Associate Degree
Program: Occupational; 2-Year Principally Bachelor's Creditable
Accreditation: NW, ADNUR, MAC, POLYT

01 President ... Dr. Jack BERMINGHAM
11 Vice President for Administration ... Mr. Larry YOK
05 Vice Pres for Academic Affairs ... Mr. Jeff WAGNITZ
30 VP Inst Advancement/Cmty Rels ... Dr. Lisa SKAR
32 Vice Pres for Student Services ... Ms. Toni CASTRO
20 Dean of Instruction-Vocational ... Ms. Alice MADSEN
20 Dean of Instruction-Academics ... Dr. Rolita EZEONU
24 Dean Instructional Resources ... Ms. Monica LUCE
51 Int Dean of Extended Learning ... Dr. James PEYTON
35 Assoc Dean Student Programs ... Mr. Jonathan BROWN
84 Assoc Dean for Enrollment Services ... Ms. Kate BLIGH
37 Director Financial Aid ... Ms. Lorraine ODOM
26 Director Communications & Marketing ... Mr. Jason PRENOVOST
15 Exec Director of Human Resources ... Ms. Beth BROOKS
21 Director Financial Services ... Ms. Shirley BEAN
13 Exec Dir Administrative Technology ... Mr. Dennis COLGAN
18 Director Plant Operations ... Mr. Barry HOLLDORF
19 Director Security & Safety ... Mr. Rich NOYER
41 Director Athletics ... Mr. John DUNN
44 Director Resources & Development ... Mr. Rod STEPHENSON
09 Director Institutional Research ... Ms. Tonya BENTON
38 Director of Student Counseling ... Mr. Lance GIBSON
40 Bookstore Manager ... Ms. Laura NOLE
96 Director of Purchasing ... Ms. Dianna THIELE
06 Interim Registrar ... Ms. Debbie FAISON
07 Director of Admissions ... Ms. L. Michelle KUWASAKI
22 Dir Multicultural Svcs/Stdnt Devel ... Ms. Yoshiko HARDEN-ABE

Interface College (F)

178 South Stevens Street, Spokane WA 99201
County: Spokane Identification: 667047
Unit ID: 235495
Telephone: (509) 467-1727 Carnegie Class: Not Classified
FAX Number: (509) 467-3804 Calendar System: Semester
URL: www.interface.edu
Established: 1982 Annual Undergrad Tuition & Fees: $12,120
Enrollment: 175 Coed
Affiliation or Control: Proprietary IRS Status: Proprietary
Highest Offering: Associate Degree
Program: Occupational
Accreditation: CNCE

01 President ... Dave WILSON
03 Vice President ... Walt LEATHERS
37 Director of Financial Aid ... Rick SINCLAIR
07 Asst Director of Admissions ... Kathy HAMMONDS

International Academy of Design and Technology (G)

645 Andover Park West, Seattle WA 98188-3319
County: King Identification: 666265
Unit ID: 446808
Telephone: (206) 575-1865 Carnegie Class: Spec/Arts
FAX Number: (206) 575-1724 Calendar System: Semester
URL: www.iadtseattle.com
Established: 2004 Annual Undergrad Tuition & Fees: N/A
Enrollment: 519 Coed
Affiliation or Control: Proprietary IRS Status: Proprietary
Highest Offering: Baccalaureate
Program: Fine Arts Emphasis
Accreditation: ACICS

01 President ... Mr. Khaled SAKALLA

† Branch campus of International Academy of Design and Technology, Tampa, FL.

ITT Technical Institute (H)

1615 75th Street SW, Everett WA 98203-6261
County: Snohomish Identification: 666326
Unit ID: 414531
Telephone: (425) 583-0200 Carnegie Class: Spec/Tech
FAX Number: (425) 485-3438 Calendar System: Quarter
URL: www.itt-tech.edu
Established: 2003 Annual Undergrad Tuition & Fees: N/A
Enrollment: 549 Coed
Affiliation or Control: Proprietary IRS Status: Proprietary
Highest Offering: Baccalaureate
Program: Technical Emphasis
Accreditation: ACICS

† Branch campus of ITT Technical Institute, Seattle, WA.

ITT Technical Institute (I)

12720 Gateway Drive, Suite 100, Seattle WA 98168-2610
County: King FICE Identification: 008443
Unit ID: 235529
Telephone: (206) 244-3300 Carnegie Class: Spec/Tech
FAX Number: (206) 246-7635 Calendar System: Quarter
URL: www.itt-tech.edu
Established: 1932 Annual Undergrad Tuition & Fees: N/A
Enrollment: 494 Coed
Affiliation or Control: Proprietary IRS Status: Proprietary
Highest Offering: Baccalaureate
Program: Technical Emphasis

Accreditation: ACICS

ITT Technical Institute (A)

13518 East Indiana Avenue,
Spokane Valley WA 99216-1589

County: Spokane FICE Identification: 030718
Unit ID: 235510
Telephone: (509) 926-2900 Carnegie Class: Spec/Tech
FAX Number: (509) 926-2908 Calendar System: Quarter
URL: www.itt-tech.edu
Established: 1985 Annual Undergrad Tuition & Fees: N/A
Enrollment: 755 Coed
Affiliation or Control: Proprietary IRS Status: Proprietary
Highest Offering: Baccalaureate
Program: Technical Emphasis
Accreditation: ACICS

Lake Washington Technical College (B)

11605 132nd Avenue, NE, Kirkland WA 98034-8506

County: King FICE Identification: 005373
Unit ID: 235699
Telephone: (425) 739-8100 Carnegie Class: Assoc/Pub-S-MC
FAX Number: (425) 739-8299 Calendar System: Quarter
URL: www.lwtc.edu
Established: 1949 Annual Undergrad Tuition & Fees (In-State): $3,462
Enrollment: 5,130 Coed
Affiliation or Control: State IRS Status: 170(c)1
Highest Offering: Associate Degree
Program: Occupational; Technical Emphasis
Accreditation: NW, ACFEI, DA, DH, MAC, OTA, PTAA

01 President ... Dr. David M. WOODALL
04 Executive Asst to President ... Ms. Debbie Z. ALMSTEDT
88 Accreditation Liaison Officer ... Dr. Brinton SPRAGUE
05 Vice Pres Instructional Svcs ... Dr. Sara BURNS
53 Dean Gen Educ/Hospitality & Svcs ... Mr. Douglas J. EMORY
76 Dean Health Occup Programs ... Ms. Maria MACEDO
72 Dean Applied Design Programs ... Ms. Nancy DICK
08 Associate Dean Learning Resources ... Mr. Ed SARGENT
76 Director Phys Therapist Asst Pgm ... Ms. Molly VERSCHUYL
76 Director Occupational Therapy ... Ms. Kay BRITTINGHAM
88 Director Funeral Services ... Mr. Jack NORRELL
66 Director Nursing Programs ... Ms. Colleen HEWES
27 Chief Information Officer ... Mr. Mike POTTER
18 Director Facilities & Operations ... Mr. Tim WHEELER
21 Controller ... Ms. Debbie DEBEAUCHAMP
88 Food Service Operations Manager ... Mr. Eric SAKAI
96 Purchasing Manager ... Ms. Betty CONWELL
56 Associate Dean Extended Learning ... Ms. Lin ZHOU
26 Director Marketing ... Ms. Regine ADAMS
102 Executive Director Foundation ... Ms. Laurie AUSTIN
32 Vice President Student Services ... Mr. Dennis LONG
89 Principal/Dean High School Programs ... Ms. Kim INFINGER
37 Director Financial Aid ... Mr. Bill CHANEY
38 Dir Student Dev & Retention ... Ms. Ruby HAYDEN
103 Director Workforce Development ... Ms. Demetra BIROS
88 Director TRiO Student Support Svcs ... Dr. Patricia HUNTER
06 Director Enroll Services/Registrar ... Vacant
88 Director Title III ... Ms. Christina HARTER
88 Manager Student Programs ... Ms. Sheila WALTON
40 Manager Bookstore ... Mr. Greg LEPAGE
85 Exec Dir Global & Extended Learning ... Ms. Myung PARK
88 Associate Dean Grants ... Ms. Joy HOWLAND
30 Executive Dir College Advancement ... Ms. Terry BYINGTON
15 Executive Director Human Resources ... Mr. Gregory W. ROBERTS

† Granted candidacy at the Baccalaureate level.

Lower Columbia College (C)

PO Box 3010, Longview WA 98632-0310

County: Cowlitz FICE Identification: 003782
Unit ID: 235750
Telephone: (360) 442-2000 Carnegie Class: Assoc/Pub-R-M
FAX Number: (360) 442-2109 Calendar System: Quarter
URL: www.lowercolumbia.edu
Established: 1934 Annual Undergrad Tuition & Fees (In-State): $3,806
Enrollment: 5,247 Coed
Affiliation or Control: State IRS Status: 170(c)1
Highest Offering: Associate Degree
Program: Occupational; 2-Year Principally Bachelor's Creditable; Technical Emphasis
Accreditation: NW, ADNUR, MAC

01 President ... Mr. Christopher C. BAILEY
05 Vice President of Instruction ... Ms. Laura BRENER
11 Vice President Administrative Svcs ... Mr. Nolan WHEELER
32 Vice President for Student Success . Ms. Lisa MATYE EDWARDS
103 Dean Workforce/Continuing Educ ... Mr. Brendan GLASER
20 Dean Instructional Programs ... Mr. Jon KERR
20 Dean Instructional Programs ... Mr. Kyle HAMMON
76 Associate Dean Allied Health/Nurse ... Ms. Karen JOINER
09 Director Institutional Research ... Ms. Wendy HALL
18 Director of Campus Services ... Mr. Richard HAMILTON
102 Director of Foundation ... Ms. Margit BRUMBAUGH
41 Athletic Director ... Mr. Kirc J. ROLAND
21 Controller ... Mr. Joe QUIRK
26 Director of College Relations ... Ms. Sue GROTH
15 Director of Personnel Services ... Mr. Nolan WHEELER
37 Financial Aid Officer ... Ms. Marisa GREEAR
08 Director of Library Services ... Mr. Jon KERR
13 Director of Information Technology ... Mr. Brandon RAY
40 Director of Bookstore ... Ms. Debbie CLEVELAND
07 Director of Admissions/Registrar ... Ms. Lynn LAWRENCE
10 Chief Business Officer ... Mr. Nolan WHEELER
84 Director Enrollment Management ... Ms. Lisa MATYE EDWARDS
96 Director of Purchasing ... Ms. Sherry GOHN
04 Executive Assistant ... Ms. Linda J. CLARK

Northwest Aviation College (D)

506 23rd Street NE, Auburn WA 98002-1699

County: King FICE Identification: 041352
Unit ID: 234526
Telephone: (253) 854-4960 Carnegie Class: Not Classified
FAX Number: (253) 931-0768 Calendar System: Quarter
URL: www.NorthwestAviationCollege.edu
Established: 1969 Annual Undergrad Tuition & Fees: $77475.61
Enrollment: 64 Coed
Affiliation or Control: Proprietary IRS Status: Proprietary
Highest Offering: Associate Degree
Program: Occupational; 2-Year Principally Bachelor's Creditable; Technical Emphasis
Accreditation: ACCSC

01 President/Director of Education ... Mr. Michael KOPP
03 Vice President ... Mr. Shawn PRATT
20 Assistant Director of Education ... Ms. Candace LYNN

Northwest College of Art (E)

16301 Creative Drive, NE, Poulsbo WA 98370-8651

County: Kitsap FICE Identification: 026021
Unit ID: 377546
Telephone: (360) 779-9993 Carnegie Class: Spec/Arts
FAX Number: (360) 779-9933 Calendar System: Semester
URL: www.nca.edu
Established: 1982 Annual Undergrad Tuition & Fees: $18,200
Enrollment: 124 Coed
Affiliation or Control: Proprietary IRS Status: Proprietary
Highest Offering: Baccalaureate
Program: Fine Arts Emphasis
Accreditation: ACCSC

01 President ... Craig N. FREEMAN
06 Registrar ... John PAWLEY, JR.
37 Financial Aid Director ... Heidi TOWNSEND
08 Library Services ... Brian MACKIN

Northwest Indian College (F)

2522 Kwina Road, Bellingham WA 98226-9278

County: Whatcom FICE Identification: 021800
Unit ID: 380377
Telephone: (360) 676-2772 Carnegie Class: Tribal
FAX Number: (360) 738-0136 Calendar System: Quarter
URL: www.nwic.edu
Established: 1978 Annual Undergrad Tuition & Fees: $6,292
Enrollment: 1,526 Coed
Affiliation or Control: Tribal Control IRS Status: 501(c)3
Highest Offering: Baccalaureate
Program: Occupational; 2-Year Principally Bachelor's Creditable
Accreditation: NW

01 President ... Ms. Cheryl CRAZY BULL
05 Vice Pres Instruction/Student Svcs ... Ms. Carole RAVE
11 Vice President Campus Development ... Mr. David OREIRO
45 VP for Research/Sponsored Programs ... Ms. Barbara ROBERTS
04 Exec Assistant to the President ... Ms. Tami JULIUS
32 Dean for Student Life ... Vacant
106 Dean Instruction/Distant Learning ... Mr. Justin GUILLORY
35 Assoc Dean for Student Life ... Ms. Crystal BAGBY
20 Assoc Dean for Instruction ... Ms. Bernice PORTERVINT
15 Human Resources Manager ... Mr. Mark POLIN
96 Purchasing Manager ... Mr. Charles ROBERTS

Northwest Institute of Literary Arts (G)

5577 Vanbarr Place Suite S1, Freeland WA 98249

County: Island Identification: 666775
Telephone: (360) 331-0307 Carnegie Class: Not Classified
FAX Number: N/A Calendar System: Semester
URL: www.writeonwhidbey.org/mfa
Established: 2005 Annual Graduate Tuition & Fees: $11,000
Enrollment: N/A Coed
Affiliation or Control: Independent Non-Profit IRS Status: 501(c)3
Highest Offering: Master's; No Undergraduates
Program: Professional
Accreditation: DETC

01 Program Director ... Mr. Wayne UDE
32 Student Services Coordinator ... Ms. Asharaine MACHALA

Northwest School of Wooden Boatbuilding (H)

42 N Water Street, Port Hadlock WA 98339-8706

County: Jefferson FICE Identification: 041550
Unit ID: 236124
Telephone: (360) 385-4948 Carnegie Class: Not Classified
FAX Number: (360) 385-5089 Calendar System: Other
URL: www.nwboatschool.org
Established: 1981 Annual Undergrad Tuition & Fees: $17,400
Enrollment: 57 Coed
Affiliation or Control: Independent Non-Profit IRS Status: 501(c)3
Highest Offering: Associate Degree
Program: Occupational
Accreditation: ACCSC

01 Executive Director ... Mr. Bill MAHLER
05 Chief Instructor ... Mr. Tim LEE
35 Student Services Administrator ... Ms. Laura ALLEN

Northwest University (I)

PO Box 579, Kirkland WA 98083-0579

County: King FICE Identification: 003783
Unit ID: 236133
Telephone: (425) 822-8266 Carnegie Class: Bac/Diverse
FAX Number: (425) 827-0148 Calendar System: Semester
URL: www.northwestu.edu
Established: 1934 Annual Undergrad Tuition & Fees: $23,030
Enrollment: 1,148 Coed
Affiliation or Control: Assemblies Of God Church IRS Status: 501(c)3
Highest Offering: Master's
Program: Liberal Arts And General
Accreditation: NW, ACBSP, NURSE

01 President ... Dr. Joseph CASTLEBERRY
05 Provost ... Dr. Jim HEUGEL
03 Executive Vice President ... Mr. Dan NEARY
10 Senior Vice President for Finance ... Mr. Dan NEARY
32 Vice Pres Student Development ... Dr. Paul BANAS
26 Assoc Vice President for Marketing ... Mr. Merlin QUIGGLE
102 Asst Vice Pres for Development ... Mr. Jason MILES
84 Asst Vice Pres Enrollment Services ... Mrs. Rose SMITH
42 Dean of the Chapel ... Rev. Phil RASMUSSEN
20 Dean of Academic Services ... Mr. Jim JESSUP
06 Registrar ... Mrs. Sandy HENDRICKSON
07 Director of Admissions ... Mrs. Jessica VELASCO
37 Director Student Financial Aid ... Mr. Roger WILSON
31 Resident Dean Extended Community ... Mr. Scott BROWN
41 Athletic Director ... Mr. Gary MCINTOSH
08 College Librarian ... Mr. Adam EPP
38 Director of Counseling Services ... Ms. Teresa REGAN
29 Director of Alumni Services ... Mr. Dustin SHIRLEY
15 Director Human Resources ... Ms. Victoria CLARK
00 Director Student Success ... Mrs. Amy JONES
30 Chief Development ... Mr. Dan NEARY
18 Chief Facilities/Physical Plant ... Mr. Steve SANKEY

† Granted candidacy at the Doctorate level.

Olympic College (J)

1600 Chester Avenue, Bremerton WA 98337-1699

County: Kitsap FICE Identification: 003784
Unit ID: 236188
Telephone: (360) 792-6050 Carnegie Class: Assoc/Pub4
FAX Number: (360) 475-7151 Calendar System: Quarter
URL: www.olympic.edu
Established: 1946 Annual Undergrad Tuition & Fees (In-State): $3,542
Enrollment: 8,916 Coed
Affiliation or Control: State IRS Status: 501(c)3
Highest Offering: Baccalaureate
Program: Occupational; 2-Year Principally Bachelor's Creditable
Accreditation: NW, ACFEI, ADNUR, MAC, NURSE, PTAA

01 President ... Dr. David C. MITCHELL
05 Vice President of Instruction ... Ms. Mary GARGUILE
11 Vice President of Administration ... Vacant
32 Vice President of Student Services ... Vacant
30 Exec Dir Institutional Advancement ... Dr. Joan HANTEN
16 Exec Director Human Resource Svcs ... Ms. Linda YERGER
56 Director of Extended Learning ... Vacant
04 Exec Assistant to the President ... Ms. Allison SMITH
37 Director Financial Aid ... Dr. Joseph KOROMA
27 Director of Communications ... Ms. Jennifer HAYES
84 Dn Enroll Svcs/Registrar/Dir Admiss ... Ms. Dianna LARSEN
18 Chief Facilities/Physical Plant ... Mr. William WILKIE
21 Director of Business Services ... Ms. Janell WHITELEY
96 Procurement Officer ... Ms. Diana LAKE
28 Multicultural Services Manager ... Vacant
40 Director of Auxiliary Services ... Mr. Denis SNYDER
36 Director Student Placement ... Ms. Patricia TRIGGS
103 Dean Workforce Development ... Ms. Amy HATFIELD
08 Dean Library-Media ... Ms. Ruth M. ROSS
35 Dean of Student Development ... Dr. Kimberly MCNAMARA
50 Dean Business & Technology ... Dr. Norma WHITACRE
81 Dean Math/Engineer/Sci/Health ... Dr. Judi BROWN
79 Dean Humanities/Social Science ... Dr. Gina HUSTON
09 Assoc Dean Planning/Assess/Research ... Vacant

Pacific Lutheran University (K)

Tacoma WA 98447-0003

County: Pierce FICE Identification: 003785
Unit ID: 236230
Telephone: (253) 531-6900 Carnegie Class: Master's M
FAX Number: (253) 535-8320 Calendar System: 4/1/4
URL: www.plu.edu
Established: 1890 Annual Undergrad Tuition & Fees: $30,950
Enrollment: 3,457 Coed
Affiliation or Control: Evangelical Lutheran Church In America
IRS Status: 501(c)3

Highest Offering: Master's
Program: Liberal Arts And General; Teacher Preparatory; Professional
Accreditation: NW, BUS, CS, ENG, MFCD, MUS, NURSE, SW, TED

01 President ... Dr. Loren J. ANDERSON
05 Provost/Dean Graduate Studies ... Dr. Steven STARKOVICH
10 Vice President Finance & Operations ... Dr. Sheri J. TONN
30 Vice Pres Development/Univ Rels ... Dr. Steve J. OLSON
32 Vice Pres Stdnt Life/Dean of Stdnts ... Dr. Laura F. MAJOVSKI
07 Vice Pres Admission/Enrollment Svcs ... Mr. Karl A. STUMO
21 Assoc Vice Pres Finance/Controller ... Mr. Robert K. RILEY
20 Asst Provost for Curriculum ... Dr. Jan P. LEWIS
08 Assoc Provost for Information Tech ... Dr. Chris D. FERGUSON
27 Exec Dir University Communications ... Mr. Greg W. BREWIS
42 University Pastor ... Rev. Dennis G. SEPPER
42 University Pastor ... Rev. Nancy J. CONNOR
57 Dean School of Arts & Communication ... Dr. Cameron D. BENNETT
50 Dean of School of Business ... Dr. James L. BROCK
53 Dean School of Educ/Movement Study ... Dr. Frank M. KLINE
66 Dean School of Nursing ... Dr. Terry W. MILLER
79 Dean of Humanities ... Dr. James M. ALBRECHT
88 Dean of Natural Sciences ... Dr. Matthew J. SMITH
83 Dean of Social Sciences ... Dr. Norris A. PETERSON
88 Dean of Student Academic Success ... Dr. Patricia E. ROUNDY
35 Dean Stdnt Dev/Dir of Stdnt Involve ... Dr. Eva R. JOHNSON
58 Assoc Dean Grad & Summer Programs ... Dr. Laura J. POLCYN
88 Exec Dir Wang Ctr Intl Programs ... Dr. Neal W. SOBANIA
41 Athletic Director ... Ms. Laurie L. TURNER
06 Registrar ... Ms. Kristin H. PLAEHN
39 Asst Dean of Stdnts/Dir of Res Life ... Mr. Tom A. HUELSBECK
18 Director Facilities Management ... Mr. David L. KOHLER
29 Exec Dir Constituent Relations ... Ms. Lauralee HAGEN
19 Director of Campus Safety & Info ... Mr. Greg V. PREMO
36 Director of Career Development ... Ms. Ruth D. ROGERS
38 Director Counseling Center ... Dr. Mark M. ANDERSON
23 Director of Health Services ... Vacant
15 Director of Human Resource Services ... Ms. Teri P. PHILLIPS
90 Dir of Information Systems ... Ms. Sue L. JENNINGS
37 Director of Student Financial Aid ... Ms. Kay W. SOLTIS
40 Director of Bookstore ... Vacant
09 Systems and Data Analyst ... Ms. Deirdre E. MCGOLDRICK

Pacific Northwest University of Health Sciences (A)

111 University Parkway, Suite 202, Yakima WA 98901
County: Yakima FICE Identification: 041305
Unit ID: 455406
Telephone: (509) 452-5100 Carnegie Class: Not Classified
FAX Number: (509) 452-5101 Calendar System: Semester
URL: www.pnwu.org
Established: 2005 Annual Graduate Tuition & Fees: $45,650
Enrollment: 44,650 Coed
Affiliation or Control: Independent Non-Profit IRS Status: 501(c)3
Highest Offering: Doctorate; No Undergraduates
Program: Professional
Accreditation: @OSTEO

01 Acting President ... Dr. Lloyd H. BUTLER
88 Dean Col of Osteopathic Medicine ... Dr. Robyn PHILLIPS
05 Chief Academic Officer ... Dr. Robert E. SUTTON
30 Vice Pres University Advancement ... Ms. Gretchen EICKMEYER
10 Chief Financial Officer ... Ms. Ann O'BRIEN

Peninsula College (B)

1502 East Lauridsen Boulevard,
Port Angeles WA 98362-6698
County: Clallam FICE Identification: 003786
Unit ID: 236258
Telephone: (360) 452-9277 Carnegie Class: Assoc/Pub4
FAX Number: (360) 457-8100 Calendar System: Quarter
URL: www.pc.ctc.edu
Established: 1961 Annual Undergrad Tuition & Fees (In-District): $2,490
Enrollment: 7,571 Coed
Affiliation or Control: State/Local IRS Status: 501(c)3
Highest Offering: Baccalaureate
Program: Occupational; 2-Year Principally Bachelor's Creditable
Accreditation: NW, ADNUR

01 President ... Dr. Thomas A. KEEGAN
05 Vice President Instruction ... Dr. Mary O'NEIL-GARRETT
11 Vice President Administrative Svcs ... Ms. Deborah FRAZIER
32 Vice President Student Services ... Mr. Jack HULS
45 VP Institutional Effectiveness ... Dr. Paula DOHERTY
51 Director Continuing Education ... Mr. Bob LAWRENCE-MARKARIAN
88 Dean Basic Skills ... Dr. Evelyn SHORT
35 Dean of Student Services ... Ms. Maria PENA
13 Director Information Technology ... Mr. Steven BAXTER
37 Director Financial Aid ... Ms. Krista FRANCIS
04 Executive Asst to the President ... Ms. Tina HERSCHELMAN
27 Public Information Officer ... Ms. Phyllis L. VAN HOLLAND
15 Director Human Resources ... Ms. Bonnie H. CAUFFMAN
85 Director of International Programs ... Ms. Nicole A. CASARES
102 Exec Director of the Foundation ... Ms. Mary HUNCHBERGER
35 Director Student Programs ... Mr. Rick ROSS
09 Director of Institutional Research ... Vacant
18 Physical Plant Director ... Mr. Rick CROOT
40 Bookstore Manager ... Mrs. Patty MCCRAY-ROBERTS
06 Enrollment Services Manager ... Ms. Cindy LAUDERBACK

Pierce College District (C)

9401 Farwest Drive SW, Lakewood WA 98498-1999
County: Pierce FICE Identification: 005000
Unit ID: 235237
Telephone: (253) 964-6500 Carnegie Class: Assoc/Pub-S-MC
FAX Number: N/A Calendar System: Quarter
URL: www.pierce.ctc.edu
Established: 1967 Annual Undergrad Tuition & Fees (In-State): $3,407
Enrollment: 14,261 Coed
Affiliation or Control: State IRS Status: 501(c)3
Highest Offering: Associate Degree
Program: Occupational; 2-Year Principally Bachelor's Creditable
Accreditation: NW, ADNUR, DH

01 District Chancellor ... Dr. Michele JOHNSON
12 President at Puyallup ... Dr. Patrick SCHMITT
12 President at Fort Steilacoom ... Ms. Denise YOCHUM
05 Vice Pres Learning Stdnt Success-FS ... Dr. Carol GREEN
05 Int VP Learning & Stdnt Success-Puy ... Mr. Bill MCMEEKIN
10 Vice Pres Administrative Services ... Ms. Joann WISZMANN
30 Vice President of Advancement ... Ms. Suzy AMES
15 Vice President for Human Resources ... Ms. Jan BUCHOLZ
13 Dean of Institutional Technology ... Mr. Mike STOCKE
06 Registrar/Dir Enrollment Svcs-Dist ... Ms. Anne WHITE
08 Dean of Library ... Dr. Debra GILCHRIST
26 Dir Marketing and Communications ... Mr. Brian BENEDETTI
36 Dir Student Development-District ... Ms. Agnes STEWARD
35 Dir Student Programs-Ft Steilacoom ... Mr. Cameron COX
41 Director of Athletics ... Mr. Duncan STEVENSON
18 Director of Facilities & Const Mgt ... Mr. Jim TAYLOR
32 Dir of Student Life-Puyallup ... Dr. Mari KRUGER
85 Director of International Education ... Dr. Pat CAVENDISH
19 District Manager Campus Safety ... Mr. Chris MACKERSIE
21 Director of Budget and Finance ... Mr. Bill VON HASSELN
37 Director Student Financial Aid ... Mr. Martin DANIELS
84 Director Enrollment Services-Puy ... Ms. Els DEMING
09 Institutional Researcher ... Ms. Kris CUMMINGS
49 Chair Arts & Humanities Div-FS ... Mr. Michael DARCHER
88 Chair Trans Education Div-Dist ... Ms. Lori GRIFFIN
76 Chair Nat Sci & Allied Health- FS ... Mr. Ronald MAY
76 Chair Nat Sci & Allied Health-Puy ... Ms. Roya SABETI
83 Chair Bus & Social Science Div-Puy ... Mr. Thomas BROXSON
83 Chair Bus & Social Science Div-FS ... Mr. Greg BRAZELL
79 Chair Arts & Humanities Div-Puy ... Ms. Ann SALAK
29 Alumni Relations Manager ... Ms. Paula HENSON-WILLIAMS
96 Procurement Officer ... Mr. Curtis LEE

Pima Medical Institute-Seattle (D)

9709 3rd Avenue NE, Suite 400, Seattle WA 98115-2052
County: King Identification: 666172
Unit ID: 368629
Telephone: (206) 322-6100 Carnegie Class: Assoc/PrivFP
FAX Number: (206) 324-1985 Calendar System: Other
URL: www.pmi.edu
Established: 1989 Annual Undergrad Tuition & Fees: $590
Enrollment: 580 Coed
Affiliation or Control: Proprietary IRS Status: Proprietary
Highest Offering: Associate Degree
Program: Occupational; 2-Year Principally Bachelor's Creditable
Accreditation: ABHES, OTA, PTAA, RAD

01 Director ... Mr. Carey HOCHMAN

Renton Technical College (E)

3000 NE Fourth Street, Renton WA 98056-4123
County: King FICE Identification: 010434
Unit ID: 236382
Telephone: (425) 235-2352 Carnegie Class: Assoc/Pub-S-SC
FAX Number: (425) 235-7832 Calendar System: Quarter
URL: www.rtc.edu
Established: 1942 Annual Undergrad Tuition & Fees (In-State): $5,392
Enrollment: 6,247 Coed
Affiliation or Control: State IRS Status: 501(c)3
Highest Offering: Associate Degree
Program: Occupational; Technical Emphasis
Accreditation: NW, ACFEI, DA, MAC, SURGT

01 President ... Mr. Steven J. HANSON
10 VP Finance/Administration ... Ms. Melinda M. MERRELL
05 Vice President Instruction ... Mr. Martin R. HEILSTEDT
32 Vice President Student Services ... Mr. Jon A. POZEGA
97 Dean Basic Studies ... Ms. Jodi NOVOTNY
76 Dean Allied Health ... Ms. Heather M. STEPHEN-SELBY
72 Dean Apprentice/Trade & Industry ... Ms. Gay KIESLING
50 Dean Bus/Educ/Hum Svcs/Gen Educ ... Ms. Peggy MOE
72 Dean Automotive/Tech/Distance Educ ... Mr. Dante J. LEON
102 College Rels/Foundation Director ... Ms. Susanna WILLIAMS
13 Director Technology ... Ms. Mary Kay WEGNER
07 Director Admissions/Registration ... Ms. Becky RIVERMAN
46 Director Research/Development ... Mr. Chris JOHNSON
08 Director Library ... Mr. Eric E. PALO
21 Director Financial Services ... Mr. Mark JOHNSON
15 Director Human Resources Develop ... Ms. Glenda K. MULLOWNEY
37 Director Financial Aid ... Ms. Debbie SOLOMON
27 Public Information Specialist ... Ms. Kathy L. CHAVERS
18 Director Plant Operations ... Mr. Barry A. BAKER
40 Bookstore Manager ... Mr. Jose A. PERDOMO
19 Director Public Safety ... Mr. Elman MCCLAIN

103 Director Workforce Development ... Ms. Maggie SUTTHOFF
88 Associate Dean Culinary Arts ... Mr. Doug MEDBURY

Saint Martin's University (F)

5300 Pacific Avenue, SE, Lacey WA 98503-1293
County: Thurston FICE Identification: 003794
Unit ID: 236452
Telephone: (360) 491-4700 Carnegie Class: Master's S
FAX Number: (360) 459-4124 Calendar System: Semester
URL: www.stmartin.edu
Established: 1895 Annual Undergrad Tuition & Fees: $26,677
Enrollment: 1,811 Coed
Affiliation or Control: Roman Catholic IRS Status: 501(c)3
Highest Offering: Master's
Program: Liberal Arts And General; Teacher Preparatory; Professional
Accreditation: NW, ENG, TEAC

00 Chancellor ... Abbot Neal G. ROTH, OSB
01 President ... Dr. Roy F. HEYNDERICKX
05 Provost & Vice President ... Dr. Joseph D. BESSIE
10 Vice President of Finance ... Ms. Susan D. HELTSLEY
30 Interim Vice Pres Inst Advancement ... Mr. Lee GOLDEN
85 Vice Pres Intl Programs/Development ... Ms. Josephine YUNG
26 VP of Marketing/Communications ... Ms. Jennifer FELLINGER
32 Dean Student Services ... Ms. Melanie RICHARDSON
84 Dean Enrollment Management ... Vacant
07 Dean Admission/Stdnt Financial Svcs ... Mr. Juan FLORES
21 Treasurer ... Fr. Bede CLASSICK
37 Financial Aid Director ... Ms. Shelle RIEHL
29 Director Alumni Relations ... Vacant
06 Registrar ... Ms. Mary Conley LAW
13 Dir Integrated Technology Systems ... Dr. Michael EXTINE
18 Director Facilities Management ... Mr. Alan TYLER
44 Dir of Development/Planned Giving ... Ms. Katie WOJKE
36 Director of Career Placement ... Ms. Ann ADAMS
41 Athletic Director ... Mr. Bob GRISHAM
49 Dean Col of Arts & Sciences ... Dr. Eric APFELSTADT
81 Dean of Science & Math ... Dr. Katherine PORTER
83 Dean of Social Sciences ... Dr. Rex CASILLAS
53 Dean of Education ... Dr. Joyce WESTGARD
50 Dean of Business ... Dr. Richard BEER
54 Dean of Engineering ... Dr. Zella KAHN-JETTER
56 Director Extension Programs ... Mr. Cruz ARROYO
08 Library Director ... Mr. Scot HARRISON
42 Director Campus Ministry ... Ms. Susan LEYSTER
39 Director of Housing/Residence Life ... Mr. Tim MCCLAIN
38 Director Counseling Center ... Ms. Jan BERNEY
09 Director Institutional Grants/Rsrch ... Vacant
15 Director of Human Resources ... Ms. Cynthia JOHNSON
89 Director of Freshmen Studies ... Dr. Sharon TAYLOR
40 Manager Bookstore ... Mr. Mark MORRIS

*Seattle Community Colleges (G)

1500 Harvard Avenue, Seattle WA 98122-3803
County: King FICE Identification: 010106
Unit ID: 236498
Telephone: (206) 934-4100 Carnegie Class: N/A
FAX Number: (206) 934-3883
URL: www.seattlecolleges.edu

01 Chancellor ... Dr. Jill WAKEFIELD
05 VC Educ/Plng/e-Lrng/Workforce Educ ... Dr. Carin S. WEISS
10 Chief Financial/Information Ofcr ... Dr. Alan WARD
15 Chief Human Resources Officer ... Mr. Charles E. SIMS
26 Public Information Officer ... Ms. Patricia PAQUETTE
30 Interim Exec Dir for Advancement ... Ms. Evelyn YENSON
12 President South Seattle Cmty Col ... Mr. Gary OERTLI
12 President North Seattle Cmty Col ... Mr. Mark MITSUI
12 President Seattle Central Cmty Col ... Dr. Paul KILLPATRICK

*North Seattle Community College (H)

9600 College Way N, Seattle WA 98103-3599
County: King FICE Identification: 009704
Unit ID: 236072
Telephone: (206) 934-3600 Carnegie Class: Assoc/Pub-U-MC
FAX Number: (206) 934-3606 Calendar System: Quarter
URL: www.northseattle.edu
Established: 1970 Annual Undergrad Tuition & Fees (In-State): $3,435
Enrollment: 6,855 Coed
Affiliation or Control: State IRS Status: 170(c)1
Highest Offering: Associate Degree
Program: Occupational; 2-Year Principally Bachelor's Creditable
Accreditation: NW, ADNUR, MAC

02 President ... Mr. Mark MITSUI
05 Vice President for Instruction ... Dr. Mary Ellen O'KEEFFE
32 Int Vice Pres Student Development ... Ms. Marci MYER
11 Vice President Admin Services ... Dr. Monty MONTERECY
36 Exec Dean Career/Workforce Educ ... Mr. Steve MILLER
79 Dean Art/Humanities/Social Sciences ... Vacant
81 Dean Math & Science ... Mr. Peter LORTZ
17 Dean Health & Human Services ... Dr. Robert FINEMAN
50 Dean Business/Eng Info Tech ... Ms. Terry COX
35 Dean Stdnt Svc/Registrar/Admissions ... Ms. Marci MYER
08 Dean Library & Media Services ... Ms. Sharon SIMES
84 Assoc Dean Enrollment Services ... Ms. Alice MELLING
88 Assoc Dean Basic/Transitional Stds ... Ms. Kim CHAPMAN
56 Assoc Dean e-Learning ... Dr. Tom BRAZIUNAS
30 Director of Development ... Ms. Anne ZACOVIC

26 Director Public Relations/Marketing .... Ms. Carol SUMMERS
06 Registrar & Director of Admissions .... Ms. Betsy ABTS
51 Director Continuing Education .... Ms. Heidi STUBER
37 Director Financial Aid Services .... Ms. Suzanne SCHELDT
35 Director Student Programs .... Mr. Jeffrey VASQUEZ
103 Director Workforce Education .... Mr. John BOWERS
09 Dir Institutional Effectiveness .... Dr. Jack BAUTSCH
104 Director International Programs .... Ms. Mari ACOB-NASH
15 Director Personnel Services .... Mr. David BITTENBENDER
18 Mgr Facilities Planning/Operations .... Mr. Bruce KIESER
38 Lead Counselor .... Dr. Lydia MINATOYA
45 Director Strategic Initiatives .... Mr. Gary GORLAND

*Seattle Central Community College (A)

1701 Broadway, Seattle WA 98122-2400
County: King FICE Identification: 003787
Unit ID: 236513
Telephone: (206) 587-3800 Carnegie Class: Assoc/Pub-U-MC
FAX Number: (206) 344-4390 Calendar System: Quarter
URL: seattlecentral.edu
Established: 1966 Annual Undergrad Tuition & Fees (In-State): $3,542
Enrollment: 10,364 Coed
Affiliation or Control: State IRS Status: 170(c)1
Highest Offering: Associate Degree
Program: Occupational; 2-Year Principally Bachelor's Creditable
Accreditation: NW, ACFEI, ADNUR, DH, OPD, SURGT

02 President .... Dr. Paul KILLPATRICK
05 Vice Pres of Instruction & Student .... Dr. Warren BROWN
11 Vice Pres Administrative Services .... Mr. Michael PHAM
103 Exec Dean Workforce Education .... Mr. Al GRISWOLD
51 Exec Dean Continuing/Prof Educ .... Dr. A. Barretto OGILVIE
09 Exec Dir Strategic Initiatives & IR .... Dr. Cherisa YARKIN
35 Dean of Student Resources & Support ......Ms. Brigid MCDEVITT
37 Director of Financial Aid .... Ms. Noel MCBRIDE
102 Executive Director Fund Development .... Vacant
27 Director Communications .... Ms. Laura MANSFIELD
08 Exec Dean Instructional Resources .... Dr. Wai-Fong LEE
49 Dean Basic Studies .... Dr. Alison STEVENS
50 Dean Business IT & Creative Arts .... Ms. Jody LAFLEN
76 Dean of Allied Health .... Ms. Ona CANFIELD
81 Interim Dean Science & Mathematics .... Dr. Wendy ROCKHILL
83 Dean Humanities/Social Sciences .... Dr. Kenneth LAWSON
00 Dean International Education .... Dr. Andrea INSLEY
35 Dean Student Life & Engagement .... Ms. Lexie EVANS
12 Assoc Dean Seattle Culinary Academy .... Ms. Linda CHAUNCEY
13 Assoc Dean Information Technology .... Ms. Harriet WASSERMAN
88 Director Facilities & Capital Proj .... Mr. Jeffery R. WATTS
12 Asst Dean Seattle Maritime Academy .... Dr. Carl ELLIS
51 Director Cmty Educ/Evening Pgm .... Mr. Jeff WEST
06 Assoc Dean Enrollment/Registrar .... Ms. Diane COLEMAN
19 Director Security/Safety .... Mr. Robert HUSS
18 Director Facilities .... Dr. Jeff KEEVER

† Granted candidacy at the Baccalaureate level.

*South Seattle Community College (B)

6000 16th Avenue, SW, Seattle WA 98106-1499
County: King FICE Identification: 009706
Unit ID: 236504
Telephone: (206) 934-5300 Carnegie Class: Assoc/Pub4
FAX Number: (206) 934-5393 Calendar System: Quarter
URL: www.southseattle.edu
Established: 1969 Annual Undergrad Tuition & Fees (In-State): $3,650
Enrollment: 8,351 Coed
Affiliation or Control: State IRS Status: 501(c)3
Highest Offering: Baccalaureate
Program: Occupational; 2-Year Principally Bachelor's Creditable
Accreditation: NW, ACFEI

02 President .... Mr. Gary L. OERTU
05 Exec Vice Pres Instruction/Admn Svc ......Dr. Kurt R. BUTTLEMAN
32 Int Vice President Student Services .... Ms. Kim K. MANDERBACH
07 Interim Dean Admissions/Registrar ...... Ms. Maureen M. SHADAIR
45 Dean Instructional Resources .... Ms. Mary Jo WHITE
75 Executive Dean Technical Education .... Mr. Malcom P. GROTHE
88 Exec Dn Apprenticeshp/Special Trng .... Ms. Holly MOORE
97 Dean Basic and Transitional Studies .... Ms. Donna MILLER-PARKER
20 Dean of Academic Programs .... Dr. Chad E. HICKOX
35 Dean Student Life .... Ms. Cessa HEARD-JOHNSON
88 Dean Hosp & Service Occupations .... Mr. Mike E. RYAN
88 Dean Transportation .... Mr. Bennett C. TAVES
72 Interim Dean of Technical Education .... Ms. Kim ALEXANDER
06 Int Registrar/Dean Enrollment Svcs ..... Ms. Maureen M. SHADAIR
51 Director Continuing Education .... Ms. Luisa MOTTEN
103 Dir Worksource Dev/Employment Svcs ...... Mr. Duncan BURGESS
37 Dir Student Financial Assistance .... Ms. Patricia L. BILLINGS
27 Interim Director Communications .... Ms. Candace DEHLER
15 Director Personnel Services .... Ms. Kathryn A. VEDVICK
09 Director Institutional Research .... Ms. Marsha D. BROWN
13 Director Computer Services .... Vacant
18 Director Facilities/Plng/Operations .... Mr. Bear L. HOLMES
30 Exec Dir Foundation/College Advance .... Ms. Elizabeth A. PLUHTA
28 Director of Diversity .... Mr. Ricardo LEYVA-PUEBLA
19 Manager Safety/Security .... Mr. James E. LEWIS
40 Manager Bookstore .... Mr. Joel BOUCHEY

Seattle Institute of Oriental Medicine (C)

916 NE 65th Street, Seattle WA 98115-5542
County: King FICE Identification: 032803
Unit ID: 439914
Telephone: (206) 517-4541 Carnegie Class: Spec/Health
FAX Number: N/A Calendar System: Trimester
URL: www.siom.edu
Established: 1994 Annual Undergrad Tuition & Fees: $18,300
Enrollment: 39 Coed
Affiliation or Control: Proprietary IRS Status: Proprietary
Highest Offering: Master's; No Lower Division
Program: Professional
Accreditation: ACUP

01 President .... Dr. Paul KARSTEN
05 Academic Dean .... Mr. Craig MITCHELL

Seattle Pacific University (D)

3307 Third Avenue W, Seattle WA 98119-1997
County: King FICE Identification: 003788
Unit ID: 236577
Telephone: (206) 281-2111 Carnegie Class: Master's L
FAX Number: (206) 281-2115 Calendar System: Quarter
URL: www.spu.edu
Established: 1891 Annual Undergrad Tuition & Fees: $29,976
Enrollment: 4,117 Coed
Affiliation or Control: Free Methodist IRS Status: 501(c)3
Highest Offering: Doctorate
Program: Liberal Arts And General; Teacher Preparatory; Professional
Accreditation: NW, BUS, CLPSY, DIETD, ENG, MFCD, MUS, NURSE, TED

01 President .... Dr. Philip W. EATON
05 Vice President for Academic Affairs .... Dr. Les L. STEELE
11 VP Administration/Univ Relations .... Mrs. Marjorie R. JOHNSON
10 Vice Pres for Business & Planning .Mr. Donald W. MORTENSON
30 Vice President for Univ Advancement .... Mr. Thomas W. BOX
20 Asc VP Acad Affs/Curriculum Assess .... Dr. Cynthia J. PRICE
13 Assoc VP Information/Data Mgmt .... Ms. Janet L. WARD
32 Assoc Vice Pres/Dean Student Life .... Dr. Jeffrey C. JORDAN
21 Assoc VP for Business & Finance .... Mr. Craig G. KISPERT
13 Asst VP of Technology Services .... Mr. David W. TINDALL
18 Asst VP for Facility Management .... Mr. David B. CHURCH
41 Assistant Vice President Endowment .... Mr. Gordon A. NYGARD
50 Dean School of Business & Economics .... Mr. Jeffrey B. VAN DUZER
53 Dean School of Education .... Dr. Rick EIGENBROOD
66 Dean School of Health Sciences .... Dr. Lucille M. KELLEY
49 Dean College of Arts & Sciences .... Dr. Bruce D. CONGDON
88 Dean School of Psych/Fam & Cmty .... Dr. Michael D. ROE
73 Dean School of Theology .... Dr. Douglas M. STRONG
102 Exec Dir Corp/Fdtn/Major Gifts .... Mr. John H. WEST
15 Director of Human Resources .... Mr. Gary E. WOMELSDUFF
36 Director Career Development Center .... Dr. Jacqui S. SMITH-BATES
08 University Librarian .... Mr. Michael PAULUS
38 Director Student Counseling Center .... Dr. Steven A. MAYBELL
07 Director Undergraduate Admissions .... Mr. Jobe S. KORB-NICE
07 Dir Graduate Admissions/Marketing .... Dr. John L. GLANCY
06 University Registrar .... Mrs. Ruth L. ADAMS
09 Director of Institutional Research .... Mr. Jerald L. FINCH
27 Director University Communications ...... Mrs. Jennifer J. GILNETT
37 Director Student Financial Services .... Mr. Jordan L. GRANT
27 News & Media Relations Manager .... Mrs. Tracy C. NORLEN
45 Assoc Director Projects & Planning .... Mr. Wayne H. ELLING
31 Director of University Services .... Mr. Murray J. LAWSON
19 Director of Safety & Security .... Mr. Mark REID
44 Director of Annual Giving .... Mr. Dean O. CARRELL
29 Director of Alumni Relations .... Mr. Kenneth E. CORNELL
41 Director of Athletics .... Ms. Erin E. O'CONNELL
42 Dir Univ Ministry/Ctr for Worship .... Dr. Stephen M. NEWBY
28 Director of the John Perkins Center .... Mr. Tali HAIRSTON
35 Director Student Programs .... Mr. Dale N. ANDERSON
23 Nurse Manager .... Ms. Jean BROWN

The Seattle School of Theology and Psychology (E)

2501 Elliot Avenue, Seattle WA 98121-1177
County: King FICE Identification: 034664
Unit ID: 441131
Telephone: (206) 876-6100 Carnegie Class: Spec/Health
FAX Number: (206) 876-6195 Calendar System: Trimester
URL: www.theseattleschool.edu
Established: 2001 Annual Graduate Tuition & Fees: $14,214
Enrollment: 275 Coed
Affiliation or Control: Independent Non-Profit IRS Status: 501(c)3
Highest Offering: Master's; No Undergraduates
Program: Religious Emphasis
Accreditation: @THEOL, TRACS

01 President .... Dr. Keith R. ANDERSON
04 Assistant to the President .... Vacant
05 Sr Vice Pres Academic Affs/CAO .... Dr. J. Derek MCNEIL
10 Chief Financial Officer .... Mr. Phil BISHOP
20 Assistant Academic Dean .... Ms. Stephanie NEIL
08 Dir Library Svcs/Inst Assessment .... Ms. Cheryl GOODWIN
06 Dir Academic Services/Registrar .... Ms. Kristin HOUSTON
07 Director of Recruitment .... Ms. Nicole GREENWALD

13 Director Computer & Info Services .... Mr. Jason BEST
37 Dir of Student Financial Services .... Ms. Isabelle MORA
15 Human Resources .... Mrs. Amy WILSON
18 Facilities Manager .... Mr. Nathan SWEET

Seattle University (F)

901 12th Avenue, Seattle WA 98122-1090
County: King FICE Identification: 003790
Unit ID: 236595
Telephone: (206) 296-6000 Carnegie Class: Master's L
FAX Number: N/A Calendar System: Quarter
URL: www.seattleu.edu
Established: 1891 Annual Undergrad Tuition & Fees: $32,400
Enrollment: 7,817 Coed
Affiliation or Control: Roman Catholic IRS Status: 501(c)3
Highest Offering: Doctorate
Program: Liberal Arts And General; Teacher Preparatory; Professional
Accreditation: NW, BUS, CACREP, DMS, ENG, LAW, @MIDWF, NURSE, SPAA, SW, TED, THEOL

01 President .... Rev. Stephen V. SUNDBORG, SJ
05 Provost .... Dr. Isiaah CRAWFORD
03 Executive Vice President .... Dr. Tim LEARY
43 Vice Pres and University Counsel .... Ms. Mary S. PETERSEN
10 Vice President Finance & Business .... Vacant
30 Vice Pres University Advancement .... Ms. Mary Kay MCFADDEN
32 Vice President Student Development .... Dr. Jacob DIAZ
88 Vice President Mission & Ministry .... Rev. Peter ELY, SJ
45 Vice President University Planning .... Dr. Robert DULLEA
84 Vice President for Enrollment Svcs .... Ms. Marilyn CRONE
15 Vice President Human Resources .... Mr. Gerald HUFFMAN
49 Dean of Arts & Sciences .... Dr. David POWERS
50 Dean of Business & Economics .... Dr. Joseph M. PHILLIPS
53 Dean of Education .... Dr. Sue A. SCHMITT
66 Dean of Nursing .... Dr. Azita EMAMI
54 Dean of Science & Engineering .... Dr. Michael QUINN
79 Dean Matteo Ricci College .... Vacant
61 Dean of Law .... Mr. Mark NILES
73 Dean of Theology & Ministry .... Dr. Mark MARKULY
08 University Librarian .... Mr. John P. POPKO
20 Assoc Provost Academic Affairs .... Dr. Jacquelyn MILLER
20 Assoc Provost Academic Affairs .... Dr. Charles LAWRENCE
27 Chief Information Officer/AVP .... Vacant
26 Asst VP/Director Public Relations .... Vacant
21 Assoc VP Finance & Business .... Mr. James L. ADOLPHSON
18 Assoc VP Facilities Administration .... Mr. Robert SCHWARTZ
13 Chief Technology Officer .... Mr. Daniel DUFFY
29 Asst VP/Sr Dir Advance Initiatives .... Ms. Carlene BUTY
44 Asst VP/Director of Development .... Ms. Sarah FINNEY
30 Assoc VP University Advancement .... Mr. Mark BURNETT
35 Assoc Vice Pres Student Development .... Dr. Michele MURRAY
35 Asst Vice Pres Student Development .... Dr. Alvin STURDIVANT
42 Director Campus Ministry .... Fr. Mike BAYARD, SJ
45 Asst VP for Planning .... Dr. Robert DUNIWAY
06 Registrar .... Ms. Joyce ALLEN
07 Dean of Admissions .... Ms. Melore NIELSEN
37 Director Student Financial Services .... Vacant
19 Director Public Safety .... Mr. Michael L. SLETTEN
85 Director International Student Ctr .... Mr. Ryan GREENE
41 Athletic Director .... Mr. Bill HOGAN
36 Executive Director Career Services .... Ms. Bethany KREITL
38 Director Counseling Center .... Dr. Susan HAWKINS
28 Dir Multicultural Student Affairs .... Ms. Monica NIXON
39 Director Housing & Residence Life .... Vacant

Shoreline Community College (G)

16101 Greenwood Avenue N, Shoreline WA 98133-5696
County: King FICE Identification: 003791
Unit ID: 236610
Telephone: (206) 546-4101 Carnegie Class: Assoc/Pub-S-SC
FAX Number: (206) 546-4630 Calendar System: Quarter
URL: www.shoreline.edu
Established: 1964 Annual Undergrad Tuition & Fees (In-State): $4,015
Enrollment: 7,174 Coed
Affiliation or Control: State IRS Status: 170(c)1
Highest Offering: Associate Degree
Program: Occupational; 2-Year Principally Bachelor's Creditable
Accreditation: NW, ADNUR, DH, MLTAD

01 President .... Mr. Lee D. LAMBERT
05 Vice President Academic Affairs .... Mr. John P. BACKES
11 Vice Pres Administrative Svcs .... Mr. Daryl J. CAMPBELL
15 VP Human Resources/Legal Affairs .... Mr. Stephen SMITH
27 Spec Asst to Pres/Public Info/Mkt .... Mr. Jim HILLS
09 Asst Director Inst Effectiveness .... Mr. Joseph DUGGAN
96 Special Asst to President Budget .... Ms. Holly M. WOODMANSEE
04 Exec Asst to the President .... Ms. Lori YONEMITSU
85 Exec Dir International Pgms .... Ms. Thalia SAPLAD
51 Director Cntr for Bus & Cont Educ .... Mr. Dave CUNNINGHAM
72 Director Technology Support Service .... Mr. Gary KALBFLEISCH
84 Dir Recruit & Enroll Svcs/Registrar .... Mr. Ted HAASE
18 Director Facilities .... Mr. Bob ROEHL
19 Director Safety & Security .... Ms. Robin BLACKSMITH
66 Program Director Nursing .... Ms. Georgia PIERCE
37 Director Financial Aid .... Mr. Ted HAASE
38 Dir Advis/Counsel/High School Pgm .... Dr. Yvonne L. TERRELL-POWELL
29 Exec Dir Community/Alumni Relations .... Ms. Jane MCNABB
40 Director Auxiliary Services .... Ms. Mary E. KELEMEN
88 Director Essential Skills .... Mr. William SPERLING

72 Interim Dean Library/Media/Tech ... Mr. Robert FRANCIS
35 Dean Student Affairs ... Dr. Tonya M. DRAKE
103 Dean Workforce Education ... Mr. Dave CUNNINGHAM
31 Dean Capital Projects/Cmty Rels ... Ms. Gillian O. LEWIS
79 Dean Humanities Division ... Dr. Norma W. GOLDSTEIN
83 Int Dean Global Stds/Trans/Honors ... Mr. Robert FRANCIS
88 Dean Student Enroll/Environ Init ... Dr. Susan H. HOYNE

Skagit Valley College (A)

2405 College Way, Mount Vernon WA 98273-5899
County: Skagit FICE Identification: 003792
Unit ID: 236638
Telephone: (360) 416-7600 Carnegie Class: Assoc/Pub-R-L
FAX Number: (360) 416-7890 Calendar System: Quarter
URL: www.skagit.edu
Established: 1926 Annual Undergrad Tuition & Fees (In-State): $4,200
Enrollment: 7,200 Coed
Affiliation or Control: State IRS Status: 501(c)3
Highest Offering: Associate Degree
Program: Occupational; 2-Year Principally Bachelor's Creditable
Accreditation: NW, ACFEI, ADNUR, MAC

01 President ... Dr. Gary TOLLEFSON
05 Vice President Educational Services ... Dr. Mick DONAHUE
10 Vice Pres Administrative Services ... Ms. Mary Alice GROBINS
12 Vice President of Whidbey Campus ... Dr. Mick DONAHUE
32 Dean of Student Services ... Dr. David PAUL
13 Dean Technology/eLearning/Library ... Mr. Tom BATES
75 Dean Workforce Education ... Ms. Laura CAILLOUX
20 Dean Academic Education ... Dr. Joan YOUNGQUIST
37 Financial Aid Officer ... Mr. Steve EPPERSON
16 Exec Director of Human Resources ... Ms. Sue WILLIAMSON
18 Director of Physical Plant ... Mr. Dave SCOTT
27 Director of Public Information ... Ms. Arden AINLEY
104 Director of International Programs ... Ms. Christa SCHULZ
40 Bookstore Manager ... Ms. Kim HALL
41 Director of Athletics ... Mr. Gary KNUTZEN
09 Director of Institutional Research ... Dr. Maureen PETTITT

South Puget Sound Community College (B)

2011 Mottman Road, SW, Olympia WA 98512-6292
County: Thurston FICE Identification: 005372
Unit ID: 236656
Telephone: (360) 754-7711 Carnegie Class: Assoc/Pub-R-L
FAX Number: (360) 664-0780 Calendar System: Quarter
URL: www.spscc.ctc.edu
Established: 1962 Annual Undergrad Tuition & Fees (In-State): $3,062
Enrollment: 6,807 Coed
Affiliation or Control: State IRS Status: 501(c)3
Highest Offering: Associate Degree
Program: Occupational; 2-Year Principally Bachelor's Creditable
Accreditation: NW, ACFEI, ADNUR, DA, MAC

01 President ... Dr. Gerald PUMPHREY
04 Exec Assistant to the President ... Ms. Diana TOLEDO
05 Vice President for Instruction ... Ms. Dorna BULLPITT
32 Vice President for Student Services ... Dr. Rhonda COATS
11 Vice Pres Administrative Services ... Ms. Nancy MCKINNEY
16 Chief Human Resources Officer ... Ms. Sheila EMERY
07 Dean of Enrollment Svcs/Registrar ... Ms. Kathy RHODES
30 Exec Director College Foundation ... Ms. Cecelia LOVELESS
18 Dean of Facilities Planning & Opers ... Ms. Penny KOAL
35 Dean of Student Life ... Dr. Dave RECTOR
37 Dean of Student Financial Services ... Ms. Carla IDOHL-CORWIN
08 Dir of Library/Media & eLearning ... Dr. Elizabeth HILL
19 Director of Security ... Mr. Lonnie HATMAN
40 Director of Auxiliary Services ... Mr. Bryce WINKELMAN
26 Dean of College Relations ... Ms. Kellie BRASETH
27 Chief Information Officer ... Mr. Bob BILLINGS
72 Dean of Applied Technology ... Dr. Brent CHAPMAN
88 Dean of Instruc Planning & Develop ... Ms. Lorna PATTERSON
76 Dean of Natural & Applied Sciences ... Dr. Allen MASON
79 Dean of Humanities/Communications ... Ms. Mary SOLTMAN
83 Dean of Social Sciences & Business ... Dr. Debbie TEED
28 Director of Diversity & Equity ... Ms. Eileen YOSHINA
09 Director of Institutional Research ... Ms. Darby KAIKKONEN
10 Chief Business Officer ... Ms. Nancy MCKINNEY

Tacoma Community College (C)

6501 S 19th Street, Tacoma WA 98466-6100
County: Pierce FICE Identification: 003796
Unit ID: 236753
Telephone: (253) 566-5000 Carnegie Class: Assoc/Pub-U-MC
FAX Number: (253) 566-5376 Calendar System: Quarter
URL: www.tacomacc.edu
Established: 1965 Annual Undergrad Tuition & Fees (In-State): $3,543
Enrollment: 12,177 Coed
Affiliation or Control: State IRS Status: 501(c)3
Highest Offering: Associate Degree
Program: Occupational; 2-Year Principally Bachelor's Creditable
Accreditation: NW, ADNUR, DMS, EMT, RAD

01 President ... Dr. Pamela TRANSUE
05 Vice Pres Academic/Student Affairs ... Dr. Timothy STOKES
11 Vice Pres Administrative Services ... Ms. Silvia BARAJAS
30 Vice Pres Institutional Advancement ... Mr. Dan SMALL
32 Assoc Vice Pres Student Services ... Ms. Mary CHIKWINYA
51 Dean of Enter/Econ Devel/Cont Ed ... Dr. Lisa EDWARDS
50 Dean Business & Workforce Education ... Mr. Charlie CRAWFORD
88 Director K-12 Ptnshps/Stdnt Conduct ... Ms. Dolores HAUGEN
07 Dean for Entry & Enrollment Svcs ... Mr. Steve ASHPOLE
88 Director of Advising ... Ms. Terri JONES
13 Director for Information/Tech ... Mr. Gary SIGMEN
46 Dir Inst Effective/Instr Assessment ... Mr. Scott MARSH
18 Director Facilities/Physical Plant ... Mr. Clint STEELE
35 Director of Student Life ... Mr. Dave PELKEY
37 Director Student Financial Aid ... Ms. Kim MATISON

Trinity Lutheran College (D)

2802 Wetmore Avenue, Everett WA 98201
County: Snohomish FICE Identification: 021067
Unit ID: 235769
Telephone: (425) 249-4800 Carnegie Class: Bac/Diverse
FAX Number: (425) 249-4801 Calendar System: 4/1/4
URL: www.tlc.edu
Established: 1944 Annual Undergrad Tuition & Fees: $21,760
Enrollment: 160 Coed
Affiliation or Control: Independent Non-Profit IRS Status: 501(c)3
Highest Offering: Baccalaureate
Program: Liberal Arts And General; Religious Emphasis
Accreditation: NW

01 President ... Mr. John REED
05 Academic Dean ... Dr. Jeff MALLINSON
10 Vice President Finance ... Mr. Tom RAMSEY
32 Dean of Students ... Vacant
30 Associate Director of Development ... Mr. Lance GEORGESON
06 Registrar ... Sir Charles NELSON
08 Director of Educ Tech & Library ... Mr. Seong Heon LEE
37 Director of Financial Aid ... Ms. Shanna PYZER
29 Alumni Relations Coordinator ... Ms. Stacie MALLINSON
31 Director of Community Life ... Vacant
13 IT Administrator ... Mr. Clay CAMPBELL
21 Accounting Manager ... Mrs. Miwa EASTON

University of Puget Sound (E)

1500 N Warner St., Tacoma WA 98416-0002
County: Pierce FICE Identification: 003797
Unit ID: 236328
Telephone: (253) 879-3100 Carnegie Class: Bac/A&S
FAX Number: (253) 879-3500 Calendar System: Semester
URL: www.pugetsound.edu
Established: 1888 Annual Undergrad Tuition & Fees: $38,720
Enrollment: 2,867 Coed
Affiliation or Control: Independent Non-Profit IRS Status: 501(c)3
Highest Offering: Doctorate
Program: Liberal Arts And General; Teacher Preparatory; Professional
Accreditation: NW, MUS, OT, PTA, TED

01 President ... Dr. Ronald R. THOMAS
04 Exec Assistant to the President ... Ms. Mary Elizabeth COLLINS
05 Academic VP/Dean of University ... Dr. Kristine M. BARTANEN
10 Vice Pres Finance & Admin ... Ms. Sherry B. MONDOU
26 Vice President University Relations ... Mr. David BEERS
84 Vice President for Enrollment ... Dr. George H. MILLS
32 VP Student Affairs/Dean of Students ... Mr. Mike SEGAWA
21 Assoc VP Accounting/Budget Svcs ... Ms. Janet S. HALLMAN
15 Assoc Vice Pres Human Resources ... Ms. Rosa Beth GIBSON
21 Assoc Vice Pres Business Services ... Mr. John M. HICKEY
18 Assoc Vice Pres Facilities Services ... Mr. Bob KIEF
37 Assoc VP for Student Financial Svcs ... Ms. Maggie A. MITTUCH
26 Executive Dir of Communications ... Ms. Gayle MCINTOSH
13 Chief Technology Officer ... Mr. William MORSE
20 Associate Academic Dean ... Dr. Alyce DEMARAIS
20 Associate Academic Dean ... Ms. Sarah MOORE
20 Associate Academic Dean ... Ms. Lisa L. FERRARI
06 Registrar ... Mr. Brad TOMHAVE
08 Library Director ... Ms. Jane CARLIN
41 Director of Athletics ... Ms. Amy E. HACKETT
29 Director Alumni & Parent Relations ... Ms. Allison CANNADY-SMITH
85 Director International Programs ... Mr. Roy ROBINSON
53 Dean School of Education ... Dr. John WOODWARD
50 Dir School of Business/Leadership ... Dr. Jim MCCULLOUGH
64 Director of School of Music ... Dr. Keith C. WARD
88 Director of Occupational Therapy ... Dr. George TOMLIN
88 Director of Physical Therapy ... Dr. Kathleen HUMMEL-BERRY
09 Director of Institutional Research ... Ms. Ellen PETERS
28 Chief Diversity Officer ... Dr. Kim BOBBY

University of Washington (F)

Seattle WA 98195-0001
County: King FICE Identification: 003798
Unit ID: 236948
Telephone: (206) 543-2100 Carnegie Class: RU/VH
FAX Number: (206) 543-9285 Calendar System: Quarter
URL: www.washington.edu
Established: 1861 Annual Undergrad Tuition & Fees (In-State): $10,346
Enrollment: 42,446 Coed
Affiliation or Control: State IRS Status: 501(c)3
Highest Offering: Doctorate
Program: Liberal Arts And General; Teacher Preparatory; Professional
Accreditation: NW, ARCPA, AUD, BUS, BUSA, CEA, CLPSY, CONST, DENT, DIETC, EMT, ENG, FOR, HSA, IPSY, JOUR, LAW, LIB, LSAR, MED, MIDWF, MT, MUS, NURSE, OPE, OT, PDPSY, PH, PHAR, PLNG, PTA, SCPSY, SP, SPAA, SW

01 President ... Mr. Michael K. YOUNG
12 Chancellor Bothell Campus ... Dr. Kenyon S. CHAN
12 Chancellor Tacoma Campus ... Dr. Patricia SPAKES
05 Provost & Executive Vice President ... Dr. Phyllis M. WISE
10 Sr Vice Pres Finance/Facilities ... Ms. V'Ella WARREN
28 VP Minority Affs/V Prov Diversity ... Dr. Sheila EDWARDS LANGE
17 Exec VP Med Affs/CEO UW Med/Dean ... Dr. Paul G. RAMSEY
30 Vice Pres for Univ Advancement ... Dr. Connie KRAVAS
15 Vice President Human Resources ... Ms. Mindy KORNBERG
13 Interim VP & Vice Prov UW Info Tech ... Ms. Kelli TROSVIG
26 Vice President for External Affairs ... Mr. Randy HODGINS
46 Vice Provost Research ... Dr. Mary E. LIDSTROM
51 V Provost UW Prof & Cont Education ... Dr. David P. SZATMARY
45 Vice Prov Planning & Budgeting ... Mr. Paul JENNY
20 Executive V Provost Acad Affs ... Mr. Douglas J. WADDEN
20 Vice Prov/Dean Undergrad Acad Affs ... Dr. Ed TAYLOR
32 VP & Vice Provost Student Life ... Mr. Eric GODFREY
88 V Provost for Academic Personnel ... Dr. Cheryl A. CAMERON
88 V Prov/UW Ctr for Commercialization ... Ms. Linden RHOADS
86 Director Federal Relations ... Ms. Christy D. GULLION
43 Division Chief Attorney General ... Mr. Gary L. IKEDA
06 University Registrar ... Ms. Virjean EDWARDS
29 Exec Dir & Assoc VP Alum Assoc ... Mr. Paul RUCKER
17 Exec Dir UW Medical Ctr Admin ... Mr. Stephen P. ZIENIEWICZ
17 Exec Dir Harborview Med Ctr ... Ms. Eileen WHALEN
37 Asst Vice Pres Student Life/Dir Fin ... Ms. S. Kay LEWIS
86 Director State Relations ... Ms. Margaret A. SHEPHERD
07 Director of Admissions ... Dr. Philip BALLINGER
09 AVP Inst Research & Data Mgmt ... Mr. Todd B. MILDON
36 Director Career Center ... Ms. Susan TERRY
13 CFO UW Information Technology ... Mr. Bill FERRIS
18 Assoc Vice Pres Facilities Services ... Mr. Charles KENNEDY
92 Director Honors Program ... Dr. James J. CLAUSS
41 Director Athletics ... Mr. Scott WOODWARD
08 Dean Libraries ... Ms. Lizabeth A. WILSON
96 Assoc Director Purchasing Services ... Mr. Mark CONLEY
58 Vice Prov/Dean Graduate School ... Dr. Gerald J. BALDASTY
49 Dean Arts & Sciences ... Dr. Ana Mari CAUCE
47 Dean Col of Built Environments ... Dr. Daniel FRIEDMAN
50 Dean Business School ... Dr. Jim JIAMBALVO
54 Dean Engineering ... Dr. Matthew O'DONNELL
61 Dean Law School ... Dr. Kellye Y. TESTY
70 Dean Social Work ... Dr. Edwina UEHARA
52 Interim Dean Dentistry ... Dr. Timothy A. DEROUEN
63 Dean Medicine ... Dr. Paul G. RAMSEY
66 Dean Nursing ... Dr. Marla SALMON
67 Dean Pharmacy ... Dr. Thomas BAILLIE
69 Dean School of Public Health ... Dr. Howard FRUMKIN
53 Dean Education ... Dr. Tom STRITIKUS
80 Dean of Public Affairs ... Dr. Sandra O. ARCHIBALD
88 Dean Information School ... Dr. Harry BRUCE
88 Dean Col of the Environment ... Dr. Lisa GRAUMLICH

Walla Walla Community College (G)

500 Tausick Way, Walla Walla WA 99362-9267
County: Walla Walla FICE Identification: 005006
Unit ID: 236887
Telephone: (509) 522-2500 Carnegie Class: Assoc/Pub-R-L
FAX Number: (509) 527-4480 Calendar System: Quarter
URL: www.wwcc.edu
Established: 1967 Annual Undergrad Tuition & Fees (In-State): $3,917
Enrollment: 5,438 Coed
Affiliation or Control: State IRS Status: 170(c)1
Highest Offering: Associate Degree
Program: Occupational; 2-Year Principally Bachelor's Creditable; Technical Emphasis
Accreditation: NW, ADNUR

01 President ... Dr. Steven L. VANAUSDLE
11 VP of Administrative Services ... Mr. James R. PETERSON
05 Vice President of Academic Educ ... Dr. Marleen RAMSEY
32 Vice President of Student Services ... Dr. Clinton GABBARD
10 Vice Pres of Financial Services ... Mrs. Davina K. FOGG
20 Vice Pres of Instruction-Workforce ... Dr. Mindy STEVENS
30 Director of Resource Development ... Mr. Doug BAYNE
07 Director of Admissions/Registrar ... Mr. Carlos E. DELGADILLO
38 Director Student Development Center ... Mrs. Wendy C. SAMITORE
37 Financial Aid Director ... Ms. Danielle HODGEN
35 Director of Student Activities ... Dr. David D. CHASE
08 Int Director of Library Services ... Mrs. Stacy PREST
12 Director of Clarkston Campus ... Dr. Janet V. DANLEY
41 Athletic Director ... Mr. Jeffrey E. REINLAND
15 Director of Human Resources ... Mrs. Sharon M. HARTFORD
18 Director of Plant Facilities ... Vacant
106 Director of eLearning ... Mrs. Sandra K. MADSEN
88 Director of Transitional Studies ... Ms. Darlene SNIDER
66 Director of Nursing Education ... Mrs. Marilyn D. GALUSHA
51 Director of Correctional Education ... Dr. Joe A. SMALL
28 Director of Multicultural Svcs ... Vacant
40 Bookstore Manager ... Ms. Alecia ANGELL
31 Coordinator of Community Education ... Mrs. Nancy E. KRESS
09 Director of Institutional Research ... Ms. Jamie FOUTY
27 Director Marketing & Communications ... Vacant

Walla Walla University (H)

204 S College Avenue, College Place WA 99324-1198
County: Walla Walla FICE Identification: 003799
Unit ID: 236896
Telephone: (509) 527-2615 Carnegie Class: Master's M
FAX Number: (509) 527-2397 Calendar System: Quarter
URL: www.wallawalla.edu
Established: 1892 Annual Undergrad Tuition & Fees: $23,670

Enrollment: 1,791 Coed
Affiliation or Control: Seventh-day Adventist IRS Status: 501(c)3
Highest Offering: Master's
Program: Liberal Arts And General; Teacher Preparatory; Professional
Accreditation: **NW**, ACBSP, ACFEI, ENG, MUS, SW

01 President .... Dr. John MCVAY
05 Vice Pres Academic Administration .... Dr. Ginger KETTING-WELLER
10 Vice Pres Financial Administration .... Mr. Steve ROSE
32 Vice Pres Student Life and Mission .... Mr. Ken ROGERS
30 Vice Pres University Advancement .... Dr. Dennis CARLSON
84 Vice Pres Marketing and Enrollment .... Ms. Jodi WAGNER
28 Asst to President for Diversity .... Dr. Pedrito MAYNARD-REID
04 Executive Asst Office of President .... Ms. Deirdre BENWELL
20 Associate Vice Pres Academic Admin .... Dr. Scott LIGMAN
21 Associate Vice Pres Financial Admin .... Mr. Glenn CARTER
08 Director of Libraries .... Ms. Carolyn GASKELL
06 Registrar .... Ms. Carolyn DENNEY
42 Chaplain .... Mr. Paddy MCCOY
29 Director of Alumni Relations .... Ms. Nicole BATTEN
14 Director Information Services .... Mr. Scott MCFADDEN
37 Director Student Financial Services .... Ms. Cassie RAGENOVICH
15 Director Human Resources .... Mr. Shane VOSHELL
18 Director of Plant Services .... Mr. Jerry MASON
26 Director of University Relations .... Ms. Rosa JIMENEZ
33 Dean of Men .... Mr. John FOOTE
34 Dean of Women .... Ms. Misty PUYMON
58 Dean of Graduate Programs .... Dr. Joseph GALUSHA
66 Dean of School of Nursing .... Ms. Lucille KRULL
73 Dean of School of Theology .... Dr. David THOMAS
54 Dean of School of Engineering .... Mr. Larry AAMODT
07 Director of Admissions .... Mr. Dallas WEIS
09 Director of Institutional Research .... Dr. James FISHER
36 Director Career Center .... Ms. Nelle CORNELISON
38 Director Student Counseling .... Mr. Don WALLACE

Washington State University (A)

PO Box 645910, Pullman WA 99164-5910
County: Whitman FICE Identification: 003800
Unit ID: 236939
Telephone: (509) 335-3564 Carnegie Class: RU/VH
FAX Number: N/A Calendar System: Semester
URL: www.wsu.edu
Established: 1890 Annual Undergrad Tuition & Fees (In-District): $10,799
Enrollment: 26,308 Coed
Affiliation or Control: State/Local IRS Status: 501(c)3
Highest Offering: Doctorate
Program: Liberal Arts And General; Teacher Preparatory; Professional
Accreditation: **NW**, BUS, BUSA, CEA, CIDA, CLPSY, CONST, COPSY, CS, DIETC, DIETD, ENG, FOR, HSA, IPSY, LSAR, MUS, NURSE, PHAR, SP, VET

01 President .... Dr. Elson S. FLOYD
05 Provost/Executive Vice President .... Dr. Warwick M. BAYLY
10 VP Business and Finance .... Mr. Roger D. PATTERSON
43 Div Chief State Attorney Gen Office .... Ms. Sharyl KAMMERZELL
03 Assoc Executive Vice President .... Dr. Larry G. JAMES
20 Vice Provost for Faculty Affairs .... Dr. Frances MCSWEENEY
106 Exec Dir Ctr for Distance/Prof Educ .... Dr. David CILLAY
84 VP Student Affairs & Enrollment .... Mr. John FRAIRE
27 VP Information Systems & CIO .... Dr. Viji MURALI
46 VP Research/Dean Grad School .... Dr. Howard D. GRIMES
12 Chancellor WSU Spokane .... Dr. Brian L. PITCHER
12 Chancellor WSU Tri-Cities .... Dr. Vicky CARWEIN
12 Chancellor WSU Vancouver .... Dr. Harold A. DENGERINK
47 Dean Agric/Human Natl Res Sci .... Dr. Daniel BERNARDO
50 Dean Business & Economics .... Dr. Eric SPANGENBERG
53 Dean Education .... Dr. A.G RUD
54 Dean Engineering & Architecture .... Dr. Candis CLAIBORN
66 Dean Nursing .... Dr. Patricia BUTTERFIELD
67 Dean Pharmacy .... Dr. Gary POLLACK
57 Dean Liberal Arts .... Dr. Doug EPPERSON
60 Dean Communication .... Dr. Lawrence E. PINTAK
81 Dean Sciences .... Dr. Daryll DEWALD
74 Dean Veterinary Medicine .... Dr. Bryan K. SLINKER
92 Dean Honors College .... Dr. Libby WALKER
45 Assoc VP & Chief Budget Office .... Ms. Joan KING
71 Dean University College .... Dr. Mary F. WACK
08 Dean Libraries .... Mr. Joseph STARRATT
06 Registrar .... Ms. Julia POMERENK
07 Director Admissions .... Ms. Wendy PETERSON
09 Interim Director Inst Research .... Ms. Fran HERMANSON
18 Assoc VP Facilities Services .... Ms. Olivia YANG
37 Director Financial Aid .... Ms. Chio FLORES
41 Director Intercollegiate Athletics .... Mr. William H. MOOS
86 Assoc VP Government Relations .... Ms. Colleen KERR
88 Director Internal Audit .... Ms. Heather LOPEZ
56 Director Extension .... Dr. Daniel BERNARDO

Wenatchee Valley College (B)

1300 Fifth Street, Wenatchee WA 98801-1799
County: Chelan FICE Identification: 003801
Unit ID: 236975
Telephone: (509) 682-6800 Carnegie Class: Assoc/Pub-R-M
FAX Number: (509) 682-6541 Calendar System: Quarter
URL: www.wvc.edu
Established: 1939 Annual Undergrad Tuition & Fees (In-State): $3,647
Enrollment: 3,358 Coed
Affiliation or Control: State IRS Status: 501(c)3
Highest Offering: Associate Degree
Program: Occupational; 2-Year Principally Bachelor's Creditable
Accreditation: **NW**, ADNUR, MAC, MLTAD

01 President .... Mr. James RICHARDSON
05 Vice President of Instruction .... Dr. Walt TRIBLEY
11 VP of Administrative Services .... Ms. Suzie BENSON
38 Vice President Student Development .... Mr. Marco AZURDIA
49 Interim Dean of Liberal Arts .... Dr. Walt TRIBLEY
12 Dean Omak Campus .... Vacant
103 Assoc Dean Workforce Education .... Ms. Mary WATSON
23 Assoc Dean of Allied Health & Nurs .... Ms. Jenny CAPELO
15 Director Human Resources .... Ms. Reagan BELLAMY
45 Director Institution Effectiveness .... Dr. Susan MURRAY
27 Director Public Information .... Ms. Kathi R. SHANNON
32 Director Student Programs/Outreach .... Mr. Kelly KETCHAM
37 Director Financial Aid .... Mr. Kevin BERG
18 Facilities & Operations Manager .... Mr. Greg RANDALL
06 Registrar .... Mr. Bruce MAXWELL
13 Director of Technology .... Vacant
20 Director of Basic Skills .... Mr. Larry RUDDELL
10 Chief Business Officer .... Mr. Jonah NICHOLAS

Western Washington University (C)

516 High Street, Bellingham WA 98225-5950
County: Whatcom FICE Identification: 003802
Unit ID: 237011
Telephone: (360) 650-3000 Carnegie Class: Master's L
FAX Number: (360) 650-3022 Calendar System: Quarter
URL: www.wwu.edu
Established: 1893 Annual Undergrad Tuition & Fees (In-State): $7,716
Enrollment: 14,979 Coed
Affiliation or Control: State IRS Status: 501(c)3
Highest Offering: Beyond Master's But Less Than Doctorate
Program: Liberal Arts And General; Teacher Preparatory; Professional
Accreditation: **NW**, ART, BUS, CACREP, CORE, CS, ENGT, MUS, NRPA, SP, TED

01 President .... Dr. Bruce SHEPARD
05 Vice Pres Academic Affairs/Provost .... Dr. Catherine A. RIORDAN
10 Vice Pres Financial Affairs .... Mr. Richard D. VAN DEN HUL
32 VP Stdnt Affs/Acad Support Svcs .... Dr. Eileen V. COUGHLIN
26 Vice Pres for University Relations .... Mr. Steve SWAN
30 Vice Pres University Advancement .... Ms. Stephanie BOWERS
35 Asst Vice Pres Student Affairs .... Dr. Kunle OJIKUTU
13 Vice Prov Info/Chief Info Officer .... Dr. John D. LAWSON
58 Vice Prov Research/Dean Grad School .... Dr. Moheb A. GHALI
53 Vice Prov Undergraduate Education .... Dr. Steven L. VANDERSTAAY
22 Vice Provost Equal Opportunity .... Dr. Sue GUENTER-SCHLESINGER
51 Vice Provost Extended Education .... Dr. Earl F. GIBBONS
35 Dean of Students .... Mr. Theodore W. PRATT, JR.
15 Director Human Resources .... Ms. Chyerl WOLFE-LEE
06 Registrar .... Mr. David BRUNNEMER
07 Director of Admissions .... Ms. Karen COPETAS
36 Director Career Services Center .... Ms. Tina LOUDON
37 Director Financial Aid .... Ms. Clara CAPRON
29 Executive Director Alumni Relations .... Ms. Deborah DEWEES
27 Director University Communications .... Mr. Paul COCKE
44 Dir Plan Giving/Sr Advisor to Pres .... Vacant
08 Dean of Libraries .... Mr. Christopher N. COX
39 Director University Residences .... Mr. Willy HART
04 Sr Executive Assistant to President .... Dr. Paul DUNN
09 Director of Institutional Research .... Dr. Ming ZHANG
18 Director of Facilities Management .... Mr. John A. FURMAN
19 Chief of Public Safety .... Mr. Randy STEGMEIER
41 Athletic Director .... Ms. Lynda GOODRICH
92 Director of Honors Program .... Dr. George MARIZ
96 Purchasing Manager .... Ms. Sally MCKECHNIE
79 Dean College of Humanities/Soc Sci .... Dr. Brent CARBAJAL
72 Dean College of Science/Technology .... Vacant
50 Dean College Business & Economics .... Dr. Brian K. BURTON
65 Dean Huxley Col of the Environment .... Dr. Bradley F. SMITH
57 Dean College Fine & Performing Arts .... Dr. Daniel G. GUYETTE
53 Dean Woodring College of Education .... Dr. Francisco RIOS
12 Dean Fairhaven College .... Dr. Roger GILMAN

Whatcom Community College (D)

237 W Kellogg Road, Bellingham WA 98226-8003
County: Whatcom FICE Identification: 010364
Unit ID: 237039
Telephone: (360) 383-3000 Carnegie Class: Assoc/Pub-R-M
FAX Number: (360) 383-4000 Calendar System: Quarter
URL: www.whatcom.ctc.edu
Established: 1970 Annual Undergrad Tuition & Fees (In-State): $3,800
Enrollment: 4,378 Coed
Affiliation or Control: State IRS Status: 501(c)3
Highest Offering: Associate Degree
Program: Occupational; 2-Year Principally Bachelor's Creditable; Technical Emphasis
Accreditation: **NW**, ADNUR, MAC, PTAA

01 President .... Dr. Kathi HIYANE-BROWN
05 Vice President for Instruction .... Dr. Ronald LEATHERBARROW
11 VP for Administrative Services .... Mr. Ray WHITE
20 Vice Pres for Educational Services .... Ms. Patricia ONION
103 Dean for Workforce Education .... Ms. Linda MAIER
08 Library Director .... Ms. Linda LAMBERT
31 Director of Community Education .... Mr. Greg MARSHALL
10 Director for Business & Finance .... Mr. Brian PHELPS
06 Registrar .... Mr. Michael SINGLETARY
07 Coordinator of Admissions Outreach .... Ms. Laine JOHNSTON
37 Director of Financial Aid .... Mr. Jack WOLLENS
32 Director Student/Athletic Pgms .... Mr. Kris BAIER
85 Director of International Programs .... Mr. Kelly KESTER
27 Exec Director for Comm/Marketing .... Vacant
40 Bookstore Manager .... Mr. Jon SPORES
18 Facilities Director .... Mr. Brian KEELEY
04 Exec Assistant to the President .... Ms. Keri PARRIERA
15 Director Human Resources .... Ms. Becky RAWLINGS
09 Director for Institutional Research .... Dr. Anne Marie KARLBERG
102 Executive Director for Advancement .... Ms. Anne BOWEN
27 Chief Public Information Officer .... Mr. Nate LANGSTRAAT

Whitman College (E)

345 Boyer Avenue, Walla Walla WA 99362-2083
County: Walla Walla FICE Identification: 003803
Unit ID: 237057
Telephone: (509) 527-5411 Carnegie Class: Bac/A&S
FAX Number: (509) 527-5859 Calendar System: Semester
URL: www.whitman.edu
Established: 1882 Annual Undergrad Tuition & Fees: $40,496
Enrollment: 1,555 Coed
Affiliation or Control: Independent Non-Profit IRS Status: 501(c)3
Highest Offering: Baccalaureate
Program: Liberal Arts And General
Accreditation: **NW**

01 President .... Dr. George S. BRIDGES
05 Provost/Dean of Faculty .... Dr. Timothy KAUFMAN-OSBORN
30 Vice President for Development .... Mr. John W. BOGLEY
32 Dean of Students .... Mr. Charles E. CLEVELAND
07 Dean of Admission/Financial Aid .... Mr. Tony A. CABASCO
20 Associate Dean of Faculty .... Dr. Lisa R. PERFETTI
10 Treasurer/Chief Financial Officer .... Mr. Peter W. HARVEY
20 Assistant Dean of Faculty .... Dr. Michelle Y. JANNING
04 Executive Assistant to President .... Ms. Jennifer A. CASPER
06 Registrar .... Dr. Ronald F. URBAN
37 Director of Financial Aid Services .... Ms. Marilyn K. PONTI
08 Librarian .... Mrs. Dalia L. CORKRUM
09 Director of Institutional Research .... Dr. Neal J. CHRISTOPHERSON
38 Director Student Counseling .... Dr. Richard N. JACKS
29 Director Alumni Affairs .... Ms. Polly C. SCHMITZ
15 Director Human Resources .... Ms. Cindy L. MATERN
18 Chief Facilities/Physical Plant .... Mr. Daniel L. PARK
13 Chief Information Officer .... Mr. Dan M. TERRIO
19 Director of Security .... Mr. Terry E. THOMPSON
23 Director Health Services .... Ms. Claudia L. NESS
27 Director of Communications .... Ms. Ruth S. WARDWELL
36 Director of Career Center .... Ms. Susan M. BUCHANAN
39 Director Residence Life & Housing .... Ms. Nancy J. TAVELLI
41 Athletic Director .... Mr. Dean C. SNIDER

Whitworth University (F)

300 W Hawthorne Road, Spokane WA 99251-0001
County: Spokane FICE Identification: 003804
Unit ID: 237066
Telephone: (509) 777-1000 Carnegie Class: Master's M
FAX Number: (509) 777-4763 Calendar System: 4/1/4
URL: www.whitworth.edu
Established: 1890 Annual Undergrad Tuition & Fees: $31,830
Enrollment: 2,699 Coed
Affiliation or Control: Presbyterian Church (U.S.A.) IRS Status: 501(c)3
Highest Offering: Master's
Program: Liberal Arts And General; Teacher Preparatory; Professional
Accreditation: **NW**, MUS, NURSE, TED

01 President .... Dr. Beck A. TAYLOR
05 Executive VP Academic Affairs .... Dr. Michael K. LE ROY
10 VP Finance & Administration .... Dr. Brian L. BENZEL
30 VP Institutional Advancement .... Dr. Scott A. MCQUILKIN
32 VP for Student Life .... Dr. Kathleen H. STORM
84 VP Admissions & Financial Aid .... Mr. Greg ORWIG
88 Assoc VP Intercultural Relations .... Dr. Lawrence A. BURNLEY
15 Assoc VP Human Resources .... Ms. Dolores J. HUMISTON
42 Dean of Spiritual Life .... Dr. Terry P. MCGONIGAL
53 Dean of School of Education .... Dr. Dennis W. STERNER
08 Director of Library .... Dr. Hans E. BYNAGLE
20 Assoc Dean Faculty Devel/Schlrshp .... Dr. Michael T. INGRAM
06 Registrar .... Ms. Beverly S. KLEEMAN
35 Associate Dean of Students .... Dr. Dick G. MANDEVILLE
20 Associate Dean of Instruction .... Dr. Randall B. MICHAELIS
91 Director of Information Systems .... Mr. Kenneth BROWN
90 Director of Instructional Resources .... Mr. Kenneth D. PECKA
21 Assoc VP Finance & Administration .... Ms. Luz I. MERKEL
29 Director of Alumni Relations .... Mr. Aaron P. MCMURRAY
51 Dean of Continuing Studies .... Dr. Terry D. RATCLIFF
07 Director of Admissions .... Ms. Marianne W. HANSEN
58 Director of Grad & Cont Studies .... Ms. Cheryl D. VAWTER
18 Director of Physical Plant .... Mr. Ed W. KELLY
23 Director of Health Center .... Ms. Kristiana L. HOLMES
41 Director of Athletics .... Mr. Aaron LEETCH
37 Director of Financial Aid .... Ms. Wendy Z. OLSON
35 Director of Student Activities .... Ms. Dayna L. COLEMAN
39 Director of Student Housing .... Mr. Alan B. JACOB
40 Manager of Bookstore .... Ms. Nancy G. LOOMIS
26 Director of Communications .... Ms. Nancy G. HINES
38 Director of Counseling Services .... Ms. Janelle R. THAYER
09 Director of Institutional Research .... Mr. Gary D. WHISENAND
50 Dean Sch Global Commerce Mgmt .... Dr. Robert C. BEATTY

Yakima Valley Community College (A)

PO Box 22520, S 16th Ave & Nob Hill,
Yakima WA 98907-2520
County: Yakima FICE Identification: 003805
Unit ID: 237109
Telephone: (509) 574-4600 Carnegie Class: Assoc/Pub-R-M
FAX Number: (509) 574-6860 Calendar System: Quarter
URL: www.yvcc.edu
Established: 1928 Annual Undergrad Tuition & Fees (In-State): $384,9.9
Enrollment: 2,762 Coed
Affiliation or Control: State IRS Status: 170(c)1
Highest Offering: Associate Degree
Program: Occupational; 2-Year Principally Bachelor's Creditable
Accreditation: NW, ADNUR, DH, MAC, SURGT

01 President ... Dr. Linda KAMINSKI
05 Vice Pres Instruction/Student Svcs ... Mr. Tomas YBARRA
10 Vice Pres Administrative Services ... Ms. Teresa HOLLAND
12 Dean Grandview Campus ... Mr. Bryce HUMPHREYS
72 Director Tech Services ... Mr. Scott TOWSLEY
32 Dean Student Services ... Ms. Leslie BLACKABY
49 Dean Arts & Sciences ... Dr. Carli SCHIFFNER
75 Dean Workforce Education ... Ms. Paulette LOPEZ
08 Library Director ... Ms. Joan WEBER
37 Director Student Financial Aid ... Ms. Laura PENDLETON
26 Community Relations Coordinator ... Ms. Nicole HOPKINS
15 Director Human Resources ... Mr. Mark ROGSTAD
18 Director Facilities/Physical Plant ... Mr. Jeff WOOD
96 Purchasing Manager ... Ms. Claudia HOFFBAUER
35 Student Life Coordinator ... Ms. Kelly ROBBINS
97 Dean Basic Skills ... Ms. Kerrie ABB

WEST VIRGINIA

Alderson Broaddus College (B)

101 College Hill Drive, Philippi WV 26416-4600
County: Barbour FICE Identification: 003806
Unit ID: 237118
Telephone: (304) 457-1700 Carnegie Class: Bac/Diverse
FAX Number: (304) 457-6239 Calendar System: Semester
URL: www.ab.edu
Established: 1871 Annual Undergrad Tuition & Fees: $22,740
Enrollment: 632 Coed
Affiliation or Control: American Baptist IRS Status: 501(c)3
Highest Offering: Master's
Program: 2-Year Principally Bachelor's Creditable; Liberal Arts And General; Teacher Preparatory; Professional
Accreditation: NH, #ARCPA, NUR, TEAC

01 President ... Mr. Richard A. CREEHAN
05 Provost/Exec VP for Academic Affs ... Dr. Joan L. PROPST
10 Vice President for Business/Finance ... Ms. Diana L. CRICKARD
30 Vice Pres Institutional Advancement ... Ms. J. Nikky LUNA
44 Asst VP Adv/Major Gifts/Donor Rels ... Dr. Carl W. GITTINGS
84 Vice President Enrollment Mgmt ... Ms. Tanya L. SHELTON
32 Director of Student Affairs ... Vacant
13 Director of Information Technology ... Mr. Byron A. SAYRES
35 Dir of Student Engagement/Orient ... Ms. Koreen VILLERS
42 Chaplain ... Dr. James M. STINESPRING
08 Director of Library Services ... Mr. David E. HOXIE
41 Athletic Director ... Mr. J. D. LONG
37 Director of Financial Aid ... Mr. Brian A. WEINGART
26 Director of Mktg/Communications ... Vacant
29 Director of Alumni Relations ... Mr. Nathan PRICE
06 Registrar ... Ms. Saundra E. HOXIE
102 Dir Foundation/Corporate Giving ... Vacant
24 Director Learning Resources Center ... Ms. Della M. COLANTONE
18 Chief Facilities/Physical Plant ... Mr. Chad E. PLYMALE
09 Director of Institutional Research ... Ms. Julia M. MORRIS
40 Director of Campus Services ... Mr. Ed BURDA
21 Director of Accounting Services ... Ms. Jill BAKER
07 Director of Admissions ... Mr. Matt SHIFLETT
38 Personal Counseling Coordinator ... Mr. Chad HOSTETLER
39 Coord Student Activit/Conferences ... Vacant

American Public University System (C)

111 W Congress Street, Charles Town WV 25414-1621
County: Jefferson FICE Identification: 035393
Unit ID: 449339
Telephone: (877) 468-6268 Carnegie Class: Master's L
FAX Number: (304) 724-3780 Calendar System: Other
URL: www.apus.edu
Established: 1991 Annual Undergrad Tuition & Fees: $6,000
Enrollment: 39,296 Coed
Affiliation or Control: Proprietary IRS Status: Proprietary
Highest Offering: Master's
Program: 2-Year Principally Bachelor's Creditable; Liberal Arts And General; Professional
Accreditation: NH, ACBSP, DETC

01 President/CEO ... Dr. Wallace E. BOSTON
05 Exec Vice President & Provost ... Dr. Karan H. POWELL
10 Exec VP & CFO ... Mr. Harry T. WILKINS
26 Exec VP Programs & Marketing ... Ms. Carol S. GILBERT
03 Exec VP/Chief Operations Officer ... Dr. Sharon VAN WYK
11 Senior VP/Chief Admin Officer ... Mr. Pete W. GIBBONS
13 Senior VP/Chief Information Officer ... Mr. W. Dale YOUNG
06 VP/Registrar ... Ms. Lyn GEER
84 VP Enrollment Mgt & Student Support ... Ms. Terry GRANT
20 VP/Academic Operations Officer ... Dr. Gwen HALL
88 VP Cmty Col Relations & Outreach ... Dr. John HOUGH
46 VP Research & Development ... Dr. Phil ICE
86 VP Regulatory & Govt Relations ... Dr. Russell KITCHNER
88 VP Strategic Initiatives ... Mr. Phil MCNAIR
18 VP Facilities & Real Estate ... Mr. Joseph SLADKI
09 VP Institutional Research & Assess ... Dr. Jennifer STEPHENS-HELM
08 VP Library and Educ. Materials ... Dr. Fred STIELOW
88 VP Military Relations ... Mr. Jim SWEIZER
15 Assoc VP Human Resources ... Ms. Amy PANZARELLA
72 Assoc VP Science & Tech Relations ... Dr. James REILLY
37 Assoc VP Financial Aid Svcs ... Mr. Gary SPOALES
27 Assoc VP Corporate Communications ... Mr. Chris SYMANOSKIE
88 Assoc VP Institutional Advancement ... Ms. Lynn C. WRIGHT
43 Director Legal Affairs ... Mr. Thomas BECKETT

Appalachian Bible College (D)

161 College Drive, Mt. Hope WV 25880
County: Raleigh FICE Identification: 007544
Unit ID: 237136
Telephone: (304) 877-6428 Carnegie Class: Spec/Faith
FAX Number: (304) 877-5082 Calendar System: Semester
URL: www.abc.edu
Established: 1950 Annual Undergrad Tuition & Fees: $11,782
Enrollment: 305 Coed
Affiliation or Control: Independent Non-Profit IRS Status: 501(c)3
Highest Offering: Master's
Program: Liberal Arts And General; Teacher Preparatory; Religious Emphasis
Accreditation: NH, BI

01 President ... Dr. Daniel L. ANDERSON
05 Vice President for Academics ... Mr. Daniel S. HANSHEW
10 Vice President for Business ... Mr. Kenneth E. LILLY
30 Vice President for Development ... Rev. Jonathan A. RINKER
32 Vice President for Student Services ... Rev. David E. CHILDS
42 Vice Pres for Extension Ministries ... Mr. David J. HOLLOWAY
33 Dean of Men ... Mr. John M. SHARP
34 Dean of Women ... Mrs. Linda J. CHILDS
06 Registrar ... Dr. Charles N. BETHEL
07 Director of Admissions ... Mr. Scott T. ROSS
08 Librarian ... Mr. David W. DUNKERTON
37 Director of Financial Aid ... Mrs. Cindi A. TURNER
04 Admin Assistant to the President ... Mrs. Elisabeth I. GOLDEN
26 Director of Public Relations ... Mr. Jarod K. BURRER

Bethany College (E)

Main Street, Bethany WV 26032-0417
County: Brooke FICE Identification: 003808
Unit ID: 237181
Telephone: (304) 829-7000 Carnegie Class: Bac/A&S
FAX Number: (304) 829-7700 Calendar System: 4/1/4
URL: www.bethanywv.edu
Established: 1840 Annual Undergrad Tuition & Fees: $23,854
Enrollment: 1,026 Coed
Affiliation or Control: Christian Church (Disciples Of Christ)
IRS Status: 501(c)3
Highest Offering: Master's
Program: Liberal Arts And General; Teacher Preparatory
Accreditation: NH, SW, TED

01 President of the College ... Dr. Scott D. MILLER
03 Executive VP & General Counsel ... Mr. William R. KIEFER
05 Vice President of Academic Affairs ... Dr. Darin E. FIELDS
30 Vice President for Advancement ... Mr. Sven M. DE JONG
04 Executive Asst to the President ... Ms. Deidra R. HALL-NUZUM
100 Assistant to the President ... Dr. Mort GAMBLE
32 Dean of Students ... Mr. Gerald STEBBINS
37 Director of Financial Aid ... Ms. Sheila NELSON-HENSLEY
41 Director of Athletics & Recreation ... Mr. Tim WEAVER
20 Asc VP Acad Affs/Dir Rsrch & Effect ... Dr. Gary H. KAPPEL
88 Director of McCann Learning Center ... Dr. Christina SAMPSON
88 Director of Student Support Service ... Ms. Tracy DEPEW
89 Director of First Year Experience ... Dr. Katrina COOPER
88 Director of International Programs ... Vacant
36 Director of Student Placement ... Mr. John OSBOURNE
23 Director of the Byrd Health Center ... Mrs. Carol TYLER
27 Director of Communications ... Ms. Rebecca ROSE
29 Director of Alumni/Parent Relations ... Ms. Michele REJONIS
88 Director of Advancement Services ... Ms. Shirley KEMP
88 Director of Sports Information ... Mr. Brian ROSE
88 Director of Church Relations ... Dr. Larry GRIMES
18 Director of Physical Plant ... Mr. Theodore D. WILLIAMS
10 Director of Financial Affairs ... Mr. Daniel T. PAJAK
21 Director of Business Services ... Ms. Saralyn DAGUE
19 Director of Safety & Security ... Mr. Gary MORGAN
15 Director of Personnel Services ... Ms. Merlinda LEES
39 Director of Residence Life ... Mr. Jonathan GEYER
35 Director of Student Activiites ... Ms. Heather MULLENDORE
42 Chaplain ... Rev. Scott THAYER
08 Director of the Libraries ... Mrs. Heather MAY-RICCIUTI
88 Director of Network Operations ... Mr. Ron SHAW
88 Director of Info Tech Operations ... Mr. Thomas V. FURBEE
88 Public Services Librarian ... Mr. Trevor ONEST
06 Registrar ... Mrs. Susan DOTY
06 Dir of Student Records & Retention ... Ms. Stephanie KAPPEL
38 College Counselor ... Ms. Renee STOCK
88 General Manager Conference Center ... Ms. Donna WHITE
88 Director of Dining Services ... Mrs. Necol M. DUNSON
40 Manager of the Bookstore ... Ms. Ann CRAFT
07 Director of Enrollment ... Mr. Robert ZITZELSBERGER

Davis & Elkins College (F)

100 Campus Drive, Elkins WV 26241-3996
County: Randolph FICE Identification: 003811
Unit ID: 237358
Telephone: (304) 637-1900 Carnegie Class: Bac/Diverse
FAX Number: (304) 637-1413 Calendar System: 4/1/4
URL: www.dewv.edu
Established: 1904 Annual Undergrad Tuition & Fees: $22,000
Enrollment: 751 Coed
Affiliation or Control: Presbyterian Church (U.S.A.) IRS Status: 501(c)3
Highest Offering: Baccalaureate
Program: Liberal Arts And General; Teacher Preparatory; Business Emphasis
Accreditation: NH, ADNUR, IACBE, TEAC, THEA

01 President ... Dr. G. T. SMITH
05 Provost and Dean of the Faculty ... Dr. Victor L. THACKER
84 VP for Enrollment Management ... Mr. Kevin H. WILSON
10 Director of Financial Operations ... Ms. Greta J. TROASTLE
30 Vice President College Advancement . Ms. Patricia J. SCHUMANN
32 Dean of Students ... Mr. Scott D. GODDARD
08 Assistant Director Booth Library ... Ms. Kathleen DOIG
06 Registrar ... Dr. Stephanie C. HAYNES
37 Director Financial Planning ... Mr. Matthew A. SUMMERS
26 Director of Communications ... Ms. Carol M. SCHULER
15 Director Human Resources ... Ms. M. J. COREY
18 Chief Facilities/Physical Plant ... Mr. Ronald J. SELDERS
20 Associate Provost ... Dr. Joseph M. ROIDT
42 Chaplain ... Dr. Robert R. MCCUTCHEON
41 Director of Athletics ... Mr. Ron PALMER
19 Director of Campus Safety/Security ... Mr. Michael R. JORDAN
44 Director of Advancement Operations ... Ms. Karen L. WILMOTH
04 Executive Asst to the President ... Ms. Robin PRICE

Everest Institute (G)

5514 Big Tyler Road, Cross Lanes WV 25313-1399
County: Kanawha FICE Identification: 010356
Unit ID: 237604
Telephone: (304) 776-6290 Carnegie Class: Assoc/PrivFP
FAX Number: (304) 776-6262 Calendar System: Other
URL: www.everest-institute.com
Established: 1968 Annual Undergrad Tuition & Fees: $25,000
Enrollment: 463 Coed
Affiliation or Control: Proprietary IRS Status: Proprietary
Highest Offering: Associate Degree
Program: Occupational
Accreditation: ACCSC

01 President ... Ms. Aimee SWITZER
05 Director of Education ... Ms. Jennifer RICHMOND
07 Director of Admission ... Ms. Karen WILKINSON
10 Director of Finance ... Mr. Matt LANE
36 Director Career Services ... Ms. Jennifer WHITTINGTON

Future Generations Graduate School (H)

400 Road Less Traveled, Franklin WV 26807-9201
County: Pendleton Identification: 666714
Telephone: (304) 358-2000 Carnegie Class: Not Classified
FAX Number: (304) 358-3008 Calendar System: Other
URL: www.future.edu
Established: 2003 Annual Graduate Tuition & Fees: $17,500
Enrollment: 16 Coed
Affiliation or Control: Independent Non-Profit IRS Status: 501(c)3
Highest Offering: Master's; No Undergraduates
Program: Liberal Arts And General
Accreditation: NH

01 President ... Mr. Jason CALDER
05 Dean ... Dr. Mike RECHLIN

Huntington Junior College (I)

900 Fifth Avenue, Huntington WV 25701-2004
County: Cabell FICE Identification: 009047
Unit ID: 237437
Telephone: (304) 697-7550 Carnegie Class: Assoc/PrivFP
FAX Number: (304) 697-7554 Calendar System: Quarter
URL: www.huntingtonjuniorcollege.edu
Established: 1936 Annual Undergrad Tuition & Fees: $6,825
Enrollment: 1,040 Coed
Affiliation or Control: Proprietary IRS Status: Proprietary
Highest Offering: Associate Degree
Program: 2-Year Principally Bachelor's Creditable; Technical Emphasis
Accreditation: NH, MAC

01 President ... Carolyn A. SMITH
03 Director ... Dr. Catherine E. SNODDY
05 Academic Affairs Director ... Linda J. WEST

ITT Technical Institute (A)

5183 US Route 60, Bldg 1, Suite 40,
Huntington WV 25705
County: Cabell Identification: 666709
Unit ID: 456418
Telephone: (304) 733-8700 Carnegie Class: Not Classified
FAX Number: N/A Calendar System: Other
URL: www.itt-tech.edu
Established: N/A Annual Undergrad Tuition & Fees: N/A
Enrollment: 312 Coed
Affiliation or Control: Proprietary IRS Status: Proprietary
Highest Offering: Associate Degree
Program: Technical Emphasis
Accreditation: ACICS

† Branch campus of ITT Technical Institute, Orange, CA.

Martinsburg Institute (B)

341 Aikens Center, Martinsburg WV 25404
County: Berkeley Identification: 667035
Telephone: (304) 263-6262 Carnegie Class: Not Classified
FAX Number: (866) 703-6611 Calendar System: Other
URL: www.martinsburginstitute.edu
Established: 1980 Annual Undergrad Tuition & Fees: $3,000
Enrollment: 775 Coed
Affiliation or Control: Proprietary IRS Status: Proprietary
Highest Offering: Associate Degree
Program: Occupational; 2-Year Principally Bachelor's Creditable; Technical Emphasis
Accreditation: DETC

01 President .... Paul VIBOCH
05 Chief Academic Officer .... Stella GARLICK
07 Director of Admissions .... Laurie MAURO
06 Registrar .... Rita CLAYPOLE

Mountain State College (C)

1608 16th Street, Parkersburg WV 26101
County: Wood FICE Identification: 005008
Unit ID: 237598
Telephone: (304) 485-5487 Carnegie Class: Assoc/PrivFP
FAX Number: (304) 485-3524 Calendar System: Quarter
URL: www.msc.edu
Established: 1888 Annual Undergrad Tuition & Fees: $8,100
Enrollment: 281 Coed
Affiliation or Control: Proprietary IRS Status: Proprietary
Highest Offering: Associate Degree
Program: Occupational; 2-Year Principally Bachelor's Creditable; Business Emphasis
Accreditation: ACICS

01 President .... Mrs. Judith SUTTON

Mountain State University (D)

410 Neville Street, Beckley WV 25801
County: Raleigh FICE Identification: 003807
Unit ID: 237154
Telephone: (304) 253-7351 Carnegie Class: Master's L
FAX Number: (304) 929-1600 Calendar System: Semester
URL: www.mountainstate.edu
Established: 1933 Annual Undergrad Tuition & Fees: $7,350
Enrollment: 5,550 Coed
Affiliation or Control: Independent Non-Profit IRS Status: 501(c)3
Highest Offering: Doctorate
Program: Occupational; 2-Year Principally Bachelor's Creditable; Liberal Arts And General; Teacher Preparatory; Professional; Business Emphasis
Accreditation: NH, ACFEI, ANEST, ARCPA, DMS, MAC, NUR, OTA, PTAA, RAD, SW

01 President .... Dr. Charles H. POLK
45 Senior Vice Pres/ Spec Asst to Pres .... Ms. Kelli L. MAYS
03 Exec Vice Pres Administration .... Dr. Cynthia D. ALEXANDER
12 Exec Vice Pres Beckley Campus .... Dr. Roslyn CLARK-ARTIS
106 Exec Vice Pres Distance Ed .... Mr. James G. SILOSKY
10 VP of Finance/Chief Financial Ofcr .... Ms. Michele SARRETT
43 Vice President of Legal Affairs .... Mr. Jon REED
26 VP Marketing/Business Development .... Ms. Susan BACKOFEN
76 Dean School Health Sciences .... Ms. Karen BOWLING
49 Dean of the Sch of Arts & Sci .... Dr. Vincent BEACH
58 Dean of Graduate Studies .... Dr. William WHITE
50 Int Dean School Business/Technology .... Dr. Marjorie SMITH
66 Dean of School of Nursing .... Dr. Sheila GARLAND
32 Dean of Students .... Ms. Mandy WRISTON
88 Assoc Dean Sch Ldrship & Prof Dev .... Dr. Ruth WYLIE
15 Sr Officer of Human Resources .... Ms. M. Kay STUMP
106 Dean Online & Individual Learning .... Dr. James OWSTON
88 Sr Ofcr School of Experiential Lrng .... Dr. Mark MILLER
66 Sr Academic Ofcr Grad Nursing .... Dr. Jessica SHARP
12 Exec Director of Florida Campus .... Mr. Randy WHITE
12 Exec Director Center Twnsh Campus .... Mr. Mark CICCARELLI
12 Exec Director NC Campus .... Mr. Dallas BRAGG
27 Chief Information Officer .... Vacant
26 Director Media & Public Relations .... Vacant
29 Dir Alumni Relations/Annual Giving .... Ms. Beth PERRY
40 Dir Univ Bookstores/Auxiliary Svcs .... Mr. Glenn JOHNSON
19 Dir of Security & Campus Operations .... Mr. Everette STEELE
96 Director of Purchasing .... Mr. Scott MANGUM
08 Dir Library/Technical Resources .... Ms. Judy ALTIS
88 Coordinator of Assessment .... Ms. Angela SPELOCK
88 Director of Information Analysis .... Ms. Kim KEATON
06 Registrar .... Dr. Rhonda SHEPPERD
06 Associate Registrar .... Ms. Angie RIFFE
41 Athletic Director .... Mr. Robert BOLEN, III
37 Director of Financial Aid .... Ms. Joann ROSS
36 Dir Practicum Ctr & Career Services .... Vacant
84 Director of Admissions .... Ms. Cynthia JUSTUS
07 Director of Recruiting & Training .... Ms. Iris MCGEE
05 Chief Academic Officer .... Dr. Roslyn ARTIS
18 General Manager Facilities .... Mr. Andy BIHL
28 Director International Student Svcs .... Mr. Charles LOWRY

National College (E)

421 Hilltop Drive, Princeton WV 24740
County: Tazewell Identification: 666499
Telephone: (304) 487-3845 Carnegie Class: Not Classified
FAX Number: (304) 487-3852 Calendar System: Quarter
URL: www.ncbt.edu
Established: 1886 Annual Undergrad Tuition & Fees: $9,790
Enrollment: 197 Coed
Affiliation or Control: Proprietary IRS Status: Proprietary
Highest Offering: Baccalaureate
Program: Occupational; Business Emphasis
Accreditation: ACICS, MAC

01 President .... Mr. Frank LONGAKER
03 Vice President .... Ms. Lenora DOWNING
05 Campus Director .... Mr. Denver RIFFE

Ohio Valley University (F)

1 Campus View Drive, Vienna WV 26105-8000
County: Wood FICE Identification: 003819
Unit ID: 237640
Telephone: (304) 865-6000 Carnegie Class: Bac/Diverse
FAX Number: (304) 865-6001 Calendar System: Semester
URL: www.ovu.edu
Established: 1958 Annual Undergrad Tuition & Fees: $16,150
Enrollment: 482 Coed
Affiliation or Control: Churches Of Christ IRS Status: 501(c)3
Highest Offering: Master's
Program: Liberal Arts And General; Teacher Preparatory
Accreditation: NH, IACBE, @TEAC

01 President .... Dr. Harold SHANK
03 Executive Vice President .... Mr. Steve MORGAN
05 Vice Pres for Academic Affairs .... Dr. Jim BULLOCK
30 Vice Pres for Advancement .... Vacant
10 Senior Vice Pres for Finance .... Vacant
29 Sr Vice Pres Alumni Services .... Mr. Jack THORN
84 Vice President for Enrollment .... Mr. Larry LYONS
43 General Counsel .... Dr. Becky D. MATHIS-STUMP
28 Asst to Pres for Minority Relations .... Mr. Harry OGLETREE
18 Director of Campus Operations .... Mr. Eric BUCKLIN
37 Director Student Financial Aid .... Mr. Dennis W. COX
06 Registrar .... Mrs. Sarah BARTON
36 Director of Career Services .... Mrs. Kathy MULLER
32 Student Life Officer .... Mr. Jason DOUGHERTY
08 Library Director .... Mr. Rodney WOOTEN
83 Dean Col Behav Scies/Biblical Stds .... Dr. Michael MOSS
41 Director of Athletics .... Mr. Dennis COX

Salem International University (G)

223 W Main Street, Box 500, Salem WV 26426-0500
County: Harrison FICE Identification: 003820
Unit ID: 237783
Telephone: (304) 326-1109 Carnegie Class: Master's M
FAX Number: (304) 326-1246 Calendar System: Semester
URL: www.salemu.edu
Established: 1888 Annual Undergrad Tuition & Fees: $14,700
Enrollment: 828 Coed
Affiliation or Control: Proprietary IRS Status: Proprietary
Highest Offering: Master's
Program: Occupational; 2-Year Principally Bachelor's Creditable; Liberal Arts And General; Teacher Preparatory; Professional; Nursing Emphasis
Accreditation: NH

00 Chancellor/CEO .... Mr. James W. BROOKS
01 President .... Mr. John LUOTTO
03 Executive Vice President .... Dr. Cecil E. KIRKLAND
05 Provost/CAO .... Dr. Debra HARRISON
10 VP Finance/CFO .... Mr. Dan NELANT
07 VP Admissions & Enrollment Mgmt .... Mr. Andrew ANDERSON
27 VP Information Technology/CIO .... Mr. Pieter BRESLER
06 Registrar .... Ms. Rebecca HALL
53 Dean School of Education .... Dr. Craig MCCLELLAN
49 Dean School of Arts & Sciences .... Dr. Larry ZBACH
66 Director Nursing Education .... Dr. Theresa COWAN
50 Dean Business .... Dr. John CAVENDISH
08 Dean Library Services .... Dr. Phyllis D. FREEDMAN
19 Director Campus Security .... Mr. Ross LODGE
18 Director Physical Plant & Maint .... Mr. John BOWERS
41 Athletic Director .... Mr. Keith BULLION
15 Human Resources .... Ms. Sue ROBISON

University of Charleston (H)

2300 Maccorkle Avenue, SE, Charleston WV 25304-1099
County: Kanawha FICE Identification: 003818
Unit ID: 237312
Telephone: (304) 357-4800 Carnegie Class: Bac/Diverse
FAX Number: (304) 357-4715 Calendar System: Semester
URL: www.ucwv.edu
Established: 1888 Annual Undergrad Tuition & Fees: $25,000
Enrollment: 1,518 Coed
Affiliation or Control: Independent Non-Profit IRS Status: 501(c)3
Highest Offering: Doctorate
Program: Liberal Arts And General; Teacher Preparatory; Professional; Fine Arts Emphasis
Accreditation: NH, ADNUR, NUR, PHAR, RAD, TEAC

01 President .... Dr. Edwin H. WELCH
05 Provost & Dean of Faculty .... Dr. Letha ZOOK
10 Vice Pres Administration & Finance .... Mrs. Cleta M. HARLESS
27 Vice President for Communications .... Mrs. Jennie FERRETTI
30 Vice Pres for Development .... Mr. Ben BEAKES
06 Registrar .... Dr. Michael C. LEVY
29 Alumni Director .... Ms. Bridgette BORST
08 Director of Library .... Mr. John ADKINS
32 Dean of Students .... Ms. Bethany MEIGHEN
37 Associate Director Financial Aid .... Ms. Nina MORTON
35 Coordinator of Student Programs .... Ms. Meghan SPARROW
40 Bookstore Manager .... Ms. Sara STURGEN
18 Director Plant & Property .... Mr. Tim EULER
19 Director Security .... Mr. Jack L. RINCHICH
41 Athletic Director .... Mr. Thomas NOZICA
88 Director of Colleague Program .... Dr. Barbara WRIGHT
85 Coord International Student Pgms .... Ms. Audrey PITONAK
13 Director of University Computing .... Mr. Tim EULER
21 Director of Operations .... Vacant
09 Director of Institutional Research .... Ms. Lisa DAWKINS
15 Director Personnel Services .... Ms. Tammy HOLSTINE
21 Associate Business Officer .... Mr. Steve DAVIS
49 Chair Division Arts & Sciences .... Dr. Barbara WRIGHT
50 Chair Division Business .... Dr. Robert BLISS
76 Chair Division Health Sciences .... Vacant
50 Dean Graduate School of Business .... Dr. Bart MORRISON
67 Dean School of Pharmacy .... Dr. Michelle EASTON

Valley College - Beckley Campus (I)

713 South Oakwood Avenue, Beckley WV 25801
County: Raleigh FICE Identification: 030844
Unit ID: 377652
Telephone: (304) 252-9547 Carnegie Class: Not Classified
FAX Number: (304) 252-1694 Calendar System: Other
URL: www.vct.edu
Established: 1983 Annual Undergrad Tuition & Fees: $9,500
Enrollment: 68 Coed
Affiliation or Control: Proprietary IRS Status: Proprietary
Highest Offering: Associate Degree
Program: Occupational; Business Emphasis
Accreditation: CNCE

01 Executive Director .... Ms. Beth GARDNER

Valley College - Martinsburg Campus (J)

287 Aikens Center, Martinsburg WV 25404-6203
County: Berkeley FICE Identification: 026094
Unit ID: 377661
Telephone: (304) 263-0979 Carnegie Class: Assoc/PrivFP
FAX Number: (304) 263-2413 Calendar System: Other
URL: www.vct.edu
Established: 1983 Annual Undergrad Tuition & Fees: $8,800
Enrollment: 60 Coed
Affiliation or Control: Proprietary IRS Status: Proprietary
Highest Offering: Associate Degree
Program: Occupational; Business Emphasis
Accreditation: ACICS

01 Executive Director .... Mr. Terry LUSHBAUGH

Valley College - Princeton Campus (K)

616 Harrison Street, Princeton WV 24740
County: Mercer FICE Identification: 030842
Unit ID: 377670
Telephone: (304) 425-2323 Carnegie Class: Not Classified
FAX Number: (304) 425-5890 Calendar System: Other
URL: www.vct.edu
Established: 1986 Annual Undergrad Tuition & Fees: $9,500
Enrollment: 36 Coed
Affiliation or Control: Proprietary IRS Status: Proprietary
Highest Offering: Associate Degree
Program: Occupational; Business Emphasis
Accreditation: CNCE

01 Executive Director .... Ms. Beth GARDNER
03 Associate Director .... Mr. Tony RIFFE

West Virginia Business College (L)

116 Pennsylvania Avenue, Nutter Fort WV 26301-4516
County: Harrison Identification: 666507
Unit ID: 237978

Telephone: (304) 624-7695 Carnegie Class: Assoc/PrivFP
FAX Number: (304) 622-2149 Calendar System: Quarter
URL: www.wvbc.edu
Established: 1881 Annual Undergrad Tuition & Fees: $9,500
Enrollment: 75 Coed
Affiliation or Control: Proprietary IRS Status: Proprietary
Highest Offering: Associate Degree
Program: Occupational
Accreditation: ACICS

01 Director Mr. Robert WRIGHT

† Branch campus of West Virginia Business College, Wheeling, WV.

West Virginia Business College (A)

1052 Main Street, Wheeling WV 26003-2702
County: Ohio FICE Identification: 010861
Unit ID: 405526
Telephone: (304) 232-0361 Carnegie Class: Assoc/PrivFP
FAX Number: (304) 232-0363 Calendar System: Quarter
URL: www.wvbc.edu
Established: 1881 Annual Undergrad Tuition & Fees: $18,000
Enrollment: 200 Coed
Affiliation or Control: Proprietary IRS Status: Proprietary
Highest Offering: Associate Degree
Program: Occupational
Accreditation: ACICS

01 Director Mr. James S. WEIR

*West Virginia Council for Community & Technical College Education (B)

1018 Kanawha Boulevard E, Suite 700,
Charleston WV 25301-2800
County: Kanawha Identification: 666993
Telephone: (304) 558-0265 Carnegie Class: N/A
FAX Number: (304) 558-1646
URL: www.wvctcs.org

01 Chancellor James L. SKIDMORE

*Blue Ridge Community and Technical College (C)

400 W Stephen Street, Martinsburg WV 25401
County: Berkeley FICE Identification: 039573
Unit ID: 446774
Telephone: (304) 260-4380 Carnegie Class: Assoc/Pub-R-M
FAX Number: (304) 260-4376 Calendar System: Semester
URL: www.blueridgectc.edu
Established: 1974 Annual Undergrad Tuition & Fees (In-State): $3,120
Enrollment: 3,813 Coed
Affiliation or Control: State IRS Status: 501(c)3
Highest Offering: Associate Degree
Program: Occupational; 2-Year Principally Bachelor's Creditable
Accreditation: NH, ADNUR

02 President Dr. Peter G. CHECKOVICH
05 Vice President of Curriculum Dr. George PERRY
50 Associate VP of Business and Tech Mr. Randall C. MILLER
103 VP Economic and Workforce Devel Dr. Ann M. SHIPWAY
84 VP of Enrollment Management Ms. Leslie SEE
06 Registrar Ms. Angie M. KINDER
07 Director of Access Ms. Brenda NEAL
10 Chief Financial Officer Ms. Ann PRICE
15 VP of Administration and HR Dr. Trudie HOLDER
14 Director of IT Mr. Michael BYERS
38 Director of Student Success Mr. James L. MCDOUGLE
37 Director of Financial Aid Ms. Doris GLENN

*Bridgemont Community and Technical College (D)

619 2nd Avenue, Montgomery WV 25136
County: Fayette FICE Identification: 040473
Unit ID: 445674
Telephone: (304) 734-6600 Carnegie Class: Assoc/Pub-S-SC
FAX Number: (304) 734-6630 Calendar System: Semester
URL: www.bridgemont.edu
Established: 2004 Annual Undergrad Tuition & Fees (In-District): $3,484
Enrollment: 931 Coed
Affiliation or Control: State/Local IRS Status: 501(c)3
Highest Offering: Associate Degree
Program: Occupational; 2-Year Principally Bachelor's Creditable
Accreditation: NH, DH, ENGT

02 President Dr. Beverly Jo HARRIS
05 Vice Pres for Academic Affairs Dr. Kristin MALLORY
10 Chief Financial Officer Ms. Patricia HUNT
06 Registrar Ms. Connie KEIFFER
37 Director of Financial Aid Ms. Mary BLIZZARD
35 Director of Student Services Ms. Jeanne SMITH
26 Director of Institutional Marketing Mr. Jack NUCKOLS
13 Director of Computer Services Mr. Thomas MINNICH
09 Director of Institutional Research Mr. James F. FAUVER
08 Interim Director of Library Ms. Alena Jewel RUCKER
51 Director of Extended/Continuing Ed Ms. Kathy LEFTWICH
18 Director of Physical Plant Mr. George BOSSIE
78 Director Career Svcs/Cooperative Ed Mr. Cantrell L. MILLER
22 Dir Affirm Action/Equal Opportunity Ms. Jennifer MCINTOSH
29 Director of Alumni Relations Mr. Jack NUCKOLS
07 Director of Admissions Ms. Joyce SURBAUGH
15 Director Personnel Services Mr. Gene LOPEZ
21 Associate Business Officer Ms. Cathy AQUINO
28 Director of Diversity Ms. Jennifer MCINTOSH
30 Chief Development Mr. Jack NUCKOLS
32 Chief Student Life Officer Ms. Jeanne SMITH
36 Director Student Placement Mr. Cantrell MILLER
96 Director of Purchasing Mr. John POWELL
84 Director Enrollment Management Ms. Joyce SURBAUGH

*Eastern West Virginia Community and Technical College (E)

316 Eastern Drive, Moorefield WV 26836-1155
County: Hardy FICE Identification: 041190
Unit ID: 438708
Telephone: (304) 434-8000 Carnegie Class: Assoc/Pub-R-S
FAX Number: (304) 434-7001 Calendar System: Semester
URL: www.eastern.wvnet.edu
Established: 1999 Annual Undergrad Tuition & Fees (In-State): $2,184
Enrollment: 645 Coed
Affiliation or Control: State IRS Status: Exempt
Highest Offering: Associate Degree
Program: Occupational; 2-Year Principally Bachelor's Creditable; Technical Emphasis
Accreditation: NH

02 President Dr. Charles TERRELL
13 Dir Information Systems/Technology Mr. Tim RIGGLEMAN
10 Exec Dean for Financial & Operation Ms. Penny REARDON
32 Dean for Academic & Student Service Mr. Robert EAGLE
32 Assoc Dean Academic & Student Svcs Ms. Sherry BECKER-GORBY
103 Director of Workforce Education Ms. Sherry WATTS
75 Dean of Career/Technical/Workforce Mr. Ward MALCOLM

*Kanawha Valley Community & Technical College (F)

PO Box 1000; Cole Complex 102, Institute WV 25112
County: Kanawha FICE Identification: 040386
Unit ID: 445018
Telephone: (304) 766-4093 Carnegie Class: Assoc/Pub-R-S
FAX Number: (304) 766-5714 Calendar System: Semester
URL: www.kvctc.edu
Established: 1953 Annual Undergrad Tuition & Fees (In-District): $3,082
Enrollment: 1,995 Coed
Affiliation or Control: State/Local IRS Status: Exempt
Highest Offering: Associate Degree
Program: Occupational; 2-Year Principally Bachelor's Creditable
Accreditation: NH, ADNUR, NMT

02 President Dr. Joseph L. BADGLEY
10 Vice President Finance Dr. Patricia HUNT
32 Vice President of Student Services Ms. Susan SPANGLER
04 Special Assistant to President Vacant
05 Int Vice President Academic Affairs Mrs. Megan LORENZ
103 Vice Pres Workforce Economic Devel Mrs. Laura L. MCCULLOUGH
06 Registrar Mr. J. P. OWENS
07 Director of Admissions Ms. Michelle D. WICKS
37 Associate Director of Financial Aid Ms. Carla BLANKENBEUHLER
26 PR Associate and Webmaster Mrs. Kristin LEDFORD
16 Human Resources Representative Ms. Michelle BISSELL
51 Director of Continuing Education Mrs. Kim SOVINE
21 Business Manager Mrs. Kristi WILLIAMS
96 Chief Purchasing Officer Mr. John POWELL

*Mountwest Community and Technical College (G)

PO Box 1539, Huntington WV 25716
County: Cabell FICE Identification: 040414
Unit ID: 444954
Telephone: (304) 696-4623 Carnegie Class: Assoc/Pub-R-M
FAX Number: (304) 522-3023 Calendar System: Semester
URL: www.mctc.edu
Established: 1975 Annual Undergrad Tuition & Fees (In-District): $2,952
Enrollment: 2,856 Coed
Affiliation or Control: State/Local IRS Status: 501(c)3
Highest Offering: Associate Degree
Program: Occupational; 2-Year Principally Bachelor's Creditable
Accreditation: NH, ACBSP, MAC, PTAA

02 President Dr. Keith J. COTRONEO
03 Vice President/CFO Mr. Herbert J. KARLET
05 Executive Dean Ms. Carol A. PERRY
32 Dean of Student Services Ms. Billie K. BROOKS
51 Dean Continuing & Corp Education Mr. Steven L. BROWN
76 Assoc Dean Allied Health Technology Ms. Jean M. CHAPPELL
103 Exec Director Workforce Development Mr. Steven L. BROWN
15 Director Employee Development Ms. Stephanie A. NEAL
27 Chief Information Officier Mrs. Terri L. TOMBLIN-BYRD

*New River Community and Technical College (H)

221 George Street, Suite 2, Beckley WV 25801
County: Raleigh FICE Identification: 039603
Unit ID: 447582
Telephone: (304) 929-5472 Carnegie Class: Assoc/Pub-R-M
FAX Number: (304) 929-5478 Calendar System: Semester
URL: www.newriver.edu
Established: 2003 Annual Undergrad Tuition & Fees (In-State): $3,080
Enrollment: 3,047 Coed
Affiliation or Control: State IRS Status: 501(c)3
Highest Offering: Associate Degree
Program: Occupational; 2-Year Principally Bachelor's Creditable
Accreditation: NH

02 President Dr. Ted D. SPRING
05 Exec Vice Pres and Chief Acad Ofcr Dr. Harry R. FAULK
12 Campus Dean-Nicholas County Mr. Fred B. CULLER
12 Campus Dean-Beckley Ms. Carolyn G. SIZEMORE
12 Campus Dean-Greenbrier Mr. Roger D. GRIFFITH
12 Campus Dean-Mercer County Mr. Steve WISE
30 VP Inst Advancement/Workforce Educ Mr. William J. LOOPE
45 Director of Inst Effectiveness Ms. Renae R. MCGINNIS
10 Vice Pres Financial/Admin Affairs Mr. Stephen BENSON
06 Registrar Ms. Donna M. LEWIS
08 Staff Librarian Mr. Robert H. COSTON
13 Vice Pres/Chief Technology Officer Dr. David J. AYERSMAN
15 Director of HR/Process Improvement Ms. Leah A. TAYLOR
27 Director of Communications Ms. Elizabeth M. BELCHER
37 Director of Financial Aid Ms. Patricia HARMON
84 Director of Enrollment Services Ms. Tracy L. EVANS
96 Director of Purchasing Ms. Twana JACKSON
88 Controller Ms. Heike I. SOEFFKER-CULICERTO
26 Director of Public Relations Ms. Barbara A. ELLIOTT
53 Dir Ctr for Teaching Excellence Mr. Ralph C. PAYNE
04 Exec Secretary to the President Ms. Lori A. MIDKIFF

*Pierpont Community & Technical College (I)

1201 Locust Avenue, Fairmont WV 26554-2470
County: Marion FICE Identification: 040385
Unit ID: 443492
Telephone: (304) 367-4692 Carnegie Class: Not Classified
FAX Number: (304) 367-4881 Calendar System: Semester
URL: www.pierpont.edu
Established: 1974 Annual Undergrad Tuition & Fees (In-State): $3,500
Enrollment: 2,946 Coed
Affiliation or Control: State IRS Status: 501(c)3
Highest Offering: Associate Degree
Program: Occupational; 2-Year Principally Bachelor's Creditable
Accreditation: NH, ACFEI, MLTAD, NAIT, PTAA

02 President Dr. Doreen LARSON
10 VP for Finance and Administration Mr. Dale R. BRADLEY
05 Interim VP for Academic Affairs Ms. Leslie LOVETT
86 VP for Organization and Development Mr. Stephen E. LEACH
103 VP Workforce & Economic Development Mr. Paul SCHREFFLER
26 VP for Community Engagement Ms. Sarah L. HENSLEY
97 Int Dean Sch of Academic Studies Ms. Linda KING
88 Dean Sch of Business/Aviation/Tech Dr. Gerald BACZA
76 Dean School of Health Careers Dr. Rosemarie ROMESBURG
88 Dean School of Human Services Dr. Beth NEWCOME

*Southern West Virginia Community and Technical College (J)

P. O. Box 2900, Mount Gay WV 25637-2900
County: Logan FICE Identification: 003816
Unit ID: 237817
Telephone: (304) 792-7098 Carnegie Class: Assoc/Pub-R-M
FAX Number: (304) 792-7046 Calendar System: Trimester
URL: www.southernwv.edu
Established: 1971 Annual Undergrad Tuition & Fees (In-State): $2,304
Enrollment: 2,565 Coed
Affiliation or Control: State IRS Status: 501(c)3
Highest Offering: Associate Degree
Program: Occupational; 2-Year Principally Bachelor's Creditable; Technical Emphasis
Accreditation: NH, ADNUR, DH, MLTAD, RAD, SURGT

02 President Ms. Joanne J. TOMBLIN
03 Executive Vice President Vacant
10 Chief Financial Officer Mr. Samuel LITTERAL
05 Vice President for Academic Affairs Vacant
103 VP Economic Workforce & Comm Dev Ms. Allyn S. BARKER
32 Interim VP for Student Services Ms. Allyn S. BARKER
14 Chief Information Officer Mr. George BESHEARS
30 Vice President for Development Mr. Ronald E. LEMON
27 Vice President for Communications Ms. Cynthia L. CRIGGER
15 Human Resources Director Ms. Patricia CLAY
04 Assistant to the President Ms. Emma L. BAISDEN
101 Assistant to the Board of Governors Ms. Emma L. BAISDEN
20 Dean Career and Techncial Programs Ms. Pamela L. ALDERMAN
20 Dean University Transfer Programs Dr. Cindy L. MCCOY
12 Director Wyoming Campus Operations Mr. David LORD
12 Director Wmson Campus Operations Ms. Rita G. ROBERSON
12 Director Logan Campus Operations Mr. Randy SKEENS

12 Director Boone Campus Operations ... Mr. William COOK
76 Chair Allied Health & Nursing Dept ... Ms. Alyce PATTERSON-DIAZ
50 Chair Business Department ... Dr. Gail HALL
72 Chair Technology & Engineering Dept . Ms. Carol A. HOWERTON
81 Chair Science Department ... Mr. Guy LOWES, JR.
88 Chair Transitional Studies ... Mr. Steven LACEK
83 Chair Social Sciences Department ... Dr. Charles WOOD, II
81 Chair Mathematics Department ... Ms. Melinda D. SAUNDERS
79 Chair Humanities Department ... Mr. George H. MORRISON
06 Interim Registrar ... Ms. Teri WELLS
37 Director Student Financial Asst ... Ms. Cindy POWERS
08 Director of Libraries ... Ms. Kimberly L. MAYNARD
105 Graphics and Web Design ... Mr. Marcus GIBBS
96 Director of Purchasing ... Ms. Melissa CREAKMAN

*West Virginia Northern Community College (A)

1704 Market Street, Wheeling WV 26003-3643

County: Ohio FICE Identification: 009054
Unit ID: 238014
Telephone: (304) 233-5900 Carnegie Class: Assoc/Pub-R-M
FAX Number: (304) 232-4651 Calendar System: Semester
URL: www.wvncc.edu
Established: 1972 Annual Undergrad Tuition & Fees (In-State): $2,478
Enrollment: 4,070 Coed
Affiliation or Control: State IRS Status: 501(c)3
Highest Offering: Associate Degree
Program: Occupational; 2-Year Principally Bachelor's Creditable
Accreditation: NH, ACFEI, ADNUR, MAC, SURGT

02 President ... Dr. Martin OLSHINSKY
05 Vice President Academic Affairs ... Dr. Vicki RILEY
10 CFO & VP Administrative Services ... Mr. Stephen LIPPIELLO
103 Vice Pres Econonic/Workforce Dev ... Mr. J. Michael KOON
32 Vice President Student Services ... Mrs. Janet FIKE
31 Dean Community Relations ... Mr. Robert DEFRANCIS
72 Dean Information Technology ... Mrs. Sue PELLEY
09 Dir Inst Research/Info Systems ... Vacant
18 Director of Facilities ... Mr. Jim BALLER
29 Director Alumni Association ... Mr. Zac WYCHERLEY
06 Registrar ... Mrs. Nancy GLENN
15 Director Human Resources ... Mrs. Peggy CARMICHAEL
30 Exec to the Pres for Development ... Mrs. Emily FISHER
36 Director Career Planning/Placement ... Mr. Zac WYCHERLEY
12 Campus Dean Weirton ... Vacant
12 Campus Dean Wheeling ... Vacant
12 Campus Dean New Martinsville ... Mr. Larry TACKETT
32 Director Student Union Activities ... Mrs. Shannon PAYTON
07 Associate Director Admissions ... Mr. Richard MCCRAY

*West Virginia Higher Education Policy Commission (B)

1018 Kanawha Boulevard E, Ste 700,
Charleston WV 25301-2887

County: Kanawha FICE Identification: 033440
Unit ID: 237941
Telephone: (304) 558-2101 Carnegie Class: N/A
FAX Number: (304) 558-5719
URL: www.hepc.wvnet.edu

01 Chancellor ... Dr. Brian E. NOLAND
05 Chancellor Comm/Tech College Educ ... Mr. James L. SKIDMORE
46 Vice Chanc for Science & Research ... Dr. Paul L. HILL
100 Chief of Staff ... Ms. Ashley L. SCHUMAKER
20 Director Academic Affairs ... Dr. Kathy BUTLER
10 Chief Financial Officer ... Mr. Richard B. DONOVAN
43 General Counsel ... Mr. Bruce R. WALKER
46 Sr Director of Policy & Planning ... Mr. Robert E. ANDERSON
32 Dir Student/Educational Services ... Mr. Daniel E. CROCKETT
37 Dir State Financial Aid Programs ... Vacant
11 Director Administrative Services ... Vacant

*Bluefield State College (C)

219 Rock Street, Bluefield WV 24701-2198

County: Mercer FICE Identification: 003809
Unit ID: 237215
Telephone: (304) 327-4000 Carnegie Class: Bac/Diverse
FAX Number: (304) 325-7747 Calendar System: Semester
URL: www.bluefieldstate.edu
Established: 1895 Annual Undergrad Tuition & Fees (In-State): $4,908
Enrollment: 2,063 Coed
Affiliation or Control: State IRS Status: 501(c)3
Highest Offering: Baccalaureate
Program: Liberal Arts And General; Teacher Preparatory
Accreditation: NH, ACBSP, ADNUR, ENGT, NURSE, RAD, TED

02 President ... Dr. Albert L. WALKER
05 Int Vice Pres Academic Affs/Provost ... Dr. Robin WARE
10 Vice Pres Financial/Admin Affairs ... Ms. Shelia JOHNSON
32 Vice President Student Affairs ... Mr. John C. CARDWELL
04 Dir Inst/Media Rels/Asst to Pres ... Mr. James A. NELSON
88 Executive Director Title III ... Dr. Felica WILLIAMS
06 Registrar ... Mr. Ray MULL
08 Director Library Services ... Ms. Joanna THOMPSON
24 Chief Technology Officer ... Dr. Thomas E. BLEVINS
91 Director of Computer Services ... Mr. Tom G. COOK
36 Director of Placement ... Mr. Thomas HARRISON
07 Director of Admissions ... Mr. Kenneth MANDEVILLE
37 Director of Financial Aid ... Mr. Thomas ILSE
15 Director of Human Resources ... Ms. Christina BROGDON
18 Admin Asst Senior of Physical Plant ... Ms. Diana GIBSON
19 Director Public Safety ... Mr. Richard AKERS
09 Director of Institutional Research ... Dr. Tracey ANDERSON
38 Director of Counseling ... Dr. Cravor JONES
29 Director Alumni Affairs ... Ms. Deirdre GUYTON
40 Manager Bookstore ... Ms. Virginia RICHARDSON
41 Athletic Director ... Mr. Terry BROWN
50 Dean School of Business ... Dr. Steve BOURNE
49 Dean School of Arts and Sciences ... Dr. David HAUS
54 Dean School of Eng Tech/Comp Sci ... Mr. Frank HART
53 Dean School of Education ... Dr. Thomas BLEVINS
66 Dean School Nursing/Allied Health ... Ms. Angela LAMBERT
66 ADN Program Director ... Ms. Sandra WYNN
66 BSN Program Director ... Ms. Beth PRITCHETT
88 Program Dir of Radiologic Tech ... Ms. Melissa HAYE
61 Program Dir Criminal Justice ... Mr. Michael LILLY
28 Director of Multicultural Affs ... Dr. Sapphire CUREG
96 Director of Purchasing ... Mr. Paul RUTHERFORD
30 Director of Advancement/Planning ... Ms. Karen HARVEY

*Concord University (D)

PO Box 1000, Athens WV 24712-1000

County: Mercer FICE Identification: 003810
Unit ID: 237330
Telephone: (304) 384-3115 Carnegie Class: Bac/Diverse
FAX Number: (304) 384-9044 Calendar System: Semester
URL: www.concord.edu
Established: 1872 Annual Undergrad Tuition & Fees (In-State): $5,446
Enrollment: 2,822 Coed
Affiliation or Control: State IRS Status: 501(c)3
Highest Offering: Master's
Program: Liberal Arts And General; Teacher Preparatory; Professional
Accreditation: NH, SW, TED

02 President ... Dr. Gregory F. ALOIA
05 VP & Academic Dean ... Dr. John David SMITH
30 Interim VP for Advancement ... Mrs. Alicia BESENYEI
20 Associate Dean ... Dr. George TOWERS
20 Associate Dean ... Dr. Kendra BOGGESS
32 VP Student Aff/Dir of Retention ... Dr. Marjie FLANIGAN
10 VP for Business & Finance ... Dr. Charles L. BECKER
07 VP for Admissions & Financial Aid ... Vacant
12 Director of the Beckley Center ... Dr. William A. O'BRIEN
06 Registrar ... Mrs. Carolyn COX
08 Director of Libraries ... Dr. Stephen ROWE
39 Dir Res Life & Fac/Int Dean of Stdn ... Mr. Rick DILLON
37 Director of Student Financial Aid ... Mrs. Debra TURNER
84 Director of Enrollment Management ... Mr. Kent GAMBLE
29 Director of Alumni Relations ... Ms. Sarah TURNER
31 Director Bonner Scholars Program ... Mrs. Kathy BALL
14 Director of Computer Center ... Mr. John SPENCER
16 Human Resources Director ... Mr. Marshall CAMPBELL
18 Director Physical Plant ... Mr. Jeffrey SHUMAKER
19 Director of Public Safety ... Chief Mark STELLA
36 Director of Career Services ... Ms. Tammy MONK
38 Director of Counseling ... Ms. Sandy GRIM
40 Bookstore Manager ... Mr. Christopher SMALLWOOD
41 Athletic Director ... Mr. Kevin GARRETT
21 Financial Reporting Officer ... Ms. Elizabeth J. CAHILL
96 Interim Purchasing Agent ... Mr. Gary HYLTON
09 Director of Institutional Research ... Mr. John SPENCER
24 Ctr for Academic Technologies ... Mr. Steve MEADOWS
26 Public Relations/Mktg Specialist ... Mr. Lance MCDANIEL
25 Director of Grants and Contracts ... Mr. Scott INGHRAM

*Fairmont State University (E)

1201 Locust Avenue, Fairmont WV 26554-2470

County: Marion FICE Identification: 003812
Unit ID: 237367
Telephone: (304) 367-4000 Carnegie Class: Master's S
FAX Number: (304) 367-4789 Calendar System: Semester
URL: www.fairmontstate.edu
Established: 1865 Annual Undergrad Tuition & Fees (In-State): $5,327
Enrollment: 4,709 Coed
Affiliation or Control: State IRS Status: 501(c)3
Highest Offering: Master's
Program: Liberal Arts And General; Teacher Preparatory; Business Emphasis
Accreditation: NH, ACBSP, ADNUR, ENGR, ENGT, NURSE, TED

02 Interim President FSU ... Dr. Maria C. ROSE
05 Interim Provost/VP Academic Affairs . Dr. Christina M. LAVORATA
10 Vice Pres Admin & Fiscal Affairs ... Mr. Enrico A. PORTO
30 Vice President for Inst Advancement ... Mrs. Devanna CORLEY
27 VP/Chief Information Officer ... Mr. David A. TAMM
25 Vice Pres Research & Grad Studies ... Vacant
32 Senior VP Enrollment/Student Svcs ... Dr. Quentin R. JOHNSON
04 Asst to the President/Director Rel ... Mrs. Amantha L. COLE
20 Assoc Provost for Academic Affs ... Dr. Christina M. LAVORATA
18 Asst Vice Pres for Facilities ... Mr. James B. DECKER
16 Asst VP HR/Campus Community ... Mrs. Cynthia S. CURRY
06 Registrar ... Ms. Evie BRANTMAYER
49 Dean College of Liberal Arts ... Dr. Deanna J. SHIELDS
72 Dean College of Science and Tech ... Dr. Anthony F. GILBERTI
50 Dean School of Business ... Dr. Richard C. HARVEY
53 Dean School of Education ... Dr. Van O. DEMPSEY
57 Dean School of Fine Arts ... Mr. Peter LACH
66 Dean School of Nursing ... Dr. M. Sharon BONI
07 Director of Admissions & Recruiting ... Mrs. Lori A. SCHOONMAKER
29 Director Alumni Relations ... Mrs. Emily L. SWAIN
91 Dir of Applications Develop Svcs ... Mr. Andy RAISOVICH
41 Director of Athletics ... Mr. James ELLIOTT
19 Director of Emergency Mgmt/Police ... Mr. Jack A. CLAYTON
38 Director of Counseling ... Ms. Kat STEVENS
37 Director Financial Aid/Scholarships ... Ms. Cynthia K. HUDOK
39 Director of Housing ... Mr. Daniel L. GOCKLEY
09 Director of Institutional Research ... Mr. William D. FINLEY
08 Director of Library Services ... Ms. Thelma J. HUTCHINS
96 Director of Procurement ... Mrs. Monica J. COCHRAN
26 Director of Public Relations ... Ms. Amy E. PELLEGRIN
36 Director of Student Development ... Ms. Sally V. FRY
90 Director of Solutions Center ... Ms. Kelly L. PRYOR
23 Director of Student Health Services ... Ms. Yolanda S. KIRCHARTZ

*Glenville State College (F)

200 High Street, Glenville WV 26351-1292

County: Gilmer FICE Identification: 003813
Unit ID: 237385
Telephone: (304) 462-7361 Carnegie Class: Bac/Diverse
FAX Number: (304) 462-7610 Calendar System: Semester
URL: www.glenville.edu
Established: 1872 Annual Undergrad Tuition & Fees (In-State): $2,444
Enrollment: 1,443 Coed
Affiliation or Control: State IRS Status: 501(c)3
Highest Offering: Baccalaureate
Program: Liberal Arts And General; Teacher Preparatory
Accreditation: NH, TED

02 President ... Dr. Peter B. BARR
05 Provost & Senior Vice President ... Dr. John PEEK
32 Dean of Student Affairs ... Mr. Jerry L. BURKHAMMER
10 Exec Vice Pres Business & Finance . Mr. Robert O. HARDMAN, II
26 Sr Vice Pres for External Relations ... Mr. James SPEARS
30 VP Advancement/Exec Dir GSC Found ... Mr. Dennis J. POUNDS
84 Vice Pres for Enrollment Management ... Mr. D. Duane CHAPMAN
04 Executive Assistant to President ... Ms. Teresa G. STERNS
53 Dean of Teacher Education ... Dr. Kevin G. CAIN
15 Director of Human Resources ... Mr. David M. STALNAKER
37 Director of Financial Aid ... Ms. Karen D. LAY
14 Director of Data Management ... Mr. Neal L. BENSON
18 Director of Physical Plant ... Mr. Joe J. WILMOTH
19 Director of Public Safety ... Mr. Daniel R. BELL
41 Director of Athletics ... Ms. Janet BAILEY
23 Director for Campus Health ... Ms. Julia R. BARR
08 Director of Library ... Ms. Gail L. WESTBROOK
06 Associate Registrar ... Ms. Ann REED
27 Director of Public Relations ... Vacant
21 Controller ... Mr. Richard D. ACCORD
36 Director Academic Support Center ... Vacant
96 Director of Purchasing ... Ms. Joyce E. RIDDLE
29 Director of Alumni Affairs ... Ms. Debra A. NAGY
35 Director of Student Activities ... Ms. Roxanne BRIGHT

*Marshall University (G)

1 John Marshall Drive, Huntington WV 25755-0001

County: Cabell FICE Identification: 003815
Unit ID: 237525
Telephone: (304) 696-3170 Carnegie Class: Master's L
FAX Number: (304) 696-6565 Calendar System: Semester
URL: www.marshall.edu
Established: 1837 Annual Undergrad Tuition & Fees (In-State): $5,648
Enrollment: 14,196 Coed
Affiliation or Control: State IRS Status: 501(c)3
Highest Offering: Doctorate
Program: Occupational; 2-Year Principally Bachelor's Creditable; Liberal Arts And General; Teacher Preparatory; Professional
Accreditation: NH, ADNUR, ANEST, BUS, BUSA, CLPSY, CYTO, DIETD, DIETI, ENG, ENGR, JOUR, MAC, MED, MLTAD, MT, MUS, NUR, SP, SW, TED

02 President ... Dr. Stephen J. KOPP
05 Provost/Sr VP Academic Affairs ... Dr. Gayle L. ORMISTON
43 Sr VP/Exec Affairs & Gen Counsel ... Mr. F. Layton COTTRILL
63 Vice Pres Health Svc/Dean Medicine ... Dr. Charles H. MCKOWN
102 CEO MU Foundation Inc ... Dr. Ron AREA
10 Interim Sr VP for Finance/Admin ... Ms. Karen KIRTLEY
46 VP Research ... Mr. John MAHER
86 VP Federal Programs/Dir CEO RCBI ... Ms. Charlotte WEBER
12 VP South Charleston/VP Regional Op ... Mr. Kemp W. WINFREE
53 Dean GSEPD ... Dr. Teresa EAGLE
26 Sr VP Communication/Chief of Staff ... Mr. Matt TURNER
29 Vice President Alumni Relations ... Ms. Tish LITTLEHALES
13 VP Information Technology/CIO ... Dr. Jan I. FOX
44 Vice President Major Gifts ... Mr. Lance WEST
28 VP Multicultural Affairs ... Dr. Shari CLARKE
20 Assoc Vice Pres Academic Affairs ... Dr. Frances S. HENSLEY
21 Associate Vice President Finance ... Vacant
14 Asst VP Information Technology ... Dr. Arnold R. MILLER
11 Interim Chief Financial Officer ... Ms. Mary Ellen HEUTON
07 Dir Admission Undergrad/Grad Pgms ... Ms. Tammy JOHNSON
32 Dean Student Affairs ... Mr. Stephen W. HENSLEY
08 Dean of Libraries ... Vacant
58 Dean Graduate College ... Dr. Donna SPINDEL
49 Dean College Liberal Arts ... Dr. David PITTENGER
50 Dean College of Business ... Dr. Chong KIM
57 Dean College of Fine Arts ... Mr. Donald L. VAN HORN

Code	Title	Name
67	Dean School of Pharmacy	Dr. Kevin W. YINGLING
66	Dean College of Health Prof	Dr. Michael PREWITT
53	Interim Dean College of Education	Vacant
54	Dean Col of Info Tech/Engr	Dr. Betsey DULIN
60	Dean Sch Journalism/Mass Comm	Dr. Corley F. DENNISON
81	Dean College of Science	Dr. Charles SOMERVILLE
41	Director of Athletics	Mr. Mike HAMRICK
06	Registrar	Ms. Roberta FERGUSON
37	Director Student Financial Aid	Ms. Kathy BIALK
36	Director Career Services	Ms. Denise HOGSETT
15	Director Human Resource Services	Ms. Michelle DOUGLAS
19	Director of Public Safety	Mr. James E. TERRY
96	Director of Purchasing	Mr. Dennis MEADOWS
18	Director of Physical Plant	Mr. Mark CUTLIP
39	Director Residence Services	Mr. John YAUN
09	Asst to the Pres/Dir Inst Rsch/Plng	Mr. Michael J. MCGUFFEY
85	Exec Dir Ctr for Intl Programs	Dr. Clark EGNOR
40	Manager of Bookstore	Mr. Mike CAMPBELL
22	Director Equity Programs	Ms. Debra HART
88	Director Recruitment	Ms. Elizabeth WOLFE

*Shepherd University (A)

PO Box 5000, Shepherdstown WV 25443-5000

County: Jefferson — FICE Identification: 003822 — Unit ID: 237792
Telephone: (304) 876-5000 — Carnegie Class: Master's S
FAX Number: (304) 876-3101 — Calendar System: Semester
URL: www.shepherd.edu
Established: 1871 — Annual Undergrad Tuition & Fees (In-State): $5,554
Enrollment: 4,234 — Coed
Affiliation or Control: State — IRS Status: 501(c)3
Highest Offering: Master's
Program: Liberal Arts And General; Teacher Preparatory
Accreditation: NH, IACBE, MUS, NUR, SW, TED

Code	Title	Name
02	President	Dr. Suzanne SHIPLEY
05	Vice President Academic Affairs	Dr. Richard HELLDOBLER
10	Vice Pres Finance & Administration	Mr. Rick STAISLOFF
32	Vice President Student Affairs	Dr. Thomas SEGAR
30	Vice President Advancement	Dr. Diane MELBY
84	Vice Pres Enrollment Management	Ms. Kimberly SCRANAGE
43	General Counsel	Mr. K. Alan PERDUE
04	Assistant to the President	Ms. Shelli DRONSFIELD
26	Exec Director Univ Communications	Ms. Valerie OWENS
09	Director Institutional Research	Ms. Sara MAENE
81	Dean Sch of Natural Sciences/Math	Dr. Colleen NOLAN
79	Dean School of Arts & Humanities	Mr. Dow BENEDICT
50	Dean Sch of Bus/Social Sciences	Dr. Ann M. LEGREID
53	Dean Sch Educ/Profess Studies	Dr. Virginia HICKS
58	Interim Dean Grad Studies/Cont Ed	Dr. Scott BEARD
88	Dean Teaching & Learning	Dr. Laura RENNINGER
21	Comptroller	Ms. Shelley THARP
39	Asst VP Stdnt Aff/Director Res Life	Vacant
15	Director Human Resources	Dr. Marie DEWALT
13	Director Info Technology Services	Mr. Robert SPIKER
06	Registrar	Ms. Tracy SEFFERS
07	Director of Admissions	Mr. Randall FRIEND
37	Director Student Financial Aid	Ms. Sandra OERLY-BENNETT
19	Dir Public Safety/Univ Police Chief	Mr. Scott BECKNER
53	Director Teacher Education	Dr. Douglas KENNARD
18	Director Physical Plant	Mr. Dan YANNA
40	Director Auxiliary Services	Mr. James VIGIL
41	Athletics Director	Mr. B.J PUMROY
96	Director of Purchasing	Ms. Debra LANGFORD
38	Director Student Counseling	Ms. Barbara BYERS
29	Director Alumni Relations	Ms. Alexis REED
92	Director Honors Program	Dr. Sally BRASHER
44	Director Annual Giving	Ms. Julia KRALL

*West Liberty University (B)

PO Box 295, West Liberty WV 26074-0295

County: Ohio — FICE Identification: 003823 — Unit ID: 237932
Telephone: (304) 336-5000 — Carnegie Class: Bac/Diverse
FAX Number: (304) 336-8403 — Calendar System: Semester
URL: www.westliberty.edu
Established: 1837 — Annual Undergrad Tuition & Fees (In-State): $5,266
Enrollment: 2,738 — Coed
Affiliation or Control: State — IRS Status: 501(c)3
Highest Offering: Master's
Program: Liberal Arts And General; Teacher Preparatory; Professional; Business Emphasis
Accreditation: NH, DH, IACBE, MT, MUS, NURSE, TED

Code	Title	Name
02	President	Mr. Robin C. CAPEHART
05	Vice Provost	Vacant
43	Vice President & General Counsel	Mr. John L. DAVIS
32	Vice President of Student Affairs	Vacant
10	Executive VP & CFO	Mr. John E. WRIGHT
11	Provost	Vacant
88	VP for Community Engagement	Mr. Jeff KNIERIM
81	Dean College of Sciences	Dr. Robert KREISBERG
49	Dean College Liberal Arts	Dr. Brian CRAWFORD
57	Dean College Arts & Comm	Dr. William M. BARONAK
53	Dean College of Education	Dr. Keely O. CAMDEN
66	Dir of Nursing Programs	Dr. Donna J. LUKICH
50	Dean College of Business	Dr. Loren A. WENZEL
35	Assoc Dean Student Services	Ms. Marcella SNYDER
06	Ex Dir Enr Svc/Regr/Dir FA/Dean Std	Mr. Scott A. COOK
15	Vice President of Human Resources	Mr. James L. STULTZ
13	Chief Technology Officer	Mr. James T. CLARK
09	Dir of Inst Research & Assessment	Ms. Paula J. TOMASIK
41	Director of Athletics	Mr. James W. WATSON
07	Director of Admissions	Ms. Brenda M. KING
51	Director of Cont Educ/Special Pgm	Vacant
08	Director of Library	Ms. Cheryl R. HARSHMAN
26	Director of University Engagement	Ms. Tammi SECRIST
29	Director of Alumni Association	Mr. Ron A. WITT
37	Director Student Financial Aid	Mr. Scott A. COOK
30	VP of Institutional Advancement	Mr. Jason W. KOEGLER
31	Director of Auxiliary Services	Mr. John L. DAVIS
18	Chief of Operations	Mr. Patrick J. HENRY
38	Director of Counseling	Ms. Bridgette DAWSON
92	Director of the Honors Program	Dr. Peter L. STAFFEL
93	Minority Student Coordinator	Vacant
88	Director Dental Hygiene Programs	Ms. Margaret J. SIX
88	Dir Clinical Lab Science Program	Dr. William C. WAGENER
20	Associate Academic Officer	Vacant
21	Associate Business Officer	Ms. Cindy R. MCGEE
84	Assoc Dean Enrollment Services	Ms. Brenda M. KING
23	Director of Health Services	Ms. Cheryl BENNINGTON
88	Vice President of Broadcasting	Mr. Reid AMOS
88	Director Physican Assistant Program	Dr. Allan M. BEDASHI
21	Controller	Ms. Stephanie L. HOOPER
04	Executive Asst to the President	Dr. John P. MCCULLOUGH
85	Coord International Student Rec	Ms. Mihaela A. SZABO
88	Marketing Director	Ms. Stefanie K. TROUTEN
44	Director of Major Gifts	Ms. Angela R. ZAMBITO

*West Virginia School of Osteopathic Medicine (C)

400 N Lee Street, Lewisburg WV 24901-1196

County: Greenbrier — FICE Identification: 011245 — Unit ID: 237880
Telephone: (304) 645-6270 — Carnegie Class: Spec/Med
FAX Number: (304) 645-4859 — Calendar System: Semester
URL: www.wvsom.edu
Established: 1972 — Annual Graduate Tuition & Fees: $19,950
Enrollment: 793 — Coed
Affiliation or Control: State — IRS Status: 501(c)3
Highest Offering: First Professional Degree; No Undergraduates
Program: Professional
Accreditation: OSTEO

Code	Title	Name
02	President	Dr. Michael D. ADELMAN
05	Vice Pres Academic Affairs & Dean	Dr. Lorence L. PENCE
10	Vice Pres Finance & Administration	Mr. Larry WARE
11	Vice Pres for Administration	Dr. James W. NEMITZ
17	Assoc Dean Graduate Med Education	Vacant
20	Asst Dean Graduate Med Educ	Mr. William SHIRES
20	Assoc Dean Predoctoral Clinical Ed	Dr. Robert W. FOSTER
20	Asst Dean Predoctoral Clinical Educ	Ms. Stephanie SCHULER
20	Assoc Dean Preclinical Education	Dr. John SCHRIEFER
20	Assoc Dean Osteopathic Med Educ	Dr. Karen M. STEELE
20	Assoc Dean Problem-Based Learning	Dr. Malcolm MODRZAKOWSKI
20	Assoc Dean Assessment/Educ Devel	Dr. Elaine SOPER
32	Assoc Dean Student Affairs	Dr. Meg MCKEON
37	Director Financial Aid/Registrar	Ms. Sharon L. HOWARD
26	Director Communications	Vacant
15	Director of Hum Res/Affirm Action	Ms. Leslie BICKSLER
08	Director of Library	Ms. Annie MCMILLION
96	Director of Purchasing	Ms. Pam OCHALA
06	Registrar	Ms. Jennifer SEAMS
07	Director of Admissions	Ms. Donna VARNEY
29	Director Alumni Relations	Ms. Shannon WARREN

*West Virginia State University (D)

PO Box 1000, Institute WV 25112-1000

County: Kanawha — FICE Identification: 003826 — Unit ID: 237899
Telephone: (304) 766-3000 — Carnegie Class: Bac/A&S
FAX Number: (304) 768-9842 — Calendar System: Semester
URL: www.wvstateu.edu
Established: 1891 — Annual Undergrad Tuition & Fees (In-State): $5,038
Enrollment: 3,190 — Coed
Affiliation or Control: State — IRS Status: 501(c)3
Highest Offering: Master's
Program: Liberal Arts And General; Teacher Preparatory
Accreditation: NH, ACBSP, SW, TED

Code	Title	Name
02	President	Dr. Hazo W. CARTER, JR.
10	Vice President for Finance	Mr. Robert PARKER
05	Provost and VP for Academic Affairs	Dr. R. Charles BYERS
32	Vice President Student Affairs	Mr. Bryce S. CASTO
45	Vice President Planning/Advancement	Dr. John M. BERRY
20	Asst Vice Pres Academic Affairs	Dr. John TEEUWISSEN
35	Asst Vice Pres Student Affairs	Mr. Joseph ODEN, JR.
45	Asst Vice Pres Planning/Advancement	Mr. Jonathan ADLER
11	Spec Asst to Pres/Strategic Plng	Dr. Cassandra WHYTE
86	Spec Asst to Pres Rsch/Pub Svc	Dr. Orlando F. MCMEANS
100	Exec Asst to Pres & Chief of Staff	Dr. Gregory D. EPPS
79	Dean College of Arts & Humanities	Dr. Barbara LADNER
81	Dean College of Natural Sci/Math	Dr. Katherine HARPER
107	Dean Col of Professional Studies	Dr. Robert L. HARRISON, JR.
50	Dean Col of Business Admin/Soc Sci	Dr. Abainesh MITIKU
53	Chrmn Department of Education	Dr. Sandra ORR
70	Chairman Department Sociology	Dr. Gail MOSBY
64	Chairman Music Department	Ms. Brenda VANDERFORD
68	Chrmn Health & Human Performance	Mrs. Debra ANDERSON-CONLIFFE
26	Chief Public Relations Officer	Ms. Patricia DICKINSON
14	Director Computer Services	Mr. Robert H. HUSTON
09	Dir Instl Effective/Rsrch/Assessmt	Dr. Barry PELPHREY
18	Director Physical Facilities	Mr. Phillip H. JUDD
06	Director Records & Registration	Ms. Donna L. HUNTER
19	Director of Public Safety	Chief Joseph SAUNDERS
10	Director of Fiscal Affairs	Mr. Lawrence J. SMITH
08	Director of the Library	Mr. David CLENDINNING
37	Interim Director Financial Aid	Ms. Sally MARCUS BURGER
29	Director Alumni Relations	Mr. Phillip BRIGHT
15	Director of Human Resources	Miss Barbara ROWELL
36	Dir Career Services & Coop Educ	Ms. Sandhya (Sandy) G. MAHARAJ
07	Interim Director of Admissions	Ms. Trina D. SWEENEY
38	Director New Student Programs	Mrs. Sharon S. BANKS
96	Director of Purchasing	Mrs. Janis A. BENNETT
88	Interim Director of Recruiting	Mr. Christopher D. JACKSON
09	Coord of Institutional Research	Dr. Danny R. CANTRELL

*West Virginia University (E)

1500 University Avenue, Morgantown WV 26506-0002

County: Monongalia — FICE Identification: 003827 — Unit ID: 238032
Telephone: (304) 293-0111 — Carnegie Class: RU/H
FAX Number: (304) 293-5883 — Calendar System: Semester
URL: www.wvu.edu
Established: 1867 — Annual Undergrad Tuition & Fees (In-State): $5,406
Enrollment: 28,898 — Coed
Affiliation or Control: State — IRS Status: 501(c)3
Highest Offering: Doctorate
Program: Liberal Arts And General; Teacher Preparatory; Professional
Accreditation: NH, ART, AUD, BUS, BUSA, CACREP, CIDA, CLPSY, COPSY, CORE, CS, DENT, DH, DIETD, DIETI, DMS, ENG, ENGR, FOR, IPSY, JOUR, LAW, LSAR, MED, MT, MUS, NMT, NURSE, OT, PA, PH, PHAR, PTA, RAD, RADMAG, RTT, SP, SPAA, SW, TED, THEA

Code	Title	Name
02	President	Dr. James P. CLEMENTS
05	Provost & VP Acad Affairs	Dr. Michele G. WHEATLY
10	Vice President for Admin & Finance	Mr. Narvel G. WEESE, JR.
26	Vice Pres University Relations	Ms. Christine M. MARTIN
17	Chancellor of Health Sciences	Dr. Christopher C. COLENDA
32	Vice President Student Affairs	Mr. Kenneth D. GRAY
46	Vice Pres Research & Econ Develop	Dr. Curt M. PETERSON
15	Vice President for Human Resources	Ms. Margaret R. PHILLIPS
76	Sr Assoc Vice Pres/Health Sciences	Mr. Fred R. BUTCHER
20	Sr Assoc Provost Academic Affairs	Dr. Russell K. DEAN
20	Assoc Provost Academic Personnel	Dr. Cecil B. WILSON
88	Director Rural Health	Ms. Jodie JACKSON
100	Chief of Staff	Mr. John J. COLE
88	Exec Officer for Policy Development	Dr. Jennifer L. FISHER
88	Exec Officer for Social Justice	Ms. Jennifer A. MCINTOSH
43	VP Legal Affairs/General Counsel	Mr. William H. HUTCHENS, III
88	Chief Financial Officer	Ms. Wendy L. KING
21	Sr Assoc Vice Pres for Finance	Mr. Daniel A. DURBIN
56	Assoc Prov Extension/Public Svcs	Dr. David E. MILLER
102	President WVU Foundation	Mr. R. Wayne KING
20	Assoc Provost Academic Programs	Dr. Elizabeth A. DOOLEY
13	Assoc Provost IT/CIO	Mr. Rehan KHAN
18	Interim Assoc VP Facilities & Svcs	Mr. Randy HUDAK
35	Asst Vice Pres Student Affairs	Mr. Michael A. ELLINGTON
88	Asst VP Hlth Sci & Tech Academy	Ms. Ann M. CHESTER
88	Associate Vice President Marketing	Ms. Tricia L. PETTY
84	Associate VP Enroll Mgmt Svcs	Ms. Brenda S. THOMPSON
45	Assoc Vice Pres Planning & Treasury	Ms. Elizabeth P. REYNOLDS
25	Asst VP Office of Sponsored Pgms	Mr. Alan B. MARTIN
09	Director of Institutional Research	Ms. Roberta A. DEAN
39	Director Housing & Residence Life	Mr. G. Corey FARRIS
41	Director Intercollegiate Athletics	Mr. Oliver F. LUCK
23	Director of Health Services	Dr. Jan E. PALMER
24	Director of Radio & TV Services	Mr. John E. DUWALL
27	Asst VP News/Information Services	Ms. Rebecca B. LOFSTEAD
29	Exec Director Alumni Association	Mr. Stephen L. DOUGLAS
37	Director Financial Aid	Ms. Kaye C. WIDNEY
07	Director Admissions & Records	Ms. Marilyn S. POTTS
06	Registrar	Mr. Steve ROBINSON
08	Dean of Library Services	Ms. Frances L. O'BRIEN
38	Asst VP Student Wellness	Dr. Catherine A. YURA
21	Director Financial Services	Ms. Lisa A. LIVELY
19	Chief of Police/Univ Police Dept	Capt. Bob E. ROBERTS
96	Interim Dir Purchasing/Cont & Pay	Mr. Joe FISHER
88	Assoc VP Intl & Global Outreach	Dr. David C. STEWART
50	Dean Business and Economics	Dr. Jose V. SARTARELLI
49	Dean of Arts & Sciences	Dr. Robert H. JONES
57	Dean College Creative Arts	Dr. Paul K. KREIDER
53	Dean Human Resources/Education	Dr. Dee HOPKINS
61	Dean of Law	Dr. Joyce E. MCCONNELL
63	Dean of Medicine	Dr. Arthur J. ROSS
52	Dean of Dentistry	Dr. David A. FELTON
54	Dean of Engr/Mineral Resources	Dr. Eugene V. CILENTO
47	Dean of Agriculture & Forestry	Dr. Cameron R. HACKNEY
67	Dean of Pharmacy	Dr. Patricia A. CHASE
60	Dean of Journalism	Dr. Maryanne REED
68	Dean Physical Education	Dr. Dana D. BROOKS
66	Dean of Nursing	Dr. Georgia L. NARSAVAGE
56	Dean Extended Learning	Dr. Susan D. DAY-PERROOTS
36	Director Career Services	Mr. David L. DURHAM
88	Assoc Provost Intl Acad Affairs	Dr. Michael LASTINGER
88	Assoc VP Acad Strategic Plng	Dr. Nigel N. CLARK
88	Assoc Provost Graduate Acad Affairs	Dr. Jonathan CUMMINGS

5 Interim Dean of Students ... Mr. G. Corey FARRIS
8 Director of Internal Audit ... Mr. William R. QUIGLEY

Potomac State College of West Virginia University (A)

Keyser WV 26726-2698
County: Mineral | FICE Identification: 003829
Unit ID: 237701
Telephone: (304) 788-6800 | Carnegie Class: Assoc/Pub2in4
FAX Number: (304) 788-6940 | Calendar System: Semester
URL: www.potomacstatecollege.edu
Established: 1901 | Annual Undergrad Tuition & Fees (In-State): $3,058
Enrollment: 1,836 | Coed
Affiliation or Control: State | IRS Status: 501(c)3
Highest Offering: Associate Degree
Program: Occupational; 2-Year Principally Bachelor's Creditable
Accreditation: &NH

02 Campus Provost ... Dr. Kerry S. ODELL
10 Senior Business Planning Officer ... Mr. Harlan N. SHREVE
05 Dean for Curriculum & Instruction ... Dr. Douglas R. WILMES
32 Dean of Student Affairs ... Mr. William M. LETRENT
84 Director of Enrollment Services ... Mrs. Beth E. LITTLE
08 Librarian ... Mrs. Jill M. GARDNER
27 Public Information Officer ... Mrs. Rene M. TREZISE
41 Athletic Director ... Mr. Shawn A. WHITE
18 Dir of Facilities/Physical Plant ... Mr. Michael A. SIMPSON
37 Financial Aid/Veterans Coordinator ... Mrs. Beth E. LITTLE
14 Information Technology Coordinator ... Mr. Geoffrey L. CHENGER
29 Coordinator of Alumni Affairs ... Mrs. Libby M. NICHOLS

West Virginia University at Parkersburg (B)

300 Campus Drive, Parkersburg WV 26104-8647
County: Wood | FICE Identification: 003828
Unit ID: 237686
Telephone: (304) 424-8000 | Carnegie Class: Bac/Assoc
FAX Number: (304) 424-8315 | Calendar System: Semester
URL: www.wvup.edu
Established: 1971 | Annual Undergrad Tuition & Fees (In-State): $2,268
Enrollment: 4,453 | Coed
Affiliation or Control: State | IRS Status: 501(c)3
Highest Offering: Baccalaureate
Program: Occupational; 2-Year Principally Bachelor's Creditable; Liberal Arts And General; Teacher Preparatory; Technical Emphasis
Accreditation: NH, ADNUR, SURGT, TED

02 President ... Dr. Marie FOSTER GNAGE
05 Sr Vice President Academic Affairs ... Dr. Rhonda TRACY
32 Vice President for Student Services ... Mr. Anthony UNDERWOOD
103 Vice Pres Workforce/Community Educ ... Mrs. Mary Beth BUSCH
10 Chief Financial Officer ... Mr. Vincent MENSAH
30 Director Marketing/Communications ... Mrs. Katie WOOTTON
18 Director Facilities & Services ... Mr. David WHITE
15 Director Human Resources ... Mrs. Peggy JAMESON
14 Director Computer Services ... Mr. Jeff WILBUR
04 Executive Assistant to President ... Mrs. Patsy BEE
04 Special Asst to President ... Mrs. Debra L. RICHARDS
12 Director Jackson County Center ... Mr. John GORRELL
09 Dir Inst Rsrch/Outcomes Assessment ... Mr. Jeremy STARKEY
08 Director of Library ... Mr. Stephen HUPP
06 Registrar ... Mrs. Leslie SIMS
37 Director of Financial Aid ... Mr. August KAFER
35 Director Student Activities ... Mr. Tom YENCHA
36 Director Student Placement ... Vacant
96 Director of Purchasing ... Vacant
50 Chair Business/Economics/Math Div ... Vacant
53 Chair Education/Humanities Division ... Ms. Cindy GISSY
76 Chair Health Sciences Division ... Mrs. Rose BEEBE
83 Chair Social Science/Languages Div ... Mrs. Denise MCCLUNG
72 Chair Science/Technology Division ... Mr. David THOMPSON

West Virginia University Institute of Technology (C)

405 Fayette Pike, Montgomery WV 25136-2436
County: Fayette | FICE Identification: 003825
Unit ID: 237950
Telephone: (304) 442-3071 | Carnegie Class: Bac/Diverse
FAX Number: (304) 442-3059 | Calendar System: Semester
URL: www.wvutech.edu
Established: 1895 | Annual Undergrad Tuition & Fees (In-State): $5,872
Enrollment: 1,211 | Coed
Affiliation or Control: State | IRS Status: 501(c)3
Highest Offering: Baccalaureate
Program: 2-Year Principally Bachelor's Creditable; Liberal Arts And General
Accreditation: &NH, ENG, ENGT

02 Campus Provost ... Dr. Scott M. HURST
05 Associate Provost ... Mr. Garth THOMAS
10 Chief Business Officer ... Mr. Solomon ADDICO
84 Dir Enrollment Mgmt ... Vacant
32 Dean of Students ... Mr. Richard CARPINELLI
07 Dir Admissions/Recruitment ... Ms. Reeta PIIRALA-SKOGLUND
50 Dean Bus/Humanities & Social Sci ... Dr. Stephen W. BROWN
54 Dean LCN College of Engr & Science ... Dr. Faris A. MALHAS
26 Dir Comm & Integrated Marketing ... Mr. Brian R. BOLYARD
41 Athletic Director ... Mr. Frank PERGOLIZZI
15 Director Human Resources ... Mr. Kevin A. LAWHON
18 Director Facilities Mgmt/Planning ... Mr. Rick LINIO
39 Director of Residence Life ... Mr. Charles A. DAVIS
19 Director of Public Safety ... Mr. Donald G. POMEROY
37 Director of Financial Aid ... Vacant
36 Director of Career Services ... Mr. Cantrell L. MILLER
08 Director of the Library ... Dr. Barbara E. CRIST
85 International Student Advisor ... Ms. Anne K. REPAIRE
40 Bookstore Manager ... Ms. Sarah J. SIMMONS
06 Registrar ... Ms. Anne K. REPAIRE

West Virginia Junior College (D)

1000 Virginia Street E, Charleston WV 25301-2817
County: Kanawha | FICE Identification: 010573
Unit ID: 237987
Telephone: (304) 345-2820 | Carnegie Class: Assoc/PrivFP
FAX Number: (304) 345-1425 | Calendar System: Quarter
URL: www.wvjc.edu
Established: 1892 | Annual Undergrad Tuition & Fees: $11,475
Enrollment: 220 | Coed
Affiliation or Control: Proprietary | IRS Status: Proprietary
Highest Offering: Associate Degree
Program: 2-Year Principally Bachelor's Creditable
Accreditation: ACICS

01 Executive Director ... Mr. Thomas A. CROUSE

West Virginia Junior College (E)

148 Willey Street, Morgantown WV 26505-5596
County: Monongalia | FICE Identification: 005007
Unit ID: 237996
Telephone: (304) 296-8282 | Carnegie Class: Assoc/PrivFP
FAX Number: (304) 581-6990 | Calendar System: Quarter
URL: www.wvjcmorgantown.edu
Established: 1922 | Annual Undergrad Tuition & Fees: $12,150
Enrollment: 209 | Coed
Affiliation or Control: Proprietary | IRS Status: Proprietary
Highest Offering: Associate Degree
Program: 2-Year Principally Bachelor's Creditable; Business Emphasis
Accreditation: ACICS

01 President & CEO ... Ms. Patricia A. CALLEN
05 Academic Director ... Ms. Leanne CARDOSA
36 Career Services ... Ms. Carissa COLLINS
06 Director of Student Records/Account . Ms. Savannah MCCONNELL

West Virginia Wesleyan College (F)

59 College Avenue, Buckhannon WV 26201-2699
County: Upshur | FICE Identification: 003830
Unit ID: 237969
Telephone: (304) 473-8000 | Carnegie Class: Bac/Diverse
FAX Number: (304) 472-2571 | Calendar System: Semester
URL: www.wvwc.edu
Established: 1890 | Annual Undergrad Tuition & Fees: $24,964
Enrollment: 1,432 | Coed
Affiliation or Control: United Methodist | IRS Status: 501(c)3
Highest Offering: Master's
Program: Liberal Arts And General; Teacher Preparatory; Professional
Accreditation: NH, MUS, NUR, TED

01 President ... Dr. Pamela M. BALCH
05 VP Academic Affs/Dean Faculty ... Dr. Larry R. PARSONS
10 Vice Pres Administration & Finance ... Dr. Barry R. PRITTS
09 Vice Pres Institutional Advancement ... Vacant
32 VP Student Devel/Enrollment Mgmt ... Ms. Julia A. KEEHNER
27 Vice Pres/Chief Information Officer ... Mr. R. Duwane SQUIRES
42 Dean of the Chapel ... Rev. Angela Gay KINKEAD
58 Dean of Graduate Stds/Extended Lrng ... Dr. Kathleen M. LONG
102 Director Foundation/Government Rels ... Ms. Nicki BENTLEY-COLTHART
07 Director of Admission ... Mr. John WALTZ
11 Director of Administrative Services ... Mr. Keith NICHOLS
37 Director Financial Planning ... Ms. Susan GEORGE
29 Director of Alumni Affairs ... Mrs. Kristi WILKERSON
08 Director of Library Services ... Ms. Paula L. MCGREW
30 Dir of Institutional Advancement ... Mr. Robert N. SKINNER, II
06 Dir Acad & Career Svcs/Registrar ... Ms. Alice J. CREASMAN
39 Director Campus Life ... Mrs. Alisa LIVELY
09 Director of Institutional Research ... Ms. Tammy L. CRITES
15 Director of Personnel ... Ms. Vickie J. CROWDER
18 Director of the Physical Plant ... Vacant
30 Director Development Operations ... Ms. Rose Ellen LOUDIN
08 Director of the Learning Center ... Dr. Shawn M. KUBA
41 Director of Athletics ... Mr. Ken TYLER
21 Comptroller ... Mr. Randall W. CRITES
40 Director of Bookstore ... Ms. Jennifer DALTON
92 Director Honors Program ... Mr. Doug VAN GUNDY
93 Director Intercultural Relations ... Vacant
44 Director of Planned & Major Gifts ... Rev. David R. PETERS
38 Dir of Counseling & Wellness Center ... Mr. Michael KUBA
31 Dir of Leadership Development ... Ms. LeeAnn BROWN

Wheeling Jesuit University (G)

316 Washington Avenue, Wheeling WV 26003-6295
County: Ohio | FICE Identification: 003831
Unit ID: 238078
Telephone: (304) 243-2000 | Carnegie Class: Bac/Diverse
FAX Number: (304) 243-2243 | Calendar System: Semester
URL: www.wju.edu
Established: 1954 | Annual Undergrad Tuition & Fees: $25,640
Enrollment: 1,372 | Coed
Affiliation or Control: Roman Catholic | IRS Status: 501(c)3
Highest Offering: Doctorate
Program: Liberal Arts And General; Professional
Accreditation: NH, ACBSP, #NMT, NURSE, PTA, TEAC

01 President ... Mr. Richard Allen BEYER
03 University Vice President ... Rev. James J. FLEMING
05 Vice President for Academic Affairs ... Dr. Stephen D. STAHL
10 Vice President for Business/Finance ... Vacant
30 VP for Institutional Advancement ... Mr. James HOLT
84 Vice President for Enrollment Mgmt ... Mr. Larry VALLAR
88 Vice President for Sponsored Pgm ... Mr. J. Davitt MCATEER
32 Dean for Student Development ... Ms. Christine OHL-GIGLIOTTI
90 Assoc VP for Info Tech Services ... Mr. Daniel T. FEELEY
37 Director Financial Aid ... Ms. Christie L. TOMCZYK
21 Controller ... Mr. Stephen CRINITI
21 Senior Accountant ... Mr. Donald YAQUINTA
06 Registrar ... Mr. Rick WEST
08 Librarian ... Ms. Kelly MUMMERT
91 Systems Administrator ... Mr. Richard M. KLEMPA
42 Director of Campus Ministry ... Mr. Jamey BROGAN
41 Athletic Director ... Mr. Danny SANCOMB
18 Director of Physical Plant ... Mr. Larry A. SKRZYPEK
85 International Student Advisor ... Mrs. Eileen P. VIGLIETTA
15 Director of Human Resources ... Mr. Donald KAMINSKI
44 Dir Planned Giving/Major Gifts ... Mr. Joseph BUCH
45 Director of Research ... Ms. Lauri STAHL

WISCONSIN

Alverno College (H)

3400 S 43rd Street, Box 343922,
Milwaukee WI 53234-3922
County: Milwaukee | FICE Identification: 003832
Unit ID: 238193
Telephone: (414) 382-6000 | Carnegie Class: Master's S
FAX Number: (414) 382-6354 | Calendar System: Semester
URL: www.alverno.edu
Established: 1887 | Annual Undergrad Tuition & Fees: $21,063
Enrollment: 2,759 | Female
Affiliation or Control: Independent Non-Profit | IRS Status: 501(c)3
Highest Offering: Master's
Program: Liberal Arts And General; Teacher Preparatory; Professional
Accreditation: NH, MUS, NURSE, TED

01 President ... Dr. Mary J. MEEHAN
10 Sr Vice Pres Finance & Mgmt Svcs ... Mr. James OPPERMANN
05 Sr Vice Pres Academic Affairs ... Sr. Kathleen O'BRIEN
30 Vice President College Advancement ... Ms. Julie QUINLAN BRAME
20 Exec Director Academic Services ... Sr. Marlene NEISES
84 VP Marketing & Enrollment Mgmt ... Ms. Susan SMITH
32 Assoc Vice Pres/Dean of Students ... Ms. Virginia WAGNER
07 Director Admissions Communications ... Ms. Julie BOULWARE
20 Associate Vice President Academic ... Dr. Kathy LAKE
20 Associate Vice President Academic ... Dr. Jeanna ABROMEIT
06 Registrar ... Ms. Patricia HARTMANN
08 Director Library ... Ms. Carol BRILL
36 Director Career Development ... Ms. Joanna PATTERSON
13 Exec Dir Information Technology ... Ms. Anita EIKENS
37 Director Student Financial Plng ... Mr. Dan GOYETTE
29 Director Alumnae Relations ... Ms. Mary FRIESEKE
38 Director Advising ... Ms. Katherine BUNDALO
51 Dir Institute Educational Outreach .. Ms. Judith REISETTER-HART
15 Director Human Resources ... Ms. Sharon WILCOX
41 Director of Athletics ... Mr. Brad DUCKWORTH
42 Campus Minister ... Ms. Connie POPP
96 Purchasing Agent ... Ms. Anne MCCARRON
09 Director of Institutional Research ... Dr. Glen ROGERS
27 Chief Information Officer ... Mr. Jim HILBY
50 Dean School of Business ... Mr. Dan HORTON
66 Dean School of Nursing ... Ms. Patricia SCHROEDER
53 Dean of School of Education ... Sr. Mary DIEZ
49 Dean School of Arts & Sciences ... Dr. Sandra GRAHAM
50 Director Master of Business Admin ... Dr. Patricia JENSEN
79 Assoc Dean Humanities Division ... Dr. Mimi CZARNIK
81 Asc Dean Natl Science/Math/Tech Div ... Dr. Angela FREY
83 Assoc Dean Behavioral Sciences Div ... Dr. Sandra GRAHAM
60 Assoc Dean Arts/Comm/Tech Div ... Dr. Patricia GEENEN
28 Sp Asst to VP Acad Affs/Multclt Iss ... Dr. Celia JACKSON
04 Assistant to the President ... Ms. Jill DESMOND
101 Executive Assistant ... Ms. Joan WALTER-SCHUMACHER

Anthem College-Milwaukee (I)

440 South Executive Drive, Ste 200,
Brookfield WI 53005-4283
County: Waukesha | Identification: 666613
Unit ID: 450155
Telephone: (262) 641-9944 | Carnegie Class: Not Classified
FAX Number: (262) 641-9955 | Calendar System: Other
URL: www.hightechinstitute.edu
Established: 2006 | Annual Undergrad Tuition & Fees: N/A
Enrollment: 365 | Coed
Affiliation or Control: Proprietary | IRS Status: Proprietary
Highest Offering: Associate Degree
Program: Occupational
Accreditation: ABHES, SURTEC

01 Campus President .... Ms. Jennifer PAUGH

† Branch campus of Anthem College, Maryland Heights, MO.

Bellin College, Inc. (A)

3201 Eaton Road, Green Bay WI 54311

County: Brown | Identification: 006639 | Unit ID: 238324

Telephone: (920) 433-6699 | Carnegie Class: Spec/Health

FAX Number: (920) 433-1923 | Calendar System: Semester

URL: www.bellincollege.edu

Established: 1909 | Annual Undergrad Tuition & Fees: $19,500

Enrollment: 329 | Coed

Affiliation or Control: Independent Non-Profit | IRS Status: 501(c)3

Highest Offering: Master's

Program: Professional; Nursing Emphasis

Accreditation: NH, NURSE, RAD

01 President & CEO of the College .... Dr. V. Jane MUHL
32 Vice President Student Services .... Ms. Joann M. WOELFEL
10 Vice President Business & Finance .... Mr. Joseph E. KEEBAUGH
05 Vice President Academic Affairs .... Dr. Connie J. BOERST
30 Vice President Development & PR .... Mr. Matt G. RENTMEESTER
06 Registrar .... Ms. Vicky M. SCHAULAND
37 Director Financial Aid .... Ms. Lena C. GOODMAN
07 Director of Recruitment .... Dr. Penelope P. CROGHAN

Beloit College (B)

700 College Street, Beloit WI 53511-5595

County: Rock | FICE Identification: 003835 | Unit ID: 238333

Telephone: (608) 363-2000 | Carnegie Class: Bac/A&S

FAX Number: (608) 363-2718 | Calendar System: Semester

URL: www.beloit.edu

Established: 1846 | Annual Undergrad Tuition & Fees: $36,674

Enrollment: 1,308 | Coed

Affiliation or Control: Independent Non-Profit | IRS Status: 501(c)3

Highest Offering: Baccalaureate

Program: Liberal Arts And General; Teacher Preparatory

Accreditation: NH

01 President .... Dr. Scott BIERMAN
05 Provost .... Dr. Ann DAVIES
11 Vice President Administration .... Mr. John M. NICHOLAS
84 Vice President Enrollment Services .... Ms. Nancy BENEDICT
30 Vice President External Affairs .... Mr. Jeff PUCKETT
32 Dean of Students .... Dr. Christina KLAWITTER
06 Registrar .... Ms. Mary BOROS-KAZAI
07 Director of Admissions .... Mr. James S. ZIELINSKI
09 Director of Institutional Research .... Dr. Cynthia B. GRAY
08 Chief Information Officer .... Ms. Megan E. FITCH
15 Director of Human Resources .... Ms. Lori RHEAD
29 Sr Dir Alumni & Parent Relations .... Ms. Ruth VATER
26 Director of Communications .... Mr. Jason HUGHES
39 Director Resident Life/Conferences .... Mr. John F. WINKELMANN
18 Director of Physical Plant .... Mr. Michael BRADY
36 Director of Career Services .... Ms. Angela DAVIS
38 College Counselor .... Vacant
40 Bookstore Director .... Mr. Peter FRONK
37 Financial Aid Director .... Ms. Jane H. HESSIAN
41 Athletic Director .... Ms. Peggy CARL
28 Dir Intercult Pgm/Asst Dean Stdnts .... Mr. Cecil YOUNGBLOOD

Bryant & Stratton College (C)

310 W Wisconsin Avenue, Suite 500 E,
Milwaukee WI 53203

County: Milwaukee | FICE Identification: 005009 | Unit ID: 239929

Telephone: (414) 276-5200 | Carnegie Class: Assoc/PrivFP4

FAX Number: (414) 276-3930 | Calendar System: Semester

URL: www.bryantstratton.edu

Established: 1863 | Annual Undergrad Tuition & Fees: $15,120

Enrollment: 1,068 | Coed

Affiliation or Control: Proprietary | IRS Status: Proprietary

Highest Offering: Baccalaureate

Program: Occupational; Professional; Business Emphasis

Accreditation: &M, MAC

01 Director/Business Office Director .... Mr. Peter J. PAVONE
07 Admissions Director .... Ms. Kathryn M. COTEY
05 Dean of Academic Affairs .... Ms. Catherine R. REBHOLZ
20 Dean of Academic Administration .... Mr. Brian R. SPORLEDER
36 Director of Career Services .... Ms. Betty A. ERBY
37 Financial Aid Manager .... Mr. Kevin MCSHANE

† Regional accreditation is carried under the parent institution (corporate office) in Buffalo, NY.

Cardinal Stritch University (D)

6801 N Yates Road, Milwaukee WI 53217-3985

County: Milwaukee | FICE Identification: 003837 | Unit ID: 238430

Telephone: (414) 410-4000 | Carnegie Class: DRU

FAX Number: (414) 410-4239 | Calendar System: Semester

URL: www.stritch.edu

Established: 1937 | Annual Undergrad Tuition & Fees: $23,330

Enrollment: 5,842 | Coed

Affiliation or Control: Roman Catholic | IRS Status: 501(c)3

Highest Offering: Doctorate

Program: 2-Year Principally Bachelor's Creditable; Liberal Arts And General; Teacher Preparatory; Professional

Accreditation: NH, ACBSP, ADNUR, NUR, NURSE, TED

01 President .... Dr. James P. LOFTUS
00 Chancellor .... Sr. Camille KLIEBHAN
04 Admin Asst to the President .... Ms. Lynn M. LARKIN
03 Executive Vice President/CFO .. Mr. Thomas W. VANHIMBERGEN
05 Executive VP Academic Affairs .... Dr. Anthea L. BOJAR
42 Dir Mission Effectiveness/Identity .... Fr. James G. GANNON
84 Vice Pres Enrollment Management .... Mr. John P. MUELLER
10 Vice President Finance & Controller .... Ms. Tammy M. HOWARD
13 Vice Pres for Info Technology/CIO .... Mr. TJ RAINS
26 Vice President of Public Relations .... Vacant
30 Vice President for Advancement .... Mr. Michael J. BRAUER
30 Assoc VP for University Advancement . Ms. Judy M. HAUGSLAND
32 Vice Pres for Student Development .. Ms. Christine M. ROBINSON
21 Asst VP for Business & Finance .... Ms. Janet MCKNIGHT
15 Director of Human Resources .... Ms. Deborah R. JOHNSON
49 Dean College of Arts & Sciences .... Dr. Daniel J. SCHOLZ
50 Dean College of Business & Mgmt .... Dr. Clara BRENNAN
53 Dean College of Education & Ldrship .... Dr. Freda R. RUSSELL
66 Dean College of Nursing .... Dr. Ruth M. WAITE
06 Registrar .... Ms. Christine L. GLYNN
21 Bursar .... Ms. Lisa M. CARLSON
20 Director of Academic Affairs .... Ms. Nancy A. DAWKINS
85 Director of International Programs .... Ms. Laine M. PHILIPPA
39 Director of Residence Life .... Mr. Joseph R. NISWONGER
41 Director of Athletics .... Mr. Patrick J. CLEMENS
07 Director of Admissions .... Mr. Kirk D. MESSER
08 Director of Library .... Mr. David W. WEINBERG-KINSEY
37 Director of Financial Aid .... Mr. Ben J. BAERBOCK
36 Director of Career Services .... Mr. Tom E. KIPP
09 Director of Institutional Research .... Vacant
18 Director of Facilities .... Mr. John B. GLYNN
91 Director of Enterprise Systems .... Ms. Susan L. INGLES
19 Director of Security .... Mr. Andrew DE RUBERTIS
44 Director Major Gifts/Planned Giving .... Mr. Chris J. LANGE
29 Dir Alumni Relations/Annual Giving .... Mr. Joel F. CENCIUS

Carroll University (E)

100 N East Avenue, Waukesha WI 53186-5593

County: Waukesha | FICE Identification: 003838 | Unit ID: 238458

Telephone: (262) 547-1211 | Carnegie Class: Master's S

FAX Number: (262) 524-7646 | Calendar System: Semester

URL: www.carrollu.edu

Established: 1846 | Annual Undergrad Tuition & Fees: $25,248

Enrollment: 3,398 | Coed

Affiliation or Control: Presbyterian Church (U.S.A.) | IRS Status: 501(c)3

Highest Offering: Doctorate

Program: Liberal Arts And General; Teacher Preparatory; Professional

Accreditation: NH, #ARCPA, NURSE, PTA

01 President .... Dr. Doug N. HASTAD
05 Provost .... Dr. Joanne PASSARO
10 Vice President for Finance .... Mr. Ron LOSTETTER
84 Vice President for Enrollment .... Mr. James V. WISEMAN
30 Vice President for Advancement .... Mr. Stephen KUHN
09 Vice Provost .... Vacant
32 Dean of Students .... Dr. Theresa BARRY
13 Chief Information Officer .... Ms. Debra JENKINS
06 Registrar .... Ms. Ann HANDFORD
44 Sr Advancement Ofcr for Development .... Ms. Gina M. EHLER
26 Director of Public Relations .... Ms. Claire M. BEGLINGER
15 Director of Human Resources .... Ms. Barbara A. CHRISTUS
08 Director of Library Services .... Dr. Lelan E. MCLEMORE
37 Director of Student Financial Svcs .... Ms. Dawn M. SCOTT
41 Athletic Director .... Mr. Joe BAKER
88 Director of Part-Time Studies .... Vacant
28 Director of Cultural Diversity .... Ms. Dolores O. BROWN
29 Director Alumni Relations .... Ms. Gina M. EHLER
96 Director of Purchasing .... Ms. Char RICHARDS
07 Director of Admissions .... Ms. Kelly J. HEIMAN
18 Chief Facilities/Physical Plant .... Mr. Chris A. PASBRIG
38 Director Student Counseling .... Ms. Angie R. BRANNAN

Carthage College (F)

2001 Alford Park Drive, Kenosha WI 53140-1994

County: Kenosha | FICE Identification: 003839 | Unit ID: 238476

Telephone: (262) 551-8500 | Carnegie Class: Bac/A&S

FAX Number: (262) 551-6208 | Calendar System: 4/1/4

URL: www.carthage.edu

Established: 1847 | Annual Undergrad Tuition & Fees: $31,300

Enrollment: 3,235 | Coed

Affiliation or Control: Evangelical Lutheran Church In America | IRS Status: 501(c)3

Highest Offering: Master's

Program: Liberal Arts And General; Teacher Preparatory

Accreditation: NH, MUS, SW

01 President .... Dr. F. Gregory CAMPBELL
11 Sr VP Administration/Business .... Mr. William R. ABT
05 Provost .... Dr. Julio C. RIVERA
51 Vice President for Adult Education .... Mr. Michael WEST
20 Sr Vice Pres Academic Resources .... Mr. Brad J. ANDREWS
90 Vice Pres Academic Information Svcs .... Mr. Todd KELLEY
30 Assoc Vice Pres for College Rels .... Ms. Elaine L. WALTON
27 Assoc Vice Pres for Communications .... Mr. Robert J. ROSEN
21 Associate Vice President Business .... Mr. William D. HOARE
07 Assoc Vice Pres for Admissions .... Mr. Dean CLARK
04 Special Assistant to President .... Mr. Paul R. HEGLAND
42 Dean of Siebert Chapel .... Vacant
20 Associate Dean of the College .... Dr. David STEEGE
06 Registrar .... Ms. Abby HANNA
36 Director Career Center .... Ms. Jean FREDERICK
91 Director Administrative Computing .... Mr. Richard HUENINK
88 Director of Conferences .... Mr. Kevin SLONAC
19 Director of Campus Security .... Mr. John KLABECHEK, IV
37 Director Student Financial Aid .... Mr. Vatistas VATISTAS
44 Asst Dir Alumni Rels/Annual Giving .... Ms. Lauren HANSEN
14 Director of Computer Center .... Mrs. Carol SABBAR
41 Athletic Director .... Dr. Robert R. BONN
58 Director of Graduate Program .... Dr. Paul ZAVADA
10 Chief Business Officer .... Mr. David MISSURELLI
18 Chief Facilities/Physical Plant .... Mr. William D. HOARE
35 Director Student Affairs .... Ms. Nina FLEMING
38 Director Student Counseling .... Ms. Deborah BETSWORTH
92 Director of Honors Program .... Dr. Paul ULRICH
07 Director of Admissions .... Ms. Michelle HAMILTON
40 Bookstore Manager .... Mrs. Pam ROBERS
29 Asst Director of Alumni Relations .... Mrs. Mardell FISHER

College of Menominee Nation (G)

PO Box 1179, Keshena WI 54135-1179

County: Menominee | FICE Identification: 031251 | Unit ID: 413617

Telephone: (800) 567-2344 | Carnegie Class: Tribal

FAX Number: (715) 799-1336 | Calendar System: Semester

URL: www.menominee.edu

Established: 1992 | Annual Undergrad Tuition & Fees: $7,350

Enrollment: 615 | Coed

Affiliation or Control: Tribal Control | IRS Status: 501(c)3

Highest Offering: Baccalaureate

Program: Occupational; 2-Year Principally Bachelor's Creditable; Teacher Preparatory; Business Emphasis

Accreditation: NH, ADNUR

01 President .... Dr. Verna M. FOWLER
05 Vice President Academic Affairs .... Dr. Donna POWLESS
10 Vice President of Finance .... Ms. Laurie REITER
32 Vice President Student Services .... Mr. Gary BESAW
12 Vice Pres of CMN Green Bay Campus .... Ms. Kathy DENOR
30 Advancement Director .... Ms. Irene KIEFER
20 Dean of Instruction .... Dr. Diana MORRIS
26 Dean External Relations .... Dr. Holly YOUNGBEAR-TIBBETS
04 Assistant to the President .... Ms. Melinda COOK
75 Dean of Technical Education .... Mrs. Deanna BISLEY
31 Dean of Community Programs .... Mr. Chad WAUKECHON
66 Dean of Nursing .... Ms. Linda TAYLOR
25 Director of Sponsored Programs .... Mrs. Jill MARTIN
13 IT Director .... Ms. Renita WILBER
15 Human Resources Director .... Ms. Gail SWANKE
21 Business Manager .... Mr. Victor ESCALANTE
37 Director Financial Aid .... Ms. Nicole FISH
18 Director of Operations .... Mr. Richard WARRINGTON
06 Registrar .... Mrs. Juanita WAUKAU-WILBER
07 Admissions Director .... Ms. Tessa JAMES
09 Director Institutional Research .... Mr. Ronald JURGENS
88 Voc Rehab Director .... Mr. Norman SHAWANOKASIC
08 Library Director .... Ms. Maria ESCALANTE
88 Campus Planner .... Mr. Joel KROENKE
40 Director of Bookstore .... Ms. Verna DELEON

Columbia College of Nursing (H)

4425 N Port Washington Rd, Milwaukee WI 53212-1099

County: Milwaukee | Identification: 006640 | Unit ID: 238573

Telephone: (414) 326-2330 | Carnegie Class: Not Classified

FAX Number: (414) 236-2331 | Calendar System: Semester

URL: www.ccon.edu

Established: 1901 | Annual Undergrad Tuition & Fees: $23,640

Enrollment: 153 | Coed

Affiliation or Control: Independent Non-Profit | IRS Status: 501(c)3

Highest Offering: Baccalaureate

Program: Liberal Arts And General; Professional; Nursing Emphasis

Accreditation: NH, NURSE

01 Dean & CEO .... Dr. Jill M. WINTERS
03 Assistant Dean .... Ms. Christina ITALIANO
05 Associate Dean of Academic Affairs .... Ms. Susan COLE

Concordia University Wisconsin (I)

12800 N Lake Shore Drive, Mequon WI 53097-2402

County: Ozaukee | FICE Identification: 003842 | Unit ID: 238616

Telephone: (262) 243-5700 | Carnegie Class: Master's L

FAX Number: (262) 243-4351 | Calendar System: 4/1/4

URL: www.cuw.edu

Established: 1881 | Annual Undergrad Tuition & Fees: $23,260

Enrollment: 7,485 | Coed

Affiliation or Control: Lutheran Church - Missouri Synod | IRS Status: 501(c)3

Highest Offering: Doctorate

Program: Liberal Arts And General; Teacher Preparatory; Professional

Accreditation: NH, IACBE, MAC, NURSE, OT, @PHAR, PTA, SW

01 President ... Rev Dr. Patrick T. FERRY
11 Executive VP & Chief Oper Ofcr ... Mr. Allen J. PROCHNOW
05 Senior Vice President of Academics ... Dr. William R. CARIO
32 Vice President of Student Life ... Dr. Andrew J. LUPTAK
07 Vice Pres of Enrollment Services ... Mr. Kenneth K. GASCHK
30 Sr Vice Pres of Advancement ... Mr. Duane H. HILGENDORF
88 Vice President Academic Operations ... Dr. Michael D. BESCH
13 Vice Pres of Information Technology ... Mr. Thomas G. PHILLIP
26 Vice President of Marketing ... Ms. Anita CLARK
10 VP Finance & CFO ... Ms. Joan M. SCHOLZ
20 Assistant Vice Pres of Academics ... Rev Dr. Randy L. FERGUSON
44 Assistant Vice Pres of Advancement ... Rev Dr. Roy PETERSON
42 Campus Pastor ... Rev. Steven N. SMITH
36 Director Counseling ... Mr. David T. ENTERS
37 Financial Aid Officer ... Mr. Steve P. TAYLOR
06 Registrar ... Dr. Steven MONTREAL
50 Dean School of Business ... Dr. David BORST
88 Dean School Human Services ... Dr. Ruth S. GRESLEY
49 Dean School Arts/Sciences ... Dr. Gaylund K. STONE
53 Dean School of Education ... Dr. Michael UDEN
35 Dean Student Affairs ... Mr. Steve W. CROOK
08 Library Director ... Mr. Christian HIMSEL
09 Institutional Research ... Dr. Tamara R. FERRY
29 Director of Alumni Relations ... Ms. Nicole TILOT
39 Director Student Housing ... Ms. Barbara A. WILSON
41 Athletic Director ... Dr. Rob M. BARNHILL
88 Chair Faculty Senate ... Dr. James BURKEE
36 Director Career Services ... Ms. Kim DUNISCH
40 Director Bookstore ... Ms. Laurie COHEN
19 Director Campus Safety ... Mr. Mario VALDES
18 Superintendent Buildings & Grounds ... Mr. Steve V. HIBBARD
15 Director Human Resources ... Ms. Barb R. BANNER
24 Director Instructional Technology ... Mr. Sean B. YOUNG
26 Public Relations Officer ... Mr. Jeff J. BANDURSKI
28 Minority Student Group Advisor ... Mr. Adam WALKER
86 Asst to President for Govern & Plng ... Dr. Ross STUEBER

DeVry University - Milwaukee Center (A)

411 E Wisconsin Avenue, Ste 300,
Milwaukee WI 53202-4400

County: Milwaukee — Identification: 666225
Unit ID: 238935
Telephone: (414) 278-7677 — Carnegie Class: Spec/Bus
FAX Number: (414) 278-0137 — Calendar System: Semester
URL: www.devry.edu
Established: 1995 — Annual Undergrad Tuition & Fees: $15,294
Enrollment: 346 — Coed
Affiliation or Control: Proprietary — IRS Status: Proprietary
Highest Offering: Master's
Program: Occupational; Professional; Business Emphasis
Accreditation: &NH

01 Campus Director ... Jeunet DAVENPORT

† Regional accreditation is carried under the parent institution in Downers Grove, IL.

DeVry University - Waukesha Center (B)

N 14 W23833 Stone Ridge Dr, Ste 450,
Waukesha WI 53188-1157

County: Waukesha — Identification: 666226
Unit ID: 439260
Telephone: (262) 347-2911 — Carnegie Class: Not Classified
FAX Number: (262) 798-9912 — Calendar System: Semester
URL: www.devry.edu
Established: 1992 — Annual Undergrad Tuition & Fees: $15,294
Enrollment: 175 — Coed
Affiliation or Control: Proprietary — IRS Status: Proprietary
Highest Offering: Master's
Program: Professional; Business Emphasis
Accreditation: &NH

01 Center Dean ... Kate PELCHAT

† Regional accreditation is carried under the parent institution in Downers Grove, IL.

Edgewood College (C)

1000 Edgewood College Drive, Madison WI 53711-1997

County: Dane — FICE Identification: 003848
Unit ID: 238661
Telephone: (608) 663-4861 — Carnegie Class: DRU
FAX Number: (608) 663-3291 — Calendar System: 4/1/4
URL: www.edgewood.edu
Established: 1927 — Annual Undergrad Tuition & Fees: $22,850
Enrollment: 1,687 — Coed
Affiliation or Control: Roman Catholic — IRS Status: 501(c)3
Highest Offering: Doctorate
Program: Liberal Arts And General; Teacher Preparatory; Professional
Accreditation: NH, ACBSP, MFCD, NURSE, TED

01 President ... Dr. Daniel J. CAREY
05 VP Academic Affs/Academic Dean ... Dr. Mary KELLY-POWELL
32 VP Student Devel/Dean of Students ... Dr. Margaret R. BALISTRERI-CLARKE
84 Vice Pres for Planning & Enrollment ... Dr. Scott FLANAGAN
10 Vice President Business & Finance ... Mr. Michael GUNS
30 Vice Pres Inst Advancement/Dir Dev ... Mr. John USELMAN
13 VP for Institutional Technology ... Mr. Walter WENTZ
20 Associate Academic Dean ... Dr. Kenneth MACUR
58 Dean Grad Adult/Profess Studies ... Dr. Scott CAMPBELL
06 Registrar ... Ms. Michelle KELLY
08 Library Director ... Dr. Sylvia CONTRERAS
36 Director for Career Counseling Svcs ... Ms. Shawn JOHNSON-WILLIAMS
29 Alumni Director ... Ms. Kathleen O'CONNOR
26 Director Public Relations ... Mr. Edward TAYLOR
15 Director of Human Resources ... Ms. Annie STROUD
18 Director Facilities & Operations ... Ms. Susan SERRAULT
35 Director Student Activities ... Ms. Beth JOHN
38 Director Student Counseling ... Ms. Stephanie GRAHAM
07 Director of Admissions ... Ms. Christine BENEDICT
21 Controller ... Ms. Jane WILHELM
28 Director of Diversity ... Ms. Pearl LEONARD-ROCK
37 Director Student Financial Aid ... Ms. Kari GRIBBLE
09 Director of Institutional Research ... Ms. Yang ZHANG

Herzing University (D)

5218 E Terrace Drive, Madison WI 53718-8340

County: Dane — FICE Identification: 009621
Unit ID: 240392
Telephone: (608) 249-6611 — Carnegie Class: Bac/Assoc
FAX Number: (608) 249-8593 — Calendar System: Semester
URL: www.herzing.edu
Established: 1948 — Annual Undergrad Tuition & Fees: $16,560
Enrollment: 903 — Coed
Affiliation or Control: Proprietary — IRS Status: Proprietary
Highest Offering: Master's
Program: Technical Emphasis
Accreditation: NH, ADNUR, MAAB

01 President ... Ms. Renee HERZING
10 CFO & Vice President of Finance ... Mr. Ryan O'DESKY
05 Academic Dean ... Mr. Brian WILLISON
37 Director of Educational Funding ... Mr. Donald FINCH
06 Director of Registration ... Ms. Ginger SCHMELZER
07 Director of Admissions ... Mr. Matthew SCHNEIDER
36 Director of Career Development ... Mr. Jeff WESTRA

ITT Technical Institute (E)

470 Security Boulevard, Green Bay WI 54313-9705

County: Brown — Identification: 666317
Unit ID: 440165
Telephone: (920) 662-9000 — Carnegie Class: Spec/Tech
FAX Number: (920) 662-9384 — Calendar System: Quarter
URL: www.itt-tech.edu
Established: 2003 — Annual Undergrad Tuition & Fees: N/A
Enrollment: 924 — Coed
Affiliation or Control: Proprietary — IRS Status: Proprietary
Highest Offering: Baccalaureate
Program: Technical Emphasis
Accreditation: ACICS

† Branch campus of ITT Technical Institute, Greenfield, WI.

ITT Technical Institute (F)

6300 West Layton Avenue, Greenfield WI 53220-4612

County: Milwaukee — FICE Identification: 030875
Unit ID: 238892
Telephone: (414) 282-9494 — Carnegie Class: Spec/Tech
FAX Number: (414) 282-9698 — Calendar System: Quarter
URL: www.itt-tech.edu
Established: 1989 — Annual Undergrad Tuition & Fees: N/A
Enrollment: 1,264 — Coed
Affiliation or Control: Proprietary — IRS Status: Proprietary
Highest Offering: Baccalaureate
Program: Technical Emphasis
Accreditation: ACICS

Lac Courte Oreilles Ojibwa Community College (G)

13466 W Trepania Road, Hayward WI 54843-2181

County: Sawyer — FICE Identification: 025322
Unit ID: 260372
Telephone: (715) 634-4790 — Carnegie Class: Tribal
FAX Number: (715) 634-5049 — Calendar System: Semester
URL: www.lco.edu
Established: 1982 — Annual Undergrad Tuition & Fees: $3,840
Enrollment: 525 — Coed
Affiliation or Control: Tribal Control — IRS Status: 501(c)3
Highest Offering: Associate Degree
Program: Occupational; 2-Year Principally Bachelor's Creditable
Accreditation: NH, MAC

01 President ... Dr. Danielle HORNETT
05 Academic Dean ... Dr. Sue GLIDDEN
32 Dean Student Services/Enroll Mgmt ... Mr. Raymond BURNS
10 Controller ... Ms. Anita HACKER
06 Registrar ... Mrs. Annette WIGGINS
37 Financial Aid Director ... Ms. Diane MCKNIGHT
46 Director Planning/Research & Devel ... Dr. Ann MARTIN
15 Human Resource Director ... Mr. Peter WHITENECK

Lakeland College (H)

PO Box 359, Sheboygan WI 53082-0359

County: Sheboygan — FICE Identification: 003854
Unit ID: 238980
Telephone: (920) 565-1000 — Carnegie Class: Master's L
FAX Number: (920) 565-1206 — Calendar System: Semester
URL: www.lakeland.edu
Established: 1862 — Annual Undergrad Tuition & Fees: $20,230
Enrollment: 3,936 — Coed
Affiliation or Control: United Church Of Christ — IRS Status: 501(c)3
Highest Offering: Master's
Program: Liberal Arts And General
Accreditation: NH, TEAC

01 President ... Dr. Stephen A. GOULD
05 Vice Pres Academic Affairs ... Dr. Margaret L. ALBRINCK
11 Senior Vice Pres Administration ... Mr. Daniel W. ECK
30 Vice President for Advancement ... Dr. Kenneth D. STRMISKA
10 Vice President Finance/CFO ... Mr. Joseph D. BOTANA, II
32 Vice President Student Development ... Mr. Nathan D. DEHNE
56 Interim VP Kellett Adult Education ... Ms. Erin K. KOHL
35 Dean of Students ... Ms. Sandra L. GIBBONS-VOLLBRECHT
43 VP Intl Programs/General Counsel ... Mr. Anthony E. FESSLER
06 Registrar ... Ms. Susan A. GOULD
09 Director of Institutional Research ... Mr. David STEIN
08 Director of Library Services ... Ms. Ann K. PENKE
07 Director of Admissions ... Mr. Nick A. SPAETH
37 Director of Financial Aid ... Ms. Patty L. TAYLOR
85 International Student Advisor ... Mr. Pei Patrick LIU
27 Director of Communications ... Mr. David D. GALLIANETTI
41 Athletic Director ... Ms. Jane A. BOUCHE
21 Controller ... Ms. Sharon L. ROOB
29 Director of Alumni Relations ... Ms. Lisa B. VIHOS
36 Director of Career Development ... Ms. Lisa M. STEPHAN

Lakeside School of Massage Therapy (I)

1726 North First Street, Milwaukee WI 53212

County: Milwaukee — FICE Identification: 030074
Unit ID: 238421
Telephone: (414) 372-4345 — Carnegie Class: Not Classified
FAX Number: N/A — Calendar System: Other
URL: www.lakeside.edu
Established: N/A — Annual Undergrad Tuition & Fees: $10,025
Enrollment: 85 — Coed
Affiliation or Control: Independent Non-Profit — IRS Status: 501(c)3
Highest Offering: Associate Degree
Program: Occupational
Accreditation: COMTA

01 CEO ... Dr. Carole OSTENDORF
11 Chief Operating Officer/Campus Coor ... Ms. Sue MILLER
05 Director of Education ... Ms. JeraiLyn JONES

Lawrence University (J)

711 E. Boldt Way, Appleton WI 54911

County: Outagamie — FICE Identification: 003856
Unit ID: 239017
Telephone: (920) 832-7000 — Carnegie Class: Bac/A&S
FAX Number: (920) 832-6606 — Calendar System: Other
URL: www.lawrence.edu
Established: 1847 — Annual Undergrad Tuition & Fees: $38,205
Enrollment: 1,565 — Coed
Affiliation or Control: Independent Non-Profit — IRS Status: 501(c)3
Highest Offering: Baccalaureate
Program: Liberal Arts And General
Accreditation: NH, MUS

01 President ... Dr. Jill BECK
04 Executive Asst to the President ... Ms. Laurie PETRICK
05 Provost and Dean of the Faculty ... Dr. David BURROWS
10 VP Business & Operations ... Mr. Brian RISTE
30 VP Development/Alumni Rels ... Mr. Calvin D. HUSMANN
32 VP Student Affairs & Dean ... Ms. Nancy D. TRUESDELL
29 VP Alumni/Constituency Engagement ... Mr. Mark D. BRESEMAN
44 Assoc VP Major & Planned Giving ... Ms. Barbara J. STACK
21 Assoc VP of Business & Operations ... Ms. Dawn ROST
64 Dean Conservatory of Music ... Mr. Brian G. PERTL
36 Dean of Career Services ... Ms. Mary T. MEANY
09 Director of Research Administration ... Dr. William F. SKINNER
26 Director of Communications ... Ms. Sheree O. ROGERS
07 Director of Admissions ... Mr. Kenneth L. ANSELMENT
37 Director of Financial Aid ... Ms. Sara C. HOLMAN
35 Dean Student Academic Services ... Mr. Geoff GAJEWSKI
20 Associate Dean of the Faculty ... Ms. Ruth M. LANOUETTE
28 Asst Dean Students Multicul Affs ... Ms. Pa Lee MOUA
06 Registrar ... Ms. Anne S. NORMAN
08 Librarian ... Mr. Peter J. GILBERT
30 Director of Development ... Ms. Stacy J. MARA
41 Athletic Director ... Mr. Michael W. SZKODZINSKI
36 Director of the Career Center ... Ms. Kathleen M. HEINZEN
13 Director Information Tech Svcs ... Mr. Steven M. ARMSTRONG
15 Director of Human Resources ... Ms. Sandy ISSELMANN
18 Director of Facility Services ... Mr. Daniel R. MEYER
38 Director Counseling Services ... Ms. Kathleen F. FUCHS

Madison Media Institute-College of Media Arts (A)

2702 Agriculture Drive, Madison WI 53718-6787

County: Dane FICE Identification: 010913
Unit ID: 364168
Telephone: (608) 663-2000 Carnegie Class: Assoc/PrivFP
FAX Number: (608) 442-0141 Calendar System: Semester
URL: www.mediainstitute.edu
Established: 1969 Annual Undergrad Tuition & Fees: $16,000
Enrollment: 580 Coed
Affiliation or Control: Proprietary IRS Status: Proprietary
Highest Offering: Baccalaureate
Program: Occupational; 2-Year Principally Bachelor's Creditable; Technical Emphasis
Accreditation: ACCSC

01 President Mr. Chris HUTCHINGS
07 Admissions Director Mr. Nile MCKIBBEN

Maranatha Baptist Bible College & Seminary (B)

745 W Main Street, Watertown WI 53094-7600

County: Jefferson FICE Identification: 023172
Unit ID: 239071
Telephone: (920) 261-9300 Carnegie Class: Bac/Diverse
FAX Number: (920) 261-9109 Calendar System: Semester
URL: www.mbbc.edu
Established: 1968 Annual Undergrad Tuition & Fees: $12,260
Enrollment: 822 Coed
Affiliation or Control: Independent Non-Profit IRS Status: 501(c)3
Highest Offering: Master's
Program: Liberal Arts And General; Teacher Preparatory; Professional; Religious Emphasis
Accreditation: NH

01 President Dr. Martin MARRIOTT
04 Administrative Assistant COO Dr. Darryl L. STURGILL
05 Vice President for Academic Affairs Dr. John R. BROCK
30 Vice President for Inst Advancement Dr. Jim H. HARRISON
10 Vice President for Business Affairs Mr. Mark W. STEVENS
32 Dean of Students Mr. Doug G. RICHARDS
06 Registrar Dr. David L. HERSHBERGER
07 Director of Admissions Dr. James H. HARRISON
30 Director of Development Mr. John DAVIS
09 Director of Institutional Research Dr. Matthew DAVIS
15 Director Personnel Services Dr. Darryl L. STURGILL
18 Chief Facilities/Physical Plant Dr. Werner LUMM
26 Chief Public Relations Officer Dr. Jeff CRUM
41 Athletic Director Mr. Robert THOMPSON
08 Librarian Miss Lois OETKEN
29 Director Alumni Relations Mr. John DAVIS
37 Director Student Financial Aid Mr. Randy HIBBS

Marian University (C)

45 S National Avenue, Fond Du Lac WI 54935-4699

County: Fond Du Lac FICE Identification: 003861
Unit ID: 239080
Telephone: (920) 923-7600 Carnegie Class: Master's L
FAX Number: (920) 923-7154 Calendar System: Semester
URL: www.marianuniversity.edu
Established: 1936 Annual Undergrad Tuition & Fees: $22,470
Enrollment: 2,881 Coed
Affiliation or Control: Roman Catholic IRS Status: 501(c)3
Highest Offering: Doctorate
Program: Liberal Arts And General; Teacher Preparatory; Professional
Accreditation: NH, IACBE, NURSE, SW, TED

01 President Dr. Steven R. DISALVO
05 Exec VP Academic & Student Affairs Dr. Edward H. OGLE
84 VP Enrollment Management Ms. Stacey L. AKEY
88 VP for Mission & Retention Ms. Kate CANDEE
30 Vice President for Advancement Mr. Paul M. NEUBERGER
42 Director of Campus Ministry Sr. Marie SCOTT, CSA
10 Dir Business & Finance/Controller Ms. Mary K. KOSMER
32 Dean of Students Ms. Kerry STRUPP
55 Dean of PACE Sr. Donna INNES, CSA
53 Dean School of Education Dr. Sue A. STODDART
66 Dean School of Nursing Dr. Julie A. LUETSCHWAGER
49 Dean Arts/Humanities & Letters Dr. James VAN DYKE
50 Dean School of Business Dr. Jeffrey G. REED
81 Dean of Math/Sciences Dr. Lance C. URVEN
83 Dean Social/Behavioral Science Dr. Larry REYNOLDS
88 Dean School of Criminal Justice Dr. Michelle MAJEWSKI
58 Dean Graduate Studies Vacant
08 Director of Libraries Ms. Mary Ellen GORMICAN
18 General Manager/Facilities Mr. Layne D. SESSIONS
06 Registrar Ms. Cheryl A. TEICHMILLER
09 Director of Institutional Research Dr. Sylvia K. REED
37 Director of Financial Aid Ms. Pamela WARREN
26 Director University Relations Ms. Lisa L. KIDD
29 Director Alumni Relations Mr. Stephen A. MATZ
07 Senior Director of Admission Ms. Shannon S. LALUZERNE
16 Director of Human Resources Ms. Cathy T. FLOOD
41 Director of Athletics Mr. Doug R. HAMMONDS
88 Dean Advising/Academic Services Ms. Cathy M. MATHWEG
23 Director of Health Services Ms. Connie DIENER
36 Director Career & Grad School Svcs Ms. Ashly G. GARNER
88 Director of Campus Dining Services Ms. Nikki A. KRAMER
13 Director of Information Technology Mr. Keith L. FALK
40 Director of Bookstore Ms. Mary MANGAN-FLOOD
38 Director of Counseling Ms. Ellen MERCER
92 Director Honors Program Dr. Abbey E. ROSEN
88 Director of Inst Assessment Ms. Jennifer K. KRUEGER
04 Executive Assistant to President Ms. Carey C. GARDIN
35 Dir Student Activities/Greek Life Ms. Julie A. GNIEWEK
39 Director of Student Services Ms. Dee HARMSEN
104 Coordinator of Study Abroad Ms. Ann UMBREIT
25 Director Research & Sponsored Grnts Mr. Marc D. HEIMERL

Marquette University (D)

PO Box 1881, Milwaukee WI 53201-1881

County: Milwaukee FICE Identification: 003863
Unit ID: 239105
Telephone: (414) 288-7700 Carnegie Class: DRU
FAX Number: (414) 288-3300 Calendar System: Semester
URL: www.mu.edu
Established: 1881 Annual Undergrad Tuition & Fees: $15,911
Enrollment: 10,590 Coed
Affiliation or Control: Roman Catholic IRS Status: 501(c)3
Highest Offering: Doctorate
Program: Liberal Arts And General; Teacher Preparatory; Professional
Accreditation: NH, ARCPA, BUS, BUSA, CLPSY, COPSY, DENT, ENG, JOUR, LAW, MIDWF, MT, NURSE, PTA, SP, TED, THEA

01 President Rev. Scott R. PILARZ, SJ
03 Senior Vice President Mr. Gregory J. KLIEBHAN
05 Provost Dr. John J. PAULY
10 Vice President Finance Mr. John C. LAMB
11 Vice President Administration Mr. Arthur F. SCHEUBER
32 Vice President for Student Affairs Dr. L. Christopher MILLER
30 Vice Pres University Advancement Ms. Julie A. TOLAN
27 Vice President Public Affairs Ms. Rana H. ALTENBURG
43 Vice President/General Counsel Ms. Cynthia M. BAUER
26 Vice Pres Marketing/Communication Ms. Patricia L. GERAGHTY
35 Assoc Vice Pres Student Affairs Dr. Linda J. LEE
15 Asst Vice Pres/Dir Human Resources Mr. Octavio CASTRO
39 Asst Vice Pres/Dean Residence Life Dr. James P. MCMAHON
88 Sr Assoc VP Development Mr. Timothy RIPPINGER
20 Vice Prov Undergrad Pgms/Teaching Dr. Gary MEYER
58 V Prov Research/Dean Graduate Sch Dr. Jeanne HOSSENLOPP
90 Assoc Vice Prov Educational Tech Mr. G. Jon PRAY
88 Assoc Vice Prov Acad Support Pgm Ms. Anne D. DEAHL
28 Sr Advisor Prov Diversity Init Dr. William WELBURN
06 Registrar Ms. Georgia D. MCRAE
49 Interim Dean of Arts & Sciences Rev. Philip J. ROSSI, SJ
50 Dean of Business Administration Dr. Linda M. SALCHENBERGER
52 Dean of Dentistry Dr. William K. LOBB
54 Dean of Engineering Dr. Robert BISHOP
60 Dean of Communication Dr. Lori BERGEN
76 Dean of Health Sciences Dr. William CULLINAN
61 Dean of the Law School Mr. Joseph D. KEARNEY
66 Dean of Nursing Dr. Margaret CALLAHAN
53 Dean College of Education Dr. William A. HENK
107 Dean Col of Professional Studies Dr. Robert J. DEAHL
08 Dean of Libraries Ms. Janice WELBURN
07 Dean of Admissions Mr. Robert BLUST
35 Dean of Students Dr. Stephanie QUADE
25 Exec Director of Research Support Mr. Keith OSTERHAGE
104 Dir Office International Education Mr. Terence MILLER
37 Director of Financial Aid Ms. Susan M. TEERINK
36 Director Career Services Center Ms. Laura F. KESTNER
41 Athletic Director Mr. Steven COTTINGHAM
23 Exec Dir Student Health Services Dr. Carolyn S. SMITH
38 Director of Counseling Center Dr. Michael J. ZEBROWSKI
42 Vice Pres of Univ Mission/Ministry Ms. Stephanie J. RUSSELL
13 Chief Information Officer Ms. Kathy J. LANG
18 Director Facilities Services Mr. Ronald L. RIPLEY
19 Director Public Safety Mr. Lawrence R. RICKARD
40 Director Marquette Spirit Shop Mr. James K. GRAEBERT
96 Director of Purchasing Ms. Jenny ALEXANDER
29 Exec Director of Alumni Association Mr. Timothy J. SIMMONS

Medical College of Wisconsin (E)

PO Box 26509, Milwaukee WI 53226-0509

County: Milwaukee FICE Identification: 024535
Unit ID: 239169
Telephone: (414) 955-8296 Carnegie Class: Spec/Med
FAX Number: (414) 955-6560 Calendar System: Other
URL: www.mcw.edu
Established: 1893 Annual Graduate Tuition & Fees: $46,851
Enrollment: 820 Coed
Affiliation or Control: Independent Non-Profit IRS Status: 501(c)3
Highest Offering: Doctorate; No Undergraduates
Program: Professional
Accreditation: NH, DENT, MED, PDPSY, PH

01 President & CEO Dr. John R. RAYMOND, SR.
11 Sr Vice Pres Finance/Administration Mr. Glenn Allen BOLTON
05 Int Dean/Executive Vice President Dr. Joseph E. KERSCHNER
88 Dean Grad Sch Biomedical Science Dr. Ravi P. MISRA
30 Vice Pres Institutional Advancement Mr. James W. HEALD
15 Vice President Human Resources Ms. Sherri DUCHARME-WHITE
86 Vice Pres Government/Community Affs Ms. Kathryn A. KUHN
100 Chief of Staff Ms. Mara LORD
44 Assoc Vice President Development Ms. Pamela J. GARVEY
28 VP Corporate Compliance Risk Mgmt Mr. Daniel WICKEHAM
26 Assoc Vice Pres Public Affairs Mr. Richard N. KATSCHKE
20 Senior Assoc Dean Education Dr. Karen MARCDANTE
22 Assoc Dean Student Affs/Diversity Dr. Dawn BRAGG
32 Assoc Dean for Student Affairs Dr. Richard L. HOLLOWAY
63 Assoc Dean Graduate Med Educ Dr. Kenneth B. SIMONS
46 Senior Associate Dean Research Dr. David D. GUTTERMAN
20 Associate Dean Curriculum Dr. Philip N. REDLICH
45 Assoc Dean Educ Support/Evaluation Dr. Deborah E. SIMPSON
21 Director Budget Administration Ms. Deidre ERWIN
13 Director Application Development Ms. Rebecca L. MORRISON
08 Director Medical Libraries Ms. Mary B. BLACKWELDER
07 Director Admissions Ms. Jennifer L. HALUZAK
06 Registrar Ms. Lesley A. MACK
18 Dir Facil Engineering/Maintenance Mr. Jeffrey BORNEMANN
37 Director Student Financial Services Ms. Linda L. PASCHAL
25 Director Grants & Contracts Ms. April HAVERTY
29 Exec Director Alumni Relations Mr. William A. SCHULTZ
21 Director Business Services Ms. Paulette PECARD
88 Medical Dir Clinical Informatics Dr. Rick D. GILLIS
40 Manager of Bookstore Ms. Cathy GRANFIELD

Midwest College of Oriental Medicine (F)

6232 Bankers Road, Racine WI 53403-9747

County: Racine FICE Identification: 030612
Unit ID: 383020
Telephone: (800) 593-2320 Carnegie Class: Spec/Health
FAX Number: (262) 554-7475 Calendar System: Quarter
URL: www.acupuncture.edu
Established: 1979 Annual Undergrad Tuition & Fees: $14,652
Enrollment: 132 Coed
Affiliation or Control: Proprietary IRS Status: Proprietary
Highest Offering: Master's; No Lower Division
Program: Professional
Accreditation: ACUP

01 President Dr. William J. DUNBAR
11 Administrative Director Dr. Robert CHELNICK
05 Academic Dean/Research Director Dr. Alan URETZ
88 Projects Director Dr. Kristine L. LA POINT
37 Director of Financial Aid Ms. Jennifer L. RHYNER
07 Admissions Coord/Transfer Credit Ms. Kelly A. WESTERLUND
06 Records Officer/Registrar Ms. Amy L. BENISH
32 Dean of Students/Librarian Mr. John BALLARINI
35 Associate Dean of Students Ms. Olga GAJDOSIK
09 Research Director Mr. Jin Hua XIE
63 Dean of Biomedicine Science Dr. Donald L. MARTIN
85 Dean of Foreign Students Dr. Duckin SUH
17 Internship Director Dr. Helen WU
09 Clinic Tracking/Inst Evaluation Ms. Deirdre M. DUNBAR
86 Compliance Officer Mr. Harry S. HEIFETZ
91 Information Systems Mr. William H. LEHMAN
26 Marketing/Student Affairs Mr. Chris A. KRAJNIAK
37 Financial Aid Processor Ms. Stephanie M. PITTMAN

Milwaukee Institute of Art & Design (G)

273 E Erie Street, Milwaukee WI 53202-6003

County: Milwaukee FICE Identification: 020771
Unit ID: 239309
Telephone: (414) 847-3200 Carnegie Class: Spec/Arts
FAX Number: (414) 291-8077 Calendar System: Semester
URL: www.miad.edu
Established: 1974 Annual Undergrad Tuition & Fees: $28,650
Enrollment: 700 Coed
Affiliation or Control: Independent Non-Profit IRS Status: 501(c)3
Highest Offering: Baccalaureate
Program: Liberal Arts And General; Fine Arts Emphasis
Accreditation: NH, ART

01 President Mr. Neil J. HOFFMAN
05 VP of Academic Affairs Mr. David MARTIN
84 VP for Enrollment Management Ms. Mary C. SCHOPP
04 Executive Assistant to President Ms. Dagmar L. CARNDUFF
09 Assoc VP Academic Plng/Assessment Ms. Cynthia LYNCH
32 Dean of Students Mr. Tony J. NOWAK
30 Director of Development Mr. Ryan DANIELS
37 Executive Director of Financial Aid Ms. Carol MASSE
07 Executive Director of Admissions Ms. Stacey STEINBERG
26 Director of Communications Ms. Vivian M. ROTHSCHILD
08 Director of Library Services Ms. Cynthia D. LYNCH
36 Director of Career Services Mr. Duane P. SEIDENSTICKER
51 Dir Pre-College & Adult Learning Ms. Jill F. KUNSMANN
19 Director Security/Safety Mr. Keith A. KOTOWICZ
06 Director of Registration Services Ms. Jean WEIMER
21 Controller/Business Manager Ms. Brenda JONES
38 Director of College Advising Ms. Rebecca BALISTRERI
18 Building Maintenance Manager Mr. Michael A. GOETZ
29 Dir Cultural & Alumni Relations Ms. Melissa RICHARDS
15 Director of Human Resources Ms. Edie MCCLELLAN
20 Director of Academic Operations Ms. Marie KAMINSKI

Milwaukee School of Engineering (H)

1025 N Broadway, Milwaukee WI 53202-3109

County: Milwaukee FICE Identification: 003868
Unit ID: 239318
Telephone: (414) 277-7300 Carnegie Class: Master's S
FAX Number: (414) 277-7454 Calendar System: Quarter
URL: www.msoe.edu

Established: 1903 Annual Undergrad Tuition & Fees: $30,990
Enrollment: 2,679 Coed
Affiliation or Control: Independent Non-Profit IRS Status: 501(c)3
Highest Offering: Master's
Program: Professional; Technical Emphasis
Accreditation: NH, CONST, ENG, ENGT, NURSE, PERF

01 President ....Dr. Hermann VIETS
05 Vice President Academics ....Dr. Fred BERRY
10 Vice President Finance/Treasurer ....Mr. Armund M. JANTO
30 Vice President of Development ....Mr. A. Frank HABIB
18 Facility Manager ....Vacant
32 Vice President Student Life ....Mr. Patrick J. COFFEY
84 Vice Pres of Enrollment Management ....Mr. Timothy VALLEY
09 Dean of Institutional Research ....Mr. Leonard A. VANDEN BOOM
25 Dean Grants & Projects ....Mr. Thomas E. BRAY
48 Chair Architectural Engr Dept ....Dr. Deborah JACKMAN
50 Chair School of Business ....Mr. Steve BIALEK
54 Chair Electrical Engr/CPU Sci Dept ....Dr. Owe G. PETERSEN
97 Chair General Studies Department ....Dr. David KENT
81 Chair Mathematics Department ....Dr. Karl H. DAVID
54 Chair Mechanical Engineering Dept ....Dr. Matthew A. PANHANS
81 Chair Physics/Chemistry Dept ....Dr. Matey KALTCHEV
66 Chair Nursing Department ....Dr. Debra JENKS
21 Controller & Assistant Treasurer ....Mr. Patrick J. AUGUSTINE
06 Registrar ....Ms. Mary F. NIELSEN
26 Director Marketing Public Affairs ....Ms. Sandra L. EVERTS
27 Director Public & Media Relations ....Ms. JoEllen BURDUE
15 Director of Human Resources ....Mr. Kevin A. MORIN
37 Director of Financial Aid ....Mr. Steve MIDTHUN
21 Asst Director Financial Services ....Ms. Debra A. DANNECKER
44 Director of Development ....Mr. Jonathan V. KOWALSKI, JR.
38 Director of Counseling ....Mr. Joseph P. MELOY
88 Director Learning Resource Center ....Mr. Brian E. BURKE
35 Director Student Activities ....Mr. Richard GAGLIANO
39 Director Residence Halls ....Mr. William E. BREESE
41 Director Athletics ....Mr. Dan I. HARRIS
23 Director of Health Services ....Ms. Kathryn J. DECHAMPS
08 Director of Library & Info Services ....Mr. Gary S. SHIMEK
24 Director University Media Services ....Mr. Kent A. PETERSON
19 Director of Public Safety ....Mr. William P. FADROWSKI
88 Director Fluid Power Institute ....Mr. Tom S. WANKE
13 Dir Computer/Communications Svcs ....Mr. Nigel LONGWORTH
07 Director of Admissions ....Ms. Dana GRENNIER
36 Director Student Placement ....Ms. Mary SPENCER
88 Asst Director of Student Life ....Mr. Nick SEIDLER
40 Bookstore Manager ....Mr. David P. ABRAHAMSON

Mount Mary College (A)

2900 N Menomonee River Parkway,
Milwaukee WI 53222-4597
County: Milwaukee FICE Identification: 003869
Unit ID: 239390
Telephone: (414) 258-4810 Carnegie Class: Master's S
FAX Number: (414) 256-1224 Calendar System: Semester
URL: www.mtmary.edu
Established: 1913 Annual Undergrad Tuition & Fees: $22,540
Enrollment: 1,963 Female
Affiliation or Control: Roman Catholic IRS Status: 501(c)3
Highest Offering: Master's
Program: Liberal Arts And General; Teacher Preparatory; Professional
Accreditation: NH, CIDA, DIETC, DIETI, OT, SW

01 President ....Dr. Eileen SCHWALBACH
05 Vice Pres Academic/Student Affairs ....Dr. David NIXON
10 Vice Pres Finance & Administration ....Mr. Reyes GONZALEZ
30 Vice Pres External Relations ....Ms. Donna GASTEVICH
84 Vice Pres Enrollment Services ....Mr. David WEGENER
88 Vice President Mission/ Identity ....Sr. Joan PENZENSTADLER, SSND
20 Assoc Dean Academic Affairs ....Dr. Wendy MCCREDIE
32 Assoc Dean for Student Affairs ....Ms. Martha NELSON
58 Assoc Dean Graduate Education ....Dr. Doug MICKELSON
66 Dean Nursing Program ....Dr. Jill WINTERS
88 Exec Dir Women's Leadership Inst ....Ms. Yvonne LUMSDEN-DILL
21 Controller ....Mr. Fredric LEX
102 Senior Director of Development ....Ms. Cynthia ECHOLS
44 Annual Giving Officer ....Ms. Sophia KINTIS
26 Senior Dir of Public Relations/Mktg ....Ms. Susan SEILER
27 Senor Manager of Media Relations ....Ms. Susan SHIMSHAK
29 Director of Alumnae Relations ....Ms. Susan NIEBERLE
06 Registrar ....Dr. Mary KARR
09 Director of Inst Research ....Ms. Maya EVANS
08 Director of Library ....Ms. Julie KAMIKAWA
13 Director of Information Technology ....Mr. Praveen KRISHNAMURTI
37 Director Financial Aid ....Ms. Debra DUFF
35 Director of Student Engagement ....Ms. Amy DANIELSON
39 Residence Life Director ....Ms. Beth SCHOENWETTER
36 Dir of Advising/Career Development ....Ms. Michelle SMALLEY
104 Dir International Studies ....Ms. Nan METZGER
15 Director of Human Resources ....Ms. Teri COX
41 Athletic Director ....Ms. Janae MAGNUSON
42 Director Campus Ministry ....Vacant
18 Director Buildings & Grounds ....Sr. Georgeann KRZYZANOWSKI, SSND
19 Director of Security ....Mr. Paul LESHOK
105 Website and Photo Manager ....Ms. Eichelle THOMPSON

Nashotah House (B)

2777 Mission Road, Nashotah WI 53058-9793
County: Waukesha FICE Identification: 003874
Unit ID: 239424
Telephone: (262) 646-6500 Carnegie Class: Spec/Faith
FAX Number: (262) 646-6504 Calendar System: Semester
URL: www.nashotah.edu
Established: 1842 Annual Graduate Tuition & Fees: $12,000
Enrollment: 119 Coed
Affiliation or Control: Protestant Episcopal IRS Status: 501(c)3
Highest Offering: Doctorate; No Undergraduates
Program: Professional; Religious Emphasis
Accreditation: THEOL

01 President & Dean ....Rt.Rev. Edward L. SALMON
03 Provost ....Mr. Richard LONGABAUGH
73 Seminary Sub-Dean ....Rev. J. Douglas MCGLYNN
11 Assoc Dean of Admin & Development ....Vacant
05 Associate Dean for Academic Affairs ....Dr. Garwood P. ANDERSON
32 Assoc Dean Student Affs/Dir Admiss ....Dr. Carol K. KLUKAS
08 Library Director ....Mr. David G. SHERWOOD
26 Director of Communications ....Rev. Steven SCHLOSSBERG
30 Dir Development & Alumni Relations ....Vacant
18 Chief Facilities/Physical Plant ....Mr. Charlie RICHARDS
40 Bookstore Director ....Ms. Charlotte BOOTH

Northland College (C)

1411 Ellis Avenue, Ashland WI 54806-3999
County: Ashland FICE Identification: 003875
Unit ID: 239512
Telephone: (715) 682-1699 Carnegie Class: Bac/A&S
FAX Number: (715) 682-1308 Calendar System: Other
URL: www.northland.edu
Established: 1892 Annual Undergrad Tuition & Fees: $26,566
Enrollment: 556 Coed
Affiliation or Control: United Church Of Christ IRS Status: 501(c)3
Highest Offering: Baccalaureate
Program: Liberal Arts And General; Teacher Preparatory
Accreditation: NH

01 President ....Dr. Michael MILLER
05 Interim VP of Academic Affairs ....Mr. Alan BREW
30 Vice President Institutional Advanc ....Mr. Marc BARBEAU
10 VP Finance & Administration ....Mr. Robert JACKSON
84 Vice President for Enrollment ....Mr. Rick J. SMITH
26 Vice President of Marketing ....Mr. David WAHLBERG
32 Dean of Student Life ....Ms. Michele MEYER
20 Academic Dean ....Mr. Alan BREW
07 Director of Admissions ....Vacant
06 Registrar ....Ms. Kathy TRAYNOR
08 Library Director ....Ms. Julia WAGGONER
29 Sr Advanc Officer Alumni Relations ....Vacant
13 Director of IT ....Mr. Ray GREGOR
41 Athletic Director ....Mr. Steve WAMMER
15 Director Human Resources ....Mr. Paul SKORACZEWSKI
35 Dir Career Educ & Retention ....Ms. Patti FENNER-LEINO
18 Director of Facilities ....Mr. Thomas HMIELEWSKI
37 Director of Student Financial Aid ....Ms. Deb MORRISSEY
21 Controller ....Ms. Lori BENNETTS
44 Senior Advancement Officer ....Ms. Kristy LIPHART
09 Institutional Research Specialist ....Ms. Petra HOFSTEDT
04 Exec Assistant to the President ....Ms. Lisa MCGINLEY
39 Director of Residential Life ....Mr. Jared FRIESEN

Northland International University (D)

W10085 Pike Plains Road, Dunbar WI 54119-9285
County: Marinette FICE Identification: 038725
Unit ID: 239503
Telephone: (715) 324-6900 Carnegie Class: Bac/Diverse
FAX Number: (715) 324-6214 Calendar System: Semester
URL: www.ni.edu
Established: 1976 Annual Undergrad Tuition & Fees: $12,880
Enrollment: 617 Coed
Affiliation or Control: Baptist IRS Status: 501(c)3
Highest Offering: Doctorate
Program: 2-Year Principally Bachelor's Creditable; Teacher Preparatory; Professional; Religious Emphasis
Accreditation: TRACS

00 Chancellor ....Dr. Les OLLILA
01 President ....Dr. Matthew OLSON
05 Vice President Academic Affairs/CAO ....Dr. Antone GOYAK
10 Vice Pres Financial Affairs/CFO ....Mr. Cary SMITH
11 Vice Pres Operational Affairs/COO ....Mr. Hugh MCCOY
32 Vice President Student Affairs ....Mr. Paul WHITT
26 Vice Presdident for Advancement ....Mr. Steve WHIGHAM
30 Vice Pres for Business Development ....Mr. Peter SULLIVAN
13 Chief Information Officer ....Mr. Greg BUCKLAND
06 Registrar ....Dr. Kevin PRIEST
07 Admissions Director ....Mr. Trevor GEARHART
09 Dir Institutional Effectiveness ....Mr. Chad HAYHURST
37 Director Student Financial Aid ....Mrs. Mandy MCLAIN
08 Head Librarian ....Mr. Van CARPENTER
41 Athletic Director ....Mr. Peter WEHRY

Ottawa University Wisconsin (E)

245 South Executive Drive, Brookfield WI 53005-4204
County: Waukesha Identification: 666084
Unit ID: 428259
Telephone: (262) 879-0200 Carnegie Class: Bac/Diverse
FAX Number: (262) 879-0096 Calendar System: Other
URL: www.ottawa.edu/wi
Established: 1992 Annual Undergrad Tuition & Fees: $10,560
Enrollment: 405 Coed
Affiliation or Control: American Baptist IRS Status: 501(c)3
Highest Offering: Master's
Program: Liberal Arts And General
Accreditation: &NH

01 President ....Mr. Kevin EICHNER
12 Campus Executive ....Dr. Wade MAULAND
05 Univ Provost/Chief Academic Officer ....Dr. Terry HAINES
10 Vice Pres Administration/CFO ....Mr. J. Clark RIBORDY
26 Mgr Public Relations & Publications ....Ms. Paula PAINE
30 Vice Pres University Advancement ....Mr. Paul BEAN
86 VP Regulatory/Governmental Affairs ....Dr. Donna LEVENE
88 Vice President for APOS ....Dr. Brian SANDUSKY
21 Director Finance/Controller ....Ms. Brenda GUENTHER
21 Director Business Operations ....Mr. Tom CORLEY
15 Director Human Resources ....Ms. Joanna WALTERS
37 Director Financial Aid ....Mr. Howard FISCHER
06 University Registrar ....Ms. Karen ADAMS
21 Business Administrator ....Mr. Brian PATTERSON
07 Executive Enrollment Advisor ....Ms. Leigh-Anne IVERSON-SOMMERS
88 Vice President for APOS ....Mr. Brian MESSER

† Regional accreditation is carried under the parent institution in Ottawa, KS.

Rasmussen College - Appleton (F)

3500 E. Destination Drive, Appleton WI 54915
County: Calumet Identification: 667059
Unit ID: 45057101
Telephone: (920) 750-5900 Carnegie Class: Not Classified
FAX Number: (920) 750-5901 Calendar System: Quarter
URL: www.rasussen.edu
Established: 1900 Annual Undergrad Tuition & Fees: $16,340
Enrollment: 44 Coed
Affiliation or Control: Proprietary IRS Status: Proprietary
Highest Offering: Baccalaureate
Program: Occupational; 2-Year Principally Bachelor's Creditable
Accreditation: &NH

01 Campus Director ....Bill PANELLA

† Regional accreditation is carried under the parent institution in Lake Elmo, MN.

Rasmussen College - Green Bay (G)

904 South Taylor Street, Suite 100, Green Bay WI 54303
County: Brown Identification: 667063
Unit ID: 450571
Telephone: (920) 593-8400 Carnegie Class: Not Classified
FAX Number: (920) 593-8401 Calendar System: Quarter
URL: www.rasmussen.edu
Established: 1900 Annual Undergrad Tuition & Fees: $16,340
Enrollment: 914 Coed
Affiliation or Control: Proprietary IRS Status: Proprietary
Highest Offering: Baccalaureate
Program: Occupational; 2-Year Principally Bachelor's Creditable
Accreditation: &NH

01 Campus Director ....Jon OTTERBACHER

† Regional accreditation is carried under the parent institution in Lake Elmo, MN.

Rasmussen College - Wausau (H)

1101 Westwood Drive, Wausau WI 54401
County: Marathon Identification: 667068
Unit ID: 45057102
Telephone: (715) 841-8000 Carnegie Class: Not Classified
FAX Number: (715) 841-8001 Calendar System: Quarter
URL: www.rasmussen.edu
Established: 1900 Annual Undergrad Tuition & Fees: $16,340
Enrollment: 444 Coed
Affiliation or Control: Proprietary IRS Status: Proprietary
Highest Offering: Baccalaureate
Program: Occupational; 2-Year Principally Bachelor's Creditable
Accreditation: &NH, MAAB

01 Campus Director ....Sue WILLIAMS

† Regional accreditation is carried under the parent institution in Lake Elmo, MN.

Ripon College (I)

300 Seward Street, PO Box 248, Ripon WI 54971-0248
County: Fond du Lac FICE Identification: 003884
Unit ID: 239628
Telephone: (920) 748-8115 Carnegie Class: Bac/A&S
FAX Number: (920) 748-7243 Calendar System: Semester
URL: www.ripon.edu
Established: 1851 Annual Undergrad Tuition & Fees: $28,689
Enrollment: 1,043 Coed
Affiliation or Control: Independent Non-Profit IRS Status: 501(c)3
Highest Offering: Baccalaureate
Program: Liberal Arts And General; Teacher Preparatory
Accreditation: NH

01 President ....David C. JOYCE

04 Admin Assistant to President ... Pamela KLINGER
05 Vice President & Dean of Faculty ... Gerald E. SEAMAN
30 Vice President for Advancement ... Wayne P. WEBSTER
10 Vice President for Finance ... Mary M. DEREGNIER
32 Vice President Dean of Students ... Christophor M. OGLE
07 VP/Dean Admission/Fin Aid & Mktg ... Steven M. SCHUETZ
06 Assoc Dean of Faculty/Registrar ... Michele A. WITTLER
36 Assoc Dean Students/Dir Career Dev ... Thomas M. VAUBEL
88 Exec Dir Ethical Leadership Program ... Lindsay BLUMER
07 Director of Admissions ... Leigh D. MLODZIK
21 Controller ... Lori A. SCHULZE
08 User Services Librarian ... Andrew PRELLWITZ
35 Dir Student Activities/Orientation ... Melissa L. BEMUS
88 Director Student Support Svcs ... Daniel J. KRHIN
39 Interim Director of Residence Life ... Jessica L. JOANIS
26 Dir Publication/Institutional Image ... Richard T. DAMM
26 Dir Media & Public Relations ... Cody PINKSTON
44 Director of Development-Major Gifts ... Larry P. MALCHOW
14 Dir Information Technology Services ... Ronald I. HAEFNER
88 General Manager Food Service ... Sarjit SINGH
18 Director Physical Plant ... Brian SKAMRA
41 Director of Athletics ... Julie H. JOHNSON
102 Dir Foundation & Gov Relations ... Terri HOLZMAN
29 Dir Annual Fund/Alumni Relations ... Nancy HINTZ
15 Human Resource Administrator ... Jennifer FRANZ
38 Director of Counseling Services ... Cynthia S. VIERTEL
40 Bookstore Manager ... Rose BALSER

Sacred Heart School of Theology (A)

7335 S Highway 100, Box 429,
Hales Corners WI 53130-0429

County: Milwaukee — FICE Identification: 020780
Unit ID: 239637
Telephone: (414) 425-8300 — Carnegie Class: Spec/Faith
FAX Number: (414) 529-6999 — Calendar System: Semester
URL: www.shst.edu
Established: 1933 — Annual Graduate Tuition & Fees: $14,550
Enrollment: 145 — Coed
Affiliation or Control: Roman Catholic — IRS Status: 501(c)3
Highest Offering: Master's; No Undergraduates
Program: Professional; Religious Emphasis
Accreditation: NH, THEOL

01 President-Rector ... Rev. Jan DE JONG, SCJ
10 VP Finance ... Ms. Sally A. SMITS
03 Vice Rector/VP External Affairs ... Rev. Thomas L. KNOEBEL
05 VP Academic Affairs ... Rev. Raul GOMEZ RUIZ, SDS
42 VP Human and Spiritual Formation ... Rev. Peter R. SCHUESSLER, SDS
20 VP Pastoral Formation ... Rev. Robert W. SCHIAVONE
08 Director Acad Information Services ... Mr. Eugene ENGELDINGER
07 Director of Recruitment/Admissions ... Rev. Thomas L. KNOEBEL
06 Registrar ... Ms. Rose M. KOPENEE
26 Director Communications ... Mr. Jonathan DRAYNA
18 Director Plant Operations ... Mr. Michael J. ERATO
04 Admin Asst to President-Rector .. Ms. Josephine A. CALCAGNINO
13 Information Systems Coordinator ... Mr. Thomas WEIS

Saint Francis Seminary (B)

3257 South Lake Drive, St. Francis WI 53235

County: Milwaukee — Identification: 667023
Telephone: (414) 747-6400 — Carnegie Class: Not Classified
FAX Number: (484) 747-6442 — Calendar System: Other
URL: www.sfs.edu
Established: 1856 — Annual Graduate Tuition & Fees: N/A
Enrollment: N/A — Coed
Affiliation or Control: Roman Catholic — IRS Status: 501(c)3
Highest Offering: Master's; No Undergraduates
Program: Religious Emphasis
Accreditation: THEOL

01 Rector ... Bishop Donald J. HYING

Saint Norbert College (C)

100 Grant Street, De Pere WI 54115-2099

County: Brown — FICE Identification: 003892
Unit ID: 239716
Telephone: (920) 403-3181 — Carnegie Class: Bac/A&S
FAX Number: (920) 403-4008 — Calendar System: Semester
URL: www.snc.edu
Established: 1898 — Annual Undergrad Tuition & Fees: $29,395
Enrollment: 2,150 — Coed
Affiliation or Control: Roman Catholic — IRS Status: 501(c)3
Highest Offering: Master's
Program: Liberal Arts And General; Teacher Preparatory; Professional
Accreditation: NH

01 President ... Mr. Thomas KUNKEL
05 Vice Pres Acad Affs/Dean of Col ... Dr. Jeffrey FRICK
10 Vice President Business & Finance ... Ms. Eileen JAHNKE
30 Vice Pres Institutional Advancement ... Mr. Phil OSWALD
32 Vice Pres Mission & Student Affairs ... Rev. Jay J. FOSTNER
84 Vice Pres Enrollment Mgmt/ Comm ... Ms. Bridget KRAGE O'CONNER
44 Assoc Vice Pres Inst Advancement ... Mr. Patrick WAGNER
09 Assoc VP Institutional Effective ... Dr. Robert RUTTER
20 Associate Academic Dean ... Dr. Kevin QUINN
36 Director Career Services ... Ms. Mandy NYCZ
35 Associate Dean Student Life ... Ms. Cynthia BARNETT
07 Exec Director of Admissions ... Mr. Edward LAMM
29 Director Alumni & Parent Relations ... Mr. Todd DANEN
21 Director of Finance ... Mr. Curt KOWALESKI
37 Director of Financial Aid ... Mr. Jeffrey A. ZAHN
26 Director Communications/Marketing ... Mr. Drew VAN FOSSEN
08 Director of Library ... Dr. Kristin D. VOGEL
15 Director Human Resources ... Mr. Gary A. UMHOEFER
41 Director Physical Educ/Athletics ... Mr. Tim BALD
38 Director Student Counseling Center ... Mr. Kevin MILLER
06 Registrar ... Mr. Richard L. GUILD
14 Dir Technology Support Services ... Mr. Tom G. SMITH
104 Director of VIE & Study Abroad ... Mr. Joseph D. TULLBANE
28 Dir Multicultural Student Services ... Ms. Bridgit MARTIN
18 Director Facilities/Physical Plant ... Mr. John J. BARNES
40 Manager Bookstore Operations ... Ms. Monica WITTROCK

Sanford-Brown College-Milwaukee (D)

6737 W. Washington Street, Ste 2355,
West Allis WI 53214

Identification: 666306
Unit ID: 448789
Telephone: (414) 771-2200 — Carnegie Class: Assoc/PrivFP
FAX Number: (414) 771-9860 — Calendar System: Semester
URL: www.sanfordbrown.edu/Milwaukee
Established: 2005 — Annual Undergrad Tuition & Fees: N/A
Enrollment: 1,232 — Coed
Affiliation or Control: Proprietary — IRS Status: Proprietary
Highest Offering: Associate Degree
Program: Occupational
Accreditation: ACICS, MAAB, RAD

01 Campus President ... Mr. Steve GUILL

† Branch campus of Sanford-Brown Institute, Jacksonville, FL.

Silver Lake College (E)

2406 S Alverno Road, Manitowoc WI 54220-9319

County: Manitowoc — FICE Identification: 003850
Unit ID: 239743
Telephone: (920) 684-6691 — Carnegie Class: Bac/Diverse
FAX Number: (920) 684-7082 — Calendar System: Semester
URL: www.sl.edu
Established: 1935 — Annual Undergrad Tuition & Fees: $21,580
Enrollment: 720 — Coed
Affiliation or Control: Roman Catholic — IRS Status: 501(c)3
Highest Offering: Master's
Program: Liberal Arts And General; Teacher Preparatory; Professional
Accreditation: NH, MUS, NURSE

01 President ... Dr. George F. ARNOLD
05 VPAA/Admissions/Dean of Faculty ... Dr. Julie MAYROSE
10 VP of Finance & Business ... Ms. Debra WIGAND
32 VP of Student Life/Dean of Students ... Mr. Matthew THIELEN
30 VP/ Advancement/External Relations ... Mr. Jake CZARNIK-NEIMEYER
42 Director of Campus Ministry ... Mr. Tommy NELSON
06 Registrar ... Sr. Janice STINGLE
08 Head Librarian ... Sr. Ritarose STAHL
37 Director Student Financial Aid ... Vacant
29 Dir Alumni/Parent Rels/Chaplain ... Deacon Paul GLEICHNER
18 Director of Facilities ... Mr. Dale FETTERER
91 Computing Coordinator ... Vacant
13 Director Technology Services ... Sr. Rosita M. BUNGE
15 Director Human Resources ... Ms. Jan GRAUNKE
36 Dir Career Res/Experiential Lrng ... Ms. Jan L. ALGOZINE
21 Associate Business Officer ... Ms. Melissa DIENER
26 Director Marketing/Communications ... Ms. Tonia DEROUIN
20 Associate Academic Officer ... Ms. Vicki ANSORGE
09 Director of Institutional Research ... Mrs. Sheila NYSSE
28 Director of Diversity ... Sr. Carmen Marie DIAZ
19 Director of Campus Security ... Mr. Randall AMMERMAN
44 Director of Annual Fund/Major Gifts ... Ms. Roxanna STRAWN
07 Interim Director of Admissions ... Ms. Cynthia ST. JOHN
41 Athletic Director ... Mr. Mike FLENTJE

*University of Wisconsin System (F)

1220 Linden Dr, 1720 Van Hise Hall,
Madison WI 53706-1559

County: Dane — FICE Identification: 003894
Unit ID: 240435
Telephone: (608) 262-2321 — Carnegie Class: N/A
FAX Number: (608) 262-3985
URL: www.wisconsin.edu

01 President ... Kevin P. REILLY
05 Int Sr Vice Pres Academic Affairs ... Mark NOOK
11 Sr VP Administration/Fiscal Affairs ... Michael L. MORGAN
10 Vice President Finance ... Deborah A. DURCAN
16 Associate Vice Pres Human Resources ... Alan N. CRIST
09 Assoc VP Policy Analysis/Research ... Heather H. KIM
91 Assoc VP Learning/Information Tech ... Ed MEACHEN
45 Assoc VP Budget & Planning ... Freda J. HARRIS
43 General Counsel ... Tomas L. STAFFORD

*University of Wisconsin-Madison (G)

500 Lincoln Drive, Madison WI 53706-1380

County: Dane — FICE Identification: 003895
Unit ID: 240444
Telephone: (608) 262-1234 — Carnegie Class: RU/VH
FAX Number: (608) 262-0123 — Calendar System: Semester
URL: www.wisc.edu
Established: 1848 — Annual Undergrad Tuition & Fees (In-State): $9,490
Enrollment: 42,595 — Coed
Affiliation or Control: State — IRS Status: 501(c)3
Highest Offering: Doctorate
Program: Liberal Arts And General; Teacher Preparatory; Professional
Accreditation: NH, ARCPA, ART, AUD, BUS, BUSA, CIDA, CLPSY, COPSY, CORE, DIETD, DIETI, DMS, ENG, FOR, IPSY, LAW, LIB, LSAR, MED, MT, MUS, NURSE, OT, PH, PHAR, PLNG, PTA, RAD, SCPSY, SP, SW, THEA, VET

02 Chancellor ... Dr. Carolyn (Biddy) MARTIN
05 Provost Academic Affairs ... Dr. Paul M. DELUCA
11 Vice Chancellor Administration ... Mr. Darrell BAZZELL
13 CIO/Vice Provost Info Technology ... Mr. Bruce MAAS
43 Director of Admin Legal Services ... Ms. Lisa H. RUTHERFORD
100 Chancellor's Chief of Staff ... Ms. Becci MENGHINI
58 VC Research/Dean Graduate School ... Dr. Martin T. CADWALLADER
49 Dean College Letters & Science ... Dr. Gary SANDEFUR
63 Dean Medicine and Public Health ... Dr. Robert N. GOLDEN
53 Dean School of Education ... Dr. Julie K. UNDERWOOD
50 Interim Dean of School of Business ... Dr. Joan SCHMIT
67 Dean School of Pharmacy ... Dr. Jeanette C. ROBERTS
54 Dean of College of Engineering ... Dr. Paul S. PEERCY
30 Vice Chanc University Relations ... Mr. Vince SWEENEY
32 Dean of Students ... Ms. Lori BERQUAM
47 Int Dean Agriculture/Life Science ... Dr. William F. TRACY
66 Dean of School of Nursing ... Dr. Katharyn A. MAY
59 Dean of Human Ecology ... Dr. Robin A. DOUTHITT
74 Dean of Veterinary Medicine ... Dr. Daryl D. BUSS
61 Dean of the Law School ... Dr. Margaret RAYMOND
18 Assoc Vice Chanc Facil Plng/Mgmt ... Mr. Alan FISH
82 Dean International Studies ... Dr. Gilles BOUSQUET
88 Int Director Environmental Studies ... Dr. Gregg MITMAN
41 Director Intercollegiate Athletics ... Mr. Barry L. ALVAREZ
88 Director of Physical Plant ... Mr. John HARROD
84 Assoc Vice Chanc Enrollment Mgmt ... Ms. Joanne E. BERG
88 Director of Arboretum ... Mr. Kevin D. MCSWEENEY
88 Director State Lab of Hygiene ... Dr. Charles BROKOPP
88 Director of Wisconsin Union ... Mr. Mark C. GUTHIER
07 Director of Admissions ... Ms. Adele BRUMFIELD
08 Director of Libraries ... Mr. Kenneth L. FRAZIER
26 Director University Communications ... Ms. Amy TOBUREN
102 President UW Foundation ... Dr. Michael M. KNETTER
29 Director of Alumni Association ... Ms. Paula E. BONNER
37 Director Student Financial Services ... Ms. Susan FISCHER
38 Director of Counseling Services ... Dr. Danielle OAKLEY
16 Director Human Resources ... Mr. Robert LAVIGNA
39 Director of University Housing ... Mr. Paul N. EVANS
51 Int Dean Continuing Studies ... Dr. James CAMPBELL
19 Director of University Police ... Ms. Susan RISELING
88 Director of Archives ... Mr. David NULL
28 Vice Provost Diversity and Climate ... Dr. Damon WILLIAMS
20 Assoc Vice Chanc Faculty/Staff Pgms ... Dr. Steve STERN
23 Director University Health Service ... Dr. Sarah A. VAN ORMAN
88 Assoc Vice Chanc Teaching/Learning ... Dr. Aaron BROWER
88 Director of Space Management ... Mr. Douglas N. ROSE
17 President Hospital & Clinics ... Ms. Donna KATEN-BAHENSKY
21 Dir Auxiliary Operations Analysis ... Ms. Donna HALLERAN
10 Asst Vice Chanc Business Services ... Mr. Donald L. MINER
88 Asst Vice Chanc Extended Pgms ... Mr. Peyton SMITH
25 Assoc Dean/Graduate/Research Svcs . Mr. James F. KNICKMEYER
06 Registrar ... Mr. Scott OWCZAREK
88 Secretary of the Faculty ... Mr. David E. MUSOLF
88 Secretary of Academic Staff ... Ms. Donna L. SILVER
88 Director of Recreational Sports ... Mr. Dale CARRUTHERS
15 Director of Academic Personnel ... Mr. Stephen R. LUND
15 Director Classified Personnel ... Mr. Mark WALTERS
85 Director Intl Student Services ... Ms. Laurie COX
22 Dir Office of Equity & Diversity ... Mr. Luis A. PINERO
96 Director of Purchasing ... Mr. Michael R. HARDIMAN
09 Dir Instl Rsrch/Acad Plng/Analysis ... Dr. Jocelyn L. MILNER
88 Special Asst to Provost ... Dr. Eden INOWAY-RONNIE
86 Sr Special Asst to Chanc Fed Rels .. Ms. Rhonda D. NORSETTER

*University of Wisconsin-Eau Claire (H)

105 Garfield Avenue, PO Box 4004,
Eau Claire WI 54702-4004

County: Eau Claire — FICE Identification: 003917
Unit ID: 240268
Telephone: (715) 836-2637 — Carnegie Class: Master's M
FAX Number: (715) 836-2902 — Calendar System: Semester
URL: www.uwec.edu
Established: 1916 — Annual Undergrad Tuition & Fees (In-State): $8,023
Enrollment: 11,409 — Coed
Affiliation or Control: State — IRS Status: 501(c)3
Highest Offering: Doctorate
Program: Liberal Arts And General; Teacher Preparatory; Professional
Accreditation: NH, BUS, CS, JOUR, MUS, NURSE, SP, SW

02 Chancellor ... Dr. Brian L. LEVIN-STANKEVICH
05 Prov/Vice Chanc Academic Affairs ... Dr. Patricia A. KLEINE
10 Asst Chanc Budget & Finance ... Mr. David GESSNER
32 Vice Chanc Student Affairs ... Dr. Beth A. HELLWIG
46 Asst VC Research/Sponsored Pgm ... Dr. Karen G. HAVHOLM
18 Asst Chanc Facil/Ex Dir Comm ... Mr. Michael J. RINDO
20 Assoc Vice Chanc Academic Affairs ... Dr. Michael R. WICK
45 Asst to Chanc Strategic Planning ... Ms. Mary Jane BRUKARDT
22 Asst to Chanc Affirmative Action ... Ms. Teresa O'HALLORAN
102 Executive Director Foundation ... Ms. Kimera WAY

32 Dean of Students .... Dr. Brian A. CARLISLE
07 Exec Dir Enrol Svcs/Admin/ Admission .... Ms. Kristina C. ANDERSON
04 Special Assistant to the Chancellor .... Mr. Michael J. RINDO
28 Director of Multicultural Affairs .... Mr. Jesse L. DIXON
08 Director of Libraries .... Mr. John H. POLLITZ
14 Dir Learning & Technology Services .... Mr. Craig A. MEY
13 Chief Information Officer .... Mr. Chip ECKARDT
15 Director of Human Resources .... Ms. Donna J. WEBER
37 Director of Financial Aid .... Ms. Kathleen A. SAHLHOFF
38 Director of Counseling .... Ms. Lynn WILSON
06 Registrar .... Mr. James BARRETT
36 Assoc Director Career Services .... Ms. Staci L. HEIDTKE
18 Director of Facilities Mgmt .... Mr. Terry L. CLASSEN
19 Director of University Police .... Mr. David W. SPRICK
23 Director of Student Health Services .... Ms. Laura G. CHELLMAN
39 Director of Housing/Residence Life .... Mr. Charles H. MAJOR
41 Director of Athletics .... Mr. J. Scott KILGALLON
51 Int Director Continuing Education .... Mr. Doug PEARSON
85 Director International Education .... Dr. Karl F. MARKGRAF
29 Director Alumni Relations .... Mr. John BACHMEIER
92 Director of Honors Program .... Dr. Jefford B. VAHLBUSCH
21 Director of Budget & Finance .... Mr. Mark REEVES
26 Chief Public Relations Officer .... Mr. Michael J. RINDO
09 Institutional Planner .... Mr. Andrew J. NELSON
49 Dean of Arts & Sciences .... Dr. Marty WOOD
66 Int Dean Nursing/Health Sciences .... Dr. Mary C. ZWYGART-STAUFFACHER
53 Dean of Education/Human Sciences .... Dr. Gail SCUKANEC
50 Dean of Business .... Ms. Diane HOADLEY
97 Int Dean of Undergraduate Studies .... Dr. Robert KNIGHT

*University of Wisconsin-Green Bay (A)

2420 Nicolet Drive, Green Bay WI 54311-7001
County: Brown FICE Identification: 003899
Unit ID: 240277
Telephone: (920) 465-2000 Carnegie Class: Master's S
FAX Number: (920) 465-2032 Calendar System: Semester
URL: www.uwgb.edu
Established: 1965 Annual Undergrad Tuition & Fees (In-State): $6,977
Enrollment: 6,636 Coed
Affiliation or Control: State IRS Status: 501(c)3
Highest Offering: Master's
Program: Liberal Arts And General; Teacher Preparatory; Professional
Accreditation: NH, DIETD, DIETI, MUS, NURSE, SW

02 Chancellor .... Dr. Thomas K. HARDEN
05 Provost/Vice Chancellor .... Dr. Julia E. WALLACE
10 Vice Chanc Business & Finance .... Mr. Thomas D. MAKI
30 Asst Chanc University Advancement .... Dr. Beverly CARMICHAEL
32 Dean of Students .... Dr. Brenda AMENSON-HILL
14 Assoc Provost Information Services .... Ms. Kathy PLETCHER
20 Assoc Provost for Academic Affairs .... Dr. Timothy SEWALL
31 Assoc Provost Outreach/Adult Access .... Dr. Steve VANDENAVOND
58 Dean Professional/Graduate Studies .... Dr. Sue JOSEPH MATTISON
49 Dean Liberal Arts & Sciences .... Dr. Scott FURLONG
43 Legal Counsel .... Vacant
07 Director of Admissions .... Ms. Pam HARVEY-JACOBS
15 Director of Human Resources .... Ms. Sheryl VAN GRUENSVEN
18 Dir Facilities Management/Planning .... Mr. Paul PINKSTON
19 Interim Director Public Safety .... Mr. Jeffrey GROSS
41 Director Athletics .... Mr. Ken BOTHOF
21 Controller .... Mr. Kelly FRANZ
09 Director Institutional Research .... Dr. Deborah FURLONG
84 Dean Enrollment & Acad Svcs .... Mr. Michael STEARNEY
88 Asst Dean Professional Stds & Rsch .... Mr. Mike MARINETTI
49 Assoc Dean Lib Arts & Sciences .... Dr. Donna RITCH
82 Director of International Education .... Mr. Brent BLAHNIK
46 Director of Institute for Research .... Ms. Lidia NONN
37 Director Financial Aid .... Mr. James P. ROHAN
39 Director of Residence Life .... Mr. Glenn GRAY
40 Manager Bookstore .... Mr. Patrick SORELLE
24 Director Media Svcs/Telecomm .... Mr. William HUBBARD
23 Director Health Services .... Ms. Amy HENNIGES
96 Director of Institutional Support .... Ms. Linda DUPUIS
38 Director Counseling Services .... Mr. Gregory L. SMITH
100 Special Asst to Chancellor .... Mr. Dan SPIELMANN
27 Director University Communications .... Mr. Christopher SAMPSON
36 Director Career Services .... Ms. Linda G. PEACOCK-LANDRUM
29 Director Alumni Relations .... Mr. Mark BRUNETTE
35 Director Student Life .... Ms. Lisa TETZLOFF
06 Registrar .... Ms. Amanda HRUSKA

*University of Wisconsin-La Crosse (B)

1725 State Street, La Crosse WI 54601-3788
County: La Crosse FICE Identification: 003919
Unit ID: 240329
Telephone: (608) 785-8000 Carnegie Class: Master's L
FAX Number: (608) 785-6868 Calendar System: Semester
URL: www.uwlax.edu
Established: 1909 Annual Undergrad Tuition & Fees (In-State): $8,310
Enrollment: 9,948 Coed
Affiliation or Control: State IRS Status: 501(c)3
Highest Offering: Doctorate
Program: Liberal Arts And General; Teacher Preparatory; Professional
Accreditation: NH, ANEST, ARCPA, BUS, MUS, NRPA, OT, PH, PTA, RADDOS, RTT

02 Chancellor .... Dr. Joe GOW
05 Provost/Vice Chancellor .... Dr. Kathleen ENZ FINKEN
30 Asst Chancellor Advancement .... Mr. Greg REICHERT
10 Vice Chancellor Admin & Finance .... Dr. Bob HETZEL
100 Chief of Staff & AA Officer .... Dr. Carmen R. WILSON
50 Dean of Business Administration .... Dr. William G. COLCLOUGH, III
53 Int Director School of Education .... Dr. Marcie WYCOFF-HORN
79 Dean of Liberal Studies .... Dr. Ruthann E. BENSON
76 Interim Dean Science Health .... Dr. Bruce RILEY
58 Assoc V Chan Acad/Dir Univ Grad Std .... Dr. Vijendra K. AGARWAL
32 Asst Chancellor & Dean of Students .... Dr. Paula M. KNUDSON
27 Chief Information Officer .... Dr. Mohamed ELHINDI
15 Exec Director of Human Resources .... Dr. Jennifer B. WILSON
51 Int Director Continuing Educ/Exten .... Ms. Penny TIEDT
08 Director of Library .... Ms. Anita K. EVANS
85 Director International Education .... Mr. Jay M. LOKKEN
07 Director ES/Admissions .... Ms. Kathryn C. KIEFER
06 Registrar .... Dr. Christine S. BAKKUM
37 Director ES/Financial Aid .... Ms. Louise L. JANKE
38 Exec Director Counseling/Testing .... Dr. Bridgette C. HENSLEY
36 Director of Career Services .... Ms. Karla E. STANEK
41 Athletic Director .... Mr. Joshua WHITMAN
26 Director Public Relations .... Vacant
29 Director Alumni Relations .... Ms. Janie M. SPENCER
23 Director Student Health Center .... Dr. Brian K. ALLEN
09 Director Institutional Research .... Ms. Debra K. VALINE
19 Director Protective Services .... Mr. Scott W. ROHDE
18 Director Physical Plant .... Mr. Hank M. KLOS
28 Assoc Dean Campus Climate/Diversity .... Ms. Barbara E. STEWART

*University of Wisconsin-Milwaukee (C)

PO Box 413, Milwaukee WI 53201-0413
County: Milwaukee FICE Identification: 003896
Unit ID: 240453
Telephone: (414) 229-1122 Carnegie Class: RU/H
FAX Number: (414) 229-6329 Calendar System: Semester
URL: www.uwm.edu
Established: 1885 Annual Undergrad Tuition & Fees (In-State): $8,698
Enrollment: 30,470 Coed
Affiliation or Control: State IRS Status: 501(c)3
Highest Offering: Doctorate
Program: Liberal Arts And General; Teacher Preparatory; Professional
Accreditation: NH, BUS, CLPSY, COPSY, CS, CYTO, ENG, LIB, MT, MUS, NURSE, OT, PLNG, PTA, SCPSY, SP, SW

02 Chancellor .... Dr. Michael R. LOVELL
05 Int Prov/Vice Chanc Academic Affs .... Dr. Johannes BRITZ
10 Vice Chanc Finance & Admin Affs .... Ms. Christy L. BROWN
26 Vice Chanc Univ Rels/Communications .... Mr. Thomas L. LULJAK
46 Vice Chanc Research/Dean Grad Sch .... Dr. Colin G. SCANES
32 Vice Chancellor Student Affairs .... Dr. Michael R. LALIBERTE
30 Vice Chancellor Development .... Ms. Patricia A. BORGER
20 Assoc Vice Chanc Academic Affairs .... Dr. Devarajan VENUGOPALAN
20 Assoc Vice Chanc Academic Affairs .... Dr. Ruth WILLIAMS
28 Assoc Vice Chancellor Diversity .... Vacant
88 Assoc Vice Chancellor .... Dr. Patricia ARREDONDO
04 Senior Advisor to the Chancellor .... Mr. David H. GILBERT
76 Dean College Health Sciences .... Dr. Chukuka S. ENWEMEKA
48 Dean Architecture & Urban Planning .... Dr. Robert C. GREENSTREET
50 Dean School Business Administration .... Dr. Timothy L. SMUNT
53 Dean of School of Education .... Dr. Carol COLBECK
54 Int Dean Col Engr & Applied Science .... Dr. Tien-Chien JEN
57 Dean Peck School of the Arts .... Dr. Wade HOBGOOD
88 Dean of Freshwater Science .... Dr. David GARMAN
89 Actg Dean School of Public Health .... Dr. Susan DEAN-BARR
58 Dean Graduate School/Research .... Dr. Colin G. SCANES
49 Dean College Letters & Science .... Dr. Richard G. MEADOWS
62 Dean School Information Studies .... Dr. Dietmar WOLFRAM
66 Dean of College of Nursing .... Dr. Sally LUNDEEN
70 Dean Helen Bader Sch Social Welfare .... Dr. Stan STOJKOVIC
51 Int Dean School of Continuing Educ .... Dr. Patricia ARREDONDO
35 Interim Dean of Students .... Mr. Thomas G. MCGINNITY
22 Act Dir Equity/Diversity Services .... Ms. Patricia VILLARREAL
13 Dir Univ Info Technology Svcs .... Mr. Bruce MAAS
08 Director of the Library .... Ms. Ewa BARCZYK
43 Director Legal Affairs .... Ms. Robin VAN HARPEN
07 Dir of Admissions/Enrollment Svcs .... Ms. Beth L. WECKMUELLER
15 Director of Human Resources .... Mr. Karl SPARKS
18 Director Facility Services .... Mr. David A. DANIELSON
19 Director University Police .... Mr. Michael J. MARZION
25 Director Office Sponsored Research .... Ms. Peggy VANCO
23 Director Health Center .... Dr. Julia BONNER
09 Dir Assessment/Institutional Rsrch .... Dr. Gesele DURHAM
85 Director Center for Intl Education .... Dr. Patrice S. PETRO
37 Director Student Financial Aid .... Ms. Jane HOJAN-CLARK
39 Director of Residence Life .... Mr. Scott S. PEAK
41 Athletic Director .... Mr. Richard COSTELLO
40 Director Bookstore .... Mr. Erik G C. HEMMING
36 Director Career Development Center .... Mr. Tom BACHHUBER
27 Dir Univ Communications & Media Rel .... Ms. Laura GLAWE
21 Dir Business & Financial Services .... Mr. Mustafa YUNDEM
29 Director Alumni Relations .... Ms. Andrea M. SIMPSON
96 Director of Purchasing .... Mr. James E. SKORLINSKI
09 Coordinator Resource Analysis .... Mr. Donald A. WEILL

*University of Wisconsin-Oshkosh (D)

800 Algoma Boulevard, Oshkosh WI 54901-3551
County: Winnebago FICE Identification: 003920
Unit ID: 240365
Telephone: (920) 424-1234 Carnegie Class: Master's L
FAX Number: (920) 424-7317 Calendar System: Semester
URL: www.uwosh.edu
Established: 1871 Annual Undergrad Tuition & Fees (In-State): $7,284
Enrollment: 13,415 Coed
Affiliation or Control: State IRS Status: 501(c)3
Highest Offering: Doctorate
Program: Liberal Arts And General; Teacher Preparatory; Professional
Accreditation: NH, BUS, CACREP, CS, #JOUR, MUS, NURSE, SW

02 Chancellor .... Dr. Richard H. WELLS
05 Provost & Vice Chancellor .... Dr. Lane R. EARNS
20 Associate Vice Chancellor .... Dr. Perry R. RETTIG
20 Asst Vice Chanc Curricular Affairs .... Dr. Carleen VANDE ZANDE
20 Int Asst Vice Chanc Acad Support .... Ms. Irma BURGOS
51 Asst Vice Chanc Lifelong Learning .... Dr. Karen HEIKEL
32 Vice Chancellor Student Affairs .... Dr. Petra ROTER
10 Vice Chancellor Administrative Svcs .... Mr. Thomas G. SONNLEITNER
21 Associate Vice Chanc Admin Svcs .... Ms. Lori M. WORM
06 Registrar .... Ms. Lisa M. DANIELSON
22 Affirmative Action Officer .... Ms. Pamela LASSITER
09 Director of Institutional Research .... Mr. Michael W. WATSON
38 Director of Counseling Center .... Dr. Joseph J. ABHOLD
14 Executive Director Info Technology .... Mr. Nick DVORACEK
50 Dean Business .... Dr. William TALLON
66 Dean Nursing .... Dr. Rosemary SMITH
53 Dean Education & Human Services .... Dr. Frederick L. YEO
49 Dean Letters & Sciences .... Dr. John J. KOKER
102 Pres Univ of Wisc Oshkosh Foundatn .... Mr. Arthur H. RATHJEN
29 Director of Alumni Association .... Ms. Christine M. GANTNER
37 Director of Financial Aid .... Ms. Beatriz D. CONTRERAS
26 Exec Director Integrated Marketing .... Vacant
25 Director Grants/Faculty Development .... Ms. Linda S. FREED
35 Dean of Students .... Dr. Sharon KIPETZ
58 Director Graduate Studies .... Mr. Gregory WYPISZYNSKI
07 Director of Admissions .... Ms. Jill M. ENDRIES
15 Int Director of Human Resources .... Mr. Timothy DANIELSON
18 Facilities/Physical Plant Director .... Mr. Steven A. ARNDT
36 Director of Career Services .... Ms. Jaime PAGE-STADLER
96 Director of Purchasing .... Vacant
92 Director University Honors Program .... Dr. Roberta S. MAGUIRE
08 Director Library .... Mr. Patrick J. WILKINSON

*University of Wisconsin-Parkside (E)

900 Wood Road, Box 2000, Kenosha WI 53141-2000
County: Kenosha FICE Identification: 005015
Unit ID: 240374
Telephone: (262) 595-2345 Carnegie Class: Bac/A&S
FAX Number: (262) 595-2202 Calendar System: Semester
URL: www.uwp.edu
Established: 1968 Annual Undergrad Tuition & Fees (In-State): $6,954
Enrollment: 5,160 Coed
Affiliation or Control: State IRS Status: 501(c)3
Highest Offering: Master's
Program: Liberal Arts And General; Teacher Preparatory; Professional
Accreditation: NH, BUS

02 Chancellor .... Deborah L. FORD
05 Provost/Vice Chancellor .... Dr. Terry BROWN
10 Vice Chanc Admin/Fiscal Affairs .... William W. STREETER
32 Vice Chanc Stdnt Svc/Dean of Stdnts .... Stephen P. MCLAUGHLIN
30 Int Vice Chanc Univ Rels/Advance .... Karen COY-ROMANO
20 Associate Provost .... Dennis ROME
28 Senior Diversity Officer .... Edward TWYMAN
50 Dean School of Business & Tech .... Fred EBEID
49 Int Dean College of Arts/Sciences .... Dean YOHNK
31 Dir Cmty Engagement/Civic Learning .... Vacant
08 Director of the Library .... Vanaja MENON
13 Chief Information Officer .... Jose NORIEGA
92 Director of Honors Program .... Gary M. WOOD
93 Director Minority Student Services .... Damian EVANS
21 Dir Business Services/Controller .... Scott MENKE
15 Director Human Resources .... Sylvia CORONADO-ROMERO
19 Dir Campus Police/Public Safety .... James HELLER
51 Director Continuing Education .... Vacant
37 Director Financial Aid .... Randall MCCREADY
26 Director of Public Information .... Dave BUCHANAN
29 Alumni/Development Activities Coord .... Vacant
06 Registrar .... Rhonda KIMMEL
36 Director of Advising/Career Center .... Susan HAWKINS-WILDING
09 Director Inst Rsrch/Assessment Svcs .... William BLANCHARD
88 Director Assessment .... Kim KELLEY
18 Director Facilities Management .... Donald A. KOLBE
94 Director of Women's Studies .... Mary LENARD
96 Director of Purchasing .... Robert FINK
35 Interim Director of Student Life .... Steve WALLNER
38 Director Student Health/Counseling .... Sandra LEICHT
40 Manager Bookstore .... Krista MULLHOLLAND
84 Int Director Enrollment Management .... DeAnn L. POSSEHL

*University of Wisconsin-Platteville (F)

1 University Plaza, Platteville WI 53818-3099
County: Grant FICE Identification: 003921
Unit ID: 240462
Telephone: (608) 342-1491 Carnegie Class: Master's L
FAX Number: (608) 342-1232 Calendar System: Semester

URL: www.uwplatt.edu
Established: 1866 Annual Undergrad Tuition & Fees (In-State): $6,372
Enrollment: 7,942 Coed
Affiliation or Control: State IRS Status: 501(c)3
Highest Offering: Master's
Program: Liberal Arts And General; Teacher Preparatory; Professional
Accreditation: NH, ENG, MUS, NAIT, TED

02 Chancellor ... Mr. Dennis J. SHIELDS
05 Provost & Vice Chancellor ... Dr. Mittie NIMOCKS
103 Spec Asst to Chanc/Chief of Staff ... Mr. Bill TREZEVANT
11 Asst Chanc Administrative Services ... Mr. Robert G. CRAMER
32 Int Asst Chancellor Student Affairs ... Ms. Joanne WILSON
58 Assoc Vice Chanc/Grad School Dean ... Dr. David P. VAN BUREN
30 Asst Chanc Univ Advance/Foundation ... Mr. Dennis R. COOLEY
06 Registrar ... Mr. David S. KIECKHAFER
07 Dir Admissions and Enrollment Svcs ... Ms. Angela M. UDELHOFEN
37 Director of Financial Aid ... Ms. Elizabeth TUCKER
09 Director of Institutional Research ... Mr. Mark R. MAILLOUX
38 Director Student Counseling ... Mr. Roger J. MEYER
26 Dir Univ Info/Comm/Public Rels ... Mr. Paul ERICKSON
41 Director Intercollegiate Athletics ... Mr. Mark D. MOLESWORTH
39 Director of Student Housing ... Ms. Rhonda L. VINEY
15 Director Personnel Services ... Ms. Jeanne DURR
19 Director Security/Safety ... Mr. Scott E. MARQUARDT
92 Director of Honors Program ... Dr. Nancy L. TURNER
93 Director of Minority Students ... Mr. Carlos A. WILEY
96 Director of Purchasing ... Ms. Linda L. SCHAAF
08 Interim Director of Library ... Ms. Zora J. SAMPSON
18 Director of Physical Plant ... Mr. Pete DAVIS
36 Director of Placement Services ... Ms. Diana J. TRENDT
51 Director Continuing Education ... Ms. Marian G. MACIEJ-HINER
29 Coordinator Alumni Relations ... Ms. Kimberly G. SCHMELZ
49 Int Dean Col Liberal Arts/Education ... Ms. Laura ANDERSON
54 Dean Col of Engr/Math/Science ... Dr. Richard D. SHULTZ
47 Int Dean Business Life Sci/Agric ... Dr. Susan L. HANSEN

*University of Wisconsin-River Falls (A)

410 S Third Street, River Falls WI 54022-5013
County: Pierce FICE Identification: 003923
Unit ID: 240471
Telephone: (715) 425-3911 Carnegie Class: Master's M
FAX Number: (715) 425-4487 Calendar System: Semester
URL: www.uwrf.edu
Established: 1874 Annual Undergrad Tuition & Fees (In-State): $7,276
Enrollment: 6,688 Coed
Affiliation or Control: State IRS Status: 501(c)3
Highest Offering: Beyond Master's But Less Than Doctorate
Program: Liberal Arts And General; Teacher Preparatory; Professional
Accreditation: NH, BUS, JOUR, MUS, SP, SW

02 Chancellor ... Dr. Dean A. VAN GALEN
05 Vice Chancellor & Provost ... Dr. Fernando P. DELGADO
10 Vice Chancellor Admin/Finance ... Mr. Joseph HARBOUK
20 Associate VC Academic Affairs ... Dr. Michael MILLER
47 Dean Agricult/Food/Environ Sci ... Dr. Dale GALLENBERG
53 Dean Education/Profess Studies ... Dr. Larry SOLBERG
49 Dean of Arts & Sciences ... Dr. Bradley J. CASKEY
50 Dean Business & Economics ... Dr. Glenn T. POTTS
58 Director Graduate Studies ... Dr. Michael MILLER
04 Special Assistant to Chancellor ... Dr. Blake W. FRY
30 Exec Director for Advancement ... Mr. Chris MUELLER
07 Director of Admissions ... Mr. Mark R. MEYDAM
06 Registrar ... Mr. Dan VANDE YACHT
08 Director of Library ... Ms. Valerie I. MALZACHER
46 Int Director Grants & Research ... Ms. Molly VAN WAGNER
21 Budget Director ... Vacant
13 Chief Information Officer ... Mr. Stephen REED
22 Director Affirmative Action ... Ms. Andriel DEES
32 Chief Student Life Officer ... Mr. Paul SHEPHERD
41 Athletic Director ... Mr. Roger TERNES
40 Manager Bookstore ... Ms. Sherry REHNELT
37 Director Financial Assistance ... Ms. Barbara J. STINSON
39 Director Residential Services ... Ms. Sandra SCOTT-DUEX
15 Director of Human Resources ... Ms. Donna ROBOLE
18 Director Facilities Management ... Mr. Michael J. STIFTER
45 Director Campus Planning ... Mr. Dale K. BRAUN
19 Director of Public Safety ... Mr. Richard TRENDE
21 Controller ... Mr. Terry N. HALVORSON
26 Chief Public Relations Officer ... Mr. Blake FRY
96 Director Purchasing Services ... Mr. Terry HALVORSON
88 Int Dir Academic Success Center ... Dr. Jennifer WILLIS-RIVERA
35 Dir Student Services & Programs ... Mr. Gregg M. HEINSELMAN
85 Director International Programs ... Mr. Brent D. GREENE
29 Director Alumni Relations ... Mr. Daniel E. MCGINTY
09 Director of Institutional Research ... Vacant
92 Director Honors Program ... Ms. Nanette J. JORDAHL
28 Director of Diversity ... Ms. Andriel DEES
38 Director Student Counseling ... Ms. Alice REILLY-MYKLEBUST
84 Director Enrollment Management ... Vacant
56 Director Outreach Programs ... Ms. Katrina LARSEN

*University of Wisconsin-Stevens Point (B)

2100 Main Street, Stevens Point WI 54481-3871
County: Portage FICE Identification: 003924
Unit ID: 240480
Telephone: (715) 346-0123 Carnegie Class: Master's M
FAX Number: (715) 346-4841 Calendar System: Semester
URL: www.uwsp.edu
Established: 1894 Annual Undergrad Tuition & Fees (In-State): $6,848
Enrollment: 9,500 Coed
Affiliation or Control: State IRS Status: 501(c)3
Highest Offering: Doctorate
Program: Liberal Arts And General; Teacher Preparatory; Professional
Accreditation: NH, ART, CIDA, DANCE, DIETD, ENG, FOR, MT, MUS, SP, @SW, THEA

02 Chancellor ... Dr. Bernie PATTERSON
05 Provost & Vice Chancellor ... Dr. Mark NOOK
10 Vice Chancellor Business Affairs ... Mr. Gregory M. DIEMER
32 Vice Chancellor Student Affairs ... Dr. Al THOMPSON
20 AVC for Tech/Lrng/Academic Pgms ... Dr. Greg SUMMERS
04 Exec Assistant to Chancellor ... Mr. Rob MANZKE
15 AVC Person/Bdgt/Grants/Summer Pgms ... Dr. Katie JORE
51 Int Exec Dir UWSP Continuing Ed ... Mr. John BIRRENKOTT
07 Director Admissions ... Ms. Catherine GLENNON
37 Interim Director of Financial Aid ... Mr. Paul WATSON
19 Director Safety & Loss Control ... Mr. Jeff KARCHER
30 Int Vice Chanc Univ Advancement ... Ms. Kathy BUENGER
29 Director of Alumni Affairs ... Ms. Laura GEHRMAN-ROTTIER
26 Director University Relations/Comm ... Mr. Stephen WARD
16 Director of Personnel ... Mr. Robert TABOR
38 Director Counseling Center ... Dr. Stacey GERKEN
13 Dir of Information Technology ... Mr. David DUMKE
22 Director Equity & Affirm Act ... Ms. Mai VANG
08 Director University Library ... Dr. Kathy DAVIS
06 Registrar ... Mr. Dan KELLOGG
18 Chief Facilities/Physical Plant ... Mr. Bob OEHLER
36 Director Student Placement ... Dr. Angie KELLOGG
96 Director of Purchasing ... Ms. Katie SCHROTH
57 Dean Col of Fine Arts & Communic ... Mr. Jeff MORIN
49 Dean College of Letters & Science ... Dr. Christopher CIRMO
65 Dean Coll of Natural Resources ... Dr. Christine L. THOMAS
107 Dean Col of Professional Studies ... Dr. Marty LOY
09 Director of Institutional Research ... Dr. Shari ELLERTSON
28 Director of Multicultural Affairs ... Mr. Ron STREGE
35 Director Student Affairs ... Dr. Bob TOMLINSON

*University of Wisconsin-Stout (C)

712 Broadway Street South, Menomonie WI 54751-2458
County: Dunn FICE Identification: 003915
Unit ID: 240417
Telephone: (715) 232-1122 Carnegie Class: Master's L
FAX Number: (715) 232-1416 Calendar System: Semester
URL: www.uwstout.edu
Established: 1891 Annual Undergrad Tuition & Fees (In-State): $8,284
Enrollment: 9,339 Coed
Affiliation or Control: State IRS Status: 501(c)3
Highest Offering: Beyond Master's But Less Than Doctorate
Program: Liberal Arts And General; Teacher Preparatory; Professional
Accreditation: NH, ART, CIDA, CONST, CORE, DIETD, DIETI, ENG, MFCD, TED

02 Chancellor ... Dr. Charles W. SORENSEN
05 Provost & Vice Chancellor ... Dr. Julie A. FURST-BOWE
11 Vice Chanc for Admin/Student Life ... Mr. Edward NIESKES
20 Associate Vice Chancellor ... Dr. Janice M. COKER
30 Vice Chanc Univ Advance/Mktg ... Vacant
35 Asst VC Student Life Svcs ... Mr. Phil LYONS
28 Asst Vice Chanc for Diversity ... Dr. Richard TAFALLA
22 Asst to Chanc Affirmative Action ... Ms. Donna M. WEBER
10 Director Budget/Plng/Analysis ... Dr. Meridith WENTZ
50 Dean College of Management ... Dr. R. Eugene KLIPPEL
49 Dean Col Arts/Humanities/Social Sci ... Dr. John E. MURPHY
53 Dean Col of Educ/Hlth/Human Sci ... Dr. Mary HOPKINS-BEST
81 Dean Col of Science/Tech/Engr/Math ... Dr. Jeff ANDERSON
32 Dean of Students ... Ms. Joan THOMAS
06 Registrar ... Mr. Larry GRAVES
84 Director Enrollment Management ... Dr. Pamela HOLSINGER-FUCHS
36 Director Career Services ... Ms. Amy LANE
08 Director University Library ... Mr. Paul ROBERTS
04 Special Assistant to the Chancellor ... Ms. Lori HASENBERG
37 Director Student Financial Aid ... Ms. Beth BOISEN
26 Director University Communications ... Mr. Doug MELL
21 Director Business/Financial Svcs ... Mr. Ed NIESKES
13 Chief Information Officer ... Mr. Doug J. WAHL
76 Exec Director Health & Safety ... Mr. James UHLIR
15 Director Human Resources ... Mr. James W. ARGO
38 Director Counseling Center ... Dr. John ACHTER
88 Director Outreach Services ... Mr. Christopher SMITH
23 Director Student Health Services ... Ms. Janice LAWRENCE-RAMAEKER
40 Director Bookstore ... Ms. Cathy CLOSE
44 Director of the Annual Fund ... Ms. Jennifer RUDIGER
85 Director International Education ... Mr. Hong ROST
18 Director Physical Plant ... Mr. Theodore HENDZEL
96 Director Procurement/Materials Mgmt ... Mr. Brent TILTON
39 Director University Housing ... Mr. Scott GRIESBACH
41 Director Athletics ... Mr. Duey NAATZ
29 Director Alumni Relations ... Ms. Sue PITTMAN
19 Dir of Safety & Risk Management ... Mr. Dean A. SANKEY
19 Coordinator University Police ... Ms. Lisa A. WALTER

*University of Wisconsin-Superior (D)

Belknap and Catlin, PO Box 2000,
Superior WI 54880-4500
County: Douglas FICE Identification: 003925
Unit ID: 240426
Telephone: (715) 394-8101 Carnegie Class: Master's S
FAX Number: (715) 394-8454 Calendar System: Semester
URL: www.uwsuper.edu
Established: 1893 Annual Undergrad Tuition & Fees (In-State): $7,371
Enrollment: 2,856 Coed
Affiliation or Control: State IRS Status: 501(c)3
Highest Offering: Beyond Master's But Less Than Doctorate
Program: Liberal Arts And General; Teacher Preparatory; Professional
Accreditation: NH, MUS, SW

02 Chancellor ... Dr. Renee WACHTER
11 Vice Chanc Administration & Finance ... Ms. Janet K. HANSON
30 Asst Chanc Inst Advancement ... Ms. Jill R. SCHOER
32 Dean of Students ... Ms. Vicki HAJEWSKI
10 Controller/Dir of Financial Svcs ... Ms. Jill N. LAUGHLIN
15 Director Human Resources ... Ms. Peggy A. FECKER
18 Director Facilities Management ... Mr. Tom FENNESSEY
26 Director Marketing & Communications ... Ms. Lynne M. WILLIAMS
06 Registrar ... Dr. Diane J. DOUGLAS
08 Librarian ... Ms. Debra L. NORDGREN
07 Interim Asst Director of Admissions ... Mr. Lee PARKER
41 Athletic Director ... Mr. Steve NELSON
37 Director Student Financial Aid ... Ms. Anne E. PODGORAK
14 Director Administrative Info Svcs ... Ms. Mary SCHOELER
51 Dir Center Cont Educ/Online Svcs ... Ms. Faith C. HENSRUD
88 Dir Distance Learning & Cont Educ ... Mr. Peter D. NORDGREN
40 Director Bookstore ... Mr. Vaughn N. RUSSOM
29 Director Alumni Relations ... Mr. Thomas K. BERGH
38 Director Advisement ... Dr. Mary Lee VANCE
28 Director of Diversity ... Mr. Alvin (Chip) BEAL
84 Director Enrollment Management ... Dr. Jane BIRKHOLZ
09 Policy & Planning Analyst ... Ms. LeAnn BROWN

*University of Wisconsin-Whitewater (E)

800 W Main, Whitewater WI 53190-1790
County: Walworth FICE Identification: 003926
Unit ID: 240189
Telephone: (262) 472-1234 Carnegie Class: Master's L
FAX Number: (262) 472-1518 Calendar System: Semester
URL: www.uww.edu
Established: 1868 Annual Undergrad Tuition & Fees (In-State): $7,196
Enrollment: 11,557 Coed
Affiliation or Control: State IRS Status: 501(c)3
Highest Offering: Beyond Master's But Less Than Doctorate
Program: Liberal Arts And General; Teacher Preparatory; Professional
Accreditation: NH, ART, BUS, CACREP, MUS, SP, SW, TED, THEA

02 Chancellor ... Dr. Richard J. TELFER
05 Prov/Vice Chanc Academic Affs ... Dr. Beverly KOPPER
32 Vice Chancellor Student Affairs ... Dr. Thomas R. RIOS
30 VC Univ Advance/Foundation Pres ... Mr. Jonathan ENSLIN
11 Vice Chanc Administrative Affs ... Mr. Jeff (Dean) ARNOLD
20 Interim Associate Vice Chancellor ... Dr. John F. STONE
13 Asst Vice Chanc Tech/Info Resource ... Dr. Elena POKOT
84 Asst Vice Chanc Enroll/Retention ... Mr. Matt ASCHENBRENER
09 Director of Institutional Research ... Dr. Chunju CHEN
20 AVC Multicult Affs/Stdnt Success ... Dr. Richard MCGREGORY
37 Director of Financial Aid ... Ms. Carol A. MILLER
10 Chief Business Officer ... Mr. Jeff (Dean) ARNOLD
26 Chief Public Relations Officer ... Ms. Sara KUHL
21 Director of Budget ... Ms. Aimee C. MCCANN
07 Director of Admissions ... Vacant
06 Registrar ... Ms. Jodi M. HARE-PAYNTER
36 Director of Career Services ... Mr. Ron BUCHHOLZ
15 Director Human Resources/Diversity ... Ms. Judith M. TRAMPF
85 Int Dir Center for Global Education ... Mr. John D. CHENOWETH
44 Exec Dir University Development ... Ms. Kate LOFTUS
18 Director Facility Planning/Mgmt ... Mr. Greg SWANSON
38 Exec Dir Univ Health/Counseling Svc ... Dr. Richard L. JAZDZEWSKI
96 Director of Purchasing ... Mr. Michael T. HIRSCHFIELD
28 Director of Diversity ... Dr. Elizabeth OGUNSOLA
92 Director of Honors Program ... Dr. Marjorie RHINE
88 Int Dir Acad Advising/Explor Ctr ... Ms. Pamela TANNER
35 Associate Dean Student Life ... Ms. Mary Beth MACKIN
57 Dean Arts/Communication ... Dr. Mark MCPHAIL
50 Dean of Business & Economics ... Dr. Christine CLEMENTS
53 Dean Education/Professional Studies ... Dr. Katharina E. HEYNING
49 Dean Letters & Sciences ... Dr. Mary PINKERTON
58 Dean Grad Stds/Continuing Educ ... Dr. John STONE

*University of Wisconsin Colleges (F)

780 Regent Street, Suite 130, Madison WI 53715-2635
County: Dane FICE Identification: 003897
Unit ID: 240055
Telephone: (608) 262-3786 Carnegie Class: Assoc/Pub2in4
FAX Number: (608) 262-7872 Calendar System: Semester
URL: www.uwc.edu
Established: 1964 Annual Undergrad Tuition & Fees (In-State): $4,503
Enrollment: 14,378 Coed
Affiliation or Control: State IRS Status: 501(c)3
Highest Offering: Associate Degree
Program: 2-Year Principally Bachelor's Creditable
Accreditation: NH

02 Chancellor ... Dr. Raymond CROSS
05 Provost/Vice Chancellor ... Dr. Gregory P. LAMPE
11 Vice Chancellor Admin & Fin Svcs ... Mr. Steven C. WILDECK
32 Assoc VC Stdt Svcs & Enroll Mgmt ... Dr. Richard BARNHOUSE
12 Int Vice Chanc/Provost UW-Extension ... Dr. Greg HUTCHINS
20 Associate Vice Chancellor ... Dr. Lisa SEALE

13 Asst Vice Chanc Info/Instruct Tech ... Ms. Marsha HENFER
15 Director Human Resources ... Ms. Pam DOLLARD
06 Registrar ... Mr. Larry GRAVES
37 Director Financial Aid ... Mr. William TRIPPETT
26 Exec Director University Relations ... Ms. Teri H. VENKER
86 Director of Government Relations ... Ms. Rosemary POTTER
12 Dean UW Baraboo/Sauk County ... Dr. Tom PLEGER
12 Dean UW Barron County ... Dr. Paul W. CHASE
12 Dean UW Fond Du Lac ... Dr. John SHORT
12 Interim Dean UW Fox Valley ... Dr. Andrew KEOGH
12 Dean UW Manitowoc ... Dr. Charles E. CLARK
12 Dean UW Marathon County ... Dr. Keith MONTGOMERY
12 Dean UW Marinette ... Ms. Paula LANGTEAU
12 Dean UW Marshfield/Wood Co. ... Dr. Patricia L. STUHR
12 Dean UW Richland ... Dr. Patrick HAGEN
12 Interim Dean UW Rock County ... Dr. Kim KOSTKA
12 Dean UW Sheboygan ... Dr. Al HARDERSEN
12 Dean UW Washington County ... Dr. Paul PRICE
12 Dean UW Waukesha ... Dr. Harry P. MUIR, JR.
28 Director of Diversity ... Dr. Stephan GILCHRIST

Viterbo University (A)

900 Viterbo Drive, La Crosse WI 54601-8802
County: La Crosse FICE Identification: 003911
Unit ID: 240107
Telephone: (608) 796-3000 Carnegie Class: Master's L
FAX Number: (608) 796-3050 Calendar System: Semester
URL: www.viterbo.edu
Established: 1890 Annual Undergrad Tuition & Fees: $21,870
Enrollment: 3,321 Coed
Affiliation or Control: Roman Catholic IRS Status: 501(c)3
Highest Offering: Master's
Program: Liberal Arts And General; Teacher Preparatory; Professional
Accreditation: NH, ACBSP, DIETC, DIETI, MUS, NURSE, SW, TED

01 President ... Dr. Richard B. ARTMAN
05 Vice President for Academic Affairs ... Dr. Barbara M. GAYLE
32 Vice President Student Development ... Dr. Diane L. BRIMMER
10 Vice Pres Administration/Finance ... Mr. Todd M. ERICSON
30 Vice Pres Institutional Advancement ... Mr. Gary L. KLEIN
26 Vice Pres Communications Marketing ... Mr. Patrick G. KERRIGAN
07 Dean of Admission ... Mr. Robert L. FORGET
42 Chaplain ... Fr. Conrad A. TARGONSKI
66 Dean School of Nursing ... Dr. Silvana F. RICHARDSON
53 Dean School of Education ... Dr. Sue S. BATELL
49 Dean School Letters & Sciences ... Dr. Glena G. TEMPLE
57 Dean School of Fine Arts ... Dr. Timothy B. SCHORR
50 Dean School of Business ... Dr. Thomas E. KNOTHE
58 Dean Graduate/Prof/Adult Education ... Vacant
88 Director of Ethics in Leadership ... Dr. Richard L. KYTE
06 Registrar ... Ms. Amy S. GLEASON
08 Director of Library ... Ms. Gretel L. STOCK KUPPERMAN
14 Director of Computer Services ... Mr. Tom L. HAUSMANN
41 Athletic Director ... Mr. Barry J. FRIED
37 Director of Financial Aid ... Ms. Terry W. NORMAN
29 Director Alumni/Parent Relations ... Ms. Kathleen A. DUERWACHTER
36 Director Career Planning/Placement . Ms. Beth D. DOLDER-ZIEKE
15 Director of Human Resources ... Vacant
09 Director Institutional Research ... Ms. Naomi R. STENNES-SPIDAHL
18 Director Facilities/Physical Plant ... Mr. Eugene M. MCCURDY
21 Assistant Vice President Finance ... Mr. Eugene R. ALBERTS
38 Director of Counseling ... Ms. Lesley A. STUGELMAYER
39 Director of Residence Life ... Ms. Vickie L. UNFERTH
53 Director Grad Studies in Education ... Ms. Rhonda M. RABBITT
88 Dir Faculty Dev/Internship Coord ... Dr. Theresa MOORE
88 Director of Global Education ... Mr. Shaojie JIANG
19 Campus Safety & Security Director ... Mr. David J. PLEASANTS
07 Associate Director of Admissions ... Ms. Jessica K. MILLER
07 Associate Director of Admissions ... Mr. Eric R. SCHMIDT
04 Executive Administrative Assistant ... Ms. Diane M. HAUGEN

Wisconsin Lutheran College (B)

8800 W Bluemound Road, Milwaukee WI 53226-4699
County: Milwaukee FICE Identification: 021366
Unit ID: 240338
Telephone: (414) 443-8800 Carnegie Class: Bac/A&S
FAX Number: (414) 443-8514 Calendar System: Semester
URL: www.wlc.edu
Established: 1973 Annual Undergrad Tuition & Fees: $21,960
Enrollment: 840 Coed
Affiliation or Control: Independent Non-Profit IRS Status: 501(c)3
Highest Offering: Master's
Program: Liberal Arts And General
Accreditation: NH

01 President ... Dr. Daniel W. JOHNSON
05 Provost & VP of Academic Affairs ... Dr. John D. KOLANDER
32 Vice President Student Affairs ... Dr. Dennis L. MILLER
10 Vice Pres Finance & Administration ... Mr. Gary SCHMID
26 Assoc VP of Public Affairs ... Mrs. Vicki HARTIG
30 Vice Pres Development ... Mr. Craig RUSSOW
21 Asst VP Finance ... Mrs. Diane HOEHNKE
84 Dean of Student Retention ... Mr. Joel P. MISCHKE
06 Registrar ... Mr. Brett VALERIO
08 Director of Library Services ... Mrs. Starla C. SIEGMANN
37 Director Student Financial Aid ... Mrs. Linda L. LOEFFEL
42 Campus Pastor ... Rev. Nathan STROBEL
53 Director Teacher Education ... Prof. James HOLMAN
39 Director Residential Life/Housing ... Mrs. Judy K. EGGERS
07 Executive Director of Admissions ... Mr. Jeff WEBER
41 Athletic Director ... Mr. Edward NOON
35 Director of Student Life ... Vacant
88 Director of Arts Programming ... Mr. Daniel SCHMAL
27 Director of Information Technology ... Mr. John MEYER
29 Director of Alumni Relations ... Mrs. Lisa LEFFEL
24 Director of Media Services ... Vacant
44 Director of Planned Giving ... Mrs. Kris METZGER
09 Information Systems Analyst ... Mrs. Olya FINNEGAN
44 Director Corp Foundation Relations ... Ms. Sharon PATTERSON
15 VP of Human Resources ... Mr. Steven SCHROEDER
18 Chief Facilities/Physical Plant ... Mr. Gary SCHMID

Wisconsin School of Professional Psychology (C)

9120 W Hampton Avenue, Suite 212, Milwaukee WI 53225-4960
County: Milwaukee FICE Identification: 022713
Unit ID: 240213
Telephone: (414) 464-9777 Carnegie Class: Spec/Health
FAX Number: (414) 358-5590 Calendar System: Semester
URL: www.wspp.edu
Established: 1979 Annual Graduate Tuition & Fees: $24,750
Enrollment: 82 Coed
Affiliation or Control: Independent Non-Profit IRS Status: 501(c)3
Highest Offering: Doctorate; No Undergraduates
Program: Professional
Accreditation: NH, CLPSY

01 President ... Dr. Kathleen M. RUSCH
05 Dean ... Dr. Dale A. BESPALEC
04 Assistant to the President ... Ms. Sheri LINDGREN
17 Director Clinical Training ... Dr. Susan DVORAK

*Wisconsin Technical College System (D)

PO Box 7874, Madison WI 53707-7874
County: Dane Identification: 666185
Telephone: (608) 266-1207 Carnegie Class: N/A
FAX Number: (608) 266-1285
URL: www.wtcsystem.edu

01 President ... Mr. Daniel CLANCY
05 Vice President Academic Programs ... Ms. Kathleen CULLEN
10 Vice President Finance ... Mr. Jim ZYLSTRA

*Blackhawk Technical College (E)

PO Box 5009, Janesville WI 53547-5009
County: Rock FICE Identification: 005390
Unit ID: 238397
Telephone: (608) 758-6900 Carnegie Class: Assoc/Pub-R-M
FAX Number: (608) 757-7740 Calendar System: Semester
URL: www.blackhawk.edu
Established: 1912 Annual Undergrad Tuition & Fees (In-District): $3,643
Enrollment: 3,337 Coed
Affiliation or Control: State/Local IRS Status: 501(c)3
Highest Offering: Associate Degree
Program: Occupational
Accreditation: NH, ACFEI, ADNUR, DA, DMS, MAC, MLTAD, PTAA, RAD

02 President ... Dr. Thomas C. ECKERT
05 Vice President Learning ... Dr. Sharon A. KENNEDY
11 Vice President Finance/College Oper ... Ms. Renea L. RANGUETTE
16 Vice President Human Resources ... Mr. Brian B. GOHLKE
32 Vice President Student Services ... Mr. Edward G. ROBINSON
09 Dir Institutional Effectiveness ... Mr. Michael J. GAGNER
04 Asst to President/Board Liaison ... Ms. Jacqueline J. PINS
14 Chief Information Officer ... Mr. Steven E. DAVIDSON
26 Director Marketing & Communications ... Mr. Len E. WALKER
20 Dean Academic Support Division ... Ms. Mona L. ANTONELLI
97 Dean General Education ... Dr. Gabrielle BANICK
76 Dean Health/Human Svcs ... Ms. Nancy R. LIGHTFIELD
88 Dean Public Safety ... Mr. Mark I. BROWN
66 Associate Degree Nursing Coord ... Ms. Ruth L. WHEATON-COX
47 Dean Trans/Agric/Appren ... Mr. Kirke E. PLANK
72 Dean Mfg/Construction/Aviation ... Mr. Kirke E. PLANK
50 Dean Business and Econ Dev ... Mr. Donald S. SMITH
21 Controller ... Mr. Richard L. SHIKOSKI
25 Manager Grants Administration ... Mr. Andrew S. MCGRATH
37 Financial Aid Coordinator ... Ms. Sue ULLRICK
06 Director Student Development ... Ms. Kerry K. FROEHLICH-MUELLER
18 Facilities Manager ... Mr. Jeffrey R. AMUNDSON
96 Manager Purchasing/Fac Design ... Ms. Kelly J. DEMPSEY
51 Continuing Education Coord ... Mr. Mark V. TRILLER
08 Librarian ... Ms. Janet C. WHITE

*Chippewa Valley Technical College (F)

620 W Clairemont Avenue, Eau Claire WI 54701-6162
County: Eau Claire FICE Identification: 005304
Unit ID: 240116
Telephone: (715) 833-6200 Carnegie Class: Assoc/Pub-R-M
FAX Number: (715) 833-6470 Calendar System: Semester
URL: www.cvtc.edu
Established: 1912 Annual Undergrad Tuition & Fees (In-District): $3,863
Enrollment: 6,062 Coed
Affiliation or Control: Local IRS Status: 501(c)3
Highest Offering: Associate Degree
Program: Occupational; 2-Year Principally Bachelor's Creditable
Accreditation: NH, ADNUR, DH, DMS, MAC, MLTAD, PNUR, PTAA, RAD, SURGT

02 President ... Bruce A. BARKER
05 Vice President Education ... Ellen M. KIRKING
11 Vice President Operations ... Tom G. HUFFCUTT
32 Vice President Student Services ... Margo A. KEYS
12 River Falls Campus Manager ... John R. KLEVEN
12 Chippewa Falls Campus Manager ... Timothy M. SHEPARDSON
12 Menomonie Campus Manager ... Roxann S. VANDERWYST
12 Nanorite Innovation Center Manager ... Pam D. OWEN
88 Dean Manufacturing/Nano Programs ... Mark R. HENDRICKSON
46 Dir of Research/Special Projects ... Margaret A. DICKENS
88 Dean Energy/Transp/Ag & Constructn ... Aliesha R. CROWE
06 Registrar ... Tessa A. PERCHINSKY
07 Director of Enrollment Services ... Sue M. BREHM
37 Financial Aid Officer ... Mary E. GORUD
26 Public Communications Manager ... Carla S. LEUCK
31 Director of Community Relations ... Doug A. OLSON
10 Director of Budget & Finance ... Kirk L. MOIST
88 Director of Staff Development ... Roger J. STANFORD
13 Director of Info Technology ... Tom J. LANGE
88 Customer Service Center Spec/Mgr ... Karen L. CALLAWAY
35 Student Life Specialist ... Alisa S. SCHLEY
96 Purchasing Agent ... Doug D. DEKAN
21 Budget Manager ... Tracy M. DRIER
19 Safety/Security and Risk Manager ... Carrie L. HALLQUIST
28 Diversity/Equal Opportunity Spec ... Michael A. OJIBWAY
50 Dean Business ... Beth A. HEIN
35 Student Services Grants/Operations ... Natalyn M. MARLAIRE
35 Student Services Learning Support ... Kristen A. RANEY
102 Dir of CVTC Foundation/Alumni Assoc ... Heidi L. FISHER
25 Grants/Development Specialist ... Vacant
88 Assessment & Curriculum Specialist ... Philip V. PALSER
88 Coord of Curriculum & Assessment ... Julia E. RAEHPOUR
88 Emergency Services Dean ... Judi A. ANIBAS
18 Facilities Manager ... Vacant
15 Human Resources Director ... Mary K. CASEY
21 Business Office Manager ... Sara J. NICK
76 Dean Health ... Shelly Y. OLSON

*Fox Valley Technical College (G)

1825 N Bluemound Drive, Appleton WI 54914-1643
County: Outagamie FICE Identification: 009744
Unit ID: 238722
Telephone: (920) 735-5600 Carnegie Class: Assoc/Pub-R-L
FAX Number: (920) 735-2582 Calendar System: Semester
URL: www.fvtc.edu
Established: 1967 Annual Undergrad Tuition & Fees (In-District): $4,000
Enrollment: 11,110 Coed
Affiliation or Control: State/Local IRS Status: 501(c)3
Highest Offering: Associate Degree
Program: Occupational; 2-Year Principally Bachelor's Creditable
Accreditation: NH, ACFEI, ADNUR, DA, DH, MAC, OTA

02 President ... Dr. Susan A. MAY
11 Vice Pres Administrative Services ... Ms. Jill MCEWEN
32 VP Student/Community Development ... Ms. Patti JORGENSEN
04 Assistant to the President ... Ms. Vicky VAN HOUT
05 VP Instructional Services ... Mr. Christopher MATHENY
76 Exec Dean Business/Health/Service ... Ms. Donna ELLIOTT
72 Ex Dn Mnfctng/Transp/Info/Agri Tech ... Mr. Jerry EYLER
97 Dean General Studies ... Ms. Carol MAY
19 Executive Dean Public Safety ... Ms. Patricia ROBINSON
102 Exec Dir FVTC Foundation/Cmty Rels ... Ms. Alyce DUMKE
12 Oshkosh Campus Director ... Ms. Melissa KOHN
10 Chief Financial Officer ... Ms. Amy VAN STRATEN
13 Chief Information Officer ... Mr. Troy KOHL
22 Affirmative Action Officer ... Vacant
21 Bursar Student Financial Services ... Ms. Stacy DORAN
35 Director Student Affairs ... Ms. Denise MARTINEZ
06 Registrar ... Mr. Brian BUSS
26 Director of College Marketing ... Ms. Barb DREGER
88 Director of Compensation & Benefits ... Ms. Barb KIEFFER
88 Director Venture Center ... Ms. Amy PIETSCH
15 Director Employee Rels/Staff Dev ... Ms. Deb GORMAN
88 Director Instructional Dev/Delivery ... Ms. Karen ALESCH
88 Director Articulated Programs ... Ms. Marge RUBIN
46 Director College Effectiveness ... Dr. Patti FROHRIB
36 Specialist-Student Employment Svcs ... Mr. Bruce WEILAND
35 Coordinator of Student Life ... Ms. Vicky BARKE

*Gateway Technical College (H)

3520 30th Avenue, Kenosha WI 53144-1690
County: Kenosha FICE Identification: 005389
Unit ID: 238759
Telephone: (262) 564-2200 Carnegie Class: Assoc/Pub-R-L
FAX Number: (262) 564-2201 Calendar System: Semester
URL: www.gtc.edu
Established: 1912 Annual Undergrad Tuition & Fees (In-District): $2,940
Enrollment: 8,170 Coed
Affiliation or Control: State/Local IRS Status: 501(c)3
Highest Offering: Associate Degree
Program: Occupational
Accreditation: NH, ADNUR, DA, MAC, PTAA, SURGT

02 President ... Mr. Bryan D. ALBRECHT
05 Exec VP/Prov/Chief Academic Officer ... Ms. Zina HAYWOOD
12 Dean Racine Campus ... Mr. Ray KOUKARI
12 Dean Elkhorn Campus ... Mr. Michael O'DONNELL

10 Vice President/Provost Finance Mr. Mark ZLEVOR
32 Vice President/Student Life Mr. Terry SIMMONS
06 Registrar Ms. Chrystal MOEZ
09 Assoc VP Institutional Research Ms. Anne WHYNOTT
15 Director Personnel Services Mr. William WHYTE
26 Marketing Director Ms. Jayne HERRING
36 Director Student Placement Ms. Sheri EISCH
07 Director of Admissions Ms. Susan ROBERTS
18 Chief Facilities/Physical Plant Mr. Mark ZLEVOR
21 Associate Business Officer Ms. Beverly HANSEN
37 Director Student Financial Aid Ms. Janice RIUTTA
28 Director of Diversity Ms. Debbie MILLER
29 Dir Alumni Relations/Foundation Mr. Ken VETROVEC
20 Associate VP Academic Affairs Mr. John THIBODEAU

*Lakeshore Technical College (A)

1290 North Avenue, Cleveland WI 53015-1414
County: Manitowoc FICE Identification: 009194
Unit ID: 239008
Telephone: (920) 693-1000 Carnegie Class: Assoc/Pub-R-M
FAX Number: (920) 693-1363 Calendar System: Semester
URL: www.gotoltc.com
Established: 1912 Annual Undergrad Tuition & Fees (In-District): $3,355
Enrollment: 2,331 Coed
Affiliation or Control: State/Local IRS Status: 501(c)3
Highest Offering: Associate Degree
Program: Occupational; 2-Year Principally Bachelor's Creditable
Accreditation: NH, ADNUR, RAD

02 President Dr. Michael LANSER
04 Executive Assistant Ms. Allison WEBER
05 Vice President of Instruction Mr. Deryl DAVIS-FULMER
13 Vice President of Student Services Dr. Douglas GOSSEN
103 Vice President Workforce Solutions Mr. Peter THILLMAN
15 Director Human Resources Ms. Kathy KOTAJARVI
10 Director Financial Services Ms. Cindy DROSS
09 Director Research & Planning Ms. Kim PAHL
26 Dir Marketing & College Relations Ms. Julie MIRECKI
28 Diversity Coordinator Ms. Nicole YANG
47 Dean Agric/Trade & Industry/Appr Mr. Michael THOMPSON
50 Dean Business & Technology Dr. Allyn FRENCH
97 Dean General Education/Basic Skills Ms. Lynn RETZAK
76 Dean Health & Human Services Dr. Barbara DODGE
19 Dean Public Safety Mr. Richard HOERTH
07 Student Services Manager Mr. Scott LIEBURN
37 Financial Aid Manager Ms. Corey GIVENS
32 Student Success Manager Ms. Foua HANG
18 Physical Plant Manager Mr. Bryan KOESER
08 Library Services Manager Ms. Karla ZAHN
22 Affirm Action Officer Ms. Kathy KOTAJARVI
40 Bookstore Manager Ms. Kelly WOLFERT
13 Chief Information Officer Mr. Jack ZHANG
30 Director of Development Ms. Katie WILLINGER
29 Director Alumni Relations Ms. Katie WILLINGER

*Madison Area Technical College (B)

3550 Anderson Street, Madison WI 53704-2599
County: Dane FICE Identification: 004007
Unit ID: 238263
Telephone: (608) 246-6100 Carnegie Class: Assoc/Pub-R-L
FAX Number: (608) 246-6880 Calendar System: Semester
URL: www.matcmadison.edu
Established: 1912 Annual Undergrad Tuition & Fees (In-District): $3,676
Enrollment: 18,220 Coed
Affiliation or Control: State/Local IRS Status: 501(c)3
Highest Offering: Associate Degree
Program: Occupational; 2-Year Principally Bachelor's Creditable
Accreditation: NH, ACFEI, ADNUR, DH, MAC, MLTAD, OPTT, OTA, @PTAA, RAD, SURGT

02 President Dr. Bettsey L. BARHORST
05 VP Learner Success/Chief Acad Ofcr Mr. Terrance WEBB
03 Vice Pres Infrastructure Services Mr. Roger PRICE
20 Vice President Student Development Dr. Keith T. CORNILLE
20 Associate Vice Pres Learner Success Vacant
28 Assoc VP Diversity/Comm Rel Ms. Maria G. BANUELOS
10 Chief Finance Officer/Controller Mr. Edwin NOEHRE
13 Chief Information Officer Mr. Igor STEINBERG
15 Executive Director Human Resources Mr. Charles E. MCDOWELL
84 Exec Dir Enrollment Management Ms. Diane K. WALLESER
25 Director Grants/Special Projects Dr. Edward G. CLARKE
41 Athletic Director Mr. Stephen C. HAUSER
09 Dir Inst Research & Effectiveness Mr. Ali R. ZARRINNAM
32 Director Student Life Ms. Renee M. ALFANO
38 Director Testing and Assessment Mr. James A. MERRITT
26 Exec Asst Community Devel/Comm Ms. Ellen FOLEY
21 Assistant Controller Mr. Jeffrey KUHN
18 Facilities Director Mr. Michael M. STARK
08 Director Library Services Ms. Julie GORES
84 Enrollment Services Manager Ms. Jennifer L. HOEGE
40 Bookstore Manager Mr. Scott HEIMAN
37 Associate Manager Financial Aid Ms. Marcia FORBES
86 Int Public Affs/Govt Relations Mgr Mr. Timothy L. CASPER
22 Diversity Recruitment/Employ Coord Ms. Malika S. MONGER
102 Admin Foundation & Alumni Relations Mr. Robert J. DINNDORF
38 Int Assoc Dean Student Development Dr. Geraldo VILA CRUZ
88 Dean Constr/Manuf/Appren/Trans Mr. Kenneth J. STARKMAN
47 Dn Ag/Eng/Appld Tech/Info/Bus Tech Mr. David L. SHONKWILER
50 Dean Business/Applied Arts Ms. Turina R. BAKKEN
49 Dean Arts & Sciences Dr. Todd H. STEBBINS
76 Dean Health & Safety Education Dr. Mark C. LAUSCH
51 Dean Adult & Continuing Education Ms. Kathleen A. RADIONOFF
19 Dean Human/Protective Services Mr. Richard F. RAEMISCH

*Mid-State Technical College (C)

500 32nd Street N, Wisconsin Rapids WI 54494-5599
County: Wood FICE Identification: 005380
Unit ID: 239220
Telephone: (715) 422-5300 Carnegie Class: Assoc/Pub-R-M
FAX Number: (715) 422-5345 Calendar System: Semester
URL: www.mstc.edu
Established: 1967 Annual Undergrad Tuition & Fees (In-District): $5,000
Enrollment: 2,560 Coed
Affiliation or Control: State/Local IRS Status: 501(c)3
Highest Offering: Associate Degree
Program: 2-Year Principally Bachelor's Creditable; Technical Emphasis
Accreditation: NH, ADNUR, MAC, SURGT

02 President Dr. Susan BUDJAC
05 Vice President Academic Affairs Dr. Ann Marie KRAUSE
32 VP Student Affairs/Information Tech Ms. Connie WILLFAHRT
10 Vice President Finance Mr. Nelson D. DAHL
15 Vice President Human Resources Mr. Richard O'SULLIVAN
50 Dean General Education & Business Dr. John HIGGS
75 Dean Technical/Industrial Mr. Alan JAVOROSKI
76 Dean Service & Health Careers Ms. Janet NEWMAN
97 Dean General Education Vacant
12 Dean Stevens Point Campus Mr. Steven SMITH
12 Dean Marshfield Campus Ms. Brenda DILLENBURG
26 Director of Communications Ms. Elizabeth MORAN
30 Director College Advancement Ms. Patty FAIRCHILD
102 Foundation and Alumni Director Ms. Chris MAGUIRE
18 Director of Facilities/Procurement Mr. Larry CIHLAR
07 Director of Admissions Ms. Mandy LANG
35 Director Student Support Ms. Nancy SCHAPERKOTTER
96 Director of Purchasing Mr. Ed BUSHMAN
06 Student Records Manager Ms. Denise KINNEY
08 Library Services Manager Ms. Maria HERNANDEZ
37 Financial Aid Supervisor Ms. Mary Jo GREEN

*Milwaukee Area Technical College (D)

700 W State Street, Milwaukee WI 53233-1443
County: Milwaukee FICE Identification: 003866
Unit ID: 239248
Telephone: (414) 297-6600 Carnegie Class: Assoc/Pub-U-MC
FAX Number: (414) 297-7990 Calendar System: Semester
URL: www.matc.edu
Established: 1912 Annual Undergrad Tuition & Fees (In-District): $4,796
Enrollment: 29,370 Coed
Affiliation or Control: Local IRS Status: 501(c)3
Highest Offering: Associate Degree
Program: Occupational; 2-Year Principally Bachelor's Creditable
Accreditation: NH, ACFEI, ADNUR, CVT, DH, DIETT, FUSER, MAC, MLTAD, OTA, PNUR, PTAA, RAD, SURGT

02 President Dr. Michael L. BURKE
05 Provost Dr. Vicki J. MARTIN
32 Int Vice Pres Student Services Mr. Al PINCKNEY
10 Vice President of Finance Dr. James WILLIAMS
43 Vice President & Legal Counsel Ms. Janice FALKENBERG
15 Assoc Vice Pres Human Resource Ms. Donna GOODWIN
13 Assoc VP Information Technology Mr. Michael WALSH
23 Dean Health Occupation Dr. Dessie LEVY
49 Int Dean Liberal Arts & Sciences Dr. Evonne CARTER
50 Int Dean Business & Graphic Arts Dr. Mohammad DAKWAR
24 General Manager Public Television Mr. Ellis BROMBERG
11 Director Operations Mr. Richard DRIES
35 Director Student Life Mr. Archie GRAHAM
08 Director of Library Mr. Jeff JACKSON
37 Interim Director Student Finances Mr. Jerry MANZ
90 Director Technical Services Mr. Michael GAVIN
21 Controller Ms. Terri GAYHART
19 Director Public Safety Mr. Bradford HINES
06 Registrar Ms. Sarah ADAMS
09 Director Institutional Research Dr. Thomas PILARZYK
84 Director Recruitment Ms. Brunetta SOWARD
29 Director Alumni Relations Ms. Christine MCGEE
38 Int Director Student Counseling Dr. Daniel BURRELL
26 Chief Public Relations Officer Ms. Kathleen HOHL
96 Procurement Manager Ms. Kristin SEIMITS
41 Coordinator Athletics Mr. Randy CASEY

*Moraine Park Technical College (E)

235 N National Avenue, Fond Du Lac WI 54935-2897
County: Fond Du Lac FICE Identification: 009256
Unit ID: 239372
Telephone: (920) 922-8611 Carnegie Class: Assoc/Pub-R-L
FAX Number: (920) 929-2471 Calendar System: Semester
URL: www.morainepark.edu
Established: 1967 Annual Undergrad Tuition & Fees (In-District): $3,544
Enrollment: 8,466 Coed
Affiliation or Control: State/Local IRS Status: 501(c)3
Highest Offering: Associate Degree
Program: Occupational; 2-Year Principally Bachelor's Creditable; Technical Emphasis
Accreditation: NH, ACFEI, ADNUR, MAC, MLTAD, RAD, SURGT

02 President L. Gayle HYTREK
05 VP Academics & Student Affairs Daniel R. ENSALACO
15 Vice President Human Resources Kathleen M. BROSKE
30 VP Marketing/College Advancement Sharon N. HOLMES
13 CIO/Vice Pres Inform Technology Jim BLAKESLEE
10 Vice Pres Finance & Facilities Bonnie BAERWALD
84 Vice Pres of Enrollment Management Bethany M. RAFFAELLI
88 VP Strategic Advancement Josh B. BULLOCK
06 Registrar Amanda HRUSKA
07 Recruitment & Retention Associate Sally A. RUBACK
12 WB & Online Campus/Cmty Partner Peter J. RETTLER
12 Beaver Dam Campus/Cmty Prtnr Karen COLEY
20 Executive Dean of Instruction James V. EDEN
24 Exec Dean Instructional Support Gerald R. EDGREN, III
08 Learning Resource Center Associate Charlene M. PETTIT
40 Auxiliary Services Associate Jon A. SHAPIRO
18 Facilities Associate Timothy J. FLOOD
22 Employment/Affirmative Action Assoc Beth A. MENDOZA
76 Exec Dean Hlth Sciences/Public Svcs Kathy S. VANEERDEN
88 Dean of Health Sciences/Public Svcs Kristin M. FINNEL
96 Purchasing Associate Charles E. BIRRINGER
37 Student Financials Partner Karen A. ZUEHLKE

*Nicolet Area Technical College (F)

Box 518, Rhinelander WI 54501-0518
County: Oneida FICE Identification: 005384
Unit ID: 239442
Telephone: (715) 365-4410 Carnegie Class: Assoc/Pub-R-S
FAX Number: (715) 365-4445 Calendar System: Semester
URL: www.nicoletcollege.edu
Established: 1967 Annual Undergrad Tuition & Fees (In-State): $3,356
Enrollment: 1,455 Coed
Affiliation or Control: State IRS Status: 501(c)3
Highest Offering: Associate Degree
Program: Occupational; 2-Year Principally Bachelor's Creditable
Accreditation: NH, ADNUR, MAC

02 President Ms. Elizabeth BURMASTER
03 Vice President Ms. Roxanne M. LUTGEN
05 Vice President Dr. Kenneth E. URBAN
88 Dean of Trade & Industry Ms. Brigitte PARSONS
49 Dn Instr Lib Arts/Early Chldhd Educ Ms. Rose PRUNTY
50 Dean Instr Bus/Institutional Effect Mr. Chuck KOMP
76 Dean Instr Health Occupations Ms. Lenore MANGLES
103 Dean Workforce/Econ Devel/Security Mr. Ron SKALLERUD
16 Director of Human Resources Dr. Dan GROLEAU
21 Dir of Accounting/Business Services Mr. John VAN DE LOO
88 Director Child Dev Lab Day Care Ms. Michelle CONRATH
18 Director of Facilities Mr. Pete VANNEY
07 Dir Admissions/PK-16 Pathways Ms. Susan KORDULA
26 Dir Communications/Col Cmty Init Ms. Sandy KINNEY
37 Director Financial Aid Ms. Jill PRICE
93 Director Multicultural Services Ms. Rachelle ASHLEY
36 Director Eval/Plcmnt/Disabil Svcs Mr. Todd ALLGOOD
88 Director Academic Success Ms. Rose PRUNTY
88 Director Protective Services Mr. Jason GOELDNER
06 Registrar/Dir Enrollment Services Ms. Kyle GRUENING
08 Director Library Services Mr. Todd MOUNTJOY
13 Manager of IT Operations Mr. Greg MILJEVICH
103 Director Workforce Tr/Econ Develop Ms. Sandy BISHOP
102 Director Foundation Ms. Roxanne LUTGEN

*Northcentral Technical College (G)

1000 W Campus Drive, Wausau WI 54401-1880
County: Marathon FICE Identification: 005387
Unit ID: 239460
Telephone: (715) 675-3331 Carnegie Class: Assoc/Pub-R-M
FAX Number: (715) 675-9776 Calendar System: Semester
URL: www.ntc.edu
Established: 1912 Annual Undergrad Tuition & Fees (In-District): $3,672
Enrollment: 5,120 Coed
Affiliation or Control: Local IRS Status: 501(c)3
Highest Offering: Associate Degree
Program: Occupational; 2-Year Principally Bachelor's Creditable
Accreditation: NH, ADNUR, DH, MAC, MLTAD, RAD, SURGT

02 President Dr. Lori A. WEYERS
05 Vice President for Learning Mrs. Shelly MONDEIK
15 Vice President of Human Resources Mrs. Jeannie M. WORDEN
32 Vice President of Student Services Mrs. Laurie BOROWICZ
10 Vice President of Finance & CFO Ms. Jane KITTEL
13 Chief Information Officer Mr. Chet A. STREBE
18 Director of Facilities Mr. Rob ELLIOTT
26 Director of Marketing & PR Mrs. Katrina FELCH
19 Dean Public Safety Mr. Bryce KOLPACK
97 Dean General Studies Mrs. Rachelle PHAKITTHONG
75 Dean Tech/Trades/Agric/Cmty Svcs Ms. Vicky PIETZ
50 Dean Business/International Educ Mr. Russ ROTHAMER
103 Dean Workforce Learning Solutions Mr. Mark BOROWICZ
12 Director East & Southeast Campuses Mr. Larry KIND
12 Dir North/West & Southwest Campuses Ms. Bobbi DAMROW
88 Director of Continuous Improvement Mr. Nick BLANCHETTE
22 Employment Coord/Affirm Action Ofcr Ms. Amy M. LANG
88 Director Organizational Development Mr. Dan DOUGHERTY
35 Director of Student Relations Mr. Shawn P. SULLIVAN
85 Assoc Dean International Education Ms. Bonita S. BISSONETTE
06 Lead Registrar Mr. James D. BLIESE
88 Dean K-16 Relations/Student Success Mrs. Laurie SAGER BOROWICZ
84 Director Enrollment Management Ms. Sarah DILLON

Northeast Wisconsin Technical College (A)

PO Box 19042, 2740 W Mason Street, Green Bay WI 54307-9042
County: Brown FICE Identification: 005301
Unit ID: 239488
Telephone: (920) 498-5400 Carnegie Class: Assoc/Pub-R-L
FAX Number: (920) 498-6260 Calendar System: Semester
URL: www.nwtc.edu
Established: 1913 Annual Undergrad Tuition & Fees (In-District): $3,710
Enrollment: 9,708 Coed
Affiliation or Control: State/Local IRS Status: 501(c)3
Highest Offering: Associate Degree
Program: Occupational; 2-Year Principally Bachelor's Creditable; Technical Emphasis
Accreditation: NH, ADNUR, DA, DH, DMS, ENGT, MAC, MLTAD, PTAA, RAD, SURGT

02	President	Dr. H. Jeffrey RAFN
05	Vice President for Learning	Ms. Lori SUDDICK
32	Vice President for Student Services	Dr. Pamela PHILLIPS
30	Vice Pres of College Advancement	Vacant
15	Vice President of Human Resources	Ms. Sandy RYCZKOWSKI
13	Chief Information Officer	Vacant
10	Chief Financial Officer	Mr. Jim BLUMREICH
12	Dean Marinette Campus	Mr. Patrick O'HARA
12	Dean Sturgeon Bay Campus	Vacant
50	Dn Business/Information Technology	Mr. Randy SMITH
76	Dean Health Science	Ms. Kay TUPALA
72	Dean Trade & Technical	Mr. Mark WEBER
97	Dean General Education	Ms. Michele SCHMIDT
31	Dean Community/Regional Lrning Svcs	Mrs. Sally L. MARTIN
20	Dean Learning Support Services	Ms. Anne KAMPS
103	Dean Corp Training & Economic Devel	Ms. Laurie RADKE
38	Dean of Student Success	Ms. Bridgett GOLMAN
28	Director of College Diversity	Dr. Alem ASRES
06	Registrar & Dean Enrollment Svcs	Mr. Mark FRANKS
84	Dir Assessment/Enrollment/Retention	Ms. Sally LANGAN
37	Director Financial Aid	Ms. Emily YSEBAERT
09	Director Planning and Development	Ms. Karen J. SMITS
96	Director of Purchasing	Mr. Mark CICHON
102	Foundation Director	Ms. Sandy KRAFT
40	Director Bookstore	Ms. Bonita ZIMA
07	Director of Admissions	Mr. Mark FRANKS
26	Chief Public Relations Officer	Vacant
18	Manager Facilities	Mr. Daniel J. SEIDL
24	Media Services Manager	Mr. John SIEMERING
08	Library Services Manager	Ms. Kim LAPLANTE
104	Manager International Education	Ms. Kelly HOLTMEIER

*Southwest Wisconsin Technical College (B)

1800 Bronson Boulevard, Fennimore WI 53809-9778
County: Grant FICE Identification: 007669
Unit ID: 239910
Telephone: (608) 822-3262 Carnegie Class: Assoc/Pub-R-M
FAX Number: (608) 822-6019 Calendar System: Semester
URL: www.swtc.edu
Established: 1967 Annual Undergrad Tuition & Fees (In-District): $3,848
Enrollment: 3,262 Coed
Affiliation or Control: State/Local IRS Status: 501(c)3
Highest Offering: Associate Degree
Program: Occupational; 2-Year Principally Bachelor's Creditable
Accreditation: NH, ADNUR, MAC, @PTAA

02	President	Dr. Duane M. FORD
10	Director of Fiscal Services	Mr. Caleb WHITE
05	Chief Academic Officer	Dr. Joyce CZAJKOWSKI
47	Agriculture & Industry Dean	Mr. Andrew CALHOUN
50	Business & Management Dean	Dr. Joyce CZAJKOWSKI
76	Health & Service Occupations Dean	Ms. Kathleen E. GARRITY
97	General Studies/Support Svcs Dean	Mr. Kevin M. HOFF
13	Director of Information Technology	Dr. Jaime KLEIN
15	Director of Human Resources	Ms. Laura BODENBENDER
26	Director of External Relations	Mr. Derek DACHELET
30	Director Institutional Advancement	Ms. Barbara TUCKER
32	Director of Student Services	Mr. Caleb WHITE
37	Student Financial Assistance Mgr	Ms. Joy A. KITE
18	Director of Facilities	Mr. Doug PEARSON
102	Foundation Manager	Ms. Heather FIFRICK
88	Human Resources Assistant	Ms. Connie HABERKORN
88	Administrative Asst Admin Services	Ms. Helen LAUFENBERG
88	Fire EMS & Early Childhood Coord	Ms. Rita LUNA
88	Criminal Justice & Drivers Ed Coord	Ms. Kris WUBBEN
04	Executive Asst to Board/President	Ms. Karen M. CAMPBELL
21	Finance Accountant/Payroll Suprvsr	Ms. Mary UREN

*Waukesha County Technical College (C)

800 Main Street, Pewaukee WI 53072-4696
County: Waukesha FICE Identification: 005294
Unit ID: 240125
Telephone: (262) 691-5566 Carnegie Class: Assoc/Pub-S-MC
FAX Number: (262) 691-5593 Calendar System: Semester
URL: www.wctc.edu
Established: 1923 Annual Undergrad Tuition & Fees (In-District): $3,371
Enrollment: 8,102 Coed
Affiliation or Control: State/Local IRS Status: 501(c)3
Highest Offering: Associate Degree
Program: Occupational; 2-Year Principally Bachelor's Creditable; Technical Emphasis
Accreditation: NH, ACFEI, ADNUR, DH, EMT, MAC, SURGT

02	President	Dr. Barbara A. PRINDIVILLE
03	Executive VP	Ms. Kaylen BETZIG
45	VP Strategic Effectiveness & Advanc	Dr. Margaret A. ELLIBEE
05	VP Learning	Ms. Denine ROOD
10	Chief Financial Officer	Ms. Cary A. TESSMANN
32	Associate VP Student Services	Ms. Deborah WALLENDAL
75	Dean Industrial & Engineering Tech	Mr. Douglas J. KANALY
76	Dean Service Occupations	Mr. Greg WEST
76	Dean Health Occupations	Ms. Sandra STEARNS
50	Dean Business Division	Mr. Bradley PIAZZA
103	Dean Corp & Community Training	Dr. Joseph WEITZER
97	Dean Academic Foundations/Gen Ed	Ms. Susan MINNICK
20	Dean Teaching/Learning/Curriculum	Vacant
15	Assoc VP Human Resource Svcs	Mr. David BROWN
06	Registrar	Ms. Jacki VANDYKE
30	Director College Advancement	Vacant
38	Director Counsel/Retent/Spec Svcs	Ms. Deborah JILBERT
14	Chief Information Officer	Mr. Rodney NOBLES
40	Bookstore Manager	Mr. Rick MILLER
18	Director Facilities Services	Mr. Jeffrey LEVERENZ
41	Athletic Director	Vacant
35	Director Student Development	Ms. Susanne FENSKE
90	Director Academic Technologies	Mr. Randall COOROUGH
08	Director of Library Services	Vacant
88	Mgr Executive Operations Pres Ofc	Mr. James F. REHAGEN
26	Dir Marketing & Public Relations	Ms. Susan STERN
07	Manager Admissions & Assessment	Ms. Kathleen KAZDA
37	Manager Financial Aid	Mr. Timothy K. JACOBSON
35	Student Life Coordinator	Mr. Paul BUTRYMOWICZ
28	Recruitment Supervisor	Ms. Trisha L. HORNBURG
25	Manager of Grants & Contracts	Ms. Linda J. MILLER
23	Safety/Enviro & Health Coord	Mr. Jayson R. SCHERER
24	Media Services Coordinator	Mr. Donald DUGAN
96	Purchasing Specialist	Ms. Victoria NASH
36	Career Development Services	Ms. Barbara SUYAMA

*Western Technical College (D)

400 N Seventh Street, La Crosse WI 54601-3368
County: La Crosse FICE Identification: 003840
Unit ID: 240170
Telephone: (608) 785-9200 Carnegie Class: Assoc/Pub-R-M
FAX Number: (608) 785-9205 Calendar System: Semester
URL: www.westerntc.edu
Established: 1912 Annual Undergrad Tuition & Fees (In-District): $3,740
Enrollment: 4,200 Coed
Affiliation or Control: State/Local IRS Status: 501(c)3
Highest Offering: Associate Degree
Program: Occupational; 2-Year Principally Bachelor's Creditable; Technical Emphasis
Accreditation: NH, ADNUR, DA, DH, EEG, MAC, MLTAD, OTA, PTAA, RAD, SURGT

02	President	Dr. J. Lee RASCH
10	Vice President Finance/Operations	Mr. Michael C. PIEPER
05	Vice President for Instruction	Dr. Peg BOUDREAU
32	VP Student Support Svc/Col Rels	Dr. Denise T. VUJNOVICH
45	Vice Pres Strategic Effectiveness	Ms. Connie HOVELAND-BELDEN
12	Admin Regional Learning Centers	Ms. Mary Ann HERLITZKE
102	Executive Director Foundation	Ms. Lynn RUDIG
14	Director Computer/Telecomm Svcs	Mr. Bruce E. MATHEW
37	Financial Aid Manager	Ms. Jerolyn R. GRANDALL
21	Business Services Director	Ms. Amy SCHMIDT
26	Director Marketing & Communications	Ms. Amy L. THORNTON
56	Director Economic Development	Ms. Patti BALACEK
38	Director Counseling Support Svcs	Dr. Karen N. GLEASON
29	Director Alumni Relations	Ms. Sally EMERSON
07	Manager Admissions/Registration	Ms. Jayne E. WELLS
35	Manager of Campus Activities	Ms. Shelley MCNEELY
08	Manager Library Services	Mr. Ron EDWARDS
24	Manager Instructional Media Center	Ms. Joan PIERCE
40	Bookstore Manager	Mr. David R. WIGNES
72	Dean Industrial Technologies	Mr. William BRENDEL
76	Dean Health & Public Safety	Ms. Diane NEEFE
97	Dean General Education	Dr. Douglas STRAUSS
50	Dean Business Education	Mr. Gary BROWN

*Wisconsin Indianhead Technical College (E)

505 Pine Ridge Drive, Shell Lake WI 54871-9300
County: Washburn FICE Identification: 011824
Unit ID: 240198
Telephone: (715) 468-2815 Carnegie Class: Assoc/Pub-R-M
FAX Number: (715) 468-2819 Calendar System: Semester
URL: www.witc.edu
Established: 1968 Annual Undergrad Tuition & Fees (In-State): $3,579
Enrollment: 4,118 Coed
Affiliation or Control: State IRS Status: Exempt
Highest Offering: Associate Degree
Program: Occupational; 2-Year Principally Bachelor's Creditable; Technical Emphasis
Accreditation: NH, ADNUR, MAC, OTA

02	President	Dr. Robert M. MEYER
10	Assc Vice Pres Finance/Bus Svcs/CFO	Mr. Steven DECKER
05	Vice President Academic Affairs	Dr. Diane VERTIN
32	Vice President Student Affairs	Mr. Steve BITZER
09	Assoc VP Instl Effectiveness	Ms. Ellen RILEY HAUSER
20	Vice President Instruct Technology	Mr. Joe HUFTEL
51	Vice President Cont Educ/Foundation	Mr. Craig FOWLER
15	Assc VP Hum Res/Employee Rels	Ms. Cher VINK
14	Sr Director Information Technology	Mr. James DAHLBERG
37	Director Financial Aid	Mr. Terry KLEIN
06	Registrar	Mr. Shane EVENSON
08	Director Learning Resources	Mr. Matthew ROSENDAHL
84	Director Enrollment	Ms. Laura SULLIVAN
26	Director Marketing & Recruitment	Ms. Kathy MAAS

WYOMING

Casper College (F)

125 College Drive, Casper WY 82601-2458
County: Natrona FICE Identification: 003928
Unit ID: 240505
Telephone: (307) 268-2110 Carnegie Class: Assoc/Pub-R-M
FAX Number: (307) 268-2682 Calendar System: Semester
URL: www.caspercollege.edu
Established: 1945 Annual Undergrad Tuition & Fees (In-District): $2,136
Enrollment: 4,611 Coed
Affiliation or Control: Local IRS Status: 501(c)3
Highest Offering: Associate Degree
Program: Occupational; 2-Year Principally Bachelor's Creditable
Accreditation: NH, ACBSP, ADNUR, ART, MLTAD, MUS, OTA, RAD, THEA

01	President	Dr. Walter H. NOLTE
05	Vice President Academic Affairs	Dr. Carmen SIMONE
32	Vice President Student Services	Dr. Joanna ANDERSON
11	Vice Pres Administrative Services	Ms. Lynnde COLLING
51	Dean of Continuing Education	Dr. Laura DRISCOLL
15	Director Human Resources	Vacant
07	Director Admissions/Student Records	Mrs. Alison MCNULTY
26	Director College Relations	Mr. Rich FUJITA
18	Director Physical Plant	Mr. Michael SAWYER
38	Director Student Counseling	Vacant
08	Director of the Library	Ms. Patricia AUFLICK
13	Interim Dir Information Technology	Vacant
36	Director Placement	Ms. Janet DEVRIES
39	Director of Housing	Ms. Barb MERYHEW
41	Athletic Director	Mr. William LANDEN
24	Director of Media Services	Mr. Todd WYKERT
19	Director Campus Security	Mr. Lance JONES
102	Director Foundation	Ms. Paulann T. DOANE
09	Institutional Researcher	Mrs. Lynn FLETCHER
37	Director of Student Financial Aid	Mr. Darry VOIGT
21	Dir Financial Services/Controller	Mrs. Robyn LANDEN
96	Purchasing Coordinator	Mr. Paul CHRISTMAN

Central Wyoming College (G)

2660 Peck Avenue, Riverton WY 82501-1520
County: Fremont FICE Identification: 007289
Unit ID: 240514
Telephone: (307) 855-2000 Carnegie Class: Assoc/Pub-R-M
FAX Number: (307) 855-2095 Calendar System: Semester
URL: www.cwc.edu
Established: 1966 Annual Undergrad Tuition & Fees (In-District): $2,208
Enrollment: 2,432 Coed
Affiliation or Control: Local IRS Status: 501(c)3
Highest Offering: Associate Degree
Program: Occupational; 2-Year Principally Bachelor's Creditable
Accreditation: NH, ADNUR

01	President	Dr. JoAnne Y. MCFARLAND
05	Vice Pres Academic Services	Mr. Jason WOOD
32	Vice President for Student Services	Dr. Mohammed A. WAHEED
10	Exec Vice Pres Admin Svcs/CFO	Mr. Jay NIELSON
30	Dean for Inst Advancement	Mr. Dane GRAHAM
13	Chief Information Officer	Mr. John WOOD
18	Chief Facilities/Physical Plant	Mr. Wayne ROBINSON
08	Director of Library Services	Ms. Cory DALY
27	Director of Public Information	Ms. Carolyn AANESTAD
15	Human Resources Director	Vacant
21	Finance Officer	Ms. Lindy PASKETT
19	Director of Campus Safety/Security	Mr. Steve BARLOW
96	Director of Purchasing	Ms. Suzie KOEHN
84	Asst Dean for Enrollment Services	Ms. Jacquelyn BURNS
103	Dean for Workforce & Cmty Educ	Ms. Lynne MCAULIFFE
41	Director of Athletics	Mr. Serol STAUFFENBERG
06	Assistant Registrar	Ms. Connie NYBERG
49	Dean for Arts & Sciences	Dr. Mark NORDEEN
50	Dean for Commerce/Allied Health	Ms. Charlotte DONELSON

Eastern Wyoming College (H)

3200 W C Street, Torrington WY 82240-1699
County: Goshen FICE Identification: 003929
Unit ID: 240596
Telephone: (307) 532-8200 Carnegie Class: Assoc/Pub-R-S
FAX Number: (307) 532-8229 Calendar System: Semester
URL: ewc.wy.edu/
Established: 1948 Annual Undergrad Tuition & Fees (In-District): $2,280
Enrollment: 1,793 Coed
Affiliation or Control: State/Local IRS Status: 501(c)3
Highest Offering: Associate Degree
Program: Occupational; 2-Year Principally Bachelor's Creditable
Accreditation: NH

01 President ... Dr. Thomas J. ARMSTRONG
04 Exec Asst to President/Board ... Ms. Holly L. BRANHAM
05 Vice President for Learning ... Dr. Dee LUDWIG
10 VP for Finance and Admin Services ... Mr. Robert COX
32 VP for Student Services ... Dr. Rex COGDILL
20 Assoc VP for Outreach & Learning ... Mr. Mike DURFEE
30 Dir of Institutional Development ... Mr. Oliver SUNDBY
08 Director of Library Services ... Mrs. Casey DEBUS
41 Director of College Athletics ... Mr. Verl E. PETSCH
26 Director of College Relations ... Ms. Tami AFDAHL
09 Director of Institutional Research ... Ms. Kimberly RUSSELL
18 Director of Physical Plant ... Mr. Keith JARVIS
39 Director of Residence Life ... Ms. Kellee GOODER
37 Director of Financial Aid ... Ms. Molly WILLIAMS
38 Director Counseling & Testing ... Mrs. Debbie OCHSNER
15 Director Human Resources ... Mr. Tom MCDOWELL
21 Business Office Director ... Ms. Karen PARRIOTT

Institute of Business and Medical Careers (A)

1854 Dell Range Boulevard, Cheyenne WY 82009

County: Laramie Identification: 666738
Telephone: (307) 433-8363 Carnegie Class: Not Classified
FAX Number: (307) 638-2348 Calendar System: Semester
URL: www.ibmc.edu
Established: 1987 Annual Undergrad Tuition & Fees: N/A
Enrollment: N/A Coed
Affiliation or Control: Proprietary IRS Status: Proprietary
Highest Offering: Associate Degree
Program: Occupational
Accreditation: ACICS

01 Director ... Mr. Archie RANDALL

† Branch campus of Institute of Business and Medical Careers, Fort Collins, CO.

Laramie County Community College (B)

1400 E College Drive, Cheyenne WY 82007-3299

County: Laramie FICE Identification: 009259
Unit ID: 240620
Telephone: (307) 778-5222 Carnegie Class: Assoc/Pub-R-M
FAX Number: (307) 778-1399 Calendar System: Semester
URL: www.lccc.wy.edu
Established: 1968 Annual Undergrad Tuition & Fees (In-District): $2,544
Enrollment: 5,193 Coed
Affiliation or Control: State/Local IRS Status: 501(c)3
Highest Offering: Associate Degree
Program: Occupational; 2-Year Principally Bachelor's Creditable
Accreditation: NH, ADNUR, DH, DMS, EMT, PTAA, RAD, SURGT

01 Interim President ... Dr. Miles LAROWE
05 Vice Pres of Instructional Services ... Dr. Marlene TIGNOR
10 Vice Pres of Administration/Finance ... Ms. Carol HOGLUND
32 Vice President of Student Services ... Vacant
13 Chief Information Officer ... Mr. Chad MARLEY
103 Vice Pres of Workforce & Cmty Devel ... Mr. Stan TORVIK
16 Asst Vice Pres Human Resources ... Ms. Peggie KRESL-HOTZ
102 Exec Director of LCCC Foundation ... Ms. Sabrina LANE
12 Dean of Albany County Campus ... Dr. Lynn STALNAKER
08 Librarian ... Ms. Karen LANGE
37 Director of Financial Aid ... Vacant
84 Dean of Enrollment Management ... Ms. Jenny HARGETT
26 Director of Public Relations ... Ms. Lisa MURPHY
18 Director of Physical Plant ... Mr. Timothy MACNAMARA
21 Director of Accounting Services ... Mr. Herry ANDREWS
29 Director of Alumni Relations ... Ms. Brenda LAIRD
09 Manager of Institutional Research ... Ms. Ann MURRAY
96 Director of Contracting/Procurement ... Mr. Jerry HARRIS
07 Director of Admissions ... Ms. Holly ALLISON
06 Registrar ... Ms. Stacy MAESTAS
35 Dir Campus Living & Learning ... Ms. Jenny RIGG
36 Dir Advising & Career Services ... Ms. Chrissy RENFRO
38 Dir Counseling & Camp Wellness ... Ms. Dianne LOWE-CARPENTER
28 Coord International/Diversity Svcs ... Ms. Sara FLEENOR
49 Dean of Arts & Humanities ... Ms. Kathleen URBAN
50 Dean of Business/Agric/ComputerTech ... Dr. Dean BARTOW
69 Dean of Health Sciences & Wellness ... Vacant
83 Dean of Ed Natural & Social Science ... Mrs. Phyllis JONES

Northern Wyoming Community College District (C)

PO Box 1500, 3059 Coffeen Avenue, Sheridan WY 82801-1500

County: Sheridan FICE Identification: 003930
Unit ID: 240666
Telephone: (307) 674-6446 Carnegie Class: Assoc/Pub-R-M
FAX Number: (307) 674-4293 Calendar System: Semester
URL: www.sheridan.edu
Established: 1948 Annual Undergrad Tuition & Fees (In-District): $2,302
Enrollment: 3,888 Coed
Affiliation or Control: Local IRS Status: 501(c)3
Highest Offering: Associate Degree
Program: Occupational; 2-Year Principally Bachelor's Creditable
Accreditation: NH, ADNUR, DH

01 President ... Dr. Paul R. YOUNG
05 VP Academic Affairs ... Dr. Jon H. CONNOLLY
10 VP Admin & Finance/CFO ... Ms. Cheryl A. HEATH
12 VP Gillette College ... Dr. Mark G. ENGLERT
30 VP Development ... Ms. Susan BIGELOW
20 Asst VP Academic Affairs ... Dr. James BAKER
06 Dean Enrollment Services ... Ms. Sharon K. ELWOOD
32 Dean of Students ... Ms. Carol GARCIA
49 Dean Arts & Sciences ... Ms. Ardath L. LUNBECK
76 Dean Health Sciences ... Ms. Trudy R. MUNSICK
75 Dean Ag & Technical Careers ... Dr. Ami N. ERICKSON
15 Director Human Resources ... Mr. Kevin PRICE
26 Dir Marketing/College Information ... Ms. Wendy M. SMITH
37 Director Financial Aid Services ... Ms. Amanda STEINMETZ
13 Dir Information Technology Services ... Mr. Brady R. FACKRELL
21 Controller ... Ms. Karen BURTIS
39 Director Housing & Residential Ed ... Ms. Larissa BONNET
84 Director Enrollment Services ... Mr. Zane S. GARSTAD
88 Director Veteran Services ... Mr. Brett K. BURTIS
18 Director Facilities/Physical Plant ... Mr. Kent A. ANDERSEN
18 Director Gillette Facilities ... Mr. Mark ANDERSEN
106 Dir Distance & Distributive Learn ... Mr. Stoney GADDY
103 Dir Workforce Development & CE ... Ms. Karen ST. CLAIR
08 Librarian ... Ms. Katrina BROWN

Northwest College (D)

231 W 6th Street, Powell WY 82435

County: Park FICE Identification: 003931
Unit ID: 240657
Telephone: (307) 754-6000 Carnegie Class: Assoc/Pub-R-S
FAX Number: (307) 754-6245 Calendar System: Semester
URL: www.northwestcollege.edu
Established: 1946 Annual Undergrad Tuition & Fees (In-District): $2,330
Enrollment: 2,173 Coed
Affiliation or Control: State/Local IRS Status: 501(c)3
Highest Offering: Associate Degree
Program: Occupational; 2-Year Principally Bachelor's Creditable
Accreditation: NH, ADNUR, MUS

01 President ... Dr. Paul PRESTWICH
05 Interim Vice Pres Academic Affairs ... Ms. Ronda PEER
32 Vice Pres Student Affairs ... Dr. Sean FOX
11 Vice Pres Administrative Services ... Mr. Kim MILLS
26 Vice Pres for College Relations ... Mr. Mark KITCHEN
102 Foundation Executive Director ... Ms. Shelby WETZEL
20 Dean Student Learning/Acad Support ... Dr. Matthew EWERS
103 Dean Extended Campus/Workforce ... Ms. Ronda PEER
08 Library Director ... Dr. Susan RICHARDS
10 Finance Director ... Mr. Sheldon FLOM
15 Human Resources Director ... Ms. Jill ANDERSON
14 Computing Services Director ... Mr. Casey DEARCORN
18 Facilities Director ... Mr. David PLUTE
06 Registrar/Admissions Director ... Mr. Brad HAMMOND
37 Financial Aid/Scholarships Director ... Mr. Shaman QUINN
39 Residence and Campus Life Director ... Mr. Dee HAVIG

University of Wyoming (E)

Dept 3434, 1000 E University Avenue, Laramie WY 82071-3434

County: Albany FICE Identification: 003932
Unit ID: 240727
Telephone: (307) 766-1121 Carnegie Class: RU/H
FAX Number: (307) 766-2271 Calendar System: Semester
URL: www.uwyo.edu
Established: 1886 Annual Undergrad Tuition & Fees (In-State): $4,125
Enrollment: 13,806 Coed
Affiliation or Control: State IRS Status: 501(c)3
Highest Offering: Doctorate
Program: Liberal Arts And General; Teacher Preparatory; Professional
Accreditation: NH, BUS, CACREP, CLPSY, CS, DIETD, ENG, LAW, MUS, NURSE, PHAR, SP, SW, TED

01 President ... Dr. Thomas BUCHANAN
05 Provost ... Dr. Myron B. ALLEN
10 Vice President Administration ... Mr. Doug VINZANT
46 Vice President Research & Econ Dev ... Dr. William A. GERN
32 Vice President Student Affairs ... Dr. Sara L. AXELSON
13 Vice President Information Tech ... Mr. Robert R. AYLWARD
30 Vice Pres Institutional Advancement ... Mr. W. Ben BLALOCK, III
88 Vice President Special Projects ... Dr. Carol FROST
43 University Counsel ... Ms. Susan WEIDEL
86 Director Govt & Community Affairs ... Mr. Don RICHARDS
41 Director Intercollegiate Athletics ... Mr. Tom BURMAN
20 Associate VP Academic Affairs ... Dr. Andrew C. HANSEN
20 Associate VP Academic Affairs ... Dr. Nicole BALLENGER
56 Assoc VP Acad Affs/Dean Outreach ... Dr. Margaret MURDOCK
11 Assoc Vice Pres Operations ... Mr. Mark A. COLLINS
21 Assoc VP Fiscal Administration ... Ms. Janet S. LOWE
15 Assoc Vice Pres Human Resources ... Ms. Laura ALEXANDER
21 Asst Vice Pres Budget/Inst Analysis ... Ms. Arley WILLIAMS
88 Assoc Vice President Research ... Ms. Dorothy C. YATES
35 AVP Student Affairs/Dn of Students ... Dr. David COZZENS
88 Assoc VP Institutional Advancement ... Mr. John D. STARK
28 Assoc Vice Pres Diversity/EPO ... Ms. Nell RUSSELL
47 Dean of Agriculture ... Dr. Frank D. GALEY
49 Dean of Arts & Sciences ... Dr. B. Oliver WALTER
50 Dean of Business ... Dr. Brent HATHAWAY
53 Dean of Education ... Dr. Kay A. PERSICHITTE
54 Dean of Engineering ... Dr. Robert ETTEMA
76 Dean of Health Sciences ... Dr. Joseph F. STEINER
61 Dean of Law ... Mr. Stephen D. EASTON
08 Dean of Libraries ... Ms. Maggie FARRELL
12 Dean UW/Casper College Center ... Dr. Brent PICKETT
88 Director School of Energy Resources ... Dr. Mark NORTHAM
07 Director Admission ... Mr. Noah BUCKLEY
36 Director Advising/Career Services ... Ms. Evelyn J. CHYTKA
29 Director Alumni Relations ... Mr. Keener FRYE
88 Director American Heritage Center ... Mr. Mark GREENE
88 Director Art Museum ... Ms. Susan MOLDENHAUER
88 Director Auxiliary Services ... Ms. Carolyn SMITH
88 Director Campus Recreation ... Mr. Patrick MORAN
88 Dir Ellbogen Ctr Teaching/Learning ... Dr. Margaret SKINNER
45 Director Facilities Planning ... Mr. Roger BAALMAN
65 Director Haub Sch Env/Nat Resources ... Dr. Ingrid BURKE
92 Director Honors Program ... Dr. Duncan HARRIS
18 Director Physical Plant ... Mr. James SCOTT
26 Director Inst Communications ... Vacant
06 Registrar ... Dr. Tammy AAGARD
39 Exec Dir Res Life/Dining/Stdnt Un ... Mr. Patrick N. CALL
37 Actg Director Student Financial Aid ... Dr. Tammy AAGARD
23 Director Student Health Services ... Dr. Joanne E. STEANE
38 Actg Director Univ Counseling Ctr ... Dr. Keith EVASHEVSKI
19 Chief University Police Dept ... Mr. Troy LANE

Western Wyoming Community College (F)

PO Box 428, Rock Springs WY 82902-0428

County: Sweetwater FICE Identification: 003933
Unit ID: 240693
Telephone: (307) 382-1600 Carnegie Class: Assoc/Pub-R-M
FAX Number: (307) 382-1636 Calendar System: Semester
URL: www.wwcc.wy.edu
Established: 1959 Annual Undergrad Tuition & Fees (In-District): $1,082
Enrollment: 4,097 Coed
Affiliation or Control: State/Local IRS Status: 501(c)3
Highest Offering: Associate Degree
Program: Occupational; 2-Year Principally Bachelor's Creditable
Accreditation: NH, ADNUR

01 President ... Dr. Karla N. LEACH
05 Vice President of Student Learning ... Vacant
32 VP of Student Success Services ... Dr. Jackie FREEZE
11 Vice President of Administration ... Mr. Marty KELSEY
88 Associate VP for Administration ... Ms. Carla BUDD
21 Controller ... Ms. Debbie BAKER
07 Director of Admissions ... Mr. Joseph MUELLER
06 Registrar ... Ms. Kay LEUM
37 Director Student Financial Aid ... Vacant
08 Director of Library Services ... Ms. Janice GROVER-ROOSA
18 Director of Physical Resources ... Vacant
39 Director Housing/Student Activities ... Mr. Dustin CONOVER
40 Bookstore Manager ... Ms. Natalie LANE
35 Director Student Development Center ... Ms. Kim DRANE
41 Athletic Director ... Dr. Lu SWEET
92 Director of Honors Program ... Mr. Richard KEMPA
09 Director of Institutional Research ... Dr. Sandra CALDWELL
15 Director Personnel Services ... Mr. Marty KELSEY
26 Coord of Marketing/Public Info ... Ms. Allyson CROSS
30 Director Community College Relation ... Mr. David TATE
36 Director Student Placement ... Mr. Mark REMBACZ
10 Chief Business Officer ... Ms. Debbie BAKER
20 Associate VP of Student Learning ... Dr. Sandy CALDWELL
88 Associate VP for Student Success ... Ms. Laurie WATKINS
38 Director Student Counseling ... Ms. Kim DRANE
96 Director of Purchasing ... Ms. Tammy REGISTER

Wyoming Technical Institute (G)

4373 N 3rd Street, Laramie WY 82072-9519

County: Albany FICE Identification: 009157
Unit ID: 240718
Telephone: (307) 742-3776 Carnegie Class: Assoc/PrivFP
FAX Number: (307) 721-4854 Calendar System: Other
URL: www.wyotech.edu
Established: 1966 Annual Undergrad Tuition & Fees: $29,250
Enrollment: 3,392 Coed
Affiliation or Control: Proprietary IRS Status: Proprietary
Highest Offering: Associate Degree
Program: Occupational
Accreditation: ACCSC

01 President ... Mr. Wm. Guy WARPNESS
05 Director of Education ... Mr. Caleb PERRITON
07 Director of Admissions ... Mr. Glenn HALSEY
37 Director of Financial Aid ... Ms. Thecla WOOLCOTT
32 Director of Student Services ... Mr. Kyle MORRIS
36 Director of Career Services ... Mr. Martin AXLUND
06 Registrar ... Ms. Revalee WEERHEIM
84 Admissions Manager ... Mr. Greg TAYLOR
39 Housing Manager ... Mr. Gabe LUCERO
04 Admin Assistant to the President ... Ms. Courtney SCHELL

US SERVICE SCHOOLS

Air Force Institute of Technology (H)

2950 Hobson Way, Wright Patterson AFB OH 45433-7765

County: Greene FICE Identification: 003009
Unit ID: 200697
Telephone: (937) 255-2321 Carnegie Class: DRU
FAX Number: (937) 656-7600 Calendar System: Quarter

URL: www.afit.edu
Established: 1919 Annual Graduate Tuition & Fees: $16,512
Enrollment: 802 Coed
Affiliation or Control: Federal IRS Status: Exempt
Highest Offering: Doctorate; No Undergraduates
Program: Professional; Technical Emphasis
Accreditation: NH, ENG

01 Commandant .... BGen. Walter GIVHAN
03 Vice Commandant .... Capt. Timothy DUENING, USN
05 Actg Director of Academic Affairs .... Dr. Marlin U. THOMAS
54 Dean Graduate School of Engr & Mgt .... Dr. Marlin U. THOMAS
20 Associate Dean for Academic Affairs .... Dr. Paul J. WOLF
46 Dean for Research .... Dr. Heidi R. RIES
10 Chief Financial Officer .... Ms. Ann M. MARBURGER
09 Director Institutional Research .... Dr. William F. ADAMS
06 Director Admissions/Registrar .... Mr. Robert J. LAVERRIERE
32 Dean of Students .... Col. Keith M. BOYER
26 Dir Communications & Information .... LtCol. Lance CARMACK
08 Director D'Azzo Research Library .... Dr. Laurene E. ZAPROROZHETZ
15 Director Personnel Services .... Ms. Leanne HEAGLE
18 Chief Facilities/Physical Plant .... Mr. Daniel W. ROHRBACH
29 Manager Alumni Affairs .... Ms. Kathleen E. SCOTT
35 Director Student Services .... Mr. Richard GAMMON
85 Director of Intl Student Affairs .... Ms. Annette D. ROBB
40 Bookstore Supervisor .... Ms. Evelyn HALL

Air University (A)

55 LeMay Plaza South, Maxwell AFB AL 36112-6335
County: Montgomery FICE Identification: 001001
Telephone: (334) 953-5613 Carnegie Class: Not Classified
FAX Number: (334) 953-2749 Calendar System: Other
URL: www.au.af.mil
Established: 1946 Annual Undergrad Tuition & Fees: N/A
Enrollment: 47,222 Coed
Affiliation or Control: Federal IRS Status: Exempt
Highest Offering: Doctorate
Program: Professional
Accreditation: SC

01 Commander .... LtGen. Allen G. PECK
03 Vice Commander .... MajGen. David S. FADOK
05 Chief Academic Officer .... Dr. Bruce T. MURPHY
06 Registrar .... Mr. Lloyd L. WILSON

† Parent institution of Community College of the Air Force, School of Advanced Air and Space Studies, and the Air Force Institute of Technology

Community College of the Air Force (B)

100 South Turner Blvd,
Maxwell-Gunter AFB AL 36114-3011
County: Montgomery FICE Identification: 012308
Unit ID: 100636
Telephone: (334) 649-5000 Carnegie Class: Assoc/Pub-Spec
FAX Number: (334) 649-5100 Calendar System: Other
URL: www.maxwell.af.mil
Established: 1972 Annual Undergrad Tuition & Fees: N/A
Enrollment: 321,000 Coed
Affiliation or Control: Federal IRS Status: Exempt
Highest Offering: Associate Degree
Program: Occupational; 2-Year Principally Bachelor's Creditable
Accreditation: &SC, PTAA

01 Commandant .... LtCol. Jonathan T. HAMILL
03 Vice Commandant .... CMSgt. James PEPIN
05 Dean Academic Affairs .... Dr. James LARKINS
04 Superintendent .... SMSgt. Rhonda BALL
20 Assoc Dean Academic Programs .... Mr. Donald HOUSE
09 Assoc Dean Campus Relations .... Mr. William NICHOLAS
32 Director of Student Services .... Mrs. Teresa AMATUZZI
88 Director of Academic Operations .... SMSgt. Rhonda BALL

† Regional accreditation is carried under the parent institution, Air University, Maxwell AFB, AL.

Defense Language Institute (C)

Presido of Monterey CA 93944-3229
County: Monterey FICE Identification: 001195
Unit ID: 428222
Telephone: (831) 242-5291 Carnegie Class: Not Classified
FAX Number: (831) 242-6495 Calendar System: Other
URL: www.dliflc.edu
Established: 1941 Annual Undergrad Tuition & Fees: N/A
Enrollment: 3,800 Coed
Affiliation or Control: Federal IRS Status: Exempt
Highest Offering: Associate Degree
Program: Occupational; 2-Year Principally Bachelor's Creditable
Accreditation: WJ

01 Commandant .... Col. Danial PICK
05 Provost .... Dr. Donald FISCHER
20 Associate Provost .... Dr. Jielu ZHAO
46 Dean Program Eval Research Testing .... Dr. Deniz BILGIN

† Associate Arts in Foreign Language authorized by US Congress in December 2001 and approved by ACCJC/WASC in June 2002.

The Judge Advocate General's Legal Center & School (D)

600 Massie Road, Charlottesville VA 22903-1781
County: Albermarle Identification: 666974
Telephone: (434) 971-3300 Carnegie Class: Not Classified
FAX Number: (434) 971-3338 Calendar System: Quarter
URL: www.jagcnet.army.mil/tjaglcs
Established: 1951 Annual Graduate Tuition & Fees: $118
Enrollment: 118 Coed
Affiliation or Control: Federal IRS Status: Exempt
Highest Offering: Master's; No Undergraduates
Program: Professional
Accreditation: LAW

01 Commander/Commandant .... BGen. John W. MILLER, II
05 Dean .... Col. David DINER
20 Associate Dean of Academics .... Mr. Maurice A. LESCAULT, JR.

Marine Corps University (E)

2076 South Street, Quantico VA 22134-5067
County: Prince William Identification: 666745
Unit ID: 438513
Telephone: (703) 784-2105 Carnegie Class: Not Classified
FAX Number: (703) 784-1271 Calendar System: Semester
URL: www.mcu.usmc.mil
Established: 1989 Annual Graduate Tuition & Fees: N/A
Enrollment: 525 Coed
Affiliation or Control: Federal IRS Status: Exempt
Highest Offering: Master's; No Undergraduates
Program: Professional; Technical Emphasis
Accreditation: SC

01 President .... MajGen. Thomas M. MURRAY
05 Vice President for Academic Affairs .... Dr. Jerre W. WILSON
20 Director Academic Support Division .... Mr. Joel S. WESTA
09 Director of Institutional Research .... Mr. Robert E. LISTON

National Defense University (F)

Fort Lesley J. McNair, Washington DC 20319-5066
FICE Identification: 031893
Unit ID: 423494
Telephone: (202) 685-3937 Carnegie Class: Not Classified
FAX Number: (202) 685-3935 Calendar System: Semester
URL: www.ndu.edu
Established: 1976 Annual Graduate Tuition & Fees: N/A
Enrollment: 1,250 Coed
Affiliation or Control: Federal IRS Status: Exempt
Highest Offering: Master's; No Undergraduates
Program: Professional
Accreditation: M

01 President .... VAdm. Ann E. RONDEAU
03 Senior Vice President .... Vacant
05 Vice Pres Academic Affairs .... Dr. John W. YAEGER
26 Director Public Affairs .... Mr. David THOMAS
20 Deputy Vice Pres Academic Affairs .... Dr. Brenda F. ROTH
27 Chief Information Officer .... Col. Joe ADAMS
08 Head Librarian .... Ms. Helen (Meg) TULLOCH
45 Acting Director Resource Management .... Mr. John GARDNER
23 Director Health Fitness .... Mr. Tony SPINOSA
25 Director Contracting .... Ms. Jenifer CUOZZO
43 General Counsel .... Ms. Mollie MURPHY
06 Registrar .... Mr. Larry JOHNSON
15 Director Personnel .... Ms. Marcia MILLER
102 President NDU Foundation ..BGen. William J. LESZCZYNSKI, JR.
85 Director International Fellows .... Mr. John CHARLTON
18 Chief Facilities/Physical Plant .... Mr. Charles FANSHAW
11 Acting Director of Operations .... Ms. Jeanette TOLBERT
28 Director of Diversity .... Ms. Carol STINER
86 Director University Outreach .... Vacant
09 Director of Institutional Research .... Vacant

National Intelligence University (G)

200 MacDill Boulevard, Washington DC 20340-5100
Identification: 666393
Unit ID: 131380
Telephone: (202) 231-3344 Carnegie Class: Not Classified
FAX Number: (202) 231-3294 Calendar System: Quarter
URL: www.dia.mil
Established: 1962 Annual Undergrad Tuition & Fees: N/A
Enrollment: 624 Coed
Affiliation or Control: Federal IRS Status: Exempt
Highest Offering: Master's
Program: Professional
Accreditation: M

01 President .... Dr. David R. ELLISON
03 Deputy to the President .... Col. Randall H. WILLIAMSON
04 Executive Assistant to President .... Ms. Jessica M. STEINRUCK
05 Provost .... Dr. Susan M. STUDDS
88 Dir Ctr for External/Internatl Pgms .... Mr. Lorenzo S. HIPONIA
46 Dir Ctr for Strategic Intel Rsrch .... Dr. Cathryn Q. THURSTON
09 Dir Outcomes Assess/Inst Research .... Dr. Felicia BRADSHAW
10 Chief Operating Officer .... Mr. Kevin C. TALIAFERRO
11 Director of Operations .... Mr. Stephen J. KERDA
19 Security Officer .... Ms. Thelma FLAMER

06 Registrar .... Mr. Eric H. STUPAR
07 Director of Admissions .... Ms. Julea REESE
90 Director Eductional Technology .... Ms. Elvia E. CORTES
08 Director Library Services .... Ms. Denise CAMPBELL
58 Dean School of Intelligence Studies .... Dr. Vance R. SKARSTEDT
20 Associate Dean .... Col. Douglas KIELY
12 Director NSA Campus .... Mr. Tom BYCZKOWSKI
12 Director NGA Campus .... Mr. Timothy J. CHRISTENSON
58 Dean School of Science & Tech Intel .... Dr. Brian R. SHAW

Naval Postgraduate School (H)

1 University Circle, Room M10, Monterey CA 93943-5100
County: Monterey FICE Identification: 001310
Unit ID: 119678
Telephone: (831) 656-2441 Carnegie Class: Master's L
FAX Number: (831) 656-2921 Calendar System: Quarter
URL: www.nps.edu
Established: 1909 Annual Undergrad Tuition & Fees: N/A
Enrollment: 2,503 Coed
Affiliation or Control: Federal IRS Status: Exempt
Highest Offering: Doctorate
Program: Professional
Accreditation: WC, BUS, ENG, SPAA

01 President .... ADM. Daniel T. OLIVER
100 Chief of Staff .... Col. Zoe HALE
05 Executive Vice President & Provost .... Dr. Leonard A. FERRARI
10 Vice Pres Finance/Administration .... Ms. Colleen A. NICKLES
46 Vice President/Dean of Research .... Dr. Karl VAN BIBBER
13 Vice Pres Information Resources/CIO .... Dr. Christine M. HASKA
20 Vice Provost for Academic Affairs .... Dr. Orrin Douglas MOSES
54 Int Dean Grad Sch Engr/Applied Sci .... Dr. Phillip A. DURKEE
82 Dean Sch of Intl Graduate Studies .... Dr. James J. WIRTZ
50 Dean Grad Sch Bus/Public Policy .... Dr. William R. GATES
72 Dean Grad Sch Oper & Info Sciences .... Dr. Peter P. PURDUE
10 Comptroller .... Mr. Kevin K. LITTLE
18 Director Facilities/Support Svcs .... Mr. Peter G. DAUSEN
08 Assoc Prov Library & Info Resources ..Ms. Eleanor S. UHLINGER
06 Registrar .... Mr. Mike ANDERSEN
15 Director Human Resources .... Ms. Julie CARPENTER
29 Director of Alumni Relations .... Mr. Kari L. MIGLAW
19 Sr Lecturer NPS/Chief Security Ofcr .... CAPT. Robert SIMERAL, RET.
88 Senior Intelligence Officer .... Capt. Jennith E. HOYT
09 Exec Dir Inst Plng/Communications .... Dr. Fran HORVATH
28 EEO Director .... Ms. Deborah A. BAITY
56 Dir Office of Continuous Learning .... Mr. Tom M. MASTRE
07 Director of Admissions .... Ms. Sue DOOLEY
88 Deputy Comptroller .... Mr. Jack L. SHISIDO
88 Director of Programs .... CDR. Mary J. SIMS

Naval War College (I)

686 Cushing Road, Newport RI 02841-1207
County: Newport FICE Identification: 003413
Unit ID: 432320
Telephone: (401) 841-3089 Carnegie Class: Not Classified
FAX Number: (401) 841-1297 Calendar System: Trimester
URL: www.usnwc.edu
Established: 1884 Annual Graduate Tuition & Fees: N/A
Enrollment: N/A Coed
Affiliation or Control: Federal IRS Status: Exempt
Highest Offering: Master's; No Undergraduates
Program: Professional
Accreditation: EH

01 President .... RADM. John N. CHRISTENSON
04 Exec Assistant to the President .... LT. Robert J. DAFOE
05 Provost .... Amb. MaryAnn PETERS, RET.
20 Senior Executive Associate/Provost .... Mr. Richard R. MENARD
20 Associate Provost .... Prof. William R. SPAIN
100 Chief of Staff .... CAPT. Russell KNIGHT
20 Dean of Academic Affairs .... Prof. John GAROFANO
09 Dean Center for Warfare Studies .... Prof. Robert J. RUBEL
32 Dean of Students .... CAPT. Raymond F. KELEDEI
08 Director Library Services .... Prof. Terrance J. METZ
56 Dir College of Distance Education .... Dr. Jay HICKEY
06 Registrar .... CAPT. Raymond F. KELEDEI
46 Chairman Strategy & Policy .... Dr. John MAURER
88 Chairman National Security Affairs .... Dr. David COOPER
88 Chairman Joint Military Operations .... CAPT. Alan ABRAMSON
10 Chief Business Officer .... Mr. Robert SAMPSON
15 Director Personnel Services .... CDR. Mary E. SMITH
18 Chief Facilities/Physical Plant .... Ms. Beth LEINBERRY
26 Chief Public Relations Officer .... CDR. Carla M. MCCARTHY
27 Chief Information Officer .... Mr. Joseph PANGBORN
19 Director of Security .... Mr. Leonard COLEMAN
29 Director Alumni Affairs .... Prof. Julia A. GAGE
88 Director Writing Center .... Dr. Donna CONNOLLY
88 Director International Programs .... Vacant
88 Dean Col Operatnl/Strtgc Ldrshp .... RADM. James KELLY, RET.

School of Advanced Air and Space Studies (J)

600 Chennault Circle, Maxwell AFB AL 36112-6424
County: Montgomery Identification: 666746
Telephone: (334) 953-5155 Carnegie Class: Not Classified
FAX Number: (334) 953-3015 Calendar System: Other
URL: www.au.af.mil/au/saass
Established: 1991 Annual Graduate Tuition & Fees: N/A
Enrollment: 58 Coed

Affiliation or Control: Federal IRS Status: Exempt
Highest Offering: Master's; No Undergraduates
Program: Professional
Accreditation: &SC

01 Commandant .... Col. Timothy SCHULTZ
03 Vice Commandant .... Dr. Stephen D. CHIABOTTI

† Regional accreditation is carried under the parent institution, Air University, Maxwell AFB, AL.

Uniformed Services University of the Health Sciences (A)

4301 Jones Bridge Road, Bethesda MD 20814-4799
County: Montgomery FICE Identification: 021610
Unit ID: 164137
Telephone: (301) 295-3013 Carnegie Class: Not Classified
FAX Number: (301) 295-3431 Calendar System: Quarter
URL: www.usuhs.mil
Established: 1972 Annual Graduate Tuition & Fees: N/A
Enrollment: 929 Coed
Affiliation or Control: Federal IRS Status: Exempt
Highest Offering: Doctorate; No Undergraduates
Program: Professional
Accreditation: M, ANEST, CLPSY, ENGR, MED, NURSE, PH

01 President .... Dr. Charles L. RICE
03 Senior Vice President .... Dr. Dale C. SMITH
05 Sr Vice Pres University Programs .... Dr. Patrick SCULLEY
10 Vice Pres Finance & Administration .... Mr. Stephen C. RICE
26 Vice Pres External Affairs .... Mr. William BESTER
46 Vice President for Research .... Dr. Steven KAMINSKY
88 VP Affiliation/Internat'l Affairs .... Dr. Jeffrey LONGACRE
04 Exec Assistant to the President .... Ms. Mary L. SCHWARTZ
100 Chief of Staff .... Mr. Robert J. THOMPSON
63 Dean School of Medicine .... Dr. Larry W. LAUGHLIN
63 Vice Dean School of Medicine .... Dr. John MCMANIGLE
58 Assoc Dean Graduate Education .... Dr. Eleanor S. METCALF
07 Assoc Dean Admiss & Recruiting SOM .... CAPT. Margaret CALLOWAY
88 Assoc Dean Graduate Medical Educ .... CAPT. Jerri CURTIS
32 Assoc Dean Student Affairs .... Dr. Richard M. MACDONALD
88 Assistant Dean Clinical Sciences .... COL. Lisa MOORES
66 Dean Graduate School of Nursing .... Dr. Ada Sue HINSHAW
20 Associate Dean Acad Affairs GSN .... Dr. Carol A. ROMANO
46 Director AFRRI .... COL. Mark MELANSON
27 Chief Information Officer .... Mr. Timothy RAPP
43 General Counsel .... Mr. John E. BAKER
76 Sr Exec Dir Cont Health Profess Ed .... CAPT. Karen BIGGS
06 Registrar .... Ms. Gail HEWITT-CLARK
15 Director Civilian Human Res .... Mr. Darryl BROWN
08 University Librarian .... Ms. Janice J. MULLER
18 Director of Facilities .... Ms. Cheryl KING
96 Director of Contracting .... Mr. Anthony REVENIS

United States Air Force Academy (B)

2304 Cadet Drive, Suite 2400,
USAF Academy CO 80840-5025
County: El Paso FICE Identification: 001369
Unit ID: 128328
Telephone: (719) 333-3070 Carnegie Class: Bac/A&S
FAX Number: (719) 333-3647 Calendar System: Semester
URL: www.academyadmissions.com
Established: 1954 Annual Undergrad Tuition & Fees: N/A
Enrollment: 4,619 Coed
Affiliation or Control: Federal IRS Status: Exempt
Highest Offering: Baccalaureate
Program: Liberal Arts And General; Professional
Accreditation: NH, BUS, CS, DENT, ENG

United States Army Command and General Staff College (C)

1 Reynolds Avenue, Building 111,
Fort Leavenworth KS 66027-1352
County: Leavenworth FICE Identification: 001947
Unit ID: 156055
Telephone: (913) 684-3097 Carnegie Class: Not Classified
FAX Number: (913) 684-2906 Calendar System: Trimester
URL: www.cgsc.army.mil
Established: 1881 Annual Undergrad Tuition & Fees: N/A
Enrollment: 1,005 Coed
Affiliation or Control: Federal IRS Status: Exempt
Highest Offering: Master's
Program: Professional
Accreditation: NH

01 Commandant .... LtGen. David G. PERKINS
03 Deputy Commandant .... BGen. Sean B. MACFARLAND
04 Assistant Deputy Commandant .... Col. Tom R. WEAFER
05 Dean of Academics .... Dr. Wendell KING
100 Chief of Staff .... Col. Michael JOHNSON
58 Director Graduate Degree Programs .... Dr. Robert BAUMANN
08 Director of Library .... Mr. Ed BURGESS
32 Director CGSS School .... Col. Jeffrey R. SPRINGMAN
06 Registrar .... Mr. Kenneth A. NORRIS
26 Chief Public Relations Officer .... Mr. Harry SARLES

United States Army War College (D)

122 Forbes Avenue, Carlisle PA 17013-5050
County: Cumberland Identification: 666235
Telephone: (717) 245-4711 Carnegie Class: Not Classified
FAX Number: (717) 245-4721 Calendar System: Other
URL: www.carlisle.army.mil
Established: N/A Annual Graduate Tuition & Fees: N/A
Enrollment: N/A Coed
Affiliation or Control: Federal IRS Status: 501(c)3
Highest Offering: Master's; No Undergraduates
Program: Professional
Accreditation: M

01 Commandant .... MajGen. Gregg F. MARTIN
05 Dean Academics .... Dr. William T. JOHNSEN

United States Coast Guard Academy (E)

15 Mohegan Avenue, New London CT 06320-8100
County: New London FICE Identification: 001415
Unit ID: 130624
Telephone: (860) 444-8444 Carnegie Class: Bac/Diverse
FAX Number: (860) 444-8288 Calendar System: Semester
URL: www.cga.edu
Established: 1876 Annual Undergrad Tuition & Fees: N/A
Enrollment: 1,017 Coed
Affiliation or Control: Federal IRS Status: Exempt
Highest Offering: Baccalaureate
Program: Occupational; Technical Emphasis
Accreditation: EH, BUS, ENG

01 Superintendent .... RADM. Sandra L. STOSZ
03 Assistant Superintendent .... Capt. James RENDON
45 Planning Officer .... LCDR. Alan G. LAPENNA
05 Dean of Academics .... Dr. Kurt J. COLELLA
20 Associate Dean .... Capt. Richard SANDERS
45 Assoc Dean Acad Support Services .... Dr. Evelyn A. ELLIS
07 Director of Admissions .... Capt. Stephan FINTON
32 Commandant of Cadets .... Capt. John O'CONNOR
06 Registrar .... Mr. Donald E. DYKES
08 Librarian .... Ms. Patricia A. DARAGAN
10 Comptroller .... CDR. Robert MCKENNA
26 Public Affairs Officer .... CWO Kimberly SMITH
09 Institutional Research .... Dr. Leonard M. GIAMBRA
46 Director of Research .... Capt. Richard B. GAINES
13 Head of Information Services .... CDR. Andrew J. SORENSON
15 Personnel Management Specialist .... Mrs. Sunnie ROBINSON
16 Chief Personnel/Administration .... Capt. John M. FITZGERALD
18 Chief Facilities Engineer .... CDR. Gregory S. GESELE
19 Security Chief .... MCPO John M. APPICELLI
22 Civil Rights Officer .... Vacant
23 Chief Health Services .... CDR. Joseph L. PEREZ
29 President Alumni Association .... CDR. James SYLVESTER
38 Chief Cadet Counselor .... Dr. Robert MURRAY
40 Bookstore Manager .... Ms. Lauri KERP
41 Director of Athletics .... Mr. Robert J. ARKEILPANE
42 Command Chaplain .... Capt. Brian K. FINCH
43 Staff Legal Officer .... CDR. James P. PRUETT
85 International Cadet Advisor .... Dr. Alina M. ZAPALSKA
28 Director of Diversity .... Mr. Antonio FARIAS
88 Director Leadership Development Ctr .... Capt. Andrea M. MARCILLE

† There is a one-time entrance fee of $3,000 to cover uniform, laptop, and supplies.

United States Merchant Marine Academy (F)

300 Steamboat Road, Kings Point NY 11024-1634
County: Nassau FICE Identification: 002892
Unit ID: 197027
Telephone: (516) 773-5000 Carnegie Class: Bac/Diverse
FAX Number: (516) 773-5509 Calendar System: Trimester
URL: www.usmma.edu
Established: 1943 Annual Undergrad Tuition & Fees: $2,850
Enrollment: 1,035 Coed
Affiliation or Control: Federal IRS Status: Exempt
Highest Offering: Master's
Program: Liberal Arts And General; Professional
Accreditation: M, ENG

01 Superintendent & Dean .... RADM. Philip H. GREENE, JR.
03 Deputy Superintendent .... RADM. Christopher MCMAHON
11 Assistant Supt Administration .... Capt. John J. JOCHMANS
05 Academic Dean/Asst Supt Acad Affs .... Dr. Shashi KUMAR
18 Asst Supt for Facilities .... Capt. Theodore DOGONNIUCK
20 Assistant Dean .... Dr. Gary A. LAMBARDO
32 Commandant Midshipmen .... Capt. William FELL
100 Chief of Staff .... Capt. Eric York WALLISCHECK
30 Director Office of External Affairs .... Capt. Robert LARSEN
07 Director of Admissions .... Capt. Robert JOHNSON
06 Registrar/Director Inst Research .... Dr. Howard ENGLISH
08 Chief Librarian .... Dr. George J. BILLY
13 Director Computer/Information Mgmt .... Mr. Howard WIENER
27 Director Public Information .... Mr. Martin P. SKROCKI
15 Director Human Resources .... Mr. LaVar M. WILLIAMS
21 Asst Chief Financial Officer .... Ms. Kelly A. FLANAGAN
29 Director Alumni Relations .... Mr. Peter RACKETT

35 Director Student Affairs .... Ms. Mary CUNNINGHAM
36 Dir of Prof Develop/Career Services .... Capt. Richard EGAN
37 Director Student Financial Aid .... Ms. Sdenka RIOS
96 Director of Purchasing .... Mr. Jay TEDESCO
44 Director Alumni Foundation .... Mr. Eugene MCCORMICK

United States Military Academy (G)

West Point NY 10996-5000
County: Orange FICE Identification: 002893
Unit ID: 197036
Telephone: (845) 938-4041 Carnegie Class: Bac/A&S
FAX Number: (845) 938-3021 Calendar System: Semester
URL: www.westpoint.edu
Established: 1802 Annual Undergrad Tuition & Fees: N/A
Enrollment: 4,686 Coed
Affiliation or Control: Federal IRS Status: Exempt
Highest Offering: Baccalaureate
Program: Liberal Arts And General; Professional
Accreditation: M, CS, ENG

01 Superintendent .... LtGen. David H. HUNTOON, JR.
05 Dean of Academic Board .... BGen. Timothy TRAINOR
20 Vice Dean of Education .... Dr. Jean BLAIR
32 Commandant of Cadets .... BGen. Theodore D. MARTIN
100 Chief of Staff .... Col. Charles A. STAFFORD
88 Garrison Commander .... Col. Michael TARSA
07 Director of Admissions .... Col. Deborah MCDONALD
37 Director Student Financial Aid .... Mr. Tom REMO
06 Assoc Dean Operations/Registrar .... Dr. James DALTON
45 Assoc Dean Academic Research .... LtCol. John GRAHAM
09 Institutional Research & Assessment .... Maj. Randall HOBERECHT
13 Chief Information Officer .... LtCol. Charles GRINDLE
10 Director of Resource Management .... Mrs. Deborah A. POOL
26 Public Affairs Officer .... LtCol. Brian TRIBUS
08 Interim Librarian .... LtCol. Scott SMITH
29 President Association of Graduates . Col. Robert MCCLURE, RET.
38 Dir Center for Personal Development .... LtCol. Edwin SUPPLEE
20 Assoc Dean Academic Affairs .... Dr. Bruce KEITH
41 Director Intercollegiate Athletics .... Mr. Boo CORRIGAN
18 Chief Facilities/Physical Plant .... Mr. Matthew TALABER
15 Dir Ctr for Teaching Excellence .... Dr. Mark EVANS
72 Chief Info & Educational Tech Div .... LtCol. Ronald DODGE
35 Dir Ctr for Enchanced Performance .... LtCol. Carl J. OHLSON

United States Naval Academy (H)

121 Blake Road, Annapolis MD 21402-5000
County: Anne Arundel FICE Identification: 030430
Unit ID: 164155
Telephone: (410) 293-1000 Carnegie Class: Bac/A&S
FAX Number: (410) 293-3734 Calendar System: Semester
URL: www.usna.edu
Established: 1845 Annual Undergrad Tuition & Fees: N/A
Enrollment: 4,606 Coed
Affiliation or Control: Federal IRS Status: Exempt
Highest Offering: Baccalaureate
Program: Liberal Arts And General; Professional
Accreditation: M, CS, ENG

01 Superintendent .... VADM. Michael H. MILLER
32 Commandant of Midshipmen .... Capt. Robert E. CLARK, II
05 Academic Dean & Provost .... Dr. Andrew T. PHILLIPS
20 Vice Academic Dean .... Dr. Michael C. HALBIG
07 Dean of Admissions .... Capt. Bruce J. LATTA
20 Associate Dean for Faculty .... Dr. Boyd A. WAITE
20 Assoc Dean for Academic Affairs .... Dr. Frederic I. DAVIS
08 Assoc Dean Information Svcs/Library .... Mr. James RETTIG
10 Deputy for Finance .... Vacant
100 Chief of Staff .... Capt. Steven S. VAHSEN
11 CO Naval Support Activity Annapolis .... Capt. Thomas L. REESE
06 Registrar .... Dr. Christopher A. DAVIS
26 Public Affairs Officer .... CDR. William MARKS
29 Exec Director Alumni Association .... Capt. George P. WATT, JR.
21 Comptroller .... CDR. Todd W. HAUGE
14 Chief Information Officer .... CDR. Louis J. GIANNOTTI
88 Director Academic Center .... Dr. Bruce J. BUKOWSKI
09 Director Institutional Research .... Capt. Glenn F. GOTTSCHALK
18 Public Works Officer .... Capt. Donald B. CAMPBELL
41 Athletic Director .... Mr. Chet GLADCHUK
42 Command Chaplain .... Capt. Michael PARISI
30 Director Officer Development .... Capt. Norman E. WEAKLAND
15 Director Human Resources .... Mr. William COFFIN
28 Director of Diversity .... Capt. Roger ISOM

AMERICAN SAMOA

American Samoa Community College (I)

PO Box 2609, Pago Pago AS 96799-2609
County: American Samoa FICE Identification: 010010
Unit ID: 240736
Telephone: (684) 699-9155 Carnegie Class: Assoc/Pub-S-SC
FAX Number: (684) 699-6259 Calendar System: Semester
URL: www.amsamoa.edu
Established: 1970 Annual Undergrad Tuition & Fees (In-State): $1,540
Enrollment: 2,207 Coed
Affiliation or Control: State IRS Status: 501(c)3
Highest Offering: Associate Degree
Program: Occupational; 2-Year Principally Bachelor's Creditable

Accreditation: WJ

01 President .... Dr. Seth P. GALEA'I
05 Vice Pres Academic/Student Affairs .... Dr. Kathleen KOLHOFF
11 Vice Pres Administrative Svcs/Finan .... Mr. Mikaele ETUALE
32 Dean of Student Services .... Dr. Emilia LE'I
51 Dir of Adult Educ/Lit Ext Learning .... Mr. Tauvela FALE
20 Dean of Academic Affairs .... Dr. Irene HELSHAM
08 Director of Library Services .... Dr. Stephen LIN
25 Dir Land Grant/Cmty & Natural Res .... Dr. Daniel F. AGA
45 Dir Institutional Effectiveness .... Mrs. Rosevonne PATO
37 Director Financial Aid .... Ms. Arleen SEWELL
88 Dir Teacher Education Program .... Dr. Lina GALEA'I-SCANLAN
10 Chief Financial Officer .... Ms. Emey SILAFAU
88 Director of SAMPAC .... Mrs. Okenaisa FAUOLO-MANILA
88 Director of Upward Bound Program .... Mrs. Elizabeth LEUMA
102 Dir of ASCC Research Foundation .... Mr. John AH SUE
88 Director of Small Business Devel .... Mr. Herbert THWEATT
06 Registrar .... Mrs. Sifagatogo TUITASI
15 Director Human Resources .... Mrs. Komiti EMMSLEY
26 Press Officer .... Mr. James KNEUBUHL
72 Acting Dean Trades & Technology .... Mr. Sal POLOAI
27 Chief Information Officer .... Ms. Grace TULAFONO
38 Director of Student Support Svcs .... Mrs. Repeka ALAIMOANA-NUUSA

FEDERATED STATES OF MICRONESIA

College of Micronesia-FSM (A)

PO Box 159 Kolonia, Pohnpei FM 96941-0159

FICE Identification: 010343
Unit ID: 243638
Telephone: (691) 320-2480 Carnegie Class: Assoc/Pub-R-M
FAX Number: (691) 320-2479 Calendar System: Semester
URL: www.comfsm.fm
Established: 1963 Annual Undergrad Tuition & Fees (In-State): $3,791
Enrollment: 2,699 Coed
Affiliation or Control: State IRS Status: 501(c)3
Highest Offering: Associate Degree
Program: Occupational; 2-Year Principally Bachelor's Creditable
Accreditation: #WJ

01 President .... Mr. Spensin JAMES
05 Vice Pres Instructional Affairs .... Mrs. Jean THOULAG
32 Vice Pres Support/Student Affairs .... Mr. Ringlen P. RINGLEN
56 VP Coop Research/Ext (Land Grant) .... Mr. Walter James CURRIE
11 Vice Pres Dept of Admin Services .... Mr. Joesph HABUCHMAI
10 Comptroller .... Mr. Danilo DUMANTAY
12 Director Chuuk Campus .... Mr. Joakim PETER
12 Director Pohnpei Campus .... Ms. Penny WEILBACHER
12 Director Kosrae Campus .... Mr. Kalwin KEPHAS
12 Director Yap Campus .... Ms. Lourdes ROBOMAN
12 Director FSM-FMI Campus .... Mr. Matthias EWARMAI
45 Director Research & Planning .... Mr. Jimmy HICKS
15 Director Human Resources .... Ms. Rencelly NELSON
20 Director Academic Programs .... Mrs. Karen SIMION
07 Director Admissions & Records .... Vacant
08 Director Learning Res Center .... Ms. Sue CALDWELL
75 Director Vocational Programs .... Vacant
18 Director Physical Plant/Maintenance .... Mr. Francisco MENDIOLA
06 Registrar .... Mr. Joey ODUCADO
09 Director of Institutional Research .... Vacant
21 Business Officer Manager .... Ms. Pelma PALIK
37 Director Student Financial Aid .... Mr. Eddie HALEYALIG
38 Counselor .... Ms. Penselyn ETSE
26 Director Devel/Public Relations .... Mr. Joseph SAIMON
13 Director Information Technology .... Mr. Gordon SEGAL
35 Director Residential/Campus Life .... Mr. Reedson ABRAHAM

GUAM

Guam Community College (B)

PO Box 23069, Barrigada GU 96921-3069

County: Guam FICE Identification: 015361
Unit ID: 240745
Telephone: (671) 735-5531 Carnegie Class: Assoc/Pub-R-S
FAX Number: (671) 734-5238 Calendar System: Semester
URL: www.guamcc.edu
Established: 1977 Annual Undergrad Tuition & Fees (In-District): $4,224
Enrollment: 2,543 Coed
Affiliation or Control: State/Local IRS Status: 501(c)3
Highest Offering: Associate Degree
Program: Occupational; 2-Year Principally Bachelor's Creditable; Technical Emphasis
Accreditation: WJ, MAC

01 President .... Dr. Mary Y. OKADA
05 Vice President Academic Affairs .... Dr. R. Ray D. SOMERA
10 Vice President Finance & Admin .... Ms. Carmen K. SANTOS
10 Controller .... Mr. Edwin E. LIMTUATCO
75 Dean Trades & Professional Services .... Mr. Reilly A. RIDGELL
72 Dean Technology & Student Services .... Dr. Michelle M. SANTOS
26 Asst Dir Communications & Promo .... Ms. Jayne T. FLORES
29 Asst Dir Dev & Alumni Relations .... Ms. Lolita C. REYES
04 Private Secretary .... Ms. Esther A. MUNA
101 Admin Secretary II BOT-Pres Ofc .... Ms. Lourdes V. BAUTISTA
06 Coordinator Admissions/Registration .... Mr. Patrick L. CLYMER
45 Asst Dir Planning & Development .... Ms. Doris U. PEREZ
103 Asst Dir Cont Ed & Workforce Dev .... Mr. Victor RODGERS
88 Assoc Dean Trades & Prof Svcs .... Dr. Geraldine S. JAMES
32 Assoc Dean Student Support Svcs .... Ms. Joanne A. IGE
15 Administrator Human Resources .... Ms. Joann W. MUNA
18 Coordinator Facilities Maintenance .... Mr. Jose C. QUITUGUA
08 Librarian .... Ms. Christine B. MATSON
20 Admin Ofcr VP's Ofc-Academic Affs .... Ms. Ava M. GARCIA
09 Institutional Researcher .... Ms. Marlena O. MONTAGUE
09 Prgm Spc AIER .... Ms. Priscilla C. JOHNS
46 Asst Dir AIER .... Dr. Virginia C. TUDELA
88 Pgm Spc Project Aim TRIO .... Ms. Christine B. SISON
35 Pgm Spc Ctr Student Involvement .... Ms. Barbara B. LEON GUERRERO
23 School Health Counselor .... Ms. Maria Cecilia H. DELOS SANTOS
37 Coordinator Student Financial Aid .... Ms. Micki L. LONSDALE
88 Pgm Spc Adult Ed/GED .... Mr. Huan F. HOSEI
26 Pgm Spc Communications & Promo .... Mr. Wesley T. GIMA
29 Pgm Spc Dev & Alumni Relations .... Ms. Bonnie Mae M. DATUIN
96 Supply Management Administrator .... Ms. Joleen M. EVANGELISTA
14 Data Processing Administrator .... Mr. Francisco C. CAMACHO
51 Pgm Spc Continuing Educ .... Ms. Terry L. BARNHART
51 Pgm Spc Continuing Educ .... Ms. Rowena Ellen PEREZ
40 Bookstore Manager .... Vacant
55 Pgm Spc Night Administrator .... Mr. John F. PAYNE
19 Safety Admin Envir Safety Ofc .... Mr. Gregorio T. MANGLONA
88 Adjunct Assoc Dean TSS .... Dr. Michael L. CHAN
88 Pgm Spc Accomodative Svcs .... Ms. Kasinda C. LUDWIG

Pacific Islands University (C)

172 Kinneys Road, Mangilao GU 96913

County: Guam FICE Identification: 034383
Unit ID: 439862
Telephone: (671) 734-1812 Carnegie Class: Spec/Faith
FAX Number: (671) 734-1813 Calendar System: Semester
URL: piu.edu
Established: 1976 Annual Undergrad Tuition & Fees: $12,130
Enrollment: 85 Coed
Affiliation or Control: Independent Non-Profit IRS Status: 501(c)3
Highest Offering: Master's
Program: Liberal Arts And General; Religious Emphasis
Accreditation: TRACS

01 President/CEO .... Dr. David L. OWEN
05 Academic Vice President .... Dr. Cristel WOOD
10 Vice President of Administration .... Mr. Nino PATE
20 Dean of the Seminary .... Vacant
44 VP of Advancement .... Vacant
32 Vice President of Student Life .... Mr. Robert WATT
08 Librarian .... Ms. Lisa COLLINS
06 Registrar .... Ms. Urte SCHERER

University of Guam (D)

UOG Station, Mangilao GU 96923-1800

County: Guam FICE Identification: 003935
Unit ID: 240754
Telephone: (671) 735-2990 Carnegie Class: Master's S
FAX Number: (671) 734-2296 Calendar System: Semester
URL: www.uog.edu
Established: 1952 Annual Undergrad Tuition & Fees (In-State): $5,058
Enrollment: 3,639 Coed
Affiliation or Control: State IRS Status: 501(c)3
Highest Offering: Master's
Program: Occupational; Liberal Arts And General; Teacher Preparatory; Professional
Accreditation: WC, IACBE, NUR, SW, TED

01 President .... Dr. Robert A. UNDERWOOD
05 Sr VP Academic & Student Affairs .... Dr. Helen J D. WHIPPY
10 Vice Pres Administration & Finance .... Mr. David M. O'BRIEN
58 AVP Graduate Studies/Research & SP .... Dr. John A. PETERSON
43 University Legal Counsel .... Ms. Victorina M Y. RENACIA
88 Institutional Compliance Officer .... Ms. Elaine FACULO-GOGUE
04 Executive Assistant to President .... Ms. Louise M. TOVES
26 Director Integrated Mktg Comm .... Ms. Cathleen MOORE-LINN
45 Chief Planning Officer .... Mr. David S. OKADA
29 Director Dev & Alumni Affairs .... Mr. Norman ANALISTA
102 Exec. Director Endowment Foundation .... Mr. Mark B. MENDIOLA
88 Dir Academic Assess/Inst Research .... Ms. Deborah D. LEON GUERRERO
49 Dean Col of Lib Arts & Social Sci .... Dr. James D. SELLMANN
47 Dean Col of Natural & Applied Sci .... Dr. Lee S. YUDIN
50 Dean Sch Bus & Pub Admin .... Dr. Anita B. ENRIQUEZ
53 Actg Dean School of Education .... Dr. Patrick LEDDY
66 Actg Dir Sch of Nursing & Hlth Sci .... Ms. Kathryn WOOD
84 Dean Enroll Mgmt & Student Services .... Dr. Julie ULLOA-HEATH
06 Registrar .... Ms. Remy B. CRISTOBAL
37 Director Financial Aid .... Mr. Mark A. DUARTE
32 Student Life Officer .... Ms. Sallie MCDONALD
88 Director Guam CEDDERS .... Dr. Heidi E. SAN NICOLAS
08 Director Learning Resources .... Ms. Christine K. SCOTT-SMITH
14 Dir Info Tech Resource/Computer Ctr .... Dr. Luan P. NGUYEN
88 Director Micronesia Area Res Center .... Dr. John A. PETERSON
88 Director Marine Laboratory .... Dr. Laurie RAYMUNDO
88 Dir Watr Env Rsrch Inst Wstrn Pac .... Dr. Gary R W. DENTON
88 Dir Ctr for Island Sustainability .... Dr. Frank CAMACHO
51 Actg Dir Prof/International Pgm .... Mr. Larry G. GAMBOA
88 Director TRIO Programs .... Mr. Yoichi K. RENGIIL
15 Actg Chief Human Resources Officer .... Ms. Elaine FACULO-GOGUE
18 Chief Plant Fac Ofcr Fac & Util .... Mr. Sonny P. PEREZ
41 Field House/Athletics Director .... Mr. Bob O. PELKEY
19 Chief of Safety .... Mr. William PALOMO
40 Director Bookstore & Auxillary Svcs .... Ms. Ann S.A. LEON GUERRERO
21 Comptroller .... Ms. Zeny ASUNCION-NACE

MARSHALL ISLANDS

College of the Marshall Islands (E)

PO Box 1258, Majuro MH 96960-1258

County: Marshalls FICE Identification: 030224
Unit ID: 376695
Telephone: (692) 625-5427 Carnegie Class: Assoc/Pub-R-S
FAX Number: (692) 625-7203 Calendar System: Semester
URL: www.cmi.edu
Established: 1989 Annual Undergrad Tuition & Fees (In-State): $4,415
Enrollment: 869 Coed
Affiliation or Control: State IRS Status: 501(c)3
Highest Offering: Associate Degree
Program: 2-Year Principally Bachelor's Creditable
Accreditation: WJ

01 President .... Dr. Kenneth WOODBURY, JR.
05 VP Academic & Student Affairs .... Dr. Meg MALMBERG
11 Chief Administrative Officer .... Ms. Ellia SABLAN-ZEBEDY
20 Interim Dean of Academic Affairs .... Mr. Donald HESS
32 Dean Student & Community Services .... Mr. Kenson ALIK
46 Dean of Coop Research & Extension .... Ms. Diane C. MYAZOE
06 Registrar .... Ms. Monica GORDON
07 Director of Admissions & Records .... Ms. Rosita V. CAPELLE
08 Director of Library Services .... Mr. John PAGOLU
15 Human Resources Director .... Mr. Robert W. WILLSON
10 Comptroller/Chief Financial Officer .... Ms. Josie Rose O. CAJIPE
51 Director Continuing/Adult Education .... Ms. Tone HERKINOS
18 Director Physical Plant .... Mr. Tont PROUT
88 Dir Stdnt Support Svcs/Upward Bound .... Vacant
45 VP for Research & Planning .... Mr. James MULIK
13 Director Information & Technology .... Mr. Peter MACHWALENG
88 Director Nuclear Institute .... Ms. Mary L. SILK
53 Chair Education/Marshallese Stds .... Mr. Max VOELZKE
37 Financial Aid Director .... Ms. Jacinta SAMUEL
49 Chair Liberal Arts .... Ms. Janet HESS
50 Chair Business & IT .... Vacant
66 Chair Nursing .... Ms. Florence L. PETER
81 Chair Mathematics/Science .... Mr. Donald HESS
04 Special Assistant to the President .... Dr. Steve MALMBERG
19 Director Security/Safety .... Mr. Daved DEBRUM
38 Director of Student Engagement .... Ms. Rachel SALOMON
09 Director of Institutional Research .... Mr. Peter CAMMISH

NORTHERN MARIANAS

Northern Marianas College (F)

PO Box 501250, Saipan MP 96950-1250

FICE Identification: 030330
Unit ID: 240790
Telephone: (670) 234-5498 Carnegie Class: Bac/Assoc
FAX Number: (670) 234-0759 Calendar System: Semester
URL: www.nmcnet.edu
Established: 1976 Annual Undergrad Tuition & Fees (In-District): $3,820
Enrollment: 1,231 Coed
Affiliation or Control: State/Local IRS Status: 501(c)3
Highest Offering: Baccalaureate
Program: 2-Year Principally Bachelor's Creditable; Liberal Arts And General; Teacher Preparatory
Accreditation: WC, #WJ

01 President .... Dr. Sharon Y. HART
05 Dean of Academic Programs & Svcs .... Ms. Barbara K. MERFALEN
32 Dean of Student Services .... Mr. Leo PANGELINAN
31 Acting Dean Community Pgms & Svcs .... Mr. David J. ATTAO
10 Chief Financial & Admin Officer .... Mr. Rogelio L. MADRIAGA
13 Acg Dir of Information Technology .... Mr. Eric ABRAGAN
09 Dir Institutional Effectiveness .... Mr. Galvin S. DELEON GUERRERO
30 Director Institutional Advancement .... Mr. Frankie M. ELIPTICO
08 Director Library Services .... Mr. Matthew PASTULA
51 Director of Adult Basic Education .... Ms. Lorraine T. CABRERA
07 Director Admissions & Records .... Ms. Cynthia DELEON GUERRERO
38 Director of Counseling Services .... Dr. Timothy BAKER
06 Registrar .... Ms. Rosaline CEPEDA
37 Director of Financial Aid .... Ms. Daisy M. PROPST
96 Procurement Manager .... Ms. Anita C. CAMACHO
15 Human Resources Manager .... Mr. John F. MANALO
21 Chief Accountant .... Ms. Solita K. BARNES
36 Career Planning/Placement Coord .... Ms. Ana B. SANTOS
11 Facilities Manager .... Mr. John GUERRERO
18 Maintenance Manager .... Mr. George DAVID
26 Marketing Manager/Public Relations .... Mr. Frankie ELIPTICO
29 NMC Alumni Association .... Mr. Jack O. KIYOSHI

PALAU

Palau Community College (A)

PO Box 9, Koror PW 96940-0009

County: Koror FICE Identification: 011009
Unit ID: 243647
Telephone: (680) 488-2470 Carnegie Class: Assoc/Pub-R-S
FAX Number: (680) 488-2447 Calendar System: Semester
URL: www.palau.edu
Established: 1969 Annual Undergrad Tuition & Fees: $4,155
Enrollment: 694 Coed
Affiliation or Control: Federal IRS Status: Exempt
Highest Offering: Associate Degree
Program: Occupational; 2-Year Principally Bachelor's Creditable
Accreditation: WJ

01 President .... Dr. Patrick U. TELLEI
05 Vice President Education & Training .... Vacant
11 Vice Pres Administration & Finance .... Mr. Jay OLEGERIIL
46 Vice Pres Cooperative Rsrch/Exten .... Mr. Thomas TARO
04 Exec Assistant to the President .... Mr. Todd NGIRAMENGIOR
32 Dean of Students .... Mr. Sherman DANIEL
20 Dean of Academic Affairs .... Mr. Tutii CHILTON
51 Dean of Continuing Education .... Mr. William WALLY
30 Director of Development .... Ms. Alvina O. MARCIL
07 Director Admissions & Financial Aid .... Mrs. Dahlia M. KATOSANG
06 Registrar .... Ms. Lesley B. ADACHI
15 Director of Human Resources .... Mr. Jay OLEGERIIL
18 Director of Physical Plant .... Mr. Clement KAZUMA
13 Director of Computer Systems .... Mr. Bruce RIMIRCH
08 Librarian .... Ms. Jessica P. BROOKS
35 Director of Student Life .... Ms. Hilda NGIRALMAU
10 Chief Business Officer .... Ms. Lorenza JOSEPH
09 Institutional Researcher .... Ms. Ligaya SARA
38 Counselor .... Ms. Maurine ALEXANDER
38 Counselor .... Mr. Winfred RECHEIUNGEL
38 Counselor .... Ms. Glendalynn NGIRMERIIL
91 System Analyst .... Ms. Grace ALEXANDER
26 Public Relations Manager .... Ms. Adora NOBUO
40 Bookstore/Supply Supervisor .... Mr. Gibson TOWAI

PUERTO RICO

American University of Puerto Rico (B)

Box 2037, Bayamon PR 00960-2037

County: Bayamon FICE Identification: 011941
Unit ID: 241100
Telephone: (787) 620-2040 Carnegie Class: Bac/Diverse
FAX Number: (787) 785-7377 Calendar System: Other
URL: www.aupr.edu
Established: 1963 Annual Undergrad Tuition & Fees: $5,080
Enrollment: 3,334 Coed
Affiliation or Control: Independent Non-Profit IRS Status: 501(c)3
Highest Offering: Master's
Program: Liberal Arts And General; Teacher Preparatory; Business Emphasis
Accreditation: M

01 Acting President .... Prof. Juan C. NAZARIO-TORRES
05 Vice President Acad Student Affairs .... Dr. Consuelo CASTRO-MELENDEZ
10 Vice Pres Finance & Admin Affairs .... Mr. Juan C. NAZARIO-TORRES
32 Dean Student Affairs .... Prof. Tamara FELIX-RODRIGUEZ
06 Registrar .... Prof. Maria RODRIGUEZ-PAZ
07 Admissions Officer .... Ms. Keren LLANOS
08 Learning Resources Center Director .... Mrs. Doris ROBLES
35 Dir Student Affairs/Public Rels .... Mrs. Nereida CRISTOBAL
37 Director Financial Aid .... Mrs. Yahaira MELENDEZ
21 Director Accounting .... Mrs. Magda CANCEL
38 Director Guidance Counseling .... Mrs. Luz S. HERNANDEZ
24 Director Educational Media .... Ms. Carol SANTIAGO
41 Athletic Director .... Mr. Manfredo VEGA
14 Director Computer Center .... Mr. Juan L. RIVERA
15 Director Personnel Services .... Mrs. Lillian BELEN-NAZARIO
12 Director Bayamon Campus .... Dr. Josephine RESTO-OLIVO
12 Director Manati Campus .... Prof. Rosa RODRIGUEZ
09 Dir Research/Institutional Planning .... Vacant
18 Chief Facilities/Physical Plant .... Mr. Efrain LUGO
36 Director of Student Placement .... Vacant
84 Director Enrollment Management .... Mrs. Mariela CRUZ
96 Director of Purchasing .... Mrs. Celeste TRAVERSO
92 Director of Honors Program .... Prof. Claribel RODRIGUEZ
30 Chief Development .... Mr. Jaime GONZALEZ
20 Associate Academic Officer .... Prof. Milagros RIVERA
14 Director Acad Computer Center .... Mr. Jorge TORRES-VARGAS
53 Dept Chair School of Education .... Dr. Jose RAMIREZ
50 Dept Chair Business Admin/Sec Sci .... Prof. Norma ORTIZ
49 Department Chair Arts & Sciences .... Prof. Carmen T. LANDRON

Atenas College (C)

101 Paseo de las Atenas, Manati PR 00674

FICE Identification: 035443
Unit ID: 440651
Telephone: (787) 884-3838 Carnegie Class: Not Classified
FAX Number: (787) 884-6754 Calendar System: Semester
URL: www.atenascollege.edu
Established: 1996 Annual Undergrad Tuition & Fees: $4,898
Enrollment: 1,395 Coed
Affiliation or Control: Independent Non-Profit IRS Status: 501(c)3
Highest Offering: Baccalaureate
Program: Liberal Arts And General
Accreditation: ACCSC

01 President .... Ms. Maria L. HERNANDEZ NUNEZ

Atlantic College (D)

9 Colton and Tapia Street, Guaynabo PR 00969

County: Guaynabo FICE Identification: 025054
Unit ID: 241216
Telephone: (787) 720-1022 Carnegie Class: Bac/Diverse
FAX Number: (787) 720-1092 Calendar System: Quarter
URL: www.atlanticcollege.edu
Established: 1983 Annual Undergrad Tuition & Fees: $6,255
Enrollment: 1,318 Coed
Affiliation or Control: Independent Non-Profit IRS Status: 501(c)3
Highest Offering: Baccalaureate
Program: 2-Year Principally Bachelor's Creditable; Liberal Arts And General; Professional
Accreditation: ACICS

01 President .... Dr. Teresa DE DIOS-UNANUE
11 Dean of Administration .... Prof. Heriberto MARTINEZ-ABREU
05 Dean of Academics .... Prof. Ivette CARBONELL
26 Dean of Technology & Marketing .... Prof. Heriberto MARTINEZ-DE DIOS
81 Dean of Science and Digital Arts .... Prof. Frances GRAU
06 Registrar .... Ms. Edna I. GUTIERREZ
38 Dir Student Counseling/ Placement .... Mrs. Maria C. LOPEZ-CEPERO
37 Director Financial Aid .... Mrs. Janice RIVERA
08 Head Librarian .... Mrs. Tania DÍAZ
07 Officer of Admissions .... Mrs. Margarita FIGUEROA
21 Bursar's Officer .... Mrs. María del C MONTESINO
15 Officer of Personnel Services .... Mrs. Urania GONZALEZ

Bayamon Central University (E)

PO Box 1725, Bayamon PR 00960-1725

County: Bayamon FICE Identification: 005022
Unit ID: 241225
Telephone: (787) 786-3030 Carnegie Class: Master's M
FAX Number: (787) 740-2200 Calendar System: Semester
URL: www.ucb.edu.pr
Established: 1961 Annual Undergrad Tuition & Fees: $8,140
Enrollment: 2,479 Coed
Affiliation or Control: Roman Catholic IRS Status: 501(c)3
Highest Offering: Master's
Program: Liberal Arts And General; Teacher Preparatory; Professional
Accreditation: M, CORE, @TEAC

01 President .... Dr. Lillian NEGRON
05 Academic Dean .... Dr. Pura ECHANDI
11 Administrative Dean .... Mrs. Rosimar FERRER
32 Dean of Students .... Mrs. Niza ZAYAS
49 Dir College Liberal Arts/Science .... Dr. Oscar CRUZ
53 Dir Col of Education and Behaviora .... Dr. Caroline GONZALEZ
50 Dir Business Development & Tech .... Prof. Nidia COLON
08 Director Learning Resources .... Mrs. Annette VALENTIN
15 Director of Human Resources .... Mrs. Elaine NUNEZ
30 Director Institutional Development .... Mr. Pedro BERMUDEZ
07 Director of Admissions .... Mrs. Christine HERNANDEZ
37 Director Student Financial Aid .... Mrs. Edna ORTIZ
38 Director Guidance Center .... Mrs. Milagros M. RIVERA
06 Registrar .... Mr. Victor COLON
35 Director Transition Services (STAE) .... Mrs. Myrna PEREZ
90 Dir Center for Faculty Development .... Mr. Jorge DIAZ
68 Director of Sports Facilities .... Mr. Edwin MORALES
13 Director of Information System .... Mr. William FRATICELLI
18 Director Physical Facilities .... Eng. Eliezer GARCIA
26 Public Relations Officer .... Mrs. Niza ZAYAS
96 Purchase Officer .... Mrs. Jessica OJEDA
09 Specialist Institutional Research .... Vacant
66 Nursing Program Coordinator .... Prof. Floridalia VIDAL
20 Associate Academic Dean .... Dr. Luz C. VALENTIN
29 Alumni Relations .... Prof. Josean FELICIANO
84 Director Enrollment Management .... Mrs. Cristine HERNANDEZ

Caribbean University (F)

Box 493, Bayamon PR 00960-0493

County: Bayamon FICE Identification: 012525
Unit ID: 241377
Telephone: (787) 780-0070 Carnegie Class: Master's M
FAX Number: (787) 785-0101 Calendar System: Semester
URL: www.caribbean.edu
Established: 1969 Annual Undergrad Tuition & Fees: $4,470
Enrollment: 1,892 Coed
Affiliation or Control: Independent Non-Profit IRS Status: 501(c)3
Highest Offering: Master's
Program: Liberal Arts And General; Teacher Preparatory
Accreditation: #M, @TEAC

01 President/CEO .... Dr. Ana E. CUCURELLA-ADORNO
03 Executive Director .... Mr. Victor T. ADORNO
05 Vice President of Academic Affairs .... Dr. Carlos BONET
45 Vice President of Planning and Info .... Mr. Jorge RIEFKOHL
11 Dean Administration Affairs .... Mr. Israel RODRIGUEZ
32 Dean Student Affairs .... Mr. Javier DELGADO
13 IT Director .... Mr. Luis RODRIGUEZ
15 Human Resources Director .... Mrs. Lourdes LUACES
37 Director Student Financial Aid .... Mrs. Anna SANCHEZ
06 Registrar .... Mrs. Kendra ORTIZ
08 Librarian/Director Audio-Visual .... Mrs. Carmen L. APONTE
36 Director Student Placement .... Mrs. Jannett TORRES
07 Director of Admissions .... Dr. Ida ALVARADO
12 Director of Carolina Campus .... Prof. Glorimary CRUZ
12 Director of Ponce Campus .... Dr. Marta HERNANDEZ
12 Director Vega Baja Campus .... Ms. Lilliam MATOS
20 Provost .... Dr. Luis MOJICA
71 Director Special Service Program .... Mrs. Maryliz AUBRET
26 Public Relations Director .... Mr. Gabriel VELEZ SUAU
49 Director Department Arts/Science .... Ms. Maria COLON
50 Director Dept Business Admin/Sec Sc .... Dra. Denise COBIAN
76 Health Services .... Ms. Mara MEDINA
54 Director Department of Engineering .... Dr. Orlando CUNDUMI
66 Director Department of Nursing .... Dr. Mariluz MARRERO
53 Director Department Education .... Prof. Nydia PAGAN
77 Director of Computer Science .... Ms. Maria COLON
35 Associate Dean Student Affairs .... Mrs. Virginia MEDINA
18 Chief Facilities/Physical Plant .... Mr. Angel LUGO
43 Legal Advisor .... Mr. Rafael SANTIAGO
38 Director Student Counseling .... Dr. Ida Y. ALVARADO
41 Athletic Director .... Mr. Jaime VAZQUEZ
58 Asst Dean Graduate Studies .... Dr. Duay RIVERA
22 Director of Compliance .... Mrs. Elena GARCIA
27 Marketing Director .... Mr. Ricardo NIEVES
84 Director Enrollment Management .... Mrs. Emmeline LOPEZ

Carlos Albizu University (G)

Box 9023711, San Juan PR 00902-3711

County: San Juan FICE Identification: 010724
Unit ID: 241331
Telephone: (787) 725-6500 Carnegie Class: Spec/Health
FAX Number: (787) 721-7187 Calendar System: Semester
URL: www.albizu.edu
Established: 1966 Annual Undergrad Tuition & Fees: $4,790
Enrollment: 909 Coed
Affiliation or Control: Independent Non-Profit IRS Status: 501(c)3
Highest Offering: Doctorate
Program: Professional
Accreditation: M, CLPSY

00 President Board of Trustees .... Dr. Jorge GONZALEZ
01 President .... Dr. Ileana RODRIGUEZ-GARCIA
12 Chancellor of San Juan Campus .... Dr. Jose J. CABIYA-MORALES
12 Int Chancellor of Miami Campus .... Dr. Carmen ROCA
11 Spec Asst to Chanc for Admin Affs .... Mr. Luis ECHEGARAY
05 Spec Asst to Chanc for Acad Affs .... Dr. Jaime VERAY
88 Special Assistant to Vice President .... Ms. Sylvia LOPEZ
10 Director of Finance .... Mrs. Maria FIGUEROA
07 Dir Student Services & Admissions .... Mr. Carlos RODRIGUEZ-IRIZARRY
46 Director Research Training .... Dr. Lymaries PADILLA-COTTO
88 Director General Psychology Program .... Dr. Jaime VERAY
51 Director Continuing Education Ofc .... Mrs. Constancia RAMOS-ROMAN
88 Director Internship .... Dr. Aida GARCIA
37 Director Student Financial Aid .... Mrs. Doris QUERO-MENDEZ
08 Librarian .... Ms. Yolanda ROSARIO-ROSARIO
06 Registrar .... Mr. Victor BONILLA-RODRIGUEZ
88 Dir Industrial/Org Psych Program .... Dr. Miguel MARTINEZ-LUGO
13 Information Technology Director .... Mr. Hugo SOLANO
88 Administrator Community Svcs Clinic .... Mr. Rafael ORTIZ
31 Director Community Services Clinic .... Dr. Jose RODRIGUEZ-QUINONES
88 Director PhD Clinical Program .... Dr. Sean SAYERS
88 Dir PsyD Clinical Psychology Pgm .... Dr. Gladys ALTIERI-RAMIREZ
15 Director of Human Resources .... Mrs. Carmen ACEVEDO-RIOS
30 Director Development .... Ms. Angeles PEREZ-TORO
88 Director Clinical Training .... Dr. Noel QUINTERO-JIMENEZ
88 Director Bachelor's Program .... Dr. Jaime VERAY
38 President Student Counseling .... Mr. Ricardo DEL RIO-MORALES
18 Chief Facilities/Physical Plant .... Mr. John FERNANDEZ
26 Public Relations Officer .... Rochely ESCALANTE
29 Director Alumni Relations .... Ms. Angeles PEREZ

Center for Advanced Studies On Puerto Rico and the Caribbean (H)

PO Box 902-3970, Old San Juan PR 00902-3970

County: San Juan FICE Identification: 021660
Unit ID: 241793
Telephone: (787) 723-4481 Carnegie Class: Spec/Other
FAX Number: (787) 723-4810 Calendar System: Semester
URL: www.ceaprc.edu
Established: 1976 Annual Graduate Tuition & Fees: $4,000
Enrollment: 500 Coed
Affiliation or Control: Independent Non-Profit IRS Status: 501(c)3
Highest Offering: Doctorate; No Undergraduates
Program: Professional; Fine Arts Emphasis
Accreditation: M

01 Chancellor .... Mr. Miguel A. RODRIGUEZ-LOPEZ
05 Academic Dean .... Dr. Jaime L. RODRIGUEZ-CANCEL
06 Registrar .... Mrs. Mayra I. RAMIREZ
08 Head Librarian .... Mr. Francis J. MOJICA

10 Administration Dean ....Mrs. Lizzette CARRILLO
04 Chancellor's Assistant ....Ms. Clarissa SANTIAGO-TORO
07 Admissions and Marketing Officer ......Mrs. Monica D. GONZALEZ
37 Financial Aid Officer ....Mrs. Lillian M. OLIVER

Centro de Estudios Multidisciplinarios (A)

Calle 13 #1206, Ext San Agustin, Rio Piedras PR 00926
County: San Juan FICE Identification: 021891
Unit ID: 241517
Telephone: (787) 765-4210 Carnegie Class: Assoc/PrivNFP
FAX Number: (787) 765-4277 Calendar System: Semester
URL: www.cempr.edu
Established: 1980 Annual Undergrad Tuition & Fees: $10,000
Enrollment: 1,367 Coed
Affiliation or Control: Independent Non-Profit IRS Status: 501(c)3
Highest Offering: Baccalaureate
Program: Occupational; 2-Year Principally Bachelor's Creditable; Nursing Emphasis
Accreditation: ACCSC

01 President ....Mr. Juan C. PAGANI-SOTO
05 Academic Dean ....Dr. Nereida NALES
07 Director of Admissions ....Mr. Juan RESTO TORRES
06 Registrar ....Mrs. Margarita RIVERA
10 Finance Director ....Mr. Carlos RODRIGUEZ
12 Branch Director ....Mrs. Laura M. DELGADO
15 Human Resources Director ......Mrs. Lilliana M. LOPEZ-MEDERO

Colegio Biblico Pentecostal De Puerto Rico (B)

PO Box 901, Saint Just PR 00978-0901
County: Trujillo Alto FICE Identification: 023355
Unit ID: 241614
Telephone: (787) 761-0808 Carnegie Class: Spec/Faith
FAX Number: (787) 748-9220 Calendar System: Semester
URL: www.cbp.edu
Established: 1956 Annual Undergrad Tuition & Fees: $3,150
Enrollment: 262 Coed
Affiliation or Control: Church Of God IRS Status: 501(c)3
Highest Offering: Baccalaureate
Program: Religious Emphasis
Accreditation: BI

01 President ....Francisco ORTIZ
05 Academic Dean ....Jenniffer E. CORITRERA
06 Registrar ....Caroline FIGAROA
10 Director of Finances ....Angel LAVOY
32 Dean of Students ....Javier SALGADO
37 Financial Aid Director ....Miriam JUARBE
08 Librarian ....Leticia SOSA

Colegio de las Ciencias Artes y Television (C)

51 Dr. Veve St, Degutau St Corner, Bayamon PR 00960
County: Bayamon FICE Identification: 031576
Unit ID: 430935
Telephone: (787) 779-2500 Carnegie Class: Assoc/PrivFP
FAX Number: (787) 995-2525 Calendar System: Semester
URL: ccat.edu
Established: 1993 Annual Undergrad Tuition & Fees: $5,995
Enrollment: 488 Coed
Affiliation or Control: Proprietary IRS Status: Proprietary
Highest Offering: Associate Degree
Program: Occupational
Accreditation: ACCSC

01 President ....Mr. Jorge GARCIA

Colegio Universitario de San Juan (D)

180 Jose R. Oliver Street, San Juan PR 00918
County: San Juan FICE Identification: 010567
Unit ID: 241720
Telephone: (787) 480-2379 Carnegie Class: Bac/Assoc
FAX Number: (787) 250-7395 Calendar System: Semester
URL: www.cunisanjuan.edu
Established: 1972 Annual Undergrad Tuition & Fees (In-District): $2,950
Enrollment: 1,720 Coed
Affiliation or Control: Local IRS Status: 501(c)3
Highest Offering: Baccalaureate
Program: Occupational; 2-Year Principally Bachelor's Creditable
Accreditation: M, ADNUR

01 Acting Chancellor ....Ms. Deborah DRAHUS-CAPO
45 Dir Planning/Inst Research/Ext Rels ....Mrs. Haydee ZAYAS
04 Administrative Asst to the Chanc ....Prof. Omar RIVERA
10 Acting Dean Administrative Affairs ....Mr. Cruz CORRALIZA-TORRES
05 Dean Academic Affairs ....Ms. Mercy FALERO
32 Dean Student Affairs ....Mrs. Virgen PAGAN
06 Registrar ....Mrs. Kennia SANTOS
08 Head Librarian ....Mrs. Sheila VERA
84 Director of Enrollment Management ....Mr. Victor RIVERA
07 Director of Admissions ....Mrs. Sandra RIVERA
38 Counselor ....Mrs. Mara MALAVE
37 Director Student Financial Aid ....Ms. Gloria MIRABAL
13 Director Info Systems/Telecomm ....Mr. Zacarias POURIET
50 Director Business Administration . Ms. Marie A. OLIVER TORRES
51 Dir Continuing Educ/Extension Pgm ....Vacant
55 Director of Evening Division ....Mr. Jose Luis ROMAN
76 Director Health Related Science ....Prof. Luz D. ORTEGA
72 Manager Science & Technology ....Prof. Ramon RIVERA
97 Manager General Education ....Ms. Carmen J. RODRIGUEZ
09 Coordinator Institutional Research ....Prof. Ailin MARTINEZ
15 Analyst Human Resources ....Ms. Jocely TORRES
36 Student Placement Officer ....Ms. Rosa AQUINO
66 Nursing Program Coordinator ....Prof. Brunilda ROMAN

Columbia Centro Universitario (E)

PO Box 8517, Caguas PR 00726-8517
County: Caguas FICE Identification: 008902
Unit ID: 241304
Telephone: (787) 743-4041 Carnegie Class: Master's S
FAX Number: (787) 746-5616 Calendar System: Semester
URL: www.columbiaco.edu
Established: 1966 Annual Undergrad Tuition & Fees: $9,435
Enrollment: 1,551 Coed
Affiliation or Control: Proprietary IRS Status: Proprietary
Highest Offering: Master's
Program: Business Emphasis
Accreditation: M

01 President ....Mr. Alex A. DEJORGE
05 VP Academic Affairs ....Mrs. Carmen J. LOPEZ
03 Senior VP of Operations ....Mrs. Carmen M. RIVERA
10 VP Finance and Administration ....Mrs. Daritza MULERO
32 VP Student Affairs ....Mrs. Brendaliz ZAYAS
26 VP Marketing and Communication ....Ms. Ana R. BURGOS
12 Chancellor of Caguas Campus ....Mr. Alex R. DEJORGE
12 Chancellor of Yauco Branch ....Ms. Rosario PADILLA
35 Dean Student Affairs ....Mr. Luis LOPEZ
20 Dean Academic Affairs ....Mrs. Myrna TORRES
08 Institutional Librarian ....Ms. Luz NEGRON
11 Administrative Support Director ....Ms. Carmen I. ROJAS
37 Financial Aid Director ....Mrs. Virginia GUANG
07 Director of Admissions ....Mrs. Xiomara SANCHEZ
06 Registrar ....Ms. Wilmarie TORRES
38 Student Counselor ....Ms. Ingrid CARRION
15 Director Human Resources ....Ms. Elsie M. TORRES
36 Director Student Placement ....Ms. Iris TIZOL
18 Facilities & Development Director ....Mr. Jesus M. RIVERA

Columbia Centro Universitario (F)

Box 3062, Yauco PR 00698-3062
County: Yauco Identification: 666036
Unit ID: 404806
Telephone: (787) 856-0845 Carnegie Class: Spec/Health
FAX Number: (787) 267-2335 Calendar System: Semester
URL: www.columbiaco.edu
Established: 1986 Annual Undergrad Tuition & Fees: $6,050
Enrollment: 553 Coed
Affiliation or Control: Proprietary IRS Status: Proprietary
Highest Offering: Baccalaureate
Program: Occupational; Nursing Emphasis
Accreditation: &M

01 Director ....Mrs. Rosario PADILLA

† Regional accreditation is carried under the parent institution in Caguas, PR.

Conservatory of Music of Puerto Rico (G)

951 Ponce de Leon Ave. Miramar, Santurce PR 00907
County: San Juan FICE Identification: 010819
Unit ID: 241766
Telephone: (787) 751-0160 Carnegie Class: Spec/Arts
FAX Number: (787) 758-8268 Calendar System: Semester
URL: www.cmpr.edu
Established: 1959 Annual Undergrad Tuition & Fees (In-State): $3,730
Enrollment: 441 Coed
Affiliation or Control: State IRS Status: 501(c)3
Highest Offering: Master's
Program: Music Emphasis
Accreditation: M

01 Chancellor ....Prof. Maria DEL CARMEN GIL
05 Dean of Academic Affairs ....Ms. Melanie SANTANA
11 Dean of Administration ....Mr. Juan Carlos HERNANDEZ
32 Dean Student Affairs/Financial Aid ......Mr. Michael RAJABALLEY
88 Dean of Preparatory School ....Mr. Germán CESPEDES
07 Director of Admissions ....Vacant
08 Librarian ....Mrs. Damaris CORDERO
20 Associate Dean of Studies ....Mr. Brian COLE
30 Development & Public Relations Dir ....Ms. Lissette GONZÁLEZ
15 Human Resources Director ....Ms. Alba DÁNILA
38 Counselor ....Mrs. Pilar RUIBAL

Dominican Study Center of the Caribbean (H)

PO Box 1968, Bayamon PR 00960-1968
County: Bayamon Identification: 666337
Telephone: (787) 787-1826 Carnegie Class: Not Classified
FAX Number: (787) 798-2712 Calendar System: Semester
URL: www.cedoc.edu
Established: 1980 Annual Undergrad Tuition & Fees: $5,100
Enrollment: 70 Coed
Affiliation or Control: Independent Non-Profit IRS Status: 501(c)3
Highest Offering: Master's
Program: Religious Emphasis
Accreditation: THEOL

01 Dean ....Rev Dr. Yamil A. SAMALOT-RIVERA, OP
05 Associate Dean ....Dr. Oscar CRUZ-CUEVAS

EDIC College (I)

PO Box 9120, Caguas PR 00726-9120
County: Caguas FICE Identification: 030219
Unit ID: 376321
Telephone: (787) 744-8519 Carnegie Class: Assoc/PrivFP
FAX Number: (787) 743-0855 Calendar System: Semester
URL: www.ediccollege.com
Established: 1987 Annual Undergrad Tuition & Fees: $6,350
Enrollment: 972 Coed
Affiliation or Control: Proprietary IRS Status: Proprietary
Highest Offering: Associate Degree
Program: Occupational
Accreditation: ACICS

01 President ....Mr. Jose A. CARTAGENA
05 Academic Dean ....Mrs. Loida R. RAMIREZ
11 Administrator ....Mrs. Milagros CARTAGENA

EDP College of Puerto Rico (J)

PO Box 192303, San Juan PR 00919-2303
County: San Juan FICE Identification: 021651
Unit ID: 243832
Telephone: (787) 765-3560 Carnegie Class: Bac/Diverse
FAX Number: (787) 777-0025 Calendar System: Semester
URL: www.edpcollege.edu
Established: 1968 Annual Undergrad Tuition & Fees: $5,900
Enrollment: 1,079 Coed
Affiliation or Control: Proprietary IRS Status: Proprietary
Highest Offering: Master's
Program: Occupational; Business Emphasis
Accreditation: M

01 President ....Mrs. Gladys T. NIEVES
00 Chancellor ....Dr. Elsa RODRIGUEZ
10 Vice President Finance ....Mr. Luis RIVERA
09 VP Institutional/International Rels ....Dr. Marilyn PASTRANA
05 VP Academic Planning and Inst Dev ....Dr. Rosa H. ALICEA
13 VP Technology/Distance Education ....Prof. Mayra RIVERA
14 Inst Information Systems Dir ....Mr. Angel RIVERA
06 Registrar ....Mrs. Glenda RODRIGUEZ
08 Librarian ....Mrs. Igrí ENRIQUEZ
21 Finance Dean ....Mrs. Marie Luz PASTRANA
32 Student Services Dean ....Dr. Leila M. ANDINO
18 Director Facilities/Physical Plant ....Mr. Jorge RAMOS
88 Director of CaSa ....Mrs. Maria COLON
07 Director of Admissions ....Mrs. Enid CARTAGENA

EDP College of Puerto Rico (K)

PO Box 1674, 49 Betances Street, San Sebastian PR 00685-1674
County: San Sebastian Identification: 666488
Unit ID: 241836
Telephone: (787) 896-2137 Carnegie Class: Bac/Diverse
FAX Number: (787) 896-0066 Calendar System: Semester
URL: www.edpcollege.edu
Established: 1978 Annual Undergrad Tuition & Fees: $5,520
Enrollment: 1,012 Coed
Affiliation or Control: Proprietary IRS Status: Proprietary
Highest Offering: Baccalaureate
Program: Occupational; Nursing Emphasis
Accreditation: &M

01 President ....Ing. Gladys NIEVES VAZQUEZ
03 Vice Pres for International Affs ....Dra. Marilyn PASTRANA MURIEL
12 Chancellor ....Dra. Melba RIVERA DELGADO
13 Technology Director ....Prof. Angel F. RIVERA BAEZ
09 Data Base Administrator ....Prof. Veronica RIVERA MOLINA
88 Assc Dir Stdnt & Acad Affair Virtua ....Mrs. Carmen QUINTANA HERNANDEZ
14 Computer Center Director ....Prof. Jose A. ARCE COLON
05 Academic Affairs Dean ....Prof. Juan AVILES FONT
50 Acad Area Director - Administration ....Prof. Noelia JIMENEZ
97 Acad Area Director - Art & Gen Educ ....Prof. Aracelia SOTO MENDEZ
66 Acad Area Director - Nursing ....Prof. Carmen ROSA ARCE
76 Acad Area Director - Health ....Prof. Lilliam ALERS SOTO
32 Student Affairs Dean ....Prof. Mildred QUINONES VELEZ
35 Acad & Stdnt Activities Coordinate ....Mrs. Pilar CORDERO DE VIDAL
46 Assoc Dean Institutional Develop ... Prof. Nydia N. RIVERA-VERA
38 Counselor ....Prof. Maria E. DELGADO ALTIERI
08 Librarian ....Prof. Marisol GIRAUD MEJIAS
26 Marketing & Promotion Director ....Mrs. Rosa E. GONZALEZ NIEVES
06 Registar ....Prof. Nydia T. MENDEZ VARGAS
37 Financial Aid Director ....Mrs. Luz E. RIVERA CRESPO

07 Assoc Director of CASA — Mrs. Zenaida OLAVARRIA RODRIGUEZ
106 Assc Dir Tech Devel & Dist Learning — Mrs. Ileana ORTIZ FLORES
88 Practice's Students Coordinator — Prof. Edith RAMIREZ HERNANDEZ
18 General Affairs Coordinator — Mr. Reinaldo MARIN CRESPO
88 Bursars Office Coordinator — Prof. Julio MENDEZ FERREIRA
15 Human Resources Officer — Mrs. Aurea TORRES SEGARRA

† Regional accreditation is carried under the parent institution in San Juan, PR.

Escuela de Artes Plasticas de Puerto Rico (A)

PO Box 9021112, San Juan PR 00902-1112

County: San Juan — FICE Identification: 025694
Unit ID: 241951
Telephone: (787) 725-8120 — Carnegie Class: Spec/Arts
FAX Number: (787) 725-8111 — Calendar System: Semester
URL: www.eap.edu
Established: 1966 — Annual Undergrad Tuition & Fees (In-State): $4,779
Enrollment: 522 — Coed
Affiliation or Control: State — IRS Status: 501(c)3
Highest Offering: Baccalaureate
Program: Liberal Arts And General; Teacher Preparatory; Fine Arts Emphasis
Accreditation: M, ART

01 Acting Chancellor — Dr. Loida E. RODRÍGUEZ SÁNCHEZ
11 Dean of Administration — Dr. Eduardo BERRIOS TORRES
05 Acting Dean Acad/Student Affairs — Dr. María M. VÁZQUEZ ANDINO
06 Registrar — Ms. Ileana MALDONADO
07 Officer of Admissions — Ms. Nitza MELÉNDEZ
13 Director Information Technology — Ms. Limaris SOTO
37 Director Student Financial Aid — Mr. Alfred DIAZ
36 Counselor Stdnt Affairs/Placement — Ms. Ivette MUÑOZ
45 Director of Planning Office — Mr. Carlos E. RIVERA
09 Assistant Institutional Research — Dr. Shirley A. TAVARES
10 Chief Financial Officer — Ms. Wanda CRUZ
18 Coord Facilities/Physical Plant — Mr. Edwin ALICEA
56 Coordinator Extension Program — Ms. Kyryhan M. RODRÍGUEZ RODRÍGUEZ
38 Counselor Stdnt Life/Counseling — Dr. Yadira ORTIZ COLÓN
88 Coordinator Cultural Activities — Mr. Adrián O. RIVERA NEGRÓN
105 Director Web Services — Mr. Celso E. PORTELA IRIGOYEN
96 Officer of Purchasing — Ms. Delia N. SÁNCHEZ BÁEZ
20 Asst Dean Acad/Student Affairs — Ms. Milagros LUGO AMADOR
15 Director Personnel Services — Vacant
28 Director of Projects — Prof. Haydeé VENEGAS ÁVILA
53 Director Education — Prof. Grisselle SOTO
97 Director General Studies — Prof. María BERRY
88 Director Fashion/Apparel Design — Prof. Ana COLORADO
88 Director Industrial/Product Design — Prof. Alfredo MONTALVO
88 Dir Design/Visual Communications — Prof. Luis BRIGANTTY
88 Director Painting — Prof. Ivelisse JIMÉNEZ
88 Director Sculpture — Prof. Adelino GONZÁLEZ VÉLEZ

Evangelical Seminary of Puerto Rico (B)

Ponce De Leon Avenue 776, San Juan PR 00925-2207

County: San Juan — FICE Identification: 006823
Unit ID: 243498
Telephone: (787) 763-6700 — Carnegie Class: Spec/Faith
FAX Number: (787) 751-0847 — Calendar System: Semester
URL: www.se-pr.edu
Established: 1919 — Annual Undergrad Tuition & Fees: $4,370
Enrollment: 233 — Coed
Affiliation or Control: Interdenominational — IRS Status: 501(c)3
Highest Offering: Doctorate
Program: Professional
Accreditation: M, THEOL

01 President — Dr. Sergio OJEDA-CARCAMO
05 Academic Dean/Chaplain — Dr. Jose R. IRIZARRY MERCADO
10 Director Administration & Finances — Ms. Myrna E. PEREZ-LOPEZ
06 Registrar — Miss Mari Lillian RIVERA
08 Head Librarian — Mrs. Sonia ARRILLAGA MONTALVO
30 Director of Development/Planning — Ms. Ruth M. DIAZ
37 Student Financial Aid — Ms. Lourdes JESUS CESAREO

Huertas Junior College (C)

PO Box 8429, Caguas PR 00726-8429

County: Caguas — FICE Identification: 022608
Unit ID: 242112
Telephone: (787) 746-1400 — Carnegie Class: Assoc/PrivFP
FAX Number: (787) 747-0170 — Calendar System: Semester
URL: www.huertas.edu
Established: 1945 — Annual Undergrad Tuition & Fees: $9,600
Enrollment: 1,853 — Coed
Affiliation or Control: Proprietary — IRS Status: Proprietary
Highest Offering: Associate Degree
Program: Occupational; 2-Year Principally Bachelor's Creditable; Technical Emphasis
Accreditation: M

01 President — Edwin RAMOS
03 Vice President — Maria del Mar LOPEZ
05 Dean of Academic Services — Ruben HERNANDEZ
06 Registrar — Krishna MARQUEZ
08 Head Librarian — Glenda PEREZ
10 Dean Administrative Fiscal Services — Camille LAMBOY
32 Dean of Student Services — Eva VEGA
38 Director Student Counseling — Marcelino COLON
88 Counselor — Evelyn COTTO
30 Planning and Development Director — Amarilys GARCIA
22 Compliance Officer — Raul HERNANDEZ
21 Director of Finance & Federal Funds — Celestino CRUZ
15 Human Resources — Sarai GONZALEZ

Humacao Community College (D)

PO Box 9139, Humacao PR 00792-9139

County: Humacao — FICE Identification: 023406
Unit ID: 242121
Telephone: (787) 852-1430 — Carnegie Class: Assoc/PrivNFP
FAX Number: (787) 850-1577 — Calendar System: Quarter
Established: 1978 — Annual Undergrad Tuition & Fees: $5,328
Enrollment: 610 — Coed
Affiliation or Control: Independent Non-Profit — IRS Status: 501(c)3
Highest Offering: Baccalaureate
Program: Occupational; Business Emphasis
Accreditation: ACICS

01 President — Lic. Jorge E. MOJICA
03 Executive Vice President — Prof. Aida E. RODRIGUEZ
05 Exec Director/Chief Academic Ofcr — Mrs. Gladys E. FLECHA
55 Director of Evening Session — Prof. Ada BAEZ
37 Director Student Financial Aid — Mrs. Cheryle PEREZ
36 Student Placement Officer — Mr. Luis GARCIA
07 Director Admissions — Vacant
06 Registrar — Mr. Israel LOPEZ
08 Head Librarian — Mrs. Lourdes ELIZA
10 Treasury Officer (Finance) — Mrs. Diana RODRIGUEZ
38 Student Counselor — Mr. Angel MORALES
11 Chief College Administrator — Mrs. Marianne BERRIOS
04 Adm Asst to Pres/Dir Personnel — Mrs. Nilda E. RODRIGUEZ

ICPR Junior College (E)

558 Munoz Rivera Avenue, Hato Rey PR 00919-0304

County: San Juan — FICE Identification: 011940
Unit ID: 243841
Telephone: (787) 753-6000 — Carnegie Class: Assoc/PrivFP
FAX Number: (787) 622-3416 — Calendar System: Semester
URL: www.icprjc.edu
Established: 1946 — Annual Undergrad Tuition & Fees: $9,495
Enrollment: 1,743 — Coed
Affiliation or Control: Proprietary — IRS Status: Proprietary
Highest Offering: Associate Degree
Program: Occupational; 2-Year Principally Bachelor's Creditable; Business Emphasis
Accreditation: M

01 President/Chief Executive Officer — Mrs. Olga RIVERA
05 Director Hato Rey Campus — Mrs. Maria de los M. RIVERA
20 Academic Coordinator Hato Rey — Mr. Josue CINTRON
06 Registrar Hato Rey — Mrs. María C. VELEZ
07 Director of Admissions Hato Rey — Mr. Ismael TAPIA
08 Librarian Hato Rey — Mrs. Lucy COLON
10 Chief Accounting/Finance Officer — Mr. Noel ORTIZ
37 Director Student Financial Aid — Mrs. Velma APONTE
38 Guidance Officer Hato Rey — Mrs. Yarelis COLON
12 Director Mayaguez Campus — Dr. Luz M. ORTIZ
20 Academic Coordinator Mayaguez — Dr. Mayra RUIZ
12 Director Arecibo Campus — Mrs. Ivette CHARRIEZ
20 Academic Coordinator Arecibo — Mrs. Edith RAMOS
06 Registrar Mayaguez — Mrs. Olga NEGRON
06 Registrar Arecibo — Mrs. Glenda PADIN
07 Director of Admissions Mayaguez — Mrs. Aracelis GASTON
07 Director of Admissions Arecibo — Mr. Eduardo SEDA
26 Director of Admissions & Marketing — Mr. Isander VELAZQUEZ
20 Director of Academic Affairs — Mrs. Maribel BAYONA
13 Information System Director — Mr. Nelson MEJIAS
08 Librarian Mayaguez — Mrs. Jessica CARO
08 Librarian Arecibo — Mrs. Irma JIMENEZ
38 Guidance Officer Mayaguez — Mrs. Barbarita CUMPIANO
38 Guidance Officer Arecibo — Mrs. Milagros AGUILAR
15 Human Resource Director — Mrs. Daisy CASTRO
88 Institutional Compliance Director — Mrs. Lizzette VARGAS
12 Campus Director Manati — Mr. Fernando GONZALEZ
20 Academic Coordinator Manati — Mrs. Maribel TORRES
38 Guidance Officer Manati — Mrs. Yetzayra LOPEZ
06 Registrar — Mrs. Vanessa TRINIDAD

*Inter American University of Puerto Rico Central Office (F)

GPO Box 363255, San Juan PR 00936-3255

County: San Juan — FICE Identification: 008242
Unit ID: 242671
Telephone: (787) 766-1912 — Carnegie Class: N/A
FAX Number: (787) 751-3375
URL: www.inter.edu

01 President — Mr. Manuel J. FERNOS
03 Exec Director President's Office — Mr. Tomas M. JIMENEZ
05 Vice Pres Academic Affairs/Planning — Mr. Agustin ECHEVARRIA
10 VP Financial Affairs/Services — Mr. Luis ESQUILIN
42 Vice President Religious Affairs — Rudo. Norberto DOMINGUEZ
20 Associate VP Academic Affairs — Dr. Rafael CABRERA
21 Assoc VP Financial Affairs/Services — Ms. Olga LUNA
32 Associate Vice Pres Student Affairs — Dr. Elba ENCARNACION
04 Exec Assistant to the President — Mrs. Sonnybel ZENO
26 Exec Dir Public Rels & Marketing — Ms. Rosa MELENDEZ
30 Executive Director Development — Mr. Eduardo LAMADRID
09 Exec Director Inst Research — Dr. Elizabeth SCALLEY
14 Director Information Management — Mrs. Jossie SALGUERO
43 Director Legal Services — Mrs. Lorraine JUARBE
43 Director Federal Legal Services — Mr. Vladimir ROMAN

*Inter American University of Puerto Rico Aguadilla Campus (G)

Box 20000, Aguadilla PR 00605-9001

County: Aguadilla — FICE Identification: 003939
Unit ID: 242626
Telephone: (787) 891-0925 — Carnegie Class: Master's S
FAX Number: (787) 882-3020 — Calendar System: Other
URL: www.aguadilla.inter.edu
Established: 1957 — Annual Undergrad Tuition & Fees: $5,578
Enrollment: 4,650 — Coed
Affiliation or Control: Independent Non-Profit — IRS Status: 501(c)3
Highest Offering: Master's
Program: Occupational; Liberal Arts And General; Teacher Preparatory; Professional
Accreditation: M, NUR, @TEAC

02 Chancellor — Dr. Elie AGESILAS
05 Dean of Studies — Prof. Nilsa M. ROMAN
32 Dean of Student Affairs — Mrs. Ana C. LAUSELL
13 Director Information and Technology — Mr. Asdrubal JIMENEZ
90 Information Systems Administrator — Mr. Jossue MORALES
11 Dean of Administrative Affairs — Mr. Israel AYALA
20 Associate Dean of Studies — Mrs. Marisol HILERIO
30 Development Director — Miss Sacha M. RUIZ
08 Library Director — Mrs. Monserrate YULFO
07 Admissions Director — Mrs. Doris PEREZ
06 Registrar — Mrs. Maria PEREZ
37 Financial Aid Director — Mrs. Gloria CORTES
21 Bursar — Mrs. Yanira GONZALEZ
16 Human Resources Director — Mr. Jose R. AREIZAGA
96 Purchasing Officer — Ms. Wanda VARGAS
35 Student Support Services Director — Mrs. Ivonne ACEVEDO
81 Director of Science and Technology — Prof. Rosa GONZALEZ
79 Director of Education & Hum Studies — Mrs. Ramonita ROSA
50 Director Economic Science & Admin — Prof. Elidine GONZALEZ
53 Dir of Social & Behavioral Sciences — Prof. Ricardo BADILLO
42 Chaplain — Mr. Francisco GONZALEZ
88 Director of Upward Bound Program — Ms. Mayra ROZADA
92 Dir Campus Learning Center Title V — Ms. Yamilette PROSPER
18 Dir Building Maintenance/Univ Guard — Mr. Jose CABAN
38 Director of Counseling Office — Ms. Gladys ACEVEDO
41 Sports Director — Ms. Yolanda PAGAN
84 Enrollment Manager — Prof. Myriam MARCIAL

*Inter American University of Puerto Rico Arecibo Campus (H)

PO Box 4050, Arecibo PR 00614-4050

County: Arecibo — FICE Identification: 005026
Unit ID: 242635
Telephone: (787) 878-5475 — Carnegie Class: Master's S
FAX Number: (787) 880-1624 — Calendar System: Semester
URL: www.arecibo.inter.edu
Established: 1957 — Annual Undergrad Tuition & Fees: $4,596
Enrollment: 5,340 — Coed
Affiliation or Control: Independent Non-Profit — IRS Status: 501(c)3
Highest Offering: Master's
Program: Occupational; Liberal Arts And General; Teacher Preparatory
Accreditation: M, ANEST, NUR, SW, @TEAC

02 Chancellor — Dr. Rafael RAMIREZ-RIVERA
05 Dean of Academic Affairs — Dr. Victor CONCEPCION
11 Dean of Administrative Affairs — Ms. Wanda PEREZ
32 Dean of Student Affairs — Prof. Ilvis AGUIRRE
20 Assoc Dean of Academic Affairs — Prof. Wanda BALSEIRO
08 Educational Resources Center Dir — Mrs. Sara ABREU
10 Bursar — Mr. Victor MALDONADO
37 Student Financial Aid Director — Mr. Ramon DE JESUS
06 Registrar — Mrs. Carmen RODRIGUEZ
07 Director of Admissions — Mrs. Provi MONTALVO
04 Executive Assistant to Chancellor — Mrs. Enid ARBELO
56 Distance Learning Director — Prof. Aida ALVAREZ
45 Planning Director — Mrs. Enid ARBELO
42 Religious Life Director — Mr. Amilcar SOTO
15 Personnel Director — Mrs. Maritza SANTOS
41 Athletic Department — Ms. Ileana MORALES
50 Director Econ & Adms Sciences Dept — Prof. Elba TORO
51 Continuing Education Director — Mrs. Mariel LLERANDI
53 Director of Education Department — Prof. Magda VAZQUEZ
66 Director of Nursing Department — Dr. Frances CORTES
79 Dir of Humanities Department — Prof. Maria L. DELGADO
81 Director of Sciences & Tech Dept — Prof. Hector PAGAN
83 Director of Social Sciences Dept — Prof. Lourdes CARRION
30 Development Director — Vacant
38 Director Student Counseling — Ms. Nydia DELGADO
14 Director of Computing Center — Mr. Jose SEGARRA
58 Director Graduate Program in Educ — Dra. Ramonita DIAZ
18 Chief Facilities/Physical Plant — Mr. Jose SANCHEZ

84 Director Enrollment Management ... Mrs. Carmen MONTALVO
88 Dir Graduate Program Anesthesia ... Prof. Josue RAMOS
96 Purchasing Officer ... Mrs. Sonia VILLAIZAN
92 Coordinator Honor Program ... Ms. Vilmaris VAZQUEZ

Inter American University of Puerto Rico Barranquitas Campus (A)

PO Box 517, Barranquitas PR 00794-0517

County: Barranquitas | FICE Identification: 005027 | Unit ID: 242644
Telephone: (787) 857-3600 | Carnegie Class: Bac/Diverse
FAX Number: (787) 857-2244 | Calendar System: Semester
URL: www.br.inter.edu
Established: 1957 | Annual Undergrad Tuition & Fees: $5,500
Enrollment: 2,217 | Coed
Affiliation or Control: Independent Non-Profit | IRS Status: 501(c)3
Highest Offering: Master's
Program: 2-Year Principally Bachelor's Creditable; Liberal Arts And General
Accreditation: M, @TEAC

02 Chancellor ... Dr. Irene FERNANDEZ
05 Dean Academic Affairs ... Dr. Patricia ALVAREZ
09 Director of Institutional Research ... Mr. Jose E. ORTIZ
10 Bursar Director ... Mr. Antonio J. ROSARIO
06 Registrar ... Mrs. Sandra MORALES
32 Dean Student Affairs ... Mrs. Aramilda CARTAGENA
11 Dean Administrative Affairs ... Mr. Jose E. ORTIZ-ZAYAS
08 Librarian ... Mrs. Clanbette RODRIGUEZ
38 Director Upward Bound Program ... Mrs. Saraliz GONZALEZ
84 Director Recruitment/Promotion ... Mrs. Ana Isabel COLON
37 Financial Aid Director ... Mr. Eduardo FONTANEZ
71 Adult Program Director ... Mrs. Lydia ARCE
07 Director of Admissions ... Mr. Edgardo CINTRON
53 Dir Education/Social Sci/Humanities ... Dr. Sifilonena CINTRON
81 Dir Natural Sciences/Technology ... Prof. Wilson LOZANO
88 Director Admin & Economics Sciences ... Prof. Carmen I. GONZALEZ
51 Director Continuing Education ... Mrs. Aixa SERRANO
29 Director Alumni Relations ... Mrs. Aramilda CARTAGENA
15 Director Personnel Services ... Mr. Victor SANTIAGO
30 Chief Development ... Dr. Patricia ALVAREZ
18 Chief Facilities/Physical Plant ... Mr. Jose E. ORTIZ-ZAYAS

*Inter American University of Puerto Rico Bayamon Campus (B)

500 Road 830, Bayamon PR 00957

County: Bayamon | FICE Identification: 005028 | Unit ID: 242705
Telephone: (787) 279-1912 | Carnegie Class: Bac/Diverse
FAX Number: (787) 279-2205 | Calendar System: Semester
URL: bayamon.inter.edu
Established: 1912 | Annual Undergrad Tuition & Fees: $4,596
Enrollment: 5,148 | Coed
Affiliation or Control: Independent Non-Profit | IRS Status: 501(c)3
Highest Offering: Master's
Program: Technical Emphasis
Accreditation: M, OPTR

02 Chancellor ... Prof. Juan F. MARTINEZ
11 Dean of Administration ... Mr. Luis M. CRUZ
32 Dean Student Affairs ... Mrs. Gema C. TORRES
06 Registrar ... Mr. Eddie AYALA
05 Dean of Studies ... Dr. Carlos OLIVARES
46 Dean of Research ... Dr. Armando RODRIGUEZ
88 Student Services Director ... Mr. Carlos ALICEA
08 Library Director ... Mrs. Sandra ROSA
88 Planning Office Coordinator ... Dr. Francisco N. MONTALVO
13 Systems Information Director ... Mr. Edwin RIVERA
15 Human Resources Director ... Mrs. Migdalia ORTIZ
88 Associate Administrative Officer ... Mr. Serafin RIVERA
26 Public Relations Officer ... Vacant
37 Financial Aid Director ... Vacant
41 Athletic Department Director ... Mr. Reynaldo ROLON
04 Assistant to Chancellor ... Mr. Antonio L. PANTOJA
18 Chief Facilities/Physical Plant ... Eng. Jose A. FUENTES
78 Educational Program Director ... Mrs. Maritza ZAMBRANA
81 Director Mathematics/Sciences ... Dr. Omar CUETO
38 Director Counseling Office ... Mrs. Magali PALMER
42 Director Religious Life Office ... Rvda. Carmen I. PEREZ
50 Dir Business Administration Dept ... Prof. Esther MOURE
75 Director Tech Institute ... Mrs. Liza FREYTES
88 Director Liberal Arts/Language Dept ... Prof. Laura RIOS
77 Director Computer Sciences Dept ... Prof. Jose RODRIGUEZ
21 Director Bursars Office ... Mrs. Lourdes ORTIZ
60 Director Communications Dept ... Prof. Ruth E. HERNANDEZ
88 Director Student Support Services ... Mrs. Zoraida CRUZ
88 President Academic Senate ... Prof. Maria J. VIZCARRONDO
35 Student Activities Director ... Mrs. Cybel BETANCOURT
23 Infirmary ... Mrs. Maria ROSADO
84 Director Enrollment Services ... Miss Ivette NIEVES
20 Associate Academic Officer ... Dra. Irma ALVARADO
36 Student Placement Coordinator ... Vacant
92 Honor Program Coordinator ... Mrs. Magaly PALMER
88 Budget Technician ... Miss Marta I. ACEVEDO
35 Student Affairs Assistant ... Mrs. Grace GOMEZ
09 Director of Institutional Research ... Vacant
29 Dir Alumni Relations/Devel Officer ... Mr. Jaime COLON
88 Dean School of Aeronautics ... Prof. Jorge CALAF
54 Dean School of Engineering ... Prof. Javier QUINTANA
55 Assoc Dean Studies II-Evening Pgm ... Vacant
54 Director Electrical Engr Dept ... Prof. Ruben FLORES
54 Director Industrial Engr Dept ... Dr. Heriberto BARRIERA
54 Director Mechanical Engr Dept ... Prof. Eduardo LAY
76 Director of Health Services ... Dra. Evelyn CROUCH

*Inter American University of Puerto Rico Fajardo Campus (C)

Call Box 70003, Fajardo PR 00738-7003

County: Fajardo | FICE Identification: 022828 | Unit ID: 242680
Telephone: (787) 863-2390 | Carnegie Class: Bac/Diverse
FAX Number: (787) 860-3470 | Calendar System: Semester
URL: fajardo.inter.edu
Established: 1960 | Annual Undergrad Tuition & Fees: $6,300
Enrollment: 2,357 | Coed
Affiliation or Control: Independent Non-Profit | IRS Status: 501(c)3
Highest Offering: Master's
Program: Liberal Arts And General; Fine Arts Emphasis
Accreditation: M, @SW, @TEAC

02 Chancellor ... Dr. Ismael SUAREZ-HERRERO
05 Dean Academic Affairs ... Dr. Paula SAGARDIA OLIVERAS
11 Dean Administrative Affairs ... Ms. Lydia E. SANTIAGO ROSADO
32 Dean for Student Affairs ... Ms. Hilda VELAZQUEZ
06 Registrar ... Mrs. Abigail RIVERA
07 Director of Admissions ... Mrs. Ada CARABALLO
37 Director Student Financial Aid ... Mrs. Marilyn MARTINEZ
08 Librarian ... Ms. Angie COLON
15 Director of Personnel Office ... Mrs. Maria A. RAMOS
09 Planning Director ... Ms. Hilda L. ORTIZ
41 Athletic Director ... Mr. Jose RUIZ
18 Physical Plant Supervisor ... Mrs. Milagros RONDÓN
42 Chaplain/Director Campus Ministry ... Rev. Rafael HIRALDO
50 Chairperson Business Department ... Prof. Wilfredo DEL VALLE
53 Chairperson Educ & Social Sci Dept ... Dr. Porfirio MONTES
79 Chairperson Humanities Dept ... Prof. Lourdes PEREZ DEL VALLE
81 Chairperson Math/Science Dept ... Prof. Irma MORALES
84 Director Enrollment Management ... Ms. Veronica VELAZQUEZ

*Inter American University of Puerto Rico Guayama Campus (D)

Call Box 10004, Guayama PR 00785

County: Guayama | FICE Identification: 022827 | Unit ID: 242699
Telephone: (787) 864-2222 | Carnegie Class: Bac/Diverse
FAX Number: (787) 866-5006 | Calendar System: Semester
URL: www.guayama.inter.edu
Established: 1956 | Annual Undergrad Tuition & Fees: $4,558
Enrollment: 2,336 | Coed
Affiliation or Control: Independent Non-Profit | IRS Status: 501(c)3
Highest Offering: Master's
Program: 2-Year Principally Bachelor's Creditable; Liberal Arts And General
Accreditation: M, @TEAC

02 Chancellor ... Prof. Carlos E. COLON-RAMOS
06 Registrar ... Mr. Luis A. SOTO
08 Librarian ... Mrs. Edny SANTIAGO
10 Bursar ... Ms. Teresa MANAUTOU
05 Dean of Studies ... Dr. Angela DE JESUS
11 Dean of Administration ... Mr. Nestor A. LEBRON
32 Dean of Students ... Dr. Rosa J. MARTINEZ
07 Director Admissions ... Mrs. Laura FERRER
37 Director Financial Aid ... Mr. Jose A. VECHINI
29 Director Alumni Relations ... Dr. Rosa J. MARTINEZ
51 Director Continuing Education ... Mrs. Dianne RIVERA
15 Human Resources Officer ... Mrs. Maria MARES
18 Chief Facilities/Physical Plant ... Mr. Benjamin AYALA
45 Chief Plng Officer/Research & Devel ... Mrs. Nitza J. TORRES
30 Chief Devel/Dir Annual Plan Giv ... Vacant
42 Chaplain Director ... Rvda. Estebania BAEZ
84 Director Enrollment Management ... Mrs. Eileen RIVERA
96 Director of Purchasing ... Mrs. Maria VAZQUEZ
31 Dir of Community & New Student Rels ... Mrs. Luz ORTIZ
23 Director Health Services ... Mrs. Arcilia RIVERA
66 Director Nursing Program ... Mrs. Marisol VELAZQUEZ
88 Dir Adult Higher Education Program ... Mrs. Carmen G. RIVERA
50 Dir Dept Business Admin/Econ Sci ... Dr. Rosalia MORALES
53 Dir Dept Education/Soc Sci/Hum Std ... Dr. Ray ROBLES
81 Dir Dept Natural & Applied Science ... Prof. Carmen TORRES

*Inter American University of Puerto Rico Metropolitan Campus (E)

PO Box 191293, San Juan PR 00919-1293

County: San Juan | FICE Identification: 003940 | Unit ID: 242653
Telephone: (787) 250-1912 | Carnegie Class: DRU
FAX Number: (787) 250-0742 | Calendar System: Semester
URL: metro.inter.edu
Established: 1962 | Annual Undergrad Tuition & Fees: $5,103
Enrollment: 10,681 | Coed
Affiliation or Control: Independent Non-Profit | IRS Status: 501(c)3
Highest Offering: Doctorate
Program: 2-Year Principally Bachelor's Creditable; Liberal Arts And General; Teacher Preparatory; Professional
Accreditation: M, ADNUR, MT, NUR, SW, @TEAC

02 Chancellor ... Prof. Marilina L. WAYLAND
05 Dean of Studies ... Prof. Migdalia TEXIDOR
32 Dean of Students ... Dr. Carmen OQUENDO
10 Dean of Administration ... Mr. Jimmy CANCEL
11 Dean of Faculty Cs Economics & Adm ... Prof. Fredrick VEGA
53 Dean of Education & Behavioral Sci ... Dr. Carmen COLLAZO
83 Director School of Psychology ... Dr. Jaime SANTIAGO
79 Dean Faculty of Humanities ... Dr. Olga VILLAMIL
66 Director of Nursing ... Dr. Aurea AYALA
72 Director of Medical Technology ... Dr. Ida A. MEJIAS
81 Dean Faculty of Science & Technolog ... Dr. Izander ROSADO
06 Registrar ... Ms. Lisette RIVERA
84 Enrollment Management ... Mr. Luis E. RUIZ
20 Associate Dean of Studies ... Ms. Blanca M. GONZALEZ
08 Director of Ctr for Access to Info ... Mrs. Rosa PIMENTEL
15 Human Resources Officer ... Vacant
37 Director of Financial Aid ... Mrs. Glenda DIAZ
18 Dir Conservation & General Services ... Mr. Roberto BERMUDEZ-TORRES
38 Dir Student Placement/Guidanc/Couns ... Ms. Beatriz RIVERA
83 Director School of Social Work ... Dr. Elizabeth MIRANDA
58 Director School of Education ... Dr. Maria D. RUBERO
88 Director International Rel Office ... Prof. Ramon AYALA
73 Dir School of Theology ... Dr. Angel VELEZ
88 Dir School of Criminal Justice ... Prof. Luis ACEVEDO
26 Public Relations Officer ... Vacant
14 Director Informatic/Telecomm Center ... Mr. Eduardo ORTIZ
36 Director Student Placement ... Mrs. Adabel-Vanessa COLON
07 Director of Admissions ... Ms. Janies OLIVIERI
09 Dean Inst Research/External Rsrch ... Dr. Debora HERNANDEZ
21 Associate Dean of Administration ... Mr. Jose L. DEJESUS
30 Development & Fund Raising ... Prof. Armando CARDONA
96 Purchasing Officer ... Mrs. Patricia GONZALEZ
92 Coordinator of Honors Program ... Prof. William ARIAS
88 Bursar ... Ms. Carmen RIVERA

*Inter American University of Puerto Rico Ponce Campus (F)

104 Turpo Industrial Park Road, #1, Mercedita PR 00715-1602

County: Ponce | FICE Identification: 005029 | Unit ID: 242662
Telephone: (787) 284-1912 | Carnegie Class: Bac/Diverse
FAX Number: (787) 841-0103 | Calendar System: Semester
URL: ponce.inter.edu
Established: 1962 | Annual Undergrad Tuition & Fees: $4,596
Enrollment: 6,460 | Coed
Affiliation or Control: Independent Non-Profit | IRS Status: 501(c)3
Highest Offering: Master's
Program: 2-Year Principally Bachelor's Creditable; Liberal Arts And General; Teacher Preparatory
Accreditation: M, @PTAA, @TEAC

02 Chancellor ... Dr. Vilma E. COLON
05 Dean of Studies ... Vacant
32 Dean of Students ... Mrs. Edda COSTAS
11 Dean of Administrative Affairs ... Eng. Victor A. FELIBERTY
08 Actg Dir Education Resource Center ... Mrs. Ana MATOS
35 Director Student Services ... Mrs. Miriam MARTINEZ
10 Bursar ... Mrs. Nilda RODRIGUEZ
06 Registrar ... Mrs. Maria del C PEREZ
84 Director Enrollment Management ... Mrs. Miriam MARTINEZ
30 Director of Development ... Mrs. Eunice CORDERO
07 Director of Admissions ... Mr. Franco L. DIAZ
09 Learning Resources Center ... Mrs. Alma I. RIOS
15 Human Resource Officer ... Mrs. Ivonne COLLAZO
19 Supervisor of University Guard ... Mr. Reinaldo ROSADO
37 Director Student Financial Aid ... Mrs. Debra MARTINEZ
41 Athletic Director ... Mr. Raul HERNANDEZ
58 Director of Graduate Programs ... Mrs. Jacqueline ALVAREZ
50 Director Business & Administration ... Prof. Maria P. GALARZA
51 Director Continuing Education ... Mrs. Maria MUNOZ
79 Dir Humanistics & Pedagogical Stds ... Dr. Orlando GONZALEZ
81 Actg Director Mathematics/Sciences ... Prof. Lourdes DIAZ
83 Dir Social/Behavioral Science ... Dr. Manuel E. BAHAMONDE
76 Director Health Science ... Prof. Gerardo RIVERA
38 Dir Univ Integration Services Ofc ... Mr. Hector MARTINEZ
14 Director Computer Center ... Mr. Antonio RAMOS
26 Public Relations Officer ... Mr. Rolando J. MENDEZ
04 Chief Executive Assistant ... Mrs. Diana RIVERA
88 Dir Marketing & Student Promotion ... Mrs. Yinaira SANTIAGO
106 Actg Dir Distance Education Program ... Dr. Omayra CARABALLO
88 Accreditation/Certification Officer ... Mrs. Evelyn CASTILLO
45 Director of Evaluation & Planning ... Mr. Anselmo ALVAREZ

*Inter American University of Puerto Rico San German Campus (G)

PO Box 5100, San German PR 00683-9801

County: San German | FICE Identification: 003938 | Unit ID: 242617
Telephone: (787) 264-1912 | Carnegie Class: Master's M
FAX Number: (787) 892-6350 | Calendar System: Semester
URL: www.sg.inter.edu
Established: 1912 | Annual Undergrad Tuition & Fees: $5,916
Enrollment: 5,408 | Coed
Affiliation or Control: Independent Non-Profit | IRS Status: 501(c)3
Highest Offering: Doctorate
Program: Occupational; 2-Year Principally Bachelor's Creditable; Liberal Arts And General; Teacher Preparatory; Professional
Accreditation: M, MT, RAD, @TEAC

02 Chancellor ..... Prof. Agnes MOJICA
05 Dean of Studies ..... Dr. Nyvia ALVARADO
11 Dean of Administration ..... Mrs. Frances CARABALLO
32 Dean of Students ..... Mr. Efrain ANGLERO
20 Associate Dean of Studies ..... Prof. Carmen TORRES
21 Auxiliary Dean of Administration ..... Mrs. Marisol GONZALEZ
15 Director of Human Resources ..... Mrs. Evelyn TORES
18 Chief Facilities/Physical Plant ..... Mr. Jose A. RIVERA
37 Director Financial Aid ..... Mrs. Maria Ines LUGO
06 Registrar ..... Vacant
07 Director of Admissions ..... Mrs. Mildred CAMACHO
08 Director of Library ..... Mrs. Doris ASENCIO
38 Acting Director Student Counseling ..... Mrs. Daisy PEREZ
09 Dir Plng Evaluation/Inst Studies ..... Miss Maria MORALES-MARTINEZ
19 Director of Security ..... Mr. Victor BONILLA
14 Director of Computer Center ..... Mr. Rogelio TORO-ZAPATA
41 Athletic Director ..... Prof. Francisco ACEVEDO
39 Acting Manager of Student Housing ..... Mrs. Erlinda VEGA
40 Bookstore Manager ..... Vacant
42 Dir Chaplaincy/Spiritual Well-being ..... Rev. Sara SALIVA
04 Special Assistant of the Chancellor ..... Mrs. Tary GARCIA
35 Manager of Student Services ..... Mrs. Maria Gil MARTINEZ
51 Director of Continuing Education ..... Mrs. Eva GARCIA
58 Director Graduate Programs ..... Dr. Carlos IRIZARRY
88 Manager of Food Services ..... Vacant
17 Director of Medical Services ..... Vacant
88 Auxiliary Dean of Students ..... Mrs. Janet RIVERA
30 Chief Development Officer ..... Miss Leticia MARTINEZ
92 Coordinator of Honors Program ..... Prof. Ricardo LOPES
96 Director of Purchasing ..... Mr. Israel CRUZ
10 Acting Director Bursar's Office ..... Mr. Carlos SEGARRA

*Inter American University of Puerto Rico School of Law (A)

PO Box 70351, San Juan PR 00936-8351

County: San Juan | Identification: 666813
Unit ID: 242723
Telephone: (787) 751-1912 | Carnegie Class: Spec/Law
FAX Number: (787) 751-2975 | Calendar System: Semester
URL: www.derecho.inter.edu
Established: 1961 | Annual Graduate Tuition & Fees: $14,403
Enrollment: 874 | Coed
Affiliation or Control: Independent Non-Profit | IRS Status: 501(c)3
Highest Offering: First Professional Degree; No Undergraduates
Program: Professional
Accreditation: M, LAW

02 Dean ..... Mr. Luis M. NEGRON-PORTILLO
05 Dean of Academic Affairs ..... Ms. Evelyn BENVENUTTI-TORO
32 Dean of Students ..... Mrs. Marilucy GONZALEZ-BAEZ
11 Dean of Administration ..... Mr. Heriberto SOTO
06 Registrar ..... Mrs. Maria de Lourdes RIVERA
08 Head Librarian ..... Mr. Hector Ruben SANCHEZ
61 Director of Legal Aid Clinic ..... Mrs. Rosabelle PADIN
37 Director of Financial Aid ..... Mr. Ricardo CRESPO
07 Director of Admissions ..... Mrs. Angela TORRES
18 Chief Facilities/Physical Plant ..... Mr. Jose A. RIVERA
96 Director of Purchasing ..... Mrs. Yajahira VIDAL
88 Director of Bursar Office ..... Mr. Samuel SANCHEZ

*Inter American University of Puerto Rico School of Optometry (B)

500 John Will Harris Road, Bayamon PR 00957-6257

County: San Juan | Identification: 666601
Unit ID: 404222
Telephone: (787) 765-1915 | Carnegie Class: Spec/Health
FAX Number: (787) 767-3920 | Calendar System: Semester
URL: www.optonet.inter.edu
Established: 1981 | Annual Graduate Tuition & Fees: $25,000
Enrollment: 217 | Coed
Affiliation or Control: Independent Non-Profit | IRS Status: 501(c)3
Highest Offering: First Professional Degree; No Undergraduates
Program: Professional
Accreditation: M, OPT

02 Dean ..... Dr. Andres PAGAN
05 Dean for Academic Affairs ..... Dr. Jose M. DE JESUS
11 Dean of Administration ..... Mr. Francisco RIVERA
32 Dean of Student Affair ..... Dra. Iris CABELLO
42 Director Religious Life ..... Dra. Ileana VARGAS
07 Director Admissions ..... Mr. Jose A. COLON
30 Director Development ..... Mrs. Maria J. AULET
88 Director Basic Sciences ..... Dr. John MORDI
20 Director Academic Affairs ..... Dr. Angel F. ROMERO
88 Dean of Clinical Affairs ..... Dra. Damaris PAGAN
08 Library Director ..... Mrs. Wilma MARRERO
90 Director of Computing ..... Mr. Elias SANTIAGO
21 Bursar's Officer ..... Mr. Eduardo SALICHS
15 Director Human Resources ..... Ms. Milagros RODRIGUEZ
37 Director Financial Aid ..... Mrs. Lourdes M. NIEVES

John Dewey College (C)

427 Barbosa Avenue, Third Floor, Hato Rey PR 00910-9538

County: San Juan | FICE Identification: 031121
Unit ID: 431309
Telephone: (787) 753-0039 | Carnegie Class: Not Classified
FAX Number: (787) 764-6303 | Calendar System: Other
URL: www.jdc.edu
Established: N/A | Annual Undergrad Tuition & Fees: $8,553
Enrollment: 684 | Coed
Affiliation or Control: Independent Non-Profit | IRS Status: 501(c)3
Highest Offering: Baccalaureate
Program: Occupational
Accreditation: ACICS

01 President/CEO ..... Mr. Carlos A. QUINONES

Mech-Tech College (D)

PO Box 6118, Caguas PR 00726

County: Caguas | FICE Identification: 030255
Unit ID: 414461
Telephone: (787) 744-1060 | Carnegie Class: Not Classified
FAX Number: (787) 744-1035 | Calendar System: Quarter
URL: www.mechtech.edu
Established: 1984 | Annual Undergrad Tuition & Fees: $8,754
Enrollment: 3,659 | Coed
Affiliation or Control: Proprietary | IRS Status: Proprietary
Highest Offering: Associate Degree
Program: Occupational; 2-Year Principally Bachelor's Creditable; Technical Emphasis
Accreditation: CNCE

01 President ..... Mr. Edwin J. COLON COSME
03 Chief of Operations ..... Miss Yadexy SIERRA CONCEPCIÓN
32 Vice President of Student Affairs ..... Mrs. Carmen RIVERA LABOY
05 Vice President of Academic Affairs ..... Mr. Carlos MARTÍNEZ GARCÍA
45 Vice resident of Planning & Develop ..... Mr. José ALGORRI NAVARRO
11 Vice President of Administration ..... Mrs. Aguilda GÓMEZ
10 Comptroller ..... Mr. Edwin RODRÍGUEZ
06 Registrar ..... Mrs. Blanca RIVERA SANTIAGO
37 Financial Aid Director ..... Mrs. Jessica CRUZ BONILLA
07 Admissions Director ..... Miss Rocío ROSARIO
36 Placement Director ..... Mrs. María RAMÓN
20 Dean of Academic Affairs ..... Dr. Delma SANTIAGO
35 Dean of Student Affairs ..... Mrs. Aurea ROQUE
08 Library Director ..... Mrs. Carmen AVILES
12 Director Bayamón Branch Campus ..... Mrs. Rosa PEÑA
12 Director of Ponce Branch Campus ..... Mr. Carlos CRUZ GORRITZ
12 Director Vega Baja Branch Campus ..... Mr. David COLLAZO
12 Director Mayaguez Branch Campus ..... Mr. James RODRÍGUEZ
13 Vicepresident Information Technolog ..... Mr. Luis CAMACHO

National College of Business and Technology (E)

MSC 452, PO Box 4035, Arecibo PR 00614

County: Arecibo | Identification: 666489
Unit ID: 242981
Telephone: (787) 879-5044 | Carnegie Class: Bac/Assoc
FAX Number: (787) 879-5047 | Calendar System: Trimester
URL: www.ncbt.edu
Established: 1984 | Annual Undergrad Tuition & Fees: $6,590
Enrollment: 1,787 | Coed
Affiliation or Control: Proprietary | IRS Status: Proprietary
Highest Offering: Baccalaureate
Program: Occupational
Accreditation: ACICS

01 President ..... Dr. Francisco NUNEZ
05 Exec & Academic Affairs Director ..... Ms. Lydia COLLAZO
37 Vice Pres Financial Aid/Compliance ..... Mr. Desi LOPEZ

National College of Business and Technology (F)

Box 2036, Highway 2, Natl Col Bldg, Bayamon PR 00960-2036

County: Bayamon | FICE Identification: 022606
Unit ID: 242972
Telephone: (787) 780-5134 | Carnegie Class: Bac/Assoc
FAX Number: (787) 740-7360 | Calendar System: Trimester
URL: www.ncbt.edu
Established: 1982 | Annual Undergrad Tuition & Fees: $6,590
Enrollment: 3,000 | Coed
Affiliation or Control: Proprietary | IRS Status: Proprietary
Highest Offering: Master's
Program: Occupational
Accreditation: @M, ACICS, @TEAC

01 President ..... Dr. Carmen Z. CLAUDIO
11 Vice Pres Administrative Affairs ..... Mr. Jose CORDOVA
37 Vice Pres Financial Aid/Compliance ..... Mr. Desi LOPEZ
06 Registrar ..... Ms. Glorimar RODRIGUEZ
08 Head Librarian ..... Mr. Angel RODRIGUEZ
07 Director Admissions ..... Ms. Sucette RUBIO
37 Institutional Dir Financial Aid ..... Ms. Damaris RODRIGUEZ
09 Dir Institutional Effectiveness ..... Ms. Daliana RIVERA

Ponce Paramedical College (G)

1213 Acacia Street Villa Flores URB, Ponce PR 00716-2901

County: Ponce | FICE Identification: 025349
Unit ID: 243072
Telephone: (787) 848-1589 | Carnegie Class: Assoc/PrivFP
FAX Number: (787) 259-0169 | Calendar System: Other
URL: www.popac.edu
Established: 1983 | Annual Undergrad Tuition & Fees: $13,300
Enrollment: 4,813 | Coed
Affiliation or Control: Proprietary | IRS Status: Proprietary
Highest Offering: Associate Degree
Program: Occupational; 2-Year Principally Bachelor's Creditable
Accreditation: ACCSC

01 President ..... Mrs. María PAGÁN
04 Executive Assistant ..... Mr. Angel QUINONES
05 Academic Dean ..... Mrs. Rosa E. CRUZ
06 Registrar ..... Mrs. Ivette OLIVERAS
37 Director Student Financial Aid ..... Mrs. Amarilis ROCHE

Ponce School of Medicine (H)

PO Box 7004, Ponce PR 00732-7004

County: Ponce | FICE Identification: 024824
Unit ID: 243081
Telephone: (787) 840-2575 | Carnegie Class: Assoc/PrivNFP4
FAX Number: (787) 840-9756 | Calendar System: Semester
URL: www.psm.edu
Established: 1977 | Annual Graduate Tuition & Fees: $24,359
Enrollment: 607 | Coed
Affiliation or Control: Independent Non-Profit | IRS Status: 501(c)3
Highest Offering: Doctorate; No Undergraduates
Program: Professional
Accreditation: M, CLPSY, #MED

01 President/Dean ..... Dr. Joxel GARCIA
05 Assoc Dean Faculty/Clinical Affairs ..... Dr. Raul ARMSTRONG
46 Assoc Dean Research/Graduated Stds ..... Dr. Jose A. TORRES
11 Exec Dean Administration & Finance ..... Mr. Reinaldo DIAZ

The Pontifical Catholic University of Puerto Rico (I)

2250 Las Americas Avenue, Suite 564, Ponce PR 00717-9997

County: Ponce | FICE Identification: 003936
Unit ID: 241410
Telephone: (787) 841-2000 | Carnegie Class: DRU
FAX Number: (787) 651-2034 | Calendar System: Semester
URL: www.pucpr.edu
Established: 1948 | Annual Undergrad Tuition & Fees: $5,278
Enrollment: 8,203 | Coed
Affiliation or Control: Roman Catholic | IRS Status: 501(c)3
Highest Offering: Doctorate
Program: Liberal Arts And General; Teacher Preparatory; Professional
Accreditation: M, CORE, LAW, MT, NUR, SW, @TEAC

00 Chancellor ..... M.Rev. Felix LAZARO
01 President ..... Dr. Jorge I. VELEZ AROCHO
04 Executive Assistant to President ..... Lcdo. Jose A. FRONTERA
03 Vice Chancellor ..... Vacant
05 Vice President Academic Affairs ..... Dr. Leandro COLON
10 Vice President of Finance ..... Mrs. Irma I. RODRIGUEZ
32 Vice President for Student Affairs ..... Prof. Freddie MARTINEZ
20 Assoc Vice Pres Academic Affairs ..... Vacant
35 Asst to Vice Pres Student Affairs ..... Prof. Myriam D. LOPEZ
09 Vice President Inst Rsrch/Dev Plng ..... Dr. Felix CORTES
12 Interim Rector Arecibo Branch ..... Dr. Edwin HERNANDEZ
12 Rector Mayaguez Branch ..... Dr. Mei-Ling VELAZQUEZ
06 Registrar ..... Prof. Ivan E. DAVILA
07 Director of Admissions ..... Dr. Ana O. BONILLA
08 Director of the Library ..... Mrs. Magda VARGAS
37 Director of Student Aid ..... Mrs. Rosalia MARTINEZ
36 Director of Placement Services ..... Mrs. Bethzaida PEREZ
14 Director Computer Center ..... Mr. Moises CABRERA
89 Director of Freshmen ..... Dr. Maria D. FERRER
55 Director of Evening Studies ..... Dra. Adalecia HASSELL
24 Director Educational Technology ..... Miss Gilda RIVERA
79 Dean of Arts & Humanities ..... Prof. Alfonso SANTIAGO
81 Dean of Sciences ..... Prof. Carmen VELAZQUEZ
61 Dean of the School of Law ..... Lic. Angel GONZALEZ
50 Dean Business Administration ..... Dr. Jaime L. SANTIAGO-CANET
53 Dean of Education ..... Dr. Myriam ZAYAS
58 Dean Institute of Graduate Studies ..... Dr. Hernan VERA
48 Organizing Dean School of Arquit ..... Mr. Abel MISLA
51 Coord Continuing Education Inst ..... Mrs. Karen G. MORALES
27 Communications ..... Mrs. Irem POVENTUD
29 Alumni Relations Officer ..... Mrs. Maria S. MASCARO
15 Director Human Resources ..... Mr. Wilfredo CORNIER
40 Director Bookstore ..... Mrs. Ashley VELEZ
41 Athletic Director ..... Prof. Louis ARCHEVAL
42 Chaplain ..... Rev. Juan IÑIGO
31 Director Auxiliary Enterprises ..... Mr. Julio FELIU
26 Director Public Relations ..... Mrs. Irem POVENTUD
38 Director Student Counseling ..... Miss Carmen GONZALEZ
18 Physical Plant/Safety & Security ..... Mr. Julio PALMER
21 Treasurer Bursar's Office ..... Mr. Juan E. ROMAN
28 Director of Diversity ..... Vacant
84 Coord Institutional Recruitment ..... Mrs. Linnette MILETTI
96 Director of Purchasing ..... Mrs. Zoraida VELAZQUEZ
88 Acreditation Liaison Officer ..... Dr. Carmen J. ACOSTA-FUMERO
88 Coordinator of Outcomes Assessment ..... Prof. Maria MUÑIZ
30 Chief Development ..... Ing. Armando RODRIGUEZ

Pontifical Catholic University of Puerto Rico-Arecibo Campus (A)

Box 144045, Arecibo PR 00614-4045

County: Arecibo — Identification: 666603
Unit ID: 241395
Telephone: (787) 881-1212 — Carnegie Class: Master's S
FAX Number: (787) 881-0777 — Calendar System: Semester
URL: www.arecibo.pucpr.edu
Established: 1960 — Annual Undergrad Tuition & Fees: $6,750
Enrollment: 675 — Coed
Affiliation or Control: Roman Catholic — IRS Status: 501(c)3
Highest Offering: Master's
Program: Occupational; 2-Year Principally Bachelor's Creditable; Liberal Arts And General; Teacher Preparatory; Business Emphasis
Accreditation: M, @TEAC

01 President ... Prof. Marcelina VELEZ DE SANTIAGO
00 Chancellor ... Dr. Jose Arnaldo TORRES
05 Dean/Chief Academic Officer ... Dr. Wiefredo LOPEZ MARA
07 Admissions ... Mrs. Rosa SANTIAGO MENDEZ

Pontifical Catholic University of Puerto Rico-Mayaguez Campus (B)

Box 1326, Mayaguez PR 00681-1326

County: Mayaguez — Identification: 666605
Unit ID: 243586
Telephone: (787) 834-5151 — Carnegie Class: Bac/Diverse
FAX Number: (787) 833-8478 — Calendar System: Semester
URL: www.pucpr.edu
Established: 1960 — Annual Undergrad Tuition & Fees: $6,150
Enrollment: 1,518 — Coed
Affiliation or Control: Roman Catholic — IRS Status: 501(c)3
Highest Offering: Master's
Program: 2-Year Principally Bachelor's Creditable; Liberal Arts And General; Professional
Accreditation: M, @TEAC

01 Chancellor ... Prof. Mei-Ling VELAZQUEZ-SEPULVEDA
05 Dean of Academic Affairs ... Dr. Frank Jimmy SIERRA-CORTES
11 Dean of Administration ... Prof. Nilsa SOTO-CRUZ
32 Dean of Student Affairs ... Prof. Astrid J. RODRIGUEZ-MONTALVO
06 Registrar ... Mrs. Iris CRUZ-JIMENEZ
07 Admissions Officer ... Ms. Jenniffer BIGAS-GONZALEZ
37 Student Financial Aid Officer ... Mrs. Marilyn MARTI

San Juan Bautista School of Medicine (C)

PO Box 4968, Carretera 172, Caguas PR 00726-4968

County: San Juan — FICE Identification: 031773
Unit ID: 430670
Telephone: (787) 743-3038 — Carnegie Class: Spec/Med
FAX Number: (787) 746-3093 — Calendar System: Semester
URL: www.sanjuanbautista.edu
Established: 1978 — Annual Graduate Tuition & Fees: $22,800
Enrollment: 272 — Coed
Affiliation or Control: Proprietary — IRS Status: Proprietary
Highest Offering: First Professional Degree; No Undergraduates
Program: Professional
Accreditation: M, MED

01 President/Dean ... Dr. Yocasta BRUGAL-MENA
10 Chief Financial Officer ... Mr. José A. COLÓN

*Sistema Universitario Ana G. Mendez (D)

Apartado 21345, Rio Piedras PR 00928-1341

County: San Juan — FICE Identification: 029078
Unit ID: 242060
Telephone: (787) 751-0178 — Carnegie Class: N/A
FAX Number: (787) 766-1706
URL: www.suagm.edu

01 President ... Mr. Jose F. MENDEZ
03 Executive Vice President ... Mr. Jose F. MENDEZ, JR.
05 Vice President for Academic Affairs ... Mr. Jorge L. CRESPO
10 Vice Pres Financial Affairs ... Mr. Alfonso L. DAVILA
26 Vice Pres Student/Marketing Affairs . Mr. Francisco BARTOLOMEI
45 Vice President Planning & Research ... Mr. Jorge CRESPO
11 Vice Pres Administrative Affairs ... Mr. Jesus A. DIAZ
15 Vice President Human Resources ... Dr. Victoria DE JESUS
13 Chief Information Officer ... Sr. Kenneth MALDONADO
26 Director Public Relations ... Ms. Maria MARTINEZ
04 Exec Assistant to President ... Ms. Lydia I. MASSARI

*Universidad del Este (E)

PO Box 2010, Carolina PR 00984-2010

County: San Juan — FICE Identification: 003941
Unit ID: 243346
Telephone: (787) 257-7373 — Carnegie Class: Master's L
FAX Number: (787) 776-1220 — Calendar System: Semester
URL: www.suagm.edu/une
Established: 1949 — Annual Undergrad Tuition & Fees: $5,294
Enrollment: 13,700 — Coed
Affiliation or Control: Independent Non-Profit — IRS Status: 501(c)3
Highest Offering: Master's
Program: Occupational; 2-Year Principally Bachelor's Creditable; Liberal Arts And General; Teacher Preparatory
Accreditation: M, @ACBSP, ACFEI, RAD, @TEAC

02 Chancellor ... Mr. Alberto MALDONADO-RUIZ
05 Vice Chancellor Academic Affairs ... Dr. Mildred HUERTAS
11 Vice Chanc Admin Affs/Ofce of Chanc ... Mrs. Maria S. DIAZ
32 Vice Chancellor Student Affairs ... Mrs. Georgina LEON
24 Vice Chanc Information Resources ... Mrs. Carmen ORTEGA
46 Vice Chanc External Resources ... Mrs. Mayra M. FERRAN
20 Assoc VC Licensing/Accreditation ... Ms. Nilda I. ROSADO
88 Assoc Vice Chanc Admin Affairs ... Mrs. Magalie ALVARADO
35 Assoc Vice Chanc Student Affairs ... Dr. Nahomy CURET
84 Assoc VC Enrollment Management ... Mrs. Magda A. OSTOLAZA
38 Assoc VC for Multidisciplinary Svcs ... Mrs. Migdalia TORRES
23 AVC Stdnt Quality of Life/Wellness . Mrs. Carmen G. VELAZQUEZ
07 Asst Vice Chan Admiss/Financial Aid ... Mr. Ramon FUENTES
09 Asst Vice Chanc Instl Effectiveness ... Vacant
36 Director Employment Placement ... Mr. Juan HERNANDEZ
30 Asst VC for University Advancement ... Mrs. Maria I. DE GUZMAN
15 Asst Vice Pres Human Resources ... Mr. Jorge RODRIGUEZ
10 Assistant Vice President of Budget ... Mr. Jorge A. TORRES
18 Physical Plant/Operations Manager ... Mr. Edgar D. RODRIGUEZ
06 Registrar ... Mrs. Elisa QUILES
37 Director of Financial Aid ... Mrs. Eigna I. DE JESUS
08 Director of Library ... Mrs. Elsa MARIANI
26 Director Public Relations ... Mrs. Ivonne D. ARROYO
29 Director Alumni & Fund Raising ... Ms. Gisela NEGRON
88 Dean Intl Sch Hosp/Culinary Arts ... Mr. Ivan O. PUIG
107 Assoc Dean Professional Studies ... Vacant
13 Information/Telecommunications Dir ... Mr. Nestor MAS
41 Athletic Director ... Mr. Julio FIGUEROA
19 Safety & Security Director ... Mr. Nazario LUGO

*Universidad Del Turabo (F)

Estacion Universidad, Box 3030, Gurabo PR 00778-3030

County: Gurabo — FICE Identification: 011719
Unit ID: 243601
Telephone: (787) 743-7979 — Carnegie Class: DRU
FAX Number: (787) 744-5394 — Calendar System: Semester
URL: www.suagm.edu
Established: 1972 — Annual Undergrad Tuition & Fees: $4,924
Enrollment: 14,949 — Coed
Affiliation or Control: Independent Non-Profit — IRS Status: 501(c)3
Highest Offering: Doctorate
Program: Liberal Arts And General; Teacher Preparatory; Professional
Accreditation: M, BUS, DIETC, ENG, NURSE, @SP, @TEAC

02 Chancellor ... Dr. Dennis ALICEA
11 Vice Chancellor of Admin Affairs ... Dr. Gladys BETANCOURT
05 Vice Chancellor Academic Affairs ... Dr. Roberto LORAN
32 Vice Chancellor of Student Affairs ... Mrs. Ana M. ORTEGA
08 Vice Chancellor Information Res ... Dr. Sarai LASTRA
92 Vice Chancellor Honors Program ... Ms. Maricarmen SANTOS
88 Asst Vice Chanc Eval & Development ..Dra. Maria del C. SANTOS
21 Asst Vice Chanc Admin Affairs ... Mrs. Edna ORTA
23 Dean Education ... Dra. Angela CANDELARIO
50 Dean Business Administration ... Dr. Marcelino RIVERA
54 Dean Engineering ... Dr. Jack T. ALLISON
72 Dean Science & Technology ... Dr. Teresa LIPSETT
83 Dean Social Sciences & Humanities ... Mr. Marco A. GIL DE LA MADRID
58 Dean of Graduate Studies ... Dr. Sharon CANTRELL
06 Registrar ... Mrs. Zoraida ORTIZ
27 Director of Marketing ... Ms. Rosa Enid TOLEDO
37 Director Office of Financial Aid ... Mrs. Carmen J. RIVERA
26 Director Public Relations ... Ms. Iris SERRANO
18 Chief Facilities/Physical Plant ... Eng. Mayra RODRIGUEZ
29 Coordinator Alumni Relations ... Ms. Maricruz ROLON
30 Chief Development Officer ... Ms. Alba RIVERA
96 Director of Purchasing ... Mr. Jose BERRIOS
07 Director of Admissions ... Mrs. Virginia GONZALEZ
09 Director of Institutional Research ... Ms. Blanca ACEVEDO
15 Director Personnel Services ... Mrs. Iris BERRIOS
36 Assoc Vice Chanc Student Placement ... Ms. Betsy VIDAL
84 Director Enrollment Management ... Ms. Maria V. FIGUEROA
10 Chief Business Officer ... Ms. Jessica M. PERRY
38 Assoc Vice Chanc Student Counseling ... Ms. Betsy VIDAL

*Universidad Metropolitana (G)

PO Box 21150, Rio Piedras PR 00928-1150

County: San Juan — FICE Identification: 025875
Unit ID: 241739
Telephone: (787) 766-1717 — Carnegie Class: Master's L
FAX Number: (787) 759-7663 — Calendar System: Quarter
URL: www.suagm.edu/umet
Established: 1980 — Annual Undergrad Tuition & Fees: $6,270
Enrollment: 12,693 — Coed
Affiliation or Control: Independent Non-Profit — IRS Status: 501(c)3
Highest Offering: Doctorate
Program: Liberal Arts And General; Teacher Preparatory; Professional; Business Emphasis
Accreditation: M, ADNUR, NUR, @TEAC

02 Chancellor ... Dr. Federico M. MATHEU
05 Vice Chancellor Academic Affairs ... Dr. Omar PONCE
32 Vice Chanc for Student Affairs ... Mrs. Carmen ROSADO
88 Vice Chanc of International Affairs ... Dr. Zaida VEGA
09 Vice Chanc Institutional Assessment ... Dr. Nellie PAGAN
09 Asst Vice Chanc for Eval/Devel ... Prof. Adanid PRIETO
88 Asst Vice Chanc for Admin Affairs ... Prof. Mildred ARBONA
15 Asst Vice Pres for Human Resources ... Mrs. Marisol MUNOZ
53 Dean of Education ... Dr. Judith GONZALEZ
49 Dean of Liberal Arts ... Dr. Eloisa GORDON
76 Dean of Health Science ... Dr. Lourdes MALDONADO
81 Dean of Science & Technology ... Dr. Karen GONZALEZ
88 Dean of Environmental Affairs ... Dr. Carlos PADIN
13 Asst Vice Chanc Info Resources ... Mr. Carlos FUENTES
51 Assoc Dean of Continuing Education ... Ms. Lorna MARTINEZ
50 Dean of Business Administration ... Prof. Juan OTERO
72 Assoc Dean of Technical Studies ... Prof. Felipe ROSA
66 Director of Nursing ... Mr. Josue PACHECO
107 Assoc Dean of Professional Studies ... Ms. Melissa GUILLIANI
79 Associate Dean of Humanities ... Prof. Martin CRUZ
83 Assoc Dean of Social Sciences ... Vacant
27 Assoc Dean of Communications ... Mr. Alfredo NIEVES
72 Director Educational Production ... Mr. Luis MARTINEZ
06 Registrar ... Mrs. Beatriz NIEVES
08 Head Librarian ... Mrs. Maria de los A. LUGO
38 Vice Chanc Student Counseling ... Mrs. Carmen ROSADO
26 Director Public Relations Officer ... Ms. Yvonne GUADALUPE
29 Vice Chanc Alumni Relations ... Ms. Belissa AQUINO
18 Chief Facilities/Physical Plant ... Mr. Jaime DOMINGUEZ
07 Director of Admissions ... Mr. Julio RODRIGUEZ
41 Athletic Director ... Mr. Ariel ORTIZ
45 Asst Vice President of Planning ... Mrs. Mariela COLLAZO
10 Asst Vice President of Business ... Ms. Aixa ALDARONDO
11 Assoc Vice Chanc Admin Affairs . Mrs. Maria DEL P. CHARNECO
76 Director of Respiratory Therapy ... Mrs. Linette CLAUDIO
53 Assoc Dean of Education ... Dr. Daisy RODRIGUEZ
53 Assoc Dean of Education ... Dr. Beverly PEREZ

Universal Career Community College (H)

PO Box 902288, San Juan PR 00902-2888

County: San Juan — FICE Identification: 033263
Unit ID: 436784
Telephone: (787) 728-7211 — Carnegie Class: Not Classified
FAX Number: (787) 728-7233 — Calendar System: Semester
URL: www.universalcareer.org
Established: 1978 — Annual Undergrad Tuition & Fees: $9,431
Enrollment: 1,335 — Coed
Affiliation or Control: Proprietary — IRS Status: Proprietary
Highest Offering: Associate Degree
Program: Occupational
Accreditation: ACCSC

01 President ... Richard D'COSTA

Universal Technology College of Puerto Rico (I)

Apartado 1955, Victoria Station, Aguadilla PR 00605-1955

County: Aguadilla — FICE Identification: 030297
Unit ID: 376385
Telephone: (787) 882-2065 — Carnegie Class: Assoc/PrivNFP
FAX Number: (787) 891-2370 — Calendar System: Semester
URL: www.unitecpr.edu
Established: 1987 — Annual Undergrad Tuition & Fees: $4,630
Enrollment: 1,750 — Coed
Affiliation or Control: Independent Non-Profit — IRS Status: 501(c)3
Highest Offering: Associate Degree
Program: Occupational; 2-Year Principally Bachelor's Creditable; Technical Emphasis
Accreditation: ACCSC

01 Chief Executive Officer ... Mrs. Keila LOPEZ
11 Administrative Manager ... Mr. Ivan F. ROMAN
04 Executive Secretary ... Mrs. Marilyn GONZALEZ
05 Chief Academic Officer ... Vacant
06 Registrar ... Ms. Maria ALVAREZ
08 Head Librarian ... Ms. Airlyn VAZQUEZ
10 Controller ... Mr. Alexis ROSADO
12 Director of Branch Campus ... Ms. Nelida CARDONA
14 Director Computer Center ... Mr. Zain CORDERO
16 Chief Personnel ... Mrs. Daisy VEGA
18 Chief Facilities/Physical Plant ... Mr. Danily NIEVES
32 Director Student Affairs ... Vacant
36 Director Student Placement ... Mrs. Ada MORALES
09 Director of Institutional Research ... Mrs. Evelyn TORRES
37 Director Student Financial Aid ... Mr. Samuel HERNANDEZ
38 Director Student Counsel ... Mrs. Dalia SANTIAGO
96 Purchasing Officer ... Mrs. Dolores MITJANS
23 Healthcare Services ... Mr. Silverio JIMENEZ
07 Coordinator of Admissions ... Mrs. Teresita RIVERA
50 Director of Business Administration ... Mrs. Sandra GONZALEZ
72 Director of Industrial Technology ... Mr. Eduardo FIGUEROA

Universidad Adventista de las Antillas (J)

Box 118, Mayaguez PR 00681-0118

County: Mayaguez — FICE Identification: 005019
Unit ID: 241191
Telephone: (787) 834-9595 — Carnegie Class: Bac/Diverse
FAX Number: (787) 834-9597 — Calendar System: Semester
URL: www.uaa.edu
Established: 1961 — Annual Undergrad Tuition & Fees: $10,680
Enrollment: 1,171 — Coed
Affiliation or Control: Seventh-day Adventist — IRS Status: 501(c)3

Highest Offering: Master's
Program: 2-Year Principally Bachelor's Creditable; Liberal Arts And General; Teacher Preparatory; Professional
Accreditation: M, NUR

01 President ... Dr. Obed JIMENEZ
05 Vice President for Academic Affairs ... Dr. Jose D. GOMEZ
10 Vice President Financial Affairs ... Mr. Misael JIMENEZ
32 Vice President for Students Affairs ... Mrs. Rosa DEL VALLE
26 VP Institutional Advancement ... Dr. Aurea ARAUJO
06 Registrar ... Mrs. Ana D. TORRES
07 Director of Admissions ... Mrs. Yolanda FERRER
08 Librarian ... Mrs. Aixa VEGA
33 Dean of Men ... Prof. Claudio GOMEZ
34 Dean of Women ... Mrs. Felicita CRUZ
38 Counselor ... Mrs. Ivelisse PEREZ
09 Official Institutional Research ... Mrs. Magda HERNANDEZ
88 Director of Special Projects ... Mr. Juan CASADO
37 Director of Student Financial Aid ... Mrs. Awilda MATOS
29 Director of Recruitment and Alumni ... Miss Lorell VARELA
30 Chief Development ... Sr. Juan CASADO
96 Director of Purchasing ... Mr. Obed RODRIGUEZ
18 Chief Facilities/Physical Plant ... Mr. Abel RODRIGUEZ

Universidad Central Del Caribe (A)

PO Box 60-327, Bayamon PR 00960-6032
County: Bayamon FICE Identification: 021633
Unit ID: 243568
Telephone: (787) 798-3001 Carnegie Class: Spec/Med
FAX Number: (787) 798-6836 Calendar System: Semester
URL: www.uccaribe.edu
Established: 1976 Annual Undergrad Tuition & Fees: $6,636
Enrollment: 485 Coed
Affiliation or Control: Independent Non-Profit IRS Status: 501(c)3
Highest Offering: Doctorate
Program: Professional
Accreditation: M, MED, RAD

01 President ... Dr. Jose Ginel RODRIGUEZ
05 Dean for Academic Affairs ... Dr. Nereida DIAZ-RODRIGUEZ
11 Dean Administrative Affairs ... Ms. Emilia SOTO
32 Dean Student Affairs ... Dr. Omar PEREZ
17 Dean of Medicine ... Dr. Jose G. RODRIGUEZ
63 Associate Dean of Medicine ... Mrs. Zilka RIOS
53 Asst Dean Professional Services ... Ms. Emilia SOTO
06 Registrar ... Ms. Nilda MONTANEZ-LOPEZ
07 Director of Admissions ... Ms. Irma L. CORDERO
37 Director Student Financial Aid ... Ms. Lisandra VIERA
10 Director of Finances ... Mrs. Iris J. FONT
08 Librarian ... Ms. Mildred RIVERA
51 Director of Continuing Education ... Dr. Frances GARCIA
38 Counselor ... Ms. Yari M. NARRERO
46 Dean of Research and Graduate Pgms ... Dr. Luis A. CUBANO
20 Dean for Clinical & Faculty Affairs ... Dr. Harry MERCADO

Universidad Pentecostal Mizpa (B)

PO Box 20966, San Juan PR 00928-0966
County: San Juan FICE Identification: 031983
Unit ID: 441690
Telephone: (787) 720-4476 Carnegie Class: Spec/Faith
FAX Number: (787) 720-2012 Calendar System: Semester
URL: www.colmizpa.edu
Established: 1937 Annual Undergrad Tuition & Fees: $3,400
Enrollment: 1,192 Coed
Affiliation or Control: Pentecostal Church of God IRS Status: 501(c)3
Highest Offering: Baccalaureate
Program: Religious Emphasis
Accreditation: BI

01 President ... Mr. Angel A. RIVERA
05 Dean of Academic Affairs ... Vacant
11 Dean Administration/Finance ... Mr. Elisamuel RODRIGUEZ
32 Dean of Student Affairs ... Mr. Jorge BURGOS
42 Director Christian Service ... Ms. Aida DIAZ
18 Director of Physical & Facilities ... Vacant
06 Registrar ... Ms. Sara MARTINEZ
08 Librarian ... Mr. Julio RAMOS
37 Student Financial Aid Officer ... Mrs. Myriam JUARBE
26 Chief Public Relations Officer ... Vacant

Universidad Politecnica De Puerto Rico (C)

Ponce de Leon 377, Box 192017, San Juan PR 00919
County: San Juan FICE Identification: 021000
Unit ID: 243577
Telephone: (787) 622-8000 Carnegie Class: Spec/Engg
FAX Number: (787) 763-8919 Calendar System: Trimester
URL: www.pupr.edu
Established: 1966 Annual Undergrad Tuition & Fees: $7,460
Enrollment: 5,167 Coed
Affiliation or Control: Independent Non-Profit IRS Status: 501(c)3
Highest Offering: Master's
Program: Liberal Arts And General
Accreditation: M, ENG, ENGR, IACBE

01 President ... Mr. Ernesto VAZQUEZ-BARQUET
84 Vice Pres/Enrollment Management ... Mr. Carlos PEREZ
05 Chief Academic Officer ... Dr. Miguel A. RIESTRA
06 Registrar ... Mrs. Mayra I. LOPEZ
07 Director Admissions ... Mrs. Teresa CARDONA
08 Head Librarian ... Mrs. Mirta COLON
37 Director Financial Aid ... Mr. Sergio VILLOLDO
09 Director of Institutional Research ... Dr. Miguel A. RIESTRA
10 Chief Business Officer ... Mr. Ernesto VÁZQUEZ-MARTÍNEZ
15 Director Personnel Services ... Ms. Ana CASTELLANO
18 Chief Facilities/Physical Plant ... Mr. Herminio ROMERO
29 Alumni Relations ... Mrs. Ana M. DAPENA
35 Director Student Affairs ... Mr. Carlos PEREZ
36 Director Student Placement ... Mrs. Angie ESCALANTE
38 Director Student Counseling ... Ms. Sidnia VÉLEZ
21 Associate Business Officer ... Mrs. Olga CANCEL

*University of Puerto Rico-Central Administration (D)

1187 Flamboyan Street, San Juan PR 00926-1117
County: San Juan FICE Identification: 003942
Unit ID: 243160
Telephone: (787) 250-0000 Carnegie Class: N/A
FAX Number: (787) 759-6917
URL: www.upr.edu

01 President ... Dr. Miguel A. MUÑOZ-MUÑOZ
03 Executive Director ... Dr. Ivette SANTIAGO
05 Vice President for Academic Affairs ... Prof. Ibis L. APONTE-AVELLANET
09 Vice President for Research ... Dr. José A. LASALDE-DOMINICCI
32 Vice Pres Student Affairs ... Vacant
12 Chancellor Rio Piedras Campus ... Dr. Ana R. GUADALUPE
12 Acting Chancellor Mayaguez Campus ... Dr. Jorge RIVERA-SANTOS
12 Chanc Medical Sciences Campus ... Dr. Rafael RODRÍGUEZ-MERCADO
12 Chanc University College at Cayey ... Dr. Juan N. VARONA-ECHEANDÍA
12 Chanc University Col Humacao ... Dr. Carmen HERNÁNDEZ-CRUZ
12 Chanc Univ College at Bayamon ... Dr. Arturo AVILÉS-GONZÁLEZ
12 Chanc Univ College at Ponce ... Dr. Fernando RODRÍGUEZ-RODRÍGUEZ
12 Chanc Univ College at Carolina ... Prof. Trinidad FERNÁNDEZ-MIRANDA
12 Chanc Univ College at Utuado ... Dr. Iris M. MERCADO-OCASIO
12 Chanc Univ College Aguadilla ... Prof. Ivelice CARDONA-CORTÉS
12 Chanc Univ College at Arecibo ... Prof. Juan RAMÍREZ-SILVA
30 Dir Devel & Alumni Affairs Office ... Ms. Sandra M. TORRES-CLEMENTE
18 Dir Ctrl Designer Construction Ofc ... Mr. Adrián LÓPEZ-NUNCI
10 Director Finance Office ... Mr. Charles A. CORDERO-ARMSTRONG
15 Director Human Resources Office ... Mrs. Edna SCHARRON
11 Director Administrative Service ... Ms. Miriam D. MARTÍNEZ
13 Director Information Systems Office ... Mrs. Alina DÍAZ
37 Director Student Financial Aid ... Mr. Hernán VAZQUEZTELL
43 Director Legal Affairs Office ... Ms. Martha L. VÉLEZ
88 Administrator Botanical Garden ... Dr. Rafael F. DÁVILA-LÓPEZ
27 University Press & Communications ... Mr. Iván N. RÍOS-HERNÁNDEZ
101 Exec Secretary University Board ... Dr. Myrna MAYOL
21 Director Budget Office ... Mr. Willie ROSARIO

*University of Puerto Rico-Aguadilla (E)

PO Box 6150, Aguadilla PR 00604-6150
County: Aguadilla FICE Identification: 012123
Unit ID: 243106
Telephone: (787) 890-2681 Carnegie Class: Bac/Diverse
FAX Number: (787) 891-3455 Calendar System: Semester
URL: www.uprag.edu
Established: 1972 Annual Undergrad Tuition & Fees (In-State): $2,722
Enrollment: 3,000 Coed
Affiliation or Control: State IRS Status: 501(c)3
Highest Offering: Baccalaureate
Program: Occupational; 2-Year Principally Bachelor's Creditable; Liberal Arts And General
Accreditation: M, ACBSP, TED

02 Acting Chancellor ... Prof. Ivelice CARDONA
05 Interim Dean Academic Affairs ... Dr. Sonia RIVERA
11 Interim Dean Administrative Affairs ... Mr. Hector VELEZ
32 Dean Student Affairs ... Prof. Pablo A. RAMIREZ-MENDEZ
06 Registrar ... Mrs. Zaida SERRANO
07 Admissions Officer ... Mrs. Melba SERRANO
08 Head Librarian ... Prof. Cande GOMEZ
14 Director of Computer Center ... Mr. Carlos JIMENEZ
16 Interim Head of Personnel ... Mr. Miguel AROCHO
19 Director of Security/Safety ... Vacant
37 Director Student Financial Aid ... Mrs. Carmen E. SANTIAGO
51 Director Continuing Education ... Dr. Ana E. CUEBAS
38 Director Student Counseling ... Prof. Elba I. ROMAN
45 Dir Planning/Inst Research Office ... Mr. Gerardo JAVARIZ
18 Chief Facilities/Physical Plant ... Vacant
29 Director Alumni Relations ... Mrs. Jeannette AQUINO
96 Purchasing Supervisor ... Mrs. Widylia MEDINA

*University of Puerto Rico at Arecibo (F)

Call Box 4010, Arecibo PR 00614-4010
County: Arecibo FICE Identification: 007228
Unit ID: 243115
Telephone: (787) 815-0000 Carnegie Class: Bac/Diverse
FAX Number: (787) 880-2245 Calendar System: Semester
URL: www.upra.edu
Established: 1967 Annual Undergrad Tuition & Fees (In-State): $2,795
Enrollment: 3,957 Coed
Affiliation or Control: State IRS Status: 501(c)3
Highest Offering: Baccalaureate
Program: Occupational; Liberal Arts And General
Accreditation: M, ACBSP, ADNUR, NUR, TED

02 Chancellor ... Dr. Juan RAMIREZ SILVA
05 Dean of Academic Affairs ... Dr. Manuel SAPONARA
11 Dean of Administrative Affairs ... Prof. Juan PEREZ
32 Dean of Student Affairs ... Prof. Deomedes PAGAN
09 Dir Planning/Institutional Research ... Dr. Soriel SANTIAGO
06 Registrar ... Mrs. Widilia RODRIGUEZ ROSA
07 Director of Admissions ... Mrs. Magay MENDEZ
08 Head Librarian ... Prof. Victor MALDONADO
15 Director Human Resources ... Mr. Luis F. LARACUENTE
38 Director Student Counseling ... Prof. Leticia MERCADE
04 Assistant to the Chancellor ... Dr. Gisela CORDERO
51 Dir Continuing Education/Prof Stds ... Mr. Benjamin SOTO TRUJILLO
37 Director Student Financial Aid ... Ms. Myrta ORTIZ
41 Athletic Director ... Prof. Jose COLON
13 Computing & Information Management ... Prof. Luis COLON
20 Assoc Dean of Academic Affairs ... Prof. Edith CUEVAS SOTO
26 Chief Public Relations Officer ... Prof. Nereidin FELICIANO
29 Director Alumni Relations ... Ms. Hilda ANTOMMARCHI
92 Director Honors Program ... Prof. Idia RODRIGUEZ
96 Director of Purchasing ... Mrs. Rosaura QUINTANA
18 Chief Facilities/Physical Plant ... Mr. Flor SERRANO
21 Associate Business Officer ... Mr. Ramon FALU

*University of Puerto Rico at Bayamon (G)

Carr. 174 #170 Industrial Minillas,
Bayamon PR 00959-1911
County: Bayamon FICE Identification: 010975
Unit ID: 243133
Telephone: (787) 993-0000 Carnegie Class: Bac/Diverse
FAX Number: (787) 993-8900 Calendar System: Semester
URL: www.uprb.edu
Established: 1971 Annual Undergrad Tuition & Fees (In-State): $2,842
Enrollment: 4,992 Coed
Affiliation or Control: State IRS Status: 501(c)3
Highest Offering: Baccalaureate
Program: Liberal Arts And General
Accreditation: M, ACBSP, TED

02 Chancellor ... Dr. Arturo AVILÉS-GONZÁLEZ
05 Dean Academic Affairs ... Dr. Edna MIRANDA-RODRÍGUEZ
32 Dean Student Affairs ... Mr. Nelson VÁZQUEZ-ESPEJO
06 Registrar ... Ms. Carmen CINTRON-OTERO
07 Director Admissions ... Mrs. Carmen MONTES-BURGOS
08 Director Learning Resources ... Prof. Maria de los Angeles ZAVALA-COLÓN
11 Dean Administrative Affairs ... Mr. Abdiel MARTÍNEZ-BARRIOS
15 Director Human Resources ... Mrs. Idalia MORELL-MARRERO
35 Director Student Activities ... Mrs. Maribelle PERGOLA-RIVERA
36 Director Student Placement ... Prof. Judith DIAZ-DIAZ
37 Director Student Financial Aid ... Mr. Héctor CUADRADO-GARCÍA
38 Director Student Counseling ... Mrs. Miguelina GONZÁLEZ-CRUZ
81 Director Biology/Coord Chemistry ... Dr. Orlando GONZÁLEZ-GONZÁLEZ
50 Director Business Administration ... Prof. Lydia UBARRI-DE LEÓN
51 Director Continuing Education ... Dr. Jorge ORTIZ-ALVAREZ
09 Director Planning & Inst Research ... Mr. Javier ZAVALA-QUIÑONES
53 Director of Education ... Dr. Carmen A. RIVERA-TORRES
54 Director of Engineering ... Prof. Jesús ORTIZ-CINTRÓN
68 Director Physical Education ... Prof. Carlos MARICHAL-LUGO
79 Director Humanities ... Dr. Luis H. PABÓN-BATLLE
83 Director Social Sciences ... Dr. Elizabeth CRESPO-KEBLER
77 Director Computer Science ... Prof. Antonio HUERTAS-BERMÚDEZ
75 Director Secretarial Sciences ... Prof. Nancy JIMÉNEZ-PÉREZ
72 Director Electronics ... Prof. Jesús ORTIZ-CINTRÓN
23 Director Health Services ... Dr. Jorge L. TORRES-SÁNCHEZ
96 Director of Purchasing ... Mr. Agustin GRATEROLE-ROSARIO
88 Director Special Services ... Dr. Fermando FERNANDEZ-MARTÍNEZ
81 Director of Physics ... Dr. Javier AVALOS-SÁNCHEZ
88 Director English ... Dr. Luis PABÓN-BATLLE
88 Director Spanish ... Dr. Luis H. PABÓN-BATLE
81 Director Mathematics ... Prof. Angel MORERA-GONZÁLEZ
18 Coord Facilities/Physical Plant ... Mr. Samuel SÁEZ-HERNÁNDEZ

*University of Puerto Rico-Carolina University College (H)

PO Box 4800, Carolina PR 00984-4800
County: San Juan FICE Identification: 030160
Unit ID: 243142
Telephone: (787) 257-0000 Carnegie Class: Bac/Diverse
FAX Number: (787) 750-7940 Calendar System: Quarter
URL: www.uprc.edu
Established: 1974 Annual Undergrad Tuition & Fees (In-State): $4,350
Enrollment: 4,004 Coed
Affiliation or Control: State IRS Status: 501(c)3
Highest Offering: Baccalaureate
Program: Occupational; 2-Year Principally Bachelor's Creditable; Liberal Arts And General

Accreditation: M

02 Chancellor ... Prof. Trinidad FERNANDEZ-MIRANDA
05 Dean of Academic Affairs ... Dra. Ana E. FALCON
11 Dean Administrative Affairs ... Mr. Rafael GEIRBOLINI
32 Dean Student Affairs ... Dr. Gerardo PERFECTO
06 Registrar ... Mr. Abelardo MARTINEZ
16 Human Resources ... Mrs. Elizabeth NEGRON
09 Director of Planning/Inst Research ... Prof. Carmen L. CRUZ
08 Director Learning Resources Center ... Prof. Stanley PORTELA
51 Director Continuing Education ... Prof. Luis RIVERA
07 Admissions Officer ... Mrs. Celia MENDEZ
14 Coord/Dir Computer Sys Center ... Mr. Christian TOLEDO
37 Financial Aid Officer ... Mrs. Carmen M. MARRERO
22 Affirmative Action Officer ... Mrs. Rosa QUINONES
29 Alumni Affairs Officer ... Mrs. Luisa BATLLE
88 Director Graphic Arts/Advertising ... Prof. Orlando TORRES
50 Director Banking/Finance/Insurance ... Prof. Mario MAURA
81 Director Natural Sciences ... Prof. Marisol RODRIGUEZ
88 Director Secretarial Sciences ... Prof. Tomas R. CLEMENTE
83 Director Social Sciences ... Dra. Carmen A. BALSA
68 Director Physical Education ... Dra. Awilda NUNEZ
88 Director Auto Tech/Mech Engineering ... Prof. Walbert MARCANO
79 Director Humanities ... Prof. Jose RIVERA
88 Director Spanish ... Prof. Jose QUINONES
88 Director English ... Prof. Katheryn ROBINSON
88 Dean Hotel Administration School ... Prof. Miguel E. PEREZ
23 Director Health Care ... Dr. Jesus M. AYUSO
19 Security Officer ... Mr. Gregory BERMUDEZ
18 Supt Operations & Maintenance ... Ing. Herman MUNIZ
41 Athletic Director ... Mr. Arcadio OCASIO
96 Director of Purchasing ... Mrs. Lourdes Z. ORTIZ
10 Chief Business Officer ... Mrs. Sarahi GUADALUPE

*University of Puerto Rico at Cayey (A)

205 Antonio R Barcelo Avenue, Cayey PR 00736
County: Cayey FICE Identification: 007206
Unit ID: 243151
Telephone: (787) 738-2161 Carnegie Class: Bac/Diverse
FAX Number: (787) 738-8039 Calendar System: Semester
URL: web1.oss.cayey.upr.edu/main/
Established: 1967 Annual Undergrad Tuition & Fees (In-State): $4,350
Enrollment: 3,631 Coed
Affiliation or Control: State IRS Status: 501(c)3
Highest Offering: Baccalaureate
Program: Liberal Arts And General; Teacher Preparatory; Professional
Accreditation: #M, TED

02 Chancellor ... Dr. Juan N. VARONA
05 Dean of Academic Affairs ... Dr. Jose A. MOLINA
11 Dean of Administration Affairs ... Prof. Angel RIVERA
32 Dean of Student Affairs ... Dr. Ivonne BAYRON
08 Director Library ... Dr. Duay RIVERA
06 Interim Registrar ... Mrs. Daisy RAMOS
15 Director Human Resources ... Mr. Jose R. POLO
56 Head Extension Division ... Dr. Enid CARABALLO
37 Director Student Financial Aid ... Mr. William RIOS
38 Director Student Counseling ... Prof. Carilu PEREZ
36 Interim Director Student Placement ... Mrs. Rosa ORTIZ
14 Director Computer Center ... Mr. Ramon MARTINEZ
45 Director Planning & Development ... Prof. Irmannette TORRES-LUGO
07 Director Admissions ... Mrs. Enerida RODRIGUEZ
18 Director Facilities/Physical Plant ... Mr. Edwin MELENDEZ
23 Director Health Services ... Dr. Sandra LISBOA
19 Director Security/Safety ... Mr. Carlos GUTIERREZ
92 Director Honor Program ... Prof. Samuel FIGUEROA
88 Director External Resources ... Prof. Gladys RAMOS
20 Associate Academic Officer ... Dr. Carlos R. CASANOVA
20 Associate Academic Officer ... Dr. Glorivee ROSARIO
20 Associate Academic Officer ... Prof. Ricardo COLON
04 Assistant to the Chancellor ... Prof. Gladys RAMOS
04 Assistant to the Chancellor ... Prof. Ismael QUILES
41 Director Athletic ... Prof. Efrain COLON
26 Chief Public Relations Officer ... Mr. Angel R. ROSA
29 Director Alumni Relations ... Mrs. Gema C. FIGUEROA
44 Director Annual or Planned Giving ... Mrs. Gema C. FIGUEROA
96 Director Purchasing ... Mrs. Candida COLON
43 Director Legal Services ... Mr. Pedro CRUZ
88 Student Ombudsman ... Prof. Evelyn COLLAZO
53 Education ... Dr. Edwin FLORES
79 Humanities ... Prof. Harry HERNANDEZ
83 Social Sciences ... Dr. Luis GALANES
88 Hispanic Studies ... Prof. Jose PEREZ
88 English ... Dr. Nelson VICENTE
81 Chemistry ... Dr. Juan ESTEVEZ
65 Natural Science ... Vacant
88 Biology ... Dr. Vivian MESTEY
94 Women's Studies ... Dr. Sarah MALAVE
09 Director Assess & Inst Research ... Prof. Irmannette TORRES-LUGO
10 Chief Business Officer ... Mr. Jose COLON
88 Director Budgeting ... Mr. Gonzalo COLON
81 Mathematics-Physics ... Prof. Rolando CID
50 Business Administration ... Prof. Edfel RIVERA
72 Technology & Office Administration ... Dr. Rochellie MARTINEZ
68 Physical Education ... Prof. Efrain COLON

*University of Puerto Rico-Humacao (B)

Bo. Tejas Estacion Postal CUH, Humacao PR 00791
County: Humacao FICE Identification: 003943
Unit ID: 243179
Telephone: (787) 850-0000 Carnegie Class: Bac/Diverse
FAX Number: (787) 852-4638 Calendar System: Semester
URL: www.uprh.edu
Established: 1962 Annual Undergrad Tuition & Fees (In-State): $2,290
Enrollment: 4,676 Coed
Affiliation or Control: State IRS Status: 501(c)3
Highest Offering: Baccalaureate
Program: Occupational; 2-Year Principally Bachelor's Creditable; Liberal Arts And General; Teacher Preparatory
Accreditation: M, ACBSP, ADNUR, ENGT, NUR, #OTA, PTAA, SW, TED

02 Chancellor ... Dra. Carmen H. HERNANDEZ
05 Int Dean Academic Affairs ... Dra. Ida RODRIGUEZ
11 Int Dean Administrative Affairs ... Mrs. Mariolga ROTGER
04 Assistant to the Chancellor ... Vacant
32 Dean Student Affairs ... Dr. David FERRER
26 Director Public Relations ... Vacant
20 Assistant Dean Academic Affairs ... Prof. Carmen S. ALBINO
20 Assistant Dean Academic Affairs ... Dra. Helena MENDEZ
30 Director University Development ... Prof. Luis R. RODRIGUEZ
06 Registrar ... Mr. Jorge ACEVEDO
07 Director of Admissions ... Mrs. Elizabeth GERENA
08 Director of the Library ... Mr. Felix BAEZ
13 Dir Computer/Commun & Info Mgmt ... Ms. Milagros MORALES
15 Acting Director Human Resources ... Ms. Maria ROSA
10 Director of Finance ... Mrs. Ines SANCHEZ
37 Asst Financial Aid Officer ... Mr. Larry CRUZ
38 Director Interdis/Intreg Dev Std ... Sra. Josefina SANCHEZ
56 Dir Continuing Education/Extension ... Dr. Maria E. PENA
23 Director Health Services ... Dr. Arnaldo REYES
18 Chief Facilities/Physical Plant ... Mr. Omar MUNIZ
19 Director Security/Safety ... Mr. Carlos FIGUEROA
96 Director of Purchasing ... Mrs. Ana H. RODRIGUEZ
22 Dir Equal Employ Oppty/Stdnt Ombdpn ... Mrs. Ivette IRIZARRY
41 Athletic Director ... Mr. W. Elmer GONZALEZ
26 Coordinator External Resources ... Prof. Gladys DEJESUS

*University of Puerto Rico-Mayaguez Campus (C)

PO Box 9000, Mayaguez PR 00681-9000
County: Mayaguez FICE Identification: 003944
Unit ID: 243197
Telephone: (787) 832-4040 Carnegie Class: DRU
FAX Number: (787) 834-3031 Calendar System: Semester
URL: www.uprm.edu
Established: 1911 Annual Undergrad Tuition & Fees (In-State): $2,300
Enrollment: 13,221 Coed
Affiliation or Control: State IRS Status: 501(c)3
Highest Offering: Doctorate
Program: Occupational; Liberal Arts And General; Teacher Preparatory; Professional
Accreditation: M, ENG, NUR, TED

02 President ... Dr. Jorge I. VELEZ-AROCHO
05 Dean of Academic Affairs ... Dr. Mildred CHAPARRO
11 Dean Administration ... Prof. Jose A. FRONTERA-AGENJO
32 Dean of Students ... Dr. Victor SIBERIO TORRES
49 Dean of Arts & Sciences ... Dr. Moises ORENGO AVILES
54 Dean of Engineering ... Dr. Ramon E. VASQUEZ ESPINOSA
47 Dean of Agricultural Sciences ... Dr. John FERNANDEZ VAN CLEVE
50 Dean Business Administration ... Prof. Eva Z. QUINONES
58 Director of Graduate Studies ... Dr. Anand D. SHARMA
14 Director Computer Center ... Eng. Victor DIAZ
06 Registrar ... Mrs. Briseida MELENDEZ
08 Director of the Library ... Prof. Jose A. MARI-MUTT
07 Director of Admissions ... Ms. Norma TORRES
37 Director Student Financial Aid ... Mrs. Ana I. RODRIGUEZ
36 Director Student Placement ... Mrs. Nancy NIEVES
26 Director of Information ... Mrs. Margarita SANTORI
45 Director Inst Research/Planning ... Dr. Antonio GONZALEZ
29 Director Alumni Association ... Miss Yomarachaliff LUCIANO-FIGUEROA
15 Director of Personnel Services ... Mr. Luis AROCHO
18 Director of Physical Resources ... Eng. Roberto AYALA
35 Director Student Affairs ... Dr. Victor SIBERIO
38 Director Student Counseling ... Dr. Nidia LOPEZ
21 Director of Financial Services ... Mr. Dario TORRES
96 Director of Purchasing ... Vacant
51 Director Continuing Education ... Dr. Rebecca ORAMA
19 Director Security/Safety ... Mr. Roberto TORRES
23 Director Health Services ... Mrs. Rosie TORRES
41 Athletic Director ... Mr. Hector B. FIGUEROA
43 Director Legal Services ... Lic. Elvia M. CAMAYD-VELEZ

*University of Puerto Rico-Medical Sciences Campus (D)

PO Box 365067, San Juan PR 00936-5067
County: San Juan FICE Identification: 024600
Unit ID: 243203
Telephone: (787) 758-2525 Carnegie Class: Spec/Med
FAX Number: (787) 767-0755 Calendar System: Semester
URL: www.rcm.upr.edu
Established: 1950 Annual Undergrad Tuition & Fees (In-State): $4,374
Enrollment: 2,371 Coed
Affiliation or Control: State IRS Status: 501(c)3
Highest Offering: Doctorate
Program: Professional
Accreditation: M, CYTO, DA, DENT, DIETI, HSA, MED, MIDWF, MT, NMT, NURSE, OT, PH, PHAR, PTA, RAD, SP

02 Chancellor ... Dr. Rafael RODRIGUEZ-MERCADO
05 Dean of Academic Affairs ... Dr. Ilka C. RIOS
32 Dean of Students ... Dr. Maria HERNANDEZ
11 Dean of Administration ... Mr. Eleuterio POMALES
63 Interim Dean of School of Medicine ... Dr. Pedro J. SANTIAGO-BORRERO
52 Dean of School of Dental Medicine ... Dr. Humberto VILLA
69 Dean of Grad School Public Health ... Dr. Jose CORDERO
67 Dean of School of Pharmacy ... Dr. Wanda MALDONADO
76 Dean School of Health Professions ... Dr. Estela ESTAPE
66 Dean of School of Nursing ... Dr. Maria CASTRO
100 Chief of Staff ... Dr. Lyvia ALVAREZ
20 Associate Academic Officer ... Dr. Juanita VILLAMIL
13 Director Information Technology ... Prof. Sandra SANTOS
43 Director Legal Services ... Mr. Raul BANDAS
27 Chief Information Officer ... Ms. Melba GUZMAN
06 Registrar ... Mr. Reinaldo POMALES
08 Library Director ... Dr. Irma QUINONES
09 Director Inst & Academic Research ... Dr. Wanda BARRETO
24 Director Educational Media ... Prof. Efrain FLORES
35 Director Student Affairs ... Mrs. Rosa VELEZ
07 Director of Admissions ... Mrs. Margarita RIVERA
38 Director of Student Counseling ... Prof. Blanca AMOROS
37 Director of Student Financial Aid ... Mrs. Cruz Zoraida FIGUEROA
10 Chief Financial Officer ... Mrs. Maribel HERNANDEZ
15 Director Personnel Services ... Mr. Nelson RIVERA
18 Chief Facilities/Physical Plant ... Mr. Julio A. COLLAZO
96 Director of Purchasing ... Mr. Jose CARDONA
19 Director Security Office ... Mr. William FIGUEROA

*University of Puerto Rico at Ponce (E)

PO Box 7186, Ponce PR 00732-7186
County: Ponce FICE Identification: 009652
Unit ID: 243212
Telephone: (787) 844-8181 Carnegie Class: Bac/Diverse
FAX Number: (787) 844-8679 Calendar System: Semester
URL: www.uprp.edu
Established: 1970 Annual Undergrad Tuition & Fees (In-State): $8,557
Enrollment: 3,233 Coed
Affiliation or Control: State IRS Status: 501(c)3
Highest Offering: Baccalaureate
Program: Occupational; Liberal Arts And General
Accreditation: M, ACBSP, PTAA, TED

02 Chancellor ... Dr. Fernando A. RODRIGUEZ
04 Assistant to the Chancellor ... Mrs. Reina M. GONZALEZ
05 Dean Academic Affairs ... Prof. Lizzette A. ROIG
11 Dean Administrative Affairs ... Mr. Harry BENGOCHEA
32 Dean Student Affairs ... Prof. Felix A. CUEZAS
20 Associate Academic Dean ... Prof. Pier LECONTE
45 Dir Inst Research/Planning Officer ... Prof. Ivonne VILARINO
08 Director Library ... Prof. Saulo COTTO
06 Registrar ... Mr. Francisco TORO
38 Director of Student Counseling ... Dr. Margarita VILLAMIL
07 Director of Admissions ... Mrs. Acmin VELAZQUEZ
37 Director of Financial Aid ... Mrs. Ada HERENCIA
15 Director of Personnel Services ... Mr. Juan C. LEON
88 Director of Cultural Activities ... Mr. Jose L. PONS
14 Director of Computer Center ... Prof. Juan VEGA
18 Chief Facilities/Physical Plant ... Mr. Alberto GARCIA
40 Director Bookstore ... Prof. Roberto COLON
41 Athletic Director ... Mrs. Lesbia COLON
23 Director Health Services ... Dr. Daniela GONZALEZ
29 Director Alumni Relations ... Miss Grisobelle VIRELLA
30 Chief Development ... Vacant
19 Director of Security/Traffic ... Mr. German PIMENTEL
88 Coordinator Security/Safety ... Mr. Francisco HERNANDEZ
22 Coordinator Affirmative Action ... Mrs. Erica RODRIGUEZ

*University of Puerto Rico-Rio Piedras Campus (F)

PO Box 23300, Rio Piedras PR 00931-3300
County: San Juan FICE Identification: 007108
Unit ID: 243221
Telephone: (787) 763-3877 Carnegie Class: RU/H
FAX Number: (787) 764-8799 Calendar System: Semester
URL: www.uprrp.edu
Established: 1903 Annual Undergrad Tuition & Fees (In-State): $2,216
Enrollment: 17,539 Coed
Affiliation or Control: State IRS Status: 501(c)3
Highest Offering: Doctorate
Program: Liberal Arts And General; Teacher Preparatory; Professional
Accreditation: #M, ACBSP, CORE, DIETD, LAW, LIB, PLNG, SPAA, SW, TED

02 Chancellor ... Dr. Ana R. GUADALUPE
05 Dean Academic Affairs ... Dr. Astrid CUBANO
11 Dean of Administration ... Mr. Alberto FELICIANO
32 Dean of Students ... Dr. Mayra CHARRIEZ
38 Director of Student Counseling ... Mrs. Raquel LOPEZ
20 Associate Dean Academic Affairs ... Prof. Leticia M. FERNANDEZ
30 Int Dir Devel & Alumni Relations ... Vacant
06 Registrar ... Mr. Juan M. APONTE
08 Acting Director of Library System ... Dr. Snejanka PENKOVA
15 Acting Director of Personnel ... Mrs. Aida ROSARIO
07 Director of Admissions ... Mrs. Cruz Belinda VALENTIN
14 Director of Computer Center ... Dr. Marialina BARCELO
50 Dean Business Administration ... Dr. Paul LATORTUE

48 Dean of Architecture .... Prof. Francisco RODRIGUEZ
81 Dean of Natural Sciences .... Dr. Brad WEINER
83 Dean of Social Sciences .... Dr. Carlos E. SEVERINO
61 Dean of Law .... Ms. Vivian NEPTUNE
97 Dean of General Studies .... Dr. Luis FERRAO
79 Dean of Humanities .... Dr. Jorge L. RAMOS-ESCOBAR
58 Dean Graduate Studies/Research .... Dr. Haydee SEIJO
53 Dean of Education .... Dr. Juanita RODRIGUEZ
35 Associate Dean Student Affairs .... Prof. Gloria DIAZ
62 Director Grad Sch Library/Info Sci .... Dr. Luisa VIGO
60 Director School of Communication .... Dr. Eliseo COLON
58 Dir Graduate Sch of Planning .... Dr. Elias R. GUTIERREZ
51 Dir Continuing Educ/Extension .... Mrs. Melba MARTINEZ
09 Director of Institutional Research .... Prof. Zulyn RODRIGUEZ
18 Chief Planning/Physical Devel Ofc .... Ing. Raul CINTRON
26 Chief Public Relations Officer .... Mrs. Rosa RIVERA
37 Director of Student Financial Aid .... Mrs. Ana HERNANDEZ
96 Director of Purchasing .... Mrs. Ivonne MATIENZO-CARRERO

*University of Puerto Rico at Utuado (A)

PO Box 2500, Utuado PR 00641-0500
County: Utuado FICE Identification: 029384
Unit ID: 243188
Telephone: (787) 894-2828 Carnegie Class: Bac/Diverse
FAX Number: (787) 894-2877 Calendar System: Semester
URL: www.uprutuado.edu/cormo.htm
Established: 1979 Annual Undergrad Tuition & Fees (In-State): $2,944
Enrollment: 1,528 Coed
Affiliation or Control: State IRS Status: 501(c)3
Highest Offering: Baccalaureate
Program: Occupational; 2-Year Principally Bachelor's Creditable; Liberal Arts And General
Accreditation: #M, ACBSP, TED

02 Chancellor .... Prof. Eladio GONZALEZ
05 Chief Academic Officer .... Dr. Eneida RODRIGUEZ
10 Chief Business Officer .... Dr. Luis TAPIA
32 Chief Student Life Officer .... Prof. Carolyn MERCADO
08 Head Librarian .... Prof. Regina OQUENDO
09 Director Institutional Research .... Dr. Luz MENDEZ
06 Registrar .... Mrs. Marilia SANTIAGO
07 Director of Admission .... Mrs. Livette REYES
15 Director Personnel Services .... Mrs. Rebecca CUEVAS
38 Director Student Counseling .... Vacant
37 Director Student Financial Aid .... Mrs. Carmen GONZALEZ
14 Director Computer Center .... Mrs. Maricelis RIVERA
18 Chief Facilities/Physical Plant .... Vacant
19 Director Security/Safety .... Mr. Miguel TORRES
41 Director of Athletics .... Mr. Miguel RODRIGUEZ
47 Director of Agriculture .... Dr. Marisol DÁVILA
50 Dir Office Systems/Business Admin .... Mrs. Debra GONZALEZ
96 Director of Purchasing .... Mrs. Luz MARTINEZ
51 Director Continuing Education .... Prof. Gelsy COLON
53 Director Education .... Dr. Mariela CORDERO
88 Director Natural Sciences .... Mr. Jorge TORRES
79 Director Humanities/Spanish/English .... Prof. Hector REYES

University of the Sacred Heart (B)

Box 12383 Loiza Station, Santurce PR 00914-0383
County: San Juan FICE Identification: 003937
Unit ID: 243443
Telephone: (787) 728-1515 Carnegie Class: Master's M
FAX Number: (787) 728-1692 Calendar System: Semester
URL: www.sagrado.edu
Established: 1935 Annual Undergrad Tuition & Fees: $5,170
Enrollment: 5,083 Coed
Affiliation or Control: Roman Catholic IRS Status: 501(c)3
Highest Offering: Master's
Program: Occupational; Liberal Arts And General; Teacher Preparatory; Professional
Accreditation: M, NUR, SW

01 President .... Dr. Jose J. RIVERA
84 Dir Inst Plng/Assessmt/Enroll Mgmt .... Prof. Lilia PLANELL
05 Dean Academic/Student Affairs .... Dr. Lydia ESPINET
11 Dean of Administration .... Mr. Jose L. RICCI
30 Dean of Development .... Prof. Adlin RIOS
20 Associate Academic Dean .... Prof. Yezmin HERNANDEZ
32 Associate Students Dean .... Prof. Pedro FRAILE
09 Director of Inst Research Office .... Dr. Carmen PADIAL
07 Director of Admissions .... Prof. Lilia PLANELL
06 Registrar .... Ms. Mildred PINEIRO
26 Chief Public Relations Officer .... Mrs. Maria E. MADRID
21 Director of Budgeting .... Mrs. Lourdes BERTRAN
91 Director Admin Computer Center .... Ms. Carmen CINTRON
18 Chief Facilities/Physical Plant .... Mr. Jose L. RICCI
15 Director Personnel Services .... Ms. Sol A. GOMILA
29 Director Alumni Relations .... Mrs. Elizabeth VARGAS
08 Head Librarian .... Mrs. Sonia DIAZ
37 Director of Financial Aid .... Vacant
39 Director Student Housing .... Ms. Livia D. PASTRANA
41 Athletic Director .... Mr. Jose L. BURGOS
42 Chaplain .... Vacant
10 Director Finance Office .... Mrs. Marissel FLORES
50 Director Business Administration .... Prof. José V. PAGÁN
53 Director Education Department .... Dr. Migdalia OQUENDO
60 Director Communication Department .... Prof. Elmer GONZALEZ
83 Director Social Science Department .... Vacant
81 Director Natural Sciences .... Prof. Francisco FERRER

79 Dir Fac Intdspln Human/Social Stds .... Prof. Isabel YAMÍN
21 Internal Auditor .... Mr. Ricardo AGUIRRE
24 Dir Center for FAC/Rchmnt/Educ Tech .... Mrs. Sylvia ALVAREZ
51 Assoc Director Continuing Education .... Mrs. Elvia AGOSTO
19 Coordinator Security/Safety .... Mr. Jose LOZADA
21 Coord Inst Devel Center for CFRET .... Mr. Wally ALVARANZA
88 Coord Edu Tech CFRET/FAC/Rchmnt .... Ms. Sylvia ALVAREZ
24 Coord Multimedia Product of CFRET .... Mr. Benigno ROSA

VIRGIN ISLANDS

University of the Virgin Islands (C)

2 John Brewers Bay, Saint Thomas VI 00802-9990
FICE Identification: 003946
Unit ID: 243665
Telephone: (340) 776-9200 Carnegie Class: Bac/Diverse
FAX Number: (340) 693-1005 Calendar System: Semester
URL: www.uvi.edu
Established: 1962 Annual Undergrad Tuition & Fees (In-State): $4,594
Enrollment: 2,733 Coed
Affiliation or Control: State IRS Status: 501(c)3
Highest Offering: Master's
Program: Liberal Arts And General; Teacher Preparatory; Professional
Accreditation: M, ADNUR, NUR

01 President .... Dr. David HALL
100 Chief of Staff .... Dr. Noreen M. MICHAEL
88 Special Asst to the President .... Dr. Haldene DAVIES
05 Provost .... Dr. Karl WRIGHT
20 Director of Academic Affairs .... Ms. Maria FLEMING
46 VP Research/Public Service .... Dr. Henry H. SMITH
84 Vice Provost Access/Enroll Services .... Dr. Judith EDWIN
07 Dir Admissions/Recruitment .... Dr. Xuri M. ALLEN
06 Registrar .... Ms. Heather HOGARTH-SMITH
37 Director of Financial Aid .... Ms. Cheryl A. ROBERTS
41 Athletics Director .... Mr. Peter SAUER
09 Dir Institutional Research/Planning .... Vacant
27 Chief Information Officer .... Ms. Tina M. KOOPMANS
08 Manager of Library/Fac Tech Svcs .... Ms. Judith ROGERS
12 Campus Exec Admin-St Thomas .... Ms. Dianne PIPER
32 Assc Campus Adm Stdnt Aff-St Thomas .... Dr. Doris BATTISTE
36 Counseling Supervisor-St Thomas .... Ms. Verna RIVERS
40 Bookstore Manager-St Thomas .... Mr. Mervin V. TAYLOR
12 Campus Exec Admin-St Croix .... Mr. Claude C. STEELE
32 Assoc Campus Adm Stdnt Aff-St Croix .... Ms. Miriam OSBORNE-ELLIOTT
36 Counseling Supervisor-St Croix .... Ms. Doris FARRINGTON-HEPBURN
40 Bookstore Manager-St Croix .... Ms. Laurel A. HECKER
19 Chief of Security .... Mr. Roderick C. PULLEN
18 Plant Maintenance Manager .... Mr. Charles MARTIN
30 VP Institutional Advancement .... Ms. Dionne V. JACKSON
29 Director of Alumni Affairs .... Ms. Linda SMITH
44 Director of Major Gifts .... Mr. Mitchell NEAVES
26 Director Public Relations .... Ms. Patrice JOHNSON
10 VP Administration & Finance .... Mr. Vincent SAMUEL
21 Controller .... Ms. Peggy SMITH
15 Director of Human Resources .... Ms. Bettina MILLER
96 Purchasing Supervisor .... Mr. Eric CHRISTIAN

Index of Key Administrators

A

ABUZNEID, Abdelshakour, A .... 203-576-4113 ..... 94 D abuzneid@bridgeport.edu
ACCAPADI, Mamta .... 541-737-8748 .... 418 F mamta.accapadi@oregonstate.edu
ACCARDI, Michael .... 978-837-5062 .... 242 D accardim@merrimack.edu
ACCIARDO, Linda, A .... 401-874-2116 .... 454 E lindaa@advance.uri.edu
ACCOMANDO, Annette ...... 337-521-8954 .... 212 B annette.accomando@southlouisiana.edu
ACCORD, Richard, D .... 304-462-4107 .... 543 F richard.accord@glenville.edu
ACCORNERO, Christina ..... 864-644-5226 .... 461 B caccornero@swu.edu
ACEBO, Kayla, K .... 918-631-3288 .... 413 F kayla-acebo@utulsa.edu
ACERNO, Louis .... 212-752-1530 .... 338 C louis.acerno@limcollege.edu
ACEVEDO, Blanca .... 787-743-7979 .... 565 F ut_bacevedo@suagm.edu
ACEVEDO, Francisco .... 787-264-1912 .... 563 G facevedo@sg.inter.edu
ACEVEDO, Gladys .... 787-891-0925 .... 562 G gacevedo@aguadilla.inter.edu
ACEVEDO, Ivonne .... 787-891-0925 .... 562 G iaecheva@ns.inter.edu
ACEVEDO, Jorge .... 787-850-9380 .... 567 B jorge.acevedo4@upr.edu
ACEVEDO, Luis .... 787-250-1912 .... 563 E laacevedo@metro.inter.edu
ACEVEDO, Marta, I .... 787-279-1912 .... 563 B macevedo@bayamon.inter.edu
ACEVEDO-RIOS, Carmen ... 787-725-6500 .... 560 G cacevedo@albizu.edu
ACEVES, Salvador, D .... 415-422-6136 ..... 76 B acevess@usfca.edu
ACEVES, William, C .... 619-239-0391 ..... 37 D waceves@cwsl.edu
ACFALLE, Valerie .... 713-973-3122 .... 486 A vacfalle@devry.edu
ACHACOSO, Michelle .... 512-863-1939 .... 495 G achacosm@southwestern.edu
ACHAMPONG, Francis, K .. 724-430-4200 .... 439 F fka3@psu.edu
ACHAMPONG, Francis, K .. 724-430-4200 .... 440 A fka3@psu.edu
ACHARYA, Suresh .... 269-749-7666 .... 257 D sacharya@olivetcollege.edu
ACHEMIRE, Roy .... 918-293-4724 .... 410 E roy.achemire@okstate.edu
ACHENBACH, USMS, Gerard .... 231-995-1203 .... 256 G gachenbach@nmc.edu
ACHESON, Carol .... 503-253-3443 .... 417 H cacheson@ocom.edu
ACHS, Carol .... 480-461-7742 ..... 15 K carol.achs@mcmail.maricopa.edu
ACHTER, John .... 715-232-2468 .... 552 C achterj@uwstout.edu
ACHTERBERG, Cheryl, L ... 614-292-2461 .... 398 H achterberg.1@osu.edu
ACIERNO, Kevin, K .... 440-964-4245 .... 393 E kacierno@kent.edu
ACIERNO, Lou .... 212-343-1234 .... 341 B lacierno@mcny.edu
ACIPELLA, Jennifer .... 212-924-5900 .... 357 A japicella@swedishinstitute.edu
ACK, Nicole .... 360-867-5371 .... 533 I ackn@evergreen.edu
ACKER, Casey .... 979-830-4146 .... 482 A casey.acker@blinn.edu
ACKER, Don .... 724-339-7542 .... 437 E dacker@nbi.edu
ACKERKNECHT, Steven, M 518-255-5214 .... 354 E ackerksm@cobleskill.edu
ACKERLEY, Roseanne .... 513-487-3234 .... 391 E rackerley@huc.edu
ACKERMAN, Ben .... 812-330-6087 .... 175 H backerma@ivytech.edu
ACKERMAN, Debbie .... 217-732-3155 .... 156 G dackerman@lincolncollege.edu
ACKERMAN, Deborah .... 503-253-3443 .... 417 H dackerman@ocom.edu
ACKERMAN, Denise .... 845-758-7625 .... 323 F ackerman@bard.edu
ACKERMAN, Judy .... 240-567-5010 .... 224 E judy.ackerman@montgomerycollege.edu
ACKERMAN, Kate .... 617-217-9225 .... 231 C kackerman@baystate.edu
ACKERMAN, Kathy .... 828-286-3636 .... 371 A kackerman@isothermal.edu
ACKERMAN, Mary .... 320-762-4673 .... 265 I marya@alextech.edu
ACKERMAN, Randall, R ..... 717-749-6116 .... 440 A rra14@psu.edu
ACKERMAN, Robert, M ..... 313-577-3933 .... 260 D ackerman@wayne.edu
ACKERMANN, Arthur, J ..... 314-935-5582 .... 292 J ackermann@wustl.edu
ACKLAND, Terri .... 520-494-5227 ..... 13 F terri.ackland@centralaz.edu
ACKLEN, Joyce .... 615-687-6905 .... 466 G jacklen@abcnash.edu
ACKLEY, Brian .... 607-844-8222 .... 357 H ackleyb@TC3.edu
ACKLEY, Lavon .... 229-430-0415 .... 123 I lackley@albanytech.edu
ACKLEY, Tonya, J .... 814-362-7592 .... 449 B tja7@pitt.edu
ACKLIN, Anthony, E .... 515-574-1368 .... 185 F acklin@iowacentral.edu
ACOB-NASH, Mari .... 206-934-7804 .... 536 H mari.acob-nash@seattlecolleges.edu
ACORACE, Joan .... 603-668-6706 .... 304 E jacorace@ccsnh.edu
ACOSTA, Araceli .... 210-924-4338 .... 481 G araceli.acosta@bua.edu
ACOSTA, Daniel .... 513-558-3326 .... 403 D daniel.acosta@uc.edu
ACOSTA, Jacqueline .... 317-738-8758 .... 171 C jacosta@franklincollege.edu
ACOSTA, Jesse .... 903-566-7044 .... 506 C jacosta@uttyler.edu
ACOSTA, Lydia, M .... 954-262-6202 .... 114 B lacosta@nsu.nova.edu
ACOSTA, Michael, E .... 210-434-6711 .... 491 G meacosta@lake.ollusa.edu
ACOSTA, Pilar .... 407-708-2432 .... 117 G acostap@seminolestate.edu
ACOSTA, R. Alexander ...... 305-348-1118 .... 119 B
ACOSTA, Reynold .... 407-303-8016 .... 108 D reynold.acosta@fhchs.edu
ACOSTA-FUMERO, Carmen, J .... 787-841-2000 .... 564 I cacosta@email.pucpr.edu
ACQUAAH, George .... 301-860-3610 .... 228 A gacquaah@bowiestae.edu
ACQUAH, Emmanuel, T ..... 410-651-8414 .... 227 E etacquah@umes.edu
ACREE, Beth .... 520-621-3432 ..... 19 B acree@email.arizona.edu
ACREE, Jenny .... 785-243-1435 .... 191 H jacree@cloud.edu
ACREY, Autry .... 903-769-5739 .... 488 M autry.acrey@jarvis.edu
ACTON, Anne .... 617-422-7282 .... 243 G aacton@library.nesl.edu
ACTON, Arthur, J .... 814-393-2337 .... 442 A aacton@clarion.edu
ACTON, James .... 312-567-5000 .... 153 B jacton@iit.edu
ACTOR, Lisa .... 801-832-2731 .... 512 F lactor@westminstercollege.edu
ACUESTA, Sylvia .... 718-636-3750 .... 346 D sacuesta@pratt.edu
ACUFF, Robert, V .... 423-439-8174 .... 473 E acuffr@etsu.edu
ADACHI, Lesley, B .... 680-488-2471 .... 560 A lbadachi@gmail.com
ADACHI, Themy .... 510-430-3285 ..... 57 D themy@mills.edu
ADADE, Anthony, K .... 252-335-3203 .... 377 D akadade@mail.ecsu.edu
ADADEVOH, Vidal .... 205-453-6300 ..... 99 D
ADAIR, Adam .... 870-612-2009 ..... 25 E adam.adair@uaccb.edu
ADAIR, Troy .... 973-278-5400 .... 307 G
ADAIR, Troy .... 212-986-4343 .... 323 J taa@Berkeleycollege.edu
ADAIR, Wendy, H .... 713-313-7455 .... 499 G adairw@tsu.edu
ADAIR, Wm. Matt .... 580-327-8545 .... 409 C wmadair@nwosu.edu
ADALIAN, Paul .... 541-552-6833 .... 419 A adalianp@sou.edu
ADAM, Audrey .... 508-286-5839 .... 246 D adam_audrey@wheatonma.edu
ADAM, Baba .... 530-895-2987 ..... 31 E adamba@butte.edu
ADAM, Charles, A .... 563-333-6151 .... 188 D AdamCharlesA@sau.edu
ADAM, Cynthia .... 315-312-5555 .... 354 A adam@oswego.edu
ADAM, Don .... 512-313-3000 .... 483 G don.adam@concordia.edu
ADAMACHE, Kimberly, E ... 303-369-5151 ..... 86 I kim@plattcolorado.edu
ADAMCHICK, Georgina ..... 716-926-8942 .... 335 F gadamchick@hilbert.edu
ADAMCIK, Barbara .... 208-282-2171 .... 143 D adambarb@isu.edu
ADAMES, Jose .... 201-447-7190 .... 307 F jadames@bergen.edu
ADAMEZ, Alma .... 361-354-2369 .... 482 I adamez@coastalbend.edu
ADAMKIEWICZ, Marsha ..... 586-791-6610 .... 248 G marsha.adamkiewicz@baker.edu
ADAMO, Clare .... 860-632-3009 ..... 92 E library@holyapostles.edu
ADAMO, Paul, J .... 607-436-2535 .... 353 E adamopj@oneonta.edu
ADAMONIS, Roberta .... 305-892-7594 .... 111 K roberta.adamonis@jwu.edu
ADAMS, Al .... 281-487-1170 .... 498 E aadams@txchiro.edu
ADAMS, Alison, B .... 253-752-2020 .... 533 J communications@faithseminary.edu
ADAMS, Amy .... 614-236-6242 .... 386 C adams@capital.edu
ADAMS, Andrea .... 434-582-2681 .... 520 F ahepburn@liberty.edu
ADAMS, Andrea .... 816-802-3468 .... 283 I aadams@kcai.edu
ADAMS, Ann .... 312-503-0054 .... 160 D a-adams@northwestern.edu
ADAMS, Ann .... 541-917-4353 .... 416 H adamsa@linnbenton.edu
ADAMS, Ann .... 360-438-4382 .... 536 F aadams@stmartin.edu
ADAMS, Ann Clay .... 404-687-4524 .... 127 C adamsa@ctsnet.edu
ADAMS, Barbara, B .... 847-866-3939 .... 151 B barbara.adams@garrett.edu
ADAMS, Barbara, S .... 757-455-3352 .... 529 F badams@vwc.edu
ADAMS, Beth .... 218-855-8186 .... 266 C badams@clcmn.edu
ADAMS, Betty .... 713-797-7000 .... 496 E bnadams@pvamu.edu
ADAMS, Billy .... 254-647-3234 .... 492 E badams@rangercollege.edu
ADAMS, Bobby .... 252-335-0821 .... 369 D badams@albemarle.edu
ADAMS, Brett, C .... 443-352-4250 .... 226 E bcadams@stevenson.edu
ADAMS, Bridgett .... 229-217-4148 .... 134 C badams@moultrietech.edu
ADAMS, Carey, H .... 417-836-5247 .... 286 F careyadams@missouristate.edu
ADAMS, Carol, H .... 585-292-2341 .... 341 H cadams@monroecc.edu
ADAMS, Carol, J .... 314-968-6907 .... 293 A caroladams05@webster.edu
ADAMS, Clinton .... 909-469-5423 ..... 78 D cadams@westernu.edu
ADAMS, Cynthia .... 620-365-5116 .... 190 A adams@allencc.edu
ADAMS, David .... 301-696-3400 .... 223 C adamsd@hood.edu
ADAMS, David, R .... 626-584-5462 ..... 48 A dadams@fuller.edu
ADAMS, Dean .... 270-384-8036 .... 203 H adamsd@lindsey.edu
ADAMS, DeAnna .... 901-843-3885 .... 472 I registrar@rhodes.edu
ADAMS, Debbie .... 423-697-3300 .... 474 D
ADAMS, Denise .... 530-895-2329 ..... 31 E adamsde@butte.edu
ADAMS, Dennis, R .... 865-694-6448 .... 475 F dadams@pstcc.edu
ADAMS, Diane .... 415-955-2133 ..... 27 F dadams@alliant.edu
ADAMS, Diane .... 407-569-1336 .... 107 G diane.adams@fcc.edu
ADAMS, Don .... 210-485-0088 .... 479 B dadams@alamo.edu
ADAMS, Dorenda .... 334-229-4324 ...... 1 C dadams@alasu.edu
ADAMS, Dreidre .... 859-622-2977 .... 200 D dreidre.adams@eku.edu
ADAMS, Ed .... 704-337-2257 .... 375 G adamse@queens.edu
ADAMS, Eileen .... 407-569-1315 .... 107 G eileen.adams@fcc.edu
ADAMS, Elisa .... 617-578-7100 .... 235 D eadams@gibbsboston.edu
ADAMS, Elizabeth, T .... 818-677-2969 ..... 35 D elizabeth.t.adams@csun.edu
ADAMS, Ellen .... 718-631-6269 .... 329 A eadams@qcc.cuny.edu
ADAMS, Gary .... 218-733-2005 .... 267 B g.adams@lsc.edu
ADAMS, Gary .... 972-241-3371 .... 484 D gadams@dallas.edu
ADAMS, Grantley .... 860-738-6333 ..... 90 F gadams@nwcc.commnet.edu
ADAMS, Guy .... 916-789-8600 ..... 49 L guy_adams@heald.edu
ADAMS, Hiuko .... 404-627-2681 .... 126 A hiukongari.adams@beulah.org
ADAMS, J. Michael .... 201-692-7100 .... 310 B president@fdu.edu
ADAMS, J. Milton .... 434-924-5118 .... 525 B jma@virginia.edu
ADAMS, J. Milton .... 434-924-3728 .... 525 B jma@virginia.edu
ADAMS, Jacob .... 909-607-3318 ..... 40 C jacob.adams@cgu.edu
ADAMS, Jamele .... 781-736-3600 .... 233 A jadams@brandeis.edu
ADAMS, James, E .... 325-942-2071 .... 480 E james.adams@angelo.edu
ADAMS, JR., James, P ..... 859-257-6654 .... 206 H james.adams@uky.edu
ADAMS, Jan .... 903-510-3287 .... 502 E jada@tjc.edu
ADAMS, Jane, A .... 352-392-4574 .... 120 B jane-adams@ufl.edu
ADAMS, Jason .... 303-762-6936 ..... 83 I jason.adams@denverseminary.edu
ADAMS, Jeff .... 479-788-7221 ..... 24 D jadams@uafortsmith.edu
ADAMS, Jeffrey, R .... 717-872-3703 .... 443 C jeffrey.adams@millersville.edu
ADAMS, Jennifer .... 925-424-1002 ..... 39 A jradams@laspositascollege.edu
ADAMS, Jennifer .... 614-236-6170 .... 386 C jadams@capital.edu
ADAMS, Joe .... 202-685-7375 .... 557 F adamsj@ndu.edu
ADAMS, Johanna, L .... 302-295-1192 ..... 97 A johanna.l.adams@wilmu.edu
ADAMS, John .... 303-937-4200 ..... 82 A jadams@chu.edu
ADAMS, John .... 512-313-3000 .... 483 G john.adams@concordia.edu
ADAMS, Josh .... 707-527-4492 ..... 68 E jadams@santarosa.edu
ADAMS, Julie .... 973-655-5459 .... 311 G adamsju@mail.montclair.edu
ADAMS, Karen .... 785-242-5200 ..... 17 C
ADAMS, Karen .... 785-242-5200 .... 195 G
ADAMS, Karen .... 785-242-5200 .... 195 F karen.adams@ottawa.edu
ADAMS, Karen .... 785-242-5200 .... 178 E
ADAMS, Karen .... 785-242-5200 .... 549 E
ADAMS, Karen, H .... 812-856-5596 .... 173 B kadams@indiana.edu
ADAMS, Katherine .... 601-974-1124 .... 275 D adamska@millsaps.edu
ADAMS, Kathryn .... 573-442-2211 .... 290 G
ADAMS, Keith .... 318-345-9266 .... 210 I kadams@ladelta.edu
ADAMS, Kelly, L .... 315-792-3047 .... 359 C kadams@utica.edu
ADAMS, Ken .... 412-359-1000 .... 448 D
ADAMS, Kent .... 620-672-5641 .... 196 A kenta@prattcc.edu
ADAMS, Kevin .... 718-270-6050 .... 328 D kadams@mec.cuny.edu
ADAMS, Larry, J .... 717-780-2306 .... 430 E ljadams@hacc.edu
ADAMS, LaVerne .... 731-668-7240 .... 478 F laverne.adams@wtbc.edu
ADAMS, Lesley .... 315-781-3671 .... 335 G ladams@hws.edu
ADAMS, Linda .... 706-379-3111 .... 139 F leadams@yhc.edu
ADAMS, Linda, T .... 336-334-7965 .... 377 F ltadams@ncat.edu
ADAMS, Lisa .... 413-565-1000 .... 231 B ladams@baypath.edu
ADAMS, Lita .... 413-748-3695 .... 245 C ladams@spfldcol.edu
ADAMS, Mark .... 936-294-1158 .... 501 A marka@shsu.edu
ADAMS, Mary .... 956-364-4337 .... 499 J mary.adams@harlingen.tstc.edu
ADAMS, Mary, A .... 303-991-1575 ..... 80 H mary.adams@americansentinel.edu
ADAMS, Mary Beth .... 205-934-3254 ...... 8 G marybeth@uab.edu
ADAMS, Melvin .... 207-775-3052 .... 218 F madams@meca.edu
ADAMS, Melvin .... 614-236-6901 .... 386 C
ADAMS, Merrill .... 505-566-3371 .... 320 D adamsm@sanjuancollege.edu
ADAMS, Michael .... 505-454-5368 .... 318 E madams@luna.edu
ADAMS, Michael, B .... 415-476-4753 ..... 74 E madams@aaeod.ucsf.edu
ADAMS, Michael, F .... 706-542-1214 .... 138 C presuga@uga.edu
ADAMS, Michael, J .... 888-777-7675 .... 533 J mjadams@faithseminary.edu
ADAMS, Michelle .... 773-291-6359 .... 147 D madams@ccc.edu
ADAMS, Misti .... 318-357-5961 .... 216 B chelettem@nsula.edu
ADAMS, N. Scott .... 828-713-2520 .... 367 C sadams@montreat.edu
ADAMS, Natasha, A .... 302-857-6009 ..... 95 F nadams@desu.edu
ADAMS, Neale, J .... 515-574-1284 .... 185 F adams_n@iowacentral.edu
ADAMS, Patricia, A .... 504-280-7477 .... 213 E paadams@uno.edu
ADAMS, Patrick .... 516-876-3194 .... 353 D adamsp@oldwestbury.edu
ADAMS, Paul, S .... 570-408-4114 .... 451 G paul.adams@wilkes.edu
ADAMS, Perrie, M .... 214-648-2258 .... 507 D perrie.adams@utsouthwestern.edu
ADAMS, Philip .... 309-438-5677 .... 153 C pmadams@ilstu.edu
ADAMS, Phillip, D .... 757-823-8323 .... 521 K pdadams@nsu.edu
ADAMS, Ray, L .... 417-268-6042 .... 279 D radams@gobbc.edu
ADAMS, Rebecca, G .... 336-334-3578 .... 379 A rebecca_adams@uncg.edu
ADAMS, Regine .... 425-739-8389 .... 535 B regine.adams@lwtc.edu

ADAMS, Richard, E ... 212-749-2802 ... 339 I
radams@msmnyc.edu
ADAMS, Ricky ... 334-244-3930 ... 2 A
radams7@aum.edu
ADAMS, Rita ... 704-272-5352 ... 373 F
r-adams@spcc.edu
ADAMS, Rita, S ... 618-393-2982 ... 152 E
adamsr@iecc.edu
ADAMS, Robert, A ... 510-436-2501 ... 62 D
radams@peralta.edu
ADAMS, Robert, H ... 501-569-3202 ... 24 E
rhadams@ualr.edu
ADAMS, Robert, J ... 386-226-6119 ... 105 B
robert.adams@erau.edu
ADAMS, Rodney ... 843-525-8219 ... 461 E
radams@tcl.edu
ADAMS, Ronald, L ... 541-737-3101 ... 418 F
ronald.lynn.adams@oregonstate.edu
ADAMS, Ruth, L ... 206-281-2548 ... 537 D
radams@spu.edu
ADAMS, Sarah ... 618-252-5400 ... 164 G
sarah.adams@sic.edu
ADAMS, Sarah ... 414-297-6595 ... 554 D
adamss@matc.edu
ADAMS, Shawn ... 404-627-2681 ... 126 A
shawn.adams@beulah.org
ADAMS, Sheila, V ... 662-329-7299 ... 276 B
sadams@nsgslp.muw.edu
ADAMS, Shirley, M ... 860-832-3836 ... 91 D
sadams@charteroak.edu
ADAMS, Stacey ... 513-727-3216 ... 396 F
ADAMS, Steven, L ... 309-438-5451 ... 153 C
sladams@ilstu.edu
ADAMS, Susan ... 740-340-9464 ... 399 E
adams.709@osu.edu
ADAMS, Susan ... 919-760-8631 ... 366 G
adamss@meredith.edu
ADAMS, Susan, W ... 817-257-7926 ... 498 F
s.adams@tcu.edu
ADAMS, Susanne, H ... 910-755-7302 ... 368 C
adamss@brunswickcc.edu
ADAMS, Tracy, R ... 205-853-1200 ... 5 C
tadams@jeffstateonline.com
ADAMS, Vic ... 606-242-0416 ... 203 A
vic.adams@kctcs.edu
ADAMS, Vickie ... 256-782-5006 ... 4 L
vadams@jsu.edu
ADAMS, William, D ... 217-333-4238 ... 167 B
wdadams@illinois.edu
ADAMS, William, D ... 207-859-4604 ... 217 G
wadams@colby.edu
ADAMS, William, E ... 714-459-1140 ... 78 C
weadams@wsulaw.edu
ADAMS, William, F ... 937-255-3636 ... 556 H
william.adams@afit.edu
ADAMS-DUNFORD, Jane ... 828-227-7234 ... 379 E
jdunford@wcu.edu
ADAMS-GASTON, Javaune 614-292-9334 ... 398 H
adams-gaston.1@osu.edu
ADAMS-KEANE, Helen ... 518-445-3206 ... 322 D
hadam@albanylaw.edu
ADAMS-WENDLING,
Linda, M ... 785-827-5541 ... 194 D
linda.adams-wendling@kwu.edu
ADAMSKI, M. Patricia ... 516-463-6800 ... 335 H
patricia.adamski@hofstra.edu
ADAMSON, Bonnie, J ... 910-630-7192 ... 366 H
adamson@methodist.edu
ADAMSON, Richard ... 320-363-3164 ... 271 F
radamson@csbsju.edu
ADAMUS, Anne M, G ... 248-204-2208 ... 254 E
aadamus@ltu.edu
ADAMUS LIOTTA,
Sheila, M ... 401-865-2259 ... 453 F
sadamus@providence.edu
ADARKWA, Joshua ... 510-261-8500 ... 61 F
joshua.adarkwa@patten.edu
ADAUTO, III, Ricardo ... 915-747-5555 ... 505 E
radauto@utep.edu
ADCOX, Jay, D ... 870-235-4102 ... 23 I
jdadcox@saumag.edu
ADCOX, Kathy, S ... 252-451-8274 ... 372 B
kadcox@nash.cc.nc.us
ADCOX, William ... 713-792-2275 ... 506 D
william.adcox@uth.tmc.edu
ADDERLEY, Cedric ... 614-236-6204 ... 386 C
cadder1@capital.edu
ADDERLEY-KELLY,
Beatrice ... 202-806-5431 ... 98 B
bkelly@howard.edu
ADDICO, Solomon ... 304-442-3246 ... 545 C
solomon.addico@mail.wvu.edu
ADDINGTON, Gary ... 719-384-6859 ... 86 F
gary.addington@ojc.edu
ADDIS, Robin ... 724-437-4600 ... 441 B
addis@wvjmorgantown.edu
ADDISON, Jennifer, D ... 276-739-2458 ... 528 D
jaddison@vhcc.edu
ADDISON, Lynn ... 912-583-3285 ... 126 C
laddison@bpc.edu
ADDISON REID, Barbara ... 617-349-8507 ... 230 D
baddison@lesley.edu
ADDISON REID, Barbara ... 617-349-8507 ... 236 G
baddison@lesley.edu
ADDUCI, James ... 219-473-4325 ... 170 D
jadduci@ccsj.edu
ADDY, Cathryn, L ... 860-255-3601 ... 91 C
caddy@txcc.commnet.edu
ADEGBOYE, David, S ... 504-286-5327 ... 214 I
dadegboye@suno.edu
ADELAINE, Michael ... 605-688-4988 ... 466 B
michael.adelaine@sdstate.edu
ADELANI, Lateef ... 314-340-3319 ... 282 I
adelanil@hssu.edu
ADELBERG, Robert ... 718-261-5800 ... 324 D
radelberg@bramsonort.edu
ADELEKE, Anthony ... 317-543-4797 ... 177 H
aadeleke@martin.edu
ADELHOCH, Paula ... 201-360-4021 ... 310 F
padelhoch@hccc.edu
ADELMAN, Michael, D ... 304-647-6200 ... 544 C
madelman@osteo.wvsom.edu
ADELSBERG, Lester ... 504-762-3224 ... 210 G
ladels@dcc.edu
ADELSPERGER, Donna ... 219-989-2436 ... 178 G
adelsper@purduecal.edu
ADEN-FOX, Nancy ... 402-472-0400 ... 300 H
naden1@unl.edu
ADER, Elaine ... 916-558-2062 ... 56 D
adere@scc.losrios.edu
ADERA, Rosette, B ... 570-941-6645 ... 450 B
aderar2@scranton.edu
ADERA, Tilahuan ... 575-646-2810 ... 319 D
tadera@nmsu.edu
ADERHOLD, Mary ... 770-537-5719 ... 139 B
mary.aderhold@westgatech.edu
ADERO, Chad ... 301-846-2531 ... 222 G
cadero@frederick.edu
ADESEGUN, T.N. Nokware 404-270-5897 ... 137 E
tadesequ@spelman.edu
ADESIDA, Ilesanmi ... 217-333-2150 ... 167 B
iadesida@illinois.edu
ADEWUMI, Michael, A ... 814-863-4030 ... 438 F
m2a@psu.edu
ADEY, Penelope, S ... 518-388-6109 ... 358 E
adeyp@union.edu
ADKINS, Cathy, L ... 828-689-1395 ... 366 F
cadkins@mhc.edu
ADKINS, Deborah ... 417-269-8910 ... 281 B
daadkin@coxcollege.edu
ADKINS, Ernest ... 480-517-8202 ... 10 C
ernest.adkins@riosalado.edu
ADKINS, Gregory ... 606-326-2043 ... 201 B
greg.adkins@kctcs.edu
ADKINS, John ... 304-357-4779 ... 541 H
johnadkins@ucwv.edu
ADKINS, John, R ... 812-298-2348 ... 177 A
jadkins@ivytech.edu
ADKINS, Kay ... 530-741-6707 ... 80 E
kadkins@yccd.edu
ADKINS, Michael, T ... 804-257-5752 ... 529 D
mtadkins@vuu.edu
ADKINS, Robert ... 724-503-1001 ... 451 A
radkins@washjeff.edu
ADKINS, Sheldon ... 405-425-5250 ... 409 E
sheldon.adkins@oc.edu
ADKINS, Toni ... 931-393-1762 ... 475 C
tadkins@mscc.edu
ADKINSON, Stacy, J ... 260-399-7700 ... 180 E
sadkinson@sf.edu
ADKISON, Linda ... 816-654-7313 ... 283 J
ladksion@kcumb.edu
ADKISON, Steven ... 541-962-3511 ... 418 C
sadkison@eou.edu
ADLEMAN, Rick ... 970-248-1525 ... 82 B
radleman@mesastate.edu
ADLER, Ar ... 212-749-2802 ... 339 I
aadler@msmnyc.edu
ADLER, Brian, D ... 580-774-3063 ... 412 F
brian.adler@swosu.edu
ADLER, Brian, U ... 229-928-1361 ... 131 B
ADLER, Carol ... 505-224-4609 ... 317 J
cadler@cnm.edu
ADLER, Charles, L ... 240-895-4343 ... 226 A
cladler@smcm.edu
ADLER, Doug ... 308-398-7325 ... 297 C
dadler@cccneb.edu
ADLER, Douglas, L ... 308-398-7325 ... 297 C
dadler@cccneb.edu
ADLER, Jackie ... 254-867-3620 ... 500 B
jackie.adler@tstc.edu
ADLER, Joel ... 804-523-5454 ... 526 F
jadler@reynolds.edu
ADLER, Jonathan ... 304-766-4152 ... 544 D
adlerj@wvstateu.edu
ADLER, Karl, P ... 914-594-4600 ... 343 F
karl_adler@nymc.edu
ADLER, Shmuel ... 773-463-7738 ... 165 F
sadler@telshe.edu
ADLER, Steven ... 858-534-1709 ... 74 D
sadler@ucsd.edu
ADLER, Wendy ... 508-541-1542 ... 234 B
wadler@dean.edu
ADLEY, Jerald ... 662-254-3636 ... 276 C
jerald.adley@mvsu.edu
ADLING, Jennifer ... 806-742-3844 ... 501 D
jennifer.adling@ttu.edu
ADOLPHSON, James, I ... 206-296-6150 ... 537 F
jamesa@seattleu.edu
ADORNO, Margaret ... 909-621-8147 ... 63 A
margaret.adorno@pomona.edu
ADORNO, Victor, T ... 787-780-0070 ... 560 F
vadorno@caribbean.edu
ADOVASIO, James, M ... 814-824-2545 ... 436 C
jadovasio@mercyhurst.edu
ADRIAN, Janet ... 913-360-7117 ... 190 F
jadrian@benedictine.edu
ADRIAN, Loretta, P ... 714-241-6152 ... 40 J
ladrian@coastline.edu
ADY, Tina ... 254-526-1903 ... 482 F
martina.ady@ctcd.edu
AEDER, Scott ... 517-321-0242 ... 252 B
aederent@comcast.net
AEILTS, Larry ... 734-973-3480 ... 260 B
laeilts@wccnet.edu
AELION, C. Marjorie ... 413-545-2526 ... 237 C
maelion@schoolph.umass.edu
AESCHLIMANN,
Rodney, L ... 775-784-1113 ... 303 A
rod@admin.edu
AFDAHL, Gordon ... 812-535-5125 ... 179 C
gafdahl@smwc.edu
AFDAHL, Tami ... 307-532-8206 ... 555 H
tami.afdahl@ewc.wy.edu
AFFENITO, Sandra ... 860-231-5769 ... 93 H
saffenito@sjc.edu
AFFLECK, Arthur, G ... 910-672-1661 ... 377 E
aaffleck@uncfsu.edu
AFFLECK, Mary Ann ... 860-906-5010 ... 89 L
maffleck@ccc.commnet.edu
AFFLECK-GRAVES,
John, F ... 574-631-4700 ... 180 D
affleck-graves.1@nd.edu
AFFRE, Mara ... 208-426-1630 ... 142 F
maraaffre@boisestate.edu
AFGHANI, Carmen ... 386-763-2790 ... 114 E
carmen.afghani@palmer.edu
AFROOKHTEH, Afshin ... 714-816-0366 ... 72 I
aafrookhteh@tuiu.edu
AFSAHI, Armin ... 858-534-3902 ... 74 D
aafsahi@ucsd.edu
AFTON, Lee Ann, M ... 931-598-1238 ... 472 J
lafton@sewanee.edu
AGA, Daniel, F ... 684-699-1575 ... 558 I
d.aga@amsamoa.edu
AGAFONOV, Alexander ... 718-522-9073 ... 323 D
agafonov@asa.edu
AGAN, James, L ... 678-839-6611 ... 138 D
jagan@westga.edu
AGAR, John, R ... 610-359-5082 ... 426 G
jagar@dccc.edu
AGARWAL, Vijendra ... 507-389-5998 ... 267 H
vijendra.agarwal@mnsu.edu
AGARWAL, Vijendra, K ... 608-785-8124 ... 551 B
agarwal.vije@uwlax.edu
AGAZZI, David ... 847-543-2631 ... 147 H
dagazzi@clcillinois.edu
AGBAYANI, Amefil ... 808-956-4567 ... 141 B
agbayani@hawaii.edu
AGBOOLA, Isaac ... 202-651-5224 ... 97 E
isaac.agboola@gallaudet.edu
AGEE, Anne, S ... 617-287-5220 ... 237 D
anne.agee@umb.edu
AGEE, Doug, A ... 636-584-6714 ... 281 I
daagee@eastcentral.edu
AGEE, Patty, A ... 660-263-3900 ... 279 J
pagee@cccb.edu
AGEE, Steve ... 405-208-5276 ... 410 A
sagee@okcu.edu
AGER, Christina ... 215-572-2115 ... 422 B
ager@arcadia.edu
AGERTER, David, C ... 507-284-3293 ... 262 G
agerter.david@mayo.edu
AGESILAS, Elie ... 787-891-0925 ... 562 G
eagesilas@aguadilla.inter.edu
AGGERS, Steve ... 310-287-4513 ... 55 F
aggerss@wlac.edu
AGGREH, Julia ... 215-951-2990 ... 444 C
aggrehj@philau.edu
AGGREY, Kwesi ... 919-530-6230 ... 378 A
kaggrey@nccu.edu
AGHA-JAFFAR, Tamara ... 913-288-7689 ... 193 J
taghajaf@kckcc.edu
AGHO, Austin, O ... 317-274-4702 ... 174 B
aagho@iupui.edu
AGJMURATI, Nick ... 212-592-2000 ... 350 F
nagjmurati@sva.edu
AGLER, Deborah, S ... 260-422-5561 ... 172 L
dsagler@indianatech.edu
AGNE, Anissa ... 904-620-2698 ... 120 C
anissa.agne@unf.edu
AGNELLI, John ... 718-429-6600 ... 359 E
john.agnelli@vaughn.edu
AGNELLO-VAZQUEZ,
Jacqueline ... 914-633-2548 ... 336 E
jagnellovazquwz@iona.eduiona.edu
AGNELLO-VELEY,
Josephine ... 860-343-5751 ... 90 D
jagnello-veley@mxcc.commnet.edu
AGNESE, JR., Louis, J ... 210-829-3900 ... 503 F
agnese@uiwtx.edu
AGNESS, Annette ... 315-792-7342 ... 356 B
annette.agness@sunyit.edu
AGNETTA, Daniel ... 269-471-3302 ... 252 C
agnetta@andrews.edu
AGNETTA, Daniel, E ... 269-471-3302 ... 247 H
agnetta@andrews.edu
AGNEW, Alice ... 814-824-2362 ... 436 C
AGNEW, Donna ... 847-578-8316 ... 163 A
donna.agnew@rosalindfranklin.edu
AGNEW, F. Raymond ... 518-327-6317 ... 345 H
ragnew@paulsmiths.edu
AGNEW, Herbert (Herby) ... 478-445-5771 ... 129 F
herbert.agnew@gcsu.edu
AGNEW, Ina ... 918-293-4761 ... 410 E
ina.agnew@okstate.edu
AGNEW, Robyn, R ... 864-379-8701 ... 457 G
ragnew@erskine.edu
AGOSTA, Frank ... 212-592-2000 ... 350 F
fagosta@sva.edu
AGOSTA, William ... 814-472-3035 ... 446 B
wagosta@francis.edu
AGOSTINI, Dennis, E ... 814-866-8156 ... 433 C
dagostini@lecom.edu
AGOSTO, Elvia ... 787-728-1515 ... 568 B
eagosto@sagrado.edu
AGPAWA, Paul ... 707-476-4389 ... 42 A
paul-agpawa@redwoods.edu
AGRAS, James, R ... 412-359-1000 ... 448 E
jagras@triangle-tech.edu
AGRAS, James, R ... 412-359-1000 ... 448 D
AGRAS, James, R ... 412-359-1000 ... 448 F
jagras@triangle-tech.edu
AGRAS, Rudy, K ... 412-359-1000 ... 448 D
AGRAWAL, Ashok ... 314-513-4214 ... 289 B
aagrawal@stlcc.edu
AGRAWAL, C. Mauli ... 210-458-4426 ... 506 B
mauli.agrawal@utsa.edu
AGRAWAL, Gail, B ... 319-335-9034 ... 182 C
gail-agrawal@uiowa.edu
AGRE, Peter ... 919-668-2370 ... 363 I
peter.agre@duke.edu
AGRE-KIPPENHAN, Susan 503-883-2409 ... 416 G
AGRELA, Ramona ... 949-824-5962 ... 73 H
ragrela@uci.edu
AGRELLA, Robert, F ... 707-527-4431 ... 68 E
ragrella@santarosa.edu
AGRONOW, Sam ... 925-631-4754 ... 64 F
sja7@stmarys-ca.edu
AGUE, Paul, E ... 619-201-8701 ... 65 D
Paul.Ague@sdcc.edu
AGUERO, Robert ... 210-485-0165 ... 479 B
raguero@alamo.edu
AGUIAR, Ara ... 310-287-4238 ... 55 F
aguiara@wlac.edu
AGUIAR, Jenny ... 508-541-1519 ... 234 B
jaguiar@dean.edu
AGUILA, Nayda, G ... 617-964-1100 ... 230 B
naguila@ants.edu
AGUILAR, Carmen ... 508-678-2811 ... 239 F
carmen.aguilar@bristolcc.edu
AGUILAR, Cheryl, M ... 909-607-1232 ... 40 D
cheryl.aguilar@cmc.edu
AGUILAR, Hector ... 512-223-7663 ... 481 B
haguilar@austincc.edu
AGUILAR, Margie ... 915-842-0422 ... 488 D
AGUILAR, Maria ... 312-261-3207 ... 159 D
maria.aguilar@nl.edu
AGUILAR, Milagros ... 787-878-6000 ... 562 E
maguilar@icprjc.edu
AGUILERA, Rafael ... 806-894-9611 ... 494 C
raguilera@southplainscollege.edu
AGUILLARD, Joe ... 318-487-7401 ... 209 B
aguillard@lacollege.edu
AGUILLON, Idalia ... 509-865-8688 ... 534 D
aguillon_i@heritage.edu
AGUIRRE, Arturo ... 213-487-0110 ... 45 C
info@dula.edu
AGUIRRE, Carlos ... 210-486-4951 ... 479 C
caguirre57@alamo.edu
AGUIRRE, Faith ... 713-313-4289 ... 499 G
aguirref@tsu.edu
AGUIRRE, Ilvis ... 787-878-5475 ... 562 H
iaguirre@arecibo.inter.edu
AGUIRRE, Juan Carlos ... 956-872-6782 ... 494 D
jcaguirre@southtexascollege.edu
AGUIRRE, Ray ... 408-270-6468 ... 67 B
ray.aguirre@sjeccd.edu
AGUIRRE, Ricardo ... 787-728-1515 ... 568 B
raguirre@sagrado.edu
AGUIRRE, Richard ... 574-535-7571 ... 171 D
rraguirre@goshen.edu
AGUIRRE, Tina ... 760-355-6347 ... 50 K
tina.aguirre@imperial.edu
AGUIRRE-ACUNA, Maria ... 325-235-7349 ... 500 C
maria.aguirre@tstc.edu
AGUNDEZ, Adrian ... 661-763-7737 ... 72 C
aagundez@taftcollege.edu
AGUSTA, Diana ... 802-860-2733 ... 513 A
agusta@champlain.edu
AH SUE, John ... 684-699-9155 ... 558 I
j.ahsue@amsamoa.edu
AHANONU, Chuck ... 662-254-3618 ... 276 C
cahan@mvsu.edu

AHEARN, Michael, J .... 978-867-4004.... 235 E
michael.ahearn@gordon.edu
AHERN, Carrie, A .... 605-256-5663.... 465 G
carrie.ahern@dsu.edu
AHERN, Frank .... 352-392-9092.... 120 B
ahern@ulf.edu
AHERN, Jack .... 413-545-2710.... 237 C
jfa@ipo.umass.edu
AHERN, James .... 812-429-9884.... 176 I
jahern@ivytech.edu
AHERN, Joseph, F .... 845-758-7178.... 323 F
ahern@bard.edu
AHERN, Martin .... 617-984-1635.... 244 C
mahern@quincycollege.edu
AHERN, Michael .... 620-227-9359.... 192 B
mfahern@dc3.edu
AHERN, Susan .... 603-228-1541.... 306 G
susan.ahern@law.unh.edu
AHERN, Susan, K .... 713-221-8009.... 503 D
aherns@uhd.edu
AHERN, Tim .... 319-752-2731.... 188 G
tahern@scciowa.edu
AHERNE, John .... 845-341-4710.... 345 E
john.aherne@sunyorange.edu
AHLBURG, Dennis, A .... 210-999-8401.... 502 C
dennis.ahlburg@trinity.edu
AHLEMANN, Tina .... 843-574-6142.... 461 G
tina.ahlemann@tridenttech.edu
AHLQUIST, Michelle .... 320-762-4918.... 265 I
michellea@alextech.edu
AHMADI, Goodarz .... 315-268-6446.... 329 C
ahmadi@clarkson.edu
AHMED, Abu .... 803-210-9798.... 455 D
ahmeda@benedict.edu
AHMED, Andrea .... 520-383-8401...... 18 L
aahmed@tocc.cc.az.us
AHMED, Ansar .... 202-274-6612...... 99 F
aahmed@udc.edu
AHMED, Ismael .... 313-593-5030.... 259 E
inahmed@umd.umich.edu
AHMED, Juzar .... 812-465-7160.... 180 F
juzar@usi.edu
AHMED, Mirza, F .... 313-496-2674.... 260 C
fahmed1@wcccd.edu
AHMED, Mustaq .... 419-358-3237.... 385 B
ahmedm@bluffton.edu
AHMED, Zahir .... 573-986-6863.... 290 D
zahmed@semo.edu
AHN, Young Jin .... 714-533-1495...... 70 B
admission@southbaylo.edu
AHNER, Yolanda .... 915-831-7724.... 486 E
yahner@epcc.edu
AHO, Duane .... 906-487-7349.... 251 C
duane.aho@finlandia.edu
AHO, Leslie .... 978-368-2305.... 230 F
leslie.aho@auc.edu
AHO, Marie, M .... 906-227-2981.... 256 F
mariaho@nmu.edu
AHOLA, Scott .... 605-642-6359.... 465 F
scott.ahola@bhsu.edu
AHOUSE, Michele, L .... 781-309-6768.... 236 I
mahouse@mariancourt.edu
AHRENS, Jennifer .... 478-240-5143.... 134 F
jahrens@oftc.edu
AHUJA, Sunil .... 440-365-5222.... 395 C
aichele@stfrancis.edu
AICHELE, Christina, M .... 815-740-3363.... 167 C
caichele@stfrancis.edu
AICINENA, Steve .... 432-552-2675.... 507 C
aicinena_s@utpb.edu
AIELLO, Frank, C .... 302-356-6752...... 97 A
frank.c.aiello@wilmu.edu
AIGNER, David .... 505-424-2302.... 318 C
daigner@iaia.edu
AIKEN, Deborah, J .... 401-825-2100.... 453 B
daiken@ccri.edu
AIKEN, George .... 415-433-9200...... 68 F
gaiken@saybrook.edu
AIKEN, Katherine, G .... 208-885-6426.... 144 B
kaiken@uidaho.edu
AIKEN, Ryan .... 413-775-1309.... 240 B
aikenr@gcc.mass.edu
AIKEN, Wallace .... 330-382-7428.... 393 F
waiken@kent.edu
AIKEN, William, C .... 910-592-8081.... 373 D
baiken@sampsoncc.edu
AIKENS, Barbara .... 609-984-1141.... 316 A
baikens@tesc.edu
AILSTOCK, M. Stephen .... 410-777-2230.... 221 B
smailstock@aacc.edu
AINLAY, Stephen, C .... 518-388-6101.... 358 E
ainlays@union.edu
AINLEY, Arden .... 360-416-7716.... 538 A
arden.ainley@skagit.edu
AINSLEY, Sharon .... 610-647-4400.... 431 B
sainsley@immaculata.edu
AINSLIE, Carolyn, N .... 609-258-1447.... 313 A
ainslic@princeton.edu
AINSWORTH, Emma, L .... 662-685-4771.... 273 H
eainsworth@bmc.edu
AINSWORTH, Jerlad .... 423-425-4666.... 477 D
jerald-ainsworth@utc.edu
AINSWORTH, Patricia .... 978-542-6446.... 239 B
painsworth@salemstate.edu
AIREY, Patricia .... 540-985-8376.... 520 D
pjairey@jchs.edu
AISTRUP, Joseph .... 785-532-6900.... 194 B
jaistrup@ksu.edu
AITCHISON, Bridget .... 765-677-2389.... 174 E
bridget.aitchison@indwes.edu
AITCHISON, Cecile .... 313-593-5131.... 259 E
cecilea@umd.umich.edu
AITKEN, Renee .... 614-251-4761.... 398 F
aitkenr@ohiodominican.edu
AITSON-ROESSLER,
Mechelle .... 405-733-7308.... 411 I
maitson-roessler@rose.edu
AIYETORO, Adjoa, A .... 501-569-3000...... 24 E
aaaiyetoro@ualr.edu
AIZENSTAT, Stephen .... 805-969-3626...... 60 K
saizenstat@pacifica.edu
AJI, Aron, R .... 563-333-6053.... 188 D
AjiAronR@sau.edu
AJNAL, Mohammad .... 225-292-5464.... 207 D
AJOHDA, Sadia .... 912-583-3216.... 126 C
sajohda@bpc.edu
AKAJUOBI, Cajetan .... 334-229-4316....... 1 C
cakajuobi@alasu.edu
AKAKPO, Koffi .... 419-755-4702.... 397 B
kakakpo@ncstatecollege.edu
AKANDE, Benjamin, O .... 314-968-5951.... 293 A
akandeb@webster.edu
AKAO, Gina .... 775-850-0700.... 302 E
gakao@morrison.neumont.edu
AKCHIN, Lisa, G .... 410-455-2889.... 227 D
akchin@umbc.edu
AKE, Barbara .... 321-433-7579.... 101 J
akeb@brevardcc.edu
AKED, Michael, A .... 434-924-4245.... 525 B
maa8q@virginia.edu
AKEKE, Peter .... 508-588-9100.... 240 E
AKENS, Cathy .... 305-919-5943.... 119 B
akens@fiu.edu
AKENS, Jeff .... 916-388-2800...... 37 F
jakens@cc.edu
AKERMAN, Kate .... 617-217-9006.... 231 C
kakerman@baystate.edu
AKERMAN, Patricia .... 320-308-5966.... 269 D
pakerman@sctcc.edu
AKERS, Elaine .... 909-384-8273...... 65 C
eakers@sbccd.cc.ca.us
AKERS, Mary Anne .... 443-885-3225.... 224 F
maryanne.akers@morgan.edu
AKERS, Phil .... 503-352-3096.... 419 E
philakers@pacificu.edu
AKERS, Richard .... 304-327-4181.... 543 C
rakers@bluefieldstate.edu
AKERS, Shawn, D .... 434-592-5451.... 520 F
sdakers@liberty.edu
AKERSON, Joni .... 320-308-6158.... 269 D
jakerson@sctcc.edu
AKEY, Stacey, L .... 920-923-7652.... 548 C
sakey@marianuniversity.edu
AKHAVI, Seyed .... 212-594-4000.... 357 G
sakhavi@tcicollege.edu
AKIN, Charles .... 903-729-0256.... 502 D
cakin@tvcc.edu
AKIN, Daniel, L .... 919-761-2222.... 376 G
dakin@sebts.edu
AKIN, Hudson .... 765-285-1633.... 169 D
hakin@bsu.edu
AKIN, Joeleen .... 404-471-6170.... 123 G
jakin@agnesscott.edu
AKIN, Renea .... 270-534-3461.... 203 B
renea.akin@kctcs.edu
AKINLEYE, Johnson, O .... 910-962-3876.... 379 C
akinleyej@uncw.edu
AKINS, Erick .... 210-486-2778.... 479 E
eakins@alamo.edu
AKINS, Richie .... 912-478-5393.... 131 A
rakins@georgiasouthern.edu
AKKAWI, Kayed .... 312-935-6025.... 162 E
kakkawi@robertmorris.edu
AKL, Fred, A .... 610-499-4036.... 451 F
faakl@widener.edu
AKMAL, Hassan .... 818-932-3127...... 44 N
hakmal@devry.edu
AKMAN, Jeffrey, S .... 202-741-2880...... 97 F
akman@gwu.edu
AKOJIE, Patricia, A .... 270-686-4200.... 198 G
patricia.akojie@brescia.edu
AKRIDGE, Jay, T .... 765-494-8391.... 178 F
akridge@purdue.edu
AKRIE, Germeka .... 434-848-1864.... 523 G
gakrie@saintpauls.edu
AKST JONES, Ellen .... 641-472-7000.... 187 B
eajones@mum.edu
AKSU, Mert .... 313-994-6620.... 259 C
aksumn@udmercy.edu
AKUJIEZE, Justin .... 773-995-2404.... 146 D
jakujieze@csu.edu
AKUKWE, Chinue .... 202-274-7110...... 99 F
cakukwe@udc.edu
AL-AMIN, John .... 805-986-5813...... 77 C
jalamin@vcccd.edu
AL-HASSAN, Marilyn .... 909-915-3771...... 29 B
malhassan@argosy.edu
AL-HASSAN, Marilyn .... 909-915-3771...... 29 E
malhassan@argosy.edu
AL-HASSAN, Marilyn .... 909-915-3771...... 29 D
malhassan@argosy.edu
AL-HASSAN, Marilyn .... 909-915-3771...... 29 C
malhassan@argosy.edu
AL-HAZZAM DAWASARI,
Elizabeth .... 480-860-2700...... 14 G
edawsari@taliesin.edu
AL-JARRAH, Radwan, A .... 580-774-7152.... 412 F
radwan.aljarrah@swosu.edu
ALADE, Ayodele, J .... 410-651-6327.... 227 E
ajalade@umes.edu
ALAIMO, Joseph .... 570-408-4512.... 451 G
joseph.alaimo@wilkes.edu
ALAIMO, Kathleen .... 773-298-3090.... 163 G
alaimo@sxu.edu
ALAIMOANA-NUUSA,
Repeka .... 684-699-9155.... 558 I
r.nuusa@amsamoa.edu
ALAM, Maria .... 901-678-2886.... 474 C
malam@memphis.edu
ALAMI, Osama .... 804-827-1111.... 525 E
oalami@vcu.edu
ALAN, Patricia .... 772-462-5604.... 110 L
palan@irsc.edu
ALANDER, Link .... 832-813-6832.... 490 C
link.s.alander@lonestar.edu
ALANGAR, Sadhana .... 734-929-9089.... 249 H
sadhana@cleary.edu
ALARCIO, Rebecca .... 805-922-6966...... 26 K
ralarcio@hancockcollege.edu
ALARID, Jandee .... 409-772-9868.... 507 B
jalarid@utmb.edu
ALASIO, Claire .... 732-571-3463.... 311 F
calasio@monmouth.edu
ALAWIYE, Osman .... 320-308-3023.... 269 C
oalawiye@stcloudstate.edu
ALBANESE, Linda .... 516-678-5000.... 341 F
lalbanese@molloy.edu
ALBANESE, Marc .... 610-282-1100.... 426 I
marc.albanese@desales.edu
ALBANESE, Robert, C .... 815-753-2755.... 160 A
rca@niu.edu
ALBANO, Mark, A .... 212-746-6329.... 360 B
maa2034@med.cornell.edu
ALBANO, Ralph .... 202-319-5218...... 97 C
albano@cua.edu
ALBARRAN, Agustin .... 619-644-7600...... 49 A
agustin.albarran@gcccd.edu
ALBAYYARI, J .... 260-481-6391.... 174 A
albayyaj@ipfw.edu
ALBEE, David .... 415-257-1308...... 45 B
david.albee@dominican.edu
ALBER, Antone, F .... 716-888-2160.... 325 G
albera@canisius.edu
ALBERICO, Ralph, A .... 540-568-3828.... 520 C
alberira@jmu.edu
ALBERLE-CANNATA,
Denise .... 800-806-1917...... 92 F
DAlberle-Cannata@lincolncollegene.edu
ALBERS, Jhett .... 605-642-6885.... 465 F
jhett.albers@bhsu.edu
ALBERS, Joe .... 641-423-2530.... 186 D
ALBERS, Lisa .... 714-449-7466...... 70 G
lalbers@scco.edu
ALBERS, Sarah .... 785-442-6008.... 193 D
salbers@highlandcc.edu
ALBERS, Tim .... 970-943-2119...... 89 B
talbers@western.edu
ALBERT, Angela .... 407-708-2499.... 117 G
alberta@seminolestate.edu
ALBERT, David .... 860-768-4482...... 95 A
dalbert@hartford.edu
ALBERT, George .... 412-291-6313.... 422 D
galbert@aii.edu
ALBERT, J, L .... 404-413-4519.... 131 C
jalbert@gsu.edu
ALBERT, Juline .... 712-274-6400.... 189 H
juline.albert@witcc.edu
ALBERT, Karen .... 215-951-2847.... 444 C
albertk@philau.edu
ALBERT, Katrice, A .... 225-578-5736.... 212 F
kalber2@lsu.edu
ALBERT, Laurie .... 919-508-2025.... 375 D
lalbert@peace.edu
ALBERT, Louis .... 520-206-6752...... 17 I
lalbert@pima.edu
ALBERT, Marianne .... 724-222-5330.... 438 E
malbert@penncommercial.edu
ALBERT, OP, Peg .... 517-264-7000.... 258 D
palbert@sienaheights.edu
ALBERT, Rachel, E .... 207-834-7510.... 220 D
realbert@maine.edu
ALBERT, Rita .... 561-237-7231.... 113 D
ralbert@lynn.edu
ALBERT, Robert .... 606-783-2174.... 204 E
r.albert@moreheadstate.edu
ALBERT-GREEN, DeEadra .. 512-313-3000.... 483 G
deeadra.green@concordia.edu
ALBERTA, Richard .... 415-282-7600...... 28 B
richardalberta@actcm.edu
ALBERTELLI, Denise .... 718-409-4946.... 356 C
dalbertelli@sunymaritime.edu
ALBERTER, Marilyn, A .... 814-269-7059.... 449 D
alberter@pitt.edu
ALBERTS, David .... 724-938-4324.... 441 G
alberts@calu.edu
ALBERTS, Eugene, R .... 608-796-3849.... 553 A
eralberts@viterbo.edu
ALBERTS, Kristin, R .... 904-256-7180.... 111 J
kalbert@ju.edu
ALBERTS, Trev .... 402-554-2305.... 301 B
talberts@unomaha.edu
ALBERTSON, Eugene .... 336-887-3000.... 365 J
ealbertson@laureluniversity.edu
ALBERTSON, Kathy, S .... 912-478-5951.... 131 A
katalb@georgiasouthern.edu
ALBERTSON, Kay, H .... 919-735-5151.... 374 F
kha@waynecc.edu
ALBERTSON, Mark, R .... 336-278-6572.... 364 A
albertso@elon.edu
ALBERTSON, Ron .... 503-517-7421.... 420 A
ron.albertson@reed.edu
ALBES, Beth .... 314-529-9380.... 284 F
balbes@maryville.edu
ALBIN, John .... 212-650-3811.... 327 E
jalbi@hunter.cuny.edu
ALBIN, Martha .... 918-456-5511.... 409 A
albinml@nsuok.edu
ALBIN-HILL, Jill .... 708-524-6980.... 150 A
jalbin@dom.edu
ALBINA, Adam, R .... 603-641-7266.... 305 H
aalbina@anselm.edu
ALBINI, Marisa .... 401-333-7150.... 453 B
malbini@ccri.edu
ALBINO, Carmen, S .... 787-850-9303.... 567 B
carmen.albino@upr.edu
ALBINSON, Erik .... 319-399-8741.... 183 C
ealbinso@coe.edu
ALBISTON, Steven, K .... 208-524-3000.... 143 C
steven.albiston@my.eitc.edu
ALBON, Darrell, J .... 740-368-3070.... 400 F
djalbon@owu.edu
ALBORN, Timothy .... 718-960-8675.... 327 C
timothy.alborn@lehman.cuny.edu
ALBRECHT, Bryan, D .... 262-564-3000.... 553 H
albrechtb@gtc.edu
ALBRECHT, Catherine .... 419-772-2130.... 398 G
c-albrecht@onu.edu
ALBRECHT, Christal, M .... 904-632-5094.... 109 E
christal.albrecht@fscj.edu
ALBRECHT, Don, D .... 806-651-2050.... 498 D
dalbrecht@mail.wtamu.edu
ALBRECHT, James, M .... 253-535-7317.... 535 K
albrecjm@plu.edu
ALBRECHT, Jana .... 309-438-2231.... 153 C
jalbre2@ilstu.edu
ALBRECHT, Jon .... 813-257-3375.... 122 H
jalbrecht@ut.edu
ALBRECHT, Shauna .... 406-265-3711.... 295 G
albrecht@msun.edu
ALBRECHT, Stan, L .... 435-797-7172.... 511 B
stan.albrecht@usu.edu
ALBRECHT, William, G .... 337-475-5816.... 215 G
walbrecht@mcneese.edu
ALBRIGHT, Geri .... 205-929-6315....... 5 E
galbright@lawsonstate.edu
ALBRIGHT, Janet .... 530-242-7555...... 69 D
jalbright@shastacollege.edu
ALBRIGHT, Mike .... 845-341-4728.... 345 E
mike.albright@sunyorange.edu
ALBRINCK, Margaret, L .... 920-565-1290.... 547 H
albrinckm@lakeland.ede
ALBRITTEN, Arna, T .... 229-430-4638.... 123 H
arna.albritten@asurams.edu
ALBRITTON, Jan, B .... 318-257-3036.... 215 F
usjba@latech.edu
ALBRITTON, Rosie, L .... 936-261-1510.... 496 E
rlalbritton@pvamu.edu
ALBRITTON, Sheila .... 423-697-4710.... 474 D
ALBRUSCATO, Tony .... 847-285-2612...... 19 C
tony.abruscato@phoenix.edu
ALBURCHER, Ronald .... 650-723-2300...... 71 F
ALBURY, Mark .... 802-485-2305.... 514 A
malbury@norwich.edu
ALCAINO, Ricardo .... 805-893-4504...... 74 F
ricardo.alcaino@oeo.ucsb.edu
ALCALA, Celena .... 310-287-4290...... 55 F
alcalac@wlac.edu
ALCALA, Juana, J .... 406-243-2049.... 295 A
juana.alcala@umontana.edu
ALCARAZ, Arturo .... 951-222-3871...... 64 B
arturo.alcaraz@rcc.edu
ALCIVAR, Doris .... 973-684-5571.... 312 E
dalcivar@pccc.edu
ALCOCK, Sherry, B .... 563-387-1862.... 187 A
alcock@luther.edu
ALCORN, Gena .... 309-341-5327.... 146 A
galcorn@sandburg.edu
ALCORTA, Joe, H .... 325-670-1594.... 487 D
jalcorta@hsutx.edu
ALDACO, Michael .... 510-235-7800...... 43 B
maldaco@contracosta.edu
ALDAMA, Ben .... 479-986-6939...... 22 H
baldama@nwacc.edu
ALDARONDO, Aixa .... 787-766-1717.... 565 G
aialdarondo@suagm.edu

ALDAY, Katherine, E .... 770-423-6290 .... 132 H kalday@kennesaw.edu

ALDEN, Alison .... 617-253-6512 .... 242 A aalden@mit.edu

ALDEN, Michael, F .... 573-882-2055 .... 291 D aldenm@missouri.edu

ALDEN, III, Raymond, W .. 815-753-0493 .... 160 A ralden@niu.edu

ALDEN, Robin .... 575-461-4413 .... 318 F robina@mesalands.edu

ALDEN, W. Lesley .... 267-502-2608 .... 423 B les.alden@anc-gc.org

ALDENDERFER, Mark, S ... 209-228-7742 .... 74 B

ALDERMAN, Charles, W ... 334-844-6406 .... 1 G aldercw@auburn.edu

ALDERMAN, Debra .... 206-268-4100 .... 530 F dalderman@antioch.edu

ALDERMAN, Norman, M ... 863-667-5129 .... 118 A nmalderman@seu.edu

ALDERMAN, Pamela, L .... 304-896-7302 .... 542 J pama@southern.wvnet.edu

ALDERMAN, Steve .... 713-646-1812 .... 494 E salderman@stcl.edu

ALDERSON, Philip, O .... 314-977-9801 .... 289 F palderso@slu.edu

ALDERSON, Ynez .... 432-552-2795 .... 507 C alderson_y@utpb.edu

ALDERTON, Karen, S .... 814-371-6920 .... 427 H mainc@dbcollege.com

ALDRICH, Adrian, M .... 630-637-5201 .... 159 F amaldrich@noctrl.edu

ALDRICH, Allison, S .... 315-268-6590 .... 329 C aldricas@clarkson.edu

ALDRICH, B.J .... 907-474-7043 .... 10 J bjaldrich@alaska.edu

ALDRICH, Dan .... 949-824-7915 .... 73 H dan.aldrich@uci.edu

ALDRICH, Kimberly, J .... 269-337-7302 .... 253 F Kim.Aldrich@kzoo.edu

ALDRICH, Maria .... 704-894-2113 .... 363 F maaldrich@davidson.edu

ALDRICH, Michael .... 808-675-3850 .... 139 I michael.aldrich@byuh.edu

ALDRICH, Susan, C .... 315-267-2162 .... 354 C aldricsc@potsdam.edu

ALDRIDGE, Betty, J .... 706-721-2592 .... 130 B baldridg@georgiahealth.edu

ALDRIDGE, Dale .... 229-225-5293 .... 137 D daldridge@southwestgatech.edu

ALDRIDGE, Doug .... 417-626-1234 .... 287 F aldridge.doug@occ.edu

ALDRIDGE, Jim .... 404-669-2404 .... 135 E jim.aldridge@point.edu

ALDRIDGE, Karen .... 847-628-2464 .... 154 I kaldridge@judsonu.edu

ALDRIDGE, Kenny .... 803-981-7021 .... 463 G kaldridge@yorktech.edu

ALDRIDGE, R. Mark .... 817-202-6355 .... 495 C aldridge@swau.edu

ALDRIDGE, Shelley .... 859-253-3637 .... 200 E shelley.aldridge@frontier.edu

ALDRIDGE, Susan .... 501-760-4204 .... 22 F saldridge@npcc.edu

ALDRIDGE, Susan, C .... 301-985-7077 .... 227 F president-office@umuc.edu

ALDRIDGE, Terrance .... 803-536-7757 .... 460 G taldridge@scsu.eu

ALDRIDGE, Wanda .... 678-717-3731 .... 129 D waldridge@gsc.edu

ALDRIDGE, William, D .... 202-885-8686 .... 100 A caldridge@wesleyseminary.edu

ALEEM, Marsha .... 229-333-5954 .... 138 F mlaleem@valdosta.edu

ALEJANDRO, Felix .... 404-270-2828 .... 128 G falejandro@devry.edu

ALEKSA, Linda .... 757-388-2900 .... 523 J

ALERS SOTO, Lilliam .... 787-896-2252 .... 561 K lalers@edpcollege.edu

ALESCH, Karen .... 920-831-4397 .... 553 G alesch@fvtc.edu

ALESH, Tammy .... 719-632-7626 .... 85 C talesh@intellitec.edu

ALESSANDRINI, Jo-Ann, G .... 508-831-6676 .... 247 B alessandrini@wpi.edu

ALESSANDRO, Lisa .... 216-221-8584 .... 405 D lisaalessand@vmcad.edu

ALEWEL, Teresa Fine .... 660-543-4221 .... 291 B alewel@ucmo.edu

ALEWINE, Jerry .... 864-941-8536 .... 460 D alewine.j@ptc.edu

ALEX-ASSENSOH, Yvette ... 812-855-3849 .... 173 C yalex@indiana.edu

ALEXANDER, Adrian, W .... 918-631-2356 .... 413 F adrian-alexander@utulsa.edu

ALEXANDER, SJ, Andrew, F .... 402-280-2779 .... 297 H alexa@creighton.edu

ALEXANDER, Anthony .... 660-359-3948 .... 287 D aalexander@mail.ncmissouri.edu

ALEXANDER, Bertha, P .... 813-974-2393 .... 120 D bertha@admin.usf.edu

ALEXANDER, Beth, A .... 317-940-6378 .... 170 C balexand@butler.edu

ALEXANDER, Bill .... 254-526-1402 .... 482 F bill.alexander@ctcd.edu

ALEXANDER, Brenda .... 203-332-5160 .... 90 B balexander@hcc.commnet.edu

ALEXANDER, Bruce, D .... 203-432-8611 .... 95 D bruce.alexander@yale.edu

ALEXANDER, Charles .... 510-841-9230 .... 79 F calexander@wrightinst.edu

ALEXANDER, Charles .... 803-536-7017 .... 460 G calexander@scsu.edu

ALEXANDER, Christine, D . 717-291-4168 .... 429 E christine.alexander@fandm.edu

ALEXANDER, Cindy .... 864-294-3324 .... 458 D cindy.alexander@furman.edu

ALEXANDER, Colins .... 256-726-8471 .... 6 C calexander@oakwood.edu

ALEXANDER, Cynthia, D .... 304-253-7351 .... 541 D cindya@mountainstate.edu

ALEXANDER, Dana, C .... 805-565-6237 .... 78 F dalexand@westmont.edu

ALEXANDER, David, C .... 208-467-8521 .... 143 I president@nnu.edu

ALEXANDER, Debra .... 989-328-1276 .... 256 A debraj@montcalm.edu

ALEXANDER, Dewayne .... 615-547-1348 .... 467 I dalexander@cumberland.edu

ALEXANDER, Donna .... 804-594-1500 .... 526 G dalexander@jtcc.edu

ALEXANDER, Donna, R .... 813-253-6272 .... 122 H dalexander@ut.edu

ALEXANDER, Edward .... 904-470-8202 .... 105 A edward.alexander@ewc.edu

ALEXANDER, Eugene .... 516-561-0050 .... 325 F

ALEXANDER, F, K .... 562-985-4121 .... 35 A csulb-president@csulb.edu

ALEXANDER, Fred .... 601-977-7813 .... 277 F vpstudent@worldnet.att.net

ALEXANDER, Gary, D .... 636-797-3000 .... 283 H galexand@jeffco.edu

ALEXANDER, George .... 239-590-7045 .... 119 A galexand@fgcu.edu

ALEXANDER, Glenda, K .... 901-448-1601 .... 477 C galexan6@uthsc.edu

ALEXANDER, Glenna, R .... 785-827-5541 .... 194 D kglennaa@kwu.edu

ALEXANDER, Grace .... 680-488-2471 .... 560 A gracea@palau.edu

ALEXANDER, Gwendolyn ... 620-341-5203 .... 192 D galexan1@emporia.edu

ALEXANDER, Jacklan .... 305-626-3718 .... 108 H jalexand@fmuniv.edu

ALEXANDER, Jay .... 908-835-2329 .... 317 C jayalex@warren.edu

ALEXANDER, Jenny .... 414-288-7362 .... 548 D jenny.alexander@marquette.edu

ALEXANDER, Jill .... 973-748-9000 .... 308 A jill_alexander@bloomfield.edu

ALEXANDER, John .... 847-491-8100 .... 160 D j-alexander8@md.northwestern.edu

ALEXANDER, Joseph, W .... 405-744-2325 .... 410 C joseph.alexander@okstate.edu

ALEXANDER, Juan .... 937-708-5720 .... 405 G jalexander2@wilberforce.edu

ALEXANDER, Karen .... 252-335-0821 .... 369 D kalexander@albemarle.edu

ALEXANDER, Karla .... 260-399-7700 .... 180 E kalexander@sf.edu

ALEXANDER, Kevin, L .... 714-449-7450 .... 70 G kalexander@scco.edu

ALEXANDER, Kim .... 828-286-3636 .... 371 A kalexander@isothermal.edu

ALEXANDER, Kim .... 206-934-6660 .... 537 B kim.alexander@seattlecolleges.edu

ALEXANDER, Kimberly .... 570-484-2955 .... 443 A kalexand@lhup.edu

ALEXANDER, Laura .... 307-766-2215 .... 556 E lalexan5@uwyo.edu

ALEXANDER, Lex .... 336-272-7102 .... 364 D lex.alexander@greensborocollege.edu

ALEXANDER, Linda .... 913-971-3529 .... 195 A lalexand@mnu.edu

ALEXANDER, Livingston .... 814-362-7501 .... 449 B lalexand@pitt.edu

ALEXANDER, Lynn, M .... 731-881-7490 .... 477 E lalexand@utm.edu

ALEXANDER, M. Christopher .... 704-894-2337 .... 363 F chalexander@davidson.edu

ALEXANDER, Makisha .... 909-868-4060 .... 44 J malexander@devry.edu

ALEXANDER, Marijo .... 507-433-0606 .... 269 A malexand@riverland.edu

ALEXANDER, Mary .... 615-514-2787 .... 472 C admissions@nossi.edu

ALEXANDER, Maura .... 215-780-1266 .... 446 G malexander@salus.edu

ALEXANDER, Maurine .... 680-488-3036 .... 560 A maurinea@palau.edu

ALEXANDER, Michael, B ... 617-243-2221 .... 236 F malexander@lasell.edu

ALEXANDER, Michael, D ... 601-635-2111 .... 274 C malexander@eccc.edu

ALEXANDER, Michelle .... 940-552-6291 .... 507 E malexander@vernoncollege.edu

ALEXANDER, P. Paul .... 617-541-5386 .... 241 D palexander@rcc.mass.edu

ALEXANDER, Pati .... 817-531-4214 .... 502 A palexander@txwes.edu

ALEXANDER, Paul .... 714-879-3901 .... 50 G palexander@hiu.edu

ALEXANDER, Pearl .... 404-894-0300 .... 130 D pearl.alexander@ohr.gatech.edu

ALEXANDER, Renee, T .... 607-255-3693 .... 331 C rta3@cornell.edu

ALEXANDER, Robert .... 209-946-2322 .... 75 D aalexander@pacific.edu

ALEXANDER, Sam .... 303-871-2705 .... 88 E Samuel.Alexander@du.edu

ALEXANDER, Seth .... 617-253-6083 .... 242 A seth.alexander@mit.edu

ALEXANDER, Sharon, E .... 406-243-2900 .... 295 A sharon.alexander@umontana.edu

ALEXANDER, Shawn .... 602-274-4300 .... 13 A salexander@brymanschool.edu

ALEXANDER, Sheldon .... 919-761-2100 .... 376 G salexander@sebts.edu

ALEXANDER, Sherry .... 918-343-7867 .... 411 H salexander@rsu.edu

ALEXANDER, Sheryl .... 650-949-6149 .... 47 H alexandersheryl@fhda.edu

ALEXANDER, State .... 704-216-6067 .... 366 D salexan@livingstone.edu

ALEXANDER, State, W .... 704-216-6067 .... 366 D salexan@livingstone.edu

ALEXANDER, Susan, L .... 651-962-6031 .... 272 E slalexander@stthomas.edu

ALEXANDER, Suzanne, T .. 410-334-2900 .... 229 E salexander@worwic.edu

ALEXANDER, Terry .... 404-527-4536 .... 126 F talexander@carver.edu

ALEXANDER, Thomas .... 413-662-5440 .... 238 F thomas.alexander@mcla.edu

ALEXANDER, Tiffany .... 252-985-5137 .... 375 C talexander@ncwc.edu

ALEXANDER, Timothy .... 321-253-2929 .... 106 A talexand@cci.edu

ALEXANDER, Walter .... 256-372-4871 .... 1 A walter.alexander@aamu.edu

ALEXANDER, William .... 205-226-4736 .... 2 C walexand@bsc.edu

ALEXANDER, William .... 757-823-2961 .... 521 K whalexander@ncu.edu

ALEXANDER, William, B ... 215-898-7021 .... 448 I wba2@pobox.upenn.edu

ALEXANDER, Willie .... 954-201-7471 .... 102 A walexand@broward.edu

ALEXANDER, Yvonne .... 501-370-5271 .... 23 B yalexander@philander.edu

ALEXANDER-HARVEY, Annie .... 863-784-7104 .... 117 I annie.alexander-harvey@southflorida.edu

ALEXANDER-WALLACE, Linda .... 718-518-4432 .... 327 D lalexander@hostos.cuny.edu

ALEXANDERSON, Walt .... 706-737-1763 .... 125 C walexanderson@aug.edu

ALEXANDRE, Laurien .... 323-666-8181 .... 383 J lalexandre@antioch.edu

ALEXANDROU, Cyprian .... 315-858-0450 .... 336 A cyprian@hts.edu

ALEXIOU, Mildred .... 845-398-4310 .... 349 H malexiou@stac.edu

ALEXIS, Eloise .... 404-270-5040 .... 137 E ealexis@spelman.edu

ALEXIS, Marnelle .... 312-922-1884 .... 157 C

ALEXO, Kenneth .... 973-408-3067 .... 309 F kalexojr@drew.edu

ALEXOPULOS, Jenny .... 918-561-8257 .... 410 D jenny.alexopulos@okstate.edu

ALFANO, Michael .... 212-998-4090 .... 344 B michael.alfano@nyu.edu

ALFANO, Renee, M .... 608-243-4539 .... 554 B ralfano@matcmadison.edu

ALFARO, Fela .... 214-860-2454 .... 484 I falfaro@dcccd.edu

ALFARO, Jose .... 561-732-4424 .... 117 A jalfaro@svdp.edu

ALFARO, Vanessa .... 305-222-2812 .... 107 E valfaro@careercollege.edu

ALFARO-LOPEZ, Maria .... 216-347-1595 .... 392 M mlopez@jcu.edu

ALFIERI, Linda, L .... 315-255-1743 .... 325 H alfieri@cayuga-cc.edu

ALFONSO, August .... 361-698-1300 .... 485 F aalfonso@delmar.edu

ALFONSO, Jorge .... 305-821-3333 .... 109 A jalfonso@mm.fnc.edu

ALFONSO, Peter .... 401-874-4576 .... 454 E peteralfonso@uri.edu

ALFORD, Bobby, R .... 713-798-5906 .... 481 H balford@bcm.edu

ALFORD, Deborah .... 618-235-2700 .... 165 B deborah.alford@swic.edu

ALFORD, Frederick .... 860-297-2157 .... 94 C frederick.alford@trincoll.edu

ALFORD, Hannah .... 310-434-3472 .... 68 D alford_hannah@smc.edu

ALFORD, Larry .... 215-204-8231 .... 447 G larry.alford@temple.edu

ALFORD, Linda, G .... 251-578-1313 .... 6 E lalford@rstc.edu

ALFORD, Marie .... 562-985-8403 .... 35 A malford@csulb.edu

ALFORD, Michelle .... 630-652-8500 .... 149 B malford@devry.edu

ALFORD, Mike, J .... 972-860-8146 .... 484 G mja3320@dcccd.edu

ALFORD, Randall, L .... 321-674-7397 .... 108 E rlalford@fit.edu

ALFORD, Tarome .... 413-748-3508 .... 245 C talford@spfldcol.edu

ALFRED, Valarie .... 256-362-4489 .... 7 H valfred@talladega.edu

ALFULTIS, Michael .... 860-405-9010 .... 94 E michael.alfultis@uconn.edu

ALGER, Gary .... 203-582-3289 .... 93 E gary.alger@quinnipiac.edu

ALGER, Jonathan .... 848-932-7697 .... 314 B alger@oldqueens.rutgers.edu

ALGER, Lennie, I .... 757-594-7863 .... 517 I lalger@cnu.edu

ALGIER, Anne-Marie .... 585-275-9390 .... 358 I anne-marie.algier@rochester.edu

ALGOE, Eric, S .... 740-368-3351 .... 400 F esalgoe@owu.edu

ALGORRI NAVARRO, José .... 787-744-1060 .... 564 D jalgorri@mechtech.edu

ALGOZINE, Jan, L .... 920-686-6192 .... 550 E Jan.Algozine@sl.edu

ALI, Abe .... 661-336-5141 .... 52 L abeali@kccd.edu

ALI, Adel .... 218-281-8268 .... 272 A adelali@umn.edu

ALI, Aneesah .... 773-702-5671 .... 166 D aali@uchicago.edu

ALI, Hesham .... 402-554-2380 .... 301 B hali@unomaha.edu

ALI, Masoom .... 516-572-7113 .... 342 C masoom.ali@ncc.edu

ALI, Mohammad .... 937-376-6235 .... 386 H mail@centralstate.edu

ALI, Nicholas, D .... 412-531-4433 .... 426 F info@deantech.edu

ALI, Omowali .... 410-276-0306 .... 226 D oali@host.sdc.edu

ALI, Raagini .... 650-543-3722 .... 57 B rali@menlo.edu

ALI, Richard, D .... 412-531-4433 .... 426 F info@deantech.edu

ALI, Rita .... 309-694-5561 .... 152 B rali@icc.edu

ALI, Yasmin .... 718-951-2407 .... 326 G yali@brooklyn.cuny.edu

ALIBERTI, Fred .... 518-629-7210 .... 336 C f.aliberti@hvcc.edu

ALICANDRO, Jean .... 860-832-1664 .... 91 G alicandro@ccsu.edu

ALICEA, Carlos .... 510-780-4500 .... 53 I calicea@lifewest.edu

ALICEA, Carlos .... 787-279-1912 .... 563 B calicea@bayamon.inter.edu

ALICEA, Dennis .... 787-743-7979 .... 565 F ut_dalicea@suagm.edu

ALICEA, Edwin .... 787-725-8120 .... 562 A ealicea@eap.edu

ALICEA, Jose .... 617-541-5307 .... 241 D jalicea@rcc.mass.edu

ALICEA, Joseph .... 718-518-4377 .... 327 D jalicea@hostos.cuny.edu

ALICEA, Marisa .... 312-362-8772 .... 148 F malicea@depaul.edu

ALICEA, Mercedes .... 212-694-1000 .... 324 C malicea@boricuacollege.edu

ALICEA, Priscilla .... 401-232-6715 .... 453 A palicea@bryant.edu

ALICEA, Rosa, H .... 787-765-3560 .... 561 J ralicea@edpcollege.edu

ALICEA, Victor, G .... 212-694-1000 .... 324 C valicea@boricuacollege.edu

ALICEA-MALDONADO, Rafael .... 585-345-6820 .... 334 F ralicea-maldonado@genesee.edu

ALIK, Kenson .... 629-625-5979 .... 559 E kalik@cmi.edu

ALINTUCK, Eve .... 603-358-2101 .... 307 A ealintuck@keene.edu

ALISHIO, Kip, C .... 513-529-4634 .... 396 D alishikc@muohio.edu

ALIX, Francis .... 617-349-8550 .... 230 D alix@lesley.edu

ALIX, Jeff .... 419-289-5093 .... 384 D jalix@ashland.edu

ALKIRE, Garry, R .... 308-635-6032 .... 301 E galkire@wncc.edu

ALKIRE, Leonica .... 701-854-8005 .... 383 A leonicaa@sbci.edu

ALLADA, Venkata .... 573-341-4573 .... 292 A allada@mst.edu

ALLADIN, Helen .... 212-243-5150 .... 334 E alladin@gts.edu

ALLAEI, Sara, K .... 317-274-3261 .... 174 B sallaei@iupui.edu

ALLAIRE, Pierre, N ... 904-620-2151 ... 120 C
pallaire@unf.edu
ALLAN, Carol ... 413-265-2289 ... 233 E
allanc@elms.edu
ALLAN, Janet, D ... 410-706-6741 ... 227 C
allan@son.umaryland.edu
ALLAN, Linda ... 412-809-5100 ... 444 F
allan@pti.edu
ALLAN, Mark ... 215-951-1395 ... 432 G
allanm@lasalle.edu
ALLAN, Peter ... 760-245-4271 ... 77 E
ALLAN-LINDBLOM,
Ronald ... 412-392-8101 ... 444 H
rlindblom@pointpark.edu
ALLANACH, Barbara ... 630-829-6047 ... 145 D
ballanach@ben.edu
ALLARD, Don ... 919-761-2310 ... 376 G
dallard@sebts.edu
ALLARD, Ingrid ... 518-262-5919 ... 322 E
allardi@mail.amc.edu
ALLARD, Jessica ... 802-862-9616 ... 512 H
jallard@burlington.edu
ALLARD, Lee, R ... 903-510-2305 ... 502 E
lall2@tjc.edu
ALLARD, Michael ... 518-828-4181 ... 330 E
allard@sunycgcc.edu
ALLAUX, Michele, M ... 401-254-3592 ... 454 C
mallaux@rwu.edu
ALLBRIGHT, A. Rodney ... 281-756-3598 ... 479 G
ara@alvincollege.edu
ALLBRIGHT, Jacque ... 512-245-2521 ... 501 C
ja14@txstate.edu
ALLBRITTEN, Jeff ... 478-471-2712 ... 133 E
jeff.allbritten@maconstate.edu
ALLBRITTEN, William, L ... 270-809-6851 ... 204 F
bill.allbritten@murraystate.edu
ALLCORN, Terry ... 407-569-1162 ... 107 G
terry.allcorn@fcc.edu
ALLCORN, Terry, A ... 417-268-6062 ... 279 D
tallcorn@gobbc.edu
ALLEE, Craig ... 706-233-7260 ... 136 E
callee@shorter.edu
ALLEE, Kelly ... 217-234-5215 ... 155 H
kallee@lakeland.cc.il.us
ALLEMAN, Vickie ... 713-942-3466 ... 504 D
alleman@stthom.edu
ALLEN, Al ... 386-822-8808 ... 121 E
aallen@stetson.edu
ALLEN, Algia ... 972-563-9573 ... 502 D
aallen@tvcc.edu
ALLEN, Andrew, T ... 619-260-4553 ... 76 A
andrewt@sandiego.edu
ALLEN, Ann ... 217-854-5506 ... 145 F
aalle@blackburn.edu
ALLEN, Ann, M ... 217-854-5506 ... 145 F
aalle@blackburn.edu
ALLEN, Anna, M ... 215-951-1374 ... 432 G
aallen@lasalle.edu
ALLEN, Anthony ... 718-933-6700 ... 341 G
aallen@monroecollege.edu
ALLEN, Anthony, W ... 816-414-3700 ... 286 A
aallen@mbts.edu
ALLEN, B. Connie ... 919-516-4001 ... 376 B
bcallen@st-aug.edu
ALLEN, Benjamin, J ... 319-273-2566 ... 182 D
ben.allen@uni.edu
ALLEN, Bill ... 252-985-5111 ... 375 C
ballen@ncwc.edu
ALLEN, Bob ... 260-484-4400 ... 169 G
roallen@brownmackie.edu
ALLEN, Bonita ... 334-876-9242 ... 4 B
ballen@wccs.edu
ALLEN, Bonnie ... 406-243-6800 ... 295 A
bonnie.allen@umontana.edu
ALLEN, Brenda ... 336-750-2200 ... 380 A
allenba@wssu.edu
ALLEN, Brian ... 815-939-5258 ... 160 F
ballen@olivet.edu
ALLEN, Brian, K ... 608-785-8558 ... 551 B
allen.bria@uwlax.edu
ALLEN, JR., Calvin, H ... 540-665-4587 ... 523 K
callen@su.edu
ALLEN, Carl ... 212-799-5000 ... 337 H
ALLEN, Carol, M ... 443-412-2144 ... 223 B
caallen@harford.edu
ALLEN, Carolyn, H ... 479-575-6702 ... 24 C
challen@uark.edu
ALLEN, Catherine ... 605-361-0200 ... 464 A
callen@sf.coloradotech.edu
ALLEN, Charles ... 650-949-6150 ... 47 F
allencharles@fhda.edu
ALLEN, Charles ... 650-949-6150 ... 47 G
allencharles@fhda.edu
ALLEN, SJ, Charles, H ... 203-254-4000 ... 92 B
executive@fairfield.edu
ALLEN, Chaunda ... 225-578-4339 ... 212 F
calle18@lsu.edu
ALLEN, Cindy ... 517-787-0800 ... 253 E
allencynthiaa@jccmi.edu
ALLEN, Craig ... 817-257-7865 ... 498 F
c.allen@tcu.edu
ALLEN, Cynthia, A ... 757-789-1768 ... 526 D
callen@es.vccs.edu

ALLEN, Dale ... 508-854-4337 ... 241 C
dallen@qcc.mass.edu
ALLEN, Dana, G ... 757-683-3097 ... 521 L
dallen@odu.edu
ALLEN, Daniel, J ... 815-836-5244 ... 156 D
allendj@lewisu.edu
ALLEN, Daniel, T ... 267-502-2636 ... 423 B
daniel.allen@anc-gc.org
ALLEN, Darren ... 205-929-6361 ... 5 E
dallen@lawsonstate.edu
ALLEN, David ... 817-923-1921 ... 495 E
dallen@swbts.edu
ALLEN, David ... 508-678-2811 ... 239 F
david.allen@bristolcc.edu
ALLEN, David ... 956-665-2404 ... 506 A
elemaster@utpa.edu
ALLEN, David, D ... 330-325-6461 ... 397 C
dallen@neoucom.edu
ALLEN, David, W ... 916-339-1500 ... 58 D
dallen@mticollege.edu
ALLEN, Dee Dee ... 501-450-1228 ... 22 A
allendd@hendrix.edu
ALLEN, Derick, A ... 573-840-9649 ... 290 J
dallen@trcc.edu
ALLEN, Diane, D ... 410-548-3374 ... 228 D
ddallen@salisbury.edu
ALLEN, Donna, Y ... 870-235-4012 ... 23 I
dyallen@saumag.edu
ALLEN, Doug ... 814-838-7673 ... 429 B
ALLEN, Douglas, W ... 320-222-5202 ... 268 I
douglas.allen@ridgewater.edu
ALLEN, OP,
Elizabeth Anne ... 615-297-7545 ... 466 H
sreanne@aquinascollege.edu
ALLEN, Erin ... 704-991-0261 ... 374 A
eallen4640@stanly.edu
ALLEN, Faye ... 864-646-1797 ... 461 F
fallen@tctc.edu
ALLEN, Faye ... 281-998-6150 ... 493 F
faye.allen@sjcd.edu
ALLEN, Forrest ... 432-685-4580 ... 490 G
fallen@midland.edu
ALLEN, Fred ... 619-644-7158 ... 49 A
fred.allen@gcccd.edu
ALLEN, Gary, K ... 573-882-9200 ... 291 C
allengk@umsystem.edu
ALLEN, Gary, K ... 573-882-9200 ... 291 D
allengk@missouri.edu
ALLEN, Gregg, N ... 207-780-5097 ... 220 G
gregg@usm.maine.edu
ALLEN, Hengameh, G ... 919-516-4488 ... 376 B
hallen@st-aug.edu
ALLEN, Hilary ... 919-760-8548 ... 366 G
allenh@meredith.edu
ALLEN, Hilary ... 601-484-8699 ... 275 C
hallen@mcc.cc.ms.us
ALLEN, Ivan, H ... 478-988-6833 ... 133 H
iallen@middlegatech.edu
ALLEN, Jack ... 254-647-3234 ... 492 E
jallen@rangercollege.edu
ALLEN, JR., James ... 301-387-3059 ... 222 H
james.allen@garrettcollege.edu
ALLEN, JR., James ... 301-387-3006 ... 222 H
james.allen@garrettcollege.edu
ALLEN, Janel, S ... 812-464-1756 ... 180 F
jallen@usi.edu
ALLEN, Janine ... 503-581-8166 ... 415 F
jallen@corban.edu
ALLEN, Jason ... 502-897-4142 ... 205 H
jallen@sbts.edu
ALLEN, Jay ... 601-928-6250 ... 275 G
jay.allen@mgccc.edu
ALLEN, Jeanetta, C ... 205-348-2976 ... 8 F
jeanetta.allen@ua.edu
ALLEN, Jeff ... 816-604-3063 ... 285 H
jeff.allen@mcckc.edu
ALLEN, Jeffrey ... 612-332-3361 ... 261 F
jallen@aii.edu
ALLEN, Jeffrey ... 724-463-0222 ... 424 B
jallen@crbc.net
ALLEN, Jeffrey ... 814-536-5168 ... 424 C
jallen@crbc.net
ALLEN, Jen ... 706-419-1119 ... 127 F
jennifer.allen@covenant.edu
ALLEN, Jennie ... 909-447-2502 ... 40 E
jallen@cst.edu
ALLEN, Jerry ... 510-594-3641 ... 31 J
jallen@cca.edu
ALLEN, Jo ... 919-760-8511 ... 366 G
jallen@meredith.edu
ALLEN, Joanne ... 559-438-4222 ... 49 G
joanne_allen@heald.edu
ALLEN, Jodi ... 270-789-5092 ... 199 C
jmallen@campbellsville.edu
ALLEN, John ... 217-824-4004 ... 155 H
john.d.allen@doc.illinois.gov
ALLEN, John, C ... 435-797-1195 ... 511 B
john.allen@usu.edu
ALLEN, John, M ... 718-270-2680 ... 352 D
jallen@downstate.edu
ALLEN, Johnny, L ... 662-720-7226 ... 276 D
jlallen@nemcc.edu
ALLEN, Joseph, L ... 864-242-5100 ... 455 E

ALLEN, Joyce ... 206-296-2000 ... 537 F
jallen@seattleu.edu
ALLEN, Judy ... 207-288-5015 ... 217 H
jallen@coa.edu
ALLEN, Julian, O ... 404-413-4723 ... 131 C
joallen@gsu.edu
ALLEN, Kanya ... 270-707-3827 ... 202 A
kanya.allen@kctcs.edu
ALLEN, Karen, H ... 919-742-2715 ... 368 H
kallen@cccc.edu
ALLEN, Katherine ... 313-593-5300 ... 259 E
ALLEN, Katherine, M ... 443-518-4604 ... 223 D
kallen@howardcc.edu
ALLEN, Kathy ... 941-487-4230 ... 119 D
kallen@ncf.edu
ALLEN, Kellie, L ... 606-326-2044 ... 201 B
kellie.allen@kctcs.edu
ALLEN, Kent ... 405-425-5140 ... 409 E
kent.allen@oc.edu
ALLEN, Kimberly ... 207-602-2462 ... 220 H
kallen@une.edu
ALLEN, Kirsten ... 316-322-3192 ... 191 D
kallen@butlercc.edu
ALLEN, Lana ... 662-329-7409 ... 276 B
thebookend@bkstr.com
ALLEN, Laura ... 360-385-4948 ... 535 H
laura@nwboatschool.org
ALLEN, Lawrence, R ... 864-656-7640 ... 456 E
lalln@clemson.edu
ALLEN, Linda, A ... 319-296-4201 ... 185 C
linda.allen@hawkeyecollege.edu
ALLEN, Linda, D ... 617-373-2307 ... 244 A
ALLEN, Lonny ... 419-448-3359 ... 402 E
lallen@tiffin.edu
ALLEN, Lori ... 575-527-7727 ... 319 G
allen@nmsu.edu
ALLEN, Lori ... 312-942-8708 ... 163 B
lori_j_allen@rush.edu
ALLEN, Mark ... 719-384-6830 ... 86 F
mark.allen@ojc.edu
ALLEN, Mark ... 918-293-4830 ... 410 E
mark.allen@okstate.edu
ALLEN, Mark, R ... 570-408-4103 ... 451 G
mark.allen@wilkes.edu
ALLEN, Mary, E ... 302-477-2175 ... 96 H
mallen@widener.edu
ALLEN, Mary Louise ... 610-896-1183 ... 430 G
mlallen@haverford.edu
ALLEN, Max ... 910-962-3030 ... 379 C
allenm@uncw.edu
ALLEN, Melissa ... 607-431-4130 ... 335 B
allenm2@hartwick.edu
ALLEN, Michael ... 615-898-2840 ... 473 F
michael.allen@mtsu.edu
ALLEN, Michael, L ... 901-678-2077 ... 474 C
mlallen@memphis.edu
ALLEN, Michael, S ... 202-319-5286 ... 97 C
allen@cua.edu
ALLEN, Michele ... 816-604-4023 ... 285 I
michele.allen@mcckc.edu
ALLEN, Moira ... 214-828-8210 ... 497 A
mallen@bcd.tamhsc.edu
ALLEN, Myron, B ... 307-766-4286 ... 556 E
allen@uwyo.edu
ALLEN, Nancy ... 919-684-2965 ... 363 I
nancy.allen@duke.edu
ALLEN, Nancy ... 325-942-2165 ... 480 E
nancy.allen@angelo.edu
ALLEN, Nancy, T ... 303-871-2007 ... 88 E
nallen@du.edu
ALLEN, Owen ... 336-887-3000 ... 365 J
oallen@laureluniversity.edu
ALLEN, Patricia ... 718-951-5074 ... 326 G
pallen@brooklyn.cuny.edu
ALLEN, Patrick ... 518-631-9875 ... 358 F
allenp@uniongraduatecollege.edu
ALLEN, Patrick ... 503-554-2142 ... 415 I
pallen@georgefox.edu
ALLEN, Paul ... 740-654-6711 ... 400 B
allenp1@ohio.edu
ALLEN, Preston, C ... 805-756-1226 ... 33 F
pallen@calpoly.edu
ALLEN, Ray ... 410-225-2289 ... 224 C
rallen@mica.edu
ALLEN, Rebecca, A ... 812-374-5154 ... 175 J
rallen@ivytech.edu
ALLEN, Rhonda ... 530-898-5029 ... 34 A
rallen@csuchico.edu
ALLEN, Robert ... 980-598-1905 ... 365 G
robert.allen@jwu.edu
ALLEN, Rosemary ... 502-863-8146 ... 200 G
rosemary_allen@georgetowncollege.edu
ALLEN, Rusty ... 620-947-3121 ... 196 E
rustya@tabor.edu
ALLEN, Samira ... 845-848-7407 ... 332 C
samira.allen@dc.edu
ALLEN, JR., Samuel ... 603-641-7492 ... 305 H
sallen@anselm.edu
ALLEN, Scott, T ... 203-596-4590 ... 93 D
scallen@post.edu
ALLEN, Seth ... 909-621-8134 ... 63 A
seth.allen@pomona.edu
ALLEN, Seth ... 704-334-6882 ... 367 E
sallen@nlts.edu

ALLEN, Sharon ... 928-428-8342 ... 14 C
sharon.allen@eac.edu
ALLEN, Sharon, S ... 812-246-3301 ... 176 H
sallen62@ivytech.edu
ALLEN, Sheila, W ... 706-542-3461 ... 138 C
sallen01@uga.edu
ALLEN, Shelli ... 816-604-3175 ... 285 H
shelli.allen@mcckc.edu
ALLEN, Stacey ... 505-566-3515 ... 320 D
allens@sanjuancollege.edu
ALLEN, Stanley, T ... 609-258-3737 ... 313 A
stallen@princeton.edu
ALLEN, Stephen ... 435-865-8223 ... 511 A
allen@suu.edu
ALLEN, Steve ... 606-539-4219 ... 206 G
steve.allen@ucumberlands.edu
ALLEN, Susan ... 478-445-5650 ... 129 F
susan.allen@gcsu.edu
ALLEN, Susan ... 864-646-1402 ... 461 F
sallen2@tctc.edu
ALLEN, Susan, K ... 603-862-3600 ... 306 E
suzy.allen@unh.edu
ALLEN, Ted ... 503-554-2161 ... 415 I
tallen@georgefox.edu
ALLEN, Teresa ... 912-688-6026 ... 134 H
tallen@ogeecheetech.edu
ALLEN, Terry, D ... 859-257-8927 ... 206 H
tallen@uky.edu
ALLEN, Theresa ... 978-837-5308 ... 242 D
theresa.allen@merrimack.edu
ALLEN, Thomas ... 845-437-7267 ... 359 D
thallen@vassar.edu
ALLEN, Tom ... 443-334-2955 ... 226 E
tallen@stevenson.edu
ALLEN, Tom ... 864-977-7135 ... 460 A
tom.allen@ngu.edu
ALLEN, Tony, M ... 731-989-6055 ... 468 K
tallen@fhu.edu
ALLEN, W. Clayton ... 903-510-2507 ... 502 E
call2@tjc.edu
ALLEN, William, R ... 530-898-5623 ... 34 A
ballen@csuchico.edu
ALLEN, Wise, E ... 510-466-7202 ... 61 H
wallen@peralta.edu
ALLEN, Xuri, M ... 340-693-1224 ... 568 C
xallen@uvi.edu
ALLEN, Zachery ... 701-224-2524 ... 382 B
zachery.allen@bismarckstate.edu
ALLEN-COLLINS, Lynette ... 215-572-2173 ... 422 B
collins@arcadia.edu
ALLEN-COVINO, Carol ... 973-278-5400 ... 307 G
cja@berkeleycollege.edu
ALLEN GRANT, Tameiko ... 904-731-4949 ... 105 H
taallen@cci.edu
ALLEN-JONES, Vara ... 907-786-6471 ... 10 I
afvda@uaa.alaska.edu
ALLEN-MEARES, Paula ... 312-413-3350 ... 166 F
pameares@uic.edu
ALLEN RYAN, Jenny ... 801-274-3280 ... 512 E
jallenryan@wgu.edu
ALLEN-SHARPE,
Regina, C ... 302-356-6790 ... 97 A
regina.a.sharpe@wilmu.edu
ALLER, Gary ... 202-448-6968 ... 97 E
gary.aller@gallaudet.edu
ALLETTO, Philip ... 912-525-5000 ... 136 B
palletto@scad.edu
ALLEVA, Joe ... 225-578-3600 ... 212 F
athletics@lsu.edu
ALLEY, Ashlee, E ... 620-229-6362 ... 196 C
ashlee.alley@sckans.edu
ALLEY, Brien ... 402-363-5624 ... 301 F
balley@york.edu
ALLEY, Carolyn ... 828-694-1730 ... 368 B
carolyna@blueridge.edu
ALLEY, Jerome ... 303-867-1155 ... 89 F
Alley@Taft.edu
ALLEY, Kathryn, E ... 605-394-6952 ... 466 A
kate.jansak@sdsmt.edu
ALLEY, Keith ... 209-228-4439 ... 74 B
KAlley@UCMerced.edu
ALLEY, Kristen ... 660-359-3948 ... 287 D
kalley@mail.ncmissouri.edu
ALLEY, Teresa, A ... 276-964-7266 ... 528 A
teresa.alley@sw.edu
ALLGOOD, John ... 225-214-6975 ... 214 B
john.allgood@ololcollege.edu
ALLGOOD, Todd ... 715-365-4509 ... 554 F
tallgood@nicoletcollege.edu
ALLIAS, Tami, L ... 412-578-8898 ... 424 G
tlallias@carlow.edu
ALLIGOOD, Bennye, J ... 352-395-5182 ... 117 E
bennye.alligood@sfcollege.edu
ALLIGOOD, Phillip, N ... 252-334-2014 ... 367 A
phillip.alligood@macuniversity.edu
ALLINA, Babette ... 401-454-6317 ... 454 B
ballina@risd.edu
ALLING, Anne, B ... 860-832-1760 ... 91 G
allinganb@ccsu.edu
ALLING, David, C ... 860-628-4751 ... 92 F
dalling@lincolncollegene.edu
ALLING, Emily ... 802-258-9221 ... 513 F
ealling@marlboro.edu
ALLIS, Celeste, H ... 336-342-4261 ... 373 B
allisc@rockinghamcc.edu

AMBROSI, Marc, D .... 585-720-0660.... 325 C
mdambrosi@bryantstratton.edu
AMBROSIO, Anthony, L .... 620-341-5103.... 192 D
aambrosi@emporia.edu
AMBROSON, Gene .... 712-274-5293.... 187 D
ambroson@morningside.edu
AMBRUSO, Diane .... 717-299-7754.... 447 H
ambruso@stevenscollege.edu
AMBUR, Roberta, S .... 605-677-5661.... 465 E
roberta.ambur@usd.edu
AMBURGEY, Jeff, S .... 859-985-3082.... 198 F
jeff_amburgey@berea.edu
AMBUSKE, Joe .... 937-484-1346.... 405 A
jambuske@urbana.edu
AMEER, Inge-Lise .... 603-643-3113.... 305 A
inge-lise.ameer@dartmouth.edu
AMEIGH, Michael .... 315-312-3500.... 354 A
ameigh@oswego.edu
AMELANG, Mary Ann .... 281-425-6256.... 489 J
mamelang@lee.edu
AMELING, Brian, F .... 864-488-8200.... 459 A
bameling@limestone.edu
AMELSBERG, James .... 641-585-8164.... 189 E
amelsbergj@waldorf.edu
AMEN, Barbara, A .... 503-777-7259.... 420 A
barbara.amen@reed.edu
AMEND, John .... 402-554-2242.... 301 B
jamend@unomaha.edu
AMENDOLA, Shawnya .... 513-241-4338.... 383 L
shawnya.amendola@antonellicollege.edu
AMENSON-HILL, Brenda ... 920-465-2159.... 551 A
hillb@uwgb.edu
AMENT, Rebecca, R .... 740-588-1322.... 407 A
bament@zanestate.edu
AMENTA, Paula .... 847-214-7717.... 150 D
pamenta@elgin.edu
AMENTA, Peter, S .... 732-235-6300.... 316 G
amenta@umdnj.edu
AMERMAN, Jordan .... 928-350-4109..... 18 C
jamerman@prescott.edu
AMERO, Carolina .... 678-466-4217.... 127 A
carolinaamero@clayton.edu
AMERSHEK, Tom .... 620-235-4775.... 195 I
tamershe@pittstate.edu
AMERSON, Philip, A .... 847-866-3901.... 151 B
philip.amerson@garrett.edu
AMES, Carole .... 517-355-1734.... 255 D
cames@msu.edu
AMES, Christopher .... 410-778-7202.... 229 D
cames2@washcoll.edu
AMES, Kim .... 330-869-3600.... 385 F
kames@brownmackie.edu
AMES, Lynda, J .... 518-564-3310.... 354 B
amеslj@plattsburgh.edu
AMES, Mark .... 405-382-9950.... 412 B
m.ames@sscok.edu
AMES, Orrin .... 334-983-6556....... 8 B
oames@troy.edu
AMES, Pam .... 714-997-6712..... 39 C
ames@chapman.edu
AMES, Susan, E .... 315-445-4277.... 338 B
amesse@lemoyne.edu
AMES, Suzy .... 253-864-3262.... 536 C
sames@pierce.ctc.edu
AMES, Trevor, R .... 612-624-6244.... 272 D
amesx001@umn.edu
AMES, W. Edward .... 407-582-5528.... 122 I
eames@valenciacollege.edu
AMEY, Carol, J .... 859-858-3511.... 198 B
camey@asbury.edu
AMICK, Michael .... 218-855-8268.... 266 C
mamick@clcmn.edu
AMICK, Patricia, A .... 816-604-1130.... 285 D
patricia.amick@mcckc.edu
AMICO, Theresa .... 727-725-2688.... 105 J
TAmico@cci.edu
AMIDAN, Angela .... 870-574-4519..... 24 A
aamidan@sautech.edu
AMIDON, Howard .... 978-921-4242.... 242 F
hamidon@montserrat.edu
AMIDON, Jacob, E .... 585-785-1418.... 334 A
amidonje@flcc.edu
AMIDON, James, L .... 765-361-6364.... 181 C
amidonj@wabash.edu
AMIENYI, Osa .... 870-972-2468..... 20 C
osami@astate.edu
AMIGUN, Kola .... 404-527-4537.... 126 F
AMIN, Sejal .... 630-652-8450.... 149 B
samin@devry.edu
AMIN GUTIERREZ DE PINERES,
Sheila .... 972-883-6706.... 505 D
pineres@utdallas.edu
AMIRIDIS, Michael .... 803-777-2808.... 462 A
provost@sc.edu
AMIRTHARAJ, Merlin .... 704-991-0207.... 374 A
mamirtharaj5283@stanly.edu
AMKRAUT, Brian, D .... 216-464-4050.... 394 H
bamkraut@siegalcollege.edu
AMLANER, Charles, J .... 770-423-6738.... 132 H
camlaner@kennesaw.edu
AMLER, Robert, W .... 914-594-4531.... 343 F
robert_amler@nymc.edu
AMMAR, Mohamed .... 310-314-6030..... 29 J

AMMAR, Salwa .... 718-862-7440.... 339 H
salwa.ammar@manhattan.edu
AMMERMAN, Amy .... 281-998-6150.... 493 F
amy.ammerman@sjcd.edu
AMMERMAN, Randall .... 920-686-6179.... 550 E
Randall.Ammerman@sl.edu.
AMMERMAN, Richard .... 973-655-5460.... 311 G
ammermanr@mail.montclair.edu
AMMERMAN, Rocky .... 218-683-8540.... 268 E
rocky.ammerman@northlandcollege.edu
AMMIRATI, Theresa, P .... 860-439-2050..... 91 E
tpamm@conncoll.edu
AMMON, Janice, S .... 609-497-7890.... 312 F
chapel@ptsem.edu
AMMONS, Don .... 704-922-6240.... 370 D
ammons.don@gaston.edu
AMMONS, James, H .... 850-599-3225.... 118 G
james.ammons@famu.edu
AMMONS, Linda, L .... 302-477-2278...... 96 H
llammons@widener.edu
AMOA, Kwesi .... 718-270-6450.... 328 D
kamoa@mec.cuny.edu
AMODIO, Francis .... 845-561-0800.... 342 A
francis.amodio@msmc.edu
AMODIO, Greg, J .... 412-396-5589.... 428 C
amodiog@duq.edu
AMOO, Judith, L .... 308-635-6702.... 301 E
amooj@wncc.edu
AMORE, Gregg, S .... 610-282-1100.... 426 I
gregg.amore@desales.edu
AMOROS, Blanca .... 787-758-2525.... 567 D
blanca.amoros@upr.edu
AMOROSO, James .... 631-451-4236.... 356 D
amorosj@sunysuffolk.edu
AMORY, Deborah .... 518-587-2100.... 355 F
deborah.amory@esc.edu
AMOS, Anthea .... 850-484-4436.... 114 G
aamos@pensacolastate.edu
AMOS, Maureen, T .... 773-442-5000.... 159 H
m-amos@neiu.edu
AMOS, Ralph .... 310-206-8962..... 74 A
ralphamos@support.ucla.edu
AMOS, Reid .... 304-336-5500.... 544 B
ramos@westliberty.edu
AMOS PALMER,
Susan, M .... 651-793-1823.... 267 D
sueamos.palmer@metrostate.edu
AMOTT, Teresa, L .... 309-341-7210.... 155 E
tamott@knox.edu
AMOUZEGAR, Mahyar .... 909-869-2600..... 33 G
AMPARO, Frank .... 623-935-8872..... 15 H
frank.amparo@estrellamountain.edu
AMPERSAND, Stephen ...... 410-287-1003.... 222 A
sampersand@cecil.edu
AMPUERO, Rosemary .... 212-774-0739.... 340 D
rampuero@mmm.edu
AMREIN, Mark .... 901-751-1086.... 19 C
mark.amrein@phoenix.edu
AMRIKHAS, Violet .... 818-947-2533..... 55 E
amrikhv@lavc.edu
AMRIR, Daouia .... 310-577-3000..... 79 K
admissions@yosan.edu
AMROZOWICZ, Barbara .... 716-896-0700.... 359 F
amrozowicz@villa.edu
AMSELMI, Michael, A .... 410-704-4008.... 220 E
manselmi@towson.edu
AMSPAUGH, Melissa, A .... 440-525-7357.... 394 F
mamspaugh@lakelandcc.edu
AMSTEY, Frederica .... 585-389-2887.... 342 D
famstey2@naz.edu
AMSTUTZ, Margaret, A ...... 706-542-0054.... 138 C
mamstutz@uga.edu
AMSTUTZ, Marilyn .... 402-449-2849.... 298 B
mamstutz@graceu.edu
AMUNDSON, Elizabeth, A . 202-994-4900..... 97 F
amundson@gwu.edu
AMUNDSON, Jeffrey, R ..... 608-757-7766.... 553 E
jamundson@blackhawk.edu
AMYOT, Maribeth .... 513-745-3445.... 406 E
amyotm@xavier.edu
AMYX, Tim .... 615-230-3614.... 476 A
tim.amyx@volstate.edu
AN, Nana .... 202-885-2729..... 97 B
nanaan@american.edu
ANAHITA, Sine .... 907-474-6515..... 10 J
sine.anahita@alaska.edu
ANALISTA, Norman .... 671-735-2586.... 559 D
nanalista@uguam.uog.edu
ANAND, Brij, B .... 718-990-6350.... 348 G
anandb@stjohns.edu
ANANDALINGAM,
G. Anand .... 301-405-2308.... 227 B
ganand@rhsmith.umd.edu
ANANOU, Simeon .... 724-738-2522.... 443 E
simeon.ananou@sru.edu
ANASAGASTI, Rogelio .... 713-718-5001.... 487 G
rogelio.anasagasti@hccs.edu
ANASTASIO, Denise .... 847-543-2444.... 147 H
danastasio@clcillinois.edu
ANASTASSIOU, Pamela, L . 928-523-2109..... 17 A
pamela.anastassiou@nau.edu
ANAWALT, Deborah .... 410-263-2371.... 225 G
debbie.anawalt@sjca.edu
ANAYA, Angela .... 505-888-8898.... 320 H
financialaid@acupuncturecollege.edu

ANAYA, Jose .... 310-660-6464...... 45 D
janaya@elcamino.edu
ANCELL, Jack .... 434-949-1066.... 527 H
jack.ancell@southside.edu
ANCH, Vincent, M .... 816-604-1411.... 285 D
vincent.anch@mcckc.edu
ANCHOR, Rebecca, E .... 585-245-5100.... 353 C
anchor@geneseo.edu
ANCI, Diane .... 413-538-2515.... 242 G
danci@mtholyoke.edu
ANCI, Diane .... 413-538-2773.... 242 G
danci@mtholyoke.edu
ANCONA, Jorge .... 949-824-9741...... 73 H
jancona@uci.edu
ANCTIL, Robin .... 641-844-5571.... 185 H
robin.anctil@iavalley.edu
ANCTIL, Robin .... 641-844-5571.... 185 J
robin.anctil@iavalley.edu
ANDALMAN, Julia .... 214-658-8807.... 508 A
jandalman@wadecollege.edu
ANDE, Taiwo, A .... 540-654-1282.... 524 H
tande@umw.edu
ANDERECK, Barbara, S ...... 740-368-3773.... 400 F
bsandere@owu.edu
ANDERLEY, Gerald, M .... 651-962-6531.... 272 E
gmanderley@stthomas.edu
ANDERMAN, Lynea .... 610-892-1524.... 441 C
landerman@pit.edu
ANDERS, Lee .... 620-862-5252.... 190 D
andle@barclaycollege.edu
ANDERS, Peter, J .... 717-872-3433.... 443 C
peter.anders@millersville.edu
ANDERS, Steven .... 641-784-5178.... 184 H
anders@graceland.edu
ANDERSEN, Belinda .... 212-982-3456.... 345 G
ANDERSEN, Catherine .... 202-651-5484...... 97 E
catherine.anderson@gallaudet.edu
ANDERSEN, Charles, N ...... 208-496-1124.... 142 G
andersenc@byui.edu
ANDERSEN, Jim .... 209-384-6396...... 57 C
andersen.j@mccd.edu
ANDERSEN, Kathy .... 717-728-2503.... 425 A
kathyandersens@centralpenn.edu
ANDERSEN, Kent, A .... 307-674-6446.... 556 C
kandersen@sheridan.edu
ANDERSEN, Laura, A .... 269-337-7248.... 253 F
Laura.Andersen@kzoo.edu
ANDERSEN, Margaret .... 302-831-2101...... 96 F
mla@udel.edu
ANDERSEN, Mark .... 307-686-0254.... 556 C
mandersen@sheridan.edu
ANDERSEN, Mary .... 719-775-8873...... 86 A
mary.andersen@morgancc.edu
ANDERSEN, Mike .... 831-656-2845.... 557 H
manderse@nps.edu
ANDERSEN, Patricia, M ..... 605-394-1261.... 466 A
patricia.andersen@sdsmt.edu
ANDERSEN, Richard .... 757-822-1970.... 528 C
randersen@tcc.edu
ANDERSEN, Robert .... 309-298-2446.... 168 A
r-andersen@wiu.edu
ANDERSEN, Shelly .... 406-657-2044.... 295 F
sandersen@msubillings.edu
ANDERSEN, Sherry .... 508-362-2131.... 240 A
sanderse@capecod.edu
ANDERSEN, Thomas Ove .. 828-884-8320.... 362 D
ove.andersen@brevard.edu
ANDERSON, Aime .... 662-562-3305.... 276 E
aanderson@northwestms.edu
ANDERSON, Al .... 406-275-4833.... 296 F
al_anderson@skc.edu
ANDERSON, Alex .... 215-780-1270.... 446 G
alex@salus.edu
ANDERSON, Alice .... 219-989-2335.... 178 G
Andersag@purduecal.edu
ANDERSON, Amy .... 813-253-7264.... 110 I
aanderson@hccfl.edu
ANDERSON, Amy .... 269-782-1367.... 258 E
aanderson@swmich.edu
ANDERSON, Amy, A .... 212-749-2802.... 339 I
admission@msmnyc.edu
ANDERSON, Andrew .... 207-780-5585.... 220 G
aanders@usm.maine.edu
ANDERSON, Andrew .... 317-573-8973.... 541 G
aanderson@salemu.edu
ANDERSON, Angela .... 970-521-6659...... 86 E
angela.anderson@njc.edu
ANDERSON, Angela, D ...... 301-322-0699.... 225 F
andersad@pgcc.edu
ANDERSON, Angela, R ...... 252-328-6747.... 377 C
andersona@ecu.edu
ANDERSON, Antje .... 402-461-7351.... 298 C
aanderson@hastings.edu
ANDERSON, Art .... 406-496-4399.... 296 C
aanderson@mtech.edu
ANDERSON, Arthur .... 406-496-4399.... 296 D
aanderson@mtech.edu
ANDERSON, Barbara .... 206-708-4995.... 200 E
barbara.anderson@frontier.edu
ANDERSON, Barry, L .... 901-334-5806.... 471 C
banderson@memphisseminary.edu
ANDERSON, Becky .... 210-308-8584.... 489 D
ANDERSON, Benjamin, J .. 828-298-3325.... 380 C
benjand@warren-wilson.edu

ANDERSON, Beth .... 937-376-6588.... 386 H
banderson@centralstate.edu
ANDERSON, Beth .... 218-322-2451.... 267 A
beth.anderson@itascacc.edu
ANDERSON, Beth .... 423-461-8316.... 471 H
banderson@milligan.edu
ANDERSON, Betty, H .... 337-475-5127.... 215 G
anderson@mcneese.edu
ANDERSON, Betty, L .... 573-629-3055.... 282 H
banderson@hlg.edu
ANDERSON, Bobby .... 209-386-6730...... 57 C
robert.anderson@mccd.edu
ANDERSON, Brett, B .... 970-491-7530...... 83 A
brett.anderson@colostate.edu
ANDERSON, Bridges .... 334-222-6591........ 5 F
banderson@lbwcc.edu
ANDERSON, Bridgette .... 845-431-8655.... 332 E
banderso@sunydutchess.edu
ANDERSON, Bruce, W .... 651-635-8051.... 261 I
bw-anderson@bethel.edu
ANDERSON, C. Colt .... 202-541-5219...... 99 G
canderson@wtu.edu
ANDERSON, Carl, A .... 202-526-3799...... 98 E
ANDERSON, Carol .... 617-951-2350.... 243 C
carol.anderson@necb.edu
ANDERSON, Carole, A .... 614-292-9755.... 398 H
anderson.32@osu.edu
ANDERSON, Carolyn .... 513-569-4755.... 387 F
carolyn.anderson@cincinnatistate.edu
ANDERSON, Carsbia .... 831-646-4191...... 57 G
canderson@mpc.edu
ANDERSON, Cary, M .... 610-660-1045.... 446 C
cander01@sju.edu
ANDERSON, Cathy .... 605-394-4034.... 466 E
cathy.anderson@wdt.edu
ANDERSON, Cathy .... 302-736-2410...... 96 G
andersca@wesley.edu
ANDERSON, Cathy .... 801-581-6940.... 510 L
cathy.anderson@hsc.utah.edu
ANDERSON, JR., Charles . 606-436-5721.... 201 H
chuck.anderson@kctcs.edu
ANDERSON, Charles, A ...... 717-221-1300.... 430 E
caanderson@hacc.edu
ANDERSON, Charlise .... 731-410-6722.... 469 M
canderson@lanecollege.edu
ANDERSON, Cheryl .... 210-829-3837.... 503 F
cheryla@uiwtx.edu
ANDERSON, Cheryl, A .... 315-255-1743.... 325 H
cheryl.anderson@cayuga-cc.edu
ANDERSON, Chris, S .... 906-487-3539.... 255 E
csanders@mtu.edu
ANDERSON, Christi .... 806-894-9611.... 494 C
canderson@southplainscollege.edu
ANDERSON, Christina .... 815-394-4388.... 162 H
canderson@rockford.edu
ANDERSON, Clara .... 907-474-5441...... 10 J
cranderson7@alaska.edu
ANDERSON, Corey, R .... 541-684-7354.... 417 F
canderson@northwestchristian.edu
ANDERSON, Craig .... 651-846-1365.... 269 E
craig.anderson@saintpaul.edu
ANDERSON, Cynthia, E ...... 330-941-3101.... 406 F
ceanderson@ysu.edu
ANDERSON, D. Craig .... 503-399-6565.... 414 J
craig.anderson@chemeketa.edu
ANDERSON, D. Craig .... 804-752-7270.... 522 F
canderson@rmc.edu
ANDERSON, Dale, N .... 206-281-2483.... 537 D
dale@spu.edu
ANDERSON, Dale, O .... 301-405-5648.... 227 B
danderso@umd.edu
ANDERSON, Dan, J .... 515-574-2813.... 185 F
anderson_dan@iowacentral.edu
ANDERSON, Daniel, J .... 336-278-7410.... 364 A
andersd@elon.edu
ANDERSON, Daniel, L .... 304-877-6428.... 540 D
president@abc.edu
ANDERSON, Danny .... 901-722-3204.... 473 B
danderson@sco.edu
ANDERSON, Danny, J .... 785-864-3661.... 196 F
djand@ku.edu
ANDERSON, Daryl .... 718-779-1430.... 346 B
danderson1@mail.plazacollege.edu
ANDERSON, Dave .... 609-984-1164.... 316 A
danderson@tesc.edu
ANDERSON, David .... 651-450-3655.... 266 I
danders@inverhills.edu
ANDERSON, David .... 405-682-1611.... 409 F
danderson@occc.edu
ANDERSON, JR., David ..... 949-451-5226...... 70 E
dandersonjr@ivc.edu
ANDERSON, David, R .... 507-786-3000.... 271 H
anderson@stolaf.edu
ANDERSON, Dawn, L .... 619-260-7733...... 76 A
dawn@sandiego.edu
ANDERSON, Deborah .... 812-429-1387.... 176 I
danderson128@ivytech.edu
ANDERSON, Deborah .... 575-769-4081.... 317 K
deborah.anderson@clovis.edu
ANDERSON, Deborah .... 906-786-5802.... 249 D
andersod@baycollege.edu
ANDERSON, Debra .... 701-328-2962.... 381 C
debra.a.anderson@ndus.edu

ANDRADE, Cherie ... 808-536-5555 ... 139 G candrade@argosy.edu
ANDRADE, Kim ... 405-422-1267 ... 411 G andradek@redlandscc.edu
ANDRAKO, Margaret, A ... 412-321-8383 ... 423 G
ANDREA, Robert ... 518-437-5011 ... 351 E randrea@uamail.albany.edu
ANDREADIS, Clea ... 781-280-3911 ... 240 F andreadisc@middlesex.mass.edu
ANDREADIS, Nicholas ... 269-387-3230 ... 260 F nick.andreadis@wmich.edu
ANDREASEN, Niels-Erik, A 269-471-3100 ... 247 H neaa@andrews.edu
ANDREATTA, Britt ... 805-962-8179 ... 28 L
ANDRECHAK, Mike ... 217-333-4493 ... 167 B mandrech@illinois.edu
ANDREI, Michael, G ... 716-839-8472 ... 331 G mandrei@daemen.edu
ANDREINI, Janelle, S ... 402-465-2414 ... 299 J jsa@nebrwesleyan.edu
ANDREJCZYK, Rose, L ... 413-205-3248 ... 229 G rose.andrejczyk@aic.edu
ANDREOLA, Michael ... 740-284-5843 ... 390 M mandreola@franciscan.edu
ANDRESEN, Julie, A ... 573-629-4001 ... 282 H jandresen@hlg.edu
ANDRESEN, Kirsten ... 310-338-1998 ... 56 E kandresen@lmu.edu
ANDRESEN, Sharla ... 541-383-7208 ... 414 I sandresen@cocc.edu
ANDRESS-MARTIN, Holly . 583-288-6421 ... 281 D
ANDREU, Angel, E ... 585-292-3031 ... 341 H aandreu@monroecc.edu
ANDREU, Frank ... 305-821-3333 ... 109 A fandreu@mm.fnc.edu
ANDREU, Frank ... 305-821-3333 ... 109 C fandreu@mm.fnc.edu
ANDREU, Frank ... 305-821-3333 ... 109 B fandreu@mm.fnc.edu
ANDREW, Aletha ... 919-735-5151 ... 374 F raandrew@waynecc.edu
ANDREW, Damon ... 334-670-3712 ... 8 B dandrew@troy.edu
ANDREW, Matt ... 314-968-6955 ... 293 A matthewandrew91@webster.edu
ANDREW, Sylvia, R ... 505-863-7501 ... 321 D sandrew@gallup.unm.edu
ANDREWS, Aaron ... 870-759-4105 ... 26 B aandrews@wbcoll.edu
ANDREWS, Adrianne ... 413-585-3358 ... 245 B aandrews@smith.edu
ANDREWS, Adrienne ... 530-642-5644 ... 56 C
ANDREWS, Arthur, W ... 919-866-5688 ... 374 E awandrews@waketech.edu
ANDREWS, Ashley ... 518-891-2915 ... 344 E aandrews@nccc.edu
ANDREWS, Bev ... 269-467-9945 ... 251 D bandrews@glenoaks.edu
ANDREWS, Beverly ... 269-467-9945 ... 251 D bandrews@glenoaks.edu
ANDREWS, Brad, J ... 262-551-5850 ... 546 F bandrews@carthage.edu
ANDREWS, Brett ... 918-335-6250 ... 411 B bandrews@okwu.edu
ANDREWS, Carolyn ... 806-291-3400 ... 508 B andrewsc@wbu.edu
ANDREWS, Chip, L ... 770-534-6759 ... 126 B candrews@brenau.edu
ANDREWS, Cyndi ... 503-594-3025 ... 415 A cyndia@clackamas.edu
ANDREWS, Cynthia, H ... 804-828-0177 ... 525 E candrews@vcu.edu
ANDREWS, Danny ... 806-291-3600 ... 508 B andrewsd@wbu.edu
ANDREWS, David, W ... 410-516-7820 ... 223 F davidandrews@jhu.edu
ANDREWS, Dewayne ... 405-271-3223 ... 413 D dewayne-andrews@ouhsc.edu
ANDREWS, Don ... 423-697-4747 ... 474 D
ANDREWS, Donald, R ... 225-771-5640 ... 214 H jazandrews@yahoo.com
ANDREWS, Douglas, M ... 863-784-7177 ... 117 I doug.andrews@southflorida.edu
ANDREWS, Evelyn ... 510-574-1100 ... 44 D eandrews@devry.edu
ANDREWS, George ... 305-237-3316 ... 113 H gandrews@mdc.edu
ANDREWS, Gregg, L ... 330-339-3391 ... 394 B gandrews@kent.edu
ANDREWS, Herry ... 307-778-1231 ... 556 B handrews@lccc.wy.edu
ANDREWS, Jacqueline ... 845-257-3227 ... 352 B andrewsj@newpaltz.edu
ANDREWS, James, G ... 973-642-8593 ... 315 C james.andrews@shu.edu
ANDREWS, Janet ... 816-995-2808 ... 288 C janet.andrews@researchcollege.edu
ANDREWS, Jeff ... 601-318-6741 ... 278 E jeff.andrews@wmcarey.edu
ANDREWS, Jeffrey ... 601-318-6741 ... 278 E jeff.andrews@wmcarey.edu
ANDREWS, John, L ... 562-624-9530 ... 79 H jandrews@cci.edu
ANDREWS, Karen, B ... 770-423-6555 ... 132 H kandrews@kennesaw.edu
ANDREWS, Karren ... 541-880-2203 ... 416 C andrews@klamathcc.edu
ANDREWS, Keenan, L ... 312-553-5926 ... 146 H kandrews@ccc.edu
ANDREWS, Laura, B ... 603-283-2128 ... 303 F landrews@antiochne.edu
ANDREWS, Lenora ... 716-286-8708 ... 344 D laa@niagara.edu
ANDREWS, Leslie, A ... 859-858-2206 ... 198 A
ANDREWS, Linda ... 713-798-4606 ... 481 H landrews@bcm.edu
ANDREWS, Linda ... 434-544-8324 ... 520 H andrews@lynchburg.edu
ANDREWS, Loretta ... 406-447-4508 ... 294 A landrews@carroll.edu
ANDREWS, M. Dewayne ... 405-271-2332 ... 413 D dewayne-andrews@ouhsc.edu
ANDREWS, Mamie ... 727-725-2688 ... 105 J maandrews@cci.edu
ANDREWS, Margaret ... 810-762-3420 ... 259 F mmandrew@umflint.edu
ANDREWS, Mark ... 770-228-7367 ... 137 B mandrews@sctech.edu
ANDREWS, Mitch ... 903-510-2034 ... 502 E mand@tjc.edu
ANDREWS, Nancy ... 919-684-2455 ... 363 I nancy.andrews@mc.duke.edu
ANDREWS, Richard ... 916-691-7423 ... 56 B andrewr@crc.losrios.edu
ANDREWS, Robert ... 510-885-4297 ... 34 C robert.andrews@csueastbay.edu
ANDREWS, Sabrina, L ... 330-972-6959 ... 403 B sabrin7@uakron.edu
ANDREWS, Sarah ... 415-257-1333 ... 45 B sarah.andrews@dominican.edu
ANDREWS, Sona ... 541-346-1000 ... 418 B sonia_andrews@ous.edu
ANDREWS, Susan ... 309-677-3296 ... 145 H susancan@bradley.edu
ANDREWS, Tim ... 913-360-7367 ... 190 F tandrews@benedictine.edu
ANDREWS, Todd, G ... 401-863-6331 ... 452 J todd_andrews@brown.edu
ANDREWS, Todd, J ... 860-727-6937 ... 92 C tandrews@goodwin.edu
ANDREWS, Wayne, D ... 606-783-2022 ... 204 E w.andrews@moreheadstate.edu
ANDRIATCH, Michael ... 585-395-5809 ... 352 F mandriat@brockport.edu
ANDRIS, Mary Kate ... 757-455-2136 ... 529 F mandris@vwc.edu
ANDRITSIS, Michael, A ... 810-766-4060 ... 248 C mike.andritsis@baker.edu
ANDRITZ, Mary, H ... 317-940-9735 ... 170 C mandritz@butler.edu
ANDROUIN, George ... 904-620-4222 ... 120 C gandroui@unf.edu
ANDRUS, David ... 361-698-1207 ... 485 F dandrus@delmar.edu
ANDRUS, Michael ... 704-334-6882 ... 367 E mandrus@nlts.edu
ANDRUSKI, Michael ... 909-815-5271 ... 29 B mandruski@argosy.edu
ANDRUSKI, Mike ... 909-915-3762 ... 29 E mandruski@argosy.edu
ANDRYSZA, Erick ... 440-526-1660 ... 405 C erick.andrysza@vatterott-college.edu
ANDRZEJEWSKI, Margaret 716-827-2564 ... 358 B andrzejewskim@trocaire.edu
ANDUJAR-WENDLAND, Sandra ... 212-686-9040 ... 360 E s.andujar@woodtobecoburn.edu
ANEMA, Laurie ... 708-974-5343 ... 159 A anema@morainevalley.edu
ANER, Max ... 954-965-7272 ... 107 F maner@careercollege.edu
ANG, Helen, C ... 773-442-5110 ... 159 H h-ang@neiu.edu
ANGE, Crystal ... 252-940-6216 ... 367 I crystala@beaufortccc.edu
ANGEL, Daniel, D ... 415-442-6570 ... 48 E dangel@ggu.edu
ANGEL, David, P ... 508-793-7320 ... 233 C dangel@clarku.edu
ANGELES, Orlando ... 704-922-6462 ... 370 D angeles.orlando@gaston.edu
ANGELES, Rocio ... 805-893-6189 ... 74 F rangeles@ltsc.ucsb.edu
ANGELI, Raymond ... 570-961-7850 ... 433 A angelir@lackawanna.edu
ANGELIS, Peter ... 310-825-4941 ... 74 A pangelis@ha.ucla.edu
ANGELL, Alecia ... 509-527-3683 ... 538 G alecia.angell@wwcc.edu
ANGELL, Lance, R ... 270-707-3709 ... 202 A lance.angell@kctcs.edu
ANGELL, Mary ... 505-473-6317 ... 320 F mary.angell@santafeuniversity.edu
ANGELL, Townsend ... 503-777-7283 ... 420 A townsend.angell@reed.edu
ANGELO, Caroline ... 706-355-5013 ... 124 H cangelo@athenstech.edu
ANGELO, Dan ... 909-384-4400 ... 65 C dangelo@sbccd.cc.ca.us
ANGELONE, Lenora ... 724-938-4439 ... 441 G angelone@calu.edu
ANGELONI, Lisa ... 609-771-2131 ... 308 G angeloni@tcnj.edu
ANGELOS, Craig ... 561-297-3199 ... 118 H cangelos@fau.edu
ANGELOTTI, Linda ... 408-855-5123 ... 78 A linda.angelotti@wvm.edu
ANGEMI, Karen ... 909-621-8384 ... 49 D karen_angemi@hmc.edu
ANGER, Donna ... 907-474-6131 ... 10 J dmanger@alaska.edu
ANGER, Paul ... 928-428-6260 ... 14 C paul.anger@eac.edu
ANGERINE, Roger, L ... 606-878-4801 ... 202 F rogerl.angerine@kctcs.edu
ANGION, Stanford ... 334-874-5700 ... 3 A sangion@concordiaselma.edu
ANGIS, Victoria ... 802-468-1231 ... 515 C victoria.angis@castleton.edu
ANGLE, J. Scott ... 706-542-3924 ... 138 C caesdean@uga.edu
ANGLE, Nick ... 517-629-0305 ... 247 E nangle@albion.edu
ANGLE, Ray ... 919-962-4481 ... 378 D rayangle@email.unc.edu
ANGLE, Steven, R ... 937-775-3035 ... 406 C steven.angle@wright.edu
ANGLE, Timothy, R ... 662-915-7621 ... 277 G tangle@olemiss.edu
ANGLERO, Efrain ... 787-892-4470 ... 563 G eanglero@sg.inter.edu
ANGLET, Carol ... 630-942-2461 ... 147 G anglet@cod.edu
ANGLIM, Sean ... 315-568-3092 ... 342 H sanglim@nycc.edu
ANGLIN, A. J ... 417-625-9394 ... 286 E anglin-a@mssu.edu
ANGLIN, Marcus ... 213-763-7227 ... 55 D anglimj@lattc.edu
ANGLIN, Mark ... 209-575-2000 ... 80 B anglinm@mjc.edu
ANGLIN, Pamela, D ... 903-785-7661 ... 492 B panglin@parisjc.edu
ANGLIN, William, G ... 978-542-6542 ... 239 B wanglin@salemstate.edu
ANGRISANI, Vincent ... 718-997-5600 ... 328 F vincent.angrisani@qc.cuny.edu
ANGST, JR., Arthur, H ... 516-876-3094 ... 353 D angsta@oldwestbury.edu
ANGSTADT, Peter ... 541-956-7000 ... 420 B pangstadt@roguecc.edu
ANGSTER, Sherrie ... 626-966-4576 ... 28 E studentservices@agu.edu
ANGULO, Susan, B ... 305-628-6566 ... 116 G sangulo@stu.edu
ANIBAS, Judi, A ... 715-855-7532 ... 553 F janibas@cvtc.edu
ANID, Nada ... 516-686-7931 ... 343 D nanid@nyit.edu
ANKE, Sharla, M ... 724-287-8711 ... 423 F sharla.anke@bc3.edu
ANKENBAUER, Mark, K ... 313-577-2017 ... 260 D dq0800@wayne.edu
ANKENY, Mark ... 503-352-1431 ... 419 E anke9541@pacificu.edu
ANKER, Bill, E ... 816-604-1002 ... 285 D bill.anker@mcckc.edu
ANKER, Laura, M ... 516-876-3460 ... 353 D ankerl@oldwestbury.edu
ANKER, Perryne ... 310-824-1586 ... 26 D
ANKER, Steve ... 661-255-1050 ... 32 C sanker@calarts.edu
ANKERSEN, Lynne ... 843-574-6137 ... 461 G lynne.ankersen@tridenttech.edu
ANKETELL, Dilip, M ... 713-313-7948 ... 499 G anketellm@tsu.edu
ANKROM, Jeff, A ... 937-327-6231 ... 406 B jankrom@wittenberg.edu
ANKTON, Darlene, S ... 760-747-3990 ... 41 E dankton@coleman.edu
ANKUDA, Pamela ... 802-728-1530 ... 515 G pankuda@vtc.vsc.edu
ANNA, Gary, M ... 309-677-3150 ... 145 H gma@bradley.edu
ANNAL, Charles ... 603-271-2722 ... 304 B
ANNAN, Jack ... 970-521-6690 ... 86 E jack.annan@njc.edu
ANNARELLI, James, J ... 727-864-8421 ... 104 K annarejj@eckerd.edu
ANNETT, JR., Bruce, J ... 248-204-2200 ... 254 E bannett@ltu.edu
ANNETTE, Harold ... 218-322-2353 ... 267 A harold.annette@itascacc.edu
ANNING, Peter ... 408-855-5125 ... 78 A peter.anning@wvm.edu
ANNIS, David, L ... 405-325-2300 ... 413 C dannis@ou.edu
ANNIS, Dominique, A ... 815-740-3365 ... 167 C dannis@stfrancis.edu
ANNIS, Patricia, O ... 207-942-6781 ... 217 B pannis@bts.edu
ANNIS, Robert, L ... 609-921-7100 ... 313 G annis@rider.edu
ANNUNZIATO, Frank ... 215-204-7366 ... 447 G frank.annunziato@temple.edu
ANORUO, Ambrose ... 361-593-2809 ... 498 A ambrose.anoruo@tamuk.edu
ANOUBI, Amjad ... 504-865-5107 ... 215 C aamjad@tulane.edu
ANSARI, Parviz ... 856-256-4850 ... 314 A ansari@rowan.edu
ANSARI, Shahid ... 781-239-4277 ... 230 G sansari@babson.edu
ANSARY, Omid ... 717-948-6541 ... 439 I axa8@psu.edu
ANSBOURY, Pamela ... 210-485-0307 ... 479 B pansboury@alamo.edo
ANSEL, Stuart ... 718-252-7800 ... 357 J sansel@touro.edu
ANSELMENT, Kenneth, L ... 920-832-6992 ... 547 J ken.anselment@lawrence.edu
ANSELMO, John ... 718-855-3661 ... 336 D janselmo@idc.edu
ANSLEY, Rhett ... 903-589-4003 ... 490 B ransley@lonmorris.edu
ANSLEY, Sharon, L ... 228-896-9727 ... 273 G
ANSON, Regan ... 402-872-2429 ... 299 H ranson@peru.edu
ANSORGE, Vicki ... 920-686-6203 ... 550 E Vicki.Ansorge@sl.edu
ANSTROM, Deborah ... 828-298-3325 ... 380 C purchasing@warren-wilson.edu
ANTCZAK, Frederick ... 616-331-2495 ... 252 A antczakf@gvsu.edu
ANTCZAK, Laura ... 954-201-7894 ... 102 A lantczak@broward.edu
ANTEL, Jaime ... 215-335-0800 ... 434 G jantell@lincolntech.com
ANTEL, John ... 713-743-8330 ... 503 B jantel@uh.edu
ANTEL, John, J ... 713-743-9101 ... 503 A antel@uh.edu
ANTEL, Lisa ... 203-596-4585 ... 93 D lantel@post.edu
ANTENEN, James ... 210-826-7595 ... 508 B antenenj@wbu.edu
ANTER, Dave ... 310-314-6076 ... 29 J
ANTHONY, Booker, T ... 910-672-1347 ... 377 E banthony@uncfsu.edu
ANTHONY, Cromartie ... 973-877-1873 ... 310 A cromartie@essex.edu
ANTHONY, Cynthia ... 205-929-3510 ... 5 E canthony@lawsonstate.edu
ANTHONY, David, D ... 540-665-4581 ... 523 K admit@su.edu
ANTHONY, Jonetta, C ... 219-981-4404 ... 176 E janthony@ivytech.edu
ANTHONY, Kathy ... 610-526-6045 ... 430 D kanthony@harcum.edu
ANTHONY, Kelly, L ... 440-964-4267 ... 393 E kanthon2@kent.edu
ANTHONY, Linda ... 410-843-8217 ... 272 F Linda.Anthony@laureate.net
ANTHONY, Lorraine ... 518-587-2100 ... 355 F lorraine.anthony@esc.edu
ANTHONY, Mark, E ... 724-357-2235 ... 442 E anthony@iup.edu
ANTHONY, Neil ... 465-289-2291 ... 175 K nanthony@ivytech.edu
ANTHONY, Patrick ... 404-385-7344 ... 130 D patrick.anthony@dopp.gatech.edu
ANTHONY, Sharon ... 215-572-2850 ... 422 B anthony@arcadia.edu
ANTHONY, Wayne ... 229-732-5935 ... 124 C wayneanthony@andrewcollege.edu
ANTHWAL, Sunny ... 845-398-4061 ... 349 H sunny@stac.edu
ANTI, Karen ... 413-265-2272 ... 233 E anitk@elms.edu
ANTILLA, Margaret ... 503-338-2428 ... 415 B mantilla@clatsopcc.edu
ANTILLON, Susan ... 386-506-3656 ... 103 J antills@DaytonaState.edu
ANTKOWIAK, Alex ... 410-337-6060 ... 222 I alex.antkowiak@goucher.edu
ANTMAN, Karen, H ... 617-638-5300 ... 232 G kha4@bu.edu
ANTOINE, Kevin ... 718-270-1738 ... 352 D kevin.antoine@downstate.edu
ANTOINE, Linda, B ... 225-771-4580 ... 214 H linda_antoine@subr.edu
ANTOINE, Mary Elizabeth .. 404-270-2903 ... 128 G mantoine@devry.edu
ANTOKHIN, Kathleen ... 510-649-2469 ... 39 F kantokhin@gtu.edu
ANTOMMARCHI, Hilda ... 787-815-0000 ... 566 F hantommarchi@upra.edu
ANTON, Annette, M ... 415-422-2692 ... 76 B anton@usfca.edu
ANTON, Janis, K ... 312-777-8508 ... 153 A janton@aii.edu
ANTONACCI, Heather ... 407-215-9705 ... 110 H heathera@orl.herzing.edu
ANTONELLI, Mona, L ... 608-757-7655 ... 553 E mantonelli@blackhawk.edu

ARICK, Larry, J ... 901-432-7727 ... 469 A
larick@hst.edu

ARILSON, Barbara ... 440-375-7000 ... 394 E
barilson@lec.edu

ARIOLA, Victor ... 310-527-7105 ... 46 C

ARIOSTO, Robert ... 609-894-9311 ... 308 C
rariosto@bcc.edu

ARITA, Kathy ... 509-793-2016 ... 531 D
kathyar@bigbend.edu

ARIZA, Cristina ... 210-829-3870 ... 503 F
mariza@ulwtx.edu

ARIZA, Diana, M ... 203-582-8200 ... 93 E
diane.ariza@quinnipiac.edu

ARIZA, Ricardo ... 402-280-2469 ... 297 H
ariza@creighton.edu

ARJUNE, Ricky, B ... 904-620-2502 ... 120 C
rarjune@unf.edu

ARKEILPANE, Robert, J ... 860-444-8603 ... 558 E

ARLINGTON, David, L ... 716-851-1987 ... 333 C
arlington@ecc.edu

ARMACOST, Susan ... 513-727-3463 ... 396 F

ARMAN, Jesse ... 303-220-1200 ... 81 F
jesse.arman@cffp.edu

ARMBRISTER, Clayton, D ... 410-516-8068 ... 223 F
carmbri1@jhu.edu

ARMBRUSTER, Jane, A ... 716-878-4658 ... 353 A
armbruja@buffalostate.edu

ARMBRUSTER, Shirley ... 559-278-2795 ... 34 D
shirleya@csufresno.edu

ARMENDARIZ, Luis ... 520-917-3939 ... 13 D
larmendariz@cc.edu

ARMENIA, Rita ... 516-877-3308 ... 322 A
registrar@adelphi.edu

ARMENT, Tamara ... 937-294-0592 ... 401 H
tamara@saa.edu

ARMENTA, Richard, R ... 512-223-7795 ... 481 B
rarmenta@austincc.edu

ARMENTI, JR., Angelo ... 724-938-4400 ... 441 G
armenti@calu.edu

ARMENTROUT, Barbara ... 434-223-6220 ... 519 B
barmentrout@email.hsc.edu

ARMENTROUT, Renae ... 319-385-6242 ... 186 A
rarmentrout@iwc.edu

ARMES, Christi ... 916-638-1616 ... 49 K
christi_armes@heald.edu

ARMES, Paul, W ... 806-291-3400 ... 508 B
armesp@wbu.edu

ARMESTO, Laura, S ... 412-365-1157 ... 425 B
larmesto@chatham.edu

ARMEY, K. Annette ... 214-333-5113 ... 484 C
annettea@dbu.edu

ARMINANA, Ruben ... 707-664-2156 ... 37 B
ruben.arminana@sonoma.edu

ARMINI, Michael, A ... 617-373-5718 ... 244 A

ARMINIAK, Anthony ... 734-374-3227 ... 260 C
aarmini1@wcccd.edu

ARMITAGE, Jacquelyn ... 603-668-6660 ... 305 C

ARMON, Paula ... 270-534-3492 ... 203 B
paula.armon@kctcs.edu

ARMONT, Bob ... 417-862-9533 ... 282 D
barmont@globaluniversity.edu

ARMOO, A. Kobina ... 410-238-9000 ... 99 D

ARMOR, Thomas, W ... 317-738-8045 ... 171 C
tarmor@franklincollege.edu

ARMOUR, Angela ... 802-654-2527 ... 514 B
aarmour@smcvt.edu

ARMOUR, Catherine ... 202-639-1803 ... 97 D
carmour@corcoran.org

ARMOUR, Janet, Y ... 662-842-5192 ... 274 G
jyamour@iccms.edu

ARMOUR, Mary Alice ... 724-805-2209 ... 446 E
maryalice.armour@email.stvincent.edu

ARMOUR, Robert ... 606-546-1799 ... 206 F
rarmour@unionky.edu

ARMOUR, Robin ... 925-439-2181 ... 43 D
rarmour@losmedanos.edu

ARMOZA, Marcela ... 718-260-4999 ... 328 E
marmoza@citytech.cuny.edu

ARMS, Gina ... 719-389-6323 ... 81 L
garms@coloradocollege.edu

ARMSTEAD, Beth ... 505-287-6628 ... 319 H
barmstea@nmsu.edu

ARMSTRONG, Amy ... 830-792-7405 ... 494 A
anarmstrong@schreiner.edu

ARMSTRONG, Andrew, V ... 540-636-2900 ... 517 H
armstrong@christendom.edu

ARMSTRONG, Booker, S ... 816-604-6732 ... 285 E
booker.armstrong@mcckc.edu

ARMSTRONG, Brian, J ... 713-313-6861 ... 499 G
armstrong_bj@tsu.edu

ARMSTRONG, Cam ... 601-925-3830 ... 275 E
armstr01@mc.edu

ARMSTRONG, Colleen ... 719-549-3005 ... 87 B
colleen.armstrong@pueblocc.edu

ARMSTRONG, Cynthia, P ... 318-797-5272 ... 213 D
carmstro@lsus.edu

ARMSTRONG, Dave ... 719-389-6870 ... 81 L
darmstrong@coloradocollege.edu

ARMSTRONG, David ... 706-865-2134 ... 138 A
darmstrong@truett.edu

ARMSTRONG, David, A ... 216-373-5214 ... 397 E
darmstrong@ndc.edu

ARMSTRONG, David, M ... 816-501-2423 ... 279 C
david.armstrong@avila.edu

ARMSTRONG, Deborah ... 252-536-4221 ... 370 F
armstrongd@halifaxcc.edu

ARMSTRONG, Diane ... 419-893-1986 ... 391 G
darmstro@heidelberg.edu

ARMSTRONG, Donald ... 716-614-5950 ... 344 C
hr@niagaracc.suny.edu

ARMSTRONG, JR.,
Donald, J ... 325-235-7414 ... 500 C
donnie.armstrong@tstc.edu

ARMSTRONG, Doreen ... 520-206-4622 ... 17 I
darmstrong@pima.edu

ARMSTRONG, Elizabeth ... 619-388-2721 ... 65 G
earmstrong@sdccd.edu

ARMSTRONG, Eric ... 541-684-4644 ... 419 F
earmstrong@pioneerpacific.edu

ARMSTRONG, Franca ... 315-792-5321 ... 341 E
farmstrong@mvcc.edu

ARMSTRONG, Hayward ... 502-897-4315 ... 205 H
harmstrong@sbts.edu

ARMSTRONG, Heather ... 419-755-4386 ... 399 C
armstrong.286@osu.edu

ARMSTRONG, J. David ... 954-201-7401 ... 102 A
darmstro@broward.edu

ARMSTRONG,
Jacquelyn, B ... 404-627-2681 ... 126 A
jacquelyn.armstrong@beulah.org

ARMSTRONG, Jane ... 973-328-5181 ... 309 B
jarmstrong@ccm.edu

ARMSTRONG, Jeff ... 563-288-6002 ... 184 D
jarmstrong@eicc.edu

ARMSTRONG, Jeffrey, D ... 805-756-1111 ... 33 F
presidentsoffice@calpoly.edu

ARMSTRONG, John ... 540-261-4119 ... 524 C
john.armstrong@svu.edu

ARMSTRONG, Kelli, J ... 617-552-0585 ... 232 D
kelli.armstrong.1@bc.edu

ARMSTRONG, Kenneth ... 860-244-7606 ... 89 J
karmstrong@commnet.edu

ARMSTRONG, Kim ... 309-796-5006 ... 145 E
armstrongk@bhc.edu

ARMSTRONG, Lee, F ... 334-844-5176 ... 1 G
armstlf@auburn.edu

ARMSTRONG, Lori, B ... 410-704-3570 ... 228 E
larmstrong@towson.edu

ARMSTRONG, Mary Beth ... 205-665-6720 ... 9 C
armstrom@montevallo.edu

ARMSTRONG, Myeisha ... 760-757-2121 ... 57 E
marmstrong@miracosta.edu

ARMSTRONG, Nancy, A ... 419-772-2251 ... 398 G
n-armstrong@onu.edu

ARMSTRONG, Neal, E ... 512-232-3305 ... 505 B
neal_armstrong@mail.utexas.edu

ARMSTRONG, Pamla ... 580-559-5239 ... 407 J
parmstro@ecok.edu

ARMSTRONG, Patricia, G ... 716-645-6136 ... 351 G
pga2@buffalo.edu

ARMSTRONG, Peggy ... 817-598-6249 ... 508 C
armstrong@wc.edu

ARMSTRONG, Peter ... 402-465-2153 ... 299 J
parmstro@nebrwesleyan.edu

ARMSTRONG, Raul ... 787-840-2575 ... 564 H

ARMSTRONG, Rhonda ... 765-455-9343 ... 173 E
rkarmstr@iuk.edu

ARMSTRONG, Richard ... 607-778-5018 ... 324 G
armstrong_r@sunybroome.edu

ARMSTRONG, Scott ... 815-825-2086 ... 155 C
scott.armstrong@kishwaukeecollege.edu

ARMSTRONG, Shane ... 310-377-5501 ... 56 F
sarmstrong@marymountpv.edu

ARMSTRONG, Shelly ... 231-591-2065 ... 251 B
armstros@ferris.edu

ARMSTRONG, Sherri ... 419-530-4842 ... 404 F
sherri.armstrong@utoledo.edu

ARMSTRONG, Shirley ... 229-430-3511 ... 123 I
sarmstrong@albanytech.edu

ARMSTRONG, Steve ... 620-223-2700 ... 192 G
stevea@fortscott.edu

ARMSTRONG, Steven, M ... 920-832-6769 ... 547 J
steven.m.armstrong@lawrence.edu

ARMSTRONG, Suzanne ... 757-221-7647 ... 517 J
smarmstrong@wm.edu

ARMSTRONG, Terry ... 925-685-1230 ... 43 C
tarmstro@dvc.edu

ARMSTRONG, Thom, M ... 760-252-2411 ... 30 F
tarmstrong@barstow.edu

ARMSTRONG, Thomas, J ... 307-532-8202 ... 555 H
tom.armstrong@ewc.wy.edu

ARMSTRONG, Timothy ... 903-769-5717 ... 488 M
timothyw_armstrong@jarvis.edu

ARMSTRONG, William, L ... 303-963-3350 ... 81 K
warmstrong@ccu.edu

ARMSTRONG-WILLIAMS,
Dlynn ... 706-864-1869 ... 134 D
dfarmstrong@northgeorgia.edu

ARMUL, Jack ... 321-674-7297 ... 108 E
jarmul@fit.edu

ARMUSEWICZ, Allison ... 716-614-6238 ... 344 C
aarmusewicz@niagaracc.suny.edu

ARN, Diana ... 501-977-2001 ... 25 G
arn@uaccm.edu

ARNDT, Steven, A ... 920-424-0220 ... 551 D
arndt@uwosh.edu

ARNDT, Wayne, S ... 732-987-2237 ... 310 D
arndt@georgian.edu

ARNELL, Terri, J ... 941-359-7592 ... 115 K
tarnell@ringling.edu

ARNER, Thomas ... 802-828-2800 ... 515 D
arnert@ccv.edu

ARNESON, Rosemary ... 540-654-1000 ... 524 H
rarneso3@umw.edu

ARNESON, Rosemary, H ... 205-665-6100 ... 9 C
arnesonr@montevallo.edu

ARNETT, Brad, K ... 770-484-1204 ... 133 D
lru@lru.edu

ARNETT, Caleb ... 816-322-0110 ... 279 H
caleb.arnett@calvary.edu

ARNETT, David ... 417-833-2551 ... 279 I
darnett@cbcag.edu

ARNETT, Harold ... 785-442-6125 ... 193 D
harnett@highlandcc.edu

ARNETT, Kathy ... 417-833-2551 ... 279 I
karnett@cbcag.edu

ARNETT, Ron, W ... 606-474-3151 ... 200 J
rarnett@kcu.edu

ARNEY, Jo ... 602-429-1012 ... 19 D
jo.arney@wintu.edu

ARNN, III, Larry, P ... 517-607-2301 ... 252 E
president@hillsdale.edu

ARNO, Marlene ... 716-851-1431 ... 333 C
arno@ecc.edu

ARNO, Rachel ... 617-423-4630 ... 231 E
rarno@bfit.edu

ARNOLD, Becky, P ... 802-656-2010 ... 514 F
becky.arnold@uvm.edu

ARNOLD, Carolyn ... 510-723-6965 ... 38 L
carnold@chabotcollege.edu

ARNOLD, Christina ... 616-234-3532 ... 251 G
carnold@grcc.edu

ARNOLD, Danny, R ... 936-468-3101 ... 495 H
arnolddr@sfasu.edu

ARNOLD, David ... 575-492-2124 ... 321 H
darnold@usw.edu

ARNOLD, Donna, C ... 619-482-6371 ... 71 C
darnold@swccd.edu

ARNOLD, Doug ... 206-268-4200 ... 530 F
darnold@antioch.edu

ARNOLD, George ... 402-431-6100 ... 298 F
gcarnold@kaplan.edu

ARNOLD, George, F ... 920-686-6138 ... 550 E
George.Arnold@sl.edu

ARNOLD, Harvey, E ... 772-462-6210 ... 110 L
harnold@irsc.edu

ARNOLD, J. David ... 309-467-6322 ... 150 H
arnold@eureka.edu

ARNOLD, Jane ... 412-536-1786 ... 432 F
jane.arnold@laroche.edu

ARNOLD, Jeanne, J ... 616-331-3296 ... 252 A
arnoljea@gvsu.edu

ARNOLD, Jeff (Dean) ... 262-472-1922 ... 552 E
arnoldd@uww.edu

ARNOLD, Jim ... 415-485-9506 ... 41 I
jim.arnold@marin.edu

ARNOLD, John ... 325-236-7408 ... 500 C
john.arnold@tstc.edu

ARNOLD, Joseph ... 657-278-3256 ... 34 E
jarnold@fullerton.edu

ARNOLD, Joshua ... 706-233-7233 ... 136 E
jarnold@shorter.edu

ARNOLD, Kelley, M ... 912-583-2241 ... 126 C
karnold@bpc.edu

ARNOLD, Kelley, M ... 912-583-3263 ... 126 C
karnold@bpc.edu

ARNOLD, Kenneth, L ... 707-253-3331 ... 58 F
karnold@napavalley.edu

ARNOLD, Lorene ... 260-399-7700 ... 180 E
larnold@sf.edu

ARNOLD, Lorin ... 856-256-4290 ... 314 A
arnold@rowan.edu

ARNOLD, Lory ... 573-442-2211 ... 290 G

ARNOLD, Mary, M ... 651-641-8268 ... 263 C
arnold@csp.edu

ARNOLD, Melody ... 575-492-2102 ... 321 H
marnold@usw.edu

ARNOLD, Michael, A ... 302-831-1195 ... 96 F
marnold@udel.edu

ARNOLD, Molly, K ... 309-438-2181 ... 153 C
mkarnol@ilstu.edu

ARNOLD, Philip, M ... 518-255-5228 ... 354 E
arnoldpm@cobleskill.edu

ARNOLD, Robert ... 815-836-5488 ... 156 D
arnoldro@lewisu.edu

ARNOLD, Robert ... 765-983-1217 ... 171 B
boba@earlham.edu

ARNOLD, Ronald, M ... 312-935-6646 ... 162 E
rarnold@robertmorris.edu

ARNOLD, Sally ... 978-232-2029 ... 234 F
sarnold@endicott.edu

ARNOLD, Shirley, E ... 828-884-8329 ... 362 D
arnoldse@brevard.edu

ARNOLD, Stephen ... 409-984-6249 ... 500 H
stephen.arnold@lamarpa.edu

ARNOLD, Sue ... 281-487-1170 ... 498 E
sarnold@txchiro.edu

ARNOLD, Tai, M ... 518-587-2100 ... 355 F
tai.arnold@esc.edu

ARNOLD, Tisha ... 870-575-8946 ... 25 B
arnoldt@uapb.edu

ARNOLD, III, W. Ellis ... 501-450-1223 ... 22 A
arnold@hendrix.edu

ARNONE, Harriet ... 516-686-7517 ... 343 D
harnone@nyit.edu

ARNOULD, Karen, A ... 810-762-3344 ... 259 F
karnould@umflint.edu

ARNS, Freida, P ... 541-485-1780 ... 417 E
freidaarns@newhope.edu

ARNST, Scott ... 810-762-3123 ... 259 F
sarnst@umflint.edu

AROCHO, Luis ... 787-265-3883 ... 567 C
mmorales@uprm.edu

AROCHO, Miguel ... 787-890-2681 ... 566 E
miguel.arocho1@upr.edu

AROMANDO, Drew, C ... 609-896-5178 ... 313 G
aromando@rider.edu

ARON, Lester ... 973-972-4321 ... 316 C
aronle@umdnj.edu

ARONOFSKY, David, J ... 406-243-4742 ... 295 A
david.aronofsky@umontana.edu

ARONSON, Donna ... 507-457-6900 ... 271 G
daronson@smumn.edu

ARONSON, Ed ... 541-881-5875 ... 420 E
earonson@tvcc.cc

ARONSON, Linda ... 508-849-3458 ... 230 C
laronson@annamaria.edu

ARONSON, Roberta, C ... 412-396-1818 ... 428 C
aronson@duq.edu

ARORA, Alka ... 805-893-2920 ... 74 F
alka.arora@sa.ucsb.edu

ARORA, Poonam ... 651-523-2051 ... 264 C
parora01@hamline.edu

ARORA SINGH, Alka ... 623-845-3968 ... 15 J
alka.arora.singh@gcmail.maricopa.edu

AROS, Jesus ... 361-570-4186 ... 503 E
arosj@uhv.edu

ARP, Alissa ... 541-552-8173 ... 419 A
arpa@sou.edu

ARP, Daniel, J ... 541-737-6400 ... 418 F
honors.college@oregonstate.edu

ARP, Mary ... 217-641-4201 ... 154 G
marp@jwcc.edu

ARP, William ... 225-771-3092 ... 214 H
william_arp@subr.edu

ARPEY, Sharon, A ... 518-580-5590 ... 351 B
sarpey@skidmore.edu

ARPINO, Donald ... 617-879-7899 ... 238 E
darpino@massart.edu

ARPS, Joyce ... 903-593-8311 ... 499 A
jarps@texascollege.edu

ARQUETTE, Mary ... 419-824-3969 ... 395 D
marquette@lourdes.edu

ARRA, Linda, N ... 610-330-5115 ... 433 B
arral@lafayette.edu

ARRAMBIDE, J. Mike ... 719-884-5000 ... 86 D
jmarrambide@nbc.edu

ARREDONDO, Marisol ... 714-628-7339 ... 39 C
arredond@chapman.edu

ARREDONDO, Patricia ... 414-229-4503 ... 551 C
arredond@uwm.edu

ARREDONDO, Patricia ... 414-227-3326 ... 551 C
arredond@uwm.edu

ARRIGO, Paul ... 281-425-6447 ... 489 J
parrigo@lee.edu

ARRILLAGA MONTALVO,
Sonia ... 787-763-6700 ... 562 B
sarrillaga@se-pr.edu

ARRINGTON, Alfred ... 870-575-8316 ... 25 B
arringtona@uapb.edu

ARRINGTON, Barbara, A ... 603-862-3105 ... 306 E
barbara.arrington@unh.edu

ARRINGTON, Cedric ... 256-372-5254 ... 1 A
cedric.arrington@aamu.edu

ARRINGTON, Doris, B ... 860-906-5085 ... 89 L
darrington@ccc.commnet.edu

ARRINGTON, Harriette ... 757-925-6302 ... 527 E
harrington@pdc.edu

ARRINGTON, Jeff ... 325-674-6802 ... 478 H
arringtonj@acu.edu

ARRINGTON, Michelle ... 601-266-6698 ... 278 A
michelle.arrington@usm.edu

ARRINGTON, Pamela ... 334-241-9577 ... 8 B
parrington@troy.edu

ARRINGTON, Teresa, R ... 662-685-4771 ... 273 H
tarrington@bmc.edu

ARRINGTON-JONES,
Angela ... 773-291-6297 ... 147 D
aarrington@ccc.edu

ARRIOLA, Benjamin ... 915-778-4001 ... 494 G

ARROCHA, Ashley ... 831-647-4128 ... 57 F
ashley.arrocha@miis.edu

ARROSSA, Monty, J ... 208-732-6267 ... 143 B
marrossa@csi.edu

ARROYO, Alan, A ... 757-352-4261 ... 523 B
alanarr@regent.edu

ARROYO, Cruz ... 253-964-4688 ... 536 F
carroyo@stmartin.edu

ARROYO, Ethel ... 847-318-8550 ... 160 C
earroyo@nc.edu

ARROYO, Ivonne, D ... 787-257-7323 ... 565 E
iarroyo@suagm.edu

ARROYO, Luz ... 561-273-6500 ... 117 J
larroyovazquez@southuniversity.edu

ATKINSON, J. Scott ... 585-395-5847 ... 352 F satkinso@brockport.edu
ATKINSON, Jane, M ... 503-768-7200 ... 416 F
ATKINSON, Joseph, C ... 202-526-3799 ... 98 E
ATKINSON, Kacey ... 561-273-6500 ... 117 J katkinson@southuniversity.edu
ATKINSON, Linda ... 301-784-5000 ... 221 A latkinson@allegany.edu
ATKINSON, Michael, J ... 812-749-1239 ... 178 D matkinson@oak.edu
ATKINSON, Rose ... 406-768-6317 ... 294 F ratkinson@fpcc.edu
ATKINSON, Stacy, R ... 843-857-4298 ... 457 A satkinson@coker.edu
ATKINSON, Susan ... 714-449-7442 ... 70 G satkinson@scco.edu
ATKINSON, Tim ... 386-752-1822 ... 108 C tim.atkinson@fgc.edu
ATKINSON, Timothy, N ... 501-450-3451 ... 25 H tatkinson@uca.edu
ATKINSON, Vicki ... 847-925-6208 ... 151 E vatkinso@harpercollege.edu
ATKINSTON, Judith ... 856-415-2115 ... 310 E jatkinson@gccnj.edu
ATLAS, Gordan ... 607-871-2924 ... 322 F atlas@alfred.edu
ATLAS, Jamie ... 615-794-4254 ... 472 D jatlas@omorecollege.edu
ATNIP, Gilbert, W ... 812-941-2208 ... 174 D gatnip@ius.edu
ATO, Gladys ... 510-217-4752 ... 29 F gato@argosy.edu
ATOR-JAMES, Carrie ... 740-753-6336 ... 392 A atorjames_c@hocking.edu
ATTALLA, Lory ... 603-228-1541 ... 306 G lory.attalla@law.unh.edu
ATTANASIO, Ann ... 410-617-7745 ... 224 A aattanasio@loyola.edu
ATTANASIO, John, B ... 214-768-2620 ... 494 F jba@smu.edu
ATTANASIO, Laurel ... 908-835-2305 ... 317 C attanasio@warren.edu
ATTAO, David, J ... 670-234-5498 ... 559 F dattao@nmcnet.edu
ATTARDO, Salvatore ... 903-886-5166 ... 497 E salvatore_attardo@tamu-commerce.edu
ATTAWAY, Vicki ... 760-921-5544 ... 61 B vattaway@paloverde.edu
ATTEBERY, Philip ... 903-586-2501 ... 481 F bmatsem@bmats.edu
ATTERBURY, George, B ... 415-422-6606 ... 76 B gbatterbury@usfca.edu
ATTIA, Magdy ... 704-378-1140 ... 365 H mattia@jcsu.edu
ATTIG, Ann, M ... 719-884-5000 ... 86 D amattig@nbc.edu
ATTOH, Samuel, A ... 773-508-2975 ... 157 A sattoh@luc.edu
ATTOH, Samuel, A ... 773-508-8948 ... 157 A sattoh@luc.edu
ATTRIDGE, Harold, W ... 203-432-5304 ... 95 D harold.attridge@yale.edu
ATTY, Alexander ... 570-561-1818 ... 446 D datty@gmail.com
ATWATER, Brent ... 336-272-7102 ... 364 D brent.atwater@greensborocollege.edu
ATWATER, Ken ... 813-253-7050 ... 110 I katwater@hccfl.edu
ATWATER, Randy ... 719-638-6580 ... 84 E ratwater@cci.edu
ATWATER, Tony ... 757-823-8670 ... 521 K president@nsu.edu
ATWELL, Scott ... 850-644-2761 ... 119 C satwell@fsu.edu
ATWOOD, Beverlee ... 208-882-1566 ... 143 G batwood@nsa.edu
ATWOOD, Beverly, A ... 270-707-3721 ... 202 A beverly.atwood@kctcs.edu
ATWOOD, Joyce ... 740-774-7200 ... 399 H atwoodj@ohio.edu
ATWOOD, Lorraine ... 802-831-1204 ... 515 A latwood@vermontlaw.edu
ATWOOD, Roy, A ... 208-882-1566 ... 143 G dratwood@nsa.edu
AU, Peggy ... 510-628-8038 ... 54 B peggyau@lincolnuca.edu
AU, Sau Fong ... 718-951-5476 ... 326 G sau@brooklyn.cuny.edu
AUBELE, Emily ... 814-676-6591 ... 442 B eaubele@clarion.edu
AUBIN, Mary Ann ... 314-792-6109 ... 283 K aubin@kenrick.edu
AUBRECHT, Donald ... 724-589-2222 ... 448 A daubrecht@thiel.edu
AUBRET, Maryliz ... 787-780-0070 ... 560 F maubret@caribbean.edu
AUBREY, Leonard ... 516-686-1100 ... 343 D laubrey@nyit.edu
AUBUT, Irene ... 603-271-6077 ... 304 G iaubut@ccsnh.edu
AUCLAIR, Billye, W ... 508-849-3359 ... 230 C bauclair@annamaria.edu
AUCOIN, Judi, F ... 205-726-2728 ... 6 G jfaucoin@samford.edu
AUCOIN, Paul, G ... 205-726-2732 ... 6 G pgaucoin@samford.edu
AUCOIN, Toni ... 337-262-5962 ... 209 D taucoin@acadiana.edu
AUDET, Sharon ... 908-737-3190 ... 311 B saudet@kean.edu
AUDET, Suzanne ... 508-999-9138 ... 237 E saudet@umassd.edu
AUDUS, Kenneth, L ... 785-864-3591 ... 196 F audus@ku.edu
AUDYATIS, Todd ... 508-531-1287 ... 238 B taudyatis@bridgew.edu
AUER, Margaret ... 313-993-1090 ... 259 C auerme@udmercy.edu
AUER, Matthew ... 812-855-3550 ... 173 C mauer@indiana.edu
AUERBACH, Michael ... 843-953-5991 ... 457 B auerbachmh@cofc.edu
AUFLICK, Patricia ... 307-268-2276 ... 555 F pauflick@caspercollege.edu
AUGENSPEIN, Amee ... 260-459-4567 ... 175 A aaugenspein@ibcfortwayne.edu
AUGOSTINI, Christopher, L ... 202-687-7330 ... 98 A cla4@georgetown.edu
AUGSBURGER, Arol, R ... 312-949-7700 ... 152 D aaugsburger@ico.edu
AUGSBURGER, Lance, A ... 515-964-0601 ... 184 G augsburgerl@faith.edu
AUGUST, Bonne ... 718-260-5560 ... 328 E baugust@citytech.cuny.edu
AUGUST-SCHWARTZ, Suzanne ... 510-869-6511 ... 64 J saugustschwartz@samuelmerritt.edu
AUGUSTIN, Monica, L ... 408-554-6908 ... 68 C mlaugustin@scu.edu
AUGUSTINE, Julie ... 718-270-5082 ... 328 D jaugustine@mec.cuny.edu
AUGUSTINE, Patrick, J ... 414-277-7127 ... 548 H augustine@msoe.edu
AUGUSTINE, Robert, M ... 217-581-2220 ... 150 C rmaugustine@eiu.edu
AUGUSTINE-PLAISANCE, Lu-Ann ... 718-409-7302 ... 356 C laugustine@sunymaritime.edu
AUGUSTINE-PLAISANCE, LuAnn ... 718-409-7304 ... 356 C laugustine@sunymaritime.edu
AUGUSTUS, Edward ... 508-793-2011 ... 233 D
AULD, Sandra ... 908-709-7030 ... 316 B auld@ucc.edu
AULET, Maria, J ... 787-765-1915 ... 564 B mjaulet@inter.edu
AULL, JR., Zeke ... 251-460-6609 ... 9 E zaull@usouthal.edu
AULSTON, Earl ... 775-673-7162 ... 302 J eaulston@tmcc.edu
AULT, Allen ... 859-622-3565 ... 200 D allen.ault@eku.edu
AULT, Brian ... 410-848-7000 ... 224 D bault@mcdaniel.edu
AULT, Jill, K ... 530-226-4103 ... 69 H jault@simpsonu.edu
AUM, Seok Joo ... 213-487-0110 ... 45 C provost@dula.edu
AUMAN, Timothy, L ... 336-758-5210 ... 380 B aumantl@wfu.edu
AUMANN, Trish ... 636-422-2244 ... 289 E paumann@stlcc.edu
AUNE, Jeff ... 952-446-4152 ... 263 E aunej@crown.edu
AUNE, Michael ... 510-524-5264 ... 60 F maune@plts.edu
AUNE, Regina, C ... 956-326-2574 ... 497 B regina.aune@tamiu.edu
AUNGST, Donald ... 563-425-5286 ... 189 C aungstd@uiu.edu
AURE, Aaron ... 605-688-6195 ... 466 B aaron.aure@sdstate.edu
AURICCHIO, Gail ... 516-739-1545 ... 343 C gail@nyctcm.edu
AURICCHIO, Michele ... 518-464-8804 ... 333 F mauricchio@excelsior.edu
AURIEMMA, Lisa ... 207-859-1233 ... 219 G libdir@thomas.edu
AURORA, Rosleen ... 818-785-2726 ... 38 G
AUSBAND, Avrohom ... 718-601-3523 ... 361 H
AUSBORN, Dawn ... 910-630-7610 ... 366 H dausborn@methodist.edu
AUSBORN, Scot ... 312-935-4232 ... 153 F sausborn@icsw.edu
AUSBURY, Brad ... 417-862-9533 ... 282 D bausbury@globaluniversity.edu
AUSEL, Jill ... 412-365-1244 ... 425 B jausel@chatham.edu
AUSEN, Orrin, J ... 507-344-7350 ... 261 H oausen@blc.edu
AUSMUS, Ryan ... 620-225-0186 ... 192 B rausmus@dc3.edu
AUST, Kandyce ... 860-768-2409 ... 95 A aust@hartford.edu
AUST, Kristen ... 315-652-6500 ... 325 A kristen_aust@bryantstratton.edu
AUST-KEEFER, Mary Beth ... 937-328-6023 ... 387 G austkeeferm@clarkstate.edu
AUSTAD, Dianne, M ... 319-368-6464 ... 187 E daustad@mtmercy.edu
AUSTENSEN, Roy, A ... 219-464-6758 ... 181 A roy.austensen@valpo.edu
AUSTER, Julie ... 914-395-2365 ... 350 C jauster@sarahlawrence.edu
AUSTIN, Anne ... 870-612-2058 ... 25 E anne.austin@uaccb.edu
AUSTIN, April ... 404-270-5153 ... 137 E aprila@spelman.edu
AUSTIN, Barbara ... 219-785-5634 ... 178 H baustin@pnc.edu
AUSTIN, Beth ... 816-604-3182 ... 285 H beth.austin@mcckc.edu
AUSTIN, Betty ... 256-372-5364 ... 1 A austin.betty@aamu.edu
AUSTIN, Brian ... 865-471-3273 ... 467 E baustin@cn.edu
AUSTIN, Charles ... 803-705-4967 ... 455 D austinc@benedict.edu
AUSTIN, Dale, F ... 616-395-7950 ... 252 F austin@hope.edu
AUSTIN, Deborah ... 717-264-4141 ... 452 B daustin@wilson.edu
AUSTIN, Diane ... 617-243-2124 ... 236 F daustin@lasell.edu
AUSTIN, Dominica ... 404-799-4500 ... 126 E doaustin@brownmackie.edu
AUSTIN, Faires ... 334-386-7180 ... 3 H faustin@faulkner.edu
AUSTIN, James ... 760-757-2121 ... 57 E jaustin@miracosta.edu
AUSTIN, James ... 802-387-6786 ... 513 E jaustin@landmark.edu
AUSTIN, Janice ... 574-289-7001 ... 176 C jaustin@ivytech.edu
AUSTIN, Janice ... 415-485-9316 ... 41 I janice.austin@marin.edu
AUSTIN, Joseph, M ... 207-780-5158 ... 220 G austin@usm.maine.edu
AUSTIN, Kelly, M ... 814-269-7991 ... 449 D kaustin@pitt.edu
AUSTIN, L. Bruce ... 847-214-7366 ... 150 D baustin@elgin.edu
AUSTIN, Laurie ... 718 960 8706 ... 327 C laurie.austin@lehman.cuny.edu
AUSTIN, Laurie ... 425-739-8200 ... 535 B laurie.austin@lwtc.edu
AUSTIN, Marlisa ... 502-213-5073 ... 202 B marlisa.austin@kctcs.edu
AUSTIN, Meredith ... 502-447-1000 ... 206 A maustin@spencerian.edu
AUSTIN, Michael ... 316-942-4291 ... 195 C austinm@newmanu.edu
AUSTIN, Philip ... 860-679-2413 ... 94 E philip.austin@uconn.edu
AUSTIN, Philip, E ... 860-679-2594 ... 94 F paustin@uchc.edu
AUSTIN, Robert, C ... 806-371-5024 ... 479 H rcaustin@actx.edu
AUSTIN, Suzanne, E ... 205-934-6290 ... 8 G seaustin@uab.edu
AUSTIN, Tiffany ... 845-675-4581 ... 344 G tiffany.austin@nyack.edu
AUSTIN, Timothy, R ... 508-793-2541 ... 233 D taustin@holycross.edu
AUSTIN, Tracey, M ... 603-526-3886 ... 304 A taustin@colby-sawyer.edu
AUSTIN, William ... 908-689-7618 ... 317 C will@warren.edu
AUTERO, Esa ... 954-545-4500 ... 117 H academics@sfbc.edu
AUTREY, Denny ... 713-634-0011 ... 495 E dautrey@swbts.edu
AUTRY, Elisa ... 575-492-2597 ... 319 B eautry@nmjc.edu
AUTRY, Timothy, J ... 803-535-5549 ... 456 D tautry@claflin.edu
AUVENSHINE, Donnie ... 325-649-8408 ... 488 A dauvenshine@hputx.edu
AUXIER, David ... 941-363-7218 ... 118 E auxierd@scf.edu
AVALONE, Valarie, L ... 585-292-3021 ... 341 H vavalone@monroecc.edu
AVALOS, Juan ... 949-582-4566 ... 70 F javalos@saddleback.edu
AVALOS, Yesenia ... 773-838-7984 ... 147 E yavalos@ccc.edu
AVALOS-SÁNCHEZ, Javier ... 787-993-8863 ... 566 G javier.avalos@upr.edu
AVANT, Cheryl ... 573-681-5162 ... 284 B avantc@lincolnu.edu
AVANT, Linda ... 918-293-4678 ... 410 E linda.avant@okstate.edu
AVANT, Toni, D ... 662-915-7174 ... 277 G tavant@olemiss.edu
AVEILLE, Candido ... 305-821-3333 ... 109 A caveille@mm.fnc.edu
AVELLANET, Maida ... 813-879-6000 ... 106 F mavellanet@cci.edu
AVEN, Ross ... 601-925-3228 ... 275 E aven@mc.edu
AVENDANO, John ... 815-802-8110 ... 154 J president@kcc.edu
AVENT, Sherri, M ... 336-334-7973 ... 377 F avent@ncat.edu
AVERILL, Kristine ... 503-495-2900 ... 19 C kristine.averill@phoenix.edu
AVERILL, Leslie ... 802-651-5907 ... 513 A averill@champlain.edu
AVERILL, Sue ... 330-672-2220 ... 393 D saveril2@kent.edu
AVERILLL, Don ... 619-644-7576 ... 48 I don.averill@gcccd.edu
AVERRE, Amy ... 207-941-7187 ... 218 A averrea@husson.edu
AVERSA, Ann ... 212-854-5561 ... 323 G aaversa@barnard.edu
AVERSA, Elizabeth, S ... 205-348-4610 ... 8 F eaversa@slis.ua.edu
AVERY, Alice, M ... 203-371-7927 ... 93 G averya@sacredheart.edu
AVERY, Annalea ... 208-524-3000 ... 143 C annalea.avery@my.eitc.edu
AVERY, Annette ... 417-873-7312 ... 281 H aavery@drury.edu
AVERY, Barbara ... 323-259-2661 ... 59 H bavery@oxy.edu
AVERY, Brigid ... 616-632-2494 ... 248 A brigid.avery@aquinas.edu
AVERY, Donald ... 478-289-2015 ... 128 J davery@ega.edu
AVERY, Earl, L ... 781-891-2907 ... 231 F eavery@bentley.edu
AVERY, Faith ... 513-721-7944 ... 391 C favery@gbs.edu
AVERY, James ... 731-661-5329 ... 476 G javery@uu.edu
AVERY, Joshua ... 513-721-7944 ... 391 C javery@gbs.edu
AVERY, Kathy ... 918-293-4988 ... 410 E kathy.avery@okstate.edu
AVERY, Lisa ... 509-533-3694 ... 532 F
AVERY, Margery, L ... 585-567-9350 ... 336 B margery.avery@houghton.edu
AVERY, Michael, R ... 513-721-7944 ... 391 C president@gbs.edu
AVERY, Paula ... 310-377-5501 ... 56 F pavery@marymountpv.edu
AVERY, Reginald, S ... 410-951-3838 ... 228 B ravery@coppin.edu
AVERY, Robert, H ... 401-254-3236 ... 454 C ravery@rwu.edu
AVERY, Susan ... 508-289-2500 ... 247 A savery@whoi.edu
AVERY, Teresa ... 501-337-5000 ... 21 D tavery@otcweb.edu
AVERY, Vanessa ... 860-509-9552 ... 92 D vaw@hartsem.edu
AVERYHART-FULLARD, Vera ... 773-291-6308 ... 147 D vfullard@ccc.edu
AVILÉS-GONZÁLEZ, Arturo ... 787-993-8850 ... 566 G arturo.aviles@upr.edu
AVILÉS-GONZÁLEZ, Arturo ... 787-993-0000 ... 566 D arturo.aviles@upr.edu
AVILA, Arcadio ... 562-860-2451 ... 38 J aavila@cerritos.edu
AVILA, Celi ... 915-532-3737 ... 508 E cavila@westerntech.edu
AVILA, Emily ... 775-850-0700 ... 302 E eavila@morrison.neumont.edu
AVILA, Glenna ... 661-255-1050 ... 32 C glenna@calarts.edu
AVILA, Lauri ... 928-428-8915 ... 14 C lauri.avila@eac.edu
AVILA, Linda, C ... 310-794-0691 ... 74 A lcavila@saa.ucla.edu
AVILA, Mike ... 909-607-9224 ... 40 C mike.avila@cgu.edu
AVILA, Pedro ... 559-934-2128 ... 77 H pedroavila@whccd.edu
AVILA, Susan ... 510-594-3661 ... 31 J savila@cca.edu
AVILES, Carmen ... 787-744-1060 ... 564 D cre_caguas@mechtech.edu
AVILES, Gladys, M ... 248-204-4123 ... 254 E gaviles@ltu.edu
AVILES FONT, Juan ... 787-896-2252 ... 561 K javiles@edpcollege.edu
AVILLION, Dianne ... 850-729-4901 ... 114 A avilliond@nwfsc.edu
AVISSAR, Roni ... 305-421-4000 ... 122 F avissar@miami.edu
AVITABLE, Mathew ... 718-270-7424 ... 352 D mavitable@downstate.edu
AW, Fanta ... 202-885-3357 ... 97 B fanta@american.edu
AWAKUNI, Gene, I ... 808-454-4750 ... 141 C awakuni@uhwo.hawaii.edu
AWBREY, Susan, M ... 248-370-4955 ... 257 C awbrey@oakland.edu
AWE, Jacqueline ... 912-358-3114 ... 136 C awej@savannahstate.edu
AWERBUCH, Janice ... 718-982-2266 ... 327 A Janice.Awerbuch@csi.cuny.edu

B

BADINELLI, Sigrid 415-433-9200 68 F
sbadinelli@saybrook.edu
BADOLATO, Greg 617-266-1400 231 G
BADOLATO, Michael 781-280-3710 240 F
badolatom@middlesex.mass.edu
BADOVINAC, Amanda 406-496-4828 296 D
abadovinac@mtech.edu
BADOVINAC, Amanda 406-496-4828 296 C
abadovinac@mtech.edu
BADOVINAC, John 406-496-4249 296 D
jbadovinac@mtech.edu
BADOVINAC, John, C 406-496-4249 296 C
jbadovinac@mtech.edu
BAEDER, Terrence 773-256-0756 157 B
tbaeder@lstc.edu
BAEHR, Marie 319-399-8616 183 C
mbaehr@coe.edu
BAEHRE-KOLOVANI, Edna, V 707-253-3360 58 F
ebaehre@napavalley.edu
BAENEN, Michael 617-627-3300 245 F
michael.baenen@tufts.edu
BAENNINGER, MaryAnn 320-363-5505 262 H
mbaenninger@csbsju.edu
BAER, Candace 401-454-6426 454 B
cbaer@risd.edu
BAER, Catherine, E 845-437-5401 359 D
cabaer@vassar.edu
BAER, Eugen 315-781-3300 335 G
baer@hws.edu
BAER, Karim 415-575-6176 32 D
kbaer@ciis.edu
BAER, Linda 219-989-2670 178 G
baer@purduecal.edu
BAER, Robert 309-677-2255 145 H
rbb@bradley.edu
BAER, Robert 203-857-7369 90 G
rbaer@ncc.commnet.edu
BAERBOCK, Ben, J 414-410-4050 546 D
bjbaerbock@stritch.edu
BAERWALD, Bonnie 920-929-2131 554 E
bbaerwald@morainepark.edu
BAESLACK, III, William, A 216-368-4346 386 E
william.baeslack@case.edu
BAESSLER, Laura 937-382-6661 405 H
laura_baessler@wilmington.edu
BAETHKE, Mark 515-965-7312 183 E
mdbaethke@dmacc.edu
BAEZ, Ada 787-285-5457 562 D
BAEZ, Estebania 787-864-2222 563 D
ebaez@inter.edu
BAEZ, Felix 787-850-9305 567 B
felix.baez1@upr.edu
BAEZ, Thomas 210-458-4140 506 B
thomas.baez@utsa.edu
BAEZ MILAN, Tony 724-653-2183 427 F
tbaez@dec.edu
BAEZA-ORTEGO, Gilda 575-538-6350 321 I
baesaortegog@wnmu.edu
BAFFA, Joe 714-556-3610 76 E
joe.baffa@vanguard.edu
BAFFORD, Karen, M 585-266-0430 333 E
kbafford@cci.edu
BAGADIONG, Neil, S 812-314-8533 175 J
nbagadio@ivytech.edu
BAGALE, Edward, J 313-593-5140 259 E
ebagale@umich.edu
BAGBY, Crystal 360-676-2772 535 F
cbagby@nwic.edu
BAGBY, Don 254-710-8200 481 I
don_bagby@baylor.edu
BAGBY MATTHEWS, Susan 707-527-4266 68 E
sbagbymatthews@santarosa.edu
BAGDAZIAN, Robert, A 805-525-4417 72 E
rbagdazian@thomasaquinas.edu
BAGEANT, Laura 410-704-2636 228 E
lbageant@towson.edu
BAGEL, George 770-534-6265 126 B
gbagel@brenau.edu
BAGENTS, Bill 256-766-6610 4 C
bbagents@hcu.edu
BAGG, Eva 562-938-4736 54 E
ebagg@lbcc.edu
BAGG, Mary Beth 317-788-3220 180 C
bagg@uindy.edu
BAGGER, Jonathan, A 410-516-8094 223 F
bagger@jhu.edu
BAGGETT, Cody 217-641-4360 154 G
cbaggett@jwcc.edu
BAGGETT, Kim 352-638-9727 101 H
kbaggett@beaconcollege.edu
BAGGETT, Magda 910-630-7225 366 H
mbaggett@methodist.edu
BAGGIO, Bobbe, G 215-951-1238 432 G
baggio@lasalle.edu
BAGGOT, Joseph 507-222-4075 262 B
jbaggot@carleton.edu
BAGGOTT, Jake 618-453-1378 164 I
jbaggott@siu.edu
BAGGS, David 843-863-7513 456 B
dbaggs@csuniv.edu
BAGGSON, Gulizar 479-619-2203 22 H
gbaggson@nwacc.edu

BAGILEO, Nick, J 202-526-3799 98 E
BAGLEY, David, K 585-395-2122 352 F
dbagley@brockport.edu
BAGLEY, Elizabeth 203-254-4000 92 B
ebagley@fairfield.edu
BAGLEY, Elizabeth 404-471-6339 123 G
ebagley@agnesscott.edu
BAGLEY, Jo, K 817-515-4507 496 A
jo.bagley@tccd.edu
BAGLEY, Michelle 360-992-2472 532 A
mbagley@clark.edu
BAGLEY, Pat 931-372-3149 474 B
pbagley@tntech.edu
BAGLEY, Phyllis 646-312-1190 326 D
phyllis_bagley@baruch.cuny.edu
BAGLEY, Vera, L 301-322-0801 225 F
vbagley@pgcc.edu
BAGNALL, James 928-428-8414 14 C
jim.bagnall@eac.edu
BAGNELL, Philip, C 423-439-6315 473 E
bagnell@etsu.edu
BAGNELL, William 252-328-6858 377 C
bagnellw@ecu.edu
BAGNO, Sherry 847-578-3262 163 A
sherry.bagno@rosalindfranklin.edu
BAGNOLI, Joe 859-985-3208 198 F
joe_bagnoli@berea.edu
BAGRANOFF, Nancy, A 804-289-8550 525 A
nbagrano@richmond.edu
BAGSTAD, Kristi 563-588-6314 183 B
kristi.bagstad@clarke.edu
BAGWELL, Andrea 202-274-5400 99 F
abagwell@udc.edu
BAGWELL, Elizabeth, R 828-232-5117 378 C
bbagwell@unca.edu
BAGWELL, Jack 803-327-8021 463 G
bagwell@yorktech.edu
BAGWELL, Linda 817-598-6274 508 C
lbagwell@wc.edu
BAGWELL, Lydia 575-527-7560 319 G
lbagwell@nmsu.edu
BAHAMONDE, Manuel, E 787-284-1912 563 F
mbahamon@ponce.inter.edu
BAHAR, Sonya 314-516-7150 291 F
bahars@umsl.edu
BAHARANYI, Ntam 334-727-8659 8 C
nbaharanyi@tuskegee.edu
BAHK, Solomon 213-385-2322 79 E
BAHL, Katie 563-588-6510 183 B
katie.bahl@clarke.edu
BAHLS, Steven, C 309-794-7208 145 B
stevenbahls@augustana.edu
BAHNEY, Steve 217-245-1488 155 H
steve.bahney@doc.illinois.gov
BAHR, Alice, H 410-543-6133 228 D
ahbahr@salisbury.edu
BAHR, Christine, M 618-537-6810 157 G
cmbahr@mckendree.edu
BAHR, Christopher 979-230-3119 482 B
christopher.bahr@brazosport.edu
BAHR, Janet 918-456-5511 409 A
bahr@nsuok.edu
BAHR, John, M 914-337-9300 331 A
john.bahr@concordia-ny.edu
BAHR, Paul 716-677-9500 325 B
pcbahr@bryantstratton.edu
BAI, Yifeng 973-748-9000 308 A
yifeng_bai@bloomfield.edu
BAIA, Larissa 603-668-6706 304 E
lbaia@ccsnh.edu
BAIER, Henry, D 734-764-3402 259 D
hbaier@umich.edu
BAIER, Kris 360-383-3003 539 D
kbaier@whatcom.ctc.edu
BAIER, Valerie, A 570-326-3761 440 K
vbaier@pct.edu
BAIERL, Kenneth, W 574-520-4560 174 C
kbaierl@iusb.edu
BAIGENT, Peter 631-632-6700 352 C
peter.baigent@stonybrook.edu
BAIGENT, Peter, M 631-632-6700 352 C
peter.baigent@stonybrook.edu
BAILEY, Alison 309-438-2947 153 C
baileya@ilstu.edu
BAILEY, Ann 662-325-3555 276 A
housing@saffairs.msstate.edu
BAILEY, Birdie, I 256-765-4311 9 D
bibailey@una.edu
BAILEY, Bliss 334-844-3500 1 G
bailebn@auburn.edu
BAILEY, Cassy 785-594-8484 190 C
cassy.bailey@bakeru.edu
BAILEY, Cheryl 701-355-8180 383 E
cbailey@mail.cdln.lib.nd.us
BAILEY, Chris 360-736-9391 531 H
cbailey@centralia.edu
BAILEY, Chris, C 570-372-4149 447 D
baileycj@susqu.edu
BAILEY, Christopher, C 360-442-2101 535 C
cbailey@lowercolumbia.edu
BAILEY, Clint 252-328-2606 377 C
baileyrc@ecu.edu
BAILEY, Craig 605-394-4034 466 E
craig.bailey@wdt.edu

BAILEY, Darlene 816-781-7700 293 D
baileyd@william.jewell.edu
BAILEY, David 303-361-7381 83 E
david.bailey@ccaurora.edu
BAILEY, DeLane 205-391-2373 7 A
dbailey@sheltonstate.edu
BAILEY, Dennis, A 850-644-8136 119 C
dbailey@fsu.edu
BAILEY, Dexter 631-632-4490 352 C
dexter.bailey@stonybrook.edu
BAILEY, Dixon 325-734-3651 500 C
dixon.bailey@tstc.edu
BAILEY, Donald Russell 401-865-1188 453 F
drbailey@providence.edu
BAILEY, Dudley (Skip), L 585-292-2833 341 H
dbailey@monroecc.edu
BAILEY, Ed 231-995-1314 256 G
ebailey@nmc.edu
BAILEY, Georgianna 248-213-1610 250 G
gbailey@devry.edu
BAILEY, Guy 806-742-2121 501 D
guy.bailey@ttu.edu
BAILEY, Helen 423-869-6387 470 C
hbailey@lmunet.edu
BAILEY, Howard, E 270-745-2791 207 C
howard.bailey@wku.edu
BAILEY, Jana, K 606-539-4234 206 G
jana.bailey@ucumberlands.edu
BAILEY, Jane 203-596-4638 93 D
jbailey@post.edu
BAILEY, Janet 304-462-4102 543 F
janet.bailey@glenville.edu
BAILEY, Janice 765-459-0561 176 A
jabailey@ivytech.edu
BAILEY, Jaye 203-392-5552 91 I
baileyj10@southernct.edu
BAILEY, Jayn, L 740-368-3036 400 F
jlbailey@owu.edu
BAILEY, Jeff 870-972-3077 20 C
jbailey@astate.edu
BAILEY, Jenna 901-383-6501 99 D
jenna.bailey@strayer.edu
BAILEY, Jeremy 330-339-3391 394 B
jbailey4@kent.edu
BAILEY, Jessica, M 336-750-3277 380 A
baileyjm@wssu.edu
BAILEY, Jessie 636-978-7488 292 F
BAILEY, John 808-675-3458 139 I
baileyj@byuh.edu
BAILEY, Joseph, A 585-345-6900 334 F
jabailey@genesee.edu
BAILEY, Judith, A 802-485-2065 514 A
judyb@norwich.edu
BAILEY, Julie 432-264-5030 487 I
jbailey@howardcollege.edu
BAILEY, Kathy 864-977-7170 460 A
kim.bailey@ngu.edu
BAILEY, Kelly 805-525-4417 72 E
kbailey@thomasaquinas.edu
BAILEY, Kelly 918-495-7225 411 C
kbailey@oru.edu
BAILEY, Ken 409-740-4400 497 D
baileyk@tamug.edu
BAILEY, Kevin 850-474-2214 121 C
baileyk@uwf.edu
BAILEY, Kim 816-322-0110 279 H
kim.bailey@calvary.edu
BAILEY, Larry, G 662-246-6301 275 F
lbailey@msdelta.edu
BAILEY, Lisa 909-652-6532 39 B
lisa.bailey@chaffey.edu
BAILEY, Lora, B 731-426-7552 469 M
lbbailey@lanecollege.edu
BAILEY, Maggie 619-849-2535 62 L
maggiebailey@pointloma.edu
BAILEY, Mara, Z 402-465-2222 299 J
mbailey@nebrwesleyan.edu
BAILEY, Margaret, A 803-934-3192 459 F
mbailey@morris.edu
BAILEY, Mark 205-853-1200 5 C
mbailey@jeffstateonline.com
BAILEY, Mark, L 214-841-3676 485 E
mbailey@dts.edu
BAILEY, Marvin 317-447-6601 172 F
marvin.bailey@harrison.edu
BAILEY, Mary, H 910-672-1390 377 E
mhbailey@uncfsu.edu
BAILEY, Mary Kaye 702-651-4362 302 G
mary.kaye.bailey@csn.edu
BAILEY, Michael, L 804-342-1497 529 D
mbailey@vuu.edu
BAILEY, Michelle 563-441-4152 184 E
BAILEY, Mike 620-417-1019 196 B
mike.bailey@sccc.edu
BAILEY, Patricia, A 870-508-6102 20 E
pbailey@asumh.edu
BAILEY, Patrick, E 410-951-6399 228 B
pbailey@coppin.edu
BAILEY, Patrick, X 504-865-3434 213 F
pbailey@loyno.edu
BAILEY, Paul 678-466-4377 127 A
paulbailey@clayton.edu
BAILEY, Peter, A 302-295-1191 97 A
peter.a.bailey@wilmu.edu

BAILEY, JR., Philip, S 805-756-2226 33 F
pbailey@calpoly.edu
BAILEY, Randy 816-584-6229 287 H
randy.bailey@park.edu
BAILEY, Richard 281-998-6150 493 F
richard.bailey@sjcd.edu
BAILEY, Richard, L 717-361-1181 428 E
baileyrl@etown.edu
BAILEY, Risha, D 919-530-7639 378 A
rdbailey@nccu.edu
BAILEY, Robyn 847-635-1444 160 E
rbailey@oakton.edu
BAILEY, Scott 706-272-4435 127 G
sbailey@daltonstate.edu
BAILEY, Scott 706-865-2134 138 A
sbailey@truett.edu
BAILEY, Shannon 330-339-3391 394 B
smbailey@kent.edu
BAILEY, Steve 434-381-6110 524 E
sbailey@sbc.edu
BAILEY, Stuart, A 512-492-3033 480 F
sbailey@aoma.edu
BAILEY, Teresa 757-825-3693 528 B
baileyt@tncc.edu
BAILEY, Terry 706-272-2611 127 G
tbailey@daltonstate.edu
BAILEY, Thelathia, B 803-313-7042 462 D
tbailey@gwm.sc.edu
BAILEY, William 252-493-7434 372 E
wbailey@email.pittcc.edu
BAILEY, William, D 814-393-2306 442 A
wbailey@clarion.edu
BAILEY-AYE, Regena 785-654-2416 190 A
rbailey@allencc.edu
BAILEY CLARK, Denise 301-934-7724 222 C
dbclark@csmd.edu
BAILEY-FOUGNIER, Dennis 831-479-6317 31 F
debailey@cabrillo.edu
BAILEY-OCHOA, Celia 409-772-8909 507 B
cebailey@utmb.edu
BAILIE, Nate 256-824-2721 9 A
nathan.bailie@uah.edu
BAILIN, Debra, M 802-626-6210 515 F
debra.bailin@lyndonstate.edu
BAILLIE, Harold 570-941-7520 450 B
baillieh1@scranton.edu
BAILLIE, Joan 856-351-2645 315 A
baillie@salemcc.edu
BAILLIE, Thomas 206-543-5050 538 F
tbaillie@uw.edu
BAILO, Carole Anne 480-212-1704 18 F
BAILON, Kathy 213-624-1200 46 L
kbailon@fidm.edu
BAILY, Kim 310-660-3281 45 D
kbaily@elcamino.edu
BAILY, Scott 970-491-7655 83 A
scott.baily@colostate.edu
BAIMA, Thomas, A 847-566-6401 167 D
tbaima@usml.edu
BAIN, Andrew, C 410-951-4231 228 B
acbain@coppin.edu
BAIN, Donald, E 585-385-8010 348 F
dbain@sjfc.edu
BAIN, Jeff, N 931-363-9872 470 E
jbain@martinmethodist.edu
BAIN, Kenneth, R 973-655-3276 311 G
baink@mail.montclair.edu
BAIN, Larry 620-223-2700 192 G
larryb@fortscott.edu
BAIN, Michael, L 404-669-2097 135 E
michael.bain@point.edu
BAINE, Mindy 863-680-3949 109 D
mbaine@flsouthern.edu
BAINES, Moses 318-357-3162 211 G
BAINES, Robert, A 603-887-7410 303 G
robert.baines@chestercollege.edu
BAINES, Walt 480-245-7965 14 K
walt.baines@ibconline.edu
BAINTER, Bradley 309-298-1808 168 A
bl-bainter@wiu.edu
BAIR, Ava 719-336-1574 85 K
ava.bair@lamarcc.edu
BAIR, Carolyn 773-929-8500 149 C
cbair@devry.edu
BAIR, Ginny, V 218-477-2581 268 A
ginny.bair@mnstate.edu
BAIR, Miles, C 309-556-3077 153 E
mbair@iwu.edu
BAIR, Susanne, P 716-878-4324 353 A
bairsp@buffalostate.edu
BAIRAKTARIS, Karen 423-893-2039 478 C
karen.bairaktaris@vc.edu
BAIRD, David, L 714-895-8125 41 A
dbaird@gwc.cccd.edu
BAIRD, Davis 508-793-7673 233 C
dbaird@clarku.edu
BAIRD, Debra 256-216-6617 1 F
debra.baird@athens.edu
BAIRD, Denise, M 317-738-8270 171 C
dbaird@franklincollege.edu
BAIRD, Jeffrey 215-951-2620 444 C
bairdj@philau.edu

BALDWIN, Christine, A ..... 714-850-4800..... 89 F
Baldwin@TaftU.edu
BALDWIN, Cynthia, A .... 814-867-4088.... 438 F
cab71@psu.edu
BALDWIN, David, N .... 508-626-4645.... 238 D
dbaldwin@framingham.edu
BALDWIN, Deborah, J .... 501-569-3296..... 24 E
djbaldwin@ualr.edu
BALDWIN, Gail .... 601-643-8322.... 274 A
gail.baldwin@colin.edu
BALDWIN, Hazel, N .... 434-223-6117.... 519 B
hbaldwin@email.hsc.edu
BALDWIN, Jackie .... 856-227-7200.... 308 E
jbaldwin@camdencc.edu
BALDWIN, James, L .... 814-362-7602.... 449 B
jlb20@pitt.edu
BALDWIN, Joelle .... 616-632-2076.... 248 A
baldwjoe@aquinas.edu
BALDWIN, Linda .... 909-594-5611..... 58 A
lbaldwin@mtsac.edu
BALDWIN, Mary Sue .... 205-726-4097....... 6 G
msbaldwi@samford.edu
BALDWIN, R. Chad .... 636-584-6609.... 281 I
rcbaldwin@eastcentral.edu
BALDWIN, Robert, D .... 301-784-5000.... 221 A
rbaldwin@allegany.edu
BALDWIN, Sarah .... 503-554-2321.... 415 I
sbaldwin@georgefox.edu
BALDWIN, Stan .... 601-925-3321.... 275 E
sbaldwin@mc.edu
BALDWIN, Thomas .... 218-281-8340.... 272 A
tbaldwin@umn.edu
BALDWIN, Troy .... 504-816-4504.... 208 I
tbaldwin@dillard.edu
BALDWIN, Veria .... 606-589-3018.... 203 A
cookie.baldwin@kctcs.edu
BALDWIN, William .... 212-678-3052.... 357 F
wjb12@tc.columbia.edu
BALDWIN-DIMEO, Caren .. 603-526-3714.... 304 A
cbaldwin-dimeo@colby-sawyer.edu
BALDYGO, Robert .... 540-234-9261.... 525 G
baldygor@brcc.edu
BALENTINE, Kim .... 417-626-1234.... 287 F
kbalentine@occ.edu
BALES, Eugene, F .... 785-227-3380.... 190 G
balese@bethanylb.edu
BALES, Jamie .... 623-245-4600..... 18 M
jbales@uticorp.com
BALES, John, G .... 760-480-8474..... 78 E
bales@wscal.edu
BALES, John Anthony .... 208-885-5953.... 144 B
jbales@uidaho.edu
BALES, Kay .... 765-285-5344.... 169 D
kbales@bsu.edu
BALES, Michael .... 276-964-7323.... 528 A
michael.bales@sw.edu
BALES, William, J .... 615-898-5818.... 473 F
joe.bales@mtsu.edu
BALESTRERI, Bob .... 415-485-9414..... 41 I
bob.balestreri@marin.edu
BALESTRERI, Teresa, A ..... 314-516-5002.... 291 F
tkb@umsl.edu
BALESTRIERI, Carmela ...... 718-982-3032.... 327 A
carmela.balestrieri@csi.cuny.edu
BALEY, Heather .... 503-244-0726.... 414 D
heatherbaley@achs.edu
BALFANTZ, Gary .... 906-635-2275.... 254 C
gbalfantz@lssu.edu
BALFOUR, Alan .... 404-894-3380.... 130 D
alan.balfour@coa.gatech.edu
BALFOUR, David .... 802-773-5900.... 513 B
dbalfour@csj.edu
BALGAS, Diana .... 510-885-3983..... 34 C
diana.balgas@csueastbay.edu
BALGE, Daniel, N .... 507-354-8221.... 265 B
balgedn@mlc-wels.edu
BALIK, Daniel, J .... 651-696-6265.... 265 A
balik@macalester.edu
BALINT, Bill .... 724-357-4000.... 442 E
wsbalint@iup.edu
BALISTRERI, Rebecca .... 414-847-3262.... 548 G
beckybalistreri@miad.edu
BALISTRERI-CLARKE,
Margaret, R .... 608-663-2212.... 547 C
balistr@edgewood.edu
BALKCOM, Paris .... 312-980-9200.... 153 G
pbalkcom@iadtchicago.edu
BALKE, William .... 859-323-9093.... 206 H
cwbalk2@uky.edu
BALL, Betty .... 303-477-7240..... 84 I
bettyb@heritage-education.com
BALL, Charles .... 574-239-8318.... 172 J
cball@hcc-nd.edu
BALL, Daniel, W .... 864-388-8300.... 458 J
dball@lander.edu
BALL, Dave .... 319-296-4204.... 185 C
david.ball@hawkeyecollege.edu
BALL, Deborah, L .... 734-647-1637.... 259 D
dball@umich.edu
BALL, Diane .... 239-513-1122.... 110 K
dball@hodges.edu
BALL, Donald .... 352-365-3532.... 112 M
balld@lscc.edu
BALL, Drexel, B .... 803-535-5263.... 456 D
dball@claflin.edu
BALL, Elizabeth .... 573-875-7403.... 280 E
eqball@ccis.edu
BALL, Gerald, D .... 828-689-1242.... 366 F
gball@mhc.edu
BALL, James, D .... 410-386-8192.... 221 G
jball@carrollcc.edu
BALL, Jason .... 561-297-3440.... 118 H
jball@fau.edu
BALL, Jennifer .... 502-495-1040.... 199 H
jball@daymarcollege.edu
BALL, John .... 504-568-4500.... 213 A
jball@lsuhsc.edu
BALL, Karen .... 559-791-2420...... 53 A
kball@portervillecollege.edu
BALL, Karen .... 717-720-4050.... 441 E
kball@passhe.edu
BALL, Kathy .... 304-384-6009.... 543 D
bonner@concord.edu
BALL, Kim .... 704-894-2521.... 363 F
kiball@davidson.edu
BALL, Margaret, A .... 405-208-5060.... 410 A
mball@okcu.edu
BALL, Margaret, T .... 718-817-3010.... 334 C
mball@fordham.edu
BALL, Michael .... 859-246-6512.... 201 D
michael.ball@kctcs.edu
BALL, Molly, A .... 309-457-2323.... 158 G
maball@monm.edu
BALL, Monte .... 330-339-3391.... 394 B
mball15@kent.edu
BALL, Rhonda .... 334-649-5000.... 557 B
BALL, Sam .... 253-833-9111.... 534 C
sball@greenriver.edu
BALL, Scott .... 423-236-2881.... 473 A
sball@southern.edu
BALL, Shelley .... 865-471-3235.... 467 E
sball@cn.edu
BALL, Terri .... 913-367-6204.... 193 D
tball@highlandcc.edu
BALL, Terri .... 913-367-6204.... 193 E
tball@highlandcc.edu
BALL, Terry .... 801-422-2736.... 509 D
terry_ball@byu.edu
BALL, Thomas, G .... 724-458-2163.... 430 B
tgball@gcc.edu
BALL, Travis .... 903-886-5060.... 497 E
travis_ball@tamu-commerce.edu
BALL, William, S .... 513-558-0026.... 403 D
william.s.ball@uc.edu
BALL-DAVIS, Marsha .... 860-906-5127...... 89 L
mball-davis@ccc.commnet.edu
BALL-PARKER, Gayle .... 310-243-2801...... 34 B
gball@csudh.edu
BALL-WILLIAMSON,
Carrie .... 662-862-8123.... 274 G
cbball@iccms.edu
BALLABAN, David, C .... 610-921-7256.... 421 D
dballaban@alb.edu
BALLAGH DE TOVAR,
Jane .... 913-621-8791.... 192 C
jane@donnelly.edu
BALLAM, Gary, O .... 816-654-7562.... 283 J
gballam@kcumb.edu
BALLANCE, Ronald, J .... 757-671-7171.... 518 G
administration@ecpi.edu
BALLANTINE, Clay .... 413-559-5590.... 235 G
BALLANTYNE, Sherri .... 425-564-2229.... 531 B
sballant@bellevuecollege.edu
BALLANTYNE, Trina .... 201-216-8165.... 315 E
tballant@stevens.edu
BALLARD, Brandi .... 940-552-6291.... 507 E
bballard@vernoncollege.edu
BALLARD, Carol .... 863-680-6236.... 109 D
cballard@flsouthern.edu
BALLARD, Carol .... 334-670-3187....... 8 B
csupri@troy.edu
BALLARD, Donna .... 662-476-5054.... 274 D
dballard@eastms.edu
BALLARD, Gail .... 231-876-3145.... 248 F
gail.ballard@baker.edu
BALLARD, Glenda .... 903-223-3073.... 498 C
glenda.ballard@tamut.edu
BALLARD, J. Barry .... 501-337-5000...... 21 D
bballard@otcweb.edu
BALLARD, Jennifer .... 870-512-7861...... 20 F
jennifer_ballard@asun.edu
BALLARD, Jennifer .... 503-883-2509.... 416 G
jballard@linfield.edu
BALLARD, Jill, M .... 814-362-5091.... 449 B
jballard@pitt.edu
BALLARD, Katie .... 270-686-4529.... 202 E
katie.ballard@kctcs.edu
BALLARD, Lowell, W .... 630-752-5222.... 168 F
lowell.ballard@wheaton.edu
BALLARD, Lynne .... 802-860-2781.... 513 A
ballard@champlain.edu
BALLARD, Margaret .... 617-745-3876.... 234 C
margaret.ballard@enc.edu
BALLARD, Phillip .... 870-862-8131...... 23 G
pballard@southark.edu
BALLARD, Robin .... 309-694-8511.... 152 B
rballard@icc.edu
BALLARD, Steve .... 252-328-6212.... 377 C
chancellor@ecu.edu
BALLARD, Terri .... 412-536-1251.... 432 F
terri.ballard@laroche.edu
BALLARD, Vinson .... 601-979-3704.... 275 A
vinson.ballard@jsums.edu
BALLARD, William, H .... 318-869-5127.... 208 F
bballard@centenary.edu
BALLARD, William, P .... 802-656-2240.... 514 F
william.ballard@uvm.edu
BALLARD GORMAN,
Shannon .... 518-244-3142.... 348 A
ballas@sage.edu
BALLARD-THROWER,
Rhea .... 202-806-8047...... 98 B
rballard@law.howard.edu
BALLARINI, John .... 262-554-6110.... 548 F
jaballarini@yahoo.com
BALLENGEE, Greg, A .... 740-351-3574.... 401 I
gballengee@shawnee.edu
BALLENGER, Grady, W ...... 386-822-7515.... 121 E
gballeng@stetson.edu
BALLENGER, Nicole .... 307-766-4286.... 556 E
nicoleb@uwyo.edu
BALLENGER, P, J .... 256-824-6565....... 9 A
John.Ballenger@uah.edu
BALLENGER, Sheryl .... 706-295-6336.... 130 C
sballeng@highlands.edu
BALLENTINE, Angela .... 252-492-2061.... 374 D
ballentine@vgcc.edu
BALLENTINE, Howard .... 302-736-2529...... 96 G
ballentine@wesley.edu
BALLER, Jim .... 304-214-8960.... 543 A
jballer@wvncc.edu
BALLESTEROS, E. Michael 207-974-4869.... 218 H
mballesteros@emcc.edu
BALLESTEROS, Victor .... 972-438-6932.... 492 C
vballesteros@parkercc.edu
BALLEW, Marcy .... 903-875-7335.... 491 B
marcy.ballew@navarrocollege.edu
BALLEW-SAFEWRIGHT,
Michelle .... 865-981-8194.... 470 F
michelle.ballew@maryvillecollege.edu
BALLIET, Cliff .... 607-778-5222.... 324 G
balliet_c@sunybroome.edu
BALLIET, Emil .... 817-461-8741.... 480 H
eballiet@abconline.org
BALLING, John, D .... 503-370-6004.... 421 C
jballing@willamette.edu
BALLINGER, Gary .... 812-514-8455.... 173 A
gballinger@indstatefoundation.org
BALLINGER, Kevin .... 714-432-5531...... 41 B
sballinger@occ.cccd.edu
BALLINGER, Marcia .... 440-365-5222.... 395 C
BALLINGER, Marcia, J .... 440-365-5222.... 395 C
BALLINGER, Philip .... 206-221-2305.... 538 F
philipba@uw.edu
BALLOM, Consuelo .... 708-709-3781.... 161 C
cballom@prairiestate.edu
BALLOM, Kenneth .... 217-333-2121.... 167 B
ballom@illinois.edu
BALLOU, Dawn .... 617-732-2077.... 241 F
dawn.ballou@mcphs.edu
BALLOU, Kathryn .... 913-344-6084.... 190 C
Kathryn.Ballou@bakeru.edu
BALLOU, Trenna .... 435-722-6900.... 510 J
BALMER, Stephanie .... 717-245-1287.... 427 E
balmers@dickinson.edu
BALMOS, Donald .... 254-299-8602.... 490 E
dbalmos@mclennan.edu
BALOG, John, A .... 904-256-7067.... 111 J
jbalog@ju.edu
BALOG, Scott .... 850-201-8632.... 121 F
BALOGA, Monica .... 321-674-7298.... 108 E
mbaloga@fit.edu
BALOGH, Deborah Ware .... 317-788-3212.... 180 C
dbalogh@uindy.edu
BALOGUN, Joseph, A .... 773-995-3987.... 146 D
ja-balogun@csu.edu
BALOGUN, Lateef .... 252-536-7253.... 370 F
balogunl@halifaxcc.edu
BALON, Michelle, J .... 727-816-3213.... 114 F
balonm@phcc.edu
BALOUBI, Desire' .... 919-546-8307.... 376 D
dbaloubi@shawu.edu
BALOUGH, Sandra, A .... 814-472-3151.... 446 B
sbalough@francis.edu
BALRAM, Arlette .... 212-686-9040.... 360 E
abalram@woodtobecoburn.edu
BALSA, Carmen, A .... 787-257-0000.... 566 H
carmen.balsa@upr.edu
BALSAM, Carl, E .... 773-244-5610.... 159 G
cbalsam@northpark.edu
BALSAMO, Michael .... 586-445-7141.... 254 F
balsamom@macomb.edu
BALSANO, Gregory, R .... 562-903-4704...... 30 H
greg.balsano@biola.edu
BALSEIRO, Wanda .... 787-878-5475.... 562 H
wbalsciro@arecibo.inter.edu
BALSER, Deborah, B .... 314-516-5146.... 291 F
balserd@umsl.edu
BALSER, Jeffrey .... 615-322-2151.... 477 F
jeff.balser@vanderbilt.edu
BALSER, Jeffrey, R .... 615-936-3030.... 477 F
jeff.balser@vanderbilt.edu
BALSER, Rose .... 920-748-8137.... 549 I
bookstore@ripon.edu
BALSER, Teresa, C .... 352-392-1961.... 120 B
tcbalser@ufl.edu
BALSLEY, Richard .... 229-317-6930.... 128 A
rich.balsley@darton.edu
BALTES, Mary .... 813-935-5700.... 115 J
marybaltes@remingtoncollege.edu
BALTIERRA, Annabelle .... 661-255-1050...... 32 C
abaltierra@calarts.edu
BALTIMORE, Lester .... 516-877-3142.... 322 A
baltimore@adelphi.edu
BALTRUS, Susan, C .... 207-795-2846.... 217 F
baltruss@cmhc.org
BALZA, Stephen, J .... 507-354-8221.... 265 B
balzasj@mlc-wels.edu
BALZANO, Wanda .... 336-758-4455.... 380 B
balzanow@wfu.edu
BALZER, Brenda .... 443-334-2176.... 226 E
bbalzer@stevenson.edu
BALZER, Jackie .... 503-725-5429.... 418 G
jbalzer@pdx.edu
BALZER, Robert, G .... 909-869-3268...... 33 G
RGbalzer@csupomona.edu
BALZER, William .... 419-372-0623.... 385 C
wbalzer@bgsu.edu
BALZER, William, K .... 419-372-0623.... 385 D
wbalzer@bgsu.edu
BAMBARA, Cynthia, S .... 301-784-5000.... 221 A
cbambara@allegany.edu
BAMBERGER, Gregory .... 610-683-4095.... 442 F
gbamberg@kutztown.edu
BAMBHROLIA, Savita .... 609-586-4800.... 311 C
bambhros@mccc.edu
BAMBINA, Antonia, D .... 812-461-5357.... 180 F
adbambina@usi.edu
BAMBURG, Jill .... 206-780-6213.... 530 I
jill.bamburg@bgi.edu
BAME, Kevin .... 618-453-6214.... 164 I
kbame@siu.edu
BAME, Kevin .... 618-453-2474.... 164 I
kbame@siu.edu
BAMFORD, Carol, M .... 515-263-6129.... 184 I
cbamford@grandview.edu
BAMFORD, Penny .... 510-869-6744...... 64 J
pbamford@samuelmerritt.edu
BAMONTE, Paul .... 718-409-6079.... 356 C
pbamonte@sunymaritime.edu
BAMONTE, Paul .... 718-409-7254.... 356 C
pbamonte@sunymaritime.edu
BANA, Mark .... 303-914-6220...... 87 C
Mark.Bana@rrcc.edu
BANACH, Michael .... 718-940-5584.... 349 A
mbanach@sjcny.edu
BANACH, Patricia, S .... 860-465-5000...... 91 H
banachp@easternct.edu
BANAHAN, Richard .... 314-644-9766.... 289 C
rbanahan@stlcc.edu
BANAS, Paul .... 425-889-5234.... 535 I
paul.banas@northwestu.edu
BANASZAK, Larry .... 614-823-1693.... 400 G
lbanaszak@otterbein.edu
BANASZAK, Lori .... 253-589-5788.... 532 B
lori.banaszak@cptc.edu
BANASZAK HOLL,
Mark, M .... 734-763-1290.... 259 D
mbanasza@umich.edu
BANAVAR, Jayanth, R .... 301-405-2316.... 227 B
banavar@umd.edu
BANBURY, Doug .... 740-392-6868.... 396 H
mbanbury@mvnu.edu
BANDA, Magda .... 708-656-8000.... 159 C
magna.banda@morton.edu
BANDAS, Mark .... 615-322-6400.... 477 F
mark.bandas@vanderbilt.edu
BANDAS, Raul .... 787-758-2525.... 567 D
BANDELIN, Janis, M .... 864-294-2191.... 458 D
janis.bandelin@furman.edu
BANDO, Chris .... 609-201-8767...... 65 D
BANDOIAN, Nancy .... 617-989-4476.... 246 C
bandoiann@wit.edu
BANDRE, Mark .... 785-594-8420.... 190 C
mark.bandre@bakeru.edu
BANDS, Kathleen .... 301-696-3400.... 223 C
bands@hood.edu
BANDSTRA, Travis .... 708-239-4854.... 165 I
travis.bandstra@trnty.edu
BANDURSKI, Jeff, J .... 262-243-5700.... 546 I
jeffrey.bandurski@cuw.edu
BANDY, Charles .... 276-964-7319.... 528 A
greg.bandy@sw.edu
BANDY, JR., John, M .... 404-413-4600.... 131 C
jbandy@gsu.edu
BANDY, Kanoe .... 661-763-7779...... 72 C
kbandy@taftcollege.edu
BANDY, Kenneth .... 417-328-1759.... 290 E
kbandy@sbuniv.edu
BANDY, Mark .... 515-727-2100.... 186 G
mbandy@hamiltonia.edu
BANDY-NEAL, LaMel .... 615-327-6767.... 471 A
lbneal@mmc.edu
BANDYOPADHYAY,
Santanu .... 714-484-7311...... 59 C
sbandyopadhyay@cypresscollege.edu

BANE, Denise 973-748-9000 308 A
denise_bane@bloomfield.edu
BANERJEE, Nantoo 269-471-6615 252 C
banerjee@andrews.edu
BANERJI, Debashish 323-663-2167 75 E
BANES, Edna, J 804-355-0671 524 F
ebanes@upsem.edu
BANESS KING, Deborah 708-456-0300 166 C
dbanessk@triton.edu
BANEY, Mary Ellen 412-396-6575 428 C
baney@duq.edu
BANEY, Todd 704-922-6485 370 D
baney.todd@gaston.edu
BANG, Barbara 701-671-2277 382 E
barbara.bang@ndscs.edu
BANG, Sam 626-584-5398 48 A
sbang@fuller.edu
BANGASSER, Karen 605-331-6684 466 D
karen.bangasser@usiouxfalls.edu
BANGASSER, Kathy 815-599-3448 152 A
kathy.bangasser@highland.edu
BANGASSER, Susan 909-384-8650 65 C
sbangasser@sbccd.cc.ca.us
BANGERT, Darci, M 515-574-1035 185 F
bangert@iowacentral.edu
BANGERT, Stephanie 510-869-6512 64 J
sbangert@samuelmerritt.edu
BANGERT-DROWNS,
Robert 518-442-4988 351 E
rbangert@uamail.albany.edu
BANGHART, Brad 530-225-3957 69 D
bbanghart@shastacollege.edu
BANICK, Gabrielle 608-757-6320 553 E
gbanick@blackhawk.edu
BANIK, Deb 303-292-0015 83 H
BANIS, William, J 847-491-5360 160 D
w-banis@northwestern.edu
BANISTER, Mickey, D 405-425-5200 409 E
mickey.banister@oc.edu
BANISTER, Stephen 701-858-3855 381 G
stephen.banister@minotstateu.edu
BANJAC, Joyce 636-797-3000 283 H
jbanjac@jeffco.edu
BANKEN, Mary Jo 573-882-6211 291 D
bankenm@missouri.edu
BANKER, Tollie 330-339-3391 394 B
tbanker@kent.edu
BANKEY, Michael 567-661-7736 400 H
michael_bankey@owens.edu
BANKHEAD, Brad 970-945-8691 82 C
BANKIRER, Marcia 303-923-4222 81 A
mbankirer@argosy.edu
BANKIRER, Marcia 303-248-2701 144 G
mbankirer@argosy.edu
BANKOLE-MEDINA,
Katherine 410-951-3431 228 B
kbankole@coppin.edu
BANKS, Cerri 413-538-2481 242 G
cbanks@mtholyoke.edu
BANKS, Christopher 213-613-2200 70 H
christopher_banks@sciarc.edu
BANKS, Dacia, L 315-684-6289 354 F
banksdl@morrisville.edu
BANKS, Darrell, L 859-233-8207 206 E
dbanks@transy.edu
BANKS, Dee 404-237-7573 125 F
dbanks@bauder.edu
BANKS, Ivan 610-399-2271 441 H
ivan.banks@cheyney.edu
BANKS, Jared 816-501-2900 279 C
jared.banks@avila.edu
BANKS, Julie, M 937-229-3233 404 A
julie.banks@notes.udayton.edu
BANKS, Kathryn, M 252-638-7367 369 E
banksk@cravencc.edu
BANKS, Kay 803-321-5146 459 G
kay.banks@newberry.edu
BANKS, Kevin 504-286-5290 214 I
kbanks@suno.edu
BANKS, Kevin, M 813-974-6677 120 D
kevinbanks@usf.edu
BANKS, Kimberly 904-256-7501 111 J
kbanks@ju.edu
BANKS, Larry 801-375-5125 510 F
lbanks@rmuohp.edu
BANKS, Lynne 814-472-3002 446 B
lbanks@francis.edu
BANKS, Martha 256-228-6001 6 A
banksm@nacc.edu
BANKS, Mary 239-590-1172 119 A
mbanks@fgcu.edu
BANKS, McRae 336-334-5338 379 A
mcbanks@uncg.edu
BANKS, Melissa 912-443-3380 136 D
mbanks@savannahtech.edu
BANKS, Michael, L 636-922-8356 288 E
mbanks@stchas.edu
BANKS, Michelle, R 901-678-2713 474 C
mbanks@memphis.edu
BANKS, Nicole, P 561-862-4310 114 D
banksn@palmbeachstate.edu
BANKS, Pat, A 404-627-2681 126 A
pat.banks@beulah.org
BANKS, Racheal, B 205-665-6215 9 C
banksrb@montevallo.edu
BANKS, Ronald 502-597-5948 203 D
ron.banks@kysu.edu
BANKS, Sharon, S 304-766-3078 544 D
banksss@wvstateu.edu
BANKS, Wayne 870-574-4493 24 A
wbanks@sautech.edu
BANKS, JR., Willie 706-583-0271 138 C
willieb@uga.edu
BANKS, Yvonne, R 651-631-5221 270 E
yrbanks@nwc.edu
BANKS-DEAVER,
Yolanda, E 919-530-7432 378 A
ybanks@nccu.edu
BANKSTON, Marsha 805-893-8653 74 F
marsha.bankston@sa.ucsb.edu
BANKSTON, Patrick 219-980-6562 173 F
pbanks@iun.edu
BANKSTON, Tony 309-556-3031 153 E
iwuadmit@iwu.edu
BANNAN, Denise, A 810-766-4272 248 C
denise.bannan@baker.edu
BANNER, Barb, R 262-243-5700 546 I
barbara.banner@cuw.edu
BANNER, Josephina, E 610-558-5548 437 C
bannerj@neumann.edu
BANNICK, Linda, J 214-333-5151 484 C
lindab@dbu.edu
BANNISTER, Darlene 830-792-7357 494 A
bannistr@schreiner.edu
BANNISTER, Darlene, A 830-792-7357 494 A
bannistr@schreiner.edu
BANNISTER, Edith 253-833-9111 534 C
ajensen@greenriver.edu
BANNISTER, Edith 253-833-9111 534 C
ebannister@greenriver.edu
BANNISTER, Geoff 808-544-0202 140 B
cwright@hpu.edu
BANNISTER, Mark 785-628-5339 192 F
markbannister@fhsu.edu
BANNON, Douglas, F 319-398-5517 186 H
doug.bannon@kirkwood.cc.ia.us
BANOCY-PAYNE, Marge 850-201-6070 121 F
banocym@tcc.fl.edu
BANOS, Anne 504-865-5201 215 C
apbanos@tulane.edu
BANREY, Vincent 718-270-6046 328 D
vbanrey@mec.cuny.edu
BANSAVICH, John 415-422-5529 76 B
bansavich@usfca.edu
BANTA, Paul, J 314-984-7444 289 D
pbanta@stlcc.edu
BANTA, Trudy, W 317-274-4111 174 B
tbanta@iupui.edu
BANTLE, John (Jack), A 937-775-3336 406 C
jack.bantle@wright.edu
BANTZ, Charles 317-274-4417 173 B
cbantz@iupui.edu
BANTZ, Charles 317-274-4417 173 C
cbantz@iupui.edu
BANTZ, Charles, R 317-274-4417 174 B
cbantz@iupui.edu
BANTZ, Don 907-564-8201 10 D
BANUELOS, Maria, G 608-246-6460 554 B
mbanuelos@matcmadison.edu
BANWARTH, Gregory 508-362-2131 240 A
gbanwarth@capecod.edu
BANZ, Clint, J 215-368-7538 424 A
BAPTISTE, Jo Rae 808-245-8323 141 H
jorae@hawaii.edu
BAPTISTE, Lloyd 225-216-8201 209 I
baptistel@mybrcc.edu
BARABE, Cathy 559-934-2147 77 H
cathybarabe@whccd.edu
BARABINO, Joseph 305-348-2494 119 B
joseph.barabino@fiu.edu
BARAJAS, Daniel 928-344-7769 12 C
daniel.barajas@azwestern.edu
BARAJAS, Leticia 213-763-7071 55 D
barajal@lattc.edu
BARAJAS, Silvia 253-566-5050 538 C
sbarajas@tacomacc.edu
BARAKAT, Nabeel, M 310-233-4351 54 I
barakanm@lahc.edu
BARALLE, Ralph 636-227-2100 284 E
ralph.baralle@logan.edu
BARAN-CENTENO,
Barbara, J 210-458-4037 506 B
barbara.centeno@utsa.edu
BARANN, Kristine 313-425-3700 248 D
kristine.barann@baker.edu
BARANOWSKI, Thomas 732-987-2219 310 D
baranowskit@georgian.edu
BARAZZONE, Esther, L 412-365-1160 425 B
barazzone@chatham.edu
BARBA, Robert 413-775-1606 240 B
barba@gcc.mass.edu
BARBA, Steve 603-535-2722 307 B
sbarba@plymouth.edu
BARBADILLO, Julie 253-943-2800 533 B
jbarbadillo@devry.edu
BARBAGALLO, Tim, M 267-502-2605 423 B
tim.barbagallo@anc-gc.org
BARBARAK, Thomas 314-256-8886 279 A
barbarak@ai.edu
BARBARI, Mary Pat 312-235-3539 164 D
m.barbari@shimer.edu
BARBATIS, Peter 718-289-5864 326 F
peter.barbatis@bcc.cuny.edu
BARBEAU, Leigh 312-752-2130 155 B
liegh.barbeau@kendall.edu
BARBEAU, Marc 715-682-1811 549 C
mbarbeau@northland.edu
BARBEE, Brent 910-410-1809 372 G
brentb@richmondcc.edu
BARBEE, Cathey 719-389-6351 81 L
cbarbee@coloradocollege.edu
BARBEE, Chris, W 616-331-3590 252 A
barbeec@gvsu.edu
BARBER, Billy 252-789-0303 371 E
bbarber@martincc.edu
BARBER, Catherine 985-858-2977 210 H
cbarber@ftcc.edu
BARBER, Deborah, G 803-323-2191 463 D
barberdg@winthrop.edu
BARBER, Elizabeth 812-749-1242 178 D
bbarber@oak.edu
BARBER, Ella 972-273-3009 485 B
ebarber@dcccd.edu
BARBER, Glynis 410-951-3078 228 B
gbarber@coppin.edu
BARBER, Jacques 516-877-4800 322 A
jbarber@adelphi.edu
BARBER, Jeff 434-582-2100 520 F
jbarber2@liberty.edu
BARBER, Jennifer 916-278-6295 35 E
jbarbar@csus.edu
BARBER, Jerald 870-777-5722 25 F
jerald.barber@uacch.edu
BARBER, John 410-276-0306 226 D
jbarber@host.sdc.edu
BARBER, Keith 229-391-4900 123 F
kbarber@abac.edu
BARBER, Kimberly 850-644-6127 119 C
kabarber@admin.fsu.edu
BARBER, Marcia, A 315-470-6611 355 A
mabarber@esf.edu
BARBER, Michael 406-247-5776 295 F
mbarber@msubillings.edu
BARBER, SJ, Michael 314-977-2701 289 F
barbermd@slu.edu
BARBER, SJ, Michael, D 314-977-2701 289 F
barbermd@slu.edu
BARBER, Michael, J 406-247-5750 295 F
mbarber@msubillings.edu
BARBER, Peggy 276-964-7556 528 A
peggy.barber@sw.edu
BARBER, Ray, G 812-749-1213 178 D
ocuexec@oak.edu
BARBER, Sharon 563-441-3176 186 E
sbarber@kucampus.edu
BARBER, Susan 405-208-5287 410 A
sbarber@okcu.edu
BARBER, Tamara 701-224-5476 382 B
tamara.barber@bismarckstate.edu
BARBER, William 800-672-3060 376 E
BARBER, William 313-845-9607 252 D
wbarber@hfcc.edu
BARBERA, Anthony 516-876-3135 353 D
barberaa@oldwestbury.edu
BARBERENA, Celia 510-723-6640 38 L
cbarberena@chabotcollege.edu
BARBERICH, Judith 610-282-1100 426 I
judy.barberich@desales.edu
BARBERO, Christina 914-633-2462 336 E
CBarbero@iona.edu
BARBICH, Michelle 814-732-1457 442 D
mbarbich@edinboro.edu
BARBIERI, Dean 925-969-3559 52 B
dbarbieri@jfku.edu
BARBIERI, Lina 610-282-1100 426 I
lina.barbieri@desales.edu
BARBOSA, Isaac 409-880-8195 500 E
ibarbosa@lit.edu
BARBOSA, Miguel 570-422-3547 442 C
mbarbosa@po-box.esu.edu
BARBOUR, Cheryl 303-546-3565 86 B
cheryl@naropa.edu
BARBOUR, Heather 401-341-2225 454 D
heather.barbour@salve.edu
BARBOUR, Kathryn, A 410-827-5806 222 B
kbarbour@chesapeake.edu
BARBOUR, Monica 313-993-1951 259 C
barboumm@udmercy.edu
BARBOUR, Sandy 510-642-5316 73 E
athletic.director@berkeley.edu
BARCALOW, Douglas 260-399-7700 180 E
dbarcalow@sf.edu
BARCELO, Marialina 787-763-3730 567 F
marialina.barcelo@upr.edu
BARCELO, Nancy (Rusty) 505-747-2140 320 A
nbarcelo@nnmc.edu
BARCHI, Robert, L 215-955-6617 448 B
robert.barchi@jefferson.edu
BARCKHOLTZ, Benjamin 406-657-1714 295 F
benjamin.barckholtz@msubillings.edu
BARCLAY, Donald, A 209-658-4444 74 B
dbarclay@UCMerced.edu
BARCLAY, Ken 805-756-2476 33 F
kbarclay@calpoly.edu
BARCLAY, Kent 978-232-2282 234 F
kbarclay@endicott.edu
BARCLAY, Lynn 413-369-4044 233 F
BARCLAY, Ray 386-822-7255 121 E
rbarclay@stetson.edu
BARCLIFT, Mark 417-862-9533 282 D
mbarclift@globaluniversity.edu
BARCO, James, M 770-534-6160 126 B
jbarco@brenau.edu
BARCZYK, Ewa 414-229-4781 551 C
ewa@uwm.edu
BARD, Sharon, K 704-463-3428 375 E
sharon.bard@fsmail.pfeiffer.edu
BARDEN, Brian, D 570-662-4813 443 B
bbarden@mansfield.edu
BARDEN, John, H 512-404-4827 481 D
jbarden@austinseminary.edu
BARDEN, Nancy 303-644-4034 86 A
nancy.barden@morgancc.edu
BARDEN, Thomas 419-530-6033 404 F
thomas.barden@utoledo.edu
BARDES, Charles 212-746-1067 360 B
clbardes@med.cornell.edu
BARDILL MOSCARITOLO,
Lisa 914-773-3860 345 F
lbardillmoscaritolo@pace.edu
BARDOWELL, Cheryl 909-389-3260 65 B
cbardowe@craftonhills.edu
BARE, Benita 276-944-6800 518 I
bbare@ehc.edu
BARE, James, S 516-739-1545 343 C
admin_dean@nyctcm.edu
BARE, Michael 714-241-6104 40 J
mbare@coastline.edu
BAREFIELD, Frank 334-556-2235 4 A
fbarefield@wallace.edu
BAREFIELD, Kevin 662-685-4771 273 H
kbarefield@bmc.edu
BAREFOOT, Clark 405-691-3800 408 H
cbarefoot@macu.edu
BARELMAN, Jason 402-375-7327 299 I
jabarel1@wsc.edu
BARENDS, Bobbi, J 302-855-1690 96 B
bbutch@dtcc.edu
BARENDS, Frans 404-894-5000 130 D
frans.barends@business.gatech.edu
BARFIELD, Craig 919-760-8516 366 G
craigb@meredith.edu
BARFIELD, Eakle 406-657-2309 295 F
ebarfield@msubillings.edu
BARFIELD, Gary 931-393-1620 475 C
jnichols@mscc.edu
BARFIELD, Mason 678-466-4672 127 A
masonbarfield@clayton.edu
BARFIELD, Virginia, C 803-786-5150 459 B
gbarfield@ltss.edu
BARFOOT, D. Scott 214-841-3666 485 E
sbarfoot@dts.edu
BARGAR, Robin 312-369-8222 148 B
rbargar@colum.edu
BARGAS, Peter 661-362-2836 56 G
pbargas@masters.edu
BARGAS, Terry 303-632-2300 83 C
tbargas@coloradotech.edu
BARGE, Scott 574-535-7110 171 D
scottcb@goshen.edu
BARGEN, Kris 517-321-0242 252 B
kbargen@glcc.edu
BARGER, Brett 636-949-4366 284 C
bbarger@lindenwood.edu
BARGER, David 203-582-8956 93 E
david.barger@quinnipiac.edu
BARGER, Debbie 828-327-7000 368 G
dbarger@cvcc.edu
BARGER, Debbie, M 515-263-6012 184 I
dbarger@grandview.edu
BARGER, Debra, E 530-898-6105 34 A
dbarger@csuchico.edu
BARGER, Eric 503-943-7337 420 G
barger@up.edu
BARGER, Kyle 215-248-6325 435 B
kbarger@ltsp.edu
BARGER, Lynn, I 814-269-2092 449 D
lbarger@pitt.edu
BARGER, Melanie 573-592-6050 293 C
Melanie.Barger@westminster-mo.edu
BARGER, Peter, S 630-637-5362 159 F
psbarger@noctrl.edu
BARGER, Sara, E 205-348-1040 8 F
sbarger@bama.ua.edu
BARGER, Stu, C 425-388-9142 533 H
sbarger@everett.edu
BARGER, Terri 405-422-1406 411 G
bargert@redlandscc.edu
BARHNOUSE, Carrie 434-592-4204 520 F
cldunbar@liberty.edu
BARHORST, Bettsey, L 608-246-6676 554 B
bbarhorst@matcmadison.edu
BARI, Maria 508-849-3313 230 C
mbari@annamaria.edu

BARID, Cathy .... 859-291-0800.... 199 F
cbaird@daymarcollege.edu
BARILLO, Madeline, K .... 203-857-7039.... 90 G
mbarillo@ncc.commnet.edu
BARIMANI, Adel .... 610-436-2828.... 443 F
abarimani@wcupa.edu
BARINOWSKI, Sandra .... 256-824-2771.... 9 A
sandra.patterson@uah.edu
BARIOLA, Kristi .... 662-246-6376.... 275 F
kbariola@msdelta.edu
BARISH, Robert, A .... 318-675-5000.... 213 B
rbaris@lsuhsc.edu
BARKALOW, Susan, L .... 252-451-8258.... 372 B
barkalow@nash.cc.nc.us
BARKAN, Chester .... 516-364-0808.... 343 A
cbarkan@nycollege.edu
BARKE, Vicky .... 920-735-2468.... 553 G
barke@fvtc.edu
BARKELOO, Mary, E .... 308-635-6033.... 301 E
barkeloo@wncc.edu
BARKER, Allyn, S .... 304-896-7404.... 542 J
allynb@southern.wvnet.edu
BARKER, Allyson .... 256-782-5002.... 4 L
abarker@jsu.edu
BARKER, Anna, M .... 301-790-2800.... 223 A
barkera@hagerstowncc.edu
BARKER, Beverly .... 386-312-4110.... 116 D
beverlybarker@sjrstate.edu
BARKER, Brent .... 334-386-7231.... 3 H
bbarker@faulkner.edu
BARKER, Bruce, A .... 715-833-6221.... 553 F
bbarker@cvtc.edu
BARKER, Catherine, A .... 816-235-1375.... 291 E
barkerca@umkc.edu
BARKER, David, F .... 502-852-4676.... 207 A
david.barker@louisville.edu
BARKER, James, F .... 864-656-3413.... 456 E
jbarker@clemson.edu
BARKER, Jeffrey, H .... 864-596-9091.... 457 E
jeff.barker@converse.edu
BARKER, Joe .... 830-591-7284.... 495 B
joe.barker@swtjc.cc.tx.us
BARKER, John, D .... 864-294-2106.... 458 D
john.barker@furman.edu
BARKER, John, F .... 716-286-8220.... 344 D
jfb@niagara.edu
BARKER, Joshua .... 252-398-6319.... 363 E
barkej@chowan.edu
BARKER, Keith .... 860-486-2686.... 94 E
keith.barker@uconn.edu
BARKER, Lee .... 773-256-3000.... 158 A
lbarker@meadville.edu
BARKER, Lorie .... 559-791-2370.... 53 A
lbarker@portervillecollege.edu
BARKER, Neva .... 909-621-8306.... 69 A
neva.barker@scrippscollege.edu
BARKER, Stan .... 541-463-5608.... 416 D
barkers@lanecc.edu
BARKER, Tom .... 937-433-3410.... 390 I
tbarker@edaff.com
BARKETT, Pamela .... 864-294-2217.... 458 D
pam.barkett@furman.edu
BARKHYMER,
Margarette, C .... 614-823-1456.... 400 G
mbarkhymer@otterbein.edu
BARKIS, Marita .... 816-235-1219.... 291 E
barkism@umkc.edu
BARKLEY, Alan .... 203-332-5967.... 90 B
abarkley@hcc.commnet.edu
BARKLEY, Eric .... 573-288-6363.... 281 D
ebarkley@culver.edu
BARKLEY, Phillip, L .... 352-392-1161.... 120 B
pbarkley@ufl.edu
BARKLEY, Robert, S .... 864-656-5463.... 456 E
rbrtbkl@clemson.edu
BARKLEY, Susan, E .... 972-238-6943.... 485 C
sbarkley@dcccd.edu
BARKLEY-GIFFIN,
Adrienne .... 618-985-3741.... 154 E
adriennebarkley@jalc.edu
BARKMAN, Jeff .... 731-989-6051.... 468 K
facilities@fhu.edu
BARKMEIER, Becky .... 507-389-2015.... 267 H
becky.barkmeier@mnsu.edu
BARKO, Valerie .... 618-985-3741.... 154 E
valeriebarko@jalc.edu
BARKSCHAT, Kate .... 828-894-3092.... 371 A
kbarkschat@isothermal.edu
BARKSDALE, Gary .... 859-622-5094.... 200 D
gary.barksdale@eku.edu
BARKSDALE, Jeffrey, M .... 334-244-3539.... 2 A
jbarksdale@aum.edu
BARKSDALE, Kevin .... 602-639-7500.... 14 I
BARKWILL, Joseph .... 516-463-6623.... 335 H
joseph.barkwill@hofstra.edu
BARLAAM, Maria .... 718-289-5608.... 326 F
maria.barlaam@bcc.cuny.edu
BARLETT, Alisa .... 605-856-5880.... 465 A
alisa.barlett@sintegleska.edu
BARLETT, Paul .... 913-234-0632.... 191 G
paul.barlett@cleveland.edu
BARLETTA, Frank .... 212-229-5660.... 342 E
barlettf@newschool.edu
BARLIEB, Deborah .... 610-683-4204.... 442 F
barlieb@kutztown.edu

BARLOW, Cathy .... 910-962-3389.... 379 C
barlowc@uncw.edu
BARLOW, Charlene .... 859-344-3348.... 206 D
charlene.barlow@thomasmore.edu
BARLOW, David .... 910-672-1659.... 377 E
dbarlow@uncfsu.edu
BARLOW, Elizabeth, A .... 713-743-0644.... 503 B
ebarlow@uh.edu
BARLOW, Gloria .... 570-408-4440.... 451 G
gloria.barlow@wilkes.edu
BARLOW, Jerry, N .... 504-282-4455.... 213 H
jbarlow@nobts.edu
BARLOW, Jill, M .... 978-468-7111.... 235 F
jbarlow@gcts.edu
BARLOW, John .... 207-326-2485.... 219 D
john.barlow@mma.edu
BARLOW, Kevin .... 281-283-3065.... 503 C
barlowk@uhcl.edu
BARLOW, Linda .... 903-693-2067.... 492 A
lbarlow@panola.edu
BARLOW, Marlene, T .... 215-968-8000.... 423 E
barlowm@bucks.edu
BARLOW, Michael .... 270-706-8614.... 201 F
Michael.Barlow@kctcs.edu
BARLOW, Sandy .... 270-534-3244.... 203 B
sandy.barlow@kctcs.edu
BARLOW, Steve .... 307-855-2143.... 555 G
barlow@cwc.edu
BARLOW, Thomas, M .... 813-879-6000.... 106 F
tbarlow@cci.edu
BARLOW, William .... 440-775-8273.... 397 F
bill.barlow@oberlin.edu
BARLOW-KELLEY, Jill .... 207-288-5015.... 217 H
jbk@coa.edu
BARNA, Peter .... 718-636-3744.... 346 D
provost@pratt.edu
BARNABY, Mike .... 218-855-8039.... 266 C
mbarnaby@clcmn.edu
BARNARD, Cheryl, A .... 860-231-5267.... 93 H
cbarnard@sjc.edu
BARNARD, Melinda .... 707-664-3236.... 37 B
melinda.barnard@sonoma.edu
BARNARD, Monica .... 806-720-7232.... 490 D
monica.barnard@lcu.edu
BARNARD, Susan .... 201-447-7938.... 307 F
sbarnard@bergen.edu
BARNARD, Tom .... 217-351-2582.... 161 B
tbarnard@parkland.edu
BARNDS, W. Kent .... 309-794-7314.... 145 B
wkentbarnds@augustana.edu
BARNER, John, C .... 812-488-2362.... 180 B
jb295@evansville.edu
BARNER, Kristin, M .... 662-329-7293.... 276 B
kbarner@dev.muw.edu
BARNES, Amy .... 540-458-8920.... 530 A
abarnes@wlu.edu
BARNES, Andre .... 415-239-3151.... 39 H
abarnes@ccsf.edu
BARNES, Andrew .... 718-636-3570.... 346 D
awbarnes@pratt.edu
BARNES, April .... 859-622-3855.... 200 D
april.barnes@eku.edu
BARNES, Brian, M .... 907-474-7649.... 10 J
bmbarnes@alaska.edu
BARNES, Carolyn .... 940-898-3456.... 502 B
cbarnes@twu.edu
BARNES, Charles .... 314-529-9504.... 284 F
cbarnes@maryville.edu
BARNES, Cheryl .... 404-756-4006.... 124 I
cbarnes@atlm.edu
BARNES, Clarence, D .... 509-313-3404.... 534 A
barnes@jepson.gonzaga.edu
BARNES, Dan .... 312-662-4041.... 144 C
barnes@adler.edu
BARNES, Edwin, A .... 909-869-3020.... 33 G
eabarnes@csupomona.edu
BARNES, Elendar .... 718-270-4982.... 328 D
elendar@mec.cuny.edu
BARNES, Elizabeth, A .... 248-689-8282.... 260 A
bbarnes@walshcollege.edu
BARNES, Emanuel .... 601-877-6147.... 273 C
ebarnes@alcorn.edu
BARNES, Fred .... 310-665-6968.... 60 B
fbarnes@otis.edu
BARNES, Gary, W .... 806-651-2095.... 498 D
gbarnes@mail.wtamu.edu
BARNES, George .... 601-885-7002.... 274 E
gebarnes@hindscc.edu
BARNES, Harold, B .... 815-224-0450.... 153 D
harold_barnes@ivcc.edu
BARNES, III, James, H .... 651-638-6230.... 261 I
j-barnes@bethel.edu
BARNES, John .... 831-459-2973.... 75 A
barnes@ucsc.edu
BARNES, John, J .... 920-403-3255.... 550 C
john.barnes@snc.edu
BARNES, Julianna .... 619-660-4301.... 48 J
julianna.barnes@gcccd.edu
BARNES, Karen .... 601-925-3241.... 275 E
misscoll@bkstr.com
BARNES, Katharine, T .... 401-863-1914.... 452 J
katharine_barnes@brown.edu
BARNES, Kathleen .... 978-232-2292.... 234 F
kbarnes@endicott.edu

BARNES, Kelly .... 706-295-6842.... 130 F
kbarnes@gntc.edu
BARNES, Kenneth, J .... 716-851-1157.... 333 B
barnesk@ecc.edu
BARNES, Kimberly .... 989-386-6622.... 255 F
kbarnes@midmich.edu
BARNES, Melissa .... 360-538-4095.... 534 B
mbarnes@ghc.edu
BARNES, Michael, W .... 918-631-2359.... 413 F
michael-barnes@utulsa.edu
BARNES, Patty .... 281-487-1170.... 498 E
pbarnes@txchiro.edu
BARNES, Peter .... 404-727-0419.... 129 A
peter.barnes@emory.edu
BARNES, Randall .... 619-388-3488.... 65 F
rbarnes@sdccd.edu
BARNES, Randy .... 619-388-7350.... 65 H
rbarnes@sdccd.edu
BARNES, Rita .... 931-372-3797.... 474 B
ritabarnes@tntech.edu
BARNES, Russell .... 713-348-4350.... 492 J
rcb@rice.edu
BARNES, Scott .... 434-797-8409.... 526 C
sbarnes@dcc.vccs.edu
BARNES, Scott .... 435-797-2060.... 511 B
scott.barnes@usu.edu
BARNES, Sharon, E .... 817-257-7095.... 498 F
s.barnes@tcu.edu
BARNES, Shelly .... 219-785-5279.... 178 H
sbarnes@pnc.edu
BARNES, Solita, K .... 670-284-5698.... 559 F
solb@nmcnet.edu
BARNES, Ted .... 254-295-4678.... 504 A
tbarnes@umhb.edu
BARNES, Tina .... 859-291-0800.... 199 F
tbarnes@daymarcollege.edu
BARNES, Wilson, C .... 678-915-5481.... 137 C
wbarnes@spsu.edu
BARNES-RHOADES,
Dianne .... 434-848-1805.... 523 G
drhoades@saintpauls.edu
BARNES-TEAMER, Toya .... 504-816-4916.... 208 I
tbteamer@dillard.edu
BARNES WHYTE, Susan .... 503-883-2517.... 416 G
swhyte@linfield.edu
BARNET, John .... 914-961-8313.... 349 I
jbarnet@svots.edu
BARNETT, Alan .... 660-359-3948.... 287 D
abarnett@mail.ncmissouri.edu
BARNETT, Alan .... 731-286-3259.... 475 A
barnett@dscc.edu
BARNETT, Beth .... 201-684-7529.... 313 D
bbarnett@ramapo.edu
BARNETT, Carolyn, M .... 904-256-7640.... 111 J
cbarnett3@ju.edu
BARNETT, Carrie .... 801-281-7630.... 510 I
carrie.barnett@stevenshenager.edu
BARNETT, Charlie .... 662-720-7375.... 276 D
cbarnett@nemcc.edu
BARNETT, Cynthia .... 920-403-3057.... 550 C
cynthia.barnett@snc.edu
BARNETT, David .... 434-592-3751.... 520 F
dbarnett@liberty.edu
BARNETT, David, L .... 770-534-6257.... 126 B
dbarnett@brenau.edu
BARNETT, Gina .... 415-565-4614.... 73 G
barnettg@uchastings.edu
BARNETT, Howard .... 918-594-8001.... 410 D
howard.barnett@okstate.edu
BARNETT, JR., Howard, G .... 918-594-8000.... 410 G
BARNETT, Jacqualine .... 717-720-4038.... 441 H
jbarnett@paisshe.edu
BARNETT, Jahnae, H .... 573-592-4216.... 293 F
jbarnett@williamwoods.edu
BARNETT, James, R .... 850-474-2005.... 121 C
jbarnett@uwf.edu
BARNETT, Jay .... 606-337-1142.... 199 E
jbarnett@ccbbc.edu
BARNETT, Karl .... 214-459-2218.... 480 G
kbarnett@argosy.edu
BARNETT, Kimberly .... 719-502-2012.... 86 G
kimberly.barnett@ppcc.edu
BARNETT, Kurt .... 216-501-3101.... 40 G
kurt.barnett@cleveland.edu
BARNETT, Larry, E .... 619-260-7777.... 76 A
larryb@sandiego.edu
BARNETT, Margaret, J .... 540-868-7123.... 526 H
mbarnett@lfcc.edu
BARNETT, Michael .... 803-754-4100.... 457 D
BARNETT, Mike .... 785-328-4251.... 192 F
mbarnett@fhsu.edu
BARNETT, Robert .... 810-766-6878.... 259 F
rbarnett@umflint.edu
BARNETT, Roy .... 601-477-4120.... 275 B
petey.barnett@jcjc.edu
BARNETT, Sharon .... 660-359-3948.... 287 D
sbarnett@mail.ncmissouri.edu
BARNETT, Theresa .... 903-463-8753.... 487 A
tbarnett@grayson.edu
BARNETT, Timothy, L .... 217-206-6581.... 167 A
barnett.timothy@uis.edu
BARNETTE, Andrew .... 724-925-4047.... 451 E
barnettea@wccc.edu

BARNETTE, F. Gary .... 229-317-6728.... 128 A
gary.barnette@darton.edu
BARNETTE, Lindsey .... 904-470-8100.... 105 A
lindsey.barnette@ewc.edu
BARNETTE, Vivian, D .... 336-334-7727.... 377 F
vdbarnet@ncat.edu
BARNEY, Alfred .... 678-891-2360.... 130 G
alfred.barney@gpc.edu
BARNEY, Carl .... 800-972-5149.... 509 K
BARNEY, James, N .... 317-916-7827.... 175 I
jbarney6@ivytech.edu
BARNEY, Patti .... 954-201-7520.... 102 A
pbarney@broward.edu
BARNEY, Rick .... 502-585-9911.... 205 I
rbarney@spalding.edu
BARNHART, Amy .... 937-775-5721.... 406 C
amy.barhart@wright.edu
BARNHART, Bruce .... 724-938-4407.... 441 G
barnhart@calu.edu
BARNHART, Daniel .... 443-352-4304.... 226 E
dbarnhart@stevenson.edu
BARNHART, Mary Jo .... 724-437-4600.... 441 B
mbarnhart@piht.edu
BARNHART, Mitch .... 859-257-8015.... 206 H
mbarn@uky.edu
BARNHART, Ross .... 719-549-3365.... 87 B
ross.barnhart@pueblocc.edu
BARNHART, Roy, R .... 724-852-3241.... 451 B
rbarnhar@waynesburg.edu
BARNHART, Terry, L .... 671-735-5571.... 559 B
terry.barnhart@guamcc.edu
BARNHILL, Carol .... 870-972-2028.... 20 C
cbarnhil@astate.edu
BARNHILL, Holly .... 310-689-3200.... 42 F
hbarnhill@kaplan.edu
BARNHILL, John .... 850-644-1224.... 119 C
jbarnhill@admin.fsu.edu
BARNHILL, Kristopher, C .... 864-488-4602.... 459 A
kbarnhill@limestone.edu
BARNHILL, Rob, M .... 262-243-5700.... 546 I
rob.barnhill@cuw.edu
BARNHILL, Tapp .... 802-254-6370.... 515 D
barnhilt@ccv.edu
BARNHOUSE, Richard .... 608-262-3786.... 552 F
richard.barnhouse@uwc.edu
BARNITZ, LaTrobe .... 814-676-6591.... 442 B
lbarnitz@clarion.edu
BARNUM, Martin .... 847-566-6401.... 167 D
mbarnum@usml.edu
BARNUM, Marty .... 847-566-6401.... 167 D
mbarnum@usml.edu
BARNWELL, Larry .... 864-977-7161.... 460 A
larry.barnwell@ngu.edu
BARNWELL, Vollie .... 828-251-6700.... 378 C
vbarnwel@unca.edu
BARON, Joshua, D .... 845-575-3000.... 340 C
josh.baron@marist.edu
BARON, Kit .... 626-396-2322.... 29 G
BARON, Melissa, M .... 724-946-7927.... 451 C
baronmm@westminster.edu
BARON, Sara .... 757-352-4182.... 523 B
sbaron@regent.edu
BARON, Stephanie .... 425-640-1049.... 533 E
stephanie.baron@edcc.edu
BARON, Stuart .... 302-622-8000.... 95 E
BARONA, Ron .... 561-912-2166.... 106 G
rbarona@evergladesuniversity.edu
BARONAK, William, M .... 304-336-8061.... 544 B
wbaronak@westliberty.edu
BARONE, OSF,
Ann Carmen .... 419-824-3703.... 395 D
acarmen@lourdes.edu
BARONE, Janet .... 703-237-6200.... 523 I
BARONE, Michael .... 716-673-3323.... 352 A
michael.barone@fredonia.edu
BARONE-PRICCI, Erica .... 570-955-1461.... 433 A
priccie@lackawanna.edu
BARONIO, Lisa Birley .... 940-565-2900.... 504 B
lisa.baronio@unt.edu
BAROODY, Daniel, A .... 607-735-1870.... 333 A
dbaroody@elmira.edu
BAROUDI, George .... 516-299-3790.... 338 F
george.baroudi@liu.edu
BARQUINERO, James, M .... 203-365-4763.... 93 G
barquineroj@sacredheart.edu
BARR, Ann .... 503-352-7200.... 419 E
ann.barr@pacificu.edu
BARR, Carol .... 413-545-6330.... 237 C
cbarr@provost.umass.edu
BARR, Donald, E .... 610-436-2825.... 443 F
dbarr2@wcupa.edu
BARR, Jared .... 813-988-5131.... 107 I
barrj@floridacollege.edu
BARR, Julia, R .... 304-462-4114.... 543 F
julia.barr@glenville.edu
BARR, K. Jill .... 410-455-1337.... 227 D
jbarr@umbc.edu
BARR, Kevin .... 812-237-3600.... 173 A
kevin.barr@indstate.edu
BARR, Krispin, W .... 336-721-2627.... 376 C
krispin.barr@salem.edu
BARR, Mary, G .... 812-877-8258.... 179 A
mary.g.barr@rose-hulman.edu

BARR, Peter, B ... 304-462-4110 ... 543 F
peter.barr@glenville.edu
BARR, Robin ... 386-506-4473 ... 103 J
barrr@DaytonaState.edu
BARR, Rodena ... 303-256-9306 ... 85 H
rbarr@jwu.edu
BARR, Sarah ... 402-465-2193 ... 299 J
sbarr@nebrwesleyan.edu
BARR, Suzy ... 843-574-6181 ... 461 G
suzy.barr@tridenttech.edu
BARR, Victor ... 865-974-2196 ... 477 B
vbarr@utk.edu
BARRACLOUGH, Diana ... 610-499-4153 ... 451 F
dbarraclough@widener.edu
BARRAM, Dirk ... 503-554-2822 ... 415 I
dbarram@georgefox.edu
BARRANTES, Jane ... 408-554-5416 ... 68 C
jbarrantes@scu.edu
BARRAR, Elena ... 610-558-5516 ... 437 C
barrare@neumann.edu
BARRAS, Janet, F ... 678-359-5022 ... 131 D
janetb@gdn.edu
BARRATT, Marguerite ... 202-994-6130 ... 97 F
barratt@gwu.edu
BARREDA, Albert ... 956-882-7575 ... 505 C
albert.barreda@utb.edu
BARREDA, Albert ... 956-882-7575 ... 499 H
albert.barreda@utb.edu
BARREE, Zita ... 434-223-6265 ... 519 B
zbarree@hsc.edu
BARREIRO, Antonio ... 303-256-9314 ... 85 H
tbarreiro@jwu.edu
BARRENTINE, Debra, A ... 256-228-6001 ... 6 A
barrentined@nacc.edu
BARRENTINE, Roger, A ... 636-797-3000 ... 283 H
rbarrent@jeffco.edu
BARRERA, Adriana, D ... 213-891-2081 ... 54 F
barrerad@laccd.edu
BARRERA, Merrynoll ... 408-934-4900 ... 49 I
merrynoll_barrera@heald.edu
BARRERA, Rosa ... 316-284-5241 ... 190 H
rbarrera@bethelks.edu
BARRETO, Mary Jo ... 803-323-2233 ... 463 D
mannm@winthrop.edu
BARRETO, Wanda ... 787-758-2480 ... 567 D
wanda.barreto@upr.edu
BARRETT, Albertha, W ... 404-413-3507 ... 131 C
abarrett@gsu.edu
BARRETT, Bill ... 657-278-2425 ... 34 E
bbarrett@fullerton.edu
BARRETT, Brian, D ... 817-515-6965 ... 496 A
brian.barrett@tccd.edu
BARRETT, Carolyn ... 904-256-7090 ... 111 J
cbarret@ju.edu
BARRETT, Christina ... 413-236-2112 ... 239 E
BARRETT, David ... 620-242-0412 ... 194 H
barrettd@mcpherson.edu
BARRETT, David ... 860-509-9519 ... 92 D
dbarrett@hartsem.edu
BARRETT, Dawn ... 617-879-7100 ... 238 E
dbarrett@massart.edu
BARRETT, Denise ... 662-846-1967 ... 200 E
denise.barrett@frontier.edu
BARRETT, James ... 715-836-3887 ... 550 H
barretjd@uwec.edu
BARRETT, Joan ... 417-447-6914 ... 287 G
barrettj@otc.edu
BARRETT, John ... 770-426-2616 ... 133 B
jbarrett@life.edu
BARRETT, Josie, L ... 512-448-8726 ... 493 B
josieb@stedwards.edu
BARRETT, Juanita ... 773-244-4892 ... 159 G
jbarrett@northpark.edu
BARRETT, Karen, D ... 757-823-2808 ... 521 K
kdbarrett@nsu.edu
BARRETT, Karinda ... 850-201-6209 ... 121 F
barrettk@tcc.fl.edu
BARRETT, Kim, E ... 858-534-6655 ... 74 D
graduatedean@ucsd.edu
BARRETT, Kimberly, A ... 205-665-6020 ... 9 C
barrettka@montevallo.edu
BARRETT, Laura ... 919-344-2517 ... 124 E
laura.barrett@armstrong.edu
BARRETT, Lawrence, M ... 207-974-4691 ... 218 H
lbarrett@emcc.edu
BARRETT, Leah, A ... 585-395-2772 ... 352 F
lbarrett@brockport.edu
BARRETT, Linda ... 620-242-0457 ... 194 H
barrettl@mcpherson.edu
BARRETT, Linda ... 401-874-2509 ... 454 E
lindab@uri.edu
BARRETT, Michael ... 850-644-1768 ... 119 C
mgbarrett@admin.fsu.edu
BARRETT, Nancy ... 928-777-3713 ... 14 D
nancy.barrett@erau.edu
BARRETT, Pam, J ... 770-534-6176 ... 126 B
pbarrett@brenau.edu
BARRETT, Robert, T ... 803-536-8980 ... 460 G
rbarrett1@scsu.edu
BARRETT, Rosemary ... 845-341-4200 ... 345 E
rosemary.barrett@sunyorange.edu
BARRETT, Sarah ... 781-768-7162 ... 244 D
sarah.barrett@regiscollege.edu
BARRETT, Sharon ... 215-335-0800 ... 434 G
sbarrett@lincolntech.com
BARRETT, Sheri ... 913-360-7431 ... 190 F
sbarrett@benedictine.edu
BARRETT, Stephen ... 817-735-2261 ... 504 C
sbarrett@hsc.unt.edu
BARRETT, Susan ... 215-596-7626 ... 450 A
s.barrett@usciences.edu
BARRETT, Thomas ... 312-467-2317 ... 146 C
tbarrett@thechicagoschool.edu
BARRETT, Thomas, M ... 240-895-4466 ... 226 A
tmbarrett@smcm.edu
BARRETT, Timothy, M ... 315-445-4155 ... 338 B
barrettm@lemoyne.edu
BARRETT, Valoree ... 785-227-3311 ... 190 G
barrettr@bethanylb.edu
BARRETT-JONES,
Kathleen, A ... 785-827-5541 ... 194 D
kbj@kwu.edu
BARRICK, Mary Grace ... 707-476-4264 ... 42 A
marygrace-barrick@redwoods.edu
BARRIE, John ... 845-848-7500 ... 332 C
john.barrie@dc.edu
BARRIENTOS, Joseph ... 808-544-0267 ... 140 B
jbarrientos@hpu.edu
BARRIER, Jeremy ... 256-766-6610 ... 4 C
jbarrier@hcu.edu
BARRIER, Patricia, A ... 507-284-3627 ... 262 F
barrier.patricia@mayo.edu
BARRIERA, Heriberto ... 787-279-1912 ... 563 B
hbarriera@bayamon.inter.edu
BARRILLEAUX, Allayne ... 985-448-4011 ... 216 A
laynie.barrilleaux@nicholls.edu
BARRINEAU, Annette, W ... 386-312-4072 ... 116 D
annettebarrineau@sjrstate.edu
BARRINGER, Judy ... 212-659-7215 ... 338 A
BARRINGER, Tony ... 239-590-7849 ... 119 A
tbarring@fgcu.edu
BARRINGTON, Ruth, A ... 401-825-2184 ... 453 B
rbarrington@ccri.edu
BARRIOS, Eugenio ... 212-220-1266 ... 326 E
ebarrios@bmcc.cuny.edu
BARRIOS, Francisco ... 573-651-2154 ... 290 D
fbarrios@semo.edu
BARRIS, Julie ... 814-472-3012 ... 446 B
jbarris@francis.edu
BARRISH, David, J ... 804-523-5069 ... 526 F
dbarrish@reynolds.edu
BARRITT, Eric ... 248-364-6150 ... 257 C
barritt@oakland.edu
BARRON, Brad, E ... 864-294-2033 ... 458 D
brad.barron@furman.edu
BARRON, Bruce ... 909-382-4091 ... 65 A
BARRON, Caulyne ... 602-648-5750 ... 14 B
cbarron@dunlap-stone.edu
BARRON, OMV, Dan ... 858-653-6740 ... 52 C
BARRON, Dave ... 334-670-3657 ... 8 B
wdbarron@troy.edu
BARRON, David ... 918-343-7553 ... 411 H
dbarron@rsu.edu
BARRON, Dianne ... 334-670-3189 ... 8 B
dlbarron@troy.edu
BARRON, Eric, J ... 850-644-1085 ... 119 C
ebarron@fsu.edu
BARRON, Glenda, O ... 254-298-8600 ... 496 B
glenda.barron@templejc.edu
BARRON, Katie ... 970-542-3108 ... 86 A
katie.barron@morgancc.edu
BARRON, Maria, V ... 954-308-2180 ... 100 I
mbarron@aii.edu
BARRON, Michael ... 319-335-1548 ... 182 C
michael-barron@uiowa.edu
BARRON, Paul, L ... 504-865-5261 ... 215 C
pbarron@tulane.edu
BARROS, Michael ... 808-845-9135 ... 141 G
mbarros@hawaii.edu
BARROSO, Diana ... 305-593-1223 ... 102 D
dbarroso@albizu.edu
BARROTT, Jim ... 423-697-3211 ... 474 D
BARROW, Carla ... 229-225-5077 ... 137 D
cbarrow@southwestgatech.edu
BARROW, Christine, E ... 301-322-0419 ... 225 F
barowce@pgcc.edu
BARROW, Deborah, L ... 940-397-4212 ... 491 A
debbie.barrow@mwsu.edu
BARROW, Jerry ... 706-369-5763 ... 124 H
jbarrow@athenstech.edu
BARROW, Linda, M ... 770-531-6331 ... 132 J
lbarrow@laniertech.edu
BARROW, Lisa ... 252-527-6223 ... 371 D
lbarrow@lenoircc.edu
BARROWS, Barbara ... 641-585-8143 ... 189 E
barbara.barrows@waldorf.edu
BARROWS, David ... 217-206-6530 ... 167 A
barrows.david@uis.edu
BARROWS, Karen, A ... 585-475-2396 ... 347 G
kab7050@rit.edu
BARROWS, Karen, A ... 585-475-2396 ... 347 G
karen.barrows@rit.edu
BARROWS, Mert ... 620-223-2700 ... 192 G
mertb@fortscott.edu
BARROWS, Nancy ... 503-821-8910 ... 419 D
nancy@pnca.edu
BARROWS, Robert ... 617-228-2241 ... 239 G
rbarrows@bhcc.mass.edu
BARRRIS, Brad ... 706-236-2272 ... 125 G
bbarris@berry.edu
BARRUS, Kent, L ... 208-496-7205 ... 142 G
barrusk@byui.edu
BARRY, A. David ... 337-482-6219 ... 216 D
dbarry@louisiana.edu
BARRY, Ann Marie ... 847-635-1699 ... 160 E
annmarie@oakton.edu
BARRY, Christine ... 713-525-3156 ... 504 D
cbarry@stthom.edu
BARRY, Donna, M ... 973-655-4361 ... 311 G
barryd@mail.montclair.edu
BARRY, Ernie ... 214-768-2004 ... 494 F
ebarry@smu.edu
BARRY, Joanne ... 607-753-2302 ... 353 B
joanne.barry@cortland.edu
BARRY, John ... 254-710-1412 ... 481 I
john_barry@baylor.edu
BARRY, Julie ... 614-947-6065 ... 391 A
barryj@franklin.edu
BARRY, Kevin, G ... 302-295-1170 ... 97 A
kevin.g.barry@wilmu.edu
BARRY, Laura ... 201-559-3504 ... 310 C
barryl@felician.edu
BARRY, Lisa ... 303-280-7491 ... 84 C
lbarry@devry.edu
BARRY, Liz ... 858-566-1200 ... 43 J
lbarry@disd.edu
BARRY, Robert ... 314-977-3434 ... 289 F
rbarry2@slu.edu
BARRY, Theresa ... 262-524-7334 ... 546 E
tbarry@carrollu.edu
BARRY, Thomas, E ... 214-768-4320 ... 494 F
tbarry@smu.edu
BARSAM, Steven, N ... 636-529-0000 ... 288 G
snbarsam@slchcmail.com
BARSHAFSKY, Deborah, L 706-721-7134 ... 130 B
debb@georgiahealth.edu
BARSKY, David ... 760-750-4329 ... 36 B
djbarsky@csusm.edu
BARTA, Barbara ... 614-234-1788 ... 396 G
bbarta@mccn.edu
BARTA, Erin ... 626-529-8456 ... 60 G
ebarta@pacificoaks.edu
BARTA, Gary ... 319-335-9435 ... 182 C
gary-barta@uiowa.edu
BARTA, Lou ... 217-641-4215 ... 154 G
lbarta@jwcc.edu
BARTANEN, Kristine, M ... 253-879-3205 ... 538 E
acadvp@pugetsound.edu
BARTEAU, Mark, A ... 302-831-4007 ... 96 F
barteau@udel.edu
BARTEE, Robert, D ... 402-559-4203 ... 301 A
bbartee@unmc.edu
BARTEL, Alexa ... 843-383-8126 ... 457 A
abartel@coker.edu
BARTEL, Brad ... 615-898-2953 ... 473 F
brad.bartel@mtsu.edu
BARTEL, Kevin, J ... 580-774-3705 ... 412 F
kevin.bartel@swosu.edu
BARTEL, LeRoy ... 972-825-4827 ... 495 D
lbartel@sagu.edu
BARTEL, Steven, J ... 605-256-5146 ... 465 G
steve.bartel@dsu.edu
BARTEL, Tonia ... 660-831-4105 ... 286 I
bartelt@moval.edu
BARTELL, William ... 605-331-6703 ... 466 D
bill.bartell@usiouxfalls.edu
BARTELMAY, Ryan ... 312-752-2454 ... 155 B
ryan.bartelmay@kendall.edu
BARTELS, Dennis ... 614-416-6200 ... 385 E
dbartels@bradfordschoolcolumbus.edu
BARTELS, Jean ... 912-478-5322 ... 131 A
jbartels@georgiasouthern.edu
BARTELS, Paige ... 802-440-4336 ... 512 G
pbartels@bennington.edu
BARTELS, Richard ... 606-337-1164 ... 199 E
rbartels@ccbbc.edu
BARTELS, Roy ... 325-574-7629 ... 508 F
rbartels@wtc.edu
BARTELS, Sharon, J ... 770-962-7580 ... 132 A
sbartels@gwinnetttech.edu
BARTELS, Suzanne, M ... 860-701-5155 ... 93 B
bartels_s@mitchell.edu
BARTELSON, Gretchen, G .. 712-324-5061 ... 188 A
gbartelson@nwicc.edu
BARTELT, Andrew, H ... 314-505-7013 ... 280 H
bartelta@csl.edu
BARTFIELD, Joel ... 518-262-7302 ... 322 E
bartfi@mail.amc.edu
BARTGES, Ellyn ... 320-308-0125 ... 269 C
elbartges@stcloudstate.edu
BARTH, Brad ... 701-671-2131 ... 382 E
brad.barth@ndscs.edu
BARTH, Cynthia ... 410-225-4223 ... 224 C
cbarth@mica.edu
BARTH, Doug ... 785-594-4526 ... 190 C
doug.barth@bakeru.edu
BARTH, Michael ... 406-496-4233 ... 296 C
mbarth@mtech.edu
BARTH, Richard ... 410-706-7794 ... 227 C
rbarth@ssw.umaryland.edu
BARTH, Tom ... 910-962-7766 ... 379 C
bartht@uncw.edu
BARTHELEMY, Jennifer ... 618-544-8657 ... 152 G
barthelemyj@iecc.edu
BARTHELL, John ... 405-974-2481 ... 413 B
jbarthell@ucok.edu
BARTHELMAS, Frederick ... 518-587-2100 ... 355 F
rick.barthlemas@esc.edu
BARTHELMES, David ... 810-762-3324 ... 259 F
dwbarth@umflint.edu
BARTHOLE, Cynthia ... 732-987-2280 ... 310 D
bartholec@georgian.edu
BARTHOLMEY, Theresa ... 660-263-3900 ... 279 J
tbart@cccb.edu
BARTHOLOMEW, Nanette .. 757-826-1883 ... 516 H
BARTHOLOMEW-FEIS,
Dixee ... 712-749-2131 ... 182 G
bartholomew@bvu.edu
BARTKOVICH, Jeffrey, P ... 585-292-3018 ... 341 H
jbartkovich@monroecc.edu
BARTL, Noelle ... 575-562-2412 ... 318 A
noelle.bartl@enmu.edu
BARTLE, Gamin ... 973-408-3106 ... 309 F
gbartle@drew.edu
BARTLEBAUGH, Brenda ... 318-797-5303 ... 213 D
brenda.bartlebaugh@lsus.edu
BARTLETT, Annemarie, M .. 610-660-1299 ... 446 C
abartlet@sju.edu
BARTLETT, Beth ... 828-251-6506 ... 378 C
bbartlet@unca.edu
BARTLETT, Kimberly ... 714-484-7104 ... 59 C
kbartlett@cypresscollege.edu
BARTLETT, Leeanna ... 214-828-8353 ... 497 A
lbartlett@bcd.tamhsc.edu
BARTLETT, Raymond ... 713-743-8780 ... 503 A
rbartlett@uh.edu
BARTLETT, Rebecca ... 802-258-9226 ... 513 F
rbartlet@marlboro.edu
BARTLETT, Stacy ... 404-669-4000 ... 135 E
stacy.bartlett@point.edu
BARTLETT, Walter, C ... 336-599-1181 ... 372 D
bartlew@piedmontcc.edu
BARTLEY, Mary, E ... 515-961-1511 ... 188 F
mimi.bartley@simpson.edu
BARTLEY, Patricia, A ... 773-256-0717 ... 157 B
pbartley@lstc.edu
BARTLEY, Ron ... 843-921-6901 ... 460 B
rbartley@netc.edu
BARTLING, Kaitlyn ... 641-648-4611 ... 185 I
kaitlyn.bartling@iavalley.edu
BARTNETT, Jane ... 718-409-7277 ... 356 C
jbartnett@sunymaritime.edu
BARTO, Christopher ... 212-752-1530 ... 338 C
christopher.barto@limcollege.edu
BARTOL, Michelle, M ... 814-641-3432 ... 431 L
bartolm@juniata.edu
BARTOLD, Melissa ... 312-225-1700 ... 152 D
mbartold@ico.edu
BARTOLI, Andrea ... 703-993-4453 ... 519 A
abartoli@gmu.edu
BARTOLINI, Brian, J ... 401-865-1554 ... 453 F
bbartoli@providence.edu
BARTOLO, Tony ... 423-478-6208 ... 474 E
tbartolo@clevelandstatecc.edu
BARTOLOMEI, Francisco ... 787-751-0178 ... 565 D
fjbartolomei@suagm.edu
BARTOLOMEO, Maria ... 718-368-5563 ... 328 B
mbartolomeo@kbcc.cuny.edu
BARTOLOTTA, Charles ... 631-451-4790 ... 356 E
bartolc@sunysuffolk.edu
BARTOLOZZI, Richard ... 847-735-6016 ... 155 F
bartolozzi@lakeforest.edu
BARTON, Aimee ... 216-791-5000 ... 388 B
aimee.barton@case.edu
BARTON, Bill ... 912-871-1690 ... 134 H
bbarton@ogeecheetech.edu
BARTON, Carissa ... 303-745-6244 ... 84 D
cbarton@cci.edu
BARTON, Carolina ... 949-214-3093 ... 42 K
carolina.barton@cui.edu
BARTON, Charles "Lennie" 919-760-8375 ... 366 G
bartonl@meredith.edu
BARTON, Connie ... 530-242-7719 ... 69 D
cbarton@shastacollege.edu
BARTON, Cynthia ... 910-695-3718 ... 373 E
bartonc@sandhills.edu
BARTON, Delores ... 404-270-5376 ... 137 E
dbarton@spelman.edu
BARTON, Gayle, R ... 610-328-7679 ... 447 E
gbarton1@swarthmore.edu
BARTON, George ... 915-747-5640 ... 505 E
gbarton@utep.edu
BARTON, J. Mark ... 479-394-7622 ... 23 E
mbarton@rmcc.edu
BARTON, Jacqueline, K ... 626-395-3646 ... 32 E
jkbarton@caltech.edu
BARTON, James ... 530-242-7912 ... 69 D
jbarton@shastacollege.edu
BARTON, John, D ... 248-218-2026 ... 257 F
jbarton@rc.edu
BARTON, Kyle ... 409-766-1100 ... 507 B
kbarton@utmb.edu
BARTON, Laurence ... 610-526-1301 ... 421 G
laurence.barton@theamericancollege.edu

BARTON, Michelle ... 760-744-1150 ... 61 C
mbarton@palomar.edu

BARTON, Nancy ... 203-837-8588 ... 92 A
bartonn@wcsu.edu

BARTON, Pat ... 678-466-4185 ... 127 A
patbarton@clayton.edu

BARTON, Patricia ... 510-136-1220 ... 50 F
barton@hnu.edu

BARTON, Sarah ... 304-865-6034 ... 541 F
sarah.barton@ovu.edu

BARTON, Todd ... 727-726-1153 ... 103 B

BARTOW, Dean ... 307-778-1154 ... 556 B
dbartow@lccc.wy.edu

BARTOW, Margaret, F ... 301-846-2490 ... 222 G
mbartow@frederick.edu

BARTRAM, Lydia ... 561-297-0180 ... 118 H
lbartram@fau.edu

BARTREM, Richard ... 423-442-2001 ... 469 B
bartrem@hiwassee.edu

BARTSCH, Jonathan ... 617-236-8800 ... 235 B
jbartsch@fisher.edu

BARTSCH, Kathy, R ... 512-471-2302 ... 505 B
kbartsch@po.utexas.edu

BARTSCHER, Patricia, B ... 415-338-2998 ... 36 F
pattyb@sfsu.edu

BARTUNEK, Darrin ... 801-818-8900 ... 510 E
darrin.bartunek@provocollege.edu

BARTUS, Thomas, J ... 609-258-7720 ... 313 A
tbartus@princeton.edu

BARWICK, Daniel ... 620-331-4100 ... 193 G
dbarwick@indycc.edu

BARZACCHINI, Mike ... 847-925-6510 ... 151 E
mbarzacc@harpercollege.edu

BARZILAY, Janet ... 310-824-1586 ... 26 D
jbarzilay@ajrca.org

BASCH, Hersch ... 718-438-1002 ... 340 H

BASEGGIO, Brock ... 970-521-6623 ... 86 E
brock.baseggio@njc.edu

BASER, Ric, N ... 918-595-7980 ... 412 H
rbaser@tulsacc.edu

BASFORD, Jerry, L ... 801-581-7793 ... 510 L
jbasford@sa.utah.edu

BASFORD, Stacey, L ... 315-386-7204 ... 355 D
basfords@canton.edu

BASH, Cassaundra ... 574-936-8898 ... 168 I
cassaundra.bash@ancilla.edu

BASH, Tamela, S ... 419-772-2027 ... 398 G
t-bash@onu.edu

BASHAM, Robert ... 660-626-2395 ... 278 F
rbasham@atsu.edu

BASHANT, Wendy ... 941-487-4250 ... 119 D
wbashant@ncf.edu

BASHARA, Teri ... 318-678-6000 ... 209 J
tbashara@bpcc.edu

BASHAW, Deb ... 501-279-4454 ... 21 H
dbashaw@harding.edu

BASHAW, Edward ... 479-968-0490 ... 20 G
ebashaw@atu.edu

BASHAW, Pat ... 501-279-4315 ... 21 H
pbashaw@harding.edu

BASHFORD, Joanne ... 305-237-7445 ... 113 H
jbashfor@mdc.edu

BASHFORD, Mike ... 870-574-4480 ... 24 A
mbashfor@sautech.edu

BASILE, Carole, G ... 314-516-5109 ... 291 F
basilec@umsl.edu

BASILE, Elizabeth ... 718-368-4539 ... 328 B
ebasile@kbcc.cuny.edu

BASINGER, Randall, G ... 717-796-5375 ... 436 D
rbasinge@messiah.edu

BASINGER, Scott, F ... 713-798-4100 ... 481 H
scottb@bcm.edu

BASINSKI, Judith, B ... 716-878-4011 ... 353 A
basinsjb@buffalostate.edu

BASIRATMAND, Mehran ... 561-297-0230 ... 118 H
mehran@fau.edu

BASKETT, Carolyn, R ... 816-604-1166 ... 285 D
carolyn.baskett@mcckc.edu

BASKIN, Richard ... 678-359-5018 ... 131 D
rbaskin@gdn.edu

BASKIN, William ... 914-251-6485 ... 354 D
bill.baskin@purchase.edu

BASKO, Aaron, M ... 410-543-6161 ... 228 D
ambasko@salisbury.edu

BASLER, Julie ... 303-369-5151 ... 86 I
jbasler@plattcolorado.edu

BASLER, Michael, J ... 314-792-6115 ... 283 K
basler@kenrick.edu

BASLER, Sandra, K ... 636-797-3000 ... 283 H
sbasler@jeffco.edu

BASLER, Thomas, G ... 843-792-9211 ... 459 C
basler@musc.edu

BASNIGHT, Beth ... 617-323-6662 ... 242 C
beth_basnight@mspp.edu

BASOM, Richard ... 717-361-4762 ... 428 E
basomr@etown.edu

BASOM, Richard, E ... 717-361-4762 ... 428 E
basomr@etown.edu

BASS, Carey, A ... 386-312-4249 ... 116 D
careybass@sjrstate.edu

BASS, Charles ... 619-260-4819 ... 76 A
charlesb@sandiego.edu

BASS, Donna ... 334-222-6591 ... 5 F
dbass@lbwcc.edu

BASS, George ... 218-935-0417 ... 273 A
bassge@wetcc.org

BASS, Harry, S ... 252-335-3189 ... 377 D
hsbass@mail.ecsu.edu

BASS, Jimmy ... 910-962-3571 ... 379 C
bassj@uncw.edu

BASS, Mary, T ... 252-823-5166 ... 370 A
bassm@edgecombe.edu

BASS, Scott, A ... 202-885-2127 ... 97 B
provost@american.edu

BASS, Wanda, S ... 334-493-3573 ... 5 F
wsbass@lbwcc.edu

BASSANO, Theodore ... 610-607-6265 ... 445 B
tbassano@racc.edu

BASSEL, Cynthia, B ... 214-648-2510 ... 507 D
cynthia.bassel@utsouthwestern.edu

BASSETT, Cheryl ... 810-762-0553 ... 256 C
cheryl.bassett@edtech.mcc.edu

BASSETT, Claire, M ... 713-798-4712 ... 481 H
bassett@bcm.edu

BASSETT, Dorothy, E ... 412-396-5839 ... 428 C
bassettd@duq.edu

BASSETT, Heidi, M ... 972-860-7255 ... 484 H
HBassett@dcccd.edu

BASSETT, Joanne ... 901-333-5020 ... 475 H
jbassett@southwest.tn.edu

BASSETT, John, E ... 509-865-8600 ... 534 D
bassett_j@heritage.edu

BASSETT, Kay ... 509-865-8658 ... 534 D
bassett_k@heritage.edu

BASSETT, Matthew, D ... 315-445-4450 ... 338 B
bassetmd@lemoyne.edu

BASSETT, Robert ... 714-997-6715 ... 39 C
bassett@chapman.edu

BASSETT, Susan ... 412-268-8555 ... 424 H
susanb@andrew.cmu.edu

BASSETTE, Lynda, D ... 607-436-2407 ... 353 E
bassetld@oneonta.edu

BASSETTI, Mimi ... 215-572-2941 ... 422 B
bassetti@arcadia.edu

BASSHAM, Donna ... 417-255-7243 ... 286 G
donnabassham@missouristate.edu

BASSHAM, Kathy ... 817-598-6427 ... 508 C
kbassham@wc.edu

BASSHAM, Mia, W ... 570-740-0420 ... 435 C
mbassham@luzerne.edu

BASSI, Susan, E ... 309-556-3151 ... 153 E
sbassi@iwu.edu

BASSI-COOK, Teresa ... 724-838-4295 ... 447 B
bassi@setonhill.edu

BASSINGER, Donnie ... 828-726-2286 ... 368 D
dbassinger@cccti.edu

BASSIS, Michael, S ... 801-832-2550 ... 512 F
mbassis@westminstercollege.edu

BASSO, Sharon, K ... 610-758-4156 ... 434 E
sbr2@lehigh.edu

BASSO, Susan ... 814-863-6188 ... 438 F
smb43@psu.edu

BASTECKI-PEREZ, Victoria ... 215-641-6482 ... 436 G
vbasteck@mc3.edu

BASTIAN, Joni ... 618-537-6555 ... 157 G
jjbastian@mckendree.edu

BASTIN, Judy ... 316-322-3235 ... 191 D
jbastin@butlercc.edu

BASTIN, Stephanie ... 502-597-6878 ... 203 D
stephanie.bastin@kysu.edu

BASTION, Tamela ... 570-662-4857 ... 443 B
tbastion@mansfield.edu

BASTIONY, Peter ... 305-949-9500 ... 105 F
pbastiony@cci.edu

BASTON, Michael ... 718-482-5180 ... 328 C
mbaston@lagcc.cuny.edu

BASU, Andra, M ... 610-921-7634 ... 421 D
abasu@alb.edu

BASU, Radha ... 408-554-4154 ... 68 C
rbasu@scu.edu

BASU, Raj ... 918-594-8016 ... 410 G
raj.basu@okstate.edu

BASU, Sam, N ... 973-720-2964 ... 317 D
basus@wpunj.edu

BATAILLON, Pamela ... 402-559-9567 ... 301 A
pdbataillon@unmc.edu

BATCHELDER, Rick ... 518-562-4106 ... 329 D
rick.batchelder@clinton.edu

BATCHELLER, Tamara ... 313-578-0436 ... 259 C
batchets@udmercy.edu

BATCHELOR, Gerald ... 731-425-2619 ... 475 B
gbatchelor@jscc.edu

BATCHELOR, Susan ... 618-545-3331 ... 155 A
sbatchelor@kaskaskia.edu

BATCHELOR, Susan ... 215-955-2867 ... 448 B
susan.mcfadden@jefferson.edu

BATCHELOR, William, D ... 334-844-3209 ... 1 G
wdb0007@auburn.edu

BATE, Carol ... 315-229-5906 ... 349 E
cbate@stlawu.edu

BATE, Jeff ... 801-375-5125 ... 510 F
jbate@rmuohp.edu

BATE, Joel, C ... 208-732-6836 ... 143 B
jbate@csi.edu

BATELL, Sue, S ... 608-796-3380 ... 553 A
ssbatell@viterbo.edu

BATEMAN, Bethany ... 877-638-8573 ... 387 A
bbateman@ChancellorU.edu

BATEMAN, Bradley, W ... 740-587-6243 ... 389 H
batemanb@denison.edu

BATEMAN, Heather ... 269-749-7189 ... 257 D
hbateman@olivetcollege.edu

BATEMAN, Linda ... 260-665-4124 ... 180 A
batemanl@trine.edu

BATEMAN, JR., Rick ... 337-491-2641 ... 212 C
rick.bateman@sowela.edu

BATEMAN, William, K ... 989-837-4448 ... 257 A
batemanw@northwood.edu

BATENHORST, Jim Ann ... 806-894-9611 ... 494 C
jbatenho@southplainscollege.edu

BATENHORST, Mandy ... 580-349-1396 ... 410 B
mandyb@opsu.edu

BATES, Alan ... 256-840-4129 ... 7 B
abates@snead.edu

BATES, Becky ... 612-332-3361 ... 261 F
bbates@aii.edu

BATES, Brad, J ... 513-529-7286 ... 396 D
batesbj@muohio.edu

BATES, Brent ... 660-596-7252 ... 290 F
bbates@sfccmo.edu

BATES, Carol ... 906-487-7258 ... 251 C
carol.bates@finlandia.edu

BATES, Carol ... 251-809-1500 ... 5 B
carol.bates@jdcc.edu

BATES, Damien ... 928-317-5892 ... 12 C
damien.bates@azwestern.edu

BATES, Deborah ... 740-389-4636 ... 395 G
batesd@mtc.edu

BATES, Donald ... 713-221-8179 ... 503 D
batesdon@uhd.edu

BATES, Doug ... 931-372-3408 ... 474 B
dbates@tntech.edu

BATES, Evola, C ... 225-771-4680 ... 214 G
evola_bates@sus.edu

BATES, Gwendolyn ... 617-824-8580 ... 234 D
gwendolyn_bates@emerson.edu

BATES, Janice ... 610-647-4400 ... 431 B
jbates@immaculata.edu

BATES, Jennifer ... 315-279-5646 ... 337 K
jbates@mail.keuka.edu

BATES, Jennifer ... 503-777-7289 ... 420 A
batesj@reed.edu

BATES, Joan ... 423-478-6205 ... 474 E
jbates@clevelandstatecc.edu

BATES, Julie ... 501-660-1000 ... 20 B
jbates@asusystem.edu

BATES, Leslie ... 937-769-1345 ... 383 J
lbates@antioch.edu

BATES, Lynette ... 909-558-4561 ... 54 D
lbates@llu.edu

BATES, Mark, R ... 440-775-8477 ... 397 F
mark.bates@oberlin.edu

BATES, Mary Lou, W ... 518-580-5588 ... 351 B
mbates@skidmore.edu

BATES, Michael ... 731-426-7560 ... 469 M
mbates@lanecollege.edu

BATES, Michael, D ... 816-235-6910 ... 291 E
batesmd@umkc.edu

BATES, Mike ... 503-375-7003 ... 415 F
mbates@corban.edu

BATES, Patrick, M ... 585-292-2820 ... 341 H
pbates@monroecc.edu

BATES, Ren ... 859-246-4605 ... 201 D
ren.bates@kctcs.edu

BATES, Rodger ... 541-463-5269 ... 416 D
batesr@lanecc.edu

BATES, Starnell ... 803-822-3235 ... 459 D
batess@midlandstech.edu

BATES, Suzanne ... 330-263-2365 ... 388 E
sbates@wooster.edu

BATES, Tom ... 281-756-3561 ... 479 G
tbates@alvincollege.edu

BATES, Tom ... 360-416-7745 ... 538 A
tom.bates@skagit.edu

BATES, Vincent ... 978-632-6600 ... 240 G
v_bates@mwcc.mass.edu

BATES, Winfrey ... 270-858-6501 ... 202 F
winfrey.bates@kctcs.edu

BATH, Michael, J ... 906-227-2151 ... 256 F
mbath@nmu.edu

BATHE, David, A ... 765-269-5600 ... 176 B
dbathe@ivytech.edu

BATIC, Marjorie ... 317-955-6150 ... 177 G
mbatic@marian.edu

BATIE, Larry ... 205-929-1517 ... 5 H
lbatie@miles.edu

BATIG, Miria, T ... 216-361-2741 ... 387 A
mbatig@chancelloru.edu

BATKIN, Norton ... 845-758-7598 ... 323 F
batkin@bard.edu

BATLLE, Luisa ... 787-257-0000 ... 566 H

BATSCHE, Catherine, J ... 813-974-7196 ... 120 D
cbatsche@usf.edu

BATSON, Barbara ... 479-575-2806 ... 24 C
bbatson@uark.edu

BATSON, Judy ... 540-351-1513 ... 526 H
jbatson@lfcc.edu

BATSON, Marie ... 251-442-2370 ... 9 B
mariet@mail.umobile.edu

BATSON, Rebecca ... 302-857-7887 ... 95 F
rbatson@desu.edu

BATSON-BOREL, Dawn ... 305-626-3150 ... 108 H
dawn.batson@fmuniv.edu

BATT, Ellen ... 208-459-5814 ... 143 A
ebatt@collegeofidaho.edu

BATT, Marylou ... 617-349-8564 ... 236 G
mbatt@lesley.edu

BATTA, Rajan ... 716-645-2771 ... 351 G
seasdean@eng.buffalo.edu

BATTAGLIA, Janet, M ... 540-464-7213 ... 529 A
battagliajm@vmi.edu

BATTAGLIA, Joseph ... 516-877-3345 ... 322 A
battaglia@adelphi.edu

BATTALORA, Elizabeth ... 318-473-6459 ... 212 G
ebattalora@lsua.edu

BATTEN, Glenn, T ... 910-277-5556 ... 376 A
battengt@sapc.edu

BATTEN, Melissa ... 843-349-5228 ... 458 G
melissa.batten@hgtc.edu

BATTEN, Nicole ... 509-527-2644 ... 538 H
nicole.batten@wallawalla.edu

BATTEN-MICKENS, Meloyde ... 202-651-5337 ... 97 E
meloyde.batten-mickens@gallaudet.edu

BATTERSBY, Gerard ... 313-883-8552 ... 257 G
battersby.gerard@shms.edu

BATTERSON, Brett ... 312-431-2391 ... 162 I
bbatterson@roosevelt.edu

BATTERSON, Bruce ... 402-872-2224 ... 299 H
bbatterson@peru.edu

BATTIATA, Ross ... 727-786-4707 ... 102 F
rbattiata@careerpathtraining.com

BATTISTA, Elizabeth ... 718-855-3661 ... 336 D
ebattista@idc.edu

BATTISTA, Vincent, C ... 718-855-3661 ... 336 D
vcbattista@idc.edu

BATTISTE, Doris ... 340-693-1121 ... 568 C
dbattis@uvi.edu

BATTISTE, Leilani ... 415-241-2294 ... 39 H
lbattist@ccsf.edu

BATTISTEL, George ... 503-768-7807 ... 416 F
georgeb@lclark.edu

BATTISTELLA, Diane ... 630-829-6415 ... 145 D
dbatistella@ben.edu

BATTLE, Angela ... 515-271-2999 ... 184 A

BATTLE, Bruce ... 661-362-3432 ... 41 G
bruce.battle@canyons.edu

BATTLE, Donna ... 919-546-8491 ... 376 D
dbattle@shawu.edu

BATTLE, Stanley, F ... 203-392-5250 ... 91 I
battles2@southernct.edu

BATTLE-BRYANT, Rebecca 803-535-1231 ... 460 C
battle-bryantr@octech.edu

BATTLE-MERCER, Delois ... 252-536-7242 ... 370 F
mercerd@halifaxcc.edu

BATTLES, Denise ... 970-351-2877 ... 88 F
denise.battles@unco.edu

BATTRAW, Danny ... 928-428-8605 ... 14 C
danny.battraw@eac.edu

BATTS, Harold ... 256-427-7164 ... 4 J
harold.batts@drakestate.edu

BATTSON, Harry ... 478-445-4477 ... 129 F
harry.battson@gcsu.edu

BATTURS, Beth Anne ... 410-777-7352 ... 221 B
babatturs@aacc.edu

BATTY, Philip ... 616-331-8648 ... 252 A
hattyp@gvsu.edu

BATTY-HERBERT, Kimberly ... 863-784-7329 ... 117 I
battyhek@southflorida.edu

BATY, David ... 860-412-7317 ... 91 A
dbaty@qvcc.commnet.edu

BAUDER, Jeff ... 410-287-6060 ... 222 A
jbauder@cecil.edu

BAUDER, Sarah, J ... 301-314-8279 ... 227 B
sbauder@umd.edu

BAUER, Carl, J ... 636-584-6701 ... 281 I
bauerj@eastcentral.edu

BAUER, Cynthia, M ... 414-288-7343 ... 548 D
cindy.bauer@marquette.edu

BAUER, Daniel, C ... 314-367-8700 ... 288 I
dbauer1@stlcop.edu

BAUER, Daniel, L ... 502-272-8240 ... 198 E
dbauer@bellarmine.edu

BAUER, JR., David, C ... 252-638-7234 ... 369 E
bauerd@cravencc.edu

BAUER, David, T ... 507-354-8221 ... 265 B
bauerdt@mlc-wels.edu

BAUER, Don ... 620-365-5116 ... 190 A
bauer@allencc.edu

BAUER, Frank ... 724-938-5717 ... 441 G
bauer_f@calu.edu

BAUER, Jackie ... 320-308-5486 ... 269 D
jbauer@sctcc.edu

BAUER, James ... 313-664-7412 ... 250 A
jbauer@collegeforcreativestudies.edu

BAUER, James ... 989-729-3403 ... 249 A
jim.bauer@baker.edu

BAUER, James, M ... 305-284-2270 ... 122 F
jbauer@miami.edu

BAUER, James, R ... 503-370-6112 ... 421 C
jbauer@willamette.edu

BAUER, Jan, L ... 847-543-2750 ... 147 H
jbauer@clcillinois.edu

BAUER, Jason, K ... 515-263-2887 ... 184 I
jbauer@grandview.edu

BEARCE, John 702-651-7454 302 G
john.bearce@csn.edu
BEARD, Glenda 919-530-5326 378 A
gbeard@nccu.edu
BEARD, John, P 843-349-6441 456 G
johnb@coastal.edu
BEARD, Lisa 407-843-3984 110 B
lbeard@fortiscollege.edu
BEARD, Lori 614-221-7770 396 B
BEARD, Mary, A 716-851-1675 333 C
beard@ecc.edu
BEARD, Rebecca 432-335-6404 491 F
bbeard@odessa.edu
BEARD, Richard, L 717-867-6363 434 C
rbeard@lvc.edu
BEARD, Russell 425-564-4200 531 B
russ.beard@bellevuecollege.edu
BEARD, Scott 304-876-5370 544 A
sbeard@shepherd.edu
BEARD, Timothy, L 727-816-3413 114 F
beardt@phcc.edu
BEARDEN, Ginna 559-442-4600 72 A
ginna.bearden@fresnocitycollege.edu
BEARDMORE, Kevin 270-686-4504 202 E
kevin.beardmore@kctcs.edu
BEARDMORE, Melissa, A 410-777-2532 221 B
mabeardmore@aacc.edu
BEARDSLEE, Bill 603-899-4188 305 B
beardsleeb@franklinpierce.edu
BEARDSLEY, Kathleen 215-572-2838 422 B
beardsley@arcadia.edu
BEARE, Paul 559-278-0210 34 D
pbeare@csufresno.edu
BEARMAN, Alan 785-670-1855 197 D
alan.bearman@washburn.edu
BEARROWS, Thomas, R 312-996-7762 166 F
bearrows@uillinois.edu
BEARROWS, Thomas, R 217-333-0563 166 E
bearrows@uillinois.edu
BEARS TAIL, Daryl 701-255-3285 383 D
dbearstail@uttc.edu
BEARSS, Carrie 810-989-5501 258 B
cbearss@sc4.edu
BEARY, Richard 407-823-5242 120 A
richard.beary@ucf.edu
BEASCA, Jeffrey 714-533-3946 37 C
jeffb@calums.edu
BEASIMER, Linda, M 845-431-8979 332 E
beasimer@sunydutchess.edu
BEASLEY, Beth, M 217-544-6464 163 F
BEASLEY, Dan, S 901-678-2438 474 C
dbeasley@memphis.edu
BEASLEY, David 870-972-2085 20 C
dbeasley@astate.edu
BEASLEY, David 870-972-2088 20 C
dbeasley@astate.edu
BEASLEY, Jack, D 757-446-5035 518 F
beaslejd@evms.edu
BEASLEY, Lori 405-974-3507 413 B
lbeasley@ucok.edu
BEASLEY, Maisha 925-631-4108 64 F
meb10@stmarys-ca.edu
BEASLEY, Pete 352-629-1941 115 G
Pete.Beasley@Rasmussen.edu
BEASLEY, Susan, S 434-832-7742 526 A
beasleys@cvcc.vccs.edu
BEASLEY, Thomas 619-482-6309 71 C
tbeasley@swccd.edu
BEATA, Anthony 239-280-2577 101 C
tony.beata@avemaria.edu
BEATRICE, Jonelle 330-941-1450 406 F
jabeatrice@ysu.edu
BEATSON, Bonnie 808-235-7374 142 C
beatson@hawaii.edu
BEATTIE, George, A 218-723-6562 262 I
gbeattie@css.edu
BEATTIE, Kamara 309-794-7721 145 B
kamybeattie@augustana.edu
BEATTIE, Linda 502-585-9911 205 I
lbeattie@spalding.edu
BEATTIE, Martha, J 603-646-2258 305 A
martha.j.beattie@dartmouth.edu
BEATTY, Anthony 859-257-8200 206 H
abeat2@uky.edu
BEATTY, Del 435-652-7514 512 A
beatty@dixie.edu
BEATTY, Fred 334-241-5477 8 B
fbeatty@troy.edu
BEATTY, Heather, P 336-841-9309 365 A
hbeatty@highpoint.edu
BEATTY, Jaye 760-630-1555 52 J
jbeatty@kaplan.edu
BEATTY, Kimberly 757-822-2430 528 C
kbeatty@tcc.edu
BEATTY, Krista, M 740-593-4330 399 G
mccallum@ohio.edu
BEATTY, Lisa, L 563-588-8000 184 F
lbeatty@emmaus.edu
BEATTY, Paul 406-496-4198 296 D
pbeatty@mtech.edu
BEATTY, Paul, V 406-496-4198 296 C
pbeatty@mtech.edu
BEATTY, Robert, C 509-777-4585 539 F
rbeatty@whitworth.edu
BEATTY, Scott 207-741-5832 219 A
sbeatty@smccme.edu
BEATTY, Tracy 269-965-3931 253 H
beattyt@kellogg.edu
BEATY, Beirne 423-478-6206 474 E
bbeaty@clevelandstatecc.edu
BEATY, Katherine, M 309-677-3107 145 H
kbeaty@bradley.edu
BEATY, Vivian 313-845-9663 252 D
vbeaty@hfcc.edu
BEAUCHAMP, Denise 610-526-6665 430 D
dbeauchamp@harcum.edu
BEAUCHAMP, CSC,
E. William 503-943-7101 420 G
beaucham@up.edu
BEAUCHAMP, Eddie 678-407-5381 130 A
ebeauchamp@ggc.edu
BEAUCHAMP, Lance 904-256-7067 111 J
lbeauch@ju.edu
BEAUCHAMP, Mary Jo 812-749-1399 178 D
mbeauchamp@oak.edu
BEAUCHAMP, Nancy, F 205-853-1200 5 C
nbeauchamp@jeffstateonline.com
BEAUCHAMP, Robin, L 401-254-3244 454 C
rbeauchamp@rwu.edu
BEAUDIN, Giselda 407-646-2466 116 B
gbeaudin@rollins.edu
BEAUDOIN, Amy, L 606-679-8501 202 F
amy.beaudoin@kctcs.edu
BEAUDRY, Marjorie 810-985-7000 249 B
marjorie.beaudry@baker.edu
BEAUDRY, Sharon, L 603-526-3741 304 A
sbeaudry@colby-sawyer.edu
BEAUJON, Francis 530-257-6181 53 G
fbeaujon@lassencollege.edu
BEAULIEU, Adrian, G 401-865-2114 453 F
abeaulie@providence.edu
BEAULIEU, Ellen 617-928-4790 243 A
ebeaulieu@mountida.edu
BEAULIEU, Gary, R 317-940-9624 170 C
gbeaulie@butler.edu
BEAUMONT, Marilyn 252-493-7340 372 E
mbeaumont@email.pittcc.edu
BEAUPRE, Judy 312-410-8998 146 C
jbeaupre@tcsedsystem.edu
BEAUPRE, Walter 302-736-2436 96 G
security@wesley.edu
BEAUPRE WHITE, Renee 802-287-8376 513 D
beauprer@greenmtn.edu
BEAUPRE', Eugene, L 513-745-4271 406 E
beaupre@xavier.edu
BEAUREGARD, Debbie 603-228-1541 306 G
dbeauregard@piercelaw.edu
BEAUREGARD, Jill 320-589-6036 272 C
beaureja@morris.umn.edu
BEAUREGARD, Michelle 401-232-6722 453 A
mbeaureg@bryant.edu
BEAUREGARD, Mike 954-587-7100 113 E
mike.beauregard@medvance.edu
BEAUREGARD, Mike 305-220-4120 115 D
cdir@ptcmatt.com
BEAUREGARD, Stephen 508-565-1375 245 D
sbeauregard@stonehill.edu
BEAUVAIS, Laura 401-874-4341 454 E
beauvais@uri.edu
BEAVER, James 541-552-8093 419 A
BeaverJ@sou.edu
BEAVER, Jeff, S 864-388-8208 458 J
jbeaver@lander.edu
BEAVER, John 979-209-7300 482 A
john.beaver@blinn.edu
BEAVER, Marie 573-592-4260 293 E
mbeaver@williamwoods.edu
BEAVER, Mark, P 804-758-6764 527 G
mbeaver@rappahannock.edu
BEAVER, Shirley 515-643-6615 187 C
sbeaver@mercydesmoines.org
BEAVER-JONES, Caitlin 727-786-4707 102 F
cbjones@cfi.edu
BEAVERS, Bobby, J 937-512-2748 401 J
bobby.beavers@sinclair.edu
BEAVERS, Dennis 314-264-1580 478 A
dennis.beavers@vatterott-college.edu
BEAVERS, Dennis 316-264-1580 167 F
dennis.beavers@vatterott-college.edu
BEAVERS, Dennis 314-264-1580 405 C
dennis.beavers@vatterott-college.edu
BEAVERS, Dennis 314-264-1580 292 C
dennis.beavers@vatterott.edu
BEAVERS, Dennis 314-264-1580 292 H
dennis.beavers@vatterott-college.edu
BEAVERS, Dennis 314-264-1580 292 G
dennis.beavers@vatterot-college.edu
BEAVERS, Dennis 314-264-1580 292 I
dennis.beavers@vatterott-college.edu
BEAVERS, Dennis 314-264-1580 292 D
dennis.beavers@vatterott-college.edu
BEAVERS, Dennis 314-264-1500 292 E
dennis.beavers@vatterott-college.edu
BEAVERS, Dennis 314-264-1580 301 D
dennis.beavers@vatterott-college.edu
BEAVERS, Dennis 314-264-1580 189 D
dennis.beavers@vatterott-college.edu
BEAVERS, Dennis 314-264-1580 414 A
dennis.beavers@vatterott-college.edu
BEAVERS, Dennis 314-264-1580 414 B
dennis.beavers@vatterott-college.edu
BEAVERS, Judy 517-321-0242 252 B
jbeavers@glcc.edu
BEAVERS, Judy 615-547-1210 467 I
jbeavers@cumberland.edu
BEAVERS, Philip, E 517-321-0242 252 B
pbeavers@glcc.edu
BEAZER, Ken 435-865-8354 511 A
beazer@suu.edu
BEBB, J, L 518-783-2328 350 I
jbebb@siena.edu
BEBBER, Glenda, H 704-233-8242 380 D
gbebber@wingate.edu
BEBENSEE, Mark, A 843-953-5156 456 C
mark.bebensee@citadel.edu
BECENTI, Deloris 505-786-4180 318 H
dbecenti@navajotech.edu
BECERRA, Cynthia 209-478-0800 50 I
cbecerra@humphreys.edu
BECERRA, Rosina 310-206-7411 74 A
rbecerra@conet.ucla.edu
BECERRA-BARCKHOLTZ,
Beatriz 956-882-8292 505 C
beatriz.becerra@utb.edu
BECERRA-FERNANDEZ,
Irma 305-348-2000 119 B
Irma.Fernandez@fiu.edu
BECHARD, Matthew 785-243-1435 191 H
mbechard@cloud.edu
BECHER, Amy 724-589-2182 448 A
abecher@thiel.edu
BECHER, Eric 606-218-5282 207 B
ericbecher@pc.edu
BECHER, Gregory, J 805-525-4417 72 E
gbecher@thomasaquinas.edu
BECHERER, Bob 618-468-3700 156 C
rbecherer@lc.edu
BECHERER, Jack, J 815-921-4003 162 F
j.becherer@rockvalleycollege.edu
BECHILL, Cynthia 248-457-2746 252 G
cbechill@iadtdetroit.com
BECHMAN, William 718-405-3212 330 A
william.bechman@mountsaintvincent.edu
BECHTEL, Brian 816-604-3036 285 H
brian.bechtel@mcckc.edu
BECHTEL, Janice, L 419-783-2444 389 G
jbechtel@defiance.edu
BECHTEL-WHERRY,
Lori, J 814-949-5012 438 H
ljb3@psu.edu
BECHTOLD, Brad 864-294-3166 458 D
brad.bechtold@furman.edu
BECK, Angela 256-533-7387 3 D
angela.beck@vc.edu
BECK, Anne, D 313-664-7473 250 A
abeck@collegeforcreativestudies.edu
BECK, Barbara, E 518-580-5800 351 B
bbeck@skidmore.edu
BECK, Carina 406-994-4353 295 E
cbeck@montana.edu
BECK, Cherie 517-371-5140 259 B
beckc@cooley.edu
BECK, Curt 601-968-5919 273 F
BECK, Deborah 803-777-3957 462 A
dbeck@gwm.sc.edu
BECK, Deborah, C 803-777-3957 462 A
dbeck@sc.edu
BECK, Erika 702-992-2500 302 I
erika.beck@nsc.nevada.edu
BECK, Fred 904-620-2900 120 C
fbeck@unf.edu
BECK, Gerald, L 208-732-6601 143 B
jbeck@csi.edu
BECK, Jeff 319-352-8491 189 F
jeff.beck@wartburg.edu
BECK, Jen 512-245-2152 501 C
jb32@txstate.edu
BECK, Jennifer 225-768-1779 214 B
jbeck@ololcollege.edu
BECK, Jill 920-832-6525 547 J
jill.beck@lawrence.edu
BECK, Jocelyn, M 610-799-1155 434 D
jbeck@lccc.edu
BECK, John 517-750-1200 258 F
jbeck@arbor.edu
BECK, Kenneth, L 606-474-3135 200 J
kbeck@kcu.edu
BECK, Lynn 209-946-2680 75 D
lbeck@pacific.edu
BECK, Margaret, Z 941-752-5597 118 E
beckm@scf.edu
BECK, Marilyn, C 256-306-2555 2 E
mcb@calhoun.edu
BECK, Maryann, M 334-833-4522 4 E
mbeck@huntingdon.edu
BECK, Maureen, A 443-334-2231 226 E
mbeck@stevenson.edu
BECK, Morgan 620-223-2700 192 G
morganb@fortscott.edu
BECK, Rhonda 859-257-4758 206 H
rsbeck0@uky.edu
BECK, Richard 918-343-7615 411 H
rbeck@rsu.edu
BECK, Robin, H 215-898-7581 448 I
beck@isc.upenn.edu
BECK, Ronda 517-371-5140 259 B
beckr@cooley.edu
BECK, Stacie 480-423-6536 16 D
BECK-DUDLEY, Caryn 850-644-3090 119 C
cbeckdudley@cob.fsu.edu
BECK-LITTLE, Rebecca 704-406-4358 364 B
rbeck-little@gardner-webb.edu
BECKAGE, Cathy 570-702-8990 431 K
cbeckage@johnson.edu
BECKEL, Dave 740-389-6786 399 D
beckel.1@osu.edu
BECKEMEYER, Wendy 412-365-1139 425 B
wbeckemeyer@chatham.edu
BECKENBAUGH, Lisa 913-758-6120 197 B
beckenbaughb@stmary.edu
BECKENHAUER,
Charles, D 254-710-3821 481 I
charles_beckenhauer@baylor.edu
BECKER, Amanda 352-588-8464 116 E
amanda.becker@saintleo.edu
BECKER, Art, C 480-423-6616 16 D
art.becker@sccmail.maricopa.edu
BECKER, Barbara 817-272-3071 505 A
bbecker@uta.edu
BECKER, Bart 425-564-3081 531 B
bart.becker@bellevuecollege.edu
BECKER, Brian 815-753-8980 160 A
bbecker@niu.edu
BECKER, Carol 212-854-9847 330 F
cbecker@columbia.edu
BECKER, Charles, L 304-384-5190 543 D
beckerc@concord.edu
BECKER, Christopher, F 714-703-1900 42 G
cbecker@concorde.edu
BECKER, Craig 212-229-5660 342 E
beckerc@newschool.edu
BECKER, Dennis, M 303-871-3897 88 E
dbecker@du.edu
BECKER, Elizabeth, M 708-209-3020 148 C
elizabeth.becker@cuchicago.edu
BECKER, Frederick, W 570-326-3761 440 K
fbecker@pct.edu
BECKER, J. Thomas 215-951-2945 444 C
beckert@philau.edu
BECKER, Janet 740-654-6711 400 B
becker@ohio.edu
BECKER, Janine 570-408-8009 451 G
janine.becker@wilkes.edu
BECKER, Jim 812-855-4884 173 C
jambecke@indiana.edu
BECKER, Jonathan 845-758-7378 323 F
jbecker@bard.edu
BECKER, Joyce, D 573-651-2189 290 D
jbecker@semo.edu
BECKER, Joyce, K 443-352-4031 226 E
jbecker@stevenson.edu
BECKER, Karen 815-802-8405 154 J
kbecker@kcc.edu
BECKER, Karl, D 215-222-4200 445 F
kbecker@walnuthillcollege.edu
BECKER, Kurt 718-260-3608 346 C
kbecker@poly.edu
BECKER, Larry 951-785-2460 53 D
lbecker@lasierra.edu
BECKER, Laurie 507-453-1462 267 F
lbecker@southeastmn.edu
BECKER, Linda 402-486-2507 300 D
libecker@ucollege.edu
BECKER, Lois, S 904-256-7030 111 J
lbecker1@ju.edu
BECKER, Mark, P 404-413-1300 131 C
mbecker@gsu.edu
BECKER, Mary 507-457-1503 271 G
mbecker@smumn.edu
BECKER, Maureen 540-458-8913 530 A
mbecker@wlu.edu
BECKER, Mike 925-439-2181 43 D
mbecker@losmedanos.edu
BECKER, Pete, D 708-209-3092 148 C
pete.becker@cuchicago.edu
BECKER, Raymond 215-567-7080 422 C
rbecker@aii.edu
BECKER, Richard, A 561-868-3137 114 D
beckerr@palmbeachstate.edu
BECKER, Roger 402-872-2218 299 H
rbecker@peru.edu
BECKER, Ron 201-761-6415 314 F
rbecker@spc.edu
BECKER, S. Ann 321-674-8780 108 E
abecker@fit.edu
BECKER, Sharon 870-972-3025 20 C
skbecker@astate.edu
BECKER, Sheila, R 563-556-5110 187 G
beckers@nicc.edu
BECKER, Tom 402-486-2511 300 D
tobecker@ucollege.edu
BECKER-GORBY, Sherry 304-434-8000 542 E
sherrybg@eastern.wvnet.edu
BECKER-RICHARDS, Joicy 609-497-7900 312 F
joicy.becker@ptsem.edu
BECKETT, Alice 415-503-6251 66 A
abeckett@sfcm.edu

BECKETT, Keith 330-263-2500 388 E kbeckett@wooster.edu
BECKETT, Thomas 304-724-3700 540 C tbeckett@apus.edu
BECKETT, Thomas, A 203-432-1414 95 D thomas.beckett@yale.edu
BECKFORD, Ian 212-875-4504 323 E ibeckford@bankstreet.edu
BECKFORD, John, S 864-294-2007 458 D john.beckford@furman.edu
BECKLER, Bob 863-638-1019 123 B pastorbob@slwcog.com
BECKLES, Anthony 434-592-3234 520 F abeckles@liberty.edu
BECKLEY, Clark 913-234-0609 191 G clark.beckley@cleveland.edu
BECKLEY, David, L 662-252-2491 277 C dbeckley@rustcollege.edu
BECKLEY, Gemma 662-252-8000 277 C gbeckley@rustcollege.edu
BECKMAN, Connie, L 570-662-4831 443 B cbeckman@mansfield.edu
BECKMAN, Donald, C 503-370-6315 421 C dbeckman@willamette.edu
BECKMAN, Jean 812-488-2589 180 B jb37@evansville.edu
BECKMAN, John 212-998-6848 344 B john.beckman@nyu.edu
BECKMAN, Nancy 773-481-8525 147 F nbeckman@ccc.edu
BECKMAN, Phyllis 225-359-9235 209 K pbeckman@catc.edu
BECKMAN, Phyllis 225-359-9356 209 K pbeckman@catc.edu
BECKMAN-WELLS, Patricia 818-733-2600 58 J
BECKMANN, Terry, J 207-786-8339 217 C tbeckman@bates.edu
BECKNER, Scott 304-876-5374 544 A sbeckner@shepherd.edu
BECKS, Crystal 661-654-3012 33 H cbecks@csub.edu
BECKSTED, Scott, M 315-470-4992 355 A smbeckst@esf.edu
BECKSTRAND, Kennan, T 585-292-5627 325 D ktbeckstrand@bryantstratton.edu
BECKSTROM, Brian, A 319-352-8217 189 F brian.beckstrom@wartburg.edu
BECKSTROM, Robert, A 440-365-5222 395 C
BECKUM, Randy 913-971-3461 195 A rbeckum@mnu.edu
BECKWITCH, Peter 517-437-7341 252 E peter.beckwitch@hillsdale.edu
BECKWITH, Cynthia, A 909-621-8512 49 D cynthia_beckwith@hmc.edu
BECKWITH, George 909-806-3347 58 I ebeckwit@nu.edu
BECKWITH, James 802-447-6342 514 D jbeckwith@svc.edu
BECKWITH, Robert 510-466-7269 62 D rbeckwith@peralta.edu
BECKWITH, Steven V, W 510-987-9436 73 D steven.beckwith@ucop.edu
BECVAR, Laurie, J 605-677-6287 465 E laurie.becvar@usd.edu
BECVAR, Laurie, J 605-677-6926 465 E laurie.becvar@usd.edu
BEDARD, Martha 505-277-4241 321 C mbedard@unm.edu
BEDARD, Richard, F 413-205-3532 229 G richard.bedard@aic.edu
BEDASHI, Allan, M 304-336-5100 544 B abedashi@westliberty.edu
BEDDALL, Tina 559-278-2191 34 D tina_beddall@csufresno.edu
BEDDARD, Wesley 252-940-6226 367 I wesleyb@beaufortccc.edu
BEDDOW, Lucinda 256-306-2784 2 E lmb@calhoun.edu
BEDELL, Frank 803-754-4100 457 D
BEDELL, Kevin 617-552-3590 232 D kevin.bedell.1@bc.edu
BEDENBAUGH, Diana, L 864-488-4589 459 A dbedenbaugh@limestone.edu
BEDFORD, Allen 267-502-2567 423 B allenbedford@brynathyn.edu
BEDFORD, April 504-280-1278 213 E awhatley@uno.edu
BEDFORD, John 405-208-5322 410 A jbedford@okcu.edu
BEDFORD, Laura 315-792-3179 359 C lbedford@utica.edu
BEDFORD, Norm 702-774-8000 302 K norm.bedford@unlv.edu
BEDI, Param, S 570-577-1557 423 D param.bedi@bucknell.edu
BEDI, Stephen, S 765-998-5203 179 F stbedi@taylor.edu
BEDICS, Stuart 610-282-1100 426 I stuart.bedics@desales.edu
BEDINI, Ken 860-465-5247 91 H bedini@easternct.edu
BEDITZ, Stephen 518-437-4702 351 E sbeditz@uamail.albany.edu
BEDNAR, Cynthia 610-436-2231 443 F cbednar@wcupa.edu
BEDNARZ, Bridgette 254-968-9271 496 F bednarz@tarleton.edu
BEDNEY, Elynda, A 269-471-6040 247 H bedney@andrews.edu
BEDOLLA, Daniel 312-935-6614 162 E dbedolla@robertmorris.edu
BEDOYA, Theresa 410-225-2434 224 C tbedoya@mica.edu
BEDTKE, James 507-457-1458 271 G jbedtke@smumn.edu
BEDWELL, Pamela 478-757-2544 133 E pamela.bedwell@maconstate.edu
BEE, Allan, C 530-898-6322 34 A abee@csuchico.edu
BEE, Patsy 304-424-8200 545 B patsy.bee@mail.wvu.edu
BEE, Richard 562-903-4728 30 H richard.e.bee@biola.edu
BEEBE, Barbara, R 301-784-5000 221 A bbeebe@allegany.edu
BEEBE, Gayle, D 805-565-6024 78 F president@westmont.edu
BEEBE, Norman 413-775-1333 240 B beebe@gcc.mass.edu
BEEBE, Robert, D 909-593-3511 75 C rbeebe@laverne.edu
BEEBE, Rose 304-424-8286 545 B rose.beebe@mail.wvu.edu
BEEBE, Thomas, E 203-932-7147 95 B tbeebe@newhaven.edu
BEECH, Glenn, J 412-675-9163 439 H gxb2@psu.edu
BEECHAM, Sarah 706-649-1858 127 E sbeecham@columbustech.edu
BEECHER, Brian 847-214-7595 150 D bbeecher@elgin.edu
BEECHER, Carla 801-863-8568 511 C carla.beecher@uvu.edu
BEECHING, Angela Myles 617-585-1118 243 E angela.beeching@necmusic.edu
BEEKMAN, Ann 407-569-1309 107 G ann.beekman@fcc.edu
BEEKMAN, Peter, A 315-268-4021 329 C pbeekman@clarkson.edu
BEEKMAN, William, R 517-353-9818 255 D bookman@mcu.odu
BEELEN, Joan 616-957-6027 249 F jrb44@calvinseminary.edu
BEELER, Jeremy 908-835-2301 317 C jbeeler@warren.edu
BEELER, Shannon 303-477-7240 84 I shannonb@heritage-education.com
BEEMAN, Greg 845-675-4417 344 G greg.beeman@nyack.edu
BEEMAN, Robert 651-523-2326 264 C rbeemanjr01@hamline.edu
BEEMER, Elizabeth 937-376-6444 386 H ebeemer@centralstate.edu
BEEMER, Matthew 904-596-2473 122 A mbeemer@tbc.edu
BEEMER, Pamela 847-467-1466 160 D p-beemer@northwestern.edu
BEEN, Sharon, A 501-882-8836 20 D sabeen@asub.edu
BEENE, Connie 913-768-1900 191 A cbeene@brownmackie.edu
BEENE, Lonnie, P 903-434-8157 491 D lbeene@ntcc.edu
BEENER, Robert, R 814-472-3100 446 B rbeener@francis.edu
BEENK, Rose 775-831-1314 303 E rbeenk@sierranevada.edu
BEER, Bernard 212-960-5353 346 F beer@yu.edu
BEER, Linda 507-389-7351 269 F linda.beer@southcentral.edu
BEER, Patrick 478-387-4720 130 E
BEER, Richard 360-486-8784 536 F jrbeer@stmartin.edu
BEERS, David 253-879-3902 538 E dbeers@pugetsound.edu
BEERS, George, S 650-949-7077 47 H beersgeorge@foothill.edu
BEERS, Josh 717-560-8240 433 D jbeers@lbc.edu
BEERS, Maggie 415-338-3613 36 F mbeers@sfsu.edu
BEERS, Peter 717-560-8267 433 D pbeers@lbc.edu
BEERS, Robert 406-657-1124 296 E robert.beers@rocky.edu
BEERS, Stephen, T 479-524-7252 22 C sbeers@jbu.edu
BEERS, Susan 714-992-7046 59 D sbeers@fullcoll.edu
BEESON, Duane, L 712-707-7116 188 B beeson@nwciowa.edu
BEESON, Patricia, E 412-624-4223 449 A beeson@pitt.edu
BEESON, Robert 239-489-9267 104 L rbeeson@edison.edu
BEESON, Teresa 740-774-6300 389 C tbeeson@daymargroup.edu
BEETS, A. Ray 319-296-4042 185 C aurel.beets@hawkeyecollege.edu
BEEZHOLD, Philip, D 616-526-6481 249 E pdb2@calvin.edu
BEG, Christina 216-397-1998 392 M cbeg@jcu.edu
BEGANY, James 724-357-2220 442 E jbegany@iup.edu
BEGAY, Janice 785-749-8419 193 B janice.begay@bie.edu
BEGGS, Donald, L 316-978-3001 197 F don.beggs@wichita.edu
BEGGS, Marck 870-230-5272 21 I beggsm@hsu.edu
BEGIN-RICHARDSON, Janet 508-831-5060 247 B jbrich@wpi.edu
BEGLEY, John, B 270-384-8505 203 H begleyj@lindsey.edu
BEGLEY, Mary Ann 415-338-2722 36 F begley@sfsu.edu
BEGLEY, Teresa, J 812-374-5127 175 J tbegley@ivytech.edu
BEGLEY, Thomas 518-276-2525 347 D begley@rpi.edu
BEGLINGER, Claire, M 262-524-7242 546 E cbegling@carrollu.edu
BEHAN, C. Joseph 315-655-7284 325 I jbehan@cazenovia.edu
BEHAN KRAUS, Carolyn, A 203-773-8521 89 H cbehan@albertus.edu
BEHE, Phil 252-399-6528 362 A pbehe@barton.edu
BEHELER, Ann 559-791-2307 53 A abeheler@portervillecollege.edu
BEHEN, Joseph 312-499-4272 164 A jbehen@saic.edu
BEHLING, Laura, L 317-940-9278 170 C lbehling@butler.edu
BEHM, Bonnie Lee 610-519-6456 450 G bonnie.behm@villanova.edu
BEHM, Rhonda, K 651-641-8894 263 C rbehm@csp.edu
BEHMER, Scott 412-304-0732 429 A sbehmer@cci.edu
BEHN, Julie, J 408-944-6121 60 L julie.behn@palmer.edu
BEHNER, Beth 907-450-8200 10 H beth.behner@alaska.edu
BEHR, Fred, C 507-786-3636 271 H behr@stolaf.edu
BEHR, John 914-961-8313 349 I jbehr@svots.edu
BEHR, Kate, E 914-337-9300 331 A kate.behr@concordia-ny.edu
BEHRE, William 609-771-2797 308 G behre@tcnj.edu
BEHRENDT, William, M 214-648-6342 507 D william.behrendt@utsouthwestern.edu
BEHRENS, Ann 217-228-5432 161 E behrens@quincy.edu
BEHRENS, James 516-572-7700 342 C james.behrens@ncc.edu
BEHRENS, Troy, T 214-768-2288 494 F tbehrens@smu.edu
BEHRENTS, Rolf, G 314-577-8600 289 F behrents@slu.edu
BEHRINGER, Marilyn 559-638-3641 72 B marilyn.behringer@reedleycollege.edu
BEHRMAN, William 407-569-1307 107 G president@fcc.edu
BEHUL, Paula 561-297-3004 118 H pbehul@fau.edu
BEICHLEY, Barbara 641-844-5747 185 J barbara.beichley@iavalley.edu
BEIDLEMAN, David, C 717-361-1493 428 E beidlemand@etown.edu
BEIER, Nancy, A 410-777-2834 221 B nabeier@aacc.edu
BEIERSCHMITT, Bill 918-338-8030 411 H bbeierschmitt@rsu.edu
BEIKIRCH, Dale 432-685-4516 490 G dbeikirch@midland.edu
BEIL, Cheryl 202-994-6712 97 F cbeil@gwu.edu
BEIL, Don 202-651-5005 97 E don.beil@gallaudet.edu
BEIL, William 724-589-2115 448 A bbeil@thiel.edu
BEILBY, Rod 530-741-6838 80 E rbeilby@yccd.edu
BEINHOFF, Lisa 575-835-5615 319 A lbeinhoff@admin.nmt.edu
BEIRNE, Jay 617-578-7170 235 D jbeirne@gibbsboston.edu
BEISEL, William 440-525-7171 394 F bbeisel@lakelandcc.edu
BEISWANGER, Robert, C 716-839-8218 331 G rbeiswan@daemen.edu
BEITEL, Amy 724-463-0222 424 B abeitel@crbc.net
BEITEL, Leland 443-334-2838 226 E lbeitel@stevenson.edu
BEITEY, George 619-388-7860 65 H gbeitey@sdccd.edu
BEITL, Thomas, R 330-972-8643 403 B tbeitl@uakron.edu
BEITNER, Veronica 616-632-2458 248 A beitnver@aquinas.edu
BEITTEL, Lisa, B 508-421-5913 238 A Lisa.Beittel@umassmed.edu
BEITZEL, Vernon, L 540-464-7211 529 A beitzelvl@vmi.edu
BEJAR, Elizabeth 305-348-2151 119 B elizabeth.bejar@fiu.edu
BEJNAROWICZ, Ewa 312-553-3193 146 H ebejnarowicz@ccc.edu
BEJOIAN, Lynne 212-226-7300 346 E lbejoian@pbcny.edu
BEJOU, David 252-335-3311 377 D dbejou@mail.ecsu.edu
BEKKEN, Joseph 208-769-3368 143 H jmbekken@nic.edu
BEKRITSKY, Brett 845-848-7405 332 C brett.bekritsky@dc.edu
BEKURS, Dana 337-482-6272 216 D dana@louisiana.edu
BELAND, Thomas 802-773-5900 513 B tbeland@csj.edu
BELANGER, OFM, Brian, C 518-783-5047 350 I bbelanger@siena.edu
BELANGER, David, J 413-585-2530 245 B dbelange@smith.edu
BELANGER, Kathleen 502-447-1000 206 A kbelanger@spencerian.edu
BELANGER, Lisa 860-768-4666 95 A belanger@hartford.edu
BELARDO, Lynette 212-686-9244 323 A
BELARMINO, Lee 209-954-5300 66 D lbelarmino@deltacollege.edu
BELATTE, Patrick 802-485-2185 514 A pbelatte@norwich.edu
BELAUSKAS, August, J 847-566-6401 167 D gbelauskas@usml.edu
BELCHER, Alan 704-463-3452 375 E alan.belcher@fsmail.pfeiffer.edu
BELCHER, C. Gary 512-313-3000 483 G charles.belcher@concordia.edu
BELCHER, Carol 843-574-6230 461 G carol.belcher@tridenttech.edu
BELCHER, Chris 918-495-6529 411 C cbelcher@oru.edu
BELCHER, David, O 828-227-7100 379 E dbelcher@wcu.edu
BELCHER, Elizabeth, M 304-929-5464 542 H ebelcher@newriver.edu
BELCHER, Keith, E 912-279-5922 127 B kbelcher@ccga.edu
BELCHER, Ken 540-231-6000 529 B
BELCHER, Michael 209-946-2537 75 D mbelcher@pacific.edu
BELCHER, Michael 978-934-3929 237 F michael_belcher@uml.edu
BELCHER, Nicholas 617-850-1297 236 A nbelcher@hchc.edu
BELCHER, Steven 239-590-1404 119 A sbelcher@fgcu.edu
BELCHER, Tim 540-365-4366 518 J tbelcher@ferrum.edu
BELDAN, Chris 717-290-8755 433 F cbeldan@lancasterseminary.edu
BELDON, William 360-992-2103 532 A wbeldon@clark.edu
BELEN-NAZARIO, Lillian 787-620-2040 560 B lbelen@aupr.edu
BELENKY, Neil 336-334-4822 370 E nmbelenky@gtcc.edu
BELETTE, Magdiel 305-593-1223 102 D mbelette@albizu.edu
BELEVICH, Darla 518-743-2269 322 B belevicd@sunyacc.edu
BELEW, Paul, D 214-648-6062 507 D paul.belew@utsouthwestern.edu
BELEW, Valerie, S 615-353-3342 475 D valerie.belew@nscc.edu
BELFERMAN, Matthew 724-335-5336 437 H mbelferman@oaa.edu
BELFIORE, Phil, J 814-824-2268 436 C pbelfiore@mercyhurst.edu
BELIN, Jackie 908-526-1200 313 E jbelin@raritanval.edu
BELINSKI, Victor 909-594-5611 58 A vbelinski@mtsac.edu
BELINSKY, Joseph 330-339-3391 394 B jbelinsky@kent.edu
BELISLE, William, R 504-284-5539 214 I wbelisle@suno.edu
BELK, Peter 913-469-8500 193 I pbelk@jccc.edu
BELK, Wesley, C 864-429-8728 462 G wcbelk@mailbox.sc.edu
BELKIN, Betsey 440-646-8184 405 B bbelkin@ursuline.edu

BELKIN, Michelle .... 561-273-6500.... 117 J
mbelkin@southuniversity.edu
BELKNAP, Mary, R .... 425-637-1010.... 531 I
mbelknap@cityu.edu
BELKNAP, Peggy .... 928-536-6231..... 17 B
peggy.belknap@npc.edu
BELKO, Dawn .... 763-424-0715.... 268 D
dbelko@nhcc.edu
BELL, Amy .... 870-743-3000..... 22 G
abell@northark.edu
BELL, Andrea .... 740-264-5591.... 390 F
abell@egcc.edu
BELL, Barrett .... 815-226-3372.... 162 H
bbell@rockford.edu
BELL, Brett .... 619-388-7810..... 65 H
bbell@sdccd.edu
BELL, Bruce, K .... 434-592-3862.... 520 F
bkbell@liberty.edu
BELL, C. Leary .... 843-208-8245.... 462 C
cbell@uscb.edu
BELL, Chris .... 940-552-6291.... 507 E
cbell@vernoncollege.edu
BELL, Christopher A, R ...... 207-768-9511.... 220 F
chris.bell@umpi.edu
BELL, Damon .... 909-384-8992..... 65 C
dbell@sbccd.cc.ca.us
BELL, Daniel, R .... 304-462-4132.... 543 F
dan.bell@glenville.edu
BELL, David, A .... 216-368-1723.... 386 E
david.a.bell@case.edu
BELL, David, D .... 614-823-1300.... 400 G
dbell@otterbein.edu
BELL, David, E .... 406-243-2122.... 295 A
david1.bell@umontana.edu
BELL, Dean .... 312-322-1791.... 165 C
dbell@spertus.edu
BELL, Deborah .... 863-784-7251.... 117 I
belld@southflorida.edu
BELL, Denise .... 850-973-9481.... 113 J
belld@nfcc.edu
BELL, Denise .... 508-793-2397.... 233 D
dbell@holycross.edu
BELL, Diana .... 256-824-3142....... 9 A
diana.bell@uah.edu
BELL, Donald .... 253-752-2020.... 533 J
fsinfo@faithseminary.edu
BELL, Elaine .... 313-993-1588.... 259 C
belles@udmercy.edu
BELL, Elizabeth, E .... 630-466-7900.... 167 G
ebell@waubonsee.edu
BELL, Genniver .... 850-561-2989.... 118 G
genniver.bell@famu.edu
BELL, Geraldine .... 205-929-1715....... 5 H
gbell@mail.miles.edu
BELL, Glenn .... 310-314-6064..... 29 J
BELL, Glenn, R .... 251-380-3099....... 7 F
bell@shc.edu
BELL, Gregory, J .... 570-321-4395.... 435 D
BELL, Gretchen, M .... 336-599-1181.... 372 D
bellg@piedmontcc.edu
BELL, Harold .... 404-270-5269.... 137 E
hbell@spelman.edu
BELL, Hershey .... 814-866-5177.... 433 C
hbell@lecom.edu
BELL, Jeff, W .... 903-923-3221.... 500 A
jeff.bell@marshall.tstc.edu
BELL, Jennifer .... 856-256-4410.... 314 A
bellj@rowan.edu
BELL, John, D .... 801-422-3037.... 509 D
john_bell@byu.edu
BELL, Jorge .... 415-239-3382..... 39 H
jbell@ccsf.edu
BELL, Jorge .... 415-550-4416..... 39 H
jbell@ccsf.edu
BELL, Julie .... 217-228-5432.... 161 E
bellju@quincy.edu
BELL, Juliette, B .... 937-376-6431.... 386 H
jbell@centralstate.edu
BELL, Karen .... 617-266-1400.... 231 G
BELL, Karen .... 845-257-2800.... 352 B
bellk@newpaltz.edu
BELL, Kathleen .... 651-779-3438.... 266 D
kathy.bell@century.edu
BELL, Kathleen .... 317-931-2305.... 170 E
kbell@cts.edu
BELL, Kelli .... 740-593-4797.... 399 G
bellk@ohio.edu
BELL, Kelly, A .... 864-662-6064.... 455 C
kbell@andersonuniversity.edu
BELL, Kim .... 412-392-3921.... 444 H
kbell@pointpark.edu
BELL, Kimberly .... 818-386-5639..... 62 F
kbell@pgi.edu
BELL, Lauren, C .... 804-752-7268.... 522 F
lbell@rmc.edu
BELL, Leia .... 860-727-6967..... 92 C
lbell@goodwin.edu
BELL, Lillie, F .... 318-357-6171.... 216 B
bell@nsula.edu
BELL, Linda .... 610-896-1014.... 430 G
lbell@haverford.edu
BELL, Linda, F .... 610-758-3181.... 434 E
lfn0@lehigh.edu

BELL, Lisa, G .... 859-246-6564.... 201 D
lisag.bell@kctcs.edu
BELL, Lynn .... 334-556-2223........ 4 A
lbell@wallace.edu
BELL, Marcus, V .... 803-376-5700.... 455 B
mbell@allenuniversity.edu
BELL, Margaret, G .... 410-857-2203.... 224 D
mbell@mcdaniel.edu
BELL, Marty .... 217-228-5432.... 161 E
bellma@quincy.edu
BELL, Melleta .... 432-837-8388.... 501 B
mbell@sulross.edu
BELL, Michael .... 847-259-1840.... 146 F
mbell@christianlifecollege.edu
BELL, Miji .... 919-530-6295.... 378 A
mbell@nccu.edu
BELL, Mike .... 907-796-6140...... 11 A
mike.bell@uas.alaska.edu
BELL, Norma, G .... 205-853-1200........ 5 C
ngbell@jeffstateonline.com
BELL, Pam .... 314-264-1852.... 405 C
pam.bell@vatterott-college.edu
BELL, Pam .... 314-264-1852.... 478 A
pam.bell@vatterott-college.edu
BELL, Pam .... 314-264-1852.... 167 F
pam.bell@vatterott-college.edu
BELL, Pam .... 314-264-1852.... 189 D
pam.bell@vatterott-college.edu
BELL, Pam .... 904-620-2372.... 120 C
pbell@unf.edu
BELL, Pam .... 314-264-1852.... 292 D
pam.bell@vatterott-college.edu
BELL, Pam .... 314-264-1852.... 292 G
pam.bell@vatterott-college.edu
BELL, Pam .... 314-264-1852.... 292 C
pam.bell@vatterott.edu
BELL, Pam .... 314-264-1852.... 292 H
pam.bell@vatterott-college.edu
BELL, Pam .... 314-264-1852.... 292 I
pam.bell@vatterott-college.edu
BELL, Pam .... 314-264-1852.... 301 D
pam.bell@vatterott-college.edu
BELL, Pam .... 314-264-1852.... 414 A
pam.bell@vatterott-college.edu
BELL, Pam .... 314-264-1852.... 414 B
pam.bell@vatterott-college.edu
BELL, Pamela .... 314-587-2433.... 284 A
BELL, Patty .... 903-983-8678.... 489 F
pbell@kilgore.edu
BELL, Paul .... 405-325-4411.... 413 C
pbell@ou.edu
BELL, Pegge, L .... 305-899-3800.... 101 F
pbell@mail.barry.edu
BELL, Priscilla, J .... 208-769-3303.... 143 H
pjbell@nic.edu
BELL, Rebecca .... 432-685-4556.... 490 G
rbell@midland.edu
BELL, Richard, S .... 803-938-3715.... 462 F
richbell@uscsumter.edu
BELL, Robert, H .... 626-585-7071...... 61 E
rhbell@pasadena.edu
BELL, Robert, R .... 931-372-3241.... 474 B
rbell@tntech.edu
BELL, Robert, W .... 864-379-8885.... 457 G
rbell@erskine.edu
BELL, Roberta .... 615-322-4359.... 477 F
roberta.bell@vanderbilt.edu
BELL, Scott .... 907-474-6265...... 10 J
svbell2@alaska.edu
BELL, Sharon, B .... 401-874-2378.... 454 E
sbbell@mail.uri.edu
BELL, Steed .... 785-242-5200.... 195 F
steed.bell@ottawa.edu
BELL, Stephen .... 847-543-2238.... 147 H
sbell@clcillinois.edu
BELL, Stephen .... 610-558-5549.... 437 C
bells@neumann.edu
BELL, Steven, D .... 757-683-4419.... 521 L
sdbell@odu.edu
BELL, Steven, K .... 724-847-6530.... 429 G
skbell@geneva.edu
BELL, Stuart, R .... 785-864-3881.... 196 F
sbell@ku.edu
BELL, Tommy .... 260-481-5443.... 174 A
belljt@ipfw.edu
BELL, Trudy .... 805-546-3206...... 43 F
tbell@cuesta.edu
BELL, Zoe .... 302-736-2566...... 96 G
bell@wesley.edy
BELL ADAMS, Sandra .... 718-262-2363.... 329 B
sadams@york.cuny.edu
BELL-GARRISON,
Eileen, K .... 509-313-6533.... 534 A
bellgarrison@gonzaga.edu
BELL-JOHNSON, Lilly .... 870-584-4471...... 25 C
lbell@cccua.edu
BELL-LUCAS, Sara .... 919-530-5129.... 378 A
bellucas@nccu.edu
BELLACK, Janis, P .... 617-726-8002.... 242 E
jbellack@mghihp.edu
BELLAFIORE, April .... 508-678-2811.... 239 F
april.bellafiore@bristolcc.edu
BELLAGIO, Mae Rose .... 707-546-4000...... 45 G
mrbellagio@empirecollege.com

BELLAH, Eric .... 865-981-8225.... 470 F
eric.bellah@maryvillecollege.edu
BELLAIRS, Bart .... 985-549-2253.... 216 C
bart.bellairs@selu.edu
BELLALTA, Maria .... 617-262-5000.... 232 B
Maria.Bellalta@the-bac.edu
BELLAMEY, Tim, H .... 618-634-3219.... 164 C
timb@shawneecc.edu
BELLAMY, Antoinette, P ..... 910-630-7257.... 366 H
abellamy@methodist.edu
BELLAMY, James .... 317-917-3628.... 177 H
jbellamy@martin.edu
BELLAMY, Reagan .... 509-682-6445.... 539 B
rbellamy@wvc.edu
BELLAMY, Sandra .... 212-694-1000.... 324 C
sbellamy@boricuacollege.edu
BELLANCA, Rose .... 734-973-3491.... 260 B
rbellanca@wccnet.edu
BELLANCA, Rose, B .... 561-478-5555.... 257 A
bellanca@northwood.edu
BELLANI, Raj .... 401-454-6593.... 454 B
rbellani@risd.edu
BELLAS, Peter .... 661-362-3144...... 41 G
peter.bellas@canyons.edu
BELLAVANCE, Leslie .... 607-871-2412.... 322 F
bellavance@alfred.edu
BELLAVIA, Rand .... 716-829-7616.... 332 F
bellavia@dyc.edu
BELLE, Walton, M .... 804-257-5885.... 529 D
BELLE-ISLE,
G. Christopher .... 585-292-2271.... 341 H
cbelleisle@monroecc.edu
BELLEFEUILLE, Barbara, K 706-886-6831.... 137 G
academic@tfc.edu
BELLEFEUILLE, Kate .... 315-498-2291.... 345 D
BELLER, Wendy .... 217-228-5432.... 161 E
bellewe@quincy.edu
BELLFIELD, Nicole .... 813-880-8064.... 111 B
nbellfield@online.academy.edu
BELLICINI, Pierre, A .... 814-866-8121.... 433 C
pbellicini@lecom.edu
BELLIN, Derek, C .... 212-517-0453.... 340 D
dbellin@mmm.edu
BELLINA, Amy .... 732-571-3607.... 311 F
abellina@monmouth.edu
BELLING, Karen .... 630-752-5021.... 168 F
karen.belling@wheaton.edu
BELLINGER, Danny .... 404-653-7806.... 134 A
dbelling@morehouse.edu
BELLINGER, Eunice .... 585-345-6975.... 334 F
embellinger@genesee.edu
BELLINGER, Larry, L .... 214-828-8322.... 497 A
lbellinger@bcd.tamhsc.edu
BELLIVEAU, Cynthia, L .... 802-656-3890.... 514 F
cynthia.belliveau@uvm.edu
BELLMAN, Ben .... 740-420-5933.... 398 C
BELLO, Chippi .... 503-594-3099.... 415 A
chippi@clackamas.edu
BELLO, Diane .... 631-632-6175.... 352 C
diane.bello@stonybrook.edu
BELLO, Jonathan .... 951-343-4721...... 31 G
jbello@calbaptist.edu
BELLO-BRUNSON,
Jane, M .... 219-464-6769.... 181 A
jane.bellobrunson@valpo.edu
BELLOLI, Ronald .... 928-724-6677...... 14 A
rbelloli@dinecollege.edu
BELLONA, Steven, J .... 315-859-4502.... 335 A
sbellona@hamilton.edu
BELLONI, Francis, L .... 914-594-4110.... 343 F
francis_belloni@nymc.edu
BELLOVICH, Steven, J .... 918-631-2478.... 413 F
steven-bellovich@utulsa.edu
BELLOWS, Charlene, M ...... 508-831-5577.... 247 B
cbellows@wpi.edu
BELLOWS, Kathryn, S .... 202-687-5867...... 98 A
bellowsk@georgetown.edu
BELLSOM, Lou .... 773-380-6880.... 168 D
lbellsom@westwood.edu
BELLUCCI, Anthony .... 973-642-8094.... 315 C
anthony.bellucci@shu.edu
BELLUCCI, Debbie .... 413-755-4334.... 241 E
dbellucci@stcc.edu
BELLUCCI, Keith .... 617-732-2145.... 241 F
keith.bellucci@mcphs.edu
BELLUM, Kim .... 605-882-5284.... 464 D
bellumk@lakeareatech.edu
BELMODIS, Cassie .... 503-399-5159.... 414 J
cassie.belmodis@chemeketa.edu
BELOBRAJDIC, Scott .... 618-650-2298.... 165 A
sbelobr@siue.edu
BELOTE, David, J .... 731-881-7525.... 477 E
dbelote@utm.edu
BELOTE, Eve .... 757-789-1767.... 526 D
ebelote@es.vccs.edu
BELOTE, Michael, R .... 478-301-2850.... 133 F
michael.r.belote@mercer.edu
BELOW, Debbie .... 573-651-2590.... 290 D
dbelow@semo.edu
BELSITO, Paul .... 508-767-7321.... 230 E
pbelsito@assumption.edu
BELSKY, Jeff .... 412-809-5100.... 444 F
belsky@pti.edu

BELSKY, Martin, H .... 330-972-7331.... 403 B
belsky@uakron.edu
BELSTRA, James, E .... 708-239-4720.... 165 I
jim.belstra@trnty.edu
BELT, Carol .... 618-634-3277.... 164 C
carolb@shawneecc.edu
BELTON, Ada, A .... 803-705-4327.... 455 D
beltona@benedict.edu
BELTON, Annie, R .... 803-536-8406.... 460 G
zs_abelton@scsu.edu
BELTON, Betty .... 817-735-2241.... 504 C
bbelton@hsc.unt.edu
BELTON, Gale .... 404-297-9522.... 128 B
beltong@dekalbtech.org
BELTON, Ray, L .... 318-670-9312.... 215 A
rbelton@susla.edu
BELTRAN, Dulce .... 305-237-2222.... 113 H
dbeltran@mdc.edu
BELTRAN, Fernando .... 209-667-3108...... 36 C
fbeltran@csustan.edu
BELTRAN, Jacque .... 847-566-6401.... 167 D
jbeltran@usml.edu
BELTRAN, Philip .... 408-554-5082...... 68 C
pjbeltran@scu.edu
BELWOOD, Marilyn .... 660-831-4085.... 286 I
belwoodmf@moval.edu
BELYEA, Daniel .... 207-974-4664.... 218 H
dbelyea@emcc.edu
BELYEA, Elizabeth .... 916-691-7367...... 56 B
belyeae@crc.losrios.edu
BELZ, Mike .... 651-846-3410.... 261 E
mbelz@argosy.edu
BELZER, Rita, A .... 716-270-5355.... 333 C
belzer@ecc.edu
BEMELEN, Jeff .... 303-871-3256...... 88 E
jbemelen@du.edu
BEMIS, Carol .... 574-807-7370.... 169 F
bemisc@bethelcollege.edu
BEMIS, Kathleen .... 503-883-2449.... 416 G
kbemis@linfield.edu
BEMIS, Scot, R .... 781-736-4464.... 233 A
bemis@brandeis.edu
BEMUS, Melissa, L .... 920-748-8112.... 549 I
bemusm@ripon.edu
BEN-AVI, Simon .... 212-353-4285.... 331 B
benavi@cooper.edu
BEN-SHOSHAN, Lisa .... 215-635-7300.... 430 A
lbenshoshan@gratz.edu
BENAICHA, Hedi .... 401-456-8053.... 454 A
hbenaicha@ric.edu
BENALLY, Curtis, R .... 505-368-3624...... 14 A
crbenally@dinecollege.edu
BENALLY, Steven .... 505-786-4110.... 318 H
sbenally@navajotech.edu
BENALLY, Suzanne .... 303-546-3523...... 86 B
sbenally@naropa.edu
BENAMATI, Dennis .... 716-338-1126.... 337 E
dennisbenamati@mail.sunyjcc.edu
BENANAV, Jay .... 612-330-1792.... 261 G
benanav@augsburg.edu
BENARD, Mary .... 619-388-3523...... 65 F
mbenard@sdccd.edu
BENATAN, Ethan .... 503-699-6325.... 416 I
ebenatan@marylhurst.edu
BENAVIDES, Adolfo .... 254-968-9350.... 496 F
benavides@tarleton.edu
BENAVIDES, Elma, F .... 512-863-1441.... 495 G
benavide@southwestern.edu
BENAVIDES, Lewis .... 940-898-3555.... 502 B
lbenavides@twu.edu
BENAVIDES-FRANKE,
Joanna .... 361-825-6052.... 497 F
joanna.benavides-franke@tamucc.edu
BENBOW, Camilla, P .... 615-322-8407.... 477 F
camilla.benbow@vanderbilt.edu
BENCA, Melissa .... 212-774-4860.... 340 D
mbenca@mmm.edu
BENCH, Patricia .... 661-763-7757...... 72 C
pbench@taftcollege.edu
BENCHOFF, Bryan .... 740-593-0061.... 399 G
BENDA, Gary .... 815-836-5222.... 156 D
bendaga@lewisu.edu
BENDAPUDI, Neeli .... 785-864-7573.... 196 F
neeli@ku.edu
BENDECK, Yvette .... 281-283-3022.... 503 C
bendeck@uhcl.edu
BENDELE, Jennifer .... 419-227-3141.... 404 D
jennifer@unoh.edu
BENDER, Chris .... 619-482-6564...... 71 C
cbender@swccd.edu
BENDER, Claire, E .... 507-284-3293.... 262 G
bender.claire@mayo.edu
BENDER, David .... 610-396-6090.... 439 A
dsb@psu.edu
BENDER, David, L .... 989-837-4374.... 257 A
bender@northwood.edu
BENDER, Gretchen .... 949-582-4565...... 70 F
gbender@saddleback.edu
BENDER, James, E .... 651-631-5493.... 270 E
jebender@nwc.edu
BENDER, Jennie, M .... 606-474-3226.... 200 J
jbender@kcu.edu
BENDER, Joe .... 812-855-6017.... 173 C
jbender@bncollege.com

BENSON, Stephen ..... 304-929-5486 .... 542 H
sbenson@newriver.edu
BENSON, Suzie ..... 509-682-6505 .... 539 B
sbenson@wvc.edu
BENSON, Vaughn ..... 402-375-7245 .... 299 I
vabenso1@wsc.edu
BENSON, Verlyn, R ..... 269-471-3413 .... 247 H
vbenson@andrews.edu
BENSON, Wade, M ..... 706-379-3111 .... 139 F
wadeb@yhc.edu
BENSON-CLAYTON, Taffye 252-328-6804 .... 377 C
claytont@ecu.edu
BENSON-NICOL, Nancy ..... 479-979-1307 .... 26 A
nbenson@ozarks.edu
BENSON-TYUS, Hasanna ... 202-462-2101 .... 98 C
benson@iwp.edu
BENTE, James ..... 630-942-2409 .... 147 G
bentej@cod.edu
BENTIVEGNA, Saverio, S .. 914-594-3368 .... 343 F
saverio_bentivegna@nymc.edu
BENTLEY, Charles ..... 909-593-3511 .... 75 C
cbentley@laverne.edu
BENTLEY, Dean ..... 404-727-6039 .... 129 A
dean.bentley@emory.edu
BENTLEY, Gloria, A ..... 563-588-7027 .... 186 I
gloria.bentley@loras.edu
BENTLEY, Jane ..... 708-974-5703 .... 159 A
jane.bentley@morainevalley.edu
BENTLEY, Pamela ..... 270-706-8728 .... 201 F
pamela.bentley@kctcs.edu
BENTLEY, Rick ..... 317-917-5921 .... 175 I
rbentley3@ivytech.edu
BENTLEY, Sarah ..... 512-492-3034 .... 480 F
sbentley@aoma.edu
BENTLEY, Tony ..... 309-347-5448 .... 146 A
abentley@sandurg.edu
BENTLEY-COLTHART,
Nicki ..... 304-472-8488 .... 545 F
bentley-colthart@wvwc.edu
BENTON, Andrew, K ..... 310-506-4451 .... 61 G
andrew.benton@pepperdine.edu
BENTON, Debra, M ..... 740-593-4260 .... 399 G
bentond@ohio.edu
BENTON, James ..... 828-659-0444 .... 371 G
jimbenton@mcdowelltech.edu
BENTON, Katherine ..... 405-382-9263 .... 412 B
k.benton@sscok.edu
BENTON, Patrena, N ..... 405-466-3241 .... 408 G
pnbenton@lunet.edu
BENTON, Ronald, W ..... 303-963-3221 .... 81 K
rbenton@ccu.edu
BENTON, Sherry ..... 352-392-1575 .... 120 B
benton@counsel.ufl.edu
BENTON, Tonya ..... 206-878-3710 .... 534 E
tbenton@highline.edu
BENTON-MESTAS, Andrea . 719-587-8333 .... 80 F
andrea@adams.edu
BENTZ, Hank ..... 812-265-2580 .... 176 G
hbentz@ivytech.edu
BENULIS, Joan, R ..... 585-385-8010 .... 348 F
jbenulis@sjfc.edu
BENVENGER, Deborah, A .. 215-871-6711 .... 444 B
admissions@pcom.edu
BENVENISTE,
Lawrence, M ..... 404-727-6377 .... 129 A
larry_benveniste@bus.emory.edu
BENVENUTTI, MaryBeth .... 510-464-3232 .... 62 C
mbenvenutti@peralta.edu
BENVENUTTI-TORO,
Evelyn ..... 787-751-1912 .... 564 A
ebenven@inter.edu
BENWAY, Elizabeth ..... 508-830-5086 .... 239 A
ebenway@maritime.edu
BENWELL, Deirdre ..... 509-527-2066 .... 538 H
deirdre.benwell@wallawalla.edu
BENZ, Deborah ..... 507-457-5069 .... 270 B
dbenz@winona.edu
BENZ, Kathleen ..... 661-362-3032 .... 41 G
kathleen.benz@canyons.edu
BENZEL, Brian, L ..... 509-777-3208 .... 539 F
bbenzel@whitworth.edu
BENZENBERG, Darlene ..... 845-561-0800 .... 342 A
darlene.benzenberg@msmc.edu
BEODEKER, Robert ..... 631-548-2514 .... 356 F
beodekr@sunysuffolk.edu
BEOKU-BETTS,
Josephine, A ..... 561-297-2057 .... 118 H
beokubet@fau.edu
BEQUETTE, Angela, L ..... 919-866-5394 .... 374 E
albequette@waketech.edu
BEQUETTE, Barry ..... 601-877-6137 .... 273 C
bequette@alcorn.edu
BEQUETTE, Michael ..... 507-285-7256 .... 269 B
mike.bequette@roch.edu
BEQUETTE, Walter ..... 251-344-1203 .... 3 I
BERALDI, Thomas ..... 603-645-9695 .... 306 B
t.beraldi@snhu.edu
BERAN, Connie ..... 512-313-3000 .... 483 G
connie.beran@concordia.edu
BERAN, Paul, B ..... 479-788-7007 .... 24 D
pberan@uafortsmith.edu
BERAN, Wayne, B ..... 361-570-4811 .... 503 E
beranw@uhv.edu
BERARD, Wayne-Daniel, S 508-213-2121 .... 243 J
wayne-daniel.berard@nichols.edu

BERARDI, William ..... 508-678-2811 .... 239 F
william.berardi@bristolcc.edu
BERDAR, Charles ..... 904-256-7484 .... 111 J
cberdar@ju.edu
BERENBACK, Steven ..... 401-454-6156 .... 454 B
sberenba@risd.edu
BERENBAUM, Devorah ..... 718-645-0536 .... 341 D
mirrer@thejnet.com
BERENBAUM, Osher ..... 917-645-0536 .... 341 D
mirrer@thejnet.com
BERENBAUM, Rachel ..... 718-645-0536 .... 341 D
mirrer@thejnet.com
BERENDT, Sherri ..... 312-427-2737 .... 154 F
6berendt@jmls.edu
BERENS, Theresa ..... 252-335-0821 .... 369 D
theresa_berens@albemarle.edu
BERENSON, Jennifer, K ..... 540-375-2204 .... 523 D
berenson@roanoke.edu
BERENSON, Jerry, A ..... 610-526-5160 .... 423 C
jberenso@brynmawr.edu
BERESFORD, Jack, F ..... 619-594-5204 .... 36 E
jack.beresford@sdsu.edu
BERESFORD, Vince ..... 714-556-3610 .... 76 E
vince.beresford@vanguard.edu
BEREZNIAK, Ronald ..... 941-756-0690 .... 433 C
rberezniak@lecom.edu
BERG, Alicia, M ..... 312-369-7102 .... 148 B
aberg@colum.edu
BERG, Amy ..... 607-753-5942 .... 353 B
amy.berg@cortland.edu
BERG, Dale ..... 520-326-1600 .... 18 B
BERG, Denise ..... 570-662-4853 .... 443 B
dberg@mansfield.edu
BERG, Diana ..... 952-888-4777 .... 270 F
dberg@nwhealth.edu
BERG, Eric ..... 218-723-6630 .... 262 I
eberg@css.edu
BERG, Gary ..... 805-437-8580 .... 33 I
gary.berg@csuci.edu
BERG, Jerry ..... 815-226-4060 .... 162 H
jberg@rockford.edu
BERG, Joanne, E ..... 608-262-3964 .... 550 G
jeberg@em.wisc.edu
BERG, John ..... 215-972-2007 .... 440 I
jberg@pafa.edu
BERG, John, A ..... 314-935-7311 .... 292 J
jberg@wustl.edu
BERG, Kevin ..... 509-682-6815 .... 539 B
kberg@wvc.edu
BERG, Linda, K ..... 651-290-6321 .... 273 B
linda.berg@wmitchell.edu
BERG, Luciane ..... 337-550-1308 .... 212 H
BERG, Michele ..... 386-323-8025 .... 105 B
michele.berg@erau.edu
BERG, Michele ..... 386-323-8025 .... 105 C
michele.berg@erau.edu
BERG, Paula ..... 701-228-5451 .... 382 C
paula.berg@dakotacollege.edu
BERG, Richard, R ..... 717-290-8704 .... 433 F
rberg@lancasterseminary.edu
BERG, Roger ..... 913-621-8744 .... 192 C
rberg@donnelly.edu
BERG, Scott, M ..... 413-748-3859 .... 245 C
sberg@spfldcol.edu
BERG, Shelton, G ..... 305-284-2241 .... 122 F
sberg@miami.edu
BERG, Stacey, L ..... 832-824-4588 .... 481 H
sberg@bcm.edu
BERG, Tamara ..... 507-457-5460 .... 270 B
tberg@winona.edu
BERG, Temma ..... 717-337-6788 .... 429 H
tberg@gettysburg.edu
BERG, Terry ..... 806-371-5008 .... 479 H
tlberg@actx.edu
BERGAMO, Anne, M ..... 856-691-8600 .... 309 C
abergamo@cccnj.edu
BERGAN, Maureen ..... 251-380-3498 .... 7 F
mbergan@shc.edu
BERGEN, Lori ..... 414-288-3588 .... 548 D
lori.bergen@marquette.edu
BERGEN, Michael ..... 718-951-5186 .... 326 G
mbergen@brooklyn.cuny.edu
BERGEN, Randy, S ..... 618-664-7021 .... 151 D
randy.bergen@greenville.edu
BERGEON, Caitlin ..... 503-821-8881 .... 419 D
cbergeon@pnca.edu
BERGER, Amy, C ..... 818-677-2932 .... 35 D
amy.berger@csun.edu
BERGER, Ann, P ..... 703-723-4465 .... 99 D
ann.berger@strayer.edu
BERGER, Aron ..... 845-426-3276 .... 360 G
ydm@thejnet.com
BERGER, David ..... 212-960-5253 .... 361 I
dberger@yu.edu
BERGER, David, O ..... 314-505-7040 .... 280 H
bergerd@csl.edu
BERGER, Edward, E ..... 620-665-3505 .... 193 F
bergere@hutchcc.edu
BERGER, Patrice ..... 402-472-5425 .... 300 H
pberger1@unl.edu
BERGER, Pearl ..... 212-960-5363 .... 361 I
berger@yu.edu
BERGER, Pearl ..... 212-960-5344 .... 346 F
dpearl@yu.edu

BERGER, Scott ..... 320-762-4475 .... 265 I
scottb@alextech.edu
BERGER, Susan, A ..... 315-655-7122 .... 325 I
sberger@cazenovia.edu
BERGER, Susan, A ..... 315-655-7126 .... 325 I
sberger@cazenovia.edu
BERGER, Vance, J ..... 423-775-7212 .... 467 D
bergerva@bryan.edu
BERGER-SWEENEY,
Joanne, E ..... 617-627-3864 .... 245 F
joanne.berger-sweeney@tufts.edu
BERGERON, Bette ..... 618-650-3350 .... 165 A
bberger@siue.edu
BERGERON, Brad ..... 312-332-0707 .... 165 H
BERGERON, Florence ..... 617-353-3608 .... 232 G
fbergero@bu.edu
BERGERON, Gabe ..... 617-262-5000 .... 232 B
gabe.bergeron@the-bac.edu
BERGERON, Iva, G ..... 217-786-2792 .... 156 I
iva.bergeron@llcc.edu
BERGERON, Jack ..... 517-483-1478 .... 254 D
bergerj@lcc.edu
BERGERON, Katherine ..... 401-863-2573 .... 452 J
katherine_bergeron@brown.edu
BERGERON, Mindy ..... 925-969-3385 .... 52 B
bergeron@jfku.edu
BERGERON, Stephanie, W . 248-689-8282 .... 260 A
sbergeron@walshcollege.edu
BERGERS, Barbara ..... 616-331-3255 .... 252 A
bergersb@gvsu.edu
BERGERSON, Catherine ..... 239-489-9206 .... 104 L
mcbergerson@edison.edu
BERGES, Cherry, L ..... 270-824-8677 .... 202 C
cherry.berges@kctcs.edu
BERGESON, John ..... 651-638-6112 .... 261 I
j-bergeson@bethel.edu
BERGESON, Rachel ..... 631-632-6740 .... 352 C
rachel.bergeson@stonybrook.edu
BERGFELD, Julie ..... 314-529-9620 .... 284 F
jbergfeld@maryville.edu
BERGFELD, Steve ..... 312-915-6449 .... 157 A
sbergfeld@luc.edu
BERGGREN, Jeffrey, C ..... 260-359-4016 .... 172 K
jberggren@huntington.edu
BERGGREN, Kent, E ..... 208-524-3000 .... 143 C
kent.berggren@my.eitc.edu
BERGGREN, Marie, N ..... 510-287-3306 .... 73 D
marie.berggren@ucop.edu
BERGGREN, Stacey, L ..... 208-467-8994 .... 143 I
BERGH, David ..... 802-635-1200 .... 515 E
david.bergh@jsc.edu
BERGH, Thomas, K ..... 715-394-8081 .... 552 D
tbergh@uwsuper.edu
BERGHOFF, Carolyn ..... 312-225-6288 .... 167 E
cberghoff@vandercook.edu
BERGHORN, George ..... 517-483-1319 .... 254 D
berghorg@lcc.edu
BERGKAMP, Sheila ..... 620-227-9201 .... 192 B
sbergkamp@dc3.edu
BERGLAND, Arne ..... 805-493-3152 .... 32 H
bergland@clunet.edu
BERGLAND, Yvonne, P ..... 619-388-2509 .... 65 G
ybergland@sdccd.edu
BERGLER, Michael ..... 949-214-3187 .... 42 K
michael.bergler@cui.edu
BERGMAN, Beverly ..... 478-471-2721 .... 133 E
beverly.bergman@maconstate.edu
BERGMAN, Bruce ..... 308-535-3676 .... 298 I
bergmanb@mpcc.edu
BERGMAN, Dave ..... 606-539-4167 .... 206 G
dave.bergman@ucumberlands.edu
BERGMAN, Ethan ..... 509-963-1975 .... 531 G
bergmane@cwu.edu
BERGMAN, Matthew ..... 217-228-5432 .... 161 E
bergmma@quincy.edu
BERGMAN, Michael ..... 413-528-7432 .... 231 A
bergman@simons-rock.edu
BERGMAN, Sarah ..... 907-852-3333 .... 10 G
sarah.bergman@ilisagvik.edu
BERGMAN, Sherrie, S ..... 207-725-3281 .... 217 E
sbergman@bowdoin.edu
BERGMAN, JR.,
William, T ..... 215-204-6550 .... 447 G
William.Bergman@temple.edu
BERGMANN, Hans ..... 203-582-8960 .... 93 E
hans.bergmann@quinnipiac.edu
BERGMANN, Ronald ..... 718-960-8421 .... 327 C
ron.bergmann@lehman.cuny.edu
BERGMANN, Ronald, F ..... 310-243-3720 .... 34 B
rbergmann@csudh.edu
BERGMANN, Tom ..... 847-947-5516 .... 159 D
tbergmann@nl.edu
BERGMEIER, Tyler ..... 603-752-1113 .... 304 I
tbergmeier@ccsnh.edu
BERGQUIST, Viola ..... 320-308-5177 .... 269 D
vbergquist@sctcc.edu
BERGSTROM, Chip ..... 617-217-9070 .... 231 C
cbergstrom@baystate.edu
BERGSTROM, Mark, A ..... 231-843-5804 .... 260 E
mabergstrom@westshore.edu
BERGSTROM, Paula ..... 870-574-4488 .... 24 A
pbergstr@sautech.edu
BERGSTROM, Scott, J ..... 208-496-1136 .... 142 G
bergstroms@byui.edu

BERGSTROM, Tracey ..... 361-582-2535 .... 507 G
tracey.bergstrom@victoriacollege.edu
BERGVALL, Dennis, P ..... 843-953-6914 .... 456 C
dennis.bergvall@citadel.edu
BERHANE, Kiflu ..... 903-927-3249 .... 509 A
kberhane@wileyc.edu
BERHE, Annette ..... 901-435-1351 .... 470 B
annette.berhe@loc.edu
BERICH, Anthony ..... 724-836-9949 .... 449 C
acb62@pitt.edu
BERINGER, Connie ..... 650-738-4202 .... 67 G
beringer@smccd.edu
BERK, Alvin ..... 718-270-1763 .... 352 D
alvin.berk@downstate.edu
BERK, Anne-Marie, P ..... 217-424-3593 .... 158 F
aberk@millikin.edu
BERK, Bradford, C ..... 585-275-3407 .... 358 I
bradford_berk@urmc.rochester.edu
BERK, Steven, L ..... 806-743-3000 .... 501 E
steven.berk@ttuhsc.edu
BERKELAND, Rondell ..... 218-723-7033 .... 262 I
rberkela@css.edu
BERKEY, Dennis, D ..... 508-831-5200 .... 247 B
dberkey@wpi.edu
BERKEY, Dolores ..... 814-269-2082 .... 449 D
berkey@pitt.edu
BERKHOF, Robert, A ..... 616-526-6091 .... 249 E
berk@calvin.edu
BERKICH, Carla ..... 361-825-2703 .... 497 F
carla.berkich@tamucc.edu
BERKMAN, Jennifer, R ..... 410-543-6262 .... 228 D
jrberkman@salisbury.edu
BERKMAN, Ronald, M ..... 216-687-3544 .... 388 C
ronald.berkman@csuohio.edu
BERKNER, Paul, D ..... 207-859-4460 .... 217 G
pberkner@colby.edu
BERKO, Andrew ..... 516-671-0379 .... 360 A
aberko@webb-institute.edu
BERKOFF, Lyudmila ..... 312-777-7620 .... 144 H
lberkoff@argosy.edu
BERKOW, Daniel ..... 209-667-3381 .... 36 C
dberkow@csustan.edu
BERKOWITZ, Justin ..... 407-673-7406 .... 113 B
BERLETH, Frank ..... 570-454-6172 .... 435 G
frank.berleth@mccann.edu
BERLIN, Robert, Y ..... 781-736-3720 .... 233 A
drb@brandeis.edu
BERLINER, Donna ..... 630-942-2475 .... 147 G
berliner@cod.edu
BERLINER, Herman, A ..... 516-463-5402 .... 335 H
herman.a.berliner@hofstra.edu
BERLYN, Mark, A ..... 314-516-6515 .... 291 F
berlynm@umsl.edu
BERMAN, Audrey ..... 510-869-6129 .... 64 J
aberman@samuelmerritt.edu
BERMAN, Francine ..... 518-276-4873 .... 347 D
bermaf@rpi.edu
BERMAN, Harris ..... 617-636-2177 .... 245 F
harris.berman@tufts.edu
BERMAN, Joel ..... 954-262-2130 .... 114 B
jb@nsu.nova.edu
BERMAN, Lou Ann ..... 903-566-7052 .... 506 C
lberman@uttyler.edu
BERMAN, Marc ..... 619-961-4271 .... 72 F
mberman@tjsl.edu
BERMAN, Mark ..... 413-662-5062 .... 238 F
m.berman@mcla.edu
BERMAN, Mark, R ..... 413-205-3366 .... 229 G
mark.berman@aic.edu
BERMAN, Mary Jane ..... 513-529-1943 .... 396 D
bermanmj@muohio.edu
BERMAN, Michael ..... 805-437-2099 .... 33 I
BERMAN, Morris, S ..... 714-449-7455 .... 70 G
mberman@scco.edu
BERMAN, Paula ..... 617-277-3915 .... 232 F
BERMAN, Richard ..... 507-222-4295 .... 262 B
rberman@carleton.edu
BERMAN-MARTIN, Gail, L 508-999-8660 .... 237 E
gberman@umassd.edu
BERMANN, Todd ..... 706-864-1450 .... 134 D
tberrman@northgeorgia.edu
BERMINGHAM, Jack ..... 206-878-3710 .... 534 E
jberming@highline.edu
BERMONT, Rebecca ..... 401-454-6918 .... 454 B
bbermont@risd.edu
BERMUDEZ, Angela ..... 432-837-8193 .... 501 B
bermudez@sulross.edu
BERMUDEZ, Gregory ..... 787-257-0000 .... 566 H
gregory.bermudez@upr.edu
BERMUDEZ, Jose Luis ..... 979-845-5141 .... 497 C
jbermudez@tamu.edu
BERMUDEZ, Megan ..... 610-921-7510 .... 421 D
mbermudez@alb.edu
BERMUDEZ, Pedro ..... 787-786-3030 .... 560 E
pbermudez@ucb.edu.pr
BERMUDEZ-TORRES,
Roberto ..... 780-250-1912 .... 563 E
rbermudez@metro.inter.edu
BERNA, Francis, J ..... 215-951-1346 .... 432 G
berna@lasalle.edu
BERNABE, Arnaldo ..... 718-518-6888 .... 327 D
abernabe@hostos.cuny.edu
BERNAD, Manuel, A ..... 858-499-0202 .... 41 E
manuelb@coleman.edu

BESTUL, Michael 216-397-4261 392 M mbestul@jcu.edu
BETANCOURT, Cybel 787-279-1912 563 B cbetancourt@bayamon.inter.edu
BETANCOURT, Gladys 787-743-7979 565 F ut-gbetancou@suagm.edu
BETECK, Ellis, B 410-651-6621 227 E ebbeteck@umes.edu
BETHEA, Edward 843-661-8060 458 A ed.bethea@fdtc.edu
BETHEL, Charles, N 304-877-6428 540 D registrar@abc.edu
BETHKE, Jeffrey 312-362-6986 148 F jbethke@depaul.edu
BETHMAN, Brenda 816-235-1643 291 E bethmanb@umkc.edu
BETHSCHEIDER, John 281-756-3619 479 G jbethschei@alvincollege.edu
BETHSCHEIDER, John 281-756-5601 479 G jbethscheider@alvincollege.edu
BETHUNE, Andrew, J 989-964-4071 258 A ajbethune@svsu.edu
BETHUNE, Brian 216-987-4125 389 A brian.bethune@tri-c.edu
BETHUNE, Lawrence, E 617-266-1400 231 G
BETHUNE-WALKER, Nicole 813-664-4260 104 G nbethune-walker@devry.edu
BETIT, Brent 802-387-6797 513 E bbetit@landmark.edu
BETKER, Pam 303-762-6898 83 I pam.betker@denverseminary.edu
BETORI, John 567-661-7575 400 H john_betori@owens.edu
BETSEY, Charles 202-806-6800 98 B cbetsey@howard.edu
BETSWORTH, Deborah 262-551-5725 546 F dbetsworth@carthage.edu
BETT, Sheri 724-838-4209 447 B bett@setonhill.edu
BETTENCOURT, Jessica 760-252-2411 30 F jbettencourt@barstow.edu
BETTENCOURT, Patrick 209-575-6149 80 B bettencourtp@mjc.edu
BETTING, Laurie 701-777-6055 381 D laurie.betting@email.und.edu
BETTINGER, Jill 315-786-2238 337 F jbettinger@sunyjefferson.edu
BETTISON-VARGA, Lori 909-621-8148 69 A president@scrippscollege.edu
BETTS, Albert 856-256-4200 314 A betts@rowan.edu
BETTS, Denver 256-233-8115 1 F denver.betts@athens.edu
BETTS, Jane 731-661-5353 476 G jbetts@uu.edu
BETTS, Keith 912-344-2514 124 E keith.betts@armstrong.edu
BETTS, Russell 312-567-3800 153 B betts@iit.edu
BETZ, A. Lorris 801-581-5701 510 L president@utah.edu
BETZ, Don 918-456-5511 409 A betz@nsuok.edu
BETZ, Jon 505-566-3505 320 D betzj@sanjuancollege.edu
BETZ, Kimberly 651-690-8890 271 E kkbetz@stkate.edu
BETZ, Leslie 309-556-3161 153 E iwureg@iwu.edu
BETZ, Norma 732-255-0400 312 D nbetz@ocean.edu
BETZ, Randy 757-569-6064 527 E rbetz@pdc.edu
BETZ-BOGOLY, Cynthia 973-748-9000 308 A Cynthia_Betz-Bogoly@bloomfield.edu
BETZIG, Kaylen 262-691-5198 555 C kbetzig@wctc.edu
BEU, Pat 605-394-1999 466 A pat.beu@sdsmt.edu
BEUKELMAN, Doug, D 712-707-7121 188 B dougb@nwciowa.edu
BEUSS, Ben 360-538-4082 534 B bbeus@ghc.edu
BEUSSMAN, Victoria 507-786-3325 271 H beussman@stolaf.edu
BEUTEL, Carmela 201-761-6472 314 F cbeutel@spc.edu
BEUTEL, Charles, M 815-740-5037 167 C cbeutel@stfrancis.edu
BEUTLER, Randy, L 580-774-3766 412 F randy.beutler@swosu.edu
BEVAN, Larry 724-222-5330 438 E lbevan@penncommercial.edu
BEVERAGE, JR., Morris, W 440-525-7118 394 F mbeverage@lakelandcc.edu
BEVERIDGE, Thomas 805-565-6017 78 F tbeverld@westmont.edu
BEVERLY, Aleza, D 765-641-4251 169 A adbeverly@anderson.edu
BEVERLY, Nancy, M 423-652-4728 469 L nmbeverly@king.edu
BEVERLY, Pearle 254-710-6939 481 I pearle_beverly@baylor.edu
BEVERLY, Roger, D 423-585-2620 476 B roger.beverly@ws.edu
BEVERSLUIS, Claudia 616-526-6102 249 E cbeversl@calvin.edu
BEVILACQUA, Linda 305-899-3010 101 F lbevilacqua@mail.barry.edu
BEVINS, P. Scott 276-376-1066 525 C pb8q@uvawise.edu
BEWSEY, Jeff 828-227-7322 379 E bewsey@wcu.edu
BEY, George, J 601-974-1385 275 D beygj@millsaps.edu
BEYAR, Renee 860-434-5232 93 A rbeyar@lymeacademy.edu
BEYDLER, Julie 970-542-3126 86 A julie.beydler@morgancc.edu
BEYER, Bryan 803-754-4100 457 D
BEYER, David 425-388-9573 533 H dbeyer@everettcc.edu
BEYER, Kirk, D 507-933-6075 264 B kbeyer@gustavus.edu
BEYER, Paul, N 443-997-5600 223 F pbeyer@jhu.edu
BEYER, Richard Allen 304-243-2233 545 G
BEYER-HERMSEN, Leslie 740-389-6786 399 D beyer-hermsen.1@osu.edu
BEYER HOUPT, Julia 740-587-6636 389 H houpt@denison.edu
BEYL, Caula 865-974-7303 477 B cbeyl@utk.edu
BEYL, Tracy 717-396-7833 440 J tbeyl@pcad.edu
BEYRER, Kim 916-558-2607 56 D beyrerk@scc.losrios.edu
BEYROUTY, Craig 970-491-6274 83 A craig.beyrouty@colostate.edu
BEZA, Mary 573-681-5561 284 B bezam@lincolnu.edu
BEZBATCHENKO, Ann, E 312-915-8902 157 A abezbat@luc.edu
BEZET, Jared 561-912-1211 106 G jbezet@evergladesuniversity.edu
BEZJIAN, Ilene 626-812-3085 30 E ibezjian@apu.edu
BEZOTTE, Christine 607-735-1852 333 A cbezotte@elmira.edu
BHADA, Farokh 401-232-6005 453 A fbhada@bryant.edu
BHAGAT, Heemanshu 626-571-8811 76 D heemanshub@uwest.edu
BHANDARI, Rohinton 415-955-2027 27 A mbhandari@alliant.edu
BHANDARI, Rupa 415-565-8909 73 G bhandari@uchastings.edu
BHARGAVA, Vivek 601-877-6450 273 C vivek@alcorn.edu
BHARUCHA, Jamshed 212-353-4240 331 B president@cooper.edu
BHASIN, Sheena, R 202-408-2400 99 D sheena.bhasin@strayer.edu
BHATIA, Tarun 415-955-2006 27 A tbhatia@alliant.edu
BHATTACHARYA, Somnath 561-297-3638 118 H sbhatt@fau.edu
BIA, Johnson 520-206-5001 17 I jbia@pima.edu
BIAFORA, Frank 727-873-4292 121 B fbiafora@mail.usf.edu
BIAGIOTTI, Eugene 610-647-4400 431 B ebiagiotti@immaculata.edu
BIALEK, Steve 414-277-7364 548 H bialek@msoe.edu
BIALK, Kathy 304-696-2281 543 G bialkk@marshall.edu
BIANCAMANO, John 860-679-1145 94 F jbiancamano@uchc.edu
BIANCAMANO, John, J 740-593-2626 399 G biancama@ohio.edu
BIANCHI, Amy, M 617-333-2236 234 A abianchi@curry.edu
BIANCHI, Ashley 901-843-3810 472 I bianchia@rhodes.edu
BIANCHI, Julius 805-493-3483 32 H bianchi@clunet.edu
BIANCHI, Mark 732-987-2678 310 D bianchim@georgian.edu
BIANCO, Amy 845-848-4065 332 C amy.bianco@dc.edu
BIASELLA, Tina 330-499-9600 393 I tbiasell@kent.edu
BIBB, Joy 214-459-2223 480 G jbibb@argosy.edu
BIBB, Shawn 408-924-1500 37 A shawn.bibb@sjsu.edu
BIBBENS, Matthew, G 909-607-8966 40 D matthew.bibbens@cmc.edu
BIBEAU, Shelley 651-846-1683 269 E shelley.bibeau@saintpaul.edu
BIBEAU, Susan 860-701-5000 93 B bibeau_s@mitchell.edu
BIBI, Khalid, W 716-888-8293 325 G bibi@canisius.edu
BIBLE, Doug 501-329-6872 21 C dbible@cbc.edu
BIBLE, J. Brice 740-597-3246 399 G bibleb@ohio.edu
BICAK, Charles, J 308-865-8209 300 G bicakc@unk.edu
BICE, Cynthia 636-949-4618 284 C cbice@lindenwood.edu
BICE, Diane, K 810-762-7491 253 I dbice@kettering.edu
BICE, JR., Gary, L 716-673-3341 352 A gary.bice@fredonia.edu
BICE, Patricia 914-251-6360 354 D patricia.bice@purchase.edu
BICHARA, Kamal 330-339-3391 394 B kbichara@kent.edu
BICKEL, Linda, S 573-681-5247 284 B bickell@lincolnu.edu
BICKEL, Sarah, L 928-523-6116 17 A sarah.bickel@nau.edu
BICKEL, Teri 301-846-2446 222 G tbickel@frederick.edu
BICKELL, Kris 203-576-4851 94 D ubonline@bridgeport.edu
BICKERS, Eugene, N 213-740-1114 76 C bickers@usc.edu
BICKFORD, David 480-557-1946 19 C david.bickford@phoenix.edu
BICKFORD, Deborah, J 937-229-2245 404 A deborah.bickford@notes.udayton.edu
BICKFORD, George 312-553-5896 146 H gbickford@ccc.edu
BICKFORD, Jeffrey 978-556-3745 241 B jbickford@necc.mass.edu
BICKFORD, Sonja 406-791-5389 296 H sbickford01@ugf.edu
BICKING, Michael, D 610-436-3478 443 F mbicking@wcupa.edu
BICKLEY, Carol, A 803-321-5124 459 G carol.bickley@newberry.edu
BICKNELL, Brian 617-423-4630 231 E bbicknell@bfit.edu
BICKSLER, Leslie 304-647-6279 544 C lbicksler@osteo.wvsom.edu
BIDDAR, Patricia, S 908-709-7509 316 B biddar@ucc.edu
BIDDINGS-MURO, Regina, D 219-989-2552 178 G reginab@purduecal.edu
BIDDISCOMBE, John, S 860-685-2895 95 C jbiddiscombe@wesleyan.edu
BIDDIX, David, K 828-765-7351 371 F dbiddix@mayland.edu
BIDDLE, Chris 615-226-3990 471 I cbiddle@nadcedu.com
BIDDY, Scott 510-642-7374 73 E fsb@berkeley.edu
BIDOGLIO, Ana 714-459-1106 78 C abidoglio@wsulaw.edu
BIDOSHI, Kristin, A 518-388-6234 358 E bidoshik@union.edu
BIDWELL, Lorena, L 269-471-6124 247 H lorena@andrews.edu
BIEBER, Ann, D 610-799-1581 434 D abieber@lccc.edu
BIEBER, Deborah 773-256-3000 158 A dbieber@meadville.edu
BIEBER, Kori 541-956-7196 420 B kbieber@roguecc.edu
BIEBIGHAUSER, Victor, K 334-395-8800 7 C vbiebighauser@southuniversity.edu
BIEBIGHAUSER, Victor, K 334-395-8800 136 H vbiebighauser@southuniversity.edu
BIEBUYCK, Bill 563-588-6405 183 B bill.biebuyck@clarke.edu
BIEBUYCK, Brent 586-445-7119 254 F Biebuyckb@macomb.edu
BIEGEL, Peter, J 904-632-3131 109 E pbiegel@fscj.edu
BIEGEN, M. Sharon 314-516-5711 291 F sharon_biegen@umsl.edu
BIEHN, Christopher, M 973-408-3997 309 F cbiehn@drew.edu
BIEL, Alan 814-732-2856 442 D abiel@edinboro.edu
BIELEC, John 215-895-1434 427 G jbielec@drexel.edu
BIELECKI, Donald, P 716-286-8679 344 D dpb@niagara.edu
BIELEN, Paul 707-524-1608 68 E pbielen@santarosa.edu
BIELER, Glenn, M 410-516-8631 223 F gbieler1@jhu.edu
BIELMAN, Jess 503-517-1140 421 A jbielman@warnerpacific.edu
BIELSKI, Bradley, A 859-344-3305 206 D bradley.bielski@thomasmore.edu
BIELSKI, Olen 413-572-8178 239 C obielski@wsc.ma.edu
BIENENFELD, Sheila 408-924-5300 37 A sheila.bienenfeld@sjsu.edu
BIENERT, Bonnie 847-628-2083 154 I bbienert@judsonu.edu
BIENFANG, Kim 763-433-1483 265 J kim.bienfang@anokaramsey.edu
BIENZ, Richard 260-399-7700 180 E rbienz@sf.edu
BIER, Alice, G 718-951-5189 326 G abier@brooklyn.cuny.edu
BIER, Debbie 412-521-6200 445 H debbie.bier@rosedaletech.org
BIER, Jill 815-825-2086 155 C jill.bier@kishwaukeecollege.edu
BIERBAUER, Charles 803-777-4105 462 A bierbauer@sc.edu
BIERBAUM, Rosina, M 734-764-2550 259 D rbierbau@umich.edu
BIERLICH, Sue 714-432-5562 41 B sbierlich@occ.cccd.edu
BIERMA, Lyle, D 616-957-6605 249 F lbierma@calvinseminary.edu
BIERMAN, Derik 402-844-7060 300 A derek@norteast.edu
BIERMAN, Scott 608-363-2201 546 B biermans@beloit.edu
BIERMANN, Mark 765-998-4734 179 F mlbiermann@taylor.edu
BIERMANN, Theodore 734-432-5515 254 G tbiermann@madonna.edu
BIERNACKI, Steve 505-566-3284 320 D biernackis@sanjuancollege.edu
BIERNBAUM, Dana 309-298-1800 168 A dm-biernbaum@wiu.edu
BIERYLA, John 570-389-4297 441 F jbieryla@bloomu.edu
BIES, James, B 605-274-4124 463 H jim.bies@augie.edu
BIESECKER, James 717-337-6700 429 H jbieseck@gettysburg.edu
BIETZ, Gordon 423-236-2801 473 A bietz@southern.edu
BIGARD, Heather 217-854-3231 145 F heather.bigard@blackburn.edu
BIGAS-GONZALEZ, Jenniffer 787-834-5151 565 B jbigas@email.pucpr.edu
BIGBY, Angela, D 702-968-2046 303 D abigby@roseman.edu
BIGELOW, Gary 704-216-3900 373 C gary.bigelow@rccc.edu
BIGELOW, Holly 507-280-3509 269 B holly.bigelow@roch.edu
BIGELOW, Scott 910-521-6351 379 B scott.bigelow@uncp.edu
BIGELOW, Susan 307-674-6446 556 C sbigelow@sheridan.edu
BIGGANE, Michael, J 716-851-1416 333 C biggane@ecc.edu
BIGGER, Kimberly 870-248-4000 21 A kim.bigger@blackrivertech.edu
BIGGER, Roberta, H 864-597-4040 463 F biggerrh@wofford.edu
BIGGERS, Carla, D 409-944-1200 486 H cbiggers@gc.edu
BIGGERS, Darlene 281-283-3000 503 C biggers@uhcl.edu
BIGGERS, Leisa 310-660-3593 45 D lbiggers@elcamino.edu
BIGGERSTAFF, Debra 814-827-4422 449 E biggers@pitt.edu
BIGGERSTAFF, Patrick 704-233-8247 380 D dpbigg@wingate.edu
BIGGIO, Nancy 205-726-4267 6 G ncbiggio@samford.edu
BIGGS, Becca 503-821-8892 419 D beca@pnca.edu
BIGGS, Bonnie 206-726-5045 532 G bbiggs@cornish.edu
BIGGS, Deborah, L 989-774-7547 249 G biggs1dl@cmich.edu
BIGGS, Jocelyn 336-517-2167 362 C jbiggs@bennett.edu
BIGGS, Karen 301-295-0962 558 A karen.biggs@usuhs.mil
BIGGS, Kristen 231-843-5875 260 E
BIGGS, Patsy 501-370-4002 19 F patsy.biggs@arkansasbaptist.edu
BIGGS, Sheila 260-480-4223 176 D sbiggs@ivytech.edu
BIGGS, Shirley, A 803-535-5268 456 D sbiggs@claflin.edu
BIGGS, Sue, A 325-670-1314 487 D sbiggs@hsutx.edu
BIGGS, Susan 802-447-6389 514 D sbiggs@svc.edu
BIGHAM, William, L 937-766-7810 386 F bbigham@cedarville.edu
BIGLEY, Karen 409-740-4830 497 D bigleyk@tamug.edu
BIGLIENI, Lindy 417-269-3401 281 B admissions@coxcollege.edu
BIGLIN, Edward 925-631-4433 64 F ebiglin@stmarys-ca.edu
BIGNALL, Douglas 313-883-8750 257 G bignall.douglas@shms.edu
BIGNEY, Tracy 207-973-3234 219 I bigney@maine.edu
BIHL, Andy 304-253-7351 541 D abihl@mountainstate.edu

BIHLMEYER, Earl, F ... 504-988-1930 ... 215 C ebihlme@tulane.edu
BIKLEN, Douglas, P ... 315-443-4751 ... 357 B dpbiklen@syr.edu
BILBRUCK, Tom ... 661-362-3235 ... 41 G tom.bilbruck@canyons.edu
BILDER, Kevin ... 480-517-8464 ... 16 C kevin.bilder@riosalado.edu
BILDERBACK, Rebecca ... 620-365-5116 ... 190 A bilderback@allencc.edu
BILELLA, Jamieson, A ... 973-655-4352 ... 311 G bilellaj@mail.montclair.edu
BILES, Deron ... 817-923-1921 ... 495 E dbiles@swbts.edu
BILES, Lantz ... 931-221-7786 ... 473 D bilesl@apsu.edu
BILGER, Cindy, L ... 570-577-1631 ... 423 D cbilger@bucknell.edu
BILGER, Jackie ... 570-321-4309 ... 435 D bilger@lycoming.edu
BILGIN, Deniz ... 831-242-5291 ... 557 C deniz.bilgin@monterey.army.mil
BILIONIS, Louis, D ... 513-556-0121 ... 403 D louis.bilionis@uc.edu
BILLARD, Edmund Thomas ... 623-572-3220 ... 16 F ebillard@midwestern.edu
BILLARD, Trisha ... 516-876-3053 ... 353 D billardt@oldwestbury.edu
BILLEAUDEAU, Kim, A ... 337-262-5300 ... 216 D kimberlyb@louisiana.edu
BILLEAUX, David ... 361-825-2393 ... 497 F david.billeaux@tamucc.edu
BILLECI, Celesta ... 805-893-3437 ... 74 F celesta.billeci@sa.ucsb.edu
BILLEN, Isabelle ... 405-733-7356 ... 411 I ibillen@rose.edu
BILLER, Gary, M ... 309-298-1814 ... 168 A gm-biller@wiu.edu
BILLESBACH, Thomas ... 660-562-1277 ... 287 E tombill@nwmissouri.edu
BILLHARTZ, Scott, L ... 618-537-6869 ... 157 G slbillhartz@mckendree.edu
BILLI, John, E ... 734-936-5214 ... 259 D jbilli@umich.edu
BILLIE, Marie, H ... 410-651-7502 ... 227 E mhbillie@umes.edu
BILLIG, Michael ... 717-291-4152 ... 429 E michael.billig@fandm.edu
BILLINGS, Amanda ... 812-330-6064 ... 175 H abillings7@ivytech.edu
BILLINGS, Bob ... 360-596-5353 ... 538 B bbillings@spscc.ctc.edu
BILLINGS, Chuck ... 415-485-3263 ... 45 B cbillings@dominican.edu
BILLINGS, Debra ... 810-766-4278 ... 248 C debra.billings@baker.edu
BILLINGS, Frank ... 516-572-8160 ... 342 C frank.billings@ncc.edu
BILLINGS, Patricia, L ... 206-934-6882 ... 537 B patricia.billings@seattlecolleges.edu
BILLINGSLEY, Anna, B ... 540-654-1056 ... 524 H abilling@umw.edu
BILLINGSLEY, Dale, B ... 502-852-5209 ... 207 A dbbill01@louisville.edu
BILLINGSLEY, Linda ... 318-487-7630 ... 209 B billingsley@lacollege.edu
BILLINGTON, Suzanne K, L ... 208-885-5867 ... 144 B suzib@uidaho.edu
BILLMAN, Cynthia ... 314-362-9191 ... 282 E cbillman@bjc.org
BILLS, Andy ... 336-841-4538 ... 365 A abills@highpoint.edu
BILLS, Joyce ... 918-465-1777 ... 408 A jbills@eosc.edu
BILLS, Linda, G ... 814-332-3362 ... 421 E linda.bills@allegheny.edu
BILLS-WINDT, Caryn, A ... 312-413-8145 ... 166 F cabw@uic.edu
BILLUPS, Vory ... 404-225-4474 ... 125 A vbillups@atlantatech.edu
BILLY, Anthony ... 505-863-7500 ... 321 D abilly@gallup.unm.edu
BILLY, Beth ... 251-809-1555 ... 5 B beth.billy@jdcc.edu
BILLY, George, J ... 516-773-5501 ... 558 F billyg@usmma.edu
BILMONT, John ... 415-241-2230 ... 39 H jbilmont@ccsf.edu
BILODEAU, Denise ... 978-232-2102 ... 234 F bilodeau@endicott.edu
BILODEAU, Gene ... 970-824-1103 ... 82 D gene.bilodeau@cncc.edu
BILODEAU, Ken ... 401-454-6371 ... 454 B kbilodea@risd.edu
BILOTTA, Barbara, J ... 716-880-2265 ... 340 E barbara.bilotta@medaille.edu
BILSKY, Steven ... 215-898-6121 ... 448 I athdir@pobox.upenn.edu
BILYEU, David, D ... 541-383-7563 ... 414 I dbilyeu@cocc.edu
BIMONTE-YERGANIAN, Maria ... 203-582-3446 ... 93 E maria.bimonte@quinnipiac.edu
BIMROSE, Irene ... 309-692-4092 ... 158 C ibimrose@midstate.edu
BINA, Shawn ... 218-235-2170 ... 270 A s.bina@vcc.edu
BINA, III, William, F ... 478-301-5570 ... 133 F bina_wf@mercer.edu
BINARD, Kris ... 970-204-8362 ... 84 H kris.binard@frontrange.edu
BINAU, Brad, A ... 614-235-4136 ... 402 G bbinau@TLSohio.edu
BINDER, George ... 985-867-2229 ... 214 F gbinderfinaid@sjasc.edu
BINDER, Jan ... 602-285-7869 ... 16 B jan.binder@pcmail.maricopa.edu
BINDER, Richard ... 602-216-3129 ... 11 F rbinder@argosy.edu
BINDER, Richard ... 770-671-1200 ... 81 A jbinder@argosy.edu
BINDER, Ronald, S ... 814-362-7630 ... 449 B binder@pitt.edu
BINDEWALD, Kurt ... 504-865-3226 ... 213 F kjbindew@loyno.edu
BINDSEIL, Kenneth ... 617-984-1643 ... 244 C kbindseil@quincycollege.edu
BINEK, Gordy ... 701-224-5697 ... 382 B gordon.binek@bismarckstate.edu
BINESH, Behzad ... 714-744-7099 ... 39 C binesh@chapman.edu
BINFORD, Gail ... 406-247-3000 ... 296 A gbinford@msubillings.edu
BING, Richard ... 212-998-2391 ... 344 B richard.bing@nyu.edu
BINGAMAN, Kristen ... 541-962-3512 ... 418 C kristen.bingaman@eou.edu
BINGAMON, Cindy ... 314-837-6777 ... 288 F cbingamon@slcconline.edu
BINGEL, Laurie, A ... 618-235-2700 ... 165 B laurie.bingel@swic.edu
BINGER, LeAnn, M ... 804-862-6247 ... 523 C lbinger@rbc.edu
BINGER, LeAnn, S ... 804-862-6247 ... 523 C lbinger@rbc.edu
BINGER, Nancy ... 847-628-2510 ... 154 I nbinger@judsonu.edu
BINGHAM, C. Sam ... 864-503-5073 ... 463 A sbingham@uscupstate.edu
BINGHAM, Charlotte ... 806-742-3627 ... 501 E charlotte.bingham@ttu.edu
BINGHAM, Charlotte ... 806-742-3627 ... 501 D charlotte.bingham@ttu.edu
BINGHAM, Daniel ... 406-444-6800 ... 295 C daniel.bingham@umhelena.edu
BINGHAM, James (Jim), L ... 913-588-4900 ... 197 A jbingham@kumc.edu
BINGHAM, Jean, M ... 312-567-5077 ... 153 B bingham@iit.edu
BINGHAM, Jeff ... 405-425-5152 ... 409 E jeff.bingham@oc.edu
BINGHAM, Nelson ... 765-983-1211 ... 171 B nelsonb@earlham.edu
BINGHAM, Nelson ... 765-983-1205 ... 171 B nelsonb@earlham.edu
BINGHAM, Rachel ... 801-524-8129 ... 510 A rbingham@ldsbc.edu
BINGHAM, Roger, B ... 812-374-5222 ... 175 J rbingham@ivytech.edu
BINGHAM, Rosie, P ... 901-678-2114 ... 474 C rbingham@memphis.edu
BINGHAM, Thomas, R ... 808-956-6460 ... 141 B bingham@hawaii.edu
BINION, Jim ... 940-552-6291 ... 507 E jbinion@vernoncollege.edu
BINK, Cynthia ... 718-260-5030 ... 328 E cbink@citytech.cuny.edu
BINKERD, James ... 707-638-5883 ... 72 H jim.binkerd@tu.edu
BINKLEY, Mark ... 662-325-0939 ... 276 A binkley@aoce.msstate.edu
BINKLEY, Yildiz, B ... 615-963-5212 ... 474 A ybinkley@tnstate.edu
BINKOWSKI, Marcella ... 215-637-7700 ... 430 H smbinkowski@holyfamily.edu
BINNEY, Craig ... 508-565-1107 ... 245 D cbinney@stonehill.edu
BINNICKER, Paul ... 816-833-0524 ... 184 H binnicke@graceland.edu
BINNICKER, Taul ... 816-833-0524 ... 282 F binnicke@graceland.edu
BINNS, Andrew, N ... 215-898-7225 ... 448 I provost-ed@upenn.edu
BINSFELD, Douglas ... 651-450-3370 ... 266 I dbinsfe@inverhills.edu
BINSTOCK, Alvin, G ... 701-483-2328 ... 381 E alvin.binstock@dickinsonstate.edu
BINSTOCK, Neal, F ... 412-397-6290 ... 445 G binstock@rmu.edu
BINTNER, Leslie ... 515-244-4221 ... 181 D bintnerl@aib.edu
BIO, Cathy ... 808-984-9277 ... 142 B cbio@hawaii.edu
BIONDI, SJ, Lawrence ... 314-977-7777 ... 289 F biondi@slu.edu
BIOTEAU, Cynthia, A ... 801-957-4226 ... 512 C cbioteau@slcc.edu
BIR, Chad ... 317-955-6040 ... 177 G cbir@marian.edu
BIRCH, Andrea, C ... 770-718-5325 ... 126 B abirch@brenau.edu
BIRCH, Barbara ... 212-960-5373 ... 361 I birch@yu.edu
BIRCH, Brian ... 801-863-8361 ... 511 C brian.birch@uvu.edu
BIRCH, Laura, A ... 217-420-6661 ... 158 F lbirch@millikin.edu
BIRCHAK, Chris ... 713-221-8007 ... 503 D birchakc@uhd.edu
BIRCHWOOD, Rachel ... 845-451-1459 ... 331 F r_birchw@culinary.edu
BIRCKBICHLER, Carrie, J ... 724-738-2150 ... 443 E carrie.birckbichler@sru.edu
BIRCKHEAD, Barry, D ... 678-915-4102 ... 137 C bbirckhe@spsu.edu
BIRD, Brandon ... 206-726-5024 ... 532 G bbird@cornish.edu
BIRD, Craig ... 210-924-4338 ... 481 G craig.bird@bua.edu
BIRD, Eric ... 617-879-7878 ... 238 E ebird@massart.edu
BIRD, Lee, E ... 405-744-5328 ... 410 C lee.bird@okstate.edu
BIRD, Lori ... 419-267-1266 ... 397 D lbird@northweststate.edu
BIRD, Lyly ... 909-537-7096 ... 36 A lbird@csusb.edu
BIRD, Margaret ... 406-338-5421 ... 293 F margie_bird@bfcc.org
BIRD, Nicole ... 909-868-4227 ... 44 J nbird@devry.edu
BIRD, Su Ann ... 229-931-2110 ... 136 G sbird@southgatech.edu
BIRD, SuAnn ... 229-931-2110 ... 136 G sbird@southgatech.edu
BIRD, Tammy ... 703-339-1850 ... 99 D tsb@strayer.edu
BIRD, Veronica ... 610-917-1422 ... 450 D rabird@vfcc.edu
BIRDINE, Phil ... 580-477-7700 ... 414 C phil.birdine@wosc.edu
BIRDSALL, Lynne ... 802-586-7711 ... 514 E lbirdsall@sterlingcollege.edu
BIRDSELL, David ... 646-660-6700 ... 326 D david_birdsell@baruch.cuny.edu
BIRDSONG, Jeff ... 918-540-6348 ... 408 J jbirdsong@neo.edu
BIRDSONG, Ronnie ... 575-562-4490 ... 318 A ronnie.birdsong@enmu.edu
BIRDSONG-MADDEX, Shelley ... 814-863-4308 ... 438 F sbm18@psu.edu
BIRDWELL, Cindy, A ... 517-264-7194 ... 258 D cbirdwell@sienaheights.edu
BIRDWELL, Mervin ... 318-487-5446 ... 210 C mbirdwell@ltc.edu
BIRDWHISTELL, Terry, P ... 859-257-1466 ... 206 H tlbird@uky.edu
BIRELINE, David ... 949-214-3209 ... 42 K david.bireline@cui.edu
BIREN, Susan, J ... 781-736-3451 ... 233 A birren@brandeis.edu
BIRGE, Benjamin ... 301-985-7682 ... 227 F bbirge@umuc.edu
BIRGE, James, F ... 603-899-4129 ... 305 B birgej@franklinpierce.edu
BIRGE, Susan, N ... 203-254-4000 ... 92 B sbirge@fairfield.edu
BIRGEN, Mariah, H ... 319-352-8565 ... 189 F mariah.birgen@wartburg.edu
BIRGEN, Mike ... 606-626-2681 ... 465 H Mike.Birgen@northern.edu
BIRGENEAU, Robert, J ... 510-642-7464 ... 73 E chancellor@berkeley.edu
BIRK, Michelle, L ... 618-235-2700 ... 165 B michelle.birk@swic.edu
BIRKE, Richard ... 503-370-6046 ... 421 C rbirke@willamette.edu
BIRKEDAHL, Patrice ... 510-659-6208 ... 59 I pbirkedahl@ohlone.edu
BIRKEDAHL, Walter ... 510-659-6216 ... 59 I wbirkedahl@ohlone.edu
BIRKENHOLTZ, Kenneth, I ... 515-961-1512 ... 188 F ken.birkenholtz@simpson.edu
BIRKEY, Robert, M ... 574-535-7403 ... 171 D bobmb@goshen.edu
BIRKHEAD, Clarence ... 704-337-2532 ... 375 G birkheadc@queens.edu
BIRKHEAD, Mary ... 610-282-1100 ... 426 I mary.birkhead@desales.edu
BIRKHOLZ, Amberleigh ... 708-209-3629 ... 148 C amberleigh.birkholz@cuchicago.edu
BIRKHOLZ, Jane ... 715-394-8306 ... 552 D jbirkhol@uwsuper.edu
BIRKNER, Linda, M ... 501-977-2006 ... 25 G birkner@uaccm.edu
BIRKS, Cynthia ... 404-527-4520 ... 126 F cbirks@carver.edu
BIRKS, Marvin ... 225-216-8244 ... 209 I birksm@mybrcc.edu
BIRKY, Ian, T ... 610-758-3880 ... 434 E itb0@lehigh.edu
BIRMINGHAM, John ... 630-353-9010 ... 149 A jbirmingham@devry.edu
BIRMINGHAM, Jolene ... 312-226-6294 ... 156 E jbirmingham@lexingtoncollege.edu
BIRMINGHAM, Stacy, G ... 724-458-3841 ... 430 B sgbirmingham@gcc.edu
BIRNBACH, David, J ... 305-284-2002 ... 122 F dbirnbach@miami.edu
BIRNBAUM, Ben ... 617-552-3353 ... 232 D ben.birnbaum@bu.edu
BIRNBAUM, David ... 510-987-9725 ... 74 F david.birnbaum@ucop.edu
BIRNBAUM, Roger ... 323-856-7600 ... 28 D
BIRO, Susan ... 410-386-8419 ... 221 G sbiro@carrollcc.edu
BIRON, Jackie ... 510-780-4500 ... 53 I jbiron00@lifewest.edu
BIRON, Louise ... 518-255-5532 ... 354 E bironl@cobleskill.edu
BIROS, Demetra ... 425-739-8315 ... 535 B demetra.biros@lwtc.edu
BIRRENKOTT, John ... 715-346-3838 ... 552 B jbirrenk@uwsp.edu
BIRRINGER, Charles, E ... 920-924-3420 ... 554 E cbirringer@morainepark.edu
BIRX, Donald, L ... 814-898-6160 ... 439 E dlb69@psu.edu
BISAHA, Andrew ... 619-275-4700 ... 46 K andrew182@aol.com
BISARYA, Alvin ... 312-553-2500 ... 146 G abisarya@ccc.edu
BISBEY, CDP, Michele ... 412-536-1255 ... 432 F michele.bisbey@laroche.edu
BISCH, Debbie ... 620-227-9209 ... 192 B debbieb@dc3.edu
BISCHOFF, Jeannette ... 916-660-7000 ... 69 F jbischoff@sierracollege.edu
BISCHOFF, Margaretha ... 956-872-8310 ... 494 D etybuh@southtexascollege.edu
BISCHOFF, Richard, W ... 216-368-5445 ... 386 E richard.bischoff@case.edu
BISCHOFF, William, D ... 316-978-6152 ... 197 F bill.bischoff@wichita.edu
BISCONTI, Ursula ... 941-694-1122 ... 307 G uhn@berkeleycollege.edu
BISCONTI, Ursula ... 914-694-1122 ... 323 J uhn@berkeleycollege.edu
BISESE, Stephen, D ... 804-289-8615 ... 525 A sbisese@richmond.edu
BISESI, Linda ... 415-565-4645 ... 73 G bisesil@uchastings.edu
BISH, Courtney, D ... 315-386-7513 ... 355 D bishc@canton.edu
BISH, Kevin ... 859-858-2272 ... 198 A
BISHARD, Althea ... 757-352-4047 ... 523 B althbis@regent.edu
BISHEL, Mary Ann ... 219-989-2510 ... 178 G bishelm@purduecal.edu
BISHIRJIAN, Richard, J ... 303-884-6777 ... 89 G rjb@yorktownuniversity.edu
BISHOP, Carol, M ... 607-746-4584 ... 355 E bishopcm@delhi.edu
BISHOP, Catherine ... 405-325-1701 ... 413 C cbishop@ou.edu
BISHOP, Catherine, F ... 405-325-1543 ... 413 D cbishop@ou.edu
BISHOP, Christine, C ... 850-729-4901 ... 114 A bishopc@nwfsc.edu
BISHOP, Christopher ... 970-675-3251 ... 82 D christopher.bishop@cncc.edu
BISHOP, Christopher ... 888-384-0849 ... 27 G cjbishop@allied.edu
BISHOP, David ... 806-785-9285 ... 508 B bishop@wbu.edu
BISHOP, Donald ... 574-631-7505 ... 180 D dbishop1@nd.edu
BISHOP, Eric ... 928-524-7400 ... 17 B eric.bishop@npc.edu
BISHOP, George ... 850-872-3803 ... 110 E gbishop@gulfcoast.edu
BISHOP, Ginger ... 828-328-7335 ... 366 B ginger.bishop@lr.edu
BISHOP, Indra ... 619-260-7898 ... 76 A ibishop@sandiego.edu
BISHOP, Jack ... 509-963-1945 ... 531 G bishopj@cwu.edu
BISHOP, Jeffrey ... 314-977-6663 ... 289 F
BISHOP, Jim ... 260-484-4400 ... 169 G jbishop@brownmackie.edu
BISHOP, Kelley, D ... 517-355-9510 ... 255 D bishopke@csp.msu.edu
BISHOP, Kristin ... 276-656-0315 ... 527 D
BISHOP, Kristy, A ... 816-604-1165 ... 285 D kristy.bishop@mcckc.edu
BISHOP, Lewis ... 540-986-1800 ... 521 J lbishop@national-college.edu
BISHOP, Lisa, J ... 812-888-4274 ... 181 B bishop@vinu.edu
BISHOP, Mary ... 305-593-1223 ... 102 D mbishop@albizu.edu
BISHOP, Mauri ... 202-885-8526 ... 100 A mbishop@wesleyseminary.edu
BISHOP, Nancy ... 803-778-6638 ... 455 G bishopnw@cctech.edu

BISHOP, Nathaniel, L .... 540-985-8484.... 520 D
nlbishop@carilionclinic.org
BISHOP, Patricia, J .... 407-823-6432.... 120 A
patricia.bishop@ucf.edu
BISHOP, Patty .... 925-631-4793.... 64 F
pbishop@stmarys-ca.edu
BISHOP, Paul .... 805-965-0581...... 68 B
pwbishop@sbcc.edu
BISHOP, Phil .... 206-876-6100.... 537 E
pbishop@theseattleschool.edu
BISHOP, Rex .... 706-754-7790.... 134 E
rbishop@northgatech.edu
BISHOP, Richard .... 860-832-2201...... 91 G
bishopr@ccsu.edu
BISHOP, Robert .... 414-288-6591.... 548 D
robert.bishop@marquette.edu
BISHOP, Sandy .... 715-365-4564.... 554 F
sbishop@nicoletcollege.edu
BISHOP, Shannon .... 828-694-1717.... 368 B
s_bishop@blueridge.edu
BISHOP, Steve .... 417-447-8802.... 287 G
bishops@otc.edu
BISHOP, Steve .... 417-447-8202.... 287 G
bishops@otc.edu
BISHOP, Steve .... 601-276-2000.... 277 E
bishop@smcc.edu
BISHOP, Terri .... 510-848-0177...... 19 C
terri.bishop@apollogrp.edu
BISHOP, Wesley, T .... 504-286-5325.... 214 I
wbishop@suno.edu
BISHOP, William .... 504-861-5431.... 213 F
wgbishop@loyno.edu
BISHOP, Wilsie, S .... 423-439-4811.... 473 E
bishopws@etsu.edu
BISHOP-CLARK, Cathy ...... 513-727-3200.... 396 F
BISHOP STUART, Aimee ... 419-251-1802.... 395 H
aimee.bishopstuart@mercycollege.edu
BISKUP, Susan .... 570-408-4355.... 451 G
susan.biskup@wilkes.edu
BISKUPIAK, Walter, H .... 406-447-5420.... 294 A
bbiskupi@carroll.edu
BISLEY, Deanna .... 800-567-2344.... 546 G
dbisley@menominee.edu
BISMARK, Jeanie .... 870-235-4078...... 23 I
mjbismark@saumag.edu
BISSELL, Michelle .... 304-204-4096.... 542 F
mbissell@kvctc.edu
BISSELL, Sally, B .... 419-783-2350.... 389 G
sbissell@defiance.edu
BISSELL, Sandra .... 315-781-3312.... 335 G
bissell@hws.edu
BISSELL PAULSON, Lisa .. 707-965-7362...... 60 J
lpaulson@puc.edu
BISSET, Matthew, S .... 727-864-8222.... 104 K
bissetms@eckerd.edu
BISSET, William, J .... 718-862-7200.... 339 H
william.bisset@manhattan.edu
BISSETTE, Callie .... 252-399-6336.... 362 A
cbissette@barton.edu
BISSETTE, S. Rex .... 252-246-1274.... 375 B
rbissette@wilsoncc.edu
BISSEY, Bret, S .... 973-972-8093.... 316 C
bisseybs@umdnj.edu
BISSONETTE, Bonita, S ..... 715-675-3331.... 554 G
bissonet@ntc.edu
BISWAS, Harun .... 678-466-4240.... 127 A
harunbiswas@clayton.edu
BITIKOFER, Scott .... 407-646-2121.... 116 B
sbitikofer@rollins.edu
BITNER, Hannah .... 816-322-0110.... 279 H
hannah.bitner@calvary.edu
BITNER, Teddy .... 816-322-0110.... 279 H
teddy.bitner@calvary.edu
BITTENBENDER, David .... 206-934-7792.... 536 H
david.bittenbender@seattlecolleges.edu
BITTERBAUM, Erik, J .... 607-753-2201.... 353 B
erik.bitterbaum@cortland.edu
BITTERSFELD, Y .... 718-692-0208.... 361 B
BITTINGER, Dale .... 410-455-2278.... 227 D
bittinger@umbc.edu
BITTLE, Carolyn .... 910-410-1751.... 372 G
carolynb@richmondcc.edu
BITTORF, David, C .... 301-790-2800.... 223 A
bittorfd@hagerstowncc.edu
BITZER, Steve .... 715-682-4591.... 555 E
Steve.Bitzer@witc.edu
BIVENS, Leon, J .... 410-651-6681.... 227 E
ljbivens@umes.edu
BIXBY, David, E .... 626-815-5334...... 30 E
dbixby@apu.edu
BIXBY, Harold .... 724-589-2130.... 448 A
hbixby@thiel.edu
BIXEL, Gil .... 850-484-1575.... 114 G
gbixel@pensacolastate.edu
BIXLER, Cindy .... 386-226-7959.... 105 B
cynthia.bixler@erau.edu
BIXLER, Donald .... 618-453-2411.... 164 I
ombuds@siu.edu
BIXLER, Kirk, J .... 317-738-8801.... 171 C
kbixler@franklincollege.edu
BIXLER, Sean .... 212-854-6030.... 323 G
sbixler@barnard.edu
BIZON, Walter, G .... 248-204-3020.... 254 E
wbizon@ltu.edu

BJELLAND, David .... 320-762-4407.... 265 I
davidb@alextech.edu
BJERKE, Jean .... 909-593-3511...... 75 C
jbjerke@laverne.edu
BJERKLIE, Joseph, R .... 207-834-8621.... 220 D
joseph.bjerklie@maine.edu
BJOKNE, Daniel, H .... 515-964-0601.... 184 G
bjokned@faith.edu
BJORGO, Lori .... 512-892-2835.... 478 I
BJORK, Ross .... 270-745-5276.... 207 C
ross.bjork@wku.edu
BJORKLUND, Robert, B .... 651-638-6396.... 261 I
robert-bjorklund@bethel.edu
BJORKMAN, David, J .... 801-581-6436.... 510 L
david.bjorkman@hsc.utah.edu
BJORKMAN, Karen .... 419-530-7842.... 404 F
karen.bjorkman@utoledo.edu
BJORN, Thorr, D .... 401-874-5245.... 454 E
tbjorn@mail.uri.edu
BJUR, Richard .... 775-784-4040.... 303 A
bjur@unr.edu
BLACK, Aaron .... 314-392-2292.... 286 C
blacka@mobap.edu
BLACK, Adam .... 801-863-6378.... 511 C
blackad@uvu.edu
BLACK, Angel .... 303-837-0825...... 81 B
ablack@aii.edu
BLACK, Barbara .... 573-681-5970.... 284 B
blackb@lincolnu.edu
BLACK, Bettye, R .... 405-466-3294.... 408 G
brblack@lunet.edu
BLACK, Britt .... 630-752-5072.... 168 F
britt.black@wheaton.edu
BLACK, Chesley .... 980-598-1050.... 365 G
chesley.black@jwu.edu
BLACK, Christopher, B .... 260-422-5561.... 172 L
cbblack@indianatech.edu
BLACK, David, R .... 610-341-5890.... 428 D
president@eastern.edu
BLACK, Dehavalyn .... 336-517-2264.... 362 C
dblack@bennett.edu
BLACK, Dennis, R .... 716-645-2982.... 351 G
dblack@buffalo.edu
BLACK, Diane .... 251-442-2209...... 9 B
dianeb@mail.umobile.edu
BLACK, Dorothy .... 731-352-4000.... 467 C
blackd@bethelu.edu
BLACK, Dwayne .... 972-686-7337.... 479 I
bigdbook@flash.net
BLACK, Eliza, E .... 803-934-3264.... 459 F
eblack@morris.edu
BLACK, Ellen .... 843-349-5211.... 458 G
ellen.black@hgtc.edu
BLACK, Heather .... 412-365-1281.... 425 B
hblack@chatham.edu
BLACK, Jane .... 740-695-9500.... 384 J
jblack@btc.edu
BLACK, Jason .... 205-726-3673...... 6 G
jjblack@samford.edu
BLACK, Jeff .... 410-263-2371.... 225 G
BLACK, Jennifer .... 314-744-7695.... 286 C
Blackjm@mobap.edu
BLACK, Jerry, D .... 937-775-2411.... 406 C
jerry.black@wright.edu
BLACK, John, B .... 478-289-2027.... 128 J
jblack@ega.edu
BLACK, John Paul .... 252-527-6223.... 371 D
jblack@lenoircc.edu
BLACK, Joshua .... 864-941-8540.... 460 D
black.j@ptc.edu
BLACK, Julie .... 479-394-7622...... 23 E
jblack@rmcc.edu
BLACK, Kedric .... 801-863-8536.... 511 C
kedric.black@uvu.edu
BLACK, Laurie .... 802-258-3273.... 514 C
laurie.black@worldlearning.org
BLACK, Lendley, C .... 218-726-7106.... 272 B
chan@d.umn.edu
BLACK, Lynda, K .... 336-838-6148.... 375 A
lynda.black@wilkescc.edu
BLACK, Lynn, C .... 308-398-7400.... 297 C
lblack@cccneb.edu
BLACK, Mark .... 615-966-5709.... 470 D
mark.black@lipscomb.edu
BLACK, Maryann .... 919-668-3792.... 363 I
maryann.black@duke.edu
BLACK, Michael .... 805-922-6966...... 26 K
mblack@pcpa.org
BLACK, Michael .... 404-894-2486.... 130 D
mike.black@housing.gatech.edu
BLACK, Michael, E .... 210-567-7103.... 506 E
blackm@uthscsa.edu
BLACK, Nanette .... 801-274-3280.... 512 E
nanette.black@wgu.edu
BLACK, Rochelle, A .... 248-370-3682.... 257 C
black@oakland.edu
BLACK, Rose Ann .... 718-779-1430.... 346 B
rblack@plazacollege.edu
BLACK, Shaun, C .... 315-445-4569.... 338 B
blacksc@lemoyne.edu
BLACK, Sul .... 803-705-4334.... 455 D
blacks@benedict.edu
BLACK, Tanja .... 864-429-8728.... 462 G
trblack@mailbox.sc.edu

BLACK, Thomas .... 650-723-1550...... 71 F
thomas.black@stanford.edu
BLACK, Timothy, R .... 541-346-5023.... 419 B
timblack@uoregon.edu
BLACK, Vicki .... 435-652-7718.... 512 A
vblack@dixie.edu
BLACK, Wilhemena .... 305-284-3064.... 122 F
wblack@miami.edu
BLACK, William, N .... 215-204-4760.... 447 G
william.black@temple.edu
BLACK-GOLD, Tonia .... 704-637-4393.... 363 C
tblackgo@catawba.edu
BLACKABY, Leslie .... 509-574-6806.... 540 A
lblackaby@yvcc.edu
BLACKARD, David .... 704-847-5600.... 376 H
dblackard@ses.edu
BLACKBOURN, Richard, L 662-325-3717.... 276 A
rlb277@msstate.edu
BLACKBURN, Alison, A .... 617-627-6272.... 245 F
alison.blackburn@tufts.edu
BLACKBURN, Anyssa .... 865-573-4517.... 469 J
ablackburn@johnsonU.edu
BLACKBURN, Bonita .... 580-559-5769.... 407 J
bblkburn@ecok.edu
BLACKBURN, Cheryl .... 425-388-9572.... 533 H
cblackburn@everettcc.edu
BLACKBURN, David .... 716-286-8405.... 344 D
deb@niagara.edu
BLACKBURN, David, T .... 270-809-2703.... 204 F
david.blackburn@murraystate.edu
BLACKBURN, J, R .... 740-753-7045.... 392 A
blackburn_j@hocking.edu
BLACKBURN, J. Blair .... 214-333-5122.... 484 C
blair@dbu.edu
BLACKBURN, James .... 315-279-5215.... 337 K
jblackbu@mail.keuka.edu
BLACKBURN, John, A .... 540-458-8651.... 530 A
blackburnj@wlu.edu
BLACKBURN, Judith, S .... 410-706-2949.... 227 C
jblackburn@umaryland.edu
BLACKBURN, Kellye .... 404-215-2703.... 134 A
kblackbu@morehouse.edu
BLACKBURN, Kristi, V .... 310-233-4021...... 54 I
blackbkv@lahc.edu
BLACKBURN, Peggy .... 336-917-5329.... 376 C
peggy.blackburn@salem.edu
BLACKBURN, Steven .... 860-509-9560...... 92 D
sblackburn@hartsem.edu
BLACKBURN, Vincent .... 410-951-3699.... 228 B
vblackburn@coppin.edu
BLACKER, James .... 540-374-4310...... 99 D
james.blacker@strayer.edu
BLACKER-BRUNO,
Shannon .... 215-641-5554.... 430 C
bruno.s@gmc.edu
BLACKFORD, Nate, J .... 660-541-5127.... 287 E
nate@nwmissouri.edu
BLACKHURST, Anne, E .... 218-477-2415.... 268 A
blackhurst@mnstate.edu
BLACKKETTER, Donald, M 406-496-4129.... 296 C
dblack@mtech.edu
BLACKKETTER, Donald, M 208-885-6470.... 144 B
dblack@uidaho.edu
BLACKLAW, Stuart .... 734-973-3488.... 260 B
sblacklaw@wccnet.edu
BLACKMAN, Don .... 954-446-6192.... 100 E
dblackman@aiufl.edu
BLACKMAN, Ronda .... 828-277-5521.... 376 F
rblackman@southcollegenc.edu
BLACKMER, Jean .... 508-373-9546.... 231 D
jean.blackmer@becker.edu
BLACKMON, Bruce .... 910-410-1723.... 372 G
bblackmon@richmondcc.edu
BLACKMON, Chianti .... 301-447-6932.... 225 A
blackmon@msmary.edu
BLACKMON, Luke .... 843-863-8004.... 456 B
lblackmon@csuniv.edu
BLACKMON, Lyn .... 843-383-8016.... 457 A
lblackmon@coker.edu
BLACKMON, Mark .... 765-983-1416.... 171 B
blackma@earlham.edu
BLACKMON, Terry, W .... 731-426-7601.... 469 M
tblackmon@lanecollege.edu
BLACKMON, Velma, B .... 252-335-3294.... 377 D
vbblackmon@mail.ecsu.edu
BLACKNEY, Kenneth .... 215-895-1505.... 427 G
ksb@drexel.edu
BLACKSHEAR, Amanda .... 770-960-1298.... 132 C
ablackshear@ict-ils.edu
BLACKSHEAR, Jim .... 505-863-7639.... 321 D
jblackshear@gallup.unm.edu
BLACKSHEAR, Regina .... 314-340-3502.... 282 I
blackshear@hssu.edu
BLACKSMITH, Lourdes .... 630-466-7900.... 167 G
lblacksmith@waubonsee.edu
BLACKSMITH, Robin .... 206-546-4503.... 537 G
rblacksmith@shoreline.edu
BLACKSTAD, Ana .... 425-352-8359.... 531 F
ablackstad@cascadia.edu
BLACKSTON, Barbara .... 931-221-6163.... 473 D
blackstonb@apsu.edu
BLACKSTON, Michael .... 559-438-4222...... 49 G
michael_blackston@heald.edu
BLACKSTONE, Tondelaya .... 410-951-4265.... 228 B
tblackstone@coppin.edu

BLACKWELDER, Mary, B ... 414-955-8323.... 548 E
blackwel@mcw.edu
BLACKWELL, Albert .... 843-525-8282.... 461 E
ablackwell@tcl.edu
BLACKWELL, Amy .... 864-294-3496.... 458 D
amy.blackwell@furman.edu
BLACKWELL, Ann .... 601-266-4568.... 278 A
ann.blackwell@usm.edu
BLACKWELL, Billie Jo .... 908-852-1400.... 308 F
blackwellb@centenarycollege.edu
BLACKWELL, Courtney ...... 212-799-5000.... 337 H
BLACKWELL, David .... 870-584-4471...... 25 C
dblackwell@cccua.edu
BLACKWELL, Deborah .... 704-355-5970.... 363 B
debbie.blackwell@carolinascollege.edu
BLACKWELL, Erik .... 757-499-7900.... 517 A
emblackwell@bryantstratton.edu
BLACKWELL, Jeannine .... 859-257-3629.... 206 H
jblack@uky.edu
BLACKWELL, Jennifer, D ... 410-546-6928.... 228 D
jdblackwell@salisbury.edu
BLACKWELL, John, N .... 785-827-5541.... 194 D
jblackwell@kwu.edu
BLACKWELL, Joyce, A .... 803-536-7180.... 460 G
jblackwe@scsu.edu
BLACKWELL, Mary, D .... 623-845-3305...... 15 J
m.blackwell@gcmail.maricopa.edu
BLACKWELL, Melanie .... 760-948-1947...... 66 I
melanie.blackwell@sjvc.edu
BLACKWELL, Michael .... 803-754-4100.... 457 D
BLACKWELL, Samuel .... 803-780-1239.... 463 B
blackwell@voorhees.edu
BLACKWELL, Scott .... 601-266-4783.... 278 A
edward.blackwell@usm.edu
BLACKWOOD, Clay .... 425-640-1233.... 533 E
clay.blackwood@edcc.edu
BLACKWOOD, James .... 706-880-8050.... 132 I
jblackwood@lagrange.edu
BLACKWOOD, Jothany, L .. 559-442-4600...... 72 A
jothany.blackwood@fresnocitycollege.edu
BLACKWOOD, Kathy .... 650-358-6790...... 67 D
blackwoodk@smccd.edu
BLACKWOOD, Phyllis .... 254-299-8659.... 490 E
pblackwood@mclennan.edu
BLACKWOOD, Rodney, B .. 806-720-7402.... 490 D
rod.blackwood@lcu.edu
BLAES, Ziuta .... 337-521-8896.... 212 B
ziuta.blaes@southlouisiana.edu
BLAESING, Ron .... 334-244-3758...... 2 A
rblaesin@aum.edu
BLAGG, Oneida .... 978-934-3565.... 237 F
oneida_blagg@uml.edu
BLAGG, Rosalyn, R .... 870-508-6128...... 20 E
rblagg@asumh.edu
BLAGUSZEWSKI,
Edward, F .... 413-545-0444.... 237 C
edblag@admin.umass.edu
BLAHNIK, Brent .... 920-465-2190.... 551 A
blahnikb@uwgb.edu
BLAHNIK, Sheryl .... 217-875-7200.... 162 D
sblahnik@richland.edu
BLAICH, Charles, F .... 765-361-6311.... 181 C
blaichc@wabash.edu
BLAIFEDER, Mark .... 212-217-4020.... 333 G
mark_blaifeder@fitnyc.edu
BLAIN, Judy .... 931-221-7691.... 473 D
blainj@apsu.edu
BLAINE, Louise .... 641-673-1038.... 189 I
blainel@wmpenn.edu
BLAINE-WALLACE,
William .... 207-786-8272.... 217 C
wblainew@bates.edu
BLAIR, Andrew, R .... 412-624-5749.... 449 A
blair@pitt.edu
BLAIR, Anothony, L .... 717-866-5775.... 428 I
ablair@evangelical.edu
BLAIR, Brian .... 202-885-2842...... 97 B
bblair@american.edu
BLAIR, Christine .... 903-693-2075.... 492 A
cblair@panola.edu
BLAIR, Cinnamon .... 505-277-1806.... 321 C
cblair@salud.unm.edu
BLAIR, Janice, L .... 818-767-0888...... 79 D
janice.blair@woodbury.edu
BLAIR, Jean .... 845-938-3615.... 558 G
Jean.Blair@usma.edu
BLAIR, Jeff .... 614-251-4735.... 398 F
blairj@ohiodominican.edu
BLAIR, Joffery .... 843-208-8118.... 462 C
jofferyb@mailbox.sc.edu
BLAIR, John, P .... 270-745-6520.... 207 C
jp.blair@wku.edu
BLAIR, Kimberly, P .... 540-365-4211.... 518 J
kblair@ferrum.edu
BLAIR, Larry .... 415-749-4560...... 65 I
lblair@sfai.edu
BLAIR, Linda .... 502-447-1000.... 206 A
lblair@spencerian.edu
BLAIR, Marilou, C .... 716-851-1411.... 333 C
blair@ecc.edu
BLAIR, Maureen .... 309-438-8611.... 153 C
meblair@ilstu.edu
BLAIR, Michael, R .... 563-387-1040.... 187 A
blairmic@luther.edu

BLEZIEN, Paul .... 916-577-2200...... 79 C
pblezien@jessup.edu
BLICE, Taylor, G .... 412-578-8712.... 424 G
blicetg@carlow.edu
BLICHARZ, Marcia .... 609-771-2848.... 308 G
blicharz@tcnj.edu
BLIESE, James, D .... 715-675-3331.... 554 G
bliese@ntc.edu
BLIESE, Richard .... 651-641-3211.... 264 J
rbliese@luthersem.edu
BLIFFEN, John .... 901-375-4400.... 471 E
johnbliffen@midsouthcc.org
BLIGEN, Erica .... 615-525-2800.... 466 I
ebligen@argosy.edu
BLIGH, Kate .... 206-878-3710.... 534 E
kbligh@highline.edu
BLILEY, Sean .... 814-732-2870.... 442 D
sbliley@edinboro.edu
BLIMLING, Gregory, S .... 848-932-8576.... 314 B
blimling@oldqueens.rutgers.edu
BLIND, Thomas .... 908-737-4835.... 311 B
tblind@kean.edu
BLINN, Robert .... 618-545-3244.... 155 A
rblinn@kaskaskia.edu
BLISS, Chris .... 415-703-9545...... 31 J
cbliss@cca.edu
BLISS, Emily, J .... 910-962-1112.... 379 C
blisse@uncw.edu
BLISS, Ethan, L .... 765-658-4268.... 170 I
ethanbliss@depauw.edu
BLISS, Frances .... 413-265-2314.... 233 E
blissf@elms.edu
BLISS, Lawrence .... 510-885-2139...... 34 C
lawrence.bliss@csueastbay.edu
BLISS, Michael, B .... 808-675-3705.... 139 I
blissm@byuh.edu
BLISS, Patricia, J .... 315-445-4141.... 338 B
blisspj@lemoyne.edu
BLISS, Robert .... 304-357-4865.... 541 H
robertbliss@ucwv.edu
BLISS, Robert, M .... 314-516-6874.... 291 F
rmbliss@umsl.edu
BLISS, Steve .... 912-525-5167.... 136 B
sbliss@scad.edu
BLISS-FURR, Carol .... 617-541-5394.... 241 D
cbliss@rcc.mass.edu
BLISSERT, Julie, H .... 315-312-2265.... 354 A
julie.blissert@oswego.edu
BLITT, William, J .... 972-377-1730.... 483 D
bblitt@collin.edu
BLITZ, Y .... 248-968-3360.... 261 A
BLITZER, Donna, M .... 831-459-3983...... 75 A
dblitzer@ucsc.edu
BLIVEN, Gail .... 651-690-6845.... 271 E
gnbliven@stkate.edu
BLIZINSKI, Robert .... 760-674-3777...... 41 H
rblizinski@collegeofthedesert.edu
BLIZZARD, Mary .... 304-558-4614.... 542 D
mblizzard@wvctcs.org
BLOCH, Ellin .... 626-284-2777...... 27 D
ebloch@alliant.edu
BLOCK, Beverly .... 417-625-9319.... 286 E
BLOCK, Gene, D .... 310-825-2151...... 74 A
chancellor@conet.ucla.edu
BLOCK, Jayme, E .... 410-543-6156.... 228 D
jeblock@salisbury.edu
BLOCK, Jeff .... 406-444-5560.... 295 C
jeff.block@umhelena.edu
BLOCK, Ken, W .... 419-772-2036.... 398 G
k-block@onu.edu
BLOCK, Kenneth .... 419-772-2008.... 398 G
k-block@onu.edu
BLOCK, Peggy .... 270-534-3464.... 203 B
peggy.block@kctcs.edu
BLOCK, Regina, M .... 815-740-5045.... 167 C
rblock@stfrancis.edu
BLOCKER, Peggy, J .... 303-765-3114...... 84 K
pblocker@iliff.edu
BLOCKER, Robert, L .... 203-432-4160...... 95 D
robert.blocker@yale.edu
BLOCKER, William, W .... 312-329-2082.... 158 H
bill.blocker@moody.edu
BLOCKSIDGE, Charles .... 412-350-1199.... 425 H
cblocksidge@ccac.edu
BLODGETT, Bruce, M .... 315-255-1743.... 325 H
blodgett@cayuga-cc.edu
BLODGETT, Martha Lee ..... 850-474-2712.... 121 C
mblodget@uwf.edu
BLODGETT, Patricia, A .... 603-358-2280.... 307 A
pblodget@keene.edu
BLODGETT, Steve .... 507-786-3316.... 271 H
blodgett@stolaf.edu
BLOECHLE, Michael .... 217-206-7757.... 167 A
bloechle.michael@uis.edu
BLOEM, Russell, J .... 616-526-6651.... 249 E
rjb42@calvin.edu
BLOEMENDAAL, Mark, R .. 712-707-7127.... 188 B
markb@nwciowa.edu
BLOEMENDAAL-GRUETT,
Joan .... 320-629-5116.... 268 G
gruettj@pinetech.edu
BLOEMKER, Geraldine, A .. 610-499-4107.... 451 F
gabloemker@widener.edu

BLOHM, Jason .... 402-941-6435.... 299 A
blohm@midlandu.edu
BLOHM, John, I .... 804-828-0880.... 525 E
jiblohm@vcu.edu
BLOHOWIAK, Shelly .... 847-578-8355.... 163 A
shelly.blohowiak@rosalindfranklin.edu
BLOK, Tamara, L .... 818-767-0888...... 79 D
tamara.blok@woodbury.edu
BLOMBERG, Thomas .... 850-644-7365.... 119 C
tgblomberg@aol.com
BLOME, Christian .... 812-888-4313.... 181 B
cblome@vinu.edu
BLOMGREN, Rebecca, F ..... 336-272-7102.... 364 D
blomgrenr@greensborocollege.edu
BLOMGREN, Richard .... 828-298-3325.... 380 C
rickb@warren-wilson.edu
BLOMQUIST, Eric .... 212-817-7150.... 327 B
eblomquist@gc.cuny.edu
BLOMQUIST, William, A ... 317-274-3976.... 174 B
blomquis@iupui.edu
BLONDE, Mitchell, P .... 517-264-7146.... 258 D
mblonde@sienaheights.edu
BLONDIN, Mark .... 401-739-5000.... 453 E
mblondin@neit.edu
BLONDIN, Monica, M .... 508-831-5469.... 247 B
mmlucey@wpi.edu
BLONIARZ, Peter .... 518-442-5115.... 351 E
pbloniarz@uamail.albany.edu
BLOOD, Janet .... 207-974-4606.... 218 H
jblood@emcc.edu
BLOOD, Rick .... 802-241-2541.... 515 B
rick.blood@vsc.edu
BLOOD, Timothy .... 510-574-1212...... 44 D
tblood@devry.edu
BLOODGOOD, Jane .... 785-587-2800.... 194 F
janebloodgood@matc.net
BLOODWORTH, JR.,
William, A .... 706-737-1440.... 125 C
wbloodwo@aug.edu
BLOOM, Bill .... 505-925-8595.... 321 G
wbloom@unm.edu
BLOOM, Joel .... 973-596-3000.... 312 C
BLOOM, Joel, S .... 973-596-6476.... 312 C
joel.s.bloom@njit.edu
BLOOM, John, S .... 214-841-3590.... 485 E
jbloom@dts.edu
BLOOM, Kathy .... 319-385-6209.... 186 A
kathy.bloom@iwc.edu
BLOOM, Richard .... 928-777-3837...... 14 D
richard.bloom@erau.edu
BLOOM, Steven .... 617-243-2440.... 236 F
sbloom@lasell.edu
BLOOM, Sue Ann .... 814-827-4472.... 449 E
sbloom@pitt.edu
BLOOM, Vicki .... 574-520-4448.... 174 C
vdbloom@iusb.edu
BLOOMBERG, Sandra .... 201-200-3321.... 312 B
sbloomberg@njcu.edu
BLOOMBERG, Steven .... 405-682-7814.... 409 F
smbloomberg@occc.edu
BLOOMER, Sherman, H ...... 541-737-4811.... 418 F
sherman.bloomer@oregonstate.edu
BLOOMFIELD, Susan, R .... 919-866-5452.... 374 E
srbloomfield@waketech.edu
BLOOMFIELD-MARTINEZ,
Amber .... 913-621-8733.... 192 C
amber@donnelly.edu
BLOOMINGDALE, Mary, E 641-422-4351.... 187 F
bloommar@niacc.edu
BLOSS, Kim, K .... 870-235-4055...... 23 I
kkbloss@saumag.edu
BLOSSER, Kim .... 540-234-9261.... 525 G
blosserk@brcc.edu
BLOUGH, David, K .... 251-460-6161........ 9 E
dblough@usouthal.edu
BLOUIN, Robert, A .... 919-966-1122.... 378 D
bob_blouin@unc.edu
BLOUNT, Brian, K .... 804-355-0671.... 524 F
bblount@upsem.edu
BLOUNT, Cameron .... 662-562-3354.... 276 E
cblount@northwestms.edu
BLOUNT, Joanna .... 574-936-8898.... 168 I
joanna.blount@ancilla.edu
BLOUNT, Nicole .... 404-880-8751.... 126 I
nblount@cau.edu
BLOUNT, Sally, E .... 847-491-2840.... 160 D
sallyblount@kellogg.northwestern.edu
BLOW, Trevor .... 954-783-7339.... 106 D
tblow@cci.edu
BLOWERS, Kelsy .... 218-683-8543.... 268 E
kelsy.blowers@northlandcollege.edu
BLOXOM, Donald, R .... 318-797-5360.... 213 D
dbloxom@lsus.edu
BLOYED, Carolyn .... 541-962-3519.... 418 C
cbloyed@eou.edu
BLOZOWSKY, Jason .... 570-454-6172.... 435 G
jason.blozowsky@mccann.edu
BLUBAUGH, Sharon .... 574-936-8898.... 168 I
sharon.blubaugh@ancilla.edu
BLUE, Debbie .... 405-878-2273.... 409 D
debbie.blue@okbu.edu
BLUE, Deborah, G .... 559-244-5901...... 71 I
deborah.blue@scccd.edu
BLUE, II, John, E .... 256-549-8607........ 3 J
jblue@gadsdenstate.edu

BLUE, Lynn .... 616-331-3327.... 252 A
bluel@gvsu.edu
BLUESTONE, Jeffrey, A ...... 415-476-4451...... 74 E
jeff.bluestone@ucsf.edu
BLUM, Brian .... 808-675-3378.... 139 I
blumb@byuh.edu
BLUM, Christopher .... 603-880-8308.... 306 C
cblum@thomasmorecollege.edu
BLUM, Robert .... 817-272-2771.... 505 A
rwblum@uta.edu
BLUM, Susan .... 631-444-8250.... 352 C
susan.blum@stonybrook.edu
BLUM, Thomas, L .... 914-395-2203.... 350 C
tblum@sarahlawrence.edu
BLUMBERG, Audrey, S .... 516-877-3159.... 322 A
blumberg@adelphi.edu
BLUMBERG, Bruce, K .... 803-938-3838.... 462 F
bruceb@uscsumter.edu
BLUMBERG, Elizabeth .... 781-239-2762.... 240 D
eblumberg@massbay.edu
BLUMBERG, James, J .... 734-384-4249.... 255 G
jblumberg@monroeccc.edu
BLUME, Jane .... 360-738-3105.... 531 C
jblume@btc.ctc.edu
BLUME, Steven, W .... 800-431-8488...... 29 A
sblume@aptc.edu
BLUME, Thomas .... 503-943-7371.... 420 G
blume@up.edu
BLUME, Travis .... 765-289-2291.... 175 K
tblume@ivytech.edu
BLUME, Wendy .... 856-227-7200.... 308 E
wblume@camdencc.edu
BLUMENFELD, Jessica ...... 563-763-2702.... 114 E
jessica.blumenfeld@palmer.edu
BLUMENSTEIN, Robert ...... 610-282-1100.... 426 I
robert.blumenstein@desales.edu
BLUMENTHAL, Bernard, G 215-951-1201.... 432 G
blumenth@lasalle.edu
BLUMENTHAL, George, R . 831-459-2058...... 75 A
chancellor@ucsc.edu
BLUMENTHAL, Jon .... 651-604-4101.... 265 D
BLUMENTHAL, Marjory, S 202-687-6400...... 98 A
blumentm@georgetown.edu
BLUMER, Lindsay .... 920-748-8316.... 549 I
blumerl@ripon.edu
BLUMHARDT, Jon .... 808-845-9125.... 141 G
jon@hcc.hawaii.edu
BLUMREICH, Jim .... 920-498-5701.... 555 A
jim.blumreich@nwtc.edu
BLUNDELL, Keith .... 361-582-2535.... 507 G
keith.blundell@victoriacollege.edu
BLUNT, Grace .... 508-767-7172.... 230 E
gblunt@assumption.edu
BLUNT, Lisa .... 406-874-6214.... 294 H
bluntl@milescc.edu
BLUST, Robert .... 414-288-7004.... 548 D
roby.blust@marquette.edu
BLUTREICH, Peter .... 336-750-3471.... 380 A
housing@wss.edu
BLY, Marie .... 603-752-1113.... 304 I
mbly@ccsnh.edu
BLYSKAL, Karen .... 732-255-0400.... 312 D
kblyskal@ocean.edu
BLYTHE, Earving, L .... 540-231-4227.... 529 B
blythe@vt.edu
BLYTHE, Gretchen, S .... 816-604-2251.... 285 G
gretchen.blythe@mcckc.edu
BLYTHE, Janett .... 270-534-3079.... 203 B
janett.blythe@kctcs.edu
BLYTHE, Tina .... 617-262-5000.... 232 B
tina.blythe@the-bac.edu
BLYTHE-SMITH, Karen .... 256-549-8357........ 3 J
ksmith@gadsdenstate.edu
BOADA, Maria .... 412-291-6247.... 422 D
mboada@aii.edu
BOAL, John, R .... 574-372-5100.... 171 E
boaljr@grace.edu
BOALS-GILBERT, Beverly .. 870-972-3052...... 20 C
bboals@astate.edu
BOARD, A. Jill .... 760-384-6212...... 52 N
jboard@cerrocoso.edu
BOARDLEY, Thomaice .... 301-860-3394.... 228 A
tboardley@bowiestate.edu
BOARDLEY SUBER,
Dianne .... 919-516-4200.... 376 B
dbsuber@st-aug.edu
BOARDMAN, Gregory, E .... 650-725-1808...... 71 F
gboardman@stanford.edu
BOAT, Thomas, F .... 513-558-7333.... 403 D
thomas.boat@uc.edu
BOATMUN, Tim .... 580-745-2370.... 412 C
tboatmun@se.edu
BOATRIGHT, Jeremiah .... 325-574-7943.... 508 F
jboatright@wtc.edu
BOATRIGHT-WELLS,
Sue Ella .... 276-523-7489.... 527 A
sboatright@me.vccs.edu
BOATWRIGHT, Betty, R ..... 803-536-8556.... 460 G
bboatwright@scsu.edu
BOATWRIGHT, Tamara ...... 678-359-5259.... 131 D
tamarab@gdn.edu
BOAZ, Matthew, L .... 513-529-7157.... 396 D
boazml@muohio.edu

BOB-PENNYPACKER,
Beaulah .... 928-524-7326...... 17 B
beaulah.bob-pennypacker@npc.edu
BOBAK, Karen, A .... 315-568-3864.... 342 H
kbobak@nycc.edu
BOBART, David .... 410-837-4331.... 229 A
dbobart@ubalt.edu
BOBB, June .... 718-997-5780.... 328 F
june.bobb@qc.cuny.edu
BOBBETT, Tricia .... 417-667-8181.... 280 I
tbobbett@cottey.edu
BOBBIN, Michael, J .... 904-256-7055.... 111 J
mbobbin@ju.edu
BOBBIN, Steffi .... 617-559-8640.... 235 I
sbobbin@hebrewcollege.edu
BOBBITT, David .... 951-571-6341...... 63 J
david.bobbitt@mvc.edu
BOBBITT, Donald, R .... 817-272-2103.... 505 A
dbobbitt@uta.edu
BOBBY, Kim .... 253-879-3991.... 538 E
kbobby@pugetsound.edu
BOBER, Delia .... 216-987-4402.... 389 A
delia.bober@tri-c.edu
BOBICH, Marni .... 909-607-8533...... 62 H
marni_bobich@pitzer.edu
BOBINSKI, Michael, A .... 513-745-3414.... 406 E
bobinski@xavier.edu
BOBINSKY, Steven .... 928-777-4210...... 14 D
steven.bobinsky@erau.edu
BOBO, David .... 205-853-1200........ 5 C
dbobo@jeffstateonline.com
BOBZIEN, Deana .... 309-854-1810.... 145 E
bobziend@bhc.edu
BOCAIN, David, F .... 951-827-2304...... 74 C
vpap@ucr.edu
BOCCHINFUSO-COHEN,
Rita .... 559-278-2381...... 34 D
ritab@csufresno.edu
BOCCHINO, Bud .... 713-798-2195.... 481 H
bocchino@bcm.edu
BOCCIA, Lenore .... 215-222-4200.... 445 F
lboccia@walnuthillcollege.edu
BOCIAN, Terry, M .... 616-632-2475.... 248 A
bociater@aquinas.edu
BOCK, Jim .... 610-328-8529.... 447 E
jbock1@swarthmore.edu
BOCK, Lisa, L .... 336-862-7986.... 372 F
llbock@randolph.edu
BOCK, Mike .... 260-665-4878.... 180 A
bockm@trine.edu
BOCKELMAN, Gary, R .... 513-487-3207.... 391 E
gbockelman@huc.edu
BODDY, Michael .... 314-252-3132.... 281 J
mboddy@eden.edu
BODE, Brian .... 913-288-7667.... 193 J
bbode@kckcc.edu
BODE, Lori .... 636-949-4925.... 284 C
lbode@lindenwood.edu
BODEN, Alison .... 609-258-6244.... 313 A
aboden@princeton.edu
BODEN, Janet .... 773-256-0744.... 157 B
jboden@lstc.edu
BODENBENDER, Laura .... 608-822-2315.... 555 B
BODIE, Cindy, H .... 336-882-3370.... 363 A
cbodie@ceds.edu
BODIE, Darryl, A .... 336-882-3370.... 363 A
dbodie@ceds.edu
BODIFORD, John, W .... 386-312-4041.... 116 D
waynebodiford@sjrstate.edu
BODIKER, Susan .... 202-274-5685...... 99 F
sbodiker@udc.edu
BODIN, Kate .... 503-297-5544.... 417 G
kbodin@ocac.edu
BODIN, Susan .... 804-627-5300.... 516 J
BODINE, Jordan .... 575-492-2143.... 321 H
jbodine@usw.edu
BODINER, Jeffrey .... 614-456-4600.... 393 B
jbodiner@teccollege.com
BODISON, Sacared, A .... 301-314-8091.... 227 B
sbodison@umd.edu
BODMAN, Andrew, R .... 909-537-5024...... 36 A
abodman@csusb.edu
BODNAR, Richard .... 718-997-5191.... 328 F
richard.bodnar@qc.edu
BODONI, June .... 978-867-4217.... 235 E
june.bodoni@gordon.edu
BODRATTI, Robert .... 518-828-4181.... 330 E
bodratti@sunycgcc.edu
BODRI, Michael .... 706-864-1958.... 134 D
msbodri@northgeorgia.edu
BODUR, Niyazi .... 516-686-7724.... 343 D
nbodur@nyit.edu
BODY, Dorothy, H .... 814-732-5555.... 442 D
dbody@edinboro.edu
BOE, Eugene .... 218-739-3375.... 264 K
eboe@lbs.edu
BOECKERMANN, Gabriele . 513-569-1550.... 387 F
gabriele.boeckermann@cincinnatistate.edu
BOEDEKER, Katrina .... 260-399-7700.... 180 E
kboedeker@sf.edu
BOEDER, John, C .... 507-354-8221.... 265 B
boederjc@mlc-wels.edu
BOEGEL, Tom .... 415-239-3360...... 39 H
tboegel@ccsf.edu

BOEH, Scott 405-271-2359 413 D scott-boeh@ouhsc.edu
BOEH, Thomas 559-244-5641 34 D tboeh@csufresno.edu
BOEHLER, Ted 714-241-6213 40 J tboehler@coastline.edu
BOEHLER, Ted 714-241-6143 40 J tboehler@coastline.edu
BOEHLER, Ted 714-241-6209 40 J tboehler@coastlin.edu
BOEHM, Beth, A 502-852-3975 207 A baboeh01@louisville.edu
BOEHM, Christopher 205-552-1222 3 B chris.boehm@ecacolleges.com
BOEHM, Christopher, H 610-921-7700 421 D cboehm@alb.edu
BOEHM, JR., Edward, G 570-945-8500 432 C edward.boehm@keystone.edu
BOEHM, J, J 989-964-4055 258 A jjboehm@svsu.edu
BOEHM, Michael 937-769-1795 383 J
BOEHM, Michael, J 614-292-5881 398 H boehm.1@osu.edu
BOEHMAN, Joseph, R 804-289-8000 525 A jboehman@richmond.edu
BOEHME, Michael, J 320-234-8509 268 I mike.boehme@ridgewater.edu
BOEHMER, Robert, G 706-542-2558 138 C bboehmer@uga.edu
BOEHNE, Cheryl 618-545-3184 155 A cboehne@kaskaskia.edu
BOEHNE, Rhonda 618-545-3022 155 A rboehne@kaskaskia.edu
BOEHNINGER, Candice 740-593-4100 399 G
BOEHNKE, Barbara 716-888-2937 325 G boehnkeb@canisius.edu
BOEKER, Cathy 979-830-4455 482 A cboeker@blinn.edu
BOELE, Erin 599-278-2345 34 D eboele@csufresno.edu
BOELK, Nicole 989-729-3435 249 A nicole.boelk@baker.edu
BOENKER, Norma 260-399-7700 180 E nboenker@sf.edu
BOER, Larry 708-239-4608 165 I larry.boer@trnty.edu
BOERGER, Leah 859-371-9393 198 D lboerger@beckfield.edu
BOERGERMANN, Gary 918-343-7625 411 H gboergermann@rsu.edu
BOERNER, Anne 503-297-5544 417 G aboerner@ocac.edu
BOERSIG, Pam 612-332-3361 261 F pboersig@aii.edu
BOERSMA, Paul, H 616-395-7145 252 F boersma@hope.edu
BOERST, Connie, J 920-433-6622 546 A connie.boerst@bellincollege.edu
BOESCH, Donald, F 410-221-2001 227 A boesch@umces.edu
BOESDORFER, Nancy, A 217-443-8856 148 E nboes@dacc.edu
BOETSCH, Larry 540-458-8145 530 A lboetsch@wlu.edu
BOETTCHER, Marlene, F 719-384-6824 86 F marlene.boettcher@ojc.edu
BOETTGER, Jennifer 319-895-4153 183 D jboettger@cornellcollege.edu
BOEZAART, Arn 616-331-6905 252 A boezaara@gvsu.edu
BOGAGE, Alan 410-386-8339 221 G abogage@carrollcc.edu
BOGAN, Gerri 706-821-8262 135 C gbogan@paine.edu
BOGAN, Ivory 601-984-1400 277 H bogan@umc.edu
BOGAN, Jeffrey, S 706-864-7999 134 D jboggan@northgeorgia.edu
BOGAN, Jeremy 518-454-5155 330 C boganj@strose.edu
BOGAN, Kim 619-849-2481 62 L kimbogan@pointloma.edu
BOGAN, Yolanda 850-599-3145 118 G yolanda.bogan@famu.edu
BOGART, Denise 229-333-5709 138 F dbogart@valdosta.edu
BOGART, Marti, S 630-637-5355 159 F msbogart@noctrl.edu
BOGART, William, T 865-981-8101 470 F tom.bogart@maryvillecollege.edu
BOGDAN, Sharon 410-532-5332 225 D sbogdan@ndm.edu
BOGDANOVICH, Holly 562-860-2451 38 J hbogdanovich@cerritos.edu
BOGDON, Leonard 973-720-2303 317 D bogdonl@wpunj.edu
BOGDONOFF, Malinda 530-741-6700 80 C
BOGEN, Janice, M 215-503-4335 448 B janice.bogen@jefferson.edu
BOGENSCHILD, Thomas 505-277-4032 321 C tbogen@unm.edu
BOGER, John, C 919-962-4417 378 D jcboger@email.unc.edu
BOGER-HAWKINS, Caitlin 860-738-6441 90 F cboger-hawkins@nwcc.commnet.edu
BOGERT, Brian 570-408-4015 451 G brian.bogert@wilkes.edu
BOGGAN, Laura, K 423-652-4707 469 L lkboggan@king.edu
BOGGER, Tommy 757-823-2004 521 K tlbogger@nsu.edu
BOGGESS, Kendra 304-384-5243 543 D kendra@concord.edu
BOGGIE, Mark 520-515-5451 13 G boggiem@cochise.edu
BOGGIO, P, J 508-213-2483 243 J pamela.boggio@nichols.edu
BOGGS, Allan 937-775-3224 406 C allan.boggs@wright.edu
BOGGS, Beverly 931-221-6540 473 D boggsb@apsu.edu
BOGGS, Bonnie, B 734-384-4268 255 G bboggs@monroeccc.edu
BOGGS, Doyle, W 864-597-4182 463 F boggsdw@wofford.edu
BOGGS, Emily 740-774-6300 389 C eboggs@daymarcollege.edu
BOGGS, Gretchen, M 410-250-1088 227 E contedoc@ezy.net
BOGGS, Jill 260-665-4122 180 A boggsj@trine.edu
BOGGS, John 281-998-6150 493 G john.boggs@sjcd.edu
BOGGS, Keith 303-404-5155 84 H keith.boggs@frontrange.edu
BOGGS, Larry 662-862-8252 274 G laboggs@iccms.edu
BOGGS, Paul, R 903-233-3981 489 K paulboggs@letu.edu
BOGGS, Rainie 859-253-3637 200 E rainie.boggs@frontier.edu
BOGGS, Tex 310-578-1080 28 K tboggs1@antioch.edu
BOGH, Wayne 909-389-3309 65 B wbogh@craftonhills.edu
BOGHOSIAN, Brue 510-987-9452 28 G
BOGLE, Barry, J 915-831-7116 486 E bbogle@epcc.edu
BOGLE, Darcy 661-763-7889 72 C dbogle@taftcollege.edu
BOGLE, Yvonne 413-782-1594 246 D ybogle@wne.edu
BOGLEY, John, W 509-527-5979 539 E bogleyj@whitman.edu
BOGNER, Drew 516-678-5000 341 F dbogner@molloy.edu
BOGOMILSKY, Moshe 718-434-0784 325 J
BOGOMOLNY, Robert, L 410-837-4866 229 A rbogomolny@ubalt.edu
BOGORAD, Deborah 845-434-5750 356 H dbogorad@sullivan.suny.edu
BOGRIS, Claudia 973-655-3291 311 G bogrisc@mail.montclair.edu
BOGUSLAWSKI, OP, Steven 202-495-3831 98 D president@dhs.edu
BOHACH, Gregory 662-325-3006 276 A gbohach@dafvm.msstate.edu
BOHACZ, Candy 269-467-9945 251 D cbohacz@glenoaks.edu
BOHAKER, Linda, A 618-374-5495 161 D linda.bohaker@principia.edu
BOHAM, Kenneth, A 828-726-2211 368 D kboham@cccti.edu
BOHAN, Ken 562-907-4261 79 B kbohan@whittier.edu
BOHANNON, Betsy 859-622-1500 200 D betsy.bohannon@eku.edu
BOHANON, Janet 770-531-6315 132 J jbohanon@laniertech.edu
BOHASKA, Chris 410-225-2490 224 C cbohaska@mica.edu
BOHEN, Mark 215-335-0800 434 G mbohen@lincolntech.com
BOHLAND, James 703-518-2700 529 B jayjon@vt.edu
BOHLANDER, Brad 970-491-6621 82 I brad.bohlander@colostate.edu
BOHLEKE, Briant 717-334-6286 435 A bbohleke@ltsg.edu
BOHLEKE, Chuck 434-961-5348 527 F cbohleke@pvcc.edu
BOHLEN, Jan 248-340-0600 248 E jan.bohlen@baker.edu
BOHLMAN, Bonnie, G 701-483-2370 381 E bonnie.bohlman@dickinsonstate.edu
BOHN, Bill 541-506-6090 415 C bbohn@cgcc.cc.or.us
BOHN, Michael, R 303-492-7930 88 B mike.bohn@colorado.edu
BOHNEN, Evan 740-376-4446 395 F evan.bohnen@marietta.edu
BOHNENBLUST, Delyna 620-421-6700 194 E delynab@labette.edu
BOHNET, Sandra 269-488-4409 253 G sbohnet@kvcc.edu
BOHNETT, Sally 419-251-8985 395 H sally.bohnett@mercycollege.edu
BOHNY, David 973-618-3440 308 D dbohny@caldwell.edu
BOHREN, Karen 231-591-2607 251 B bksferrisstate@bncollege.com
BOICE, Daniel 563-876-3353 183 G dboice@dwci.edu
BOIES, Brandy 540-868-7161 526 H bboies@lfcc.edu
BOIES, Chris 540-868-7129 526 H cboies@lfcc.edu
BOILINI, Laura, L 386-312-4199 116 D lauraboilini@sjrstate.edu
BOISE, Craig 216-687-2300 388 C c.boise@law.csuohio.edu
BOISEN, Beth 715-232-1695 552 C boisenb@uwstout.edu
BOISJOLY, Russell, P 716-673-4813 352 A russell.boisjoly@fredonia.edu
BOISSELLE, Dave 757-352-4757 523 B daviboi@regent.edu
BOISSELLE, Vincent 315-781-3549 335 G boisselle@hws.edu
BOISSONEAULT, Susan 508-678-2811 239 F susan.boissoneault@bristolcc.edu
BOISVERT, David 603-897-8502 305 G dboisvert@rivier.edu
BOITNOTT, Tina 903-886-5110 497 E tina_boitnott@tamu-commerce.edu
BOITOS, Linda, R 928-541-7777 16 I lboitos@ncu.edu
BOJAR, Anthea, L 414-410-4006 546 D albojar@stritch.edu
BOKOWSKI, Debrah 503-675-3961 416 I dbokowski@marylhurst.edu
BOKSAN, George 610-861-1421 436 I megjb01@moravian.edu
BOKTOR, Monir 949-794-9090 71 E mboktor@stanbridge.edu
BOLA, William 207-206-2365 220 H wbola@une.edu
BOLA, William 207-602-2365 220 H wbola@une.edu
BOLAND, Carolyn 513-244-4717 388 D carolyn_boland@mail.msj.edu
BOLAND, Catherine 928-350-4001 18 C cboland@prescott.edu
BOLAND, Jean, L 315-684-6036 354 F bolandjl@morrisville.edu
BOLAND, Kristine 419-783-2469 389 G kboland@defiance.edu
BOLAND, Mary, G 808-956-8522 141 B mgboland@hawaii.edu
BOLAND, Mary Kate 610-647-4400 431 B mboland@immaculata.edu
BOLAND, Patrick, O 203-857-7032 90 G pboland@ncc.commnet.edu
BOLAND-CHASE, Ann 590-961-4728 435 F chase@marywood.edu
BOLAR, Gretchen, S 951-827-7312 74 C gretchen.bolar@ucr.edu
BOLD, Jessica 770-938-4711 133 A
BOLDEN, John 313-496-2536 260 C jbolden1@wcccd.edu
BOLDER, Catherine, M 973-972-4855 316 C bolder@umdnj.edu
BOLDREY, Penny 989-358-7297 247 G boldreyp@alpenacc.edu
BOLDT, Amy 505-254-7575 320 G
BOLDT, Deborah 505-428-1704 320 E deborah.boldt@sfcc.edu
BOLDT, William 702-895-5895 302 K william.boldt@unlv.edu
BOLDUC, Darlene, R 802-626-6490 515 F darlene.bolduc@lyndonstate.edu
BOLDUC, Michael, C 561-237-7180 113 D mbolduc@lynn.edu
BOLEK, Catherine 410-651-6714 227 E csbolek@umes.edu
BOLEMAN, Roger, P 320-589-6150 272 C bolemarp@morris.umn.edu
BOLEN, III, Robert 304-253-7351 541 D bobbolen@mountainstate.edu
BOLENDER, James, P 619-260-4792 76 A bolender@sandiego.edu
BOLENDER, Melanie 740-366-1351 386 G
BOLES, Jessica, A 918-540-6217 408 J jboles@neo.edu
BOLEY, Paula 765-289-2291 175 K pboley@ivytech.edu
BOLEY, Stacie 318-798-6868 208 B
BOLGER, Eric 417-690-2278 280 C bolger@cofo.edu
BOLHOUSE, Lana 405-878-2081 409 D lana.bolhouse@okbu.edu
BOLICK-FLOSS, Annie 707-826-3341 36 D amb2@humboldt.edu
BOLIG, Kimberly, L 570-326-3761 440 K kbolig@pct.edu
BOLIN, Alexis 408-848-4742 48 B 0282mgr@fheg.follett.com
BOLIN, Lisa 615-327-3927 469 I bolin@guptoncollege.edu
BOLIN-REECE, Mary, C 859-257-8701 206 H mcreec01@uky.edu
BOLING, Charles 276-739-2514 528 D cboling@vhcc.edu
BOLING, Cindy 405-974-3342 413 B cboling@ucok.edu
BOLING, Gena 573-876-7106 290 G gboling@stephens.edu
BOLL, Jackie 714-992-7040 59 D jboll@fullcoll.edu
BOLL, John 614-251-4567 398 F bollj@ohiodominican.edu
BOLL, Julie 217-228-5432 161 E bollju@quincy.edu
BOLLARD, Kathleen 303-860-5600 88 A Kathleen.Bollard@cu.edu
BOLLE, Brian, E 636-797-3000 283 H bbolle@jeffco.edu
BOLLEN, Kathryn, A 585-785-1228 334 A bollenka@flcc.edu
BOLLENBACH, Evelyn 405-945-3317 410 F
BOLLENBAUGH, Mick 541-684-7345 417 F mbbaugh@northwestchristian.edu
BOLLERER, Fred 202-639-1736 97 D fbollerer@corcoran.org
BOLLIER, John, H 203-432-6754 95 D john.bollier@yale.edu
BOLLING, Phyllis 973-596-3420 312 C phyllis.bolling@njit.edu
BOLLING-CLAY, Sharon 770-394-8300 124 F dbolling@aii.edu
BOLLINGER, Brian 316-295-5568 192 H bollinger@friends.edu
BOLLINGER, Bruce 701-231-6177 381 H bruce.bollinger@ndsu.edu
BOLLINGER, Gary 402-486-2502 300 D gabollin@ucollege.edu
BOLLINGER, Lee, C 212-854-9970 330 F bollinger@columbia.edu
BOLLINGER, Mary 603-888-1311 305 G mbollinger@rivier.edu
BOLLINGER, Richard 903-223-3068 498 C rbolinger@tamut.edu
BOLLINGER, Robert, D 218-755-4147 266 B rbollinger@bemidjistate.edu
BOLLMAN, Lois 612-659-6305 267 E lois.bollman@minneapolis.edu
BOLLMAN-DALANSKY, Terri, L 814-641-3424 431 L bollmat@juniata.edu
BOLLMANN, Janice, A 314-286-4805 288 B jabollmann@ranken.edu
BOLMAN, Dave 602-383-8228 19 A dbolman@uat.edu
BOLMIDA, Peter 937-512-3028 401 J peter.bolmida@sinclair.edu
BOLOWSKI, Mary 201-200-3041 312 B
BOLSINGER, Judith, A 412-578-6027 424 G bolsingerja@carlow.edu
BOLSTER, Jeff 619-849-2480 62 L jeffbolster@pointloma.edu
BOLSTER, Sharon 480-203-7258 11 C
BOLSTRIDGE, Ronald 207-755-5246 218 G rbolstr@cmcc.edu
BOLT, Barb 814-868-9900 428 H barbb@erieit.edu
BOLT, Carolyn 212-517-0454 340 D cbolt@mmm.edu
BOLT, Dave 559-925-3222 77 J davebolt@whccd.edu
BOLT, Gita 504-861-2657 213 F gbolt@loyno.edu
BOLT, Susan, K 810-762-9787 253 I sbolt@kettering.edu
BOLT, Tracy, L 443-334-2270 226 E tbolt@stevenson.edu
BOLTE, Jenny, L 540-674-3652 527 B jbolte@nr.edu
BOLTE, Michael 831-459-2991 75 A bolte@ucolick.org
BOLTON, Cathy 940-552-6291 507 E cbolton@vernoncollege.edu
BOLTON, David 417-328-1538 290 E dbolton@sbuniv.edu
BOLTON, Glenn Allen 414-955-8704 548 E abolton@mcw.edu
BOLTON, Harry 707-654-1192 32 I hbolton@csum.edu
BOLTON, Lance 719-502-2200 86 G lance.bolton@ppcc.edu
BOLTON, Lance 970-521-6607 86 E lance.bolton@njc.edu
BOLTON, Melenie 256-378-2047 2 F mbolton@cacc.edu
BOLTON, Sarah, R 413-597-4171 246 G sarah.r.bolton@williams.edu
BOLTON, Stanley 803-822-3523 459 D boltons@midlandstech.edu
BOLTON, Tama 831-477-3548 31 F tabolton@cabrillo.edu
BOLTON, Tonya, D 870-759-4130 26 B tbolton@wbcoll.edu
BOLYAI, Stephen 973-720-2233 317 D bolyais@wpunj.edu

BOLYARD, Adrienne, M ..... 206-726-5021.... 532 G
abolyard@cornish.edu

BOLYARD, Brian, R .... 304-442-1062.... 545 C
brian.bolyard@mail.wvu.edu

BOMAN, Margaret .... 717-948-6424.... 439 I
myb9@psu.edu

BOMAN, Victoria .... 205-247-8837........ 7 G
vbowen@stillman.edu

BOMBA, Jody, L .... 909-593-3511...... 75 C
jbomba@laverne.edu

BOMBARDIER, Patricia ..... 413-265-2281.... 233 E
bombardierp@elms.edu

BOMBERGER, Sherry .... 717-757-1100.... 452 I
sherry.bomberger@yti.edu

BOMMERSBACH, Mimi, L . 530-898-6345...... 34 A
mbommersbach@csuchico.edu

BOMOTTI, Gerry .... 702-895-3571.... 302 K
gerry.bomotti@unlv.edu

BONA, Dennis .... 269-965-3931.... 253 H
bonad@kellogg.edu

BONA, Mike .... 706-245-7226.... 128 K
mbona@ec.edu

BONACCI, Andrew .... 413-572-5394.... 239 C
abonacci@wsc.ma.edu

BONACIC, Patricia .... 310-900-1600...... 45 E
bonacic_v@compton.edu

BONAGURA, Giancarlo ...... 212-772-4475.... 327 E
bonagura@hunter.cuny.edu

BONAGURO, John, A .... 270-745-7003.... 207 C
john.bonaguro@wku.edu

BONAHUE, Edward .... 352-395-5843.... 117 E
ed.bohahue@sfcollege.edu

BONANDO, John, S .... 724-738-2728.... 443 E
john.bonando@sru.edu

BONANNO, Barbara .... 726-926-8924.... 335 F
bbonnano@hilbert.edu

BONANNO, Janice, M .... 617-228-2436.... 239 G
jbonanno@bhcc.mass.edu

BONANNO, Joseph .... 812-855-4440.... 173 C
jbonanno@indiana.edu

BONANO, Anthony .... 718-260-3915.... 346 C
abonano@poly.edu

BONAPARTE, Donna .... 781-239-6434.... 230 G
dbonaparte@babson.edu

BONAPARTE, Wallace, T ... 843-792-1568.... 459 C
bonaparw@musc.edu

BONAUDI, William, C .... 509-793-2001.... 531 D
billb@bigbend.edu

BONCUORE, Cheryl .... 312-752-2646.... 155 B
cheryl..boncuore@kendall.edu

BOND, Bill, E .... 406-756-3818.... 294 D
bbond@fvcc.edu

BOND, Bradley .... 815-753-9403.... 160 A
bbond@niu.edu

BOND, Byron, D .... 734-487-0427.... 250 H
byron.bond@emich.edu

BOND, Cheryl .... 601-928-6213.... 275 G
cheryl.bond@mgccc.edu

BOND, Cindy, R .... 208-732-6454.... 143 B
cbond@csi.edu

BOND, Emma .... 601-426-6346.... 277 D
ebond@southeasternbaptist.edu

BOND, Inge .... 408-741-2166...... 78 B
inge.bond@westvalley.edu

BOND, Jan .... 561-297-3025.... 118 H
jbond@fau.edu

BOND, Kathy, E .... 337-475-5613.... 215 G
kbond@mcneese.edu

BOND, Lavell .... 601-528-8424.... 275 G
lavell.bond@mgccc.edu

BOND, Martha .... 315-781-3780.... 335 G
mbond@hws.edu

BOND, Meredith, R .... 216-687-9321.... 388 C
m.bond40@csuohio.edu

BOND, Peter .... 972-883-2301.... 505 D
pbond@utdallas.edu

BOND, Sandra .... 540-831-5248.... 522 D
smbond@radford.edu

BOND, Sheree .... 601-928-6230.... 275 G
sheree.bond@mgccc.edu

BOND, Susan, E .... 610-359-1222.... 426 G
sbond@dccc.edu

BOND, Toney .... 910-296-2505.... 371 B
tbond@jamessprunt.edu

BONDAVALLI, Bonnie .... 815-836-5242.... 156 D
bondavbo@lewisu.edu

BONDAVALLI, Bruno .... 773-878-3439.... 163 D
bbondavalli@staugustine.edu

BONDI, Tony .... 626-229-1300...... 53 H

BONDS, Denisha .... 910-521-6270.... 379 B
denisha.bonds@uncp.edu

BONDS, Dorothea .... 214-648-7500.... 507 D
dorothea.bonds@utsouthwestern.edu

BONDS, Jess .... 209-478-0800...... 50 I
jbonds@humphreys.edu

BONDS, Nechell, T .... 757-683-3685.... 521 L
nbonds@odu.edu

BONDS, Nell .... 870-743-3000...... 22 G
nbonds@northark.edu

BONDS, Thomas .... 662-862-8131.... 274 G
tabonds@iccms.edu

BONDS, TJ .... 770-394-8300.... 124 F
tbonds@aii.edu

BONDUM, Victoria .... 315-228-7481.... 329 H
vbondum@colgate.edu

BONDURANT, Glenda, P ... 252-246-1333.... 375 B
gbondurant@wilsoncc.edu

BONDURANT, William, S .. 606-474-3234.... 200 J
bbondurant@kcu.edu

BONE, Andrew .... 503-399-6593.... 414 J
andrew.bone@chemeketa.edu

BONE, Don .... 215-573-3444.... 448 I
donbone@upenn.edu

BONE, Larry .... 501-244-5139...... 19 F
larry.bone@arkansasbaptist.edu

BONELLI, Vicky .... 618-544-8657.... 152 G
bonelliv@iecc.edu

BONES, Rafael .... 413-572-8277.... 239 C
rbones@wsc.ma.edu

BONET, Carlos .... 787-780-0070.... 560 F
cbonet@caribbean.edu

BONEWALD, Karen, I .... 603-526-3748.... 304 A
kbonewald@colby-sawyer.edu

BONFANTI, Philip .... 662-325-8853.... 276 A
pgb13@msstate.edu

BONFIGLIO, Robert, A .... 585-245-5618.... 353 C
bonfig@geneseo.edu

BONGARD, Joseph, W .... 610-785-6271.... 446 A
vicerectorscs@adphils.org

BONGARTEN, Bruce, C ...... 315-470-6510.... 355 A
bcbongarten@esf.edu

BONGARTZ, Michael .... 816-235-1515.... 291 E
bongartzm@umkc.edu

BONGO, Catherine, N .... 973-655-7137.... 311 G
bongoc@mail.montclair.edu

BONHOMME, Mary .... 321-674-8883.... 108 E
bonhomme@fit.edu

BONI, Bethyn .... 315-568-3252.... 342 H
bboni@nycc.edu

BONI, M. Sharon .... 304-367-0205.... 543 E
sharon.boni@fairmontstate.edu

BONICELLI, Paul .... 757-352-4127.... 523 B

BONIEWSKI, Vladia .... 518-381-1322.... 350 E
boniewvc@sunysccc.edu

BONIFER, Duane .... 270-384-8043.... 203 H
boniferd@lindsey.edu

BONIFORTI, Alfredo, II ...... 561-237-7173.... 113 D
aboniforti@lynn.edu

BONIFORTI, Chris, G .... 561-237-7163.... 113 D
cboniforti@lynn.edu

BONILLA, Ana, O .... 787-841-2000.... 564 I
abonilla@email.pucpr.edu

BONILLA, Charles .... 312-369-8611.... 148 B
cbonilla@colum.edu

BONILLA, J. C .... 718-260-3201.... 346 C
jbonilla@poly.edu

BONILLA, Kathleen .... 559-489-2221...... 72 A
kathy.bonilla@fresnocitycollege.edu

BONILLA, Mary Kay .... 406-771-5123.... 296 B
mbonilla@msugf.edu

BONILLA, Matthew, F .... 212-346-1200.... 345 F
mbonilla@pace.edu

BONILLA, Vicky .... 808-791-5050.... 140 F

BONILLA, Victor .... 787-892-4675.... 563 G
vicbonil@sg.inter.edu

BONILLA-RODRIGUEZ,
Victor .... 787-725-6500.... 560 G
vbonilla@albizu.edu

BONIN, Charles, G .... 207-768-9550.... 220 F
charles.bonin@umpi.edu

BONINI, Robin .... 906-487-7225.... 251 C
robin.bonini@finlandia.edu

BONK, Kenneth, J .... 540-831-5332.... 522 D
kjbonk@radford.edu

BONK, Sharon, B .... 617-423-4630.... 231 E
sbonk@bfit.edu

BONK, Theresa, A .... 412-339-6020.... 440 B
tab19@psu.edu

BONKOWSKI, Marie .... 517-841-4528.... 248 I
marie.bonkowski@baker.edu

BONN, Cynthia, L .... 401-874-7100.... 454 E
deanofadmission@uri.edu

BONN, Robert, R .... 262-551-5942.... 546 F
rbonn@carthage.edu

BONNE, Connie .... 563-441-2450.... 186 E
cbonne@kucampus.edu

BONNEAU, Elizabeth .... 508-849-3459.... 230 C
ebonneau@annamaria.edu

BONNER, A. Frank .... 704-406-4236.... 364 B
fbonner@gardner-webb.edu

BONNER, Beverly, J .... 865-882-4550.... 475 G
bonner@roanestate.edu

BONNER, Bryant .... 210-486-4787.... 479 C
wbonner2@alamo.edu

BONNER, Carol, E .... 617-521-2088.... 245 A
carol.bonner@simmons.edu

BONNER, Davita .... 386-481-2143.... 101 I
bonnerd@cookman.edu

BONNER, Debera .... 804-524-5276.... 529 C
dbonner@vsu.edu

BONNER, Ellen-Marie .... 630-617-3034.... 150 F
bonnere@elmhurst.edu

BONNER, Gary .... 951-343-4251...... 31 G
gbonner@calbaptist.edu

BONNER, Gloria, L .... 615-898-2622.... 473 F
gbonner@mtsu.edu

BONNER, Hugh, W .... 315-464-6560.... 352 E
bonnerh@upstate.edu

BONNER, James .... 215-572-2187.... 422 B
bonner@arcadia.edu

BONNER, John, B .... 425-276-9520.... 533 H
jbonner@everettcc.edu

BONNER, Judy, L .... 205-348-4892........ 8 F
judy.bonner@ua.edu

BONNER, Julia .... 414-229-4716.... 551 C
jbonner@uwm.edu

BONNER, Paula, E .... 608-262-9630.... 550 G
pbonner@waastaff.com

BONNER, Thomas, P .... 651-696-6295.... 265 A
bonner@macalester.edu

BONNER, William, L .... 803-754-3950.... 463 E

BONNER, Yahosh .... 308-641-6608.... 301 E
bonnerk@wncc.edu

BONNET, Larissa .... 307-674-6446.... 556 C
lbonnet@sheridan.edu

BONNET, Steve .... 319-363-0481.... 186 D

BONNETTE, Margaree .... 803-793-5175.... 457 F
bonnettem@denmarktech.edu

BONNETTE, Thomas .... 802-860-2705.... 513 A
bonnette@champlain.edu

BONNEY, Kristin .... 231-876-3118.... 248 F
kristin.bonney@baker.edu

BONNEY-BAKER, Janet .... 901-572-2446.... 467 A
janet.bonney@bchs.edu

BONNIN, Linda, H .... 901-678-3949.... 474 C
lmichael@memphis.edu

BONNSTETTER, Bret .... 847-925-6224.... 151 E
bbonnste@harpercollege.edu

BONO, John .... 831-459-4747...... 75 A
jbono@ucsc.edu

BONOFIGLIO, Carrie .... 517-338-3314.... 249 H
cbono@cleary.edu

BONONES, Patrick .... 404-471-6396.... 123 G
pbonones@agnesscott.edu

BONSANG, Stacy .... 781-595-6768.... 236 I
sbonsang@mariancourt.edu

BONSIGNORE, Diana .... 770-650-3000...... 99 D

BONSIGNORE, Francis .... 516-299-3017.... 339 A
francis.bonsignore@liu.edu

BONTATIBUS, Donna .... 860-343-5805...... 90 D
dbontatibus@mxcc.commnet.edu

BONTE, Troy .... 724-503-1001.... 451 A
tbonte@washjeff.edu

BONTINELLI, Stasi .... 303-751-8700...... 81 D
bontinelli@bel-rea.com

BONTRAGER, Cindy, A .... 785-532-6767.... 194 B
cab@ksu.edu

BONTRAGER, Katherine, A 859-572-6132.... 205 E
bontragerk1@nku.edu

BONTRAGER, Kimberlee .... 423-869-6314.... 470 C
kimberlee.bontrager@lmunet.edu

BONUCHI, Molly, A .... 308-635-6112.... 301 E
bonuchim@wncc.edu

BONURA, Rocky .... 310-660-3670...... 45 D
abonura@elcamino.edu

BONVENUTO, Chris .... 310-434-4508...... 68 D
bonvenuto_chris@smc.edu

BONVILLAIN, Thomas .... 985-449-7173.... 216 A
tom.bonvillain@nicholls.edu

BONVILLIAN, Gary .... 229-226-1621.... 137 F
gbonvillian@thomasu.edu

BONVILLIAN, William, B .... 202-789-1828.... 242 A
bonvill@mit.edu

BOOCKER, David .... 402-554-2338.... 301 B
dboocker@unomaha.edu

BOODROOKAS, George, J ... 209-575-6498...... 80 B
boodrookasg@yosemite.cc.ca.us

BOOHER, Doug .... 812-855-9529.... 173 C
dbooher@indiana.edu

BOOHER, Mark .... 805-922-6966...... 26 K
mbooher@pcpa.org

BOOK, Cheryl, A .... 612-343-4163.... 270 C
cabook@northcentral.edu

BOOK, Connie .... 336-278-5661.... 364 A
cbook@elon.edu

BOOK, Peggy .... 909-607-1138...... 69 A
peggy.book@scrippscollege.edu

BOOK, Wes .... 612-343-4143.... 270 C
wcbook@northcentral.edu

BOOKER, Kevin .... 404-653-7893.... 134 A
kbooker@morehouse.edu

BOOKER, Marc .... 602-557-4609...... 19 C
marc.booker@phoenix.edu

BOOKER, Marc .... 205-934-2420........ 8 G
mbooker@uab.edu

BOOKER, Mary .... 909-621-8205...... 63 A
mary.booker@pomona.edu

BOOKER, Sid .... 814-732-2810.... 442 D
sbooker@edinboro.edu

BOOKER, Steve .... 407-646-2395.... 116 B
sbooker@rollins.edu

BOOKER, Tony .... 574-936-8898.... 168 I
tony.booker@ancilla.edu

BOOKMAN, Douglas .... 800-672-3060.... 376 E

BOOKMAN, Mark .... 310-476-9777...... 28 F
mbookman@ajula.edu

BOOKMEYER, Paul, G .... 816-942-8400.... 279 C
paul.bookmeyer@avila.edu

BOOKOUT, James .... 334-670-3108........ 8 B
jbookout@troy.edu

BOOKOUT, Jeff .... 870-358-8614...... 20 F
jeff_bookout@asun.edu

BOOM, Bill .... 320-363-3996.... 271 F
bboom@csbsju.edu

BOOMER, Peggy, A .... 940-397-4604.... 491 A
peggy.boomer@mwsu.edu

BOOMS, Carole .... 734-432-5811.... 254 G
cbooms@madonna.edu

BOONE, Chimene .... 434-381-6420.... 524 E
cboone@sbc.edu

BOONE, Christine, R .... 803-536-8449.... 460 G
cboone@scsu.edu

BOONE, Dan .... 615-248-1251.... 476 E
dboone@trevecca.edu

BOONE, Debbie .... 334-291-4927........ 2 G
debbie.boone@cv.edu

BOONE, J. Allen .... 901-843-3760.... 472 I
boone@rhodes.edu

BOONE, James, T .... 662-915-7546.... 277 G
pboone@olemiss.edu

BOONE, John, B .... 919-866-5923.... 374 E
jbboone@waketech.edu

BOONE, Katherine, B .... 410-455-3768.... 227 D
kboone@umbc.edu

BOONE, Kathleen, C .... 716-839-8301.... 331 G
kboone@daemen.edu

BOONE, LaShanda, R .... 314-340-3301.... 282 I
boonel@hssu.edu

BOONE, Loren .... 320-308-3151.... 269 C
ljboone@stcloudstate.edu

BOONE, Lynn .... 870-338-6474...... 25 D

BOONE, Morell .... 734-487-9751.... 250 H
morell.boone@emich.edu

BOONE, Phil .... 325-674-2659.... 478 H
phil.boone@acu.edu

BOONE, Rebecca .... 318-357-5621.... 216 B
booner@nsula.edu

BOONE, Tracie .... 704-272-5324.... 373 F
tboone@spcc.edu

BOONE JONES, Cary .... 801-863-8037.... 511 C
jonesca@uvu.edu

BOOP, David .... 219-866-6116.... 179 B
dboop@saintjoe.edu

BOOR, Kathryn, J .... 607-255-3111.... 331 C
kjb4@cornell.edu

BOORD, Peggy, L .... 904-632-3251.... 109 E
pboord@fscj.edu

BOOREN, Diane .... 303-457-2757...... 84 F
dbooren@cci.edu

BOOROM, Richard .... 510-220-1947...... 29 F
rboorom@argosy.edu

BOOROS, Deborah .... 610-282-1100.... 426 I
deborah.booros@desales.edu

BOOS, Jean .... 843-355-4167.... 463 C
boosj@wiltech.edu

BOOS, Manfred, B .... 708-209-3088.... 148 C
manfred.boos@cuchicago.edu

BOOSINGER, Timothy, R ..... 334-844-5771........ 1 G
provost@auburn.edu

BOOSTER, Richard .... 541-683-5141.... 415 J
dbooster@gutenberg.edu

BOOTH, Ann .... 718-982-2391.... 327 A
Ann.Booth@csi.cuny.edu

BOOTH, Austin .... 716-645-0983.... 351 G
abooth@buffalo.edu

BOOTH, Charlotte .... 262-646-6529.... 549 B
cbooth@nashotah.edu

BOOTH, Derrick .... 916-484-8361...... 56 A
boothd@arc.losrios.edu

BOOTH, Eric .... 512-313-3000.... 483 G
eric.booth@concordia.edu

BOOTH, George, E .... 302-855-1662...... 96 B
gbooth@dtcc.edu

BOOTH, James, M .... 713-525-6960.... 504 D
booth@stthom.edu

BOOTH, Jane, E .... 212-854-0286.... 330 F
jeb@gc.columbia.edu

BOOTH, Julie .... 530-541-4660...... 53 F
booth@ltcc.edu

BOOTH, Kim .... 435-613-5207.... 511 E
kim.booth@ceu.edu

BOOTH, LaQuita .... 334-229-4124........ 1 C
lbooth@alasu.edu

BOOTH, Melanie .... 503-636-3941.... 416 I
mbooth@marylhurst.edu

BOOTH, Paige .... 512-448-8429.... 493 B
paigeb@stedwards.edu

BOOTH, Richard .... 618-374-5127.... 161 D
richard.booth@principia.edu

BOOTH, Ronnie, L .... 864-646-1773.... 461 F
rlbooth@tctc.edu

BOOTH, Scott .... 614-947-6592.... 391 A
booths@franklin.edu

BOOTH, Susan, A .... 573-629-3002.... 282 H
sbooth@hlg.edu

BOOTH, Susan, L .... 540-224-4640.... 520 D
slbooth@jchs.edu

BOOTH, Terry, L .... 803-778-6624.... 455 G
boothtl@cctech.edu

BOOTHBY, Mandy .... 712-749-2123.... 182 G
boothbym@bvu.edu

BOOTHE, Alan .... 334-242-7710........ 8 B
aboothe@troy.edu

BOOTHE, Diane 208-426-1611 142 F dianeboothe@boisestate.edu
BOOTHE, Jason 435-652-7526 512 A boothe@dixie.edu
BOOTHE, M. Shane 832-252-4646 483 A shane.boothe@cbshouston.edu
BOOTMAN, Lyle 520-626-1657 19 B bootman@pharmacy.arizona.edu
BOOZANG, Kathleen 973-761-9018 315 B kathleen.boozang@shu.edu
BOOZANG, Kathleen, M 973-642-8501 315 C kathleen.boozang@shu.edu
BOOZER, Andrew 803-786-5150 459 B aboozer@ltss.edu
BOPKO, Patricia 909-652-6152 39 B patricia.bopko@chaffey.edu
BOPP, Ruthane, I 847-735-5025 155 F bopp@lakeforest.edu
BOQUET, Elizabeth 203-254-4000 92 B eboquet@fairfield.edu
BOQUET, OSB, Gregory, M 985-867-2232 214 F rector@sjasc.edu
BOQUETTE, Troy 810-762-0476 256 C troy.boquette@mcc.edu
BORASI, Raffaella 585-275-3950 358 I raffaella.borasi@rochester.edu
BORCHERS, Mitch 913-469-8500 193 I mborchers@jccc.edu
BORCHERS, Patrick, J 402-280-3009 297 H borchers@creighton.edu
BORCHERS, Timothy, A 218-477-2764 268 A tim.borchers@mnstate.edu
BORCHERT, Jill 706-233-7394 136 E jborchert@shorter.edu
BORCK, Pat 478-471-2865 133 E pat.borck@maconstate.edu
BORDAS, Stephen, J 718-817-3900 334 C bordas@fordham.edu
BORDEAUX, Lionel 605-856-5880 465 A lionel.bordeaux@sintegleska.edu
BORDELON, Deborah 708-534-8396 151 C dbordelon@govst.edu
BORDELON, Kristi 407-628-6275 121 H kbordelon@teu.edu
BORDEN, David, S 512-223-7738 481 B dborden@austincc.edu
BORDEN, John, S 212-875-4603 323 E jborden@bankstreet.edu
BORDEN, M. Paige 407-823-4765 120 A paige.borden@ucf.edu
BORDEN, Oliver 505-566-3490 320 D bordeno@sanjuancollege.edu
BORDEN, Robert 216-421-7467 387 H rborden@cia.edu
BORDEN, Sid 256-352-8213 10 B sid.borden@wallacestate.edu
BORDEN, Susan 410-263-2371 225 G susan.borden@sjca.edu
BORDEN, Vic 812-855-9893 173 C vborden@indiana.edu
BORDER, Debra 402-481-3804 297 B dborder@bryanlgh.org
BORDERS, Gayle, P 606-679-8501 202 F gayle.borders@kctcs.edu
BORDERS, Marianne 803-981-7320 463 G borders@sctechsystem.edu
BORDERS, Taliashia 815-455-8555 157 F tborders@mchenry.edu
BORDIN, Cristina, L 512-464-8893 493 B cristinb@stedwards.edu
BORDNER, Marsha, S 419-559-2326 402 D mbordner@terra.edu
BOREK, JR., John, M 901-320-9710 478 B jborek@victory.edu
BORELLI, Alyssa 425-637-1010 531 I aborelli@cityu.edu
BORELLI, Elaine 408-554-2377 68 C eborelli@scu.edu
BORELLI, Tricia 319-368-6463 187 E tborelli@mtmercy.edu
BOREN, Carla 816-584-6317 287 H carla.boren@park.edu
BOREN, David, L 405-325-3916 413 C dboren@ou.edu
BOREN, J. B 806-352-5207 508 B borenjb@wbu.edu
BOREN, Laura 918-456-5511 409 A borenld@nsuok.edu
BORER, Jim 763-424-0736 268 D jborer@nhcc.edu
BORER, Ralph, J 402-557-7355 297 A sam.borer@bellevue.edu
BORES, Gerald 503-552-2007 417 D gbores@ncnm.edu
BORG, Mary, O 904-620-2649 120 C mborg@unf.edu
BORGE, Keith 914-654-5552 330 B kborge@cnr.edu
BORGE, Valerie, L 970-247-7368 84 G borge_v@fortlewis.edu
BORGER, Mark 717-391-3598 447 H borger@stevenscollege.edu
BORGER, Patricia, A 414-229-3013 551 C pborger@uwm.edu
BORGES, Eduardo 281-649-3299 487 F eborges@hbu.edu
BORGES, Michael 510-276-3888 38 E mborges@cc.edu
BORGMAN, Cathleen, M 203-254-4081 92 B cborgman@fairfield.edu
BORGMAN, Debbie 601-928-6222 275 G debbie.borgman@mgccc.edu
BORGMAN, Kenneth, L 989-463-7314 247 F borgman@alma.edu
BORGMANN-INGWERSEN, Marian 402-465-2415 299 J mborgman@nebrwesleyan.edu
BORGOGNONI, Mary, E 716-286-8352 344 D meb@niagara.edu
BORIS, Barbara, A 610-409-3605 450 C bboris@ursinus.edu
BORIS, Patricia, A 716-673-3131 352 A patricia.boris@fredonia.edu
BORJESSON, Peggy 503-399-2537 414 J peggy.borjesson@chemeketa.edu
BORK, Ronald 402-643-7475 297 F ron.bork@cune.edu
BORKOWSKI, Donald, V 207-725-3947 217 E dborkows@bowdoin.edu
BORKOWSKI, Ellen, Y 518-388-6293 358 E borkowse@union.edu
BORKOWSKI, James 701-228-5432 382 C jim.borkowski@dakotacollege.edu
BORLAND, James 312-777-8661 153 A jborland@aii.edu
BORN, Bill 574-535-7543 171 D billjb@goshen.edu
BORN, Brad 316-284-5239 190 H bborn@bethelks.edu
BORNEMANN, Jeffrey 414-955-8793 548 E jbornema@mcw.edu
BORNER, John 315-792-7530 356 B john.borner@sunyit.edu
BORNHEIMER, Mary, E 618-537-6524 157 G mebornheimer@mckendree.edu
BORNSTEIN, Eva 718-960-8232 327 C eva.bornstein@lehman.cuny.edu
BORNSTEIN, Leah, L 928-226-4100 13 H leah.bornstein@coconino.edu
BORNSTEIN, Scott 617-824-8555 234 D scott_bornstein@emerson.edu
BORNUS, Susan 651-523-2929 264 C sbornus@hamline.edu
BORONICO, Jess 516-686-7838 343 D jboronic@nyit.edu
BOROS, Barbara 480-461-7128 15 K barbara.boros@mcmail.maricopa.edu
BOROS-KAZAI, Mary 608-363-2640 546 B boroskaz@beloit.edu
BOROSKI, Edna 843-574-6931 461 G edna.boroski@tridenttech.edu
BOROUGHS, SJ, Philip, L 202-687-4300 98 A boroughs@georgetown.edu
BOROUJERDI, Mehdi 518-694-7212 322 C mehdi.boroujerdi@acphs.edu
BOROWIAK, Mary Marcine 716-896-0700 359 F marcine@villa.edu
BOROWICK, Matthew 973-378-9847 315 B matthew.borowick@shu.edu
BOROWICZ, Laurie 715-675-3331 554 G borowiczl@ntc.edu
BOROWICZ, Mark 715-675-3331 554 G Borowicz@ntc.edu
BORRA, Andrea 631-287-8010 339 B andrea.borra@liu.edu
BORREGO, Paul 210-486-2194 479 E pborrego4@alamo.edu
BORREGO, Susan, E 310-243-3784 34 B sborrego@csudh.edu
BORREGO, Tom 316-942-4291 195 C borregot@newmanu.edu
BORRERO, Harold 707-638-5267 72 H harold.borrero@tu.edu
BORROMEO, Sharlene 619-275-4700 46 K sharlene@fashioncareerscollege.com
BORSKI, Brian 972-860-4116 484 F
BORST, Andrew 309-295-1414 168 A AJ-Borst@wiu.edu
BORST, Bridgette 304-357-4925 541 H bridgetteborst@ucwv.edu
BORST, Charlotte 562-907-4204 79 B cborst@whittier.edu
BORST, David 262-243-5700 546 I david.borst@cuw.edu
BORST, James 509-865-8652 534 D borst_j@heritage.edu
BORTHWICK, Kristen 512-492-3011 480 F registrar@aoma.edu
BORTMAN, Walter, J 818-364-7800 55 A bortmawj@lamission.admin
BORTUNK, Ayelet 305-653-8770 123 E abortunk@lecfl.com
BORTZ, Carolyn 610-861-5375 437 G cbortz@northampton.edu
BORUFF-JONES, Polly 417-873-7282 281 H pboruffjones@drury.edu
BORUM, Art 618-545-3401 155 A aborum@kaskaskia.edu
BORUS, David, M 845-437-7583 359 D daborus@vassar.edu
BORUSZEWSKI, Richard 517-371-5140 259 B boruszer@cooley.edu
BOS, James 712-722-6030 183 H jbos@dordt.edu
BOS, Saskia 212-353-4203 331 B sbos@cooper.edu
BOSACK-KOSEK, Carol, A 570-408-5963 451 G carol.bosack@wilkes.edu
BOSANAC, Bob 630-829-6688 145 D bbosanac@ben.edu
BOSCA, David 561-273-6500 117 J dbosca@southuniversity.edu
BOSCH, Matthew Antonio 763-424-0850 268 D mbosch@nhcc.edu
BOSCHINI, JR., Victor, J 817-257-7783 498 F v.boschini@tcu.edu
BOSCHMANN, Erv 765-455-9258 173 E eboschma@iupui.edu
BOSCHUNG, Milla 205-348-6250 8 F mboschun@ches.ua.edu
BOSCO, Mike 617-423-4630 231 E mbosco@bfit.edu
BOSCO, Pat, J 785-532-6237 194 B bosco@ksu.edu
BOSE, Pradeep 859-622-1761 200 D pradeep.bose@eku.edu
BOSE, Rathindra, N 713-743-9104 503 A rnbose@uh.edu
BOSE, Rathindra, N 713-743-9104 503 B rnbose@uh.edu
BOSIO, Amy 215-895-6382 427 G aab97@drexel.edu
BOSIO, Katherine 810-762-9537 253 I kbosio@kettering.edu
BOSKO, Mark 330-325-6673 397 C mbosko@neoucom.edu
BOSLAND, Judy 575-646-1720 319 D jbosland@nmsu.edu
BOSLEY, Barry 717-358-4663 429 E barry.bosley@fandm.edu
BOSLEY, Gabriele 502-272-8476 198 E gbosley@bellarmine.edu
BOSMA, Tim 707-524-1635 68 E tbosma@santarosa.edu
BOSQUE-PEREZ, Nilsa 208-885-6243 144 B uigrad@uidaho.edu
BOSS, Diane 479-936-5172 22 H dboss@nwacc.edu
BOSS, JR., Edward, A 516-299-4095 339 A edward.boss@liu.edu
BOSS, Ken 708-239-4830 165 I ken.boss@trnty.edu
BOSS, Shannon 215-780-1318 446 G sbaoss@salus.edu
BOSSA, Susan, G 617-984-1656 244 C sbossa@quincycollege.edu
BOSSE, Donald 202-319-5307 97 C bosse@cua.edu
BOSSE, Jeannine 207-859-1105 219 G sfs@thomas.edu
BOSSE, Patricia, A 410-532-5177 225 D pbosse@ndm.edu
BOSSERMAN, David 918-293-5293 410 E david.bosserman@okstate.edu
BOSSERT, Joanne 404-504-3474 135 A jbossert@oglethorpe.edu
BOSSERT, Rodney 770-423-6030 132 H rbossert@kennesaw.edu
BOSSI, Steve 619-482-6336 71 C sbossi@swccd.edu
BOSSIE, George 304-734-6663 542 D gbossie@bridgemont.edu
BOSSIO, Lora, J 530-752-6449 73 F ljbossio@ucdavis.edu
BOSSIO, Lora, J 530-752-2971 73 F ljbossio@ucdavis.edu
BOSSLE, Francis, X 443-997-6394 223 F fbossle@jhu.edu
BOSSO, Edward, H 202-651-5346 97 E edward.bosso@gallaudet.edu
BOST, Joanne 803-321-5153 459 G joanne.bost@newberry.edu
BOSTIAN, Susan 605-626-2520 465 H sbostian@northern.edu
BOSTIC, Ann 410-276-0306 226 D abostic@host.sdc.edu
BOSTIC, Deborah 717-846-5000 452 G
BOSTIC, Don 325-641-5726 492 E dbostic@rangercollege.edu
BOSTIC, Heather 314-340-3567 282 I bostich@hssu.edu
BOSTIC, Kevin 574-753-5101 176 A kbostic@ivytech.edu
BOSTIC, Peter 707-864-7000 70 A peter.bostic@solano.edu
BOSTICK, David 773-380-6820 168 D dbostick@westwood.edu
BOSTICK, Sharon, L 816-235-1531 291 E bosticks@umkc.edu
BOSTICK-ISSAC, Sharon 386-481-2957 101 I bosticks@cookman.edu
BOSTON, Cassandra 202-884-9053 99 E bostonc@trinitydc.edu
BOSTON, McKinley 575-646-7630 319 D boston@nmsu.edu
BOSTON, Pamela, F 757-823-2293 521 K pfboston@nsu.edu
BOSTON, Wallace, E 304-724-3700 540 C wboston@apus.edu
BOSTWICK, Gerald, J 513-556-4615 403 D gerald.bostwick@uc.edu
BOSWELL, Kate Fiedler 804-355-0671 524 F kboswell@upsem.edu
BOSWELL, Kathrine 817-598-6216 508 C kboswell@wc.edu
BOSWELL, Robert 303-735-1332 88 B robert.boswell@colorado.edu
BOSWORTH, Blair 216-987-4899 389 A blair.bosworth@tri-c.edu
BOSWORTH, Stephen 617-627-3050 245 F stephen.bosworth@tufts.edu
BOSWORTH, Susan, L 757-221-3584 517 J slbosw@wm.edu
BOSWORTH, Theresa 541-278-5757 414 G tbosworth@bluecc.edu
BOTA, Al 630-801-7900 167 G abota@waubonsee.edu
BOTANA, II, Joseph, D 920-565-1336 547 H botanajd@lakeland.edu
BOTELER, Trina 770-975-4000 126 H
BOTELHO, Marla 781-768-7340 244 D marla.botelho@regiscollege.edu
BOTELLO, Raymond, S 210-932-7122 498 B raymond.botello@tamusa.tamus.edu
BOTERO, Nancy 954-201-7414 102 A nbotero@broward.edu
BOTHEL, Richard 409-880-2294 500 F richard.bothel@lamar.edu
BOTHNE, Nancy 312-662-4213 144 C nbothne@adler.edu
BOTHNER, Peter, G 585-389-2196 342 D pbothne4@naz.edu
BOTHOF, Ken 920-465-2145 551 A bothofk@uwgb.edu
BOTHWELL, Jennifer 508-541-1596 234 B jbothwell@dean.edu
BOTKIN, Sarah, L 319-363-8213 187 E sbotkin@mtmercy.edu
BOTLEY, Robert, L 910-672-1151 377 E rbotley@uncfsu.edu
BOTMAN, Selma 207-780-4480 220 G selma.botman@usm.maine.edu
BOTSTEIN, Leon 914-758-7423 231 A president@bard.edu
BOTSTEIN, Leon 845-758-7423 323 F president@bard.edu
BOTTARO, Jesus 718-270-4950 328 D jbottaro@mec.cuny.edu
BOTTEMILLER, Sandi 503-768-7183 416 F sjb@lclark.edu
BOTTERUDE, Carl 323-259-1441 59 H cbotteru@oxy.edu
BOTTGER, Connie, M 402-941-6471 299 A bottger@midlandu.edu
BOTTICELLI, Jill 817-461-8741 480 H jbotticelli@abconline.org
BOTTICELLI, Marie, J 973-353-1731 314 E mbottice@andromeda.rutgers.edu
BOTTIGLIA, Christina 503-517-1888 421 B cbottiglia@westernseminary.edu
BOTTOMLY, Kim 781-283-2237 246 B kbottomly@wellesley.edu
BOTTOMS, Bette, L 312-413-2267 166 F bbottoms@uic.edu
BOTTOMS, Rebecca 336-725-8344 375 F bottomsb@pbc.edu
BOTTOMS, Robert 614-231-3095 385 A
BOTTOMS, Robert, G 847-328-9300 164 B
BOTTONE, Frances, H 605-652-4988 313 F frances.bottone@stockton.edu
BOTTORFF, Allen 772-462-7360 110 L ebottorff@irsc.edu
BOTTORFF, Margaret, B 302-831-2101 96 F bottorff@udel.edu
BOTTREL, Graham 610-526-6047 430 D gbottrel@harcum.edu
BOTTRELL, Cynthia 319-296-4470 185 C cynthia.bottrell@hawkeyecollege.edu
BOTTUM, James, R 864-656-3466 456 E jb@clemson.edu
BOTZ, Janet, M 574-631-6798 180 D botz.1@nd.edu
BOTZMAN, Thomas, J 240-895-4413 226 A tjbotzman@smcm.edu
BOUABIDI, Debra 845-574-4492 347 I moppenhe@sunyrockland.edu
BOUBEL, Diana 936-468-2206 495 H dboubel@sfasu.edu
BOUCHARD, Beth 702-434-6599 303 E bbouchard@sierranevada.edu
BOUCHARD, Christine, A 518-956-8140 351 E cbouchard@uamail.albany.edu
BOUCHE, Jane, A 920-565-1240 547 H boucheja@lakeland.edu

BOUCHELLE, Joseph .... 540-261-8428.... 524 C
joseph.bouchelle@svu.edu

BOUCHER, Carol, T .... 203-582-8733...... 93 E
carol.boucher@quinnipiac.edu

BOUCHER, Ed .... 931-372-3237.... 474 B
edboucher@tntech.edu

BOUCHER, JR., Gerald, M 252-444-7289.... 369 E
boucherg@cravencc.edu

BOUCHER, Joceline .... 207-326-2489.... 219 D
joceline.boucher@mma.edu

BOUCHER, Karen .... 405-422-1265.... 411 G
boucherk@redlandscc.edu

BOUCHER, Lynne .... 585-389-2305.... 342 D
lbouche9@naz.edu

BOUCHEY, Joel .... 206-934-6794.... 537 B
joel.bouchey@seattlecolleges.edu

BOUCIAS, Jean .... 413-775-1147.... 240 B
boucias@gcc.mass.edu

BOUCIAS, Karen .... 207-581-2905.... 220 A
boucias@maine.edu

BOUCNEAU, Nancy .... 303-477-7240...... 84 I
nancyb@heritage-education.com

BOUCQUEY, Thierry .... 909-607-3538...... 69 A
thierry.boucquey@scrippscollege.edu

BOUDINOT, F. Douglas ..... 804-828-2233.... 525 E
fdboudinot@vcu.edu

BOUDJOUK, Philip .... 701-231-6542.... 381 H
philip.boudjouk@ndsu.edu

BOUDOURIS, Jeff .... 937-512-2512.... 401 J
jeff.boudouris@sinclair.edu

BOUDREAU, Charles .... 630-466-7900.... 167 G
cboudreau@waubonsee.edu

BOUDREAU, George .... 314-256-8801.... 279 A
boudreau@ai.edu

BOUDREAU, Nancy, D ...... 203-365-7599...... 93 G
boudreaun@sacredheart.edu

BOUDREAU, Peg .... 608-785-9102.... 555 D
boudreaum@westerntc.edu

BOUDREAU-SHEA, Karen .. 617-349-8541.... 236 G
kbshea@lesley.edu

BOUDREAUX, David, E ..... 985-448-4134.... 216 A
david.boudreaux@nicholls.edu

BOUDREAUX, JoAnn .... 337-981-4010.... 214 D
joann.boudreaux@remingtoncollege.edu

BOUDREAUX, Ronald, P ... 504-280-6559.... 213 E
rpboudre@uno.edu

BOUEY, Joy .... 808-739-4619.... 140 A
jbouey@chaminade.edu

BOUFFARD, Patricia, A .... 860-738-6319...... 90 F
pbouffard@nwcc.commnet.edu

BOUIE, Archie .... 305-620-3045.... 108 H
archie.bouie@fmuniv.edu

BOUILLON, Rick .... 801-957-2077.... 512 C
rick.bouillon@slcc.edu

BOUKNIGHT, H. Randall ... 864-388-8239.... 458 J
rbouknig@lander.edu

BOUL, Sarah .... 314-719-3663.... 282 C
sboul@fontbonne.edu

BOULANGER, Jennifer .... 315-792-5308.... 341 E
jboulanger@mvcc.edu

BOULAS, Karen .... 607-962-9291.... 331 D
boulas@corning-cc.edu

BOULDIN, Randy .... 615-966-5711.... 470 D
randy.bouldin@lipscomb.edu

BOULDIN, T. Lee .... 832-252-4635.... 483 A
lee@cbshouston.edu

BOULDRY, Sandra, L .... 603-887-7409.... 303 G
sandra.bouldry@chestercollege.edu

BOULER, David, E .... 423-493-4117.... 476 C
debouler@aol.com

BOULET, Scott .... 617-349-8610.... 236 G
sboulet@lesley.edu

BOULEY, Pat .... 303-797-5635...... 80 J
pat.bouley@arapahoe.edu

BOULGER, Lynn .... 207-288-5015.... 217 H
lboulger@coa.edu

BOULTON, Matthew, W ..... 317-931-2303.... 170 E
mboulton@cts.edu

BOULWARE, Julie .... 414-382-6031.... 545 H
julie.boulware@alverno.edu

BOUMA, Glenn .... 712-722-6035.... 183 H
gbouma@dordt.edu

BOUNDY, Janice, F .... 309-655-2230.... 163 E
jan.f.boundy@osfhealthcare.org

BOUNIAEV, Mikhail .... 956-882-6701.... 505 C
mikhail.bouniaev@utb.edu

BOURA, Ahmad .... 603-899-1132.... 305 B
ahmadb@franklinpierce.edu

BOURAS, Ted .... 928-350-2101...... 18 C
tbouras@prescott.edu

BOURASSA, David .... 303-753-6046...... 87 F
dbourassa@rmcad.edu

BOURASSA, Eileen .... 503-883-2507.... 416 G
ebouras@linfield.edu

BOURDETTE, Marcia .... 575-538-6318.... 321 I
bourdettem@wnmu.edu

BOURG, Chuck .... 318-357-5581.... 216 B
bourgc@nsula.edu

BOURG, Tammy .... 985-549-2316.... 216 C
tbourg@selu.edu

BOURGAULT, Keith, R .... 207-795-2270.... 217 F
keithb@cmhc.org

BOURGEOIS, David, L .... 919-658-7747.... 367 D
dbourgeois@moc.edu

BOURGEOIS, Gene .... 512-245-2205.... 501 C
eb04@txstate.edu

BOURGEOIS, Jack, R .... 864-592-4618.... 461 C
bourgeois@sccsc.edu

BOURGEOIS, Sheryl .... 714-997-6955...... 39 C
sbourgeo@chapman.edu

BOURGEOIS, Thomas .... 662-325-3611.... 276 A
thomasb@saffairs.msstate.edu

BOURGOIN, Jim .... 207-453-5035.... 218 I
jbourgoin@kvcc.me.edu

BOURLIER, Julie .... 310-660-3383...... 45 D
jbourlier@elcamino.edu

BOURNE, Don, E .... 208-524-3000.... 143 C
don.bourne@my.eitc.edu

BOURNE, Jeffrey, T .... 540-568-6164.... 520 C
bournejt@jmu.edu

BOURNE, Linda, D .... 606-679-8501.... 202 F
linda.bourne@kctcs.edu

BOURNE, Steve .... 304-327-4087.... 543 C
sbourne@bluefieldstate.edu

BOURQUE, Alicia .... 504-865-2011.... 213 F
aabourqu@loyno.edu

BOURQUE, Alicia .... 504-865-3835.... 213 F
aabourqu@loyno.edu

BOURQUE, Daniel, F .... 617-552-6067.... 232 D
daniel.bourque@bc.edu

BOURQUE, Elizabeth, B ..... 518-580-5700.... 351 B
ebourque@skidmore.edu

BOURQUE, Jackie, R .... 804-523-5286.... 526 F
jbourque@reynolds.edu

BOURQUE, Kathleen .... 413-565-1000.... 231 B
kbourque@baypath.edu

BOURQUE, Michael, J .... 617-552-0343.... 232 D
michael.borque.2@bc.edu

BOURQUE, Nancy .... 773-697-2040.... 149 C
nbourque@devry.edu

BOUSE, Brenda, A .... 636-584-6527.... 281 I
bouseb@eastcentral.edu

BOUSKA, Denise .... 319-296-4275.... 185 C
denise.bouska@hawkeyecollege.edu

BOUSQUET, David .... 508-373-9558.... 231 D
david.bousquet@becker.edu

BOUSQUET, David .... 928-523-8483...... 17 A
david.bousquet@nau.edu

BOUSQUET, Gilles .... 608-262-9833.... 550 G
bousquet@wisc.edu

BOUSQUET, Jennifer .... 540-665-4618.... 523 K
jbousque@su.edu

BOUSQUET, Lisa, M .... 401-865-2760.... 453 F
lbousque@providence.edu

BOUTE, Brad .... 480-994-9244...... 18 I
bradb@swiha.org

BOUTELL, Heather .... 502-272-8124.... 198 E
hboutell@bellamine.edu

BOUTHILLIER, Daris .... 909-607-1554...... 40 C
daris.bouthillier@cgu.edu

BOUTIN, Karyn .... 508-588-9100.... 240 E
BOUTON, Deborah .... 704-330-6446.... 369 A
debbie.bouton@cpcc.edu

BOUTON, Deborah .... 802-635-1664.... 515 E
deborah.bouton@jsc.edu

BOUTTE, Gwen .... 504-671-5010.... 210 G
gboutt@dcc.edu

BOUTTE, Kenneth .... 504-520-5466.... 217 A
kboutte@xula.edu

BOUTTE, Kimberly .... 925-288-5800...... 49 F
kimberly_boutte@heald.edu

BOUTWELL, Ashli .... 334-556-2226........ 4 A
aboutwell@wallace.edu

BOUTWELL, Bryant .... 713-500-3762.... 506 D
bryant.boutwell@uth.tmc.edu

BOUTWELL, Gale, M .... 417-873-7211.... 281 H
gboutwel@drury.edu

BOUVET, Didier .... 401-254-3642.... 454 C
dbouvet@rwu.edu

BOUZARD, Ramona, S .... 319-352-8217.... 189 F
ramona.bouzard@wartburg.edu

BOVA, Breda .... 505-277-7611.... 321 C
bova@unm.edu

BOVA, Paul .... 802-485-2079.... 514 A
pbova@norwich.edu

BOVE, Elena, M .... 310-338-2885...... 56 E
ebove@lmu.edu

BOVE, Laurence .... 330-490-7122.... 405 E
lbove@walsh.edu

BOVE, Maria .... 802-773-5900.... 513 B
mbove@csj.edu

BOVEE, Jerry .... 801-626-7738.... 511 D
jerrybovee@weber.edu

BOVEE, Valerie, J .... 507-354-8221.... 265 B
boveevj@mlc-wels.edu

BOVENGA, Anne .... 617-876-0956.... 236 H
anne.bovenga@longy.edu

BOVIA, Marilyn .... 419-473-2700.... 389 B
mmbovia@daviscollege.edu

BOW, Bryce .... 407-569-1343.... 107 G
bryce.bow@fcc.edu

BOWAB, Lynn .... 978-681-0800.... 242 B
bowab@mslaw.edu

BOWDEN, Anita .... 508-854-4206.... 241 C
anitab@qcc.mass.edu

BOWDEN, Dorothy, J .... 256-533-7387........ 3 D
dorothy.bowden@vc.edu

BOWDEN, Russ .... 707-527-4262...... 68 E
rbowden@santarosa.edu

BOWDEN, Vicky .... 626-815-2110...... 30 E
vbowden@apu.edu

BOWDICH, William .... 505-925-8851.... 321 G
bbowdich@unm.edu

BOWDITCH, Brent .... 517-884-0101.... 255 D
bowditcb@msu.edu

BOWDLER, Michelle, D ...... 617-627-3766.... 245 F
michelle.bowdler@tufts.edu

BOWE, Adraenne .... 212-817-7020.... 327 B
abowe1@gc.cuny.edu

BOWE, Derek .... 256-726-7186........ 6 C
dbowe@oakwood.edu

BOWE, Erik, R .... 770-499-3360.... 132 H
ebowe@kennesaw.edu

BOWE, Mona .... 574-284-4587.... 179 D
mbowe@saintmarys.edu

BOWELL, Daniel .... 765-998-5241.... 179 F
dnbowell@taylor.edu

BOWEN, Alyncia .... 614-234-5177.... 396 G
abowen@mccn.edu

BOWEN, Anne .... 360-383-3323.... 539 D
abowen@whatcom.ctc.edu

BOWEN, Blannie, E .... 814-863-7494.... 438 F
bxb1@psu.edu

BOWEN, Bruce .... 801-626-6006.... 511 D
babowen@weber.edu

BOWEN, Candice .... 303-492-6893...... 88 B
candice.bowen@colorado.edu

BOWEN, Corey, J .... 410-651-8100.... 227 E
cjbowen@umes.edu

BOWEN, David .... 602-978-7431...... 18 K
david.bowen@thunderbird.edu

BOWEN, David, C .... 315-268-2327.... 329 C
dbowen@clarkson.edu

BOWEN, Gilbert, C .... 910-962-3123.... 379 C
bowengc@uncw.edu

BOWEN, Janine .... 410-337-6460.... 222 I
jbowen@goucher.edu

BOWEN, Jennifer .... 580-581-2988.... 407 D
jbowen@cameron.edu

BOWEN, Jo Anne .... 219-980-6937.... 173 F
jbowen@iun.edu

BOWEN, John .... 713-743-0209.... 503 B
jbowen@uh.edu

BOWEN, John, J .... 401-598-1900.... 453 C
jbowen@jwu.edu

BOWEN, Jose, A .... 214-768-2880.... 494 F
jabowen@smu.edu

BOWEN, Julie .... 806-291-3470.... 508 B
registrar@wbu.edu

BOWEN, Karen .... 336-599-1181.... 372 D
bowenk@piedmontcc.edu

BOWEN, Ken .... 317-921-4882.... 175 I
kbowen@ivytech.edu

BOWEN, Laura .... 704-484-4106.... 369 B
bowen@clevelandcommunitycollege.edu

BOWEN, Lauren, L .... 216-397-4374.... 392 M
bowen@jcu.edu

BOWEN, Maxine .... 662-254-3578.... 276 C
mrbowen@mvsu.edu

BOWEN, Patricia, A .... 606-693-5000.... 203 C
pbowen@kmbc.edu

BOWEN, Randy .... 716-614-6471.... 344 C
rbowen@niagaracc.suny.edu

BOWEN, Richard, M .... 928-523-8831...... 17 A
richard.bowen@nau.edu

BOWEN, Robin, E .... 978-665-3421.... 238 C
rbowen@fitchburgstate.edu

BOWEN, Samuel, J .... 320-222-6090.... 268 I
sam.bowen@ridgewater.edu

BOWEN, Sharon, G .... 931-540-2548.... 474 F
sbowen@columbiastate.edu

BOWEN, Sherri, W .... 336-734-7200.... 370 C
sbowen@forsythtech.edu

BOWEN, Stephen, H .... 404-784-8300.... 129 A
sbowen@emory.edu

BOWEN, Susan .... 229-317-6747.... 128 A
susan.bowen@darton.edu

BOWEN, Susan .... 609-586-4800.... 311 C
bowens@mccc.edu

BOWEN, Tamara .... 410-857-2223.... 224 D
tbowen@mcdaniel.edu

BOWEN, Terry .... 410-386-8494.... 221 G
tbowen@carrollcc.edu

BOWEN, Thomas .... 408-924-1200...... 37 A
thomas.bowen@sjsu.edu

BOWEN, Tyler .... 507-537-6257.... 269 G
Tyler.Bowen@smsu.edu

BOWEN, W. Ann .... 423-585-6892.... 476 B
ann.bowen@ws.edu

BOWENS, Ollie .... 662-252-8000.... 277 C
obowens@rustcollege.edu

BOWENS GELLMAN,
Laura Lee .... 973-290-4410.... 309 A
lbowens@cse.edu

BOWER, Beth .... 978-542-7757.... 239 B
bbowers@salemstate.edu

BOWER, David, A .... 812-464-1918.... 180 F
bower@usi.edu

BOWER, Eric .... 216-791-5000.... 388 B
eric.bower@case.edu

BOWER, Jami .... 678-839-6464.... 138 D
jbower@westga.edu

BOWER, Leah .... 620-672-5641.... 196 A
leahb@prattcc.edu

BOWER, Marco .... 305-593-1223.... 102 D
mbower@albizu.edu

BOWER, Mike .... 701-662-1501.... 382 D
mike.bower@lrsc.edu

BOWER, Shirley .... 585-475-5034.... 347 G
slbwml@rit.edu

BOWER, SCC, Theresa .... 973-543-6528.... 307 C
acslibrary@acs350.org

BOWERS, Amanda .... 407-628-6265.... 121 H
abowers@teu.edu

BOWERS, Bege, K .... 330-941-1560.... 406 F
bkbowers@ysu.edu

BOWERS, Blake .... 360-992-2938.... 532 A
bbowers@clark.edu

BOWERS, David, A .... 212-938-5666.... 355 B
dbowers@sunyopt.edu

BOWERS, David, D .... 619-239-0391...... 37 D
dbowers@cwsl.edu

BOWERS, David, G .... 734-929-9095.... 249 H
dbowers@cleary.edu

BOWERS, Dianne .... 770-531-6360.... 132 J
dbowers@laniertech.edu

BOWERS, Gayln, K .... 707-965-6231...... 60 J
gbowers@puc.edu

BOWERS, J. Betsy .... 850-474-2637.... 121 C
bbowers@uwf.edu

BOWERS, Jane .... 212-237-8801.... 328 A
jbowers@jjay.cuny.edu

BOWERS, John .... 270-745-4278.... 207 C
john.bowers@wku.edu

BOWERS, John .... 304-326-1341.... 541 G
jbowers@salemu.edu

BOWERS, John .... 206-934-3727.... 536 H
john.bowers@seattlecolleges.edu

BOWERS, Karen .... 209-473-5200...... 50 C
karen_bowers@heald.edu

BOWERS, Kathy .... 417-626-1234.... 287 F
kbowers@occ.edu

BOWERS, Kevin .... 618-544-8657.... 152 G
bowersk@iecc.edu

BOWERS, Marilyn, R .... 423-585-2633.... 476 B
marilyn.bowers@ws.edu

BOWERS, Marilyn, R .... 423-318-2776.... 476 B
marilyn.bowers@ws.edu

BOWERS, Michael, E .... 864-587-4220.... 461 D
bowersme@smcsc.edu

BOWERS, Michael, W .... 702-895-3301.... 302 K
michael.bowers@unlv.edu

BOWERS, Paul, E .... 330-569-5453.... 391 H
bowerspe@hiram.edu

BOWERS, Richard .... 817-598-6213.... 508 C
rbowers@wc.edu

BOWERS, Rodney .... 321-674-8080.... 108 E
rbowers@fit.edu

BOWERS, Stephanie .... 360-650-2055.... 539 C
stephanie.bowers@wwu.edu

BOWERS, Steven, P .... 904-632-3218.... 109 E
sbowers@fscj.edu

BOWERSOCK, Ally .... 540-985-9943.... 520 D
ahbowersock@jchs.edu

BOWERSOCK, Gary .... 303-273-3330...... 82 F
gbowerso@mines.edu

BOWES, William .... 706-721-2901.... 130 B
wbowes@georgiahealth.edu

BOWIE, DeWayne .... 337-482-6287.... 216 D
dkbowie@louisiana.edu

BOWIE, Jalonna .... 913-234-0681.... 191 G
jalonna.bowie@cleveland.edu

BOWIE, John .... 207-755-5432.... 218 G
jbowie@cmcc.edu

BOWIE, Linda .... 410-951-3915.... 228 B
lbowie@coppin.edu

BOWIE, Lois .... 903-593-8311.... 499 A
lbowie@texascollege.edu

BOWIE, Michelle .... 202-884-9611...... 99 E
bowiem@trinitydc.edu

BOWIE, Sandra A, M .... 601-977-7871.... 277 F
sbowie@tougaloo.edu

BOWIE, Staci, A .... 843-349-2227.... 456 G
sbowie@coastal.edu

BOWKER, Janet, L .... 814-732-2544.... 442 D
bowker@edinboro.edu

BOWKER, Wayne .... 515-271-1426.... 183 F
wayne.bowker@dmu.edu

BOWLAN, Ronald, E .... 215-503-7268.... 448 B
ron.bowlan@jefferson.edu

BOWLBY, Rebecca .... 610-647-4400.... 431 B
rbowlby@immaculata.edu

BOWLER, Connie, A .... 440-964-4345.... 393 E
cbowler@kent.edu

BOWLES, Adam .... 618-842-3711.... 152 F
bowlesa@iecc.edu

BOWLES, Anita, K .... 864-587-4221.... 461 D
bowlesa@smcsc.edu

BOWLES, Diane .... 704-378-1202.... 365 H
dbowles@jcsu.edu

BOWLES, Dympna .... 212-217-4050.... 333 G
dympna_bowles@fitnyc.edu

BOWLES, James, H .... 270-824-8588.... 202 C
james.bowles@kctcs.edu

BOWLES, Janis .... 706-507-8800.... 127 D
bowles_janis@columbusstate.edu

BOZEMAN, Carlyn ... 937-512-2781 ... 401 J
carlyn.bozeman@sinclair.edu

BOZEMAN, Joseph, C ... 443-885-3017 ... 224 F
joseph.bozeman@morgan.edu

BOZIC, Christy ... 765-455-9375 ... 173 E
cbozic@purdue.edu

BOZINSKI, Glenn ... 570-674-6434 ... 436 F
gbozinsk@misericordia.edu

BOZYLINSKY, Garrett, A ... 401-874-4599 ... 454 E
garry@uri.edu

BOZZUTO, Victoria ... 203-285-2408 ... 90 A
vbozzuto@gwcc.commnet.edu

BRAA, Tim ... 303-464-2319 ... 87 D
tbraa@westwood.edu

BRAATEN, Beth ... 719-590-6758 ... 83 D
bbraaten@coloradotech.edu

BRAATEN, Jennifer, L ... 540-365-4202 ... 518 J
jbraaten@ferrum.edu

BRAATEN, Norm ... 402-472-3171 ... 300 H
nbraaten1@unl.edu

BRAATEN, Pamela, K ... 701-788-4773 ... 381 F
Pamela.Braaten@mayvillestate.edu

BRAATZ, Jay ... 312-362-7561 ... 148 F
jbraatz@depaul.edu

BRABAZON, Jodi ... 215-574-9600 ... 431 A
jbrabazon@hussianart.edu

BRABENDER, Bob, L ... 515-574-1086 ... 185 F
brabender@iowacentral.edu

BRABHAM, Sherry, F ... 212-217-4020 ... 333 G
sherry_brabham@fitnyc.edu

BRABHAM, Susan, S ... 803-938-3795 ... 462 F
brabhams@uscsumter.edu

BRABOY, John, R ... 812-288-8878 ... 178 A
macfs@mindspring.com

BRACCI, Steven ... 310-689-3200 ... 42 F
sbracci@kaplan.edu

BRACCIANO, Susan ... 816-271-4214 ... 287 A
braccian@missouriwestern.edu

BRACE, Liz ... 828-298-3325 ... 380 C
gathering@warren-wilson.edu

BRACE, Simon ... 704-847-5600 ... 376 H
sbrace@ses.edu

BRACEY, Carol ... 951-343-4456 ... 31 G
cbracey@calbaptist.edu

BRACEY, Gerald ... 228-897-7101 ... 278 E
jerry.bracey@wmcarey.edu

BRACEY, W. Earl ... 309-298-1900 ... 168 A
we-bracey@wiu.edu

BRACHHAUS, Allison ... 318-487-7194 ... 209 B
brachhaus@lacollege.edu

BRACK, Jonathan ... 215-572-3878 ... 451 D
jbrack@wts.edu

BRACK, Tiffany ... 219-769-3321 ... 169 I
tabrack@brownmackie.edu

BRACKE, Mary ... 314-918-2519 ... 281 J
mbracke@eden.edu

BRACKEN, Damien, S ... 617-266-1400 ... 231 G

BRACKEN, Larry ... 850-484-1705 ... 114 G
lbracken@pensacolastate.edu

BRACKEN, Lisa ... 803-778-6652 ... 455 G
brackenlm@cctech.edu

BRACKER, Beverly ... 619-961-4235 ... 72 F
bbracker@tjsl.edu

BRACKETT, Edmund ... 816-584-6588 ... 287 H
edmund.brackett@park.edu

BRACKETT, Geoffrey, L ... 845-575-3000 ... 340 C
geoffrey.brackett@marist.edu

BRACKETT, Jan ... 207-725-3142 ... 217 E
jbracket@bowdoin.edu

BRACKIN, Chad ... 225-578-4736 ... 212 E
cmb@lsu.edu

BRACKLEY, Paul ... 312-329-4225 ... 158 H
paul.brackley@moody.edu

BRACY, Marion ... 504-520-7507 ... 217 A
mbracy@xula.edu

BRADAC, John, P ... 607-274-3365 ... 336 G
jbradac@ithaca.edu

BRADACH, Carmen ... 218-749-7743 ... 267 C
c.bradach@mr.mnscu.edu

BRADBERRY, J. Chris ... 402-280-2950 ... 297 H
jcbradberry@creighton.edu

BRADBERRY, Richard ... 443-885-3488 ... 224 F
richard.bradberry@morgan.edu

BRADBURY, Guy ... 252-633-4464 ... 367 D
gbradbury@moc.edu

BRADDER, Kelley, L ... 515-961-1621 ... 188 F
kelley.bradder@simpson.edu

BRADDIX, D'Andre ... 314-516-5205 ... 291 F
braddixd@umsl.edu

BRADDLEE, ... 914-674-7262 ... 340 G

BRADDS, Nancy ... 407-569-1160 ... 107 G
nancy.bradds@fcc.edu

BRADEN, Jay ... 321-939-7600 ... 121 E
jbraden@stetson.edu

BRADEN, Jeffery, P ... 919-515-2468 ... 378 B
jeff_braden@ncsu.edu

BRADEN, SJ, Michael, L ... 201-761-6014 ... 314 F
mbraden@spc.edu

BRADEN, Sandra ... 313-664-7471 ... 250 A
sbraden@collegeforcreativestudies.edu

BRADFIELD, Anna ... 508-531-1347 ... 238 B
abradfield@bridgew.edu

BRADFIELD, Brett ... 605-331-6712 ... 466 D
brett.bradfield@usiouxfalls.edu

BRADFIELD, Glynis ... 269-471-3432 ... 252 C
glynisb@andrews.edu

BRADFIELD, Katrina ... 731-661-5346 ... 476 G
kbradfie@uu.edu

BRADFIELD, Murray ... 770-671-1200 ... 124 D
mbradfield@argosy.edu

BRADFIELD, Terry ... 202-885-8631 ... 100 A
tbradfield@wesleyseminary.edu

BRADFORD, SR.,
Corey, S ... 936-261-2150 ... 496 E
csbradford@pvamu.edu

BRADFORD, David ... 870-850-4821 ... 23 H
dbradford@seark.edu

BRADFORD, Frances, C ... 757-221-7802 ... 517 J
fcbrad@wm.edu

BRADFORD, James ... 615-322-2316 ... 477 F
james.w.bradford@vanderbilt.edu

BRADFORD, Jerry ... 256-233-8278 ... 1 F
jerry.bradford@athens.edu

BRADFORD, Lawrence ... 323-953-4000 ... 54 H
bradfoll@lacitycollege.edu

BRADFORD, Linda ... 205-247-8001 ... 7 G
lbradford@stillman.edu

BRADFORD, Margaret ... 541-956-7088 ... 420 B
mbradford@roguecc.edu

BRADFORD, Michele ... 256-439-6837 ... 3 J
mbradford@gadsdenstate.edu

BRADFORD, Peggy ... 216-987-4283 ... 389 A
peggy.bradford@tri-c.edu

BRADFORD, Sarah, E ... 423-439-8304 ... 473 E
bradfors@etsu.edu

BRADFORD, Susan, E ... 713-942-3436 ... 504 D
bradfords@stthom.edu

BRADFORD-PERRY,
Emma ... 225-771-4990 ... 214 H
emma_perry@subr.edu

BRADFORD ROUSE, Teri ... 805-565-7255 ... 78 F
tbradfordrouse@westmont.edu

BRADIN, Bernice ... 617-349-8685 ... 230 D
bbradin@lesley.edu

BRADIN, Bernice ... 617-349-8685 ... 236 G
bbradin@lesley.edu

BRADLEY, Alan ... 615-297-7545 ... 466 H
alanb@aquinascollege.edu

BRADLEY, Alice ... 704-290-5832 ... 373 F
abradley@spcc.edu

BRADLEY, Brenda ... 712-274-6400 ... 189 H
brenda.bradley@witcc.edu

BRADLEY, Carol, B ... 863-667-5026 ... 118 A
cbradly@seu.edu

BRADLEY, Dale, R ... 304-367-4692 ... 542 I
Dale.Bradley@pierpont.edu

BRADLEY, Daniel, J ... 812-237-4000 ... 173 A
president@indstate.edu

BRADLEY, David, M ... 713-221-8610 ... 503 D
bradleyd@uhd.edu

BRADLEY, Dennis, J ... 814-732-1030 ... 442 D
bradley@edinboro.edu

BRADLEY, George, C ... 706-821-8230 ... 135 C
gbradley@paine.edu

BRADLEY, Jacquline ... 707-468-3110 ... 57 A
jbradley@mendocino.edu

BRADLEY, Jane ... 641-782-7081 ... 189 A
bradley@swcciowa.edu

BRADLEY, Jennifer ... 808-734-9890 ... 141 E
jbradley@hawaii.edu

BRADLEY, Jennifer ... 319-398-4913 ... 186 H
jbradley@kirkwood.edu

BRADLEY, JoAnn ... 718-270-4418 ... 352 D
jbradley@downstate.edu

BRADLEY, Joseph ... 410-617-5780 ... 224 A
jbradley@loyola.edu

BRADLEY, Judy ... 606-218-5253 ... 207 B
jbradley@pc.edu

BRADLEY, Kathy ... 717-337-6960 ... 429 H
kbradley@gettysburg.edu

BRADLEY, Kevin, L ... 812-265-2580 ... 176 G
kbradley@ivytech.edu

BRADLEY, Leah, J ... 502-895-3411 ... 204 B
lbradley@lpts.edu

BRADLEY, Marcy, K ... 607-871-2350 ... 322 F
bradlemk@alfred.edu

BRADLEY, Mark ... 360-882-2200 ... 48 D
markbradley@ggbts.edu

BRADLEY, Martha, S ... 801-585-3582 ... 510 L
martha.bradley@utah.edu

BRADLEY, Monica ... 318-274-6118 ... 215 E
bradleym@gram.edu

BRADLEY, Monty, E ... 614-823-1409 ... 400 G
mbradley@otterbein.edu

BRADLEY, Nedra ... 601-484-8674 ... 275 C
nbradley@mcc.cc.ms.us

BRADLEY, Patrick, J ... 660-543-4515 ... 291 B
pbradley@ucmo.edu

BRADLEY, Paul, A ... 651-631-5592 ... 270 E
pabradley@nwc.edu

BRADLEY, Robert, E ... 850-644-0797 ... 119 C
rbradley@tsu.edu

BRADLEY, Robert, J ... 302-292-3838 ... 96 C
bradley@dtcc.edu

BRADLEY, Roger ... 386-267-0565 ... 103 I
director@daytonacollege.edu

BRADLEY, Ryan ... 918-343-7782 ... 411 H
ryanbradley@rsu.edu

BRADLEY, Sara ... 317-738-8120 ... 171 C
sbradley@franklincollege.edu

BRADLEY, Tanya, W ... 802-626-6218 ... 515 F
tanya.bradley@lyndonstate.edu

BRADLEY, Tess ... 610-341-5827 ... 428 D
tbradley@eastern.edu

BRADLEY, Winifred ... 850-484-2014 ... 114 G
wbradley@pensacolastate.edu

BRADLEY-DOPPES, Peg ... 303-871-3399 ... 88 E
pbd@du.edu

BRADLEY-HASTY, Barbara 252-536-7203 ... 370 F
hastyba@halifaxcc.edu

BRADSHAW, Amelia, M ... 804-523-5132 ... 526 F
abradshaw@reynolds.edu

BRADSHAW, Boyd ... 636-227-2100 ... 284 E
boyd.bradshaw@logan.edu

BRADSHAW, Brent ... 972-279-6511 ... 479 I
bbradshaw@amberton.edu

BRADSHAW, Debra ... 816-268-5472 ... 287 C
dlbradshaw@nts.edu

BRADSHAW, Felicia ... 202-231-3354 ... 557 G
felicia.bradshaw@dia.mil

BRADSHAW, Gail ... 708-534-4124 ... 151 C
gbradshaw@govst.edu

BRADSHAW, George ... 909-594-5611 ... 58 A
gbradshaw@mtsac.edu

BRADSHAW, John, F ... 919-572-1625 ... 361 M
jbradshaw@apexsot.edu

BRADSHAW, Ken ... 270-534-3169 ... 203 B
ken.bradshaw@kctcs.edu

BRADSHAW, Kenny ... 901-448-5661 ... 477 C
kbradsh1@uthsc.edu

BRADSHAW, Kim ... 704-355-5584 ... 363 B
kim.bradshaw@carolinascollege.edu

BRADSHAW, Marjorie ... 913-234-0607 ... 191 G
marjorie.bradshaw@cleveland.edu

BRADSHAW, Martha, M ... 214-820-2776 ... 481 I
martha_bradshaw@baylor.edu

BRADSHAW, Sheryl ... 903-813-2444 ... 481 A
sbradshaw@austincollege.edu

BRADSHAW, Steve ... 706-295-6934 ... 130 F
sbradshaw@gntc.edu

BRADSHAW, William ... 215-204-7759 ... 447 G
william.bradshaw@temple.edu

BRADSHAW, Wilson, G ... 239-590-1055 ... 119 A
president@fgcu.edu

BRADSHAW, York ... 410-951-1288 ... 228 B
ybradshaw@coppin.edu

BRADSHER, Carl ... 434-791-5646 ... 516 D
cbradshe@averett.edu

BRADSHER, Judy, S ... 336-599-1181 ... 372 D
bradshj@piedmontcc.edu

BRADT, Jeremy ... 815-599-3486 ... 152 A
jeremy.bradt@highland.edu

BRADT, Kay ... 785-594-8414 ... 190 C
kay.bradt@bakeru.edu

BRADY, Brac ... 207-255-1290 ... 220 E
bracb@maine.edu

BRADY, Carolyn, M ... 610-861-5342 ... 437 G
cbrady@northampton.edu

BRADY, Christian ... 814-865-2631 ... 438 F
cmb44@psu.edu

BRADY, Claire ... 352-435-6308 ... 112 M
bradyc@lscc.edu

BRADY, David, M ... 203-576-4589 ... 94 D
dbrady@bridgeport.edu

BRADY, Donna, C ... 704-687-5725 ... 378 E
dcbrady@uncc.edu

BRADY, Elizabeth, A ... 415-442-7813 ... 48 E
ebrady@ggu.edu

BRADY, Henry ... 510-642-5116 ... 73 E
hbrady@econ.berkeley.edu

BRADY, James ... 509-533-3660 ... 532 F
jimb@spokanefalls.edu

BRADY, Jill ... 706-864-1760 ... 134 D
jebrady@northgeorgia.edu

BRADY, Kathleen ... 314-977-8173 ... 289 F
bradyk@slu.edu

BRADY, Linda, P ... 336-334-5266 ... 379 A
lpbrady@uncg.edu

BRADY, Michael ... 608-363-2200 ... 546 B
bradym@beloit.edu

BRADY, Reginald ... 323-953-4287 ... 54 H
bradyr@lacitycollege.edu

BRADY, Steven ... 315-464-4510 ... 352 E
bradys@upstate.edu

BRADY, Steven, D ... 314-984-7640 ... 289 D
sbrady@stlcc.edu

BRADY, Tara ... 781-768-7238 ... 244 D
tara.brady@regiscollege.edu

BRADY, Thomas, E ... 603-862-4643 ... 306 E
tom.brady@unh.edu

BRADY COYLE, Maureen ... 201-355-1124 ... 310 C
coylem@felician.edu

BRAENDEL, Carly ... 828-669-8012 ... 367 C
cbraendel@montreat.edu

BRAESE, Paul ... 828-298-3325 ... 380 C
pbraese@warren-wilson.edu

BRAEUTIGAM, Ronald, R ... 847-491-7040 ... 160 D
braeutigam@northwestern.edu

BRAGA, Eddie, D ... 407-303-9585 ... 108 D
eddie.braga@fhchs.edu

BRAGDON, Clifford, R ... 321-914-0741 ... 108 E
cbragdon@fit.edu

BRAGG, Dallas ... 704-664-3343 ... 541 D
dbragg@mountainstate.edu

BRAGG, Dawn ... 414-955-8734 ... 548 E
dbragg@mcw.edu

BRAGG, Kaye ... 310-243-3745 ... 34 B
kbragg@csudh.edu

BRAGG, Mark, S ... 423-439-4137 ... 473 E
bragg@etsu.edu

BRAGG, Martin, E ... 805-756-2511 ... 33 F
mbragg@calpoly.edu

BRAGG, Nancy, S ... 540-665-4538 ... 523 K
nbragg@su.edu

BRAGG, Sadie ... 212-220-8320 ... 326 E
sbragg@bmcc.cuny.edu

BRAHA, Habtu ... 410-951-3447 ... 228 B
hbraha@coppin.edu

BRAHAMS, Teri, T ... 865-694-6476 ... 475 F
tbrahams@pstcc.edu

BRAHM, Gary ... 949-753-4774 ... 30 I
chancellor@brandman.edu

BRAIDES, Cheryl ... 215-612-6600 ... 425 D
cbraides@chicareers.com

BRAILEY, David, J ... 860-701-7739 ... 93 B
brailey_d@mitchell.edu

BRAILOFSKY, Yosef ... 845-362-3053 ... 323 H

BRAILOW, David, G ... 317-738-8017 ... 171 C
dbrailow@franklincollege.edu

BRAIM, Barry ... 413-775-1311 ... 240 B
braim@gcc.mass.edu

BRAINARD, Mark, T ... 302-454-3962 ... 96 C
brainard@dtcc.edu

BRAINARD, Nancy ... 918-495-7119 ... 411 C
nbrainard@oru.edu

BRAISHER, Mark, H ... 405-912-9013 ... 408 D
mbraisher@hc.edu

BRAITMAN, Keli ... 816-501-4122 ... 288 D
keli.braitman@rockhurst.edu

BRAKEFIELD, Jean Ann ... 843-349-2846 ... 456 G
jeanann@coastal.edu

BRAKKE, David, F ... 540-568-3508 ... 520 C
brakkedf@jmu.edu

BRALY, JR., Cliff ... 336-272-7102 ... 364 D
bralyc@greensborocollege.edu

BRAMANTE, Paula ... 617-951-2350 ... 243 C
paula.bramante@necb.edu

BRAMBILA, Albert ... 760-921-5447 ... 61 B
abrambila@paloverde.edu

BRAMBLETT, Sandra, J ... 404-894-8874 ... 130 D
sandi.bramblett@irp.gatech.edu

BRAME, Tracey ... 616-301-6800 ... 259 B
bramet@cooley.edu

BRAMES, Luann ... 317-955-6306 ... 177 G
brames@marian.edu

BRAMLAGE, Jenell ... 419-227-3141 ... 404 D
bramlage@unoh.edu

BRAMLETT, Rebecca ... 919-962-4388 ... 378 D
rebecca_bramlett@unc.edu

BRAMLEY, A. John ... 802-656-7878 ... 514 F
john.bramley@uvm.edu

BRAMMELL, Keith ... 606-326-2426 ... 201 B
Keith.brammell@kctcs.edu

BRAMUCCI, Robert, S ... 949-582-4577 ... 70 D
rbramucci@socccd.org

BRAMWELL, Bevil ... 540-338-2700 ... 517 D
frbramwell@cdu.edu

BRAMWELL, Fitzgerald, B ... 202-806-4759 ... 98 B
fitzgerald.bramwell@howard.edu

BRANAM, Matt ... 812-877-8000 ... 179 A
matt.branam@rose-hulman.edu

BRANAN, Jean ... 858-598-1200 ... 30 A
jbranan@aii.edu

BRANCA, Matthew, P ... 570-326-3761 ... 440 K
mbranca@pct.edu

BRANCATO, Marco ... 781-239-2571 ... 240 D
mbrancato@massbay.edu

BRANCH, Deborah, G ... 252-335-3271 ... 377 D
dgbranch@mail.ecsu.edu

BRANCH, Gary ... 256-395-2211 ... 7 E
gbranch@suscc.edu

BRANCH, Gary, L ... 251-580-2202 ... 5 A
gbranch@faulknerstate.edu

BRANCH, Kevin ... 404-215-7902 ... 134 A
kbranch@morehouse.edu

BRANCH, Teresa, S ... 406-243-5225 ... 295 A
teresa.branch@umontana.edu

BRANCH-FRAPPIER,
Michele ... 803-754-4100 ... 457 D

BRANCH-GRIFFIN,
Rebecca ... 804-524-5674 ... 529 C
rbgriffi@vsu.edu

BRANCHEAU, Carrie ... 303-753-6046 ... 87 F

BRANCHINI, Ann, Z ... 860-383-5204 ... 91 B
abranchini@trcc.commnet.edu

BRANCOLINI, Kristine ... 310-338-4593 ... 56 E
kbrancol@lmu.edu

BRAND, Amy ... 601-553-3455 ... 275 C
abrand@mcc.cc.ms.us

BRAND, Frederick ... 609-984-1588 ... 316 A
fbrand@tesc.edu

BRAND, Jeffrey, S ... 415-422-6304 ... 76 B
brandj@usfca.edu

BRAND, Jonathan ... 319-895-4324 ... 183 D
jbrand@cornellcollege.edu

BRAND, Latricia ... 503-768-7743 ... 416 F lbrand@lclark.edu

BRAND, Richard ... 865-981-8011 ... 470 F richard.brand@maryvillecollege.edu

BRAND, Robert ... 978-368-2364 ... 230 F robert.brand@auc.edu

BRAND, Ronald ... 609-894-9311 ... 308 C rbrand@bcc.edu

BRANDEBERRY, Shari ... 419-434-4245 ... 406 A registrar@winebrenner.edu

BRANDEBURG, Rosanne ... 352-365-3515 ... 112 M brandebr@lscc.edu

BRANDEBURY, Amy ... 812-488-2155 ... 180 B ab288@evansville.edu

BRANDEL, Rick, L ... 928-523-6696 ... 17 A rick.brandel@nau.edu

BRANDENBURG, Aurelia ... 859-985-3173 ... 198 F aurelia_brandenburg@berea.edu

BRANDENBURG, Mark, C ... 843-953-5252 ... 456 C mark.brandenburg@citadel.edu

BRANDES, Derek ... 509-544-4914 ... 532 C dbrandes@columbiabasin.edu

BRANDES, Gregory ... 310-689-3200 ... 42 F gbrandes@kaplan.edu

BRANDES, Rand ... 828-328-7077 ... 366 B rand.brandes@lr.edu

BRANDFORD-CALVO, Dania, C ... 401-874-2018 ... 454 E brandford@uri.edu

BRANDIMORE, Kimberly ... 989-964-2793 ... 258 A kbrand@svsu.edu

BRANDIMORE, Merry Jo ... 989-964-4289 ... 258 A mjbrand@svsu.edu

BRANDING, Celeste, E ... 630-844-7520 ... 145 C cbrandin@aurora.edu

BRANDON, Alonzo, C ... 757-683-3421 ... 521 L abrandon@odu.edu

BRANDON, Dave, E ... 217-424-3612 ... 158 F dbrandon@millikin.edu

BRANDON, David, A ... 734-764-9416 ... 259 D dabran@umich.edu

BRANDON, Deborah, L ... 909-869-3427 ... 33 G dlbrandon@csupomona.edu

BRANDON, Eileen ... 706-721-2515 ... 130 B ebrandon@georgiahealth.edu

BRANDON, Elvis ... 615-230-3375 ... 476 A elvis.brandon@volstate.edu

BRANDON, Eric ... 828-328-7301 ... 366 B eric.brandon@lr.edu

BRANDON, John, R ... 419-289-5034 ... 384 D jbrandon@ashland.edu

BRANDON, Kevin ... 708-209-3127 ... 148 C kevin.brandon@cuchicago.edu

BRANDON, Lisa, K ... 618-537-6865 ... 157 G lkbrandon@mckendree.edu

BRANDON, Maureen ... 970-247-7264 ... 84 G brandon_m@fortlewis.edu

BRANDON, Sonia ... 970-248-1884 ... 82 B sbrandon@mesastate.edu

BRANDSEN, Cheryl ... 616-526-8538 ... 249 E brac@calvin.edu

BRANDSTETTER, Matthew ... 916-649-2400 ... 31 C

BRANDSTETTER, Mike ... 253-680-7229 ... 531 A mbrandstetter@bates.ctc.edu

BRANDT, Allan, M ... 617-496-1464 ... 235 H brandt@fas.harvard.edu

BRANDT, Barry, M ... 712-707-7284 ... 188 B brandt@nwciowa.edu

BRANDT, Elaine ... 573-897-5000 ... 284 D

BRANDT, Jay, J ... 561-237-7947 ... 113 D jbrandt@lynn.edu

BRANDT, John ... 540-261-4478 ... 524 C john.brandt@svu.edu

BRANDT, John ... 731-661-5015 ... 476 G jbrandt@uu.edu

BRANDT, Martin ... 631-420-2333 ... 356 A martin.brandt@farmingdale.edu

BRANDT, Thompson, A ... 815-599-3450 ... 152 A thompson.brandt@highland.edu

BRANDT, Troy, A ... 515-574-1985 ... 185 F brandt@iowacentral.edu

BRANDT, William ... 973-278-5400 ... 307 G wab@Berkeleycollege.edu

BRANDT, William ... 973-278-5400 ... 323 J wab@Berkeleycollege.edu

BRANDT, William, A ... 724-946-6216 ... 451 C brandtwa@westminster.edu

BRANDT-RAUF, Paul ... 312-996-5939 ... 166 F pwb1@uic.edu

BRANDT STOVER, Cynthia ... 510-430-2380 ... 57 D cbrandtstover@mills.edu

BRANHAM, Celeste ... 207-778-7087 ... 220 C cbranham@maine.edu

BRANHAM, Holly, L ... 307-532-8303 ... 555 H holly.branham@ewc.wy.edu

BRANHAM, Jim ... 512-786-4484 ... 507 H jim.branham@vc.edu

BRANHAM, Keith ... 574-289-7001 ... 176 C kbranham2@ivytech.edu

BRANHAM, LaTonya ... 937-376-6611 ... 386 H lbranham@centralstate.edu

BRANHAM, Lorraine ... 315-443-3627 ... 357 B lbranham@syr.edu

BRANIGAN, David ... 814-863-9150 ... 438 F deb7@psu.edu

BRANKLE, Steve ... 479-524-7209 ... 22 C SBrankle@jbu.edu

BRANNAN, Angie, R ... 262-524-7335 ... 546 E abrannan@carrollu.edu

BRANNAN, Colleen, E ... 607-436-2748 ... 353 E brannace@oneonta.edu

BRANNAN, Leigh ... 334-386-7071 ... 3 H lbrannan@faulkner.edu

BRANNEN, Andy ... 912-287-5858 ... 135 B abrannen@okefenokeetech.edu

BRANNER, Wade, H ... 540-464-7253 ... 529 A brannerwh@vmi.edu

BRANNOCK, Kathleen ... 518-783-2919 ... 350 I

BRANNON, Jennifer ... 478-934-3138 ... 133 G jbrannon@mgc.edu

BRANNON, Jennifer ... 478-374-6221 ... 133 G jbrannon@mgc.edu

BRANNON, Melanie ... 704-357-8020 ... 361 N mbrannon@aii.edu

BRANNON, Tony, L ... 270-809-3328 ... 204 F tony.brannon@murraystate.edu

BRANSFORD, Denise, A ... 312-341-2040 ... 162 I dbrandsford@roosevelt.edu

BRANSKY, David ... 805-654-6400 ... 77 D dbransky@vcccd.edu

BRANSON, Cathy ... 606-487-3148 ... 201 H Cathy.Branson@kctcs.edu

BRANSON, David ... 207-775-3052 ... 218 E dbranson@meca.edu

BRANSON, Lisa ... 703-414-4029 ... 518 B lbranson@devry.edu

BRANSON, Mark ... 312-662-4121 ... 144 C

BRANSON, Mark ... 336-249-8186 ... 369 F mbranson@davidsonccc.edu

BRANSON, Salinda Jo ... 309-649-6217 ... 165 D jo.branson@src.edu

BRANSON, Tracy ... 724-805-2962 ... 446 E tracy.branson@email.stvincent.edu

BRANSON, Walter, J ... 260-481-6804 ... 174 A branson@ipfw.edu

BRANSTETTER, Jeffrey, C ... 402-280-2709 ... 297 H jbranstetter@creighton.edu

BRANSTETTER, Marie ... 913-288-7211 ... 193 J marie@kckcc.edu

BRANT, Christine ... 734-432-5620 ... 254 G cbrant@madonna.edu

BRANT, David ... 310-506-4730 ... 61 G david.brant@pepperdine.edu

BRANT, Felicia ... 202-274-5000 ... 99 F fbrant@udc.edu

BRANT, Joseph ... 410-234-4640 ... 225 E

BRANT, Keith, E ... 925-631-4219 ... 64 F keb5@stmarys-ca.edu

BRANT, Kelly ... 419-772-2073 ... 398 G k-brant@onu.edu

BRANTINGHAM, James ... 323-660-6166 ... 40 G james.brantingham@cleveland.edu

BRANTLEY, Clarence, E ... 248-341-2101 ... 257 B cebrantl@oaklandcc.edu

BRANTLEY, Clinton ... 478-757-5138 ... 139 A cbrantley@wesleyancollege.edu

BRANTLEY, Don ... 970-675-3307 ... 82 D don.brantley@cncc.edu

BRANTLEY, Kyle ... 601-925-7634 ... 275 E brantley@mc.edu

BRANTLEY, Martha, S ... 818-779-8041 ... 53 B mbrantley@kingsuniversity.edu

BRANTLEY, Marty ... 504-865-5724 ... 215 C mbrantle@tulane.edu

BRANTLY, Linda ... 978-762-4000 ... 241 A lbrantly@northshore.edu

BRANTMAYER, Evie ... 304-367-4141 ... 543 E evie.brantmayer@fairmontstate.edu

BRANTNER, Doug ... 316-677-9507 ... 197 E dbrantner@watc.edu

BRANTZ, Malcolm ... 303-797-5739 ... 80 J malcolm.brantz@arapahoe.edu

BRAS, Duane ... 616-222-3000 ... 254 A dbras@kuyper.edu

BRAS, Rafael ... 404-385-5700 ... 130 D provost@gatech.edu

BRASCHERS, Randolph ... 978-934-4000 ... 237 F Randolph_Braschers@uml.edu

BRASE, Don ... 503-399-5184 ... 414 J don.brase@chemeketa.edu

BRASE, Heather ... 314-744-5342 ... 286 C Matlock@mobap.edu

BRASE, Ruby, F ... 217-424-5071 ... 158 F rbrase@millikin.edu

BRASE, Wendell, C ... 949-824-5107 ... 73 H wcbrase@uci.edu

BRASEL, Steve ... 312-329-4194 ... 158 H steve.brasel@moody.edu

BRASETH, Kellie ... 360-596-5214 ... 538 B kbraseth@spscc.ctc.edu

BRASFIELD, Kathleen, L ... 325-942-2264 ... 480 E kathleen.brasfield@angelo.edu

BRASHAR, Neil ... 606-436-5721 ... 201 H neil.brashear@kctcs.edu

BRASHEAR, Kandy ... 615-217-9347 ... 468 B kbrashear@daymarinstitute.edu

BRASHER, Christine ... 337-482-1394 ... 216 D cbrasher@louisiana.edu

BRASHER, Melinda ... 512-313-3000 ... 483 G melinda.brasher@concordia.edu

BRASHER, Sally ... 304-876-5244 ... 544 A sbrasher@shepherd.edu

BRASIER, Terry ... 704-922-6537 ... 370 D brasier.terry@gaston.edu

BRASINGTON, Diane, F ... 804-523-5130 ... 526 F dbrasington@reynolds.edu

BRASINGTON, Dyan, L ... 410-704-3780 ... 228 E dbrasington@towson.edu

BRASLEY, Stephanie, L ... 323-242-5512 ... 55 C braslesl@lasc.edu

BRASSARD, Kevin, F ... 508-213-2213 ... 243 J kevin.brassard@nichols.edu

BRASSARD, Richard, G ... 281-487-1170 ... 498 E rbrassard@txchiro.edu

BRASSAW, Lori ... 435-613-5328 ... 511 E lori.brassaw@ceu.edu

BRASSEUR, Gary ... 989-686-9000 ... 250 F gvbrasse@delta.edu

BRASSORD, James, D ... 413-542-2202 ... 230 A jdbrassord@amherst.edu

BRASTETER, Christina ... 856-256-5173 ... 314 A brasteter@rowan.edu

BRASWELL, Clara ... 478-825-6347 ... 129 C braswellc@fvsu.edu

BRASWELL, Don ... 718-518-4340 ... 327 D dbraswell@hostos.cuny.edu

BRASWELL, James ... 281-476-2771 ... 493 E james.braswell@sjcd.edu

BRASWELL, Lee ... 704-355-6937 ... 363 B lee.braswell@carolinas.org

BRASWELL, Matthew, D ... 717-780-2376 ... 430 E mdbraswe@hacc.edu

BRASWELL, Randy ... 912-260-4407 ... 136 F randy.braswell@sgc.edu

BRASWELL, Rosanne, R ... 864-833-8700 ... 460 E rbraswell@presby.edu

BRASWELL, Theresa ... 484-365-7429 ... 434 H tbraswell@lincoln.edu

BRATCHER, Richard, W ... 434-395-2630 ... 520 G bratcherrw@longwood.edu

BRATCHER, Winnie ... 502-863-8024 ... 200 G winnie_bratcher@georgetowncollege.edu

BRATER, Craig ... 317-274-8416 ... 173 B dbrater@iupui.edu

BRATER, D. Craig ... 317-274-8416 ... 173 C dbrater@iupui.edu

BRATER, D. Craig ... 317-274-8157 ... 174 B dbrater@iupui.edu

BRATHWAITE, Joy, E ... 330-471-8238 ... 395 E jbrathwaite@malone.edu

BRATSCH, John ... 559-730-3776 ... 42 B johnbr@cos.edu

BRATSCH-PRINCE, Dawn ... 515-294-6410 ... 182 B deprince@iastate.edu

BRATT, Jonathan ... 585-594-6830 ... 347 F bratt_jonathan@roberts.edu

BRATT, Kenneth, D ... 616-526-6296 ... 249 E kbratt@calvin.edu

BRATTIN, Emily ... 816-802-3561 ... 283 I

BRATTON, Chris ... 617-267-6100 ... 244 G

BRATTON, Phyllis, K ... 701-252-3467 ... 381 A pbratton@jc.edu

BRATUS, Karen ... 313-425-3732 ... 248 D karen.bratus@baker.edu

BRAUCH, Jeffrey, A ... 757-352-4040 ... 523 B jeffbra@regent.edu

BRAUCHLE, Ken ... 812-237-2334 ... 173 A ken.brauchle@indstate.edu

BRAUER, Cynthia, A ... 757-221-1693 ... 517 J cabra1@wm.edu

BRAUER, David, F ... 270-831-9625 ... 201 I david.brauer@kctcs.edu

BRAUER, Douglas ... 217-875-7200 ... 162 D dbrauer@richland.edu

BRAUER, Jeanna ... 417-667-8181 ... 280 I jbrauer@cottey.edu

BRAUER, Michael, J ... 414-410-4201 ... 546 D mjbrauer@stritch.edu

BRAUER, Susan ... 773-697-2297 ... 149 C sbrauer@devry.edu

BRAUER, William, L ... 757-594-7040 ... 517 I wbrauer@cnu.edu

BRAUGHTON, Michael, L ... 317-788-3214 ... 180 C mbraughton@uindy.edu

BRAUKMAN, Mark ... 303-986-2320 ... 82 E markb@csha.net

BRAUN, Abraham ... 845-425-1370 ... 345 B

BRAUN, Dale, K ... 715-425-3840 ... 552 A dale.k.braun@uwrf.edu

BRAUN, Dennis ... 508-767-7541 ... 230 E dbraun@assumption.edu

BRAUN, Elizabeth ... 610-328-8365 ... 447 E lbraun1@swarthmore.edu

BRAUN, Eric ... 603-428-2241 ... 305 E ebraun@nec.edu

BRAUN, Eric ... 740-351-3257 ... 401 I ebraun@shawnee.edu

BRAUN, Kathy, E ... 603-641-4160 ... 306 F kathy.braun@unh.edu

BRAUN, Keith, V ... 727-816-3336 ... 114 F braunk@phcc.edu

BRAUN, Lynn ... 206-780-6221 ... 530 I lynn.braun@bgi.edu

BRAUN, Mark ... 507-933-7541 ... 264 B mbraun@gustavus.edu

BRAUN, Neil ... 212-346-1962 ... 345 F nbraun@pace.edu

BRAUN, Steve ... 503-280-8500 ... 415 E sbraun@cu-portland.edu

BRAUN, Thomas, W ... 412-648-1938 ... 449 A twb3@pitt.edu

BRAUN PASTERNACK, Carol ... 805-893-2706 ... 74 F c.pasternack@summersessions.ucsb.edu

BRAUNGARD, Elizabeth, A ... 717-361-1525 ... 428 E braungarde@etown.edu

BRAUNINGER, Mike ... 504-280-6590 ... 213 E rbraunin@uno.edu

BRAUNSCHWEIGER, Nanci ... 805-962-8179 ... 28 L

BRAVAIS-SLYMAN, Karine ... 312-777-8674 ... 153 A kbravais-slyman@aii.edu

BRAVEMAN, Daan ... 585-389-2004 ... 342 D dbravem7@naz.edu

BRAVERMAN, David ... 413-748-3100 ... 245 C dbraverman@spfldcol.edu

BRAVERMAN, Lisa, R ... 212-217-3334 ... 333 G lisa_braverman@fitnyc.edu

BRAVERMAN, Marsha ... 215-972-2014 ... 440 I mbraverman@pafa.edu

BRAVMAN, John, C ... 570-577-1511 ... 423 D john.bravman@bucknell.edu

BRAWNER, Dan ... 615-383-4848 ... 478 E dbrawner@watkins.edu

BRAWNER, Jeff ... 901-751-8453 ... 471 D jbrawner@mabts.edu

BRAXTON, Jean, P ... 757-823-8701 ... 521 K jpbraxton@nsu.edu

BRAXTON, Phyllis ... 818-719-6422 ... 55 B braxtopd@piercecollege.edu

BRAXTON, Sallie, W ... 540-286-8016 ... 524 H sbraxton@umw.edu

BRAY, Carol ... 478-289-2088 ... 128 J cbray@ega.edu

BRAY, D. John ... 716-829-7818 ... 332 F brayjd@dyc.edu

BRAY, Jane, S ... 717-872-3379 ... 443 C jane.bray@millersville.edu

BRAY, Jason ... 918-586-4541 ... 410 D jason.bray@okstate.edu

BRAY, Tammy ... 541-737-3220 ... 418 F tammy.bray@oregonstate.edu

BRAY, Thomas, E ... 414-277-7416 ... 548 H bray@msoe.edu

BRAYMER, Meta, R ... 540-286-8014 ... 524 H mbraymer@umw.edu

BRAYTON, Kelley ... 310-434-3465 ... 68 D brayton_kelley@smc.edu

BRAZ, Meredith ... 603-646-2246 ... 305 A meredith.braz@dartmouth.edu

BRAZA, Peter, A ... 904-620-1350 ... 120 C pbraza@unf.edu

BRAZALOVICS, Jennifer ... 440-449-6508 ... 405 B jbrazalovics@ursuline.edu

BRAZEAU, Gayle ... 207-221-4366 ... 220 H gbrazeau@une.edu

BRAZELL, Greg ... 253-964-6696 ... 536 C gbrazell@pierce.ctc.edu

BRAZIEL, Maureen ... 718-260-3860 ... 346 C mbraziel@poly.edu

BRAZIER, Elise ... 512-313-3000 ... 483 G elise.brazier@concordia.edu

BRAZILE, Orella ... 318-670-9315 ... 215 A obrazile@susla.edu

BRAZINA, Paul, R ... 215-951-1040 ... 432 G brazina@lasalle.edu

BRAZIUNAS, Tom ... 206-934-3619 ... 536 H tom.braziunas@seattlecolleges.edu

BRAZZEL, Thomas ... 979-830-4041 ... 482 A Thomas.Brazzel@blinn.edu

BRAZZIL, Nancy, A ... 512-471-1232 ... 505 B nab@po.utexas.edu

BRAZZILE, Evette, C ... 817-515-7733 ... 496 A evette.brazzile@tccd.edu

BRAZZLE, Reggie ... 281-290-2899 ... 490 C reggie.l.brazzle@lonestar.edu

BREAU, Walter, C ... 413-265-2222 ... 233 E breauw@elms.edu

BREAULT, Susan ... 860-412-7362 ... 91 A sbreault@qvcc.commnet.edu

BREAUX, Aminta, H ... 717-872-3594 ... 443 C aminta.breaux@millersville.edu

BREAUX, Arleene ... 479-788-7006 ... 24 D abreaux@uafortsmith.edu

BREAUX, Consuella ... 318-274-3135 ... 215 E breauxc@gram.edu

BRECCIAROLI, T. J ... 814-472-3029 ... 446 B tbrecciaroli@francis.edu

BRECKENRIDGE, Jim ... 650-843-3520 ... 61 A jbreckenridge@paloaltou.edu

BRECKENRIDGE, Joyce ... 412-237-3110 ... 425 H jbreckenridge@ccac.edu

BRECKENRIDGE, Mary, B ... 216-373-5310 ... 397 E mbreckenridge@ndc.edu

BREDFELDT, Becky .... 620-227-9240 .... 192 B
becajo@dc3.edu
BREDFELDT, Gary .... 717-560-8297 .... 433 D
gbredfeldt@lbc.edu
BREDLAU, Peter, S .... 484-664-3120 .... 437 B
bredlau@muhlenberg.edu
BREE, Gretchen .... 217-732-3155 .... 156 G
gbree@lincolncollege.edu
BREECE, James .... 207-973-3212 .... 219 I
breece@maine.edu
BREEDEN, Ann Lloyd .... 804-289-8732 .... 525 A
abreeden@richmond.edu
BREEDEN, Kathy .... 931-540-2555 .... 474 F
mbreeden@columbiastate.edu
BREEDEN, Susan, D .... 804-289-8400 .... 525 A
sbreeden@richmond.edu
BREEDING, MaLesa .... 325-674-2700 .... 478 H
breedingm@acu.edu
BREEDLOVE, Debbie .... 479-788-7052 .... 24 D
dbreedlo@uafortsmith.edu
BREEDLOVE, Paul .... 541-880-2239 .... 416 C
breedlove@klamathcc.edu
BREEN, Anne, L .... 603-271-6310 .... 304 G
abreen@ccsnh.edu
BREEN, Catherine .... 617-495-9047 .... 235 H
catherine_breen@harvard.edu
BREEN, Greg .... 858-653-6740 .... 52 C
BREEN, Patricia .... 312-410-8971 .... 146 C
pbreen@thechicagoschool.edu
BREER, Lynn .... 217-234-5401 .... 155 H
mbreer@lakeland.cc.il.us
BREERWOOD, Adam .... 601-403-1132 .... 277 A
abreerwood@prcc.edu
BREESE, Jeffrey .... 816-501-4370 .... 288 D
jeffrey.breese@rockhurst.edu
BREESE, Steven .... 757-594-8825 .... 517 I
sbreese@cnu.edu
BREESE, William, E .... 414-277-7401 .... 548 H
breese@msoe.edu
BREGOLI, Marilyn .... 617-731-7081 .... 244 B
bregolim@pmc.edu
BREHLER, Elizabeth .... 336-506-4138 .... 367 G
brehlere@alamancecc.edu
BREHM, Larry .... 209-946-2401 .... 75 D
lbrehm@pacific.edu
BREHM, Laura .... 406-243-2593 .... 295 A
laura.brehm@mso.umt.edu
BREHM, Richard .... 540-423-9042 .... 526 E
rbrehm@germanna.edu
BREHM, Sue, M .... 715-833-6245 .... 553 F
sbrehm@cvtc.edu
BREIDENBACH,
Elizabeth, E .... 207-778-7385 .... 220 C
ebreiden@maine.edu
BREINER, Ozzie .... 610-758-3500 .... 434 E
lb05@lehigh.edu
BREISCH, Leah .... 610-282-1100 .... 426 I
leah.breisch@desales.edu
BREITBARTH, Jonathan, S 651-641-8796 .... 263 C
breitbarth@csp.edu
BREITBORDE,
Lawrence, B .... 309-341-7216 .... 155 E
lbreitbo@knox.edu
BREITENBACH, Ed .... 231-777-0295 .... 256 D
BREITENBERG, Mark .... 510-594-3649 .... 31 J
mbreitenberg@cca.edu
BREITMAN, Paul .... 609-258-2676 .... 313 A
breitman@princeton.edu
BREITMEYER, Chris .... 636-922-8281 .... 288 E
cbreitmeyer@stchas.edu
BREJA, Lisa .... 641-844-5576 .... 185 H
lisa.breja@iavalley.edu
BREKKE, Alice .... 701-777-3511 .... 381 D
alice.brekke@email.und.edu
BREKKE, Tom .... 218-723-6717 .... 262 I
tbrekke@css.edu
BREKKEN, Kathryn, C .... 702-651-7535 .... 302 G
kc.brekken@csn.edu
BRELAND, Byron .... 562-938-3903 .... 54 E
bbreland@lbcc.edu
BRELAND, Garry, M .... 601-318-6101 .... 278 E
garry.breland@wmcarey.edu
BRELLIS, Matthew .... 631-687-4561 .... 349 B
mbrellis@sjcny.edu
BRELLIS, Matthew .... 631-447-5396 .... 349 A
mbrellis@sjcny.edu
BRELSFORD, George .... 301-387-3748 .... 222 H
george.brelsford@garrettcollege.edu
BREMER, Cris, M .... 559-489-2220 .... 72 A
crism.bremer@fresnocitycollege.edu
BREMER, Geoff .... 828-669-8012 .... 367 C
BREMER, John, H .... 928-524-7381 .... 17 B
john.bremer@npc.edu
BRENAN, Lindsey .... 212-678-3004 .... 357 F
brenan@exchange.tc.columbia.edu
BRENDEL, William .... 608-785-9175 .... 555 D
brendelw@westerntc.edu
BRENER, Laura .... 360-442-2501 .... 535 C
lbrener@lowercolumbia.edu
BRENN, James, E .... 803-535-5326 .... 456 D
jbrenn@claflin.edu
BRENNAN, Adriana .... 908-737-2586 .... 311 B
adicecil@kean.edu
BRENNAN, Bill .... 815-479-7510 .... 157 F
bbrennan@mchenrye.du
BRENNAN, Blair .... 308-432-6044 .... 299 G
bbrennan@csc.edu
BRENNAN, Christopher .... 732-246-5604 .... 312 A
cbrennan@nbts.edu
BRENNAN, Christopher, J . 978-656-3152 .... 240 F
brennanc@middlesex.mass.edu
BRENNAN, Christopher, P . 727-864-8311 .... 104 K
brennacp@eckerd.edu
BRENNAN, Clara .... 414-410-4004 .... 546 D
cbrennan@stritch.edu
BRENNAN, Cynthia .... 201-684-7695 .... 313 D
brennanc@ramapo.edu
BRENNAN, Deb .... 308-398-7305 .... 297 C
dbrennan@cccneb.edu
BRENNAN, Fran .... 781-595-6768 .... 236 I
fbrennan@mariancourt.edu
BRENNAN, James, F .... 202-319-5244 .... 97 C
brennan@cua.edu
BRENNAN, Jonathan, R .... 607-746-4670 .... 355 E
brennajr@delhi.edu
BRENNAN, Joseph, A .... 716-645-6969 .... 351 G
brennanj@buffalo.edu
BRENNAN, Kara .... 914-633-2410 .... 336 E
kbrennan@iona.edu
BRENNAN, Keith .... 561-732-4424 .... 117 A
kbrennan@svdp.edu
BRENNAN, Kelly .... 914-654-5294 .... 330 B
kbrennan@cnr.edu
BRENNAN, Kevin .... 215-717-6437 .... 448 H
kbrennan@uarts.edu
BRENNAN, Kwi .... 973-748-9000 .... 308 A
kwi_brennan@bloomfield.edu
BRENNAN, Leah .... 860-701-5061 .... 93 B
brennan_l@mitchell.edu
BRENNAN, Lipa .... 718-438-2727 .... 361 J
rlb@novominsk.com
BRENNAN, Mary Rosita .... 201-559-6024 .... 310 C
brennanr@felician.edu
BRENNAN, Nicole .... 617-912-9120 .... 232 E
nbrennan@bostonconservatory.edu
BRENNAN, Rick .... 708-974-5388 .... 159 A
brennan@morainevalley.edu
BRENNAN, Robert, J .... 301-447-7432 .... 225 A
brennan@msmary.edu
BRENNAN, Shannon .... 570-622-7622 .... 436 A
sbrennan@mccannschool.edu
BRENNAN, Terrence .... 972-881-5734 .... 483 D
tbrennan@collin.edu
BRENNAN, Thomas .... 215-951-1516 .... 432 G
brennan@lasalle.edu
BRENNAN, Thomas, H .... 401-341-3232 .... 454 D
brennant@salve.edu
BRENNAN, Timothy, G .... 716-829-7801 .... 332 F
brennant@dyc.edu
BRENNAN, William, J .... 207-326-2220 .... 219 D
bill.brennan@mma.edu
BRENNEMAN, James, E .... 574-535-7501 .... 171 D
president@goshen.edu
BRENNEMANN, Kyle, R .... 573-629-3008 .... 282 H
kbrennemann@hlg.edu
BRENNEN, David .... 859-257-8319 .... 206 H
dabr223@uky.edu
BRENNEN, Kathleen .... 828-227-7398 .... 379 E
kbrennen@wcu.edu
BRENNER, Christina .... 415-354-9324 .... 32 B
cbrenner@baychef.com
BRENNER, David, A .... 858-534-1501 .... 74 D
dbrenner@ucsd.edu
BRENNER, Paul .... 212-237-8968 .... 328 A
pbrenner@jjay.cuny.edu
BRENNER-BUDER,
Barbara .... 415-451-2817 .... 66 B
bbrenner@sfts.edu
BRENT, Alicia .... 831-647-6541 .... 57 F
alicia.brent@miis.edu
BRENT, Daniel .... 617-323-6662 .... 242 C
dan_brent@mspp.edu
BRENTLINGER, Dustin .... 419-448-2062 .... 391 G
dbrentli@heidelberg.edu
BRENTON, Angela, L .... 501-569-3244 .... 24 E
albrenton@ualr.edu
BRENTON, George, W .... 410-857-2714 .... 224 D
gbrenton@mcdaniel.edu
BRENTON, Robin, A .... 410-857-2297 .... 224 D
rbrenton@mcdaniel.edu
BRENZEL, Jeffrey .... 203-432-9321 .... 95 D
jeff.brenzel@yale.edu
BRESALIER, Alex .... 516-364-0808 .... 343 A
executive_assistant@nycollege.edu
BRESCIA, Robert .... 918-610-0027 .... 411 A
rbrescia@communitycarecollege.edu
BRESCIA, Robert .... 918-298-8200 .... 407 F
BRESCIANI, Dean .... 701-231-7211 .... 381 H
dean.bresciani@ndsu.edu
BRESEE, Mikel .... 313-664-7421 .... 250 A
mbresee@collegeforcreativestudies.edu
BRESEMAN, Mark, D .... 920-832-6519 .... 547 J
mark.d.breseman@lawrence.edu
BRESHEARS, Pearlene .... 417-328-1729 .... 290 E
pbreshears@sbuniv.edu
BRESKO, Lynn .... 336-256-1283 .... 379 A
lynn_bresko@uncg.edu
BRESLAUER, George, W .... 510-642-1961 .... 73 E
bresl@berkeley.edu
BRESLER, Pieter .... 304-326-1609 .... 541 G
pbresler@salemu.edu
BRESLIN, Beau .... 518-580-8111 .... 351 B
bbreslin@skidmore.edu
BRESLIN, Eileen, T .... 210-567-5800 .... 506 E
breslin@uthscsa.edu
BRESLIN, Kathleen, A .... 610-359-5131 .... 426 G
kbreslin@dccc.edu
BRESLIN, Lisa .... 410-857-2225 .... 224 D
lbreslin@mcdaniel.edu
BRESNAHAN, Carol .... 407-646-2355 .... 116 B
cbresnahan@rollins.edu
BRESSETT, Ashley, J .... 315-268-4314 .... 329 C
abressett@clarkson.edu
BRESSETTE, Andy .... 706-236-2229 .... 125 G
abressette@berry.edu
BRESSI-STOPPE, Elizabeth 215-895-1104 .... 450 A
ebs@usciences.edu
BRESSINGTON, Cheryl .... 308-865-8655 .... 300 G
bresstonc@unk.edu
BRESSINGTON, Cheryl .... 308-865-8388 .... 300 G
bressingtonc@unk.edu
BRESSLER, Coleen .... 402-844-7006 .... 300 A
coleen@northeast.edu
BRESSLER, Darlene .... 765-677-2147 .... 174 E
darlene.bressler@indwes.edu
BRESSLER, Gregory, W .... 973-655-5457 .... 311 G
bresslerg@mail.montclair.edu
BRETHERICK, Jim .... 941-487-4570 .... 119 D
jbretherick@ncf.edu
BRETL, Jim .... 402-280-2722 .... 297 H
bretlj@creighton.edu
BRETT, Anne .... 417-269-3402 .... 281 B
abrett@coxcollege.edu
BRETT, Jennifer .... 203-576-4122 .... 94 D
acup@bridgeport.edu
BRETTI, Anthony .... 912-478-5966 .... 131 A
tbretti@georgiasouthern.edu
BRETTSCHNEIDER,
Marla, B .... 603-862-4676 .... 306 E
marla.brettschneider@unh.edu
BRETZ, Brenda, K .... 717-245-1587 .... 427 E
bretz@dickinson.edu
BREUDER, Robert, L .... 630-942-2200 .... 147 G
breuder@cod.edu
BREUER, Catherine, L .... 952-487-8243 .... 268 C
catherine.breuer@normandale.edu
BREUER, Isaac .... 718-963-9770 .... 358 H
yab@utsb.org
BREVETT, Renford A, B .... 484-365-7215 .... 434 H
rbrevett@lincoln.edu
BREW, Alan .... 715-682-1226 .... 549 C
abrew@northland.edu
BREW, Alan .... 715-682-1329 .... 549 C
abrew@northland.edu
BREWER, Brent .... 269-782-1411 .... 258 E
bbrewer@swmich.edu
BREWER, Clay .... 618-985-3741 .... 154 E
claybrewer@jalc.edu
BREWER, Dawn, M .... 812-888-4225 .... 181 B
dbrewer@vinu.edu
BREWER, Deborah .... 716-614-5911 .... 344 C
dbrewer@niagaracc.suny.edu
BREWER, Douglas .... 217-333-3061 .... 167 B
d-brewer@illinois.edu
BREWER, Frank .... 301-405-1105 .... 227 B
fbrewer@umd.edu
BREWER, J. Frank .... 301-405-3205 .... 227 B
fbrewer@umd.edu
BREWER, James, L .... 870-460-1074 .... 25 A
brewer@uamont.edu
BREWER, Jane, T .... 843-549-6314 .... 462 E
jtbrewer@mailbox.sc.edu
BREWER, Janet .... 501-760-4313 .... 22 F
jbrewer@npcc.edu
BREWER, Janet, L .... 765-641-4272 .... 169 A
jlbrewer@anderson.edu
BREWER, Jason .... 386-763-2781 .... 114 E
jason.brewer@palmer.edu
BREWER, Jerry, T .... 803-777-4172 .... 462 A
jerry-brewer@sc.edu
BREWER, John .... 801-863-8320 .... 511 C
brewerjc@uvu.edu
BREWER, JR., John, B .... 301-447-5280 .... 225 A
brewer@msmary.edu
BREWER, Kristina .... 260-665-4161 .... 180 A
brewerk@trine.edu
BREWER, Michael, H .... 484-664-3400 .... 437 B
brewer@muhlenberg.edu
BREWER, Michelle .... 318-678-6017 .... 209 J
mbrewer@bpcc.edu
BREWER, Mondy, R .... 806-720-7803 .... 490 D
mondy.brewer@lcu.edu
BREWER, Nathan .... 618-664-6752 .... 151 D
nathan.brewer@greenville.edu
BREWER, Patricia .... 513-487-1182 .... 402 I
patricia.brewer@myunion.edu
BREWER, Randy .... 404-627-2681 .... 126 A
Randy.Brewer@beulah.org
BREWER, Reta .... 785-832-8622 .... 193 B
reta.brewer@bie.edu
BREWER, Rick .... 843-863-7505 .... 456 B
rbrewer@csuniv.edu
BREWER, Robert .... 336-272-7102 .... 364 D
rbrewer@greensborocollege.edu
BREWER, Ryan .... 205-329-7865 .... 3 B
ryan.brewer@ecacolleges.com
BREWER, Stacey .... 864-596-9050 .... 457 E
stacey.brewer@converse.edu
BREWER, Susan .... 870-460-1050 .... 25 A
brewers@uamont.edu
BREWER, Theresa .... 617-427-0060 .... 241 D
tbrewer@rcc.mass.edu
BREWER, Tim .... 704-878-3264 .... 371 H
tbrewer@mitchellcc.edu
BREWINGTON, Donald, E . 512-505-3054 .... 488 B
debrewington@htu.edu
BREWINGTON, Mazie .... 209-384-6108 .... 57 C
mazie.brewington@mccd.edu
BREWIS, Greg, W .... 253-535-7430 .... 535 K
brewisgw@plu.edu
BREWSTER, Carrie .... 925-631-4643 .... 64 F
cbrewste@stmarys-ca.edu
BREWSTER, Edward .... 360-538-4000 .... 534 B
brewster@ghc.edu
BREWSTER, Geoffrey .... 918-610-8303 .... 411 D
geoffrey.brewster@ptstulsa.edu
BREWSTER, Twania .... 312-850-7035 .... 147 C
tbrewster3@ccc.edu
BREY, Amanda .... 805-966-3888 .... 31 A
amanda.brey@brooks.edu
BREYER, Eugene .... 513-569-1564 .... 387 F
eugene.breyer@cincinnatistate.edu
BREZEL, Allen .... 404-872-3593 .... 125 B
abrezel@johnmarshall.edu
BREZINA, Katherine, S .... 401-341-2159 .... 454 D
katherine.brezina@salve.edu
BREZINA, Mike .... 661-362-3302 .... 41 G
mike.brezina@canyons.edu
BREZINSKI, Donald .... 603-645-9688 .... 306 B
d.brezinski@snhu.edu
BREZLER, Kristin, D .... 301-766-3681 .... 223 G
kbrezler@kaplan.edu
BRHEL, Richard, D .... 216-432-8965 .... 387 A
rbhel@ChancellorU.edu
BRIAN, Thomas, J .... 918-631-2200 .... 413 F
thomas-brian@utulsa.edu
BRIANT, Clyde, L .... 401-863-7408 .... 452 J
clyde_briant@brown.edu
BRIAR-LAWSON,
Katharine .... 518-442-5324 .... 351 E
kbriarlawson@uamail.albany.edu
BRIARE, Bill .... 503-594-3110 .... 415 A
billb@clackamas.edu
BRICE, Albie .... 919-761-2100 .... 376 G
abrice@sebts.edu
BRICE, Diane .... 806-371-5028 .... 479 H
kdbrice@actx.edu
BRICE, Michelle .... 312-662-4113 .... 144 C
BRICE-FINCH, Jacqueline .. 410-651-6508 .... 227 E
jbricefinch@umes.edu
BRICELAND, Cynthia .... 724-503-1001 .... 451 A
cbriceland@washjeff.edu
BRICHER, Gary .... 202-884-9133 .... 99 E
bricherg@trinitydc.edu
BRICK, George .... 575-624-8023 .... 319 C
brick@nmmi.edu
BRICK, III,
Harold (Ben), B .... 402-449-2893 .... 298 B
gu-library@graceu.edu
BRICK, Robert .... 979-209-7206 .... 482 A
rbrick@blinn.edu
BRICKER, J. Douglas .... 412-396-6361 .... 428 C
bricker@duq.edu
BRICKER, Susan .... 805-654-6457 .... 77 D
sbricker@vcccd.edu
BRICKER THOMPSON,
Jason, A .... 330-569-6094 .... 391 H
brickerja@hiram.edu
BRICKETTO, Matthew, M ... 610-436-3301 .... 443 F
mbricketto@wcupa.edu
BRICKHOUSE, Nancy .... 302-831-1656 .... 96 F
nbrick@udel.edu
BRICKHOUSE, Wendy, W .. 252-335-0821 .... 369 D
wbrickhouse@albemarle.edu
BRICKLE, Colleen .... 952-487-8158 .... 268 C
colleen.brickle@normandale.edu
BRICKNER-WOOD, Larry .. 603-862-1165 .... 306 E
larry.brickner-wood@unh.edu
BRIDDELL, Jocelyn .... 860-439-2834 .... 91 E
jocelyn.briddell@conncoll.edu
BRIDGE, David .... 605-394-2251 .... 466 A
BRIDGE, Louise .... 801-863-8689 .... 511 C
bridgelo@uvu.edu
BRIDGEMAN, Doris .... 601-977-7836 .... 277 F
dbridgeman@tougaloo.edu
BRIDGEMAN, Robert .... 352-638-9761 .... 101 H
bbridgeman@beaconcollege.edu
BRIDGENS, Marc, E .... 570-326-3761 .... 440 K
mbridgen@pct.edu
BRIDGEO, Kim .... 978-837-5938 .... 242 D
kim.bridgeo@merrimack.edu
BRIDGER, Donald .... 303-458-4206 .... 87 E
dbridger@regis.edu
BRIDGERS, Amy .... 252-399-6397 .... 362 A
abbridgers@barton.edu
BRIDGES, Avie .... 714-564-6910 .... 63 F
bridges_avie@sac.edu

BRIDGES, Barbara 818-785-2726 38 G
BRIDGES, Brian 740-593-2431 399 G
bridgesb@ohio.edu
BRIDGES, Ceil, L 870-235-4079 23 I
clbridges@saumag.edu
BRIDGES, Clarence, E 312-413-5946 166 F
cbridges@uic.edu
BRIDGES, Daniel 323-343-3080 35 B
dbridges@cslanet.calstatela.edu
BRIDGES, Darryl, L 843-661-1225 458 C
dbridges@fmarion.edu
BRIDGES, David 229-391-5050 123 F
dbridges@abac.edu
BRIDGES, Deborah, K 504-280-6173 213 E
dkbridge@uno.edu
BRIDGES, Dennis 309-556-3345 153 E
dbridges@iwu.edu
BRIDGES, George, S 509-527-5132 539 E
bridges@whitman.edu
BRIDGES, Joey 704-406-4647 364 B
jbridges@gardner-webb.edu
BRIDGES, Kermit, S 972-825-4652 495 D
president@sagu.edu
BRIDGES, LaDonna 508-626-4906 238 D
lbridges@framingham.edu
BRIDGES, Ruth 254-298-8309 496 B
ruth.bridges@templejc.edu
BRIDGES, Shelton 502-451-0815 206 B
sbridges@sullivan.edu
BRIDGES, Shelton 502-451-0815 206 C
sbridges@sullivan.edu
BRIDGES, Steven, J 812-465-7048 180 F
sjbridge@usi.edu
BRIDGES, Tharsteen 334-874-5700 3 A
tbridges@concordiaselma.edu
BRIDGESMITH, Larry 615-966-7145 470 D
larry.bridgesmith@lipscomb.edu
BRIDGMAN, Christa, L 828-298-3325 380 C
cbridgma@warren-wilson.edu
BRIDWELL, Chadd, J 210-436-3126 493 C
cbridwell@stmarytx.edu
BRIDWELL, Virginia 425-564-2198 531 B
virginia.bridwell@bellevuecollege.edu
BRIELL, Scott, A 770-538-4706 126 B
sbriell@brenau.edu
BRIEN, Jane 845-758-4294 323 F
brien@bard.edu
BRIER, Bonnie 212-998-4095 344 B
bonnie.brier@nyu.edu
BRIER, Stephen, F 503-370-6022 421 C
sbrier@willamette.edu
BRIERE, Daniel, H 317-788-3277 180 C
dbriere@uindy.edu
BRIGANTTY, Luis 787-725-8120 562 A
lbrigantty0007@eap.edu
BRIGDON, Beth, P 706-721-3840 130 B
bbrigdon@georgiahealth.edu
BRIGGANCE, Richard 615-327-6666 471 A
rbriggance@mmc.edu
BRIGGS, Betty, S 903-510-2371 502 E
bbri@tjc.edu
BRIGGS, Catherine 609-894-9311 308 C
cbriggs@bcc.edu
BRIGGS, Cordell 951-571-6320 64 B
cordell.briggs@rcc.edu
BRIGGS, Darcy 303-797-5623 80 J
darcy.briggs@arapahoe.edu
BRIGGS, De Armond 641-472-1162 187 B
dbriggs@mum.edu
BRIGGS, Douglas, S 540-636-2900 517 H
dougb@christendom.edu
BRIGGS, Jeff 785-628-4200 192 F
jbriggs@fhsu.edu
BRIGGS, Jennifer 812-429-1433 176 I
jbriggs@ivytech.edu
BRIGGS, Jerryl 937-376-6387 386 H
jbriggs@centralstate.edu
BRIGGS, Julia 210-486-2510 479 E
jbriggs@alamo.edu
BRIGGS, Julie, A 585-245-5616 353 C
briggsja@geneseo.edu
BRIGGS, Karen 662-476-5041 274 D
kbriggs@eastms.edu
BRIGGS, Karen, M 215-670-9230 438 D
kmbriggs@peirce.edu
BRIGGS, Kennon 919-807-7100 367 F
briggsk@nccommunitycolleges.edu
BRIGGS, LaNae, R 803-786-3856 457 C
lrbriggs@columbiasc.edu
BRIGGS, LaVerne 804-524-5011 529 C
lbriggs@vsu.edu
BRIGGS, Lawrence 509-359-6685 533 D
lbriggs@ewu.edu
BRIGGS, Lea 605-229-8468 464 I
lea.briggs@presentation.edu
BRIGGS, Lynn 509-359-2227 533 D
lbriggs@ewu.edu
BRIGGS, Mary, K 276-944-6836 518 I
mkbriggs@ehc.edu
BRIGGS, Michelle, A 570-321-4190 435 D
briggs@lycoming.edu
BRIGGS, Patricia 802-831-1234 515 A
dmyette@vermontlaw.edu
BRIGGS, Pertrina 630-743-0695 168 C
pbriggs@westwood.edu
BRIGGS, Peter, F 517-353-1720 255 D
pbriggs@msu.edu
BRIGGS, Sarah, F 517-629-0244 247 E
sbriggs@albion.edu
BRIGGS, Stephen, R 706-236-2281 125 G
sbriggs@berry.edu
BRIGGS, Susan 406-683-7031 295 B
s_briggs@umwestern.edu
BRIGGS, Thyra 909-607-4408 49 D
thyra_briggs@hmc.edu
BRIGGS, William 657-278-3355 34 E
wbriggs@fullerton.edu
BRIGGS KITTREDGE,
Cynthia 512-472-4133 494 B
ckittredge@ssw.edu
BRIGHAM, Allegra 662-329-7100 276 B
BRIGHAM, Bettie Ann 610-341-5823 428 D
bbrigham@eastern.edu
BRIGHAM, David, R 215-972-2056 440 I
skesskler@pafa.edu
BRIGHAM, Jeffrey 617-964-1100 230 B
BRIGHT, Brett, O 903-923-3240 500 A
brett.bright@marshall.tstc.edu
BRIGHT, Caroline, O 240-895-3000 226 A
cobright@smcm.edu
BRIGHT, Don 719-336-1527 85 K
don.bright@lamarcc.edu
BRIGHT, Harry 641-472-1178 187 B
hbright@mum.edu
BRIGHT, James (Phillip) 731-881-7845 477 E
pbright@utm.edu
BRIGHT, Kimberly 719-336-1590 85 K
kimberly.bright@lamarcc.edu
BRIGHT, Kristina 573-592-4257 293 E
kbright@williamwoods.edu
BRIGHT, Marvin, L 631-451-4737 356 D
brightm@sunysuffolk.edu
BRIGHT, Phillip 304-766-3322 544 D
pbright@wvstateu.edu
BRIGHT, Roxanne 304-462-4111 543 F
roxanne.bright@glenville.edu
BRIGHT, Steve 434-544-8208 520 H
bright@lynchburg.edu
BRIGHTBILL, Ashley, E 330-287-7507 399 A
brightbill.10@osu.edu
BRILEY, Brantley 252-527-6223 371 D
bbriley@lenoircc.edu
BRILEY, Jana 912-478-1652 131 A
janawms@georgiasouthern.edu
BRILEY, Terry 615-966-5714 470 D
terry.briley@lipscomb.edu
BRILL, Ann 309-341-7130 155 E
abrill@knox.edu
BRILL, Ann, M 785-864-4755 196 F
abrill@ku.edu
BRILL, Carol 414-382-6054 545 H
carol.brill@alverno.edu
BRILLER, Vladimir 718-636-4245 346 D
vbriller@pratt.edu
BRILLHART, David 740-366-9183 399 E
brillhart.5@osu.edu
BRILLHART, David 740-366-9319 386 G
brillhart.5@osu.edu
BRIMAGE, Yira 602-285-7229 16 B
yira.brimage@pcmail.maricopa.edu
BRIMHALL, Carrie 218-736-1504 267 G
carrie.brimhall@minnesota.edu
BRIMHALL, Joseph 503-251-5712 420 H
jebrimhall@uws.edu
BRIMI, Barbara 865-251-1800 472 K
bbrimi@southcollegetn.edu
BRIMMER, Diane, L 608-796-3801 553 A
dlbrimmer@viterbo.edu
BRIMMER, Donald, L 607-735-1900 333 A
dbrimmer@elmira.edu
BRINDLE, Denise 508-213-2372 243 J
denise.brindle@nichols.edu
BRINDLEY, Rob 330-339-3391 394 B
rbrindley@kent.edu
BRINGAZE, Tammy 413-572-5491 239 C
tbringaze@wsc.ma.edu
BRINGER, Michael 573-288-6300 281 D
mbringer@culver.edu
BRINGHURST, Steve 435-652-7901 512 A
brings@dixie.edu
BRINGLE, Jennifer 336-721-2831 376 C
jennifer.bringle@salem.edu
BRINGLE, Mary, L 828-884-8142 362 D
mbringle@brevard.edu
BRINGSJORD, Elizabeth 518-320-1356 351 D
elizabeth.bringsjord@suny.edu
BRINING, Patricia, N 856-691-8600 309 C
pbrining@cccnj.edu
BRINK, Erik, D 213-821-1900 76 C
ebrink@usc.edu
BRINK, SC, Mary Louise 631-423-0483 350 G
mlbrink@icseminary.edu
BRINK, Matthew 302-831-2392 96 F
mbrink@udel.edu
BRINKER, Cynthia, S 812-464-1774 180 F
cbrinker@usi.edu
BRINKERHOFF, Cal 760-252-2411 30 F
cbrinkerhoff@barstow.edu
BRINKLEY, Buffy 225-359-9213 209 K
bbrinkley@catc.edu
BRINKLEY, Frankie, M 252-335-3787 377 D
fmbrinkley@mail.ecsu.edu
BRINKLEY, William, R 713-798-5263 481 H
brinkley@bcm.edu
BRINKMAN, Cathy 818-364-7723 55 A
brinkmanc@lamission.edu
BRINN, Tracy 423-461-8736 471 H
tnbrinne@milligan.edu
BRINNEMAN, Charlotte 859-525-6510 205 D
cbrinneman@ncbt.edu
BRINNEMAN, Charlotte 859-525-6510 204 H
cbrinneman@national-college.edu
BRINNEMAN, Charlotte 859-525-6510 205 A
cbrinneman@national-college.edu
BRINNEMAN, Charlotte 859-525-6510 204 G
cbrinneman@national-college.edu
BRINSON, Anne 317-921-4831 175 G
aebrinson@ivytech.edu
BRINSON, Donna 770-781-6963 132 J
dbrinson@laniertech.edu
BRINSON, Kristy 910-296-1429 371 B
kbrinson@jamessprunt.edu
BRINSON, Leigh 312-935-4408 162 E
lbrinson@robertmorris.edu
BRINSON, Marla 732-906-4233 311 E
mbrinson@middlesexcc.edu
BRINSON, Reginald 404-880-8779 126 I
rbrinson@cau.edu
BRINSON, Willie, L 919-735-5151 374 F
wlbrinson@waynecc.edu
BRIONES, Eloisa 650-738-4227 67 G
briones@smccd.edu
BRISBANE, Frances, L 631-444-2139 352 C
frances.brisbane@stonybrook.edu
BRISCO, Thomas, V 325-670-1211 487 D
tbrisco@hsutx.edu
BRISCOE, Doris 573-288-6511 281 D
dbriscoe@culver.edu
BRISCOE, Stephen, A 641-269-4570 185 A
briscoe@grinnell.edu
BRISKEY, Marvin 614-947-6002 391 A
briskeym@franklin.edu
BRISKI, Colleen 562-997-5351 44 G
cbriski@devry.edu
BRISSON, E. Carson 804-355-0671 524 F
cbrisson@upsem.edu
BRISSON, Jerry 314-529-9356 284 F
jbrisson@maryville.edu
BRISSON, Michelle 973-408-3454 309 F
mbrisson@drew.edu
BRISTLE, Shawn 928-758-3926 16 G
sbristle@mohave.edu
BRISTOL, Cecelia, M 815-226-4083 162 H
cbristol@rockford.edu
BRISTOL, David 919-513-6210 378 B
david_bristol@ncsu.edu
BRISTOL, Jon 315-472-6603 325 E
jbristol@bryantstratton.edu
BRISTOL, Louis 860-738-6328 90 F
lbristol@nwcc.commnet.edu
BRISTOR, Valerie 561-297-3357 118 H
bristor@fau.edu
BRISTOW, Aimee 573-592-5364 293 C
Aimee.Bristow@westminster-mo.edu
BRISTOW, Vance 662-325-3707 276 A
vbristow@foundation.msstate.edu
BRITIGAN, Bradley, E 402-559-4000 301 A
bradley.britigan@unmc.edu
BRITO, Aurora 718-289-5910 326 F
aurora.brito@bcc.cuny.edu
BRITO, Herbert 912-525-6928 136 B
hbrito@scad.edu
BRITO, Sandra 508-362-2131 240 A
sbrito@capecod.edu
BRITT, Ann, R 252-789-0222 371 E
abritt@martincc.edu
BRITT, Anthony 252-328-4781 377 C
britta@ecu.edu
BRITT, Denise 404-752-1500 134 B
dbritt@msm.edu
BRITT, Helen 904-470-8210 105 A
h.britt@ewc.edu
BRITT, James 312-629-6869 164 A
jbrittjr1@saic.edu
BRITT, Julianne 781-891-3456 231 F
jbritt@bentley.edu
BRITT, Nathan 509-865-8591 534 D
britt_n@heritage.edu
BRITT, Rosemary 704-272-5342 373 F
rbritt@spcc.edu
BRITTAIN, Andrew 808-236-5288 140 B
abrittain@hpu.edu
BRITTAIN, Frederick, L 207-778-7303 220 C
brittain@maine.edu
BRITTAIN, Jack, W 801-587-3836 510 L
jack.brittain@utah.edu
BRITTAIN, Lee 936-468-3206 495 H
lbrittain@sfasu.edu
BRITTAIN, Linda, D 717-264-4141 452 B
lbrittain@wilson.edu
BRITTEN, Richard, S 937-778-7814 390 G
rbritten@edisonohio.edu
BRITTENHAM, Marti 505-224-4340 317 J
mbrittenham@cnm.edu
BRITTINGHAM, Kay 425-739-8178 535 B
kay.brittingham@lwtc.edu
BRITTON, Brian, J 401-232-6051 453 A
bbritton@bryant.edu
BRITTON, Dana, J 717-766-2511 436 D
dbritton@messiah.edu
BRITTON, Keith, E 803-938-3882 462 F
kbritton@uscsumter.edu
BRITTON, Malcolm, E 719-884-5000 86 D
mebritton@nbc.edu
BRITTON, Mark 620-441-5595 192 A
britton@cowley.edu
BRITTON, Sharon, R 419-372-0689 385 D
sbritto@bgsu.edu
BRITTON, Terry 405-733-7300 411 I
tbritton@rose.edu
BRITZ, Johannes 412-229-4501 551 C
britz@uwm.edu
BRIZENDINE, Emily 510-602-6767 34 C
emily.brizendine@csueastbay.edu
BRKOVICH, LeAnna 814-536-5168 424 C
lbrkovich@crbc.net
BROADBENT, Hilary 505-888-8898 320 H
hbroadbent@msn.com
BROADDUS, Henry, R 757-221-3980 517 J
hrbroa@wm.edu
BROADDUS, Virginia 202-884-9291 99 E
broaddusv@trinitydc.edu
BROADED,
C. Montgomery 317-940-8312 170 C
mbroaded@butler.edu
BROADHEAD, Fenton, L 208-496-1123 142 G
broadheadf@byui.edu
BROADIE, II, Paul 845-341-4020 345 E
paul.broadie@sunyorange.edu
BROADUS, Alicia 330-684-8901 403 C
broadus@uakron.edu
BROADWATER, Bonnie 301-387-3050 222 H
bonnie.broadwater@garrettcollege.edu
BROADWATER, Larry 865-251-1800 472 K
lbroadw@southcollegetn.edu
BROADWAY, Michael, J 906-227-2700 256 F
mbroadwa@nmu.edu
BROCATO, Christian 617 951 2360 243 C
christian.brocato@necb.edu
BROCATO, MaryAnne 662-332-8750 275 F
mbrocato@msdelta.edu
BROCK, Amber 229-226-1621 137 F
abrock@thomasu.edu
BROCK, David, W 480-245-7969 14 K
david.brock@ibconline.edu
BROCK, Deborah 540-891-3046 526 E
dbrock@germanna.edu
BROCK, Deborah, M 804-828-8036 525 E
dmbrock@vcu.edu
BROCK, Donna 404-880-8337 126 I
dbrock@cau.edu
BROCK, Gary 419-251-1780 395 H
gary.brock@mercycollege.edu
BROCK, III, Harry, B 205-726-4071 6 G
bbrock@samford.edu
BROCK, J, C 727-341-4495 116 F
brock.jc@spcollege.edu
BROCK, James, L 253-535-7445 535 K
brockjl@plu.edu
BROCK, Jeanette 239-513-1122 110 K
jbrock@hodges.edu
BROCK, John, R 920-206-2320 548 B
jbrock@mbbc.edu
BROCK, Kathy 218-736-1500 267 G
kathy.brock@minnesota.edu
BROCK, Kishia 480-517-8567 16 C
kishia.brock@riosalado.edu
BROCK, Lynn, A 937-766-7846 386 F
brockl@cedarville.edu
BROCK, Marcius 507-389-6266 267 H
marcius.brock@mnsu.edu
BROCK, Michael 610-989-1246 450 E
mbrock@vfmac.edu
BROCK, Michelle 704-272-5357 373 F
mbrock@spcc.edu
BROCK, Nancy, R 802-258-3357 514 C
Nancy.brock@worldlearning.org
BROCK, Nikki 336-917-5473 376 C
nikki.brock@salem.edu
BROCK, Regan 419-251-8968 395 H
regan.brock@mercycollege.edu
BROCK, Summer 252-399-6383 362 A
sebrock@barton.edu
BROCK, Teresa 817-598-6348 508 C
tbrock@wc.edu
BROCK, Todd 270-686-9551 198 G
todd.brock@brescia.edu
BROCKBANK, Kevin 406-444-6775 295 C
kevin.brockbank@umhelena.edu
BROCKENBROUGH,
Karl, B 301-860-3470 228 A
kbrockenbrough@bowiestate.edu
BROCKETT, Lori 760-750-4405 36 B
brockett@csusm.edu

BROCKGREITENS, Kathy ... 636-922-8229 ... 288 E kbrockgreitens@stchas.edu
BROCKIE, Clarena ... 406-353-2607 ... 294 E cbrockie@mail.fbcc.edu
BROCKIE, Dixie ... 406-353-2607 ... 294 E dbrockie@mail.fbcc.edu
BROCKIE, Kimberly ... 406-353-2607 ... 294 E kbrockie@mail.fbcc.edu
BROCKINGTON, Joseph, L ... 269-337-7133 ... 253 F Joe.Brockington@kzoo.edu
BROCKINTON, W. Joseph . 864-644-5142 ... 461 B jbrockinton@swu.edu
BROCKMAN, Diane ... 660-596-7205 ... 290 F dbrockman@sfccmo.edu
BROCKMYER, Richard, A .. 801-832-2516 ... 512 F rbrockmyer@westminstercollege.edu
BROCKWAY, David, J ... 601-318-6199 ... 278 E david.brockway@wmcarey.edu
BROCKWELL, Gerri, S ... 423-323-0226 ... 475 E gsbrockwell@northeaststate.edu
BROD, Catherine ... 847-925-6278 ... 151 E cbrod@harpercollege.edu
BRODA, Joanna ... 212-346-1652 ... 345 F jbroda@pace.edu
BRODAK, Elizabeth ... 970-248-1029 ... 82 B ebrodak@mesastate.edu
BRODE, Andrea, M ... 602-791-6186 ... 305 B brodea@franklinpierce.edu
BRODERHAUSEN, Cathryn 843-863-7523 ... 456 B cbroderhausen@csuniv.edu
BRODERICK, Christopher .. 503-725-3773 ... 418 G christopher.broderick@pdx.edu
BRODERICK, Deborah ... 212-998-6825 ... 344 B deborah.broderick@nyu.edu
BRODERICK, Jo ... 978-921-4242 ... 242 F jbroderick@montserrat.edu
BRODERICK, John, R ... 757-683-3159 ... 521 L jbroderi@odu.edu
BRODERICK, JR., John, T 603-513-5100 ... 306 G john.broderick@law.unh.edu
BRODERICK, Katherine, S . 202-274-7332 ... 99 F sbroderick@udc.edu
BRODERICK, Marc ... 703-993-8756 ... 519 A mbroder1@gmu.edu
BRODERICK, Mark, C ... 410-617-2713 ... 224 A mbroder@loyola.edu
BRODERICK, Marybeth ... 845-848-7824 ... 332 C marybeth.broderick@dc.edu
BRODERICK, Michael ... 860-231-5430 ... 93 H mbroderick@sjc.edu
BRODERICK, Terry ... 704-688-2701 ... 375 G broderit@queens.edu
BRODERICK, Victor, K ... 217-786-2414 ... 156 I victor.broderick@llcc.edu
BRODEUR, Thomas ... 860-832-2531 ... 91 G brodeur@ccsu.edu
BRODHEAD, Richard, H ... 919-684-2424 ... 363 I president@duke.edu
BRODIE, Carol ... 209-946-2261 ... 75 D cbrodie@pacific.edu
BRODIE, Janet ... 909-621-8880 ... 40 C janet.farrell-brodie@cgu.edu
BRODIE, Marilyn ... 408-298-2181 ... 67 C marilyn.brodie@sjcc.edu
BRODIGAN, Becky ... 207-721-5235 ... 217 E rbrodiga@bowdoin.edu
BRODMERKEL, Darcy ... 570-674-6466 ... 436 F dbrodmer@misericordia.edu
BRODRICK, Tracy ... 970-248-1422 ... 82 B tbrodrick@mesastate.edu
BRODSKY, Mikhail ... 510-208-2803 ... 54 B president@lincolnuca.edu
BRODSKY, Stephen ... 212-346-1274 ... 345 F sbrodksy@pace.edu
BRODY, Charmain ... 610-398-5300 ... 434 F cbrody@lincolntech.com
BRODY, Gerald, D ... 512-863-1582 ... 495 G brodyj@southwestern.edu
BRODY, Lynne ... 512-863-1214 ... 495 G brodyl@southwestern.edu
BRODY, Michael ... 503-777-7521 ... 420 A brodym@reed.edu
BRODY, Susan, S ... 617-262-5000 ... 232 B sue.brody@the-bac.edu
BRODZINSKI, Deborah ... 312-935-6659 ... 162 E dbrody@robertmorris.edu
BRODZINSKI, James ... 773-298-3601 ... 163 G brodzinski@sxu.edu
BROERING, Naomi ... 619-574-6909 ... 60 E nbroering@pacificcollege.edu
BROESTL, Mary, K ... 419-559-2317 ... 402 D mbroestl@terra.edu
BROGAN, Frank, T ... 850-245-0466 ... 118 F chancellor@flbog.edu
BROGAN, Jamey ... 304-243-2385 ... 545 G jbrogan@wju.edu
BROGAN, John, J ... 712-707-7200 ... 188 B jbrogan@nwciowa.edu
BROGAN, Michael, S ... 716-839-8227 ... 331 G mbrogan@daemen.edu
BROGDEN, Jeff, D ... 919-658-7171 ... 367 D jbrogden@moc.edu
BROGDEN, Susan ... 513-244-4524 ... 388 D susan_brogden@mail.msj.edu
BROGDON, Christina ... 304-327-4049 ... 543 C cbrogdon@bluefieldstate.edu
BROGE, Jason ... 989-275-5000 ... 253 K jason.broge@kirtland.edu
BROGGER, Ann ... 361-572-6414 ... 507 G jessie.brogger@victoriacollege.edu
BROIDA, Judith ... 410-888-9048 ... 226 F jbroida@tai.edu
BROKAW, Melinda, S ... 319-399-8617 ... 183 C mbrokaw@coe.edu
BROKAW, Michelle ... 617-217-9228 ... 231 C mbrokaw@baystate.edu
BROKENSHIRE, Catherine . 312-980-9216 ... 153 G cbrokenshire@iadtchicago.edu
BROKKEN, Patty ... 319-385-6391 ... 186 A pbrokken@iwc.edu
BROKOPP, Charles ... 608-890-1569 ... 550 G cdb@mail.slh.wisc.edu
BROLLEY, Francis, R ... 815-224-0524 ... 153 D fran_brolley@ivcc.edu
BROLLEY, Francis, R ... 815-224-0466 ... 153 D fran_brolley@ivcc.edu
BROM, Donald ... 215-637-7700 ... 430 H dbrom@holyfamily.edu
BROMAN, Erica ... 413-552-2747 ... 240 C ebroman@hcc.edu
BROMANDER, Lowell ... 651-523-2225 ... 264 C lbromander@hamline.edu
BROMBACH, Ruth, C ... 651-690-6666 ... 271 E rcbrombach@stkate.edu
BROMBERG, Ellis ... 414-297-6600 ... 554 D brombere@matc.edu
BROMBERGER, Brian ... 504-861-5550 ... 213 F bbromber@loyno.edu
BROMFIELD, Robert, L ... 415-422-2786 ... 76 B rlbromfield@usfca.edu
BROMFIELD, Wayne, A ... 570-577-1149 ... 423 D wayne.bromfield@bucknell.edu
BROMILOW, Neil, F ... 336-278-5490 ... 364 A bromilow@elon.edu
BROMLEY, Dennis ... 801-957-4357 ... 512 C dennis.bromley@slcc.edu
BROMLEY, Michael, D ... 203-576-4641 ... 94 D mbromley@bridgeport.edu
BROMMELSIEK, Margaret . 816-235-6092 ... 291 E brommelsiekm@umkc.edu
BROMSTAD, Peter, J ... 770-720-5521 ... 135 F pjb@reinhardt.edu
BROND, David, L ... 302-831-3358 ... 96 F dbrond@udel.edu
BRONDER, James, S ... 419-227-3141 ... 404 D jsbronde@unoh.edu
BRONET, Frances ... 541-346-3631 ... 419 B fbronet@uoregon.edu
BRONFMAN, Jane ... 860-906-5103 ... 89 L jbronfman@ccc.commnet.edu
BRONK, Leslie ... 612-977-4222 ... 262 A leslie.bronk@capella.edu
BRONK, Lisa ... 315-792-3006 ... 359 C lbronk@utica.edu
BRONNER, Gwethalyn ... 847-543-2685 ... 147 H gbronner@clcillinois.edu
BRONNER, Jennifer ... 740-826-8131 ... 396 I jbronner@muskingum.edu
BRONOSKE, Bruce, L ... 253-752-2020 ... 533 J registrar@faithseminary.edu
BRONSON, Jennifer ... 412-365-1862 ... 425 B jbronson@chatham.edu
BRONSTEIN, Chaim ... 212-960-5400 ... 346 F bronstein@yu.edu
BRONSTEIN, Susan ... 716-338-1035 ... 337 E susanbronstein@mail.sunyjcc.edu
BROOKBANK, Julie ... 605-995-3026 ... 464 E julie.brookbank@mitchelltech.edu
BROOKE, Judith ... 321-674-8053 ... 108 E jbrooke@fit.edu
BROOKE, Patrick, T ... 630-752-5126 ... 168 F patrick.brooke@wheaton.edu
BROOKE, JR., Paul, P ... 806-743-3223 ... 501 E paul.brooke@ttuhsc.edu
BROOKER, Nancy ... 330-287-1302 ... 399 A brooker.1@osu.edu
BROOKER, Sarah ... 717-564-4112 ... 432 A sbrooker@kaplan.edu
BROOKET, Jenn ... 517-264-7159 ... 258 D jbrooket@sienaheights.edu
BROOKEY, Lauren, F ... 918-595-7977 ... 412 H lbrookey@tulsacc.edu
BROOKNER, Laurie ... 415-565-8813 ... 73 G brookner@uchastings.edu
BROOKOVER, Cecile ... 504-520-7563 ... 217 A cbrookov@xula.edu
BROOKS, Arthur, L ... 937-382-6661 ... 405 H art_brooks@wilmington.edu
BROOKS, Beth ... 206-878-3710 ... 534 E bbrooks@highline.edu
BROOKS, Beth, A ... 708-763-6975 ... 162 C beth.brooks@resu.edu
BROOKS, Billie, K ... 304-696-3004 ... 542 G hendersb@mctc.edu
BROOKS, Bob ... 325-670-1426 ... 487 D Bob.Brooks@hsutx.edu
BROOKS, Bryan ... 972-825-4821 ... 495 D BBrooks@sagu.edu
BROOKS, Carlton ... 719-502-2003 ... 86 G carlton.brooks@ppcc.edu
BROOKS, Carol, A ... 810-762-7870 ... 253 I cbrooks@kettering.edu
BROOKS, Carolyn ... 323-856-7742 ... 28 D cbrooks@afi.com
BROOKS, Charles ... 803-705-4358 ... 455 D brooksc@benedict.edu
BROOKS, Cindy, L ... 610-799-1121 ... 434 D cbrooks@lccc.edu
BROOKS, Craig ... 719-336-1674 ... 85 K craig.brooks@lamarcc.edu
BROOKS, Cynthia ... 615-963-7410 ... 474 A cbrooks@tnstate.edu
BROOKS, Dana, D ... 304-293-8026 ... 544 E dbrooks@mail.wvu.edu
BROOKS, Danny, K ... 205-226-4699 ... 2 C dbrooks@bsc.edu
BROOKS, Darlene, D ... 901-843-3901 ... 472 I brooksd@rhodes.edu
BROOKS, DeeAnna ... 803-323-2225 ... 463 D brooksd@winthrop.edu
BROOKS, Delores, J ... 708-974-5376 ... 159 A brooks@morainevalley.edu
BROOKS, II, Earl, D ... 260-665-4101 ... 180 A brookse@trine.edu
BROOKS, Fred ... 252-451-8233 ... 372 B fbrooks@nash.cc.nc.us
BROOKS, Gail ... 562-951-4455 ... 33 E gbrooks@calstate.edu
BROOKS, Glee, R ... 530-226-4188 ... 69 H gbrooks@simpsonu.edu
BROOKS, Glenn ... 734-432-5541 ... 254 G gabrooks@madonna.edu
BROOKS, II, H. Gordon ... 337-482-6224 ... 216 D gbrooks@louisiana.edu
BROOKS, Henry, M ... 410-651-6206 ... 227 E hmbrooks@umes.edu
BROOKS, James ... 386-481-2716 ... 101 I brooksj@cookman.edu
BROOKS, James, J ... 541-346-3221 ... 419 B fawww@uoregon.edu
BROOKS, James, W ... 304-326-1500 ... 541 G jwb@salemu.edu
BROOKS, Jessica, P ... 680-488-2471 ... 560 A jessicab@palau.edu
BROOKS, John ... 678-466-4232 ... 127 A johnbrooks@clayton.edu
BROOKS, John, I ... 910-672-1060 ... 377 E jibrooks@uncfsu.edu
BROOKS, Julia ... 503-223-2245 ... 416 E jbrooks@westernculinary.com
BROOKS, Juliette ... 201-692-7050 ... 310 B juliette_brooks@fdu.edu
BROOKS, Justin, P ... 619-239-0391 ... 37 D jbrooks@cwsl.edu
BROOKS, Keith ... 410-706-7131 ... 227 C kbrooks@umaryland.edu
BROOKS, Kent ... 580-477-7764 ... 414 C kent.brooks@wosc.edu
BROOKS, L. Rayburn ... 864-941-8301 ... 460 D brooks.r@ptc.edu
BROOKS, Larry ... 701-228-5457 ... 382 C larry.brooks@dakotacollege.edu
BROOKS, LaShundia ... 281-899-1240 ... 492 G lashundia.brooks@remingtoncollege.edu
BROOKS, Laura ... 410-234-4559 ... 225 E
BROOKS, Lois ... 541-737-0739 ... 418 F lois.brooks@oregonstate.edu
BROOKS, Lyvette ... 215-751-8046 ... 426 B lbrooks@ccp.edu
BROOKS, Marilyn, A ... 804-257-5846 ... 529 D mabrooks2@vuu.edu
BROOKS, Mark ... 229-931-2246 ... 136 G mbrooks@southgatech.edu
BROOKS, Mark, D ... 270-901-1117 ... 201 E mark.brooks@kctcs.edu
BROOKS, Nancy, S ... 515-294-8757 ... 182 B nsbrook@iastate.edu
BROOKS, Page, M ... 504-282-4455 ... 213 H pbrooks@nobts.edu
BROOKS, Patricia ... 662-621-4168 ... 273 I pbrooks@coahomacc.edu
BROOKS, Paul ... 972-825-4616 ... 495 D pbrooks@sagu.edu
BROOKS, Randy, M ... 217-424-6205 ... 158 F rbrooks@millikin.edu
BROOKS, Robert ... 617-928-4602 ... 243 A rbrooks@mountida.edu
BROOKS, Roger, L ... 860-439-2030 ... 91 E roger.brooks@conncoll.edu
BROOKS, Roger, L ... 804-289-8491 ... 525 A rbrooks@richmond.edu
BROOKS, Ronnie ... 615-963-5671 ... 474 A rbrooks@tnstate.edu
BROOKS, Sherry ... 906-635-2216 ... 254 C sbrooks@lssu.edu
BROOKS, Sherry, L ... 906-635-2216 ... 254 C sbrooks1@lssu.edu
BROOKS, Steven ... 954-776-4456 ... 112 H
BROOKS, Susan, H ... 704-687-5770 ... 378 E sbrooks@uncc.edu
BROOKS, Susan, W ... 317-921-4896 ... 175 G swbrooks@ivytech.edu
BROOKS, Susie, A ... 651-631-5312 ... 270 E sabrooks2@nwc.edu
BROOKS, Telaekah ... 202-884-9519 ... 99 E brookst@trinitydc.edu
BROOKS, Tim ... 617-627-3986 ... 245 F tim.brooks@tufts.edu
BROOKS, Tim ... 314-977-7221 ... 289 F tbrooks5@slu.edu
BROOKS, Tom ... 828-339-4202 ... 373 H tbrooks@southwesterncc.edu
BROOKS, Tyrone, W ... 208-885-5255 ... 144 B tyroneb@uidaho.edu
BROOKS, Vera ... 410-462-8500 ... 221 D vbrooks@bccc.edu
BROOKS, Walter ... 609-586-4800 ... 311 C brooksw@mccc.edu
BROOKS, Wanda ... 504-816-4039 ... 208 I wbrooks@dillard.edu
BROOKS, Wendy ... 989-358-7299 ... 247 G brooksw@alpenacc.edu
BROOKS, Wesley, H ... 319-352-8260 ... 189 F wes.brooks@wartburg.edu
BROOKS BLAIR, Sarah, D 937-529-2201 ... 403 A sblair@united.edu
BROOKSHIRE, Kathy ... 601-484-8612 ... 275 C kbrooksh@mcc.cc.ms.us
BROOKSHIRE, Sue ... 252-940-6328 ... 367 I sueb@beaufortcc.edu
BROOM, Cheryl ... 760-795-2121 ... 57 E cbroom@miracosta.edu
BROOM, Mahailier, L ... 318-670-9345 ... 215 A mbroom@susla.edu
BROOMALL, James, K ... 302-831-2795 ... 96 F jbroom@udel.edu
BROOME, Betty ... 325-649-8041 ... 488 A bbroome@hputx.edu
BROOME, JR., David, E ... 704-687-5732 ... 378 E debroome@uncc.edu
BROOME, Marion, E ... 317-274-1486 ... 174 B mbroome@iupui.edu
BROOMHEAD, Keiko ... 617-989-4034 ... 246 C broomheadk@wit.edu
BROPHY, Ann ... 314-968-6922 ... 293 A annbrophy26@webster.edu
BROPHY, Bonni ... 972-599-3143 ... 483 D bbrophy@collin.edu
BROPHY, E, J ... 256-824-6144 ... 9 A william.brophy@uah.edu
BROPHY, George ... 860-768-4608 ... 95 A brophy@hartford.edu
BROPHY, Michael, S ... 310-377-5501 ... 56 F mbrophy@marymountpv.edu
BRORSON, Susan ... 218-281-8186 ... 272 A sbrorson@umn.edu
BROSCH, Lisa ... 630-617-6466 ... 150 F lbrosch@elmhurst.edu
BROSCHART, Jim ... 607-431-4026 ... 335 B broschartj@hartwick.edu
BROSE, Jack ... 740-593-1660 ... 399 G
BROSE, John, A ... 740-593-2247 ... 399 G brose@ohio.edu
BROSIUS, Jo ... 859-622-2474 ... 200 D jo.brosius@eku.edu
BROSKE, Kathleen, M ... 920-924-2139 ... 554 E kbroske@morainepark.edu
BROSKI, Annette ... 315-792-5411 ... 341 E abroski@mvcc.edu
BROSKY, Lisa ... 502-213-2400 ... 202 B lisa.brosky@kctcs.edu
BROSNAN, Joseph, S ... 215-489-2203 ... 426 H Joseph.Brosnan@delval.edu
BROSNIHAN, Kathleen ... 508-626-4575 ... 238 D kbrosnihan@framingham.edu
BROSSEAU, Gayle ... 323-265-8973 ... 54 G brossegd@elac.edu
BROSSETTE, Alicia ... 214-768-2030 ... 494 F abrosset@smu.edu
BROSSMANN, William, D . 517-321-0242 ... 252 B wbrossmann@glcc.edu
BROSTROM, Nathan, E ... 510-987-9029 ... 73 D nathan.brostrom@ucop.edu
BROSZ, Jeff ... 952-545-2000 ... 270 J Jeff.Brosz@Rasmussen.edu
BROTHERS, Gregory, A ... 713-646-1888 ... 494 E gbrothers@stcl.edu
BROTHERS, James, F ... 937-229-2829 ... 404 A James.Brothers@notes.udayton.edu
BROTHERS, Wes ... 740-477-7757 ... 398 C wbrothers@ohiochristian.edu
BROTHERTON, Thomas, S 712-852-5224 ... 185 G tbrotherton@iowalakes.edu
BROTHWELL, Debbie ... 510-885-4135 ... 34 C debbie.brothwell@csueastbay.edu
BROUCEK, Willard ... 605-626-2401 ... 465 H broucekw@northern.edu
BROUDE, Nancy ... 617-587-5585 ... 243 D brouden@neco.edu
BROUDER, Gerald, T ... 573-875-7200 ... 280 E gbrouder@ccis.edu
BROUGH, Amy, F ... 860-297-5315 ... 94 C amy.brough@trincoll.edu
BROUGHTON, Donnie ... 813-879-6000 ... 106 F dbrought@cci.edu

BROUGHTON, Nancy 218-879-0837 266 F
sam@fdltcc.edu

BROUGHTON, Phyllis, J 252-789-0247 371 E
pbroughton@martincc.edu

BROUGHTON, Sandy, S 732-255-0400 312 D
sbroughton@ocean.edu

BROUILLETTE, Domenick, R 816-604-1370 285 D
domenick.brouillette@mcckc.edu

BROUILLETTE, Jim 928-314-9565 12 C
james.brouillette@azwestern.edu

BROUK, Judy 636-422-2240 289 E
jbrouk@stlcc.edu

BROUK, Susan 660-263-4110 287 B
susanbr@macc.edu

BROUNK, Thomas, M 314-935-5955 292 J
tom_brounk@wustl.edu

BROUSSARD, Camille 212-431-2354 343 E
cbroussard@nyls.edu

BROUSSARD, JR., Leroy 337-482-6473 216 D
lxb9416@louisiana.edu

BROUSSARD, Michael 337-550-1292 212 H

BROUSSARD, William 318-869-5087 208 F
wbroussard@centenary.edu

BROUSSEAU, Mike 403-538-2107 19 C
mike.brousseau@phoenix.edu

BROUWER, Penelope 609-777-5693 316 A
pbrouwer@tesc.edu

BROUWER, Peter, S 315-267-2515 354 C
brouweps@potsdam.edu

BROUWERS, Mariette 541-737-2131 418 F
mariette.brouwers@oregonstate.edu

BROWDER, Steven, K 317-738-8301 171 C
sbrowder@franklincollege.edu

BROWER, Aaron 608-262-5246 550 G
ambrower@wisc.edu

BROWER, Anita 919-546-8261 376 D
abrower@shawu.edu

BROWER, Bob 619-849-2216 62 L
bobbrower@pointloma.edu

BROWER, Carol 718-982-3088 327 A
Carol.Brower@csi.cuny.edu

BROWER, David 517-355-5020 255 D
brower@msu.edu

BROWER, Laura 805-654-6460 77 D
lbrower@vcccd.edu

BROWER, Paul, O 508-213-2271 243 J
paul.brower@nichols.edu

BROWER, Pearl 907-852-3333 10 G
pearl.brower@ilisagvik.edu

BROWER, Roderick 910-678-8232 370 B
browerr@faytechcc.edu

BROWER-GARRETT, Paulette 718-982-2681 327 A
Paulette.BrowerGarrett@csi.cuny.edu

BROWN, A, R 718-982-2335 327 A
aramona.brown@csi.cuny.edu

BROWN, Aaron 951-222-8645 64 B
aaron.brown@rcc.edu

BROWN, Adrienne 912-358-4166 136 C
brownad@savannahstate.edu

BROWN, Albert, F 740-588-1210 407 A
abrown@zanestate.edu

BROWN, Alfreda 330-672-2442 393 D
abbrown@kent.edu

BROWN, Alice 361-593-3991 498 A
alice.brown@tamuk.edu

BROWN, Alistair 630-620-2101 160 B
abrown@seminary.edu

BROWN, Amanda 850-747-6223 101 G
ambrown@baymedical.org

BROWN, Amy 704-463-3046 375 E
amy.brown@fsmail.pfeiffer.edu

BROWN, Angela, C 254-968-9128 496 F
abrown@tarleton.edu

BROWN, Angela, P 731-425-2347 475 B
abrown@jscc.edu

BROWN, Angelo 770-391-6176 128 F
abrown9@devry.edu

BROWN, Anne 617-228-3267 239 G
abrown@bhcc.mass.edu

BROWN, Anthony 252-335-3277 377 D
abrown@mail.ecsu.edu

BROWN, Arthur, E 212-217-3650 333 G
arthur_brown@fitnyc.edu

BROWN, B, T 252-536-7245 370 F
brownbt@halifaxcc.edu

BROWN, B, T 252-536-7256 370 F
brownbt@halifaxcc.edu

BROWN, Barbara 678-891-2720 130 G
bbrown@gpc.edu

BROWN, Barry 617-573-8298 245 E
bbrown@suffolk.edu

BROWN, Barry 617-573-8220 245 E
bbrown@suffolk.edu

BROWN, Bernetta, H 252-335-3596 377 D
bhbrown@mail.ecsu.edu

BROWN, Beth 229-420-8000 132 I
egbrown@lagrange.edu

BROWN, Bill 913-469-8500 193 I
bbrown@jccc.edu

BROWN, Bill 386-752-1822 108 C
bill.brown@fgc.edu

BROWN, Bill 229-732-5919 124 C
billbrown@andrewcollege.edu

BROWN, Bill 863-638-7228 123 B
bill.brown@warner.edu

BROWN, Bill 919-760-2367 366 G
brownw@meredith.edu

BROWN, Bill 417-328-1601 290 E
bbrown@sbuniv.edu

BROWN, Bob 903-886-5024 497 E
bob_brown@tamu-commerce.edu

BROWN, Bobbie 806-742-3661 501 D
bobbie.brown@ttu.edu

BROWN, Bonita, J 336-334-4244 379 A
bjbrown3@uncg.edu

BROWN, Braden 405-382-9277 412 B
b.brown@sscok.edu

BROWN, Brandon 706-821-8233 135 C
bbrown@paine.edu

BROWN, Breighan 269-782-1294 258 E
bbrown02@swmich.edu

BROWN, Brenda 309-796-4815 145 E
brownb@bhc.edu

BROWN, Brenda 405-224-3140 413 E
bbrown@usao.edu

BROWN, Brenda, L 478-988-6851 133 H
bbrown@middlegatech.edu

BROWN, Brent, K 801-581-3003 510 L
brent.brown@osp.utah.edu

BROWN, Bruce, E 276-223-4726 528 F
wcbrowb@wcc.vccs.edu

BROWN, Buddy 301-934-7728 222 C
bbrown@csmd.edu

BROWN, Calvin 205-348-5966 8 F
cbrown@alumni.ua.edu

BROWN, Canter 478-825-6156 129 C
brownc@fvsu.edu

BROWN, JR., Canter 478-825-6156 129 C
brownc@fvsu.edu

BROWN, Carl 614-947-6080 391 A
brownca@franklin.edu

BROWN, Carlton, E 404-880-8566 126 I
cbrown@cau.edu

BROWN, Carly 412-747-7800 99 D

BROWN, Carmen 803-584-3446 462 E
cdbrown@mailbox.sc.edu

BROWN, Carmhiel, J 215-955-8051 448 B
carmhiel.brown@jeffersonhospital.org

BROWN, Carol 860-701-5068 93 B
brown_c@mitchell.edu

BROWN, Carol 559-791-2316 53 A
cbrown@portervillecollege.edu

BROWN, Carol 518-891-2915 344 E
president@nccc.edu

BROWN, Carol 901-333-4462 475 H
cbrown@southwest.tn.edu

BROWN, Carol, J 309-341-7980 155 E
cbrown@knox.edu

BROWN, Carolanne 561-803-2050 114 C
carolanne_brown@pba.edu

BROWN, Carolyn, H 252-399-6357 362 A
chbrown@barton.edu

BROWN, Carolyn, S 816-604-1204 285 D
carolyn.brown@mcckc.edu

BROWN, Carolyn, S 801-524-8160 510 A
cs-brown@ldsbc.edu

BROWN, Carrie 936-468-3971 495 H
brownch@sfasu.edu

BROWN, Cassandra 205-226-4643 2 C
clbrown@bsc.edu

BROWN, Cathy, R 850-474-3127 121 C
cbrown@uwf.edu

BROWN, Chad 740-588-1260 407 A
cbrown@zanestate.edu

BROWN, Charity 559-453-2236 47 K
charityb@fresno.edu

BROWN, Charlene 406-791-5271 296 H
cbrown02@ugf.edu

BROWN, Charles 502-456-6773 206 C
cbrown@sullivan.edu

BROWN, Charles 915-532-3737 508 E
cbrown@westerntech.edu

BROWN, Charles, L 561-297-3988 118 H
clbrown@fau.edu

BROWN, Charles, R 410-455-2207 227 D
chbrown@umbc.edu

BROWN, Cheryl-Ann 321-674-7581 108 E
cbrown@fit.edu

BROWN, Chris 510-276-3888 38 E
cbrown@cc.edu

BROWN, Chris, A 989-463-7347 247 F
cabrown@alma.edu

BROWN, Christine 207-602-2371 220 H
sbrown@une.edu

BROWN, Christopher, D 570-577-3164 423 D
chris.brown@bucknell.edu

BROWN, Christopher, M 517-355-6509 255 D
brownc28@msu.edu

BROWN, Christy, L 414-229-4461 551 C
clb52@uwm.edu

BROWN, Cindy 417-455-5540 281 C
cbrown@crowder.edu

BROWN, Clarence 909-594-5611 58 A
cbrown@mtsac.edu

BROWN, Clay 870-460-1028 25 A
browncl@uamont.edu

BROWN, Colleen 408-924-6070 37 A
colleen.brown@sjsu.edu

BROWN, Constance 516-561-0050 325 F

BROWN, Constance 212-854-2011 323 G
cbrown@barnard.edu

BROWN, Curressia 662-254-3051 276 C
cbrown@mvsu.edu

BROWN, Cynthia 706-754-7714 134 E
cbrown@northgatech.edu

BROWN, Cynthia, F 413-662-5242 238 F
c.brown@mcla.edu

BROWN, Cynthia, L 508-213-2215 243 J
cindy.brown@nichols.edu

BROWN, Dale 308-535-8112 298 I
brownd@mpcc.edu

BROWN, Dan 707-965-7150 60 J
dabrown@puc.edu

BROWN, Dan 502-863-7035 200 G
dan_brown@georgetowncollege.edu

BROWN, Daniel 512-245-3579 501 C
sp15@txstate.edu

BROWN, Daniel, A 361-593-3290 498 A
daniel.brown@tamuk.edu

BROWN, Daniel, E 808-974-7468 141 A
dbrown@hawaii.edu

BROWN, Daniel, W 203-582-8927 93 E
daniel.brown@quinnipiac.edu

BROWN, Daniella 516-364-0808 343 A
Dbrown@nycollege.edu

BROWN, daniella 516-364-0808 343 A
dbrowni@nycollege.edu

BROWN, Danielle 407-275-9696 102 G

BROWN, Danita 203-857-7004 90 G
dbrown@ncc.commnet.edu

BROWN, Danita, M 765-494-1239 178 F
dmbrown@purdue.edu

BROWN, Darlene 215-248-7158 425 C
brown@chc.edu

BROWN, Darrell 317-613-4800 169 B

BROWN, Darryl 301-295-3412 558 A
dbrown@usuhs.mil

BROWN, David 262-691-5346 555 C
dbrown@wctc.edu

BROWN, David 617-369-3870 244 G
dbrown@smfa.edu

BROWN, David 314-434-4044 281 A
david.brown@covenantseminary.edu

BROWN, David 910-668-7731 491 C
dbrown@nctc.edu

BROWN, OSB, David 704-461-6733 362 B
davidbrown@bac.edu

BROWN, David, H 845-437-5315 359 D
brown@vassar.edu

BROWN, Dawn, K 817-515-6697 496 A
dawn.brown@tccd.edu

BROWN, Deanie 217-206-6222 167 A
brown.deanie@uis.edu

BROWN, Debbi 808-984-3204 142 B
debbi@hawaii.edu

BROWN, Deborah 512-863-1944 495 G
brownd@southwestern.edu

BROWN, Deborah 615-217-9347 468 B
dbrown@daymarinstitute.edu

BROWN, Delbert, W 585-245-5566 353 C
brown@geneseo.edu

BROWN, Dennis 915-831-6471 486 E
dbrown49@epcc.edu

BROWN, DeShanna 404-270-5128 137 E
dbrown56@spelman.edu

BROWN, Diane, M 484-365-8055 434 H
dbrown@lincoln.edu

BROWN, Dianne 361-593-2111 498 A
dianne.brown@tamuk.edu

BROWN, Dina 978-556-3701 241 B
dbrown@necc.mass.edu

BROWN, Dolly 813-621-0041 105 G
dbrown@cci.edu

BROWN, Dolores, O 262-524-7378 546 E
dobrown@carrollu.edu

BROWN, Donald 202-462-2101 98 C
brown@iwp.edu

BROWN, Donna 479-248-7236 21 G
registrar@ecollege.edu

BROWN, Donna 660-626-2790 278 F
dbrown@atsu.edu

BROWN, Donna, L 218-477-2721 268 A
donna.brown@mnstate.edu

BROWN, Donnie 806-291-3596 508 B
brownd@wbu.edu

BROWN, Doug, M 505-277-6148 321 C
browndm@mgt.unm.edu

BROWN, Drew 914-674-7385 340 G
dbrown@mercy.edu

BROWN, Eleanor, J 718-855-3661 336 D
ebrown@idc.edu

BROWN, Eric, A 843-355-4170 463 C
browne@wiltech.edu

BROWN, Erica 302-736-2485 96 G
browner@wesley.edu

BROWN, Erica 205-226-4733 2 C
ebrown@bsc.edu

BROWN, JR., Ermen 701-766-1342 380 E
ermen.brown@littlehoop.edu

BROWN, Ethel 678-891-2526 130 G
ebrown@gpc.edu

BROWN, Ethel, M 404-413-1300 131 C
ebrown@gsu.edu

BROWN, Evelyn 731-426-7532 469 M
ebrown@lanecollege.edu

BROWN, Faith 802-322-1616 513 C
faith.brown@goddard.edu

BROWN, Felicia 252-335-3642 377 D
fdbrown@mail.ecsu.edu

BROWN, Fletcher 860-628-4751 92 F
fbrown@lincolncollegene.edu

BROWN, Fran 248-476-1122 255 C
fbrown@mispp.edu

BROWN, Francis, H 801-581-8767 510 L
fbrown@mines.utah.edu

BROWN, Frank 850-201-8499 121 F
brownf@tcc.fl.edu

BROWN, Frankie, M 316-978-3065 197 F
frankie.brown@wichita.edu

BROWN, Fred 970-339-6640 80 G
fred.brown@aims.edu

BROWN, Gary 608-785-9167 555 D
browng@westerntc.edu

BROWN, Gary, M 814-725-6118 436 C
gbrown@mercyhurst.edu

BROWN, Genevieve 936-294-1101 501 A
brown@shsu.edu

BROWN, Giles 903-463-8620 487 A
browng@grayson.edu

BROWN, Glenna, G 205-934-2090 8 G
glenna@uab.edu

BROWN, Greg 760-366-5290 43 E
gbrown@cmccd.edu

BROWN, Gregory, N 212-854-2003 323 G
gbrown@barnard.edu

BROWN, Guilbert, L 703-993-8743 519 A
gbrowne@gmu.edu

BROWN, Gwen 203-857-7145 90 G
gbrown@ncc.commnet.edu

BROWN, H. David 816-271-4327 287 A
browndav@missouriwestern.edu

BROWN, Heather 213-477-2966 57 H
hbrown@msmc.la.edu

BROWN, Hilrie 615-383-4848 478 E
hbrown@watkins.edu

BROWN, J. Kevin 863-784-7424 117 I
kevin.brown@southflorida.edu

BROWN, J.J, J 828-262-2060 377 B
brownjjl@appstate.edu

BROWN, Jack 859-371-9393 198 D
jbrown@beckfield.edu

BROWN, Jacqueline, L 301-322-0918 225 F
jbrown@pgcc.edu

BROWN, Jamere 573-681-5113 284 B
brownj@lincolnu.edu

BROWN, James 508-854-4324 241 C
jbrown@qcc.mass.edu

BROWN, James 570-389-4410 441 F
jbrown@bloomu.edu

BROWN, James 570-662-4805 443 B
jbrown@mansfield.edu

BROWN, James, C 315-792-3001 359 C
jbrown@utica.edu

BROWN, James, V 610-399-2331 441 H
jbrown@cheyney.edu

BROWN, James, W 319-895-4485 183 D
jbrown@cornellcollege.edu

BROWN, James, W 757-455-5730 529 F
bbrown@vwc.edu

BROWN, Jane, B 617-373-4810 244 A

BROWN, Janet, M 219-464-5289 181 A
janet.brown@valpo.edu

BROWN, Jasmin, K 910-630-7034 366 H
jabrown@methodist.edu

BROWN, Jean 206-281-2583 537 D
jbrown@spu.edu

BROWN, Jean, K 716-829-2210 351 G
UBNursingDean@buffalo.edu

BROWN, Jeff 801-832-2900 512 F
jbrown@westminstercollege.edu

BROWN, Jeffrey, D 573-629-3015 282 H
jbrown@hlg.edu

BROWN, SR., Jeffrey, S 757-594-7053 517 I
jsbrown@cnu.edu

BROWN, Jennifer 785-738-9085 195 D
jbrown@ncktc.edu

BROWN, Jennifer, A 334-244-3413 2 A
jbrown@aum.edu

BROWN, Jennifer, A 617-287-5420 237 D
jennifer.brown@umb.edu

BROWN, Jeremy 970-248-1962 82 B
jbrown@mesastate.edu

BROWN, Jeremy, D 631-244-3200 332 D
president@dowling.edu

BROWN, Jesse, M 260-359-4028 172 K
jbrown@huntington.edu

BROWN, Jessyca 254-659-7818 487 E
jbrown@hillcollege.edu

BROWN, Jim 770-229-3455 137 B
jbrown@sctech.edu

BROWN, Joann 318-274-6153 215 E
brownj@gram.edu

BROWN, JoAnn 318-670-6651 215 A jwarren@susla.edu

BROWN, JoAnn 409-832-2956 500 E jcbrown@lit.edu

BROWN, Joanna 413-552-2253 240 C jbrown@hcc.edu

BROWN, Joanne 409-832-2956 500 E jcbrown@lit.edu

BROWN, Joanne 510-649-2422 48 H jbrown@gtu.edu

BROWN, Joe, C 740-420-0428 398 C jbrown@ohiochristian.edu

BROWN, Johanna 810-762-0409 256 C johanna.brown@mcc.edu

BROWN, John 619-482-6320 71 C jbrown@swccd.edu

BROWN, John 215-489-2413 426 H John.Brown@delval.edu

BROWN, John, H 706-507-8800 127 D brown_john9@columbusstate.edu

BROWN, John-Michael 314-837-6777 288 F jbrown@slcconline.edu

BROWN, Jonathan 206-878-3710 534 E jbrown@highline.edu

BROWN, Joseph 828-884-8282 362 D joseph.brown@brevard.edu

BROWN, Joseph 910-246-4957 373 E brownj@sandhills.edu

BROWN, Joyce 443-885-3015 224 F joyce.brown@morgan.edu

BROWN, Joyce, F 212-217-4000 333 G joyce_brown@fitnyc.edu

BROWN, JT 563-588-7810 186 I jt.brown@loras.edu

BROWN, Judi 360-475-7700 535 J jbrown@olympic.edu

BROWN, Julia 662-472-9011 274 F jubrown@holmescc.edu

BROWN, Julie 651-255-6111 271 I jbrown@unitedseminary.edu

BROWN, June, E 918-631-2361 413 F june-brown@utulsa.edu

BROWN, Karen 607-962-9221 331 D kbrown7@corning-cc.edu

BROWN, Karen, A 607-436-2524 353 E brownka@oneonta.edu

BROWN, Kate 603-899-1090 305 B 0212mgr@fhet.follett.com

BROWN, Kathie 814-677-1322 427 H occ@dbcollege.com

BROWN, Kathleen 502-776-1443 205 G

BROWN, Kathleen 202-541-5216 99 G brown@wtu.edu

BROWN, Kathleen, M 574-284-4557 179 D kbrown@saintmarys.edu

BROWN, Kathryn, A 814-677-1322 428 B occ@dbcollege.com

BROWN, Kathryn, F 612-624-3533 272 D brown059@umn.edu

BROWN, Katrina 307-674-6446 556 C kbrown@sheridan.edu

BROWN, Keith 440-365-5222 395 C

BROWN, Keith, A 318-342-5422 216 E kbrown@ulm.edu

BROWN, Keith, A 205-853-1200 5 C kbrown@jeffstateonline.com

BROWN, Kelly 405-224-3140 413 E kbrown@usao.edu

BROWN, Kelvin 252-335-0821 369 D klbrown@albemarle.edu

BROWN, Kendal, N 712-290-8737 433 F kbrown@lancasterseminary.edu

BROWN, Kennard, D 901-448-4797 477 C kbrown@uthsc.edu

BROWN, Kenneth 509-777-4486 539 F kbrown@whitworth.edu

BROWN, Kent 573-681-5042 284 B brownk@lincolnu.edu

BROWN, Kevin 423-236-2874 473 A kbrown@southern.edu

BROWN, Kevin 541-784-5149 184 H brown@graceland.edu

BROWN, Kevin 843-349-5398 458 G kevin.brown@hgtc.edu

BROWN, Kevin, A 919-866-5475 374 E kabrown@waketech.edu

BROWN, Kevin, H 425-637-1010 531 I khbrown@cityu.edu

BROWN, Kim 940-668-7731 491 C kbrown@nctc.edu

BROWN, Kim, S 757-455-3275 529 F kbrown@vwc.edu

BROWN, Kimberly, A 630-515-6044 158 E kbrown@midwestern.edu

BROWN, Kimberly, S 850-474-2200 121 C kimbrown@uwf.edu

BROWN, Kristen 626-395-8395 32 E kbrown@caltech.edu

BROWN, Kristen 336-272-7102 364 D kristen.brown@greensborocollege.edu

BROWN, Kristy 317-738-8051 171 C kbrown@franklincollege.edu

BROWN, LaSonya 704-378-1044 365 H lbrown@jcsu.edu

BROWN, Laura, S 607-255-5180 331 C lsb7@cornell.edu

BROWN, Lauren 704-357-8020 361 N laubrown@aii.edu

BROWN, Lauri 615-297-7545 466 H brownl@aquinascollege.edu

BROWN, LeAnn 715-394-8355 552 D lbrown20@uwsuper.edu

BROWN, LeeAnn 304-473-8160 545 F brown_l@wvwc.edu

BROWN, Leon, R 804-706-5020 526 G lbrown@jtcc.edu

BROWN, JR., Leonard, E 717-245-1736 427 E brownl@dickinson.edu

BROWN, Levy 252-527-6223 371 D lbrown@lenoircc.edu

BROWN, Lewis 605-688-4161 466 B lewis.brown@sdstate.edu

BROWN, Linda 660-359-3948 287 D lbrown@mail.ncmissouri.edu

BROWN, Linda 580-628-6240 409 B linda.brown@north-ok.edu

BROWN, Linda, J 218-299-4206 263 B linbrown@cord.edu

BROWN, Lindsey 406-265-4190 295 G lindsey.brown@msun.edu

BROWN, Lisa 563-441-4016 184 E lbrown@eicc.edu

BROWN, Lisa, M 216-397-4184 392 M lmbrown@jcu.edu

BROWN, Llatetra, D 443-518-4766 223 D llatetrabrown@howardcc.edu

BROWN, Lloyd 978-368-2230 230 F lloyd.brown@auc.edu

BROWN, Lori 814-817-4459 449 E lbrown@pitt.edu

BROWN, Lori, A 973-313-6132 315 B lori.brown@shu.edu

BROWN, Lougene 706-507-8902 127 D brown_lougene@columbusstate.edu

BROWN, Lucille 203-285-2114 90 A lbrown@gwcc.commnet.edu

BROWN, Luther 662-846-4312 274 B lbrown@deltastate.edu

BROWN, Lynn 207-893-6603 219 F lbrown@sjcme.edu

BROWN, Lynn, M 904-620-2115 120 C lmbrown@unf.edu

BROWN, Lynne 212-998-2350 344 B lynne.brown@nyu.edu

BROWN, II, M.Christopher 601-877-6100 273 C president@alcorn.edu

BROWN, Mae, W 858-534-3156 74 D mbrown@ucsd.edu

BROWN, Manning 570-586-2400 422 F mbrown@bbc.edu

BROWN, Marcia, W 973-353-5541 314 E mwbrown@andromeda.rutgers.edu

BROWN, Marcus 217-875-7200 162 D mbrown@richland.edu

BROWN, Margie 318-397-6128 210 J mabrown@myneltc.edu

BROWN, Margo 904-819-6474 107 A mbrown@flagler.edu

BROWN, Marie 404-292-7900 128 G mbrown1@devry.edu

BROWN, Marinell 859-442-1120 201 G marinell.brown@kctcs.edu

BROWN, Mario 901-321-3529 467 G mbrown11@cbu.edu

BROWN, Mark 712-324-5061 188 A mbrown@nwicc.edu

BROWN, Mark, C 703-247-2500 99 D mbrown@strayer.edu

BROWN, Mark, I 608-743-4526 553 E mbrown55@blackhawk.edu

BROWN, Marnika 616-632-2455 248 A brownmar@aquinas.edu

BROWN, Marsha, D 206-934-5136 537 B marsha.brown@seattlecolleges.edu

BROWN, Mary 217-544-6464 163 F

BROWN, Mary, L 864-596-9094 457 E mary.brown@converse.edu

BROWN, Mary Lee 215-898-7260 448 I marylb@pobox.upenn.edu

BROWN, Matthew, S 405-744-9164 410 C brownms@okstate.edu

BROWN, Max, D 312-942-6886 163 B maxbrown@rush.edu

BROWN, Melanie, A 386-312-4202 116 D melaniebrown@sjrstate.edu

BROWN, Melvin, L 973-353-5872 314 E melbrown@rci.rutgers.edu

BROWN, Merv, R 208-496-2010 142 G brownme@byui.edu

BROWN, Michael 928-717-7709 19 E michael.brown@yc.edu

BROWN, Michael 323-660-6166 40 G michael.brown@cleveland.edu

BROWN, Michael, E 202-994-6241 97 F brownm@gwu.edu

BROWN, Michael, J 765-361-6384 181 C

BROWN, Michael, S 406-444-6880 295 C brownms@umhelena.edu

BROWN, Michael, T 805-893-2944 74 F michael.brown@els.ucsb.edu

BROWN, Michaela 910-672-1287 377 E mbrown38@uncfsu.edu

BROWN, Michele 847-635-1724 160 E mbrown@oakton.edu

BROWN, Michelle, H 215-898-7233 448 I mbnevers@sfs.upenn.edu

BROWN, Mike 574-936-8898 168 I mike.brown@ancilla.edu

BROWN, Mike 903-463-8772 487 A mbrown@grayson.edu

BROWN, Mikell 804-594-1509 526 G mbrown@jtcc.edu

BROWN, Mindy 503-594-3041 415 A mindyb@clackamas.edu

BROWN, Monte 919-684-0317 363 I monte.brown@duke.edu

BROWN, Nancy 801-957-4247 512 C nancy.brown@slcc.edu

BROWN, Nancy, B 423-318-2709 476 B nancy.brown@ws.edu

BROWN, Nicci, C 704-233-8126 380 D brown@wingate.edu

BROWN, Norman 202-319-5044 97 C brownn@cua.edu

BROWN, O. Ted 270-809-6937 204 F ted.brown@murraystate.edu

BROWN, Pamela 718-260-5008 328 E pbrown@citytech.cuny.edu

BROWN, Pamela 843-574-6246 461 G

BROWN, Pamela, J 740-593-2583 399 G brownp@ohio.edu

BROWN, Pamela, S 217-228-5520 145 G pbrown@brcn.edu

BROWN, Patricia, R 716-839-8484 331 G pbrown@daemen.edu

BROWN, Patrick 253-680-7014 531 A pbrown@bates.ctc.edu

BROWN, Patty 423-697-2437 474 D

BROWN, Paul 254-659-7860 487 E pbrown@hillcollege.edu

BROWN, Paul, M 404-880-8790 126 I pbrown@cau.edu

BROWN, Paul, P 856-225-6005 314 C peyton@camden.rutgers.edu

BROWN, Paul, R 740-588-1200 407 A pbrown@zanestate.edu

BROWN, Paul, R 610-758-6725 434 E prb207@lehigh.edu

BROWN, Peg, A 319-296-4283 185 C peg.brown@hawkeyecollege.edu

BROWN, Perry 406-243-4689 295 A perry.brown@umontana.edu

BROWN, Perry, J 406-243-4689 295 A perry.brown@umontana.edu

BROWN, Peter, M 914-594-4560 343 F peter_brown@nymc.edu

BROWN, Philip, R 207-768-2708 218 J pbrown@nmcc.edu

BROWN, Phillip 219-989-2240 178 G brown@purduecal.edu

BROWN, Phillip, M 618-650-3415 165 A phbrown@siue.edu

BROWN, Quincy, D 706-880-8297 132 I qbrown@lagrange.edu

BROWN, R. McKenna 804-828-8471 525 E mbrown@vcu.edu

BROWN, Rachel 215-204-7981 447 G rachel.brown@temple.edu

BROWN, Rae Linda 310-338-5217 56 E raelinda.brown@lmu.edu

BROWN, Randy 408-848-4852 48 B rbrown@gavilan.edu

BROWN, Ray 573-592-5238 293 C Ray.Brown@westminster-mo.edu

BROWN, Ray 918-343-7622 411 H rbrown@rsu.edu

BROWN, Raymond, A 610-527-0200 445 I bbrown@rosemont.edu

BROWN, Raymond, A 817-257-7490 498 F r.brown@tcu.edu

BROWN, Rebecca 214-333-5426 484 C rebeccab@dbu.edu

BROWN, Rebekkah, L 484-664-3247 437 B rbrown@muhlenberg.edu

BROWN, Renee, D 419-559-2367 402 D rbrown@terra.edu

BROWN, Rhonda, L 215-204-7303 447 G rhonda.brown@temple.edu

BROWN, Richard 423-425-4393 477 D richard-brown@utc.edu

BROWN, Richard 856-415-2205 310 E rbrown@gccnj.edu

BROWN, Richard, B 801-581-6912 510 L brown@coe.utah.edu

BROWN, Richard, W 530-226-4728 69 H rbrown@simpsonu.edu

BROWN, Ricky 252-493-7423 372 E rbrown@email.pittcc.edu

BROWN, Rita 510-723-6618 38 L rbrown@chabotcollege.edu

BROWN, Robert 410-386-8224 221 G rbrown@carrollcc.edu

BROWN, Robert 312-553-6029 146 H rbrown@ccc.edu

BROWN, Robert 505-224-4608 317 J rbrown@cnm.edu

BROWN, Robert 803-793-5155 457 F brownr@denmarktech.edu

BROWN, Robert, A 617-353-2200 232 G rabrown@bu.edu

BROWN, Robert, C 479-968-0237 20 G rcbrown@atu.edu

BROWN, Robert, C 216-368-4306 386 E robert.c.brown@case.edu

BROWN, Robert, D 919-515-2883 378 B robert_brown@ncsu.edu

BROWN, Robert, K 918-781-7218 407 B brownr@bacone.edu

BROWN, Robert, L 803-981-7375 463 G rbrown@yorktech.edu

BROWN, Robert, M 336-315-7317 379 A rmbrown2@uncg.edu

BROWN, Robert, M 251-460-6151 9 E rbrown@usouthal.edu

BROWN, Robin, C 970-491-2682 83 A robin.brown@colostate.edu

BROWN, Rock 406-265-3765 295 G rock.brown@msun.edu

BROWN, Rodney, J 801-422-2007 509 D rod_brown@byu.edu

BROWN, Roger 901-435-1535 470 B roger_brown@loc.edu

BROWN, Roger, G 423-425-4141 477 D roger-brown@utc.edu

BROWN, Roger, H 617-266-1400 231 G

BROWN, Ron 254-295-4517 504 A rbrown@umhb.edu

BROWN, Ronald 281-290-2754 490 C ronald.w.brown@lonestar.edu

BROWN, Ronald, C 512-245-2205 501 C rb04@txstate.edu

BROWN, Ronald, G 405-878-5161 412 A rgbrown@stgregorys.edu

BROWN, Ronald, H 919-516-4190 376 B rhbrown@st-aug.edu

BROWN, Ronald, T 313-577-2200 260 D rtbrown@wayne.edu

BROWN, Rosann 814-641-3133 431 L brownr@juniata.edu

BROWN, Ryan 757-352-4106 523 B rbrown@regent.edu

BROWN, Sabrina 540-654-1617 524 H sbrown9@umw.edu

BROWN, Samuel 203-575-8022 90 E sbrown@nvcc.commnet.edu

BROWN, Sandra 858-534-3526 74 D

BROWN, Sandra 605-668-1555 464 F sbrown@mtmc.edu

BROWN, Saundra, E 812-941-2394 174 D sebrown2@ius.edu

BROWN, Scott 315-228-7425 329 H sbrown@colgate.edu

BROWN, Scott 513-785-3227 396 E brownsj3@muohio.edu

BROWN, Scott 425-889-5287 535 I scott.brown@northwestu.edu

BROWN, Shanita 615-327-6223 471 A sbrown@mmc.edu

BROWN, Shannon 828-726-2288 368 D sbrown@cccti.edu

BROWN, Sharon, A 610-625-7847 436 I mesab01@moravian.edu

BROWN, Sharon, S 937-778-7821 390 G sbrown@edisonohio.edu

BROWN, Shirley, F 828-652-0676 371 G shirleyb@mcdowelltech.edu

BROWN, Shondae 256-395-2211 7 E sbrown@suscc.edu

BROWN, Simon 215-751-8039 426 B sbrown@ccp.edu

BROWN, Sloane 918-540-6393 408 J scbrown@neo.edu

BROWN, Stacy 305-534-7050 121 G stacyb@talmudicu.edu

BROWN, Stan 229-317-6721 128 A stan.brown@darton.edu

BROWN, Stephan 352-588-8331 116 E stephan.brown@saintleo.edu

BROWN, Stephanie 954-262-7456 114 B browstep@nsu.nova.edu

BROWN, Stephanie 417-447-2653 287 G browns@otc.edu

BROWN, Stephen, E 248-204-2300 254 E sbrown@ltu.edu

BROWN, Stephen, G 530-221-4275 69 C sbrown@shasta.edu

BROWN, Stephen, W 304-442-3105 545 C stephen.brown@mall.wvu.edu

BROWN, Steve 570-586-2400 422 F sbrown@bbc.edu

BROWN, Steve 202-639-1764 97 D sbrown@corcoran.org

BROWN, Steve 407-345-2826 104 D sbrown2@devry.edu

BROWN, Steve 724-805-2534 446 E steve.brown@email.stvincent.edu
BROWN, Steve, D 423-439-4841 473 E browsd02@etsu.edu
BROWN, Steven 802-287-8912 513 D browns@greenmtn.edu
BROWN, Steven, F 620-341-5278 192 D sbrown10@emporia.edu
BROWN, Steven, L 304-696-3431 542 G brown175@mctc.edu
BROWN, Sue, A 918-595-7884 412 H sbrown3@tulsacc.edu
BROWN, Sue, C 309-655-2206 163 E sue.c.brown@osfhealthcare.org
BROWN, Susan 802-860-2754 513 A brown@champlain.edu
BROWN, Susan 509-359-6403 533 D sbrown@ewu.edu
BROWN, Susan, M 859-233-8225 206 E subrown@transy.edu
BROWN, Sylvia 252-744-6422 377 C brownsy@ecu.edu
BROWN, T. Rhett 704-233-8022 380 D rhbrown@wingate.edu
BROWN, Tammy 225-359-9201 209 K tbrown@catc.edu
BROWN, Ted 516-299-2229 339 A ted.brown@liu.edu
BROWN, Ted, R 931-363-9802 470 E tbrown@martinmethodist.edu
BROWN, Teresa 404-225-4700 125 A tbrown@atlantatech.edu
BROWN, Teresa 615-230-3377 476 A teresa.brown@volstate.edu
BROWN, Teresa, L 401-456-8240 454 A tlbrown@ric.edu
BROWN, Terrence 901-751-8453 471 D tbrown@mabts.edu
BROWN, Terry 304-327-4191 543 C tbrown@bluefieldstate.edu
BROWN, Terry 262-595-2261 551 E terry.brown@uwp.edu
BROWN, Therese 303-404-5535 84 H therese.brown@frontrange.edu
BROWN, Thomas 702-651-4002 302 G thomas.brown@csn.edu
BROWN, Thomas 540-231-3787 529 B tbrown@vt.edu
BROWN, Tim 843-574-6424 461 G tim.brown@tridenttech.edu
BROWN, Timothy 616-392-8555 260 G tim.brown@westernsem.edu
BROWN, Travis 954-446-6169 100 E tbrown@aiufl.edu
BROWN, Troy 513-562-8771 384 A tbrown@artacademy.edu
BROWN, Troy, D 317-274-7711 174 B tdbrown@iupui.edu
BROWN, Venessa 618-650-5867 165 A vbrown@siue.edu
BROWN, Venessa 618-482-6912 165 A vbrown@siue.edu
BROWN, Vicki, R 540-985-9784 520 D vrbrown@jchs.edu
BROWN, Victor 937-298-3399 394 D victor.brown@kcma.edu
BROWN, Vince 209-954-5059 66 D vbrown@deltacollege.edu
BROWN, Violet 610-896-1000 430 G vbrown@haverford.edu
BROWN, Walter 909-868-4004 44 J wbrown@devry.edu
BROWN, Walter, E 412-648-3185 449 A walter.brown@ia.pitt.edu
BROWN, Wanda, C 336-633-0286 372 F wcbrown@randolph.edu
BROWN, Warren 206-587-5481 537 A wbrown@sccd.ctc.edu
BROWN, Warren 210-341-1366 491 E wbrown@ost.edu
BROWN, Wes, S 912-260-4312 136 F wes.brown@sgc.edu
BROWN, Wes, S 912-260-4430 136 F wes.brown@sgc.edu
BROWN, Wilfred, E 805-893-4155 74 F wbrown@housing.ucsb.edu
BROWN, Will, M 843-355-4116 463 C brownw@wiltech.edu
BROWN, William 520-494-5340 13 F william.brown@centralaz.edu
BROWN, William, E 937-766-7900 386 F bbrown@cedarville.edu
BROWN, William, H 704-894-2143 363 F wibrown@davidson.edu
BROWN, William, J 717-867-6180 434 C wbrown@lvc.edu
BROWN, William (Bill) 859-846-5358 204 D bbrown@midway.edu
BROWN, Willie 601-979-4299 275 A willie.g.brown@jsums.edu
BROWN, Willie, T 256-539-0834 4 F deanac@hbc1.edu
BROWN, Willie, T 256-539-0834 4 F deaninst@hbc1.edu
BROWN, Winston, D 504-520-7577 217 A wbrown@xula.edu
BROWN, Yvette 305-899-3600 101 F ybrown@mail.barry.edu
BROWN, Zachary 607-431-4547 335 B brownz@hartwick.edu
BROWN, Zachary, M 309-692-4092 158 C zbrown@midstate.edu
BROWN-CARMEN, Vivian 904-470-8081 105 A vivian.browncarmen@ewc.edu
BROWN-CORNELIUS, Denise 502-272-8270 198 E dbrowncornelius@bellarmine.edu
BROWN-GUILLORY, Elizabeth 713-313-1180 499 G brown_guillorye@tsu.edu
BROWN-HART, Denise 910-672-1856 377 E dbrownhart@uncfsu.edu
BROWN-HAYWOOD, Felicia, L 717-948-6180 439 I flb1@psu.edu
BROWN-SOW, Lynette 215-751-8859 426 B lbrown@ccp.edu
BROWN-WADE, Glenda 205-929-1404 5 H plac@mail.miles.edu
BROWN-WELTY, Sharon 559-278-2448 34 D sharonb@csufresno.edu
BROWNBACK, H, O 618-235-2700 165 B h.brownback@swic.edu
BROWNE, Brian 718-990-2762 348 G browneb@stjohns.edu
BROWNE, Dorothy, C 757-823-8668 521 K dcbrowne@nsu.edu
BROWNE, Doug 620-417-1201 196 B doug.browne@sccc.edu
BROWNE, Jennifer 631-287-8304 339 B jennifer.browne@liu.edu
BROWNE, Joan, M 202-806-7513 98 B jmbrowne@howard.edu
BROWNE, Kevin, M 209-228-4567 74 B KBrowne@UCMerced.edu
BROWNE, Nancy, E 305-595-9500 100 D nancy@amcollege.edu
BROWNE, Patrick 503-256-3180 420 H pbrowne@uws.edu
BROWNE, Richard, M 305-595-9500 100 D richard@amcollege.edu
BROWNE, Timm 562-907-4211 70 B tbrowne@whittier.edu
BROWNELL, Claire 303-871-4876 88 E cbrownel@du.edu
BROWNELL, Lauren 318-342-6787 216 E brownell@ulm.edu
BROWNELL, Winifred, E 401-874-4101 454 E winnie@uri.edu
BROWNER, Stephanie 859-985-3490 198 F stephanie_browner@berea.edu
BROWNER, Stephanie 212-229-5100 342 E
BROWNIE, Ronald 605-626-2568 465 H ronald.brownie@northern.edu
BROWNING, David, A 214-860-2015 484 I dbrowning@dcccd.edu
BROWNING, Douglas, D 301-846-2442 222 G dbrowning@frederick.edu
BROWNING, Eric 740-392-6868 396 H eric.browning@mvnu.edu
BROWNING, Gari 510-659-6200 59 I gbrowning@ohlone.edu
BROWNING, John 619-594-6648 36 E browning@mail.sdsu.edu
BROWNING, Julie 713-348-2575 492 J jmb@rice.edu
BROWNING, Katherine 301-387-3097 222 H katherine.browning@garrettcollege.edu
BROWNING, Marguerite 909-621-8125 49 D maggie_browning@hmc.edu
BROWNING, Midge 618-374-5776 161 D midge.browning@principia.edu
BROWNING, Rebecca 858-598-1200 30 A rbrowning@aii.edu
BROWNING, Roger 618-393-2982 152 E browningr@iecc.edu
BROWNING, Skye 620-229-6223 196 C skye.browning@sckans.edu
BROWNLEE, David, W 610-558-5628 437 C dbrownle@neumann.edu
BROWNLEE, Jamie 714-556-3610 76 E jbrownlee@vanguard.edu
BROWNLEE, L. Lang 317-788-3382 180 C lbrownlee@uindy.edu
BROWNLEE, Reb 814-262-3842 441 A rbrownlee@pennhighlands.edu
BROWNLEE, Sibyl, M 508-929-8077 239 D sbrownlee@worcester.edu
BROXSON, Thomas 253-840-8338 536 C tbroxson@pierce.ctc.edu
BROYLES, Ken 423-461-8734 471 H kbroyles@milligan.edu
BROYLES, Stephen 940-668-7731 491 C sbroyles@nctc.edu
BROZ, Betty, P 615-353-3258 475 D betty.broz@nscc.edu
BROZ, Roger 612-659-6805 267 E roger.broz@minneapolis.edu
BROZA, Dave 651-638-6459 261 I d-broza@bethel.edu
BROZIK, Linda, J 605-256-5136 465 G linda.brozik@dsu.edu
BRUBACHER, Don 517-607-3130 252 E don.brubacher@hillsdale.edu
BRUBAKER, Andy 706-880-8773 132 I abrubaker@lagrange.edu
BRUBAKER, Beryl, H 540-432-4170 518 E brubakeb@emu.edu
BRUBAKER, Clifford, E 412-383-6560 449 A cliffb@pitt.edu
BRUBAKER, David 585-567-9484 336 B david.brubaker@houghton.edu
BRUBAKER, Donald, C 818-779-8069 53 B dbrubaker@kingsuniversity.edu
BRUBAKER, Glenn, R 607-587-4750 355 C brubakgr@alfredstate.edu
BRUBAKER, Jackie 870-733-6741 22 E jbrubaker@midsouthcc.edu
BRUBAKER, Karl 620-327-8216 193 C karlb@hesston.edu
BRUBAKER, Kevin 503-375-7030 415 F kbrubaker@corban.edu
BRUBAKER, Linda 708-216-7826 157 A lbrubaker@lumc.edu
BRUBAKER, Lisa 719-219-9636 81 J l.brubaker@att.net
BRUBAKER, Lori, L 260-422-5561 172 L llbrubaker@indianatech.edu
BRUCE, Aaron, I 619-594-5201 36 E abruce@mail.sdsu.edu
BRUCE, Alex, M 931-598-1919 472 J ambruce@sewanee.edu
BRUCE, Ben 334-386-7257 3 H bbruce@faulkner.edu
BRUCE, Charles, W 405-744-7440 410 C charles.bruce@okstate.edu
BRUCE, Charlotte 618-395-7777 152 H brucec@iecc.edu
BRUCE, Debra 509-542-4604 532 C dbruce@columbiabasin.edu
BRUCE, Gonzalo 620-341-5374 192 D gbruce@emporia.edu
BRUCE, Harry 206-616-0985 538 F harryb@uw.edu
BRUCE, J. Michael 812-866-7039 171 F bruce@hanover.edu
BRUCE, Jimmie 210-486-4905 479 C jbruce10@alamo.edu
BRUCE, Joanna, E 706-886-6831 137 G jbruce@tfc.edu
BRUCE, Kathy 217-351-2280 161 B kbruce@parkland.edu
BRUCE, Lisa 619-961-4209 72 F lbruce@tjsl.edu
BRUCE, Marilyn 912-478-5211 131 A marilynb@georgiasouthern.edu
BRUCE, Patricia, S 601-974-1127 275 D brucesp@millsaps.edu
BRUCE, Rob 919-962-2646 378 D rob_bruce@unc.edu
BRUCE, Roberta 575-624-7127 318 B roberta.bruce@roswell.enmu.edu
BRUCE, Terry 619-393-2982 152 E brucet@iecc.edu
BRUCE, Thomas, W 607-255-9929 331 C twb22@cornell.edu
BRUCE, Tom, S 765-641-4232 169 A tsbruce@anderson.edu
BRUCE, Will 805-922-6966 26 K wbruce@hancockcollege.edu
BRUCE, William, P 615-327-3927 469 I pbruce@guptoncollege.edu
BRUCE-SANFORD, Gail 303-556-6433 85 N brucesan@mscd.edu
BRUCKER, Denise 518-743-2329 322 B bruckerd@sunyacc.edu
BRUCKER, Denise 518-381-1314 350 E bruckedk@sunysccc.edu
BRUCKI, Mark, J 248-204-2300 254 E mbrucki@ltu.edu
BRUCKNER, Michael, S 484-664-3230 437 B bruckner@muhlenberg.edu
BRUDER, Carolyn 337-482-6454 216 D cbruder@louisiana.edu
BRUDER, Edward, C 717-815-1314 452 F ebruder@ycp.edu
BRUDNOK, Celine, R 724-805-2720 446 E celine.brudnok@email.stvincent.edu
BRUDVIG, James 845-758-7429 323 F brudvig@bard.edu
BRUDVIG, Jon, L 701-483-2330 381 E jon.brudvig@dickinsonstate.edu
BRUECK, Joshua 217-641-4320 154 G jbrueck@jwcc.edu
BRUECKEN, John 515-271-1471 183 F john.bruecken@dmu.edu
BRUEGGEMAN, Cheryl 513-936-1735 403 F cheryl.brueggeman@uc.edu
BRUEGGEMEIER, Robert, W 614-292-5711 398 H brueggemeier.1@osu.edu
BRUEHL, Allen, A 508-767-7311 230 E abruehl@assumption.edu
BRUEN, Christina, M 508-910-6633 237 E cbruen@umassd.edu
BRUENGINSEN, Gail 585-266-0430 333 E gbrueningsen@cci.edu
BRUESS, Brian 651-690-6778 271 E bjbruess@stkate.edu
BRUFLODT, Lori, L 563-589-0219 189 G lbruflodt@wartburgseminary.edu
BRUGA, Leslie 216-391-6937 387 A LBruga@ChancellorU.edu
BRUGAL-MENA, Yocasta 787-743-3038 565 C ybrugal@sanjuanbautista.edu
BRUGGEMAN, Bob 903-223-3153 498 C bob.bruggeman@tamut.edu
BRUGGEMAN, John, H 513-487-3269 391 E jbruggeman@huc.edu
BRUGGEMAN, Joyce 760-750-4040 36 B jbruggem@csusm.edu
BRUGGER, Janet 877-442-0505 88 G janet.brugger@rockies.edu
BRUGH, Larry, W 814-886-6320 437 A lbrugh@mtaloy.edu
BRUGH, Suzanne 814-262-6463 441 A sbrugh@pennhighlands.edu
BRUGMAN, Donna, M 617-984-1776 244 C dbrugman@quincycollege.edu
BRUHN, Tobias 215-968-8223 423 E bruhnt@bucks.edu
BRUI, Breena 850-484-2044 114 G bbruni@pensacolastate.edu
BRUKARDT, Mary Jane 715-836-2320 550 H brukarmj@uwec.edu
BRULE, Lise, M 203-392-5722 91 I brulel1@southernct.edu
BRUM, Joseph, P 401-865-2416 453 F joebrum@providence.edu
BRUMAGIN, Ruth 570-288-8400 429 C ruthb@marcogrp.com
BRUMBACH, Alicia 717-815-1309 452 F brumbach@ycp.edu
BRUMBAUGH, Margit 360-442-2131 535 C mbrumbaugh@lowercolumbia.edu
BRUMELOW, Harvey 404-627-2681 126 A harvey.brumelow@beulah.org
BRUMFIEL, Byron 618-395-3011 152 E brumfielb@iecc.edu
BRUMFIELD, Adele 608-262-0464 550 G abrumfield@admissions.wisc.edu
BRUMFIELD, Rick 253-833-9111 534 C rbrumfield@greenriver.edu
BRUMFIELD, Wendell, W 318-342-5215 216 E wbrumfie@ulm.edu
BRUMITT, Jane 312-629-6184 164 A jbrumitt@saic.edu
BRUMLEY, Larry, D 478-301-5700 133 F brumley_ld@mercer.edu
BRUMMEL, Joe 641-628-5232 183 A brummelj@central.edu
BRUMMELS, Lin 402-375-7321 299 I librumm1@wsc.edu
BRUMMER, Bert 757-221-1218 517 J eabrum@wm.edu
BRUMMETT, Ronald, L 303-273-3297 82 F rbrummet@mines.edu
BRUMMETT, Ronald, L 303-273-3377 82 F rbrummet@mines.edu
BRUMMETT, Tracy 912-427-5861 124 A tbrummett@altamahatech.edu
BRUN, James 859-371-9393 198 D jbrun@beckfield.edu
BRUNDAGE, Ken 814-871-7551 429 F brundage001@gannon.edu
BRUNDAGE, Thomas 661-722-6300 28 J tbrundage@avc.edu
BRUNDO-SHARRAR, Tricia, A 402-280-3058 297 H sharrar@creighton.edu
BRUNE, Carolyn 847-574-5154 155 G cbrune@lfgsm.edu
BRUNE, William 260-399-7700 180 E wbrune@sf.edu
BRUNEAU, Patrice 803-323-2266 463 D bruneaup@winthrop.edu
BRUNEL, Robert 912-260-4221 136 F robert.brunel@sgc.edu
BRUNELLE, Laura 508-929-8649 239 D lbrunelle@worcester.edu
BRUNELLI, Leslie, G 803-777-7478 462 A lgbrunel@gwm.sc.edu
BRUNEN, Meredith 479-619-4176 22 H mbrunen@nwacc.edu
BRUNER, Darl, L 208-467-8843 143 I dlbruner@nnu.edu
BRUNER, Greg 815-939-5249 160 F gbruner@olivet.edu
BRUNER, Joe, W 859-858-3511 198 B joe.bruner@asbury.edu
BRUNER, Michael 651-779-3288 266 D mike.bruner@century.edu
BRUNER, Richard, K 334-833-4540 4 E netdoctor@huntingdon.edu
BRUNER, Robert, F 434-924-7481 525 B rfb9k@virginia.edu

BRUNET EAGAN, Kathleen 973-328-5052 309 B
keagan@ccm.edu
BRUNET-KOCH, Cameron 231-348-6601 256 E
ckoch@ncmich.edu
BRUNETTE, Mark 920-465-2586 551 A
brunettm@uwgb.edu
BRUNGARDT, Cherie 970-521-6787 86 E
cherie.brungardt@njc.edu
BRUNGARDT, Kevin 620-276-9539 193 A
kevin.brungardt@gcccks.edu
BRUNING, Merribeth 870-245-5154 22 I
bruningm@obu.edu
BRUNKE, Mark 206-393-3504 530 G
mbrunke@argosy.edu
BRUNKOW, Alan 402-761-8259 300 C
abrunkow@southeast.edu
BRUNNEMER, David 360-650-7732 539 C
david.brunnemer@wwu.edu
BRUNNER, David 513-244-8485 387 D
David.Brunner@ccuniversity.edu
BRUNNER, Diane 419-473-2700 389 B
dbrunner@daviscollege.edu
BRUNNER, Jon, L 239-590-7950 119 A
jbrunner@fgcu.edu
BRUNNER, Karen, L 865-882-4606 475 G
brunnerkl@roanestate.edu
BRUNNER, Mark 573-876-2381 290 G
mbrunner@stephens.edu
BRUNNER, Mary, K 810-989-5512 258 B
mbrunner@sc4.edu
BRUNNER, Matthew, S 540-851-5271 522 D
msbrunner@radford.edu
BRUNNER, Penelope, W 518-783-2307 350 I
pbrunner@siena.edu
BRUNNER, Roger 907-450-8080 10 H
roger.brunner@alaska.edu
BRUNNER, Tim 419-473-2700 389 B
tbrunner@daviscollege.edu
BRUNO, Bonnie 336-278-6603 364 A
bbruno2@elon.edu
BRUNO, Frank, W 303-492-7523 88 B
frank.bruno@colorado.edu
BRUNO, Gene 800-290-4226 469 C
gbruno@hchs.edu
BRUNO, Joanne, Z 201-200-3003 312 B
jbruno@njcu.edu
BRUNO, John 314-889-1401 282 C
jbruno@fontbonne.edu
BRUNO, Kristin 818-240-1000 48 C
kbruno@glendale.edu
BRUNO, Laura 718-262-2165 329 B
lbruno@york.cuny.edu
BRUNO, Mary 386-506-3618 103 J
brunom@DaytonaState.edu
BRUNO, Michael, S 201-216-5338 315 E
mbruno@stevens.edu
BRUNO, Nick, J 318-342-1000 216 E
bruno@ulm.edu
BRUNO, Tania 212-280-1404 358 G
tbruno@uts.columbia.edu
BRUNOLD, Timothy 213-740-6753 76 C
admdean@usc.edu
BRUNS, Bradley, J 636-584-6583 281 I
bjbruns@eastcentral.edu
BRUNS, Clara 802-322-1603 513 C
clara.bruns@goddard.edu
BRUNS, Dale 570-408-4600 451 G
dale.bruns@wilkes.edu
BRUNS, Sandy 712-324-5061 188 A
sandy@nwicc.edu
BRUNSEN, James 815-753-1554 160 A
jbrunsen@niu.edu
BRUNSON, Kathleen, D 815-753-1300 160 A
kbrunson@niu.edu
BRUNSON, Mary Nelle 936-468-2707 495 H
mbrunson@sfasu.edu
BRUNSON, Teesa 803-780-1194 463 B
tbrunson@voorhees.edu
BRUNSSEN, Jeremy 402-572-8500 298 F
jbrunssen@kaplan.edu
BRUNTMYER, Eric 214-333-5160 484 C
eric@dbu.edu
BRUNTON, Mark 702-579-3528 302 C
mbrunton@kaplan.edu
BRUNTZ, Crystal 816-501-3600 279 C
crystal.bruntz@avila.edu
BRUSATI, Gerianne 845-341-4060 345 E
gerianne.brusati@sunyorange.edu
BRUSATTI, Louis, T 512-448-8643 493 B
louisb@stedwards.edu
BRUSH, C. Beeler 434-223-6145 519 B
bbrush@email.hsc.edu
BRUSH, Diana 814-393-2323 442 A
dbrush@clarion.edu
BRUSH, Richard 401-598-4621 453 C
dbrush@jwu.edu
BRUSH, Tressa 912-201-8000 136 H
tbrush@southuniversity.edu
BRUSKI, Kathleen 989-358-7335 247 G
bruskik@alpenacc.edu
BRUSS, Carl 908-709-7485 316 B
bruss@ucc.edu
BRUSS, Dan, R 507-344-7315 261 H
danbruss@blc.edu
BRUSSELL, Carlotta 859-336-5082 205 F
cbrussell@sccky.edu
BRUSTEIN, William, I 614-292-5881 398 H
brustein.1@osu.edu
BRUSZEWSKI, Roger 717-872-3043 443 C
roger.bruszewski@millersville.edu
BRUTON, John, W 540-365-4332 518 J
jbruton@ferrum.edu
BRUUN-HORRIGAN, Christina 937-484-1320 405 A
cbruunhorrigan@urbana.edu
BRUXVOORT, Debra 641-628-7671 183 A
bruxvoortb@central.edu
BRUYN, Kimberly, A 616-732-1165 250 E
kbruyn@davenport.edu
BRY, Jay, D 978-665-3298 238 C
jbry@fitchburgstate.edu
BRYAN, Barbara, J 954-201-2202 102 A
bbryan@broward.edu
BRYAN, Derek 336-917-5472 376 C
derek.bryan@salem.edu
BRYAN, Doreen 662-476-5060 274 D
dbryan@eastms.edu
BRYAN, Doug 704-406-4398 364 B
dbryan@gardner-webb.edu
BRYAN, G. William 214-841-3792 485 E
bbryan@dts.edu
BRYAN, Jerold, M 801-524-8102 510 A
jerry@ldsbc.edu
BRYAN, Jerry 580-477-7754 414 C
jerry.bryan@wosc.edu
BRYAN, Jessica 603-271-6311 304 G
jbryan@ccsnh.edu
BRYAN, John, S 678-466-4351 127 A
johnbryan@clayton.edu
BRYAN, Marsha 508-626-4737 238 D
mbryan@framingham.edu
BRYAN, JR., Norman, B 864-833-2820 460 E
nbryan@presby.edu
BRYAN, Paul 215-893-5257 426 E
paul.bryan@curtis.edu
BRYAN, Paula, K 419-586-0352 406 D
paula.bryan@wright.edu
BRYAN, Penelope 714-444-4141 79 B
pbryan@law.whittier.edu
BRYAN, Robert 216-987-4684 389 A
bob.bryan@tri-c.edu
BRYAN, Robert, G 865-539-7198 475 F
jbryan@pstcc.edu
BRYAN, Sandy 520-417-4098 13 G
bryans@cochise.edu
BRYAN, Sibley 706-453-0378 124 H
sbryan@athenstech.edu
BRYAN, Susan 417-865-2811 282 A
bryans@evangel.edu
BRYAN, Sylvia 850-729-5362 114 A
bryans@nwfsc.edu
BRYAN, Terry 832-252-4676 483 A
terry.bryan@cbshouston.edu
BRYAN, Virginia, S 318-678-6000 209 J
gbryan@bpcc.edu
BRYAN, Wes 714-895-8101 41 A
wbryan@gwc.cccd.edu
BRYAN, William, V 570-963-2690 440 F
wvb3@psu.edu
BRYAN-PETERSON, Maggie 716-673-3569 352 A
maggie.bryan-peterson@fredonia.edu
BRYANT, America 650-843-3411 61 A
a.bryant@paloaltou.edu
BRYANT, Angela, V 229-928-1378 131 B
BRYANT, Brenda 313-927-1502 255 A
bbryant@marygrove.edu
BRYANT, Brenda 540-887-7220 520 I
bbryant@mbc.edu
BRYANT, Bruce, K 425-637-1010 531 I
brucebryant@cityu.edu
BRYANT, Carlton 800-782-2422 33 B
cbryant@mail.cnuas.edu
BRYANT, Cherie 207-741-5726 219 A
cbryant@smccme.edu
BRYANT, Clint 706-737-1626 125 C
cbryant@aug.edu
BRYANT, Daniel, C 740-376-4718 395 F
dan.bryant@marietta.edu
BRYANT, David, A 407-303-9305 108 D
david.bryant@fhchs.edu
BRYANT, David, A 580-349-1302 410 B
dbryant@opsu.edu
BRYANT, Debbie 870-460-1034 25 A
bryant@uamont.edu
BRYANT, Felicia 856-227-7200 308 E
fbryant@camdencc.edu
BRYANT, Fred 361-593-3922 498 A
kffcb00@tamuk.edu
BRYANT, Gerald 417-447-7553 287 G
bryantg@otc.edu
BRYANT, Greg 615-329-8566 468 G
gbryant@fisk.edu
BRYANT, Jack 405-422-1256 411 G
bryantj@redlandscc.edu
BRYANT, Jackie 716-827-4347 358 B
bryantj@trocaire.edu
BRYANT, III, James, S 803-535-1330 460 C
bryantj@octech.edu
BRYANT, Jason 417-624-7070 284 G
jbryant@messengercollege.edu
BRYANT, Jay 602-978-7294 18 K
jay.bryant@thunderbird.edu
BRYANT, John 309-556-3449 153 E
jbryant@iwu.edu
BRYANT, Joy, L 864-644-5385 461 B
jbryant@swu.edu
BRYANT, Karen 618-842-3711 152 F
bryantk@iecc.edu
BRYANT, Kashina 207-513-3602 218 C
kabryant@kaplan.edu
BRYANT, Kevin 503-517-1220 421 A
kmbryant@warnerpacific.edu
BRYANT, Kimberly 215-895-1121 450 A
k.bryant@usciences.edu
BRYANT, Leisa 662-325-7353 276 A
lbryant@audit.msstate.edu
BRYANT, Leonora, C 336-433-5570 377 F
leonora@ncat.edu
BRYANT, Lori 918-293-5294 410 E
lori.bryant@okstate.edu
BRYANT, Margie 202-687-3698 98 A
bryantm@georgetown.edu
BRYANT, Matthew 706-419-1651 127 F
bryant@covenant.edu
BRYANT, Micki 714-564-6079 63 F
bryant_micki@sac.edu
BRYANT, Morgan 601-925-3354 275 E
mbryant@mc.edu
BRYANT, Paul 318-274-6018 215 E
bryantp@gram.edu
BRYANT, Paul 309-467-6377 150 H
pbryant@eureka.edu
BRYANT, Penny, J 314-367-8700 288 I
pbryant@stlcop.edu
BRYANT, Randal, E 412-268-8821 424 H
randy.bryant@cs.cmu.edu
BRYANT, Scott 903-923-2173 486 D
sbryant@etbu.edu
BRYANT, Sheila, M 931-221-7178 473 D
bryantsm@apsu.edu
BRYANT, Stephanie 803-754-4100 457 D
BRYANT, Steve 601-583-4100 273 D
BRYANT, Tanika 803-793-5192 457 F
bryantt@denmarktech.edu
BRYANT, Theresa 757-822-1184 528 C
tbryant@tcc.edu
BRYANT, Toni 830-792-7229 494 A
tlbryant@schreiner.edu
BRYANT, Vickie 817-461-8741 480 H
vbryant@abconline.org
BRYANT, William, C 208-524-3000 143 C
bill.bryant@my.eitc.edu
BRYANT-ALLEN, Tina 336-599-1181 372 D
bryantt@piedmontcc.edu
BRYANT-LOWERY, Francis, T 404-614-6337 132 D
fblowery@itc.edu
BRYANT-WEBB, Jocelyn 410-951-3926 228 B
jbryant@coppin.edu
BRYCE, Jeanne 928-428-8261 14 C
jeanne.bryce@eac.edu
BRYCE, Mark 928-428-8231 14 C
mark.bryce@eac.edu
BRYD, John 803-323-3374 463 D
brydj@winthrop.edu
BRYDEN, David, L 336-841-9101 365 A
dbryden@highpoint.edu
BRYDON, Lucinda, C 607-746-4603 355 E
brydonlm@delhi.edu
BRYENTON, John 270-686-4615 202 E
john.bryenton@kctcs.edu
BRYER, Erin 412-365-1262 425 B
ebryer@chatham.edu
BRYNE, Kathryn 617-243-2176 236 F
kbryne@lasell.edu
BRYNTESON, Susan 302-831-2231 96 F
susanb@udel.edu
BRYNTESSON, Hilary 267-502-4819 423 B
hilary.bryntesson@brynathyn.edu
BRYSON, Barbara 713-348-5151 492 J
bwbryson@rice.edu
BRYSON, Cynthia 713-771-5336 132 C
cbryson@ict-ils.edu
BRYSON, J. Richard 740-389-4636 395 G
brysonr@mtc.edu
BRYSON, Lance 717-477-1451 443 D
jlbrys@ship.edu
BRYSON, Suzanne 828-251-6128 378 C
sbryson@unca.edu
BRYSON, Terri 256-306-2583 2 E
tbb@calhoun.edu
BRYSON, Terri 256-890-4703 2 E
tbb@calhoun.edu
BRZEZINSKI, Michael, A 765-494-9399 178 F
mbrzezinski@purdue.edu
BRZEZINSKI, Michael, A 765-494-5770 178 F
mbrzezinski@purdue.edu
BRZORAD, Joe 828-328-7606 366 B
john.brzorad@lr.edu
BRZOZOWSKI, Samantha 615-383-4848 478 E
sbrzozowski@watkins.edu
BUBB, Daniel, K 509-313-6948 534 A
bubb@gonzaga.edu
BUBB, Kevin 517-483-9764 254 D
bubbk@lcc.edu
BUBNIKOVICH, Barbara 651-675-4700 264 H
bbubnikovich@twincitiesculinary.com
BUBNOVA, Elena 775-673-8239 302 J
ebubnova@tmcc.edu
BUCARO, S. Ted 937-229-4122 404 A
ted.bucaro@udayton.edu
BUCCHI, Joyce 724-836-9902 449 C
jeb14@pitt.edu
BUCCILLI, Michael 203-285-2144 90 A
mbuccilli@gwcc.commnet.edu
BUCELL, Michael 814-732-2252 442 D
bucell@edinboro.edu
BUCH, Joseph 304-243-2000 545 G
BUCHA, Edward, R 724-738-2183 443 E
edward.bucha@sru.edu
BUCHANAN, Carrie 970-943-2101 89 B
cbuchanan@western.edu
BUCHANAN, Dave 262-595-2404 551 E
dave.buchanan@uwp.edu
BUCHANAN, David 865-471-3222 467 E
dbuchanan@cn.edu
BUCHANAN, Doug 806-742-2121 501 D
douglas.buchanan@ttu.edu.
BUCHANAN, Frank, L 817-515-5154 496 A
frank.buchanan@tccd.edu
BUCHANAN, George 845-431-8673 332 E
george.buchanan@sunydutchess.edu
BUCHANAN, Harvey 850-644-3444 119 C
buchanan@otc.fsu.edu
BUCHANAN, Janelle, M 806-720-7476 490 D
janelle.buchanan@lcu.edu
BUCHANAN, Jennifer, N 850-644-6876 119 C
jbuchanan@admin.fsu.edu
BUCHANAN, Joan 321-433-5533 101 J
buchananj@brevardcc.edu
BUCHANAN, Ken 828-898-8809 366 A
buchanank@lmc.edu
BUCHANAN, Linda, R 319-385-6284 186 A
linda.buchanan@iwc.edu
BUCHANAN, Nancy 914-633-2483 336 E
NBuchanan@iona.edu
BUCHANAN, Pam 251-442-2372 9 B
pamb@umobile.edu
BUCHANAN, Pamela 828-227-7640 379 E
pbuchanan@wcu.edu
BUCHANAN, Richard 801-878-1400 303 D
rbuchanan@roseman.edu
BUCHANAN, Rollie, O 516-876-4873 353 D
buchananr@oldwestbury.edu
BUCHANAN, Sally 334-556-2244 4 A
sbuchanan@wallace.edu
BUCHANAN, Saundra 541-506-6050 415 C
sbuchanan@cgcc.cc.or.us
BUCHANAN, Sharmane 954-446-6137 100 E
sbuchanan@aiufl.edu
BUCHANAN, Susan, M 509-527-5183 539 E
buchansm@whitman.edu
BUCHANAN, Tenielle 615-966-5264 470 D
tenielle.buchanan@lipscomb.edu
BUCHANAN, Thomas 307-766-4121 556 F
tombuch@uwyo.edu
BUCHANAN, Timothy, M 724-938-5887 441 G
buchanan@calu.edu
BUCHANAN, Tony 407-301-4928 478 G
tony.buchanan@earthlink.net
BUCHANAN, Trey 512-313-3000 483 G
trey.buchanan@concordia.edu
BUCHDAHL, David 802-885-8360 515 D
buchdahd@mail.ccv.vsc.edu
BUCHELI, Hernan 650-508-3512 59 G
hbucheli@ndnu.edu
BUCHER, John, E 440-775-6727 397 F
john.bucher@oberlin.edu
BUCHER, Karen, H 540-868-7132 526 H
kbucher@lfcc.edu
BUCHER, Mary, L 315-386-7228 355 D
bucher@canton.edu
BUCHER, Oskar 541-684-7273 417 F
oskar@northwestchristian.edu
BUCHHEIT, Peter, J 814-362-7670 449 B
pjb4@pitt.edu
BUCHHOLTZ, Gina 701-224-5702 382 B
gina.buchholtz@bismarckstate.edu
BUCHHOLZ, Richard 405-422-6204 411 G
richard.buchholz@redlandscc.edu
BUCHHOLZ, Robert 336-278-5500 364 A
rbuchholz@elon.edu
BUCHHOLZ, Ron 262-472-1498 552 E
buchholr@uww.edu
BUCHHOLZ, Stephen 605-394-4034 466 E
stephen.buchholz@wdt.edu
BUCHMAN, Ashley 870-358-8636 20 F
ashley_buchman@asun.edu
BUCHMAN, Irene 212-217-4590 333 G
irene_buchman@fitnyc.edu
BUCHMAN, Lorne, M 626-396-2301 29 G
lorne.buchman@artcenter.edu
BUCHOLC, Stanley 978-665-3215 238 C
sbucholc@fitchburgstate.edu

BUNCE, Larry 816-235-1045 291 E buncel@umkc.edu

BUNCH, Kirsten, H 828-694-1809 368 B kristenb@blueridge.edu

BUNCH, Martha, M 336-272-7102 364 D bunchm@greensborocollege.edu

BUNCH, Meredith, N 309-692-4092 158 C mbunch@midstate.edu

BUNCH, Meredith, N 309-692-4092 158 C munch@midstate.edu

BUNCH, Thomas, G 817-202-6207 495 C buncht@swau.edu

BUNCH, Wayne 918-687-6747 407 H wayne.bunch@connorsstate.edu

BUNCH, Wes 828-327-7000 368 G wbunch@cvcc.edu

BUNCH, Wilma, C 417-269-3051 281 B wbunch@coxcollege.edu

BUNDALO, Katherine 414-382-6398 545 H kathy.bundalo@alverno.edu

BUNDERS, Lisa, L 563-588-7135 186 I lisa.bunders@loras.edu

BUNDRICK, David, R 417-865-2811 282 A bundrickd@evangel.edu

BUNDY, Barbara 213-624-1200 46 L bbundy@fidm.edu

BUNDY, David 626-584-5221 48 A bundy@fuller.edu

BUNDY, James, A 203-432-1505 95 D james.bundy@yale.edu

BUNDY, Lewis 510-215-0277 29 F lbundy@argosy.edu

BUNDY, O. Keith 605-256-5146 465 G keith.bundy@dsu.edu

BUNDY, III, O. Richard 802-656-2010 514 F richard.bundy@uvm.edu

BUNDY, Penny 269-387-2000 260 F penny.bundy@wmich.edu

BUNGE, Rosita, M 920-686-6143 550 E Rosita.Bunge@sl.edu

BUNGE, Sacha 415-338-2204 36 F sbunge@sfsu.edu

BUNIS, David, A 781-736-3993 233 A dbunis@brandeis.edu

BUNKER, Jeffery, N 801-422-4530 509 D jeff_bunker@byu.edu

BUNKER, Laurel 651-638-6372 261 I l-bunker@bethel.edu

BUNKER, Matt 801-957-4838 512 C matt.bunker@slcc.edu

BUNKOWSKE, Heidi 619-388-3911 65 F hbunkows@sdccd.edu

BUNN, Dumont, C 478-988-6800 133 H dbunn@middlegatech.edu

BUNN, Sandra, J 912-279-5965 127 B sbunn@ccga.edu

BUNNELL, David 620-235-4878 195 I dbunnell@pittstate.edu

BUNNELL, Robert 219-989-2540 178 G bunnellr@purduecal.edu

BUNNELL, Robin 541-888-7339 420 C rbunnell@socc.edu

BUNNELL, Tom 603-228-1541 306 G tom.bunnell@law.unh.edu

BUNNELL-RIIYNE, Melinda, A 301-369-2800 221 F melindabunnell@capitol-college.edu

BUNNING, Galen, B 785-227-3380 190 G bunningg@bethanylb.edu

BUNSELMEYER, Leonard 620-792-9393 190 E bunselmeyerl@bartonccc.edu

BUNTEN, Margie, J 714-895-8315 41 A mbunten@gwc.cccd.edu

BUNTEN, Tricia 218-726-6995 272 B

BUNTING, Cheryl 602-749-4542 13 M cbunting@devry.edu

BUNTON, Tim, M 217-443-8780 148 E tbunton@dacc.edu

BUNTYN, Carolyn 915-831-2224 486 E cbuntyn@epcc.edu

BUNYARD, Magen 903-923-2325 486 D mbunyard@etbu.edu

BUNYI, Beth 760-630-1555 52 J bbunyi@kaplan.edu

BUOL, Deborah, L 563-589-3223 189 B dbuol@dbq.edu

BUOSCIO, Amy 708-237-5050 160 C abuoscio@nc.edu

BURBA, Randy 714-997-6763 39 C burba@chapman.edu

BURBAGE, Gary 252-940-6233 367 I garyb@beaufortccc.edu

BURCH, Beth 503-253-3443 417 H bburch@ocom.edu

BURCH, Brad, E 336-334-4822 370 E beburch@gtcc.edu

BURCH, C. Vicki 731-668-7240 478 F vicki.burch@wtbc.edu

BURCH, Carl 501-450-1377 22 A burch@hendrix.edu

BURCH, Chuck, S 704-406-4342 364 B cburch@gardner-webb.edu

BURCH, Doug 801-622-1573 510 G doug.burch@stevenshenager.edu

BURCH, Franki 704-406-4414 364 B fburch@gardner-webb.edu

BURCH, John 270-789-5015 199 C jrburch@campbellsville.edu

BURCH, John 850-201-8535 121 F burchj@tcc.fl.edu

BURCH, Rhonda 812-866-7014 171 F burch@hanover.edu

BURCH, Susan 406-756-3839 294 D sburch@fvcc.edu

BURCH, Terese, A 815-395-5088 163 C terriburch@sacn.edu

BURCH-SIMS, G. Pamela 615-963-7437 474 A psims@tnstate.edu

BURCHAM, Daniel 231-591-3578 251 B burchamd@ferris.edu

BURCHAM, David, W 310-258-5404 56 E david.burcham@lmu.edu

BURCHAM, CFRE, Timothy, R 859-256-3100 201 A tim.burcham@kctcs.edu

BURCHARD, Bob, P 573-875-7410 280 E rpburchard@ccis.edu

BURCHARD, Elizabeth, B 802-443-5201 513 G eboudah@middlebury.edu

BURCHARD, Eric 740-593-1804 399 G

BURCHARD, Faye, C 573-875-7400 280 E fcburchard@ccis.edu

BURCHELL, Iain 214-645-0316 507 D iain.burchell@utsouthwestern.edu

BURCHETT, Amy 432-264-5063 487 I aburchett@howardcollege.edu

BURCHETT, Bonnie, L 423-439-4446 473 E bonnie@etsu.edu

BURCHETT, Lance 941-359-7674 115 K lburchet@ringling.edu

BURCHFIELD, Bill 814-868-9900 428 H burchfield@erieit.edu

BURCHFIELD, James 406-243-5521 295 A james.burchfield@umontana.edu

BURCHFIELD, Nettie, L 985-549-2068 216 C nburchfield@selu.edu

BURD, Barbara 843-349-2401 456 G bburd@coastal.edu

BURD, Gail 520-621-1856 19 B gburd@email.arizona.edu

BURDA, Bradley 541-885-1180 418 E bradley.burda@oit.edu

BURDA, Ed 304-457-6238 540 B burdaep@ab.edu

BURDEN, Kathlyn 770-228-7362 137 B kburden@sctech.edu

BURDEN, Paul 708-342-3360 149 L pburden@devry.edu

BURDEN, Regina 931-393-1690 475 C rburden@mscc.edu

BURDETTE, David, A 989-774-3334 249 G burde1da@cmich.edu

BURDETTE, Ilona 859-336-5082 205 F iburdette@sccky.edu

BURDGE, Amber 620-431-2820 195 B

BURDICK, Evelyn, P 708-209-3259 148 C evelyn.burdick@cuchicago.edu

BURDICK, Jack 937-395-8112 394 D jack.burdick@kcma.edu

BURDICK, Jonathan 585-275-6805 358 I jonathan.burdick@rochester.edu

BURDICK, Mary Ellen 315-684-6461 354 F burdicme@morrisville.edu

BURDICK, Phil 847-925-6183 151 E pburdick@harpercollege.edu

BURDICK, Rebekah 864-231-2073 455 C rburdick@andersonuniversity.edu

BURDSALL, Dawn, M 610-660-1333 446 C dburdsal@sju.edu

BURDUE, JoEllen 414-277-7117 548 H burdue@msoe.edu

BURDZINSKI, Donna, R 727-816-3767 114 F burdzid@phcc.edu

BURDZINSKI, Kenneth, R 727-816-3412 114 F burdzink@phcc.edu

BURFORD, Kristina 501-450-1362 22 A burford@hendrix.edu

BURG, Mary, G 785-864-3131 196 F mburg@ku.edu

BURGARD, Bambi 816-802-3455 283 I bburgard@kcai.edu

BURGARD, Jim, E 504-280-6698 213 E jburgard@uno.edu

BURGAY, Stephen, P 617-353-1168 232 G burgay@bu.edu

BURGDORF, Barry, D 512-499-4563 504 E bburgdorf@utsystem.edu

BURGE, Dale, L 620-241-0723 191 F dale.burge@centralchristian.edu

BURGE, Legand, L 334-727-8976 8 C lburge@tuskegee.edu

BURGENER, Kelly, T 208-496-1140 142 G burgenerk@byui.edu

BURGER, Arnold 615-329-8516 468 G aburger@fisk.edu

BURGER, Cindy, L 717-766-2511 436 D cburger@messiah.edu

BURGER, Lisa 701-777-4463 381 D lisa.burger@email.und.edu

BURGER, Michael 334-244-3380 2 A mburger1@aum.edu

BURGER, Rosemary 570-340-6054 435 F burger@marywood.edu

BURGES, Jena 707-826-4192 36 D jb139@humboldt.edu

BURGESON, John 320-308-3081 269 C jcburgeson@stcloudstate.edu

BURGESON, Sharron 760-921-5444 61 B sharron.burgeson@paloverde.edu

BURGESS, Barbara 409-882-3342 500 G bobbie.burgess@lsco.edu

BURGESS, Brenda, K 580-774-3015 412 F brenda.burgess@swosu.edu

BURGESS, Charlotte, G 909-748-8281 75 F char_burgess@redlands.edu

BURGESS, Dale 404-270-2919 128 G dburgess@devry.edu

BURGESS, Dawn 619-388-7681 65 H dburgess@sdccd.edu

BURGESS, Douglas 513-556-9900 403 D douglas.burgess@uc.edu

BURGESS, Duncan 206-934-6882 537 B duncan.burgess@seattlecolleges.edu

BURGESS, Ed 913-758-3033 558 C burgesse@leavenworth.army.mil

BURGESS, Jay 603-428-2254 305 E jburgess@nec.edu

BURGESS, Karen 864-239-5301 455 F kaburgess@brownmackie.edu

BURGESS, Marcus 803-535-5348 456 D mburgess@claflin.edu

BURGESS, Marrlee 585-389-2884 342 D mburges4@naz.edu

BURGESS, Melissa 213-613-2200 70 H melissa_burgess@sciarc.edu

BURGESS, Nancy, E 301-583-7011 225 F burgesne@pgcc.edu

BURGESS, Nelda 770-537-5721 139 B nelda.burgess@westgatech.edu

BURGESS, Norma 615-966-6146 470 D norma.burgess@lipscomb.edu

BURGESS, Shane 520-621-7621 19 B

BURGESS, Terrence 619-388-3453 65 F tburgess@sdccd.edu

BURGESS, Timothy, P 706-542-1361 138 C timb@uga.edu

BURGESS, Valerie 603-880-8308 306 C tmc@thomasmorecollege.edu

BURGETT, Paul, J 585-274-3326 358 I pburgett@admin.rochester.edu

BURGETT, Shelley, J 606-679-8501 202 F shelly.burgett@kctcs.edu

BURGGRAF, JR., Thomas, F 970-641-2237 89 B tburggraf@western.edu

BURGGRAFF, Dennis 727-726-1153 103 B dennisburggraff@clearwater.edu

BURGGRAFF, Lucy 800-672-3060 376 E

BURGGRAFF, Philip 727-726-1153 103 B

BURGGREN, Warrewn 940-565-2550 504 B warren.burggren@unt.edu

BURGHER, Karl 812-237-8449 173 A karl.burgher@indstate.edu

BURGHER, Louis, W 402-552-2586 297 D burgherlouis@clarksoncollege.edu

BURGIE-BRYANT, Willette 484-384-2942 428 D wburgie@eastern.edu

BURGIE-BRYANT, Willette, A 484-384-2942 438 C wburgie@eastern.edu

BURGIN, Jeffery 256-372-5233 1 A jeffery.burgin@aamu.edu

BURGIN, Vicky 251-442-2269 9 B vickyb@mail.umobile.edu

BURGMAN, Raymonda 941-487-4225 119 D rburgman@ncf.edu

BURGMEIER, Julie 563-588-6374 183 B julie.bergmeier@clarke.edu

BURGNER, Ryan, C 308-635-6798 301 E burgnerr@wncc.edu

BURGOS, Ana, R 787-258-1501 561 E aburgos@columbiaco.edu

BURGOS, Henry 860-906-5007 89 L hburgos@ccc.commnet.edu

BURGOS, Irma 920-424-3080 551 D burgos@uwosh.edu

BURGOS, Jorge 787-720-4476 566 B decanatoestudiantes@colmizpa.edu

BURGOS, Jose, L 787-728-1515 568 B jburgos@sagrado.edu

BURGOS, Maida 305-821-3333 109 A mburgos@mm.fnc.edu

BURGOS, Maida 305-821-3333 109 B mburgos@mm.fnc.edu

BURGOS, Michael 858-642-8207 58 I mburgos@nu.edu

BURHENN, Herbert 423-425-4635 477 D herbert-burhenn@utc.edu

BURI, David 360-359-4958 533 D dburi@ewu.edu

BURICH, Lawrence, R 815-740-3427 167 C lburich@stfrancis.edu

BURIK, Larry 909-607-2226 62 H larry_burik@pitzer.edu

BURISH, Thomas, G 574-631-6631 180 D burish.2@nd.edu

BURK, Ann, M 308-432-6311 299 G aburk@csc.edu

BURK, Hasan, K 703-591-7042 528 H

BURK, Jan 972-721-5221 502 F jburk@udallas.edu

BURK, Jill 254-968-9089 496 F burk@tarleton.edu

BURK, Kathleen 972-721-5331 502 F kathburk@udallas.edu

BURK, Kelly 765-983-1501 171 B burkke@earlham.edu

BURK, Thomas 973-328-5037 309 B tburk@ccm.edu

BURK, William 716-338-1265 337 E billburk@mail.sunyjcc.edu

BURKARD, Donald, C 843-953-1432 457 B burkardd@cofc.edu

BURKE, OSB, Adrian 812-357-6515 179 E aburke@saintmeinrad.edu

BURKE, Andrew, J 575-527-7650 319 G aburke@nmsu.edu

BURKE, Barbara 718-260-5173 328 E bburke@citytech.cuny.edu

BURKE, Barbara 831-647-3513 57 F barbara.burke@miis.edu

BURKE, Barbara, A 217-581-2319 150 C baburke2@eiu.edu

BURKE, Brenda, L 804-828-7372 525 E blburke@vcu.edu

BURKE, Brian, E 414-277-7266 548 H burke@msoe.edu

BURKE, Brian, W 413-545-2204 237 C bwburke@external.umass.edu

BURKE, Carson 330-923-9959 390 J cburke@fortiscollege.edu

BURKE, Christy 740-376-4708 395 F christy.burke@marietta.edu

BURKE, Colleen 215-572-2785 422 B burke@arcadia.edu

BURKE, Connie 617-739-1700 243 F conburke@aii.edu

BURKE, Dale 808-544-9394 140 B dburke@hpu.edu

BURKE, David 626-812-3016 30 E dburke@apu.edu

BURKE, Debbie 918-587-6789 413 A dburke@twsweld.com

BURKE, Debra 325-574-7988 508 F dburke@wtc.edu

BURKE, Derek, A 252-398-6369 363 E burked@chowan.edu

BURKE, Diane 505-224-3750 317 J dburke4@cnm.edu

BURKE, Diane, M 315-279-5688 337 K dburke@mail.keuka.edu

BURKE, Donald, S 412-624-3001 449 A donburke@pitt.edu

BURKE, Ellen 607-735-1774 333 A eburke@elmira.edu

BURKE, George 216-687-3910 388 C g.burke@csuohio.edu

BURKE, Greg 318-357-5251 216 B burkeg@nsula.edu

BURKE, Ingrid 307-766-5080 556 E burke@uwyo.edu

BURKE, Janice, P 215-503-9606 448 B janice.burke@jefferson.edu

BURKE, Jeanmarie, R 315-568-3869 342 H jburke@nycc.edu

BURKE, Joe 620-421-6700 194 E joeburke@labette.edu

BURKE, John 724-852-3307 451 B jburke@waynesburg.edu

BURKE, John 845-848-4079 332 C john.burke@dc.edu

BURKE, John 513-727-3232 396 F

BURKE, Jonathan 949-376-6000 53 E jburke@lagunacollege.edu

BURKE, Jonathan, L 816-604-6620 285 E jon.burke@mcckc.edu

BURKE, Joseph, D 256-228-6001 6 A burkej@nacc.edu

BURKE, Joy 570-662-4804 443 B jburke@mansfield.edu

BURKE, Judith, A 765-285-1847 169 D jmoore@bsu.edu

BURKE, Kathleen, M 202-973-2083 97 F kmburke@gwu.edu

BURKE, Keri 503-883-2269 416 G

BURKE, SJ, Kevin, F 510-549-5040 68 C kburke@jstb.edu

BURKE, Kristin 617-824-8608 234 D kristin_burke@emerson.edu

BURKE, Larry, R 541-485-1780 417 E larryburke@newhope.edu

BURKE, JR., Lewis 270-901-1033 201 E lewis.burke@kctcs.edu

BURRIS, Deborah, J .... 314-516-5695.... 291 F
dburris@umsl.edu
BURRIS, Janssen .... 225-214-1947.... 214 B
janssen.burris@ololcollege.edu
BURRIS, Rolanda .... 847-628-1069.... 154 I
rburris@judsonu.edu
BURRISS, April .... 978-232-2272.... 234 F
aburriss@endicott.edu
BURROUGHS, Brenda .... 734-995-4678.... 250 B
burrob@cuaa.edu
BURROUGHS, Cynthia ...... 501-370-5337...... 23 B
cburroughs@philander.edu
BURROUGHS, Derrick .... 731-426-2540.... 469 M
dburroughs@lanecollege.edu
BURROUGHS, Lillian .... 610-902-8251.... 423 H
lillian.burroughs@cabrini.edu
BURROUGHS, W. Jeffrey .. 808-675-3923.... 139 I
burrougj@byuh.edu
BURROUGHS-DAVIS,
Robin .... 603-526-3752.... 304 A
rdavis@colby-sawyer.edu
BURROW, Jack .... 256-306-2545....... 2 E
jburrow@calhoun.edu
BURROW, Jeanavon .... 706-865-2134.... 138 A
jburrow@truett.edu
BURROWS, Angie .... 570-372-4120.... 447 D
burrows@susqu.edu
BURROWS, Carmen .... 757-825-2939.... 528 B
burrowsc@tncc.edu
BURROWS, David .... 920-832-6528.... 547 J
david.burrows@lawrence.edu
BURROWS, SC,
Joanne, M .... 563-588-6385.... 183 B
joanne.burrows@clarke.edu
BURROWS-SCHUMACHER,
Molly, A .... 563-588-4981.... 186 I
molly.burrowsschumacher@loras.edu
BURRUS, Ken .... 509-533-7220.... 532 D
kburrus@ccs.spokane.edu
BURRUS, Ken .... 509-533-7220.... 532 E
kburrus@ccs.spokane.edu
BURRUS, Ken .... 509-533-3630.... 532 F
kburrus@ccs.spokane.edu
BURRUS, Patricia .... 252-399-6417.... 362 A
pburrus@barton.edu
BURRUSS, John, W .... 713-798-6265.... 481 H
jburruss@bcm.edu
BURSAVICH, Gregory, F .... 336-316-2841.... 364 E
bursavichgf@guilford.edu
BURSI, Lee .... 217-786-2446.... 156 I
lee.bursi@llcc.edu
BURSON, Max .... 316-295-5521.... 192 H
mburson@friends.edu
BURSTEIN, Mark .... 609-258-3112.... 313 A
burstein@princeton.edu
BURSTON, Gwen .... 336-770-3317.... 379 D
burstong@uncsa.edu
BURSZTYN, Jacob .... 732-367-1060.... 307 H
jbursztyn@bmg.edu
BURT, Bruce, E .... 937-229-2131.... 404 A
bruce.burt@notes.udayton.edu
BURT, Cecil .... 601-554-5506.... 277 A
jcburt@prcc.edu
BURT, Charles .... 617-745-3725.... 234 C
charles.burt@enc.edu
BURT, DeAnna .... 231-777-5244.... 248 J
deanna.burt@baker.edu
BURT, Jennifer, A .... 435-586-1997.... 511 A
burt@suu.edu
BURT, Mickey, G .... 563-884-5451.... 114 E
mickey.burt@palmer.edu
BURT, Mickey, G .... 563-884-5451.... 188 C
mickey.burt@palmer.edu
BURT, Mickey, G .... 563-884-5451...... 60 L
mickey.burt@palmer.edu
BURT, R. Andrew .... 563-441-4303.... 184 E
aburt@eicc.edu
BURT, R.J .... 360-867-6568.... 533 I
burtr@evergreen.edu
BURT, Robert .... 510-885-2534...... 34 C
bob.burt@csueastbay.edu
BURT, Theresa, E .... 215-926-2010.... 447 G
theresa.burt@temple.edu
BURT, Woodrow, W .... 573-629-3252.... 282 H
wburt@hlg.edu
BURT, Yolanda .... 216-687-2246.... 388 C
y.burt@csuohio.edu
BURT-GRACIK, Melissa ..... 619-849-2253...... 62 L
melissaburtgracik@pointloma.edu
BURTCH, Polly .... 314-968-6954.... 293 A
burtch@webster.edu
BURTIS, Brett, K .... 307-674-6446.... 556 C
bburtis@sheridan.edu
BURTIS, Karen .... 307-674-6446.... 556 C
kburtis@sheridan.edu
BURTLEY, Harold .... 219-980-6778.... 173 F
hburtley@iun.edu
BURTNER, Jeff, R .... 540-338-1770.... 522 A
BURTON, Alan .... 580-745-2731.... 412 C
aburton@se.edu
BURTON, Ben .... 317-921-4712.... 175 G
bburton@ivytech.edu
BURTON, Brian, K .... 360-650-3896.... 539 C
brian.burton@wwu.edu
BURTON, Caroyn .... 434-381-6510.... 524 E
cburton@sbc.edu
BURTON, Chris .... 405-691-3800.... 408 H
cburton@macu.edu
BURTON, Chuck .... 817-531-5813.... 502 A
cburton@txwes.edu
BURTON, Clen .... 225-675-8270.... 211 J
cburton@rpcc.edu
BURTON,
Crompton (Hub), B .... 740-376-4402.... 395 F
hub.burton@marietta.edu
BURTON, Dan .... 513-244-8167.... 387 D
dan.burton@ccuniversity.edu
BURTON, Donald, N .... 602-648-5750...... 14 B
dburton@dunlap-stone.edu
BURTON, E. James .... 615-898-2764.... 473 F
eburton@mtsu.edu
BURTON, Gene .... 765-285-1832.... 169 D
gburton@bsu.edu
BURTON, Gregory, A .... 973-761-9362.... 315 B
gregory.burton@shu.edu
BURTON, Heather .... 540-868-7201.... 526 H
hburton@lfcc.edu
BURTON, Homer .... 270-247-8521.... 204 C
hburton@midcontinent.edu
BURTON, Jennus, L .... 928-523-2708...... 17 A
jennus.burton@nau.edu
BURTON, Jenny .... 303-292-0015...... 83 H
BURTON, Liz .... 541-962-3359.... 418 C
eburton@eou.edu
BURTON, Lonnie .... 806-291-3635.... 508 B
burtonl@wbu.edu
BURTON, Marjorie .... 440-775-5782.... 397 F
marjorie.burton@oberlin.edu
BURTON, Pam .... 303-762-6948...... 83 I
pam.burton@denverseminary.edu
BURTON, Patrice .... 708-596-2000.... 164 F
pburton@ssc.edu
BURTON, Raymond .... 804-523-5374.... 526 F
BURTON, Robert .... 808-984-3245.... 142 B
reburton@hawaii.edu
BURTON, Terrance .... 508-999-8664.... 237 E
tburton@umassd.edu
BURTON, Thomas .... 315-498-6061.... 345 D
burtont@sunyocc.edu
BURTON, Timothy, P .... 516-877-3385.... 322 A
burton@adelphi.edu
BURTON, Wayne, M .... 978-762-4000.... 241 A
wburton@northshore.edu
BURTON-GRAHAM, Laura 410-337-6439.... 222 I
lburtong@goucher.edu
BURTT, Alison .... 202-885-8657.... 100 A
aburtt@wesleyseminary.edu
BURTT, Edward, H .... 740-368-3886.... 400 F
ehburtt@owu.edu
BURWELL, Elissia .... 903-769-5763.... 488 M
elissia_burwell@jarvis.edu
BURWELL, Tim .... 828-262-2070.... 377 B
burwellth@appstate.edu
BURZACHECHI, Nancilee .. 412-237-8182.... 425 H
nancilee@ccac.edu
BURZICHELLI, Dominick ... 856-415-2292.... 310 E
dburzichelli@gccnj.edu
BURZINSKI, Jody .... 620-421-6700.... 194 E
jodyb@labette.edu
BUSAM, Leah .... 513-745-4892.... 406 E
BUSBOOM, Jacquie .... 352-435-5027.... 112 M
busboomj@lscc.edu
BUSBOOM, Margo .... 402-461-7494.... 298 C
mbusboom@hastings.edu
BUSBY, Adam .... 707-967-2404...... 43 G
a_busby@culinary.edu
BUSBY, Bruce .... 260-481-6140.... 174 A
busbyb@ipfw.edu
BUSBY, Michael .... 615-963-7631.... 474 A
busby@tnstate.edu
BUSBY, Ralph .... 936-468-2401.... 495 H
rbusby@sfasu.edu
BUSBY, Teresa .... 601-446-1211.... 274 A
teresa.busby@colin.edu
BUSCH, Beverly .... 732-356-1595.... 315 D
bbusch@somerset.edu
BUSCH, C. Lawrence .... 419-772-2362.... 398 G
c-busch@onu.edu
BUSCH, Caroline, C .... 804-752-7300.... 522 F
cbusch@rmc.edu
BUSCH, Gregory .... 419-755-4570.... 397 B
gbusch@ncstatecollege.edu
BUSCH, Kari .... 507-433-0526.... 269 A
kbusch@riverland.edu
BUSCH, Mary, E .... 317-788-3303.... 180 C
busch@uindy.edu
BUSCH, Mary Beth .... 304-424-8271.... 545 B
marybeth.busch@mail.wvu.edu
BUSCH, Nancy .... 718-817-4400.... 334 C
busch@fordham.edu
BUSCHART, W. David .... 303-762-6907...... 83 I
david.buschart@denverseminary.edu
BUSCHE, Donald .... 949-582-4795...... 70 F
dbusche@saddleback.edu
BUSCHER, Frank .... 901-321-3230.... 467 G
fbuscher@cbu.edu
BUSE, Beth, H .... 651-201-1799.... 265 H
beth.buse@so.mnscu.edu
BUSE, Dustin .... 218-683-8616.... 268 E
dustin.buse@northlandcollege.edu
BUSE, Jon .... 319-273-2331.... 182 D
jon.buse@uni.edu
BUSE, Kathleen .... 973-618-3411.... 308 D
kbuse@caldwell.edu
BUSE, William .... 212-799-5000.... 337 H
BUSEL, Yaakov .... 732-985-6533.... 313 B
BUSER, Boyd, R .... 606-218-5411.... 207 B
bbuser@pc.edu
BUSER, David .... 619-388-7663...... 65 H
dbuser@sdccd.edu
BUSH, Brian .... 405-425-1062.... 409 E
brian.bush@oc.edu
BUSH, Carolyn .... 606-436-5721.... 201 H
carolyn.bush@kctcs.edu
BUSH, Cathy .... 440-525-7112.... 394 F
cbush@lakelandcc.edu
BUSH, Christina .... 530-346-6792...... 30 D
cbush@aesa.com
BUSH, Darren .... 760-750-4826...... 36 B
dbush@csusm.edu
BUSH, David .... 972-825-4888.... 495 D
dbush@sagu.edu
BUSH, David .... 435-797-1012.... 511 B
david.bush@usu.edu
BUSH, Edward .... 951-222-8000...... 64 B
BUSH, Elizabeth .... 770-394-8300.... 124 F
ebush@aii.edu
BUSH, Frank .... 843-383-8007.... 457 A
fbush@coker.edu
BUSH, Gary .... 256-372-4747....... 1 A
gary.bush@aamu.edu
BUSH, Gary, W .... 678-915-5501.... 137 C
gbush@spsu.edu
BUSH, Jeffrey, A .... 504-862-8385.... 215 C
jbush@tulane.edu
BUSH, Jim .... 509-865-8570.... 534 D
bush_j@heritage.edu
BUSH, Katherine .... 845-437-5900.... 359 D
kabush@vassar.edu
BUSH, Keith .... 218-751-8670.... 270 G
it@oakhills.edu
BUSH, Kristen .... 540-231-6994.... 529 B
khbush@vt.edu
BUSH, Lisa, F .... 828-254-1921.... 367 H
lbush@abtech.edu
BUSH, Lonica .... 409-933-8413.... 483 B
lbush@com.edu
BUSH, Norma .... 425-602-3043.... 530 K
nbush@bastyr.edu
BUSH, Rachel .... 229-732-5962.... 124 C
rachelbush@andrewcollege.edu
BUSH, Robert .... 318-473-6414.... 212 G
rbush@lsua.edu
BUSH, Tim .... 520-319-3300...... 12 L
tbush@brownmackie.edu
BUSHER, Edward, J .... 937-328-6095.... 387 G
bushere@clarkstate.edu
BUSHEY, Jane .... 480-245-7930...... 14 K
jane.bushey@ibconline.edu
BUSHEY, Stephanie .... 516-463-6853.... 335 H
stephanie.bushey@hofstra.edu
BUSHMAN, David .... 301-447-8399.... 225 A
bushman@msmary.edu
BUSHMAN, Ed .... 715-422-5308.... 554 C
ed.bushman@mstc.edu
BUSHNELL, Elizabeth, J ..... 260-982-5242.... 177 F
ejbushnell@manchester.edu
BUSHNELL, Lynn, M .... 203-582-8651...... 93 E
lynn.bushnell@quinnipiac.edu
BUSHNELL, Rebecca, W .... 215-898-7320.... 448 I
bushnell@falcon.sas.upenn.edu
BUSHNER, Therese .... 410-462-8003.... 221 D
tbushner@bccc.edu
BUSHONG, Sara .... 419-372-2856.... 385 C
sbushon@bgsu.edu
BUSHWAY, Deb .... 612-977-4149.... 262 A
deb.bushway@capella.edu
BUSHWAY, Deborah .... 612-977-4149.... 262 A
deborah.bushway@capella.edu
BUSHWAY, Deborah .... 888-227-3552.... 262 A
deborah.bushway@capella.edu
BUSHWAY, Deborah .... 612-977-5478.... 262 A
deborah.bushway@capella.edu
BUSIC, David .... 816-268-5400.... 287 C
BUSICK, Dawn .... 417-447-8902.... 287 G
busickd@otc.edu
BUSKEY, Cynthia .... 404-880-8550.... 126 I
cbuskey@cau.edu
BUSROE, Andrew .... 606-368-6113.... 197 H
andrewbusroe@alc.edu
BUSS, Brian .... 920-735-5792.... 553 G
buss@fvtc.edu
BUSS, Daryl, D .... 608-263-6716.... 550 G
bussd@svm.vetmed.wisc.edu
BUSSANI, Nancy .... 408-924-1120...... 37 A
nancy.bussani@sjsu.edu
BUSSARD, Patsy, G .... 276-964-7332.... 528 A
pat.bussard@sw.edu
BUSSE, Barbara .... 310-338-7430...... 56 E
bbusse@lmu.edu
BUSSELL, Helena .... 817-531-4405.... 502 A
hbussell@txwes.edu
BUSSELL, Jim .... 252-789-0268.... 371 E
jbussell@martincc.edu
BUSSELL, Paige .... 903-468-3209.... 497 E
paige_bussell@tamu-commerce.edu
BUSSELL, Rachelle .... 909-558-4544...... 54 D
rbussell@llu.edu
BUSSERT, Ronald .... 918-594-8004.... 410 G
ron.bussert@okstate.edu
BUSSEY, Brenda .... 508-929-8455.... 239 D
bbussey@worcester.edu
BUSTA, Joseph, F .... 251-460-7616........ 9 E
jbusta@usouthal.edu
BUSTAMANTE, Camilla ..... 505-747-5454.... 320 A
cbustamante@nnmc.edu
BUSTAMANTE, Chris .... 480-517-8118...... 16 C
chris.bustamente@riosalado.edu
BUSTARD, James .... 217-351-2211.... 161 B
jbustard@parkland.edu
BUSTILLO, Pamela .... 408-273-2696...... 58 G
pbustillo@nhu.edu
BUSTOS, Phillip .... 505-224-4741.... 317 J
pbustos@cnm.edu
BUSTROM, Carla .... 612-977-5302.... 262 A
carla.bustrom@capella.edu
BUSZEK, Thomas .... 269-687-5641.... 258 E
tbuszek@swmich.edu
BUTALA, Dick .... 612-977-5770.... 262 A
richard.butala@capella.edu
BUTCHER, Claudette .... 918-293-5256.... 410 E
claudette.butcher@okstate.edu
BUTCHER, Fred, R .... 304-293-1536.... 544 E
fbutcher@hsc.wvu.edu
BUTCHER, Lisa .... 276-523-2400.... 527 A
lbutcher@me.vccs.edu
BUTCHER, Michael .... 912-279-5815.... 127 B
mbutcher@ccga.edu
BUTCHER, Sean .... 706-233-7491.... 136 E
sbutcher@shorter.edu
BUTCHER, Thomas, A .... 616-331-2067.... 252 A
butchert@gvsu.edu
BUTCHER, Tina .... 706-507-8265.... 127 D
butcher_tina@columbusstate.edu
BUTCHER, Tom .... 513-721-7944.... 391 C
tbutcher@gbs.edu
BUTDORFF, Carla .... 419-747-5401.... 397 B
196mgr@fheg.follett.com
BUTIN, Dan .... 978-837-5338.... 242 D
dan.butin@merrimack.edu
BUTKOVICH, Michelle .... 248-204-2111.... 254 E
mbutkovic@ltu.edu
BUTLER, Adam .... 615-269-9900.... 469 K
abutler@kaplan.edu
BUTLER, Allen, P .... 815-455-8999.... 157 F
abutler@mchenry.edu
BUTLER, Ann .... 910-592-8081.... 373 D
abutler@sampsoncc.edu
BUTLER, Barbara .... 707-664-2397...... 37 B
barbara.butler@sonoma.edu
BUTLER, Beautrice .... 210-486-4173.... 479 C
bbutler@alamo.edu
BUTLER, Broderick, F .... 713-313-1347.... 499 G
butlerbf@tsu.edu
BUTLER, Bryant .... 601-968-5930.... 273 F
bbutler@belhaven.edu
BUTLER, Cass .... 816-221-1300.... 281 F
cbutler@devry.edu
BUTLER, Cathy .... 562-908-3427...... 63 H
cbutler@riohondo.edu
BUTLER, Cindy, A .... 816-604-1527.... 285 D
cindy.butler@mcckc.edu
BUTLER, Connie .... 402-643-7332.... 297 F
connie.butler@cune.edu
BUTLER, D. Martin .... 816-268-5421.... 287 C
dbutler@nts.edu
BUTLER, Elizabeth, S .... 847-328-9300.... 164 B
elizabeth.butler@seabury.edu
BUTLER, Frank, A .... 859-257-1841.... 206 H
fbutler@uky.edu
BUTLER, Gillian .... 530-752-2000...... 73 F
gbutler@ucdavis.edu
BUTLER, Greg .... 601-477-4113.... 275 B
greg.butler@jcjc.edu
BUTLER, Greg, L .... 412-291-6456.... 422 D
gbutler@aii.edu
BUTLER, Harry, P .... 248-204-3925.... 254 E
hbutler@ltu.edu
BUTLER, Heidi .... 610-861-5453.... 437 G
hbutler@northampton.edu
BUTLER, Jack .... 931-372-3227.... 474 B
jbutler@tntech.edu
BUTLER, Janice, R .... 570-577-3973.... 423 D
janice.butler@bucknell.edu
BUTLER, Jennifer .... 708-656-8000.... 159 C
jennifer.butler@morton.edu
BUTLER, Joan .... 972-825-4650.... 495 D
jbutler@sagu.edu
BUTLER, SJ, John, T .... 617-552-1602.... 232 D
john.butler@bc.edu
BUTLER, Johnnella, E .... 404-270-5021.... 137 E
jebutler@spelman.edu
BUTLER, Kathleen .... 860-231-5322...... 93 H
kbutler@sjc.edu
BUTLER, Kathleen, P .... 325-235-7311.... 500 C
kathleen.butler@tstc.edu

C

CABRERA, Rafael ... 787-766-1912 ... 562 F rcabrera@inter.edu

CABUNGCAL, Christi ... 614-947-6542 ... 391 A cabungcc@franklin.edu

CACACE, Marie ... 301-447-5360 ... 225 A cacace@msmary.edu

CACCIA, Stephen, P ... 603-271-6982 ... 304 G scaccia@ccsnh.edu

CACCIATORE, Lawrence ... 212-353-4250 ... 331 B caciatl@cooper.edu

CACKOWSKI, Sandra ... 713-525-2162 ... 504 D sandy2@stthom.edu

CADDY, Kurt ... 417-328-1900 ... 290 E kcaddy@sbuniv.edu

CADE, Eulanda ... 402-872-2230 ... 299 H ecade@peru.edu

CADE, John ... 615-963-5107 ... 474 A jcade@tnstate.edu

CADE, Michelle ... 313-927-1485 ... 255 A mcade4052@marygrove.edu

CADE, Tinina, Q ... 804-289-8032 ... 525 A tcade@richmond.edu

CADENA, Rosa ... 617-236-8800 ... 235 B rcadena@fisher.edu

CADIEUX, Cynthia ... 757-822-5185 ... 528 C ccadieux@tcc.edu

CADLAON, Carlos ... 770-279-0507 ... 129 E gcuesol@yahoo.com

CADLE, Julie ... 229-732-5927 ... 124 C juliecadle@andrewcollege.edu

CADLE, Robin ... 361-570-4120 ... 503 E cadler@uhv.edu

CADLE, Wendi ... 479-619-3149 ... 22 H wcadle@nwacc.edu

CADMAN, Harry ... 919-760-8011 ... 366 G cadmanh@meredith.edu

CADMAN, Lesley, A ... 212-517-3929 ... 351 C

CADWALLADER, Martin, T 608-262-1044 ... 550 G cadwallader@grad.wisc.edu

CADWALLADER, Meghan .. 617-912-9211 ... 232 E mcadwallader@bostonconservatory.edu

CADWALLADER, Sarah ... 620-431-2820 ... 195 B scadwallader@neosho.edu

CADWELL BROWN, Carrie, S ... 413-585-2027 ... 245 B ccadwell@smith.edu

CADY, Karen ... 978-542-7503 ... 239 B kcady@salemstate.edu

CADY, Paul, S ... 208-282-3475 ... 143 D cady@pharmacy.isu.edu

CADY MELZER, Deborah, M ... 315-445-4525 ... 338 B cadymedm@lemoyne.edu

CAESAR, Jemma ... 713-221-8006 ... 503 D caesarj@uhd.edu

CAETANO, Raul ... 214-648-1500 ... 507 D raul.caetano@utsouthwestern.edu

CAFARO, Thomas, R ... 508-213-2294 ... 243 J tom.cafaro@nichols.edu

CAFFARELLI, Joseph ... 973-720-2714 ... 317 D caffarellij@wpunj.edu

CAFFEY, Walter ... 617-573-8647 ... 245 E wcaffey@suffolk.edu

CAFFO, Betty, J ... 302-356-6723 ... 97 A betty.j.caffo@wilmu.edu

CAFONCELLI, Kathy, L ... 610-921-7600 ... 421 D kcafoncelli@alb.edu

CAFONE, James, M ... 973-761-9139 ... 315 B james.cafone@shu.edu

CAGE, Beverly ... 361-698-1279 ... 485 F bacage@delmar.edu

CAGE, Patrick ... 773-995-3524 ... 146 D pcage@csu.edu

CAGE, Stephanie ... 615-340-3553 ... 468 G scage@fisk.edu

CAGGIANO, Marion ... 973-655-3417 ... 311 G caggianom@mail.montclair.edu

CAGIGAL, Josefina ... 305-348-2233 ... 119 B cagigalj@fiu.edu

CAGIGAS, Gloria, C ... 724-946-7368 ... 451 C cagigagc@westminster.edu

CAGLE, David ... 815-802-8128 ... 154 J dcagle@kcc.edu

CAGLE, Michael, R ... 903-886-5421 ... 497 E michael_cagle@tamu-commerce.edu

CAGLE, Susie ... 918-781-7280 ... 407 B cagles@bacone.edu

CAGLE-PAGE, Jonna ... 281-425-6209 ... 489 J jcagle@lee.edu

CAGLEY, Karen ... 405-325-4088 ... 413 C kcagley@ou.edu

CAHALAN, Jodi ... 515-271-1369 ... 183 F jodi.cahalan@dmu.edu

CAHALAN, SJ, Patrick, J ... 310-338-5921 ... 56 E pcahalan@lmu.edu

CAHEN, Robert ... 440-525-7097 ... 394 F bcahen@lakelandcc.edu

CAHILL, Elizabeth, A ... 603-526-3729 ... 304 A ecahill@colby-sawyer.edu

CAHILL, Elizabeth, J ... 304-384-6003 ... 543 D lcahill@concord.edu

CAHILL, Heather ... 413-205-3972 ... 229 G heather.cahill@aic.edu

CAHILL, Linda ... 434-961-5304 ... 527 F lcahill@pvcc.edu

CAHILL, Margaret, D ... 651-962-6131 ... 272 E mdcahill@stthomas.edu

CAHILL, Mark ... 702-651-4350 ... 302 G mark.cahill@csn.edu

CAHILL, Michael, T ... 718-780-7943 ... 324 F michael.cahill@brooklaw.edu

CAHILL, Regina ... 212-594-4000 ... 357 G rcahill@tcicollege.edu

CAHILL, Richard ... 859-985-3451 ... 198 F richard_cahill@berea.edu

CAHILL, Stanley ... 978-542-6400 ... 239 B scahill@salemstate.edu

CAHOE, William, B ... 765-285-1486 ... 169 D wcahoe@bsu.edu

CAHOON, Ann ... 907-852-3333 ... 10 G ann.cahoon@ilisagvik.edu

CAHOON, Kirsten ... 507-786-3268 ... 271 H cahoon@stolaf.edu

CAHOY, William ... 320-363-3182 ... 271 F bcahoy@csbsju.edu

CAI, Hui-Yan ... 262-554-2010 ... 158 D midwestmedicine@cs.com

CAI, Maoyi ... 512-444-8082 ... 499 B

CAI, Maoyi ... 512-444-8082 ... 499 B cai@texastcm.edu

CAIL, Don, P ... 405-271-2121 ... 413 D don-cail@ouhsc.edu

CAILLOUET, Rachel ... 713-798-4300 ... 481 H rachelc@bcm.edu

CAILLOUX, Laura ... 360-416-7729 ... 538 A laura.cailloux@skagit.edu

CAIN, Chad ... 626-584-5352 ... 48 A adm-fpo2@dept.fuller.edu

CAIN, Cheryl ... 361-593-2138 ... 498 A cheryl.cain@tamuk.edu

CAIN, Dan ... 760-366-5295 ... 43 E dcain@cmccd.edu

CAIN, Darrell ... 317-917-5702 ... 175 I dcain@ivytech.edu

CAIN, Dawn ... 918-456-5511 ... 409 A cain@nsuok.edu

CAIN, Jason ... 334-493-3573 ... 5 F jcain@lbwcc.edu

CAIN, Jerry, B ... 847-628-2001 ... 154 I jcain@judsonu.edu

CAIN, Jessica ... 425-388-9274 ... 533 H jcain@everettcc.edu

CAIN, John ... 405-733-7458 ... 411 I jcain@rose.edu

CAIN, Joshua ... 252-985-5145 ... 375 C jmcain@ncwc.edu

CAIN, Kevin, G ... 304-462-4119 ... 543 F kevin.cain@glenville.edu

CAIN, Michael ... 716-829-2100 ... 351 G vphs@buffalo.edu

CAIN, Michael, E ... 716-829-3955 ... 351 G mcain@buffalo.edu

CAIN, Rhea ... 317-738-8100 ... 171 C rcain@franklincollege.edu

CAIN, Sandra ... 508-541-1658 ... 234 B scain@dean.edu

CAIN, Sanford ... 910-678-8287 ... 370 B cains@faytechcc.edu

CAIN, Shelly ... 309-796-5052 ... 145 E cains@bhc.edu

CAIN, Stephen, D ... 240-567-1796 ... 224 E stephen.cain@montgomerycollege.edu

CAIN, Thomas ... 404-527-4520 ... 126 F tcain@carver.edu

CAINE, Randy ... 808-236-5811 ... 140 B rcaine@hpu.edu

CAINES, Royce ... 864-644-5343 ... 461 B rcaines@swu.edu

CAIRE, Cynthia, D ... 504-865-3388 ... 213 F caire@loyno.edu

CAIRES, Matthew ... 406-994-2826 ... 295 E

CAIRNS, James ... 412-237-3024 ... 425 H jcairns@ccac.edu

CAIRNS, Jill ... 207-834-7602 ... 220 D jillb@maine.edu

CAIRNS, Melissa ... 602-275-7133 ... 18 D melissa@rsiaz.edu

CAIRNS, Michael ... 415-433-9200 ... 68 F mcairns@saybrook.edu

CAIRNS, Michael, A ... 231-591-3770 ... 251 B cairnsm@ferris.edu

CAIRNS, Schanie ... 303-937-4042 ... 82 A scairns@chu.edu

CAIRO, Jim, R ... 504-568-4246 ... 213 A jcairo@lsuhsu.edu

CAIROL, Miguel ... 718-260-5600 ... 328 E mcairol@citytech.cuny.edu

CAIRY, Timothy, J ... 610-499-1193 ... 451 F tjcairy@widener.edu

CAISON, Anthony, M ... 919-866-6101 ... 374 E amcaison@waketech.edu

CAJAYON, Felicito ... 213-891-2056 ... 54 F cajayof@email.laccd.edu

CAJIPE, Josie Rose, O ... 692-625-4931 ... 559 E jcajipe@cmi.edu

CAJKA, Karen, L ... 423-439-4135 ... 473 E cajka@etsu.edu

CAL, John ... 305-348-4001 ... 119 B john.cal@fiu.edu

CALABRESE, Nancy ... 410-263-2371 ... 225 G nancy.calabrese@sjca.edu

CALABRIA, Patrick ... 631-420-2400 ... 356 A patrick.calabria@farmingdale.edu

CALABRO, Barbara ... 239-939-4766 ... 118 D bcalabro@swfc.edu

CALABRO, Richard ... 505-224-3565 ... 317 J rcalabro@cnm.edu

CALABRO, Stephen ... 239-939-4766 ... 118 D scalabro@swfc.edu

CALAF, Jorge ... 787-279-1912 ... 563 B jcalaf@bayamon.inter.edu

CALAMAI, Anthony, G ... 828-262-3076 ... 377 B calamaiag@appstate.edu

CALAMAIO, Caprice ... 913-234-0733 ... 191 G caprice.calamaio@cleveland.edu

CALAMARE, Susan, S ... 617-422-7387 ... 243 G scalamare@admin.nesl.edu

CALAME, Catherine ... 516-299-2719 ... 339 A catherine.calame@liu.edu

CALAME, Wanda ... 334-683-2304 ... 5 G wcalame@marionmilitary.edu

CALAMETTI, Jeffrey, D ... 251-442-2242 ... 9 B jeffc@mail.umobile.edu

CALAMIA, John, J ... 504-865-3946 ... 213 F calamia@loyno.edu

CALANDRELLA, Drew ... 530-898-6131 ... 34 A dcalandrella@csuchico.edu

CALAPA, Joseph, P ... 508-626-4523 ... 238 D joec@framingham.edu

CALARESO, Jack, P ... 508-849-3333 ... 230 C jcalareso@annamaria.edu

CALARESO, Joe ... 305-595-9500 ... 100 D admissions@amcollege.edu

CALAWAY, Terry, A ... 913-469-8500 ... 193 I tcalaway@jccc.edu

CALCADO, Antonio ... 732-445-2166 ... 314 B acalcado@facilities.rutgers.edu

CALCAGNI, Thomas ... 406-994-4571 ... 295 E tcalcagni@montana.edu

CALCAGNINO, Josephine, A ... 414-425-8300 ... 550 A jcalcagnino@shst.edu

CALDARELLO, Beth ... 816-941-4030 ... 281 E bcaldarello@devry.edu

CALDER, Jason ... 706-247-6484 ... 540 H

CALDER, Marie ... 508-457-1313 ... 243 B mcalder@ngs.edu

CALDERBANK, Robert ... 919-668-2728 ... 363 I natscidean@duke.edu

CALDERHEAD, John ... 719-389-6854 ... 81 L John.Calderhead@ColoradoCollege.edu

CALDERON, Ann Marie ... 615-230-3401 ... 476 A annmarie.calderon@volstate.edu

CALDERON, Janet ... 407-303-6108 ... 108 D janet.calderon@fhchs.edu

CALDERON, Larry, A ... 954-262-7300 ... 114 B lc@nsu.nova.edu

CALDERON, Nancy ... 408-554-2397 ... 68 C ntcalderon@scu.edu

CALDERON, Raoul ... 641-472-7000 ... 187 B rcalderon@mum.edu

CALDERON, Victor ... 305-573-1600 ... 100 K vcalderon@atienterprises.edu

CALDERSON, Carl ... 619-201-8780 ... 65 D Carl.Calderson@sdcc.edu

CALDON, Heather ... 760-252-2411 ... 30 F hcaldon@barstow.edu

CALDWELL, Adonna ... 901-572-2592 ... 467 A adonna.caldwell@bchs.edu

CALDWELL, Agnes ... 517-265-5161 ... 247 D acaldwell@adrian.edu

CALDWELL, Angela ... 870-248-4000 ... 21 A angelac@blackrivertech.edu

CALDWELL, Avery ... 619-684-8794 ... 59 A acaldwell@newschoolarch.edu

CALDWELL, Brinda, W ... 828-254-1921 ... 367 H bcaldwell@abtech.edu

CALDWELL, Cheryl ... 417-255-7960 ... 286 G cherylcaldwell@missouristate.edu

CALDWELL, Chico ... 478-825-6888 ... 129 C caldwellc@fvsu.edu

CALDWELL, Daniel ... 601-318-6115 ... 278 E daniel.caldwell@wmcarey.edu

CALDWELL, David ... 508-286-3403 ... 246 E dcaldwel@wheatoncollege.edu

CALDWELL, David ... 970-351-2707 ... 88 F david.caldwell@unco.edu

CALDWELL, David ... 615-248-1311 ... 476 E dcaldwell@trevecca.edu

CALDWELL, Diana ... 574-936-8898 ... 168 I diana.caldwell@ancilla.edu

CALDWELL, Gail ... 256-726-7024 ... 6 C gcaldwell@oakwood.edu

CALDWELL, Helen ... 704-378-1014 ... 365 H hcaldwell@jcsu.edu

CALDWELL, Herbert ... 217-245-3271 ... 152 C herbert.caldwell@ic.edu

CALDWELL, Jacqueline, H . 918-631-2691 ... 413 F jacqueline-caldwell@utulsa.edu

CALDWELL, James ... 303-280-7411 ... 84 C jcaldwell@devry.com

CALDWELL, James ... 215-780-1306 ... 446 G jcaldwell@salus.edu

CALDWELL, Janet ... 615-327-6851 ... 471 A jcaldwell@mmc.edu

CALDWELL, Jeff ... 405-733-7395 ... 411 I jcaldwell@rose.edu

CALDWELL, Lin, D ... 310-434-4200 ... 68 D caldwell_lin@smc.edu

CALDWELL, Linda ... 251-580-2247 ... 5 A lcaldwell@faulknerstate.edu

CALDWELL, Mike ... 801-832-2592 ... 512 F mcaldwell@westminstercollege.edu

CALDWELL, Nina ... 314-529-9485 ... 284 F ncaldwell@maryville.edu

CALDWELL, Patrice ... 575-562-2315 ... 318 A patrice.caldwell@enmu.edu

CALDWELL, Sandra ... 307-382-1720 ... 556 F scaldwell@wwcc.wy.edu

CALDWELL, Sandy ... 307-382-1720 ... 556 F scaldwel@wwcc.wy.edu

CALDWELL, Stefanie ... 312-935-4055 ... 162 E scoleman@robertmorris.edu

CALDWELL, Steve ... 662-472-2312 ... 274 F scaldwell@holmescc.edu

CALDWELL, Sue ... 691-320-2480 ... 559 A scaldwell@comfsm.fm

CALDWELL, Susan ... 606-589-0310 ... 203 A susan.caldwell@kctcs.edu

CALDWELL, Vicki ... 704-878-3206 ... 371 H vcaldwell@mitchellcc.edu

CALDWELL, Ward, W ... 570-326-3761 ... 440 K wcaldwel@pct.edu

CALE, Lynn ... 252-446-0436 ... 370 A calel@edgecombe.edu

CALE, JR., William, G ... 256-765-4211 ... 9 D wgcale@una.edu

CALEB, Peter ... 212-749-2802 ... 339 I library@msmnyc.edu

CALENDA, Marianne ... 717-361-1196 ... 428 E calendam@etown.edu

CALERO, Pamela ... 352-873-5808 ... 103 D calerop@cf.edu

CALERO, Teofilo ... 773-878-2998 ... 163 D tcalero@staugustine.edu

CALFAS, Karen, J ... 858-822-7552 ... 74 D kcalfas@ucsd.edu

CALFEE, Laura ... 512-499-8787 ... 503 A lcalfee@uh.edu

CALHOUN, Andrew ... 608-822-2303 ... 555 B

CALHOUN, Barbara, S ... 770-423-6258 ... 132 H bcalhoun@kennesaw.edu

CALHOUN, Deborah, C ... 803-934-3216 ... 459 F dcalhoun@morris.edu

CALHOUN, Jeff ... 847-317-8730 ... 166 B jcalhoun@tiu.edu

CALHOUN, Larry ... 478-289-2250 ... 137 A lcalhoun@southeasterntech.edu

CALHOUN, Larry, D ... 423-439-2068 ... 473 E calhoun@etsu.edu

CALHOUN, Linda ... 270-686-4400 ... 202 E linda.calhoun@kctcs.edu

CALHOUN, M.Grace ... 773-508-7465 ... 157 A athdir@luc.edu

CALHOUN, Mary Lynne ... 704-687-8992 ... 378 E mlcalhou@uncc.edu

CALHOUN, Matthew ... 602-222-9300 ... 11 I mcalhoun@arizonacollege.edu

CALHOUN, Matthew ... 601-276-2000 ... 277 E mattc@smcc.edu

CALHOUN, Mike ... 502-863-8046 ... 200 G mike_calhoun@georgetowncollege.edu

CALHOUN, Patricia ... 870-512-7898 ... 20 F patricia_calhoun@asun.edu

CALHOUN, Ralph ... 901-435-1276 ... 470 B ralph_calhoun@loc.edu

CALHOUN, Sandra ... 970-491-6321 ... 83 A sandy.calhoun@colostate.edu

CALHOUN, Sandy ... 970-491-6321 ... 83 A sandy.calhoun@colostate.edu

CALHOUN, JR., Thomas, C ... 256-765-4709 ... 9 D tcalhoun@una.edu

CALHOUN, Thomas, G ... 703-993-2541 ... 519 A tcalhou2@gmu.edu

CALHOUN, Tony ... 731-426-7658 ... 469 M tcalhoun@lanecollege.edu

CALHOUN, Valerie, A ... 717-290-8713 ... 433 F vcalhoun@lancasterseminary.edu

CALHOUN, W. Rochelle ... 518-580-5760 ... 351 B rcalhoun@skidmore.edu

CALHOUN-BROWN, Allison ... 404-413-2067 ... 131 C acalhounbrown@gsu.edu

CALHOUN-FRENCH, Diane ... 502-213-2120 ... 202 B diane.calhoun-french@kctcs.edu

CALIA, Georgina, N ... 718-817-3112 ... 334 C calia@fordham.edu

CALIENDO, Amy, A ... 215-670-9114 ... 438 D aacaliendo@peirce.edu

CALIENDO, Evelyn ... 847-467-3622 ... 160 D evelyn-caliendo@northwestern.edu

CALIFF, Robert, M ... 919-668-8820 ... 363 I calif001@mc.duke.edu

CALINGO, Luis ... 415-458-3759 ... 45 B luis.calingo@dominican.edu

CAMPBELL, Jane, S ... 712-362-7947 ... 185 G
jcampbell@iowalakes.edu

CAMPBELL, Janet, M ... 989-328-1208 ... 256 A
janetc@montcalm.edu

CAMPBELL, Jennifer, D ... 561-868-3280 ... 114 D
campbejd@palmbeachstate.edu

CAMPBELL, Jeremy ... 704-216-3577 ... 373 C
jermey.campbell@rccc.edu

CAMPBELL, Jerry ... 510-204-0707 ... 39 F
jcampbell@cdsp.edu

CAMPBELL, Jerry, D ... 909-447-2552 ... 40 E
jcampbell@cst.edu

CAMPBELL, Jo ... 419-530-5472 ... 404 F
jo.campbell@utoledo.edu

CAMPBELL, Joann, N ... 904-620-2002 ... 120 C
jcampbel@unf.edu

CAMPBELL, Joanne ... 479-248-7236 ... 21 G
jcampbell@ecollege.edu

CAMPBELL, John ... 954-446-6344 ... 100 E
jcampbell@aiuniv.edu

CAMPBELL, John, T ... 843-953-7144 ... 457 B
campbelljt@cofc.edu

CAMPBELL, Jonathan ... 870-230-5098 ... 21 I
campbej@hsu.edu

CAMPBELL, Jonathan ... 248-689-8282 ... 260 A
jcampbel@walshcollege.edu

CAMPBELL, Joseph, A ... 215-895-2807 ... 427 G
jac47@drexel.edu

CAMPBELL, Joyce ... 501-244-4980 ... 19 F
joyce.campbell@arkansasbaptist.edu

CAMPBELL, Judy ... 386-506-4403 ... 103 J
campbelju@DaytonaState.edu

CAMPBELL, K. Celeste ... 405-744-6876 ... 410 C
celeste.campbell@okstate.edu

CAMPBELL, Karen, M ... 608-822-2300 ... 555 B

CAMPBELL, Kathy ... 503-399-5018 ... 414 J
kathy.campbell@chemeketa.edu

CAMPBELL, Kathy ... 269-488-4722 ... 253 G
kcampbell@kvcc.edu

CAMPBELL, Keith, E ... 404-413-4465 ... 131 C
kcampbell@gsu.edu

CAMPBELL, Kelly ... 415-380-1678 ... 48 D
kellycampbell@ggbts.edu

CAMPBELL, Kelly, J ... 620-417-1181 ... 196 B
kelly.campbell@sccc.edu

CAMPBELL, Ken, B ... 208-732-6243 ... 143 B
kcampbell@csi.edu

CAMPBELL, Keni ... 907-796-6569 ... 11 A
keni.campbell@uas.alaska.edu

CAMPBELL, Keshia ... 757-727-5641 ... 519 C
keshia.campbell@hamptonu.edu

CAMPBELL, Kevin ... 325-674-2765 ... 478 H
kevin.campbell@acu.edu

CAMPBELL, Kim ... 614-234-5144 ... 396 G
kcampbell@mccn.edu

CAMPBELL, Kimberly ... 405-491-6335 ... 412 D
kcampbel@snu.edu

CAMPBELL, Kirby, D ... 318-342-5147 ... 216 E
kcampbell@ulm.edu

CAMPBELL, Kirk ... 909-558-4748 ... 54 D
kpcampbell@llu.edu

CAMPBELL, Lauren ... 215-637-7700 ... 430 H
lcampbell@holyfamily.edu

CAMPBELL, Lea ... 713-221-5548 ... 503 D
campbellc@uhd.edu

CAMPBELL, Linda, J ... 408-554-4806 ... 68 C
lcampbell@scu.edu

CAMPBELL, Lisa ... 714-992-7085 ... 59 D
lcampbell@fullcoll.edu

CAMPBELL, Lisa ... 775-623-4824 ... 302 H
lisac@gwmail.gbcnv.edu

CAMPBELL, Lisa, M ... 724-287-8711 ... 423 F
lisa.campbell@bc3.edu

CAMPBELL, Lori ... 423-585-6933 ... 476 B
lori.campbell@ws.edu

CAMPBELL, Luke ... 479-986-0385 ... 19 C
luke.campbell@phoenix.edu

CAMPBELL, Margareta ... 707-546-4000 ... 45 G
mcampbell@empirecollege.com

CAMPBELL, Mark ... 617-266-1400 ... 231 G

CAMPBELL, Marshall ... 304-384-5276 ... 543 D
mcampbell@concord.edu

CAMPBELL, Martin ... 870-230-5150 ... 21 I
campbem@hsu.edu

CAMPBELL, Mary, B ... 314-935-3617 ... 292 J
marycampbell@wustl.edu

CAMPBELL, Mary, B ... 864-488-8280 ... 459 A
mcampbell@limestone.edu

CAMPBELL, Mary, K ... 213-740-9464 ... 76 C
mcampbell@caps.usc.edu

CAMPBELL, Megan ... 301-369-2800 ... 221 F
megan@capitol-college.edu

CAMPBELL, Michael ... 760-384-6159 ... 52 N
michael.campbell@cerrocoso.edu

CAMPBELL, Michael, A ... 423-585-2682 ... 476 B
mike.campbell@ws.edu

CAMPBELL, Michele ... 580-745-2512 ... 412 C
mcampbell@se.edu

CAMPBELL, Mike ... 304-696-2456 ... 543 G
marshallbkstr@fheg.follett.com

CAMPBELL, Milt ... 641-673-1074 ... 189 I
campbellm@wmpenn.edu

CAMPBELL, Mitchell, L ... 916-558-2426 ... 56 D
campbem@scc.losrios.edu

CAMPBELL, Nicole ... 315-386-7123 ... 355 D
campbelln@canton.edu

CAMPBELL, Nina ... 412-392-3990 ... 444 H
ncampbell@pointpark.edu

CAMPBELL, Pamela ... 281-998-6150 ... 493 D
pamela.campbell@sjcd.edu

CAMPBELL, Pat ... 806-742-2155 ... 501 D
pat.campbell@ttu.edu

CAMPBELL, Patricia ... 617-627-3331 ... 245 F
patricia.campbell@tufts.edu

CAMPBELL, Patricia ... 509-542-4761 ... 532 C
pcambell@columbiabasin.edu

CAMPBELL, Phyllis ... 731-352-4046 ... 467 C
campbellp@bethelu.edu

CAMPBELL, Phyllis ... 731-352-4020 ... 467 C
campbellp@bethelu.edu

CAMPBELL, Ralph ... 623-935-8051 ... 15 H
ralph.campbell@estrellamountain.edu

CAMPBELL, Rebecca, J ... 409-882-3318 ... 500 G
becky.campbell@lsco.edu

CAMPBELL, Rebecca, R ... 724-838-4276 ... 447 B
rcampbell@setonhill.edu

CAMPBELL, Regina ... 704-362-2345 ... 363 G
rcampbell@devry.edu

CAMPBELL, Renee ... 479-636-9222 ... 22 H
rcampbell@nwacc.edu

CAMPBELL, Ric ... 845-758-7154 ... 323 F
rcampbell@bard.edu

CAMPBELL, Richard ... 207-780-4484 ... 220 G
dcamp@usm.maine.edu

CAMPBELL, Rick ... 503-699-4453 ... 416 I
rcampbell@marylhurst.edu

CAMPBELL, Rickie, N ... 276-523-2400 ... 527 A
rcampbell@me.vccs.edu

CAMPBELL, Rina ... 559-453-2289 ... 47 K
rina.campbell@fresno.edu

CAMPBELL, Robert, D ... 212-817-7300 ... 327 B
rcampbell@gc.cuny.edu

CAMPBELL, Ron ... 847-317-8000 ... 166 B
rcampbel@tiu.edu

CAMPBELL, Rose, M ... 309-796-5043 ... 145 E
campbellr@bhc.edu

CAMPBELL, Rupert ... 718-940-5844 ... 349 B
rcampbell@sjcny.edu

CAMPBELL, Rupert ... 718-940-5844 ... 349 A
rcampbell@sjcny.edu

CAMPBELL, Rusty ... 615-844-5269 ... 468 J
rcampbell@fwbbc.edu

CAMPBELL, Ruth ... 573-681-5483 ... 284 B
campbelr@lincolnu.edu

CAMPBELL, Sandra ... 870-460-1080 ... 25 A
campbell@uamont.edu

CAMPBELL, Sara ... 215-596-7510 ... 450 A
s.campbell@usciences.edu

CAMPBELL, Sarah ... 415-451-2830 ... 66 B
scampbell@sfts.edu

CAMPBELL, Scott ... 608-663-2377 ... 547 C
sacampbell@edgewood.edu

CAMPBELL, Shannon ... 601-477-4022 ... 275 B
shannon.campbell@jcjc.edu

CAMPBELL, Shoshanna, M 718-780-7501 ... 324 F
shoshanna.campbell@brooklaw.edu

CAMPBELL, Stanley, R ... 859-238-5271 ... 199 D
stan.campbell@centre.edu

CAMPBELL, Stephanie ... 318-357-5351 ... 216 B
campbells@nsula.edu

CAMPBELL, Stephen ... 216-368-5555 ... 386 E
stephen.campbell@case.edu

CAMPBELL, Stephen, S ... 757-594-7663 ... 517 I
stephen.campbell@cnu.edu

CAMPBELL, Steven ... 423-323-0205 ... 475 E
srcampbell@northeaststate.edu

CAMPBELL, Susan ... 802-443-5391 ... 513 G
scampbel@middlebury.edu

CAMPBELL, Susan ... 207-780-4547 ... 220 G
scamp@usm.maine.edu

CAMPBELL, Susan ... 773-702-4065 ... 166 D
smc1@uchicago.edu

CAMPBELL, Susan, G ... 817-257-4690 ... 498 F
s.g.campbell@tcu.edu

CAMPBELL, Susan, M ... 717-815-1305 ... 452 F
scampbel@ycp.edu

CAMPBELL, Suzanne, H ... 203-254-4150 ... 92 B
scampbell@fairfield.edu

CAMPBELL, Suzanne, P ... 814-886-6385 ... 437 A
suzanne.campbell@mtaloy.edu

CAMPBELL, Thomas, F ... 214-905-3001 ... 505 D
thomas.f.campbell@utdallas.edu

CAMPBELL, Thomas, L ... 610-282-1100 ... 426 I
thomas.campbell@desales.edu

CAMPBELL, Timothy, M ... 443-334-2838 ... 226 E
tmcampbell@stevenson.edu

CAMPBELL, Tom ... 714-628-2516 ... 39 C
tcampbell@chapman.edu

CAMPBELL, Wes ... 407-345-2823 ... 104 D
wcampbell@devry.edu

CAMPBELL, William (Bill) .. 916-638-1616 ... 49 K
bill_campbell@heald.edu

CAMPBELL, Yanka ... 410-238-9000 ... 99 D

CAMPBELL JACKSON,
Candace ... 330-972-7075 ... 403 B
candac7@uakron.edu

CAMPBELL LOUNSBURY,
Susan ... 404-657-8883 ... 138 E
susan.campbell@usg.edu

CAMPBELL-PRICE, Kerry ... 707-527-4246 ... 68 E
kcampbell-price@santarosa.edu

CAMPEAU, Tony ... 406-496-4632 ... 296 C
tcampeau@mtech.edu

CAMPEAU, Tony ... 406-496-4632 ... 296 D
tcampeau@mtech.edu

CAMPER, Diane ... 731-286-3338 ... 475 A
camper@dscc.edu

CAMPER, Yolanda ... 318-342-1651 ... 216 E
camper@ulm.edu

CAMPERI, Marcelo, F ... 415-422-6496 ... 76 B
camperi@usfca.edu

CAMPFIELD, Ruth ... 817-598-6388 ... 508 C
rcampfield@wc.edu

CAMPION, James, R ... 518-828-4181 ... 330 E
campion@sunycgcc.edu

CAMPION, William, J ... 254-647-3234 ... 492 E
bcampion@rangercollege.edu

CAMPO, Carlos ... 757-352-4015 ... 523 B
ccampo@regent.edu

CAMPO, Carol ... 858-598-1200 ... 30 A
ccampo@aii.edu

CAMPO, Juan, E ... 805-893-3945 ... 74 F
jcampo@religion.ucsb.edu

CAMPO, Kathleen ... 516-299-2503 ... 338 F
kathy.campo@liu.edu

CAMPO, Regina, Z ... 717-337-6207 ... 429 H
rcampo@gettysburg.edu

CAMPOS, Becky ... 714-997-6943 ... 39 C
bcampos@chapman.edu

CAMPOS, Darcie, R ... 708-534-5000 ... 151 C
dcampos@govst.edu

CAMPOS, Jesus ... 956-872-8330 ... 494 D
jhcampos@southtexascollege.edu

CAMPOS, Joseph ... 980-598-1101 ... 365 G
joseph.campos@jwu.edu

CAMPOS, Luis ... 505-224-4565 ... 317 J
lcampos@cnm.edu

CAMPOS, Pete ... 505-454-2555 ... 318 E
pcampos@luna.edu

CAMPOS, Tom ... 210-486-0606 ... 479 F
tcampos1@alamo.edu

CAMPOY, Renee, W ... 270-809-3817 ... 204 F
renee.campoy@coe.murraystate.edu

CAMSTRA, Margaret ... 740-366-9233 ... 399 E
camstra.7@osu.edu

CAMSTRA, Margaret ... 740-366-9233 ... 386 G
mcamstra@cotc.edu

CAMUTI, Alice ... 931-372-3232 ... 474 B
acamuti@tntech.edu

CANACARIS, Diana ... 865-981-8198 ... 470 F
diana.canacaris@maryvillecollege.edu

CANADA, Allison, M ... 410-334-2918 ... 229 E
acanada@worwic.edu

CANADA, Britt ... 325-574-7671 ... 508 F
bcanada@wtc.edu

CANADA, Greg ... 415-565-4885 ... 73 G
canadag@uchastings.edu

CANADA, Mark ... 910-521-6431 ... 379 B
mark.canada@uncp.edu

CANADAY, Joseph ... 215-596-7524 ... 450 A
j.canaday@usciences.edu

CANADAY, Michael ... 386-312-4091 ... 116 D
mikecanaday@sjrstate.edu

CANADAY, William ... 937-708-5755 ... 405 G
wcanaday@wilberforce.edu

CANALES, Jason, G ... 413-662-5413 ... 238 F
jason.canales@mcla.edu

CANALES, Luis ... 270-809-4152 ... 204 F
lcanales@murraystate.edu

CANALES, Luzelma ... 956-872-6760 ... 494 D
luzelma@southtexascollege.edu

CANALS, Alex ... 718-933-6700 ... 341 G
acanals@monroecollege.edu

CANAS, Carlos ... 305-626-3698 ... 108 H
carlos.canas@fmuniv.edu

CANAS, Renee ... 702-579-3544 ... 302 C
rcanas@kaplan.edu

CANAVAN, Terry ... 631-499-7100 ... 338 D
tcanavan@libi.edu

CANCEL, Jimmy ... 787-250-1912 ... 563 E
jcancel@metro.inter.edu

CANCEL, Magda ... 787-620-2040 ... 560 B
mcancel@aupr.edu

CANCEL, Olga ... 787-754-8000 ... 566 C
ocancel@pupr.edu

CANCETTY, Alba ... 718-289-5889 ... 326 F
alba.cancetty@bcc.cuny.edu

CANCHOLA, Rebecca ... 915-779-8031 ... 483 F
rcanchola@computercareercenter.com

CANCILLA, Mike ... 256-549-8311 ... 3 J
mcancilla@gadsdenstate.edu

CANDEE, Kate ... 920-923-8727 ... 548 C
kcandee@marianuniversity.edu

CANDELARIA, J. Randel ... 336-734-7216 ... 370 C
rcandelaria@forsythtech.edu

CANDELARIO, Angela ... 787-743-7979 ... 565 F
ut_acandelar@suagm.edu

CANDELAS, Saul, C ... 915-831-2354 ... 486 E
scandel8@epcc.edu

CANDELERIA, James ... 602-274-4300 ... 13 A
jcandeleria@brymanschool.edu

CANDIA, Patricia ... 361-664-2981 ... 482 I
candia@coastalbend.edu

CANDIELLO, Mario ... 410-532-5389 ... 225 D
mcandiello@ndm.edu

CANDIOTTI, Alan ... 973-408-3362 ... 309 F
acandiot@drew.edu

CANDLER, Brandy ... 812-298-2286 ... 177 A
bcandler@ivytech.edu

CANDLER, George, B ... 212-327-7801 ... 347 H
candler@rockefeller.edu

CANDREVA, Anne, M ... 412-578-6043 ... 424 G
candrevaam@carlow.edu

CANEDAY, Lois ... 651-757-4031 ... 263 A
lcaneday@cva.edu

CANEDO, Agnes, F ... 509-963-3049 ... 531 G
canedoa@cwu.edu

CANEIRO-LIVINGSTON,
Graciela ... 563-588-6406 ... 183 B
graciela.caneiro-livingston@clarke.edu

CANEPA, Janet, A ... 203-254-4280 ... 92 B
jcanepa@fairfield.edu

CANEPA, Thomas ... 513-556-2495 ... 403 D
tom.canepa@uc.edu

CANEPI, Karen ... 702-968-2033 ... 303 D
kcanepi@roseman.edu

CANER, Emir ... 706-865-2134 ... 138 A
ecaner@truett.edu

CANFIELD, Anne ... 816-802-3426 ... 283 I
acanfield@kcai.edu

CANFIELD, Cheri ... 847-318-8550 ... 160 C
ccanfield@nc.edu

CANFIELD, Kathleen ... 847-925-6283 ... 151 E
kcanfiel@harpercollege.edu

CANFIELD, Merle ... 607-753-5565 ... 353 B
merle.canfield@cortland.edu

CANFIELD, Michael ... 703-284-1512 ... 521 A
michael.canfield@marymount.edu

CANFIELD, Ona ... 206-587-4349 ... 537 A
OCanfield@sccd.ctc.edu

CANGI, Ellen ... 813-253-7995 ... 110 I
ecangi@hccfl.edu

CANHAM, Raymond, P ... 972-238-6248 ... 485 C
canham@dcccd.edu

CANIA, Lisa, M ... 315-229-5585 ... 349 E
lcania@stlawu.edu

CANIA, Salvatore, J ... 315-268-7978 ... 329 C
scania@clarkson.edu

CANICK, Simon ... 651-290-6360 ... 273 B
simon.canick@wmitchell.edu

CANIDA, II, Robert, L ... 910-522-5790 ... 379 B
canida@uncp.edu

CANIGLIA, Alan ... 717-291-4168 ... 429 E
alan.caniglia@fandm.edu

CANIGLIA, Alan, S ... 717-291-3985 ... 429 E
alan.caniglia@fandm.edu

CANIZARES, Claude, R ... 617-253-3206 ... 242 A
crc@mit.edu

CANNADA, Robert, C ... 601-923-1600 ... 115 I
rcannada@rts.edu

CANNADA, JR., Robert, C 601-923-1600 ... 277 B
rcannada@rts.edu

CANNADA, JR., Robert, C 704-366-5066 ... 375 H
rcannada@rts.edu

CANNADA, JR., Robert, C 703-222-7871 ... 523 A

CANNADAY, Billy, K ... 434-982-5207 ... 525 B
bkc2p@Virginia.EDU

CANNADAY SAULNY,
Helen ... 202-994-6710 ... 97 F
saulnyh@gwu.edu

CANNADY, Sonya, Y ... 919-516-4482 ... 376 B
scannady@st-aug.edu

CANNADY-SMITH, Allison 253-879-3450 ... 538 E
acannadysmith@pugetsound.edu

CANNAN, Erin ... 845-758-7454 ... 323 F
cannan@bard.edu

CANNELL, Stephen ... 269-488-4241 ... 253 G
scannell@kvcc.edu

CANNEY, Catherine, E ... 978-665-3181 ... 238 C
ccanney@fitchburgstate.edu

CANNEY, Jane, W ... 651-962-6120 ... 272 E
jwcanney@stthomas.edu

CANNICI, James, P ... 972-883-2575 ... 505 D
cannici@utdallas.edu

CANNIFF, James, F ... 617-228-2435 ... 239 G
jfcanniff@bhcc.mass.edu

CANNING, Fran ... 603-228-1541 ... 306 G
fran.canning@law.unh.edu

CANNING, Ian ... 860-343-5710 ... 90 D
icanning@mxcc.commnet.edu

CANNING, John, B ... 401-232-6020 ... 453 A
jcanning@bryant.edu

CANNING, Marcia ... 415-476-5003 ... 74 E
mcanning@legal.ucsf.edu

CANNING, Mary ... 415-442-7885 ... 48 E
mcanning@ggu.edu

CANNING, Patricia ... 215-248-7144 ... 425 C
canningp@chc.edu

CANNION, Anthony, E ... 757-823-8053 ... 521 K
aecannion@nsu.edu

CANNIZZARO, Jennifer ... 802-258-3283 ... 514 C
jennifer.cannizzaro@worldlearning.org

CANNON, Blake ... 870-612-2057 ... 25 E
blake.cannon@uaccb.edu

CANNON, Brenda ... 931-393-1546 ... 475 C
bcannon@mscc.edu

CANNON, Bunnie ... 225-578-0302 ... 212 F
bcannon@lsu.edu

CARDWELL, Thomas 402-228-3468 300 C
tcardwel@southeast.edu
CAREAGA, Andrew, P 573-341-4183 292 A
acareaga@mst.edu
CAREAGA, Juana 305-809-3322 108 F
juana.careaga@fkcc.edu
CAREN, William, L 585-245-5619 353 C
caren@geneseo.edu
CARET, Robert, L 617-287-7050 237 B
rcaret@umassp.edu
CAREW, William 863-680-4305 109 D
wcarew@flsouthern.edu
CAREY, Amy, B 651-631-5220 270 E
abcarey@nwc.edu
CAREY, Chris 423-236-2828 473 A
carey@southern.edu
CAREY, Chris, J 858-499-0202 41 E
webmaster@coleman.edu
CAREY, Daniel, J 608-663-2262 547 C
dcarey@edgewood.edu
CAREY, Debra 718-270-4293 352 D
debra.carey@downstate.edu
CAREY, Debra 718-780-4997 338 E
dcarey@chpnet.org
CAREY, Ernie 801-863-8237 511 C
ecarey@uvu.edu
CAREY, Francis, J 716-839-8478 331 G
fcarey@daemen.edu
CAREY, Jay 503-838-8481 419 C
careywj@wou.edu
CAREY, Kate 614-823-3209 400 G
kcarey@otterbein.edu
CAREY, Kathy 828-327-7000 368 G
kcarey@cvcc.edu
CAREY, Kim 503-594-0760 415 A
kimc@clackamas.edu
CAREY, Linda 302-831-3676 96 F
llc@udel.edu
CAREY, Lisa 501-760-4129 22 F
lcarey@npcc.edu
CAREY, Marita 404-876-1227 126 D
marita.carey@bccr.edu
CAREY, Michael 718-862-8000 339 H
michael.carey@manhattan.edu
CAREY, Patricia, M 860-439-2508 91 E
pmcar@conncoll.edu
CAREY, Patti 305-809-3299 108 F
patti.carey@fkcc.edu
CAREY, Paula 508-854-4244 241 C
pcarey@qcc.mass.edu
CAREY, Peter, M 716-878-6332 353 A
careypm@buffalostate.edu
CAREY, Russell, C 401-863-9846 452 J
russell_carey@brown.edu
CAREY, Sandra 859-246-6203 201 D
sandra.carey@kctcs.edu
CAREY, Seamus 203-396-8020 93 G
careys@sacredheart.edu
CAREY, Susan 530-895-2378 31 E
careysu@butte.edu
CAREY, Thomas, P 207-786-6254 217 C
tcarey@bates.edu
CAREY, Timothy 973-655-5210 311 G
careyt@mail.montclair.edu
CAREY, Yvonne 434-961-5245 527 F
ycarey@pvcc.edu
CAREY-FLETCHER, Kathi 240-567-7674 224 E
kc.carey-fletcher@montgomerycollege.edu
CAREY-MCDONALD, Jan 435-586-7735 511 A
careymcdonald@suu.edu
CARFAGNA, Angelo 201-692-7025 310 B
angelo@fdu.edu
CARFAGNA, John 216-397-4321 392 M
jcarfagna@jcu.edu
CARGILE, Kenneth, R 731-989-6000 468 K
kcargile@fhu.edu
CARGILL, Jennifer, S 225-578-2217 212 F
cargill@lsu.edu
CARGILL, Jim, A 406-377-9408 294 C
jcargill@dawson.edu
CARIDEO, James, J 717-221-1300 430 E
jcaride@hacc.edu
CARIDI, James, A 614-251-4595 398 F
caridij@ohiodominican.edu
CARIGNAN, Steven 413-528-7207 231 A
scarignan@simons-rock.edu
CARILLI, Vincent 570-941-7680 450 B
carilliv2@scranton.edu
CARINO, Annie 718-260-3020 346 C
acarino@poly.edu
CARIO, William, R 262-243-5700 546 I
william.cario@cuw.edu
CARISSIMI, Kathleen 513-585-2064 387 C
CARISSIMI, Laura, K 440-365-5222 395 C
CARITHERS, Bart 605-626-3007 465 H
CARITO, Phyllis 518-828-4181 330 E
carito@sunycgcc.edu
CARKEEK, Susan 434-924-4475 525 B
sc9ym@virginia.edu
CARKUM, Duane 504-520-7490 217 A
dcarkum@xula.edu
CARL, Ashley 813-253-7158 110 I
acarl@hccfl.edu
CARL, Cathy 845-431-8635 332 E

CARL, Cherie 804-333-6716 527 G
ccarl@rappahannock.edu
CARL, Harold, F 903-233-4400 489 K
haroldcarl@letu.edu
CARL, Peggy 608-363-2296 546 B
carlp@beloit.edu
CARL, III, William, J 412-362-5610 444 G
wcarl@pts.edu
CARLANDER, Jay, R 410-677-3625 228 D
jrcarlander@salisbury.edu
CARLBERG, Laurie, J 440-365-5222 395 C
CARLBLOM, Shelia 765-677-2191 174 E
sheila.carlblom@indwes.edu
CARLEO, A. Susan 818-947-2321 55 E
carleoas@lavc.edu
CARLETON, Dia 570-662-4893 443 B
dcarleton@mansfield.edu
CARLETON, Mary Ruth 619-594-4562 36 E
maryruth.carleton@sdsu.edu
CARLETTA, Charles, F 518-276-6212 347 D
carlec@rpi.edu
CARLEY, Michael 559-791-2275 53 A
mcarley@portervillecollege.edu
CARLI, Gale 510-742-3102 59 I
gcarli@ohlone.edu
CARLILE, Galyn 541-880-2287 416 C
carlile@klamathcc.edu
CARLIN, Erin 717-620-0103 452 I
erin.carlin@yti.edu
CARLIN, Gale 215-248-7199 425 C
carling@chc.edu
CARLIN, Hiedi 417-625-9329 286 E
carlin-h@mssu.edu
CARLIN, Jane 253-879-3118 538 E
jcarlin@pugetsound.edu
CARLIN, John 540-365-4300 518 J
jcarlin@ferrum.edu
CARLIN, Melanie 217-357-9117 162 E
mcarlin@robertmorris.edu
CARLIN, Terrence, C 814-732-1752 442 D
carlin@edinboro.edu
CARLIN, Virginia 312-669-5161 150 E
vcarlin@ellis.edu
CARLINO, Michelle, A 610-799-1186 434 D
mcarlino@lccc.edu
CARLISLE, Brian, A 715-836-5626 550 H
carlisba@uwec.edu
CARLISLE, David, M 323-563-4987 39 D
davidcarlisle@cdrewu.edu
CARLISLE, Elizabeth 812-749-1241 178 D
lcarlisle@oak.edu
CARLISLE, Jerry, H 501-882-8835 20 D
jhcarlisle@asub.edu
CARLISLE, Margaret, K 785-539-3571 194 G
carlisle@mccks.edu
CARLISLE, Susan 502-213-5200 202 B
susan.carlisle@kctcs.edu
CARLISLE, Thomas, T 270-707-3889 202 A
taylor.carlisle@kctcs.edu
CARLO, Jennifer 412-578-6087 424 G
CARLO, Luis 646-378-6171 344 G
luis.carlo@nyack.edu
CARLOCK, Myra 731-352-4000 467 C
carlockm@bethelu.edu
CARLOCK, Robert 618-437-5321 162 B
carlock@rlc.edu
CARLON, Peter, D 817-272-2261 505 A
carlon@uta.edu
CARLSEN, Guy, F 718-489-5468 348 E
gcarlsen@stfranciscollege.edu
CARLSON, Annie 828-669-8012 367 C
CARLSON, C. Robert 630-682-6002 153 B
carlson@iit.edu
CARLSON, Cathy 507-222-4080 262 B
ccarlson@carleton.edu
CARLSON, Charles 914-637-2757 336 E
ccarlson@iona.edu
CARLSON, Chris 951-222-8000 63 I
chris.carlson@rcc.edu
CARLSON, Clint 256-782-5820 4 L
ccarlson@jsu.edu
CARLSON, Curtis, K 308-865-8529 300 G
carlsonck@unk.edu
CARLSON, Cynthia, B 847-735-5036 155 F
ccarlson@lakeforest.edu
CARLSON, David, H 618-453-2522 164 I
dcarlson@lib.siu.edu
CARLSON, David, S 979-862-3389 496 G
dscarlson@tamhsc.edu
CARLSON, Dawn 813-880-8045 111 B
dcarlson@online.academy.edu
CARLSON, Deborah 402-354-7023 299 E
deb.carlson@methodistcollege.edu
CARLSON, Denise, M 402-354-7256 299 E
denise.carlson@methodistcollege.edu
CARLSON, Dennis 509-527-2635 538 H
dennis.carlson@wallawalla.edu
CARLSON, Douglas 618-437-5321 162 B
carlson@rlc.edu
CARLSON, Douglas 415-476-4527 74 E
doug.carlson@ucsf.edu
CARLSON, Douglas, W 712-707-7055 188 B
carlson@nwciowa.edu

CARLSON, Gerald 317-940-6375 170 C
gcarlson@butler.edu
CARLSON, Gerald, P 337-482-6678 216 D
gcarlson@louisiana.edu
CARLSON, Herbert, F 724-738-2545 443 E
herbert.carlson@sru.edu
CARLSON, Jean 914-831-0416 330 D
jcarlson@cw.edu
CARLSON, Jeffrey 708-524-6814 150 A
jcarlson@dom.edu
CARLSON, Jim 406-586-3585 294 I
jim.carlson@montanabiblecollege.edu
CARLSON, Jon, C 216-707-8076 398 E
jcarlson@ocpm.edu
CARLSON, Karen, A 218-299-3734 263 B
carlsonk@cord.edu
CARLSON, Kathleen 773-298-3305 163 G
carlson@sxu.edu
CARLSON, Kerri 612-659-6204 267 E
kerri.carlson@minneapolis.edu
CARLSON, Kurt 919-497-3325 366 E
kcarlson@louisburg.edu
CARLSON, Libby, L 662-846-4268 274 B
lcarlson@deltastate.edu
CARLSON, Lisa, M 414-410-4230 546 D
lmcarlson@stritch.edu
CARLSON, Malinda, L 217-245-3011 152 C
mcarlson@ic.edu
CARLSON, Nancy 303-914-6389 87 C
nancy.carlson@rrcc.edu
CARLSON, Paul 815-802-8652 154 J
pcarlson@kcc.edu
CARLSON, Paul 323-953-4000 54 H
carlsopr@lacitycollege.edu
CARLSON, Paula, J 507-786-3632 271 H
carlsonp@stolaf.edu
CARLSON, Rich 402-486-2508 300 D
ricarlso@ucollege.edu
CARLSON, Rosa, F 559-791-2316 53 A
rcarlson@portervillecollege.edu
CARLSON, Rose 505-287-6622 319 H
rcarlson@nmsu.edu
CARLSON, Stanley, E 563-884-5684 188 C
stan.carlson@palmer.edu
CARLSON, Steven, T 574-372-5100 171 E
carlsost@grace.edu
CARLSON, Terry 641-683-5243 185 D
tcarlson@indianhills.edu
CARLSON, Tracey 423-614-6000 470 A
tcarlson@leeuniversity.edu
CARLSON HURST,
Marjorie, F 330-471-8244 395 E
mcarlson@malone.edu
CARLSTROM, Lester, H 773-244-5597 159 G
lcarlstrom@northpark.edu
CARLTON, Dennis 409-740-4417 497 D
carltond@tamug.tamu.edu
CARLTON, LeAnn, K 816-654-7213 283 J
lcarlton@kcumb.edu
CARLTON, William "Bee" 912-279-5892 127 B
wcarlton@ccga.edu
CARLUCCI, Carl 832-842-5550 503 B
ccarlucci@uh.edu
CARLUCCI, Carl, P 832-842-5550 503 A
ccarlucci@uh.edu
CARLUCCIO, Lance 617-928-4502 243 A
lcarluccio@mountida.edu
CARMACK, Connie, K 540-375-2230 523 D
carmack@roanoke.edu
CARMACK, Lance 937-255-6565 556 H
CARMAN, Kevin, R 225-578-4201 212 F
zocarm@lsu.edu
CARMEL, Julie 508-929-8754 239 D
jcarmel@worcester.edu
CARMEN, Beth Anne 614-236-6211 386 C
bcarmen@capital.edu
CARMEN, Kim 318-675-5000 213 B
kcarme@lsuhsc.edu
CARMER, Gregory, W 978-867-4012 235 E
greg.carmer@gordon.edu
CARMICAL, Beth 910-272-3343 373 A
bcarmical@robeson.edu
CARMICHAEL, Ann, C 803-584-3446 462 E
anncar@mailbox.sc.edu
CARMICHAEL, Beverly 920-465-2074 551 A
carmichb@uwgb.edu
CARMICHAEL, Brenda 620-343-4600 192 E
bcarmichael@fhtc.edu
CARMICHAEL, Georgia 713-718-5466 487 G
georgia.carmichael@hccs.edu
CARMICHAEL, John 360-867-6100 533 I
carmichj@evergreen.edu
CARMICHAEL, Paul 860-343-5787 90 D
pcarmichael@mxcc.commnet.edu
CARMICHAEL, Peggy 304-214-8901 543 A
pcarmichael@wvncc.edu
CARMICHAEL, Stacy 228-896-2503 275 G
stacy.carmichael@mgccc.edu
CARMICHAEL, William 202-408-2400 99 D
CARMINE, Kevin 718-319-7965 327 D
kcarmine@hostos.cuny.edu
CARMODY, Margaret 877-246-9388 149 L
mcarmody@devry.edu

CARMODY, Patricia 507-537-6206 269 G
Patricia.Carmody@smsu.edu
CARMODY, Richard 805-922-6966 26 K
rcarmody@hancockcollege.edu
CARMONA, Gloria 760-355-6244 50 K
gloria.carmona@imperial.edu
CARNAGHI, Jan 317-955-6154 177 G
jcarnaghi@marian.edu
CARNAGHI, Jill, E 314-935-5022 292 J
jill.carnaghi@wustl.edu
CARNAGHI, John, R 850-644-4444 119 C
jcarnaghi@admin.fsu.edu
CARNAGHI, Laura 859-282-9999 203 G
lcarnaghi@lincolntech.com
CARNAHAN, Allison, G 260-422-5561 172 L
gcarnahan@indianatech.edu
CARNAHAN, D. Francette 254-867-3984 499 I
francette.carnahan@systems.tstc.edu
CARNAHAN, Scott 503-883-2229 416 G
scarnah@linfield.edu
CARNAROLI, Craig 215-898-6693 448 I
carnarol@pobox.upenn.edu
CARNDUFF, Dagmar, L 414-847-3211 548 G
dagmarcarnduff@miad.edu
CARNE, Kim 906-786-5802 249 D
carnek@baycollege.edu
CARNEGIE, Kay 503-399-5058 414 J
kay.carnegie@chemeketa.edu
CARNES, John 210-486-4015 479 C
jcarnes@alamo.edu
CARNES, Kathy, M 252-493-7220 372 E
kcarnes@email.pittcc.edu
CARNES, Peter 508-565-1206 245 D
pcarnes@stonehill.edu
CARNEVALE, David 562-907-4284 79 B
dcarneva@whittier.edu
CARNEY, Angela, P 727-736-5082 117 F
angela_carney@schiller.edu
CARNEY, Bruce 919-962-2198 378 D
bruce_carney@unc.edu
CARNEY, Conferlete 727-712-5742 116 F
carney.conferlete@spcollege.edu
CARNEY, Diane, E 412-291-6250 422 D
dcarney@aii.edu
CARNEY, Edward 856-227-7200 308 E
ecarney@camdencc.edu
CARNEY, Gary 610-861-1300 436 I
CARNEY, Ginny 218-335-4200 264 I
ginny.carney@lltc.edu
CARNEY, III, John, F 573-341-4116 292 A
jfc3@mst.edu
CARNEY, Karen 508-793-3371 233 D
kcarney@holycross.edu
CARNEY, Leslie 407-646-1528 116 B
lcarney@rollins.edu
CARNEY, OSF, Margaret 716-375-2222 348 C
mcarney@sbu.edu
CARNEY, Martin 216-421-7424 387 H
mcarney@cia.edu
CARNEY, Paul 314-968-6974 293 A
paulcarney89@webster.edu
CARNEY, Sheila, A 412-578-6424 424 G
carneysa@carlow.edu
CARNEY, Tim 513-244-4426 388 D
tim_carney@mail.msj.edu
CARNEY, Timothy 202-319-5619 97 C
carneyt@cua.edu
CARNEY-DEBORD, Nan 740-587-6428 389 H
carneydebord@denison.edu
CARNEY-HALL, Karla 501-450-1222 22 A
carney-hall@hendrix.edu
CARNLEY, Raymond 864-833-8006 460 E
rcarnley@presby.edu
CARNWATH, Thomas 215-717-6640 448 H
tcarnwath@uarts.edu
CARNZ, Scott 206-239-2320 530 H
scarnz@aii.edu
CARO, Jessica 787-832-6000 562 E
jcaro@icprjc.edu
CARO, Mary Ellen 609-984-1130 316 A
mcaro@tesc.edu
CAROL, Claudia, C 512-448-8538 493 B
claudiac@stedwards.edu
CAROL, Steven 484-365-8064 434 H
scarol@lincoln.edu
CAROLAN, Tammy 563-425-5337 189 C
carolant@uiu.edu
CAROLLA, Jeff 908-835-2320 317 C
jcarollo@warren.edu
CARONA, Charles 214-333-5200 484 C
charlesc@dbu.edu
CARONE, Joseph 567-661-7190 400 H
joseph_carone@owens.edu
CAROTHERS, Amy 775-784-6620 303 A
acarothers@unr.edu
CAROTHERS, Harry, G 303-963-3228 81 K
hcarothers@ccu.edu
CAROTHERS, John 775-784-1394 303 A
jcarothers@adv.unr.edu
CAROTHERS, Margaret 909-621-8208 62 H
margaret_carothers@pitzer.edu
CAROTHERS, Michael 703-257-5515 516 F
CARP, Richard, M 925-631-4443 64 F
rmcarp@gmail.com

CARRUTH, Ron 678-891-2515 130 G
Ron.Carruth@gpc.edu
CARRUTHERS, Anthony 508-856-6074 238 A
anthony.carruthers@umassmed.edu
CARRUTHERS, Becky 575-769-4913 317 K
becky.carruthers@clovis.edu
CARRUTHERS, Brian, A 864-242-5100 455 E
CARRUTHERS, Dale 608-262-8256 550 G
dcarruthers@recsports.wisc.edu
CARRUTHERS, Deborah 713-221-8220 503 D
carruthersd@uhd.edu
CARRUTHERS, Garrey, E 575-646-4083 319 D
garreyc@nmsu.edu
CARRUTHERS, Judith 802-468-1339 515 C
judith.carruthers@castleton.edu
CARRY, Ainsley 334-844-8880 1 G
azc0018@auburn.edu
CARSCALLEN, Carey 269-471-6003 247 H
ccarey@andrews.edu
CARSON, Barrett, H 404-894-1868 130 D
barrett.carson@dev.gatech.edu
CARSON, Beth 516-299-2589 339 A
beth.carson@liu.edu
CARSON, Brenda, B 601-635-2111 274 C
bcarson@eccc.edu
CARSON, Carolyn, N 865-694-6554 475 F
ccarson@pstcc.edu
CARSON, Connie, L 864-294-2202 458 D
connie.carson@furman.edu
CARSON, Cristi 207-780-4104 220 G
ccarson@usm.maine.edu
CARSON, Daniel 713-348-3350 492 J
dcarson@rice.edu
CARSON, David 912-344-2506 124 E
david.carson@armstrong.edu
CARSON, Denise, K 785-227-3380 190 G
carsond@bethanylb.edu
CARSON, Dwayne 434-592-4138 520 F
decarson@liberty.edu
CARSON, Elizabeth, M 815-395-5102 163 C
bethcarson@sacn.edu
CARSON, Jay, T 412-397-5870 445 G
carsonj@rmu.edu
CARSON, Kenneth, P 724-847-6605 429 G
kpcarson@geneva.edu
CARSON, Lesley 517-265-5161 247 D
lcarson@adrian.edu
CARSON, Pat 740-351-3460 401 I
pcarson@shawnee.edu
CARSON, Paula, P 337-482-5754 216 D
plp6475@louisiana.edu
CARSON, Randal 303-923-4120 81 A
rcarson@argosy.edu
CARSON, Rebecca 310-506-4558 61 G
rebecca.carson@pepperdine.edu
CARSON, Rick 602-433-1333 13 E
rcarson@cc.edu
CARSON, Sylvia 678-915-7222 137 C
sylvia@spsu.edu
CARSON, Tom 601-635-2111 274 C
tcarson@eccc.edu
CARSON, Virginia, M 912-260-4394 136 F
virginia.carson@sgc.edu
CARSON, William 443-885-3110 224 F
william.carson@morgan.edu
CARSTARPHEN, Minnie 334-876-9345 4 B
mcarstarphen@wccs.edu
CARSTENS, Janese 406-247-5786 295 F
janese.carstens@msubillings.edu
CARSTENS, Jeffrey 402-375-7213 299 I
jecarst1@wsc.edu
CARSTENS, Lisa, P 757-455-3268 529 F
lcarstens@vwc.edu
CARSTENSEN, Lundie 619-201-8705 65 D
Lundie.Carstensen@sdcc.edu
CARSWELL, Linda 828-438-6000 374 G
lcarswell@wpcc.edu
CARSWELL, Pamela 386-752-1822 108 C
pamela.carswell@fgc.edu
CART, Robert 973-655-7212 311 G
cartr@mail.montclair.edu
CARTABUKE, Jacqueline 516-877-6004 322 A
jcartabuke@adelphi.edu
CARTAGENA, Aramilda 787-857-3600 563 A
acartagena@br.inter.edu
CARTAGENA, Carlos 520-417-4119 13 G
cartagec@cochise.edu
CARTAGENA, Enid 787-765-3560 561 J
ecartagena@edpcollege.edu
CARTAGENA, Jose, A 787-744-8519 561 I
jcartagena@ediccollege.com
CARTAGENA, Milagros 787-744-8519 561 I
mcartagena@ediccollege.com
CARTEE, Dawn, H 912-871-1638 134 H
dcartee@ogeecheetech.edu
CARTEE, Len 816-501-3629 279 C
len.cartee@avila.edu
CARTENSEN, Nicole 305-581-1233 45 I
CARTER, Alfred 601-979-1325 275 A
alfred.j.carter@jsums.edu
CARTER, Allison, A 906-487-2335 255 E
allison@mtu.edu
CARTER, Andrew, V 580-327-8632 409 C
avcarter@nwosu.edu
CARTER, Angela, M 336-334-4822 370 E
amcarter@gtcc.edu
CARTER, Anthony, D 704-687-2461 378 E
acarte1@uncc.edu
CARTER, Bernadette 610-399-2302 441 H
bcarter@cheyney.edu
CARTER, Bessie 405-945-3211 410 F
CARTER, Beth 352-588-8480 116 E
beth.carter@saintleo.edu
CARTER, Betsy, L 517-321-0242 252 B
betsycarter@glcc.edu
CARTER, Brenda, C 214-491-6271 483 D
bcarter@collin.edu
CARTER, Brian 202-686-0876 99 A
brian.carter@potomac.edu
CARTER, Cathy 773-697-2215 149 C
ccarter@devry.edu
CARTER, Charles, K 252-335-0821 369 D
ckcarter@albemarle.edu
CARTER, Chris 925-631-4200 64 F
ccarter@stmarys-ca.edu
CARTER, Cindy 641-585-8130 189 E
carterc@waldorf.edu
CARTER, Clark 843-863-8008 456 B
ccarter@csuniv.edu
CARTER, Clay 252-940-6357 367 I
clayc@beaufortccc.edu
CARTER, Cynthia 229-931-2057 136 G
ccarter@southgatech.edu
CARTER, Cynthia 254-968-9877 496 F
carter@tarleton.edu
CARTER, Cynthia, A 906-786-5802 249 D
carterc@baycollege.edu
CARTER, D. Michael 435-586-7738 511 A
carter_m@suu.edu
CARTER, Dan 406-657-2266 295 F
dcarter@msubillings.edu
CARTER, Danielle, J 216-397-4185 392 M
dcarter@jcu.edu
CARTER, David 806-743-2300 501 E
david.carter@ttuhsc.edu
CARTER, Deb 717-391-1349 447 H
dcarter@stevenscollege.edu
CARTER, Deborah 517-264-7100 258 D
dcarter2@sienaheights.edu
CARTER, Derek 302-857-6030 95 F
dcarter@desu.edu
CARTER, Donald, D 979-845-1145 497 C
d-carter@tamu.edu
CARTER, Donald, M 315-859-4582 335 A
CARTER, Drake 701-224-5545 382 B
fred.carter@bismarckstate.edu
CARTER, Elaine 610-399-0991 441 H
ecarter@cheyney.edu
CARTER, Eloise 334-727-8953 8 C
ecarter@tuskegee.edu
CARTER, Evonne 414-297-7990 554 D
cartere@matc.edu
CARTER, Gary, L 731-661-5204 476 G
gcarter@uu.edu
CARTER, Glenda, F 903-927-3336 509 A
gcarter@wileyc.edu
CARTER, Glenn 509-527-2202 538 H
glenn.carter@wallawalla.edu
CARTER, H. Steven 252-638-7400 369 E
carters@cravencc.edu
CARTER, Hasani 973-275-2385 315 B
hasani.carter@shu.edu
CARTER, JR., Hazo, W 304-766-3111 544 D
carterhw@wvstateu.edu
CARTER, Herbert 910-892-3178 364 F
hcarter@heritagebiblecollege.edu
CARTER, Holly 706-729-2306 125 C
hcarter1@aug.edu
CARTER, Isaac 305-628-6740 116 G
icarter@stu.edu
CARTER, Jacque 402-826-8253 298 A
jacque.carter@doane.edu
CARTER, James, F 270-809-4894 204 F
jim.carter@murraystate.edu
CARTER, Jane 828-669-8012 367 C
jcarter@montreat.edu
CARTER, Janet 912-427-5876 124 A
jcarter@altamahatech.edu
CARTER, Janice 415-442-7248 48 E
jcarter@ggu.edu
CARTER, JaPrince, L 804-342-3895 529 D
jlcarter@vuu.edu
CARTER, Jessica 276-656-0312 527 D
CARTER, John 847-866-3995 151 B
john.carter@garrett.edu
CARTER, John, B 413-542-2771 230 A
jbcarter@amherst.edu
CARTER, John, M 601-477-4161 275 B
john.carter@jcjc.edu
CARTER, John, P 212-854-1458 330 F
jpc11@columbia.edu
CARTER, Joyce, M 937-229-2554 404 A
joyce.carter@udayton.edu
CARTER, Judy 478-825-6250 129 C
carterj02@fvsu.edu
CARTER, Julien, C 512-232-9161 505 B
julien.carter@austin.utexas.edu
CARTER, Junko 401-454-6558 454 B
jcarter@risd.edu
CARTER, Karen 541-506-6010 415 C
kcarter@cgcc.cc.or.us
CARTER, Kathryn 978-934-2741 237 F
kathryn_carter@uml.edu
CARTER, Kathy 217-875-7200 162 D
kcarter@richland.edu
CARTER, Kermit 256-306-2613 2 E
klc@calhoun.edu
CARTER, Kyle, R 910-521-6201 379 B
chancellor@uncp.edu
CARTER, Lana 719-549-3253 87 B
lana.carter@pueblocc.edu
CARTER, Laurie, A 212-799-5000 337 H
CARTER, Lawrence, E 404-215-2608 134 A
lcarter@morehouse.edu
CARTER, Lawrence, L 517-321-0242 252 B
lcarter@glcc.edu
CARTER, Leon 810-766-2190 248 H
leon.carter@baker.edu
CARTER, Linda 816-604-3081 285 H
linda.carter@mcckc.edu
CARTER, Linda 606-539-4230 206 G
linda.carter@ucumberlands.edu
CARTER, Linda 336-334-5696 379 A
linda_carter@uncg.edu
CARTER, Linnie 252-536-7239 370 F
carterl@halifaxcc.edu
CARTER, Lisa 617-427-0060 241 D
ljenkins@rcc.mass.edu
CARTER, Luther, F 843-661-1210 458 C
lcarter@fmarion.edu
CARTER, Mark 660-596-7221 290 F
mcarter@sfccmo.edu
CARTER, Mark 619-849-2961 62 L
markcarter@pointloma.edu
CARTER, Max, L 336-316-2445 364 E
mcarter@guilford.edu
CARTER, Melody 478-825-6397 129 C
carterm0@fvsu.edu
CARTER, Melody 478-825-6959 129 C
carterm0@fvsu.edu
CARTER, Michael 270-789-5001 199 C
mvcarter@campbellsville.edu
CARTER, Michael 661-255-1050 32 C
mcarter@calarts.edu
CARTER, Michael 937-512-2975 401 J
michael.carter@sinclair.edu
CARTER, Michele 254-526-1668 482 F
michele.carter@ctcd.edu
CARTER, Michele, G 317-278-2665 174 B
CARTER, Mike 918-495-7150 411 C
mcarter@oru.edu
CARTER, Natasha 706-396-7591 135 C
ncarter@paine.edu
CARTER, Niaomi 703-878-2800 99 D
CARTER, Nichole 978-632-6600 240 G
n_carter@mwcc.mass.edu
CARTER, Nick 617-964-1100 230 B
ncarter@ants.edu
CARTER, Parris 937-708-5611 405 G
pcarter@wilberforce.edu
CARTER, Patricia 305-626-3190 108 H
pcarter@fmuniv.edu
CARTER, Perna 803-780-1269 463 B
pcarter@voorhees.edu
CARTER, Petrina 434-791-5629 516 D
pcarter@averett.edu
CARTER, Phil 770-830-2180 139 B
phil.carter@westgatech.edu
CARTER, Phillip 615-547-1307 467 I
pcarter@cumberland.edu
CARTER, R. Daphne 843-661-1188 458 C
rcarter@fmarion.edu
CARTER, R. Lee 919-508-2049 375 D
rlcarter@peace.edu
CARTER, Richard 309-298-1929 168 A
r-carter@wiu.edu
CARTER, Richard 309-298-2501 168 A
r-carter@wiu.edu
CARTER, Richard, E 858-642-8110 58 I
rcarter@nu.edu
CARTER, Ronald, L 909-558-4542 54 D
rcarter@llu.edu
CARTER, Ronald, L 704-378-1006 365 H
rcarter@jcsu.edu
CARTER, Rosalyn, Y 954-762-5640 118 H
rcarter@fau.edu
CARTER, Sandra 864-225-7653 458 B
sandracarter@forrestcollege.edu
CARTER, Saundra, M 202-274-5531 99 F
scarter@udc.edu
CARTER, Shelia 312-369-7994 148 B
scarter@colum.edu
CARTER, Shirley 336-887-3000 365 J
scarter@laureluniversity.edu
CARTER, Shirley, P 336-889-2262 363 A
scarter@ceds.edu
CARTER, Shree 714-556-3610 76 E
scarter@vanguard.edu
CARTER, Spencer, D 269-471-3395 247 H
scarter@andrews.edu
CARTER, Steven 310-577-3000 79 K
scarter@yosan.edu
CARTER, Tamara 573-592-4358 293 E
tamara.carter@williamwoods.edu
CARTER, Tammy 478-757-3408 126 G
tcarter@centralgatech.edu
CARTER, Tara 815-825-2086 155 C
tara.carter@kishwaukeecollege.edu
CARTER, Taysha 479-619-4396 22 H
tcarter@nwacc.edu
CARTER, Thacher 541-962-3524 418 C
tcarter@eou.edu
CARTER, Tiffany 773-291-6317 147 D
tcarter63@ccc.edu
CARTER, Tom 256-331-5263 6 B
tom.carter@nwscc.edu
CARTER, Virginia, M 610-359-5394 426 G
gcarter@dccc.edu
CARTER, Warrick, L 312-369-7200 148 B
wcarter@colum.edu
CARTER, William, E 713-718-8708 487 G
william.carter@hccs.edu
CARTER, William, H 361-593-2830 498 A
william.carter@tamuk.edu
CARTER, Yolanda 502-863-7967 200 G
yolanda_carter@georgetowncollege.edu
CARTER, Zina 979-532-6417 508 J
zinac@wcjc.edu
CARTER-CHAPMAN, Renee, M 907-786-6486 10 I
anrmc@uaa.alaska.edu
CARTER-COLEY, Stacey 919-718-7213 368 H
scarter@cccc.edu
CARTER-DUBOIS, Marie, H 530-752-2063 73 F
mhcarter@ucdavis.edu
CARTER-STEVENS, Marilyn 718-862-7958 339 H
marilyn.carter@manhattan.edu
CARTER-TELLISON, Katrina 561-237-7210 113 D
kcarter-tellison@lynn.edu
CARTER-WAREN, Mary 305-628-6653 116 G
mwaren@stu.edu
CARTHELL, Sidney, G 270-809-6836 204 F
sg.carthell@murraystate.edu
CARTIER, Jolie, L 619-239-0391 37 D
jcartier@cwsl.edu
CARTIER, Missy, M 559-323-2100 66 C
mcartier@sjcl.edu
CARTIER, Mose 410-951-3636 228 B
mcartier@coppin.edu
CARTLEDGE, Maureen 210-486-7173 479 E
mcartledge@alamo.edu
CARTLEDGE, Vince, E 740-284-5191 390 M
vcartledge@franciscan.edu
CARTMELL, Brandy, D 731-881-7050 477 E
bcartmel@utm.edu
CARTMILL, Larry 816-942-5474 84 I
larryc@heritage-education.com
CARTMILL, Larry 816-942-5474 283 A
larryc@heritage-education.com
CARTMILL, Mark 859-985-3922 198 F
cartmillm@berea.edu
CARTNAL, Ryan 805-546-3946 43 F
rcartnal@cuesta.edu
CARTNEY, Michael 605-882-5284 464 D
cartneym@lakeareatech.edu
CARTOLANO, Joseph 718-631-6231 329 A
jcartolano@qcc.cuny.edu
CARTON, Shirley 702-651-7341 302 G
shirley.carton@csn.edu
CARTSONIS, George, A 248-341-2122 257 B
gacartso@oaklandcc.edu
CARTWRIGHT, Alexander 716-645-3321 351 G
vpr@buffalo.edu
CARTWRIGHT, Cindy 716-664-5100 337 D
cindycartwright@jamestownbusinesscollege.edu
CARTWRIGHT, Peggy 909-652-6115 39 B
peggy.cartwright@chaffey.edu
CARTWRIGHT, Rhonda, D 512-448-8403 493 B
rhondac@stedwards.edu
CARTWRIGHT, Rick, E 260-399-7700 180 E
rcartwright@sf.edu
CARTY, Karenann 718-933-6700 341 G
kcarty@monroecollege.edu
CARTY, Melva 202-686-0876 99 A
melva.carty@potomac.edu
CARTY, Raymond, W 573-629-3265 282 H
rcarty@hlg.edu
CARULLO, Susan, H 843-792-2071 459 C
carullos@musc.edu
CARUOLO, Wayne 303-914-6577 87 C
wayne.caruolo@rrcc.edu
CARUSO, Anne-Marie 617-989-4174 246 C
carusoa@wit.edu
CARUSO, David, A 603-283-2436 303 F
dcaruso@antiochne.edu
CARUSO, Elizabeth, S 585-395-2414 352 F
lcaruso@brockport.edu
CARUSO, Janet 516-572-7599 342 C
janet.caruso@ncc.edu
CARUSO, Kelly 337-948-0239 209 D
kcaruso@acadiana.edu

CASTILLO, Victor 312-850-7427 147 C vcastillo4@ccc.edu
CASTILLO-FRICK, Iliana 305-237-0294 113 H ifrick@mdc.edu
CASTILOW, Nancy 402-554-3509 301 B ncastilow@unomaha.edu
CASTLE, Blanche 978-368-2269 230 F blanche.castle@auc.edu
CASTLE, Carolyn 859-985-3050 198 F carolyn_castle@berea.edu
CASTLE, Clinton 218-683-8600 268 E clinton.castle@northlandcollege.edu
CASTLE, David 740-699-2333 400 A castle@ohio.edu
CASTLE, Don 606-487-3354 201 H don.castle@kctcs.edu
CASTLE, Josh 802-322-1672 513 C josh.castle@goddard.edu
CASTLE, Lyle, W 208-282-7852 143 D castlyle@isu.edu
CASTLE, Ruthie 662-562-3213 276 E rcastle@northwestms.edu
CASTLEBERRY, Gina 931-553-0071 471 G gina.castleberry@miller-motte.com
CASTLEBERRY, Jeff 405-208-5000 410 A jcastleberry@okcu.edu
CASTLEBERRY, Joseph 425-889-4202 535 I joseph.castleberry@northwestu.edu
CASTLEBERRY, Rita, J 580-327-8601 409 C rjcastleberry@nwosu.edu
CASTLEBERRY, Robert 580-559-5377 407 J rcastleberry@ecok.edu
CASTLEBURY, Lisa 541-684-7219 417 F lcastlebury@northwestchristian.edu
CASTLEGRANT, Dave 734-878-1765 249 H dcastlegrant@cleary.edu
CASTLEMAN, Janet, L 401-865-2816 453 F jcastlem@providence.edu
CASTNER, Clarey 402-458-1100 300 H ccastner@nufoundation.org
CASTNER, David, H 906-635-2452 254 C dcastner@lssu.edu
CASTO, Bryce, S 304-766-3140 544 D castosb@wvstateu.edu
CASTON, Everett 662-329-7142 276 B ecaston@edhs.muw.edu
CASTONGUAY, Suzette 937-769-1375 383 K scastonguay@antioch.edu
CASTONGUAY, Suzette 937-769-1375 383 J scastonguay@antioch.edu
CASTOR, Peter 717-560-8219 433 D
CASTOR, Tammy 661-362-3516 41 G tammy.castor@canyons.edu
CASTORA, Susan, L 757-446-5812 518 F castorsl@evms.edu
CASTORENA, Christina 425-388-9282 533 H ccastore@everettcc.edu
CASTRO, Adam 973-748-9000 308 A adam_castro@bloomfield.edu
CASTRO, Andrea 530-938-5209 42 C castro@siskiyous.edu
CASTRO, Daisy 787-753-6335 562 E dcastro@icprjc.edu
CASTRO, David, J 303-797-5704 80 J david.castro@arapahoe.edu
CASTRO, Donna 505-426-2240 318 I dcastro@nmhu.edu
CASTRO, Ernesto 305-418-4220 115 B ecastro@pupr.edu
CASTRO, Francia, L 212-694-1000 324 C fcastro@boricuacollege.edu
CASTRO, Griselda 530-752-8787 73 F gcastro@ucdavis.edu
CASTRO, Ida, L 570-504-9647 425 F
CASTRO, Joseph, I 415-502-7786 74 E joseph.castro@ucsf.edu
CASTRO, Kaye, A 239-687-5336 101 B kcastro@avemarialaw.edu
CASTRO, Maria 787-758-2525 567 D maria.castro14@upr.edu
CASTRO, Michelle, A 412-396-4266 428 C castrom@duq.edu
CASTRO, Octavio 414-288-5629 548 D octavio.castro@marquette.edu
CASTRO, Patricia 702-651-5684 302 G patricia.castro@csn.edu
CASTRO, Toni 206-878-3710 534 E tcastro@highline.edu
CASTRO-MELENDEZ, Consuelo 787-620-2040 560 B castromelendez@aupr.edu
CASTRONOVO, Neil, R 508-767-7274 230 E ncastron@assumption.edu
CASTRUITA, Javier 408-741-2042 77 K javier_castruita@wvm.edu
CASWELL, Robert, S 207-780-4200 220 G caswell@usm.maine.edu
CATALANA, Paul, V 864-294-2180 458 D paul.catalana@furman.edu
CATALANO, George 607-777-3583 351 F catalano@binghamton.edu
CATALANO, James, M 201-216-9901 309 G
CATALANO, John 803-313-7001 462 D jcatalano@gwm.sc.edu
CATALANO, Rita 724-805-2274 446 E rita.catalano@email.stvincent.edu
CATALANO, Steven 718-489-5309 348 E scatalano@stfranciscollege.edu
CATALLOZZI, Lori, A 617-228-2048 239 G lacatallozzi@bhcc.mass.edu
CATALON, Linda, H 225-771-2520 214 G linda_catalon@sus.edu
CATANESE, Anthony, J 321-674-7232 108 E catanese@fit.edu
CATANESE, Robert 914-831-0316 330 D ccatanese@cw.edu
CATANIA, Guy 412-392-3952 444 H gcatania@pointpark.edu
CATANIA, Raymond, P 773-298-3031 163 G catania@sxu.edu
CATANZARO, James, L 423-697-4455 474 D
CATAU, John, C 417-836-5022 286 F johncatau@missouristate.edu
CATE, Richard, H 802-656-0219 514 F richard.cate@uvm.edu
CATE, Rodney 940-397-4198 491 A rodney.cate@mwsu.edu
CATELL, Mike 540-423-9074 526 E mcatell@germanna.edu
CATELLA, Rosanne 440-934-3101 398 B rcatella@ohiobusinesscollege.edu
CATER, Gloria, H 617-541-5144 241 D gcater@rcc.mass.edu
CATER, Judy 760-744-1150 61 C jcater@palomar.edu
CATES, Carolyn 901-320-9743 478 B cates@victory.edu
CATES, Chris 865-471-3245 467 E ccates@cn.edu
CATES, Janet 615-966-1788 470 D janet.cates@lipscomb.edu
CATES, Jo 312-369-7125 148 B jcates@colum.edu
CATES, Paul 615-966-1781 470 D paul.cates@lipscomb.edu
CATES, Truett 903-813-2309 481 A tcates@austincollege.edu
CATH, Tom 219-464-5005 181 A tom.cath@valpo.edu
CATHCART, Chris 404-237-7573 125 F ccathcart@bauder.edu
CATHCART, Scott 760-744-1150 61 C scathcart@palomar.edu
CATHCART, Susan, D 248-276-8230 248 E susan.cathcart@baker.edu
CATHELINE, Jim 724-964-8811 437 D jcatheline@ncstrades.com
CATHERMAN, David 504-394-7744 214 A dcatherman@olhcc.edu
CATHERMAN, Laura 661-654-2497 33 H lcatherman@csub.edu
CATHEY, Ron 318-257-4336 215 F rcathey@latech.edu
CATHEY, William, N 775-784-1740 303 A billca@unr.edu
CATHIE, Julie 530-541-4660 53 F cathie@ltcc.edu
CATIGGAY, James 415-422-6216 76 B catiggay@usfca.edu
CATILLAZ, Michael, J 585-245-5519 353 C catillaz@geneseo.edu
CATLETT, Jennifer 865-471-3530 467 E jcatlett@cn.edu
CATLETT, Lowell 575-646-3748 319 D agdean@nmsu.edu
CATLIN, Diane 559-453-2252 47 K diane.catlin@fresno.edu
CATLIN, Linda 800-955-2527 282 G
CATO, James, C 352-392-7622 120 B jccato@ufl.edu
CATRON, Jonathan 864-644-5662 461 B jcatron@swu.edu
CATRON, LaKeysha 937-376-6657 386 H lcatron@centralstate.edu
CATRON, Sue 918-456-5511 409 A catrons@nsuok.edu
CATRON-WOOD, Rhonda, K 276-223-4772 528 F wccatrr@wcc.vccs.edu
CATT, Helen 229-430-3506 123 I hcatt@albanytech.edu
CATT, Stephen, R 724-287-8711 423 F stephen.catt@bc3.edu
CATT, Susan 812-330-6079 175 H scatt@ivytech.edu
CATTANACH, John, R 315-516-4100 291 F cattanachj@umsl.edu
CATTELINO, Ronald, E 816-802-3431 283 I rcattelino@kcai.edu
CATTERSON, Anna 620-365-5116 190 A catterson@allencc.edu
CATTOOR, Chad 314-505-7304 280 H cattoorc@csl.edu
CAUCE, Ana Mari 206-543-5340 538 F cauce@uw.edu
CAUDA, Lisa 585-475-7721 347 G lisa.cauda@rit.edu
CAUDILL, Alicia 678-717-3877 129 D acaudill@gsc.edu
CAUDILL, Dave 678-915-3168 137 C dcaudill@spsu.edu
CAUDILL, Gene 606-783-2066 204 E g.caudill@moreheadstate.edu
CAUDILL, Helene, L 512-448-8648 493 B helenec@stedwards.edu
CAUDILL, Jeff 615-844-5250 468 J jcaudill@fwbbc.edu
CAUDILL, Pamela, S 215-573-6706 448 I caudill@pobox.upenn.edu
CAUDILL, Patricia 606-436-5721 201 H pat.caudill@kctcs.edu
CAUDLE, Donald, R 252-823-5166 370 A caudled@edgecombe.edu
CAUDLE, Patricia, M 909-748-8171 75 F pat_caudle@redlands.edu
CAUFFMAN, Bonnie, H 360-417-6212 536 B bcauffman@pencol.edu
CAUGHEY, Martha 850-484-1604 114 G mcaughey@pensacolastate.edu
CAUGHMAN, Gretchen 706-721-4014 130 B gcaughma@georgiahealth.edu
CAUGHMAN, S. Wright 404-778-3774 129 A scaughm@emory.edu
CAULEY, Phil 828-227-2923 379 E cauley@wcu.edu
CAULFIELD, Jack 508-213-2398 243 J jack.caulfield@nichols.edu
CAULFIELD, Richard 907-796-6256 11 A provost@uas.alaska.edu
CAULFIELD, Thomas, M 217-351-2477 161 B tcaulfield@parkland.edu
CAULLEY, Barbara 650-508-3601 59 G bcaulley@ndnu.edu
CAUPP, Jeffrey, G 480-245-7973 14 K jeff.caupp@ibconline.edu
CAUSEY, Brian, C 336-633-4165 372 F bccausey@randolph.edu
CAUSEY, Bruce 256-306-2569 2 E bcausey@calhoun.edu
CAUSEY, Joy 229-317-6886 128 A joy.causey@darton.edu
CAUSEY, Katherine 901-435-1259 470 B katherine_causey@loc.edu
CAUSEY, Mary Frances 928-350-1112 18 C mcausey@prescott.edu
CAUSEY, Rebecca 850-484-1795 114 G rcausey@pensacolastate.edu
CAUWELS, Beth 805-565-6101 78 F bcauwels@westmont.edu
CAVACO, Frank 617-964-1100 230 B fcavaco@ants.edu
CAVAHAUGH, Brian 716-829-7878 332 F cavanaub@dyc.edu
CAVALIER, Donald, R 218-281-8585 272 A cavalier@umn.edu
CAVALIER, Philip Acree 309-467-6301 150 H pcavalier@eureka.edu
CAVALIER, Sandra 301-846-2485 222 G scavalier@frederick.edu
CAVALIERI, Correne 718-779-1430 346 B ccavalieri@plazacollege.edu
CAVALIERI, Cristina, G 215-503-9496 448 B cristina.cavalieri@jefferson.edu
CAVALIERI, Thomas, A 856-566-6996 316 I cavalita@umdnj.edu
CAVALLARO, Claire 657-278-4021 34 E ccavallaro@fullerton.edu
CAVALLARO, Gregory, M 540-464-7328 529 A gcav@vmiaa.org
CAVALLARO, Vito 212-938-5500 355 B vito@sunyopt.edu
CAVALLI, Mario 914-606-6844 360 D mario.cavalli@sunywcc.edu
CAVALLUZZI, Marty, R 425-640-1557 533 E marty.cavalluzzi@edcc.edu
CAVAN, John, J 434-949-1003 527 H john.cavan@southside.edu
CAVANAGH, David 802-635-1289 515 E david.cavanagh@jsc.edu
CAVANAGH, Kevin 914-633-2120 336 E kcavanagh@iona.edu
CAVANAGH, Stephen 413-545-5093 237 C
CAVANAUGH, Amy 503-943-7201 420 G cavanaug@up.edu
CAVANAUGH, SSJ, Cecelia, J 215-753-3623 425 C ccavanau@chc.edu
CAVANAUGH, Erica 701-766-1305 380 E erica.cavanaugh@littleloop.edu
CAVANAUGH, John, C 717-720-4010 441 E jcavanaugh@passhe.edu
CAVANAUGH, Kyle 919-684-2826 363 I kyle.cavanaugh@duke.edu
CAVANAUGH, Mary Anne 803-641-3563 462 B maryanc@usca.edu
CAVANAUGH, Patrick, D 209-946-2345 75 D pcavanaugh@pacific.edu
CAVANAUGH, Rachel 516-299-3641 338 F rachel.cavanaugh@liu.edu
CAVAZOS, Cyndi 210-434-6711 491 G cacavazos@lake.ollusa.edu
CAVAZOS, Henry 409-772-3004 507 B hcavazos@utmb.edu
CAVAZOS, Rebecca 956-664-4680 494 D beckyc@southtexascollege.edu
CAVE, Robert 909-621-8122 49 D robert_cave@hmc.edu
CAVENAUGH, Andy 910-296-2480 371 B acavenaugh@jamessprunt.edu
CAVENDAR, Joe 256-835-5463 3 J jcavendar@gadsdenstate.edu
CAVENDISH, John 304-326-1258 541 G jcavendish@salemu.edu
CAVENDISH, Pat 253-964-7327 536 C pcavendish@pierce.ctc.edu
CAVENY, Deanna, M 843-953-5527 457 B cavenys@cofc.edu
CAVIGGIOLA, Brian 765-677-2102 174 E brian.caviggiola@indwes.edu
CAVIN, JR., Elmo, M 806-743-3080 501 E elmo.cavin@ttuhsc.edu
CAVINS-TULL, Kathryn 817-257-7820 498 F k.cavins@tcu.edu
CAVIS, Mark 906-487-7315 251 C mark.cavis@finlandia.edu
CAVITT, Deborah 817-531-4298 502 A dcavitt@txwes.edu
CAVOSI-O'DEA, Marybeth 610-799-1166 434 D modea@lccc.edu
CAWLEY, Frank 805-756-1161 33 F fcawley@calpoly.edu
CAWLEY, Steve 305-284-3515 122 F s.cawley@miami.edu
CAWOOD, J. Scott 215-702-4281 444 A scawood@pbu.edu
CAWTHON, Donald, L 254-968-9227 496 F cawthon@tarleton.edu
CAWTHON, James 574-936-8898 168 I jim.cawthon@ancilla.edu
CAWTHORN, Shawna 270-745-6463 207 C shawna.cawthorn@wku.edu
CAYAN, Sally 217-479-7123 157 D sally.cayan@mac.edu
CAYER, Cynthia, B 860-832-1741 91 G cayerc@ccsu.edu
CAYLOR, Deborah, Z 540-458-8730 530 A dcaylor@wlu.edu
CAYSE, Dan 513-569-1624 387 F dan.cayse@cincinnatistate.edu
CAYWOOD, Janet 620-278-4280 196 D jcaywood@sterling.edu
CAZALET, JR., David, J 606-679-8501 202 F david.cazalet@kctcs.edu
CAZAUBON, Steve 504-762-3050 210 G scazau@dcc.edu
CAZZETTA, Vinnie 845-341-4726 345 E vinnie.cazzetta@sunyorange.edu
CEASAR, Ted 760-355-6312 50 K ted.ceasar@imperial.edu
CEBALLOS, Adis 213-251-3636 29 H aceballos@aii.edu
CEBELAK, Jane, P 772-462-7544 110 L jcebelak@irsc.edu
CEBRICK, Daniel, T 570-208-5870 432 E dtcebric@kings.edu
CEBRZYNSKI, Gerard, J 847-735-5104 155 F cebrzynski@lakeforest.edu
CECALA, Diana 843-349-5207 458 G dianna.cecala@hgtc.edu
CECCANECCHIO, Domenic 215-895-1554 427 G dc444@drexel.edu
CECCHINI, Bernard 315-568-3127 342 H bcecchini@nycc.edu
CECCHINI, Dan 541-383-7700 414 I dcecchini@cocc.edu
CECERE, Janice 973-748-9000 308 A janice_cecere@bloomfield.edu
CECERO, Diane, M 585-292-2108 341 H dcecero@monroecc.edu
CECH, John 406-444-0314 294 J jcech@montana.edu
CECIL, Dale 270-686-4239 198 G dale.cecil@brescia.edu
CECIL, David, J 859-233-8239 206 E financialaid@transy.edu
CECIL, Jackie 606-886-3863 201 C jackie.cecil@kctcs.edu
CECIL, Jamie, N 717-867-6228 434 C cecil@lvc.edu
CECIL, Kathy 813-253-7027 110 I kcecil@hccfl.edu
CECIL, Patrick, A 502-895-3411 204 B pcecil@lpts.edu
CEDAR, Leslie 512-471-3800 505 B cedar@alumni.utexas.edu
CEDEL, Thomas 512-313-3000 483 G thomas.cedel@concordia.edu
CEDENO, Derena 717-764-9550 426 D dcedeno@csb.edu
CEDERGREN, Cindy 218-683-8611 268 E cindy.cedergren@northlandcollege.edu
CEDILLO, Arnulfo 415-485-9375 41 I arnulfo.cedillo@marin.edu
CEDRONE, David, C 617-994-6904 237 A dmcedrone@bhe.mass.edu

CHANDLER, Derrall .... 619-388-3537..... 65 F
dchandler@sdccd.edu
CHANDLER, Dianne .... 765-973-8232.... 173 D
dschandl@iue.edu
CHANDLER, Dianne, S ...... 765-973-8232.... 173 D
dschandl@iue.edu
CHANDLER, G. Thomas ..... 803-777-5032.... 462 A
tchandler@sc.edu
CHANDLER, Grant .... 269-373-7800.... 253 G
gchandler@kvcc.edu
CHANDLER, Jarrett, T .... 704-216-3451.... 373 C
jerry.chandler@rccc.edu
CHANDLER, John, M .... 319-399-8622.... 183 C
jchandle@coe.edu
CHANDLER, Kathy .... 205-652-3421...... 10 A
kchandler@uwa.edu
CHANDLER, Keith .... 615-329-8665.... 468 G
kchandler@fisk.edu
CHANDLER, Kim .... 651-696-6366.... 265 A
kchandle@macalester.edu
CHANDLER, Maria .... 803-641-3317.... 462 B
mariac@usca.edu
CHANDLER, Mary, M .... 315-445-4462.... 338 B
richermm@lemoyne.edu
CHANDLER, Nancy, W .... 334-347-2623....... 3 G
nchandler@escc.edu
CHANDLER, Norma .... 602-787-7073...... 16 A
norma.chandler@pvmail.maricopa.edu
CHANDLER, Rebecca .... 310-338-5118...... 56 E
rchandler@lmu.edu
CHANDLER, Rick .... 212-650-3258.... 327 E
rick.chandler@hunter.cuny.edu
CHANDLER, Roger .... 251-575-3156......... 1 B
rchandler@ascc.edu
CHANDLER, Sabrina, J ...... 914-606-6880.... 360 D
sabrina.johnson.chandler@sunywcc.edu
CHANDLER, Shelly .... 352-787-7660.... 101 H
schandler@beaconcollege.edu
CHANDLER, Stanford .... 770-975-4000.... 126 H
CHANDLER, Sue .... 404-297-9522.... 128 B
chandles@dekalbtech.edu
CHANDLER, Timothy, J ..... 330-672-2220.... 393 D
tchandl1@kent.edu
CHANEY, Bill .... 425-739-8119.... 535 B
bill.chaney@lwtc.edu
CHANEY, C. Steven .... 916-348-4689...... 45 H
stevec@chaneyassociates.com
CHANEY, Carmela .... 626-571-8811...... 76 D
carmelac@uwest.edu
CHANEY, L, D .... 903-785-7661.... 492 B
dchaney@parisjc.edu
CHANEY, Matthew .... 231-591-2617.... 251 B
chaneym@ferris.edu
CHANEY, Rob .... 850-201-6085.... 121 F
chaneyr@tcc.fl.edu
CHANEY, William .... 901-320-9700.... 478 B
bchaney@victory.edu
CHANG, Chaw-ye .... 610-436-3043.... 443 F
cchang@wcupa.edu
CHANG, Christopher .... 845-687-5096.... 358 C
changc@sunyulster.edu
CHANG, Cindy .... 818-719-6425..... 55 B
changck@piercecollege.edu
CHANG, Gilberto .... 239-513-1135.... 123 D
gchang@wolford.edu
CHANG, Hubert .... 562-902-3317...... 71 A
hurbertchang@scuhs.edu
CHANG, Jong Sik .... 770-279-0507.... 129 E
changjongsik@hotmail.com
CHANG, Lay, N .... 540-231-5422.... 529 B
laynam@vt.edu
CHANG, Lillian .... 808-947-4788.... 142 D
wmi@worldmedicineinstitute.com
CHANG, Lin .... 719-549-2110...... 83 B
lin.chang@colostate-pueblo.edu
CHANG, Lon .... 704-357-8020.... 361 N
lchang@aii.edu
CHANG, Mari .... 808-993-0540.... 141 F
changm@hawaii.edu
CHANG, Nancy, H .... 817-515-5222.... 496 A
nancy.chang@tccd.edu
CHANG, Otto, H .... 260-481-0219.... 174 A
chango@ipfw.edu
CHANG, Patrick .... 201-684-7456.... 313 D
pchang@ramapo.edu
CHANG, Peter, M .... 703-333-5904.... 530 B
CHANG, Shi-Kuo .... 847-679-3135.... 155 D
changsk@ksi.edu
CHANG, Susan .... 630-652-8360.... 149 B
schang@devry.edu
CHANG, Tim .... 323-259-2531...... 59 H
tchang@oxy.edu
CHANG, Wendy .... 860-493-0125...... 91 F
CHANG, Wendy .... 203-392-7460...... 91 I
changw@southernct.edu
CHANGNON, Susan, J ...... 724-287-8711.... 423 F
susan.changnon@bc3.edu
CHANLATTE, Ruben, D ...... 817-257-5022.... 498 F
r.chanlatte@tcu.edu
CHANLER, Annette .... 318-371-3035.... 211 F
achanler@ltc.edu
CHANNELL, Pat .... 510-276-3888...... 38 E
pchannell@cc.edu
CHANNING, Eric .... 602-850-8000...... 17 H
echanning@phoenixseminary.edu
CHANT, Loreen, M .... 305-892-7039.... 111 K
loreen.chant@jwu.edu
CHANZIT, Gwen .... 303-871-4790...... 88 E
gchanzit@du.edu
CHAO, Gloria .... 212-220-8304.... 326 E
gchao@bmcc.cuny.edu
CHAPA, Catherine .... 210-486-3731.... 479 D
cchapa@alamo.edu
CHAPA, Marl, F .... 956-882-8277.... 505 C
mari.chapa@utb.edu
CHAPA, Paul .... 210-999-8328.... 502 C
Paul.Chapa@trinity.edu
CHAPA, Yolanda, M .... 512-223-9154.... 481 B
ymc@austincc.edu
CHAPARRO, Luis .... 915-831-2132.... 486 E
lchapa13@epcc.edu
CHAPARRO, Mildred .... 787-265-3807.... 567 C
chaparro@uprm.edu
CHAPDELAINE, Andrea, E . 610-921-7643.... 421 D
achapdelaine@alb.edu
CHAPDELAINE, Karen .... 772-462-7465.... 110 L
kchapdel@irsc.edu
CHAPDELAINE, Roland ...... 213-763-7052...... 55 D
chapder@lattc.edu
CHAPEL, Edward, V .... 973-655-4040.... 311 G
chapele@mail.montclair.edu
CHAPELL, Bryan .... 314-434-4044.... 281 A
kathy.woodard@covenantseminary.edu
CHAPIN, Frank .... 513-875-3344.... 387 B
frank.chapin@chatfield.edu
CHAPIN, John .... 850-201-8760.... 121 F
chapinj@tcc.fl.edu
CHAPIN, William .... 518-891-2915.... 344 E
wchapin@nccc.edu
CHAPKIS, Wendy .... 207-780-4966.... 220 G
chapkis@maine.edu
CHAPLIN, Elyse .... 714-564-6277...... 63 F
chaplin_elyse@sac.edu
CHAPLIN, Patricia .... 313-927-1249.... 255 A
pchaplin@marygrove.edu
CHAPMAN, April .... 707-836-2904...... 68 E
achapman@santarosa.edu
CHAPMAN, Bethany .... 254-295-4167.... 504 A
bchapman@umhb.edu
CHAPMAN, Brent .... 360-596-5219.... 538 B
bchapman@spscc.ctc.edu
CHAPMAN, Brian, R .... 713-221-8003.... 503 D
chapmanb@uhd.edu
CHAPMAN, Brian Keith .... 678-891-3337.... 130 G
bchapman@gpc.edu
CHAPMAN, Bryce .... 314-744-7631.... 286 C
chapmanb@mobap.edu
CHAPMAN, Carol, R .... 303-273-3280...... 82 F
crchapma@mines.edu
CHAPMAN, Carrie .... 314-837-6777.... 288 F
cchapman@slcconline.edu
CHAPMAN, Clint .... 816-781-7700.... 293 D
chapmanc@william.jewell.edu
CHAPMAN, D. Duane .... 304-462-4128.... 543 F
donald.chapman@glenville.edu
CHAPMAN, Dale, T .... 618-468-2001.... 156 C
dchapman@lc.edu
CHAPMAN, Dana, L .... 904-256-7682.... 111 J
dchapma@ju.edu
CHAPMAN, David, W .... 205-726-2771........ 6 G
dwchapma@samford.edu
CHAPMAN, Elaine .... 626-585-7608...... 61 E
efchapman@pasadena.edu
CHAPMAN, Elaine, F .... 626-585-7065...... 61 E
efchapman@pasadena.edu
CHAPMAN, Emily .... 312-499-4184.... 164 A
echapman@saic.edu
CHAPMAN, Grant .... 314-246-8755.... 293 A
chapman@webster.edu
CHAPMAN, Jeff .... 785-827-5541.... 194 D
jeff.chapman@kwu.edu
CHAPMAN, John .... 919-572-1625.... 361 M
jchapman@apexsot.edu
CHAPMAN, Judy .... 406-657-2188.... 295 F
jchapman@msubillings.edu
CHAPMAN, Katrina .... 651-638-6043.... 261 I
k-chapman@bethel.edu
CHAPMAN, Kendall, P .... 601-643-8364.... 274 A
ken.chapman@colin.edu
CHAPMAN, Kim .... 206-934-4521.... 536 H
kim.chapman@seattlecolleges.edu
CHAPMAN, Leslie, T .... 847-735-5030.... 155 F
chapman@lakeforest.edu
CHAPMAN, Linda .... 618-468-4000.... 156 C
lchapman@lc.edu
CHAPMAN, Lisa, M .... 919-718-7295.... 368 H
CHAPMAN, Mary .... 515-697-7702.... 183 E
mlchapman@dmacc.edu
CHAPMAN, Richard, L .... 615-898-2988.... 473 F
rchapman@mtsu.edu
CHAPMAN, Richard, N .... 843-661-1281.... 458 C
rchapman@fmarion.edu
CHAPMAN, Robyn, F .... 828-327-7000.... 368 G
rchapman@cvcc.edu
CHAPMAN, Ronald, K .... 801-422-4007.... 509 D
ronald_chapman@byu.edu
CHAPMAN, Sharon, H .... 803-938-3810.... 462 F
hamptons@uscsumter.edu
CHAPMAN, Staci .... 773-380-6840.... 168 D
schapman@westwood.edu
CHAPMAN, Susan, E .... 508-929-8034.... 239 D
schapman@worcester.edu
CHAPMAN, Terry .... 704-216-3700.... 373 C
terry.chapman@rccc.edu
CHAPMAN, Tim .... 503-253-3443.... 417 H
tchapman@ocom.edu
CHAPMAN, Warren .... 312-355-0420.... 166 F
wchapman@uic.edu
CHAPP, Belena .... 215-568-4515.... 436 H
bchapp@moore.edu
CHAPPELL, Cindy .... 619-849-2531...... 62 L
cindychappell@pointloma.edu
CHAPPELL, David .... 910-362-7073.... 368 E
dchappell@cfcc.edu
CHAPPELL, Debnam .... 203-254-4000...... 92 B
dchappell@fairfield.edu
CHAPPELL, Dorothy, F .... 630-752-5627.... 168 F
dorothy.chappell@wheaton.edu
CHAPPELL, Jean, M .... 304-696-4645.... 542 G
jean.chappell@mctc.edu
CHAPPELL, Julie .... 540-887-7225.... 520 I
jchappel@mbc.edu
CHAPPELL, Ka'thy, G .... 804-204-1209.... 516 G
kchappell@btsr.edu
CHAPPELL, Marilyn, J .... 818-779-8047...... 53 B
mchappell@kingsuniversity.edu
CHAPPELL, Paul, G .... 818-779-8259...... 53 B
pchappell@kingsuniversity.edu
CHAPPELL-WILLIAMS,
Lynette .... 607-255-3976.... 331 C
lc75@cornell.edu
CHAPPLE, Bernard .... 904-470-8176.... 105 A
bchapple@ewc.edu
CHAPPLE, Reginald .... 610-917-1457.... 450 D
rechapple@vfcc.edu
CHAPUT, JR., Maury, L ...... 410-777-2324.... 221 B
mlchaput@aacc.edu
CHARD, David, J .... 214-768-5465.... 494 F
dchard@smu.edu
CHARDKOFF, Richard, B ... 318-342-1540.... 216 E
chardkoff@ulm.edu
CHARETTE, Reno .... 406-657-2011.... 295 F
rcharette@msubillings.edu
CHARETTE, Sharon .... 401-739-5000.... 453 E
scharette@neit.edu
CHARGIN, Jan .... 408-848-4724...... 48 B
jbchargin@gavilan.edu
CHARLES, Curtis .... 910-672-2247.... 377 E
ccharles@uncfsu.ed
CHARLES, Cynthia .... 504-816-4263.... 208 I
ccharles@dillard.edu
CHARLES, Harvey .... 928-523-1308...... 17 A
harvey.charles@nau.edu
CHARLES, Jeffrey, R .... 408-554-4607...... 68 C
jcharles@scu.edu
CHARLES, Joanne .... 740-351-3560.... 401 I
jcharles@shawnee.edu
CHARLES, Kevin, E .... 603-862-1098.... 306 E
kevin.charles@unh.edu
CHARLES, Kristin .... 415-239-3677...... 39 H
kcharles@ccsf.edu
CHARLES, Misha, J .... 603-358-2111.... 307 A
mcharles1@keene.edu
CHARLES, Mitch .... 925-522-7777...... 37 G
mpcharles@cc.edu
CHARLESTON, Kathleen ...... 217-353-2024.... 161 B
kcharleston@parkland.edu
CHARLIER, Hara .... 540-234-9261.... 525 G
charlierh@brcc.edu
CHARLSON, Elaine, M .... 713-743-9103.... 503 A
echarlson@uh.edu
CHARLSON, Elaine, M .... 713-743-9103.... 503 B
echarlson@uh.edu
CHARLTON, John .... 202-685-4242.... 557 F
charltonj@ndu.edu
CHARLTON, Patricia, A .... 702-651-5667.... 302 G
patty.charlton@csn.edu
CHARMOLI, Audrey .... 231-876-3100.... 248 F
audrey.charmoli@baker.edu
CHARNEY, Dennis, S .... 212-241-5674.... 342 B
CHARNEY, Len .... 617-262-5000.... 232 B
len.charney@the-bac.edu
CHARNOW, Rebecca .... 212-749-2802.... 339 I
rcharnow@msmnyc.edu
CHAROENSIRI, Kanitta ...... 540-231-5313.... 529 B
charkx@vt.edu
CHARON, Joseph .... 413-662-5284.... 238 F
joseph.charon@mcla.edu
CHARPENTIER, Heather ...... 518-743-2342.... 322 B
charpentierh@sunyacc.edu
CHARRIEZ, Ivette .... 787-878-6000.... 562 E
icharriez@icprjc.edu
CHARRIEZ, Mayra .... 787-767-0344.... 567 F
mbcestudiantes@uprrp.edu
CHARRON, Michael .... 507-457-1606.... 271 G
mcharron@smumn.edu
CHARTER, Caryn .... 734-487-3090.... 250 H
ccharter@emich.edu
CHARTIER, Lark .... 337-482-6243.... 216 D
lark@louisiana.edu
CHARTON, Jacques .... 415-485-3227...... 45 B
charton@dominican.edu
CHARUHAS, Mary, S .... 847-543-2402.... 147 H
mcharuhas@clcillinois.edu
CHARVILLE, Mark, R .... 419-372-0638.... 385 D
markrc@bgsu.edu
CHASE, Anne .... 859-985-3266.... 198 F
anne_chase@berea.edu
CHASE, Brian, J .... 970-491-0007...... 83 A
brian.chase@colostate.edu
CHASE, Bruce, W .... 540-831-5278.... 522 D
bchase@radford.edu
CHASE, Cheryl .... 641-269-3450.... 185 A
chaseche@grinnell.edu
CHASE, David .... 203-857-7058...... 90 G
dchase@ncc.commnet.edu
CHASE, David, D .... 509-527-4261.... 538 G
david.chase@wwcc.edu
CHASE, David, T .... 973-267-9404.... 313 C
CHASE, Diane .... 407-823-6197.... 120 A
diane.chase@ucf.edu
CHASE, Geoffrey, W .... 619-594-2873...... 36 E
gchase@mail.sdsu.edu
CHASE, Gregory, M .... 336-734-7246.... 370 C
gchase@forsythtech.edu
CHASE, Horace, W .... 731-425-2610.... 475 B
hchase@jscc.edu
CHASE, James .... 315-364-3207.... 360 C
jimc@wells.edu
CHASE, Jared .... 785-227-3380.... 190 G
chasej@bethanylb.edu
CHASE, Marilyn, O .... 317-788-2192.... 180 C
chase@uindy.edu
CHASE, Mary, E .... 402-280-2162.... 297 H
marychase@creighton.edu
CHASE, Mary Jane .... 801-832-2301.... 512 F
mjchase@westminstercollege.edu
CHASE, MaryEtta .... 801-957-4799.... 512 C
maryetta.chase@slcc.edu
CHASE, Michael .... 602-749-4539...... 13 M
mchase@devry.edu
CHASE, Michael, K .... 423-775-7327.... 467 D
mchase5606@bryan.edu
CHASE, Patricia, A .... 304-293-5101.... 544 E
pachase@hsc.wvu.edu
CHASE, Paul, W .... 715-234-8176.... 552 F
paul.chase@uwc.edu
CHASE, Ryan .... 480-517-8314...... 16 C
ryan.chase@riosalado.edu
CHASE PADULA, Allison ...... 401-254-3042.... 454 C
achasepadula@rwu.edu
CHASIS, Jocelyn .... 410-455-3636.... 227 D
jocelyn_chasis@umbc.edu
CHASON, Foster .... 423-585-2681.... 476 B
foster.chason@ws.edu
CHASON, Michael, D .... 229-391-5055.... 123 F
mchason@abac.edu
CHASTAIN, Andrea, J .... 913-288-7270.... 193 J
chastain@kckcc.edu
CHASTAIN, Lesa, M .... 417-268-6091.... 279 D
ir@gobbc.edu
CHASTAIN, Lisa .... 478-934-3082.... 133 G
lchastain@mgc.edu
CHASTAIN, Wes .... 828-835-4265.... 374 C
wchastain@tricountycc.edu
CHASTANT, Jane .... 713-623-2040.... 480 J
jchastant@aii.edu
CHASTEEN, Jon, R .... 405-789-7661.... 412 E
jon.chasteen@swcu.edu
CHATAS, Geoffrey .... 614-292-9232.... 398 H
chatas.1@osu.edu
CHATELAIN, Joel, A .... 504-280-6953.... 213 E
jchatela@uno.edu
CHATELAIN, Rose, D .... 504-568-4802.... 213 A
rtowns@lsuhsc.edu
CHATELLE, Shane .... 518-891-2915.... 344 E
schatelle@nccc.edu
CHATFIELD, Brenda, L .... 785-890-3641.... 195 E
bchatfield@nwktc.edu
CHATFIELD, Denson .... 219-980-6501.... 173 F
dchat@iun.edu
CHATHAM, April .... 214-692-8080.... 480 I
achatham@aii.edu
CHATHAM, David, W .... 864-833-8299.... 460 E
dchatham@presby.edu
CHATMAN, Cheryl, T .... 651-603-6151.... 263 C
chatman@csp.edu
CHATMAN, Emanuel, D .... 301-736-3631.... 224 B
emanuel.chatman@msbbcs.edu
CHATMAN, Robert .... 803-536-7200.... 460 G
zs_rchatman@scsu.edu
CHATMAN, Stephanie .... 601-979-2100.... 275 A
stephanie.i.chatman@jsums.edu
CHATMON, Angelo, V .... 804-257-5856.... 529 D
achatmon@vuu.edu
CHATTERJEE-SUTTON,
Eva .... 802-440-4330.... 512 G
ecs@bennington.edu
CHATTERTON, Jim .... 603-623-0313.... 305 F
jimchatterton@nhia.edu
CHATTERTON, Stephen, A . 208-282-2515.... 143 D
chatstep@isu.edu
CHATTIN, Duane, H .... 812-888-4164.... 181 B
dchattin@vinu.edu

CHATY, Karen ... 707-468-3065 ... 57 A
kchaty@mendocino.edu
CHAUDHARY, Khalid, M ... 615-963-7676 ... 474 A
kchaudhary@tnstate.edu
CHAUHDRI, Aamer ... 502-456-6509 ... 206 B
achauhdri@sctd.edu
CHAUNCEY, Linda ... 206-344-4386 ... 537 A
lchauncey@sccd.ctc.edu
CHAURET, Christian ... 765-455-9371 ... 173 E
cchauret@iuk.edu
CHAUVIN, Marc ... 985-732-6640 ... 211 C
CHAVARIA, Fred ... 415-239-3174 ... 39 H
fchavari@ccsf.edu
CHAVERS, Kathy, L ... 425-235-5842 ... 536 E
kchavers@rtc.edu
CHAVES, William ... 509-359-2347 ... 533 D
wchaves@ewu.edu
CHAVEZ, April ... 575-769-4061 ... 317 K
april.chavez@clovis.edu
CHAVEZ, Chris ... 404-270-2718 ... 128 G
cchavez2@devry.edu
CHAVEZ, Connie ... 575-461-4413 ... 318 F
conniec@mesalands.edu
CHAVEZ, David, E ... 540-665-4551 ... 523 K
dchavez@su.edu
CHAVEZ, Dennis, J ... 607-777-2428 ... 351 F
dchavez@binghamton.edu
CHAVEZ, Ernest ... 505-224-4639 ... 317 J
emchavez@cnm.edu
CHAVEZ, Gloriann ... 909-389-3248 ... 65 B
gchavez@sbccd.cc.ca.us
CHAVEZ, Gloriann ... 909-384-8665 ... 65 C
gchavez@sbccd.cc.ca.us
CHAVEZ, Guadalupe ... 956-872-3499 ... 494 D
gchavez@southtexascollege.edu
CHAVEZ, Israel ... 563-588-8000 ... 184 F
ichavez@emmaus.edu
CHAVEZ, Lisa, M ... 323-343-3500 ... 35 B
lchavez@cslanet.calstatela.edu
CHAVEZ, Mario, J ... 308-635-6186 ... 301 E
chavezm@wncc.edu
CHAVEZ, Michael ... 661-654-3181 ... 33 H
mchavez@csub.edu
CHAVEZ, Michael ... 432-685-4507 ... 490 G
mchavez@midland.edu
CHAVEZ, Miguel ... 330-490-7341 ... 405 E
mchavez@walsh.edu
CHAVEZ, Olga ... 915-831-3322 ... 486 E
ochave30@epcc.edu
CHAVEZ, Orquedia ... 916-649-2400 ... 31 C
CHAVEZ, Stella, M ... 661-654-2241 ... 33 H
schavez@csub.edu
CHAVEZ-AGUILAR,
Antonia Amie ... 575-737-6200 ... 321 F
aca@unm.edu
CHAVIANO-MORAN,
Rosa, M ... 973-972-1103 ... 316 D
chaviaro@umdnj.edu
CHAVIRA, Jessica ... 325-235-7342 ... 500 C
jessica.chavira@tstc.edu
CHAVIRA, Rejoice ... 909-389-3456 ... 65 B
rchavira@craftonhills.edu
CHAVIS, Donna ... 843-921-6907 ... 460 B
dchavis@netc.edu
CHAVIS, Gordon ... 407-823-3004 ... 120 A
gchavis@ucf.edu
CHAVIS, Kimberly ... 773-602-5501 ... 147 B
kboyd@ccc.edu
CHAVIS, Linda ... 317-352-8736 ... 170 H
lchavis@crossroads.edu
CHAVIS, Tim ... 248-204-3700 ... 254 E
tchavis@ltu.edu
CHAWKIN, Ken ... 641-472-4037 ... 187 B
kchawkin@mum.edu
CHAYA, Ramon, C ... 585-345-6999 ... 334 F
rcchaya@genesee.edu
CHEAGLE, Dorothy, S ... 803-934-3227 ... 459 F
dcheagle@morris.edu
CHEAL, Catheryn, L ... 248-370-4566 ... 257 C
cheal@oakland.edu
CHEATEM, Michelle ... 410-617-5171 ... 224 A
micheatem@loyola.edu
CHEATHAM, Frank ... 270-789-5231 ... 199 C
fdcheatham@campbellsville.edu
CHEATHAM, George ... 703-284-1560 ... 521 A
george.cheatham@marymount.edu
CHEATHAM, Kathy ... 205-329-7853 ... 3 B
kathy.cheatham@ecacolleges.com
CHEATHAM, Thomas, J ... 615-898-2613 ... 473 F
thomas.cheatham@mtsu.edu
CHEBATOR, Paul, J ... 617-552-3470 ... 232 D
paul.chebator.1@bc.edu
CHECCHIO, Debbie ... 276-326-4243 ... 516 I
dchecchio@bluefield.edu
CHECCIO, Albert, R ... 213-740-2211 ... 76 C
checcio@usc.edu
CHECHOWICH, Faye ... 765-998-4571 ... 179 F
fychechow@taylor.edu
CHECK, Andrea, G ... 260-422-5561 ... 172 L
agcheck@indianatech.edu
CHECK, Elizabeth ... 636-797-3000 ... 283 H
echeck@jeffco.edu
CHECK, Theresa ... 513-569-1493 ... 387 F
theresa.check@cincinnatistate.edu
CHECKETTS, Max, L ... 808-675-3455 ... 139 I
checkettsm@byuh.edu
CHECKOVICH, Irene, C ... 508-531-1231 ... 238 B
icheckovich@bridgew.edu
CHECKOVICH, Peter, G ... 304-260-4380 ... 542 C
pcheckov@blueridgectc.edu
CHECOV, Elissa ... 770-962-7580 ... 132 A
echecov@gwinnetttech.edu
CHEE, Kathleen ... 808-544-0292 ... 140 B
kchee@hpu.edu
CHEEK, Claude ... 516-299-3780 ... 338 F
claude.cheek@liu.edu
CHEEK, Claude ... 516-299-3780 ... 338 H
claude.cheek@liu.edu
CHEEK, Debbie, Q ... 843-921-6945 ... 460 B
dcheek@netc.edu
CHEEK, Eric, A ... 336-334-7810 ... 377 F
echeek@ncat.edu
CHEEK, Jimmy, G ... 865-974-3265 ... 477 B
chancellor@utk.edu
CHEEK, King ... 516-364-0808 ... 343 A
cheek@nycollege.edu
CHEEK, JR., Lee ... 678-717-3688 ... 129 D
lcheek@gsc.edu
CHEEK, Richard ... 405-878-2249 ... 409 D
richard.cheek@okbu.edu
CHEEK, Sherrie ... 662-472-2312 ... 274 F
scheek@holmescc.edu
CHEEKS, Roger ... 757-352-4486 ... 523 B
rogeche@regent.edu
CHEERS, Karen, T ... 276-739-2490 ... 528 D
kcheers@vhcc.edu
CHEESEBRO, Dorothy ... 336-770-3321 ... 379 D
cheesebrod@uncsa.edu
CHEETHAM, William, C ... 315-445-4400 ... 338 B
cheethwc@lemoyne.edu
CHELBERG, Gene ... 415-405-3728 ... 36 F
chelberg@sfsu.edu
CHELETTE, Newton ... 661-722-6300 ... 28 J
nchelette@avc.edu
CHELINE, OSB, Paschal ... 503-845-3269 ... 417 A
paschal.cheline@mtangel.edu
CHELLMAN, Laura, G ... 715-836-5954 ... 550 H
chellmlg@uwec.edu
CHELNICK, Robert ... 773-975-1295 ... 158 D
krisbob1@cs.com
CHELNICK, Robert ... 773-975-1295 ... 548 F
krisbob1@cs.com
CHELSEN, Paul, O ... 630-752-5026 ... 168 F
Paul.Chelsen@wheaton.edu
CHELTE, Anthony, F ... 501-569-3356 ... 24 E
afchelte@ualr.edu
CHEMA, Thomas, V ... 330-569-5120 ... 391 H
chematv@hiram.edu
CHEMERINSKY, Erwin ... 949-824-7722 ... 73 H
echemerinsky@law.uci.edu
CHEN, Alex ... 501-450-3445 ... 25 H
achen@uca.edu
CHEN, Bill ... 626-571-8811 ... 76 D
billchen@uwest.edu
CHEN, Chau-Kuang ... 615-327-6848 ... 471 A
ckchen@mmc.edu
CHEN, Chunju ... 262-472-1276 ... 552 E
chenc@uww.edu
CHEN, Daxing (Michael) ... 210-431-5009 ... 493 C
mchen@stmarytx.edu
CHEN, Desiree ... 630-617-3033 ... 150 F
chend@elmhurst.edu
CHEN, Ekron ... 626-571-5110 ... 54 C
ekron@les.edu
CHEN, Hui-Ling ... 603-222-4203 ... 305 H
hchen@anselm.edu
CHEN, Jack ... 516-877-3334 ... 322 A
jchen@adelphi.edu
CHEN, James, M ... 502-852-6879 ... 207 A
jim.chen@louisville.edu
CHEN, Jane ... 212-472-1500 ... 343 G
jchen@nysid.edu
CHEN, Julie ... 978-934-2992 ... 237 F
Julie_Chen@uml.edu
CHEN, Karen ... 323-731-2383 ... 60 I
esl@psuca.edu
CHEN, Liana ... 408-260-0208 ... 47 D
accounting@fivebranches.edu
CHEN, Mary M, Y ... 302-454-3968 ... 96 C
mchen@dtcc.edu
CHEN, May, K ... 510-981-2820 ... 62 A
mchen@peralta.edu
CHEN, Mei-Shya ... 913-588-1259 ... 197 A
mchen-su@kumc.edu
CHEN, Nellie ... 212-349-4330 ... 334 G
nchen@globe.edu
CHEN, Qi ... 312-777-7600 ... 144 H
qchen@argosy.edu
CHEN, Sheying ... 212-346-1555 ... 345 F
schen@pace.edu
CHEN, Steve ... 518-629-7311 ... 336 C
s.chen@hvcc.edu
CHEN, Tracy ... 617-327-6777 ... 242 C
tracy_chen@mspp.edu
CHEN, Tsuey-Hwa ... 612-977-5732 ... 262 A
tsuey-hwa.chen@capella.edu
CHEN, Wen-Hsin ... 617-989-4029 ... 246 C
chenw@wit.edu
CHEN, Xiangming ... 860-297-5170 ... 94 C
xiangming.chen@trincoll.edu
CHEN, Xueying ... 334-291-4979 ... 2 G
xueying.chen@cv.edu
CHEN, Yanping ... 703-516-0035 ... 524 G
yanping.chen@umtweb.edu
CHEN, Yemeng ... 516-739-1545 ... 343 C
president@nyctcm.edu
CHEN, Yong-Zhuo ... 814-362-7633 ... 449 B
yong@pitt.edu
CHEN MA, Biehwa ... 415-371-0002 ... 60 A
CHEN-ORTEGA, Cathy ... 303-546-3517 ... 86 B
cchenortega@naropa.edu
CHENAIL, Ronald ... 954-262-5389 ... 114 B
ron@nsu.nova.edu
CHENAULT, Shirley ... 817-598-6337 ... 508 C
chenault@wc.edu
CHENAULT, Venida ... 785-830-2770 ... 193 B
venida.chenault@bie.edu
CHENAUX, H. Eliot ... 361-825-2612 ... 497 F
eliot.chenaux@tamucc.edu
CHENCO, William ... 610-917-1430 ... 450 D
bachenco@vfcc.edu
CHENETTE, Jonathan ... 845-437-5300 ... 359 D
jochenette@vassar.edu
CHENEVERT, Peter, S ... 207-859-5530 ... 217 G
pschenev@colby.edu
CHENEVERT, Renee ... 727-873-4475 ... 121 B
rcheneve@mail.usf.edu
CHENEY, Christine ... 775-784-4345 ... 303 A
cheney@unr.edu
CHENEY, John ... 413-542-2331 ... 230 A
jycheney@amherst.edu
CHENEY, Susan ... 630-888-3500 ... 161 F
Susan.Cheney@rasmussen.edu
CHENEY, Victor ... 904-819-6213 ... 107 A
vcheney@flagler.edu
CHENG, Alex ... 662-915-7407 ... 277 G
acheng@olemiss.edu
CHENG, Rita ... 618-453-2341 ... 164 I
rcheng@siu.edu
CHENG, Stephen Z, D ... 330-972-7500 ... 403 B
cheng@uakron.edu
CHENG, Yan ... 954-763-9840 ... 101 A
dean@atom.edu
CHENGER, Geoffrey, L ... 304-788-6970 ... 545 A
glchenger@mail.wvu.edu
CHENIER, Spencer ... 202-806-5057 ... 90 D
schenier@howard.edu
CHENOWETH, Gregg ... 815-939-5213 ... 160 F
gchenowe@olivet.edu
CHENOWETH, Jeff ... 410-752-4710 ... 221 E
jchenoweth@bic.edu
CHENOWETH, John, D ... 262-472-1592 ... 552 E
chenowej@uww.edu
CHENOWETH, Kevin ... 740-699-2335 ... 400 A
chenowet@ohio.edu
CHERAGHI, S. Hossein ... 413-782-1272 ... 246 D
cheraghi@wne.edu
CHERECK, Deborah, T ... 541-346-3235 ... 419 B
dchereck@uoregon.edu
CHEREWICK, Daniel, P ... 248-341-2011 ... 257 B
dpchere@oaklandcc.edu
CHERIYAN, Ajith ... 631-370-3300 ... 350 D
acheriyan@sbmelville.edu
CHERMACK, Jerry ... 954-262-4419 ... 114 B
chermack@nsu.nova.edu
CHERMONTE, Debra, J ... 440-775-8411 ... 397 F
debra.chermonte@oberlin.edu
CHERN, James ... 973-746-2323 ... 311 G
chernj@mail.montclair.edu
CHERNAK, Robert, A ... 202-994-7210 ... 97 F
rac@gwu.edu
CHERNOW, Barbara ... 631-632-6340 ... 352 C
barbara.chernow@stonybrook.edu
CHERNOWSKI, Mary Ann ... 716-827-2435 ... 358 B
cherowskim@trocaire.edu
CHERREY, Cynthia ... 609-258-3000 ... 313 A
CHERREY, Cynthia ... 504-865-5180 ... 215 C
ccherrey@tulane.edu
CHERRIN, Bruce, E ... 505-277-1740 ... 321 C
cherrin@unm.edu
CHERRINGTON, R. Brent ... 801-524-8190 ... 510 A
rb-cherrington@ldsbc.edu
CHERRY, Charles, D ... 252-335-3593 ... 377 D
cdcherry@mail.ecsu.edu
CHERRY, Doris ... 270-831-9771 ... 201 I
doris.cherry@kctcs.edu
CHERRY, Evonne ... 254-647-3234 ... 492 E
echerry@rangercollege.edu
CHERRY, Jewel, B ... 336-734-7297 ... 370 C
jcherry@forsythtech.edu
CHERRY, Mark ... 321-433-7031 ... 101 J
cherrym@brevardcc.edu
CHERRY, Matthew ... 617-585-6681 ... 230 D
mcherry@aiboston.edu
CHERRY, Michelle ... 305-809-3237 ... 108 F
michelle.cherry@fkcc.edu
CHERRY, Stephanie ... 319-296-2320 ... 185 C
stephanie.cherry@hawkeyecollege.edu
CHERRY, Virginia, R ... 804-862-6208 ... 523 C
vcherry@rbc.edu
CHERUBIN, Daniel ... 212-772-4161 ... 327 E
dcherubi@hunter.cuny.edu
CHERUBINI, Angela ... 914-395-2567 ... 350 C
acherubini@sarahlawrence.edu
CHERUBINO, Thomas ... 908-709-7546 ... 316 B
cherubino@ucc.edu
CHESBRO, Patricia ... 970-786-4484 ... 10 I
afprc@uaa.alaska.edu
CHESBROUGH, Ronald, D ... 402-461-7394 ... 298 C
rchesbrough@hastings.edu
CHESLAK, Monica ... 212-472-1500 ... 343 G
mcheslak@nysid.edu
CHESLEY, Laurie ... 616-234-4230 ... 251 G
lchesley@grcc.edu
CHESNEY, Alan, P ... 410-778-7706 ... 229 D
achesney2@washcoll.edu
CHESNEY, Linda, H ... 718-262-5119 ... 329 B
chesney@york.cuny.edu
CHESNEY, Scott ... 603-862-1870 ... 306 E
scott.chesney@unh.edu
CHESNEY, Thom, D ... 972-860-4809 ... 484 F
CHESNUT, Robert, W ... 217-581-2125 ... 150 C
rwchesnut@eiu.edu
CHESSER, Ron ... 501-760-4230 ... 22 F
rchesser@npcc.edu
CHESSER, Trace ... 502-459-3535 ... 206 C
tchesser@sullivan.edu
CHESSON, JR., Andrew, L ... 318-675-5000 ... 213 B
achess@lsuhsc.edu
CHESTER, Ann, M ... 304-293-1651 ... 544 E
achester@hsc.wvu.edu
CHESTER, Brandi ... 870-248-4000 ... 21 A
brandic@blackrivertech.edu
CHESTER, Cathie, L ... 607-871-2300 ... 322 F
fchester@alfred.edu
CHESTER, Claudia ... 925-969-3108 ... 52 B
cchester@jfku.edu
CHESTER, Steven ... 860-343-5864 ... 90 D
schester@mxcc.commnet.edu
CHESTER, Timothy, M ... 310-506-4501 ... 61 G
tim.chester@pepperdine.edu
CHESTERFIELD,
Alverne, W ... 410-651-6253 ... 227 E
awchesterfield@umes.edu
CHESTERFIELD, Gail ... 765-289-2291 ... 175 K
gchester@ivytech.edu
CHESTERMAN, Gregg ... 760-366-5294 ... 43 E
gchesterman@cmccd.edu
CHESTNUT, Jacki, L ... 612-874-3729 ... 265 E
jacki_chestnut@mcad.edu
CHEUNG, Alvin ... 916-631-8108 ... 33 C
CHEUNG, Enos ... 718-939-5100 ... 338 D
echeung@libi.edu
CHEUNG, Lillian ... 651-631-0204 ... 261 D
lcheung@aaaom.edu
CHEVALIER, Cherie ... 503-244-6111 ... 419 G
cheric.chevalicr@pcc.cdu
CHEVALIER, JR., Joseph ... 404-756-5773 ... 134 B
jchevalier@msm.edu
CHEVES, Brad, E ... 214-768-2666 ... 494 F
bcheves@smu.edu
CHEW, Catherine ... 252-638-7200 ... 369 E
chewc@cravencc.edu
CHEW, Dan ... 925-288-5800 ... 49 F
dan_chew@heald.edu
CHEW, Kenneth ... 812-237-3939 ... 173 A
kenneth.chew@indstate.edu
CHEWNING, Michelle ... 336-506-4410 ... 367 G
michelle.chewning@alamancecc.edu
CHEYDLEUR, James ... 714-459-1139 ... 78 C
jcheydleur@wsulaw.edu
CHEZUM, Kelly, O ... 315-268-4483 ... 329 C
chezumk@clarkson.edu
CHI, Ching ... 408-260-0208 ... 47 D
chingchi@fivebranches.edu
CHI, Selina ... 323-265-8154 ... 54 G
chiss@elac.edu
CHIA, Samuel ... 214-841-3956 ... 485 E
schia@dts.edu
CHIABOTTI, Stephen, D ... 334-953-5155 ... 557 J
stephen.chiabotti@maxwell.af.mil
CHIACCHIERINI, Chris ... 503-253-3443 ... 417 H
cc@ocom.edu
CHIAL, Sally ... 612-977-5299 ... 262 A
sally.chial@capella.edu
CHIANG, Amber ... 661-395-4251 ... 52 M
amchiang@bakersfieldcollege.edu
CHIANG, Theresa, Y ... 210-567-2004 ... 506 E
chiangt@uthscsa.edu
CHIANG, Theresa, Y ... 210-567-2628 ... 506 E
chiangt@uthscsa.edu
CHIAPPINI, Thomas ... 330-494-6170 ... 402 A
tchiappini@starkstate.edu
CHIARA, Mary Jo, B ... 718-940-5574 ... 349 A
mchiara@sjcny.edu
CHIARAMONTE, Susan ... 877-248-6724 ... 14 J
schiaramonte@hmu.edu
CHIARAVALLE, Paul ... 312-369-7363 ... 148 B
pchiaravalle@colum.edu
CHICHESTER, Susan, E ... 585-245-5577 ... 353 C
sue@geneseo.edu
CHICKERING, F. William ... 609-896-5111 ... 313 G
wchickering@rider.edu
CHICOINE, David, L ... 605-688-4111 ... 466 B
david.chicoine@sdstate.edu

CHIELLI, Jack, A 570-408-4770 451 G jack.chielli@wilkes.edu
CHIEVES, Kevin 912-443-5491 136 D kchieves@savannahtech.edu
CHIGAWA, Steven 808-235-7457 142 C chigawa@hawaii.edu
CHIGOGIDZE, Alex 718-982-2430 327 A alex.chigogidze@csi.cuny.edu
CHIGOS, Lisa 619-961-4326 72 F lchigos@tjsl.edu
CHIGWEDERE, Shingai 972-929-9390 486 B schigwedere@devry.edu
CHIH, Lo-Li 808-974-7595 141 A loli@hawaii.edu
CHIKWEM, John, O 484-365-8253 434 H jchikwem@lincoln.edu
CHIKWINYA, Mary 253-566-5127 538 C mchikwinya@tacomacc.edu
CHILD, Elizabeth 202-884-9238 99 E childe@trinitydc.edu
CHILDERS, Amber 501-337-5000 21 D amber@otcweb.edu
CHILDERS, Karen 909-389-3392 65 B kchilder@craftonhills.edu
CHILDERS, Steven, L 407-366-9493 115 I schilders@rts.edu
CHILDRESS, Herb 617-262-5000 232 B herb.childress@the-bac.edu
CHILDRESS, Jamie, P 336-386-3279 374 B childressj@surry.edu
CHILDRESS, John 615-322-2631 477 F john.childress@vanderbilt.edu
CHILDRESS, Layton 417-447-8102 287 G childrel@otc.edu
CHILDRESS, Thomas, C 704-637-4394 363 C tchildre@catawba.edu
CHILDREY, Cynthia, A 928-523-5021 17 A cynthia.childrey@nau.edu
CHILDS, David, E 304-877-6428 540 D david.childs@abc.edu
CHILDS, Dena 870-543-5959 23 H dchilds@seark.edu
CHILDS, Kimberly, M 936-468-2805 495 H kchilds@sfasu.edu
CHILDS, LInda, J 304-877-6428 540 D linda.childs@abc.edu
CHILDS, Liz 801-863-8460 511 C childsli@uvu.edu
CHILDS, Mick 740-446-4367 391 B mchilds@gallipoliscareercollege.edu
CHILDS, Paige 864-941-8688 460 D childs.p@ptc.edu
CHILDS, Randal, V 919-530-5264 378 A rchilds@nccu.edu
CHILDS, Richard, G 410-864-4274 226 B rchilds@stmarys.edu
CHILDS, Sidney 419-372-2677 385 C sidneyc@bgsu.edu
CHILDS, Susan, T 919-508-2033 375 D schilds@peace.edu
CHILDS, Tim 269-687-5651 258 E tchilds@swmich.edu
CHILES, Jessica, N 903-589-4033 490 B jchiles@lonmorris.edu
CHILES, Rebecca 318-797-5082 213 D rebecca.chiles@lsus.edu
CHILLO, Joseph 617-730-7019 243 I joseph.chillo@newbury.edu
CHILTON, Brad 254-968-9354 496 F chilton@tarleton.edu
CHILTON, Bruce, D 845-758-7335 323 F chilton@bard.edu
CHILTON, Tutii 680-488-2471 560 A tutiichilton@gmail.com
CHIMENTI, Vito, R 215-670-9297 438 D vrchimenti@peirce.edu
CHIMERA, Anthony 312-662-4031 144 C achimera@adler.edu
CHIN, Calvin 646-557-4552 328 A chin@jjay.cuny.edu
CHIN, Deborah 203-932-7020 95 B dchin@newhaven.edu
CHIN, Diane 603-427-7630 304 C dchin@ccsnh.edu
CHIN, Elaine 408-924-3601 37 A elaine.chin@sjsu.edu
CHIN, Jean, E 706-542-8715 138 C jchin@uhs.uga.edu
CHIN, Penny, J 516-876-3137 353 D chinp@oldwestbury.edu
CHIN, Sonia 619-849-2958 62 L soniachin@pointloma.edu
CHIN, Steve 718-488-1389 338 H steve.chin@liu.edu
CHIN, Wayman 617-876-0956 236 H wayman.chin@longy.edu
CHIN KEE FATT, Camille 718-780-7963 324 F camille.chinkeefatt@brooklaw.edu
CHINARIS, Tim 334-386-7214 3 H tchinaris@faulkner.edu
CHINDEMI, Craig, T 716-888-8208 325 G chindemc@canisius.edu
CHING, David, M 310-233-4091 54 I chingdm@lahc.edu
CHING-RAPPA, Myrtle 808-956-4399 141 B chingrapp@hawaii.edu
CHINN-JOINTER, June 901-435-1507 470 B june_chinn-jointer@loc.edu
CHINNASWAMY, Sainath 508-678-2811 239 F sainath.chinnaswamy@bristolcc.edu
CHINNIAH, Nim 773-702-8118 166 D nim.chinniah@uchicago.edu
CHINNICI, OFM, Joseph 510-848-5232 47 I jchinnici@fst.edu
CHINWAH, Lovette 937-376-6453 386 H lchinwah@centralstate.edu
CHIPMAN, Nelson 412-392-4306 444 H nchipman@pointpark.edu
CHIPMAN, Sue 478-471-2732 133 E sue.chipman@maconstate.edu
CHIPPS, Michael 308-535-3720 298 I chippsm@mpcc.edu
CHIPREAN, Kristina, B 724-738-2052 443 E kristina.chiprean@sru.edu
CHIRPICH, MaryJo 218-755-2040 266 B mchirpich@bemidjistate.edu
CHISCHILLY, April 505-786-4114 318 H achischilly@navajotech.edu
CHISEM, Lori 205-929-3409 5 E lchisem@lawsonstate.edu
CHISHOLM, Arnett 734-973-3540 260 B achisholm@wccnet.edu
CHISHOLM, Barbara 334-727-8535 8 C chisholm@mytu.tuskegee.edu
CHISHOLM, Brendan, H 508-856-4031 238 A brendan.chisholm@umassmed.edu
CHISHOLM, Bruce 336-599-1181 372 D chishob@piedmontcc.edu
CHISHOLM, Margery 617-724-6446 242 E mchischolm@mghihp.edu
CHISHOLM, Mark, P 505-277-5115 321 C markchis@unm.edu
CHISHOLM, Michael, T 503-725-2500 418 G chisholm@pdx.edu
CHISHOLM, Pam 802-828-2800 515 D chisholp@ccv.edu
CHISLER, Christi, R 909-869-3805 33 G
CHISMAR, William, G 808-956-8866 141 B chismar@hawaii.edu
CHISOLM, Roxanne 662-472-2312 274 F rchisolm@holmescc.edu
CHISSOE, David, H 405-789-7661 412 E david.chissoe@swcu.edu
CHISUM, Virginia, E 432-335-6415 491 F vchisum@odessa.edu
CHITRE, Manoj 909-607-9828 40 C manoj.chitre@cgu.edu
CHITTIM, Del 863-667-5008 118 A dchittim@seu.edu
CHITTUM, Amanda 803-593-9231 455 A chittum@atc.edu
CHITWOOD, Ashley 504-671-6607 210 G achitw@dcc.edu
CHITWOOD, Charles 405-491-6455 412 D cchitwood@snu.edu
CHITWOOD, James 847-969-4915 144 G jchitwood@argosy.edu
CHITWOOD, James 847-969-4915 145 A jchitwood@argosy.edu
CHITWOOD, Jim 410-462-8237 221 D jchitwood@bccc.edu
CHITWOOD, Linda, F 662-915-5526 277 G lchitwoo@olemiss.edu
CHIU, Edward 978-934-4814 237 F Edward_Chiu@uml.edu
CHIU, Yuwen 415-282-7600 28 B yuwenchiu@actcm.edu
CHIUDIONI, Kathy 317-841-6400 175 B kchiudioni@ibcindianapolis.edu
CHLIWNIAK, Luba 520-206-7100 17 I lchliwniak@pima.edu
CHMURA, Michael 781-239-4549 230 G mchmura@babson.edu
CHMURA, Thomas, J 774-455-7270 237 B tchmura@umassp.edu
CHO, Hyun Sung 770-279-0507 129 E revdrcho@gcuniv.edu
CHO, Karen 808-235-7404 142 C kcho@hawaii.edu
CHO, Katherine H, S 213-413-9500 71 B dean@scusoma.edu
CHOATE, Brad, E 479-575-6800 24 C choate@uark.edu
CHOATE, Edward 417-836-6616 286 F edchoate@missouristate.edu
CHOATE, Jim 319-398-7612 186 H jchoate@kirkwood.edu
CHOATE, Michael, J 972-883-2943 505 D mchoate@utdallas.edu
CHOATE, Regina 575-492-2774 319 B rchoate@nmjc.edu
CHOBOT, Karen, M 701-671-2385 382 E karen.chobot@ndscs.edu
CHOCKLEY, Cheri 573-635-6600 285 B cheri@metrobusinesscollege.edu
CHOCKLEY, Randy 573-635-6600 285 B chockrl@metrobusinesscollege.edu
CHODOSH, Hiram 801-581-6571 510 L chodoshh@law.utah.edu
CHOI, Bo Yoon 213-487-0110 45 C officemanager@dula.edu
CHOI, Byong Kie 770-279-0507 129 E bkcdhoi@gmail.com
CHOI, Haesan 562-926-1023 63 B haesanchoi@yahoo.com
CHOI, Henry 714-533-1495 70 B advising@southbaylo.edu
CHOI, Jeff 937-708-5512 405 G jchoi@wilberforce.edu
CHOI, Ji Mi 718-260-3392 346 C jchoi@poly.edu
CHOI, Kyunam 714-525-0088 48 G qchoi3@yahoo.com
CHOI, Linda 773-702-7040 166 D lchoi@uchicago.edu
CHOI, Sun Hee 718-639-3975 129 E eastersun@hanmail.net
CHOI, Sun Young 213-385-2322 79 E
CHOICE, Thomas, L 815-825-2086 155 C tom.choice@kishwaukeecollege.edu
CHOJNICKI, Linda, M 413-782-1315 246 D lchojnic@wne.edu
CHOLETTE, Beth, K 585-245-5716 353 C cholette@geneseo.edu
CHOLICK, Fred, A 785-532-6266 194 B fcholick@ksu.edu
CHOMA, Michael 724-339-7542 437 E thedean@teacher.com
CHOMIAK, Renee DeLong 562-860-2451 38 J rdlchomiak@cerritos.edu
CHONCEK, Christopher 412-392-3905 444 H cchoncek@pointpark.edu
CHONG, Bruce 912-201-8106 136 H bchong@southuniversity.edu
CHONG, James, D 770-279-0507 129 E basicsoccer@gmail.com
CHONG, Jocelyn 310-434-4547 68 D chong_jocelyn@smc.edu
CHONG, Joyce 707-664-2427 37 B joyce.chong@sonoma.edu
CHONG, Philip 800-782-2422 33 B pchong@prodigy.net
CHONG, Philip 800-782-2422 33 B pchong@mail.cnuas.edu
CHONG, Salvacion 808-942-1000 140 H salvacion.chong@remingtoncollege.edu
CHONKO, Arthur, J 740-587-6456 389 H chonko@denison.edu
CHOO, Jeff 617-327-6777 242 C jeff_choo@mspp.edu
CHOO, Taecheong 213-381-2221 64 I tchoo@samra.edu
CHOONOO, John 646-312-2196 326 D john_choonoo@baruch.cuny.edu
CHOONOO, Ralph 201-447-7991 307 F rchoonoo@bergen.edu
CHOPIN, Connie 337-262-5962 209 D cchopin@acadiana.edu
CHOPKA, John, A 717-766-2511 436 D jchopka@messiah.edu
CHOPP, Rebecca, S 610-328-8314 447 E rchopp1@swarthmore.edu
CHORBAJIAN, Gil 518-694-7394 322 C gil.chorbajian@acphs.edu
CHORNEY, Doris 215-965-4051 436 H dchorney@moore.edu
CHOROSZY, Melisa, N 775-784-6181 303 A choroszy@admin.unr.edu
CHOSA, Robin 906-353-4600 253 J rchosa@kbocc.org
CHOTAS, Chrysanne, N 802-656-3192 514 F chrysanne.chotas@uvm.edu
CHOTTINER, Gregg 212-217-3400 333 G gregg_chottiner@fitnyc.edu
CHOU, Lexer 808-455-0248 142 A achou@hawaii.edu
CHOU, Peter 626-448-0023 51 H
CHOU, Victoria 312-996-5641 166 F vchou@uic.edu
CHOUINARD, Mary 909-537-5077 36 A mchouina@csusb.edu
CHOW, Fred 408-741-2635 78 B fred.chow@westvalley.edu
CHOW, Raymond 650-358-6742 67 D chow@smccd.edu
CHOW, Timothy 812-877-8910 179 A timothy.chow@rose-hulman.edu
CHOWDHURY, Faruque 908-737-3300 311 B fchowdhu@kean.edu
CHOWEN, Jodi 808-675-3260 139 I jodi.chowen@byuh.edu
CHOWN, David 563-425-5284 189 C chownd@uiu.edu
CHOWN, Deborah 413-775-1832 240 B chown@gcc.mass.edu
CHOWN, Peggy 563-425-5283 189 C chownp@uiu.edu
CHOWNING, John, E 270-789-5520 199 C jechowning@campbellsville.edu
CHOY, Jonathan 562-903-4742 30 H jonathan.choy@biola.edu
CHOY, Lance, M 650-723-1983 71 F lchoy@stanford.edu
CHREST, Erin 410-225-2493 224 C echrest@mica.edu
CHRESTAY, Joan, F 610-660-1226 446 C joan.chrestay@sju.edu
CHRESTMAN, Charles, V 910-272-3230 373 A cchrestman@robeson.edu
CHRETIEN, Enrica 718-982-2365 327 A
CHRISMAN, Dana 319-208-5017 188 G dchrisman@scciowa.edu
CHRISMAN, Rick 518-580-8340 351 B rchrisma@skidmore.edu
CHRISNER, Carl 417-862-9533 282 D cchrisner@globaluniversity.edu
CHRISOPE, Linda 314-392-2231 286 C chrislc@mobap.edu
CHRISPENS, Pamela 951-785-2002 53 D pchrispe@lasierra.edu
CHRIST, Andrew 201-200-3191 312 B achrist@njcu.edu
CHRIST, Carol, T 413-585-2100 245 B cchrist@smith.edu
CHRIST, Sharon 717-771-4048 440 G sem1@psu.edu
CHRIST, Suzanne 618-545-3069 155 A schrist@kaskaskia.edu
CHRISTAL, Melodie, E 785-670-1876 197 D melodie.christal@washburn.edu
CHRISTEL, Mark, A 330-263-2483 388 E mchristel@wooster.edu
CHRISTENBERRRY, Reid, J 678-891-2830 130 G Reid.Christenberry@gpc.edu
CHRISTENBURY, Elizabeth, S 704-894-2700 363 F bechristenbury@davidson.edu
CHRISTENER, Louise 805-378-1407 77 B lchristener@vcccd.edu
CHRISTENSEN, Angela 612-659-6229 267 E angela.christensen@minneapolis.edu
CHRISTENSEN, April 660-263-3900 279 J aprilc@cccb.edu
CHRISTENSEN, Barbara, W 650-574-6560 67 D christensen@smccd.edu
CHRISTENSEN, Bill 641-472-1156 187 B bchristensen@mum.edu
CHRISTENSEN, Charles 419-448-3268 402 E christensenc@tiffin.edu
CHRISTENSEN, Chris 913-469-8500 193 I cchris20@jccc.edu
CHRISTENSEN, Dale, A 214-828-8250 497 A dchristensen@bcd.tamhsc.edu
CHRISTENSEN, Edward 732-571-3649 311 F echriste@monmouth.edu
CHRISTENSEN, Holly 912-510-3303 127 B hchristensen@ccga.edu
CHRISTENSEN, John, E 402-554-2311 301 B johnchristensen@unomaha.edu
CHRISTENSEN, John, M 410-263-2371 225 G john.christensen@sjca.edu
CHRISTENSEN, Jolene, D 507-933-7538 264 B jolene@gustavus.edu
CHRISTENSEN, Kathleen, E 512-223-1909 481 B kchriste@austincc.edu
CHRISTENSEN, Kay 208-282-5482 143 D chrikay@isu.edu
CHRISTENSEN, Keith, J 563-387-1506 187 A chriskei@luther.edu
CHRISTENSEN, Laure 816-584-6810 287 H laure.christensen@park.edu
CHRISTENSEN, Lisa 651-846-1733 269 E lisa.christensen@saintpaul.edu
CHRISTENSEN, Lisa, M 802-258-9259 513 F lmchrist@marlboro.edu
CHRISTENSEN, Matt 707-253-3340 58 F mchristensen@napavalley.edu
CHRISTENSEN, Nicolette, D 215-572-2907 422 B christen@arcadia.edu
CHRISTENSEN, Rocky 660-263-3900 279 J rockyc@cccb.edu
CHRISTENSEN, Rocky 660-263-3900 279 J
CHRISTENSEN, Scott 972-438-6932 492 C schstnsn@parkercc.edu
CHRISTENSEN, Thomas 719-255-4550 88 C tchriste@uccs.edu
CHRISTENSEN, Tracie 310-794-2308 74 A traciec@support.ucla.edu
CHRISTENSEN, William 435-652-7887 512 A christenb@dixie.edu
CHRISTENSON, John, N 401-841-2266 557 I
CHRISTENSON, Larry 478-445-5160 129 F larry.christenson@gcsu.edu
CHRISTENSON, Timothy, J 571-557-4594 557 G timothy.christenson2@dia.mil
CHRISTENSON-JONES, Marybeth 763-576-4706 266 A mchristenson@anokatech.edu
CHRISTESON, Tracy 210-999-7328 502 C tracy.christeson@trinity.edu

CHRISTIAN, Beth .... 570-389-4102.... 441 F
bchristi@bloomu.edu
CHRISTIAN, Donal .... 718-270-6113.... 328 D
dchristian@mec.cuny.edu
CHRISTIAN, Donald .... 512-313-3000.... 483 G
donald.christian@concordia.edu
CHRISTIAN, Donald, P ...... 845-257-3288.... 352 B
president@newpaltz.edu
CHRISTIAN, Eric .... 340-693-1491.... 568 C
echrist@uvi.edu
CHRISTIAN, Linda .... 800-962-7682.... 293 B
lchristian@wma.edu
CHRISTIAN, Samantha .... 914-674-7841.... 340 G
CHRISTIAN, Sonya .... 541-463-5120.... 416 D
christians@lanecc.edu
CHRISTIAN, Susan, C .... 609-895-5768.... 313 G
christian@rider.edu
CHRISTIANO, Patricia .... 914-674-7622.... 340 G
pchristiano@mercy.edu
CHRISTIANO, Susan .... 518-762-4651.... 334 D
schristi@fmcc.suny.edu
CHRISTIANSEN, Claudia ...... 620-431-2820.... 195 B
cchristiansen@neosho.edu
CHRISTIANSEN, David, J .. 814-898-6160.... 439 E
djc21@psu.edu
CHRISTIANSEN, Douglas ... 615-322-6702.... 477 F
douglas.christiansen@vanderbilt.edu
CHRISTIANSEN,
Jeanne, M .... 208-885-7941.... 144 B
jeannec@uidaho.edu
CHRISTIANSEN, Kari .... 218-855-8060.... 266 C
kchristi@clcmn.edu
CHRISTIANSEN, Kayla .... 903-589-4061.... 490 B
kchristiansen@lonmorris.edu
CHRISTIE, Cynthia, L .... 203-582-3656...... 93 E
cynthia.christie@quinnipiac.edu
CHRISTIE, Marla .... 828-726-2202.... 368 D
mchristie@cccti.edu
CHRISTIE, Marla .... 828-726-2203.... 368 D
mchristie@cccti.edu
CHRISTIE, N. Bradley .... 864-379-8872.... 457 G
nbc@erskine.edu
CHRISTIE, Pamela, L .... 989-837-4212.... 257 A
christie@northwood.edu
CHRISTIE, Ray, L .... 989-774-7062.... 249 G
chris2r@cmich.edu
CHRISTIE, Tori .... 712-325-3293.... 186 B
tchristie@iwcc.edu
CHRISTISON, Dominic .... 610-799-1560.... 434 D
dchristison@lccc.edu
CHRISTL, Richard, I .... 559-442-4600...... 72 A
richard.christl@fresnocitycollege.edu
CHRISTMAN,
Harold (Bud), G .... 828-689-1102.... 366 F
bchristman@mhc.edu
CHRISTMAN, Paul .... 307-268-2633.... 555 F
pchristman@caspercollege.edu
CHRISTMAN, Rick .... 740-474-7217.... 398 C
CHRISTMAN, Vanessa .... 610-526-6594.... 423 C
vchristma@brynmawr.edu
CHRISTMANN, Dan .... 505-287-6673.... 319 H
tazman1@nmsu.edu
CHRISTMAS, Erica, G .... 803-938-3851.... 462 F
mcleodeg@uscsumter.edu
CHRISTMON, Kenneth, C .. 260-481-6605.... 174 A
christmk@ipfw.edu
CHRISTNER, Richard .... 231-591-2163.... 251 B
christnr@ferris.edu
CHRISTOFFERSON,
Kimberlee, K .... 724-946-7247.... 451 C
christkk@westminster.edu
CHRISTOFFERSON,
Martin, G .... 607-844-8222.... 357 H
christm@tc3.edu
CHRISTOPHER, Andrea, D . 717-749-6138.... 440 A
axc8@psu.edu
CHRISTOPHER, Curtis .... 740-420-2847.... 398 C
cchristopher@ohiochristian.edu
CHRISTOPHER, Dan .... 518-631-9843.... 358 F
christopherd@uniongraduatecollege.edu
CHRISTOPHER, Doris .... 478-752-4278.... 129 F
doris.christopher@gcsu.edu
CHRISTOPHER, Greg, T ...... 417-268-6009.... 279 D
gchristopher@gobbc.edu
CHRISTOPHER,
Gregory, A .... 419-372-7052.... 385 C
gachris@bgsu.edu
CHRISTOPHER, Jennifer .... 201-360-4061.... 310 F
jchristopher@hccc.edu
CHRISTOPHER, Mario .... 312-332-0707.... 165 H
CHRISTOPHER, Marv .... 707-654-1050...... 32 I
mchristopher@csum.edu
CHRISTOPHER, Renny .... 805-437-8994...... 33 I
renny.christopher@csuci.edu
CHRISTOPHER, Robert .... 563-333-6260.... 188 D
ChristopherRobert@sau.edu
CHRISTOPHER, Ronald, J . 716-880-2485.... 340 E
ronald.j.christopher@medaille.edu
CHRISTOPHER-HICKS,
Joann .... 410-951-3933.... 228 B
jchristopher-hicks@coppin.edu
CHRISTOPHERSON,
Carolyn .... 831-459-4886...... 75 A
carolync@ucsc.edu
CHRISTOPHERSON, Karen 707-468-3091...... 57 A
kchristo@mendocino.edu
CHRISTOPHERSON,
Michelle .... 218-281-8679.... 272 A
mchristo@umn.edu
CHRISTOPHERSON,
Neal, J .... 509-527-5056.... 539 E
christnj@whitman.edu
CHRISTUS, Barbara, A .... 262-524-7124.... 546 E
bchristus@carrollu.edu
CHRISTY, Benjamin, C .... 716-878-6326.... 353 A
christy@buffalostate.edu
CHRISTY, David, P .... 805-756-2705...... 33 F
dchristy@calpoly.edu
CHRISTY, Gregory, E .... 712-707-7100.... 188 B
president@nwciowa.edu
CHRISTY, John, R .... 256-961-7763........ 9 A
christy@nsstc.uah.edu
CHRISTY, Jon, A .... 563-387-1016.... 187 A
chrijo01@luther.edu
CHRISTY, Kathy .... 417-447-6963.... 287 G
christyk@otc.edu
CHRISTY, Kathy .... 724-463-0222.... 424 B
CHRISTY, Michelle, D .... 617-324-9022.... 242 A
mchristy@mit.edu
CHRITE, E. LaBrent .... 973-655-4304.... 311 G
chritee@mail.montclair.edu
CHRUSZCZYK, Cynthia, A . 305-899-3125.... 101 F
cchruszczyk@mail.barry.edu
CHRYSANTHOU, Juanita ... 916-558-2139...... 56 D
CHRYSSIS, George, C .... 617-423-4630.... 231 E
gchryssis@bfit.edu
CHRZASTEK, OP, Brian ..... 202-495-3842...... 98 D
bchrzastek@dhs.edu
CHU, Don .... 760-750-4311...... 36 B
dchu@csusm.edu
CHU, Dragon .... 512-444-8082.... 499 B
CHU, Jason, Y .... 425-558-0299.... 533 C
jchu@digipen.edu
CHUDNOFSKY, Robert ...... 707-778-3628...... 68 E
rchudnofsky@santarosa.edu
CHUDNOVSKY, Marina ...... 847-324-5588.... 168 H
CHUDY, Beverly .... 716-926-8940.... 335 F
bchudy@hilbert.edu
CHUKS, Samuel .... 251-405-7021........ 2 D
schuks@bishop.edu
CHULVICK, Charles, E .... 908-526-1200.... 313 E
cchulvic@raritanval.edu
CHUMAN, Jerilyn .... 949-582-4573...... 70 F
jchuman@saddleback.edu
CHUMLEY, Heidi .... 913-588-7201.... 197 A
hchumley@kumc.edu
CHUMLEY, Josh .... 508-614-4020...... 19 C
josh.chumley@phoenix.edu
CHUN, Dawn .... 760-355-6286...... 50 K
dawn.chun@imperial.edu
CHUN, Edna .... 336-334-5167.... 379 A
e_chun@uncg.edu
CHUN, Leanne .... 808-455-0676.... 142 A
leannech@hawaii.edu
CHUNG, Bernie .... 610-896-1106.... 430 G
bchung@haverford.edu
CHUNG, Byron .... 415-865-0198...... 30 B
bchung@aii.edu
CHUNG, Jin .... 213-252-5100...... 26 C
CHUNG, Jo Kam .... 770-279-0507.... 129 E
chungjok@gcuniv.edu
CHUNG, Munghwa .... 213-381-2221...... 64 I
mchung@samra.edu
CHUNG, Peggy .... 718-779-1430.... 346 B
pchung@plazacollege.edu
CHUNG, Rhea .... 213-763-7149...... 55 D
chungj@lattc.edu
CHUNG, Sean .... 240-684-2542.... 227 F
enroll@umuc.edu
CHUNG, Silvan .... 808-845-9404.... 141 G
silvan@hawaii.edu
CHUNG, Wing-Kit .... 503-977-4250.... 419 G
wchung@pcc.edu
CHUNN, Robert, P .... 813-253-7260.... 110 I
rchunn@hccfl.edu
CHUPP, Tim .... 616-222-3000.... 254 A
tchupp@kuyper.edu
CHURCH, Cathy .... 928-350-4100...... 18 C
cchurch@prescott.edu
CHURCH, Daniel, K .... 425-602-3003.... 530 K
dchurch@bastyr.edu
CHURCH, Darline .... 706-754-7704.... 134 E
dchurch@northgatech.edu
CHURCH, David, B .... 206-281-2602.... 537 D
dchurch@spu.edu
CHURCH, Ginger .... 864-596-9055.... 457 E
ginger.church@converse.edu
CHURCH, Jennifer, H .... 517-264-7143.... 258 D
jhchurch@sienaheights.edu
CHURCH, John .... 610-989-1450.... 450 E
jchurch@vfmac.edu
CHURCH, Jonathan .... 215-572-4017.... 422 B
church@arcadia.edu
CHURCH, Lori .... 843-349-2751.... 456 G
lchurch@coastal.edu
CHURCH, Melinda .... 614-247-4573.... 398 H
church.104@osu.edu
CHURCH, Roy, A .... 440-365-5222.... 395 C
CHURCH, Vicki .... 503-682-1862.... 419 F
vchurch@pioneerpacific.edu
CHURCH-GONZALES,
Hunter .... 559-730-3805...... 42 B
hunterc@cos.edu
CHURCHILL, Brian .... 508-830-5051.... 239 A
bchurchill@maritime.edu
CHURCHILL, Carol, A .... 989-386-6602.... 255 F
cchurchill@midmich.edu
CHURCHILL, Clifford, W .... 772-546-5534.... 110 J
cliffchurchill@hsbc.edu
CHURCHILL, Mark .... 617-585-1130.... 243 E
mark.churchill@necmusic.edu
CHURCHILL, Monte .... 956-447-6631.... 494 D
mchurch@southtexascollege.edu
CHURCHILL, Robert .... 573-884-9080.... 291 D
churchillr@missouri.edu
CHURCHILL, Sally, J .... 734-763-5553.... 259 D
sjc@umich.edu
CHURCHILL, Sarah .... 860-434-5232...... 93 A
schurchill@lymeacademy.edu
CHURCHILL, Steve .... 510-524-5264...... 60 F
schurchill@plts.edu
CHURCHWELL, Dennis ...... 806-894-9611.... 494 C
dchurchwell@southplainscollege.edu
CHUSID, Eileen .... 212-410-8127.... 343 B
echusid@nycpm.edu
CHUTE, Patricia .... 516-686-3939.... 343 D
pchute@nyit.edu
CHYCINSKI, Jodi .... 616-331-2025.... 252 A
chycinsj@gvsu.edu
CHYKA, Robert, D .... 716-880-2343.... 340 E
robert.d.chyka@medaille.edu
CHYR, Fred, A .... 909-593-3511...... 75 C
fchyr@laverne.edu
CHYTKA, Evelyn, J .... 307-766-2398.... 556 E
jchytka@uwyo.edu
CIABOCCHI, Elizabeth .... 516-299-3990.... 338 F
liz.ciabocchi@liu.edu
CIACCIO, Dolores .... 631-420-2411.... 356 A
CIACIUCH, Denis .... 419-267-1407.... 397 D
dciaciuch@northweststate.edu
CIAMBOR, Thaddeus, J ...... 585-292-2310.... 341 H
tciambor@monroecc.edu
CIANCHETTA, Susan, A ...... 410-827-5811.... 222 B
scianchetta@chesapeake.edu
CIANCI, Karen .... 559-453-2273...... 47 K
karen.cianci@fresno.edu
CIANELLI, Shannon, N .... 301-766-3708.... 223 G
scianelli@kaplan.edu
CIARALDI, Penne .... 802-828-4060.... 515 D
ciaraldp@ccv.edu
CIARAVINO, Asia .... 210-434-6711.... 491 G
ahciaravino@lake.ollusa.edu
CIBIRKA, Roman, M .... 706-721-3096.... 130 B
rcibirka@georgiahealth.edu
CIBUZAR, Jean .... 202-651-5282...... 97 E
jean.cibuzar@gallaudet.edu
CICALA, RSM, Joseph, J .... 610-796-8211.... 421 F
joe.cicala@alvernia.edu
CICCARELLI, Mark .... 724-774-2400.... 541 D
mciccarelli@mountainstate.edu
CICCARINO,
Christopher, M .... 973-761-9576.... 311 A
christopher.ciccarino@shu.edu
CICCAZZO, Michele .... 305-348-5344.... 119 B
Michele.Ciccazzo@fiu.edu
CICERO, John .... 312-281-3376.... 162 I
jcicero@roosevelt.edu
CICHOCKI, Eileen .... 707-468-3067...... 57 A
ecichock@mendocino.edu
CICHOMSKA, Grace, J .... 708-524-6288.... 150 A
gcichomska@dom.edu
CICHON, Mark .... 920-498-5759.... 555 A
mark.cichon@nwtc.edu
CICHONSKI, Michael .... 413-552-2567.... 240 C
mcichonski@hcc.edu
CICHY, Evelina .... 815-825-2086.... 155 C
ejcichy@kishwaukeecollege.edu
CICIRELLI, Anna .... 201-761-6036.... 314 F
acicirelli@spc.edu
CICIRELLO, Pam .... 501-812-2774...... 23 C
pcicirello@pulaskitech.edu
CICOTELLO, David .... 615-898-2111.... 473 F
david.cicotell@mtsu.edu
CID, Carmen, R .... 860-465-5295...... 91 H
cid@easternct.edu
CID, Rolando .... 787-738-2161.... 567 A
rolando.cid@upr.edu
CIDDIO, Steve, A .... 505-662-0337.... 321 E
sac@unm.edu
CIESLICA, Jeanmarie, O ..... 716-888-2711.... 325 G
cieslicj@canisius.edu
CIFONE, Rocky .... 949-582-4773...... 70 F
rcifone@saddleback.edu
CIGANOVIC, Denny, D .... 843-953-5692.... 457 B
ciganovicd@cofc.edu
CIGARROA, Francisco, G ... 512-499-4201.... 504 E
chancellor@utsystem.edu
CIGELMAN, M. Susan .... 515-244-4221.... 181 D
cigelmans@aib.edu
CIHA, Lisa .... 319-399-8669.... 183 C
lciha@coe.edu
CIHLAR, Larry .... 715-422-5308.... 554 C
larry.cihlar@mstc.edu
CILENTO, Eugene, V .... 304-293-4157.... 544 E
gene.cilento@mail.wvu.edu
CILIBERTI, Anne .... 973-720-3179.... 317 D
ciliberta@wpunj.edu
CILIBERTI, Scott .... 415-575-6143...... 32 D
sciliberti@ciis.edu
CILIBERTI, Scott .... 415-369-5365...... 48 E
sciliberti@ggu.edu
CILL, Donna .... 973-972-9793.... 316 H
cilldm@umdnj.edu
CILLAY, David .... 509-335-5454.... 539 A
dcillay@wsu.edu
CILLO, Robert .... 303-546-3506...... 86 B
bcillo@naropa.edu
CIMBOLIC, Peter .... 614-251-4690.... 398 F
cimbolicp@ohiodominican.edu
CIMILLUCA, Maria, T .... 717-291-4372.... 429 E
maria.cimilluca@fandm.edu
CIMINELLI, Mary .... 972-273-3130.... 485 B
marygciminelli@dcccd.edu
CIMINO, Chris .... 865-974-9880.... 477 B
cimino@utk.edu
CIMINO, James .... 510-885-2263...... 34 C
jim.cimino@csueastbay.edu
CIMMINO, Michael .... 407-277-0311.... 106 G
mcimmino@evergladesuniversity.edu
CIMORELLI, Nick .... 843-863-7581.... 456 B
ncimorel@csuniv.edu
CINAR, Ali .... 312-567-3637.... 153 B
cinar@iit.edu
CINCLAIR, Richard, J .... 972-860-7156.... 484 H
RCinclair@dcccd.edu
CINI, Marie .... 240-684-2800.... 227 F
mcini@umuc.edu
CINNAMON, Gary .... 760-750-4675...... 36 B
cinnamon@csusm.edu
CINTORINO, Salvatore .... 860-832-1889...... 91 G
cintorino@ccsu.edu
CINTRON, Carmen .... 787-728-1515.... 568 B
crcintron@sagrado.edu
CINTRON, Doris .... 212-650-5471.... 326 H
dcintron@ccny.cuny.edu
CINTRON, Edgardo .... 787-857-3600.... 563 A
ecintron@br.inter.edu
CINTRON, Josue .... 787-753-6000.... 562 E
jcintron@icprjc.edu
CINTRON, Maribel .... 305-573-1600.... 100 K
mcintron@atienterprises.edu
CINTRON, Nancy, A .... 718-960-8366.... 327 C
nancy.cintron@lehman.cuny.edu
CINTRON, Raul .... 787-763-4215.... 567 F
raul.cintron@uprrp.edu
CINTRON, Rene .... 504-671-6138.... 210 G
rcintr@dcc.edu
CINTRON, Sifilonena .... 787-857-3600.... 563 A
CINTRON-OTERO, Carmen 787-993-8922.... 566 G
carmen.cintron2@upr.edu
CIOC, Mark .... 831-459-4908...... 75 A
cioc@ucsc.edu
CIOCE, Michael .... 609-894-9311.... 308 C
mcioce@bcc.edu
CIOLEK, Anne .... 716-375-2102.... 348 C
aciolek@sbu.edu
CIOLINO, Salvatore .... 717-337-6582.... 429 H
sciolino@gettysburg.edu
CIOPPA, Lee .... 212-799-5000.... 337 H
CIORRA, Anthony, J .... 718-817-4802.... 334 C
ciorra@fordham.edu
CIOSEK, Edward .... 413-748-3108.... 245 C
eciosek@spfldcol.edu
CIOTOLI, Carlo .... 212-443-1297.... 344 B
carlo.ciotoli@nyu.edu
CIPFL, Joseph, J .... 618-537-6462.... 157 G
jjcipfl@mckendree.edu
CIPOLLA, Anthony .... 845-848-7814.... 332 C
anthony.cipolla@dc.edu
CIPRES, Elizabeth .... 949-451-5410...... 70 E
ecipres@ivc.edu
CIPRIANI, Colleen .... 614-234-5828.... 396 G
ccipriani@mccn.edu
CIPRIANO, Eli .... 713-743-8901.... 503 A
ecipriano@uh.edu
CIPRIANO, Matt, J .... 215-968-8255.... 423 E
cipriano@bucks.edu
CIPRO, Cheryl .... 914-395-2525.... 350 C
ccipro@sarahlawrence.edu
CIPULLO, Donald, D .... 973-655-5105.... 311 G
cipullod@mail.montclair.edu
CIRAC, Maxine .... 775-423-4281.... 303 B
mcirac@wnc.edu
CIRASA, Robert .... 732-255-0356.... 311 B
rcirasa@kean.edu
CIRAULO, Paul .... 212-517-0531.... 340 D
pciraulo@mmm.edu
CIRBEE, Carolann .... 540-338-2700.... 517 D
ccirbee@cdu.edu
CIRI, Michael .... 907-796-6452...... 11 A
michael.ciri@uas.alaska.edu
CIRILLO, Susan .... 978-542-6232.... 239 B
scirillo@salemstate.edu
CIRMO, Christopher .... 715-346-4224.... 552 B
ccirmo@uwsp.edu
CISAR, Mary .... 507-786-3015.... 271 H
cisar@stolaf.edu

CISCO, OSB, Bede .... 812-357-6611.... 179 E
bcisco@saintmeinrad.edu
CISKANIK, John, F .... 540-636-2900.... 517 H
ciskanik@christendom.edu
CISNEROS, Maria .... 504-671-5022.... 210 G
mcisne@dcc.edu
CISNEROS, Suzanna .... 806-743-2143.... 501 E
suzanna.cisneros@ttuhsc.edu
CISNEROS, Teo .... 210-924-4338.... 481 G
teo.cisneros@bua.edu
CISSELL, Jason, A .... 502-272-8329.... 198 E
jcissell@bellarmine.edu
CITRON, Chaim .... 323-937-3763..... 79 J
CITRON, Lois .... 212-962-0002.... 342 G
CIUFFO, Patricia .... 212-463-0400.... 357 J
patricia.ciuffo@touro.edu
CIUFULESCU, Sally .... 620-331-4100.... 193 G
sciufulescu@indycc.edu
CIULLO, Carol .... 888-254-4238.... 517 D
cciullo@cdu.edu
CLABORN, Dave .... 740-389-6786.... 399 D
claborn.17@osu.edu
CLACK, Olivia .... 870-574-4481...... 24 A
oclack@sautech.edu
CLADER, Linda, L .... 510-204-0730...... 39 F
lclader@cdsp.edu
CLAFFEY, JR., George, F .. 860-832-3890...... 91 D
gclaffey@charteroak.edu
CLAFFEY, Marian, A .... 773-508-7473.... 157 A
mclaffe@luc.edu
CLAGETT, Craig, A .... 410-386-8163.... 221 G
cclagett@carrollcc.edu
CLAGETT, Susan, W .... 512-471-7753.... 505 B
clagett@mail.utexas.edu
CLAGGETT, Mindy .... 937-298-3399.... 394 D
mindy.claggett@kcma.edu
CLAGHORN, Patricia .... 856-468-5000.... 310 E
pclaghorn@gccnj.edu
CLAIBORN, Candis .... 509-335-5593.... 539 A
claiborn@wsu.edu
CLAIBORNE, Brenda .... 561-297-2011.... 118 H
CLAIRE, Michael .... 650-574-6222...... 67 F
clairem@smccd.edu
CLAIRMONT, Corky .... 406-275-4946.... 296 F
corwin_clairmont@skc.edu
CLAMURRO, William, H .... 620-341-5899.... 192 D
wclamurr@emporia.edu
CLANCY, Amanda .... 303-678-3736...... 84 H
amanda.clancy@frontrange.edu
CLANCY, Barbara .... 781-768-7243.... 244 D
barbara.clancy@regiscollege.edu
CLANCY, Daniel .... 608-266-7983.... 553 D
daniel.clancy@wtcsystem.edu
CLANCY, Michael .... 616-698-7111.... 250 E
mclancy@davenport.edu
CLANCY, Pauline .... 617-296-8300.... 236 E
pauline_clancy@laboure.edu
CLANCY, SJ, Tim, R .... 509-313-6701.... 534 A
clancy@gonzaga.edu
CLANG, Heather .... 617-349-8769.... 236 G
hclang@lesley.edu
CLANTON, Ann .... 251-575-3156........ 1 B
aclanton@ascc.edu
CLANTON, Janet .... 573-897-5000.... 284 D
CLANTON, Karen .... 256-824-6013........ 9 A
karen.clanton@uah.edu
CLAPP, Jason .... 319-363-8213.... 187 E
jclapp@mtmercy.edu
CLAPP, Kenneth, W .... 704-637-4446.... 363 C
kclapp@catawba.edu
CLAPPER, Cara .... 260-459-4550.... 175 A
cclapper@ibcfortwayne.edu
CLAPPER, Mark, A .... 717-361-1499.... 428 E
clapperm@etown.edu
CLAPPER, Stacie, J .... 740-588-1321.... 407 A
sclapper@zanestate.edu
CLAPPER-DEWELL,
Theophylact .... 315-858-3914.... 336 A
frtheophylact@jordanville.org
CLARD, Bob .... 310-506-6190...... 61 G
bob.clark@pepperdine.edu
CLARDY, Betsy, B .... 409-772-1991.... 507 B
bbclardy@utmb.edu
CLARE, Judith .... 401-232-6090.... 453 A
jclare@bryant.edu
CLARIDA, Traci .... 801-818-8900.... 510 E
traci.clarida@provocollege.edu
CLARIDAY, Sandra .... 423-746-5249.... 476 D
sclariday@twcnet.edu
CLARK, Al, E .... 251-460-7051........ 9 E
aclark@usouthal.edu
CLARK, Alfred, P .... 909-593-3511...... 75 C
aclark@laverne.edu
CLARK, Alice, M .... 662-915-7482.... 277 G
vcrsp@olemiss.edu
CLARK, Allen .... 940-565-2085.... 504 B
allen.clark@unt.edu
CLARK, Anita .... 262-243-5700.... 546 I
anita.clark@cuw.edu
CLARK, Ann, B .... 860-727-6761...... 92 C
aclark@goodwin.edu
CLARK, Annette .... 314-977-8172.... 289 F
aclark43@slu.edu
CLARK, Annie .... 603-880-8308.... 306 C
aclark@thomasmorecollege.edu
CLARK, Benita, I .... 919-866-7894.... 374 E
biclark@waketech.edu
CLARK, Bettye .... 404-880-8667.... 126 I
bclark@cau.edu
CLARK, Beverly .... 228-896-2512.... 275 G
beverly.clark@mgccc.edu
CLARK, Billy, L .... 225-928-7770.... 208 G
CLARK, Bonnie, M .... 727-816-3129.... 114 F
clarkb@phcc.edu
CLARK, Bradd .... 337-482-6986.... 216 D
deanclark@louisiana.edu
CLARK, Brenda .... 912-525-6119.... 136 B
bclark@scad.edu
CLARK, Brian .... 401-427-6920.... 454 B
bclark@risd.edu
CLARK, Bridget .... 845-398-4016.... 349 H
bclark@stac.edu
CLARK, Brock .... 228-497-7634.... 275 G
brock.clark@mgccc.edu
CLARK, Brooks .... 530-226-4763...... 69 H
bclark@simpsonu.edu
CLARK, Bryon .... 580-745-2064.... 412 C
bclark@se.edu
CLARK, Carmenita Renee ... 301-937-8448.... 226 H
cclark@tesst.com
CLARK, Carol .... 904-398-4141.... 121 D
CLARK, Carol .... 931-221-7570.... 473 D
clarkc@apsu.edu
CLARK, Carol, D .... 931-221-7570.... 473 D
clarkc@apsu.edu
CLARK, Carol, M .... 404-413-1509.... 131 C
cclark@gsu.edu
CLARK, Carolyn .... 213-763-5316...... 55 D
cwalker@lattc.edu
CLARK, Cate .... 303-464-2306...... 87 D
cclark@redstone.edu
CLARK, Charles .... 228-896-3809.... 275 G
charles.clark@mgccc.edu
CLARK, Charles, E .... 920-683-4710.... 552 F
charles.clark@uwc.edu
CLARK, Charles, L .... 309-341-7399.... 155 E
clclark@knox.edu
CLARK, Cherry .... 919-466-4400...... 99 D
CLARK, Chip .... 903-566-7431.... 506 C
cclark@uttyler.edu
CLARK, Chris .... 618-634-3233.... 164 C
chrisc@shawneecc.edu
CLARK, Christopher .... 334-833-4498........ 4 E
cclark@huntingdon.edu
CLARK, Craig, R .... 607-587-3101.... 355 C
clarkcr@alfredstate.edu
CLARK, Cynthia, A .... 860-628-4751...... 92 F
cclark@lincolncollegene.edu
CLARK, Dana .... 570-740-0422.... 435 C
dclark@luzerne.edu
CLARK, Daniel .... 616-234-4354.... 251 G
dbclark@grcc.edu
CLARK, Daniel .... 425-602-3064.... 530 K
dclark@bastyr.edu
CLARK, David .... 559-638-3641...... 72 B
david.clark@reedleycollege.edu
CLARK, David .... 651-638-6553.... 261 I
d-clark@bethel.edu
CLARK, David .... 212-346-1590.... 345 F
dclark@pace.edu
CLARK, David .... 701-224-5434.... 382 B
david.clark@bismarckstate.edu
CLARK, David, K .... 651-638-6371.... 261 I
d-clark@bethel.edu
CLARK, Dean .... 262-551-6000.... 546 F
dean@carthage.edu
CLARK, Debbie .... 309-457-2125.... 158 G
dclark@monm.edu
CLARK, Debbie .... 706-771-4049.... 125 D
dclark@augustatech.edu
CLARK, Deborah .... 404-225-4714.... 125 A
dclark@atlantatech.edu
CLARK, Deborah .... 802-586-7711.... 514 E
dclark@sterlingcollege.edu
CLARK, Debra .... 970-943-7005...... 89 B
dclark@western.edu
CLARK, Denise .... 301-405-6266.... 227 B
djclark@umd.edu
CLARK, Dennis .... 510-261-8500...... 61 F
dennis.clark@patten.edu
CLARK, Dennis .... 815-802-8606.... 154 J
dclark@kcc.edu
CLARK, Diana .... 269-782-2110.... 258 E
dclark@swmich.edu
CLARK, Diane .... 318-371-3035.... 211 F
dclark@ltc.edu
CLARK, Donald .... 207-602-2274.... 220 H
dclark@une.edu
CLARK, Donald, A .... 417-836-5509.... 286 F
donclark@missouristate.edu
CLARK, Douglas, E .... 540-365-4551.... 518 J
dclark@ferrum.edu
CLARK, Douglas, R .... 951-785-2244...... 53 D
dclark@lasierra.edu
CLARK, E. Culpepper .... 706-542-4989.... 138 C
cully@uga.edu
CLARK, Ed .... 507-389-6651.... 267 H
edmund.clark@mnsu.edu
CLARK, Elaine, L .... 207-581-1493.... 220 A
elaine.clark@maine.edu
CLARK, Elizabeth .... 617-541-5332.... 241 D
eclark@rcc.mass.edu
CLARK, Erin .... 516-364-0808.... 343 A
eclark@nycollege.edu
CLARK, Frank, A .... 252-492-2061.... 374 D
clark@vgcc.edu
CLARK, Frank, C .... 843-792-2211.... 459 C
clarkf@musc.edu
CLARK, G. Reynolds .... 412-624-4200.... 449 A
clark@pitt.edu
CLARK, Gail .... 765-987-1439.... 171 B
clarkga@earlham.edu
CLARK, Gary, C .... 405-744-6384.... 410 C
gary.clark@okstate.edu
CLARK, Gary, E .... 864-294-3460.... 458 D
gary.clark@furman.edu
CLARK, Gaye .... 910-410-1804.... 372 G
agclark@richmondcc.edu
CLARK, Geno .... 706-396-8118.... 135 C
gclark@paine.edu
CLARK, George .... 509-963-2323.... 531 G
clarkg@cwu.edu
CLARK, Ginger .... 813-253-7022.... 110 I
gclark@hccfl.edu
CLARK, Harold, E .... 504-286-5119.... 214 I
hclark@suno.edu
CLARK, Helen .... 252-446-0436.... 370 A
clarkh@edgecombe.edu
CLARK, Irvin .... 912-358-3118.... 136 C
clarki@savannahstate.edu
CLARK, J. Milton .... 909-537-5032...... 36 A
mclark@csusb.edu
CLARK, Jackie .... 910-521-6264.... 379 B
jackie.clark@uncp.edu
CLARK, Jacqueline .... 718-262-5213.... 329 B
jclark@york.cuny.edu
CLARK, James .... 218-333-6600.... 268 F
jim.clark@ntcmn.edu
CLARK, James, A .... 334-844-4765........ 1 G
clarkj3@auburn.edu
CLARK, James, L .... 816-322-0110.... 279 H
president@calvary.edu
CLARK, James, R .... 256-824-2679........ 9 A
james.clark@uah.edu
CLARK, James, R .... 806-651-2585.... 498 D
jclark@mail.wtamu.edu
CLARK, James, T .... 304-336-8043.... 544 B
clarkj@westliberty.edu
CLARK, Jamie, K .... 740-588-1222.... 407 A
jclark@zanestate.edu
CLARK, Janet .... 812-535-5182.... 179 C
jclark@smwc.edu
CLARK, Jayne, V .... 215-572-3846.... 451 D
jclark@wts.edu
CLARK, Jeanian .... 540-868-7122.... 526 H
jclark@lfcc.edu
CLARK, Jeffrey, A .... 518-580-5929.... 351 B
jclark@skidmore.edu
CLARK, Jennifer, R .... 312-915-7819.... 157 A
jclark7@luc.edu
CLARK, Jerry .... 601-984-5012.... 277 H
jclark@umc.edu
CLARK, Jerry, W .... 336-334-4822.... 370 E
jwclark@gtcc.edu
CLARK, Jill .... 712-325-3285.... 186 B
jclark@iwcc.edu
CLARK, Jim .... 859-622-1509.... 200 D
james.clark@eku.edu
CLARK, Jimmy .... 479-979-1484...... 26 A
jclark@ozarks.edu
CLARK, Joan .... 914-633-2046.... 336 E
jclark@iona.edu
CLARK, John .... 603-577-6529.... 304 J
clark@dwc.edu
CLARK, John, L .... 419-372-0657.... 385 D
jlclark@bgsu.edu
CLARK, John, P .... 603-535-2750.... 307 B
jpclark@plymouth.edu
CLARK, John, S .... 865-694-6601.... 475 F
jclark@pstcc.edu
CLARK, Justin .... 806-742-2020.... 501 D
justin.clark@ttu.edu.
CLARK, Karen .... 254-299-8689.... 490 E
kclark@mclennan.edu
CLARK, Karen .... 765-973-8257.... 173 D
krclark@iue.edu
CLARK, Karen .... 574-520-4845.... 174 C
kbclark@iusb.edu
CLARK, Katherine .... 704-357-8020.... 361 N
kmclark@aii.edu
CLARK, Kathleen .... 808-543-8022.... 140 B
kclark@hpu.edu
CLARK, Kellie, E .... 708-709-3725.... 161 C
kclark@prairiestate.edu
CLARK, Kevin, D .... 610-519-4330.... 450 G
kevin.d.clark@villanova.edu
CLARK, Kim .... 814-868-9900.... 428 H
clarkk@erieit.edu
CLARK, Kim, B .... 208-496-1111.... 142 G
clarkk@byui.edu
CLARK, Kira .... 303-530-2100...... 81 E
dclark@bcmt.org
CLARK, Kristin .... 714-432-5897...... 41 B
kclark@occ.cccd.edu
CLARK, Kyle .... 806-742-4250.... 501 D
kyle.clark@ttu.edu
CLARK, Kym .... 432-264-5124.... 487 I
kclark@howardcollege.edu
CLARK, L. Nathan, N .... 775-856-2266.... 301 H
nclark@ccnn4u.com
CLARK, Laron, J .... 757-727-5356.... 519 C
laron.clark@hamptonu.edu
CLARK, Larry .... 425-352-8633.... 531 F
lclark@cascadia.edu
CLARK, Larry, D .... 620-341-5372.... 192 D
lclark@emporia.edu
CLARK, Lawrence, S .... 910-962-7301.... 379 C
clarkl@uncw.edu
CLARK, Lela .... 910-521-6262.... 379 B
lela.clark@uncp.edu
CLARK, Lesa, C .... 757-683-4406.... 521 L
lclark@odu.edu
CLARK, Linda, J .... 360-442-2100.... 535 C
lclark@lowercolumbia.edu
CLARK, Lloyd .... 502-863-7074.... 200 G
lloyd_clark@georgetowncollege.edu
CLARK, Loretta .... 615-383-3230.... 466 H
clarkl@dominicancampus.org
CLARK, Margie .... 517-483-1461.... 254 D
clarkm@lcc.edu
CLARK, Marilyn .... 909-599-5433...... 54 A
mclark@lifepacific.edu
CLARK, Marlin .... 801-957-4004.... 512 C
marlin.clark@slcc.edu
CLARK, Martin .... 937-395-8607.... 394 D
martin.clark@khnetwork.org
CLARK, Mary .... 501-977-2011...... 25 G
clark@uaccm.edu
CLARK, MaryAnn .... 516-299-2486.... 339 A
maryann.clark@liu.edu
CLARK, OSB, Matthew .... 985-867-2245.... 214 F
mrclark@sjasc.edu
CLARK, Michael .... 910-521-6815.... 379 B
michael.clark@uncp.edu
CLARK, Michael, P .... 949-824-4501...... 73 H
mpclark@uci.edu
CLARK, Nancy .... 386-740-1215.... 100 F
CLARK, Nancy, L .... 225-578-2735.... 212 F
nclark@lsu.edu
CLARK, Naoma .... 940-397-4544.... 491 A
naoma.clark@mwsu.edu
CLARK, Nathaniel .... 323-357-3674...... 39 D
nathanielclark@cdrewu.edu
CLARK, Nick .... 662-476-5075.... 274 D
nclark@eastms.edu
CLARK, Nigel, N .... 304-293-4813.... 544 E
nigel.clark@mail.wvu.edu
CLARK, Pam .... 989-686-9225.... 250 F
pamelaclark@delta.edu
CLARK, Patrick .... 408-453-9900...... 50 E
pclark@henley-putnam.edu
CLARK, Paul .... 704-463-3076.... 375 E
paul.clark@fsmail.pfeiffer.edu
CLARK, Paul, E .... 610-921-7708.... 421 D
pclark@alb.edu
CLARK, Perry .... 440-834-3761.... 393 G
pclark@kent.edu
CLARK, R. Kent .... 559-278-5333...... 34 D
rkclark@csufresno.edu
CLARK, R. Yvette .... 617-873-0171.... 233 B
Yvette.Clark@cambridgecollege.edu
CLARK, Richard .... 404-894-1940.... 130 D
rick.clark@admiss.gatech.edu
CLARK, Richard .... 702-895-1469.... 302 K
richard.clark@unlv.edu
CLARK, Rick .... 562-907-4986...... 79 B
rclark@whittier.edu
CLARK, Robert .... 404-880-6623.... 126 I
rclark@cau.edu
CLARK, Robert, A .... 207-941-7138.... 218 A
clarkr@husson.edu
CLARK, Robert, E .... 940-397-4179.... 491 A
robert.clark@mwsu.edu
CLARK, II, Robert, E .... 410-293-7005.... 558 H
rclarkii@usna.edu
CLARK, Robert, M .... 913-897-8400.... 196 F
rmclark@ku.edu
CLARK, Rodney .... 508-678-2811.... 239 F
rodney.clark@bristolcc.edu
CLARK, Ron .... 309-649-6303.... 165 D
ronald.clark@src.edu
CLARK, Ron, M .... 972-238-6277.... 485 C
rclark@dcccd.edu
CLARK, S. Kay .... 615-366-4411.... 473 C
kay.clark@tbr.edu
CLARK, III, Samuel, J .... 910-630-7020.... 366 H
sclark@methodist.edu
CLARK, Sandra, G .... 443-412-2342.... 223 B
sclark@harford.edu
CLARK, Sara, M .... 417-836-6105.... 286 F
saraclark@missouristate.edu
CLARK, Sarah .... 619-201-8702...... 65 D
Sarah.Clark@sdcc.edu

CLEMMER, Robert .... 540-234-9261.... 525 G
clemmerr@brcc.edu
CLEMMONS, Sarah .... 850-718-2213.... 102 H
clemmonss@chipola.edu
CLEMO, Lorrie, A .... 315-312-2290.... 354 A
lorrie.clemo@oswego.edu
CLEMONS, Brian .... 816-781-7700.... 293 D
clemonsb@william.jewell.edu
CLEMONS, Cheryl .... 270-686-4250.... 198 G
cheryl.clemons@brescia.edu
CLEMONS, Chuck .... 352-395-5200.... 117 E
chuck.clemons@sfcollege.edu
CLEMONS, Lai-L .... 620-229-6168.... 196 C
lai-l.clemons@sckans.edu
CLEMONS, Linda .... 813-253-7160.... 110 I
lclemons@hccfl.edu
CLEMONS, Lorenzo .... 312-850-7167.... 147 C
lclemons4@ccc.edu
CLEMONS, Tammy .... 859-985-3524.... 198 F
clemonst@berea.edu
CLEMONS, Teresa .... 806-651-2647.... 498 D
tclemons@mail.wtamu.edu
CLENDENIN, Larry .... 505-984-6060.... 320 C
admissions@sjcsf.edu
CLENDINNING, David .... 304-766-3239.... 544 D
bdclendinning@wvstateu.edu
CLENNON, Hopeton, C ...... 610-861-1411.... 436 I
chclennon@moravian.edu
CLERKIN, Elizabeth .... 440-775-8450.... 397 F
liz.clerkin@oberlin.edu
CLEROU, Diane .... 559-244-5977...... 71 I
diane.clerou@scccd.edu
CLESCERI, Michael .... 815-479-7833.... 157 F
mclesceri@mchenry.edu
CLEVELAND, SR., Alvin, A 334-872-2533........ 6 H
aclevesr@aol.com
CLEVELAND, Arthur .... 951-343-4215...... 31 G
acleveland@calbaptist.edu
CLEVELAND, Ashley .... 913-234-0648.... 191 G
ashley.cleveland@cleveland.edu
CLEVELAND, Ashley .... 323-660-6166...... 40 G
ashley.cleveland@cleveland.edu
CLEVELAND, III, Carl, S ... 323-660-6166...... 40 G
carl.clevelandiii@cleveland.edu
CLEVELAND, III, Carl, S ... 913-234-0600.... 191 G
carl.clevelandiii@cleveland.edu
CLEVELAND, Charles, E .... 509-527-5158.... 539 E
clevelan@whitman.edu
CLEVELAND, Christy, H ..... 859-846-5485.... 204 D
ccleveland@midway.edu
CLEVELAND, Debbie .... 360-442-2241.... 535 C
dcleveland@lowercolumbia.edu
CLEVELAND, Essie .... 501-812-2212...... 23 C
ecleveland@pulaskitech.edu
CLEVELAND, Iesha, M .... 919-536-7202.... 369 G
clevelai@durhamtech.edu
CLEVENGER, Aaron .... 386-226-6037.... 105 B
aaron.clevenger@erau.edu
CLEVENGER, Brian .... 217-206-6709.... 167 A
clevenger.brian@uis.edu
CLEVENGER, Julie .... 217-786-2365.... 156 I
julie.clevenger@llcc.edu
CLEVENGER, Timothy, R .... 541-346-7036.... 419 B
trc@uoregon.edu
CLEVERING, Peter .... 708-239-4770.... 165 I
peter.clevering@trnty.edu
CLIATT, Cass .... 609-258-6108.... 313 A
ccliatt@princeton.edu
CLICK, Ben, A .... 240-895-4253.... 226 A
baclick@smcm.edu
CLICK, Sally, E .... 317-940-9854.... 170 C
sclick@butler.edu
CLICK, Stanley .... 606-759-7141.... 202 D
stanley.click@kctcs.edu
CLICK, Stanley, W .... 606-783-1538.... 202 D
stanley.click@kctcs.edu
CLICKNER, David .... 518-629-8068.... 336 C
d.clickner@hvcc.edu
CLIFFORD, Christopher ...... 205-934-8229........ 8 G
cbcliff@uab.edu
CLIFFORD, Joan .... 518-244-2410.... 348 A
cliffj3@sage.edu
CLIFFORD, Michael .... 310-377-5501...... 56 F
mclifford@marymountpv.edu
CLIFFORD, Patrick .... 732-235-8544.... 317 A
CLIFFORD, Paul .... 252-328-6072.... 377 C
cliffordp@ecu.edu
CLIFT, Carla .... 256-551-3120........ 4 J
carla.clift@drakestate.edu
CLIFT, Edward .... 818-767-0888...... 79 D
edward.clift@woodbury.edu
CLIFTON, Gaye, B .... 336-342-4261.... 373 B
cliftong@rockinghamcc.edu
CLIFTON, Mary .... 315-652-6500.... 325 A
mclifton@bryantstratton.edu
CLIFTON, Mary .... 315-472-6603.... 325 E
mclifton@bryantstratton.edu
CLIFTON, Maurice .... 570-504-7000.... 425 F
CLIFTON, Warren .... 318-869-5108.... 208 F
wclifton@centenary.edu
CLINARD, Rhonda .... 931-363-9820.... 470 E
rclinard@martinmethodist.edu
CLINE, Dave .... 678-915-7495.... 137 C
dcline@spsu.edu
CLINE, Glen, E .... 607-587-3917.... 355 C
clinege@alfredstate.edu
CLINE, Glenda .... 765-966-2656.... 176 F
gcline@ivytech.edu
CLINE, J. Robert .... 864-231-2077.... 455 C
bcline@andersonuniversity.edu
CLINE, Janet, H .... 816-604-2326.... 285 G
janet.cline@mcckc.edu
CLINE, Joshua .... 276-326-4208.... 516 I
jcline@bluefield.edu
CLINE, Kimberly, R .... 914-674-7307.... 340 G
kcline@mercy.edu
CLINE, Margaret .... 573-341-6995.... 292 A
cline@mst.edu
CLINE, Patricia .... 931-553-0071.... 471 G
patricia.cline@miller-motte.com
CLINE, Robert, J .... 814-871-5615.... 429 F
cline001@gannon.edu
CLINE, Tamara .... 530-283-0202...... 47 B
tcline@frc.edu
CLINE, Thomas, G .... 847-491-5608.... 160 D
t-cline@northwestern.edu
CLINE, Tricia .... 785-628-4091.... 192 F
tcline@fhsu.edu
CLINEFELTER, David .... 612-312-2356.... 272 F
david.clinefelter@waldenu.edu
CLINGMAN, A. Michele ...... 575-492-2545.... 319 B
mclingman@nmjc.edu
CLINK, Wendy .... 954-201-7533.... 102 A
wclink@broward.edu
CLINTON, Adele .... 956-364-4302.... 499 J
adele.clinton@harlingen.tstc.edu
CLINTON, Antwan, D .... 202-238-2661...... 98 B
aclinton@howard.edu
CLINTON, Christine, M ...... 814-886-6380.... 437 A
cclinton@mtaloy.edu
CLINTON, Don .... 903-693-2055.... 492 A
dclinton@panola.edu
CLINTON, Jack .... 503-494-8801.... 418 D
CLINTON, John .... 405-974-3773.... 413 B
jclinton@ucok.edu
CLINTON, John .... 717-477-1377.... 443 D
jeclin@sufoundation.org
CLINTON, Joseph .... 845-848-7700.... 332 C
joseph.clinton@dc.edu
CLINTON, Linda, T .... 903-886-5139.... 497 E
linda_clinton@tamu-commerce.edu
CLINTON, Ron .... 903-434-8186.... 491 D
rclinton@ntcc.edu
CLIPPERTON, Ken .... 402-941-6005.... 299 A
clipperton@midlandu.edu
CLISH, Colleen .... 651-523-2468.... 264 C
cclish01@hamline.edu
CLITES, Mona .... 301-784-5000.... 221 A
mclites@allegany.edu
CLOCK, Joyce .... 218-733-5930.... 267 B
j.clock@lsc.edu
CLODFELTER, Elaine .... 704-272-5302.... 373 F
eclodfelter@spcc.edu
CLODFELTER, JR.,
Roger, D .... 336-841-9156.... 365 A
rclodfel@highpoint.edu
CLOETE, Marion, E .... 619-239-0391...... 37 D
mcloete@cwsl.edu
CLOKEY, Michael .... 505-428-1214.... 320 E
michael.clokey@sfccc.edu
CLONINGER, Mindy, E ...... 620-235-4241.... 195 I
mcloning@pittstate.edu
CLOONAN, Michele .... 617-521-2806.... 245 A
michele.cloonan@simmons.edu
CLOOS, Kevin, P .... 716-673-3452.... 352 A
kevin.cloos@fredonia.edu
CLOPTON, John, D .... 319-296-4004.... 185 C
john.clopton@hawkeyecollege.edu
CLOSE, Cathy .... 715-232-1235.... 552 C
closec@uwstout.edu
CLOSE, Cindy .... 330-494-6170.... 402 A
cclose@starkstate.edu
CLOSE, Steve .... 443-334-2690.... 226 E
sclose@stevenson.edu
CLOSIUS, Phil .... 410-837-4458.... 229 A
pclosius@ubalt.edu
CLOSTERMAN, Jane, E ...... 573-882-2411.... 291 C
clostermanj@umsystem.edu
CLOTFELTER, James, H ..... 336-334-5426.... 379 A
james_clotfelter@uncg.edu
CLOTHIER, Timothy, S ...... 620-341-5440.... 192 D
jheasley@emporia.edu
CLOUD, Andy .... 432-837-8179.... 501 B
wacloud@sulross.edu
CLOUD, Rodney .... 334-387-3877........ 1 D
rodneycloud@amridgeuniversity.edu
CLOUD, Sybil .... 850-718-2223.... 102 H
clouds@chipola.edu
CLOUD, Yvonne .... 870-245-5299...... 22 I
cloudy@obu.edu
CLOUGH, Kathleen .... 510-580-3504...... 79 G
kclough@cci.edu
CLOUGH, Kenneth .... 518-438-3111.... 340 B
kclough@mariacollege.edu
CLOUGH, Lisa .... 505-661-4695.... 321 E
lclough@unm.edu
CLOUGH, Susan .... 970-542-3127...... 86 A
susan.clough@morgancc.edu
CLOUGH, JR., Victor, W ... 804-333-6705.... 527 G
vclough@rappahannock.edu
CLOUGHERTY, Helen .... 832-813-6514.... 490 C
helen.clougherty@lonestar.edu
CLOUGHERTY, Robert, J ... 518-587-2100.... 355 F
robert.clougherty@esc.edu
CLOUNCH, Teresa .... 785-594-8473.... 190 C
teresa.clounch@bakeru.edu
CLOUSE, Christine .... 623-572-3286...... 16 F
cclous@midwestern.edu
CLOUSE, Cindy, D .... 606-679-8501.... 202 F
cindy.clouse@kctcs.edu
CLOUSE, Dave .... 731-989-6019.... 468 K
dclouse@fhu.edu
CLOUSE, Jim, W .... 432-837-8777.... 501 B
jclouse@sulross.edu
CLOVER, Richard, D .... 502-852-3297.... 207 A
richard.clover@louisville.edu
CLOW, Todd .... 517-437-7341.... 252 E
todd.clow@hillsdale.edu
CLOW, William .... 205-665-6206........ 9 C
wclow@montevallo.edu
CLOWER, John .... 706-864-1818.... 134 D
jclower@northgeorgia.edu
CLOWERS, Laurie, C .... 919-866-5929.... 374 E
lcclowers@waketech.edu
CLOYD, J. Timothy .... 501-450-1351...... 22 A
cloyd@hendrix.edu
CLUBB, Patricia, L .... 512-232-7742.... 505 B
pclubb@mail.utexas.edu
CLUBB, Sandy Hatfield ...... 515-271-2889.... 184 A
sandra.clubb@drake.edu
CLUFF, Richard .... 480-461-7095...... 15 K
richard.cluff@mcmail.maricopa.edu
CLULOW, Frank .... 603-752-1113.... 304 I
fclulow@ccsnh.edu
CLUNIS, Tamara, T .... 806-371-5429.... 479 H
ttclunis@actx.edu
CLUSS, Bob .... 802-443-5025.... 513 G
rcluss@middlebury.edu
CLUTE, Richard .... 815-479-7588.... 157 F
rclute@mchenry.edu
CLUTTER, Michael, L .... 706-542-4741.... 138 C
mclutter@warnell.uga.edu
CLUTTER, Sam .... 724-357-2141.... 442 E
Samuel.Clutter@iup.edu
CLUTTER, William .... 850-644-6860.... 119 C
wclutter@admin.fsu.edu
CLYBURN, Michael .... 423-869-6223.... 470 C
michael.clyburn@lmunet.edu
CLYDE, William .... 718-862-7303.... 339 H
william.clyde@manhattan.edu
CLYDE, JR., William .... 516-299-2241.... 339 A
william.clyde@liu.edu
CLYMER, Patrick, L .... 671-735-5561.... 559 B
gcc.registrar@guamcc.edu
CLYMER, Ron .... 203-575-8044...... 90 E
rclymer@nvcc.commnet.edu
COACHMAN, Kenneth .... 205-929-1457........ 5 H
kcoachman@mail.miles.edu
COAKLEY, Jim .... 615-226-3990.... 471 I
jcoakley@nadcedu.com
COAKLEY, Toni .... 580-477-7751.... 414 C
toni.coakley@wosc.edu
COALTER, Milton, J .... 804-355-0671.... 524 F
jcoalter@upsem.edu
COAN, John .... 413-265-2275.... 233 E
coanj@elms.edu
COARTNEY, Jorge, W .... 540-831-7802.... 522 D
jcoartne@radford.edu
COASH, Julia .... 203-773-8973...... 89 H
jcoash@albertus.edu
COAT, Christopher .... 814-827-4470.... 449 E
coat@pitt.edu
COATE, Letitia .... 707-664-2836...... 37 B
letitia.coate@sonoma.edu
COATES, Brett .... 757-352-4753.... 523 B
bretcoa@regent.edu
COATES, Clifton, L .... 202-274-6413...... 99 F
ccoates@udc.edu
COATES, Dennis .... 561-297-3629.... 118 H
coates@fau.edu
COATES, James .... 708-596-2000.... 164 F
jcoates@ssc.edu
COATES, Jo Ann .... 724-480-3401.... 426 A
joann.coates@ccbc.edu
COATES, Thomas, E .... 716-878-6114.... 353 A
coateste@buffalostate.edu
COATES, Tom .... 906-635-6670.... 254 C
tcoates@lssu.edu
COATIE, Robert, M .... 305-348-2436.... 119 B
coatier@fiu.edu
COATS, Carol .... 580-745-2134.... 412 C
ccoats@se.edu
COATS, Jeffrey .... 334-347-2623........ 3 G
jcoats@escc.edu
COATS, Patrick, K .... 804-355-0671.... 524 F
pcoats@upsem.edu
COATS, Rhonda .... 360-596-5231.... 538 B
rcoats@spscc.ctc.edu
COATSWORTH, John .... 212-854-4604.... 330 F
jhc2125@columbia.edu
COAUETTE, Chad .... 320-762-4403.... 265 I
chadc@alextech.edu
COAUETTE, Chad .... 763-576-4707.... 266 A
ccoauette@anokatech.edu
COAXUM, Tom .... 704-216-6328.... 366 D
tcoaxum@livingstone.edu
COBALLES-VEGA, Carmen . 718-518-6611.... 327 D
ccvega@hostos.cuny.edu
COBANE, Craig .... 270-745-2085.... 207 C
craig.cobane@wku.edu
COBARRUBIAS, Maria .... 201-200-2349.... 312 B
mcobarrubias@njcu.edu
COBB, Beverly .... 937-298-3399.... 394 D
beverly.cobb@kcma.edu
COBB, Charles .... 270-706-8566.... 201 F
charles.cobb@kctcs.edu
COBB, Charles, G .... 828-262-3045.... 377 B
cobbcg@appstate.edu
COBB, Cindy .... 303-861-1151...... 83 G
ccobb@concorde.edu
COBB, Edythe .... 901-435-1731.... 470 B
edythe_cobb@loc.edu
COBB, James .... 931-372-3234.... 474 B
jimcobb@tntech.edu
COBB, Katharine .... 718-997-5775.... 328 F
katharine.cobb@qc.cuny.edu
COBB, Kathy .... 321-433-7100.... 101 J
cobbk@brevardcc.edu
COBB, Keith .... 714-484-7116...... 59 C
kcobb@cypresscollege.edu
COBB, Kim, S .... 256-549-8236........ 3 J
kcobb@gadsdenstate.edu
COBB, Larry .... 334-229-4844........ 1 C
cobb@alasu.edu
COBB, Myreon, K .... 419-434-4544.... 404 B
mcobb@findlay.edu
COBB, Stephen, H .... 270-809-3391.... 204 F
steve.cobb@murraystate.edu
COBB, Steve .... 907-786-4878...... 10 I
ansrc@uaa.alaska.edu
COBEIGH, Lee .... 215-785-0111.... 440 H
COBIAN, Denise .... 787-780-0070.... 560 F
dcobian@caribbean.edu
COBIAN, Oscar .... 323-241-5328...... 55 C
cobianom@lasc.edu
COBLE, Bridgette .... 303-556-3664...... 85 N
bcoble@mscd.edu
COBLE, Tammi .... 252-222-6081.... 368 F
coblet@carteret.edu
COBLENTZ, Laban .... 518-276-6211.... 347 D
coblel@rpi.edu
COBLENTZ, Pablo .... 208-426-1616.... 142 F
pablocoblentz@boisestate.edu
COBLER, Paula .... 361-570-4350.... 503 E
coblerp@uhv.edu
COBURN, Kari, C .... 702-895-3771.... 302 K
kari@nevada.edu
COBURN, Kevin .... 802-287-8926.... 513 D
commsgmc@greenmtn.edu
COBURN, Mary, B .... 850-644-5590.... 119 C
mcoburn@fsu.edu
COBURN, Nancy, A .... 325-674-2932.... 478 H
coburnn@acu.edu
COBURN, Oakley, H .... 864-597-4300.... 463 F
coburnoh@wofford.edu
COCA, John .... 505-454-3405.... 318 I
johncoca@nmhu.edu
COCCHI, Wayne .... 514-287-5004.... 388 G
COCCHIARELLA, Frank, L .. 603-535-2260.... 307 B
frankc@plymouth.edu
COCCHIOLA, Phil .... 860-244-7652...... 89 J
pcocchiola@commnet.edu
COCCO-MITTEN, Melissa ... 415-503-6231...... 66 A
mcocco@sfcm.edu
COCHRAN, Amber .... 478-274-7761.... 134 G
acochran@oftc.edu
COCHRAN, Angela .... 269-965-3931.... 253 H
cochrana@kellogg.edu
COCHRAN, Barry, A .... 260-359-4035.... 172 K
bcochran@huntington.edu
COCHRAN, Bob .... 503-594-6790.... 415 A
bobc@clackamas.edu
COCHRAN, Connie, L .... 713-313-7606.... 499 G
cochrancl@tsu.edu
COCHRAN, Daniel, J .... 574-239-8409.... 172 J
dcochran@hcc-nd.edu
COCHRAN, Douglas .... 541-737-4085.... 418 F
career.services@oregonstate.edu
COCHRAN, Edward, E .... 724-503-1001.... 451 A
ecochran@washjeff.edu
COCHRAN, Geri .... 336-770-1457.... 379 D
cochrang@uncsa.edu
COCHRAN, Glenn .... 508-626-4636.... 238 D
gcochran@framingham.edu
COCHRAN, Jerome .... 412-624-4247.... 449 A
cochran@pitt.edu
COCHRAN, John .... 303-556-3245...... 85 N
cochranj@mscd.edu
COCHRAN, Kevin .... 860-231-5522...... 93 H
kcochran@sjc.edu
COCHRAN, Linda .... 601-923-1661.... 277 B
lcochran@rts.edu
COCHRAN, Mark, J .... 501-686-2540...... 24 B
mjcochran@uasys.edu
COCHRAN, Maryjo .... 334-670-3869........ 8 B
macochran@troy.edu

COLE, Brenda ..... 956-872-5584 .... 494 D
bcole@southtexascollege.edu

COLE, Brian ..... 248-218-2040 .... 257 F
bcole1@rc.edu

COLE, Brian ..... 787-751-0160 .... 561 G
bcole@cmpr.gobierno.pr

COLE, Bruce ..... 704-922-6413 .... 370 D
cole.bruce@gaston.edu

COLE, Christopher, L ..... 804-523-5843 .... 526 F
ccole@reynolds.edu

COLE, Christy, C ..... 434-381-6530 .... 524 E
ccole@sbc.edu

COLE, Dan ..... 402-363-5609 .... 301 F
dcole@york.edu

COLE, David ..... 305-229-4833 .... 104 B
dcole@keller.edu

COLE, David, C ..... 662-862-8001 .... 274 G
dccole@iccms.edu

COLE, Dayton, T ..... 828-262-2751 .... 377 B
coledt@appstate.edu

COLE, Donald, R ..... 662-915-7474 .... 277 G
dcole@olemiss.edu

COLE, Elyne ..... 217-333-6677 .... 167 B
egcole@illinois.edu

COLE, Frances, E ..... 252-398-6452 .... 363 E
colefr@chowan.edu

COLE, Holly ..... 603-428-2440 .... 305 E
hcole@nec.edu

COLE, Jack ..... 717-766-2511 .... 436 D
jcole@messiah.edu

COLE, Jim ..... 478-301-2994 .... 133 F
cole_jm@mercer.edu

COLE, Joey ..... 501-812-2243 ...... 23 C
jcole@pulaskitech.edu

COLE, John, J ..... 304-293-8673 .... 544 E
jay.cole@mail.wvu.edu

COLE, John, P ..... 478-757-6630 .... 133 E
john.cole@maconstate.edu

COLE, Judith ..... 813-879-6000 .... 106 F
jcole@cci.edu

COLE, Judith, M ..... 617-253-8231 .... 242 A
judycole@mit.edu

COLE, Karen ..... 913-588-7300 .... 197 A
kcole@kumc.edu

COLE, Kathryn, B ..... 601-857-3502 .... 274 E
Kathryn.Cole@hindscc.edu

COLE, Kathy ..... 251-981-3771 .... 2 H
kathy.cole@columbiasouthern.edu

COLE, Ken ..... 803-313-7068 .... 462 D
colekt@gwm.sc.edu

COLE, Kristie, C ..... 864-231-2067 .... 455 C
kcole@andersonuniversity.edu

COLE, Laura, L ..... 815-740-3657 .... 167 C
lcole@stfrancis.edu

COLE, Lisa ..... 318-257-4325 .... 215 F
lcole@latech.edu

COLE, Lucinda ..... 910-410-1817 .... 372 G
lucindac@richmondcc.edu

COLE, Maenecia ..... 252-335-0821 .... 369 D
mlewis@albemarle.edu

COLE, Mark ..... 315-312-3627 .... 354 A
rcole2@oswego.edu

COLE, Marsha, A ..... 803-777-4111 .... 462 A
marshac@carolinaalumni.org

COLE, Michael ..... 216-421-7413 .... 307 H
mcole@cia.edu

COLE, Milton, T ..... 610-519-4220 .... 450 G
milton.cole@villanova.edu

COLE, Nadara, L ..... 662-720-7277 .... 276 D
ncole@nemcc.edu

COLE, Nathan ..... 614-456-4600 .... 393 B
ncole@teccollege.com

COLE, Patricia ..... 205-226-4907 .... 2 C
pcole@bsc.edu

COLE, Rebecca, S ..... 937-775-2350 .... 406 C
rebecca.cole@wright.edu

COLE, Richard ..... 732-906-4153 .... 311 E
RCole@middlesexcc.edu

COLE, Richard ..... 631-244-1113 .... 332 D
coler@dowling.edu

COLE, Robert ..... 401-254-3149 .... 454 C
rcole@rwu.edu

COLE, Robert ..... 610-647-4400 .... 431 B
rcole@immaculata.edu

COLE, Sericia ..... 501-370-5379 ...... 23 B
scole@philander.edu

COLE, Sherri ..... 330-363-4381 .... 384 G
scole@aultman.com

COLE, Stephanie, A ..... 716-286-8319 .... 344 D
scole@niagara.edu

COLE, Stephen, W ..... 845-575-3000 .... 340 C
stephen.cole@marist.edu

COLE, Steve ..... 870-584-4471 ...... 25 C
scole@cccua.edu

COLE, Susan ..... 414-326-2304 .... 546 H
scole@ccon.edu

COLE, Susan, A ..... 973-655-4212 .... 311 G
coles@mail.montclair.edu

COLE, Vicki, D ..... 540-224-6752 .... 520 D
vdcole@jchs.edu

COLE, W. Scott ..... 407-823-2482 .... 120 A
scott.cole@ucf.edu

COLE, Wayne ..... 563-441-4011 .... 184 E
wcole@eicc.edu

COLE, Wendy, P ..... 484-664-3433 .... 437 B
cole@muhlenberg.edu

COLE, Xavier ..... 410-617-5171 .... 224 A
xcole@loyola.edu

COLE DILLON, Ce, S ..... 773-995-2019 .... 146 D
ccdillon@csu.edu

COLEAL, Sharlene ..... 661-362-3405 ...... 41 G
sharlene.coleal@canyons.edu

COLEGROVE, Michael ..... 606-539-4230 .... 206 G
michael.colegrove@ucumberlands.edu

COLELLA, Kurt, J ..... 860-444-8275 .... 558 E
kurt.j.colella@uscg.mil

COLELLA, Laurie ..... 508-831-4922 .... 247 B
lcolella@wpi.edu

COLELLI, Leonard, A ..... 724-938-4169 .... 441 G
colelli@calu.edu

COLEMAN, Alberta ..... 870-633-4480 ...... 21 F
alberta.coleman@eacc.edu

COLEMAN, Alvin ..... 870-633-4480 ...... 21 F
acoleman@eacc.edu

COLEMAN, Anne Marie ..... 401-874-5270 .... 454 E
amc@uri.edu

COLEMAN, Barbara ..... 212-875-4472 .... 323 E
bcoleman@bankstreet.edu

COLEMAN, Carole ..... 928-344-7521 ...... 12 C
carole.coleman@azwestern.edu

COLEMAN, Catherine, T ..... 870-633-4480 ...... 21 F
ccoleman@eacc.edu

COLEMAN, Cheryl, C ..... 913-288-7471 .... 193 J
ccoleman@kckcc.edu

COLEMAN, Christopher ..... 901-761-5730 .... 478 A
christopher.coleman@vatterott-college.edu

COLEMAN, Clarence, D ..... 757-823-8408 .... 521 K
cdcoleman@nsu.edu

COLEMAN, Clinton, R ..... 443-885-3022 .... 224 F
clinton.coleman@morgan.edu

COLEMAN, Craig, S ..... 412-397-4302 .... 445 G
colemanc@rmu.edu

COLEMAN, David ..... 781-239-2463 .... 240 D
dcoleman@massbay.edu

COLEMAN, Dayna, L ..... 509-777-4565 .... 539 F
dcoleman@whitworth.edu

COLEMAN, Deanna ..... 269-927-8190 .... 254 B
colemand@lakemichigancollege.edu

COLEMAN, Deborah, D ..... 614-287-3670 .... 388 G
dcoleman@cscc.edu

COLEMAN, Denise ..... 708-239-4706 .... 165 I
denise.coleman@trnty.edu

COLEMAN, Diane ..... 206-587-3842 .... 537 A
dcoleman@sccd.ctc.edu

COLEMAN, Don ..... 423-323-3191 .... 475 E
dscoleman@northeaststate.edu

COLEMAN, Elizabeth ..... 802-440-4300 .... 512 G
ecoleman@bennington.edu

COLEMAN, Ellen ..... 302-736-2508 ...... 96 G
colemael@wesley.edu

COLEMAN, F. Paul ..... 607-431-4449 .... 335 B
colemanf@hartwick.edu

COLEMAN, Frances, N ..... 662-325-7661 .... 276 A
fcoleman@library.msstate.edu

COLEMAN, Gerald ..... 610-399-2222 .... 441 H
geraldcoleman@cheyney.edu

COLEMAN, Hardin ..... 617-353-3213 .... 232 G
hardin@bu.edu

COLEMAN, James ..... 713-348-4002 .... 402 J
james.s.coleman@rice.edu

COLEMAN, Jamie ..... 208-467-8768 .... 143 I
jcoleman@nnu.edu

COLEMAN, Jay, T ..... 319-352-8264 .... 189 F
todd.coleman@wartburg.edu

COLEMAN, Jeff ..... 435-797-1223 .... 511 B
jeff.coleman@usu.edu

COLEMAN, Joe ..... 904-256-7550 .... 111 J
jcolema@ju.edu

COLEMAN, Joseph, L ..... 386-481-2626 .... 101 I
colemanj@cookman.edu

COLEMAN, Joyce ..... 815-280-6626 .... 154 H
jcoleman@jjc.edu

COLEMAN, Joyce ..... 661-395-4614 ...... 52 M

COLEMAN, Laura, L ..... 906-786-5802 .... 249 D
colemanl@baycollege.edu

COLEMAN, Leonard ..... 401-841-4068 .... 557 I

COLEMAN, Linda ..... 610-519-4074 .... 450 G
linda.coleman@villanova.edu

COLEMAN, Lisa, M ..... 617-495-1540 .... 235 H
lisa_coleman@harvard.edu

COLEMAN, Lorn, B ..... 773-442-4680 .... 159 H
l-coleman@neiu.edu

COLEMAN, Lynn, C ..... 443-518-4918 .... 223 D
lcoleman@howardcc.edu

COLEMAN, Mardell ..... 352-395-4474 .... 117 E
mardell.coleman@sfcollege.edu

COLEMAN, Marion, A ..... 717-358-7194 .... 429 E
marion.coleman@fandm.edu

COLEMAN, Mark, E ..... 704-403-1754 .... 362 E
mark.coleman@carolinashealthcare.org

COLEMAN, Mary ..... 617-349-8458 .... 236 G
mcolema5@lesley.edu

COLEMAN, Mary, E ..... 718-289-5128 .... 326 F
mary.coleman@bcc.cuny.edu

COLEMAN, Mary Sue ..... 734-764-6270 .... 259 D
marysuec@umich.edu

COLEMAN, Michael ..... 313-664-7676 .... 250 A
mcoleman@collegeforcreativestudies.edu

COLEMAN, Michael, J ..... 540-231-5530 .... 529 B
colemanm@vt.edu

COLEMAN, Mick ..... 612-659-6107 .... 267 E
mick.coleman@minneapolis.edu

COLEMAN, Mychal ..... 208-885-3478 .... 144 B
coleman@uidaho.edu

COLEMAN, Pamela ..... 860-244-7602 ...... 89 J
pcoleman@commnet.edu

COLEMAN, Reggie ..... 405-491-6366 .... 412 D
rcoleman@snu.edu

COLEMAN, Richard, A ..... 812-888-4280 .... 181 B
rcoleman@vinu.edu

COLEMAN, Rob ..... 562-907-4271 ...... 79 B
rcoleman@whittier.edu

COLEMAN, Robert, F ..... 979-761-9008 .... 315 B
robert.coleman@shu.edu

COLEMAN, Robert, F ..... 973-761-9016 .... 311 A
robert.coleman@shu.edu

COLEMAN, S. Michelle ..... 415-575-6160 ...... 32 D
mcoleman@ciis.edu

COLEMAN, Sean ..... 412-365-1164 .... 425 B
scoleman1@chatham.edu

COLEMAN, Stephanie ..... 828-298-3325 .... 380 C
bookstore@warren-wilson.edu

COLEMAN, Stephen, F ..... 607-735-1804 .... 333 A
scoleman@elmira.edu

COLEMAN, Steve, B ..... 864-941-8373 .... 460 D
coleman.s@ptc.edu

COLEMAN, Tammy ..... 870-584-4471 ...... 25 C
tcoleman@cccua.edu

COLEMAN, Teresa ..... 912-538-3103 .... 137 A
tcoleman@southeasterntech.edu

COLEMAN, Thereisa ..... 512-505-3147 .... 488 B
thcoleman@htu.edu

COLEMAN, Tonya, R ..... 678-359-5435 .... 131 D
tonya_c@gdn.edu

COLEMAN, Vera ..... 831-646-4006 ...... 57 G
vcoleman@mpc.edu

COLEMAN, Vicki ..... 336-334-7782 .... 377 F

COLEMAN-HULL, June ..... 620-341-5407 .... 192 D
jcoleman@emporia.edu

COLEMAN-LEE, Barbara ..... 973-972-8385 .... 316 E
leeba@umdnj.edu

COLEMER, Dena ..... 507-389-7272 .... 269 F
dena.colemer@southcentral.edu

COLEN, Alan, H ..... 913-288-7117 .... 193 J
acolen@kckcc.edu

COLENDA, Christopher, C . 304-293-4511 .... 544 E
ccolenda@hsc.wvu.edu

COLENDER, Shelly ..... 800-469-0236 .... 211 E

COLES, Alicia ..... 757-873-2423 .... 521 B

COLES, Allen ..... 803-705-4679 .... 455 D
colesa@benedict.edu

COLES, Julius ..... 404-215-6040 .... 134 A
jcoles@morehouse.edu

COLES, Patricia ..... 847-317-7033 .... 166 B
pcoles@tiu.edu

COLES, Roger, L ..... 989-774-6099 .... 249 G
coles1rl@cmich.edu

COLEY, Donavon, O ..... 478-825-6520 .... 129 C
coleyd@fvsu.edu

COLEY, Karen ..... 920-887-4426 .... 554 E
kcoley@morainepark.edu

COLEY, Kathryn, S ..... 631-420-2400 .... 356 A
kathy.coley@farmingdale.edu

COLEY, Norman ..... 701-483-2175 .... 381 E
norman.coley@dickinsonstate.edu

COLEY, Ron, T ..... 510-643-1430 ...... 73 E
rcoley@berkeley.edu

COLEY, Soraya ..... 661-654-2154 ...... 33 H
scoley@csub.edu

COLEY, Thomas, G ..... 574-289-7001 .... 176 C

COLFORD, Francis, X ..... 973-972-7981 .... 316 C
colforfx@umdnj.edu

COLGAN, Dennis ..... 206-878-3710 .... 534 E
dcolgan@highline.edu

COLGAN, William ..... 802-225-3342 .... 513 H
will.colgan@neci.edu

COLICCHIO, Damian ..... 201-559-6021 .... 310 C
colicchiod@felician.edu

COLIFLOWER, Natalie ..... 406-638-3148 .... 294 G
coliflowern@lbhc.cc.mt.us

COLIJN, G. Jan ..... 609-652-4542 .... 313 F
jan.colijn@stockton.edu

COLIP, Mark ..... 312-949-7405 .... 152 D
mcolip@ico.edu

COLKER, Lee ..... 412-291-6220 .... 422 D
lcolker@aii.edu

COLLA, JR., Stanley, A ..... 607-871-2144 .... 322 F
colla@alfred.edu

COLLADA, Tere ..... 305-237-1135 .... 113 H
mcollado@mdc.edu

COLLADO, Ana ..... 305-262-4748 .... 106 J

COLLADO, Diosa ..... 312-777-8584 .... 153 A
dcollado@aii.edu

COLLADO, Raquel ..... 718-780-4565 .... 338 H
Raquel.Collado@liu.edu

COLLADO, Shirley ..... 802-443-5382 .... 513 G
scollado@middlebury.edu

COLLAND, Ronna ..... 724-836-9906 .... 449 C
rsc5@pitt.edu

COLLAR, Doug ..... 419-448-2157 .... 391 G
dcollar@heidelberg.edu

COLLARD, Lori ..... 218-723-6602 .... 262 I
lcollard@css.edu

COLLAZO, Carmen ..... 787-250-1912 .... 563 E
ccollazo@metro.inter.edu

COLLAZO, David ..... 787-807-0575 .... 564 D
dcollazo@mechtech.edu

COLLAZO, Evelyn ..... 787-738-2161 .... 567 A
evlyn.collazo@upr.edu

COLLAZO, Ivonne ..... 787-284-1912 .... 563 F
icollazo@ponce.inter.edu

COLLAZO, Julio, A ..... 787-758-2525 .... 567 D
julio.collazo@upr.edu

COLLAZO, Lydia ..... 787-780-5134 .... 564 E
lcollazo@nationalcollegepr.edu

COLLAZO, Mariela ..... 787-766-1717 .... 565 G
mcollazo@suagm.edu

COLLEN, Dan ..... 707-826-3666 ...... 36 D
dgc7001@humboldt.edu

COLLER, Barry, S ..... 212-327-7490 .... 347 H
collerb@rockefeller.edu

COLLERAN, Jeanne ..... 216-397-4460 .... 392 M
jcolleran@jcu.edu

COLLETTE, Mark ..... 508-849-3370 .... 230 C
mcollette@annamaria.edu

COLLEY, Debra, A ..... 716-286-8560 .... 344 D
dcolley@niagara.edu

COLLIE, Pamela, J ..... 276-328-0128 .... 525 C
pjc9w@uvawise.edu

COLLIE, Susan, A ..... 501-882-8967 ...... 20 D
sacollie@asub.edu

COLLIER, Adrienne ..... 585-395-2109 .... 352 F
acollier@brockport.edu

COLLIER, Barbara ..... 662-915-7275 .... 277 G
bcollier@olemiss.edu

COLLIER, Barbara ..... 323-226-4911 ...... 55 G
bcollier@dhs.lacounty.gov

COLLIER, Barry, S ..... 317-940-8421 .... 170 C
bcollier@butler.edu

COLLIER, Billie ..... 850-644-5054 .... 119 C
bcollier@mailer.fsu.edu

COLLIER, Charles ..... 615-547-1310 .... 467 I
ccollier@cumberland.edu

COLLIER, Chris ..... 573-876-7207 .... 290 G
ccollier@stephens.edu

COLLIER, Cindy ..... 661-395-4281 ...... 52 M
ccollier@bakersfieldcollege.edu

COLLIER, Diondrae ..... 408-273-2688 ...... 58 G
dcollier@nhu.edu

COLLIER, Elizabeth ..... 615-361-7555 .... 468 C
ecollier@daymarinstitute.edu

COLLIER, Harvest, L ..... 573-341-4390 .... 292 A
hcollier@mst.edu

COLLIER, Jackie ..... 859-622-1260 .... 200 D
jackie.collier@eku.edu

COLLIER, Jay ..... 402-375-7325 .... 299 I
jacolli1@wsc.edu

COLLIER, Jo ..... 918-781-3353 .... 407 B
collierj@bacone.edu

COLLIER, John ..... 850-410-6161 .... 118 G
john.collier@famu.edu

COLLIER, John ..... 850-410-6161 .... 119 C
jcollier2@fsu.edu

COLLIER, Kristen, L ..... 937-327-7523 .... 406 B
kcollier@wittenberg.edu

COLLIER, Linda, J ..... 610-359-5230 .... 426 G
lcollier@dccc.edu

COLLIER, Lisa ..... 618-545-3081 .... 155 A
lcollier@kaskaskia.edu

COLLIER, Roger ..... 918-449-6521 .... 409 A
collier@nsuok.edu

COLLIER, Scott ..... 704-290-5872 .... 373 F
scollier@spcc.edu

COLLIER, Sharon ..... 870-633-4480 ...... 21 F
scollier@eacc.edu

COLLIER, Warner ..... 361-698-2177 .... 485 F
wcollier@delmar.edu

COLLIER, Willyerd, R ..... 479-575-4019 ...... 24 C
wcollier@uark.edu

COLLIER-WHITE, Nelva, G 410-651-7700 .... 227 E
ngcollier@umes.edu

COLLIN, Lor ..... 530-541-4660 ...... 53 F
collin@ltcc.edu

COLLING, Lynnde ..... 307-268-2247 .... 555 F
lcolling@caspercollege.edu

COLLINGS, Richard ..... 510-436-1327 ...... 50 F
collings@hnu.edu

COLLINGWOD, Tracy ..... 716-673-3327 .... 352 A
tracy.collingwood@fredonia.edu

COLLINS, Aaron ..... 251-981-3771 .... 2 H
aaron.collins@columbiasouthern.edu

COLLINS, Amy ..... 678-717-3824 .... 129 D
acollins@gsc.edu

COLLINS, Andrea ..... 804-524-5973 .... 529 C
acollins@vsu.edu

COLLINS, Anthony, G ..... 315-268-6444 .... 329 C
president@clarkson.edu

COLLINS, Brad, M ..... 405-878-5102 .... 412 A
bmcollins@stgregorys.edu

COLLINS, Bryan ..... 516-299-2847 .... 339 A
bryan.collins@liu.edu

COLLINS, Buddy ..... 662-862-8271 .... 274 G
bacollins@iccms.edu

COLLINS, Candis ..... 757-457-7176 .... 516 C
candis.collins@atlanticuniv.edu

COMICI, Erio ... 314-264-1740 ... 478 A
erioc@vatterott-college.edu
COMISH, Alice ... 225-768-1734 ... 214 B
acomish@ololcollege.edu
COMMISSO, Louis ... 516-918-3609 ... 324 E
lcommisso@bcl.edu
COMMON, Easter ... 601-977-7879 ... 277 F
ecommon@tougaloo.edu
COMMONS, Mary ... 803-593-9231 ... 455 A
commons@atc.edu
COMO, Michael ... 303-861-1151 ... 83 G
mcomo@concorde.edu
COMPAAN, Korey ... 916-577-2200 ... 79 C
kcompaan@jessup.edu
COMPARY, Kristin ... 361-593-3606 ... 498 A
kristin.compary@tamuk.edu
COMPAS, Krystal ... 417-873-7258 ... 281 H
kcompas@drury.edu
COMPHER, Jeff ... 815-753-7370 ... 160 A
jcompher@niu.edu
COMPIER, Don ... 816-483-9600 ... 289 H
COMPTON, Betsy ... 205-652-3892 ... 10 A
bcompton@uwa.edu
COMPTON, D. Chad ... 808-675-3790 ... 139 I
chad.compton@byuh.edu
COMPTON, Jennifer ... 517-264-3175 ... 247 D
COMPTON, Kathy, M ... 570-586-2400 ... 422 F
kcompton@bbc.edu
COMPTON, Kerry ... 510-748-2204 ... 62 B
kcompton@peralta.edu
COMRIE, Andrew ... 520-621-3512 ... 19 B
comrie@email.arizona.edu
COMSTOCK, Alysha ... 708-524-6296 ... 150 A
acomstock@dom.edu
COMSTOCK, Jamie, M ... 317-940-9903 ... 170 C
jcomstoc@butler.edu
CONARD, T. Hunt ... 518-580-5940 ... 351 B
hconard@skidmore.edu
CONAWAY, Kathleen, M ... 814-332-4799 ... 421 E
kathleen.conaway@allegheny.edu
CONAWAY, Tamatha ... 312-329-6685 ... 146 C
tconaway@thechicagoschool.edu
CONBOY, Katie ... 508-565-1311 ... 245 D
kconboy@stonehill.edu
CONCA, Lorraine ... 434-961-6541 ... 527 F
lconca@pvcc.edu
CONCEPCION, George ... 718-982-2029 ... 327 A
George.Concepcion@csi.cuny.edu
CONCEPCION, Victor ... 787-878-5475 ... 562 H
vconcepcion@arecibo.inter.edu
CONCHA, Lee ... 847-578-8848 ... 163 A
lee.concha@rosalindfranklin.edu
CONCHA-BUCKHEART,
Mona ... 775-673-7623 ... 302 J
mbuckheart@tmcc.edu
CONCO, Paul, W ... 757-569-6712 ... 527 E
pconco@pdc.edu
CONDE, Jean ... 650-508-3513 ... 59 G
jconde@ndnu.edu
CONDE-FRAZIER,
Elizabeth ... 215-324-0746 ... 428 D
ocondefr@eastern.edu
CONDENI, Karen, P ... 419-772-2260 ... 398 G
k-condeni@onu.edu
CONDER, Ken ... 425-564-2250 ... 531 B
k.conder@bellevuecollege.edu
CONDINO, Francis ... 724-357-2132 ... 442 E
fcondino@iup.edu
CONDIT, Lucas ... 239-280-2541 ... 101 C
luke.condit@avemaria.edu
CONDON, Charlie ... 276-935-4349 ... 516 A
ccondon@asl.edu
CONDON, Debra, A ... 610-799-1938 ... 434 D
dcondon@lccc.edu
CONDON, Eileen ... 314-968-7152 ... 293 A
econdon@webster.edu
CONDON, Jacquelyn, S ... 309-457-2113 ... 158 G
jackiec@monm.edu
CONDON, Jennifer, M ... 515-574-1190 ... 185 F
condon@iowacentral.edu
CONDON, Michael, A ... 214-768-2802 ... 494 F
mikec@smu.edu
CONDON, Patricia ... 508-678-2811 ... 239 F
patricia.condon@bristolcc.edu
CONDON, Sara, A ... 515-574-1005 ... 185 F
condon_s@iowacentral.edu
CONDON, Tami ... 269-471-3591 ... 247 H
alumni@andrews.edu
CONDON, Terry ... 617-287-7800 ... 237 D
terry.condon@umb.edu
CONDRA, Shawn, M ... 785-539-3571 ... 194 G
scondra@mccks.edu
CONDRON, Dan ... 707-664-2732 ... 37 B
condrond@sonoma.edu
CONE, Allen, J ... 323-265-8913 ... 54 G
coneaj@elac.edu
CONE, Cynthia ... 270-706-8406 ... 201 F
cynthia.cone@kctcs.edu
CONE, Fabian ... 954-446-6118 ... 100 E
fcone@aiufl.edu
CONE, Janet, R ... 828-251-6922 ... 378 C
jcone@unca.edu
CONELLI, Maria, A ... 718-951-3180 ... 326 G
MConelli@brooklyn.cuny.edu

CONEWAY, Raydor ... 478-553-2065 ... 134 F
rconeway@oftc.edu
CONEY, Lennetta ... 810-762-0269 ... 256 C
lennetta.coney@mcc.edu
CONGDON, Bruce, D ... 206-281-2899 ... 537 D
bcongdon@spu.edu
CONGDON, Frank ... 215-951-2902 ... 444 C
congdonf@philau.edu
CONGER, Lora ... 918-610-8303 ... 411 D
lora.conger@ptstulsa.edu
CONGLETON, Dawn, L ... 434-223-6203 ... 519 B
dcongleton@email.hsc.edu
CONGLETON, O. Mort ... 919-866-5926 ... 374 E
omcongleton@waketech.edu
CONGRESSI, Karyn ... 386-752-1822 ... 108 C
karyn.congressi@fgc.edu
CONIGLIO, Michael ... 706-880-8184 ... 132 I
mconiglio@lagrange.edu
CONINE, Chris ... 423-614-8102 ... 470 A
cconine@leeuniversity.edu
CONISON, Jay ... 219-465-7834 ... 181 A
jay.conison@valpo.edu
CONJAR, Catarin ... 610-647-4400 ... 431 B
cconjar@immaculata.edu
CONKLIN, Barbara ... 252-399-6570 ... 362 A
baconklin@barton.edu
CONKLIN, D. David ... 845-431-8980 ... 332 E
conklin@sunydutchess.edu
CONKLIN, David ... 716-488-3026 ... 337 D
david.conklin@jamestownbusinesscollege.edu
CONKLIN, Deborah, M ... 260-481-6118 ... 174 A
conklin@ipfw.edu
CONKLIN, Denise ... 405-912-9005 ... 408 D
dconklin@hc.edu
CONKLIN, Eileen ... 915-831-4432 ... 486 E
econklin@epcc.edu
CONKLIN, Kathleen ... 517-371-5140 ... 259 B
conklink@cooley.edu
CONKLIN, Lara, L ... 217-443-8798 ... 148 E
lconklin@dacc.edu
CONKLIN, Peter ... 603-513-1382 ... 306 H
peter.conklin@granite.edu
CONKLIN, Robin ... 845-574-4484 ... 347 I
CONLEY, Aaron ... 972-883-6402 ... 505 D
aconley@utdallas.edu
CONLEY, Bill ... 402-554-2358 ... 301 B
bconley@unomaha.edu
CONLEY, Cary ... 270-831-9610 ... 201 I
cary.conley@kctcs.edu
CONLEY, Davis, B ... 607-431-4173 ... 335 B
conleyd@hartwick.edu
CONLEY, Dennis ... 618-395-7777 ... 152 H
conleyd@iecc.edu
CONLEY, Ellen, O ... 716-888-2130 ... 325 G
conley@canisius.edu
CONLEY, Heather ... 406-657-2046 ... 295 F
heather.conley@msubillings.edu
CONLEY, John ... 518-562-4219 ... 329 D
john.conley@clinton.edu
CONLEY, Keith, A ... 828-448-3151 ... 374 G
kconley@wpcc.edu
CONLEY, Kimberley, S ... 270-831-9752 ... 201 I
kim.conley@kctcs.edu
CONLEY, Lanny ... 407-366-9493 ... 115 I
lconley@rts.edu
CONLEY, Laura, H ... 330-972-5793 ... 403 B
lhc1@uakron.edu
CONLEY, Mark ... 206-543-4139 ... 538 F
mconley@uw.edu
CONLEY, Marsha, A ... 717-866-5775 ... 428 I
mconley@evangelical.edu
CONLEY, Michael Anne ... 415-442-7281 ... 48 E
maconley@ggu.edu
CONLEY, Sean ... 802-258-9203 ... 513 F
sconley@marlboro.edu
CONLEY, Sonja ... 620-331-4100 ... 193 G
sconley@indycc.edu
CONLEY, Susanne, H ... 508-626-4926 ... 238 D
sconley@framingham.edu
CONLEY, William, J ... 508-793-3423 ... 233 D
wjconley@holycross.edu
CONLIFFE, Marcia ... 850-599-3730 ... 118 G
marcia.conliffe@famu.edu
CONLIN, Pam ... 214-768-3738 ... 494 F
pconlin@smu.edu
CONLOGUE, Jon ... 413-572-5572 ... 239 C
jconlogue@wsc.ma.edu
CONLON, Cindy, H ... 256-765-4206 ... 9 D
chconlon@una.edu
CONLON, Kevin, J ... 614-222-6171 ... 388 F
kconlon@ccad.edu
CONN, Annette, L ... 215-968-8048 ... 423 E
conna@bucks.edu
CONN, Brian ... 423-614-8621 ... 470 A
bconn@leeuniversity.edu
CONN, Bruce ... 706-236-1756 ... 125 G
bconn@berry.edu
CONN, C. Paul ... 423-614-8600 ... 470 A
pconn@leeuniversity.edu
CONN, Keith ... 757-464-4600 ... 530 E
deankconn@cie-wc.edu
CONN, Melinda ... 314-434-4044 ... 281 A
melinda.conn@covenantseminary.edu

CONN, Tom ... 973-684-5329 ... 312 E
tconn@pccc.edu
CONN, W. David ... 805-756-6005 ... 33 F
dconn@calpoly.edu
CONNAGHAN, Stephen ... 202-319-5055 ... 97 C
connaghan@cua.edu
CONNALLY, Sam ... 502-852-3698 ... 207 A
s0conn02@louisville.edu
CONNAUGHTON,
David, M ... 409-772-3446 ... 507 B
dmconnau@utmb.edu
CONNEELY, James ... 859-622-1721 ... 200 D
james.conneely@eku.edu
CONNELL, Bernadean ... 817-598-6350 ... 508 C
bconnell@wc.edu
CONNELL, Christopher ... 513-785-3171 ... 396 E
connellcm@muohio.edu
CONNELL, Dan ... 606-783-2005 ... 204 E
d.connell@moreheadstate.edu
CONNELL, John ... 706-233-7821 ... 136 E
jconnell@shorter.edu
CONNELL, Mary Kay ... 401-341-2262 ... 454 D
connellm@salve.edu
CONNELL, Matthew, J ... 570-688-2466 ... 437 G
mconnell@northampton.edu
CONNELL, Patrick ... 518-454-2833 ... 330 C
connellp@strose.edu
CONNELL, S. Jack ... 585-594-6200 ... 347 F
connell_jack@roberts.edu
CONNELL, Timothy ... 562-908-3413 ... 63 H
tconnell@riohondo.edu
CONNELLY, Carol ... 219-785-5267 ... 178 H
cconnelly@pnc.edu
CONNELLY, Edward, D ... 860-628-4751 ... 92 F
econnelly@lincolncollegene.edu
CONNELLY, Krysti, H ... 618-537-6861 ... 157 G
khconnelly@mckendree.edu
CONNELLY, Laurie ... 509-359-2372 ... 533 D
lconnelly@ewu.edu
CONNELLY, Philip ... 908-737-7020 ... 311 B
pconnell@kean.edu
CONNELLY, Robert ... 210-829-2700 ... 503 F
bobc@uiwtx.edu
CONNELLY, Robert, A ... 864-503-5230 ... 463 A
bconnelly@uscupstate.edu
CONNELLY, Terry, R ... 415-442-6514 ... 48 E
tconnelly@ggu.edu
CONNELLY-DUGGAN,
Lisa, L ... 410-888-9048 ... 226 F
lisacd@tai.edu
CONNELLY-WEIDA,
Cecelia, A ... 610-799-1630 ... 434 D
cconnellyweida@lccc.edu
CONNELY, Anne ... 610-398-5300 ... 434 F
aconnely@lincolntech.com
CONNELY, Kristen ... 425-564-2388 ... 531 B
kristen.connely@bellevuecollege.edu
CONNER, Andrea ... 641-269-3708 ... 185 A
conneran@grinnell.edu
CONNER, Arabie ... 785-242-5200 ... 195 F
arabie.conner@ottawa.edu
CONNER, B. Renee ... 301-784-5000 ... 221 A
rconner@allegany.edu
CONNER, Charlene ... 214-333-5244 ... 484 C
charlene@dbu.edu
CONNER, Courtney, L ... 276-619-4317 ... 525 C
cconner@swcenter.edu
CONNER, David ... 806-894-9611 ... 494 C
dconner@southplainscollege.edu
CONNER, Deborah, K ... 843-349-2568 ... 456 G
dconner@coastal.edu
CONNER, Jamelle ... 727-341-3358 ... 116 F
conner.jamelle@spcollege.edu
CONNER, Laurence ... 860-701-5028 ... 93 B
conner_l@mitchell.edu
CONNER, Louis, M ... 931-540-2632 ... 474 F
lconner@columbiastate.edu
CONNER, Margaret, R ... 847-317-6504 ... 166 B
mconner@tiu.edu
CONNER, Michael ... 951-487-3440 ... 58 B
mconner@msjc.edu
CONNER, Phyllis ... 402-375-7510 ... 299 I
phconne1@wsc.edu
CONNER, Rita, D ... 828-694-1825 ... 368 B
ritac@blueridge.edu
CONNER, Shelly ... 559-244-5980 ... 71 I
shelly.conner@scccd.edu
CONNER, Susan ... 517-629-0221 ... 247 E
sconner@albion.edu
CONNER, Victor ... 619-201-8710 ... 65 D
Victor.Conner@sdcc.edu
CONNERS, John, R ... 607-844-8222 ... 357 H
connerj@tc3.edu
CONNERS, Mary Ann ... 732-906-4681 ... 311 E
mconners@middlesexcc.edu
CONNERTY, Denise, A ... 215-204-0720 ... 447 G
denise.connerty@temple.edu
CONNERY, Elizabeth, A ... 570-348-6200 ... 435 F
connery@marywood.edu
CONNETT, David ... 909-469-5264 ... 78 D
dconnett@westernu.edu
CONNIFF, Brian, P ... 570-941-6284 ... 450 B
conniffb2@scranton.edu
CONNIRY, JR., Charles, J 503-554-6152 ... 415 I
cconniry@georgefox.edu

CONNOLE, Kim ... 701-627-4738 ... 380 F
kconno@fbcc.bia.edu
CONNOLLY, Adam ... 843-383-8050 ... 457 A
aconnolly@coker.edu
CONNOLLY, Ann Marie ... 313-883-8500 ... 257 G
connolly.annmarie@shms.edu
CONNOLLY, Derry ... 858-653-6740 ... 52 C
CONNOLLY, Donna ... 401-841-6499 ... 557 I
CONNOLLY, Edward ... 602-393-5900 ... 13 C
econnolly@cc.edu
CONNOLLY, Elizabeth, A ... 315-386-7325 ... 355 D
connolly@canton.edu
CONNOLLY, Jim ... 203-332-5088 ... 90 B
jconnolly@hcc.commnet.edu
CONNOLLY, John ... 718-409-5979 ... 356 C
jconnolly@sunymaritime.edu
CONNOLLY, Jon, H ... 307-674-6446 ... 556 C
jconnolly@sheridan.edu
CONNOLLY, Lettie ... 563-242-4023 ... 181 G
lettie.connolly@ashford.edu
CONNOLLY, Lidy ... 858-653-6740 ... 52 C
CONNOLLY, Lynn ... 720-496-1370 ... 84 J
lconnolly@religiousscience.org
CONNOLLY, Marie ... 509-865-8586 ... 534 D
connolly_m@heritage.edu
CONNOLLY, Meg ... 314-977-7121 ... 289 F
burnsmm@slu.edu
CONNOLLY, Melissa, A ... 516-463-4160 ... 335 H
melissa.a.connolly@hofstra.edu
CONNOLLY, Michael ... 320-363-3171 ... 271 F
mconnolly@csbsju.edu
CONNOLLY, Monika ... 949-582-4602 ... 70 F
mconnolly@saddleback.edu
CONNOLLY, Patricia, A ... 412-536-1243 ... 432 F
patricia.connolly@laroche.edu
CONNOLLY, Robert, P ... 617-287-7073 ... 237 B
rconnolly@umassp.edu
CONNOLLY, Tara ... 515-964-6447 ... 183 E
tkconnolly@dmacc.edu
CONNON, Ryan ... 207-453-5141 ... 218 I
rconnon@kvcc.me.edu
CONNOR, Adele ... 914-395-2521 ... 350 C
aconner@sarahlawrence.edu
CONNOR, Catherine, H ... 610-519-4036 ... 450 G
catherine.connor@villanova.edu
CONNOR, Edward, J ... 508-831-5286 ... 247 B
econnor@wpi.edu
CONNOR, Elizabeth ... 843-953-7691 ... 456 C
elizabeth.connor@citadel.edu
CONNOR, Erin ... 207-513-3620 ... 218 C
econnor@kaplan.edu
CONNOR, Francis, P ... 260-399-7700 ... 180 E
fconnor@sf.edu
CONNOR, Joseph ... 518-445-3224 ... 322 D
jconn@albanylaw.edu
CONNOR, Nancy, J ... 253-535-7465 ... 535 K
connornj@plu.edu
CONNOR, Pat ... 812-855-1764 ... 173 C
connorp@indiana.edu
CONNOR, Rosie ... 435-283-7160 ... 512 B
rosie.connor@snow.edu
CONNOR, Terrence ... 214-768-4909 ... 494 F
connor@smu.edu
CONNOR, Terry, D ... 859-344-3308 ... 206 D
terry.connor@thomasmore.edu
CONNORS, Anne ... 207-453-5126 ... 218 I
aconnors@kvcc.me.edu
CONNORS, Chalese ... 940-898-2373 ... 502 B
cconnors@twu.edu
CONNORS, Cheryl, C ... 401-739-5000 ... 453 E
CONNORS, Christine, M ... 617-266-1400 ... 231 G
CONNORS, John ... 215-596-8973 ... 450 A
j.connors@usciences.edu
CONNORS, Mary, B ... 716-829-7775 ... 332 F
connorsm@dyc.edu
CONNORS, Michael, W ... 773-371-5484 ... 146 B
mconnors@ctu.edu
CONNORS, Nancy, J ... 718-940-5580 ... 349 B
nconnors@sjcny.edu
CONNORS, Nancy, J ... 718-940-5580 ... 349 A
nconnors@sjcny.edu
CONNORS, Natalie ... 219-785-5498 ... 178 H
nconnors@pnc.edu
CONNORS, Patricia ... 718-488-1038 ... 338 H
patricia.connors@liu.edu
CONOLEY, Jane ... 805-893-3917 ... 74 F
jane-conoley@education.ucsb.edu
CONOLLY, Charlene ... 410-287-6060 ... 222 A
cconolly@cecil.edu
CONOVER, Dustin ... 307-382-1644 ... 556 F
dconover@wwcc.wy.edu
CONOVER, Henry ... 775-831-1314 ... 303 E
hconover@sierranevada.edu
CONOVER, Kurt ... 480-654-7777 ... 15 K
kurt.conover@mcmail.maricopa.edu
CONOVER, Randall ... 937-328-6180 ... 387 G
conoverr@clarkstate.edu
CONOVER, Robert ... 507-457-1496 ... 271 G
bconover@smumn.edu
CONOVER, Wheeler ... 606-589-3038 ... 203 A
wheeler.conover@kctcs.edu
CONRAD, Cecilia ... 909-621-8137 ... 63 A
cecilia.conrad@pomona.edu

COOMER, Roger ... 501-337-5000 ... 21 D
rcoomer@otcweb.edu
COOMER, Sue, B ... 270-384-8024 ... 203 H
coomers@lindsey.edu
COOMES, Judy ... 270-686-4532 ... 202 E
judy.coomes@kctcs.edu
COON, David, W ... 415-485-9502 ... 41 I
davidwain.coon@marin.edu
COON, Jule ... 231-591-2324 ... 251 B
coonj@ferris.edu
COON, Omayra ... 910-221-2224 ... 364 C
COON, Thomas, G ... 517-355-2308 ... 255 D
coontg@msu.edu
COONAN, Daniel ... 408-554-5344 ... 68 C
dcoonan@scu.edu
COONAN, Patrick, R ... 516-877-4511 ... 322 A
coonan@adelphi.edu
COONEN, Ned ... 847-214-7557 ... 150 D
ncoonen@elgin.edu
COONEY, Terry ... 410-704-2128 ... 228 E
tcooney@towson.edu
COONEY MINER,
Dianne, C ... 585-385-8472 ... 348 F
dcooney-miner@sjfc.edu
COONING, Peggy, J ... 615-248-1355 ... 476 E
pcooning@trevecca.edu
COONROD, Curtis, C ... 314-516-5211 ... 291 F
curt_coonrod@umsl.edu
COONS, Christopher ... 814-824-3125 ... 436 C
ccoons@mercyhurst.edu
COONS, Maria ... 847-925-6143 ... 151 E
mcoons@harpercollege.edu
COONS, Patrick ... 502-272-8056 ... 198 E
pcoons@bellarmine.edu
COONS, Robert, A ... 812-877-8246 ... 179 A
robert.a.coons@rose-hulman.edu
COONS, Roy ... 517-586-3005 ... 249 H
rcoons@cleary.edu
COOPEE, Scott, J ... 413-782-1246 ... 246 D
sjcoopee@wne.edu
COOPER, Alan ... 212-678-8065 ... 337 G
alcooper@jtsa.edu
COOPER, Amy, M ... 270-384-8053 ... 203 H
coopera@lindsey.edu
COOPER, Ann ... 985-380-2436 ... 211 K
COOPER, Ann, A ... 803-778-6636 ... 455 G
cooperaa@cctech.edu
COOPER, Anne, M ... 727-341-3323 ... 116 F
cooper.anne@spcollege.edu
COOPER, Annie, L ... 570-662-4381 ... 443 B
acooper@mansfield.edu
COOPER, Barbara, I ... 252-222-6225 ... 368 F
cooperb@carteret.edu
COOPER, Beverly ... 765-269-5200 ... 176 B
bcooper@ivytech.edu
COOPER, Brett ... 870-759-4107 ... 26 B
bcooper@wbcoll.edu
COOPER, Burns ... 907-474-7231 ... 10 J
gbcooper@alaska.edu
COOPER, Candace ... 704-878-3256 ... 371 H
ccooper@mitchellcc.edu
COOPER, Carlton ... 903-886-5568 ... 497 E
carlton_cooper@tamu-commerce.edu
COOPER, Carrie ... 601-857-3224 ... 274 E
CECooper@hindscc.edu
COOPER, Carrie ... 859-622-1778 ... 200 D
carrie.cooper@eku.edu
COOPER, Cary, W ... 409-772-2665 ... 507 B
ccooper@utmb.edu
COOPER, Cathy, E ... 330-684-8944 ... 403 C
ccooper@uakron.edu
COOPER, Claire ... 808-544-1191 ... 140 B
ccooper@hpu.edu
COOPER, Colleen, M ... 386-822-7481 ... 121 E
cmcooper@stetson.edu
COOPER, Cynthia, L ... 585-292-3015 ... 341 H
ccooper@monroecc.edu
COOPER, David ... 773-777-4220 ... 160 C
dcooper@nc.edu
COOPER, David ... 401-841-3540 ... 557 I
COOPER, David, H ... 336-278-5900 ... 364 A
dcooper8@elon.edu
COOPER, Doug ... 404-653-7882 ... 134 A
dacooper@morehouse.edu
COOPER, Douglas ... 860-486-2421 ... 94 E
douglas.cooper@uconn.edu
COOPER, Ed ... 229-430-3577 ... 123 I
ecooper@albanytech.edu
COOPER, Edy ... 708-763-6505 ... 162 C
edy.cooper@resu.edu
COOPER, Erik ... 530-741-6605 ... 80 E
ecooper@yccd.edu
COOPER, Frank ... 609-771-2357 ... 308 G
cooper@tcnj.edu
COOPER, Franklin ... 406-638-3161 ... 294 G
cooperf@lbhc.cc.mt.us
COOPER, Gail, F ... 626-588-7529 ... 61 E
gfcooper@pasadena.edu
COOPER, Gayle ... 870-612-2004 ... 25 E
gayle.cooper@uaccb.edu
COOPER, George, E ... 803-536-7013 ... 460 G
president@scsu.edu
COOPER, Hortense ... 310-660-3492 ... 45 D
hcooper@elcamino.edu

COOPER, James ... 610-409-3698 ... 450 C
jcooper@ursinus.edu
COOPER, James, E ... 334-727-8011 ... 8 C
cooper@tuskegee.edu
COOPER, James, M ... 619-239-0391 ... 37 D
jcooper@cwsl.edu
COOPER, James, W ... 678-915-4986 ... 137 C
jcooper@spsu.edu
COOPER, Jeffrey ... 215-898-1388 ... 448 I
jeffcoop@upenn.edu
COOPER, Jennifer ... 404-233-3949 ... 135 G
jcooper@richmont.edu
COOPER, Jeremy ... 785-841-9640 ... 195 H
COOPER, Joel ... 507-222-4077 ... 262 B
jcooper@carleton.edu
COOPER, John, D ... 563-333-6480 ... 188 D
COOPER, Jorsene ... 757-727-5323 ... 519 C
jorsene.cooper@hamptonu.edu
COOPER, Karen ... 603-897-8508 ... 305 G
kcooper@rivier.edu
COOPER, Karen, S ... 650-723-0198 ... 71 F
karen.cooper@stanford.edu
COOPER, Karla ... 402-826-8111 ... 298 A
karla.cooper@doane.edu
COOPER, Katrina ... 304-829-7437 ... 540 E
kcooper@bethanywv.edu
COOPER, Kelly ... 815-226-4022 ... 162 H
khaugen@rockford.edu
COOPER, Kenneth ... 845-758-7461 ... 323 F
cooper@bard.edu
COOPER, Kerrie, L ... 315-386-7616 ... 355 D
cooper@canton.edu
COOPER, SR., Lamar, E ... 214-818-1322 ... 484 A
coopsr@criswell.edu
COOPER, Lisa, A ... 229-931-2921 ... 131 B
COOPER, Lisa, J ... 215-951-2940 ... 444 C
cooperl@philau.edu
COOPER, Margaret ... 815-802-8962 ... 154 J
mcooper@kcc.edu
COOPER, Marilee ... 806-457-4200 ... 486 G
mcooper@fpctx.edu
COOPER, OSB, Mark, A ... 603-641-7100 ... 305 H
mcooper@anselm.edu
COOPER, Mark, E ... 740-368-3108 ... 400 F
mecooper@owu.edu
COOPER, Mary ... 434-223-6311 ... 519 B
mcooper@hsc.edu
COOPER, Mary Gail ... 252-536-7237 ... 370 F
cooperm@halifaxcc.edu
COOPER, Mary-Beth ... 585-475-2267 ... 347 G
mbccooper@rit.edu
COOPER, MaryKay ... 210-999-7011 ... 502 C
marykay.cooper@trinity.edu
COOPER, Matthew ... 609-984-1140 ... 316 A
mcooper@tesc.edu
COOPER, Michael ... 507-389-2523 ... 267 H
michael.cooper@mnsu.edu
COOPER, MiChielle ... 620-421-6700 ... 194 E
michiellec@labette.edu
COOPER, Miranda, D ... 423-652-4715 ... 469 L
mdcooper@king.edu
COOPER, N. John ... 412-624-1164 ... 449 A
cooper@pitt.edu
COOPER, Nani Lou, S ... 864-488-4617 ... 459 A
ncooper@limestone.edu
COOPER, Natalie ... 215-871-6560 ... 444 B
nataliecoo@pcom.edu
COOPER, Patricia, A ... 808-956-7541 ... 141 B
pcooper@hawaii.edu
COOPER, Patricia, D ... 412-578-6157 ... 424 G
pdcooper@carlow.edu
COOPER, R. Scott ... 267-502-2604 ... 423 B
rscott.cooper@anc-gc.org
COOPER, Reginald ... 870-574-4504 ... 24 A
rcooper@sautech.edu
COOPER, Rick ... 251-981-3771 ... 2 H
rick.cooper@columbiasouthern.edu
COOPER, Robert, A ... 213-740-2101 ... 76 C
racooper@usc.edu
COOPER, Ruth ... 512-313-3000 ... 483 G
ruth.cooper@concordia.edu
COOPER, Sandra ... 319-398-5630 ... 186 H
scooper@kirkwood.edu
COOPER, Sandra, M ... 813-974-8128 ... 120 D
scooper@admin.usf.edu
COOPER, Shaun ... 575-646-6030 ... 319 D
scooper@nmsu.edu
COOPER, Stephanie ... 973-300-2161 ... 315 F
scooper@sussex.edu
COOPER, Stewart, E ... 219-464-5002 ... 181 A
stewart.cooper@valpo.edu
COOPER, Tammi ... 254-295-4507 ... 504 A
tcooper@umhb.edu
COOPER, Tara, L ... 606-546-1241 ... 206 F
tcooper@unionky.edu
COOPER, Toya ... 805-565-6832 ... 78 F
tcooper@westmont.edu
COOPER, Tracey, I ... 440-525-7230 ... 394 F
tcooper@lakelandcc.edu
COOPER-WHITE,
Michael, L ... 717-334-6286 ... 435 A
mcooper@ltsg.edu
COOPERIDER, Susan ... 740-368-3376 ... 400 F
skcooper@owu.edu

COOPERSTEIN, Robert ... 408-944-6009 ... 60 L
robert.cooperstein@palmer.edu
COOPWOOD, Kenneth ... 219-980-6596 ... 173 F
kcoopwoo@iun.edu
COOROUGH, Randall ... 262-691-5168 ... 555 C
rcoorough@wctc.edu
COOTE, Polly ... 415-451-2853 ... 66 B
pcoote@sfts.edu
COOTER, Raelynn ... 215-503-6595 ... 448 B
raelynn.cooter@jefferson.edu
COOTER, Robert, B ... 502-272-7992 ... 198 E
rcooter@bellarmine.edu
COOTS, Kevin ... 606-326-2064 ... 201 B
Kevin.Coots@kctcs.edu
COPANS, Ruth, S ... 518-580-5506 ... 351 B
rcopans@skidmore.edu
COPAS, Aimee ... 701-328-4136 ... 381 C
COPAS, Lisa ... 937-393-3431 ... 401 K
lcopas@sscc.edu
COPE, Glen, H ... 314-516-5373 ... 291 F
copeg@umsl.edu
COPE, Marla ... 913-234-0687 ... 191 G
marla.cope@cleveland.edu
COPELAND, Brian ... 616-331-2257 ... 252 A
copelabr@gvsu.edu
COPELAND, David, L ... 540-464-7218 ... 529 A
copelanddl@vmi.edu
COPELAND, Elaine, J ... 803-327-7402 ... 456 F
ecopeland@clintonjuniorcollege.edu
COPELAND, Ellis ... 312-329-6684 ... 146 C
ecopeland@thechicagoschool.edu
COPELAND, John, B ... 505-323-9282 ... 508 B
copelandj@wbu.edu
COPELAND, Judson ... 405-425-5129 ... 409 E
judson.copeland@oc.edu
COPELAND, Leigh ... 843-525-8231 ... 461 E
lcopeland@tcl.edu
COPELAND, Louise ... 651-290-6439 ... 273 B
louise.copeland@wmitchell.edu
COPELAND, Maura ... 912-478-7481 ... 131 A
mconley@georgiasouthern.edu
COPELAND, Nate ... 501-279-4126 ... 21 H
nbcopeland@harding.edu
COPELAND, Robert ... 803-327-7402 ... 456 F
rcopeland@clintonjuniorcollege.edu
COPELAND, JR.,
Robert, M ... 803-327-7402 ... 456 F
rcopeland@clintonjuniorcollege.edu
COPELAND, Sandra ... 252-862-1225 ... 372 H
sandrac@roanokechowan.edu
COPELAND, Therese, A ... 812-374-5115 ... 175 J
tcopeland15@ivytech.edu
COPELIN, Michele ... 806-874-3571 ... 482 H
michele.copelin@clarendoncollege.edu
COPENAGLE, Lily ... 503-517-7916 ... 420 A
copenagl@reed.edu
COPENHAVER, Bonny ... 931-393-1735 ... 475 C
bcopenhaver@mscc.edu
COPENHAVER, Lisa, A ... 301-766-3646 ... 223 G
lcopenhaver@kaplan.edu
COPENHAVER, Michael ... 619-644-7000 ... 49 A
michael.coppenhaver@gcccd.edu
COPERTHWAITE, Corby ... 860-244-7604 ... 89 J
ccoperthwaite@commnet.edu
COPES, Marcella ... 410-951-3990 ... 228 B
mcopes@coppin.edu
COPETAS, Karen ... 360-650-3440 ... 539 C
karen.copetas@wwu.edu
COPLER, Thomas, H ... 804-752-7263 ... 522 F
tcopler@rmc.edu
COPLES, Jimmy ... 404-270-2873 ... 128 G
jcoples@devry.edu
COPLEY, Jason ... 301-369-2800 ... 221 F
jcopley@capitol-college.edu
COPLIN, Kimberly, A ... 740-587-6469 ... 389 H
coplin@denison.edu
COPLIN, Louis ... 518-629-7348 ... 336 C
l.coplin@hvcc.edu
COPONITI, Mike ... 405-224-3140 ... 413 E
mcoponiti@usao.edu
COPONITI, Mike, D ... 405-224-3140 ... 413 E
mcoponiti@usao.edu
COPPAGE, Mike ... 205-726-2020 ... 6 G
wcoppag1@samford.edu
COPPENHAVER, Dorian, H 409-772-2665 ... 507 B
dcoppenh@utmb.edu
COPPENS, Nina ... 978-934-3832 ... 237 F
Nina_Coppens@uml.edu
COPPERSMITH, Clifford, P 570-326-3761 ... 440 K
COPPI, Carla, E ... 618-453-7661 ... 164 I
ccoppi@siu.edu
COPPINGER, Debbie ... 615-460-6474 ... 467 B
debbie.coppinger@belmont.edu
COPPLE, Chad ... 618-437-5321 ... 162 B
copple@rlc.edu
COPPLE, James "Dean" ... 865-694-6536 ... 475 F
jdcopple@pstcc.edu
COPPLE, Jenna ... 589-336-5082 ... 205 F
jcopple@sccky.edu
COPPOLA, David, L ... 203-365-4809 ... 93 G
coppolad@sacredheart.edu
COPPOLA, Joseph ... 559-437-5303 ... 44 E
jcoppola@devry.edu

COPPOLA, Lynn ... 215-591-5753 ... 427 A
lcoppola@devry.edu
COPPOLA, Robert ... 978-837-5118 ... 242 D
robert.coppola@merrimack.edu
COPPOLA, Sandra ... 973-278-5400 ... 307 G
sec@berkeleycollege.edu
COPPOLA, Stephen, A ... 704-687-5965 ... 378 E
scoppola@uncc.edu
COPPOLA, Tim ... 813-889-3460 ... 111 A
tcoppola@academy.edu
CORA, Alisha, J ... 651-631-5237 ... 270 E
ajcora@nwc.edu
CORAK, Kathleen, A ... 928-226-4224 ... 13 H
kathleen.corak@coconino.edu
CORALLO, Anthony, L ... 610-758-3970 ... 434 E
alc2@lehigh.edu
CORAZZA, Anthony ... 718-368-5124 ... 328 B
acorazza@kbcc.cuny.edu
CORBA, David ... 586-286-2058 ... 254 F
corbad@macomb.edu
CORBALIS, Kathleen, J ... 609-343-4907 ... 307 D
corbalis@atlantic.edu
CORBAT, Carol ... 318-473-6431 ... 212 G
ccorbat@lsua.edu
CORBETT, Andy ... 303-352-3032 ... 83 F
andy.corbett@cccs.edu
CORBETT, Ann ... 207-621-3145 ... 220 B
annie@maine.edu
CORBETT, Idna, M ... 610-436-3416 ... 443 F
icorbett@wcupa.edu
CORBETT, Keith ... 605-688-4153 ... 466 B
keith.corbett@sdstate.edu
CORBETT, Kevin, J ... 785-864-4760 ... 196 F
kcorbett@ku.edu
CORBETT, Michele ... 619-849-2510 ... 62 L
michelecorbett@pointloma.edu
CORBETT, Mickey ... 432-837-8059 ... 501 B
mcorbett@sulross.edu
CORBIN, Rebecca ... 609-894-9311 ... 308 C
rcorbin@bcc.edu
CORBIN, Thomas ... 802-443-5504 ... 513 G
corbin@middlebury.edu
CORBIN, Ty ... 804-523-5726 ... 526 F
tcorbin@reynolds.edu
CORBIN-HUTCHINSON,
Terry ... 631-687-2629 ... 349 B
tcorbon-hutchinson@sjcny.edu
CORBINE, Theresa, C ... 315-386-7448 ... 355 D
corbine@canton.edu
CORBITT, Sandra, K ... 540-338-1776 ... 522 A
CORBITT, Timothy ... 860-832-1629 ... 91 G
corbitt@ccsu.edu
CORBOY, Lynne ... 215-780-1394 ... 446 G
lcorboy@salus.edu
CORCORAN, Janenne ... 410-386-8444 ... 221 G
jcorcoran@carrollcc.edu
CORCORAN, Jerry, M ... 815-224-0404 ... 153 D
jerry_corcoran@ivcc.edu
CORCORAN, Krista, L ... 417-268-6064 ... 279 D
kcorcoran@gobbc.edu
CORCORAN, Lisa, D ... 425-637-1010 ... 531 I
lcorcoran@city.edu
CORCORAN, Marsha, A ... 302-225-6261 ... 96 E
corcorm@gbc.edu
CORCORAN, Mary, C ... 617-552-8647 ... 232 D
mary.corcoran.1@bc.edu
CORCORAN, Michael, H ... 408-453-9900 ... 50 E
mcorcoran@henley-putnam.edu
CORCORAN, William ... 201-612-5234 ... 307 F
wcorcoran@bergen.edu
CORCORAN, William, M ... 570-208-5846 ... 432 E
wmcorcor@kings.edu
CORDANO, Mark ... 978-837-5000 ... 242 D
cordanom@merrimack.edu
CORDANO, Mark ... 607-274-3341 ... 336 G
mcordano@ithaca.edu
CORDARY, John ... 281-283-2135 ... 503 C
cordary@uhcl.edu
CORDEIRO, Paula, A ... 619-260-4540 ... 76 A
cordeiro@sandiego.edu
CORDEIRO, Wayne ... 808-853-1040 ... 140 G
CORDEIRO, Wayne ... 541-485-1780 ... 417 E
waynecordeiro@newhope.edu
CORDELL, Barbara ... 903-694-4003 ... 492 A
bcordell@panola.edu
CORDELL, David, J ... 425-640-1412 ... 533 E
dcordell@edcc.edu
CORDELL, Janice, K ... 563-387-1018 ... 187 A
cordellj@luther.edu
CORDELL, Joyce ... 915-831-6530 ... 486 E
jyamasak@cpcc.edu
CORDELL, Michelle ... 479-619-4361 ... 22 H
mcordell@nwacc.edu
CORDELL, Peggy ... 706-295-6959 ... 130 F
pcordell@gntc.edu
CORDELL, Penny ... 706-272-4498 ... 127 G
pcordell@daltonstate.edu
CORDERO, Carolina ... 704-334-6882 ... 367 E
ccordero@nlts.edu
CORDERO, Damaris ... 787-751-0160 ... 561 G
dcordero@cmpr.gobierno.pr
CORDERO, Eunice ... 787-284-1912 ... 563 F
ecordero@ponce.inter.edu
CORDERO, Gisela ... 787-815-0000 ... 566 F

CORDERO, Irma, L ... 787-740-1611 ... 566 A
icordero@uccaribe.edu
CORDERO, Jose ... 787-758-2525 ... 567 D
jose.cordero6@upr.edu
CORDERO, Maggie ... 562-860-2451 ... 38 J
mcordero@cerritos.edu
CORDERO, Mariela ... 787-894-2828 ... 568 A
mariela.cordero@upr.edu
CORDERO, Zain ... 787-882-2065 ... 565 I
mis@unitecpr.net
CORDERO-ARMSTRONG,
Charles, A ... 787-250-0000 ... 566 D
an.cordero@upr.edu
CORDERO DE VIDAL,
Pilar ... 787-896-2252 ... 561 K
pcordero@edpcollege.edu
CORDERY, Simon ... 706-864-1819 ... 134 D
sdcordery@northgeorgia.edu
CORDES, Cynthia ... 773-481-8182 ... 147 F
ccordes@ccc.edu
CORDIA, Judith ... 775-445-3295 ... 303 B
cordiaj@wnc.edu
CORDLE, David, P ... 910-962-7232 ... 379 C
cordled@uncw.edu
CORDLE, Robbie, L ... 301-687-4403 ... 228 C
rcordle@frostburg.edu
CORDOVA, Jose ... 787-780-5134 ... 564 F
jcordova@lbancapr.com
CORDOVA, Mario ... 209-384-6092 ... 57 C
mario.cordova@mccd.edu
CORDOVA, Mitchell ... 239-590-7074 ... 119 A
mcordova@fgcu.edu
CORDOVA, Ryan ... 505-747-2288 ... 320 A
rcordova@nnmc.edu
CORDOVA, Tracy, H ... 417-667-8181 ... 280 I
tcordova@cottey.edu
CORDRAY, JR., John, A ... 843-953-8259 ... 457 B
cordrayj@cofc.edu
CORDULACK, John ... 217-875-7200 ... 162 D
jcordula@richland.edu
CORE, Gordon ... 724-938-5985 ... 441 G
core@calu.edu
CORE, Justin ... 541-881-5781 ... 420 E
jcore@tvcc.cc
CORE, Ron ... 912-478-5491 ... 131 A
rcore@georgiasouthern.edu
COREN, Richard, II ... 401-825-2028 ... 453 B
rhcoren@ccri.edu
CORESSEL, James ... 419-783-2503 ... 389 G
jcoressel@defiance.edu
COREY, Barry, H ... 562-903-4701 ... 30 H
president@biola.edu
COREY, Frederick, C ... 602-496-0624 ... 12 B
frederick.corey@asu.edu
COREY, M, J ... 304-637-1344 ... 540 F
coreym@dewv.edu
COREY, Pat ... 765-269-5605 ... 176 B
pcorey@ivytech.edu
COREY, Steven, M ... 269-749-7642 ... 257 D
scorey@olivetcollege.edu
COREY, Timothy ... 570-586-2400 ... 422 F
tcorey@bbc.edu
CORGNATI, Bart ... 919-962-4592 ... 377 A
bbc@northcarolina.edu
CORIA, Elizabeth ... 562-908-3411 ... 63 H
elizabeth.coria@riohondo.edu
CORIELL, Bruce ... 719-389-6638 ... 81 L
bcoriell@coloradocollege.edu
CORINA, Laura ... 617-984-1713 ... 244 C
lcorina@quincycollege.edu
CORINO, Mark, A ... 973-618-3412 ... 308 D
mcorino@caldwell.edu
CORITRERA, Jenniffer, E ... 787-761-0640 ... 561 B
decanatoacademica@cbp.edu
CORJAY, Marcy ... 704-216-7217 ... 373 C
marcy.corjay@rccc.edu
CORKERY, John, E ... 312-987-1426 ... 154 F
7corkery@jmls.edu
CORKILL, Jim, R ... 805-893-5882 ... 74 F
jim.corkill@accounting.ucsb.edu
CORKRAN, Kenneth, F ... 508-541-1700 ... 234 B
kcorkran@dean.edu
CORKRUM, Dalia, L ... 509-527-5193 ... 539 E
corkrum@whitman.edu
CORKUM, David ... 617-552-4500 ... 232 D
david.corkum.1@bc.edu
CORLEY, Andreas ... 803-793-5122 ... 457 F
corleya@denmarktech.edu
CORLEY, Charlene ... 314-768-1234 ... 283 C
CORLEY, Devanna ... 304-367-4375 ... 543 E
CORLEY, Diane ... 512-463-1808 ... 500 D
diane.corley@tsus.edu
CORLEY, John, C ... 870-230-5179 ... 21 I
corleyj@hsu.edu
CORLEY, Teresa ... 615-794-4254 ... 472 D
tcorley@omorecollege.edu
CORLEY, Thomas ... 785-242-5200 ... 195 F
thomas.corley@ottawa.edu
CORLEY, Tom ... 785-242-5200 ... 195 G
CORLEY, Tom ... 785-242-5200 ... 178 E
CORLEY, Tom ... 785-242-5200 ... 17 C
CORLEY, Tom ... 785-242-5200 ... 549 E
CORLL, Thomas ... 432-685-5540 ... 490 G
tcorll@midland.edu

CORMACK, Barbara ... 530-283-0202 ... 47 B
bcormack@frc.edu
CORMICAN, Marty, J ... 610-499-4182 ... 451 F
mjcormican@widener.edu
CORMIER, Marilyn, E ... 802-654-2215 ... 514 B
mcormier@smcvt.edu
CORN, Melanie ... 510-594-5034 ... 31 J
mcorn@cca.edu
CORNACCHIA, Eugene, J ... 201-761-6010 ... 314 F
ecornacchia@spc.edu
CORNEJO-DARCY, Silvia ... 619-216-6795 ... 71 C
scornejo@swccd.edu
CORNEJO-DARCY, Silvia ... 619-216-6755 ... 71 C
scornejo@swccd.edu
CORNELIA, Jim ... 712-274-5234 ... 187 D
cornelia@morningside.edu
CORNELISON, Nelle ... 509-527-2664 ... 538 H
nelle.cornelison@wallawalla.edu
CORNELIUS, George, E ... 540-828-5605 ... 516 K
gcornelius@bridgewater.edu
CORNELIUS, Jerod, L ... 651-631-5320 ... 270 E
jlcornelius@nwc.edu
CORNELIUS, Michael ... 480-423-6573 ... 16 D
michael.cornelius@sccmail.maricopa.edu
CORNELIUS, Tim ... 479-619-3117 ... 22 H
tcornelius@nwacc.edu
CORNELL, David ... 760-384-6291 ... 52 N
dcornell@cerrocoso.edu
CORNELL, Dennis ... 213-740-2111 ... 76 C
dcornell@president.usc.edu
CORNELL, Dona, G ... 713-743-0949 ... 503 B
dghamilton@central.uh.edu
CORNELL, Dona, G ... 832-842-0949 ... 503 A
dhcornell@uh.edu
CORNELL, John ... 912-279-5703 ... 127 B
jcornell@ccga.edu
CORNELL, Kenneth, E ... 206-281-2405 ... 537 D
CORNELL, Linda, S ... 859-442-1123 ... 201 G
linda.cornell@kctcs.edu
CORNELL, Starr ... 248-364-6160 ... 257 C
cornell2@oakland.edu
CORNELL, Stefanie ... 510-574-1211 ... 44 D
scornell@devry.edu
CORNELL-POKU, Natasha ... 212-353-4099 ... 331 B
natasha@cooper.edu
CORNELL-SCOTT, Andrea ... 540-887-7270 ... 520 I
ascott@mbc.edu
CORNER, William, T ... 616-526-6451 ... 249 E
wtc2@calvin.edu
CORNERO, Robert ... 732-571-3424 ... 311 F
rcornero@monmouth.edu
CORNETT, Christy ... 617-369-3617 ... 244 G
ccornett@smfa.edu
CORNETT, Jeffrey, L ... 407-582-1362 ... 122 I
jcornett1@valenciacollege.edu
CORNETT, Mark ... 904-264-9122 ... 106 C
mcornett@cci.edu
CORNETT, Scott ... 606-368-6120 ... 197 H
scottcornett@alc.edu
CORNETT, Sherry, N ... 770-720-5543 ... 135 F
snc@reinhardt.edu
CORNFORD, Ernest, A ... 314-516-5092 ... 291 F
cornford@umsl.edu
CORNIA, Gary, C ... 801-422-4122 ... 509 D
gary_cornia@byu.edu
CORNIER, Wilfredo ... 787-841-2000 ... 564 I
wcornier@email.pucpr.edu
CORNILLE, Keith, T ... 608-246-6464 ... 554 B
kcornille@matcmadison.edu
CORNISH, Irene, K ... 315-859-4999 ... 335 A
icornish@hamilton.edu
CORNISH, Letitia ... 336-750-2132 ... 380 A
cornishl@wssu.edu
CORNMAN, Thomas, H ... 937-766-7770 ... 386 F
tcornman@cedarville.edu
CORNNER, Ryan ... 323-265-8967 ... 54 G
cornnerm@elac.edu
CORNOG, Evan, W ... 516-463-5213 ... 335 H
evan.cornog@hofstra.edu
CORNWELL, Grant, H ... 330-263-2311 ... 388 E
gcornwell@wooster.edu
CORNWELL, Mona, L ... 828-254-1921 ... 367 H
mcornwell@abtech.edu
CORNWELL, Shirley, A ... 937-393-3431 ... 401 K
scornwell@sscc.edu
COROMINAS, Mike ... 954-262-8840 ... 114 B
coromina@nsu.nova.edu
CORONA, Nayeli ... 619-574-6909 ... 60 E
ncorona@pacificcollege.edu
CORONA, Paul ... 847-491-8570 ... 160 D
p-corona@northwestern.edu
CORONADO, George, S ... 401-232-6001 ... 453 A
gcoronad@bryant.edu
CORONADO, Rene ... 956-882-8205 ... 505 C
rene.coronado@utb.edu
CORONADO, Ricardo ... 817-515-5234 ... 496 A
ricardo.coronado@tccd.edu
CORONADO-ROMERO,
Sylvia ... 262-595-2230 ... 551 E
sylvia.coronado-romero@uwp.edu
CORPENING, Brian, K ... 405-271-2332 ... 413 D
brian-corpening@ouhsc.edu
CORPUS, Ben ... 646-312-4570 ... 326 D
bencorpus@baruch.cuny.edu

CORR, Daniel, P ... 480-423-6317 ... 16 D
daniel.corr@sccmail.maricopa.edu
CORR, Marianne ... 574-631-6411 ... 180 D
mcorr1@nd.edu
CORRADETTI, Arthur ... 718-631-6344 ... 329 A
acorradetti@qcc.cuny.edu
CORRADO, Rebecca ... 212-217-4202 ... 333 G
rebecca_corrado@fitnyc.edu
CORRAL, David ... 661-654-2254 ... 33 H
Corral-david@aramark.com
CORRAL-NAVA, Nita ... 915-831-2302 ... 486 E
ncorraln@epcc.edu
CORRALIZA-TORRES,
Cruz ... 787-480-2386 ... 561 D
ccorraliza@sanjuancapital.com
CORRAN, Robert ... 802-656-3075 ... 514 F
robert.corran@uvm.edu
CORREA, Florinda ... 361-582-2516 ... 507 G
florinda.correa@victoriacollege.edu
CORREA, Leslie ... 808-544-0228 ... 140 B
lcorrea@hpu.edu
CORREA, Omar, G ... 309-457-2142 ... 158 G
correa@monm.edu
CORREA, Peter ... 404-965-6542 ... 124 B
pecorrea@aiuniv.edu
CORREA, Sylvia ... 256-233-8116 ... 1 F
sylvia.correa@athens.edu
CORREDERA, Enrique ... 802-656-2005 ... 514 F
enrique.corredera@uvm.edu
CORREIA, Jorge ... 781-595-6768 ... 236 I
jcorreia@mariancourt.edu
CORRELL, Brenda, J ... 417-268-6042 ... 279 D
bcorrell@gobbc.edu
CORRELL, Dennis, L ... 570-327-4761 ... 440 K
dcorrell@pct.edu
CORRELL, Jen ... 717-728-2362 ... 425 A
jencorrell@centralpenn.edu
CORRENTI, Bill ... 718-368-5066 ... 328 B
bcorrenti@kbcc.cuny.edu
CORRIE, Bruce, P ... 651-641-8226 ... 263 C
corrie@csp.edu
CORRIE, Rosie ... 575-769-4021 ... 317 K
rosie.corrie@clovis.edu
CORRIGAN, Boo ... 845-938-3701 ... 558 G
Boo.Corrigan@usma.edu
CORRIGAN, Deborah ... 518-438-3111 ... 340 B
debc@mariacollege.edu
CORRIGAN, Gary ... 567-661-2692 ... 400 H
gary_corrigan@owens.edu
CORRIGAN, Robert, A ... 415-338-1381 ... 36 F
corrigan@sfsu.edu
CORRIGAN, JR.,
Robert, F ... 713-798-6392 ... 481 H
corrigan@bcm.edu
CORRIGAN, Tom ... 617-217-9205 ... 231 C
tcorrigan@baystate.edu
CORRISS, Mary Jean ... 540-362-6332 ... 519 E
corrissmj@hollins.edu
CORSELLO, Christine ... 207-768-9601 ... 220 F
christine.corsello@umpi.edu
CORSENTINO, Leanne ... 719-549-3206 ... 87 B
leanne.corsentino@pueblocc.edu
CORSETTI, Dan ... 617-912-9125 ... 232 E
dcorsetti@bostonconservatory.edu
CORSO, Joseph ... 225-578-3312 ... 212 E
jacorso@lsu.edu
CORSO, Michael ... 973-300-2226 ... 315 F
mcorso@sussex.edu
CORSO, Teri ... 973-290-4266 ... 309 A
tcorso@cse.edu
CORSON, D.J ... 319-296-4292 ... 185 C
debra.corson@hawkeyecollege.edu
CORSON, Stephanie ... 813-621-0041 ... 105 G
scorson@cci.edu
CORSON-RIKERT, Janet, L ... 607-255-3564 ... 331 C
jlc18@cornell.edu
CORTELLINI, Melissa ... 914-674-7231 ... 340 G
MCortellini@mercy.edu
CORTES, Chris ... 559-638-3641 ... 72 B
chris.cortes@reedleycollege.edu
CORTES, Dario ... 212-986-4343 ... 323 J
dario@berkeleycollege.edu
CORTES, Dario, A ... 973-278-5400 ... 307 G
dario@berkeleycollege.edu
CORTES, Elvia, E ... 202-231-5605 ... 557 G
elvia.cortes@dia.mil
CORTES, Felix ... 787-841-2000 ... 564 I
fcortes@email.pucpr.edu
CORTES, Frances ... 787-878-5475 ... 562 H
fcortes@arecibo.inter.edu
CORTES, Gloria ... 787-891-0925 ... 562 G
gcortes@aguadilla.inter.edu
CORTES, Reinaldo ... 352-323-3691 ... 112 M
cortesr@lscc.edu
CORTES-SUAREZ, Gina ... 305-237-6034 ... 113 H
gcortes@mdc.edu
CORTESE, Joseph ... 570-504-9641 ... 425 F
CORTEZ, Jack ... 973-748-9000 ... 308 A
jack_cortez@bloomfield.edu
CORTEZ, Lori ... 989-386-6622 ... 255 F
lcortez@midmich.edu
CORTEZ, Marc ... 503-517-1876 ... 421 B
mcortez@westernseminary.edu
CORTEZ, Michele ... 909-915-3800 ... 29 B
mcortez@argosy.edu

CORTEZ, Ray ... 956-721-5303 ... 489 G
rcortez@laredo.edu
CORTEZ, Ronald ... 805-893-8291 ... 74 F
ron.cortez@vcadmin.ucsb.edu
CORTEZ, Sandra, L ... 956-721-5374 ... 489 G
sandra.cortez@laredo.edu
CORTEZ, Sylvia ... 619-849-2596 ... 62 L
sylviacortez@pointloma.edu
CORTEZ-FARAH, Terre ... 619-684-8763 ... 59 A
tcortez@newschoolarch.edu
CORTHEK, Ronald ... 219-989-2654 ... 178 G
CORTI, Tom ... 631-420-2264 ... 356 A
CORTILET-ALBRECHT,
Carol ... 219-989-2507 ... 178 G
Carol.Cortilet-Albrecht@purduecal.edu
CORTINAS, Debra ... 361-825-5743 ... 497 F
debra.cortinas@tamucc.edu
CORUM, Ilana ... 954-308-2218 ... 100 I
icorum@aii.edu
CORUM, John, D ... 308-763-2020 ... 301 E
corumj@wncc.edu
CORVEY, Jim ... 214-860-8520 ... 485 A
jcorvey@dcccd.edu
CORVEY, Rebecca, J ... 478-471-2734 ... 133 E
rebecca.corvey@maconstate.edu
CORVIN, Clay, L ... 504-282-4455 ... 213 H
claycor@wbsn.com
CORWIN, Cynthia ... 719-255-3696 ... 88 C
ccorwin@uccs.edu
CORWIN, Rhonda ... 800-955-2527 ... 282 G
CORY, Christopher ... 212-346-1117 ... 345 F
ccory@pace.edu
CORY, Gerald, A ... 888-488-4968 ... 51 G
CORY, Jeff ... 845-675-4425 ... 344 G
jeff.cory@nyack.edu
CORYAT, Catherine, A ... 973-655-4199 ... 311 G
coryatc@mail.montclair.edu
COSBY, Glen ... 509-533-3576 ... 532 F
glenc@spokanefalls.edu
COSBY, Helen ... 334-876-9234 ... 4 B
hcosby@wccs.edu
COSBY, Kevin, W ... 502-776-1443 ... 205 G
COSBY, Laura ... 268-488-4440 ... 253 G
lcosby@kvcc.edu
COSCIA, Paul ... 336-316-2395 ... 364 E
pcoscia@guilford.edu
COSDEN, Julie ... 239-280-2558 ... 101 C
julie.cosden@avemaria.edu
COSENTINO, Lauren ... 310-506-4397 ... 61 G
lauren.cosentino@pepperdine.edu
COSER, Pete ... 918-687-3299 ... 407 B
coserp@bacone.edu
COSEY, Arnel ... 504-671-5055 ... 210 G
acosey@dcc.edu
COSGROVE, John ... 570-662-4586 ... 443 B
jcosgrov@mansfield.edu
COSGROVE, John, J ... 314-539-5380 ... 289 A
jcosgrove@stlcc.edu
COSGROVE, Maryellen ... 678-717-3482 ... 129 D
mcosgrove@gsc.edu
COSIMO, Julie ... 630-829-6037 ... 145 D
jcosimo@ben.edu
COSKIE, Patti, L ... 228-392-2994 ... 278 B
patti.coskie@vc.edu
COSKY, Alicia, C ... 630-844-5116 ... 145 C
acosky@aurora.edu
COSMATO, Charley ... 540-831-6597 ... 522 D
ccosmato@radford.edu
COSO, Xuchitl ... 863-680-4390 ... 109 D
xcoso@flsouthern.edu
COSPER, Tracy ... 229-317-6838 ... 128 A
tracy.cosper@darton.edu
COSSETTE, Ed ... 207-941-7000 ... 218 A
cossettee@husson.edu
COSSICH, Marc ... 936-468-2608 ... 495 H
mcossich@sfasu.edu
COSSICH, Monique ... 936-468-2504 ... 495 H
cossichm@sfasu.edu
COSTA, Anthony, J ... 610-785-6264 ... 446 A
dirspiritcdscs@adphila.org
COSTA, Kathleen ... 925-866-1822 ... 43 C
Kcosta@dvc.edu
COSTA, Linda, J ... 732-932-7743 ... 314 B
smeds@rci.rutgers.edu
COSTA, Maria, D ... 423-439-7737 ... 473 E
costa@etsu.edu
COSTA, Nick ... 215-572-2781 ... 422 B
costan@arcadia.edu
COSTA, JR., Richard, F ... 859-371-9393 ... 198 D
rcosta@beckfield.edu
COSTA, Xavier ... 617-373-3682 ... 244 A
COSTA-BROWN, Darlene ... 508-531-1217 ... 238 B
dcosta@bridgew.edu
COSTANTINO, Andrea ... 716-645-2171 ... 351 G
costanti@buffalo.edu
COSTANTINO, Arthur ... 360-867-6296 ... 533 I
costanta@evergreen.edu
COSTANZA, Carl, F ... 847-635-1876 ... 160 E
costanza@oakton.edu
COSTANZA, Laina ... 334-387-3877 ... 1 D
lainacostanza@amridgeuniversity.edu
COSTANZO, Brian ... 570-961-7841 ... 433 A
costanzob@lackawanna.edu

COSTAS, Edda ..... 787-284-1912 .... 563 F
ecostas@ponce.inter.edu
COSTAS, Rose, L ..... 617-964-1100 .... 230 B
rcostas@ants.edu
COSTELLO, Dennis ..... 586-445-7308 .... 254 F
costellod@macomb.edu
COSTELLO, Eileen ..... 978-632-6600 .... 240 G
e_costello@mwcc.mass.edu
COSTELLO, Georgia ..... 618-235-2700 .... 165 B
georgia.costello@swic.edu
COSTELLO, Gregory, W ..... 507-344-7305 .... 261 H
costello@blc.edu
COSTELLO, Jamie ..... 617-879-7703 .... 238 E
jcostello@massart.edu
COSTELLO, Janice ..... 860-727-6919 .... 92 C
jcostello@goodwin.edu
COSTELLO, Joan ..... 651-450-3618 .... 266 I
jcostel@inverhills.edu
COSTELLO, SJ, John ..... 312-518-7535 .... 157 A
jcoste2@luc.edu
COSTELLO, Kathryn ..... 270-745-6208 .... 207 C
kathryn.costello@wku.edu
COSTELLO, Kevin ..... 617-327-6777 .... 242 C
kevin_costello@mspp.edu
COSTELLO, Mary Elizabeth 973-761-9175 .... 315 B
maryelizabeth.costello@shu.edu
COSTELLO, Richard ..... 414-229-5669 .... 551 C
rickc@uwm.edu
COSTELLO, Rob ..... 360-752-8317 .... 531 C
rcostell@btc.ctc.edu
COSTELLO, Rose, M ..... 260-481-6677 .... 174 A
costellr@ipfw.edu
COSTIGAN, Harry ..... 215-567-7080 .... 422 C
hcostigan@edmc.edu
COSTNER, Carl ..... 828-652-0614 .... 371 G
carlc@mcdowelltech.edu
COSTON, Charlotte, M ..... 716-851-1180 .... 333 B
coston@ecc.edu
COSTON, D, C ..... 701-231-7656 .... 381 H
d.c.coston@ndsu.edu
COSTON, Linda ..... 229-430-2751 .... 123 I
lcoston@albanytech.edu
COSTON, Robert, H ..... 304-647-6574 .... 542 H
rcoston@newriver.edu
COSTON-MCHUGH, Rose .. 856-227-7200 .... 308 E
rcoston-mchugh@camdencc.edu
COTA, Amalia ..... 925-288-5800 .... 49 F
amalia_cota@heald.edu
COTA, Marco ..... 909-384-8952 .... 65 C
mcota@sbccd.cc.ca.us
COTE, Deborah ..... 413-236-1022 .... 239 E
dcote@berkshirecc.edu
COTE, John, C ..... 810-766-4191 .... 248 H
john.cote@baker.edu
COTE, Matthew ..... 207-513-3660 .... 218 C
mcote@kaplan.edu
COTE, Matthew, J ..... 207-786-6066 .... 217 C
mcote@bates.edu
COTE, Roland ..... 812-855-2654 .... 173 C
cote@indiana.edu
COTE-BONANNO,
Joanne, F ..... 973-655-6234 .... 311 G
bonannoj@mail.montclair.edu
COTEY, Kathryn, M ..... 414-276-5200 .... 546 C
kmcotey@bryantstratton.edu
COTGREAVE, Bruce ..... 806-345-5565 .... 479 H
blcotgreave@actx.edu
COTHAM, Brian ..... 559-278-2111 .... 34 D
bcotham@csufresno.edu
COTHERN, John, W ..... 615-898-2852 .... 473 F
john.cothern@mtsu.edu
COTHERN, Richard ..... 912-427-5824 .... 124 A
rcothern@altamahatech.edu
COTHERN, Susan, L ..... 828-884-8373 .... 362 D
strombsl@brevard.edu
COTHRAN, Rick ..... 864-646-1701 .... 461 F
rcothran@tctc.edu
COTHRAN, Robbie ..... 864-503-5145 .... 463 A
rcothran@uscupstate.edu
COTICCHIO, Wanda ..... 478-274-7879 .... 134 G
wcoticchio@oftc.edu
COTLEUR, Mary Elizabeth .. 216-373-5316 .... 397 E
mcotleur@ndc.edu
COTNOIR, Kathleen ..... 413-565-1209 .... 231 B
kcotnoir@baypath.edu
COTNOIR, Paul ..... 508-373-9731 .... 231 D
paul.cotnoir@becker.edu
COTREL, Jack, R ..... 423-439-6900 .... 473 E
cotrel@etsu.edu
COTRELL, Charles, L ..... 210-436-3722 .... 493 C
ccotrell@stmarytx.edu
COTRONEO, Keith, J ..... 304-696-4623 .... 542 G
cotroneo@mctc.edu
COTSONES, Rena ..... 815-753-0834 .... 160 A
rcotsones@niu.edu
COTSONIS, Joachim ..... 617-850-1243 .... 236 A
jcotsonis@hchc.edu
COTTER, Anita ..... 310-825-1443 .... 74 A
acotter@registrar.ucla.edu
COTTER, Dan, J ..... 802-258-9297 .... 513 F
dcotter@marlboro.edu
COTTER, Geri, E ..... 402-465-2159 .... 299 J
gec@nebrwesleyan.edu
COTTER, James, W ..... 517-355-6532 .... 255 D
cotterj@msu.edu

COTTER, Jeff ..... 805-922-6966 .... 26 K
jcotter@hancockcollege.edu
COTTER, Michael ..... 914-594-3675 .... 343 F
michael_cotter@nymc.edu
COTTER, Robert, M ..... 513-745-3183 .... 406 E
cotter@xavier.edu
COTTERMAN, Susan ..... 740-389-4636 .... 395 G
cottermans@mtc.edu
COTTIER, Mary ..... 210-486-2597 .... 479 E
mcottier@alamo.edu
COTTINGHAM, Steven ..... 414-288-6303 .... 548 D
steve.cottingham@marquette.edu
COTTO, Evelyn ..... 787-746-1400 .... 562 C
ecotto@huertas.edu
COTTO, Marguerite, C ..... 231-995-1775 .... 256 G
mcotto@nmc.edu
COTTO, Maria ..... 337-491-2678 .... 212 C
maria.cotto@sowela.edu
COTTO, Saulo ..... 787-844-8181 .... 567 E
saulo.cotto@upr.edu
COTTON, Dwight ..... 859-336-5082 .... 205 F
dwightcotton@sccky.edu
COTTON, Fran ..... 806-894-9611 .... 494 C
fcotton@southplainscollege.edu
COTTON, Jerry, D ..... 972-860-8157 .... 484 G
jdc3420@dcccd.edu
COTTON, Pam ..... 540-986-1800 .... 205 A
pcotton@national-college.edu
COTTON, Roger, D ..... 417-268-1000 .... 279 B
rcotton@agts.edu
COTTON, S. Page ..... 765-658-4938 .... 170 I
pagecotton@depauw.edu
COTTON, Sabrina ..... 256-726-7408 .... 6 C
cotton@oakwood.edu
COTTON, Trae ..... 336-750-3200 .... 380 A
cottontt@wssu.edu
COTTON KELLY,
Montique, R ..... 419-372-7673 .... 385 C
mcotton@bgsu.edu
COTTONE, John ..... 607-753-2701 .... 353 B
john.cottone@cortland.edu
COTTONHAM, Patricia, F .. 337-482-6276 .... 216 D
pattcottonham@louisiana.edu
COTTRELL, Angela ..... 816-235-1407 .... 291 E
cottrella@umkc.edu
COTTRELL, Debbie ..... 254-295-5059 .... 504 A
dcottrell@umhb.edu
COTTRELL, Debbie, M ..... 919-508-2395 .... 375 D
dcottrell@peace.edu
COTTRELL, Janet ..... 802-865-6492 .... 513 A
cottrell@champlain.edu
COTTRELL, Karen, R ..... 757-221-1166 .... 517 J
krcott@wm.edu
COTTRELL, Leslie ..... 378-839-6452 .... 138 D
lcottrel@westga.edu
COTTRELL, Rick ..... 800-962-7682 .... 293 B
rcottrell@wma.edu
COTTRELL, Stephen, E ..... 662-325-8460 .... 276 A
wec3@msstate.edu
COTTRELL, Terrance, L ..... 815-740-5041 .... 167 C
tcottrell@stfrancis.edu
COTTRILL, F. Layton ..... 304-696-6295 .... 543 G
cottrill@marshall.edu
COTTRILL, Gary, L ..... 812-246-3301 .... 176 H
gcottril@ivytech.edu
COTTRILL, Tamra ..... 540-863-2905 .... 526 B
tcottrill@dslcc.edu
COTY, Blake ..... 229-732-5934 .... 124 C
blakecoty@andrewcollege.edu
COTY, Christie ..... 229-732-5943 .... 124 C
christiecoty@andrewcollege.edu
COTY, Mark ..... 941-782-5980 .... 433 C
mcoty@lecom.edu
COUCH, Alisha, M ..... 740-368-3099 .... 400 F
amcouch@owu.edu
COUCH, Brett ..... 513-785-3070 .... 396 E
couchbc@muohio.edu
COUCH, Carl ..... 480-423-6161 .... 16 D
carl.couch@sccmail.maricopa.edu
COUCH, Charlie ..... 970-351-2231 .... 88 F
charlie.couch@unco.edu
COUCH, Daryl, D ..... 864-644-5328 .... 461 B
dcouch@swu.edu
COUCH, JR., Gene, C ..... 336-506-4154 .... 367 G
gene.couch@alamancecc.edu
COUCH, Lisa ..... 760-384-6288 .... 52 N
lcouch@cerrocoso.edu
COUCH, Michael ..... 513-745-1000 .... 406 E
couch@xavier.edu
COUCH, Stephen, R ..... 570-385-6071 .... 440 C
src@psu.edu
COUCHEY, Evangeline ..... 845-675-4733 .... 344 G
evangeline.couchey@nyack.edu
COUCHON, William, D ..... 607-735-1830 .... 333 A
dcouchon@elmira.edu
COUDRET, Nadine, A ..... 812-465-1173 .... 180 F
NCoudret@usi.edu
COUGHENOUR, Brenda ..... 814-262-6434 .... 441 A
bcoughen@pennhighlands.edu
COUGHLEN, Cass ..... 620-341-5264 .... 192 D
ccoughli@emporia.edu
COUGHLIN, Devan ..... 904-256-7054 .... 111 J
dcoughl1@ju.edu
COUGHLIN, Eileen, V ..... 360-650-3839 .... 539 C
eileen.coughlin@wwu.edu

COUGHLIN, OFM,
F. Edward ..... 716-375-2032 .... 348 C
coughlin@sbu.edu
COUGHLIN, Kathleen ..... 210-829-6012 .... 503 F
coughlin@uiwtx.edu
COUGHLIN, Kevin ..... 239-489-9027 .... 104 L
kcoughlinr@edison.edu
COUGHLIN, Mary Ann ..... 413-748-3959 .... 245 C
mcoughlin@spfldcol.edu
COUGHLIN, Richard ..... 660-785-4106 .... 291 A
coughlin@truman.edu
COUGHLIN, Richard ..... 660-785-4038 .... 291 A
coughlin@truman.edu
COUGHLIN-LAMPHEAR,
Kim ..... 707-826-4321 .... 36 D
coughlin@humboldt.edu
COULING, Mike ..... 303-464-2300 .... 87 D
mcouling@westwood.edu
COULSTON, Susan ..... 269-782-1396 .... 258 E
scoulston@swmich.edu
COULTER, Ann ..... 641-782-7081 .... 189 A
coulter@swcciowa.edu
COULTER, Cindy ..... 828-327-7000 .... 368 G
ccoulter@cvcc.edu
COULTER, Denise ..... 215-972-2019 .... 440 I
dcoulter@pafa.edu
COULTER, Ed ..... 870-508-6101 .... 20 E
ecoulter@asumh.edu
COULTER, Kristin ..... 512-313-3000 .... 483 G
kristin.coulter@concordia.edu
COULTER, Laurie ..... 903-813-2900 .... 481 A
lcoulter@austincollege.edu
COULTER, Martha ..... 802-468-1314 .... 515 C
martha.coulter@castleton.edu
COUNCE, Bamby ..... 901-572-2853 .... 467 A
bamby.counce@bchs.edu
COUNCIL, Juanette ..... 910-672-1208 .... 377 E
jcouncil@uncfsu.edu
COUNCIL, William ..... 910-410-1823 .... 372 G
bcouncil@richmondcc.edu
COUNIHAN, Patricia, B ..... 207-581-1359 .... 220 A
counihan@maine.edu
COUNTS, John, E ..... 575-538-6238 .... 321 I
countsj@wnmu.edu
COUNTS, LaNeta ..... 404-471-6483 .... 123 G
lcounts@agnesscott.edu
COUNTY, Deb ..... 970-521-6660 .... 86 E
deb.county@njc.edu
COURCEY, Daniel, P ..... 203-285-2152 .... 90 A
dcourcey@gwcc.commnet.edu
COURCHAINE, Jeff ..... 714-892-7711 .... 41 A
jcourchaine@gwc.cccd.edu
COURSEY, Greg ..... 912-583-3221 .... 126 C
gcoursey@bpc.edu
COURSEY, Martha ..... 404-297-9522 .... 128 B
courseym@dekalbtech.edu
COURTADE, Kay ..... 515-271-1657 .... 183 F
kay.courtade@dmu.edu
COURTEMANCHE, Brian ..... 978-927-2278 .... 234 F
bcourtem@endicott.edu
COURTEY, Susan ..... 818-240-1000 .... 48 C
scourtey@glendale.edu
COURTLEY-TODD, Laura ... 305-628-6677 .... 116 G
lcourtle@stu.edu
COURTNEY, Andolyn, M ..... 716-888-2780 .... 325 G
courtnea@canisius.edu
COURTNEY, Jim ..... 773-947-6285 .... 157 E
jcourtney@mccormick.edu
COURTNEY, Justin ..... 419-772-2145 .... 398 G
j-courtney@onu.edu
COURTNEY, Regina, L ..... 214-828-8235 .... 497 A
rcourtney@bcd.tamhsc.edu
COURTNEY, Sharon, P ..... 504-988-3390 .... 215 C
sharonc@tulane.edu
COURTRIGHT, Mary Beth .. 508-588-9100 .... 240 E
COURTS, Roger ..... 513-875-3344 .... 387 B
roger.courts@chatfield.edu
COURTWAY, Tom ..... 501-450-3170 .... 25 H
tcourtway@uca.edu
COURTWRIGHT, Caren ..... 509-793-2038 .... 531 D
carenc@bigbend.edu
COURY, David ..... 850-644-6031 .... 119 C
dpcoury@admin.fsu.edu
COUSIN, Dennis ..... 504-520-7330 .... 217 A
dcousin@xula.edu
COUSINS, Stephany, C ..... 336-454-1126 .... 370 E
sccousins@gtcc.edu
COUTILISH, Theodore, G ... 734-487-2483 .... 250 H
ted.coutilish@emich.edu
COUTS, Barbara ..... 614-885-5585 .... 401 B
bcouts@pcj.edu
COUTTS, Chris ..... 540-868-7083 .... 526 H
ccoutts@lfcc.edu
COUTTS, Kimberly ..... 760-797-2121 .... 57 E
kcoutts@miracosta.edu
COUTURE, Barbara ..... 575-646-2035 .... 319 D
president@nmsu.edu
COUTURE, Charles ..... 406-243-5225 .... 295 A
charles.couture@umontana.edu
COUTURE, Daniel, R ..... 802-654-3243 .... 514 B
dcouture@smcvt.edu
COUTURE, Donna, L ..... 978-232-2026 .... 234 F
dcouture@endicott.edu
COUTURE, Janelle ..... 216-391-6937 .... 387 A
jcouture@chancelloru.edu

COUTURE, Richard ..... 607-274-3225 .... 336 G
rcouture@ithaca.edu
COVAL, Scott ..... 610-282-1100 .... 426 I
scott.coval@desales.edu
COVALT, Lindy ..... 765-966-2656 .... 176 F
lcovalt@ivytech.edu
COVAR, Tom ..... 864-388-8305 .... 458 J
tcovar@lander.edu
COVAULT, Pamela ..... 785-242-2067 .... 195 B
pcovault@neosho.edu
COVE, Lorraine, D ..... 617-573-8160 .... 245 E
lcove@acad.suffolk.edu
COVELLE, Fred ..... 617-422-7205 .... 243 G
fcovelle@nesl.edu
COVELLI-KOVACH, Andrea 215-572-4014 .... 422 B
covelli@arcadia.edu
COVENEY, Kevin, C ..... 410-778-7700 .... 229 D
kcoveney2@washcoll.edu
COVENEY, Michael, J ..... 215-572-2943 .... 422 B
coveney@arcadia.edu
COVER, Ellen Catherine ..... 941-355-9080 .... 104 J
COVER, Michael, S ..... 570-577-3348 .... 423 D
mike.cover@bucknell.edu
COVERDALE, Pat ..... 423-236-2276 .... 473 A
plcoverdale@southern.edu
COVERS, Beth, A ..... 810-762-9925 .... 253 I
bcovers@kettering.edu
COVERT, Carl ..... 903-785-7661 .... 492 B
ccovert@parisjc.edu
COVERT, Sheree, S ..... 319-352-8272 .... 189 F
sheree.covert@wartburg.edu
COVEY, Angie, E ..... 540-674-3655 .... 527 B
acovey@nr.edu
COVEY, Becky ..... 276-466-7192 .... 528 G
beckycovey@vic.edu
COVEY, Bruce ..... 404-727-6223 .... 129 A
bcovey@emory.edu
COVEY, Douglass, F ..... 404-413-1500 .... 131 C
dcovey@gsu.edu
COVILLE, Joanne ..... 909-621-8211 .... 69 A
COVILLE, Joanne ..... 805-437-8877 .... 33 I
joanne.coville@csuci.edu
COVINGTON, Bill, C ..... 512-245-2314 .... 501 C
bc18@txstate.edu
COVINGTON, Dan ..... 606-546-1285 .... 206 F
dcovin@unionky.edu
COVINGTON, Dean ..... 870-307-7206 .... 22 D
covington@lyon.edu
COVINGTON, Janet ..... 713-348-6312 .... 492 J
jcov@rice.edu
COVINGTON, Kate ..... 620-276-9642 .... 193 A
kate.covington@gcccks.edu
COVINGTON, Mary ..... 919-966-9176 .... 378 D
mary_covington@unc.edu
COVINGTON, Richard ..... 407-253-5354 .... 102 E
COVINGTON, Valerie, L ..... 757-455-3108 .... 529 F
vcovington@vwc.edu
COVINGTON-GRAHAM,
Adrainne ..... 405-945-3383 .... 410 F
COVINO, Nicholas ..... 617-327-6777 .... 242 C
nicholas_covino@mspp.edu
COVINO, William, A ..... 559-278-2636 .... 34 D
wcovino@csufresno.edu
COVITZ, Sharon, B ..... 336-734-7520 .... 370 C
scovitz@forsythtech.edu
COVONE, Nicole ..... 305-892-7043 .... 111 K
nicole.covone@jwu.edu
COWAN, Anthony ..... 901-435-1470 .... 470 B
anthony_cowan@loc.edu
COWAN, Carole, A ..... 978-656-3101 .... 240 F
cowanc@middlesex.mass.edu
COWAN, Cindy ..... 864-977-2058 .... 460 A
cindy.cowan@ngu.edu
COWAN, David ..... 507-389-2267 .... 267 H
david.cowan@mnsu.edu
COWAN, David, G ..... 713-646-1729 .... 494 E
dcowan@stcl.edu
COWAN, Kenneth, H ..... 402-559-4238 .... 301 A
kcowan@unmc.edu
COWAN, Marianne ..... 207-786-6128 .... 217 C
mcowan@bates.edu
COWAN, Michael ..... 931-372-3034 .... 474 B
mcowan@tntech.edu
COWAN, Richard, E ..... 706-233-7207 .... 136 E
rcowan@shorter.edu
COWAN, Theresa ..... 304-326-1358 .... 541 G
tcowan@salemu.edu
COWAN, Vickie, M ..... 718-862-7398 .... 339 H
vickie.cowan@manhattan.edu
COWARD, Bettye, R ..... 662-685-4771 .... 273 H
bcoward@bmc.edu
COWARD, Raymond, T ..... 435-797-1167 .... 511 B
raymond.coward@usu.edu
COWARD, William ..... 814-536-5168 .... 424 C
bcoward@crbc.net
COWARD, William ..... 814-536-5168 .... 424 B
bcoward@crbc.net
COWART, Danny ..... 479-788-7179 .... 24 D
dcowart@uafortsmith.edu
COWART, John ..... 352-395-5513 .... 117 E
john.cowart@sfcollege.edu
COWART, Julian, R ..... 903-233-4091 .... 489 K
juliancowart@letu.edu

CRAMER, Paul ..... 717-361-1400 .... 428 E
cramerp@etown.edu

CRAMER, Rick ..... 607-729-1581 .... 332 A
rcramer@davisny.edu

CRAMER, Robert, G ..... 608-342-1226 .... 551 F
cramerr@uwplatt.edu

CRAMER, Steven ..... 574-257-3313 .... 169 F
cramers@bethelcollege.edu

CRAMER, Walter ..... 203-837-8547 .... 92 A
cramerw@wcsu.edu

CRAMPTON, Anne-Marie ... 719-336-1520 .... 85 K
anne-marie.crampton@lamarcc.edu

CRAMPTON, Tom ..... 810-762-0506 .... 256 C
thomas.crampto@mcc.edu

CRAMPTON, Troy, D ..... 515-574-1114 .... 185 F
crampton@iowacentral.edu

CRANCE, Gina-Lyn ..... 610-921-7611 .... 421 D
gcrance@alb.edu

CRANCE, Mike ..... 602-337-3044 .... 12 K
mcrance@brownmackie.edu

CRANDALL, Connie ..... 605-688-5148 .... 466 B
connie.crandall@sdstate.edu

CRANDALL, Donald, W ..... 479-524-7150 .... 22 C
dcrandal@jbu.edu

CRANDALL, James ..... 530-242-7989 .... 69 D
jcrandall@shastacollege.edu

CRANDALL, Jared ..... 312-502-4795 .... 509 B
jcrandall@argosy.edu

CRANDALL, Larry ..... 801-302-2800 .... 510 C
larry.crandall@neumont.edu

CRANDALL, Laura ..... 315-470-4865 .... 355 A
ldcranda@esf.edu

CRANDALL, Paige ..... 914-395-2575 .... 350 C
pcrandall@sarahlawrence.edu

CRANDALL, Stephen, S ..... 607-871-2184 .... 322 F
fcrandall@alfred.edu

CRANDELL, Gale, M ..... 989-386-6664 .... 255 F
gcrandell@midmich.edu

CRANE, Carol ..... 480-732-7114 .... 15 G
carol.crane@cgcmail.maricopa.edu

CRANE, Charles, F ..... 210-458-7240 .... 506 B
charles.crane@utsa.edu

CRANE, Crystal, D ..... 714-895-8970 .... 41 A
ccrane@gwc.cccd.edu

CRANE, Eileen, C ..... 615-353-3545 .... 475 D
eileen.crane@nscc.edu

CRANE, Jeff ..... 270-384-8150 .... 203 H
cranej@lindsey.edu

CRANE, Melanie ..... 303-581-9955 .... 320 H
mcrane@acupuncturecollege.edu

CRANE, Peter ..... 203-432-5109 .... 95 D
peter.crane@yale.edu

CRANE, Ramona ..... 719-219-9636 .... 81 J
rlsfattire@hotmail.com

CRANE, Rob, M ..... 913-288-7283 .... 193 J
rcrane@kckcc.edu

CRANE, Robert ..... 956-380-8100 .... 493 A
rcrane@riogrande.edu

CRANE, Susan, L ..... 989-964-4350 .... 258 A
scrane@svsu.edu

CRANE-SMITH, Jeanne ..... 913-288-7362 .... 193 J
jeannecs@kckcc.edu

CRANER, Marcia, R ..... 607-777-2054 .... 351 F
mcraner@binghamton.edu

CRANER, Marcia, R ..... 607-777-6757 .... 351 F
mcraner@binghamton.edu

CRANFORD, Bill ..... 601-925-3283 .... 275 E
cranford@mc.edu

CRANFORD, Carolyn ..... 903-813-2281 .... 481 A
ccranford@austincollege.edu

CRANFORD, Shannon ..... 580-628-6229 .... 409 B
shannon.cranfor@north-ok.edu

CRANFORD, Sondra ..... 727-786-4707 .... 102 F
scranford@cfi.edu

CRANFORD, Timothy ..... 912-358-4154 .... 136 C
cranfordt@savannahstate.edu

CRANHAM, John, B ..... 919-508-2336 .... 375 D
jbcranham@peace.edu

CRANK, Edwin ..... 903-586-2518 .... 488 L
ecrank@jacksonville-college.edu

CRANK, Robert ..... 816-322-0110 .... 279 H
bob.crank@calvary.edu

CRANMORE, Jill, A ..... 217-443-8756 .... 148 E
jcranmore@dacc.edu

CRANOR, Gay Nell ..... 417-268-6097 .... 279 D
gncranor@gobbc.edu

CRANSTON, Carey ..... 708-636-7700 .... 151 A

CRANSTON, Carolyn ..... 412-362-5610 .... 444 G
ccranston@pts.edu

CRANSTON, Pam ..... 410-516-6087 .... 223 F
pcranston@jhu.edu

CRANWELL, Mary, E ..... 732-987-2285 .... 310 D
cranwell@georgian.edu

CRAPANZANO, Vincent ..... 845-398-4019 .... 349 H
vcrapanz@stac.edu

CRAPO, Eric ..... 603-887-7425 .... 303 G
eric.crapo@chestercollege.edu

CRAPP, Michael ..... 570-422-3595 .... 442 C
mcrapp@po-box.esu.edu

CRATER, Richard ..... 570-504-7305 .... 425 F

CRATTY, Frederic ..... 203-837-8665 .... 92 A
crattyf@wcsu.edu

CRAVEN, Bryan, C ..... 850-718-2375 .... 102 H
cravenb@chipola.edu

CRAVEN, Randy ..... 423-236-2732 .... 473 A
rlcraven@southern.edu

CRAVEY, Irene ..... 903-923-3312 .... 500 A
irene.cravey@marshall.tstc.edu

CRAVO, Ana, M ..... 201-761-6104 .... 314 F
acravo@spc.edu

CRAWFORD, Allison ..... 615-794-4254 .... 472 D
acrawford@omorecollege.edu

CRAWFORD, Bill, E ..... 806-354-6070 .... 479 H
wecrawford@actx.edu

CRAWFORD, Brenda ..... 712-274-5606 .... 187 D
crawford@morningside.edu

CRAWFORD, Brian ..... 304-336-8252 .... 544 B
bcrawford@westliberty.edu

CRAWFORD, Bruce ..... 205-929-6312 .... 5 E
bcrawford@lawsonstate.edu

CRAWFORD, Bryan ..... 719-562-7002 .... 87 B
bryan.crawford@pueblocc.edu

CRAWFORD, Cardon, B ..... 843-953-6966 .... 456 C
cardon.crawford@citadel.edu

CRAWFORD, Carol ..... 215-728-4700 .... 438 A
carol.crawford@jevs.org

CRAWFORD, Catherine ..... 903-923-2069 .... 486 D
ccrawford@etbu.edu

CRAWFORD, Cathy ..... 260-399-7700 .... 180 E
ccrawford@sf.edu

CRAWFORD, Charlie ..... 253-566-5091 .... 538 C
ccrawford@tacomacc.edu

CRAWFORD, Chemene, L .. 702-651-5830 .... 302 G
chemene.crawford@csn.edu

CRAWFORD, Chris ..... 785-628-4531 .... 192 F
ccrawfor@fhsu.edu

CRAWFORD, Colleen ..... 512-313-3000 .... 483 G
colleen.crawford@concordia.edu

CRAWFORD, David ..... 970-521-6643 .... 86 E
david.crawford@njc.edu

CRAWFORD, David ..... 773-947-6250 .... 157 E
dcrawford@mccormick.edu

CRAWFORD, David, S ..... 202-526-3799 .... 98 E

CRAWFORD, Debbie ..... 970-945-8691 .... 82 C

CRAWFORD, Deborah ..... 215-895-6203 .... 427 G
deborah.l.crawford@drexel.edu

CRAWFORD, Deena ..... 601-266-4829 .... 278 A
deena.crawford@usm.edu

CRAWFORD, Derrick ..... 760-750-4309 .... 36 B
crawford@csusm.edu

CRAWFORD, Diane ..... 919-546-8309 .... 376 D
dcrawford@shawu.edu

CRAWFORD, Doris, S ..... 434-528-5276 .... 529 E
dorisscott@vul.edu

CRAWFORD, Felicia ..... 269-387-3635 .... 260 F
felicia.crawford@wmich.edu

CRAWFORD, Forrest, C ..... 801-626-7420 .... 511 D
fcrawford@weber.edu

CRAWFORD, Gene, L ..... 570-577-1631 .... 423 D
gene.crawford@bucknell.edu

CRAWFORD, George, F ..... 417-865-2811 .... 282 A
crawfordc@evangel.edu

CRAWFORD, Gregory, P ..... 574-631-6456 .... 180 D
gregory_crawford@nd.edu

CRAWFORD, Holly ..... 203-392-5237 .... 91 I
crawfordh1@southernct.edu

CRAWFORD, Holly ..... 585-273-4734 .... 358 I
hcrawford@admin.rochester.edu

CRAWFORD, Iris ..... 813-463-7125 .... 100 H
ncrawford@argosy.edu

CRAWFORD, Isiaah ..... 206-296-6963 .... 537 F
crawford@seattleu.edu

CRAWFORD, J. Patrick ..... 850-474-2426 .... 121 C
pat@uwf.edu

CRAWFORD, James, E ..... 423-585-6956 .... 476 B
james.crawford@ws.edu

CRAWFORD, JR.,
James, E ..... 423-585-6956 .... 476 B
james.crawford@ws.edu

CRAWFORD, Jane, T ..... 386-312-4190 .... 116 D
janecrawford@sjrstate.edu

CRAWFORD, Janice ..... 314-977-2925 .... 289 F
crawford@slu.edu

CRAWFORD, John ..... 330-672-2760 .... 393 D
jcrawfor1@kent.edu

CRAWFORD, John, D ..... 229-333-5339 .... 138 F
jdcrawford@valdosta.edu

CRAWFORD, Jonas ..... 805-986-5870 .... 77 C
jcrawford@vcccd.edu

CRAWFORD, Kara ..... 540-261-4102 .... 524 C
kara.crawford@svu.edu

CRAWFORD, Kathryn ..... 605-394-1288 .... 466 A
kathryn.crawford@sdsmt.edu

CRAWFORD, Kevin ..... 706-245-7226 .... 128 K
kcrawford@lifespring.net

CRAWFORD, Lelia ..... 404-727-3300 .... 129 A
lcrawfo@emory.edu

CRAWFORD, Leonard ..... 310-434-4491 .... 68 D
crawford_leonard@smc.edu

CRAWFORD, Linden, G ..... 314-984-7609 .... 289 D
lcrawford@stlcc.edu

CRAWFORD, Malinda ..... 406-756-3828 .... 294 D
mcrawfor@fvcc.edu

CRAWFORD, Matt ..... 952-358-8200 .... 268 C

CRAWFORD, Nellie ..... 757-727-5221 .... 519 C
nellie.crawford@hamptonu.edu

CRAWFORD, Peggy, L ..... 207-581-1324 .... 220 A
pcrawf@maine.edu

CRAWFORD, R. Scott ..... 765-361-6355 .... 181 C
crawforr@wabash.edu

CRAWFORD, Rhia ..... 828-765-7351 .... 371 F
rcrawford@mayland.edu

CRAWFORD, Ronald, W ..... 804-355-8135 .... 516 G
rcrawford@btsr.edu

CRAWFORD, Steven, R ..... 740-587-5717 .... 389 H
crawfords@denison.edu

CRAWFORD, Susan ..... 707-527-4527 .... 68 E
scrawford@santarosa.edu

CRAWFORD, Teresa ..... 863-784-7041 .... 117 I
teresa.crawford@southflorida.edu

CRAWFORD, Tim ..... 254-295-4180 .... 504 A
tcrawford@umhb.edu

CRAWFORD, Valerie ..... 309-268-8000 .... 151 G
val.crawford@heartland.edu

CRAWFORD, Valerie, S ..... 334-244-3667 .... 2 A
vsamuel@aum.edu

CRAWFORD, Virginia ..... 601-266-5390 .... 278 A
virginia.crawford@usm.edu

CRAWFORD, Wilbur, O ..... 215-574-9600 .... 431 A
info@hussianart.edu

CRAWFORD, III,
William, H ..... 480-732-7309 .... 15 G
bill.crawford.iii@cgcmail.maricopa.edu

CRAWLEY, Cathy ..... 478-445-5149 .... 129 F
cathy.crawley@gcsu.edu

CRAWLEY, Deborah ..... 610-558-5519 .... 437 C
cawleyd@neumann.edu

CRAWLEY, Vernon, O ..... 708-974-5201 .... 159 A
crawley@morainevalley.edu

CRAWMER, Martha ..... 937-328-6031 .... 387 G
crawmerm@clarkstate.edu

CRAYS, Linda, L ..... 713-500-2080 .... 506 D
linda.l.crays@uth.tmc.edu

CRAZY BULL, Cheryl ..... 360-676-2772 .... 535 F
ccb@nwic.edu

CREA, Catharine ..... 914-594-4480 .... 343 F
catharine_crea@nymc.edu

CREAGER, Carol ..... 540-887-7310 .... 520 I
ccreager@mbc.edu

CREAGH, Curtis ..... 573-681-5079 .... 284 B
creaghc@lincolnu.edu

CREAHAN, Patricia, H ..... 716-888-2616 .... 325 G
creahan@canisius.edu

CREAKMAN, Melissa ..... 304-896-7411 .... 542 J
Melissac@southern.wvnet.edu

CREAMER, David ..... 513-529-4225 .... 396 D
creamerd@muohio.edu

CREAMER, Deborah ..... 303-765-3170 .... 84 K
dcreamer@iliff.edu

CREAMER, George ..... 617-879-7163 .... 238 E
creamer@massart.edu

CREAMER, Stephen ..... 978-762-4000 .... 241 A
Screamer@northshore.edu

CREAMER, Tia ..... 918-631-3244 .... 413 F
tia-creamer@utulsa.edu

CREAR, Alana ..... 228-392-2994 .... 278 B
alana.crear@vc.edu

CREASIA, Joan, L ..... 865-974-7584 .... 477 B
jcreasia@utk.edu

CREASMAN, Alice, J ..... 304-473-8440 .... 545 F
creasman_aj@wvwc.edu

CREASON, Paul ..... 562-938-4171 .... 54 E
pcreason@lbcc.edu

CREASON, Rita, A ..... 270-789-5233 .... 199 C
racreason@campbellsville.edu

CRECELIUS, Carolyn ..... 573-518-2100 .... 286 B
kayc@mineralarea.edu

CRECELIUS, Kathryn, J ..... 443-997-2370 .... 223 F
kcrecelius@jhu.edu

CREDILLE, John ..... 417-328-1606 .... 290 E
jcredille@sbuniv.edu

CREDLE, Sid, H ..... 757-727-5361 .... 519 C
sid.credle@hamptonu.edu

CREECH, Bill ..... 918-595-7888 .... 412 H
bcreech@tulsacc.edu

CREECH, Pat ..... 918-540-6294 .... 408 J
pcreech@neo.edu

CREED, J. Bradley ..... 205-726-2718 .... 6 G
jbcreed@samford.edu

CREED, Stephanie ..... 501-882-4547 .... 20 D
sacreed@asub.edu

CREED-DIKEOGU, Gloria ... 785-242-5200 .... 195 F
creeddikeogu@ottawa.edu

CREEGER, Joan ..... 704-216-3602 .... 373 C
joan.creeger@rccc.edu

CREEHAN, Kenneth ..... 314-968-6969 .... 293 A
creehan@webster.edu

CREEHAN, Richard, A ..... 304-457-1700 .... 540 B
creehanra@ab.edu

CREEK, Fred, A ..... 253-833-9111 .... 534 C
fcreek@greenriver.edu

CREEKMORE, Carol ..... 973-443-8607 .... 310 B
carol_creekmore@fdu.edu

CREEKMORE, Crystal ..... 575-562-2175 .... 318 A
crystal.creekmore@enmu.edu

CREEL, Ronnie ..... 334-670-3496 .... 8 B
rcreel@troy.edu

CREEL, Scott ..... 615-248-1236 .... 476 E
screel@trevecca.edu

CREEL-ERB, Angie ..... 928-344-7776 .... 12 C
angela.creel-erb@azwestern.edu

CREELY, Hilliary ..... 724-357-2223 .... 442 E
Hilliary.Creely@iup.edu

CREER, John ..... 636-949-4777 .... 284 C
jcreer@lindenwood.edu

CREFT, Dawn, H ..... 407-303-7894 .... 108 D
dawn.creft@fhchs.edu

CREGAN, CSC, Mark, T ..... 508-565-1301 .... 245 D
presidentcregan@stonehill.edu

CREGGER, Crystal, Y ..... 276-233-4762 .... 528 F
wccregc@wcc.vccs.edu

CREIGHTON, Clarinda ..... 816-584-6833 .... 287 H
clarinda.creighton@park.edu

CREIGHTON, Karen ..... 417-447-2601 .... 287 G
creightk@otc.edu

CREMAROSA, Anne ..... 805-922-6966 .... 26 K
acremarosa@hancockcollege.edu

CREMER, Doug ..... 530-895-2946 .... 31 E
cremerdo@butte.edu

CREMER, Douglas ..... 818-767-0888 .... 79 D
douglas.cremer@woodbury.edu

CREMER, Phyllis, A ..... 818-767-0888 .... 79 D
phyllis.cremer@woodbury.edu

CRENSHAW, Chris ..... 601-266-4414 .... 278 A
christopher.crenshaw@usm.edu

CRENSHAW, Christine ..... 405-744-5358 .... 410 C
christine.crenshaw@okstate.edu

CRENSHAW, Jan ..... 281-998-6150 .... 493 F
jan.crenshaw@sjcd.edu

CRENSHAW, Karen ..... 724-503-1001 .... 451 A
kcrenshaw@washjeff.edu

CREOLA, Thomas ..... 772-398-9990 .... 112 I
tcreola@keisercollege.edu

CRERAR, Gregg, R ..... 203-392-5518 .... 91 I
crerarg1@southernct.edu

CRESAP, Linda ..... 701-858-3110 .... 381 G
linda.cresap@minotstateu.edu

CRESCENZO, Mario ..... 212-650-5250 .... 326 H
mcrescenzo@ccny.cuny.edu

CRESON, Gadsby ..... 901-272-5120 .... 471 B
gcreson@mca.edu

CRESPINO, Curt, J ..... 816-235-1105 .... 291 E
crespinocj@umkc.edu

CRESPO, Jorge ..... 787-751-0178 .... 565 D
ac_jcrespo@suagm.edu

CRESPO, Jorge, L ..... 787-751-0178 .... 565 D
ac_jcrespo@suagm.edu

CRESPO, Ricardo ..... 787-751-1912 .... 564 A
rcrespo@inter.edu

CRESPO-KEBLER,
Elizabeth ..... 787-993-8864 .... 566 G
elizabeth.crespo1@upr.edu

CRESPO-LOPEZ, Sylvia ..... 212-237-8897 .... 328 A
sylopez@jjay.cuny.edu

CRESPY, Charles, T ..... 989-774-2481 .... 249 G
cresp1ct@cmich.edu

CRESSWELL-YEAGER,
Tiffany ..... 610-285-5021 .... 439 K
tjc8@psu.edu

CREW, Alicia ..... 850-644-0553 .... 119 C
acrew@admin.fsu.edu

CREW, Dwayne ..... 478-825-6301 .... 129 C
crewd@fvsu.edu

CREW, Robert ..... 318-357-5800 .... 216 B
crew@nsula.edu

CREWELL, Don ..... 626-395-6280 .... 32 E
dcrewell@caltech.edu

CREWS, Bradford, W ..... 561-297-2190 .... 118 H
bcrews2@fau.edu

CREWS, II, Lyen, C ..... 859-846-5701 .... 204 D
lcrews@midway.edu

CREWS, Micah, R ..... 423-652-4773 .... 469 L
mrcrews@king.edu

CREWS, Michele ..... 617-879-2114 .... 246 F
mcrews@wheelock.edu

CREWS, Phyllis ..... 703-709-5875 .... 522 B
pcrews@potomac.edu

CREWS, Ron ..... 910-221-2224 .... 364 C

CREWS, Sharon ..... 205-929-6307 .... 5 E
sharon.crews@lawsonstate.edu

CREWS, William, O ..... 415-380-1326 .... 48 D
billcrews@ggbts.edu

CRIBBY, William ..... 617-928-4021 .... 243 A
wcribby@mountida.edu

CRICK, James ..... 502-451-0815 .... 206 B
jcrick@sullivan.edu

CRICK, James ..... 502-451-0815 .... 206 C
jcrick@sullivan.edu

CRICKARD, Diana, L ..... 304-457-6220 .... 540 B
crickarddl@ab.edu

CRICKENBERGER, Leslie ... 706-583-2818 .... 124 H
lcrickenberger@athenstech.edu

CRIDER, Wayne ..... 706-245-7226 .... 128 K
wcrider@ec.edu

CRIGGER, Cynthia, L ..... 304-896-7412 .... 542 J
cindyc@southern.wvnet.edu

CRILLEY, Bonnie ..... 814-866-8144 .... 433 C
bcrilley@lecom.edu

CRILLY, Sam ..... 405-912-9064 .... 408 D
scrilly@hc.edu

CRIM, Kim ..... 717-846-5000 .... 452 G

CRIMMIN, Nancy, P ..... 508-767-7536 .... 230 E
ncrimmin@assumption.edu

CRIMMINS, Cindy ..... 717-815-1216 .... 452 F
ccrimmins@ycp.edu

CRIMMINS, Kate ..... 410-837-6135 .... 229 A
kcrimmins@ubalt.edu

CROUSE, Thomas, A ... 304-345-2820 ... 545 D
tom.crouse@yahoo.com
CROUSHORN, Susan ... 606-242-2014 ... 203 A
susan.croushorn@kctcs.edu
CROUTER, Ann, C ... 814-865-1420 ... 438 F
ac1@psu.edu
CROW, C. Robert ... 616-526-6165 ... 249 E
rcrow@calvin.edu
CROW, Debra ... 816-531-5223 ... 280 G
dcrow@concordecareercolleges.com
CROW, Donna, E ... 435-797-3588 ... 511 B
donna.crow@usu.edu
CROW, Krisan ... 970-945-8691 ... 82 C
CROW, Michael, G ... 912-358-4172 ... 136 C
crowm@savannahstate.edu
CROW, Michael, M ... 480-965-8972 ... 12 B
michael.crow@asu.edu
CROW, Scott ... 916-608-6500 ... 56 C
flc-pio@flc.losrios.edu
CROW, Sharon ... 386-506-3016 ... 103 J
crows@DaytonaState.edu
CROW, Steve ... 530-938-5220 ... 42 C
crow@siskiyous.edu
CROW, Susan ... 505-424-2309 ... 318 C
scrow@iaia.edu
CROW, Tony, L ... 303-458-4161 ... 87 E
tcrow@regis.edu
CROWDER, Darren ... 417-328-1817 ... 290 E
dcrowder@sbuniv.edu
CROWDER, Mike ... 806-743-3023 ... 501 E
mike.crowder@ttuhsc.edu
CROWDER, Rick ... 423-869-6306 ... 470 C
rcrowder@lmunet.edu
CROWDER, Vickie, J ... 304-473-8032 ... 545 F
crowder_v@wvwc.edu
CROWE, Aliesha, R ... 715-852-1394 ... 553 F
acrowe3@cvtc.edu
CROWE, Carl ... 410-778-7752 ... 229 D
ccrowe2@washcoll.edu
CROWE, Chuck ... 303-404-5238 ... 84 H
chuck.crowe@frontrange.edu
CROWE, Daniel ... 410-263-2371 ... 225 G
daniel.crowe@sjca.edu
CROWE, Ellen ... 773-380-6860 ... 168 D
ecrowe@westwood.edu
CROWE, Gregg ... 804-281-3902 ... 19 C
gregg.crowe@phoenix.edu
CROWE, Jason ... 314-454-7770 ... 282 E
jcrowe@bjc.org
CROWE, Lisa ... 859-622-2696 ... 200 D
lisa.crowe@eku.edu
CROWE, Richard ... 818-345-8414 ... 42 D
rcrowe@columbiacollege.edu
CROWE, Sara ... 912-583-3240 ... 126 C
scrowe@bpc.edu
CROWE, Thomas ... 847-543-2473 ... 147 H
tcrowe@clcillinois.edu
CROWE, William ... 706-542-3451 ... 138 C
georgiacenter@uga.edu
CROWELL, Perry ... 850-644-4780 ... 119 C
pcrowell@admin.fsu.edu
CROWELL, Rebecca, C ... 972-516-5011 ... 483 D
rcrowell@collin.edu
CROWELL, Scott ... 507-537-6844 ... 269 G
Scott.Crowell@smsu.edu
CROWETIPTON, Vaughn ... 864-294-2138 ... 458 D
vaughn.crowetipton@furman.edu
CROWFOOT, Rebecca ... 770-394-8300 ... 124 F
rcrowfoot@aii.edu
CROWL, Rebecca, R ... 330-363-6364 ... 384 G
rcrowl@aultman.com
CROWL, Ronald ... 330-829-2756 ... 404 C
crowlrl@mountunion.edu
CROWLEY, Christine ... 210-486-4572 ... 479 C
ccrowley5@alamo.edu
CROWLEY, Kimberly, A ... 806-354-6087 ... 479 H
kacrowley@actx.edu
CROWLEY, Rachel, C ... 812-877-8365 ... 179 A
crowley@rose-hulman.edu
CROWLEY, Tim ... 785-628-4236 ... 192 F
tcrowley@fhsu.edu
CROWLEY, Timothy, D ... 207-768-2811 ... 218 J
tcrowley@nmcc.edu
CROWLEY, Treacy ... 216-987-3245 ... 389 A
treacy.crowley@tri-c.edu
CROWNE, Deborah ... 808-544-0283 ... 140 B
dcrowne@hpu.edu
CROWTHER, Ann ... 912-279-5739 ... 127 B
acrowther@ccga.edu
CROWTHER, Elizabeth, H ... 804-758-6701 ... 527 G
ecrowther@rappahannock.edu
CROWTHER, Lori, D ... 620-792-9216 ... 190 E
crowtherl@bartonccc.edu
CROWTHER, Steven ... 910-221-2224 ... 364 C
CROWTHER, Susan ... 661-362-3098 ... 41 G
susan.crowther@canyons.edu
CROWTHERS, Jay ... 503-491-7682 ... 417 B
jay.crowthers@mhcc.edu
CROX, Walter ... 812-280-7271 ... 195 F
walter.crox@ottawa.edu
CROX, Walter ... 812-280-7271 ... 178 E
lonnie.cooper@ottawa.edu
CROY, Jason ... 706-245-7226 ... 128 K
jcroy@ec.edu

CROY, Melanie ... 432-837-8134 ... 501 B
mcroy@sulross.edu
CROYLE, Mary ... 806-743-2143 ... 501 E
mary.croyle@ttuhsc.edu
CRUDELE, Dennis ... 561-297-3266 ... 118 H
crudele@fau.edu
CRUDUP, Shaina ... 336-517-2230 ... 362 C
scrudup@bennett.edu
CRUIKSHANK, Nancy, L ... 724-738-4831 ... 443 E
nancy.cruikshank@sru.edu
CRUISE, Deborah, J ... 443-412-2233 ... 223 B
dcruise@harford.edu
CRUISE, Thomas ... 540-831-5479 ... 522 D
tcruise@radford.edu
CRUISE-HARPER, Christie ... 678-717-3749 ... 129 D
ccharper@gsc.edu
CRUISE-HARPER, Christie ... 314-529-9684 ... 284 F
ccruiseharper@maryville.edu
CRUIT, Suzanne ... 610-648-3200 ... 439 G
syk123@psu.edu
CRUM, Claude ... 606-368-6081 ... 197 H
claudecrum@alc.edu
CRUM, Janet ... 515-244-4221 ... 181 D
crumj@aib.edu
CRUM, Jeff ... 920-206-2395 ... 548 B
jcrum@mbbc.edu
CRUM, Jeffrey ... 336-725-8344 ... 375 F
crumj@pbc.edu
CRUM, Tom ... 423-697-2417 ... 474 D
CRUMBLIN, Leon ... 870-575-8360 ... 25 B
crumblinl@uapb.edu
CRUMEDY, Ron, C ... 409-944-1237 ... 486 H
rcrumedy@gc.edu
CRUMLEY, Kristie ... 410-386-8408 ... 221 G
kcrumley@carrollcc.edu
CRUMMIE, Carla, M ... 404-527-4525 ... 126 F
ccrummie@carver.edu
CRUMMIE, Robert, W ... 404-527-4520 ... 126 F
rcrummie@carver.edu
CRUMP, D'adra ... 718-636-6825 ... 349 A
dcrump@sjcny.edu
CRUMP, D'adra ... 718-940-5869 ... 349 B
dcrump@sjcny.edu
CRUMP, Linda ... 402-472-3417 ... 300 H
lcrump1@unl.edu
CRUMP, Tammy ... 704-991-0267 ... 374 A
tcrump5648@stanly.edu
CRUMP, Virginia, S ... 731-410-6709 ... 469 M
vcrump@lanecollege.edu
CRUMPACKER, Laurie ... 617-521-2250 ... 245 A
laurie.crumpacker@simmons.edu
CRUMPTON, Beth ... 478-274-7850 ... 134 G
bcrumpton@oftc.edu
CRUSCIEL, Robert ... 814-472-3021 ... 446 B
rcrusciel@francis.edu
CRUSE, David ... 517-265-5161 ... 247 D
CRUSE, Susan ... 404-727-6061 ... 129 A
scruse2@emory.edu
CRUSE, Terry Dale ... 314-392-2291 ... 286 C
cruset@mobap.edu
CRUSOE, Kris ... 541-888-2525 ... 420 C
kcrusoe@socc.edu
CRUTCHER, Ben ... 859-257-5849 ... 206 H
ben@uky.edu
CRUTCHER, Caicey, L ... 620-792-9386 ... 190 E
crutcherc@bartonccc.edu
CRUTCHER, Cheryl ... 602-243-8398 ... 16 E
cheryl.crutcher@smcmail.maricopa.edu
CRUTCHER, Gary ... 816-414-3700 ... 286 A
gcrutcher@mbts.edu
CRUTCHER, Ronald, A ... 508-286-8244 ... 246 E
crutcher_ronald@wheatoncollege.edu
CRUTCHFIELD, Victor ... 901-448-7271 ... 477 C
vcrutchfield@uthsc.edu
CRUTSINGER, Gene ... 419-448-3383 ... 402 E
crutsingerg@tiffin.edu
CRUZ, Abraham ... 212-694-1000 ... 324 C
acruz@boricuacollege.edu
CRUZ, Anthony ... 513-569-1640 ... 387 F
anthony.cruz@cincinnatistate.edu
CRUZ, Beatriz ... 718-429-6600 ... 359 E
beatriz.cruz@vaughn.edu
CRUZ, Carmen, L ... 787-257-0000 ... 566 H
carmen.cruz3@upr.edu
CRUZ, Celestino ... 787-746-1400 ... 562 C
ccruz@huertas.edu
CRUZ, Cindy ... 708-763-6538 ... 162 C
cindy.cruz@resu.edu
CRUZ, Erin ... 559-791-2332 ... 53 A
ecruz@portervillecollege.edu
CRUZ, Esteban ... 217-786-2200 ... 156 I
esteban.cruz@llcc.edu
CRUZ, Felicita ... 787-834-9595 ... 565 J
fcruz@uaa.edu
CRUZ, Glorimary ... 787-769-0007 ... 560 F
gcruz@caribbean.edu
CRUZ, Heather, A ... 716-851-1858 ... 333 B
cruzh@ecc.edu
CRUZ, Heidi ... 305-222-2815 ... 107 E
hcruz@careercollege.edu
CRUZ, Israel ... 787-264-1912 ... 563 G
icruz@sg.inter.edu
CRUZ, Janet ... 615-794-4254 ... 472 D
jcruz@omorecollege.edu

CRUZ, Jo Ann Moran ... 504-865-3244 ... 213 F
jcruz@loyno.edu
CRUZ, Joe ... 405-878-5402 ... 412 A
jccruz@stgregorys.edu
CRUZ, Johnny ... 520-621-1877 ... 19 B
cruzj@email.arizona.edu
CRUZ, Jose ... 956-872-3554 ... 494 D
jcruz@southtexascollege.edu
CRUZ, Lambert ... 602-386-4111 ... 11 H
lambert.cruz@arizonachristian.edu
CRUZ, Larry ... 787-850-9342 ... 567 B
larry.cruz@upr.edu
CRUZ, Lourdes ... 203-837-9202 ... 92 A
cruzl@wcsu.edu
CRUZ, Luis, M ... 787-279-2250 ... 563 B
lcruz@bayamon.inter.edu
CRUZ, Mariela ... 787-620-2040 ... 560 B
marielacruz@aupr.edu
CRUZ, Martin ... 787-766-1717 ... 565 G
um_mcruzsa@suagm.edu
CRUZ, Nathaniel ... 718-518-4253 ... 327 D
ncruz@hostos.cuny.edu
CRUZ, Octavio ... 408-274-6700 ... 67 A
octavio.cruz@sjeccd.org
CRUZ, Octavio ... 408-270-6423 ... 67 B
octavio.cruz@evc.edu
CRUZ, Oscar ... 787-786-3030 ... 560 E
oscruz@ucb.edu.pr
CRUZ, Pedro ... 787-738-2161 ... 567 A
pedro.cruz3@upr.edu
CRUZ, Robert ... 201-360-4051 ... 310 F
rcruz@hccc.edu
CRUZ, Rosa, E ... 787-848-1589 ... 564 G
rcruz@popac.edu
CRUZ, Rosalia ... 212-694-1000 ... 324 C
rcruz@boricuacollege.edu
CRUZ, Tony ... 760-744-1150 ... 61 C
tcruz@palomar.edu
CRUZ, Villan ... 718-933-6700 ... 341 G
Vcrux@monroecollege.edu
CRUZ, Wanda ... 787-725-8120 ... 562 A
wcruz@eap.edu
CRUZ, Zoraida ... 787-279-1912 ... 563 B
zcruz@bayamon.inter.edu
CRUZ BONILLA, Jessica ... 787-744-1060 ... 564 D
jecbo@mechtech.edu
CRUZ-CUEVAS, Oscar ... 787-786-0018 ... 561 H
ocruz@cedoc.edu
CRUZ-CULLARI,
Christopher ... 718-892-2510 ... 327 A
chris.cruzcullari@csi.cuny.edu
CRUZ GORRITZ, Carlos ... 787-709-4442 ... 564 D
ccruz@mechtech.edu
CRUZ-JIMENEZ, Iris ... 787-834-5151 ... 565 B
incruz@email.pucpr.edu
CRUZ-RICHMAN, Daisy ... 718-270-7631 ... 352 D
dcruzrichman@downstate.edu
CRUZ-URIBE, Kathryn ... 831-582-4401 ... 35 C
kcruz@csumb.edu
CRUZADO, Waded ... 406-994-2341 ... 295 E
president@montana.edu
CRYER, Byron, L ... 214-648-2590 ... 507 D
byron.cryer@utsouthwestern.edu
CRYLEN, Thomas ... 847-925-6169 ... 151 E
tcrylen@harpercollege.edu
CSIKOS, Andrew, M ... 814-269-7130 ... 449 D
csikos@pitt.edu
CUADRA, Darla ... 510-261-8500 ... 61 F
darla.cuadra@patten.edu
CUADRADO-GARCÍA,
Héctor ... 787-993-8953 ... 566 G
hector.cuadrado@upr.edu
CUARON, Berta ... 760-744-1150 ... 61 C
bcuaron@palomar.edu
CUARTA, Adrian ... 813-974-2750 ... 120 D
acuarta@admin.usf.edu
CUBANO, Astrid ... 787-751-0500 ... 567 F
astrid.cubano@upr.edu
CUBANO, Luis, A ... 787-798-3001 ... 566 A
luis.cubano@uccaribe.edu
CUBBA, Stephanie ... 213-477-2766 ... 57 H
scubba@msmc.la.edu
CUBBAGE, Alan, K ... 847-491-4886 ... 160 D
a-cubbage@northwestern.edu
CUBBERLEY, Frances, M ... 610-359-5141 ... 426 G
fcubberl@dccc.edu
CUBBIN, Michael ... 510-574-1100 ... 44 D
mcubbin@devry.edu
CUBBINS, Elaine ... 520-383-8401 ... 18 L
ecubbins@tocc.cc.az.us
CUBE, Joan ... 925-631-8317 ... 64 F
jic2@stmarys-ca.edu
CUBELIC, Chuck ... 412-809-5100 ... 444 F
cubelic@pti.edu
CUBIT, James, R ... 847-735-5054 ... 155 F
cubit@lakeforest.edu
CUCCIA, Christopher ... 718-390-4094 ... 348 G
cucciac@stjohns.edu
CUCURELLA-ADORNO,
Ana, E ... 787-780-0070 ... 560 F
president@caribbean.edu
CUDDEFORD, James ... 402-481-3135 ... 297 B
james.cuddeford@bryanlgh.org
CUDDIGAN, Janet ... 402-559-6612 ... 301 A
jcuddiga@unmc.edu

CUDDY, Colleen ... 212-746-6070 ... 360 B
czc2003@med.cornell.edu
CUDE, Ruth ... 361-354-2767 ... 482 I
rcude@coastalbend.edu
CUDHEA, Renee, M ... 518-489-7436 ... 340 B
srcudhea@mariacollege.edu
CUE, Elaine ... 270-886-1302 ... 198 H
rcue@brownmackie.edu
CUEBAS, Ana, E ... 787-890-2681 ... 566 E
ana.cuebas@upr.edu
CUELLAR, Carlos, E ... 956-326-2626 ... 497 B
ccuellar@tamiu.edu
CUELLAR, Tina ... 409-772-1983 ... 507 B
ehcuella@utmb.edu
CUELLAR, Toni ... 254-298-8333 ... 496 B
toni.cuellar@templejc.edu
CUENIN, Walter ... 781-736-3574 ... 233 A
cuenin@brandeis.edu
CUERVO, Heydee ... 305-226-9999 ... 109 B
hcuervo@mm.fnc.edu
CUETO, Omar ... 787-279-1912 ... 563 B
ocueto@bayamon.inter.edu
CUEVAS, Nuria ... 757-823-8118 ... 521 K
ncuevas@nsu.edu
CUEVAS, Rebecca ... 787-894-2828 ... 568 A
rebecca.cuevas1@upr.edu
CUEVAS SOTO, Edith ... 787-815-0000 ... 566 F
CUEZAS, Felix, A ... 787-844-2750 ... 567 E
felix.cuezas@upr.edu
CUFF, Michael ... 508-830-5037 ... 239 A
mcuff@maritime.edu
CUFFARI, Gina ... 216-447-8807 ... 19 C
gina.cuffari@phoenix.edu
CUFFE, Michael ... 919-681-5153 ... 363 I
cuffe002@mc.duke.edu
CUFFEE, Sallie ... 718-270-4984 ... 328 D
scuffee@mec.cuny.edu
CUIMAN, Leonzo ... 718-270-1972 ... 352 D
lcuiman@downstate.edu
CUKANNA, Paul-James ... 412-396-5002 ... 428 C
cukanna@duq.edu
CUKROWSKI, Ken ... 325-674-2024 ... 478 H
cukrowskie@acu.edu
CULATTA, Victor ... 408-795-5600 ... 37 A
victor.culatta@sjsu.edu
CULBERSON, Roy ... 940-498-6282 ... 491 C
rculberson@nctc.edu
CULBERT, John ... 773-325-7954 ... 148 F
jculbert@depaul.edu
CULBERTSON, Charles, R ... 540-828-5720 ... 516 K
cculbert@bridgewater.edu
CULBERTSON, Lindsay ... 903-923-2072 ... 486 D
lculbertson@etbu.edu
CULBERTSON, Paul ... 717-764-9550 ... 426 D
pculbertson@csb.edu
CULBERTSON, JR.,
Rodney, A ... 704-366-5066 ... 375 H
rculbertson@rts.edu
CULBREATH, Geri ... 912-279-5760 ... 127 B
gculbreath@ccga.edu
CULBRETH, Paul ... 717-299-7763 ... 447 H
culbreth@stevenscollege.edu
CULHAN, Timothy, P ... 859-238-5360 ... 199 D
tim.culhan@centre.edu
CULHANE, Marianne, B ... 402-280-3154 ... 297 H
mculhane@creighton.edu
CULKOWSKI, Justin, F ... 315-470-6632 ... 355 A
jfculkow@esf.edu
CULL, Cecelia ... 617-682-1525 ... 234 G
ccull@eds.edu
CULLARS, Kyle ... 478-445-1976 ... 129 F
kyle.cullars@gcsu.edu
CULLEN, Andrew ... 505-277-6465 ... 321 C
acullen@unm.edu
CULLEN, Daryl ... 415-282-7600 ... 28 B
darylcullen@actcm.edu
CULLEN, Gail ... 316-684-5335 ... 196 C
gail.cullen@sckans.edu
CULLEN, Holly ... 225-578-3872 ... 212 F
hhouk@lsu.edu
CULLEN, Jim ... 570-961-7864 ... 433 A
cullenj@lakcawanna.edu
CULLEN, Kathleen ... 608-266-9399 ... 553 D
kathleen.cullen@wtcsystem.edu
CULLEN, Keith ... 334-244-3345 ... 2 A
kcullen1@aum.edu
CULLEN, Kevin ... 302-736-2442 ... 96 G
cullenke@wesley.edu
CULLEN, Marie, D ... 330-941-1518 ... 406 F
mdcullen@ysu.edu
CULLEN, Matt ... 323-357-3438 ... 39 D
mattcullen@cdrewu.edu
CULLEN, Richard, T ... 845-451-1300 ... 331 F
r_cullen@culinary.edu
CULLER, Fred, B ... 304-883-2424 ... 542 H
fculler@newriver.edu
CULLER, Kevin, J ... 313-845-9755 ... 252 D
kjculler@hfcc.edu
CULLER, Lori, L ... 260-359-4213 ... 172 K
lculler@huntington.edu
CULLERTON, Laura ... 303-369-5151 ... 86 I
lcullerton@plattcolorado.edu
CULLEY, Christopher, M ... 614-292-0611 ... 398 H
culley.8@osu.edu

CULLEY, JR., W. Glenn ..... 434-223-6219.... 519 B
gculley@hsc.edu
CULLIGAN, Rob .... 320-363-3388.... 271 F
rculligan@csbsju.edu
CULLINAN, Carol .... 716-880-2211.... 340 E
carol.cullinan@medaille.edu
CULLINAN, Mary .... 541-552-6111.... 419 A
cullinanm@sou.edu
CULLINAN, Matthew, S ..... 336-758-3097.... 380 B
cullinan@wfu.edu
CULLINAN, William .... 414-288-5053.... 548 D
william.cullinan@marquette.edu
CULLINANE, Mary .... 508-565-3360.... 245 D
stonehillbkstr@fheg.follett.com
CULLINS, Robert, C .... 432-837-8049.... 501 B
rcullins@sulross.edu
CULLION, Suzanne .... 401-454-6331.... 454 B
scullion@risd.edu
CULLISON, Janet, L .... 443-518-4904.... 223 D
jcullison@howardcc.edu
CULLITON, Pamela .... 314-529-9520.... 284 F
pculliton@maryville.edu
CULLITON, Richard .... 860-685-2627...... 95 C
rculliton@wesleyan.edu
CULLUM, Carol, J .... 910-362-7040.... 368 E
ccullum@cfcc.edu
CULLUM, Charles .... 508-929-8038.... 239 D
ccullum2@worcester.edu
CULLUM, Douglas .... 585-594-6331.... 344 F
cullumd@nes.edu
CULLUMBER, Shari .... 317-931-3324.... 170 E
scullumber@cts.edu
CULLUP, Michael .... 521-344-1403...... 19 C
michael.cullup@phoenix.edu
CULOTTA, Cheryl, C .... 518-327-6340.... 345 H
cculotta@paulsmiths.edu
CULOTTA, Sheryl .... 860-685-2008...... 95 C
sculotta@wesleyan.edu
CULP, Kristin, J .... 937-328-6087.... 387 G
culpk@clarkstate.edu
CULP, Mark, K .... 610-861-5301.... 437 G
mculp@northampton.edu
CULPEPPER, Anthony .... 714-816-0366...... 72 I
aculpepper@tuiu.edu
CULPEPPER, Grady .... 404-756-4033.... 124 I
gculpepper@atlm.edu
CULPEPPER, R. Alan .... 678-547-6471.... 133 F
culpepper_ra@mercer.edu
CULPEPPER, Suzann .... 229-430-3510.... 123 I
sculpepper@albanytech.edu
CULUM, Samra .... 208-732-6223.... 143 B
sculum@csi.edu
CULVER, Dale .... 913-758-6122.... 197 B
hr@stmary.edu
CULVER, Dale .... 913-758-4372.... 197 B
culverd@stmary.edu
CULVER, Jay .... 863-638-2947.... 123 C
culverjr@webber.edu
CULVER, Jeff .... 303-256-9330...... 85 H
jculver@jwu.edu
CULVER, Richard, W .... 410-543-6017.... 228 D
rwculver@salisbury.edu
CULVER, Sandi .... 907-786-1464...... 10 I
smculver@uaa.alaska.edu
CULVER, Terry .... 212-217-4109.... 333 G
terry_culver@fitnyc.edu
CULVERHOUSE, Rosemary 478-757-3408.... 126 G
rculverh@centralgatech.edu
CUMBERBATCH, Ellis .... 909-607-3369...... 40 C
ellis.cumberbatch@cgu.edu
CUMBIA, Doug .... 540-868-7235.... 526 H
dcumbia@lfcc.edu
CUMBIE, Donna, L .... 252-222-6161.... 368 F
dlc@carteret.edu
CUMBY, Rick .... 423-478-6226.... 474 E
rcumby@clevelandstatecc.edu
CUMENS, Chris .... 270-901-1113.... 201 E
chris.cumens@kctcs.edu
CUMINGS, Victoria .... 503-517-1012.... 421 A
vcumings@warnerpacific.edu
CUMMING, Tammie .... 718-260-5007.... 328 E
tcumming@citytech.cuny.edu
CUMMINGS, Alice .... 216-916-7516.... 398 E
acummings@ocpm.edu
CUMMINGS, Alison .... 404-270-5344.... 137 E
acummin3@spelman.edu
CUMMINGS, SSE,
Brian, J .... 802-654-2386.... 514 B
bcummings@smcvt.edu
CUMMINGS, Carmen .... 850-599-3707.... 118 G
carmen.cummings@famu.edu
CUMMINGS, Carmen, M ... 386-312-4152.... 116 D
carmencummings@sjrstate.edu
CUMMINGS, Corlis .... 678-466-4270.... 127 A
corliscummings@clayton.edu
CUMMINGS, Cynthia .... 508-910-6402.... 237 E
ccumings2@umassd.edu
CUMMINGS, Dee Dee .... 765-983-1513.... 171 B
cummide@earlham.edu
CUMMINGS, Edmond, M .. 504-286-5258.... 214 I
ecumming@suno.edu
CUMMINGS, Helen .... 973-642-8380.... 315 C
helen.cummings@shu.edu
CUMMINGS, J. Robert ...... 706-776-0117.... 135 D
bcummings@piedmont.edu
CUMMINGS, Jenny .... 956-872-6411.... 494 D
jennyr@southtexascollege.edu
CUMMINGS, Jim .... 270-745-5327.... 207 C
jim.cummings@wku.edu
CUMMINGS, John .... 559-244-2680...... 71 I
john.cummings@scccd.edu
CUMMINGS, John, H .... 559-244-2680...... 72 A
john.cummings@scccd.edu
CUMMINGS, Jonathan .... 304-293-7173.... 544 E
jonathan.cumming@mail.wvu.edu
CUMMINGS, Joseph .... 718-489-5346.... 348 E
jcummings@stfranciscollege.edu
CUMMINGS, Joyce .... 954-308-2177.... 100 I
cummingsj@aii.edu
CUMMINGS, Kevin, R .... 914-594-4536.... 343 F
webmaster@nymc.edu
CUMMINGS, Kris .... 253-964-6529.... 536 C
kycummings@pierce.ctc.edu
CUMMINGS, Lisa .... 802-635-1382.... 515 E
lisa.cummings@jsc.edu
CUMMINGS, Lynn .... 412-392-3904.... 444 H
lcummings@pointpark.edu
CUMMINGS, Marge .... 606-337-1407.... 199 E
mcummings@ccbbc.edu
CUMMINGS, Natalie, A ...... 402-465-2123.... 299 J
nac@nebrwesleyan.edu
CUMMINGS, Pam .... 252-940-6204.... 367 I
PamC@beaufortccc.edu
CUMMINGS, Sandra, A ..... 904-620-2903.... 120 C
s.cummings@unf.edu
CUMMINGS, Terrence, M .. 803-533-3721.... 460 G
tcummings@scsu.edu
CUMMINGS, Tiffany, N ...... 434-381-6362.... 524 E
tcummings@sbc.edu
CUMMINGS, Victor .... 707-527-4615...... 68 E
vcummings@santarosa.edu
CUMMINGS, Walter .... 404-756-4052.... 124 I
wcummings@atlm.edu
CUMMINGS,
Wm. Theodore .... 281-283-3100.... 503 C
cummings@uhcl.edu
CUMMINGS-DANSON,
Gail, L .... 518 580 5370.... 351 B
gcumming@skidmore.edu
CUMMINGS-SIMMONS,
Louise .... 641-784-5110.... 184 H
lcummings@graceland.edu
CUMMINS, Cheryl .... 662-846-4405.... 274 B
ccummins@deltastate.edu
CUMMINS, David, J .... 330-972-8396.... 403 B
dcummins@uakron.edu
CUMMINS, David, J .... 440-365-5222.... 395 C
CUMMINS, F. James .... 810-766-4250.... 248 C
jim.cummins@baker.edu
CUMMINS, Richard .... 509-542-4869.... 532 C
rcummins@columbiabasin.edu
CUMMINS, Stephen .... 630-942-3007.... 147 G
cummins@cod.edu
CUMMISKEY, Raymond, V 636-797-3000.... 283 H
rcummisk@jeffco.edu
CUMOLETTI, Susan, K .... 315-652-6500.... 325 A
scumoletti@bryantstratton.edu
CUMPIANO, Barbarita .... 787-832-6000.... 562 E
bcumpiano@icprjc.edu
CUNDALL, JR., Michael .... 336-285-2030.... 377 F
mcundall@ncat.edu
CUNDARI, Alan .... 909-469-5670...... 78 D
acundari@westernu.edu
CUNDIFF, H. Lynn .... 928-757-0801...... 16 G
lcundiff@mohave.edu
CUNDIFF, Michael .... 314-984-7608.... 289 D
mcundiff@stlcc.edu
CUNDUMI, Orlando .... 787-780-0070.... 560 F
ocundumi@caribbean.edu
CUNEAZ, Jodi .... 810-766-4015.... 248 H
jodi.cuneaz@baker.edu
CUNHA, Sonia .... 973-642-8743.... 315 C
sonia.cunha@shu.edu
CUNNING, Catherine, A ..... 973-378-2661.... 311 A
catherine.cunning@shu.edu
CUNNING, Charles, J .... 864-488-4540.... 459 A
cunning@limestone.edu
CUNNINGHAM, Al .... 912-443-5827.... 136 D
acunningham@savannahtech.edu
CUNNINGHAM, Austin, J .. 972-883-2234.... 505 D
cunning@utdallas.edu
CUNNINGHAM, Bruce, W . 919-684-9007.... 363 I
bruce.cunningham@duke.edu
CUNNINGHAM, Carl, G .... 251-460-6895........ 9 E
ccunningham@usouthal.edu
CUNNINGHAM, Cecelia ..... 616-632-2816.... 248 A
cunnicec@aquinas.edu
CUNNINGHAM,
Chester, M .... 270-824-8699.... 202 C
chet.cunningham@kctcs.edu
CUNNINGHAM, Dave .... 206-546-4595.... 537 G
dcunningham@shoreline.edu
CUNNINGHAM, David .... 313-845-4106.... 252 D
CUNNINGHAM, Diana, J ... 914-594-4200.... 343 F
diana_cunningham@nymc.edu
CUNNINGHAM, Diane .... 270-707-3921.... 202 A
diane.cunningham@kctcs.edu
CUNNINGHAM, Donald ..... 865-974-4373.... 477 B
hip@utk.edu
CUNNINGHAM, Eddie .... 302-454-3922...... 96 C
ecunning@dtcc.edu
CUNNINGHAM, Eric .... 573-875-7649.... 280 E
ercunningham@ccis.edu
CUNNINGHAM, Gary .... 606-679-8501.... 202 F
gary.cunningham@kctcs.edu
CUNNINGHAM, James, E . 570-326-3761.... 440 K
jcunning@pct.edu
CUNNINGHAM, Janet, L ... 580-327-8400.... 409 C
jlcunningham@nwosu.edu
CUNNINGHAM, Janice, M 574-296-7075.... 172 L
jmcunningham@indianatech.edu
CUNNINGHAM, Joan .... 973-328-5340.... 309 B
jcunningham@ccm.edu
CUNNINGHAM, John .... 404-270-5074.... 137 E
jcunning@spelman.edu
CUNNINGHAM, Joi, M ...... 248-370-3496.... 257 C
cunning3@oakland.edu
CUNNINGHAM, Julie .... 212-817-7040.... 327 B
jcunningham@gc.cuny.edu
CUNNINGHAM, Karla, K ... 317-940-9570.... 170 C
kcunning@butler.edu
CUNNINGHAM, Kathleen .. 610-606-4635.... 424 I
ksglass@cedarcrest.edu
CUNNINGHAM, Kay .... 901-321-3430.... 467 G
kay.cunningham@cbu.edu
CUNNINGHAM, Kevin, A .. 563-884-5898.... 188 C
kevin.cunningham@palmer.edu
CUNNINGHAM, Kevin, A .. 563-884-5898.... 114 E
kevin.cunningham@palmer.edu
CUNNINGHAM, Kevin, A .. 563-884-5898...... 60 L
kevin.cunningham@palmer.edu
CUNNINGHAM, Khaneetah 314-513-4226.... 289 B
kcunningham@stlcc.edu
CUNNINGHAM, Lawrence . 918-631-2181.... 413 F
bubba-cunningham@utulsa.edu
CUNNINGHAM, Luana .... 318-487-7301.... 209 B
cunningham@lacollege.edu
CUNNINGHAM, Marina ..... 973-655-4499.... 311 G
cunninghamm@mail.montclair.edu
CUNNINGHAM, Mark .... 404-756-4654.... 124 I
mcunningham@atlm.edu
CUNNINGHAM, Mary .... 516-773-5398.... 558 F
cunninghamm@usmma.edu
CUNNINGHAM, Michael ... 619-594-5259...... 36 E
mcunningham@mail.sdsu.edu
CUNNINGHAM, Michael ... 254-647-1414.... 492 E
mcunningham@rangercollege.edu
CUNNINGHAM,
Michael, A .... 419-995-8215.... 399 B
cunningham.15@osu.edu
CUNNINGHAM,
Michael, M .... 570-326-3761.... 440 K
mcunning@pct.edu
CUNNINGHAM, Paul R, G 252-744-2201.... 377 C
cunninghamp@ecu.edu
CUNNINGHAM,
R. Michael .... 217-443-8831.... 148 E
mcunningham@dacc.edu
CUNNINGHAM, Rose .... 201-360-4158.... 310 F
rcunningham@hccc.edu
CUNNINGHAM, Sean .... 512-463-1808.... 500 D
sean.cunningham@tsus.edu
CUNNINGHAM, Shannon .. 918-540-6272.... 408 J
scunningham@neo.edu
CUNNINGHAM, Steven, D 815-753-6021.... 160 A
cunningham@niu.edu
CUNNINGHAM, Todd .... 201-234-3104...... 19 C
todd.cunningham@phoenix.edu
CUNNINGHAM, Todd .... 724-357-4000.... 442 E
todd.cunningham@iup.edu
CUNNINGHAM, William, J 215-596-8535.... 450 A
w.cunningham@usciences.edu
CUNY, John, E .... 859-238-5451.... 199 D
john.cuny@centre.edu
CUNZ, Leonard .... 908-852-1400.... 308 F
cunzl@centenarycollege.edu
CUOMO, Michele .... 718-631-6344.... 329 A
mcuomo@qcc.cuny.edu
CUOZZO, Jenifer .... 202-685-3785.... 557 F
cuozzoj@ndu.edu
CUP, Jo Beth .... 312-662-4101.... 144 C
jcup@adler.edu
CUPPARI, Antoinette .... 954-938-3083.... 103 K
acuppari@keller.edu
CUPPER, Barbara .... 415-433-6691...... 46 L
bcupper@fidm.edu
CUPPER, Barbara .... 415-675-5200...... 47 A
bcupper@fidm.edu
CUPPLES, Thomas, B .... 302-356-6761...... 97 A
thomas.b.cupples@wilmu.edu
CUPPS, Lowell .... 803-786-3686.... 457 C
lcupps@columbiasc.edu
CUPRAK, Greg .... 610-436-3200.... 443 F
gcuprak@wcupa.edu
CURAVO, Pam .... 419-824-3731.... 395 D
pcuravo@lourdes.edu
CURBO, Billy, D .... 254-659-7701.... 487 E
bdcurbo@hillcollege.edu
CURCHACK, Mark, P .... 215-572-4076.... 422 B
curchack@arcadia.edu
CURD, David .... 877-248-6724...... 14 J
CURE, Nancy .... 708-974-5712.... 159 A
cure@morainevalley.edu
CUREG, Sapphire .... 304-327-4512.... 543 C
scureg@bluefieldstate.edu
CURET, Nahomy .... 787-257-7373.... 565 E
ue_ncuret@suagm.edu
CURETON, Alan, S .... 651-631-5250.... 270 E
ascureton@nwc.edu
CURETON, Archie, L .... 585-245-5731.... 353 C
cureton@geneseo.edu
CURIA, Rich .... 714-628-4721...... 63 G
curia_rich@sccollege.edu
CURL, John .... 801-581-8788.... 510 L
jcurl@sa.utah.edu
CURL, Timothy, D .... 859-371-9393.... 198 D
tcurl@beckfield.edu
CURLEE, Michelle .... 406-477-6215.... 294 B
mcurlee@cdkc.edu
CURLER, Alan .... 918-587-6789.... 413 A
acurler@twsweld.com
CURLESS, Chris .... 805-893-4638...... 74 F
chris.curless@purc.ucsb.edu
CURLEY, Greg, M .... 814-641-3512.... 431 L
curleyg@juniata.edu
CURLEY, Lauren .... 781-239-2572.... 240 D
lcurley@massbay.edu
CURLEY, McKeever .... 505-786-4172.... 318 H
mcurley@navajotech.edu
CURLEY, Meredith .... 480-557-1588...... 19 C
meredith.curley@phoenix.edu
CURLEY, Michael, J .... 508-831-5469.... 247 B
mjcurley@wpi.edu
CURLEY, Russell, L .... 218-477-2565.... 268 A
CURLEY, Stephen, R .... 814-865-7641.... 438 F
src2@psu.edu
CURLEY, Thomas .... 413-236-2103.... 239 E
tcurley@berkshirecc.edu
CURLEY, Timothy, M .... 814-865-1086.... 438 F
tmc3@psu.edu
CURLL, Steve .... 814-371-2090.... 448 C
scurll@triangle-tech.edu
CURNS, Jeannine .... 419-448-2111.... 391 G
jcurns@heidelberg.edu
CURNUTT, Cindy .... 432-335-6601.... 491 F
ccurnutt@odessa.edu
CURNUTT, Marlin, R .... 423-585-2690.... 476 B
marlin.curnutt@ws.edu
CURRALL, Steven, C .... 530-752-4600...... 73 F
scc@ucdavis.edu
CURRAN, Catherine .... 847-969-4901.... 145 A
ccurran@argosy.edu
CURRAN, Daniel, J .... 937-229-4122.... 404 A
president@udayton.edu
CURRAN, Diana, T .... 810-762-3150.... 259 F
dtcurran@umflint.edu
CURRAN, James, W .... 404-727-8720.... 129 A
jcurran@sph.emory.edu
CURRAN, Joanne, M .... 607-436-2541.... 353 E
curranjm@oneonta.edu
CURRAN, Linda .... 303-678-3620...... 84 H
linda.curran@frontrange.edu
CURRAN, Susan .... 401-232-6020.... 453 A
scurran3@bryant.edu
CURRAN, Terrence, M .... 910-962-3137.... 379 C
currant@uncw.edu
CURRAN, OSFS,
Thomas, B .... 816-501-4250.... 288 D
thomas.curran@rockhurst.edu
CURREN, Robert, A .... 407-303-9372.... 108 D
robert.curren@fhchs.edu
CURRENT, Amy, L .... 563-589-0274.... 189 G
acurrent@wartburgseminary.edu
CURRERI, Michelle, S .... 401-874-4502.... 454 E
michelle@uri.edu
CURREY, David .... 714-997-6789...... 39 C
dcurrey@chapman.edu
CURREY, Pamela, A .... 804-828-2092.... 525 E
pacurrey@vcu.edu
CURRIE, Catherine .... 401-232-6369.... 453 A
ccurrie@bryant.edu
CURRIE, Dean, W .... 626-395-6275...... 32 E
dean.currie@caltech.edu
CURRIE, Eunice, M .... 817-272-5554.... 505 A
currie@uta.edu
CURRIE, Jacqueline .... 205-366-8894........ 7 G
jcurrie@stillman.edu
CURRIE, John .... 785-532-6912.... 194 B
ksuad@ksu.edu
CURRIE, John .... 215-887-5511.... 451 D
scotsrev@comcast.net
CURRIE, Kevin, D .... 724-738-2082.... 443 E
kevin.currie@sru.edu
CURRIE, Tammy, H .... 757-221-1909.... 517 J
thcurr@wm.edu
CURRIE, Thomas, W .... 704-337-2450.... 524 F
tcurrie@upsem.edu
CURRIE, Walter James .... 691-320-2480.... 559 A
jimc@comfsm.fm
CURRIER, Camile, W .... 318-342-5230.... 216 E
currier@ulm.edu
CURRIER, Chuck .... 630-942-2790.... 147 G
currier@cod.edu
CURRIER, Nicole .... 508-854-7515.... 241 C
ncurrier@qcc.mass.edu
CURRIN, Alicia .... 903-886-5034.... 497 E
alicia_currin@tamu-commerce.edu

CURRIN, Bruce, A .... 402-472-3105 .... 300 H
bcurrin1@unl.edu
CURRIN, Tom .... 678-915-7482 .... 137 C
tcurrin@spsu.edu
CURRISTINE, Eileen .... 609-343-6810 .... 307 D
ecurrist@atlantic.edu
CURRO, Margaret (Peg) .... 508-678-2811 .... 239 F
peg.curro@bristolcc.edu
CURRY, Agnes, B .... 860-231-5224 .... 93 H
acurry@sjc.edu
CURRY, Anne .... 205-226-4904 .... 2 C
acurry@bsc.edu
CURRY, Bonita, P .... 517-353-3243 .... 255 D
curryb@msu.edu
CURRY, Carolyn .... 302-857-6060 .... 95 F
ccurry@desu.edu
CURRY, Charles, T .... 724-738-2002 .... 443 E
charles.curry@sru.edu
CURRY, Cynthia, S .... 304-367-4000 .... 543 E
CURRY, Dean, C .... 717-766-2511 .... 436 D
dcurry@messiah.edu
CURRY, JR., H. Pete .... 717-337-6311 .... 429 H
pcurry@gettysburg.edu
CURRY, James .... 252-249-1851 .... 372 C
pbanks@pamlicocc.edu
CURRY, JR., James, L .... 770-720-5577 .... 135 F
JLC1@reinhardt.edu
CURRY, James, P .... 504-394-7744 .... 214 A
jcurry@olhcc.edu
CURRY, Jason .... 615-329-8582 .... 468 G
jcurry@fisk.edu
CURRY, Keith .... 310-900-1600 .... 45 E
curry_k@compton.edu
CURRY, Kraig .... 740-753-6106 .... 392 A
curry_k@hocking.edu
CURRY, Michael, D .... 989-837-4758 .... 257 A
currym@northwood.edu
CURRY, Ralph, W .... 906-786-5802 .... 249 D
curryr@baycollege.edu
CURRY, Robert .... 662-252-8000 .... 277 C
rcurry@rustcollege.edu
CURRY, Ruby .... 314-513-4135 .... 289 B
rcurry@stlcc.edu
CURRY, Susan .... 319-384-5452 .... 182 C
sue-curry@uiowa.edu
CURRY, Terri, A .... 712-274-5257 .... 187 D
curryte@morningside.edu
CURRY, II, Theodore, H .... 517-353-5300 .... 255 D
thcurry@msu.edu
CURRY, Tilden, J .... 615-963-7139 .... 474 A
tcurry@tnstate.edu
CURRY, Tina .... 252-536-7263 .... 370 F
curryt@halifaxcc.edu
CURRY, Vicki .... 620-365-5116 .... 190 A
curry@allencc.edu
CURRY, William, N .... 601-318-6103 .... 278 E
bill.curry@wmcarey.edu
CURRY DAMATO, Ellen, R 914-654-5854 .... 330 B
ecurry@cnr.edu
CURTIN, Brian .... 207-893-6670 .... 219 F
bcurtin@sjcme.edu
CURTIN, Kathleen, M .... 410-857-2259 .... 224 D
kcurtin@mcdaniel.edu
CURTIN, Michael, J .... 502-852-6166 .... 207 A
mjcurt01@louisville.edu
CURTIS, Allison .... 805-965-0581 .... 68 B
curtis@sbcc.edu
CURTIS, Alyce .... 617-928-4556 .... 243 A
acurtis@mountida.edu
CURTIS, Amy .... 207-879-8757 .... 218 B
CURTIS, Benjamin, J .... 607-735-1821 .... 333 A
bcurtis@elmira.edu
CURTIS, Brandon .... 276-935-4349 .... 516 A
bcurtis@asl.edu
CURTIS, Carolyn, G .... 518-629-7204 .... 336 C
c.curtis@hvcc.edu
CURTIS, Cynthia, A .... 615-460-6408 .... 467 B
cynthia.curtis@belmont.edu
CURTIS, Deborah, J .... 309-438-5415 .... 153 C
djcurti@ilstu.edu
CURTIS, Deloris, Y .... 203-332-5102 .... 90 B
dcurtis@hcc.commnet.edu
CURTIS, Ed .... 301-552-1400 .... 229 C
ecurtis@bible.edu
CURTIS, Edison .... 928-724-6727 .... 14 A
ecurtis@dinecollege.edu
CURTIS, Elaine .... 931-540-2534 .... 474 F
bcurtis@columbiastate.edu
CURTIS, Jeanne, F .... 215-898-6300 .... 448 I
curtis@isc.upenn.edu
CURTIS, Jeffrey, H .... 540-464-7104 .... 529 A
CurtisJH@vmi.edu
CURTIS, Jerri .... 301-295-3628 .... 558 A
jcurtis@usuhs.mil
CURTIS, Joseph .... 615-329-8773 .... 468 G
jcurtis@fisk.edu
CURTIS, K. Tyler .... 620-341-5440 .... 192 D
kcurtis2@emporia.edu
CURTIS, Kathleen, A .... 915-747-7280 .... 505 E
kacurtis@utep.edu
CURTIS, Kelly .... 310-377-5501 .... 56 F
kcurtis@marymountpv.edu
CURTIS, Kelly, T .... 864-488-4601 .... 459 A
kcurtis@limestone.edu

CURTIS, Mark .... 989-358-7458 .... 247 G
curtism@alpenacc.edu
CURTIS, Marvin .... 574-520-4170 .... 174 C
mcurtis@iusb.edu
CURTIS, Monty, L .... 512-863-1200 .... 495 G
curtism@southwestern.edu
CURTIS, Regina .... 413-775-1426 .... 240 B
curtis@gcc.mass.edu
CURTIS, Rosanne .... 714-415-6500 .... 77 G
rcurtis@westcoastuniversity.edu
CURTIS, Seletha, R .... 314-286-4803 .... 288 B
srcurtis@ranken.edu
CURTIS, Stephen, M .... 215-751-8028 .... 426 B
scurtis@ccp.edu
CURTIS, Sue .... 951-785-2167 .... 53 D
scurtis@lasierra.edu
CURTIS, Susan .... 336-517-2289 .... 362 C
scurtis@bennett.edu
CURTIS, Tammy .... 707-826-3626 .... 36 D
curtis@humboldt.edu
CURTIS, Ted .... 330-972-6107 .... 403 B
curtis4@uakron.edu
CURTIS, Timothy .... 928-428-8220 .... 14 C
tim.curtis@eac.edu
CURTIS, Tina .... 606-759-7141 .... 202 D
tina.curtis@kctcs.edu
CURTIS-CHAVEZ, Mark .... 216-987-5137 .... 389 A
mark.curtis-chavez@tri-c.edu
CURTIS HANE, Audrey .... 316-942-4291 .... 195 C
hanea@newmanu.edu
CURTIS POWELL, Melissa 614-235-4136 .... 402 G
mcpowell@TLSohio.edu
CURTISS, Kathleen, M .... 603-283-2361 .... 303 F
kcurtiss@antiochne.edu
CURTO, Stephen, A .... 732-224-2593 .... 308 B
scurto@brookdalecc.edu
CURVIN, Nicole .... 802-258-9261 .... 513 F
ncurvin@marlboro.edu
CUSACK, Kelly, J .... 419-372-0632 .... 385 D
kcusack@bgsu.edu
CUSACK, Kristen .... 303-360-4701 .... 83 E
kristen.cusack@ccaurora.edu
CUSACK, Mary .... 810-762-0474 .... 256 C
CUSATO, Peter .... 617-353-2148 .... 232 G
pcusato@bu.edu
CUSEO, Vincent .... 323-259-2700 .... 59 H
admission@oxy.edu
CUSHMAN, Jenifer, S .... 814-641-3181 .... 431 L
cushmaj@juniata.edu
CUSHMAN, Ron .... 417-873-7323 .... 281 H
rcushman@drury.edu
CUSHMAN, Valerie, J .... 540-458-8702 .... 530 A
vcushman@wlu.edu
CUSICK, Dianna .... 612-659-6319 .... 267 E
dianna.cusick@minneapolis.edu
CUSICK, Eileen .... 413-755-4014 .... 241 E
cusick@stcc.edu
CUSICK, Sherry .... 563-589-3721 .... 189 B
scusick@dbq.edu
CUSKER, Anne .... 812-265-2580 .... 176 G
acusker@ivytech.edu
CUSTER, Cristeen .... 507-457-2569 .... 270 B
ccuster@winona.edu
CUSTER, Laura .... 859-344-3314 .... 206 D
laura.custer@thomasmore.edu
CUSTER, Mandi .... 740-654-6711 .... 400 B
custera@ohio.edu
CUSTER, Rodney .... 605-642-6262 .... 465 F
rod.custer@bhsu.edu
CUSTER, Rodney, L .... 309-438-2583 .... 153 C
rlcuster@ilstu.edu
CUTAIA, Diana .... 617-879-2238 .... 246 F
dcutaia@wheelock.edu
CUTCHER-GERSHENFELD, Joel .... 217-333-1480 .... 167 B
joelcg@illinois.edu
CUTCHIN, Claudine .... 812-749-1443 .... 178 D
ccutchin@oak.edu
CUTCHIN, Jeff .... 618-842-3711 .... 152 F
cutchinj@iecc.edu
CUTHBERT, James, E .... 585-594-6860 .... 347 F
cuthbertj@roberts.edu
CUTHBERTSON, Rebecca, F .... 704-355-1547 .... 363 B
rebecca.cuthbertson@carolinashealthcare.org
CUTIETTA, Robert, A .... 213-740-5389 .... 76 C
musicdean@thornton.usc.edu
CUTLER, Ada Beth .... 973-655-5167 .... 311 G
cutlera@mail.montclair.edu
CUTLER, Bruce .... 925-439-2181 .... 43 D
bcutler@losmedanos.edu
CUTLER, David, A .... 802-654-2653 .... 514 B
dcutler@smcvt.edu
CUTLER, Jared .... 937-512-2789 .... 401 J
jared.cutler@sinclair.edu
CUTLER, Jerry .... 302-831-2171 .... 96 F
jcutler@udel.edu
CUTLER, Nancy .... 408-554-4915 .... 68 C
ncutler@scu.edu
CUTLER, Sally, M .... 317-940-9742 .... 170 C
scutler@butler.edu
CUTLIFF, Janice .... 270-843-6750 .... 199 G
jcutliff@daymarcollege.edu

CUTLIP, Mark .... 304-696-3253 .... 543 G
cutlipm@marshall.edu
CUTOLO, Chuck .... 516-572-7811 .... 342 C
chuck.cutolo@ncc.edu
CUTONE, Joan .... 412-536-1079 .... 432 F
joan.cutone@laroche.edu
CUTRELL, Kathy .... 336-887-3000 .... 365 J
kcutrell@laureluniversity.edu
CUTRELL, Kel Lee .... 706-778-8500 .... 135 D
kcutrell@piedmont.edu
CUTRELL, Lori .... 615-230-4834 .... 476 A
lori.cutrell@volstate.edu
CUTRER, Emily .... 760-750-4050 .... 36 B
ecutrer@csusm.edu
CUTRI, David .... 419-530-6294 .... 404 F
david.cutri@utoledo.edu
CUTRIGHT, Patricia .... 509-963-1973 .... 531 G
cutright@cwu.edu
CUTSHALL-KING, Joseph .. 518-743-2243 .... 322 B
cutshallkingj@sunyacc.edu
CUTSHAW, Kathleen, D .... 808-956-9190 .... 141 B
cutshaw@hawaii.edu
CUTSINGER, Ginger .... 269-965-3931 .... 253 H
cutsingerg@kellogg.edu
CUTSPEC, John .... 828-251-6868 .... 378 C
jcutspec@unca.edu
CUTTING, Alicia .... 603-668-6706 .... 304 E
acutting@ccsnh.edu
CUTTING, Merrill, W .... 808-955-1500 .... 140 D
merrill_cutting@heald.edu
CUTTINO, Robert, E .... 770-538-4749 .... 126 B
rcuttino@brenau.edu
CUYKENDALL, Lora, L .... 503-494-8252 .... 418 D
CUZZOLINO, Robert, G .... 215-871-6770 .... 444 B
bob@pcom.edu
CVITKOVIC, Davorka .... 510-436-1198 .... 50 F
cvitkovic@hnu.edu
CVITKOVIC, Kimberly, F .... 269-660-8021 .... 257 E
cvitkovick@millercollege.edu
CVITKOVIC, Vicky .... 847-543-6504 .... 147 H
vcvitkovic@clcillinois.edu
CWALINA, Marianne, F .... 781-891-2129 .... 231 F
mcwalina@bentley.edu
CYBORON, Robert .... 808-544-0215 .... 140 B
rcyboron@hpu.edu
CYGAN, Brian .... 570-326-3761 .... 440 K
blc1@pct.edu
CYNAR, Deana .... 908-852-1400 .... 308 F
cynar@centenarycollege.edu
CYPHERS, Christopher, J .... 212-472-1500 .... 343 G
ccyphers@nysid.edu
CYPRESS, Sharen .... 731-989-6986 .... 468 K
scypress@fhu.edu
CYPRIAN, Alecia .... 504-816-4398 .... 208 I
acyprian@dillard.edu
CYREE, Kendall, B .... 662-915-5820 .... 277 G
kbcyree@olemiss.edu
CYRUS, Cynthia .... 615-322-7311 .... 477 F
CYTERSKI-ACOSTA, Andrea .... 210-805-5864 .... 503 F
cyterski@uiwtx.edu
CYZE, Mike .... 563-588-8193 .... 183 B
mike.cyze@clarke.edu
CZAJKIEWICZ, Zbigniew .... 281-283-3703 .... 503 C
czajkiewiez@uhcl.edu
CZAJKOWSKI, Joyce .... 608-822-2419 .... 555 B
CZAPIEWSKI, Duane, J .... 701-777-3491 .... 381 D
duane.czapiewski@email.und.edu
CZARDA, Lawrence, D .... 336-272-7221 .... 364 D
lczarda@greensborocollege.edu
CZARNIK, Mimi .... 414-382-6138 .... 545 H
mimi.czarnik@alverno.edu
CZARNIK-NEIMEYER, Jake .... 920-686-6176 .... 550 E
Jake.Czarnik-Neimeyer@sl.edu
CZEKAJ, Sandra .... 219-785-5696 .... 178 H
czekajs@pnc.edu
CZEKAJ, Walter, P .... 724-938-5244 .... 441 G
czekaj@calu.edu
CZEKANSKI, Kathleen .... 215-951-1322 .... 432 G
czekanski@lasalle.edu
CZERNIAK, Walter, L .... 815-753-0783 .... 160 A
wczerniak@niu.edu
CZERWINSKI, Rick .... 540-887-7336 .... 520 I
rczerwin@mbc.edu
CZERWINSKI-ALJETS, Sue 618-468-4800 .... 156 C
sczerwin@lc.edu
CZIRAK, Steve, G .... 718-951-5504 .... 326 G
czirak@brooklyn.cuny.edu
CZOHARA, Cami .... 603-623-0313 .... 305 F
cczohara@nhia.edu
CZUBATYJ, Anna .... 586-791-6610 .... 248 G
czubatyj.anna@baker.edu
CZYZ, Vito .... 716-375-2525 .... 348 C
vczyc@sbu.edu

D

DÁNILA, Alba .... 787-751-0160 .... 561 G
adanila@cmpr.gobierno.pr
DÁVILA, Marisol .... 787-894-2828 .... 568 A
marisol.davila2@upr.edu
DÁVILA-LÓPEZ, Rafael, F .. 787-250-0000 .... 566 D
rafael.davila4@upr.edu

DA COSTA, Jacqueline .... 732-987-2425 .... 310 D
dacostaj@georgian.edu
DA GRACA, John .... 956-968-2132 .... 498 A
j-dagraca@tamuk.edu
DAAKE, Mary .... 308-865-8501 .... 300 G
daakem@unk.edu
DAAR, Karen .... 323-265-8723 .... 54 G
daarkl@elac.edu
DABIRIAN, Amir .... 657-278-5000 .... 34 E
adabirian@fullerton.edu
DABNEY, A, D .... 215-935-3879 .... 451 D
ddabney@wts.edu
DABNEY, David, O .... 419-530-8776 .... 404 F
david.dabney@utoledo.edu
DABNEY, Jerome .... 773-602-5252 .... 147 B
jdabney@ccc.edu
DABOUB, Joel .... 817-735-2204 .... 504 C
jdaboub@hsc.unt.edu
DABOVAL, Jeanne, M .... 337-475-5508 .... 215 G
jdaboval@mcneese.edu
DABROWSKI, Jan .... 503-699-6275 .... 416 I
jdabrowski@marylhurst.edu
DACAL, Anita, S .... 412-578-6343 .... 424 G
dacalas@carlow.edu
DACANAY, Emelita .... 310-578-1080 .... 28 K
edacanay@antiochla.edu
DACE, Karen, L .... 816-235-6704 .... 291 E
dacek@umkc.edu
DACHELET, Derek .... 608-822-2417 .... 555 B
DACHILLE, Nancy .... 215-248-7048 .... 425 C
ndachill@chc.edu
DACOSTA, Tracy, M .... 401-254-3541 .... 454 C
tdacosta@rwu.edu
DACUS, Kent .... 951-343-4687 .... 31 G
kdacus@calbaptist.edu
DADABHOY, Zav .... 719-549-2919 .... 83 B
zav.dadabhoy@colostate-pueblo.edu
DADDONA, Mark .... 678-466-4070 .... 127 A
markdaddona@clayton.edu
DADDONA, Sharon, N .... 860-727-6903 .... 92 C
sdaddona@goodwin.edu
DADEZ, Edward .... 352-588-8206 .... 116 E
ed.dadez@saintleo.edu
DADEZ, Teresa .... 352-588-8347 .... 116 E
teresa.dadez@saintleo.edu
DAFFER, Steve .... 405-733-7424 .... 411 I
sdaffer@rose.edu
DAFFRON, Eric .... 201-684-7532 .... 313 D
edaffron@ramapo.edu
DAFFRON, Jeanne .... 816-271-4234 .... 287 A
daffron@missouriwestern.edu
DAFFRON, SJ, Justin .... 312-915-6406 .... 157 A
jdaffro@luc.edu
DAFLER, James, E .... 724-946-7317 .... 451 C
daflerje@westminster.edu
DAFOE, Robert, J .... 401-841-7008 .... 557 I
DAGANAAR, Mark .... 913-469-8500 .... 193 I
mdaganaar@jccc.edu
DAGAVARIAN, Debra .... 609-652-4514 .... 313 F
dagavarian@stockton.edu
DAGES, John, R .... 202-994-5300 .... 97 F
dages@gwu.edu
DAGG, Carrie .... 618-842-3711 .... 152 F
daggc@iecc.edu
DAGGETT, Paula .... 210-486-0224 .... 479 F
pdaggett@alamo.edu
DAGOSTIN, Jean .... 334-983-3521 .... 4 A
jdagostin@wallace.edu
DAGRADI, Linda .... 413-205-3259 .... 229 G
linda.dagradi@aic.edu
DAGUE, Saralyn .... 304-829-7835 .... 540 E
sdague@bethanywv.edu
DAHER, Hamsa .... 248-349-5454 .... 260 A
hdaher@walshcollege.edu
DAHILL, Patricia .... 617-587-5632 .... 243 D
dahillp@neco.edu
DAHL, Carolyn, C .... 205-348-6331 .... 8 F
cdahl@ccs.ua.edu
DAHL, Christopher, C .... 585-245-5501 .... 353 C
cdahl@geneseo.edu
DAHL, James, G .... 217-424-6285 .... 158 F
jdahl@millikin.edu
DAHL, James, G .... 217-424-6284 .... 158 F
jdahl@millikin.edu
DAHL, John, C .... 260-481-6375 .... 174 A
dahl@ipfw.edu
DAHL, Margaret, W .... 706-583-8209 .... 138 C
mwd@uga.edu
DAHL, Mark .... 503-768-7339 .... 416 F
dahl@lclark.edu
DAHL, Nelson, D .... 715-422-5327 .... 554 C
nelson.dahl@mstc.edu
DAHL, Noel .... 415-703-9537 .... 31 J
ndahl@cca.edu
DAHL, Tracy .... 360-736-9391 .... 531 H
tdahl@centralia.edu
DAHL, Wendy .... 206-268-4107 .... 530 F
wdahl@antioch.edu
DAHLBERG, Albert, A .... 401-863-1885 .... 452 J
albert_a_dahlberg@brown.edu
DAHLBERG, James .... 715-468-2815 .... 555 E
jim.dahlberg@witc.edu
DAHLBERG, Margaret .... 701-845-7200 .... 382 A
margaret.dahlberg@vcsu.edu

DANIEL, Larry 904-620-2520 120 C
ldaniel@unf.edu
DANIEL, Linda 903-675-6350 502 D
ldaniel@tvcc.edu
DANIEL, Lori 256-395-2211 7 E
ldaniel@suscc.edu
DANIEL, Margaret 615-297-7545 466 H
daniel@aquinascollege.edu
DANIEL, Nancy 617-348-6513 246 A
daniel@urbancollege.edu
DANIEL, Richard 915-747-8600 505 E
rjdaniel@utep.edu
DANIEL, Robin 336-272-7102 364 D
rdaniel@greensborocollege.edu
DANIEL, Rolf, W 260-399-7700 180 E
rdaniel@sf.edu
DANIEL, Sandra, D 229-931-2275 131 B
DANIEL, Sharlene 423-775-6596 472 E
sdaniel@ogs.edu
DANIEL, Sherman 680-488-2471 560 A
shermand1961@yahoo.com
DANIEL, Stephen, P 757-683-3093 521 L
sdaniel@odu.edu
DANIEL, Thomas, E 404-656-2212 138 E
tom.daniel@usg.edu
DANIEL, Tim 701-483-2181 381 E
tim.daniel@dickinsonstate.edu
DANIEL, W. John 205-934-3474 8 G
wdaniel@uab.edu
DANIEL, Wallace, L 478-301-2110 133 F
daniel_wl@mercer.edu
DANIEL-ROBINSON, Kim 973-720-3766 317 D
danielrobinsonk@wpunj.edu
DANIELL, Steven 817-531-4900 502 A
sdaniell@txwes.edu
DANIELLE, Bob 253-943-3085 533 B
rdanielle@devry.edu
DANIELS, Anjela 501-370-5335 23 B
adaniels@philander.edu
DANIELS, Calvin 913-234-0710 191 G
calvin.daniels@cleveland.edu
DANIELS, Cathy 404-270-5002 137 E
cdaniels@spelman.edu
DANIELS, Charlotte 218-855-8014 266 C
cdaniels@clcmn.edu
DANIELS, Darrell 919-546-8230 376 D
ddaniels@shawu.edu
DANIELS, Debra, S 909-384-4470 65 C
ddaniels@sbccd.cc.ca.us
DANIELS, Dennis, E 936-261-3085 496 E
dedaniels@pvamu.edu
DANIELS, Dennis, E 936-261-5206 496 E
dedaniels@pvamu.edu
DANIELS, Gerri, L 906-227-2650 256 F
gdaniels@nmu.edu
DANIELS, Glynis 610-799-1936 434 D
gdaniels@lccc.edu
DANIELS, Herman, G 850-872-3857 110 E
hdaniels@gulfcoast.edu
DANIELS, III, Jack, E 323-241-5273 55 C
danielje@lasc.edu
DANIELS, Jennifer 949-376-6000 53 E
jdaniels@lagunacollege.edu
DANIELS, Joel 740-397-9934 386 G
jdaniels@cotc.edu
DANIELS, John, C 802-728-1250 515 G
jdaniels@vtc.vsc.edu
DANIELS, Jon, M 785-227-3380 190 G
danielsj@bethanylb.edu
DANIELS, Judy 337-550-1218 212 H
DANIELS, Kathryn 206-726-5080 532 G
kdaniels@cornish.edu
DANIELS, Kyle 585-266-0430 333 E
kdaniels@cci.edu
DANIELS, Linda 601-979-2282 275 A
linda.j.daniels@jsums.edu
DANIELS, Linda 404-656-2243 138 E
linda.daniels@usg.edu
DANIELS, Lisa 518-464-8500 333 F
ldaniels@excelsior.edu
DANIELS, Martin 253-964-6619 536 C
mdaniels@pierce.ctc.edu
DANIELS, Maurice, C 706-542-5424 138 C
sswdean@uga.edu
DANIELS, Michael 828-448-3564 374 G
mdaniels@wpcc.edu
DANIELS, Mildred, L 803-536-7171 460 G
mdanie8@scsu.edu
DANIELS, Nettie 318-274-6142 215 E
danielsn@gram.edu
DANIELS, Orangel, J 910-362-7129 368 E
odaniels@cfcc.edu
DANIELS, Pat, E 252-451-8329 372 B
pdaniels@nash.cc.nc.us
DANIELS, Patti, J 618-537-6936 157 G
pjdaniels@mckendree.edu
DANIELS, Philip 330-490-7131 405 E
pdaniels@walsh.edu
DANIELS, Randell, W 734-384-4224 255 G
rdaniels@monroeccc.edu
DANIELS, Richard 513-569-1427 387 F
richard.daniels@cincinnatistate.edu
DANIELS, Rochelle 803-822-3208 459 D
danielsr@midlandstech.edu
DANIELS, Ronald, J 410-516-4170 223 F
president@jhu.edu
DANIELS, Ronnie 606-573-3274 203 A
ronnie.daniels@kctcs.edu
DANIELS, Ryan 414-847-3237 548 G
ryandaniels@miad.edu
DANIELS, Sally 612-330-1525 261 G
daniels@augsburg.edu
DANIELS, Scott 626-815-5441 30 E
sdaniels@apu.edu
DANIELS, Shelia 772-462-7275 110 L
sdaniels@irsc.edu
DANIELS, Wanda 251-405-7003 2 D
wdaniels@bishop.edu
DANIELS, Wesley, J 843-383-8178 457 A
wdaniels@coker.edu
DANIELSON, Amy 414-443-3637 549 A
danielsa@mtmary.edu
DANIELSON, David, A 414-229-6368 551 C
danielso@uwm.edu
DANIELSON, David, D 651-631-5329 270 E
dddanielson@nwc.edu
DANIELSON, James 907-796-6534 11 A
jedanielson@uas.alaska.edu
DANIELSON, Lisa, M 920-424-3007 551 D
danielsn@uwosh.edu
DANIELSON, Mary Ann 402-280-2535 297 H
maryanndanielson@creighton.edu
DANIELSON, Ronald, L 408-554-6813 68 C
rdanielson@scu.edu
DANIELSON, Timothy 920-424-1037 551 D
danielso@uwosh.edu
DANIEU, Paul, F 716-851-1856 333 D
danieu@ecc.edu
DANIK, Stephen, R 724-480-3356 426 A
steve.danik@ccbc.edu
DANILOWICZ, Bret, S 912-478-1854 131 A
bdanilowicz@georgiasouthern.edu
DANKEL, Richard 401-232-6117 453 A
rdankel@bryant.edu
DANKO, James, M 317-940-9900 170 C
jdanko@butler.edu
DANLEY, Charrita, D 757-727-5231 519 C
charrita.danley@hamptonu.edu
DANLEY, Janet, V 509-758-1703 538 G
janet.danley@wwcc.edu
DANLEY, Judy 336-841-9244 365 A
jdanley@highpoint.edu
DANLEY, Stacy 334-229-4505 1 C
sdanley@alasu.edu
DANNA, Debra 504-864-7550 213 F
danna@loyno.edu
DANNA, John 716-851-1360 333 C
danna@ecc.edu
DANNECKER, Debra, A 414-277-7131 548 H
schreite@msoe.edu
DANNECKER, Ronald 716-829-7600 332 F
dannecrh@dyc.edu
DANNELLEY, Jenny 909-652-6231 39 B
jenny.dannelley@chaffey.edu
DANNELLY, Jason 402-941-6545 299 A
dannelly@midlandu.edu
DANNEN, Troy, A 319-273-2470 182 D
troy.dannen@uni.edu
DANNENBAUM,
Martha, C 979-458-8300 497 C
mdannenbaum@tamu.edu
DANNER, Jerry 601-979-2144 275 A
jerry.l.danner@jsums.edu
DANNER-ODENWELDER,
Tracey 765-289-2291 175 K
tdannerodenwel@ivytech.edu
DANOS, Paul 603-646-2460 305 A
paul.danos@dartmouth.edu
DANSER, Dolores, A 717-245-1589 427 E
danserd@dickinson.edu
DANT, Kittridge 270-686-4508 202 E
kitt.dant@kctcs.edu
DANTLEY, Michael, E 513-529-6722 396 D
dantleme@muohio.edu
DANTLEY, Scott, J 410-951-3828 228 B
sdantley@coppin.edu
DANTSIN, Catherine 610-861-1509 436 I
kdantsin@moravian.edu
DANVILLE, M. Lisa 860-679-2701 94 F
danville@uchc.edu
DANZELL, Linda 508-678-2811 239 F
linda.danzell@bristolcc.edu
DANZEY, Ida 310-434-4792 68 D
danzey_ida@smc.edu
DAPENA, Ana, M 787-622-8000 566 C
adapena@pupr.edu
DAPICE-WONG, Stephanie 631-665-1600 357 J
stephanie.wong@touro.edu
DAPONTE, Paul 508-565-1551 245 D
pdaponte@stonehill.edu
DAQUILA, August 201-684-7494 313 D
adaquila@ramapo.edu
DARAGAN, Patricia, A 860-444-8553 558 E
patricia.a.daragan@uscga.edu
DARANDARI, H. Sam 314-516-6423 291 F
darandarih@umsl.edu
DARBONE, Davidson 337-491-2888 212 C
david.darbone@sowela.edu
DARBUT, Jeff 480-461-7382 15 K
jeffrey.darbut@mcmail.maricopa.edu
DARBY, Barbara, A 904-766-6551 109 E
bdarby@fscj.edu
DARBY, Cindy 318-678-6000 209 J
cdarby@bpcc.edu
DARBY, Mary, A 225-771-5640 214 H
magdarby@yahoo.com
DARBY, Sue 816-412-7702 464 G
sdarby@national.edu
DARCHER, Michael 253-964-6408 536 C
mdarcher@pierce.ctc.edu
DARCY, Diane 718-482-5080 328 C
ddarcy@lagcc.cuny.edu
DARDEN, Barbara 610-683-4484 442 F
darden@kutztown.edu
DARDEN, Beth 618-634-3224 164 C
bethda@shawneecc.edu
DARDEN, James 618-634-3325 164 C
jamesda@shawneecc.edu
DARDEN, Mary 210-253-3264 483 G
mary.darden@concordia.edu
DARDIS, Anne-Marie 703-416-1441 519 F
amdardis@ipsciences.deu
DARE, Adebimpe 617-928-4763 243 A
adare@mountida.edu
DARE, Donna 314-539-5288 289 A
ddare@stlcc.edu
DARE, Stephen, A 518-388-6180 358 E
dares@union.edu
DARGA, Richard 773-995-2378 146 D
rdarga@csu.edu
DARIN, Mary, K 972-238-6230 485 C
mkdarin@dcccd.edu
DARIN, Thomas, R 585-389-2830 342 D
tdarin2@naz.edu
DARING, William 508-854-4415 241 C
wdaring@qcc.mass.edu
DARKAZALLI, Ghazi 781-595-6768 236 I
gdarkazalli@mariancourt.edu
DARLAGE, Larry, J 817-515-6200 496 A
larry.darlage@tccd.edu
DARLING, Bruce, B 510-987-9444 73 D
bruce.darling@ucop.edu
DARLING, Douglas, D 701-662-1506 382 D
doug.darling@lrsc.edu
DARLING, Joshua, J 864-488-8219 459 A
jdarling@limestone.edu
DARLINGTON, Carol 989-386-6625 255 F
cdarlington@midmich.edu
DARNALL, Steve 707-826-4202 36 D
wsd1@humboldt.edu
DARNALL BURKE, Randi 707-826-3361 36 D
darnall@humboldt.edu
DARNELL, Charles, G 309-298-1834 168 A
cg-darnell@wiu.edu
DARNELL, Darrell, L 202-994-1000 97 F
ddarnell@gwu.edu
DARNELL, Meg 212-924-5900 357 A
placement@swedishinstitute.edu
DAROSKY, Renee 312-939-4975 151 F
rdarosky@harringtoncollege.com
DAROVICH, Donna 817-515-5209 496 A
donna.darovich@tccd.edu
DARR, Brandi 724-836-7167 449 C
bsd@pitt.edu
DARR, Eric, D 717-901-5111 430 F
EDarr@HarrisburgU.edu
DARR, Steven 863-638-7230 123 B
steven.darr@warner.edu
DARRAGH, Terianne 718-982-3045 327 A
terianne.darragh@csi.cuny.edu
DARRAH, SSJ, Mary 215-248-7031 425 C
darrahm@chc.edu
DARRIGRAND, Denise, M 508-793-7423 233 C
ddarrigrand@clarku.edu
DARRINGTON,
Jessyca, M 334-229-4894 1 C
jdarrington@alasu.edu
DARROW, David 231-876-3126 248 F
david.darrow@baker.edu
DARROW, David, W 937-229-4615 404 A
David.Darrow@notes.udayton.edu
DARROW, Karen 406-756-3900 294 D
kdarrow@fvcc.edu
DARST, Robert 508-999-8989 237 E
RDarst@umassd.edu
DARST, Valerie 660-263-4110 287 B
valeried@macc.edu
DARSTEIN, Claire 716-827-2577 358 B
darsteinc@trocaire.edu
DART, Greg 435-283-7154 512 B
greg.dart@snow.edu
DARVILLE, Dennis 919-761-2100 376 G
ddarville@sebts.edu
DARVILLE, Robert, H 706-233-7335 136 E
rdarville@shorter.edu
DARWIN, Mike 205-726-4241 6 G
mdarwin@samford.edu
DARWISH, Nadia 630-829-6093 145 D
ndarwish@ben.edu
DAS, Dilip 410-951-6102 228 B
ddas@coppin.edu
DAS, Pradeep, K 404-627-2681 126 A
pradeep.das@beulah.org
DAS, Purna 219-785-5254 178 H
pdas@pnc.edu
DAS, Shelley 360-992-2952 532 A
sdas@clark.edu
DASBURG, Deanne 828-884-8129 362 D
dasburg@brevard.edu
DASENBROCK, Reed, W 808-956-8447 141 B
rdasenbr@hawaii.edu
DASEY-MORALES,
Maureen 316-978-3440 197 F
maureen.dasey-morales@witchita.edu
DASGUPTA, Nandini 510-869-8711 64 J
ndasgupta@samuelmerritt.edu
DASHER, Glenn 256-824-6200 9 A
dasherg@uah.edu
DASILVA, Frank 617-682-1565 234 G
fdasilva@eds.edu
DASILVA, Joseph 413-755-4889 241 E
DASTMOZD, Rassoul 651-846-1335 269 E
rassoul.dastmozd@saintpaul.edu
DATHER, Julie 605-668-1525 464 F
jdather@mtmc.edu
DATSKO, Robert, G 814-472-3006 446 B
rdatsko@francis.edu
DATTA, Sumana 979-845-6774 497 C
sumad@tamu.edu
DATTE, Catherine 703-339-1850 99 D
cdatte@strayer.edu
DATUIN, Bonnie Mae, M 671-735-5616 559 B
bonniemae.datuin@guamcc.edu
DAUDISTEL, Howard 915-747-8533 505 E
hdaudistel@utep.edu
DAUER, Eve 443-627-7587 272 F
eve.dauer@waldenu.edu
DAUGHADAY, David 410-617-2349 224 A
daughaday@loyola.edu
DAUGHERTY, Craig, A 740-427-5430 394 C
daugherty@kenyon.edu
DAUGHERTY, Donna 706-295-6306 130 C
ddaugher@highlands.edu
DAUGHERTY, Eleanor 773-702-5243 166 D
ebd1@uchicago.edu
DAUGHERTY, Penny, J 541-346-2971 419 B
pdaugherty@uoregon.edu
DAUGHERTY, Rex 918-293-4966 410 E
rex.daugherty@okstate.edu
DAUGHERTY, Robert, C 216-361-2760 387 A
RDaugherty@ChancellorU.edu
DAUGHERTY, Robyn 479-524-7301 22 C
rdaugherty@jbu.edu
DAUGHERTY, Tim 618-985-4872 154 E
timdaugherty@jalc.edu
DAUGHERTY, Vernon, D 828-254-1921 367 H
vdaugherty@abtech.edu
DAUGHETY, Kathy 252-399-6529 362 A
kdaughety@barton.edu
DAUGHT, Gary 423-461-8799 471 H
gfdaught@milligan.edu
DAUGHTERS, Kenneth, A 563-588-8000 184 F
kdaughters@emmaus.edu
DAUGHTREY, III,
Thomas, W 910-630-7316 366 H
tdaughtrey@methodist.edu
DAUGHTRY, Dee Dee, D 919-209-2066 371 C
dddaughtry@johnstoncc.edu
DAULTON, Jonathan, G 864-242-5100 455 E
DAUM, Kent 312-949-7013 152 D
kdaum@ico.edu
DAUM, Sarah 909-594-5611 58 A
sdaum@mtsac.edu
DAUN, Eugene 847-578-3252 163 A
eugene.daun@rosalindfranklin.edu
DAUPHINAIS, Leonard 701-477-7862 383 C
ldauphin@tm.edu
DAUSEN, Peter, G 831-656-3037 557 H
pgdausen@nps.edu
DAUTERIVE, Jerry 401-254-3444 454 C
jdauterive@rwu.edu
DAUWALDER, David, P 203-932-7267 95 B
ddauwalder@newhaven.edu
DAVAR, David 212-678-6161 337 G
dadavar@jtsa.edu
DAVAULT, Joey 405-733-7392 411 I
jdavault@rose.edu
DAVEE, Douglas 212-472-1500 343 G
ddavee@nysid.edu
DAVELAAR, Kate 616-395-7145 252 F
davelaark@hope.edu
DAVENPORT, A. Wade 610-372-4721 445 B
wdavenport@racc.edu
DAVENPORT, Brenda 314-513-4248 289 B
bdavenport@stlcc.edu
DAVENPORT, Courtney 803-780-1199 463 B
cdavenport@voorhees.edu
DAVENPORT, Daniel, D 208-885-6312 144 B
dand@uidaho.edu
DAVENPORT, Darrien 717-815-6663 452 F
ddavenp2@ycp.edu
DAVENPORT, Douglas 660-785-7200 291 A
douglas@truman.edu
DAVENPORT, Elizabeth 773-702-1234 166 D
DAVENPORT, Jeunet 414-278-7677 547 A
jdavenport@devry.edu

DAVIS, Jack 540-231-6416 529 B
davisa@vt.edu
DAVIS, James 303-871-3141 88 E
jdavis@du.edu
DAVIS, James 310-206-0011 74 A
jdavis@conet.ucla.edu
DAVIS, James 972-825-4803 495 D
jdavis@sagu.edu
DAVIS, James, A 515-294-0323 182 B
davis@iastate.edu
DAVIS, James, S 706-721-9826 130 B
jdavis@georgiahealth.edu
DAVIS, James Earl 215-204-8017 447 G
dean.ed@temple.edu
DAVIS, Janet 312-935-6805 162 E
jdavis@robertmorris.edu
DAVIS, Janice 229-931-2381 136 G
jdavis@southgatech.edu
DAVIS, Jef, C 330-941-2336 406 F
jcdavis05@ysu.edu
DAVIS, Jeff 936-468-3407 495 H
jhdavis@sfasu.edu
DAVIS, Jeff 912-871-1640 134 H
jdavis@ogeecheetech.edu
DAVIS, Jeff 541-757-8944 416 H
jeff.davis@linnbenton.edu
DAVIS, Jeffrey 706-864-1641 134 D
jldavis@northgeorgia.edu
DAVIS, Jeffrey, W 260-481-0739 174 A
davisj@ipfw.edu
DAVIS, Jennifer 302-831-2769 96 F
jjdavis@udel.edu
DAVIS, Jennifer, L 740-374-8716 405 F
jdavis@wscc.edu
DAVIS, Jerold 212-592-2000 350 F
jdavis@sva.edu
DAVIS, Jerome 212-854-9970 330 F
jd2145@columbia.edu
DAVIS, Jerome 205-226-4848 2 C
jdavis@bsc.edu
DAVIS, Jerry 619-388-3428 65 F
jdavis@sdccd.edu
DAVIS, Jerry, C 417-690-2470 280 C
pres@cofo.edu
DAVIS, Jessica 732-247-5241 312 A
jdavis@nbts.edu
DAVIS, Jim, L 701-477-7862 383 C
jdavis@tm.edu
DAVIS, Jimmy, H 731-661-5461 476 G
jdavis@uu.edu
DAVIS, Joan 214-333-6855 484 C
joan@dbu.edu
DAVIS, Joe, M 765-641-4084 169 A
jmdavis@anderson.edu
DAVIS, John 605-677-5341 465 E
john.davis@usd.edu
DAVIS, John 210-458-2233 506 B
john.davis@utsa.edu
DAVIS, John 540-423-9072 526 E
jdavis@germanna.edu
DAVIS, John 413-585-3000 245 B
jdavis@smith.edu
DAVIS, John 937-766-3455 386 F
davisjo@cedarville.edu
DAVIS, John 920-206-2371 548 B
jdavis@mbbc.edu
DAVIS, John, L 304-336-8337 544 B
jdavis@westliberty.edu
DAVIS, John, L 304-336-8024 544 B
jdavis@westliberty.edu
DAVIS, John, R 740-376-4390 395 F
john.davis@marietta.edu
DAVIS, Jonathan, M 802-626-6419 515 F
jonathan.davis@lyndonstate.edu
DAVIS, Judson, B 731-989-6023 468 K
jdavis@fhu.edu
DAVIS, Julia, T 478-301-2644 133 F
davis_jt@mercer.edu
DAVIS, Julianna 203-254-4030 92 B
jdavis@fairfield.edu
DAVIS, Julie, A 207-778-7142 220 C
jadavis@maine.edu
DAVIS, June 910-296-2424 371 B
jdavis@jamessprunt.edu
DAVIS, Karan, P 850-718-2205 102 H
davisk@chipola.edu
DAVIS, Karen 805-493-3164 32 H
kdavis@clunet.edu
DAVIS, Karen 401-863-3377 452 J
karen_davis@brown.edu
DAVIS, Karen, S 937-393-3431 401 K
ksdavis@sscc.edu
DAVIS, Kathleen 207-893-7741 219 F
kdavis@sjcme.edu
DAVIS, Kathy 715-346-4193 552 B
kdavis@uwsp.edu
DAVIS, Kathy, K 207-768-9581 220 F
kathy.k.davis@umpi.edu
DAVIS, Katie 478-274-7775 134 G
kdavis@oftc.edu
DAVIS, Kelly 479-968-0242 20 G
kdavis@atu.edu
DAVIS, Kelly 817-272-2194 505 A
kdavis@uta.edu

DAVIS, Ken, R 423-478-1131 472 F
kdavis@ptseminary.edu
DAVIS, JR., Kenneth, M 919-658-2502 367 D
kdavis@moc.edu
DAVIS, Kerry 904-819-6200 107 A
KDavis@flagler.edu
DAVIS, Kim, D 806-371-2912 479 H
kddavis@actx.edu
DAVIS, Kimely 434-832-7627 526 A
davisk@cvcc.vccs.edu
DAVIS, LaDonna 301-937-8448 226 H
ldavis@tesst.com
DAVIS, Larry 903-223-3106 498 C
larry.davis@tamut.edu
DAVIS, Larry, D 501-977-2013 25 G
davis@uaccm.edu
DAVIS, Larry, E 412-624-6337 449 A
ledavis@pitt.edu
DAVIS, Larry, J 314-516-5606 291 F
ldavis@umsl.edu
DAVIS, Laura 859-280-1236 203 F
ldavis@lextheo.edu
DAVIS, Laura 913-758-6308 197 B
davisl@stmary.edu
DAVIS, Laurie 706-864-1763 134 D
ldavis@northgeorgia.edu
DAVIS, JR., Lawrence, A 870-575-8471 25 B
davisla@uapb.edu
DAVIS, LeeAnn 386-506-3404 103 J
davisl@DaytonaState.edu
DAVIS, Len, L 516-876-3191 353 D
davisl@oldwestbury.edu
DAVIS, Lewin, B 573-288-6458 281 D
ldavis@culver.edu
DAVIS, Lily 619-849-2524 62 L
lilydavis@pointloma.edu
DAVIS, Linda 617-879-2341 246 F
ldavis@wheelock.edu
DAVIS, Linda 810-989-5765 258 B
ldavis@sc4.edu
DAVIS, Linda, P 386-822-7451 121 E
ldavis@stetson.edu
DAVIS, Lisa 570-286-3058 436 B
ld@mccannschool.com
DAVIS, Lois 503-725-4488 418 G
loisd@pdx.edu
DAVIS, Loren 253-589-5771 532 B
loren.davis@cptc.edu
DAVIS, Lori, A 502-597-6414 203 D
lori.davis@kysu.edu
DAVIS, LuAnn 402-486-2503 300 D
ludavis@ucollege.edu
DAVIS, Lynwood 301-552-1400 229 C
ldavis@bible.edu
DAVIS, M. Wayne 251-460-6132 9 E
wdavis@usouthal.edu
DAVIS, Malcolm 713-743-0583 503 B
mdavis@uh.edu
DAVIS, Marcellus 763-433-1695 265 J
marcellus.davis@anokaramsey.edu
DAVIS, Margaret 513-244-4824 388 D
maggie_davis@mail.msj.edu
DAVIS, Maria 269-749-7643 257 D
mdavis@olivetcollege.edu
DAVIS, Maria` 515-244-4221 181 D
davism@aib.edu
DAVIS, Marilyn 208-282-2507 143 D
mdavis@isu.edu
DAVIS, Marilyn, S 217-424-6379 158 F
mdavis@millikin.edu
DAVIS, Marion 480-858-9100 18 H
m.davis@scnm.edu
DAVIS, Mark 310-506-4472 61 G
mark.davis@pepperdine.edu
DAVIS, Marsha 845-758-7433 323 F
davis@bard.edu
DAVIS, Mary 828-298-3325 380 C
mdavis@warren-wilson.edu
DAVIS, Matt 505-984-6082 320 C
gi@sjcsf.edu
DAVIS, Matt 812-877-8421 179 A
matt.davis@rose-hulman.edu
DAVIS, Matthew 402-557-7232 297 A
matthew.davis@bellevue.edu
DAVIS, Matthew 920-261-9300 548 B
mdavis@mbbc.edu
DAVIS, Meagon 478-757-3803 139 A
mdavis@wesleyancollege.edu
DAVIS, Megan, W 603-862-2450 306 E
megan.davis@unh.edu
DAVIS, Melvin 601-979-1400 275 A
melvin.davis@jsums.edu
DAVIS, Michael 770-381-7200 131 F
DAVIS, Michael 312-553-2771 146 G
mdavis@ccc.edu
DAVIS, Michael, D 804-828-1305 525 E
mddavis@vcu.edu
DAVIS, Michael, G 985-448-4030 216 A
mike.davis@nicholls.edu
DAVIS, Michelle 404-880-8021 126 I
mdavis@cau.edu
DAVIS, Michelle 434-544-8228 520 H
davis@lynchburg.edu

DAVIS, Mike 386-752-1822 108 C
mike.davis@fgc.edu
DAVIS, Mitch 251-442-2334 9 B
mdavis@mail.umobile.edu
DAVIS, Mitch, E 251-442-2334 9 B
mdavis@mail.umobile.edu
DAVIS, Mitchel, W 207-725-3930 217 E
mwdavis@bowdoin.edu
DAVIS, Nan, M 903-813-3000 481 A
ndavis@austincollege.edu
DAVIS, Nancy 619-644-7000 49 A
nancy.davis@gcccd.edu
DAVIS, Nancy 919-962-2011 378 D
nancy_davis@unc.edu
DAVIS, Natalie 601-643-8354 274 A
natalie.davis@colin.edu
DAVIS, Nick 510-783-2100 49 H
nick_davis@heald.edu
DAVIS, Ora 334-387-3877 1 D
oradavis@amridgeuniversity.edu
DAVIS, Pam 423-746-5327 476 D
pdavis@twcnet.edu
DAVIS, Pamela 919-760-8360 366 G
davisp@meredith.edu
DAVIS, Pamela, B 216-368-2825 386 E
pamela.davis@case.edu
DAVIS, Patricia 207-780-5911 220 G
patdavis@usm.maine.edu
DAVIS, Patricia, A 251-380-3063 7 F
pdavis@shc.edu
DAVIS, Patrick 772-546-5534 110 J
patdavis@hsbc.edu
DAVIS, Patti 410-386-8066 221 G
pdavis@carrollcc.edu
DAVIS, Paul 641-784-5422 184 H
pjdavis@graceland.edu
DAVIS, Paul 718-270-3176 352 D
paul.davis@downstate.edu
DAVIS, Paul 936-468-1111 495 H
pdavis@sfasu.edu
DAVIS, Paula 609-343-5091 307 D
pdavis@atlantic.edu
DAVIS, Peggy 804-524-5030 529 C
pdavis@vsu.edu
DAVIS, Pete 608-342-1147 551 F
davisp@uwplatt.edu
DAVIS, Phillip, L 612-659-6300 267 E
phil.davis@minneapolis.edu
DAVIS, Rachelle 301-387-3044 222 H
rachelle.davis@garrettcollege.edu
DAVIS, Ralph 770-426-2713 133 B
rdavis@life.edu
DAVIS, Ralph, U 843-661-1110 458 C
rdavis@fmarion.edu
DAVIS, Rance 315-229-5551 349 E
rdavis@stlawu.edu
DAVIS, Randy 502-213-2122 202 B
randall.davis@kctcs.edu
DAVIS, Rene 202-872-4700 99 C
rene@sanz.edu
DAVIS, Renee 334-386-7230 3 H
rdavis@faulkner.edu
DAVIS, Rhonda 417-624-7070 284 G
rdavis@messengercollege.edu
DAVIS, Richard 317-931-2391 170 E
ddavis@cts.edu
DAVIS, TOR, Richard 740-283-6406 390 M
rdavis@franciscan.edu
DAVIS, Richard, E 954-262-1203 114 B
redavis@nsu.nova.edu
DAVIS, Richelle 207-893-7726 219 F
DAVIS, Rick 850-973-9492 113 J
davisr@nfcc.edu
DAVIS, Rick 662-246-6441 275 F
rdavis@msdelta.edu
DAVIS, Rick 703-993-8891 519 A
rdavi4@gmu.edu
DAVIS, Rob 612-874-3793 265 E
rob_davis@mcad.edu
DAVIS, Rob 216-373-6386 397 E
rdavis@ndc.edu
DAVIS, Robert 405-744-6350 410 C
robert.davis@okstate.edu
DAVIS, Robert, H 303-492-7006 88 B
robert.davis@colorado.edu
DAVIS, Rod 254-968-9071 496 F
rdavis@tarleton.edu
DAVIS, Roger 615-966-7161 470 D
roger.davis@lipscomb.edu
DAVIS, Ron 901-383-6712 99 D
rnd@strayer.edu
DAVIS, Sally 404-752-1942 134 B
sdavis@msm.edu
DAVIS, Sally 918-465-1756 408 A
sdavis@eosc.edu
DAVIS, Sandie 706-295-6339 130 C
sdavis@highlands.edu
DAVIS, Sandra 803-536-7067 460 G
sdavis@scsu.edu
DAVIS, Sandra, L 909-869-2289 33 G
sldavis@csupomona.edu
DAVIS, Scott 478-301-2024 133 F
davis_ds@mercer.edu

DAVIS, Shane 318-487-7181 209 B
davis@lacollege.edu
DAVIS, Shara 440-365-5222 395 C
DAVIS, Sharon 513-569-1475 387 F
sharon.davis@cincinnatistate.edu
DAVIS, Sharon 254-526-1346 482 F
sharon.davis@ctcd.edu
DAVIS, Sharon 214-860-8705 485 A
sdavis@dcccd.edu
DAVIS, Sherri 205-929-6357 5 E
sdavis@lawsonstate.edu
DAVIS, Sherri 606-672-2312 200 E
sherri.davis@frontier.edu
DAVIS, Sherry 254-659-7602 487 E
sdavis@hillcollege.edu
DAVIS, Stefan, S 317-274-8828 174 B
ssdavis@iupui.edu
DAVIS, Stephen 410-225-2355 224 C
sdavis@mica.edu
DAVIS, Steve 954-382-6531 122 C
sdavis@tiu.edu
DAVIS, Steve 304-357-4980 541 H
stevedavis@ucwv.edu
DAVIS, Steven, J 208-496-3305 142 G
daviss@byui.edu
DAVIS, Stuart 650-723-9406 71 F
spdavis@stanford.edu
DAVIS, Sue 225-768-1802 214 B
sue.davis@ololcollege.edu
DAVIS, Sue 713-221-8636 503 D
daviss@uhd.edu
DAVIS, Sue, E 330-941-2000 406 F
sedavis@ysu.edu
DAVIS, Susan, H 502-272-8217 198 E
sdavis@bellarmine.edu
DAVIS, Susan, Y 573-875-7210 280 E
sydavis@ccis.edu
DAVIS, Taishieka 318-670-6415 215 A
tdavis@susla.edu
DAVIS, Tammy 325-574-7695 508 F
tdavis@wtc.edu
DAVIS, Tanya 704-991-0249 374 A
tdavis5131@stanly.edu
DAVIS, Terry 619-482-6561 71 C
tdavis@swccd.edu
DAVIS, Thomas 434-791-5651 516 D
thom.davis@averett.edu
DAVIS, Thomas 803-705-4687 455 D
davist@benedict.edu
DAVIS, Thomas, A 423-775-7205 467 D
davisto@bryan.edu
DAVIS, Thomas, D 517-353-6727 255 D
tdd@msu.edu
DAVIS, Tiffany 810-766-4277 248 C
tiffany.davis@baker.edu
DAVIS, Tina 859-622-3876 200 D
tina.davis@eku.edu
DAVIS, Todd 678-359-5061 131 D
toddd@gdn.edu
DAVIS, Tom 334-670-3196 8 B
tomdavis@troy.edu
DAVIS, Tom 505-786-4113 318 H
tdavis@navajotech.edu
DAVIS, Tracie, L 574-289-7001 176 C
tldavis@ivytech.edu
DAVIS, Tracy 641-782-7081 189 A
davis@swcciowa.edu
DAVIS, Tracy 415-371-0002 60 A
DAVIS, Troy 413-265-2340 233 E
davist@elms.edu
DAVIS, Wayne 865-974-5321 477 B
wtdavis@utk.edu
DAVIS, Wayne 757-825-3513 528 B
davisw@tncc.edu
DAVIS, Wendall, M 919-530-6204 378 A
wendell.davis@nccu.edu
DAVIS, Wendy 520-515-3623 13 G
davisw@cochise.edu
DAVIS, Wendy 501-812-2273 23 C
wdavis@pulaskitech.edu
DAVIS, Wesley 701-477-7862 383 C
wdavis1@tm.edu
DAVIS, William 610-359-6500 426 G
wdavis@dccc.edu
DAVIS AUSTIN, Patricia 215-895-5844 427 G
pda@drexel.edu
DAVIS-BLAKE, Alison 734-764-1363 259 D
alisondb@umich.edu
DAVIS-BLAKE, Alison 612-624-7876 272 D
adavis-blake@csom.umn.edu
DAVIS BRAY, Nancy 478-445-0980 129 F
nancy.davisbray@gcsu.edu
DAVIS-DUKES, Janet 973-720-3096 317 D
davisdukesj@wpunj.edu
DAVIS FREEMAN,
Louisa, M 413-755-4333 241 E
ldavisfreeman@stcc.edu
DAVIS-FULMER, Deryl 920-693-1231 554 A
deryl.davisfulmer@gotoltc.edu
DAVIS GRIFFIN, Nancy 603-641-7171 305 H
ngriffin@anselm.edu
DAVIS-JOHNSON, Max 208-426-3033 142 F
maxdavisjohnson@boisestate.edu

DEAN, Barbara .... 502-942-8503.... 206 C
bsdean@sullivan.edu
DEAN, Becky .... 413-545-2211.... 237 C
becky.dean@chancellor.umass.edu
DEAN, Bill .... 806-742-3641.... 501 D
bill.dean@ttu.edu
DEAN, Delores .... 850-599-3700.... 118 G
delores.dean@famu.edu
DEAN, Dianna, G .... 512-505-3039.... 488 B
dgdean@htu.edu
DEAN, Don .... 914-323-5219.... 340 A
deand@mville.edu
DEAN, Gayle .... 505-566-3204.... 320 D
deang@sanjuancollege.edu
DEAN, Jackie .... 785-826-2607.... 194 C
jdean@k-state.edu
DEAN, James .... 919-962-3232.... 378 D
james_dean@unc.edu
DEAN, James, H .... 941-359-7524.... 115 K
jdean@ringling.edu
DEAN, James, S .... 412-531-4433.... 426 F
info@deantech.edu
DEAN, Jeffrey, L .... 856-225-2747.... 314 C
jdean@camden.rutgers.edu
DEAN, Jerome .... 617-928-4500.... 243 A
jdean@mountida.edu
DEAN, JR., Joe .... 205-226-4936........ 2 C
jdean@bsc.edu
DEAN, John, E .... 904-620-2800.... 120 C
jdean@unf.edu
DEAN, Johnie, E .... 859-846-5779.... 204 D
jdean@midway.edu
DEAN, Karol .... 310-954-4086...... 57 H
kdean@msmc.la.edu
DEAN, Kathy, L .... 251-442-2215........ 9 B
kathyd@mail.umobile.edu
DEAN, Kendall .... 801-713-0915.... 509 J
kenddean@edaff.com
DEAN, Kenneth, D .... 573-882-6597.... 291 D
deank@missouri.edu
DEAN, Laura .... 859-336-5082.... 205 F
ldean@sccky.edu
DEAN, Laura .... 303-256-9529...... 85 H
ladean@jwu.edu
DEAN, Laurie .... 575-492-2108.... 321 H
ldean@usw.edu
DEAN, LeAnn .... 320-589-6173.... 272 C
deanl@morris.umn.edu
DEAN, Leonard .... 229-248-2558.... 125 E
ldean@bainbridge.edu
DEAN, Lynne .... 210-486-4135.... 479 C
ldean12@alamo.edu
DEAN, Mark, E .... 620-792-9235.... 190 E
deanm@bartonccc.edu
DEAN, Marvin .... 810-766-4041.... 248 H
marvin.dean@baker.edu
DEAN, Mary Anne .... 781-280-3580.... 240 F
deanm@middlesex.mass.edu
DEAN, Randy .... 804-862-6249.... 523 C
rdean@rbc.edu
DEAN, Roberta, A .... 304-293-4245.... 544 E
radean@mail.wvu.edu
DEAN, Russell, K .... 304-293-7119.... 544 E
rkdean@mail.wvu.edu
DEAN, Sherry, L .... 972-238-6250.... 485 C
sherrydean@dcccd.edu
DEAN, Sheryl, L .... 810-766-4062.... 248 C
sheryl.dean@baker.edu
DEAN, Tanya .... 972-524-3341.... 495 F
DEAN, Thomas, K .... 319-335-1995.... 182 C
thomas-k-dean@uiowa.edu
DEAN, Troy .... 541-684-7293.... 417 F
tdean@northwestchristian.edu
DEAN, Wanda, H .... 540-231-7951.... 529 B
wdean@vt.edu
DEAN, Willow .... 316-677-9499.... 197 E
wdean@watc.edu
DEAN-BARR, Susan .... 414-229-3083.... 551 C
DEANE, Lynne, P .... 804-289-8064.... 525 A
ldeane@richmond.edu
DEANE, Robert .... 270-745-2548.... 207 C
robert.deane@wku.edu
DEANER, Kathy, F .... 954-308-2601.... 100 I
deanerk@aii.edu
DEANGELIS, Bill, J .... 770-720-9102.... 135 F
wjd@reinhardt.edu
DEANGELIS, Brian .... 580-559-5604.... 407 J
bdeangls@ecok.edu
DEANGELIS, Debby .... 510-885-3038...... 34 C
debby.deangelis@csueastbay.edu
DEANGELIS, Raymond .... 410-825-2196.... 453 B
rdeangelis@ccri.edu
DEANGELIS, Toni .... 719-846-5520...... 87 J
toni.deangelis@trinidadstate.edu
DEANGELO, OFM CONV,
Jude .... 202-319-5575...... 97 C
deangelo@cua.edu
DEANGELO, Mary .... 413-748-3757.... 245 C
mdeangelo@spfldcol.edu
DEANNA, Linda .... 312-996-4857.... 166 F
ldeanna@uic.edu
DEANS, Beverly .... 919-735-5151.... 374 F
bdeans@waynecc.edu

DEAR, Carley .... 601-857-3357.... 274 E
carley.dear@hindscc.edu
DEARBORN, Philip, E .... 717-560-8233.... 433 D
pdearborn@lbc.edu
DEARCORN, Casey .... 307-754-6084.... 556 D
Casey.Dearcorn@northwestcollege.edu
DEARDURFF, Dayle .... 513-861-6400.... 402 I
dayle.deardurff@myunion.edu
DEARSTYNE, JR.,
Kenneth, E .... 717-872-3475.... 443 C
kenneth.dearstyne@millersville.edu
DEARTH, John, C .... 716-673-3251.... 352 A
john.dearth@fredonia.edu
DEAS, Edwin .... 760-773-2511...... 41 H
edeas@collegeofthedesert.edu
DEAS, M. Gary .... 334-347-2623........ 3 G
gdeas@escc.edu
DEASE, Dennis, J .... 651-962-6500.... 272 E
djdease@stthomas.edu
DEASE, Mary Ann .... 203-837-8248...... 92 A
deasem@wcsu.edu
DEASON, Michael .... 972-860-4670.... 484 F
mdeason@dcccd.edu
DEATHERAGE, Adam .... 918-293-5274.... 410 E
adam.deatherage@okstate.edu
DEATHERAGE, Janet .... 312-915-6512.... 157 A
jdeathe@luc.edu
DEATLEY, Janeen, S .... 937-393-3431.... 401 K
jdeatley@sscc.edu
DEATON, Andrea, D .... 405-325-1646.... 413 C
adeaton@ou.edu
DEATON, Brady, J .... 573-882-3387.... 291 D
deatonb@missouri.edu
DEATON, Judy .... 949-675-4451...... 51 D
interior_designer@msn.com
DEATON, Sharon .... 949-675-4451...... 51 D
interior_designer@msn.com
DEATON, Taryn .... 703-812-4757.... 520 E
tdeaton@leland.edu
DEATS, Jacqueline .... 714-997-6851...... 39 C
deats@chapman.edu
DEATS, John .... 432-685-4726.... 490 G
jdeats@midland.edu
DEAVER, Christy .... 828-339-4406.... 373 H
christyd@southwesterncc.edu
DEAVER, Jennifer .... 573-876-7225.... 290 G
DEAVER, Reekitta .... 252-527-6223.... 371 D
rdeaver@lenoircc.edu
DEAVER, Robin .... 910-678-8484.... 370 B
deaverr@faytechcc.edu
DEBARROS, Angelia .... 210-485-0374.... 479 B
adebarros1@alamo.edu
DEBASIO, Nancy .... 816-995-2810.... 288 D
nancy.debasio@researchcollege.edu
DEBASIO, Nancy, O .... 816-995-2810.... 288 C
nancy.debasio@researchcollege.edu
DEBAUN, Amy .... 860-297-2305...... 94 C
amy.debaun@trincoll.edu
DEBEAUCHAMP, Debbie ..... 425-739-8232.... 535 B
deborah.debeauchamp@lwtc.edu
DEBEER, Dean .... 718-779-1430.... 346 B
ddb@plazacollege.edu
DEBELA, Kenesa .... 773-256-0716.... 157 B
kdebela@lstc.edu
DEBELLIS, Carol .... 559-453-7104...... 47 K
carol.debellis@fresno.edu
DEBENHAM, Kathie .... 801-863-8361.... 511 C
kathie.debenham@uvu.edu
DEBERNARDI, Maureen ...... 617-779-4369.... 244 E
admissionsandrecords@sjs.edu
DEBERRY, Ron .... 757-826-1883.... 516 H
DEBIAS, Patti .... 773-256-0728.... 157 B
pdebias@lstc.edu
DEBITY, Brittany .... 978-556-3615.... 241 B
bdebity@necc.mass.edu
DEBLASIO, Denise, M .... 973-655-4340.... 311 G
deblasiod@mail.montclair.edu
DEBLOIS, Benjamin, A .... 910-755-7403.... 368 C
debloisb@brunswickcc.edu
DEBLOIS, Louise .... 502-410-6200.... 200 F
DEBOARD, John .... 580-581-2237.... 407 D
jdeboard@cameron.edu
DEBOCK, Devin .... 918-293-4944.... 410 E
devin.debock@okstate.edu
DEBOER, Keith .... 616-222-1247.... 250 C
keith.deboer@cornerstone.edu
DEBOER-MORAN,
Jason, T .... 651-641-8766.... 263 C
moran@csp.edu
DEBORD, Bonnie, H .... 770-720-5502.... 135 F
bhd@reinhardt.edu
DEBOSE, Angela, W .... 813-974-4018.... 120 D
awdebose@usf.edu
DEBOSE, Henry .... 804-524-5992.... 529 C
hdebose@vsu.edu
DEBOWER, Lore .... 508-362-2131.... 240 A
ldebower@capecod.edu
DEBRAGA, Angie .... 775-775-2231.... 302 H
angied@gwmail.gbcnv.edu
DEBRAGGIO, Michael, J ...... 315-859-4654.... 335 A
mdebragg@hamilton.edu
DEBRITO, Joannie, L .... 303-963-3378...... 81 K
jdebrito@ccu.edu

DEBRIZZI, JR.,
Thomas, A .... 203-576-4690...... 94 D
tdebriz@bridgeport.edu
DEBROCK, Larry .... 217-333-2747.... 167 B
ldebrock@business.uiuc.edu
DEBRUM, Daved .... 692-625-6416.... 559 E
ddebrum@cmi.edu
DEBUHR, Larry .... 812-866-6846.... 171 F
debuhr@hanover.edu
DEBURE, Olivier .... 727-864-8421.... 104 K
debureoc@eckerd.edu
DEBURRO, Jennifer .... 207-602-2132.... 220 H
jdeburro@une.edu
DEBUS, Casey .... 307-532-8311.... 555 H
casey.debus@ewc.wy.edu
DEBUSK, Frankie .... 423-636-7300.... 476 F
fdebusk@tusculum.edu
DEBUSK, Lisa .... 907-277-1000...... 10 F
contact@chartercollege.edu
DECAIRE, Maryann .... 847-578-8810.... 163 A
maryann.decaire@rosalindfranklin.edu
DECAIRE, Maryann .... 847-578-3217.... 163 A
maryann.decaire@rosalindfranklin.edu
DECALO, Ruth .... 212-678-8915.... 337 G
rudecalo@jtsa.edu
DECAMILLIS, Susan .... 231-995-1014.... 256 G
sdecamillis@nmc.edu
DECARBO, Diane, M .... 724-658-1938.... 423 F
diane.decarbo@bc3.edu
DECARLO, Robert, L .... 516-877-3184.... 322 A
decarlo@adelphi.edu
DECARVALHO, Fatima .... 973-655-7818.... 311 G
decarvalhf@mail.montclair.edu
DECASTRO, John .... 936-294-2200.... 501 A
jdecastro@shsu.edu
DECASTRO-SALLIS,
Kishma .... 412-397-3648.... 445 G
sallis@rmu.edu
DECATUR, Jane .... 508-626-4585.... 238 D
jdecatur@framingham.edu
DECATUR, Sean .... 440-775-8410.... 397 F
sean.decatur@oberlin.edu
DECATUR, William .... 401-454-6474.... 454 B
wdecatur@risd.edu
DECELLE, Jerry .... 518-564-2082.... 354 B
decellejl@plattsburgh.edu
DECENA, Peter .... 408-924-2222...... 37 A
peter.decena@sjsu.edu
DECENZO, David, A .... 843-349-2001.... 456 G
ddecenzo@coastal.edu
DECHAMPS, Kathryn, J .... 414-277-7333.... 548 H
dechamps@msoe.edu
DECHANT, Emma .... 828-565-4095.... 370 G
edechant@haywood.edu
DECHANT, Margaret .... 361-825-5952.... 497 F
margaret.dechant@tamucc.edu
DECHARINTE, Janeen .... 815-838-0500.... 156 D
decharja@lewisu.edu
DECHELLIS, Andrea .... 973-642-8092.... 315 C
andrea.dechellis@shu.edu
DECHILLO, Neal .... 978-542-6630.... 239 B
ndechillo@salemstate.edu
DECICCIO, Albert, C .... 802-447-6333.... 514 D
adeciccio@svc.edu
DECICCO, Darlene .... 631-656-2134.... 334 B
darlene.decicco@ftc.edu
DECINQUE, Gregory, T .... 716-338-1060.... 337 E
gregdecinque@mail.sunyjcc.edu
DECK, Alisa .... 812-374-5129.... 175 J
adeck@ivytech.edu
DECK, Joseph, G .... 210-434-6711.... 491 G
jgdeck@lake.ollusa.edu
DECKER, Ann .... 772-462-7240.... 110 L
adecker@irsc.edu
DECKER, Barbara, Q .... 515-643-6601.... 187 C
bdecker@mercydesmoines.org
DECKER, Charles .... 810-989-2133.... 249 B
charles.decker@baker.edu
DECKER, Charley .... 517-265-5161.... 247 D
DECKER, David, R .... 614-947-6017.... 391 A
deckerd@franklin.edu
DECKER, Diann .... 801-818-8900.... 510 E
diann.decker@provocollege.edu
DECKER, Douglas .... 724-983-0700.... 434 A
ddecker@laurel.edu
DECKER, Douglas, S .... 724-439-4900.... 433 H
ddecker@laurel.edu
DECKER, James, B .... 304-367-4861.... 543 E
james.decker@fairmontstate.edu
DECKER, Lisa, M .... 212-752-1530.... 338 C
lisa.decker@limcollege.edu
DECKER, Nancy .... 724-983-0700.... 434 A
ndecker@laurel.edu
DECKER, Nancy, M .... 724-439-4900.... 433 H
ndecker@laurel.edu
DECKER, Pat .... 913-469-8500.... 193 I
pdecker5@jccc.edu
DECKER, Paul, W .... 818-767-0888...... 79 D
paul.decker@woodbury.edu
DECKER, Robert, W .... 201-559-6099.... 310 C
deckerr@felician.edu
DECKER, Sheryl .... 574-237-0774.... 170 B
sdecker@brownmackie.edu
DECKER, Stephanie .... 973-684-6868.... 312 E
sdecker@pccc.edu

DECKER, Steven .... 715-468-2815.... 555 E
steven.decker@witc.edu
DECKER, Susan .... 812-535-5138.... 179 C
sdecker@smwc.edu
DECKER, Timothy .... 845-298-0755.... 332 E
tdecker@sunydutchess.edu
DECKER, Vicki .... 507-457-5878.... 270 B
vdecker@winona.edu
DECLEENE, Catherine, A .... 574-284-4584.... 179 D
decleene@saintmarys.edu
DECLUE, Gary .... 217-641-4999.... 154 G
declueg@jwcc.edu
DECLUE, Stephanie .... 816-781-7700.... 293 D
declues@william.jewell.edu
DECOCK, Murray .... 315-228-7489.... 329 H
mdecock@colgate.edu
DECOLFMACKER, Robert .... 207-985-7976.... 218 D
robertdecolfmacker@landingschool.edu
DECONCILIS, Patricia, A .... 724-653-2213.... 427 F
pdecon@dec.edu
DECONTI, Katherine .... 860-297-2366...... 94 C
katherine.deconti@trincoll.edu
DECONTI, Merlin, A .... 401-598-4700.... 453 C
mdeconti@jwu.edu
DECOSTA, Jean .... 805-756-5198...... 33 F
jdecosta@calpoly.edu
DECOSTA, Melvin .... 808-735-4792.... 140 A
security@chaminade.edu
DECOSTER, Patrice .... 518-587-2100.... 355 F
pat.decoster@esc.edu
DECOTEAU, Brian .... 701-255-3285.... 383 D
bdecoteau@uttc.edu
DECOTEAU, Steve .... 701-477-7862.... 383 C
sdecoteau@tm.edu
DECOUDREAUX, Alecia, A .... 510-430-2094...... 57 D
adecoudreaux@mills.edu
DECOURCY, Alan .... 513-244-4487.... 388 D
alan_decourcy@mail.msj.edu
DECOURSEY, Paul, A .... 515-574-1055.... 185 F
decoursey@iowacentral.edu
DECOY, Dirk .... 740-695-9500.... 384 J
ddecoy@btc.edu
DECRISTOFORO, Joe, R ...... 210-458-7070.... 506 B
joe.decristoforo@utsa.edu
DECROSTA, Tony .... 970-491-5793...... 83 A
tony.decrosta@colostate.edu
DECUIR, Anthony .... 504-865-3039.... 213 F
decuir@loyno.edu
DEDAPPER, Lisa .... 208-459-5770.... 143 A
ldedapper@collegeofidaho.edu
DEDARIO, Nancy .... 716-614-5902.... 344 C
dedario@niagaracc.suny.edu
DEDE, Brenda, S .... 814-393-2337.... 442 A
bdede@clarion.edu
DEDECKER, Sherry .... 805-893-3713...... 74 F
sherry.dedecker@library.ucsb.edu
DEDEO, Patrick .... 973-720-2224.... 317 D
dedeop@wpunj.edu
DEDIEMAR, Jeanette .... 850-644-2466.... 119 C
jdediemar@fsu.edu
DEDIOS, Paul .... 714-484-7335...... 59 C
pdedios@cypresscollege.edu
DEDMAN, Tony .... 615-547-7610.... 467 I
tdedman@cumberland.edu
DEDOMINICIS, Ken .... 713-525-3119.... 504 D
ken@stthom.edu
DEDWYLDER, Jason .... 601-477-4240.... 275 B
jason.dedwylder@jcjc.edu
DEE, Edward .... 718-779-1430.... 346 B
edee@plazacollege.edu
DEE, Shawn, G .... 336-334-4822.... 370 E
sgdee@gtcc.edu
DEE, Tina .... 231-777-0660.... 256 D
tina.dee@muskegoncc.edu
DEEB, Bassam .... 716-614-6240.... 344 C
bdeeb@niagaracc.suny.edu
DEEDRICK, Gary, A .... 864-242-5100.... 455 E
DEEDS, Cher .... 330-684-8952.... 403 C
cher@uakron.edu
DEEDS, Sarene .... 417-873-7869.... 281 H
sdeeds@drury.edu
DEEDS, William, C .... 712-274-5103.... 187 D
deeds@morningside.edu
DEEGAN, James, E .... 727-864-8965.... 104 K
deeganje@eckerd.edu
DEEGAN, Jess .... 661-952-5071...... 33 H
jdeegan@csub.edu
DEEGAN, Pam .... 760-757-2121...... 57 E
pdeegan@miracosta.edu
DEEGAN, Robert, P .... 760-744-1150...... 61 C
rdeegan@palomar.edu
DEEGAN, Rosemary, L .... 610-921-7202.... 421 D
rdeegan@alb.edu
DEEGEN, Lynn .... 601-928-6212.... 275 G
lynn.deegen@mgccc.edu
DEEHAN, Theresa, L .... 973-761-9746.... 315 B
theresa.deehan@shu.edu
DEEK, Fadi, P .... 973-596-2997.... 312 C
fadi.deek@njit.edu
DEEL, Connie .... 785-594-8362.... 190 C
connie.deel@bakeru.edu
DEEL, Susan, M .... 989-463-7348.... 247 F
deel@alma.edu

DEEM, Marie 412-536-1128 432 F
marie.deem@laroche.edu

DEEMER, Kevin, L 440-964-4329 393 E
kdeemer@kent.edu

DEEMER, Kevin, L 440-964-4237 393 E
kdeemer@kent.edu

DEEN, Candace 717-872-3771 443 C
candace.deen@millersville.edu

DEEN, Delores 810-762-0567 256 C
delores.deen@mcc.edu

DEEN, Michael 903-813-2306 481 A
mdeen@austincollege.edu

DEER, Susan 845-574-4000 347 I

DEES, Andriel 715-425-3833 552 A
andriel.dees@uwrf.edu

DEES, Andriel 715-425-3711 552 A
andriel.dees@uwrf.edu

DEES, Charles 973-596-8293 312 C
charles.dees@njit.edu

DEES, Margaret 904-680-7649 107 H
mdees@fcsl.edu

DEESS, Eugene, P 973-596-3110 312 C
deess@njit.edu

DEETER, Daniel, P 574-284-4543 179 D
ddeeter@saintmarys.edu

DEETZ, Kristi, R 812-888-4358 181 B
kdeetz@vinu.edu

DEFA, Dennis 509-963-1258 531 G
defad@cwu.edu

DEFALCO, Ron, E 713-718-7586 487 G
ron.defalco@hccs.edu

DEFALUSSY, George 607-735-1978 333 A
gdefalussy@elmira.edu

DEFATTA, Jerry 601-266-5013 278 A
jerry.defatta@usm.edu

DEFEIS, Evelyn 973-684-5900 312 E
edefeis@pccc.edu

DEFELICE, OSB,
Jonathan, P 603-641-7010 305 H
jdefelice@anselm.edu

DEFELICE, Robert, A 781-891-2256 231 F
rdefelice@bentley.edu

DEFENDORF, Monica 607-962-9587 331 D
mdefendo@corning-cc.edu

DEFEO, Gregory 412-809-5100 444 F
defeo@pti.edu

DEFEO, Joseph 203-254-4025 92 B
jdefeo@fairfield.edu

DEFFENBACHER, Mark 559-453-2080 47 K
mdeffen@fresno.edu

DEFFENBAUGH,
Cynthia, B 804-289-8438 525 A
cdeffenb@richmond.edu

DEFFENBAUGH, MaryAnn 503-297-5544 417 G
mdeffenbaugh@ocac.edu

DEFFKE, Cliff 303-280-7530 84 C
cdeffke@devry.edu

DEFILIPPO, Eugene, B 617-552-4681 232 D
eugene.defilippo.2@bc.edu

DEFOE, Darren 207-221-8727 218 C
ddefoe@kaplan.edu

DEFOE, Richard 504-278-6230 211 I
rdefoe@nunez.edu

DEFOOR, Keith 706-379-5156 139 F
kdefoor@yhc.edu

DEFORD, J. Kevin 423-652-4859 469 L
jkdeford@king.edu

DEFOREST, Kristin, A 607-746-4590 355 E

DEFRANCESCO, Carolyn 336-272-7265 364 D
carolyn.defrancesco@greensborocollege.edu

DEFRANCIS, Robert 304-214-8820 543 A
rdefrancis@wvncc.edu

DEFRANCO, Agnes, L 713-743-2422 503 B
adefranco@uh.edu

DEFRANCO, Thomas 860-486-3813 94 E
thomas.defranco@uconn.edu

DEFRATES, Bruce 509-359-6329 533 D
bdefrates@ewu.edu

DEFREECE, Michele, T 607-746-4652 355 E
defreemt@delhi.edu

DEFREECE, Perri, D 607-746-4700 355 E
defreepd@delhi.edu

DEGAISH, Ann 361-825-2612 497 F
ann.degaish@tamucc.edu

DEGARMO, David, L 602-944-3335 11 D
ddegarmo@aicag.edu

DEGATEGNO, Paul, J 610-892-1411 439 B
pjd15@psu.edu

DEGAZON, Karen 212-938-5654 355 B
kdegazon@sunyopt.edu

DEGEL, Tom 406-771-4423 296 B
tdegel@msugf.edu

DEGEN, Bruno 718-270-6110 328 D
bdegen@mec.cuny.edu

DEGEN, Charlotte 413-662-5231 238 F
charlotte.degen@mcla.edu

DEGENHART, Mary Louise 314-367-8700 288 I
mary.degenhart@stlcop.edu

DEGEORGE, Christine, C 941-359-7645 115 K
ccarnegi@ringling.edu

DEGERMAN, Roger, E 218-299-3645 263 B
degerman@cord.edu

DEGEUS, Marilyn, J 816-654-7262 283 J
mdegeus@kcumb.edu

DEGIOIA, John (Jack), J 202-687-4134 98 A
president@georgetown.edu

DEGIOVANNI, Kim 301-387-3040 222 H
kim.degiovanni@garrettcollege.edu

DEGIOVINE, Christopher 518-454-5293 330 C
frchris@strose.edu

DEGLER, Suzanne, C 612-874-3799 265 E
suzanne_degler@mcad.edu

DEGN, Jason 402-399-2431 297 E
jdegn@csm.edu

DEGNAN, Susan 218-262-6710 266 H
susandegnan@hibbing.edu

DEGRAFFENREID, Pamela 828-227-7346 379 E
degraffen@wcu.edu

DEGRANGE, Karen, A 812-877-8285 179 A
karen.degrange@rose-hulman.edu

DEGRAW, Auburn 225-923-2524 207 E

DEGRAW, Julie, E 847-543-2359 147 H
jdegraw@clcillinois.edu

DEGROFT, Michael 717-299-7796 447 H
degroft@stevenscollege.edu

DEGROOT, Ophelia, H 828-689-1438 366 F
fdegroot@mhc.edu

DEGROOTE, David, K 320-308-2192 269 C
dkdegroote@stcloudstate.edu

DEGUEVARA, Maria 408-924-1116 37 A
maria.DeGuevara@sjsu.edu

DEHAAN, Laurens 415-433-9200 68 F
ldehaan@saybrook.edu

DEHAEMERS, Jennifer 816-235-1143 291 E
dehaemersj@umkc.edu

DEHAHN, Tracee 805-756-2586 33 F
tdehahn@calpoly.edu

DEHART, Dan, J 818-779-8557 53 B
ddehart@kingsuniversity.edu

DEHART, Joe 515-964-6279 183 E
jcdehart@dmacc.edu

DEHAVEN, Barbara 201-216-8762 315 E
bdehaven@stevens.edu

DEHAVEN, James 269-353-1280 253 G
jdehaven@kvcc.edu

DEHAVEN, Jane 515-244-4221 181 D
dehavenj@aib.edu

DEHAYES, Donald, H 401-874-4410 454 E
ddehayes@uri.edu

DEHLER, Candace 206-934-6875 537 B
candace.dehler@seattlecolleges.edu

DEHLIN, Catherine, L 906-227-2420 256 F
cdehlin@nmu.edu

DEHN, Paula 270-852-3117 203 E
pdehn@kwc.edu

DEHNE, Nathan, D 920-565-1588 547 H
dehneND@lakeland.edu

DEHOYOS, Diane, N 915-747-5601 505 E
dndehoyos@utep.edu

DEICHERT, Karen 724-480-3444 426 A
karen.deichert@ccbc.edu

DEICHMANN, Wendy, J 937-529-2201 403 A
wjdedwards@united.edu

DEIERLING, Tara 573-592-4248 293 E
tdeierli@williamwoods.edu

DEIGHTON, Joe 251-380-3023 7 F
jdeighton@shc.edu

DEIGNAN, Kathleen 609-258-5431 313 A
kdeignan@princeton.edu

DEIKE, Randall 212-998-4553 344 B
randall.deike@nyu.edu

DEIKE, Terri 903-233-3769 489 K
terrideike@letu.edu

DEILY, Leslie 724-266-3838 448 G
ldeily@tsm.edu

DEINNOCENTIIS, Maria 212-517-0482 340 D
mdeinnocentiis@mmm.edu

DEIRTH, Sherry 812-330-6074 175 H
sdeirth@ivytech.edu

DEIS, Elizabeth 434-223-6118 519 B

DEITCHMAN, Jay 518-629-7567 336 C
j.deitchman@hvcc.edu

DEITEMEYER, Kandi, W 252-335-0821 369 D
kdeitemeyer@albemarle.edu

DEITRICK, Becky 570-372-4015 447 D
deitrick@susqu.edu

DEITS, Will 805-986-5821 77 C
wdeits@vcccd.edu

DEJESUS, Arnoldo 585-594-6140 347 F
dejesus_arnoldo@roberts.edu

DEJESUS, Gladys 787-850-9343 567 B
gladys.dejesus@upr.edu

DEJESUS, Janie, A 814-371-2090 448 C
jdejesus@triangle-tech.edu

DEJESUS, Jose, L 787-250-1912 563 E
jdejesus@metro.inter.edu

DEJESUS-RUEFF, Richard 585-385-8229 348 F
rdejesus@sjfc.edu

DEJOHN, Fred 212-431-2880 343 E
fdejohn@nyls.edu

DEJONG, Carol 616-395-7760 252 F
cdejong@hope.edu

DEJONG, Chris 712-722-6070 183 H
cdejong@dordt.edu

DEJONG, David, N 412-624-4228 449 A
dejong@pitt.edu

DEJORGE, Alex, A 787-258-1501 561 E
adejorge@columbiaco.edu

DEJORGE, Alex, R 787-743-4041 561 E
ardejorge@columbiaco.edu

DEJULIO, Rosemary, A 718-817-3009 334 C
dejulio@fordham.edu

DEJULIO, Thomas, E 718-817-3111 334 C
tdejulio@fordham.edu

DEKALB, Jenifer 503-821-8901 419 D
jenifer@pnca.edu

DEKAN, Doug, D 715-833-6238 553 F
ddekan@cvtc.edu

DEKAY, Amy, M 716-880-2224 340 E
amy.marie.dekay@medaille.edu

DEKAY, Todd 717-358-6021 429 E
todd.dekay@fandm.edu

DEKKER, Jan 559-638-3641 72 B
jan.dekker@reedleycollege.edu

DEKLOTZ, Steve 503-493-6286 415 E
sdeklotz@cu-portland.edu

DEKOSKY, Steven, T 434-924-0311 525 B
sd3zc@virginia.edu

DEKREY, Susan 845-437-7400 359 D
sudekrey@vassar.edu

DEKRUIF, Kimberly 909-469-5342 78 D
kdekruif@westernu.edu

DEKSHENIEKS, Craig 770-426-2833 133 B
craig.deksheniecks@life.edu

DEL BALZO, Mary Beth 914-831-0463 330 D
mdelbalzo@cw.edu

DEL BELLO, Wendy 281-756-3600 479 G
wdelbello@alvincollege.edu

DEL BELLO, Wendy 281-756-3686 479 G
wdelbello@alvincollege.edu

DEL CARMEN GIL, Maria 787-763-7005 561 G
mcgil@cmpr.gobierno.pr

DEL CERRO, Gerardo 212-353-4321 331 B
cerro@cooper.edu

DEL CONTE, Chris 713-348-6920 492 J
delconte@rice.edu

DEL CONTE, Christopher 817-257-7710 498 F
delconte@tcu.edu

DEL CORE, Thomas 973-761-9284 315 B
thomas.delcore@shu.edu

DEL GIORNO, Julie 610-861-1361 436 I
jdelgiorno@moravian.edu

DEL GIUDICE, Tristan, S 814-641-3390 431 L
delgiut@juniata.edu

DEL GIZZO, Dennis, J 401-341-2200 454 D
delgizzd@salve.edu

DEL P. CHARNECO,
Maria 787-766-1717 565 G
um_mcharneco@suagm.edu

DEL PINO, Jennifer 515-961-1530 188 F
jennifer.delpino@simpson.edu

DEL RIO-MORALES,
Ricardo 787-725-6500 560 G
consejoactivo@gmail.com

DEL ROSARIO, Diana 216-987-5027 389 A
diana.del-rosario@tri-c.edu

DEL SESTO, Lisa 312-322-1726 165 C
ldelsesto@spertus.edu

DEL TONDO, Bruce 719-587-7227 80 F
bdeltond@adams.edu

DEL TORO, Debra 210-829-6001 503 F
ddeltoro@uiwtx.edu

DEL VALLE, David 515-289-9200 185 E
ddelvalle@inste.edu

DEL VALLE, Deb 513-745-3877 406 E
delvalle@xavier.edu

DEL VALLE, Dennis 623-934-7273 11 G
ddelvalle@atienterprises.com

DEL VALLE, Rosa 787-834-9595 565 J
rdelvalle@uaa.edu

DEL VALLE, Wilfredo 787-863-2390 563 C
wilfredo.delvalle@fajardo.inter.edu

DEL VECCHIO, Ron 218-281-8109 272 A
dsvedars@umn.edu

DELA ROSA, Ram 956-364-4951 499 J
ram.delarosa@harlingen.tstc.edu

DELA TEJA, Magdalena 817-515-6203 496 A
magdalena.delateja@tccd.edu

DELABY, Lisa 530-895-2937 31 E
delabyli@butte.edu

DELACH, Ruth 412-809-5100 444 F
delach@pti.edu

DELACRUZ, Marisa 646-312-2050 326 D
marisa_delacruz@baruch.cuny.edu

DELAET, Lee 314-889-4539 282 C
ldelaet@fontbonne.edu

DELAHAYA, Richard 615-963-5331 474 A
rdelahay@tnstate.edu

DELAHOUSSAYE, Yasmin 213-891-2279 54 F
delahoyj@email.laccd.edu

DELAHOYDE, Theresa 402-481-8843 297 B
tdelahoyde@bryanlgh.org

DELAHUNT, Tom 515-271-2092 184 A
tom.delahunt@drake.edu

DELAHUNTY, Jennifer 740-427-5778 394 C
delahuntyj@kenyon.edu

DELAIN, Cindy 559-730-6265 42 B
cindyd@cos.edu

DELALUE-KING, Shontay 401-232-6448 453 A
sdelalue@bryant.edu

DELAND, Jane, S 202-885-8602 100 A
jdeland@wesleyseminary.edu

DELAND, Robert 312-225-6288 167 E
rdeland@vandercook.edu

DELANEY, Anne Marie 781-239-6481 230 G
delaneya@babson.edu

DELANEY, Christopher 717-337-6235 429 H
cdelaney@gettysburg.edu

DELANEY, Connie, J 612-624-1410 272 D
delan108@umn.edu

DELANEY, Jeff 912-358-4400 136 C
delaneyj@savannahstate.edu

DELANEY, John 423-425-4534 477 D
john-delaney@utc.edu

DELANEY, John, A 904-620-2500 120 C
jdelaney@unf.edu

DELANEY, John, T 412-648-1556 449 A
jtd@pitt.edu

DELANEY, Kevin, J 310-338-5756 56 E
kevin.delaney@lmu.edu

DELANEY, Melissa 510-841-9230 79 F
mdelaney@wrightinst.edu

DELANEY, Meredith 513-558-9964 403 E
meredith.delaney@uc.edu

DELANEY, Peggy 831-459-4375 75 A
pdelaney@ucsc.edu

DELANEY, Thomas 212-992-8851 344 B
tom.delaney@nyu.edu

DELANEY, Timothy, J 740-284-5210 390 M
tdelaney@franciscan.edu

DELANEY, Timothy, R 412-624-4216 449 A
tdelaney@pitt.edu

DELANEY, Ute 845-752-3000 358 D
registrar@uts.edu

DELANO, Cigdem, E 404-752-1786 134 B
cdelano@msm.edu

DELANO, Patty 218-726-8829 272 B
pdelano@d.umn.edu

DELANOY, Debra 845-687-5088 358 C
delanoyd@sunyulster.edu

DELANSKY, Barbara 541-463-5337 416 D
delanskyb@lanecc.edu

DELAP, Joe 256-782-5004 4 L
jdelap@jsu.edu

DELAP, Melanie 256-782-5003 4 L
mdelap@jsu.edu

DELAP, Ronald 903-233-3900 489 K
ronalddelap@letu.edu

DELARCO, Karen, R 484-664-3496 437 B
delarco@muhlenberg.edu

DELAROSA, Antonio, S 765-641-4150 109 A
asdelarosa@anderson.edu

DELAROSA, Sam 312-939-4975 151 F
sdelarosa@harringtoncollege.com

DELAS, Kristina 212-312-4343 332 B
kdelas@devry.edu

DELASHMIT, Jim 248-340-0600 248 E
james.delashmit@baker.edu

DELATE, John 914-251-6320 354 D
john.delate@purchase.edu

DELAUTER, Leslie, J 215-898-5551 448 I
collegehouses@pobox.upenn.edu

DELAY, Mary, E 210-567-2010 506 E
delay@uthscsa.edu

DELBELSO, Debra 518-783-2339 350 I
ddelbelso@siena.edu

DELBRIDGE, Kristina 518-587-2100 355 F
kristina.delbridge@esc.edu

DELBUONO, Mary Gray 412-536-1300 432 F
mary.delbuono@laroche.edu

DELCAMBRE, Barry 318-345-9270 210 I
bdelcambre@ladelta.edu

DELCAMBRE, Ken 409-944-1314 486 H
kdelcamb@gc.edu

DELCAMP, Tom 215-222-4200 445 F
tdelcamp@walnuthillcollege.edu

DELCORE, Carolyn 518-564-2071 354 B
delcorcm@plattsburgh.edu

DELEHANTY, Faith 405-878-5420 412 A
fdelehanty@stgregorys.edu

DELEMEESTER, Gregory, J 740-376-4630 395 F
greg.delemeester@marietta.edu

DELENER, Nejdet 516-876-3292 353 D
delenern@oldwestbury.edu

DELEON, Gilbert 210-530-9449 488 C

DELEON, Hilda 713-798-4612 481 H
hildad@bcm.edu

DELEON, Javier 956-364-4562 499 J
javier.deleon@harlingen.tstc.edu

DELEON, Jerry 541-463-5870 416 D
deleonj@lanecc.edu

DELEON, Nicole 602-787-6606 16 A
nicole.deleon@pvmail.maricopa.edu

DELEON, Rocio 310-954-4025 57 H
rdeleon@msmc.la.edu

DELEON, Verna 800-567-2344 546 G
vdeleon@menominee.edu

DELEON, Zelma 940-565-3901 504 B
zelma.deleon@unt.edu

DELEON GUERRERO,
Cynthia 670-234-5498 559 F
cynthiad@nmcnet.edu

DELEON GUERRERO,
Galvin, S 670-234-5498 559 F
galving@nmcnet.edu

DELERME, Leslie 740-368-3152 400 F
ljdelerm@owu.edu

DELFORTE, Joseph, L .... 585-785-1227.... 334 A
delforjl@flcc.edu
DELGADILLO, Carlos, E .... 509-527-4282.... 538 G
carlos.delgadillo@wwcc.edu
DELGADO, Art .... 815-921-4092.... 162 F
a.delgado@rockvalleycollege.edu
DELGADO, Fernando, P ..... 715-425-3700.... 552 A
fernando.delgado@uwrf.edu
DELGADO, Genobeba .... 305-231-3326.... 109 C
gdelgado@mm.fnc.edu
DELGADO, Gilbert .... 954-732-6183.... 107 E
gdelgado@careercollege.edu
DELGADO, Gilbert .... 954-733-7551.... 107 D
gdelgado@careercollege.edu
DELGADO, Gilbert .... 954-965-7272.... 107 F
gdelgado@careercollege.edu
DELGADO, Irene, R .... 718-409-5879.... 356 C
idelgado@sunymaritime.edu
DELGADO, Jane Lee .... 212-220-1407.... 326 E
jdelgado@bmcc.cuny.edu
DELGADO, Javier .... 787-780-0070.... 560 F
jdelgado@caribbean.edu
DELGADO, Junior .... 413-572-5546.... 239 C
jdelgado@wsc.ma.edu
DELGADO, Laura, M .... 787-765-4210.... 561 A
DELGADO, Maria, L .... 787-878-5475.... 562 H
mdelgado@arecibo.inter.edu
DELGADO, Nydia .... 787-878-5475.... 562 H
ndelgado@arecibo.inter.edu
DELGADO, Steve .... 718-518-4314.... 327 D
sdelgado@hostos.cuny.edu
DELGADO ALTIERI,
Maria, E .... 787-896-2252.... 561 K
mdelgado@edpcollege.edu
DELGADO-LIBRERO,
M. Celeste .... 434-381-6334.... 524 E
jys@sbc.edu
DELGAUDIO, Rose .... 562-938-4397...... 54 E
rdelgaudio@lbcc.edu
DELGIORNO,
Christopher, M .... 845-575-3000.... 340 C
christopher.delgiorno@marist.edu
DELGIORNO, Daniel, R ..... 717-245-1571.... 427 E
delgiorr@dickinson.edu
DELGIUDICE, Candice .... 619-201-8741...... 65 D
Candice.DelGiudice@sdcc.edu
DELGUIDICE, Bernard, V ... 856-225-6657.... 314 C
bdelguidice@facilities.rutgers.edu
DELHOUSAYE, Darryl, L .... 602-850-8000...... 17 H
ddelhousaye@phoenixseminary.edu
DELICH, Patti .... 218-235-2157.... 270 A
p.delich@mr.mnscu.edu
DELILE, John .... 207-453-5123.... 218 I
jdelile@kvcc.me.edu
DELIN, Theresa, M .... 847-491-3293.... 160 D
t-delin@northwestern.edu
DELIO, Vincent .... 518-956-8010.... 351 E
vdelio@uamail.albany.edu
DELISA, Kenneth, J .... 860-465-5269...... 91 H
delisak@easternct.edu
DELISI, Richard .... 732-932-7496.... 314 D
richard.delisi@gse.rutgers.edu
DELISLE, David, W .... 315-268-6666.... 329 C
delisle@clarkson.edu
DELIZIO, Carissa .... 603-899-4142.... 305 B
delizioc@franklinpierce.edu
DELKER, David .... 785-826-2963.... 194 C
ddelker@k-state.edu
DELL, Erin, B .... 336-316-2196.... 364 E
edell@guilford.edu
DELL, Troy .... 301-687-4471.... 228 C
tadell@frostburg.edu
DELLA PORTA, Pamela ..... 617-951-2350.... 243 C
pamela.dellaporta@necb.edu
DELLA POSTA, Joseph, B . 315-445-4564.... 338 B
dellapjb@lemoyne.edu
DELLA VOLPE, Angela ...... 657-278-2024...... 34 E
adellavolpe@fullerton.edu
DELLAMURA, Virginia, C .. 203-857-7311...... 90 G
vdellamura@ncc.commnet.edu
DELLAPINA, Mario .... 718-960-8350.... 327 C
mario.dellapina@lehman.cuny.edu
DELLAR, Dan .... 231-843-5985.... 260 E
ddellar@westshore.edu
DELLAVECCHIA, Nancy, J . 330-672-2444.... 393 D
ndellave@kent.edu
DELLER, Jean .... 260-665-4100.... 180 A
dellerj@trine.edu
DELLHIME, Roberta, G ...... 909-748-8040...... 75 F
roberta_dellhime@redlands.edu
DELLI CARPINI,
Michael, X .... 215-898-4407.... 448 I
dean@asc.upenn.edu
DELLICARPINI, Dominic .... 717-815-1231.... 452 F
dcarpini@ycp.edu
DELLINGER, Dewey .... 704-922-6236.... 370 D
dewey.dellinger@gaston.edu
DELLINGER, Janice .... 864-503-5771.... 463 A
dellinger@uscupstate.edu
DELLINGER, Tim .... 731-424-2603.... 475 B
tdellinger1@jscc.edu
DELLIVENERI, Richard .... 303-964-3656...... 87 E
rdellive@regis.edu
DELLUTRI, Alexandra .... 708-237-5050.... 160 C
adellutri@nc.edu
DELLWO, Sarah .... 406-444-6800.... 295 C
sarah.dellwo@umhelena.edu
DELL'OMO, Gregory, G ..... 412-397-6400.... 445 G
dellomo@rmu.edu
DELL'OSA, Lydia, J .... 610-359-7322.... 426 G
ldellosa@dccc.edu
DELMAR, Cindy .... 585-345-6813.... 334 F
DELMONACO, JR., Rocco 202-687-7014...... 98 A
rd254@georgetown.edu
DELNEGRO, Ann, L .... 302-855-1687...... 96 B
delnegro@dtcc.edu
DELOACH, Adrien .... 540-831-5765.... 522 D
adeloach@radford.edu
DELOATCH, Eugene .... 443-885-3231.... 224 F
eugene.deloatch@eng.morgan.edu
DELOATCH, Lois .... 919-530-6100.... 378 A
lois.deloatch@nccu.edu
DELOATCH, Sandra, J .... 757-823-8180.... 521 K
sjdeloatch@nsu.edu
DELONG, Allen, W .... 207-725-3536.... 217 E
adelong2@bowdoin.edu
DELONG, Brian .... 718-982-2572.... 327 A
Brian.Delong@csi.cuny.edu
DELONG, Catherine .... 212-998-6270.... 344 B
catherine.delong@nyu.edu
DELONG, Cliff .... 605-455-6079.... 464 H
cdelong@olc.edu
DELONG, Mary Lou .... 617-552-3636.... 232 D
marylou.delong.1@bc.edu
DELONG, Michael, L .... 870-368-7371...... 23 A
mdelong@ozarka.edu
DELONG, Richard .... 810-766-4018.... 248 C
richard.delong@baker.edu
DELONG, Shirley .... 610-799-1743.... 434 D
sdelong3@lccc.edu
DELONY, John .... 325-674-2784.... 478 H
john.delony@acu.edu
DELORENZO, Donna .... 904-819-6255.... 107 A
dDeLorenzo@flagler.edu
DELORENZO, Michael .... 217-333-1300.... 167 B
michaeld@illinois.edu
DELORENZO, Patricia .... 410-888-9048.... 226 F
pdelorenzo@tai.edu
DELORENZO, Stephen, F .. 518-438-3111.... 340 B
steved@mariacollege.edu
DELOREY, Mark, J .... 269-387-6005.... 260 F
mark.delorey@wmich.edu
DELOS SANTOS,
Maria Cecilia, H .... 671-735-5644.... 559 B
studentsupportservices@guamcc.edu
DELOUISE, Tia .... 973-278-5400.... 323 J
tdl@berkeleycollege.edu
DELOUISE, Tia .... 973-278-5400.... 307 G
tdl@berkeleycollege.edu
DELOZIER, David .... 610-396-6056.... 439 A
dcd11@psu.edu
DELP, Kevin .... 864-242-5100.... 455 E
DELPHENICH, Pamela .... 617-253-1727.... 242 A
pdelphen@mit.edu
DELPIEAGO, Jose .... 412-281-2600.... 446 H
jdelpieago@western-school.com
DELPRATO, Darlene .... 315-792-7177.... 356 B
darlene.delprato@sunyit.edu
DELPRETE, Angela .... 440-646-8371.... 405 B
adelprete@ursuline.edu
DELPROPOST, Carol, J ...... 740-368-3059.... 400 F
cjdelpro@owu.edu
DELSO, Dusty .... 918-781-7269.... 407 B
delsod@bacone.edu
DELUCA, Daryl .... 617-358-0700.... 232 G
djdeluca@bu.edu
DELUCA, Eileen .... 239-985-2498.... 104 L
ecduluca@edison.edu
DELUCA, Mary .... 443-840-5215.... 222 D
mdeluca@ccbcmd.edu
DELUCA, Paul, M .... 608-262-1304.... 550 G
pmdeluca@wisc.edu
DELUCA, Peter, L .... 805-525-4417...... 72 E
pdeluca@thomasaquinas.edu
DELUCA, Tony .... 610-359-5110.... 426 G
tdeluca@dccc.edu
DELUCA, Vincent, J .... 212-817-7500.... 327 B
vdeluca@gc.cuny.edu
DELUCAS, Vicki .... 740-453-0762.... 400 D
delucas@ohio.edu
DELVECCHIO, Edie .... 201-200-3159.... 312 B
edelvecchio@njcu.edu
DELVENTHAL, Bruce .... 518-564-3140.... 354 B
bruce.delventhal@plattsburgh.edu
DELVISCIO, Gregory .... 607-777-2175.... 351 F
gregdelv@binghamton.edu
DELYSER, Susan .... 315-279-5247.... 337 K
sdelyser@mail.keuka.edu
DELZEIT, Greg .... 785-442-6039.... 193 D
gdelzeit@highlandcc.edu
DEMA, Anne, C .... 816-781-7700.... 293 D
demaa@william.jewell.edu
DEMARAIS, Alyce .... 253-879-3207.... 538 E
ademarais@pugetsound.edu
DEMARCO, Deborah .... 508-856-2903.... 238 A
deborah.demarco@umassmed.edu
DEMARESKI, Roger .... 609-258-8022.... 313 A
rogerd@princeton.edu
DEMAREST, David, F .... 650-724-8887...... 71 F
demarest@stanford.edu
DEMAREST, Geralyn .... 518-828-4181.... 330 E
demarest@sunycgcc.edu
DEMARK, Paul .... 707-476-4358...... 42 A
paul-demark@redwoods.edu
DEMARTE, Daniel .... 757-822-1061.... 528 C
ddemarte@tcc.edu
DEMATTEO, Jeanne .... 925-631-4123...... 64 F
jdematte@stmarys-ca.edu
DEMAYO, Andrea .... 518-244-2427.... 348 A
demaya@sage.edu
DEMBECK, Brian, B .... 443-997-3728.... 223 F
bdembeck@jhu.edu
DEMBOSKY, Deborah .... 910-630-7522.... 366 H
driley@methodist.edu
DEMCIE, Christine .... 716-829-7688.... 332 F
demciec@dyc.edu
DEMCZUK, Bernard .... 202-994-1000...... 97 F
bdemczuk@gwu.edu
DEMEDEIROS, Joe .... 512-233-1443.... 493 B
joed@stedwards.edu
DEMEDERIOS, Joe .... 617-287-5330.... 237 D
joe.demederios@umb.edu
DEMEIS, Debra .... 781-283-2322.... 246 B
ddemeis@wellesley.edu
DEMELLO, Kenneth .... 509-533-3555.... 532 F
DEMENT, Mary .... 870-762-3113...... 20 A
mdement@smail.anc.edu
DEMERCHANT, Doug, B .... 630-752-5321.... 168 F
doug.demerchant@wheaton.edu
DEMERITT, Linda, C .... 814-332-3393.... 421 E
linda.demeritt@allegheny.edu
DEMERRITT, Stan .... 806-291-3415.... 508 B
demerritt@wbu.edu
DEMERS, David .... 413-565-1000.... 231 B
ddemers@baypath.edu
DEMERS, Mary .... 207-941-7131.... 218 A
demersm@husson.edu
DEMERS, Paul .... 603-897-8537.... 305 G
pdemers@rivier.edu
DEMERS, Susan, S .... 727-791-2501.... 116 F
demers.susan@spcollege.edu
DEMERS, Suzanne .... 863-784-7041.... 117 I
suzanne.demers@southflorida.edu
DEMES, Dennis .... 561-732-4424.... 117 A
ddemes@svdp.edu
DEMETRIOU, Sophia .... 212-650-6507.... 326 H
sdemetriou@ccny.cuny.edu
DEMETRULIAS, Diana .... 650-508-3494...... 59 G
ddemetrulias@ndnu.edu
DEMICHAEL, Mark .... 765-677-2317.... 174 E
mark.demichael@indwes.edu
DEMIK, Harry .... 561-297-2429.... 118 H
hdemik@fau.edu
DEMING, Elizabeth .... 229-430-3693.... 123 I
edeming@albanytech.edu
DEMING, Els .... 253-840-8401.... 536 C
edeming@pierce.ctc.edu
DEMING, Merrill .... 909-652-6402...... 39 B
merrill.deming@chaffey.edu
DEMING, Merrill .... 909-652-6242...... 39 B
merrill.deming@chaffey.edu
DEMING, Ronald .... 731-352-4232.... 467 C
demingr@bethelu.edu
DEMITSAS, Yiani .... 260-422-5561.... 172 L
jdemitsas@indianatech.edu
DEMKO, Steve .... 216-361-2733.... 387 A
SDemko@ChancellorU.edu
DEMLEITNER, Nora, V .... 516-463-6190.... 335 H
lawnvd@hofstra.edu
DEMMINGS, Elizabeth .... 765-658-4220.... 170 I
betsydemmings@depauw.edu
DEMO, Patricia .... 530-242-7649...... 69 D
pdemo@shastacollege.edu
DEMORANVILLE, Carol .... 401-232-6227.... 453 A
cdemoran@bryant.edu
DEMORE, Maybelle .... 940-898-3585.... 502 B
mdemore@twu.edu
DEMOSS, Brian .... 209-588-5222...... 80 A
demossb@yosemite.edu
DEMOTT, Robin .... 309-341-5221.... 146 A
rdemott@sandburg.edu
DEMPSEY, Connie .... 570-961-4692...... 17 E
connie.dempsey@pennfoster.edu
DEMPSEY, Grace .... 707-826-4101...... 36 D
gdempsey@humboldt.edu
DEMPSEY, Jimmy, E .... 602-944-3335...... 11 D
jdempsey@aicag.edu
DEMPSEY, John, G .... 217-333-2500.... 167 B
jgdempse@illinois.edu
DEMPSEY, John, R .... 910-695-3700.... 373 E
dempseyj@sandhills.edu
DEMPSEY, Kelly, J .... 608-757-6328.... 553 E
kdempsey@blackhawk.edu
DEMPSEY, Marianne .... 301-447-5330.... 225 A
dempsey@msmary.edu
DEMPSEY, Michael .... 207-893-7892.... 219 F
mdempsey@sjcme.edu
DEMPSEY, Michael .... 845-848-4058.... 332 C
michael.dempsey@dc.edu
DEMPSEY, Mike .... 802-728-1302.... 515 G
mdempsey@vtc.vsc.edu
DEMPSEY, Patricia .... 410-263-2371.... 225 G
DEMPSEY, Richard .... 972-883-2141.... 505 D
rmdempsey@utdallas.edu
DEMPSEY, Ron .... 816-781-7700.... 293 D
dempseyr@william.jewell.edu
DEMPSEY, Ron, D .... 678-915-7351.... 137 C
dempsey@spsu.edu
DEMPSEY, Sarah .... 269-927-6188.... 254 B
sdempsey@lakemichigancollege.edu
DEMPSEY, Van, O .... 304-367-4241.... 543 E
van.dempsey@fairmontstate.edu
DEMPSEY, Wayne, W .... 770-531-3116.... 126 B
wdempsey@brenau.edu
DEMPSEY, William .... 610-683-4575.... 442 F
dempsey@kutztown.edu
DEMPSEY ST. JOHN,
Penny .... 303-458-3536...... 87 E
pstjohn@regis.edu
DEMPSEY-SWOPES,
Danielle .... 913-588-5048.... 197 A
ddempsey-swopes@kumc.edu
DEMPSTER, Douglas, J ..... 512-471-9601.... 505 B
ddempster@austin.utexas.edu
DEMSKI, Gary .... 574-520-4457.... 174 C
gdemski@iusb.edu
DEMUTH, Paul .... 651-423-8370.... 266 E
paul.demuth@dctc.edu
DENARD, Jeffrey, D .... 630-637-5142.... 159 F
jddenard@noctrl.edu
DENARD, Letitia .... 404-270-5143.... 137 E
ldenard@spelman.edu
DENARDO, Arlina, B .... 610-330-5055.... 433 B
denardoa@lafayette.edu
DENARDO, John .... 312-413-8202.... 166 F
jdenardo@uic.edu
DENARDO, Melissa, D .... 724-480-3439.... 426 A
melissa.denardo@ccbc.edu
DENBOER, Marten .... 909-869-3443...... 33 G
mdenboer@csupomona.edu
DENBOW, Gary, A .... 417-833-2551.... 279 I
gdenbow@cbcag.edu
DENBOW, Stephanie .... 701-349-3621.... 383 B
sdenbow@trinitybiblecollege.edu
DENBY, Eric, N .... 434-924-4019.... 525 B
end@virginia.edu
DENBY, Karlene .... 281-487-1170.... 498 E
kdenby@txchiro.edu
DENDY, Larry, C .... 252-493-7239.... 372 E
ldendy@email.pittcc.edu
DENEAULT, Henry .... 781-239-5613.... 230 G
deneault@babson.edu
DENEEN, Linda .... 218-726-7588.... 272 B
ldeneen@d.umn.edu
DENG, Yi .... 704-687-8450.... 378 E
Yi.Deng@uncc.edu
DENGERINK, Harold, A ...... 360-546-9581.... 539 A
dengerin@wsu.edu
DENGLE, Stephen, S .... 515-271-1596.... 183 F
stephen.dengle@dmu.edu
DENHAM, Cynthia .... 256-840-4133........ 7 B
cdenham@snead.edu
DENHAM, Scott, D .... 704-894-2855.... 363 F
scdenham@davidson.edu
DENHEETEN, Kathryn .... 989-775-4123.... 257 H
denheeten.katy@sagchip.edu
DENHOLM, Jack .... 701-845-7160.... 382 A
jack.denholm@vcsu.edu
DENHOLM, Patricia .... 201-447-7130.... 307 F
pdenholm@berger.edu
DENICOLIS, Antonio .... 301-431-5419.... 225 B
adenicolis@nlc.edu
DENIO, John .... 518-694-7263.... 322 C
john.denio@acphs.edu
DENIO, John .... 401-232-6140.... 453 A
jdenio@bryant.edu
DENIS, Alex .... 954-201-7405.... 102 A
adenis@broward.edu
DENISI, Angelo, S .... 504-865-5401.... 215 C
adenisi@tulane.edu
DENISON, Bronda .... 334-670-5843........ 8 B
bdenison@troy.edu
DENISON, Cathy .... 812-288-8878.... 178 A
macfs@mindspring.com
DENKER, Lee .... 402-554-2444.... 301 B
ldenker@unomaha.edu
DENLY, David .... 620-229-6104.... 196 C
david.denly@sckans.edu
DENMAN, Bob, G .... 501-569-3194...... 24 E
bgdenman@ualr.edu
DENMAN, Ellie .... 601-977-0960.... 278 C
ellie.denman@vc.edu
DENMARK, Robert, M .... 973-972-5410.... 317 B
denmarrm@umdnj.edu
DENN, Patricia .... 617-873-0278.... 233 B
Patricia.Denn@cambridgecollege.edu
DENNA, Eric .... 801-581-3100.... 510 L
eric.denna@utah.edu
DENNE, Cynthia, K .... 909-593-3511...... 75 C
cdenne@laverne.edu
DENNEE, Mary Jo, R .... 716-851-1999.... 333 B
dennee@ecc.edu
DENNEHY, Michael .... 972-860-4607.... 484 F
mdennehy@dcccd.edu
DENNEY, Carolyn .... 509-527-2811.... 538 H
carolyn.denney@wallawalla.edu

DESPO, Pamela, M .... 724-589-2195.... 448 A
pdespo@thiel.edu
DESROSIERS, Jacque .... 734-677-5306.... 260 B
jdesrosiers@wccnet.edu
DESSART, Donna .... 415-865-0198..... 30 B
ddessart@aii.edu
DESSEM, R. Lawrence .... 573-882-3246.... 291 D
dessemrl@missouri.edu
DESSOYE, Jane, F .... 570-674-6168.... 436 F
jdessoye@misericordia.edu
DESTAFANO, Cynthia, L .... 717-394-6211.... 426 C
cdestafano@csb.edu
DESTAFANO, Cynthia, L .... 717-764-6211.... 426 D
cdestafano@csb.edu
DESTEFANO, Deborah .... 202-651-5005..... 97 E
deborah.destefano@gallaudet.edu
DESTEFANO, Joanne, M .... 607-255-4242.... 331 C
jmd11@cornell.edu
DESTEFANO, Joseph .... 252-335-0821.... 369 D
jdestefano@albemarle.edu
DESTEIGUER, John .... 405-425-5094.... 409 E
john.desteiguer@oc.edu
DESTEPHEN, Daniel, E ...... 937-775-3162.... 406 C
dan.destephen@wright.edu
DESTITO, Connie .... 626-529-8202..... 60 G
cdestito@pacificoaks.edu
DESTLER, William, W .... 585-475-2394.... 347 G
bill.destler@rit.edu
DESVIGNE, LaVora .... 718-482-5114.... 328 C
ldesvigne@lagcc.cuny.edu
DETAMORE, Ed .... 317-931-2318.... 170 E
edetamore@cts.edu
DETAR, Eric .... 315-279-5378.... 337 K
edetar@mail.keuka.edu
DETEMPLE, Jon Jay .... 610-526-6119.... 430 D
jdetemple@harcum.edu
DETER, Richard, S .... 940-565-3000.... 504 B
deter@unt.edu
DETGEN, E. James .... 580-327-8645.... 409 C
ejdetgen@nwosu.edu
DETHERAGE, Larry .... 502-852-8185.... 207 A
jldeth01@louisville.edu
DETHOMASIS, FSC, Louis 612-728-5200.... 271 G
ldethoma@smumn.edu
DETILLIER, LeAnn, O .... 225-675-8270.... 211 J
ldetillier@rpcc.edu
DETISCH, John, C .... 724-925-4093.... 451 E
detischj@wccc.edu
DETORE, Anthony .... 215-836-2222.... 422 A
admissions@antonelli.edu
DETROW, David, A .... 540-432-4109.... 518 E
detrowd@emu.edu
DETTBARN, Lana, J .... 563-336-3336.... 184 B
ldettbarn@eicc.edu
DETTERICK, Mark .... 210-999-7306.... 502 C
mdetteri@trinity.edu
DETTLAFF, Christine .... 405-422-1255.... 411 G
dettlaffc@redlandscc.edu
DETURK, Sabrina .... 610-660-1289.... 446 C
sdeturk@sju.edu
DETURRIS, John .... 610-892-1543.... 441 C
jdeturris@pit.edu
DETWEILER, Bob .... 805-756-2126..... 33 F
rdetweil@calpoly.edu
DETWEILER, Sally .... 660-785-4031.... 291 A
sallydet@truman.edu
DETWILER, Nancy .... 617-745-3638.... 234 C
nancy.l.detwiler@enc.edu
DETWILER, Rita .... 434-544-8300.... 520 H
detwiler@lynchburg.edu
DETWILER, Tim .... 616-945-5300.... 250 C
tim.detwiler@cornerstone.edu
DETWILER, Timothy .... 616-222-1589.... 250 C
tim.detwiler@cornerstone.edu
DETWILER, William .... 214-768-3237.... 494 F
bdetwile@smu.edu
DETZEL, Lee, A .... 214-459-2215.... 480 G
DETZLER, Wayne, R .... 704-847-5600.... 376 H
wdetzler@ses.edu
DEUEL, Ryan, P .... 315-386-7109.... 355 D
deuelr@canton.edu
DEUSSING, Karin .... 215-935-3847.... 451 D
kdeussing@wts.edu
DEUTER, Clayton .... 605-995-7132.... 464 E
clayton.deuter@mitchelltech.edu
DEUTSCH, Thomas, A .... 312-942-5567.... 163 B
thomas_deutsch@rush.edu
DEUTSCH, Yeruchem .... 718-963-9770.... 358 H
ed@utsb.org
DEVAN, Rhonda, K .... 828-694-1716.... 368 B
r_devan@blueridge.edu
DEVANE, Larry, F .... 405-422-1260.... 411 G
devanel@redlandscc.edu
DEVANEY, Barbara, J .... 207-768-9750.... 220 F
barbara.devaney@umpi.edu
DEVANI, Jeani .... 617-217-9066.... 231 C
jdevani@baystate.edu
DEVANTIER, Paul .... 314-505-7257.... 280 H
devantierp@csl.edu
DEVASHER, Mary, E .... 615-868-6503.... 471 F
ikey@mtsa.edu
DEVAUGHN, Gerald .... 803-780-1265.... 463 B
gdevaughn@voorhees.edu
DEVAULT, Sylvia, Y .... 812-488-2239.... 180 B
sy5@evansville.edu
DEVAUX, April, A .... 585-785-1634.... 334 A
devauxaa@flcc.edu
DEVEAU, Laura, A .... 617-353-3540.... 232 G
ladeveau@bu.edu
DEVEAU, Shawn .... 409-772-9803.... 507 B
sjdeveau@utmb.edu
DEVELLE, Choury .... 562-902-3311...... 71 A
chourydevelle@scuhs.edu
DEVENNY, Marianne .... 815-455-8716.... 157 F
mdevenny@mchenry.edu
DEVENS, Philip .... 401-232-6119.... 453 A
revdev@bryant.edu
DEVER, Carolyn .... 615-322-2851.... 477 F
carolyn.dever@vanderbilt.edu
DEVER, David .... 310-434-4384...... 68 D
dever_david@smc.edu
DEVER, John, T .... 703-323-4291.... 527 C
jdever@nvcc.edu
DEVER, Michael, K .... 517-750-1200.... 258 F
miked@arbor.edu
DEVER, Susan .... 310-900-1600...... 45 E
dever_s@compton.edu
DEVEREAUX, Kent .... 206-726-5029.... 532 G
kdevereaux@cornish.edu
DEVEREAUX, Martin, C .... 561-237-7151.... 113 D
mdevereaux@lynn.edu
DEVERES, Georgette .... 909-621-8356...... 40 D
georgette.deveres@cmc.edu
DEVERSE, Nancy .... 360-538-4030.... 534 B
ndeverse@ghc.edu
DEVERTEUIL, Johanna .... 863-638-2914.... 123 C
deverteuilj@webber.edu
DEVESTERN, Diane .... 610-436-3511.... 443 F
ddevestern@wcupa.edu
DEVICO, Barbara, F .... 617-287-7008.... 237 B
bdevico@email.umassp.edu
DEVICTORIA, Carol .... 516-686-7476.... 343 D
cdevicto@nyit.edu
DEVIER, David, H .... 937-328-6026.... 387 G
devierd@clarkstate.edu
DEVILBISS, John, W .... 435-797-1358.... 511 B
john.devilbiss@usu.edu
DEVILBISS, Mark, B .... 937-327-7808.... 406 B
mdevilbiss@wittenberg.edu
DEVILLE, Helen .... 318-371-3035.... 211 F
hdeville@ltc.edu
DEVINCENTIS, Mark .... 585-340-9501.... 329 G
mdevincentis@crcds.edu
DEVINE, Flora, B .... 770-499-3562.... 132 H
fdevine@kennesaw.edu
DEVINE, Frederick, R .... 336-316-2134.... 364 E
fdevine@guilford.edu
DEVINE, Jane .... 718-482-5421.... 328 C
jane@lagcc.cuny.edu
DEVINE, Linda, W .... 813-253-6203.... 122 H
ldevine@ut.edu
DEVINE, Mary .... 218-846-3711.... 267 G
mary.devine@minnesota.edu
DEVINE, Michelle .... 989-275-5000.... 253 K
michelle.devine@kirtland.edu
DEVINE, Scott, W .... 240-895-4295.... 226 A
swdevine@smcm.edu
DEVITO, Felix .... 508-588-9100.... 240 E
DEVITO, Jennifer .... 516-918-3628.... 324 E
jdevito@bcl.edu
DEVITO, Paul, L .... 610-660-3261.... 446 C
pdevito@sju.edu
DEVITO, William, J .... 215-951-1326.... 432 G
devito@lasalle.edu
DEVITTO, John .... 704-272-5333.... 373 F
jdevitto@spcc.edu
DEVIVO, Sharon, B .... 718-429-6600.... 359 E
sharon.devivo@vaughn.edu
DEVLIN, Diane, M .... 617-627-5878.... 245 F
diane.devlin@tufts.edu
DEVLIN, George, A .... 803-705-4417.... 455 D
devling@benedict.edu
DEVLIN, Jeffrey .... 740-588-1242.... 407 A
jdevlin@zanestate.ed
DEVLIN, Susan, L .... 860-701-5161...... 93 B
devlin_s@mitchell.edu
DEVLIN, Thomas, C .... 510-642-3461...... 73 E
tcd@berkeley.edu
DEVOE, Michele .... 973-618-3484.... 308 D
mDeVoe@caldwell.edu
DEVOE HEIDMAN, Sheila . 520-515-5362...... 13 G
heidmans@cochise.edu
DEVORE, Brett .... 563-425-5248.... 189 C
devoreb@uiu.edu
DEVORE, Cynthia .... 651-793-1466.... 267 D
cynthia.devore@metrostate.edu
DEVORE, Janice, G .... 217-424-3524.... 158 F
jdevore@millikin.edu
DEVORE, Victor .... 619-660-4323...... 48 J
victor.devore@gcccd.edu
DEVORE, William .... 847-543-2640.... 147 H
bdevore@clcillinois.edu
DEVOS, Edward .... 617-327-6777.... 242 C
edward_devos@mspp.edu
DEVOSS, David, V .... 270-809-2222.... 204 F
public.safety@murraystate.edu
DEVRIES, Eileen, A .... 845-451-1323.... 331 F
e_devrie@culinary.edu
DEVRIES, II, Henry, E .... 616-526-6148.... 249 E
hdevries@calvin.edu
DEVRIES, Janet .... 307-268-2662.... 555 F
jdevries@caspercollege.edu
DEVRIES, Kathleen .... 303-914-6326...... 87 C
kathleen.devries@rrcc.edu
DEVRIES, Lora .... 712-722-6422.... 183 H
ldevries@dordt.edu
DEVRIES, Warren, R .... 410-455-3270.... 227 D
wdevries@umbc.edu
DEVRIESE, Todd .... 320-308-3093.... 269 C
tjdevriese@stcloudstate.edu
DEW, Beverley .... 804-594-1479.... 526 G
bdew@jtcc.edu
DEW, John, R .... 334-670-5991........ 8 B
jrdew@troy.edu
DEWALD, Barb .... 712-707-7192.... 188 B
bdewald@nwciowa.edu
DEWALD, Daryll .... 509-335-5548.... 539 A
daryll.dewald@wsu.edu
DEWALD, Howard .... 740-593-2850.... 399 G
DEWALD, Janice, P .... 214-828-8341.... 497 A
jdewald@bcd.tamhsc.edu
DEWALT, Ardie .... 212-220-8141.... 326 E
adewalt@bmcc.cuny.edu
DEWALT, Carol .... 603-668-6660.... 305 C
DEWALT, Marie .... 304-876-5299.... 544 A
mdewalt@shepherd.edu
DEWAN, Craig .... 315-866-0300.... 335 E
dewancp@herkimer.edu
DEWBERRY, Angela .... 404-471-6306.... 123 G
adewberry@agnesscott.edu
DEWBERRY, Loretta .... 903-593-8311.... 499 A
ldewberry@texascollege.edu
DEWBERRY, Thomas .... 541-683-5141.... 415 J
cdewberry@gutenberg.edu
DEWBRE, Dane .... 806-894-9611.... 494 C
ddewbre@southplainscollege.edu
DEWBRE, Jeri Ann .... 806-894-9611.... 494 C
jdewbre@southplainscollege.edu
DEWEERTH, Jennifer .... 315-731-5818.... 341 E
jdeweerth@mvcc.edu
DEWEES, Deborah .... 360-560-3353.... 539 C
deborah.dewees@wwu.edu
DEWEES, Julie .... 309-298-1800.... 168 A
jk-dewees@wiu.edu
DEWEESE, Jonathan .... 760-872-2000...... 43 H
jdeweese@deepsprings.edu
DEWEESE, Sam .... 812-330-6260.... 175 H
sdeweese@ivytech.edu
DEWET, Carol .... 717-291-3985.... 429 E
carol.dewet@fandm.edu
DEWEY, Amy .... 610-526-1000.... 421 G
amy.dewey@theamericancollege.edu
DEWEY, Barbara, I .... 814-865-0401.... 438 F
bid1@psu.edu
DEWEY, Gregory .... 909-593-3511...... 75 C
gdewey@laverne.edu
DEWEY, Gwen .... 206-264-9100.... 530 J
gwend@bgu.edu
DEWEY, Marvin .... 620-278-4290.... 196 D
mdewey@sterling.edu
DEWEY, Phyllis, K .... 716-926-8930.... 335 F
pdewey@hilbert.edu
DEWEY, Susan .... 607-844-8222.... 357 H
deweys@tc3.edu
DEWEY, Susan .... 501-977-2084...... 25 G
dewey@uaccm.edu
DEWEY, Thomas .... 707-826-3456...... 36 D
twd7001@humboldt.edu
DEWINE, Sue .... 812-866-7056.... 171 F
dewine@hanover.edu
DEWINTER, Naomi .... 231-348-6618.... 256 E
ndewinter@ncmich.edu
DEWIS, Rob .... 408-855-5327...... 78 A
rob.dewis@wvm.edu
DEWITT, Brenda, E .... 740-368-3329.... 400 F
bedewitt@owu.edu
DEWITT, Charles .... 601-968-5919.... 273 F
cdewitt@belhaven.edu
DEWITT, Dan .... 502-897-4555.... 205 H
ddewitt@sbts.edu
DEWITT, Deborah, S .... 937-327-7001.... 406 B
ddewitt@wittenberg.edu
DEWITT, Jean .... 713-221-5553.... 503 D
dewittj@uhd.edu
DEWITT, Matt .... 314-837-6777.... 288 F
mdewitt@slcconline.edu
DEWITT, Patricia, A .... 706-233-7308.... 136 E
patdewitt@shorter.edu
DEWITT, Sara .... 206-393-3531.... 530 G
sdewitt@argosy.edu
DEWITT, Siobhan, K .... 412-578-6651.... 424 G
skdewitt@carlow.edu
DEWITT-ROGERS, Johari ... 626-585-7730...... 61 E
dmdewitt-rogers@pasadena.edu
DEWOLF, William .... 617-824-8655.... 234 D
william_dewolf@emerson.edu
DEWOLFE, Sandra .... 408-270-6448...... 67 B
sandra.dewolfe@evc.edu
DEWSNUP, Vicky .... 801-622-1569.... 510 G
vicky.dewsnup@stevenshenager.edu
DEWSNUP, Vicky, L .... 801-622-1569.... 510 I
vicky.dewsnup@stevenshenager.edu
DEXTER, Ann .... 781-891-2640.... 231 F
adexter@bentley.edu
DEXTER, Brian .... 509-542-4727.... 532 C
bdexter@columbiabasin.edu
DEXTER, Karen, B .... 816-604-2217.... 285 G
karen.dexter@mcckc.edu
DEXTER, Kathleen, A .... 207-621-3153.... 220 B
dexter@maine.edu
DEXTER, Warin .... 617-353-2755.... 232 G
wdexter@bu.edu
DEXTER-HARRIS, Roz .... 904-632-3375.... 109 E
rdexter@fscj.edu
DEXTER-WILSON,
Elizabeth .... 251-380-3470........ 7 F
edexterwilson@shc.edu
DEY, Farouk .... 412-268-2064.... 424 H
fdey@andrew.cmu.edu
DEYER, Carole, A .... 586-286-2147.... 254 F
deyerc@macomb.edu
DEYOUNG, Gene .... 916-577-2200...... 79 C
gdeyoung@jessup.edu
DEYOUNG, Michael .... 702-968-2006.... 303 D
mdeyoung@roseman.edu
DEYOUNG, Paul .... 503-777-7290.... 420 A
paul.deyoung@reed.edu
DEYOUNG, Renee .... 231-439-6347.... 256 E
rdeyoung@ncmich.edu
DEYOUNG, Sandra .... 973-720-2432.... 317 D
deyoungs@wpunj.edu
DEZEMBER, Mary .... 575-835-5172.... 319 A
dezember@nmt.edu
DEZENBERG, Maria .... 253-943-2800.... 533 B
mdezenberg@devry.edu
DEZOLT, Denise .... 612-312-1286.... 272 F
denise.dezolt@waldenu.edu
DHANAK, Manhar .... 954-924-7242.... 118 H
dhanak@fau.edu
DHANKHER, Veena .... 978-630-9597.... 240 G
DHILLON, Mona .... 415-869-2900.... 236 B
mona,dhillon@hult.edu
DHILLON, Upinder, S .... 607-777-2314.... 351 F
dhillon@binghamton.edu
DHILLON, Vineeta .... 707-654-1086...... 32 I
vdhillon@csum.edu
DHINGRA, Ashok .... 727-873-4287.... 121 B
adhingra@mail.usf.edu
DHIR, Vijay, K .... 310-825-8507...... 74 A
vdhir@seas.ucla.edu
DI DONATO, Ana .... 352-588-8992.... 116 E
ana.didonato@saintleo.edu
DI FAVA, John .... 617-252-1703.... 242 A
jdifava@mit.edu
DI GATE, Russell .... 215-596-8865.... 450 A
r.digate@usciences.edu
DI GUILIO, Raymond .... 916-484-8483...... 56 A
diguilr@arc.losrios.edu
DI LULLO, Trish .... 256-233-8184........ 1 F
trish.dilullo@athens.edu
DI MARE, Lesley Ann .... 702-992-2354.... 302 I
lesley.dimare@nsc.nevada.edu
DI NALLO, Benjamin .... 201-559-3507.... 310 C
dinallob@felician.edu
DI NARDI, Jason .... 914-594-4668.... 343 F
jason_dinardi@nymc.edu
DI NUCCI, Jo Ellen .... 208-426-1200.... 142 F
jedinucc@boisestate.edu
DI PASQUALE, Ray .... 401-825-2188.... 453 B
rmdipasquale@ccri.edu
DI PAUL, Len .... 610-361-5225.... 437 C
dipaul@neumann.edu
DI RADDO, Colleen .... 302-736-2420...... 96 G
diraddo@wesley.edu
DI SARLO, Charlene .... 215-641-5576.... 430 C
disarlo.c@gmc.edu
DI THOMAS, Debbie .... 951-372-7015...... 63 I
debbie.dithomas@rcc.edu
DIAB, Dorey .... 330-494-6170.... 402 A
ddiab@starkstate.edu
DIACON, Todd .... 413-545-5703.... 237 C
tdiacon@umass.edu
DIAL, Bill .... 303-914-6298...... 87 C
bill.dial@rrcc.edu
DIAL, Cortez, K .... 804-524-5070.... 529 C
cdial@vsu.edu
DIAL, Eugene, A .... 985-448-4021.... 216 A
eugene.dial@nicholls.edu
DIAL, Sabrina, Y .... 270-809-3155.... 204 F
sabrina.dial@murraystate.edu
DIAL, Sheila .... 407-226-6438.... 104 D
sdial@devry.edu
DIAMOND, Alice .... 617-349-8550.... 236 G
adiamond@lesley.edu
DIAMOND, Beverly, E .... 843-953-5528.... 457 B
diamondb@cofc.edu
DIAMOND, Christopher, R 860-832-1934...... 91 G
diamondchr@ccsu.edu
DIAMOND, Fred .... 626-914-8691...... 39 G
fdiamond@citruscollege.edu
DIAMOND, Holly .... 313-845-9887.... 252 D
hadiamond@hfcc.edu
DIAMOND, John, N .... 479-575-2000...... 24 C
diamond@uark.edu

DIAMOND, Ladene .... 925-969-3581 ...... 52 B

DIAMOND BURROWAY, Sarah .... 606-326-2106 .... 201 B
sdiamondburrowa0001@kctc.edu

DIANDA, Lisa .... 209-473-5217 ...... 50 C
lisa_dianda@heald.edu

DIANE, Donna Lee .... 212-650-8173 .... 326 H
ddiane@ccny.cuny.edu

DIANGELO, JR., Joseph, A .... 610-660-1645 .... 446 C
jodiange@sju.edu

DIAS, James .... 518-956-8170 .... 351 E
jdias@uamail.albany.edu

DIAS, Margaret, S .... 508-999-8791 .... 237 E
mdias@umassd.edu

DIAS, Robert .... 408-270-6400 ...... 67 A
robert.dias@sjeccd.org

DIAWARA, Patricia .... 719-549-3058 ...... 87 B
Patricia.Diawara@pueblocc.edu

DIAZ, Aida .... 787-720-4476 .... 566 B
serviciocristiano@colmizpa.edu

DIAZ, Alfred .... 787-725-8120 .... 562 A
adiaz@eap.edu

DIAZ, Allison .... 980-598-1016 .... 365 G
allison.diaz@jwu.edu

DIAZ, Alphonso, V .... 765-494-9705 .... 178 F
avdiaz@purdue.edu

DIAZ, Amy .... 815-921-4283 .... 162 F
a.diaz@rockvalleycollege.edu

DIAZ, Andrea .... 401-254-3317 .... 454 C
adiaz@rwu.edu

DIAZ, Armando .... 210-567-0372 .... 506 E
diaza@uthscsa.edu

DIAZ, Carmen, L .... 860-493-0011 ...... 91 F
diazc@ct.edu

DIAZ, Carmen Marie .... 920-686-6372 .... 550 E
CarmenMarie.Diaz@sl.edu

DIAZ, Deborah .... 407-447-7300 .... 109 H
ddiaz@flatech.edu

DIAZ, Emiliano .... 916-278-5266 ...... 35 E
diaz@csus.edu

DIAZ, Fernando .... 773-995-2259 .... 146 D
fdiaz@csu.edu

DIAZ, Francisco .... 973-720-3244 .... 317 D
diazf@wpunj.edu

DIAZ, Franco, L .... 787-284-1912 .... 563 F
fldiaz@ponce.inter.edu

DIAZ, Gene .... 617-349-8426 .... 236 G
gdiaz@lesley.edu

DIAZ, Glenda .... 787-250-1912 .... 563 E
gdiaz@metro.inter.edu

DIAZ, Gloria .... 787-764-0000 .... 567 F

DIAZ, J. Lionel .... 480-731-8233 ...... 15 F
lionel.diaz@domail.maricopa.edu

DIAZ, Jackie .... 254-710-3805 .... 481 I
jackie_diaz@baylor.edu

DIAZ, Jacob .... 206-296-6155 .... 537 F
diazj@seattleu.edu

DIAZ, Janet .... 313-883-8696 .... 257 G
diaz.janet@shms.edu

DIAZ, Jesus, A .... 787-751-0178 .... 565 D
ac_jdiaz@suagm.edu

DIAZ, Jo Ann .... 843-953-5580 .... 457 B
diazv@cofc.edu

DIAZ, Jorge .... 787-786-3030 .... 560 E
jdiaz@ucb.edu.pr

DIAZ, Leticia, M .... 321-206-5602 .... 101 F
ldiaz@mail.barry.edu

DIAZ, Linda .... 201-529-7461 .... 313 D
ldiaz@ramapo.edu

DIAZ, Lourdes .... 787-284-1912 .... 563 F
ldiaz@ponce.inter.edu

DIAZ, Maria, S .... 787-257-7373 .... 565 E
ue_mdiaz@suagm.edu

DIAZ, Mark .... 305-284-2862 .... 122 F
markdiaz@miami.edu

DIAZ, Mischelle, R .... 512-448-8404 .... 493 B
mischeld@stedwards.edu

DIAZ, Paula .... 312-935-4222 .... 162 E
pdiaz@robertmorris.edu

DIAZ, Ramonita .... 787-878-5475 .... 562 H

DIAZ, Reinaldo .... 787-840-2575 .... 564 H

DIAZ, Robert .... 212-220-8305 .... 326 E
rdiaz@bmcc.cuny.edu

DIAZ, Roberto .... 215-893-5252 .... 426 E

DIAZ, Russell .... 845-848-4048 .... 332 C
russell.diaz@dc.edu

DIAZ, Ruth, M .... 787-763-6700 .... 562 B
rmdiaz@se-pr.edu

DIAZ, Sam .... 570-504-9069 .... 425 F

DIAZ, Sharon, C .... 510-869-6512 ...... 64 J
sdiaz@samuelmerritt.edu

DIAZ, Sonia .... 787-728-1515 .... 568 B
sdiaz@sagrado.edu

DIAZ, Tatiana .... 717-766-2511 .... 436 D
tdiaz@messiah.edu

DIAZ, Victor .... 787-834-3718 .... 567 C
victor@uprm.edu

DIAZ, Walter .... 956-665-3551 .... 506 A

DIAZ-BONACQUISTI, Judi 303-556-6492 ...... 85 N
jbonacqu@mscd.edu

DIAZ-DIAZ, Judith .... 787-993-8957 .... 566 G
judith.diaz2@upr.edu

DIAZ-HERRERA, Jorge, L .. 315-279-5201 .... 337 K
jdiazh@mail.keuka.edu

DIAZ-RODRIGUEZ, Nereida .... 787-798-6732 .... 566 A
nereida.diaz@uccaribe.edu

DIBB, Andrew M, T .... 267-502-2525 .... 423 B
andrew.dibb@ancts.org

DIBBERT, Douglas, S .... 919-962-7050 .... 378 D
doug_dibbert@unc.edu

DIBBINI, Murad .... 510-436-1430 ...... 50 F
dibbini@hnu.edu

DIBBLE, Emily .... 617-228-2412 .... 239 G
dibble@bhcc.mass.edu

DIBELLA, Tom .... 813-974-3305 .... 120 D
tdibella@admin.usf.edu

DIBELLO, Nan, M .... 716-686-7800 .... 355 F
nan.dibello@esc.edu

DIBENEDETTO, Eileen, M .. 212-854-7732 .... 323 G
edibened@barnard.edu

DIBENEDETTO, Steve .... 847-947-5409 .... 159 D
steve.dibenedetto@nl.edu

DIBIASIO, Daniel, A .... 419-772-2030 .... 398 G
d-dibiasio@onu.edu

DIBISCEGLIE, Lisa .... 973-618-3280 .... 308 D
ldibi@caldwell.edu

DIBLEY, Paula .... 704-216-3467 .... 373 C
paula.dibley@rccc.edu

DIBONIFAZIO, Susan .... 570-408-4000 .... 451 G
susan.dibonifazio@wilkes.edu

DIBRIGIDA, Vladimir .... 303-996-6663 ...... 82 H
director@cstcm.edu

DIBRITO, Kyle, J .... 717-221-1300 .... 430 E
kjdibrit@hacc.edu

DICAMILLO, Thomas .... 520-494-5204 ...... 13 F
tom.dicamillo@centralaz.edu

DICAPRIO, Deborah, A .... 845-575-3000 .... 340 C
deborah.dicaprio@marist.edu

DICARLO, Michael .... 318-257-2577 .... 215 F
miked@latech.edu

DICARLO, Sandra, V .... 419-372-0648 .... 385 D
sandrad@bgsu.edu

DICARO, Kim .... 313-496-2625 .... 260 C
kdicaro1@wcccd.edu

DICE, Douglas .... 989-463-7162 .... 247 F
dice@alma.edu

DICE, Frances .... 412-237-3064 .... 425 H
fdice@ccac.edu

DICESARE, Deborah, A .... 818-778-5622 ...... 55 E
dicesad@lavc.edu

DICESARE, John .... 951-343-4876 ...... 31 G
jdecesare@calbaptist.edu

DICHRISTINA, Joseph, J .. 814-332-4356 .... 421 E
joseph.dichristina@allegheny.edu

DICK, Beth .... 231-777-0314 .... 256 D

DICK, Larry .... 956-380-8179 .... 493 A
ldick@riogrande.edu

DICK, Nancy .... 425-739-8228 .... 535 B
nancy.dick@lwtc.edu

DICKASON, John .... 909-447-2512 ...... 40 E
jdickason@cst.edu

DICKENS, Brian, K .... 713-313-1379 .... 499 G
dickensbk@tsu.edu

DICKENS, Margaret, A .... 715-833-6419 .... 553 F
mdickens@cvtc.edu

DICKENS, Martha .... 828-254-1921 .... 367 H
mdickens@abtech.edu

DICKENS, Reginald .... 903-769-5723 .... 488 M
rdickens@jarvis.edu

DICKENS, Robert .... 210-458-4060 .... 506 B
robert.dickens@utsa.edu

DICKENS, Robert, E .... 775-784-1417 .... 303 A
robertd@unr.edu

DICKENS, Susan .... 651-779-3298 .... 266 D
susan.dickens@century.edu

DICKENS, Tony .... 419-720-6670 .... 401 C
tdickens@proskills.com

DICKENSON, Debra, L .... 703-726-4200 ...... 97 F
ddickens@gwu.edu

DICKER, James, W .... 610-330-5021 .... 433 B
dickerj@lafayette.edu

DICKERMAN, Christopher, M .... 610-359-5302 .... 426 G
cdickerman@dccc.edu

DICKERMAN, Robert .... 413-755-4606 .... 241 E
dickerman@stcc.edu

DICKERSON, Bill .... 281-998-6150 .... 493 D
bill.dickerson@sjcd.edu

DICKERSON, Carol .... 719-389-6671 ...... 81 L
cdickerson@coloradocollege.edu

DICKERSON, Cathy, S .... 540-375-2262 .... 523 D
cdickerson@roanoke.edu

DICKERSON, Darby .... 806-742-3990 .... 501 D

DICKERSON, Dee Ann .... 918-647-1300 .... 407 E
ddickerson@carlalbert.edu

DICKERSON, Donna .... 903-566-7447 .... 506 C
ddickerson@uttyler.edu

DICKERSON, John .... 601-849-0112 .... 274 A
john.dickerson@colin.edu

DICKERSON, Larry .... 816-802-3363 .... 283 I
ldickerson@kcai.edu

DICKERSON, Mark .... 626-387-5763 ...... 30 E
mdickerson@apu.edu

DICKERSON, Mary Ann .... 913-469-8500 .... 193 I
mdkerson@jccc.edu

DICKERSON, Russell .... 928-524-7418 ...... 17 B
russell.dickerson@npc.edu

DICKERSON, Shelltha, W .. 585-292-3010 .... 341 H
sdickerson@monroecc.edu

DICKERSON, Shirley .... 936-468-4109 .... 495 H
sdickerson@sfasu.edu

DICKERT, Gerry .... 409-984-6342 .... 500 H

DICKEY, Daryl .... 678-839-6534 .... 138 D
ddickey@westga.edu

DICKEY, Elbert, C .... 402-472-2966 .... 300 H
edickey1@unl.edu

DICKEY, Elizabeth, D .... 212-875-4595 .... 323 E
edickey@bankstreet.edu

DICKEY, Jennifer .... 313-664-7428 .... 250 A
jdickey@collegeforcreativestudies.edu

DICKEY, M. Thaxter .... 813-988-5131 .... 107 I
dickeyt@floridacollege.edu

DICKEY, Marilyn .... 850-201-6652 .... 121 F
dickeym@tcc.fl.edu

DICKEY, Matt .... 417-626-1234 .... 287 F
dickey.matt@occ.edu

DICKEY, Nancy, W .... 979-458-7200 .... 496 G
dickey@tamhsc.edu

DICKEY, Serita .... 281-998-6150 .... 493 F
serita.dickey@sjcd.edu

DICKEY, Todd, R .... 213-740-8184 ...... 76 C
svpadmin@usc.edu

DICKEY, Wanda .... 813-988-5131 .... 107 I
library@floridacollege.edu

DICKEY, Wyman .... 904-269-7086 .... 109 J

DICKHERBER, David .... 636-949-4907 .... 284 C
ddickherber@lindenwood.edu

DICKINSON, Arthur .... 717-872-3282 .... 443 C
arthur.dickinson@millersville.edu

DICKINSON, Marjorie, M .. 530-752-2619 ...... 73 F
mmdickinson@ucdavis.edu

DICKINSON, Mark, D .... 651-696-6278 .... 265 A
dickinsonm@macalester.edu

DICKINSON, Michael, B .... 607-255-9300 .... 331 C
mbd3@cornell.edu

DICKINSON, Patricia .... 304-766-3363 .... 544 D
dickinpa@wvstateu.edu

DICKINSON, Rosa, A .... 956-326-2200 .... 497 B
rosie@tamiu.edu

DICKMEYER, Nathan .... 718-482-6119 .... 328 C
ndickmeyer@lagcc.cuny.edu

DICKSON, Beverly .... 704-330-4119 .... 369 A
beverly.dickson@cpcc.edu

DICKSON, Brook, E .... 540-362-6287 .... 519 E
bdickson@hollins.edu

DICKSON, Chris, M .... 260-422-5561 .... 172 L
cmdickson@indianatech.edu

DICKSON, Eric .... 508-421-1400 .... 238 A
Eric.Dickson@umassmemorial.org

DICKSON, Janet .... 419-824-3704 .... 395 D
jdickson@lourdes.edu

DICKSON, Jo Carole .... 502-213-2411 .... 202 B
jocarole.dickson@kctcs.edu

DICKSON, John .... 727-873-4350 .... 121 B
jdickson@mail.usf.edu

DICKSON, John .... 202-639-1843 ...... 97 D

DICKSON, John, H .... 478-301-5639 .... 133 F
john.h.dickson@mercer.edu

DICKSON, Mary .... 607-778-5021 .... 324 G
dickson_m@sunybroome.edu

DICKSON, Nancy .... 724-480-3553 .... 426 A
nancy.dickson@ccbc.edu

DICKSON, Richard, P .... 504-865-5500 .... 215 C
rpd@tulane.edu

DICKSON, Risa .... 909-537-5029 ...... 36 A
rdickson@csusb.edu

DICOLA, Rose Ann .... 412-237-6517 .... 425 H
rdicola@ccac.edu

DICROCE, Deborah, M .... 757-822-1052 .... 528 C
ddicroce@tcc.edu

DIDARIO, Thomas, A .... 401-254-3531 .... 454 C
tdidario@rwu.edu

DIDIER, Kim .... 515-965-7064 .... 183 E
kmdidier@dmacc.edu

DIDIMAMOFF, Stephen .... 914-968-6200 .... 349 D
stephen.didimamoff@archny.org

DIDION, John .... 714-480-7489 ...... 63 E
didion_john@rsccd.edu

DIDION, Judy .... 419-517-8905 .... 395 D
jdidion@lourdes.edu

DIDONNA, Diane .... 219-877-3100 .... 170 A
ddidonna@brownmackie.edu

DIEBEL, Carol .... 907-474-6939 ...... 10 J
cediebel@alaska.edu

DIEBOLD, Ann .... 610-519-4560 .... 450 G
ann.diebold@villanova.edu

DIECKMAN, Stacy .... 402-844-7288 .... 300 A
stacyd@northeast.edu

DIECKMANN, Mike, F .... 850-474-2555 .... 121 C
michaeldieckmann@uwf.edu

DIECKMEYER, Diane .... 951-372-7000 ...... 64 A

DIEDRCHS, Carol, P .... 614-292-6151 .... 398 H
diedrichs.1@0osu.edu

DIEDRICK, James, K .... 404-471-6102 .... 123 G
jdiedrick@agnesscott.edu

DIEFENDORF, Wendy .... 518-244-2443 .... 348 A
diefew@sage.edu

DIEHL, Bert .... 440-525-7140 .... 394 F
rdiehl@lakelandcc.edu

DIEHL, Dave .... 301-696-3800 .... 223 C
diehld@hood.edu

DIEHL, Hope, L .... 610-359-5333 .... 426 G
hdiehl@dccc.edu

DIEHL, Jim .... 913-782-3750 .... 195 A

DIEHL, Melissa, M .... 570-577-3776 .... 423 D
melissa.diehl@bucknell.edu

DIEHL, Michele .... 215-646-7300 .... 430 C
diehl.m@gmc.edu

DIEHL, Randy, L .... 512-471-4141 .... 505 B
diehl@austin.utexas.edu

DIEHL, Shanda .... 360-992-2421 .... 532 A
sdiehl@clark.edu

DIEHL, Timothy .... 207-725-3716 .... 217 E
tdiehl@bowdoin.edu

DIEHM, Perry .... 913-971-3722 .... 195 A
pdiehm@mnu.edu

DIEKER, R. Joseph .... 319-895-4210 .... 183 D
jdieker@cornellcollege.edu

DIEKHANS, Carl .... 775-753-2265 .... 302 H
carld@gwmail.gbcnv.edu

DIEM, Richard, A .... 210-458-6463 .... 506 B
richard.diem@utsa.edu

DIEMER, Gregory, M .... 715-346-2641 .... 552 B
gdiemer@uwsp.edu

DIEMER, Rene .... 215-248-6305 .... 435 B
registrar@ltsp.edu

DIEMER, Robert .... 352-588-8974 .... 116 E
robert.diemer@saintleo.edu

DIENER, Connie .... 920-923-7615 .... 548 C
cdiener@marianuniversity.edu

DIENER, Melissa .... 920-686-6146 .... 550 E
Melissa.Diener@sl.edu

DIENHART, Mark, C .... 651-962-6920 .... 272 E
mcdienhart@stthomas.edu

DIENNO, Michele .... 513-785-3251 .... 396 E
diennomm@muohio.edu

DIENST, Tom .... 907-796-6497 ...... 11 A
tom.dienst@uas.alaska.edu

DIEPENBROCK, Amy .... 210-436-3102 .... 493 C
adiepenbrock@stmarytx.edu

DIERCKX, Heidi .... 607-735-1954 .... 333 A
hdierckx@elmira.edu

DIERENFIELD, Bruce, J .... 716-888-2683 .... 325 G
derenfb@canisius.edu

DIERICKX, George .... 269-782-1207 .... 258 E
gdierickx@swmich.edu

DIERINGER, Deanna, L .... 907-474-6629 ...... 10 J
dldieringer@alaska.edu

DIERINGER, Dennis, D .... 770-484-1204 .... 133 D
lru@lru.edu

DIERINGER, Jerome, T .... 410-704-2516 .... 228 E
jdieringer@towson.edu

DIERKS, Barbara .... 877-442-0505 ...... 88 G
barbara.dierks@rockies.edu

DIERKS, David, R .... 319-335-3305 .... 182 C
david-dierks@uiowa.edu

DIERLAM, Lois .... 914-337-9300 .... 331 A
lois.dierlam@concordia-ny.edu

DIESMAN, Julie .... 765-459-0561 .... 176 A
jdiesman@ivytech.edu

DIETER, Darryl .... 425-388-9392 .... 533 H
ddieter@everettcc.edu

DIETERLE, Sheila .... 719-336-1621 ...... 85 K
sheila.dieterle@lamarcc.edu

DIETRICH, Autumn .... 509-793-2003 .... 531 D
autumnw@bigbend.edu

DIETRICH, Darryl .... 218-723-6165 .... 262 I
ddietric@css.edu

DIETRICH, John, F .... 321-433-7090 .... 101 J
dietrichj@brevardcc.edu

DIETRICH, Robert, C .... 570-326-3761 .... 440 K
rdietric@pct.edu

DIETRICH, Robin .... 540-887-7025 .... 520 I
rdietrich@mbc.edu

DIETRICH, Sandra, L .... 919-866-5674 .... 374 E
sldietrich@waketech.edu

DIETZ, Carol, P .... 216-397-4314 .... 392 M
cdietz@jcu.edu

DIETZ, Fred, K .... 270-809-2684 .... 204 F
fred.dietz@murraystate.edu

DIETZ, James .... 657-278-2616 ...... 34 E
jdietz@fullerton.edu

DIETZ, Kenneth .... 502-852-6176 .... 207 A
kenneth.dietz@louisville.edu

DIETZ, Pam .... 620-672-5641 .... 196 A
pamd@prattcc.edu

DIETZ, Sally .... 607-274-3385 .... 336 G
sdietz@ithaca.edu

DIETZLER, Deborah, H .... 706-542-2251 .... 138 C
dietzler@uga.edu

DIEUDONNE, Jose .... 215-517-2580 .... 422 B
dieudonj@arcadia.edu

DIEUGENIO, Richard, D .... 814-865-6563 .... 438 F
rxd2@psu.edu

DIEZ, Mary .... 414-382-6214 .... 545 H
mary.diez@alverno.edu

DIEZ, Mickey, P .... 318-797-5063 .... 213 D
mdiez@lsus.edu

DIEZ, Pam .... 225-216-8068 .... 209 I
diezp@mybrcc.edu

DIFABIO, Mark .... 386-226-7055 .... 105 C
mark.difabio@erau.edu

DIFELICIANTONIO, Richard, G .... 610-409-3200 .... 450 C
rdifeliciantonio@ursinus.edu

DIFETERICI, Amanda .... 803-799-9082 .... 461 A
adifeterici@southuniversity.edu

DIFFEY, Steve .... 662-472-2312 .... 274 F
sdiffey@holmescc.edu

DIFFIE, Rita Nell .... 432-685-4503 .... 490 G
rndiffie@midland.edu

DIFFILY, Michael, E .... 603-577-6000 .... 304 J
diffily@dwc.edu

DIFFLEY, Peter .... 860-768-5425 ...... 95 A
diffley@hartford.edu

DIFILIPO, Steve .... 410-287-1021 .... 222 A
sdifilipo@cecil.edu

DIFRANCO, Heidi .... 803-641-3397 .... 462 B
heidid@usca.edu

DIFRANCO, Kathleen, J ..... 216-397-4291 .... 392 M
difranco@jcu.edu

DIFRONZO-HEITZER, Nicola, C .... 610-526-6153 .... 430 D
ndifronzo@harcum.edu

DIGBY, Joan .... 516-299-2840 .... 339 A
joan.digby@liu.edu

DIGERLANDO, Rose .... 847-214-7635 .... 150 D
rdigerlando@elgin.edu

DIGGS, Michael .... 217-875-7200 .... 162 D
mdiggs@richland.edu

DIGIACINTO, Mary, L .... 410-706-7355 .... 227 C
mdigiaci@hr.umaryland.edu

DIGIACOMO, Kris .... 702-369-9944 .... 301 G
kdigiacomo@aii.edu

DIGIACOMO, Robert .... 631-656-2154 .... 334 B
rdigiacomo@ftc.edu

DIGIANFILIPPO, Denise ..... 602-787-6693 ...... 16 A
denise.digianfilippo@pvmail.maricopa.edu

DIGIORGIO, Anthony, J .... 803-323-2225 .... 463 D
digiorgioa@winthrop.edu

DIGIRONIMO, Joseph .... 215-468-8800 .... 431 J
director@culinaryarts.edu

DIGMAN, Jo-Ann .... 314-539-5358 .... 289 A
jdigman1@stlcc.edu

DIGNAN WEIR, Joette ...... 330-972-6401 .... 403 B
jdweir@uakron.edu

DIGRANES, Jo Lynn, A ..... 918-463-2931 .... 407 H
jdigran@connorsstate.edu

DIGREGORIO, Christian .... 570-348-6234 .... 435 F
digregorio@marywood.edu

DIGREGORIO, Theresa ...... 716-614-6430 .... 344 C
digregor@niagaracc.suny.edu

DIGREORIO, Jeffrey .... 510-849-8283 ...... 48 H
jdigreorio@gtu.edu

DIGUISEPPE, Steven, A ..... 717-872-3352 .... 443 C
steve.diguiseppe@millersville.edu

DIINA-DEMPSEY, Stephanie, C .... 512-223-7736 .... 481 B
diina@austincc.edu

DIIORIO, Lisa .... 631-244-3220 .... 332 D
diioriol@dowling.edu

DIJULIA, Dominick, J .... 610-660-1707 .... 446 C
ddijulia@sju.edu

DIKEMAN, Scott .... 802-468-1214 .... 515 C
scott.dikeman@castleton.edu

DIKET, Read, M .... 601-318-6205 .... 278 E
read.diket@wmcarey.edu

DILAURO, Nanette .... 212-854-2154 .... 323 G
ndilauro@barnard.edu

DILAURO, Nanette, M .... 212-854-3711 .... 330 F
nd143@columbia.edu

DILBECK, Jack .... 270-706-8892 .... 201 F
jdilbeck0001@kctcs.edu

DILBECK, Joel .... 334-386-7259 .... 3 H
jdilbeck@faulkner.edu

DILDAY, Gwynne .... 773-702-6889 .... 166 D
egdilday@uchicago.edu

DILENO, Susan .... 440-826-2222 .... 384 H
sdileno@bw.edu

DILEO, Jeffrey .... 361-570-4201 .... 503 E
dileoj@uhv.edu

DILES, David .... 216-368-2866 .... 386 E
dxd87@case.edu

DILGER, Patrick .... 203-392-6586 ...... 91 I
dilgerp1@southernct.edu

DILGREN, Amy .... 626-529-8008 ...... 60 G
adilgren@pacificoaks.edu

DILIBERTO, James, G .... 631-691-8733 .... 336 F
dilibertoj@idti.edu

DILIBERTO, John, G .... 631-691-8733 .... 336 F
johng@idti.edu

DILISIO, James .... 410-704-2131 .... 228 E
jdilisio@towson.edu

DILL, Anna Maria .... 541-962-3774 .... 418 C
adill@eou.edu

DILL, April .... 580-477-7710 .... 414 C
april.dill@wosc.edu

DILL, Bonnie, T .... 301-405-2095 .... 227 B
btdill@umd.edu

DILL, Gary .... 575-492-2123 .... 321 H
gdill@usw.edu

DILL, Herb .... 440-375-7000 .... 394 E
hdill@lec.edu

DILL, Jane, P .... 864-644-5404 .... 461 B
jdill@swu.edu

DILL, Julia .... 573-518-2261 .... 286 B
jdill@mineralarea.edu

DILL, Randy, G .... 208-732-6600 .... 143 B
rdill@csi.edu

DILL, Rosemary .... 662-621-4201 .... 273 I
rdill@coahomacc.edu

DILL, Stephen .... 617-879-2355 .... 246 F
sdill@wheelock.edu

DILLABOUGH, Daniel, J ... 619-260-2247 ...... 76 A
dillabough@sandiego.edu

DILLANE, Robert, J .... 717-867-6060 .... 434 C
dillane@lvc.edu

DILLARD, Cara .... 804-440-1529 .... 526 F
cdillard@ccwa.vccs.edu

DILLARD, Gail .... 229-391-5128 .... 123 F
gdillard@abac.edu

DILLARD, Glenn .... 501-279-4407 ...... 21 H
gdillard@harding.edu

DILLARD, Maria, P .... 954-262-8051 .... 114 B
mdillard@nsu.nova.edu

DILLBECK, Michael .... 641-472-1187 .... 187 B
sdillbeck@mum.edu

DILLBECK, Susan .... 641-472-1187 .... 187 B

DILLE, Wayne .... 641-628-5268 .... 183 A
dille@central.edu

DILLEMUTH, Jim .... 612-659-6600 .... 267 E
jim.dillemuth@minneapolis.edu

DILLENBERG, Jack .... 480-219-6081 .... 278 F
jdillenberg@atsu.edu

DILLENBURG, Brenda .... 715-389-7011 .... 554 C
brenda.dillenburg@mstc.edu

DILLER, Elizabeth .... 740-857-1311 .... 401 F
ediller@rosedale.edu

DILLER, Tiffany .... 601-664-9500 ...... 19 C
tiffany.diller@phoenix.edu

DILLET, Brigette .... 775-423-2254 .... 303 B
bdillet@wnc.edu

DILLING, Brooke .... 303-556-6930 ...... 85 N
dillingb@mscd.edu

DILLINGHAM, Tom .... 931-393-1756 .... 475 C
tdillingham@mscc.edu

DILLINGHAM-EVANS, Donna .... 435-652-7506 .... 512 A
dillingh@dixie.edu

DILLION, Diana .... 605-856-2355 .... 465 A
diana.dillion@sintegleska.edu

DILLMAN, David .... 903-813-3000 .... 481 A
ddillman@austincollege.edu

DILLMAN, Rob .... 702-579-3518 .... 302 C
rdillman@kaplan.edu

DILLMAN, Robert, J .... 570-422-3546 .... 442 C
rdillman@po-box.esu.edu

DILLON, Alice, A .... 903-586-2518 .... 488 L
adillon@jacksonville-college.edu

DILLON, Anastacia .... 503-768-7095 .... 416 F
adillon@lclark.edu

DILLON, Andrew, P .... 512-471-3821 .... 505 B
adillon@ischool.utexas.edu

DILLON, Charles, T .... 231-843-5540 .... 260 E
ctdillon@westshore.edu

DILLON, Clotilde .... 212-594-4000 .... 357 G
cdillon@tcicollege.edu

DILLON, III, Cyrus, I .... 434-223-6197 .... 519 B
cdillon@email.hsc.edu

DILLON, Dawn, M .... 919-508-2005 .... 375 D
ddillon@peace.edu

DILLON, Francis, X .... 508-565-1344 .... 245 D
fdillon@stonehill.edu

DILLON, Glenn .... 817-735-5400 .... 504 C
gdillon@hsc.unt.edu

DILLON, Howard .... 212-217-4040 .... 333 G
howard_dillon@fitnyc.edu

DILLON, James, S .... 717-720-4100 .... 441 E
jdillon@passhe.edu

DILLON, John .... 610-683-4002 .... 442 F
dillon@kutztown.edu

DILLON, John .... 718-409-7311 .... 356 C
jdillon@sunypurchase.edu

DILLON, Kendall .... 515-271-1661 .... 183 F
kendall.dillon@dmu.edu

DILLON, Mary Jane .... 904-819-6314 .... 107 A
dillonmj@flagler.edu

DILLON, Michael .... 410-455-2111 .... 227 D
midillon@umbc.edu

DILLON, Mike .... 573-592-4209 .... 293 E
mike.dillon@williamwoods.edu

DILLON, Paul .... 201-360-4635 .... 310 F
pdillon@hccc.edu

DILLON, R. Mark .... 630-752-5016 .... 168 F
mark.dillon@wheaton.edu

DILLON, Rick .... 304-384-5231 .... 543 D
rdillon@concord.edu

DILLON, Sarah .... 715-675-3331 .... 554 G
Dillon@ntc.edu

DILLON, T. Kevin .... 713-500-3535 .... 506 D
kevin.dillon@uth.tmc.edu

DILLON, Tabitha .... 412-566-2433 .... 434 B
tdillon@paculinary.com

DILLON, Thomas .... 419-434-5777 .... 404 B
dillon@findlay.edu

DILLON HOGAN, Kate ...... 716-375-2128 .... 348 C
khogan@sbu.edu

DILLOW, Rhonda .... 618-634-3251 .... 164 C
rhondad@shawneecc.edu

DILLOW, Sarah, L .... 423-652-4739 .... 469 L
sldillow@king.edu

DILLSWORTH, Gary .... 716-926-8920 .... 335 F
gdillsworth@hilbert.edu

DILMORE, Donald, H .... 814-732-2779 .... 442 D
ddilmore@edinboro.edu

DILORENZO, Peter .... 856-227-7200 .... 308 E
pdilorenzo@camdencc.edu

DILORENZO, Thomas .... 205-934-5643 .... 8 G
tmd@uab.edu

DILORENZO, Vicki .... 518-694-7331 .... 322 C
vicki.dilorenzo@acphs.edu

DILS, Keith .... 724-357-2480 .... 442 E
Keith.Dils@iup.edu

DILUSTRO, John .... 252-398-6220 .... 363 E
dilusj@chowan.edu

DIMAGGIO, Jacqueline, R . 864-250-8179 .... 458 F
jacqui.dimaggio@gvltec.edu

DIMAIO, Judith .... 516-686-7594 .... 343 D
jdimaio@nyit.edu

DIMANTOVA, Walter .... 916-563-3237 ...... 55 J
dimantw@losrios.edu

DIMARCO, Casey .... 518-694-7278 .... 322 C
casey.dimarco@acphs.edu

DIMARCO, Erin .... 302-356-6924 ...... 97 A
erin.j.dimarco@wilmu.edu

DIMARCO, Scott, L .... 570-662-4672 .... 443 B
sdimarco@mansfield.edu

DIMARIA, Vince .... 216-987-2341 .... 389 A
vince.dimaria@tri-c.edu

DIMARIO, Joseph, X .... 847-578-8633 .... 163 A
joseph.dimario@rosalindfranklin.edu

DIMARZO, Brett .... 617-726-8439 .... 242 E
bdimarzo@mghihp.edu

DIMASI, Louis .... 802-654-2566 .... 514 B
ldimasi@smcvt.edu

DIMATTIA, Andrea .... 570-504-9634 .... 425 F

DIMAURO, JR., Alfred .... 508-831-5130 .... 247 B
fred@wpi.edu

DIMAURO, Nancy .... 718-780-1560 .... 338 E
ndimauro@chpnet.org

DIMENNA, Grey .... 732-571-3598 .... 311 F
gdimenna@monmouth.edu

DIMENT, Gregory, S .... 269-337-7149 .... 253 F
Greg.Diment@kzoo.edu

DIMIERI, Thomas, J .... 401-232-6027 .... 453 A
tdimieri@bryant.edu

DIMINO, John, L .... 215-204-7276 .... 447 G
john.dimino@temple.edu

DIMINO, Laura .... 717-901-5137 .... 430 F
ldimino@harrisburgu.edu

DIMINO, Solweig .... 973-300-2215 .... 315 F
sdimino@sussex.edu

DIMITROV, Danielle, E .... 718-982-2250 .... 327 A
danielle.dimitrov@csi.cuny.edu

DIMKOVA, Dimitrina .... 703-323-5053 .... 527 C
ddimkova@nvcc.edu

DIMMITT, Al .... 816-604-4003 .... 285 I
al.dimmitt@mcckc.edu

DIMOLA, Anne .... 631-244-3020 .... 332 D
dimolaa@dowling.edu

DIMOLITSAS, Spiros .... 202-687-3730 ...... 98 A
seniorvp@georgetown.edu

DIMON, Donna, L .... 240-567-7290 .... 224 E
donna.dimon@montgomerycollege.edu

DIMOND, David .... 914-632-5400 .... 341 G
ddimond@monroecollege.edu

DINAN, Susan .... 973-720-3657 .... 317 D
dinans@wpunj.edu

DINARDO, N. John .... 215-895-2510 .... 427 G
dinardo@drexel.edu

DINDIAL-THOMPSON, Heidi .... 727-725-2688 .... 105 J
HDindialthompson@cci.edu

DINDOFFER, Tamara, L .... 517-750-1200 .... 258 F
tammyd@arbor.edu

DINE YOUNG, Katie .... 812-866-6842 .... 171 F
kdineyoung@hanover.edu

DINEEN, Elizabeth .... 413-565-1000 .... 231 B
edineen@baypath.edu

DINEGAR, Leonard .... 303-860-5600 ...... 88 A
leonard.dinegar@cu.edu

DINELL, Brandon .... 585-720-0660 .... 325 C
bdinell@bryantstratton.edu

DINELLO, William, V .... 718-262-2330 .... 329 B
wdinello@york.cuny.edu

DINER, David .... 434-971-3303 .... 557 D
david.diner@conus.army.mil

DINER, Steven, J .... 973-353-5541 .... 314 E
chancellor-newark@newark.rutgers.edu

DINGER, Tim .... 479-524-7234 ...... 22 C
tdinger@jbu.edu

DINGLE, Terry .... 843-661-8321 .... 458 A
terry.dingle@fdtc.edu

DINGLEY, Clare .... 320-589-6030 .... 272 C
strandcd@morris.umn.edu

DINGMANN, Melissa .... 218-281-8576 .... 272 A
dingmann@umn.edu

DINIELLI, Michael .... 909-652-6257 ...... 39 B
michael.dinielli@chaffey.edu

DINIELLI, Michael .... 909-652-6904 ...... 39 B
michael.dinielli@chaffey.edu

DINKINS, Marva .... 910-879-5570 .... 368 A
mdinkins@bladencc.edu

DINKINS, Sandy .... 904-264-2172 .... 116 A
sdinkins@iws.edu

DINNAN, Matthew, A .... 203-254-4000 ...... 92 B
madinnan@fairfield.edu

DINNDORF, Robert, J .... 608-246-6440 .... 554 B
rdinndorf@matcmadison.edu

DINNEEN, Peter .... 303-329-3000 ...... 84 B
pdinneen@keller.edu

DINNO, Christopher .... 707-664-2870 ...... 37 B
christopher.dinno@sonoma.edu

DINSE, Jayne .... 507-389-7269 .... 269 F
jayne.dinse@southcentral.edu

DINTINO, Dennis .... 718-260-3770 .... 346 C
ddintino@poly.edu

DINUZZO, Theresa, M .... 904-620-2602 .... 120 C
tdinuzzo@unf.edu

DINWIDDIE, Mollie, D .... 660-543-4140 .... 291 B
dinwiddie@ucmo.edu

DINWIDDIE-BOYD, Elza ... 914-654-5522 .... 330 B
edinwiddie@cnr.edu

DIOGUARDI, Brian, K .... 716-625-6300 .... 324 K
bkdioguardi@bryantstratton.edu

DION, Kent .... 406-377-9416 .... 294 C
kent_d@dawson.edu

DIONNE, Woody .... 802-635-1280 .... 515 E
woody.dionne@jsc.edu

DIORIO, Mary Ann .... 860-255-3474 ...... 91 C
mdiorio@txcc.commnet.edu

DIPADOVA, Audra .... 949-582-4616 ...... 70 F
adipadova@saddleback.edu

DIPADOVA-STOCKS, Laurie .... 816-559-5617 .... 287 H
laurie.dipadovastocks@park.edu

DIPALMA, Allen, A .... 412-624-7415 .... 449 A
dipalma@pitt.edu

DIPETRO, David .... 412-396-5140 .... 428 C
dipetro@duq.edu

DIPIERRO, John .... 269-965-3931 .... 253 H
dipierroj@kellogg.edu

DIPIETRO, Joe .... 865-974-2241 .... 477 A
utpresident@tennessee.edu

DIPIETRO, Joseph, A .... 865-974-7342 .... 477 A
dipietro@tennessee.edu

DIPIETRO, Stephen .... 609-894-9311 .... 308 C
sdipietr@bcc.edu

DIPILLO, Mary Lou .... 330-941-3215 .... 406 F

DIPIPPA, John, M .... 501-324-9434 ...... 24 E
jmdipippa@ualr.edu

DIPIRO, Joseph, T .... 803-777-4151 .... 462 A
joseph.dipiro@sc.edu

DIPIRO, Joseph, T .... 843-792-8450 .... 459 C
dipiroj@musc.edu

DIPLOCK, Peter .... 860-486-2238 ...... 94 E
peter.diplock@uconn.edu

DIPUCCIO, Denise .... 910-962-3685 .... 379 C
dipucciod@uncw.edu

DIRADDO, Colleen .... 484-384-2943 .... 438 C
cdiraddo@eastern.edu

DIRE, James .... 808-245-8229 .... 141 H
dire@hawaii.edu

DIRECTOR, Stephen, W .... 617-373-2170 .... 244 A

DIRIKER, Veronique, L .... 410-651-8142 .... 227 E
vdiriker@umes.edu

DIRKS, Dennis .... 562-903-4816 ...... 30 H
dennis.dirks@biola.edu

DIRKS, Nicholas, B .... 212-854-8296 .... 330 F
nbd7@columbia.edu

DIRKSCHNEIDER, Carla .... 402-552-6295 .... 297 D
dirkschneider@clarksoncollege.edu

DIRKSE, John .... 661-654-3420 ...... 33 H
jdirkse@csub.edu

DIRKSEN, Carolyn .... 423-614-8118 .... 470 A
cdirksen@leeuniversity.edu

DIRKSEN, Dawn .... 866-323-0233 ...... 63 D

DIRLAM, David .... 513-487-3234 .... 391 E
ddirlam@huc.edu

DIRSCHEL, Kathleen, M .... 914-964-4282 .... 329 E

DIRST, Eric .... 630-515-4510 .... 149 A
edirst@devry.edu

DISABATINO, Gail .... 864-656-2161 .... 456 E
gaild@clemson.edu

DISAIA, Kenneth, F .... 401-598-2346 .... 453 C
kdisaia@jwu.edu

DISALVIO, Philip .... 617-287-7925 .... 237 D
philip.disalvio@umb.edu

DISALVO, Stephen .... 314-529-9521 .... 284 F
sdisalvo@maryville.edu

DISALVO, Steven, R .... 920-923-7617 .... 548 C
sdisalvo@marianuniversity.edu

DISANTI, Francis, J .... 610-660-1506 .... 446 C
disanti@sju.edu

DISATE, Nancy .... 303-861-1151 ...... 83 G
ndisate@concorde.edu

DISCHINO, Maureen .... 617-989-4009 .... 246 C
dischinom@wit.edu

DISHMAN, Laurie .... 615-547-1278 .... 467 I
ldishman@cumberland.edu

DISHMAN, Leslie, B .... 985-448-4415 .... 216 A
leslie.dishman@nicholls.edu

DISHMAN, Marcie .... 919-718-7491 .... 368 H
mdishman@cccc.edu

DISHNER, Annette, H .... 252-451-8236 .... 372 B
adishner@nash.cc.nc.us

DISKIN, Becca, L .... 417-659-5422 .... 286 E
diskin-b@mssu.edu

DOERPINGHAUS, Helen, I 803-777-2808 462 A
doerp@sc.edu
DOERR, Judith, E 520-515-5400 13 G
doerrj@cochise.edu
DOERR, Pamela 941-359-4200 121 A
DOERZAPH, Ron 309-677-2919 145 H
rd@bradley.edu
DOFFONEY, Ned 714-808-4797 59 B
ndoffoney@nocccd.edu
DOGBEVIA, Moses 402-461-7466 298 C
mdogbevia@hastings.edu
DOGGETT, Jeffrey 978-837-5207 242 D
doggettj@merrimack.edu
DOGGETT, Laine 240-895-4514 226 A
ledoggett@smcm.edu
DOGONNIUCK, Theodore 516-773-5000 558 F
DOHERTY, Arthur 541-278-5850 414 G
adoherty@bluecc.edu
DOHERTY, Brian 941-487-4300 119 D
bdoherty@ncf.edu
DOHERTY, Brian, E 413-265-2372 233 E
dohertyb@elms.edu
DOHERTY, Cynthia, A 717-221-1300 430 E
cadohert@hacc.edu
DOHERTY, Dan 897-339-6336 80 G
dan.doherty@aims.edu
DOHERTY, Eileen 773-298-5060 163 G
edoherty@sxu.edu
DOHERTY, Frank, J 540-568-6830 520 C
dohertfj@jmu.edu
DOHERTY, Katherine 603-752-1113 304 I
kdoherty@ccsnh.edu
DOHERTY, Kevin 312-369-7162 148 B
kdoherty@colum.edu
DOHERTY, Kristal 864-646-1795 461 F
kdoherty@tctc.edu
DOHERTY, Mary Jane 781-768-7015 244 D
mj.doherty@regiscollege.edu
DOHERTY, Ned 415-955-2120 27 F
ndoherty@alliant.edu
DOHERTY, Paul 425-640-1713 533 E
paul.doherty@edcc.edu
DOHERTY, Paula 360-417-6275 536 B
pdoherty@pencol.edu
DOHERTY, Sharon 651-690-6783 271 E
sldoherty@stkate.edu
DOHERTY, Steve 269-488-4442 253 G
sdoherty@kvcc.edu
DOHMAN, Gloria 701-671-2619 382 E
gloria.dohman@ndscs.edu
DOHNALIK, Judith 254-298-8600 496 B
j.dohnalik@templejc.edu
DOIG, Kathleen 304-637-1359 540 F
doigk@dewv.edu
DOIGUCHI, Farah 808-845-9120 141 G
farah@hawaii.edu
DOKE, Tim 214-648-7144 507 D
tim.doke@utsouthwestern.edu
DOKEY, Denise 225-768-0818 214 B
denise.dokey@ololcollege.edu
DOKTOR, Caryn, G 212-799-5000 337 H
DOLAK, James 970-491-4752 83 A
jim.dolak@colostate.edu
DOLAMORE, Joan 617-243-2497 236 F
jdolamore@lasell.edu
DOLAN, Barbara 605-394-2649 466 A
barbara.dolan@sdsmt.edu
DOLAN, Carol 912-358-4014 136 C
dolanc@savannahstate.edu
DOLAN, Daniel 212-237-8900 328 A
ddolan@jjay.cuny.edu
DOLAN, Donna, M 617-521-2111 245 A
donna.dolan@simmons.edu
DOLAN, Gayle 617-277-3915 232 F
DOLAN, John, F 215-951-1024 432 G
dolanj@lasalle.edu
DOLAN, Julie, L 203-254-4000 92 B
jdolan@fairfield.edu
DOLAN, Linda 320-762-4439 265 I
lindad@alextech.edu
DOLAN, Mary, K 315-267-4816 354 C
dolanmk@potsdam.edu
DOLAN, Serafina 212-772-4451 327 E
serafina.dolan@hunter.cuny.edu
DOLAN, Teresa, A 352-723-5800 120 B
tdolan@dental.ufl.edu
DOLAN, Tim 435-283-7152 512 B
tim.dolan@snow.edu
DOLAN, Tina, M 781-283-3501 246 B
cdolan@wellesley.edu
DOLAN, SJ, William, S 315-445-4110 338 B
dolanws@lemoyne.edu
DOLANSKY, Brian, P 914-606-6284 360 D
brian.dolansky@sunywcc.edu
DOLCI, Elizabeth 802-635-1482 515 E
liz.dolci@jsc.edu
DOLDER-ZIEKE, Beth, D 608-796-3828 553 A
bdzieke@viterbo.edu
DOLDO, Frank 315-786-2250 337 F
fdoldo@sunyjefferson.edu
DOLE, Karen, F 641-422-4327 187 F
dolekare@niacc.edu
DOLE, Wanda 501-569-8803 24 E
wvdole@ualr.edu

DOLEAC, Marge, O 503-845-3555 417 A
marge.doleac@mtangel.edu
DOLHEIMER, Mary, E 717-815-1274 452 F
mdolheim@ycp.edu
DOLIBER, Joy 561-237-7233 113 D
jdoliber@lynn.edu
DOLINAY, Petro 215-885-2360 435 E
pdolinay@manor.edu
DOLINSKY, Beverly 978-232-2194 234 F
bdolinsk@endicott.edu
DOLINSKY, Claudia 305-593-1223 102 D
cdolinsky@albizu.edu
DOLINSKY, Diane 570-702-8907 431 K
ddolinsky@johnson.edu
DOLIVE, Mark 817-515-3083 496 A
mark.dolive@tccd.edu
DOLL, Caroline 805-437-3232 33 I
caroline.doll@csuci.edu
DOLL, Tammy 620-417-1131 196 B
tammy.doll@sccc.edu
DOLLA, Marie 718-779-1430 346 B
mdolla@plazacollege.edu
DOLLAR, Marek 513-529-4036 396 D
dollarm@muohio.edu
DOLLAR, Mark, E 423-652-6320 469 L
medollar@king.edu
DOLLARD, Heidi 413-545-6133 237 C
hdollard@oit.umass.edu
DOLLARD, John, D 512-232-9205 505 B
dollard@mail.utexas.edu
DOLLARD, Pam 608-890-1066 552 F
pam.dollard@uwc.edu
DOLLARHIDE, Kenneth 908-737-0430 311 B
kdollarh@kean.edu
DOLLASE, Beth 816-654-7282 283 J
bdollase@kcumb.edu
DOLLENMAYER, Lisa 727-726-1153 103 B
lisadollenmayer@clearwater.edu
DOLLHOPF, Mark, R 203-432-1941 95 D
mark.dollhopf@yale.edu
DOLLING, David 202-994-6080 97 F
dolling@gwu.edu
DOLLING, Lisa 201-216-5405 315 E
ldolling@stevens.edu
DOLLINS, David 207-255-1318 220 E
david.dollins@maine.edu
DOLLY, Patricia, A 248-232-4500 257 B
padolly@oaklandcc.edu
DOLSEN, David, H 620-229-6298 196 C
david.dolsen@sckans.edu
DOMAN, Earle, F 417-836-5526 286 F
earledoman@missouristate.edu
DOMANN, Jessica 713-942-5036 504 D
domannj@sthom.edu
DOMAS, Matthew 662-562-3205 276 E
gmdomas@northwestms.edu
DOMAS, Matthew, S 662-562-3235 276 E
gmdomas@northwestms.edu
DOMBROWSKI, Teresa, A 630-515-6479 158 E
tdombr@midwestern.edu
DOMCHEK, Dennis, A 610-861-1360 436 I
domchek@moravian.edu
DOMENECH, Manuel 432-335-5360 501 E
manuel.domenech@ttuhsc.edu
DOMENITZ, Linda 860-906-5153 89 L
ldomenitz@ccc.commnet.edu
DOMERACKI, Kristin 713-942-9505 487 H
kdomeracki@hgst.edu
DOMES, Chris, E 703-284-1502 521 A
chris.domes@marymount.edu
DOMHOLDT, Elizabeth 218-723-6012 262 I
bdomhold@css.edu
DOMIANO, Sam, B 985-549-3312 216 C
sdomiano@selu.edu
DOMICK, Timothy 845-574-4122 347 I
tdomick@sunyrockland.edu
DOMIN, Greg 706-507-8704 127 D
domin_gregory@columbusstate.edu
DOMINELLI, Angela 518-694-7333 322 C
angela.dominelli@acphs.edu
DOMINGO, Benjamin, J 315-684-6078 354 F
domingbj@morrisville.edu
DOMINGO, Jannette 212-237-8757 328 A
jdomingo@jjay.cuny.edu
DOMINGUEZ, Armando 956-364-4341 499 J
armando.dominguez@harlingen.tstc.edu
DOMINGUEZ, Carmen 305-237-3374 113 H
cdoming3@mdc.edu
DOMINGUEZ, Carmen 661-259-7800 41 G
DOMINGUEZ, Jaime 787-766-1717 565 G
jdominguez@suagm.edu
DOMINGUEZ,
Jeronimo, C 505-277-2215 321 C
dominguz@unm.edu
DOMINGUEZ, Leo 432-837-8596 501 B
leodo@sulross.edu
DOMINGUEZ, Leo, G 432-837-8033 501 B
leodo@sulross.edu
DOMINGUEZ, Maria 575-538-6611 321 I
dominguezm@wnmu.edu
DOMINGUEZ, Mary 831-755-6714 49 C
mdomingu@hartnell.edu
DOMINGUEZ, Norberto 787-296-0453 562 F
dominguez@inter.edu

DOMINIAK, Dorothy 773-256-0726 157 B
ddominia@lstc.edu
DOMINIAK, Tracy 716-677-9500 325 B
tdominiak@bryantstratton.edu
DOMINICK, James, L 704-687-8495 378 E
jdomini5@uncc.edu
DOMINY, Michele 845-758-7420 323 F
dominy@bard.edu
DOMINY, Robert 478-757-3579 126 G
rdominy@centralgatech.edu
DOMKE-DAMONTE,
Darla, J 843-349-2129 456 G
ddamonte@coastal.edu
DOMPE, Rudy 818-719-6440 55 B
domperf@piercecollege.edu
DOMPIERRE, Michael, B 636-922-8355 288 E
mdompierre@stchas.edu
DOMZALSKI, James 570-740-0342 435 C
jdomzalski@luzerne.edu
DOMZALSKI, Jim 570-740-0342 435 C
jdomzalski@luzerne.edu
DONAGHUE, Joanne 860-434-5232 93 A
jdonaghue@lymeacademy.edu
DONAHOE, Patrick 406-994-4531 295 E
uccpd@montana.edu
DONAHOU, Andy 502-897-4011 205 H
adonahou@sbts.edu
DONAHUE, Ann 740-366-9123 399 E
donahue.5@osu.edu
DONAHUE, Ann, E 603-641-4123 306 F
annie.donahue@unh.edu
DONAHUE, Bob 614-947-6010 391 A
donahueb@franklin.edu
DONAHUE, Colin, J 818-677-2561 35 D
colin.donahue@csun.edu
DONAHUE, Eileen, B 203-432-5850 95 D
eileen.donahue@yale.edu
DONAHUE, Gabriel, M 973-290-4055 309 A
gdonahue@cse.edu
DONAHUE, Gerard, J 610-660-1016 446 C
gdonahue@sju.edu
DONAHUE, James, A 510-649-2410 48 H
president@gtu.edu
DONAHUE, James, P 423-652-6002 469 L
jpd@king.edu
DONAHUE, Janice, M 423-585-6921 476 B
janice.donahue@ws.edu
DONAHUE, Linda, V 802-654-2563 514 B
ldonahue@smcvt.edu
DONAHUE, Mark 281-899-1240 492 G
mark.donahue@remingtoncollege.edu
DONAHUE, Mick 360-416-7732 538 A
mick.donahue@skagit.edu
DONAHUE, Mick 360-679-5333 538 A
mick.donahue@skagit.edu
DONAHUE, Patrick 812-855-4269 173 C
donahued@indiana.edu
DONAHUE, Sally, C 617-495-1580 235 H
sdonahue@fas.harvard.edu
DONAHUE, Sandy 207-948-3131 219 H
sdonahue@unity.edu
DONAHUE, Tim 503-977-4338 419 G
tdonahue@pcc.edu
DONALD, Samuel 850-599-2644 118 G
samuel.donald@famu.edu
DONALDSON, Anthony 951-343-4841 31 G
adonaldson@calbaptist.edu
DONALDSON, Charles 501-569-3328 24 E
cwdonaldson@ualr.edu
DONALDSON, Charles, W 501-569-3328 24 E
cwdonaldson@ualr.edu
DONALDSON, Colleen 585-395-5118 352 F
cdonaldo@brockport.edu
DONALDSON, Cynthia 334-222-6591 5 F
cldonaldson@lbwcc.edu
DONALDSON, Dan 816-584-6846 287 H
daniel.donaldson@park.edu
DONALDSON, Glen 618-546-5659 155 H
glen.donaldson@doc.illinois.gov
DONALDSON, James, A 202-806-6700 98 B
jdonaldson@howard.edu
DONALDSON, Janice, W 904-620-2476 120 C
jdonalds@unf.edu
DONALDSON, Jennifer 858-598-1200 30 A
jdonaldson@aii.edu
DONALDSON, Jody 319-398-7186 186 H
jdonald@kirkwood.edu
DONALDSON, John, A 406-265-3520 295 G
jdonaldson@msun.edu
DONALDSON, Monde 251-414-2291 7 F
mdonaldson@shc.edu
DONALDSON, Penny 785-442-6054 193 D
pdonaldson@highlandcc.edu
DONALDSON, Scott 510-780-4500 53 I
sdonalds@lifewest.edu
DONALDSON, Stewart 909-607-3707 40 C
stewart.donaldson@cgu.edu
DONALDSON, Tracey 215-968-8091 423 E
donaldso@bucks.edu
DONAT, Kim 812-237-2215 173 A
kim.donat@indstate.edu
DONAT, Patricia 706-864-1840 134 D
pldonat@northgeorgia.edu
DONATH, Ben 712-749-2181 182 G
donath@bvu.edu

DONATO, CSC, John, J 503-943-7207 420 G
donato@up.edu
DONATUCCI, Nancy 724-339-7542 437 E
gradeservices@nbi.edu
DONAUDY, Tom 561-297-2663 118 H
tdonaudy@fau.edu
DONAVANT, Susan, H 804-752-7222 522 F
sdonavan@rmc.edu
DONCASTER, Bill 617-349-8525 230 D
wdoncast@lesley.edu
DONCASTER, Bill 617-349-8525 236 G
wdoncast@lesley.edu
DONCEVIC, John, G 724-847-6692 429 G
jgdoncev@geneva.edu
DONCITS, Diane 651-641-3472 264 J
ddoncits@luthersem.edu
DONCSECZ, Joseph, J 814-865-1355 438 F
jjd7@psu.edu
DONDERO, Eileen 239-590-7967 119 A
edondero@fgcu.edu
DONEGAN, Helen 407-317-7725 120 A
helen.donegan@ucf.edu
DONEGAN, John, P 734-487-3591 250 H
jdonega1@emich.edu
DONELAN, William 305-243-7873 122 F
w.donelan@miami.edu
DONELSON, Barbara, W 202-885-8552 100 A
bdonelson@wesleyseminary.edu
DONELSON, Charlotte 307-855-2154 555 G
donelson@cwc.edu
DONELSON, Frances, A 918-781-7263 407 B
donelsonf@bacone.edu
DONELSON, Rollin 336-334-5963 379 A
rollin_donelson@uncg.edu
DONELSON, Tery 573-875-7490 280 E
tldonelson@ccis.edu
DONESKY, Grant 206-726-5043 532 G
gdonesky@cornish.edu
DONEY, J.R 620-417-1101 196 B
jr.doney@sccc.edu
DONEY, Lisa 770-947-3817 139 B
lisa.doney@westgatech.edu
DONGES, James 812-855-3684 173 C
jdonges@indiana.edu
DONGES, John 434-592-3508 520 F
jcdonges@liberty.edu
DONHAM, Marilyn 734-973-3630 260 B
mdonham@wccnet.edu
DONHARDT, Gary, L 901-678-2231 474 C
donhardt@memphis.edu
DONIGER, Lauri 508-565-1086 245 D
ldoniger@stonehill.edu
DONIN, Robert, B 603-646-0101 305 A
robert.b.donin@dartmouth.edu
DONINI, Joseph 845-398-4040 349 H
jdonini@stac.edu
DONIUS, Mary Alice 914-654-5803 330 B
mdonius@cnr.edu
DONIUS, Robert, M 716-375-2600 348 C
rdonius@sbu.edu
DONKERSLOOT, Norman 616-392-8555 260 G
norman@westernsem.edu
DONLAN, Michael 540-891-3016 526 E
mdonlan@germanna.edu
DONLEY, Bob 515-201-3904 102 A
bdonley@iastate.edu
DONLEY, Laurie 330-339-3391 394 B
ldonley@kent.edu
DONN, Denise, C 209-954-5114 66 D
dcdonn@deltacollege.edu
DONNA, Jerry, A 217-581-3714 150 C
jdonna@eiu.edu
DONNELL, Dorothy 662-252-8400 277 C
ddonnell@rustcollege.edu
DONNELL, Floyd, D 812-374-5223 175 J
fdonnell@ivytech.edu
DONNELL, Joseph 701-349-3621 383 B
jdonnell@trinitybiblecollege.edu
DONNELL, Kathy, S 951-487-3002 58 B
kdonnell@msjc.edu
DONNELL, Richard, H 731-424-5883 469 M
rdonnell@lanecollege.edu
DONNELL, Robert 314-264-1000 292 E
robert.donnell@vatterott.edu
DONNELL, Shauna 479-968-0343 20 G
sdonnell@atu.edu
DONNELL, Shauna, H 479-968-0343 20 G
sdonnell@atu.edu
DONNELLA, II, Joseph, A 717-337-6280 429 H
donnella@gettysburg.edu
DONNELLAN, Barbara 617-369-3832 244 G
bdonnellan@mfa.org
DONNELLY, Crystal 610-892-1536 441 C
cdonnelly@pit.edu
DONNELLY, Daniel, K 412-396-5081 428 C
donnelly@duq.edu
DONNELLY, Eileen, G 302-356-6812 97 A
eileen.g.donnelly@wilmu.edu
DONNELLY, Gloria 215-762-4943 427 G
gd27@drexel.edu
DONNELLY, Jerry 503-978-5870 419 G
jdonnell@pcc.edu
DONNELLY, Jim 336-249-8186 369 F
jdonnelly@davidsonccc.edu

DOUGHERTY, Gail, E ... 717-764-9550 ... 426 D gdougherty@csb.edu
DOUGHERTY, Gail, I ... 717-764-9550 ... 426 C gdougherty@csb.edu
DOUGHERTY, James, M ... 330-344-6050 ... 397 C jdougherty@agmc.org
DOUGHERTY, Jason ... 304-865-6084 ... 541 F jason.dougherty@ovu.edu
DOUGHERTY, John ... 816-654-7303 ... 283 J jdougherty@kcumb.edu
DOUGHERTY, John, M ... 607-871-2108 ... 322 F dougherty@alfred.edu
DOUGHERTY, Lynne ... 516-463-6740 ... 335 H lynne.dougherty@hofstra.edu
DOUGHERTY, Mark, A ... 814-269-7115 ... 449 D mdougher@pitt.edu
DOUGHERTY, Michael ... 303-273-3554 ... 82 F mike.dougherty@is.mines.edu
DOUGHERTY, Shanin, L ... 570-326-3761 ... 440 K sdougher@pct.edu
DOUGHERTY, Steve ... 706-754-7701 ... 134 E sdougherty@northgatech.edu
DOUGHERTY, Tom, P ... 484-664-3110 ... 437 B tdougher@muhlenberg.edu
DOUGHERTY, Tracy, D ... 806-371-5106 ... 479 H tsdougherty@actx.edu
DOUGHERTY, Troy, J ... 208-496-9225 ... 142 G doughertyt@byui.edu
DOUGHTY, Bruce ... 303-457-2757 ... 84 F bdoughty@cci.edu
DOUGHTY, JR., Clyde ... 516-686-1133 ... 343 D cdoughty@nyit.edu
DOUGHTY, Corine ... 714-432-5628 ... 41 B cdoughty@occ.cccd.edu
DOUGHTY, JR., David, C ... 757-594-7365 ... 517 I doughty@cnu.edu
DOUGHTY, Kathryn ... 603-646-2215 ... 305 A kathryn.doughty@dartmouth.edu
DOUGHTY, Venita ... 303-762-6933 ... 83 I venita.doughty@denverseminary.edu
DOUGLAS, Alicia, R ... 816-501-4306 ... 288 D alicia.douglas@rockhurst.edu
DOUGLAS, Ashley ... 785-243-1435 ... 191 H adouglas@cloud.edu
DOUGLAS, Beth ... 717-867-6210 ... 434 C douglas@lvc.edu
DOUGLAS, Brian ... 774-455-7563 ... 237 B bdouglas@umassp.edu
DOUGLAS, Carmen ... 334-229-4667 ... 1 C cdouglas@alasu.edu
DOUGLAS, Chris ... 859-223-9608 ... 205 J cdouglas@spencerian.edu
DOUGLAS, Davison, M ... 757-221-3790 ... 517 J dmdoug@wm.edu
DOUGLAS, Delano ... 804-524-5214 ... 529 C ddouglas@vsu.edu
DOUGLAS, Diane, J ... 715-394-8218 ... 552 D ddougla2@uwsuper.edu
DOUGLAS, Gay ... 860-486-3426 ... 94 E gay.douglas@uconn.edu
DOUGLAS, Georgia, I ... 630-752-5779 ... 168 F georgia.douglass@wheaton.edu
DOUGLAS, James, M ... 713-313-1122 ... 499 G douglasj@tsu.edu
DOUGLAS, Jeffrey, A ... 309-341-7491 ... 155 E jdouglas@knox.edu
DOUGLAS, Jim ... 508-213-2333 ... 243 J jim.douglas@nichols.edu
DOUGLAS, Karen ... 325-793-4881 ... 490 F douglas.karen@mcm.edu
DOUGLAS, Katherine, P ... 607-962-9232 ... 331 D kdouglas@corning-cc.edu
DOUGLAS, Kelly, C ... 619-260-7974 ... 76 A kdouglas@sandiego.edu
DOUGLAS, Kimberly ... 626-395-6416 ... 32 E kdouglas@its.caltech.edu
DOUGLAS, Kris ... 765-677-2710 ... 174 E kris.douglas@indwes.edu
DOUGLAS, Kristen ... 770-537-5754 ... 139 B kristen.douglas@westgatech.edu
DOUGLAS, Laura ... 515-248-7206 ... 183 E lldouglas@dmacc.edu
DOUGLAS, Malcolm, C ... 847-574-5166 ... 155 G mdouglas@lfgsm.edu
DOUGLAS, Mary ... 419-824-3880 ... 395 D mdouglas@lourdes.edu
DOUGLAS, Michelle ... 304-696-2597 ... 543 G douglasm@marshall.edu
DOUGLAS, Minnie, L ... 562-408-6969 ... 26 H
DOUGLAS, Renee ... 231-591-5968 ... 251 B douglar3@ferris.edu
DOUGLAS, Scott, C ... 828-254-1921 ... 367 H sdouglas@abtech.edu
DOUGLAS, Shawn ... 478-471-0779 ... 133 E shawn.douglas@maconstate.edu
DOUGLAS, Sherry, L ... 308-432-6230 ... 299 G sdouglas@csc.edu
DOUGLAS, Stephen, L ... 304-293-4731 ... 544 E stephen.douglas@mail.wvu.edu
DOUGLAS, Tanya ... 317-543-4895 ... 177 H tdouglas@martin.edu
DOUGLAS-JOHNSON, Abegail ... 201-360-4011 ... 310 F ajohnson@hccc.edu

DOUGLASS, Barbara ... 860-738-6406 ... 90 F bdouglass@nwcc.commnet.edu
DOUGLASS, Brent ... 540-887-7201 ... 520 I bdouglass@mbc.edu
DOUGLASS, Claudia, B ... 989-774-3631 ... 249 G dougl1cb@cmich.edu
DOUGLASS, David, A ... 503-370-6447 ... 421 C ddouglas@willamette.edu
DOUGLASS, Debbie ... 559-730-3736 ... 42 B debbied@cos.edu
DOUGLASS, James ... 507-433-0611 ... 269 A jdouglas@riverland.edu
DOUGLASS, Jill ... 505-428-1351 ... 320 E jill.douglass@sfcc.edu
DOUGLASS, Scott, R ... 302-831-2200 ... 96 F douglass@udel.edu
DOUGLIS, Evan ... 518-276-6460 ... 347 D douglis@rpi.edu
DOUILLARD, Paul ... 718-405-3258 ... 330 A paul.douillard@mountsaintvincent.edu
DOUKAS, Peter, H ... 215-707-4990 ... 447 G peter.doukas@temple.edu
DOULIS, Peter ... 215-871-6900 ... 444 B peterd@pcom.edu
DOUMA, Debbie ... 850-484-1848 ... 114 G ddouma@pensacolastate.edu
DOUTHAT, James, E ... 570-321-4101 ... 435 D douthat@lycoming.edu
DOUTHIT, Tricia ... 303-273-3383 ... 82 F tdouthit@mines.edu
DOUTHITT, Robin, A ... 608-262-4847 ... 550 G douthitt@wisc.edu
DOVCI, Andrew ... 440-365-5222 ... 395 C
DOVE, John ... 606-886-3863 ... 201 C john.dove@kctcs.edu
DOVE, Robert, B ... 901-843-3800 ... 472 I dove@rhodes.edu
DOVE, Wendy ... 406-771-4399 ... 296 B wendy.dove@msugf.edu
DOVER, Gordon ... 901-272-6852 ... 471 B gdover@mca.edu
DOVERVAN, Darnell ... 954-783-7339 ... 106 D ddovervan@cci.edu
DOVI, John ... 703-821-8570 ... 524 D jdovi@stratford.edu
DOVI, Sharon ... 607-844-8222 ... 357 H dovis@TC3.edu
DOW, Brenda ... 315-792-7110 ... 356 B dowb@sunyit.edu
DOW, Dennis, C ... 650-508-3578 ... 59 G ddow@ndnu.edu
DOW, Larry ... 860-297-2157 ... 94 C larry.dow@trincoll.edu
DOW, Sarah ... 617-585-1296 ... 243 E sarah.dow@necmusic.edu
DOW, Steven, R ... 402-465-2255 ... 299 J sdow@nebrwesleyan.edu
DOW-MCDONALD, Jennifer ... 810-762-0533 ... 256 C jennifer.dow@mcc.edu
DOW-ROYER, Cathy, A ... 413-205-3321 ... 229 G cathy.dow-royer@aic.edu
DOW-SIMPSON, Evelyn ... 505-224-5217 ... 317 J evdow@cnm.edu
DOWD, Deirdre, M ... 516-876-3191 ... 353 D dowdd@oldwestbury.edu
DOWD, Dennis, C ... 214-333-5338 ... 484 C denny@dbu.edu
DOWD, John, P ... 843-661-1295 ... 458 C jdowd@fmarion.edu
DOWD, Julia, A ... 415-422-2531 ... 76 B dowd@usfca.edu
DOWD, Sarah ... 803-778-6668 ... 455 G dowdss@cctech.edu
DOWDAL, Bridgid, E ... 651-290-6405 ... 273 B bridgid.dowdal@wmitchell.edu
DOWDELL, John, J ... 419-289-5732 ... 384 D jdowdell@ashland.edu
DOWDEN, G. Blair ... 260-359-4050 ... 172 K bdowden@huntington.edu
DOWDEY, Don ... 432-837-8124 ... 501 B ddowdey@sulross.edu
DOWDLE, Deedie, K ... 334-844-9999 ... 1 G dowdldk@auburn.edu
DOWDLE, Maureen ... 203-332-5130 ... 90 B mdowdle@hcc.commnet.edu
DOWDLE, Rita ... 662-562-3206 ... 276 E rbdowdle@northwestms.edu
DOWDY, Kathleen, B ... 806-371-5389 ... 479 H kbdowdy@actx.edu
DOWDY, Lawrence, A ... 610-436-6974 ... 443 F ldowdy@wcupa.edu
DOWDY, Mickey ... 252-328-9595 ... 377 C dowdym@ecu.edu
DOWDY, Phyllis ... 910-695-3739 ... 373 E dowdyp@sandhills.edu
DOWE, Peter ... 585-395-2531 ... 352 F pdowe@brockport.edu
DOWELL, Chanda ... 309-854-1721 ... 145 E dowellc@bhc.edu
DOWELL, David ... 562-985-4128 ... 35 A ddowell@csulb.edu
DOWELL, Elise ... 212-678-8950 ... 337 G eldowell@jtsa.edu

DOWELL, Marcia, A ... 317-940-9257 ... 170 C mdowell@butler.edu
DOWELL, Marsha ... 864-503-5328 ... 463 A mdowell@uscupstate.edu
DOWER, Julia ... 603-542-7744 ... 304 H jdower@ccsnh.edu
DOWER, Karyn ... 209-381-6585 ... 57 C karyn.dower@mccd.edu
DOWLAND, Pam ... 812-357-6515 ... 179 E pdowland@saintmeinrad.edu
DOWLESS, Donald, V ... 706-233-7201 ... 136 E chimes@shorter.edu
DOWLING, Amy, S ... 570-321-4134 ... 435 D dowling@lycoming.edu
DOWLING, Earl ... 630-942-3416 ... 147 G dowlinge@cod.edu
DOWLING, Joseph, B ... 714-895-8158 ... 41 A jdowling@gwc.cccd.edu
DOWLING, Thomas, E ... 863-297-1051 ... 115 A tdowling@polk.edu
DOWLING, Victoria, A ... 618-537-2154 ... 157 G vadowling@mckendree.edu
DOWNES, Amanda ... 302-736-2318 ... 96 G downesam@wesley.edu
DOWNES, John ... 770-426-2646 ... 133 B jdownes@life.edu
DOWNES, Timothy ... 404-727-6532 ... 129 A timothy.downes@emory.edu
DOWNEY, Geraldine ... 212-854-0151 ... 330 F gd20@columbia.edu
DOWNEY, Jim ... 757-352-4891 ... 523 B jdowney@regent.edu
DOWNEY, John ... 704-337-2227 ... 375 G downeyj@queens.edu
DOWNEY, John, A ... 540-234-9261 ... 525 G downeyj@brcc.edu
DOWNEY, Nancy ... 207-859-4503 ... 217 G ndowney@colby.edu
DOWNEY, Nora ... 610-785-6582 ... 446 A financeopsscs@adphila.org
DOWNEY, Robert, F ... 724-938-4299 ... 441 G downey_r@calu.edu
DOWNING, Amy ... 617-730-7174 ... 243 I amy.downing@newbury.edu
DOWNING, Andre ... 502-456-6509 ... 206 B adowning@sctd.edu
DOWNING, Arthur ... 646-312-1020 ... 326 D arthur_downing@baruch.cuny.edu
DOWNING, Charlotte ... 585-292-2000 ... 341 H
DOWNING, Darrell ... 641-683-4253 ... 185 D ddowning@indianhills.edu
DOWNING, Irvine ... 956-882-4238 ... 505 C irv.downing@utb.edu
DOWNING, Kimberly ... 513-556-5028 ... 403 D kimberly.downing@uc.edu
DOWNING, Lenora ... 540-986-1800 ... 521 E downing@ncbt.edu
DOWNING, Lenora ... 540-986-1800 ... 541 E ldowning@national-college.edu
DOWNING, Lenora, S ... 540-986-1800 ... 521 J ldowning@national-college.edu
DOWNING, Lenora, S ... 540-986-1800 ... 521 F downing@ncbt.edu
DOWNING, Linda ... 407-582-1238 ... 122 I ldowning@valenciacollege.edu
DOWNING, Michael ... 508-336-8700 ... 453 C mdowning@jwu.edu
DOWNING, Rossann ... 816-604-4071 ... 285 I rossann.downing@mcckc.edu
DOWNING, Sherry ... 513-862-2743 ... 391 D
DOWNING, Teresa ... 603-899-4105 ... 305 B downingt@franklinpierce.edu
DOWNS, Amanda ... 662-720-7246 ... 276 D adowns@nemcc.edu
DOWNS, Fred ... 516-572-7214 ... 342 C fred.downs@ncc.edu
DOWNS, Kim ... 802-443-5208 ... 513 G kdowns@middlebury.edu
DOWNS, Ronald, J ... 502-231-5221 ... 204 A downsron@louisvillebiblecollege.org
DOWNS, Timothy, M ... 716-286-8342 ... 344 D downs@niagara.edu
DOWNS, Timothy, M ... 814-871-7549 ... 429 F downs@gannon.edu
DOWNS, Tom ... 631-244-3348 ... 332 D downst@dowling.edu
DOWNS, Wil ... 812-237-4114 ... 173 A wil.downs@indstate.edu
DOWSE, Bruce ... 308-535-3605 ... 298 I dowseb@mpcc.edu
DOWSETT, Carol ... 989-729-3405 ... 249 A carol.dowsett@baker.edu
DOXEY, Scott, Y ... 540-261-8577 ... 524 C scott.doxey@svu.edu
DOXIE-DIXON, Eloise ... 504-520-7515 ... 217 A edixon@xula.edu
DOYAL, Renee ... 972-792-7450 ... 486 C rdoyal@devry.edu
DOYLE, Amanda ... 337-482-6730 ... 216 D amandad@louisiana.edu
DOYLE, Bethany ... 724-852-3289 ... 451 B bdoyle@waynesburg.edu
DOYLE, Catherine ... 585-389-2123 ... 342 D cdoyle0@naz.edu

DOYLE, Cathleen, H ... 410-777-2902 ... 221 B chdoyle@aacc.edu
DOYLE, Christine, M ... 610-355-7151 ... 426 G cdoyle@dccc.edu
DOYLE, Creig ... 603-535-2331 ... 307 B cwdoyle@plymouth.edu
DOYLE, Denise ... 210-829-6003 ... 503 F ddoyle@uiwtx.edu
DOYLE, Diana ... 303-797-5701 ... 80 J diana.doyle@arapahoe.edu
DOYLE, Duane ... 270-843-6750 ... 199 G ddoyle@daymarcollege.edu
DOYLE, Duane ... 870-512-7863 ... 20 F duane_doyle@asun.edu
DOYLE, Eileen ... 212-229-8930 ... 342 E doylee@newschool.edu
DOYLE, Gerald ... 312-567-5203 ... 153 B doyle@iit.edu
DOYLE, James, P ... 530-346-6792 ... 30 D jpdoyle@aesa.com
DOYLE, James, R ... 312-362-8854 ... 148 F jdoyle@depaul.edu
DOYLE, Janice, B ... 301-445-1901 ... 227 A jdoyle@usmd.edu
DOYLE, Jeanette, M ... 508-831-5260 ... 247 B jmdoyle@wpi.edu
DOYLE, Jeff ... 254-710-1011 ... 481 I jeff_doyle@baylor.edu
DOYLE, Leslie ... 314-889-4503 ... 282 C ldoyle@fontbonne.edu
DOYLE, Lori ... 215-895-2100 ... 427 G lori.n.doyle@drexel.edu
DOYLE, Mary ... 831-459-4906 ... 75 A mdoyle1@ucsc.edu
DOYLE, OFM, Mathias, F ... 518-783-2333 ... 350 I mdoyle@siena.edu
DOYLE, Michael, H ... 563-588-7823 ... 186 I michael.doyle@loras.edu
DOYLE, Patrick ... 970-248-1847 ... 82 B pdoyle@mesastate.edu
DOYLE, Sheila ... 607-777-3844 ... 351 F sdoyle@binghamton.edu
DOYLE, CSC, Thomas ... 574-631-7394 ... 180 D tdoyle@nd.edu
DOYLE, William, H ... 651-638-6306 ... 261 I w-doyle@bethel.edu
DOYNE, Diane ... 312-369-7524 ... 148 B ddoyne@colum.edu
DOYON, Jane ... 508-531-1244 ... 238 B jdoyon@bridgew.edu
DOZIER, Belinda ... 270-886-1302 ... 198 H bdozier@brownmackie.edu
DOZIER, Cheryl ... 912-358-4000 ... 136 C ssupresident@savannahstate.edu
DOZIER, Jack ... 417-447-7570 ... 287 G dozierj@otc.edu
DOZIER, Luann, D ... 504-865-5794 ... 215 C ldozier@tulane.edu
DRABEK, Walter, J ... 716-888-2449 ... 325 G drabek@canisius.edu
DRABIER, Renee ... 817-735-2146 ... 504 C rdrabier@hsc.unt.edu
DRABIK, Mary, A ... 954-545-4500 ... 117 H mdrabik@sfbc.edu
DRABIK, Thomas ... 954-545-4500 ... 117 H
DRAEGER, Darren ... 415-388-1133 ... 48 D darren.draeger@lifeway.com
DRAGAN, Kimberly ... 860-738-6418 ... 90 F kdragan@nwcc.commnet.edu
DRAGHI, Mary Kathleen ... 814-871-7430 ... 429 F draghi002@gannon.edu
DRAGICH, Dennis ... 716-614-5980 ... 344 C ddragich@niagaracc.suny.edu
DRAGO, Dan ... 217-362-6419 ... 158 F ddrago@millikin.edu
DRAGO, Linda, S ... 412-396-5181 ... 428 C drago@duq.edu
DRAGOO, Ana ... 830-591-7330 ... 495 B amdragoo@swtjc.cc.tx.us
DRAHUS-CAPO, Deborah ... 787-751-3374 ... 561 D ddrahus@sanjuancapital.com
DRAIN, Cecil, B ... 804-828-7247 ... 525 E cbdrain@vcu.edu
DRAIN, Jerome ... 404-756-4443 ... 124 I jdrain@atlm.edu
DRAIN, Timothy, S ... 903-510-2458 ... 502 E tdra@tjc.edu
DRAKE, Autumn ... 405-912-9096 ... 408 D adrake@hc.edu
DRAKE, Brent, M ... 765-494-6136 ... 178 F bmdrake@purdue.edu
DRAKE, Carlene ... 909-558-4581 ... 54 D cdrake@llu.edu
DRAKE, Carolyn, C ... 559-244-2604 ... 72 A carolyn.drake@fresnocitycollege.edu
DRAKE, Charles, E ... 405-744-6494 ... 410 C cedrake@okstate.edu
DRAKE, Chris ... 972-273-3301 ... 485 B cdrake@dcccd.edu
DRAKE, James, A ... 321-433-7000 ... 101 J drakej@brevardcc.edu
DRAKE, Janet, M ... 701-845-7302 ... 382 A jan.drake@vcsu.edu

DRAKE, Kay, L ... 859-238-5467 ... 199 D
kay.drake@centre.edu
DRAKE, Linda, R ... 949-824-4016 ... 73 H
lrdrake@uci.edu
DRAKE, Margaret ... 661-722-6300 ... 28 J
mdrake@avc.edu
DRAKE, Marianne ... 413-662-5224 ... 238 F
m.drake@mcla.edu
DRAKE, Michael, V ... 949-824-5111 ... 73 H
chancellor@uci.edu
DRAKE, Peter ... 212-966-0300 ... 342 F
info@nyaa.edu
DRAKE, Ricky ... 334-229-4241 ... 1 C
rdrake@alasu.edu
DRAKE, Ricky ... 334-229-5104 ... 1 C
rdrake@alasu.edu
DRAKE, Roger, D ... 270-384-8040 ... 203 H
draker@lindsey.edu
DRAKE, Steve ... 618-283-4170 ... 155 H
DRAKE, Susan, K ... 217-243-9071 ... 152 C
sdrake@ic.edu
DRAKE, Tom ... 575-769-4994 ... 317 K
tom.drake@clovis.edu
DRAKE, Tonya, M ... 206-546-6910 ... 537 G
tdrake@shoreline.edu
DRAKE, JR., William, B ... 859-846-5310 ... 204 D
bdrake@midway.edu
DRAKE-DEESE, Kent ... 603-358-2346 ... 307 A
kdrakedeese@keene.edu
DRAKEFORD, Carolyn ... 803-705-4423 ... 455 D
drakefordc@benedict.edu
DRAKULICH, J. Scott ... 973-877-3370 ... 310 A
drakulich@essex.edu
DRALE, Christina, S ... 501-569-3204 ... 24 E
csdrale@ualr.edu
DRANE, Kim ... 307-382-1645 ... 556 F
kdrane-n@wwcc.wy.edu
DRANGER, Phyllis ... 219-785-5343 ... 178 H
pdranger@pnc.edu
DRANGMEISTER, Cheryl ... 505-428-1162 ... 320 E
cheryl.drangmeister@sfcc.edu
DRAPEAU, Guy ... 860-297-4210 ... 94 C
guy.drapeau@trincoll.edu
DRAPEAU, Robert, F ... 401-874-2109 ... 454 E
drapeau@uri.edu
DRAPELICK, Tony ... 802-258-3361 ... 514 C
tony.drapelick@worldlearning.org
DRAPER, Ann ... 831-459-5358 ... 75 A
ann@ucsc.edu
DRAPER, Charles ... 312-322-1742 ... 165 C
cdraper@spertus.edu
DRAPER, David ... 310-377-5501 ... 56 F
ddraper@marymountpv.edu
DRAPER, David, E ... 419-434-4202 ... 406 A
president@winebrenner.edu
DRAPER, Dennis ... 310-338-7504 ... 56 E
ddraper@lmu.edu
DRAPER, James ... 603-358-2492 ... 307 A
jdraper@keene.edu
DRAPER, Mary ... 727-726-1153 ... 103 B
DRAPER, Mary, C ... 727-726-1153 ... 103 B
marydraper@clearwater.edu
DRAPER, Nancy, J ... 405-912-9024 ... 408 D
ndraper@hc.edu
DRAPER, Randall, W ... 303-492-2695 ... 88 B
randall.draper@colorado.edu
DRASKOVIC, Inez ... 585-785-1322 ... 334 A
draskoi@flcc.edu
DRASS, Mike ... 302-736-2545 ... 96 G
drassmi@wesley.edu
DRAUDE, Barbara, J ... 615-904-8189 ... 473 F
barbara.draude@mtsu.edu
DRAUDT, Wayne, J ... 815-836-5235 ... 156 D
draudtwa@lewisu.edu
DRAUGALIS, JoLaine ... 405-271-6484 ... 413 D
jolaine-draugalis@ouhsc.edu
DRAUGHON, Bill ... 305-348-3961 ... 119 B
draughon@fiu.edu
DRAUGHON, Katherine, A ... 812-465-7107 ... 180 F
kdraughon@usi.edu
DRAUS, David, A ... 612-330-1033 ... 261 G
draus@augsburg.edu
DRAVES, Patricia, H ... 330-823-2690 ... 404 C
dravesph@mountunion.edu
DRAYER, Kevin, S ... 315-255-1743 ... 325 H
drayer@cayuga-cc.edu
DRAYFAHL, Perry, M ... 610-499-1291 ... 451 F
pmdrayfahl@widener.edu
DRAYNA, Jonathan ... 414-425-8300 ... 550 A
jdrayna@shst.edu
DRAYTON, Ronald ... 803-738-7606 ... 459 D
draytonr@midlandstech.edu
DREBLOW, Lewis, M ... 740-826-8050 ... 396 I
dreblow@muskingum.edu
DREES, Betty, M ... 816-235-1808 ... 291 E
dreesb@umkc.edu
DREFFS, Daryl, A ... 603-668-2211 ... 306 B
d.dreffs@snhu.edu
DREGER, Barb ... 920-735-4776 ... 553 G
dreger@fvtc.edu
DREGIER, Denise, M ... 443-412-2428 ... 223 B
ddregier@harford.edu
DREHER, John ... 404-627-2681 ... 126 A
john.dreher@beulah.org
DREHER, Karolina ... 610-796-8218 ... 421 F
karolina.dreher@alvernia.edu
DREHER, Melanie ... 312-942-7117 ... 163 B
melanie_dreher@rush.edu
DREIBELBIS, Elizabeth, M ... 717-846-5000 ... 452 G
DREIBELBIS, John, A ... 717-846-5000 ... 452 G
DREIFUSS, Susan, B ... 410-843-8852 ... 272 F
Susan.Dreifuss@waldenu.edu
DREISBACH, Joseph, H ... 570-941-7560 ... 450 B
dreisbachj1@scranton.edu
DREISSEN, Dan ... 701-662-1508 ... 382 D
dan.dreissen@lrsc.edu
DREITH, Michael, L ... 325-574-6501 ... 508 F
mdreith@wtc.edu
DREITZ, Donetta ... 620-417-1061 ... 196 B
donetta.dreitz@sccc.edu
DRELL, Persis ... 650-926-8704 ... 71 F
persis@slac.stanford.edu
DRENKOW, Daniel, D ... 605-274-5251 ... 463 H
dan.drenkow@augie.edu
DRENNEN, Carol, K ... 440-964-4234 ... 393 E
cdrennen@kent.edu
DRENNEN, Michelle ... 859-341-5627 ... 199 B
mdrennen@brownmackie.edu
DRENNON, Marsha, K ... 660-596-7223 ... 290 F
mdrennon@sfccmo.edu
DRESCHER, Kurt, W ... 978-468-7111 ... 235 F
kdrescher@gcts.edu
DRESSELHAUS, Mark ... 316-942-4291 ... 195 C
dresselhausm@newmanu.edu
DRESSEN, Dan ... 507-786-3962 ... 271 H
dressen@stolaf.edu
DRESSER, Charles, E ... 312-329-4267 ... 158 H
cdresser@moody.edu
DRESSER-RECKTENWALD,
Wendy ... 607-587-4025 ... 355 C
dressews@alfredstate.edu
DRESSMAN, Michael, R ... 713-221-8003 ... 503 D
dressmanM@uhd.edu
DREVON, CSC, Charles, D 574-239-8392 ... 172 J
cdrevon@hcc-nd.edu
DREW, Daniel, J ... 716-888-2569 ... 325 G
drewd@canisius.edu
DREW, Don ... 405-425-5577 ... 409 E
don.drew@oc.edu
DREW, John ... 617-827-6047 ... 237 D
john.drew@umb.edu
DREW, Rus ... 706-568-2022 ... 127 D
drew_rus@columbusstate.edu
DREW, Todd ... 402-872-2222 ... 299 H
tdrew@peru.edu
DREWELOW, Lonna ... 319-368-6468 ... 187 E
drewelow@mtmercy.edu
DREWENSKI, Shirley ... 708-596-2000 ... 164 F
sdrewenski@ssc.edu
DREWETT, Jerry, S ... 318-257-2769 ... 215 F
uajsd@latech.edu
DREWS, David ... 517-265-5161 ... 247 D
ddrews@adrian.edu
DREXLER, Brad ... 610-796-8216 ... 421 F
bradley.drexler@alvernia.edu
DREXLER, Jim ... 706-419-1408 ... 127 F
drexler@covenant.edu
DREYER, Allen, R ... 570-586-2400 ... 422 F
adreyer@bbc.edu
DREYER, Brenda ... 605-626-2552 ... 465 H
brenda.dreyer@northern.edu
DREYER, CSC, Chris, J ... 574-239-8383 ... 172 J
cdreyer@hcc-nd.edu
DREYER, Thomas, F ... 585-395-5205 ... 352 F
tdreyer@brockport.edu
DREYFUS, Lawrence, A ... 816-235-2576 ... 291 E
dreyfusl@umkc.edu
DREYFUS, Mark, B ... 757-671-7171 ... 518 G
president@ecpi.edu
DREYFUSS, Simeon ... 503-699-3961 ... 416 I
sdreyfuss@marylhurst.edu
DREYFUSS, Teresa ... 562-908-3404 ... 63 H
tdreyfuss@riohondo.edu
DRICI, Zahia ... 309-556-3760 ... 153 E
zdrici@iwu.edu
DRICKEY, Nancy ... 503-883-2201 ... 416 G
ndricke@linfield.edu
DRIER, Tracy, M ... 715-833-6498 ... 553 F
tdrier@cvtc.edu
DRIES, Richard ... 414-297-6572 ... 554 D
driesr@matc.edu
DRIESSNER, Johnnie ... 503-493-6549 ... 415 E
jdriessner@cu-portland.edu
DRIFKA, Amy ... 612-977-5368 ... 262 A
amy.drifka@capella.edu
DRIGGERS, Jon ... 803-799-9082 ... 461 A
jdriggers@southuniversity.edu
DRIGGERS, Kimberly, A ... 910-277-5561 ... 376 A
driggers@sapc.edu
DRIGGS, Bob ... 319-398-5516 ... 186 H
bdriggs@kirkwood.edu
DRILLING, Peter ... 716-652-8900 ... 326 A
pdrilling@cks.edu
DRIMMER, Alan ... 480-557-1696 ... 19 C
alan.drimmer@phoenix.edu
DRIMMER, Alan ... 602-943-2311 ... 19 D
alan.drimmer@wintu.edu
DRINAN, Helen, G ... 617-521-2070 ... 245 A
helen.drinan@simmons.edu
DRINKARD, Gretchen ... 314-454-7055 ... 282 E
gdrinkard@bjc.org
DRINKO, J. Randall ... 216-781-9400 ... 388 A
instruct@cie-wc.edu
DRINKO, Randy ... 757-464-4600 ... 530 E
instruct@cie-wc.edu
DRINKWATER, L. Ray ... 804-706-5064 ... 526 G
ldrinkwater@jtcc.edu
DRINNON, Henry ... 423-585-2629 ... 476 B
henry.drinnon@ws.edu
DRISCOLL, Daniel, R ... 630-889-6546 ... 159 E
ddriscoll@nuhs.edu
DRISCOLL, Eileen, G ... 207-948-3131 ... 219 H
edriscoll@unity.edu
DRISCOLL, Frederick ... 617-989-4135 ... 246 C
driscollf@wit.edu
DRISCOLL, Karen ... 360-992-2260 ... 532 A
kdriscoll@clark.edu
DRISCOLL, Laura ... 307-268-2733 ... 555 F
ldriscoll@caspercollege.edu
DRISCOLL, Lisa ... 508-849-3398 ... 230 C
ldriscoll@annamaria.edu
DRISCOLL, Lori ... 850-769-1551 ... 110 E
ldriscoll@gulfcoast.edu
DRISCOLL, Marcy, P ... 850-644-6885 ... 119 C
mdriscol@fsu.edu
DRISCOLL, Marsha ... 218-755-3984 ... 266 B
mdriscoll@bemidjistate.edu
DRISCOLL, Mary, C ... 716-375-7673 ... 348 C
mdriscol@sbu.edu
DRISCOLL, Michael ... 908-709-7113 ... 316 B
michael.driscoll@ucc.edu
DRISCOLL, Michael ... 907-786-1050 ... 10 I
provost@uaa.alaska.edu
DRISCOLL, Micheline ... 718-368-5436 ... 328 B
mdriscoll@kbcc.cuny.edu
DRISCOLL, Michelle ... 815-802-8524 ... 154 J
mdriscoll@kcc.edu
DRISCOLL, Paul, M ... 909-748-8159 ... 75 F
paul_driscoll@redlands.edu
DRISCOLL, JR., Robert, G 401-865-2090 ... 453 F
rdriscol@providence.edu
DRISCOLL, Robert, L ... 770-720-5504 ... 135 F
rld@reinhardt.edu
DRISCOLL, Terry ... 757-221-3332 ... 517 J
ecdris@wm.edu
DRISCOLL, William ... 617-745-6704 ... 234 C
william.driscoll@enc.edu
DRISKELL, Lavon ... 662-685-4771 ... 273 H
ldriskell@bmc.edu
DRISKILL, Jerry ... 318-671-4001 ... 214 E
DRISKO, Connie, L ... 706-721-2117 ... 130 B
cdrisko@georgiahealth.edu
DRIVER, C. Berry ... 817-923-1921 ... 495 E
bdriver@swbts.edu
DRIVER, Doug ... 970-943-7010 ... 89 B
ddriver@western.edu
DRIVER, Lisa, C ... 252-493-7354 ... 372 E
ldriver@email.pittcc.edu
DRIVER, Louise ... 501-882-8845 ... 20 D
oldriver@asub.edu
DRIVER-LINN, Erin ... 617-384-9033 ... 235 H
erin_driver-linn@harvard.edu
DRNEK, James ... 216-687-3977 ... 388 C
j.drnek@csuohio.edu
DROBNICKI, John ... 718-262-2025 ... 329 B
drobnicki@york.cuny.edu
DRODDY, Jason ... 225-578-5745 ... 212 F
jdroddy@lsu.edu
DROEGEMEIER, Kelvin ... 405-325-3806 ... 413 C
kkd@ou.edu
DROEL, Bill ... 708-974-5221 ... 159 A
droel@morainevalley.edu
DROGE, Michael ... 816-584-6202 ... 287 H
michael.droge@park.edu
DROLETTE, Frances ... 781-736-8302 ... 233 A
drolette@brandeis.edu
DROMPP, Michael, R ... 901-843-3795 ... 472 I
drompp@rhodes.edu
DRONE-SILVERS, Scott ... 217-234-5338 ... 155 H
dsilvers@lakeland.cc.il.us
DRONEY, Michael ... 330-494-6170 ... 402 A
mdroney@starkstate.edu
DRONSFIELD, Shelli ... 304-876-5107 ... 544 A
sdronsfi@shepherd.edu
DROOG, Sue ... 712-722-6017 ... 183 H
sdroog@dordt.edu
DROPKIN, Keith ... 617-423-4630 ... 231 E
kdropkin@bfit.edu
DROSS, Cindy ... 920-693-1385 ... 554 A
cindy.dross@gotoltc.edu
DROST, Donald ... 732-906-2568 ... 311 E
ddrost@middlesexcc.edu
DROST, Jim ... 641-673-1104 ... 189 I
drostj@wmpenn.edu
DROSTE, Pamela ... 843-574-6129 ... 461 G
pamela.droste@tridenttech.edu
DROTMAN, Barbara ... 203-857-7077 ... 90 G
bdrotman@ncc.commnet.edu
DROUART, Eric ... 802-681-2898 ... 514 D
edrouart@svc.edu
DROUGHT, Joe ... 815-921-4353 ... 162 F
i.drought@rockvalleycollege.edu
DROUIN, Amy ... 816-501-4628 ... 288 D
amy.drouin@rockhurst.edu
DROUIN, Nancy ... 207-216-4434 ... 219 C
ndrouin@yccc.edu
DROVER, Lisa, M ... 202-541-5228 ... 99 G
drover@wtu.edu
DROWN, Steven, A ... 530-754-6295 ... 73 F
sadrown@ucdavis.edu
DROZ, Elizabeth ... 607-777-2804 ... 351 F
droz@binghamton.edu
DRUCE, Zack ... 719-336-6660 ... 85 K
zach.druce@lamarcc.edu
DRUCKER, David ... 508-541-1508 ... 234 B
ddrucker@dean.edu
DRUCKER, Sheldon ... 201-692-2875 ... 310 B
drucker@fdu.edu
DRUCKREY, Melissa ... 601-979-2123 ... 275 A
melissa.l.druckrey@jsums.edu
DRUDING, Marlene ... 856-225-6020 ... 314 C
mdruding@camden.rutgers.edu
DRUEKE, Tim ... 803-323-2228 ... 463 D
DRUGOVICH, Margaret, L ... 607-431-4990 ... 335 B
president@hartwick.edu
DRUIN, Cathy ... 502-456-6509 ... 206 B
cdruin@sctd.edu
DRUMGOOLE, W, P ... 903-675-6220 ... 502 D
wdrumgoole@tvcc.edu
DRUMLUK, Sandy ... 607-844-8222 ... 357 H
drumlus@tc3.edu
DRUMM, Kathy ... 704-330-6717 ... 369 A
kathy.drumm@cpcc.edu
DRUMM, Kevin ... 607-778-5100 ... 324 G
DRUMM, Rene' ... 423-236-2766 ... 473 A
rdrumm@southern.edu
DRUMMER, Carlee ... 847-635-1671 ... 160 E
cdrummer@oakton.edu
DRUMMER, Carol, J ... 516-463-4876 ... 335 H
carol.j.drummer@hofstra.edu
DRUMMER FRANCIS,
Raydora, S ... 315-470-4815 ... 355 A
rsdrumme@esf.edu
DRUMMOND, Carl, N ... 260-481-5750 ... 174 A
drummond@ipfw.edu
DRUMMOND, Darl, E ... 847-543-2048 ... 147 H
ddrummond@clcillinois.edu
DRUMMOND, Gordon ... 480-212-1704 ... 18 F
DRUMMOND, Lew ... 205-391-2347 ... 7 A
ldrummondr@sheltonstate.edu
DRUMMOND, Marcy, J ... 213-763-7036 ... 55 D
drummomj@lattc.edu
DRUMMOND, Mary Bea ... 918-594-8223 ... 410 D
mary_bea.drummond@okstate.edu
DRUMMOND, R. Wayne ... 402-472-9212 ... 300 H
wdrummond2@unl.edu
DRUMMOND, Sarah, B ... 617-964-1100 ... 230 B
sdrummond@ants.edu
DRUMMY, Michael ... 714-997-6919 ... 39 C
mdrummy@chapman.edu
DRURY, Joel ... 405-422-1257 ... 411 G
druryj@redlandscc.edu
DRURY, Timothy ... 718-405-3239 ... 330 A
timothy.drury@mountsaintvincent.edu
DRUSE, Rick ... 620-227-9264 ... 192 B
rdruse@dc3.edu
DRY, Shana ... 803-313-7008 ... 462 D
drysf@gwm.sc.edu
DRYDEN, Barbara ... 386-226-6300 ... 105 B
dbfinaid@erau.edu
DRYE, Felix, M ... 919-536-7217 ... 369 G
dryef@durhamtech.edu
DRYER, Christy ... 410-287-6060 ... 222 A
cdryer@cecil.edu
DRYER, Norma ... 956-665-7021 ... 506 A
dryern@utpa.edu
DRYER, Peter ... 276-326-4281 ... 516 I
pdryer@bluefield.edu
DRYGAS, Emily ... 907-474-6631 ... 10 J
emily.drygas@alaska.edu
DU, Fang ... 330-829-8175 ... 404 C
dufang@mountunion.edu
DUARTE, Angelina ... 415-485-9505 ... 41 I
angelina.duarte@marin.edu
DUARTE, Lamar ... 210-486-3600 ... 479 D
pacsfa8@alamo.edu
DUARTE, Mark, A ... 671-735-2266 ... 559 D
mduarte@uguam.uog.edu
DUARTE, Melanie ... 617-912-9160 ... 232 E
mduarte@bostonconservatory.edu
DUBACH, John, F ... 413-545-2211 ... 237 C
dubach@chancellor.umass.edu
DUBANOSKI, Richard, A ... 808-956-6570 ... 141 B
dickd@hawaii.edu
DUBAY, Rene ... 406-444-0334 ... 294 J
rdubay@montana.edu
DUBBERT, Becky ... 970-675-3301 ... 82 D
becky.dubbert@cncc.edu
DUBBINK, Mary, T ... 724-334-6041 ... 440 B
mtd13@psu.edu
DUBE, CarolAnne ... 207-974-4817 ... 218 H
cadube@emcc.edu
DUBEAU, Peter ... 410-225-2371 ... 224 C
pdubeau@mica.edu

DUBEY, Marty 256-551-3136 4 J
marty.dubey@drakestate.edu
DUBIEL, Julia 805-962-8179 28 L
jdubiel@antioch.edu
DUBIN, Bruce 303-373-2008 87 G
DUBIN, Bruce 817-735-2244 504 C
bdubin@hsc.unt.edu
DUBINSKY, Zalman 973-267-8005 313 C
zalmandubinsky@gmail.com
DUBLE, Troy 706-419-1122 127 F
duble@covenant.edu
DUBLON, Felice 312-629-6800 164 A
fdublon@saic.edu
DUBMAN, Shirley 636-797-3000 283 H
sdubman@jeffco.edu
DUBOIS, Arthur 203-575-8056 90 E
adubois@nvcc.commnet.edu
DUBOIS, Glenn 804-819-4903 525 F
gdubois@vccs.edu
DUBOIS, Keith 207-780-5250 220 G
dubois@usm.maine.edu
DUBOIS, Melinda, C 585-245-5736 353 C
dubois@geneseo.edu
DUBOIS, Philip, L 704-687-5729 378 E
pdubois@uncc.edu
DUBOIS, Priscilla 540-985-9701 520 D
pldubois@jchs.eud
DUBOIS, Raymond 713-792-6161 507 A
DUBOIS, Shelly 480-515-7648 149 A
sdubois@devry.edu
DUBOIS, Toni 714-992-7074 59 D
tdubois@fullcoll.edu
DUBOSE, Cheryl 843-355-4162 463 C
dubosec@wiltech.edu
DUBOSE, Lisa 567-661-7314 400 H
lisa_dubose@owens.edu
DUBOSE, Lisa 567-661-7263 400 H
lisa_dubose@owens.edu
DUBOSE, Richard, A 270-745-5405 207 C
rick.dubose@wku.edu
DUBOSE, Rosa, L 904-680-7753 107 H
rdubose@fcsl.edu
DUBRAY, Kirsten 916-484-8175 56 A
dubrayk@arc.losrios.edu
DUBRAY, Robert, R 412-365-1641 425 B
rdubray@chatham.edu
DUBUC-PEDERSEN, Danielle 402-354-7259 299 E
danielle.dubuc-pedersen@methodistcollege.edu
DUBUIS, Dina 734-432-5309 254 G
ddubuis@madonna.edu
DUBY, Paul, B 906-227-2670 256 F
pduby@nmu.edu
DUCHARME-WHITE, Sherri 414-955-4145 548 E
sducharm@mail.mcw.edu
DUCHATELET, Martine 219-989-3194 178 G
duchatel@purduecal.edu
DUCHON, Maire, I 718-862-7166 339 H
maire.duchon@manhattan.edu
DUCHSCHERER, Eric, D 315-267-2350 354 C
duchsced@potsdam.edu
DUCIOAME, Lynn 940-397-4676 491 A
lynn.ducioame@mwsu.edu
DUCK, Patricia, M 724-836-9689 449 C
pmd1@pitt.edu
DUCKETT, Dwaine, B 510-987-0301 73 D
dwaine.duckett@ucop.edu
DUCKETT, Randy, R 803-641-3487 462 B
randyd@usca.edu
DUCKSWORTH, Stephanie 407-261-0319 107 L
sducksworth@fcnh.com
DUCKWORTH, Brad 414-382-6323 545 H
brad.duckworth@alverno.edu
DUCKWORTH, Cory, L 801-863-6158 511 C
duckwoco@uvu.edu
DUCKWORTH, Tony 918-444-3926 409 A
duckwo01@nsuok.edu
DUCLOS-BARRETT, Victoria 401-341-2345 454 D
duclosv@salve.edu
DUCOFFE, Robert 574-520-4133 174 C
ducoffe@iusb.edu
DUCOTE, Christopher, M 334-551-1566 3 F
chris.ducote@vc.edu
DUCRAY, Sarah 202-651-5000 97 E
sarah.ducray@gallaudet.edu
DUCUENNOIS, Sara 954-262-2103 114 B
ducuenno@nsu.nova.edu
DUDA, Laura 570-504-1588 433 A
dudal@lackawanna.edu
DUDA, Mark 570-961-7852 433 A
dudam@lackawanna.edu
DUDA, Stephen 570-504-1734 433 A
dudas@lackawanna.edu
DUDA, Teri 201-967-9667 307 G
td@berkeleycollege.edu
DUDAK, Nancy, J 610-519-7300 450 G
nancy.dudak@villanova.edu
DUDAS, Bertalan 814-866-8142 433 C
bdudas@lecom.edu
DUDAS, Maryann 724-838-4275 447 B
dudas@setonhill.edu
DUDAS, Philip 651-905-3542 261 J
pdudas@browncollege.edu
DUDEK, Scott 305-573-1600 100 K
sdudek@atienterprises.edu
DUDGEON, David 305-899-3727 101 F
ddudgeon@mail.barry.edu
DUDLEY, Brad, D 310-506-6825 61 G
brad.dudley@pepperdine.edu
DUDLEY, Christopher, H 336-841-4530 365 A
cdudley@highpoint.edu
DUDLEY, Deborah, L 315-267-2113 354 C
dudleydl@potsdam.edu
DUDLEY, Erastus, C 334-833-4582 4 E
tdudley@huntingdon.edu
DUDLEY, Erlene 573-592-4291 293 E
edudley@williamwoods.edu
DUDLEY, Jacklyn, K 270-809-4126 204 F
jackie.dudley@murraystate.edu
DUDLEY, Kim 225-675-8270 211 J
kdudley@rpcc.edu
DUDLEY, Lavoyd, R 318-274-6227 215 E
dudleyr@gram.edu
DUDLEY, Manuel 336-334-4822 370 E
mcdudley@gtcc.edu
DUDLEY, JR., Phillip, L 402-469-1449 298 C
pdudley@hastings.edu
DUDLEY, Sharese 219-980-6791 173 F
shaadudl@iun.edu
DUDLEY, Valerie 610-660-1015 446 C
vdudley@sju.edu
DUDLEY, Waller, T 540-458-8470 530 A
wdudley@wlu.edu
DUDLEY, William, C 413-597-4352 246 G
william.c.dudley@williams.edu
DUDLEY-ESHBACH, Janet, E 410-543-6011 228 D
jdudleyeshbach@salisbury.edu
DUDOLSKI, Robert 573-288-6571 281 D
rdudolski@culver.edu
DUDT, Susan 770-426-2700 133 B
sdudt@life.edu
DUEKER, Arlene 618-545-3131 155 A
adueker@kaskaskia.edu
DUELL, Charles 970-542-3158 86 A
charles.duell@morgancc.edu
DUENAS, Felicia 323-241-5376 55 C
duenasmv@lasc.edu
DUENAS, Hector 305-273-4499 103 C
hector@cbt.edu
DUENING, USN, Timothy 937-255-2195 556 H
timothy.duening@afit.edu
DUERKSEN, Deanne 620-947-3121 196 E
deanned@tabor.edu
DUERWACHTER, Kathleen, A 608-796-3072 553 A
kaduerwachter@viterbo.edu
DUESING, Jason, G 817-923-1921 495 E
jduesing@swbts.edu
DUESTERHAUS, Molly 864-596-9614 457 E
molly.duesterhaus@converse.edu
DUETT, Belinda, G 334-833-4519 4 E
bduett@huntingdon.edu
DUEWEKE, Anne, T 269-337-7418 253 F
Anne.Dueweke@kzoo.edu
DUEWEKE, Pauline 586-791-6610 248 G
pauline.dueweke@baker.edu
DUFAULT-HUNTER, David 626-815-2022 30 E
ddhunter@apu.edu
DUFF, Debra 414-256-1258 549 A
duffd@mtmary.edu
DUFF, John, A 727-864-8318 104 K
duffja@eckerd.edu
DUFF, Patricia 978-934-2369 237 F
patricia_duff@uml.edu
DUFF, Patrick 330-684-8920 403 C
pduff@uakron.edu
DUFFEL, Harry 901-751-8453 471 D
hduffel@mabts.edu
DUFFEL-JONES, Mona 504-816-4024 208 I
mduffeljones@dillard.edu
DUFFETT, Robert, G 605-995-2601 464 B
roduffet@dwu.edu
DUFFEY, Patrick 903-813-2361 481 A
pduffey@austincollege.edu
DUFFIE, James, E 561-868-3077 114 D
duffiej@palmbeachstate.edu
DUFFIE, Robert 361-582-2469 507 G
robert.duffie@victoriacollege.edu
DUFFIELD, Beth 931-540-2554 474 F
bduffield@columbiastate.edu
DUFFY, Andrew 215-895-6468 427 G
andrew.duffy@drexel.edu
DUFFY, Arwen 626-396-2311 29 G
arwen.duffy@artcenter.edu
DUFFY, Brian 215-972-2030 440 I
bduffy@pafa.edu
DUFFY, Brian 901-320-9768 478 B
bduffy@victory.edu
DUFFY, Charles 707-468-3011 57 A
cduffy@mendocino.edu
DUFFY, Christopher, L 215-670-9174 438 D
cduffy@peirce.edu
DUFFY, Daniel 206-296-5550 537 F
duffyd@seattleu.edu
DUFFY, Daniel 918-660-3090 413 D
daniel-duffy@ouhsc.edu
DUFFY, Dolly 574-631-2788 180 D
eduffy@nd.edu
DUFFY, James 717-337-6240 429 H
jpduffy@gettysburg.edu
DUFFY, James, P 757-683-5421 521 L
jduffy@odu.edu
DUFFY, Kevin 401-598-1760 453 C
kduffy@jwu.edu
DUFFY, Kristine 315-498-2222 345 D
duffyk@sunyocc.edu
DUFFY, Larry, K 580-477-7705 414 C
larry.duffy@wosc.edu
DUFFY, Lawrence 907-474-7464 10 J
lkduffy@alaska.edu
DUFFY, Mary Ellen 610-921-7515 421 D
mduffy@alb.edu
DUFFY, Michael 517-265-5161 247 D
mduffy@adrian.edu
DUFFY, Pamela, A 619-239-0391 37 D
pduffy@cwsl.edu
DUFFY, Rachelle, M 517-265-5161 247 D
rduffy@adrian.edu
DUFFY, Rochelle 413-528-7201 231 A
registr@simons-rock.edu
DUFFY, Trent 740-699-2338 400 A
duffyt@ohiou.edu
DUFFY, William 563-425-5354 189 C
duffyw@uiu.edu
DUFFY JOHNSON, Bernice 919-530-5235 378 A
bduffyj@nccu.edu
DUFFY TURNER, Marlo 918-594-8500 410 D
mduffy@osugiving.com
DUFORE, Timothy, R 330-972-7238 403 B
tdufore@uakron.edu
DUFOUR, Graciela 815-836-5270 156 D
dufourgr@lewisu.edu
DUFRESNE-REYES, Alice 408-848-4791 48 B
adufresnereyes@gavilan.edu
DUGAL, Gerald, M 978-837-5446 242 D
gerald.dugal@merrimack.edu
DUGAN, Brendan, J 718-489-5416 348 E
bdugan@stfranciscollege.edu
DUGAN, Christine, M 717-245-1180 427 E
duganc@dickinson.edu
DUGAN, Donald 262-691-5309 555 C
ddugan@wctc.edu
DUGAN, James 602-870-9222 13 M
jdugan@devry.edu
DUGAN, Jim 480-515-7648 149 A
jdugan@devry.edu
DUGAN, John 646-312-3320 326 D
john_dugan@baruch.cuny.edu
DUGAN, Marnie 309-341-5230 146 A
mdugan@sandburg.edu
DUGAN, Melinda, E 215-887-5511 451 D
mdugan@wts.edu
DUGAN, Michael 216-381-1680 397 E
mdugan@ndc.edu
DUGAN, Robert 850-474-3135 121 C
rdugan@uwf.edu
DUGAN, Robert, E 617-573-8536 245 E
rdugan@suffolk.edu
DUGAN, Thomas, F 718-270-2626 352 D
tdugan@downstate.edu
DUGAS, Ross 952-888-4777 270 F
rdugas@nwhealth.edu
DUGATKIN, David 845-257-3802 352 B
dugatkind@newpaltz.edu
DUGDALE, Kathy 218-733-5990 267 B
k.dugdale@lsc.edu
DUGGAN, Joseph 206-546-6949 537 G
jduggan@shoreline.edu
DUGGAN, Michael, B 617-573-8468 245 E
mduggan@suffolk.edu
DUGGAN, Roberta 707-826-5833 36 D
duggan@humboldt.edu
DUGGAN, Sean 806-742-2661 501 D
s.duggan@ttu.edu
DUGGAN, Theresa 516-299-2783 339 A
theresa.duggan@liu.edu
DUGGAN-GOLD, Lori 516-877-3262 322 A
duggangold@adelphi.edu
DUGGAR, Jan 215-627-7700 430 H
jduggar@holyfamily.edu
DUGGER, Jim 901-435-1680 470 B
jim_dugger@loc.edu
DUGGER, Karen 410-704-5456 228 E
kdugger@towson.edu
DUGGINS, Rick 336-917-5405 376 C
rick.duggins@salem.edu
DUGUID, Stephanie 601-643-8341 274 A
stephanie.duguid@colin.edu
DUHON, Gail 616-222-1431 250 C
gail.duhon@cornerstone.edu
DUHON, Stacey 318-274-6120 215 E
duhons@gram.edu
DUIGNAN, Kevin 845-398-4017 349 H
kduignan@stac.edu
DUIN, Diane 406-896-5841 295 F
dduin@msubillings.edu
DUISTERMARS, Blaine 712-325-3292 186 B
bduistermars@iwcc.edu
DUJARDIAN, Tamara 407-628-5870 106 B
tdujardian@cci.edu
DUKE, Carol 425-602-3083 530 K
cduke@bastyr.edu
DUKE, Charles 828-262-2234 377 B
dukecr@appstate.edu
DUKE, Kenneth 828-884-8144 362 D
dukekm@brevard.edu
DUKE, Lisa, A 770-423-6333 132 H
lduke8@kennesaw.edu
DUKE, Lori 919-760-2291 366 G
dukel@meredith.edu
DUKE, Phyllis 908-737-5000 311 B
pduke@kean.edu
DUKE, Shalamon 310-287-4423 55 F
dukesa@wlac.edu
DUKE, Steven 336-758-5938 380 B
dukest@wfu.edu
DUKE, Susan, I 716-851-1169 333 B
dukesi@ecc.edu
DUKE, Todd 765-973-8611 173 D
mtduke@iue.edu
DUKES, Charlene, M 301-322-0400 225 F
cdukes@pgcc.edu
DUKES, Gary 503-838-8221 419 C
dukesg@wou.edu
DUKES, Kenya 919-878-9900 99 D
DUKES, Melinda 423-636-7305 476 F
mdukes@tusculum.edu
DUKES, Michael 601-965-5980 273 F
mdukes@belhaven.edu
DUKES, Mona 843-355-4121 463 C
dukesm@wiltech.edu
DUKES, Mona, B 843-355-4121 463 C
dukesm@wiltech.edu
DUKES, Randy, J 504-286-5118 214 I
rdukes@suno.edu
DUKETT, William 724-503-1001 451 A
wdukett@washjeff.edu
DULABAUM, Mary 847-628-2089 154 I
mdulabaum@judsonu.edu
DULAN, Garland 256-726-7005 6 C
gdulan@oakwood.edu
DULAN, Silas 785-594-8364 190 C
silas.dulan@bakerU.edu
DULANEY, Jeri 979-627-0286 482 A
jeri.dulaney@blinn.edu
DULANEY, Malik 972-721-5064 502 F
mdulaney@udallas.edu
DULAY, Sarah 708-237-5050 160 C
sdulay@nc.edu
DULIN, Betsey 304-746-2087 543 G
bdulin@marshall.edu
DULIN, Bill 828-327-7000 368 G
bdulin@cvcc.edu
DULIN, Scott 617-236-8800 235 B
sdulin@fisher.edu
DULING, Ennis 802-468-1239 515 C
ennis.duling@castleton.edu
DULING, Sandra 802-468-1396 515 C
sandy.duling@castleton.edu
DULL, Calvin, R 336-838-6208 375 A
calvin.dull@wilkescc.edu
DULL, Charles 216-987-4677 389 A
charles.dull@tri-c.edu
DULLEA, Daniel, E 315-268-6428 329 C
ded@clarkson.edu
DULLEA, Robert 206-296-2590 537 F
dullea@seattleu.edu
DUMANTAY, Danilo 691-320-2480 559 A
comptroller@comfsm.fm
DUMAS, Carrie, M 404-752-1733 134 B
cdumas@msm.edu
DUMAS, Dan 502-897-4131 205 H
ddumas@sbts.edu
DUMAS, Maureen 401-598-2350 453 C
MDumas@jwu.edu
DUMAS, Roxanne 617-879-2208 246 F
rdumas@wheelock.edu
DUMAUAL, Roberto 718-522-9073 323 D
rdumaual@asa.edu
DUMERVE, Steeve 813-621-0072 117 D
sdumerve@sbtampa.com
DUMESTRE, Marcel 612-728-5100 271 G
mdumestr@smunm.edu
DUMKE, Alyce 920-735-5695 553 G
dumke@fvtc.edu
DUMKE, David 715-346-4171 552 B
ddumke@uwsp.edu
DUMM, Pamela 502-213-2109 202 B
pamela.dumm@kctcs.edu
DUMMER, Robin, K 530-226-4733 69 H
rdummer@simpsonu.edu
DUMOND, Debra 207-216-4400 219 C
ddumond@yccc.edu
DUMONT, Cathy 207-859-1167 219 G
alumni@thomas.edu
DUMONT, Monica, L 207-216-4311 219 C
mdumont@yccc.edu
DUMONT, Paul, E 972-860-7786 484 E
pdumont@dcccd.edu
DUMONT, Ronald 201-692-2811 310 B
ronald_dumont@fdu.edu

DUPUIS, Glenda .... 409-984-6316 .... 500 H
glenda.dupuis@lamarpa.edu
DUPUIS, Linda .... 920-465-2522 .... 551 A
dupuisl@uwgb.edu
DUPUIS, Phyllis .... 337-262-5962 .... 209 D
pdupuis@acadiana.edu
DUPUIS, Phyllis .... 337-521-8953 .... 212 B
phyllis.dupuis@southlouisiana.edu
DUPUY, Edward .... 912-525-5838 .... 136 B
edupuy@scad.edu
DURAJ, Jonathan .... 937-327-7814 .... 406 B
jduraj@wittenberg.edu
DURAL, Dalton .... 337-269-0620 .... 207 F
daltond@bluecliffcollege.com
DURAN, Benjamin, T .... 209-384-6101 .... 57 C
duran.b@mccd.edu
DURAN, Charlene .... 719-846-5559 .... 87 J
charlene.duran@trinidadstate.edu
DURAN, Dolly .... 305-892-7039 .... 111 K
dolly.duran@jwu.edu
DURAN, Dorothy .... 712-325-3202 .... 186 B
dduran@iwcc.edu
DURAN, Margret .... 806-743-2300 .... 501 E
margret.duran@ttuhsc.edu
DURAN, Richard .... 805-986-5808 .... 77 C
rduran@vcccd.edu
DURAN, Veronica .... 520-494-5260 .... 13 F
veronica.duran@centralaz.edu
DURAND, Bonita, R .... 716-878-4102 .... 353 A
durandbr@buffatostate.edu
DURANT, Benjamin .... 252-335-8792 .... 377 D
bdurant@mail.ecsu.edu
DURANT, Brian .... 518-743-2236 .... 322 B
durantb@sunyacc.edu
DURANT, Ivonne .... 727-786-4707 .... 102 F
idurant@cfi.edu
DURANT, Joseph .... 843-661-8086 .... 458 A
joe.durant@fdtc.edu
DURANT, Joyce, M .... 843-661-1300 .... 458 C
jdurant@fmarion.edu
DURANT, Leroy, A .... 803-535-5341 .... 456 D
ldurant@claflin.edu
DURANT, Linda, S .... 610-499-4123 .... 96 H
lsdurant@widener.edu
DURANT, Linda, S .... 610-499-4123 .... 451 F
lsdurant@widener.edu
DURANT, Natalie .... 860-512-3223 .... 90 C
ndurant@mcc.commnet.edu
DURANT, Zoe, W .... 580-581-2288 .... 407 D
zoed@cameron.edu
DURANTE, Angela .... 773-298-3191 .... 163 G
durante@sxu.edu
DURANTI, Alessandro .... 310-825-4017 .... 74 A
aduranti@college.ucla.edu
DURBIN, Bryce .... 706-238-7887 .... 125 G
bdurbin@berry.edu
DURBIN, Daniel, A .... 304-293-4008 .... 544 E
dan.durbin@mail.wvu.edu
DURBIN, Mark .... 407-569-1160 .... 107 G
mark.durbin@fcc.edu
DURCAN, Deborah, A .... 608-262-1311 .... 550 F
ddurcan@uwsa.edu
DURDEN, Drew .... 478-289-2090 .... 128 J
ddurden@ega.edu
DURDEN, Lori .... 912-486-7607 .... 134 H
DURDEN, William, G .... 717-245-1322 .... 427 E
durden@dickinson.edu
DUREE, Christopher .... 641-844-5720 .... 185 H
christopher.duree@iavalley.edu
DUREE, Christopher, A .... 641-844-5720 .... 185 J
christopher.duree@iavalley.edu
DUREN, Andrew, M .... 708-974-5203 .... 159 A
duren@morainevalley.edu
DUREN, Deborah .... 573-876-7212 .... 290 G
debd@stephens.edu
DURFEE, Carissa .... 617-989-4086 .... 246 C
durfeec@wit.edu
DURFEE, Mike .... 307-532-8346 .... 555 H
mike.durfee@ewc.wy.edu
DURFIELD, Jonathan .... 832-813-6615 .... 490 C
jonathan.durfield@lonestar.edu
DURGANS, Kenneth, B .... 317-278-3820 .... 174 B
kdurgans@iupui.edu
DURGIN, William .... 315-792-7200 .... 356 B
william.durgin@sunyit.edu
DURHAM, David, L .... 304-293-8220 .... 544 E
david.durham@mail.wvu.edu
DURHAM, Ed .... 410-287-1010 .... 222 A
edurham@cecil.edu
DURHAM, Gesele .... 414-229-3305 .... 551 C
gerdurham@uwm.edu
DURHAM, Jerry .... 319-226-2015 .... 181 E
durhamjd@ihs.org
DURHAM, John .... 252-328-6105 .... 377 C
durhamj@ecu.edu
DURHAM, John, R .... 610-519-7164 .... 450 G
john.durham@villanova.edu
DURHAM, Lisa .... 704-378-1135 .... 365 H
ldurham@jcsu.edu
DURHAM, Lynn .... 404-894-8261 .... 130 D
lynn.durham@carnegie.gatech.edu
DURHAM, Mark .... 406-683-7509 .... 295 B
m_durham@umwestern.edu

DURHAM, Rhonda .... 501-882-4442 .... 20 D
rsdurham@asub.edu
DURHAM, Ron .... 559-278-4062 .... 34 D
rdurham@csufresno.edu
DURIN, Lynne .... 815-825-2086 .... 155 C
lynne.durin@kishwaukeecollege.edu
DURINGER, Robert, A .... 406-243-4662 .... 295 A
robert.duringer@umontana.edu
DURISH, Aubrey, L .... 815-740-5047 .... 167 C
adurish@stfrancis.edu
DURKEE, Phillip, A .... 831-656-2517 .... 557 H
padurkee@nps.edu
DURKEE, Robert, K .... 609-258-6428 .... 313 A
durkee@princeton.edu
DURKEE, Wayne, E .... 919-536-7230 .... 369 G
durkeew@durhamtech.edu
DURKIN, Karen .... 856-415-2284 .... 310 E
kdurkin@gccnj.edu
DURKIN, Melissa .... 859-282-9999 .... 203 G
mdurkin@lincolntech.com
DURKIN, Rebecca .... 847-578-8351 .... 163 A
rebecca.durkin@rosalindfranklin.edu
DURKLE, Robert, F .... 937-229-4411 .... 404 A
robert.durkle@notes.udayton.edu
DURNEY, L. John .... 845-398-4116 .... 349 H
ldurney@stac.edu
DURNFORD, Ronald, R .... 504-520-5031 .... 217 A
rdurnfor@xula.edu
DURNIN, Ellen .... 203-392-5356 .... 91 I
durnine1@southernct.edu
DURNING, Lucinda .... 212-851-0627 .... 330 F
cdurning@columbia.edu
DUROCHER, Becky, L .... 985-448-4510 .... 216 A
becky.leblanc-durocher@nicholls.edu
DUROCHER, Jennifer .... 203-773-8577 .... 89 H
jdurocher@albertus.edu
DUROSS, Frank .... 315-792-5526 .... 341 E
fduross@mvcc.edu
DURR, David .... 501-812-2351 .... 23 C
ddurr@pulaskitech.edu
DURR, Elaine .... 336-278-5229 .... 364 A
edurr@elon.edu
DURR, Jeanne .... 608-342-1176 .... 551 F
durrj@uwplatt.edu
DURR, Kimberly, H .... 618-650-2477 .... 165 A
kdurr@siue.edu
DURR, Michael .... 315-792-7340 .... 356 B
durrm1@sunyit.edu
DURRENCE, J. Larry .... 270-686-4508 .... 202 E
DURRETT, Duane .... 940-627-2690 .... 508 C
ddurrett@wc.edu
DURSI, Joseph, F .... 914-594-4234 .... 343 F
joseph_dursi@nymc.edu
DURSI, Joseph, F .... 914-594-4487 .... 343 F
joseph_dursi@nymc.edu
DURSKY, Jill .... 641-673-1046 .... 189 I
durskyj@wmpenn.edu
DURSO, Thomas .... 218-637-7700 .... 430 H
tdurso@holyfamily.edu
DURST, Devoiry .... 732-414-2834 .... 317 F
DURST, Maribeth .... 352-588-8244 .... 116 E
maribeth.durst@saintleo.edu
DURST, Richard, W .... 440-826-2424 .... 384 H
rdurst@bw.edu
DURST, Steve .... 231-591-2254 .... 251 B
dursts@ferris.edu
DURY, Carl, G .... 615-353-3615 .... 475 D
carl.dury@nscc.edu
DUSENBURY, Renata .... 919-546-8200 .... 376 D
rdusenbury@shawu.edu
DUSENBURY, Renata .... 919-546-8395 .... 376 D
rdusenbury@shawu.edu
DUSHDUROVA, Valida .... 505-690-2671 .... 321 E
valida@unm.edu
DUSING, Roger .... 816-584-6386 .... 287 H
roger.dusing@park.edu
DUSINI, Paul .... 802-865-6451 .... 513 A
dusini@champlain.edu
DUSSAULT, Patrick, H .... 402-472-6951 .... 300 H
pdussault1@unl.edu
DUSSOURD, Ellen, A .... 716-645-2258 .... 351 G
dussourd@buffalo.edu
DUST, Nancy .... 870-368-2006 .... 23 A
ndust@ozarka.edu
DUSTER, Murrell, J .... 773-442-5449 .... 159 H
m-duster@neiu.edu
DUSTERHOFT, Bruce .... 407-569-1363 .... 107 G
bruce.dusterhoft@fcc.edu
DUTCHER, Debra .... 518-327-6082 .... 345 H
ddutcher@paulsmiths.edu
DUTCHER, Donald .... 315-866-0300 .... 335 E
dutcherdm@herkimer.edu
DUTCHER, James .... 518-255-5337 .... 354 E
dutchejm@cobleskill.edu
DUTCHER, Robin .... 802-828-2835 .... 515 D
dutcherr@ccu.edu
DUTFIELD, Stewart .... 518-828-4181 .... 330 E
stewart.dutfield@sunycgcc.edu
DUTKA, Mela .... 410-778-7752 .... 229 D
mdutka2@washcoll.edu
DUTLER, Sue .... 312-935-2210 .... 162 E
sdutler@robertmorris.edu
DUTREMBLE, Kathy .... 850-484-1630 .... 114 G
kdutremble@pensacolastate.eduedu

DUTREMBLE, Kathy .... 850-484-1547 .... 114 G
kdutremble@pensacolastate.edu
DUTRISAC, Gordon .... 425-558-0299 .... 533 C
gordon@digipen.edu
DUTSCHKE, Dennis .... 215-527-2901 .... 422 B
dutschke@arcadia.edu
DUTTA, Debasish .... 217-333-6715 .... 167 B
ddutta@illinois.edu
DUTTO, Larry .... 559-730-3808 .... 42 B
larryd@cos.edu
DUTTON, Chrys, M .... 619-594-6323 .... 36 E
cdutton@mail.sdsu.edu
DUTTON, Dennis .... 620-278-4275 .... 196 D
ddutton@sterling.edu
DUTTON, Jill, M .... 517-780-4547 .... 248 I
jill.dutton@baker.edu
DUTTON, Mary Pat .... 913-758-6110 .... 197 B
registrar@stmary.edu
DUTTON, Shelley, A .... 703-284-1549 .... 521 A
shelley.dutton@marymount.edu
DUTTON, Yunge H, K .... 507-457-1709 .... 271 G
ydutton@smumn.edu
DUTTON COX, Deborah .... 207-859-4393 .... 217 G
ddutton@colby.edu
DUVAL, Denise .... 312-935-4241 .... 153 F
dduval@icsw.edu
DUVAL, Derethia .... 415-338-2208 .... 36 F
derethia@sfsu.edu
DUVAL, Michael, W .... 806-371-5159 .... 479 H
mwduval@actx.edu
DUVAL, Roger .... 207-948-3131 .... 219 H
rduval@unity.edu
DUVALL, Darlene .... 575-439-3711 .... 319 E
duvall@nmsua.nmsu.edu
DUVALL, Helen .... 409-933-8482 .... 483 B
hduvall1@com.edu
DUWALL, John, E .... 304-293-7171 .... 544 E
john.duwall@mail.wvu.edu
DUZENSKI, Ted .... 706-595-0166 .... 125 D
tduzensk@augustatech.edu
DUZIK, David, B .... 402-465-2144 .... 299 J
dduzik@nebrwesleyan.edu
DUZIK, Don .... 712-274-6400 .... 189 H
don.duzik@witcc.edu
DVORACEK, Nick .... 920-424-7363 .... 551 D
dvoracek@uwosh.edu
DVORACSEK, Jo .... 727-341-6108 .... 116 F
dvoracsek.joe@spcollege.edu
DVORAK, Robert .... 415-380-1358 .... 48 D
robertdvorak@ggbts.edu
DVORAK, Susan .... 414-466-9777 .... 553 C
sdvorak@wspp.edu
DVORSKE, Tom .... 337-475-5510 .... 215 G
tdvorske@mcneese.edu
DWIGHT, Beverly, J .... 413-782-2210 .... 246 D
bdwight@wne.edu
DWIRE, Steven, W .... 518-454-5464 .... 330 C
dwires@strose.edu
DWORACZYK, Bill .... 214-768-3140 .... 494 F
billd@smu.edu
DWORAK, Joseph, V .... 651-638-6400 .... 261 I
j-dworak@bethel.edu
DWORKIN, James, B .... 219-785-5331 .... 178 H
jdworkin@pnc.edu
DWORSHAK, Lydia .... 701-483-2092 .... 381 E
lydia.dworshak@dickinsonstate.edu
DWOSKIN-SITZER, Paula .. 212-824-2224 .... 335 C
psitzer@huc.edu
DWYER, Daniel, J .... 406-243-6670 .... 295 A
daniel.dwyer@umontana.edu
DWYER, Gregory .... 914-337-9300 .... 331 A
gregory.dwyer@concordia-ny.edu
DWYER, James, P .... 989-964-4209 .... 258 A
jdwyer@svsu.edu
DWYER, Katelyn .... 617-296-8300 .... 236 E
katelyn_dwyer@laboure.edu
DWYER, Ken .... 508-854-4579 .... 241 C
krd@qcc.mass.edu
DWYER, Patricia .... 302-736-2352 .... 96 G
pdwyer@wesley.edu
DWYER, Sharon .... 805-648-8976 .... 77 D
sdwyer@vcccd.edu
DWYER, JR., Thomas, L .... 401-598-1410 .... 453 C
tdwyer@jwu.edu
DWYER, Thomas, P .... 804-752-7244 .... 522 F
tdwyer@rmc.edu
DYAL, Donald .... 806-742-2261 .... 501 D
donald.dyal@ttu.edu
DYAR, Jeanne .... 601-403-1330 .... 277 A
jdyar@prcc.edu
DYBATA, Christine .... 615-525-2800 .... 466 I
cdybata@argosy.edu
DYBDAHL, Tammy .... 303-753-6046 .... 87 F
tdybdahl@rmcad.edu
DYBEN, Andrea .... 561-803-2062 .... 114 C
andrea_dyben@pba.edu
DYBING, Olivia .... 617-348-6359 .... 246 A
dybing@urbancollege.edu
DYBWAD, Peter .... 510-841-9230 .... 79 F
pdybwad@wrightinst.edu
DYCHES, David .... 435-283-7058 .... 512 B
david.dyches@snow.edu
DYCK, Catherine .... 575-234-9219 .... 319 F
cdyck@cavern.nmsu.edu

DYCKMAN, Lise .... 415-575-6181 .... 32 D
ldyckman@ciis.edu
DYE, Danny, L .... 502-231-5221 .... 204 A
lbcpartner@louisvillebiblecollege.org
DYE, Hank, C .... 865-974-8184 .... 477 A
hank.dye@tennessee.edu
DYE, Joanna .... 309-796-5442 .... 145 E
dyej@bhc.edu
DYE, John .... 330-337-6403 .... 383 H
college@awc.edu
DYE, Larry .... 580-628-6217 .... 409 B
larry.dye@north-ok.edu
DYE, Michael .... 940-397-4278 .... 491 A
michael.dye@mwsu.edu
DYE, Ryan, D .... 563-333-6389 .... 188 D
DyeRyanD@sau.edu
DYE, Teresa .... 651-730-5100 .... 264 A
tdye@globeuniversity.edu
DYER, Amelia, G .... 703-461-1724 .... 522 C
adyer@vts.edu
DYER, Chris .... 417-255-7255 .... 286 G
cdyer@missouristate.edu
DYER, Cynthia, M .... 515-961-1519 .... 188 F
cyd.dyer@simpson.edu
DYER, Duane .... 909-447-2596 .... 40 E
ddyer@cst.edu
DYER, Edgar, L .... 843-349-2628 .... 456 G
dyer@coastal.edu
DYER, Gail, A .... 401-865-2463 .... 453 F
gdyer@providence.edu
DYER, John, C .... 214-841-3538 .... 485 E
jdyer@dts.edu
DYER, Kent .... 484-664-3140 .... 437 B
dyer@muhlenberg.edu
DYER, Kristyn, M .... 508-793-2418 .... 233 D
kdyer@holycross.edu
DYER, Nicole, L .... 419-289-5309 .... 384 D
ndyer@ashland.edu
DYER, Peggy, D .... 918-595-8100 .... 412 H
pdyer@tulsacc.edu
DYER, Robin .... 704-484-4128 .... 369 B
dyer@clevelandcommunitycollege.edu
DYER, Rodney .... 865-471-3235 .... 467 E
rdyer@cn.edu
DYER, Ruth .... 785-532-6224 .... 194 B
rdyer@ksu.edu
DYER, Steve .... 818-767-0888 .... 79 D
steve.dyer@woodbury.edu
DYER, Tom .... 206-283-4500 .... 144 G
tdyer@argosy.edu
DYER, Tom .... 206-393-3503 .... 530 G
tdyer@argosy.edu
DYJAK, Mary Lou .... 413-748-3271 .... 245 C
mdyjak@spfldcol.edu
DYK, Brian .... 303-477-7240 .... 84 I
briand@heritage-education.com
DYKE, Frances, L .... 541-346-3003 .... 419 B
fdyke@uoregon.edu
DYKEMA, Mark .... 717-545-4747 .... 432 D
DYKENS, Amy .... 660-248-6213 .... 279 K
amdykens@centralmethodist.edu
DYKES, Allison .... 404-727-8878 .... 129 A
allison.dykes@emory.edu
DYKES, Bill, G .... 513-851-3800 .... 402 C
bill.dykes@templebaptist.edu
DYKES, Danny .... 601-643-8403 .... 274 A
danny.dykes@colin.edu
DYKES, Donald, E .... 860-444-8213 .... 558 E
donald.e.dykes@uscga.edu
DYKSHOORN, Sharon .... 712-274-6400 .... 189 H
sharon.dykshoorn@witcc.edu
DYKSTRA, Arlen, R .... 314-392-2201 .... 286 C
adykstra@mobap.edu
DYKSTRA, Doug .... 808-235-7402 .... 142 C
dykstra@hawaii.edu
DYKSTRA, Frank .... 520-515-5311 .... 13 G
poncho@cochise.edu
DYKSTRA, Joel .... 575-624-8203 .... 319 C
dykstra@nmmi.edu
DYKZEUL, Carin .... 503-682-3903 .... 419 F
cdykzeul@pioneerpacific.edu
DYLAK, Sandy .... 914-251-6953 .... 354 D
sandy.dylak@purchase.edu
DYMEK, Cheryle .... 270-707-3707 .... 202 A
cheryle.dymek@kctcs.edu
DYMENT, Christine .... 508-588-9100 .... 240 E
DYMOWSKI, Tom .... 210-829-3131 .... 503 F
dymowski@uiwtx.edu
DYMSKI, M, L .... 617-349-8208 .... 236 G
mld@lesley.edu
DYNAK, David .... 303-556-2279 .... 88 D
david.dynak@ucdenver.edu
DYSARD, Nancy, J .... 443-412-2408 .... 223 B
ndysard@harford.edu
DYSSON, Melissa, J .... 217-245-3080 .... 152 C
mdyson@ic.edu
DZAU, Victor .... 919-684-2255 .... 363 I
victor.dzau@duke.edu
DZIADON, Ann, H .... 850-474-3063 .... 121 C
adziadon@uwf.edu
DZIAK, SJ, Ted .... 504-865-2304 .... 213 F
dziak@loyno.edu
DZIEDZIAK, Michael .... 610-341-1376 .... 428 D
mdzidzi@eastern.edu

E

EBER, Richard .... 417-667-8181.... 280 I
reber@cottey.edu
EBERHARDT, David .... 205-226-4731........ 2 C
deberhar@bsc.edu
EBERHARDT, Everett, V ..... 703-323-3266.... 527 C
eeberhardt@nvcc.edu
EBERHARDT, Paul .... 641-648-4611.... 185 I
paul.eberhardt@iavalley.edu
EBERHARDT, Ronald, E ..... 724-925-4071.... 451 E
eberhardtr@wccc.edu
EBERHART, Becky, J .... 847-866-3938.... 151 B
becky.eberhart@garrett.edu
EBERHART, Cathy .... 563-884-5114.... 188 C
cathy.eberhart@palmer.edu
EBERHART, Cathy .... 202-686-0876...... 99 A
cathy.eberhart@potomac.edu
EBERHART, Cathy .... 703-709-5875.... 522 B
cathy.eberhart@potomac.edu
EBERLE, Debra, A .... 812-941-2200.... 174 D
deberle@ius.edu
EBERLE, Jeanette .... 863-638-2978.... 123 C
eberleja@webber.edu
EBERLE, OSB, Peter .... 503-845-3304.... 417 A
peter.eberle@mtangel.edu
EBERLE, Sarah .... 512-313-3000.... 483 G
sarah.eberle@concordia.edu
EBERLEIN, Tim .... 800-342-7342...... 14 H
tim.eberlein@golfacademy.edu
EBERLY, Marian .... 973-300-2257.... 315 F
meberly@sussex.edu
EBERSOLD, E. Douglas ...... 573-592-4339.... 293 E
doug.ebersold@williamwoods.edu
EBERSOLD, Julie, A .... 417-836-5654.... 286 F
julieebersold@missouristate.edu
EBERSOLE, Bradley .... 225-216-8068.... 209 I
ebersoleb@mybrcc.edu
EBERSOLE, Erin, R .... 610-647-4400.... 431 B
eebersole@immaculata.edu
EBERSOLE, John, F .... 518-464-8524.... 333 F
jebersole@excelsior.edu
EBERSOLE, Ken .... 978-867-4500.... 235 E
ken.ebersole@gordon.edu
EBERSOLE, Kenney .... 352-371-2833.... 104 I
academicdean@dragonrises.edu
EBERSOLE, Susan .... 212-749-2802.... 339 I
sebersole@msmnyc.edu
EBERSOLE, Tim .... 717-477-1218.... 443 D
tmeber@ship.edu
EBERT, Derry .... 303-963-3338...... 81 K
debert@ccu.edu
EBERT, Lisa .... 718-982-2254.... 327 A
Lisa.Ebert@csi.cuny.edu
EBERT, Sharon .... 570-961-7860.... 433 A
eberts@lackawanna.edu
EBERTZ, Susan J, S .... 563-589-0265.... 189 G
library@wartburgseminary.edu
EBHOTEMEN, Richard .... 219-785-5247.... 178 H
rebhotemen@pnc.edu
EBNER, Timothy, J .... 801-581-5808.... 510 L
tebner@sa.utah.edu
EBNER-SMITH, Maria, E .... 248-370-4423.... 257 C
ebnersmi@oakland.edu
EBONG, Imeh, D .... 904-620-2700.... 120 C
i.ebong@unf.edu
EBRAHIMPOUR, Maling .... 727-873-4786.... 121 B
mebrahimpour@mail.usf.edu
EBSEN, David, W .... 541-885-1600.... 418 E
david.ebsen@oit.edu
EBSTEIN, Gemma, F .... 860-685-2535...... 95 C
gebstein@wesleyan.edu
EBY, Larry .... 302-225-6289...... 96 E
ebyl@gbc.edu
EBY, Tim, J .... 314-516-6765.... 291 F
ebyt@umsl.edu
ECCLES, John, G .... 434-544-8226.... 520 H
eccles@lynchburg.edu
ECCLES, Tom .... 845-758-7598.... 323 F
ccs@bard.edu
ECHANDI, Pura .... 787-786-3030.... 560 E
pechandi@ucb.edu.pr
ECHEGARAY, Luis .... 787-725-6500.... 560 G
lechegaray@sju.albizu.edu
ECHENHOFER, George .... 215-568-9215.... 436 E
gechenhofer@mccworks.org
ECHEVARRI, Rick .... 215-780-1410.... 446 G
rech@salus.edu
ECHEVARRIA, Agustin .... 787-763-5845.... 562 F
aecheva@inter.edu
ECHEVARRIA, Fabian .... 209-478-0800...... 50 I
ECHOLS, Carolyn, J .... 410-276-0306.... 226 D
cechols@host.sdc.edu
ECHOLS, Connie, C .... 530-226-4178...... 69 H
cechols@simpsonu.edu
ECHOLS, Cynthia .... 414-443-3639.... 549 A
echolsc@mtmary.edu
ECHOLS, Mike .... 402-557-7851.... 297 A
mike.echols@bellevue.edu
ECHOLS TOBE, Dorothy ...... 201-684-7621.... 313 D
dechols@ramapo.edu
ECK, Daniel, W .... 920-565-6589.... 547 H
eckdw@lakeland.edu
ECK, Debra .... 717-334-6286.... 435 A
deck@ltsg.edu
ECK, Don .... 503-654-8000.... 419 F
deck@pioneerpacific.edu
ECK, James, C .... 919-497-3201.... 366 E
jeck@louisburg.edu
ECK, Katherine, D .... 610-285-5057.... 439 K
kde1@psu.edu
ECK, Stephen .... 405-425-5118.... 409 E
stephen.eck@oc.edu
ECK, Tim .... 801-626-6352.... 511 D
teck@weber.edu
ECKARD, Shannon .... 704-504-5409...... 19 C
shannon.eckard@phoenix.edu
ECKARDT, Chip .... 715-836-2381.... 550 H
eckardpp@uwec.edu
ECKARDT, Jill .... 561-297-3904.... 118 H
jeckardt@fau.edu
ECKARDT, Michael .... 207-581-3465.... 220 A
michael.eckardt@maine.edu
ECKARDT, Paula, J .... 212-924-5900.... 357 A
pje@swedishinstitute.edu
ECKARDT, William, C .... 212-924-5900.... 357 A
wce@swedishinstitute.edu
ECKEL, Terri .... 928-776-2129...... 19 E
terri.eckel@yc.edu
ECKELHOEFER, Miriam ...... 617-876-0956.... 236 H
miriam.eckelhoefer@longy.edu
ECKELS, Robert, T .... 417-836-6865.... 286 F
bobeckels@missouristate.edu
ECKEN, Lou .... 989-463-7245.... 247 F
ecken@alma.edu
ECKERD, Tom .... 541-440-4600.... 420 F
Tom.Eckerd@umpqua.edu
ECKERT, Gerald, C .... 717-872-3775.... 443 C
jerry.eckert@millersville.edu
ECKERT, Jason, C .... 937-229-2045.... 404 A
Jason.Eckert@notes.udayton.edu
ECKERT, Phyllis .... 702-579-3539.... 302 C
peckert@kaplan.edu
ECKERT, Thomas, C .... 608-757-7770.... 553 E
tom.eckert@blackhawk.edu
ECKHARDT, Marjorie, N ..... 847-866-3902.... 151 B
meckhardt@garrett.edu
ECKLES, James, E .... 901-843-3745.... 472 I
ecklesj@rhodes.edu
ECKLES, Robert .... 212-410-8007.... 343 B
reckles@nycpm.edu
ECKLES, Robert .... 212-410-8480.... 343 B
reckles@nycpm.edu
ECKLEY, Lloydean, M .... 512-245-2158.... 501 C
le11@txstate.edu
ECKLIN, Laura .... 707-253-3369...... 58 F
lecklin@napavalley.edu
ECKLUND, Timothy, R .... 716-878-3506.... 353 A
eckluntr@buffalostate.edu
ECKMAN, James, P .... 402-449-2809.... 298 B
gupres@graceu.edu
ECKMAN, John .... 503-725-5401.... 418 G
eckman@pdx.edu
ECKMAN, Steven .... 386-506-3180.... 103 J
eckmans@DaytonaState.edu
ECKMAN, Steven, W .... 402-363-5621.... 301 F
seckman@york.edu
ECKRICH, Steve, E .... 541-737-4323.... 418 F
stevee@osubookstore.com
ECKSTEIN, Mark .... 716-829-8349.... 332 F
ecksteln@dyc.edu
ECKSTEIN, Rebecca, R .... 740-368-3025.... 400 F
rreckste@owu.edu
ECONOMOU, James, S .... 310-825-7943...... 74 A
jeconomou@conet.ucla.edu
ECSEDY, Brenda .... 617-879-2225.... 246 F
becsedy@wheelock.edu
ECUNG, Antonia .... 559-791-2308...... 53 A
aecung@portervillecollege.edu
EDAMATSU, Phyllis, Y .... 302-857-7023...... 95 F
edamatsu@desu.edu
EDBURG, Lisa .... 573-518-2294.... 286 B
lisae@mineralarea.edu
EDDIE, Walter .... 914-632-5400.... 341 G
weddiel@monroecollege.edu
EDDINGER, Frederick, G ..... 717-872-3275.... 443 C
frederick.eddinger@millersville.edu
EDDINGER, Pam .... 805-378-1407...... 77 B
peddinger@vcccd.edu
EDDINGER, Terry, W .... 336-882-3370.... 363 A
teddinger@ceds.edu
EDDINGTON, Chris .... 405-208-5000.... 410 A
ceddington@okcu.edu
EDDINGTON, Natalie, D .... 410-706-2176.... 227 C
neddingt@rx.umaryland.edu
EDDINS, Trevell .... 847-214-7391.... 150 D
teddins@elgin.edu
EDDINS-FOLENSBEE,
Florence, F .... 713-798-4768.... 481 H
florence@bcm.edu
EDDLEMAN, Bill .... 573-651-2062.... 290 D
weddleman@semo.edu
EDDLEMAN, Bill .... 573-651-2192.... 290 D
weddleman@semo.edu
EDDLEMAN, Donna, M .... 435-586-7712.... 511 A
eddleman@suu.edu
EDDY, Alex .... 513-244-8145.... 387 D
alex.eddy@ccuniversity.edu
EDDY, Jean .... 401-454-6419.... 454 B
jeddy@risd.edu
EDDY, Laura, M .... 620-341-5465.... 192 D
leddy@emporia.edu
EDDY, Walter, D .... 973-655-7894.... 311 G
eddyw@mail.montclair.edu
EDELBROCK, Craig, S .... 610-648-3202.... 439 G
cse1@psu.edu
EDELBROCK, Robert .... 877-442-0505...... 88 G
robert.edelbrock@rockies.edu
EDELEN, Charles .... 812-941-2400.... 174 D
cedelen@ius.edu
EDELMAN, David .... 805-687-1099...... 47 C
EDELSON, Paul .... 631-632-7052.... 352 C
paul.edelson@stonybrook.edu
EDELSON, Robert, E .... 302-356-6781...... 97 A
robert.e.edelson@wilmu.edu
EDELSTEIN, Ronald, A .... 323-563-4980...... 39 D
ronaldedelstein@cdrewu.edu
EDEN, Bradford, L .... 219-464-5099.... 181 A
brad.eden@valpo.edu
EDEN, Gene, F .... 610-799-1146.... 434 D
geden@lccc.edu
EDEN, James, V .... 262-335-5705.... 554 E
jeden@morainepark.edu
EDEN, Karen, S .... 563-884-5613.... 188 C
karen.eden@palmer.edu
EDEN, Peter, A .... 802-387-6730.... 513 E
petereden@landmark.edu
EDENFIELD, Joe .... 757-569-6744.... 527 E
jedenfield@pdc.edu
EDENS, Byron .... 423-493-4288.... 476 C
edensb@tntemple.edu
EDENS, Gary .... 915-747-7471.... 505 E
gedens@utep.edu
EDENS, Michael, H .... 504-282-4455.... 213 H
medens@nobts.edu
EDENS, Mike .... 903-693-2021.... 492 A
medens@panola.edu
EDENS, Ruth .... 617-964-1100.... 230 B
redens@ants.edu
EDER, Sheila .... 973-972-5449.... 316 C
edersh@umdnj.edu
EDERER, Jeff .... 303-256-9400...... 85 H
jederer@jwu.edu
EDGAR, Kimberly, S .... 615-898-2622.... 473 F
kimberly.edgar@mtsu.edu
EDGAR, Wendy .... 952-446-4138.... 263 E
edgarw@crown.edu
EDGE, James, N .... 417-268-6008.... 279 D
jedge@gobbc.edu
EDGE, Johnnie .... 478-553-2124.... 134 F
jedge@oftc.edu
EDGECOMBE, Nydia .... 718-518-4180.... 327 D
nedgecombe@hostos.cuny.edu
EDGERLY, Chelona .... 217-228-5432.... 161 E
edgerch@quincy.edu
EDGERTON, Teresa .... 402-486-2540.... 300 D
teedgert@ucollege.edu
EDGETTE, Bill .... 903-813-2240.... 481 A
bedgette@austincollege.edu
EDGEWORTH, Lori .... 419-251-1784.... 395 H
lori.edgeworth@mercycollege.edu
EDGINGTON, Rick .... 580-628-6220.... 409 B
rick.edgingt@north-ok.edu
EDGINGTON, Steve .... 714 879 3901...... 50 G
sedgington@hiu.edu
EDGREN, III, Gerald, R .... 920-924-3184.... 554 E
gedgren@morainepark.edu
EDICK, Nancy .... 402-554-2719.... 301 B
nedick@unomaha.edu
EDIDIN, Aron .... 941-487-4360.... 119 D
edidin@ncf.edu
EDIE, Shawn .... 781-768-7452.... 244 D
shawn.edie@regiscollege.edu
EDINBURGH, Mary .... 518-587-2100.... 355 F
mary.edinburgh@esc.edu
EDINGER, Denise .... 617-296-8300.... 236 E
denise_edinger@laboure.edu
EDINGTON, Mary .... 253-833-9111.... 534 C
medington@greenriver.edu
EDINGTON, Pamela .... 203-857-7309...... 90 G
pedington@ncc.commnet.edu
EDKINS, Ivonna .... 562-427-0861...... 44 G
iedkins@devry.edu
EDLER, Thomas .... 314-454-8515.... 282 E
tedler@bjc.org
EDLESTON, Robert, J .... 785-587-2800.... 194 F
robertedleston@matc.net
EDLEY, JR., Christopher .... 510-642-6483...... 73 E
edley@berkeley.edu
EDLUND, Kristy .... 303-762-6886...... 83 I
kristy.edlund@denverseminary.edu
EDMAN, Neal, A .... 724-946-7110.... 451 C
nedman@westminster.edu
EDMAN, Patricia .... 612-374-5800.... 263 I
pedman@dunwoody.edu
EDMAN, Sally .... 712-707-7321.... 188 B
sedman@nwciowa.edu
EDMINSTER, Warren .... 270-809-3166.... 204 F
warren.edminster@murraystate.edu
EDMISTEN, Steve, G .... 479-979-1380...... 26 A
sgedmist@ozarks.edu
EDMOND, Steven .... 512-505-3130.... 488 B
ssedmond@htu.edu
EDMONDS, Charles, W .... 570-321-4347.... 435 D
edmonds@lycoming.edu
EDMONDS, Gail, N .... 410-337-6150.... 222 [illegible]
gedmonds@goucher.edu
EDMONDS, James, Q .... 731-989-6092.... 468 K
jedmonds@fhu.edu
EDMONDS, Kerry .... 540-362-6630.... 519 E
kedmonds@hollins.edu
EDMONDS, Lawson, C .... 205-652-3545...... 10 A
ledmonds@uwa.edu
EDMONDS, Mabel .... 253-589-5510.... 532 B
mabel.edmonds@cptc.edu
EDMONDS, Melody .... 931-668-7010.... 475 C
medmonds@mscc.edu
EDMONDS, Michelle, K .... 434-949-1006.... 527 H
michelle.edmonds@southside.edu
EDMONDS, Mike .... 719-389-6684...... 81 L
medmonds@coloradocollege.edu
EDMONDS, William, A .... 724-938-4404.... 441 G
edmonds@calu.edu
EDMONDS TURNER,
Linda .... 617-348-6390.... 246 A
turner@urbancollege.edu
EDMONDSON, Angie, S .... 276-944-6108.... 518 I
aedmonds@ehc.edu
EDMONDSON, Charles, M 607-871-2101.... 322 F
edmondson@alfred.edu
EDMONDSON, Mary Lou .. 212-650-7808.... 326 H
edmondson@ccny.cuny.edu
EDMONDSON,
Melanie, M .... 443-334-2272.... 226 E
medmondson@stevenson.edu
EDMONDSON, Ricks .... 817-515-7726.... 496 A
ricks.edmondson@tccd.edu
EDMONDSON, William .... 814-871-7298.... 429 F
edmondso002@gannon.edu
EDMONSON, Frances .... 731-425-2654.... 475 B
fedmonson@jscc.edu
EDMONSON, Michele .... 661-362-3435...... 41 G
michele.edmonson@canyons.edu
EDMUNDSON, John .... 928-314-9500...... 12 C
john.edmundson@azwestern.edu
EDNEY, Kristyn .... 972-761-6884.... 485 C
kkedney@dcccd.edu
EDNEY, Norris .... 601-877-6120.... 273 C
nedney@alcorn.edu
EDOUARD, Randall .... 607-777-2791.... 351 F
redouard@binghamton.edu
EDRICH, Terri .... 972-860-4825.... 484 F
tedrich@dcccd.edu
EDRY, Ariel .... 305-534-7050.... 121 G
EDSALL, Denese .... 954-201-7502.... 102 A
dedsall@broward.edu
EDSALL, Paul .... 724-838-4236.... 447 B
edsall@setonhill.edu
EDSCORN, Steven, R .... 901-334-5812.... 471 C
sedscorn@memphisseminary.edu
EDSTROM, Julie, A .... 612-330-1740.... 261 G
edstrom@augsburg.edu
EDUARDO, Marcelo .... 601-925-3214.... 275 E
eduardo@mc.edu
EDWARDS, Alan, E .... 330-740-5672.... 397 C
aedwards@forumhealth.org
EDWARDS, Alan, T .... 252-493-7777.... 372 E
aedwards@email.pittcc.edu
EDWARDS, Anne .... 609-894-9311.... 308 C
aedwards@bcc.edu
EDWARDS, Annette, E .... 757-569-6708.... 527 E
aedwards@pdc.edu
EDWARDS, Bahola .... 432-685-4520.... 490 G
bahola@midland.edu
EDWARDS, Barbara .... 314-286-4870.... 288 B
bedwards@ranken.edu
EDWARDS, Barbara .... 303-556-4331...... 88 D
barbara.edwards@ucdenver.edu
EDWARDS, Benee .... 334-420-4291........ 7 I
btedwards@trenholmstate.edu
EDWARDS, Betty .... 334-420-4321........ 7 I
bedwards@trenholmstate.edu
EDWARDS, Betty .... 405-733-7380.... 411 I
eedwards@rose.edu
EDWARDS, Brad .... 803-321-5152.... 459 G
brad.edwards@newberry.edu
EDWARDS, Bruce .... 305-899-3050.... 101 F
bedwards@mail.barry.edu
EDWARDS, Bruce, L .... 419-372-7302.... 385 C
edwards@bgsu.edu
EDWARDS, Bud .... 334-745-6437........ 7 E
bedwards@suscc.edu
EDWARDS, Candace .... 410-386-8505.... 221 G
cedwards@carrollcc.edu
EDWARDS, Carlton, G .... 804-257-5851.... 529 D
cgedwards@vuu.edu
EDWARDS, Carol .... 806-742-0700.... 501 D
carol.edwards@ttu.edu
EDWARDS, Cathy .... 214-860-8685.... 485 A
cedwards@dcccd.edu
EDWARDS, Charles .... 630-844-3847.... 145 C
cedwards@aurora.edu
EDWARDS, JR., Charles .... 515-271-3194.... 184 A
charles.edwards@drake.edu
EDWARDS, JR., Charles .... 515-271-2871.... 184 A
charles.edwards@drake.edu
EDWARDS, Cynthia .... 404-297-9522.... 128 B
edwardsc@dekalbtech.edu

EISENHAUER, Walt 570-484-2168 443 A weisenha@lhup.edu
EISENHUTH, Wayne 507-222-4427 262 B weisenhu@carleton.edu
EISENMAN, Ann 563-244-7040 184 C aeisenman@eicc.edu
EISENMAN, Elaine 781-239-4355 230 G eeisenman@babson.edu
EISENMAN, Gordon 706-737-1400 125 C geisenman@aug.edu
EISENMANN, Linda 508-286-8212 246 E eisenmann_linda@wheatonma.edu
EISENMENGER, Paul 847-317-7087 166 B peisenme@tiu.edu
EISENSTADT, Robert, C 318-342-1151 216 E eisenstadt@ulm.edu
EISENSTEIN, Bruce 215-895-2359 427 G bruce.a.eisenstein@drexel.edu
EISENSTEIN, Laya 718-268-4700 347 B
EISENSTEIN, Paul 614-823-1609 400 G peisenstein@otterbein.edu
EISENTRAGER, Pete 816-235-2665 291 E eisentragerp@umkc.edu
EISERLOH, Matt 972-438-6932 492 C meiserloh@parkercc.edu
EISGRUBER, Christopher, L 609-258-3026 313 A eisgrube@princeton.edu
EISINGER, Robert 912-525-5801 136 B reisinge@scad.edu
EISLER, David, L 231-591-2500 251 B eislerd@ferris.edu
EISMAN, Gerald 415-338-1082 36 F geisman@sfsu.edu
EISMEIER, Elizabeth, A 845-437-5500 359 D eismeier@vassar.edu
EISNAUGLE, Eva 704-463-3424 375 E eva.eisnaugle@fsmail.pfeiffer.edu
EISNER, SND, Janet 617-735-9825 234 E president@emmanuel.edu
EITEL, Keith 817-923-1921 495 E keitel@swbts.edu
EITH, Gary, L 440-525-7084 394 F geith@lakelandcc.edu
EITT, Gretchen 703-526-5800 516 B geitt@argosy.edu
EJIAGA, Romanus 504-286-5384 214 I rejiaga@suno.edu
EJIGU, Gebeyehu 708-534-4120 151 C gejigu@govst.edu
EJIGU, Gebeyehu 708-534-8044 151 C gejigu@govst.edu
EKARD, Megan 619-849-2298 62 L meganekard@pointloma.edu
EKBOLM, Kathleen 508-541-1530 234 B deanbkstr@fheg.follett.com
EKE, Kenoye 318-274-2245 215 E
EKELAND, Mark 605-688-6895 466 B mark.ekeland@sdstate.edu
EKEY, William, M 443-412-2344 223 B bekey@harford.edu
EKURE, Ebuta 803-705-4431 455 D ekuree@benedict.edu
EL-AASSER, Mohamed, S 610-758-2981 434 E mse0@lehigh.edu
EL-BERMAWY, Mohamed 573-288-6344 281 D melbermawy@culver.edu
EL FATTAL, David 562-860-2451 38 J delfattal@cerritos.edu
EL-GAYAR, Omar, F 605-256-5799 465 G omar.el-gayar@dsu.edu
EL-HAGGAN, Ahmed 410-951-3850 228 B elhaggan@coppin.edu
EL-HAQQ, Mahdi 410-276-0306 226 D emahdi@host.sdc.edu
EL-HOUT, Eman 909-915-2100 29 I
EL MOHANDES, Ayman 402-559-4950 301 A aelmohandes@unmc.edu
EL-REWINI, Hesham 701-777-3412 381 D rewini@engr.und.edu
EL-SAYED, Jacqueline, A 810-762-7992 253 I jelsayed@kettering.edu
EL SHAYEB, Tarek 270-745-4857 207 C tarek.elshayeb@wku.edu
ELACHI, Charles 818-354-5673 32 E charles.elachi@jpl.nasa.gov
ELAM, Becky 951-487-3011 58 B belam@msjc.edu
ELAM, Demar 334-387-3877 1 D demarelam@amridgeuniversity.edu
ELAM, Harry, J 650-723-2300 71 F helam@stanford.edu
ELAM, Jacqueline 661-255-1050 32 C jelam@calarts.edu
ELAM, John, W 614-825-6255 383 I jelam@aiam.edu
ELAM, Joyce 305-348-2751 119 B elamj@fiu.edu
ELAM, Michael 409-933-8271 483 B melam@com.edu
ELAM, Richard, L 540-868-7042 526 H relam@lfcc.edu
ELAM, Terry 434-592-3966 520 F tlelam@liberty.edu
ELAM, Terry, D 706-771-4005 125 D telam@augustatech.edu
ELAND, Tom 612-659-6286 267 E thomas.eland@minneapolis.edu
ELBAUM, Ruth 847-866-3921 151 B ruth.elbaum@garrett.edu
ELBE, Joyce 845-848-7900 332 C joyce.elbe@dc.edu
ELBE, Mike 217-641-4308 154 G melbe@jwcc.edu
ELBEL, Jacqueline 972-438-6932 492 C jelbel@parkercc.edu
ELBERT, Dennis, J 701-777-2135 381 D delbert@business.und.edu
ELBOUSHI, Toni, C 323-563-4800 39 D tonielboushi@cdrewu.edu
ELBOW, Gary 806-742-2184 501 D gary.elbow@ttu.edu
ELCOMBE, Ron 507-453-2501 270 B relcombe@winona.edu
ELDAYRIE, Elias, G 352-392-4577 120 B eldayrie@ufl.edu
ELDE, Robert, P 612-624-2244 272 D elde@umn.edu
ELDER, Anissa 404-816-4533 132 B aelder@atl.herzing.edu
ELDER, Connie 619-660-4400 48 J connie.elder@gcccd.edu
ELDER, Dana 509-359-6305 533 D delder@ewu.edu
ELDER, Darla 814-732-2743 442 D delder@edinboro.edu
ELDER, Eric 310-314-6101 29 J
ELDER, Laura 770-531-6318 132 J lelder@laniertech.edu
ELDER, Stephen 719-389-6741 81 L selder@coloradocollege.edu
ELDER, Tom 903-832-5565 496 C thomas.elder@texarkanacollege.edu
ELDERT, John 617-266-1400 231 G
ELDERTON, R. Brian 215-951-1540 432 G elderton@lasalle.edu
ELDREDGE, Brad 406-756-3619 294 D beldredge@fvcc.edu
ELDREDGE, Kristen 303-837-0825 81 B keldredge@aii.edu
ELDREDGE, Shirley 423-472-7141 474 E seldredge@clevelandstatecc.edu
ELDRIDGE, Amy 312-935-4232 153 F eldridge@icsw.edu
ELDRIDGE, Bruce, T 757-455-5719 529 F beldridge@vwc.edu
ELDRIDGE, Jon 541-552-6221 419 A eldridgj@sou.edu
ELDRIDGE, Jonathan 541-552-6223 419 A eldridgj@sou.edu
ELDRIDGE, Joseph, T 202-885-3336 97 B eldridg@american.edu
ELDRIDGE, Karen 865-981-8207 470 F karen.eldridge@maryvillecollege.edu
ELDRIDGE, Kim 479-524-7424 22 C keldridge@adm.jbu.edu
ELDRIDGE, Linda, P 859-846-5340 204 D leldridge@midway.edu
ELDRIDGE, Maurice, G 610-328-8312 447 E meldrid1@swarthmore.edu
ELDRIDGE, Paul 303-963-3093 81 K peldridge@ccu.edu
ELDRIDGE, Randy 239-513-1122 110 K reldridge@hodges.edu
ELENICH, Richard 906-487-2763 255 E rjelenic@mtu.edu
ELEY, Curt 972-883-2270 505 D curt.eley@utdallas.edu
ELEY, Greg 765-998-5224 179 F greley@taylor.edu
ELFLAND, Carolyn, W 919-962-7244 378 D carolyn_elfland@unc.edu
ELFRINK, Ann Marie 918-495-6001 411 C aelfrink@oru.edu
ELFRINK, Stephanie 314-529-9370 284 F selfrink@maryville.edu
ELGER, William, R 409-266-2006 507 B welger@utmb.edu
ELGINBEHI, Iman 845-434-5750 356 H ielginbehi@sullivan.suny.edu
ELGIRUS, Marie Lourdes 781-239-3140 240 D melgirus@massbay.edu
ELHINDI, Mohamed 608-785-8309 551 B Melhindi@uwlax.edu
ELIADES, Shari 803-313-7062 462 D seliades@gwm.sc.edu
ELIADI, Carol 617-373-5680 241 F carol.eliadi@mcphs.edu
ELIAS, Helen 619-388-3709 65 F helias@sdccd.edu
ELIAS, Miguel 719-542-3181 85 E melias@intelliteccollege.edu
ELIAS, Stephanny, J 617-333-2010 234 A selias0104@curry.edu
ELIASSON-CREEK, Fia 253-833-9111 534 C feliasson-creek@greenriver.edu
ELICK, Cynthia, M 260-481-6204 174 A elick@ipfw.edu
ELICKER, Beth 207-775-3052 218 E belicker@meca.edu
ELICKER, Kreig 716-338-1040 337 E kreigelicker@mail.sunyjcc.edu
ELIPTICO, Frankie 670-234-5498 559 F frankiee@nmcnet.edu
ELIPTICO, Frankie, M 670-284-5498 559 F frankiee@nmcnet.edu
ELIQUE, Jose 702-895-3668 302 K chiefofpolice@unlv.edu
ELIZA, Lourdes 787-852-1430 562 D
ELIZALDE, Velma 361-354-2304 482 I velmae@coastalbend.edu
ELIZALDE, Velma 361-354-2707 482 I velmae@coastalbend.edu
ELIZANDRO, John 516-686-7605 343 D jelizand@nyit.edu
ELIZONDO, Javier 210-924-4338 481 G javier.elizondo@bua.edu
ELIZONDO, Laura, M 956-326-2225 497 B laura@tamiu.edu
ELIZONDO, Maria 956-664-4600 494 D marye@southtexascollege.edu
ELKESHK, Abed 718-405-3300 330 A abed.elkeshk@mountsaintvincent.edu
ELKIN, Rob 617-912-9112 232 E relkin@bostonconservatory.edu
ELKINGTON, John, A 808-675-3542 139 I elkingtj@byuh.edu
ELKINS, Becki, S 319-895-4595 183 D belkins@cornellcollege.edu
ELKINS, Donna 502-213-7112 202 B donna.elkins@kctcs.edu
ELKINS, Geoffrey, W 864-488-8347 459 A ekins-geoffrey@aramark.com
ELKINS, Jolene 910-672-1084 377 E jelkins@uncfsu.edu
ELKINS, Leah 513-241-4338 383 L leah.elkins@antonellicollege.edu
ELKINS, Mark 904-596-2445 122 A melkins@tbc.edu
ELKINS, Mary Jane 434-949-1063 527 H maryjane.elkins@southside.edu
ELKINS, Mary Jane 434-949-1051 527 H maryjane.elkins@southside.edu
ELKINS, Paula, S 706-886-6831 137 G pelkins@tfc.edu
ELKINS, Penny, L 678-547-6556 133 F elkins_pl@mercer.edu
ELKINS, Shawn 217-228-5350 161 E elkinsh@quincy.edu
ELKINS, Susan 931-372-3394 474 B selkins@tntech.edu
ELKINS, Vicki 580-477-7728 414 C vicki.elkins@wosc.edu
ELKS, Martha 404-752-1881 134 B melks@msm.edu
ELLARD, Mark 205-387-0511 2 B mellard@bscc.edu
ELLARD, Peter, C 518-783-2307 350 I pellard@siena.edu
ELLEFSON, David 775-753-2385 302 H davide@gwmail.gbcnv.edu
ELLENBERG, George, B 850-474-2077 121 C GEllenberg@uwf.edu
ELLENBERG, Meems 203-576-4542 94 D mellenb@bridgeport.edu
ELLENBERG, Todd, M 305-284-6047 122 F tellenberg@miami.edu
ELLENBERGER, Sheila, J 740-826-8260 396 I sheilaj@muskingum.edu
ELLENBURG, Phillip 615-966-6219 470 D phil.ellenburg@lipscomb.edu
ELLENS, S. Dean 630-617-3059 150 F ellenss@elmhurst.edu
ELLENS, Timothy, L 616-526-6475 249 E tje6@calvin.edu
ELLENSON, David 212-824-2201 391 E dellenson@huc.edu
ELLENSTEIN, Peter 620-331-4100 193 G pellenstein@ingefestival.org
ELLERMAN, Larry, M 318-342-5350 216 E ellerman@ulm.edu
ELLERTSON, Christopher, J 210-999-7207 502 C cellerts@trinity.edu
ELLERTSON, Shari 715-346-2385 552 B sellerts@uwsp.edu
ELLIBEE, Margaret, A 262-691-5207 555 C mellibee@wctc.edu
ELLIEHAUSEN-SLOBOZIEN, Kathryn 717-291-4215 429 E kathy.elliehausenslobozien@fandm.edu
ELLING, Wayne, H 206-281-2599 537 D elling@spu.edu
ELLINGER, Amanda 540-985-8513 520 D amellinger@carilionclinic.org
ELLINGER, John, M 419-372-2006 385 C johne@bgsu.edu
ELLINGHUYSEN, Scott 507-457-5050 270 B sellinghuysen@winona.edu
ELLINGSON, Mike 701-231-7307 381 H michael.ellingson@ndsu.edu
ELLINGSON, Scott, D 218-299-3004 263 B sellings@cord.edu
ELLINGTON, Christi 770-229-3442 137 B cellington@sctech.edu
ELLINGTON, Curt 870-762-3116 20 A cellington@smail.anc.edu
ELLINGTON, Keri 317-738-8086 171 C kellington@franklincollege.edu
ELLINGTON, Michael, A 304-293-4409 544 E michael.ellington@mail.wvu.edu
ELLINGTON, Ross 850-645-6900 119 C wellington@admin.fsu.edu
ELLINOR, Ben 941-359-4200 121 A
ELLINWOOD, Dawn 413-559-5412 235 G
ELLIOT, Autumn 406-265-3770 295 G autumn.elliot@msun.edu
ELLIOTT, Angela, P 563-333-6339 188 D ElliottAngelaP@sau.edu
ELLIOTT, Barbara 215-596-7558 450 A b.elliott@usciences.edu
ELLIOTT, Barbara, A 304-929-6727 542 H belliott@newriver.edu
ELLIOTT, Brian 503-588-9207 415 F belliott@corban.edu
ELLIOTT, Clara 413-552-2219 240 C celliott@hcc.edu
ELLIOTT, Clifton, R 843-355-4138 463 C elliottr@wiltech.edu
ELLIOTT, Craig 510-869-6627 64 J celliott@samuelmerritt.edu
ELLIOTT, Dan 417-268-6023 279 D delliott@gobbc.edu
ELLIOTT, David 603-526-3718 304 A delliott@colby-sawyer.edu
ELLIOTT, David, R 570-340-6075 435 F delliott@marywood.edu
ELLIOTT, Diane 717-361-1198 428 E elliottd@etown.edu
ELLIOTT, Donna 920-735-5638 553 G elliott@fvtc.edu
ELLIOTT, Emily 603-752-1113 304 I eelliott@ccsnh.edu
ELLIOTT, Gregg 719-587-7011 80 F greggelliott@adams.edu
ELLIOTT, Heather 419-423-2211 385 H helliott@brownmackie.edu
ELLIOTT, Holly 205-391-2211 7 A helliott@sheltonstate.edu
ELLIOTT, Jacquelyn 870-743-3000 22 G jelliott@northark.edu
ELLIOTT, James 620-947-3121 196 E jime@tabor.edu
ELLIOTT, James 304-367-4220 543 E rusty.elliott@fairmontstate.edu
ELLIOTT, Jeffrey 703-416-1441 519 F jelliott@ipsciences.edu
ELLIOTT, John 662-846-4040 274 B jelliott@deltastate.edu
ELLIOTT, John 646-312-3030 326 D john_elliott@baruch.cuny.edu
ELLIOTT, John, P 412-624-6127 449 A jelliott@bc.pitt.edu
ELLIOTT, Julie 610-341-1583 428 D jelliott@eastern.edu
ELLIOTT, Justin 574-522-0397 172 A justin.elliott@harrison.edu
ELLIOTT, Kathy 405-744-4188 410 C kathy.elliott@okstate.edu
ELLIOTT, Ken 828-327-7000 368 G kelliott@cvcc.cedu
ELLIOTT, Kiersten 310-434-4173 68 D elliott_kiersten@smc.edu
ELLIOTT, Larry 802-786-6996 515 D elliottl@ccv.edu
ELLIOTT, Lynn 310-377-5501 56 F lelliott@marymountpv.edu
ELLIOTT, Mark 330-499-9600 393 I mellio12@kent.edu
ELLIOTT, Melissa, J 940-552-6291 507 E mjelliott@vernoncollege.edu
ELLIOTT, Michael, S 870-297-4261 94 C michael.elliott@trincoll.edu
ELLIOTT, Patrick 201-761-7302 314 F pelliott@spc.edu
ELLIOTT, Peter, A 863-297-1081 115 A pelliott@polk.edu
ELLIOTT, Rennae 256-726-7533 6 C elliott@oakwood.edu
ELLIOTT, Richard 718-482-5501 328 C richard@lagcc.cuny.edu
ELLIOTT, Rita 815-226-3374 162 H relliott@rockford.edu
ELLIOTT, Rob 715-675-3331 554 G elliottr@ntc.edu
ELLIOTT, Scott, D 601-484-8619 275 C selliott@mcc.cc.ms.us
ELLIOTT, Stanley, J 919-658-2502 367 D selliott@moc.edu
ELLIOTT, Timothy 281-476-1878 493 E timothy.elliott@sjcd.edu
ELLIOTT, Tracy 941-752-5399 118 E elliott@scf.edu
ELLIOTT, Trish 602-387-7000 19 C trish.elliott@apollogrp.edu
ELLIOTT, Wyley 479-936-5174 22 H welliott@nwacc.edu

ELLIOTT CAIN, Pam ... 515-294-6218 ... 182 B
pelliott@iastate.edu
ELLIOTT-LONG, Karina ... 512-651-4700 ... 464 G
kelliott-long@national.edu
ELLIOTT-NELSON, Linda ... 928-344-7516 ... 12 C
linda.elliott-nelson@azwestern.edu
ELLIS, Annette, M ... 903-923-3313 ... 500 A
annette.ellis@marshall.tstc.edu
ELLIS, Barbara, J ... 336-256-7856 ... 377 F
ellis@ncat.edu
ELLIS, Bonnie ... 425-352-8125 ... 531 F
bellis@cascadia.edu
ELLIS, Bonny, R ... 717-780-2583 ... 430 E
brellis@hacc.edu
ELLIS, Brent ... 517-750-1200 ... 258 F
bellis@arbor.edu
ELLIS, Bret, R ... 801-626-7660 ... 511 D
bretellis@weber.edu
ELLIS, Brian ... 405-325-6211 ... 413 C
be@ou.edu
ELLIS, Bridget ... 252-399-6371 ... 362 A
bbellis@barton.edu
ELLIS, Butch ... 714-879-3901 ... 50 G
bellis@hiu.edu
ELLIS, Carl ... 206-782-2647 ... 537 A
cellis@sccd.ctc.edu
ELLIS, Charity ... 281-283-2019 ... 503 C
ellisc@uhcl.edu
ELLIS, Craig, D ... 717-764-9550 ... 426 C
cellis@csb.edu
ELLIS, Craig, D ... 717-764-9550 ... 426 D
cellis@csb.edu
ELLIS, David ... 503-768-7691 ... 416 F
dgellis@lclark.edu
ELLIS, David, A ... 513-529-3638 ... 396 D
ellisda2@muohio.edu
ELLIS, Denise ... 402-826-8251 ... 298 A
denise.ellis@doane.edu
ELLIS, Donna ... 570-674-6266 ... 436 F
dellis@misericordia.edu
ELLIS, Eric ... 541-881-5599 ... 420 E
eellis@tvcc.cc
ELLIS, Evelyn, A ... 860-444-8361 ... 558 E
evelyn.a.ellis@uscg.mil
ELLIS, Evelynn ... 603-646-3146 ... 305 A
evelynn.ellis@dartmouth.Edu
ELLIS, Evelynn ... 603-646-3197 ... 305 A
evelynn.ellis@dartmouth.edu
ELLIS, Gail ... 617-573-8144 ... 245 E
gellis@acad.suffolk.edu
ELLIS, George, W ... 813-974-5454 ... 120 D
gellis@usf.edu
ELLIS, Gerald ... 816-943-7460 ... 281 E
gellis@devry.edu
ELLIS, Graham ... 502-272-8218 ... 198 E
gellis@bellarmine.edu
ELLIS, Heidi, B ... 903-813-2235 ... 481 A
hellis@austincollege.edu
ELLIS, James, G ... 213-740-6422 ... 76 C
dean@marshall.usc.edu
ELLIS, Jennifer, A ... 401-456-8099 ... 454 A
jellis@ric.edu
ELLIS, Jessica ... 864-294-2164 ... 458 D
jessica.ellis@furman.edu
ELLIS, John ... 518-454-5166 ... 330 C
ellisj@strose.edu
ELLIS, OSA, Kail, C ... 610-519-4521 ... 450 G
kail.ellis@villanova.edu
ELLIS, Kenneth ... 443-885-3177 ... 224 F
kenneth.ellis@morgan.edu
ELLIS, Kimberly ... 409-944-1234 ... 486 H
kellis@gc.edu
ELLIS, Larry ... 607-729-1581 ... 332 A
financialaid@davisny.edu
ELLIS, Larry, E ... 803-321-5229 ... 459 G
larry.ellis@newberry.edu
ELLIS, Leann ... 817-515-7701 ... 496 A
leann.ellis@tccd.edu
ELLIS, Lee ... 618-374-5030 ... 161 D
lee.ellis@principia.edu
ELLIS, Lunette ... 434-848-6471 ... 523 G
lellis@saintpauls.edu
ELLIS, Machelle ... 580-371-2371 ... 408 I
mellis@mscok.edu
ELLIS, Marjorie, R ... 828-262-2180 ... 377 B
ellismr@appstate.edu
ELLIS, Meredith ... 607-274-3185 ... 336 G
mellis@ithaca.edu
ELLIS, Michelle ... 330-972-5860 ... 403 B
mellis@uakron.edu
ELLIS, Mike ... 423-614-8304 ... 470 A
mellis@leeuniversity.edu
ELLIS, Pamela ... 828-765-7351 ... 371 F
pellis@mayland.edu
ELLIS, Pat ... 315-229-5392 ... 349 E
pellis@stlawu.edu
ELLIS, Patricia ... 443-352-4034 ... 226 E
pellis@stevenson.edu
ELLIS, Rebecca ... 310-314-6035 ... 29 J
ELLIS, Robin ... 831-479-6298 ... 31 F
roellis@cabrillo.edu
ELLIS, Rodney ... 404-225-4609 ... 125 A
rellis@atlantatech.edu
ELLIS, Roger ... 636-949-4839 ... 284 C
ELLIS, Ronald, L ... 951-343-4210 ... 31 G
rellis@calbaptist.edu
ELLIS, Rose, R ... 203-857-7202 ... 90 G
rellis@ncc.commnet.edu
ELLIS, Sabrina ... 212-650-7226 ... 326 H
sellis@ccny.cuny.edu
ELLIS, Samuel ... 207-216-4436 ... 219 C
sellis@yccc.edu
ELLIS, Shannon ... 775-784-6196 ... 303 A
elliss@admin.unr.edu
ELLIS, Sharon ... 678-359-5158 ... 131 D
sharone@gdn.edu
ELLIS, Shirley ... 912-583-3287 ... 126 C
sellis@bpc.edu
ELLIS, Tom, M ... 423-425-4687 ... 477 D
tom-ellis@utc.edu
ELLIS, Wade ... 760-773-2513 ... 41 H
wellis@collegeofthedesert.edu
ELLIS, Wendy ... 802-287-8210 ... 513 D
ellisw@greenmtn.edu
ELLIS, William, N ... 325-649-8049 ... 488 A
wellis@hputx.edu
ELLIS DUKE, Rhea, V ... 570-945-8311 ... 432 C
rhea.ellis@keystone.edu
ELLISON, Barbara ... 614-416-6230 ... 385 E
bellison@bradfordschoolcolumbus.edu
ELLISON, David, R ... 202-231-3344 ... 557 G
david.ellison@dia.mil
ELLISON, Diane ... 585-475-7284 ... 347 G
dmeges@rit.edu
ELLISON, Gary ... 325-793-4610 ... 490 F
gellison@mcm.edu
ELLISON, Jenny ... 205-970-9203 ... 7 D
jellison@sebc.edu
ELLISON, Jimmy ... 325-674-2305 ... 478 H
jimmy.ellison@acu.edu
ELLISON, Kate ... 352-371-2833 ... 104 I
faa@dragonrises.edu
ELLISON, Kimberly ... 513-732-5221 ... 403 E
kimberly.ellison@uc.edu
ELLISON, Lori ... 239-513-1135 ... 123 D
lellison@wolford.edu
ELLISON, Maderia ... 928-532-6743 ... 17 B
maderia.ellison@npc.edu
ELLISON, Marjorie ... 573-288-6541 ... 281 D
mellison@culver.edu
ELLISON, Mark, A ... 704-403-1616 ... 362 E
mark.ellison@carolinashealthcare.org
ELLISON, Michael ... 817-531-7565 ... 502 A
mellison@txwes.edu
ELLISON, Pamela ... 216-987-4459 ... 389 A
pamela.ellison@tri-c.edu
ELLISON, Richard ... 530-898-3590 ... 34 A
reellison@csuchico.edu
ELLISON, Ron ... 503-842-8222 ... 420 D
ellison@tillamookbay.cc
ELLISOR, Kimberly, M ... 843-661-1190 ... 458 C
kellisor@fmarion.edu
ELLMORE, Philip, T ... 609-626-3546 ... 313 F
philip.ellmore@stockton.edu
ELLRICH, Phillip ... 618-545-3149 ... 155 A
pellrich@kaskaskia.edu
ELLWANGER, Carolyn ... 712-274-6400 ... 189 H
carolyn.ellwanger@witcc.edu
ELLWEIN, Todd, W ... 641-423-2530 ... 186 F
tellwein@kaplan.edu
ELLWOOD, David ... 617-495-1122 ... 235 H
david_ellwood@harvard.edu
ELLZEY, Janet, L ... 512-471-7020 ... 505 B
jellzey@mail.utexas.edu
ELMAN, Erin ... 215-717-6372 ... 448 H
eelman@uarts.edu
ELMAN, Jeffrey ... 858-534-6073 ... 74 D
deansocsci@ucsd.edu
ELMER, Wally, J ... 315-445-4280 ... 338 B
elmer@lemoyne.edu
ELMOGZHZY, Yehia ... 732-255-0400 ... 312 D
yelmogzhzy@ocean.edu
ELMORE, Beth ... 909-593-3511 ... 75 C
belmore@laverne.edu
ELMORE, Cecilia ... 573-341-6798 ... 292 A
elmorec@mst.edu
ELMORE, Chris ... 336-272-7102 ... 364 D
chris.elmore@greensborocollege.edu
ELMORE, Dana ... 601-925-3371 ... 275 E
elmore@mc.edu
ELMORE, Donna ... 803-535-1374 ... 460 C
elmored@octech.edu
ELMORE, Garland, C ... 317-274-4507 ... 174 B
elmore@iupui.edu
ELMORE, Kenneth ... 617-353-4126 ... 232 G
kennmore@bu.edu
ELMORE, Lela ... 352-395-5420 ... 117 E
lela.elmore@sfcollege.edu
ELMORE, Rheena ... 251-580-2145 ... 5 A
relmore@faulknerstate.edu
ELMORE, Ron ... 336-272-7102 ... 364 D
relmore@greensborocollege.edu
ELMORE, Troy, A ... 270-384-8144 ... 203 H
elmoret@lindsey.edu
ELNESS, Jodi, M ... 320-308-5087 ... 269 D
jelness@sctcc.edu
ELNICK, William ... 215-572-2172 ... 422 B
elnick@arcadia.edu
ELOFIR, Stacey ... 410-704-4414 ... 228 E
selofir@towson.edu
ELPERS, Stephanie ... 217-245-3030 ... 152 C
stephanie.elpers@ic.edu
ELROD, David ... 706-272-4473 ... 127 G
delrod@daltonstate.edu
ELROD, Roger ... 408-924-6112 ... 37 A
rogere@sbcglobal.net
ELSASS, Priscilla ... 508-793-7676 ... 233 C
pelsass@clarku.edu
ELSASS, Susan, C ... 603-577-6580 ... 304 J
elsass@dwc.edu
ELSBECK, George, J ... 607-431-4320 ... 335 B
elsbeckg@hartwick.edu
ELSE, Iwalani ... 218-723-6583 ... 262 I
ielse@css.edu
ELSE, Robert ... 805-965-0581 ... 68 B
else@sbcc.edu
ELSEA, Kathy ... 660-785-4130 ... 291 A
kelsea@truman.edu
ELSEN, Jake ... 410-644-6400 ... 226 G
ELSEN, Jake ... 602-548-1955 ... 15 C
ELSENBAUMER, Ron ... 817-272-1021 ... 505 A
elsenbaumer@uta.edu
ELSENER, Daniel, J ... 317-955-6100 ... 177 G
delsener@marian.edu
ELSENRATH, Gregory, M ... 314-421-0949 ... 290 H
financialaid@siba.edu
ELSEROAD, Arleen ... 949-451-5416 ... 70 E
aelseroad@ivc.edu
ELSIK, Heather ... 361-593-4191 ... 498 A
heather.elsik@tamuk.edu
ELSLEY, Judy ... 801-626-6186 ... 511 D
jelsley@weber.edu
ELSTAD, Pamela ... 218-723-2380 ... 267 B
p.elstad@lsc.edu
ELSTER, Janette ... 315-568-3053 ... 342 H
jelster@nycc.edu
ELSTON, Randy, L ... 931-540-2521 ... 474 F
relston@columbiastate.edu
ELSTON, Sheryl ... 219-877-3100 ... 170 A
selston@brownmackie.edu
ELSTON, Timothy, G ... 803-321-5197 ... 459 G
timothy.elston@newberry.edu
ELSWICK, Clark ... 575-562-4352 ... 318 A
clark.elswick@enmu.edu
ELTON, Nathan, J ... 704-894-2492 ... 363 F
naelton@davidson.edu
ELUKA, Johnny ... 336-315-7800 ... 99 D
ELWELL, Frank ... 918-343-7683 ... 411 H
felwell@rsu.edu
ELWELL, Jeffery, S ... 334-244-3600 ... 2 A
jelwell@aum.edu
ELWOOD, Sharon, K ... 307-674-6446 ... 556 C
elwood@sheridan.edu
ELY, Aiden ... 916-608-6500 ... 56 C
ELY, Eileen, E ... 253-833-9111 ... 534 C
eely@greenriver.edu
ELY, Janice ... 310-660-3109 ... 45 D
jely@elcamino.edu
ELY, Neal ... 925-424-1182 ... 39 A
nely@laspositascollege.edu
ELY, SJ, Peter ... 206-296-6158 ... 537 F
ely@seattleu.edu
ELY, Tami ... 276-376-1057 ... 525 C
tsd5p@uvawise.edu
ELY, Tim ... 610-526-6053 ... 430 D
tely@harcum.edu
ELZEY, Thomas, J ... 843-953-5092 ... 456 C
telzey@citadel.edu
ELZY, Cheryl, A ... 309-438-3481 ... 153 C
caelzy@ilstu.edu
EMAMI, Azita ... 206-296-5660 ... 537 F
emamia@seattleu.edu
EMAMI, Morteza ... 801-626-6853 ... 511 D
memami@weber.edu
EMANUEL, Catherine, B ... 770-720-9232 ... 135 F
cbe@reinhardt.edu
EMANUEL, Tom ... 217-244-8671 ... 167 B
emanuel@illinois.edu
EMBERTON, Sherilyn ... 903-923-2040 ... 486 D
academicaffairs@etbu.edu
EMBLETON, Kathleen ... 215-717-6972 ... 448 H
kembleton@uarts.edu
EMBREE, Angela ... 515-271-1843 ... 184 A
angela.embree@drake.edu
EMBREE, Katie ... 212-678-3991 ... 357 F
embree@tc.edu
EMBREE, Sean, P ... 603-641-4132 ... 306 F
sean.embree@unh.edu
EMBRY, Kathleen ... 312-980-9252 ... 153 G
kembry@iadtchicago.edu
EMBRY, Maria ... 831-443-1700 ... 50 A
maria_embry@heald.edu
EMCH, Laura ... 419-372-2945 ... 385 C
lemch@bgsu.edu
EMDY, Jim ... 831-476-9424 ... 47 E
librarian@fivebranches.edu
EMENGER, Nancy, E ... 801-626-6017 ... 511 D
nemenger@weber.edu
EMEOTT, Robert, E ... 407-366-9493 ... 115 I
remeott@rts.edu
EMERSON, Brian ... 216-373-5177 ... 397 E
bemerson@ndc.edu
EMERSON, Colleen ... 401-341-2331 ... 454 D
emersonc@salve.edu
EMERSON, Nate ... 507-453-2711 ... 267 F
nemerson@southeastmn.edu
EMERSON, Sally ... 608-789-6083 ... 555 D
emersons@westerntc.edu
EMERSON, Stephen, G ... 610-896-1021 ... 430 G
semerson@haverford.edu
EMERSON, Steve ... 951-343-4415 ... 31 G
semerson@calbaptist.edu
EMERSON, Wendy, R ... 336-734-7540 ... 370 C
wemerson@forsythtech.edu
EMERSON, Yolanda ... 562-908-3405 ... 63 H
yemerson@riohondo.edu
EMERSON CLAPP, Susan ... 413-528-7253 ... 231 A
sclapp@simons-rock.edu
EMERT, Chuck ... 619-201-8995 ... 70 J
cemert@socalsem.edu
EMERY, John ... 661-654-2157 ... 33 H
jemery@csub.edu
EMERY, Kathleen ... 407-226-6491 ... 104 D
kemery@devry.edu
EMERY, Kathy, S ... 615-353-3259 ... 475 D
kathy.emery@nscc.edu
EMERY, Lea ... 914-251-6105 ... 354 D
lea.emery@purchase.edu
EMERY, Monica ... 716-375-2400 ... 348 C
memery@sbu.edu
EMERY, Rebecca, A ... 410-543-6075 ... 228 D
raemery@salisbury.edu
EMERY, Robert ... 518-445-2339 ... 322 D
remer@albanylaw.edu
EMERY, Scott ... 510-594-3753 ... 31 J
semery@cca.edu
EMERY, Sheila ... 360-596-5360 ... 538 B
semery@spscc.ctc.edu
EMERZIAN, Janice ... 559-638-3641 ... 72 B
janice.emerzian@scccd.com
EMERZIAN, Janice ... 559-442-8237 ... 72 A
janice.emerzian@fresnocitycollege.edu
EMETT, Ray ... 801-957-4403 ... 512 C
ray.emett@slcc.edu
EMFINGER, Susan ... 410-455-2766 ... 227 D
emfinger@umbc.edu
EMIHOVICH, Catherine, H ... 352-392-0728 ... 120 B
cemihovich@coe.ufl.edu
EMILIO, Linda ... 909-469-8421 ... 78 D
lemilio@westernu.edu
EMIRU, Tadael ... 651-450-3572 ... 266 I
temiru@inverhills.edu
EMLET, Jerry, D ... 860-727-6906 ... 92 C
jemlet@goodwin.edu
EMM, William ... 315-498-2530 ... 345 D
emmw@sunyocc.edu
EMMA, Janine ... 732-729-3818 ... 309 D
jemma@devry.edu
EMMANUEL, Narbeth, R ... 618-650-2020 ... 165 A
nemmanu@siue.edu
EMMERLING, Andrew ... 717-757-1100 ... 452 I
drew.emmerling@yti.edu
EMMERSON, Richard, K ... 718-862-7345 ... 339 H
richard.emmerson@manhattan.edu
EMMERT, Michelle ... 909-469-5616 ... 78 D
memmert@westernu.edu
EMMICK, Joseph, R ... 765-361-6367 ... 181 C
emmickj@wabash.edu
EMMIL, Bruce ... 701-224-5758 ... 382 B
bruce.emmil@bismarckstate.edu
EMMONS, Carol-Ann ... 312-567-3827 ... 153 B
emmons@iit.edu
EMMONS, Sarah ... 859-233-8120 ... 206 E
semmons@transy.edu
EMMONS, Todd, C ... 508-854-7530 ... 241 C
temmons@qcc.mass.edu
EMMSLEY, Komiti ... 684-699-9155 ... 558 I
k.emmsley@amsamoa.edu
EMOND, Gean Ann ... 850-484-1728 ... 114 G
gemond@pensacolastate.edu
EMOND, Susie ... 989-964-6067 ... 258 A
semond@svsu.edu
EMORY, Cynthia ... 301-696-3566 ... 223 C
emory@hood.edu
EMORY, Douglas, J ... 425-739-8311 ... 535 B
doug.emory@lwtc.edu
EMORY, Fran ... 252-222-6144 ... 368 F
emoryf@carteret.edu
EMORY, Julie, W ... 252-398-6252 ... 363 E
emoryj@chowan.edu
EMORY, Nate ... 301-784-5000 ... 221 A
nemory@allegany.edu
EMRICH, Paula ... 704-334-6882 ... 367 E
pemrich@nlts.edu
EMSLIE, Gordon ... 270-745-2297 ... 207 C
gordon.emslie@wku.edu
EMSWELLER, David, W ... 419-434-4578 ... 404 B
emsweller@findlay.edu
EMSWELLER, David, W ... 419-434-4570 ... 404 B
emsweller@findlay.edu
ENCARNACION, Elba ... 787-766-1912 ... 562 F
eencarnacion@inter.edu
ENDER, Barbara, A ... 724-738-2004 ... 443 E
barbara.ender@sru.edu
ENDER, Kenneth, L ... 847-925-6390 ... 151 E
kender@harpercollege.edu

ENDER, Steven, C .... 616-234-3901..... 251 G
sender@grcc.edu
ENDERS, Naulayne, R .... 606-474-3276.... 200 J
nenders@kcu.edu
ENDERS, Thomas .... 562-985-5462...... 35 A
tenders@csulb.edu
ENDICOTT, Daniel, D .... 904-620-2019.... 120 C
dendicot@unf.edu
ENDICOTT, Patricia .... 812-749-1435.... 178 D
pendicott@oak.edu
ENDICOTT, Wanda .... 620-235-4776.... 195 I
wendicot@pittstate.edu
ENDRASKE, Mark .... 281-649-3148.... 487 F
mendraske@hbu.edu
ENDRIES, Jill, M .... 920-424-0228.... 551 D
endries@uwosh.edu
ENDRIJONAS, Erika .... 805-986-5814..... 77 C
eendrijonas@vcccd.edu
ENDSLEY, Douglas .... 210-829-6004.... 503 F
douge@uiwtx.edu
ENDY, Michael .... 817-598-6211.... 508 C
mendy@wc.edu
ENDY, Stephanie .... 718-960-8107.... 327 C
stephanie.endy@lehman.cuny.edu
ENEBO, Jeanette, E .... 701-231-7537.... 381 H
j.enebo@ndsu.edu
ENEGUESS, Katharine .... 603-752-1113.... 304 I
keneguess@ccsnh.edu
ENERSON, Diane .... 585-389-2380.... 342 D
deners09@naz.edu
ENG, Carla .... 605-668-1514.... 464 F
ceng@mtmc.edu
ENG, Edwin .... 559-244-5910...... 71 I
ed.eng@scccd.edu
ENG, William .... 646-312-5046.... 326 D
william_eng@baruch.cuny.edu
ENGBRECHT, Dennis .... 574-257-3305.... 169 F
engbred@bethelcollege.edu
ENGBROCK, M. Jeff .... 409-944-1215.... 486 H
mengbroc@gc.edu
ENGEBRETSON, Pam .... 651-779-3994.... 266 D
pam.engebretson@century.edu
ENGEL, Deidre .... 712-279-5448.... 182 E
deidre.engel@briarcliff.edu
ENGEL, Heather .... 585-475-2627.... 347 G
ncedar@rit.edu
ENGEL, Kirk .... 510-654-2934...... 46 J
kengel@expression.edu
ENGEL, Richard, R .... 530-752-9960...... 73 F
rrengel@ucdavis.edu
ENGEL, Scott, A .... 630-942-2233.... 147 G
engels@cod.edu
ENGELBACH, Karl, M .... 530-754-7237...... 73 F
kmengelbach@ucdavis.edu
ENGELBRECHT, Laci .... 217-479-7041.... 157 D
ENGELBRECHT, Sharon .... 417-626-1234.... 287 F
engelbrecht.sharon@occ.edu
ENGELBRIDE, Edward .... 518-320-1286.... 351 D
edward.engelbride@suny.edu
ENGELDINGER, Eugene ..... 414-425-8300.... 550 A
gengeldinger@shst.edu
ENGELDINGER, Ronald ..... 503-228-6528.... 414 E
engeldin@aii.edu
ENGELEN, John, T .... 404-727-5311.... 129 A
john.engelen@emory.edu
ENGELHARDT, Jon .... 254-710-3111.... 481 I
jon_engelhardt@baylor.edu
ENGELHART, Rene .... 916-646-2774...... 64 J
rengelhart@samuelmerritt.edu
ENGELKEMEYER, Susan ...... 508-999-9288.... 237 E
sengelkemeyer@umassd.edu
ENGELLS, Thomas .... 409-772-1503.... 507 B
tengells@utmb.edu
ENGELMAN, Denisa, A ...... 580-774-3212.... 412 F
denisa.engelman@swosu.edu
ENGELMAN, Mark, D .... 580-774-3269.... 412 F
mark.engelman@swosu.edu
ENGELMEYER, Renee .... 507-285-7183.... 269 B
renee.engelmeyer@roch.edu
ENGELSEN, Karen .... 805-986-5847...... 77 C
kengelsen@vcccd.edu
ENGER, Lee .... 217-228-5432.... 161 E
engerle@quincy.edu
ENGH, SJ, Michael, E .... 408-554-4100...... 68 C
mengh@scu.edu
ENGH, Peter, M .... 508-213-2390.... 243 J
peter.engh@nichols.edu
ENGLAND, David .... 225-768-1711.... 214 B
david.england@ololcollege.edu
ENGLAND, David .... 615-966-6210.... 470 D
david.england@lipscomb.edu
ENGLAND, David, C .... 860-255-3500...... 91 C
ENGLAND, Ken .... 205-726-2355........ 6 G
kwenglan@samford.edu
ENGLAND, Pamela .... 504-816-4871.... 208 I
pengland@dillard.edu
ENGLAND, Robert, E .... 330-337-6403.... 383 H
college@awc.edu
ENGLAND, Robert, E .... 330-337-6403.... 383 H
reengland@awc.edu
ENGLAND, Sid .... 530-752-2432...... 73 F
asengland@ucdavis.edu
ENGLAND, Tony .... 276-466-7873.... 528 G
tonyengland@vic.edu

ENGLAND, Tresa .... 970-675-3285...... 82 D
tresa.england@cncc.edu
ENGLE, Chris .... 810-762-0242.... 256 C
chris.engle@mcc.edu
ENGLE, Kevin, E .... 330-684-8948.... 403 C
kengle@uakron.edu
ENGLE, Marcia, J .... 540-432-4148.... 518 E
marcy.engle@emu
ENGLE, Patricia, A .... 810-762-9773.... 253 I
pengle@kettering.edu
ENGLEBRECHT, JoAnn .... 940-898-2684.... 502 B
jenglebrecht@twu.edu
ENGLEHARDT, Elaine, E .... 801-863-6464.... 511 C
elainee@uvu.edu
ENGLEHARDT, Richard ...... 606-693-5000.... 203 C
ENGLER, Jennifer, A .... 612-624-8344.... 272 D
engle009@umn.edu
ENGLERT, Mark, G .... 307-686-0254.... 556 C
menglert@sheridan.edu
ENGLERT, Richard .... 215-204-8873.... 447 G
richard.englert@temple.edu
ENGLERT, Richard, M .... 215-204-8873.... 447 G
richard.englert@temple.edu
ENGLERT, William, C .... 310-233-4301...... 54 I
englerbc@lahc.edu
ENGLESTATTER, Pauline .... 301-447-5600.... 225 A
englesta@msmary.edu
ENGLETT, Mickey .... 850-729-5371.... 114 A
englettm@nwfsc.edu
ENGLIN, Peter, D .... 515-294-5636.... 182 B
penglin@iastate.edu
ENGLISH, Alison .... 714-556-3610...... 76 E
aenglish@vanguard.edu
ENGLISH, Andrew .... 412-291-6423.... 422 D
aenglish@aii.edu
ENGLISH, Anna .... 404-460-2462.... 135 E
anna.english@point.edu
ENGLISH, Carl, J .... 716-372-7978.... 345 C
cenglish@obi.edu
ENGLISH, Clara, S .... 863-667-5249.... 118 A
csenglish@seu.edu
ENGLISH, Claude .... 816-584-6492.... 287 H
claude.english@park.edu
ENGLISH, Denise, K .... 352-365-3541.... 112 M
englishd@lscc.edu
ENGLISH, Eva .... 406-353-2607.... 294 E
eenglish@mail.fbcc.edu
ENGLISH, Evon .... 361-825-5787.... 497 F
evon.english@tamucc.edu
ENGLISH, Hope .... 806-291-3430.... 508 B
hope@wbu.edu
ENGLISH, Howard .... 516-773-5244.... 558 F
englishh@usmma.edu
ENGLISH, John, R .... 785-532-5590.... 194 B
jenglish@ksu.edu
ENGLISH, Linda .... 970-945-8691...... 82 C
ENGLISH, Matthew .... 503-280-8516.... 415 E
menglish@cu-portland.edu
ENGLISH, Millie .... 910-277-5227.... 376 A
englishmb@sapc.edu
ENGLISH, Patry .... 407-708-2144.... 117 G
englishp@seminolestate.edu
ENGLISH, Raymond, A ...... 440-775-5666.... 397 F
ray.english@oberlin.edu
ENGLISH, Robert, E .... 812-237-2307.... 173 A
robert.english@indstate.edu
ENGLISH, Suzanne .... 419-434-4425.... 404 B
english@findlay.edu
ENGLISH, Zachary .... 407-277-0311.... 106 G
zenglish@evergladesuniversity.edu
ENGLISH-WHITMAN,
Shirley .... 603-899-1131.... 305 B
engliss@franklinpierce.edu
ENGLN, Jay .... 719-389-6772...... 81 L
Jay.Engln@ColoradoCollege.edu
ENGLUND, Melissa, M ...... 215-895-6395.... 427 G
englunmm@drexel.edu
ENGQUIST, John .... 218-751-8670.... 270 G
johnengquist@oakhills.edu
ENGSTROM, Janet .... 708-732-7427.... 200 E
janet.engstrom@frontier.edu
ENGSTROM, Larry .... 775-784-6145.... 303 A
engstrom@unr.edu
ENGSTROM, Royce, C .... 406-243-2311.... 295 A
royce.engstrom@umontana.edu
ENICKS, Charles, R .... 601-984-1140.... 277 H
cenicks@umc.edu
ENKE, Wendy .... 314-918-2629.... 281 J
wenke@eden.edu
ENLOE, Donald .... 303-871-2463...... 88 E
denloe@du.edu
ENNASSEF, Abdelilan .... 973-328-5155.... 309 B
aennassef@ccm.edu
ENNEKING, Thomas .... 317-955-6010.... 177 G
tenneking@marian.edu
ENNEN, Rita .... 701-483-2883.... 381 E
rita.ennen@dickinsonstate.edu
ENNIS, Daniel .... 843-349-2746.... 456 G
dennis@coastal.edu
ENNIS, Daniel, G .... 410-516-2373.... 223 F
danielgennis@jhu.edu
ENNIS, Jackie .... 252-399-6571.... 362 A
jennis@barton.edu

ENNIS, James .... 707-864-7104...... 70 A
james.ennis@solano.edu
ENNIS, Kim .... 205-387-0511........ 2 B
kennis@bscc.edu
ENNIS, Matt .... 941-752-5574.... 118 E
ennism@scf.edu
ENNIST, Phyllis .... 937-529-2201.... 403 A
pjennist@united.edu
ENNS-REMPEL, Kevin .... 559-453-2300...... 47 K
kevin.enns.rempel@fresno.edu
ENOCH, Hollace, J .... 804-257-5841.... 529 D
hjenoch@vuu.edu
ENOS, Elizabeth .... 781-239-2751.... 240 D
eenos@massbay.edu
ENOS, Jonathan, C .... 717-291-3982.... 429 E
jon.enos@fandm.edu
ENOS, Ronald .... 623-572-3270...... 16 F
renosx@midwestern.edu
ENOS, Stacey .... 828-298-3325.... 380 C
senos@warren-wilson.edu
ENRIGHT, Jacquelyn, K ..... 301-369-2800.... 221 F
jke@capitol-college.edu
ENRIGHT, Judy .... 507-433-0636.... 269 A
jenright@riverland.edu
ENRIGHT, Mia .... 508-531-1242.... 238 B
menright@bridgew.edu
ENRIGHT, Patrick .... 973-328-5700.... 309 B
penright@ccm.edu
ENRIQUEZ, Anita, B .... 671-735-2553.... 559 D
abe@uguam.uog.edu
ENRIQUEZ, Igrí .... 787-765-3560.... 561 J
enriquez@edpcollege.edu
ENRIQUEZ, Jon .... 518-782-6598.... 350 I
jenriquez@siena.edu
ENSALACO, Daniel, R .... 920-924-3317.... 554 E
densalaco@morainepark.edu
ENSELEIN, Elizabeth .... 410-225-2363.... 224 C
benselei@mica.edu
ENSENBERGER, Matthew ... 847-925-6586.... 151 E
mensenbe@harpercollege.edu
ENSER, Pamela, E .... 315-386-7042.... 355 D
enserp@canton.edu
ENSEY, Dianne .... 806-457-4200.... 486 G
densey@fpctx.edu
ENSING, Kim .... 805-922-6966...... 26 K
kensing@hancockcollege.edu
ENSLE, Kay, E .... 814-676-6591.... 442 B
kensle@clarion.edu
ENSLEY, Carol .... 916-278-7737...... 35 E
censley@csus.edu
ENSLEY, Dana .... 706-379-5336.... 139 F
ddensley@yhc.edu
ENSLEY, Kevin .... 817-923-1921.... 495 E
kensley@swbts.edu
ENSLIN, Jonathan .... 262-472-1482.... 552 E
enslinj@uww.edu
ENSMAN, JR., Richard, G . 585-345-6809.... 334 F
rgensman@genesee.edu
ENSOR, Pat .... 713-221-8011.... 503 D
ensorp@uhd.edu
ENSWORTH, Scott, F .... 724-480-3364.... 426 A
scott.ensworth@ccbc.edu
ENTERLINE, Keri .... 954-783-7339.... 106 D
kenterline@cci.edu
ENTERS, David, T .... 262-243-5700.... 546 I
dave.enters@cuw.edu
ENTESSARI, Abbass .... 305-623-1441.... 108 H
aentessa@fmuniv.edu
ENTREKIN, Cindy .... 256-215-4251........ 2 F
centrekin@cacc.edu
ENTRIKIN, Nicholas .... 574-631-5204.... 180 D
Entrikin.1@nd.edu
ENTRIKIN, Nicholas, J ...... 310-825-4921...... 74 A
nentrikin@international.ucla.edu
ENTRINGER, Chris, E .... 563-556-5110.... 187 G
entringc@nicc.edu
ENTWISLE, Barbara .... 919-962-1319.... 378 D
bentwisle@email.unc.edu
ENTWISTLE, David, E .... 801-581-7480.... 510 L
david.entwistle@hsc.utah.edu
ENTZ, Mary .... 515-791-1721.... 183 E
mjentz@dmacc.edu
ENTZ, Ryan .... 316-322-3190.... 191 D
rentz1@butlercc.edu
ENTZMINGER, Robert, L ... 501-450-1273...... 22 A
entzminger@hendrix.edu
ENWEMEKA, Chukuka, S .. 414-229-4712.... 551 C
enwemeka@uwm.edu
ENYARD, Richard .... 573-876-7172.... 290 G
renyard@stephens.edu
ENYART, Marcia .... 918-540-6378.... 408 J
menyart@neo.edu
ENYEDI, Alexander .... 269-387-4350.... 260 F
alex.enyedi@wmich.edu
ENZ FINKEN, Kathleen ...... 608-785-8042.... 551 B
enzfinke.kath@uwlax.edu
ENZOR, Sharon, B .... 662-685-4771.... 273 H
senzor@bmc.edu
EOFF, Robert, H .... 901-678-5649.... 474 C
rheoff@memphis.edu
EOFF, Shirley .... 325-942-2722.... 480 E
shirley.eoff@angleo.edu
EPEMA, Michael .... 712-722-6080.... 183 H
epema@dordt.edu

EPES, JR., Hansford, M .... 704-894-2227.... 363 F
haepes@davidson.edu
EPHLIN, Edward, C .... 903-875-7361.... 491 B
ed.ephlin@navarrocollege.edu
EPLAWY, Rick .... 440-375-7225.... 394 E
replawy@lec.edu
EPLEY, David .... 520-795-0787...... 12 A
president@asaom.edu
EPLING, Linda .... 859-246-6584.... 201 D
linda.epling@kctcs.edu
EPP, Adam .... 425-889-5263.... 535 I
adam.epp@northwestu.edu
EPP, Helmut, P .... 312-362-8760.... 148 F
hepp@depaul.edu
EPP, Ken .... 503-517-1815.... 421 B
kepp@westernseminary.edu
EPP, Stephanie Ann .... 309-438-2586.... 153 C
saepp@ilstu.edu
EPPERHART, David, H .... 870-230-5146...... 21 I
epperd@hsu.edu
EPPERLY, Ronald .... 276-656-0205.... 527 D
repperly@ph.vccs.edu
EPPERSON, Doug .... 509-335-4582.... 539 A
epperson@wsu.edu
EPPERSON, II, Richard, P 434-223-6153.... 519 B
repperson@email.hsc.edu
EPPERSON, Russell .... 731-989-6349.... 468 K
repperson@fhu.edu
EPPERSON, Shonte .... 903-927-3260.... 509 A
sepperson@wileyc.edu
EPPERSON, Steve .... 360-416-7771.... 538 A
steve.epperson@skagit.edu
EPPICH, David .... 505-566-3318.... 320 D
eppichd@sanjuancollege.edu
EPPINETTE, Chance, W ..... 318-342-5021.... 216 E
eppinette@ulm.edu
EPPINGER, Beth .... 479-788-7348...... 24 D
beppinge@uafortsmith.edu
EPPLER, Michelle .... 402-557-7010.... 297 A
michelle.eppler@bellevue.edu
EPPLEY, Doug .... 814-472-3017.... 446 B
depple‍y@francis.edu
EPPLING, Chris .... 706-865-2134.... 138 A
ceppling@truett.edu
EPPS, Bruce .... 614-236-6461.... 386 C
bepps@capital.edu
EPPS, Carol .... 864-596-9595.... 457 E
carol.epps@converse.edu
EPPS, Gregory, D .... 304-766-3249.... 544 D
epps@wvstateu.edu
EPPS, Joanne, A .... 215-204-8993.... 447 G
joanne.epps@temple.edu
EPPS, Ronald .... 254-299-8647.... 490 E
repps@mclennan.edu
EPPS, Valerie .... 202-274-5210...... 99 F
vepps@udc.edu
EPSTEIN, Chaim, L .... 718-438-1002.... 340 H
EPSTEIN, Irving .... 309-556-3760.... 153 E
iepstein@iwu.edu
EPSTEIN, Joanne .... 352-335-2332.... 100 B
EPSTEIN, Meryl .... 602-331-7500...... 12 D
mepstein@aii.edu
EPSTEIN, Scott .... 616-554-5691.... 250 E
sepstein@davenport.edu
EPSTEIN, Shelley .... 309-677-3260.... 145 H
sepstein@bradley.edu
EPTING, James, B .... 864-977-7018.... 460 A
jimmy.epting@ngu.edu
ERARDI, Scott, M .... 860-832-2032...... 91 G
erardis@ccsu.edu
ERARIO, Vince .... 678-264-8808.... 133 B
vince.erario@life.edu
ERATO, Michael, J .... 414-425-8300.... 550 A
merato@shst.edu
ERB, Brian, I .... 706-236-2234.... 125 G
berb@berry.edu
ERB, Daniel, E .... 336-841-4595.... 365 A
derb@highpoint.edu
ERB, Jennifer .... 610-799-1034.... 434 D
0617mgr@sheg.follett.com
ERBERT, Daniel .... 970-339-6602...... 80 G
daniel.erbert@aims.edu
ERBES, Fred, S .... 712-274-5168.... 187 D
erbes@morningside.edu
ERBY, Betty, A .... 414-276-5200.... 546 C
baerby@bryantstratton.edu
ERCHUL, James, C .... 612-330-1758.... 261 G
erchul@augsburg.edu
ERCK, Lisa .... 916-631-8108...... 33 C
ERCKERT, Joseph .... 215-489-2397.... 426 H
Joseph.Erckert@delval.edu
ERDICE, Stephanie .... 717-477-7447.... 443 D
smerdice@ship.edu
ERDMAN, Anne, C .... 269-927-8127.... 254 B
erdman@lakemichigancollege.edu
ERDMAN, Howard .... 208-792-2456.... 143 F
herdman@lcsc.edu
ERDMAN, Larry .... 269-927-8138.... 254 B
erdmanl@lakemichigancollege.edu
ERDMANN, David .... 407-646-2317.... 116 B
derdmann@rollins.edu
ERDMANN, James .... 215-503-6595.... 448 B
james.erdmann@jefferson.edu

ESQUIVEL, Ruben, E .... 214-648-0448.... 507 D
ruben.esquivel@utsouthwestern.edu

ESQUIVEL-GONZALEZ, Olga .... 614-292-5688.... 398 H
esquivel-gonzale.1@osu.edu

ESQUIVEL-SWINSON, Adela .... 805-922-6966..... 26 K
aesquivel-swinson@hancockcollege.edu

ESRY, Kip .... 800-955-2527.... 282 G

ESSAR, Andrea .... 507-457-1888.... 271 G
aessar@smumn.edu

ESSARY, Larry .... 919-508-2386.... 375 D
lessary@peace.edu

ESSARY, Melissa .... 919-865-4651.... 362 F
essary@law.campbell.edu

ESSARY, Reba, J .... 205-348-7917....... 8 F
ressary@fa.ua.edu

ESSELSTROM, Beth .... 218-726-7171.... 272 B
besselst@d.umn.edu

ESSEX, Nathan, L .... 901-333-4200.... 475 H
nessex@southwest.tn.edu

ESSIG, Lori .... 605-995-2614.... 464 B
loessig@dwu.edu

ESTA, Daniel .... 847-578-3257.... 163 A
daniel.esta@rosalindfranklin.edu

ESTABROOK, Madeleine, A .... 617-373-2772.... 244 A

ESTAPE, Estela .... 787-758-2525.... 567 D
estela.estape@upr.edu

ESTAPHAN, Charles, F ...... 508-793-2514.... 233 D
cestapha@holycross.edu

ESTEBAN, A. Gabriel .... 973-761-9691.... 315 B
gabriel.esteban@shu.edu

ESTEN, Phil, L .... 612-624-6142.... 272 D
esten@umn.edu

ESTEP, Charles, R .... 864-379-8869.... 457 G
estep@erskine.edu

ESTEP, Kimberly .... 423-636-7305.... 476 F
kestep@tusculum.edu

ESTEP, Kimberly, K .... 615-353-3326.... 475 D
kimberly.estep@nscc.edu

ESTEP, Leon, F .... 334-387-3877....... 1 D
leonestep@amridgeuniversity.edu

ESTEP, Tim .... 704-337-2460.... 375 G
estept@queens.edu

ESTEPP, J. Mark .... 276-964-7315.... 528 A
mark.estepp@sw.edu

ESTER, Joyce .... 661-395-4223..... 52 M

ESTERBERG, Kristin .... 978-542-6246.... 239 B
kesterberg@salemstate.edu

ESTERHUIZEN, Amy, H ...... 563-556-5110.... 187 G
esterhuizena@portal.nicc.edu

ESTERS, Randy .... 318-335-3944.... 210 F
randy.esters@ltc.edu

ESTES, David, C .... 210-434-6711.... 491 G
dcestes@lake.ollusa.edu

ESTES, Eric .... 440-775-8462.... 397 F
eric.estes@oberlin.edu

ESTES, Jessica .... 270-686-4567.... 202 E
jessica.estes@kctcs.edu

ESTES, Lalita, W .... 903-927-3304.... 509 A
lestes@wileyc.edu

ESTES, Lane .... 205-226-4640....... 2 C
lestes@bsc.edu

ESTES, Michael .... 601-984-1130.... 277 H
mestes@umc.edu

ESTES, Susan .... 650-574-6404..... 67 F
estes@smccd.edu

ESTES-LEWIS, Karyn .... 207-513-3640.... 218 C
kestes@kaplan.edu

ESTESS, Larry, M .... 318-342-5140.... 216 E
estess@ulm.edu

ESTESS, Larry, M .... 318-342-5205.... 216 E
estess@ulm.edu

ESTEVEZ, Juan .... 787-738-2161.... 567 A
juan.estevez@upr.edu

ESTEVEZ MARTINEZ, Jacqueline .... 212-938-5500.... 355 B
jmartinez@sunyopt.edu

ESTEY, Diana, L .... 336-841-9205.... 365 A
destey@highpoint.edu

ESTILL, Donna .... 620-223-2700.... 192 G
donnae@fortscott.edu

ESTILL, Sandi, L .... 606-759-7141.... 202 D
sandi.estill@kctcs.edu

ESTLACK, Scarlet .... 806-874-3571.... 482 H
scarlet.estlack@clarendoncollege.edu

ESTOCK, Steven .... 575-562-2632.... 318 A
steven.estock@enmu.edu

ESTOFF, Charles, W .... 716-851-1114.... 333 B
estoff@ecc.edu

ESTRADA, Donna .... 985-858-5731.... 210 H
destrada@ftcc.edu

ESTRADA, George .... 530-242-7930..... 69 D
gestrada@shastacollege.edu

ESTRADA, George .... 203-576-4330..... 94 D
gestrada@bridgeport.edu

ESTRADA, James .... 860-832-2553..... 91 G
james.estrada@ccsu.edu

ESTRADA-HAMBY, Lisa .... 940-397-4076.... 491 A
lisa.hamby@mwsu.edu

ESTRELLA, Fred .... 928-523-9998..... 17 A
fred.estrella@nau.edu

ESTRELLADO, Michelles .... 310-752-4700..... 29 J

ESTREMERA, Miguel, A ..... 973-353-5089.... 314 E
miguele@andromeda.rutgers.edu

ESTRIDGE, Gwen .... 303-300-8740..... 81 H
gwen.estridge@collegeamerica.com

ESTRIN, Elena .... 212-349-4330.... 334 G
eestrin@globe.edu

ESTRY, Douglas .... 517-353-5380.... 255 D
estry@msu.edu

ESZTERHAS, Gabriel .... 646-660-6660.... 326 D
gabriel_eszterhas@baruch.cuny.edu

ETAUGH, Claire .... 309-677-2380.... 145 H
cetaugh@bradley.edu

ETCHELLS, Timothy .... 802-443-5707.... 513 G
tetchell@middlebury.edu

ETCHEMENDY, John, W .... 650-724-4074..... 71 F
etch@stanford.edu

ETESAMNIA, Hamid .... 909-748-8063..... 75 F
hamid_etesamnia@redlands.edu

ETHEREDGE, Tiffany .... 803-799-9082.... 461 A
tetheredge@southuniversity.edu

ETHIER, Richard .... 802-241-2536.... 515 B
rje10150@hemlock.vsc.edu

ETHINGTON, Robert .... 707-527-4573..... 68 E
rethington@santarosa.edu

ETRE-PEREZ, Pam .... 505-224-3974.... 317 J
petreperez@cnm.edu

ETSCHMAIER, Gale .... 619-594-1643..... 36 E
gale.etschmaier@sdsu.edu

ETSE, Penselyn .... 691-320-2480.... 559 A
petse@comfsm.fm

ETSITTY, Marie, R .... 928-724-6670..... 14 A
metsitty@dinecollege.edu

ETTARO, Barbara .... 814-863-1030.... 438 F
bxm7@psu.edu

ETTEMA, Robert .... 307-766-4253.... 556 E
rettema@uwyo.edu

ETTER, Alan .... 202-274-5314..... 99 F
aetter@udc.edu

ETTER, Stephanie .... 305-273-4499.... 103 C
setter@cbt.edu

ETTLE, Violeta .... 202-885-2720..... 97 B
vi@american.edu

ETTLING, John .... 518-564-2010.... 354 B
president_office@plattsburgh.edu

ETTORE, JD .... 620-223-2700.... 192 G
jde@fortscott.edu

ETUALE, Mikaele .... 684-699-9155.... 558 I
m.etuale@amsamoa.edu

EUBANK, Charlotte .... 573-840-9662.... 290 J
ceubank@trcc.edu

EUBANK, Gary .... 937-529-2201.... 403 A
geubank@united.edu

EUBANK, Jeff .... 215-702-4202.... 444 A
jeubank@pbu.edu

EUBANK, Jeffrey, M .... 816-604-6645.... 285 E
jeff.eubank@mcckc.edu

EUBANKS, Audrey, C .... 251-442-2218....... 9 B
aeubanks@mail.umobile.edu

EUBANKS, David, L .... 865-573-4517.... 469 J
deubanks@johnsonU.edu

EUBANKS, Gail .... 912-443-5443.... 136 D
geubanks@savannahtech.edu

EUBANKS, Gregory .... 205-247-8145....... 7 G
geubanks@stillman.edu

EUBANKS, Karla, C .... 912-427-5899.... 124 A
keubanks@altamahatech.edu

EUBANKS, Kathleen, L .... 508-999-8086.... 237 E
keubanks@umassd.edu

EUBANKS, Philip, A .... 865-573-4517.... 469 J
peubanks@johnsonU.edu

EUBANKS, Ranelle .... 870-460-1233..... 25 A
eubanksr@uamont.edu

EUDY, Kim .... 619-260-7967..... 76 A
keudy@sandiego.edu

EUDY, Kristina .... 704-991-0235.... 374 A
keudy5611@stanly.edu

EULER, Tim .... 304-357-4363.... 541 H
timeuler@ucwv.edu

EULER, Tim .... 304-357-4363.... 541 H
timeuler@ucwv.edu

EULIANO, Guy .... 814-838-7673.... 429 B
geuliano@tsbi.org

EUNICE, E, E .... 850-201-6446.... 121 F
eunicee@tcc.fl.edu

EURE, Darius .... 252-335-3307.... 377 D
deure@mail.ecsu.edu

EUSTROM, Jim .... 503-399-5076.... 414 J
jim.eustrom@chemeketa.edu

EVAN, Joseph .... 570-208-5895.... 432 E
josephevan@kings.edu

EVANGELISTA, Joleen, M .. 671-735-5540.... 559 B
materialsmanagement@guamcc.edu

EVANGELISTA, Nancy .... 607-871-2649.... 322 F
fevangel@alfred.edu

EVANS, Alana .... 906-487-7358.... 251 C
alana.evans@finlandia.edu

EVANS, Andrew .... 781-283-2305.... 246 B

EVANS, Angela, J .... 770-423-6300.... 132 H
aevans@kennesaw.edu

EVANS, Anita, K .... 608-785-8805.... 551 B
evans.anit@uwlax.edu

EVANS, Annette .... 706-542-7066.... 138 C
amevans@uga.edu

EVANS, Atlas, D .... 617-726-5164.... 242 E
aevans3@mghihp.edu

EVANS, Beth .... 718-990-6999.... 348 G
evansb@stjohns.edu

EVANS, Beverly, A .... 717-815-1228.... 452 F
behinger@ycp.edu

EVANS, Brian .... 559-253-2235..... 27 B
bevans@alliant.edu

EVANS, Brian .... 502-863-8040.... 200 G
brian_evans@georgetowncollege.edu

EVANS, Brian, K .... 801-422-3760.... 509 D
brian_evans@byu.edu

EVANS, Carol, A .... 231-995-1705.... 256 G
cevans@nmc.edu

EVANS, Carolyn, L .... 601-977-7764.... 277 F
cevans@tougaloo.edu

EVANS, Cheryl .... 580-628-6201.... 409 B
cheryl.evans@north-ok.edu

EVANS, Cheryl, O .... 585-385-8015.... 348 F
cevans@sjfc.edu

EVANS, Chet .... 941-756-0690.... 433 C
cevans@lecom.edu

EVANS, Christopher, G ...... 303-757-0059..... 89 G
chris@yorktownuniversity.edu

EVANS, Damian .... 262-595-2540.... 551 E
damian.evans@uwp.edu

EVANS, Dan .... 740-533-4600.... 399 G
evansd1@ohio.edu

EVANS, Dave .... 619-388-2737..... 65 G
devans@sdccd.edu

EVANS, David .... 229-391-2647.... 134 C
devans@moultrietech.edu

EVANS, David .... 972-860-8261.... 484 G
devans@dcccd.edu

EVANS, David .... 972-273-3561.... 485 B
devans@dcccd.edu

EVANS, David .... 512-404-4802.... 481 D
devans@austinseminary.edu

EVANS, David, C .... 215-368-7538.... 424 A

EVANS, David, R .... 712-749-2243.... 182 G
evansd@bvu.edu

EVANS, Deborah, L .... 610-861-1340.... 436 I
debevans@moravian.edu

EVANS, Diane, T .... 936-261-2202.... 496 E
dtevans@pvamu.edu

EVANS, Eileen, B .... 269-387-2363.... 260 F
eileen.evans@wmich.edu

EVANS, Elizabeth, J .... 217-424-6335.... 158 F
eevans@millikin.edu

EVANS, Eric, D .... 781-981-7000.... 242 A
eevans@ll.mit.edu

EVANS, Erik .... 570-389-4047.... 441 F
eevans@bloomu.edu

EVANS, Frederick, M .... 803-516-4930.... 460 G
fevans6@scsu.edu

EVANS, Gail .... 415-338-2206..... 36 F
gevans@sfsu.edu

EVANS, George .... 618-545-2751.... 155 A
gevans@kaskaskia.edu

EVANS, JR., Gilbert, L ...... 386-312-4127.... 116 D
gilbertevans@sjrstate.edu

EVANS, Gregory .... 815-455-8564.... 157 F
gevans@mchenry.edu

EVANS, J. David .... 770-423-6194.... 132 H
devans@kennesaw.edu

EVANS, Jack .... 706-721-3964.... 130 B
jaevans@georgiahealth.edu

EVANS, Jack .... 813-253-7604.... 110 I
jevans@hccfl.edu

EVANS, Jack .... 972-524-3341.... 495 F

EVANS, JR., Jack .... 972-524-3341.... 495 F

EVANS, James, D .... 636-949-4900.... 284 C
jevans@lindenwood.edu

EVANS, Jane .... 740-695-9500.... 384 J
jevans@btc.edu

EVANS, Janet, D .... 412-392-3824.... 444 H
jevans@pointpark.edu

EVANS, Janie .... 802-287-8203.... 513 D
evansj@greenmtn.edu

EVANS, Jeannette, H .... 315-684-6067.... 354 F
evansjh@morrisville.edu

EVANS, Jeffrey, L .... 313-593-5110.... 259 E
jlevan@umd.umich.edu

EVANS, Jennifer .... 510-420-5400..... 38 A
jlevans@cc.edu

EVANS, Jennifer, M .... 717-867-6271.... 434 C
jevans@lvc.edu

EVANS, Joe, W .... 405-224-3140.... 413 E
jwevans@usao.edu

EVANS, John .... 336-506-4367.... 367 G
john.evans@alamancecc.edu

EVANS, Jon .... 714-459-1164..... 78 C
jonevans@wsulaw.edu

EVANS, Joseph .... 410-706-8501.... 227 C
jevans@af.umaryland.edu

EVANS, Joy .... 678-717-3800.... 129 D
jevans@gsc.edu

EVANS, Julia .... 909-607-3689..... 40 C
julia.evans@cgu.edu

EVANS, Julie .... 701-777-6345.... 381 D
jae@email.und.edu

EVANS, K. James .... 814-362-7650.... 449 B
kje2@pitt.edu

EVANS, Kamira .... 610-892-1566.... 441 C
kevans@pit.edu

EVANS, Karen, V .... 610-921-7630.... 421 D
kevans@alb.edu

EVANS, Karyn .... 937-393-3431.... 401 K
kevans@sscc.edu

EVANS, Katherine .... 973-761-9500.... 315 B
katherine.evans@shu.edu

EVANS, Kenneth, R .... 405-325-2070.... 413 C
evansk@ou.edu

EVANS, Lana .... 419-267-1225.... 397 D
levans@northweststate.edu

EVANS, Laurie .... 313-664-1501.... 250 A
levans@collegeforcreativestudies.edu

EVANS, Leigh .... 478-553-2054.... 134 F
levans@oftc.edu

EVANS, Lexie .... 206-587-3890.... 537 A
leevan@sccd.ctc.edu

EVANS, Linda .... 803-641-3342.... 462 B
lindae@usca.edu

EVANS, Lisa .... 828-254-1921.... 367 H
levans@abtech.edu

EVANS, Liz .... 412-392-5945.... 444 H
eevans@pointpark.edu

EVANS, III, Louis, D .... 713-221-2766.... 503 D
evansl@uhd.edu

EVANS, Marisa, L .... 814-886-6336.... 437 A
mevans@mtaloy.edu

EVANS, Mark .... 845-938-5502.... 558 G
Mark.Evans@usma.edu

EVANS, Mark .... 330-672-2972.... 393 D
mevans@kent.edu

EVANS, Mark .... 434-793-6822.... 521 F
evans@ncbt.edu

EVANS, Mary .... 315-859-4346.... 335 A

EVANS, Maya .... 414-258-4810.... 549 A
evans@mtmary.edu

EVANS, Mercedes .... 617-879-7060.... 238 E
msevans@massart.edu

EVANS, Michael .... 334-420-4302....... 7 I
mevans@trenholmstate.edu

EVANS, Michael .... 817-461-8741.... 480 H
mevans@abconline.org

EVANS, Michael, L .... 314-362-6289.... 282 E
mevans@bjc.org

EVANS, Michael, L .... 806-743-2738.... 501 E
michael.evans@ttuhsc.edu

EVANS, Mike .... 765-289-2291.... 175 K
mevans@ivytech.edu

EVANS, Nicole .... 614-251-4603.... 398 F
evansn@ohiodominican.edu

EVANS, Oliver .... 616-451-2787.... 251 B
evanso@ferris.edu

EVANS, Paul, N .... 608-262-6982.... 550 G
paul.evans@housing.wisc.edu

EVANS, JR., R. Lee .... 334-844-8348....... 1 G
evansrl@auburn.edu

EVANS, Renee .... 201-761-7806.... 314 F
wknapp@spc.edu

EVANS, Richard, W .... 585-785-1300.... 334 A
evansrw@flcc.edu

EVANS, Rick .... 818-677-2906..... 35 D
rick.evans@csun.edu

EVANS, Rob .... 740-654-6711.... 400 B

EVANS, Robert .... 501-660-1000..... 20 C
revans@astate.edu

EVANS, Robert .... 501-660-1000..... 20 B
revans@asusystem.edu

EVANS, Roberta .... 406-243-4911.... 295 A
roberta.evans@umontana.edu

EVANS, Sam .... 773-947-6288.... 157 E
sevans@mccormick.edu

EVANS, Sam .... 270-745-4664.... 207 C
sam.evans@wku.edu

EVANS, Sarah .... 317-931-2377.... 170 E
sevans@cts.edu

EVANS, Scott .... 440-375-7000.... 394 E
sevans@lec.edu

EVANS, Sharlotte .... 706-821-3965.... 233 B
Sharlotte.Evans@cambridgecollege.edu

EVANS, Sharon .... 309-298-1552.... 168 A
sa-evans@wiu.edu

EVANS, Sharon .... 708-534-3148.... 151 C
sevans@govst.edu

EVANS, Shirley .... 410-276-0306.... 226 D
sevans@host.sdc.edu

EVANS, Sidney, S .... 540-458-8754.... 530 A
sevans@wlu.edu

EVANS, Steve .... 281-425-6887.... 489 J
sevans@lee.edu

EVANS, Susan .... 239-590-1057.... 119 A
sevans@fgcu.edu

EVANS, Susan, T .... 757-221-1585.... 517 J
stevan@wm.edu

EVANS, Tamara .... 718-997-5790.... 328 F
tamara.evans@qc.cuny.edu

EVANS, Thomas .... 973-408-3379.... 309 F
tevans@drew.edu

EVANS, Thomas, A .... 515-281-6527.... 182 A
taevans@iastate.edu

EVANS, Thomas, M .... 512-448-8607.... 493 B
tome@stedwards.edu

EVANS, Thomas, S .... 315-443-9732.... 357 B
tevans02@syr.edu

F

FAIST, Tom ... 614-222-6174 ... 388 F tfaist@ccad.edu
FAITH, Helen ... 503-251-5709 ... 420 H hfaith@uws.edu
FAITH, Lani ... 503-517-1369 ... 421 A lfaith@warnerpacific.edu
FAITHFUL, Mark ... 252-638-7283 ... 369 E faithfum@cravencc.edu
FAIX, Peter, K ... 412-397-6271 ... 445 G faix@rmu.edu
FAJACK, Deidra ... 859-572-5489 ... 205 E fajackd@nku.edu
FAJARDO, Juan Carlos ... 718-631-6611 ... 329 A jfajardo@qcc.cuny.edu
FAJEN, Larry ... 816-331-5700 ... 288 A lfajen@pcitraining.edu
FAKHRI RAVARI, Saeed ... 949-480-4230 ... 69 I sfakhriravari@soka.edu
FALA, Grace, M ... 814-641-3467 ... 431 L fala@juniata.edu
FALARDEAU, George ... 626-396-2201 ... 29 G george.falardeau@artcenter.edu
FALASTER, Marilyn ... 618-985-3741 ... 154 E marilynfalaster@jalc.edu
FALAVOLITO, Steven, J ... 412-531-4433 ... 426 F info@deantech.edu
FALBO, Mary Anna ... 716-896-0700 ... 359 F falbo@villa.edu
FALCK-YI, Suzanne ... 641-585-8225 ... 189 E falckyis@waldorf.edu
FALCO, James ... 815-479-7728 ... 157 F jfalco@mchenry.edu
FALCO, Jim ... 815-455-8680 ... 157 F jfalco@mchenry.edu
FALCON, Ana, E ... 787-769-2043 ... 566 H ana.falcon@upr.edu
FALCON, Greg ... 817-451-0017 ... 492 I greg.falcon@remingtoncollege.edu
FALCON, Kim ... 918-495-6928 ... 411 C kfalcon@oru.edu
FALCON-CHANDLER, Carole ... 406-353-2607 ... 294 E cfalconchan@hotmail.com
FALCONER, James ... 860-434-5232 ... 93 A jfalconer@lymeacademy.edu
FALCONETTI, Angela, M ... 386-506-3962 ... 103 J falcona@DaytonaState.edu
FALCONI, Stefano ... 617-521-2877 ... 245 A stefano.falconi@simmons.edu
FALDER, Mike ... 765-998-5538 ... 179 F mcfalder@taylor.edu
FALDUTO, Ellen ... 330-263-2230 ... 388 E efalduto@wooster.edu
FALE, Tauvela ... 684-699-9155 ... 558 I t.fale@amsamoa.edu
FALEN, Geoff ... 719-389-6424 ... 81 L Geoff.Falen@ColoradoCollege.edu
FALER, Kurt ... 630-889-6463 ... 159 E kfaler@nuhs.edu
FALERO, Mercy ... 787-480-2382 ... 561 D mfalero@sanjuancapital.com
FALES, Michael, F ... 269-749-7624 ... 257 D mfales@olivetcollege.edu
FALESE, Joseph, T ... 815-836-5275 ... 156 D falesejo@lewisu.edu
FALEY, Heather ... 802-440-4423 ... 512 G hfaley@bennington.edu
FALK, Adam, F ... 413-597-4233 ... 246 G adam.f.falk@williams.edu
FALK, Cheryl ... 503-399-5145 ... 414 J cheryl.falk@chemeketa.edu
FALK, Dan ... 620-229-6267 ... 196 C dan.falk@sckans.edu
FALK, Israel ... 845-356-7064 ... 361 A
FALK, Jessica ... 620-229-6155 ... 196 C jessica.falk@sckans.edu
FALK, Joyce ... 619-849-2534 ... 62 L joycefalk@pointloma.edu
FALK, Keith, L ... 920-923-8594 ... 548 C kfalk@marianuniversity.edu
FALK, Stephanie, A ... 717-867-6696 ... 434 C falk@lvc.edu
FALKE, Steve, J ... 814-863-0205 ... 438 F sfalke@bncollege.com
FALKENBERG, Janice ... 414-297-8718 ... 554 D falkenjm@matc.edu
FALKENBERG, Taunji ... 503-229-0492 ... 416 A taunji_falkenberg@heald.edu
FALKENHAGEN, George ... 989-358-7442 ... 247 G falkenh@alpenacc.edu
FALKENRATH, Rex ... 801-832-2588 ... 512 F rfalkenrath@westminstercollege.edu
FALKENSTEIN, Jay ... 609-894-9311 ... 308 C jfalkens@bcc.edu
FALKENSTERN, Sharon ... 814-676-6591 ... 442 A sfalkenstern@clarion.edu
FALKENSTIEN, Sarah, N ... 909-748-8044 ... 75 F sarah_falkenstien@redlands.edu
FALKIEWICZ, Linda, K ... 313-577-3550 ... 260 D ab4753@wayne.edu
FALKINBURG, Joyce, L ... 410-543-6056 ... 228 D jlfalkinburg@salisbury.edu
FALKNER, Jeff ... 641-784-5341 ... 184 H falkner@graceland.edu
FALKNER, Thomas, M ... 410-857-2248 ... 224 D tfalkner@mcdaniel.edu
FALKOFSKE, James ... 320-308-5171 ... 269 D jfalkofske@sctcc.edu
FALKOWSKI, William, G ... 716-270-2942 ... 333 C falkowski@ecc.edu
FALKS, Delisa, F ... 979-458-5311 ... 497 C delisa@tamu.edu
FALL, Diane ... 309-796-4840 ... 145 E falld@bhc.edu
FALL, Stephany ... 850-599-3203 ... 118 G stephany.fall@famu.edu
FALLACARO, Anthony ... 203-596-4531 ... 93 D afallacaro@post.edu
FALLERT, Danelle ... 323-265-8797 ... 54 G fallerdj@elac.edu
FALLIN, Terri ... 417-667-8181 ... 280 I tfallin@cottey.edu
FALLING, Cary ... 405-425-5290 ... 409 E cary.falling@oc.edu
FALLING, Sali, K ... 765-285-5162 ... 169 D sfalling@bsu.edu
FALLIS, James, E ... 928-523-5353 ... 17 A james.fallis@nau.edu
FALLIS, Sue ... 925-631-4856 ... 64 F sfallis@stmarys-ca.edu
FALLO, Thomas, M ... 310-660-3111 ... 45 D tfallo@elcamino.edu
FALLON, Greg ... 973-684-5895 ... 312 E gfallon@pccc.edu
FALLON, Melissa, A ... 607-436-3368 ... 353 E fallonma@oneonta.edu
FALLON, Patricia, C ... 617-521-2018 ... 245 A patricia.fallon@simmons.edu
FALLON, Thomas ... 978-556-3866 ... 241 B tfallon@necc.mass.edu
FALLONE, Deborah, A ... 914-323-5224 ... 340 A deborah.fallone@mville.edu
FALLS, Meda ... 731-925-5722 ... 475 B mfalls@jscc.edu
FALLS, Mike ... 704-484-4129 ... 369 B fallsm@clevelandcommunitycollege.edu
FALLS, Sarah ... 212-472-1500 ... 343 G sfalls@nysid.edu
FALOTICO, Michael ... 312-777-7735 ... 144 H mfalotico@argosy.edu
FALOTICO, Michael ... 312-777-7735 ... 144 G mfalotico@argosy.edu
FALSO, Frank ... 570-422-3333 ... 442 C ffalso@esufoundation.org
FALTYN, Timothy, W ... 918-463-2931 ... 407 H
FALU, Ramon ... 787-815-0000 ... 566 F
FALVEY, Mary ... 323-343-4300 ... 35 B mfalvey@calstatela.edu
FALWELL, Colbie, M ... 501-882-8824 ... 20 D cmmoody@asub.edu
FALWELL, JR., Jerry ... 434-582-2957 ... 520 F jlfjr@liberty.edu
FALWELL, Jonathan ... 434-582-2000 ... 520 F jonfalwell@liberty.edu
FALZERANO, Christine ... 718-260-3025 ... 346 C cfalzera@poly.edu
FAMA, Melissa ... 978-632-6600 ... 240 G m_fama@mwcc.mass.edu
FAMBLE, JR., Freddie ... 325-793-4906 ... 490 F ffamble@mcm.edu
FAMULA, Michelle, S ... 530-752-6559 ... 73 F msfamula@ucdavis.edu
FAMULARE, Dominick, F ... 518-388-6168 ... 358 E famularn@union.edu
FAN, Lori ... 309-677-2245 ... 145 H llw@bradley.edu
FANCHER, Karen, J ... 503-255-0332 ... 417 C kfancher@multnomah.edu
FANDOZZI, Melissa ... 518-828-4181 ... 330 E melissa.fandozzi@sunycgcc.edu
FANEK, Sami ... 407-851-2525 ... 106 E sfanek@cci.edu
FANELLI, Greg ... 361-570-4820 ... 503 E fanellig@uhv.edu
FANEUFF, Ken ... 706-379-5202 ... 139 F kfaneuff@yhc.edu
FANFAIR STEURY, Michelle ... 574-535-7746 ... 171 D michellefs@goshen.edu
FANFANX, Lerick ... 617-745-3869 ... 234 C lerick.fanfanx@enc.edu
FANG, John ... 714-533-1495 ... 70 B johnfang@southbaylo.edu
FANNAN, Lisa, L ... 816-604-2314 ... 285 G lisa.fannan@mcckc.edu
FANNER, Sjohonton ... 940-552-6291 ... 507 E sfanner@vernoncollege.edu
FANNIN, John, A ... 269-782-1262 ... 258 E jfannin@swmich.edu
FANNIN, Larry ... 801-878-1053 ... 303 D lfannin@roseman.edu
FANNIN, William, R ... 432-552-2110 ... 507 C fannin_w@utpb.edu
FANSHAW, Charles ... 202-685-3929 ... 557 F fanshawc@ndu.edu
FANSLER, A. Gigi ... 217-732-3155 ... 156 G gfansler@lincolncollege.edu
FANT, Charlotte ... 662-915-7792 ... 277 G cfant@olemiss.edu
FANT, Gene ... 731-661-5520 ... 476 G gfant@uu.edu
FANT, Greg ... 575-646-2127 ... 319 D gfant@nmsu.edu
FANTE, Cheryl ... 352-854-2322 ... 103 D fantec@cf.edu
FANTER, Jeff ... 317-921-4502 ... 175 G jfanter@ivytech.edu
FANTINI, Beatriz ... 802-258-3343 ... 514 C beatriz.fantini@worldlearning.org
FANTOZZI, Joseph ... 212-650-7865 ... 326 H jfantozzi@ccny.cuny.edu
FANUTTI, Carol ... 716-827-2462 ... 358 B fanuttic@trocaire.edu
FAOUR, Sheila ... 318-675-5000 ... 213 B sfaour@lsuhsc.edu
FAOUR, William, G ... 423-624-0077 ... 467 F billf@chattanoogacollege.edu
FAPOHUNDA, Eleanor ... 631-420-2198 ... 356 A
FARAHANI, Gohar ... 301-846-2451 ... 222 G gfarahani@frederick.edu
FARAHI, Dawood ... 908-737-7000 ... 311 B dfarahi@kean.edu
FARAKISH, Negar ... 908-412-3590 ... 316 B negar.farakish@ucc.edu
FARAN, Ellen, W ... 617-253-4078 ... 242 A ewfaran@mit.edu
FARANDA, John, P ... 909-621-8153 ... 40 D john.faranda@cmc.edu
FARARA, Joseph ... 802-635-1272 ... 515 E joe.farara@jsc.edu
FARBANIEC, David ... 845-257-3196 ... 352 B farbanid@newpaltz.edu
FARBROTHER, Barry ... 386-226-6817 ... 105 C barry.farbrother@erau.edu
FARE, Bridget, M ... 412-396-6052 ... 428 C fareb@duq.edu
FARELLA, Adriana ... 202-319-5300 ... 97 C farella@cua.edu
FARES, Ted ... 575-562-2511 ... 318 A ted.fares@enmu.edu
FARHA, Darron, C ... 219-464-6702 ... 181 A darron.farha@valpo.edu
FARHANG, Ahad ... 718-951-5669 ... 326 G afarhang@brooklyn.cuny.edu
FARIA, Geraldine ... 718-951-5214 ... 326 G gfaria@brooklyn.cuny.edu
FARIA, Pamela ... 617-243-2221 ... 236 F pfaria@lasell.edu
FARIAS, Antonio ... 860-701-6702 ... 558 E antonio.farias@uscg.edu
FARIAS, Jaime, D ... 915-831-2394 ... 486 E jfarias@epcc.edu
FARIDIAN, Fred ... 909-884-8891 ... 42 I ffaridian@concorde.edu
FARINHOLT, Phil ... 910-362-7014 ... 368 E pfarinholt@cfcc.edu
FARINOS, Jose, L ... 772-462-7611 ... 110 L jfarinos@irsc.edu
FARIS, Kimberly ... 903-463-8650 ... 487 A farisk@grayson.edu
FARISH, Donald, J ... 401-254-3201 ... 454 C
FARISH, Guy ... 440-826-2478 ... 384 H gfarish@bw.edu
FARKAS, Abraham ... 707-524-1508 ... 68 E afarkas@santarosa.edu
FARKAS, Scott, M ... 937-382-6661 ... 405 H scott_farkas@wilmington.edu
FARLAND, William, H ... 970-491-7194 ... 83 A william.farland@colostate.edu
FARLEY, Andre ... 706-793-2030 ... 135 C afarley@paine.edu
FARLEY, Barbara ... 612-330-1024 ... 261 G farleyb@augsburg.edu
FARLEY, Christy ... 928-523-0185 ... 17 A christy.farley@nau.edu
FARLEY, Erik, S ... 745-587-6605 ... 389 H farleye@denison.edu
FARLEY, James ... 602-386-4175 ... 11 H james.farley@arizonachristian.edu
FARLEY, Jean ... 617-296-8300 ... 236 E jean_farley@laboure.edu
FARLEY, Jerry, B ... 785-670-1556 ... 197 D jerry.farley@washburn.edu
FARLEY, Karen ... 563-336-3323 ... 184 B kfarley@eicc.edu
FARLEY, Kay ... 785-670-1049 ... 197 D kay.farley@washburn.edu
FARLEY, Kenneth ... 626-395-6005 ... 32 E farley@gps.caltech.edu
FARLEY, Lee ... 559-442-8231 ... 72 A lee.farley@fresnocitycollege.edu
FARLEY, Mark ... 202-274-5183 ... 99 F mfarley@udc.edu
FARLEY, Mike ... 719-549-2314 ... 83 B mike.farley@colostate-pueblo.edu
FARLEY, Patrick ... 301-891-4551 ... 229 B pfarley@wau.edu
FARLEY, Penelope, L ... 410-778-7224 ... 229 D pfarley2@washcoll.edu
FARLEY, Thomas, R ... 757-455-3263 ... 529 F tfarley@vwc.edu
FARLEY, Tim ... 925-631-4830 ... 64 F tif5@stmarys-ca.edu
FARLEY, Troy ... 616-331-3311 ... 252 A farleytr@gvsu.edu
FARMER, Anne ... 708-209-3237 ... 148 C anne.farmer@cuchicago.edu
FARMER, Berkwood, M ... 937-775-4859 ... 406 C berkwood.farmer@wright.edu
FARMER, Carla ... 417-667-8181 ... 280 I cfarmer@cottey.edu
FARMER, David ... 910-695-3911 ... 373 E farmerdj@sandhills.edu
FARMER, David, M ... 401-874-6222 ... 454 E thedean@gso.uri.edu
FARMER, JR., John, J ... 973-353-5561 ... 314 E jofarmer@andromeda.rutgers.edu
FARMER, Joyce ... 610-282-1100 ... 426 I joyce.farmer@desales.edu
FARMER, Karla ... 620-223-2700 ... 192 G karlaf@fortscott.edu
FARMER, Ken, R ... 513-721-7944 ... 391 C kfarmer@gbs.edu
FARMER, Larry, G ... 704-637-4227 ... 363 C lfarmer@catawba.edu
FARMER, Linda ... 541-684-4644 ... 419 F lfarmer@pioneerpacific.edu
FARMER, Lorna ... 908-852-1400 ... 308 F farmer@centenarycollege.edu
FARMER, Pam ... 864-977-7009 ... 460 A pam.farmer@ngu.edu
FARMER, Patricia ... 603-358-2370 ... 307 A pfarmer@keene.edu
FARMER, Patricia J, B ... 315-229-5265 ... 349 E pfarmer@stlawu.edu
FARMER, Randy, L ... 214-648-2344 ... 507 D randy.farmer@utsouthwestern.edu
FARMER, Richard ... 617-578-7100 ... 235 D rfarmer@gibbsboston.edu
FARMER, Scott ... 337-482-5393 ... 216 D sfarmer@louisiana.edu
FARMER, Stephen, M ... 919-966-3992 ... 378 D smfarmer@email.unc.edu
FARMER, Steve ... 601-968-5929 ... 273 F sfarmer@belhaven.edu
FARMER, Steve ... 419-227-3141 ... 404 D wfarmer@unoh.edu
FARMER, Vickie, L ... 319-895-4243 ... 183 D vfarmer@cornellcollege.edu
FARMER, William, C ... 562-860-2451 ... 38 J wfarmer@cerritos.edu
FARMER-NEAL, Rochonda ... 254-710-1453 ... 481 I rochonda_farmer-neal@baylor.edu
FARMER NOONAN, Erin ... 617-735-9991 ... 234 E farmer@emmanuel.edu
FARNESKI, Anna ... 201-684-6844 ... 313 D afarnesk@ramapo.edu
FARNEY, Ashlee ... 312-922-1884 ... 157 C afarney@maccormac.edu
FARNHAM, Bruce ... 619-660-4347 ... 48 J bruce.farnham@gcccd.edu
FARNHAM, Margaret, L ... 614-235-4136 ... 402 G mfarnham@TLSohio.edu
FARNLACHER, Jeanne, K ... 614-257-4682 ... 390 B jfarnlacher@devry.edu
FARNSWORTH, Briant, J ... 801-863-8006 ... 511 C briant.farnsworth@uvu.edu
FARNSWORTH, Scott ... 928-776-2234 ... 19 E scott.farnsworth@yc.edu
FARO, Michael, E ... 585-594-6130 ... 347 F farom@roberts.edu
FAROL, Dorothy ... 714-997-6611 ... 39 C farol@chapman.edu
FARQUHARSON, Janice, E ... 309-624-8980 ... 163 E janice.farquharson@osfhealthcare.org
FARR, Betty ... 603-428-2480 ... 305 E bfarr@nec.edu
FARR, C. Stephen ... 478-757-3700 ... 139 A sfarr@wesleyancollege.edu
FARR, Harbin ... 912-449-7530 ... 138 G hfarr@waycross.edu
FARR, Harbin ... 912-449-7545 ... 138 G hfarr@waycross.edu
FARR, Lamar ... 215-953-5999 ... 99 D lamar.farr@strayer.edu
FARR, Lamar ... 864-250-7000 ... 99 D
FARR, Lum ... 318-368-3179 ... 210 L lfarr@ltc.edu
FARR, Matthew ... 609-894-9311 ... 308 C mfarr@bcc.edu
FARR, Pamela ... 912-287-5842 ... 135 B pfarr@okefenokeetech.edu
FARR, Ralph, E ... 409-747-3810 ... 507 B rfarr@utmb.edu
FARR, Sharon ... 573-288-6633 ... 281 D sfarr@culver.edu
FARRA, Taline ... 617-587-5624 ... 243 D farrat@neco.edu
FARRAR, James, D ... 540-458-8465 ... 530 A jdfarrar@wlu.edu
FARRAR, Jazaer ... 708-596-2000 ... 164 F jfouad-farrar@ssc.edu
FARRAR, Margaret, E ... 309-794-7313 ... 145 B margaretfarrar@augustana.edu

FEEHERY, Peggy, C ... 770-720-5548 ... 135 F
prc@reinhardt.edu
FEELER, Billy ... 432-685-4626 ... 490 G
bfeeler@midland.edu
FEELEY, Daniel, T ... 304-243-2383 ... 545 G
feeley@wju.edu
FEELEY, John ... 970-204-8131 ... 84 H
john.feeley@frontrange.edu
FEENEY, David, F ... 508-678-2811 ... 239 F
david.feeney@bristolcc.edu
FEENSTRA, Ronald, J ... 616-957-7193 ... 249 F
feenro@calvinseminary.edu
FEERER, Pam ... 620-252-7357 ... 191 I
pamf@coffeyville.edu
FEEZOR, Karen ... 828-328-7392 ... 366 B
karen.feezor@lr.edu
FEFFERMAN, Robert, A ... 773-702-7950 ... 166 D
psd-dean@uchicago.edu
FEGAN, Kevin, G ... 972-293-5449 ... 257 A
fegan@northwood.edu
FEGELY, Neal, R ... 610-526-1501 ... 421 G
neal.fegely@theamericancollege.edu
FEGLEY, Jill ... 252-638-7233 ... 369 E
fegleyj@cravencc.edu
FEHLAU, Fred ... 626-396-2290 ... 29 G
fred.fehlau@artcenter.edu
FEHLEN, Mike ... 419-448-2517 ... 391 G
mfehlen@heidelberg.edu
FEHLER, Tim, G ... 864-294-3347 ... 458 D
tim.fehler@furman.edu
FEHLMAN, John, C ... 330-471-8236 ... 395 E
jfehlman@malone.edu
FEHN, Bruce, C ... 848-932-5661 ... 314 B
fehn@oldqueens.rutgers.edu
FEHN, Heather ... 609-771-2101 ... 308 G
hfehn@tcnj.edu
FEHOKO, Lisa ... 808-675-3701 ... 139 I
lisa.fehoko@byuh.edu
FEHRENBACH, Leslie, A ... 848-932-1352 ... 314 B
fehrenbach@oldqueens.rutgers.edu
FEICHTER, Kathryn ... 330-966-5452 ... 402 A
kfeichter@starkstate.edu
FEICK, Andrew ... 610-409-3598 ... 450 C
afeick@ursinus.edu
FEIDER, Lynn, A ... 803-786-5150 ... 459 B
lfeider@ltss.edu
FEIER, Julie ... 970-943-2061 ... 89 B
jfeier@western.edu
FEIERSTEIN, Barry ... 301-502-8639 ... 19 C
barry.feierstein@phoenix.edu
FEIERTAG, Jason ... 484-664-3140 ... 437 B
feiertag@muhlenberg.edu
FEIGELSTOCK, Yitzchok ... 516-225-4700 ... 346 K
rcli@mlb.edu
FEIGENBAUM, Maurice ... 973-684-6036 ... 312 E
mfeigenbaum@pccc.edu
FEIGERT, Kendra, M ... 717-867-6126 ... 434 C
feigert@lvc.edu
FEIL, Kevin, D ... 717-815-6818 ... 452 F
kfeil@ycp.edu
FEIMSTER, Torrey ... 704-378-1111 ... 365 H
tfeimster@jcsu.edu
FEIN, Cheri ... 212-217-4700 ... 333 G
cheri_fein@fitnyc.edu
FEIN, Jason ... 973 408 3648 ... 309 F
jfein@drew.edu
FEIN, Michael, T ... 434-832-7751 ... 526 A
feinm@cvcc.vccs.edu
FEIN, Oliver, T ... 212-746-4030 ... 360 B
ofein@med.cornell.edu
FEINAUER, John ... 540-261-4091 ... 524 C
john.feinauer@svu.edu
FEINBERG, David, T ... 310-267-9315 ... 74 A
dfeinberg@mednet.ucla.edu
FEINER, Barbara, A ... 314-935-9842 ... 292 J
barbara.a.feiner@wustl.edu
FEINERMAN, Frances ... 413-236-2102 ... 239 E
ffeinerm@berkshirecc.edu
FEINGOLD, Marilyn ... 856-374-4932 ... 308 E
mfeingold@camdencc.edu
FEINSTEIN, Andrew, H ... 909-869-3464 ... 33 G
andyf@csupomona.edu
FEINSTEIN, David ... 212-964-2830 ... 340 I
FEINSTEIN, Jerald, L ... 301-548-5500 ... 99 D
FEITZ, David, A ... 801-321-7210 ... 510 K
dfeitz@utahsbr.edu
FEKARIS, Cynthia ... 212-594-4000 ... 357 G
cfekaris@tcicollege.edu
FEKE, Donald, L ... 216-368-4389 ... 386 E
dlf4@case.edu
FEKETE, Michael ... 815-836-5549 ... 156 D
feketemi@lewisu.edu
FELCH, Katrina ... 715-675-3331 ... 554 G
felch@ntc.edu
FELD, Steven ... 803-321-3353 ... 459 G
steve.feld@newberry.edu
FELD-GORE, Jeffrey ... 503-768-7178 ... 416 F
jfeldgore@lclark.edu
FELDBLUM, Miriam ... 909-621-8017 ... 63 A
miriam.feldblum@pomona.edu
FELDER, Barbara, M ... 803-535-1218 ... 460 C
felderb@octech.edu
FELDER, Luther ... 706-821-8295 ... 135 C
lfelder@paine.edu
FELDER, Nigel ... 937-376-6566 ... 386 H
nfelder@centralstate.edu
FELDER-DEAS, Altoya, A ... 803-934-3167 ... 459 F
afdeas@morris.edu
FELDHAUS, Joseph, H ... 513-745-3908 ... 406 E
feldhausjl@xavier.edu
FELDHUES, Nicole ... 412-396-5675 ... 428 C
feldhuesn@duq.edu
FELDHUS, Karima ... 949-451-5336 ... 70 E
kfeldhus@ivc.edu
FELDMAN, Aharon ... 410-484-7200 ... 225 C
FELDMAN, Barbara ... 201-200-3001 ... 312 B
bfeldman@njcu.edu
FELDMAN, Barry ... 860-486-3826 ... 94 E
barry.feldman@uconn.edu
FELDMAN, Cecile, A ... 973-972-4633 ... 316 D
feldman@umdnj.edu
FELDMAN, Dan ... 781-736-8405 ... 233 A
feldman@brandeis.edu
FELDMAN, Harriet ... 212-346-1956 ... 345 F
hfeldman@pace.edu
FELDMAN, Jacqueline ... 978-632-6600 ... 240 G
j_feldman@mwcc.mass.edu
FELDMAN, Jerome ... 212-938-5540 ... 355 B
jfeldman@sunyopt.edu
FELDMAN, Mary Jane ... 716-614-5926 ... 344 C
feldman@niagaracc.suny.edu
FELDMAN, Robert, S ... 413-545-4173 ... 237 C
feldman@sbs.umass.edu
FELDMAN, Stuart ... 212-851-1192 ... 357 J
sfeldman@touro.edu
FELDMANN, Deborah ... 510-594-3606 ... 31 J
dfeldmann@cca.edu
FELDMANN, Jacob ... 718-645-0536 ... 341 D
FELDMEIER, Theresa ... 614-236-6813 ... 386 C
tfeldmei@capital.edu
FELDSCHER, Donald ... 215-489-4978 ... 426 H
Donald.Feldscher@delval.edu
FELDT, Tina ... 318-869-5424 ... 208 F
tfeldt@centenary.edu
FELDZYNSKI, Tom ... 303-632-2300 ... 83 C
tfeldzynski@coloradotech.edu
FELIBERTY, Victor, A ... 787-284-1912 ... 563 F
vfeliber@ponce.inter.edu
FELICE, Susan ... 708-656-8000 ... 159 C
susan.felice@morton.edu
FELICIANA, Jerrye, B ... 301-736-3631 ... 224 B
jerrye.feliciana@msbbcs.edu
FELICIANO, Alberto ... 787-764-0033 ... 567 F
alberto.feliciano@upr.edu
FELICIANO, Idali ... 517-265-5161 ... 247 D
ifeliciano@adrian.edu
FELICIANO, Josean ... 787-786-3030 ... 560 E
jfeliciano@ucb.edu.pr
FELICIANO, Nereidin ... 787-815-0000 ... 566 F
nereidin.feliciano@gmail.com
FELICIANO, Orlando ... 847-317-8072 ... 166 B
feliciano@tiu.edu
FELICIANO, Patsy ... 813-974-3827 ... 120 D
pfelicia@admin.usf.edu
FELIO, John, R ... 518-783-2471 ... 350 I
jfelio@siena.edu
FELIU, Julio ... 787-841-2000 ... 564 I
jfeliu@email.pucpr.edu
FELIX-MATA, Bertha ... 559-934-2217 ... 77 I
berthafelixmata@whccd.edu
FELIX-RODRIGUEZ,
Tamara ... 787-620-2040 ... 560 B
tdrodriguez@aupr.edu
FELKER, Sharon ... 618-634-3270 ... 164 C
sharonf@shawneecc.edu
FELKER, Sharon, M ... 303-963-3369 ... 81 K
sfelker@ccu.edu
FELKNOR, Bruce ... 312-629-6128 ... 164 A
bfelknor@saic.edu
FELL, Janet ... 732-923-4645 ... 311 F
jfell@monmouth.edu
FELL, Katherine, R ... 419-434-4510 ... 404 B
fell@findlay.edu
FELL, Stephanie ... 918-631-2241 ... 413 F
stephanie-fell@utulsa.edu
FELL, William ... 514-773-5665 ... 558 F
fellw@usmma.edu
FELLEGY, Anna ... 218-879-0878 ... 266 F
afellegy@fdltcc.edu
FELLENBERG, William ... 201-200-3598 ... 312 B
wfellenberg@njcu.edu
FELLINGER, Jennifer ... 360-491-4700 ... 536 F
jfellinger@stmartin.edu
FELLMER, Jennine ... 641-472-1190 ... 187 B
alumni@mum.edu
FELLOWS, Maureen, O ... 315-470-6621 ... 355 A
mfellows@esf.edu
FELSER, Francis, J ... 716-250-7500 ... 324 H
fjfelser@bryantstratton.edu
FELSHEIM, Mark ... 763-488-2465 ... 266 G
mark.felsheim@hennepintech.edu
FELSKE, Julie, L ... 989-837-4436 ... 257 A
felske@northwood.edu
FELSOVALYI, Erzsebet ... 973-748-9000 ... 308 A
elizabeth_felsovalyi@bloomfield.edu
FELSTEN, Marsha, E ... 610-799-1219 ... 434 D
mfelsten@lccc.edu
FELT, K.C ... 208-282-3755 ... 143 D
feltkc@isu.edu
FELT, Suzanne ... 208-524-3000 ... 143 C
suzanne.felt@my.eitc.edu
FELTES, Carol ... 212-327-8909 ... 347 H
cfeltes@rockvax.rockefeller.edu
FELTMANN, Charles ... 636-227-2100 ... 284 E
charles.feltmann@logan.edu
FELTON, David, A ... 304-293-2521 ... 544 E
david.felton@hsc.wvu.edu
FELTON, Herman ... 704-216-6044 ... 366 D
hfelton@livingstone.edu
FELTON, James ... 828-227-2276 ... 379 E
jafelton@wcu.edu
FELTON, Judith ... 860-343-5816 ... 90 D
jfelton@mxcc.commnet.edu
FELTON, Rob ... 503-554-2129 ... 415 I
rfelton@georgefox.edu
FELTON, Terence ... 708-456-0300 ... 166 C
tfelton@triton.edu
FELTS, Bennie, L ... 919-941-2920 ... 375 E
bennie.felts@fsmail.pfeiffer.edu
FELTS, Ronald ... 661-726-1911 ... 73 C
FELTY, Donna, H ... 423-652-4752 ... 469 L
dhfelty@king.edu
FELVER, Eric, L ... 912-279-5770 ... 127 B
efelver@ccga.edu
FEMINO, Donald ... 978-232-5201 ... 234 F
dfemino@endicott.edu
FENDERS, Nancy ... 207-941-7153 ... 218 A
fendersn@husson.edu
FENDRICH, Carlotta ... 719-549-2904 ... 83 B
carlotta.fendrich@colostate-pueblo.edu
FENESY, Kim ... 973-972-4440 ... 316 D
fenesy@umdnj.edu
FENESY, Kim, E ... 973-972-1699 ... 316 D
fenesy@umdnj.edu
FENG, Janet ... 281-649-3748 ... 487 F
jfeng@hbu.edu
FENG, Xiaomei ... 203-365-7511 ... 93 G
fengx@sacredheart.edu
FENING, June ... 513-727-3440 ... 396 F
FENLASON, Laurie ... 413-585-2170 ... 245 B
lfenlaso@smith.edu
FENN, Patricia ... 732-255-0400 ... 312 D
pfenn@ocean.edu
FENNELL, Angelia ... 903-593-8311 ... 499 A
afennell@texascollege.edu
FENNELL, Barbara ... 432-686-4250 ... 490 G
bfennell@midland.edu
FENNELL, Catherine ... 610-896-1221 ... 430 G
cfennell@haverford.edu
FENNELL, Catherine ... 610-527-0200 ... 445 I
fennell@roesmont.edu
FENNELL, Dustin ... 480-423-6277 ... 16 D
dustin.fennell@sccmail.maricopa.edu
FENNELL, Dwight ... 903-593-8311 ... 499 A
dfennell@texascollege.edu
FENNELL, Francis, L ... 773-508-3505 ... 157 A
ffennel@luc.edu
FENNELL, Shirley ... 919-546-8227 ... 376 D
sfennell@shawu.edu
FENNER-LEINO, Patti ... 715-682-1230 ... 549 C
pfen-lei@northland.edu
FENNERN, Nicole ... 507-457-1781 ... 271 G
nfennern@smumn.edu
FENNESSEY, Tom ... 715-394-8122 ... 552 D
tfenness@uwsuper.edu
FENNESSY, Mary ... 732-255-0400 ... 312 D
mfennessy@ocean.edu
FENNING, Robert, L ... 757-683-3464 ... 521 L
rfenning@odu.edu
FENSKE, David, E ... 215-895-2479 ... 427 G
def23@drexel.edu
FENSKE, Susanne ... 262-691-5295 ... 555 C
sfenske@wctc.edu
FENSTAD, Terry ... 413-572-5276 ... 239 C
tfenstad@wsc.ma.edu
FENTER, Glen, F ... 870-733-6722 ... 22 E
gfenter@midsouthcc.edu
FENTON, James, W ... 419-772-2070 ... 398 G
j-fenton@onu.edu
FENTON, Walter ... 618-664-6500 ... 151 D
walter.fenton@greenville.edu
FENTON, William, E ... 502-272-8059 ... 198 E
wfenton@bellarmine.edu
FENTON-MACE, Christina ... 570-945-8162 ... 432 C
christina.mace@keystone.edu
FENTRESS, Connie ... 757-789-1728 ... 526 D
cfentress@es.vccs.edu
FENTRESS, Craig, M ... 301-790-2800 ... 223 A
fentressc@hagerstowncc.edu
FENTRESS, Lisa, I ... 757-455-3337 ... 529 F
lfentress@vwc.edu
FENTRESS, Mike ... 360-752-8320 ... 531 C
mfentress@btc.ctc.edu
FENVES, Gregory, L ... 512-471-1166 ... 505 B
fenves@mail.utexas.edu
FENWICK, Garland ... 540-423-9046 ... 526 E
gfenwick@germanna.edu
FENWICK, Leslie, T ... 202-806-7340 ... 98 B
lfenwick@howard.edu
FEOLA, Ralph, J ... 315-792-5444 ... 341 E
rfeola@mvcc.edu
FERALDI, Corey ... 803-641-3280 ... 462 B
coreyf@usca.edu
FERALDI, Patricia, A ... 716-673-3553 ... 352 A
patricia.feraldi@fredonia.edu
FERBER, Maragaret, C ... 585-389-2020 ... 342 D
mferber6@naz.edu
FERBRACHE, Jeanne ... 402-559-3937 ... 301 A
jferbrache@unmc.edu
FERCHLAND-PARELLA,
Joanne ... 954-262-2114 ... 114 B
ferchlan@nsu.nova.edu
FERDEN, Patricia ... 507-457-5330 ... 270 B
pferden@winona.edu
FERDINAND, Amy ... 973-655-4367 ... 311 G
ferdinanda@mail.montclair.edu
FEREBEE, Ryan, A ... 757-594-7033 ... 517 I
ryan.ferebee@cnu.edu
FEREIRA, James, A ... 651-638-6300 ... 261 I
j-fereira@bethel.edu
FERENBACH, Gregory ... 703-247-2500 ... 99 D
gregory.ferenbach@strayer.edu
FERGERSON, Nicole ... 775-831-1314 ... 303 E
nfergerson@sierranevada.edu
FERGUSON, Angela, M ... 704-403-1614 ... 362 E
angela.ferguson@carolinashealthcare.org
FERGUSON, Annette ... 806-874-3571 ... 482 H
annette.ferguson@clarendoncollege.edu
FERGUSON, Bennett ... 678-359-5023 ... 131 D
benf@gdn.edu
FERGUSON, Charity, F ... 270-384-8100 ... 203 H
fergusonc@lindsey.edu
FERGUSON, Chen ... 513-785-7703 ... 396 E
fergusc@muohio.edu
FERGUSON, Chris, D ... 253-535-7505 ... 535 K
cdf@plu.edu
FERGUSON, Christy ... 716-286-8345 ... 344 D
clf@niagara.edu
FERGUSON, Constance, M ... 315-268-6475 ... 329 C
cmferguson@clarkson.edu
FERGUSON, Darla ... 321-433-7080 ... 101 J
fergusond@brevardcc.edu
FERGUSON, David ... 508-999-8100 ... 237 E
dferguson1@umassd.edu
FERGUSON, David ... 419-434-4398 ... 404 B
ferguson@findlay.edu
FERGUSON, Devin ... 972-825-4700 ... 495 D
dferguson@sagu.edu
FERGUSON, Douglas, J ... 610-359-7399 ... 426 G
dferguson@dccc.edu
FERGUSON, F. Joel ... 831-459-2412 ... 75 A
fjf@ucsc.edu
FERGUSON, Gail ... 940-397-4273 ... 491 A
gail.ferguson@mwsu.edu
FERGUSON, Janice, Y ... 716-625-6300 ... 324 K
jyferguson@bryantstratton.edu
FERGUSON, Jason ... 773-821-2601 ... 146 D
jfergu20@csu.edu
FERGUSON, Jason ... 503-229-0492 ... 416 A
jason_ferguson@heald.edu
FERGUSON, Jessame, E ... 410-857-2741 ... 224 D
jferguson@mcdaniel.edu
FERGUSON, Joe, C ... 402-844-7236 ... 300 A
joe@northeast.edu
FERGUSON, Joseph, F ... 510-780-4500 ... 53 I
jferguson@lifewest.edu
FERGUSON, Joseph, S ... 361-570-4390 ... 503 E
fergusonj@uhv.edu
FERGUSON, Judy ... 281-649-3450 ... 487 F
jferguson@hbu.edu
FERGUSON, Julie ... 973-972-4640 ... 316 F
fergusje@umdnj.edu
FERGUSON, Keith, D ... 615-353-3604 ... 475 D
keith.ferguson@nscc.edu
FERGUSON, Ken ... 573-681-5265 ... 284 B
fergusonk@lincolnu.edu
FERGUSON, Kimberly ... 404-270-5133 ... 137 E
kfergu15@spelman.edu
FERGUSON, Larry ... 606-326-2232 ... 201 B
larry.ferguson@kctcs.edu
FERGUSON, Larry, W ... 803-323-2216 ... 463 D
fergusonl@winthrop.edu
FERGUSON, Lee ... 214-333-5363 ... 484 C
lee@dbu.edu
FERGUSON, Lisa, M ... 740-283-6450 ... 390 M
lferguson@franciscan.edu
FERGUSON, Lori ... 580-349-1566 ... 410 B
lorif@opsu.edu
FERGUSON, Lorrie ... 540-863-2823 ... 526 B
lferguson@dslcc.edu
FERGUSON, Mary ... 812-237-2877 ... 173 A
mary.ferguson@indstate.edu
FERGUSON, Mla ... 605-455-6000 ... 464 H
mferguson@olc.edu
FERGUSON, Nancy ... 513-727-3431 ... 396 F
FERGUSON, Nicole ... 775-831-1314 ... 303 E
nferguson@sierranevada.edu
FERGUSON, Noreen ... 248-204-3106 ... 254 E
nferguson@ltu.edu
FERGUSON, Pam ... 405-751-8343 ... 409 E
pam.ferguson@oc.edu
FERGUSON, Pamela ... 973-720-2615 ... 317 D
FERGUSON, Paul ... 912-478-7288 ... 131 A
pferguson@georgiasouthern.edu

FICK, Verlyn ..... 520-515-5414 ..... 13 G
fickv@cochise.edu
FICKE, Joan, C ..... 973-655-4368 ..... 311 G
fickej@mail.montclair.edu
FICKENSCHER, II, Carl, C 260-452-2131 ..... 170 G
carl.fickenscher@ctsfw.edu
FICKESS, Jordan ..... 305-892-7039 ..... 111 K
jordan.fickess@jwu.edu
FICTUM, Daniel ..... 718-260-5931 ..... 328 E
dfictum@citytech.cuny.edu
FIDERIO, Janet ..... 603-283-2107 ..... 303 F
jfiderio@antiochne.edu
FIDLER, Jane, P ..... 617-333-2355 ..... 234 A
jfidler0803@curry.edu
FIEDLER, Daniel ..... 903-233-3561 ..... 489 K
danielfiedler@letu.edu
FIEDLER, Kay ..... 207-948-3131 ..... 219 H
kfiedler@unity.edu
FIEDLER, Peter ..... 617-353-6500 ..... 232 G
pfiedler@bu.edu
FIEDLER, Thomas ..... 617-353-3488 ..... 232 G
tfiedler@bu.edu
FIEGE, William ..... 540-891-3040 ..... 526 E
wfiege@germanna.edu
FIELD, Darryl ..... 215-591-5880 ..... 427 A
dfield@devry.edu
FIELD, Hilary ..... 617-585-1701 ..... 243 E
hilary.field@necmusic.edu
FIELD, Jay ..... 562-938-4280 ..... 54 E
jfield@lbcc.edu
FIELD, Juliana ..... 617-423-4630 ..... 231 E
jfield@bfit.edu
FIELD, Lindsey ..... 435-283-7164 ..... 512 B
lindsey.field@snow.edu
FIELD, Martha ..... 413-775-1421 ..... 240 B
field@gcc.mass.edu
FIELD, Stephen, G ..... 585-594-6150 ..... 347 F
fields@roberts.edu
FIELD, Susan ..... 218-683-8678 ..... 268 E
susan.field@northlandcollege.edu
FIELDER, Marsha ..... 517-265-5161 ..... 247 D
mfielder@adrian.edu
FIELDING, Ahn ..... 707-476-4140 ..... 42 A
ahn-fielding@redwoods.edu
FIELDING, Chad ..... 870-230-5420 ..... 21 I
fieldic@hsu.edu
FIELDING, William ..... 256-782-5773 ..... 4 L
fielding@jsu.edu
FIELDS, Ann ..... 641-673-1076 ..... 189 I
fieldsa@wmpenn.edu
FIELDS, Ann, Z ..... 901-722-3230 ..... 473 B
annfields@sco.edu
FIELDS, Beverly ..... 806-457-4200 ..... 486 G
bfields@fpctx.edu
FIELDS, Brad ..... 610-225-5032 ..... 428 D
bfields@eastern.edu
FIELDS, Charlene ..... 303-876-7100 ..... 464 G
cfields@national.edu
FIELDS, Christopher ..... 614-947-6803 ..... 391 A
fieldsc@franklin.edu
FIELDS, Darin, E ..... 304-829-7313 ..... 540 E
dfields@bethanywv.edu
FIELDS, Dennis ..... 717-545-4747 ..... 432 D
FIELDS, Edward ..... 502-597-6163 ..... 203 D
edward.fields@kysu.edu
FIELDS, Gene ..... 337-482-9246 ..... 216 D
gene.fields@louisiana.edu
FIELDS, Jay ..... 803-793-5286 ..... 457 F
fieldsj@denmarktech.edu
FIELDS, Jeff ..... 276-656-0222 ..... 527 D
jfields@ph.vccs.edu
FIELDS, JoElla ..... 405-945-9106 ..... 410 F
FIELDS, John ..... 229-430-4711 ..... 123 H
john.fields@asurams.edu
FIELDS, Lee, M ..... 252-334-2080 ..... 367 A
lee.fields@macuniversity.edu
FIELDS, Leonard, B ..... 563-562-3263 ..... 187 G
fieldsl@nicc.edu
FIELDS, Marcia, C ..... 573-840-9666 ..... 290 J
FIELDS, Marcia, C ..... 573-840-9675 ..... 290 J
mfields@trcc.edu
FIELDS, Melea ..... 562-902-3344 ..... 71 A
meleafields@scuhs.edu
FIELDS, Michael ..... 954-262-5053 ..... 114 B
fieldsm@nsu.nova.edu
FIELDS, Michael ..... 707-668-5663 ..... 43 I
FIELDS, Peter ..... 406-994-4221 ..... 295 E
pfields@msubobcats.com
FIELDS, Petra ..... 704-991-0231 ..... 374 A
pfields7679@stanly.edu
FIELDS, Ron ..... 651-747-4085 ..... 266 D
ron.fields@century.edu
FIELDS, Stan, D ..... 816-604-1578 ..... 285 D
stan.fields@mcckc.edu
FIELDS, Todd, E ..... 972-881-5174 ..... 483 D
tfields@collin.edu
FIELDS, Valarie ..... 803-516-4969 ..... 460 G
vfields1@scsu.edu
FIEMS, Richard ..... 309-796-5915 ..... 145 E
fiemsr@bhc.edu
FIENBERG, Nona ..... 603-358-2772 ..... 307 A
nfienber@keene.edu
FIENE, Jay ..... 909-537-5600 ..... 36 A
jfiene@csusb.edu

FIENE, John, L ..... 402-554-3670 ..... 301 B
jfiene@unomaha.edu
FIENMAN, Barbara ..... 978-921-4242 ..... 242 F
bfienman@montserrat.edu
FIENSY, David, A ..... 606-474-3263 ..... 200 J
dfiensy@kcu.edu
FIERBAUGH, Lee ..... 423-461-8719 ..... 471 H
lfierbaugh@milligan.edu
FIERKE, Kimberly ..... 607-431-4000 ..... 335 B
FIERO, Diane ..... 661-362-3424 ..... 41 G
diane.fiero@canyons.edu
FIERO, Tom, D ..... 517-750-1200 ..... 258 F
tfiero@arbor.edu
FIFE, Jerry ..... 615-343-6688 ..... 477 F
jerry.fife@vanderbilt.edu
FIFE, Kaaren ..... 913-288-7281 ..... 193 J
kfife@kckcc.edu
FIFE, Linda, L ..... 443-412-2377 ..... 223 B
lfife@harford.edu
FIFER, Tom ..... 660-831-4219 ..... 286 I
fifert@moval.edu
FIFIELD, Mary, L ..... 617-228-2400 ..... 239 G
mfifield@bhcc.mass.edu
FIFRICK, Heather ..... 608-822-2366 ..... 555 B
FIGA, Jan ..... 815-226-4165 ..... 162 H
jfiga@rockford.edu
FIGARELLE, Thomas ..... 406-771-4412 ..... 296 B
thomas.figarelle@msugf.edu
FIGARI, Charles, A ..... 713-500-8400 ..... 506 D
charles.a.figari@uth.tmc.edu
FIGAROA, Caroline ..... 787-761-0640 ..... 561 B
registraduria@cbp.edu
FIGGS, Joel ..... 785-243-1435 ..... 191 H
jfiggs@cloud.edu
FIGHERA, Christine ..... 714-992-7025 ..... 59 D
cfighera@fullcoll.edu
FIGUEIRA, Joseph, F ..... 406-496-4456 ..... 296 C
jfigueira@mtech.edu
FIGUEIRA, Russell, J ..... 610-526-1200 ..... 421 G
russell.figueira@theamericancollege.edu
FIGUEREDO, Danilo, H ..... 973-748-9000 ..... 308 A
danilo_figueredo@bloomfield.edu
FIGUEROA, Ana, M ..... 973-290-4434 ..... 309 A
afigueroa@cse.edu
FIGUEROA, Carlos ..... 787-850-9367 ..... 567 B
carlos.figueroa7@upr.edu
FIGUEROA, Cruz Zoraida ... 787-758-2525 ..... 567 D
zoraida.figueroa@upr.edu
FIGUEROA, Eduardo ..... 787-882-2065 ..... 565 I
FIGUEROA, Elsa ..... 708-456-0300 ..... 166 C
efiguero@triton.edu
FIGUEROA, Fernando ..... 361-698-1205 ..... 485 F
ffigueroa@delmar.edu
FIGUEROA, Gema, C ..... 787-738-2161 ..... 567 A
gema.figueroa@upr.edu
FIGUEROA, Hector, B ..... 787-265-3866 ..... 567 C
h_figueroa@rumad.uprm.edu
FIGUEROA, Ivan ..... 903-769-5700 ..... 488 M
ivan.figueroa@jarvis.edu
FIGUEROA, Julio ..... 787-257-7373 ..... 565 E
ue_jfigueroa@suagm.edu
FIGUEROA, Marc ..... 909-621-8224 ..... 69 A
marc.figueroa@scrippscollege.edu
FIGUEROA, Margarita ..... 787-720-1022 ..... 560 D
admisiones@atlanticcollege.edu
FIGUEROA, Maria ..... 787-725-6500 ..... 560 G
mafigueroa@albizu.edu
FIGUEROA, Maria, V ..... 787-743-7979 ..... 565 F
ut_mfigueroa@suagm.edu
FIGUEROA, Rachel ..... 330-499-9600 ..... 393 I
rfiguero@kent.edu
FIGUEROA, Roberto ..... 518-464-8800 ..... 333 F
rfigueroa@excelsior.edu
FIGUEROA, Samuel ..... 787-738-2161 ..... 567 A
samuel.figueroa5@upr.edu
FIGUEROA, Vitaliano ..... 702-651-4609 ..... 302 G
vitaliano.figueroa@csn.edu
FIGUEROA, William ..... 787-758-2525 ..... 567 D
william.figueroa3@upr.edu
FIGUEROA-MARTINEZ,
Agnes ..... 425-564-4128 ..... 531 B
agnes.figueroa@bellevuecollege.edu
FIGURA, Rebecca ..... 734-487-1300 ..... 250 H
rebecca.figura@emich.edu
FIIGUEROA, Ken ..... 407-888-4000 ..... 113 A
kfigueroa@orlando.chefs.edu
FIKE, David, J ..... 313-927-1208 ..... 255 A
dfike@marygrove.edu
FIKE, Esther ..... 954-492-5353 ..... 102 J
dhigley@citycollege.edu
FIKE, Esther ..... 407-831-9816 ..... 102 I
efike@citycollege.edu
FIKE, Harry ..... 301-387-3104 ..... 222 H
harry.fike@garrettcollege.edu
FIKE, Janet ..... 304-214-8837 ..... 543 A
jfike@wvncc.edu
FIKE, Jeffrey ..... 540-828-5395 ..... 516 K
jfike@bridgewater.edu
FIKE, Linda, K ..... 301-387-3049 ..... 222 H
linda.fike@garrettcollege.edu
FILAN, Sonia ..... 480-461-7446 ..... 15 K
sonia.filan@mcmail.maricopa.edu
FILARDI, Salvatore ..... 508-999-8058 ..... 237 E
sfilardi@umassd.edu

FILBRY, Sandra ..... 516-463-4335 ..... 335 H
sandra.filbry@hofstra.edu
FILBY, Robert, G ..... 740-284-5472 ..... 390 M
rfilby@franciscan.edu
FILE, Carter ..... 620-665-3509 ..... 193 F
FILE, David, C ..... 319-385-6245 ..... 186 A
dfile@iwc.edu
FILE, James ..... 404-527-4520 ..... 126 F
jfile@carver.edu
FILEMYR, Ann ..... 505-424-2354 ..... 318 C
afilemyr@iaia.edu
FILIPELLI, Steve ..... 516-877-4963 ..... 322 A
filipelli@adelphi.edu
FILIPIAK, Joseph, M ..... 312-915-7671 ..... 157 A
jfilipi@luc.edu
FILIPIC, Matthew, V ..... 937-775-2002 ..... 406 C
matthew.filipic@wright.edu
FILIPP, Robert ..... 773-442-5300 ..... 159 H
r-filipp@neiu.edu
FILIPPIDIS, Barbara ..... 512-448-8558 ..... 493 B
barbaraf@stedwards.edu
FILIPPONE, Anne ..... 610-902-8407 ..... 423 H
anne.ferry@cabrini.edu
FILIPPONE, Gregg, S ..... 716-851-1073 ..... 333 B
filipponeg@ecc.edu
FILIPPONE, Robin ..... 716-270-5237 ..... 333 C
filippone@ecc.edu
FILLINGER, Barbara ..... 734-973-3560 ..... 260 B
bfilling@wccnet.edu
FILLIPPI, Carolyn ..... 315-229-5267 ..... 349 E
cfillippi@stlawu.edu
FILLMER, Larry ..... 334-844-6140 ..... 1 G
fillmjl@auburn.edu
FILLNER, Russ ..... 406-444-6800 ..... 295 C
russ.fillner@umhelena.edu
FILLPOT, Jim ..... 909-652-6460 ..... 39 B
jim.fillpot@chaffey.edu
FILORAMO, Dorothy ..... 845-848-7400 ..... 332 C
dorothy.filoramo@dc.edu
FILOSA, Bruce ..... 718-951-5366 ..... 326 G
bfilosa@brooklyn.cuny.edu
FILOWSKI, Melissa ..... 509-865-8544 ..... 534 D
filowski_m@heritage.edu
FILPUS-LUYCKX, Mary ..... 706-737-1492 ..... 125 C
mfilpusl@aug.edu
FILSON, Cori ..... 518-580-5355 ..... 351 B
cfilson@skidmore.edu
FILTZ, William, J ..... 229-333-5701 ..... 138 F
bfiltz@valdosta.edu
FINALY, Roy ..... 619-477-6310 ..... 73 A
rfinaly@usuniversity.edu
FINALY, Tom ..... 619-477-6310 ..... 73 A
tf@usuniversity.edu
FINCANNON, Angie ..... 765-998-5311 ..... 179 F
anfincann@taylor.edu
FINCH, Brian, K ..... 860-444-8480 ..... 558 E
Bryan.K.Finch@uscg.mil
FINCH, Christopher ..... 201-559-6084 ..... 310 C
finchc@felician.edu
FINCH, Daniel ..... 419-720-6670 ..... 401 C
dfinch@proskills.com
FINCH, Donald ..... 608-249-6611 ..... 547 D
donnie@msn.herzing.edu
FINCH, Irene ..... 207-741-5715 ..... 219 A
ifinch@smccme.edu
FINCH, J. Howard ..... 205-726-2364 ..... 6 G
hfinch@samford.edu
FINCH, Jack, L ..... 740-377-2520 ..... 402 F
jfinch1@zoominternet.net
FINCH, Jerald, L ..... 206-281-2577 ..... 537 D
j_finch@spu.edu
FINCH, Mary Ellen ..... 314-529-9400 ..... 284 F
mfinch@maryville.edu
FINCH, R. Lynette ..... 252-451-8244 ..... 372 B
lfinch@nash.cc.nc.us
FINCH, Thomas ..... 315-786-2235 ..... 337 F
tfinch@sunyjefferson.edu
FINCH, Tony ..... 662-720-7304 ..... 276 D
tfinch@nemcc.edu
FINCH, Tracy ..... 870-972-2031 ..... 20 C
tfinch@astate.edu
FINCH, Veronica, M ..... 757-683-3689 ..... 521 L
vfinch@odu.edu
FINCHER, David, B ..... 660-263-3900 ..... 279 J
academics@cccb.edu
FINCHER, Wade ..... 501-882-8866 ..... 20 D
wade@asub.edu
FINCK, Kathy ..... 802-225-3258 ..... 513 H
kathy.finck@neci.edu
FINCK, Konrad ..... 312-329-4066 ..... 158 H
konrad.finck@moody.edu
FINDLEY, Brenda ..... 706-867-2705 ..... 134 D
bkfindley@northgeorgia.edu
FINDLEY, Donna ..... 478-387-4846 ..... 130 E
FINDLEY, Pamela, L ..... 256-782-5151 ..... 4 L
pfindley@jsu.edu
FINDT, William ..... 910-879-5502 ..... 368 A
wfindt@bladencc.edu
FINE, Ricka, K ..... 410-777-1868 ..... 221 B
rkfine@aacc.edu
FINE, Robert ..... 773-508-2398 ..... 157 A
rfine@luc.edu
FINEGAN, SC, Carol, M ..... 718-405-3349 ..... 330 A
carol.finegan@mountsaintvincent.edu

FINEGAN, James, M ..... 814-871-7000 ..... 429 F
finegan001@gannon.edu
FINEGAN, James, M ..... 814-871-7681 ..... 429 F
finegan001@gannon.edu
FINEGAN, Kathleen ..... 816-501-3621 ..... 279 C
kathleen.finegan@avila.edu
FINEGOLD, David, L ..... 732-445-5993 ..... 314 D
dfinegold@smlr.rutgers.edu
FINEIS, Jill ..... 802-586-7711 ..... 514 E
jfineis@sterlingcollege.edu
FINEMAN, Robert ..... 206-934-3791 ..... 536 H
robert.fineman@seattlecolleges.edu
FINEOUT-OVERHOLT,
Ellen ..... 903-923-2210 ..... 486 D
FINESHRIBER, Mara ..... 801-274-3280 ..... 512 E
mfineshriber@wgu.edu
FINESILVER, Jennifer ..... 317-632-5553 ..... 177 E
jfinesilver@lincolntech.com
FINFROCK, Randal, M ..... 724-925-4060 ..... 451 E
finfrockr@wccc.edu
FINGER, Mary ..... 312-362-8666 ..... 148 F
mfinger@depaul.edu
FINK, Brenda ..... 626-914-8830 ..... 39 G
bfink@citruscollege.edu
FINK, Charles, R ..... 631-423-0483 ..... 350 G
cfink@icseminary.edu
FINK, Ernest ..... 718-409-7341 ..... 356 C
efink@sunymaritime.edu
FINK, Gayle, M ..... 301-860-3403 ..... 228 A
gfink@bowiestate.edu
FINK, Jonathon ..... 503-725-9944 ..... 418 G
jon.fink@pdx.edu
FINK, Joseph, W ..... 412-624-9510 ..... 449 A
fink@pitt.edu
FINK, Michael ..... 909-652-6453 ..... 39 B
michael.fink@chaffey.edu
FINK, Michael ..... 912-525-5879 ..... 136 B
mfink@scad.edu
FINK, Robert ..... 262-595-2207 ..... 551 E
robert.fink@uwp.edu
FINKBEINER, Nicole ..... 269-965-3931 ..... 253 H
finkbeinern@kellogg.edu
FINKE, Barbara ..... 816-802-3434 ..... 283 I
bfinke@kcai.edu
FINKE, John ..... 317-955-6202 ..... 177 G
jfinke@marian.edu
FINKEL, Lee ..... 602-557-1595 ..... 19 C
lee.finkel@phoenix.edu
FINKELMAN, Jay ..... 626-284-2777 ..... 27 D
jfinkelman@alliant.edu
FINKELSTEIN, Barbara, E .. 508-588-9100 ..... 240 E
FINKELSTEIN, Eric, M ..... 718-990-2417 ..... 348 G
finkelse@stjohns.edu
FINKELSTEIN, Jon ..... 478-934-3335 ..... 133 G
jkfinkelstein@mgc.edu
FINKELSTEIN, Larry, A ..... 617-373-2462 ..... 244 A
FINKELSTEIN, Monte ..... 850-201-8488 ..... 121 F
finkelsm@tcc.fl.edu
FINKELSTEIN, Richard ..... 540-654-1052 ..... 524 H
rfinkels@umw.edu
FINKENBINE, Roy ..... 313-993-3250 ..... 259 C
finkenre@udmercy.edu
FINKLEA, Tim ..... 202-686-0876 ..... 99 A
tim.finklea@potomac.edu
FINKS, Frederick, J ..... 419-289-5050 ..... 384 D
ffinks@ashland.edu
FINLAY, Barbara, A ..... 540-338-1776 ..... 522 A
FINLAYSON, Alexander ..... 215-572-3823 ..... 451 D
sfinlayson@wts.edu
FINLAYSON, Deborah ..... 806-742-0502 ..... 501 D
deborah.finlayson@ttu.edu
FINLAYSON, Jeanne ..... 508-565-1337 ..... 245 D
jfinlayson@stonehill.edu
FINLEY, Adam ..... 817-598-8831 ..... 508 C
afinley@wc.edu
FINLEY, Bill, R ..... 785-890-3641 ..... 195 E
bfinley@nwktc.edu
FINLEY, David ..... 260-665-4224 ..... 180 A
finleyd@trine.edu
FINLEY, Jane ..... 251-442-2219 ..... 9 B
jfinley@umobile.edu
FINLEY, Jenna ..... 970-351-2721 ..... 88 F
jenna.finley@unco.edu
FINLEY, Jennifer ..... 828-277-5521 ..... 376 F
jfinley@southcollegenc.edu
FINLEY, Lucinda, M ..... 716-645-3594 ..... 351 G
finleylu@buffalo.edu
FINLEY, Michelle ..... 918-495-6203 ..... 411 C
mfinley@oru.edu
FINLEY, Rebecca ..... 215-503-9000 ..... 448 B
rebecca.finley@jefferson.edu
FINLEY, Tony ..... 501-279-4242 ..... 21 H
tfinley@harding.edu
FINLEY, William, D ..... 304-367-4842 ..... 543 E
william.finley@fairmontstate.edu
FINLINSON, Norm ..... 801-422-6424 ..... 509 D
norm_finlinson@byu.edu
FINN, Alicia, A ..... 603-641-7600 ..... 305 H
afinn@anselm.edu
FINN, Barbara ..... 678-260-3551 ..... 136 E
bfinn@shorter.edu
FINN, Bob, D ..... 509-313-6100 ..... 534 A
finn@gonzaga.edu

FITZENBERGER, Jennifer ... 520-621-9017 ..... 19 B
jfitzen@email.arizona.edu

FITZGERALD, Ann ... 574-936-8898 .... 168 I
ann.fitzgerald@ancilla.edu

FITZGERALD, Charles, B ... 434-924-3245 .... 525 B
cbf2w@virginia.edu

FITZGERALD, David ... 602-557-2387 ..... 19 C
david.fitzgerald@phoenix.edu

FITZGERALD, Deborah, K .. 617-253-3450 .... 242 A
dkfitz@mit.edu

FITZGERALD, Ed ... 618-252-5400 .... 164 G
eddie.fitzgerald@sic.edu

FITZGERALD, Ed ... 765-973-8222 .... 173 D
efitzger@iue.edu

FITZGERALD, Erin ... 860-493-0013 ..... 91 F
fitzgeralde@ct.edu

FITZGERALD, Faith, M ... 757-823-8407 .... 521 K
fmfitzgerald@nsu.edu

FITZGERALD, Hiram, E ... 517-353-8977 .... 255 D
fitzger9@msu.edu

FITZGERALD, Ione ... 312-461-0600 .... 144 D
ifitzgerald@aaart.edu

FITZGERALD, Janice ... 314-513-4238 .... 289 B
jfitzgerald@stlcc.edu

FITZGERALD, Jeanne, R ... 570-389-4070 .... 441 F
jfitzger@bloomu.edu

FITZGERALD, Joanne ... 518-631-9842 .... 358 F
fitzerj@uniongraduatecollege.edu

FITZGERALD, John, M ... 860-444-8200 .... 558 E
John.M.Fitzgerald@uscg.mil

FITZGERALD, Karen, L ... 419-866-0261 .... 402 B
klfitzgerald@stautzenberger.com

FITZGERALD, Kathy ... 914-323-5464 .... 340 A
kathy.fitzgerald@mville.edu

FITZGERALD, Laura ... 716-896-0700 .... 359 F
fitzgeraldl@villa.edu

FITZGERALD, Laureen, A .. 518-438-3111 .... 340 B
lfitz@mariacollege.edu

FITZGERALD, Liz ... 802-225-3261 .... 513 H
liz.fitzgerald@neci.edu

FITZGERALD, Maureen, F . 818-677-5674 ..... 35 D
maureen.fitzgerald@csun.edu

FITZGERALD, Mike ... 618-833-3399 .... 164 C
mikef@shawneecc.edu

FITZGERALD, Paul ... 312-662-4214 .... 144 C

FITZGERALD, Paul ... 814-868-9900 .... 428 H
paulf@erieit.edu

FITZGERALD, SJ, Paul, J .. 203-254-4000 ..... 92 B
pfitzgerald@fairfield.edu

FITZGERALD, Robert, E ... 309-298-1949 .... 168 A
re-fitzgerald@wiu.edu

FITZGERALD, Robert, F ... 401-863-2500 .... 452 J
robert_fitzgerald@brown.edu

FITZGERALD, Ronald ... 207-768-2806 .... 218 J
rfitzgerald@nmcc.edu

FITZGERALD, Sean, P ... 419-372-0464 .... 385 C
sfitzge@bgsu.edu

FITZGERALD, Susan ... 860-768-4011 ..... 95 A
fitzgeral@hartford.edu

FITZGERALD, Thomas ... 617-850-1212 .... 236 A
tfitzgerald@hchc.edu

FITZGERALD MILLER,
Judith ... 573-882-0278 .... 291 D
millerjud@missouri.edu

FITZGERLAD, Darren ... 800-962-7682 .... 293 B
dfitzgerald@wma.edu

FITZGIBBON, Heather, M .. 330-263-2576 .... 388 E
hfitzgibbon@wooster.edu

FITZGIBBON, John ... 831-582-3000 ..... 35 C
jfitzgibbon@csumb.edu

FITZGIBBON, John ... 831-582-4749 ..... 35 C
jfitzgibbon@csumb.edu

FITZGIBBON, William ... 713-743-3453 .... 503 B
fitz@uh.edu

FITZGIBBONS,
Dorothy Anne ... 516-678-5000 .... 341 F
dfitzgibbons@molloy.edu

FITZHUGH, Linda, H ... 903-233-4310 .... 489 K
lindafitzhugh@letu.edu

FITZMAURICE, Patricia ... 212-752-1530 .... 338 C
patricia.fitzmaurice@limcollege.edu

FITZPATRICK, Beata ... 510-642-7464 ..... 73 E
bfitzpatrick@berkeley.edu

FITZPATRICK, Bridget ... 570-961-7818 .... 433 A
fitzpatrickb@lackawanna.edu

FITZPATRICK, George ... 480-444-1112 ..... 18 E

FITZPATRICK, James ... 270-686-4332 .... 198 G
james.fitzpatrick@brescia.edu

FITZPATRICK, James, D ... 203-254-4000 ..... 92 B
jfitzpatrick@fairfield.edu

FITZPATRICK, Jane ... 606-783-2599 .... 204 E
j.fitzpatrick@moreheadstate.edu

FITZPATRICK, John, C ... 718-429-6600 .... 359 E
john.fitzpatrick@vaughn.edu

FITZPATRICK, Joy ... 425-388-9220 .... 533 H
jfitzpat@everettcc.edu

FITZPATRICK, M. Louise ... 610-519-4909 .... 450 G
louise.fitzpatrick@villanova.edu

FITZPATRICK, SC,
Margaret, M ... 845-398-4013 .... 349 H
mfitzpat@stac.edu

FITZPATRICK, Mary Anne .. 803-777-7798 .... 462 A
fitzpatm@gwm.sc.edu

FITZPATRICK, Pat ... 718-390-3131 .... 359 G
pfitzpat@wagner.edu

FITZPATRICK, Sharon ... 405-945-3292 .... 410 F

FITZPATRICK, Susan ... 906-635-2831 .... 254 C
sfitzpatrick@lssu.edu

FITZPATRICK, Timothy, J .. 352-392-2061 .... 120 B
timf@ufl.edu

FITZSIMMONS, Joanne ... 518-445-2324 .... 322 D
jfitz@albanylaw.edu

FITZSIMMONS, John ... 207-629-4000 .... 218 F
jfitzsimmons@mccs.me.edu

FITZSIMMONS, Peter ... 408-270-6130 ..... 67 A
peter.fitzsimmons@sjeccd.org

FITZSIMMONS, Stephanie . 732-224-2369 .... 308 B
sfitzsimmons@brookdalecc.edu

FITZSIMMONS, Tracy ... 540-665-4505 .... 523 K
tfitzsim@su.edu

FITZSIMMONS, William, R 617-495-1557 .... 235 H
wrf@fas.harvard.edu

FITZSIMONS, Connie ... 310-660-3715 ..... 45 D
cfitzsimons@elcamino.edu

FITZSIMONS, Debra ... 949-582-4665 ..... 70 D
dfitzsimons@socccd.org

FITZWATER, Valerie ... 972-825-4753 .... 495 D
vfitzwater@sagu.edu

FIVECOAT, Frederick ... 610-892-1519 .... 441 C
ffivecoat@pit.edu

FIX, John ... 256-824-6605 ..... 9 A
john.fix@uah.edu

FIXEN, Randall ... 701-662-1513 .... 382 D
randy.fixen@lrsc.edu

FIXEN, Randall ... 701-662-1518 .... 382 D
randy.fixen@lrsc.edu

FJORTOFT, Nancy, F ... 630-515-6072 .... 158 E
nfjort@midwestern.edu

FLACHMANN, Michael ... 661-654-2121 ..... 33 H
mflachmann@csub.edu

FLACK, Anna ... 631-451-4008 .... 356 D
flacka@sunysuffolk.edu

FLACK, Bobby, L ... 301-447-5220 .... 225 A
flack@msmary.edu

FLACK, Felecia, J ... 906-227-1272 .... 256 F
fflack@nmu.edu

FLACK, Lisa ... 217-228-5432 .... 161 E
flackli@quincy.edu

FLACK, Wayne, R ... 218-299-3362 .... 263 B
flack@cord.edu

FLADELAND, Diane ... 701-355-8140 .... 383 E
dflade@umary.edu

FLAGEL, Andrew ... 703-993-2395 .... 519 A
aflagel@gmu.edu

FLAGG, Aaron ... 860-768-5236 ..... 95 A
aflagg@hartford.edu

FLAGG, Mary ... 610-372-4721 .... 445 B
mflagg@racc.edu

FLAGGERT, James ... 703-821-8570 .... 524 D
jflaggert@stratford.edu

FLAGLER, William ... 703-764-5043 .... 527 C
wflagler@nvcc.edu

FLAGSTAD, Lois ... 605-642-6599 .... 465 F
lois.flagstad@bhsu.edudu

FLAHARTY, Sue ... 910-938-6251 .... 369 C
flahartys@coastalcarolina.edu

FLAHERTY, Eileen, P ... 716-851-1844 .... 333 D
flaherty@ecc.edu

FLAHERTY, Jane ... 979-845-8588 .... 497 C
jflaherty@tamu.edu

FLAHERTY, John ... 212-817-7769 .... 327 B
jflaherty@gc.cuny.edu

FLAHERTY, Pamela ... 781-280-3631 .... 240 F
flahertyp@middlesex.mass.edu

FLAHERTY, Richard, A ... 617-746-5412 .... 244 E

FLAHERTY, Rob ... 785-594-8319 .... 190 C
rob.flaherty@bakeru.edu

FLAHIVE, Roger ... 973-328-5011 .... 309 B
rflahive@ccm.edu

FLAIG, Sue ... 813-253-7132 .... 110 I
sflaig@hccfl.edu

FLAKE, Bryant ... 435-586-7725 .... 511 A
flake@suu.edu

FLAKE, Forrest ... 801-422-3861 .... 509 D
forrest_flake@byu.edu

FLAKE, Sandra, M ... 530-898-6101 ..... 34 A
sflake@csuchico.edu

FLAKE, Susan, R ... 704-272-5331 .... 373 F
sflake@spcc.edu

FLAMER, LaTonya ... 336-517-2111 .... 362 C
lflamer@bennett.edu

FLAMER, Thelma ... 202-231-2768 .... 557 G
thelma.flamer@dia.mil

FLAMM, Mara ... 215-717-6621 .... 448 H
mflamm@uarts.edu

FLANAGAN, Alyce ... 256-352-8295 ..... 10 B
alyce.malcolm@wallacestate.edu

FLANAGAN, Elizabeth, A ... 540-231-7676 .... 529 B
betsyf@vt.edu

FLANAGAN, Hilary ... 216-397-4432 .... 392 M
hflanagan@jcu.edu

FLANAGAN, J. Kelly ... 801-422-3142 .... 509 D
kelly_flanagan@byu.edu

FLANAGAN, James ... 212-247-3434 .... 339 G
jflanagan@mandl.edu

FLANAGAN, James, L ... 770-484-1204 .... 133 D
lru@lru.edu

FLANAGAN, James, P ... 603-641-6025 .... 305 H
jflanagan@anselm.edu

FLANAGAN, Jason ... 281-487-1170 .... 498 E
jflanagan@txchiro.edu

FLANAGAN, Jeanne ... 518-485-3902 .... 330 C
flanagaj@strose.edu

FLANAGAN, Jerry, E ... 802-654-3000 .... 514 B
jflanagan@smcvt.edu

FLANAGAN, Joan ... 815-479-7884 .... 157 F
jflanaga@mchenry.edu

FLANAGAN, John ... 973-642-8404 .... 315 C
john.flanagan@shu.edu

FLANAGAN, Joseph, V ... 716-375-2302 .... 348 C
jflan@sbu.edu

FLANAGAN, Kathleen ... 310-338-4482 ..... 56 E
flanagan@lmu.edu

FLANAGAN, Kelly, A ... 516-773-5375 .... 558 F
flanagank@usmma.edu

FLANAGAN, Lori ... 314-516-5661 .... 291 F
flanagamlo@umsl.edu

FLANAGAN, Mary Jane ... 989-774-3131 .... 249 G
flana1mj@cmich.edu

FLANAGAN, Maureen, P ... 215-574-9600 .... 431 A
mflanagan@hussianart.edu

FLANAGAN, Michael ... 610-399-2360 .... 441 H
mflanagan@cheyney.edu

FLANAGAN, Scott ... 608-663-2294 .... 547 C
sflanagan@edgewood.edu

FLANAGAN, Tim ... 707-476-4381 ..... 42 A
tim-flanagan@redwoods.edu

FLANAGAN, Timothy, J ... 508-626-4575 .... 238 D
tflanagan@framingham.edu

FLANAGAN-HERSTEK,
Katherine, M ... 570-675-9225 .... 440 E
kfh2@psu.edu

FLANARY, Barry ... 802-442-5427 .... 514 D
bflanary@svc.edu

FLANDERS, Lorene ... 678-839-6369 .... 138 D
lflanders@westga.edu

FLANIGAN, Jean, C ... 423-439-4337 .... 473 E
flanigan@etsu.edu

FLANIGAN, Marjie ... 304-384-6035 .... 543 D
Mflanigan@concord.edu

FLANIGAN, Patricia ... 949-582-4733 ..... 70 F
pflanigan@saddleback.edu

FLANIGAN, Raaven ... 859-291-0800 .... 199 F
rflanigan@daymarcollege.edu

FLANIGAN, JR.,
Robert, D ... 404-270-5072 .... 137 E
rflaniga@spelman.edu

FLANIK, Greg, G ... 440-826-2700 .... 384 H
gflanik@bw.edu

FLANNAGAN, Dorothy, A .. 210-458-6878 .... 506 B
dorothy.flannagan@utsa.edu

FLANNELY, SC, Jean ... 718-405-3230 .... 330 A
jean.flannely@mountsaintvincent.edu

FLANNERY, Bob ... 903-923-2076 .... 486 D
bflannery@etbu.edu

FLANNERY, Brenda ... 507-389-1866 .... 267 H
brenda.flannery@mnsu.edu

FLANNERY, Chad ... 618-252-5400 .... 164 G
chad.flannery@sic.edu

FLANNERY, Katherine ... 215-951-2965 .... 444 C
flanneryk@philau.edu

FLANNERY, Kathleen ... 620-231-7000 .... 195 I

FLANNERY, Maura, C ... 718-990-1860 .... 348 G
flannerm@stjohns.edu

FLANNERY, Patrick ... 517-607-2239 .... 252 E
patrick.flannery@hillsdale.edu

FLANNERY, Teresa (Terry) . 202-885-2163 ..... 97 B
flannery@american.edu

FLANNIGAN, Suzanne ... 831-770-7090 ..... 49 C
sflannigan@hartnell.edu

FLANZRAICH, Gerri ... 516-686-1158 .... 343 D
gflanzra@nyit.edu

FLATHMAN, Christian ... 912-478-6397 .... 131 A
cflathman@georgiasouthern.edu

FLATT, Bonnie ... 503-251-5712 .... 420 H
bflatt@uws.edu

FLATTERY, Patrick ... 218-723-6042 .... 262 I
pflatter@css.edu

FLAUM, JR., Leonard ... 210-458-4120 .... 506 B
leonard.flaum@utsa.edu

FLAVIN, Stephen, P ... 508-831-5095 .... 247 B
sflavin@wpi.edu

FLAX, Carol ... 419-772-2047 .... 398 G
c-flax@onu.edu

FLAX, Christine ... 443-334-2639 .... 226 E
cflax@stevenson.edu

FLAX-HYMAN, Cheryl, L ... 850-747-3215 .... 110 E
cflax-hyman@gulfcoast.edu

FLEAGLE, Steven, R ... 319-384-0595 .... 182 C
steve-fleagle@uiowa.edu

FLECHA, Gladys, E ... 787-852-1430 .... 562 D

FLECK, Lorraine ... 540-375-2299 .... 523 D
fleck@roanoke.edu

FLECKENSTEIN,
Marilynn, P ... 716-286-8352 .... 344 D
mpf@niagara.edu

FLECKENSTEIN, Susan, M . 810-762-9864 .... 253 I
sflecken@kettering.edu

FLEENER, Harry ... 850-718-2310 .... 102 H
fleenerh@chipola.edu

FLEENER, Jayne ... 919-515-2011 .... 378 B

FLEENOR, Rick ... 606-539-4154 .... 206 G
rick.fleenor@ucumberlands.edu

FLEENOR, Sara ... 307-778-1221 .... 556 B
sfleenor@lccc.wy.edu

FLEET, Frances ... 419-448-3326 .... 402 E
ffleet@tiffin.edu

FLEGE, Kelly, A ... 319-273-5885 .... 182 D
kelly.flege@uni.edu

FLEISCHER, Stephen ... 323-343-4800 ..... 35 B
sfleischer@cslanet.calstatela.edu

FLEISCHER, Vicki ... 973-642-8512 .... 315 C
vicki.fleischer@shu.edu

FLEISCHMAN, Jean ... 978-542-7765 .... 239 B
jfleischman@salemstate.edu

FLEISCHMAN, Linda, M ... 315-279-5204 .... 337 K
lfleisch@mail.keuka.edu

FLEISCHMANN, Kenneth ... 314-977-3948 .... 289 F
fleiske@slu.edu

FLEISHER, Craig ... 912-279-5854 .... 127 B
cfleisher@ccga.edu

FLEIT, Jody ... 617-587-5511 .... 243 D
fleitj@neco.edu

FLEMING, Allyson ... 615-327-6235 .... 471 A
afleming@mmc.edu

FLEMING, Carol ... 828-254-1921 .... 367 H
cfleming@abtech.edu

FLEMING, Carry ... 614-251-4718 .... 398 F
flemingc@ohiodominican.edu

FLEMING, Dan, A ... 814-393-2361 .... 442 A
dfleming@clarion.edu

FLEMING, David ... 269-782-1201 .... 258 E
dfleming@swmich.edu

FLEMING, Debra ... 440-646-8120 .... 405 B
dfleming@ursuline.edu

FLEMING, Elizabeth ... 413-565-1000 .... 231 B
lfleming@baypath.edu

FLEMING, Elizabeth, A ... 864-596-9050 .... 457 E
betsy.fleming@converse.edu

FLEMING, Erika ... 305-428-5700 .... 113 I
efleming@aii.edu

FLEMING, Graham ... 510-642-7540 ..... 73 E
fleming@berkeley.edu

FLEMING, Honoree ... 802-468-1344 .... 515 C
honoree.fleming@castleton.edu

FLEMING, J. Christopher ... 361-825-5934 .... 497 F
christopher.fleming@tamucc.edu

FLEMING, James ... 605-642-6270 .... 465 F
james.fleming@bhsu.edu

FLEMING, James ... 503-352-1510 .... 419 E
jfleming@pacificu.edu

FLEMING, James, J ... 304-243-2224 .... 545 G

FLEMING, Jami ... 877-442-0505 ..... 88 G
jami.fleming@rockies.edu

FLEMING, Jennifer ... 479-498-6020 ..... 20 G
jfleming@atu.edu

FLEMING, Julie, C ... 770-720-5527 .... 135 F
jcf@reinhardt.edu

FLEMING, Kay ... 618-985-3741 .... 154 E
kayfleming@jalc.edu

FLEMING, Kevin ... 951-372-7000 ..... 64 A

FLEMING, Maria ... 340-692-4183 .... 568 C
mflemin@uvi.edu

FLEMING, Mark, J ... 610-861-1472 .... 436 I
memjf01@moravian.edu

FLEMING, Michael ... 404-222-2588 .... 134 A
mfleming@morehouse.edu

FLEMING, Mike, R ... 618-235-2700 .... 165 B
mike.fleming@swic.edu

FLEMING, Nina ... 262-551-5800 .... 546 F
nfleming@carthage.edu

FLEMING, Patricia, A ... 574-284-4575 .... 179 D
pfleming@saintmarys.edu

FLEMING, Paul, C ... 504-864-7490 .... 213 F
pcflemin@loyno.edu

FLEMING, Richard ... 443-550-6021 .... 222 C
rfleming@csmd.edu

FLEMING, Rita ... 501-686-2920 ..... 24 B
rfleming@uasys.edu

FLEMING, Robert ... 617-824-8670 .... 234 D
robert_fleming@emerson.edu

FLEMING, Saundra ... 773-878-4699 .... 163 D
sfleming@staugustine.edu

FLEMING, Scott, S ... 202-687-3455 ..... 98 A
ssf2@georgetown.edu

FLEMING, Shannon ... 501-370-5378 ..... 23 B
sfleming@philander.edu

FLEMING, Sherie ... 256-378-2021 ..... 2 F
sfleming@cacc.edu

FLEMING, Siobhan ... 832-813-6764 .... 490 C
siobhan.fleming@lonestar.edu

FLEMING, Stephen ... 404-894-5217 .... 130 D
fleming@gatech.edu

FLEMING, Terri ... 317-554-8322 .... 169 H
tfleming@brownmackie.edu

FLEMING, Tom, O ... 310-338-2714 ..... 56 E
tfleming@lmu.edu

FLEMING, Trish ... 215-836-2222 .... 422 A
tfleming@antonelli.edu

FLEMING, Vickie ... 919-497-3203 .... 366 E
vfleming@louisburg.edu

FLEMING, William ... 312-942-6832 .... 163 B
bill_p_fleming@rush.edu

FLEMING, William ... 919-962-4651 .... 377 A
wafleming@northcarolina.edu

FLEMING, William, A ... 910-962-3160 .... 379 C
flemingw@uncw.edu

FLEMING, William, B ... 561-803-2001 ... 114 C william_fleming@pba.edu
FLEMING, JR., William M, B ... 561-803-2012 ... 114 C bill_fleming@pba.edu
FLEMION, Meg ... 419-434-4510 ... 404 B flemion@findlay.edu
FLEMMING, Carole ... 773-834-2500 ... 165 G
FLEMMING, Sondra, G ... 214-860-2146 ... 484 I sflemming@dcccd.edu
FLEMON, Marc ... 405-466-3445 ... 408 G mflemon@lunet.edu
FLENIKEN, Tracey ... 940-668-7731 ... 491 C tfleniken@nctc.edu
FLENTJE, H. Edward ... 620-341-5333 ... 192 D president@emporia.edu
FLENTJE, Mike ... 920-686-6204 ... 550 E Mike.Flentje@sl.edu
FLESH, Barbara ... 636-797-3000 ... 283 H bflesh@jeffco.edu
FLESHLER, David ... 216-368-2399 ... 386 E david.fleshler@case.edu
FLESNER, Brian ... 402-826-8218 ... 298 A brian.flesner@doane.edu
FLETCHALL, Craig, N ... 620-792-9378 ... 190 E fletchallc@bartonccc.edu
FLETCHER, Anthony, S ... 972-860-7645 ... 484 H AnthonyFletcher@dcccd.edu
FLETCHER, Bill ... 615-898-2500 ... 473 F bfletch@mtsu.edu
FLETCHER, Bridget ... 314-977-7778 ... 289 F fletchb@slu.edu
FLETCHER, Christopher ... 305-809-3147 ... 108 F chrisopher.fletcher@fkcc.edu
FLETCHER, Courtney ... 402-559-4333 ... 301 A cfletcher@unmc.edu
FLETCHER, Heidi, L ... 410-532-5105 ... 225 D hfletcher@ndm.edu
FLETCHER, James, A ... 208-282-2404 ... 143 D fletjame@isu.edu
FLETCHER, Janice ... 617-243-2145 ... 236 F jfletcher@lasell.edu
FLETCHER, John ... 252-328-5817 ... 377 C fletcherjo@ecu.eddu
FLETCHER, Lynn ... 307-268-2211 ... 555 F lfletcher@caspercollege.edu
FLETCHER, Nikia ... 419-755-4813 ... 397 B nfletcher@ncstatecollege.edu
FLETCHER, Randy ... 217-351-2236 ... 161 B rfletcher@parkland.edu
FLETCHER, Richard, L ... 440-826-2323 ... 384 H rfletche@bw.edu
FLETCHER, Scott ... 503-768-6001 ... 416 F graddean@lclark.edu
FLETCHER, Thomas ... 570-389-5161 ... 441 F tfletche@bloomu.edu
FLETCHER, Wayne ... 714-415-6500 ... 77 G wfletcher@westcoastuniversity.edu
FLETCHER, Wesla ... 843-525-8293 ... 461 E wfletcher@tcl.edu
FLETCHER, William, A ... 843-953-5114 ... 456 C bill.fletcher@citadel.edu
FLETCHER, William, A ... 352-846-3903 ... 120 B afletcher@ufl.edu
FLEURIET, Cathy, A ... 512-245-8113 ... 501 C cf07@txstate.edu
FLEURY, Jane ... 518-631-9851 ... 358 F fleuryj@uniongraduatecollege.edu
FLEURY, Traci ... 704-971-8500 ... 363 D
FLEWELLING, Colleen ... 570-372-4567 ... 447 D flewelling@susqu.edu
FLEWELLING, Colleen ... 570-372-4183 ... 447 D flewelling@susq.edu
FLICK, Kenneth ... 843-525-8238 ... 461 E kflick@tcl.edu
FLICK, Matt ... 937-294-0592 ... 401 H flick@saa.edu
FLICKINGER, Catherine ... 516-686-7516 ... 343 D
FLICKINGER, Craig ... 734-432-5725 ... 254 G cflickinger@madonna.edu
FLICKINGER, Donald ... 231-591-3532 ... 251 B flickind@ferris.edu
FLIEGE, Cheryl ... 309-694-5599 ... 152 B cfliege@icc.edu
FLIER, Jeffrey, S ... 617-432-1501 ... 235 H jeffrey_flier@hms.harvard.edu
FLIKEID, Ben ... 651-730-5100 ... 264 A bflikeid@globeuniversity.edu
FLIKKEMA, Melvin, J ... 616-222-3000 ... 254 A mflikkema@kuyper.edu
FLINN, Amy ... 254-298-8364 ... 496 B alflinn@templejc.edu
FLINN, Deborah ... 860-832-3873 ... 91 D
FLINN, Gordon, B ... 530-226-4735 ... 69 H gflinn@simpsonu.edu
FLINN, Nancy ... 510-436-1054 ... 50 F flinn@hnu.edu
FLINN, Ronald, T ... 517-355-3366 ... 255 D flinn@msu.edu
FLINT, David ... 603-668-6706 ... 304 E dflint@ccsnh.edu
FLINT, Juanita ... 972-860-4694 ... 484 F juanitazf@dcccd.edu
FLINTOFT, Rebecca ... 303-273-3050 ... 82 F rebecca.flintoft@is.mines.edu
FLIPPO, Angela, D ... 870-759-4117 ... 26 B aflippo@wbcoll.edu
FLIS, Denise ... 405-208-5848 ... 410 A dflis@okcu.edu
FLOCCHINI, Randy ... 775-674-7688 ... 302 J rflocchini@tmcc.edu
FLOCCO, Nicholas ... 215-248-7182 ... 425 C
FLOCH, Jacob ... 406-496-4500 ... 296 C jfloch@mtech.edu
FLOCKEN, Lise ... 760-757-2121 ... 57 E lflocken@miracosta.edu
FLOM, Sheldon ... 307-754-6284 ... 556 D Sheldon.Flom@northwestcollege.edu
FLOMENHAFT, Marion ... 516-678-5000 ... 341 F mflomenhaft@molloy.edu
FLOOD, Cathy, T ... 920-923-8082 ... 548 C cflood@marianuniversity.edu
FLOOD, Flora ... 256-726-7287 ... 6 C fflood@oakwood.edu
FLOOD, Margo ... 828-298-3325 ... 380 C mflood@warren-wilson.edu
FLOOD, Thomas ... 718-489-5443 ... 348 E thomasflood@stfranciscollege.edu
FLOOD, Tim ... 619-644-7141 ... 49 A tim.flood@gcccd.edu
FLOOD, Tim ... 619-644-7653 ... 49 A tim.flood@gcccd.edu
FLOOD, Timothy, J ... 920-929-2136 ... 554 E tflood@morainepark.edu
FLOOR, Gregory ... 617-850-1285 ... 236 A gfloor@hchc.edu
FLOR, Doug ... 706-880-8923 ... 132 I dflor@lagrange.edu
FLORA, Allen ... 301-696-3811 ... 223 C flora@hood.edu
FLORCZAK, Gregory, P ... 716-880-2200 ... 340 E gregory.p.florczak@medaille.edu
FLORCZAK, Joan, E ... 203-576-4665 ... 94 D joan@bridgeport.edu
FLORENCE, Bob, K ... 816-604-6546 ... 285 E bob.florence@mcckc.edu
FLORENCE, Christopher ... 314-434-4044 ... 281 A chris.florence@covenantseminary.edu
FLORENDO, Chava ... 541-552-6128 ... 419 A florendch@sou.edu
FLORENTINE, Dennis ... 908-835-2326 ... 317 C dflorentine@warren.edu
FLORER, Timothy, M ... 847-649-3980 ... 149 G tflorer@keller.edu
FLORES, Anthony ... 510-464-3592 ... 62 C aflores@peralta.edu
FLORES, Ben ... 915-747-7974 ... 505 E bflores@utep.edu
FLORES, Caren ... 510-783-2100 ... 49 H caren_flores@heald.edu
FLORES, Chio ... 509-335-9711 ... 539 A cflores@wsu.edu
FLORES, Deanna, L ... 407-303-1851 ... 108 D deanna.flores@fhchs.edu
FLORES, Edwin ... 787-738-2161 ... 567 A edwin.flores@upr.edu
FLORES, Efrain ... 787-758-2525 ... 567 D efrain.flores@upr.edu
FLORES, Elizabeth ... 915-747-7872 ... 505 E lizaf@utep.edu
FLORES, Esmerelda, M ... 210-434-6711 ... 491 G flore@lake.ollusa.edu
FLORES, Fatima ... 561-912-2166 ... 106 G fflores@evergladesuniversity.edu
FLORES, Fernando ... 915-831-6391 ... 486 E fernief@epcc.edu
FLORES, Greg ... 503-725-4971 ... 418 G gregory.flores@pdx.edu
FLORES, Gustavo ... 707-664-4388 ... 37 B gustavo.flores@sonoma.edu
FLORES, Hector ... 585-475-4476 ... 347 G
FLORES, Henry ... 210-436-3214 ... 493 C hflores@stmarytx.edu
FLORES, Jacob, C ... 956-721-5148 ... 489 G jacob.flores@laredo.edu
FLORES, Javier ... 432-264-5015 ... 487 I jflores@howardcollege.edu
FLORES, Jayne, T ... 671-735-5638 ... 559 B pio@guamcc.edu
FLORES, Juan ... 360-486-8860 ... 536 F jflores@stmartin.edu
FLORES, Kat ... 541-888-7293 ... 420 C kflores@socc.edu
FLORES, Kathy ... 253-680-7178 ... 531 A kflores@bates.ctc.edu
FLORES, Marissel ... 787-728-1515 ... 568 B mcflores@sagrado.edu
FLORES, Mike ... 210-486-3930 ... 479 D rflores@alamo.edu
FLORES, Rebecca ... 661-395-4534 ... 52 M
FLORES, Robert ... 909-599-5433 ... 54 A rflores@lifepacific.edu
FLORES, Roberto ... 863-453-6661 ... 117 I robert.flores@southflorida.edu
FLORES, Roy ... 520-206-4747 ... 17 I royflores@pima.edu
FLORES, Ruben ... 210-486-0941 ... 479 F rflores5@alamo.edu
FLORES, Ruben ... 787-279-1912 ... 563 B rflores@bayamon.inter.edu
FLORES, Rudy ... 530-895-2429 ... 31 E floresru@butte.edu
FLORES, Saundra ... 619-275-4700 ... 46 K saundra@fashioncareerscollege.com
FLORES, Susan ... 956-364-4443 ... 499 J susan.flores@harlingen.tstc.edu
FLORES, Suzana ... 312-777-8616 ... 153 A sflores@aii.edu
FLORES, Viviana ... 201-327-8877 ... 309 H vflores@eastwick.edu
FLORES, William, V ... 713-221-8001 ... 503 D president@uhd.edu
FLORES-CHURCH, Adriana ... 562-860-2451 ... 38 J achurch@cerritos.edu
FLORES-MEDINA, Donna ... 505-454-5328 ... 318 E dfmedina@luna.edu
FLOREY, Nancy, E ... 717-361-1406 ... 428 E floreyne@etown.edu
FLORIAN, Greg, E ... 217-875-7200 ... 162 D gflorian@richland.edu
FLORIAN, Jim ... 520-621-1634 ... 19 B florianj@email.arizona.edu
FLORIO, SJ, Philip, J ... 718-817-4503 ... 334 C pflorio2@fordham.edu
FLORY, Lowell ... 800-287-8822 ... 169 E florylo@bethanyseminary.edu
FLOT, Rob ... 847-735-5200 ... 155 F flot@lakeforest.edu
FLOTTE, Terence, R ... 508-856-8000 ... 238 A terry.flotte@umassmed.edu
FLOUHOUSE, Steve ... 606-326-2055 ... 201 B steve.flouhouse@kctcs.edu
FLOURNOY, Bonita ... 404-756-4025 ... 124 I bflournoy@atlm.edu
FLOURNOY, Jacob, W ... 501-686-2901 ... 24 B jwflournoy@uasys.edu
FLOWERS, Damon ... 734-677-5322 ... 260 B dflowers@wccnet.edu
FLOWERS, George ... 334-844-4700 ... 1 G flowegt@auburn.edu
FLOWERS, Marshall ... 828-669-8012 ... 367 C mflowers@montreat.edu
FLOWERS, Paury ... 610-957-6149 ... 447 E pflower1@swarthmore.edu
FLOWERS, Robert ... 315-781-3827 ... 335 G flowers@hws.edu
FLOWERS, Robert ... 817-531-4461 ... 502 A rflowers@txwes.edu
FLOYD, Arlene ... 330-941-2333 ... 406 F afloyd@ysu.edu
FLOYD, Brenda, L ... 940-898-3505 ... 502 B bfloyd@twu.edu
FLOYD, Carey ... 580-371-2371 ... 408 I cfloyd@mscok.edu
FLOYD, Carlton ... 619-260-7455 ... 76 A cfloyd@sandiego.edu
FLOYD, Charlsie ... 636-949-4909 ... 284 C cfloyd@lindenwood.edu
FLOYD, Cindy ... 619-574-6909 ... 60 E cmfloyd@pacificcollege.edu
FLOYD, Cynthia ... 334-291-4905 ... 2 G cynthia.floyd@cv.edu
FLOYD, David J, W ... 225-765-2437 ... 212 F rulife1@lsu.edu
FLOYD, Donna ... 510-235-7800 ... 43 B dfloyd@contracosta.edu
FLOYD, Donna ... 925-685-1230 ... 43 C dfloyd@dvc.edu
FLOYD, Elizabeth ... 864-225-7653 ... 458 B lizfloyd@forrestcollege.edu
FLOYD, Elson, S ... 509-335-4200 ... 539 A presidentsoffice@wsu.edu
FLOYD, Gregg, S ... 330-672-2422 ... 393 D gfloyd@kent.edu
FLOYD, James, J ... 909-621-8351 ... 40 D james.floyd@cmc.edu
FLOYD, Jennifer ... 606-539-4497 ... 206 G jennifer.floyd@ucumberlands.edu
FLOYD, Joshua ... 276-944-6138 ... 518 I jfloyd@ehc.edu
FLOYD, Linda ... 706-295-6511 ... 130 F lfloyd@gntc.edu
FLOYD, Lydia ... 404-880-8454 ... 126 I lfloyd@cau.edu
FLOYD, Polly, K ... 850-263-3261 ... 101 E pkfloyd@baptistcollege.edu
FLOYD, Richard ... 610-409-3200 ... 450 C rfloyd@ursinus.edu
FLOYD, Shirley ... 910-642-7141 ... 373 G sfloyd@sccnc.edu
FLOYD, Virgina ... 404-752-1953 ... 134 B vfloyd@msm.edu
FLUEGEMAN, Tere ... 949-582-4920 ... 70 D tfluegeman@soccd.org
FLUELLEN, William ... 561-912-2166 ... 106 G wfluellen@evergladesuniversity.edu
FLUET, Gregoire, J ... 860-632-3010 ... 92 E rector@holyapostles.edu
FLUGUM, Deborah ... 818-677-2301 ... 35 D deborah.flugum@csun.edu
FLUHARTY, Steven, J ... 215-898-7236 ... 448 I vpr@pobox.upenn.edu
FLUKE, Donald, W ... 574-372-5100 ... 171 E dwfluke@grace.edu
FLUKE, Lauri, A ... 405-878-2020 ... 409 D lauri.fluke@okbu.edu
FLUKER, Rod ... 409-933-8619 ... 483 B rfluker@com.edu
FLUKER, Zillah ... 334-229-5679 ... 1 C zfluker@alasu.edu
FLUNKER, Thomas, G ... 507-344-7577 ... 261 H tom.flunker@blc.edu
FLUSKEY, Sara, B ... 716-880-2259 ... 340 E sara.b.fluskey@medaille.edu
FLYER, Robert ... 440-365-5222 ... 395 C
FLYNN, Charles, L ... 718-405-3232 ... 330 A charles.flynn@mountsaintvincent.edu
FLYNN, Chris ... 540-231-6557 ... 529 B flynnc@vt.edu
FLYNN, Jackie ... 412-391-7021 ... 450 F admissions@vettechinstitute.edu
FLYNN, Joan ... 410-617-5161 ... 224 A jflynn@loyola.edu
FLYNN, John, J ... 212-769-5055 ... 347 E
FLYNN, Karen ... 203-932-7317 ... 95 B kflynn@newhaven.edu
FLYNN, Kathy, A ... 319-296-4218 ... 185 C kathleen.flynn@hawkeyecollege.edu
FLYNN, Kevin ... 781-239-2549 ... 240 D kflynn@massbay.edu
FLYNN, Linda ... 979-830-4251 ... 482 A lflynn@blinn.edu
FLYNN, Mari ... 570-945-8335 ... 432 C mari.flynn@keystone.edu
FLYNN, Maria ... 270-534-3140 ... 203 B maria.flynn@kctcs.edu
FLYNN, Marilyn, L ... 213-740-8311 ... 76 C mflynn@usc.edu
FLYNN, Maura ... 716-926-8822 ... 335 F mflynn@hilbert.edu
FLYNN, Michael ... 561-912-2166 ... 106 G mflynn@evergladesuniversity.edu
FLYNN, Molly ... 716-829-7809 ... 332 F flynnm@dyc.edu
FLYNN, Monty ... 315-498-2538 ... 345 D flynnm@sunyocc.edu
FLYNN, Richard, B ... 413-748-3241 ... 245 C rflynn@spfldcol.edu
FLYNN, Thomas, F ... 610-796-8203 ... 421 F tom.flynn@alvernia.edu
FLYNN, Thomas, V ... 505-565-1413 ... 245 D tflynn@stonehill.edu
FLYNN SAULNIER, Christine ... 718-982-2315 ... 327 A Christine.Saulnier@csi.cuny.edu
FLYNT, Hilde ... 228-392-2994 ... 278 B hilde.flynt@vc.edu
FOCHT, Jeffrey, W ... 610-861-5434 ... 437 G jfocht@northampton.edu
FOCKLER, Debra ... 509-359-6348 ... 533 D dfockler@ewu.edu
FOECKLER, Michael, S ... 540-636-2900 ... 517 H foeckler@christendom.edu
FOEHL, Brooks, L ... 413-597-4408 ... 246 G Brooks.L.Foehl@williams.edu
FOERST, Cara Herrick ... 973-642-8726 ... 315 C cara.foerst@shu.edu
FOFT, Susan ... 707-864-7000 ... 70 A susan.foft@solano.edu
FOGARINO, Shirley ... 510-981-2852 ... 62 A sfogarino@peralta.edu
FOGARTY, John ... 850-644-1346 ... 119 C jfogarty@fsu.edu
FOGARTY, Raymond ... 401-232-6407 ... 453 A rfogarty@bryant.edu
FOGARTY, Tammy ... 561-912-2166 ... 106 G tfogarty@evergladesuniversity.edu
FOGARTY, Thomas, J ... 717-221-1300 ... 430 E tjfogart@hacc.edu
FOGARTY, Timothy, P ... 814-393-2235 ... 442 A tfogarty@clarion.edu
FOGARTY, William ... 413-552-2221 ... 240 C bfogarty@hcc.edu
FOGEL, Henry ... 312-341-3782 ... 162 I hfogel@roosevelt.edu
FOGELGREN, John, A ... 302-454-3922 ... 96 C fogelgre@dtcc.edu
FOGERSON, Linda ... 760-757-2121 ... 57 E lfogerson@miracosta.edu
FOGERTY, Karen ... 617-912-9108 ... 232 E kfogerty@bostonconservatory.edu
FOGERTY, Rebecca, R ... 302-831-8065 ... 96 F bfogerty@udel.edu
FOGG, Christine ... 231-777-5239 ... 248 J christine.fogg@baker.edu
FOGG, Davina, K ... 509-527-4201 ... 538 G davina.fogg@wwcc.edu
FOGG, Richard ... 785-587-2800 ... 194 F richardfogg@matc.net
FOGLE, Rick, A ... 724-836-9916 ... 449 C fogle@pitt.edu
FOGLEMAN, David ... 318-670-9590 ... 215 A dfogleman@susla.edu

FOHRMAN, Jonathan .... 619-388-2873 ...... 65 G
jfohrma@sdccd.edu
FOISY, Brian .... 701-858-3331 .... 381 G
brian.foisy@minotstateu.edu
FOLBERG, Robert .... 248-370-3634 .... 257 C
rfolberg@oakland.edu
FOLDA, Joe .... 719-549-2730 ...... 83 B
joe.folda@colostate-pueblo.edu
FOLDA, John, T .... 402-643-4052 .... 300 B
sggs@stgregoryseminary.edu
FOLDS, Jim .... 912-260-4387 .... 136 F
jim.folds@sgc.edu
FOLEY, Anne .... 312-369-7477 .... 148 B
afoley@colum.edu
FOLEY, Beth .... 435-797-1437 .... 511 B
beth.foley@usu.edu
FOLEY, Bill .... 925-631-4052 ...... 64 F
wfoley@stmarys-ca.edu
FOLEY, Brian, P .... 703-822-6697 .... 527 C
bfoley@nvcc.edu
FOLEY, C. Brad .... 541-346-5661 .... 419 B
bfoley@uoregon.edu
FOLEY, Chris, J .... 317-274-0402 .... 174 B
cfoley@iupui.edu
FOLEY, Cindy .... 310-544-6405 ...... 64 H
cindy.foley@usw.salvationarmy.org
FOLEY, Constance, L .... 724-738-2003 .... 443 E
constance.foley@sru.edu
FOLEY, Don .... 907-474-7317 ...... 10 J
djfoley@alaska.edu
FOLEY, Ellen .... 608-243-4334 .... 554 B
foley@matcmadison.edu
FOLEY, Erin .... 410-532-3586 .... 225 D
efoley@ndm.edu
FOLEY, Erin .... 541-885-1013 .... 418 E
erin.foley@oit.edu
FOLEY, Fred, J .... 215-951-1543 .... 432 G
foley@lasalle.edu
FOLEY, Gary, A .... 803-535-1264 .... 460 C
foleyg@octech.edu
FOLEY, Henry .... 814-865-6332 .... 438 F
hcf2@psu.edu
FOLEY, Jeffrey, W .... 706-737-1445 .... 125 C
jwfoley@aug.edu
FOLEY, Jeremy, N .... 352-375-4683 .... 120 B
jeremy@gators.uaa.ufl.edu
FOLEY, Jim .... 406-243-0211 .... 295 A
jim.foley@umontana.edu
FOLEY, John .... 508-793-7444 .... 233 C
jfoley@clarku.edu
FOLEY, Linda .... 402-354-7050 .... 299 E
linda.foley@methodistcollege.edu
FOLEY, Lisa .... 530-541-4660 ...... 53 F
foley@ltcc.edu
FOLEY, Mark, R .... 251-442-2201 .... 9 B
markfoley@mail.umobile.edu
FOLEY, Michael .... 570-348-6233 .... 435 F
foley@marywood.edu
FOLEY, Neil .... 845-341-4180 .... 345 E
neil.foley@sunyorange.edu
FOLEY, Phyllis .... 615-230-4828 .... 476 A
phyllis.foley@volstate.edu
FOLEY, Robert .... 802-773-5900 .... 513 B
rfoley@csj.edu
FOLEY, Robert, A .... 978-665-3195 .... 238 C
rfoley@fitchburgstate.edu
FOLEY, Ryan .... 912-688-6061 .... 134 H
rfoley@ogeecheetech.edu
FOLEY, Sandra .... 701-858-3497 .... 381 G
sandy.foley@minotstateu.edu
FOLEY, J.D., Thomas, P ... 814-886-6411 .... 437 A
tfoley@mtaloy.edu
FOLEY, Tim .... 310-544-6461 ...... 64 H
tim.foley@usw.salvationarmy.org
FOLEY, Tim .... 704-216-3650 .... 373 C
tim.foley@rccc.edu
FOLEY, Timothy .... 251-626-3303 .... 8 D
tfoley@ussa.edu
FOLGER, Pamela, M .... 217-424-6294 .... 158 F
pmfolger@millikin.edu
FOLK, Joseph .... 330-499-9600 .... 393 I
jfolk@kent.edu
FOLKENDT, Kurt .... 858-513-9240 .... 181 G
research@ashford.edu
FOLKERT, Eva Dean .... 616-395-7956 .... 252 F
folkert@hope.edu
FOLKMAN, Eric .... 937-769-1833 .... 383 K
FOLKS, Kay .... 260-481-6103 .... 174 A
folksp@ipfw.edu
FOLKS, Lonnie .... 609-652-4877 .... 313 F
lonnie.folks@stockton.edu
FOLLICK, David .... 516-299-3389 .... 339 A
david.follick@liu.edu
FOLLICK, Edwin .... 714-533-1495 ...... 70 B
edfollick@southbaylo.edu
FOLLICK, Edwin .... 714-533-3946 ...... 37 C
efollick@calums.edu
FOLLINS, Craig .... 773-291-6313 .... 147 D
cfollins@ccc.edu
FOLLOSCO, David .... 818-710-2944 ...... 55 B
follosd@piercecollege.edu
FOLSE, Victoria .... 309-556-3051 .... 153 E
vfolse@iwu.edu
FOLSOM, B. Kevin .... 214-874-3441 .... 485 E
kfolsom@dts.edu
FOLSOM, Scott, D .... 801-585-1158 .... 510 L
scott.folsom@dps.utah.edu
FOLT, Carol, L .... 603-646-2404 .... 305 A
carol.l.folt@dartmouth.edu
FOLTIN, Craig .... 216-987-4705 .... 389 A
craig.foltin@tri-c.edu
FOLZ, James .... 518-828-4181 .... 330 E
folz@sunycgcc.edu
FOMBELLE, Douglas, W .... 215-641-4801 .... 261 I
d-fombelle@bethel.edu
FONDETTO, Gina .... 973-642-8377 .... 315 C
gina.fondetto@shu.edu
FONDILLER, Jennifer .... 212-854-2014 .... 323 G
jfondill@barnard.edu
FONG, Bobby .... 610-409-3587 .... 450 C
bfong@ursinus.edu
FONG, Franklin .... 510-848-5232 ...... 47 I
ffong@fst.edu
FONG, Harry, M .... 408-554-4398 ...... 68 C
hfong@scu.edu
FONG, Jennifer, C .... 818-947-2433 ...... 55 E
fongjc@lavc.edu
FONG, Lindy .... 323-780-6738 ...... 54 G
fonglw@elac.edu
FONG, Margarita .... 914-633-2246 .... 336 E
mfong@iona.edu
FONG, Norman .... 916-631-8108 ...... 33 C
FONG, Yaa-Yin .... 808-956-8259 .... 140 J
yaayin@hawaii.edu
FONGER, Ron .... 503-493-6510 .... 415 E
rfonger@cu-portland.edu
FONKEN, David .... 512-223-4606 .... 481 B
fonken@austincc.edu
FONS, August .... 575-492-2721 .... 319 B
afons@nmjc.edu
FONSECA, James, W .... 740-453-0762 .... 399 G
fonseca@ohio.edu
FONSECA, Mimi .... 503-517-1100 .... 421 A
mfonseca@warnerpacific.edu
FONT, Iris, J .... 787-740-4282 .... 566 A
ifont@uccaribe.edu
FONTAINE,
Christopher, W .... 903-233-4071 .... 489 K
chrisfontaine@letu.edu
FONTAINE, Dorrie, K .... 434-924-0141 .... 525 B
dkf2u@virginia.edu
FONTAINE, Mike .... 502-968-7191 .... 199 A
mfontaine@brownmackie.edu
FONTAINE, Timothy .... 603-668-6706 .... 304 E
tfontaine@ccsnh.edu
FONTAINE, Yvette, M .... 619-260-7691 ...... 76 A
yvettef@sandiego.edu
FONTANEZ, Eduardo .... 787-857-3600 .... 563 A
efontanez@br.inter.edu
FONTANILLA, Linda .... 805-546-3116 ...... 43 F
linda_fontanilla@cuesta.edu
FONTANO, Dominick .... 718-390-3164 .... 359 G
dfontano@wagner.edu
FONTENETTE, Edward, J .... 870-575-8410 ...... 25 B
fontenettee@uapb.edu
FONTENOT, Dale .... 409-880-8305 .... 500 F
dale.fontenot@lamar.edu
FONTENOT, MSC, Helen ... 504-394-7744 .... 214 A
hfontenot@olhcc.edu
FONTENOT, Janet, S .... 618-235-2700 .... 165 B
janet.fontenot@swic.edu
FONTENOT, Karen .... 985-549-2101 .... 216 C
kfontenot@selu.edu
FONTENOT, Patrick .... 210-486-4431 .... 479 C
pfontenot@alamo.edu
FONTES, Mary .... 218-793-2460 .... 268 E
mary.fontes@northlandcollege.edu
FONTEYN, Paul, J .... 802-287-8201 .... 513 D
fonteynp@greenmtn.edu
FONTHAM, Elizabeth .... 504-559-1388 .... 213 A
efonth@lsuhsc.edu
FONTOURA, Ana .... 914-654-5456 .... 330 B
afontoura@cnr.edu
FONVILLE, John, A .... 252-638-7220 .... 369 E
fonvillj@cravencc.edu
FONZO, Crescenzo .... 201-761-6402 .... 314 F
cfonzo@spc.edu
FOO, Lori .... 808-454-4742 .... 141 C
lori@uhwo.hawaii.edu
FOOSE, David .... 913-234-0650 .... 191 G
david.foose@cleveland.edu
FOOTE, Clarinda, L .... 870-307-7327 ...... 22 D
cfoote@lyon.edu
FOOTE, Jeffrey, C .... 518-255-5300 .... 354 E
footjc@cobleskill.edu
FOOTE, Joe, S .... 405-325-2721 .... 413 C
jfoote@ou.edu
FOOTE, John .... 509-527-2111 .... 538 H
john.foote@wallawalla.edu
FOOTE, Monica, W .... 718-939-5100 .... 338 D
mfoote@libi.edu
FOOTE, Stephanie .... 803-641-3321 .... 462 B
stephanief@usca.edu
FOOTE, Tom, J .... 708-209-3142 .... 148 C
tom.foote@cuchicago.edu
FOOTER, Nancy .... 817-735-2527 .... 504 C
nancy.footer@unt.edu
FOOTER, Nancy .... 940-565-2717 .... 504 B
nfooter@unt.edu
FOPMA, Wes .... 712-722-6020 .... 183 H
wfopma@dordt.edu
FORAKER, Wayne .... 480-557-3285 ...... 19 C
wayne.foraker@phoenix.edu
FORBES, Carol, M .... 612-330-1184 .... 261 G
forbes@augsburg.edu
FORBES, David .... 406-243-4621 .... 295 A
david.forbes@umontana.edu
FORBES, Don, L .... 320-363-2490 .... 262 H
dforbes@csbsju.edu
FORBES, Donald .... 320-363-2490 .... 271 F
dforbes@csbsju.edu
FORBES, Gerald .... 580-559-5208 .... 407 J
gforbes@ecok.edu
FORBES, J. T .... 812-855-5700 .... 173 C
forbesjt@indiana.edu
FORBES, J. T .... 812-855-5394 .... 173 B
jtforbes@indiana.edu
FORBES, Karen, J .... 610-330-5005 .... 433 B
forbesk@lafayette.edu
FORBES, Kathleen .... 843-574-6600 .... 461 G
kathleen.forbes@tridenttech.edu
FORBES, Kathryn, P .... 603-862-1505 .... 306 E
kathie.forbes@unh.edu
FORBES, Lindi, D .... 620-421-6700 .... 194 E
lindif@labette.edu
FORBES, Marcia .... 608-246-6607 .... 554 B
mforbes@matcmadison.edu
FORBES, Maribeth .... 781-595-6768 .... 236 I
mforbes@mariancourt.edu
FORBES, Robert, P .... 678-915-3291 .... 137 C
rforbes@spsu.edu
FORBES, Sharon .... 708-237-5050 .... 160 C
sforbes@nc.edu
FORBES, Shawna .... 313-496-2758 .... 260 C
sforbes1@wcccd.edu
FORBES, Shawna .... 313-496-2587 .... 260 C
sforbes1@wcccd.edu
FORBES, Suzetta, R .... 906-932-4231 .... 251 E
suef@gogebic.edu
FORBES, Tonya, P .... 919-866-5595 .... 374 E
tpforbes@waketech.edu
FORBES-BOYTE, Kari, L .... 605-256-5270 .... 465 G
kari.forbes-boyte@dsu.edu
FORBES ISAIS, Geraldine .. 505-277-2879 .... 321 C
gforbes@unm.edu
FORBESS, Timothy .... 937-529-2201 .... 403 A
tforbess@united.edu
FORBIS, Brenda .... 912-344-2904 .... 124 E
brenda.forbis@armstrong.edu
FORBUSH, Dan .... 518-580-5746 .... 351 B
dforbush@skidmore.edu
FORCE, Bruce .... 918-293-5456 .... 410 E
bruce.force@okstate.edu
FORCE, Darcy .... 817-202-6629 .... 495 C
dforce@swau.edu
FORCH, Paul, J .... 434-924-3586 .... 525 B
pjf8t@virginia.edu
FORD, Amy .... 580-559-5725 .... 407 J
aford@ecok.edu
FORD, Beth .... 216-373-5351 .... 397 E
bford@ndc.edu
FORD, Brian .... 703-821-8570 .... 524 D
bford@stratford.edu
FORD, Carol .... 601-643-8626 .... 274 A
carol.ford@colin.edu
FORD, Charles, W .... 270-247-8521 .... 204 C
cford@midcontinent.edu
FORD, JR., Charles, W ..... 336-750-2400 .... 380 A
fordcw@wssu.edu
FORD, Charlotte .... 205-226-4740 .... 2 C
cford@bsc.edu
FORD, Claudia .... 401-454-6725 .... 454 B
cford@risd.edu
FORD, Deborah, L .... 262-595-2211 .... 551 E
deborah.ford@uwp.edu
FORD, Dow .... 601-403-1214 .... 277 A
dford@prcc.edu
FORD, Duane, M .... 608-822-2301 .... 555 B
FORD, Gayle .... 201-200-3156 .... 312 B
gford@njcu.edu
FORD, Gillian, F .... 814-332-2155 .... 421 E
gford@allegheny.edu
FORD, Glenn .... 870-633-4480 ...... 21 F
gford@eacc.edu
FORD, III, Harrison .... 843-661-8231 .... 458 A
harrison.ford@fdtc.edu
FORD, Iris, C .... 240-895-4554 .... 226 A
icford@smcm.edu
FORD, James .... 503-682-3903 .... 419 F
jford@pioneerpacific.edu
FORD, Jean .... 734-384-4274 .... 255 G
jford@monroeccc.edu
FORD, Jeff .... 417-447-6930 .... 287 G
fordj@otc.edu
FORD, Jimmy .... 502-852-7155 .... 207 A
jimmy.ford@louisville.edu
FORD, John .... 985-448-4040 .... 216 A
john.ford@nicholls.edu
FORD, John, L .... 404-727-4364 .... 129 A
jford2@emory.edu
FORD, Josanne .... 215-569-9215 .... 436 E
jford@mccworks.org
FORD, Joseph .... 212-261-1702 .... 343 D
jford@nyit.edu
FORD, Kari .... 940-668-7731 .... 491 C
kford@nctc.edu
FORD, Kathy .... 909-469-5542 ...... 78 D
kford@westernu.edu
FORD, Kevan .... 216-325-6919 .... 387 A
kford@chancelloru.edu
FORD, Kimberly .... 330-337-6403 .... 383 H
college@awc.edu
FORD, Laura, C .... 309-794-7452 .... 145 B
lauraford@augustana.edu
FORD, Linda .... 918-610-8303 .... 411 D
linda.ford@ptstulsa.edu
FORD, Lynne, E .... 843-953-6531 .... 457 B
fordl@cofc.edu
FORD, Madeline .... 718-518-4211 .... 327 D
mford@hostos.cuny.edu
FORD, Mark, C .... 913-971-3614 .... 195 A
mford@mnu.edu
FORD, Mary .... 603-513-1370 .... 306 H
mary.ford@granite.edu
FORD, Mary, E .... 573-629-3046 .... 282 H
mford@hlg.edu
FORD, Michael .... 312-341-2098 .... 162 I
mford@roosevelt.edu
FORD, Michael, B .... 503-768-7000 .... 416 F
mford@lclark.edu
FORD, Michelle .... 802-764-2139 .... 513 H
michelle.ford@neci.edu
FORD, Nadine, Y .... 919-516-4131 .... 376 B
nford@st-aug.edu
FORD, Nancy .... 620-365-5116 .... 190 A
ford@allencc.edu
FORD, Pamela, R .... 318-257-3031 .... 215 F
prford@latech.edu
FORD, Ralph .... 908-709-7142 .... 316 B
ford@ucc.edu
FORD, Regina .... 714-484-7344 ...... 59 C
rford@cypresscollege.edu
FORD, Ricky .... 662-720-7302 .... 276 D
rgford@nemcc.edu
FORD, Roberta .... 706-641-5047 .... 127 D
ford_roberta@columbusstate.edu
FORD, Sean, P .... 937-778-7969 .... 390 G
sford@edisonohio.edu
FORD, Sylverna, V .... 901-678-2201 .... 474 C
sford@memphis.edu
FORD, Timothy .... 207-602-2334 .... 220 H
tford@une.edu
FORD, Tom, B .... 330-569-5954 .... 391 H
fordtb@hiram.edu
FORD, Victoria, A .... 740-376-4725 .... 395 F
vicki.ford@marietta.edu
FORD, W. Glenn .... 503-883-2458 .... 416 G
gford@linfield.edu
FORD, Wendy .... 330-494-6170 .... 402 A
wford@starkstate.edu
FORD, William .... 215-968-8285 .... 423 E
fordw@bucks.edu
FORD, William .... 407-628-5870 .... 106 B
wford@cci.edu
FORD FISHER, Margaret ... 713-718-8010 .... 487 G
margaret.fordfisher@hccs.edu
FORD-KEE, Dianthia .... 484-365-7391 .... 434 H
dfkee@lincoln.edu
FORDE, Althea .... 718-960-8066 .... 327 C
althea.forde@lehman.cuny.edu
FORDE, Dermot, M .... 419-372-9475 .... 385 C
dforde@bgsu.edu
FORDE, Rita, C .... 215-871-6500 .... 444 B
hr@pcom.edu
FORDHAM, Diana .... 731-425-2607 .... 475 B
dfordham@jscc.edu
FORDIS, JR., C. Michael .. 713-798-3395 .... 481 H
fordis@bcm.edu
FORDOSKI, Dori .... 814-371-2090 .... 448 C
dfordoski@triangle-tech.edu
FORDYCE, Richard, A .... 660-263-3900 .... 279 J
rfordyce@cccb.edu
FORE, Janet, S .... 574-284-5281 .... 179 D
jfore@saintmarys.edu
FORE, Marilyn .... 843-349-5208 .... 458 G
marilyn.fore@hgtc.edu
FOREMAN, Artie .... 601-635-2111 .... 274 C
aforeman@eccc.edu
FOREMAN, David .... 530-898-5103 ...... 34 A
dforeman@csuchico.edu
FOREMAN, David, M .... 570-577-3200 .... 423 D
david.foreman@bucknell.edu
FOREMAN, Dorine, M .... 845-368-7202 .... 350 A
FOREMAN, Hank, T .... 828-262-7525 .... 377 B
foremanht@appstate.edu
FOREMAN, Karen, N .... 540-868-7109 .... 526 H
kforeman@lfcc.edu
FOREMAN, Ronald, R .... 845-368-7210 .... 350 A
FOREMAN, Todd, D .... 607-436-2081 .... 353 E
orematd@oneonta.edu
FOREST, Laura Ann .... 334-844-6444 .... 1 G
laf0009@auburn.edu
FOREST, Rebecca .... 978-632-6600 .... 240 G
r_forest@mwcc.mass.edu

FOUTY, Dennis .... 832-842-4603.... 503 B
dfouty@uh.edu
FOUTY, Jamie .... 509-527-4642.... 538 G
jamie.fouty@wwcc.edu
FOWLE, Marilyn .... 361-593-2410.... 498 A
marilyn.fowle@tamuk.edu
FOWLE, Teri .... 281-998-6151.... 493 D
teri.fowle@sjcd.edu
FOWLER, Alex .... 508-999-8025.... 237 E
afowler@umassd.edu
FOWLER, Angela .... 803-981-7339.... 463 G
afowler@yorktech.edu
FOWLER, Carlton .... 816-604-4101.... 285 I
carlton.fowler@mcckc.edu
FOWLER, Cass .... 386-506-3101.... 103 J
fowlerma@DaytonaState.edu
FOWLER, Craig .... 828-227-7282.... 379 E
cfowler@wcu.edu
FOWLER, Craig .... 715-234-7082.... 555 E
Craig.Fowler@witc.edu
FOWLER, David, G .... 601-815-1149.... 277 H
dfowler@umc.edu
FOWLER, Dwight .... 610-341-1388.... 428 D
dfowler@eastern.edu
FOWLER, Gerard .... 314-977-2479.... 289 F
fowlerga@slu.edu
FOWLER, Gregory, T .... 928-523-1186..... 17 A
gt.fowler@nau.edu
FOWLER, Gregory, W .... 801-274-3280.... 512 E
gfowler@wgu.edu
FOWLER, James .... 508-541-1547.... 234 B
jfowler@dean.edu
FOWLER, James, F .... 910-642-7141.... 373 G
jfowler@sccnc.edu
FOWLER, Jeffrey .... 314-977-2849.... 289 F
fowlerjl@slu.edu
FOWLER, Jeffrey, L .... 314-977-2540.... 289 F
fowlerjl@slu.edu
FOWLER, Julie, H .... 903-983-8281.... 489 F
jfowler@kilgore.edu
FOWLER, Kelly .... 559-489-2352..... 72 A
kelly.fowler@fresnocitycollege.edu
FOWLER, Liesl, A .... 309-794-7211.... 145 B
lieslfowler@augustana.edu
FOWLER, Lindi .... 864-977-7200.... 460 A
lindi.fowler@ngu.edu
FOWLER, Lisa .... 678-891-2995.... 130 G
Lisa.Fowler@gpc.edu
FOWLER, Marc .... 616-222-1443.... 250 C
marc.fowler@cornerstone.edu
FOWLER, Matt .... 618-262-8641.... 152 I
fowlerm@iecc.edu
FOWLER, Mike .... 502-451-0815.... 206 C
mfowler@sullivan.edu
FOWLER, Ned, H .... 828-254-1921.... 367 H
nfowler@abtech.edu
FOWLER, Pamela, W .... 734-763-4119.... 259 D
pfowler@umich.edu
FOWLER, Paul .... 404-727-0512.... 129 A
pgfowle@emory.edu
FOWLER, Peter .... 617-989-4082.... 246 C
fowlerp@wit.edu
FOWLER, Richard .... 315-472-6603.... 325 E
rfowler@bryantstratton.edu
FOWLER, S. Kevin .... 903-510-2419.... 502 E
kfow@tjc.edu
FOWLER, Sandra, S .... 334-683-5108...... 5 D
sfowler@judson.edu
FOWLER, Sandy .... 530-674-9199..... 37 E
sfowler@cambridge.edu
FOWLER, Shaanette .... 330-490-7320.... 405 E
sfowler@walsh.edu
FOWLER, Tammy .... 870-972-3024..... 20 C
tlfowler@astate.edu
FOWLER, Verna, M .... 800-567-2344.... 546 G
vfowler@menominee.edu
FOWLER, Vivia, L .... 478-757-5229.... 139 A
vfowler@wesleyancollege.edu
FOWLER, Walter, B .... 412-365-1105.... 425 B
wfowler@chatham.edu
FOWLER-HILL, Sandra .... 425-388-9216.... 533 H
sfowler-hill@everettcc.edu
FOWLES, Gareth .... 561-237-7601.... 113 D
gfowles@lynn.edu
FOWLES, Michelle, R .... 818-947-2437..... 55 E
fowlesmr@lavc.edu
FOWLKES, Bruce, M .... 309-467-6423.... 150 H
bfowlkes@eureka.edu
FOWLKES, Carolyn, J .... 312-939-0111.... 150 B
caroline@eastwest.edu
FOWLKES, Dane .... 903-923-2068.... 486 D
dfowlkes@etbu.edu
FOWLKES, Deborah, W .... 303-492-8484..... 88 B
deborah.fowlkes@colorado.edu
FOWLKES, Keith .... 276-376-4578.... 525 C
jkf7e@uvawise.edu
FOX, Amanda, T .... 205-665-6038...... 9 C
foxat@montevallo.edu
FOX, Andrea, D .... 404-752-1510.... 134 B
afox@msm.edu
FOX, Ann .... 316-942-4291.... 195 C
foxa@newmanu.edu
FOX, Anthony .... 989-386-6622.... 255 F
aefox@midmich.edu
FOX, Barbara .... 301-552-1400.... 229 C
bfox@bible.edu
FOX, Barbara, R .... 301-552-1400.... 229 C
bfox@bible.edu
FOX, Brenda .... 903-463-8631.... 487 A
foxb@grayson.edu
FOX, Carl .... 406-994-4145.... 295 E
carl.fox1@montana.edu
FOX, Carole, M .... 512-463-1808.... 500 D
carole.fox@tsus.edu
FOX, Chris .... 412-261-2647.... 432 B
cfox@kaplan.edu
FOX, Christie, L .... 435-797-3940.... 511 B
clfox@cc.usu.edu
FOX, Christopher .... 617-369-3894.... 244 G
cfox@mfa.org
FOX, D. Jeff .... 208-732-6220.... 143 B
jfox@csi.edu
FOX, David .... 937-708-5253.... 405 G
dfox@wilberforce.edu
FOX, Debbie .... 225-768-1727.... 214 B
Deborah.Fox@ololcollege.edu
FOX, Deborah .... 785-442-6002.... 193 D
dfox@highlandcc.edu
FOX, Delcy .... 518-783-8300.... 350 I
fox@siena.edu
FOX, Don .... 303-273-3231..... 82 F
dfox@mines.edu
FOX, Donnie, S .... 606-337-1530.... 199 E
dfox@ccbbc.edu
FOX, Doug .... 615-226-3990.... 471 I
dfox@nadcedu.com
FOX, Douglas .... 325-942-2333.... 480 E
doug.fox@angelo.edu
FOX, Douglas .... 405-974-2649.... 413 B
dfox@ucok.edu
FOX, Jan, I .... 304-696-6671.... 543 G
fox@marshall.edu
FOX, Jeanne .... 574-257-3386.... 169 F
foxj@bethelcollege.edu
FOX, Joe .... 516-364-0808.... 343 A
itsupport@nycollege.edu
FOX, John .... 229-931-6884.... 131 B
FOX, John, T .... 404-778-4432.... 129 A
john_fox@emory.org
FOX, OP, Joseph .... 202-495-3858..... 98 D
vpadvance@dhs.edu
FOX, Karen .... 617-364-3510.... 232 C
kfox@boston.edu
FOX, Karen, L .... 717-560-8254.... 433 D
kfox@lbc.edu
FOX, Karla .... 860-486-1868..... 94 E
karla.fox@uconn.edu
FOX, Katheryn .... 850-436-8444.... 123 A
katheryn.fox@vc.edu
FOX, Kelly .... 303-860-5600..... 88 A
Kelly.Fox@cu.edu
FOX, Lori .... 212-678-3438.... 357 F
lfox@exchange.tc.columbia.edu
FOX, Lynn .... 209-946-2421..... 75 D
lfox@pacific.edu
FOX, Marie .... 650-949-6149..... 47 G
foxmarie@fhda.edu
FOX, Mark .... 704-484-4101.... 369 B
foxm@clevelandcommunitycollege.edu
FOX, Mark .... 423-461-8760.... 471 H
mpfox@milligan.edu
FOX, OP, Mary Michael .... 615-297-7545.... 466 H
srmmichael@aquinascollege.edu
FOX, Marye Anne .... 858-534-3135..... 74 D
chancellor@ucsd.edu
FOX, Michael, J .... 757-221-1693.... 517 J
mjfox1@wm.edu
FOX, Nili .... 513-487-3243.... 391 F
nfox@huc.edu
FOX, P. Michael .... 585-395-2504.... 352 F
mfox@brockport.edu
FOX, Pamela .... 540-887-7026.... 520 I
pfox@mbc.edu
FOX, Patricia .... 315-731-5753.... 341 E
pfox@mvcc.edu
FOX, Patricia .... 740-654-6711.... 400 B
fox@ohio.edu
FOX, Phyllis .... 423-461-8708.... 471 H
pfox@milligan.edu
FOX, Rebecca, M .... 305-284-4330.... 122 F
rfox@miami.edu
FOX, Richard .... 718-368-4799.... 328 B
rfox@kbcc.cuny.edu
FOX, Robert .... 502-852-6745.... 207 A
bob.fox@louisville.edu
FOX, Robert .... 215-468-8800.... 431 J
admissions@culinaryarts.edu
FOX, BSG, Ronald, A .... 847-328-9300.... 164 B
ron.fox@seabury.edu
FOX, Rusty .... 817-515-3015.... 496 A
rusty.fox@tccd.edu
FOX, Sean .... 307-754-6102.... 556 D
Sean.Fox@northwestcollege.edu
FOX, Shari .... 615-794-4254.... 472 D
sfox@omorecollege.edu
FOX, Susan, E .... 804-355-0671.... 524 F
sfox@upsem.edu
FOX, Theresa .... 575-769-4030.... 317 K
theresa.fox@clovis.edu
FOX, Thomas .... 909-706-3548..... 78 D
tfox@westernu.edu
FOX, Timothy .... 410-617-2863.... 224 A
tfox@loyola.edu
FOX, Todd .... 954-783-7339.... 106 D
tfox@cci.edu
FOX, William .... 315-229-5892.... 349 E
wfox@stlawu.edu
FOX-FORRESTER, Susan ... 432-837-8178.... 501 B
sforrester@sulross.edu
FOX KUHLKEN, Pam .... 619-335-0441..... 62 E
pamfox@juno.com
FOXMAN, Philip, R .... 814-332-5383.... 421 E
phil.foxman@allegheny.edu
FOXMAN, Ruth .... 860-231-5221..... 93 H
rfoxman@sjc.edu
FOXMAN, Steven, H .... 610-499-4141.... 451 F
shfoxman@widener.edu
FOXWORTH, Jessica, L .... 601-877-6479.... 273 C
jfoxworth@alcorn.edu
FOY, Jocelyn, L .... 919-530-5218.... 378 A
jfoy@nccu.edu
FOZARD, John, D .... 405-691-3800.... 408 H
ecox@macu.edu
FOZARD, Jonathan .... 405-945-3284.... 410 F
FRABONI, David, J .... 404-413-3405.... 131 C
dfraboni@gsu.edu
FRADEN, Rena .... 860-297-2130..... 94 C
rena.fraden@trincoll.edu
FRADKIN, Bernard .... 951-222-8038..... 64 B
bernie.fradkin@rcc.edu
FRAGE, Gary .... 229-430-3593.... 123 I
gfrage@albanytech.edu
FRAGNOLI, Kristen, M .... 585-292-3369.... 341 H
kfragnoli@monroecc.edu
FRAGOSO, Marcos .... 210-805-3014.... 503 F
fragoso@uiwtx.edu
FRAHER, Michael, P .... 845-437-5320.... 359 D
mifraher@vassar.edu
FRAIER, Whitney .... 636-949-4975.... 284 C
wfraier@lindenwood.edu
FRAILE, Pedro .... 787-727-3583.... 568 B
pfraile@sagrado.edu
FRAILING, Mallory .... 517-265-5161.... 247 D
FRAINIER, Janine, L .... 317-940-9228.... 170 C
jfrainie@butler.edu
FRAIRE, John .... 509-335-5900.... 539 A
jfraire@wsu.edu
FRAIRE, Virginia, M .... 512-223-6019.... 481 B
vfraire@austincc.edu
FRALEY, Doug .... 606-487-3086.... 201 H
doug.fraley@kctcs.edu
FRALEY, F. Allen .... 330-471-8237.... 395 E
afraley@malone.edu
FRALIC, Bradley, W .... 216-368-2126.... 386 E
bradley.fralic@case.edu
FRALICKER, Tamara .... 618-395-7777.... 152 H
fralickert@iecc.edu
FRAME, Adrienne .... 850-644-2860.... 119 C
aframe@admin.fsu.edu
FRAME, J. Davidson .... 703-516-0035.... 524 G
davidson.frame@umtweb.edu
FRAME, Randall, L .... 484-384-2980.... 438 C
rframe@eastern.edu
FRAMPTON, John .... 845-687-5288.... 358 C
framptoj@sunyulster.edu
FRANCE, Lucy .... 406-243-5710.... 295 A
lucy.france@umontana.edu
FRANCE, Melissa, H .... 918-631-2516.... 413 F
melissa-france@utulsa.edu
FRANCE, Nancy .... 503-838-8327.... 419 C
francen@wou.edu
FRANCE, Richard .... 302-736-2321..... 96 G
franceri@wesley.edu
FRANCES, Duran .... 505-925-8585.... 321 G
fduran@unm.edu
FRANCHI, Gary .... 719-549-3053..... 87 B
Gary.Franchi@pueblocc.edu
FRANCIOSI, Adrienne .... 617-243-2400.... 236 F
afranciosi@lasell.edu
FRANCIS, Amy .... 419-783-2376.... 389 G
afrancis@defiance.edu
FRANCIS, Andrew .... 978-368-2901.... 230 F
andrew.francis@auc.edu
FRANCIS, Billy .... 501-337-5000..... 21 D
bfrancis@otcweb.edu
FRANCIS, Charles .... 559-324-6461..... 72 A
charles.francis@fresnocitycollege.edu
FRANCIS, JR., D. Morgan . 336-838-6102.... 375 A
morgan.francis@wilkescc.edu
FRANCIS, Diana .... 219-473-4211.... 170 D
dfrancis@ccsj.edu
FRANCIS, Donald .... 301-846-2458.... 222 G
dfrancis@frederick.edu
FRANCIS, Eddie .... 504-286-5343.... 214 I
efrancis@suno.edu
FRANCIS, Gerald, L .... 336-278-7900.... 364 A
francis@elon.edu
FRANCIS, Heather .... 972-825-4627.... 495 D
hfrancis@sagu.edu
FRANCIS, James, M .... 630-617-3041.... 150 F
jimf@elmhurst.edu
FRANCIS, Jeff .... 972-825-4731.... 495 D
JFrancis@sagu.edu
FRANCIS, Jeffrey .... 918-631-2546.... 413 F
jeffrey-francis@utulsa.edu
FRANCIS, Karen .... 603-623-0313.... 305 F
kfrancis@nhia.edu
FRANCIS, Krista .... 360-417-6394.... 536 B
kfrancis@pencol.edu
FRANCIS, Laurel .... 714-432-5670..... 41 B
lfrancis@occ.cccd.edu
FRANCIS, Laurie .... 201-447-7117.... 307 F
lfrancis@bergen.edu
FRANCIS, Leon .... 610-558-5584.... 437 C
francisl@neumann.edu
FRANCIS, MaEsther .... 903-769-5740.... 488 M
maesther_francis@jarvis.edu
FRANCIS, Michael, R .... 801-863-8818.... 511 C
francimi@uvu.edu
FRANCIS, Monty, E .... 214-860-2178.... 484 I
mfrancis@dcccd.edu
FRANCIS, Norman, C .... 504-520-7541.... 217 A
nfrancis@xula.edu
FRANCIS, Paige .... 479-619-4337..... 22 H
pfrancis@nwacc.edu
FRANCIS, Patricia, L .... 607-436-2846.... 353 E
francipl@oneonta.edu
FRANCIS, Randall .... 502-863-7962.... 200 G
randall_francis@georgetowncollege.edu
FRANCIS, Raymond, W .... 989-774-3888.... 249 G
franc1rw@cmich.edu
FRANCIS, Robert .... 215-895-6966.... 427 G
raf47@drexel.edu
FRANCIS, Robert .... 206-546-4797.... 537 G
bfrancis@shoreline.edu
FRANCIS, Sally, K .... 541-737-4881.... 418 F
sally.francis@oregonstate.edu
FRANCIS, William .... 641-269-4901.... 185 A
francisb@grinnell.edu
FRANCISCHETTI, Jessica ... 406-657-1041.... 296 E
francisj@rocky.edu
FRANCISCO, Eva Lynn .... 904-819-6460.... 107 A
efrancisco@flagler.edu
FRANCISCO, Patricia .... 619-594-6181..... 36 E
patricia.francisco@sdsu.edu
FRANCKO, David, A .... 205-348-8280...... 8 F
dfrancko@ua.edu
FRANCO, Barry .... 843-574-6796.... 461 G
barry.franco@tridenttech.edu
FRANCO, Juan .... 402-472-3755.... 300 H
jfranco2@unl.edu
FRANCO, Kerry .... 562-908-3476..... 63 H
foundation@riohondo.edu
FRANCO, Larry .... 201-360-4191.... 310 F
lfranco@hccc.edu
FRANCO, Maria .... 386-226-6225..... 14 D
maria.franco@erau.edu
FRANCO, Maria .... 386-226-6225.... 105 C
maria.franco@erau.edu
FRANCO, Maria .... 386-226-6225.... 105 B
francom@erau.edu
FRANCO, Michael, R .... 410-225-2594.... 224 C
mfranco@mica.edu
FRANCO, Onorina .... 575-538-6174.... 321 I
francoo@wnmu.edu
FRANCO, Raymond .... 607-753-2518.... 353 B
raymond.franco@cortland.edu
FRANCO, Rita .... 209-478-0800..... 50 I
rfranco@humphreys.edu
FRANCO, Robert .... 808-734-9514.... 141 E
bfranco@hawaii.edu
FRANCO, Vivian .... 559-278-6111..... 34 D
vivian_franco@csufresno.edu
FRANCOIS, K. Michael .... 936-261-1009.... 496 E
kmfrancois@pvamu.edu
FRANCOIS, Mary Ann, J .... 504-286-5340.... 214 I
mfrancoi@suno.edu
FRANCOIS, Willie, L .... 225-771-4410.... 214 H
willie_francois@subr.edu
FRANCOIS-SEENY, Denise 610-861-5066.... 437 G
dfrancois@northampton.edu
FRANCOS, Richard .... 516-463-6613.... 335 H
richard.francos@hofstra.edu
FRANCOVALLE, Charlotte .. 212-787-5300.... 322 G
info@amda.edu
FRANCOVALLE, Charlotte .. 212-787-5300..... 27 H
info@amda.edu
FRANDSEN, Michael .... 517-629-0315.... 247 E
mfrandsen@albion.edu
FRANK, Anthony, A .... 970-491-6211..... 83 A
presofc@colostate.edu
FRANK, Brad .... 612-977-5736.... 262 A
brad.frank@capella.edu
FRANK, Brian .... 727-341-4143.... 116 F
frank.brian@spcollege.edu
FRANK, Christine, D .... 312-942-8735.... 163 B
christine_frank@rush.edu
FRANK, David .... 541-346-4198.... 419 B
dfrank@uoregon.edu
FRANK, Greg .... 757-822-7260.... 528 C
gfrank@tcc.edu
FRANK, Isabel .... 718-817-4602.... 334 C
frank@fordham.edu
FRANK, Jonathan .... 312-793-7150.... 150 G
jfrank@erikson.edu

FREEDMAN, Victoria .... 212-430-3179.... 361 I
vfreedman@aecom.yu.edu
FREEH, Mary Beth .... 610-606-4605.... 424 I
mafreeh@cedarcrest.edu
FREEL, Lisa .... 301-846-2468.... 222 G
lfreel@frederick.edu
FREELAND, Kay .... 770-426-2944.... 133 B
freeland@life.edu
FREELAND, Richard, M ..... 617-994-6901.... 237 A
freeland@bhe.mass.edu
FREELANDER, Chichi .... 405-491-6396.... 412 D
cfreelan@snu.edu
FREELEN, Robert .... 858-642-8131...... 58 I
rfreelen@nu.edu
FREELIN, Dawn .... 478-757-5170.... 139 A
dfreelin@wesleyancollege.edu
FREELOVE, Bob .... 805-565-6058...... 78 F
bfreelove@westmont.edu
FREELS, Ean .... 319-208-5015.... 188 G
efreels@scciowa.edu
FREEMAN, Alston .... 803-934-3179.... 459 F
afreeman@morris.edu
FREEMAN, Andrew, W .... 585-292-2231.... 341 H
afreeman@monroecc.edu
FREEMAN, Angela .... 404-880-8757.... 126 I
afreeman@cau.edu
FREEMAN, Carol Ann .... 845-675-4794.... 344 G
carol_ann.freeman@nyack.edu
FREEMAN, Charles .... 559-925-3145...... 77 I
charlesfreeman@whccd.edu
FREEMAN, Charles .... 559-925-3145...... 77 J
charlesfreeman@whccd.edu
FREEMAN, Chris .... 310-578-1080...... 28 K
cfreeman@antiochla.edu
FREEMAN, Chris .... 803-786-3886.... 457 C
bookstore@columbiasc.edu
FREEMAN, Craig, N .... 360-779-9993.... 535 E
cfreeman@nca.edu
FREEMAN, Dave .... 530-242-2220...... 69 D
dfreeman@shastacollege.edu
FREEMAN, Dave, W .... 706-737-1590.... 125 C
dfreema4aug.edu
FREEMAN, DJ .... 620-947-3121.... 196 E
djf@tabor.edu
FREEMAN, Eddie .... 817-272-2106.... 505 A
efreeman@uta.edu
FREEMAN, Elijah, T .... 252-789-0276.... 371 E
efreeman@martincc.edu
FREEMAN, Everette, J .... 229-430-4605.... 123 H
everette.freeman@asurams.edu
FREEMAN, Ginger, C .... 615-898-2922.... 473 F
freeman@mtsu.edu
FREEMAN, Irving .... 724-552-2880.... 433 C
ifreeman@lecom.edu
FREEMAN, Iva, M .... 312-752-2530.... 155 B
iva.freeman@kendall.edu
FREEMAN, Jackie .... 435-652-7612.... 512 A
freeman@dixie.edu
FREEMAN, Jeannie .... 916-568-3039...... 55 J
freemaj@losrios.edu
FREEMAN, Julie .... 607-436-2125.... 353 E
freemanj@oneonta.edu
FREEMAN, Karen, J .... 315-786-2234.... 337 F
kfreeman@sunyjefferson.edu
FREEMAN, Kavita .... 202-884-9412...... 99 E
freemank@trinitydc.edu
FREEMAN, Kenneth .... 314-968-5990.... 293 A
kennethfreeman@webster.edu
FREEMAN, Larry .... 910-521-6601.... 379 B
larry.freeman@uncp.edu
FREEMAN, Lisa .... 413-572-5204.... 239 C
lfreeman@wsc.ma.edu
FREEMAN, Lisa, C .... 815-753-1000.... 160 A
FREEMAN, Mabel, G .... 614-292-3324.... 398 H
freeman.9@osu.edu
FREEMAN, Mark, A .... 610-526-6599.... 423 C
mfreeman@brynmawr.edu
FREEMAN, Melanie, H .... 662-329-7222.... 276 B
mfreeman@hr.muw.edu
FREEMAN, Nicole .... 617-369-3659.... 244 G
nfreeman@mfa.org
FREEMAN, Pam .... 620-417-2102.... 196 B
pam.freeman@sccc.edu
FREEMAN, Pat, B .... 336-334-4822.... 370 E
pbfreeman@gtcc.edu
FREEMAN, Robert .... 312-777-8710.... 153 A
rfreeman@aii.edu
FREEMAN, Roger .... 763-433-1378.... 265 J
roger.freeman@anokaramsey.edu
FREEMAN, Russell .... 773-577-8100.... 148 D
FREEMAN, Sharon .... 662-246-6256.... 275 F
sfreeman@msdelta.edu
FREEMAN, Sheila, D .... 662-685-4771.... 273 H
sfreeman@bmc.edu
FREEMAN, Stanley .... 910-272-3503.... 373 A
sfreeman@robeson.edu
FREEMAN, Stella .... 937-395-8006.... 394 D
stella.freeman@kcma.edu
FREEMAN, Steve .... 270-534-3363.... 203 B
steve.freeman@kctcs.edu
FREEMAN, William .... 314-862-3456.... 282 C
wfreeman@fontbonne.edu
FREEMAN, Yancy .... 423-425-4662.... 477 D
yancy-freeman@utc.edu
FREEMAN-GALLANT,
Corey .... 518-580-5720.... 351 B
cfreeman@skidmore.edu
FREER, Douglas, R .... 909-869-3310...... 33 G
drfreer@csupomona.edu
FREER, Peter .... 704-463-3066.... 375 E
peter.freer@fsmail.pfeiffer.edu
FREER, Steven .... 845-687-5200.... 358 C
freers@sunyulster.edu
FREER, Wayne .... 845-687-5053.... 358 C
freerw@sunyulster.edu
FREESE, Rachelle .... 800-955-2527.... 282 G
rfreese@grantham.edu
FREEZE, Jackie .... 307-382-1639.... 556 F
jfreeze@wwcc.wy.edu
FREGIA, Bertha .... 409-880-8355.... 500 E
bertha.fregia@lit.edu
FREGIA, Bertha .... 409-880-8375.... 500 F
bertha.fregia@lamar.edu
FREGIA, Olin .... 903-769-5813.... 488 M
olin_fregia@jarvis.edu
FREHSE, Sandra .... 518-454-5244.... 330 C
frehses@strose.edu
FREIBERGER, Amy, M .... 918-631-3727.... 413 F
amy-freiberger@utulsa.edu
FREIBURGER, Lisa .... 616-234-4025.... 251 G
lfreiburger@grcc.edu
FREIBURGHAUS, Stacy, J . 208-467-8766.... 143 I
sjfreiburghaus@nnu.edu
FREIJE, Margaret .... 508-793-2541.... 233 D
mfreije@holycross.edu
FREILER, Dan .... 717-396-7833.... 440 J
dfreiler@pcad.edu
FREILICH, Yosef .... 718-601-3523.... 361 H
RabbiFreilich@yahoo.com
FREISER, Jean .... 858-635-4063...... 27 E
jfreiser@alliant.edu
FREITAG, Paul, A .... 612-343-4455.... 270 C
pafreita@northcentral.edu
FREITAG, Thomas .... 215-641-6538.... 436 G
tfreitag@mc3.edu
FREITAS, Frances Anne ..... 330-382-3805.... 393 F
ffreitas@kent.edu
FREITAS, Rockne .... 808-956-6405.... 140 J
rfreitas@hawaii.edu
FREJOSKY, Joe .... 423-493-4225.... 476 C
frejosj@tntemple.edu
FREJOSKY, Pam .... 423-493-4100.... 476 C
frejosky@tntemple.edu
FREMONT, II, Ron, H .... 909-869-4379...... 33 G
rfremont@csupomona.edu
FRENCH, Allyn .... 920-693-1871.... 554 A
allyn.french@gotoltc.edu
FRENCH, Amy .... 270-686-6415.... 198 G
amy.french@brescia.edu
FRENCH, Barbara .... 415-476-6296...... 74 E
bfrench@ucsf.edu
FRENCH, Daphne .... 912-260-4232.... 136 F
daphne.french@sgc.edu
FRENCH, JR., George, T .... 205-929-1428........ 5 H
gtfrench@aol.com
FRENCH, Joy .... 303-724-2516...... 88 D
joy.french@ucdenver.edu
FRENCH, Kathy .... 602-285-7503...... 16 B
kathy.french@pcmail.maricopa.edu
FRENCH, Marjie, M .... 210-458-4228.... 506 B
marjie.french@utsa.edu
FRENCH, Meghan, Q .... 212-346-1025.... 345 F
mfrench@pace.edu
FRENCH, Paige .... 540-515-3749.... 516 K
pfrench@bridgewater.edu
FRENCH, CSSP, Raymond . 412-396-4827.... 428 C
french@duq.edu
FRENCH, Richard, G .... 781-283 3583.... 246 B
rfrench@wellesley.edu
FRENCH, Robert, C .... 315-470-6511.... 355 A
rcfrench@esf.edu
FRENCH, William, R .... 609-497-7789.... 312 F
bill.french@ptsem.edu
FRENDEWEY, JR., James . 906-487-2259.... 255 E
jimf@mtu.edu
FRENDIAN, Michel .... 312-893-7145.... 150 G
mfrendian@erikson.edu
FRENK, Julio .... 617-495-2936.... 235 H
jfrenk@hsph.harvard.edu
FRENZEL, Michelle .... 218-755-2020.... 266 B
mfrenzel@bemidjistate.edu
FRERE, Leslie .... 219-866-6116.... 179 B
lfrere@saintjoe.edu
FRERICHS, Chris .... 515-961-1711.... 188 F
chris.frerichs@simpson.edu
FRESCH, Cathy .... 814-871-5842.... 429 F
fresch001@gannon.edu
FRESH, Frederick .... 404-270-5185.... 137 E
ffresh@spelman.edu
FRESHOUR, Brett .... 330-490-7171.... 405 E
bfreshour@walsh.edu
FRESHWATER, Laurie, A .... 252-222-6281.... 368 F
lap@carteret.edu
FRESHWATER, Thomas, A . 910-962-3100.... 379 C
freshwatert@uncw.edu
FRESQUEZ, Anthony .... 605-455-6093.... 464 H
afresquez@olc.edu
FRESQUEZ, Julie .... 951-343-4302...... 31 G
jfresque@calbaptist.edu
FREUDENBURG, Gene .... 269-387-8237.... 260 F
gene.freudenburg@wmich.edu
FREUND, Deborah, A .... 909-621-8025...... 40 C
debbie.freund@cgu.edu
FREW, Erin .... 719-549-2207...... 83 B
erin.frew@colostate-pueblo.edu
FREY, Angela .... 414-382-6206.... 545 H
angela.frey@alverno.edu
FREY, Cathy .... 802-485-2327.... 514 A
frey@norwich.edu
FREY, Don .... 360-736-9391.... 531 H
dfrey@centralia.edu
FREY, Donald .... 402-280-2300.... 297 H
donaldfrey@creighton.edu
FREY, Isabel, D .... 516-463-6800.... 335 H
isabel.d.frey@hofstra.edu
FREY, Joan, L .... 502-410-6200.... 200 F
FREY, Len .... 870-972-3035...... 20 C
lfrey@astate.edu
FREY, Lori .... 717-264-4141.... 452 B
lfrey@wilson.edu
FREY, Mary .... 860-768-4392...... 95 A
mfrey@hartford.edu
FREY, Melissa .... 503-589-7652.... 414 J
melissa.frey@chemeketa.edu
FREY, Phil .... 503-399-2535.... 414 J
phil.frey@chemeketa.edu
FREY, Rodney .... 316-284-5315.... 190 H
rodfrey@bethelks.edu
FREY, Ruth .... 847-328-9300.... 164 B
ruth.frey@seabury.edu
FREY, Sandy .... 636-797-3000.... 283 H
sfrey@jeffco.edu
FREYBURGER, James .... 912-201-8109.... 136 H
jfreyburger@southuniversity.edu
FREYRE, Francoise .... 212-746-6565.... 360 B
ffreyre@med.cornell.edu
FREYTAG, Carol .... 419-755-4214.... 399 C
freytag.7@osu.edu
FREYTES, Elvin, R .... 212-966-0300.... 342 F
elvin@nyaa.edu
FREYTES, Liza .... 787-279-1912.... 563 B
lfreytes@bayamon.inter.edu
FRIAS, Frank .... 626-529-8064...... 60 G
ffrias@pacificoaks.edu
FRIAS, Mary Lou .... 508-531-1252.... 238 B
mfrias@bridgew.edu
FRICK, Caroline .... 706-754-7722.... 134 E
cfrick@northgatech.edu
FRICK, Jeffrey .... 562-926-1023...... 63 B
jeffreyfrick@gmail.com
FRICK, Jeffrey .... 920-403-3001.... 550 C
jeffrey.frick@snc.edu
FRICK, Lillian, K .... 989-386-6605.... 255 F
lfrick@midmich.edu
FRICKE, Bob .... 419-227-3141.... 404 D
rlfricke@unoh.edu
FRICKE, David .... 732-906-2519.... 311 E
dfricke@middlesexcc.edu
FRICKX, Gretchen .... 312-939-4975.... 151 F
gfrickx@harringtoncollege.com
FRID, Sarah .... 760-921-5469...... 61 B
sfrid@paloverde.edu
FRIDAY, Mary Ann .... 410-857-2219.... 224 D
mfriday@mcdaniel.edu
FRIDAY-STROUD,
Shawnta .... 850-599-3565.... 118 G
shawnta.friday-stroud@famu.edu
FRIDDELL, Melinda .... 229-226-1621.... 137 F
mfriddell@thomasu.edu
FRIDGE, Rob .... 417-873-7527.... 281 H
rfridge@drury.edu
FRIE, Vinetta .... 225-216-8504.... 209 I
friev@mybrcc.edu
FRIEBEL, Thomas .... 718-368-6646.... 328 B
tfriebel@kbcc.cuny.edu
FRIED, Barry, J .... 608-796-3811.... 553 A
bjfried@viterbo.edu
FRIED, Linda, P .... 212-305-9300.... 330 F
lpfried@columbia.edu
FRIED, Ray .... 325-235-7302.... 500 C
ray.fried@tstc.edu
FRIED-GOODNIGHT,
Maud .... 856-691-8600.... 309 C
mgoodnight@cccnj.edu
FRIEDBERG, Connie .... 412-809-5100.... 444 F
friedberg@pti.edu
FRIEDBERG, Jason, D .... 570-577-3333.... 423 D
jason.friedberg@bucknell.edu
FRIEDBERG, Susan, L .... 630-953-1300.... 149 B
sfriedberg@devry.edu
FRIEDEL, Kristin, M .... 315-859-4637.... 335 A
kfriedel@hamilton.edu
FRIEDENBERG, Samantha . 610-799-1754.... 434 D
sfriedenberg@lccc.edu
FRIEDERICH, Larry, V .... 618-235-2700.... 165 B
larry.friederich@swic.edu
FRIEDERICHS, Marla, J ..... 651-962-6151.... 272 E
mjfriederich@stthomas.edu
FRIEDHOFF, Scott .... 330-263-2118.... 388 E
sfriedhoff@wooster.edu
FRIEDLAND, Michael .... 561-297-4341.... 118 H
mfriedl@fau.edu
FRIEDLANDER, Jack .... 805-965-0581...... 68 B
friedlan@sbcc.edu
FRIEDLINE, Patrick .... 312-329-4414.... 158 H
patrick.friedline@moody.edu
FRIEDMAN, Aaron .... 612-626-4949.... 272 D
alfried@umn.edu
FRIEDMAN, Aaron .... 612-626-3700.... 272 D
alfried@umn.edu
FRIEDMAN, Al .... 425-388-9399.... 533 H
afriedman@everettcc.edu
FRIEDMAN, Anita, S .... 757-683-5789.... 521 L
asfriedm@odu.edu
FRIEDMAN, Avraham .... 847-982-2500.... 151 H
friedman@htc.edu
FRIEDMAN, Beth .... 402-354-7236.... 299 E
beth.friedman@methodistcollege.edu
FRIEDMAN, Daniel .... 206-616-2442.... 538 F
dsfx@uw.edu
FRIEDMAN, Danielle .... 212-431-2843.... 343 E
dfriedman@nyls.edu
FRIEDMAN, David .... 410-484-7200.... 225 C
FRIEDMAN, Eric .... 201-360-4646.... 310 F
efriedman@hccc.edu
FRIEDMAN, Frank .... 434-977-1620.... 527 F
ffriedman@pvcc.edu
FRIEDMAN, Jay, R .... 716-645-3313.... 351 G
jf5@buffalo.edu
FRIEDMAN, Joel .... 401-825-2003.... 453 B
jafriedman@ccri.edu
FRIEDMAN, Judith Ann ..... 310-287-4244...... 55 F
friedmja@wlac.edu
FRIEDMAN, Kathryn, A .... 401-874-7439.... 454 E
kfriedman@uri.edu
FRIEDMAN, Larry, S .... 610-558-5522.... 437 C
lfriedma@neumann.edu
FRIEDMAN, Lauren .... 203-575-8139...... 90 E
lfriedman@nvcc.commnet.edu
FRIEDMAN, Mark .... 573-681-5316.... 284 B
friedmanm@lincolnu.edu
FRIEDMAN, Melissa .... 212-280-6001.... 337 G
mefriedman@jtsa.edu
FRIEDMAN, Robert .... 212-960-5269.... 346 F
friedman@yu.edu
FRIEDMAN, Robert .... 212-960-5269.... 361 I
rfriedm2@yu.edu
FRIEDMAN, Scott .... 847-925-6266.... 151 E
sfriedma@harpercollege.edu
FRIEDMAN, Stephen, J ..... 212-346-1097.... 345 F
president@pace.edu
FRIEDMAN, William .... 312-369-7623.... 148 B
bfriedman@colum.edu
FRIEDMAN, Yaakov .... 847-982-2500.... 151 H
FRIEDMAN-LOMBARDO,
Jaclyn .... 973-655-7599.... 311 G
friedmanlj@mail.montclair.edu
FRIEDMANN, Mina .... 212-217-3560.... 333 G
mina_friedmann@fitnyc.edu
FRIEDNER, Julia .... 615-217-9347.... 468 B
jfriedner@daymarinstitute.edu
FRIEDRICH, Brian, L .... 402-643-7364.... 297 F
brian.friedrich@cune.edu
FRIEDRICH, Dan .... 605-256-5555.... 465 G
dan.friedrich@dsu.edu
FRIEDRICH,
Glenn (Fred), E .... 512-471-3723.... 505 B
fred.friedrich@austin.utexas.edu
FRIEDRICH, Katherine .... 409-933-8150.... 483 B
kfriedrich@com.edu
FRIEDRICHSEN,
Steven, W .... 909-706-3911...... 78 D
sfriedrichsen@westernu.edu
FRIEL, Kathern, R .... 302-573-5497...... 96 C
friel@dtcc.edu
FRIEL, Terri, L .... 312-281-3320.... 162 I
tfriel@roosevelt.edu
FRIEL, Thomas .... 215-641-5565.... 430 C
friel.t@gmc.edu
FRIEL, Wm. Jake .... 724-287-8711.... 423 F
jake.friel@bc3.edu
FRIEND, Dane, K .... 713-798-1544.... 481 H
dfriend@bcm.edu
FRIEND, David .... 402-457-2770.... 298 H
djfriend@mccneb.edu
FRIEND, Dean .... 717-846-5000.... 452 G
FRIEND, Gwyn .... 312-362-6961.... 148 F
gfriend@depaul.edu
FRIEND, Jennifer .... 937-461-5174.... 396 C
jennifer.friend@staffmiamijacobs.edu
FRIEND, Joanie .... 314-539-5157.... 289 A
jfriend4@stlcc.edu
FRIEND, Randall .... 304-876-5212.... 544 A
rfriend@shepherd.edu
FRIEND, Vivian, M .... 727-816-3427.... 114 F
friendv@phcc.edu
FRIERSON, Henry, T .... 352-392-6622.... 120 B
hfrierson@ufl.edu
FRIERSON, Muriel .... 856-256-4367.... 314 A
frierson@rowan.edu
FRIERY, Gary .... 281-998-6150.... 493 F
gary.friery@sjcd.edu
FRIES, James .... 505-454-3269.... 318 I
president_office@nmhu.edu
FRIES, Jane .... 970-542-3106...... 86 A
jane.fries@morgancc.edu
FRIESEKE, Mary .... 414-382-6098.... 545 H
mary.frieseke@alverno.edu

FULLER, Tony .... 276-739-2575.... 528 D
mmcbride@vhcc.edu
FULLER, Vivian .... 410-943-1171.... 226 D
vfuller@host.sdc.edu
FULLERTON, Darren, S ...... 417-625-3135.... 286 E
fullerton-d@mssu.edu
FULLERTON, Fred, C .... 208-467-8530.... 143 I
ffullerton@nnu.edu
FULLMER, Paul .... 717-867-6135.... 434 C
fullmer@lvc.edu
FULMER, David .... 918-495-6549.... 411 C
dfulmer@oru.edu
FULMER, Gregory, L .... 717-291-3993.... 429 E
greg.fulmer@fandm.edu
FULMER, Hal .... 334-670-3112........ 8 B
hfulmer@troy.edu
FULMER, Judy .... 334-670-3102........ 8 B
jfulmer@troy.edu
FULMER, Shannon .... 214-692-8080.... 480 I
sfulmer@aii.edu
FULMORE, Robbin .... 757-683-3701.... 521 L
rfulmore@odu.edu
FULOP, Timothy .... 814-886-6302.... 437 A
tfulop@mtaloy.edu
FULP, Andrew .... 912-525-5000.... 136 B
afulp@scad.edu
FULTON, Deborah, M .... 540-231-0735.... 529 B
dfulton@vt.edu
FULTON, Delores .... 336-725-8344.... 375 F
fultond@pbc.edu
FULTON, Donna .... 541-880-2233.... 416 C
fulton@klamathcc.edu
FULTON, Erica .... 870-575-8491...... 25 B
fultone@uapb.edu
FULTON, Jerry .... 915-831-6359.... 486 E
jfulton@epcc.edu
FULTON, Jodie .... 541-956-7200.... 420 B
jfulton@roguecc.edu
FULTON, Kathy .... 254-298-8426.... 496 B
kath.library@templejc.edu
FULTON, Malikah .... 973-642-8742.... 315 C
malikah.fulton@shu.edu
FULTON, Richard .... 808-235-7443.... 142 C
fulton@hawaii.edu
FULTON, Ronnie .... 941-744-1244.... 107 K
FULTON, Tamara .... 352-787-7660.... 101 H
tfulton@beaconcollege.edu
FULTZ, Angela .... 606-759-7141.... 202 D
angela.fultz@kctcs.edu
FULTZ, Larenda .... 731-286-3234.... 475 A
fultz@dscc.edu
FUNCHES, LaTrista .... 561-912-1211.... 106 G
lfunches@evergladesuniversity.edu
FUNDERBURK, Dana .... 618-664-7015.... 151 D
dana.funderburk@greenville.edu
FUNDERBURK, Debra ...... 618-545-3100.... 155 A
dfunderburk@kaskaskia.edu
FUNDERBURK, Jerome ..... 704-216-6200.... 366 D
jfunderburk@livingstone.edu
FUNG, Haang .... 718-260-3560.... 346 C
hfung@poly.edu
FUNG, Henry, Y .... 713-500-9069.... 506 D
henry.y.fung@uth.tmc.edu
FUNG, Hsin-Ming .... 213-613-2200...... 70 H
ming@sciarc.edu
FUNIGIELLO, Tony .... 716-827-2481.... 358 B
funigielloa@trocaire.edu
FUNK, Carla .... 321-674-6129.... 108 E
cfunk@fit.edu
FUNK, Cynthia .... 615-322-2750.... 477 F
cindy.funk@vanderbilt.edu
FUNK, David .... 503-255-0332.... 417 C
dfunk@multnomah.edu
FUNK, Nancy .... 530-242-7689...... 69 D
nfunk@shastacollege.edu
FUNK, Robert .... 215-646-7300.... 430 C
funk.r@gmc.edu
FUNK, Tracy .... 317-921-4371.... 175 I
tfunk@ivytech.edu
FUNK-BAXTER, Kathryn .... 361-825-2321.... 497 F
kathryn.funk-baxter@tamucc.edu
FUNK-BAXTER, Kathryn .... 361-825-2183.... 497 F
kathryn.funk-baxter@tamucc.edu
FUNKE, Kathy, W .... 812-465-7050.... 180 F
kfunke@usi.edu
FUNKEY, George, E .... 303-273-3155...... 82 F
george.funkey@is.mines.edu
FUQUA, Amy .... 605-642-6397.... 465 F
amy.fuqua@bhsu.edu
FUQUA, Douglas .... 808-983-4138.... 140 C
dfuqua@tokai.edu
FUQUA, JR., Jacques, L ... 334-244-3224........ 2 A
jfuqua2@aum.edu
FUQUA, Jeff .... 615-794-4254.... 472 D
jfuqua@omorecollege.edu
FUQUA, Stacy .... 432-552-2809.... 507 C
fuqua_s@utpb.edu
FUQUAY, Melissa .... 757-352-4270.... 523 B
mfuquay@regent.edu
FURBEE, Thomas, V .... 304-829-7749.... 540 E
tfurbee@bethanywv.edu
FURDA, Eric, J .... 215-898-2886.... 448 I
furda@admissions.upenn.edu
FURE-SLOCUM, Carolyn .... 507-222-4003.... 262 B
cfureslo@carleton.edu
FURGAL, Charles, A .... 508-286-8213.... 246 E
cfurgal@wheatoncollege.edu
FURLANI, Thomas .... 716-645-7979.... 351 G
furlani@ccr.buffalo.edu
FURLONG, Bill .... 937-224-0061.... 395 A
bfurlong@swcollege.net
FURLONG, Deborah .... 920-465-2374.... 551 A
furlongd@uwgb.edu
FURLONG, Matthew .... 409-772-5113.... 507 B
mfurlong@utmb.edu
FURLONG, Scott .... 920-465-2336.... 551 A
furlongs@uwgb.edu
FURMAN, John, A .... 360-650-3496.... 539 C
john.furman@wwu.edu
FURNER, Jennifer .... 315-279-5264.... 337 K
jfurner@mail.keuka.edu
FURNISH, Shearle .... 330-941-3409.... 406 F
sfurnish@ysu.edu
FURNSTAHL, Doug .... 218-235-2119.... 270 A
d.furnstahl@vcc.edu
FURQUERON, Cherry .... 432-264-5603.... 487 I
cfurqueron@howardcollege.edu
FURR, Timothy, L .... 320-222-5735.... 268 I
tim.furr@ridgewater.edu
FURROW, Louise .... 626-815-5328........ 30 E
lfurrow@apu.edu
FURSE, Cynthia, M .... 801-581-7236.... 510 L
cfurse@ece.utah.edu
FURST, Michele .... 617-879-7366.... 238 E
mfurst@massart.edu
FURST-BOWE, Julie, A ...... 715-232-2421.... 552 C
furst-bowej@uwstout.edu
FURTADO, Maria .... 727-864-8331.... 104 K
furtadm@eckerd.edu
FURTAW, Paul .... 215-596-7570.... 450 A
p.furtaw@usciences.edu
FURTEK, Diane, H .... 413-205-3212.... 229 G
diane.furtek@aic.edu
FURTON, Kenneth .... 305-348-2866.... 119 B
kenneth.furton@fiu.edu
FURTWENGLER, Scott ...... 281-998-6150.... 493 G
scott.furtwengler@sjcd.edu
FURUKAWA, Karen .... 707-527-4302...... 68 E
kfurukawa-schlereth@santarosa.edu
FURUKAWA, Tom .... 323-265-8669...... 54 G
furukat@elac.edu
FURUKAWA-SCHLERETH,
Laurence .... 707-664-2310...... 37 B
laurence.furukawa-schlereth@sonoma.edu
FURUSETH, Owen, J .... 704-687-4253.... 378 E
ojfuruse@uncc.edu
FURUSHIMA, Randall .... 808-853-1040.... 140 G
randallf@pacrim.edu
FURUTO, Brian .... 808-845-9235.... 141 G
bfuruto@hawaii.edu
FURUTO, Sandra .... 808-956-7487.... 140 J
yano@hawaii.edu
FURUYAMA, Ron .... 310-434-4370...... 68 D
furuyama_ron@smc.edu
FUSCHETTI, Deborah, M .... 863-784-7139.... 117 I
deborah.fuschetti@southflorida.edu
FUSCO, Cathy .... 415-433-9200...... 68 F
cfusco@saybrook.edu
FUSCO, David, J .... 814-641-3604.... 431 L
fusco@juniata.edu
FUSCO, Jane, E .... 401-456-8468.... 454 A
jfusco@ric.edu
FUSCO, Steven .... 732-987-2602.... 310 D
fuscos@georgian.edu
FUSCO, Valerie .... 315-792-7111.... 356 B
valerie.fusco@sunyit.edu
FUSCO, William, J .... 707-664-2639...... 37 B
bill.fusco@sonoma.edu
FUSE-HALL, Rosalind .... 850-599-3225.... 118 G
rosalind.fuse-hall@famu.edu
FUSS, Kevin, J .... 815-825-2086.... 155 C
kevin.fuss@kishwaukeecollege.edu
FUSSELL, Carl .... 408-554-4024...... 68 C
cfussell@scu.edu
FUSSELL, Paula, V .... 352-392-1075.... 120 B
pvarnes@ufl.edu
FUTATO, Mark, D .... 407-366-9493.... 115 I
mfutato@rts.edu
FUTCH, Lynn .... 912-871-1606.... 134 H
lfutch@ogeecheetech.edu
FUTHEY, Carol .... 970-248-1881...... 82 B
cfuthey@mesastate.edu
FUTHEY, Tracy .... 919-684-8111.... 363 I
futhey@duke.edu
FUTRELL, Norman .... 773-291-6279.... 147 D
nfutrell1@ccc.edu
FUTRELL, Tamara, Y .... 540-458-8766.... 530 A
tfutrell@wlu.edu
FUTRELLE, Carole .... 828-884-8280.... 362 D
futrelcw@brevard.edu
FUZY, Bob .... 864-587-4295.... 461 D
fuzyb@smcsc.edu
FYE, Christa, D .... 434-223-6286.... 519 B
cfye@hsc.edu
FYFE, Brenda, S .... 314-968-6913.... 293 A
fyfebr@webster.edu
FYFE, Dorothy, R .... 718-270-2258.... 352 D
dfyfe@downstate.edu
FYFE, John .... 415-442-6540...... 48 E
jfyfe@ggu.edu
FYFFE, Richard .... 641-269-3351.... 185 A
fyffe@grinnell.edu
FYLES, Susan .... 415-485-3283...... 45 B
sfyles@dominican.edu
FYOCK, Debra, R .... 412-648-1458.... 449 A
dfyock@bc.pitt.edu

G

GÓMEZ, Aguilda .... 787-744-1060.... 564 D
agomez@mechtech.edu
GAALSWYK, Terry, B .... 308-635-6103.... 301 E
gaalswy2@wncc.edu
GAARDER, David, K .... 972-883-6374.... 505 D
dkg053000@utdallas.edu
GABA, Barbara .... 908-965-6091.... 316 B
gaba@ucc.edu
GABBARD, Billie, J .... 727-816-3116.... 114 F
gabbarb@phcc.edu
GABBARD, Clinton .... 509-527-4300.... 538 G
clinton.gabbard@wwcc.edu
GABBARD, Jene .... 281-649-3747.... 487 F
vgabbard@hbu.edu
GABBARD, Kurt, A .... 512-404-4816.... 481 D
kgabbard@austinseminary.edu
GABBARD, Ruth .... 859-371-9393.... 198 D
rgabbard@beckfield.edu
GABBE, Steve, G .... 614-292-1200.... 398 H
gabbe.1@osu.edu
GABBERT, Jill .... 312-942-6302.... 163 B
jill_gabbert@rush.edu
GABBERT, Paula, S .... 864-294-2064.... 458 D
paula.gabbert@furman.edu
GABEHART, Alan, D .... 318-798-4131.... 213 D
agabehar@lsus.edu
GABEL, Ann-Marie .... 562-938-4540...... 54 E
agabel@lbcc.edu
GABEL, Barb .... 419-448-2183.... 391 G
bgabel@heidelberg.edu
GABEL, Joan .... 573-882-6688.... 291 D
gabelj@missouri.edu
GABEL, Stephen, H .... 773-702-0790.... 166 D
sgabel@uchicago.edu
GABELMAN, Kenneth .... 914-674-7379.... 340 G
kgabelman@mercy.edu
GABER, Ron .... 660-626-2236.... 278 F
rgaber@atsu.edu
GABER, Sharon .... 479-575-2151...... 24 C
sgaber@uark.edu
GABERT, Glen, E .... 201-360-4003.... 310 F
ggabert@hccc.edu
GABERT, Susan, S .... 603-641-7231.... 305 H
sgabert@anselm.edu
GABIANELLI, Barbara, A ... 203-576-4134...... 94 D
bag@bridgeport.edu
GABIS, Mark .... 270-926-1188.... 199 H
mgabis@daymargroup.com
GABIS, Mark .... 270-926-1188.... 199 G
mgabis@daymargroup.com
GABIS, Mark .... 270-926-1188.... 389 C
mgabis@daymargroup.com
GABIS, Mark .... 270-926-1188.... 468 A
mgabis@daymargroup.com
GABIS, Mark, A .... 270-926-1188.... 468 B
mgabis@daymargroup.com
GABIS, Mark, A .... 270-926-1188.... 468 C
mgabis@daymargroup.com
GABIS, Mark, A .... 270-926-1188.... 389 F
mgabis@daymargroup.com
GABIS, Mark, A .... 270-926-1188.... 200 B
mgabis@daymargroup.com
GABIS, Mark, A .... 270-926-1188.... 199 K
mgabis@daymargroup.com
GABIS, Mark, A .... 270-926-1188.... 199 J
mgabis@daymargroup.com
GABIS, Mark, A .... 270-926-1188.... 199 I
mgabis@daymargroup.com
GABIS, Mark, A .... 270-926-1188.... 199 F
mgabis@daymargroup.com
GABIS, Mark, A .... 270-926-1188.... 200 A
mgabis@daymargroup.com
GABLE, Carol .... 315-229-5563.... 349 E
cgable@stlawu.edu
GABLE, Marsha .... 714-564-6230...... 63 F
gable_marsha@sac.ed
GABLER, David, L .... 210-458-5105.... 506 B
david.gabler@utsa.edu
GABONAY, Paul, W .... 317-788-3290.... 180 C
gabonay@uindy.edu
GABOVITCH, Rhonda .... 508-678-2811.... 239 F
rhonda.gabovitch@bristolcc.edu
GABRIEL, George, E .... 703-323-3129.... 527 C
ggabriel@nvcc.edu
GABRIEL, Lisa .... 281-283-3032.... 503 C
gabriel@uhcl.edu
GABRIEL, Paul, E .... 773-508-3622.... 157 A
pgabrie@luc.edu
GABRIEL, Rochelle .... 973-748-9000.... 308 A
rochelle_gabriel@bloomfield.edu
GABRIELE, Carol .... 508-849-3380.... 230 C
cgabriele@annamaria.edu
GABRIELE, Gary, A .... 610-519-5860.... 450 G
gary.gabriele@villanova.edu
GABRIELSE, Ken .... 405-878-2305.... 409 D
ken.gabrielse@okbu.edu
GABRIELSON, Kerry .... 719-846-5643...... 87 J
kerry.gabrielson@trinidadstate.edu
GABRIELSON, Linda .... 802-828-2800.... 515 D
linda.gabrielson@ccv.edu
GABY, Dennis .... 714-449-7459...... 70 G
dgaby@scco.edu
GACHETTE, Yves, M .... 716-878-4521.... 353 A
gachetym@buffalostate.edu
GACHUPIAN, Raymond ..... 505-346-2354.... 321 B
rgachupian@sipi.bia.edu
GACIOCH, Dennis, M .... 860-768-4007...... 95 A
gacioch@hartford.edu
GACKENHEIMER, Lois, M . 561-683-1400.... 100 C
GACKLE, Joel .... 714-556-3610...... 76 E
joel.gackle@vanguard.edu
GACSEH, Mary .... 573-364-8464.... 285 C
mary@metrobusinesscollege.edu
GADBERRY, Brad .... 770-531-6319.... 132 J
bgadberry@laniertech.edu
GADD, Bethany .... 330-382-7430.... 393 F
bgadd@kent.edu
GADD, Dale .... 574-807-7322.... 169 F
gaddd@bethelcollege.edu
GADD, Elisabeth .... 864-646-1812.... 461 F
egadd@tctc.edu
GADD, Keeley .... 859-623-8956.... 205 D
kgadd@educorp.edu
GADDE, Sandee, A .... 989-463-7146.... 247 F
gadde@alma.edu
GADDIE, Faith .... 717-396-7833.... 440 J
fgaddie@pcad.edu
GADDIS, Glendi .... 210-999-7011.... 502 C
ggaddis@trinity.edu
GADDY, Margo, H .... 910-576-6222.... 372 A
gaddym@montgomery.edu
GADDY, Stoney .... 307-674-6446.... 556 C
sgaddy@sheridan.edu
GADIKIAN, Randolph Lee . 716-673-3181.... 352 A
randolph.gadikian@fredonia.edu
GADSBY, Peter .... 845-758-7457.... 323 F
gadsby@bard.edu
GADSON, John .... 404-297-9522.... 128 B
gadsonj@dekalbtech.edu
GADSON, Mark, P .... 410-810-5735.... 229 D
mgadson2@washcoll.edu
GADZINSKI, James, G ...... 906-227-2971.... 256 F
jgadzins@nmu.edu
GAEDE, Rhonda, K .... 256-824-6573........ 9 A
Rhonda.Gaede@uah.edu
GAEKLE, Robert .... 219-785-5220.... 178 H
rgaekle@pnc.edu
GAER-CARLTON, Kathy ..... 509-963-1211.... 531 G
gaerk@cwu.edu
GAERTE, Phyllis, E .... 585-567-9620.... 336 B
phyllis.gaerte@houghton.edu
GAERTNER, Gregory .... 312-329-4125.... 158 H
greg.gaertner@moody.edu
GAETA, Alexa .... 404-471-6423.... 123 G
agaeta@agnesscott.edu
GAETA, James .... 512-863-1259.... 495 G
gaetaj@southwestern.edu
GAETA, Michael .... 503-253-3443.... 417 H
president@ocom.edu
GAETJENS, Stuart .... 931-393-1663.... 475 C
ssgaetjens@mscc.edu
GAETZ, Ivan, K .... 303-458-3556...... 87 E
igaetz@regis.edu
GAFFIN, Douglas, D .... 405-325-3521.... 413 C
ddgaffin@ou.edu
GAFFNER, Lori .... 618-664-7120.... 151 D
lori.gaffner@greenville.edu
GAFFNEY, Dick .... 910-221-2224.... 364 C
GAFFNEY, Eva .... 508-531-1335.... 238 B
egaffney@bridgew.edu
GAFFNEY, FSC, James ...... 815-836-5230.... 156 D
brjgaff@lewisu.edu
GAFFNEY, Kevin .... 610-921-7520.... 421 D
kgaffney@alb.edu
GAFFNEY, Michelle .... 330-823-7288.... 404 C
gaffnemi@mountunion.edu
GAFFNEY, II, Paul, G .... 732-571-3402.... 311 F
president@monmouth.edu
GAFFNEY, Paul, J .... 512-863-1379.... 495 G
gaffneyp@southwestern.edu
GAFFNEY, Tony .... 407-851-2525.... 106 E
tgaffney@cci.edu
GAGAN, Kelly .... 585-389-2411.... 342 D
kgagan8@naz.edu
GAGE, Amy .... 651-690-6829.... 271 E
agage@stkate.edu
GAGE, Brent .... 205-934-4073........ 8 G
bgage@uab.edu
GAGE, Brent, A .... 815-753-5600.... 160 A
bagage@niu.edu
GAGE, Chris .... 812-866-7028.... 171 F
gage@hanover.edu
GAGE, Chris .... 972-883-2055.... 505 D
ccg034000@utdallas.edu
GAGE, Colin, C .... 816-235-1430.... 291 E
gagec@umkc.edu
GAGE, J. Scott .... 978-837-5468.... 242 D
j.scott.gage@merrimack.edu

GAMBAIANA, Mark 660-785-4133 291 A
markg@truman.edu

GAMBARO, Jennifer 415-503-6230 66 A
jmg@sfcm.edu

GAMBILL, Debra 405-878-5396 412 A
dsgambill@stgregorys.edu

GAMBILL, Todd 502-863-8004 200 G
todd_gambill@georgetowncollege.edu

GAMBINO, Ellen 845-431-8966 332 E
gambino@sunydutchess.edu

GAMBLE, Barbara 256-830-2626 3 H
bgamble@faulkner.edu

GAMBLE, Brad 417-328-1823 290 E
bgamble@sbuniv.edu

GAMBLE, Carol 704-637-4411 363 C
cgamble@catawba.edu

GAMBLE, Gregory 856-479-9077 314 C
gambleg@camden.rutgers.edu

GAMBLE, Joan 419-559-2252 402 D
jgamble@terra.edu

GAMBLE, Kay 334-556-2397 4 A
kgamble@wallace.edu

GAMBLE, Kent 304-384-5316 543 D
kgamble@concord.edu

GAMBLE, Mort 304-829-7111 540 E
mgamble@bethanywv.edu

GAMBLE, Patrick, K 907-450-8000 10 H
ua.president@alaska.edu

GAMBLE, Sarah 615-966-6061 470 D
sarah.gamble@lipscomb.edu

GAMBLE, Steven 575-562-2121 318 A
steven.gamble@enmu.edu

GAMBLE, Thomas, J 814-824-2311 436 C
tgamble@mercyhurst.edu

GAMBOA, David 310-243-3819 34 B
dgamboa@csudh.edu

GAMBOA, Kathy 775-828-7720 19 C
kathy.gamboa@phoenix.edu

GAMBOA, Larry, G 671-735-2600 559 D
lgamboa@uguam.uog.edu

GAMBOA, Noel 718-262-2372 329 B
ngamboa@york.cuny.edu

GAMBON, Lynn 704-290-5855 373 F
lgambon@spcc.edu

GAMBRELL, Richard 423-425-5316 477 D
richard-gambrell@utc.edu

GAMBRO, John, S 815-740-3829 167 C
jgambro@stfrancis.edu

GAMEL, Henry 636-651-1600 289 I
hgamel@sbc-fenton.com

GAMELLI, Richard 708-216-9222 157 A
rgamell@lumc.edu

GAMES, Cheryl, A 440-964-4567 393 E
cgames1@kent.edu

GAMEZ, J. Felix 956-721-5357 489 G
fgamez@laredo.edu

GAMINO, Eliseo 559-934-2974 77 I
eliseogamino@whccd.edu

GAMMELL, William, J 860-493-0003 91 F
gammellw@ct.edu

GAMMON, Marcia 480-245-7918 14 K
marcia.gammon@ibconline.edu

GAMMON, Richard 937-255-6800 556 H
richard.gammon@afit.edi

GAMPERT, Richard 718-518-6692 327 D
rgampert@hostos.cuny.edu

GAMSU, Lisa 212-854-6031 323 G
lgamsu@barnard.edu

GAN, Sonny 626-571-5110 54 C
sonnygan@les.edu

GANA, Karen 315-568-3184 342 H
kgana@nycc.edu

GANDHI, Ketan 609-894-9311 308 C
kgandhi@bcc.edu

GANDIA, Melodee 516-299-4090 338 F
melodee.gandia@liu.edu

GANDRE, James 312-341-3615 162 I
jgandre@roosevelt.edu

GANDU, Bobby 316-978-3162 197 F
bobby.gandu@wichita.edu

GANDY, Beverly 310-506-4451 61 G
berverly.gandy@pepperdine.edu

GANDY, Rex, F 361-593-3106 498 A
rex.gandy@tamuk.edu

GANDY, Sue 215-717-6030 448 H
sgandy@uarts.edu

GANES, Andy 510-261-8500 61 F
andy.ganes@patten.edu

GANESAN, Arasu 330-325-2511 397 C
aganesan@neoucom.edu

GANESAN, Arasu 910-672-1477 377 E
nganesan@uncfsu.edu

GANESCU, Virgil, C 717-221-1300 430 E
vcganesc@hacc.edu

GANESH, Jaishankar 856-225-6217 314 C
jganesh@camden.rutgers.edu

GANG, Tom 707-468-3141 57 A
tgang@mendocino.edu

GANGEL, Jeffrey, S 706-886-6831 137 G
jgangel@tfc.edu

GANGER, Karen 269-467-9945 251 D
kganger@glenoaks.edu

GANGES, Tendaji, W 810-762-3365 259 F
tganges@umflint.edu

GANGL, Doris 320-363-5353 262 H
dgangl@csbsju.edu

GANGLOFF, Larry 618-395-7777 152 H
gangloffl@iecc.edu

GANGONE, Lynn 303-871-6801 88 E
lynn.gangone@du.edu

GANGSTEAD, Sandra 478-445-4092 129 F
sandra.gangstead@gcsu.edu

GANIO, John 845-687-5092 358 C
ganioj@sunyulster.edu

GANN, John 903-223-3114 498 C
john.gann@tamut.edu

GANN, Johnny 254-647-3234 492 E
jgann@rangercollege.edu

GANN, Michael 662-846-4675 274 B
mgann@deltastate.edu

GANN, Pamela, B 909-621-8111 40 D
pamela.gann@cmc.edu

GANN, Robert 310-660-3015 45 D
bgann@elcamino.edu

GANN, Sandra, K 336-342-4261 373 B
ganns@rockinghamcc.edu

GANNETT-MALICK, Lynn 205-970-9218 7 D
lynngm@sebc.edu

GANNON, Avi 718-982-2208 327 A
Avi.Gannon@csi.cuny.edu

GANNON, Cindy 573-651-2229 290 D
cmgannon@semo.edu

GANNON, Debbie, K 515-263-6020 184 I
dgannon@grandview.edu

GANNON, James, G 414-410-4151 546 D
jggannon@stritch.edu

GANNON, Kim 512-245-2371 501 C
kg33@txstate.edu

GANNON, Lauren 978-837-5250 242 D
gannonl@merrimack.edu

GANNON, Marcy 301-934-7560 222 C
marcyg@csmd.edu

GANNON, Susan 908-737-3461 311 B
sgannon@kean.edu

GANSBERG, Alan, L 818-401-1032 42 D
agansberg@columbiacollege.edu

GANSCHOW, Darby 605-677-6623 465 E
darby.ganschow@usd.edu

GANSKE, Kathryn, M 540-678-4381 523 K
kganske@su.edu

GANSON, Lisa 781-239-3111 240 D
lganson@massbay.edu

GANSZ, David 937-778-7951 390 G
dgansz@edisonohio.edu

GANT, Jocelind, E 814-393-2109 442 A
jgant@clarion.edu

GANTHER, Felicia 847-543-2288 147 H
fganther@clcillinois.edu

GANTMAN, Amy 310-665-6851 60 B
agantman@otis.edu

GANTNER, Christine, M 920-424-3414 551 D
gantner@uwosh.edu

GANTNER, Myrna 678-839-6445 138 D
mgantner@westga.edu

GANTOS, JR., Charles, J 336-278-5555 364 A
gantos@elon.edu

GANTT, Aubra, J 817-515-7778 496 A
aubra.gantt@tccd.edu

GANTT, Bernard 718-289-5883 326 F
bernard.gantt@bcc.cuny.edu

GANTT, Bernard 718-289-5887 326 F
bernard.gantt@bcc.cuny.edu

GANTT, Kevin 913-758-6230 197 B
ganttk@stmary.edu

GANZ, Rick, H 509-313-4242 534 A
ganz@gonzaga.edu

GAO, Qizhi 316-691-8822 194 A
admin@kccm.edu

GAONA, Selin 816-604-4190 285 I
selin.gaona@mcckc.edu

GARAFOLA, David 972-438-6932 492 C
dgarafola@parkercc.edu

GARAND, Bob 843-661-8326 458 A
bob.garand@fdtc.edu

GARANT, Carl 614-222-3237 388 F
cgarant@ccad.edu

GARANZINI, SJ, Michael, J 312-915-6400 157 A
mgaranz@luc.edu

GARBADE, Henry 843-208-8087 462 C
hgarbade@uscb.edu

GARBARINO, James 816-444-0669 288 D
bookstore@rockhurst.edu

GARBART, Hadley 410-225-2231 224 C
hgarbart@mica.edu

GARBE, John 585-389-2038 342 D
jgarbe6@naz.edu

GARBE, Theresa 423-461-8718 471 H
tmgarbe@milligan.edu

GARBER, Alan, M 617-496-5100 235 H
alan_garber@harvard.edu

GARBER, Christopher, W 260-982-5027 177 F
cwgarber@manchester.edu

GARBER, Darrell 610-683-4253 442 F
garber@kutztown.edu

GARBER, Gail 860-486-5519 94 E
gail.garber@uconn.edu

GARBER, Greg 724-589-2000 448 A
ggarber@thiel.edu

GARBER, Kevin, S 913-971-3275 195 A
ksgarber@mnu.edu

GARBER, Philip 847-214-7285 150 D
pgarber@elgin.edu

GARBER, Sandy 928-776-2117 19 E
sandy.garber@yc.edu

GARBER BAX, Sharlene 660-543-4114 291 B
bax@ucmo.edu

GARBINI, Dennis, J 973-761-9011 315 B
dennis.garbini@shu.edu

GARBIOGLU, Ibrahim 412-323-2323 425 H
igarbioglu@ccac.edu

GARCEAU, Linda, R 423-439-4289 473 E
garceaul@etsu.edu

GARCERA, Felix 661-654-3283 33 H
fgarcera@csub.edu

GARCES, Gabriel 407-447-7300 109 H
ggarces@flatech.edu

GARCIA, A. Ramon 719-549-2149 83 B
aramon.garcia@colostate-pueblo.edu

GARCIA, Abigail 602-331-7500 12 D

GARCIA, Adam 775-784-4689 303 A
adam_garcia@police.unr.edu

GARCIA, Adrienne 813-253-7014 110 I
agarcia@hccfl.edu

GARCIA, Aida 787-725-6500 560 G
agarcia@sju.albizu.edu

GARCIA, Albert 916-558-2337 56 D
garciaaj@scc.losrios.edu

GARCIA, Alberto 787-848-0810 567 E
agarcia@uprp.edu

GARCIA, Alexandra 210-434-6711 491 G
amgarcia08@lake.ollusa.edu

GARCIA, Alfredo 505-260-6180 318 I
a_garcia@nmhu.edu

GARCIA, Alice 708-709-3519 161 C
agarcia@prairiestate.edu

GARCIA, Amarilys 787-746-1400 562 C
agarcia@huertas.edu

GARCIA, Angelica 925-631-4165 64 F
mag6@stmarys-ca.edu

GARCIA, Ava, M 671-735-5527 559 B
gccavp@guamcc.edu

GARCIA, Bob 989-463-7299 247 F
garciab@alma.edu

GARCIA, Brenda, W 575-439-3697 319 E
brenda@nmsua.nmsu.edu

GARCIA, Brett 540-261-4503 524 C
brett.garcia@svu.edu

GARCIA, Camilo, F 443-518-4781 223 D
cgarcia@howardcc.edu

GARCIA, Carol 718-779-1430 346 B
cgarcia@plazacollege.edu

GARCIA, Carol 307-674-6446 556 C
cgarcia@sheridan.edu

GARCIA, Cathy 619-594-4723 36 E
cgarcia@mail.sdsu.edu

GARCIA, Christian 305-284-5451 122 F
christian@miami.edu

GARCIA, Dan, D 806-651-2031 498 D
ddgarcia@mail.wtamu.edu

GARCIA, David 330-672-1001 393 D
tgarcia5@kent.edu

GARCIA, Delia 305-348-3598 119 B
garciade@fiu.edu

GARCIA, Della 602-243-8124 16 E
della.garcia@smcmail.maricopa.edu

GARCIA, Diana 630-743-0680 168 C
dgarcia@westwood.edu

GARCIA, Dianne 505-566-3162 320 D
garciad@sanjuancollege.edu

GARCIA, Elena 787-780-0070 560 F
egarcia@caribbean.edu

GARCIA, Eliezer 787-786-3030 560 E
egarcia@ucb.edu.pr

GARCIA, Elizabeth 860-439-2624 91 E
elizabeth.garcia@conncoll.edu

GARCIA, Elizabeth 610-282-1100 426 I
elizabeth.garcia@desales.edu

GARCIA, JR., Enrique 361-698-1293 485 F
egarcia@delmar.edu

GARCIA, Eugene, E 602-496-1152 12 B
eugene.garcia@asu.edu

GARCIA, Eva 787-264-1912 563 G
egarcia@sg.inter.edu

GARCIA, Florence 406-768-6312 294 F
fgarcia@fpcc.edu

GARCIA, Frances 787-786-2412 566 A
fgarcia@uccaribe.edu

GARCIA, Gerard 973-972-3251 316 C
garciage@umdnj.edu

GARCIA, Gilda 940-565-2711 504 B
ggarcia@unt.edu

GARCIA, Gloria 718-982-2410 327 A
Gloria.Garcia@csi.cuny.edu

GARCIA, Heather 870-612-2048 25 E
heather.garcia@uaccb.edu

GARCIA, Helen 915-566-9621 508 E
hgarcia@westerntech.edu

GARCIA, Irene 559-737-3775 42 B
ireneg@cos.edu

GARCIA, Irma 718-489-5490 348 E
igarcia@stfranciscollege.edu

GARCIA, Janet, K 605-221-3234 464 C
jgarcia@kilian.edu

GARCIA, Joann 760-252-2411 30 F
jgarcia@barstow.edu

GARCIA, Joe 312-996-9450 166 E
jggarcia@uic.edu

GARCIA, Jorge 831-443-1700 50 A
jorge_garcia@heald.edu

GARCIA, Jorge 787-779-2500 561 C
ccat@coqui.edu

GARCIA, Jose 210-932-6286 498 B
jgarcia@tamusa.tamus.edu

GARCIA, Joxel 787-840-2575 564 H

GARCIA, Joyce 323-265-8732 54 G
garciajb@elac.edu

GARCIA, Juan 817-515-4507 496 A
juan.garcia@tccd.edu

GARCIA, Juan 956-364-4604 499 J
juan.garcia@harlingen.tstc.edu

GARCIA, Juliet, V 956-882-8201 499 H
president@utb.edu

GARCIA, Juliet, V 956-882-8201 505 C
president@utb.edu

GARCIA, Julio 408-273-2690 58 G
jgarcia@nhu.edu

GARCIA, Kellie 661-654-2266 33 H
kgarcia@csub.edu

GARCIA, Kim, L 408-274-6700 67 A
kim.garcia@sjeccd.org

GARCIA, Leslie 503-494-5657 418 D

GARCIA, Louie 415-276-1027 30 B
lgarcia@aii.edu

GARCIA, Luis 787-285-5457 562 D

GARCIA, Maria 305-595-9500 100 D
registrar@amcollege.edu

GARCIA, Martin 432-685-4734 490 G
mgarcia@midland.edu

GARCIA, Melissa 956-721-5189 489 G
melissagarcia@laredo.edu

GARCIA, Miguel 203-285-2358 90 A
mgarcia@gwcc.commnet.edu

GARCIA, Mildred 310-243-3301 34 B
president@csudh.edu

GARCIA, Mirna 312-341-2309 162 I
mtgarcia@roosevelt.edu

GARCIA, Myra 718-390-3121 359 G
myra.garcia@wagner.edu

GARCIA, Orlando 305-348-3357 119 B
orlando.garcia@fiu.edu

GARCIA, Oscar 830-591-7234 495 B
o_garcia@swtjc.cc.tx.us

GARCIA, Pete 305-348-0504 119 B
pete.garcia@fiu.edu

GARCIA, Peter 925-685-1230 43 C
pgarcia@dvc.edu

GARCIA, Racquel 212-247-3434 339 G

GARCIA, Raul 847-635-1637 160 E
rgarcia@oakton.edu

GARCIA, Rene 305-237-3519 113 H
rgarcia@mdc.edu

GARCIA, Rick 310-338-6047 56 E
rgarcia@lmu.edu

GARCIA, Robert, P 214 860-2064 484 I
rgarcia@dcccd.edu

GARCIA, Roberto 719-389-6348 81 L
rgarcia@coloradocollege.edu

GARCIA, Ron 505-454-3251 318 I
garcia_rs@nmhu.edu

GARCIA, Rosemarie, M 505-428-1201 320 E
rosemarie.garcia@sfcc.edu

GARCIA, Rudy 505-224-4342 317 J
rudyg@cnm.edu

GARCIA, Sandra, L 361-593-3344 498 A

GARCIA, Sarah 208-769-3341 143 H
sarah_garcia@nic.edu

GARCIA, Skip 312-996-9450 166 F
jggarcia@uic.edu

GARCIA, Steve 760-245-4271 77 E
Steve.Garcia@vvc.edu

GARCIA, Steven, N 909-621-8030 40 C
steve.garcia@cgu.edu

GARCIA, Sunshine 323-660-6166 40 G
sunshine.garcia@cleveland.edu

GARCIA, Susan, P 740-587-6592 389 H
garcia@denison.edu

GARCIA, Tania 805-437-8452 33 I
tania.garcia@csuci.edu

GARCIA, Tary 787-264-1912 563 G
tdgarcia@sg.inter.edu

GARCIA, Val 661-763-7945 72 C
vgarcia@taftcollege.edu

GARCIA, Veronica 619-477-6310 73 A
vgarcia@usuniversity.edu

GARCIA, Veronica 503-614-7800 419 G
veronica.garcia6@pcc.edu

GARCIA, Veronica 956-882-4322 505 C
veronica.m.garcia@utb.edu

GARCIA, Vonda 760-750-4852 36 B
vgarcia@csusm.edu

GARCIA, William 973-596-5320 312 C
william.garcia@njit.edu

GARCIA, Yessika 212-686-9040 360 E
ygarcia@woodtobecoburn.edu

GARRITY, Collette ... 212-343-1234 ... 341 B
cgarrity@mcny.edu
GARRITY, Cynthia, A ... 504-866-7426 ... 213 I
registrar@nds.edu
GARRITY, Kathleen, E ... 608-822-2471 ... 555 B
GARRITY, Michael ... 708-456-0300 ... 166 C
mgarrit1@triton.edu
GARRITY, Patricia ... 603-899-4221 ... 305 B
garrityp@franklinpierce.edu
GARRITY, Robert, M ... 239-280-2424 ... 101 C
robert.garrity@avemaria.edu
GARRITY, Ryan ... 225-768-1719 ... 214 B
ryan.garrity@ololcollege.edu
GARRO, Anthony, J ... 508-999-8024 ... 237 E
agarro@umassd.edu
GARROTT, Marci ... 214-860-8680 ... 485 A
mgarrott@dcccd.edu
GARST, Stephanie, P ... 540-375-2323 ... 523 D
garst@roanoke.edu
GARSTAD, Zane, S ... 307-674-6446 ... 556 C
zgarstad@sheridan.edu
GARSTECKI, Marcus ... 308-535-3603 ... 298 I
garsteckim@mpcc.edu
GARTEN, Ann ... 310-660-3406 ... 45 D
agarten@elcamino.edu
GARTEN, Ann, M ... 310-660-3670 ... 45 D
agarten@elcamino.edu
GARTEN-SHUMAN, John .. 510-869-6727 ... 64 J
jgartens@samuelmerritt.edu
GARTENMAYER, Charles ... 913-360-7583 ... 190 F
cgartenmayer@benedictine.edu
GARTH, Bryant, G ... 213-738-6710 ... 71 D
deansoffice@swlaw.edu
GARTH, Mark ... 617-427-0060 ... 241 D
mgarth@rcc.mass.edu
GARTHOFF, Jerry ... 207-621-3067 ... 220 B
garthoff@maine.edu
GARTIN, Stanton ... 970-521-6650 ... 86 E
stanton.gartin@njc.edu
GARTNER, Lia ... 212-229-5192 ... 342 E
gartnerl@newschool.edu
GARTNER, Maggie ... 979-845-4427 ... 497 C
molona@tamu.edu
GARTNER, Mary ... 301-687-4212 ... 228 C
mgartner@frostburg.edu
GARTON, Jilda ... 404-894-4819 ... 130 D
jilda.garton@gtrc.gatech.edu
GARTRELL, William ... 626-396-2316 ... 29 G
bill.gartrell@artcenter.edu
GARUS, Marcella Marie ... 716-896-0700 ... 359 F
smgarus@villa.edu
GARVER, Julie ... 360-867-6453 ... 533 I
GARVER, Phil ... 423-236-2852 ... 473 A
garver@southern.edu
GARVEY, Anne, L ... 612-330-1168 ... 261 G
garvey@augsburg.edu
GARVEY, Carol ... 712-274-5178 ... 187 D
garvey@morningside.edu
GARVEY, Diane ... 985-492-2009 ... 216 A
diane.garvey@nicholls.edu
GARVEY, Hugh ... 217-786-2304 ... 156 I
hugh.garvey@llcc.edu
GARVEY, James ... 603-428-2477 ... 305 E
jgarvey@nec.edu
GARVEY, John, H ... 202-319-5100 ... 97 C
cua-president@cua.edu
GARVEY, JR., Joseph, X ... 570-348-6222 ... 435 F
jxgarvey@marywood.edu
GARVEY, Judy ... 714-241-6230 ... 40 J
jgarvey@coastline.edu
GARVEY, Kathleen, M ... 508-373-9455 ... 231 D
kathleen.garvey@becker.edu
GARVEY, Kevin ... 914-606-6940 ... 360 D
kevin.garvey@sunywcc.edu
GARVEY, Pamela, J ... 414-955-4700 ... 548 E
pgarvey@mcw.edu
GARVEY-NIX, Ruth, C ... 812-941-2420 ... 174 D
rgarvey@ius.edu
GARVIE, Joyce, A ... 580-327-8530 ... 409 C
jagarvie@nwosu.edu
GARVIN, Maureen ... 912-525-5829 ... 136 B
mgarvin@scad.edu
GARVIN, Natara ... 615-329-8504 ... 468 G
ngarvin@fisk.edu
GARWOOD, Shana ... 212-982-3456 ... 345 G
GARWOOD, Victoria ... 412-675-9072 ... 439 H
vkg2@psu.edu
GARY, Chandra ... 219-981-4438 ... 176 E
cgary@ivytech.edu
GARY, JR., Charles ... 219-980-6793 ... 173 F
cfgary@iun.edu
GARY, James, B ... 972-883-6284 ... 505 D
gary@utdallas.edu
GARY, Lula, J ... 803-934-3257 ... 459 F
lgary@morris.edu
GARY, Susan ... 704-337-2305 ... 375 G
garys@queens.edu
GARY, SR., William, H ... 703-323-2399 ... 527 C
wgary@nvcc.edu
GARZA, Ana Lisa ... 210-486-2300 ... 479 E
agarza2@alamo.edu
GARZA, Andres ... 312-996-2969 ... 166 F
agarza@uic.edu
GARZA, Cutberto ... 617-552-3260 ... 232 D
bert.garza.1@bc.edu
GARZA, Felipe ... 361-593-2611 ... 498 A
felipe.garza@tamuk.edu
GARZA, Fena ... 713-718-7748 ... 487 G
fena.garza@hccs.edu
GARZA, Lori ... 512-892-2640 ... 495 A
GARZA, Noemi ... 956-872-2681 ... 494 D
ngarza24@southtexascollege.edu
GARZA, Nora, R ... 956-721-5868 ... 489 G
nrgarza@laredo.edu
GARZA, Raul ... 703-556-8888 ... 523 H
GARZA, Rebecca, J ... 214-860-2618 ... 484 I
rgarza@dcccd.edu
GARZA, Robert ... 210-486-3100 ... 479 D
robogrz@alamo.edu
GARZA, Saul ... 432-839-8697 ... 501 B
sgarza@sulross.edu
GARZA, JR., Victor ... 408-274-7900 ... 67 B
victor.garza@evc.edu
GARZA, Wanda ... 956-872-2770 ... 494 D
wgarza@southtexascollege.edu
GARZA-RODERICK, Jessie 209-833-7900 ... 66 D
jgarza-roderick@deltacollege.edu
GASAWAY, Debbie ... 870-460-1622 ... 25 A
gasaway@uamont.edu
GASAWAY, R. Clinton ... 765-361-6375 ... 181 C
gasawayc@wabash.edu
GASCHK, Kenneth, K ... 262-243-5700 ... 546 I
ken.gaschk@cuw.edu
GASCICH, Misty ... 620-331-4100 ... 193 G
mgascich@indycc.edu
GASIOR, Donna ... 773-298-3165 ... 163 G
gasior@sxu.edu
GASKELL, Carolyn ... 509-527-2133 ... 538 H
carolyn.gaskell@wallawalla.edu
GASKILL, Gayle ... 651-690-6857 ... 271 E
ggaskill@stkate.edu
GASKIN, Beth ... 912-525-5806 ... 136 B
egaskin@scad.edu
GASKIN, Evelyn ... 480-927-0000 ... 19 C
GASKIN, Lori ... 408-741-2668 ... 78 B
lori.gaskin@westvalley.edu
GASKIN-FITCHUE, Leah ... 937-376-2946 ... 401 A
lfitchue@payne.edu
GASKINS, Frances ... 252-527-6223 ... 371 D
fgaskins@lenoircc.edu
GASKINS, Jennifer ... 704-233-8117 ... 380 D
jgaskins@wingate.edu
GASKINS, Laverne, L ... 229-333-5351 ... 138 F
llgaskin@valdosta.edu
GASKINS, Leebrian ... 956-326-2310 ... 497 B
lgaskins@tamiu.edu
GASOSKE, Betsy ... 314-434-4044 ... 281 A
betsy.gasoske@covenantseminary.edu
GASPAR, Leigh ... 781-891-2874 ... 231 F
lgaspar@bentley.edu
GASPAR, Timothy ... 419-383-5858 ... 404 F
terry.gaspar@utoledo.edu
GASPARD, Harold ... 504-671-5420 ... 210 G
hgaspa@dcc.edu
GASPARIAN, Albert ... 714-895-8334 ... 41 A
agasparian@gwc.cccd.edu
GASPARRO, Paul ... 405-382-9203 ... 412 B
p.gasparro@sscok.edu
GASPER, Joseph ... 570-740-0372 ... 435 C
jgasper@luzerne.edu
GASPER, William ... 213-763-7043 ... 55 D
gasperw@lattc.edu
GASPER, William ... 617-638-4590 ... 232 G
wgasper@bu.edu
GASS, Beverley, A ... 336-334-4822 ... 370 E
abgass@gtcc.edu
GASSAWAY, Kathy ... 530-938-5200 ... 42 C
gassaway@siskiyous.edu
GASSEAU, Michelle ... 617-243-2150 ... 236 F
mgaseau@lasell.edu
GASSEL, Robert, K ... 313-593-5410 ... 259 E
bgassel@umd.umich.edu
GASSER, Heather ... 208-885-6616 ... 144 B
hgasser@uidaho.edu
GASSER, Ray ... 208-885-6571 ... 144 B
rgasser@uidaho.edu
GASSER, Stephanie ... 520-325-0123 ... 18 J
registrar@theartcenter.edu
GASSNER, Sheila ... 573-681-5084 ... 284 B
gassners@lincolnu.edu
GASSNER, Taryn, E ... 302-857-1829 ... 96 A
tgassner@dtcc.edu
GAST, Alice, P ... 610-758-3156 ... 434 E
apg206@lehigh.edu
GAST, Kristen ... 770-962-7580 ... 132 A
kgast@gwinnetttech.edu
GAST, Steve ... 712-279-1707 ... 182 E
steve.gast@briarcliff.edu
GAST, Valerie ... 757-479-3706 ... 517 E
vgast@baptistseminary.edu
GASTENVELD, Paula, M ... 434-736-2085 ... 527 H
paula.gastenveld@southside.edu
GASTER, Buddy ... 580-745-2030 ... 412 C
bgaster@se.edu
GASTEVICH, Donna ... 414-256-1217 ... 549 A
gastevid@mtmary.edu
GASTON, Aracelis ... 787-832-6000 ... 562 E
agaston@icprjc.edu
GASTON, Carmen ... 503-943-8506 ... 420 G
kwong@up.edu
GASTON, David ... 785-864-3624 ... 196 F
adgaston@ku.edu
GASTON, Della, J ... 336-342-4261 ... 373 B
gastond@rockinghamcc.edu
GASTON, Garrett ... 216-649-8800 ... 398 E
ggaston@ocpm.edu
GASTON, John, C ... 229-333-5832 ... 138 F
jgaston@valdosta.edu
GASTON, Kenneth ... 410-651-7550 ... 227 E
klgaston@umes.edu
GASTON, Lori ... 704-894-2208 ... 363 F
logaston@davidson.edu
GASTON-MARSH, Latonia, D ... 716-878-4618 ... 353 A
marshld@buffalostate.edu
GATCH, Denise, D ... 941-752-5325 ... 118 E
gatch@scf.edu
GATCHELL, Michael, D ... 864-294-2475 ... 458 D
mike.gatchell@furman.edu
GATELY, Kevin ... 781-280-3225 ... 240 F
gatelyk@middlesex.mass.edu
GATELY, Kevin ... 603-897-8232 ... 305 G
kgately@rivier.edu
GATENBY, Sarah, J ... 408-554-4642 ... 68 C
sgatenby@scu.edu
GATES, Anne ... 330-263-2545 ... 388 E
agates@wooster.edu
GATES, Cynthia, K ... 405-878-2401 ... 409 D
cynthia.gates@okbu.edu
GATES, Geoffrey ... 602-749-4541 ... 13 M
ggates@devry.edu
GATES, Kathryn, F ... 662-915-7206 ... 277 G
kfg@olemiss.edu
GATES, Leigh ... 312-939-4975 ... 151 F
lgates@harringtoncollege.com
GATES, Lori ... 503-842-8222 ... 420 D
gates@tillamookbay.cc
GATES, Pamela, S ... 989-774-3342 ... 249 G
gates1ps@cmich.edu
GATES, Reginald ... 817-515-5001 ... 496 A
reginald.gates@tccd.edu
GATES, Sheila, R ... 301-766-3677 ... 223 G
sgates@kaplan.edu
GATES, Steve ... 479-936-5168 ... 22 H
sgates@nwacc.edu
GATES, William, R ... 831-656-2754 ... 557 H
bgates@nps.edu
GATES BLACK, Joy ... 817-515-4501 ... 496 A
joy.gatesblack@tccd.edu
GATES-MILINER, Elaine ... 619-574-6909 ... 60 E
egates@pacificcollege.edu
GATEWOOD, Algie ... 503-978-5302 ... 419 G
agatewoo@pcc.edu
GATEWOOD, David ... 949-451-5650 ... 70 E
dgatewood@ivc.edu
GATEWOOD-JASHO, Gay-linn ... 404-880-8892 ... 126 I
gjasho@cau.edu
GATHARD, James ... 718-933-6700 ... 341 G
jgathard@monroecollege.edu
GATHERS, Avis ... 803-793-5241 ... 457 F
gathersa@denmarktech.edu
GATHII, James ... 518-445-3304 ... 322 D
jgath@albanylaw.edu
GATHJE, Pete ... 901-334-5832 ... 471 C
pgathje@memphisseminary.edu
GATHMAN, Allen ... 573-651-2361 ... 290 D
agathman@semo.edu
GATHRO, Richard ... 202-220-1300 ... 344 G
richard.gathro@nyack.edu
GATLEY, Ian ... 973-596-3220 ... 312 C
ian.gatley@njit.edu
GATLIN, Kerry, P ... 256-765-4401 ... 9 D
kpgatlin@una.edu
GATLIN, Lavonne ... 256-765-4787 ... 9 D
lgatlin@una.edu
GATRELL, Jay ... 812-237-3087 ... 173 A
jay.gatrell@indstate.edu
GATTA, JR., George ... 631-451-4611 ... 356 D
gattag@sunysuffolk.edu
GATTA, John, J ... 931-598-1248 ... 472 J
jogatta@sewanee.edu
GATTAS, Joyce, M ... 619-594-5124 ... 36 E
gattas@mail.sdsu.edu
GATTEN, Jeffrey ... 661-255-1050 ... 32 C
jgatten@calarts.edu
GATTERDAM, Hans ... 817-272-3275 ... 505 A
hgatt@uta.edu
GATTI, Robert, M ... 614-823-1250 ... 400 G
rgatti@otterbein.edu
GATTIN, Leroy ... 501-977-2033 ... 25 G
gattin@uaccm.edu
GATTIN, Tom ... 870-230-5135 ... 21 I
gattint@hsu.edu
GATTO, Teri ... 201-355-1309 ... 310 C
gattot@felician.edu
GATTON, Pam ... 903-983-8207 ... 489 F
pgatton@kilgore.edu
GATTON, Philip, S ... 618-453-4172 ... 164 I
philg@pso.siu.edu
GATTON, Steven, J ... 903-233-4466 ... 489 K
stevegatton@letu.edu
GATTY, Janie ... 724-335-5336 ... 437 H
director@oaa.edu
GATZKE, Donald ... 817-272-2801 ... 505 A
gatzke@uta.edu
GAUBATZ, Ronnie ... 314-529-9536 ... 284 F
rgaubatz@maryville.edu
GAUBERT, Judith ... 985-867-2240 ... 214 F
jgaubert@sjasc.edu
GAUCHAT, Urs, P ... 973-596-3079 ... 312 C
urs.p.gauchat@njit.edu
GAUCHEL, Steph, L ... 617-627-4640 ... 245 F
steph.gauchel@tufts.edu
GAUDINO, James, L ... 509-963-2111 ... 531 G
gaudino@cwu.edu
GAUDIO, Arthur, R ... 413-782-2201 ... 246 D
agaudio@law.wne.edu
GAUDIO, Melissa ... 570-408-4358 ... 451 G
melissa.gaudio@wilkes.edu
GAUGH, Sherri ... 505-566-4007 ... 320 D
gaughs@sanjuancollege.edu
GAUGHAN, Cheryl ... 619-849-2499 ... 62 L
cherylgaughan@pointloma.edu
GAUGHF, Natalie, W ... 601-815-4236 ... 277 H
nwgaughf1@umc.edu
GAUL, Julie, M ... 412-578-6042 ... 424 G
gauljm@carlow.edu
GAUL, Veera ... 401-598-1001 ... 453 C
vgual@jwu.edu
GAULDEN, JR., Corbett, F 325-942-2337 ... 480 E
corbett.gaulden@angelo.edu
GAULT, Brian, C ... 601-923-1671 ... 277 B
bgault@rts.edu
GAULT, Carrie, J ... 724-458-2134 ... 430 B
cjgault@gcc.edu
GAULT, Kevin ... 727-726-1153 ... 103 B
kevingault@clearwater.edu
GAULT, Ron ... 931-393-1582 ... 475 C
rgault@mscc.edu
GAULT, Sandra ... 816-235-6234 ... 291 E
gaults@umkc.edu
GAUME, Curtis, C ... 716-888-2300 ... 325 G
gaume@canisius.edu
GAUNA, Lucy ... 210-486-4408 ... 479 C
lgauna5@alamo.edu
GAUNT, John, C ... 785-864-4281 ... 196 F
jgaunt@ku.edu
GAUNT, Marianne, I ... 732-932-7505 ... 314 B
gaunt@rci.rutgers.edu
GAUNT, Victoria, F ... 410-864-4234 ... 226 B
GAURMER, Terry ... 303-458-1629 ... 87 E
tgaurmer@regis.edu
GAUS, Gregory, J ... 630-515-7307 ... 158 E
ggausx@midwestern.edu
GAUS, Gregory, J ... 623-572-3400 ... 16 F
ggausx@midwestern.edu
GAUSE, William, C ... 973-972-7697 ... 316 F
gausewc@umdnj.edu
GAUSS, Nancy ... 970-943-2053 ... 89 B
ngauss@western.edu
GAUSVIK, Tom ... 706-542-2621 ... 138 C
tgausvik@uga.edu
GAUTHIER, Laureen ... 802-225-3205 ... 513 H
laureen.gauthier@neci.edu
GAUTHIER, Raymond, C ... 503-682-3903 ... 419 F
rgauthier@pioneerpacific.edu
GAUTIER, Ed, E ... 985-549-2064 ... 216 C
egautier@selu.edu
GAUTNEY, Michael, B ... 256-765-4274 ... 9 D
mbgautney@una.edu
GAUTRIEAU, Karen ... 513-241-4338 ... 383 L
karen.gautrieau@antonellicollege.edu
GAUTSCHI, David ... 212-636-6111 ... 334 C
gautschi@fordham.edu
GAUVIN, Keith ... 203-596-4612 ... 93 D
kgauvin@post.edu
GAVAL, Kathleen, D ... 610-660-1204 ... 446 C
kgaval@sju.edu
GAVALETZ, Tami ... 618-374-5187 ... 161 D
tami.gavaletz@principia.edu
GAVANUS, Michael ... 215-248-7163 ... 425 C
gavanusmi@chc.edu
GAVAZZI, Stephen, M ... 419-755-4221 ... 399 C
gavazzi.1@osu.edu
GAVER, Bob ... 402-363-5721 ... 301 F
bagaver@york.edu
GAVIN, Carrie ... 850-599-3076 ... 118 G
carrie.gavin@famu.edu
GAVIN, Jack ... 732-571-3536 ... 311 F
gavin@monmouth.edu
GAVIN, M. F. Chip ... 207-973-3335 ... 219 I
chip.gavin@maine.edu
GAVIN, Michael ... 414-297-6760 ... 554 D
gavinmj@matc.edu
GAVIN, Mike ... 828-286-3636 ... 371 A
mgavin@isothermal.edu
GAVIN, Todd ... 803-822-3233 ... 459 D
gavint@midlandstech.edu
GAVIN-WILLIAMS, Barbara ... 908-709-7511 ... 316 B
gavin@ucc.edu
GAVLICK, Christopher ... 914-251-6916 ... 354 D
christopher.gavlick@purchase.edu

GAVLIK, Deborah 567-661-7510 400 H
deborah_gavlik@owens.edu
GAW, Kevin, E 404-413-1835 131 C
kgaw@gsu.edu
GAWEL, Gary, P 912-478-0268 131 A
gpgawel@georgiasouthern.edu
GAWELEK, Mary Ann 724-838-4216 447 B
gawelek@setonhill.edu
GAWENDA, Mateusz 312-922-1884 157 C
mgawenda@maccormac.edu
GAWENDA, Peter 956-882-6791 505 C
peter.gawenda@utb.edu
GAWLIK, Gail 815-740-5041 167 C
ggawlik@stfrancis.edu
GAWNE, Jenna 603-887-7442 303 G
GAWRONSKI, JR., Michael 845-341-4284 345 E
michael.gawronski@sunyorange.edu
GAWTHROP, Larry 810-762-0235 256 C
larry.gawthrop@mcc.edu
GAY, Bill 760-355-6124 50 K
bill.gay@imperial.edu
GAY, Bob 212-229-5150 342 E
gayr@newschool.edu
GAY, Cliff 478-289-2025 128 J
cgay@ega.edu
GAY, John 410-888-9048 226 F
jgay@tai.edu
GAY, Judith, R 215-751-8355 426 B
jgay@ccp.edu
GAY, Kathleen 318-678-6000 209 J
kgay@bpcc.edu
GAY, Melvin, L 704-330-4203 369 A
mel.gay@cpcc.edu
GAY, Vergel, L 979-458-7001 496 D
vgay@tamus.edu
GAYESKI, Diane 607-274-3895 336 G
gayeski@ithaca.edu
GAYHART, Terri 414-297-6663 554 D
gayhartt@matc.edu
GAYLE, Barbara, M 608-796-3080 553 A
bmgayle@viterbo.edu
GAYLEN, Nancy, I 217-424-6244 158 F
ngaylen@millikin.edu
GAYLOR, Sue, S 570-321-4219 435 D
gaylor@lycoming.edu
GAYMER, Dawn 260 387 4200 260 F
dawn.gaymer@wmich.edu
GAYNOR, Deborah 717-264-4141 452 B
dgaynor@wilson.edu
GAYNOR, Dona, E 321-674-8102 108 E
dgaynor@fit.edu
GAYNOR, Julie 940-397-4353 491 A
julie.gaynor@mwsu.edu
GAYNOR, Kimberly 281-649-3025 487 F
kgaynor@hbu.edu
GAYNOR, Michael 610-519-4000 450 G
michael.gaynor@villanova.edu
GAYNOR, Suzanne 607-431-4670 335 B
gaynors@hartwick.edu
GAYTON, Linda 973-684-6104 312 E
lgayton@pccc.edu
GAZA, Roberto 305-223-4561 116 C
gaza@sjvcs.edu
GAZZALE, Bob 323-856-7600 28 D
GAZZOLA, Kim 617-873-0689 233 B
Kim.Gazzola@cambridgecollege.edu
GBENEDIO, Pender 803-750-2510 99 D
pender.gbenedio@strayer.edu
GEADELMANN, Patricia, L 319-273-6144 182 D
patricia.geadelmann@uni.edu
GEALT, Michael 501-569-3545 24 E
magealt@ualr.edu
GEANOUS, Elizabeth 814-838-7673 429 B
GEAR, Jill 419-434-4429 404 B
gear@findlay.edu
GEAR, Lisa, L 213-738-6834 71 D
admissions@swlaw.edu
GEARAN, Mark, D 315-781-3309 335 G
gearan@hws.edu
GEARHART, G. David 479-575-4148 24 C
gdgearh@uark.edu
GEARHART, Gregory, L 717-691-6007 436 D
gearhart@messiah.edu
GEARHART, Rob 607-274-1909 336 G
rgearhart@ithaca.edu
GEARHART, Trevor 715-324-6900 549 D
trevor.gearhart@ni.edu
GEARHART, William, H 401-456-8200 454 A
wgearhart@ric.edu
GEARIN, Christopher, A 314-434-2212 283 B
GEARY, Colette 914-654-5363 330 B
cgeary@cnr.edu
GEARY, Leslie, H 203-576-4625 94 D
lgeary@bridgeport.edu
GEARY, Melanie 303-534-6290 82 I
melanie.geary@colostate.edu
GEARY, JR., Raymond, R 814-362-5198 449 B
rgeary@pitt.edu
GEARY, Wes 303-404-5024 84 H
wes.geary@frontrange.edu
GEASEY, David, W 607-436-3314 353 E
geaseydw@oneonta.edu

GEASON, Robin 985-447-0924 211 L
rgeason@ltc.edu
GEBAR, Shelley 913-588-1698 197 A
sgebar@kumc.edu
GEBB, Billie Anne 859-253-3637 200 E
billieanne.gebb@frontier.edu
GEBEL, Karen 319-296-2320 185 C
karen.gebel@hawkeyecollege.edu
GEBER, David 212-749-2802 339 I
dgeber@msmnyc.edu
GEBHARD, Susan 336-917-5783 376 C
susan.gebhard@salem.edu
GEBHARDT, Lynita, J 708-709-3585 161 C
lgebhardt@prairiestate.edu
GEBHARDT, Virginia 660-263-4110 287 B
virginig@macc.edu
GEBHART, Daniel, L 260-481-6322 174 A
gebhartd@ipfw.edu
GEBHART, Jennifer, L 937-775-5611 406 C
jennifer.gebhart@wright.edu
GEBRETENSAE, Hanna 617-348-6358 246 A
gebretensae@urbancollege.edu
GEDDES, Leonard 828-328-7024 366 B
leonard.geddes@lr.edu
GEDDINGS, Scarlet 803-535-1243 460 C
geddingss@octech.edu
GEDDIS, Janet 610-558-5540 437 C
geddisj@neumann.edu
GEDEON, Tai 973-642-8744 315 C
tai-gedeo@shu.edu
GEDNALSKE, Julie 605-331-6683 466 D
julie.gednalske@usiouxfalls.edu
GEE, Albert, R 936-261-1730 496 E
argee@pvamu.edu
GEE, Billy 706-272-4461 127 G
bgee@daltonstate.edu
GEE, Carmelita 708-763-6941 162 C
carmelita.gee@resu.edu
GEE, Claudine 502-597-6976 203 D
claudine.gee@kysu.edu
GEE, E. Gordon 614-292-2424 398 H
gee.2@osu.edu
GEE, Henry 562-908-3489 63 H
hgee@riohondo.edu
GEE, Henry 408-274-7900 67 B
henry.gee@evc.edu
GEE, Jeffrey 434-223-6164 519 B
jgee@email.hsc.edu
GEE, Robert 508-457-1313 243 B
bgee@ngs.edu
GEE, Terry 619-594-2853 36 E
tgee@mail.sdsu.edu
GEEHAN, Margaret, M 518-629-7117 336 C
m.geehan@hvcc.edu
GEENEN, Patricia 414-382-6258 545 H
pat.geenen@alverno.edu
GEENENS, Dave 913-360-7633 190 F
dgeenens@benedictine.edu
GEER, Anne, R 585-385-8070 348 F
ageer@sjfc.edu
GEER, Lyn 703-330-5398 540 C
lgeer@apus.edu
GEER, Walter 617-928-4710 243 A
wgeer@mountida.edu
GEFELL, Michele, D 315-786-2271 337 F
mgefell@sunyjefferson.edu
GEFFERT, Bryn 413-542-2212 230 A
GEFFNER, Linda, O 860-231-5208 93 H
lgeffner@sjc.edu
GEGENHEIMER BALDASSARO, Sarah 202-994-5152 97 F
sarahgb@gwu.edu
GEGG-LAPLUME, Tamara 314-968-6982 293 A
laplume@webster.edu
GEGGIE, Steven 847-317-8178 166 B
sgeggie@tiu.edu
GEHANI, Narain 973-596-5488 312 C
narain.gehani@njit.edu
GEHEBER, Leah 225-768-1746 214 B
lgeheber@ololcollege.edu
GEHLER, Jan, L 480-423-6310 16 D
jan.gehler@sccmail.maricopa.edu
GEHLHAR, Jim 252-328-4829 377 C
gehlhar@ecu.edu
GEHLHAUSEN, Keith 812-488-2943 180 B
kg77@evansville.edu
GEHLING, William 617-627-3232 245 F
bill.gehling@tufts.edu
GEHR, Theresa 614-287-2642 388 G
tgehr@cscc.edu
GEHRELS, David 903-586-5261 490 B
dgehrels@lonmorris.edu
GEHRET, Steve 423-636-5096 476 F
sgehret@tusculum.edu
GEHRICH, Michael, D 317-381-6000 181 B
mgehrich@vinu.edu
GEHRING, Dale 701-858-3375 381 G
dale.gehring@minotstateu.edu
GEHRINGER, Margie 515-271-7498 183 F
margie.gehringer@dmu.edu
GEHRLS, Janet 563-441-2455 186 E
jgehrls@kucampus.edu
GEHRMAN-ROTTIER, Laura 715-346-3811 552 B
lgehrman@uwsp.edu

GEIB, Bethany 740-857-1311 401 F
bgeib@rosedale.edu
GEIER, Cathy 202-884-9545 99 E
geierc@trinitydc.edu
GEIER, Connie 606-626-2415 465 H
geierc@northern.edu
GEIER, Nikki 620-276-9531 193 A
nikki.geier@gcccks.edu
GEIER, Peter, E 614-292-2635 398 H
geier.10@osu.edu
GEIGER, David 610-341-1468 428 D
dgeiger@eastern.edu
GEIGER, Douglas 914-323-5235 340 A
GEIGER, Jim 937-327-7430 406 B
jgeiger@wittenberg.edu
GEIGER, Kimberly 423-775-6597 472 E
GEIGER, Martha 513-558-0087 403 E
geigerml@ucmail.uc.edu
GEIGER, Robin 502-597-7014 203 D
robin.geiger@kysu.edu
GEIGER, William 903-566-7081 506 C
wgeiger@uttyler.edu
GEIGER, Yolanda 803-376-5736 455 B
ygeiger@allenuniversity.edu
GEIGLE, Michele, Z 727-736-5082 117 F
michele_geigle@schiller.edu
GEILING, Betty, C 914-337-9300 331 A
elizabeth.geiling@concordia-ny.edu
GEILING, Bryan, K 610-989-1351 450 E
bgeiling@vfmac.edu
GEIMAN, John, E 410-706-3822 227 C
jgeiman@af.umaryland.edu
GEIMER, Jill 312-332-0707 165 H
GEIRBOLINI, Rafael 787-769-9965 566 H
rafael.gierbolini@upr.edu
GEISER, Jeff 575-562-2153 318 A
jeff.geiser@enmu.edu
GEISLER, Michael 802-443-5275 513 G
geisler@middlebury.edu
GEISLER, Rowena 561-273-6500 117 J
rgeisler@southuniversity.edu
GEIST, Alan 937-766-7768 386 F
geista@cedarville.edu
GEIST, Betsy 206-268-4904 530 F
bgeist@antioch.edu
GEIST, Edward, V 203-576-4956 94 D
edwgeist@bridgeport.edu
GELAYE, Enku 413-254-2300 237 C
egelaye@stuaf.umass.edu
GELBKE, Konrad 517-355-9671 255 D
gelbke@nscl.msu.edu
GELCH, Deborah 617-243-2390 236 F
dgelch@lasell.edu
GELDART, David 617-369-3230 244 G
dgeldart@mfa.org
GELDENHUYS, Tammie 620-331-4100 193 G
tgeldenhuys@indycc.edu
GELDER, Alvern 616-957-6045 249 F
af094@calvinseminary.edu
GELDER, Minna 503-589-7870 414 J
minna.gelder@chemeketa.edu
GELDWORTH, Lipa 718-853-8500 357 I
GELERNTER, Mark 303-556-5938 88 D
mark.gelernter@ucdenver.edu
GELETA, Nomsa 814-732-2724 442 D
ngeleta@edinboro.edu
GELETKA, Catherine, M 419-289-5306 384 D
cgeletka@ashland.edu
GELFAND, Jack 315-312-2888 354 A
jack.gelfand@oswego.edu
GELFAND, M 732-364-1220 307 E
GELFER, Miriam 617-682-1518 234 G
mgelfer@eds.edu
GELFMAN, Arnold, J 732-224-2749 308 B
agelfman@brookdalecc.edu
GELINAS, Cynthia, B 803-641-2841 462 B
cindyg@usca.edu
GELINAS, Cynthia, B 803-641-3609 462 B
cindyg@usca.edu
GELINAS, David 704-894-2698 363 F
dagelinas@davidson.edu
GELL, Barry 518-255-5440 354 E
gellbf@cobleskill.edu
GELLE, Mark 507-786-3294 271 H
gelle@stolaf.edu
GELLER, Jack 218-281-8248 272 A
gelle045@umn.edu
GELLER, L. Randy 541-346-3082 419 B
gcounsel@uoregon.edu
GELLER, Mark 800-371-6105 16 H
mark@nationalparalegal.edu
GELLER, Mary, A 320-363-5601 262 H
mgeller@csbsju.edu
GELLES, Richard, J 215-898-5511 448 I
gelles@sp2.upenn.edu
GELLIN, Marcia, A 716-851-1113 333 B
gellin@ecc.edu
GELLMAN-DANLEY, Barbara 740-245-7205 404 E
bdanley@rio.edu
GELMAN, Sheldon, R 212-960-0820 361 I
srgelman@yu.edu
GELO, Daniel, J 210-458-4359 506 B
daniel.gelo@utsa.edu

GELSINGER, Sue 610-372-4721 445 B
sgelsinger@racc.edu
GELTCH, Wendy 863-297-1083 115 A
wgeltch@polk.edu
GELVIN, Karen 316-323-6915 191 D
kgelvin@butlercc.edu
GELY, Gilda, G 616-234-3920 251 G
ggely@grcc.edu
GEMME, Terese 203-392-5499 91 I
gemmet1@southernct.edu
GEMPERLINE, Paul 252-328-6012 377 C
gemperlinep@ecu.edu
GEMPESAW, Bobby 513-529-6721 396 D
gempescm@muohio.edu
GENANDT, James 620-431-2820 195 B
GENAO, Janet 813-879-6000 106 F
jgenao@cci.edu
GENCO, Rosemarie 973-720-2107 317 D
gencor@wpunj.edu
GENDERNALIK-COOPER, Mary, L 540-654-1000 524 H
mgendern@umw.edu
GENDRON, Dennis 615-963-5301 474 A
dgendron@tnstate.edu
GENDRON, Josee 530-242-7574 69 D
jgendron@shastacollege.edu
GENECIN, Paul 203-432-0076 95 D
paul.genecin@yale.edu
GENEE, Murray 718-405-3733 330 A
murray.genee@mountsaintvincent.edu
GENEGA, Paul 973-748-9000 308 A
paul_genega@bloomfield.edu
GENELIN, Nancy 507-389-7228 269 F
nancy.genelin@southcentral.edu
GENERALS, Donald 609-586-4800 311 C
generald@mccc.edu
GENESE, Carol 718-933-6700 341 G
cgenese@monroecollege.edu
GENET, Robert 717-846-5000 452 G
GENGARO, Nicholas 973-642-8859 315 C
nicholas.gengaro@shu.edu
GENIG, Dennis 734-995-7393 250 B
genigd@cuaa.edu
GENIK, Chris 213-613-2200 70 H
chris@sciarc.edu
GENIK, Christopher 619-684-8762 59 A
cgenik@newschoolarch.edu
GENNA, Angela 602-285-7357 16 B
angela.genna@pcmail.maricopa.edu
GENNARO, Gwen 719-255-3153 88 C
ggennaro@uccs.edu
GENNARO, Susan 617-552-4250 232 D
susan.gennaro.1@bc.edu
GENO, Rita, B 802-468-1203 515 C
rita.geno@castleton.edu
GENOUS, Zandra 847-543-2420 147 H
zgenous@clcillinois.edu
GENOVESE, Louis 973-877-3040 310 A
genovese@essex.edu
GENSHAFT, Judy, L 813-974-2791 120 D
jgensha@usf.edu
GENSLER, Charlotte 505-224-4551 317 J
cgensler@cnm.edu
GENSON, Barrett 239-590-1520 119 A
bgenson@fgcu.edu
GENT, Jerri 814-676-6591 442 B
jgent@clarion.edu
GENTHNER, Patricia 585-389-2002 342 D
pgenthn5@naz.edu
GENTHON, Paulette 402-556-4456 300 E
info@ucha.com
GENTILE, Dina, M 610-789-6700 445 A
dgentile@prismcareerinstitute.edu
GENTILE, Jackie 413-528-7239 231 A
jgentile@simons-rock.edu
GENTILE, Kathy, J 314-516-6383 291 F
gentilek@umsl.edu
GENTILE, Patricia 609-463-4507 307 D
pgentile@atlantic.edu
GENTILE, Sam, A 702-458-9650 303 C
GENTILLON, Jeanne 818-386-5606 62 F
jgentillon@pgi.edu
GENTLES, Lori 415-405-2650 36 F
lgentles@sfsu.edu
GENTLEWARRIOR, Sabrina 508-531-1429 238 B
sgentlewarrior@bridgew.edu
GENTNER, Lisa, K 812-246-3301 176 H
lgentner@ivytech.edu
GENTRY, Bradley, D 217-786-2278 156 I
brad.gentry@llcc.edu
GENTRY, Jerry, H 270-831-9622 201 I
jerry.gentry@kctcs.edu
GENTRY, Jodi, D 352-392-4626 120 B
jodi-gentry@ufl.edu
GENTRY, Margaret 315-859-4615 335 A
mgentry@hamilton.edu
GENTRY, Richard, E 956-326-2266 497 B
rgentry@tamiu.edu
GENTRY, Vickie 318-357-6288 216 B
gentry@nsula.edu
GENTRY, W. Marichal 203-432-2907 95 D
marichal.gentry@yale.edu
GENTRY-BARTH, Danielle 513-585-0359 387 C

GENTRY-EPLEY, Beth .... 816-781-7700.... 293 D
gentry-epleyb@william.jewell.edu
GENTRY-WRIGHT, Susan, C .... 864-833-8100.... 460 E
sgentry-w@presby.edu
GENTSCH, James .... 205-652-3361...... 10 A
jgentsch@uwa.edu
GENTUL, Jack .... 973-596-3466.... 312 C
jack.gentul@njit.edu
GENTZLER, Randall .... 410-617-2345.... 224 A
rdgentzler@loyola.edu
GENUA, Kathy .... 516-918-3626.... 324 E
kgenua@bcl.edu
GENUNG, Bruce .... 760-750-7305...... 36 B
bgenung@csusm.edu
GEOCARIS, Diane, F .... 949-824-2880...... 73 H
dfgeocar@uci.edu
GEOFFROY, Gregory, L ..... 515-294-2042.... 182 B
geoffroy@iastate.edu
GEOGHEGAN, Jeffrey, P .... 860-679-3162...... 94 F
geoghegan@uchc.edu
GEOGHEGAN, Michael ...... 513-569-1586.... 387 F
michael.geoghegan@cincinnatistate.edu
GEORGE, Abraham .... 706-507-8111.... 127 D
george_abraham@columbusstate.edu
GEORGE, Archie, A .... 208-885-7995.... 144 B
archie@uidaho.edu
GEORGE, Barbara .... 805-546-3279...... 43 F
bgeorge@cuesta.edu
GEORGE, Betty .... 520-621-3175...... 19 B
george@ogc.arizona.edu
GEORGE, Carol, S .... 937-766-7900.... 386 F
georgec@cedarville.edu
GEORGE, Chris .... 303-871-4883...... 88 E
Chris.George@du.edu
GEORGE, Christi .... 205-652-3840...... 10 A
cjw@uwa.edu
GEORGE, Dennis, K .... 270-745-8723.... 207 C
dennis.george@wku.edu
GEORGE, Douglas, J .... 716-652-8900.... 326 A
dgeorge@cks.edu
GEORGE, Ellen .... 309-999-4580.... 152 B
egeorge@icc.edu
GEORGE, Francis .... 847-566-6401.... 167 D
GEORGE, Gene .... 316-322-3338.... 191 D
ggeorge@butlercc.edu
GEORGE, Janice, S .... 620-421-6700.... 194 E
janicec@labette.edu
GEORGE, Kristina .... 320-308-5980.... 269 D
kgeorge@sctcc.edu
GEORGE, LePra .... 312-669-5273.... 150 E
lgeorge@ellis.edu
GEORGE, Lynda .... 859-257-3172.... 206 H
lgeorge@uky.edu
GEORGE, Marie, A .... 610-902-8200.... 423 H
marie.a.george@cabrini.edu
GEORGE, Neil, J .... 314-968-6915.... 293 A
georgenj@webster.edu
GEORGE, JR., Orlando, J .. 302-739-4053...... 96 A
pres@dtcc.edu
GEORGE, R. Dillard .... 757-683-4156.... 521 L
rdgeorge@odu.edu
GEORGE, Robert .... 941-782-5657.... 433 C
rgeorge@lecom.edu
GEORGE, Russell .... 970 675-3201.... 82 D
russell.george@cncc.edu
GEORGE, Sandra, B .... 562-951-4700...... 33 E
sgeorge@calstate.edu
GEORGE, Sarah, B .... 801-581-6927.... 510 L
sgeorge@umnh.utah.edu
GEORGE, Sharon, A .... 603-641-7084.... 305 H
sgeorge@anselm.edu
GEORGE, Sheila .... 212-924-5900.... 357 A
sgeorge@swedishinstitute.edu
GEORGE, Susan .... 304-473-8080.... 545 F
george@wvwc.edu
GEORGE, Tami .... 910-272-3541.... 373 A
tgeorge@robeson.edu
GEORGE, Thomas .... 678-891-2500.... 130 G
thomas.george@gpc.edu
GEORGE, Thomas, F .... 314-516-5252.... 291 F
tfgeorge@umsl.edu
GEORGE, Timothy, F .... 205-726-2632........ 6 G
tfgeorge@samford.edu
GEORGE, Varghese, T .... 706-721-0801.... 130 B
vgeorge@georgiahealth.edu
GEORGE, Viji, D .... 914-337-9300.... 331 A
viji.george@concordia-ny.edu
GEORGE, W. Michael .... 205-348-7219........ 8 F
michael.george@ua.edu
GEORGE-TAYLOR, Mosunmola .... 423-697-2552.... 474 D
GEORGENES, George .... 617-850-1317.... 236 A
gag@hchc.edu
GEORGES, Anthony, C .... 314-516-5508.... 291 F
tony_georges@umsl.edu
GEORGESON, Lance .... 425-249-4752.... 538 D
lance.georgeson@tlc.edu
GEORGO, Maria .... 352-787-7660.... 101 H
mgeorgo@beaconcollege.edu
GEPPI, Steve .... 410-386-8524.... 221 G
sgeppi@carrollcc.edu
GERA, Holly, P .... 973-655-5234.... 311 G
gerah@mail.montclair.edu

GERAC, Anna .... 802-728-1586.... 515 G
agerac@vtc.edu
GERACI, Joseph .... 516-877-3156.... 322 A
geraci@adelphi.edu
GERACI, Richard, V .... 575-624-8400.... 319 C
cmdt@nmmi.edu
GERAGHTY, Patricia, L ...... 414-288-3423.... 548 D
patricia.geraghty@marquette.edu
GERALD, Trudy .... 619-388-3522...... 65 F
tgerald@sdccd.edu
GERAMI, Keyvan .... 314-286-3670.... 288 B
kgerami@ranken.edu
GERARD, Ada .... 916-638-1616...... 49 K
ada_gerard@heald.edu
GERARD, Pamela, S .... 563-588-7818.... 186 I
pam.gerard@loras.edu
GERARD, Phillip, R .... 864-242-5100.... 455 E
GERASSIMIDES, Gus .... 859-985-3158.... 198 F
gus_gerassimides@berea.edu
GERATY, Brent G, T .... 269-471-6530.... 247 H
bgeraty@andrews.edu
GERBASI, Iris .... 714-997-6676...... 39 C
gerbasi@chapman.edu
GERBER, Cheryl .... 724-946-7102.... 451 C
gerberca@westminster.edu
GERBER, Elizabeth, L .... 815-599-3421.... 152 A
liz.gerber@highland.edu
GERBER, Joanna .... 310-578-1080...... 28 K
jgerber@antiochla.edu
GERBER, Linda .... 503-977-4357.... 419 G
linda.gerber@pcc.edu
GERBER, Michael, A .... 718-780-7923.... 324 F
michael.gerber@brooklaw.edu
GERBINO, Philip, P .... 215-596-8970.... 450 A
pgerbino@usciences.edu
GERBOTH, Karen, L .... 937-327-6141.... 406 B
kgerboth@wittenberg.edu
GERDEMAN, Penny .... 419-434-4558.... 404 B
gerdeman@findlay.edu
GERDES, Darin .... 843-574-3220.... 456 B
dgerdes@csuniv.edu
GERDES, Neil, W .... 773-752-5757.... 146 E
ngerdes@ctschicago.edu
GERDES, Neil, W .... 773-256-3000.... 158 A
ngerdes@meadville.edu
GERDICH, Michael .... 724-805-2895.... 446 E
michael.gerdich@email.stvincent.edu
GERDING, Melissa, D .... 610-519-4044.... 450 G
melissa.gerding@villanova.edu
GERE, Nicholas .... 207-602-2011.... 220 H
ngere@une.edu
GEREAUX, Teresa, T .... 540-375-2282.... 523 D
gereaux@roanoke.edu
GEREMIA, Kenneth .... 413-528-7291.... 231 A
kgeremia@simons-rock.edu
GERENA, Elizabeth .... 787-850-9301.... 567 B
elizabeth.gerena@upr.edu
GERETY, RSM, Jane .... 401-341-2337.... 454 D
jane.gerety@salve.edu
GERETY, Mason .... 928-523-2012...... 17 A
mason.gerety@nau.edu
GERETY, Mason .... 928-523-3657...... 17 A
mason.gerety@nau.edu
GERHARD, Karen .... 563-588-6444.... 183 B
karen.gerhard@clarke.edu
GERHARDT, Mark .... 605-995-7174.... 464 E
mark.gerhardt@mitchelltech.edu
GERHARDT, Winifred .... 440-826-2222.... 384 H
wgerhard@bw.edu
GERHART, Phillip, M .... 812-488-2651.... 180 B
pg3@evansville.edu
GERHARTER, Janelle .... 402-844-7063.... 300 A
janelle@northeast.edu
GERIG, Bev .... 541-917-4857.... 416 H
gerigb@linnbenton.edu
GERIGUIS, David .... 951-785-2002...... 53 D
dgerigui@lasierra.edu
GERIK, Debbie .... 254-659-7704.... 487 E
debgerik@hillcollege.edu
GERING, Jon .... 660-785-4248.... 291 A
jgering@truman.edu
GERITY, Patrick, E .... 724-925-4219.... 451 E
gerityk@wccc.edu
GERITY, Peter, F .... 575-835-5227.... 319 A
vpaa@admin.nmt.edu
GERKEN, Keith .... 907-796-6496...... 11 A
william.gerken@uas.alaska.edu
GERKEN, Stacey .... 715-346-3553.... 552 B
sgerken@uwsp.edu
GERKIN, David .... 623-845-4762...... 15 J
david.gerkin@gcmail.maricopa.edu
GERKIN, Jeffrey, G .... 865-974-3131.... 477 B
jgerkin@utk.edu
GERL, Beth, R .... 410-871-3199.... 224 D
bgerl@mcdaniel.edu
GERLACH, David, M .... 315-386-7082.... 355 D
gerlach@canton.edu
GERLACH, Jeanne, M .... 817-272-5476.... 505 A
gerlach@uta.edu
GERLICA, Reg .... 313-845-9605.... 252 D
rgerlica@hfcc.edu
GERLICH, Bella .... 907-474-7224...... 10 J
GERLING, Angela .... 573-592-5245.... 293 C
Angela.Gerling@westminster-mo.edu

GERMAIN, George, F .... 989-328-1275.... 256 A
georgeg@montcalm.edu
GERMAN, Dana .... 540-654-2246.... 524 H
dgerman@umw.edu
GERMAN, Deborah .... 407-266-1000.... 120 A
deborah.german@ucf.edu
GERMAN, Lisa .... 256-352-8306...... 10 B
lisa.german@wallacestate.edu
GERMAN, JR., Robert (Chip) .... 717-871-5844.... 443 C
robert.german@millersville.edu
GERMAN, Steve .... 806-720-7353.... 490 D
steve.german@lcu.edu
GERMANO, William .... 212-353-4274.... 331 B
germano@cooper.edu
GERMANY, Sylvia .... 256-726-8218........ 6 C
germany@oakwood.edu
GERN, William, A .... 307-766-5353.... 556 E
willger@uwyo.edu
GERNAND, Peg .... 812-280-7271.... 178 E
peg.gernand@ottawa.edu
GERNERT, Maureen, C ...... 203-837-8266...... 92 A
gernertm@wcsu.edu
GERNES, Todd, S .... 508-565-1840.... 245 D
tgernes@stonehill.edu
GERRICK, W. Greg .... 419-289-5657.... 384 D
ggerrick@ashland.edu
GERRITY, Nancy .... 405-682-7587.... 409 F
ngerrity@occc.edu
GERRY, Frank .... 207-973-3375.... 219 I
fgerry@maine.edu
GERRY, Thomas .... 518-828-4181.... 330 E
gerry@sunycgcc.edu
GERSEY, Martin, L .... 574-520-5522.... 174 C
mgersey@iusb.edu
GERSH, Stan .... 818-932-3010...... 44 N
sgersh@devry.edu
GERSHEN, Jay Alan .... 330-325-2511.... 397 C
GERSHON, I. Richard .... 662-915-6900.... 277 G
igershon@olemiss.edu
GERSHOWITZ, Whitney .... 804-862-6461.... 523 C
wgershowitz@rbc.edu
GERSICH, Frank .... 309-457-2119.... 158 G
fgersich@monm.edu
GERST, Bernard .... 410-704-3383.... 228 E
bgerst@towson.edu
GERSTEIN, Dean .... 909-607-9406...... 40 C
dean.gerstein@cgu.edu
GERSTEN, Karen .... 312-752-2000.... 155 B
karen.gersten@kendall.edu
GERSTER, Patrick .... 408-288-3785...... 67 C
patrick.gerster@sjcc.edu
GERSZEWSKI, Raymond, H .... 701-788-4770.... 381 F
Ray.Gerszewski@mayvillestate.edu
GERTS, John .... 231-843-5850.... 260 E
jkgerts@westshore.edu
GERTSMAN, Josh .... 253-833-9111.... 534 C
jgerstman@greenriver.edu
GERTSON, Katherine .... 212-799-5000.... 337 H
GERTZ, Genie .... 510-659-6272...... 59 I
ggertz@ohlone.edu
GERTZ, Tanya, M .... 563-387-1536.... 187 A
gertta01@luther.edu
GERVAIS, Carly .... 504-278-6421.... 211 I
cgervais@nunez.edu
GERVAIS, Noelle .... 310-338-7880...... 56 E
ngervais@lmu.edu
GERVASI, Robert .... 217-228-5432.... 161 E
gervasi@quincy.edu
GERVIN, Dennis .... 209-588-5107...... 80 A
gervind@yosemite.edu
GERVIN, Dennis .... 209-588-5115...... 80 A
gervind@yosemite.edu
GESELE, Gregory, S .... 860-701-6727.... 558 E
Gregory.S.Gesele@uscg.mil
GESO, Cristina, A .... 215-895-1674.... 427 G
cag58@drexel.edu
GESSELL, Donna .... 706-864-1543.... 134 D
dgessell@northgeorgia.edu
GESSFORD, Sheryl .... 916-485-6045...... 56 A
gessfos@arc.losrios.edu
GESSLER, Klaus .... 845-431-8939.... 332 E
gessler@sunydutchess.edu
GESSNER, David .... 715-836-5182.... 550 H
gessnedp@uwec.edu
GESSNER, James, C .... 570-389-4105.... 441 F
jgessner@bloomu.edu
GESSNER, James, R .... 218-722-4000.... 263 H
jimg@dbumn.edu
GESTRINE, Beverley .... 360-736-9391.... 531 H
bgestrine@centralia.edu
GESTRING, Sheila .... 605-677-5255.... 465 E
sheila.gestring@usd.edu
GETCHELL, Charles .... 203-582-8631...... 93 E
charles.getchell@quinnipiac.edu
GETCHELL, Stephanie, L .... 919-530-7824.... 378 A
slgetchell@nccu.edu
GETER, Travaras .... 718-405-3234.... 330 A
travaras.geter@mountsaintvincent.edu
GETTER, Angela .... 662-254-3490.... 276 C
angela.getter@mvsu.edu
GETTING, Kris, A .... 651-962-6168.... 272 E
kagetting@stthomas.edu

GETTY, Larry, R .... 785-628-4513.... 192 F
lgetty@fhsu.edu
GETZ, Karen .... 724-266-3838.... 448 G
kgetz@tsm.edu
GETZ, Kathleen, A .... 312-915-6115.... 157 A
kgetz@luc.edu
GETZ, Rae .... 605-394-4034.... 466 E
rae.getz@wdt.edu
GETZ, Roger .... 302-736-2455...... 96 G
getz@wesley.edu
GETZEN, Bruce .... 808-245-8355.... 141 H
bgetzen@hawaii.edu
GEU, Thomas .... 605-677-5443.... 465 E
thomas.geu@usd.edu
GEUDER, Maridith, W .... 662-325-7454.... 276 A
geuderm@ur.msstate.edu
GEYE, Trina .... 254-968-9400.... 496 F
geye@tarleton.edu
GEYER, Dennis .... 916-278-3901...... 35 E
dgeyer@csus.edu
GEYER, Enid .... 518-262-6008.... 322 E
geyere@mail.amc.edu
GEYER, Enid .... 518-262-5586.... 322 E
geyere@mail.amc.edu
GEYER, Jonathan .... 304-829-7645.... 540 E
jgeyer@bethanywv.edu
GEYER, Mariann .... 412-392-3805.... 444 H
mgeyer@pointpark.edu
GHAHRAMANI, Saeed .... 413-782-1218.... 246 D
sghahram@wne.edu
GHALI, Moheb, A .... 360-650-3170.... 539 C
moheb.ghali@wwu.edu
GHAN, Landon .... 417-268-6113.... 279 D
lghan@gobbc.edu
GHAN, Mark .... 775-445-4237.... 303 B
mark_ghan@wnc.edu
GHANEM, Salma, I .... 989-774-1885.... 249 G
ghane1si@cmich.edu
GHANNADIAN, Frank .... 813-253-6221.... 122 H
fghannadian@ut.edu
GHARAHBAGHIAN, Mohsen .... 858-499-0202...... 41 E
mohseng@coleman.edu
GHARIB, Morteza .... 626-395-6365...... 32 E
vpr@caltech.edu
GHAZARIAN, Esther, A ..... 781-768-7280.... 244 D
esther.ghazarian@regiscollege.edu
GHAZVINI, Mariam .... 510-592-9688...... 59 F
mariam@npu.edu
GHEE, Harry .... 910-323-5614.... 362 G
GHILANI, Mary .... 570-740-0456.... 435 C
mghilani@luzerne.edu
GHIO, Frederick, W .... 401-456-8201.... 454 A
fghio@ric.edu
GHIORSE, Emily, A .... 401-865-2392.... 453 F
GHISELLI, Nina .... 415-955-2164...... 27 F
nghiselli@alliant.edu
GHOLKAR, Girija, V .... 212-678-8023.... 337 G
gigholkar@jtsa.edu
GHOLSON, Shari .... 270-534-3372.... 203 B
shari.gholson@kctcs.edu
GHOLSTON, Brandon .... 770-394-8300.... 124 F
bgholston@aii.edu
GHORAYEB, Samir .... 409-984-6484.... 500 H
samir.ghorayeb@lamarpa.edu
GHORI, Aisha .... 312-467-2309.... 146 C
aghori@thechicagoschool.edu
GHOSH, Jayati .... 415-485-3238...... 45 B
jayati.ghosh@domincan.edu
GHOSH, Sibdas .... 415-482-3583...... 45 B
sibdas.ghosh@dominican.edu
GHOUS, Mostafa .... 707-864-7000...... 70 A
mostafa.ghous@solano.edu
GHRIGA, Mohammed .... 718-488-1159.... 338 H
mohammed.ghriga@liu.edu
GIACCHETTI, Richard .... 408-554-4982...... 68 C
rgiacchetti@scu.edu
GIACCHINO, Mike .... 305-949-9500.... 105 F
mgiacchino@cci.edu
GIACOBBE, Jeff .... 973-655-5373.... 311 G
giacobbej@mail.montclair.edu
GIACOMELLI, Marie, A .... 217-793-4201.... 162 E
mgiacomelli@robertmorris.edu
GIACOMINO, Dennis .... 419-267-1356.... 397 D
dgiacomino@northweststate.edu
GIACONA, Nick .... 505-984-6110.... 320 C
ngiacona@sjcsf.edu
GIAMARTINO, Gary, A .... 618-650-3823.... 165 A
ggiamar@siue.edu
GIAMBELLUCA, Russell ...... 209-667-3077...... 36 C
rgiambelluca@csustan.edu
GIAMBRA, Leonard, M .... 860-701-6679.... 558 E
leonard.m.giambra@uscg.mil
GIAMPAOLI, Michael, J ...... 203-576-4168...... 94 D
gmichael@bridgeport.edu
GIAMPAPA, Heather .... 215-780-1391.... 446 G
hgiampapa@salus.edu
GIAMPIETRO, Michael .... 413-565-1000.... 231 B
mgiampietro@baypath.edu
GIANCHETTA, Larry, D .... 406-243-4831.... 295 A
larry.gianchetta@business.umt.edu
GIANCOLA, John .... 703-414-4021.... 518 B
jgiancola@devry.edu

GILBREATH, Bill .... 972-279-6511 .... 479 I
bgilbreath@amberton.edu

GILBRIDE, Anna Margaret . 440-646-8104 .... 405 B
amgilbride@ursuline.edu

GILCHRIST, Bryan .... 305-809-3279 .... 108 F
bryan.gilchrist@fkcc.edu

GILCHRIST, Cathine .... 610-399-2353 .... 441 H
cgilchrist@cheyney.edu

GILCHRIST, Cheryl, B .... 502-852-8139 .... 207 A
cbgilc01@louisville.edu

GILCHRIST, Debbie .... 956-665-2140 .... 506 A
gilchrist@utpa.edu

GILCHRIST, Debra .... 253-964-6553 .... 536 C
dgilchrist@pierce.ctc.edu

GILCHRIST, James, A .... 269-387-5430 .... 260 F
james.gilchrist@wmich.edu

GILCHRIST, James, A .... 269-387-2382 .... 260 F
james.gilchrist@wmich.edu

GILCHRIST, Joseph .... 239-513-1122 .... 110 K
jgilchrist@hodges.edu

GILCHRIST, Lou Ann .... 660-785-4111 .... 291 A
lcg@truman.edu

GILCHRIST, Stephan .... 608-262-0277 .... 552 F
stephan.gilchrist@uwex.uwc.edu

GILCHRIST, Willie, J .... 252-335-3228 .... 377 D
wjgilchrist@mail.ecsu.edu

GILCREASE, Kathy, J .... 936-294-1012 .... 501 A
gilcrease@shsu.edu

GILCRIST, Robin .... 907-796-6141 ...... 11 A
robin.gilcrist@uas.alaska.edu

GILDAWIE, Janice .... 413-528-7698 .... 231 A
jgildawie@simons-rock.edu

GILDAY, Colleen .... 513-487-3215 .... 391 E
cgilday@huc.edu

GILDERHUS, Kiki .... 303-753-6046 ...... 87 F

GILDERSLEEVE,
Elizabeth, T .... 781-283-2376 .... 246 B
egilders@wellesley.edu

GILES, Don .... 859-336-5082 .... 205 F
dongiles@sccky.edu

GILES, Doug .... 812-330-6066 .... 175 H
dgiles@ivytech.edu

GILES, JR., Henry, C .... 864-592-4616 .... 461 C
gilesh@sccsc.edu

GILES, Karen .... 513-618-1923 .... 387 E
kgiles@ccms.edu

GILES, Pam .... 276-523-2400 .... 527 A
pgiles@me.vccs.edu

GILES, Roger, W .... 870-235-4008 ...... 23 I
rwgiles@saumag.edu

GILES, Timothy, W .... 904-620-4200 .... 120 C
timothy.giles@unf.edu

GILES-GEE, Helen, F .... 603-358-2000 .... 307 A
gilesgee@keene.edu

GILFILLAN, Candace .... 505-566-3035 .... 320 D
gilfillanc@sanjuancollege.edu

GILFILLAN, Margaret .... 412-392-3994 .... 444 H
mgilfillan@pointpark.edu

GILGOUR, Joe .... 660-596-7393 .... 290 F
jgilgour@sfccmo.edu

GILION, Millie .... 417-455-5480 .... 281 C
mgilion@crowder.edu

GILJE, Stephen, A .... 607-777-6136 .... 351 F
sgilje@binghamton.edu

GILKER, Bill .... 817-760-5504 .... 487 E
wmgilker@hillcollege.edu

GILKERSON, Tammeil .... 408-270-6474 ...... 67 B
tammeil.gilkerson@evc.edu

GILKEY, Mary .... 540-423-9820 .... 526 E
mgilkey@germanna.edu

GILKEY, Shane, L .... 740-593-9813 .... 399 G
gilkeys@ohio.edu

GILL, Allison .... 978-837-5174 .... 242 D
gilla@merrimack.edu

GILL, Ann, M .... 970-491-5421 ...... 83 A
ann.gill@colostate.edu

GILL, Anne, M .... 617-989-4193 .... 246 C
gilla@wit.edu

GILL, Barbara .... 603-887-7412 .... 303 G

GILL, Barbara, A .... 301-314-8350 .... 227 B
bgill@umd.edu

GILL, Barbara, J .... 850-201-6570 .... 121 F
gillb@tcc.fl.edu

GILL, Chris .... 314-719-8057 .... 282 C
cgill@fontbonne.edu

GILL, Chris, G .... 509-313-3827 .... 534 A
gill@its.gonzaga.edu

GILL, D. Christopher .... 573-288-6322 .... 281 D
cgill@culver.edu

GILL, Dennis .... 541-881-5915 .... 420 E
dgill@tvcc.cc

GILL, Diane, E .... 717-531-4103 .... 439 L
deg9@psu.edu

GILL, Don .... 503-223-2245 .... 416 E
dgill@westernculinary.com

GILL, Jamie, W .... 727-864-8337 .... 104 K
gilljw@eckerd.edu

GILL, Janet .... 712-274-6400 .... 189 H
janet.gill@witcc.edu

GILL, Jeffery, A .... 574-372-5100 .... 171 E
gillja@grace.edu

GILL, Keith .... 202-885-3190 ...... 97 B
gill@american.edu

GILL, Lanae .... 313-993-1230 .... 259 C
gilla@udmercy.edu

GILL, Lee, A .... 330-972-7522 .... 403 B
lee16@uakron.edu

GILL, Mary .... 712-749-2123 .... 182 G
gill@bvu.edu

GILL, Michele .... 308-345-3600 .... 298 I
gillm@mpcc.edu

GILL, Nancy .... 805-437-8456 ...... 33 I
nancy.gill@csuci.edu

GILL, Randolph, E .... 619-201-8960 ...... 70 J
rgill@socalsem.edu

GILL, Robert .... 301-624-2719 .... 222 G
bgill@frederick.edu

GILL, Russell .... 480-515-7648 .... 149 A
rgill@devry.edu

GILL, Sandra .... 630-829-6216 .... 145 D
sgill@ben.edu

GILL, Steven .... 609-258-3466 .... 313 A
sgill@princeton.edu

GILL-JACOBSON,
Roseanne .... 419-824-3829 .... 395 D
rgill-jacobson@lourdes.edu

GILLAHAN, Sheilah .... 731-286-3316 .... 475 A
gillahan@dscc.edu

GILLAN, Darlene .... 617-879-7050 .... 238 E
dgillan@massart.edu

GILLAN, Maria .... 973-684-5904 .... 312 E
mgillan@pccc.edu

GILLARD, Natalie .... 575-461-4413 .... 318 F
natalieg@mesalands.edu

GILLARDI, Michael .... 401-598-1450 .... 453 C
mgillardi@jwu.edu

GILLASPIE, Ray .... 270-824-8592 .... 202 C
ray.gillaspie@kctcs.edu

GILLE, Chaudron .... 678-717-3835 .... 129 D
cgille@gsc.edu

GILLEAN, Jack .... 501-450-3170 ...... 25 H
jgillean@uca.edu

GILLECE, Nancy, E .... 301-696-3710 .... 223 C
gillece@hood.edu

GILLELAND, Drew .... 541-552-6319 .... 419 A
gilliland@sou.edu

GILLEN, Ann .... 209-946-2135 ...... 75 D

GILLEN, Dan .... 319-296-4268 .... 185 C
daniel.gillen@hawkeyecollege.edu

GILLEN, Dan .... 641-844-5539 .... 185 J
dan.gillen@iavalley.edu

GILLEN, Edward .... 203-582-8471 ...... 93 E
edward.gllen@quinnipiac.edu

GILLEN, Jonathan .... 541-881-5842 .... 420 E
jgillen@tvcc.cc

GILLEN-CARYL, Shawn ...... 315-498-2537 .... 345 D
gillencs@sunyocc.edu

GILLER, Patricia .... 312-777-8562 .... 153 A
pgiller@aii.edu

GILLERMAN, Sharon .... 213-749-4241 ...... 50 D
sgillerman@huc.edu

GILLES, Barbara, L .... 412-578-6123 .... 424 G
gillesbl@carlow.edu

GILLESPIE, Bart .... 678-839-6582 .... 138 D
bgillesp@westga.edu

GILLESPIE, Christine .... 215-968-8718 .... 423 E
gillespi@bucks.edu

GILLESPIE, David, M .... 301-687-4396 .... 228 C
dgillespie@frostburg.edu

GILLESPIE, Donald, A .... 718-817-3190 .... 334 C
gillespie@fordham.edu

GILLESPIE, Gregory .... 928-717-7778 ...... 19 E
greg.gillespie@yc.edu

GILLESPIE, Jason .... 513-244-8442 .... 387 D
jason.gillespie@ccuniversity.edu

GILLESPIE, Joseph, E .... 610-558-5641 .... 437 C
gillespj@neumann.edu

GILLESPIE, SJ, Kevin .... 312-915-7619 .... 157 A
kgillespie2@luc.edu

GILLESPIE, Maggie .... 570-389-4950 .... 441 F
mgillesp@bloomu.edu

GILLESPIE, Michael .... 212-220-8323 .... 326 E
mgillespie@bmcc.cuny.edu

GILLESPIE, Nancy, N .... 260-399-7700 .... 180 E
ngillespie@sf.edu

GILLESPIE, Pamela .... 212-650-7271 .... 326 H
prgcc@ccny.cuny.edu

GILLESS, J. Keith .... 510-642-7171 ...... 73 E
gilless@nature.berkeley.edu

GILLET, Henri .... 312-413-7636 .... 166 F
gillet@uic.edu

GILLETT, Charisse .... 859-280-1254 .... 203 F
cgillett@lextheo.edu

GILLETT, William .... 603-668-2211 .... 306 B
w.gillett@snhu.edu

GILLETTE, Donna .... 207-947-4591 .... 217 D
dgillette@bealcollege.edu

GILLETTE, Jack .... 617-349-8401 .... 236 G
jgillett@lesley.edu

GILLETTE, Kimberly .... 218-282-8442 .... 272 A
gillette@umn.edu

GILLETTE, Lynn .... 775-831-1314 .... 303 E
lgillette@sierranevada.edu

GILLETTE, Maureen, D .... 773-442-5500 .... 159 H
m-gillette@neiu.edu

GILLETTE, Susan .... 410-706-5353 .... 227 C
sgillett@umaryland.edu

GILLETTE, Vivian .... 701-255-3285 .... 383 D
vgillette@uttc.edu

GILLEY, Michael .... 276-523-2400 .... 527 A
mgilley@me.vccs.edu

GILLIAM, Cynthia .... 832-813-6512 .... 490 C
cynthia.f.gilliam@lonestar.edu

GILLIAM, David .... 918-587-6789 .... 413 A
dgilliam@twsweld.com

GILLIAM, JR., Franklin, D 310-206-7568 ...... 74 A
fgilliam@conet.ucla.edu

GILLIAM, Fred .... 615-966-5887 .... 470 D
fred.gilliam@lipscomb.edu

GILLIAM, Janice, H .... 423-323-0201 .... 475 E
jgilliam@northeaststate.edu

GILLIAM, Jerry .... 270-707-3741 .... 202 A
jerry.gilliam@kctcs.edu

GILLIAM, Juanita .... 410-951-3055 .... 228 B
jgilliam@coppin.edu

GILLIAM, Kevin, E .... 616-538-2330 .... 251 F
kgilliam@gbcol.edu

GILLIAM, Michael .... 615-361-7555 .... 468 C
mgilliam@daymarinstitute.edu

GILLIAM, Thomas, J .... 850-484-1700 .... 114 G
tgilliam@pensacolastate.edu

GILLIAM, Tom .... 850-484-1500 .... 114 G
tgilliam@pensacolastate.edu

GILLICK, Megan .... 410-617-2290 .... 224 A
mgillick@loyola.edu

GILLIGAN, Pamela .... 781-768-7181 .... 244 D
pamela.gilligan@regiscollege.edu

GILLIGAN, Patrick, K .... 740-427-5643 .... 394 C
gilliganp@kenyon.edu

GILLIGAN, Thomas, J .... 402-466-4774 .... 298 A
thomas.gilligan@doane.edu

GILLIGAN, Thomas, W .... 512-471-5058 .... 505 B
dean.gilligan@mccombs.utexas.edu

GILLIGAN, William .... 617-824-8190 .... 234 D
william_gilligan@emerson.edu

GILLILAND, Christie .... 253-833-9111 .... 534 C
cgilliland@greenriver.edu

GILLILAND, Jane, A .... 607-587-3979 .... 355 C
gillilja@alfredstate.edu

GILLING RAYNOR,
Beatrice .... 718-951-6545 .... 326 G
braynor@brooklyn.cuny.edu

GILLIS, Arthur .... 337-521-8913 .... 212 B
agillis@southlouisiana.edu

GILLIS, Chester .... 202-687-4259 ...... 98 A
gillisc@georgetown.edu

GILLIS, Graham .... 501-450-3181 ...... 25 H
ggillis@uca.edu

GILLIS, Ida .... 219-980-6853 .... 173 F
ilgillis@iun.edu

GILLIS, Rick, D .... 414-955-6333 .... 548 E
rgillis@mcw.edu

GILLISPIE, Charley, E .... 219-464-5215 .... 181 A
charley.gillispie@valpo.edu

GILLISS, Buster .... 701-224-5512 .... 382 B
buster.gilliss@bismarckstate.edu

GILLISS, Catherine .... 919-684-3786 .... 363 I
catherine.gilliss@duke.edu

GILLMAN, Howard .... 213-740-2531 ...... 76 C
dean@college.usc.edu

GILLMAN, Patricia .... 660-596-7379 .... 290 F
pgillman@sfccmo.edu

GILLMAN, Rick .... 219-464-6718 .... 181 A
rick.gillman@valpo.edu

GILLMING, Kenneth, D .... 617-364-3510 .... 232 C
kgillming@boston.edu

GILLOGLY, Brenda .... 479-394-7622 ...... 23 E
bgillogly@rmcc.edu

GILLOOLY, Patrick .... 617-258-9276 .... 242 A
gillooly@mit.edu

GILLUM, Danny .... 620-227-9269 .... 192 B
dgillum@dc3.edu

GILLUS, Raynaldo .... 937-376-6205 .... 386 H
rgillus@centralstate.edu

GILMAN, Frederick, J .... 412-268-5124 .... 424 H
gilman@andrew.cmu.edu

GILMAN, Jean .... 314-977-3415 .... 289 F
jgilman2@slu.edu

GILMAN, Josephine .... 301-387-3091 .... 222 H
josephine.gilman@garrettcollege.edu

GILMAN, Mary, A .... 864-597-4010 .... 463 F
gilmanaf@wofford.edu

GILMAN, Regis .... 828-227-7397 .... 379 E
rgilman@wcu.edu

GILMAN, Roger .... 360-650-3681 .... 539 C
roger.gilman@wwu.edu

GILMAN, Sarah, S .... 808-455-0497 .... 141 C

GILMARTIN, Maureen, A ...... 410-827-5842 .... 222 B
mgilmartin@chesapeake.edu

GILMARTIN, Michael .... 831-646-4039 ...... 57 G
mgilmartin@mpc.edu

GILMER, Elizabeth .... 478-289-2037 .... 128 J
egilmer@ega.edu

GILMER, Francene .... 859-257-1564 .... 206 H
fgi222@uky.edu

GILMER, Garrett .... 419-372-2081 .... 385 C
ggilmer@bgsu.edu

GILMER, Randy, G .... 276-328-0312 .... 525 C
rgg8z@uvawise.edu

GILMORE, Becky .... 913-360-7578 .... 190 F
bgilmore@benedictine.edu

GILMORE, Calvin, L .... 336-272-7102 .... 364 D
gilmorec@greensborocollege.edu

GILMORE, Daniel .... 808-735-4831 .... 140 A
dgilmore@chaminade.edu

GILMORE, Don .... 661-362-2811 ...... 56 G
dgilmore@masters.edu

GILMORE, Elizabeth .... 575-758-8914 .... 318 G
info@midwiferycollege.org

GILMORE, Grover, C .... 216-368-2270 .... 386 E
gcg@case.edu

GILMORE, Jennifer, D .... 812-888-5332 .... 181 B
jgilmore@vinu.edu

GILMORE, John, W .... 609-497-7705 .... 312 F
john.gilmore@ptsem.edu

GILMORE, Kevin, P .... 913-971-3294 .... 195 A
kgilmore@mnu.edu

GILMORE, Laurie, A .... 518-438-3111 .... 340 B
laurieg@mariacollege.edu

GILMORE, Maureen .... 585-266-0430 .... 333 E
mgilmore@cci.edu

GILMORE, Rick .... 816-271-4527 .... 287 A
gilmore@missouriwestern.edu

GILMORE, Robert .... 914-323-5376 .... 340 A
robert.gilmore@mville.edu

GILMORE, Sherri .... 802-485-2001 .... 514 A
sgilmore@norwich.edu

GILMORE, Stephanie .... 717-245-1063 .... 427 E
gilmores@dickinson.edu

GILMOUR, Allan .... 313-577-2230 .... 260 D
Allan.Gilmour@wayne.edu

GILMOUR, Davie, J .... 570-326-3761 .... 438 F
djg120@psu.edu

GILMOUR, Davie Jane .... 570-326-3761 .... 440 K
dgilmour@pct.edu

GILMOUR, Joseph, E .... 570-408-4000 .... 451 G
joseph.gilmour@wilkes.edu

GILNER, David .... 513-487-3273 .... 391 E
dgilner@huc.edu

GILNETT, Jennifer, J .... 206-281-2974 .... 537 D
jgilnett@spu.edu

GILOT, Sandra .... 973-618-3353 .... 308 D
sgilot@caldwell.edu

GILOTH, Copper, F .... 413-545-4833 .... 237 C
giloth@oit.umass.edu

GILPATRICK, Russell .... 623-572-3804 ...... 16 F
rgilpa@midwestern.edu

GILPIN, Sue .... 309-268-8139 .... 151 G
sue.gilpin@heartland.edu

GILREATH, Charles .... 979-845-8160 .... 497 C
charles-gilreath@tamu.edu

GILROY, Janice .... 914-606-6610 .... 360 D
janice.gilroy@sunywcc.edu

GILROY, Jim .... 575-737-6224 .... 321 F
gilroy@unm.edu

GILROY, Maryellen .... 518-783-2328 .... 350 I
mgilroy@siena.edu

GILSON, David .... 216-791-5000 .... 388 B
david.gilson@case.edu

GILSON, Ken .... 562-903-4870 ...... 30 H
ken.gilson@biola.edu

GILSON, William, C .... 505-662-0339 .... 321 E
wgilson@unm.edu

GILSRUD, Linda, J .... 218-755-3966 .... 266 B
lgilsrud@bemidjistate.edu

GILSTRAP, Don .... 316-978-3586 .... 197 F
don.gilstrap@wichita.edu

GILT, Thomas, N .... 330-287-1486 .... 399 A
gilt.1@osu.edu

GILTNER, Beverly, S .... 214-333-5303 .... 484 C
beverly@dbu.edu

GILTZ, Scott .... 503-594-3440 .... 415 A
scottg@clackamas.edu

GIMA, Wesley, T .... 671-735-3025 .... 559 B
gcc.itcinfo@guamcc.edu

GIMENEZ, Clara .... 802-831-1323 .... 515 A
cgimenez@vermontlaw.edu

GIMENEZ, Rochelle, P .... 860-465-5279 ...... 91 H
gimenezr@easternct.edu

GIN, David .... 510-430-3264 ...... 57 D
dgin@mills.edu

GINDELE, Linda, K .... 513-556-1301 .... 403 D
linda.gindele@uc.edu

GINDER, Amy .... 775-445-3240 .... 303 B
aginder@wnc.edu

GINDER, Bernice .... 732-445-1749 .... 314 B
ginder@rutgers.edu

GINDER, Greg .... 317-955-6018 .... 177 G
gginder@marian.edu

GINDER, Terry .... 212-217-4260 .... 333 G
terry_ginder@fitnyc.edu

GINES, Joan, E .... 801-585-9144 .... 510 L
joan.gines@utah.edu

GINES, Scott .... 361-593-2414 .... 498 A
scott.gines@tamuk.edu

GINESE, Joseph .... 508-213-2112 .... 243 J
joseph.ginese@nichols.edu

GINEVAN, Douglas, W .... 207-786-6093 .... 217 C
dginevan@bates.edu

GINGERELLA, David .... 978-556-3924 .... 241 B
dgingerella@necc.mass.edu

GINGERICH, Jeffrey .... 610-902-8302 .... 423 H
jpg722@cabrini.edu

GINGERICH, Orval, J .... 612-330-1383 .... 261 G
gingerio@augsburg.edu

GLENN, Nancy .... 304-214-8852 .... 543 A
nglenn@wvncc.edu

GLENN, Nannette .... 214-459-2296 .... 480 G
nglenn@argosy.edu

GLENN, Robert, K .... 256-233-8201 .... 1 F
bob.glenn@athens.edu

GLENN, Sharon .... 706-771-4146 .... 125 D
sglenn@augustatech.edu

GLENN, Thomas .... 312-996-5133 .... 166 F
teglenn@uic.edu

GLENN, William .... 575-527-7776 .... 319 G
bglenn@nmsu.edu

GLENN-SUMMITT, Peggy .. 918-456-5511 .... 409 A
glennsum@nsuok.edu

GLENNON, Catherine .... 715-346-2441 .... 552 B
cglennon@uwsp.edu

GLESSNER, Lisa .... 724-805-2933 .... 446 E
lisa.glessner@email.stvincent.edu

GLEZERMAN, David, R .... 215-204-7269 .... 447 G
david.glezerman@temple.edu

GLICK, Kristel .... 772-546-5534 .... 110 J
kristelglick@hsbc.edu

GLICK, Michael, L .... 716-829-2836 .... 351 G
sdm-dean@buffalo.edu

GLICK, Steven .... 330-263-2590 .... 388 E
sglick@wooster.edu

GLICK, William, H .... 713-348-5928 .... 492 J
glickb@rice.edu

GLICKMAN, Gena .... 860-512-3100 .... 90 C
gglickman@mcc.commnet.edu

GLICKSTEIN, Shelley .... 310-314-6047 ...... 29 J

GLIDDEN, Stacey, T .... 978-468-7111 .... 235 F
sglidden@gcts.edu

GLIDDEN, Sue .... 715-634-4790 .... 547 G
sglidden@lco.edu

GLIDEWELL, Chris .... 618-536-3345 .... 164 H
cglide@siu.edu

GLIDWELL, Bob .... 417-328-1550 .... 290 E
bglidwell@sbuniv.edu

GLIEM, Valerie .... 727-864-8408 .... 104 K
gliemvm@eckerd.edu

GLIER, Nancy .... 513-562-6265 .... 384 A
nglier@artacademy.edu

GLIHA, John .... 530-895-2906 ...... 31 E
glihajo@butte.edu

GLINDEMANN, Kent, E .... 276-223-4885 .... 528 F
wcglink@wcc.vccs.edu

GLINES, Carol, A .... 563-333-6329 .... 188 D
GlinesCarolA@sau.edu

GLINES, Debbie .... 404-237-7573 .... 125 F
dglines@bauder.edu

GLINES, Marsha, A .... 561-237-7881 .... 113 D
mglines@lynn.edu

GLINIECKI, Anita .... 203-332-5224 ...... 90 B
agliniecki@hcc.commnet.edu

GLISSON, Michael .... 602-286-8030 ...... 15 I
micheal.glisson@gwmail.maricopa.edu

GLISSON, Tony, L .... 270-745-5360 .... 207 C
tony.glisson@wku.edu

GLOBIS, Roxanne .... 609-633-9658 .... 316 A
rglobis@tesc.edu

GLOCK, Jon, W .... 563-588-8000 .... 184 F
jglock@emmaus.edu

GLOD, Carol, A .... 978-542-7044 .... 239 B
cglod@salemstate.edu

GLODO, Michael, J .... 407-366-9493 .... 115 I
mglodo@rts.edu

GLOEGE, Martin .... 303-280-7476 ...... 84 C
mgloege@devry.edu

GLOGOWSKI, Maryruth, F . 716-878-6314 .... 353 A
glogowmf@buffalostate.edu

GLORE, Susan, J .... 410-871-3305 .... 224 D
sglore@mcdaniel.edu

GLORIA, Jackie .... 858-566-1200 ...... 43 J
jgloria@disd.edu

GLOSSER, Wade, W .... 816-654-7717 .... 283 J
bglosser@kcumb.edu

GLOSTER, II, Arthur .... 401-232-6196 .... 453 A
agloster@bryant.edu

GLOSTER, Sandra .... 803-780-1019 .... 463 B
sdgloster@voorhees.edu

GLOTZBACH, Philip, A .... 518-580-5700 .... 351 B
pglotzba@skidmore.edu

GLOVEN, Greta .... 303-765-3109 ...... 84 K
ggloven@iliff.edu

GLOVER, Charles .... 215-702-4301 .... 444 A
bookstore@pbu.edu

GLOVER, David .... 757-727-5259 .... 519 C
david.glover@hamptonu.edu

GLOVER, Devon, H .... 208-524-3000 .... 143 C
devon.glover@my.eitc.edu

GLOVER, Diane, F .... 919-718-7231 .... 368 H
dglover@cccc.edu

GLOVER, Glenda, B .... 601-979-2411 .... 275 A
glenda.b.glover@jsums.edu

GLOVER, Jamie, L .... 580-581-2987 .... 407 D
jglover@cameron.edu

GLOVER, Joseph .... 352-392-2404 .... 120 B
jglover@aa.ufl.edu

GLOVER, Joseph, M .... 812-941-2028 .... 174 D
joglover@ius.edu

GLOVER, Josh .... 515-244-4221 .... 181 D
gloverj@aib.edu

GLOVER, Nathaniel .... 904-470-8010 .... 105 A
n.glover@ewc.edu

GLOVER, Paula .... 660-263-4110 .... 287 B
paulag@macc.edu

GLOVER-BROWN,
Michelle .... 516-876-2787 .... 353 D
brownmi@oldwestbury.edu

GLOWKA, Arthur, W .... 770-720-5628 .... 135 F
awg@reinhardt.edu

GLUCK, Daniel .... 916-577-2200 ...... 79 C
dgluck@jessup.edu

GLUCKOWSKY, Moshe, M 718-774-3430 .... 325 J

GLUSKER, Marjorie .... 914-606-6585 .... 360 D
marge.glusker@sunywcc.edu

GLYNN, Christine, L .... 414-410-4083 .... 546 D
clglynn@stritch.edu

GLYNN, John, B .... 414-410-4313 .... 546 D
jbglynn@stritch.edu

GLYNN, Patrick, M .... 314-434-2212 .... 283 B
pglynn@hickeycollege.edu

GMEINER, Rebecca .... 678-466-4145 .... 127 A
rebeccagmeiner@clayton.edu

GMELCH, Walter, H .... 415-422-2108 ...... 76 B
whgmelch@usfca.edu

GNADE, Bruce .... 972-883-6636 .... 505 D
gnade@utdallas.edu

GNADINGER, Cindy, G .... 502-272-8259 .... 198 E
cgnadinger@bellarmine.edu

GNAGE, David, C .... 717-749-6061 .... 440 A
dcg12@psu.edu

GNAN, Peter, D .... 708-209-3192 .... 148 C
pete.gnan@cuchicago.edu

GNASSO, Emil, A .... 610-758-3200 .... 434 E
emg3@lehigh.edu

GNIADY, Carol .... 504-762-3018 .... 210 G
cgniad@dcc.edu

GNIEWEK, Julie, A .... 920-923-8080 .... 548 C
jagniewek78@marianuniversity.edu

GNIOT, Phillip .... 606-783-2097 .... 204 E
p.gniot@moreheadstate.edu

GOAD, Frank .... 859-858-3511 .... 198 B
frank.goad@asbury.edu

GOAD, Philip .... 256-766-6610 .... 4 C
pgoad@hcu.edu

GOAD, William .... 405-425-1870 .... 409 E
bill.goad@oc.edu

GOAN, Bradley, L .... 859-233-8300 .... 206 E
bgoan@transy.edu

GOBAR, Angela .... 601-979-0663 .... 275 A
angela.m.gobar@jsums.edu

GOBBI, Laura .... 510-430-2112 ...... 57 D
lgobbi@mills.edu

GOBBLE, Sheryl .... 619-388-7428 ...... 65 H
sgobble@sdccd.edu

GOBEN, Allen .... 309-268-8100 .... 151 G
allen.goben@heartland.edu

GOBER, Chris, G .... 636-922-8211 .... 288 E
cgober@stchas.edu

GOBER, T. Kale .... 870-230-5072 ...... 21 I
gobertk@hsu.edu

GOBLE, Daniel .... 203-837-8851 ...... 92 A
gobled@wcsu.edu

GOBLET, Lois, E .... 518-255-5524 .... 354 E
gobletle@cobleskill.edu

GOCALA, John, J .... 330-941-3527 .... 406 F
jjgocala@ysu.edu

GOCHENAUR, Heather, K .. 260-982-5873 .... 177 F
hkgochenaur@manchester.edu

GOCHENAUR, Jack, A .... 260-982-5245 .... 177 F
jagochenaur@manchester.edu

GOCHNAUER, Richard, D .. 302-356-6795 ...... 97 A
richard.d.gochnauer@wilmu.edu

GOCIAL, Tammy .... 314-529-6893 .... 284 F
tgocial@maryville.edu

GOCKE, Philip .... 417-833-2551 .... 279 I
pgocke@cbcag.edu

GOCKEN, Drew .... 515-965-7120 .... 183 E
rdgocken@dmacc.edu

GOCKLEY, Daniel, L .... 304-367-4216 .... 543 E
dan.gockley@fairmontstate.edu

GODAR, Mark, E .... 641-269-3300 .... 185 A
godar@grinnell.edu

GODBOLD, Heidi .... 719-638-6580 ...... 84 E
hgodbold@cci.edu

GODBOUT, Muriel .... 315-364-3356 .... 360 C
mgodbout@wells.edu

GODDARD, Diane, H .... 785-864-4904 .... 196 F
dgoddard@ku.edu

GODDARD, Scott, D .... 304-637-1352 .... 540 F
goddards@dewv.edu

GODDING, Jesse .... 972-825-4811 .... 495 D
jgodding@sagu.edu

GODEK, Christine .... 212-237-8628 .... 328 A
cgodek@jjay.cuny.edu

GODEK, Jim .... 949-376-6000 ...... 53 E
jgodek@lagunacollege.edu

GODENZI, Alberto, A .... 617-552-4020 .... 232 D
alberto.godenzi.1@bc.edu

GODES, Iris .... 508-854-4260 .... 241 C
igodes@qcc.mass.edu

GODFREY, Abby .... 215-591-5700 .... 427 A
agodfrey@devry.edu

GODFREY, Blanton .... 919-515-6500 .... 378 B
blanton_godfrey@ncsu.edu

GODFREY, Christian, J .... 208-524-3000 .... 143 C
christian.godfrey@my.eitc.edu

GODFREY, Christine .... 415-257-1365 ...... 45 B
christine.godfrey@dominican.edu

GODFREY, Cornelia, B .... 617-422-7401 .... 243 G
cgodfrey@admin.nesl.edu

GODFREY, Eric .... 206-543-0128 .... 538 F
egodfrey@uw.edu

GODFREY, Herbert, G .... 570-208-5834 .... 432 E
hggodfre@kings.edu

GODFREY, Kenneth, G .... 906-227-1826 .... 256 F
kgodfrey@nmu.edu

GODFREY, Kevin .... 610-796-8365 .... 421 F
kevin.godfrey@alvernia.edu

GODFREY, Robert .... 928-524-7431 ...... 17 B
robert.godfrey@npc.edu

GODFREY, W. Robert .... 760-480-8474 ...... 78 E
bvansolkema@wscal.edu

GODFREY-DAWSON,
Angela, R .... 252-335-0821 .... 369 D
adawson@albemarle.edu

GODIN, Norm .... 951-222-8000 ...... 64 B

GODIN, Roger, A .... 717-291-3989 .... 429 E
roger.godin@fandm.edu

GODINA, Estela .... 312-226-6294 .... 156 E
busofc1@lexingtoncollege.edu

GODINO, Trish .... 603-271-6984 .... 304 G
tgodino@ccsnh.edu

GODLESKI, Mark, G .... 315-445-4520 .... 338 B
godlesmg@lemoyne.edu

GODLEY, Linda .... 601-304-4300 .... 273 C
godley@alcorn.edu

GODO, James .... 630-637-5809 .... 159 F
jwgodo@noctrl.edu

GODOW, JR., Rew .... 843-574-6788 .... 461 G

GODSEY, Jim .... 507-288-4563 .... 263 D
library@crossroadscollege.edu

GODSEY, R. Kirby .... 478-301-5750 .... 133 F
godsey_rk@mercer.edu

GODWIN, Donald .... 619-260-4588 ...... 76 A
donald.godwin@sandiego.edu

GODWIN, Donald .... 505-272-3241 .... 321 C
dgodwin@salud.unm.edu

GODWIN, Jack .... 916-278-6686 ...... 35 E
jgodwin@csus.edu

GODWIN, Joseph, H .... 616-331-2400 .... 252 A
godwinj@gvsu.edu

GODWIN, Michael, R .... 662-325-1332 .... 276 A
mgodwin@utc.msstate.edu

GODWIN, Ronald, S .... 434-582-7600 .... 520 F
rgodwin@liberty.edu

GODWIN, Wendell .... 580-559-5274 .... 407 J
wgodwin@ecok.edu

GODZWA, Alicia .... 540-362-6660 .... 519 E
agodzwa@hollins.edu

GOEB, Rick, A .... 218-755-4022 .... 266 B
rgoeb@bemidjistate.edu

GOEBEL, Jeffrey, D .... 218-477-2069 .... 268 A
goebelj@mnstate.edu

GOEBEL, Ken .... 603-358-2378 .... 307 A
kgoebel@keene.edu

GOECKER, James, A .... 812-877-8894 .... 179 A
james.goecker@rose-hulman.edu

GOEDDE, Tony, G .... 419-434-4556 .... 404 B
goedde@findlay.edu

GOEDEKE, Allen .... 336-841-9191 .... 365 A
agoedeke@highpoint.edu

GOEDERT, JoAnn .... 301-445-1921 .... 227 A
sansbury@usmd.edu

GOEL, Meeta .... 970-945-8691 ...... 82 C

GOELDNER, Jason .... 715-365-4534 .... 554 F
jgoeldner@nicoletcollege.edu

GOELLNER, Marilyn .... 814-732-1778 .... 442 D
mgoellner@edinboro.edu

GOELOE-ALSTON,
Hendrina .... 718-270-1191 .... 352 D
hgoeloe-alston@downstate.edu

GOELZHAUSER,
Michael, J .... 812-464-1717 .... 180 F
mjgoelzh@usi.edu

GOEN, Jennifer .... 239-590-1020 .... 119 A
jgoen@fgcu.edu

GOEPPINGER, Kathleen, H 630-515-7300 .... 158 E
drgoeppinger@midwestern.edu

GOEPPINGER, Kathleen, H 623-572-3400 ...... 16 F
kgoepp@midwestern.edu

GOERING, Doug .... 907-474-7730 ...... 10 J
djgoering@alaska.edu

GOERING, Fred .... 316-284-5250 .... 190 H
fgoering@bethelks.edu

GOERING, Wynn .... 505-277-2611 .... 321 C
wgoering@unm.edu

GOERING, Wynn, M .... 505-277-0896 .... 321 C
wgoering@unm.edu

GOERTEMILLER, Paul .... 903-510-2389 .... 502 E
pgoe@tjc.edu

GOERTLER, Reed .... 707-638-5259 ...... 72 H
reed.goertler@tu.edu

GOERTZ, Christine .... 563-884-5159 .... 188 C
christine.goertz@palmer.edu

GOERTZ, Christine, G .... 563-884-5159 ...... 60 L
christine.goertz@palmer.edu

GOERTZ, Christine, G .... 563-884-5159 .... 114 E
christine.goertz@palmer.edu

GOERTZEN, Leroy .... 253-759-6104 .... 415 F
lgoertzen@nbs.edu

GOERTZEN, Ryan .... 918-836-6886 .... 412 G
rgoertzen@mail.spartan.edu

GOERZEN, Les .... 316-284-5261 .... 190 H
lgoerzen@bethelks.edu

GOETHE, Corey .... 989-386-6622 .... 255 F
cgoethe@midmich.edu

GOETSCH, David, L .... 850-863-6501 .... 114 A
goetsch@nwfsc.edu

GOETSCH, Lori, A .... 785-532-7402 .... 194 B
lgoetsch@ksu.edu

GOETSCH, Steven .... 203-837-8286 ...... 92 A
goetschs@wcsu.edu

GOETSCHIUS, Susan, C .... 607-871-2170 .... 322 F
goetschius@alfred.edu

GOETT, Felica .... 303-937-4200 ...... 82 A
fgoett@chu.edu

GOETZ, Bruce, P .... 303-273-3225 ...... 82 F
bgoetz@mines.edu

GOETZ, Michael, A .... 414-847-3305 .... 548 G
mikegoetz@miad.edu

GOETZ, William, G .... 701-328-2963 .... 381 C

GOETZE, David .... 810-989-5761 .... 258 B
dpgoetze@sc4.edu

GOETZMAN, David .... 719-587-7820 ...... 80 F
degoetzm@adams.edu

GOEWERT, Ed .... 618-374-5109 .... 161 D

GOFF, Allen .... 836-686-1444 .... 105 I
agoff@cci.edu

GOFF, Anton .... 301-860-3571 .... 228 A
agoff@bowiestate.edu

GOFF, Billie Jean .... 607-753-4728 .... 353 B
billie.goff@cortland.edu

GOFF, Catherine .... 509-359-6362 .... 533 D
cgoff@ewu.edu

GOFF, David, W .... 870-236-6901 ...... 21 E
dgoff@crc.edu

GOFF, Gary .... 865-882-4501 .... 475 G
goffdg@roanestate.edu

GOFF, Jay, W .... 573-341-4378 .... 292 A
goffjw@mst.edu

GOFF, Karen .... 732-987-2601 .... 310 D
kgoff@georgian.edu

GOFF, Kathleen .... 413-542-2226 .... 230 A
kgoff@amherst.edu

GOFF, Melissa, L .... 501-450-5371 ...... 25 H
mgoff@uca.edu

GOFF, Michelle .... 478-289-2095 .... 128 J
mgoff@ega.edu

GOFF, Patricia, A .... 401-865-1031 .... 453 F
pgoff@providence.edu

GOFF, Susan .... 707-468-3131 ...... 57 A
sgoff@mendocino.edu

GOFF-CREWS, Kimberley .... 773-702-7770 .... 166 D
kgoffcrews@uchicago.edu

GOFFENA-BEYER, Tricia .... 928-350-2002 ...... 18 C
tgoffena@prescott.edu

GOFFNETT, Chris .... 989-386-6622 .... 255 F
cgoffnett@midmich.edu

GOFORTH, Craig .... 828-689-1405 .... 366 F
cgoforth@mhc.edu

GOGGIN, Megan .... 312-226-6294 .... 156 E
pr@lexingtoncollege.edu

GOGGIN, Paul .... 614-287-2424 .... 388 G
pgoggin@cscc.edu

GOGGIN, Trudi .... 708-524-6824 .... 150 A
tgoggin@dom.edu

GOGNAT, Tim .... 937-327-7457 .... 406 B
tgognat@wittenberg.edu

GOGOL, Miriam .... 914-674-3033 .... 340 G
mgogol@mercy.edu

GOGUE, Jay .... 334-844-4650 .... 1 G
president@auburn.edu

GOHLKE, Brian, B .... 608-757-7773 .... 553 E
bgohlke@blackhawk.edu

GOHLKE, Michael .... 630-844-6509 .... 145 C
mgohlke@aurora.edu

GOHMANN, Jennifer .... 502-585-9911 .... 205 I
jgohmann@spalding.edu

GOHN, Sherry .... 360-442-2216 .... 535 C
sgohn@lowercolumbia.edu

GOIN, Jay .... 972-385-1055 ...... 19 C
jay.goin@phoenix.edu

GOIN, JR., Randy, A .... 850-245-0466 .... 118 F
randy.goin@flbog.edu

GOINES, Shirley, M .... 479-968-0399 ...... 20 G
sgoines@atu.edu

GOINGS, Amy .... 253-589-5782 .... 532 B
amy.goings@cptc.edu

GOINGS, Eric .... 918-335-6257 .... 411 B
egoings@okwu.edu

GOINGS, James .... 918-335-6263 .... 411 B
jgoings@okwu.edu

GOINS, David .... 409-882-3367 .... 500 G
david.goins@lsco.edu

GOINS, Jessica, D .... 864-488-4590 .... 459 A
jgoins@limestone.edu

GOINS, Scott, E .... 337-475-5329 .... 215 G
sgoins@mcneese.edu

GOKE, Evelyn .... 906-487-7272 .... 251 C
evelyn.goke@finlandia.edu

GOKE-PARIOLA, Abiodun . 704-337-2492 .... 375 G
g-p@queens.edu

GONZALES, Junius .... 915-747-5725 .... 505 E jjxgonzales@utep.edu
GONZALES, Katharine .... 504-394-7744 .... 214 A kgonzales@olhcc.edu
GONZALES, Lucinda, A ..... 972-860-7668 .... 484 H LucindaGonzales@dcccd.edu
GONZALES, Maria .... 865-882-4628 .... 475 G gonzalesmr@roanestate.edu
GONZALES, Mark .... 408-274-7900 ..... 67 B mark.gonzales@evc.edu
GONZALES, Mona .... 785-749-8448 .... 193 B mona.gonzales@bie.edu
GONZALES, Oscar .... 713-718-7561 .... 487 G oscar.gonzales@hccs.edu
GONZALES, Patricia .... 575-737-6200 .... 321 F patrodr@unm.edu
GONZALES, Rhonda .... 719-549-2315 ..... 83 B rhonda.gonzales@colostate-pueblo.edu
GONZALES, Ron .... 505-454-5305 .... 318 E rgonzales@luna.edu
GONZALES, Roxanne .... 303-458-1844 ..... 87 E rmgonzales@regis.edu
GONZALES, Rudy .... 337-521-8949 .... 212 B rudy.gonzales@southlouisiana.edu
GONZALES, Samuel, M ...... 210-458-4595 .... 506 B samuel.gonzales@utsa.edu
GONZALES, Sandra, M ...... 602-944-3335 ..... 11 D sgonzales@aicag.edu
GONZALES, Steven .... 480-677-6750 ..... 13 F steven.gonzales@centralaz.edu
GONZALES-MCKOSKY, Latricia .... 505-438-8884 .... 320 H latricia@acupuncturecollege.edu
GONZALEZ, Alex .... 505-277-4792 .... 321 C agonzale@unm.edu
GONZALEZ, Alex .... 574-252-8256 .... 169 F alex.gonzalez@bethelcollege.edu
GONZALEZ, Alexander .... 916-278-7737 ..... 35 E alexg@csus.edu
GONZALEZ, Alfredo, G ...... 323-343-3830 ..... 35 B alfredo@cslanet.calstatela.edu
GONZALEZ, Angel .... 787-841-2000 .... 564 I agonzalez@email.pucpr.edu
GONZALEZ, Angie .... 956-364-4500 .... 499 J angie.gonzalez@harlingen.tstc.edu
GONZALEZ, Antonio .... 787-265-3877 .... 567 C antonio@uprm.edu
GONZALEZ, Bethaida .... 315-443-3259 .... 357 B bgonzale@syr.edu
GONZALEZ, Blanca, M ...... 787-250-1912 .... 563 E bmgonzalez@metro.inter.edu
GONZALEZ, Brenda .... 806-291-3564 .... 508 B gonzalezb@wbu.edu
GONZALEZ, Carla .... 313-664-7457 .... 250 A cgonzalez@collegeforcreativestudies.edu
GONZALEZ, Carmen .... 787-841-2000 .... 564 I cgonzalez@email.pucpr.edu
GONZALEZ, Carmen .... 787-894-2828 .... 568 A carmen.gonzalez19@upr.edu
GONZALEZ, Carmen, I ...... 787-857-3600 .... 563 A cigonzalez@br.inter.edu
GONZALEZ, Carolina, E .... 973-290-4345 .... 309 A cgonzalez01@cse.edu
GONZALEZ, Caroline .... 787-786-3030 .... 560 F cagonzalez@ucb.edu.pr
GONZALEZ, Cheryl, N .... 904-620-2507 .... 120 C cheryl.gonzalez@unf.edu
GONZALEZ, Cisco .... 616-222-3000 .... 254 A cgonzalez@kuyper.edu
GONZALEZ, Clara .... 954-322-4460 .... 112 B
GONZALEZ, Daniela .... 787-844-8621 .... 567 E dgonzalez@uprp.edu
GONZALEZ, Debra .... 787-894-2828 .... 568 A debra.gonzalez1@upr.edu
GONZALEZ, Diana .... 515-242-6116 .... 182 A
GONZALEZ, Eladio .... 787-894-2828 .... 568 A eladio.gonzalez1@upr.edu
GONZALEZ, Eleazar .... 956-721-5142 .... 489 G elegon@laredo.edu
GONZALEZ, Elidine .... 787-891-0925 .... 562 G egonzale@aguadilla.inter.edu
GONZALEZ, Elma, D .... 936-261-2124 .... 496 E edgonzalez@pvamu.edu
GONZALEZ, Elmer .... 787-728-1515 .... 568 B elmer@sagrado.edu
GONZALEZ, Esther .... 336-917-5579 .... 376 C esther.gonzalez@salem.edu
GONZALEZ, Fernando .... 787-884-6000 .... 562 E fgonzalez@icprjc.edu
GONZALEZ, Francisco .... 787-891-0925 .... 562 G fgonzale@aquadilla.inter.edu
GONZALEZ, George .... 281-998-6150 .... 493 D george.gonzalez@sjcd.edu
GONZALEZ, Gerardo .... 812-856-8001 .... 173 C gonzalez@indiana.edu
GONZALEZ, Gladys .... 305-626-3677 .... 108 H gladys.gonzalez@fmuniv.edu
GONZALEZ, Griselda .... 212-217-4000 .... 333 G griselda_gonzalez@fitnyc.edu
GONZALEZ, Hector .... 609-894-9311 .... 308 C hgonzale@bcc.edu
GONZALEZ, Herman .... 623-845-3562 ..... 15 J herman.gonzalez@gcmail.maricopa.edu
GONZALEZ, Iris, P .... 785-670-1470 .... 197 D iris.gonzalez@washburn.edu
GONZALEZ, J, E .... 727-873-4716 .... 121 B jegon@mail.usf.edu
GONZALEZ, Jaime .... 787-620-2040 .... 560 B trodriguez@aupr.edu
GONZALEZ, Jean .... 714-867-5009 ..... 70 C
GONZALEZ, Jeffery .... 305-348-2731 .... 119 B jeff@fiu.edu
GONZALEZ, Jorge .... 323-259-2634 ..... 59 H jgonzale@oxy.edu
GONZALEZ, Jorge .... 787-725-6500 .... 560 G jorgegonzalez4@pfizer.com
GONZALEZ, Jorge .... 601-977-0960 .... 278 C jorge.gonazlez@vc.edu
GONZALEZ, Jose .... 914-323-5445 .... 340 A gonzalezjr@mville.edu
GONZALEZ, Juan, C .... 512-471-1133 .... 505 B juan.gonzalez@austin.utexas.edu
GONZALEZ, Judith .... 787-766-1717 .... 565 G jugonzalez@suagm.edu
GONZALEZ, Karen .... 787-766-1717 .... 565 G um_kgonzalez@suagm.edu
GONZALEZ, Linda .... 915-831-2566 .... 486 E lgonz265@epcc.edu
GONZALEZ, Lizbeth .... 603-882-6923 .... 304 F lgonzalez@ccsnh.edu
GONZALEZ, Lori .... 574-252-8526 .... 169 F lori.gonzalez@bethelcollege.edu
GONZALEZ, Lori, S .... 859-323-1100 .... 206 H lsgonz01@uky.edu
GONZALEZ, Luis .... 724-357-2330 .... 442 E Luis.Gonzalez@iup.edu
GONZALEZ, Luz .... 559-278-3013 ..... 34 D luz_gonzalez@csufresno.edu
GONZALEZ, Maria .... 305-273-4499 .... 103 C registrar@cbt.edu
GONZALEZ, Marilyn .... 787-882-2065 .... 565 I secretaria_ejecutiva@unitecpr.net
GONZALEZ, Marisol .... 787-264-1912 .... 563 G margonza@sg.inter.edu
GONZALEZ, Mary .... 361-593-2111 .... 498 A kamlp00@tamuk.edu
GONZALEZ, Mauricio .... 904-620-2600 .... 120 C mgonzale@unf.edu
GONZALEZ, Monica, D ...... 787-723-4481 .... 560 H mgonzalez@ceaprc.org
GONZALEZ, Nichole .... 716-375-2572 .... 348 C ngonzalez@sbu.edu
GONZALEZ, Noelia .... 209-667-3337 ..... 36 C ngonzalez@csustan.edu
GONZALEZ, Norma .... 210-486-4208 .... 479 C ngonzales43@alamo.edu
GONZALEZ, Orlando .... 787-284-1912 .... 563 F ochevere@ponce.inter.edu
GONZALEZ, Patricia .... 787-250-1912 .... 563 E pgonzalez@metro.inter.edu
GONZALEZ, Pepe .... 415-485-3242 ..... 45 B
GONZALEZ, R. Louie .... 219-932-3600 .... 176 E lgonzale@ivytech.edu
GONZALEZ, Raul, D .... 818-947-2606 ..... 55 E gonzalrd@lavc.edu
GONZALEZ, Reina, M .... 787-840-8108 .... 567 E reina.gonzalez@upr.edu
GONZALEZ, Reyes .... 414-256-1228 .... 549 A gonzaler@mtmary.edu
GONZALEZ, Roberto .... 310-434-4912 ..... 68 D gonzalez_roberto@smc.edu
GONZALEZ, Rocelia, T .... 904-620-2870 .... 120 C rrgonz@unf.edu
GONZALEZ, Rosa .... 787-891-0925 .... 562 G rgonzale@aguadilla.inter.edu
GONZALEZ, Ruben, L .... 516-876-3275 .... 353 D gonzalezr@oldwestbury.edu
GONZALEZ, Rudy .... 210-212-6080 .... 495 E rgonzalez@swbts.edu
GONZALEZ, Ruth .... 860-738-6315 ..... 90 F rgonzalez@nwcc.commnet.edu
GONZALEZ, Sandra .... 787-882-2065 .... 565 I
GONZALEZ, Sarai .... 787-746-1400 .... 562 C sgonzalez@huertas.edu
GONZALEZ, Saraliz .... 787-857-3600 .... 563 A sgonzalez@br.inter.edu
GONZALEZ, Sergio, M .... 305-284-4111 .... 122 F smgonzalez@miami.edu
GONZALEZ, Sophia .... 210-486-2247 .... 479 E fklein@alamo.edu
GONZALEZ, Stacy .... 515-244-2209 .... 348 A gonzas@sage.edu
GONZALEZ, Thomasa .... 609-652-4724 .... 313 F t.gonzalez@stockton.edu
GONZALEZ, Tina .... 212-799-5000 .... 337 H
GONZALEZ, Urania .... 787-720-1022 .... 560 D Administracion@atlanticcollege.edu
GONZALEZ, Virginia .... 787-743-7979 .... 565 F ut_vgonzalez@suagm.edu
GONZALEZ, W. Elmer .... 787-850-9345 .... 567 B elmer.gonzalez@upr.edu
GONZALEZ, Yanira .... 787-891-0925 .... 562 G ygonzalezez@aguadilla.inter.edu
GONZALEZ-BAEZ, Marilucy .... 787-751-1912 .... 564 A marigonza@inter.edu
GONZALEZ DE SCOLLARD, Edith .... 212-817-7520 .... 327 B egonzalez@gc.cuny.edu
GONZALEZ-GENERALS, Joann .... 973-618-3589 .... 308 D jgonzalez@caldwell.edu
GONZALEZ-LOPEZ, Taima 305-418-4220 .... 115 B tgonzalez@pupr.edu
GONZALEZ NIEVES, Rosa, E .... 787-896-2252 .... 561 K rgonzalez@edpcollege.edu
GONZALEZ-SCARANO, Francisco .... 210-567-4432 .... 506 E scarano@uthscsa.edu
GOOCH, Cynthia .... 402-457-2649 .... 298 H cgooch@mccneb.edu
GOOCH, Gene .... 254-299-8679 .... 490 E ggooch@mclennan.edu
GOOCH, Janet .... 660-785-4383 .... 291 A jquinzek@truman.edu
GOOCH, Mary, E .... 936-261-1066 .... 496 E megooch@pvamu.edu
GOOCH, Michael .... 212-312-4428 .... 332 B mgooch@devry.edu
GOOD, Barry .... 406-243-7851 .... 295 D barry.good@umontana.edu
GOOD, Barry .... 406-243-7811 .... 295 A barry.good@umontana.edu
GOOD, Chad .... 847-543-2477 .... 147 H cgood@clcillinois.edu
GOOD, Gayle .... 586-445-7302 .... 254 F goodg@macomb.edu
GOOD, Jennifer .... 334-244-3481 .... 2 A jgood@aum.edu
GOOD, Joseph, C .... 843-792-4063 .... 459 C goodj@musc.edu
GOOD, Julie .... 505-428-1653 .... 320 E julie.good@sfcc.edu
GOOD, Kathy .... 864-596-9622 .... 457 E kathy.good@converse.edu
GOOD, Laura, E .... 330-823-6050 .... 404 C goodle@mountunion.edu
GOOD, Michael, L .... 352-273-7500 .... 120 B mgood@ufl.edu
GOOD, Rhonda .... 717-337-6015 .... 429 H rgood@gettysburg.edu
GOOD, Rhonda, L .... 717-766-2511 .... 436 D rgood@messiah.edu
GOOD, William .... 309-854-1831 .... 145 E goodb@bhc.edu
GOOD LUCK, Aldean .... 406-638-3118 .... 294 G goodlucka@lbhc.cc.mt.us
GOODACRE, Charles, J ..... 909-558-4683 ..... 54 D cgoodacre@llu.edu
GOODALE, Brian .... 518-587-2100 .... 355 F brian.goodale@esc.edu
GOODALL, Debbie .... 816-604-5280 .... 285 F debbie.goodall@mcckc.edu
GOODALL, Donetta .... 832-813-6597 .... 490 C donetta.p.goodall@lonestar.edu
GOODARZI, Shirin, M .... 410-777-2148 .... 221 B smgoodarzi@aacc.edu
GOODCUFF, Esther .... 516-877-3681 .... 322 A goodcuff@adelphi.edu
GOODE, Debbie .... 580-581-2255 .... 407 D debbieg@cameron.edu
GOODE, Greg, J .... 425-602-3006 .... 530 K ggoode@bastyr.edu
GOODE, Mark .... 714-432-5898 ..... 41 B mgoode@occ.cccd.edu
GOODE, Tammy .... 423-585-6845 .... 476 B tammy.goode@ws.edu
GOODELL, Neil, E .... 928-523-3937 ..... 17 A neil.goodell@nau.edu
GOODELL-LACKEY, Shirley, J .... 802-654-2586 .... 514 B sgoodell-lackey@smcvt.edu
GOODEN, Charles, H .... 314-340-5030 .... 282 I goodenc@hssu.edu
GOODEN, John .... 334-229-4240 .... 1 C jsgooden@alasu.edu
GOODEN, Winston, E .... 626-584-5501 ..... 48 A gooden@fuller.edu
GOODER, Kellee .... 307-532-8336 .... 555 H kellee.gooder@ewc.wy.edu
GOODFELLOW, Sandy .... 615-383-1340 .... 468 J alex@fwbbc.edu
GOODGAME, Henry .... 404-215-2658 .... 134 A hgoodgame@morehouse.edu
GOODHAND, Melony .... 501-686-5670 ..... 24 F mjgoodhand@uams.edu
GOODHEART, Harriet, K .... 610-660-1532 .... 446 C hgoodhea@sju.edu
GOODHIND, Deb .... 413-545-5542 .... 237 C dgoodhind@admin.umass.edu
GOODHUE, Bill .... 607-436-2532 .... 353 E goodhucw@oneonta.edu
GOODHUE, Robert, M .... 774-455-7191 .... 237 B rgoodhue@umassp.edu
GOODHUE LYNCH, Mary . 508-588-9100 .... 240 E
GOODIN, Ruth .... 925-439-2181 ..... 43 D rgoodin@losmedanos.edu
GOODING, Betsy .... 903-434-8137 .... 491 D bgooding@ntcc.edu
GOODING, Marjory .... 626-395-8808 ..... 32 E marjory.gooding@caltech.edu
GOODING, Mary, B .... 229-333-7444 .... 138 F mbgooding@valdosta.edu
GOODLING, Barry, G .... 717-796-5064 .... 436 D bgoodlin@messiah.edu
GOODLING, Eileen, J .... 716-338-1025 .... 337 E eileengoodling@mail.sunyjcc.edu
GOODLIVE, Kathy .... 707-476-4151 ..... 42 A kathy-goodlive@redwoods.edu
GOODMAN, Alan .... 413-559-5378 .... 235 G
GOODMAN, Brent, S .... 805-756-2204 ..... 33 F bgoodman@calpoly.edu
GOODMAN, Brittney, G ...... 218-477-2923 .... 268 A brittney.goodman@mnstate.edu
GOODMAN, Clay .... 623-935-8456 ..... 15 H clay.goodman@estrellamountain.edu
GOODMAN, Debbie .... 229-225-3978 .... 137 D dgoodman@southwestgatech.edu
GOODMAN, Elizabeth, A ... 636-227-2100 .... 284 E elizabeth.goodman@logan.edu
GOODMAN, George, A .... 636-227-2100 .... 284 E george.goodman@logan.edu
GOODMAN, Grayson .... 407-303-1631 .... 108 D grayson.goodman@fhchs.edu
GOODMAN, Guy .... 309-694-8970 .... 152 B ggoodman@icc.edu
GOODMAN, Jacque .... 641-844-5640 .... 185 H Jacque.Goodman@iavalley.edu
GOODMAN, Jacque .... 641-844-7106 .... 185 J jacque.goodman@iavalley.edu
GOODMAN, Jacqueline, K 315-267-2116 .... 354 C goodmajk@potsdam.edu
GOODMAN, James .... 808-455-0228 .... 142 A goodmanj@hawaii.edu
GOODMAN, Jeremy .... 617-739-1700 .... 243 F jgoodman@aii.edu
GOODMAN, Jerry, C .... 713-798-7234 .... 481 H jgoodman@bcm.edu
GOODMAN, Julie .... 308-432-6487 .... 299 G jgoodman@csc.edu
GOODMAN, Larry, J .... 312-942-7073 .... 163 B larry_j_goodman@rush.edu
GOODMAN, Lena, C .... 920-433-6638 .... 546 A lena.goodman@bellincollege.edu
GOODMAN, Marc, P .... 310-506-4670 ..... 61 G marc.goodman@pepperdine.edu
GOODMAN, Marshall .... 863-667-7053 .... 120 D mgoodman@poly.usf.edu
GOODMAN, Michael .... 504-988-6135 .... 215 C mgoodman@tulane.edu
GOODMAN, Patricia .... 859-442-1173 .... 201 G patricia.goodman@kctcs.edu
GOODMAN, Patricia .... 603-882-6923 .... 304 F pgoodman@ccsnh.edu
GOODMAN, Rachel .... 641-472-7000 .... 187 B rgoodman@mum.edu
GOODMAN, Rhonna .... 914-323-5277 .... 340 A goodmanr@mville.edu
GOODMAN, Richard, H ...... 503-494-5078 .... 418 D
GOODMAN, Robert, M ...... 732-932-9000 .... 314 D execdean@cook.rutgers.edu
GOODMAN, Sharon .... 910-410-1734 .... 372 G sharong@richmondcc.edu
GOODMAN, Steven .... 315-464-6563 .... 352 E goodmans@upstate.edu
GOODMAN, Sylvia .... 405-789-6400 .... 412 D sgoodman@snu.edu
GOODMAN, Timothy, D ...... 478-289-2034 .... 128 J goodman@ega.edu
GOODMAN, Veronica .... 803-535-5540 .... 456 D vgoodman@claflin.edu
GOODMAN, William, L .... 651-638-6400 .... 261 I w-goodman@bethel.edu
GOODMAN, Willie .... 404-527-5735 .... 132 D wgoodman@itc.edu
GOODNER, Jason .... 229-732-5929 .... 124 C jasongoodner@andrewcollege.edu
GOODNOUGH, Doug .... 517-264-7141 .... 258 D dgoodnou@sienaheights.edu
GOODNOW, Jean .... 989-686-9201 .... 250 F jeangoodnow@delta.edu
GOODRICH, Blaine .... 517-841-4522 .... 248 I blaine.goodrich@baker.edu
GOODRICH, Deborah, J ..... 607-587-4215 .... 355 C goodridj@alfredstate.edu
GOODRICH, James, A .... 323-343-2800 ..... 35 B
GOODRICH, Jim .... 858-635-4495 ..... 27 E jgoodrich@alliant.edu
GOODRICH, Joan .... 802-440-4300 .... 512 G goodrich@bennington.edu
GOODRICH, Joy, P .... 804-354-5210 .... 529 D jgoodrich@vuu.edu
GOODRICH, Larry .... 972-825-4820 .... 495 D lgoodrich@sagu.edu
GOODRICH, Lynda .... 360-650-3109 .... 539 C lynda.goodrich@wwu.edu
GOODRICH, Mark .... 415-338-2723 ..... 36 F goodrich@sfsu.edu
GOODRICH PELLETIER, Monica .... 508-213-2108 .... 243 J monica.goodrich-pelletier@nichols.edu

GOUGH, Christopher .... 203-332-5022..... 90 B
cgough@hcc.commnet.edu

GOUGH, Darby .... 816-501-3660.... 279 C
darby.gough@avila.edu

GOUGH, Ellen .... 636-422-2030.... 289 E
egough@stlcc.edu

GOUGH, Miriam .... 207-221-8728.... 218 C
mgough@kaplan.edu

GOUGH, Paul .... 605-773-3455.... 465 D
paulg@sdbor.edu

GOUGH, Richard .... 910-695-3703.... 373 E
goughr@sandhills.edu

GOUKER, Dan .... 702-651-4163.... 302 G
dan.gouker@csn.edu

GOULD, Amanda .... 413-565-1000.... 231 B
agould@baypath.edu

GOULD, Bryan .... 360-867-6170.... 533 I
gouldb@evergreen.edu

GOULD, Charles, W .... 843-661-8000.... 458 A
charles.gould@fdtc.edu

GOULD, Claudia .... 215-898-5911.... 448 I
info@icaphila.org

GOULD, David .... 505-880-2877.... 317 H

GOULD, Holly .... 617-369-4041.... 244 G
hgould@smfa.edu

GOULD, Ingrid, E .... 773-782-8846.... 166 D
i-gould@uchicago.edu

GOULD, Jerry .... 757-826-1883.... 516 H

GOULD, Jessica .... 617-730-7091.... 243 I
jessica.gould@newbury.edu

GOULD, Karen, L .... 718-951-5671.... 326 G
bcpresident@brooklyn.cuny.edu

GOULD, Larry .... 928-317-6475..... 17 A
larry.gould@nau.edu

GOULD, Lawrence, V .... 785-628-4241.... 192 F
lgould@fhsu.edu

GOULD, Robert, J .... 802-287-8207.... 513 D
gouldr@greenmtn.edu

GOULD, Stephen, A .... 920-565-1201.... 547 H
gouldst@lakeland.edu

GOULD, Susan, A .... 920-565-1514.... 547 H
gouldsu@lakeland.edu

GOULD, Thomas, E .... 919-536-7200.... 369 G
gouldt@durhamtech.edu

GOULDING, Laurel .... 701-662-1513.... 382 D
laurel.goulding@lrsc.edu

GOULDING, Ruth .... 619-239-0391..... 37 D
rgoulding@cwsl.edu

GOULET, Camille, A .... 213-891-2188..... 54 F
gouletca@laccd.edu

GOULET, Richard .... 978-556-3981.... 241 B
rgoulet@necc.mass.edu

GOULET, Stephen, P .... 508-793-7598.... 233 C
sgoulet@clarku.edu

GOULETTE, Thomas .... 603-524-3207.... 304 D
tgoulette@ccsnh.edu

GOUNARD, Jean, F .... 716-878-5331.... 353 A
gounarjf@buffalostate.edu

GOUNDIE, Tedd .... 207-786-6219.... 217 C
tgoundie@bates.edu

GOUPEL, Sharon .... 951-781-2727..... 64 C

GOURDINE, Raji .... 334-876-9292....... 4 B
rgourdine@wccs.edu

GOURLEY, Dick, R .... 901-448-6036.... 477 C
dgourley@uthsc.edu

GOURLEY, Pamela, L .... 276-944-6122.... 518 I
pgourley@ehc.edu

GOURNEAU, Bill .... 701-477-7862.... 383 C
bgourneau@tm.edu

GOURNEAU, Haven .... 406-768-6329.... 294 F
hgourneau@fpcc.edu

GOUSE, Richard, I .... 401-739-5000.... 453 E

GOUTTIERRE, Thomas, E .. 402-554-2376.... 301 B
teg@unomaha.edu

GOVAN, Shawn, L .... 708-709-3518.... 161 C
sgovan@prairiestate.edu

GOVAN, JR., Tom .... 708-596-2000.... 164 F
tgovan@ssc.edu

GOVE, Marilyn .... 949-480-4131..... 69 I
mgove@soka.edu

GOVE, Ryan, K .... 913-588-6681.... 197 A
rgove@kumc.edu

GOVEA, Hector .... 432-552-2740.... 507 C
govea_h@utpb.edu

GOVEA, Sam .... 972-860-4216.... 484 F
sgovea@dcccd.edu

GOVER, Bruce .... 606-679-8501.... 202 F
bruce.gover@kctcs.edu

GOVERT, OSF,
M. Mary Evelyn .... 260-399-7700.... 180 E
mgovert@sf.edu

GOVINDAN, Indira .... 201-692-2060.... 310 B
govindan@fdu.edu

GOVITZ, Leanne .... 989-686-9490.... 250 F
leannegovitz@delta.edu

GOVITZ, Scott .... 989-386-6624.... 255 F
sgovitz@midmich.edu

GOVONI, Mark .... 215-951-2700.... 444 C
govonim@philau.edu

GOW, Joe .... 608-785-8004.... 551 B
gow.joe@uwlax.edu

GOWDY, Lisa .... 517-780-4567.... 248 I
lisa.gowdy@baker.edu

GOWER, J. Michael .... 212-960-5475.... 361 I
gower@yu.edu

GOWER, Michael, E .... 615-898-2540.... 473 F
mike.gower@mtsu.edu

GOWER, Paula .... 405-682-1611.... 409 F
pgower@occc.edu

GOWER, Stephanie .... 205-453-6300..... 99 D

GOWN, Jacob .... 310-476-9777..... 28 F
jgown@ajula.edu

GOWRON, Leah .... 831-647-3558..... 57 F
leah.gowron@miis.edu

GOYAK, Antone .... 715-324-6900.... 549 D
antone.goyak@ni.edu

GOYETTE, Barbara .... 410-263-2371.... 225 G
barbara.goyette@sjca.edu

GOYETTE, Dan .... 414-382-6040.... 545 H
dan.goyette@alverno.edu

GOYETTE, John, J .... 805-525-4417..... 72 E
jgoyette@thomasaquinas.edu

GOYETTE, Karen .... 619-961-4261..... 72 F
kgoyette@tjsl.edu

GOYETTE, Kelly .... 859-344-3619.... 206 D
kelly.goyette@thomasmore.edu

GOZA, Molly .... 501-370-5204..... 23 B
mgoza@philander.edu

GOZUM, Allan .... 630-829-6418.... 145 D
agozum@ben.edu

GOZZO, James .... 518-694-7255.... 322 C
james.gozzo@acphs.edu

GRAAGE, Eric .... 401-454-6525.... 454 B
egraage@risd.edu

GRABAN, Jennifer, L .... 812-488-1178.... 180 B
jg54@evansville.edu

GRABER, David .... 402-375-7257.... 299 I
dagrabe1@wsc.edu

GRABER, Doug .... 620-947-3121.... 196 E
dougg@tabor.edu

GRABER, Thomas .... 570-208-5900.... 432 E
thomasgraber@kings.edu

GRABER, Tony .... 316-284-5233.... 190 H
tgraber@bethelks.edu

GRABLE, Lynda .... 478-445-7305.... 129 F
lynda.grable@gcsu.edu

GRABOIS, Neil .... 212-229-5400.... 342 E
graboisn@newschool.edu

GRABOWSKA, Lynette .... 605-367-6122.... 466 C
lynette.grabowska@southeasttech.edu

GRABOWSKI, Janice, T ..... 724-925-4123.... 451 E
grabowskij@wccc.edu

GRABOWSKI, John, F .... 410-777-2231.... 221 B
jfgrabowski@aacc.edu

GRABOWSKI, Mark .... 417-328-1556.... 290 E
mgrabowski@sbuniv.edu

GRABOWSKI, Rod .... 813-974-8848.... 120 D
rgrabowski@admin.usf.edu

GRABOWSKI, Rodney .... 904-620-2113.... 120 C
rgrabows@unf.edu

GRABUS, Scott .... 215-572-2847.... 422 B
grabuss@arcadia.edu

GRACA, Michael .... 508-286-3503.... 246 E
mgraca@wheatonma.edu

GRACA, Thomas, J .... 972-860-7218.... 484 H
TomGraca@dcccd.edu

GRACE, Chris .... 562-903-4708..... 30 H
chris.grace@biola.edu

GRACE, Coy, F .... 870-633-4480..... 21 F
cgrace@eacc.edu

GRACE, Dennis .... 239-280-1613.... 101 C
dennis.grace@avemaria.edu

GRACE, Ellen .... 561-868-3135.... 114 D
gracee@palmbeachstate.edu

GRACE, Gary, S .... 319-352-8276.... 189 F
gary.grace@wartburg.edu

GRACE, Glenda .... 718-518-4154.... 327 D
ggrace@hostos.cuny.edu

GRACE, Michelle, M .... 847-543-2274.... 147 H
mgrace@clcillinois.edu

GRACE, Nabil, F .... 248-204-2500.... 254 E
ngrace@ltu.edu

GRACE, Ted, W .... 618-453-4408.... 164 I
tgrace@siu.edu

GRACIE, Larry, W .... 252-249-1851.... 372 C
lgracie@pamlicocc.edu

GRACY, Robert, W .... 210-458-4341.... 506 B
robert.gracy@utsa.edu

GRACYALNY, David .... 410-225-2220.... 224 C
dgracyal@mica.edu

GRACYK, June .... 440-684-6083.... 405 B
jgracyk@ursuline.edu

GRADISHER, Michael .... 352-588-7560.... 116 E
michael.gradisher@saintleo.edu

GRADY, Akeembra .... 301-624-2851.... 222 G
agrady@frederick.edu

GRADY, Amber .... 870-512-7890..... 20 F
amber_grady@asun.edu

GRADY, Bruce .... 919-546-8574.... 376 D
bgrady@shawu.edu

GRADY, David, L .... 319-335-3114.... 182 C
david-grady@uiowa.edu

GRADY, Dennis, O .... 540-831-5724.... 522 D
dgrady4@radford.edu

GRADY, Donald .... 815-753-1811.... 160 A
dgrady@niu.edu

GRADY, J. Thomas .... 508-678-2811.... 239 F
tom.grady@bristolcc.edu

GRADY, Janet, L .... 814-269-2078.... 449 D
jgrady@pitt.edu

GRADY, Kevin .... 814-269-7005.... 449 D
kgrady@pitt.edu

GRADY, Lea, W .... 910-296-1812.... 371 B
lgrady@jamessprunt.edu

GRADY, Lynne .... 706-379-3111.... 139 F
lbgrady@yhc.edu

GRADY, Paul .... 310-233-4112..... 54 I
gradyp@lahc.edu

GRADY, Sarah .... 718-409-7262.... 356 C
sgrady@sunymaritime.edu

GRADY, Suzanne .... 845-257-3245.... 352 B
gradys@newpaltz.edu

GRADY, OSF, Thomas ..... 718-489-5367.... 348 E
tgrady@stfranciscollege.edu

GRAEBERT, James, K .... 414-288-3048.... 548 D
james.graebert@marquette.edu

GRAEM, David .... 903-675-6364.... 502 D
dgraem@tvcc.edu

GRAESSER, William .... 765-966-2656.... 176 F
bgraesse@ivytech.edu

GRAF, Debby .... 208-376-7731.... 142 E
dgraf@boisebible.edu

GRAF, Elizabeth .... 219-866-6195.... 179 B
bethg@saintjoe.edu

GRAF, Nancy .... 316-295-5888.... 192 H
ngraf@friends.edu

GRAF, Tom .... 936-294-2525.... 501 A
tpg001@shsu.edu

GRAFF, Irene .... 310-660-3593..... 45 E
igraff@elcamino.edu

GRAFF, Irene .... 310-660-3515..... 45 D
igraff@elcamino.edu

GRAFF, Jonathan .... 575-624-8291.... 319 C
graff@nmmi.edu

GRAFFICE, Anne .... 330-823-2030.... 404 C
graffiaz@mountunion.edu

GRAFTON, Kenneth, A .... 701-231-6693.... 381 H
k.grafton@ndsu.edu

GRAFTON, Phillip, C .... 937-766-7834.... 386 F
graftonp@cedarville.edu

GRAFTON, Steve, C .... 734-763-9730.... 259 D
sgrafton@umich.edu

GRAGG, JR., Derrick, L .... 734-487-1050.... 250 H
derrick.gragg@emich.edu

GRAGG, Douglas, L .... 502-895-3411.... 204 B
dgragg@lpts.edu

GRAGG, Margaret .... 520-322-6330..... 12 F

GRAGG, T. Dewayne .... 903-875-7376.... 491 B
dewayne.gragg@navarrocollege.edu

GRAHAM, Amie, E .... 757-594-7672.... 517 I
amie.graham@cnu.edu

GRAHAM, Angela .... 540-863-2806.... 526 B
agraham@dslcc.edu

GRAHAM, Archie .... 414-297-6870.... 554 D
grahama@matc.edu

GRAHAM, Bernard .... 570-408-4280.... 451 G
bernard.graham@wilkes.edu

GRAHAM, Bruce .... 312-996-1040.... 166 F
bgraham@uic.edu

GRAHAM, Carlos .... 573-681-5971.... 284 B
grahamc@lincolnu.edu

GRAHAM, Catherine .... 310-338-2753..... 56 E
cgraham@lmu.edu

GRAHAM, Charles, W .... 405-325-0311.... 413 C
charles.w.graham-1@ou.edu

GRAHAM, Christina, L .... 814-362-7654.... 449 B
cgraham5@pitt.edu

GRAHAM, Christine .... 941-907-2262.... 106 G
chgraham@evergladesuniversity.edu

GRAHAM, Chuck .... 352-335-2332.... 100 B

GRAHAM, Dane .... 307-855-2250.... 555 G
dgraham@cwc.edu

GRAHAM, David .... 305-892-7022.... 111 K
david.graham@jwu.edu

GRAHAM, Deborah, L .... 314-516-4165.... 291 F
gramhamdeb@umsl.edu

GRAHAM, Duncan .... 559-730-3823..... 42 B
duncang@cos.edu

GRAHAM, Jack, R .... 330-672-0790.... 393 D
jgraham@kent.edu

GRAHAM, James, F .... 660-543-4279.... 291 B
graham@ucmo.edu

GRAHAM, Janielle .... 773-995-2067.... 146 D
jgraham@csu.edu

GRAHAM, Jeanne .... 906-932-4231.... 251 E
jeanneg@gogebic.edu

GRAHAM, Jeanne, P .... 906-932-4231.... 251 E
jeanneg@gogebic.edu

GRAHAM, Jeffrey .... 956-665-2112.... 506 A
grahamja@utpa.edu

GRAHAM, Jennifer .... 254-298-8592.... 496 B
jennifer.graham@templejc.edu

GRAHAM, Jerry, W .... 254-968-9877.... 496 F
graham@tarleton.edu

GRAHAM, Joan, E .... 585-475-6079.... 347 G
jegirp@rit.edu

GRAHAM, Joe, M .... 704-233-8148.... 380 D
graham@wingate.edu

GRAHAM, John .... 718-270-5110.... 328 D
jgraham@mec.cuny.edu

GRAHAM, John .... 845-938-5868.... 558 G
John.Graham@usma.edu

GRAHAM, III, John .... 412-346-2100.... 444 D
jgrahamiii@pia.edu

GRAHAM, John, D .... 812-855-1432.... 173 C
grahamjd@indiana.edu

GRAHAM, John, M .... 512-471-4716.... 505 B
john.graham@athletics.utexas.edu

GRAHAM, John-Bauer .... 256-782-5255........ 4 L
jgraham@jsu.edu

GRAHAM, Judith .... 617-228-3296.... 239 G
jgraham@bhcc.mass.edu

GRAHAM, Karen .... 714-744-7672..... 39 C
kgraham@chapman.edu

GRAHAM, Kathleen .... 570-577-3200.... 423 D
kathy.graham@bucknell.edu

GRAHAM, Keith .... 570-740-0307.... 435 C
kgraham@luzerne.edu

GRAHAM, Kevin .... 321-674-8111.... 108 E
kgraham@fit.edu

GRAHAM, Kevin, C .... 217-425-4663.... 158 F
kgraham@millikin.edu

GRAHAM, Kim .... 805-922-6966..... 26 K
kgraham@hancockcollege.edu

GRAHAM, Ladd .... 714-415-6500..... 77 G
lgraham@westcoastuniversity.edu

GRAHAM, LeRoy .... 802-443-5770.... 513 G
leroyg@middlebury.edu

GRAHAM, JR., Louis, W .. 617-253-2808.... 242 A
graham@mit.edu

GRAHAM, Margaret, P .... 434-223-6167.... 519 B
bgraham@email.hsc.edu

GRAHAM, MariAnn .... 651-962-5000.... 272 E
magraham@stthomas.edu

GRAHAM, Mark, R .... 276-944-6104.... 518 I
mgraham@ehc.edu

GRAHAM, Mary, S .... 601-928-6280.... 275 G
mary.graham@mgccc.edu

GRAHAM, Melody .... 319-368-6482.... 187 E
melody@mtmercy.edu

GRAHAM, SJ, Michael, J .. 513-745-3502.... 406 E

GRAHAM, Mickey .... 580-477-7782.... 414 C
mckey.graham@wosc.edu

GRAHAM, Nancy .... 724-847-6550.... 429 G
ngraham@geneva.edu

GRAHAM, Nicole .... 305-892-7554.... 111 K
nicole.graham@jwu.edu

GRAHAM, Philip .... 858-795-5210..... 67 H
pgraham@sandfordburnham.org

GRAHAM, Robert, J .... 724-852-3456.... 451 B
rgraham@waynesburg.edu

GRAHAM, Roy .... 803-934-3298.... 459 F
roygraham@morris.edu

GRAHAM, Sandra .... 414-382-6366.... 545 H
sandra.graham@alverno.edu

GRAHAM, Stephanie .... 608-663-4861.... 547 C
srgraham@edgewood.edu

GRAHAM, Stephanie .... 909-607-6722..... 49 D
stephanie_graham@hmc.edu

GRAHAM, Steven, W .... 573-884-3360.... 291 C
grahams@umsystem.edu

GRAHAM, Susie .... 812-330-6247.... 175 H
sgraham31@ivytech.edu

GRAHAM, Terri .... 402-461-7431.... 298 C
tgraham@hastings.edu

GRAHAM, Troy .... 901-320-9763.... 478 B
tgraham@victory.edu

GRAHAM, William .... 212-410-8008.... 343 B
wgraham@nycpm.edu

GRAHAM, William, A .... 617-495-4513.... 235 H
wgraham@hds.harvard.edu

GRAHAM, Wray .... 901-375-4400.... 471 E
wraygraham@midsouthcc.org

GRAHAM-CORNELL,
Michael .... 203-254-4088..... 92 B
mgraham-cornell@fairfield.edu

GRAHAM-HANDLEY, Tad . 212-625-6000.... 323 C

GRAHAM SAYLORS,
Rebekah .... 828-898-8828.... 366 A
grahamr@lmc.edu

GRAHN, Lance, R .... 501-450-3126..... 25 H
lanceg@uca.edu

GRAINGER, Kristen .... 503-370-6209.... 421 C
kgrainge@willamette.edu

GRAJEK, Michael, A .... 330-569-5272.... 391 H
GrajekMA@hiram.edu

GRAJEK, Michael, A .... 330-569-5124.... 391 H
grajekma@hiram.edu

GRAMBERG, Anne-Katrin .. 334-844-4026........ 1 G
gramban@auburn.edu

GRAMENZ, Gary .... 559-453-2291..... 47 K
gary.gramenz@fresno.edu

GRAMLICH, Nicole .... 314-768-7806.... 286 D
ngramlich@missouricollege.com

GRAMLING, Keith, E .... 504-865-3240.... 213 F
gramling@loyno.edu

GRAMLING, Tim .... 816-303-7799.... 280 D
tgramling@ctukansascity.com

GRAMMER, Jill .... 303-444-0202..... 86 B
jgrammer@naropa.edu

GRAMMER, Robert .... 615-460-6417.... 467 B
robert.grammer@belmont.edu

GRAMS, Ed, J .... 574-289-7001.... 176 C
egrams@ivytech.edu

GRAY, Paul 626-815-3869 30 E
pgray@apu.edu
GRAY, Rebecca 254-968-9473 496 F
rgray@tarleton.edu
GRAY, Rebecca 843-953-5633 457 B
grayrj@cofc.edu
GRAY, Reginald 214-379-5409 492 D
rgray@pqc.edu
GRAY, Richard, D 860-486-3455 94 E
richard.gray@uconn.edu
GRAY, Robert, R 804-257-5842 529 D
rrgray@vuu.edu
GRAY, Rosemary 731-881-3506 477 E
rgray20@utm.edu
GRAY, Sandra, C 859-858-3511 198 B
president@asbury.edu
GRAY, Sarah 309-649-6265 165 D
sarah.gray@src.edu
GRAY, Shaun 207-741-5580 219 A
sgray@smccme.edu
GRAY, Sheryl 865-471-3240 467 E
sgray@cn.edu
GRAY, Shonda 443-885-3430 224 F
shonda.gray@morgan.edu
GRAY, Susan 478-289-2027 128 J
sgray@ega.edu
GRAY, Taylor, C 702-651-7627 302 G
taylor.gray@csn.edu
GRAY, Tim 319-208-5022 188 G
tgray@scciowa.edu
GRAY, Toni 806-354-6083 479 H
tbgray@actx.edu
GRAY, Warren 606-589-3070 203 A
warren.gray@kctcs.edu
GRAY, Warren, S 401-865-1602 453 F
wgray@providence.edu
GRAY, Wilbur, E 717-728-2511 425 A
billgray@centralpenn.edu
GRAY, William 417-777-5062 279 E
bgray@texascountytech.edu
GRAY-LACKEY, Denise 502-213-7202 202 B
denise.graylackey@kctcs.edu
GRAY-LITTLE, Bernadette 785-864-3131 196 F
graylittle@ku.edu
GRAY PAYTON, Pamela 619-260-4681 76 A
grayp@sandiego.edu
GRAYBEAL, Clay 207-221-4509 220 H
cgraybeal@une.edu
GRAYBEAL, Jerry, G 801-626-8114 511 D
jgraybeal@weber.edu
GRAYBEAL, Susan, E 423-354-2471 475 E
segraybeal@northeaststate.edu
GRAYSON, Chinester 334-874-5700 3 A
cgrayson@concordiaselma.edu
GRAYSON, Denise, R 605-256-5152 465 G
denise.grayson@dsu.edu
GRAYSON, Lorenzo 251-405-7170 2 D
lgrayson@bishop.edu
GRAYSON, Paul 212-774-0727 340 D
pgrayson@mmm.edu
GRAZIANO, Joanne 516-299-2999 339 A
joanne.graziano@liu.edu
GRAZIANO, Vincent, S 412-391-6710 423 A
vgraziano@bradfordpittsburgh.edu
GRAZIOTTI, Michael 305-892-5374 111 K
michael.graziotti@jwu.edu
GRBOVIC, Vesna 312-777-8668 153 A
vgrbovic@aii.edu
GREAF, Eileen 330-941-2364 406 F
egreaf@ysu.edu
GREALISH, William 617-578-7178 235 D
wgrealish@gibbsboston.edu
GREANEY, Elizabeth 703-526-5831 516 B
egreaney@argosy.edu
GREANEY, KC 707-521-7940 68 E
kgreaney@santarosa.edu
GREAR, Nancy, C 585-389-2801 342 D
ngrear2@naz.edu
GREASLEY, Philip 859-257-3381 206 H
greasle@uky.edu
GREATHOUSE, Jan 615-248-7782 476 E
jgreathouse@trevecca.edu
GREAVES, Christopher 718-997-3930 328 F
christopher.greaves@qc.cuny.edu
GREAVES, Curtis, K 757-823-8173 521 K
cgreaves@nsu.edu
GREAZEL, Nicholaus 847-566-6401 167 D
ngreazel@usml.edu
GREB, Christine 215-951-2808 444 C
grebc@philau.edu
GREBEL, David, A 817-257-7130 498 F
d.grebel@tcu.edu
GREBING, Karen 573-651-2433 290 D
kgrebing@semo.edu
GRECO, Anne 215-751-8217 426 B
agreco@ccp.edu
GRECO, Carol 804-627-5300 516 J
GRECO, Frank, M 412-365-1133 425 B
greco@chatham.edu
GRECO, Gary 860-738-6397 90 F
ggreco@nwcc.commnet.edu
GRECO, Joseph 610-543-2500 99 D
GRECO, Juneann 570-340-6004 435 F
greco@marywood.edu

GRECO, Michelle 504-671-6001 210 G
mgreco@dcc.edu
GRECO, Peter, L 303-458-4050 87 E
pgreco@regis.edu
GRECO, Sal 516-299-3796 338 F
sal.greco@liu.edu
GREDER, Darcy, L 309-556-3541 153 E
dgreder@iwu.edu
GREDY, John, W 937-766-3200 386 F
jgredy@cedarville.edu
GREEAR, Marisa 360-442-2391 535 C
mgreear@lowercolumbia.edu
GREEN, Alberta 318-342-5338 216 E
agreen@ulm.edu
GREEN, Allen 914-395-2249 350 C
agreen@sarahlawrence.edu
GREEN, Alus 201-360-4047 310 F
agreen@hccc.edu
GREEN, Amber 619-644-7631 49 A
amber.green@gcccd.edu
GREEN, Andy 256-782-5268 4 L
agreen@jsu.edu
GREEN, Ann, F 828-694-1709 368 B
anng@blueridge.edu
GREEN, Audrey 661-362-3424 41 G
audrey.green@canyons.edu
GREEN, Barbara 518-743-2250 322 B
greenb@sunyacc.edu
GREEN, Barbara, C 626-395-6351 32 E
barbarag@caltech.edu
GREEN, Calvin 903-593-8311 499 A
cgreen@texascollege.edu
GREEN, Carla 804-527-1000 99 D
GREEN, Carla, D 913-288-7273 193 J
cgreen@kckcc.edu
GREEN, Carol 903-233-4010 489 K
carolgreen@letu.edu
GREEN, Carol 253-964-6584 536 C
cgreen@pierce.ctc.edu
GREEN, Cathy 603-513-5101 306 G
cathy.green@law.unh.edu
GREEN, Charles 919-843-9834 378 D
green@unc.edu
GREEN, Charles, D 319-335-5026 182 C
charles-green@uiowa.edu
GREEN, Christopher 805-546-3902 43 F
cgreen@cuesta.edu
GREEN, Clarence 660-562-1254 287 E
cgreen@nwmissouri.edu
GREEN, Constance, C 503-842-8222 420 D
green@tillamookbay.cc
GREEN, Cullen 807-832-2245 512 F
cgreen@westminstercollege.edu
GREEN, Danny 919-760-8026 366 G
greend@meredith.edu
GREEN, David, A 217-786-2406 156 I
david.green@llcc.edu
GREEN, David, M 818-947-2679 55 E
greendm@lavc.edu
GREEN, Denise, O 989-774-3700 249 G
green1do@cmich.edu
GREEN, Dianne 313-845-9611 252 D
dgreen@hfcc.edu
GREEN, Don 657-278-2413 34 E
dgreen@fullerton.edu
GREEN, Donald 616-643-5737 251 B
greend@ferris.edu
GREEN, Donald 231-591-2548 251 B
greend@ferris.edu
GREEN, Donald 973-290-4290 309 A
security@cse.edu
GREEN, JR., Donald, W 904-632-3105 109 E
dgreen@fscj.edu
GREEN, Donna 562-985-8403 35 A
dgreen4@csulb.edu
GREEN, Donna 602-242-6265 12 H
dgreen@brooklinecollege.edu
GREEN, Ed 408-855-5021 78 A
ed.green@wvm.edu
GREEN, Elaine 215-248-7063 425 C
greene@chc.edu
GREEN, Eleanor, M 979-845-5051 497 C
emgreen@tamu.edu
GREEN, Elizabeth, B 617-358-4218 232 G
ebgreen@bu.edu
GREEN, Ellen 843-574-6147 461 G
ellen.green@tridenttech.edu
GREEN, Ellen, R 806-371-5131 479 H
ergreen@actx.edu
GREEN, Eric 575-439-3806 319 E
egreen@nmsua.nmsu.edu
GREEN, Finley, L 423-652-4865 469 L
flgreen@king.edu
GREEN, Gary, M 336-734-7200 370 C
ggreen@forsythtech.edu
GREEN, Hope 773-380-6840 168 D
hgreen@westwood.edu
GREEN, Jean, M 217-228-5432 161 E
greenje@quincy.edu
GREEN, Jeff, W 256-549-8317 3 J
jgreen@gadsdenstate.edu
GREEN, Jeffrey 312-662-4401 144 C
jgreen@adler.edu

GREEN, Jenny 607-729-1581 332 A
jgreen@davisny.edu
GREEN, Jerry 718-817-4170 334 C
jgreen@fordham.edu
GREEN, Jim 360-992-2408 532 A
jgreen@clark.edu
GREEN, Joe 806-743-2870 501 E
joe.green@ttuhsc.edu
GREEN, John, C 610-683-4114 442 F
jgreen@kutztown.edu
GREEN, Jonathan, D 309-556-3101 153 E
provost@iwu.edu
GREEN, Joyce 803-536-8551 460 G
jgreen@scsu.edu
GREEN, Judith 201-684-7523 313 D
jgreen2@ramapo.edu
GREEN, Julia 207-941-7129 218 A
greenj@husson.edu
GREEN, Karen 484-664-3182 437 B
green@muhlenberg.edu
GREEN, Keith, A 717-901-5123 430 F
KGreen@HarrisburgU.edu
GREEN, Kristina 207-893-7799 219 F
kgreen@sjcme.edu
GREEN, Kurt 530-541-4660 53 F
green@ltcc.edu
GREEN, Lawrence 610-399-2417 441 H
lgreen@cheyney.edu
GREEN, Lillie, F 757-727-5057 519 C
lillie.green@hamptonu.edu
GREEN, Lorry 864-977-7124 460 A
lorry.green@ngu.edu
GREEN, Mark, A 618-235-2700 165 B
mark.green@swic.edu
GREEN, Mary 269-965-3931 253 H
greenm@kellogg.edu
GREEN, Mary Beth 334-222-6591 5 F
mbgreen@lbwcc.edu
GREEN, Mary Jo 715-422-5504 554 C
maryjo.green@mstc.edu
GREEN, Matthew 805-546-3924 43 F
mgreen@cuesta.edu
GREEN, Matthew, T 919-508-2016 375 D
mtgreen@peace.edu
GREEN, Melanie, H 804-627-5300 516 J
GREEN, Melissa 707-476-4153 42 A
melissa-green@redwoods.edu
GREEN, Melissa 567-661-7000 400 H
melissa_green3@owens.edu
GREEN, Michael, R 717-867-6208 434 C
mgreen@lvc.edu
GREEN, Michael, S 518-629-4554 336 C
m.green@hvcc.edu
GREEN, Mike 615-966-6000 470 D
mike.green@lipscomb.edu
GREEN, Moishe 845-352-5852 360 G
GREEN, Monica 951-372-7000 64 A
GREEN, Myrtes 205-929-6305 5 E
mdgreen@lawsonstate.edu
GREEN, Nancy, L 765-966-2656 176 F
ngreen12@ivytech.edu
GREEN, Neila 718-982-2123 327 A
Neila.Green@csi.cuny.edu
GREEN, Nichol 601-928-6264 275 G
nichol.green@mgccc.edu
GREEN, Paul 509-327-2443 19 C
paul.green@phoenix.edu
GREEN, Paula 626-914-8873 39 G
pgreen@citruscollege.edu
GREEN, Paula, L 508-849-3344 230 C
pgreen@annamaria.edu
GREEN, Queen 334-229-4357 1 C
qgreen@alasu.edu
GREEN, Rachel, T 904-819-6223 107 A
rgreen@flagler.edu
GREEN, Ragan 478-275-7865 134 G
rgreen@oftc.edu
GREEN, Ramona 903-223-3058 498 C
ramona.green@tamut.edu
GREEN, Rebecca 760-355-6499 50 K
becky.green@imperial.edu
GREEN, Rhonda, T 209-575-6664 80 B
greenr@yosemite.cc.ca.us
GREEN, Richard 312-261-2300 159 D
richard.green@nl.edu
GREEN, Robert, L 540-464-7321 529 A
greenrl@vmi.edu
GREEN, Ronald, F 843-953-7416 456 C
ron.green@citadel.edu
GREEN, Ronnie 402-472-2871 300 F
rgreen@nebraska.edu
GREEN, Ronnie, D 402-472-2871 300 H
rgreen2@unl.edu
GREEN, Ruvain 845-352-5852 360 G
GREEN, Sandy, B 864-488-8348 459 A
sgreen@limestone.edu
GREEN, Sean-Michael 845-575-3800 340 C
sean-michael.green@marist.edu
GREEN, Sharon, F 318-670-9337 215 A
sgreen@susla.edu
GREEN, Shirley 602-787-6604 16 A
shirley.green@pvmail.maricopa.edu
GREEN, Stanton 732-571-3419 311 F
sgreen@monmouth.edu

GREEN, Steve 478-988-6890 133 H
sgreen@middlegatech.edu
GREEN, Susan 802-635-1308 515 E
susan.green@jsc.edu
GREEN, Tim 256-549-8601 3 J
tgreen@gadsdenstate.edu
GREEN, Timothy, M 615-248-1387 476 E
tgreen@trevecca.edu
GREEN, Tracey 315-498-2532 345 D
GREEN, Tracy 804-523-5789 526 F
tgreen@reynolds.edu
GREEN, Vannessa 718-951-5842 326 G
vgreen@brooklyn.cuny.edu
GREEN, Wandra, B 816-235-1601 291 E
greenwb@umkc.edu
GREEN, William 507-786-3060 271 H
greenw@stolaf.edu
GREEN, William 423-614-8240 470 A
wgreen@leeuniversity.edu.edu
GREEN, William, S 305-284-2006 122 F
wgreen@miami.edu
GREEN-QUARLES, Ryanne 916-361-1660 38 C
rgreen@cc.edu
GREEN WARE, Nikisha 601-979-1472 275 A
nikisha.g.ware@jsums.edu
GREENAN, Jennie 309-692-4092 158 C
jgreenan@midstate.edu
GREENAN, Linda 202-687-5677 98 A
greenanl@georgetown.edu
GREENAN, Martin 317-543-3618 177 H
mgreenan@martin.edu
GREENBAUM, Michael, B 212-678-8800 337 G
migreenbaum@jtsa.edu
GREENBAUM, Steve 215-885-2360 435 E
sgreenbaum@manor.edu
GREENBERG, Barbara, L 973-972-1796 316 D
greenbbl@umdnj.edu
GREENBERG, Douglas 732-932-7896 314 D
execdean@sas.rutgers.edu
GREENBERG, Jeffrey 215-591-5738 427 A
jgreenberg@devry.edu
GREENBERG, Judith, G 617-422-7245 243 G
jgreenbe@faculty.nesl.edu
GREENBERG, Kenneth, S 617-573-8265 245 E
kgreenbe@suffolk.edu
GREENBERG, Mark, L 215-895-2200 427 G
mlg25@drexel.edu
GREENBERG, Raymond, S 843-792-2211 459 C
greenber@musc.edu
GREENBERG, Robert 212-772-5195 327 E
robert.greenberg@hunter.cuny.edu
GREENBERG, Roberta 718-933-6700 341 G
rgreenbe@monroecollege.edu
GREENBERG, Scott, B 508-626-4550 238 D
sgreenberg@framingham.edu
GREENBERG, Stephen, B 713-798-8878 481 H
stepheng@bcm.edu
GREENBERG, Yeshaya 305-534-7050 121 G
GREENBLATT, Kathy 410-225-2219 224 C
greenblatt@mica.edu
GREENBURG, Erik 703-376-6150 19 C
erik.greenburg@phoenix.edu
GREENE, Barbara 704-484-4040 369 B
greeneb@clevelandcommunitycollege.edu
GREENE, Brent, D 715-425-4891 552 A
brent.d.greene@uwrf.edu
GREENE, Carolyn, H 205-940-7800 8 A
cgreene@edaff.com
GREENE, Chanel 908-852-1400 308 F
greenec@centenarycollege.edu
GREENE, D. Gayle 919-532-5522 374 E
dggreene@waketech.edu
GREENE, David, A 773-702-1377 166 D
davidgreene@uchicago.edu
GREENE, Gail 865-471-3532 467 E
ggreene@cn.edu
GREENE, Gloria 256-824-6000 9 A
gloria.green@uah.edu
GREENE, Heidi 302-736-2300 96 G
greene@cchs.k12.de.us
GREENE, James 386-506-4429 103 J
greenej@DaytonaState.edu
GREENE, James 202-319-5247 97 C
greene@cua.edu
GREENE, Jane, D 864-379-8715 457 G
GREENE, Jeff, W 606-474-3298 200 J
jgreene@kcu.edu
GREENE, Jessica, A 617-552-3111 232 D
jessica.greene.2@bc.edu
GREENE, John, W 615-322-2426 477 F
john.greene@vanderbilt.edu
GREENE, Joseph, J 401-598-1038 453 C
JGreene@jwu.edu
GREENE, Karen, L 614-234-5685 396 G
kgreene@mccn.edu
GREENE, Ken, S 252-334-2019 367 A
ken.greene@macuniversity.edu
GREENE, Kenneth 973-443-8084 310 B
greene@fdu.edu
GREENE, Kristin 978-837-5120 242 D
kristin.greene@merrimack.edu
GREENE, Lori, A 773-508-3079 157 A
lgreene@luc.edu

GRIBBONS, Barry ... 661-362-5500 ... 41 G
barry.gribbons@canyons.edu
GRIBOU, Julius, M ... 210-458-4110 ... 506 B
julius.gribou@utsa.edu
GRICE, Len ... 870-733-6743 ... 22 E
lgrice@midsouthcc.edu
GRICE, Vivian, D ... 803-641-3550 ... 462 B
viviang@usca.edu
GRIECO, Chrysanthy, M ... 973-761-9005 ... 315 B
chrysanthy.grieco@shu.edu
GRIEGER, Ingrid ... 914-633-2038 ... 336 E
igrieger@iona.edu
GRIEGO, Brenda ... 702-968-1619 ... 303 D
bgriego@roseman.edu
GRIEGO, Elizabeth, B ... 209-946-2365 ... 75 D
egriego@pacific.edu
GRIEP, Laura ... 253-833-9111 ... 534 C
lgriep@geenriver.edu
GRIER, Arthur ... 404-225-4504 ... 125 A
agrier@atlantatech.edu
GRIER, Douglas, L ... 630-466-7900 ... 167 G
dgrier@waubonsee.edu
GRIER, Ed, A ... 804-827-0072 ... 525 E
egrier@vcu.edu
GRIER, Judith, M ... 757-789-1753 ... 526 D
jgrier@es.vccs.edu
GRIESBACH, Scott ... 715-232-2131 ... 552 C
griesbachs@uwstout.edu
GRIESSE, Sarah ... 612-330-1489 ... 261 G
griesse@augsburg.edu
GRIEVE, Cathy ... 303-871-2397 ... 88 E
cgrieve@du.edu
GRIEVE, Kim ... 419-824-3834 ... 395 D
kgrieve@lourdes.edu
GRIFFENBERG, Bill ... 843-661-8261 ... 458 A
bill.griffenberg@fdtc.edu
GRIFFETH, Hank ... 478-757-3510 ... 126 G
hgriffeth@centralgatech.edu
GRIFFETH, Hank ... 478-445-2301 ... 126 G
hgriffeth@centralgatech.edu
GRIFFIN, Adrian ... 718-260-5050 ... 328 E
agriffin@citytech.cuny.edu
GRIFFIN, Archie ... 614-292-9820 ... 398 H
griffin@ohiostatealumni.org
GRIFFIN, Barbara ... 202-806-2100 ... 98 B
bgriffin@howard.edu
GRIFFIN, Brian ... 919-658-7763 ... 367 D
bgriffin@moc.edu
GRIFFIN, Bruce ... 510-659-6514 ... 59 I
bgriffin@ohlone.edu
GRIFFIN, Carol ... 907-796-6258 ... 11 A
carol.griffin@uas.alaska.edu
GRIFFIN, Cathy ... 908-526-1200 ... 313 E
cgriffin@raritanval.edu
GRIFFIN, Clifton, P ... 410-548-3894 ... 228 D
cpgriffin@salisbury.edu
GRIFFIN, D. Joseph ... 617-373-2121 ... 244 A
GRIFFIN, Dale, M ... 405-878-2377 ... 409 D
dale.griffin@okbu.edu
GRIFFIN, Daniel ... 312-329-4425 ... 158 H
Daniel.Griffin@moody.edu
GRIFFIN, David ... 425-637-1010 ... 531 I
dgriffin@cityu.edu
GRIFFIN, Deborah ... 510-659-6151 ... 59 I
dgriffin@ohlone.edu
GRIFFIN, Don, Q ... 415-239-3303 ... 39 H
dgriffin@ccsf.edu
GRIFFIN, Donitha ... 334-876-9302 ... 4 B
dgriffin@wccs.edu
GRIFFIN, Elaine ... 615-966-5818 ... 470 D
elaine.griffin@lipscomb.edu
GRIFFIN, Ellen ... 415-338-1666 ... 36 F
elleng@sfsu.edu
GRIFFIN, Ervin, V ... 252-536-7217 ... 370 F
griffing@halifaxcc.edu
GRIFFIN, Gary ... 815-939-5296 ... 160 F
ggriffin@olivet.edu
GRIFFIN, Jacquelyn, H ... 864-977-7081 ... 460 A
jackie.griffin@ngu.edu
GRIFFIN, James ... 401-598-1563 ... 453 C
jgriffin@jwu.edu
GRIFFIN, Jeff, D ... 504-816-8018 ... 213 H
jgriffin@nobts.edu
GRIFFIN, Jennie ... 601-979-2522 ... 275 A
jennie.b.griffin@jsums.edu
GRIFFIN, Jo ... 405-425-5119 ... 409 E
jo.griffin@oc.edu
GRIFFIN, Joan ... 805-493-3555 ... 32 H
griffin@clunet.edu
GRIFFIN, Joel ... 864-941-8446 ... 460 D
griffin.j@ptc.edu
GRIFFIN, Joseph, E ... 530-226-4157 ... 69 H
jgriffin@simpsonu.edu
GRIFFIN, Karen ... 813-253-7002 ... 110 I
kgriffin@hccfl.edu
GRIFFIN, Larry ... 901-375-4400 ... 471 E
larrygriffin@midsouthcc.org
GRIFFIN, Lee, G ... 225-578-3811 ... 212 F
lgriffin@lsufoundation.org
GRIFFIN, Leslie ... 662-846-4400 ... 274 B
lgriffin@deltastate.edu
GRIFFIN, Linner ... 252-328-1418 ... 377 C
griffinl@ecu.edu
GRIFFIN, Lisa ... 229-217-4144 ... 134 C
lgrifin@moultrietech.edu
GRIFFIN, Lori ... 253-912-3633 ... 536 C
lgriffin@pierce.ctc.edu
GRIFFIN, Lynn ... 843-383-8071 ... 457 A
lgriffin@coker.edu
GRIFFIN, Mark ... 973-353-1458 ... 314 E
markg@andromeda.rutgers.edu
GRIFFIN, Marsha ... 732-356-1595 ... 315 D
mgriffin@somerset.edu
GRIFFIN, Michael ... 415-575-6154 ... 32 D
admissions@ciis.edu
GRIFFIN, Michael, J ... 305-899-3085 ... 101 F
mgriffin@mail.barry.edu
GRIFFIN, Patricia, L ... 785-628-5377 ... 192 F
pgriffin@fhsu.edu
GRIFFIN, Patrick ... 845-431-8924 ... 332 E
griffin@sunydutchess.edu
GRIFFIN, Patsy ... 770-531-6326 ... 132 J
pgriff@laniertech.edu
GRIFFIN, Paul, A ... 503-255-0332 ... 417 C
pgriffin@multnomah.edu
GRIFFIN, Paul, F ... 315-684-6081 ... 354 F
griffipf@morrisville.edu
GRIFFIN, Randy, R ... 541-881-5595 ... 420 E
rgriffin@tvcc.cc
GRIFFIN, Rick ... 619-644-7868 ... 49 A
rick.griffin@gcccd.edu
GRIFFIN, Robert, S ... 804-758-6731 ... 527 G
rgriffin@rappahannock.edu
GRIFFIN, Sallie ... 601-877-6377 ... 273 C
sgriffin@alcorn.edu
GRIFFIN, Stephen ... 504-865-5910 ... 215 C
sgriffin@tulane.edu
GRIFFIN, Susan ... 513-745-3311 ... 406 E
0565mgr@fheg.follett.com
GRIFFIN, Tamara ... 870-612-2022 ... 25 E
tamara.griffin@uaccb.edu
GRIFFIN, Thomas, H ... 919-515-5036 ... 378 B
tommy_griffin@ncsu.edu
GRIFFIN, Tim ... 719-502-2320 ... 86 G
tim.griffin@ppcc.edu
GRIFFIN, Timothy ... 201-216-5325 ... 315 E
tgriffin@stevens.edu
GRIFFIN, Walt, R ... 864-488-4616 ... 459 A
wgriffin@limestone.edu
GRIFFIN, William ... 910-678-8564 ... 370 B
griffinw@faytechcc.edu
GRIFFIN-SOBEL, Joyce ... 212-772-4000 ... 327 E
GRIFFIS, Mary, E ... 660-543-4359 ... 291 B
griffis@ucmo.edu
GRIFFIS, William, I ... 912-478-5253 ... 131 A
bgriffis@georgiasouthern.edu
GRIFFITH, Barry ... 336-725-8344 ... 375 F
griffb@pbc.edu
GRIFFITH, Becki, S ... 281-425-6399 ... 489 J
bgriffit@lee.edu
GRIFFITH, Cynthia ... 804-594-1576 ... 526 G
cgriffith@jtcc.edu
GRIFFITH, Debbie ... 828-232-5066 ... 378 C
dgriffit@unca.edu
GRIFFITH, Dennis, J ... 330-369-3200 ... 402 H
tbcmail@tbc-trumbullbusiness.com
GRIFFITH, Dennis, R ... 937-393-3431 ... 401 K
dgriffith@soucc.sscc.edu
GRIFFITH, Dennison, W ... 614-222-3220 ... 388 F
dgriffith@ccad.edu
GRIFFITH, Ivelaw, L ... 718-262-2780 ... 329 B
provost@york.cuny.edu
GRIFFITH, Janice, C ... 617-573-8120 ... 245 E
jgriffith@suffolk.edu
GRIFFITH, Jeffrey ... 505-272-2321 ... 321 C
jkgriffith@salud.unm.edu
GRIFFITH, John ... 610-526-5160 ... 423 C
jgriffith@brynmawr.edu
GRIFFITH, John, V ... 864-833-8222 ... 460 E
griffith@presby.edu
GRIFFITH, Jolene ... 641-782-7081 ... 189 A
griffith@swcciowa.edu
GRIFFITH, Kathy ... 740-392-6868 ... 396 H
kathy.griffity@mvnu.edu
GRIFFITH, Kelley ... 317-955-6090 ... 177 G
kelleygr@marian.edu
GRIFFITH, Kippi, R ... 512-448-8405 ... 493 B
kippig@stedwards.edu
GRIFFITH, Larry ... 765-361-6212 ... 181 C
griffitl@wabash.edu
GRIFFITH, Larry, K ... 724-847-6585 ... 429 G
lkgriffith@geneva.edu
GRIFFITH, Mark ... 716-829-7551 ... 332 F
griffith@dyc.edu
GRIFFITH, Maxine, F ... 212-854-6524 ... 330 F
mfg30@columbia.edu
GRIFFITH, Mike ... 541-880-2244 ... 416 C
griffith@klamathcc.edu
GRIFFITH, Patricia, A ... 740-774-7200 ... 399 H
griffith@ohio.edu
GRIFFITH, Roger, D ... 304-647-6563 ... 542 H
rgriffith@newriver.edu
GRIFFITH, Ross, A ... 336-758-5244 ... 380 B
GRIFFITH, Sally ... 847-925-6793 ... 151 E
sgriffit@harpercollege.edu
GRIFFITH, Steven, J ... 515-961-1720 ... 188 F
steve.griffith@simpson.edu
GRIFFITH, Susan ... 956-665-2383 ... 506 A
sgriffith@utpa.edu
GRIFFITHS, Andy ... 207-288-5015 ... 217 H
agriffiths@coa.edu
GRIFFITHS, Deborah, H ... 252-451-8336 ... 372 B
debg@nash.cc.nc.us
GRIFFITHS, Fredrick ... 413-542-2123 ... 230 A
GRIFFITHS, Jose-Marie ... 401-232-6060 ... 453 A
jgriffiths@bryant.edu
GRIFFITHS, Kelly, A ... 334-683-2372 ... 5 G
kgriffiths@marionmilitary.edu
GRIFFITHS, Lloyd, J ... 703-993-1500 ... 519 A
lgriff@gmu.edu
GRIFFITHS, Slade ... 620-441-6584 ... 192 A
griffiths@cowley.edu
GRIFFUS, Randall ... 706-272-4440 ... 127 G
rgriffus@daltonstate.edu
GRIGALUNAS, Jon ... 708-456-0300 ... 166 C
jgrigalu@triton.edu
GRIGG, Daniel, G ... 817-257-7524 ... 498 F
d.grigg@tcu.edu
GRIGG, Daniel, J ... 336-334-4822 ... 370 E
djgrigg@gtcc.edu
GRIGG, Eddie, G ... 704-334-6882 ... 367 E
egrigg@nlts.edu
GRIGGS, Carmen, S ... 617-912-9121 ... 232 E
cgriggs@bostonconservatory.edu
GRIGGS, Cindy ... 859-371-9393 ... 198 D
cgriggs@beckfield.edu
GRIGGS, Deborah ... 334-420-4260 ... 7 I
dgriggs@trenholmstate.edu
GRIGGS, Donald, R ... 843-953-5540 ... 457 B
griggsd@cofc.edu
GRIGGS, Gary, B ... 831-459-2464 ... 75 A
griggs@es.ucsc.edu
GRIGGS, Judith, R ... 412-396-6661 ... 428 C
griggs@duq.edu
GRIGGS, Michelle ... 815-394-5112 ... 162 H
mgriggs@rockford.edu
GRIGGS, Robert, J ... 218-755-2015 ... 266 B
rgriggs@bemidjistate.edu
GRIGGS, Ronald, K ... 740-427-5667 ... 394 C
griggs@kenyon.edu
GRIGGS, Ronald, K ... 740-427-5632 ... 394 C
griggs@kenyon.edu
GRIGGS, Thomas, J ... 906-786-5802 ... 249 D
griggst@baycollege.edu
GRIGGS-GRIFFIN, Ebony ... 859-344-4069 ... 206 D
ebony.griggs-griffin@thomasmore.edu
GRIGSBY, Beth ... 712-279-5504 ... 182 E
beth.grigsby@briarcliff.edu
GRIGSBY, Bryon, L ... 540-665-4525 ... 523 K
bgrigsby@su.edu
GRIGSBY, Lindle, D ... 972-860-7199 ... 484 H
LGrigsby@dcccd.edu
GRIGSBY, Mark ... 918-540-6275 ... 408 J
mgrigsby@neo.edu
GRIJALVA, Luis-Pablo ... 936-261-9300 ... 496 E
lpgrijalva@pvamu.edu
GRIJALVA, Sara ... 575-835-5133 ... 319 A
sjgrijalva@admin.nmt.edu
GRILL, Joshua, L ... 570-577-3200 ... 423 D
josh.grill@bucknell.edu
GRILL, Stephen, A ... 574-372-5100 ... 171 E
grillsa@grace.edu
GRILLI, Eugene, P ... 330-941-1331 ... 406 F
epgrilli@ysu.edu
GRILLI, Joseph ... 570-740-0243 ... 435 C
jgrilli@luzerne.edu
GRILLO, Mary Ann ... 212-226-5500 ... 323 C
mgrillo@aii.edu
GRILLO, Robert ... 305-348-2738 ... 119 B
robert.grillo@fiu.edu
GRILLOT, Larry, R ... 405-325-3821 ... 413 C
lrgrillot@ou.edu
GRIM, Sandy ... 304-384-5290 ... 543 D
counseling_center@concord.edu
GRIMARD, Rocky ... 210-349-4173 ... 491 E
orc@ost.edu
GRIMES, Charles, R ... 330-471-8438 ... 395 E
cgrimes@malone.edu
GRIMES, Darrell ... 806-894-9611 ... 494 C
dgrimes@southplainscollege.edu
GRIMES, Debbie, J ... 205-391-2233 ... 7 A
dgrimes@sheltonstate.edu
GRIMES, Deborah ... 252-527-6223 ... 371 D
dgrimes@lenoircc.edu
GRIMES, Donnie ... 606-539-4197 ... 206 G
donnie.grimes@ucumberlands.edu
GRIMES, Howard, D ... 509-335-6412 ... 539 A
grimes@wsu.edu
GRIMES, Judith ... 816-271-5991 ... 287 A
grimes@missouriwestern.edu
GRIMES, Larry ... 304-829-7420 ... 540 E
lgrimes@bethanywv.edu
GRIMES, Lee ... 956-872-7271 ... 494 D
lgrimes@southtexascollege.edu
GRIMES, Mark ... 812-749-1368 ... 178 D
mgrimes@oak.edu
GRIMES, Paul ... 620-235-4598 ... 195 I
paul.grimes@pittstate.edu
GRIMES, Robert ... 212-636-6300 ... 334 C
rgrimes@fordham.edu
GRIMES, Robert (Bud), D ... 731-881-7615 ... 477 E
bgrimes@utm.edu
GRIMES, Steve ... 918-540-6226 ... 408 J
sgrimes@neo.edu
GRIMES, Terri, A ... 815-599-3514 ... 152 A
terri.grimes@highland.edu
GRIMES, Tresmaine ... 914-633-2206 ... 336 E
tgrimes@iona.edu
GRIMES, William, S ... 512-505-3021 ... 488 B
wsgrimes@htu.edu
GRIMM, Carol, M ... 218-477-2327 ... 268 A
grimm@mnstate.edu
GRIMM, Dan ... 954-731-8880 ... 103 F
GRIMM, Gary ... 503-370-6814 ... 421 C
ggrimm@willamette.edu
GRIMM, Keith ... 503-370-6210 ... 421 C
kgrimm@willamette.edu
GRIMM, Randy ... 816-322-0110 ... 279 H
randy.grimm@calvary.edu
GRIMM, Rich ... 731-661-5102 ... 476 G
rgrimm@uu.edu
GRIMM, Robert, J ... 610-683-4120 ... 442 F
grimm@kutztown.edu
GRIMM, Tony ... 815-935-4992 ... 160 F
tgrimm@olivet.edu
GRIMMER, Karen, D ... 618-374-5152 ... 161 D
karen.grimmer@principia.edu
GRIMMER, Kevin, M ... 315-792-7520 ... 356 B
grimmek@sunyit.edu
GRIMMER, Nicholas, J ... 305-684-6030 ... 354 F
grimmenj@morrisville.edu
GRIMMETTE, Ronald, D ... 312-850-7450 ... 147 C
rgrimmette@ccc.edu
GRIMSLEY, Deloris ... 973-877-3056 ... 310 A
dgrimsle@essex.edu
GRIMSLEY, Linda ... 229-430-4635 ... 123 H
linda.grimsley@asurams.edu
GRIMSON, W. Eric, L ... 617-253-9742 ... 242 A
welg@mit.edu
GRINDEL, Cecelia, M ... 404-413-1100 ... 131 C
cgrindel@gsu.edu
GRINDELL, Monique ... 503-352-1566 ... 419 E
grindelm@pacificu.edu
GRINDLE, Charles ... 845-938-2729 ... 558 G
8ocio@usma.edu
GRINNAN, Susan ... 804-706-5035 ... 526 G
sgrinnan@jtcc.edu
GRINNELL, Jimmy, E ... 704-687-4585 ... 378 E
jegrinne@uncc.edu
GRINNELL, Mike ... 509-542-4898 ... 532 C
mgrinnell@columbiabasin.edu
GRINO, Placido ... 713-798-8085 ... 481 H
grino@bcm.edu
GRIPP, Kristine ... 216-791-5000 ... 388 B
kristine.gripp@case.edu
GRIPPIN, Margaret ... 518-255-5516 ... 354 E
grippim@cobleskill.edu
GRISCOM, William, E ... 717-299-7722 ... 447 H
griscom@stevenscollege.edu
GRISHAM, Bob ... 360-438-4372 ... 536 F
bgrisham@stmartin.edu
GRISHAM, Elizabeth ... 417-255-7240 ... 286 G
elizabethgrisham@missouristate.edu
GRISHAM, Linda ... 781-239-3147 ... 240 D
lgrisham@massbay.edu
GRISI, Mark, P ... 215-968-8391 ... 423 E
grisim@bucks.edu
GRISSETT, Jendia ... 334-386-7264 ... 3 H
jgrissett@faulkner.edu
GRISSOM, Cytha, D ... 717-477-1444 ... 443 D
cdgris@ship.edu
GRISSOM, Randy ... 505-428-1252 ... 320 E
randy.grissom@sfcc.edu
GRISWOLD, Al ... 206-587-5482 ... 537 A
agriswold@sccd.ctc.edu
GRISWOLD, Anna, M ... 814-863-0507 ... 438 F
amg5@psu.edu
GRISWOLD, Cecilia ... 660-359-3948 ... 287 D
cgriswold@mail.ncmissouri.edu
GRISWOLD, Emmett ... 229-430-3396 ... 123 I
egriswold@albanytech.edu
GRISWOLD, Mac ... 713-348-6163 ... 492 J
griswold@rice.edu
GRISWOLD, Richard, M ... 617-262-5000 ... 232 B
richard.griswold@the-bac.edu
GRITTON, Mark ... 559-934-2455 ... 77 I
markgritton@whccd.edu
GRITZAN, Walt ... 330-339-3391 ... 394 B
wgritzan@kent.edu
GRIZANTI, Vincent ... 716-896-0700 ... 359 F
vgrizanti@villa.edu
GRIZZLE, Debra, F ... 706-245-7226 ... 128 K
dgrizzle@ec.edu
GRIZZLE, Jeff ... 870-512-7866 ... 20 F
jeff_grizzle@asun.edu
GRIZZLE, Jerry, W ... 575-624-8001 ... 319 C
supt@nmmi.edu
GROAT, Gary ... 415-380-1330 ... 48 D
garygroat@ggbts.edu
GROB, Keith ... 859-622-3840 ... 200 D
admissions@eku.edu
GROBER, David, J ... 724-589-2842 ... 448 A
dgrober@thiel.edu

GROBINS, Mary Alice .... 360-416-7719.... 538 A
maryalice.grobins@skagit.edu
GROBSMITH, Elizabeth, S . 928-523-2230...... 17 A
liz.grobsmith@nau.edu
GRODE-HANKS, Carol ...... 605-995-7103.... 464 E
carol.grode-hanks@mitchelltech.edu
GROELING, Jeff .... 260-744-8746.... 179 F
jfgroeling@taylor.edu
GROENEMAN, Ryan .... 636-797-3000.... 283 H
rgroenem@jeffco.edu
GROENER, Michael .... 323-259-2646...... 59 H
groenerm@oxy.edu
GROENINGER, Sandra .... 847-543-2345.... 147 H
sgroeninger@clcillinois.edu
GROENWALD, Susan, L .... 630-512-8900.... 280 A
sgroenwald@chamberlain.edu
GROFF, Keith .... 614-947-6122.... 391 A
groffk@franklin.edu
GROFF, Rodney .... 717-728-2258.... 425 A
rodgroff@centralpenn.edu
GROGAN, Anne .... 617-349-8155.... 236 G
agrogan@lesley.edu
GROGAN, Fred, L .... 816-604-2044.... 285 G
fred.grogan@mcckc.edu
GROGAN, Margaret .... 909-621-8075...... 40 C
margaret.grogan@cgu.edu
GROGAN, Rita .... 408-855-5072...... 78 A
rita.grogan@wvm.edu
GROGAN LAVIN,
Bernadette .... 718-990-1980.... 348 G
lavinb@stjohns.edu
GROGG, Sam, L .... 516-877-4125.... 322 A
sgrogg@adelphi.edu
GROH, Sara .... 315-228-6134.... 329 H
sgroh@colgate.edu
GROH BECK, Genelle .... 507-457-1421.... 271 G
ggroh@smumn.edu
GROHAM, Jean .... 251-580-2293........ 5 A
jgroham@faulknerstate.edu
GROHMAN, Adam .... 516-299-2256.... 339 A
adam.grohman@liu.edu
GROLEAU, Dan .... 715-365-4450.... 554 F
dgroleau@nicoletcollege.edu
GROLEAU, Ron, W .... 815-224-0482.... 153 D
ron_groleau@ivcc.edu
GROM, Nancy, S .... 412-531-4433.... 426 F
info@deantech.edu
GROMAN, Beth .... 260-399-7700.... 180 E
bgroman@sf.edu
GROMATZKY, Steven .... 913-360-7511.... 190 F
sgromatzky@benedictine.edu
GRONA, Marion .... 940-552-6291.... 507 E
mgrona@vernoncollege.edu
GRONBECK-TEDESCO,
Susan .... 785-864-6161.... 196 F
slgt@ku.edu
GRONDAHL, Mary, M .... 518-454-5150.... 330 C
grondahm@strose.edu
GRONER, Steve .... 618-532-2049.... 155 A
sgroner@kaskaskia.edu
GRONNIGER, Eileen, C ...... 785-442-6010.... 193 D
egronniger@highlandcc.edu
GRONO, Anthony .... 718-817-4943.... 334 C
grono@fordham.edu
GROOM, David .... 503-255-0332.... 417 C
dgroomjr@multnomah.edu
GROOME, Jean, M .... 336-734-7292.... 370 C
jgroome@forsythtech.edu
GROOMS, Craig .... 814-732-2761.... 442 D
eup_admissions@edinboro.edu
GROOMS, David .... 808-984-3376.... 142 B
grooms@hawaii.edu
GROOMS, Jean, M .... 843-792-3433.... 459 C
groomsj@musc.edu
GROOMS, Jerri, H .... 931-540-2538.... 474 F
jgrooms@columbiastate.edu
GROOP, Judith, M .... 717-691-6035.... 436 D
jgroop@messiah.edu
GROOT, Joycelyn .... 714-241-6323...... 40 J
jgroot@coastline.edu
GROOTERS, Stacy .... 508-565-1324.... 245 D
sgrooters@stonehill.edu
GROOVER, Brenda .... 417-864-7220.... 282 B
bgroover@cci.edu
GROOVER, Diane .... 520-206-4592...... 17 I
dgroover@pima.edu
GROOVER, Joann, V .... 803-938-3789.... 462 F
groover@vm.sc.edu
GROOVER, John .... 912-486-7602.... 134 H
jgroover@ogeecheetech.edu
GROOVER, R. Edwin .... 404-669-2065.... 135 E
eddie.groover@point.edu
GROPEN, Laura .... 760-744-1150...... 61 C
lgropen@palomar.edu
GROPP, Douglas, M .... 214-528-8600.... 492 F
GROPP, Jonathan .... 864-622-6011.... 455 C
jgropp@andersonuniversity.edu
GROPPER, Idania, R .... 904-620-1707.... 120 C
igropper@unf.edu
GROS, Kathy, R .... 504-865-3552.... 213 F
kgros@loyno.edu
GROSBY, Karen .... 954-262-5716.... 114 B
grosby@nsu.nova.edu
GROSETH, Jaynee .... 406-994-2401.... 295 E
jgroseth@montana.edu
GROSETH, Rolf, S .... 406-657-2300.... 295 F
rolf.groseth@msubillings.edu
GROSHANS, David, E .... 308-635-6105.... 301 E
groshans@wncc.edu
GROSHONG, Matt .... 425-564-5608.... 531 B
matt.groshon@bellevuecollege.edu
GROSOVSKY, Andrew .... 617-287-5775.... 237 D
andrew.grosovsky@umb.edu
GROSPITCH, Eric .... 816-235-8955.... 291 E
grospitche@umkc.edu
GROSS, Anne .... 303-871-3382...... 88 E
agross@du.edu
GROSS, Barbara, L .... 818-677-2121...... 35 D
barbara.gross@csun.edu
GROSS, Bernard, M .... 301-459-8686.... 226 D
rbernard@host.sdc.edu
GROSS, Bill .... 605-274-4311.... 463 H
bill.gross@augie.edu
GROSS, Bryan, J .... 203-576-4552...... 94 D
bgross@bridgeport.edu
GROSS, Carla, E .... 717-691-6027.... 436 D
cgross@messiah.edu
GROSS, Daryl, J .... 315-443-8705.... 357 B
djgross@syr.edu
GROSS, David .... 217-545-8080.... 164 H
dgross@siu.edu
GROSS, Dolores .... 915-831-2122.... 486 E
dgross2@epcc.edu
GROSS, James .... 651-748-2609.... 266 D
james.gross@century.edu
GROSS, Jeffrey .... 920-465-2300.... 551 A
grossj@uwgb.edu
GROSS, Karen .... 802-447-6319.... 514 D
kgross@svc.edu
GROSS, Laura .... 518-255-5626.... 354 E
grossll@cobleskill.edu
GROSS, Mary Margaret ...... 610-861-1350.... 436 I
registrar@moravian.edu
GROSS, Michael .... 508-362-2131.... 240 A
mgross@capecod.edu
GROSS, Michael .... 732-987-2373.... 310 D
gross@georgian.edu
GROSS, Michelle .... 410-951-3610.... 228 B
mgross@coppin.edu
GROSS, Monika .... 301-860-4091.... 228 A
mgross@bowiestate.edu
GROSS, Nancy, L .... 609-497-7880.... 312 F
nancy.gross@ptsem.edu
GROSS, Natalie .... 914-337-0700.... 350 C
ngross@sarahlawrence.edu
GROSS, Scott .... 606-436-5721.... 201 H
scott.gross@kctcs.edu
GROSS, Susan .... 212-431-2828.... 343 E
sgross@nyls.edu
GROSS, Susan .... 212-431-2888.... 343 E
sgross@nyls.edu
GROSS, Tim .... 770-426-2611.... 133 B
tim.gross@life.edu
GROSSBERG, Richard .... 718-951-5296.... 326 G
richardg@brooklyn.cuny.edu
GROSSE, Eric, F .... 202-419-4168...... 99 D
eric.grosse@strayer.edu
GROSSE, Mike .... 502-451-0815.... 206 C
mgrosse@sullivan.edu
GROSSE, Mike .... 502-456-0004.... 206 B
mgrosse@sullivan.edu
GROSSET, Jane, M .... 215-751-8085.... 426 B
jgrosset@ccp.edu
GROSSI, OSB, Anthony ...... 724-537-4554.... 446 E
anthony.grossi@email.stvincent.edu
GROSSI, Deann .... 312-777-8665.... 153 A
dgrossi@aii.edu
GROSSI, Joseph, P .... 617-353-4330.... 232 G
jgrossi@bu.edu
GROSSINGER, Harvey .... 202-651-5000...... 97 E
harvey.grossinger@gallaudet.edu
GROSSKOPF, John .... 850-973-1601.... 113 J
grosskopfj@nfcc.edu
GROSSMAN, Claudio .... 202-274-4004...... 97 B
grossman@american.edu
GROSSMAN, David .... 760-252-2411...... 30 F
dgrossman@barstow.edu
GROSSMAN, Divina .... 305-348-7752.... 119 B
divina.grossman@fiu.edu
GROSSMAN, LuAnn .... 605-331-6738.... 466 D
luann.grossman@usiouxfalls.edu
GROSSMAN, Miriam .... 845-425-1370.... 345 B
GROSZ, Dale .... 701-671-2188.... 382 E
dale.grosz@ndscs.edu
GROSZ, Ken .... 701-228-5431.... 382 C
ken.grosz@dakotacollege.edu
GROSZ, Kenneth .... 701-228-5431.... 381 G
ken.grosz@dakotacollege.edu
GROTE, Linda .... 205-391-2253........ 7 A
lgrote@sheltonstate.edu
GROTGEN, John .... 229-333-5940.... 138 F
jgrotgen@valdosta.edu
GROTH, Cary .... 775-784-6900.... 303 A
cgroth@unr.edu
GROTH, Sue .... 360-442-2110.... 535 C
sgroth@lowercolumbia.edu
GROTHE, Cathy .... 712-749-2120.... 182 G
grothec@bvu.edu
GROTHE, Malcom, P .... 206-934-5303.... 537 B
malcolm.grothe@seattlecolleges.edu
GROTHOUS, Tom .... 419-227-3141.... 404 D
trgrot@unoh.edu
GROTRIAN, James .... 402-457-2335.... 298 H
jgrotrian@mccneb.edu
GROUSOSKY, David, P .... 412-396-6699.... 428 C
grousosk@duq.edu
GROUT, David .... 574-372-5100.... 171 E
groutd@grace.edu
GROUT, John .... 706-236-2233.... 125 G
jgrout@berry.edu
GROVA, Beverly .... 831-755-6810...... 49 C
bgrova@hartnell.edu
GROVE, Dana .... 913-469-8500.... 193 I
dgrove@jccc.edu
GROVE, Daryl .... 563-425-5311.... 189 C
groved@uiu.edu
GROVE, Doug .... 714-556-3610...... 76 E
dgrove@vanguard.edu
GROVE, Helen .... 937-512-2522.... 401 J
helen.grove@sinclair.edu
GROVE, Kathryne .... 303-871-7436...... 88 E
Kathryne.Grove@du.edu
GROVE, Kathy, M .... 641-422-4382.... 187 F
grovekat@niacc.edu
GROVE, Laurie .... 717-396-7188.... 447 H
grove@stevenscollege.edu
GROVE, Luke, J .... 515-574-1035.... 185 F
grove@iowacentral.edu
GROVE, Russell .... 208-376-7731.... 142 E
russellg@boisebible.edu
GROVE, Shannon, D .... 814-886-6391.... 437 A
sgrove@mtaloy.edu
GROVE-MARKWOOD,
Robert .... 207-942-6781.... 217 B
rgrove-markwood@bts.edu
GROVER, Arthur .... 215-951-1300.... 432 G
grover77@lasalle.edu
GROVER, Barbara .... 801-957-4434.... 512 C
barbara.grover@slcc.edu
GROVER, Carol, N .... 315-279-5252.... 337 K
cgrover@mail.keuka.edu
GROVER, Herbert .... 806-291-1118.... 508 B
groverh@wbu.edu
GROVER, Joan .... 480-654-7702...... 15 K
joni.grover@mcmail.maricopa.edu
GROVER, Rajiv .... 901-678-3633.... 474 C
rgrover@memphis.edu
GROVER-ROOSA, Janice ...... 307-382-1701.... 556 F
jgrover@wwcc.wy.edu
GROVES, Allen, W .... 434-924-7429.... 525 B
awg8vd@virginia.edu
GROVES, Betsy, A .... 508-856-2265.... 238 A
betsy.groves@umassmed.edu
GROVES, Danford .... 910-272-3335.... 373 A
dgroves@robeson.edu
GROVES, Denise .... 254-968-9121.... 496 F
registrar@tarleton.edu
GROVES, Eric .... 619-849-2520...... 62 L
ericgroves@pointloma.edu
GROVES, Glenn .... 215-567-7080.... 422 C
ggroves@edmc.edu
GROVES, Greg .... 318-397-6167.... 210 J
ggroves@myneltc.edu
GROVES, Jason .... 325-674-2646.... 478 H
jason.groves@acu.edu
GROVES, Jay .... 309-438-5631.... 153 C
jrgrove@ilstu.edu
GROVES, Kathleen, H .... 585-395-2317.... 352 F
kgroves@brockport.edu
GROVES, Kathy .... 573-592-1106.... 293 E
kathy.groves@williamwoods.edu
GROVES, Mike .... 970-245-8101...... 85 D
mgrove@intelliteccollege.edu
GROVES, Monica, R .... 651-631-5380.... 270 E
mrgroves@nwc.edu
GROVES, Robert .... 517-884-1008.... 255 D
grovesr@msu.edu
GROW, David .... 801-274-3280.... 512 E
dgrow@wgu.edu
GROWDEN, Melissa, A .... 517-264-7614.... 258 D
mgrowden@sienaheights.edu
GROWDON, James, F .... 610-785-6252.... 446 A
academicdcdscs@adphila.org
GROWNEY, Kathy .... 603-668-2211.... 306 B
k.growney@snhu.edu
GROWNS, Richard, O .... 501-977-2024...... 25 G
growns@uaccm.edu
GROZA, Adam .... 415-380-1448...... 48 D
adamgroza@ggbts.edu
GROZEN BIERI, Deborah .. 617-266-1400.... 231 G
GRUBB, Geoffrey, J .... 419-824-3818.... 395 D
ggrubb@lourdes.edu
GRUBB, Lillie .... 620-223-2700.... 192 G
lillieg@fortscott.edu
GRUBBS, Lisa .... 985-447-7244.... 216 A
lisa.grubbs@nicholls.edu
GRUBE, Dave .... 616-222-1412.... 250 C
dave.grube@cornerstone.edu
GRUBE, M. Marshall .... 423-439-4219.... 473 E
grube@etsu.edu
GRUBE, Sean .... 816-501-4843.... 288 D
sean.grube@rockhurst.edu
GRUBER, Christopher, J .... 704-894-2710.... 363 F
chgruber@davidson.edu
GRUBER, Donna .... 419-434-4540.... 404 B
gruber@findlay.edu
GRUBER, Thomas .... 504-671-6480.... 210 G
tgrube@dcc.edu
GRUBIAK, Michael .... 360-736-9391.... 531 H
mgrubiak@centralia.edu
GRUBIS, Sharon .... 727-864-7677.... 104 K
grubissm@eckerd.edu
GRUBY, Elizabeth .... 773-878-3752.... 163 D
egruby@staugustine.edu
GRUEN, Kris .... 802-322-1721.... 513 C
kris.gruen@goddard.edu
GRUENBERGER, Moses .... 718-854-2290.... 324 A
GRUENDYKE, Randall .... 765-998-5205.... 179 F
rngruendyke@taylor.edu
GRUENING, Jennifer .... 309-677-4939.... 145 H
jgruening@bradley.edu
GRUENING, Kyle .... 715-365-4481.... 554 F
gruening@nicoletcollege.edu
GRUENLOH, Gwen .... 719-336-1572...... 85 K
gwen.gruenloh@lamarcc.edu
GRUETT, Jon .... 314-968-6903.... 293 A
gruettjo@webster.edu
GRUETZEMACHER,
Richard, R .... 423-425-4007.... 477 D
richard-gruetzemacher@utc.edu
GRUGEL, Kenneth, E .... 814-393-2315.... 442 A
kgrugel@clarion.edu
GRUHLER, Sarah .... 360-992-2406.... 532 A
sgruhler@clark.edu
GRUICHICH, Dawn .... 480-732-7050...... 15 G
dawn.gruichich@cgcmail.maricopa.edu
GRULKE, Kimmi .... 928-226-4343...... 13 H
kimmi.grulke@coconino.edu
GRUMBLES, Owen Kent ..... 336-316-2499.... 364 E
grumblesok@gulford.edu
GRUMET, Barbara .... 718-260-5345.... 328 E
bgrumet@citytech.cuny.edu
GRUNBLATT, Akiva .... 718-268-4700.... 347 B
GRUND, Faye .... 419-520-2602.... 384 D
fgrund@ashland.edu
GRUNDBERG, Andy .... 202-639-1847...... 97 D
agrundberg@corcoran.org
GRUNDEN, Cynthia .... 773-907-4810.... 147 A
cgrunden@ccc.edu
GRUNDEN, Jennifer, J .... 302-857-1040...... 96 D
jgrunden@dtcc.edu
GRUNDER, John .... 831-647-6512...... 57 F
john.grunder@miis.edu
GRUNDER, Mark .... 989-358-7317.... 247 G
grunderm@alpenacc.edu
GRUNDHAUSER, Tony .... 651-523-2219.... 264 C
agrundhauser01@hamline.edu
GRUNDIG, John .... 863-680-6212.... 109 D
jgrundig@flsouthern.edu
GRUNDY, Diane, H .... 724-458-2049.... 430 B
dhgrundy@gcc.edu
GRUNDY, Jeffrey, W .... 973-596-2451.... 312 C
jeffrey.w.grundy@njit.edu
GRUNDY, Marc, A .... 423-236-2834.... 473 A
magrundy@southern.edu
GRUNER, Bradley, W .... 702-651-5920.... 302 G
bradley.gruner@csn.edu
GRUNER, Celeste, A .... 704-216-3459.... 373 C
celeste.gruner@rccc.edu
GRUNEWALD, Mark, A .... 540-458-8502.... 530 A
grunewaldm@wlu.edu
GRUNINGER, Sandra .... 212-686-9040.... 360 E
sgruninger@woodtobecoburn.edu
GRUNOW, Tamie, L .... 989-686-9042.... 250 F
tlgrunow@delta.edu
GRUNWALD, Gerald .... 215-503-8982.... 448 B
gerald.grunwald@jefferson.edu
GRUNWALD, James, R .... 507-354-8221.... 265 B
grunwajr@mlc-wels.edu
GRUPAS, Angela .... 314-984-7388.... 289 D
agrupas@stlcc.edu
GRUS, Shannon, M .... 636-584-6505.... 281 I
smgrus@eastcentral.edu
GRUSH, Joseph .... 815-753-0495.... 160 A
jgrush@niu.edu
GRUSHINSKI, Alberta .... 570-945-8373.... 432 C
alberta.grushinski@keystone.edu
GRUSKA, Julie .... 320-363-3197.... 271 F
jgruska@csbsju.edu
GRUSKA, Julie, E .... 320-363-3395.... 262 H
jgruska@csbsju.edu
GRUSZKA, William .... 404-413-4469.... 131 C
billgruszka@gsu.edu
GRUVER, Barry, L .... 609-497-7705.... 312 F
barry.gruver@ptsem.edu
GRUVER, Wendy .... 903-886-5140.... 497 E
wendy_gruver@tamu-commerce.edu
GRUWELL, Mark, A .... 712-362-0439.... 185 G
mgruwell@iowalakes.edu
GRZESIAK, Michael, P .... 724-503-1001.... 451 A
mgrzesiak@washjeff.edu
GRZYBOWSKI, Mark, J ...... 815-224-0437.... 153 D
mark_grzybowski@ivcc.edu
GSCHWEND, Richard .... 217-875-7200.... 162 D
rqschwend@richland.edu

GSTALDER, Steven ... 203-773-0129 ... 89 H
sgstalder@albertus.edu
GUADAGNINO, Beatrice ... 954-545-4500 ... 117 H
cfo@sfbc.edu
GUADAGNINO, Joseph ... 954-545-4500 ... 117 H
jguadagnino@sfbc.edu
GUADALUPE, Ana, R ... 787-764-0000 ... 566 D
anlupe@uprrp.edu
GUADALUPE, Ana, R ... 787-751-4166 ... 567 F
anlupe@uprrp.edu
GUADALUPE, Sarahi ... 787-769-9965 ... 566 H
sarahi.guadalupe@upr.edu
GUADALUPE, Yvonne ... 787-766-1717 ... 565 G
yguadalupe@suagm.edu
GUADAMUZ, Tatiana ... 510-261-8500 ... 61 F
tatiana.Gaudamuz@patten.edu
GUAJARDO, Dan ... 918-495-7703 ... 411 C
dguajardo@oru.edu
GUAL, Karen ... 954-382-6441 ... 122 C
kgual@tiu.edu
GUALTIERI, Karen ... 845-574-4226 ... 347 I
kgualtie@sunyrockland.edu
GUAN, Sharon ... 773-325-7726 ... 148 F
xguan@depaul.edu
GUANCI-THERRIEN,
Patricia ... 603-641-7202 ... 305 H
pguanci@anselm.edu
GUANG, Virginia ... 787-743-4041 ... 561 E
vguang@columbiaco.edu
GUARASCI, Richard ... 718-390-3131 ... 359 G
guarasci@wagner.edu
GUARDINO, Richard, V ... 516-463-4069 ... 335 H
richard.v.guardino@hofstra.edu
GUARIGLIA, Carolyn, L ... 315-255-1743 ... 325 H
guarigliac@cayuga-cc.edu
GUARIGLIA, Daniel, M ... 716-286-8431 ... 344 D
dmg@niagara.edu
GUASCONI, Joseph ... 973-378-2643 ... 315 B
joseph.guasconi@shu.edu
GUAY, Sheila ... 401-323-6324 ... 453 A
sguay@bryant.edu
GUBAN, Philip ... 440-943-7600 ... 401 G
pguban@dioceseofcleveland.org
GUBBINS, Jean, E ... 216-368-5557 ... 386 E
jeg2@case.edu
GUC, Jeremy ... 248-689-8282 ... 260 A
jguc@walshcollege.edu
GUCKAVAN, Joseph ... 215-641-5520 ... 430 C
guckavan.j@gmc.edu
GUCKERT, Donald, J ... 319-335-1201 ... 182 C
don-guckert@uiowa.edu
GUDBRANSON, Margaret .. 216-421-8016 ... 387 H
mgudbranson@cia.edu
GUDENAU, Henry ... 254-867-3690 ... 500 B
henry.gudenau@tstc.edu
GUDMUNDSON, Donald ... 970-351-2764 ... 88 F
donald.gudmundson@unco.edu
GUEDEA CARRENO,
Lisa, G ... 574-535-7425 ... 171 D
lisagc@goshen.edu
GUELDENZOPH, Derek ... 507-786-3775 ... 271 H
derekg@stolaf.edu
GUELFO, Tammy ... 404-627-2681 ... 126 A
Tammy.Guelfo@beulah.org
GUELICH, Julie ... 952-487-8156 ... 268 C
julie.guelich@normandale.edu
GUEMPEL, Stephen ... 337-550-1301 ... 212 H
GUENARD, Erik, M ... 906-932-4231 ... 251 E
erikg@gogebic.edu
GUENGERICH, Colleen ... 575-835-5525 ... 319 A
cguengerich@admin.nmt.edu
GUENTER-SCHLESINGER,
Sue ... 360-650-3307 ... 539 C
sue.guenter-schlesinger@wwu.edu
GUENTHER, Brenda ... 785-242-5200 ... 549 E
GUENTHER, Brenda ... 785-242-5200 ... 178 E
GUENTHER, Brenda ... 785-242-5200 ... 17 C
GUENTHER, Brenda ... 785-242-5200 ... 195 F
brenda.guenther@ottawa.edu
GUENTHER, Brenda ... 785-242-5200 ... 195 G
GUENTHER, Ronald, E ... 217-333-3631 ... 167 B
rguenthe@illinois.edu
GUERCIO, Greg ... 254-867-3801 ... 500 B
greg.guercio@tstc.edu
GUERIN, David ... 318-257-4854 ... 215 F
dguerin@latech.edu
GUERIN, Fae ... 908-835-2302 ... 317 C
guerin@warren.edu
GUERIN, Keith ... 908-526-1200 ... 313 E
kguerin@raritanval.edu
GUERIN, Michael, W ... 909-869-3065 ... 33 G
mguerin@csupomona.edu
GUERIN, Thomas, B ... 513-556-2389 ... 403 D
tom.guerin@uc.edu
GUERRA, Blanca ... 210-567-2621 ... 506 E
guerrabe@uthscsa.edu
GUERRA, Dahlia ... 956-665-2175 ... 506 A
guerrad@utpa.edu
GUERRA, Elizabeth ... 909-469-5418 ... 78 D
guerra@westernu.edu
GUERRA, Esmeralda ... 956-665-2100 ... 506 A
engdc@utpa.edu
GUERRA, John ... 239-287-5196 ... 119 A
jguerra@fgcu.edu
GUERRA, Jorge ... 954-201-8800 ... 102 A
jguerra@broward.edu
GUERRA, Juan, M ... 512-245-2820 ... 501 C
jg76@txstate.edu
GUERRA, Kimberly ... 510-261-8500 ... 61 F
kim.guerra@patten.edu
GUERRA, Luis ... 510-436-1516 ... 50 F
guerra@hnu.edu
GUERRA, Manuel ... 503-365-4684 ... 414 J
manuel.guerra@chemeketa.edu
GUERRA, Michael ... 559-489-2232 ... 72 A
michael.guerra@fresnocitycollege.edu
GUERRA, Olga ... 610-527-0200 ... 445 I
oguerra@rosemont.edu
GUERRA, Olivia ... 972-860-8065 ... 484 G
oguerra@dcccd.edu
GUERRA, Ron ... 336-841-9363 ... 365 A
rguerra@highpoint.edu
GUERRA, Sabra ... 254-968-9770 ... 496 F
sguerra@tarleton.edu
GUERREIRO, Mario, H ... 417-268-1000 ... 279 B
mguerreiro@agts.edu
GUERRERO, Alfred, A ... 310-287-4314 ... 55 F
guerreraa@wlac.edu
GUERRERO, Blas ... 925-439-2181 ... 43 D
bguerrero@losmedanos.edu
GUERRERO, Carmen ... 805-986-5824 ... 77 C
cguerrero@vcccd.edu
GUERRERO, Daniel, G ... 310-206-6382 ... 74 A
dguerrero@athletics.ucla.edu
GUERRERO, Dolores ... 361-593-4410 ... 498 A
dolores.guerrero@tamuk.edu
GUERRERO, Jennifer ... 609-984-1588 ... 316 A
jguerrero@tesc.edu
GUERRERO, John ... 670-234-5498 ... 559 F
johng@nmcnet.edu
GUERRERO, Ricky ... 318-342-1982 ... 216 E
ulm@campuscornerinc.com
GUERRERO, Sherrie, L ... 909-652-6131 ... 39 B
sherrie.guerrero@chaffey.edu
GUERRERO, Tammy ... 219-989-2675 ... 178 G
guerrero@purduecal.edu
GUERRIERI, Rose, A ... 330-675-8866 ... 394 A
rguerrie@kent.edu
GUERRIERO, Franco ... 740-654-6711 ... 400 B
guerrief@ohio.edu
GUERRIERO, Steven ... 215-248-7120 ... 425 C
guerrieros@chc.edu
GUERRIERO, William ... 480-732-7012 ... 15 G
william.guerriero@cgcmail.maricopa.edu
GUERRISI, Theresa, L ... 717-780-2576 ... 430 E
tlguerri@hacc.edu
GUERTIN, Donna ... 413-565-1000 ... 231 B
dguertin@baypath.edu
GUESS, Melissa ... 660-359-3948 ... 287 D
mguess@mail.ncmissouri.edu
GUEST, James ... 402-472-7488 ... 300 H
jguest2@unl.edu
GUEST, Joshua ... 662-472-2312 ... 274 F
jguest@holmescc.edu
GUETTI, Joan ... 973-761-9022 ... 315 B
joan.guetti@shu.edu
GUEVARA, Christine ... 505-473-6652 ... 320 F
christine.guevara@santafeuniversity.edu
GUEVARA, Julia ... 616-331-2400 ... 252 A
guevaraj@gvsu.edu
GUEVARA, Yamil ... 813-663-0100 ... 99 D
GUEVERRA, Jonathan ... 202-274-7177 ... 99 F
jgueverra@udc.edu
GUFFEY, Larry, D ... 256-228-6001 ... 6 A
ldguffey@nacc.edu
GUFFEY, Paula, J ... 606-679-8501 ... 202 F
paula.guffey@kctcs.edu
GUFFEY, Ryan ... 636-949-4475 ... 284 C
rguffey@lindenwood.edu
GUGE, Gail ... 909-748-8070 ... 75 F
gail_guge@redlands.edu
GUGE, Misty ... 828-627-4506 ... 370 G
mguge@haywood.edu
GUGELCHUK, Gary ... 909-469-5381 ... 78 D
gugelchuk@westernu.edu
GUGENHEIMER, Yirmiya ... 718-853-8500 ... 357 I
GUGERTY, SSND,
Catherine ... 410-617-2997 ... 224 A
cgugerty@loyola.edu
GUGGENHEIM, Joan ... 609-586-4800 ... 311 C
guggenhj@mccc.edu
GUGGENMOS, Karl, J ... 401-598-2244 ... 453 C
kguggenmos@jwu.edu
GUGLIELMO, David ... 757-822-1177 ... 528 C
dguglielomo@tcc.edu
GUGLIELMONI, Mark, J ... 203-254-4080 ... 92 B
mguglielmoni@fairfield.edu
GUICHARD-ASHBROOK,
Danielle ... 617-253-3795 ... 242 A
danielle@mit.edu
GUIDA, Nancy, J ... 212-431-2325 ... 343 E
nguida@nyls.edu
GUIDO, Diane ... 626-812-3034 ... 30 E
dguido@apu.edu
GUIDO, OP, Joseph, J ... 401-865-2687 ... 453 F
jguido@providence.edu
GUIDRY, Stephen ... 954-783-7339 ... 106 D
sguidry@cci.edu
GUILBAUD, Sergeo ... 718-780-1681 ... 338 E
sguilbau@chpnet.org
GUILBAULT, Melodi ... 863-638-7122 ... 123 B
melodi.guilbault@warner.edu
GUILBAULT, Susie ... 909-607-7821 ... 40 C
susie.guilbault@cgu.edu
GUILBE, Robert ... 718-782-2200 ... 324 C
rguilbe@boricuacollege.edu
GUILBEAULT, Nancy, G ... 612-330-1169 ... 261 G
guilbeau@augsburg.edu
GUILBERT, Debra, A ... 740-368-3394 ... 400 F
daguilbe@owu.edu
GUILBERT, Debra, R ... 614-251-4557 ... 398 F
guilberd@ohiodominican.edu
GUILD, Richard, L ... 920-403-3216 ... 550 C
rick.guild@snc.edu
GUILER, Douglas ... 352-365-3526 ... 112 M
guilerd@lscc.edu
GUILER, Jeff ... 614-236-6508 ... 386 C
jguiler@capital.edu
GUILFOILE, Patrick, G ... 218-755-2016 ... 266 B
pguilfoile@bemidjistate.edu
GUILFORD, Arthur, M ... 941-359-4200 ... 121 A
GUILFORD, Arthur, M ... 941-359-4340 ... 120 D
aguilford@sar.usf.edu
GUILFORD, Renate, H ... 703-993-2299 ... 519 A
rguilfor@gmu.edu
GUILIANO, Edward ... 516-686-7650 ... 343 D
edwardg@nyit.edu
GUILL, Steve ... 414-771-2200 ... 550 D
GUILLAUME, JR.,
Alfred, J ... 574-520-4183 ... 174 C
guillaum@iusb.edu
GUILLEN, Alfonso ... 956-364-4600 ... 499 J
al.guillen@harlingen.tstc.edu
GUILLEN, George ... 281-283-3950 ... 503 C
guillen@uhcl.edu
GUILLEN, Patrick ... 310-243-3893 ... 34 B
pguillen@csudh.edu
GUILLETTE, Natalie, L ... 802-656-4183 ... 514 F
natalie.guillette@uvm.edu
GUILLIANI, Melissa ... 787-766-1717 ... 565 G
mguilliani@suagm.edu
GUILLIOT, Jessie ... 650-543-3896 ... 57 B
jguilliot@menlo.edu
GUILLORY, Angela ... 225-578-2171 ... 212 F
angelagu@lsu.edu
GUILLORY, Ann, V ... 201-559-6154 ... 310 C
guillorya@felician.edu
GUILLORY, Justin ... 360-676-2772 ... 535 F
jguillory@nwic.edu
GUILLORY, Sharon, E ... 337-475-5748 ... 215 G
eguillory@mcneese.edu
GUILLORY, Tonya, L ... 202-806-5990 ... 98 B
tguillory@howard.edu
GUILMETTE, Ronald ... 978-837-5555 ... 242 D
ronald.guilmette@merrimack.edu
GUILMETTE, Winfield, L ... 610-409-3591 ... 450 C
wguilmette@ursinus.edu
GUIM, George ... 408-273-2765 ... 58 G
gguim@nhu.edu
GUIMOND, John, M ... 413-265-2294 ... 233 E
guimondj@elms.edu
GUIMOND, Kathy, A ... 505-277-1933 ... 321 C
kguimo@unm.edu
GUINAN, JR., Mark, A ... 607-871-2909 ... 322 F
guinan@alfred.edu
GUINAN, Mary ... 702-895-5090 ... 302 K
mary.guinan@unlv.edu
GUINN, Raines ... 303-457-2757 ... 84 F
rguinn@cci.edu
GUINN, Stephen ... 913-667-5700 ... 191 E
sguinn@cbts.edu
GUINN, Traci, L ... 989-774-3945 ... 249 G
guinn1tl@cmich.edu
GUION, John ... 916-278-7322 ... 35 E
jguion@csus.edu
GUISEPPI, Lori ... 407-478-0500 ... 110 H
lorig@orl.herzing.edu
GUITER, Kristin ... 202-639-1867 ... 97 D
kguiter@corcoran.org
GUIZADO, Roy ... 909-469-5445 ... 78 D
roygpac@westernu.edu
GUKENBERGER, Vickie ... 630-942-8425 ... 147 G
gukenbergerv@cod.edu
GUKICH, Doris, B ... 863-638-7261 ... 123 B
doris.gukich@warner.edu
GULARI, Esin ... 864-656-3202 ... 456 E
egulari@clemson.edu
GULARTE, Mary Anne ... 925-485-5235 ... 38 L
mgularte@clpccd.org
GULARTE, Mary Anne ... 925-485-5235 ... 38 K
mgularte@clpccd.org
GULAS, Charles ... 314-529-9625 ... 284 F
cgulas@maryville.edu
GULBIS, George ... 419-772-3100 ... 398 G
g-gulbis@onu.edu
GULEBIAN, Bryan ... 404-870-8980 ... 139 C
GULEFF, Virginia ... 707-468-3014 ... 57 A
vguleff@mendocino.edu
GULICK, James, K ... 215-951-1535 ... 432 G
gulick@lasalle.edu
GULINO, Tracy ... 858-566-1200 ... 43 J
tgulino@disd.edu
GULLATT, David ... 318-257-3712 ... 215 F
gullattd@latech.edu
GULLEDGE, Jim, E ... 704-463-3366 ... 375 E
jim.gulledge@fsmail.pfeiffer.edu
GULLETT, J. Dan ... 731-286-3237 ... 475 A
gullett@dscc.edu
GULLETT, J. Dan ... 731-286-3327 ... 475 A
gullett@dscc.edu
GULLEY, Jeff ... 260-484-4400 ... 169 G
jgulley@brownmackie.edu
GULLEY, Lawrence ... 662-254-3306 ... 276 C
gulley@mvsu.edu
GULLEY, S. Beverly ... 773-298-3221 ... 163 G
gulley@sxu.edu
GULLEY, Shawn, M ... 504-286-5348 ... 214 I
sgulley@suno.edu
GULLEY, Yancey ... 706-355-5175 ... 124 H
ygulley@athenstech.edu
GULLICKSON, Janet ... 509-434-5060 ... 532 E
jgullickson@ccs.spokane.edu
GULLICKSON, Janet ... 509-434-5060 ... 532 D
jgullickson@ccs.spokane.edu
GULLICKSON, Marcia, A ... 563-387-1400 ... 187 A
gullicma@luther.edu
GULLION, Christy, D ... 202-624-1424 ... 538 F
cgullion@uw.edu
GULLO, Safawo ... 256-726-7054 ... 6 C
sgullo@oakwood.edu
GULLY, Andrew ... 781-736-4213 ... 233 A
agully@brandeis.edu
GULLY, Constance, G ... 314-340-3321 ... 282 I
gullyc@hssu.edu
GULSTAD, Rita ... 660-248-6211 ... 279 K
rgulstad@centralmethodist.edu
GUM, Tory ... 847-628-2082 ... 154 I
tgum@judsonu.edu
GUMA, Susan ... 914-395-2374 ... 350 C
sguma@sarahlawrence.edu
GUMBRIS, Janet ... 508-531-1246 ... 238 B
jgumbris@bridgew.edu
GUMBS, Jean ... 718-270-6222 ... 328 D
jgumbs@mec.cuny.edu
GUMBS, Marva ... 202-994-6495 ... 97 F
mgumbs@gwu.edu
GUMM, Eric ... 325-674-2000 ... 478 H
gummj@acu.edu
GUMMIG, Shanna ... 816-414-3700 ... 286 A
sgummig@mbts.edu
GUMPPER, Marianne, L ... 203-254-4184 ... 92 B
mgumpper@fairfield.edu
GUMZ, Diane ... 503-777-7560 ... 420 A
diane.gumz@reed.edu
GUNBY, Stephanie ... 404-816-4533 ... 132 B
sgunby@atl.herzing.edu
GUNDEN, Randy ... 574-535-7007 ... 171 D
randygg@goshen.edu
GUNDERMAN, Lisa ... 501-977-2025 ... 25 G
gunderman@uaccm.edu
GUNDERSEN, Ryan ... 702-579-3548 ... 302 C
Rgundersen@kaplan.edu
GUNDERSON, Garth, M ... 208-496-3000 ... 142 G
gundersong@byui.edu
GUNDERSON, Gayle, C ... 303-963-3252 ... 81 K
ggunderson@ccu.edu
GUNDERSON, Greg ... 314-968-5911 ... 293 A
greggunderson86@webster.edu
GUNDERSON, Jeff ... 415-749-4559 ... 65 I
jgunderson@sfai.edu
GUNDERSON, Shirley ... 402-399-2435 ... 297 E
GUNDRUM, Peggy ... 847-214-7399 ... 150 D
pgundrum@elgin.edu
GUNEL, Esther ... 734-487-3116 ... 250 H
esther.gunel@emich.edu
GUNN, Cathy ... 606-783-2040 ... 204 E
c.gunn@moreheadstate.edu
GUNN, Christopher, S ... 928-523-2261 ... 17 A
christopher.gunn@nau.edu
GUNN, Daniel, P ... 207-778-7276 ... 220 C
dpgunn@maine.edu
GUNN, E. Anthony ... 336-342-4261 ... 373 B
gunnt@rockinghamcc.edu
GUNN, George, A ... 530-221-4275 ... 69 C
ggunn@shasta.edu
GUNN, Karen ... 801-957-4366 ... 512 C
karen.gunn@slcc.edu
GUNN, Michael, C ... 605-394-2414 ... 466 A
michael.gunn@sdsmt.edu
GUNN, Stanley, T ... 512-223-1200 ... 481 B
sgunn@austincc.edu
GUNN, Tim ... 972-438-6932 ... 492 C
tgunn@parkercc.edu
GUNNELS, Robert ... 870-574-4541 ... 24 A
rgunnels@sautech.edu
GUNNER, Jeanne ... 714-744-7627 ... 39 C
gunner@chapman.edu
GUNNING, Kathleen ... 570-372-4320 ... 447 D
gunning@susqu.edu
GUNNING, Mary Jo ... 570-961-4724 ... 435 F
gunning@marywood.edu
GUNNOE, JR., Charles ... 616-632-2151 ... 248 A
gunnocha@aquinas.edu
GUNS, Michael ... 608-663-4861 ... 547 C
mguns@edgewood.edu

GUNSALUS, Robert ... 408-551-1691 ... 68 C
rgunsalus@scu.edu

GUNSAULUS, Stephan ... 805-546-3279 ... 43 F
sgunsaul@cuesta.edu

GUNSELMAN, Ken ... 402-363-5704 ... 301 F
kgunselman@york.edu

GUNSHOL, Frances ... 443-334-2063 ... 226 E
fgunshol@stevenson.edu

GUNSOLLEY, Joanne ... 785-227-3380 ... 190 G
gunsolleyj@bethanylb.edu

GUNST, Richard ... 630-515-3136 ... 149 A
rgunst@devry.edu

GUNTER, Deby ... 406-771-4392 ... 296 B
dgunter@msugf.edu

GUNTER, Ellen ... 334-291-4918 ... 2 G
ellen.gunter@cv.edu

GUNTER, Gail, P ... 662-329-7333 ... 276 B
ggunter@library.muw.edu

GUNTER, Joan ... 985-549-2301 ... 216 C
joan.gunter@selu.edu

GUNTER, Kathy ... 334-244-3343 ... 2 A
kgunter1@aum.edu

GUNTER, Mary ... 479-968-0398 ... 20 G
mgunter@atu.edu

GUNTER, Pat ... 541-956-7158 ... 420 B
pgunter@roguecc.edu

GUNTER, Philip, L ... 229-333-5950 ... 138 F
pgunter@valdosta.edu

GUNTER, Randy ... 404-880-8787 ... 126 I
rgunter@cau.edu

GUNTER, Randy ... 910-576-6222 ... 372 A
gunterr@montgomery.edu

GUNTER, Steve ... 828-765-7351 ... 371 F
sgunter@mayland.edu

GUNTER-SMITH,
Pamela, J ... 973-408-3073 ... 309 F
pgunter@drew.edu

GUNTHER, Harry, B ... 949-824-6510 ... 73 H
harry.gunther@uci.edu

GUNTHER, Janet ... 270-707-3833 ... 202 A
janet.gunther@kctcs.edu

GUNTHER, Michael ... 661-362-3536 ... 41 G
michael.gunther@canyons.edu

GUNTHORPE, Sydney ... 505-224-3824 ... 317 J
sydney@cnm.edu

GUO, Lan ... 816-781-7700 ... 293 D
guol@william.jewell.edu

GUPCHUP, Girish, V ... 618-650-5163 ... 165 A
ggupchu@siue.edu

GUPTA, Mahendra, R ... 314-935-6344 ... 292 J
guptam@wustl.edu

GUPTA, Rakesh ... 516-877-4629 ... 322 A
gupta@adelphi.edu

GUPTA, Sunil ... 212-346-8449 ... 326 E
sbgupta@bmcc.cuny.edu

GUPTIL, Chris ... 707-864-7199 ... 70 A
Chris.guptl@solano.edu

GURA, Daniel, T ... 813-253-6277 ... 122 H
dgura@ut.edu

GURANOWSKI, Vicki ... 212-217-4100 ... 333 G
vicki_guranowski@fitnyc.edu

GUREK, Shannon, D ... 413-542-2802 ... 230 A
sdqurek@amherst.edu

GURGANUS, Lynn ... 205-665-6030 ... 9 C
gurganus@montevallo.edu

GURLAND, Jerome, S ... 413-782-1508 ... 246 D
jgurland@wne.edu

GURLER, Dan ... 415-575-6125 ... 32 D
dgurler@ciis.edu

GURNON, R, G ... 508-830-5001 ... 239 A
rgurnon@maritime.edu

GURROLA, Jeannette ... 909-607-8632 ... 40 C
jeanette.gurrola@cgu.edu

GURROLA, Virginia ... 559-791-2222 ... 53 A
vgurrola@portervillecollege.edu

GUSEMAN, Dennis ... 760-750-4242 ... 36 B
dguseman@csusm.edu

GUSSIN, Louise ... 410-888-9048 ... 226 F
lgussin@tai.edu

GUST, Jonathan ... 610-519-6508 ... 450 G
jonathan.gust@villanova.edu

GUSTAFSON, Anita, O ... 864-833-8233 ... 460 E
agustafs@presby.edu

GUSTAFSON, Crandon ... 617-262-5000 ... 232 B
Crandon.Gustafson@the-bac.edu

GUSTAFSON, Donna, J ... 812-877-8275 ... 179 A
donna.gustafson@rose-hulman.edu

GUSTAFSON, Eric, P ... 508-849-3298 ... 230 C
egustafson@annamaria.edu

GUSTAFSON, Eric, T ... 704-847-5600 ... 376 H
egustafson@ses.edu

GUSTAFSON, Liz ... 510-580-6715 ... 79 G
lgustafson@cci.edu

GUSTAFSON, Peter, A ... 812-877-8230 ... 179 A
peter.a.gustafson@rose-hulman.edu

GUSTAFSON, Ralph ... 651-638-6122 ... 261 I
r-gustafson@bethel.edu

GUSTAFSON, Rita ... 661-654-3405 ... 33 H
rgustafson@csub.edu

GUSTAFSON, Thomas, J ... 802-656-4450 ... 514 F
thomas.gustafson@uvm.edu

GUSTAFSON, William ... 516-299-2824 ... 339 A
William.Gustafson@liu.edu

GUSTAVSON, David, B ... 318-795-4279 ... 213 D
dgustavs@lsus.edu

GUSTAVSON, Julie ... 206-264-9100 ... 530 J
julieg@bgu.edu

GUSTINE, Adam ... 847-317-7034 ... 166 B
agustine@tiu.edu

GUSTITUS, Carole, R ... 570-348-6247 ... 435 F
gustitusc@marywood.edu

GUSTWILLER, Douglas ... 812-488-2678 ... 180 B
dg57@evansville.edu

GUSZCZA, Susie, C ... 617-373-2101 ... 244 A

GUTELIUS, Harry ... 610-341-1729 ... 428 D
hguteliu@eastern.edu

GUTENBERGER,
Thomas, C ... 804-287-8052 ... 525 A
tgutenbe@richmond.edu

GUTER, Donald, J ... 713-646-1819 ... 494 E
dguter@stcl.edu

GUTERMAN, Jeff ... 814-362-7587 ... 449 B
guterman@pitt.edu

GUTERMAN, Neil ... 773-702-1420 ... 166 D
nguterman@uchicago.edu

GUTH, Ginny ... 847-628-1151 ... 154 I
gguth@judsonu.edu

GUTHIER, Mark, C ... 608-262-4463 ... 550 G
mcguthier@wisc.edu

GUTHMAN, John, C ... 516-463-6791 ... 335 H
john.c.guthman@hofstra.edu

GUTHRIE, Anne Marie ... 315-279-5412 ... 337 K
aguthrie@mail.keuka.edu

GUTHRIE, Chris ... 615-322-9800 ... 477 F
chris.guthrie@vanderbilt.edu

GUTHRIE, Doug ... 202-994-6380 ... 97 F
guthrie@gwu.edu

GUTHRIE, Edward, L ... 302-356-6870 ... 97 A
edward.l.guthrie@wilmu.edu

GUTHRIE, George ... 910-521-6509 ... 379 B
george.guthrie@uncp.edu

GUTHRIE, Grant ... 601-318-6193 ... 278 E
grant.guthrie@wmcarey.edu

GUTHRIE, Gregory ... 641-472-1125 ... 187 B
gguthrie@mum.edu

GUTHRIE, Henrietta, C ... 803-535-1210 ... 460 C
guthrieh@octech.edu

GUTHRIE, Pamella ... 260-563-8828 ... 176 A
pguthrie@ivytech.edu

GUTHRIE, Tara ... 919-775-5401 ... 368 H

GUTHRIE, Vicki ... 859-336-5082 ... 205 F
vguthrie@sccky.edu

GUTHRO, Clement, P ... 207-859-5104 ... 217 G
cpguthro@colby.edu

GUTIERREZ, Amanda ... 620-242-0424 ... 194 H
gutierra@mcpherson.edu

GUTIERREZ, Anthony ... 805-546-3289 ... 43 F
agutierr@cuesta.edu

GUTIERREZ, Brian, G ... 817-257-7815 ... 498 F
brian.gutierrez@tcu.edu

GUTIERREZ, Carlos ... 787-738-2161 ... 567 A
carlos.gutierrez1@upr.edu

GUTIERREZ, Diana ... 989-686-9434 ... 250 F
dvgutier@delta.edu

GUTIERREZ, Edna, I ... 787-720-1022 ... 560 D
registrador@atlanticcollege.edu

GUTIERREZ, Elias, R ... 787-765-5244 ... 567 F
eliasgutierrez@yahoo.com

GUTIERREZ, Isela ... 208-524-3000 ... 143 C
isela.gutierrez@my.eitc.edu

GUTIERREZ, Jaime, P ... 520-621-1501 ... 19 B
jaimeg@email.arizona.edu

GUTIERREZ, Juan, F ... 626-585-7315 ... 61 E
jfgutierrez@pasadena.edu

GUTIERREZ, Keri ... 956-364-4114 ... 499 J
keri.gutierrez@harlingen.tstc.edu

GUTIERREZ, Manuel ... 956-380-8115 ... 493 A
mgutierrez@riogrande.edu

GUTIERREZ, Mary ... 361-593-2601 ... 498 A
sm698@bncollege.com

GUTIERREZ, Michael ... 518-437-1802 ... 324 I
magutierrez@bryantstratton.edu

GUTIERREZ, Michael, J ... 972-860-7196 ... 484 H
MGutierrez@dcccd.edu

GUTIERREZ, Muriel ... 786-972-9083 ... 107 E
mgutierrez@careercollege.edu

GUTIERREZ, Nancy, A ... 704-687-2247 ... 378 E
ngutierr@uncc.edu

GUTIERREZ, Roberto ... 419-995-8357 ... 392 L
gutierrez.r@rhodesstate.edu

GUTIERREZ, Silvia ... 626-584-5579 ... 48 A
silviagutierrez@fuller.edu

GUTIERREZ, Susan ... 707-664-2287 ... 37 B
susan.gutierrez@sonoma.edu

GUTIERREZ, Tiffany ... 518-694-7254 ... 322 C
tiffany.gutierrez@acphs.edu

GUTIERREZ, Tim ... 505-277-0963 ... 321 C
tguiterr@unm.edu

GUTIERREZ-KEETON,
Rebecca, L ... 909-869-3305 ... 33 G
rgkeeton@csupomona.edu

GUTKNECHT, Leah, K ... 319-273-0028 ... 182 D
leah.gutknecht@uni.edu

GUTMAN, Gretchen ... 765-285-1020 ... 169 D
gkgutman@bsu.edu

GUTMANN, Amy ... 215-898-7221 ... 448 I
president@upenn.edu

GUTMANN, Mark ... 407-843-3984 ... 110 B
mgutmann@fortiscollege.edu

GUTOSKEY, David, P ... 410-543-6040 ... 228 D
dpgutoskey@salisbury.edu

GUTSTEIN, Daniel ... 410-225-4254 ... 224 C
dgutstein@mica.edu

GUTTENTAG, Christoph, O ... 919-684-2898 ... 363 I
christoph.guttentag@duke.edu

GUTTERIDGE, Thomas ... 419-530-4612 ... 404 F
thomas.gutteridge@utoledo.edu

GUTTERMAN, David, D ... 414-955-8495 ... 548 E
dgutte@mcw.edu

GUTTMAN, Minerva ... 201-692-2890 ... 310 B
minerva_guttman@fdu.edu

GUTTMAN, Stephen, J ... 610-758-4204 ... 434 E
sjg2@lehigh.edu

GUTTRY, Melonie ... 530-541-4660 ... 53 F
guttry@ltcc.edu

GUTWEIN, Sharon, S ... 515-964-0601 ... 184 G
gutweins@faith.edu

GUVENDIREN, Ali ... 781-239-2557 ... 240 D
aguvendiren@massbay.edu

GUY, Dave ... 330-337-4203 ... 393 H
dguy@kent.edu

GUY, Elmer ... 505-786-4112 ... 318 H
eguy@navajotech.edu

GUY, Karen, I ... 402-844-7073 ... 300 A
karen@northeast.edu

GUY, Renee ... 914-606-7612 ... 360 D
renee.guy@sunywcc.edu

GUY, Yvonne ... 661-255-1050 ... 32 C
yguy@calarts.edu

GUY-SHEFTALL, Beverly ... 404-270-5624 ... 137 E
bsheftall@spelman.edu

GUYDEN, Janet, A ... 318-274-7374 ... 215 E
guydenj@gram.edu

GUYDOSH, Raymond ... 518-564-3185 ... 354 B
guydosrm@plattsburgh.edu

GUYER, Kim ... 402-898-1000 ... 297 G
kim_g@creativecenter.edu

GUYER- WOOD, Jennifer ... 507-389-1794 ... 267 H
jennifer.guyer-wood@mnsu.edu

GUYET, Alan ... 615-322-8333 ... 477 F
alan.r.guyet@vanderbilt.edu

GUYETTE, Daniel, G ... 360-650-6144 ... 539 C
dan.guyette@wwu.edu

GUYN, Kathy ... 606-589-3098 ... 203 A
kathy.guyn@kctcs.edu

GUYTON, Deirdre ... 304-327-4569 ... 543 C
dguyton@bluefieldstate.edu

GUYTON, Don ... 713-743-8000 ... 503 A
dguyton@uh.edu

GUYTON, Duffy ... 901-751-8453 ... 471 D
dguyton@mabts.edu

GUZDAR, Farida ... 443-518-3823 ... 223 D
fguzdar@howardcc.edu

GUZELIMIAN, Ara ... 212-799-5000 ... 337 H

GUZICK, David, S ... 352-733-1700 ... 120 B
dguzick@ufl.edu

GUZIE, Candice ... 575-646-1720 ... 319 D
cguzie@nmsu.edu

GUZMAN, Ana, M ... 210-486-3960 ... 479 D
aguzman@alamo.edu

GUZMAN, Ana (Cha) ... 210-486-3963 ... 479 B
aguzman@alamo.edu

GUZMAN, Andre ... 509-793-2031 ... 531 D
Andreg@bigbend.edu

GUZMAN, Ben ... 949-451-5604 ... 70 E
rguzman@ivc.edu

GUZMAN, Elizabeth ... 312-939-0111 ... 150 B
elizabeth@eastwest.edu

GUZMAN, Evelyn ... 718-951-4796 ... 326 G
eguzman@brooklyn.cuny.edu

GUZMAN, Frances ... 559-730-3778 ... 42 B
francesg@cos.edu

GUZMAN, Juan ... 308-865-8127 ... 300 G
guzmanj@unk.edu

GUZMAN, Keyla ... 732-356-1595 ... 315 D
kguzman@somerset.edu

GUZMAN, Melba ... 787-758-2525 ... 567 D
melba.guzman@upr.edu

GUZMAN, Sandra, Q ... 956-665-2741 ... 506 A
sandraq@utpa.edu

GUZMAN, Tobias ... 970-351-1944 ... 88 F
tobias.guzman@unco.edu

GUZZARDO, Joseph ... 609-777-3083 ... 316 A
jguzzardo@tesc.edu

GUZZO, Linda ... 860-906-5132 ... 89 L
lguzzo@ccc.commnet.edu

GWALTNEY, Darrell ... 615-460-6405 ... 467 B
darrell.gwaltney@belmont.edu

GWINN, Lois ... 205-366-8868 ... 7 G
lgwinn@stillman.edu

GYLLIN, John ... 407-708-4722 ... 117 G
gyllinj@seminolestate.edu

GYMER-KOCH, Jana ... 763-566-7777 ... 265 F
jkoch@msbcollege.edu

GYOLAI, Kevin ... 651-450-3526 ... 266 I
kgyolai@inverhills.edu

GYURE, James, F ... 814-263-7048 ... 449 D
gyure@pitt.edu

H

HA, Jee Won ... 714-517-1945 ... 30 G
admission@bcu.edu

HAAB, Melissa ... 251-575-3156 ... 1 B
mhaab@ascc.edu

HAACK, Jaclyn ... 303-300-8740 ... 81 H
jaclyn.haack@collegeamerica.com

HAACK, Joel ... 319-273-2725 ... 182 D
joel.haack@uni.edu

HAACK, Julie, A ... 563-333-6314 ... 188 D
HaackJulieA@sau.edu

HAACK, Kim ... 617-912-9150 ... 232 E
khaack@bostonconservatory.edu

HAAG, Brandon, A ... 678-717-3885 ... 129 D
bhaag@gsc.edu

HAAG, JanDee ... 719-549-3220 ... 87 B
Jandee.Haag@pueblocc.edu

HAAG, Jerry, T ... 254-710-2561 ... 481 I
jerry_haag@baylor.edu

HAAG, Justin ... 308-432-6213 ... 299 G
jhaag@csc.edu

HAAK, Sarah, E ... 336-841-9571 ... 365 A
shaak@highpoint.edu

HAAKE, Megan, L ... 859-238-5516 ... 199 D
megan.haake@centre.edu

HAALAND, Tami ... 406-657-2948 ... 295 F
honors@msubillings.edu

HAAN, Fred ... 712-722-6050 ... 183 H
fred@dordt.edu

HAAN, Stanley, L ... 616-526-6442 ... 249 E
haan@calvin.edu

HAAR, Jean ... 507-389-5445 ... 267 H
jean.haar@mnsu.edu

HAAR, Murray ... 605-274-4113 ... 463 H
murray.haar@augie.edu

HAAR, Scott ... 417-862-5700 ... 279 G
shaar@bryancolleges.edu

HAAS, Carol, A ... 989-774-5251 ... 249 G
haas1ca@cmich.edu

HAAS, Evelyn ... 612-861-7554 ... 261 C
ev@alfredadler.edu

HAAS, Frank ... 808-734-9518 ... 141 E
fhaas@hawaii.edu

HAAS, Jan, M ... 215-702-4312 ... 444 A
jhaas@pbu.edu

HAAS, Julie ... 913-469-8500 ... 193 I
jhaas@jccc.edu

HAAS, Mitch ... 503-251-5728 ... 420 H
mhaas@uws.edu

HAAS, Nate ... 970-351-1763 ... 88 F
nate.haas@unco.edu

HAAS, Ocki ... 417-865-2811 ... 282 A
haaso@evangel.edu

HAAS, Patricia ... 215-503-5511 ... 448 B
patricia.haas@jefferson.edu

HAAS, Sarah ... 573-518-2307 ... 286 B
shaas@mineralarea.edu

HAAS, Stephen ... 800-371-6105 ... 16 H
shaas@nationalparalegal.edu

HAAS, Thomas, J ... 616-331-2100 ... 252 A
president@gvsu.edu

HAASE, Arthur, H ... 812-888-4448 ... 181 B
ahaase@vinu.edu

HAASE, Ryan ... 620-862-5252 ... 190 D
rhaase@barclaycollege.edu

HAASE, Ted ... 206-546-4704 ... 537 G
thaase@shoreline.edu

HAATVEDT, Chad ... 218-322-2444 ... 267 A
chad.haatvedt@itascacc.edu

HABA, Jerry ... 972-721-5018 ... 502 F
dhaba@udallas.edu

HABBEN, Dorothy, E ... 718-990-1611 ... 348 G
habbend@stjohns.edu

HABECKER, Eugene, B ... 765-998-5201 ... 179 F
president@taylor.edu

HABEGER, Christian, M ... 864-379-8813 ... 457 G

HABEGGER, Arman, J ... 419-434-4791 ... 404 B
habegger@findlay.edu

HABEGGER, Toni ... 509-359-6373 ... 533 D
thabegger@ewu.edu

HABEL, Leah ... 406-771-4327 ... 296 B
lhabel@msugf.edu

HABER, Carol ... 504-865-5225 ... 215 C
chaber@tulane.edu

HABER, Melanie ... 860-512-2803 ... 90 C
mhaber@mcc.commnet.edu

HABER, Sheldon, R ... 425-602-3040 ... 530 K
shaber@bastyr.edu

HABERAECKER, Heather, J ... 312-996-2860 ... 166 F
hjh2@uic.edu

HABERER, Kathy ... 618-468-4126 ... 156 C
khaberer@lc.edu

HABERER, Ronald, J ... 716-888-2812 ... 325 G
habererr@canisius.edu

HABERICH, Klaus ... 614-947-6026 ... 391 A
haberich@franklin.edu

HABERKORN, Connie ... 608-822-2314 ... 555 B

HABERLE, Charles, J ... 401-865-1154 ... 453 F
chaberle@providence.edu

HABERMANN, Robert, J ... 979-830-4189 ... 482 A
bhaberman@blinn.edu

HABERMAS, Mary ... 479-524-7153 ... 22 C
mhaberma@jbu.edu

HABETZ, Pauline, M ... 713-500-8425 ... 506 D
pauline.m.habetz@uth.tmc.edu

HABIB, A. Frank ... 414-277-7259 ... 548 H
habib@msoe.edu

HABLE, Jim .... 415-282-7600 ..... 28 B
jimhable@actcm.edu
HABSCHMIDT, Cathy .... 765-983-1772 ..... 171 B
habscca@earlham.edu
HABTEMARIAM, Tsegaye .. 334-727-8174 ..... 8 C
HABUCHMAI, Joesph .... 691-320-2480 ..... 559 A
jhabuchmai@comfsm.fm
HABUKI, Daniel, Y .... 949-480-4005 ..... 69 I
habuki@soka.edu
HACHTEL, John .... 540-665-4922 ..... 523 K
jhachtel@su.edu
HACK, Dick .... 718-409-7331 ..... 356 C
dhack@sunymaritime.edu
HACK, Mary, C .... 609-984-1661 ..... 316 A
mhack@tesc.edu
HACK, Tyler, D .... 718-270-6071 ..... 328 D
thack@mec.cuny.edu
HACKEMER, Kurt .... 605-677-6497 ..... 465 E
kurt.hackemer@usd.edu
HACKER, Anita .... 715-634-4790 ..... 547 G
ahacker@lco.edu
HACKER, Carol, J .... 781-239-4220 ..... 230 G
hackerc@babson.edu
HACKER, Cheryl .... 740-351-3283 ..... 401 I
chacker@shawnee.edu
HACKER, David .... 909-469-5408 ..... 78 D
dhacker@westernu.edu
HACKET, JR., William, C .. 863-667-5004 ..... 118 A
wchacket@seu.edu
HACKETT, Amy, E .... 253-879-3140 ..... 538 E
ahackett@pugetsound.edu
HACKETT, Eleanor, A .... 914-606-6745 ..... 360 D
eleanor.hackett@sunywcc.edu
HACKETT, Gail .... 816-235-1107 ..... 291 E
hackettg@umkc.edu
HACKETT, Karen .... 650-508-3756 ..... 59 G
khackett@ndnu.edu
HACKETT, Matthew .... 859-572-5198 ..... 205 E
hackettm2@nku.edu
HACKETT, Royce .... 229-931-2074 ..... 131 B
HACKETT, Timothy .... 510-436-2464 ..... 62 D
thackett@peralta.edu
HACKETT, Tom .... 706-507-8968 ..... 127 D
hackett_tom@columbusstate.edu
HACKING, George, B .... 802-626-6200 ..... 515 F
george.hacking@lyndonstate.edu
HACKLE, Dale .... 850-973-1616 ..... 113 J
hackled@nfcc.edu
HACKNEY, Cameron, R ..... 304-293-2395 ..... 544 E
chackney@mail.wvu.edu
HACKNEY, Susan .... 706-295-6972 ..... 130 F
shackney@gntc.edu
HADDAD, Abdallah .... 843-349-2938 ..... 456 G
abdallah@coastal.edu
HADDEN, Diane .... 701-777-6284 ..... 381 D
diane.hadden@email.und.edu
HADDOCK, Ed .... 407-679-0100 ..... 110 C
ehaddock@fullsail.com
HADDOCK, Gregory .... 660-562-1145 ..... 287 E
haddock@nwmissouri.edu
HADDOCK, Jennifer .... 870-743-3000 ..... 22 G
jhaddock@northark.edu
HADDOCK, Jorge .... 703-993-1875 ..... 519 A
jhaddock@gmu.edu
HADDON, Phoebe, A .... 410-706-2041 ..... 227 C
phaddon@law.umaryland.edu
HADDOX, Chuck .... 502-897-4617 ..... 205 H
chaddox@sbts.edu
HADDUCK, Kevin .... 620-947-3121 ..... 196 E
kevinh@tabor.edu
HADEN, David, W .... 617-824-8620 ..... 234 D
david_haden@emerson.edu
HADEN, Laura .... 570-208-5698 ..... 432 E
laurahaden@kings.edu
HADEN, Patrick, C .... 213-740-4154 ..... 76 C
phaden@usc.edu
HADER, John .... 312-553-5962 ..... 146 H
jhader@ccc.edu
HADERLIE, Brian .... 336-334-4822 ..... 370 E
bmhaderlie@gtcc.edu
HADFIELD, Janice, M .... 402-466-4774 ..... 298 A
janice.hadfield@doane.edu
HADGIS, Nicholas, J .... 610-499-1103 ..... 451 F
njhadgis@widener.edu
HADIMI, Chala, J .... 617-262-5000 ..... 232 B
chala.hadimi@the-bac.edu
HADJEZ, Claudia .... 305-899-3970 ..... 101 F
chadjez@mail.barry.edu
HADLEY, Craig .... 207-992-1953 ..... 218 A
hadleyc@husson.edu
HADLEY, Deborah, L .... 919-866-5696 ..... 374 E
dlhadley@waketech.edu
HADLEY, H. Roger .... 909-558-4481 ..... 54 D
rhadley@llu.edu
HADLEY, James .... 602-279-9700 ..... 11 E
HADLEY, June, M .... 818-779-8424 ..... 53 B
jhadley@kingsuniversity.edu
HADLEY, Kim .... 479-524-7117 ..... 22 C
KHadley@jbu.edu
HADLEY, Linda .... 706-568-2044 ..... 127 D
hadley_linda@columbusstate.edu
HADLEY, Nan .... 417-823-3477 ..... 290 B
nhadley@forest.edu
HADLEY TORRES, Nola ..... 510-981-2935 ..... 62 A
nhadley@peralta.edu
HADLOCK, Eddie, L .... 940-668-7731 ..... 491 C
ehadlock@nctc.edu
HADLOCK, Heather .... 214-333-5340 ..... 484 C
heather@dbu.edu
HADRA, Becky, L .... 301-784-5000 ..... 221 A
bhadra@allegany.edu
HADSELL, Heidi .... 860-509-9502 ..... 92 D
hadsell@hartsem.edu
HADWICK, Jim .... 775-850-0700 ..... 302 E
jhadwick@morrison.neumont.edu
HADWIN, Julie .... 803-584-3446 ..... 462 E
jhadwin@mailbox.sc.edu
HAEFNER, Jeremy, A .... 585-475-6399 ..... 347 G
jahpro@rit.edu
HAEFNER, Ronald, I .... 920-748-8320 ..... 549 I
haefnerr@ripon.edu
HAEFNER, Stephen, R .... 570-326-3761 ..... 440 K
shaefner@pct.edu
HAEGER, John, D .... 928-523-3232 ..... 17 A
john.haeger@nau.edu
HAEGER, Loredana .... 801-957-6321 ..... 512 C
loredana.haeger@slcc.edu
HAEHL, Sherry, L .... 910-814-5582 ..... 362 F
haehl@campbell.edu
HAELEN, Robert .... 518-320-1100 ..... 351 D
HAESLOOP, Mary .... 650-508-3651 ..... 59 G
mhaesloop@ndnu.edu
HAEUSER, Patricia, N .... 928-523-7777 ..... 17 A
patricia.haeuser@nau.edu
HAFELI, Mary .... 845-257-3860 ..... 352 B
hafelim@newpaltz.edu
HAFER, Greg .... 417-626-1234 ..... 287 F
ghafer@occ.edu
HAFFAR, Warren .... 215-572-2094 ..... 422 B
haffarw@arcadia.edu
HAFFEY, Jim .... 662-226-0830 ..... 274 F
jhaffey@holmescc.edu
HAFFNER, Christopher, D . 904-819-6225 ..... 107 A
haffnerc@flagler.edu
HAFFORD, Patrick .... 617-989-4870 ..... 246 C
haffordp@wit.edu
HAFKEMEYER, Susan, P ... 563-588-7769 ..... 186 I
sue.hafkemeyer@loras.edu
HAFNER, Arthur, W .... 765-285-5277 ..... 169 D
ahafner@bsu.edu
HAFNER, JR., David, T ..... 808-956-4636 ..... 141 B
hafner@hawaii.edu
HAFNER, Donald, L .... 617-552-4173 ..... 232 D
donald.hafner.1@bc.edu
HAFNER, Greg .... 641-673-2168 ..... 189 I
hafnerg@wmpenn.edu
HAFNER, Lars, A .... 941-752-5201 ..... 118 E
hafnerl@scf.edu
HAFT, Mary .... 260-399-7700 ..... 180 E
mhaft@sf.edu
HAFT, Susan .... 740-245-7276 ..... 404 E
shaft@rio.edu
HAFT, Tami .... 208-769-7729 ..... 143 H
tami_haft@nic.edu
HAGAN, Abdalla, F .... 903-927-3343 ..... 509 A
afhagan@wileyc.edu
HAGAN, Chris .... 217-228-5432 ..... 161 E
HAGAN, G. Michael .... 605-336-6588 ..... 465 B
gmhagan@sfseminary.edu
HAGAN, Linda .... 248-689-8282 ..... 260 A
lhagan@walshcollege.edu
HAGAN, Michael .... 217-351-2457 ..... 161 B
mhagan@parkland.edu
HAGAN, Pam .... 864-592-4634 ..... 461 C
haganp@sccsc.edu
HAGAN, Rick .... 619-260-4624 ..... 76 A
rhagan@sandiego.edu
HAGAN, Waldon .... 757-822-1227 ..... 528 C
whagan@tcc.edu
HAGAN, Willie .... 657-278-2115 ..... 34 E
whagan@fullerton.edu
HAGANS, Elbert .... 606-487-3178 ..... 201 H
elbert.hagans@kctcs.edu
HAGANS, Karen .... 419-289-5067 ..... 384 D
khagans@ashland.edu
HAGANS, Lori, R .... 405-878-2708 ..... 409 D
lori.hagans@okbu.edu
HAGAR, Teresa .... 303-963-3283 ..... 81 K
tahager@ccu.edu
HAGARA, Kimberly .... 409-747-3277 ..... 507 B
kkhagara@utmb.edu
HAGBERG, Stewart .... 801-818-8900 ..... 510 E
stewarth@provocollege.edu
HAGE, Gloria .... 734-487-1055 ..... 250 H
ghage@emich.edu
HAGEDORN, Christine .... 215-968-8034 ..... 423 E
hagedorn@bucks.edu
HAGEDORN, Valerie, A ..... 412-531-4433 ..... 426 F
info@deantech.edu
HAGEMAN, James, H .... 989-774-3094 ..... 249 G
hagem1jh@cmich.edu
HAGEMAN, Kristin .... 651-773-1780 ..... 266 D
kristin.hageman@century.edu
HAGEMANN, Julie .... 630-652-8314 ..... 149 B
jhagemann@devry.edu
HAGEMANN, Ryan .... 541-346-5767 ..... 418 B
ryan_hagemann@ous.edu
HAGEMEYER, Gwen .... 812-535-5285 ..... 179 C
ghagemeyer@smwc.edu
HAGEN, Berta .... 218-285-2207 ..... 268 H
bhagen@rrcc.mnscu.edu
HAGEN, Cheryl, M .... 734-462-4400 ..... 258 C
chagen@schoolcraft.edu
HAGEN, Gary, D .... 701-788-4754 ..... 381 F
Gary.Hagen@mayvillestate.edu
HAGEN, Lauralee .... 253-535-7203 ..... 535 K
hagen@plu.edu
HAGEN, Lise .... 617-541-5328 ..... 241 D
lhagen@rcc.mass.edu
HAGEN, Patrick .... 608-647-6186 ..... 552 F
patrick.hagen@uwc.edu
HAGEN, Peter .... 609-652-4504 ..... 313 F
hagenp@stockton.edu
HAGEN, Randi .... 904-819-6322 ..... 107 A
rhagen@flagler.edu
HAGEN, Stan .... 503-838-8174 ..... 419 C
hagens@wou.edu
HAGEN, Susan .... 205-226-4660 ..... 2 C
shagen@bsc.edu
HAGEN-FOLEY, Tim .... 989-275-5000 ..... 253 K
tim.hagen-foley@kirtland.edu
HAGENBAUGH, Stacie ..... 413-585-2582 ..... 245 B
shagenba@smith.edu
HAGENBUCH, Brian .... 607-431-4518 ..... 335 B
hagenbuchb@hartwick.edu
HAGER, Amy .... 660-263-4110 ..... 287 B
amyh@macc.edu
HAGER, Melissa .... 609-652-4295 ..... 313 F
melissa.hager@stockton.edu
HAGER, Michael .... 319-273-2333 ..... 182 D
michael.hager@uni.edu
HAGER, Tim .... 515-964-6409 ..... 183 E
tjhager@dmacc.edu
HAGERMAN, Bonnie, K ..... 301-696-3550 ..... 223 C
hagerman@hood.edu
HAGERMAN, Brandi, F ..... 336-633-0213 ..... 372 F
bfhagerman@randolph.edu
HAGERMANN, P. Donald .. 302-356-6844 ..... 97 A
p.donald.hagermann@wilmu.edu
HAGERTY, Michael .... 617-266-1400 ..... 231 G
HAGERTY, Stephen .... 212-243-5150 ..... 334 E
hagerty@gts.edu
HAGG, Scott .... 707-826-4400 ..... 36 D
skh7001@humboldt.edu
HAGGANS, Mary, S .... 417-667-8181 ..... 280 I
mhaggans@cottey.edu
HAGGARD, Bill .... 828-251-6742 ..... 378 C
bhaggard@unca.edu
HAGGARD, Cynthia .... 815-921-4402 ..... 162 F
c.haggard@rockvalleycollege.edu
HAGGARD, David .... 541-684-7218 ..... 417 F
dhaggard@northwestchristian.edu
HAGGERTY, Christina .... 815-455-8727 ..... 157 F
chaggerty@mchenry.edu
HAGGERTY, Dennis .... 609-894-9311 ..... 308 C
dhaggert@bcc.edu
HAGGERTY, Donald, F ..... 914-968-6200 ..... 349 D
donald.haggerty@archny.org
HAGGERTY, Gary .... 617-266-1400 ..... 231 G
HAGGERTY, Janet, A .... 918-631-2714 ..... 413 F
janet-haggerty@utulsa.edu
HAGGINS, Debra, L .... 757-727-5340 ..... 519 C
debra.haggins@hamptonu.edu
HAGGINS, Tanya .... 216-201-9025 ..... 394 G
HAGGRAY, M. Annette ..... 443-412-2244 ..... 223 B
ahaggray@harford.edu
HAGGRAY, Shelby, M .... 202-885-8614 ..... 100 A
shaggray@wesleyseminary.edu
HAGHIGHI, Shawn .... 636-949-4726 ..... 284 C
shaghighi@lindenwood.edu
HAGLER, Cathy .... 618-453-2474 ..... 164 I
chagler@siu.edu
HAGLER, James .... 478-471-2778 ..... 133 E
james.hagler@maconstate.edu
HAGLIN, Reid .... 218-879-0822 ..... 266 F
rhaglin@fdltcc.edu
HAGON, Sean, P .... 617-585-1100 ..... 243 E
sean.hagon@necmusic.edu
HAGOOD, Nesbitt .... 505-425-3418 ..... 318 I
nwhagood@nmhu.edu
HAGOVSKY, Beth .... 610-660-1072 ..... 446 C
bhagovsk@sju.edu
HAGSTROM, Steven, W ..... 817-515-6637 ..... 496 A
steven.hagstrom@tccd.edu
HAGUE, Barth, A .... 316-978-6288 ..... 197 F
barth.hague@wichita.edu
HAGUE, Stephen, T .... 410-323-6211 ..... 222 F
fts@faiththeological.org
HAH, Megan .... 626-289-7719 ..... 26 J
HAHKA, Curt .... 906-487-7380 ..... 251 C
curt.hahka@finlandia.edu
HAHN, Jacqueline .... 808-885-9226 ..... 140 I
HAHN, Karen .... 352-588-8522 ..... 116 E
karen.hahn@saintleo.edu
HAHN, Kathy .... 828-328-7402 ..... 366 B
kathy.hahn@lr.edu
HAHN, Linda .... 215-568-9215 ..... 436 E
lhahn@mccworks.org
HAHN, Marc .... 207-602-2340 ..... 220 H
mhahn@une.edu
HAHN, Marc .... 207-221-2340 ..... 220 H
mhahn@une.edu
HAHN, Mary Joan .... 509-313-4220 ..... 534 A
hahn@gonzaga.edu
HAHN, Norman, P .... 757-825-2952 ..... 528 B
hahnn@tncc.edu
HAHN, Roger .... 816-268-5412 ..... 287 C
rlhahn@nts.edu
HAHN, Sarah .... 212-650-7060 ..... 326 H
shahn@ccny.cuny.edu
HAHN, Stephen .... 973-720-2565 ..... 317 D
hahns@wpunj.edu
HAHS, Sharon, K .... 773-442-5400 ..... 159 H
s-hahs@neiu.edu
HAID, William, R .... 858-534-5448 ..... 74 D
whaid@ucsd.edu
HAIDER, Rita .... 740-351-3127 ..... 401 I
rhaider@shawnee.edu
HAIDLE, Shirley, J .... 208-467-8523 ..... 143 I
sjhaidle@nnu.edu
HAIGHT, Charles .... 413-538-2756 ..... 242 G
chaight@mtholyoke.edu
HAIGHT, Donald .... 707-638-5270 ..... 72 H
donald.haight@tu.edu
HAIGHT, Heather, R .... 315-684-6046 ..... 354 F
haighthr@morrisville.edu
HAIGHT, Larry, L .... 530-226-4110 ..... 69 H
lhaight@simpsonu.edu
HAIGLER, Anna, D .... 803-536-7047 ..... 460 G
ahaigler@scsu.edu
HAIL, Amy .... 207-221-4228 ..... 220 H
ahail@une.edu
HAILE, Bob, A .... 309-649-6331 ..... 165 D
bob.haile@src.edu
HAILE, Christine, E .... 518-437-4920 ..... 351 E
chaile@uamail.albany.edu
HAILEY, Maryann .... 903-875-7305 ..... 491 B
maryann.hailey@navarrocollege.edu
HAILEY, Robert, C .... 504-862-8064 ..... 215 C
rhailey@tulane.edu
HAILU, Elias .... 713-313-7879 ..... 499 G
hailu_ex@tsu.edu
HAIN, C. Stuart .... 610-328-8575 ..... 447 E
chain1@swarthmore.edu
HAIN, Judith, E .... 973-655-5293 ..... 311 G
hainj@mail.montclair.edu
HAIN, Peggy, S .... 402-465-2137 ..... 299 J
phain@nebrwesleyan.edu
HAIN, Tom .... 432-552-2782 ..... 507 C
hain_t@utpb.edu
HAIN, Tony .... 810-762-9616 ..... 253 I
thain@kettering.edu
HAINES, Chris .... 602-243-8257 ..... 16 E
chris.haines@smcmail.maricopa.edu
HAINES, Chuck .... 805-893-8541 ..... 74 F
chuck.haines@bap.ucsb.edu
HAINES, Ena .... 212-678-3486 ..... 357 F
ena@tc.columbia.edu
HAINES, Gerald, C .... 301-790-2800 ..... 223 A
hainesg@hagerstowncc.edu
HAINES, Malcolm .... 757-727-5477 ..... 519 C
malcolm.haines@hamptonu.edu
HAINES, Terry .... 913-266-8601 ..... 17 C
HAINES, Terry .... 913-266-8601 ..... 195 F
terry.haines@ottawa.edu
HAINES, Terry .... 913-266-8601 ..... 195 G
HAINES, Terry .... 913-266-8601 ..... 178 E
donna.levene@ottawa.edu
HAINES, Terry .... 913-266-8601 ..... 549 E
HAINEY, Dale, E .... 817-202-6519 ..... 495 C
haineyd@swau.edu
HAINGRAY, Donald .... 585-567-9287 ..... 336 B
donald.haingray@houghton.edu
HAINLINE, Benjamin .... 580-628-6250 ..... 409 B
ben.hainline@north-ok.edu
HAINSTOCK, Brian .... 215-717-6614 ..... 448 H
bhainstock@uarts.edu
HAIR, Bill .... 254-710-3591 ..... 481 I
bill_hair@baylor.edu
HAIR, Shannon .... 434-797-2222 ..... 526 C
HAIRE, Connie, M .... 828-339-7018 ..... 373 H
connie@southwesterncc.edu
HAIRSTON, Creasie .... 312-996-3219 ..... 166 F
cfh@uic.edu
HAIRSTON, Gregory, G ..... 336-750-2125 ..... 380 A
hairstong@wssu.edu
HAIRSTON, Jewel, E .... 804-524-5871 ..... 529 C
jhairston@vsu.edu
HAIRSTON, Lathan .... 870-862-8131 ..... 23 G
lhairston@southark.edu
HAIRSTON, Marie .... 415-565-4703 ..... 73 G
hairston@uchastings.edu
HAIRSTON, Tali .... 206-281-2455 ..... 537 D
tali@spu.edu
HAISCH, Craig .... 503-883-2217 ..... 416 G
chaisch@linfield.edu
HAISEN, Michael .... 808-735-4785 ..... 140 A
mhalsen@chominade.edu
HAISLETT, Judith .... 575-562-2221 ..... 318 A
judith.haislett@enmu.edu
HAISLIP, Jackie, F .... 252-789-0259 ..... 371 E
jhaislip@martincc.edu
HAISMA, Dale .... 616-632-3037 ..... 248 A
haismdal@aquinas.edu

HALL, Nathan ... 417-833-2551 ... 279 I
HALL, Norman, D ... 618-664-7119 ... 151 D
norm.hall@greenville.edu
HALL, Palmer, H ... 210-436-3441 ... 493 C
phall@stmarytx.edu
HALL, Pamela ... 313-845-9603 ... 252 D
phall@hfcc.edu
HALL, Pat ... 620-862-5252 ... 190 D
pat.hall@barclaycollege.edu
HALL, Patricia ... 479-394-7622 ... 23 E
phall@rmcc.edu
HALL, Patricia, G ... 909-748-8019 ... 75 F
patricia_hall@redlands.edu
HALL, Patrick ... 814-827-4512 ... 449 E
phall2@pitt.edu
HALL, Philip, D ... 843-792-8979 ... 459 C
hallpd@musc.edu
HALL, Rachelle ... 623-845-3231 ... 15 J
rachelle.hall@gcmail.maricopa.edu
HALL, Ralph, G ... 972-758-3831 ... 483 D
rhall@collin.edu
HALL, Randolph, W ... 213-740-6709 ... 76 C
rwhall@usc.edu
HALL, Randy ... 864-597-4351 ... 463 F
halljr@wofford.edu
HALL, Rebecca ... 304-326-1304 ... 541 G
rhall@salemu.edu
HALL, Renardo, A ... 217-424-6395 ... 158 F
rhall@millikin.edu
HALL, Ricardo, D ... 305-284-5353 ... 122 F
rdhall@miami.edu
HALL, Richard ... 405-208-5050 ... 410 A
rhall@okcu.edu
HALL, Richard (Bubba) ... 520-515-5477 ... 13 G
hallr@cochise.edu
HALL, Robert ... 716-829-7657 ... 332 F
hallrm@dyc.edu
HALL, Robert, C ... 914-323-5230 ... 340 A
bob.hall@mville.edu
HALL, Ron ... 865-251-1800 ... 472 K
rhall@southcollegetn.edu
HALL, Russell ... 806-894-9611 ... 494 C
rhall@southplainscollege.edu
HALL, Ryan ... 513-732-5301 ... 403 E
hallrn@email.uc.edu
HALL, Sandra Betts ... 334-833-4349 ... 4 E
shall@huntingdon.edu
HALL, Sandy ... 325-674-2273 ... 478 H
halls@acu.edu
HALL, Sarah, S ... 859-238-5471 ... 199 D
sarah.hall@centre.edu
HALL, Sheila ... 215-567-7080 ... 422 C
shall@aii.edu
HALL, Steven, A ... 617-353-2251 ... 232 G
sahall@bu.edu
HALL, Susan ... 856-415-2185 ... 310 E
shall@gccnj.edu
HALL, Susan, H ... 214-378-1814 ... 484 E
shall@dcccd.edu
HALL, Susie ... 850-201-6049 ... 121 F
halls@tcc.fl.edu
HALL, Teresa ... 410-704-2332 ... 228 E
thall@towson.edu
HALL, Terrill ... 248-218-2042 ... 257 F
thall@rc.edu
HALL, Terry ... 415-561-1908 ... 39 H
thall@ccsf.edu
HALL, Thomas, H ... 864-242-5100 ... 455 E
HALL, Tim ... 308-535-3612 ... 298 I
hallt@mpcc.edu
HALL, Timothy, L ... 931-221-7566 ... 473 D
hallt@apsu.edu
HALL, Timothy, W ... 816-235-1020 ... 291 E
halltw@umkc.edu
HALL, Tom ... 904-256-7715 ... 111 J
thall5@ju.edu
HALL, Tom ... 806-291-3750 ... 508 B
hallt@wbu.edu
HALL, Tracy ... 314-644-9280 ... 289 C
thall80@stlcc.edu
HALL, Tracy ... 845-434-5750 ... 356 H
thall@sullivan.suny.edu
HALL, Tracy ... 360-867-6205 ... 533 I
hallt@evergreen.edu
HALL, Tracy, A ... 336-316-2349 ... 364 E
thall@guilford.edu
HALL, Trevor ... 863-638-7286 ... 123 B
trevor.hall@warner.edu
HALL, Troy ... 610-574-6909 ... 60 E
twhall@pacificcollege.edu
HALL, Walter ... 404-364-8543 ... 135 A
whall@oglethorpe.edu
HALL, Wayne ... 502-852-6111 ... 207 A
whall@louisville.edu
HALL, Wendy ... 360-442-2491 ... 535 C
whall@lowercolumbia.edu
HALL, William ... 714-997-6891 ... 39 C
whall@chapman.edu
HALL, William ... 607-871-2137 ... 322 F
fhall@alfred.edu
HALL, JR., William, A ... 859-858-3511 ... 198 B
bill.hall@asbury.edu
HALL, William, B ... 401-341-2132 ... 454 D
hallb@salve.edu
HALL, William, C ... 617-984-1760 ... 244 C
whall@quincycollege.edu
HALL CARNES, Ginger ... 210-486-3884 ... 479 D
vcarnes@alamo.edu
HALL-HOLT, Christy ... 507-786-3995 ... 271 H
hallholt@stolaf.edu
HALL-NUZUM, Deidra, R ... 304-829-7115 ... 540 E
dhall-nuzum@bethanywv.edu
HALL-PITTSLEY, Sigrid ... 336-750-3148 ... 380 A
allensh@wssu.edu
HALL SMITH, Willa ... 202-797-3670 ... 8 C
HALLADAY, Charles ... 561-842-8324 ... 113 C
challiday@lincolntech.com
HALLAHAN, Kerry, R ... 314-505-7000 ... 280 H
hallahank@csl.edu
HALLAM, Donna ... 813-874-0094 ... 103 G
HALLAM, Steve ... 315-279-5213 ... 337 K
shallam@mail.keuka.edu
HALLAS, Vicki ... 718-405-3332 ... 330 A
vicki.hallas@mountsaintvincent.edu
HALLBERG, Robert ... 773-298-3109 ... 163 G
hallberg@sxu.edu
HALLBLADE, Shirley ... 904-620-2616 ... 120 C
shirley.hallblade@unf.edu
HALLE, Kevin ... 402-375-7234 ... 299 I
kehalle1@wsc.edu
HALLEEN, Jan ... 952-888-4777 ... 270 F
jhalleen@nwhealth.edu
HALLEN, Margaret, C ... 847-866-3987 ... 151 B
margaret.hallen@garrett.edu
HALLER, Bryan ... 212-220-8013 ... 326 E
bhaller@bmcc.cuny.edu
HALLER, Hal ... 770-484-1204 ... 133 D
library@lru.edu
HALLER, James, P ... 864-587-4208 ... 461 D
hallerje@smcsc.edu
HALLER, John, G ... 610-660-1305 ... 446 C
jhaller@sju.edu
HALLER, John, R ... 320-308-5922 ... 269 D
jhaller@sctcc.edu
HALLERAN, Donna ... 608-265-3443 ... 550 G
dhalleran@vc.wisc.edu
HALLERAN, Michael ... 757-221-1993 ... 517 J
halleran@wm.edu
HALLETT, David ... 503-399-5172 ... 414 J
david.hallett@chemeketa.edu
HALLETT, Malinda, A ... 412-291-6286 ... 422 D
mhallett@aii.edu
HALLETT, Tom ... 708-209-3350 ... 148 C
tom.hallett@cuchicago.edu
HALLICK, Lesley, M ... 503-352-2123 ... 419 E
president@pacificu.edu
HALLIDAY, Nancy, E ... 516-463-5740 ... 335 H
nancy.halliday@hofstra.edu
HALLIDAY, Robert, M ... 315-792-3122 ... 359 C
rhalliday@utica.edu
HALLIGAN, Meg, F ... 563-333-6311 ... 188 D
HalliganMegF@sau.edu
HALLIS, John ... 412-578-8741 ... 424 G
hallisjx@carlow.edu
HALLISEY, Diane, M ... 617-521-2001 ... 245 A
diane.hallisey@simmons.edu
HALLMAN, Janet, S ... 253-879-8620 ... 538 E
jhallman@pugetsound.edu
HALLMAN, Raymond ... 215-248-7007 ... 425 C
hallmanr@chc.edu
HALLMAN, Thomas, L ... 803-641-3434 ... 462 B
tomh@usca.edu
HALLMARK, James ... 806-651-2044 ... 498 D
jhallmark@mail.wtamu.edu
HALLOCK, Addison ... 860-632-3036 ... 92 E
rector@holyapostles.edu
HALLOCK, Hilton ... 603-428-2235 ... 305 E
hhallock@nec.edu
HALLOCK, Meghan ... 508-849-3641 ... 230 C
mhallock@annamaria.edu
HALLORAN, Beth ... 641-269-3200 ... 185 A
halloran@grinnell.edu
HALLORAN, Florence ... 770-962-7580 ... 132 A
fhalloran@gwinnetttech.edu
HALLORAN, Sybil, C ... 804-828-6125 ... 525 E
schallor@vcu.edu
HALLORAN, Tom ... 781-595-6768 ... 236 I
thalloran@mariancourt.edu
HALLQUIST, Carrie, L ... 715-833-6670 ... 553 F
challquist1@cvtc.edu
HALLSMITH, George ... 802-322-1754 ... 513 C
george.hallsmith@goddard.edu
HALLSTROM, Lilian ... 808-543-8088 ... 140 B
lhallstrom@hpu.edu
HALLSTROM, Peggy ... 605-626-3011 ... 465 H
hallstrp@northern.edu
HALLUM, Ann ... 415-338-2231 ... 36 F
glider@sfsu.edu
HALONEN, Jane, S ... 850-474-2688 ... 121 C
jhalonen@uwf.edu
HALPERIN, Edward, C ... 502-852-1499 ... 207 A
meddean@louisville.edu
HALPERIN, Michael ... 607-735-1895 ... 333 A
registrar@elmira.edu
HALPERIN, Avrohom ... 516-239-9002 ... 350 H
HALPERN, Jane, L ... 410-704-2466 ... 228 E
jhalpern@towson.edu
HALPERN, Linda, C ... 540-568-2852 ... 520 C
halperlc@jmu.edu
HALPERN, Meredith ... 212-772-4070 ... 327 E
meredith.halpern@hunter.cuny.edu
HALPERN, Mike ... 208-769-3310 ... 143 H
mike_halpern@nic.edu
HALPIN, Eamon ... 318-473-6545 ... 212 G
ehalpin@lsua.edu
HALPIN, Eamon ... 318-427-4469 ... 212 G
ehalpin@lsua.edu
HALPIN-ROBBINS, Kathleen ... 413-565-1000 ... 231 B
khrobbins@baypath.edu
HALSEY, Cindy ... 843-470-8396 ... 461 E
chalsey@tcl.edu
HALSEY, Glenn ... 307-755-9820 ... 556 G
ghalsey@wyotechstaff.edu
HALSEY, Mark, D ... 845-758-7267 ... 323 F
halsey@bard.edu
HALSEY, Timothy ... 805-966-3888 ... 31 A
timothy.halsey@brooks.edu
HALSMER, Dominic ... 918-495-6004 ... 411 C
dhalsmer@oru.edu
HALSTEAD, John, R ... 585-395-2361 ... 352 F
halstead@brockport.edu
HALSTEAD, Joyce ... 229-225-5062 ... 137 D
jhalstead@southwestgatech.edu
HALSTEAD, Lois, A ... 312-942-7117 ... 163 B
lois_a_halstead@rush.edu
HALSTEAD, Michele ... 845-257-3295 ... 352 B
halsteam@newpaltz.edu
HALSTED, Steve ... 406-771-4367 ... 296 B
shalsted@msugf.edu
HALTER, Robert ... 317-274-7746 ... 174 B
rhalter@iupui.edu
HALTERMAN, Lauren, C ... 410-827-5818 ... 222 B
lhalterman@chesapeake.edu
HALTERMAN, Rick ... 423-236-2871 ... 473 A
halterman@southern.edu
HALTTUNEN, Lynda ... 760-744-1150 ... 61 C
lhalttunen@palomar.edu
HALUPA, Colleen ... 903-923-3442 ... 500 A
colleen.halupa@marshall.tstc.edu
HALUSCHAK, Rich ... 626-396-2308 ... 29 G
rich.haluschak@artcenter.edu
HALUSHKA, Perry, V ... 843-792-3012 ... 459 C
halushpv@musc.edu
HALUSKA, Jan ... 423-236-2738 ... 473 A
haluska@southern.edu
HALUZAK, Jennifer, L ... 414-955-8246 ... 548 E
jhaluzak@mcw.edu
HALVERSEN, Laurie ... 707-965-7080 ... 60 J
lhalversen@puc.edu
HALVERSON, Andrea, R ... 651-631-5121 ... 270 E
arhalverson@nwc.edu
HALVERSON, Tom, L ... 605-256-5165 ... 465 G
tom.halverson@dsu.edu
HALVERSTADT, Adrian ... 620-862-5252 ... 190 D
adrian.halverstadt@barclaycollege.edu
HALVERSTADT, David ... 360-538-4234 ... 534 B
dhalverst@ghc.edu
HALVORSON, Daisy ... 605-668-1566 ... 464 F
dhalvorson@mtmc.edu
HALVORSON, J. Derek ... 866-323-0233 ... 63 D
HALVORSON, Paula ... 785-460-5497 ... 191 J
paula.halvorson@colbycc.edu
HALVORSON, Stephen, J ... 704-366-5066 ... 375 H
shalvorson@rts.edu
HALVORSON, Terry ... 715-425-3265 ... 552 A
terry.n.halvorson@uwrf.edu
HALVORSON, Terry, N ... 715-425-3265 ... 552 A
terry.n.halvorson@uwrf.edu
HAM, Carol Ann ... 229-317-6734 ... 128 A
carolann.ham@darton.edu
HAM, Clay ... 217-732-3168 ... 156 F
cham@lincolnchristian.edu
HAM, Gary ... 978-762-4000 ... 241 A
gham@northshore.edu
HAM, Hal ... 361-593-2819 ... 498 A
kahh000@tamuk.edu
HAM, Karen, L ... 315-267-2344 ... 354 C
hamkl@potsdam.edu
HAM, Scott, D ... 317-940-8112 ... 170 C
sdham@butler.edu
HAMAKER, Michelle ... 308-865-8517 ... 300 G
hamakerm@unk.edu
HAMAN, Linda ... 636-227-2100 ... 284 E
linda.haman@logan.edu
HAMANN, Dick, T ... 407-708-2258 ... 117 G
hamannd@seminolestate.edu
HAMANN, Gregory, J ... 541-917-4200 ... 416 H
hamanng@linnbenton.edu
HAMANN, Julie, A ... 419-372-0669 ... 385 D
jrogers@bgsu.edu
HAMANN, Melanie ... 573-840-9767 ... 290 J
mhamann@trcc.edu
HAMBERGER, Barnett ... 212-998-2310 ... 344 B
bwh1@nyu.edu
HAMBEY, Anthony ... 205-226-4850 ... 2 C
ahambey@bsc.edu
HAMBLEN, Jon ... 916-660-7382 ... 69 F
jhamblen@sierracollege.edu
HAMBLIN, Carolyn ... 928-875-9116 ... 16 G
chamblin@mohave.edu
HAMBLIN, John ... 541-463-5686 ... 416 D
hamblinj@lanecc.edu
HAMBLIN, Veronica ... 660-263-3900 ... 279 J
vhamblin@cccb.edu
HAMBLIN-FOX, Jeannie ... 765-966-2656 ... 176 F
jhamblin@ivytech.edu
HAMBLING, William ... 574-284-4552 ... 179 D
whamblin@saintmarys.edu
HAMBRICK, Genie ... 404-687-4530 ... 127 C
hambrickg@ctsnet.edu
HAMBRIGHT, M. Karen ... 912-279-5879 ... 127 B
khambright@ccga.edu
HAMBROCK, Daniel ... 651-793-1712 ... 267 D
daniel.hambrock@metrostate.edu
HAMBURG, Gail ... 509-793-2002 ... 531 D
gailh@bigbend.edu
HAMBURG, Gary ... 773-834-2059 ... 165 G
ghamburg@ttic.edu
HAMBURG, Jo Ann ... 845-341-4903 ... 345 E
joann.hamburg@sunyorange.edu
HAMBURGER, Daniel ... 630-725-1930 ... 149 A
dhamburger@devry.edu
HAMBY, Dan ... 270-707-3790 ... 202 A
dan.hamby@kctcs.edu
HAMBY, David, E ... 918-631-2309 ... 413 F
david-hamby@utulsa.edu
HAMBY, Eileen ... 386-506-3939 ... 103 J
hambye@DaytonaState.edu
HAMBY, Karen, G ... 205-726-2643 ... 6 G
kghamby@samford.edu
HAME, Frederic ... 321-674-8020 ... 108 E
fmh@fit.edu
HAMEL, Carolyn ... 508-999-8032 ... 237 E
chamel@umassd.edu
HAMEL, Dale, M ... 508-626-4580 ... 238 D
dhamel@framingham.edu
HAMEL, James ... 978-665-3584 ... 238 C
jhamel@fitchburgstate.edu
HAMEL, John ... 617-573-8460 ... 245 E
jhamel@suffolk.edu
HAMEL, Kayte ... 815-825-2086 ... 155 C
kayte.hamel@kishwaukeecollege.edu
HAMEL, Thomas ... 847-635-1660 ... 160 E
thamel@oakton.edu
HAMELINE, Walter ... 718-390-3488 ... 359 G
whamelin@wagner.edu
HAMEN, Laurie, M ... 630-637-5155 ... 159 F
lahamen@noctrl.edu
HAMER, Ronald, J ... 518-454-2060 ... 330 C
hamerj@strose.edu
HAMES, Anne ... 731-352-4066 ... 467 C
hamesa@bethelu.edu
HAMES, Becky ... 731-352-4046 ... 467 C
hamesb@bethelu.edu
HAMIL, Bobby ... 678-466-4050 ... 127 A
bobbyhamil@clayton.edu
HAMILL, Anne ... 410-837-4763 ... 229 A
ahamill@ubalt.edu
HAMILL, Jonathan, T ... 334-649-5000 ... 557 B
HAMILL, Paul, J ... 607-274-1326 ... 336 G
hamill@ithaca.edu
HAMILL, Robert, P ... 740-392-6868 ... 396 H
robert.hamill@mvnu.edu
HAMILTON, Alana, R ... 423-323-3191 ... 475 F
arhamilton@northeaststate.edu
HAMILTON, Alice ... 785-442-6025 ... 193 D
ahamilton@highlandcc.edu
HAMILTON, Allana, R ... 423-279-7632 ... 475 E
arhamilton@northeaststate.edu
HAMILTON, Ann ... 714-556-3610 ... 76 E
OfficeVPSA@vanguard.edu
HAMILTON, Barbara ... 870-837-4003 ... 24 A
bhamilto@sautech.edu
HAMILTON, Barbara ... 601-318-6524 ... 278 E
barbara.hamilton@wmcarey.edu
HAMILTON, Ben ... 912-583-3280 ... 126 C
bhamilton@bpc.edu
HAMILTON, Bill ... 850-484-1304 ... 114 G
bhamilton@pensacolastate.edu
HAMILTON, Billy Jo ... 813-974-3039 ... 120 D
BJHamilton@usf.edu
HAMILTON, Bob ... 412-237-3108 ... 425 H
rhamilton@ccac.edu
HAMILTON, Carol ... 310-434-4403 ... 68 D
hamilton_carol@smc.edu
HAMILTON, Catherine ... 617-558-1788 ... 243 H
chamilton@nesa.edu
HAMILTON, Cecilia ... 305-348-2560 ... 119 B
cecilia.hamilton@fiu.edu
HAMILTON, Charlene ... 337-482-6243 ... 216 D
personnel@louisiana.edu
HAMILTON, Cheresa, Y ... 904-620-2455 ... 120 C
chamilto@unf.edu
HAMILTON, Chris ... 402-354-7065 ... 299 E
chris.hamilton@methodistcollege.edu
HAMILTON, Donna, B ... 301-405-9354 ... 227 B
dhamil@umd.edu
HAMILTON, Dwight ... 616-331-2242 ... 252 A
hamiltdw@gvsu.edu
HAMILTON, JR., Elbert ... 713-629-8940 ... 507 F
HAMILTON, Eldrie ... 318-274-6321 ... 215 E
hamiltoneb@gram.edu
HAMILTON, Ethan ... 619-849-2621 ... 62 L
ethanhamilton@pointloma.edu

HANDLEY, Shellee .... 630-889-6733.... 159 E
shandley@nuhs.edu
HANDOJO, Jeanne .... 626-584-5366..... 48 A
jeanne@fuller.edu
HANDS, Ashanti .... 619-388-2699..... 65 G
ahands@sdccd.edu
HANDS, Colette .... 773-244-5737.... 159 G
chands@northpark.edu
HANDY, Cromwell .... 334-229-4309....... 1 C
chandy@alasu.edu
HANDY, Cynthia, H .... 404-752-1654.... 134 B
cynthia@msm.edu
HANDY, James, L .... 214-860-2067.... 484 I
jhandy@dcccd.edu
HANDY, Linda, B .... 317-788-3349.... 180 C
handy@uindy.edu
HANDY, Lori, J .... 317-921-4780.... 175 I
lhandy1@ivytech.edu
HANDY, Ray .... 207-221-4213.... 220 H
rhandy@une.edu
HANDY, Ty .... 850-729-5360.... 114 A
handyt@nwfsc.edu
HANDZLIK, Deborah .... 716-896-0700.... 359 F
dhandzlik@villa.edu
HANDZLIK, Diane, M .... 716-896-0700.... 359 F
dianeh@villa.edu
HANE, Jennifer .... 719-255-3180..... 88 C
jhane@uccs.edu
HANEBERG, Erin .... 316-295-5513.... 192 H
haneberg@friends.edu
HANEFIELD, Robert .... 580-581-2415.... 407 D
rhanefield@cameron.edu
HANELLY, William .... 570-484-2002.... 443 A
whanelly@lhup.edu
HANES, Jack, A .... 270-745-6519.... 207 C
jack.hanes@wku.edu
HANES, Madlyn .... 814-863-0327.... 438 F
mqh3@psu.edu
HANES, Sheila .... 562-947-8755..... 71 A
sheilahanes@scuhs.edu
HANEWICH, Sheila, K .... 219-866-6157.... 179 B
sheilah@saintjoe.edu
HANEY, Joyce, A .... 814-863-0274.... 438 F
jzh8@psu.edu
HANEY, Lee Anna .... 828-694-1885.... 368 B
leeannah@blueridge.edu
HANEY, Michele .... 303-914-6215..... 87 C
Michele.Haney@rrcc.edu
HANEY, Pamela .... 708-974-4300.... 159 A
HANEY, Regina .... 806-457-4200.... 486 G
rhaney@fpctx.edu
HANEY, Richard, J .... 847-543-2635.... 147 H
rhaney@clcillinois.edu
HANFORD, Karen .... 909-469-5243..... 78 D
khanford@westernu.edu
HANG, Foua .... 920-693-1387.... 554 A
foua.hang@gotoltc.edu
HANIFIN, Leo, E .... 313-993-1216.... 259 C
hanifinl@udmercy.edu
HANIGAN, Sherri .... 402-826-8586.... 298 A
sherri.hanigan@doane.edu
HANINCIK, Amanda .... 610-921-7529.... 421 D
ahanincik@alb.edu
HANK, Jack, L .... 210-434-6711.... 491 G
jlhank@lake.ollusa.edu
HANK, Vigil .... 505-925-8581.... 321 G
vigilh@unm.edu
HANKERSON, Brian .... 954-486-7728.... 122 E
HANKIN, Joseph, N .... 914-606-6707.... 360 D
joseph.hankin@sunywcc.edu
HANKINS, Lori .... 904-826-0084.... 122 G
lhankins@usa.edu
HANKINS, Orlando, E .... 919-516-4860.... 376 B
HANKINS, Paul .... 662-846-4100.... 274 B
phankins@deltastate.edu
HANKINS, Robert .... 615-353-3572.... 475 D
robert.hankins@nscc.edu
HANKINS, Stephen, J .... 864-242-5100.... 455 E
HANKS, Bob .... 928-541-7777..... 16 I
bhanks@ncu.edu
HANKS, Bob .... 503-534-4061.... 416 I
bhanks@marylhurst.edu
HANKS, Charles .... 256-761-6206....... 7 H
chanks@talladega.edu
HANKS, Martha .... 803-822-3434.... 459 D
hanksm@midlandstech.edu
HANKS, Sue .... 719-549-2142..... 83 B
s.hanks@colostate-pueblo.edu
HANLEIN, Jeanette .... 973-655-7066.... 311 G
hanleinj@mail.montclair.edu
HANLEY, Bob, L .... 864-231-2075.... 455 C
bhanley@andersonuniversity.edu
HANLEY, Darla, S .... 617-266-1400.... 231 G
HANLEY, Glenn .... 512-245-2392.... 501 C
gh18@txstate.edu
HANLEY, Jim .... 215-204-4494.... 447 G
jim.hanley@temple.edu
HANLEY, OSFS, John .... 610-282-1100.... 426 I
john.hanley@desales.edu
HANLEY, Peggy .... 318-274-6546.... 215 E
peggy@gram.edu
HANLEY, Sally, B .... 814-332-2996.... 421 E
sally.hanley@allegheny.edu
HANLEY, Theodore .... 337-521-8951.... 212 B
theodore.hanley@southlouisiana.edu
HANLIN, Shawn .... 541-888-1546.... 420 C
shanlin@socc.edu
HANLON, Erin .... 617-296-8300.... 236 E
erin_hanlon@laboure.edu
HANLON, Joyce .... 617-730-7074.... 243 I
joyce.hanlon@newbury.edu
HANLON, Marcia, C .... 630-844-5416.... 145 C
mhanlon@aurora.edu
HANLON, Philip, J .... 734-764-9292.... 259 D
hanlon@umich.edu
HANLON, Rob .... 479-936-5116..... 22 H
rhanlon@nwacc.edu
HANN, Dan .... 928-344-7515..... 12 C
dan.hann@azwestern.edu
HANN, Julia .... 478-445-1549.... 129 F
julia.hann@gcsu.edu
HANNA, Abby .... 262-551-6100.... 546 F
ahanna@carthage.edu
HANNA, Alexis .... 440-375-7000.... 394 E
ahanna@lec.edu
HANNA, Bashar, W .... 215-489-2324.... 426 H
bashar.hanna@delval.edu
HANNA, C. Phil .... 270-384-8102.... 203 H
hannap@lindsey.edu
HANNA, Dorothy, A .... 785-827-5541.... 194 D
dahanna@kwu.edu
HANNA, Jeffery, G .... 540-458-8459.... 530 A
jhanna@wlu.edu
HANNA, Kimberly .... 575-461-4413.... 318 F
kimberlyh@mesalands.edu
HANNA, Laura .... 817-531-4480.... 502 A
lhanna@txwes.edu
HANNA, Mae .... 513-732-5332.... 403 E
hannamh@email.uc.edu
HANNA, Mark .... 806-371-5401.... 479 H
mlhanna@actx.edu
HANNA, Michael .... 315-781-3574.... 335 G
hanna@hws.edu
HANNA, Nancy .... 323-563-4960..... 39 D
nhanna@cdrewu.edu
HANNA, Peter .... 562-947-8755..... 71 A
peterhanna@scuhs.edu
HANNA, Roger .... 970-675-3212..... 82 D
roger.hanna@cncc.edu
HANNA, Tara .... 914-337-9300.... 331 A
tara.hanna@concordia-ny.edu
HANNABURY, Stephen, P .... 781-292-2401.... 235 C
stephen.hannabury@olin.edu
HANNAFIN, Robert .... 516-299-2210.... 339 A
robert.hannafin@liu.edu
HANNAH, Marcus .... 334-876-9360....... 4 B
mhannah@wccs.edu
HANNAH, Mary .... 218-751-8670.... 270 G
registrar@oakhills.edu
HANNAH, Roddy .... 570-586-2400.... 422 F
rhannah@bbc.edu
HANNAH, Russ .... 870-972-3303..... 20 C
rhannah@astate.edu
HANNAHS, Mitch .... 618-544-8657.... 152 G
hannahsm@iecc.edu
HANNAM, Paula .... 610-799-1718.... 434 D
phannam@lccc.edu
HANNAM, Susan, E .... 724-738-2982.... 443 E
susan.hannam@sru.edu
HANNAN, Steven, M .... 419-289-5007.... 384 D
shannan@ashland.edu
HANNAR, Christine .... 636-949-4965.... 284 C
channar@lindenwood.edu
HANNEMAN, Richard .... 402-457-2739.... 298 H
rhanneman@mccneb.edu
HANNER, Mary Beth .... 518-464-8500.... 333 F
mhanner@excelsior.edu
HANNIGAN, Jennifer .... 903-675-6327.... 502 D
jhannigan@tvcc.edu
HANNIGAN, Jim .... 610-566-1776.... 452 A
jhannigan@williamson.edu
HANNIGAN, Terence .... 718-862-8000.... 339 H
terence.hannigan@manhattan.edu
HANNO, Barbara .... 406-586-3585.... 294 I
barbara.hanno@montanabiblecollege.edu
HANNO, Dennis .... 781-239-5660.... 230 G
dhanno@babson.edu
HANNON, Bernard .... 765-285-1186.... 169 D
bmhannon@bsu.edu
HANNON, Charles .... 724-503-1001.... 451 A
channon@washjeff.edu
HANNON, Dennis, A .... 860-465-5208..... 91 H
hannond@easternct.edu
HANNON, Jim, M .... 563-333-6359.... 188 D
HannonJamesM@ambrose.sau.edu
HANNON, Kristin .... 330-966-5459.... 402 A
khannon@starkstate.edu
HANNON, Patrick, K .... 770-537-5749.... 139 B
pat.hannon@westgatech.edu
HANNON, Ron .... 408-848-4895..... 48 B
rhannon@gavilan.edu
HANNUM, Judy, A .... 508-793-2431.... 233 D
jhannum@holycross.edu
HANOFEE, Rose .... 845-434-5750.... 356 H
rhanofee@sullivan.suny.edu
HANOLD, John, W .... 814-863-0768.... 438 F
jhh6@psu.edu
HANOUSEK, Mandy .... 208-885-5369.... 144 B
hanousek@uidaho.edu
HANRAHAN, Susan, N .... 870-972-3112..... 20 C
hanrahan@astate.edu
HANRAHAN, Thomas .... 718-399-4308.... 346 D
hanrahan@pratt.edu
HANRAHAN, Thomas, M .... 717-867-6030.... 434 C
hanrahan@lvc.edu
HANS, John .... 651-905-3474.... 261 J
jhans@browncollege.edu
HANSBURY, Kevin .... 302-736-2586..... 96 G
hansbuke@wesley.edu
HANSEL, Marie, C .... 708-709-3766.... 161 C
mhansel@prairiestate.edu
HANSEL, Sheila .... 713-646-1799.... 494 E
shansel@stcl.edu
HANSELL, Phyllis .... 973-761-9015.... 315 B
phyllis.hansell@shu.edu
HANSEN, Allan .... 310-287-4307..... 55 F
hansenas@wlac.edu
HANSEN, Andrew, C .... 307-766-4286.... 556 E
hansen@uwyo.edu
HANSEN, Anne, P .... 775-445-3235.... 303 B
anne@wnc.edu
HANSEN, Beverly .... 262-564-3160.... 553 H
hansenb@gtc.edu
HANSEN, Carl, F .... 707-826-3731..... 36 D
ch1@humboldt.edu
HANSEN, Carl, K .... 575-624-8011.... 319 C
hansenc@nmmi.edu
HANSEN, Cheryl .... 503-534-4005.... 416 I
chansen@marylhurst.edu
HANSEN, Chris .... 423-236-2915.... 473 A
chansen@southern.edu
HANSEN, Christian .... 203-576-4642..... 94 D
registrar@bridgeport.edu
HANSEN, Corinne .... 605-642-6215.... 465 F
corinne.hansen@bhsu.edu
HANSEN, D, A .... 208-496-3303.... 142 G
hansena@byui.edu
HANSEN, David .... 843-574-6021.... 461 G
david.hansen@tridenttech.edu
HANSEN, David .... 605-677-5047.... 465 D
dhansen@sdbor.edu
HANSEN, Douglas .... 801-957-4084.... 512 C
douglas.hansen@slcc.edu
HANSEN, Dwight .... 605-642-6146.... 465 F
dwight.hansen@bhsu.edu
HANSEN, Eileen .... 515-643-6612.... 187 C
ehansen@mercydesmoines.org
HANSEN, Eric .... 978-665-4095.... 238 C
ehansen@fitchburgstate.edu
HANSEN, Erica, L .... 516-671-7373.... 360 A
ehansen@webb-institute.edu
HANSEN, Gregg .... 978-468-7111.... 235 F
ghansen@gcts.edu
HANSEN, J. Mark .... 773-702-8798.... 166 D
jhansen@uchicago.edu
HANSEN, James, R .... 334-844-5860....... 1 G
honors@auburn.edu
HANSEN, Jim .... 909-384-8958..... 65 C
jhansen@sbccd.cc.ca.us
HANSEN, Julie .... 641-673-1096.... 189 I
hansenj@wmpenn.edu
HANSEN, Kathy .... 909-537-5142..... 36 A
hansen@csusb.edu
HANSEN, Kenneth .... 402-559-5301.... 301 A
hansenkl@unmc.edu
HANSEN, Kent, A .... 909-558-2644..... 54 D
khansen@claysonlaw.com
HANSEN, Kevin .... 801-626-8022.... 511 D
khansen@weber.edu
HANSEN, Kinsey .... 432-264-5127.... 487 I
khansen@howardcollege.edu
HANSEN, Lauren .... 262-551-5816.... 546 F
HANSEN, Linda, L .... 406-768-6327.... 294 F
lhansen@fpcc.edu
HANSEN, Lynn .... 407-823-2362.... 120 A
lynn.hansen@ucf.edu
HANSEN, Marianne, W .... 509-777-4347.... 539 F
mhansen@whitworth.edu
HANSEN, Mary Mincer .... 515-271-1424.... 183 F
mary.hansen@dmu.edu
HANSEN, Matt, B .... 563-333-6258.... 188 D
HansenMattB@sau.edu
HANSEN, Patricia .... 212-774-0748.... 340 D
phansen@mmm.edu
HANSEN, Peter .... 210-436-3324.... 493 C
phansen@stmarytx.edu
HANSEN, Richard .... 513-861-6400.... 402 I
richard.hansen@myunion.edu
HANSEN, Sue .... 217-854-3231.... 145 F
sue.hansen@blackburn.edu
HANSEN, Susan, L .... 608-342-1547.... 551 F
hansens@uwplatt.edu
HANSEN, Ted, P .... 440-510-1112.... 386 A
tphansen@bryantstratton.edu
HANSEN, Terry .... 432-264-5160.... 487 I
thansen@howardcollege.edu
HANSEN, Tiffany .... 619-574-6909..... 60 E
thansen@pacificcollege.edu
HANSEN, Tim .... 408-962-6400..... 30 C
thansen@aii.edu
HANSEN, Timothy, R .... 847-578-8734.... 163 A
tim.hansen@rosalindfranklin.edu
HANSEN, Vagn, K .... 256-765-4288....... 9 D
vkhansen@una.edu
HANSEN-KIEFFER,
Kristin, M .... 717-796-5234.... 436 D
khansen@messiah.edu
HANSHEW, Daniel, S .... 304-877-6428.... 540 D
dan.hanshew@abc.edu
HANSMAN, Erin, M .... 573-592-1116.... 293 E
ehansman@williamwoods.edu
HANSMANN, Marilyn .... 507-285-7214.... 269 B
marilyn.hansmann@roch.edu
HANSOM, Connie .... 615-297-7545.... 466 H
hansomc@aquinascollege.edu
HANSON, Andrew .... 208-792-2218.... 143 F
ahanson@lcsc.edu
HANSON, Anita .... 218-879-0805.... 266 F
anita@fdltcc.edu
HANSON, Barbara .... 281-476-1501.... 493 E
barbara.hanson@sjcd.edu
HANSON, Brenda .... 406-756-3812.... 294 D
bhanson@fvcc.edu
HANSON, Catherine .... 979-230-3632.... 482 B
catherine.hanson@brazosport.edu
HANSON, Charles, D .... 810-762-7812.... 253 I
chanson@kettering.edu
HANSON, Christina, R .... 717-766-2511.... 436 D
chanson@messiah.edu
HANSON, Clint .... 603-880-8308.... 306 C
tmc@thomasmorecc.edu
HANSON, Daniel .... 402-872-2239.... 299 H
dhanson@peru.edu
HANSON, Denise .... 319-226-2012.... 181 E
hansondl@ihs.org
HANSON, Gail, S .... 202-885-3484..... 97 B
gsher@american.edu
HANSON, Gary, A .... 310-506-4607..... 61 G
gary.hanson@pepperdine.edu
HANSON, Glenn .... 910-642-7141.... 373 G
ghanson@sccnc.edu
HANSON, Hans, M .... 515-271-2222.... 184 A
hans.hanson@drake.edu
HANSON, Janet, K .... 715-394-8014.... 552 D
jhanson@uwsuper.edu
HANSON, Jeanette .... 316-295-5485.... 192 H
jeanette@friends.edu
HANSON, Jenifer, A .... 319-368-6469.... 187 E
jhanson@mtmercy.edu
HANSON, Karen .... 812-855-9011.... 173 C
provost@indiana.edu
HANSON, Karen .... 812-855-5752.... 173 B
provost@indiana.edu
HANSON, Kent .... 218-793-2461.... 268 E
kent.hanson@northlandcollege.edu
HANSON, Kirk, O .... 408-554-7898..... 68 C
kohanson@scu.edu
HANSON, Kristina .... 281-487-1170.... 498 E
khanson@txchiro.edu
HANSON, Laurie, R .... 563-336-3351.... 184 B
lhanson@eicc.edu
HANSON, Linda .... 507-389-2986.... 267 H
linda.hanson@mnsu.edu
HANSON, Linda, N .... 651-523-2202.... 264 C
president@hamline.edu
HANSON, Lisa .... 309-341-5212.... 146 A
lhanson@sandburg.edu
HANSON, Myron, L .... 406-243-5373.... 295 A
mick.hanson@umontana.edu
HANSON, Perry .... 781-736-4588.... 233 A
phanson@brandeis.edu
HANSON, Richard, A .... 218-755-2011.... 266 B
rhanson@bemidjistate.edu
HANSON, Rick, D .... 816-501-4275.... 288 D
rick.hanson@rockhurst.edu
HANSON, Sara .... 402-354-7111.... 299 E
sara.hanson@methodistcollege.edu
HANSON, Shirley, M .... 701-788-4767.... 381 F
Shirley.M.Hanson@mayvillestate.edu
HANSON, Steven, J .... 425-235-2235.... 536 E
shanson@rtc.edu
HANSON, Susan .... 909-469-5329..... 78 D
shanson@westernu.edu
HANSON, Susanah .... 724-266-3838.... 448 G
shanson@tsm.edu
HANSON HEGG, Breanne .... 651-523-2012.... 264 C
bhansonhegg01@hamline.edu
HANSON HUBER, Tonya .... 952-487-8213.... 268 C
tonya.huber@normandale.edu
HANSTEIN, Andrea .... 714-992-7014..... 59 D
ahanstein@fullcoll.edu
HANTEN, Joan .... 360-475-7120.... 535 J
jhanten@olympic.edu
HANTZ, Joan .... 406-477-6215.... 294 B
jhantz@cdkc.edu
HANTZSCHEL, Linda, J .... 516-463-6903.... 335 H
linda.j.hantzschel@hofstra.edu
HANUSA, Matthew .... 303-280-7600..... 84 C
mhanusa@devry.edu
HANUSCIN, R. Douglas .... 419-755-4871.... 397 B
dhanusci@ncstatecollege.edu
HANYPSIAK, Krista, L .... 716-645-3020.... 351 G
klh5@buffalo.edu
HAO, Lan .... 626-914-8521..... 39 G
lhao@citruscollege.edu

HARMER, Paula .... 303-964-5199..... 87 E
pharmer@regis.edu
HARMON, Brian .... 718-488-1418.... 338 H
brian.harmon@liu.edu
HARMON, Bruce .... 719-590-6852..... 83 D
bharmon@coloradotech.edu
HARMON, Christopher ...... 717-337-6810.... 429 H
charmon@gettysburg.edu
HARMON, Debbie .... 503-883-2607.... 416 G
dharmon@linfield.edu
HARMON, Deborah, L .... 828-254-1921.... 367 H
dharmon@abtech.edu
HARMON, Debra, J .... 217-732-3155.... 156 G
dharmon@lincolncollege.edu
HARMON, Dorinda, Q .... 843-953-5934.... 457 B
harmond@cofc.edu
HARMON, Eva .... 828-726-2715.... 368 D
eharmon@cccti.edu
HARMON, Jeff .... 479-788-7125..... 24 D
jharmon@uafortsmith.edu
HARMON, Jeff, M .... 208-732-6210.... 143 B
jharmon@csi.edu
HARMON, Jerry .... 575-562-2443.... 318 A
jerry.harmon@enmu.edu
HARMON, Justin .... 603-862-1463.... 306 E
justin.harmon@unh.edu
HARMON, Justin .... 609-258-0840.... 313 A
jharmon@princeton.edu
HARMON, Kate .... 503-244-0726.... 414 D
kateharmon@achs.edu
HARMON, Kathy, M .... 937-229-4303.... 404 A
Kathy.Harmon@udayton.edu
HARMON, Kevin .... 701-858-4363.... 381 G
kevin.harmon@minotstateu.edu
HARMON, Ladelle .... 828-652-0626.... 371 G
ladelleh@mcdoweltech.edu
HARMON, LaVerne, T .... 302-356-6938..... 97 A
laverne.t.harmon@wilmu.edu
HARMON, Lindsay .... 312-461-0600.... 144 D
lharmon@aaart.edu
HARMON, Mark .... 706-776-0108.... 135 D
mharmon@piedmont.edu
HARMON, Martino .... 419-995-8133.... 392 L
harmon.m@rhodesstate.edu
HARMON, Melanie, B .... 260-982-5211.... 177 F
mbharmon@manchester.edu
HARMON, Patricia .... 304-929-5460.... 542 H
pharmon@newriver.edu
HARMON, Sherri .... 317-632-5553.... 177 E
sharmon@lincolntech.com
HARMON, Steve, K .... 956-326-2180.... 497 B
harmon@tamiu.edu
HARMON, W. Ken .... 770-423-6023.... 132 H
wharmon3@kennesaw.edu
HARMON, William .... 713-718-6041.... 487 G
william.harmon@hccs.edu
HARMON JACOBS, Jane .. 206-268-4822.... 530 F
jharmonjacobs@antioch.edu
HARMONY, Stephena .... 513-745-5710.... 403 F
stephena.harmony@uc.edu
HARMS, JR., Alfred .... 407-823-2232.... 120 A
alfred.harms@ucf.edu
HARMS, Jeff .... 507-223-7252.... 268 B
jeff.harms@mnwest.edu
HARMS, Mason .... 641-585-8137.... 189 E
harmsm@waldorf.edu
HARMS, Steve .... 513-721-7944.... 391 C
sharms@gbs.edu
HARMSEN, Dee .... 920-923-8530.... 548 C
dharmsen@marianuniversity.edu
HARMSEN,
Frederika (Fraka) .... 530-898-6121..... 34 A
fharmsen@csuchico.edu
HARNER, Kristy .... 423-614-8110.... 470 A
kharner@leeuniversity.edu
HARNER, Mike .... 517-607-2303.... 252 E
mike.harner@hillsdale.edu
HARNEY, Joseph .... 212-854-1540.... 330 F
jh2087@columbia.edu
HARNISH, Eric .... 661-362-3400..... 41 G
eric.harnish@canyons.edu
HARNUM, Donald, P .... 609-896-5054.... 313 G
harnum@rider.edu
HAROLD, Martin .... 858-653-6740..... 52 C
HARP, Brittaney .... 859-371-9393.... 198 D
bharp@beckfield.edu
HARP, Debbie .... 606-539-4259.... 206 G
debbie.harp@ucumberlands.edu
HARP, Deborah .... 312-893-7114.... 150 G
dharp@erikson.edu
HARP, Jeff .... 405-974-2800.... 413 B
jharp@ucok.edu
HARP, John, W .... 319-895-4234.... 183 D
jharp@cornellcollege.edu
HARP-STEPHENS, Becky ... 859-246-6498.... 201 D
becky.harp@kctcs.edu
HARPER, Allyson, R .... 612-874-3775.... 265 E
allyson_harper@mcad.edu
HARPER, Cheri .... 502-895-3411.... 204 B
charper@lpts.edu
HARPER, David .... 229-209-5239.... 124 C
dahar@andrewcollege.edu
HARPER, David .... 828-298-3325.... 380 C
dharper@warren-wilson.edu

HARPER, Deborah .... 607-274-3136.... 336 G
dharper@ithaca.edu
HARPER, Derry .... 850-245-0466.... 118 F
derry.harper@flbog.edu
HARPER, Donna, L .... 540-568-3705.... 520 C
harperdl@jmu.edu
HARPER, Doreen, C .... 205-934-5360........ 8 G
dcharper@uab.edu
HARPER, E. Royster .... 734-764-5132.... 259 D
harperer@umich.edu
HARPER, Elizabeth .... 703-323-3398.... 527 C
eharper@nvcc.edu
HARPER, Jane .... 765-269-5640.... 176 B
jharper@ivytech.edu
HARPER, Jane .... 817-515-6686.... 496 A
jane.harper@tccd.edu
HARPER, Janice, A .... 919-530-7297.... 378 A
jharper@nccu.edu
HARPER, Jay, A .... 540-654-1241.... 524 H
jharper@umw.edu
HARPER, Jimmy .... 423-614-8420.... 470 A
jharper@leeuniversity.edu
HARPER, Joann .... 706-245-7226.... 128 K
jharper@ec.edu
HARPER, John .... 813-974-1686.... 120 D
jharper@admin.usf.edu
HARPER, John, C .... 508-531-1352.... 238 B
jharper@bridgew.edu
HARPER, Julie .... 248-218-2096.... 257 F
jharper@rc.edu
HARPER, Katherine .... 304-766-3142.... 544 D
harperkl@wvstateu.edu
HARPER, Kristin .... 205-226-4720........ 2 C
kharper@bsc.edu
HARPER, Larisa .... 740-588-1252.... 407 A
HARPER, Lisa .... 405-974-2553.... 413 B
lharper@ucok.edu
HARPER, Lisa, D .... 859-858-3511.... 198 B
lisa.harper@asbury.edu
HARPER, Lisa, M .... 903-510-2147.... 502 E
lhar@tjc.edu
HARPER, Loretta, F .... 801-585-0928.... 510 L
loretta.harper@utah.edu
HARPER, Marjoree .... 318-678-6000.... 209 J
mharper@bpcc.edu
HARPER, Mary, J .... 812-464-1767.... 180 F
mjharper@usi.edu
HARPER, Mary Ann .... 501-337-5000...... 21 D
mharper@otcweb.edu
HARPER, Norma .... 843-863-7765.... 456 B
nharper@csuniv.edu
HARPER, Ollie .... 601-979-2260.... 275 A
ollie.l.harper@jsums.edu
HARPER, Pam .... 270-706-8434.... 201 F
pam.harper@kctcs.edu
HARPER, Patricia .... 816-654-7162.... 283 J
pharper@kcumb.edu
HARPER, Paul .... 740-753-7135.... 392 A
harper_p@hocking.edu
HARPER, Paul, J .... 361-575-8944.... 503 E
harperj@uhv.edu
HARPER, Randy .... 870-574-4590..... 24 A
rharper@sautech.edu
HARPER, Robert .... 559-278-2482..... 34 D
roberth@csufresno.edu
HARPER, Robert .... 903-769-5793.... 488 M
robert_harper@jarvis.edu
HARPER, Rosie .... 601-977-7818.... 277 F
rharper@tougaloo.edu
HARPER, Sandra, S .... 225-768-1710.... 214 B
sandra.harper@ololcollege.edu
HARPER, Vernon .... 570-408-4149.... 451 G
vernon.harper@wilkes.edu
HARPER, Wanda .... 573-681-5017.... 284 B
harperw@lincolnu.edu
HARPER, Yolanda .... 901-320-9700.... 478 B
yharper@victory.edu
HARPER HAGAN, Mary, T 718-990-2505.... 348 G
harperm@stjohns.edu
HARPER-MARINICK,
Maria .... 480-731-8101..... 15 F
maria.harper@domail.maricopa.edu
HARPEST, Todd, R .... 419-783-2312.... 389 G
tharpest@defiance.edu
HARPHAM, Jennifer .... 757-822-1360.... 528 C
jharpham@tcc.edu
HARPINE, Layne .... 252-638-7372.... 369 E
harpinel@cravencc.edu
HARPS, Trynette Lottie ...... 231-777-0559.... 256 D
trynette.lottie-harps@muskegoncc.edu
HARPST, Steve .... 845-341-4230.... 345 E
steve.harpst@sunyorange.edu
HARPSTER, G. F. (Jody) .... 717-477-1030.... 443 D
gfharp@ship.edu
HARR, Jon, P .... 423-323-0231.... 475 E
jpharr@northeaststate.edu
HARR, Kathleen .... 785-354-5853.... 190 C
kharr@stormontvail.org
HARR, Lois .... 718-862-7142.... 339 H
lois.harr@manhattan.edu
HARRADINE, Andy, A .... 315-267-3011.... 354 C
andy@potsdam.edu
HARRAL, Judy .... 361-825-5936.... 497 F
judy.harral@tamucc.edu

HARRAL, Kevin .... 650-949-7223..... 47 H
harralkevin@foothill.edu
HARRAR, William, R .... 570-389-4255.... 441 F
wharrar@bloomu.edu
HARRED, Jack .... 903-886-5509.... 497 E
jack_harred@tamu-commerce.edu
HARREL, Peggy, F .... 812-465-7015.... 180 F
pharrel@usi.edu
HARRELL, Ann .... 361-592-1615.... 482 I
artpsyfx@coastalbend.edu
HARRELL, Brandan .... 229-931-2801.... 136 G
bharrell@southgatech.edu
HARRELL, Bryant, L .... 860-727-6756..... 92 C
bharrell@goodwin.edu
HARRELL, Charlie, R .... 252-823-5166.... 370 A
harrellc@edgecombe.edu
HARRELL, Diana .... 512-245-1555.... 501 C
dh32@txstate.edu
HARRELL, Frank (Doug) ..... 504-865-5352.... 215 C
fharrel@tulane.edu
HARRELL, Ivan, L .... 410-777-2830.... 221 B
ilharrell@aacc.edu
HARRELL, Jerry, H .... 317-921-4447.... 175 I
jeharrel@ivytech.edu
HARRELL, Kip .... 602-978-7304..... 18 K
kip.harrell@thunderbird.edu
HARRELL, Lee .... 740-368-3052.... 400 F
jlharrell@owu.edu
HARRELL, Lou .... 336-334-5091.... 379 A
mwharrel@uncg.edu
HARRELL, P. Randy .... 252-398-6209.... 363 E
harrer@chowan.edu
HARRELL, Pamela, J .... 919-209-2048.... 371 C
pjharrell@johnstoncc.edu
HARRELL, Ronald .... 270-706-8580.... 201 F
ron.harrell@kctcs.edu
HARRELL, Wanda .... 423-585-6976.... 476 B
wanda.harrell@ws.edu
HARRELSON, Jerry, W .... 336-316-2333.... 364 E
jharrelson@guilford.edu
HARRELSON, Laura .... 407-888-4000.... 113 A
lharrelson@orlando.chefs.edu
HARRES, JR., Burt, H .... 727-816-3490.... 114 F
harresb@phcc.edu
HARREYS, M. Seamus .... 617-373-4095.... 244 A
HARRI, Robert .... 563-387-2103.... 187 A
harrro01@luther.edu
HARRICK, Kristie .... 205-970-9244........ 7 D
kharrick@sebc.edu
HARRIENDORF, SC,
Cecilia .... 718-405-3215.... 330 A
cecilia.harriendorf@mountsaintvincent.edu
HARRIGAN, Maureen .... 410-234-4520.... 225 E
HARRIGAN, Theresa, A ...... 617-552-3430.... 232 D
theresa.harrigan.1@bc.edu
HARRIGER, Sherill .... 863-638-7235.... 123 B
sherill.harriger@warner.edu
HARRILL, Thad .... 828-286-3636.... 371 A
tharrill@isothermal.edu
HARRIMAN, Mark .... 661-654-2635..... 33 H
mharriman@csub.edu
HARRING, Kathleen, E .... 484-664-3424.... 437 B
harring@muhlenberg.edu
HARRING-HENDON,
Janice .... 773-442-4000.... 159 H
j-harringhendon@neiu.edu
HARRINGTON, Angela .... 201-447-7071.... 307 F
aharrington@bergen.edu
HARRINGTON, Anne, E .... 603-641-7465.... 305 H
aharrington@anselm.edu
HARRINGTON, Antivan ...... 407-843-3984.... 110 B
aharrington@fortiscollege.edu
HARRINGTON, Bonnie .... 215-751-8253.... 426 B
bharrington@ccp.edu
HARRINGTON, Daphne ...... 617-521-2754.... 245 A
daphne.harrington@simmons.edu
HARRINGTON, CM,
Donald, J .... 718-990-6301.... 348 G
pres@stjohns.edu
HARRINGTON, James .... 540-887-7333.... 520 I
jharring@mbc.edu
HARRINGTON, Janet .... 617-670-4413.... 235 B
jharrington@fisher.edu
HARRINGTON, John, D ..... 207-768-9585.... 220 F
john.harrington@umpi.edu
HARRINGTON, Kate .... 774-455-7163.... 237 B
kharrington@umassp.edu
HARRINGTON, Kristen ...... 617-879-2260.... 246 F
kharrington@wheelock.edu
HARRINGTON,
L. Katharine .... 213-740-7849..... 76 C
vpap@usc.edu
HARRINGTON, Lynn .... 708-974-5704.... 159 A
harrington@morainevalley.edu
HARRINGTON, Mary, M ..... 662-915-7387.... 277 G
ccmary@olemiss.edu
HARRINGTON, Melissa ..... 406-496-4108.... 296 C
mharrington@mtech.edu
HARRINGTON, Melissa ..... 406-496-4108.... 296 D
mharrington@mtech.edu
HARRINGTON, Melody .... 405-878-5310.... 412 A
maharrington@stgregorys.edu
HARRINGTON, Michael ...... 631-420-2053.... 356 A
michael.harrington@farmingdale.edu

HARRINGTON, Pamela ...... 401-454-6318.... 454 B
pharring@risd.edu
HARRINGTON, Paul .... 651-641-3216.... 264 J
pharrington001@luthersem.edu
HARRINGTON, Robert .... 417-625-3191.... 286 E
harrington-r@mssu.edu
HARRINGTON, Shawn, M . 860-231-5314..... 93 H
sharrington@sjc.edu
HARRINGTON, Sherre Lee 706-236-2285.... 125 G
sharrington@berry.edu
HARRINGTON, Thea .... 570-945-8516.... 432 C
thea.harrington@keystone.edu
HARRINGTON, Thomas ...... 504-280-1154.... 213 E
trharrin@uno.edu
HARRINGTON, Thomas ...... 520-206-4772...... 17 I
teharrington@pima.edu
HARRIS, Allatia .... 281-459-7140.... 493 F
allatia.harris@sjcd.edu
HARRIS, Amelia, J .... 276-376-4557.... 525 C
ajh7a@uvawise.edu
HARRIS, Andrew .... 508-531-1295.... 238 B
andrew.harris@bridgew.edu
HARRIS, Andrew, M .... 940-565-2055.... 504 B
aharris@unt.edu
HARRIS, Angela .... 706-272-4476.... 127 G
aharris@daltonstate.edu
HARRIS, Anjour, B .... 804-828-2021.... 525 E
abharris@vcu.edu
HARRIS, Ann .... 573-681-5074.... 284 B
harrisa@lincolnu.edu
HARRIS, Ann .... 503-725-4441.... 418 G
harrisa@pdx.edu
HARRIS, April .... 256-824-6085........ 9 A
april.harris@uah.edu
HARRIS, Arlita .... 405-491-6350.... 412 D
aharris@snu.edu
HARRIS, Benjamin, G .... 812-246-3301.... 176 H
bharris88@ivytech.edu
HARRIS, Bennie, L .... 615-966-5687.... 470 D
bennie.harris@lipscomb.edu
HARRIS, Bernice .... 303-556-3786..... 83 F
bernice.harris@ccd.edu
HARRIS, Beth .... 203-287-3023..... 93 C
paierartlibrary@snet.net
HARRIS, Beth, A .... 773-702-7243.... 166 D
ba-harris@uchicago.edu
HARRIS, Bethany, W .... 434-949-1007.... 527 H
bethany.harris@southside.edu
HARRIS, Betsy, A .... 207-768-2791.... 218 J
bharris@nmcc.edu
HARRIS, Bette Ann .... 617-724-6138.... 242 E
baharris@mghihp.edu
HARRIS, Beverly .... 620-331-4100.... 193 G
bharris@indycc.edu
HARRIS, Beverly Jo .... 304-734-6601.... 542 D
jharris@bridgemont.edu
HARRIS, Brenda .... 325-670-1262.... 487 D
bharris@hsutx.edu
HARRIS, Brent .... 254-295-8642.... 504 A
bharris@umhb.edu
HARRIS, Brice, W .... 916-568-3021..... 55 J
harrisbw@losrios.edu
HARRIS, Camille .... 312-939-4975.... 151 F
HARRIS, Celia, D .... 781-736-3015.... 233 A
cdharris@brandeis.edu
HARRIS, Charles .... 334-420-4232........ 7 I
charris@trenholmstate.edu
HARRIS, Charles, S .... 434-791-5701.... 516 D
csharris@averett.edu
HARRIS, Charlotte .... 937-775-2821.... 406 C
charlotte.harris@wright.edu
HARRIS, Charlotte, M .... 205-348-6690........ 8 F
charris@fa.ua.edu
HARRIS, Chelsy .... 719-502-3033..... 86 G
chelsy.harris@ppcc.edu
HARRIS, Chris .... 949-214-3169..... 42 K
chris.harris@cui.edu
HARRIS, Chris .... 440-375-7000.... 394 E
charris1@lec.edu
HARRIS, Chris .... 601-635-2111.... 274 C
charris@eccc.edu
HARRIS, Chriss .... 419-755-4753.... 397 B
charris@ncstatecollege.edu
HARRIS, Christina .... 215-568-9215.... 436 E
charris@mccworks.org
HARRIS, Clark .... 810-762-0500.... 256 C
clark.harris@mcc.edu
HARRIS, Clayton .... 216-987-4325.... 389 A
clayton.harris@tri-c.edu
HARRIS, Cliff .... 313-664-7403.... 250 A
charris@collegeforcreativestudies.edu
HARRIS, Craig .... 716-926-8888.... 335 F
charris@hilbert.edu
HARRIS, Craig .... 540-857-6479.... 528 E
charris@virginiawestern.edu
HARRIS, D. Steve .... 229-317-6780.... 128 A
steve.harris@darton.edu
HARRIS, Dan, I .... 414-277-7230.... 548 H
harris@msoe.edu
HARRIS, Darrell, A .... 904-264-2172.... 116 A
dharris@iws.edu
HARRIS, David .... 501-812-2205..... 23 C
dharris@pulaskitech.edu
HARRIS, David .... 718-268-4700.... 347 B

HARRIS, David, J 269-660-8021 257 E harrisd@millercollege.edu
HARRIS, David, P 909-558-7600 54 D dpharris@llu.edu
HARRIS, David, W 505-277-7520 321 C dwharris@unm.edu
HARRIS, Debbie 804-751-9191 523 E dharris@rsht.edu
HARRIS, Delphia 901-435-1380 470 B delphia_harris@loc.edu
HARRIS, Denise 716-926-8727 335 F dharris@hilbert.edu
HARRIS, Dennis 405-422-1283 411 G harrisd@redlandscc.edu
HARRIS, Dina 574-520-4131 174 C dlharris@iusb.edu
HARRIS, Don 541-346-1702 419 B cio@uoregon.edu
HARRIS, Duncan 307-766-4110 556 E dharris@uwyo.edu
HARRIS, Earl 951-343-4449 31 G eharris@calbaptist.edu
HARRIS, Ed 303-871-2647 88 E ed.harris@du.edu
HARRIS, Erica 606-539-4241 206 G erica.harris@ucumberlands.edu
HARRIS, SR., Forrest, E 615-256-1463 466 G harrisfe@abcnash.edu
HARRIS, Freda, J 608-262-6423 550 F fharris@uwsa.edu
HARRIS, G. Duncan 860-512-3203 90 C gharris@mcc.commnet.edu
HARRIS, Gail 423-746-5208 476 D gharris@twcnet.edu
HARRIS, George, G 704-330-1181 365 H gharris@jcsu.edu
HARRIS, George, G 704-378-1181 365 H gharris@jcsu.edu
HARRIS, Gheretta, R 248-341-2081 257 B grharris@oaklandcc.edu
HARRIS, Goddess 937-224-0061 395 A gharris@swcollege.net
HARRIS, Greg 770-426-2836 133 B gharris@life.edu
HARRIS, Greg 503-584-7153 414 J greg.harris@chemeketa.edu
HARRIS, Gregory 617-573-8406 245 E gharris@suffolk.edu
HARRIS, Gregory 803-533-3740 460 G gharri17@scsu.edu
HARRIS, Gregory, C 704-378-1101 365 H gcharris@jcsu.edu
HARRIS, Helen 225-216-8089 209 I harrish@mybrcc.edu
HARRIS, Hubert, B 804-524-8989 529 C hharris@vsu.edu
HARRIS, Hugh, W 610-330-5330 433 B harrish@lafayette.edu
HARRIS, Jackie 417-624-7070 284 G jharris@messengercollege.edu
HARRIS, James 903-593-8311 499 A jharris@texascollege.edu
HARRIS, James, T 706-721-2619 130 B jharris@georgiahealth.edu
HARRIS, III, James, T 610-499-4101 96 H jtharris@widener.edu
HARRIS, III, James, T 610-499-4101 451 F jtharris@widener.edu
HARRIS, Jay, H 260-481-6785 174 A harrishj@ipfw.edu
HARRIS, Jerrold, R 570-389-4129 441 F jharris@bloomu.edu
HARRIS, Jerry 307-778-1280 556 B jharris@lccc.wy.edu
HARRIS, Jessica 907-564-8275 10 D jharris08@alaskapacific.edu
HARRIS, Jo-Anne 610-399-2247 441 H jharris@cheyney.edu
HARRIS, Joel, C 843-953-6841 456 C joel.harris@citadel.edu
HARRIS, John 903-923-2181 486 D jharris@etbu.edu
HARRIS, John, D 979-830-4150 482 A jharris@blinn.edu
HARRIS, Joseph 601-426-6346 277 D jharris@southeasternbaptist.edu
HARRIS, Judy 252-493-7252 372 E jharris@email.pittcc.edu
HARRIS, Kandace 919-546-8435 376 D kharris@shawu.edu
HARRIS, Kathy 618-544-8657 152 G harrisk@iecc.edu
HARRIS, Kay 601-266-5858 278 A elizabeth.harris@usm.edu
HARRIS, Kendall, T 936-261-9900 496 E ktharris@pvamu.edu
HARRIS, Kim 865-882-4695 475 G harriskb@roanestate.edu
HARRIS, Kimberly 972-758-3804 483 D kharris@collin.edu
HARRIS, Kip, B 208-496-9200 142 G harrisk@byui.edu
HARRIS, Kristin 940-855-2203 507 E kharris@vernoncollege.edu
HARRIS, Lakecia 334-244-3903 2 A lharri18@aum.edu
HARRIS, Lamel 559-730-3912 42 B lamelh@cos.edu
HARRIS, Lesa, C 270-809-3750 204 F lesa.harris@murraystate.edu
HARRIS, Lisa 208-426-1630 142 F lisaharris@boisestate.edu
HARRIS, Lisa 763-433-1292 265 J lisa.harris@anokaramsey.edu
HARRIS, Lois, A 206-726-5181 532 G lharris@cornish.edu
HARRIS, Margie, R 402-552-3470 297 D harris@clarksoncollege.edu
HARRIS, Marie Joan 816-501-3758 279 C marie.harris@avila.edu
HARRIS, Mary 575-492-2162 321 H mharris@usw.edu
HARRIS, Mary 317-931-2300 170 E mharris@cts.edu
HARRIS, Mary, A 202-274-5498 99 F mharris@udc.edu
HARRIS, Mary, E 512-223-7705 481 B mharris3@austincc.edu
HARRIS, Mary, M 309-298-1888 168 A mm-harris@wiu.edu
HARRIS, Matthew 419-289-5090 384 D mharris@ashland.edu
HARRIS, Meco 312-939-0111 150 B meco@eastwest.edu
HARRIS, Michael 202-806-1002 98 B micharris@howard.edu
HARRIS, Michael 316-634-0066 197 C
HARRIS, Michael 765-455-9225 173 E micharis@iuk.edu
HARRIS, Michael 856-256-4650 314 A harrismi@rowan.edu
HARRIS, Michael, E 336-734-7764 370 C mharris@forsythtech.edu
HARRIS, Mike 334-874-5700 3 A mharris@concordiaselma.edu
HARRIS, Nancy 323-856-7600 28 D
HARRIS, Natalie 502-968-7191 199 A nharris@brownmackie.edu
HARRIS, Nick, L 504-816-4704 208 I nharris@dillard.edu
HARRIS, Obadiah 323-663-2167 75 E
HARRIS, Ozzie 404-727-2616 129 A ozzie.harris@emory.edu
HARRIS, P. Al 912-344-3300 124 E al.harris@armstrong.edu
HARRIS, Patricia 662-252-8000 277 C pharris@rustcollege.edu
HARRIS, Patrick 706-355-5160 124 H pharris@athenstech.edu
HARRIS, Patty 651-290-6358 273 B patty.harris@wmitchell.edu
HARRIS, Paul 585-475-4992 347 G pahdar@rit.edu
HARRIS, Peggy 850-973-1621 113 J harrisp@nfcc.edu
HARRIS, Peggy 785-594-8492 190 C peggy.harris@bakeru.edu
HARRIS, Peter 860-512-3213 90 C pharris@mcc.commnet.edu
HARRIS, Randall 601-857-3280 274 E Randall.Harris@hindscc.edu
HARRIS, Randolph 252-862-1302 372 H harrisr@roanokechowan.edu
HARRIS, Richard 919-735-5151 374 F rharris@waynecc.edu
HARRIS, Richard 877-804-1424 273 F rharris@belhaven.edu
HARRIS, Richard, C 516-671-2215 360 A rharris@webb-institute.edu
HARRIS, Rob 417-328-1827 290 E rharris@sbuniv.edu
HARRIS, Robert, L 607-255-8536 331 C rlh10@cornell.edu
HARRIS, Sandra 757-822-7183 528 C sharris@tcc.edu
HARRIS, Sara 620-421-6700 194 E sarah@labette.edu
HARRIS, Scott 405-319-8471 409 D scott.harris@okbu.edu
HARRIS, Sedgwick 618-545-3033 155 A sharris@kaskaskia.edu
HARRIS, Simone 985-448-4521 216 A simone.harris@nicholls.edu
HARRIS, Stephen, A 615-248-1245 476 E sharris@trevecca.edu
HARRIS, Susan, G 434-924-7081 525 B sgh4c@virginia.edu
HARRIS, JR., Thomas 229-430-4650 123 H thomas.harris@asurams.edu
HARRIS, Thomas, G 910-893-1278 362 F harris@campbell.edu
HARRIS, Thomas, W 859-257-1933 206 H tom.harris@uky.edu
HARRIS, Tom 951-571-6160 63 I tom.harris@rcc.edu
HARRIS, Tom 951-571-6160 63 J tom.harris@mvc.edu
HARRIS, Tosca 620-365-5116 190 A harris@allencc.edu
HARRIS, Tracy, A 301-322-0014 225 F tharris@pgcc.edu
HARRIS, Troy 805-565-6848 78 F tharris@westmont.edu
HARRIS, Valorie 618-468-4100 156 C vharris@lc.edu
HARRIS, Virginia, M 203-371-7958 93 G harrisv@sacredheart.edu
HARRIS, Wayne 757-727-5071 519 C wayne.harris@hamptonu.edu
HARRIS, Wesley, L 617-253-0911 242 A weslhar@mit.edu
HARRIS, Whitney Stewart 651-201-1746 265 H whitney.harris@so.mnscu.edu
HARRIS, William, H 334-229-4200 1 C wharris@alasu.edu
HARRIS, William, L 859-257-9100 206 H wlharr2@uky.edu
HARRIS, Willie, J 434-848-6492 523 G wharris@saintpauls.edu
HARRIS, Wilma, K 479-979-1215 26 A wkharris@ozarks.edu
HARRIS, Yonie 805-893-2771 74 F yonie.harris@sa.ucsb.edu
HARRIS BANE, Holly 330-972-7508 403 B harrisb@uakron.edu
HARRIS-HOOKER, Sandra 404-752-1725 134 B sharris-hooker@msm.edu
HARRIS-JOLLY, Stephanie 229-430-4667 123 H stephanie.harris-jolley@asurams.edu
HARRIS PAOLILLO, Linda 212-752-1530 338 C linda.harris@limcollege.edu
HARRIS REED, Terri 609-258-6110 313 A thr@princeton.edu
HARRISON, II, A.J 415-884-3100 41 I al.harrison@marin.edu
HARRISON, B. Keith 251-460-6261 9 E kharriso@usouthal.edu
HARRISON, B. Timothy 618-537-6962 157 G btharrison@mckendree.edu
HARRISON, Barbara 713-348-5836 492 J barbara.harrison@rice.edu
HARRISON, Bobbie, J 972-238-6130 485 C bjharrison@dcccd.edu
HARRISON, Carol 301-934-7552 222 C carolh@csmd.edu
HARRISON, Carolyn 740-245-7204 404 E carolynh@rio.edu
HARRISON, Connie 810-989-2124 249 B connie.harrison@baker.edu
HARRISON, David 803-641-3376 462 B davidh@usca.edu
HARRISON, David, T 614-287-2402 388 G dth@cscc.edu
HARRISON, David, W 540-857-6126 528 E dharrison@virginiawestern.edu
HARRISON, Debra 304-326-1247 541 G dharrison@salemu.edu
HARRISON, Dianne, F 831-582-3532 35 C dharrison@csumb.edu
HARRISON, Don 770-534-6136 126 B dharrison@brenau.edu
HARRISON, Frances, L 770-423-6203 132 H fharris4@kennesaw.edu
HARRISON, Frank 901-448-2360 477 C fharrsio@uthsc.edu
HARRISON, Fred, H 501-686-2515 24 B fhharrison@uasys.edu
HARRISON, Gloria, M 909-389-3200 65 B gharris@craftonhills.edu
HARRISON, Gordon 678-407-5496 130 A gharrison@ggc.edu
HARRISON, Hope, S 864-379-6546 457 G harrison@erskine.edu
HARRISON, James 805-525-4417 72 E jharrison@thomasaquinas.edu
HARRISON, James, H 920-206-2327 548 B jharrison@mbbc.edu
HARRISON, James, M 228-897-7131 278 E james.harrison@wmcarey.edu
HARRISON, Janice 508-565-1096 245 D jharrison@stonehill.edu
HARRISON, Jennifer 405-682-1611 409 F jharrison@occc.edu
HARRISON, Jim 478-553-2108 134 F jharrison@oftc.edu
HARRISON, Jim, H 920-206-2327 548 B jharrison@mbbc.edu
HARRISON, Judy 870-230-5358 21 I harrisj@hsu.edu
HARRISON, Judy 281-998-6150 493 G judy.harrison@sjcd.edu
HARRISON, Karen, D 918-465-1829 408 A kdharrison@eosc.edu
HARRISON, Kate 573-592-5261 293 C kate.harrison@westminster-mo.edu
HARRISON, Kim, W 931-363-9876 470 E kharrison@martinmethodist.edu
HARRISON, Kylee, J 620-417-1103 196 B kylee.harrison@sccc.edu
HARRISON, Lacey 229-226-1621 137 F lharrison@thomasu.edu
HARRISON, Lisa 205-226-4912 2 C lharriso@bsc.edu
HARRISON, Lonnie 575-492-2168 321 H lharrison@usw.edu
HARRISON, Matthew 773-995-2867 146 D
HARRISON, Monnie 660-626-2325 278 F mharrison@atsu.edu
HARRISON, Nathaniel 225-771-2430 214 H nathaniel_harrison@subr.edu
HARRISON, Paul, D 740-245-7200 404 E harrison@rio.edu
HARRISON, Richard 903-983-8212 489 F rharrison@kilgore.edu
HARRISON, Robert 508-856-8863 237 B rharrison@email.umassp.edu
HARRISON, Robert 269-927-8600 254 B harrison@lakemichigancollege.edu
HARRISON, JR., Robert, L 304-766-3313 544 D harrisonr@wvstateu.edu
HARRISON, Rodney, A 816-414-3700 286 A rharrison@mbts.edu
HARRISON, Ruth 928-776-2163 19 E ruth.harrison@yc.edu
HARRISON, Ruth, G 413-597-3166 246 G ruth.g.harrison@williams.edu
HARRISON, Scot 360-438-8808 536 F sharrison@stmartin.edu
HARRISON, Scott 517-371-5140 259 B harrisos@cooley.edu
HARRISON, Sheryl, E 404-872-3593 125 B sharrison@johnmarshall.edu
HARRISON, Stan 423-746-5239 476 D sharrison@twcnet.edu
HARRISON, Steve 843-349-6405 456 G harrison@coastal.edu
HARRISON, Suzan 727-864-8863 104 K harrisms@eckerd.edu
HARRISON, Tammiko 601-979-2345 275 A tammiko.l.harrison@jsums.edu
HARRISON, Tammy 501-569-3492 24 E twharrison@ualr.edu
HARRISON, Teresa 757-925-6782 527 E tharrison@pdc.edu
HARRISON, Thomas 304-327-4011 543 C tharrison@bluefieldstate.edu
HARRISON, Tim 805-654-6400 77 D tharrison@vcccd.edu
HARRISON, Todd 801-601-4951 509 B tharrison@argosy.edu
HARRISON, Tracey 601-925-3239 275 E tharriso@mc.edu
HARRISON, W. Darryl 404-669-2098 135 E darryl.harrison@point.edu
HARRISON, Walter 860-768-4417 95 A horky@hartford.edu
HARRISON, Wendy 303-273-3529 82 F wharriso@mines.edu
HARRISON, Wendy 757-569-6792 527 E wharrison@pdc.edu
HARROD, John 608-263-3077 550 G jharrod@fpm.wisc.edu
HARROD, Joseph, C 502-897-4215 205 H jharrod@sbts.edu
HARROD, Robert, C 937-382-6661 405 H chip_harrod@wilmington.edu
HARROLD, Cindy 620-429-3896 191 I cindyh@coffeyville.edu
HARROLD, Francis, B 320-308-4790 269 C fbharrold@stcloudstate.edu
HARROLD, Frank 801-626-6232 511 D frankharrold@weber.edu
HARROP, Maureen 217-786-2255 156 I maureen.harrop@llcc.edu
HARROZ, JR., Joseph 405-325-4699 413 C jharroz@ou.edu
HARSHA, Brad 419-783-2365 389 G bharsha@defiance.edu
HARSHA, Phil 417-836-4408 286 F
HARSHAW, Clay, E 336-316-2329 364 E charshaw@guilford.edu
HARSHBARGER, Bruce 478-445-5169 129 F bruce.harshbarger@gcsu.edu
HARSHMAN, Cheryl, R 304-336-8035 544 B harshmac@westliberty.edu
HARSHMAN, Cris 828-254-1921 367 H charshman@abtech.edu
HARSHMAN, Ellen, F 314-977-3833 289 F harshman@slu.edu
HARSTAD, Sarah, A 507-344-7321 261 H
HARSTINE, Stan 316-295-5871 192 H harstine@friends.edu
HART, Aaron 317-274-7200 174 B aarohart@iupui.edu
HART, Allen 413-542-2337 230 A deanstudents@amherst.edu
HART, Anne 239-280-1669 101 C anne.hart@avemaria.edu
HART, Arma 501-244-0717 19 F arma.hart@arkansasbaptist.edu
HART, Brad 912-538-3121 137 A brhart@southeasterntech.edu
HART, Charles 601-643-8358 274 A charles.hart@colin.edu

HART, Chris 410-837-5739 229 A chart@ubalt.edu

HART, Chris 502-585-9911 205 I chart@spalding.edu

HART, Christi 503-491-6961 417 B christi.hart@mhcc.edu

HART, Christina 772-462-4703 110 L chart@irsc.edu

HART, Craig, H 801-422-3567 509 D craig_hart@byu.edu

HART, Curt 605-995-2152 464 B cuhart@dwu.edu

HART, Darrell, E 435-797-1952 511 B darrell.hart@usu.edu

HART, David 410-225-2321 224 C dhart@mica.edu

HART, Dean 707-826-5107 36 D dh40@humboldt.edu

HART, Deanna 562-860-2451 38 J dhart@cerritos.edu

HART, Debra 304-696-2597 543 G hart70@marshall.edu

HART, Delmar 717-545-4747 432 D

HART, Eyvonne 912-486-7784 134 H ehart@ogeecheetech.edu

HART, Frank 304-327-4120 543 C frankh@bluefieldstate.edu

HART, Haven 843-349-2300 456 G hhart@coastal.edu

HART, J. Tyler, T 804-862-6223 523 C jhart@rbc.edu

HART, JR., James 800-342-7342 458 E james.hart@golfacademy.edu

HART, James, R 904-264-2172 116 A president@iws.edu

HART, Jana, D 479-979-1221 26 A jhart@ozarks.edu

HART, Jodi 561-868-3465 114 D hartj@palmbeachstate.edu

HART, John, E 937-229-4333 404 A john.hart@notes.udayton.edu

HART, Karen 248-218-2011 257 F khart@rc.edu

HART, Kathleen 209-954-5047 66 D khart@deltacollege.edu

HART, Kathy, S 919-515-2143 378 B kathy_hart@ncsu.edu

HART, Kelly 413-572-8519 239 C khart@westfield.ma.edu

HART, Kerry 970-542-3105 86 A kerry.hart@morgancc.edu

HART, Lisa 330-499-9600 393 I lhart@kent.edu

HART, Martin 860-512-2903 90 C mhart@mcc.commnet.edu

HART, Mary 619-388-7614 65 H mhart@sdccd.edu

HART, Peter, L 978-232-2058 234 F lehart@endicott.edu

HART, Quentin 319-296-4463 185 C quentin.hart@hawkeyecollege.edu

HART, Rahmon 412-396-1117 428 C hartr1214@duq.edu

HART, Richard, H 909-558-4540 54 D rhart@llu.edu

HART, Rick 423-425-2270 477 D rick-hart@utc.edu

HART, Robert 508-793-2224 233 D rhart@holycross.edu

HART, Roderick, P 512-471-5646 505 B rod.hart@austin.utexas.edu

HART, Sharon, Y 670-234-5498 559 F president@nmcnet.edu

HART, Susan 205-934-5833 8 G slhart@uab.edu

HART, Tara 973-761-9593 315 B tara.hart@shu.edu

HART, Tom 314-246-7576 293 A harttr@webster.edu

HART, Trois 260-399-7700 180 E thart@sf.edu

HART, Willy 360-650-2950 539 C willy.hart@wwu.edu

HART-SCHUTTE, Julie 605-995-7135 464 E julie.schutte@mitchelltech.edu

HART-THORE, Dawn 504-278-6332 211 I dhart@nunez.edu

HARTBURG, Sonya 330-297-7319 390 K

HARTE, Meghan 407-646-2599 116 B mharte@rollins.edu

HARTENBURG, Dale 706-721-3356 130 B dhartenburg@georgiahealth.edu

HARTER, Christina 425-739-8225 535 B chris.harter@lwtc.edu

HARTER, Donald, L 315-792-3191 359 C dharter@utica.edu

HARTER, Eric 502-456-6506 206 C eharter@sullivan.edu

HARTER, James 419-251-1786 395 H james.harter@mercycollege.edu

HARTER, James, L 419-251-1786 395 H james.harter@mercycollege.edu

HARTFIELD, Rick 601-925-3275 275 E hartfiel@mc.edu

HARTFORD, Colleen, C 601-857-3364 274 E colleen.hartfield@hindscc.edu

HARTFORD, Sharon, M 509-527-4323 538 G sharon.hartford@wwcc.edu

HARTGE, Steve, P 314-286-3669 288 B sphartge@ranken.edu

HARTHORN, Karen, M 651-962-6353 272 E kmharthorn@stthomas.edu

HARTIG, Jeanne 312-567-3000 153 B jhartig@iit.edu

HARTIG, Vicki 414-443-8846 553 B vicki.hartig@wlc.edu

HARTIGAN, Ellen 718-631-6351 329 A ehartigan@qcc.cuny.edu

HARTIGAN, William, J 401-865-2166 453 F hartigan@providence.edu

HARTIN, Linda, A 334-222-6591 5 F lhartin@lbwcc.edu

HARTING, William 317-955-6015 177 G bharting@marian.edu

HARTING, William 317-955-6016 177 G bharting@marian.edu

HARTKE, Emily 217-234-5259 155 H ehartke@lakeland.cc.il.us

HARTLEROAD, LeAnn 618-395-7777 152 E hartleroadl@iecc.edu

HARTLESS, Sharon 434-582-7600 520 F shartles@liberty.edu

HARTLEY, Carolyn 219-980-6971 173 F cjhartle@iun.edu

HARTLEY, Christina 401-454-6794 454 B chartley@risd.edu

HARTLEY, Gary 916-608-6500 56 C

HARTLEY, Greg, L 916-348-4689 45 H ghartley@epic.edu

HARTLEY, Lorraine 216-987-2424 389 A lorraine.hartley@tri-c.edu

HARTLEY, Meredith 504-861-5888 213 F mhartley@loyno.edu

HARTLEY, Nancy, K 970-491-5841 83 A nancy.hartley@colostate.edu

HARTLEY, Rebecca 205-665-6360 9 C hartleyrs@montevallo.edu

HARTLEY, Stacey, M 419-372-0719 385 D staceyh@bgsu.edu

HARTLEY, Stephanie, J 601-923-1657 277 B shartley@rts.edu

HARTLEY, William, B 714-772-3330 28 I whar838361@aol.com

HARTLINE, Beverly 202-274-5027 99 F bhartline@udc.edu

HARTMAN, Brandi, P 864-488-4606 459 A bhartman@limestone.edu

HARTMAN, Bryan 518-564-3824 354 B hartmabg@plattsburgh.edu

HARTMAN, Chad, M 336-841-9000 365 A chartman@highpoint.edu

HARTMAN, Cheryl, J 605-221-3100 464 C chartman@kilian.edu

HARTMAN, Christine, M 717-337-6276 429 H chartman@gettysburg.edu

HARTMAN, Dean, A 706-880-8246 132 I dhartman@lagrange.edu

HARTMAN, Eric, G 931-598-1229 472 J ehartman@sewanee.edu

HARTMAN, Freda 480-557-3049 19 C freda.hartman@phoenix.edu

HARTMAN, Heather, S 770-718-5328 126 B hhartman@brenau.edu

HARTMAN, Jackie, L 785-532-6221 194 B jlh1980@ksu.edu

HARTMAN, James, P 215-951-2966 444 C

HARTMAN, Joel, L 407-823-6778 120 A joel.hartman@ucf.edu

HARTMAN, Joseph 972-825-4774 495 D jhartman@sagu.edu

HARTMAN, Kathy 802-831-1232 515 A khartman@vermontlaw.edu

HARTMAN, Laurie 315-792-7400 356 B laurie.hartman@sunyit.edu

HARTMAN, Luke 540-432-4000 518 E luke.hartman@emu.edu

HARTMAN, Nancy 513-244-8447 387 D nancy.hartman@ccuniversity.edu

HARTMAN, Nathan 859-344-3602 206 D nathan.hartman@thomasmore.edu

HARTMAN, Robert 740-477-7843 398 C rhartman@ohiochristian.edu

HARTMAN, Robin 714-879-3901 50 G rhartman@hiu.edu

HARTMAN, Sherry, L 208-467-8588 143 I slhartman@nnu.edu

HARTMAN, Thomas 303-923-4155 81 A thartman@argosy.edu

HARTMANN, Anita 907-474-7231 10 J amharmann@alaska.edu

HARTMANN, Patricia 414-382-6072 545 H pat.hartmann@alverno.edu

HARTMANN, Shari 714-459-1120 78 C shartmann@wsulaw.edu

HARTMANN, Wendy 636-584-6712 281 I wahartm@eastcentral.edu

HARTNER, Joseph 610-606-4631 424 I jhartner@cedarcrest.edu

HARTNETT, Deborah 212-650-8638 326 H dhartnett@ccny.cuny.edu

HARTOG, III, John 515-964-0601 184 G hartogj3@faith.edu

HARTOG, William, M 540-458-8710 530 A bhartog@wlu.edu

HARTON, Mary Kay 928-344-7580 12 C marykay.harton@azwestern.edu

HARTS, Stanley, H 910-962-3057 379 C hartss@uncw.edu

HARTSFIELD, Jason, H 610-921-7529 421 D jhartsfield@alb.edu

HARTSFIELD, LaTanya 404-237-7573 125 F lhartsfield@bauder.edu

HARTSOCK, James 240-629-7902 222 G jhartsock@frederick.edu

HARTSOE, Janice 678-717-3822 129 D jhartsoe@gsc.edu

HARTUNG, Jason 661-362-2207 56 G jhartung@masters.edu

HARTUNIAN, Vaughn 626-873-2181 58 C

HARTVIGSEN, Jake 941-487-4150 119 D jhartvigsen@ncf.edu

HARTWELL, Robert, E 516-877-4231 322 A hartwell@adelphi.edu

HARTZ, James 270-686-4630 202 E jim.hartz@kctcs.edu

HARTZ, Jan 949-753-4774 30 I hartz@brandman.edu

HARTZ, Jason, M 517-265-5161 247 D shelfer@adrian.edu

HARTZEL, Ruth Ann 724-847-5673 429 G rhartzel@geneva.edu

HARTZLER, Christi 407-823-4663 120 A christi.hartzler@ucf.edu

HARTZLER, Murray, G 843-661-1237 458 C mhartzler@fmarion.edu

HARTZOG, Gail, C 850-718-2342 102 H hartzogg@chipola.edu

HARVENER, Lisa 586-791-6610 248 G lisa.harvener@baker.edu

HARVEY, Addie 901-435-1704 470 B addie_harvey@loc.edu

HARVEY, Barron, H 202-806-1500 98 B bharvey@howard.edu

HARVEY, Brian, J 417-864-7220 282 B bharvey@cci.edu

HARVEY, Bryan, C 413-545-6238 237 C harvey@provost.umass.edu

HARVEY, Cheryl 248-457-2765 252 G

HARVEY, David 941-487-4511 119 D dharvey@ncf.edu

HARVEY, David, T 765-658-4359 170 I harvey@depauw.edu

HARVEY, Diana 801-957-4278 512 C diana.harvey@slcc.edu

HARVEY, Gayle, S 217-581-3511 150 C gsharvey@eiu.edu

HARVEY, Iris, E 330-672-7882 393 D iharvey1@kent.edu

HARVEY, JR., James 478-757-3467 126 G jharvey@centralgatech.edu

HARVEY, James, D 352-854-2322 103 D harveyj@cf.edu

HARVEY, John 803-754-4100 457 D

HARVEY, John 325-793-4751 490 F jharvey@mcm.edu

HARVEY, Karen 304-327-4031 543 C kharvey@bluefieldstate.edu

HARVEY, Keith 218-744-7522 267 C k.harvey@mr.mnscu.edu

HARVEY, Kelly 252-536-7219 370 F harveyk@halifaxcc.edu

HARVEY, Kim, M 636-797-3000 283 H kharvey@jeffco.edu

HARVEY, Laurie 516-686-7711 343 D lharve05@nyit.edu

HARVEY, Leah 651-793-1333 267 D leah.harvey@metrostate.edu

HARVEY, Leah 651-793-1777 267 D Leah.Harvey@metrostate.edu

HARVEY, Linda 718-780-7966 324 F linda.harvey@brooklaw.edu

HARVEY, Lydia 907-564-8218 10 D lydiah@alaskapacific.edu

HARVEY, Marcus 816-604-4121 285 I marcus.harvey@mcckc.edu

HARVEY, Maria 601-979-2107 275 A maria.l.harvey@jsums.edu

HARVEY, Mary, J 773-702-8806 166 D mj-harvey@uchicago.edu

HARVEY, Patricia, A 804-863-1629 523 C pharvey@rbc.edu

HARVEY, Pauline 907-442-3400 10 J pharvey1@alaska.edu

HARVEY, Peter, W 509-527-5145 539 E harvey@whitman.edu

HARVEY, Richard, C 304-367-4395 543 E richard.harvey@fairmontstate.edu

HARVEY, Roberta 856-256-5140 314 A harvey@rowan.edu

HARVEY, Sarah, J 260-359-4010 172 K sharvey@huntington.edu

HARVEY, Scott 864-646-1556 461 F sharvey@tctc.edu

HARVEY, Stu 405-682-7849 409 F sharvey@occc.edu

HARVEY, Valtroud 410-923-4500 99 D valtroud.harvey@strayer.edu

HARVEY, William, R 757-727-5231 519 C presidentsoffice@hamptonu.edu

HARVEY-JACOBS, Pam 920-465-2111 551 A harveyp@uwgb.edu

HARVEY-LEE, Peggy, A 585-292-2252 341 H pharvey-lee@monroecc.edu

HARVEY-SAHAK, Judy, B 909-621-8973 69 A judy.harveysahak@scrippscollege.edu

HARVEY-SMITH, Alicia, B 410-462-8302 221 D abharvey-smith@bccc.edu

HARVIN, Lillian 510-869-8785 64 J lharvin@samuelmerritt.edu

HARVIN, Nancy 845-451-1299 331 F n_harvin@culinary.edu

HARVIN, Peter, B 864-231-2017 455 C pharvin@andersonuniversity.edu

HARVITH, John 412-624-4380 449 A harvith@pitt.edu

HARWARD, L. Kay 801-581-3490 510 L kharward@sa.utah.edu

HARWOOD, Debra 704-991-0206 374 A dharwood5544@stanly.edu

HARWOOD, Michael, D 701-231-7559 381 H michael.harwood@ndsu.edu

HARWOOD, Scott 518-891-2915 344 E sharwood@nccc.edu

HASAN, Zia 803-535-5219 456 D hasan@claflin.edu

HASBROUCK, Norman, G 724-938-1561 441 G hasbrouck@calu.edu

HASELDEN, Gregory, W 864-379-8812 457 G haselden@erskine.edu

HASELOFF, Gregory, K 859-858-3511 198 B greg.haseloff@asbury.edu

HASELTON, Blake 502-852-5597 207 A blake.haselton@louisville.edu

HASENBERG, Lori 715-232-2441 552 C hasenbergl@uwstout.edu

HASENOEHRL, Mary 208-792-2458 143 F mlhasenoehrl@lcsc.edu

HASFURTHER, Victor 435-879-4801 512 A hasfurther@dixie.edu

HASH, Jennifer 303-722-5724 85 L jhash@lincolntech.com

HASH, Joseph 707-476-4212 42 A joe-hash@redwoods.edu

HASHIMOTO, Brenna 808-956-2974 140 J hbrenna@hawaii.edu

HASINGER, Guenther 808-956-8566 141 B hasinger@hawaii.edu

HASKA, Christine, M 831-656-3411 557 H cmhaska@nps.edu

HASKAMP, Misty 573-875-7582 280 E mrhaskamp@ccis.edu

HASKELL, Benjamin, E 207-941-7176 219 E haskellb@nescom.edu

HASKELL, Chester, D 408-541-0100 41 C chaskell@cogswell.edu

HASKELL, Richard 781-239-3191 240 D rhaskell@massbay.edu

HASKETT, Tammy 828-227-7222 379 E haskett@wcu.edu

HASKINS, Brenda 985-448-4518 216 A brenda.haskins@nicholls.edu

HASKINS, Dana, R 972-860-7269 484 H DRHaskins@dcccd.edu

HASKINS, Dennis, E 931-363-9889 470 E dhaskins@martinmethodist.edu

HASKINS, Eileen, T 401-598-1035 453 C ehaskins@jwu.edu

HASKINS, Mike 843-953-6461 457 B haskinsm@cofc.edu

HASKINS, Nena 574-936-8898 168 I nena.haskins@ancilla.edu

HASKINS, Richard 412-392-8097 444 H rhaskins@pointpark.edu

HASKVITZ, Esther 518-244-4590 348 A haskev@sage.edu

HASL, Rudolph, C 619-961-4215 72 F hasl@tjsl.edu

HASLAG, Daniel 573-592-5282 293 C Dan.Haslag@westminster-mo.edu

HASLAM, Laurie 980-598-1312 365 G laurie.haslam@jwu.edu

HASLANGER, Sally 617-253-8844 242 A shaslang@mit.edu

HASLEM, Lori 309-341-7214 155 E lhaslem@knox.edu

HASLER, Brian, K 812-237-7778 173 A brian.hasler@indstate.edu

HASLIM, Hue 602-429-1078 19 D hue.haslim@wintu.edu

HASLINGER, Robert, W 419-559-2386 402 D rhaslinger@terra.edu

HASLUND, Steve 281-487-1170 498 E shaslund@txchiro.edu

HASS, Marjorie 903-813-3001 481 A mhass@austincollege.edu

HASSAN, Nidia 903-510-2883 502 E
nhas@tjc.edu
HASSAN, Sharon, E 301-322-0749 225 F
hassanse@pgcc.edu
HASSAN, Sherry, P 626-585-7529 61 E
sphassan@pasadena.edu
HASSEL, George, E 610-499-4182 451 F
gehassel.sr@widener.edu
HASSELER, Susan, S 717-766-2511 436 D
shasseler@messiah.edu
HASSELL, Adalecia 787-841-2000 564 I
ahassell@email.pucpr.edu
HASSELL, Cheryl 918-343-7539 411 H
chassell@rsu.edu
HASSELL, Coletta 678-891-2455 130 G
Coletta.Hassell@gpc.edu
HASSELL, Dayna 973-748-9000 308 A
dayna_hassell@bloomfield.edu
HASSELTINE, Donald, A 717-245-1029 427 E
hasseltd@dickinson.edu
HASSENZAHL, David 412-365-1842 425 B
dhassenzahl@chatham.edu
HASSEON, Chantel 904-731-4949 105 H
cwhidbee@cci.edu
HASSETT, A. Tracy 508-831-5473 247 B
thassett@wpi.edu
HASSIEB, Farouk 609-292-2108 316 A
fhassieb@tesc.edu
HASSINGER, Mary, C 573-876-7213 290 G
mhassinger@stephens.edu
HASSINGER, Steven 717-728-2262 425 A
stevehassinger@centralpenn.edu
HASSLER, Ardoth 202-687-1973 98 A
hasslera@georgetown.edu
HASSON, Amy, S 410-548-3316 228 D
ashasson@salisbury.edu
HASSON, Eileen 631-420-2369 356 A
hassone@farmingdale.edu
HASTAD, Doug, N 262-524-7246 546 E
dhastad@carrollu.edu
HASTED, Grigor 517-437-7341 252 E
grigor.hasted@hillsdale.edu
HASTIE, John 607-778-5196 324 G
hastie_j@sunybroome.edu
HASTINGS, Dana, M 785-532-6221 194 B
dhasting@ksu.edu
HASTINGS, Daniel, E 617-253-6056 242 A
hastings@mit.edu
HASTINGS, Donald, B 518-580-5768 351 B
dhasting@skidmore.edu
HASTINGS, Edward, T 610-361-5293 437 C
hastinge@neumann.edu
HASTINGS, Jan 818-401-1030 42 D
jhastings@columbiacollege.edu
HASTINGS, Janel, H 909-607-8191 49 D
janel_hastings@hmc.edu
HASTINGS, Kevin, J 309-341-7438 155 E
khasting@knox.edu
HASTINGS, Michael 207-581-1476 220 A
mhastings@umit.maine.edu
HASTINGS, Nancy 312-329-4415 158 H
HASTINGS, Rebecca 425-352-8256 531 F
rhastings@cascadia.edu
HASTINGS, Susan 651-255-6120 271 I
shastings@unitedseminary.edu
HASTINGS-CANDELORO, Valerie, J 302-225-6246 96 E
hastinv@gbc.edu
HASTINGS-SHEPPARD, Lisa, C 302-739-4623 96 A
lhasting@dtcc.edu
HATAIER, Maria 212-678-3779 357 F
mrt2112@tc.columbia.edu
HATANAKA, Janice 562-985-5252 35 A
jhatanak@csulb.edu
HATCH, Adam 808-544-0839 140 B
ahatch@hpu.edu
HATCH, Barbara 781-239-2629 240 D
bhatch@massbay.edu
HATCH, Blaine 928-524-7440 17 B
blaine.hatch@npc.edu
HATCH, SHCJ, Jeanne Marie 610-527-0200 445 I
jhatch@rosemont.edu
HATCH, Jennifer 717-764-9550 426 D
jhatch@csb.edu
HATCH, Joy, A 804-819-4990 525 F
jhatch@vccs.edu
HATCH, Joyce, M 413-545-1581 237 C
hatch@admin.umass.edu
HATCH, Mark 719-389-6805 81 L
mhatch@coloradocollege.edu
HATCH, Mary 847-214-7421 150 D
mhatch@elgin.edu
HATCH, Nathan, O 336-758-5211 380 B
hatch@wfu.edu
HATCH, Paul 218-262-6731 266 H
paulhatch@hibbing.edu
HATCHER, Brian 410-617-5026 224 A
bhatcher@loyola.edu
HATCHER, George 919-546-8353 376 D
ghatcher@shawu.edu
HATCHER, Graham 205-391-5836 7 A
ghatcher@sheltonstate.edu
HATCHER, Kevin, L 909-537-5011 36 A
khatcher@csusb.edu
HATCHER, Oeida 434-544-8344 520 H
hatcher@lynchburg.edu
HATCHER, Robert 212-817-7020 327 B
rhatcher@gc.cuny.edu
HATCHER, Wayne 870-248-4000 21 A
wayne.hatcher@blackrivertech.edu
HATCHETT, Paul 270-707-3795 202 A
phatchett0001@kctcs.edu
HATER, Karen 407-646-2345 116 B
khater@rollins.edu
HATFIELD, Amy 360-475-7841 535 J
ahatfield@olympic.edu
HATFIELD, Barbara, S 318-473-6446 212 G
bhatfield@lsua.edu
HATFIELD, Chad 914-961-8313 349 I
hatfield@svots.edu
HATFIELD, Heather 865-539-7331 475 F
hrhatfield@pstcc.edu
HATFIELD, Karen 352-588-8460 116 E
karen.hatfield@saintleo.edu
HATFIELD, Misty, F 803-938-3728 462 F
hatfielm@uscsumter.edu
HATFIELD, Penny 501-450-3128 25 H
pennye@uca.edu
HATFIELD, Renee 503-222-3225 415 H
rhatfiel@cci.edu
HATFIELD, Sharon, L 540-985-8263 520 D
slhatfield@jchs.edu
HATHAWAY, Brent 307-766-4194 556 E
bhathaway@uwyo.edu
HATHAWAY, Gretchel, L 518-388-8327 358 E
hathawag@union.edu
HATHAWAY, Jeffrey 860-486-2725 94 E
jeffrey.hathaway@uconn.edu
HATHAWAY, Joel 314-434-4044 281 A
joel.hathaway@covenantseminary.edu
HATHAWAY, Karry, L 443-412-2401 223 B
khathaway@harford.edu
HATHAWAY, Nick 405-325-3916 413 C
nhathaway@ou.edu
HATHAWAY, William 757-352-4294 523 B
willhat@regent.edu
HATHAWAY-CLARK, Bill 303-458-4066 87 E
whathawa@regis.edu
HATHCOCK, Michele 828-254-1921 367 H
mhathcock@abtech.edu
HATHMAN, Laurie, E 816-501-4144 288 D
laurie.hathman@rockhurst.edu
HATHORN, Janine, M 540-458-8671 530 A
jhathorn@wlu.edu
HATMAN, Lonnie 360-596-5300 538 B
lhatman@spscc.ctc.edu
HATRAK, Gregory 914-961-8313 349 I
ghatrak@svots.edu
HATTAUER, Edward, A 718-990-6384 348 G
hattauee@stjohns.edu
HATTAWAY, Trey 903-983-8218 489 F
thattaway@kilgore.edu
HATTEBERG, Gregory, A 214-841-3704 485 E
alumni@dts.edu
HATTEN, Angie 309-692-4092 158 C
ahatten@midstate.edu
HATTER, John, L 812-374-5119 175 J
jhatter@ivytech.edu
HATTERMAN, Dawn, K 816-604-3223 285 H
HATTERMANN, Troy 309-694-5156 152 B
troy.hattermann@icc.edu
HATTLESTAD, Neil, W 501-450-3122 25 H
neilh@uca.edu
HATTMAN, Melissa 314-516-5708 291 F
hattmanm@umsl.edu
HATTO, Susan 989-328-1254 256 A
susanf@montcalm.edu
HATTON, Karl 270-247-8521 204 C
khatton@midcontinent.edu
HATTON, Martin 662-329-7138 276 B
mhatton@as.muw.edu
HATTON, Martin 662-329-7110 276 B
mhatton@as.muw.edu
HATTON, Nora 859-336-5082 205 F
nhatton@sccky.edu
HATUEY, Josie 617-348-6507 246 A
hatuey@urbancollege.edu
HATZENBUEHLER, Linda 208-282-4899 143 D
hatzlind@isu.edu
HAU, Hoang 562-907-4244 79 B
hhau@whittier.edu
HAUB, Mark 865-251-1800 472 K
mhaub@southcollegetn.edu
HAUCK, Duane, D 701-231-7867 381 H
duane.hauck@ndsu.edu
HAUCK, Gary 989-328-1234 256 A
garyh@montcalm.edu
HAUCK, Steven 605-882-5284 464 D
haucks@lakeareatech.edu
HAUF, Todd 701-483-2570 381 E
todd.hauf@dickinsonstate.edu
HAUG, Darin, L 816-654-7203 283 J
dhaug@kcumb.edu
HAUG, Marsha, L 610-436-3411 443 F
mhaug@wcupa.edu
HAUG-BELVIN, Theresa 573-651-5166 290 D
tbelvin@semo.edu
HAUGABROOK, Adrian, K 617-879-2008 246 F
ahaugabrook@wheelock.edu
HAUGE, Todd, W 410-293-1600 558 H
hauge@usna.edu
HAUGEN, Catherine (Kate) 701-231-7052 381 H
kate.haugen@ndsu.edu
HAUGEN, Daniel 612-861-7554 261 C
haugen@alfredadler.edu
HAUGEN, Diane, M 608-796-3001 553 A
dmhaugen@viterbo.edu
HAUGEN, Dolores 253-566-6090 538 C
dhaugen@tacomacc.edu
HAUGEN, Donna, M 516-572-7809 342 C
donna.haugen@ncc.edu
HAUGEN, Doug 530-938-5295 42 C
haugend@siskiyous.edu
HAUGEN, Jane, A 320-363-5388 262 H
jhaugen@csbsju.edu
HAUGEN, Linda 907-443-8401 10 J
llhaugen@alaska.edu
HAUGEN, Nancy 510-869-6511 64 J
nhaugen@samuelmerritt.edu
HAUGEN, Regina 270-384-8300 203 H
haugenr@lindsey.edu
HAUGHIE, Jennifer, A 301-790-2800 223 A
fisherj@hagerstowncc.edu
HAUGHT, Kenneth 701-483-2330 381 E
ken.haught@dickinsonstate.edu
HAUGHT, Paul, A 901-321-3579 467 G
phaught@cbu.edu
HAUGHTON, Chantaye 410-276-0306 226 D
chaughton@host.sdc.edu
HAUGSLAND, Judy, M 414-410-4202 546 D
jmhaugsland@stritch.edu
HAUK, Gary, S 404-727-6021 129 A
gary.hauk@emory.edu
HAUKAP, Erica 513-585-3502 387 C
HAUKE, Raymond, A 620-341-5173 192 D
rhauke@emporia.edu
HAULOTTE, Erin 847-947-5491 159 D
erin.haulotte@nl.edu
HAUNGS, Megan 415-282-7600 28 B
meganhaungs@actem.edu
HAUPERT, Vincent, D 260-359-4089 172 K
vhaupert@huntington.edu
HAURY, Clifford, W 404 001 5000 527 F
chaury@pvcc.edu
HAUS, David 304-327-4155 543 C
dhaus@bluefieldstate.edu
HAUS, Teri 970-943-2196 89 B
thaus@western.edu
HAUSAM, Wiley 914-251-6196 354 D
wiley.hausam@purchase.edu
HAUSAMMANN, Marilyn 617-495-8635 235 H
marilyn_hausammann@harvard.edu
HAUSCARRIAGUE, Elizabeth 925-685-1230 43 C
ehauscarriague@dvc.edu
HAUSCHILDT, Jim 816-932-2532 289 G
jhaushildt@saintlukescollege.edu
HAUSE, Jeffrey 402-280-3581 297 H
jeffreyhause@creighton.edu
HAUSER, Carol 513-529-3131 396 D
hauserca@muohio.edu
HAUSER, Chuck 252-940-6371 367 I
chuckh@beaufortccc.edu
HAUSER, John 336-838-6149 375 A
john.hauser@wilkescc.edu
HAUSER, Joseph, H 901-722-3228 473 B
jhauser@sco.edu
HAUSER, Robert 217-244-2807 167 B
r-hauser@illinois.edu
HAUSER, Stephen 215-702-4217 444 A
shauser@pbu.edu
HAUSER, Stephen, C 608-246-2101 554 B
shauser@matcmadison.edu
HAUSFATHER, Sam 314-529-9466 284 F
shausfather@maryville.edu
HAUSLADEN, Stephanie 559-438-4222 49 G
stephanie_hausladen@heald.edu
HAUSMANN, Tom, L 608-796-3860 553 A
tlhausmann@viterbo.edu
HAUSS, Kevin 212-431-2136 343 E
khauss@nyls.edu
HAUSSLER, Alicia 308-398-7335 297 C
ahaussler@cccneb.edu
HAUST, Rebecca 518-762-4651 334 D
rebecca.haust@fmcc.suny.edu
HAUVER, Dottie 508-793-2327 233 D
dhauver@holycross.edu
HAVEARD, Melanie, J 850-474-2540 121 C
mhaveard@uwf.edu
HAVELY, Candace 319-296-4229 185 C
candace.havely@hawkeyecollege.edu
HAVEN, Jan, C 870-633-4480 21 F
jhaven@eacc.edu
HAVENS, Brandi 806-874-3571 482 H
brandi.havens@clarendoncollege.edu
HAVENS, Luisa, M 915-747-5890 505 E
lmhavens@utep.edu
HAVERLACK, Sandra, J 540-863-2822 526 B
shaverlack@dslcc.edu
HAVERLY, Jeffrey, A 404-669-2086 135 E
jeff.haverly@point.edu
HAVERLY, Mark 660-596-7407 290 F
mhaverly@sfccmo.edu
HAVERSAT, Walt 803-799-9082 461 A
whaversat@southuniversity.edu
HAVERSTICK, III, Henry, W 718-780-7906 324 F
henry.haverstick@brooklaw.edu
HAVERTY, April 414-955-4844 548 E
ahaverty@mcw.edu
HAVERTY, Dan 574-239-8350 172 J
dhaverty@hcc-nd.edu
HAVHOLM, Karen, G 715-836-3405 550 H
havholkg@uwec.edu
HAVIG, Dee 307-754-6412 556 D
Dee.Havig@northwestcollege.edu
HAVILAND, Bobbie 620-365-5116 190 A
haviland@allencc.edu
HAVIS, Allan 858-534-4004 74 D
ahavis@ucsd.edu
HAVLOVIC, Stephen 607-587-3913 355 C
havlovics@alfredstate.edu
HAVRAN, Natalie, M 609-652-4384 313 F
natalie.havran@stockton.edu
HAWES, Heather 404-270-5068 137 E
hhawes@spelman.edu
HAWES, Matthew 860-628-4751 92 F
mhawes@lincolncollegene.edu
HAWES, Matthew 800-955-2527 282 G
mhawes@grantham.edu
HAWES, Matthew 315-866-0300 335 E
hawesmr@herkimer.edu
HAWGOOD, Samuel 415-476-2342 74 E
sam.hawgood@ucsf.edu
HAWK, Jeanine 408-270-6426 67 A
jeanine.hawk@sjeccd.org
HAWK, Linda 760-750-4950 36 B
lhawk@csusm.edu
HAWK, R. Neil 910-521-6209 379 B
neil.hawk@uncp.edu
HAWK, Thomas, R 215-751-8029 426 B
thawk@ccp.edu
HAWK, Tricia 785-227-3380 190 G
hawkt@bethanylb.edu
HAWKES, Peter 570-422-3494 442 C
phawkes@po-box.esu.edu
HAWKEY, Earl, W 402-472-2025 300 H
ehawkey1@unl.edu
HAWKEY, Philip, A 909-593-3511 75 C
phawkey@laverne.edu
HAWKINS, Andre 772-462-7100 110 L
ahawkins@irsc.edu
HAWKINS, Angela 415-476-5997 74 E
Angela.Hawkins@ucsf.edu
HAWKINS, Audrey 903-675-6357 502 D
ahawkins@tvcc.edu
HAWKINS, Ben 910-893-1380 362 F
hawkinsb@campbell.edu
HAWKINS, Billy, C 256-761-6212 7 H
bhawkins@talladega.edu
HAWKINS, Calvin, H 620-241-0723 191 F
calvin.hawkins@centralchristian.edu
HAWKINS, Carol 407-708-2488 117 G
hawkinsc@seminolestate.edu
HAWKINS, Carson 731-661-5018 476 G
chawkins@uu.edu
HAWKINS, Charles 951-487-3073 58 B
chawkins@msjc.edu
HAWKINS, Cheryl 734-462-4400 258 C
chawkins@schoolcraft.edu
HAWKINS, Christie 405-744-4244 410 C
christie.hawkins@okstate.edu
HAWKINS, Cynthia 386-481-2402 101 I
hawkinsc@cookman.edu
HAWKINS, Daryl 610-341-5822 428 D
dhawkins@eastern.edu
HAWKINS, David 916-631-8108 33 C
HAWKINS, DeLores 515-964-6514 183 E
dwhawkins@dmacc.edu
HAWKINS, Don 205-970-9213 7 D
dhawkins@sebc.edu
HAWKINS, Donna 215-646-7300 430 C
hawkins.d@gmc.edu
HAWKINS, Gabriel 407-673-7406 113 B
HAWKINS, Gains, B 410-651-7169 227 E
gbhawkins@umes.edu
HAWKINS, Greg 901-986-5969 273 F
stlife@belhaven.edu
HAWKINS, H. Gregory 423-636-7305 476 F
ghawkins@tusculum.edu
HAWKINS, Hilda, J 252-536-6399 370 F
hawkinsh@halifaxcc.edu
HAWKINS, Irene 302-857-6261 95 F
ihawkins@desu.edu
HAWKINS, JR., Jack 334-670-3200 8 B
jhawkins@troy.edu
HAWKINS, James, M 850-599-3379 118 G
james.hawkins@famu.edu
HAWKINS, JoAnn 443-518-4974 223 D
jhawkins@howardcc.edu
HAWKINS, Jonathan 615-547-1239 467 I
jhawkins@cumberland.edu

HAWKINS, Julia 606-783-5189 204 E j.hawkins@moreheadstate.edu

HAWKINS, Katherine 540-831-6514 522 D khawkins3@radford.edu

HAWKINS, Leigh, T 336-342-4261 373 B hawkinsl@rockinghamcc.edu

HAWKINS, Lewis 770-394-8300 124 F rhawkins@aii.edu

HAWKINS, Mark 312-362-5562 148 F mhawkin1@depaul.edu

HAWKINS, Mary 502-326-2863 200 C mhawkins2@devry.edu

HAWKINS, Mary, B 402-557-7005 297 A mary.hawkins@bellevue.edu

HAWKINS, Mary, M 303-871-4758 88 E mhawkins@du.edu

HAWKINS, JR., Melvin 803-822-3592 459 D hawkinsm@midlandstech.edu

HAWKINS, Michele 561-297-3245 118 H mhawkins@fau.edu

HAWKINS, Patricia 404-965-8118 124 B phawkins@aiuniv.edu

HAWKINS, Paul, M 386-312-4134 116 D mikehawkins@sjrstate.edu

HAWKINS, Regina 312-553-2515 146 G rhawkins@ccc.edu

HAWKINS, Robert, S 706-542-8176 138 C rhawkins@uga.edu

HAWKINS, Ronald, E 434-592-4030 520 F rehawkin@liberty.edu

HAWKINS, Susan 206-296-6090 537 F shawkins@seattleu.edu

HAWKINS, Tara 775-673-7206 302 J thawkins@tmcc.edu

HAWKINS, Tiffany 580-774-3233 412 F tiffany.hawkins@swosu.edu

HAWKINS, Vernon, L 922-860-4221 484 F vhawkins@dcccd.edu

HAWKINS, Warren, H 903-927-3390 509 A whawkins@wileyc.edu

HAWKINS, William 603-899-4237 305 B

HAWKINS, William 860-231-5405 93 H bhawkins@sjc.edu

HAWKINS-WILDING, Susan 262-595-2040 551 E susan.hawkins-wilding@uwp.edu

HAWKINSON, Kenneth 309-298-1066 168 A ks-hawkinson@wiu.edu

HAWKRIDGE, Fred, M 804-828-1674 525 E fmhawkri@vcu.edu

HAWKS, Kathy 651-361-3450 265 C khawks@mcnallysmith.edu

HAWKS, Sue, W 910-642-7141 373 G shawks@sccnc.edu

HAWKSHEAD, Richard 404-965-6574 124 B rhawkshead@aiuniv.edu

HAWLEY, Beth 417-864-7220 282 B bhawley@cci.edu

HAWLEY, Dennis, W 570-577-1911 423 D dennis.hawley@bucknell.edu

HAWLEY, Donna, J 316-978-3015 197 F donna.hawley@wichita.edu

HAWLEY, Dwight 630-620-2129 160 B dhawley@seminary.edu

HAWLEY, Eric 435-797-8146 511 B eric.hawley@usu.edu

HAWLEY, Harold 843-349-5279 458 G harold.hawley@hgtc.edu

HAWLEY, Kent 217-641-4570 154 G khawley@jwcc.edu

HAWLEY, Michael, E 314-286-4846 288 B mehawley@ranken.edu

HAWLEY, Stephanie 512-223-7637 481 B shawley@austincc.edu

HAWLEY, Thomas 605-626-2524 465 H thawley@northern.edu

HAWLEY, Thomas, A 231-843-5803 260 E tahawley@westshore.edu

HAWORTH, Karen 847-947-5246 159 D khaworth@nl.edu

HAWORTH-HOEPPNER, Susan 616-632-2974 248 A haworsus@aquinas.edu

HAWS, Pamela, M 817-272-3365 505 A haws@uta.edu

HAWSEY, David, S 276-944-6133 518 I dhawsey@ehc.edu

HAWSEY, Vicki 256-352-8180 10 B vicki.hawsey@wallacestate.edu

HAWTHORNE, Camille 724-946-7110 451 C hawthorc@westminster.edu

HAWTHORNE, Marge 740-695-9500 384 J mhawthor@btc.edu

HAWTHORNE, Mary Jane 731-352-4046 467 C hawthornemj@bethelu.edu

HAWTHORNE, Michael, R 910-521-6637 379 B michael.hawthorne@uncp.edu

HAWTHORNE, Philip 918-465-1786 408 A phawthorne@eosc.edu

HAWTIN, Mary, L 810-989-5546 258 B mhawtin@sc4.edu

HAWXHURST, Joan 269-337-7384 253 F Joan.Hawxhurst@kzoo.edu

HAXTON, Lori 660-626-2410 278 F lhaxton@atsu.edu

HAY, April 812-237-2020 173 A april.hay@indstate.edu

HAY, Ellen 309-794-7724 145 B ellenhay@augustana.edu

HAY, George 312-467-2560 146 C ghay@tcsedsystem.edu

HAY, Judy 406-771-5133 296 B jhay@msugf.edu

HAY, Kuni 408-741-2052 78 B kuni.hay@westvalley.edu

HAY, Margaret 269-782-1306 258 E mhay@swmich.edu

HAY, Meredith 520-621-1856 19 B mhay@email.arizona.edu

HAY, Michael, D 503-491-7211 417 B michael.hay@mhcc.edu

HAY, Sharon, L 401-865-2750 453 F sharhay@providence.edu

HAY, William 605-856-5880 465 A william.hay@sintegleska.edu

HAYASHI, Adam 847-635-1862 160 E ahayashi@oakton.edu

HAYASHIDA, Peter, A 951-827-5203 74 C peter.hayashida@ucr.edu

HAYASHINO, Carole 916-278-7043 35 E caroleh@csus.edu

HAYDEN, Brian 724-480-3460 426 A brian.hayden@ccbc.edu

HAYDEN, Cathy, C 601-857-3322 274 E cchayden@hindscc.edu

HAYDEN, Donna, G 601-877-6182 273 C dhayden@alcorn.edu

HAYDEN, Hart 803-822-3676 459 D haydenh@midlandstech.edu

HAYDEN, John, D 215-836-2222 422 A john.hayden@antonelli.edu

HAYDEN, Mary 573-876-7105 290 G mhayden@stephens.edu

HAYDEN, Roger 410-704-2487 228 E rhayden@towson.edu

HAYDEN, Ruby 425-739-8208 535 B ruby.hayden@lwtc.edu

HAYDEN-MILES, Marie 631-420-2171 356 A marie.hayden-miles@farmingdale.edu

HAYDOCK, Joseph 559-297-4500 51 B jhaydock@it-email.com

HAYDON, Darrell 510-885-2749 34 C darrell.haydon@csueastbay.edu

HAYDUK, Steven 864-644-5294 461 B shayduk@swu.edu

HAYE, Melissa 304-327-4145 543 C mhaye@bluefieldstate.edu

HAYEN, Christopher 518-388-6911 358 E hayenc@union.edu

HAYES, Ann, C 717-867-6416 434 C hayes@lvc.edu

HAYES, Ann, K 573-651-2552 290 D ahayes@semo.edu

HAYES, Anne, M 610-566-1776 452 A ahayes@williamson.edu

HAYES, Barbara, E 713-313-4277 499 G hayes_be@tsu.edu

HAYES, Becky 912-201-8029 136 H bhayes@southuniversity.edu

HAYES, Billy 251-981-3771 2 H billy.hayes@columbiasouthern.edu

HAYES, Blair 301-985-7940 227 F diversity-initiatives@umuc.edu

HAYES, Charlene, M 410-516-8113 223 F chayes13@jhu.edu

HAYES, Chuck 810-762-0501 256 C chuck.hayes@mcc.edu

HAYES, Clint, R 606-679-8501 202 F clint.hayes@kctcs.edu

HAYES, Collette, M 302-454-3959 96 C cmhayes@dtcc.edu

HAYES, Connie 434-947-8116 522 E chayes@randolphcollege.edu

HAYES, Dale 772-462-7809 110 L dhayes@irsc.edu

HAYES, Dan 434-791-7252 516 D dhayes@averett.edu

HAYES, Daniel, J 315-267-2147 354 C hayesdj@potsdam.edu

HAYES, David, M 518-388-6233 358 E hayesd@union.edu

HAYES, Debra, L 330-972-7210 403 B dlhayes@uakron.edu

HAYES, Denise 909-621-8355 40 B denise_hayes@cuc.claremont.edu

HAYES, Diane 802-831-1308 515 A dhayes@vermontlaw.edu

HAYES, Eric 773-291-6384 147 D ehayes10@ccc.edu

HAYES, Erik, Z 812-877-8230 179 A erik.hayes@rose-hulman.edu

HAYES, Gaye 229-928-1273 131 B

HAYES, Gaynelle, H 409-944-1206 486 H ghayes@gc.edu

HAYES, George 212-431-2820 343 E ghayes@nyls.edu

HAYES, Glenn 731-352-4206 467 C hayesg@bethelu.edu

HAYES, Greg 816-235-1015 291 E hayesgr@umkc.edu

HAYES, Homer, M 903-510-3203 502 E bhay2@tjc.edu

HAYES, Ingrid 256-824-6857 9 A ingrid.hayes@uah.edu

HAYES, Jack, W 516-463-6750 335 H jack.w.hayes@hofstra.edu

HAYES, Jeannie 606-242-0309 203 A jhayes0114@kctcs.edu

HAYES, Jeff 678-359-5008 131 D jeff@gdn.edu

HAYES, Jeff 863-638-7256 123 B jeff.hayes@warner.edu

HAYES, Jennifer 360-475-7106 535 J jhayes@olympic.edu

HAYES, Jerry 413-572-5260 239 C jhayes@wsc.ma.edu

HAYES, Jessica 516-299-2480 339 A jessica.hayes@liu.edu

HAYES, Jessica 516-299-1451 339 A jessica.hayes@liu.edu

HAYES, Joanne 541-440-4600 420 F joanne.hayes@umpqua.edu

HAYES, Joe 907-474-7081 10 J uaf-fyalum@alaska.edu

HAYES, Joe, F 864-977-1367 460 A joe.hayes@ngu.edu

HAYES, John, W 503-352-2141 419 E jhayes@pacificu.edu

HAYES, Julie, C 413-545-4169 237 C jhayes@hfa.umass.edu

HAYES, Julie, L 336-272-7102 364 D jlhayes@greensborocollege.edu

HAYES, Kelly 631-656-2157 334 B khayes@ftc.edu

HAYES, Lance, R 512-448-8750 493 B lanceh@stedwards.edu

HAYES, Linda 650-306-3201 67 E hayes@smccd.edu

HAYES, Marshall 815-825-2086 155 C marshall.hayes@kishwaukeecollege.edu

HAYES, Michelle 603-862-1370 306 E michelle.hayes@unh.edu

HAYES, Mike 423-614-8406 470 A mhayes@leeuniversity.edu

HAYES, Nancy, K 415-338-2521 36 F nkhayes@sfsu.edu

HAYES, Nila 417-836-5632 286 F nilahayes@missouristate.edu

HAYES, Phebe, A 337-482-6829 216 D phayes@louisiana.edu

HAYES, Randall 501-312-0007 23 D randall.hayes@remingtoncollege.edu

HAYES, Ray 205-348-8343 8 E crhayes@uasystem.ua.edu

HAYES, Rhonda, M 252-335-3103 377 D rmhayes@mail.ecsu.edu

HAYES, Richard, L 251-380-2738 9 E rlhayes@usouthal.edu

HAYES, Rob 617-266-1400 231 G

HAYES, Robin, A 501-882-8936 20 D rahayes@asub.edu

HAYES, Samantha 270-852-3130 203 F shays@kwc.edu

HAYES, Sandra, J 207-725-3770 217 E shayes@bowdoin.edu

HAYES, Sandra, L 408-554-1784 68 C shayes@scu.edu

HAYES, Scotty 903-832-5565 496 C scotty.hayes@texarkanacollege.edu

HAYES, Sherman, L 910-962-3271 379 C hayess@uncw.edu

HAYES, Stephanie, A 804-524-5997 529 C shayes@vsu.edu

HAYES, Suzanne 518-587-2100 355 F suzanne.hayes@esc.edu

HAYES, Theresa 323-464-2777 27 I thayes@ca.aada.org

HAYES, Valerie, O 814-732-2167 442 D vhayes@edinboro.edu

HAYES, Verdel, I 336-723-0371 370 C vhayes@forsythtech.edu

HAYES, Wendy 937-376-6470 386 H whayes@centralstate.edu

HAYES, William 336-750-2142 380 A hayeswl@wssu.edu

HAYES-MORRISON, Ruth 352-371-2833 104 I admissions@dragonrises.edu

HAYFORD, Jack, W 818-779-8040 53 B mclemens@kingsuniversity.edu

HAYGOOD, Jennifer 919-807-7100 367 F haygoodj@nccommunitycolleges.edu

HAYHURST, Chad 715-324-6900 549 D chad.hayhurst@ni.edu

HAYHURST, David, T 619-594-6061 36 E hayhurst@engineering.sdsu.edu

HAYHURST, Neil 641-844-5670 185 J neil.hayhurst@iavalley.edu

HAYLOCK, Ryan 706-291-2121 136 E rhaylock@shorter.edu

HAYMAN, Gregory 916-558-2544 56 D haymang@scc.losrios.edu

HAYMET, Anthony, D 858-534-2827 74 D thaymet@ucsd.edu

HAYMON, JR., Elmer 412-237-2543 425 H ehaymon@ccac.edu

HAYNER, Kate 510-869-4780 64 J khayner@samuelmerritt.edu

HAYNER, Leon 407-646-2649 116 B lhayner@rollins.edu

HAYNER, Stephen, A 404-687-4514 127 C hayners@ctsnet.edu

HAYNES, Alexis 315-279-5674 337 K ahaynes@mail.keuka.edu

HAYNES, Amy, M 330-684-8932 403 C hamy@uakron.edu

HAYNES, Angela, N 919-516-4064 376 B ahaynes@st-aug.edu

HAYNES, Brian 678-466-5433 127 A brianhaynes@clayton.edu

HAYNES, Carl, E 607-844-8222 357 H haynesc@tc3.edu

HAYNES, Carolyn 513-529-2021 396 D haynesca@muohio.edu

HAYNES, Charlene, M 864-379-8773 457 G haynes@erskine.edu

HAYNES, Curtis, A 215-248-6322 435 B chaynes@ltsp.edu

HAYNES, David, A 540-985-4020 520 D dahaynes@jchs.edu

HAYNES, Douglas, M 949-824-2798 73 H dhaynes@uci.edu

HAYNES, Felix 813-757-2110 110 I fhaynes@hccfl.edu

HAYNES, Fred 541-917-4589 416 H fred.haynes@linnbenton.edu

HAYNES, Hal 701-483-2090 381 E hal.haynes@dickinsonstate.edu

HAYNES, Harriett, C 612-624-5862 272 D haynes@umn.edu

HAYNES, John, G 806-743-7841 501 E john.g.haynes@ttuhsc.edu

HAYNES, John, K 404-215-2609 134 A jhaynes@morehouse.edu

HAYNES, Karen, S 760-750-4040 36 B pres@csusm.edu

HAYNES, Lisa 616-331-7204 252 A haynesl@gvsu.edu

HAYNES, Martha, B 906-227-2610 256 F haynes@nmu.edu

HAYNES, Michael 817-735-2520 504 C mhaynes@hsc.unt.edu

HAYNES, Pamela, J 336-888-9055 365 A phaynes@highpoint.edu

HAYNES, Patricia, A 636-922-8427 288 E phaynes@stchas.edu

HAYNES, Penny, A 518-381-1374 350 E haynespa@sunysccc.edu

HAYNES, Peter, F 225-578-9903 212 F pfhaynes@vetmed.lsu.edu

HAYNES, Robert (Mike) 254-968-9080 496 F rhaynes@tarleton.edu

HAYNES, Sandra 303-556-2978 85 N hayness@mscd.edu

HAYNES, Stephanie, C 304-637-1335 540 F hayness@dewv.edu

HAYNES, Tina 704-216-4561 373 C tina.haynes@rccc.edu

HAYNIE, Janice 910-672-1211 377 E jhaynie@uncfsu.edu

HAYNIE, Todd 928-428-8320 14 C todd.haynie@eac.edu

HAYS, Antoinette, M 781-768-7122 244 D antoinette.hays@regiscollege.edu

HAYS, Cheryl, M 412-268-6382 424 H chays@andrew.cmu.edu

HAYS, Christi 703-821-8570 524 D chays@stratford.edu

HAYS, Danny 870-245-5526 22 I haysd@obu.edu

HAYS, Ida Mae 804-204-1218 516 G imhays@btsr.edu

HAYS, Ina, R 636-584-6565 281 I haysir@eastcentral.edu

HAYS, Joel 602-386-4127 11 H joel.hays@arizonachristian.edu

HAYS, Karen 732-906-2515 311 E khays@middlesexcc.edu

HAYS, Larry 314-529-9390 284 F lhays@maryville.edu

HAYS, Laura 580-349-1354 410 B lola@opsu.edu

HAYS, Patricia, H 401-456-8803 454 A phays@ric.edu

HAYS, Regina, M 618-650-3324 165 A rmhays@siue.edu

HAYS, Richard 919-660-3411 363 I richard.hays@duke.edu

HAYS, Stacie 712-274-5254 187 D hays@morningside.edu

HAYS, Stephanie 215-574-9600 431 A shays@hussianart.edu

HAYS, Wm. Randy 859-238-5471 199 D randy.hays@centre.edu

HAYSBERT, JoAnn, W 405-466-3201 408 G jwhaysbert@lunet.edu

HAYTER, Christopher, A ..... 614-823-1348 .... 400 G
chayter@otterbein.edu
HAYTER, Richard ..... 972-721-5227 .... 502 F
rhayter@udallas.edu
HAYTER, Sonya ..... 417-269-3469 .... 281 B
shayter@coxcollege.edu
HAYWARD, Craig ..... 831-477-5656 .... 31 F
crhaywar@cabrillo.edu
HAYWARD, Craig ..... 831-479-5656 .... 31 F
crhaywar@cabrillo.edu
HAYWARD, Jayanne ..... 717-867-6321 .... 434 C
hayward@lvc.edu
HAYWARD, John ..... 419-251-1314 .... 395 H
john.hayward@mercycollege.edu
HAYWARD, Maysa ..... 732-255-0400 .... 312 D
mhayward@ocean.edu
HAYWARD, Pierre, D ..... 302-831-2113 .... 96 F
phayward@udel.edu
HAYWARD-WYZIK, Lisa ..... 603-542-7744 .... 304 H
lwyzik@ccsnh.edu
HAYWOOD, Carl ..... 210-829-3935 .... 503 F
carl@uiwtx.edu
HAYWOOD, Chanta ..... 919-530-7395 .... 378 A
chaywood@nccu.edu
HAYWOOD, Donna ..... 661-362-3133 .... 41 G
donna.haywood@canyons.edu
HAYWOOD, Michele ..... 910-576-6222 .... 372 A
haywoodm@montgomery.edu
HAYWOOD, Zina ..... 262-564-3104 .... 553 H
haywoodz@gtc.edu
HAYWORTH, Kimberly, K ..... 517-750-1200 .... 258 F
kimh@arbor.edu
HAZAM, Bruce ..... 207-288-5015 .... 217 H
bhazam@coa.edu
HAZARD, Laurie, L ..... 401-232-6746 .... 453 A
lhazard@bryant.edu
HAZARD, Victor, A ..... 859-257-3754 .... 206 H
vahaz2@uky.edu
HAZEL, Julie ..... 719-502-3005 .... 86 G
julie.hazel@ppcc.edu
HAZEL, Marianne ..... 814-768-3401 .... 443 A
mhazel@lhup.edu
HAZELBAKER, Nicole ..... 406-683-7900 .... 295 B
n_hazelbaker@umwestern.edu
HAZELWOOD, Don ..... 252-493-7608 .... 372 E
dhazelwo@email.pittcc.edu
HAZELWOOD, Renita ..... 336-386-3392 .... 374 B
hazelwoodr@surry.edu
HAZELWOOD, Rhonda ..... 336-386-3336 .... 374 B
hazelwoodr@surry.edu
HAZEN, Verna, J ..... 585-475-5520 .... 347 G
vjhsfa@rit.edu
HAZEN, Virginia, S ..... 603-646-2451 .... 305 A
virginia.s.hazen@dartmouth.edu
HAZLETT, Brian ..... 410-704-2588 .... 228 E
bhazlett@towson.edu
HAZLETT, Margaret, L ..... 207-725-3490 .... 217 E
mhazlett@bowdoin.edu
HAZZARD, Douglas ..... 904-256-7100 .... 111 J
dhazzar@ju.edu
HAZZARD, Mike ..... 270-706-8686 .... 201 F
mikew.hazzard@kctcs.edu
HAZZARD, Nancy, J ..... 315-498-2119 .... 345 D
hazzardn@sunyocc.edu
HAZZARD, Terry ..... 251-405-7285 .... 2 D
thazzard@bishop.edu
HE, Huot ..... 301-548-5500 .... 99 D
HE, Yuxin ..... 512-454-1188 .... 480 F
info@aoma.edu
HEACOCK, Maureen ..... 937-769-1846 .... 383 K
mheacock@antioch.edu
HEACOCK, Ronald, C ..... 518-743-2237 .... 322 B
heacockr@sunyacc.edu
HEAD, Elizabeth ..... 904-620-2111 .... 120 C
ehead@unf.edu
HEAD, Elizabeth, M ..... 904-620-2111 .... 120 C
ehead@unf.edu
HEAD, John, D ..... 706-233-7342 .... 136 E
jhead@shorter.edu
HEAD, Linda ..... 832-813-6816 .... 490 C
linda.head@lonestar.edu
HEAD, Robert, L ..... 815-226-4010 .... 162 H
rhead@rockford.edu
HEAD, Steve ..... 281-618-5440 .... 490 C
steve.head@lonestar.edu
HEADING-GRANT,
Wanda, R ..... 802-656-8426 .... 514 F
wanda.heading-grant@uvm.edu
HEADLEE, Dianne ..... 918-540-6388 .... 408 J
dheadlee@neo.edu
HEADLEY, Allan ..... 903-886-5159 .... 497 E
allan_headley@tamu-commerce.edu
HEADLEY, Larry ..... 816-414-3700 .... 286 A
lheadley@mbts.edu
HEADLEY, William, R ..... 619-260-7919 .... 76 A
wheadley@sandiego.edu
HEADRICK, Alissa ..... 605-361-0200 .... 464 A
aheadrick@sf.coloradotech.edu
HEADRICK, Darrell, L ..... 804-752-7374 .... 522 F
dheadric@rmc.edu
HEADRICK, Dennis ..... 402-323-3427 .... 300 C
dheadric@southeast.edu
HEADRICK, Robert ..... 479-248-7236 .... 21 G
bheadrick@ecollege.edu
HEAFNER, Lori ..... 843-349-7871 .... 458 G
lori.hardin@hgtc.edu
HEAGLE, Leanne ..... 937-255-6565 .... 556 H
leanne.heagle@afit.edu
HEALD, James, W ..... 414-955-4400 .... 548 E
jheald@mcw.edu
HEALEY, Stephen, E ..... 203-576-4271 .... 94 D
healey@bridgeport.edu
HEALEY, Tom ..... 810-762-0417 .... 256 C
thomas.healey@mcc.edu
HEALY, Amy ..... 518-255-5111 .... 354 E
healyak@cobleskill.edu
HEALY, David ..... 617-928-4516 .... 243 A
dhealy@mountida.edu
HEALY, Gayle ..... 518-629-7326 .... 336 C
g.healy@hvcc.edu
HEALY, Ingrid ..... 903-813-2423 .... 481 A
ihealy@austincollege.edu
HEALY, Jack ..... 660-248-6320 .... 279 K
jhealy@centralmethodist.edu
HEALY, James ..... 508-856-2007 .... 238 A
james.healy@umassmed.edu
HEALY, John, W ..... 952-885-5436 .... 270 F
jhealy@nwhealth.edu
HEALY, Kevin ..... 612-338-6537 .... 261 G
healyk@augsburg.edu
HEALY, Kit ..... 641-472-1219 .... 187 B
khealy@mum.edu
HEALY, Mark ..... 530-938-5591 .... 42 C
healy@siskiyous.edu
HEALY, Mary ..... 812-749-1277 .... 178 D
mhealy@oak.edu
HEALY, Mary Louise ..... 410-704-4931 .... 228 E
mhealy@towson.edu
HEALY, JR., Nicholas, J ..... 239-280-2511 .... 101 C
nhealy@avemaria.edu
HEALY, Patrick, J ..... 203-582-8643 .... 93 E
patrick.healy@quinnipiac.edu
HEALY, Paul, F ..... 215-717-6161 .... 448 H
phealy@uarts.edu
HEALY, Rose Mary ..... 973-278-5400 .... 307 G
rmh@berkeleycollege.edu
HEALY, Rose Mary ..... 973-278-5400 .... 323 J
rmh@berkeleycollege.edu
HEALY, William, L ..... 863-680-4140 .... 109 D
whealy@flsouthern.edu
HEANEY, Margaret ..... 603-752-1113 .... 304 I
pheaney@ccsnh.edu
HEANEY, Roma, E ..... 313-593-5353 .... 259 E
rheaney@umich.edu
HEAP, Jeffrey ..... 815-280-2401 .... 154 H
jheap@jjc.edu
HEAPS, Doug, L ..... 704-357-8020 .... 361 N
dheaps@aii.edu
HEARD, Alvin ..... 323-563-9326 .... 39 D
alvinheard@cdrewu.edu
HEARD, JR., Ernest, W ..... 615-460-6424 .... 467 B
ernest.heard@belmont.edu
HEARD, John ..... 660-626-2397 .... 278 F
jheard@atsu.edu
HEARD, Michael ..... 229-217-4207 .... 134 C
mheard@moultrietech.edu
HEARD, Pamela, K ..... 973-353-5805 .... 314 E
pkheard@andromeda.rutgers.edu
HEARD-JOHNSON, Cessa . 206-934-6749 .... 537 B
cessa.heard.johnson@seattlecolleges.edu
HEARIN, Rick ..... 301-314-7236 .... 227 B
rhearin@umd.edu
HEARIT, Keith, M ..... 269-387-2354 .... 260 F
keith.hearit@wmich.edu
HEARN, Deyna ..... 310-434-4435 .... 68 D
hearn_deyna@smc.edu
HEARN, Kevin ..... 716-286-8405 .... 344 D
khearn@niagara.edu
HEARN, JR., Robert, W ..... 302-855-1684 .... 96 B
rhearn@dtcc.edu
HEARN, Sabrina ..... 205-934-9176 .... 9 A
shearn@uasystem.ua.edu
HEARN, Sabrina, B ..... 205-934-9176 .... 8 E
shearn@uasystem.ua.edu
HEARNS, Rene ..... 814-732-1052 .... 442 D
rhearns@edinboro.edu
HEAROD, Marguerite ..... 405-382-9950 .... 412 B
m.hearod@sscok.edu
HEARON, Holly ..... 317-931-2306 .... 170 E
hhearon@cts.edu
HEARON, Michael ..... 678-731-0555 .... 19 C
michael.hearon@phoenix.edu
HEARTFIELD, Judy ..... 254-526-1472 .... 482 F
judy.heartfield@ctcd.edu
HEARTLEIN, Karrie ..... 309-341-7340 .... 155 E
kheartle@knox.edu
HEARTT, Justine ..... 916-278-5992 .... 35 E
hearttj@csus.edu
HEASLEY, Ronald, P ..... 717-361-1558 .... 428 E
heasleyrp@etown.edu
HEATER, Margaret ..... 585-343-0055 .... 334 F
meheater@genesee.edu
HEATH, Aaron ..... 816-322-0110 .... 279 H
aaron.heath@calvary.edu
HEATH, Ann ..... 610-647-4400 .... 431 B
aheath@immaculata.edu
HEATH, Bill ..... 863-638-2953 .... 123 C
heathwl@webber.edu
HEATH, Bob ..... 417-626-1234 .... 287 F
heath.bob@occ.edu
HEATH, Cheryl, A ..... 307-674-6446 .... 556 C
cheath@sheridan.edu
HEATH, David, A ..... 212-938-5650 .... 355 B
dheath@sunyopt.edu
HEATH, Diann ..... 785-825-5422 .... 191 B
dheath@brownmackie.edu
HEATH, Erin, L ..... 651-628-3323 .... 270 E
elheath@nwc.edu
HEATH, Fred, M ..... 512-495-4350 .... 505 B
fheath@austin.utexas.edu
HEATH, Gregory ..... 616-538-2330 .... 251 F
gheath@gbcol.edu
HEATH, Hildy ..... 415-405-4256 .... 36 F
hheath@spsu.edu
HEATH, Jeffrey, D ..... 864-242-5100 .... 455 E
HEATH, Joan, L ..... 512-245-2133 .... 501 C
jh06@txstate.edu
HEATH, Jonathan ..... 772-546-5534 .... 110 J
jonathanheath@hsbc.edu
HEATH, Kathy ..... 207-326-2339 .... 219 D
kathy.heath@mma.edu
HEATH, Kerri ..... 310-506-7586 .... 61 G
kerri.heath@pepperdine.edu
HEATH, Marie ..... 904-470-8141 .... 105 A
HEATH, Mary-Teresa ..... 518-828-4181 .... 330 E
mary-teresa.heath@sunycgcc.edu
HEATH, Mona ..... 217-333-3303 .... 167 B
mbh@illinois.edu
HEATH, Nicole ..... 918-302-3617 .... 408 A
nheath@eosc.edu
HEATH, Raymond, P ..... 570-348-6246 .... 435 F
heath@marywood.edu
HEATH, Richard, C ..... 410-777-2204 .... 221 B
rcheath@aacc.edu
HEATH, Robert ..... 205-366-8851 .... 7 G
rheath@stillman.edu
HEATH, Susan, D ..... 801-832-2283 .... 512 F
sheath@westminstercollege.edu
HEATH-THORNTON,
Debra ..... 610-225-5055 .... 428 D
dheath@eastern.edu
HEATHERLY, David, L ..... 910-938-6789 .... 369 C
heatherlyd@coastalcarolina.edu
HEATHERSHAW, Susan ..... 605-455-6051 .... 464 H
sheathershaw@olc.edu
HEATON, Donnio ..... 641-472-7000 .... 187 D
dheaton@mum.edu
HEATON, Monica ..... 563-425-5773 .... 189 C
heatonm@uiu.edu
HEATON, Scott ..... 209-946-2541 .... 75 D
sheaton@pacific.edu
HEATON, Tim ..... 605-688-5117 .... 466 B
tim.heaton@sdstate.edu
HEATON, JR., William ..... 714-449-7464 .... 70 G
wheaton@scco.edu
HEATON-DUNLAP, Anne ..... 650-543-3804 .... 57 B
adunlap@menlo.edu
HEATOR, Martin ..... 734-462-4400 .... 258 C
mheator@schoolcraft.edu
HEATWOLE, Deirdre ..... 774-455-7300 .... 237 B
dheatwole@umassp.edu
HEATWOLE, Deirdre ..... 774-455-7300 .... 237 D
DHeatwole@umassp.edu
HEAVENER, Bill ..... 407-679-0100 .... 110 C
bheavener@fullsail.com
HEAVENER, Mac ..... 904-596-2400 .... 122 A
macheavener@tbc.edu
HEBARD, John ..... 907-474-6831 .... 10 J
jahebard@alaska.edu
HEBBARD, Don ..... 972-279-6511 .... 479 I
dhebbard@amberton.edu
HEBBARD, Matthew ..... 956-872-2147 .... 494 D
mshebbar@southtexascollege.edu
HEBDON, Catherine ..... 907-277-1000 .... 10 F
contact@chartercollege.edu
HEBERER, Janet ..... 402-844-7021 .... 300 A
janet@northeast.edu
HEBERLE, Julia, F ..... 610-921-7581 .... 421 D
jheberle@alb.edu
HEBERLING, Michael ..... 810-766-4374 .... 248 C
mike.heberling@baker.edu
HEBERT, Barbara, B ..... 985-549-3894 .... 216 C
bhebert@selu.edu
HEBERT, Bill ..... 985-380-2436 .... 211 K
HEBERT, Carolyn ..... 860-832-3804 .... 91 D
chebert@charteroak.edu
HEBERT, Corell ..... 337-354-4700 .... 19 C
corell.hebert@phoenix.edu
HEBERT, Debborah ..... 707-654-1182 .... 32 I
dhebert@csum.edu
HEBERT, Gaston ..... 512-448-8597 .... 493 B
gastonh@stedwards.edu
HEBERT, Helen, D ..... 336-334-5371 .... 379 A
helen_dennison@uncg.edu
HEBERT, Jaimie ..... 936-294-1001 .... 501 A
HEBERT, Joseph ..... 281-998-6150 .... 493 G
joseph.hebert@sjcd.edu
HEBERT, MSC, Marjorie ..... 504-394-7744 .... 214 A
mhebert@olhcc.edu
HEBERT, Mark ..... 502-852-3133 .... 207 A
mark.hebert@louisville.edu
HEBERT, Michelle ..... 978-681-0800 .... 242 B
mhebert@mslaw.edu
HEBERT, Rudolph ..... 413-572-5699 .... 239 C
rudy@wsc.ma.edu
HEBERT, Sally ..... 505-925-8502 .... 321 G
shebert@unm.edu
HEBERT, III, Stanley ..... 510-885-4238 .... 34 C
stanley.hebert@csueastbay.edu
HEBERT, Susan, K ..... 906-786-5802 .... 249 D
heberts@baycollege.edu
HECHT, Boruch ..... 973-267-9404 .... 313 C
boruch.hecht@gmail.com
HECHT, George, E ..... 541-346-2290 .... 419 B
ghecht@uoregon.edu
HECHT, Laura ..... 661-654-2124 .... 33 H
lhecht@csub.edu
HECHT, Pinchas ..... 718-645-0536 .... 341 D
phecht@thejnet.com
HECK, Barbara, H ..... 410-778-7805 .... 229 D
bheck2@washcoll.edu
HECK, Catherine, J ..... 740-283-6498 .... 390 M
check@franciscan.edu
HECK, Paul ..... 773-878-3194 .... 163 D
pheck@staugustine.edu
HECK, Thomas, R ..... 701-252-3467 .... 381 A
theck@jc.edu
HECK, Traci ..... 918-595-8634 .... 412 H
theck@tulsacc.edu
HECKAMAN, Daniel, A ..... 218-477-2300 .... 268 A
daniel.heckaman@mnstate.edu
HECKAMAN, Judith, M ..... 717-560-8278 .... 433 D
jheckaman@lbc.edu
HECKARD, Bonnie ..... 734-462-4400 .... 258 C
bheckard@schoolcraft.edu
HECKEL, David ..... 704-463-3124 .... 375 E
david.heckel@fsmail.pfeiffer.edu
HECKELER, Dave ..... 775-850-0700 .... 302 E
dheckeler@morrison.neumont.edu
HECKENDORN, Miles, J ..... 320-308-3453 .... 269 C
mjheckendorn@stcloudstate.edu
HECKENLAIBLE, Anna ..... 605-361-0200 .... 464 A
ahecken@sf.coloradotech.edu
HECKER, Jeffrey, E ..... 207-581-1954 .... 220 A
jeff.hecker@umit.maine.edu
HECKER, Laurel, A ..... 340-692-3160 .... 568 C
lhecker@uvi.edu
HECKERT, L. Randall ..... 330-471-8280 .... 395 E
rheckert@malone.edu
HECKLER, Mark, A ..... 219-464-5115 .... 181 A
mark.heckler@valpo.edu
HECKMAN, Mary Ellen ..... 610-372-4721 .... 445 B
mheckman@racc.edu
HECKMAN, Richard, A ..... 717-245-1308 .... 427 E
heckman@dickinson.edu
HECTOR, Gerald ..... 704-378-1190 .... 365 H
ghector@jcsu.edu
HEDBERG, Mary, A ..... 989-964-4062 .... 258 A
hedberg@svsu.edu
HEDBERG, Nancy ..... 503-375-7010 .... 415 F
nhedberg@corban.edu
HEDBERG, Rick ..... 701-858-3042 .... 381 G
rick.hedberg@minotstateu.edu
HEDBERG, Ulf ..... 202-250-2642 .... 97 E
ulf.hedberg@gallaudet.edu
HEDDERICK, Malgorzata ..... 617-253-9358 .... 242 A
malrh@mit.edu
HEDDLESTON, George ..... 937-775-7098 .... 406 C
george.heddleston@wright.edu
HEDDLESTON, Patrick, D .. 330-823-6572 .... 404 C
heddlepd@mountunion.edu
HEDEEN, Deborah, L ..... 208-282-2783 .... 143 D
hededebo@isu.edu
HEDGE, Clarence, A ..... 405-466-3419 .... 408 G
cahedge@lunet.edu
HEDGE, Dennis ..... 605-688-6197 .... 466 B
dennis.hedge@sdstate.edu
HEDGECOCK, Wally ..... 210-524-2100 .... 19 C
wally.hedgecock@phoenix.edu
HEDGEMAN, Denita ..... 901-435-1729 .... 470 B
denita_hedgeman@loc.edu
HEDGEPETH, Martha, E ..... 919-497-3430 .... 366 E
mhedgepeth@louisburg.edu
HEDGES, Amy, M ..... 859-371-9393 .... 198 D
ahedges@beckfield.edu
HEDGES, Denise, C ..... 417-667-8181 .... 280 I
dhedges@cottey.edu
HEDGES, Douglas ..... 609-343-4911 .... 307 D
hedges@atlantic.edu
HEDGES, Jerris, R ..... 808-692-0881 .... 141 B
jerris@hawaii.edu
HEDGES, Mark, C ..... 270-852-3242 .... 203 E
mhedges@kwc.edu
HEDGES, Mimi ..... 573-442-2211 .... 290 G
mhedges@stephens.edu
HEDGES, Tammy, L ..... 901-678-5314 .... 474 C
thedges@memphis.edu
HEDLIN, Carol ..... 907-796-6016 .... 11 A
carol.hedlin@uas.alaska.edu
HEDLUN, Randy ..... 417-862-9533 .... 282 D
rhedlun@globaluniversity.edu
HEDLUND, Helene ..... 218-846-3724 .... 267 G
helene.hedlund@minnesota.edu
HEDLUND, Joyce, B ..... 207-454-1001 .... 219 B
jhedlund@wccc.me.edu

HEDMAN, Shawn .... 507-537-6292.... 269 G Shawn.Hedman@smsu.edu
HEDRICK, Erica .... 978-927-2217.... 234 F ehedrick@endicott.edu
HEDRICK, Jennifer .... 303-457-2757..... 84 F jhedrick@cci.edu
HEDRICK, Liz .... 405-208-5857.... 410 A lhedrick@okcu.edu
HEDRICK, Van .... 940-668-7347.... 491 C vhedrick@nctc.edu
HEEKE, JR., David .... 989-774-3046.... 249 G heeke1dw@cmich.edu
HEEN, Shellee .... 808-544-0290.... 140 B sheen@hpu.edu
HEENAN, Christine .... 617-495-1703.... 235 H christine_heenan@harvard.edu
HEENAN, Elizabeth, A .... 215-951-1240.... 432 G heenan@lasalle.edu
HEEREN, Matthew .... 660-626-2064.... 278 F mheeren@atsu.edu
HEERMAN, Heather .... 508-565-1325.... 245 D hheerman@stonehill.edu
HEERMANN, Keith .... 417-862-9533.... 282 D kheermann@globaluniversity.edu
HEERSINK, Heather .... 719-587-7759..... 80 F heather_heersink@adams.edu
HEETER-BASS, Janet, A ..... 740-826-8080.... 396 I jheeter@muskingum.edu
HEETLAND, David, L .... 847-866-3970.... 151 B david.heetland@garrett.edu
HEEVNER, Howard .... 814-863-2052.... 438 F hwh10@psu.edu
HEFFELFINGER, Sara .... 928-777-3710..... 14 D heffels@erau.edu
HEFFELFINGER, Scott .... 610-372-4721.... 445 B sheffelfinger@racc.edu
HEFFERIN, Cathy, D .... 336-633-0208.... 372 F cdhefferin@randolph.edu
HEFFERN, Robert .... 606-539-4525.... 206 G robert.heffern@ucumberlands.edu
HEFFERNAN, Cathy .... 402-457-2715.... 298 H cheffernan@mccneb.edu
HEFFERNAN, Robert, J ...... 848-932-7305.... 314 B heffernan@instlres.rutgers.edu
HEFFERNAN, Thomas, J .... 561-237-7270.... 113 D theffernan@lynn.edu
HEFFLEY, David, P .... 215-699-5700.... 433 G dheffley@LSB.edu
HEFFNER, David, B .... 570-321-4278.... 435 D heffner@lycoming.edu
HEFFNER, Emily .... 215-591-5700.... 427 A eheffner@devry.edu
HEFFRON, Jay .... 949-480-4028..... 69 I heffron@soka.edu
HEFLEY, Jacqueline, D .... 512-404-4826.... 481 D jhefley@austinseminary.edu
HEFLIN, David .... 605-361-0200.... 464 A dheflin@ctuonline.edu
HEFLIN, Sherry .... 717-815-1257.... 452 F sheflin@ycp.edu
HEFNER, David, S .... 706-721-6569.... 130 B dhefner@georgiahealth.edu
HEFNER, Dennis, L .... 716-673-3456.... 352 A dennis.hefner@fredonia.edu
HEGARTY, Kevin, P .... 512-471-1422.... 505 B hegarty@mail.utexas.edu
HEGARTY, Staci .... 815-534-3300.... 161 G Staci.Hegarty@rasmussen.edu
HEGDE, Raju .... 909-389-3362..... 65 B rhegde@craftonhills.edu
HEGEDUS, Mary Ellen .... 574-239-8391.... 172 J mhegedus@hcc-nd.edu
HEGEL, Barbara .... 907-796-6457..... 11 A barbara.hegel@uas.alaska.edu
HEGEMAN, Diane .... 303-797-5702..... 80 J diane.hegeman@arapahoe.edu
HEGGEMEYER, Terri .... 402-844-7263.... 300 A roseann@northeast.edu
HEGLAND, Paul, R .... 262-551-5858.... 546 F paul@carthage.edu
HEGLAR, Pamela .... 229-430-3504.... 123 I pheglar@albanytech.edu
HEGMAN, John, P .... 404-471-6109.... 123 G jhegman@agnesscott.edu
HEGMANN, Edward, H .... 540-654-1039.... 524 H ehegmann@umw.edu
HEGRANES, Colleen .... 651-690-8844.... 271 E cahegranes@stkate.edu
HEICHELBECK, Tamie .... 618-664-7000.... 151 D tamie.heichelbeck@greenville.edu
HEIDA, Debbie .... 706-236-2207.... 125 G dheida@berry.edu
HEIDBREDER, Kay, K .... 540-231-6293.... 529 B heidbred@vt.edu
HEIDE, Gale .... 406-586-3585.... 294 I gale.heide@montanabiblecollege.edu
HEIDEMAN, Carl, E .... 616-395-7670.... 252 F heideman@hope.edu
HEIDEN, Jill .... 843-661-8003.... 458 A jill.heiden@fdtc.edu
HEIDENREICH, Donald ...... 636-949-4414.... 284 C dheidenreich@lindenwood.edu
HEIDER, Cindy .... 816-271-4364.... 287 A heider@missouriwestern.edu
HEIDER, Donald, B .... 312-915-6548.... 157 A dheider@luc.edu
HEIDER, Mary Jane .... 585-345-6813.... 334 F mjheider@genesee.edu
HEIDERMAN, JR., Donald, L .... 812-265-2580.... 176 G dheiderm@ivytech.edu
HEIDERMAN, Paula .... 812-537-4010.... 176 G pheiderm@ivytech.edu
HEIDINGSFIELD, Michael, J .... 512-499-4688.... 504 E mheidingsfield@utsystem.edu
HEIDKE, Stephen .... 314-392-2372.... 286 C heidkesj@mobap.edu
HEIDRICH, Mark, W .... 240-895-4208.... 226 A mwheidrich@smcm.edu
HEIDRICK, Judy .... 785-738-9058.... 195 D jheidrick@ncktc.edu
HEIDT, Loretta, A .... 701-483-2314.... 381 E loretta.heidt@dickinsonstate.edu
HEIDTKE, Staci, L .... 715-836-5358.... 550 H heidtksl@uwec.edu
HEIER, Greg .... 402-826-8583.... 298 A greg.heier@doane.edu
HEIFETZ, Harry, S .... 262-554-2010.... 158 D harryh.21stcentury@rcn.com
HEIFETZ, Harry, S .... 262-554-2010.... 548 F harryh.21stcentury@rcn.com
HEIFNER, Bryan .... 432-335-6512.... 491 F bheifner@odessa.edu
HEIGHT, Linda, L .... 248-204-2128.... 254 E lheight@ltu.edu
HEIKEL, Karen .... 920-424-1463.... 551 D heikelk@uwosh.edu
HEIKKILA, Christina .... 910-362-7000.... 368 E
HEIL, Elissa .... 479-979-1338..... 26 A eheil@ozarks.edu
HEIL, Lina .... 619-388-2759..... 65 G lheil@sdccd.edu
HEIL, Marti .... 812-855-7137.... 173 C heilm@indiana.edu
HEIL, Mary Colleen .... 717-396-7833.... 440 J mcheil@pcad.edu
HEILE, Judi .... 513-244-4630.... 388 D judi_heile@mail.msj.edu
HEILGEIST, Peter, J .... 435-586-7948.... 511 A heilgeist@suu.edu
HEILLE, Gregory .... 314-256-8881.... 279 A heille@ai.edu
HEILMAN, Carl, R .... 620-792-9301.... 190 E heilmanc@bartonccc.edu
HEILMAN, Linda, A .... 315-386-7328.... 355 D heilmanl@canton.edu
HEILMAN, Valerie .... 701-228-5437.... 382 C valerie.heilman@dakotacollege.edu
HEILSTEDT, Martin, R .... 425-235-2369.... 536 E mheilstedt@rtc.edu
HEIM, Peggy, M .... 610-799-1532.... 434 D pheim@lccc.edu
HEIMAN, Kelly, J .... 262-524-7695.... 546 E kheiman@carrollu.edu
HEIMAN, Scott .... 608-246-6018.... 554 B sheiman@matcmadison.edu
HEIMANN, Anne .... 402-481-3908.... 297 B anne.heimann@bryanlgh.org
HEIMANN, B. Sue .... 419-289-5324.... 384 D sheimann@ashland.edu
HEIMBROCK, Kimberly ...... 859-572-5139.... 205 E heimbrockk@nku.edu
HEIMEL, Theres .... 952-944-0080.... 270 D theimel@nti.edu
HEIMERL, Marc, D .... 920-923-8796.... 548 C mdheimerl78@marianuniversity.edu
HEIMMERMANN, Daniel ..... 956-882-8252.... 505 C daniel.heimmermann@utb.edu
HEIMOVITZ, Issac .... 718-438-1002.... 340 H
HEIN, Audrey, D .... 563-333-6364.... 188 D HeinAudreyD@sau.edu
HEIN, Beth, A .... 715-852-1380.... 553 F bhein1@cvtc.edu
HEIN, Candy .... 956-326-4483.... 497 B chein@tamiu.edu
HEIN, Gail .... 908-709-7610.... 316 B hein@ucc.edu
HEIN, Holly, A .... 207-948-3131.... 219 H hein@unity.edu
HEIN, Sherril .... 909-948-7582..... 66 L sherrilh@sjvc.edu
HEIN, Steven, M .... 912-478-0831.... 131 A shein@georgiasouthern.edu
HEIN, Tierney, M .... 563-556-5110.... 187 G heint@nicc.edu
HEINDL, Michael .... 228-497-7700.... 275 G michael.heindl@mgccc.edu
HEINEMAN, William .... 978-556-3327.... 241 B wheineman@necc.mass.edu
HEINEMANN, Brian .... 760-366-5278..... 43 E bheinemann@cmccd.edu
HEINEMANN, Dovid .... 732-367-4259.... 311 D
HEINEMANN, Kenneth, G .. 808-942-1000.... 140 H careers.hnl@remingtoncollege.edu
HEINEN, Judith .... 313-927-1256.... 255 A jheinen@marygrove.edu
HEINEN, Terry .... 615-230-3227.... 476 A terry.heinen@volstate.edu
HEINITSH, Julie, C .... 828-232-2430.... 378 C jheinits@unca.edu
HEINLEIN, Chester .... 609-894-9311.... 308 C cheinlei@bcc.edu
HEINOLD, Sandra .... 361-570-4286.... 503 E heinolds@uhv.edu
HEINRICH, Carl .... 913-469-8500.... 193 I heinrich@jccc.edu
HEINRICH, George, F .... 973-972-4631.... 316 C heinrich@umdnj.edu
HEINRICH, George, F .... 973-972-4631.... 316 F heinrige@umdnj.edu
HEINRICH, Heike .... 216-687-2051.... 388 C h.heinrich@csuohio.edu
HEINRICH, Mark, A .... 205-391-5880........ 7 A mheinrich@sheltonstate.edu
HEINRICH, Matt, W .... 816-501-4064.... 288 D matt.heinrich@rockhurst.edu
HEINRICH, Peggy .... 847-214-6911.... 150 D pheinrich@elgin.edu
HEINRICH, Sam .... 916-577-2200..... 79 C sheinrich@jessup.edu
HEINRICHS, Leslee .... 503-203-6427.... 415 G lheinrichs@devry.edu
HEINRICHS, Ruth .... 619-849-2371..... 62 L ruthheinrichs@pointloma.edu
HEINS, Donald .... 607-962-9264.... 331 D dheins1@corning-cc.edu
HEINSELMAN, Gregg, M ... 715-425-4444.... 552 A gregg.heinselman@uwrf.edu
HEINSOHN, Lori .... 701-224-5690.... 382 B lori.heinsohn@bismarckstate.edu
HEINTZ, Barbara, B .... 808-933-3116.... 141 A bheintz@hawaii.edu
HEINTZ, David .... 860-628-4751..... 92 F dheintz@lincolncollegene.edu
HEINTZ, Jill .... 315-792-5584.... 341 E jheintz@mvcc.edu
HEINTZE, Michael, R .... 512-245-1977.... 501 C mh63@txstate.edu
HEINTZELMAN, Jonathan, R .... 312-915-7262.... 157 A jheintz@luc.edu
HEINY, Danielle .... 507-433-0517.... 269 A dheiny@riverland.edu
HEINZ, Anne, K .... 303-492-2202..... 88 B anne.heinz@colorado.edu
HEINZ, Heidi .... 217-854-3231.... 145 F hhein@blackburn.edu
HEINZ, Robert, A .... 804-523-5934.... 526 F rheinz@reynolds.edu
HEINZE, Edward .... 502-897-4721.... 205 H eheinze@sbts.edu
HEINZEN, Kathleen, M .... 920-832-6561.... 547 J kathleen.m.heinzen@lawrence.edu
HEINZMAN, Mary, B .... 563-333-6241.... 188 D HeinzmanMaryB@sau.edu
HEISER, Andrew .... 712-274-5493.... 187 D heiser@morningside.edu
HEISER, Gregory, M .... 405-325-3221.... 413 C gheiser@ou.edu
HEISER, Lesley .... 207-942-6781.... 217 B lheiser@bts.edu
HEISER, Mary Kate .... 301-387-3164.... 222 H kate.heiser@garrettcollege.edu
HEISEY, Bill .... 540-423-9037.... 526 E bheisey@germanna.edu
HEISEY, Jennifer, L .... 716-878-6001.... 353 A heiseyjl@buffalostate.edu
HEISEY, Nancy .... 540-432-4141.... 518 E nancy.heisey@emu.edu
HEISEY, Terry, M .... 717-866-5775.... 428 I theisey@evangelical.edu
HEISLER, John, F .... 614-885-5585.... 401 B jheisler@pcj.edu
HEISLER, JR., Robert, B ... 330-672-6317.... 393 D yheisler@kent.edu
HEISSERER, Gary .... 641-784-5265.... 184 H heissere@graceland.edu
HEISSERER, Nick .... 218-855-8038.... 266 C nheisserer@clcmn.edu
HEIST, Daniel, P .... 814-865-1359.... 438 F dph3@psu.edu
HEIST, Richard .... 386-226-6634.... 105 B richard.heist@erau.edu
HEITHAUS, Peter, A .... 314-516-5809.... 291 F peter_heithaus@umsl.edu
HEITKEMPER, Mary .... 509-313-4231.... 534 A heitkemper@gonzaga.edu
HEITMILLER, Janet .... 713-221-8678.... 503 D heitmillerj@uhd.edu
HEITZ, Tim .... 717-560-8211.... 433 D
HEITZENRATER, John .... 817-923-8459.... 483 C jwheitzenrater@gmail.com
HEITZENRATER, Kim, D ..... 931-598-1121.... 472 J kheltzen@sewanee.edu
HEITZMANN, Dennis, E ...... 814-865-0966.... 438 F deh8@psu.edu
HEIZER NEWQUIST, Lelise .... 253-833-9111.... 534 C lheizernewquist@greenriver.edu
HEIZER NEWQUIST, Leslie .... 253-833-9111.... 534 C lheizernewquist@greenriver.edu
HEJL, Cindy .... 303-556-4741..... 85 N hejlc@mscd.edu
HEKKEL, Jerry .... 206-726-5111.... 532 G jhekkel@cornish.edu
HELBERT, Lee, A .... 708-709-3639.... 161 C lhelbert@prairiestate.edu
HELBIG, Tuesdi .... 270-745-3250.... 207 C tuesdi.helbig@wku.edu
HELBING, Shirley .... 570-702-8918.... 431 K shelbing@johnson.edu
HELBLE, Joseph .... 603-646-2238.... 305 A joseph.helble@dartmouth.edu
HELD, Jeffrey .... 607-733-2300.... 359 A jheld@uscny.edu
HELD, Steve .... 636-227-2100.... 284 E steve.held@logan.edu
HELDT, Kim .... 812-749-1218.... 178 D kheldt@oak.edu
HELEKAR, Andrea .... 213-624-1200..... 46 L ahelekar@fidm.edu
HELENS, Joyce, M .... 320-308-5017.... 269 D jhelens@sctcc.edu
HELFANT, Ian .... 315-228-7220.... 329 H ihelfant@colgate.edu
HELFGOT, Steven .... 480-731-8098..... 15 F steve.helfgot@domail.maricopa.edu
HELFRICH, Christine .... 301-846-2518.... 222 G chelfrich@frederick.edu
HELFRICH, Glenda .... 806-743-2986.... 501 E glenda.helfrich@ttuhsc.edu
HELFRICH, Stephen, P .... 812-464-1782.... 180 F shelfric@usi.edu
HELGERSON, Carolyn .... 605-221-3108.... 464 C chelgerson@kilian.edu
HELGESEN, Paul .... 978-867-4730.... 235 E paul.helgesen@gordon.edu
HELGESEN, Pete .... 913-360-7476.... 190 F phelgesen@benedictine.edu
HELGESON, Richard, J .... 731-881-7380.... 477 E helgeson@utm.edu
HELLA, Lori, L .... 989-774-7194.... 249 G hella1ll@cmich.edu
HELLAND, Karen .... 541-888-7212.... 420 C khelland@socc.edu
HELLDOBLER, Richard .... 304-876-5176.... 544 A rhelldob@shepherd.edu
HELLENBRAND, Harry .... 818-677-2957..... 35 D harry.hellenbrand@csun.edu
HELLER, Caren, A .... 212-746-5767.... 360 B cah2021@med.cornell.edu
HELLER, Carrie .... 765-973-8404.... 173 D hellerc@iue.edu
HELLER, James .... 262-595-2455.... 551 E james.heller@uwp.edu
HELLER, Joshua, W .... 585-785-1335.... 334 A hellerjw@flcc.edu
HELLER, Leonard, E .... 859-218-6512.... 206 H lehell2@uky.edu
HELLER, Rebecca .... 860-701-5491..... 93 B heller_r@mitchell.edu
HELLER, Stephen .... 212-998-1035.... 344 B stephen.heller@nyu.edu
HELLER, Tracy .... 626-284-2777..... 27 D theller@alliant.edu
HELLER, Tracy .... 858-635-4763..... 27 E theller@alliant.edu
HELLER-STERN, Miriam ...... 310-476-9777..... 28 F mstern@ajula.edu
HELLERSTEIN, Laurel .... 978-232-2153.... 234 F lhellers@endicott.edu
HELLESON, Connie .... 503-777-7705.... 420 A chelleson@reed.edu
HELLIE, Thomas .... 503-883-2408.... 416 G thellie@linfield.edu
HELLIGE, Joseph .... 310-338-2733..... 56 E jhellige@lmu.edu
HELLING, Mary Kay .... 605-688-4173.... 466 B mary.helling@sdstate.edu
HELLING, Mary Kay .... 605-688-4181.... 466 B mary.helling@sdstate.edu
HELLING, Nathan, M .... 605-336-6588.... 465 B nhelling@sfseminary.edu
HELLMAN, Lawrence, K ...... 405-208-5337.... 410 A lhellman@okcu.edu
HELLMERS, Nathan, J .... 919-508-2303.... 375 D njhellmers@peace.edu
HELLMICH, David, M .... 859-246-4649.... 201 D david.hellmich@kctcs.edu
HELLMUND, Paul, C .... 413-369-4044.... 233 F hellmund@csld.edu
HELLWIG, Beth, A .... 715-836-5992.... 550 H hellwiba@uwec.edu
HELLYER, Brenda .... 281-998-6100.... 493 D brenda.hellyer@sjcd.edu
HELM, Ann .... 718-982-2100.... 327 A Ann.Helm@csi.cuny.edu
HELM, Darlene .... 225-359-9218.... 209 K dhelm@catc.edu
HELM, Hunt, C .... 502-272-8046.... 198 E hhelm@bellarmine.edu
HELM, Karen, P .... 919-515-6648.... 378 B karen_helm@ncsu.edu

HELM, Lloyd, L .... 503-255-0332 .... 417 C
lhelm@multnomah.edu
HELM, Peyton, R .... 484-664-3125 .... 437 B
pres@muhlenberg.edu
HELM, Phoebe, K .... 831-755-6900 .... 49 C
phelm@hartnell.edu
HELM, Ron, C .... 870-368-2027 .... 23 A
rhelm@ozarka.edu
HELM, Steve .... 540-831-5471 .... 522 D
shelm@radford.edu
HELMAN, Jay, W .... 970-943-2114 .... 89 B
jhelman@western.edu
HELMBRECHT, Lena .... 912-260-4314 .... 136 F
lena.helmbrecht@sgc.edu
HELMBURGER, David .... 314-977-2991 .... 289 F
HELMER, Robert, C .... 419-824-3809 .... 395 D
rhelmer@lourdes.edu
HELMER, Shannon .... 610-799-1857 .... 434 D
shelmer@lccc.edu
HELMICH, Doris .... 520-494-5406 .... 13 F
doris.helmich@centralaz.edu
HELMICK, Michael, S .... 336-342-4261 .... 373 B
HELMICK, Sarah .... 330-675-8961 .... 394 A
shelmick@kent.edu
HELMICK, Tom .... 724-852-3210 .... 451 B
thelmick@waynesburg.edu
HELMS, Bryan .... 229-732-5946 .... 124 C
bryanhelms@andrewcollege.edu
HELMS, Chris .... 828-765-7351 .... 371 F
chelms@mayland.edu
HELMS, Doris, R .... 864-656-3243 .... 456 E
biol110@clemson.edu
HELMS, Jim .... 812-537-4010 .... 176 G
jhelms@ivytech.edu
HELMS, Lance .... 912-538-3207 .... 137 A
lhelms@southeasterntech.edu
HELMS, Mark .... 704-330-6127 .... 369 A
mark.helms@cpcc.edu
HELMS, Sandra .... 309-677-2808 .... 145 H
sandy@bradley.edu
HELMS, Sherrie .... 912-583-3206 .... 126 C
shelms@bpc.edu
HELMS, Steve .... 334-222-6591 .... 5 F
shelms@lbwcc.edu
HELMSING, Debra, F .... 260-665-4240 .... 180 A
helmsingd@trine.edu
HELMSTETTER, Donald, W 651-641-8227 .... 263 C
helmstetter@csp.edu
HELMUS, D. Mark .... 317-940-9332 .... 170 C
mhelmus@butler.edu
HELOU, Ibrahim (Abe) .... 909-593-3511 .... 75 C
ahelou@laverne.edu
HELSABECK, Hank .... 503-554-2143 .... 415 I
hhelsabeck@georgefox.edu
HELSEL, Dennis .... 252-398-6484 .... 363 E
helsel@chowan.edu
HELSEN, Michael .... 616-777-5206 .... 248 C
mike.helsen@baker.edu
HELSEN, Michael, L .... 231-777-5206 .... 248 J
mike.helsen@baker.edu
HELSETH, Joe .... 423-697-2606 .... 474 D
HELSHAM, Irene .... 684-699-9155 .... 558 I
i.helsham@amsamoa.edu
HELSPER, Nancy .... 320-589-6012 .... 272 C
helsper@morris.umn.edu
HELTON, Karen .... 903-927-3369 .... 509 A
khelton@wileyc.edu
HELTON, Kasey .... 678-915-3998 .... 137 C
khelton@spsu.edu
HELTON, Patti .... 303-871-3289 .... 88 E
phelton@du.edu
HELTON, Richard, E .... 812-888-4208 .... 181 B
president@vinu.edu
HELTON, Tom .... 706-507-8909 .... 127 D
helton_tom@columbusstate.edu
HELTON, Tonja .... 813-620-1446 .... 110 A
HELTSLEY, Susan, D .... 360-438-4534 .... 536 F
sheltsley@stmartin.edu
HELVERING, Christal, R .... 765-641-4205 .... 169 A
crhelvering@anderson.edu
HELWICK, Christine .... 562-951-4500 .... 33 E
chelwick@calstate.edu
HELWIG, Christine, A .... 518-629-7343 .... 336 C
c.helwig@hvcc.edu
HELWIG, Daniel, S .... 717-815-1502 .... 452 F
dhelwig@ycp.edu
HELWIG, Denice .... 707-826-3300 .... 36 D
dh7003@humboldt.edu
HELWIG, Susan, M .... 570-674-6368 .... 436 F
shelwig@misericordia.edu
HEMANS, Peter .... 828-694-1723 .... 368 B
peterh@blueridge.edu
HEMBREE, Lois, D .... 620-421-6700 .... 194 E
loish@labette.edu
HEMENWAY, David, A .... 860-832-3904 .... 91 D
dhemenway@charteroak.edu
HEMINGWAY, Sally, A .... 478-757-5212 .... 139 A
shemingway@wesleyancollege.edu
HEMINGWAY SMITH,
Patricia, A .... 919-536-7244 .... 369 G
smithp@durhamtech.edu
HEMLICK, Lisa, M .... 610-341-5830 .... 428 D
lhemlick@eastern.edu
HEMM, Curtiss .... 802-793-0728 .... 513 H
curtiss.hemm@neci.edu
HEMMASI, Harriette .... 401-863-2162 .... 452 J
harriette_hemmasi@brown.edu
HEMMILA, Deanna, K .... 906-227-2637 .... 256 F
dhemmila@nmu.edu
HEMMING, Erik G, C .... 414-229-4201 .... 551 C
hemmingc@aux.uwm.edu
HEMMINGER, John, C .... 949-824-5796 .... 73 H
jchemmin@uci.edu
HEMMINGS, Bob .... 336-386-3276 .... 374 B
hemmingsb@surry.edu
HEMMINGSEN, Jens .... 614-236-6105 .... 386 C
jhemming@capital.edu
HEMMITT, Ernita .... 404-880-6128 .... 126 I
ehemmitt@cau.edu
HEMMITT, Ernita .... 404-880-6701 .... 126 I
ehemmitt@cau.edu
HEMPEL, Lamont, C .... 909-748-8589 .... 75 F
monty_hempel@redlands.edu
HEMPHILL, Brian, O .... 815-753-6103 .... 160 A
bhemphill@niu.edu
HEMPHILL, Dorothy, D .... 302-477-2009 .... 96 H
ddhemphill@widener.edu
HEMPHILL, Michael, R .... 318-869-5104 .... 208 F
mhemphill@centenary.edu
HEMPHILL, Ron .... 423-442-2001 .... 469 B
hemphill@hiwassee.edu
HEMPHILL, Teale .... 719-336-1591 .... 85 K
teale.hemphill@lamarcc.edu
HEMPHILL, Tockie .... 479-968-0302 .... 20 G
themphill@atu.edu
HEMPSTEAD, Laurie, A .... 518-381-1271 .... 350 E
hempstla@sunysccc.edu
HEMRICK, Robert, D .... 731-425-2636 .... 475 B
dhemrick@jscc.edu
HEMSEY, Charles .... 516-796-4800 .... 342 H
chemsey@nycc.edu
HENAHAN, David .... 518-587-2100 .... 355 F
david.henahan@esc.edu
HENAN, Carmen .... 505-424-2302 .... 318 C
chenan@iaia.edu
HENAULT, Cheri .... 860-701-5052 .... 93 B
henault_c@mitchell.edu
HENBERG, Marvin .... 208-459-5502 .... 143 A
HENCHY, Dolores .... 201-355-1133 .... 310 C
henchyd@felician.edu
HENDEE, Helen .... 706-737-1442 .... 125 C
hhendee@aug.edu
HENDEL, BVM, Kate .... 563-588-6432 .... 183 B
kate.hendel@clarke.edu
HENDERSHOT, Debra .... 256-306-2581 .... 2 E
ddg@calhoun.edu
HENDERSHOT, Lewis .... 407-303-8192 .... 108 D
lewis.hendershot@fhchs.edu
HENDERSHOT, Mike, W .... 816-604-6766 .... 285 E
mike.hendershot@mcckc.edu
HENDERSHOT,
Stephanie, N .... 412-262-6291 .... 445 G
hendershot@rmu.edu
HENDERSON, Alexa, B .... 404-880-8328 .... 126 I
ahenders@cau.edu
HENDERSON, Alisha, R .... 901-678-2230 .... 474 C
arose3@memphis.edu
HENDERSON, Allen .... 817-531-4405 .... 502 A
ahenderson@txwes.edu
HENDERSON, Andrea .... 309-298-1977 .... 168 A
ad-henderson@wiu.edu
HENDERSON, Angela .... 773-995-2215 .... 146 D
ahende22@csu.edu
HENDERSON, Ann, L .... 518-580-5719 .... 351 B
ahenders@skidmore.edu
HENDERSON, Ann, S .... 212-817-7215 .... 327 B
ahenderson@gc.cuny.edu
HENDERSON, Anne .... 410-532-5301 .... 225 D
ahenderson@ndm.edu
HENDERSON, JR.,
Arnold, R .... 617-253-4861 .... 242 A
hndrson@mit.edu
HENDERSON, Arthur .... 478-825-6400 .... 129 C
hendersona@fvsu.edu
HENDERSON, Barbara, J .... 512-448-8532 .... 493 B
barbarah@stedwards.edu
HENDERSON, Brad .... 918-540-6409 .... 408 J
bhenderson@neo.edu
HENDERSON, Brian .... 267-502-4890 .... 423 B
brian.henderson@brynathyn.edu
HENDERSON, Brian .... 770-537-6012 .... 139 B
brian.henderson@westgatech.edu
HENDERSON, Carl, E .... 443-412-2300 .... 223 B
chenderson@harford.edu
HENDERSON, Carol .... 607-274-3837 .... 336 G
cghenderson@ithaca.edu
HENDERSON, Castella .... 314-539-5354 .... 289 A
chenderson@stlcc.edu
HENDERSON, III,
Charles, M .... 401-874-4756 .... 454 E
chad@uri.edu
HENDERSON, Christine .... 773-371-5403 .... 146 B
studentservices@ctu.edu
HENDERSON, Cindy .... 815-753-4405 .... 160 A
chenderson@niu.edu
HENDERSON, Cynthia .... 903-223-3053 .... 498 C
cynthia.henderson@tamut.edu
HENDERSON, Cynthia, L .... 202-884-1723 .... 98 B
cynthia.henderson@howard.edu
HENDERSON, Cynthia, M .... 814-886-6396 .... 437 A
chenderson@mtaloy.edu
HENDERSON, Darren .... 219-473-4346 .... 170 D
dhenderson@ccsj.edu
HENDERSON, Dee .... 731-424-3520 .... 475 B
dhenderson@jscc.edu
HENDERSON, Dianna .... 913-360-7386 .... 190 F
diannah@benedictine.edu
HENDERSON, Dorothy .... 850-599-3805 .... 118 G
dorothy.henderson@famu.edu
HENDERSON, Drew .... 606-783-2068 .... 204 E
d.henderson@moreheadstate.edu
HENDERSON, Eddie, W .... 806-651-2600 .... 498 D
ehenderson@mail.wtamu.edu
HENDERSON, Eric .... 928-524-7350 .... 17 B
eric.henderson@npc.edu
HENDERSON, Ernie .... 678-839-6582 .... 138 D
ehenders@westga.edu
HENDERSON, Floyd .... 843-525-8271 .... 461 E
fhenderson@tcl.edu
HENDERSON, George, A .... 252-257-1900 .... 374 D
henderson@vgcc.edu
HENDERSON, Gregg .... 626-395-4701 .... 32 E
gregg.henderson@caltech.edu
HENDERSON, Harlan .... 937-376-6304 .... 386 H
hhenderson@centralstate.edu
HENDERSON, Howard .... 580-349-1380 .... 410 B
howardh@opsu.edu
HENDERSON, Jacqueline .... 256-439-6831 .... 3 J
jhenderson@gadsdenstate.edu
HENDERSON, James .... 856-256-4175 .... 314 A
henderson@rowan.edu
HENDERSON, James, B .... 318-678-6000 .... 209 J
jhenderson@bpcc.edu
HENDERSON, James, P .... 323-343-2000 .... 35 B
jhender3@calstatela.edu
HENDERSON, Janet .... 706-754-7761 .... 134 E
jhenders@northgatech.edu
HENDERSON, Janice .... 850-729-5392 .... 114 A
hendersonj@nwfsc.edu
HENDERSON, Janice, W .... 850-729-5392 .... 114 A
hendersonj@nwfsc.edu
HENDERSON, Kristina, L .... 678-359-5221 .... 131 D
kristinah@gdn.edu
HENDERSON, Kyle, W .... 740-427-5729 .... 394 C
hendersonk@kenyon.edu
HENDERSON, Larry .... 252-638-7260 .... 369 E
hendersl@cravencc.edu
HENDERSON, Lennijo .... 972-238-6107 .... 485 C
lhenderson@dcccd.edu
HENDERSON, Lisle .... 718-636-3664 .... 346 D
lhenderson@pratt.edu
HENDERSON, Mantra .... 662-254-3495 .... 276 C
mlhenderson@mvsu.edu
HENDERSON, Mark .... 713-525-3155 .... 504 D
hendermk@stthom.edu
HENDERSON, Marsha, S .... 716-645-2920 .... 351 G
marsha@buffalo.edu
HENDERSON, Maureen, E .... 816-501-4063 .... 288 D
maureen.henderson@rockhurst.edu
HENDERSON, Melisha .... 219-473-4229 .... 170 D
mhenderson@ccsj.edu
HENDERSON, Michelle .... 760-252-2411 .... 30 F
mhenderson@barstow.edu
HENDERSON, Mitchell .... 718-482-5534 .... 328 C
mhenderson@lagcc.cuny.edu
HENDERSON, Nancy .... 319-296-2320 .... 185 C
nancy.henderson@hawkeyecollege.edu
HENDERSON, Necedah .... 256-233-8151 .... 1 F
necedah.henderson@athens.edu
HENDERSON, Pamela .... 251-460-6133 .... 9 E
phenderson@usouthal.edu
HENDERSON, Paul .... 207-602-2302 .... 220 H
phenderson@une.edu
HENDERSON, Roald .... 312-752-2120 .... 155 B
roald.henderson@kendall.edu
HENDERSON, Ron, R .... 618-235-2700 .... 165 B
ronald.henderson@swic.edu
HENDERSON, Sandra .... 205-929-6333 .... 5 E
shenderson@lawsonstate.edu
HENDERSON, Sean .... 559-265-5711 .... 72 A
sean.henderson@fresnocitycollege.edu
HENDERSON, Sherri .... 919-760-8139 .... 366 G
hendersh@meredith.edu
HENDERSON, Stanley, E .... 313-593-5151 .... 259 E
sehender@umich.edu
HENDERSON, Sue .... 718-997-5557 .... 328 F
sue.henderson@qc.cuny.edu
HENDERSON, Tammy .... 850-484-1766 .... 114 G
thenderson@pensacolastate.edu
HENDERSON, Thomas, W .... 601-974-1070 .... 275 D
hendetw@millsaps.edu
HENDERSON, Timothy, G .... 605-394-2371 .... 466 A
tim.henderson@sdsmt.edu
HENDERSON, Toni .... 910-296-2438 .... 371 B
thenderson@jamessprunt.edu
HENDERSON, Traci .... 270-843-6750 .... 199 G
thenderson@daymarcollege.edu
HENDERSON, Trennis .... 870-245-5206 .... 22 I
hendersont@obu.edu
HENDERSON, V, C .... 501-292-0582 .... 19 F
cortez.henderson@arkansasbaptist.edu
HENDERSON, Virginia .... 601-968-5903 .... 273 F
vhenderson@belhaven.edu
HENDLER, Catherine .... 269-965-3931 .... 253 H
hendlerc@kellogg.edu
HENDLEY, W. Clark .... 402-461-7346 .... 298 C
chendley@hastings.edu
HENDREY, Elizabeth .... 718-997-5441 .... 328 F
elizabeth.hendrey@qc.cuny.edu
HENDRICK, Amy, W .... 432-335-6417 .... 491 F
ahendrick@odessa.edu
HENDRICK, Larry .... 724-537-4555 .... 446 E
larry.hendrick@email.stvincent.edu
HENDRICK, Robert, B .... 215-503-3403 .... 448 B
robert.hendrick@jefferson.edu
HENDRICK, Ruth .... 540-857-6325 .... 528 E
rhendrick@virginiawestern.edu
HENDRICKS, Cindy .... 419-372-7341 .... 385 C
cindyg@bgsu.edu
HENDRICKS, Cynthia, L .... 651-696-6145 .... 265 A
chendric@macalester.edu
HENDRICKS, Daniel .... 219-989-2323 .... 178 G
daniel.hendricks@purduecal.edu
HENDRICKS, Denisha .... 502-597-6014 .... 203 D
denisha.hendricks@kysu.edu
HENDRICKS, J. Gary .... 254-867-4898 .... 499 I
gary.hendricks@systems.tstc.edu
HENDRICKS, Jeff .... 336-278-5580 .... 364 A
jhendrick4@elon.edu
HENDRICKS, Joan, C .... 215-898-8841 .... 448 I
vetdean@vet.upenn.edu
HENDRICKS, Joanne .... 703-812-4757 .... 520 E
jhendricks@leland.edu
HENDRICKS, Julie .... 805-965-0581 .... 68 B
hendrick@sbcc.edu
HENDRICKS, Laurie, M .... 515-574-1145 .... 185 F
hendricks@iowacentral.edu
HENDRICKS, Linda .... 865-974-8170 .... 477 A
Linda.Hendricks@tennessee.edu
HENDRICKS, Mark, S .... 512-245-2925 .... 501 C
mh06@txstate.edu
HENDRICKS, Martha, S .... 937-382-6661 .... 405 H
martha_hendricks@wilmington.edu
HENDRICKS, Michael .... 202-319-5305 .... 97 C
hendricks@cua.edu
HENDRICKS, Michelle .... 515-294-7971 .... 182 B
mh2@iastate.edu
HENDRICKS, Nancy .... 956-364-4708 .... 499 J
nancy.henricks@harlingen.tstc.edu
HENDRICKS, Paul .... 623-682-8660 .... 11 H
paul.hendricks@arizonachristian.edu
HENDRICKS, Randy .... 678-839-5450 .... 138 D
rhendric@westga.edu
HENDRICKS, Steve .... 808-236-5809 .... 140 B
shendricks@hpu.edu
HENDRICKS, Sylvia .... 520-383-8401 .... 18 L
shendricks@tocc.cc.az.us
HENDRICKSON, Anthony .... 402-280-2852 .... 297 H
anthonyhendrickson@creighton.edu
HENDRICKSON, Avis, D .... 203-332-5183 .... 90 B
ahendrickson@hcc.commnet.edu
HENDRICKSON, Charles .... 575-624-8379 .... 319 C
hendrick@nmmi.edu
HENDRICKSON, Jennifer .... 678-717-3648 .... 129 D
jhendrickson@gsc.edu
HENDRICKSON, John .... 651-793-1818 .... 267 D
john.hendrickson@metrostate.edu
HENDRICKSON, John, E .... 408-741-2011 .... 77 K
john_hendrickson@wvm.edu
HENDRICKSON, Karen .... 701-231-8356 .... 381 H
karen.hendrickson@ndsu.edu
HENDRICKSON, Kristine .... 401-341-2148 .... 454 D
hendrick@salve.edu
HENDRICKSON, Mark, R .... 715-874-4601 .... 553 F
mhendrickson@cvtc.edu
HENDRICKSON, Mary .... 717-262-2018 .... 452 B
mhendrickson@wilson.edu
HENDRICKSON, Philip .... 402-643-7358 .... 297 F
philip.hendrickson@cune.edu
HENDRICKSON,
Robert, M .... 612-436-7524 .... 265 G
rhendrickson@msbcollege.edu
HENDRICKSON, Sandy .... 425-889-5232 .... 535 I
sandy.hendrickson@northwestu.edu
HENDRICKSON,
Sherell, D .... 850-474-2116 .... 121 C
shendric@uwf.edu
HENDRICKSON, Vicki, A .... 918-631-2526 .... 413 F
vicki-hendrickson@utulsa.edu
HENDRIKSMA, Jane, E .... 616-526-6116 .... 249 E
jhendrik@calvin.edu
HENDRIX, Andrew .... 803-641-3490 .... 462 B
andrewh@usca.edu
HENDRIX, Beverly .... 301-624-2711 .... 222 G
bhendrix@frederick.edu
HENDRIX, Frances .... 405-733-7394 .... 411 I
fhendrix@rose.edu
HENDRIX, Phillip, E .... 336-758-5998 .... 380 B
hendriep@wfu.edu
HENDRIX, Richard .... 201-200-3409 .... 312 B
rhendrix@njcu.edu
HENDRIX, Sarah .... 606-546-1318 .... 206 F
HENDRY, Christopher .... 508-626-4578 .... 238 D
chendry@framingham.edu
HENDRY, Daryle .... 915-831-2580 .... 486 E
dhendry@epcc.edu

HENDRYX, Julie, A .... 260-359-4200.... 172 K
jhendryx@huntington.edu
HENDZEL, Theodore .... 715-232-2190.... 552 C
hendzelt@uwstout.edu
HENEGAR, Kellie .... 618-545-3025.... 155 A
khenegar@kaskaskia.edu
HENERY, Vicki .... 567-661-7172.... 400 H
vicki_henery@owens.edu
HENFER, Marsha .... 608-263-6012.... 552 F
marsha.henfer@uwc.edu
HENFEY, John, M .... 610-660-1164.... 446 C
jhenfey@sju.edu
HENGEL, Crystal, L .... 619-239-0391...... 37 D
chengel@cwsl.edu
HENGEL, Madeline .... 612-375-1900.... 264 F
mhengel@ipr.edu
HENGST, Dianne, P .... 210-458-4157.... 506 B
dianne.hengst@utsa.edu
HENGSTERMAN, Stacey .... 518-320-1148.... 351 D
stacey.hengsterman@suny.edu
HENICK, Steven, T .... 410-777-2429.... 221 B
sthenick@aacc.edu
HENIK, John .... 319-398-5518.... 186 H
jhenik@kirkwood.edu
HENK, William, A .... 414-288-7376.... 548 D
william.henk@marquette.edu
HENKE, Donald .... 314-792-6304.... 283 K
henke@kenrick.edu
HENKE, Donald, E .... 314-792-6111.... 283 K
henke@kenrick.edu
HENKE, Elizabeth .... 734-995-7461.... 250 B
henkee@cuaa.edu
HENKE, Holger .... 718-262-5338.... 329 B
hhenke@york.cuny.edu
HENKEL, David .... 805-969-3626...... 60 K
dhenkel@pacifica.edu
HENKEL, Scott .... 612-977-5410.... 262 A
scott.henkel@capella.edu
HENKEL-JOHNSON,
Gerald .... 218-723-6023.... 262 I
gjohnson@css.edu
HENKEN, Marla .... 208-426-1979.... 142 F
marlahenken@boisestate.edu
HENKES, Jonathan, M .... 605-274-5521.... 463 H
jonathan.henkes@augie.edu
HENLEY, Barbara .... 312-996-7654.... 166 F
bhenley@uic.edu
HENLEY, Blair .... 423-636-7300.... 476 F
HENLEY, Brian, L .... 541-346-1289.... 419 B
bhenley@uoregon.edu
HENLEY, Keldon .... 870-245-5220...... 22 I
henleyk@obu.edu
HENLEY, Marilynn, D .... 602-614-2337...... 11 C
HENLEY, Marsia .... 215-751-8902.... 426 B
mhenley@ccp.edu
HENLINE, Branden, H .... 928-541-7777...... 16 I
bhenline@ncu.edu
HENNARD, Cynthia .... 802-635-1424.... 515 E
cynthia.hennard@jsc.edu
HENNEN, Jack .... 513-562-8769.... 384 A
jhennen@artacademy.edu
HENNES, Doug, E .... 651-962-6402.... 272 E
dehennes@stthomas.edu
HENNESSEY, Brendan .... 808-974-7333.... 141 A
brendanh@hawaii.edu
HENNESSEY, David .... 617-243-2478.... 236 F
dhennessey@lasell.edu
HENNESSEY, Patrick .... 914-606-6638.... 360 D
patrick.hennessey@sunywcc.edu
HENNESSEY, Richard .... 203-332-5079...... 90 B
rhennessey@hcc.commnet.edu
HENNESSEY, JR., Thomas 703-993-8703.... 519 A
thenness@gmu.edu
HENNESSY, Andrea .... 845-675-4414.... 344 G
andrea.hennessy@nyack.edu
HENNESSY, Catherine .... 516-463-6820.... 335 H
catherine.hennessy@hofstra.edu
HENNESSY, James .... 212-636-6470.... 334 C
hennessy@fordham.edu
HENNESSY, John, L .... 650-723-2481...... 71 F
hennessy@stanford.edu
HENNESSY, Michael .... 512-245-2317.... 501 C
mh17@txstate.edu
HENNIG, Gloria .... 402-643-7270.... 297 F
finaid@cune.edu
HENNIG, Kathy .... 415-487-2413...... 39 H
khenning@ccsf.edu
HENNIGAN, Paul .... 412-392-3990.... 444 H
phennigan@pointpark.edu
HENNIGES, Amy .... 920-465-2380.... 551 A
hennigea@uwgb.edu
HENNING, Amy .... 215-895-1415.... 427 G
amyh@drexel.edu
HENNING, Arnold .... 847-866-3920.... 151 B
arnold.henning@garrett.edu
HENNING, Brenda .... 575-492-2111.... 321 H
bhenning@usw.edu
HENNING, Cindy .... 706-507-8774.... 127 D
henning_cindy@columbusstate.edu
HENNING, Florence .... 330-369-3200.... 402 H
tbcmail@tbc-trumbullbusiness.com
HENNING, Kent, L .... 515-263-2802.... 184 I
khenning@grandview.edu
HENNING, Patti .... 906-786-5802.... 249 D
henningp@baycollege.edu
HENNING, Paul .... 602-944-3335...... 11 D
phenning@aicag.edu
HENNING, Richard .... 631-423-0483.... 350 G
rhenning@icseminary.edu
HENNING, Volker .... 423-236-2912.... 473 A
henning@southern.edu
HENNINGER, Edward, A .... 570-326-3761.... 440 K
ehenninger@pct.edu
HENNINGER, Frank, L .... 610-519-4160.... 450 G
frank.henninger@villanova.edu
HENNINGSEN, James .... 407-708-2270.... 117 G
henningj@seminolestate.edu
HENNIS, Anne, R .... 336-386-3451.... 374 B
hennisa@surry.edu
HENRICH, William, L .... 210-567-2050.... 506 E
henrich@uthscsa.edu
HENRICHS, Susan, M .... 907-474-7096...... 10 J
smhenrichs@alaska.edu
HENRICKS, Vern .... 785-539-3571.... 194 G
vhenricks@mccks.edu
HENRICKSEN, Richard, C .. 727-376-6911.... 122 B
rhenricksen@trinitycollege.edu
HENRICKSON, Gary .... 218-736-1506.... 267 G
gary.henrickson@minnesota.edu
HENRICKSON, Jay, A .... 701-788-4899.... 381 F
Jay.Henrickson@mayvillestate.edu
HENRICKSON, R. Paul ...... 540-375-2300.... 523 D
henricks@roanoke.edu
HENRIE, Kimberly .... 801-957-4782.... 512 C
kimberly.henrie@slcc.edu
HENRIE, Lynda, D .... 801-524-8136.... 510 A
lhenrie@ldsbc.edu
HENRIE, M. Elaine .... 620-341-5211.... 192 D
ehenrie@emporia.edu
HENRIE, M. Elaine .... 620-341-5457.... 192 D
ehenrie@emporia.edu
HENRIKSEN, Deb .... 605-642-6581.... 465 F
deb.henriksen@bhsu.edu
HENRIKSON, Bruce .... 217-351-2435.... 161 B
bhenrikson@parkland.edu
HENRIS, Dan .... 989-463-7144.... 247 F
henris@alma.edu
HENRISS, Silvia, H .... 330-287-1253.... 399 A
henriss.1@osu.edu
HENRY, Alanna, L .... 423-478-7705.... 472 F
ahenry@ptseminary.edu
HENRY, Alison .... 609-652-4831.... 313 F
alison.henry@stockton.edu
HENRY, Amy .... 404-894-7475.... 130 D
amy.henry@oie.gatech.edu
HENRY, April .... 620-654-2416.... 190 A
henry@allencc.edu
HENRY, Barbara .... 404-364-8476.... 135 A
bhenry@oglethorpe.edu
HENRY, Barbara, L .... 419-372-4825.... 385 C
bhenry@bgsu.edu
HENRY, Bill .... 559-791-2459...... 53 A
bhenry@portervillecollege.edu
HENRY, Carol, A .... 618-453-3336.... 164 I
cahenry@siu.edu
HENRY, Carole .... 757-683-4283.... 521 L
cshenry@odu.edu
HENRY, Charles, E .... 713-313-4343.... 499 G
henryce@tsu.edu
HENRY, Deena, H .... 919-209-2017.... 371 C
dhhenry@johnstoncc.edu
HENRY, Dolph .... 865-981-8141.... 470 F
dolph.henry@maryvillecollege.edu
HENRY, Donna Price .... 239-590-7156.... 119 A
dhenry@fgcu.edu
HENRY, Frank .... 406-395-4313.... 296 G
fghenry_9@hotmail.com
HENRY, Jamie .... 618-544-8657.... 152 G
henryj@iecc.edu
HENRY, Janis .... 404-965-6504.... 124 B
jhenry@aiuniv.edu
HENRY, Jeffery .... 406-395-4875.... 296 G
jhenry@stonechild.edu
HENRY, Jennifer .... 314-529-9552.... 284 F
jhenry@maryville.edu
HENRY, Jerry .... 903-223-3012.... 498 C
jerry.henry@tamut.edu
HENRY, Jon .... 207-621-3000.... 220 B
jhenry@maine.edu
HENRY, Jonathan .... 727-726-1153.... 103 B
jonathanhenry@clearwater.edu
HENRY, Keith .... 323-660-6166...... 40 G
keith.henry@cleveland.edu
HENRY, Kelly, K .... 585-292-5627.... 325 C
kkhenry@bryantstratton.edu
HENRY, Kelly, K .... 585-292-5627.... 325 D
kkhenry@bryantstratton.edu
HENRY, Kevin, C .... 717-866-5775.... 428 I
khenry@evangelical.edu
HENRY, Kim .... 318-676-7811.... 211 H
ksnider@nwltc.edu
HENRY, Kim .... 712-325-3445.... 186 B
khenry@iwcc.edu
HENRY, Larry .... 701-477-7862.... 383 C
lhenry@tm.edu
HENRY, Linda .... 913-360-7500.... 190 F
lhenry@benedictine.edu
HENRY, Marci .... 970-521-6617...... 86 E
marci.henry@njc.edu
HENRY, Margaret .... 303-871-3740...... 88 E
mhenry@du.edu
HENRY, Margaret Rose ...... 302-888-5284...... 96 C
mrhenry@dtcc.edu
HENRY, Matthew .... 903-233-3510.... 489 K
MatthewHenry@letu.edu
HENRY, Melanie .... 985-380-2436.... 211 K
mhenry@ltc.edu
HENRY, Melody .... 903-434-8148.... 491 D
mhenry@ntcc.edu
HENRY, Melody .... 406-395-4313.... 296 G
mrbhenry@hotmail.com
HENRY, Neil .... 510-642-5999...... 73 E
nhenry@berkeley.edu
HENRY, Nick .... 706-272-4435.... 127 G
nhenry@daltonstate.edu
HENRY, Patrick, J .... 304-336-8250.... 544 B
phenry@westliberty.edu
HENRY, Philip, W .... 717-477-1481.... 443 D
pwhenr@ship.edu
HENRY, Rachel .... 802-258-3111.... 514 C
rachel.henry@worldlearning.org
HENRY, Raylean .... 615-366-3917.... 473 C
raylean.henry@tbr.edu
HENRY, Rita .... 402-554-2779.... 301 B
rhenry@unomaha.edu
HENRY, Robert, H .... 405-208-5032.... 410 A
rhenry@okcu.edu
HENRY, Ronnie .... 229-317-6700.... 128 A
ronnie.henry@darton.edu
HENRY, Ronnie, A .... 229-317-6700.... 128 A
ronnie.henry@darton.edu
HENRY, Shannon, B .... 336-750-2020.... 380 A
henrysb@wssu.edu
HENRY, Stephen, S .... 406-243-5455.... 295 A
stephen.henry@umontana.edu
HENRY, Susan, P .... 802-865-4422.... 515 D
henrys@ccv.edu
HENRY, TOR, Terence .... 740-283-6216.... 390 M
thenry@franciscan.edu
HENRY, Terrance .... 419-289-5565.... 384 D
thenry@ashland.edu
HENRY, Veronica .... 631-420-2622.... 356 A
veronica.henry@farmingdale.edu
HENRY-CROWE, Susan ...... 404-727-6226.... 129 A
shenryc@emory.edu
HENRY-MITCHELL, Kim ...... 856-691-8600.... 309 C
kmitchell@cccnj.edu
HENRY-QUINN, Barbara ... 877-442-0505...... 88 G
barbara.henry-quinn@rockies.edu
HENRY ROBINSON,
Shanelle .... 914-773-3775.... 345 F
shenryrobinson@pace.edu
HENRY-SATURNE, Bordes . 978-368-2201.... 230 F
bordes.henry-saturne@auc.edu
HENSAL, Nathan .... 815-599-3599.... 152 A
nathan.hensal@highland.edu
HENSCHEL, Paul, D .... 440-525-7060.... 394 F
phenschel@lakelandcc.edu
HENSEL, Chester .... 610-876-7300.... 451 F
cahensel@widener.edu
HENSEY, Richard .... 773-256-0784.... 157 B
rhensey@lstc.edu
HENSGEN, Brian, C .... 217-442-3044.... 148 E
bhensgen@dacc.edu
HENSHAW, Debbie .... 706-649-1888.... 127 E
dhenshaw@columbustech.edu
HENSHAW, Rodney, N .... 515-271-3993.... 184 A
rod.henshaw@drake.edu
HENSLER, Douglas, A .... 316-978-3200.... 197 F
doug.hensler@wichita.edu
HENSLEY, Bridgette, C .... 608-785-8073.... 551 B
hensley.brid@uwlax.edu
HENSLEY, Ella .... 606-546-1323.... 206 F
ehensley@unionky.edu
HENSLEY, Frances, S .... 304-696-6690.... 543 G
hensleyf@marshall.edu
HENSLEY, Kimberly, S .... 815-753-8494.... 160 A
khensley@niu.edu
HENSLEY, Mary .... 512-223-7618.... 481 B
mhensley@austincc.edu
HENSLEY, Michele, R .... 540-432-4139.... 518 E
michele.hensley@emu.edu
HENSLEY, Mike .... 704-216-3651.... 373 C
mike.hensley@rccc.edu
HENSLEY, Ron .... 417-255-7255.... 286 G
ronhensley@missouristate.edu
HENSLEY, Sarah, L .... 304-367-4692.... 542 I
Sarah.Hensley@pierpont.edu
HENSLEY, Scott .... 580-745-3198.... 412 C
shensley@se.edu
HENSLEY, Shane .... 810-989-2107.... 249 B
shane.hensley@baker.edu
HENSLEY, Stephen, W .... 304-696-2269.... 543 G
hensley@marshall.edu
HENSLEY, Wanda, F .... 501-977-2028...... 25 G
hensley@uaccm.edu
HENSON, Aprella .... 803-376-5802.... 455 B
ahenson@allenuniversity.edu
HENSON, Brandi .... 405-682-1611.... 409 F
bhenson@occc.edu
HENSON, Emily .... 618-252-5400.... 164 G
emily.henson@sic.edu
HENSON, Greg .... 630-705-8250.... 160 B
ghenson@seminary.edu
HENSON, Jena .... 312-752-2182.... 155 B
jena.henson@kendall.edu
HENSON, Kevin .... 650-574-6581...... 67 F
hensonk@smccd.edu
HENSON, Mark .... 618-985-3741.... 154 E
markhenson@jalc.edu
HENSON, Michael, C .... 219-989-2468.... 178 G
henson@purduecal.edu
HENSON, Pamella, A .... 314-935-5277.... 292 J
hensonp@wustl.edu
HENSON, Scott .... 706-721-4416.... 130 B
shenson@georgiahealth.edu
HENSON, Travis .... 618-545-3177.... 155 A
thenson@kaskaskia.edu
HENSON-WILLIAMS,
Paula .... 253-864-3229.... 536 C
phenson@pierce.ctc.edu
HENSRUD, Faith, C .... 715-394-8455.... 552 D
fhensrud@uwsuper.edu
HENSS, Mark .... 217-206-7796.... 167 A
henss.mark@uis.edu
HENTHORN, Janet .... 312-235-3507.... 164 D
j.henthorn@shimer.edu
HENTHORNE, Michael .... 541-737-2416.... 418 F
michael.henthorne@oregonstate.edu
HENTON, June, M .... 334-844-4790........ 1 G
hentoju@auburn.edu
HENTSCHEL, Alain, R .... 386-312-4302.... 116 D
alainhentschel@sjrstate.edu
HENTZ, Herbert, E .... 413-775-1809.... 240 B
hentz@gcc.mass.edu
HENZEL, JR., John, R .... 706-245-7226.... 128 K
jhenzel@ec.edu
HENZY, John .... 856-415-2106.... 310 E
jhenzy@gccnj.edu
HEO, Chan .... 714-517-1945...... 30 G
HEOS, Pamela .... 517-371-5140.... 259 B
heosp@cooley.edu
HEPBURN, Deborah .... 724-832-1050.... 448 E
dhepburn@triangle-tech.edu
HEPBURN, Deborah, G .... 814-371-2090.... 448 F
dhepburn@triangle-tech.edu
HEPBURN, Deborah, G .... 814-371-2090.... 448 E
dhepburn@triangle-tech.edu
HEPBURN, Valerie .... 912-279-5705.... 127 B
president@ccga.edu
HEPERI, Vernon, L .... 801-422-2731.... 509 D
vernon_heperi@byu.edu
HEPLER, Lisa, L .... 814-393-2229.... 442 A
lhepler@clarion.edu
HEPLER, Meghan, E .... 570-321-4231.... 435 D
hepler@lycoming.edu
HEPNER, Mickey .... 405-974-2809.... 413 B
mhepner@ucok.edu
HEPPNER, Angela .... 417-624-7070.... 284 G
aheppner@messengercollege.edu
HEPPNER, Harold, H .... 406-353-2607.... 294 E
hheppner@mail.fbcc.edu
HEPPNER, Keith .... 956-380-8171.... 493 A
kheppner@riogrande.edu
HERALD, John .... 606-886-3863.... 201 C
john.herald@kctcs.edu
HERB, Amanda, K .... 740-374-8716.... 405 F
aherb@wscc.edu
HERBERT, Derek .... 970-521-6714...... 86 E
derek.herbert@njc.edu
HERBERT, George, E .... 319-335-3179.... 182 C
george-herbert@uiowa.edu
HERBERT, Jim .... 678-915-6824.... 137 C
jherbert@spsu.edu
HERBERT, Mike .... 541-888-7705.... 420 C
mherbert@socc.edu
HERBERT, Nancy .... 870-633-4480...... 21 F
nherbert@eacc.edu
HERBERT-ASHTON,
Marilyn, J .... 540-857-6372.... 528 E
mherbert-ashton@virginiawestern.edu
HERBERTZ, Anita .... 317-955-6021.... 177 G
aherbertz@marian.edu
HERBKERSMAN, Neil .... 937-512-2524.... 401 J
neil.herbkersman@sinclair.edu
HERBRAND, Laurie .... 209-228-2741...... 74 B
LHerbrand@UCMerced.edu
HERBST, Chet .... 208-792-2240.... 143 F
cgherbst@lcsc.edu
HERBST, Daniel .... 480-732-7120...... 15 G
daniel.herbst@cgcmail.maricopa.edu
HERBST, Gordon, J .... 814-732-2585.... 442 D
herbst@edinboro.edu
HERBST, Jeffrey .... 315-228-7444.... 329 H
jherbst@colgate.edu
HERBST, John, H .... 859-257-5781.... 206 H
herbst@uky.edu
HERBST, Susan .... 404-656-2274.... 138 E
susan.herbst@usg.edu
HERBST, Susan .... 860-486-2337...... 94 E
president@uconn.edu
HERBST, Susan .... 860-486-2337...... 94 F
president@uconn.edu
HERCHMER, Janice .... 716-896-0700.... 359 F
jherchmer@villa.edu
HERDEGEN, III, Robert, T 434-223-6112.... 519 B
rherdegen@hsc.edu

HERDLICK, Michael .... 419-448-3582.... 402 E
herdlickm@tiffin.edu
HEREDIA, Deborah .... 706-771-4027.... 125 D
dheredia@augustatech.edu
HEREFORD, Taylor .... 912-449-7510.... 138 G
thereford@waycross.edu
HERENCIA, Ada .... 787-844-8181.... 567 E
ada.herencia@upr.edu
HERENDEEN, Steve, A ...... 260-422-5561.... 172 L
saherendeen@indianatech.edu
HERGAN, Mark, J .... 443-352-4400.... 226 E
mhergan@stevenson.edu
HERGENROTHER,
Diane, S .... 718-990-1428.... 348 G
hergenrd@stjohns.edu
HERGERT, Erin .... 719-549-3226...... 87 B
erin.hergert@pueblocc.edu
HERGERT, Travis, J .... 641-422-4990.... 187 F
HERGOTT, Lori .... 402-461-7370.... 298 C
lhergott@hastings.edu
HERING, Leendert, R .... 619-260-5998...... 76 A
lrhering@sandiego.edu
HERINGER, David, L .... 870-307-7290...... 22 D
david.heringer@lyon.edu
HERKINOS, Tone .... 692-625-4803.... 559 E
HERLEMAN, Karl .... 305-237-0244.... 113 H
kherlema@mdc.edu
HERLIHY, James, E .... 205-665-6600........ 9 C
herlihyj@montevallo.edu
HERLIHY, Joseph, M .... 617-552-2855.... 232 D
joseph.herlihy.1@bc.edu
HERLITZKE, Mary Ann .... 608-789-6080.... 555 D
herlitzkem@westerntc.edu
HERMAN, Amber .... 336-838-6292.... 375 A
amber.herman@wilkescc.edu
HERMAN, Anne .... 503-352-2777.... 419 E
hermana@pacificu.edu
HERMAN, Arthur .... 724-459-9500.... 452 D
HERMAN, Barbara, B .... 817-257-7855.... 498 F
b.herman@tcu.edu
HERMAN, Brian, A .... 210-567-0397.... 506 E
hermanb@uthscsa.edu
HERMAN, Catherine .... 518-956-8151.... 351 E
cherman@uamail.albany.edu
HERMAN, David, E .... 716-673-3271.... 352 A
david.herman@fredonia.edu
HERMAN, Debbie .... 713-743-1000.... 503 B
daherman@central.uh.edu
HERMAN, Florence .... 732-729-3834.... 309 D
fherman@devry.edu
HERMAN, Fran .... 248-414-6900.... 255 B
fherman@mji.edu
HERMAN, Harvey .... 605-856-5880.... 465 A
harvey.herman@sintegleska.edu
HERMAN, Janet .... 260-471-7667.... 172 C
janet.herman@harrison.edu
HERMAN, Janet .... 618-842-3711.... 152 F
hermanj@iecc.edu
HERMAN, Jeanne .... 330-941-2264.... 406 F
jmherman@ysu.edu
HERMAN, Jennifer .... 719-296-6106...... 87 B
jennifer.herman@pueblocc.edu
HERMAN, Jennifer .... 716-286-8186.... 344 D
jherman@niagara.edu
HERMAN, Karen, D .... 507-538-0162.... 262 D
herman.karen@mayo.edu
HERMAN, Rick .... 951-222-8384...... 64 B
rick.herman@rcc.edu
HERMAN, Sharon, S .... 816-654-7177.... 283 J
sherman@kcumb.edu
HERMAN-BARLOW, Janet . 440-365-5222.... 395 C
HERMANCE, Patricia .... 302-736-0403...... 96 G
hermance@ccs.k12.de.us
HERMANO, Mara .... 401-454-6336.... 454 B
mhermano@risd.edu
HERMANSEN, Beckie .... 435-283-7346.... 512 B
beckie.hermansen@snow.edu
HERMANSON, Dean, E ...... 480-423-6390...... 16 D
dean.hermanson@sccmail.maricopa.edu
HERMANSON, Fran .... 509-335-4553.... 539 A
franherm@wsu.edu
HERMANSON, Steve .... 605-668-1500.... 464 F
shermanson@mtmc.edu
HERMES, John .... 405-425-1815.... 409 E
john.hermes@oc.edu
HERMES, Joseph .... 312-996-3490.... 166 F
jhermes@uic.edu
HERMES, Wayne, J .... 970-247-7432...... 84 G
hermes_w@fortlewis.edu
HERMON, Vada .... 620-227-9213.... 192 B
vhermon@dc3.edu
HERMOSILLO, Gilbert .... 760-757-2121...... 57 E
ghermosillo@miracosta.edu
HERMSEN, Albert, G .... 313-577-4982.... 260 D
ahermsen@wayne.edu
HERMSEN, Cindy, L .... 248-370-3370.... 257 C
hermsen@oakland.edu
HERNÁNDEZ-CRUZ,
Carmen .... 787-850-0000.... 566 D
carmen.hernandez1@upr.edu
HERN, Marcia, J .... 502-852-8300.... 207 A
m.hern@louisville.edu
HERNANDEZ, Abraham ..... 956-882-8281.... 505 C
abraham.hernandez@utb.edu
HERNANDEZ, Albert .... 303-765-3183...... 84 K
ahernandez@iliff.edu
HERNANDEZ, Alex .... 915-831-6383.... 486 F
aherna78@epcc.edu
HERNANDEZ, Ana .... 305-666-9242.... 103 A
ahernandez@citycollege.edu
HERNANDEZ, Ana .... 813-974-4041.... 120 D
ahernandez@usf.edu
HERNANDEZ, Ana .... 787-764-0000.... 567 F
HERNANDEZ, Annette .... 717-560-8240.... 433 D
ahernandez@lbc.edu
HERNANDEZ, Arnold .... 208-459-5868.... 143 A
ahernandez@collegeofidaho.edu
HERNANDEZ, Arthur .... 361-825-2661.... 497 F
art.hernandez@tamucc.edu
HERNANDEZ, Axel, N .... 858-499-0202...... 41 E
ahernadez@coleman.edu
HERNANDEZ, Carlos .... 201-200-3111.... 312 B
chernandez@njcu.edu
HERNANDEZ, Carmen, H .. 787-850-9375.... 567 B
carmen.hernandez@upr.edu
HERNANDEZ, Christine ...... 916-558-2438...... 56 D
HERNANDEZ, Christine ...... 787-786-3030.... 560 E
chernandez@ucb.edu.pr
HERNANDEZ, Cristine .... 787-786-3030.... 560 E
chernandez@ucb.edu.pr
HERNANDEZ, David .... 805-565-6164...... 78 F
dhernand@westmont.edu
HERNANDEZ, Debora .... 787-250-8195.... 563 E
dhernandez@metro.inter.edu
HERNANDEZ, Dino, M ...... 248-204-2306.... 254 E
dhernande@ltu.edu
HERNANDEZ, Edwin .... 787-881-1212.... 564 I
edwin_hernandez@email.pucpr.edu
HERNANDEZ, Eliza .... 210-486-4913.... 479 C
ehernandez716@alamo.edu
HERNANDEZ, Felix .... 805-922-6966...... 26 K
fhernandez@hancockcollege.edu
HERNANDEZ, Francisco .... 787-840-8894.... 567 E
fhernandez@uprp.edu
HERNANDEZ, Francisco, J 808-956-3290.... 141 B
fjh@hawaii.edu
HERNANDEZ, Frank .... 847-214-7442.... 150 D
fhernandez@elgin.edu
HERNANDEZ, Grace .... 806-742-2121.... 501 D
grace.hernandez@ttu.edu
HERNANDEZ, Harry .... 787-738-2161.... 567 A
harry.hernandez2@upr.edu
HERNANDEZ, Ivan .... 765-269-5253.... 176 B
ihernand@ivytech.edu
HERNANDEZ, Jean .... 425-640-1515.... 533 E
jean.hernandez@edcc.edu
HERNANDEZ, Jelenny .... 305-821-3333.... 109 A
jhernandez@mm.fnc.edu
HERNANDEZ, Jocceline .... 818-386-5632...... 62 F
jhernandez@pgi.edu
HERNANDEZ, John .... 714-628-4886...... 63 G
hernandez_john@sccollege.edu
HERNANDEZ, John .... 212-678-3379.... 357 F
jlh2172@tc.columbia.edu
HERNANDEZ, Jorge .... 808-739-4640.... 140 A
jhernand@chaminade.edu
HERNANDEZ, Josephine ... 973-341-1600.... 312 E
hernandez@pccc.edu
HERNANDEZ, Juan .... 787-257-7373.... 565 E
jhernandez@suagm.edu
HERNANDEZ, Juan Carlos 787-751-0160.... 561 G
jhernandez@cmpr.gobierno.pr
HERNANDEZ, Justin, J ..... 660-944-2851.... 280 F
justin@conception.edu
HERNANDEZ, Luz, S .... 787-620-2040.... 560 B
lhernandez@aupr.edu
HERNANDEZ, Magda .... 787-834-9595.... 565 J
magdah@uaa.edu
HERNANDEZ, Maria .... 715-422-5469.... 554 C
maria.hernandez@mstc.edu
HERNANDEZ, Maria .... 559-278-2182...... 34 D
maria_hernandez@csufresno.edu
HERNANDEZ, Maria .... 787-758-2525.... 567 D
maria.hernandez15@upr.edu
HERNANDEZ, Maribel .... 787-758-2525.... 567 D
maribel.hernandez1@upr.edu
HERNANDEZ, Marta .... 787-840-2955.... 560 F
mhernandez@caribbean.edu
HERNANDEZ, Michael .... 816-584-6379.... 287 H
michael.hernandez@park.edu
HERNANDEZ, Michelle .... 212-616-7278.... 335 D
michelle.hernandez@helenefuld.edu
HERNANDEZ, Noe .... 432-837-8603.... 501 B
noeh@sulross.edu
HERNANDEZ, Oscar .... 956-872-2522.... 494 D
oscarh@southtexascollege.edu
HERNANDEZ, Otto .... 606-343-4978.... 307 D
hernande@atlantic.edu
HERNANDEZ, JR., Paul .... 956-872-8372.... 494 D
phernan@southtexascollege.edu
HERNANDEZ, Paul, R .... 937-775-4001.... 406 C
paul.hernandez@wright.edu
HERNANDEZ, Raul .... 787-284-1912.... 563 F
rhernand@ponce.inter.edu
HERNANDEZ, Raul .... 787-746-1400.... 562 C
rahernandez@huertas.edu
HERNANDEZ, Richard .... 843-574-6350.... 461 G
richard.hernandez@tridenttech.edu
HERNANDEZ, Ruben .... 787-746-1400.... 562 C
rhernandez@huertas.edu
HERNANDEZ, Ruth, E .... 787-279-1912.... 563 B
rehernandez@bayamon.inter.edu
HERNANDEZ, Samuel .... 787-882-2065.... 565 I
asistencia_economica@unitecpr.net
HERNANDEZ, Sheila .... 831-582-3632...... 35 C
shernandez@csumb.edu
HERNANDEZ, Tracy .... 801-878-1035.... 303 D
thernandez@roseman.edu
HERNANDEZ, Victoria .... 305-237-3221.... 113 H
vhernand@mdc.edu
HERNANDEZ, Wanda .... 212-463-0400.... 357 J
wandau@touro.edu
HERNANDEZ, Wendie .... 254-659-7503.... 487 E
whernandez@hillcollege.edu
HERNANDEZ, Yezmin .... 787-728-1515.... 568 B
yhernandez@sagrado.edu
HERNANDEZ-HUNTER,
Anna .... 503-838-8195.... 419 C
hernana@wou.edu
HERNANDEZ LEE, Susan .. 409-740-4533.... 497 D
lees@tamug.edu
HERNANDEZ NUNEZ,
Maria, L .... 787-884-3838.... 560 C
directora_ejecutiva@atenascollege.edu
HERNDON, Godfrey .... 919-530-5063.... 378 A
gherndon@nccu.edu
HERNDON, Jim .... 602-978-7986...... 18 K
jim.herndon@thunderbird.edu
HERNDON, Joe .... 817-598-6283.... 508 C
jherndon@wc.edu
HERNDON, Kimmetha, D .. 205-726-2198........ 6 G
kherndon@samford.edu
HERNDON, OSB, Linda .... 913-360-7553.... 190 F
lherndon@benedictine.edu
HERNDON, Linda, M .... 229-226-1621.... 137 F
lherndon@thomasu.edu
HERNDON, Michael .... 601-266-4131.... 278 A
michael.herndon@usm.edu
HERNDON, Steven, T .... 937-229-3317.... 404 A
Steve.Herndon@notes.udayton.edu
HERNEY, Susan .... 562-908-3445...... 63 H
sherney@riohondo.edu
HERNON, Michael .... 740-283-6447.... 390 M
mhernon@franciscan.edu
HEROLD, Brent .... 504-568-2412.... 213 A
bherol@lsuhsc.edu
HEROLD, Dale .... 802-387-6716.... 513 E
dherold@landmark.edu
HEROLD, Irene .... 603-358-2736.... 307 A
iherold@keene.edu
HEROLD, Paul, A .... 330-972-7873.... 403 B
BoardOffice@uakron.edu
HEROLD, Paul, A .... 330-972-7873.... 403 B
paulherold@uakron.edu
HERON, David .... 954-262-5291.... 114 B
heron@nsu.nova.edu
HERON-BURKE, Alice .... 516-686-7683.... 343 D
aburke@nyit.edu
HERPICH, Matt .... 803-641-3719.... 462 B
matth@usca.edu
HERR, Audrey .... 717-872-3263.... 443 C
audrey.herr@millersville.edu
HERR, Robert .... 443-352-4402.... 226 E
rherr@stevenson.edu
HERR-VALBURG, Melissa . 605-995-2600.... 464 B
meherr@dwu.edu
HERRELL, James .... 719-384-6884...... 86 F
james.herrell@ojc.edu
HERRELL, Jim .... 719-384-6884...... 86 F
jim.herrell@ojc.edu
HERREN, James .... 310-825-1633...... 74 A
jherren@ucpd.ucla.edu
HERREN, Melissa .... 405-945-3297.... 410 F
HERRERA, Cynthia .... 805-986-5944...... 77 C
cherrera@vcccd.edu
HERRERA, Jennifer .... 828-627-4507.... 370 G
jherrera@haywood.edu
HERRERA, LaNae .... 909-447-2504...... 40 E
lherrera@cst.edu
HERRERA, Rick .... 956-364-4052.... 499 I
Rck.Herrera@harlingen.tstc.edu
HERRERA, Rick .... 956-364-4052.... 499 J
rick.herrera@systems.edu
HERRERA LINDSTROM,
Cynthia, E .... 312-413-2495.... 166 F
cynthiar@uic.edu
HERRERA-SOBEK, Maria ... 805-893-5114...... 74 F
maria.sobek@evc.ucsb.edu
HERRICK, Amy .... 312-752-2192.... 155 B
amy.herrick@kendall.edu
HERRICK, Bryan, D .... 636-797-3000.... 283 H
bherrick@jeffco.edu
HERRICK, Carol, A .... 978-867-4208.... 235 E
carol.herrick@gordon.edu
HERRICK, James, S .... 619-594-2586...... 36 E
herrick1@mail.sdsu.edu
HERRICK, Laura .... 704-463-3439.... 375 E
laura.herrick@fsmail.pfeiffer.edu
HERRICK, P. Douglas ...... 215-503-0264.... 448 B
doug.herrick@jefferson.edu
HERRIDGE, Bart .... 325-674-2300.... 478 H
bart.herridge@acu.edu
HERRIN, Andraea .... 803-780-1189.... 463 B
adoctor@voorhees.edu
HERRIN, Brice .... 229-732-5980.... 124 C
briceherrin@andrewcollege.edu
HERRIN, Jodi .... 843-521-4137.... 462 C
herrinj@uscb.edu
HERRIN, Mark .... 405-974-3141.... 413 B
mherrin@ucok.edu
HERRIN, Mary, L .... 316-978-3030.... 197 F
mary.herrin@wichita.edu
HERRIN, Scott .... 619-660-4505...... 48 J
scott.herrin@gcccd.edu
HERRIN, Timothy, D .... 704-233-8150.... 380 D
herrin@wingate.edu
HERRING, Carol, P .... 848-932-7890.... 314 B
cherring@winants.rutgers.edu
HERRING, Cassandra .... 757-727-5773.... 519 C
cassandra.herring@hamptonu.edu
HERRING, Clyde .... 865-471-3316.... 467 E
clherring@cn.edu
HERRING, Donald, R .... 910-938-6236.... 369 C
herringd@coastalcarolina.edu
HERRING, George .... 972-860-4634.... 484 F
gtherring@dcccd.edu
HERRING, Jack .... 928-350-2000...... 18 C
jherring@prescott.edu
HERRING, Jayne .... 262-564-3092.... 553 H
herringj@gtc.edu
HERRING, Jimmy, G .... 706-880-8237.... 132 I
jherring@lagrange.edu
HERRING, Mark, Y .... 803-323-2232.... 463 D
herringm@winthrop.edu
HERRING, Trellie .... 919-735-5151.... 374 F
wcc-bookstore@waynecc.edu
HERRINGER, Gretchen .... 315-228-7676.... 329 H
gherringer@colgate.edu
HERRINGTON, Glenda .... 936-468-2304.... 495 H
gherrington@sfasu.edu
HERRINGTON, Jere .... 662-562-3214.... 276 E
recruiting@northwestms.edu
HERRINGTON, Katie .... 601-477-4087.... 275 B
katie.herrington@jcjc.edu
HERRINGTON, Laurie .... 912-443-5519.... 136 D
lherrington@savannahtech.edu
HERRINGTON, William ...... 434-848-1852.... 523 G
wherrington@saintpauls.edu
HERRINGTON-HALL, Glen 651-255-6107.... 271 I
gherrington-hall@unitedseminary.edu
HERRINTON, Thomas, R ... 619-260-4553...... 76 A
herrinton@sandiegoe.edu
HERRITY, Andrew, K .... 951-343-4574...... 31 G
aherrity@calbaptist.edu
HERRLING, John, R .... 732-906-2548.... 311 E
jherrling@middlesexcc.edu
HERRLINGER, Timothy, J .. 610-799-1711.... 434 D
therrlinger@lccc.edu
HERRMANN, Anthony .... 914-323-5406.... 340 A
anthony.herrmann@mville.edu
HERRMANN, Bryan .... 320-589-6038.... 272 C
herrmanb@morris.umn.edu
HERRMANN, Jane .... 618-545-3220.... 155 A
jherrmann@kaskaskia.edu
HERRMANN, Jane .... 515-965-7130.... 183 E
jmherrmann@dmacc.edu
HERRMANN, John, L .... 740-284-5215.... 390 M
jherrmann@franciscan.edu
HERRMANN, Linda .... 815-753-9762.... 160 A
lherrmann@niu.edu
HERRMANN, Marilyn, M ... 909-558-4517...... 54 D
mherrmann@llu.edu
HERRMANN, Mark .... 907-474-7116...... 10 J
mlherrmann@alaska.edu
HERRMANN, Nira .... 212-346-1517.... 345 F
nherrmann@pace.edu
HERRMANN, William .... 718-409-2882.... 356 C
wherrmann@sunymaritime.edu
HERRNSTEIN, Kate .... 216-432-8943.... 387 A
kherrnstein@chancelloru.edu
HERROD, Lorinda .... 432-264-5028.... 487 I
lherrod@howardcollege.edu
HERROLD, Jan .... 717-815-1744.... 452 F
jherrold@ycp.edu
HERRON, Alberta, H .... 336-841-9198.... 365 A
aherron@highpoint.edu
HERRON, Anne .... 315-255-1743.... 325 H
anne.herron@cayuga-cc.edu
HERRON, Crystal .... 314-286-0236.... 288 B
cherron@ranken.edu
HERRON, Jerry .... 313-577-3469.... 260 D
jerry.herron@wayne.edu
HERRON, Margaret .... 660-785-4143.... 291 A
mherron@truman.edu
HERRON, Marla .... 785-864-5170.... 196 F
mherron@ku.edu
HERRON, Robert .... 847-317-7180.... 166 B
rherron@tiu.edu
HERRON-WILLIAMS,
Sharron .... 334-229-5176........ 1 C
HERSBERGER, Rodney, M . 661-654-3042...... 33 H
rhersberger@csub.edu
HERSCHEDE, Kathryn, J .... 859-572-5172.... 205 E
herschede@nku.edu
HERSCHELMAN, Tina .... 360-417-6201.... 536 B
thershelman@pencol.edu

HERSEN, Michel ... 503-352-7330 ... 419 E
hersenm@pacificu.edu
HERSH, Doug ... 805-965-0581 ... 68 B
hersh@sbcc.edu
HERSH, Melissa ... 802-865-5402 ... 513 A
hersh@champlain.edu
HERSHBELL, Anne ... 434-947-8158 ... 522 E
ahershbell@randolphcollege.edu
HERSHBERGER, Bernie ... 207-725-3069 ... 217 E
bhershbe@bowdoin.edu
HERSHBERGER, David, L .. 920-206-2342 ... 548 B
dhershberger@mbbc.edu
HERSHBERGER, Vinse ... 219-866-6134 ... 179 B
vinseh@saintjoe.edu
HERSHENSON, Jay ... 212-794-5318 ... 326 C
jay.hershenson@mail.cuny.edu
HERSHEY, Diane, K ... 717-771-4126 ... 440 G
dkh13@psu.edu
HERSHEY, J. David ... 717-396-7833 ... 440 J
dhershey@pcad.edu
HERSHEY, Jonathan ... 706-368-7639 ... 130 C
jhershey@highlands.edu
HERSHFIELD, Nancy ... 830-372-8000 ... 499 C
nhershfield@tlu.edu
HERSHKOWITZ, M ... 203-325-4351 ... 89 I
HERSHOCK, Martin ... 313-593-5030 ... 259 E
mhershoc@umd.umich.edu
HERSKOWITZ, Issac ... 212-463-0400 ... 357 J
issac.herskowitz@touro.edu
HERSKOWITZ, Mordechai . 732-367-1060 ... 307 H
HERSON, Moshe ... 973-267-9404 ... 313 C
rca226@aol.com
HERT, Fiona ... 616-234-3744 ... 251 G
fhert@grcc.edu
HERTEL, Gary ... 651-846-1315 ... 269 E
gary.hertel@saintpaul.edu
HERTEL, Michael ... 215-572-2972 ... 422 B
hertel@arcadia.edu
HERTEL, Ralph, E ... 412-624-7600 ... 449 A
hertel@pitt.edu
HERTENBERGER, Patricia .. 281-756-3789 ... 479 G
phertenberger@alvincollege.edu
HERTZ, Adam ... 610-328-8325 ... 447 E
ahertz1@swarthmore.edu
HERTZFELD, Patricia, A ... 508-213-2382 ... 243 J
patricia.hertzfeld@nichols.edu
HERVAS, Kevin ... 212-217-4126 ... 333 G
kevin_hervas@fitnyc.edu
HERVEY, Eurmon ... 904-470-8050 ... 105 A
eurmon.hervey0905@ewc.edu
HERZ, Carol, A ... 561-237-7821 ... 113 D
cherz@lynn.edu
HERZBERGER, Sharon, D .. 562-907-4201 ... 79 B
president@whittier.edu
HERZEK, Farley ... 760-773-2506 ... 41 H
fherzek@collegeofthedesert.edu
HERZIG, Brenda, H ... 218-726-8532 ... 272 B
bherzig@d.umn.edu
HERZING, Renee ... 608-249-6611 ... 547 D
HERZOG, Alex ... 435-613-5229 ... 511 E
alex.herzog@ceu.edu
HERZOG, Linda ... 859-622-4642 ... 200 D
linda.herzog@eku.edu
HERZOG, Marc, S ... 860-244-7601 ... 89 J
mherzog@commnet.edu
HERZOG, Serge ... 775-784-4546 ... 303 A
serge@unr.edu
HESBROOK, Mechele ... 505-428-1664 ... 320 E
mechele.hesbrook@sfcc.edu
HESCH, Kim ... 701-845-7403 ... 382 A
kim.hesch@vcsu.edu
HESHEL, Alan ... 323-937-7772 ... 38 H
HESKETT, Lauren ... 785-539-3571 ... 194 G
lheskett@mccks.edu
HESLEP, Debbie, S ... 662-846-4655 ... 274 B
dheslep@deltastate.edu
HESLEPH, Jack ... 801-957-4013 ... 512 C
jack.hesleph@slcc.edu
HESLIN, Joseph ... 802-258-9209 ... 513 F
jheslin@gradcenter.marlboro.edu
HESS, Allison, B ... 801-626-7948 ... 511 D
ahess@weber.edu
HESS, Ann ... 928-536-6257 ... 17 B
ann.hess@npc.edu
HESS, Cindy ... 502-852-1105 ... 207 A
cindy.hess@louisville.edu
HESS, Cindy, K ... 314-644-9743 ... 289 C
chess17@stlcc.edu
HESS, Clayton ... 423-869-6377 ... 470 C
clayton.hess@lmunet.edu
HESS, Craig, E ... 803-822-3216 ... 459 D
hessc@midlandstech.edu
HESS, Cynthia ... 254-968-9125 ... 496 F
hess@tarleton.edu
HESS, Donald ... 692-625-5903 ... 559 E
cmihess@yahoo.com
HESS, Donald ... 692-625-5427 ... 559 E
HESS, Gregory ... 909-621-8117 ... 40 D
gregory.hess@cmc.edu
HESS, James ... 217-875-7200 ... 162 D
jhess@richland.edu
HESS, James, D ... 918-561-1137 ... 410 D
jim.hess@okstate.edu

HESS, Janet ... 692-625-3994 ... 559 E
cmihess@yahoo.com
HESS, Kristine, M ... 402-354-7260 ... 299 E
kris.hess@methodistcollege.edu
HESS, Maren ... 724-805-2372 ... 446 E
maren.hess@stvincent.edu
HESS, Pat ... 507-786-3000 ... 271 H
hessp@stolaf.edu
HESS, Resa ... 559-791-2457 ... 53 A
resa.hess@portervillecollege.edu
HESS, Shimon ... 718-259-2525 ... 324 B
HESS, SJ, Stephen ... 201-761-7360 ... 314 F
epoiani@spc.edu
HESS, Suzanne ... 515-244-4221 ... 181 D
hesss@aib.edu
HESS, Thomas, R ... 606-218-5475 ... 207 B
thess@pc.edu
HESS, Vickie ... 413-205-3216 ... 229 G
vickie.hess@aic.edu
HESS, William ... 510-628-8013 ... 54 B
whess@lincolnuca.edu
HESS, Wilson, G ... 207-834-7504 ... 220 D
wilson.hess@maine.edu
HESS MOLL, Sandra ... 815-455-8987 ... 157 F
smoll@mchenry.edu
HESSE, Allison ... 714-556-3610 ... 76 E
allison.hesse@vanguard.edu
HESSE, Carla ... 510-642-5039 ... 73 E
chesse@berkeley.edu
HESSE, Cindy ... 303-360-4752 ... 83 E
cindy.hesse@ccaurora.edu
HESSE-BIBER, Sharlene ... 617-552-4130 ... 232 D
sharlene.hesse-biber.1@bc.edu
HESSELBERG, Bonnie ... 941-752-5530 ... 118 E
hesselb@scf.edu
HESSELL, Debra ... 617-578-7100 ... 235 D
dhessell@gibbsboston.edu
HESSELRODE, Betsy ... 731-989-6021 ... 468 K
bhesselrode@fhu.edu
HESSIAN, Jane, H ... 608-363-2663 ... 546 B
hessianj@beloit.edu
HESSINGER, Rodney, J ... 330-569-5261 ... 391 H
HessingerRJ@hiram.edu
HESSLER, Arthur, C ... 802-862-9616 ... 512 H
ahessler@burlington.edu
HESSLER, Jim ... 479-619-4313 ... 22 H
jhessler@nwacc.edu
HESSLER, Robert, L ... 308-635-6030 ... 301 E
hesslerr@wncc.edu
HESSMANN, Steven, L ... 724-983-2907 ... 440 D
sxh46@psu.edu
HESTAND, Phil ... 870-972-2318 ... 20 C
phestand@astate.edu
HESTER, Barry, C ... 318-670-6414 ... 215 A
bhester@susla.edu
HESTER, Brenda ... 606-337-4524 ... 199 E
bhester@ccbbc.edu
HESTER, Clyda ... 740-377-2520 ... 402 F
clydasteacup@windstream.net
HESTER, Colleen ... 217-479-7025 ... 157 D
president@mac.edu
HESTER, David, C ... 502-895-3411 ... 204 B
dhester@lpts.edu
HESTER, Kerri ... 916-660-7603 ... 69 F
HESTER, Lynda ... 252-473-2264 ... 369 D
lynda_hester@albemarle.edu
HESTER, Malcolm ... 606-337-1114 ... 199 E
mhester@ccbbc.edu
HESTER, Mary ... 620-242-0487 ... 194 H
hesterm@mcpherson.edu
HESTER, Mary, L ... 620-792-9366 ... 190 E
hesterm@bartonccc.edu
HESTER, Ray ... 252-536-7250 ... 370 F
hesterr@halifaxcc.edu
HESTER, Susan ... 919-530-7601 ... 378 A
shester@nccu.edu
HESTER, Yvonne ... 951-343-5067 ... 31 G
yhester@calbaptist.edu
HESTERMAN, Jeff ... 334-874-5700 ... 3 A
jhesterman@concordiaselma.edu
HESTNESS, Gregory, S ... 612-626-4734 ... 272 D
hestness@umn.edu
HESTON, Angie ... 325-646-2502 ... 488 A
HESTON, Dave ... 602-850-8000 ... 17 H
dheston@phoenixseminary.edu
HESTON, Grant ... 407-823-5988 ... 120 A
grant.heston@ucf.edu
HETH, Justin ... 630-752-5022 ... 168 F
justin.heth@wheaton.edu
HETHERINGTON,
Kathleen, B ... 443-518-4820 ... 223 D
khetherington@howardcc.edu
HETHERINGTON,
Vincent, J ... 216-707-8004 ... 398 E
vjh@ocpm.edu
HETRICK, Barbara ... 904-620-2560 ... 120 C
barbara.hetrick@unf.edu
HETRICK, Janice ... 215-637-7700 ... 430 H
jhetrick@holyfamily.edu
HETRICK, Lori, J ... 864-488-4610 ... 459 A
lhetrick@limestone.edu
HETTLEMAN, Thomas ... 410-617-1120 ... 224 A
tdhettleman@loyola.edu

HETU, Marcel ... 559-334-2960 ... 77 I
marcelhetu@whccd.edu
HETZEL, Bob ... 608-785-6491 ... 551 B
hetzel.robe@uwlax.edu
HETZEL, Sandra ... 718-818-6470 ... 349 G
HEU, Nancy ... 808-235-7435 ... 142 C
heu@hawaii.edu
HEUER, Bobbi ... 661-255-1050 ... 32 C
bheuer@calarts.edu
HEUER, John, J ... 215-898-6884 ... 448 I
heuer@hr.upenn.edu
HEUER, Kathy ... 651-757-4061 ... 263 A
kheuer@cva.edu
HEUER, Mychael ... 360-867-6189 ... 533 I
heuermy@evergreen.edu
HEUER, Timothy ... 773-508-3254 ... 157 A
theuer@luc.edu
HEUERMANN, Robert ... 651-793-1805 ... 267 D
robert.heuermann@metrostate.edu
HEUGEL, Jim ... 425-889-4098 ... 535 I
jim.heugel@northwestu.edu
HEULITT, Ken ... 312-329-2070 ... 158 H
ken.heulitt@moody.edu
HEURING, Curt ... 609-771-3269 ... 308 G
heuring@tcnj.edu
HEURING, Michael ... 406-243-2022 ... 295 A
michael.heuring@umontana.edu
HEUSNER, Warren ... 718-270-6048 ... 328 D
wheusner@mec.cuny.edu
HEUTON, Mary Ellen ... 304-696-6603 ... 543 G
heuton@marshall.edu
HEVERON, Eileen ... 858-642-8106 ... 58 I
eheveron@nu.edu
HEVRON, Danelle ... 617-544-8657 ... 152 G
hevrond@iecc.edu
HEW, Rick ... 828-726-2704 ... 368 D
rhew@caldwell.cc.nc.us
HEWELL, Sherry, D ... 270-824-8666 ... 202 C
sherry.hewell@kctcs.edu
HEWERDINE, Kevin, L ... 812-877-8184 ... 179 A
kevin.l.hewerdine@rose-hulman.edu
HEWES, Colleen ... 425-739-8244 ... 535 B
colleen.hewes@lwtc.edu
HEWES, Pollyanne ... 207-947-4591 ... 217 D
phewes@bealcollege.edu
HEWETSON, Hank ... 812-855-1763 ... 173 C
hhewetso@indiana.edu
HEWETT, Georgianne ... 512-863-1584 ... 495 G
hewettg@southwestern.edu
HEWETT, James, E ... 712-749-2248 ... 182 G
hewettj@bvu.edu
HEWETT, Kelly ... 410-334-2908 ... 229 E
khewett@worwic.edu
HEWETT, Lamar ... 803-549-6314 ... 462 E
dlhewett@mailbox.sc.edu
HEWITT, Bradley, L ... 618-650-2871 ... 165 A
bhewitt@siue.edu
HEWITT, Dawn ... 718-262-2060 ... 329 B
hewittd@york.cuny.edu
HEWITT, Emma ... 712-274-6400 ... 189 H
emma.hewitt@witcc.edu
HEWITT, Gordon, J ... 315-859-4084 ... 335 A
ghewitt@hamilton.edu
HEWITT, JR., Harold, W ... 714-997-6815 ... 39 C
hewitt@chapman.edu
HEWITT, Janine ... 860-509-9520 ... 92 D
HEWITT, Mark, S ... 781-736-2010 ... 233 A
mhewitt@brandeis.edu
HEWITT, Maureen, A ... 312-935-4232 ... 153 F
mhewitt@icsw.edu
HEWITT, Michael ... 718-951-5131 ... 326 G
mhewitt@brooklyn.cuny.edu
HEWITT, Nathaniel ... 903-923-2404 ... 509 A
nhewitt@wileyc.edu
HEWITT, Stephany ... 843-574-6922 ... 461 G
stephany.hewitt@tridenttech.edu
HEWITT BOYD, Kimberly .. 612-624-9547 ... 272 D
boyd009@umn.edu
HEWITT-CLARK, Gail ... 301-295-3101 ... 558 A
gail.hewitt-clark@usuhs.mil
HEWLETT, Fannie ... 423-697-4456 ... 474 D
HEWLETT, Mira, A ... 717-245-1267 ... 427 E
hewlettm@dickinson.edu
HEWLETT, Peggy ... 803-777-3861 ... 462 A
peggy.hewlett@sc.edu
HEWLETT, Rod ... 402-557-7125 ... 297 A
rod.hewlett@bellevue.edu
HEXTER, Ralph, J ... 530-752-4964 ... 73 F
hexter@ucdavis.edu
HEYD, Steven ... 605-742-1116 ... 465 C
sheyd@swc.tc
HEYDARI, Shahryar ... 706-778-8500 ... 135 D
sheydari@piedmont.edu
HEYER, Doreen, E ... 213-738-6801 ... 71 D
academicadmin@swlaw.edu
HEYING, Lori ... 319-363-8213 ... 187 E
lheying@mtmercy.edu
HEYING, Steve ... 210-829-6023 ... 503 F
lindaw@uiwtx.edu
HEYMAN, George ... 585-271-3657 ... 348 B
gheyman@stbernards.edu
HEYMAN, Jeffrey ... 510-466-7369 ... 61 H
jheyman@peralta.edu

HEYMAN, Jeffrey ... 510-436-2419 ... 62 D
jheyman@peralta.edu
HEYMAN, Lawrence, A ... 610-785-6235 ... 446 A
registrarscs@adphila.org
HEYNDERICKX, Roy, F ... 360-438-4307 ... 536 F
president@stmartin.edu
HEYNING, Katharina, E ... 262-472-1101 ... 552 E
heyningk@uww.edu
HEYWARD, Kerry, L ... 404-413-0500 ... 131 C
kheyward@gsu.edu
HEYWARD, Loretta ... 912-358-3049 ... 136 C
heywardl@savannahstate.edu
HIATT, Aaron ... 415-433-9200 ... 68 F
ahiatt@saybrook.edu
HIATT, Jim ... 615-248-1256 ... 476 E
Jhiatt@trevecca.edu
HIATT, Jon ... 605-331-6636 ... 466 D
jon.hiatt@usiouxfalls.edu
HIBBARD, Kristine ... 904-264-9122 ... 106 C
khibbard@cci.edu
HIBBARD, Steve, V ... 262-243-5700 ... 546 I
steve.hibbard@cuw.edu
HIBBERD, Grover ... 502-863-8091 ... 200 G
grover_hibberd@georgetowncollege.edu
HIBBERT OLENDER,
Ursula ... 315-228-7318 ... 329 H
uolender@colgate.edu
HIBBS, Joseph, L ... 856-691-8600 ... 309 C
jhibbs@cccnj.edu
HIBBS, Randy ... 920-206-2318 ... 548 B
rhibbs@mbbc.edu
HIBBS, Thomas, S ... 254-710-7689 ... 481 I
thomas_hibbs@baylor.edu
HIBLER, Dirk ... 904-819-6336 ... 107 A
dhibler@flagler.edu
HICE, Muriel ... 269-488-4410 ... 253 G
mhice@kvcc.edu
HICHWA, Richard, D ... 319-335-2106 ... 182 C
richard-hichwa@uiowa.edu
HICKE, Linda ... 847-467-4490 ... 160 D
l-hicke@northwestern.edu
HICKEY, Bill ... 320-363-5480 ... 262 H
bhickey@csbsju.edu
HICKEY, Catherine, M ... 508-999-8182 ... 237 E
chickey@umassd.edu
HICKEY, Dean ... 508-373-9520 ... 231 D
dean.hickey@becker.edu
HICKEY, Eric ... 559-278-2803 ... 27 B
ehickey@alliant.edu
HICKEY, Jay ... 401-841-6515 ... 557 I
HICKEY, John, M ... 253-879-3203 ... 538 E
hickey@pugetsound.edu
HICKEY, Kate, D ... 336-278-6572 ... 364 A
hickey@elon.edu
HICKEY, Lynn ... 210-458-4444 ... 506 B
lynn.hickey@utsa.edu
HICKEY, Melissa ... 845-675-4424 ... 344 G
melissa.hickey@nyack.edu
HICKEY, Paul, J ... 931-540-2516 ... 474 F
phickey@columbiastate.edu
HICKEY, JR., Robert, E ... 937-775-3326 ... 406 C
robert.hickey@wright.edu
HICKEY, Thomas, F ... 312-915-7796 ... 157 A
thickey@luc.edu
HICKLIN, Lee, E ... 757-499-7900 ... 517 A
lehicklin@bryantstratton.edu
HICKMAN, Carla ... 314-889-1416 ... 282 C
chickman@fontbonne.edu
HICKMAN, Heather ... 415-749-4540 ... 65 I
hhickman@sfai.edu
HICKMAN, Melissa ... 317-931-2311 ... 170 E
mhickman@cts.edu
HICKMAN, Michael ... 719-846-5691 ... 87 J
michael.hickman@trinidadstate.edu
HICKMAN, Randall ... 586-445-7866 ... 254 F
hickmanr@macomb.edu
HICKMAN, Thomas, N ... 803-323-2129 ... 463 D
hickmant@winthrop.edu
HICKMAN, Tim ... 909-558-4532 ... 54 D
thickman@llu.edu
HICKMAN, Tom ... 701-671-2354 ... 382 E
tom.hickman@ndscs.edu
HICKMAN, Tracy ... 386-752-1822 ... 108 C
tracy.hickman@fgc.edu
HICKOX, Chad, E ... 206-934-7959 ... 537 B
chad.hickox@seattlecolleges.edu
HICKOX, Charles ... 859-622-6605 ... 200 D
charles.hickox@eku.edu
HICKS, Ali ... 505-565-1290 ... 245 D
ahicks@stonehill.edu
HICKS, Barbara ... 602-331-7500 ... 12 D
bhicks@aii.edu
HICKS, Brenda, D ... 620-229-6387 ... 196 C
brenda.hicks@sckans.edu
HICKS, Brian, A ... 336-734-7191 ... 370 C
bhicks@forsythtech.edu
HICKS, Bruce ... 310-287-4307 ... 55 F
hicksbr@wlac.edu
HICKS, Cheryl ... 816-414-3700 ... 286 A
chicks@mbts.edu
HICKS, Dale, A ... 813-974-9232 ... 120 D
dhicks1@usf.edu
HICKS, David, L ... 610-292-9852 ... 445 D
bishophicks@comcast.net

HICKS, Debbie, L ... 757-455-3338 ... 529 F
dlhicks@vwc.edu
HICKS, Dennis ... 765-973-8456 ... 173 D
dehicks@iue.edu
HICKS, Ed ... 334-386-7309 ... 3 H
ehicks@faulkner.edu
HICKS, Elena ... 410-617-2251 ... 224 A
ehicks@loyola.edu
HICKS, Elizabeth, M ... 617-253-4090 ... 242 A
emhicks@mit.edu
HICKS, George ... 740-588-1379 ... 407 A
HICKS, Henry, L ... 423-236-2700 ... 473 A
hlhicks@southern.edu
HICKS, James, D ... 423-652-4782 ... 469 L
jdhicks@king.edu
HICKS, JR., James, W ... 256-533-7387 ... 3 D
jim.hicks@vc.edu
HICKS, Janine, M ... 815-740-2272 ... 167 C
jhicks@stfrancis.edu
HICKS, Jim ... 423-425-4246 ... 477 D
jim-hicks@utc.edu
HICKS, Jimmy ... 691-320-2480 ... 559 A
jhicks@comfsm.fm
HICKS, Jud ... 806-457-4200 ... 486 G
jhicks@fpctx.edu
HICKS, Julia ... 860-685-2100 ... 95 C
jhicks@wesleyan.edu
HICKS, Kenneth ... 215-248-7103 ... 425 C
hicksk@chc.edu
HICKS, Larry ... 919-962-5401 ... 378 D
larry_hicks@unc.edu
HICKS, Lawrence ... 313-593-5380 ... 259 E
hickslg@umd.umich.edu
HICKS, Loretta ... 404-297-9522 ... 128 B
hicksl@dekalbtech.edu
HICKS, M. Geoffrey ... 434-832-7641 ... 526 A
hicksg@cvcc.vccs.edu
HICKS, Marcus ... 404-297-9522 ... 128 B
hicksm@dekalbtech.edu
HICKS, Marian ... 323-660-6166 ... 40 G
marian.hicks@cleveland.edu
HICKS, Michael ... 706-821-8350 ... 135 C
mhicks@paine.edu
HICKS, Michael, G ... 574-284-4719 ... 179 D
mhicks@saintmarys.edu
HICKS, Minora ... 803-327-7402 ... 456 F
fisherlibrary@clintonjuniorcollege.edu
HICKS, Mona, L ... 561-803-2176 ... 111 C
mona_hicks@pba.edu
HICKS, Nancy, W ... 609-652-4693 ... 313 F
nancy.hicks@stockton.edu
HICKS, Renardo, L ... 803-376-5700 ... 455 B
rhicks@allenuniversity.edu
HICKS, Renee, G ... 985-493-2556 ... 216 A
renee.hicks@nicholls.edu
HICKS, Ronald ... 847-566-6401 ... 167 D
HICKS, Rosemary ... 507-285-7259 ... 269 B
rosemary.hicks@roch.edu
HICKS, Sara ... 978-837-5502 ... 242 D
hickss@merrimack.edu
HICKS, Stacey ... 209-384-6100 ... 57 C
stacey.hicks@mccd.edu
HICKS, Timothy ... 803-793-5157 ... 457 F
hickst@denmarktech.edu
HICKS, Timothy, J ... 315-859-4790 ... 335 A
thicks@hamilton.edu
HICKS, Virginia ... 304-876-5712 ... 544 A
vhicks@shepherd.edu
HICKS-GOLDSTEIN, Regan ... 302-454-3998 ... 96 C
regan@dtcc.edu
HICKSON, Cheryl, E ... 443-412-2129 ... 223 B
chickson@harford.edu
HICKSON, Melissa ... 941-554-1522 ... 100 G
mhickson@edmc.edu
HICSWA, Stefani, G ... 406-874-6158 ... 294 H
hicswas@milescc.edu
HIDALGO, Jeannie ... 305-220-4120 ... 115 D
hrdir@ptcmatt.com
HIDALGO, Lisa ... 985-858-5729 ... 210 H
lhidalgo@ftcc.edu
HIDALGO, Maria ... 505-424-2317 ... 318 C
mhidalgo@iaia.edu
HIEL, Edwin ... 619-388-3036 ... 65 F
ehiel@sdccd.edu
HIEMENZ, Karen, A ... 320-308-5017 ... 269 D
khiemenz@sctcc.edu
HIEMER, Linda ... 310-689-3200 ... 42 F
lhiemer@kaplan.edu
HIEMER, Linda ... 866-621-0124 ... 88 G
linda.hiemer@rockies.edu
HIEMSTRA, Tricia ... 805-893-2489 ... 74 F
tricia.hiemstra@hr.ucsb.edu
HIERONYMUS, Bob ... 208-882-1566 ... 143 G
bobh@nsa.edu
HIERS, Richard ... 314-434-4044 ... 281 A
richard.hiers@covenantseminary.edu
HIESIGER, Linda ... 413-585-2231 ... 245 B
lhiesige@smith.edu
HIETALA, Robert ... 406-994-5523 ... 295 E
robert.hietala@montana.edu
HIETAPELTO, Amy, B ... 773-442-6100 ... 159 H
a-hietapelto@neiu.edu
HIETT, David ... 617-746-1990 ... 236 B
david.hiett@hult.edu
HIETT, Jim ... 615-230-3350 ... 476 A
jim.hiett@volstate.edu
HIGA, Jane, H ... 805-565-6028 ... 78 F
jhiga@westmont.edu
HIGA, Milton ... 808-734-9572 ... 141 E
miltonh@hawaii.edu
HIGASHI, Guy ... 808-853-1040 ... 140 G
HIGASHI, Lori ... 808-853-1040 ... 140 G
lorih@pacrim.edu
HIGDEM, Julie ... 763-488-2453 ... 266 G
julie.higdem@hennepintech.edu
HIGDON, Hal, L ... 417-447-2602 ... 287 G
higdonh@otc.edu
HIGDON, Jo Ann ... 310-660-3107 ... 45 D
jhigdon@elcamino.edu
HIGDON, Jo Ann ... 310-660-3670 ... 45 D
jhigdon@elcamino.edu
HIGDON, JoAnn ... 310-660-3107 ... 45 E
jhigdon@elcamino.edu
HIGDON, JR., Leo, I ... 860-439-2666 ... 91 E
lhigdon@conncoll.edu
HIGGASON, Rich ... 816-604-1350 ... 285 D
rich.higgason@mcckc.edu
HIGGERSON, Mary Lou ... 440-826-2251 ... 384 H
mlhigger@bw.edu
HIGGINBOTHAM, Debra ... 940-397-4120 ... 491 A
debra.higginbotham@mwsu.edu
HIGGINBOTHAM, Eve, J ... 202-865-7470 ... 98 B
eve.higginbotham@howard.edu
HIGGINBOTHAM, James, A ... 207-725-3290 ... 217 E
jhigginb@bowdoin.edu
HIGGINBOTHAM, Judy ... 337-262-5962 ... 209 D
jhigginbotham@acadiana.edu
HIGGINBOTHAM, Karen ... 323-464-2777 ... 27 I
khigginbotham@ca.aada.org
HIGGINBOTHAM, Karen ... 212-686-0620 ... 323 A
HIGGINBOTHAM, Milton ... 870-584-4471 ... 25 C
mhigginbotham@cccua.edu
HIGGINS, Alice, J ... 512-448-8411 ... 493 B
aliceh@stedwards.edu
HIGGINS, Barbara ... 207-941-7191 ... 218 A
higginsb@husson.edu
HIGGINS, Brenda ... 660-785-4562 ... 291 A
bhiggins@truman.edu
HIGGINS, Daniel, E ... 609-896-5192 ... 313 G
dhiggins@rider.edu
HIGGINS, Dawn ... 603-271-8928 ... 304 G
dhiggins@ccsnh.edu
HIGGINS, Edna ... 228-392-2994 ... 278 B
edna.higgins@vc.edu
HIGGINS, Elizabeth ... 518-262-5831 ... 322 E
higgine@mail.amc.edu
HIGGINS, Elizabeth ... 207-780-4632 ... 220 G
bhiggins@maine.maine.edu
HIGGINS, Garland ... 502-597-6760 ... 203 D
garland.higgins@kysu.edu
HIGGINS, Joey ... 828-669-8012 ... 367 C
jhiggins@montreat.edu
HIGGINS, Kacey ... 325-670-1368 ... 487 D
Kacey.Higgins@hsutx.edu
HIGGINS, Margaret ... 401-341-2205 ... 454 D
margaret.higgins@salve.edu
HIGGINS, Mark, M ... 401-874-4244 ... 454 E
markhiggins@uri.edu
HIGGINS, Michael ... 314-434-4044 ... 281 A
mike.higgins@covenantseminary.edu
HIGGINS, Michael, J ... 203-371-7902 ... 93 G
higginsmw@sacredheart.edu
HIGGINS, Mildred ... 504-520-7517 ... 217 A
mhiggins@xula.edu
HIGGINS, Peter, J ... 678-359-5156 ... 131 D
phiggins@gdn.edu
HIGGINS, Renee ... 309-649-6050 ... 165 D
renee.higgins@src.edu
HIGGINS, Richard, J ... 518-564-2040 ... 354 B
higginrj@plattsburgh.edu
HIGGINS, Ronnell, A ... 203-432-9455 ... 95 D
ronnell.higgins@yale.edu
HIGGINS, Sandra ... 718-260-5700 ... 328 E
shiggins@citytech.cuny.edu
HIGGINS, Scott ... 828-227-7398 ... 379 E
higgins@wcu.edu
HIGGINS, Sharon ... 410-617-5025 ... 224 A
sbhiggins@loyola.edu
HIGGINS, Stephen ... 615-771-7821 ... 478 G
HIGGINS, Tammy ... 620-235-4240 ... 195 I
thiggins@pittstate.edu
HIGGINS, Terri ... 641-782-7081 ... 189 A
thiggins@swcciowa.edu
HIGGINS, Thomas, J ... 518-564-3013 ... 354 B
higgintj@plattsburgh.edu
HIGGINS-FREESE, Jonna ... 319-895-4372 ... 183 D
jhigginsfreese@cornellcollege.edu
HIGGINSON, Bonnie, S ... 270-809-3744 ... 204 F
bonnie.higginson@murraystate.edu
HIGGS, David ... 601-643-8376 ... 274 A
david.higgs@colin.edu
HIGGS, Jessica ... 309-677-2700 ... 145 H
jhiggs@bradley.edu
HIGGS, John ... 715-422-5356 ... 554 C
john.higgs@mstc.edu
HIGGS, Richard ... 864-596-9021 ... 457 E
richard.higgs@converse.edu
HIGGS, Ronnie ... 831-582-4363 ... 35 C
rhiggs@csumb.edu
HIGH, Jon ... 612-343-3544 ... 270 C
jahigh@northcentral.edu
HIGH, Katherine, N ... 865-974-4615 ... 477 A
khigh@tennessee.edu
HIGH, Kaye ... 606-759-7141 ... 202 D
kaye.high@kctcs.edu
HIGH, Sherine ... 443-627-7808 ... 272 F
Sherine.High@waldenu.edu
HIGHAM, Eugene ... 435-797-1042 ... 511 B
eugene.higham@usu.edu
HIGHAM, Pamela, S ... 814-332-3576 ... 421 E
phigham@allegheny.edu
HIGHFIELD, Richard ... 203-932-7402 ... 95 B
rhighfield@newhaven.edu
HIGHLEY, Brian ... 859-223-9608 ... 205 J
bhighley@spencerian.edu
HIGHLEY, Melinda, C ... 606-783-2033 ... 204 E
m.highley@moreheadstate.edu
HIGHLEY, Tonda, S ... 845-257-3236 ... 352 B
highleyt@newpaltz.edu
HIGHSTREET, Eve ... 856-227-7200 ... 308 E
ehighstreet@camdencc.edu
HIGHT, Donna ... 419-755-4034 ... 399 C
hight.6@osu.edu
HIGHTOWER, Darlene ... 405-744-3555 ... 410 C
darlene.hightower@okstate.edu
HIGHTOWER, Diane, D ... 724-925-4050 ... 451 E
higtowerd@wccc.edu
HIGHTOWER, Janey, W ... 540-985-8296 ... 520 D
jwhightower@jchs.edu
HIGHTOWER, Jennifer ... 713-221-8978 ... 503 D
hightowerj@uhd.edu
HIGHTOWER, Kenneth, R ... 248-370-3562 ... 257 C
hightowe@oakland.edu
HIGHTOWER, Len ... 310-303-7311 ... 56 F
lhightower@marymountpv.edu
HIGHTOWER, Michelle ... 478-445-4255 ... 129 F
michelle.hightower@gcsu.edu
HIGHTOWER, Stephanie ... 614-222-3230 ... 388 F
shightower@ccad.edu
HIGHTOWER, JR., William, H ... 276-223-4794 ... 528 F
wchighb@wcc.vccs.edu
HIGHUM, Ann, C ... 563-387-1020 ... 187 A
highuman@luther.edu
HIGINBOTHAM, Lynn ... 212-998-4444 ... 344 B
lynn.higinbotham@nyu.edu
HIGLEY, David (Skip) ... 954-492-5353 ... 102 J
dhigley@citycollege.edu
HIGLEY, Tony ... 509-434-5123 ... 532 F
thigley@ccs.spokane.edu
HIGLEY, Tony ... 509-434-5123 ... 532 E
thigley@ccs.spokane.edu
HIGLEY, Tony, D ... 509-434-5123 ... 532 D
thigley@ccs.spokane.edu
HIJLEH, Mark ... 585-567-9315 ... 336 B
mark.hijleh@houghton.edu
HILBERT, Pamela ... 252-493-7406 ... 372 E
philbert@email.pittcc.edu
HILBRANDS, Steve ... 616-538-2330 ... 251 F
shilbrands@gbcol.edu
HILBUN, Christy ... 601-477-4058 ... 275 B
christy.hilbun@jcjc.edu
HILBURN, Julius ... 405-325-5647 ... 413 D
jhilburn@ou.edu
HILBURN, Julius ... 405-325-1826 ... 413 C
jhilburn@ou.edu
HILBY, Jim ... 414-382-6327 ... 545 H
jim.hilby@alverno.edu
HILDEBRAND, Jane ... 563-387-1008 ... 187 A
hildebja@luther.edu
HILDEBRANDT, Guy ... 516-686-7751 ... 343 D
ghildebr@nyit.edu
HILDERBRAND, David ... 605-688-4723 ... 466 B
david.hilderbrand@sdstate.edu
HILDERBRANT, Pat ... 404-799-4500 ... 126 E
philderbrant@brownmackie.edu
HILDRETH, James, E ... 530-752-4460 ... 73 F
HILERIO, Marisol ... 787-891-0825 ... 562 G
mhilerio@aguadilla.inter.edu
HILES, Dawn ... 417-873-6804 ... 281 H
dhiles@drury.edu
HILES, Thomas, S ... 419-372-7706 ... 385 C
thiles@bgsu.edu
HILGENBRINK, Robert, J ... 618-235-2700 ... 165 B
robert.hilgenbrink@swic.edu
HILGENDORF, Duane, H ... 262-243-5700 ... 546 I
duane.hilgendorf@cuw.edu
HILGERSOM, Karin, M ... 541-383-7205 ... 414 I
khilgersom@cocc.edu
HILKE, David ... 412-536-1104 ... 432 F
david.hilke@laroche.edu
HILKE, Jurgen ... 301-846-2401 ... 222 G
jhilke@frederic.edu
HILL, Abbas ... 219-989-3107 ... 178 G
hillab@purduecal.edu
HILL, Adam ... 248-218-2114 ... 257 F
ahill@rc.edu
HILL, Alan, P ... 317-738-8062 ... 171 C
ahill@franklincollege.edu
HILL, Allan ... 610-436-1050 ... 443 F
ahill@wcupa.edu
HILL, Amber ... 256-824-2779 ... 9 A
sm418@bncollege.com
HILL, Amy ... 641-585-8672 ... 189 E
hilla@waldorf.edu
HILL, Andrew, E ... 904-264-2172 ... 116 A
ahill@iws.edu
HILL, Angeline ... 707-476-4364 ... 42 A
angeline-hill@redwoods.edu
HILL, Art ... 541-278-5863 ... 414 G
ahill@bluecc.edu
HILL, Ashley ... 601-477-4039 ... 275 B
ashley.hill@jcjc.edu
HILL, Brian, W ... 540-231-4000 ... 518 H
HILL, Calvin ... 508-929-8784 ... 239 D
chill@worcester.edu
HILL, Carnice ... 773-995-3521 ... 146 D
chill24@csu.edu
HILL, Catharine, B ... 845-437-7200 ... 359 D
hill@vassar.edu
HILL, Cathy, L ... 724-287-8711 ... 423 F
cathy.hill@bc3.edu
HILL, Chris ... 619-644-7163 ... 49 A
chris.hill@gcccd.edu
HILL, Chris ... 801-581-5605 ... 510 L
chill@huntsman.utah.edu
HILL, Christopher, R ... 303-871-2539 ... 88 E
Christopher.R.Hill@du.edu
HILL, Curtis ... 870-862-8131 ... 23 G
chill@southark.edu
HILL, Curtis ... 817-515-3584 ... 496 A
curtis.hill@tccd.edu
HILL, Cynthia ... 919-546-8564 ... 376 D
chill@shawu.edu
HILL, David ... 518-792-5425 ... 354 B
david.hill@plattsburgh.edu
HILL, David, R ... 903-566-7028 ... 506 C
dhill@uttyler.edu
HILL, Deana ... 570-484-2014 ... 443 A
dhill@lhup.edu
HILL, Deborah ... 435-865-8628 ... 511 A
hilld@suu.edu
HILL, Deborah, G ... 585-245-5519 ... 353 C
hilld@geneseo.edu
HILL, Deidra, W ... 301-322-0916 ... 225 F
dhill@pgcc.edu
HILL, Diana ... 770-394-8300 ... 124 F
diahill@aii.edu
HILL, Donna ... 502-213-2184 ... 202 B
donna.hill@kctcs.edu
HILL, Doris ... 651-450-3372 ... 266 I
dhill@inverhills.edu
HILL, Edward ... 216-687-2135 ... 388 C
e.hill@urban.csuohio.edu
HILL, Elizabeth ... 360-596-5416 ... 538 B
ehill@spscc.ctc.edu
HILL, Elizabeth, A ... 718-940-5989 ... 349 A
sehill@sjcny.edu
HILL, Elizabeth, A ... 718-940-5989 ... 349 B
sehill@sjcny.edu
HILL, Erin ... 302-857-6351 ... 95 F
ehill@desu.edu
HILL, Fitz ... 501-370-4000 ... 19 F
fitzhill@hotmail.com
HILL, G. Richard ... 801-626-7313 ... 511 D
grhill@weber.edu
HILL, Gladys ... 205-391-2457 ... 7 A
ghill@sheltonstate.edu
HILL, Hazel, M ... 209-954-5093 ... 66 D
hhill@deltacollege.edu
HILL, Henderson ... 931-221-6274 ... 473 D
hillh@apsu.edu
HILL, Ira ... 305-534-7050 ... 121 G
ryhill@talmudicu.edu
HILL, James, M ... 973-972-2849 ... 316 F
hilljm@umdnj.edu
HILL, Jean ... 505-454-3562 ... 318 I
jlhill@nmhu.edu
HILL, Jeff ... 312-578-3873 ... 168 B
jhill@westwood.edu
HILL, Jennifer ... 256-352-8032 ... 10 B
jennifer.hill@wallacestate.edu
HILL, Joanna ... 813-620-1446 ... 110 A
HILL, JoAnne, L ... 818-779-8040 ... 53 B
jhill@kingsuniversity.edu
HILL, John, A ... 317-955-6050 ... 177 G
jahill@marian.edu
HILL, Kelly, D ... 801-832-2565 ... 512 F
kdhill@westminstercollege.edu
HILL, Ken ... 207-288-5015 ... 217 H
khill@coa.edu
HILL, Kenneth ... 678-915-6827 ... 137 C
khill@spsu.edu
HILL, Kevin ... 212-986-4343 ... 323 J
keh@berkeleycollege.edu
HILL, Laqueta ... 870-850-8632 ... 23 H
lhill@seark.edu
HILL, Leah ... 252-985-5291 ... 375 C
lhill@ncwc.edu
HILL, Leon ... 215-641-6674 ... 436 G
hlhill@mc3.edu
HILL, Linda ... 207-941-7154 ... 218 A
hilll@husson.edu

HILL, Marie 617-587-5678 243 D
hillm@neco.edu

HILL, Marion, A 214-333-5261 484 C
marion@dbu.edu

HILL, Martha, N 410-955-7544 223 F
mnhill@son.jhmi.edu

HILL, Marty 336-887-3000 365 J
mhill@laureluniversity.edu

HILL, Mary, H 202-806-7459 98 B
marhill@howard.edu

HILL, Mathew, B 651-631-5362 270 E
mbhill@nwc.edu

HILL, Michael, B 484-365-7259 434 H
mhill@lincoln.edu

HILL, Michael, W 706-721-2661 130 B
mhill@georgiahealth.edu

HILL, Michelle, D 757-823-8531 521 K
mdhill@nsu.edu

HILL, Michelle, L 225-771-5020 214 H
michelle_hill@subr.edu

HILL, Missy 724-463-0222 424 B
mhill@crbc.net

HILL, Nancy 517-780-4569 248 I
nancy.hill@baker.edu

HILL, Nanyamka 619-660-4240 48 J
nanyamka.hill@gcccd.edu

HILL, Nelson, W 585-594-6944 347 F
hill_nelson@roberts.edu

HILL, Pamela 978-665-3515 238 C
phill@fitchburgstate.edu

HILL, Patricia, L 334-271-1670 6 D
phill@princeinstitute.edu

HILL, Paul, L 304-558-4128 543 B
hill@hepc.wvnet.edu

HILL, Ralph 870-762-3159 20 A
rhill@smail.anc.edu

HILL, Ramona, M 251-380-3092 7 F
rhill@shc.edu

HILL, Reinhold 708-534-4101 151 C
rhill@govst.edu

HILL, Richard 812-265-2580 176 G
rhill@ivytech.edu

HILL, Robert 412-624-2795 449 A
hillr@pitt.edu

HILL, Robert, A 617-353-3560 232 G
rahill@bu.edu

HILL, Robert, R 513-745-3331 406 E
hill@xavier.edu

HILL, Robert, W 936-468-3501 495 H
rhill@sfasu.edu

HILL, S. Trent 361-825-5749 497 F
trent.hill@tamucc.edu

HILL, Sam 703-878-5778 527 C
shill@nvcc.edu

HILL, Sandra, B 318-342-1145 216 E
shill@ulm.edu

HILL, Scott 540-985-4693 520 D
bshill@jchs.edu

HILL, Scott 601-635-2111 274 C
shill@eccc.edu

HILL, Seddrick 256-761-6205 7 H
sthill@talladega.edu

HILL, Shannon 661-654-3211 33 H
shill@csub.edu

HILL, Sharon, F 781-891-2108 231 F
shill@bentley.edu

HILL, Sheila 706-771-4008 125 D
shill@augustatech.edu

HILL, Sherry, A 334-271-1670 6 D
shill@princeinstitute.edu

HILL, Shirley 901-435-1452 470 B
shirley_hill@loc.edu

HILL, Steve 801-422-2153 509 D
steve_hill@byu.edu

HILL, Theresa 406-791-5262 296 H
thill01@ugf.edu

HILL, Thomas, J 215-885-2360 435 E
thill@manor.edu

HILL, Thomas, L 515-294-4420 182 B
tomhill@iastate.edu

HILL, Tim 801-422-7010 509 D
tim_hill@byu.edu

HILL, Tracy 412-578-6164 424 G
carlow@bkstr.com

HILL, Travis, R 315-859-4023 335 A
thill@hamilton.edu

HILL, Valerie, D 512-505-3060 488 B
vdhill@htu.edu

HILL, Vicki 918-647-1373 407 E
vhill@carlalbert.edu

HILL, W. Weldon 804-524-5997 529 C
whill@vsu.edu

HILL, Walter, A 334-727-8327 8 C
hillwa@tuskegee.edu

HILL, Wanda 513-921-9856 387 B
wanda.hill@chatfield.edu

HILL, Wendy, L 610-330-5066 433 B
hillw@lafayette.edu

HILL, William 732-571-3580 311 F
hill@monmouth.edu

HILL, William, E 904-256-7345 111 J
whill@ju.edu

HILL, II, William, L 215-965-4021 436 H
whill@moore.edu

HILL, Wynn, N 208-496-9204 142 G
hillw@byui.edu

HILL-CHEATOM, Petrina 716-851-1120 333 B
cheatom@ecc.edu

HILL DUIN, Ann 612-625-9259 272 D
ahduin@umn.edu

HILL-FLANAGAN,
LaVerne, M 202-274-6069 99 F
lflanagan@udc.edu

HILL GETZ, Janet 309-268-8175 151 G
janet.hill-getz@heartland.edu

HILL-MILLER, Katherine 516-299-2234 339 A
katherine.hill-miller@liu.edu

HILLARD,
James Randolph 517-353-3967 255 D
jhillard@msu.edu

HILLARD, Jan 859-572-7567 205 E
hillardj1@nku.edu

HILLBERRY, Andrew, R 248-232-4803 257 B
arhilbe@oaklandcc.edu

HILLE, Jim 817-257-7031 498 F
j.hille@tcu.edu

HILLE, John, S 814-641-3113 431 L
hillej@juniata.edu

HILLE, William, P 336-599-1181 372 D
hillep@piedmontcc.edu

HILLEBRAND, Karen 248-689-8282 260 A
khillebr@walshcollege.edu

HILLENBRAND, Bruce 845-451-1286 331 F
b_hillen@culinary.edu

HILLER, Jerry 315-279-5244 337 K
jhiller@mail.keuka.edu

HILLER, Melissa 301-687-4341 228 C

HILLER-FREUND,
Darby, L 231-995-1084 256 G
dhiller@nmc.edu

HILLERMAN, Donnie 660-359-3948 287 D
dhillerman@mail.ncmissouri.edu

HILLERY, Barbara 516-876-3915 353 D
hilleryb@oldwestbury.edu

HILLESHEIM, Gwen 312-752-2000 155 B
gwen.hillesheim@kendall.edu

HILLHOUSE, Hank 863-680-4738 109 D
rhillhouse@flsouthern.edu

HILLIAR, Mara, M 804-594-1570 526 G
mhilliar@jtcc.edu

HILLIARD, Aaron 231-777-0447 256 D
aaronhilliard@muskegoncc.edu

HILLIARD, Beth 859-256-3100 201 A
beth.hilliard@kctcs.edu

HILLIARD, Colette 903-675-6306 502 D
chilliard@tvcc.edu

HILLIARD, Danny, C 405-325-0311 413 C
dhilliard@ou.edu

HILLIARD, Dianne 775-445-3288 303 B
dianne@wnc.edu

HILLIARD, Kimberly 601-979-2255 275 A
kimberly.d.hilliard@jsums.edu

HILLIARD, Mark 615-794-4254 472 D
mhilliard@omorecollege.edu

HILLIER, Gregory 518-762-4651 334 D
ghillier@fmcc.suny.edu

HILLIER, Jim 704-991-0218 374 A
jhillier5068@stanly.edu

HILLIER, John 860-632-3007 92 E
rector@holyapostles.edu

HILLIS, John, R 405-208-5120 410 A
jrhillis@okcu.edu

HILLIS, Vicki, B 419-372-0651 385 D
vickih@bgsu.edu

HILLKIRK, R. Keith 570-385-6102 440 C
rkh5@psu.edu

HILLMAN, Greg 601-426-6346 277 D
ghillman@southeasternbaptist.edu

HILLMAN, Jason, D 580-327-8439 409 C
jdhillman@nwosu.edu

HILLMAN, Melinda 865-481-2000 475 G
hillmanmk@roanestate.edu

HILLMAN, Michel 701-328-2965 381 C
michel.hillman@ndus.edu

HILLMAN, Pamela 657-278-7030 34 E
phillman@fullerton.edu

HILLS, Gaynor 425-564-2282 531 B
gaynor.hills@bellevuecollege.edu

HILLS, Jim 206-546-4634 537 G
jhills@shoreline.edu

HILLS, Warren 231-591-3879 251 B
hillsw@ferris.edu

HILLYER, Jill 336-334-4079 379 A
jill_hillyer@uncg.edu

HILPERT, John, M 662-846-4000 274 B
jhilpert@deltastate.edu

HILSABECK, Alison 847-947-5065 159 D
ahilsabeck@nl.edu

HILT, Elizabeth 650-843-3418 61 A
ehilt@paloaltou.edu

HILTABIDDLE, Tom 818-947-2734 55 E
hiltabtr@lavc.edu

HILTE, Ken 719-502-2140 86 G
ken.hilte@ppcc.edu

HILTERBRAN, Stephen 870-543-5907 23 H
shilterbran@seark.edu

HILTON, Adriel 563-425-5221 189 C
hiltona@uiu.edu

HILTON, Carol 949-582-4872 70 F
chilton@saddleback.edu

HILTON, Don 254-647-3234 492 E
dhilton@rangercollege.edu

HILTON, III, Earl, M 336-334-7686 377 F
hiltone@ncat.edu

HILTON, James, L 434-924-1432 525 B
jlh5mc@virginia.edu

HILTON, Linda 802-241-3148 515 B
hiltonl@lsc.vsc.edu

HILTON, Linwood 404-752-1663 134 B
lhilton@msm.edu

HILTON, Richard, H 315-697-2300 359 A
rhilton@uscny.edu

HILTON, Robert, C 479-979-1203 26 A
rchilton@mail.ozarks.edu

HILTS, Deb, B 607-431-4171 335 B
hiltsd@hartwick.edu

HILYER, Billy, D 334-386-7103 3 H
bhilyer@faulkner.edu

HIMARIOS, Daniel 817-272-2881 505 A
himarios@uta.edu

HIMBEAULT-TAYLOR,
Simone 734-764-5132 259 D
shtaylor@umich.edu

HIMBER, David 212-960-5330 361 I
himber@yu.edu

HIMES, A.C. (Buddy) 936-468-2801 495 H
himesac@sfasu.edu

HIMLER, Kim, A 724-925-4116 451 E
himlerk@wccc.edu

HIMMELBERGER,
Stacey, J 315-859-4416 335 A
shimmelb@hamilton.edu

HIMMELMAN, Ken 802-440-4312 512 G
khimmelman@bennington.edu

HIMSEL, Christian 262-243-5700 546 I
christian.himsel@cuw.edu

HIMSTEDT, Lucy 812-488-2625 180 B
lh133@evansville.edu

HINCH, Virginia 509-359-2329 533 D
vhinch@ewu.edu

HINCHEE, Jeanne 423-697-4721 474 D

HINCK, Shelly, S 989-774-3951 249 G
hinck1ss@cmich.edu

HINCKER, Larry 540-231-5396 529 B
hincker@vt.edu

HINCKLEY, Richard 702-651-7488 302 G
richard.hinckley@csn.edu

HIND, Jonathan, T 315-859-4116 335 A
jhind@hamilton.edu

HINDELEH, Nitsa 314-392-2319 286 C
hindeleh@mobap.edu

HINDERS, Sally 208-769-3349 143 H
sally_hinders@nic.edu

HINDES, Victoria 408-741-2020 78 B
victoria.hindes@westvalley.edu

HINDS, Blayne, E 405-962-1620 408 G
behinds@lunet.edu

HINDS, M. Ray 813-988-5131 107 I
hindsr@floridacollege.edu

HINDS, Randy, C 770-423-6755 132 H
rhinds@kennesaw.edu

HINDS, Teri 507-457-5059 270 B
thinds@winona.edu

HINDS-BROWN, Lindsey 615-297-7545 466 H
hinds-brownl@aquinascollege.edu

HINDUS, Myra 617-266-1400 231 G

HINE, James 415-502-3037 74 E
jhine@finance.ucsf.edu

HINE, Mark, L 434-592-3240 520 F
mhine@liberty.edu

HINE, Suzanne, A 423-746-5205 476 D
shine@twcnet.edu

HINE, Terry 203-576-5072 94 A
thine@stvincentscollege.edu

HINE, William, C 217-581-6644 150 C
wchine@eiu.edu

HINES, Alexander 507-457-5597 270 B
ahines@winona.edu

HINES, Bonnie 318-473-6438 212 G
hines@lsua.edu

HINES, Bradford 414-297-6990 554 D
hinesbe@matc.edu

HINES, CharMaine 313-496-2720 260 C
chines1@wcccd.edu

HINES, Clay, T 919-866-5699 374 E
cthines@waketech.edu

HINES, Cory 214-333-5628 484 C
coryh@dbu.edu

HINES, Craig 312-662-4111 144 C
chines@adler.edu

HINES, DeAnna, J 404-413-1350 131 C
djhines@gsu.edu

HINES, Deborah-Harmon 508-856-2444 238 A
deborah-harmon.hines@umassmed.edu

HINES, Elizabeth 724-946-7031 451 C
ehines@westminster.edu

HINES, Florence, W 410-857-2273 224 D
fhines@mcdaniel.edu

HINES, Jean, C 804-289-8181 525 A
jhines@richmond.edu

HINES, Kenneth, D 919-658-7783 367 D
dhines@moc.edu

HINES, Lara 314-392-2242 286 C
robeyl@mobap.edu

HINES, Linda, K 817-515-5308 496 A
linda.hines@tccd.edu

HINES, Mary, E 412-578-6123 424 G
hinesme@carlow.edu

HINES, Nancy, A 563-333-6377 188 D
HinesNancyA@sau.edu

HINES, Nancy, G 509-777-4638 539 F
nhines@whitworth.edu

HINES, Patti 619-574-6909 60 E
phines@pacificcollege.edu

HINES, Robert, M 540-375-2326 523 D
hines@roanoke.edu

HINES, Ruth 617-427-0600 241 D
rhines@rcc.mass.edu

HINES, JR., Samuel, M 843-953-5007 456 C
sam.hines@citadel.edu

HINES, Wes 865-974-8701 477 B
jhines2@utk.edu

HINES-FRITTS,
Mary Lou, A 816-235-1107 291 E
hinesml@umkc.edu

HINEY, Delaine, S 712-362-0428 185 G
dhiney@iowalakes.edu

HING FAY, Eleanor, C 215-898-8493 448 I
hingfay@dev.upenn.edu

HINGA, Gilbert 254-968-9081 496 F
hinga@tarleton.edu

HINGELBERG, Julie 313-664-7494 250 A
julieh@collegeforcreativestudies.edu

HINKLE, Adrian 405-789-7661 412 E
Adrian.Hinkle@swcu.edu

HINKLE, Ana 907-834-1623 11 B
ahinkle@pwscc.edu

HINKLE, Barbara 724-838-4206 447 B
hinkle@setonhill.edu

HINKLE, Barbara, C 724-838-4206 447 B
hinkle@setonhill.edu

HINKLE, Bernadette 610-436-2961 443 F
bhinkle@wcupa.edu

HINKLE, George 740-753-6310 392 A
hinkle_g@hocking.edu

HINKLE, Keith 310-506-4893 61 G
keith.hinkle@pepperdine.edu

HINKLE, Lance 405-744-5237 410 C
lance.hinkle@okstate.edu

HINKLE, Lisa 312-379-1632 146 C
lhinkle@thechicagoschool.edu

HINKLE, M, L 620-665-3526 193 F
hinklem@hutchcc.edu

HINKLE, Sandy, L 573-651-2250 290 D
shinkle@semo.edu

HINKLEY, Lisa 847-735-5235 155 F
hinkley@lakeforest.edu

HINKLEY, Richard 434-592-3077 520 F
rdhinkle@liberty.edu

HINKSON, Avis 212-854-5262 323 G
ahinkson@barnard.edu

HINMAN, David 253-680-7713 531 A
dhinman@bates.ctc.edu

HINNEN, Jack 205-226-4761 2 C
jhinnen@bsc.edu

HINNEN, Marsha 251-981-3771 2 H
marsha.hinnen@columbiasouthern.edu

HINNERS, Gordon 828-689-1208 366 F
ghinners@mhc.edu

HINOJOSA, Gilberto 301-322-0656 225 F
hinojogx@pgcc.edu

HINOJOSA, Maggie 956-665-2011 506 A
williamsm@utpa.edu

HINRICHS, Jay 970-351-2362 88 F
jay.hinrichs@unco.edu

HINRICHS, Judy 425-637-1010 531 I
jhinrichs@city.edu

HINRICHS, Kathleen 620-223-2700 192 G
kathleenh@fortscott.edu

HINRICHS, Mark 520-318-2700 12 E
mhinrichs@aii.edu

HINRICHSEN, Greg 626-852-8047 39 G
ghinrichsen@citruscollege.edu

HINSHAW, Ada Sue 301-295-9002 558 A
adasue.hinshaw@usuhs.mil

HINSHAW, Dana 620-665-3322 193 F
hinshawd@hutchcc.edu

HINSHAW, Garrett, D 828-327-7000 368 G
ghinshaw@cvcc.edu

HINSHAW, Virginia, S 808-956-7651 141 B
vhinshaw@hawaii.edu

HINSON, Bobby 850-201-6071 121 F
hinsonb@tcc.fl.edu

HINSON, David 704-991-0183 374 A
hinsonld@stanly.edu

HINSON, David, J 501-450-1340 22 A

HINSON, Dianne, B 919-747-0007 374 E
dbhinson@waketech.edu

HINSON, Fred 828-227-7495 379 E
hinson@wcu.edu

HINSON, Jane 478-445-4546 129 F
jane.hinson@gcsu.edu

HINTERLONG, James, E 804-828-1036 525 E
jehinterlong@vcu.edu

HINTON, Amy, E 601-426-6346 277 D
ahinton@southeasternbaptist.edu

HINTON, Billy, C .... 713-500-8444.... 506 D
william.c.hinton@uth.tmc.edu
HINTON, Carolyn .... 601-877-6151.... 273 C
chinton@alcorn.edu
HINTON, Cheryl .... 443-352-4489.... 226 E
chinton@stevenson.edu
HINTON, Don .... 435-652-7651.... 512 A
hinton@dixie.edu
HINTON, H. Scott .... 435-797-2776.... 511 B
hinton@engineering.usu.edu
HINTON, Hortense, B .... 703-257-6664.... 527 C
hhinton@nvcc.edu
HINTON, John, A .... 252-398-6376.... 363 E
hintoj@chowan.edu
HINTON, Mary .... 845-561-0800.... 342 A
HINTON-DOYLE, June .... 516-678-5000.... 341 F
jhinton-doyle@molloy.edu
HINTON-RIVERA, Jake ...... 928-524-7662...... 17 B
jake.hinton-rivera@npc.edu
HINTZ, Carol .... 816-235-1621.... 291 E
hintzc@umkc.edu
HINTZ, Debra .... 704-406-3973.... 364 B
dhintz@gardner-webb.edu
HINTZ, Nancy .... 920-748-8346.... 549 I
HINTZ, Sharon .... 908-835-2356.... 317 C
hintz@warren.edu
HINTZ, Veronica .... 740-587-6655.... 389 H
hintz@denison.edu
HINZ, Chuck .... 319-398-5511.... 186 H
chinz@kirkwood.edu
HINZ, Chuck .... 319-398-5574.... 186 H
chinz@kirkwood.edu
HINZ, James .... 770-593-2257.... 131 E
jahinz@yahoo.com
HINZ, Laurence, A .... 505-473-6234.... 320 F
president@santafeuniversity.edu
HINZMAN, Larry .... 907-474-7331...... 10 J
ldhinzman@alaska.edu
HIOCO, Barbara, A .... 559-638-3641...... 72 B
barbara.hioco@reedleycollege.edu
HIPES, Mark .... 276-326-4340.... 516 I
mhipes@bluefield.edu
HIPOL, Ana .... 408-848-4720...... 48 B
ahipol@gavilan.edu
HIPOLITO, Veronica .... 928-226-4334...... 13 H
veronica.hipolito@coconino.edu
HIPONIA, Lorenzo, S .... 202-231-8785.... 557 G
lorenzo.hiponia@dia.mil
HIPP, Kathleen .... 603-577-6659.... 304 J
hipp@dwc.edu
HIPPLE, Andrew .... 717-757-1100.... 452 I
andy.hipple@yti.edu
HIPPLE, Miranda .... 828-298-3325.... 380 C
mhipple@warren-wilson.edu
HIPPLER, Stanley .... 337-475-5181.... 215 G
stan@mcneese.edu
HIPPOLITE WRIGHT,
Debbie .... 808-675-3799.... 139 I
debbie.hippolite.wright@byuh.edu
HIPPS, OSB, Norman, W .. 724-805-2271.... 446 E
norman.hipps@email.stvincent.edu
HIPPS, Suzanne .... 602-243-8153...... 16 E
suzanne.hipps@smcmail.maricopa.edu
HIPSKY, Martin, A .... 740-368-3113.... 400 F
mahipsky@owu.edu
HIRA, Labh, S .... 515-294-2422.... 182 B
lhira@iastate.edu
HIRA, Tahira, K .... 515-294-2042.... 182 B
tkhira@iastate.edu
HIRAK, Joe .... 802-728-1283.... 515 G
HIRALDO, Rafael .... 787-863-2390.... 563 C
rafael.hiraldo@fajardo.inter.edu
HIRAMOTO, James .... 415-955-2107...... 27 F
jhiramoto@alliant.edu
HIRAMOTO, Patti .... 831-582-3332...... 35 C
phiramoto@csumb.edu
HIRD, Lon .... 605-367-7284.... 466 C
lon.hird@southeasttech.edu
HIRE, Jack .... 740-587-5698.... 389 H
hire@denison.edu
HIRIS, Eric, J .... 240-895-4468.... 226 A
ejhiris@smcm.edu
HIRLENAN, E. Daniel .... 209-228-4411...... 74 B
dhirlenan@UCMerced.edu
HIRNER, Leo, J .... 816-604-4501.... 285 D
leo.hirner@mcckc.edu
HIROKAWA, Randy .... 808-974-7300.... 141 A
randyh@hawaii.edu
HIRSCH, Brian .... 210-999-8330.... 502 C
Brian.Hirsch@trinity.edu
HIRSCH, Deborah .... 563-876-3353.... 183 G
dhirsch@dwci.edu
HIRSCH, Deborah .... 617-928-4730.... 243 A
dhirsch@mountida.edu
HIRSCH, Jerry, A .... 413-782-1247.... 246 D
jhirsch@wne.edu
HIRSCH, Linda, R .... 563-333-6296.... 188 D
HirschLindaR@sau.edu
HIRSCH, Michael, L .... 512-505-3125.... 488 B
mlhirsch@htu.edu
HIRSCH, Michelle .... 718-489-5202.... 348 E
mhirsch@stfranciscollege.edu
HIRSCH, Robert .... 814-756-0690.... 433 C
rhirsch@lecom.edu
HIRSCH, Samuel .... 215-751-8160.... 426 B
shirsch@ccp.edu
HIRSCH, Tom .... 641-472-1170.... 187 B
thirsch@mum.edu
HIRSCH, Wendy .... 802-753-2462.... 512 G
whirsch@bennington.edu
HIRSCHBECK, Denise, R ... 314-935-5320.... 292 J
dhirschbeck@wustl.edu
HIRSCHFIELD, Michael, T . 262-472-1633.... 552 E
hirschfm@uww.edu
HIRSCHMAN, Shalom .... 212-463-0400.... 357 J
shirschman@touro.edu
HIRSCHY, Margaret .... 419-434-4260.... 406 A
hirschym@findlay.edu
HIRSH, Barbara .... 215-576-0800.... 445 C
bhirsh@rrc.edu
HIRSH, David, I .... 212-854-1656.... 330 F
dih1@columbia.edu
HIRSH, Deborah, D .... 714-438-4707...... 40 I
dhirsh@mail.cccd.edu
HIRSH, Dennis .... 614-891-5030.... 397 G
HIRSH, Louis, L .... 302-831-1209...... 96 F
louhirsh@udel.edu
HIRSHMAN, Elliot .... 619-594-5201...... 36 E
presidents.office@sdsu.edu
HIRSHON, Arnold .... 216-368-5292.... 386 E
arnold.hirshon@case.edu
HIRST, Martha .... 718-990-3250.... 348 G
hirstm@stjohns.edu
HIRST, Thomas, M .... 845-451-1904.... 331 F
t_hirst@culinary.edu
HIRT, E. Jill .... 610-861-5421.... 437 G
jhirt@northampton.edu
HIRTLE, Christopher .... 413-572-5455.... 239 C
chirtle@wsc.ma.edu
HIRTZEL, Lucas, R .... 573-629-3011.... 282 H
LHirtzel@hlg.edu
HIRTZINGER, Debbie, A .... 937-778-7961.... 390 G
dhirtzinger@edisonohio.edu
HISE, Paul .... 806-720-7279.... 490 D
paul.hise@lcu.edu
HISER, Larry, R .... 740-376-4665.... 395 F
larry.hiser@marietta.edu
HISEY, Richard, M .... 617-266-1400.... 231 G
HISKEY, Robert, M .... 419-586-0381.... 406 D
robert.hiskey@wright.edu
HISLE, W. Lee .... 860-439-2650...... 91 E
wlhis@conncoll.edu
HISLOP, Charli .... 888-384-0849...... 27 G
charli@allied.edu
HISS, Nancy .... 503-699-6242.... 416 I
nhiss@marylhurst.edu
HISSONG, Kimberly .... 315-229-5837.... 349 E
khissong@stlawu.edu
HISTAND, James, L .... 574-535-7456.... 171 D
jimlh@goshen.edu
HISTAND, Phillip, C .... 541-737-9355.... 418 F
phillip.histand@oregonstate.edu
HITCH, Elizabeth, J .... 801-321-7119.... 510 K
ehitch@utahsbr.edu
HITCHCOCK, Cheryl, Y ...... 443-885-3535.... 224 F
cheryl.hitchcock@morgan.edu
HITCHCOCK, Claude, E ..... 443-885-3938.... 224 F
claude.hitchcock@morgan.edu
HITCHCOCK, Eloise .... 615-547-1351.... 467 I
ehitchcock@cumberland.edu
HITCHCOCK, Lynn .... 225-359-9206.... 209 K
lhitchcock@catc.edu
HITCHCOCK, Susan .... 607-255-5147.... 331 C
sh54@cornell.edu
HITCHCOCK, Walter, T ...... 575-624-8183.... 319 C
hitchcock@nmmi.edu
HITCHELL, Dan .... 314-968-7442.... 293 A
danhitchell51@webster.edu
HITE, Carl .... 423-478-6200.... 474 E
chite@clevelandstatecc.edu
HITE, Elinor .... 312-662-4415.... 144 C
HITE, Joe .... 940-552-6291.... 507 E
jhite@vernoncollege.edu
HITE, Patrick .... 214-768-2146.... 494 F
phite@smu.edu
HITE, Robert, D .... 415-442-7058...... 48 E
bhite@ggu.edu
HITE, Trudy, E .... 302-356-6965...... 97 A
trudy.e.hite@wilmu.edu
HITES, Michael .... 217-244-0102.... 166 E
hites@uillinois.edu
HITESMAN, Bill .... 402-461-2400.... 297 C
bhitesman@cccneb.edu
HITLIN, Amy .... 919-760-8521.... 366 G
hitlina@meredith.edu
HITT, John, C .... 407-823-1823.... 120 A
john.hitt@ucf.edu
HITT, Richard, J .... 863-784-7036.... 117 I
richard.hitt@southflorida.edu
HITTENBERGER, Jeff .... 714-556-3610...... 76 E
officeoftheprovost@vanguard.edu
HITTLE, Dennis, M .... 309-794-7370.... 145 B
dennishittle@augustana.edu
HITZ, Randy .... 503-725-4697.... 418 G
hitz@pdx.edu
HITZEL, Joan .... 515-244-4221.... 181 D
hitzelj@aib.edu
HITZEMAN, John .... 936-294-1900.... 501 A
pur_jch@shsu.edu
HIXON, Jennifer .... 413-565-1000.... 231 B
jhixon@baypath.edu
HIXSON, Carla .... 701-224-5580.... 382 B
carla.braun@bismarckstate.edu
HIXSON, Carol .... 727-873-4400.... 121 B
carol.hixson@nelson.usf.edu
HIXSON, John .... 479-619-4341...... 22 H
jhixson@nwacc.edu
HIXSON, Paul .... 217-244-6227.... 167 B
pch@mx.uillinois.edu
HIYANE-BROWN, Kathi ...... 360-383-3330.... 539 D
khiyane-brown@whatcom.ctc.edu
HIZER, Ginny .... 513-745-5685.... 403 F
ginny.hizer@uc.edu
HJELLUM, Wilma .... 402-457-2723.... 298 H
whjellum@mccneb.edu
HLADEK, Thomas .... 718-482-5510.... 328 C
tomhl@lagcc.cuny.edu
HLADIO, Patricia, A .... 724-738-2044.... 443 E
patricia.hladio@sru.edu
HLADIS, Jirka .... 303-245-4702...... 86 B
jirka@naropa.edu
HLAVIN, Karen .... 847-543-2384.... 147 H
khlavin@clcillinois.edu
HLAVINKA, Lysa, A .... 703-247-2500...... 99 D
lh@strayer.edu
HLINAK, Matthew, J .... 708-524-6812.... 150 A
mhlinak@dom.edu
HLINKA, Karen .... 270-534-3236.... 203 B
karen.hlinka@kctcs.edu
HLUBB, Emma .... 931-424-7366.... 470 E
ehlubb@martinmethodist.edu
HLUBB, James, R .... 931-424-7379.... 470 E
jhlubb@martinmethodist.edu
HLUBEK, Andrew .... 507-537-6286.... 269 G
Andrew.Hlubek@smsu.edu
HMIELEWSKI, Christopher 507-537-7984.... 269 G
Christopher.Hmielewski@smsu.edu
HMIELEWSKI, Thomas ...... 715-682-1208.... 549 C
thmielewski@northland.edu
HO, Co .... 714-992-7021...... 59 D
cho@fullcoll.edu
HO, David .... 402-457-2716.... 298 H
dho@mccneb.edu
HO, Jenney .... 562-860-2451...... 38 J
jho@cerritos.edu
HO, John, I .... 716-645-3786.... 351 G
proho@buffalo.edu
HO, Peggy .... 773-442-5143.... 159 H
k-ho1@neiu.edu
HO, Sam .... 408-298-2181...... 67 A
sam.ho@sjeccd.org
HO, Sandra .... 603-427-7614.... 304 C
sho@ccsnh.edu
HOAD, Michael .... 813-974-4014.... 120 D
mhoad@health.usf.edu
HOADLEY, Diane .... 715-836-2500.... 550 H
hoadled@uewc.edu
HOAG, Arlene .... 337-262-5962.... 209 D
ahoag@acadiana.edu
HOAG, Arlene .... 337-262-5962.... 209 F
ahoag@ltc.edu
HOAG, David .... 847-317-7128.... 166 B
dhoag@tiu.edu
HOANG, Linh .... 808-734-9570.... 141 E
lhoang@hawaii.edu
HOARE, William, D .... 262-551-6200.... 546 F
whoare@carthage.edu
HOBAN, Elizabeth .... 973-328-5160.... 309 B
ehoban@ccm.edu
HOBAN, Kristi, M .... 817-257-7803.... 498 F
k.hoban@tcu.edu
HOBAN, Patricia, K .... 503-375-5477.... 421 C
phoban@willamette.edu
HOBAN, Theresa, M .... 315-568-3216.... 342 H
thoban@nycc.edu
HOBAUGH, Greg .... 215-572-3848.... 451 D
ghobaugh@wts.edu
HOBBIE, Lawrence .... 516-877-3165.... 322 A
hobbie@adelphi.edu
HOBBS, Bruce, R .... 208-496-3110.... 142 G
hobbsb@byui.edu
HOBBS, Clinton, G .... 706-379-3111.... 139 F
clinth@yhc.edu
HOBBS, Evelyn .... 575-527-7630.... 319 G
erhobbs@nmsu.edu
HOBBS, Harriet .... 910-879-5516.... 368 A
hhobbs@bladencc.edu
HOBBS, Jeanie .... 817-598-6267.... 508 C
hobbs@wc.edu
HOBBS, Jeffrey .... 714-432-5725...... 41 B
jhobbs@occ.cccd.edu
HOBBS, Lynn, E .... 478-934-3012.... 133 G
lhobbs@mgc.edu
HOBBS, Marcia .... 270-809-2196.... 204 F
mhobbs4@murraystate.edu
HOBBS, Nancy, A .... 734-764-7254.... 259 D
hobbsn@umich.edu
HOBBS, Pamelia, C .... 336-599-1181.... 372 D
hobbsp@piedmontcc.edu
HOBBS, Patrick, E .... 973-642-8750.... 315 C
patrick.hobbs@shu.edu
HOBBS, Patrick, J .... 973-642-8750.... 315 B
patrick.hobbs@shu.edu
HOBBS, Phillip, M .... 205-853-1200........ 5 C
mhobbs@jeffstateonline.com
HOBBS, Rose .... 518-438-3111.... 340 B
roseh@mariacollege.edu
HOBBS, Valerie .... 303-581-9955.... 320 H
vhobbs@acupuncturecollege.edu
HOBBS, Valerie .... 303-581-9955...... 87 I
HOBBY, Angela .... 229-333-5365.... 139 E
angela.hobby@wiregrass.edu
HOBBY-MEARS, Michelle .. 949-480-4134...... 69 I
mhobby@soka.edu
HOBERECHT, Randall .... 845-938-7382.... 558 G
Randall.Hobberecht@usma.edu
HOBERMAN, Chaim .... 516-225-4700.... 346 K
HOBGOOD, Wade .... 414-229-4762.... 551 C
hobgood@uwm.edu
HOBIN, Caron, T .... 413-565-1000.... 231 B
chobin@baypath.edu
HOBIN, Gail .... 617-287-5310.... 237 D
gail.hobin@umb.edu
HOBLER, Billie, J .... 419-586-0324.... 406 D
bj.hobler@wright.edu
HOBLER, Dean .... 419-227-3141.... 404 D
dahobler@unoh.edu
HOBLET, Kent, H .... 662-325-1418.... 276 A
hoblet@cvm.msstate.edu
HOBSON, James .... 703-284-1617.... 521 A
bing.hobson@marymount.edu
HOBSON, Lynn, M .... 620-341-5267.... 192 D
lhobson@emporia.edu
HOBSON, Paula Lee .... 775-674-7686.... 302 J
phobson@tmcc.edu
HOBSON, Sheila .... 301-860-3451.... 228 A
shobson@bowiestate.edu
HOBSON, Tricia .... 405-422-1263.... 411 G
hobsont@redlandscc.edu
HOBYAK, Michael, S .... 215-785-0111.... 440 H
HOCHANADEL, Gery .... 972-438-6932.... 492 C
ghochanadel@parkercc.edu
HOCHMAN, Carey .... 206-322-6100.... 536 D
chochman@pmi.edu
HOCHMAN, Leah .... 213-765-2666...... 50 D
lhochman@huc.edu
HOCHSCHILD, Joshua .... 301-447-7435.... 225 A
hochschild@msmary.edu
HOCHSTEIN, Dale .... 201-701-7027.... 314 F
dhochstein@spc.edu
HOCHSTETLER, Char .... 574-535-7541.... 171 D
chardh@goshen.edu
HOCHSTETLER, Donald ..... 508-929-8511.... 239 D
dhochstetler@worcester.edu
HOCK, Carl, E .... 856-566-6066.... 316 E
hock@umdnj.edu
HOCK, Carl, E .... 856-566-6066.... 316 I
hock@umdnj.edu
HOCK, Joan .... 215-489-2975.... 426 H
Joan.Hock@delval.edu
HOCKENBERRY, Frederick 301-846-2544.... 222 G
fhockenberry@frederick.edu
HOCKENHULL,
Benjamin, R .... 512-448-8688.... 493 B
ben@stedwards.edu
HOCKENSMITH, William ..... 805-922-6966...... 26 K
whockensmith@hancockcollege.edu
HOCKETT, Anne, B .... 336-633-0218.... 372 F
abhockett@randolph.edu
HOCKFIELD, Susan .... 617-253-0148.... 242 A
hockfield@mit.edu
HOCKMAN, Joan .... 814-371-2090.... 448 C
jhockman@triangle-tech.edu
HOCKMAN, CSC,
Richard, C .... 570-208-5890.... 432 E
rchockma@kings.edu
HOCKSTRA, Dale .... 650-543-3874...... 57 B
dhockstra@menlo.edu
HOCQUARD, Stephen, L .... 989-964-4081.... 258 A
shoc@svsu.edu
HOCUTT, Kirby .... 806-742-3355.... 501 D
kirby.hocutt@ttu.edu
HOCUTT, Martha .... 205-652-3675...... 10 A
mhocutt@uwa.edu
HODA, Rebecca .... 718-518-4249.... 327 D
rhoda@hostos.cuny.edu
HODGE, Brad, K .... 215-670-9210.... 438 D
bkhodge@peirce.edu
HODGE, David .... 334-291-4928........ 2 G
david.hodge@cv.edu
HODGE, David .... 978-478-3400.... 247 C
dhodge@zbc.edu
HODGE, David .... 513-529-2345.... 396 D
president@muohio.edu
HODGE, Derek, M .... 703-323-3267.... 527 C
dhodge@nvcc.edu
HODGE, Doug .... 731-286-3359.... 475 A
hodge@dscc.edu
HODGE, Emilia .... 352-395-4495.... 117 E
emilia.hodge@sfcollege.edu
HODGE, Evelyn .... 334-229-4139........ 1 C
ehodge@alasu.edu
HODGE, Gary, B .... 972-881-5897.... 483 D
ghodge@collin.edu

HODGE, Hortencia ... 559-438-4222 ... 49 G
hortencia_hodge@heald.edu
HODGE, Johnesa ... 313-496-2796 ... 260 C
jdimick1@wcccd.edu
HODGE, Kevin ... 214-234-4850 ... 486 F
khodge@cci.edu
HODGE, Marilyn ... 757-822-7244 ... 528 C
mhodge@tcc.edu
HODGE, Michel, A ... 718-262-2707 ... 329 B
mahodge@york.cuny.edu
HODGE, Mike ... 314-264-1740 ... 292 C
mike.hodge@vatterott.edu
HODGE, Mildred ... 860-885-2344 ... 91 B
mhodge@trcc.commnet.edu
HODGE, Rick, L ... 626-585-3001 ... 61 E
rlhodge@pasadena.edu
HODGE, Sandra ... 440-775-6200 ... 397 F
sandra.hodge@oberlin.edu
HODGE, Wendy ... 860-701-5166 ... 93 B
hodge_w@mitchell.edu
HODGEN, Barbara ... 323-464-2777 ... 27 I
bhodgen@ca.aada.org
HODGEN, Danielle ... 509-527-4301 ... 538 G
danielle.hodgen@wwcc.edu
HODGES, Carolyn, R ... 865-974-3694 ... 477 B
chodges@utk.edu
HODGES, Christopher ... 215-893-5262 ... 426 E
christopher.hodges@curtis.edu
HODGES, Dale, B ... 269-471-3321 ... 247 H
dbhodges@andrews.edu
HODGES, Daniel, K ... 540-365-4365 ... 518 J
dhodges@ferrum.edu
HODGES, Dawn ... 770-229-3293 ... 137 B
dhodges@sctech.edu
HODGES, Diane ... 219-980-6824 ... 173 F
dlhodges@iun.edu
HODGES, Donika ... 773-907-4462 ... 147 A
dhodges19@ccc.edu
HODGES, Elaine ... 843-661-8020 ... 458 A
elaine.hodges@fdtc.edu
HODGES, Gary ... 479-968-0394 ... 20 G
ghodges@atu.edu
HODGES, Heath ... 918-463-2931 ... 407 H
heath.hodges@connorsstate.edu
HODGES, James ... 510-885-3957 ... 34 C
james.hodges@csueastbay.edu
HODGES, Jeff ... 540-362-6503 ... 519 E
jhodges@hollins.edu
HODGES, Kimberly, S ... 860-701-5000 ... 93 B
hodges_k@mitchell.edu
HODGES, Nathan, L ... 270-901-1111 ... 201 E
nathan.hodges@kctcs.edu
HODGES, Omega ... 828-298-3325 ... 380 C
ohodges@warren-wilson.edu
HODGES, Rhonda ... 276-656-0256 ... 527 D
rhodges@ph.vccs.edu
HODGES, Richard, A ... 215-898-4050 ... 448 I
rhodges@sas.upenn.edu
HODGES, Ricky, C ... 336-734-7272 ... 370 C
rhodges@forsythtech.edu
HODGES, Stacey ... 601-276-2000 ... 277 E
slee@smcc.edu
HODGES, Stephen ... 617-746-1990 ... 236 B
stephen.hodges@hult.edu
HODGES, Tim ... 785-594-8365 ... 190 C
tim.hodges@bakeru.edu
HODGES, Tina ... 731-352-4032 ... 467 C
hodgest@bethelu.edu
HODGES, Zachary ... 713-718-5721 ... 487 G
zachary.hodges@hccs.edu
HODGES MOORE, Sue ... 859-572-5349 ... 205 E
moores4@nku.edu
HODGINS, Randy ... 206-221-5670 ... 538 F
rhodgins@uw.edu
HODNETT, James ... 478-387-4715 ... 130 E
HODOWANEC, Michael ... 610-372-4721 ... 445 B
mhodowanec@racc.edu
HODOWNES, Stephen ... 603-645-9730 ... 306 B
s.hodownes@snhu.edu
HODSDON, Roger ... 626-815-5080 ... 30 E
rhodsdon@apu.edu
HODSON, Andrea ... 603-283-2363 ... 303 F
ahodson@antiochne.edu
HODSON, J. Bradford ... 620-235-4757 ... 195 I
bhodson@pittstate.edu
HODSON, Luke ... 859-985-3503 ... 198 F
hodsonl@berea.edu
HODUM, Robert ... 931-372-3888 ... 474 B
rhodum@tntech.edu
HOEBER, Mark, S ... 716-851-1413 ... 333 C
hoeber@ecc.edu
HOECK, Andreas ... 303-715-3218 ... 87 H
HOEF, Ted ... 314-968-6980 ... 293 A
hoeftl@webster.edu
HOEFER, Michael, T ... 770-394-8300 ... 124 F
mhoefer@aii.edu
HOEFLER, William ... 479-968-0353 ... 20 G
whoeflerjr@atu.edu
HOEFT, Robert ... 217-333-9480 ... 167 B
rhoeft@illinois.edu
HOEGE, Jennifer, L ... 608-246-6220 ... 554 B
jlhoege@matcmadison.edu
HOEHN, Alex, J ... 718-990-2998 ... 348 G
hoehna@stjohns.edu
HOEHNE, Therese, A ... 630-844-3866 ... 145 C
thoehne@aurora.edu
HOEHNER, Robert ... 314-505-7170 ... 280 H
hoehnerr@csl.edu
HOEHNKE, Diane ... 414-443-8627 ... 553 B
diane.hoehnke@wlc.edu
HOEKSTRA, Erik ... 712-722-6333 ... 183 H
ehoekstra@dordt.edu
HOEKSTRA, Jack ... 866-323-0233 ... 63 D
HOEKSTRA, Jonathan ... 254-867-4892 ... 499 I
jonathan.hoekstra@systems.tstc.edu
HOEKSTRA, Steve, J ... 785-827-5541 ... 194 D
hoekstr@kwu.edu
HOEL, Monica, S ... 276-944-6126 ... 518 I
mshoel@ehc.edu
HOELCLE, Larene, L ... 585-345-6811 ... 334 F
lhoelcle@genesee.edu
HOELKER, Florentine, J ... 440-510-1112 ... 386 A
fjhoelker@bryantstratton.edu
HOELLE, Brian ... 317-955-6080 ... 177 G
0777mgr@fheg.follett.com
HOELLEN, Kathy, L ... 803-981-7150 ... 463 G
khoellen@yorktech.edu
HOELSCHER, Ronda ... 325-793-4857 ... 490 F
hoelscher.ronda@mcm.edu
HOELTING, Floyd, B ... 512-471-8631 ... 505 B
floydh@austin.utexas.edu
HOELTZEL, Susan ... 718-960-8731 ... 327 C
susan.hoeltzel@lehman.cuny.edu
HOEMANN, D. Lee ... 360-867-6300 ... 533 I
hoemannl@evergreen.edu
HOEPFER, Maureen, G ... 717-780-1157 ... 430 E
mhoepfer@hacc.edu
HOEPP, Michael ... 315-781-3309 ... 335 G
hoepp@hws.edu
HOEPPEL, John ... 773-442-4650 ... 159 H
j-hoeppel@neiu.edu
HOEPPNER, Stephen, A ... 651-962-6949 ... 272 E
sahoeppner@stthomas.edu
HOERITZ, Kim ... 412-396-6213 ... 428 C
hoeritzk@duq.edu
HOERSCH, Alice, L ... 215-951-1010 ... 432 G
hoersch@lasalle.edu
HOERSCH, Kathy ... 619-425-3200 ... 62 G
khoersch@pmi.edu
HOERST, Barbara ... 215-951-1386 ... 432 G
hoerst@lasalle.edu
HOERTH, Richard ... 920-693-1237 ... 554 A
rich.hoerth@gotoltc.edu
HOESCHLER, Katie ... 928-776-2067 ... 19 E
katie.hoeschler@yc.edu
HOETING, Mark ... 870-972-3033 ... 20 C
mhoeting@astate.edu
HOEY, John, T ... 508-999-8027 ... 237 E
jhoey@umassd.edu
HOFEMANN, Neva ... 408-273-2718 ... 58 G
nhofemann@nhu.edu
HOFER, OP, Andrew ... 202-495-3861 ... 98 D
ahofer@dhs.edu
HOFER, Jeanie, H ... 573-341-4208 ... 292 A
jeanie@mst.edu
HOFER, Linda ... 605-995-2956 ... 464 B
lihofer@dwu.edu
HOFER, Philip ... 909-593-3511 ... 75 C
phofer@laverne.edu
HOFER, Titus, W ... 479-248-7236 ... 21 G
titus@ecollege.edu
HOFF, Andrew ... 559-278-4004 ... 34 D
andrewh@csufresno.edu
HOFF, Andrew ... 559-278-3936 ... 34 D
andrewh@csufresno.edu
HOFF, Darren ... 763-433-1159 ... 265 J
darren.hoff@anokaramsey.edu
HOFF, Kathy ... 614-257-5013 ... 390 B
khoff@devry.edu
HOFF, Kevin, M ... 608-822-2660 ... 555 B
HOFF, Reno, R ... 503-375-7000 ... 415 F
rhoff@corban.edu
HOFFACKER, Thomas, E ... 270-809-2146 ... 204 F
tom.hoffacker@murraystate.edu
HOFFARD, Dwight ... 618-985-3741 ... 154 E
dwighthoffard@jalc.edu
HOFFBAUER, Claudia ... 509-574-4612 ... 540 A
choffbauer@yvcc.edu
HOFFBERG, Michael, C ... 610-519-4264 ... 450 G
michael.hoffberg@villanova.edu
HOFFEE, Byron, L ... 740-374-8716 ... 405 F
bhoffee@wscc.edu
HOFFER, Wallace, C ... 330-966-5450 ... 402 A
whoffer@starkstate.edu
HOFFMAN, A, P ... 334-556-2225 ... 4 A
ahoffman@wallace.edu
HOFFMAN, Agnes ... 503-725-5502 ... 418 G
hoffmana@pdx.edu
HOFFMAN, Barbara ... 319-399-8540 ... 183 C
bhoffman@coe.edu
HOFFMAN, Barbara ... 419-372-2120 ... 385 C
bahoffm@bgsu.edu
HOFFMAN, Bart ... 714-564-6800 ... 63 F
hoffman_bart@sac.edu
HOFFMAN, Beth ... 301-687-4101 ... 228 C
bhoffman@frostburg.edu
HOFFMAN, Brad ... 513-244-4416 ... 388 D
msj@bkstr.com
HOFFMAN, Carol ... 740-389-4636 ... 395 G
hoffmanc@mtc.edu
HOFFMAN, Carolyn, F ... 301-322-0561 ... 225 F
hoffmacf@pgcc.edu
HOFFMAN, Cheryl, A ... 309-833-6021 ... 165 D
cheryl.hoffman@src.edu
HOFFMAN, David ... 540-665-5457 ... 523 K
dhoffman@su.edu
HOFFMAN, Deborah ... 813-935-5700 ... 115 J
deborahhoffman@remingtoncollege.edu
HOFFMAN, Derek, M ... 717-872-3820 ... 443 C
derek.hoffman@millersville.edu
HOFFMAN, Donna ... 909-384-8987 ... 65 C
dhoffman@sbccd.cc.ca.us
HOFFMAN, Ed ... 402-471-2505 ... 299 F
ehoffman@nscs.edu
HOFFMAN, Elizabeth ... 515-294-0070 ... 182 B
bhoffman@iastate.edu
HOFFMAN, Erin ... 847-735-5207 ... 155 F
hoffman@lakeforest.edu
HOFFMAN, Gail ... 212-854-1079 ... 330 F
gh2116@columbia.edu
HOFFMAN, Jeffrey ... 626-396-2325 ... 29 G
jeffrey.hoffman@artcenter.edu
HOFFMAN, Jeffrey, L ... 315-255-1743 ... 325 H
foundation@cayuga-cc.edu
HOFFMAN, Joseph, C ... 718-409-7260 ... 356 C
jhoffman@sunymaritime.edu
HOFFMAN, Joseph, M ... 301-687-4120 ... 228 C
jhoffman@frostburg.edu
HOFFMAN, Kathy, S ... 716-851-1832 ... 333 D
hoffman@ecc.edu
HOFFMAN, Larry ... 914-395-2384 ... 350 C
lhoffman@sarahlawrence.edu
HOFFMAN, Linda ... 301-696-3919 ... 223 C
hoffmanl@hood.edu
HOFFMAN, Lorraine, B ... 530-898-6231 ... 34 A
lbhoffman@csuchico.edu
HOFFMAN, Louis ... 410-484-7200 ... 225 C
HOFFMAN, Marc, L ... 312-235-3535 ... 164 D
m.hoffman@shimer.edu
HOFFMAN, Marcia, K ... 570-577-1631 ... 423 D
marcia.hoffman@bucknell.edu
HOFFMAN, Marion, S ... 850-488-2447 ... 120 B
marionh@ufl.edu
HOFFMAN, Martin ... 609-894-9311 ... 308 C
mhoffman@bcc.edu
HOFFMAN, Mary ... 719-587-7372 ... 80 F
mchoffma@adams.edu
HOFFMAN, Melissa ... 402-354-7212 ... 299 E
melissa.hoffman@methodistcollege.edu
HOFFMAN, Michael ... 716-375-2530 ... 348 C
mhoffman@sbu.edu
HOFFMAN, Michael ... 605-995-3022 ... 464 E
mike.hoffman@mitchelltech.edu
HOFFMAN, Micki, D ... 636-584-6532 ... 281 I
mdhoffma@eastcentral.edu
HOFFMAN, Neil, J ... 414-847-3210 ... 548 G
neilhoffman@miad.edu
HOFFMAN, Patricia, A ... 916-285-9468 ... 51 E
HOFFMAN, Robert ... 507-389-5566 ... 267 H
robert.hoffman@mnsu.edu
HOFFMAN, Sandra ... 856-415-2220 ... 310 E
shoffma2@gccnj.edu
HOFFMAN, Sharon, L ... 802-287-8215 ... 513 D
hoffmans@greenmtn.edu
HOFFMAN, Shirleen, A ... 651-523-2100 ... 264 C
shoffman01@hamline.edu
HOFFMAN, Steven, A ... 859-236-6688 ... 199 D
steven.hoffman@centre.edu
HOFFMAN, Thomas ... 507-453-2770 ... 267 F
thoffman@southeastmn.edu
HOFFMAN, Wendy ... 859-846-5364 ... 204 D
whoffman@midway.edu
HOFFMAN-HARDING,
Erin ... 574-631-7074 ... 180 D
eharding@nd.edu
HOFFMAN-JOHNSON,
Gail ... 989-686-9291 ... 250 F
gailhoffman@delta.edu
HOFFMANN, Lee ... 760-744-1150 ... 61 C
lhoffmann@palomar.edu
HOFFMANN, Len ... 563-589-0322 ... 189 G
lhoffmann@wartburgseminary.edu
HOFFMANN, Lowell ... 731-286-3307 ... 475 A
hoffmann@dscc.edu
HOFFMANN, Mark ... 701-777-2492 ... 381 D
mark.hoffmann@email.und.edu
HOFFMANN, Phylis ... 501-329-6872 ... 21 C
phoffmann@cbc.edu
HOFFMANN, Susie ... 785-670-1643 ... 197 D
susie.hoffmann@washburn.edu
HOFFMANS, Kim ... 805-378-1459 ... 77 B
khoffmans@vcccd.edu
HOFFMASTER, Linda, L ... 717-764-9550 ... 426 D
lhoffmaster@csb.edu
HOFFMEYER, Ed ... 828-689-1352 ... 366 F
ehoffmeyer@mhc.edu
HOFFMEYER, Tom ... 254-710-1561 ... 481 I
tom_hoffmeyer@baylor.edu
HOFFNER, Alan ... 718-982-2381 ... 327 A
Alan.Hoffner@csi.cuny.edu
HOFFNUNG, Michele ... 203-582-8903 ... 93 E
michele.hoffnung@quinnipiac.edu
HOFFSIS, Glen, F ... 352-392-2213 ... 120 B
hoffsisg@vetmed.ufl.edu
HOFMANN, Glenn ... 978-837-5306 ... 242 D
glenn.hofmann@merrimack.edu
HOFMANN, Jacqueline ... 406-243-7908 ... 295 D
jacqueline.hofmann@umontana.edu
HOFMANN, Paul ... 419-372-2248 ... 385 C
phofmann@bgsu.edu
HOFMANN, Rob ... 802-225-3201 ... 513 H
rob.hofmann@neci.edu
HOFMEYER, Karna ... 712-324-5061 ... 188 A
khofmeyer@nwicc.edu
HOFNER, Amyjo ... 617-262-5000 ... 232 B
amyjo.hofner@the-bac.edu
HOFRENNING, Dan ... 507-786-3128 ... 271 H
dhofrenn@stolaf.edu
HOFRENNING, Ilene ... 508-626-4900 ... 238 D
ihofrenning@framingham.edu
HOFSTEDT, Petra ... 715-682-1983 ... 549 C
phofstedt@northland.edu
HOFSTETTER, Shirley, A ... 636-584-6704 ... 281 I
HOFTIEZER, David ... 609-984-1164 ... 316 A
dhoftiezer@tesc.edu
HOGAN, Andrea ... 203-932-7338 ... 95 B
ahogan@newhaven.edu
HOGAN, Beverly, W ... 601-977-7730 ... 277 F
bhogan@tougaloo.edu
HOGAN, Bill ... 206-296-5451 ... 537 F
hoganw@seattleu.edu
HOGAN, Carrie ... 518-783-2554 ... 350 I
chogan@siena.edu
HOGAN, Cheryl ... 231-843-5864 ... 260 E
clhogan@westshore.edu
HOGAN, Christopher ... 617-287-6800 ... 237 D
christopher.hogan@umb.edu
HOGAN, Heather ... 440-775-8410 ... 397 F
heather.hogan@oberlin.edu
HOGAN, Jennifer ... 810-767-2150 ... 259 F
jhogan@umflint.edu
HOGAN, Joan, P ... 828-448-6041 ... 374 G
jhogan@wpcc.edu
HOGAN, John, A ... 812-374-5115 ... 175 J
jhogan@ivytech.edu
HOGAN, John, T ... 401-865-2676 ... 453 F
jhogan@providence.edu
HOGAN, Judith ... 781-280-3816 ... 240 F
hoganj@middlesex.mass.edu
HOGAN, Kay ... 850-973-9422 ... 113 J
hogank@nfcc.edu
HOGAN, Lesley ... 253-833-9111 ... 534 C
lhogan@greenriver.edu
HOGAN, Marianna ... 212-431-2173 ... 343 E
mhogan@nyls.edu
HOGAN, Martha, A ... 972-238-6210 ... 485 C
mhogan@dcccd.edu
HOGAN, Michael, J ... 217-333-3070 ... 166 E
HOGAN, Pamela ... 603-668-2211 ... 306 B
p.hogan@snhu.edu
HOGAN, Patrick, J ... 301-445-1927 ... 227 A
pjhogan@usmd.edu
HOGAN, Paul ... 603-271-6426 ... 304 G
phogan@ccsnh.edu
HOGAN, Phyllis, E ... 317-466-2121 ... 172 L
pehogan@indianatech.edu
HOGAN, Robert ... 773-843-4524 ... 147 E
rhogan@ccc.edu
HOGAN, CSSP, Sean ... 412-396-5069 ... 428 C
hogan@duq.edu
HOGAN, Stacey, L ... 303-678-3755 ... 84 H
stacey.hogan@frontrange.edu
HOGAN, Susan, S ... 413-597-4204 ... 246 G
susan.s.hogan@williams.edu
HOGAN, Terrence ... 319-273-2332 ... 182 D
terry.hogan@uni.edu
HOGAN, Tracy ... 415-482-3507 ... 45 B
tracy.hogan@dominican.edu
HOGAN, William ... 508-999-8270 ... 237 E
whogan@umassd.edu
HOGANS, Arnesha ... 334-277-3390 ... 3 F
arnesha.hogans@vc.edu
HOGARTH-SMITH,
Heather ... 340-693-1151 ... 568 C
hhogart@uvi.edu
HOGARTY, Lisa ... 617-495-1512 ... 235 H
lisa_hogarty@harvard.edu
HOGEBOOM, Cindi ... 510-261-8500 ... 61 F
cindi.hogeboom@patten.edu
HOGELAND, Beth ... 541-917-4911 ... 416 H
hogelab@linnbenton.edu
HOGENSON, Deborah ... 952-888-4777 ... 270 F
dhogenson@nwhealth.edu
HOGG, James, E ... 770-207-3130 ... 124 H
jhogg@athenstech.edu
HOGG, Michael ... 504-862-8495 ... 215 C
mhogg@tulane.edu
HOGGE, Jane Curley ... 410-617-2131 ... 224 A
jchogge@loyola.edu
HOGLUND, Carol ... 307-778-1281 ... 556 B
choglund@lccc.wy.edu
HOGLUND, Susan ... 740-826-8081 ... 396 I
shoglund@muskingum.edu
HOGREFE, Richard ... 909-389-3205 ... 65 B
rhogrefe@craftonhills.edu

HOLLOWAY, Jerry, R .... 918-631-2539.... 413 F
jerry-holloway@utulsa.edu
HOLLOWAY, John .... 718-960-8242.... 327 C
john.holloway@lehman.cuny.edu
HOLLOWAY, Karen .... 229-931-2151.... 131 B
HOLLOWAY, Kendra .... 510-780-4500...... 53 I
khollowa@lifewest.edu
HOLLOWAY, Linda, C .... 217-581-3514.... 150 C
lcholloway2@eiu.edu
HOLLOWAY, Mary .... 803-822-3529.... 459 D
hollowaym@midlandstech.edu
HOLLOWAY, Richard, L ..... 414-955-8256.... 548 E
holloway@mcw.edu
HOLLOWAY, Stacy .... 618-985-3741.... 154 E
stacyholloway@jalc.edu
HOLLOWELL, Lorna .... 270-686-3784.... 202 E
lorna.hollowell@kctcs.edu
HOLLOWELL, Sarah .... 712-325-3207.... 186 B
shollowell@iwcc.edu
HOLLOWELL, Stephen .... 212-237-8521.... 328 A
shollowell@jjay.cuny.edu
HOLLY, Gordon, K .... 330-684-8740.... 403 C
gholly@uakron.edu
HOLLY, Krisztina .... 213-821-5002...... 76 C
z@usc.edu
HOLLY, Marty .... 208-459-5850.... 143 A
mholly@collegeofidaho.edu
HOLLY, Richard .... 815-753-1138.... 160 A
rholly@niu.edu
HOLLY, Shelly .... 918-631-2550.... 413 F
shelly-holly@utulsa.edu
HOLLY, Yvette, A .... 402-559-5678.... 301 A
yholly@unmc.edu
HOLM, Carl, D .... 906-227-2622.... 256 F
cholm@nmu.edu
HOLM, Cyndi .... 507-537-7854.... 269 G
Cyndi.Holm@smsu.edu
HOLM, Janet .... 253-589-5545.... 532 B
janet.holm@cptc.edu
HOLM, Lee .... 713-525-3500.... 504 D
lholm@stthom.edu
HOLMAN, Cheri .... 734-462-4400.... 258 C
cholman@schoolcraft.edu
HOLMAN, Dena .... 828-726-2703.... 368 D
dholman@cccti.edu
HOLMAN, Dena .... 828-726-2705.... 368 D
dholman@cccti.edu
HOLMAN, Fred, B .... 775-784-4853.... 303 A
fholman@unr.edu
HOLMAN, James .... 414-443-8566.... 553 B
james.holman@wlc.edu
HOLMAN, John .... 606-218-5194.... 207 B
jholman@pc.edu
HOLMAN, Lucy .... 606-218-5265.... 207 B
lholman@pc.edu
HOLMAN, Lucy .... 410-837-4333.... 229 A
lholman@ubalt.edu
HOLMAN, Mark .... 701-854-8024.... 383 A
markh@sbci.edu
HOLMAN, Pat .... 505-984-6144.... 320 C
HOLMAN, Sara, C .... 920-832-6583.... 547 J
sara.b.holman@lawrence.edu
HOLMANS, Jim .... 325-674-4974.... 478 H
holmansj@acu.edu
HOLMES, Arlene .... 605-642-6219.... 465 F
arlene.holmes@bhsu.edu
HOLMES, Barbara .... 501-244-5101...... 19 F
barbara.holmes@arkansasbaptist.edu
HOLMES, Barbara, J .... 202-274-6156...... 99 F
bholmes@udc.edu
HOLMES, Bear, L .... 206-934-6424.... 537 B
bear.holmes@seattlecolleges.edu
HOLMES, Beverly .... 309-341-7755.... 155 E
bholmes@knox.edu
HOLMES, Carlos .... 302-857-6062...... 95 F
cholmes@desu.edu
HOLMES, Charley .... 903-586-2501.... 481 F
holmes@bmats.edu
HOLMES, Claire .... 510-642-3734...... 73 E
claireholmes@berkeley.edu
HOLMES, Debra .... 912-279-5787.... 127 B
dholmes@ccga.edu
HOLMES, Edward, J .... 716-851-1016.... 333 B
holmese@ecc.edu
HOLMES, Ella .... 601-979-6858.... 275 A
ella.b.holmes@jsums.edu
HOLMES, Erica .... 252-536-7289.... 370 F
holmese@halifaxcc.edu
HOLMES, Erin .... 605-642-6011.... 465 F
erin.holmes@bhsu.edu
HOLMES, Frank, R .... 936-294-3625.... 501 A
holmes@shsu.edu
HOLMES, Harold, R .... 336-758-5226.... 380 B
holmes@wfu.edu
HOLMES, Heather, W .... 410-677-4865.... 228 D
hwholmes@salisbury.edu
HOLMES, Heidi .... 314-768-7808.... 286 D
hholmes@missouricollege.com
HOLMES, Jim .... 202-462-2101...... 98 C
holmes@iwp.edu
HOLMES, Joan .... 813-253-7043.... 110 I
jholmes16@hccfl.edu
HOLMES, John, D .... 402-449-2873.... 298 B
jholmes@graceu.edu

HOLMES, Johnny, B .... 901-321-3445.... 467 G
jholmes@cbu.edu
HOLMES, Judy .... 785-825-5422.... 191 B
jholmes@brownmackie.edu
HOLMES, Kenneth, M .... 203-576-4393...... 94 D
kholmes@bridgeport.edu
HOLMES, Kimberley .... 502-597-6310.... 203 D
kimberly.holmes@kysu.edu
HOLMES, Kizzy .... 478-757-5205.... 139 A
kholmes@wesleyancollege.edu
HOLMES, Kristen .... 256-352-8118...... 10 B
kristen.holmes@wallacestate.edu
HOLMES, Kristiana, L .... 509-777-4563.... 539 F
kholmes@whitworth.edu
HOLMES, Kurt .... 330-263-2011.... 388 E
kholmes@wooster.edu
HOLMES, Lisa .... 760-921-5453...... 61 B
lholmes@paloverde.edu
HOLMES, Lloyd, A .... 978-762-4000.... 241 A
lholmes@northshore.edu
HOLMES, Lorene .... 903-769-5792.... 488 M
lorene_holmes@jarvis.edu
HOLMES, Malcolm, T .... 804-523-5231.... 526 F
mholmes@reynolds.edu
HOLMES, Matt .... 610-902-8228.... 423 H
matthew.holmes@cabrini.edu
HOLMES, Michael .... 407-708-2108.... 117 G
holmesm@seminolestate.edu
HOLMES, Michelle, M .... 510-841-1905...... 27 J
mmholmes@absw.edu
HOLMES, Mildred .... 815-280-2357.... 154 H
mholmes@jjc.edu
HOLMES, Myioshi, U .... 972-860-8237.... 484 G
muh3310@dcccd.edu
HOLMES, Owen .... 657-278-5403...... 34 E
oholmes@fullerton.edu
HOLMES, Phillip, M .... 478-387-4904.... 130 E
HOLMES, R.J .... 319-895-4574.... 183 D
rjholmes@cornellcollege.edu
HOLMES, Raymond .... 434-848-6473.... 523 G
rholmes@saintpauls.edu
HOLMES, JR., Robert .... 407-882-1250.... 120 A
robert.holmes@ucf.edu
HOLMES, Robert, C .... 317-921-4718.... 175 G
bholmes@ivytech.edu
HOLMES, Robin, H .... 541-346-1137.... 419 B
savp@uoregon.edu
HOLMES, Rodney .... 480-461-7315...... 15 K
rodney.holmes@mcmail.maricopa.edu
HOLMES, Ron .... 325-793-4631.... 490 F
rholmes@mcm.edu
HOLMES, Sharon, N .... 920-924-6326.... 554 E
sholmes@morainepark.edu
HOLMES, Susan .... 956-364-4107.... 499 J
susan.holmes@harlingen.tstc.edu
HOLMES, Terrell .... 302-857-6375...... 95 F
tholmes@desu.edu
HOLMES, Tiffany .... 312-345-3760.... 164 A
tholmes@saic.edu
HOLMES, Wendy .... 845-341-4662.... 345 E
wendy.holmes@sunyorange.edu
HOLMES-MOORE,
Shanee', S .... 214-860-2138.... 484 I
sholmes@dcccd.edu
HOLMGREN, Marilyn .... 605-721-5275.... 464 G
mholmgren@national.edu
HOLMGREN, Richard, A .... 814-332-2898.... 421 E
richard.holmgren@allegheny.edu
HOLMQUIST, David .... 562-903-4886...... 30 H
dave.holmquist@biola.edu
HOLMQUIST, Eric .... 712-279-5435.... 182 E
eric.holmquist@briarcliff.edu
HOLMSTROM, Kevin .... 701-224-5776.... 382 B
kevin.holmstrom@bismarckstate.edu
HOLO, Joshua .... 213-749-4214...... 50 D
jholo@huc.edu
HOLODICK, Nicholas, A ...... 570-208-5895.... 432 E
naholodi@kings.edu
HOLOMAN, Christopher, L 716-926-8854.... 335 F
choloman@hilbert.edu
HOLOPIREK, Darnell, S ...... 620-792-9367.... 190 E
holopirekd@bartonccc.edu
HOLOWICKI, Linda .... 708-209-3170.... 148 C
linda.holowicki@cuchicago.edu
HOLPER, Mark .... 651-779-5834.... 266 D
mark.holper@century.edu
HOLS, Eric .... 703-284-1601.... 521 A
eric.hols@marymount.edu
HOLSAPPLE, Kelly .... 906-487-7230.... 251 C
kelly.holsapple@finlandia.edu
HOLSCLAW, Mick .... 916-568-3017...... 55 J
holsclm@losrios.edu
HOLSCLAW, Scott .... 870-245-5129...... 22 I
holsclaws@obu.edu
HOLSCLAW, Sheila, K .... 859-846-5310.... 204 D
sholsclaw@midway.edu
HOLSENBECK, Daniel .... 407-823-2387.... 120 A
daniel.holsenbeck@ucf.edu
HOLSINGER-FUCHS,
Pamela .... 715-232-2639.... 552 C
holsinger-fuchsp@uwstout.edu
HOLSOPPLE, Heather .... 517-265-5161.... 247 D
hholsopple@adrian.edu
HOLST, Tim .... 218-726-7571.... 272 B
tholst@umn.edu

HOLSTAD, Deb .... 320-308-3277.... 269 D
dholstad@sctcc.edu
HOLSTAD, Deb, A .... 320-308-3227.... 269 D
dholstad@sctcc.edu
HOLSTAD, Larry .... 507-457-5212.... 270 B
lholstad@winona.edu
HOLSTEIN, Charley .... 618-437-5321.... 162 B
holsteinc@rlc.edu
HOLSTEIN, David .... 561-868-3004.... 114 D
holsteid@palmbeachstate.edu
HOLSTEN, Robert, D .... 252-246-1258.... 375 B
rholsten@wilsoncc.edu
HOLSTER, Melissa .... 617-228-2271.... 239 G
mholster@bhcc.mass.edu
HOLSTINE, Tammy .... 304-357-4383.... 541 H
tammyholstine@ucwv.edu
HOLSTON, Tavarez .... 229-217-4202.... 134 C
tholston@moultrietech.edu
HOLSTON, William .... 336-841-9221.... 365 A
bookstor@highpoint.edu
HOLT, Amy .... 575-562-2467.... 318 A
amy.holt@enmu.edu
HOLT, Brooke .... 479-619-4298...... 22 H
bholt@nwacc.edu
HOLT, Bruce .... 865-981-8035.... 470 F
bruce.holt@maryvillecollege.edu
HOLT, Chad .... 252-398-6298.... 363 E
holtch@chowan.edu
HOLT, Debbie .... 859-246-6286.... 201 D
debbie.holt@kctcs.edu
HOLT, Dennis .... 573-986-6888.... 290 D
dholt@semo.edu
HOLT, Dennis .... 573-651-2135.... 290 D
dholt@semo.edu
HOLT, Diann .... 757-822-1069.... 528 C
dholt@tcc.edu
HOLT, James .... 304-243-2000.... 545 G
HOLT, Jerry .... 219-785-5200.... 178 H
jholt@pnc.edu
HOLT, Jim .... 956-548-8776.... 505 C
jim.holt@utb.edu
HOLT, Joseph .... 559-651-2500...... 66 E
HOLT, Joseph, L .... 410-778-7201.... 229 D
jholt2@washcoll.edu
HOLT, Kathy .... 303-797-5822...... 80 J
kathy.holt@arapahoe.edu
HOLT, Raymond .... 229-931-2001.... 136 G
rholt@southgatech.edu
HOLT, Roslyn, J .... 318-670-6436.... 215 A
rholt@susla.edu
HOLT, Vicki .... 704-272-5424.... 373 F
vholt@spcc.edu
HOLT, Wilford .... 334-420-4400........ 7 I
wholt@trenholmstate.edu
HOLTE, Lane .... 406-377-9404.... 294 C
lholte@dawson.edu
HOLTE, Terri .... 770-938-4711.... 133 A
HOLTEN, Kathryn .... 803-323-2275.... 463 D
holtenk@winthrop.edu
HOLTER, Joan .... 218-723-6041.... 262 I
jholer@css.edu
HOLTER, Sherer .... 509-963-2111.... 531 G
holters@cwu.edu
HOLTFRETER, David .... 217-875-7200.... 162 D
dholt@richland.edu
HOLTGREN, Shawn .... 574-257-3344.... 169 F
holtgrs@bethelcollege.edu
HOLTHAUS, Barbara .... 217-641-4104.... 154 G
bholthaus@jwcc.edu
HOLTHOUSER, David, M ...... 704-894-2220.... 363 F
daholthouser@davidson.edu
HOLTMANN, Ruth Ann .... 314-421-0949.... 290 H
holtmann@siba.edu
HOLTMEIER, Kelly .... 920-498-6384.... 555 A
kelly.holtmeier@nwtc.edu
HOLTON, Christa .... 312-777-7600.... 144 H
cholton@argosy.edu
HOLTON, Simone .... 802-387-6753.... 513 E
sholton@landmark.edu
HOLTROP, Stephen, D .... 260-359-4166.... 172 K
sholtrop@huntington.edu
HOLTSCHNEIDER,
Dennis, H .... 312-362-8890.... 148 F
president@depaul.edu
HOLTZ, Anthony, B .... 412-675-9047.... 439 H
abh16@psu.edu
HOLTZ, Barry .... 212-678-8030.... 337 G
baholtz@jtsa.edu
HOLTZ, Daniel, F .... 320-222-5205.... 268 I
daniel.holtz@ridgewater.edu
HOLTZ, Eddie .... 712-325-3426.... 186 B
eholtz@iwcc.edu
HOLTZCLAW, Barry .... 510-204-0745...... 39 F
bholtzclaw@cdsp.edu
HOLUB, Robert, C .... 413-545-2211.... 237 C
chancellor@umass.edu
HOLWAY, Carla, A .... 610-648-3258.... 439 G
cah1@psu.edu
HOLWICK, Jana .... 440-375-7252.... 394 E
jholwick@lec.edu
HOLYCROSS, Robert, L .... 205-652-3601...... 10 A
rlh@uwa.edu
HOLZBERLEIN, Anne .... 405-974-2000.... 413 B
aholzberlein@ucok.edu

HOLZEMER, William, L ..... 732-932-1738.... 314 D
holzemer@andromeda.rutgers.edu
HOLZEMER, William, L ..... 973-353-5149.... 314 E
holzemer@andromeda.rutgers.edu
HOLZER, Anna, R .... 817-515-7229.... 496 A
anna.holzer@tccd.edu
HOLZER, Charlotte .... 718-871-6187.... 357 J
charloth@touro.edu
HOLZER, Marc .... 973-353-5093.... 314 E
mholzer@rutgers.edu
HOLZHEUSER, Christina .... 361-825-5975.... 497 F
christina.holzheuser@tamucc.edu
HOLZMAN, Terri .... 920-748-8351.... 549 I
holzmant@ripon.edu
HOMAN, David .... 847-318-8550.... 160 C
dhoman@nc.edu
HOMAN, J. Michael .... 507-284-9595.... 262 D
homan.michael@mayo.edu
HOMAN, J. Michael .... 507-284-9595.... 262 F
HOMAN, Richard, V .... 215-762-3500.... 427 G
Homan-RichardV@drexel.edu
HOMAN, Sharon .... 816-501-4617.... 288 D
sharon.homan@rockhurst.edu
HOMAN, Thomas .... 218-723-2214.... 262 I
thoman@css.edu
HOMANN, Gordon .... 617-912-9154.... 232 E
ghomann@bostonconservatory.edu
HOMBURGER, John, R .... 518-564-2130.... 354 B
homburjr@plattsburgh.edu
HOME, Arlene .... 678-839-4760.... 138 D
ahome@westga.edu
HOMEIER, Debra, L .... 906-227-2092.... 256 F
dhomeier@nmu.edu
HOMER, Jessica .... 781-768-7049.... 244 D
jessica.homer@regiscollege.edu
HOMESLEY, Diane .... 678-839-6582.... 138 D
dhomesley@westga.edu
HOMIAK, JR., Albert, J ...... 302-831-7285...... 96 F
homiak@udel.edu
HOMKOW, Gary .... 516-572-7304.... 342 C
gary.homkow@ncc.edu
HOMOLKA, Karen, K .... 217-245-3094.... 152 C
khomolk@ic.edu
HOMSHER, Betsy, E .... 810-762-9540.... 253 I
bhomsher@kettering.edu
HOMSTED, Gillian .... 800-862-9616.... 512 H
ghomsted@burlington.edu
HOMYOCK, Kathleen .... 440-375-7144.... 394 E
khomyock@lec.edu
HONABACH, Dennis .... 859-572-6406.... 205 E
honabachd1@nku.edu
HONAKER, Evelyn, J .... 423-585-6972.... 476 B
evelyn.honaker@ws.edu
HONAKER, Everett .... 276-591-5699.... 524 B
HONAN, Molly .... 617-735-9876.... 234 E
honanm@emmanuel.edu
HONDROS, Jack .... 610-526-1445.... 421 G
jack.hondros@theamericancollege.edu
HONEA, Adam .... 480-557-1659...... 19 C
adam.honea@phoenix.edu
HONEA, Scott .... 979-436-0900.... 496 G
shonea@tamhsc.edu
HONEBRINK, Stephanie ...... 513-244-4892.... 388 D
stephanie_honebrink@mail.msj.edu
HONECK, Sara .... 913-588-5170.... 197 A
shoneck@kumc.edu
HONEGAN, Rhonda .... 404-270-5075.... 137 E
rhonegan@spelman.edu
HONEGGER, Rose .... 337-482-6819.... 216 D
oia@louisiana.edu
HONEMAN, Donald .... 508-793-7419.... 233 C
dhoneman@clarku.edu
HONEY, Delores .... 417-625-9696.... 286 E
honey-d@mssu.edu
HONEYCUTT, Alan .... 858-642-8190...... 58 I
ahoneycutt@nu.edu
HONEYCUTT, Tony, L .... 606-679-8501.... 202 F
tony.honeycutt@kctcs.edu
HONEYMAN, Ryan, C .... 937-778-7808.... 390 G
rhoneymanr@edisonohio.edu
HONEYWOOD, Omega .... 803-327-7402.... 456 F
ohoneywood@clintonjuniorcollege.edu
HONG, De .... 626-571-8811...... 76 D
dehong@uwest.edu
HONG, E-Sing .... 408-260-0208...... 47 D
chinesedoctoral@fivebranches.edu
HONG, Luoluo .... 808-974-7334.... 141 A
luoluo@hawaii.edu
HONG, Tran .... 949-451-5254...... 70 E
thong@ivc.edu
HONG, Tran .... 951-343-3907...... 31 G
thong@calbaptist.edu
HONHOLT, Richard .... 616-222-1954.... 250 C
richard.honholt@cornerstone.edu
HONKE, Mary, J .... 402-844-7124.... 300 A
maryh@northeast.edu
HONNELL, Cherie .... 503-494-7800.... 418 D
HONTS, Arlen .... 316-295-5800.... 192 H
ahonts@friends.edu
HOOD, Donna .... 828-286-3636.... 371 A
dhood@isothermal.edu
HOOD, Gwendolyn, D .... 205-348-5855...... 8 F
ghood@aalan.ua.edu

HOOD, Jean ... 817-272-5554 ... 505 A jmhood@uta.edu
HOOD, Jeremiah ... 312-521-6881 ... 19 C jeremiah.hood@phoenix.edu
HOOD, Jon ... 402-449-2928 ... 298 B jhood@graceu.edu
HOOD, Mary, D ... 408-554-2732 ... 68 C mhood@scu.edu
HOOD, Michael, J ... 724-357-2397 ... 442 E mhood@iup.edu
HOOD, Mike ... 903-233-4115 ... 489 K mikehood@letu.edu
HOOD, Nan, S ... 610-989-1456 ... 450 E nhood@vfmac.edu
HOOD, Pam ... 317-917-3370 ... 177 H phood@martin.edu
HOOD, Patricia ... 706-649-1883 ... 127 E phood@columbustech.edu
HOOD, Richard, J ... 318-342-1010 ... 216 E hood@ulm.edu
HOOD, Robert ... 650-306-3340 ... 67 E hoodr@smccd.edu
HOOD, Scott, W ... 207-725-3256 ... 217 E shood@bowdoin.edu
HOOD, Tim ... 815-235-6121 ... 152 A tim.hood@highland.edu
HOOD-MARTIN, Jacquie ... 773-602-5020 ... 147 B jhmartin@ccc.edu
HOOFF, McLean ... 912-525-5856 ... 136 B mhooff@scad.edu
HOOGAKKER, John ... 540-458-8446 ... 530 A
HOOGHART, Anne ... 517-264-7662 ... 258 D ahooghar@sienaheights.edu
HOOK, Amy ... 617-353-2399 ... 232 G amyhook@bu.edu
HOOK, Morgan ... 518-320-1311 ... 351 D morgan.hook@suny.edu
HOOK, Randall ... 540-828-5358 ... 516 K rhook@bridgewater.edu
HOOK, Sam ... 864-592-4630 ... 461 C hooks@sccsc.edu
HOOK, Talbort ... 808-455-0611 ... 142 A talbort@hawaii.edu
HOOKER, Brenda ... 773-995-2304 ... 146 D b-hooker@csu.edu
HOOKER, Dianna ... 406-638-3142 ... 294 G dianna@lbhc.cc.mt.us
HOOKER, Mary Kaye ... 404-237-7573 ... 125 F mahooker@bauder.edu
HOOKER-HARING, Christopher ... 484-664-3245 ... 437 B hookerh@muhlenberg.edu
HOOKS, Beth ... 919-735-5151 ... 374 F bhooks@waynecc.edu
HOOKS, Brenda ... 502-456-6504 ... 206 C bhooks@sullivan.edu
HOOKS, Gerald, D ... 478-289-2036 ... 128 J jhooks@ega.edu
HOOKS, Haley ... 229-317-6746 ... 128 A haley.hooks@darton.edu
HOOLE, Thomas ... 978-934-3509 ... 237 F thomas_hoole@uml.edu
HOOPER, Celia, R ... 336-334-5744 ... 379 A crhooper@uncg.edu
HOOPER, Debra, A ... 919-488-8500 ... 366 C dhooper@higherdigital.com
HOOPER, John ... 940-565-3858 ... 504 B john.hooper@unt.edu
HOOPER, Lynn ... 405-425-5157 ... 409 E lynn.looper@oc.edu
HOOPER, Robert, D ... 740-427-5109 ... 394 C hooperr@kenyon.edu
HOOPER, Stephanie, L ... 304-336-8990 ... 544 B stephanie.hooper@westliberty.edu
HOOPES, Clark, D ... 330-471-8427 ... 395 E choopes@malone.edu
HOOPES, Tom ... 913-360-7529 ... 190 F thoopes@benedictine.edu
HOOTEN, Al ... 936-294-1016 ... 501 A
HOOTEN, Jon ... 909-447-2558 ... 40 E jhooten@cst.edu
HOOTEN, Michael ... 806-354-5589 ... 501 E michael.hooten@ttuhsc.edu
HOOTON, Linda, J ... 205-853-1200 ... 5 C lhooton@jeffstateonline.com
HOOTS, Cathy ... 336-750-2265 ... 380 A hoots@wssu.edu
HOOVEN, Barbara ... 716-896-0700 ... 359 F bhooven@villa.edu
HOOVER, Becky, J ... 330-972-6462 ... 403 B hoover@uakron.edu
HOOVER, Chris ... 620-341-5337 ... 192 D choover@emporia.edu
HOOVER, Christine ... 614-252-8850 ... 390 C choover@devry.edu
HOOVER, Douglas ... 724-938-4096 ... 441 G hoover@calu.edu
HOOVER, James, W ... 214-841-3694 ... 485 E jhoover@dts.edu
HOOVER, Jean, B ... 717-262-2007 ... 452 B jhoover@wilson.edu
HOOVER, Jeffrey ... 717-560-8258 ... 433 D jhoover@lbc.edu
HOOVER, Jonathan ... 214-333-5475 ... 484 C jonh@dbu.edu
HOOVER, Kathleen ... 610-558-5560 ... 437 C hooverk@neumann.edu
HOOVER, Kevin ... 559-438-4222 ... 49 G kevin_hoover@heald.edu
HOOVER, Kim ... 601-984-6200 ... 277 H khoover@umc.edu
HOOVER, Linda ... 806-742-3031 ... 501 D linda.hoover@ttu.edu
HOOVER, Lisa ... 214-637-3530 ... 508 A lhoover@wadecollege.edu
HOOVER, Lisa, D ... 570-577-3757 ... 423 D lisa.hoover@bucknell.edu
HOOVER, Lorette, M ... 912-427-5800 ... 124 A lhoover@altamahatech.edu
HOOVER, Marissa ... 717-948-6316 ... 439 I mrg159@psu.edu
HOOVER, Nancy ... 503-699-6261 ... 416 I nhoover@marylhurst.edu
HOOVER, Nancy, Z ... 740-587-6629 ... 389 H hoover@denison.edu
HOOVER, Sara ... 205-226-4989 ... 2 C shoover@bsc.edu
HOOVLER, David ... 412-237-4554 ... 425 H dhoovler@ccac.edu
HOOYMAN, Jamie ... 660-359-3948 ... 287 D jhooyman@mail.ncmissouri.edu
HOOYMAN, Phyllis, K ... 616-395-7765 ... 252 F hooyman@hope.edu
HOPE, Laura ... 909-652-6113 ... 39 B laura.hope@chaffey.edu
HOPE, Maury, M ... 515-294-2126 ... 182 B mmhope@iastate.edu
HOPE, Oral ... 212-431-2300 ... 343 E ohope@nyls.edu
HOPEWELL, JR., Woodson, H ... 757-727-5303 ... 519 C woodson.hopewell@hamptonu.edu
HOPEY, Christopher, E ... 978-837-5110 ... 242 D christopher.hopey@merrimack.edu
HOPKINS, Amanda ... 407-646-2124 ... 116 B ahopkins@rollins.edu
HOPKINS, Andrea, M ... 401-874-4502 ... 454 E ahopkins@uri.edu
HOPKINS, Becky ... 323-343-3200 ... 35 B bhopkins@cslanet.calstatela.edu
HOPKINS, Christi ... 620-242-0414 ... 194 H hopkinsc@mcpherson.edu
HOPKINS, Darlene ... 910-630-7150 ... 366 H dhopkins@methodist.edu
HOPKINS, David, R ... 937-775-2312 ... 406 C david.hopkins@wright.edu
HOPKINS, Debbie ... 704-216-7211 ... 373 C debbie.hopkins@rccc.edu
HOPKINS, Dee ... 304-293-5704 ... 544 E dee.hopkins@mail.wvu.edu
HOPKINS, Denise, C ... 718-990-1323 ... 348 G hopkinsd@stjohns.edu
HOPKINS, Drew, W ... 609-984-3430 ... 316 A dhopkins@tesc.edu
HOPKINS, Dustin ... 918-781-7400 ... 407 B hopkinsd@bacone.edu
HOPKINS, Gena ... 260-459-4513 ... 175 A ghopkins@ibcfortwayne.edu
HOPKINS, Glenn, W ... 662-915-7177 ... 277 G ghopkins@olemiss.edu
HOPKINS, Hunter, H ... 412-261-2647 ... 432 B hhopkins@kaplan.edu
HOPKINS, Jane, L ... 618-664-6600 ... 151 D jane.hopkins@greenville.edu
HOPKINS, Jason ... 312-777-8651 ... 153 A jkhopkins@aii.edu
HOPKINS, Jayne, S ... 270-384-8033 ... 203 H hopkinsj@lindsey.edu
HOPKINS, Jim ... 405-224-3140 ... 413 E jhopkins@usao.edu
HOPKINS, John ... 330-263-2082 ... 388 E jhopkins@wooster.edu
HOPKINS, LC, John ... 703-416-1441 ... 519 F jhopkins@ipsciences.edu
HOPKINS, Jon ... 816-604-4062 ... 285 I jon.hopkins@mcckc.edu
HOPKINS, Joseph ... 205-726-2778 ... 6 G jhopkins@samford.edu
HOPKINS, Kathryn ... 870-777-5722 ... 25 F kathryn.hopkins@uacch.edu
HOPKINS, Laurie, B ... 803-786-3669 ... 457 C lhopkins@columbiasc.edu
HOPKINS, Marilyn ... 707-638-5276 ... 72 H marilyn.hopkins@tu.edu
HOPKINS, Mark ... 706-236-2231 ... 125 G mhopkins@berry.edu
HOPKINS, Melissa ... 910-277-5670 ... 376 A hopkinsmc@sapc.edu
HOPKINS, Nicole ... 509-574-6870 ... 540 A nhopkins@yvcc.edu
HOPKINS, Paulette ... 619-388-7813 ... 65 H phopkins@sdccd.edu
HOPKINS, Portia ... 916-577-2200 ... 79 C phopkins@jessup.edu
HOPKINS, Robert, J ... 910-277-5008 ... 376 A hopkinsb@sapc.edu
HOPKINS, Robert, P ... 212-353-4350 ... 331 B bob@cooper.edu
HOPKINS, Ronald ... 281-998-6150 ... 493 F ronald.hopkins@sjcd.edu
HOPKINS, Sara ... 615-248-1653 ... 476 E shopkins@trevecca.edu
HOPKINS, Shelli ... 918-781-7344 ... 407 B hopkinss@bacone.edu
HOPKINS, T. Hampton ... 704-355-5585 ... 363 B hampton.hopkins@carolinascollege.edu
HOPKINS, Thomas, F ... 540-464-7228 ... 529 A hopkinstf@vmi.edu
HOPKINS, Tony ... 740-453-0762 ... 400 D hopkint1@ohio.edu
HOPKINS, Tony ... 740-588-1409 ... 407 A thopkins@zanestate.edu
HOPKINS, Willie ... 718-951-3166 ... 326 G WHopkins@brooklyn.cuny.edu
HOPKINS-BEST, Mary ... 715-232-1168 ... 552 C hopkinsbestm@uwstout.edu
HOPKINS GROSS, Anne, M ... 802-447-6323 ... 514 D ahopkinsgross@svc.edu
HOPKINS-LISLE, Grace ... 207-775-3052 ... 218 E ghopkins-lisle@meca.edu
HOPP, Melissa ... 443-840-3176 ... 222 D mhopp@ccbcmd.edu
HOPP, Susan ... 503-883-2278 ... 416 G shopp@linfield.edu
HOPPA, Anthony, T ... 585-245-5516 ... 353 C thoppa@geneseo.edu
HOPPE, Dale, W ... 815-753-0205 ... 160 A dhoppe@niu.edu
HOPPE, Elizabeth ... 909-706-3497 ... 78 D shoppe@westernu.edu
HOPPE, Heather ... 419-251-8989 ... 395 H heather.hoppe@mercycollege.edu
HOPPE, Jim ... 651-696-6220 ... 265 A hoppe@macalester.edu
HOPPE, Ken ... 870-236-6901 ... 21 E khoppe@crc.edu
HOPPER, Darla ... 812-535-5110 ... 179 C dhopper@smwc.edu
HOPPER, David, R ... 757-455-3415 ... 529 F dhopper@vwc.edu
HOPPER, George, M ... 662-325-2953 ... 276 A ghopper@cfr.msstate.edu
HOPPER, Jack ... 409-880-8741 ... 500 F jack.hopper@lamar.edu
HOPPER, Karen, S ... 870-508-6110 ... 20 E khopper@asumh.edu
HOPPER, Lisa ... 501-760-4241 ... 22 F lhopper@npcc.edu
HOPPER, Marianne, F ... 512-448-8551 ... 493 B marianh@stedwards.edu
HOPPER, William ... 305-626-3701 ... 108 H william.hopper@fmuniv.edu
HOPPES, Cherron ... 415-442-6510 ... 48 E choppes@ggu.edu
HOPPIN, Andrew, S ... 952-888-4777 ... 270 F ahoppin@nwhealth.edu
HOPPLE, Dennis, M ... 570-577-1201 ... 423 D dennis.hopple@bucknell.edu
HOPPLE, Stephnie ... 928-541-7777 ... 16 I shopple@ncu.edu
HOPPMANN, Richard, A ... 803-733-1531 ... 462 A richard.hoppmann@uscmed.sc.edu
HOPSON, George, A ... 864-977-2194 ... 460 A george.hopson@ngu.edu
HOPSON, Pamela, F ... 812-465-7188 ... 180 F pfhopson@usi.edu
HOPWOOD, Dennis ... 541-962-3672 ... 418 C dhopwood@eou.edu
HOR, Annie, Y ... 209-667-3709 ... 36 C ahor@csustan.edu
HORACE, Mia ... 864-644-5144 ... 461 B mhorace@swu.edu
HORACK, John, M ... 256-824-6100 ... 9 A john.horack@uah.edu
HORADAN, Lloyd ... 478-553-2060 ... 134 F lhoradan@oftc.edu
HORADAN, Lloyd ... 478-553-2060 ... 134 G lhoradan@oftc.edu
HORAK, Janice ... 254-968-9075 ... 496 F jhorak@tarleton.edu
HORAK, Maureen ... 413-662-5205 ... 238 F m.horak@mcla.edu
HORAN, James, J ... 207-948-3131 ... 219 H jhoran@unity.edu
HORAN, Kevin ... 925-866-1822 ... 43 C khoran@srvc.net
HORAN, Michael, D ... 404-364-8322 ... 135 A mhoran@oglethorpe.edu
HORAN, Thomas ... 909-607-9302 ... 40 C thomas.horan@cgu.edu
HORAZDOVSKY, Bruce, F ... 507-284-3862 ... 262 E horazdovsky.bruce@mayo.edu
HORBACEWICZ, Jill ... 212-463-0400 ... 357 J jillh@touro.edu
HORGAN, Joan ... 518-454-5296 ... 330 C horganj@strose.edu
HORGAN, Louise, M ... 732-224-2202 ... 308 B lhorgan@brookdalecc.edu
HORGAN, Ralph, R ... 412-268-6156 ... 424 H rh44@andrew.cmu.edu
HORINEK, Jon ... 405-682-1611 ... 409 F jhorinek@occc.edu
HORISSIAN, Kevork, T ... 276-944-6763 ... 518 I khorissian@ehc.edu
HORMANN, Shana ... 206-268-5714 ... 530 F shormann@antioch.edu
HORN, Brian, S ... 727-816-3458 ... 114 F hornb@phcc.edu
HORN, Carla ... 717-757-1100 ... 452 I carla.horn@yti.edu
HORN, Cindy ... 231-591-5309 ... 251 B hornc@ferris.edu
HORN, David, G ... 978-468-7111 ... 235 F dhorn@gcts.edu
HORN, Dennis, R ... 509-313-3522 ... 534 A horn@gonzaga.edu
HORN, George ... 912-478-2897 ... 131 A ghorn@georgiasouthern.edu
HORN, Herman ... 512-245-2539 ... 501 C hh18@txstate.edu
HORN, Jamie ... 334-386-7168 ... 3 H jhorn@faulkner.edu
HORN, Jay ... 817-272-2355 ... 505 A horn@uta.edu
HORN, John, F ... 215-898-7593 ... 448 I horn3@pobox.upenn.edu
HORN, Jonathon ... 419-995-8302 ... 392 L horn.j@rhodesstate.edu
HORN, Larry ... 713-623-2040 ... 480 J lhorn@aii.edu
HORN, Larry, S ... 812-488-2775 ... 180 B lh6@evansville.edu
HORN, Mark ... 479-788-7035 ... 24 D mhorn@uafortsmith.edu
HORN, Michael ... 704-330-5963 ... 369 A michael.horn@cpcc.edu
HORN, Paul ... 212-998-3228 ... 344 B paul.horn@nyu.edu
HORN, Samuel, E ... 763-417-8250 ... 262 C
HORN, Tammy ... 859-246-6637 ... 201 D tammy.horn@kctcs.edu
HORNBACK, Carla ... 270-706-8535 ... 201 F carla.hornback@kctcs.edu
HORNBEAK, Joe, N ... 405-466-3265 ... 408 G jnhornbeak@lunet.edu
HORNBECK, Billi ... 605-455-6037 ... 464 H bhornbeck@olc.edu
HORNBERGER, Cynthia, A ... 785-670-1213 ... 197 D cynthia.hornberger@washburn.edu
HORNBERGER, Lois ... 503-352-2240 ... 419 E lhornberger@pacificu.edu
HORNBERGER, Rob ... 417-836-6444 ... 286 F robhornberger@missouristate.edu
HORNBERGER, Tiffany ... 502-863-8027 ... 200 G tiffany_hornberger@georgetowncollege.edu
HORNBUCKLE, Jami ... 606-783-2372 ... 204 E j.hornbuckle@moreheadstate.edu
HORNBURG, Trisha, L ... 262-691-5446 ... 555 C thornburg@wctc.edu
HORNDT, Christin ... 989-275-5000 ... 253 K christin.horndt@kirtland.edu
HORNE, Arthur, M ... 706-542-6446 ... 138 C ahorne@uga.edu
HORNE, Cathy ... 704-272-5337 ... 373 F chorne@spcc.edu
HORNE, Denise, M ... 252-246-1263 ... 375 B dhorne@wilsoncc.edu
HORNE, Derek ... 850-599-3868 ... 118 G derek.horne@famu.edu
HORNE, Hadie, C ... 252-246-1221 ... 375 B hhorne@wilsoncc.edu
HORNE, J. Douglas ... 801-524-8110 ... 510 A d-horne@ldsbc.edu
HORNE, Pamela, T ... 765-494-9116 ... 178 F pamhorne@purdue.edu
HORNE, JR., Rex, M ... 870-245-5400 ... 22 I president@obu.edu
HORNE, Rhonda ... 937-258-8251 ... 392 C
HORNE, Robert, E ... 215-780-1313 ... 446 G rhorne@salus.edu
HORNE, Tabitha ... 612-436-7523 ... 265 G thorne@msbcollege.edu
HORNE, Valerie ... 601-403-1211 ... 277 A vhorne@prcc.edu
HORNER, Jeff ... 719-502-2011 ... 86 G jeffrey.horner@ppcc.edu
HORNER, Jeffrey ... 719-502-2011 ... 86 G jeffrey.horner@ppcc.edu
HORNER, Jeffrey, T ... 423-798-7952 ... 476 B jeff.horner@ws.edu
HORNER, Kenneth, R ... 931-540-2533 ... 474 F khorner@columbiastate.edu
HORNER, Theresa ... 716-827-2485 ... 358 B hornert@trocaire.edu
HORNER, Theresa, M ... 814-269-7001 ... 449 D thorner@pitt.edu
HORNETT, Danielle ... 715-634-4790 ... 547 G dhornett@lco-college.edu
HORNEY, Margot, L ... 336-334-4822 ... 370 E mlhorney@gtcc.edu
HORNING, Kirsten ... 503-338-2341 ... 415 B khorning@clatsopcc.edu
HORNS, Phyllis, N ... 252-744-2265 ... 377 C hornsp@ecu.edu
HORNSBERGER, Bill ... 330-869-3600 ... 385 F whornsberger@brownmackie.edu

HORNSBY, Sharon, G ... 225-222-4351 ... 211 D
shornsby@northshorecollege.edu
HOROWITZ, Anne, B ... 215-596-7518 ... 450 A
a.horowitz@usciences.edu
HOROWITZ, Avery ... 718-252-7800 ... 357 J
averymh@touro.edu
HOROWITZ,
Boruch Avrohom ... 718-438-2018 ... 346 I
rcby26@aol.com
HOROWITZ, Elias ... 845-783-0833 ... 359 B
HOROWITZ, Michael ... 626-529-8008 ... 60 G
president@pacificoaks.edu
HOROWITZ, Sam, L ... 904-264-2172 ... 116 A
shorowitz@iws.edu
HOROWITZ, Sara ... 212-678-8838 ... 337 G
sahorowitz@jtsa.edu
HORR, Stephen, J ... 207-221-8770 ... 218 C
shorr@kaplan.edu
HORRELL, Jeffrey, L ... 603-646-2235 ... 305 A
jeffrey.l.horrell@dartmouth.edu
HORRIDGE, Blake ... 510-841-1905 ... 27 J
bhorridge@absw.edu
HORROCKS, Dianne, K ... 208-282-2592 ... 143 D
horrdian@isu.edu
HORSCH, Ellen, S ... 906-487-1737 ... 255 E
eshorsch@mtu.edu
HORSEY, Cheryl ... 215-641-5546 ... 430 C
horsey.c@gmc.edu
HORSEY, Dwight, G ... 717-872-3026 ... 443 C
dwight.horsey@millersville.edu
HORSLEY, Jeff, O ... 714-808-4822 ... 59 B
jhorsley@nocccd.edu
HORSLEY, Julia ... 252-536-7254 ... 370 F
horsleyj@halifaxcc.edu
HORSMAN, Rand ... 817-735-2690 ... 504 C
rhorsman@hsc.unt.edu
HORST, Pamela ... 907-822-3201 ... 10 C
phorst@akbible.edu
HORSTMAN, Scott ... 281-476-1501 ... 493 E
scott.horstman@sjcd.edu
HORSTMEYER, Mark ... 708-974-5275 ... 159 A
horstmeyer@morainevalley.edu
HORTON, Amy ... 847-317-7152 ... 166 B
ahorton@tiu.edu
HORTON, C, R ... 864-488-4586 ... 459 A
chorton@limestone.edu
HORTON, Carol, R ... 626-914-8886 ... 39 G
chorton@citruscollege.edu
HORTON, Claudia ... 816-833-0524 ... 184 H
horton@graceland.edu
HORTON, Claudia, D ... 816-833-0524 ... 282 F
horton@graceland.edu
HORTON, Connie ... 310-506-4210 ... 61 G
connie.horton@pepperdine.edu
HORTON, Dan ... 414-382-6238 ... 545 H
dan.horton@alverno.edu
HORTON, Gretchen ... 503-253-3443 ... 417 H
ghorton@ocom.edu
HORTON, Howard, E ... 617-951-2350 ... 243 C
howard.horton@necb.edu
HORTON, James, F ... 225-216-8402 ... 209 I
hortonj@mybrcc.edu
HORTON, Jana ... 251-575-3156 ... 1 B
jhorton@ascc.edu
HORTON, Jane, T ... 540-458-8401 ... 530 A
jhorton@wlu.edu
HORTON, Jeanine ... 918-495-7575 ... 411 C
jhorton@oru.edu
HORTON, Jeff ... 916-649-2400 ... 31 C
HORTON, Joanne, M ... 804-594-1569 ... 526 G
jhorton@jtcc.edu
HORTON, Johnna ... 507-389-7223 ... 269 F
johnna.horton@southcentral.edu
HORTON, Joseph, M ... 603-641-7600 ... 305 H
jhorton@anselm.edu
HORTON, Kimberly ... 937-769-1837 ... 383 K
khorton2@antioch.edu
HORTON, Larry, N ... 650-725-3324 ... 71 F
larry.horton@stanford.edu
HORTON, Mac ... 251-380-2272 ... 7 F
horton@shc.edu
HORTON, Muriel ... 843-574-6138 ... 461 G
muriel.horton@tridenttech.edu
HORTON, Peter ... 412-536-1050 ... 432 F
peter.horton@laroche.edu
HORTON, Stanley, W ... 360-538-4051 ... 534 B
shorton@ghc.edu
HORTON, Steve ... 318-357-4330 ... 216 B
hortons@nsula.edu
HORTON, Steve ... 318-357-5851 ... 216 B
hortons@nsula.edu
HORTON, Steven ... 281-476-1806 ... 493 E
steven.horton@sjcd.edu
HORTON, Susan ... 845-434-5750 ... 356 H
shorton@sullivan.suny.edu
HORTON, Traci ... 918-835-8288 ... 414 B
thorton@vatterott-college.edu
HORTON, JR., Walter, E ... 330-325-6499 ... 397 C
wehj@neoucom.edu
HORTON, JR., Walter, E ... 330-325-6290 ... 397 C
wehj@neoucom.edu
HORTON, William, M ... 918-595-7263 ... 412 H
bhorton@tulsacc.edu

HORVATH, Albert, G ... 814-865-6574 ... 438 F
argh12@psu.edu
HORVATH, Cathy ... 701-858-4444 ... 381 G
cathy.horvath@minotstateu.edu
HORVATH, Fran ... 831-656-2228 ... 557 H
rfhorvat@nps.edu
HORVATH, Katherine, K ... 978-468-7111 ... 235 F
khorvath@gcts.edu
HORVATH, Michael ... 678-839-6445 ... 138 D
HORVATH, Rebecca, L ... 215-951-1898 ... 432 G
horvath@lasalle.edu
HORVATH, Scott ... 317-921-4772 ... 175 I
shorvath@ivytech.edu
HORWATH, Donna ... 303-963-3365 ... 81 K
dhorwath@ccu.edu
HORWITZ, Pamela ... 314-529-9418 ... 284 F
phorwitz@maryville.edu
HOSACK, Susan, E ... 314-935-5567 ... 292 J
sue.hosack@wustl.edu
HOSCH, Jason ... 504-278-6281 ... 211 I
jhosch@nunez.edu
HOSEA, Walter ... 865-251-1800 ... 472 K
whosea@southcollegetn.edu
HOSEI, Huan, F ... 671-735-5584 ... 559 B
adulteducation@guamcc.edu
HOSELTON, Steven, A ... 312-341-2442 ... 162 I
shoselton@roosevelt.edu
HOSENEY, Jason ... 573-840-9668 ... 290 J
jhoseney@trcc.edu
HOSHIKO, Carol ... 808-734-9568 ... 141 E
hoshiko@hawaii.edu
HOSKEY, Lisa ... 607-274-3011 ... 336 G
HOSKIN, Marilyn ... 212-650-5700 ... 326 H
mhoskin@ccny.cuny.edu
HOSKINS, Deb ... 970-641-2237 ... 89 B
dhoskins@western.edu
HOSKINS, Phillip, J ... 573-882-2011 ... 291 C
hoskinsp@umsystem.edu
HOSKINS, Sheila ... 252-823-5166 ... 370 A
hoskinss@edgecombe.edu
HOSKINS, Steve ... 606-546-4151 ... 206 F
shoskins@unionky.edu
HOSKINSON, Buddy ... 859-223-9608 ... 205 J
bhoskinson@spencerian.edu
HOSKINSON, Heidi ... 316-295-5861 ... 192 H
heidi_hoskinson@friends.edu
HOSKOWITZ, Joel, M ... 410-386-8412 ... 221 G
jhoskowitz@carrollcc.edu
HOSPEDALES, Marcia ... 973-877-3353 ... 310 A
hospedales@essex.edu
HOSS, Cindy ... 620-665-3507 ... 193 F
hossc@hutchcc.edu
HOSS, Cynthia ... 800-955-2527 ... 282 G
dhoss@grantham.edu
HOSS, Neal ... 760-750-4400 ... 36 B
nhoss@csusm.edu
HOSSENLOPP, Jeanne ... 414-288-1532 ... 548 D
jeanne.hossenlopp@marquette.edu
HOSTEN-HAAS, Nicole ... 718-951-5671 ... 326 G
nicole@brooklyn.cuny.edu
HOSTETLER, Bumper, R ... 812-888-4510 ... 181 B
bhostetler@vinu.edu
HOSTETLER, Chad ... 304-457-6213 ... 540 B
hostetlercs@ab.edu
HOSTETLER, Lori, J ... 812-888-4121 ... 181 B
lhostetler@vinu.edu
HOSTETLER, Theodore, J ... 434-947-8133 ... 522 E
thostetler@randolphcollege.edu
HOSTETLER, Timothy, J ... 423-775-7262 ... 467 D
hostetti@bryan.edu
HOSTETTER, Julie, M ... 800-287-8822 ... 169 E
hosteju@bethanyseminary.edu
HOSTETTER, Larry ... 270-686-4236 ... 198 G
larry.hostetter@brescia.edu
HOSTETTER, Steve, J ... 218-751-8670 ... 270 G
stevehostetter@oakhills.edu
HOTALING, Diane, E ... 757-455-3216 ... 529 F
dhotaling@vwc.edu
HOTALING, Marcus, S ... 518-388-6161 ... 358 E
hotalinm@union.edu
HOTCHKISS, Carolyn ... 781-239-5528 ... 230 G
hotchkiss@babson.edu
HOTCHKISS, Charles ... 617-989-4831 ... 246 C
hotchkissc@wit.edu
HOTCHKISS, David ... 415-239-3000 ... 39 H
dhotchki@ccsf.edu
HOTCHKISS, Pat ... 520-515-5420 ... 13 G
hotchkis@cochise.edu
HOTLE, C. Patrick ... 573-288-6394 ... 281 D
photle@culver.edu
HOTTEL, Haven ... 910-893-1421 ... 362 F
hottelh@campbell.edu
HOTTEL, Timothy, L ... 901-448-6202 ... 477 C
thottel@uthsc.edu
HOTTENSTEIN, Kristi ... 517-264-3142 ... 247 D
kmaxwell@adrian.edu
HOTTOIS, James ... 760-921-5499 ... 61 B
jhottois@paloverde.edu
HOTTON, Bob ... 661-362-2696 ... 56 G
bhotton@masters.edu
HOTZLER, Russell, K ... 718-260-5400 ... 328 E
rhotzler@citytech.cuny.edu
HOU, Feng ... 941-752-5694 ... 118 E
fengh@scf.edu

HOUBECK, JR., Robert, L . 810-762-3410 ... 259 F
rhoubeck@umflint.edu
HOUCHINS, Shelia, E ... 270-745-4493 ... 207 C
shelia.houchins@wku.edu
HOUCK, Clarence, M ... 803-934-3235 ... 459 F
chouck@morris.edu
HOUCK, Keith, W ... 407-582-3465 ... 122 I
khouck@valenciacollege.edu
HOUCK, Maureen, B ... 516-463-6745 ... 335 H
maureen.b.houck@hofstra.edu
HOUCK, Susan ... 803-738-7610 ... 459 D
houcks@midlandstech.edu
HOUDEK, Rob ... 605-642-6562 ... 465 F
robert.houdek@bhsu.edu
HOUDESHELL, Tara ... 740-366-9223 ... 386 G
thoudesh@cotc.edu
HOUFF, Terry, E ... 540-828-5433 ... 516 K
thouff@bridgewater.edu
HOUGEN, Philip, L ... 773-256-0728 ... 157 B
phougen@lstc.edu
HOUGH, John ... 304-724-3700 ... 540 C
jhough@apus.edu
HOUGH, Melanie ... 317-921-4823 ... 175 I
mhough11@ivytech.edu
HOUGH, Susan ... 916-278-7469 ... 35 E
shough@csus.edu
HOUGH, Tony ... 803-738-7695 ... 459 D
hought@midlandstech.edu
HOUGHTON, David, C ... 405-878-3254 ... 409 D
david.houghton@okbu.edu
HOUGHTON, Gail ... 503-552-1702 ... 417 D
ghoughton@ncnm.edu
HOUGHTON, James ... 212-799-5000 ... 337 H
HOUK, Christopher ... 270-686-4241 ... 198 G
chris.houk@brescia.edu
HOUK, Suzanne, N ... 724-458-2208 ... 430 B
snhouk@gcc.edu
HOULE, Linda ... 508-362-2131 ... 240 A
lhoule@capecod.edu
HOULE, Pamela ... 508-580-5550 ... 351 B
phoule@skidmore.edu
HOULETTE, Forrest ... 502-456-6504 ... 206 C
fhoulette@sullivan.edu
HOULIHAN, Briana ... 608-240-3601 ... 19 C
briana.houlihan@phoenix.edu
HOULIHAN, Elizabeth ... 561-433-2330 ... 112 D
HOULIHAN, Janet, M ... 714-895-8307 ... 41 A
jhoulihan@gwc.cccd.edu
HOULIHAN, Robert ... 516-678-5000 ... 341 F
rhoulihan@molloy.edu
HOULIHAN, Timothy, J ... 718-489-5290 ... 348 E
thoulihan@stfranciscollege.edu
HOULKER, Megan ... 781-239-5264 ... 230 G
mhoulker@babson.edu
HOULT, Kevin ... 256-782-8122 ... 4 L
khoult@jsu.edu
HOUPIS, James ... 510-885-3711 ... 34 C
james.houpis@csueastbay.edu
HOUPT, Mark ... 217-732-3168 ... 156 F
mhoupt@lincolnchristian.edu
HOURIGAN, Christopher ... 401-598-2029 ... 453 C
CHourigan@jwu.edu
HOURIGAN, Gerard ... 216-987-4706 ... 389 A
gerard.hourigan@tri-c.edu
HOUSE, Antionette ... 434-848-6495 ... 523 G
ahouse@saintpauls.edu
HOUSE, Barbara, S ... 716-270-2662 ... 333 B
house@ecc.edu
HOUSE, Cheryl ... 520-206-4646 ... 17 I
chouse@pima.edu
HOUSE, Donald ... 334-649-5000 ... 557 B
HOUSE, J. Daniel ... 815-753-6002 ... 160 A
jhouse@niu.edu
HOUSE, Janice, M ... 805-546-3248 ... 43 F
jhouse@cuesta.edu
HOUSE, Karen ... 603-358-2045 ... 307 A
khouse@keene.edu
HOUSE, Renee ... 732-247-5241 ... 312 A
rhouse@nbts.edu
HOUSE, Seymour ... 503-845-3507 ... 417 A
seymour.house@mtangel.edu
HOUSE, Steven, D ... 336-278-6647 ... 364 A
shouse@elon.edu
HOUSE, Vicki, D ... 325-670-5892 ... 487 D
vhouse@hsutx.edu
HOUSEKNECHT, Eric, T ... 215-368-5000 ... 422 H
rhouseknecht@biblical.edu
HOUSEMAN, Susan ... 910-642-7141 ... 373 G
shouseman@sccnc.edu
HOUSENICK, Joseph ... 570-408-4631 ... 451 G
joseph.housenick@wilkes.edu
HOUSER, David ... 310-578-1080 ... 28 K
dhouser@antioch.edu
HOUSER, Frieda ... 406-444-6570 ... 294 J
fhouser@montana.edu
HOUSER, Gary ... 530-245-7337 ... 69 D
ghouser@shastacollege.edu
HOUSER, Gerald, B ... 503-370-6413 ... 421 C
jhouser@willamette.edu
HOUSER, Janet ... 303-458-4174 ... 87 E
jhouser@regis.edu
HOUSER, Kay ... 910-642-7141 ... 373 G
khouser@sccnc.edu

HOUSER, Kristin ... 661-362-3245 ... 41 G
kristin.houser@canyons.edu
HOUSER, Samuel ... 717-291-4271 ... 429 E
sam.houser@fandm.edu
HOUSH, David, P ... 573-882-7703 ... 291 D
houshd@missouri.edu
HOUSHMAND, Ali, A ... 856-256-4100 ... 314 A
houshmand@rowan.edu
HOUSHOWER, Hans ... 419-358-3234 ... 385 B
houshowerh@bluffton.edu
HOUSKA, Nila ... 712-749-2233 ... 182 G
houskan@bvu.edu
HOUSLEY, Harold ... 903-875-7511 ... 491 B
harold.housley@navarrocollege.edu
HOUSLEY, Heather, L ... 404-413-2070 ... 131 C
heatherh@gsu.edu
HOUSLEY, John ... 912-525-5080 ... 136 B
jhousley@scad.edu
HOUSTON, A. Glen ... 281-283-3000 ... 503 C
houston@uhcl.edu
HOUSTON, Adam ... 760-921-5463 ... 61 B
ahouston@paloverde.edu
HOUSTON, Alan, C ... 858-534-2247 ... 74 D
ahouston@ucsd.edu
HOUSTON, Don ... 408-855-5428 ... 78 A
don.houston@wvm.edu
HOUSTON, Dorothy ... 903-675-6235 ... 502 D
dhouston@tvcc.edu
HOUSTON, Douglas, B ... 530-741-6700 ... 80 C
HOUSTON, Kristin ... 206-876-6100 ... 537 E
khouston@theseattleschool.edu
HOUSTON, Kristina ... 312-777-7600 ... 144 H
khouston@argosy.edu
HOUSTON, Michael ... 662-621-4134 ... 273 I
mhouston@coahomacc.edu
HOUSTON, Michelle ... 631-499-7100 ... 338 D
mhouston@libi.edu
HOUSTON, Ned, R ... 802-586-7711 ... 514 E
nhouston@sterlingcollege.edu
HOUSTON, Pam ... 901-448-1164 ... 477 C
phouston@uthsc.edu
HOUSTON, Paul ... 404-894-3300 ... 130 D
paul.houston@cos.gatech.edu
HOUSTON, Richard ... 662-846-4694 ... 274 B
rhouston@deltastate.edu
HOUSTON, Teresa ... 662-846-4698 ... 274 B
thouston@deltastate.edu
HOUSTON, Terri ... 919-962-6962 ... 378 D
thouston@email.unc.edu
HOUSTON, Vinson ... 256-782-5993 ... 4 L
vhouston@jsu.edu
HOUSTON, Whitney, C ... 972-860-7396 ... 484 H
HOUSTON, William ... 662-621-4226 ... 273 I
whouston@coahomacc.edu
HOUSTON, Willie ... 937-376-6631 ... 386 H
whouston@centralstate.edu
HOUSTON-BLACK,
Barbaina, M ... 252-335-3279 ... 377 D
bmhouston-black@mail.ecsu.edu
HOUSTON-BROWN,
Clive, K ... 909-593-3511 ... 75 C
cio@laverne.edu
HOUTSMA, Lisa ... 605-336-4602 ... 464 G
lhoutsma@national.edu
HOVATTER, Angela, L ... 301-687-4301 ... 228 C
ahovatter@frostburg.edu
HOVDA, Ric, A ... 619-594-1424 ... 36 E
rhovda@mail.sdsu.edu
HOVELAND-BELDEN,
Connie ... 608-785-9877 ... 555 D
beldenc@westerntc.edu
HOVERSON, Sharon, R ... 218-299-4642 ... 263 B
hoverson@cord.edu
HOVERSTEN, Mark, E ... 208-885-5423 ... 144 B
hoverstm@uidaho.edu
HOVESTOL, Daniel ... 218-751-8670 ... 270 G
ohfinaid@oakhills.edu
HOVEY, Ann ... 714-992-7033 ... 59 D
ahovey@fullcoll.edu
HOVEY, Cherie ... 603-577-6570 ... 304 J
HOVEY, Roger, S ... 308-635-6012 ... 301 E
rhovey@wncc.edu
HOWALD, Carl ... 910-410-1900 ... 372 G
carlh@richmondcc.edu
HOWANSKY, Joe ... 337-981-4010 ... 214 D
joe.howansky@remingtoncollege.edu
HOWARD, Angela ... 708-342-3500 ... 149 L
ahoward@devry.edu
HOWARD, Angelita ... 404-627-2681 ... 126 A
HOWARD, Angelita ... 404-627-2681 ... 126 A
angelita.howard@beulah.org
HOWARD, Barbara, C ... 352-365-3520 ... 112 M
howardb@lscc.edu
HOWARD, Barry ... 615-361-7555 ... 468 C
bhoward@daymarinstitute.edu
HOWARD, Bernadette ... 808-235-7361 ... 142 C
mbhoward@hawaii.edu
HOWARD, Bill ... 520-206-4568 ... 17 I
whoward@pima.edu
HOWARD, Burgwell ... 847-467-0301 ... 160 D
b-howard@northwestern.edu
HOWARD, Carol ... 828-298-3325 ... 380 C
choward@warren-wilson.edu

HUANG, Chris .... 708-239-4759 .... 165 I chris.huang@trnty.edu
HUANG, Fay .... 941-907-2262 .... 106 G fhuang@evergladesuniversity.edu
HUANG, Gina .... 408-260-0208 .... 47 D sjstudentservices@fivebranches.edu
HUANG, Guiyou .... 802-485-2025 .... 514 A vpaa@norwich.edu
HUANG, Jefferson .... 909-621-8114 .... 40 D jefferson.huang@cmc.edu
HUANG, Lixin .... 415-282-7600 .... 28 B lixinhuang@actcm.edu
HUANG, Wen .... 713-780-9777 .... 480 A info@acaom.edu
HUARD, Etienne .... 660-944-2886 .... 280 F vocations@conception.edu
HUARD, Jenny .... 660-944-2823 .... 280 F communications@conception.edu
HUARD, Susan, D .... 603-668-6706 .... 304 E shuard@ccsnh.edu
HUBAND, David, E .... 757-446-8474 .... 518 F hubandde@evms.edu
HUBBARD, Ann .... 772-462-7570 .... 110 L ahubbard@irsc.edu
HUBBARD, Annie .... 618-634-3228 .... 164 C annieh@shawneecc.edu
HUBBARD, Brittany .... 812-941-2246 .... 174 D bchubbar@ius.edu
HUBBARD, David, W .... 903-586-2518 .... 488 L dhubbard@jacksonville-college.edu
HUBBARD, Dean, L .... 816-932-2144 .... 289 G dlhubbard@saint-lukes.org
HUBBARD, Francis .... 207-941-7144 .... 218 A hubbardfj@husson.edu
HUBBARD, James .... 309-268-8453 .... 151 G jim.hubbard@heartland.edu
HUBBARD, Janet .... 248-689-8282 .... 260 A jhubbard@walshcollege.edu
HUBBARD, Jeannette .... 726-946-7199 .... 451 C hubbarj@westminster.edu
HUBBARD, Joan .... 801-626-6403 .... 511 D jhubbard@weber.edu
HUBBARD, Laura, E .... 541-346-2817 .... 419 B lhubbard@uoregon.edu
HUBBARD, Phillip .... 610-647-4400 .... 431 B phubbard@immaculata.edu
HUBBARD, R. Glenn .... 212-854-2888 .... 330 F rgh1@columbia.edu
HUBBARD, Robert .... 203-773-8563 .... 89 H hubbard@albertus.edu
HUBBARD, Ruth .... 443-334-2203 .... 226 E rhubbard@stevenson.edu
HUBBARD, Stacey, L .... 217-424-6210 .... 158 F shubbard@millikin.edu
HUBBARD, Victoria .... 859-282-9999 .... 203 G vhubbard@lincolntech.com
HUBBARD, William .... 920-465-2510 .... 551 A hubbardw@uwgb.edu
HUBBARD, Yvonne, B .... 434-982-6000 .... 525 B yhs@virginia.edu
HUBBARD-COLE, Lady June .... 803-376-5700 .... 455 B
HUBBARD GIVEN, Mary .... 626-584-5691 .... 48 A mgiven@fuller.edu
HUBBELL, Kent, L .... 607-255-1115 .... 331 C klh4@cornell.edu
HUBBERT, Daron .... 951-552-8000 .... 31 G dhubbert@calbaptist.edu
HUBBS, Janet .... 732-255-0400 .... 312 D jhubbs@ocean.edu
HUBBS, Jocelyn .... 541-684-7345 .... 417 F jhubbs@northwestchristian.edu
HUBBS, Michael .... 225-675-8270 .... 211 J mhubbs@rpcc.edu
HUBENER, James .... 214-860-8695 .... 485 A jhubener@dcccd.edu
HUBER, Amy .... 732-356-1595 .... 315 D ahuber@somerset.edu
HUBER, Bettina .... 818-677-3277 .... 35 D bettina.huber@csun.edu
HUBER, Chip .... 616-222-1423 .... 250 C chip.huber@cornerstone.edu
HUBER, Dan .... 503-588-2722 .... 415 F dhuber@corban.edu
HUBER, Gary .... 309-796-5602 .... 145 E huberg@bhc.edu
HUBER, Gary .... 239-280-2573 .... 101 C gary.huber@avemaria.edu
HUBER, Lane .... 701-224-5714 .... 382 B lane.huber@bismarckstate.edu
HUBER, Laurie, G .... 248-232-4513 .... 257 B lghuber@oaklandcc.edu
HUBER, Lydia .... 361-572-6461 .... 507 G lydia.huber@victoriacollege.edu
HUBER, Mark, D .... 570-372-4247 .... 447 D huber@susqu.edu
HUBER, Marsha, A .... 973-408-3319 .... 309 F mhuber@drew.edu
HUBER, Patricia, B .... 540-674-3631 .... 527 B phuber@nr.edu
HUBER, Susan, J .... 651-962-6720 .... 272 E sjhuber@stthomas.edu
HUBER, Terry, W .... 812-429-1465 .... 176 I thuber@ivytech.edu
HUBERMAN, Jeffrey, H .... 309-677-2360 .... 145 H huberman@bradley.edu
HUBERMAN, Steven .... 212-463-0400 .... 357 J stevenh@touro.edu
HUBERS, Todd, K .... 616-526-6495 .... 249 E thubers@calvin.edu
HUBERT, Barbara .... 714-997-6940 .... 39 C hubert@chapman.edu
HUBERT, David .... 801-957-4280 .... 512 C david.hubert@slcc.edu
HUBIN, David, R .... 541-346-3036 .... 419 B hubin@uoregon.edu
HUBINGER, Amy, M .... 906-227-2626 .... 256 F ahubinge@nmu.edu
HUBLER, Barbara .... 415-338-2611 .... 36 F bhubler@sfsu.edu
HUBLER, Grant .... 541-956-7235 .... 420 B grant@roguecc.edu
HUBREGTSE, Joyce .... 605-221-3113 .... 464 C jhubregtse@kilian.edu
HUCH, Robert, E .... 540-261-8413 .... 524 C bob.huch@svu.edu
HUCK, Jack, J .... 402-323-3415 .... 300 C jhuck@southeast.edu
HUCKABAY, Sonia .... 559-791-2403 .... 53 A shuckaba@portervillecollege.edu
HUCKABY, Hank, M .... 404-656-2202 .... 138 E chancellor@usg.edu
HUCKEBY, Ed .... 405-789-7661 .... 412 E ed.huckeby@swcu.edu
HUCKESTEIN, Jim .... 541-917-4331 .... 416 H jim.huckestein@linnbenton.edu
HUCKESTEIN, Julie, A .... 503-399-5138 .... 414 J julie.huckestein@chemeketa.edu
HUCKINS, Heather .... 603-535-2249 .... 307 B hhuckins@plymouth.edu
HUCKMAN, Beverly, B .... 312-942-7093 .... 163 B beverly_b_huckman@rush.edu
HUCKS, Cheri, A .... 864-592-4931 .... 461 C huckscc@sccsc.edu
HUDACK, Jon .... 716-827-2547 .... 358 B hudackj@trocaire.edu
HUDAK, DeDe .... 916-577-2305 .... 79 C dhudak@jessup.edu
HUDAK, Jane, E .... 484-664-3300 .... 437 B hudak@muhlenberg.edu
HUDAK, Randy .... 304-293-3944 .... 544 E randy.hudak@mail.wvu.edu
HUDD, Robert, S .... 860-486-4806 .... 94 E robert.hudd@uconn.edu
HUDDLESTON, Gwen .... 805-654-6388 .... 77 D ghuddleston@vcccd.edu
HUDDLESTON, Jerry .... 219-879-9137 .... 176 E jhuddles@ivytech.edu
HUDDLESTON, Mark, W .... 603-862-2450 .... 306 E presidents.office@unh.edu
HUDDLESTON, Timothy .... 417-690-2209 .... 280 C thuddleston@cofo.edu
HUDDY, Michael .... 207-834-7607 .... 220 D michael.huddy@maine.edu
HUDEC, Susan .... 718-940-5854 .... 349 A shudec@sjcny.edu
HUDEC, Susan .... 718-940-5854 .... 349 B shudec@sjcny.edu
HUDGENS, Lisa .... 618-985-3741 .... 154 E lisahudgens@jalc.edu
HUDGIN, Denise .... 419-251-1324 .... 395 H denise.hudgin@mercycollege.edu
HUDGINS, Chris .... 702-895-0301 .... 302 K chris.hudgins@unlv.edu
HUDGINS, Jim .... 870-460-1018 .... 25 A hudgins@uamont.edu
HUDGINS, John .... 410-951-3528 .... 228 B jhudgins@coppin.edu
HUDGINS, V. Lavoyed .... 859-985-3240 .... 198 F hudginsv@berea.edu
HUDLOW, Penny .... 320-629-5115 .... 268 G hudlowp@pinetech.edu
HUDNUT-BEUMLER, James .... 615-343-3960 .... 477 F james.hudnut-beumler@vanderbilt.edu
HUDOCK, Virginia, S .... 803-641-3310 .... 462 B gingerh@usca.edu
HUDOK, Cynthia, K .... 304-367-4213 .... 543 E cynthia.hudok@fairmontstate.edu
HUDSICK, Walter .... 425-352-8162 .... 531 F whudsick@cascadia.edu
HUDSON, Angela .... 501-686-2504 .... 24 B ahudson@uasys.edu
HUDSON, Bill .... 816-604-1453 .... 285 D bill.hudson@mcckc.edu
HUDSON, Blake .... 540-338-1776 .... 522 A
HUDSON, Blake, W .... 423-285-1689 .... 467 D blake.hudson@bryan.edu
HUDSON, Bobby .... 615-230-3445 .... 476 A bobby.hudson@volstate.edu
HUDSON, Carol .... 406-874-6162 .... 294 H hudsonc@milescc.edu
HUDSON, Carol, I .... 406-874-6162 .... 294 H hudsonc@milescc.edu
HUDSON, David, D .... 714-895-8907 .... 41 A dhudson@gwc.cccd.edu
HUDSON, Dean, A .... 214-828-8391 .... 497 A dhudson@bcd.tamhsc.edu
HUDSON, Dean, P .... 843-349-2739 .... 456 G dhudson@coastal.edu
HUDSON, Debra .... 270-247-8521 .... 204 C dhudson@midcontinent.edu
HUDSON, Delaphine .... 562-907-4223 .... 79 B dhudson@whittier.edu
HUDSON, Delores .... 256-372-5227 .... 1 A delores.hudson@aamu.edu
HUDSON, Donald .... 812-488-2452 .... 180 B dh104@evansville.edu
HUDSON, Donald .... 609-894-9311 .... 308 C dhudson@bcc.edu
HUDSON, Earnest .... 828-227-7301 .... 379 E ehudson@wcu.edu
HUDSON, Eileen, L .... 716-888-2700 .... 325 G hudsone@canisius.edu
HUDSON, Gregory .... 662-621-4153 .... 273 I ghudson@coahomacc.edu
HUDSON, Harold .... 937-529-2201 .... 403 A hhudson@united.edu
HUDSON, Howard .... 610-399-2219 .... 441 H hhudson@cheyney.edu
HUDSON, Jackie .... 205-929-1401 .... 5 H jhudson@miles.edu
HUDSON, James, B .... 502-852-2234 .... 207 A jbhuds01@louisville.edu
HUDSON, James, M .... 765-494-0226 .... 178 F hudson35@purdue.edu
HUDSON, Jennifer, M .... 713-646-1899 .... 494 E jhudson@stcl.edu
HUDSON, Jerry .... 806-742-3385 .... 501 D jerry.hudson@ttu.edu
HUDSON, Karen .... 615-771-7821 .... 478 G khudson@williamsoncc.edu
HUDSON, Kathy .... 434-961-5446 .... 527 F khudson@pvcc.edu
HUDSON, Keith .... 270-686-4261 .... 198 G keith.hudson@brescia.edu
HUDSON, Lea Ann .... 404-471-6402 .... 123 G lhudson@agnesscott.edu
HUDSON, Lyla .... 843-792-8721 .... 459 C hudsonly@musc.edu
HUDSON, Marilyn .... 405-789-7661 .... 412 E marilyn.hudson@swcu.edu
HUDSON, Mark, A .... 217-581-3923 .... 150 C mahudson@eiu.edu
HUDSON, Maureen .... 781-280-3506 .... 240 F hudsonm@middlesex.mass.edu
HUDSON, Melissa, A .... 530-226-4974 .... 69 H mhudson@simpsonu.edu
HUDSON, Michael, J .... 630-637-5661 .... 159 F mjhudson@noctrl.edu
HUDSON, Pam .... 417-455-5506 .... 281 C phudson@crowder.edu
HUDSON, Pat .... 816-414-3700 .... 286 A phudson@mbts.edu
HUDSON, Peggy .... 618-468-5100 .... 156 C phudson@lc.edu
HUDSON, Richard .... 502-585-9911 .... 205 I rhudson@spalding.edu
HUDSON, Richard, B .... 479-575-7964 .... 24 C rhudson@uark.edu
HUDSON, Robert .... 617-353-3710 .... 232 G rhudson@bu.edu
HUDSON, Robert .... 252-399-6345 .... 362 A rdhudson@barton.edu
HUDSON, Robin .... 407-226-6423 .... 104 D rhudson@devry.edu
HUDSON, Rodeny, B .... 803-535-5470 .... 456 D rhudson@claflin.edu
HUDSON, Teresa .... 409-933-8250 .... 483 B thudson@com.edu
HUDSON, Terri, C .... 419-289-5300 .... 384 D thudson1@ashland.edu
HUDSON, Tijuana, R .... 803-535-5197 .... 456 D thudson@claflin.edu
HUDSON, Tim .... 806-742-0012 .... 501 D
HUDSON, JR., William .... 850-599-3183 .... 118 G william.hudson@famu.edu
HUDSON-MACISAAC, Kelley .... 760-744-1150 .... 61 C kmacisaac@palomar.edu
HUDSON-NOWAK, Melissa, A .... 419-372-2147 .... 385 C melhuds@bgsu.edu
HUDSON-TOMLIN, Della .... 516-877-3661 .... 322 A hudson@adelphi.edu
HUDSPETH, Donald .... 585-475-7077 .... 347 G don@acmt.hr
HUDSPETH, Harvey, L .... 806-651-2116 .... 498 D hhudspeth@mail.wtamu.edu
HUDY, Karen .... 216-421-7321 .... 387 H khudy@cia.edu
HUEBNER, Julie, A .... 630-752-5490 .... 168 F julie.huebner@wheaton.edu
HUEBNER, Kathleen .... 215-780-1361 .... 446 G kathyh@salus.edu
HUEBNER, Maryjo "MJ" .... 402-461-7398 .... 298 C mjhuebner@hastings.edu
HUEBNER, Thomas .... 205-391-2999 .... 7 A thuebner@sheltonstate.edu
HUEBNER, Valerie, O .... 207-778-7258 .... 220 C huebner@maine.edu
HUEBOTTER, Chris .... 573-288-6542 .... 281 D chuebotter@culver.edu
HUEBSCH, Pat .... 541-956-7163 .... 420 B phuebsch@roguecc.edu
HUEFTLE, Theresa .... 216-432-8986 .... 387 A THueftle@ChancellorU.edu
HUEG, Kurt .... 650-949-7349 .... 47 H huegkurt@foothill.edu
HUEGEL, Mary .... 978-232-2084 .... 234 F mhuegel@endicott.edu
HUEHN-JOHNSON, Juliana, H .... 213-740-9780 .... 76 C huehn@usc.edu
HUELSBECK, Tom, A .... 253-535-7200 .... 535 K tom.huelsbeck@plu.edu
HUELSMAN, Shelly .... 620-227-9285 .... 192 B shuelsman@dc3.edu
HUENEMANN, Kurt .... 419-448-2351 .... 391 G keh@heidelberg.edu
HUENINK, Richard .... 262-551-6200 .... 546 F rhuenink@carthage.edu
HUENNEKE, Laura .... 928-523-2599 .... 17 A laura.huenneke@nau.edu
HUERTA, David .... 559-278-8400 .... 34 D davidhu@csufresno.edu
HUERTA, Margie, C .... 575-527-7510 .... 319 G marhuert@nmsu.edu
HUERTA, Patricia .... 312-362-8601 .... 148 F phuerta@depaul.edu
HUERTAS, Carmelo, V .... 973-972-7551 .... 316 C huertarv@umdnj.edu
HUERTAS, Mildred .... 787-257-7373 .... 565 E ue_mhuertas@suagm.edu
HUERTAS, Orlando .... 305-626-3798 .... 108 H orlando.huertas@fmuniv.edu
HUERTAS-BERMÚDEZ, Antonio .... 787-993-8862 .... 566 G antonio.huertas@upr.edu
HUESER, Kyle .... 712-274-6400 .... 189 H kyle.hueser@witcc.edu
HUESING, Alan .... 903-923-2172 .... 486 D ahuesing@etbu.edu
HUESTON, Eddie, C .... 972-238-6170 .... 485 C ehueston@dcccd.edu
HUEWITT, Jerri .... 404-297-9522 .... 128 B huewittj@dekalbtech.edu
HUEY, Lindley .... 617-253-6162 .... 242 A lindley@mit.edu
HUEY, Yick Pon .... 212-924-5900 .... 357 A yph@swedishinstitute.edu
HUFF, Amy .... 931-393-1629 .... 475 C ahuff@mscc.edu
HUFF, Betty .... 901-678-5218 .... 474 C bjhuff@memphis.edu
HUFF, Dwayne .... 417-833-2551 .... 279 I dhuff@cbcag.edu
HUFF, Eugene, C .... 925-229-1000 .... 43 A ehuff@4cd.edu
HUFF, Glenda .... 325-649-8014 .... 488 A ghuff@hputx.edu
HUFF, Jane .... 606-693-5000 .... 203 C
HUFF, III, Joseph, E .... 409-944-1302 .... 486 H jhuff@gc.edu
HUFF, Kim, R .... 803-535-1204 .... 460 C huffk@octech.edu
HUFF, Marie .... 828-227-7271 .... 379 E mhuff@wcu.edu
HUFF, Randall .... 606-693-5000 .... 203 C rhuff@kmbc.edu
HUFF, Scott .... 503-978-5573 .... 419 G shuff@pcc.edu
HUFF, Thomas, F .... 804-827-5600 .... 525 E tfhuff@vcu.edu
HUFF, Tim, T .... 405-744-5459 .... 410 C tim.huff@okstate.edu
HUFF-CORZINE, Lin .... 407-882-0077 .... 120 A lin.huff-corzine@ucf.edu
HUFFARD, Evertt, W .... 901-761-1352 .... 469 A dean@hst.edu
HUFFARD, Lorri, M .... 276-223-4829 .... 528 F wchuffl@wcc.vccs.edu
HUFFCUTT, Tom, G .... 715-833-6661 .... 553 F thuffcutt@cvtc.edu
HUFFMAN, Don .... 312-662-4236 .... 144 C dhuffman@adler.edu
HUFFMAN, Gerald .... 206-296-5869 .... 537 F huffmanje@seattleu.edu
HUFFMAN, Jeffery .... 419-559-2257 .... 402 D jhuffman01@terra.edu
HUFFMAN, Jessamine .... 256-840-4151 .... 7 B jhuffman@snead.edu
HUFFMAN, Laurene, K .... 740-374-8716 .... 405 F lhuffman@wscc.edu
HUFFMAN, Linda .... 573-518-2204 .... 286 B lhuffman@mineralarea.edu
HUFFMAN, Lon .... 269-467-9945 .... 251 D lhuffman@glenoaks.edu
HUFFMAN, Mari, L .... 419-866-0261 .... 402 B mlhuffman@stautzenberger.com
HUFFMAN, Miriam, I .... 314-516-5291 .... 291 F huffmanmi@umsl.edu
HUFFMAN, Monica, R .... 660-543-4106 .... 291 B mhuffman@ucmo.edu
HUFFMAN, Pat .... 425-640-1002 .... 533 E phuffman@edcc.edu
HUFFMAN, Robin .... 260-399-7700 .... 180 E rhuffman@sf.edu

HUFFMAN, Sherri, H ... 434-797-8576 ... 526 C shuffman@dcc.vccs.edu
HUFFMAN, Tammy, S ... 740-588-1212 ... 407 A thuffman@zanestate.edu
HUFFMAN, Virginia, A ... 212-327-8300 ... 347 H huffman@rockefeller.edu
HUFFSTETLER, Edward, W 540-828-5332 ... 516 K ehuffste@bridgewater.edu
HUFFT, Anita, G ... 229-333-5959 ... 138 F ahufft@valdosta.edu
HUFNAGEL, Michele ... 724-503-1001 ... 451 A mhufnagel@washjeff.edu
HUFSTETLER, Catrice ... 770-975-4000 ... 126 H
HUFTALIN, Deneece ... 801-957-4285 ... 512 C deneece.huftalin@slcc.edu
HUFTEL, Joe ... 715-246-6561 ... 555 E joe.huftel@witc.edu
HUG-ENGLISH, Cheryl ... 775-784-6122 ... 303 A cherylh@med.unr.edu
HUGETZ, Edward ... 713-743-3419 ... 503 B ehugetz@uh.edu
HUGETZ, Edward, T ... 713-743-3419 ... 503 A ehugetz@uh.edu
HUGGETT, Monica ... 212-799-5000 ... 337 H
HUGGINS, Cynthia, E ... 207-255-1210 ... 220 E chuggins@maine.edu
HUGGINS, Desiree ... 337-262-5962 ... 209 D dhuggins@acadiana.edu
HUGGINS, Jenny ... 812-330-6025 ... 175 H jhuggins5@ivytech.edu
HUGGINS, Jonathan ... 706-236-2217 ... 125 G jhuggins@berry.edu
HUGGINS, Regina, M ... 919-866-5408 ... 374 E rmhuggins@waketech.edu
HUGHES, A. LeAnn ... 423-652-4706 ... 469 L lhughes@king.edu
HUGHES, B. Hilles ... 740-376-4645 ... 395 F hilles.hughes@marietta.edu
HUGHES, Barbara, J ... 814-641-3311 ... 431 L hughesb@juniata.edu
HUGHES, Bernice ... 229-391-5140 ... 123 F bhughes@abac.edu
HUGHES, Bonnie ... 506-865-8588 ... 534 D hughes_b@heritage.edu
HUGHES, C. Raymond ... 860-906-5012 ... 89 L rhughes@ccc.commnet.edu
HUGHES, Charles, F ... 417-690-2211 ... 280 C hughes@cofo.edu
HUGHES, Christine ... 617-824-8908 ... 234 D christine_hughes@emerson.edu
HUGHES, Chuck ... 910-962-3188 ... 379 C hughesch@uncw.edu
HUGHES, Craig ... 716-839-8246 ... 331 G
HUGHES, David ... 207-780-4946 ... 220 G dehughes@usm.maine.edu
HUGHES, David ... 785-738-9008 ... 195 D dhughes@ncktc.edu
HUGHES, David ... 501-760-4311 ... 22 F dhughes@npcc.edu
HUGHES, Deborah ... 305-220-4120 ... 115 D lmdir@ptcmatt.com
HUGHES, Derek ... 701-845-7401 ... 382 A derek.hughes@vcsu.edu
HUGHES, DeVetta ... 843-574-6199 ... 461 G devetta.hughes@tridenttech.edu
HUGHES, Dianna ... 662-252-8000 ... 277 C dr_hughes@rustcollege.edu
HUGHES, Ed ... 859-442-1175 ... 201 G ed.hughes@kctcs.edu
HUGHES, Edwin ... 973-278-5400 ... 307 G ejh@berkeleycollege.edu
HUGHES, Edwin ... 973-278-5400 ... 323 J ejh@berkeleycollege.edu
HUGHES, Elizabeth ... 312-567-5045 ... 153 B hughes@iit.edu
HUGHES, Elizabeth, B ... 417-690-2212 ... 280 C ehughes@cofo.edu
HUGHES, Erinn ... 281-649-3213 ... 487 F erhughes@hbu.edu
HUGHES, Ernie, T ... 225-771-3911 ... 214 G ernie_hughes@sus.edu
HUGHES, Frank ... 605-274-4325 ... 463 H frank.hughes@augie.edu
HUGHES, James, J ... 860-297-2376 ... 94 C james.hughes@trincoll.edu
HUGHES, James, L ... 410-706-1935 ... 227 C jhughes@umaryland.edu
HUGHES, James, W ... 732-932-5475 ... 314 D jwhughes@rci.rutgers.edu
HUGHES, Jason ... 608-363-2137 ... 546 B hughesj@beloit.edu
HUGHES, Jay ... 870-460-1053 ... 25 A hughesj@uamont.edu
HUGHES, Jennifer ... 650-574-6118 ... 67 F hughesj@smccd.edu
HUGHES, Jerry, M ... 660-543-4250 ... 291 B hughes@ucmo.edu
HUGHES, Jim ... 620-235-4154 ... 195 I jhughes@pittstate.edu
HUGHES, Joe Pat ... 580-371-2371 ... 408 I jhughes@mscok.edu
HUGHES, John, A ... 661-362-2223 ... 56 G jhughes@masters.edu
HUGHES, Joy, R ... 703-993-8728 ... 519 A jhughes@gmu.edu
HUGHES, Karla ... 606-783-2002 ... 204 E k.hughes@moreheadstate.edu
HUGHES, Kevin, M ... 757-594-7335 ... 517 I kmhughes@cnu.edu
HUGHES, Laura ... 870-460-1454 ... 25 A hughesl@uamont.edu
HUGHES, Laura ... 208-792-2224 ... 143 F lhughes@lcsc.edu
HUGHES, Lecia ... 325-793-4998 ... 490 F hughes.lecia@mcm.edu
HUGHES, Leslie ... 601-635-2111 ... 274 C lhughes@eccc.edu
HUGHES, Linda ... 402-354-7049 ... 299 E linda.hughes@methodistcollege.edu
HUGHES, Louise ... 870-612-2013 ... 25 E louise.hughes@uaccb.edu
HUGHES, Lucille ... 215-717-6144 ... 448 H lhughes@uarts.edu
HUGHES, Mark ... 301-925-3800 ... 275 E rmhughes@mc.edu
HUGHES, Mark ... 512-245-2501 ... 501 C mh66@txstate.edu
HUGHES, Marshall ... 617-541-5381 ... 241 D mhughes@rcd.mass.edi
HUGHES, Martha ... 972-273-3590 ... 485 B mhughes@dcccd.edu
HUGHES, Marvalene ... 504-816-4640 ... 208 I mhughes@dillard.edu
HUGHES, Mary, E ... 614-235-4136 ... 402 G mhughes@TLSohio.edu
HUGHES, Melany ... 308-432-6415 ... 299 G mhughes@csc.edu
HUGHES, Michael ... 415-422-2465 ... 76 B hughesm@usfca.edu
HUGHES, Michael, J ... 740-351-3539 ... 401 I mhughes@shawnee.edu
HUGHES, Michelle ... 508-588-9100 ... 240 E
HUGHES, Michelle ... 610-683-4822 ... 442 F hughes@kutztown.edu
HUGHES, Mike ... 231-591-2924 ... 251 B hughesm@ferris.edu
HUGHES, Mike, C ... 817-923-1921 ... 495 E mhughes@swbts.edu
HUGHES, Montaven ... 765-459-0561 ... 176 A mhughes@ivytech.edu
HUGHES, Myron ... 513-556-4344 ... 403 D myron.hughes@uc.edu
HUGHES, Nancy ... 405-224-3140 ... 413 E nhughes@usao.edu
HUGHES, Nancy, B ... 607-746-4573 ... 355 E hughesnb@delhi.edu
HUGHES, Patricia ... 256-551-3130 ... 4 J pat.hughes@drakestate.edu
HUGHES, Peter, D ... 518-244-2200 ... 348 A hughep@sage.edu
HUGHES, Robert ... 615-963-1836 ... 474 A rhughes@tnstate.edu
HUGHES, Robert, A ... 402-398-5527 ... 296 I robert.hughes@alegent.org
HUGHES, Ronald ... 586-445-7183 ... 254 F hughesr@macomb.edu
HUGHES, Sandra ... 843-863-7933 ... 456 B shughes@csuniv.edu
HUGHES, Scott ... 352-787-7660 ... 101 H shughes@beaconcollege.edu
HUGHES, Scott, S ... 361-593-2717 ... 498 A scott.hughes@tamuk.edu
HUGHES, Sherri, L ... 703-284-1550 ... 521 A sherri.hughes@marymount.edu
HUGHES, Stacy ... 312-915-6740 ... 157 A shughe2@luc.edu
HUGHES, Tanya, G ... 432-335-6815 ... 491 F thughes@odessa.edu
HUGHES, Tom ... 928-776-2205 ... 19 E tom.hughes@yc.edu
HUGHES, Tom ... 800-962-7682 ... 293 B athletics@wma.edu
HUGHES, W. William ... 909-558-1300 ... 54 D bhughes@llu.edu
HUGHES HANDLEY, Allyson ... 207-621-3403 ... 220 B allyson.handley@maine.edu
HUGHES-HARRIS, Cynthia 850-599-3276 ... 118 G cynthia.harris@famu.edu
HUGHEY, Andrew, C ... 713-313-7470 ... 499 G hugheyac@tsu.edu
HUGHEY, Willie, M ... 903-927-3211 ... 509 A wmhughey@wileyc.edu
HUGHLEY, Corine ... 229-430-3537 ... 123 I chughley@albanytech.edu
HUGHSTON, Patty ... 251-580-2101 ... 5 A phughston@faulknerstate.edu
HUGINE, JR., Andrew ... 256-372-5230 ... 1 A andrew.hugine@aamu.edu
HUGLE, Shelbie ... 859-246-6216 ... 201 D shelbie.hugle@kctcs.edu
HUGUENIN, Sanders ... 276-328-0120 ... 525 C jsh4ew@uvawise.edu
HUH, Andy ... 312-553-5628 ... 146 H ahuh@ccc.edu
HUHRA, Lourdene ... 847-543-2514 ... 147 H lhuhra@clcillinois.edu
HUI, Andrew ... 215-702-4203 ... 444 A ahui@pbu.edu
HUI, Timothy, K ... 215-702-4377 ... 444 A thui@pbu.edu
HUIATT, Ron ... 724-938-5775 ... 441 G huiatt@calu.edu
HUIDEKOPER, Elizabeth ... 401-863-9400 ... 452 J elizabeth_huidekoper@brown.edu
HUISH, Darrel, S ... 651-201-1454 ... 265 H darrel.huish@so.mnscu.edu
HUISH, David ... 928-524-7888 ... 17 B david.huish@npc.edu
HUISKAMP, Julie, G ... 563-562-3263 ... 187 G huiskamj@nicc.edu
HUIZINGA, Dorota ... 657-278-4831 ... 34 E dhuizinga@fullerton.edu
HUKE, Theresa ... 610-361-5249 ... 437 C huket@neumann.edu
HUKILL, Lezlie ... 806-291-3446 ... 508 B lezlieh@wbu.edu
HUKOWICZ, Elizabeth ... 413-265-2222 ... 233 E hukowicze@elms.edu
HULBERT, Stephen, T ... 985-448-4003 ... 216 A stephen.hulbert@nicholls.edu
HULETT, Matt ... 505-277-2446 ... 321 C mhulett@unm.edu
HULETT, Rosemary, D ... 704-534-7892 ... 151 C rhulett@govst.edu
HULIN, Alicia ... 337-521-8920 ... 212 B alicia.hulin@southlouisiana.edu
HULKE, Carla, J ... 507-354-8221 ... 265 B hulkecj@mlc-wels.edu
HULL, Brooks, A ... 903-813-2419 ... 481 A bhull@austincollege.edu
HULL, Deborah ... 323-731-2383 ... 60 I dhull@psuca.edu
HULL, Edward, C ... 413-545-1964 ... 237 C ehull@gw.housing.umass.edu
HULL, James, L ... 419-755-4850 ... 397 B jhull@ncstatecollege.edu
HULL, Jim ... 607-844-8222 ... 357 H hullj@TC3.edu
HULL, Jim ... 217-234-5225 ... 155 H jhull17327@lakeland.cc.il.us
HULL, JR., Joe ... 843-953-5546 ... 457 B hulljj@cofc.edu
HULL, Judy, M ... 931-372-3491 ... 474 B jmhull@tntech.edu
HULL, Karen, S ... 530-752-3383 ... 73 F kshull@ucdavis.edu
HULL, Kevin ... 312-427-2737 ... 154 F 6hull@jmls.edu
HULL, Leota, V ... 956-665-2561 ... 506 A hull@utpa.edu
HULL, Lynn ... 740-753-7036 ... 392 A hull_l@hocking.edu
HULL, Shawn ... 573-592-4389 ... 293 E shull@williamwoods.edu
HULL, Stephen, E ... 863-297-1026 ... 115 A shull@polk.edu
HULL, Teresa ... 909-652-7653 ... 39 B teresa.hull@chaffey.edu
HULL, Thomas, A ... 518-782-8000 ... 350 I thull@siena.edu
HULLETT, Lisa ... 256-352-8267 ... 10 B lisa.hullett@wallacestate.edu
HULME, Wendy ... 215-702-4509 ... 444 A whulme@pbu.edu
HULON, Jane ... 601-643-8310 ... 274 A jane.hulon@colin.edu
HULS, Jack ... 360-417-6246 ... 536 B jhuls@pencol.edu
HULSEBOSCH, Patricia ... 202-448-7036 ... 97 E patricia.hulsebosch@gallaudet.edu
HULSEY, Janet ... 706-419-1262 ... 127 F hulsey@covenant.edu
HULSEY, Tara ... 843-863-7075 ... 456 B thulsey@csuniv.edu
HULSEY, Timothy, L ... 804-828-1803 ... 525 E tlhulsey@vcu.edu
HULSMAN, J Patrick ... 716-286-8771 ... 344 D phulsman@niagara.du
HULST, Mary ... 616-526-7617 ... 249 E msh4@calvin.edu
HULSTEIN, Pamela, L ... 712-722-6689 ... 183 H hulstein@dordt.edu
HULSTINE, Thomas ... 717-544-4912 ... 433 E
HULTBERG, Jane ... 207-288-5015 ... 217 H jhultberg@coa.edu
HULTIN, Jerry, M ... 718-260-3500 ... 346 C hultin@poly.edu
HULTMAN, Ken ... 402-554-3514 ... 301 B khultman@unomaha.edu
HULTQUIST, Sharon, S ... 260-480-4280 ... 176 D shultqui@ivytech.edu
HULTSMAN, John ... 661-654-6093 ... 33 H jhultsman@csub.edu
HUMBERGER, Laura ... 406-994-4361 ... 295 E lhumberger@montana.edu
HUMBERT, Mark ... 315-312-2248 ... 354 A mark.humbert@oswego.edu
HUMBLE, Dina ... 209-575-6130 ... 80 B humbled@mjc.edu
HUME, Evelyn ... 316-295-5858 ... 192 H evelyn_hume@friends.edu
HUME, Gary ... 615-230-3600 ... 476 A gary.hume@volstate.edu
HUME, Richard ... 631-420-2080 ... 356 A richard.hume@farmingdale.edu
HUMERICK, Rosalind, M ... 386-312-4212 ... 116 D rosalindhumerick@sjrstate.edu
HUMES, Cynthia ... 909-607-8713 ... 40 D cynthia.humes@cmc.edu
HUMESTON, Howard, D ... 305-899-3139 ... 101 F dhumeston@mail.barry.edu
HUMISTON, Dolores, J ... 509-777-4320 ... 539 F dhumiston@whitworth.edu
HUMME, Larryl ... 708-239-3977 ... 165 I larryl.humme@trnty.edu
HUMMEL, Paul ... 630-466-7900 ... 167 G phummel@waubonsee.edu
HUMMEL, Scott ... 601-318-6769 ... 278 E scott.hummel@wmcarey.edu
HUMMEL-BERRY, Kathleen ... 253-879-3531 ... 538 E hummel@pugetsound.edu
HUMMER, Alissa ... 805-893-4091 ... 74 F alissa.hummer@planning.ucsb.edu
HUMMER, Jim ... 760-773-2561 ... 41 H jhummer@collegeofthedesert.edu
HUMMER, Judith, G ... 717-290-8718 ... 433 F jhummer@lancasterseminary.edu
HUMMERT, Mary Lee ... 785-864-4904 ... 196 F mlhummert@ku.edu
HUMMINGBIRD, Edward ... 505-922-6506 ... 321 B ehummingbird@sipi.bia.edu
HUMPHREY, Amy ... 865-471-2000 ... 467 E ahumphrey@cn.edu
HUMPHREY, Bonnie ... 660-831-4108 ... 286 I humphreyb@moval.edu
HUMPHREY, Dana ... 207-581-2216 ... 220 A dana.humphrey@umit.maine.edu
HUMPHREY, George, E ... 617-732-2292 ... 241 F george.humphrey@mcphs.edu
HUMPHREY, Kathy, W ... 412-648-1006 ... 449 A kathyh@pitt.edu
HUMPHREY, Laura ... 803-313-7066 ... 462 D humphrLB@mailbox.sc.edu
HUMPHREY, Lynn ... 208-426-2948 ... 142 F lynnhumphrey@boisestate.edu
HUMPHREY, Scott ... 315-792-3835 ... 359 C shumphrey@utica.edu
HUMPHREY, Shawn ... 904-448-9499 ... 112 E
HUMPHREY, Twila ... 719-502-2052 ... 86 G twila.humphrey@ppcc.edu
HUMPHREYS, Bryce ... 509-882-7049 ... 540 A bhumphreys@yvcc.edu
HUMPHREYS, David ... 310-233-4025 ... 54 I humphrd@lahc.edu
HUMPHREYS, George, G ... 270-824-1723 ... 202 C george.humphreys@kctcs.edu
HUMPHREYS, Melanie ... 630-752-5941 ... 168 F melanie.humphreys@wheaton.edu
HUMPHREYS, Robert, G ... 209-478-0800 ... 50 I rgh@humphreys.edu
HUMPHREYS, JR., Robert, G ... 209-478-0800 ... 50 I rhumphreys@humphreys.edu
HUMPHRIES, Brian, L ... 651-286-7620 ... 270 E blhumphries@nwc.edu
HUMPHRIES, Corey ... 843-574-5505 ... 456 B chumphries@csuniv.edu
HUMPHRIES, Evelyn ... 847-969-4982 ... 145 A ehumphries@argosy.edu
HUMPHRIES, Karl ... 903-875-7600 ... 491 B karl.humphries@navarrocollege.edu
HUMPHRIES, Kelly ... 864-250-7000 ... 99 D kyh@strayer.edu
HUMPHRIES, Lou ... 619-388-3473 ... 65 F lhumphri@sdccd.edu
HUMPHRIES, Mary ... 360-752-8378 ... 531 C mhumphries@btc.ctc.edu
HUMPHRIES, Tara ... 919-735-5151 ... 374 F tarah@waynecc.edu
HUNCHBERGER, Mary ... 360-417-6535 ... 536 B mhunchberger@pencol.edu
HUNDERSMARCK, Steven, F ... 260-422-5561 ... 172 L sfhundersmarck@indianatech.edu
HUNDLEY, Patrick ... 618-650-2345 ... 165 A phundle@siue.edu
HUNEYCUTT, Richy ... 252-527-6223 ... 371 D rhuneycutt@lenoircc.edu
HUNGER, Suzanne ... 406-444-2799 ... 295 C hungers@umhelena.edu
HUNGSBERG, Jill, C ... 518-388-6131 ... 358 E hungsbej@union.edu
HUNKER, Kurt ... 619-684-8787 ... 59 A khunker@newschoolarch.edu
HUNKLER, Chris ... 205-329-7900 ... 48 F chris.hunkler@golfacademy.edu
HUNKLER, Chris ... 205-329-7900 ... 110 D chris.hunkler@golfacademy.edu
HUNKLER, Chris ... 205-329-7900 ... 14 H chris.hunkler@golfacademy.edu
HUNKLER, Chris ... 205-329-7900 ... 458 E chris.hunkler@golfacademy.edu

HUNLEY, Marcha .... 513-569-1732.... 387 F
marcha.hunley@cincinnatistate.edu
HUNN, Martha, S .... 843-349-2962.... 456 G
mhunn@coastal.edu
HUNN, II, Marvin, T .... 214-841-3751.... 485 E
mhunn@dts.edu
HUNNICUTT, Lew .... 806-648-1450.... 486 G
lunnicutt@fpctx.edu
HUNNICUTT, Veronica .... 415-239-3762...... 39 H
vhunnicu@ccsf.edu
HUNSAKER, Deanna .... 660-626-2356.... 278 F
dhunsaker@atsu.edu
HUNSAKER, Miles .... 801-524-8108.... 510 A
mhunsaker@ldsbc.edu
HUNSBERGER, Gerald .... 607-431-4738.... 335 B
hunsbergerg@hartwick.edu
HUNSBERGER, Susan .... 208-459-5407.... 143 A
shunsberger@collegeofidaho.edu
HUNSICKER, Donald .... 617-262-5000.... 232 B
don.hunsicker@the-bac.edu
HUNSICKER, Jennie, I .... 610-398-5300.... 434 F
jhunsicker@lincolntech.com
HUNSINGER, Fred .... 215-340-8401.... 423 E
hunsinge@bucks.edu
HUNSINGER, Leo .... 228-392-2994.... 278 B
leo.hunsinger@vc.edu
HUNSUCKER, Scott, E .... 704-233-8220.... 380 D
scotth@wingate.edu
HUNT, Alice .... 773-752-5757.... 146 E
ahunt@ctschicago.edu
HUNT, Altavese .... 803-327-7402.... 456 F
ahunt@clintonjuniorcollege.edu
HUNT, Cammie .... 910-522-5789.... 379 B
cammie.hunt@uncp.edu
HUNT, Cathy .... 270-831-9723.... 201 I
cathy.hunt@kctcs.edu
HUNT, Daphne .... 254-968-1852.... 496 F
djhunt@tarleton.edu
HUNT, Darla .... 606-759-7141.... 202 D
darla.hunt@kctcs.edu
HUNT, David, A .... 801-422-3868.... 509 D
david_hunt@byu.edu
HUNT, Delores .... 704-406-2361.... 364 B
dhunt@gardner-webb.edu
HUNT, Denise .... 760-921-5510...... 61 B
dhunt@paloverde.edu
HUNT, Dennis .... 812-866-7017.... 171 F
huntd@hanover.edu
HUNT, Gregory, K .... 570-340-6063.... 435 F
gkhunt@marywood.edu
HUNT, J. Steven .... 503-375-7591.... 415 F
shunt@corban.edu
HUNT, James, W .... 512-863-1567.... 495 G
huntj@southwestern.edu
HUNT, Jeffrey .... 808-235-7442.... 142 C
jwhunt@hawaii.edu
HUNT, Jennifer .... 617-912-9130.... 232 E
jhunt@bostonconservatory.edu
HUNT, John .... 254-526-1116.... 482 F
John.hunt@ctcd.edu
HUNT, Judith, L .... 973-655-4301.... 311 G
huntjl@mail.montclair.edu
HUNT, Karen .... 937-327-6377.... 406 B
khunt@wittenberg.edu
HUNT, Lawerence .... 413-585-2260.... 245 B
lhunt@smith.edu
HUNT, Lisa, O .... 910-272-3501.... 373 A
lohunt@robeson.edu
HUNT, Louis, D .... 919-515-1428.... 378 B
louis_hunt@ncsu.edu
HUNT, Marilyn, L .... 910-272-3320.... 373 A
mhunt@robeson.edu
HUNT, Mark .... 334-386-7140...... 3 H
mhunt@faulkner.edu
HUNT, Marsha, D .... 301-937-8448.... 226 H
mhunt@tesst.com
HUNT, Marvin .... 913-288-7659.... 193 J
mhunt@kckcc.edu
HUNT, Mary .... 312-226-6294.... 156 E
mhunt@lexingtoncollege.edu
HUNT, Melany, L .... 626-395-6249...... 32 E
hunt@caltech.edu
HUNT, Patricia .... 304-734-6611.... 542 D
phunt@bridgemont.edu
HUNT, Patricia .... 304-204-4097.... 542 F
phunt@kvctc.edu
HUNT, Patrick, G .... 240-895-4307.... 226 A
pghunt@smcm.edu
HUNT, Paul, M .... 517-432-4499.... 255 D
pmhunt@msu.edu
HUNT, Penelepe, C .... 312-413-2992.... 166 F
phunt@uic.edu
HUNT, Peter, G .... 434-949-1005.... 527 H
peter.hunt@southside.edu
HUNT, Rene .... 662-325-0610.... 276 A
rch2@its.msstate.edu
HUNT, Roe, B .... 803-535-5471.... 456 D
rhunt@claflin.edu
HUNT, Ruston .... 678-915-7338.... 137 C
rhunt@spsu.edu
HUNT, Rusty .... 336-249-8186.... 369 F
rthunt@davidsonccc.edu
HUNT, Ryan .... 513-569-1756.... 387 F
ryan.hunt@cincinnatistate.edu
HUNT, Sharon, P .... 336-272-7102.... 364 D
shunt@greensborocollege.edu
HUNT, Susan .... 617-964-1100.... 230 B
shunt@ants.edu
HUNT, Todd, A .... 407-582-1463.... 122 I
thunt3@valenciacollege.edu
HUNT, Virginia .... 570-504-7300.... 425 F
HUNT, William, M .... 412-566-2433.... 434 B
whunt@paculinary.com
HUNT-BULL, Nicholas .... 603-668-2211.... 306 B
n.hunt-bull@snhu.edu
HUNT-CARTER, Pamela ...... 831-459-2749...... 75 A
phcarter@ucsc.edu
HUNT LAWSON, Amy .... 434-223-6149.... 519 B
ahuntlawson@hsc.edu
HUNT LOVETT, Jill .... 270-809-3763.... 204 F
jill.hunt@murraystate.edu
HUNTER, Ben, D .... 317-940-9982.... 170 C
bdhunter@butler.edu
HUNTER, Benita .... 773-838-7519.... 147 E
bhunter@ccc.edu
HUNTER, Bill .... 850-973-9448.... 113 J
hunterb@nfcc.edu
HUNTER, Bill .... 850-201-6556.... 121 F
hunterb@tcc.fl.edu
HUNTER, Bonnie, L .... 219-464-5411.... 181 A
bonnie.hunter@valpo.edu
HUNTER, Carolyn .... 513-585-2068.... 387 C
HUNTER, Charles .... 602-386-4133...... 11 H
chuck.hunter@arizonachristian.edu
HUNTER, Cynthia .... 941-752-5290.... 118 E
hunterc@scf.edu
HUNTER, DeLandra .... 678-839-6280.... 138 D
dhunter@westga.edu
HUNTER, Donna, L .... 304-766-4146.... 544 D
hunterdl@wvstateu.edu
HUNTER, Edith, T .... 212-280-1342.... 358 G
ehunter@uts.columbia.edu
HUNTER, Edward .... 215-567-7080.... 422 C
ehunter@edmc.edu
HUNTER, Erik .... 703-346-5407.... 516 B
erihunter@argosy.edu
HUNTER, Gayle .... 386-752-1822.... 108 C
gayle.hunter@fgc.edu
HUNTER, Gerald, E .... 336-750-2703.... 380 A
hunterge@wssu.edu
HUNTER, Ira .... 773-907-4800.... 147 A
ihunter@ccc.edu
HUNTER, Jack, M .... 417-836-5636.... 286 F
jackhunter@missouristate.edu
HUNTER, JR., Jairy, C .... 843-863-7500.... 456 B
jhunter@csuniv.edu
HUNTER, James, E .... 804-524-5997.... 529 C
jhunter@vsu.edu
HUNTER, Jane .... 503-768-7446.... 416 F
hunter@lclark.edu
HUNTER, Janet .... 563-387-2229.... 187 A
hunterja@luther.edu
HUNTER, Jeanne .... 814-375-4722.... 439 D
jch20@psu.edu
HUNTER, John .... 417-626-1234.... 287 F
library@occ.edu
HUNTER, Joseph, A .... 781-292-2300.... 235 C
HUNTER, Kim .... 870-245-5185...... 22 I
hunterk@obu.edu
HUNTER, Kim .... 513-244-4248.... 388 D
kim_hunter@mail.msj.edu
HUNTER, Kymm .... 803-705-4519.... 455 D
hunterk@benedict.edu
HUNTER, Larry, T .... 614-236-6641.... 386 C
lhunter2@capital.edu
HUNTER, Lonna .... 918-333-6830.... 411 B
lhunter@okwu.edu
HUNTER, Lori .... 336-334-7946.... 377 F
lhunter@ncat.edu
HUNTER, Lori .... 865-981-8121.... 470 F
lori.hunter@maryvillecollege.edu
HUNTER, Lorna, J .... 401-232-6100.... 453 A
lhunter@bryant.edu
HUNTER, Lynn .... 508-270-4005.... 240 D
lhunter@massbay.edu
HUNTER, Mark, A .... 805-756-5222...... 33 F
mhunter@calpoly.edu
HUNTER, Mary .... 925-969-3466...... 52 B
mhunter@jfku.edu
HUNTER, Pam .... 254-867-3609.... 500 B
pamelia.hunter@tstc.edu
HUNTER, Patricia .... 425-739-8361.... 535 B
patricia.hunter@lwtc.edu
HUNTER, Rebecca .... 508-793-7561.... 233 C
rhunter@clarku.edu
HUNTER, Robert, D .... 325-674-2495.... 478 H
hunterr@acu.edu
HUNTER, Rosemarie .... 801-972-3596.... 510 L
r.hunter@partners.utah.edu
HUNTER, Steve .... 360-867-6310.... 533 I
hunters@evergreen.edu
HUNTER, Susan .... 503-552-1512.... 417 D
shunter@ncnm.edu
HUNTER, Susan, J .... 207-581-1547.... 220 A
hunter@maine.edu
HUNTER, Tim, W .... 814-332-2755.... 421 E
tim.hunter@allegheny.edu
HUNTER, Tracie .... 310-377-5501...... 56 F
thunter@marymountpv.edu
HUNTER, W, B .... 602-850-8000...... 17 H
bhunter@phoenixseminary.edu
HUNTER, William (Curt) .... 319-335-0866.... 182 C
curt-hunter@uiowa.edu
HUNTER HAYES, Tracey .... 484-365-7370.... 434 H
thunterhayes@lincoln.edu
HUNTINGTON, Judith .... 914-654-5430.... 330 B
president@cnr.edu
HUNTINGTON, Mark, W ... 260-982-5051.... 177 F
mwhuntington@manchester.edu
HUNTINGTON, Robert .... 419-448-2202.... 391 G
president@heidelberg.edu
HUNTLEY, Daniel .... 512-313-3000.... 483 G
daniel.huntley@concordia.edu
HUNTLEY, Deborah .... 989-964-4144.... 258 A
dhuntley@svsu.edu
HUNTLEY, Edelma, D .... 828-262-2130.... 377 B
huntleyed@appstate.edu
HUNTLEY, Steve .... 904-264-2172.... 116 A
steve.huntley@iws.edu
HUNTLEY-SMITH, Jen .... 775-784-8262.... 303 A
jhuntleysmith@unr.edu
HUNTOON, JR., David, H . 845-938-2610.... 558 G
8sgs@usma.edu
HUNTOON, Jacqueline, E .. 906-487-2327.... 255 E
jeh@mtu.edu
HUNTSBERGER, Stephen .. 772-462-7945.... 110 L
shuntsbe@irsc.edu
HUNTSINGER, Trish .... 828-286-3636.... 371 A
thuntsing@isothermal.edu
HUNTSMAN, Deborah, C ... 330-672-3237.... 393 D
dhuntsm1@kent.edu
HUNTSMAN, Kent .... 512-863-1235.... 495 G
huntsmak@southwestern.edu
HUO, Xiaoming (Sharon) ... 931-372-3463.... 474 B
xhuo@tntech.edu
HUO, Y. Paul .... 612-659-7256.... 267 D
paul.huo@metrostate.edu
HUOPPI, Jennifer .... 860-465-4357.... 91 H
huoppij@easternct.edu
HUOT, Anne, E .... 585-395-2524.... 352 F
ahuot@brockport.edu
HUPFER, Mary, A .... 812-464-1627.... 180 F
mhupfer@usi.edu
HUPKE, Doug .... 415-405-3824...... 36 F
dhupke@sfsu.edu
HUPP, Mark .... 419-755-5665.... 397 B
mhupp@ncstatecollege.edu
HUPP, Stephen .... 304-424-8273.... 545 B
stephen.hupp@mail.wvu.edu
HUPPE, Alicia, L .... 972-377-1749.... 483 D
ahuppe@collin.edu
HUPPERT, Susan .... 515-271-1384.... 183 F
susan.huppert@dmu.edu
HURD, Cathy .... 704-378-1490.... 365 H
churd@jcsu.edu
HURD, James, R .... 850-474-2384.... 121 C
jhurd@uwf.edu
HURD, Janice .... 501-279-4403...... 21 H
jhurd@harding.edu
HURD, John .... 916-376-8888...... 79 I
jhurd@wyotech.edu
HURD, Roy .... 707-546-4000...... 45 G
rhurd@empcol.edu
HURD, Sandra, N .... 315-443-1899.... 357 B
snhurd@syr.edu
HURD, Sherie .... 707-546-4000...... 45 G
shurd@empcol.edu
HURDLE, Bill .... 478-757-4024.... 139 A
bhurdle@wesleyancollege.edu
HURDLE-WINSLOW,
B. Lynn .... 252-335-0821.... 369 D
lynnhw@albemarle.edu
HURLBERT, Janet, M .... 570-321-4082.... 435 D
hurlbjan@lycoming.edu
HURLBUT, L, E .... 540-464-7292.... 529 A
hurlbutle@vmi.edu
HURLEY, Alicia .... 212-998-6859.... 344 B
alicia.hurley@nyu.edu
HURLEY, Celia .... 919-718-7360.... 368 H
churley@cccc.edu
HURLEY, Deanne .... 440-646-8320.... 405 B
dhurley@ursuline.edu
HURLEY, Douglas, E .... 901-678-8324.... 474 C
dhurley@memphis.edu
HURLEY, Gail, A .... 814-865-5423.... 438 F
gah5@psu.edu
HURLEY, James .... 606-218-5272.... 207 B
jhurley@pc.edu
HURLEY, James, B .... 601-923-1630.... 277 B
jhurley@rts.edu
HURLEY, James, M .... 847-491-4286.... 160 D
j-hurley2@northwestern.edu
HURLEY, John .... 360-867-6500.... 533 I
hurleyj@evergreen.edu
HURLEY, John, J .... 716-888-2100.... 325 G
hurleyj@canisius.edu
HURLEY, Leah, A .... 214-648-7986.... 507 D
leah.hurley@utsouthwestern.edu
HURLEY, Marja, M .... 860-679-3483...... 94 F
hurley@nso1.uchc.edu
HURLEY, Patricia .... 818-240-1000...... 48 C
phurley@glendale.edu
HURLEY, JR., Paul, B .... 716-826-1200.... 358 B
hurleyp@trocaire.edu
HURLEY, Richard, V .... 540-654-1301.... 524 H
president@umw.edu
HURLEY, Rose .... 928-776-2211...... 19 E
rose.hurley@yc.edu
HURLEY, Tracy .... 210-932-6241.... 498 B
HURLEY, Wanda .... 601-635-2111.... 274 C
whurley@eccc.edu
HURLIMANN, John .... 701-483-2166.... 381 E
john.hurlimann@dickinsonstate.edu
HURLOCK, Timothy, J .... 860-253-3048...... 89 K
thurlock@acc.commnet.edu
HURRELL, Rockie .... 719-502-2007...... 86 G
rockie.hurrell@ppcc.edu
HURST, Carmen, A .... 765-269-5650.... 176 B
churst@ivytech.edu
HURST, Carol, P .... 540-674-3611.... 527 B
churst@nr.edu
HURST, Dan .... 727-726-1153.... 103 B
danhurst@clearwater.edu
HURST, DeWayne .... 909-607-8509...... 40 C
dewayne.hurst@cgu.edu
HURST, Floyd .... 904-620-2920.... 120 C
fhurst@unf.edu
HURST, Fred .... 928-523-6598...... 17 A
fred.hurst@nau.edu
HURST, James .... 574-520-4125.... 174 C
jhurst@iusb.edu
HURST, Jason .... 850-484-2020.... 114 G
jhurst@pensacolastate.edu
HURST, Jeffrey, J .... 801-626-7256.... 511 D
jhurst@weber.edu
HURST, Laura .... 610-660-1175.... 446 C
lannhurs@sju.edu
HURST, Richard, S .... 773-508-7465.... 157 A
rhurst@luc.edu
HURST, Scott, M .... 304-442-3246.... 545 C
scott.hurst@mail.wvu.edu
HURST, Susan .... 870-245-5567...... 22 I
hursts@obu.edu
HURST, Thomas, R .... 410-864-3613.... 226 B
thurst@stmarys.edu
HURST, Timothy .... 931-221-7671.... 473 D
hurstt@apsu.edu
HURT, Lynn .... 540-857-6244.... 528 E
lhurt@virginiawestern.edu
HURTADO, Mike .... 626-914-8870...... 39 G
mhurtado@citruscollege.edu
HURTE, Vernon .... 757-221-2300.... 517 J
vjhurt@wm.edu
HURTIG, Juliet, K .... 419-772-2032.... 398 G
j-hurtig@onu.edu
HURWITZ, Donna .... 212-774-4801.... 340 D
dhurwitz@mmm.edu
HURWITZ, T. Alan .... 202-651-5005...... 97 E
president@gallaudet.edu
HURWITZ, Valerie .... 765-983-1523.... 171 B
neverva@earlham.edu
HUSAIN, Naveed .... 718-997-3009.... 328 F
naveed.husain@qc.cuny.edu
HUSAK, William .... 310-338-5940...... 56 E
whusak@lmu.edu
HUSBY, Kristin .... 303-975-5015...... 89 E
khusby@westwood.edu
HUSEIN, Lori, A .... 310-338-7552...... 56 E
lhusein@lmu.edu
HUSELTON, Ken .... 412-323-4000.... 422 I
khuselton@mcg-btc.org
HUSHON, Kate .... 814-868-9900.... 428 H
kateh@erieit.edu
HUSK, Mark, A .... 317-921-4723.... 175 G
mhusk@ivytech.edu
HUSK, Stephanie .... 503-375-7010.... 415 F
shusk@corban.edu
HUSKEY, Dana .... 336-342-4261.... 373 B
huskeyd@rockinghamcc.edu
HUSKEY, Dave .... 402-935-9400.... 299 C
dhuskey@nechristian.edu
HUSKEY, Robin .... 903-983-8620.... 489 F
rhuskey@kilgore.edu
HUSKINS, Steve .... 423-697-4466.... 474 D
HUSMANN, Calvin, D .... 920-832-6517.... 547 J
calvin.d.husmann@lawrence.edu
HUSS, H. Fenwick .... 404-413-7000.... 131 C
hfhuss@gsu.edu
HUSS, Larry, F .... 803-754-4100.... 457 D
HUSS, Robert .... 206-587-5437.... 537 A
rhuss@sccd.ctc.edu
HUSSAIN, Asif .... 718-368-6674.... 328 B
ahussain@kbcc.cuny.edu
HUSSAIN, Nayyer .... 740-245-7358.... 404 E
nhussain@rio.edu
HUSSEY, Mark, A .... 979-862-4384.... 497 C
mhussey@tamu.edu
HUSSON, James, J .... 617-552-3441.... 232 D
james.husson.1@bc.edu
HUSSON, William, J .... 303-458-1844...... 87 E
whusson@regis.edu
HUSTED, David, S .... 972-881-5684.... 483 D
dhusted@collin.edu
HUSTED, Jean, L .... 203-582-8645...... 93 E
jean.husted@quinnipiac.edu

IKEOKWU, Francis 904-470-8000 105 A fikeokwu@ewc.edu
IKHARO, Sadiq 510-466-7336 62 D sikharo@peralta.edu
ILER, Susan 216-421-7417 387 H siler@cia.edu
ILES, Linda 530-221-4275 69 C finaid@shasta.edu
ILIFF, Dana 318-397-6119 210 J dana.iliff@myneltc.edu
ILLESCAS, Roger 603-887-7404 303 G roger.illescas@chestercollege.edu
ILLIAN, Louise, M 773-442-4670 159 H l-illian@neiu.edu
ILLIAN, Paul 800-955-2527 282 G
ILLICH, Paul 254-299-8636 490 E pillich@mclennan.edu
ILLINGWORTH, Kendra 219-866-6428 179 B kendra@saintjoe.edu
ILSE, Thomas 304-327-4022 543 C tilse@bluefieldstate.edu
ILYAS, Mohammad 302-225-6234 96 E ilyasm@gbc.edu
ILYAS, Mohammad 561-297-3426 118 H ilyas@fau.edu
IMAI, Geri 808-235-7430 142 C gerii@hawaii.edu
IMAI, Peggy, H 802-654-2222 514 B pimai@smcvt.edu
IMASUEN, Edwin 252-536-7260 370 F imasuene@halifaxcc.edu
IMBERGAMO, John 617-353-2260 232 G jimberga@bu.edu
IMBIMBO, Patricia 646-312-4683 326 D patricia_imbimbo@baruch.cuny.edu
IMBLER, John, M 918-610-8303 411 D john.imbler@ptstulsa.edu
IMBRAGULIO, Lisa 205-726-4172 6 G lcimbrag@samford.edu
IMBRESCIA, Jeffrey, D 724-653-2200 427 F jimbrescia@dec.edu
IMBRIALE, William 212-752-1530 338 C william.imbriale@limcollege.edu
IMEL, George 208-282-2902 143 D gimel@isu.edu
IMHOF, Howard 740-366-9379 386 G himhof@cotc.edu
IMHOFF, Donna 412-369-3610 425 H dimhoff@ccac.edu
IMHOFF, Jacquelyn 270-247-8521 204 C jimhoff@midcontinent.edu
IMHOFF, Maren, E 212-327-8682 347 H imhoff@rockefeller.edu
IMHOFF, Michael, A 903-813-2226 481 A mimhoff@austincollege.edu
IMHOFF, Robert, J 270-247-8521 204 C bimhoff@midcontinent.edu
IMLER, Mary Elizabeth 815-740-2622 167 C mimler@stfrancis.edu
IMMERMAN, Stephen, D 978-921-4242 242 F simmerman@montserrat.edu
IMPERATO, Anthony 718-368-5902 328 B aimperato@kbcc.cuny.edu
IMPERATO-MCGINLEY, Julianne 212-746-4745 360 B jimperat@med.cornell.edu
IMPERIALE, Michael, C 732-932-1002 314 B michaeli@rci.rutgers.edu
IMWALLE, Todd, W 937-229-3299 404 A Todd.Imwalle@notes.udayton.edu
INABINET, Chad, E 231-843-5965 260 E ceinabinet@westshore.edu
INAFUKU, Derek 808-845-9211 141 G derek@hcc.hawaii.edu
INBODY, Brian, L 620-431-2820 195 B binbody@neosho.edu
INCANDELA, Marybeth 631-420-2107 356 A marybeth.incandela@farmingdale.edu
INCH, Edward 916-278-7674 35 E edward.inch@csus.edu
INCLAN, Betty 510-981-2850 62 A binclan@peralta.edu
INFANTI, Steven, M 717-901-5146 430 F SInfanti@harrisburgu.edu
INFINGER, Kim 425-739-8274 535 B kim.infinger@lwtc.edu
INGALLS, Keith 413-748-3946 245 C kingalls@spfldcol.edu
INGALLS, Laura 202-464-6973 514 C laura.ingalls@worldlearning.org
INGARGIOLA, Janet, M 217-443-8760 148 E jingarg@dacc.edu
INGBER, Esther 212-463-0400 357 J ingbere@touro.edu
INGBER, Marc 303-556-2870 88 D mark.ingber@ucdenver.edu
INGELSON, Jeannine 563-441-4046 184 E jingleson@eicc.edu
INGERMAN, Bret 845-437-7220 359 D ingerman@vassar.edu
INGERSOLL, Barton, R 607-436-2491 353 E ingersbr@oneonta.edu
INGERSOLL, Chris 989-774-1850 249 G inger1c@cmich.edu
INGERSOLL, Julia 610-526-6132 430 D jingersoll@harcum.edu
INGERSOLL, Pat 616-234-3869 251 G pingerso@grcc.edu
INGHAM, Joanne 212-431-2876 343 E jingham@nyls.edu
INGHRAM, Scott 304-384-5271 543 D inghramcs@concord.edu
INGLE, Andrea 765-285-5974 169 D akingle@bsu.edu
INGLE, Brooke 970-247-7421 84 G bookstoremgr@fortlewis.edu
INGLE, Jeff, S 704-406-4654 364 B jingle@gardner-webb.edu
INGLE, Kent 863-667-5002 118 A kingle@seu.edu
INGLES, Roger, D 740-368-3738 400 F rdingles@owu.edu
INGLES, Susan, L 414-410-4236 546 D slingles@stritch.edu
INGLI, Robin, C 651-523-2461 264 C ringli@hamline.edu
INGLIS, Mark 216-421-7403 387 H minglis@cia.edu
INGLISH, Darla 940-397-4321 491 A darla.inglish@mwsu.edu
INGMIRE, Randall, L 785-539-3571 194 G ringmire@mccks.edu
INGOLD, Barbara, S 815-740-3369 167 C bingold@stfrancis.edu
INGOLD, Scott 305-284-4206 122 F singold@miami.edu
INGOLFSLAND, Dennis 952-446-4239 263 E ingolfsland@crown.edu
INGRAHAM, Barry 207-768-2702 218 J bingraham@nmcc.edu
INGRAHAM, Carolyn, K 706-737-1636 125 C cingraha@aug.edu
INGRAHAM, Patricia 607-777-5572 351 F pingraha@binghamton.edu
INGRAHAM, Timothy 978-468-7111 235 F tingraham@gcts.edu
INGRAM, Archinya 803-327-7402 456 F aingram@clintonjuniorcollege.edu
INGRAM, Beth 319-335-3565 182 C beth-ingram@uiowa.edu
INGRAM, Beverly 318-487-7694 209 B ingram@lacollege.edu
INGRAM, Charles 520-626-4176 19 B cingram@arizona.edu
INGRAM, Earl 334-670-3104 8 B ingram@troy.edu
INGRAM, Edie 918-540-6250 408 J eingram@neo.edu
INGRAM, Geoff 951-785-2000 53 D gingram@lasierra.edu
INGRAM, Gregory 301-891-4017 229 B gingram@wau.edu
INGRAM, Iris 805-378-1412 77 B iingram@vcccd.edu
INGRAM, J. Kevin 785-539-3571 194 G kingram@mccks.edu
INGRAM, J. LaVelle 410-455-2472 227 D jlavelle@umbc.edu
INGRAM, Jim 662-862-8047 274 G jingram@iccms.edu
INGRAM, Joyce, A 850-644-7950 119 C jingram@admin.fsu.edu
INGRAM, Lashawanda, T 315-386-7128 355 D ingraml@canton.edu
INGRAM, Lynne 256-233-8183 1 F lynne.ingram@athens.edu
INGRAM, Michael, T 509-777-4428 539 F mingram@whitworth.edu
INGRAM, Mike 423-746-5292 476 D mingram@twcnet.edu
INGRAM, Ozzie 214-333-6875 484 C ozzie@dbu.edu
INGRAM, Sherry 704-406-4303 364 B singram@gardner-webb.edu
INGRAM, Shirley, M 956-872-5051 494 D singram@southtexascollege.edu
INGRAM, Sue 417-255-7911 286 G sueingram@missouristate.edu
INGRAM, Victoria, L 540-828-5393 516 K vingram@bridgewater.edu
INGRAM, William, G 919-536-7250 369 G ingramb@durhamtech.edu
INGRAM-WALLACE, Brenda, J 610-921-7585 421 D bingramwallace@alb.edu
INGRASSIA, Maria 845-434-5750 356 H mingrassia@sullivan.suny.edu
INGS, Margaret Ann 617-824-8299 234 D margaret_ann_ings@emerson.edu
INIGUEZ-JIMENEZ, J. Alfredo 956-764-5798 489 G ainiguez@laredo.edu
INKSTER, Larry 606-546-1233 206 F linkster@unionky.edu
INMAN, Ann 812-866-7013 171 F inmana@hanover.edu
INMAN, Barbara, L 757-727-5264 519 C barbara.inman@hamptonu.edu
INMAN, Dean 870-862-8131 23 G dinman@southark.edu
INMAN, Deana 641-844-5712 185 J deana.inman@iavalley.edu
INMAN, Gerald 617-989-4252 246 C inmang@wit.edu
INMAN, John, G 724-458-2176 430 B jginman@gcc.edu
INMAN, Keith 502-852-6924 207 A akinma01@louisville.edu
INMAN, Laurel 520-795-0787 12 A admissions@asaom.edu
INMAN, Laurel 520-795-0787 12 A edu_director@asaom.edu
INMAN, Linda, D 336-334-7708 377 F ldinman@ncat.edu
INMAN, Lucille 707-546-4000 45 G linman@empirecollege.com
INMAN, Marianne, E 660-248-6221 279 K minman@centralmethodist.edu
INMAN, Richard 817-515-5206 496 A richard.inman@tccd.edu
INMAN, Stan, D 801-585-5028 510 L sinman@sa.utah.edu
INNES, CSA, Donna 920-923-8760 548 C dinnes@marianuniversity.edu
INNIGER, Jessica, M 260-422-5561 172 L jminniger@indianatech.edu
INNIS, Daniel, E 603-862-1983 306 E dan.innis@unh.edu
INNOCENT, N 803-376-5717 455 B ninnocent@allenuniversity.edu
INNOCENTI, Bethany 805-966-3888 31 A bethany.innocenti@brooks.edu
INOA, Luis 845-437-5862 359 D inoa@vassar.edu
INOKUCHI, Richard 650-738-4166 67 G inokuchi@smccd.edu
INOSHITA, Lynn 808-845-9118 141 G inoshita@hawaii.edu
INOUYE, Carolyn 805-986-5803 77 C cinouye@vcccd.edu
INOUYE, Susan, K 808-956-8155 140 J susani@hawaii.edu
INOWAY-RONNIE, Eden 608-265-5975 550 G etinoway@wisc.edu
INSANALLI, Dawn 914-637-2726 336 E DInsanalli@iona.edu
INSCHO, Edward 706-721-3278 130 B einscho@georgiahealth.edu
INSKEEP, Tony, D 910-277-5079 376 A inskeeptd@sapc.edu
INSLER, Gayle, D 516-877-3167 322 A insler@adelphi.edu
INSLEY, Andrea 206-587-3899 537 A ainsley@sccd.ctc.edu
INSLEY, Lynn 201-216-8927 315 E linsley@stevens.edu
INTEMANN, Gerald, W 724-357-2219 442 E Gerald.Intemann@iup.edu
INTILLE, Amy 617-989-4885 246 C intillea@wit.edu
INTROCASO, CDP, Candace 412-536-1204 432 F cintrocaso@laroche.edu
INZER, Monica, C 315-859-4421 335 A minzer@hamilton.edu
IOANNOU, Carin 336-770-3301 379 D IoannouC@uncsa.edu
IOCANO, Lynn 302-857-6250 95 F liocano@desu.edu
IODICE, Emilio 773-508-2760 157 A eiodice@luc.edu
IOLI, Christine 412-809-5100 444 F ioli@pti.edu
IORG, Jeff 415-380-1322 48 D jeffiorg@ggbts.edu
IORIO, Richard 800-342-7342 48 F richard.iorio@golfacademy.edu
IORIO, Sharon 316-978-3301 197 F sharon.iorio@wichita.edu
IPACH, Nichole 805-437-8893 33 I nichole.ipach@csuci.edu
IPPINECA, Carey, L 607-735-1812 333 A cippineca@elmira.edu
IRBY, Michele 573-651-5120 290 D mirby@semo.edu
IRELAND, Alan 336-750-2935 380 A irelandag@wssu.edu
IRELAND, Chris, M 801-581-3402 510 L cireland@deans.pharm.utah.edu
IRELAND, Jim, D 620-792-9339 190 E irelandj@bartonccc.edu
IRGENS, Dana 763-433-1822 265 J dana.irgens@anokaramsey.edu
IRICK, Troy, D 260-359-4066 172 K tirick@huntington.edu
IRISH, Edward, P 757-221-2425 517 J epiris@wm.edu
IRIZARRY, Carlos 787-264-1912 563 G carlos.irizarry@sg.inter.edu
IRIZARRY, Ivette 787-850-0000 567 B ivette.irizarry@upr.edu
IRIZARRY MERCADO, Jose, R 787-763-6700 562 B drirìzarry@se-pr.edu
IRLA-CHESNEY, Kathy 603-862-2120 306 E kathy.irla-chesney@unh.edu
IROFF, Jayson 954-201-7423 102 A jiroff@broward.edu
IROFF, Jayson 954-201-7410 102 A jiroff@broward.edu
IRUDAYAM, Irene 508-849-3410 230 C iIrudayam@annamaria.edu
IRVIN, Camilla 334-833-4577 4 E cirvin@huntingdon.edu
IRVIN, Dale, T 212-870-1223 344 A dirvin@nyts.edu
IRVIN, Dave 713-743-5579 503 A dirvin@uh.edu
IRVIN, Dave 713-743-5579 503 B dirvin@central.uh.edu
IRVIN, Dexter 808-974-7762 141 A ldirvin@hawaii.edu
IRVIN, Hal 540-231-7784 529 B hirvin@vt.edu
IRVIN, Howard, J 510-723-6744 38 L hirvin@chabotcollege.edu
IRVIN, Michael, E 864-503-5217 463 A mirvin@uscupstate.edu
IRVIN, ValaRay 225-771-2480 214 H valaray_irvin@subr.edu
IRVIN, Zoe, A 443-518-4742 223 D zirvin@howardcc.edu
IRVINE, Angela 802-654-2396 514 B airvine@smcvt.edu
IRVINE, David 518-262-5251 322 E irvined@mail.amc.edu
IRVINE, Shelly 540-887-7367 520 I sirvine@mbc.edu
IRVING, Jackie 610-341-5872 428 D jirving@eastern.edu
IRVING, Jean, H 530-898-5944 34 A jirving@csuchico.edu
IRWIN, Bonnie 217-581-2917 150 C dbirwin@eiu.edu
IRWIN, Darci 616-222-1439 250 C darci.irwin@cornerstone.edu
IRWIN, Dennis 740-593-1479 399 G irwind@ohio.edu
IRWIN, Graham 513-583-5000 390 A girwin@devry.edu
IRWIN, Hugh 712-325-3390 186 B hirwin@iwcc.edu
IRWIN, Joseph 404-894-0771 130 D joe.irwin@alumni.gatech.edu
IRWIN, Kathy 810-762-0415 256 C kathy.irwin@mcc.edu
IRWIN, Kevin, W 202-319-5683 97 C irwin@cua.edu
IRWIN, Lorry 845-434-5750 356 H lirwin@sullivan.suny.edu
IRWIN, Robert 864-578-8770 460 F rirwin@sherman.edu
IRWIN, Suzy 903-832-5565 496 C suzy.irwin@texarkanacollege.edu
IRWIN, Ursula 503-491-7657 417 B ursula.irwin@mhcc.edu
IRWIN, William 570-208-5900 432 E williamirwin@kings.edu
IRWIN, William, J 626-395-3727 32 E bill.irwin@cco.caltech.edu
IRWIN-CHASE, Holly 619-849-2706 62 L hollyirwinchase@pointloma.edu
IRWIN-DEVITIS, Linda 757-683-3777 521 L ldevitis@odu.edu
ISAAC, Angela 412-392-8011 444 H aisaac@pointpark.edu
ISAAC, Bina 760-862-1333 41 H bisaac@collegeofthedesert.edu
ISAAC, JR., Lawrence 505-786-4104 318 H lisaac@navajotech.edu
ISAAC, Nancy 620-431-2820 195 B nisaac@neosho.edu
ISAAC, Samantha 561-912-2166 106 G sissac@evergladesuniversity.edu
ISAACS, Becky 580-559-5243 407 J bisaacs@ecok.edu
ISAACS, Carol, B 260-481-6147 174 A isaacs@ipfw.edu
ISAACS, Jennifer, R 828-765-7351 371 F jisaacs@mayland.edu
ISAACS, Jerry 918-495-7750 411 C jisaacs@oru.edu
ISAACS, Mona 859-622-1986 200 D mona.isaacs@eku.edu
ISAACS, Yolanda 708-974-5441 159 A isaacs@morainevalley.edu
ISAACSON, Lyn, R 641-628-5266 183 A isaacsonl@central.edu
ISAACSON, Melvin 212-346-1366 345 F misaacson@pace.edu
ISAACSON, Michael, L 605-642-6788 465 F michael.isaacson@bhsu.edu
ISAAK, Larry, A 888-227-3552 262 A
ISABELLE, Geoffrey, S 315-684-6070 354 F isabelgs@morrisville.edu

JACKSON, Judy 504-282-4455 213 H
jjackson@nobts.edu
JACKSON, Judy, J 859-257-9000 206 H
jj@uky.edu
JACKSON, Judy, T 256-765-4896 9 D
jtjackson@una.edu
JACKSON, Julie 662-846-4151 274 B
jjackson@deltastate.edu
JACKSON, Karen 313-496-2759 260 C
kjackso1@wcccd.edu
JACKSON, Karen 323-469-3300 27 H
info@amda.edu
JACKSON, Karen, L 818-386-1769 62 F
kjackson@pgi.edu
JACKSON, Katherine 334-244-3704 2 A
kjackson@outreach.aum.edu
JACKSON, Kenneth 219-989-2366 178 G
kjackson@purduecal.edu
JACKSON, Kevin 254-710-1314 481 I
kevin_jackson@baylor.edu
JACKSON, Kim 509-793-2067 531 D
kimj@bigbend.edu
JACKSON, Kimberly 434-848-6492 523 G
kjackson@saintpauls.edu
JACKSON, Kimberly 404-752-1740 134 B
kjackson@msm.edu
JACKSON, Kristian 913-758-6331 197 B
jackson36@stmary.edu
JACKSON, L. Judy 413-748-5555 245 C
ljackson@spfldcol.edu
JACKSON, Laura 707-826-3132 36 D
Laura.Jackson@humboldt.edu
JACKSON, Lee, F 214-752-5530 504 B
chancellor@unt.edu
JACKSON, Lenora 404-270-5209 137 E
lenoraj@spelman.edu
JACKSON, Linda, Y 512-505-3006 488 B
lyjackson@htu.edu
JACKSON, Lisa, D 740-368-3002 400 F
ldjackso@owu.edu
JACKSON, Lorraine 516-678-5000 341 F
ljackson@molloy.edu
JACKSON, Lynn, E 309-794-7347 145 B
ljackson@augustana.edu
JACKSON, Mack 800-469-0236 211 E
mjackson@ltc.edu
JACKSON, III, Mack 985-543-4120 211 C
JACKSON, Marcia 773-291-6313 147 D
mjackson@ccc.edu
JACKSON, Marcia 757-727-5430 519 C
marcia.jackson@hamptonu.edu
JACKSON, Margaret, W 931-363-9836 470 E
mjackson@martinmethodist.edu
JACKSON, Marian, D 903-510-2759 502 E
mjac@tjc.edu
JACKSON, Mark 617-427-0060 241 D
mjackson@rcc.mass.edu
JACKSON, Marsha, D 716-851-1205 333 B
jacksonm@ecc.edu
JACKSON, Melanie, M 863-784-7015 117 I
melanie.jackson@southflorida.edu
JACKSON, Melika 803-780-1259 463 B
mjackson@voorhees.edu
JACKSON, Melissa 912-235-5223 19 C
melissa.jackson@phoenix.edu
JACKSON, Michael 405-208-5088 410 A
mjackson@okcu.edu
JACKSON, Michael, L 213-740-2421 76 C
mjackson@usc.edu
JACKSON, Michael, P 919-516-4859 376 B
mpjackson@st-aug.edu
JACKSON, Michael, S 302-831-1234 96 F
mjackson@udel.edu
JACKSON, Micheal, B 214-860-2019 484 I
mjackson1@dcccd.edu
JACKSON, Miles 360-992-2934 532 A
mjackson@clark.edu
JACKSON, Minor 217-353-2119 161 B
mjackson@parkland.edu
JACKSON, Natalie 567-661-2647 400 H
natalie_jackson3@owens.edu
JACKSON, Neal 901-321-3283 467 G
njackson@cbu.edu
JACKSON, Newton, N 904-620-2700 120 C
newton.jackson@unf.edu
JACKSON, Nikki, R 480-731-8000 15 F
nikki.jackson@domail.maricopa.edu
JACKSON, Pamela 318-342-5230 216 E
pjackson@ulm.edu
JACKSON, Pamela, E 757-683-3143 521 L
pejackso@odu.edu
JACKSON, Peggy 870-612-2030 25 E
peggy.jackson@uaccb.edu
JACKSON, Phillip 910-678-1009 370 B
jacksonp@faytechcc.edu
JACKSON, Prentiss 773-602-5517 147 B
pjackson@ccc.edu
JACKSON, Rebecca 972-721-5194 502 F
jackson@udallas.edu
JACKSON, Rhalanda 318-670-9328 215 A
rjackson@susla.edu
JACKSON, Rickey 928-289-6530 17 B
rickey.jackson@npc.edu
JACKSON, Robert 715-682-1207 549 C
rjackson@northland.edu
JACKSON, Robert, D 847-578-3248 163 A
robert.jackson@rosalindfranklin.edu
JACKSON, Roberta 212-463-0400 357 J
roberta.jackson@touro.edu
JACKSON, Ron 864-592-4817 461 C
jacksonr@sccsc.edu
JACKSON, Ronald, C 215-751-8876 426 B
rcjackson@ccp.edu
JACKSON, Rose Mary 501-882-8855 20 D
rmjackson@asub.edu
JACKSON, Rosemary 423-585-2614 476 B
rosemary.jackson@ws.edu
JACKSON, Sally 712-279-5280 182 E
sally.jackson@briarcliff.edu
JACKSON, Shanna 615-790-4419 474 F
sjackson@columbiatate.edu
JACKSON, Sharon 561-273-6500 117 J
smjackson@southuniversity.edu
JACKSON, Sharon, S 804-752-3747 522 F
sjackson@rmc.edu
JACKSON, Shawn 740-389-6786 399 D
jackson.368@osu.edu
JACKSON, Sherry 904-256-7212 111 J
sjackso@ju.edu
JACKSON, Shirley, A 518-276-6211 347 D
president@rpi.edu
JACKSON, Starlene, P 919-718-7216 368 H
sjackson@cccc.edu
JACKSON, Stephanie 803-699-5096 19 C
stephanie.jackson@phoenix.edu
JACKSON, Stephanie 202-291-9020 99 B
JACKSON, Susan 406-586-3585 294 I
susan.jackson@montanabiblecollege.edu
JACKSON, Suzanne 828-328-7080 366 B
suzanne.jackson@lr.edu
JACKSON, Tammy 651-687-9000 271 B
Tammy.Jackson@Rasmussen.edu
JACKSON, Tanya 404-237-7573 125 F
tjackson@bauder.edu
JACKSON, Theron, J 318-670-9684 215 A
tjjackson@susla.edu
JACKSON, Thomas 208-282-2665 143 D
tjackson@isu.edu
JACKSON, JR.,
Thomas, H 706-542-8090 138 C
tjackson@uga.edu
JACKSON, Tom 918-456-5511 409 A
jacks009@nsuok.edu
JACKSON, JR., Tom 502-852-6933 207 A
trjack02@louisville.edu
JACKSON, Tondaleya 803-705-4479 455 D
jacksont@benedict.edu
JACKSON, Tonya, P 919-209-2025 371 C
tpjackson@johnstoncc.edu
JACKSON, Twana 304-929-6716 542 H
tjackson@newriver.edu
JACKSON, Tyrone 228-896-2507 275 G
tyrone.jackson@mgccc.edu
JACKSON, Vera 601-979-2326 275 A
vera.j.jackson@jsums.edu
JACKSON, Vickie, G 405-466-6008 408 G
vgjackson@lunet.edu
JACKSON, Vincent 213-763-7035 55 D
vjackson@lattc.edu
JACKSON, Wayne 407-823-2716 120 A
wayne.jackson@ucf.edu
JACKSON, Weldon 404-215-2647 134 A
wjackson@morehouse.edu
JACKSON, Wendy 704-216-6158 366 D
wjackson@livingstone.edu
JACKSON, Willie, J 334-727-8514 8 C
jacksonw@tuskegee.edu
JACKSON, Wilma 402-826-8620 298 A
wilma.jackson@doane.edu
JACKSON, Zena 972-273-3482 485 B
zjackson@dcccd.edu
JACKSON-ELMOORE,
Cynthia 517-355-2326 255 D
jacks174@msu.edu
JACKSON HALLOWAY,
Melissa 919-530-6105 378 A
jacksonm@nccu.edu
JACKSON-LEE, Sophia 318-670-9355 215 A
slee@susla.edu
JACKSON THOMPSON,
Karlene 718-488-1216 338 H
karlene.thompson@liu.edu
JACOB, Alan, B 509-777-3250 539 F
ajacob@whitworth.edu
JACOB, Antony 302-292-6100 99 D
antony.jacob@strayer.edu
JACOB, Craig 602-870-9222 13 M
cjacob@devry.edu
JACOB, Mary 805-893-3753 74 F
mary.jacob@sa.ucsb.edu
JACOB, Mary, J 805-893-3753 74 F
jacob-m@sa.ucsb.edu
JACOB, Susan, R 901-448-6135 477 C
sjacob4@uthsc.edu
JACOB, Travis 208-376-7731 142 E
tjacob@boisebible.edu
JACOBI, Judy, N 219-785-5593 178 H
jjacobi@pnc.edu
JACOBOWITZ, Chanie 732-367-1060 307 H
cjacobowitz@bmg.edu
JACOBOWITZ, Sharon 516-239-9002 350 H
JACOBS, Alexandra, M 315-267-2918 354 C
jacobsam@potsdam.edu
JACOBS, Alice, M 217-443-8848 148 E
amjacobs@dacc.edu
JACOBS, Andrew, C 207-834-7671 220 D
andrew.jacobs@maine.edu
JACOBS, Arthur 302-736-2428 96 G
jacobsar@wesley.edu
JACOBS, Bonita 706-864-1993 134 D
bjacobs@northgeorgia.edu
JACOBS, Bret 504-865-3979 213 F
bljacobs@loyno.edu
JACOBS, Bruce 812-855-5650 173 C
jacobsb@indiana.edu
JACOBS, Carol 937-294-6155 393 C
cjacobs2@kaplan.edu
JACOBS, Carolyn 413-585-7950 245 B
cjacobs@smith.edu
JACOBS, Craig, M 610-892-1509 441 C
cjacobs@pit.edu
JACOBS, Dawn Ellen 951-343-4275 31 G
djacobs@calbaptist.edu
JACOBS, Dennis 408-554-4533 68 C
dcjacobs@scu.edu
JACOBS, Derya, A 412-397-2191 445 G
jacobs@rmu.edu
JACOBS, Donna, P 256-765-4252 9 D
dpjacobs@una.edu
JACOBS, Ed, C 318-257-4805 215 F
ejacobs@latech.edu
JACOBS, Ellen 402-399-2611 297 E
ejacobs@csm.edu
JACOBS, Holly, A 330-941-2340 406 F
hajacobs@ysu.edu
JACOBS, Jacqueline, W 626-585-7205 61 E
jwjacobs@pasadena.edu
JACOBS, James 586-445-7241 254 F
jacobsj@macomb.edu
JACOBS, Jane 973-761-9181 315 B
jane.jacobs@shu.edu
JACOBS, Jeanne 305-237-5006 113 H
jfjacobs@mdc.edu
JACOBS, Jeff 701-224-5441 382 B
jeffrey.jacobs@bismarckstate.edu
JACOBS, Jim 415-476-0311 74 E
jim.jacobs@ucsf.edu
JACOBS, JR., John, O 334-844-9891 1 G
jacobjo@auburn.edu
JACOBS, Joshua, E 270-809-3763 204 F
joshua.jacobs@murraystate.edu
JACOBS, Junoesque 601-977-7765 277 F
jjacobs@tougaloo.edu
JACOBS, Ken 785-628-4259 192 F
kjacobs@fhsu.edu
JACOBS, Kevin 303-315-2700 88 D
kevin.jacobs@ucdenver.edu
JACOBS, Kim 402-826-8111 298 A
kim.jacobs@doane.edu
JACOBS, Linda 517-265-5161 247 D
JACOBS, Lloyd, A 419-530-2211 404 F
lloyd.jacobs@utoledo.edu
JACOBS, Lori, A 757-594-7961 517 I
lori.jacobs@cnu.edu
JACOBS, Mark 480-965-2354 12 B
mark.jacobs@asu.edu
JACOBS, Mary, R 513-875-3344 387 B
mary.jacobs@chatfield.edu
JACOBS, Pat 661-654-2483 33 H
pjacobs@csub.edu
JACOBS, Patricia 615-460-6490 467 B
patricia.jacobs@belmont.edu
JACOBS, Raymond 512-505-3007 488 B
rajacobs@htu.edu
JACOBS, Stan, G 432-685-4551 490 G
sjacobs@midland.edu
JACOBS, Steve 303-458-3560 87 E
jjacobs@regis.edu
JACOBS, Susan 978-921-4242 242 F
sjacobs@montserrat.edu
JACOBS, Sylvia, A 404-880-8395 126 I
sjacobs@cau.edu
JACOBS, Tina 206-393-3545 530 G
tjacobs@argosy.edu
JACOBS, Todd 231-591-3817 251 B
jacobst@ferris.edu
JACOBS, Tracy 410-225-2378 224 C
tjacobs@mica.edu
JACOBS, Wayne 903-233-3860 489 K
waynejacobs@letu.edu
JACOBS ASTLE, Karen 215-503-1040 448 B
karen.astle@jefferson.edu
JACOBS ELSON, Claire 609-258-4131 313 A
celson@princeton.edu
JACOBSEN, Brandy 318-670-9371 215 A
bjacobsen@susla.edu
JACOBSEN, Cheryl, R 563-588-7107 186 I
cheryl.jacobsen@loras.edu
JACOBSEN, Jeffrey 406-994-3681 295 E
agdean@montana.edu
JACOBSEN, Jim 605-367-5461 466 C
jim.jacobsen@southeasttech.edu
JACOBSEN, Michael, V 801-863-8998 511 C
michael.jacobsen@uvu.edu
JACOBSEN, Paul, G 308-635-6144 301 E
jacobsen@wncc.edu
JACOBSEN, Richard, T 208-282-3134 143 D
jacorich@isu.edu
JACOBSMA, Kelly, G 616-395-7790 252 F
jacobsma@hope.edu
JACOBSMEYER, Adam, R 808-675-3368 139 I
adam.jacobsmeyer@byuh.edu
JACOBSMEYER, Tom, V 818-947-2336 55 E
jacobsmt@lavc.edu
JACOBSON, Adela 619-388-7356 65 H
ajacobson@sdccd.edu
JACOBSON, Adele 605-352-2662 464 B
adjacobs@dwu.edu
JACOBSON, Anne, D 804-828-1223 525 E
adjacobson@vcu.edu
JACOBSON, Beatrice, F 563-333-6100 188 D
JacobsonBeatriceF@sau.edu
JACOBSON, Bert 815-802-8242 154 J
bjacobson@kcc.edu
JACOBSON, Betsy 218-733-7618 267 B
b.jacobson@lsc.edu
JACOBSON, Carl 302-831-6070 96 F
carlj@udel.edu
JACOBSON, Evelyn, M 402-472-3751 300 H
ejacobson1@unl.edu
JACOBSON, Gabriel 585-567-9220 336 B
gabriel.jacobson@hougton.edu
JACOBSON, Gloria 773-298-3706 163 G
jacobson@sxu.edu
JACOBSON, Janet, L 712-274-5244 187 D
jacobson@morningside.edu
JACOBSON, John, E 765-285-5251 169 D
jejacobson@bsu.edu
JACOBSON, Kathy 231-777-5207 248 J
kathy.jacobson@baker.edu
JACOBSON, Larry, P 585-385-8256 348 F
ljacobson@sjfc.edu
JACOBSON, Mary 763-433-1315 265 J
mary.jacobson@anokaramsey.edu
JACOBSON, Mickey 503-228-6528 414 E
jacobsonm@aii.edu
JACOBSON, Renee, R 231-995-1256 256 G
jacobsr@nmc.edu
JACOBSON, Ron 718-817-1000 334 C
rjacobson@fordham.edu
JACOBSON, Stacy 651-690-6526 271 E
ssjacobson@stkate.edu
JACOBSON, Steven 209-946-2331 75 D
sjacobson@pacific.edu
JACOBSON, Thomas 850-644-7687 119 C
tjacobson@admin.fsu.edu
JACOBSON, Thomas 215-204-8421 447 G
jacobson.thomas@temple.edu
JACOBSON, Timothy, K 262-691-5221 555 C
tjacobson9@wctc.edu
JACOBSON, Vicky 203-576-5869 94 A
vjacobson@stvincentscollege.edu
JACOBSON-BERG, Judy 320-308-5096 269 D
jjacobsonberg@sctcc.edu
JACOBY, Brian 612-375-1900 264 F
bjacoby@lpr.edu
JACOBY, Robin, M 214-648-2288 507 D
robin.jacoby@utsouthwestern.edu
JACOMET, Terri, L 937-778-7806 390 G
tjacomet@edisonohio.edu
JACQUES, Ed 617-879-2446 246 F
ejacques@wheelock.edu
JACQUES, Kathleen, C 207-795-2858 217 F
jacqueka@cmhc.org
JACQUES, Lori 508-999-8025 237 E
ljacques@umassd.edu
JACQUES, Paul 323-856-7643 28 D
pjacques@afi.com
JACQUES, Theresa, K 906-487-2936 255 E
tjacques@mtu.edu
JACQUET, Roberta 610-902-8260 423 H
jacquet@cabrini.edu
JACQUEZ, Ricardo 575-646-2914 319 D
rjacquez@nmsu.edu
JADALLAH, Edward 843-349-2773 456 G
ejadalla@coastal.edu
JADLOS, Melissa 585-385-8164 348 F
mjadlos@sjfc.edu
JADUSHLEVER, Renee 510-430-2033 57 D
reneejad@mills.edu
JAECKEL, Andrea 734-487-3328 250 H
ajaeckel@emich.edu
JAECKEL, Roger 707-654-1127 32 I
rjaeckel@csum.edu
JAECKS, Steve 423-697-3397 474 D
JAECQUES, Chad 660-831-4172 286 I
jaecquesc@moval.edu
JAEGER, Alberta 973-300-2176 315 F
ajaeger@sussex.edu
JAEGER, David 239-590-2315 119 A
djaeger@fgcu.edu
JAEGER, Jason 480-994-9244 18 I
jasonj@swiha.org
JAEGER, Lois, A 507-344-7365 261 H
ljaeger@blc.edu

JANZEN, Dennis ... 559-453-2000 ... 47 K djanzen@fresno.edu

JAQUEZ, Martha ... 312-553-3204 ... 146 H mjaquez@ccc.edu

JARA, Mike ... 803-641-3254 ... 462 B mikej@usca.edu

JARAMILLO, Ray ... 806-665-8801 ... 482 H ray.jaramillo@clarendoncollege.edu

JARAMILLO FLEMING, Melissa ... 575-835-5880 ... 319 A mjaramillo@admin.nmt.edu

JARAMILLO-FLEMING, Melissa ... 575-835-5880 ... 319 A mjaramillo@admin.nmt.edu

JARBOE, Dan ... 870-245-5591 ... 22 I jarboed@obu.edu

JARED, Tim ... 864-622-6011 ... 455 C tjared@andersonuniversity.edu

JARETT, Sadie ... 334-874-5700 ... 3 A sjarret@concordiaselma.edu

JARGO, Jeralyn ... 651-779-3235 ... 266 D jeralyn.jargo@century.edu

JARLEY, Paul ... 702-895-3362 ... 302 K paul.jarley@unlv.edu

JARMAN, Chet ... 252-940-6241 ... 367 I chetj@beaufortccc.edu

JARMIN MILLER, Catherine ... 503-883-2494 ... 416 G cjarmin@linfield.edu

JARNAGIN, Lea ... 657-278-3211 ... 34 E ljarnagin@fullerton.edu

JAROSZ, Jonathan ... 810-424-5486 ... 259 F jarosz@umflint.edu

JARR, William ... 770-426-2632 ... 133 B wdjarr@life.edu

JARRELL, Camille, L ... 337-373-0011 ... 209 H cjarrell@lct.edu

JARRELL, Karen ... 972-883-2708 ... 505 D karenl@utdallas.edu

JARRELL, Michelle ... 205-391-2328 ... 7 A mjarrell@sheltonstate.edu

JARRELL, Sasha ... 850-729-5363 ... 114 A jarrells@nwfsc.edu

JARRELL, Sheila ... 928-776-2188 ... 19 E sheila.jarrell@yc.edu

JARRETT, Jessica ... 918-335-6334 ... 411 B founders@okwu.edu

JARRETT, Juan, A ... 413-545-0360 ... 237 C jjarrett@admin.umass.edu

JARRETT, Kathy ... 413-565-1000 ... 231 B kjarrett@baypath.edu

JARRETT-HORTIS, Frances, L ... 864-503-5195 ... 463 A fjarrett-hortis@uscupstate.edu

JARRIEL, Jenifer ... 713-798-1103 ... 481 H jenifer@bcm.edu

JARROLL, Edward ... 718-960-8764 ... 327 C edward.jarroll@lehman.cuny.edu

JARRY, Timothy ... 508-793-2515 ... 233 D tjarry@holycross.edu

JARSTFER, Amiel ... 423-869-6203 ... 470 C amiel.jarstfer@lmunet.edu

JARVIE, Greg, I ... 330-672-9494 ... 393 D gjarvie@kent.edu

JARVIS, Athena ... 405-422-1464 ... 411 G athena.jarvis@redlandscc.edu

JARVIS, Jeffrey, A ... 419-227-3141 ... 404 D jjarvis@unoh.edu

JARVIS, Keith ... 307-532-8255 ... 555 H keith.jarvis@ewc.wy.edu

JARVIS, Sam ... 610-841-3333 ... 441 D sjarvis@psb.edu

JARVIS, Shelli, W ... 703-323-3074 ... 527 C sjarvis@nvcc.edu

JARZABSKI, Kerri, P ... 413-782-1312 ... 246 D kjarzabs@wne.edu

JASHINSKI, Michelle, L ... 814-371-2090 ... 448 C mjashinski@triangle-tech.edu

JASIENIECKI, Darren ... 219-473-4292 ... 170 D djasieniecki@ccsj.edu

JASIEWICZ, James ... 574-289-7001 ... 176 C jjasiewicz1@ivytech.edu

JASINSKI, John ... 660-562-1110 ... 287 E johnj@nwmissouri.edu

JASMAN, Troy ... 712-274-6400 ... 189 H troy.jasman@witcc.edu

JASNA, Kirsten ... 505-424-2309 ... 318 C kjasna@iaia.edu

JASON, Greer ... 718-817-3080 ... 334 C jason@fordham.edu

JASON, Hoerr, U ... 610-921-7221 ... 421 D jhoerr@alb.edu

JASPERSON, Mindy ... 415-703-9551 ... 31 J mjasperson@cca.edu

JASS, Lori ... 651-635-8084 ... 261 I l-jass@bethel.edu

JASTORFF, Michael ... 605-642-6279 ... 465 F michael.jastorff@bhsu.edu

JASWAL, Faisal ... 425-564-6151 ... 531 B fjaswal@bellevuecollege.edu

JASZCZAK, John ... 215-637-7700 ... 430 H jaszczak@holyfamily.edu

JASZKA, Michael, S ... 716-286-8343 ... 344 D msj@niagara.edu

JATTKOWSKI-HUDSON, Anna, J ... 815-226-3392 ... 162 H ajattkowski-hudson@rockford.edu

JATULIS, Viltis, A ... 805-525-4417 ... 72 E vjatulis@thomasaquinas.edu

JAURIGUI, Leroy ... 952-446-4181 ... 263 E jauriguil@crown.edu

JAURON, Les ... 530-895-2266 ... 31 E jauronle@butte.edu

JAVAHERIPOUR, G, H ... 760-245-4271 ... 77 E GH.Javaheripour@vvc.edu

JAVARIZ, Gerardo ... 787-890-2681 ... 566 E gerardo.javariz@upr.edu

JAVIER, Byron, A ... 312-850-7140 ... 147 C bjavier@ccc.edu

JAVOR, Seta ... 818-767-0888 ... 79 D seta.javor@woodbury.edu

JAVOROSKI, Alan ... 715-422-5402 ... 554 C al.javoroski@mstc.edu

JAY, Andrea ... 305-348-7347 ... 119 B andrea.jay@fiu.edu

JAYARAMAN, Ruki ... 312-505-0705 ... 144 G rjayaraman@argosy.edu

JAYASURIYA, Kumara ... 765-973-8473 ... 173 D pjayasur@iue.edu

JAYASURIYA, Kumara ... 219-785-5201 ... 178 H gasteriadis@pnc.edu

JAYASURIYA, Kumara ... 219-785-5201 ... 178 H

JAYAWICKREMA, Arosha .. 860-768-4276 ... 95 A jaya@hartford.edu

JAYE, Marilyn ... 617-559-8642 ... 235 I mjaye@hebrewcollege.edu

JAYNE, Billie Jo ... 315-279-5684 ... 337 K bjjayne@keuka.edu

JAYNE, Joanne ... 718-429-6600 ... 359 E joanne.jayne@vaughn.edu

JAYNE, Lorrie ... 828-298-3325 ... 380 C ljayne@warren-wilson.edu

JAYNES, D. Thomas ... 919-536-7207 ... 369 G jaynest@durhamtech.edu

JAYNES, Kathy ... 406-265-4147 ... 295 G kjaynes@msun.edu

JAZDZEWSKI, Richard, L .. 262-472-1305 ... 552 E jazdzewr@uww.edu

JAZWIECKI, Gabrielle, E ... 203-576-4664 ... 94 D gjazwiec@bridgeport.edu

JAZZABI, Monica ... 323-343-3342 ... 35 B mjazzabi@cslanet.calstatela.edu

JEAN, Kevin, J ... 919-658-7750 ... 367 D kjean@moc.edu

JEAN, Libby ... 269-749-7655 ... 257 D ljean@olivetcollege.edu

JEAN, Martin, D ... 203-432-9681 ... 95 D martin.jean@yale.edu

JEAN-JOSPEH, Daneweise . 561-912-2166 ... 106 G djoseph@evergladesuniversity.edu

JEAN-LOUIS, Patrick ... 617-541-5388 ... 241 D pjeanlouis@rcc.mass.edu

JEAN-MARIE, Cherisna ... 615-687-6904 ... 466 G abclibrary2011@gmail.com

JEAN-PIERRE, Paul ... 718-631-6314 ... 329 A pjean-pierre@qcc.cuny.edu

JEANCAKE, Chris ... 912-427-1958 ... 124 A cjeancake@altamahatech.edu

JEANES, Opey ... 919-734-8585 ... 367 D ojeanes@moc.edu

JEANES, Opey, D ... 919-734-8585 ... 367 D ojeanes@moc.edu

JEANPIERRE, Letha ... 408-864-8976 ... 47 G jeanpierreletha@deanza.edu

JEANRENAUD, Stephane ... 704-366-5066 ... 375 H sjeanrenaud@rts.edu

JEBALI, Lisa ... 978-837-5109 ... 242 D lisa.jebali@merrimack.edu

JEBSEN, Chris ... 419-358-3254 ... 385 B jebsenc@bluffton.edu

JECH, Sue ... 507-433-0610 ... 269 A sjech@riverland.edu

JEDLICKA, Diane ... 216-373-5182 ... 397 E djedlicka@ndc.edu

JEELANI, Shaikr ... 334-727-8246 ... 8 C jeelanis@tuskegee.edu

JEFFCOAT, Harold, G ... 217-424-6208 ... 158 F hjeffcoat@millikin.edu

JEFFERS, Brenda, R ... 217-544-6464 ... 163 F

JEFFERS, Joe ... 870-245-5216 ... 22 I jeffers@obu.edu

JEFFERS, Karen ... 405-422-1442 ... 411 G jeffersk@redlandscc.edu

JEFFERSON, Adriene ... 772-462-7606 ... 110 L ajeffers@irsc.edu

JEFFERSON, Arthur ... 601-979-2484 ... 275 A arthur.jefferson@jsums.edu

JEFFERSON, Curtis ... 352-395-5175 ... 117 E curtis.jefferson@sfcollege.edu

JEFFERSON, Debrah ... 773-995-3586 ... 146 D djeffers@csu.edu

JEFFERSON, Doug ... 817-598-6247 ... 508 C djefferson@wc.edu

JEFFERSON, Henry ... 606-759-7141 ... 202 D henry.jefferson@kctcs.edu

JEFFERSON, Jeff ... 870-574-4499 ... 24 A jjeffers@sautech.edu

JEFFERSON, Patrick ... 323-241-5280 ... 55 C jefferpd@lasc.edu

JEFFERSON, Richard, P ... 617-552-3334 ... 232 D richard.jefferson.1@bc.edu

JEFFERSON, Sharon ... 850-201-8490 ... 121 F jefferss@tcc.fl.edu

JEFFERSON, Sheri ... 704-216-6010 ... 366 D sjefferson@livingstone.edu

JEFFERSON, Shirley ... 802-831-1333 ... 515 A sjefferson@vermontlaw.edu

JEFFERSON, Vivian ... 409-880-8188 ... 500 E vgjefferson@lit.edu

JEFFERSON, Willie ... 803-780-1049 ... 463 B williej@voorhees.edu

JEFFERSON-BILBY, Patricia, A ... 317-788-3260 ... 180 C jefferson@uindy.edu

JEFFERY, Charles, F ... 623-845-4001 ... 15 J charles.jeffery@gcmail.maricopa.edu

JEFFERY, Jack ... 740-774-7200 ... 399 H jefferyj@ohio.edu

JEFFERY, James, E ... 570-586-2400 ... 422 F jjeffery@bbc.edu

JEFFERY, James, R ... 269-471-3481 ... 247 H jimjeff@andrews.edu

JEFFERY, John, A ... 610-660-1060 ... 446 C jjeffery@sju.edu

JEFFERY, Kathryn ... 916-558-2100 ... 56 D jefferk@scc.losrios.edu

JEFFORD, Janet, L ... 860-727-6904 ... 92 C jjefford@goodwin.edu

JEFFRESS, Conway, A ... 734-462-4400 ... 258 C jeffress@schoolcraft.edu

JEFFREY, David ... 763-576-4725 ... 266 A djeffrey@anokatech.edu

JEFFREY, David, K ... 540-568-7044 ... 520 C jeffredk@jmu.edu

JEFFREY, Don ... 334-983-6556 ... 8 B djeffr@troy.edu

JEFFREY, Don ... 334-670-3399 ... 8 B djeffr@troy.edu

JEFFREY, Dorothy ... 816-322-0110 ... 279 H dorothy.filsinger@calvary.edu

JEFFREY, Douglas ... 517-437-7341 ... 252 E doug.jeffrey@hillsdale.edu

JEFFREY, Douglas ... 517-607-2518 ... 252 E doug.jeffrey@hillsdale.edu

JEFFREY, Russell ... 512-313-3000 ... 483 G russell.jeffrey@concordia.edu

JEFFRIES, Frankie ... 901-435-1530 ... 470 B frankie_jeffries@loc.edu

JEFFRIES, John ... 410-455-2386 ... 227 D jeffries@umbc.edu

JEFFRIES, Rosemary ... 732-987-2252 ... 310 D jeffries@georgian.edu

JEFFRIES, Shelly ... 616-632-2130 ... 248 A jeffrmic@aquinas.edu

JEFFRIES, Susan, K ... 580-327-8570 ... 409 C skjeffries@nwosu.edu

JEFFRION, William ... 504-520-6780 ... 217 A wjeffrio@xula.edu

JEFFS, Madeline ... 509-542-4765 ... 532 C mjeffs@columbiabasin.edu

JEFIMENKO, Otto ... 219-981-4291 ... 173 F ojefimen@iun.edu

JEFREMOW, George ... 212-217-4420 ... 333 G george_jefremow@fitnyc.edu

JEHLICKA, Rodger ... 217-206-6674 ... 167 A jehlicka.rodger@uis.edu

JEHNINGS, Marcia ... 860-512-2703 ... 90 C mjehnings@mcc.commnet.edu

JEKA, Mary, R ... 617-627-4220 ... 245 F mary.jeka@tufts.edu

JELENIC, Susan ... 216-265-3151 ... 386 B smjelenic@bryantstratton.edu

JELINAK, Micah ... 734-207-9581 ... 256 B mjelinak@mts.edu

JELINEK, Diane, F ... 507-284-3862 ... 262 E jelinek.diane@mayo.edu

JELINEK, John, A ... 312-329-4185 ... 158 H john.jelinek@moody.edu

JELLEMA, Jon, A ... 616-331-2400 ... 252 A jellemaj@gvsu.edu

JELLY, Katherine ... 518-587-2100 ... 355 F katherine.jelly@esc.edu

JEMIOLA, Richard ... 757-352-4028 ... 523 B richjem@regent.edu

JEMISON, Henry ... 501-370-5365 ... 23 B hjemison@philander.edu

JEMISON, Jan ... 415-565-4723 ... 73 G jemisonj@uchastings.edu

JEMMOTT, Nina ... 973-720-3093 ... 317 D jemmottn@wpunj.edu

JEN, Ezbon ... 707-524-1591 ... 68 E ejen@santarosa.edu

JEN, Tien-Chien ... 414-229-4126 ... 551 C jent@uwm.edu

JENAL, Robert, E ... 508-856-3892 ... 238 A robert.jenal@umassmed.edu

JENCKS, Doyle ... 580-477-7736 ... 414 C doyle.jencks@wosc.edu

JENDA, Overtoun ... 334-844-4184 ... 1 G jendaov@auburn.edu

JENE, Beverly ... 802-322-1650 ... 513 C beverly.jene@goddard.edu

JENERETTE, Kim ... 864-644-5504 ... 461 B kjenerette@swu.edu

JENETTE, Brian ... 213-381-3333 ... 53 C bjenette@lac.edu

JENIK, Jeff ... 803-641-3455 ... 462 B jeffj@usca.edu

JENIOUS, Anita ... 615-322-4075 ... 477 F anita.jenious@vanderbilt.edu

JENKIN, Dave ... 949-582-4479 ... 70 F djenkin@saddleback.edu

JENKINS, Anne ... 252-737-1133 ... 377 C jenkinsa@ecu.edu

JENKINS, Anthony, L ... 410-651-2200 ... 227 E

JENKINS, Anthony, L ... 231-995-1263 ... 256 G tjenkins@nmc.edu

JENKINS, Betty, A ... 803-705-4808 ... 455 D jenkinsb@benedict.edu

JENKINS, Bobby ... 580-349-1376 ... 410 B bjenkins@opsu.edu

JENKINS, Bonita ... 706-771-4019 ... 125 D bjenkins@augustatech.edu

JENKINS, Brandon ... 919-735-5151 ... 374 F bmjenkins@waynecc.edu

JENKINS, Brian ... 657-278-2423 ... 34 E bjenkins@fullerton.edu

JENKINS, Carolyn ... 404-237-7573 ... 125 F cjenkins@bauder.edu

JENKINS, Carri, P ... 801-422-4511 ... 509 D carri_jenkins@byu.edu

JENKINS, Cheryl, S ... 919-760-8338 ... 366 G jenkinsc@meredith.edu

JENKINS, Cynthia ... 618-453-1040 ... 164 I cjenk@siu.edu

JENKINS, Debbie ... 503-594-3002 ... 415 A debbiej@clackamas.edu

JENKINS, Deborah, D ... 410-334-2904 ... 229 E djenkins@worwic.edu

JENKINS, Debra ... 262-524-7120 ... 546 E djenkins@carrollu.edu

JENKINS, Dennis ... 520-494-5200 ... 13 F dennis.jenkins@centralaz.edu

JENKINS, Edward ... 205-781-7471 ... 5 H

JENKINS, G. Scott ... 336-334-7006 ... 377 F gsjenkin@ncat.edu

JENKINS, Gerald ... 440-525-7248 ... 394 F gjenkins@lakelandcc.edu

JENKINS, Helen ... 713-646-1887 ... 494 E hjenkins@stcl.edu

JENKINS, J. Marshall ... 706-236-2259 ... 125 G mjenkins@berry.edu

JENKINS, Jack ... 678-839-6419 ... 138 D jjenkins@westga.edu

JENKINS, Jacqueline, D ... 302-454-3916 ... 96 C jjenkins@dtcc.edu

JENKINS, Jan ... 479-968-0456 ... 20 G ejenkins@atu.edu

JENKINS, Jane, E ... 614-235-4136 ... 402 G jjenkins@TLSohio.edu

JENKINS, Jeffrey, L ... 812-877-8209 ... 179 A jenkins@rose-hulman.edu

JENKINS, Jessika ... 281-873-0262 ... 483 E j.jenkins@commonwealth.edu

JENKINS, Jim ... 909-594-5611 ... 58 A jjenkins@mtsac.edu

JENKINS, SR., Jimmy, R .. 704-216-6098 ... 366 D jjenkins@livingstone.edu

JENKINS, John, B ... 312-280-3500 ... 153 A jbjenkins@aii.edu

JENKINS, CSC, John, I ... 574-631-8261 ... 180 D jenkins.1@nd.edu

JENKINS, Katrina, E ... 217-245-3060 ... 152 C katrina.jenkins@ic.edu

JENKINS, Kelly ... 773-697-2078 ... 149 C kjenkins@devry.edu

JENKINS, Kevin ... 870-307-7220 ... 22 D kjenkins@lyon.edu

JENKINS, LaChanda, J ... 713-313-1362 ... 499 G jenkinslj@tsu.edu

JENKINS, Lidia ... 415-241-2286 ... 39 H ljenkins@ccsf.edu

JENKINS, Malia ... 619-201-8728 ... 65 D Malia.Jenkins@sdcc.edu

JENKINS, Mark ... 713-348-4966 ... 492 J jenky@rice.edu

JENKINS, Max, A ... 405-878-5141 ... 412 A majenkins@stgregorys.edu

JENKINS, Mike ... 903-983-8189 ... 489 F mjenkins@kilgore.edu

JENKINS, Paul ... 513-244-4351 ... 388 D paul_jenkins@mail.msj.edu

JENKINS, Richard, J ... 701-858-3299 ... 381 G dick.jenkins@minotstateu.edu

JENKINS, Robert ... 713-500-3334 ... 506 D robert.jenkins@uth.tmc.edu

JENKINS, Rod ... 972-708-7321 ... 486 I rod_jenkins@gial.edu

JENKINS, Roger, L ... 513-529-1799 ... 396 D roger.jenkins@muohio.edu

JENKINS, Ron ... 973-972-3469 ... 316 F jenkinjw@umdnj.edu

JENKINS, Ronnie, D ... 620-229-6356 ... 196 C ronnie.jenkins@sckans.edu

JENKINS, Scott ... 810-762-0502 ... 256 C scott.jenkins@mcc.edu

JENKINS, Shantelle, K 610-957-5700 426 G
sjenkins@dccc.edu
JENKINS, Sonja 478-988-6800 133 H
sjenkins@middlegatech.edu
JENKINS, Stephen 541-962-3553 418 C
stephen.jenkins@eou.edu
JENKINS, Steve 619-201-8720 65 D
Steve.Jenkins@sdcc.edu
JENKINS, Steven 740-392-6868 396 H
steven.jenkins@mvnu.edu
JENKINS, Susan 954-499-9802 104 C
sjenkins@devry.edu
JENKINS, Sylvia 708-974-5202 159 A
jenkins@morainevalley.edu
JENKINS, Tara, F 508-854-4249 241 C
tarafj@qcc.mass.edu
JENKINS, Terry 217-641-4960 154 G
tjenkins@jwcc.edu
JENKINS, Timothy, S 219-464-5411 181 A
tim.jenkins@valpo.edu
JENKINS-CARTER, D'Lonkia 318-687-9925 68 G
djenkins@sum.edu
JENKINS-MONROE, Valata 415-955-2112 27 F
vmonroe@alliant.edu
JENKINS-SCOTT, Jackie 617-879-2161 246 F
jjenkins-scott@wheelock.edu
JENKS, Debra 414-277-4516 548 H
jenks@msoe.edu
JENLINK, Christee 918-449-6000 409 A
jenlink@nsuok.edu
JENNEMAN, Eugene, A 231-995-1572 256 G
ejenneman@nmc.edu
JENNESS, Valerie 949-824-6094 73 H
jenness@uci.edu
JENNETTE, Judy 252-940-6326 367 I
judyj@beaufortccc.edu
JENNINGS, Barbara 641-844-5522 185 H
barb.jennings@iavalley.edu
JENNINGS, Bret 256-765-4658 9 D
nmjennings@una.edu
JENNINGS, Charla 870-743-3000 22 G
charlam@northark.edu
JENNINGS, Charles 209-954-5040 66 D
cjennings@deltacollege.edu
JENNINGS, Chris 213-624-1200 46 L
cjennings@fidm.edu
JENNINGS, Christal 610-205-3130 427 B
cjennings@devry.edu
JENNINGS, David, C 845-675-4616 344 G
david.jennings@nyack.edu
JENNINGS, Donna 630-353-9069 149 A
djennings@devry.edu
JENNINGS, Donna 305-237-7489 113 H
djenning@mdc.edu
JENNINGS, George-Harold 973-408-3392 309 F
gjenning@drew.edu
JENNINGS, John, C 432-335-5113 501 E
john.jennings@ttuhsc.edu
JENNINGS, John, L 903-813-2410 481 A
jjennings@austincollege.edu
JENNINGS, Patricia, L 302-295-1163 97 A
pattie.l.jennings@wilmu.edu
JENNINGS, Rita, O 252-335-0821 369 D
rjennings@albemarle.edu
JENNINGS, Ross 253-833-9111 534 C
rjennings@greenriver.edu
JENNINGS, Sandra 718-405-3260 330 A
sandra.jennings@mountsaintvincent.edu
JENNINGS, Sarah 617-369-3391 244 G
sjennings@smfa.edu
JENNINGS, Sarah, E 870-235-4040 23 I
sejennings@saumag.edu
JENNINGS, Sue, L 253-535-7588 535 K
jenninsl@plu.edu
JENNINGS, Suzanne 843-661-8161 458 A
suzanne.jennings@fdtc.edu
JENNINGS, Thomas, W 850-645-9655 119 C
tjennings@admin.fsu.edu
JENNINGS, Todd 909-537-5655 36 A
tjennin@csusb.edu
JENNINGS, William, P 818-677-2455 35 D
william.jennings@csun.edu
JENNISON, Barry 731-425-2601 475 B
bjennison@jscc.edu
JENNUM, Joe 909-594-5644 58 A
jjennum@mtsac.edu
JENNY, Paul 206-543-6277 538 F
pjenny@uw.edu
JENSEN, Betty 850-201-8235 121 F
jensenb@tcc.fl.edu
JENSEN, Carol 406-657-1022 296 E
jensenc@rocky.edu
JENSEN, Chuck 406-756-3808 294 D
cjensen@fvcc.edu
JENSEN, Clyde 503-491-7365 417 B
clyde.jensen@mhcc.edu
JENSEN, Dale 417-865-2811 282 A
jensend@evangel.edu
JENSEN, Dan 817-735-2500 504 C
djensen@hsc.unt.edu
JENSEN, Darlene 714-992-7096 59 D
djensen@fullcoll.edu
JENSEN, Doug 661-722-6300 28 J
djensen@avc.edu
JENSEN, Douglas, J 724-925-5974 451 E
jensend@wccc.edu
JENSEN, Elena 802-225-3273 513 H
elena.jensen@neci.edu
JENSEN, Gail 402-280-2870 297 H
gailjensen@creighton.edu
JENSEN, Genevieve, M 718-357-4522 349 F
gjensen@edaff.com
JENSEN, Jeffrey 305-899-3250 101 F
jjensen@mail.barry.edu
JENSEN, Jennifer 907-564-8333 10 D
jjensen@alaskapacific.edu
JENSEN, Laura 239-590-1155 119 A
ljensen@fgcu.edu
JENSEN, Laura 970-491-5939 83 A
l.jensen@colostate.edu
JENSEN, Leigh 662-325-2091 276 A
ljensen@saffairs.msstate.edu
JENSEN, Libby 978-556-3621 241 B
ljensen@necc.mass.edu
JENSEN, Patricia 414-382-6321 545 H
patricia.jensen@alverno.edu
JENSEN, Paul 708-456-0300 166 C
pjensen@triton.edu
JENSEN, Peter, E 605-677-5341 465 E
pete.jensen@usd.edu
JENSEN, Robert 714-992-7035 59 D
rjensen@fullcoll.edu
JENSEN, Robert 619-201-8698 65 D
JENSEN, Scott, R 410-547-3160 228 D
srjensen@salisbury.edu
JENSEN, Stanley 970-945-8691 82 C
JENSEN, Steve, M 563-588-8000 184 F
smjensen@emmaus.edu
JENSEN, Todd 317-299-6001 177 C
JENSEN, Travis 763-852-7502 464 G
tjensen@national.edu
JENSKI, Laura, J 605-677-5370 465 E
laura.jenski@usd.edu
JENSON, Hal, B 269-387-9000 260 F
hal.jenson@wmich.edu
JENSON, Linda 817-515-4521 496 A
linda.jenson@tccd.edu
JENT, Laura 931-393-1544 475 C
ljent@mscc.edu
JEON, Daejin 808-791-5050 140 F
JEONG, Benjamin 714-527-0691 45 J
JEONG, Peter 973-748-9000 308 A
peter_jeong@bloomfield.edu
JEPSON, Darla 815-802-8832 154 J
djepson@kcc.edu
JEREBKO, Peter, J 716-851-1221 333 B
jerebko@ecc.edu
JEREMIAH, James 563-242-4023 181 G
JEREMIAH, Jim 901-320-9700 478 B
jjeremiah@victory.edu
JEREMY, M. Jamie 269-387-8777 260 F
jamie.jeremy@wmich.edu
JEREZ, Antonio 201-327-8877 309 H
ajerez@eastwick.edu
JERGINS, Rusty 254-968-9081 496 F
jergins@tarleton.edu
JERIES, John 651-690-6533 271 E
jjeries@stkate.edu
JERKE, Bonnie, J 503-554-2330 415 I
bjerke@georgefox.edu
JERMAN, Rita, H 919-866-5701 374 E
whjerman@waketech.edu
JERMAN LIGUORI, Denise 201-447-7480 307 F
djerman@bergen.edu
JERNIGAN, Tony 301-934-7715 222 C
tjernigan@csmd.edu
JERNIGAN, William 918-495-6723 411 C
wjernigan@oru.edu
JEROME, Allison 808-735-4718 140 A
ajerome@chaminade.edu
JEROME, Evan 914-632-6700 341 G
ejerome@monroecollege.edu
JEROME, Leslie 914-632-5400 341 G
ljerome@monroecollege.edu
JEROME, Marc, M 914-632-5400 341 G
mjerome@monroecollege.edu
JEROME, Philip 574-257-3500 169 F
philip.jerome@bethelcollege.edu
JEROME, Priya 619-482-6557 71 C
pjerome@swccd.edu
JEROME, Stephen, J 718-933-6700 341 G
sjerome@monroecollege.edu
JERRY, Randy 870-862-8131 23 G
rjerry@southark.edu
JERRY, Robert, H 352-273-0600 120 B
jerryr@law.ufl.edu
JERZYK, Barbara 219-981-4436 176 E
bjerzyk@ivytech.edu
JESKO, Rhonda 575-769-4043 317 K
rhonda.jesko@clovis.edu
JESPERSEN, Christopher 706-864-1771 134 D
tcjespersen@northgeorgia.edu
JESSE, Hugh, A 406-243-2788 295 A
hugh.jesse@umontana.edu
JESSELL, Kenneth 305-348-2101 119 B
kenneth.jessell@fiu.edu
JESSEN-MARSHALL, Amy 434-381-6205 524 E
ajessen-marshall@sbc.edu
JESSIE, Jason 918-456-5511 409 A
jessiejb@nsuok.edu
JESSOGNE, Cheryl 312-499-4186 164 A
cjessogne@saic.edu
JESSOP, Craig 435-797-3046 511 B
craig.jessop@usu.edu
JESSOP, Hugh 812-855-6511 173 C
jessoph@indiana.edu
JESSUP, Dwight 617-427-7293 235 F
djessup@gcts.edu
JESSUP, Jim 916-577-1800 79 C
jjessup@jessup.edu
JESSUP, Jim 425-889-5340 535 I
jim.jessup@northwestu.edu
JESSUP, Leonard 520-621-2125 19 B
len@eller.arizona.edu
JESSUP, Rhonda, E 919-658-7754 367 D
rjessup@moc.edu
JESSUP, Tracy, C 704-406-4279 364 B
tjessup@gardner-webb.edu
JESTER, Brad 770-233-5576 137 B
bjester@sctech.edu
JESUS CESAREO, Lourdes 787-763-6700 562 B
ldjesus@se-pr.edu
JETER, Everett, M 919-536-7209 369 G
jetere@durhamtech.edu
JETER, Joni 580-371-2371 408 I
jjeter@mscok.edu
JETER, Kaye 937-376-6210 386 H
kjeter@centralstate.edu
JETT, Melissa 417-255-7955 286 G
melissajett@missouristate.edu
JETT, Susan, P 864-429-8728 462 G
jettsp@mailbox.sc.edu
JETT, Zeny 903-693-2005 492 A
zjett@panola.edu
JETTE, Tracey 406-265-3708 295 G
tracey.jette@msun.edu
JETTON, Kent 731-286-3250 475 A
jetton@dscc.edu
JEW, Carl 415-561-1875 39 H
cjew@ccsf.edu
JEWELL, JoAnn, I 814-866-8106 433 C
jjewell@lecom.edu
JEWELL, Kirk, A 405-385-5112 410 C
kjewell@osugiving.com
JEWELL, Richard, G 724-458-2500 430 B
rgjewell@gcc.edu
JEWELL, Scott 617-349-8714 230 D
sjewell@lesley.edu
JEWELL, Scott 617-349-8714 236 G
sjewell@lesley.edu
JEWELL, Steve 303-245-4686 86 B
sjewell@naropa.edu
JEWETT, Kristen 207-893-7894 219 F
kjewett@sjcme.edu
JEZ, Paul, P 804-828-4482 525 E
ppjez@vcu.edu
JEZAK, Patricia 567-661-2650 400 H
patricia_jezak@owens.edu
JEZEK, Kenda 918-495-6198 411 C
kjezek@oru.edu
JEZEK-TAUSSIG, Jennifer 314-968-5944 293 A
jezekjk@webster.edu
JEZUIT, Deborah 847-543-2339 147 H
djezuit@clcillinois.edu
JHAJ, Sukhwant, S 503-725-8996 418 G
jhaj@pdx.edu
JIAMBALVO, Jim 206-543-9132 538 F
jjiambal@uw.edu
JIANG, Jerome 626-289-7719 26 J
JIANG, Shaojie 608-796-3172 553 A
sjiang@viterbo.edu
JIGA, Anthony 212-998-2278 344 B
anthony.jiga@nyu.edu
JILBERT, Deborah 262-691-5210 555 C
djilbert@wctc.edu
JILES, Michael 770-537-5707 139 B
michael.jiles@westgatech.edu
JILOG, Jennifer 480-990-3773 15 E
JIMÉNEZ, Ivelisse 787-725-8120 562 A
ijimenez0027@eap.edu
JIMÉNEZ-PÉREZ, Nancy 787-993-8877 566 G
nancy.jimenez1@upr.edu
JIMENA-PALMER, Jaretha, J 626-448-0023 51 H
JIMENEZ, Annie 480-732-7391 15 G
a.jimenez@cgcmail.maricopa.edu
JIMENEZ, Araceli 661-726-1911 73 C
JIMENEZ, Asdrubal 787-891-0925 562 G
ajimenez@aguadilla.inter.edu
JIMENEZ, Carlos 787-890-2681 566 E
c.jimenez@upr.edu
JIMENEZ, Estevanny 301-891-4542 229 B
ejimenez@wau.edu
JIMENEZ, Eva 530-242-7560 69 D
ejimenez@shastacollege.edu
JIMENEZ, Irma 787-878-6000 562 E
ijimenez@icprjc.edu
JIMENEZ, Misael 787-834-9595 565 J
mjimenez@uaa.edu
JIMENEZ, Noelia 787-896-2252 561 K
njimenez@edpcollege.edu
JIMENEZ, Obed 787-834-9595 565 J
JIMENEZ, Oscar 432-837-8042 501 B
ojimenez@sulross.edu
JIMENEZ, Paula 305-296-9081 108 F
paula.jimenez@fkcc.edu
JIMENEZ, Rosa 509-527-2363 538 H
rosa.jimenez@wallawalla.edu
JIMENEZ, Sharon 510-567-6174 68 G
sjimenez@sum.edu
JIMENEZ, Silverio 787-882-2065 565 I
dispensario@unitecpr.net
JIMENEZ, Tomas, M 787-751-1459 562 F
tjimenez@inter.edu
JIMENO, Cheri, A 575-439-3640 319 E
cjimeno@nmsua.nmsu.edu
JIMILL, Fiona 404-816-4533 132 B
fjimill@atl.herzing.edu
JIMISON, Nancy, M 804-706-5024 526 G
njiminson@jtcc.edu
JIMISON, Sylvia 802-447-6372 514 D
sjimison@svc.edu
JIMMERSON, Judy 229-430-3514 123 I
jjimmerson@albanytech.edu
JIN, Yoo Chul 714-517-1945 30 G
JINDARYAN, Liana 818-767-0888 79 D
liana.jindaryan@woodbury.edu
JINDRA, Barbara 972-758-3821 483 D
bjindra@collin.edu
JINKINS, Michael 512-404-4822 481 D
mjinkins@austinseminary.edu
JINKINS, Michael 502-895-3411 204 B
mjinkins@lpts.edu
JINKS, Mary 865-974-6621 477 A
mary.jinks@tennessee.edu
JIRA, Pamela, A 740-588-1205 407 A
pjira@zanestate.edu
JIRAK, Randal 785-227-3380 190 G
jirakr@bethanylb.edu
JIRON, Al 954-771-0376 112 L
ajiron@knoxseminary.edu
JIROVEC, Kelly 402-826-8265 298 A
kelly.jirovec@doane.edu
JIUNTA, Marty 602-589-9860 13 J
JIWANJI, Insiya 240-684-2124 227 F
admissions@umuc.edu
JOACHIM, Gisele 973-642-8475 315 C
gisele.joachim@shu.edu
JOACHIM KITZMAN, Patricia 641-628-5271 183 A
kitzmanp@central.edu
JOANIS, Jessica, L 920-748-8186 549 I
joanisj@ripon.edu
JOASIL, Lorna 973-328-5149 309 B
ljoasil@ccm.edu
JOBE, Carol 413-205-3503 229 G
carol.jobe@aic.edu
JOBE, Carol, A 413-205-3056 229 G
carol.jobe@aic.edu
JOBE, Carol, S 413-205-3503 229 G
carol.jobe@aic.edu
JOBE, Deanna, L 319-399-8741 183 C
djobe@coe.edu
JOBE, Steve 812-866-7005 171 F
jobe@hanover.edu
JOBSON, John, E 616-395-7800 252 F
jobson@hope.edu
JOCHEMS, Jeff 417-447-7932 287 G
jochemsj@otc.edu
JOCHMANS, John, J 516-773-5595 558 F
jochmanj@usmma.edu
JODELKA, Edward 708-709-3795 161 C
ejodelka@prairiestate.edu
JODIS, Stephen, M 724-805-2358 446 E
stephen.jodis@email.stvincent.edu
JOE, Ether 336-750-3300 380 A
joee@wssu.edu
JOEL, Harry 650-358-6767 67 D
joelh@smccd.edu
JOEL, Richard, M 212-960-5300 361 I
rjoel@yu.edu
JOENS, Angela 515-643-8037 187 C
ajoens@mercydesmoines.org
JOERSCHKE, Bonnie 706-542-6147 138 C
bonniej@uga.edu
JOHANN, Randy 812-265-2580 176 G
rjohann@ivytech.edu
JOHANNES, Cheri 406-657-2158 295 F
cjohannes@msubillings.edu
JOHANNSEN, Danelle, D 712-279-3377 188 E
johanndd@stlukescollege.edu
JOHANSEN, Alfred, W 801-832-2127 512 F
ajohansen@westminstercollege.edu
JOHANSEN, Bob, L 626-815-4603 30 E
bjohansen@apu.edu
JOHANSEN, Judith 503-699-6266 416 I
president@marylhurst.edu
JOHANSEN, Ruthann, K 800-287-8822 169 E
johanru@bethanyseminary.edu
JOHANSON, Michael 808-675-3669 139 I
michael.johanson@byuh.edu

JOHANSON, Rod ... 503-517-1010 ... 421 A
rjohanson@warnerpacific.edu
JOHANSON, Rosanne ... 716-664-5100 ... 337 D
rosannejohnson@jamestownbusinesscollege.edu
JOHHSON, Joyce ... 757-825-2827 ... 528 B
johnsonj@tncc.edu
JOHN, Beth ... 608-663-4861 ... 547 C
bjohn@edgewood.edu
JOHN, Joby ... 337-482-6491 ... 216 D
jjohn@louisiana.edu
JOHN, Kathy ... 937-769-1840 ... 383 K
kjohn@antioch.edu
JOHN, JR., Leon ... 570-348-6257 ... 435 F
ljohn@marywood.edu
JOHN, Linda ... 718-982-3975 ... 327 A
Linda.John@csi.cuny.edu
JOHN, Michael, A ... 919-508-2401 ... 375 D
majohn@peace.edu
JOHN, Rebecca ... 612-330-1482 ... 261 G
rjohn@augsburg.edu
JOHN, Stephen, S ... 806-894-9611 ... 494 C
sjohn@southplainscollege.edu
JOHN, Vukich ... 719-549-3334 ... 87 B
John.Vukich@pueblocc.edu
JOHNDROW, David, A ... 570-674-6762 ... 436 F
djohndro@misericordia.edu
JOHNOSON, April ... 301-860-3831 ... 228 A
ajohnson@bowiestate.edu
JOHNS, Deborah ... 216-265-3151 ... 386 B
dmjohns@bryantstratton.edu
JOHNS, Krista ... 510-981-2933 ... 62 A
kjohns@peralta.edu
JOHNS, Lolita ... 727-786-4707 ... 102 F
ljohns@cfi.edu
JOHNS, Niki ... 870-838-2913 ... 20 A
njohns@smail.anc.edu
JOHNS, Patrick ... 218-733-5997 ... 267 B
p.johns@lsc.edu
JOHNS, Priscilla, C ... 671-735-5520 ... 559 B
assessment@guamcc.edu
JOHNS, Sheila, R ... 308-635-6366 ... 301 E
johnss23@wncc.edu
JOHNS, Xenia ... 770-228-7348 ... 137 B
xjohns@sctech.edu
JOHNS-LAUDERDALE, Wendy ... 985-549-5544 ... 216 C
wjohns@selu.edu
JOHNSEN, David, C ... 319-335-7144 ... 182 C
david-johnsen@uiowa.edu
JOHNSEN, John, H ... 315-792-3120 ... 359 C
jjohnsen@utica.edu
JOHNSEN, William, T ... 717-245-4711 ... 558 D
JOHNSON, Aaron ... 801-333-8100 ... 509 H
JOHNSON, Abe ... 972-548-6677 ... 483 D
ajohnson@collin.edu
JOHNSON, Alan, D ... 812-482-3030 ... 181 B
ajohnson@vinu.edu
JOHNSON, JR., Albert, D ... 580-581-2999 ... 407 D
ajohnson@cameron.edu
JOHNSON, Alex ... 412-237-4413 ... 425 H
ajohnson@ccac.edu
JOHNSON, Alex, F ... 617-726-8008 ... 242 E
ajohnson@mghihp.edu
JOHNSON, Alice ... 502-597-6343 ... 203 D
alice.johnson@kysu.edu
JOHNSON, Alice ... 210-486-0902 ... 479 F
ajohnson235@alamo.edu
JOHNSON, Alisa ... 207-948-3131 ... 219 H
ajohnson@unity.edu
JOHNSON, Alison ... 802-860-2747 ... 513 A
ajohnson@champlain.edu
JOHNSON, Allan ... 202-806-5042 ... 98 B
ajohnson@howard.edu
JOHNSON, Allen ... 951-343-4477 ... 31 G
ajohnson@calbaptist.edu
JOHNSON, Allison ... 816-331-5700 ... 288 A
ajohnson@pcitraining.edu
JOHNSON, Anderson ... 909-607-8235 ... 40 C
andy.johnson@cgu.edu
JOHNSON, Andrea ... 870-236-6901 ... 21 E
ajohnson@crc.edu
JOHNSON, Andy ... 912-260-4430 ... 136 F
andy.johnson@sgc.edu
JOHNSON, Angela ... 216-987-4213 ... 389 A
angela.johnson@tri-c.edu
JOHNSON, Anitra ... 219-947-8400 ... 177 D
ajohnson@kaplan.edu
JOHNSON, Ann Marie ... 207-780-4540 ... 220 G
amjohnson@usm.maine.edu
JOHNSON, Anna ... 312-427-2737 ... 154 F
6johnson@jmls.edu
JOHNSON, Anna ... 740-753-6553 ... 392 A
johnson_a@hocking.edu
JOHNSON, Anne ... 651-450-3642 ... 266 I
ajohnson@inverhills.edu
JOHNSON, Anne ... 313-927-1209 ... 255 A
ajohnson@marygrove.edu
JOHNSON, Annette, M ... 906-786-5802 ... 249 D
johnsona@baycollege.edu
JOHNSON, Annie ... 213-624-1200 ... 46 L
ajohnson@fidm.edu
JOHNSON, Arvid ... 708-524-6465 ... 150 A
ajohnson@dom.edu

JOHNSON, Barbara ... 609-777-4351 ... 316 A
bjohnson@tesc.edu
JOHNSON, Barbara, G ... 412-578-6021 ... 424 G
johnsonbg@carlow.edu
JOHNSON, Barbara, L ... 308-865-8205 ... 300 G
johnsonbl@unk.edu
JOHNSON, Barbara, L ... 802-656-4490 ... 514 F
barbara.johnson@uvm.edu
JOHNSON, Barry ... 704-406-4440 ... 364 B
bjohnson@gardner-webb.edu
JOHNSON, Barry, W ... 409-880-8458 ... 500 F
barry.johnson@lamar.edu
JOHNSON, Belinda ... 401-863-3476 ... 452 J
belinda_johnson@brown.edu
JOHNSON, Ben ... 501-370-5336 ... 23 B
bjohnson@philander.edu
JOHNSON, Ben ... 325-670-1252 ... 487 D
bjohnson@hsutx.edu
JOHNSON, Bernard ... 973-754-7192 ... 312 E
bjohnson@pccc.edu
JOHNSON, Bernice, D ... 919-530-5234 ... 378 A
bjohnson@nccu.edu
JOHNSON, Beth Ann, H ... 203-392-5250 ... 91 I
johnsonb3@southernct.edu
JOHNSON, Betty, D ... 386-822-7175 ... 121 E
bjohnson@stetson.edu
JOHNSON, Bonnie ... 641-673-1036 ... 189 I
johnsonb@wmpenn.edu
JOHNSON, Bonnie ... 815-394-5047 ... 162 H
bonjohnson@rockford.edu
JOHNSON, Brad ... 325-649-8020 ... 488 A
bjohnson@hputx.edu
JOHNSON, Brad ... 901-751-8453 ... 471 D
bjohnson@mabts.edu
JOHNSON, Brad, W ... 903-434-8102 ... 491 D
bjohnson@ntcc.edu
JOHNSON, Brandon ... 816-501-2400 ... 279 C
brandon.johnson@avila.edu
JOHNSON, Brenda ... 812-855-3403 ... 173 C
johnbren@indiana.edu
JOHNSON, Brenda ... 510-981-2830 ... 62 A
bjohnson@peralta.edu
JOHNSON, Brenda, R ... 510-780-4500 ... 53 I
bjohnson@lifewest.edu
JOHNSON, Brett ... 210-826-1000 ... 487 B
bjohnson@hallmarkcollege.edu
JOHNSON, Brian ... 931-221-7992 ... 473 D
johnsonb@apsu.edu
JOHNSON, Brian ... 727-726-1153 ... 103 B
JOHNSON, Brian ... 406-791-5290 ... 296 H
bjohnson01@ugf.edu
JOHNSON, Brian, D ... 208-885-6246 ... 144 B
johnsonb@uidaho.edu
JOHNSON, Brian, M ... 570-326-3761 ... 440 K
bmj2@pct.edu
JOHNSON, Brian, T ... 219-464-6732 ... 181 A
brian.johnson1@valpo.edu
JOHNSON, Brodie, I ... 901-320-9700 ... 478 B
bjohnson@victory.edu
JOHNSON, C. Lynn ... 320-222-5208 ... 268 I
lynn.johnson@ridgewater.edu
JOHNSON, Calvin ... 870-575-7011 ... 25 B
johnsonc@uapb.edu
JOHNSON, Calvin, M ... 334-844-4546 ... 1 G
johncal@auburn.edu
JOHNSON, Candace ... 810-766-4109 ... 248 H
candace.johnson@baker.edu
JOHNSON, Carl ... 847-317-8138 ... 166 B
cjohnson@tiu.edu
JOHNSON, Carl ... 303-871-3111 ... 88 E
cdjohnson@du.edu
JOHNSON, Carl, E ... 704-687-7217 ... 378 E
cjohns1@uncc.edu
JOHNSON, Carol ... 606-783-2022 ... 204 E
c.johnson@moreheadstate.edu
JOHNSON, Carol ... 651-690-6650 ... 271 E
cpjohnson@stkate.edu
JOHNSON, Carol ... 704-878-3225 ... 371 H
cjohnson@mitchellcc.edu
JOHNSON, Carol, B ... 386-481-2075 ... 101 I
johnsonc@cookman.edu
JOHNSON, Casie ... 507-453-2663 ... 267 F
cjohnson@southeastmn.edu
JOHNSON, Cass, H ... 614-823-1500 ... 400 G
cjohnson@otterbein.edu
JOHNSON, Catherine, M ... 614-823-1005 ... 400 G
cmjohnson@otterbein.edu
JOHNSON, Catherine, W ... 336-506-4237 ... 367 G
johnsonc@alamancecc.edu
JOHNSON, Cathi ... 901-334-5811 ... 471 C
chjohnson@memphisseminary.edu
JOHNSON, Cecelia ... 931-540-2762 ... 474 F
cjohnson@columbiastate.edu
JOHNSON, Cel ... 619-260-7878 ... 76 A
cel@sandiego.edu
JOHNSON, Celestine ... 765-459-0561 ... 176 A
cjohnson@ivytech.edu
JOHNSON, Charlene, M ... 803-536-7243 ... 460 G
cmjohnson@scsu.edu
JOHNSON, Charles ... 706-272-4434 ... 127 G
cdjohnson@daltonstate.edu
JOHNSON, Charlie ... 405-974-2315 ... 413 B
chjohnson@ucok.edu

JOHNSON, Charlotte ... 870-584-4471 ... 25 C
cjohnson@cccua.edu
JOHNSON, Charlotte, H ... 603-646-2243 ... 305 A
charlotte.h.johnson@dartmouth.edu
JOHNSON, Cheri ... 402-557-7016 ... 297 A
cheri.johnson@bellevue.edu
JOHNSON, Cheri, L ... 785-827-5541 ... 194 D
kcherib@kwu.edu
JOHNSON, Cheryl ... 618-545-3091 ... 155 A
cjohnson@kaskaskia.edu
JOHNSON, Chris ... 303-762-6924 ... 83 I
chris.johnson@denverseminary.edu
JOHNSON, Chris ... 425-235-2352 ... 536 E
cjohnson@rtc.edu
JOHNSON, Chris ... 434-592-3017 ... 520 F
cjohnson@liberty.edu
JOHNSON, Christine ... 509-434-5006 ... 532 D
cjohnson@ccs.spokane.edu
JOHNSON, Christine ... 509-434-5006 ... 532 E
cjohnson@ccs.spokane.edu
JOHNSON, Christine, P ... 941-309-4731 ... 115 K
cjohnso4@ringling.edu
JOHNSON, Christopher ... 203-254-4332 ... 92 B
cjohnson@fairfield.edu
JOHNSON, Christopher, P 208-885-6126 ... 144 B
cjohnson@uidaho.edu
JOHNSON, Cindi Beth ... 651-255-6137 ... 271 I
cbjohnson@unitedseminary.edu
JOHNSON, Cindy, K ... 816-604-1011 ... 285 D
cindy.johnson@mcckc.edu
JOHNSON, Cinthia ... 970-521-6603 ... 86 E
cinthia.johnson@njc.edu
JOHNSON, Classie, O ... 601-877-6333 ... 273 C
alcorn@bkstr.com
JOHNSON, JR., Clyde ... 443-552-1659 ... 224 C
cjohnson01@mica.edu
JOHNSON, Colleen ... 916-608-6500 ... 56 C
JOHNSON, Cornelia ... 302-454-3944 ... 96 C
cornelia@dtcc.edu
JOHNSON, Corry ... 912-449-7540 ... 138 G
cjohnson@waycross.edu
JOHNSON, Craig ... 813-253-7051 ... 110 I
cjohnson@hccfl.edu
JOHNSON, Craig ... 870-972-2852 ... 20 C
crjohnso@astate.edu
JOHNSON, Craig ... 773-244-5637 ... 159 G
crjohnson@northpark.edu
JOHNSON, Croslena ... 864-646-1568 ... 461 F
cjohnso5@tctc.edu
JOHNSON, Curtis ... 501-244-5111 ... 19 F
curtis.johnson@arkansasbaptist.edu
JOHNSON, Cuthrell ... 336-750-2230 ... 380 A
johnsonc@wssu.edu
JOHNSON, Cynthia ... 360-486-8131 ... 536 F
cjohnson@stmartin.edu
JOHNSON, D. Nichole ... 614-236-6945 ... 386 C
njohnson@capital.edu
JOHNSON, Dacia ... 218-736-1512 ... 267 G
dacia.johnson@minnesota.edu
JOHNSON, Dale ... 510-780-4500 ... 53 I
djohnson@lifewest.edu
JOHNSON, Dan ... 617-369-3620 ... 244 G
djohnson@smfa.edu
JOHNSON, Daniel ... 701-662-1515 ... 382 D
dan.johnson@lrsc.edu
JOHNSON, Daniel ... 803-584-3446 ... 462 E
johns943@mailbox.sc.edu
JOHNSON, Daniel ... 918-456-5511 ... 409 A
johnso89@nsuok.edu
JOHNSON, Daniel, R ... 203-582-8930 ... 93 E
dan.johnson@quinnipiac.edu
JOHNSON, Daniel, W ... 414-443-8952 ... 553 B
daniel.johnson@wlc.edu
JOHNSON, Darren ... 518-381-1320 ... 350 E
JOHNSON, Daryl ... 651-793-1227 ... 267 D
daryl.johnson@metrostate.edu
JOHNSON, Daryl ... 651-793-1303 ... 267 D
daryl.johnson@metrostate.edu
JOHNSON, Dave ... 503-375-7021 ... 415 F
djohnson@corban.edu
JOHNSON, David ... 716-338-1002 ... 337 E
davejohnson@mail.sunyjcc.edu
JOHNSON, David ... 606-368-6031 ... 197 H
davidjohnson@alc.edu
JOHNSON, David ... 602-240-3284 ... 48 D
davidjohnson@ggbts.edu
JOHNSON, David ... 812-855-8908 ... 173 C
dj44@indiana.edu
JOHNSON, David ... 256-824-6288 ... 9 A
david.johnson@uah.edu
JOHNSON, David ... 650-306-3336 ... 67 E
johnsond@smccd.edu
JOHNSON, David, A ... 330-494-6170 ... 402 A
djohnson@starkstate.edu
JOHNSON, David, M ... 540-365-4364 ... 518 J
djohnson@ferrum.edu
JOHNSON, David, N ... 919-209-2050 ... 371 C
dnjohnson@johnstoncc.edu
JOHNSON, David, T ... 513-562-8750 ... 384 A
president@artacademy.edu
JOHNSON, Deborah ... 419-251-1327 ... 395 H
deborah.johnson@mercycollege.edu
JOHNSON, Deborah, R ... 414-410-4222 ... 546 D
drjohnson@stritch.edu

JOHNSON, Debra ... 318-274-2560 ... 215 E
johnsond@gram.edu
JOHNSON, Debra, J ... 540-985-8492 ... 520 D
djjohnson@jchs.edu
JOHNSON, Deirdra, G ... 410-334-2902 ... 229 E
djohnson@worwic.edu
JOHNSON, Delmar, R ... 605-688-6134 ... 466 B
del.johnson@sdstate.edu
JOHNSON, Dennis ... 913-971-3279 ... 195 A
ddjohnson@mnu.edu
JOHNSON, Dennis ... 760-480-8474 ... 78 E
dejohnson@wscal.edu
JOHNSON, Dennis ... 719-549-3035 ... 87 B
dennis.johnson@pueblocc.edu
JOHNSON, Dennis ... 314-889-1452 ... 282 C
djohnson@fontbonne.edu
JOHNSON, DeWayne ... 213-637-1376 ... 78 I
dejohnson@westwood.edu
JOHNSON, Dexter ... 425-564-4261 ... 531 B
d.johnson@bellevuecollege.edu
JOHNSON, Diana ... 479-936-5135 ... 22 H
djohnson@nwacc.edu
JOHNSON, Diane ... 518-828-4181 ... 330 E
diane.johnson@sunycgcc.edu
JOHNSON, Diane, S ... 515-263-6149 ... 184 I
djohnson@grandview.edu
JOHNSON, Don, F ... 651-631-5324 ... 270 E
dfjohnson@nwc.edu
JOHNSON, Donna ... 845-431-8682 ... 332 E
djohnson@sunydutchess.edu
JOHNSON, Doris ... 972-524-3341 ... 495 F
JOHNSON, Doris, W ... 803-705-4536 ... 455 D
johnsond@benedict.edu
JOHNSON, Douglas ... 207-581-1392 ... 220 A
douglasj@maine.edu
JOHNSON, Earl ... 918-631-2633 ... 413 F
JOHNSON, Earl ... 918-631-3142 ... 413 F
earl-johnson@utulsa.edu
JOHNSON, Edward ... 716-829-7636 ... 332 F
JOHNSON, Edwin ... 406-243-2995 ... 295 A
edwin.johnson@umontana.edu
JOHNSON, Elise ... 586-498-4119 ... 254 F
johnsonem@macomb.edu
JOHNSON, Elise ... 770-824-5242 ... 139 B
elise.johnson@westgatech.edu
JOHNSON, Elizabeth, J ... 415-422-6534 ... 76 B
johnson@usfca.edu
JOHNSON, Eric ... 318-487-7134 ... 209 B
ejohnson@lacollege.edu
JOHNSON, Eric ... 402-844-7299 ... 300 A
paulsb@northeast.edu
JOHNSON, Eric, A ... 330-777-2070 ... 403 B
ejohnson@upakron.com
JOHNSON, Eric, W ... 985-549-3860 ... 216 C
ejohnson@selu.edu
JOHNSON, Erica ... 404-270-5189 ... 137 E
ESJohnson@spelman.edu
JOHNSON, Erie ... 760-379-5001 ... 52 N
eriejohn@cerrocoso.edu
JOHNSON, Erika ... 415-503-6297 ... 66 A
emj@sfcm.edu
JOHNSON, Erin ... 602-274-4300 ... 13 A
ejohnson@brymanschool.edu
JOHNSON, Estelle ... 605-668-1363 ... 464 F
ejohnson@mtmc.edu
JOHNSON, Eva, R ... 253-535-7159 ... 535 K
johnsoer@plu.edu
JOHNSON, Fatima, R ... 585-245-5620 ... 353 C
johnsonf@geneseo.edu
JOHNSON, Faye, R ... 229-226-1621 ... 137 F
fjohnson@thomasu.edu
JOHNSON, Floretha, J ... 636-922-8365 ... 288 E
fjohnson@stchas.edu
JOHNSON, Francie, H ... 757-823-9159 ... 521 K
fhjohnson@nsu.edu
JOHNSON, Frank ... 620-947-3121 ... 196 E
frankj@tabor.edu
JOHNSON, Frank ... 404-756-4013 ... 124 I
frankjohnson@atlm.edu
JOHNSON, Freddie, L ... 404-756-4442 ... 124 I
fjohnson@atlm.edu
JOHNSON, Frederick ... 412-392-6132 ... 444 H
fjohnson@pointpark.edu
JOHNSON, G. David ... 251-460-6261 ... 9 E
djohnson@usouthal.edu
JOHNSON, Gary ... 605-773-3455 ... 465 D
gary.johnson@sdbor.edu
JOHNSON, Gary ... 704-878-3250 ... 371 H
gjohnson@mitchellcc.edu
JOHNSON, Gary ... 419-434-4445 ... 404 B
gjohnson@findlay.edu
JOHNSON, Gary, F ... 540-654-1022 ... 524 H
gjohnson@umw.edu
JOHNSON, Gary, K ... 815-224-0378 ... 153 D
gary_johnson@ivcc.edu
JOHNSON, George ... 937-376-2946 ... 401 A
gjohnson@payne.edu
JOHNSON, George ... 336-279-9237 ... 364 A
gjohnson8@elon.edu
JOHNSON, Georgene, T ... 740-374-8716 ... 405 F
gjohnson@wscc.edu
JOHNSON, Gerry ... 502-213-7276 ... 202 B
gerald.johnson@kctcs.edu

JOHNSON, Paul, C .... 480-965-9235...... 12 B
paul.c.johnson@asu.edu
JOHNSON, Paulette .... 256-726-7250........ 6 C
pjohnson@oakwood.edu
JOHNSON, Paulette .... 314-644-9228.... 289 C
pjohnson@stlcc.edu
JOHNSON, Peg .... 505-428-1506.... 320 E
peg.johnson@sfcc.edu
JOHNSON, Peggy .... 281-283-3007.... 503 C
johnsonp@uhcl.edu
JOHNSON, Penny .... 408-855-5195...... 78 A
penny.johnson@wvm.edu
JOHNSON, Peter .... 701-777-2731.... 381 D
peter.johnson@email.und.edu
JOHNSON,
Pharris D. (PJ) .... 404-253-3111.... 136 B
pjohnson@scad.edu
JOHNSON, Philip .... 906-487-7201.... 251 C
philip.johnson@finlandia.edu
JOHNSON, FSC, Philip ..... 815-836-5550.... 156 D
johnsoph@lewisu.edu
JOHNSON, Philip, M .... 503-255-0332.... 417 C
pjohnson@multnomah.edu
JOHNSON, Phillip, A .... 574-631-8338.... 180 D
johnson.30@nd.edu
JOHNSON, Phyllis, E .... 701-777-6736.... 381 D
phyllis.e.johnson@research.und.edu
JOHNSON, Quentin, R .... 304-367-4000.... 543 E
JOHNSON, R, C .... 901-678-2335.... 474 C
rjohnson@memphis.edu
JOHNSON, R. Stafford, R .. 513-745-3528.... 406 E
JOHNSON, Ralph .... 256-372-5221........ 1 A
ralph.johnson@aamu.edu
JOHNSON, Ralph .... 864-977-2077.... 460 A
ralph.johnson@ngu.edu
JOHNSON, Ralph, F .... 706-542-7369.... 138 C
rfj@uga.edu
JOHNSON, Rebecca .... 770-467-6037.... 137 B
rajohnson@sctech.edu
JOHNSON, Rebecca .... 541-322-3100.... 418 F
rebecca.johnson@osucascades.edu
JOHNSON, Rebecca, D ...... 203-932-7176...... 95 B
rjohnson@newhaven.edu
JOHNSON, Rhonda .... 510-885-3419...... 34 C
rhonda.johnson@csueastbay.edu
JOHNSON, Richard .... 870-236-6901...... 21 E
rjohnson@crc.edu
JOHNSON, Richard, A .... 864-597-4090.... 463 F
johnsonra@wofford.edu
JOHNSON, Richard, G .... 805-756-1281...... 33 F
rjohnson@calpoly.edu
JOHNSON, Richard, T .... 309-677-2721.... 145 H
rtj@bradley.edu
JOHNSON, Richard, W ...... 315-268-2099.... 329 C
rjohnson@clarkson.edu
JOHNSON,
Richard (Rick), L .... 913-588-5179.... 197 A
rjohnso1@kumc.edu
JOHNSON, Rick .... 239-590-7072.... 119 A
rjohnson@wgcu.edu
JOHNSON, Rick .... 740-392-6868.... 396 H
rjohnson@mvnu.edu
JOHNSON, Rick .... 806-651-2080.... 498 D
rjohnson@mail.wtamu.edu
JOHNSON, Rick, D .... 701-231-7215.... 381 H
rick.johnson@ndsu.edu
JOHNSON, Rita .... 828-328-7235.... 366 B
rita.johnson@lr.edu
JOHNSON, Robert .... 916-691-7390...... 56 B
johnsor@crc.losrios.edu
JOHNSON, Robert .... 909-335-8863...... 42 E
bjohnson@cccollege.edu
JOHNSON, Robert .... 225-922-2800.... 209 C
rjohnson@lctcs.edu
JOHNSON, Robert .... 516-773-5755.... 558 F
johnsonr@usmma.edu
JOHNSON, Robert, E .... 913-667-5700.... 191 E
rjohnson@cbts.edu
JOHNSON, Robert, E .... 508-373-1900.... 231 D
robert.johnson@becker.edu
JOHNSON, Robert, E .... 704-687-8242.... 378 E
robejohn@uncc.edu
JOHNSON, Robert, L .... 973-972-4538.... 316 F
rjohnson@umdnj.edu
JOHNSON, JR.,
Robert, M .... 901-843-3745.... 472 I
johnsonb@rhodes.edu
JOHNSON, Robert, V .... 213-821-1900...... 76 C
rjohnson@usc.edu
JOHNSON, Roberta, L .... 515-294-2223.... 182 B
rljohnse@iastate.edu
JOHNSON, Robin .... 864-977-7064.... 460 A
robin.johnson@ngu.edu
JOHNSON, Rodney .... 803-934-3226.... 459 F
johnsonrod@morris.edu
JOHNSON, Rodney .... 937-766-4114.... 386 F
johnsnr@cedarville.edu
JOHNSON, Roger .... 870-248-4000...... 21 A
rogerj@blackrivertech.edu
JOHNSON, Roger .... 218-733-5935.... 267 B
r1.johnson@lsc.edu
JOHNSON, Ronald .... 713-500-3455.... 506 D
ronald.johnson@uth.tmc.edu
JOHNSON, Ronald, D .... 701-231-8804.... 381 H
ronald.d.johnson@ndsu.edu
JOHNSON, Ronald, W .... 310-206-0404...... 74 A
rojohnso@saonet.ucla.edu
JOHNSON, Rose .... 828-627-4516.... 370 G
rjohnson@haywood.edu
JOHNSON, Ruben .... 972-860-8160.... 484 G
rjohnson@dcccd.edu
JOHNSON, Ryan .... 501-329-6872...... 21 C
rjohnson@cbc.edu
JOHNSON, Sabrina, C .... 540-654-1046.... 524 H
sjohnson@umw.edu
JOHNSON, Samuel .... 215-568-9215.... 436 E
sjohnson@mccworks.org
JOHNSON, Sandra .... 661-726-1911...... 73 C
JOHNSON, Sandra .... 212-243-5150.... 334 E
sjohnson@gts.edu
JOHNSON, Sandra .... 516-463-6933.... 335 H
sandra.johnson@hofstra.edu
JOHNSON, Sara .... 662-862-8050.... 274 G
scjohnson@iccms.edu
JOHNSON, Sara .... 517-264-7185.... 258 D
sjohnson@sienaheights.edu
JOHNSON, Sarah .... 303-837-0825...... 81 B
sljohnson@aii.edu
JOHNSON, Scherry, F .... 972-883-2105.... 505 D
sjohnson@utdallas.edu
JOHNSON, Scott .... 336-838-6141.... 375 A
scott.johnson@wilkescc.edu
JOHNSON, Scott .... 309-438-2251.... 153 C
sdjohns@ilstu.edu
JOHNSON, Scott .... 701-228-5474.... 382 C
scott.johnson@dakotacollege.edu
JOHNSON, Scott, L .... 716-878-6210.... 353 A
johnsosl@buffalostate.edu
JOHNSON, Scott, L .... 716-878-5906.... 353 A
johnsosl@buffalostate.edu
JOHNSON, Serena .... 704-290-5844.... 373 F
sjohnson@spcc.edu
JOHNSON, Sharon .... 908-709-7085.... 316 B
johnson@ucc.edu
JOHNSON, Sharon .... 903-468-8707.... 497 E
sharon_johnson@tamu-commerce.edu
JOHNSON, Sheila .... 765-289-2291.... 175 K
sjohnson@ivytech.edu
JOHNSON, Sheila .... 812-237-8954.... 173 A
sheila.johnson@indstate.edu
JOHNSON, Sheila .... 731-668-7240.... 478 F
sheila.johnson@wtbc.edu
JOHNSON, Sheila, G .... 405-744-6321.... 410 C
sheila.johnson@okstate.edu
JOHNSON, Shelia .... 304-327-4040.... 543 C
sjohnson@bluefieldstate.edu
JOHNSON, Sherie .... 410-951-3846.... 228 B
shejohnson@coppin.edu
JOHNSON, Sonia .... 870-236-6901...... 21 E
sjohnson@crc.edu
JOHNSON, Sonja .... 616-331-6811.... 252 A
johnsoso@gvsu.edu
JOHNSON, Stacey .... 718-939-5100.... 338 D
sjohnson@libi.edu
JOHNSON, Stacey .... 210-486-3933.... 479 D
sjohnson@alamo.edu
JOHNSON, Stefanie .... 407-303-9498.... 108 D
stefanie.johnson@fhchs.edu
JOHNSON, Stephanie .... 410-455-1517.... 227 D
sjohn@umbc.edu
JOHNSON, Stephen .... 560-860-2451...... 38 J
sjohnson@cerritos.edu
JOHNSON, Stephen .... 325-674-3791.... 478 H
stephan.johnson@acu.edu
JOHNSON, Stephen .... 817-923-1921.... 495 E
sjohnson@swbts.edu
JOHNSON, Stephen, P .... 607-255-9029.... 331 C
spj2@cornell.edu
JOHNSON, Steve .... 503-552-2001.... 417 D
sjohnson@ncnm.edu
JOHNSON, Steve .... 800-422-2418.... 101 G
sjohnson@baymedical.org
JOHNSON, Steve .... 913-360-7415.... 190 F
stevej@benedictine.edu
JOHNSON, Steve .... 504-280-6303.... 213 E
sgjohnso@uno.edu
JOHNSON, Steve .... 435-652-7544.... 512 A
johnsons@dixie.edu
JOHNSON, Steven .... 212-346-1835.... 345 F
sjohnson@pace.edu
JOHNSON, Steven .... 215-489-2905.... 426 H
Steven.Johnson@delval.edu
JOHNSON, Steven, C .... 208-885-7372.... 144 B
stevejohnson@uidaho.edu
JOHNSON, Steven, D .... 607-436-3592.... 353 E
johnsosd@oneonta.edu
JOHNSON, Steven, L .... 212-346-1835.... 345 F
sjohnson@pace.edu
JOHNSON, Steven, L .... 973-655-7677.... 311 G
johnsonst@mail.montclair.edu
JOHNSON, Steven, L .... 202-806-2705...... 98 B
steven.johnson@howard.edu
JOHNSON, Steven, L .... 937-512-2525.... 401 J
steven.lee.johnson@sinclair.edu
JOHNSON, Susan .... 805-652-5536...... 77 A
sjohnson@vcccd.edu
JOHNSON, Susan .... 513-244-4503.... 388 D
susan_johnson@mail.msj.edu
JOHNSON, Susie .... 863-784-7108.... 117 I
susie.johnson@southflorida.edu
JOHNSON, Sylvester, C .... 504-865-5300.... 215 C
sylj@tulane.edu
JOHNSON, Sylvia, M .... 847-543-2404.... 147 H
cps086@clcillinois.edu
JOHNSON, Tammy .... 304-696-3161.... 543 G
johnson73@marshall.edu
JOHNSON, Ted .... 847-543-2247.... 147 H
tjohnson@clcillinois.edu
JOHNSON, Ted .... 858-822-5949...... 74 D
edjohnson@ucsd.edu
JOHNSON, Teisha .... 312-949-7407.... 152 D
tjohnson@ico.edu
JOHNSON, Tendai .... 910-672-1612.... 377 E
tejohnson@uncfsu.edu
JOHNSON, Teresa .... 731-286-3226.... 475 A
johnson@dscc.edu
JOHNSON, Terri .... 248-213-1614.... 149 A
tjohnson@devry.edu
JOHNSON, Terry, L .... 937-382-6661.... 405 H
terry_johnson@wilmington.edu
JOHNSON, Theodore, T .... 973-596-3140.... 312 C
johnson@njit.edu
JOHNSON, Thomas .... 323-343-3480...... 35 B
tjohnson@cslanet.calstatela.edu
JOHNSON, Thomas .... 712-325-3227.... 186 B
tjohnson@iwcc.edu
JOHNSON, Thomasine .... 202-319-6065...... 97 C
johnsotn@cua.edu
JOHNSON, Tim .... 318-487-7118.... 209 B
tjohnson@lacollege.edu
JOHNSON, Tim, P .... 937-766-7777.... 386 F
johnsont@cedarville.edu
JOHNSON, Timothy .... 336-334-5636.... 379 A
tjjohns3@uncg.edu
JOHNSON, Timothy .... 617-731-7116.... 244 B
johnsontim@pmc.edu
JOHNSON, Timothy, J .... 973-353-1037.... 314 E
timmerj@andromeda.rutgers.edu
JOHNSON, Tina .... 615-898-5910.... 473 F
ntjohnso@mtsu.edu
JOHNSON, Todd .... 757-683-3462.... 521 L
tjohnso@odu.edu
JOHNSON, Tonjanita .... 631-632-4418.... 352 C
tonjanita.johnson@stonybrook.edu
JOHNSON, Tony .... 903-983-8102.... 489 F
tjohnson@kilgore.edu
JOHNSON, Tony .... 401-454-6638.... 454 B
ajohnson@risd.edu
JOHNSON, Tony, W .... 843-953-5871.... 456 C
tony.johnson@citadel.edu
JOHNSON, Tonya, L .... 678-359-5011.... 131 D
tonyaj@gdn.edu
JOHNSON, Tracey .... 618-634-3271.... 164 C
traceyj@shawneecc.edu
JOHNSON, Tracie .... 615-383-4848.... 478 E
tjohnson@watkins.edu
JOHNSON, Troy .... 940-565-4602.... 504 B
tjohnson@unt.edu
JOHNSON, Trygve, D .... 616-395-7145.... 252 F
johnsont@hope.edu
JOHNSON, Tyron, S .... 407-582-1344.... 122 I
tjohnson@valenciacollege.edu
JOHNSON, Vernon .... 312-821-6300.... 144 E
JOHNSON, Vicki, M .... 731-989-6095.... 468 K
vjohnson@fhu.edu
JOHNSON, Victoria, D .... 504-865-5591.... 215 C
victoria@tulane.edu
JOHNSON, W. Stephen ..... 731-989-6632.... 468 K
sjohnson@fhu.edu
JOHNSON, W. Taylor .... 212-217-7999.... 333 G
wtaylor_johnson@fitnyc.edu
JOHNSON, Walter .... 601-979-2522.... 275 A
walter.l.johnson@jsums.edu
JOHNSON, Walter .... 864-977-7068.... 460 A
walter.johnson@ngu.edu
JOHNSON, Walter .... 919-546-8383.... 376 D
wjohnson@shawu.edu
JOHNSON, Warner, O .... 412-397-3287.... 445 G
johnsonw@rmu.edu
JOHNSON, Wayne, E .... 704-406-4331.... 364 B
wjohnson@gardner-webb.edu
JOHNSON, Wendy .... 225-675-8270.... 211 J
wjohnson@rpcc.edu
JOHNSON, Wendy .... 713-777-4433.... 508 I
wjohnson01@westwood.edu
JOHNSON, Wendy .... 937-393-3431.... 401 K
wjohnson@sscc.edu
JOHNSON, William, H .... 203-254-4000...... 92 B
wjohnson@fairfield.edu
JOHNSON, William, L .... 313-927-1226.... 255 A
wjohnson@marygrove.edu
JOHNSON, Yvonne, J .... 314-984-7665.... 289 D
yjohnson@stlcc.edu
JOHNSON-BAILEY,
Juanita .... 706-542-2846.... 138 C
jjb@uga.edu
JOHNSON-BLAKE,
Deborah .... 404-225-4491.... 125 A
djohnsonblake@atlantatech.edu
JOHNSON-CRAFT, Shirley . 928-757-0857...... 16 G
sjohnsoncraft@mohave.edu
JOHNSON-EANES,
Berenecea .... 212-237-8100.... 328 A
bjeanes@jjay.cuny.edu
JOHNSON-FANNIN,
Arcelia .... 210-883-1015.... 503 F
johnsonf@uiwtx.edu
JOHNSON HADLEY,
Erma, C .... 817-515-5100.... 496 A
erma.johnson-hadley@tccd.edu
JOHNSON-HAWKINS,
Alma .... 818-364-7635...... 55 A
johnsonal@lamission.edu
JOHNSON-HOUSTON,
Debbie, L .... 337-475-5716.... 215 G
djohnsonhouston@mcneese.edu
JOHNSON-KINCAID,
Denise .... 812-429-1430.... 176 I
ajohnson@ivytech.edu
JOHNSON-ODIM, Cheryl .. 708-524-6813.... 150 A
cjohnson-odim@dom.edu
JOHNSON-ROSS, Debora .. 410-386-4632.... 224 D
djohnson@mcdaniel.edu
JOHNSON SHAHEED,
Karen .... 301-860-3462.... 228 A
kshaheed@bowiestate.edu
JOHNSON-TAYLOR,
Don, W .... 803-321-5112.... 459 G
don.johnson-taylor@newberry.edu
JOHNSON-WEEKS,
Demetria .... 713-313-7940.... 499 G
weeks_dj@tsu.edu
JOHNSON-WHATLEY,
Jeanne .... 404-270-2803.... 128 G
jjohnson-whatley@devry.edu
JOHNSON WILLIAMS,
Nikki .... 540-362-6217.... 519 E
nwilliams@hollins.edu
JOHNSON-WILLIAMS,
Shawn .... 608-663-2312.... 547 C
johnson@edgewood.edu
JOHNSRUD, Courtney .... 406-771-4387.... 296 B
cjohnsrud@msugf.edu
JOHNSRUD, Jason, C .... 202-462-2101...... 98 C
admissions@iwp.edu
JOHNSRUD, Linda, K .... 808-956-7075.... 140 J
johnsrud@hawaii.edu
JOHNSTON, Adena .... 215-553-7952.... 427 C
ajohnston@devry.edu
JOHNSTON, Adena .... 215-591-5758.... 427 A
ajohnston@devry.edu
JOHNSTON, Alysia .... 620-251-7700.... 191 I
alysiaj@coffeyville.edu
JOHNSTON, Amy, J .... 260-480-4255.... 176 D
ajohnston18@ivytech.edu
JOHNSTON, Andrew, J ...... 615-460-6407.... 467 B
andrew.johnston@belmont.edu
JOHNSTON, Angela .... 330-263-2313.... 388 E
ajohnston@wooster.edu
JOHNSTON, Bonnie .... 415-451-2812...... 66 B
bjohnston@sfts.edu
JOHNSTON, Brian .... 216-373-5252.... 397 E
bjohnston@ndc.edu
JOHNSTON, Brian, A .... 202-319-6425...... 97 C
johnston@cua.edu
JOHNSTON, Cheryl, L .... 724-847-6577.... 429 G
cljohnst@geneva.edu
JOHNSTON, Chris .... 209-946-2967...... 75 D
cjohnston@pacific.edu
JOHNSTON, Christine, D ... 309-457-2327.... 158 G
cjohnsto@monm.edu
JOHNSTON, Daniel .... 402-354-7080.... 299 E
dan.johnston@methodistcollege.edu
JOHNSTON, Daryl .... 352-334-0300.... 117 E
daryl.johnston@sfcollege.edu
JOHNSTON, Deborah .... 907-564-8204...... 10 D
debj@alaskapacific.edu
JOHNSTON, Dexter, L .... 310-434-4549...... 68 D
johnston_dexter@smc.edu
JOHNSTON, Dusty, R .... 940-552-6291.... 507 E
drj@vernoncollege.edu
JOHNSTON, E. Bubby .... 601-635-2111.... 274 C
bjohnston@eccc.edu
JOHNSTON, Emily .... 251-460-6231........ 9 E
ejohnsto@usouthal.edu
JOHNSTON, F. Bruce .... 870-307-7247...... 22 D
bjohnston@lyon.edu
JOHNSTON, Glynn .... 386-506-6301.... 103 J
johnstong@DaytonaState.edu
JOHNSTON, Gordon, T ...... 573-840-9654.... 290 J
gordonj@trcc.edu
JOHNSTON, James, K .... 219-989-2232.... 178 G
johnston@purduecal.edu
JOHNSTON, Jed .... 402-826-8604.... 298 A
jed.johnston@doane.edu
JOHNSTON, Jeff .... 574-520-4454.... 174 C
jjohnsto@iusb.edu
JOHNSTON, Jeffrey .... 907-747-7704...... 11 A
jeff.johnston@uas.alaska.edu
JOHNSTON, Jobyna .... 563-425-5279.... 189 C
johnstonj@uiu.edu
JOHNSTON, John .... 212-217-3600.... 333 G
john_johnston@fitnyc.edu
JOHNSTON, John, E .... 517-265-5161.... 247 D
jjohnston@adrian.edu

JONES, Ericka, D ... 512-505-3040 ... 488 B
edjones@htu.edu
JONES, Faye ... 615-353-3556 ... 475 D
faye.jones@nscc.edu
JONES, Frances ... 309-677-2646 ... 145 H
fjc@bradley.edu
JONES, Freida ... 478-825-6363 ... 129 C
jonesf@fvsu.edu
JONES, Garry ... 407-679-0100 ... 110 C
gjones@fullsail.com
JONES, Garry ... 662-243-2643 ... 274 D
gjones@eastms.edu
JONES, Gary ... 618-252-5400 ... 164 G
gary.jones@sic.edu
JONES, Gena ... 806-743-2865 ... 501 E
gena.jones@ttuhsc.edu
JONES, Geoffrey ... 952-487-8191 ... 268 C
geoffrey.jones@normandale.edu
JONES, George, A ... 606-759-7141 ... 202 D
george.jones@kctcs.edu
JONES, Geraldine ... 434-848-6410 ... 523 G
gjones@saintpauls.edu
JONES, Geraldine ... 724-938-4407 ... 441 G
jones_gm@calu.edu
JONES, Gina ... 803-323-2194 ... 463 D
JONES, Gladys, J ... 601-977-7821 ... 277 F
gjones@tougaloo.edu
JONES, Glendell ... 870-972-2030 ... 20 C
gjones@astate.edu
JONES, Glenna, S ... 815-224-0230 ... 153 D
glenna_jones@ivcc.edu
JONES, Gloria ... 803-323-3900 ... 463 D
jonesg@winthrop.edu
JONES, Grace, S ... 860-383-5201 ... 91 B
gjones@trcc.commnet.edu
JONES, Grady ... 904-608-9840 ... 383 J
JONES, Gwen ... 937-512-4294 ... 401 J
gwen.jones@sinclair.edu
JONES, Gwendolyn ... 937-512-2509 ... 401 J
gwendolyn.jones@sinclair.edu
JONES, Harold ... 903-675-6256 ... 502 D
hjones@tvcc.edu
JONES, Harold, P ... 205-934-5149 ... 8 G
jonesh@uab.edu
JONES, Harriett, S ... 706-821-8219 ... 135 C
hjones@paine.edu
JONES, Indgrid ... 561-297-3959 ... 118 H
ijones7@fau.edu
JONES, J. Pernell ... 610-341-5948 ... 428 D
pjones1@eastern.edu
JONES, J. Robert ... 706-649-1837 ... 127 E
bjones@columbustech.edu
JONES, Jacquelyn, K ... 573-882-4097 ... 291 D
jonesjk@missouri.edu
JONES, Jahmil ... 214-234-4850 ... 486 F
jjones@cci.edu
JONES, James ... 843-863-7665 ... 456 B
jjones@csuniv.edu
JONES, JR., James, F ... 860-297-2086 ... 94 C
james.f.jones@trincoll.edu
JONES, James, M ... 812-888-5555 ... 181 B
jjones@vinu.edu
JONES, James, V ... 716-888-2475 ... 325 G
jones11@canisius.edu
JONES, James, W ... 405-425-5150 ... 409 E
jay.jones@oc.edu
JONES, Jamie ... 620-235-4185 ... 195 I
jjones@pittstate.edu
JONES, Jane, M ... 423-439-4211 ... 473 E
jonesj@etsu.edu
JONES, Janet ... 937-512-2514 ... 401 J
janet.jones@sinclair.edu
JONES, Jay ... 870-460-1022 ... 25 A
jonesj@uamont.edu
JONES, Jayne, W ... 479-968-0400 ... 20 G
jjones@atu.edu
JONES, Jeff ... 574-520-4252 ... 174 C
jones427@iusb.edu
JONES, Jeff ... 415-380-1488 ... 48 D
jeffjones@ggbts.edu
JONES, Jeffrey ... 570-422-3833 ... 442 C
jjones@po-box.esu.edu
JONES, Jeffrey, A ... 724-847-6512 ... 429 G
JONES, Jennifer ... 815-455-8770 ... 157 F
jjones@mchenry.edu
JONES, Jennifer ... 201-200-3005 ... 312 B
jjones@njcu.edu
JONES, Jennine ... 541-684-7244 ... 417 F
jjones@northwestchristian.edu
JONES, Jenny ... 859-246-6653 ... 201 D
jenny.jones@kctcs.edu
JONES, Jenny, E ... 512-542-7834 ... 496 G
jjones@tamhsc.edu
JONES, JeraiLyn ... 414-372-4345 ... 547 I
jerailyn@lakeside.edu
JONES, Jessica ... 815-921-4755 ... 162 F
j.jones@rockvalleycollege.edu
JONES, Jessica, S ... 252-246-1216 ... 375 B
jjones@wilsoncc.edu
JONES, Jim ... 316-942-4291 ... 195 C
jonesj@newmanu.edu
JONES, Jim ... 706-721-0011 ... 130 B
jjones@georgiahealth.edu
JONES, Jim ... 325-670-1207 ... 487 D
jjones@hsutx.edu
JONES, Jimmie, L ... 513-785-3283 ... 396 E
jonesjl@muohio.edu
JONES, Jimmy ... 202-806-1280 ... 98 B
jimmy.jones@howard.edu
JONES, JoAnna ... 252-492-2061 ... 374 D
jonesj@vgcc.edu
JONES, John ... 530-251-8877 ... 53 G
jjones@lassencollege.edu
JONES, John ... 765-677-2387 ... 174 E
john.jones@indwes.edu
JONES, John ... 803-536-4974 ... 460 G
jjones@scsu.edu
JONES, John, D ... 803-786-3966 ... 457 C
jdjones@columbiasc.edu
JONES, John, P ... 520-621-1112 ... 19 B
jpjones@email.arizona.edu
JONES, John, R ... 479-788-7912 ... 24 D
jrjones@uafortsmith.edu
JONES, John, S ... 772-546-5534 ... 110 J
johnjones@hsbc.edu
JONES, John Raymond ... 815-753-6100 ... 160 A
jrjones@niu.edu
JONES, Johnnye ... 903-593-8311 ... 499 A
jjones@texascollege.edu
JONES, Jon ... 417-268-6110 ... 279 D
jjones@gobbc.edu
JONES, Joseph ... 773-244-5648 ... 159 G
jjones@northpark.edu
JONES, Joyce ... 706-737-1411 ... 125 C
jjones@aug.edu
JONES, Judy ... 870-245-5578 ... 22 I
jonesj@obu.edu
JONES, Judy ... 979-532-6561 ... 508 J
judyj@wcjc.edu
JONES, Karen ... 828-286-3636 ... 371 A
kjones@isothermal.edu
JONES, Karen ... 717-815-1787 ... 452 F
kjones@ycp.edu
JONES, Karen, B ... 843-953-5773 ... 457 B
jonesk@cofc.edu
JONES, Karen, S ... 478-289-2012 ... 128 J
kjones@ega.edu
JONES, Katherine ... 919-735-5151 ... 374 F
kathyj@waynecc.edu
JONES, Kathleen, M ... 515-294-1840 ... 182 B
kmjones@iastate.edu
JONES, Kathryn ... 803-705-4865 ... 455 D
jonesk@benedict.edu
JONES, Kathryn, C ... 870-972-3027 ... 20 C
kjones@astate.edu
JONES, Katie ... 413-565-1000 ... 231 B
kjones@baypath.edu
JONES, Katrina ... 812-330-6042 ... 175 H
katjones@ivytech.edu
JONES, Keith ... 410-752-4710 ... 221 E
kjones@bic.edu
JONES, Ken ... 818-767-0888 ... 79 D
ken.jones@woodbury.edu
JONES, Ken, A ... 918-595-7029 ... 412 H
kjones@tulsacc.edu
JONES, Kenneth ... 205-929-1459 ... 5 H
academics@mail.miles.edu
JONES, Kent ... 256-228-6001 ... 6 A
jonesk@nacc.edu
JONES, Kevin ... 863-638-7213 ... 123 B
kevin.jones@warner.edu
JONES, Kim ... 361-593-2187 ... 498 A
krkdy00@tamuk.edu
JONES, Kim ... 731-668-7240 ... 478 F
kim.jones@wtbc.edu
JONES, Kona ... 217-875-7200 ... 162 D
kona@richland.edu
JONES, Kristen ... 406-756-3894 ... 294 D
kjones@fvcc.edu
JONES, Kristine ... 803-325-8025 ... 463 G
kjones@yorktech.edu
JONES, Kushi ... 951-343-4344 ... 31 G
kjones@calbaptist.edu
JONES, L. Ken ... 806-720-7125 ... 490 D
ken.jones@lcu.edu
JONES, Lance ... 307-268-2672 ... 555 F
ljones@caspercollege.edu
JONES, Larry, H ... 931-598-1187 ... 472 J
ljones@sewanee.edu
JONES, Larry, W ... 662-329-7282 ... 276 B
ljones@its.muw.edu
JONES, Laura, B ... 734-764-7423 ... 259 D
laurabj@umich.edu
JONES, Laurel ... 408-855-5122 ... 78 A
laurel.jones@wvm.edu
JONES, Laurene ... 609-586-4800 ... 311 C
jonesl@mccc.edu
JONES, Laurie, S ... 706-568-2005 ... 127 D
jones_laurie@columbusstate.edu
JONES, Lee ... 901-755-9399 ... 233 B
lee.jones@cambridgecollege.edu
JONES, JR., Lee ... 575-624-8250 ... 319 C
jones@nmmi.edu
JONES, Lewis ... 937-708-5684 ... 405 G
ljones@wilberforce.edu
JONES, Linda ... 312-341-2440 ... 162 I
ljones@roosevelt.edu
JONES, Linda, E ... 607-871-2767 ... 322 F
jones@alfred.edu
JONES, Linda, M ... 254-968-9104 ... 496 F
ljones@tarleton.edu
JONES, Linda Kay ... 575-538-6133 ... 321 I
jonesl6@wnmu.edu
JONES, Lirse ... 973-720-2101 ... 317 D
jonesl@wpunj.edu
JONES, Lisa ... 845-257-3216 ... 352 B
jonesl@newpaltz.edu
JONES, Lisa ... 801-832-2237 ... 512 F
ljones@westminstercollege.edu
JONES, Lisa, R ... 785-670-1712 ... 197 D
lisa.jones@washburn.edu
JONES, Marcia, A ... 913-588-4876 ... 197 A
mjones@kumc.edu
JONES, Marcus ... 318-357-5701 ... 216 B
marcusj@nsula.edu
JONES, Margaret ... 914-422-4043 ... 345 F
mjones@pace.edu
JONES, Marian ... 704-378-1074 ... 365 H
myjones@jcsu.edu
JONES, Mark, A ... 954-262-7893 ... 114 B
jonesmar@nsu.nova.edu
JONES, Marvin, L ... 410-651-6144 ... 227 E
mljones@umes.edu
JONES, Mary ... 870-575-8461 ... 25 B
jonesm@uapb.edu
JONES, Mary ... 405-491-6609 ... 412 D
mjones@snu.edu
JONES, Mary, C ... 502-213-2200 ... 202 B
maryc.jones@kctcs.edu
JONES, Mary, O ... 814-371-6920 ... 427 H
mainc@dbcollege.com
JONES, Matteel ... 843-525-8216 ... 461 E
JONES, Matthew Robert ... 317-738-8018 ... 171 C
mjones2@franklincollege.edu
JONES, Mattie ... 386-752-1822 ... 108 C
mattie.jones@fgc.edu
JONES, Maurice ... 510-748-2234 ... 62 B
majones@peralta.edu
JONES, Melanie ... 803-376-5728 ... 455 B
mjones@allenuniversity.edu
JONES, Melinda, L ... 901-678-2690 ... 474 C
mljones6@memphis.edu
JONES, Melissa ... 651-846-3406 ... 261 E
mejones@argosy.edu
JONES, Melissa, A ... 910-678-8474 ... 370 B
jonesma@faytechcc.edu
JONES, Michael ... 601-925-3819 ... 275 E
jones01@mc.edu
JONES, Michelle, M ... 570-321-4031 ... 435 D
jones@lycoming.edu
JONES, Mike ... 325-649-8830 ... 488 A
mjones@hputx.edu
JONES, Monique ... 312-935-2003 ... 162 E
mqjones@robertmorris.edu
JONES, Monique, J ... 731-426-7575 ... 469 M
mjones@lanecollege.edu
JONES, Murel, M ... 252-335-3944 ... 377 D
mmjones@mail.ecsu.edu
JONES, Nancy, A ... 816-654-7039 ... 283 J
njones@kcumb.edu
JONES, Nancy, L ... 804-524-5976 ... 529 C
nljones@vsu.edu
JONES, Ned, J ... 518-783-2423 ... 350 I
jones@siena.edu
JONES, Nicholas, P ... 410-516-4050 ... 223 F
npjones@jhu.edu
JONES, Norman ... 256-372-8653 ... 1 A
norman.jones@aamu.edu
JONES, Norman ... 215-489-2491 ... 426 H
Robert.Yapsuga@delval.edu
JONES, Pamela ... 972-241-3371 ... 484 D
pjones@dallas.edu
JONES, Pamela, R ... 716-880-2451 ... 340 E
pamela.r.jones@medaille.edu
JONES, Para ... 864-592-4655 ... 461 C
jonesp@sccsc.edu
JONES, Patricia ... 301-736-3631 ... 224 B
patricia.jones@msbbcs.edu
JONES, Patricia ... 863-297-1025 ... 115 A
pjones@polk.edu
JONES, Patricia, C ... 636-227-2100 ... 284 E
patricia.jones@logan.edu
JONES, Patrick ... 518-464-8500 ... 333 F
pjones@excelsior.edu
JONES, Patty ... 727-341-3141 ... 116 F
jones.patty@spcollege.edu
JONES, Paul, A ... 478-445-5148 ... 129 F
paul.jones@gcsu.edu
JONES, Peter ... 215-204-2044 ... 447 G
peter.jones@temple.edu
JONES, Phil ... 772-546-5534 ... 110 J
philjones@hsbc.edu
JONES, JR., Philip, M ... 704-687-2181 ... 378 E
pmjones@uncc.edu
JONES, Phyllis ... 307-778-1179 ... 556 B
pjones@lccc.wy.edu
JONES, Pocahantas ... 252-862-1222 ... 372 H
jonesp@roanokechowan.edu
JONES, R. Thomas ... 805-756-1414 ... 33 F
rtjones@calpoly.edu
JONES, Randall, T ... 901-542-3900 ... 99 D
ran@strayer.edu
JONES, Randy ... 302-857-6230 ... 95 F
ljones@desu.edu
JONES, Randy ... 805-565-7048 ... 78 F
rjones@westmont.edu
JONES, Rauchelle ... 281-283-2536 ... 503 C
jonesrau@uhcl.edu
JONES, Rene ... 870-733-6722 ... 22 E
rjones@midsouthcc.edu
JONES, Renee, P ... 910-277-5331 ... 376 A
jonesrp@sapc.edu
JONES, Richard ... 856-256-4040 ... 314 A
jonesri@rowan.edu
JONES, Richard ... 718-270-5128 ... 328 D
richardj@mec.cuny.edu
JONES, Rilla, C ... 662-720-7411 ... 276 D
rjones@nemcc.edu
JONES, Robert ... 303-762-6913 ... 83 I
robert.jones@denverseminary.edu
JONES, Robert, A ... 317-788-3304 ... 180 C
rjones@uindy.edu
JONES, Robert, H ... 304-293-4611 ... 544 E
robert.jones@mail.wvu.edu
JONES, Robert, J ... 612-624-3533 ... 272 D
jones012@umn.edu
JONES, Robert, P ... 915-831-3112 ... 486 E
rjones35@epcc.edu
JONES, Robin ... 575-769-4921 ... 317 K
robin.jones@clovis.edu
JONES, Robin ... 575-769-4954 ... 317 K
robin.jones@clovis.edu
JONES, Rockwell, F ... 740-368-3000 ... 400 F
rfjones@owu.edu
JONES, Roger ... 704-461-6665 ... 362 B
rogerjones@bac.edu
JONES, Ron ... 714-564-6319 ... 63 F
jones_ron@sac.edu
JONES, Ronald, L ... 901-272-5100 ... 471 B
rjones@mca.edu
JONES, Rosa ... 305-348-2797 ... 119 B
rosa.jones@fiu.edu
JONES, Rosalie, I ... 215-596-8697 ... 450 A
r.jones@usciences.edu
JONES, Rose, L ... 218-755-2041 ... 266 B
rjones@bemidjistate.edu
JONES, JR., Ross ... 386-312-4162 ... 116 D
rossjones@sjrstate.edu
JONES, Rubye ... 502-597-6671 ... 203 D
rubye.jones@kysu.edu
JONES, Sam ... 850-729-4929 ... 114 A
joness@nwfsc.edu
JONES, Sam ... 601-477-4038 ... 275 B
sam.jones@jcjc.edu
JONES, Samuel, B ... 843-953-6367 ... 457 B
jonessa@cofc.edu
JONES, Samuel, E ... 757-221-2565 ... 517 J
sejone@wm.edu
JONES, Samuel, T ... 731-989-6992 ... 468 K
sjones@fhu.edu
JONES, Sandra ... 870-743-3000 ... 22 G
sjones@northark.edu
JONES, Sara ... 626-463-5656 ... 19 C
sara.jones@apollogrp.edu
JONES, Sarah, L ... 540-464-7667 ... 529 A
jonessl10@vmi.edu
JONES, Scott ... 765-455-9380 ... 173 E
scotjone@iuk.edu
JONES, Serene ... 212-280-1403 ... 358 G
sjones@uts.columbia.edu
JONES, Sharon ... 503-943-7314 ... 420 G
JONES, Shawn ... 562-860-2451 ... 38 J
sjones@cerritos.edu
JONES, Sheba ... 312-662-4131 ... 144 C
sjones@adler.edu
JONES, Sheila ... 570-389-4027 ... 441 F
sjones@bloomu.edu
JONES, Sherra ... 201-216-5799 ... 315 E
sjones@stevens.edu
JONES, Sherry ... 602-275-7133 ... 18 D
sherry@rsiaz.edu
JONES, Sloan, W ... 678-717-3836 ... 129 D
sjones@gsc.edu
JONES, Stacey ... 479-788-7302 ... 24 D
sjones@uafortsmith.edu
JONES, Stanley ... 229-333-5727 ... 138 F
sjones@valdosta.edu
JONES, Stanton, L ... 630-752-5004 ... 168 F
stanton.jones@wheaton.edu
JONES, Stephen ... 864-242-5100 ... 455 E
JONES, Stephen ... 937-484-1300 ... 405 A
sjones@urbana.edu
JONES, Stephen, M ... 801-422-8271 ... 509 D
stephen_jones@byu.edu
JONES, Stephen, W ... 330-569-5128 ... 391 H
jonessw@hiram.edu
JONES, Steve ... 904-826-0084 ... 122 G
sjones@usa.edu
JONES, Steven ... 309-341-7356 ... 155 E
sjones@knox.edu
JONES, Steven, G ... 570-941-7526 ... 450 B
joness21@scranton.edu
JONES, Stuart ... 434-791-7110 ... 516 D
sdjones@averett.edu

JOYCE-BRADY, Jean .... 617-732-2178.... 241 F
jean.joyce-brady@mcphs.edu
JOYE, Teresa .... 510-649-2410...... 48 H
tjoye@gtu.edu
JOYNER, Brenda .... 504-865-2476.... 213 F
bjoyner@loyno.edu
JOYNER, Deborah .... 252-638-7264.... 369 E
joynerd@cravencc.edu
JOYNER, James, N .... 540-464-7096.... 529 A
joynerjm@vmi.edu
JOYNER, Jennifer .... 706-507-8956.... 127 D
joyner_jennifer@columbusstate.edu
JOYNER, Laurie .... 407-646-2185.... 116 B
ljoyner@rollins.edu
JOYNER, Patsy, R .... 757-569-6791.... 527 E
pjoyner@pdc.edu
JOYNER, Scott .... 912-344-2541.... 124 E
scott.joyner@armstrong.edu
JOYNER, SR., Stephen ...... 704-330-1406.... 365 H
sjoyner@jcsu.edu
JOYNER, Stephen, E .... 718-951-5114.... 326 G
sjoyner@brooklyn.cuny.edu
JOYNER-GRAHAM, JoAnn 718-270-4832.... 328 D
jjoyner@mec.cuny.edu
JOYNTON, Olin .... 989-358-7246.... 247 G
joyntono@alpenacc.edu
JOZAITIS, Judy .... 217-786-2200.... 156 I
judy.jozaitis@llcc.edu
JOZWIAK, Lisa .... 419-559-2355.... 402 D
ljozwiak01@terra.edu
JROSKI, Linda, L .... 610-330-5017.... 433 B
jroskil@lafayette.edu
JUARBE, Lorraine .... 787-763-6425.... 562 F
ljuarbe@inter.edu
JUARBE, Miriam .... 787-761-0640.... 561 B
asistenciaeconomica@cbp.edu
JUARBE, Myriam .... 787-720-4476.... 566 B
asistenciaeconomica@colmizpa.edu
JUAREZ, Benjamin .... 617-353-3334.... 232 G
bjuarez@bu.edu
JUAREZ, David .... 210-434-6711.... 491 G
djuarez4090@lake.ollusa.edu
JUAREZ, Elisa .... 520-494-5426...... 13 F
elisa.juarez@centralaz.edu
JUAREZ, Reina .... 858-534-3755...... 74 D
rjuarez@ucsd.edu
JUBIE, Kathie .... 218-879-0808.... 266 F
kjubie@fdltcc.edu
JUCHEMS, Jane, J .... 319-352-8521.... 189 F
jane.juchems@wartburg.edu
JUCHNIEWICZ, Tarcilia, M 201-559-6086.... 310 C
JUCHT, Craig .... 605-221-3110.... 464 C
cjucht@kilian.edu
JUCKIEWICZ, Robert, W .... 516-463-6900.... 335 H
robert.w.juckiewicz@hofstra.edu
JUDD, Cristle Collins .... 207-725-3578.... 217 E
cjudd@bowdoin.edu
JUDD, Deborah .... 301-846-2452.... 222 G
djudd@frederick.edu
JUDD, Kimberly .... 802-387-6723.... 513 E
kjudd@landmark.edu
JUDD, Maureen .... 617-726-6069.... 242 E
mjudd@mghihp.edu
JUDD, Phillip, H .... 304-766-3333.... 544 D
pjudd@wvstateu.edu
JUDD, T. Randy .... 435-652-7641.... 512 A
judd@dixie.edu
JUDD, Tim .... 270-789-5027.... 199 C
tmjudd@campbellsville.edu
JUDGE, Jeff .... 952-487-7272.... 268 C
jeff.judge@normandale.edu
JUDGE, Joseph .... 609-896-5121.... 313 G
jjudge@rider.edu
JUDGE, Kathleen, M .... 757-455-3298.... 529 F
kjudge@vwc.edu
JUDGE, Mark .... 321-253-2929.... 106 B
mjudge@cci.edu
JUDGE, Mark, W .... 321-253-2929.... 106 A
mjudge@cci.edu
JUDGE, Peter .... 803-323-2160.... 463 D
JUDGE, William .... 617-682-1553.... 234 G
wjudge@eds.edu
JUDY, Joyce, M .... 802-828-2800.... 515 D
judyj@ccv.edu
JUDY, Thomas, L .... 775-784-6662.... 303 A
tomj@unr.edu
JUEDES, Scott .... 781-283-1000.... 246 B
JUETTEMEYER, Tricia .... 503-228-6528.... 414 E
tjuettemeyer@aii.edu
JUGGANAIKLOO,
M. Spalding .... 208-496-7009.... 142 G
jugganaikloos@byui.edu
JUHL, Lavonne .... 501-812-2293...... 23 C
ljuhl@pulaskitech.edu
JUKOSKI, Mary Ellen .... 860-701-5027...... 93 B
jukoski_m@mitchell.edu
JULIA, Jake .... 847-491-2912.... 160 D
jjulia@northwestern.edu
JULIAN, Augusta, A .... 859-246-6501.... 201 D
augusta.julian@kctcs.edu
JULIAN, Betsy .... 707-864-7110...... 70 A
betsy.julian@solano.edu
JULIAN, Charity .... 812-749-1235.... 178 D
cjulian@oak.edu
JULIAN, James, R .... 617-287-7050.... 237 B
jjulian@email.umassp.edu
JULIAN, Leisa .... 765-285-1104.... 169 D
lijulian@bsu.edu
JULIAN, Tijuana, S .... 417-873-7215.... 281 H
tjulian@drury.edu
JULIAN, Tracey .... 423-636-7300.... 476 F
tjulian@tusculum.edu
JULIEN, Earlye, A .... 563-884-5476.... 188 C
earlye.julien@palmer.edu
JULIEN-MOLINEAUX,
Gabrielle .... 410-888-9048.... 226 F
gjulien-molineaux@tai.edu
JULIN, Paul .... 315-268-7718.... 329 C
pjulin@clarkson.edu
JULIO, Elizabeth .... 906-353-4600.... 253 J
liz@kbocc.org
JULIUS, Dan .... 907-450-8019...... 10 H
dan.julius@alaska.edu
JULIUS, David .... 815-967-7322.... 162 G
djulius@rockfordcareercollege.edu
JULIUS, James .... 760-757-2121...... 57 E
jjulius@miracosta.edu
JULIUS, Peg .... 319-398-1274.... 186 H
pjulius@kirkwood.edu
JULIUS, Peg .... 319-398-1274.... 186 H
peg.julius@kirkwood.edu
JULIUS, Tami .... 360-676-2772.... 535 F
tj@nwic.edu
JUMP, Jonathan, D .... 740-362-3440.... 396 A
jjump@mtso.edu
JUMP, Jonathan, D .... 740-363-1146.... 396 A
jjump@mtso.edu
JUMPER, Barbara .... 202-274-5140...... 99 F
bjumper@udc.edu
JUMPER, G. Robin .... 850-263-3261.... 101 E
grjumper@baptistcollege.edu
JUNCAJ, Lisa .... 718-862-7962.... 339 H
lisa.juncaj@manhattan.edu
JUNE, Jan, J .... 585-785-1273.... 334 A
juneje@flcc.edu
JUNE, Jane .... 508-854-4517.... 241 C
janej@qcc.mass.edu
JUNE, Vincent .... 678-891-2300.... 130 G
vincent.june@gpc.edu
JUNEJA, Renu .... 219-464-6880.... 181 A
renu.juneja@valpo.edu
JUNG, Barnabas .... 415-371-0002...... 60 A
JUNG, Jimmy .... 585-395-2772.... 352 F
jjung@brockport.edu
JUNG, Terence, D .... 832-252-4616.... 483 A
terry.jung@cbshouston.edu
JUNGKUNTZ, David .... 360-752-8355.... 531 C
djungkun@btc.ctc.edu
JUNGO, Rene .... 918-293-5026.... 410 E
rene.jungo@okstate.edu
JUNKANS, Lee .... 773-995-2327.... 146 D
ljunkans@csu.edu
JUNKER, Linda, K .... 301-447-5306.... 225 A
junker@msmary.edu
JUNKER, Tercio, B .... 317-937-9336.... 170 E
tjunker@cts.edu
JUNKERMAN, Charles, L .. 650-723-6866...... 71 F
clj@stanford.edu
JUNKERMAN, Lisa .... 407-646-1580.... 116 B
ljunkerman@rollins.edu
JUNKIN, Lawrence .... 410-857-2256.... 224 D
cjunkin@mcdaniel.edu
JUNN, Ellen .... 559-278-6639...... 34 D
ejunn@csufresno.edu
JUNOR, Bill .... 914-251-6460.... 354 D
bill.junor@purchase.edu
JUNSTRON, Ernie .... 412-281-2600.... 446 H
ejunstron@western-school.com
JURASEK, Richard, T .... 716-880-2202.... 340 E
richard.t.jurasek@medaille.edu
JURASINSKI, OSBM,
M. Cecilia .... 215-885-2360.... 435 E
scecilia@manor.edu
JURENA, Donna .... 402-826-8565.... 298 A
donna.jurena@doane.edu
JURENOVICH, David, M .... 210-829-6007.... 503 F
davidj@uiwtx.edu
JURGELA, Linda .... 617-735-9920.... 234 E
jurgela@emmanuel.edu
JURGENS, Ronald .... 800-567-2344.... 546 G
rjurgens@menominee.edu
JURGENS, William, K .... 321-674-8032.... 108 E
bjurgens@fit.edu
JURICH, Tom .... 502-852-5732.... 207 A
jurich@louisville.edu
JURICK, Donna, M .... 512-448-8412.... 493 B
donnaj@stedwards.edu
JURMA, William .... 308-865-8521.... 300 G
jurmaw@unk.edu
JUSIM, Stewart .... 954-752-1414.... 108 G
sjusim@aol.com
JUSKEVICE, Leigh .... 207-948-3131.... 219 H
ljuskevice@unity.edu
JUSKIEWICZ,
Mary Kathryn .... 802-728-1319.... 515 G
mjuskiewicz@vtc.edu
JUSSEAUME, Richard .... 330-490-7102.... 405 E
rjusseaume@walsh.edu
JUST, David, A .... 864-592-4805.... 461 C
justd@sccsc.edu
JUSTER, Fern, R .... 914-594-4507.... 343 F
fern_juster@nymc.edu
JUSTICE, Bobby .... 828-227-7321.... 379 E
justiceb@wcu.edu
JUSTICE, Brooke .... 270-901-1001.... 201 E
brooke.justice@kctcs.edu
JUSTICE, Gary .... 606-218-5294.... 207 B
gjustice@pc.edu
JUSTICE, George .... 573-884-4178.... 291 D
justiceg@missouri.edu
JUSTICE, Joshua .... 276-376-4514.... 525 C
jvj6e@uvawise.edu
JUSTICE, Katherine .... 281-283-2160.... 503 C
justice@uhcl.edu
JUSTICE, Lorraine .... 585-475-5436.... 347 G
JUSTICE, Melinda .... 606-886-3863.... 201 C
melinda.justice@kctcs.edu
JUSTICE, Stephen, C .... 949-451-5212...... 70 E
cjustice@ivc.edu
JUSTICE, Teresa, R .... 803-323-2460.... 463 D
justicet@winthrop.edu
JUSTIZ, Manuel, J .... 512-471-7255.... 505 B
mjustiz@mail.utexas.edu
JUSTUS, Cynthia .... 304-253-7351.... 541 D
cjustus@mountainstate.edu
JUTT, Kathy .... 260-484-4400.... 169 G
kjutt@brownmackie.edu
JUUSELA, Kari .... 617-266-1400.... 231 G
JWANIER, David .... 610-740-3790.... 424 I
djwanier@cedarcrest.edu

K

KAANOI, Aulani .... 808-739-8394.... 140 A
akaanoi@chaminade.edu
KAASA, Teri, L .... 919-536-7249.... 369 G
kaasat@durhamtech.edu
KAATRUDE, Peter, B .... 409-984-6216.... 500 H
peter.kaatrude@lamarpa.edu
KAATZ, Jeffry, M .... 951-785-2500...... 53 D
jkaatz@lasierra.edu
KAAZ, Barry .... 785-460-5429.... 191 J
barry.kaaz@colbycc.edu
KAAZ, Lisa .... 408-741-2065...... 78 B
lisa.kaaz@westvalley.edu
KABAB, Shawn .... 718-933-6700.... 341 G
skabab@monroecollege.edu
KABALA, Heather .... 724-836-9885.... 449 C
hlk3@pitt.edu
KABAT LENSCH, Ellen ...... 563-336-3331.... 184 B
ekabat@eicc.edu
KABBAZ, Michael, S .... 513-529-2075.... 396 D
mkabbaz@muohio.edu
KABETZKE, Donald .... 214-333-5305.... 484 C
donaldk@dbu.edu
KABISATPATHY, Ashok ..... 803-793-5105.... 457 F
kabisatpathya@denmarktech.edu
KACHEL, Tim .... 701-252-3467.... 381 A
kachel@jc.edu
KACHUR, John .... 412-434-6626.... 428 C
bksduquesne@bncollege.com
KACZMAREK, Christine .... 518-580-5813.... 351 B
ckaczmar@skidmore.edu
KACZOR, Adrian .... 561-912-2166.... 106 G
akaczor@evergladesuniversity.edu
KACZOROWSKI, Robert .... 856-227-7200.... 308 E
rkaczorowski@camdencc.edu
KADA, Solange .... 707-253-3313...... 58 F
skada@napavalley.edu
KADAVY, Matthew, T .... 402-465-2323.... 299 J
mtk@nebrwesleyan.edu
KADDEN, Jerome, H .... 410-484-7200.... 225 C
KADEL, Andrew .... 212-243-5150.... 334 E
kadel@gts.edu
KADEL, Jim .... 740-351-3270.... 401 I
jkadel@shawnee.edu
KADIR, Susan .... 561-868-3389.... 114 D
kadirs@palmbeachstate.edu
KADISH, Alan .... 212-463-0400...... 72 G
alan.kadish@touro.edu
KADISH, Alan .... 212-463-0400...... 72 H
alan.kadish@touro.edu
KADISH, Alan .... 914-594-4600.... 343 F
alan_kadish@nymc.edu
KADISH, Alan .... 212-463-0400.... 357 J
alan.kadish@touro.edu
KADISH, Steven, N .... 603-646-2715.... 305 A
steven.n.kadish@dartmouth.edu
KADLIK, MaryLou .... 207-602-2306.... 220 H
mkadlik@une.edu
KADUC, Maria .... 701-671-2616.... 382 E
maria.kaduc@ndscs.edu
KAEGI, Keli, A .... 413-597-4233.... 246 G
keli.a.kaegi@williams.edu
KAESS, Almabeth .... 719-384-6821...... 86 F
almabeth.kaess@ojc.edu
KAFATOS, Menas .... 714-289-2048...... 39 C
kafatos@chapman.edu
KAFELE, Fatima .... 718-488-1014.... 338 H
fatima.kafele@liu.edu
KAFER, August .... 304-424-8210.... 545 B
augie.kafer@mail.wvu.edu
KAFI, Farhoud .... 617-746-1990.... 236 B
farhoud.kafi@hult.edu
KAFTAN, John .... 315-792-3102.... 359 C
jkaftan@utica.edu
KAGAN, Aleksandra .... 718-261-5800.... 324 D
akagan@bramsonort.edu
KAGOL, Phillip .... 651-636-3305.... 270 H
phillip.kagol@rasmussen.edu
KAHALAS, Harvey .... 312-906-6596.... 153 B
kahalas@stuart.iit.edu
KAHALAS, Judith .... 617-427-0060.... 241 D
jkahalas@rcc.mass.edu
KAHAN, Abraham .... 718-782-7070.... 358 H
akahan@utsb.org
KAHAN, Miriam .... 714-415-6500...... 77 G
mkahan@westcoastuniversity.edu
KAHKEDJIAN, George .... 480-731-8102...... 15 F
george.kahkedjian@domail.maricopa.edu
KAHL, Meredith .... 843-347-2593.... 456 G
mkahl@coastal.edu
KAHL, Michael, D .... 585-389-2890.... 342 D
mkahl6@naz.edu
KAHLA, Steven .... 970-339-6683...... 80 G
steven.kahla@aims.edu
KAHLE, David, J .... 617-627-3435.... 245 F
david.kahle@tufts.edu
KAHLE, Lisa .... 607-753-5793.... 353 B
lisa.kahle@cortland.edu
KAHLER, James, W .... 808-853-1040.... 140 G
jimk@pacrim.edu
KAHLER, John .... 215-248-6397.... 435 B
jkahler@ltsp.edu
KAHLER, Kari, L .... 231-995-1228.... 256 G
kkahler@nmc.edu
KAHLER, Lewis .... 315-792-5537.... 341 E
lkahler@mvcc.edu
KAHLER, Mark .... 731-661-5543.... 476 G
mkahler@uu.edu
KAHLER, William .... 619-239-0391...... 37 D
wkahler@cwsl.edu
KAHLEY, Richard .... 301-696-3545.... 223 C
kahley@hood.edu
KAHLIG, Charla .... 254-295-5436.... 504 A
ckahlig@umhb.edu
KAHN, Alfred .... 281-283-2600.... 503 C
kahn@uhcl.edu
KAHN, Amy .... 877-798-0584...... 88 G
amy.kahn@rockies.edu
KAHN, Amy .... 585-395-2126.... 352 F
akahn@brockport.edu
KAHN, Avi .... 718-382-8702.... 360 J
KAHN, Carrie, W .... 716-270-5167.... 333 B
kahn@ecc.edu
KAHN, Fito .... 512-472-4133.... 494 B
fkahn@ssw.edu
KAHN, Henry .... 415-476-1683...... 74 E
henry.kahn@ucsf.edu
KAHN, James, R .... 212-746-0463.... 360 B
jkahn@med.cornell.edu
KAHN, Jay, V .... 603-358-2114.... 307 A
jkahn@keene.edu
KAHN, Lance, W .... 252-399-6388.... 362 A
lwkahn@barton.edu
KAHN, Patricia .... 732-224-2061.... 308 B
pkahn@brookdalecc.edu
KAHN, Robert .... 718-482-5073.... 328 C
bobkahn@lagcc.cuny.edu
KAHN, Shirley, S .... 205-934-0177...... 8 G
kahn@uab.edu
KAHN-JETTER, Zella .... 360-491-4700.... 536 F
zkahnjetter@stmartin.edu
KAHR, Audra .... 610-606-4630.... 424 I
ajhoffma@cedarcrest.edu
KAHRIG, Tammy .... 513-745-4845.... 406 E
kahrigt@xavier.edu
KAHRL, Sarah, H .... 740-427-5154.... 394 C
kahrls@kenyon.edu
KAHSAY, Million .... 303-937-4232...... 82 A
mkahsay@chu.edu
KAHWAJIAN, Z. Greg .... 626-873-2128...... 58 C
KAIDEN, Drew .... 718-488-1249.... 338 H
drew.kaiden@liu.edu
KAIKKONEN, Darby .... 360-596-5369.... 538 B
dkaikkonen@spscc.ctc.edu
KAIL, Pam .... 870-933-7900...... 20 B
pkail@asusystem.edu
KAIN, Douglas .... 209-384-6344...... 57 C
kain.d@mccd.edu
KAIN, Kassi .... 509-313-4100.... 534 A
kain@gonzaga.edu
KAIN, Michael, P .... 954-308-2622.... 100 I
mkain@aii.edu
KAINA, Steve .... 208-321-8800.... 142 H
skalina@brownmackie.edu
KAINTH, Pritpal .... 516-876-3207.... 353 D
kainthp@oldwestbury.edu
KAIRIS, Rob .... 330-499-9600.... 393 I
rkairis@kent.edu
KAISER, David, M .... 305-237-7445.... 113 H
dkaiser@mdc.edu
KAISER, Dick .... 605-394-2351.... 466 A
dick.kaiser@sdsmt.edu
KAISER, Farley .... 651-675-4700.... 264 H
fkaiser@twincitiesculinary.com

KARCH, Jason .... 406-683-7471.... 295 B
j_karch@umwestern.edu
KARCHER, Jeff .... 715-346-3901.... 552 B
jkarcher@uwsp.edu
KARCHER, Steve .... 859-985-3130.... 198 F
steve_karcher@berea.edu
KARDAN, Sal .... 213-621-2200...... 41 D
KARDONSKY, Stanley .... 716-878-4311.... 353 A
kardons@buffalostate.edu
KAREH, Krystal .... 801-840-4800.... 509 I
kkareh@cci.edu
KARGES, Teri .... 843-863-7050.... 456 B
tkarges@csuniv.edu
KARICKHOFF, Michael .... 765-459-0561.... 176 A
mkarickh@ivytech.edu
KARIM, Anwar .... 610-799-1925.... 434 D
akarim@lccc.edu
KARIM, Mohammad, A .... 757-683-3460.... 521 L
mkarim@odu.edu
KARIMKHANI, Denise .... 254-295-4636.... 504 A
karimkhani@umhb.edu
KARIMPOR, Mehdi .... 562-408-6969...... 26 H
KARIMPOUR, Mehdi .... 562-408-6969...... 26 H
KARKI, Bhagbat .... 716-888-2336.... 325 G
karkib@canisius.edu
KARL, Debbie .... 325-734-3640.... 500 C
debbie.karl@tstc.edu
KARLBERG, Anne Marie .... 360-383-3302.... 539 D
amkarlberg@whatcom.ctc.edu
KARLET, Herbert, J .... 304-696-3742.... 542 G
karlet@mctc.edu
KARLIN, Angela .... 816-501-4238.... 288 D
angela.karlin@rockhurst.edu
KARLIN, Barbara, H .... 415-442-7882...... 48 E
bkarlin@ggu.edu
KARLIN, Craig, E .... 785-628-4408.... 192 F
ckarlin@fhsu.edu
KARLIN, Jane .... 212-824-2212.... 391 E
jkarlin@huc.edu
KARLIN, Lisa, M .... 785-628-4232.... 192 F
lkarlin@fhsu.edu
KARLOFF, Michael .... 402-461-7473.... 298 C
mkarloff@hastings.edu
KARLOUTSOS, James, D ... 617-850-1290.... 236 A
jkarloutsos@hchc.edu
KARMANOVA, Tatiana .... 909-537-3986...... 36 A
tkarma@csusb.edu
KARMIS, Beth .... 312-949-7415.... 152 D
bkarmis@ico.edu
KARNES, Melinda Ann .... 716-673-3717.... 352 A
melinda.karnes@fredonia.edu
KARNES, Michael, S .... 585-753-3700.... 341 H
mkarnes@monroecc.edu
KARNES, Susan, J .... 816-781-7700.... 293 D
armstrongs@william.jewell.edu
KARNES, Valerie .... 760-384-6258...... 52 N
vkarnes@cerrocoso.edu
KARNIG, Albert, K .... 909-537-5002...... 36 A
akarnig@csusb.edu
KARNS, Jennifer, E .... 703-416-1441.... 519 F
jkarns@ipsciences.edu
KARNS, Julie, A .... 609-896-5016.... 313 G
karns@rider.edu
KARNS, Leslie .... 801-878-1402.... 303 D
lkarns@roseman.edu
KAROL, Diana .... 903-510-2127.... 502 E
dkar@tjc.edu
KAROLLE-BERG, Julia .... 216-397-4193.... 392 M
jkarolle@jcu.edu
KARON, Judith, S .... 218-726-7161.... 272 B
jkaron@d.umn.edu
KAROW, Thomas, R .... 312-341-3512.... 162 I
tkarow@roosevelt.edu
KARP, David .... 518-580-5779.... 351 B
dkarp@skidmore.edu
KARP, Emily .... 212-237-8488.... 328 A
ekarp@jjay.cuny.edu
KARP, Jeff .... 323-660-6166...... 40 G
jeff.karp@cleveland.edu
KARP, Jeff .... 913-234-0634.... 191 G
jeff.karp@cleveland.edu
KARP, Robert .... 518-564-4106.... 354 B
karprm@plattsburgh.edu
KARP, Roberta .... 518-891-2915.... 344 E
bkarp@nccc.edu
KARPALO, Nikolay .... 610-526-6012.... 430 D
facilities@harcum.edu
KARPER, Barbara, M .... 315-445-4530.... 338 B
karperbm@lemoyne.edu
KARPF, Michael .... 859-323-5126.... 206 H
mkarpf@uky.edu
KARPOVICH, Jeff, A .... 336-841-9011.... 365 A
jkarpovi@highpoint.edu
KARPP, Edward .... 818-240-1000...... 48 C
ekarpp@glendale.edu
KARR, Charles, L .... 205-348-6400........ 8 F
ckarr@eng.ua.edu
KARR, Forrest .... 907-474-6812...... 10 J
flkarr@alaska.edu
KARR, Mary .... 414-256-1251.... 549 A
karrm@mtmary.edu
KARR, Steve .... 865-471-3252.... 467 E
skarr@cn.edu
KARR, Susan .... 281-351-3644.... 490 C
susan.karr@lonestar.edu
KARRICK, Cathy .... 618-545-3182.... 155 A
ckarrick@kaskaskia.edu
KARRIKER, W. Keith .... 864-833-8220.... 460 E
kkarriker@presby.edu
KARRY, Cathy .... 313-664-7677.... 250 A
ckarry@collegeforcreativestudies.edu
KARSHMER, Judith .... 415-422-2959...... 76 B
jfkarshmer@usfca.edu
KARSTEN, Paul .... 206-517-4541.... 537 C
pkarsten@siom.edu
KARSTEN, Peter .... 989-729-3431.... 249 A
pete.karsten@baker.edu
KARSTEN, Suzanne .... 773-477-4822...... 60 E
skarsten@pacificcollege.edu
KARTHAUSER, Patricia, F .. 402-465-2551.... 299 J
pkart@nebrwesleyan.edu
KARTJE, Jean, V .... 815-825-2086.... 155 C
jean.kartje@kishwaukeecollege.edu
KARVIA, Nick .... 714-992-7009...... 59 D
nkarvia@fullcoll.edu
KARWOCKI, Michele .... 603-271-7140.... 304 G
mkarwocki@ccsnh.edu
KARWOWSKI, Sharon .... 607-844-8222.... 357 H
karwows@TC3.edu
KARY, Ken .... 785-826-2601.... 194 C
kkary@k-state.edu
KASCENSKA, John, R .... 802-626-6346.... 515 F
john.kascenska@lyndonstate.edu
KASDIN, Robert .... 212-854-9967.... 330 F
rk2052@columbia.edu
KASDORF, Michael .... 217-234-5431.... 155 H
mkasdorf@lakeland.cc.il.us
KASE, Robert .... 815-740-3367.... 167 C
rkase@stfrancis.edu
KASE, Ronald .... 201-684-7287.... 313 D
rkase@ramapo.edu
KASEM, Shahed .... 773-481-3730.... 160 C
skasem@nc.edu
KASENOW, Paul .... 270-831-9686.... 201 I
paul.kasenow@kctcs.edu
KASEY, Jack, D .... 614-293-9701.... 398 H
kasey.3@osu.edu
KASEY, Tina .... 270-686-2110.... 198 G
tina.kasey@brescia.edu
KASH, Elizabeth, F .... 516-877-3247.... 322 A
kash@adelphi.edu
KASHACK, Susan .... 707-664-2122...... 37 B
susan.kashack@sonoma.edu
KASHIMA, Stephanie .... 408-855-5319...... 78 A
stephanie.kashima@wvm.edu
KASHIRI, Anton .... 408-924-1950...... 37 A
anton.kashiri@sjsu.edu
KASHIWADA, Keith .... 808-734-9578.... 141 E
kashiwad@hawaii.edu
KASIM, Luke .... 215-751-8199.... 426 B
lkasim@ccp.edu
KASIMATIS, Margaret .... 310-338-3790...... 56 E
mkasimat@lmu.edu
KASINSKI, Nancy .... 815-753-9734.... 160 A
nancyk@niu.edu
KASKEL, Roberta .... 504-865-3835.... 213 F
rekaskel@loyno.edu
KASLER, Michael, J .... 714-484-7308...... 59 C
mkasler@cypresscollege.edu
KASLYN, SJ, Robert, J .... 202-319-5492...... 97 C
kaslyn@cua.edu
KASPARI, Brenda .... 701-355-8130.... 383 E
bkaspari@umary.edu
KASPER, Chet .... 906-248-8431.... 249 C
ckasper@bmcc.edu
KASPER, Lisa, A .... 973-655-6911.... 311 G
kasperl@mail.montclair.edu
KASSA, Zewdnesh .... 973-877-3107.... 310 A
zkassa@essex.edu
KASSAMALI, Fatma .... 909-621-8177...... 40 C
fatma.kassamali@cgu.edu
KASSEBAUM, Denise .... 303-724-7100...... 88 D
denise.kassebaum@ucdenver.edu
KASSEL, Sarah .... 541-552-6127.... 419 A
kassels@sou.edu
KASSIMIR, Ronald .... 212-229-8947.... 342 E
kassimir@newschool.edu
KASSNER, Scott .... 805-893-8000...... 74 F
skassner@ltsc.ucsb.edu
KASSNER, Tammy, J .... 205-588-2827........ 1 E
tkassner@aju.edu
KASSON, Jeff .... 614-823-1876.... 400 G
jkasson@otterbein.edu
KAST, Nancy .... 559-244-5998...... 71 I
nancy.kast@scccd.edu
KASTAN, Shira .... 305-284-2618.... 122 F
skastan@miami.edu
KASTER, James, D .... 540-458-8720.... 530 A
jdkaster@wlu.edu
KASTERN, Amanda, A .... 443-412-2345.... 223 B
akastern@harford.edu
KASTNER, Marc, A .... 617-253-8900.... 242 A
mkastner@mit.edu
KASTOR, Lisa .... 330-263-2496.... 388 E
lkastor@wooster.edu
KASUNIC, Lisa .... 330-966-5460.... 402 A
lkasunic@starkstate.edu
KASVINSKY, Peter, J .... 330-941-3091.... 406 F
pjkasvinsky@ysu.edu
KASYAN, Linda .... 910-362-7054.... 368 E
lkasyan@cfcc.edu
KASZA, John .... 248-683-0446.... 259 A
KATCHMAR, Paul .... 314-792-5510.... 341 E
pkatchmar@mvcc.edu
KATEHI, Linda, P .... 530-752-2065...... 73 F
chancellor@ucdavis.edu
KATEMAN, Mike .... 573-875-7563.... 280 E
mwkateman@ccis.edu
KATEN-BAHENSKY,
Donna .... 608-263-8025.... 550 G
dkaten-bahensky@uwhealth.org
KATER, Sue .... 602-286-8038...... 15 I
sue.kater@gwmail.maricopa.edu
KATES, Donald .... 215-780-1240.... 446 G
don@salus.edu
KATES, Jonathan, A .... 434-924-3721.... 525 B
jak7g@virginia.edu
KATES, Kenneth .... 319-356-3155.... 182 C
ken-kates@uiowa.edu
KATHMAN, Mary Jo .... 513-862-2743.... 391 D
KATHOL, Diane .... 402-481-8847.... 297 B
dkathol@bryanlgh.org
KATHOL, Lyle, J .... 402-844-7215.... 300 A
lylek@northeast.edu
KATHURIA, Navneet .... 713-798-4951.... 481 H
kathuria@bcm.edu
KATINAS, James .... 617-731-3500.... 236 A
jkatinas@hchc.edu
KATIP, William, J .... 574-372-5100.... 171 E
bill.katip@grace.edu
KATIS, David, J .... 814-393-1997.... 442 A
dkatis@clarion.edu
KATKANANT, Chanida .... 201-360-4014.... 310 F
ckatkanant@hccc.edu
KATO, Ken .... 808-845-9123.... 141 G
kato@hcc.hawaii.edu
KATO, Stephen .... 908-709-7045.... 316 B
kato@ucc.edu
KATOPES, Peter .... 718-482-5400.... 328 C
pkatopes@lagcc.cuny.edu
KATOS, Demetrios .... 617-850-1253.... 236 A
dkatos@hchc.edu
KATOSANG, Dahlia, M .... 680-488-2471.... 560 A
dahliapcc@palaunet.com
KATRENICZ, Laura .... 570-740-0384.... 435 C
lkatrenicz@luzerne.edu
KATSCHKE, Richard, N .... 414-955-4700.... 548 E
katschke@mcw.edu
KATSIAFICAS, Charles .... 909-621-8016...... 63 A
charles.katsiaficas@pomona.edu
KATSILOMETES, Bessie .... 208-373-1708.... 143 D
katsbess@isu.edu
KATSOULEAS, Thomas .... 919-660-5386.... 363 I
tom.katsouleas@duke.edu
KATT, Donald, C .... 845-687-5050.... 358 C
kattd@sunyulster.edu
KATTELMANN, Dean .... 605-688-4136.... 466 B
dean.kattelmann@sdstate.edu
KATTERMAN, Sharon .... 708-974-5271.... 159 A
katterman@morainevalley.edu
KATZ, Avi .... 800-371-6105...... 16 H
avi@nationalparalegal.edu
KATZ, Ben .... 617-928-4777.... 243 A
bkatz@mountida.edu
KATZ, Bernard .... 718-963-9770.... 358 H
bkatz@utsb.org
KATZ, Brit .... 601-974-1200.... 275 D
katzrb@millsaps.edu
KATZ, Clifford, H .... 401-874-4402.... 454 E
chkatz@uri.edu
KATZ, Craig .... 201-200-3022.... 312 B
ckatz@njcu.edu
KATZ, David .... 626-284-2777...... 27 D
kdatz@alliant.edu
KATZ, Edward, J .... 828-250-3872.... 378 C
ekatz@unca.edu
KATZ, Elya .... 718-941-8000.... 341 A
KATZ, Harry, C .... 607-255-3230.... 331 C
hck2@cornell.edu
KATZ, Helen .... 309-268-8173.... 151 G
helen.mckay-katz@heartland.edu
KATZ, Jeffrey .... 270-745-6311.... 207 C
KATZ, Jeffrey .... 845-758-7501.... 323 F
katz@bard.edu
KATZ, Jonathan, N .... 626-395-4068...... 32 E
jkatz@caltech.edu
KATZ, Louis, H .... 202-994-6600...... 97 F
lkatz@gwu.edu
KATZ, Madelyn .... 213-749-4323...... 50 D
mkatz@huc.edu
KATZ, Martin, J .... 303-871-6301.... 88 E
mkatz@du.edu
KATZ, Matthew .... 909-469-5567...... 78 D
mkatz@westernu.edu
KATZ, Paul .... 856-361-2800.... 314 A
katzp@rowan.edu
KATZ, Sally .... 860-297-2444...... 94 C
sally.katz@trincoll.edu
KATZ, Saul, W .... 718-368-5051.... 328 B
bkatz@kbcc.cuny.edu
KATZENMEYER, Scott .... 216-781-9400.... 388 A
scottk@cie-wc.edu
KATZENMEYER, Scott .... 757-464-4600.... 530 E
instruct@cie-wc.edu
KATZMAN, Carol .... 212-854-5768.... 323 G
ckatzman@barnard.edu
KATZMAN, Gerald .... 518-694-7298.... 322 C
gerald.katzman@acphs.edu
KAUCHER, Ellie .... 800-877-4723.... 233 B
Ellie.Kaucher@cambridgecollege.edu
KAUFFMAN, Brad .... 803-799-9082.... 136 H
bkauffman@southuniversity.edu
KAUFFMAN, Dana .... 703-323-3750.... 527 C
tkauffman@nvcc.edu
KAUFFMAN, JR.,
John, M .... 910-893-1200.... 362 F
kauffmanj@campbell.edu
KAUFFMAN, Peg .... 717-872-3402.... 443 C
peg.kauffman@millersville.edu
KAUFFMAN, Steve .... 312-369-7383.... 148 B
skauffman@colum.edu
KAUFFMAN, Wendy .... 910-695-3814.... 373 E
kauffmanw@sandhills.edu
KAUFFMAN, William, R .... 314-977-3719.... 289 F
kauffman@slu.edu
KAUFMAN, Angela .... 817-257-7830.... 498 F
a.kaufman@tcu.edu
KAUFMAN, Daniel, J .... 678-407-5001.... 130 A
dkaufman@ggc.edu
KAUFMAN, Donald, E .... 812-888-5343.... 181 B
dkaufman@vinu.edu
KAUFMAN, Geof .... 253-680-7105.... 531 A
KAUFMAN, Kris, A .... 716-878-3000.... 353 A
kaufmaka@buffalostate.edu
KAUFMAN, Norman .... 561-297-3061.... 118 H
nkaufman@fau.edu
KAUFMAN, Patty .... 517-841-4528.... 248 I
patty.kaufman@baker.edu
KAUFMAN, Paula .... 217-333-0790.... 167 B
ptk@illinois.edu
KAUFMAN, Paulette .... 303-751-8700...... 81 D
kaufman@bel-rea.com
KAUFMAN, Robin .... 914-251-6030.... 354 D
robin.kaufman@purchase.edu
KAUFMAN KELLY, Lisa .... 530-283-0202...... 47 B
lkelly@frc.edu
KAUFMAN-OSBORN,
Timothy .... 509-527-5397.... 539 E
kaufmatv@whitman.edu
KAUFMANN, RSM,
Barbara .... 215-641-5570.... 430 C
kaufmann.b@gmc.edu
KAUFMANN, Marta .... 215-968-8242.... 423 E
kaufmann@bucks.edu
KAUFMANN, Nancy, K .... 636-529-0000.... 288 G
nkaufmann@slchcmail.com
KAUFMANN, Sandra .... 516-876-2715.... 353 D
kaufmanns@oldwestbury.edu
KAUKE, Donna .... 815-599-3688.... 152 A
donna.kauke@highland.edu
KAUKUS, Arlene, F .... 716-645-2231.... 351 G
arleneks@buffalo.edu
KAUL, Gitanjali .... 561-297-1333.... 118 H
gkaul@fau.edu
KAULFUS, John .... 210-458-4740.... 506 B
john.kaulfus@utsa.edu
KAUMEYER, Robert .... 214-841-3705.... 485 E
bkaumeyer@dts.edu
KAUNITZ, Carol .... 732-255-0400.... 312 D
ckaunitz@ocean.edu
KAUR, Kuldeep .... 530-741-6700...... 80 C
KAUR, Rajbir .... 516-364-0808.... 343 A
kaur@nycollege.edu
KAUS, Annette .... 575-835-5333.... 319 A
akaus@admin.nmt.edu
KAUS, Cheryl .... 609-652-4512.... 313 F
cheryl.kaus@stockton.edu
KAUSHAL, Janice .... 312-935-4852.... 162 E
jkaushal@robertmorris.edu
KAUSHANSKY, Kenneth .... 631-444-9011.... 352 C
kenneth.kashansky@stonybrook.edu
KAUSHIK, Suresh, C .... 334-420-4244........ 7 I
skaushik@trenholmstate.edu
KAUTZ, Barbara, K .... 413-748-3222.... 245 C
bkautz@spfldcol.edu
KAUTZ DE ARANGO,
Kathy .... 610-341-5870.... 428 D
kkautz2@eastern.edu
KAVALER, Bernard .... 860-493-0093...... 91 F
kavalerb@ct.edu
KAVALIER, Barbara .... 408-298-2181...... 67 C
KAVANAGH, Edward .... 203-582-8618...... 93 E
edward.kavanagh@quinnipiac.edu
KAVANAGH, Kathy, J .... 914-594-4487.... 343 F
kathy_johnston@nymc.edu
KAVANAGH, Kenneth .... 239-590-7007.... 119 A
kavanagh@fgcu.edu
KAVANAUGH, Maria, A .... 508-565-1331.... 245 D
mkavanaugh@stonehill.edu
KAVANAUGH, Michael .... 714-484-7108...... 59 C
mkavanaugh@cypresscollege.edu
KAVANAUGH, Steven .... 610-896-1141.... 430 G
skavanau@haverford.edu
KAVERMAN, Don .... 314-340-3534.... 282 I
kavermad@hssu.edu

KEIFFER, Connie .... 304-734-6606.... 542 D
ckeiffer@bridgemont.edu
KEILERS, Vikki .... 903-233-4141.... 489 K
vikkikeilers@letu.edu
KEILITZ, Craig, D .... 336-841-9057.... 365 A
ckeilitz@highpoint.edu
KEILLER, James, B .... 404-627-2681.... 126 A
james.keiller@beulah.org
KEILLOR, Robin .... 503-352-2081.... 419 E
keillor@pacificu.edu
KEILSON, Suzanne .... 410-617-2608.... 224 A
skeilson@loyola.edu
KEIM, Barbara .... 636-922-8573.... 288 E
bkeim@stchas.edu
KEIM, Barry, A .... 772-462-4705.... 110 L
bkeim@irsc.edu
KEIM, Howard .... 620-327-8233.... 193 C
howardk@hesston.edu
KEIN, Chris .... 207-948-3131.... 219 H
ckein@unity.edu
KEIRN, Christy, C .... 870-508-6107.... 20 E
ckeirn@asumh.edu
KEIRSTEAD, Carol, A .... 864-242-5100.... 455 E
KEISER, Arthur .... 954-776-4476.... 112 H
artk@keiseruniversity.edu
KEISER, Kurt .... 719-587-7161...... 80 F
kjkeiser@adams.edu
KEISER, Pamela, G .... 570-577-1238.... 423 D
pamela.keiser@bucknell.edu
KEISER, Sue, T .... 662-915-7111.... 277 G
stkeiser@olemiss.edu
KEISER, Thomas .... 757-479-3706.... 517 E
tkeiser@baptistseminary.edu
KEISLER, Ruben .... 501-337-5000...... 21 D
rkeisler@otcweb.edu
KEISLING, Bruce, L .... 502-897-4807.... 205 H
bkeisling@sbts.edu
KEISTER, Tripp .... 302-736-2369...... 96 G
keistertr@wesley.edu
KEITA, Alma, G .... 229-931-2708.... 131 B
KEITES, Jim .... 352-395-5536.... 117 E
jim.keites@sfcollege.edu
KEITGES, David .... 513-529-5623.... 396 D
dkeitges@muohio.edu
KEITH, Bruce .... 845-938-6321.... 558 G
Bruce.Keith@usma.edu
KEITH, Colleen, P .... 864-587-4236.... 461 D
keithc@smcsc.edu
KEITH, Dana, S .... 205-348-4530........ 8 F
dkeith@fa.ua.edu
KEITH, Donald, W .... 205-329-7911........ 3 B
don.keith@ecacolleges.com
KEITH, Edwin, M .... 662-325-2513.... 276 A
ekeith@saffairs.msstate.edu
KEITH, Jamie, L .... 352-392-1358.... 120 B
jlkeith@ufl.edu
KEITH, Jeffrey .... 813-626-8008...... 99 D
jeffrey.keith@strayer.edu
KEITH, Jeffrey, D .... 801-422-4331.... 509 D
jeff_keith@byu.edu
KEITH, Lisa, M .... 706-233-7250.... 136 E
lkeith@shorter.edu
KEITH, Nancy .... 806-291-3766.... 508 B
keithn@wbu.edu
KEITH, Paul, D .... 832-252-4603.... 483 A
paul.keith@cbshouston.edu
KEITH, Paula, S .... 618-536-3471.... 164 H
pkeith@siu.edu
KEITH, Shelby, C .... 318-797-5221.... 213 D
skeith@lsus.edu
KEITH, Shena .... 312-915-7283.... 157 A
smcnama@luc.edu
KEITH, Tim .... 928-505-3314...... 16 G
tkeith@mohave.edu
KEIZS, Marcia, V .... 718-262-2350.... 329 B
mkeizs@york.cuny.edu
KEKEC, Adrienne .... 215-895-2502.... 427 G
abk35@drexel.edu
KELAHER, James, E .... 713-798-7880.... 481 H
jkelaher@bcm.edu
KELCHNER, Dana .... 660-596-7250.... 290 F
dkelchner@sfccmo.edu
KELCHNER, Loretta, L .... 660-263-3900.... 279 J
lkelchner@cccb.edu
KELEDEI, Raymond, F .... 401-841-6594.... 557 I
KELEMAN, Frank .... 517-629-0236.... 247 E
fkeleman@albion.edu
KELEMEN, Mary, E .... 206-546-4733.... 537 G
mkelemen@shoreline.edu
KELEMEN, Paul .... 972-273-3590.... 485 B
pkelemen@dcccd.edu
KELIN, Shebon .... 303-632-2300...... 83 C
skelin@coloradotech.edu
KELL, Christine .... 814-866-8169.... 433 C
ckell@lecom.edu
KELL, Gwen .... 707-253-3328...... 58 F
gkell@napavalley.edu
KELL, Sheila .... 561-912-2166.... 106 G
skell@evergladesuniversity.edu
KELLAM, James, W .... 410-651-6174.... 227 E
jwkellam@umes.edu
KELLAR, Deborah .... 303-762-6881...... 83 I
debbie.kellar@denverseminary.edu
KELLAR, Katharine, E .... 724-653-2221.... 427 F
kkellar@dec.edu
KELLAR, Michelle .... 641-628-7523.... 183 A
kellarm@central.edu
KELLAR, Patricia, L .... 570-208-5845.... 432 E
plkellar@kings.edu
KELLARIS, William .... 540-338-1776.... 522 A
KELLEHER, Audrey .... 877-804-1424.... 273 F
akelleher@belhaven.edu
KELLEHER, Erin, C .... 978-665-3151.... 238 C
ekelleher@fitchburgstate.edu
KELLEHER, Maureen, E .... 617-373-2333.... 244 A
KELLEHER, William, J .... 413-782-1288.... 246 D
bkelleher@wne.edu
KELLEN, Jim .... 251-405-7086........ 2 D
jkellen@bishop.edu
KELLEN, Joni, K .... 515-574-1146.... 185 F
kellen@iowacentral.edu
KELLEN, Vincent, J .... 859-257-3609.... 206 H
vkellen@uky.edu
KELLENBENZ, Joe .... 215-780-1402.... 446 G
jkellenbenz@salus.edu
KELLER, Alison .... 248-218-2268.... 257 F
akeller@rc.edu
KELLER, Bill .... 718-368-5028.... 328 B
bkeller@kbcc.cuny.edu
KELLER, Bruce .... 215-572-2922.... 422 B
kellerb@arcadia.edu
KELLER, Chaim, D .... 773-463-7738.... 165 F
KELLER, Charlotte .... 928-757-0852...... 16 G
ckeller@mohave.edu
KELLER, Christopher, J .... 570-389-4740.... 441 F
ckeller@bloomu.edu
KELLER, Cindy .... 276-656-0337.... 527 D
ckeller@ph.vccs.edu
KELLER, David .... 248-218-2150.... 257 F
dkeller@rc.edu
KELLER, Donald, G .... 716-829-7675.... 332 F
kellerd@dyc.edu
KELLER, Elizabeth .... 800-287-8822.... 169 E
kelleel@bethanyseminary.edu
KELLER, Harrison .... 512-232-8277.... 505 B
harrison.keller@po.utexas.edu
KELLER, Heather .... 573-288-6570.... 281 D
hkeller@culver.edu
KELLER, James .... 650-306-3238...... 67 E
kellerj@smccd.edu
KELLER, Joe .... 661-362-2226...... 56 G
jkeller@masters.edu
KELLER, John .... 413-265-2210.... 233 E
kellerj@elms.edu
KELLER, John, C .... 319-335-2142.... 182 C
john-keller@uiowa.edu
KELLER, Jonathan .... 617-994-6941.... 237 A
jkeller@bhe.mass.edu
KELLER, Kara .... 828-254-1921.... 367 H
kkeller@abtech.edu
KELLER, Kathleen .... 402-474-5315.... 298 E
kkeller@kaplanuniversity.edu
KELLER, Kerri, D .... 785-532-6506.... 194 B
kdkeller@ksu.edu
KELLER, Kristina .... 320-308-5538.... 269 D
kkeller@sctcc.edu
KELLER, Linda, B .... 270-852-3110.... 203 C
lkeller@kwc.edu
KELLER, Lise, K .... 336-334-5243.... 379 A
lise_keller@uncg.edu
KELLER, Marlon, D .... 215-699-5700.... 433 G
mkeller@LSB.edu
KELLER, Mary .... 732-255-0400.... 312 D
mkeller@ocean.edu
KELLER, Michael, A .... 650-723-5553...... 71 F
michael.keller@stanford.edu
KELLER, Michael, J .... 904-276-6826.... 116 D
mikekeller@sjrstate.edu
KELLER, Michael, J .... 605-677-5455.... 465 E
mike.keller@usd.edu
KELLER, Mike .... 325-236-8253.... 500 C
mike.keller@tstc.edu
KELLER, Noel .... 909-621-8090...... 49 D
noel_keller@hmc.edu
KELLER, Peter .... 570-662-4804.... 443 B
pkeller@mansfield.edu
KELLER, Rebecca .... 518-262-8105.... 322 E
kellerr@mail.amc.edu
KELLER, Robert .... 970-491-5679...... 83 A
robert.keller@colostate.edu
KELLER, Scott .... 815-280-2775.... 154 H
skeller@jjc.edu
KELLER, Stephen, H .... 413-755-4440.... 241 E
keller@stcc.edu
KELLER, Susan .... 714-459-1141...... 78 C
skeller@wsulaw.edu
KELLER, Thomas .... 636-227-2100.... 284 E
thomas.keller@logan.edu
KELLER, Travis .... 740-392-6868.... 396 H
travis.keller@mvnu.edu
KELLER, Wayne .... 505-428-1223.... 320 E
wayne.keller@sfcc.edu
KELLER, JR., Willie .... 361-698-1245.... 485 F
wkeller@delmar.edu
KELLER-MCNULTY, Sallie .. 713-348-4009.... 492 J
deng@rice.edu
KELLER-RABER, Candace .. 407-355-4809.... 104 D
ckeller-raber@devry.edu
KELLERER, Eric, J .... 208-467-8350.... 143 I
ejkellerer@nnu.edu
KELLERHER, Paul, D .... 212-749-2802.... 339 I
pkellerher@msmnyc.edu
KELLERHOUSE, James .... 518-445-3209.... 322 D
jkell@albanylaw.edu
KELLERMAN, Larry .... 218-855-8178.... 266 C
lkellerm@clcmn.edu
KELLERSBERGER, Gail .... 713-221-8047.... 503 D
kellersbergerg@uhd.edu
KELLES, Anna .... 315-568-3292.... 342 H
akelles@nycc.edu
KELLETT, Chris .... 206-726-5180.... 532 G
ckellett@cornish.edu
KELLEY, Amber, L .... 512-223-2012.... 481 B
amberk@austincc.edu
KELLEY, Aundrea .... 617-994-6979.... 237 A
akelley@bhe.mass.edu
KELLEY, Benjamin, S .... 254-710-3871.... 481 I
ben_kelley@baylor.edu
KELLEY, Bev .... 620-241-0723.... 191 F
bev.kelley@centralchristian.edu
KELLEY, Brenda .... 334-214-4815........ 2 G
brenda.kelley@cv.edu
KELLEY, JR., Charles, S ... 504-282-4455.... 213 H
ckelley@nobts.edu
KELLEY, Danny, R .... 926-261-3180.... 496 E
drkelley@pvamu.edu
KELLEY, Dave .... 503-554-2167.... 415 I
dkelley@georgefox.edu
KELLEY, Debbie, D .... 417-625-9805.... 286 E
kelley-d@mssu.edu
KELLEY, Ella .... 225-771-4845.... 214 H
ella_kelley@aol.com
KELLEY, Gary, D .... 806-651-3451.... 498 D
gkelley@mail.wtamu.edu
KELLEY, Gary, F .... 978-232-2048.... 234 F
gkelley@endicott.edu
KELLEY, Gloria .... 704-330-6441.... 369 A
gloria.kelley@cpcc.edu
KELLEY, Holly .... 904-743-1122.... 112 A
hkelley@jones.edu
KELLEY, James, W .... 336-633-0049.... 372 F
jwkelley@randolph.edu
KELLEY, Jan .... 541-485-1780.... 417 E
jankelley@newhope.edu
KELLEY, Jane .... 518-762-4651.... 334 D
jkelley@fmcc.suny.edu
KELLEY, Jeanne .... 617-353-3565.... 232 G
jkelley@bu.edu
KELLEY, Katherine, M .... 423-439-4224.... 473 E
kelleyk@etsu.edu
KELLEY, Kathleen .... 860-253-3011...... 89 K
kkelley@acc.commnet.edu
KELLEY, Kelvin, J .... 325-670-5898.... 487 D
kjkelley@hsutx.edu
KELLEY, Kevin .... 417-328-1536.... 290 E
kkelley@sbuniv.edu
KELLEY, Kim .... 706-754-7726.... 134 E
kkelley@northgatech.edu
KELLEY, Kim .... 262-595-2553.... 551 E
kelleyk@uwp.edu
KELLEY, Kimberly .... 309-268-8057.... 151 G
kim.kelley@heartland.edu
KELLEY, Kirk .... 918-335-6843.... 411 B
kkelley@okwu.edu
KELLEY, Larry .... 252-985-5281.... 375 C
lkelley@ncwc.edu
KELLEY, Laurie .... 503-943-8332.... 420 G
kelleyl@up.edu
KELLEY, Lawrence, R .... 805-756-2171...... 33 F
lkelley@calpoly.edu
KELLEY, Lisa .... 859-622-2101.... 200 D
lisa.kelley@eku.edu
KELLEY, Lucille, M .... 206-281-2608.... 537 D
lkelley@spu.edu
KELLEY, Marie, N .... 225-768-1789.... 214 B
mkelley@ololcollege.edu
KELLEY, Meredith .... 530-898-4113...... 34 A
makelley@csuchico.edu
KELLEY, Michael .... 402-280-2733.... 297 H
michaelk@creighton.edu
KELLEY, Michael .... 802-485-2135.... 514 A
vpcmdt@norwich.edu
KELLEY, Mildred .... 972-860-4195.... 484 F
mkelley1@dcccd.edu
KELLEY, Richard, D .... 631-656-2130.... 334 B
rkelley@ftc.edu
KELLEY, Ritch .... 570-586-2400.... 422 F
rkelley@bbc.edu
KELLEY, Robert, O .... 701-777-2121.... 381 D
robert.kelley@email.mail.und.edu
KELLEY, Scott, C .... 512-499-4560.... 504 E
skelley@utsystem.edu
KELLEY, Susan .... 717-531-5665.... 439 L
sqk6@psu.edu
KELLEY, Susan, E .... 407-582-2969.... 122 I
skelley@valenciacollege.edu
KELLEY, Sylvia .... 541-552-6873.... 419 A
KelleySy@sou.edu
KELLEY, Thomas .... 508-626-4614.... 238 D
tkelley@framingham.edu
KELLEY, Todd .... 262-551-5900.... 546 F
tkelley@carthage.edu
KELLEY, Tom .... 301-934-7822.... 222 C
tkelley@csmd.edu
KELLEY, Zachary .... 315-655-7174.... 325 I
jzkelley@cazenovia.edu
KELLEY-WINDERS,
Anna Faye .... 228-897-4360.... 275 G
annafaye.kelley@mgccc.edu
KELLIHER, Marsha, C .... 512-448-8593.... 493 B
marshak@stedwards.edu
KELLLY, Sarah, M .... 937-327-7800.... 406 B
smkelly@wittenberg.edu
KELLOGG, Angie .... 715-346-4323.... 552 B
akellogg@uwsp.edu
KELLOGG, Dan .... 715-346-2046.... 552 B
dkellogg@uwsp.edu
KELLOGG, Leslie .... 269-927-8167.... 254 B
souden@lakemichigancollege.edu
KELLOGG, Tonia .... 405-878-2004.... 409 D
tonia.kellogg@okbu.edu
KELLOGG-BRADLEY,
Polly .... 507-288-4563.... 263 D
pkelloggbradley@crossroadscollege.edu
KELLOM, Kolleen, E .... 320-363-5879.... 262 H
kkellom@csbsju.edu
KELLOUGH, Stephen, B .... 630-752-5087.... 168 F
stephen.kellough@wheaton.edu
KELLY, Alan, J .... 516-463-5027.... 335 H
alan.j.kelly@hofstra.edu
KELLY, Anita .... 484-664-3178.... 437 B
akelly@muhlenberg.edu
KELLY, Anna .... 401-739-5000.... 453 E
akelly@neit.edu
KELLY, Annice .... 312-369-8171.... 148 B
akelly@colum.edu
KELLY, Audrey .... 908-737-7000.... 311 B
aukelly@kean.edu
KELLY, OSB, Augustine .... 603-641-7250.... 305 H
akelly@anselm.edu
KELLY, Barbara .... 334-386-7299........ 3 H
bkelly@faulkner.edu
KELLY, Benji .... 270-789-5211.... 199 C
jbkelly@campbellsville.edu
KELLY, Bill .... 570-702-8984.... 431 K
bkelly@johnson.edu
KELLY, Brian .... 508-541-1622.... 234 B
bkelly@dean.edu
KELLY, Brian .... 510-780-4500...... 53 I
KELLY, Brian .... 805-525-4417...... 72 E
bkelly@thomasaquinas.edu
KELLY, Chris .... 620-235-4122.... 195 I
ckelly@pittstate.edu
KELLY, OSB, David .... 724-805-2644.... 446 E
david.kelly@email.stvincent.edu
KELLY, Debra .... 574-284-4542.... 179 D
dkwalsh@saintmarys.edu
KELLY, Dennis, M .... 610-902-8554.... 423 H
dmk323@cabrini.edu
KELLY, Diane .... 312-225-6288.... 167 E
dkelly@vandercook.edu
KELLY, Donald .... 901-272-5796.... 471 B
dkelly@mca.edu
KELLY, Ed, W .... 509-777-4780.... 539 F
ekelly@whitworth.edu
KELLY, Edward, J .... 423-439-8550.... 473 E
kellye@etsu.edu
KELLY, Eleanor, A .... 302-477-2273...... 96 H
eakelly@widener.edu
KELLY, Evelyn .... 252-527-6223.... 371 D
ekelly@lenoircc.edu
KELLY, Gary .... 909-607-3470...... 49 D
gary_kelly@hmc.edu
KELLY, Gary, E .... 781-891-2360.... 231 F
gkelly@bentley.edu
KELLY, George .... 610-282-1100.... 426 I
george.kelly@desales.edu
KELLY, George, N .... 615-327-6523.... 471 A
gkelly@mmc.edu
KELLY, Grace, A .... 802-654-2568.... 514 B
gkelly@smcvt.edu
KELLY, Hank .... 740-420-5924.... 398 C
hkelly@ohiochristian.edu
KELLY, Heather, A .... 302-831-2021...... 96 F
hkelly@udel.edu
KELLY, J. Michael .... 205-329-7933........ 3 B
mike.kelly@ecacolleges.com
KELLY, Jack .... 617-732-2143.... 241 F
jack.kelly@mcphs.edu
KELLY, Jack .... 717-262-2013.... 452 B
jkelly@wilson.edu
KELLY, James .... 650-543-3860...... 57 B
jkelly@menlo.edu
KELLY, RET., James .... 401-841-3674.... 557 I
KELLY, Jamie .... 617-989-4668.... 246 C
kellyj8@wit.edu
KELLY, Jane, E .... 585-389-2320.... 342 D
jkelly5@naz.edu
KELLY, Janet, H .... 478-988-6800.... 133 H
jkelly@middlegatech.edu
KELLY, Jeff .... 443-334-2331.... 226 E
jkelly@stevenson.edu
KELLY, Jeff .... 515-964-6630.... 183 E
jjkelly@dmacc.edu

KENNEDY, SSJ, Sheila .... 215-248-7023 .... 425 C
kennedys@chc.edu
KENNEDY, Tanner .... 727-864-8219 .... 104 K
kennedtl@eckerd.edu
KENNEDY, Thomas, D .... 706-236-2297 .... 125 G
tkennedy@berry.edu
KENNEDY, Tim .... 325-793-4775 .... 490 F
tkennedy@mcm.edu
KENNEDY, Timothy, J .... 704-403-4336 .... 362 E
tim.kennedy@carolinashealthcare.org
KENNEDY, Valerie .... 718-270-5000 .... 328 D
vkennedy@mec.cuny.edu
KENNEDY, Vernal, L .... 859-246-6507 .... 201 D
vernal.kennedy@kctcs.edu
KENNEDY, Vicki, D .... 864-587-4236 .... 461 D
kennedyv@smcsc.edu
KENNEDY, Wilton, C .... 540-985-8256 .... 520 D
wckennedy@jchs.edu
KENNEDY-LAMAR, Danielle .... 334-229-6969 .... 1 C
dkennedylamar@alasu.edu
KENNEDY-WITTHAR, Shawna, J .... 806-651-2227 .... 498 D
switthar@mail.wtamu.edu
KENNELL, Deena .... 308-432-6388 .... 299 G
dkennell@csc.edu
KENNELL, Scott, E .... 570-326-3761 .... 440 K
sek3@pct.edu
KENNELLY, James .... 718-289-5168 .... 326 F
james.kennelly@bcc.cuny.edu
KENNELLY, Raymond .... 815-836-5520 .... 156 D
kennelra@lewisu.edu
KENNEMER, DeAira .... 972-273-3163 .... 485 B
dkennemer@dcccd.edu
KENNER, Corry, G .... 701-662-1505 .... 382 D
corry.kenner@lrsc.edu
KENNER, Patsy .... 513-244-4621 .... 388 D
patsy_kenner@mail.msj.edu
KENNERLY, A. Chris .... 740-427-5160 .... 394 C
kennerlyc@kenyon.edu
KENNERLY, John, F .... 864-379-8747 .... 457 G
kennerly@erskine.edu
KENNEY, Anne, R .... 607-255-6875 .... 331 C
ark3@cornell.edu
KENNEY, Beth .... 301-687-4244 .... 228 C
bkenney@frostburg.edu
KENNEY, Dan .... 910-521-6227 .... 379 B
daniel.kenney@uncp.edu
KENNEY, Debra .... 914-674-7891 .... 340 G
dkenney@mercy.edu
KENNEY, Dianne .... 412-268-5075 .... 424 H
dkenney@andrew.cmu.edu
KENNEY, Gerardina .... 610-738-0496 .... 443 F
gkenney@wcupa.edu
KENNEY, Mary, W .... 505-277-9290 .... 321 C
mkenney@salud.unm.edu
KENNEY, Michael .... 734-432-5343 .... 254 G
mkenney@madonna.edu
KENNEY, Rebecca, J .... 510-748-2301 .... 62 B
jjackson@peralta.edu
KENNEY, Sue .... 443-334-2547 .... 226 E
skenney@stevenson.edu
KENNICOTT, Lisa .... 615-514-4644 .... 469 D
lkennicott@iadtnashville.com
KENNINGTON, Janet, S .... 410-334-2942 .... 229 E
jkennington@worwic.edu
KENNISON, Kimberly .... 860-768-5516 .... 95 A
kennison@hartford.edu
KENNON, John (Gil) .... 573-518-2127 .... 286 B
gil@mineralarea.edu
KENNON, Paul .... 314-340-3351 .... 282 I
kennonp@hssu.edu
KENNY, Cathleen .... 845-561-0800 .... 342 A
cathleen.kenny@msmc.edu
KENNY, Dan .... 810-985-7000 .... 249 B
dan.kenny@baker.edu
KENNY, Daryl .... 802-447-6357 .... 514 D
dkenny@svc.edu
KENNY, Ed, N .... 540-863-2880 .... 526 B
ekenny@dslcc.edu
KENNY, Eddie .... 352-588-8994 .... 116 E
edmond.kenny@saintleo.edu
KENNY, Keith (Dallas) .... 308-865-8246 .... 300 G
kennyd2@unk.edu
KENNY, Kevin .... 925-288-5800 .... 49 F
kevin_kenny@heald.edu
KENNY, Mike .... 219-473-4341 .... 170 D
mkenny@ccsj.edu
KENT, Caryn .... 518-244-2391 .... 348 A
kentc@sage.edu
KENT, David .... 414-277-7350 .... 548 H
kent@msoe.edu
KENT, Jonathan .... 607-431-4116 .... 335 B
kentj@hartwick.edu
KENT, Leigh .... 360-992-2101 .... 532 A
lkent@clark.edu
KENT, Ronald, H .... 313-577-3398 .... 260 D
ad0831@wayne.edu
KENT, Tom .... 518-793-5250 .... 322 B
kentt@sunyacc.edu
KENT-DAVIS, Linda, S .... 401-456-8031 .... 454 A
lkent@ric.edu
KENT-HUMMEL, Deena .... 937-769-1851 .... 383 K
dkent@antioch.edu

KENTON, Jay .... 541-737-3646 .... 418 B
jay_kenton@ous.edu
KENTOPP, Timothy .... 803-780-1219 .... 463 B
tkentopp@voorhees.edu
KENWORTHY, Anne, H .... 901-321-4213 .... 467 G
akenwort@cbu.edu
KENYON, Charles, B .... 716-878-4618 .... 353 A
kenyoncb@buffalostate.edu
KENYON, Kevin, S .... 765-285-8988 .... 169 D
kkenyon@bsu.edu
KENYON, Steven .... 508-678-2811 .... 239 F
steve.kenyon@bristolcc.edu
KENYON, JR., Thomas, W 732-235-9619 .... 316 C
kenyontw@umdnj.edu
KEOGH, Andrew .... 920-832-2610 .... 552 F
andrew.keogh@uwc.edu
KEOHANE, Edward, J .... 508-856-2900 .... 238 A
edward.keohane@umassmed.edu
KEOHANE, Ellen, J .... 508-793-2477 .... 233 D
ekeohane@holycross.edu
KEON, Thomas, L .... 407-823-2183 .... 120 A
tkeon@bus.ucf.edu
KEON, Thomas, L .... 219-989-2203 .... 178 G
Thomas.Keon@purduecal.edu
KEOUGH, Jeffrey .... 617-879-7369 .... 238 E
jkeough@massart.edu
KEOUGH, Patrick, J .... 252-222-6257 .... 368 F
pjk@carteret.edu
KEOUGH, Vicki, A .... 708-216-3582 .... 157 A
vkeough@luc.edu
KEPHART, Kevin .... 605-688-5642 .... 466 B
kevin.kephart@sdstate.edu
KEPHAS, Kalwin .... 691-370-3191 .... 559 A
dirksa@comfsm.fm
KEPIC, Paul .... 817-547-9600 .... 508 H
pkepic@westwood.edu
KEPIC, Paul .... 214-570-0100 .... 508 G
pkepic@westwood.edu
KEPLAN, Cary .... 415-808-3000 .... 50 B
cary_kaplan@heald.edu
KEPPEN, Jesse .... 620-431-2820 .... 195 B
KEPPLE, JR., Thomas, R .... 814-641-3101 .... 431 L
kepplet@juniata.edu
KEPPLER, Kurt, J .... 225-578-3607 .... 212 F
kkeppler@lsu.edu
KEPPNER, Dana .... 217-228-5432 .... 161 E
keppnda@quincy.edu
KERBAUGH, Jon .... 303-837-0825 .... 81 B
KERBS, Nancy .... 417-667-8181 .... 280 I
nkerbs@cottey.edu
KERBUSCH, William .... 440-826-2233 .... 384 H
bkerbusc@bw.edu
KERBY, Debra .... 660-785-4346 .... 291 A
dkerby@truman.edu
KERDA, Stephen, J .... 202-231-3068 .... 557 G
stephen.kerda@dia.mil
KERDOLFF, Russell, A .... 859-572-6455 .... 205 E
kerdolff@nku.edu
KERESTLY, Ed .... 325-674-2546 .... 478 H
ed.kerestly@acu.edu
KERFELD, Sally .... 320-222-5977 .... 268 I
sally.kerfeld@ridgewater.edu
KERICH, Julie, A .... 717-358-4743 .... 429 E
julie.kerich@fandm.edu
KERKAERT, Debra .... 507-537-6093 .... 269 G
Deb.Kerkaert@smsu.edu
KERKER, R. Michael .... 512-471-2694 .... 505 B
mkerker@austin.utexas.edu
KERKHOFF, Tom .... 217-540-3555 .... 155 H
tkerkhof@lakeland.cc.il.us
KERLEY, Jim .... 850-872-3800 .... 110 E
jkerley@gulfcoast.edu
KERLIN, Christine .... 425-388-9204 .... 533 H
ckerlin@everettcc.edu
KERLIN, Matthew, S .... 205-726-2825 .... 6 G
mskerlin@samford.edu
KERLIN, Scott .... 415-433-9200 .... 68 F
skerlin@saybrook.edu
KERMAN, Lucy, E .... 215-895-2123 .... 427 G
lucy.e.kerman@drexel.edu
KERN, Patricia .... 618-437-5321 .... 162 B
kernp@rlc.edu
KERN, Sharon .... 918-343-7537 .... 411 H
skern@rsu.edu
KERN-SIMIRENKO, Cheryl 330-972-7495 .... 403 B
cks7@uakron.edu
KERNAGIS, Ken .... 505-566-3299 .... 320 D
kernagisk@sanjuancollege.edu
KERNAN, William .... 503-838-8154 .... 419 C
kernanb@wou.edu
KERNEK, Lee .... 407-823-3812 .... 120 A
lee.kernek@ucf.edu
KERNER, Kelly .... 207-786-6247 .... 217 C
kkerner@bates.edu
KERNICK, Rhonda .... 432-264-5101 .... 487 I
rkernick@howardcollege.edu
KERNIN, Richard, P .... 716-286-8044 .... 344 D
rpk@niagara.edu
KERNS, Connie, M .... 620-792-9273 .... 190 E
kernsc@bartonccc.edu
KERP, Lauri .... 860-444-8308 .... 558 E
bookstore@uscga.edu
KERR, Andre .... 864-592-4774 .... 461 C
kerra@sccsc.edu

KERR, Anne, B .... 863-680-4100 .... 109 D
akerr@flsouthern.edu
KERR, Barbara .... 360-992-2921 .... 532 A
bkerr@clark.edu
KERR, Colleen .... 206-219-2408 .... 539 A
colleen.kerr@wsu.edu
KERR, Greg .... 620-278-4217 .... 196 D
gkerr@sterling.edu
KERR, James, M .... 419-995-8890 .... 399 B
kerr.63@osu.edu
KERR, John .... 251-414-3203 .... 7 F
jkerr@shc.edu
KERR, Johnathan, C .... 706-886-6831 .... 137 G
jkerr@tfc.edu
KERR, Jon .... 360-442-2531 .... 535 C
jkerr@lowercolumbia.edu
KERR, Marcus .... 817-531-4237 .... 502 A
mkerr@txwes.edu
KERR, Mary, E .... 216-368-2544 .... 386 E
KERR, Samuel .... 605-721-5214 .... 464 G
skerr@national.edu
KERR, Scott, A .... 330-684-8910 .... 403 C
sak@uakron.edu
KERR, Shelly, K .... 541-346-3227 .... 419 B
skerr@uoregon.edu
KERR, Steve .... 216-391-6937 .... 387 A
SKerr@ChancellorU.edu
KERR, Steve .... 801-626-7587 .... 511 D
skerr1@weber.edu
KERR, Steven .... 216-391-6937 .... 387 A
CUProvost@ChancellorU.edu
KERR, Susan .... 708-456-0300 .... 166 C
skerr@triton.edu
KERR-POINDEXTER, Monica .... 410-276-0306 .... 226 D
mpoindexter@host.sdc.edu
KERRICK, Joyce .... 570-265-0141 .... 433 A
kerrickj@lackawanna.edu
KERRICK, Sandra .... 804-751-9191 .... 523 E
skerrick@rsht.edu
KERRIGAN, John, E .... 408-554-4968 .... 68 C
jekerrigan@scu.edu
KERRIGAN, JR., John, F .. 503-883-2443 .... 416 G
kerrigan@linfield.edu
KERRIGAN, Patrick, G .... 608-796-3041 .... 553 A
pgkerrigan@viterbo.edu
KERRIS, Deborah .... 941-379-0404 .... 100 G
dkerris@argosy.edu
KERSCHNER, Alexis .... 505-224-4669 .... 317 J
akerschner@cnm.edu
KERSCHNER, Joseph, E .... 414-955-8213 .... 548 E
jkerschner@mcw.edu
KERSENBROCK, Angela, M .... 407-708-2483 .... 117 G
kersenbrocka@seminolestate.edu
KERSEY, Elizabeth, A .... 757-683-3152 .... 521 L
ekersey@odu.edu
KERSEY-MATUSIAK, Gloria .... 215-637-7700 .... 430 H
gkmatusiak@holyfamily.edu
KERSEY OTTO, Sarah .... 734-487-0400 .... 250 H
sarah.otto@emich.edu
KERSHAW, Mara .... 503-491-7219 .... 417 B
mara.kershaw@mhcc.edu
KERSTEN, David, J .... 716-847-8370 .... 326 A
dkersten@buffalodiocese.org
KERSTEN, James, B .... 515-574-1132 .... 185 F
kersten@iowacentral.edu
KERSTEN, Tiffany .... 251-626-3303 .... 8 D
tkersten@ussa.edu
KERSTETTER, Philip, P .... 919-658-7746 .... 367 D
pkerstetter@moc.edu
KERSTIENS, Michael, J .... 812-941-2596 .... 174 D
mjkersti@ius.edu
KERSTING, Monica, R .... 218-299-4557 .... 263 B
kersting@cord.edu
KERWIN, Bill .... 714-241-6257 .... 40 J
bkerwin@coastline.edu
KERWIN, Cornelius, M .... 202-885-2121 .... 97 B
president@american.edu
KERWIN, Mark .... 617-369-3281 .... 244 G
mkerwin@mfa.org
KERWOOD, Jennifer .... 413-236-2188 .... 239 E
jkerwood@berkshirecc.edu
KESERAUSKIS, Elizabeth, M .... 618-650-3605 .... 165 A
ekesera@siue.edu
KESLER, Andrew .... 818-401-1041 .... 42 D
akesler@columbiacollege.edu
KESLER, Michael .... 802-773-5900 .... 513 B
mkesler@csj.edu
KESSELMAN, Harvey .... 609-652-4514 .... 313 F
harvey.kesselman@stockton.edu
KESSENICH, Raymond, J .... 319-363-8213 .... 187 E
rkessenich@mtmercy.edu
KESSIN, Janet .... 212-799-5000 .... 337 H
KESSINGER, Kevin, S .... 765-658-4175 .... 170 I
kevinkessinger@depauw.edu
KESSLER, Gene .... 219-473-4299 .... 170 D
gkessler@ccsj.edu
KESSLER, Jeanne, D .... 785-670-1629 .... 197 D
jeanne.kessler@washburn.edu
KESSLER, Jeffrey, A .... 516-877-3660 .... 322 A
kessler@adelphi.edu

KESSLER, Karen .... 850-484-1673 .... 114 C
kkessler@pensacolastate.edu
KESSLER, Nevin, E .... 919-515-3226 .... 378 E
nevin_kessler@ncsu.edu
KESSLER, Richard .... 212-580-0210 .... 342 E
kesslerr@newschool.edu
KESSLER, Susan, B .... 386-312-4021 .... 116 D
susankessler@sjrstate.edu
KESSLER, Suzanne .... 914-251-6600 .... 354 D
suzanne.kessler@purchase.edu
KESTEN, Philip, R .... 408-554-4311 .... 68 C
pkesten@scu.edu
KESTER, Chris .... 618-664-6735 .... 151 D
chris.kester@greenville.edu
KESTER, Karen, A .... 941-752-5329 .... 118 E
kesterk@scf.edu
KESTER, Kelly .... 360-383-3245 .... 539 D
kkester@whatcom.ctc.edu
KESTER-MABON, Eric .... 701-228-5621 .... 382 C
eric.kester-mabon@dakotacollege.edu
KESTERSON, Ronald, L .... 865-694-6608 .... 475 F
rkesterson@pstcc.edu
KESTERSON, Sean, K .... 989-774-7865 .... 249 G
keste1sk@cmich.edu
KESTNER, Laura, F .... 414-288-7424 .... 548 D
laura.kestner@marquette.edu
KETCHAM, Kelly .... 509-682-6865 .... 539 B
kketcham@wvc.edu
KETCHESON, Kathi, A .... 503-725-3432 .... 418 G
ketchesonk@pdx.edu
KETCHUM, Deann .... 206-393-3530 .... 530 G
dketchum@argosy.edu
KETELS, Margo .... 563-589-3131 .... 189 B
mketels@dbq.edu
KETNER, Annette .... 619-260-2925 .... 76 A
aketner@sandiego.edu
KETO, Stephen, W .... 919-515-9224 .... 378 B
steve_keto@ncsu.edu
KETTEMAN, Greg .... 615-383-1340 .... 468 J
gketteman@fwbbc.edu
KETTENBEIL, Ken .... 313-593-5555 .... 259 E
kketten@umich.edu
KETTER, Jason .... 610-683-4112 .... 442 F
ketter@Give2KU.org
KETTERER, John, J .... 256-782-5303 .... 4 L
jkettere@jsu.edu
KETTERER, Patricia .... 212-237-8516 .... 328 A
pketterer@jjay.cuny.edu
KETTERING, III, Rocky .... 210-436-3138 .... 493 C
rkettering@stmarytx.edu
KETTERMAN, Dave, V .... 417-667-8181 .... 280 I
dketterman@cottey.edu
KETTERMAN, Jesse .... 301-687-4226 .... 228 C
jketterman@frostburg.edu
KETTING-WELLER, Ginger . 509-527-2431 .... 538 H
ginger.kettingweller@wallawalla.edu
KETTL, Donald, F .... 301-405-6355 .... 227 B
kettl@umd.edu
KETTLEWELL, Charles, L .... 214-648-3606 .... 507 D
charles.kettlewell@utsouthwestern.edu
KETTNER, Valrey, V .... 701-231-9608 .... 381 H
val.kettner@ndsu.edu
KETTNER-POLLEY, Richard .... 603-577-6610 .... 304 J
kettnerpolley@dwc.edu
KETTS, Amy .... 636-651-1600 .... 289 I
aketts@sbc-fenton.com
KETTY, Sanjay .... 330-494-1214 .... 385 I
snketty@brownmackie.edu
KETTY, Sanjay .... 415-292-8214 .... 32 B
sketty@baychef.com
KETTYLE, William, M .... 617-253-1716 .... 242 A
kett@med.mit.edu
KEUFFEL, Elizabeth .... 603-641-7203 .... 305 H
ekeuffel@anselm.edu
KEUL, Martha .... 303-280-7478 .... 84 C
mkeul@devry.edu
KEUNG, Chi-Chung .... 562-938-4723 .... 54 E
ckeung@lbcc.edu
KEUP, Mike .... 309-677-2677 .... 145 H
mkeup@bradley.edu
KEUSCH, Gerald, T .... 617-638-5234 .... 232 G
keusch@bu.edu
KEVIL, Tim .... 903-875-7443 .... 491 B
tim.kevil@navarrocollege.edu
KEY, Charlet .... 309-796-5143 .... 145 E
keyc@bhc.edu
KEY, Chris .... 770-576-4543 .... 136 A
KEY, Damon .... 610-526-1382 .... 421 G
russell.figueira@theamericancollege.edu
KEY, Danny .... 704-233-8025 .... 380 D
dkey@wingate.edu
KEY, Elizabeth .... 801-832-2202 .... 512 F
ekey@westminstercollege.edu
KEY, Henry .... 908-709-7151 .... 316 B
key@ucc.edu
KEY, Rand .... 832-813-6522 .... 490 C
rand.key@lonestar.edu
KEY, Roby, V .... 817-257-7706 .... 498 F
r.key@tcu.edu
KEY, Spencer .... 607-729-1581 .... 332 A
skey@davisny.edu
KEY, Stacy .... 479-979-1360 .... 26 A
skey@ozarks.edu

KIM, David .... 704-330-6828 .... 369 A
david.kim@cpcc.edu
KIM, Davis, S .... 703-333-5904 .... 530 B
KIM, Diane .... 916-577-2200 ..... 79 C
dkim@missouri.edu
KIM, Eunice .... 770-279-0507 .... 129 E
daltting@gmail.com
KIM, Eunice .... 312-662-4215 .... 144 C
KIM, Gamey .... 610-917-1418 .... 450 D
jgkim@vfcc.edu
KIM, Haeryon .... 970-382-6977 ..... 84 G
kim_h@fortlewis.edu
KIM, Hanjik .... 714-533-1495 ..... 70 B
hjk@southbaylo.edu
KIM, Heather .... 602-386-4136 ..... 11 H
heather.kim@arizonachristian.edu
KIM, Heather, H .... 608-262-2321 .... 550 F
hkim@uwsa.edu
KIM, Hee Kun .... 201-242-8846 .... 129 E
dockimus@naver.com
KIM, Hyunwan .... 714-525-0088 ..... 48 G
hyunwan@hotmail.com
KIM, In Soo .... 562-926-1023 ..... 63 B
iskim1123@hanmail.net
KIM, James .... 714-533-1495 ..... 70 B
james@southbaylo.edu
KIM, James .... 714-533-3946 ..... 37 C
jameskim@calums.edu
KIM, Jean .... 413-545-2333 .... 237 C
jeankim@stuaf.umass.edu
KIM, Jim, Y .... 603-646-2223 .... 305 A
jim.y.kim@dartmouth.edu
KIM, Jin .... 323-731-2383 ..... 60 I
jskim@psuca.edu
KIM, Jin, Q .... 323-731-2383 ..... 60 I
president@psuca.edu
KIM, John .... 619-684-8841 ..... 59 A
jkim@newschoolarch.edu
KIM, John, J .... 415-405-4155 ..... 36 F
johnjkim@sfsu.edu
KIM, Joshua .... 619-477-6310 ..... 73 A
jkim@usuniversity.edu
KIM, Julius .... 760-480-8474 ..... 78 E
jjkim@wscal.edu
KIM, Jung .... 415-282-7600 ..... 28 B
jungkim@actcm.edu
KIM, Keith, K .... 323-731-2383 ..... 60 I
keith@psuca.edu
KIM, Kwang-Wu .... 480-965-8561 ..... 12 B
kwang-wu.kim@asu.edu
KIM, Kwangsin .... 714-525-0088 ..... 48 G
KIM, Lauren .... 909-621-8273 ..... 69 A
registrar@ad.scrippscol.edu
KIM, Man Tae .... 714-517-1945 ..... 30 G
chiefacademic@bcu.edu
KIM, Min Sang .... 323-731-2384 ..... 60 I
mskim@psuca.edu
KIM, Min Soo .... 770-279-0507 .... 129 E
soo729@hotmail.com
KIM, Myeong .... 213-252-5100 ..... 26 C
KIM, Myo Ryoung .... 678-735-5471 .... 129 E
estherkim17@yahoo.com
KIM, Paul, C .... 770-279-0507 .... 129 E
drpaul@gcuniv.edu
KIM, Rebecca .... 847-574-5264 .... 155 G
rkim@lfgsm.edu
KIM, Sam .... 626-284-2777 ..... 27 D
skim@alliant.edu
KIM, Samuel .... 770-279-0507 .... 129 E
38317muel@hanmail.net
KIM, Sang Jo .... 714-535-3886 ..... 70 B
sjkim@southbaylo.edu
KIM, Shalom, Y .... 213-481-1313 ..... 69 E
KIM, Soo Jin .... 770-279-0507 .... 129 E
soojinkim@bellsouth.net
KIM, Young .... 703-663-8088 .... 517 B
KIM, Young Hwan .... 770-638-1383 .... 129 E
yhkim30024@yahoo.com
KIM, Young Jun .... 770-638-1383 .... 129 E
humbleofman@yahoo.co.kr
KIM, Young-Ja .... 212-217-3820 .... 333 G
youngja_kim@fitnyc.edu
KIM, Yun .... 310-453-8300 ..... 45 F
yun@emperors.edu
KIM, Yun .... 570-422-3856 .... 442 C
ykim@po-box.esu.edu
KIMATA, Stephen, A .... 434-924-4293 .... 525 B
sak@virginia.edu
KIMBALL, Amber, M .... 919-508-2028 .... 375 D
amkimball@peace.edu
KIMBALL, Cathy .... 904-731-4949 .... 105 H
ckimball@cci.edu
KIMBALL, Christopher .... 805-493-3100 ..... 32 H
ckimball@clunet.edu
KIMBALL, Elmer .... 802-654-0505 .... 515 D
elmer.kimball@ccv.edu
KIMBALL, Jon .... 617-521-2411 .... 245 A
jon.kimball@simmons.edu
KIMBALL, Joseph .... 814-824-2559 .... 436 C
jkimball@mercyhurst.edu
KIMBALL, Kevin .... 541-383-7209 .... 414 I
kekimball@cocc.edu
KIMBARK, Kris .... 409-933-8131 .... 483 B
kkimbark@com.edu

KIMBERLING, Renee .... 951-222-8150 ..... 64 B
renee.kimberling@rcc.edu
KIMBLE, Darius, Z .... 903-927-3316 .... 509 A
dkimble@wileyc.edu
KIMBLE, James, A .... 419-372-0680 .... 385 D
jkimble@bgsu.edu
KIMBROUGH, Del .... 478-825-6228 .... 129 C
kimbroughd@fvsu.edu
KIMBROUGH, Michael, J .. 913-288-7161 .... 193 J
kimbr@kckcc.edu
KIMBROUGH, Ralph .... 502-597-5117 .... 203 D
ralph.kimbrough@kysu.edu
KIMBROUGH, Scott .... 904-256-7118 .... 111 J
skimbro@ju.edu
KIMBROUGH, Walter, M ... 501-370-5314 ..... 23 B
wkimbrough@philander.edu
KIMBROW, Terry .... 501-329-6872 ..... 21 C
tkimbrow@cbc.edu
KIME, Don .... 717-262-2017 .... 452 B
dkime@wilson.edu
KIMES, Gene .... 254-295-4608 .... 504 A
gkimes@umhb.edu
KIMMEL, Howard, S .... 973-596-3574 .... 312 C
howard.kimmel@njit.edu
KIMMEL, Margaret .... 207-786-6328 .... 217 C
mkimmel@bates.edu
KIMMEL, Michael .... 216-421-7384 .... 387 H
mkimmel@cia.edu
KIMMEL, Rhonda .... 262-595-2281 .... 551 E
rhonda.kimmel@uwp.edu
KIMMEL, William .... 212-229-5620 .... 342 E
kimmelw@newschool.edu
KIMMELBLATT, Rachel .... 518-629-7736 .... 336 C
r.kimmelblatt@hvcc.edu
KIMMELMAN, Eric .... 518-762-4651 .... 334 D
ekimmelm@fmcc.suny.edu
KIMMELMAN, Scott .... 772-462-7760 .... 110 L
skimmelm@irsc.edu
KIMMENS, Randy .... 480-731-8202 ..... 15 F
randy.kimmens@domail.maricopa.edu
KIMMERLE, Robert, S .... 518-580-5733 .... 351 B
bkimmerl@skidmore.edu
KIMMINS, William, P .... 516-876-3179 .... 353 D
kimminsw@oldwestbury.edu
KIMREY, Donna .... 704-991-0285 .... 374 A
dkimrey5073@stanly.edu
KIMREY, Phil .... 205-726-2736 ...... 6 G
ppkimrey@samford.edu
KIMS, Erdene .... 718-933-6700 .... 341 G
ekims@monroecollege.edu
KIMSEY, James .... 520-494-5200 ..... 13 F
jim.kimsey@centralaz.edu
KIMSEY, Phillip .... 706-295-6350 .... 130 C
pkimsey@highlands.edu
KINANE, Denis, F .... 215-898-1038 .... 448 I
dean@dental.upenn.edu
KINANE, Michael, G .... 516-876-3212 .... 353 D
kinanem@oldwestbury.edu
KINANE, Michael, G .... 516-876-3162 .... 353 D
kinanem@oldwestbury.edu
KINARD, Sylvia .... 718-270-6896 .... 328 D
skinard@mec.cuny.edu
KINARD, Zeolean, F .... 864-941-8688 .... 460 D
kinard.z@ptc.edu
KINCADE, Luis .... 432-264-5092 .... 487 I
wkincade@howardcollege.edu
KINCAID, Johnna, K .... 713-500-3094 .... 506 D
johnna.k.kincaid@uth.tmc.edu
KINCAID, Paul, K .... 417-836-5139 .... 286 F
paulkincaid@missouristate.edu
KINCAID, Rachel, A .... 504-280-7049 .... 213 E
rakincai@uno.edu
KINCAID, Ramona .... 808-245-8336 .... 141 H
rkincaid@hawaii.edu
KINCAID, Scott, A .... 317-940-9700 .... 170 C
kincaid@butler.edu
KINCAID, Tim .... 419-559-2211 .... 402 D
tkincaid@terra.edu
KINCAID, William .... 317-931-2330 .... 170 E
bkincaid@cts.edu
KINCAID, Zach, O .... 434-381-6262 .... 524 E
zkincaid@sbc.edu
KINCHEN, Thomas, A .... 850-263-3261 .... 101 E
takinchen@baptistcollege.edu
KINCHERLOW-MARTIN,
Janet .... 256-306-2561 ...... 2 E
jkm@calhoun.edu
KIND, Jule .... 765-677-2980 .... 174 E
jule.kind@indwes.edu
KIND, Larry .... 715-675-3331 .... 554 G
Kind@ntc.edu
KIND-KEPPEL, Heather ...... 217-875-7200 .... 162 D
hkindkep@richland.edu
KINDE, Haragewen .... 909-384-8265 ..... 65 C
hkinde@sbccd.cc.ca.us
KINDE, Wayne .... 858-695-8587 ..... 50 H
wkinde@horizoncollege.org
KINDER, Angie, M .... 304-260-4380 .... 542 C
akinder@blueridgectc.edu
KINDER, L. Chad .... 580-774-7036 .... 412 F
chad.kinder@swosu.edu
KINDERS, Mark .... 918-444-2017 .... 409 A
kinders@nsuok.edu
KINDIN, Patricia, K .... 973-972-4211 .... 316 H

KINDL, Christine .... 724-938-5492 .... 441 G
kindl@calu.edu
KINDLE, Carolyn .... 618-634-3364 .... 164 C
carolynk@shawneecc.edu
KINDLE, Derek .... 202-806-2864 ..... 98 B
dkindle@howard.edu
KINDLE, Joan .... 847-925-6738 .... 151 E
jkindle@harpercollege.edu
KINDRED, Cheryl .... 480-545-8755 ..... 12 I
KINDRICK, Garvel .... 502-863-8015 .... 200 G
garvel_kindrick@georgetowncollege.edu
KINEAVY, Jacqueline .... 973-684-6300 .... 312 E
jkineavy@pccc.edu
KINERSON, Sara .... 802-635-1257 .... 515 E
sara.kinerson@jsc.edu
KINES, Teresa .... 336-249-8186 .... 369 F
tkines@davidsonccc.edu
KING, Alex, H .... 515-294-2770 .... 182 B
alexking@ameslab.gov
KING, Amanda .... 601-266-5000 .... 278 A
amanda.king@usm.edu
KING, Amy .... 815-306-2600 .... 162 A
Amy.King@rasmussen.edu
KING, Amy .... 303-871-7420 ..... 88 E
KING, Andrew, B .... 618-650-2197 .... 165 A
andking@siue.edu
KING, Andrew, R .... 914-968-6200 .... 349 D
sjsds@archny.org
KING, Angelynn .... 207-255-1234 .... 220 E
angelynn.king@maine.edu
KING, Apryl .... 216-916-7497 .... 398 E
aking@ocpm.edu
KING, Armanda .... 315-684-6038 .... 354 F
kinga@morrisville.edu
KING, Art .... 410-704-2051 .... 228 E
aking@towson.edu
KING, B, J .... 423-439-4414 .... 473 E
kingbj@etsu.edu
KING, Barbara .... 405-682-1611 .... 409 F
bking@occc.edu
KING, Barbara, E .... 570-408-4107 .... 451 G
barbara.king@wilkes.edu
KING, Baron .... 215-702-4224 .... 444 A
baronking@pbu.edu
KING, Becky, L .... 254-710-4566 .... 481 I
becky_king@baylor.edu
KING, Bernt .... 717-560-8240 .... 433 D
bking@lbc.ede
KING, Beverly .... 910-521-6295 .... 379 B
beverly.king@uncp.edu
KING, Bill .... 530-541-4660 ..... 53 F
king@ltcc.edu
KING, Bill .... 305-348-2623 .... 119 B
kingb@fiu.edu
KING, Bonnie, L .... 419-995-8310 .... 392 L
king.b@rhodesstate.edu
KING, Brad .... 501-569-3400 ..... 24 E
cbking@ualr.edu
KING, Brad .... 435-613-5246 .... 511 E
brad.king@ceu.edu
KING, Brenda, M .... 304-336-8076 .... 544 B
kingbren@westliberty.edu
KING, Brent .... 713-500-7863 .... 506 D
brent.king@uth.tmc.edu
KING, Brian .... 831-479-6302 ..... 31 F
brking@cabrillo.edu
KING, Bruce .... 510-235-7800 ..... 43 B
bking@contracosta.edu
KING, Bruce .... 507-786-3334 .... 271 H
kingb@stolaf.edu
KING, Carol .... 714-556-3610 ..... 76 E
founderslerk@vanguard.edu
KING, Carol, S .... 570-586-2400 .... 422 F
cking@bbc.edu
KING, Carole .... 202-884-9120 ..... 99 E
kingc@trinitydc.edu
KING, Carolee .... 409-772-1904 .... 507 B
caaking@utmb.edu
KING, Carolee .... 409-772-8738 .... 507 B
caaking@utmb.edu
KING, Caroline .... 941-907-2262 .... 106 G
caking@evergladesuniversity.edu
KING, Charles, G .... 423-652-4700 .... 469 L
gregking1@king.edu
KING, Charles, W .... 540-568-6434 .... 520 C
kingcw@jmu.edu
KING, Cheri .... 740-389-6786 .... 399 D
king.637@osu.edu
KING, Cheryl .... 301-295-3045 .... 558 A
cking@usuhs.mil
KING, Christopher .... 956-665-2221 .... 506 A
kingca@utpa.edu
KING, Christy .... 407-708-2103 .... 117 G
kingc@seminolestate.edu
KING, Chuck .... 303-753-6046 ..... 87 F
cking@rmcad.edu
KING, Chula, G .... 850-474-3135 .... 121 C
cking@uwf.edu
KING, Curt .... 518-587-2100 .... 355 F
curt.king@esc.edu
KING, Cynthia .... 202-651-5865 ..... 97 E
cynthia.king@gallaudet.edu
KING, Cynthia, L .... 610-861-5510 .... 437 G
cking@northampton.edu

KING, Cynthia, P 617-726-2947 242
cking@mghihp.edu
KING, D. Wayne 859-238-5550 199
wayne.king@centre.edu
KING, Dan 617-327-6777 242
dan_king@mspp.edu
KING, David 315-312-3692 354
david.king@oswego.edu
KING, David 706-721-2856 130
daking@georgiahealth.edu
KING, David, A 610-341-5929 428
dking@eastern.edu
KING, David, A 540-432-4440 518
david.king@emu.edu
KING, David, A 541-737-2676 418
ecampus@oregonstate.edu
KING, David, S 203-582-3213 93
david.king@quinnipiac.edu
KING, David, W 805-565-6036 78
dking@westmont.edu
KING, De-Anthony .... 312-662-4035 .... 144 C
KING, Deanna .... 812-298-2205 .... 177 A
dking@ivytech.edu
KING, Deborah .... 870-338-6474 ..... 25 D
KING, Deborah .... 410-276-0306 .... 226 D
dking@host.sdc.edu
KING, Deborah .... 252-399-6306 .... 362 A
dking@barton.edu
KING, Denise .... 636-922-8698 .... 288 E
dking@stchas.edu
KING, Dennis .... 828-254-1921 .... 367 H
dking@abtech.edu
KING, Dennis .... 785-628-4291 .... 192 F
dking@fhsu.edu
KING, Don .... 508-999-8575 .... 237 E
dking@umassd.edu
KING, Donald (Jr.) .... 765-285-1478 .... 169 D
jking@bsu.edu
KING, Donna .... 606-783-2011 .... 204 E
d.king@moreheadstate.edu
KING, Donna .... 903-463-8735 .... 487 A
donnaking@grayson.edu
KING, Dottie .... 812-535-5296 .... 179 C
president@smwc.edu
KING, Duane .... 918-596-2710 .... 413 F
duane-king@utulsa.edu
KING, E. Thayne .... 918-456-5511 .... 409 A
king21@nsuok.edu
KING, Eddie .... 843-208-8135 .... 462 C
eking@uscb.edu
KING, Edward, M .... 617-353-9095 .... 232 G
eking@bu.edu
KING, Elizabeth .... 316-978-3510 .... 197 F
elizabeth.king@witchita.edu
KING, Elizabeth, C .... 513-558-8547 .... 403 D
elizabeth.king@uc.edu
KING, Elston, H .... 504-286-5197 .... 214 I
eking@suno.edu
KING, Eric, B .... 903-927-3217 .... 509 A
ebking@wileyc.edu
KING, Gordon, B .... 617-557-1520 .... 245 E
gking@suffolk.edu
KING, Greg .... 305-341-6600 .... 102 B
grking@brownmackie.edu
KING, Greg .... 423-236-2983 .... 473 A
king@southern.edu
KING, Gregory .... 330-823-2282 .... 404 C
kinggl@mountunion.edu
KING, Gregory, D .... 323-343-3700 ..... 35 B
KING, Hazel .... 910-892-3178 .... 364 F
hking@heritagebiblecollege.edu
KING, Herbert .... 651-773-1794 .... 266 D
herbert.king@century.edu
KING, J, D .... 281-443-8900 .... 499 D
KING, Jackie, E .... 585-275-1051 .... 358 I
jking@admin.rochester.edu
KING, James .... 615-336-4470 .... 473 C
james.king@tbr.edu
KING, Janice .... 775-753-2361 .... 302 H
janicek@gwmail.gbcnv.edu
KING, Janice .... 530-754-1388 ..... 73 F
janking@ucdavis.edu
KING, Jeannie .... 704-337-2529 .... 375 G
kingj@queens.edu
KING, Jeff .... 706-764-3530 .... 130 F
jking@gntc.edu
KING, Jerry .... 903-675-6210 .... 502 D
jking@tvcc.edu
KING, Jessica .... 303-975-5016 ..... 89 E
jking@westwood.edu
KING, Jim .... 318-257-2445 .... 215 F
king@latech.edu
KING, Jim .... 254-295-4644 .... 504 A
jking@umhb.edu
KING, Jim, M .... 318-257-2445 .... 215 F
king@latech.edu
KING, Joan .... 509-335-9681 .... 539 A
joank@wsu.edu
KING, Jodie .... 215-248-7004 .... 425 C
kingj@chc.edu
KING, Joe, M .... 504-280-6723 .... 213 E
provost@uno.edu
KING, Joe, M .... 504-280-6000 .... 213 E
chancellor@uno.edu

KIRK, Melissa .... 718-289-5193 .... 326 F
melissa.kirk@bcc.cuny.edu
KIRK, Michael .... 860-486-3530 .... 94 E
michael.kirk@uconn.edu
KIRK, Nina .... 970-339-6622 .... 80 G
nina.kirk@aims.edu
KIRK, Rich .... 541-956-7040 .... 420 B
rkirk@roguecc.edu
KIRK, Robert, D .... 301-784-5000 .... 221 A
KIRK, Sharon .... 817-923-8459 .... 483 C
skirk@cstm.edu
KIRK, Tim .... 870-862-8131 .... 23 G
wtkirk@southark.edu
KIRK, Tom .... 334-774-5113 .... 3 G
tkirk@escc.edu
KIRKEBY, Lori .... 763-424-0713 .... 268 D
lkirkeby@nhcc.edu
KIRKENDALL, Joan .... 617-353-4365 .... 232 G
joank@bu.edu
KIRKER, William .... 516-299-2278 .... 339 A
william.kirker@liu.edu
KIRKHAM, Stephen, W .... 719-255-3075 .... 88 C
skirkham@uccs.edu
KIRKHOLM, Mark .... 712-749-2500 .... 182 G
kirkholmm@bvu.edu
KIRKING, Ellen, M .... 715-833-6326 .... 553 F
ekirking@cvtc.edu
KIRKLAND, Cecil, E .... 304-326-1519 .... 541 G
ekirkland@salemu.edu
KIRKLAND, Jennifer, E .... 540-458-8929 .... 530 A
jkirkland@wlu.edu
KIRKLAND, Joe .... 828-669-8012 .... 367 C
jkirkland@montreat.edu
KIRKLAND, Joseph .... 409-882-3926 .... 500 G
joe.kirkland@lsco.edu
KIRKLAND, Kim, D .... 317-274-2306 .... 174 B
kirkland@iupui.edu
KIRKLAND, Lee Ann .... 919-344-2614 .... 124 E
leeann.kirkland@armstrong.edu
KIRKLAND, Michael .... 229-248-2560 .... 125 E
mkirkland@bainbridge.edu
KIRKLAND, Sandie, I .... 336-334-4822 .... 370 E
sikirkland@gtcc.edu
KIRKLAND, Sara, G .... 570-372-4108 .... 447 D
kirkland@susqu.edu
KIRKLAND, Susan .... 305-899-3598 .... 101 F
skirkland@mail.barry.edu
KIRKLAND, Willie .... 504-816-4428 .... 208 I
wkirkland@dillard.edu
KIRKLAND-GORDON,
Sharon, E .... 301-314-7675 .... 227 B
skirklan@umd.edu
KIRKLAND-HARRIS,
Linda .... 757-727-5617 .... 519 C
linda.kirkland-harri@hamptonu.edu
KIRKLEY, Angela, J .... 919-508-2249 .... 375 D
akirkley@peace.edu
KIRKLIN, Anlatear .... 504-816-4170 .... 208 I
akirklin@dillard.edu
KIRKLIN, Kathleen .... 916-608-6500 .... 56 C
KIRKMAN, Duane .... 828-328-7028 .... 366 B
duane.kirkman@lr.edu
KIRKMAN, Larry .... 202-885-2058 .... 97 B
larry@american.edu
KIRKMAN, Sue .... 805-966-3888 .... 31 A
sue.kirkman@brooks.edu
KIRKMAN, Sue .... 805-585-8077 .... 31 B
sue.kirkman@brooks.edu
KIRKPATRICK, Brett, A .... 409-772-2371 .... 507 B
bkirkpat@utmb.edu
KIRKPATRICK, Dana .... 510-436-1601 .... 50 F
kirkpatrick@hnu.edu
KIRKPATRICK, Holly, R .... 215-572-4475 .... 422 B
kirkpath@arcadia.edu
KIRKPATRICK, J. Stephen . 877-442-0505 .... 88 G
stephen.kirkpatrick@rockies.edu
KIRKPATRICK, Judith, A ... 315-792-3122 .... 359 C
jkirkpatrick@utica.edu
KIRKPATRICK, Kenneth, J . 765-658-4141 .... 170 I
kjkirk@depauw.edu
KIRKPATRICK, Laura .... 931-363-9864 .... 470 E
lkirkpatrick@martinmethodist.edu
KIRKPATRICK, Lindsey .... 918-561-8468 .... 410 D
lindsey.kirkpatrick@okstate.edu
KIRKPATRICK, Lisa, L .... 512-448-8408 .... 493 B
lisak@stedwards.edu
KIRKPATRICK, Mac .... 864-388-8398 .... 458 J
mkirkpat@lander.edu
KIRKPATRICK, R. James ... 517-355-4473 .... 255 D
cnsdean@msu.edu
KIRKPATRICK, Stephen .... 516-876-3156 .... 353 D
kirkpatricks@oldwestbury.edu
KIRKSEY, Jason .... 405-744-9154 .... 410 C
jason.kirksey@okstate.edu
KIRKSEY, Kirk, A .... 214-645-8404 .... 507 D
kirk.kirksey@utsouthwestern.edu
KIRKTON, Vicki, S .... 574-535-7376 .... 171 D
vickysk@goshen.edu
KIRKWOOD, Diane .... 478-445-5596 .... 129 F
diane.kirkwood@gcsu.edu
KIRKWOOD, Rod .... 813-621-0041 .... 105 G
rkirkwoo@cci.edu
KIRKWOOD, Rod .... 863-686-1444 .... 105 I
rkirkwoo@cci.edu
KIRKWOOD, Valerie .... 509-793-2371 .... 531 D
valeriek@bigbend.edu
KIRKWOOD, William, G .... 423-439-4219 .... 473 E
kirkwood@etsu.edu
KIRMER, Lisa .... 620-343-4600 .... 192 E
lkirmer@fhtc.edu
KIRSCH, Lloyd .... 480-990-3773 .... 15 E
KIRSCH, OSB, Myron .... 724-805-2111 .... 446 E
myron.kirsch@email.stvincent.edu
KIRSCH, Rodney, P .... 814-863-4826 .... 438 F
rpk6@psu.edu
KIRSCHENMANN,
Sandra, G .... 916-568-3075 .... 55 J
kirschs@losrios.edu
KIRSCHLING, Jane, M .... 859-323-6533 .... 206 H
janek@uky.edu
KIRSH, Bruce, M .... 603-899-4080 .... 305 B
kirshb@franklinpierce.edu
KIRSHMAN, David .... 510-594-3688 .... 31 J
dkirshman@cca.edu
KIRSTEIN, Frank, W .... 716-888-8361 .... 325 G
kirstein@canisius.edu
KIRSTEIN, Kurt .... 425-637-1010 .... 531 I
kdkirstein@cityu.edu
KIRSTEN, Jan .... 732-255-0400 .... 312 D
jkirsten@ocean.edu
KIRTLAND, James, L .... 419-289-5012 .... 384 D
jkirtlan@ashland.edu
KIRTLEY, Brad, J .... 931-221-7561 .... 473 D
kirtleyb@apsu.edu
KIRTLEY, Karen .... 304-696-3328 .... 543 G
kirtley@marshall.edu
KIRTLEY, Laura .... 765-269-5160 .... 176 B
lkirtley1@ivytech.edu
KIRTMAN, Janet .... 212-346-1700 .... 345 F
jkirtman@pace.edu
KIRVES, Carol .... 270-707-3751 .... 202 A
carol.kirves@kctcs.edu
KIRWAN, David, E .... 315-267-4875 .... 354 C
kirwande@potsdam.edu
KIRWAN, William .... 301-445-1901 .... 227 A
bkirwan@usmd.edu
KIRYUKHIN, Sergey, S .... 315-858-0945 .... 336 A
ssk@hts.edu
KISARE-RESSLER, Dorca ... 717-766-2511 .... 436 D
dressler@messiah.edu
KISELICA, Mark .... 609-771-2100 .... 308 G
kiselica@tcnj.edu
KISELYUK, Ella .... 212-817-7701 .... 327 B
ekiselyuk@gc.cuny.edu
KISER, Dan .... 828-328-7154 .... 366 B
dan.kiser@lr.edu
KISER, Holly .... 817-531-4495 .... 502 A
hkiser@txwes.edu
KISER, Jennifer .... 907-852-3333 .... 10 G
jennifer.kiser@ilisagvik.edu
KISER, Joseph, B .... 276-328-0143 .... 525 C
jbk5b@uvawise.edu
KISER, Kristy .... 276-328-0220 .... 525 C
kej5c@uvawise.edu
KISER, Lee .... 828-448-6707 .... 374 G
lkiser@wpcc.edu
KISER, Leonard, R .... 336-734-7313 .... 370 C
lkiser@forsythtech.edu
KISER, Lyda, C .... 540-869-0623 .... 526 H
lkiser@lfcc.edu
KISER, Ronnie .... 276-964-7221 .... 528 A
ronnie.kiser@sw.edu
KISER, Sara, B .... 334-683-5104 .... 5 D
skiser@judson.edu
KISH-GOODLING,
Donna, M .... 484-664-3479 .... 437 B
kishgood@muhlenberg.edu
KISNER, Dawn .... 410-287-1025 .... 222 A
dkisner@cecil.edu
KISPERT, Craig, G .... 206-281-2536 .... 537 D
ckispert@spu.edu
KISPERT, John, J .... 843-661-1110 .... 458 C
jkispert@fmarion.edu
KISS, Elizabeth .... 404-471-6280 .... 123 G
president@agnesscott.edu
KISSEL, Anthony .... 352-588-8288 .... 116 E
anthony.kissel@saintleo.edu
KISSEL, Karen .... 708-534-4054 .... 151 C
kkissel@govst.edu
KISSELL, Joseph .... 570-389-4263 .... 441 F
jkissell@bloomu.edu
KISSICK, Sharon .... 910-521-6298 .... 379 B
sharon.kissick@uncp.edu
KISSLING, Paul .... 972-241-3371 .... 484 D
pkissling@dallas.edu
KISSNER, Vern .... 612-343-4447 .... 270 C
vakissne@northcentral.edu
KIST, Jennifer, S .... 814-269-7049 .... 449 D
jskist@pitt.edu
KIST, Tom .... 732-729-3813 .... 309 D
tkist@devry.edu
KISTLER, Kevin .... 661-362-3025 .... 41 G
kevin.kistler@canyons.edu
KISTLER, Ron .... 580-928-5533 .... 412 F
ron.kistler@swosu.edu
KISTNER, Warren .... 309-556-3071 .... 153 E
wkistner@iwu.edu
KITAJIMA, Lorraine, N .... 650-949-7243 .... 47 H
kitajimalorraine@fhda.edu
KITAMURA, Robert .... 805-756-7171 .... 33 F
rkitamur@calpoly.edu
KITCHEN, Augusta .... 803-780-1159 .... 463 B
akitchen@voorhees.edu
KITCHEN, Cheryl .... 419-772-2220 .... 398 G
c-kitchen@onu.edu
KITCHEN, Clifford .... 719-549-3121 .... 87 B
clifford.kitchen@pueblocc.edu
KITCHEN, Darrell, B .... 937-327-7002 .... 406 B
dkitchen@wittenberg.edu
KITCHEN, James, R .... 619-594-5211 .... 36 E
jkitchen@mail.sdsu.edu
KITCHEN, Janie .... 606-326-2163 .... 201 B
janie.kitchen@kctcs.edu
KITCHEN, Kimberly .... 814-641-3114 .... 431 L
kitchek@juniata.edu
KITCHEN, Mark .... 307-754-6405 .... 556 D
Mark.Kitchen@northwestcollege.edu
KITCHEN, Steve .... 678-915-3929 .... 137 C
skitchen@spsu.edu
KITCHEN, Todd .... 479-619-4232 .... 22 H
tkitchen@nwacc.edu
KITCHENS, Angie .... 706-737-1469 .... 125 C
akitchens@aug.edu
KITCHENS, Joann .... 701-662-1502 .... 382 D
joann.kitchens@lrsc.edu
KITCHENS, Joseph, H .... 770-720-5966 .... 135 F
jhk@reinhardt.edu
KITCHENS, Larry .... 870-236-6901 .... 21 E
lkitchens@crc.edu
KITCHENS, Larry, E .... 817-257-7121 .... 498 F
l.kitchens@tcu.edu
KITCHENS, Penny .... 478-553-2060 .... 134 F
pkitchens@oftc.edu
KITCHENS, Ronnie .... 601-426-6346 .... 277 D
rkitchens@southeasternbaptist.edu
KITCHENS, Tempie .... 770-233-6170 .... 137 B
tkitchens@sctech.edu
KITCHEYAN, Billie .... 402-878-2380 .... 298 G
billiek@littlepriest.edu
KITCHINGS, Dorcas, A .... 803-822-3584 .... 459 D
kitchingsd@midlandstech.edu
KITCHNER, Russell .... 304-724-3700 .... 540 C
rkitchner@apus.edu
KITE, Bruce .... 575-646-2446 .... 319 D
bkite@nmsu.edu
KITE, Joy, A .... 608-822-2319 .... 555 B
KITEI, Susan, C .... 610-758-3870 .... 434 E
sck0@lehigh.edu
KITHCART, Jane .... 845-687-5111 .... 358 C
kithcarj@sunyulster.edu
KITSON, Clair .... 423-236-2918 .... 473 A
cjkitson@southern.edu
KITTEL, Jane .... 715-675-3331 .... 554 G
kittelj@ntc.edu
KITTELL, Gary .... 315-464-4448 .... 352 E
kittelg@upstate.edu
KITTINGER, Fred .... 407-823-1208 .... 120 A
fred.kittinger@ucf.edu
KITTLITZ, Lenell .... 860-244-7640 .... 89 J
lkittlitz@commnet.edu
KITTRELL, Carol, N .... 251-460-7084 .... 9 E
ckittrell@usouthal.edu
KITTS, Kenneth, D .... 910-521-6224 .... 379 B
ken.kitts@uncp.edu
KIVEL, Andy .... 925-685-1230 .... 43 C
akivel@dvc.edu
KIVETZ, Robert .... 212-998-4611 .... 344 B
rsk1@nyu.edu
KIYOSHI, Jack, O .... 670-234-5498 .... 559 F
jackk@nmcnet.edu
KIZER, James .... 615-963-5171 .... 474 A
jkizer@tnstate.edu
KIZINA, Terrence, R .... 814-871-5759 .... 429 F
kizina002@gannon.edu
KJARTANSON, Mary .... 619-221-2144 .... 65 H
mkjartan@sdccd.edu
KJONAAS, Wayne .... 970-247-7525 .... 84 G
kjonaas_w@fortlewis.edu
KLAAS, Alan .... 928-692-3085 .... 16 G
aklaas@mohave.edu
KLAAS, Carlene .... 312-362-8146 .... 148 F
cklaas@depaul.edu
KLABECHEK, IV, John .... 262-551-5911 .... 546 F
jklabechek@carthage.edu
KLACIK, Michael .... 402-474-5315 .... 298 E
mklacik@kaplanuniversity.edu
KLADIVKO, Deborah .... 803-641-3577 .... 462 B
debk@usca.edu
KLAFFKE, David .... 208-467-8641 .... 143 I
dklaffke@nnu.edu
KLAG, Michael, J .... 410-955-3540 .... 223 F
mklag@jhsph.edu
KLAGGE, Jay .... 480-446-5022 .... 19 C
jay.klagge@phoenix.edu
KLAHR, Sabine .... 801-581-8876 .... 510 L
s.klahr@ic.utah.edu
KLAIBER, Robert .... 207-221-8750 .... 218 C
rklaiber@kaplan.edu
KLAICH, Daniel, J .... 775-784-4901 .... 302 F
chancellor@nevada.edu
KLAPERMAN MORROW,
Carol .... 212-998-4798 .... 344 B
carol.morrow@nyu.edu
KLAPHAAK, Kirk, K 812-941-2445 174
kklapha@ius.edu
KLAPPER, Robert .... 770-729-8400 .... 124 G
KLASEN, James 617-423-4630 231
jklasen@bfit.edu
KLASKO, Stephen, K .... 813-974-2196 .... 120 D
sklasko@health.usf.edu
KLASS, Stephen, P .... 413-597-3118 .... 246 G
stephen.p.klass@williams.edu
KLAUDER, Mark, J .... 802-447-6322 .... 514 D
mklauder@svc.edu
KLAUS, Allen, R .... 210-434-6711 .... 491 G
arklaus@lake.ollusa.edu
KLAUS, Byron, D .... 417-268-1000 .... 279 B
bklaus@agts.edu
KLAUS, Chad, L .... 609-258-5498 .... 313 A
klaus@princeton.edu
KLAUS, Dennis .... 801-957-4250 .... 512 C
dennis.klaus@slcc.edu
KLAUSER, Patricia, A .... 203-371-7978 .... 93 G
klauserp@sacredheart.edu
KLAUSMEYER, Robert .... 573-875-7304 .... 280 E
rklausmeyer@ccis.edu
KLAWE, Maria, M .... 909-921-8120 .... 49 D
klawe@hmc.edu
KLAWITTER, Christina .... 608-363-2660 .... 546 B
klawitterc@beloit.edu
KLAWUNN, Margaret, M ... 401-863-1800 .... 452 J
margaret_klawunn@brown.edu
KLAY, Kathy, A .... 937-328-6085 .... 387 G
klayk@clarkstate.edu
KLCO, JoEllen .... 330-499-9600 .... 393 I
jklco@kent.edu
KLEEMAN, Beverly, S .... 509-777-4548 .... 539 F
bkleeman@whitworth.edu
KLEEN, Betty .... 985-448-4191 .... 216 A
betty.kleen@nicholls.edu
KLEFFMAN, David, L .... 330-471-8139 .... 395 E
dkleffman@malone.edu
KLEI, Thomas, R .... 225-578-7696 .... 212 F
tklei@lsu.edu
KLEICH, Tammie .... 308-635-6072 .... 301 E
kleicht@wncc.edu
KLEIN, Andrew, O .... 508-849-3313 .... 230 C
aklein@annamaria.edu
KLEIN, Barb .... 641-648-4611 .... 185 I
barb.klein@iavalley.edu
KLEIN, Barb .... 641-844-5709 .... 185 J
barb.klein@iavalley.edu
KLEIN, Barbara, A .... 410-269-5087 .... 227 C
bklein@umaryland.edu
KLEIN, Bob, P .... 518-783-2432 .... 350 I
rklein@siena.edu
KLEIN, Craig .... 660-596-7208 .... 290 F
cklein@sfccmo.edu
KLEIN, Cynthia .... 412-809-5100 .... 444 F
klein@pti.edu
KLEIN, David, A .... 434-223-6129 .... 519 B
dklein@email.hsc.edu
KLEIN, Eileen .... 512-223-5766 .... 481 B
eklein@austincc.edu
KLEIN, Gary, L .... 608-796-3074 .... 553 A
glklein@viterbo.edu
KLEIN, Glen, J .... 517-355-5029 .... 255 D
kleing@ctlr.msu.edu
KLEIN, J. Douglass .... 518-388-6056 .... 358 E
kleind@union.edu
KLEIN, Jaime .... 608-822-2445 .... 555 B
KLEIN, James .... 541-552-6114 .... 419 A
kleinj@sou.edu
KLEIN, James, W .... 301-766-3671 .... 223 G
jklein@kaplan.edu
KLEIN, Jason, D .... 605-336-6588 .... 465 B
jklein@sfseminary.edu
KLEIN, Jim .... 502-456-6508 .... 206 C
jklein@sullivan.edu
KLEIN, Joanne, R .... 240-895-4251 .... 226 A
jrklein@smcm.edu
KLEIN, John, E .... 434-947-8140 .... 522 E
jklein@randolphcollege.edu
KLEIN, June .... 650-843-3415 .... 61 A
jklein@paloaltou.edu
KLEIN, Marjorie, S .... 814-332-5910 .... 421 E
marjorie.klein@allegheny.edu
KLEIN, Mendel .... 718-384-5460 .... 361 E
KLEIN, Michael .... 631-370-3300 .... 350 D
mklein@sbmelville.edu
KLEIN, Michelle, W .... 504-866-7426 .... 213 I
finance@nds.edu
KLEIN, Paul .... 415-749-4589 .... 65 I
paulklein@sfai.edu
KLEIN, Sandy, L .... 701-483-2371 .... 381 E
sandy.klein@dickinsonstate.edu
KLEIN, Sarah .... 718-390-3420 .... 359 G
sarah.klein@wagner.edu
KLEIN, Shelley .... 661-763-7711 .... 72 C
sklein@taftcollege.edu
KLEIN, Steve .... 503-352-2822 .... 419 E
kleinsk@pacificu.edu
KLEIN, Steven .... 325-942-2185 .... 480 E
steven.klein@angelo.edu
KLEIN, Steven, J .... 765-361-6253 .... 181 C
kleins@wabash.edu

KNIGHT, James ... 774-354-0658 ... 231 D
james.knight@becker.edu
KNIGHT, Janet ... 219-785-5557 ... 178 H
jknight@pnc.edu
KNIGHT, Jim, D ... 815-939-5201 ... 160 F
jdknight@olivet.edu
KNIGHT, John ... 312-329-8018 ... 158 H
john.knight@moody.edu
KNIGHT, JR., John, F ... 334-229-4286 ... 1 C
jknight@alasu.edu
KNIGHT, Kelly ... 207-221-8718 ... 218 C
kknight@kaplan.edu
KNIGHT, Kerri ... 229-226-1621 ... 137 F
kknight@thomasu.edu
KNIGHT, Lea Ann ... 601-643-8342 ... 274 A
leaann.knight@colin.edu
KNIGHT, Leonard ... 760-245-4271 ... 77 E
Leonard.Knight@vvc.edu
KNIGHT, Lori ... 504-816-4797 ... 208 I
lknight@dillard.edu
KNIGHT, Lydia ... 706-272-4527 ... 127 G
lknight@daltonstat.edu
KNIGHT, Mary, E ... 512-471-3727 ... 505 B
bd.knightme@austin.utexas.edu
KNIGHT, Melvin ... 973-877-3301 ... 310 A
knight@essex.edu
KNIGHT, Robert ... 715-836-4353 ... 550 H
knightrm@uwec.edu
KNIGHT, Robert ... 360-992-2101 ... 532 A
rknight@clark.edu
KNIGHT, Robin ... 478-387-4890 ... 130 E
KNIGHT, Roger, A ... 601-403-1206 ... 277 A
rknight@prcc.edu
KNIGHT, Russell ... 401-841-6436 ... 557 I
KNIGHT, Sheri ... 620-343-4600 ... 192 E
sknight@fhtc.edu
KNIGHT, Steven, H ... 601-318-6111 ... 278 E
steve.knight@wmcarey.edu
KNIGHT, Unita ... 910-296-2460 ... 371 B
uknight@jamessprunt.edu
KNIGHT, W. Hal ... 423-439-7627 ... 473 E
knighth@etsu.edu
KNIGHT, Wendy, S ... 563-557-8271 ... 187 G
knightw@nicc.edu
KNIGHT, William, E ... 419-372-7816 ... 385 C
wknight@bgsu.edu
KNIGHTON, Denise ... 662-915-7792 ... 277 G
denisek@olemiss.edu
KNIGHTON, Diana, W ... 205-929-1442 ... 5 H
diana@mail.miles.edu
KNIPE, Robert, G ... 585-345-6969 ... 334 F
rgknipe@genesee.edu
KNIPLE, Jeffrey ... 410-617-2032 ... 224 A
jwkniple@loyola.edu
KNIPPLE, Robert, W ... 814-269-2080 ... 449 D
knipple@pitt.edu
KNIPSCHIELD, Debbie ... 253-833-9111 ... 534 C
DKnipschield@greenriver.edu
KNISELY, Bertie ... 610-861-1345 ... 436 I
bertiek@moravian.edu
KNISPEL, Todd ... 406-377-9413 ... 294 C
knispelt@dawson.edu
KNISS, Fred, L ... 540-432-4105 ... 518 E
fred.kniss@emu.edu
KNOBEL, Dale, T ... 740-587-6281 ... 389 H
knobel@denison.edu
KNOBEL, David ... 954-535-8820 ... 107 E
dknobel@careercollege.edu
KNOBLICH, Julie, A ... 620-792-9275 ... 190 E
knoblichj@bartonccc.edu
KNOCH, Daniel, L ... 517-437-7341 ... 252 E
dan.knoch@hillsdale.edu
KNOCHE, Charlotte, M ... 651-641-8240 ... 263 C
knoche@csp.edu
KNODELL, Jane, E ... 802-656-1417 ... 514 F
jane.knodell@uvm.edu
KNODLE-BRAGIEL, Lisa ... 503-883-2214 ... 416 G
lbragiel@linfield.edu
KNOEBEL, Ann, G ... 210-999-7601 ... 502 C
aknoebel@trinity.edu
KNOEBEL, Thomas, L ... 414-425-8300 ... 550 A
tknoebel@shst.edu
KNOELL, Karen ... 605-995-2647 ... 464 B
kaknoell@dwu.edu
KNOETTGEN, Suzi ... 785-243-1435 ... 191 H
sknoettgen@cloud.edu
KNOFF, Gregory ... 313-664-7650 ... 250 A
gknoff@collegeforcreativestudies.edu
KNOKE, Luke ... 317-845-0300 ... 177 I
lknoke@medtechcollege.edu
KNOLL, Dorothy, A ... 913-588-4698 ... 197 A
dknoll@kumc.edu
KNOLL, Kathy ... 575-562-2611 ... 318 A
kathy.knoll@enmu.edu
KNOLLMAN, Paul, L ... 734-384-4282 ... 255 G
pknollman@monroeccc.edu
KNOOR, Robert ... 616-957-6039 ... 249 F
rknoor@calvinseminary.edu
KNOP, Joachim, W ... 202-994-6506 ... 97 F
knop@gwu.edu
KNOP-COX, Barbara ... 405-422-1401 ... 411 G
knopcoxb@redlandscc.edu
KNORR, Joseph ... 301-447-5271 ... 225 A
knorr@msmary.edu
KNORR, Stephen, C ... 573-882-2726 ... 291 C
knorrs@umsystem.edu
KNORR, Walter ... 312-413-9097 ... 166 E
wknorr@uillinois.edu
KNORTZ, Geraldine ... 802-654-2200 ... 514 B
gknortz@smcvt.edu
KNOST, Julie ... 812-855-7559 ... 173 B
knost@indiana.edu
KNOST, Julie ... 812-855-7559 ... 173 C
jknost@indiana.edu
KNOTHE, Thomas, E ... 608-796-3360 ... 553 A
teknothe@viterbo.edu
KNOTT, Allan ... 214-860-8531 ... 485 A
aknott@dcccd.edu
KNOTT, Gregory ... 305-237-0825 ... 113 H
gknott@mdc.edu
KNOTT, Jack, H ... 213-740-0350 ... 76 C
jhknott@usc.edu
KNOTT, Kevin ... 217-351-2239 ... 161 B
kknott@parkland.edu
KNOTT, Ronald ... 812-357-6544 ... 179 E
rknott@saintmeinrad.edu
KNOTT, Toni ... 559-456-2777 ... 27 B
tknott@alliant.edu
KNOTT, William ... 616-222-1918 ... 250 C
bill.knott@cornerstone.edu
KNOTTS, Ann ... 321-433-7032 ... 101 J
knottsa@brevardcc.edu
KNOTTS, Bradley ... 815-226-3398 ... 162 H
bknotts@rockford.edu
KNOTTS, Cecil ... 318-357-5965 ... 216 B
knottsc@nsula.edu
KNOTTS, David ... 636-798-2166 ... 284 C
dknotts@lindenwood.edu
KNOTTS, Debby ... 505-277-5765 ... 321 C
debby@unm.edu
KNOTTS, H. Gibbs ... 828-227-7646 ... 379 E
gknotts@wcu.edu
KNOUFF, Christine ... 859-341-5627 ... 199 B
cknouff@brownmackie.edu
KNOUSE, Christine ... 717-262-2016 ... 452 B
cknouse@wilson.edu
KNOWLES, Daniel, M ... 212-746-6464 ... 360 B
dknowles@med.cornell.edu
KNOWLES, Harley ... 423-746-5201 ... 476 D
hknowles@twcnet.edu
KNOWLES, J. Geoff ... 765-269-5681 ... 176 B
jknowles5@ivytech.edu
KNOWLES, John ... 239-687-5402 ... 101 B
jknowles@avemarialaw.edu
KNOWLES, Kriss ... 847-214-7819 ... 150 D
kknowles@elgin.edu
KNOWLES, Monica ... 360-992-2904 ... 532 A
mknowles@clark.edu
KNOWLTON, Douglas, D ... 605-256-5112 ... 465 G
doug.knowlton@dsu.edu
KNOWLTON, Eloise ... 508-767-7487 ... 230 E
eknowlton@assumption.edu
KNOX, Carol ... 510-666-8248 ... 26 G
registrar@aimc.edu
KNOX, Chris ... 559-737-6146 ... 42 B
chrisk@cos.edu
KNOX, Chrisanne ... 925-685-1230 ... 43 C
cknox@dvc.edu
KNOX, George, C ... 620-421-6700 ... 194 E
georgek@labette.edu
KNOX, Linda ... 219-989-3169 ... 178 G
Linda.Knox@purduecal.edu
KNOX, Marg ... 512-322-3774 ... 504 E
mknox@utsystem.edu
KNOX, Pamela ... 615-366-4411 ... 473 C
pamela.knox@tbr.edu
KNOX, Ruth, A ... 478-757-5212 ... 139 A
rknox@wesleyancollege.edu
KNOX, Teresa ... 918-298-8200 ... 407 F
KNOX, Teresa, L ... 918-610-0027 ... 407 G
tknox@communitycarecollege.edu
KNOX, Teresa, L ... 918-610-0027 ... 411 A
tknox@communitycarecollege.edu
KNUDSEN, Alice ... 510-430-2350 ... 57 D
aknudsen@mills.edu
KNUDSEN, H. Peter ... 406-496-4395 ... 296 C
pknudsen@mtech.edu
KNUDSEN, J. Todd ... 562-902-3358 ... 71 A
toddknudsen@scuhs.edu
KNUDSEN, Kjell ... 218-726-7281 ... 272 B
kknudsen@d.umn.edu
KNUDSEN, Ross ... 208-376-7731 ... 142 E
rknudsen@boisebible.edu
KNUDSON, Edward ... 805-378-1403 ... 77 B
eknudson@vcccd.edu
KNUDSON, Kari ... 701-224-5604 ... 382 B
kari.l.knudson@bismarckstate.edu
KNUDSON, Paula, M ... 608-785-8150 ... 551 B
knudson.paul@uwlax.edu
KNUDSON-CARL, Tara ... 402-399-2449 ... 297 E
tknudsoncarl@csm.edu
KNUESEL, Rita ... 320-363-3147 ... 271 F
rknuesel@csbsju.edu
KNUESEL, Rita ... 320-363-5503 ... 262 H
rknuesel@csbsju.edu
KNUEVE, Donald, S ... 419-783-2581 ... 389 G
dknueve@defiance.edu
KNUTEL, Phillip, G ... 781-891-3422 ... 231 F
pknutel@bentley.edu
KNUTH, Barbara, A ... 607-255-5864 ... 331 C
bak3@cornell.edu
KNUTSEN, John, D ... 510-883-2073 ... 45 A
jknutsen@dspt.edu
KNUTSON, Craig ... 405-208-5000 ... 410 A
crknutson@okcu.edu
KNUTSON, Karen ... 320-363-2736 ... 262 H
kknutson@csbsju.edu
KNUTSON, Karen, G ... 320-363-5922 ... 271 F
kknutson@csbsju.edu
KNUTSON, Victoria, P ... 713-500-9860 ... 506 D
victoria.p.knutson@uth.tmc.edu
KNUTZEN, Gary ... 360-416-7714 ... 538 A
gary.knutzen@skagit.edu
KNUTZEN, Kathleen ... 661-654-2210 ... 33 H
kknutzen@csub.edu
KO, Jeanne ... 212-472-1500 ... 343 G
jko@nysid.edu
KO, Joseph ... 510-763-7787 ... 26 F
josephko@acchs.edu
KO, Winston, T ... 530-754-8918 ... 73 F
wtko@ucdavis.edu
KOAL, Penny ... 360-596-5227 ... 538 B
pkoal@spscc.ctc.edu
KOBALLA, Thomas ... 912-478-5648 ... 131 A
tkoballa@georgiasouthern.edu
KOBAYASHI, Frank ... 408-741-2117 ... 78 B
frank.kobayashi@westvalley.edu
KOBAYASHI, JR., Paul, Y ... 808-956-7161 ... 140 J
pyk@hawaii.edu
KOBAYASHI, Vivian ... 408-541-0100 ... 41 C
vkobayashi@cogswell.edu
KOBERNA, Sharon ... 480-517-8220 ... 16 C
sharon.koberna@riosalado.edu
KOBES, Patricia ... 845-574-4000 ... 347 I
KOBOLAKIS, Evan ... 201-612-5499 ... 307 F
ekobolakis@bergen.edu
KOBRITZ, Richard ... 818-345-7921 ... 42 D
rkobritz@columbiacollege.edu
KOBULNICKY, Paul, J ... 330-941-3675 ... 406 F
pjkobulnicky@ysu.edu
KOBUS, Lee ... 732-255-0400 ... 312 D
lkobus@ocean.edu
KOBUSZEWSKI, Jeanne, K ... 563-333-6298 ... 188 D
KOBYLSKI, Janet ... 570-408-4501 ... 451 G
janet.kobylski@wilkes.edu
KOCAR, Deb ... 617-349-8800 ... 236 G
ugadm@lesley.edu
KOCER, Ken ... 605-668-1589 ... 464 F
kkocer@mtmc.edu
KOCH, Amelia ... 617-266-1400 ... 231 G
KOCH, Andrew, S ... 240-895-4905 ... 226 A
askoch@smcm.edu
KOCH, Bill ... 252-328-6166 ... 377 C
kochb@ecu.edu
KOCH, Connie ... 314-362-6289 ... 282 E
ckoch@bjc.org
KOCH, Dennis ... 903-886-5796 ... 497 E
dennis_koch@tamu-commerce.edu
KOCH, Don ... 618-634-3289 ... 164 C
donk@shawneecc.edu
KOCH, James ... 651-638-6415 ... 261 I
j-koch@bethel.edu
KOCH, Jennifer ... 716-888-2235 ... 325 G
koch25@canisius.edu
KOCH, Jo Ann ... 770-394-8300 ... 124 F
jkoch@aii.edu
KOCH, Julian, D ... 985-549-3643 ... 216 C
jdkoch@selu.edu
KOCH, Katharine ... 828-227-7677 ... 379 E
kakoch@wcu.edu
KOCH, Kathryn, E ... 989-774-6995 ... 249 G
koch1ke@cmich.edu
KOCH, Keith ... 612-977-5322 ... 262 A
keith.koch@capella.edu
KOCH, Kelly ... 989-386-6639 ... 255 F
kkoch@midmich.edu
KOCH, Linda, D ... 570-484-2022 ... 443 A
lkoch@lhup.edu
KOCH, Lindsey ... 361-570-4136 ... 503 E
kochl@uhv.edu
KOCH, Paul ... 563-333-6212 ... 188 D
KochPaulC@sau.edu
KOCH, Paul ... 831-459-5861 ... 75 A
plkoch@ucolick.ort
KOCH, Paul, C ... 563-333-6196 ... 188 D
KochPaulC@sau.edu
KOCH, Robert ... 657-278-2638 ... 34 E
KOCH, Roy ... 503-725-5257 ... 418 G
kochr@pdx.edu
KOCH, Susan ... 217-206-6634 ... 167 A
koch@uis.edu
KOCHAN, Roman ... 562-985-4047 ... 35 A
rkochan@csulb.edu
KOCHANCZYK, Kristin ... 617-262-5000 ... 232 B
kristin.kochanczyk@the-bac.edu
KOCHANEK, Lea ... 210-341-1366 ... 491 E
development@ost.edu
KOCHANOWSKI-SUTTER,
Lorraine, A ... 716-685-9631 ... 342 H
lkochanowski@nycc.edu
KOCHARD, Beverly ... 610-861-1502 ... 436
kochardb@moravian.edu
KOCHARD, Dale, A ... 610-758-5801 ... 434
dak304@lehigh.edu
KOCHER, Andy, M ... 317-788-3493 ... 180 C
akocher@uindy.edu
KOCHER, Betty, A ... 269-387-2360 ... 260 F
betty.kocher@wmich.edu
KOCHER, Bruce ... 269-488-4205 ... 253 G
bkocher@kvcc.edu
KOCHER, Charles ... 856-691-8600 ... 309 C
ckocher@cccnj.edu
KOCHER, Craig, T ... 804-289-8500 ... 525 A
ckocher@richmond.edu
KOCHER, Edward, W ... 412-396-6082 ... 428 C
kocher@duq.edu
KOCHEVAR, Brenda ... 218-749-0314 ... 267 C
b.kochevar@mr.mnscu.edu
KOCHEVAR, Deborah ... 508-887-4700 ... 245 F
deborah.kochevar@tufts.edu
KOCHEVAR, Sue ... 719-549-3280 ... 87 B
Sue.Kochevar@pueblocc.edu
KOCHIEN, Kenneth, G ... 603-526-3627 ... 304 A
kkochien@colby-sawyer.edu
KOCHIN, Frank, S ... 314-516-6311 ... 291 F
kochinf@umsl.edu
KOCHIS, Stephen, J ... 845-575-3000 ... 340 C
stephen.kochis@marist.edu
KOCHON, Barbara ... 413-565-1000 ... 231 B
bkochon@baypath.edu
KOCIAN, Bryce ... 979-532-6308 ... 508 J
brycek@wcjc.edu
KOCICH, Dennis ... 979-830-4160 ... 482 A
dkocich@blinn.edu
KOCIOLEK, Patrick ... 303-492-8464 ... 88 B
patrick.kociolek@colorado.edu
KOCOUR, Bruce ... 865-471-3240 ... 467 E
bkocour@cn.edu
KOCZON, Lenore ... 701-858-3310 ... 381 G
lenore.koczon@minotstateu.edu
KOCZUR-RICHARDSON,
Jennifer ... 219-981-1111 ... 176 E
jkoczurrichardson@ivytech.edu
KODA-KIMBLE,
Mary Anne ... 415-476-8010 ... 74 E
kodakimblem@pharmacy.ucsf.edu
KODALI, Naren ... 703-821-8570 ... 524 D
nkodali@stratford.edu
KODAMA, Be-Jay ... 808-739-8526 ... 140 A
bkodama@chaminade.edu
KODNER-WENZEL,
Andrea ... 952-487-8469 ... 268 C
KOEBEL, Dave ... 402-457-2391 ... 298 H
dkoebel@mccneb.edu
KOECHIG, Donna ... 541-463-5307 ... 416 D
koechigd@lanecc.edu
KOEGEL, Warren ... 256-782-5368 ... 4 L
wkoegel@jsu.edu
KOEGLER, Jason, W ... 304-336-8302 ... 544 B
jkoegler@westliberty.edu
KOEHLER, Al ... 636-922-8452 ... 288 E
alkoehler@stchas.edu
KOEHLER, David ... 308-635-6021 ... 301 E
koehlerd@wncc.edu
KOEHLER, Donna ... 253-589-5588 ... 532 B
donna.koehler@cptc.edu
KOEHLER, Gwendolyn ... 815-455-8783 ... 157 F
gkoehler@mchenry.edu
KOEHLER, John ... 406-791-5330 ... 296 H
jkoehler01@ugf.edu
KOEHLER, Kory ... 281-998-6150 ... 493 F
kory.koehler@sjcd.edu
KOEHLER, Kristen ... 718-390-3404 ... 359 G
Kristen.Koehler@wagner.edu
KOEHLER, Larry ... 810-232-8153 ... 256 C
larry.koehler@mcc.edu
KOEHLER, Martha, K ... 813-253-7007 ... 110 I
mkoehler@hccfl.edu
KOEHLER, Randy ... 513-244-8449 ... 387 D
randy.koehler@ccuniversity.edu
KOEHLER, Tracey ... 970-943-3038 ... 89 B
tkoehler@western.edu
KOEHN, David ... 918-444-2186 ... 409 A
koehn@nsuok.edu
KOEHN, Effie, F ... 406-243-6413 ... 295 A
effie.koehn@umontana.edu
KOEHN, Michelle ... 316-226-2002 ... 181 E
koehnml@ihs.org
KOEHN, Suzie ... 307-855-2148 ... 555 G
suzie@cwc.edu
KOEHNKE, Paul ... 704-330-6121 ... 369 A
paul.koehnke@cpcc.edu
KOELBL, James, J ... 207-221-4701 ... 220 H
jkoelbl@une.edu
KOELKER, June ... 817-257-7106 ... 498 F
j.koelker@tcu.edu
KOELLEIN, David ... 615-794-4254 ... 472 D
dkoellein@omorecollege.edu
KOELLER, C. Timothy ... 201-216-5376 ... 315 E
tkoeller@stevens.edu
KOELLER, Martin, E ... 973-761-9782 ... 315 B
martin.koeller@shu.edu
KOELLIKER, Marilynn ... 785-670-1450 ... 197 D
marilynn.koelliker@washburn.edu

KOPKE, Lael 415-749-4512 65 I
lkopke@sfai.edu
KOPLOCK, Karina 770-619-3628 128 C
kkoplock@devry.edu
KOPLOWITZ, Stephan 661-255-1050 32 C
skoplowitz@calarts.edu
KOPONEN, Glenn 845-675-4691 344 G
glenn.koponen@nyack.edu
KOPP, Courtney, A 515-574-1020 185 F
kopp@iowacentral.edu
KOPP, Mark, W 864-242-5100 455 E
KOPP, Michael 253-854-4960 535 D
KOPP, Stephen, J 304-696-2300 543 G
kopp@marshall.edu
KOPP, Sue 503-517-1032 421 A
skopp@warnerpacific.edu
KOPP, Will 614-287-2412 388 G
wkopp@cscc.edu
KOPPEL, Roberta, K 401-874-5177 454 E
bkoppel@uri.edu
KOPPEL, Sheree 502-456-6509 206 B
skoppel@sctd.edu
KOPPER, Beverly 262-472-1672 552 E
kopperb@uww.edu
KOPPI, Steve 413-538-2081 242 G
skoppi@mtholyoke.edu
KOPTEROS, Michelle, C 773-883-7279 158 D
kopter15@hotmail.com
KORAL, Jacqueline, K 203-932-7462 95 B
jkoral@newhaven.edu
KORAN, Noel 541-552-6522 419 A
korann@sou.edu
KORB, Christine 503-699-3361 416 I
ckorb@maryhurst.edu
KORB, Judy 913-469-8500 193 I
jkorb@jccc.edu
KORB, Leigh, S 662-846-4000 274 B
lkorb@deltastate.edu
KORB, Scott 906-635-2032 254 C
skorb@lssu.edu
KORB, Scott, M 906-635-2032 254 C
skorb@lssu.edu
KORB-NICE, Jobe, S 206-281-2564 537 D
jobe@spu.edu
KORBEL, Linda 847-635-1952 160 E
lkorbel@oakton.edu
KORBER, Stephanie 814-269-7074 449 D
korber@pitt.edu
KORCAN-BUZZA,
Andrea, L 724-847-6603 429 G
akorcanb@geneva.edu
KORD, JoLanna 620-341-6839 192 D
jkord@emporia.edu
KORDENBROCK, Jeffrey 859-344-3321 206 D
jeff.kordenbrock@thomasmore.edu
KORDULA, Susan 715-365-4464 554 F
skordula@nicoletcollege.edu
KOREEN, Michael 952-487-7007 268 C
michael.koreen@normandale.edu
KORENKIEWICZ, Jason 212-746-1059 360 B
jkorenki@med.cornell.edu
KORETOFF, Lisa, A 336-334-4822 370 E
lakoretoff@gtcc.edu
KORF, Abraham 305-673-5664 123 E
rabbikorf@hotmail.com
KORF, Benzion 305-653-8770 123 E
bkorf@lecfl.com
KORFIATIS, George, P 201-216-5263 315 E
gkorfiat@stevens.edu
KORINEK, Clare, M 312-915-7235 157 A
ckorine@luc.edu
KORIS, Carol 305-913-2104 111 K
carol.koris@jwu.edu
KORMAN, Thomas, P 517-750-1200 258 F
tkorman@arbor.edu
KORN, Jane 509-313-3700 534 A
jkorn@lawschool.gonzaga.edu
KORNBERG, Judith 212-986-4343 323 J
jdk@berkeleycollege.edu
KORNBERG, Judith 973-278-5400 307 G
KORNBERG, Mindy 206-685-4730 538 F
mindyk@uw.edu
KORNBERG, Sir Hans 617-353-4020 232 G
hlk@bu.edu
KORNBLUH, Mark 859-257-1246 206 H
kornbluh@uky.edu
KORNBLUH, Rebecca 909-621-8000 62 H
rebecca_kornbluh@cucmail.claremont.edu
KORNEGAY, Arthur 910-296-2575 371 B
akornegay@jamessprunt.edu
KORNEGAY, Barbara, R 919-658-7756 367 D
bkornegay@moc.edu
KORNEGAY, Carolyn, T 405-466-3411 408 G
ctkornegay@lunet.edu
KORNEGAY, Jeffrey 910-879-5574 368 A
jeffkornegay@bladencc.edu
KORNEGAY, Jeri, S 260-982-5285 177 F
jskornegay@manchester.edu
KORNEGAY, Joy 919-735-5151 374 F
jkornegay@waynecc.edu
KORNER, Barbara, O 814-865-2591 438 F
bok2@psu.edu
KORNFELD, Harriet, S 617-724-6399 242 E
hkornfeld@mghihp.edu

KORNHAUSER, Stanley 212-410-8498 343 B
skornhauser@nycpm.edu
KORNIEWICZ, Denise 701-777-4555 381 D
denise.korniewicz@email.und.edu
KORNMILLER, Brenda, L 740-374-8716 405 F
bkornmiller@wscc.edu
KORNOWSKI, Andrew 502-213-4162 202 B
andrew.kornowski@kctcs.edu
KORNUTA, Halyna, M 209-667-3082 36 C
hkornuta@csustan.edu
KOROCH, Greg, A 269-927-8161 254 B
koroch@lakemichigancollege.edu
KOROMA, Ibrahim, H 202-274-5415 99 F
ikoroma@udc.edu
KOROMA, Joseph 360-475-7160 535 J
jkoroma@olympic.edu
KOROPCHAK, John, A 618-453-4551 164 I
koropcha@siu.edu
KORPELA, Doreen 906-487-7201 251 C
doreen.korpela@finlandia.edu
KORPI, Ray 360-992-2932 532 A
rkorpi@clark.edu
KORPICS, Wayne 419-423-2211 385 H
wkorpics@brownmackie.edu
KORR, Wynne, S 217-333-2261 167 B
wkorr@illinois.edu
KORSCHGEN, Ann, J 573-882-7651 291 D
korschgena@missouri.edu
KORSE-DEVLIN, Allison 661-362-3648 41 G
allison.devlin@canyons.edu
KORSTAD, Donna 509-542-4401 532 C
dkorstad@columbiabasin.edu
KORSTAD, John 918-495-6942 411 C
jkorstad@oru.edu
KORTE, Andi 910-695-3767 373 E
kortea@sandhills.edu
KORTENHOEVEN, Steve 866-323-0233 63 D
KORVAS, Ronald 407-646-2174 116 B
rkorvas@rollins.edu
KORVAS, Thomas, F 740-593-2909 399 G
korvas@ohio.edu
KORVER, Bill 910-323-5614 362 G
KORWITTS, Kayte 312-980-4822 153 G
kkorwitts@iadtchicago.edu
KORZAN, Loren 419-227-3141 404 D
lkorzan@unoh.edu
KORZINEK, Sue 616-331-2035 252 A
korzines@gvsu.edu
KOSAK, Robbee 412-268-2136 424 H
rkosak@andrew.cmu.edu
KOSANOVIC, David 614-251-4512 398 F
kosanovd@ohiodominican.edu
KOSBOTH, Michele 617-243-2227 236 F
mkosboth@lasell.edu
KOSCHMEDER, Douglas 563-387-1167 187 A
registrar@luther.edu
KOSEL, Paul 402-554-2648 301 B
pkosel@unomaha.edu
KOSELUK, William 805-893-5252 74 F
william.koseluk@ic.ucsb.edu
KOSH, Jamie 814-472-3372 446 B
jkosh@francis.edu
KOSHEWA, Angela, D 502-852-6981 207 A
adkosh01@louisville.edu
KOSHINSKI, Robert 716-614-6227 344 C
koshinski@niagaracc.suny.edu
KOSHORK, Lori 206-726-5027 532 G
lkoshork@cornish.edu
KOSHUT, Thomas, M 256-824-6100 9 A
tom.koshut@uah.edu
KOSHUTE, Daniel 814-472-3222 446 B
dkoshute@francis.edu
KOSIEWICZ, Lisa 415-422-2710 76 B
lkosiewicz@usfca.edu
KOSIN, Mary 570-740-0395 435 C
mkosin@luzerne.edu
KOSINSKI, Mark 203-285-2077 90 A
mkosinski@gwcc.commnet.edu
KOSINSKI, Ross 623-572-3329 16 F
rkosin@midwestern.edu
KOSINSKY, James, A 708-209-3519 148 C
jim.kosinsky@cuchicago.edu
KOSKI, Lynne, D 402-844-7036 300 A
lynne@northeast.edu
KOSLOSKI, James 516-877-3974 322 A
kosloski@adelphi.edu
KOSLOSKY, Jill 620-252-7295 191 I
jillk@coffeyville.edu
KOSMER, Mary, K 920-923-8089 548 C
mkkosmer09@marianuniversity.edu
KOSMOSKI, Kathleen 912-486-7409 134 H
kkosmoski@ogeecheetech.edu
KOSMYNA, Sandy 734-847-4332 255 G
skosmyna@monroeccc.edu
KOSOWSKY, Vicki 812-535-5216 179 C
vkosowsk@smwc.edu
KOSSE, Glenn, F 502-272-8328 198 E
gkosse@bellarmine.edu
KOSSEFF, Christopher, O 973-972-4866 316 C
kosseff@umdnj.edu
KOSSES, Jennifer 617-732-2866 241 F
jennifer.kosses@mcphs.edu
KOSSUTH, Joanne 781-292-2431 235 C
joanne.kossuth@olin.edu

KOSTELECKY, Sarah 505-424-2392 318 C
skostelecky@iaia.edu
KOSTELNIK, Marjorie 402-472-2913 300 H
mkostelnik2@unl.edu
KOSTKA, Kim 608-758-6522 552 F
kim.kostka@uwc.edu
KOSTRAB, Lynn, M 330-569-5109 391 H
kostrablm@hiram.edu
KOSTRUBANIC, Robert, M 260-481-6196 174 A
kostrubr@ipfw.edu
KOSTRZEWA, Waldemar 203-575-8297 90 E
wkostrzewa@nvcc.commnet.edu
KOSTRZEWSKI, Diana 303-362-2901 83 D
dkostrzewski@coloradotech.edu
KOSTYUKOV, Victoria 718-522-9073 323 D
victoria_kostyukov@asa.edu
KOTAGAL, Nirmala 507-285-7143 269 B
nirmala.kotagal@roch.edu
KOTAJARVI, Kathy 920-693-1163 554 A
kathy.kotajarvi@gotoltc.edu
KOTARSKI, Beth 610-328-8058 447 E
bkotars1@swarthmore.edu
KOTARSKI, Vida 317-955-6203 177 G
vidako@marian.edu
KOTCAMP, Butch 740-351-3429 401 I
bkotcamp@shawnee.edu
KOTECKI, Kathy 406-657-1660 295 F
kkotecki@msubillings.edu
KOTESKEY, Kerri 406-791-5207 296 H
kkoteskey01@ugf.edu
KOTH, Tara 402-449-2831 298 B
tkoth@graceu.edu
KOTHE, Alison 765-361-6027 181 C
kothea@wabash.edu
KOTHE, DiAnn 605-367-6110 466 C
diann.kothe@southeasttech.edu
KOTHENBEUTEL, Nancy 563-336-3328 184 B
nkothenbeutel@eicc.edu
KOTILA, Paul, M 603-899-4303 305 B
kotilapm@franklinpierce.edu
KOTLER, A. Malkiel 732-367-1060 307 H
KOTLER, Aaron 732-367-1060 307 H
akotler@bmg.edu
KOTLER, Yitzchok, S 732-367-1060 307 H
KOTLIKOFF, Michael, I 607-253-3336 331 C
mik7@cornell.edu
KOTLINSKI, Michael, J 717-337-6363 429 H
mkotlinski@gettysburg.edu
KOTOWICZ, Keith, A 414-847-3301 548 G
keithkotowicz@miad.edu
KOTSAKIS, Ted 360-992-2936 532 A
tkotsakis@clark.edu
KOTSIOPULOS, Peter 308-698-5270 300 G
pkotsiopulos@nufoundation.org
KOTSIOPULOS, Peter 308-865-8474 300 G
pkotsiopulos@nufoundation.org
KOTTER, Ronald, L 812-888-4124 181 B
rkotter@vinu.edu
KOTTICH, Sarah 402-399-2427 297 E
skottich@csm.edu
KOTUBEY, Jordan 248-457-2739 252 G
KOTULSKI, Bob, L 417-268-6036 279 D
bkotulski@gobbc.edu
KOUA, Deb 515-965-7025 103 D
dkkoua@dmacc.edu
KOUBEK, Richard 225-578-5701 212 F
rkoubek@lsu.edu
KOUCOUMARIS, John, S 740-695-9500 384 J
jkoucoum@btc.edu
KOUDELIK-JONES,
Rachelle 540-857-6187 528 E
rkoudelikjones@virginiawestern.edu
KOUDOU, Nick 816-559-6182 287 H
nick.koudou@park.edu
KOUGH, Katherine 717-262-2006 452 B
kkough@wilson.edu
KOUKARI, Ray 262-619-6712 553 H
koukarir@gtc.edu
KOUKOLA, Christine, H 573-882-4523 291 D
koukolac@missouri.edu
KOULIK, Chester 845-451-1275 331 F
c_koulik@culinary.edu
KOURASIS, Betty 312-280-3500 153 A
bkourasis@aii.edu
KOURIS, Demitris 817-257-7727 498 F
d.kouris@tcu.edu
KOURY, Kevin, A 724-938-4125 441 G
koury@calu.edu
KOUTSOUTIS, Kalli 718-429-6600 359 E
kalli.koutsoutis@vaughn.edu
KOUTSOVITIS,
Christopher, S 914-337-9300 331 A
christopher.koutsovitis@concordia-ny.edu
KOVAC, Jason 913-469-8500 193 I
jasonkovac@jccc.edu
KOVAC, John 412-809-5100 444 F
kovac@pti.edu
KOVAC, Matt 724-287-8711 423 F
matt.kovac@bc3.edu
KOVACH, Kathy 912-427-1963 124 A
kkovach@altamahatech.edu
KOVACH, Paul 412-365-1140 425 B
pkovach@chatham.edu

KOVACH, Ron 219-989-2664 178
kovachr@purduecal.edu
KOVACH-ALLEN,
Katharina, E 585-345-6831 334
kekovachallen@genesee.edu
KOVACK, Ronald, J 954-771-0376 112
KOVACS, Anita, A 863-784-7123 117
anita.kovacs@southflorida.edu
KOVACS, Charles 941-359-7650 115
ckovacs@ringling.edu
KOVACS, Mark, C 315-792-3025 359
mkovacs@utica.edu
KOVACS, Paul 814-866-6641 433
pkovacs@lecom.edu
KOVAL, Volga 707-826-4143 36
volga.koval@humboldt.edu
KOVALA, Irene 623-845-3012 15
irene.kovala@gcmail.maricopa.edu
KOVALCHICK, Ann 515-271-2345 184 A
KOVALCIK, Andrew, B 412-648-0233 449 A
kandrew@pitt.edu
KOVANES, Tera, D 540-654-1042 524 H
tkovanes@umw.edu
KOVAR, Andrew 660-263-3900 279 J
akovar@cccb.edu
KOVATCH, John, E 330-972-6922 403 E
kovatch@uakron.edu
KOVATCH, Richard, A 434-982-5166 525 E
rak3e@virginia.edu
KOVATCHITCH, Marian 315-798-8125 348 D
mkovatch@secon.edu
KOVERMAN, Robert 312-369-6543 148 B
rkoverman@colum.edu
KOVEROLA, Catherine 617-349-8317 236 G
koverola@lesley.edu
KOVIC, Hong Yu 860-383-5284 91 B
hkovic@trcc.commnet.edu
KOVLER, Allen 518-828-4181 330 E
kovler@sunycgcc.edu
KOWAL, Donna, M 585-395-5400 352 F
dkowal@brockport.edu
KOWALCHUK, Elizabeth 785-864-3661 196 F
kowalchu@ku.edu
KOWALCZYK, Paul 970-491-3350 83 A
paul.kowalczyk@colostate.edu
KOWALESKI, Curt 920-403-3117 550 C
curt.kowaleski@snc.edu
KOWALEWSKI, John, L 801-626-7212 511 D
jkowalewski@weber.edu
KOWALEWSKY, Lyn 989-358-7280 247 G
kowalewl@alpenacc.edu
KOWALIK, Thomas 607-777-2792 351 F
kowalik@binghamton.edu
KOWALSKI, Alexis 312-461-0600 144 D
akowalski@aaart.edu
KOWALSKI, Beth 614-251-4576 398 F
kowalskb@ohiodominican.edu
KOWALSKI, JR.,
Edward, J 315-255-1743 325 H
kowalskie@cayuga-cc.edu
KOWALSKI, Gerard, J 706-542-1421 138 C
housing@uga.edu
KOWALSKI, JR.,
Jonathan, V 414-277-4510 548 H
kowalski@msoe.edu
KOWALSKI, Karl 907-450-8383 10 J
karl.kowalski@alaska.edu
KOWALSKI, Melanie 570-504-1583 433 A
kowalskim@lackawanna.edu
KOWALSKI, Timothy, J 540-231-4000 518 H
KOWAR, Pamela 860-255-3603 91 C
pkowar@txcc.commnet.edu
KOWEEK, Joan 518-828-4181 330 E
joan.koweek@sunycgcc.edu
KOWICH, Colleen 816-271-5650 287 A
ckowich@missouriwestern.edu
KOWNACKI, James 570-484-2460 443 A
jkownack@lhup.edu
KOWPAK, Corinne 207-216-4399 219 C
ckowpak@yccc.edu
KOWTA, Mayomi 805-437-3107 33 I
mayomi.kowta@csuci.edu
KOYE, Diane 609-984-1110 316 A
dkoye@tesc.edu
KOZACHYN, Karen 610-359-5362 426 G
kkozachy@dccc.edu
KOZACZKA, Stanley 315-655-7132 325 I
skozaczka@cazenovia.edu
KOZAK, Diane 907-786-4513 10 I
andhk1@uaa.alaska.edu
KOZAK, Gregory 847-574-5194 155 G
gkozak@lfgsm.edu
KOZAK, Laura 410-706-8138 227 C
lkoza001@umaryland.edu
KOZAKIEWICZ, Patricia 201-684-7610 313 D
pkozakie@ramapo.edu
KOZEL, Anj 612-332-3361 261 F
akozel@aii.edu
KOZERACKI, Carol 818-710-4108 55 B
kozaraca@piercecollege.edu
KOZIATEK, Caroline 203-932-7479 95 B
ckoziatek@newhaven.edu
KOZIK, Bob 518-631-9881 358 F
kozikr@uniongraduatecollege.edu

KRIDELBAUGH, Linda .... 541-888-7402.... 420 C lkridelbaugh@socc.edu

KRIEBEL, Denise A, T .... 765-641-4133.... 169 A dakriebel@anderson.edu

KRIEBEL, Richard, M .... 215-871-6527.... 444 B rickk@pcom.edu

KRIEDER, Eric, W .... 330-972-5303.... 403 B ewk@uakron.edu

KRIEG, Katherine .... 225-490-1674.... 214 B kkrieg@ololcollege.edu

KRIEG, Randall .... 207-893-6643.... 219 F rkrieg@sjcme.edu

KRIEGER, Nora .... 973-748-9000.... 308 A nora_krieger@bloomfield.edu

KRIEGER, Rob .... 973-748-9000.... 308 A rob_kriefer@bloomfield.edu

KRIEGERMEIER, Pat .... 815-455-8726.... 157 F pkriegermeier@mchenry.edu

KRIEGH, Debbie .... 541-881-5805.... 420 E dkriegh@tvcc.cc

KRIER, Jacob, C .... 507-344-7519.... 261 H jake.krier@blc.edu

KRIESE, Theresa .... 605-995-2621.... 464 B thkriese@dwu.edu

KRIETSCH, Gary .... 707-826-4111...... 36 D gdk7001@humboldt.edu

KRIGER, Tom .... 301-431-5402.... 225 B tkriger@nlc.edu

KRIIGEL, Barbara .... 313-593-5400.... 259 E bkriigel@umich.edu

KRIKAU, Paul .... 574-520-5805.... 174 C pkrikau@iusb.edu

KRIKORIAN, Gregory, H .... 717-867-6238.... 434 C krikoria@lvc.edu

KRILL, OFM, Jude Michael .... 610-558-5526.... 437 C krillj@neumann.edu

KRIMMEL, Bob, S .... 814-472-3276.... 446 B bkrimmel@francis.edu

KRIPPEL, Nancy, F .... 770-534-6119.... 126 B nkrippel@brenau.edu

KRISE, Tom .... 209-946-2141...... 75 D tkrise@pacific.edu

KRISHNAMURTHY, K .... 573-341-4154.... 292 A kkrishna@mst.edu

KRISHNAMURTI, Praveen . 414-256-0238.... 549 A krishnap@mtmary.edu

KRISHNAN, G, V .... 713-221-8478.... 503 D krishnang@uhd.edu

KRISHNAN, Kris .... 201-360-4771.... 310 F kkrishnan@hccc.edu

KRISHNAN, Ramayya .... 412-268-2159.... 424 H rk2x@andrew.cmu.edu

KRISLOV, Marvin .... 440-775-8400.... 397 F marvin.krislov@oberlin.edu

KRISMER, Marianne .... 513-569-1686.... 387 F marianne.krismer@cincinnatistate.edu

KRISS, George .... 618-537-6425.... 157 G gnkriss@mckendree.edu

KRISS, OSF, M. Elise .... 260-399-7700.... 180 E ekriss@sf.edu

KRISTENSEN, Douglas, A .. 308-865-8208.... 300 G kristensend@unk.edu

KRISTENSEN, Sheryl .... 309-692-4092.... 158 C skristensen@midstate.edu

KRISTOF, Leslie .... 954-382-5303...... 19 C leslie.kristof@phoenix.edu

KRISTOFCO, Clare, M .... 858-534-6861...... 74 D ckristofco@uscd.edu

KRISTOFCO, Clare, M .... 858-534-6861...... 74 D ss@ucsd.edu

KRISTOFCO, John, P .... 330-972-8940.... 403 B jpkrist@uakron.edu

KRISTOFF, Tricia .... 904-819-6311.... 107 A tkristoff@flagler.edu

KRISTOVICH, Bobbi .... 541-278-5933.... 414 G bkristovich@bluecc.edu

KRITICOS, Kia .... 713-525-3117.... 504 D kritick@stthom.edu

KRITIKOS, Mike .... 773-907-4777.... 147 A mkritikos@ccc.edu

KRITSCHER, Matt .... 510-723-6716...... 38 L mkritscher@chabotcollege.edu

KRITTENBRINK, Juanita .... 405-422-1253.... 411 G krittenbrinkj@redlandscc.edu

KRIVDA, Ronald, A .... 724-925-4278.... 451 E krivdar@wccc.edu

KRIVESTI, Robin .... 740-593-2665.... 399 G krivesti@ohio.edu

KRIVOSKI, James, F .... 610-330-5200.... 433 B krivoskj@lafayette.edu

KROB, Adam .... 504-865-5026.... 215 C akrob@tulane.edu

KROB, Jay, C .... 785-827-5541.... 194 D jayk@kwu.edu

KROBER, Alfred, C .... 585-594-6501.... 347 F krobera@roberts.edu

KROBER, Kent .... 314-516-4115.... 291 F kroberk@umsl.edu

KROBOTH, Patricia, D .... 412-624-3270.... 449 A pkroboth@pitt.edu

KROC, Richard .... 520-621-8543...... 19 B kroc@email.arizona.edu

KROEGER, Laura .... 859-442-1177.... 201 G laura.kroeger@kctcs.edu

KROEGER, Lillian .... 254-526-1114.... 482 F admissions.registrar@ctcd.edu

KROEKER, Dean .... 620-241-0770.... 191 F dean.kroeker@centralchristian.edu

KROENING, Mike .... 507-453-2752.... 267 F mkroening@southeastmn.edu

KROENKE, Joel .... 800-567-2344.... 546 G jkroenke@menominee.edu

KROENKE, Paul .... 309-677-2325.... 145 H pkroenke@bradley.edu

KROEZE, Nicholas, V .... 616-222-3000.... 254 A nvk@kuyper.edu

KROGH, Nancy .... 208-885-2020.... 144 B nkrogh@uidaho.edu

KROGH, Nancy, A .... 208-885-2020.... 144 B nkrogh@uidaho.edu

KROGH DUREE, Brenda ... 641-844-5733.... 185 J brenda.kroghduree@iavalley.edu

KROGH-JESPERSEN, Mary-Beth .... 570-963-2539.... 440 F mik2@psu.edu

KROGMAN, Mark, A .... 207-741-5629.... 219 A mkrogman@smccme.edu

KROH, Lynne .... 417-862-9533.... 282 D enroll@globaluniversity.edu

KROH, JR., Robert, C .... 215-951-1315.... 432 G kroh@lasalle.edu

KROHN, Paul .... 630-617-3142.... 150 F paulk@elmhurst.edu

KROLL, Charles .... 617-850-1222.... 236 A ckroll@hchc.edu

KROLL, John, R .... 773-702-1941.... 166 D xjrk@uchicago.edu

KROLOFF, Reed .... 248-645-3301.... 250 D rkroloff@cranbrook.edu

KROM, Bethany .... 507-284-3293.... 262 G krom.bethany@mayo.edu

KRONCKE, Charles .... 513-244-4273.... 388 D charles_kroncke@mail.msj.edu

KRONDAK, Anita, M .... 913-288-7274.... 193 J akrondak@kckcc.edu

KRONDORFER, Bjorn, H .... 240-895-4219.... 226 A bhkrondorfer@smcm.edu

KRONEMAN, Ann .... 517-483-1604.... 254 D kronemaa@lcc.edu

KRONENBURGER, John .... 630-942-3614.... 147 G kronenburgerj@cod.edu

KRONSTEIN, Krista .... 330-263-2498.... 388 E kkronstein@wooster.edu

KRONSTEINER, Denise ...... 480-423-6567...... 16 D denise.kronsteiner@sccmail.maricopa.edu

KROOK, Scott .... 507-285-7205.... 269 B scott.krook@roch.edu

KROPF, Kevin .... 785-594-8327.... 190 C Kevin.Kropf@bakeru.edu

KROPF, Shannon .... 901-381-3939.... 478 D shannon@visible.edu

KROPFF, Robert .... 330-972-7048.... 403 B bobk@uakron.edu

KROPP, Peter .... 330-966-5461.... 402 A pkropp@starkstate.edu

KROPP, Peter .... 330-494-6170.... 402 A pkropp@starkstate.edu

KROPP, Vicky .... 989-358-7317.... 247 G kroppv@alpenacc.edu

KROPP-ANDERSON, Pamela .... 207-973-1048.... 218 A kroppandersonp@husson.edu

KROSCH, Brandon .... 651-255-6136.... 271 I bkrosch@unitedseminary.edu

KROTSENG, Marsha .... 701-328-2979.... 381 C marsha.krotseng@ndus.edu

KROTZER, Mary Jane .... 205-366-8929........ 7 G mkrotzer@stillman.edu

KROVI, Ravi .... 330-972-7442.... 403 B krovi@uakron.edu

KRUCHOWSKI, Gary .... 218-733-7649.... 267 B g.kruchowski@lsc.edu

KRUDOP, James, D .... 334-382-2133........ 5 F jkrudop@lbwcc.edu

KRUEGER, Bryon, D .... 651-631-5392.... 270 E bdkrueger@nwc.edu

KRUEGER, C. Norman .... 434-223-6216.... 519 B nkrueger@email.hsc.edu

KRUEGER, Cheryl .... 937-775-2556.... 406 C cheryl.krueger@wright.edu

KRUEGER, Cindy .... 419-267-1233.... 397 D ckrueger@northweststate.edu

KRUEGER, Conrad .... 210-486-0915.... 479 F ckrueger@alamo.edu

KRUEGER, James, M .... 314-516-6539.... 291 F jimkrueger@umsl.edu

KRUEGER, Jennifer, K .... 920-923-8758.... 548 C jkkrueger37@marianuniversity.edu

KRUEGER, Jim .... 402-399-2332.... 297 E jkrueger@csm.edu

KRUEGER, Joni .... 605-274-4015.... 463 H joni.krueger@augie.edu

KRUEGER, Karl .... 215-248-6330.... 435 B kkrueger@ltsp.edu

KRUEGER, Kurt, J .... 949-214-3194...... 42 K kurt.krueger@cui.edu

KRUEGER, Mablene .... 312-935-6645.... 162 E mkrueger@robertmorris.edu

KRUEGER, Mary, M .... 419-372-8034.... 385 C mkruege@bgsu.edu

KRUEGER, Paul, M .... 856-566-6031.... 316 I krueger@umdnj.edu

KRUFT, Sherre .... 831-647-4123...... 57 F sherre.kruft@miis.edu

KRUG, Christopher .... 858-642-8145...... 58 I ckrug@nu.edu

KRUG, Sheila, R .... 620-229-6368.... 196 C sheila.krug@sckans.edu

KRUG, Stefan .... 617-521-3929.... 245 A stefan.krug@simmons.edu

KRUGER, Mari .... 253-840-8472.... 536 C mkruger@pierce.ctc.edu

KRUGER, Michael, J .... 704-366-5066.... 375 H mkruger@rts.edu

KRUGMAN, Richard, D ...... 303-724-0882...... 88 D richard.krugman@ucdenver.edu

KRUHLY, Leslie, L .... 215-898-7005.... 448 I kruhly@pobox.upenn.edu

KRUKONES, James, H .... 216-397-4762.... 392 M jkrukones@jcu.edu

KRULAK, Charles, C .... 205-226-4620........ 2 C ckrulak@bsc.edu

KRULL, Kimberly .... 785-243-1435.... 191 H kkrull@cloud.edu

KRULL, Lucille .... 503-251-6115.... 538 H lucy.krull@wallawalla.edu

KRULY, Kenneth, C .... 716-888-3755.... 325 G krulyk@canisius.edu

KRUMHANSL, Ezra .... 502-585-9911.... 205 I ekrumhansl@spalding.edu

KRUMM, Brenda, L .... 620-431-2820.... 195 B bkrumm@neosho.edu

KRUMPE, Keith .... 828-250-3880.... 378 C kkrumpe@unca.edu

KRUMWIEDE, Robert .... 218-726-7560.... 272 B tkrumw@d.umn.edu

KRUPANSKY, Sharla .... 270-534-3275.... 203 B sharla.krupansky@kctcs.edu

KRUPICA, Glen .... 217-854-3231.... 145 F glen.krupica@blackburn.edu

KRUPICA, Suzanne .... 217-854-3231.... 145 F suzanne.krupica@blackburn.edu

KRUPKA, Moshe .... 212-463-0400.... 357 J moshe.krupka@touro.edu

KRUPP, Jason .... 727-341-3050.... 116 F krupp.jason@spcollege.edu

KRUPP, Julie .... 419-358-3000.... 385 B kruppj@bluffton.edu

KRUPP, Robert, A .... 503-517-1838.... 421 B rakrupp@westernseminary.edu

KRUPSKI, Eric, A .... 617-422-7232.... 243 G ekrupski@admin.nesl.edu

KRUSE, Ellen .... 925-685-1230...... 43 C ekruse@dvc.edu

KRUSE, Emily .... 563-588-6436.... 183 B emily.kruse@clarke.edu

KRUSE, Janetta .... 817-598-6391.... 508 C jkruse@wc.edu

KRUSE, Mary .... 517-264-7112.... 258 D mkruse@sienaheights.edu

KRUSE, Tom, D .... 563-588-4948.... 186 I tom.kruse@loras.edu

KRUSE, Tracy, L .... 563-562-3263.... 187 G kruset@nicc.edu

KRUSE, Valerie .... 386-226-6339.... 105 B krusev@erau.edu

KRUSEE, Kelly .... 310-377-5501...... 56 F kkrusee@marymountpv.edu

KRUSEMARK, Stacy, L .... 605-256-5127.... 465 G stacy.krusemark@dsu.edu

KRUSEN, Cynthia .... 978-840-0176.... 240 G c_krusen@mwcc.mass.edu

KRUSHINSKI, Lynn .... 570-702-8955.... 431 K lkrushinski@johnson.edu

KRUSHINSKY, Linda .... 717-394-6211.... 426 C ldrushinsky@csb.edu

KRUSNIAK, Bryan .... 660-626-2364.... 278 F bkrusniak@atsu.edu

KRUTKY, Judith, B .... 440-826-2257.... 384 H jkrutky@bw.edu

KRUTZ, Ellen .... 312-369-7465.... 148 B ekrutz@colum.edu

KRUZEL, Douglas .... 734-973-3497.... 260 B kruzel@wccnet.edu

KRYGEL, Barbara .... 586-791-6610.... 248 G barbara.krygel@baker.edu

KRYLOWICZ, Brian .... 406-243-4711.... 295 A brian.krylowicz@umontana.edu

KRYSHAK, Michael .... 916-649-2400...... 31 C

KRYSIAK, Richard .... 405-744-7147.... 410 C rick.krysiak@okstate.edu

KRYSTOSEK, Brooke .... 503-493-6454.... 415 E bkrystosek@cu-portland.edu

KRZAK, Chris .... 909-593-3511...... 75 C ckrzak@laverne.edu

KRZYWICKI, Tricia .... 617-327-6777.... 242 C tricia_krzywicki@mspp.edu

KRZYZANOWSKI, SSND, Georgeann .... 414-258-4810.... 549 A krzyzag@mtmary.edu

KRZYZKOWSKI, Karen .... 215-489-2309.... 426 H Karen.Kay@delval.edu

KSENDZOVSKY, Yelena ...... 440-449-1700.... 384 faid@atsinstitute.edu

KTUL, Kathy .... 252-492-2061.... 374 ktul@vgcc.edu

KU, John .... 510-592-9688...... 59 johnku@npu.edu

KUA, Kenway, L .... 808-675-3565.... 139 kuak@byuh.edu

KUABASEK, Stephen .... 352-588-8250.... 116 E stephen.kubasek@saintleo.edu

KUANG, Connie .... 909-931-7599...... 78 H ckuang@westwood.edu

KUBA, Jodie, M .... 808-956-3993.... 141 E jodiek@hawaii.edu

KUBA, Michael .... 304-473-8090.... 545 F kuba_m@wvwc.edu

KUBA, Shawn, M .... 304-473-8560.... 545 F kuba_s@wvwc.edu

KUBACAK, James .... 254-299-8608.... 490 E jkubacak@mclennan.edu

KUBASKA, Julie .... 914-594-4550.... 343 F julie_kubaska@nymc.edu

KUBAT, Laural .... 507-389-7219.... 269 F laural.kubat@southcentral.edu

KUBAT, Robert, A .... 765-494-6133.... 178 F rkubat@purdue.edu

KUBATZKE, Trevor, A .... 989-686-9339.... 250 F trevorkubatzke@delta.edu

KUBB, Richard .... 314-529-9606.... 284 F rkubb@maryville.edu

KUBE, Thomas, A .... 480-314-2102...... 18 G

KUBEJA, Judy .... 814-732-2729.... 442 D kubeja@edinboro.edu

KUBERSKI, Chris .... 618-437-5321.... 162 B kuberski@rlc.edu

KUBERSKY, Edward .... 201-559-6117.... 310 C kuberskye@felician.edu

KUBIC, Craig .... 816-414-3700.... 286 A ckubic@mbts.edu

KUBIK, Susan, K .... 610-861-5451.... 437 G skubik@northampton.edu

KUBINAK, Lois, A .... 610-921-7612.... 421 D lkubinak@alb.edu

KUBISIAK, Mike .... 701-224-5400.... 382 B michael.kubisiak@bismarckstate.edu

KUBO, Takeo .... 408-288-3733...... 67 C takeo.kubo@sjcc.edu

KUBOW, Steven .... 908-737-0300.... 311 B skubow@kean.edu

KUCERA, Kevin .... 734-487-2390.... 250 H kkucera@emich.edu

KUCHARSKI, Chris .... 570-961-7856.... 433 A kucharskic@lackawanna.edu

KUCHENREUTHER, Brad .... 360-254-3282.... 533 G

KUCHMAS, Deborah .... 203-332-5150...... 90 B dkuchmas@hcc.commnet.edu

KUCHTA, Sheila .... 605-668-1526.... 464 F skuchta@mtmc.edu

KUCIA, John, F .... 513-745-3997.... 406 E kucia@xavier.edu

KUCINSKI, Nancy .... 325-670-1298.... 487 D nkicinski@hsutx.edu

KUCK, Ann .... 208-459-5826.... 143 A akuck@collegeofidaho.edu

KUCK, Cynthia .... 312-279-3909.... 144 G ckuck@argosy.edu

KUCKO, Jane .... 817-257-7473.... 498 F j.kucko@tcu.edu

KUCYNDA, Steve .... 660-596-7282.... 290 F skucynda@sfccmo.edu

KUDLAC, John .... 412-392-3920.... 444 H jkudlac@pointpark.edu

KUDLIK, Richard .... 714-241-6150...... 40 J rkudlik@coastline.edu

KUDRAVETZ, Douglas .... 202-885-2700...... 97 B doug@american.edu

KUEBLER, Alan, S .... 314-935-5727.... 292 J alan_kuebler@wustl.edu

KUEBLER, Elizabeth, D ...... 630-617-3069.... 150 F betsyk@elmhurst.edu

KUEFNER, Michael .... 479-899-6928...... 22 H mkuefner@nwacc.edu

KUEHLER, Robert .... 303-837-2112...... 88 A Robert.Kuehler@cu.edu

KUEHN, Lisa .... 620-252-7137.... 191 I lisak@coffeyville.edu

KUEHNER, Megan, R .... 904-620-2523.... 120 C mkuehner@unf.edu

KUENNEN, Daniel, S .... 410-651-6183.... 227 E dskuennen@umes.edu

KUENSTLER, Donna .... 432-837-8361.... 501 B dkuenstl@sulross.edu

KUFFELL, Lorne .... 205-348-7205........ 8 F lkuffel@ua.edu

KUGA, Donna, J .... 724-773-3939.... 438 I djk3@psu.edu

KUGELMANN DEKAT, Laurie .... 972-721-5322.... 502 F ldekat@udallas.edu

KUGLER, Angela .... 425-558-0299.... 533 C akugler@digipen.edu

KUGLER, Sharon .... 203-432-1128...... 95 D sharon.kugler@yale.edu

KYTE, Richard, L ... 608-796-3704 ... 553 A
rlkyte@viterbo.edu
KYZER, Melany ... 405-789-6400 ... 412 D
mkyzer@snu.edu

L

LÓPEZ-NUNCI, Adrián ... 787-250-0000 ... 566 D
adrian.lopeznunci@upr.edu
LA BELLE, Heather ... 213-615-7204 ... 146 C
hlabelle@thechicagoschool.edu
LA BRANCHE, Mark, D ... 919-497-3226 ... 366 E
mdl@louisburg.edu
LA BRIE, Mary Anne ... 603-623-0313 ... 305 F
maryannelabrie@nhia.edu
LA CHAPELLE, Jacqueline . 337-550-1282 ... 212 H
LA DOW, Carolyn ... 252-862-1316 ... 372 H
ladowc@roanokechowan.edu
LA DUKE, John, C ... 308-865-8518 ... 300 G
ladukejc@unk.edu
LA FERNEY, Sheila ... 580-477-7769 ... 414 C
sheila.laferney@wosc.edu
LA FOEUR, Mary Ann ... 703-416-1441 ... 519 F
mlafoeur@ipsciences.edu
LA PERLA-MORALES,
Joann ... 732-906-2517 ... 311 E
jlaperla@middlesexcc.edu
LA PLANTE, Brian ... 518-445-2381 ... 322 D
blapl@albanylaw.edu
LA POINT, Kristine, L ... 773-975-1295 ... 158 D
krisbob1@cs.com
LA POINT, Kristine, L ... 262-975-1295 ... 548 F
krisbob1@cs.com
LA RUE, Lacie ... 541-737-4218 ... 418 F
lacie.larue@oregonstate.edu
LAACKMAN, Donald ... 312-553-5902 ... 146 H
dlaackman@ccc.edu
LAAGER, Melinda ... 912-427-5835 ... 124 A
mlaager@altamahatech.edu
LAAKSO, Kathleen ... 901-843-3885 ... 472 I
laakso@rhodes.edu
LABARBERA, Mark ... 219-464-6894 ... 181 A
mark.labarbera@valpo.edu
LABARBERA, Paul ... 845-758-7819 ... 323 F
labarbera@bard.edu
LABATE, William ... 310-206-7323 ... 74 A
labate@ats.ucla.edu
LABAUGH, Amy, R ... 208-496-9810 ... 142 G
labaugha@byui.edu
LABAUVE-MAHER, Laura .. 847-925-6522 ... 151 E
llabauve@harpercollege.edu
LABBADIA, Gail ... 860-253-3015 ... 89 K
glabbadia@acc.commnet.edu
LABE, Dorothy ... 610-896-4923 ... 430 G
dlabe@haverford.edu
LABE, Paul, E ... 443-412-2291 ... 223 B
plabe@harford.edu
LABEFF, Toni ... 903-434-8105 ... 491 D
tlabeff@ntcc.edu
LABELLE, Alyssa ... 603-271-7731 ... 304 G
alabelle@ccsnh.edu
LABELLE, Michael ... 954-308-7400 ... 117 B
mrlabelle@sbftlaud.com
LABELLE-HAMER, Nettie ... 907-474-6167 ... 10 J
nettie.labellehamer@alaska.edu
LABINE, Nancy ... 423-478-6227 ... 474 E
nlabine@clevelandstatecc.edu
LABKOWSKI, Zalman ... 718-434-0784 ... 325 J
LABOE, Mark ... 773-325-4004 ... 148 F
mlaboe@depaul.edu
LABONTE, Kim ... 618-650-2789 ... 164 H
klabont@siue.edu
LABONTE, Kimberlee ... 617-876-0956 ... 236 H
kimberlee.labonte@longy.edu
LABONTE, Robert ... 978-632-6600 ... 240 G
r_labonte@mwcc.mass.edu
LABORDO, Darwin ... 909-869-2008 ... 33 G
dlabordo@csupomona.edu
LABRIE, John, G ... 617-373-2400 ... 244 A
LABRIE, SJ, Joseph ... 310-338-5238 ... 56 E
jlabrie@lmu.edu
LABRIE, Lori, A ... 713-313-7040 ... 499 G
labrie_la@tsu.edu
LABRIE, Lynn ... 928-317-6178 ... 12 C
lynn.labrie@azwestern.edu
LABRIOLA, Elisabeth, S ... 860-439-2064 ... 91 E
elisabeth.labriola@conncoll.edu
LABROSSE, Tonya ... 508-373-9701 ... 231 D
tonya.labrosse@becker.edu
LABROSSE, Tonya, B ... 603-899-4097 ... 305 B
labrosset@franklinpierce.edu
LABRUZZO, Anne ... 928-350-4006 ... 18 C
alabruzzo@prescott.edu
LABUDE, Mark, S ... 318-342-3610 ... 216 E
labude@ulm.edu
LABYAK, Gregory ... 618-545-3015 ... 155 A
glabyak@kaskaskia.edu
LACE, William, W ... 817-515-5242 ... 496 A
bill.lace@tccd.edu
LACEK, Steven ... 304-896-7357 ... 542 J
stevenl@southern.wvnet.edu
LACEY, Aaron ... 314-264-1802 ... 167 F
aaron.lacey@vatterott-college.edu
LACEY, Aaron ... 314-264-1802 ... 414 B
aaron.lacey@vatterott-college.edu
LACEY, Aaron ... 314-264-1802 ... 301 D
aaron.lacey@vatterott-college.edu
LACEY, Aaron ... 314-264-1802 ... 292 I
aaron.lacey@vatterott-college.edu
LACEY, Aaron ... 314-264-1802 ... 292 G
aaron.lacey@vatterott-college.edu
LACEY, Aaron ... 314-264-1802 ... 405 C
aaron.lacey@vatterott-college.edu
LACEY, LaVondra ... 312-777-8582 ... 153 A
llacey@aii.edu
LACEY, Linda ... 575-646-5746 ... 319 D
lacey@nmsu.edu
LACEY, Pete ... 810-989-5561 ... 258 B
placey@sc4.edu
LACEY, R. Alton ... 314-392-2355 ... 286 C
president@mobap.edu
LACEY-HAUN, Lora ... 816-235-1700 ... 291 E
lacey-haunc@umkc.edu
LACH, Peter ... 304-367-4219 ... 543 E
peter.lach@fairmontstate.edu
LACHANCE, Andrea ... 607-753-5430 ... 353 B
andrea.lachance@cortland.edu
LACHANCE, Beatrice ... 615-547-1244 ... 467 I
blachance@cumberland.edu
LACHANCE, Elizabeth, A ... 585-385-8410 ... 348 F
llachance@sjfc.edu
LACHAPELLE, Laurie ... 978-762-4000 ... 241 A
llachape@northshore.edu
LACHENAUER, Kathy, R ... 412-268-8524 ... 424 H
kathyl@andrew.cmu.edu
LACHER, Candis ... 509-793-2063 ... 531 D
candyl@bigbend.edu
LACHER, Didi ... 212-343-1234 ... 341 B
dlacher@mcny.edu
LACHUT, Darlene, M ... 804-745-2444 ... 516 L
dmlachut@bryantstratton.edu
LACIEN, Mark ... 219-989-2579 ... 178 G
lacien@purduecal.edu
LACK, Paul, D ... 443-334-2205 ... 226 E
lcjohnson@stevenson.edu
LACKEY, Charles ... 956-882-6552 ... 505 C
charles.lackey@utb.edu
LACKEY, David ... 570-586-2400 ... 422 F
dlackey@bbc.edu
LACKEY, Fred, G ... 251-442-2482 ... 9 B
LACKEY, Mary Lou ... 209-946-2011 ... 75 D
LACKEY, Polly, R ... 806-291-3702 ... 508 B
lackeyp@wbu.edu
LACKEY, Sharon ... 803-321-5113 ... 459 G
sharon.lackey@newberry.edu
LACKMAN, Vickie ... 253-680-7180 ... 531 A
vlackman@bates.ctc.edu
LACKNER, Andrew ... 985-871-6201 ... 215 C
alackner@tulane.edu
LACKNER, Elisabeth ... 718-631-6279 ... 329 A
elackner@qcc.cuny.edu
LACORTE, Ellen ... 610-519-4237 ... 450 G
ellen.lacorte@villanova.edu
LACOUR, Debra, R ... 979-830-4130 ... 482 A
Debra.LaCour@blinn.edu
LACOUR, Mary ... 985-549-2244 ... 216 C
mlacour@selu.edu
LACOUR, Melissa ... 504-671-6219 ... 210 G
mlacou@dcc.edu
LACOURSE, Michael ... 858-642-8107 ... 58 I
mlacourse@nu.edu
LACOURSE, Peter, W ... 231-995-1198 ... 256 G
placourse@nmc.edu
LACOURSE, William ... 410-455-2598 ... 227 D
lacourse@umbc.edu
LACRO, Erika ... 808-845-9158 ... 141 G
lacro@hawaii.edu
LACROIX, Michael, J ... 402-280-2217 ... 297 H
lacroix@creighton.edu
LACROIX, Roland ... 207-581-4053 ... 220 A
roland.j.lacroix@maine.edu
LACY, Charles, F ... 702-968-2016 ... 303 D
clacy@roseman.edu
LACY, Kirk ... 406-247-5785 ... 295 F
klacy@msubillings.edu
LACY, Linda, L ... 562-860-2451 ... 38 J
llacy@cerritos.edu
LACY, Russell ... 503-255-0332 ... 417 C
rlacy@Multnomah.edu
LACY, William, B ... 530-752-6376 ... 73 F
wblacy@ucdavis.edu
LADAGE, Marcia ... 816-932-2194 ... 289 G
meshaw@saint-lukes.org
LADAS, Lori ... 406-447-5426 ... 294 A
ladas@carroll.edu
LADD, Jack ... 432-552-2170 ... 507 C
ladd_j@utpb.edu
LADD, Sheilah, M ... 802-626-6697 ... 515 F
sheilah.ladd@lyndonstate.edu
LADD, Susan, K ... 515-271-3048 ... 184 A
susan.ladd@drake.edu
LADE, Becky ... 515-271-1485 ... 183 F
becky.lade@dmu.edu
LADENDECKER, Rob ... 213-388-9950 ... 46 E
LADERMAN, Michael, S ... 305-899-3189 ... 101 F
mladerman@mail.barry.edu
LADEWIG, Patricia, A ... 303-458-1843 ... 87 E
pladewig@regis.edu
LADHA, Amin ... 734-973-3400 ... 260 B
amin@wccnet.edu
LADIG, R, D ... 218-755-3750 ... 266 B
rladig@bemidjistate.edu
LADISCH, Christine, M ... 765-494-8210 ... 178 F
ladischc@purdue.edu
LADITKA, Doug ... 330-263-2310 ... 388 E
LADNER, Barbara ... 304-766-4113 ... 544 D
ladnerbe@wvstateu.edu
LADNER, Gail ... 985-732-6640 ... 211 C
LADNER, Hilda ... 320-589-6095 ... 272 C
hladner@morris.umn.edu
LADNER, Marilyn ... 352-854-2322 ... 103 D
ladnerm@cf.edu
LADNER, Pam ... 228-497-7642 ... 275 G
pamela.ladner@mgccc.edu
LADNER-MATHIS, Jocelyn 216-987-4537 ... 389 A
jocelyn.ladner-mathis@tri-c.edu
LADREW, Tammy ... 540-868-7056 ... 526 H
tladrew@lfcc.edu
LADUCA, Bonnie ... 651-690-8664 ... 271 E
bsladuca@stkate.edu
LADUCER, Wanda ... 701-477-7862 ... 383 C
wladucer@tm.edu
LADUSAW, William ... 831-459-2696 ... 75 A
humdean@ucsc.edu
LAEL, Robert ... 217-206-7020 ... 167 A
lael.robert@uis.edu
LAFAILLE, Pierre-Carly ... 619-321-3000 ... 29 E
plafaille@argosy.edu
LAFATA-JOHNSON,
Paulette ... 219-980-6769 ... 173 F
plafataj@iun.edu
LAFAVE, Alan ... 605-626-2497 ... 465 H
lafavea@northern.edu
LAFAVOR, Jeff ... 712-279-5423 ... 182 E
jeff.lafavor@briarcliff.edu
LAFAYETTE, Jack ... 717-391-8920 ... 421 D
jlafayette@alb.edu
LAFEVER, Michael ... 716-827-2491 ... 358 B
lafeverm@trocaire.edu
LAFEVER, Steven, D ... 316-978-3070 ... 197 F
steve.lafever@wichita.edu
LAFEVRE, Lisa ... 719-336-1551 ... 85 K
lisa.lafevre@lamarcc.edu
LAFFERTY, Carolyn ... 732-255-0400 ... 312 D
clafferty@ocean.edu
LAFFERTY, William, J ... 717-337-6912 ... 429 H
wlaffert@gettysburg.edu
LAFFEY, Brian ... 312-567-3677 ... 153 B
blaffey1@iit.edu
LAFFITTE, Ron ... 864-587-4002 ... 461 D
laffitter@smcsc.edu
LAFLAMME, Janet ... 207-893-7755 ... 219 F
jlaflamm@sjcme.edu
LAFLAMME, Martha ... 603-752-1113 ... 304 I
mlaflamme@ccsnh.edu
LAFLASH, Debra, A ... 508-854-4551 ... 241 C
dal@qcc.mass.edu
LAFLEN, Jody ... 206-287-5566 ... 537 A
jlaflen@sccd.ctc.edu
LAFLEUR, Joyce, L ... 616-632-2106 ... 248 A
laflejoy@aquinas.edu
LAFLEUR, Thomas, W ... 956-721-5816 ... 489 G
tlafleur@laredo.edu
LAFOND, Robert ... 215-637-7700 ... 430 H
rlafond@holyfamily.edu
LAFONTAINE, Joni ... 701-477-7862 ... 383 C
jlafontaine@tm.edu
LAFORGIA, John ... 507-284-2073 ... 262 D
laforgia.john@mayo.edu
LAFORGIA, John, W ... 507-284-2073 ... 262 F
LAFRANCE, Mark ... 617-243-2178 ... 236 F
mlafrance@lasell.edu
LAFUZE, Alice ... 765-983-1677 ... 171 B
lafuzal@earlham.edu
LAGASSE, Ray ... 701-777-6438 ... 381 D
raymond.lagasse@email.und.edu
LAGATTA, James, J ... 518-629-4523 ... 336 C
j.lagatta@hvcc.edu
LAGATTA, Regina ... 518-255-5524 ... 354 E
lagattrm@cobleskill.edu
LAGEORGE, Lisa ... 661-362-2205 ... 56 G
llageorge@masters.edu
LAGER, Carol ... 360-752-8323 ... 531 C
clager@btc.ctc.edu
LAGESON, David ... 541-962-3114 ... 418 C
dlageson@eou.edu
LAGGNER, Laurie ... 802-586-7711 ... 514 E
llaggner@sterlingcollege.edu
LAGRANGE, Janet ... 337-521-8900 ... 212 B
janet.lagrange@southlouisiana.edu
LAGRANGE, Linda ... 505-454-3578 ... 318 I
lagrange_l@nmhu.edu
LAGRANGE, Teresa ... 216-523-7402 ... 388 C
t.lagrange@csuohio.edu
LAGRASSA, Michael ... 508-999-9180 ... 237 E
mlagrassa@umassd.edu
LAGROW, Patricia ... 405-974-3371 ... 413 B
plagrow@ucok.edu
LAGUARDIA, John, A ... 330-972-5328 ... 403 B
jlaguardia@uakron.edu
LAGUERRE, Jowel, C ... 707-864-7112 ... 70 A
jowel.laguerre@solano.edu
LAGUERRE-BROWN,
Caroline ... 410-516-8075 ... 223 F
clbrown@jhu.edu
LAGUNA, Robert ... 512-492-3010 ... 480 F
rlaguna@aoma.edu
LAHANN, Mary ... 928-777-3803 ... 14 D
mary.lahann@erau.edu
LAHART, Amy ... 570-674-6340 ... 436 F
alahart@misericordia.edu
LAHART, Edward ... 570-504-7000 ... 425 F
LAHER, Ronald ... 610-527-0200 ... 445 [illegible]
rlaher@rosemont.edu
LAHEY, John, L ... 203-582-8700 ... 93 E
john.lahey@quinnipiac.edu
LAHM, Chris ... 417-626-1234 ... 287 F
lahm.chris@occ.edu
LAHM, Terry, D ... 614-236-6800 ... 386 C
tlahm@capital.edu
LAHR, Sheri, K ... 580-327-8550 ... 409 C
sklahr@nwosu.edu
LAI, Chun ... 215-572-3850 ... 451 D
clai@wts.edu
LAI, Mary, M ... 516-299-2502 ... 338 F
mary.lai@liu.edu
LAI HING, Kenneth ... 256-726-7112 ... 6 C
laihing@oakwood.edu
LAIBLE, Jim ... 815-967-7307 ... 162 G
jlaible@rockfordcareercollege.edu
LAIDACKER, Crystal ... 972-241-3371 ... 484 D
claidacker@dallas.edu
LAING, Katherine ... 217-333-1086 ... 166 E
klaing@illinois.edu
LAING-IDLE, Michelle, L ... 704-357-8020 ... 361 N
mlaing@aii.edu
LAINO, Nicholas ... 315-866-0300 ... 335 E
lainonf@herkimer.edu
LAIPSON, Peter ... 413-528-7239 ... 231 A
plaipson@simons-rock.edu
LAIR, Patrick ... 651-423-8399 ... 266 E
pat.lair@dctc.edu
LAIRD, Allan ... 208-459-5151 ... 143 A
alaird@collegeofidaho.edu
LAIRD, Brenda ... 307-778-1372 ... 556 B
blaird@lcccfoundation.edu
LAIRD, Kim ... 903-468-3039 ... 497 E
kim_laird@tamu-commerce.edu
LAIRD, Stephen ... 660-626-2701 ... 278 F
slaird@atsu.edu
LAIRD, William, G ... 312-915-7803 ... 157 A
wlaird@luc.edu
LAJAUNIE, Carol ... 800-962-7682 ... 293 B
clajaunie@wma.edu
LAJAUNIE, Ronald, P ... 337-482-6235 ... 216 D
rpl7290@louisiana.edu
LAJEUNESSE, Mary Ellen .. 518-629-7292 ... 336 C
m.lajeunesse@hvcc.edu
LAJINESS, Todd ... 313-883-8556 ... 257 G
lajiness.todd@shms.edu
LAJUBUTU, Oyebanjo ... 410-951-3494 ... 228 B
olajubutu@coppin.edu
LAKE, Amber ... 641-673-1078 ... 189 I
lakea@wmpenn.edu
LAKE, Diana ... 360-475-7831 ... 535 J
dlake@olympic.edu
LAKE, Doris, J ... 270-831-9617 ... 201 I
doris.capehart@kctcs.edu
LAKE, Gashaw ... 502-597-6117 ... 203 D
gashaw.lake@kysu.edu
LAKE, Jeannine ... 816-204-2158 ... 19 C
jeannine.lake@phoenix.edu
LAKE, Kathy ... 414-382-6084 ... 545 H
kathy.lake@alverno.edu
LAKE, Kathy ... 231-591-2113 ... 251 B
lakek@ferris.edu
LAKE, Michael, P ... 850-644-2478 ... 119 C
mlake@admin.fsu.edu
LAKE, Stephanie, S ... 919-866-5927 ... 374 E
sslake@waketech.edu
LAKE, Todd ... 615-460-6628 ... 467 B
todd.lake@belmont.edu
LAKE, Tracy ... 860-231-5447 ... 93 H
tlake@sjc.edu
LAKEN, Elizabeth, A ... 630-637-5680 ... 159 F
ealaken@noctrl.edu
LAKEN, Michael, J ... 630-515-6148 ... 158 E
mlaken@midwestern.edu
LAKER, Jason ... 408-924-5900 ... 37 A
jason.laker@sjsu.edu
LAKETA, Dave ... 815-740-3464 ... 167 C
dlaketa@stfrancis.edu
LAKEY, John ... 308-865-8427 ... 300 G
lakeyj@unk.edu
LAKIN, Lyn ... 785-594-4590 ... 190 C
lyn.lakin@bakeru.edu
LAKIS, James ... 570-321-4141 ... 435 D
lakis@lycoming.edu
LAKSO, James, J ... 814-641-3121 ... 431 L
lakso@juniata.edu
LALE, Tully ... 417-864-7220 ... 282 B
tlale@cci.edu
LALIBERTE, Jean ... 334-670-3608 ... 8 B
jlaliber@troy.edu

LANDRY, Mark 228-497-7809 275 G
mark.landry@mgccc.edu
LANDRY, Patrick 337-482-6402 216 D
pml@louisiana.edu
LANDRY, Ruth 337-482-5811 216 D
rwl@louisiana.edu
LANDRY, Shawntel, D 312-821-6300 144 E
LANDRY, Stephen 973-275-2299 315 B
stephen.landry@shu.edu
LANDSAW, Christy 918-456-5511 409 A
landsaw@nsuok.edu
LANDSMAN, Pat 352-365-3526 112 M
landsmap@lscc.edu
LANDSMARK, Theodore, C 617-262-5000 232 B
ted.landsmark@the-bac.edu
LANDWER, Allan, J 325-670-2222 487 D
alandwer@hsutx.edu
LANE, Amy 715-232-1469 552 C
lanea@uwstout.edu
LANE, Andy 317-339-4409 177 H
alane@martin.edu
LANE, Austin 936-273-7222 490 C
austin.lane@lonestar.edu
LANE, Barry 218-736-1524 267 G
barry.lane@minnesota.edu
LANE, Charles, E 213-740-3649 76 C
clane@caps.usc.edu
LANE, David 207-621-3448 220 B
dlane@maine.edu
LANE, David, H 410-234-4848 225 E
LANE, Deborah 205-348-8089 8 F
dlane@ur.ua.edu
LANE, Deborah 405-744-6384 410 C
debbie.lane@okstate.edu
LANE, Diane, C 410-287-6060 222 A
dlane@cecil.edu
LANE, Diane, L 217-362-6416 158 F
dlane@millikin.edu
LANE, Edwin, H 816-781-7700 293 D
lanee@william.jewell.edu
LANE, Ginny 651-999-5894 267 D
ginny.lane@metrostate.edu
LANE, Harry, W 617-373-3232 244 A
LANE, Jennifer 808-675-4971 139 I
jennifer.lane@byuh.edu
LANE, Jill 678-466-4194 127 A
jilllane@clayton.edu
LANE, Jill 618-468-4900 156 C
jlane@lc.edu
LANE, Kelly 617-369-3631 244 G
klane@mfa.org
LANE, Kimberly 216-373-5290 397 E
klane@ndc.edu
LANE, Laura 248-476-1122 255 C
llane@mispp.edu
LANE, Marguerite 516-678-5000 341 F
mlane@molloy.edu
LANE, Mark 808-455-0213 142 A
marklane@hawaii.edu
LANE, Matt 304-776-6290 540 G
mlane@cci.edu
LANE, Natalie 307-382-1673 556 F
nlane@wwcc.wy.edu
LANE, Nicole 724-222-5330 438 E
nlane@penncommercial.edu
LANE, Phyllis 360-867-6034 533 I
lanep@evergreen.edu
LANE, Robert, J 515-961-1417 188 F
bob.lane@simpson.edu
LANE, Roberta 847-578-8309 163 A
roberta.lane@rosalindfranklin.edu
LANE, Sabrina 307-778-4335 556 B
slane@lcccfoundation.edu
LANE, Sandi, J 704-403-3518 362 E
sandi.lane@carolinashealthcare.org
LANE, Shelese 404-270-5110 137 E
sjlane@spelman.edu
LANE, Thomas 989-686-9298 250 F
thlane@delta.edu
LANE, Troy 307-766-5188 556 E
tlane1@uwyo.edu
LANE COBB, Michelle 252-789-0244 371 E
mlane@martincc.edu
LANE-MARTIN, Tanya 585-345-6800 334 F
tmlanemartin@genesee.edu
LANEY, Anita 706-880-8068 132 I
alaney@lagrange.edu
LANEY, Jo 575-562-2677 318 A
jo.laney@enmu.edu
LANEY, Mary, A 386-312-4069 116 D
maryannelaney@sjrstate.edu
LANEY, Miriam 803-778-7825 455 G
laneymt@cctech.edu
LANFEAR, Jeffery 773-325-8308 148 F
jlanfear@depaul.edu
LANG, Amy, M 715-675-3331 554 G
lang@ntc.edu
LANG, Anita 201-216-5163 315 E
alang@stevens.edu
LANG, Ashley 319-385-6262 186 A
ashley.lang@iwc.edu
LANG, Celine 321-674-7111 108 E
celine@fit.edu
LANG, Christine 843-574-6162 461 G
chris.lang@tridenttech.edu
LANG, Cyndi 574-520-4490 174 C
clang@iusb.edu
LANG, Donna 409-740-4408 497 D
langd@tamug.edu
LANG, Edith 910-755-7304 368 C
lange@brunswickcc.edu
LANG, Heather 303-581-9955 320 H
heather@acupuncturecollege.edu
LANG, Janell 419-251-1614 395 H
janell.lang@mercycollege.edu
LANG, Jennifer 718-780-0383 324 F
jennifer.lang@brooklaw.edu
LANG, Kathy, J 414-288-1782 548 D
kathy.lang@marquette.edu
LANG, Mandy 715-422-5446 554 C
mandy.lang@mstc.edu
LANG, Melissa, W 757-446-6054 518 F
langmw@evms.edu
LANG, Paul, L 906-227-2920 256 F
plang@nmu.edu
LANG, Robert 907-786-1859 10 I
anrjl1@uaa.alaska.edu
LANG, Sherrie 210-486-2252 479 E
slang14@alamo.edu
LANG, Stephen, W 432-837-8061 501 B
slang@sulross.edu
LANG, Stuart 417-667-8181 280 I
slang@cottey.edu
LANGAN, Sally 920-498-5688 555 A
sally.langan@nwtc.edu
LANGAN, Terrence, G 651-962-6001 272 E
tglangan@stthomas.edu
LANGAN-YOUNG, Tammy 402-844-7733 300 A
tammy@northeast.edu
LANGDON, Deb 740-389-4636 395 G
langdond@mtc.edu
LANGDON, Lucas, O 270-686-4336 198 G
lucas.langdon@brescia.edu
LANGDON, Rita 516-299-2334 339 A
rita.langdon@liu.edu
LANGDON, Steven, D 515-643-6716 187 C
slangdon@mercydesmoines.org
LANGDON, Tennille 660-831-4157 286 I
langdont@moval.edu
LANGE, Bob 757-594-8070 517 I
robert.lange@cnu.edu
LANGE, Chris, J 414-410-4207 546 D
cjlange@stritch.edu
LANGE, Christine, M 941-359-7594 115 K
clange@ringling.edu
LANGE, Dan 541-278-5891 414 G
dlange@bluecc.edu
LANGE, Douglas, J 606-218-5988 207 B
douglaslange@pc.edu
LANGE, Janet 309-677-2523 145 H
lange@bradley.edu
LANGE, Karen 307-778-1204 556 B
klange@lccc.wy.edu
LANGE, Karen, M 651-962-6050 272 E
kmlange@stthomas.edu
LANGE, Michelle 248-689-8282 260 A
mlange@walshcollege.edu
LANGE, Mindy, W 717-691-6024 436 D
mlange@messiah.edu
LANGE, Peter 919-684-2631 363 I
peter.lange@duke.edu
LANGE, Shirley 614-236-6114 386 C
slange@capital.edu
LANGE, Steven 320-629-5100 268 G
langes@pinetech.edu
LANGE, Tom, J 715-831-7285 553 F
tlange8@cvtc.edu
LANGE, Tyana 765-455-9217 173 E
tylange@iuk.edu
LANGENBACHER, Mark 808-942-1000 140 H
mark.langenbacher@remingtoncollege.edu
LANGENBACK, Timothy 941-752-5342 118 E
langent@scf.edu
LANGENSTEIN, Deborah 980-598-1205 365 G
deborah.langenstein@jwu.edu
LANGER, Allan 401-739-5000 453 E
alanger@neit.edu
LANGER, Nathan 218-723-6010 262 I
nlanger@css.edu
LANGER, Peter 617-287-5611 237 D
peter.langer@umb.edu
LANGERUD, Steven 765-658-4280 170 I
stevelangarud@depauw.edu
LANGEVIN, John 207-602-2549 220 H
jlangevin@une.edu
LANGFERMAN, Neil 317-955-6759 177 G
nlangferman@marian.edu
LANGFORD, Allison 417-328-2093 290 E
alangford@sbuniv.edu
LANGFORD, David 201-692-9867 310 B
david_langford@fdu.edu
LANGFORD, Debra 304-876-5216 544 A
dlangfor@shepherd.edu
LANGFORD, George, M 315-443-3949 357 B
glangfor@syr.edu
LANGFORD, Harold (Hal), P 903-886-5189 497 E
hal_langford@tamu-commerce.edu
LANGFORD, James, D 325-674-2855 478 H
langford@acu.edu
LANGFORD, Mike 828-328-7302 366 B
mike.langford@lr.edu
LANGFORD, Pam 909-537-5008 36 A
plangfor@csusb.edu
LANGFORD, Pamela 909-537-7454 36 A
plangfor@csusb.edu
LANGHAM, Gay 601-643-8307 274 A
gay.langham@colin.edu
LANGHAM, Julie 706-595-0166 125 D
jlangham@augustatech.edu
LANGHAM, Lynda 936-468-2503 495 H
llangham@sfasu.edu
LANGIS, Gayle 207-893-7850 219 F
glangis@sjcme.edu
LANGKILDE, Jared 480-461-7396 15 K
jared.langkilde@mcmail.maricopa.edu
LANGLAND, Elizabeth 602-543-4506 12 B
elizabeth.langland@asu.edu
LANGLAND, Meg 573-592-5381 293 C
Meg.Langland@westminster-mo.edu
LANGLEY, Amy 256-840-4185 7 B
alangley@snead.edu
LANGLEY, Angie 662-720-7249 276 D
alangle@nemcc.edu
LANGLEY, Dawn 336-599-1181 372 D
langled@piedmontcc.edu
LANGLEY, Dorothy 903-769-2710 488 M
dorothy_langley@jarvis.edu
LANGLEY, Goldie 614-947-6509 391 A
langleyg@franklin.edu
LANGLEY, Harry, M 724-938-1523 441 G
langley@calu.edu
LANGLEY, Janet 602-286-8017 15 I
janet.langley@gwmail.maricopa.edu
LANGLEY, Janet 602-286-8287 15 I
janet.langley@gwmail.maricopa.edu
LANGLEY, Janet, R 601-974-1134 275 D
langljr@millsaps.edu
LANGLEY, Pamela 603-271-7150 304 G
plangley@ccsnh.edu
LANGLEY, Winston 617-287-5600 237 D
winston.langley@umb.edu
LANGLIE, Mary, L 516-876-3175 353 D
langliem@oldwestbury.edu
LANGLOIS, John 508-767-7045 230 E
jlanglois@assumption.edu
LANGLOIS, Judith, H 512-232-3317 505 B
langlois@mail.utexas.edu
LANGLOIS, Mary Ann 716-888-2103 325 G
langloim@canisius.edu
LANGOLF, Judi 810-989-2138 249 B
judi.langolf@baker.edu
LANGREHR, Andrew, M 314-984-7387 289 D
alangrehr@stlcc.edu
LANGRELL, Ron 507-433-0530 269 A
ron.langrell@riverland.edu
LANGSETH, Kay 402-461-7300 298 C
klangseth@hastings.edu
LANGSETH, Roger 507-535-3309 263 D
LANGSETH, Roger, W 507-288-4563 263 D
rlangseth@crossroadscollege.edu
LANGSTAFF, Kris, A 606-474-3153 200 J
klangstaff@kcu.edu
LANGSTON, II, Bill, C 863-680-3905 109 D
blangston@flsouthern.edu
LANGSTON, Carol 501-812-2211 23 C
clangston@pulaskitech.edu
LANGSTON, Diane 706-295-6357 130 C
dlangston@highlands.edu
LANGSTON, Ginna, V 918-631-2641 413 F
ruth-langston@utulsa.edu
LANGSTON, Nancy, F 804-828-5174 525 E
nlangston@vcu.edu
LANGSTON, Randall 970-351-2881 88 F
randall.langston@unco.edu
LANGSTON-SMITH, Sanette 601-977-4458 277 F
slsmith@tougaloo.edu
LANGSTRAAT, Nate 360-383-3312 539 D
nlangstraat@whatcom.ctc.edu
LANGTEAU, Paula 715-735-4339 552 F
paula.langteau@uwc.edu
LANGTON, Patricia 618-374-5106 161 D
patricia.langton@principia.edu
LANGUTH, Christine 860-383-5211 91 B
clanguth@trcc.commnet.edu
LANGVARDT, Guy 714-542-8086 52 K
glangvardt@kensington.edu
LANHAM, Allen, K 217-581-6061 150 C
aklanham@eiu.edu
LANHAM, Heather 937-778-7803 390 G
hlanham@edisonohio.edu
LANHAM, Jeff 740-245-7485 404 E
jlanham@rio.edu
LANIAK, Timothy, S 704-527-9909 235 F
tlaniak@gcts.edu
LANIER, Carolyn 203-837-8277 92 A
lanierc@wcsu.edu
LANIER, Gregory, W 850-474-2934 121 C
glanier@uwf.edu
LANIER, Marilyn 415-405-3838 36 F
mlanier@sfsu.edu
LANIER, Percy 205-929-1665 5
plani@mail.miles.edu
LANIER, Stephen, M 843-792-2211 459
lanier@musc.edu
LANIER, William 406-265-4117 295
wjlanier@msun.edu
LANIUS, Karin 740-389-6786 399
lanius.1@osu.edu
LANKA, Greg 330-494-6170 402
glanka@starkstate.edu
LANKER, Jason 716-926-8933 335
jlanker@hilbert.edu
LANKES, Susan 716-652-8900 326
slankes@cks.edu
LANKEWICZ, Linda, B 931-598-1101 472
lankewicz@sewanee.edu
LANKFORD, Donna, W 404-669-2017 135
donna.lankford@point.edu
LANKFORD, Peggy 575-538-6629 321
lankfordp@wnmu.edu
LANN, Jennifer 802-387-4767 513
jlann@landmark.edu
LANN, Patti 318-676-7811 211 H
plann@nwltc.edu
LANNERT, Mary 406-444-7378 295 C
mary.lannert@umhelena.edu
LANNING, Gale 507-453-1443 267 F
glanning@southeastmn.edu
LANNING, Patrick 503-399-5144 414 J
patrick.lanning@chemeketa.edu
LANNING, Stephanie 620-227-9409 192 B
slg@dc3.edu
LANNON, SJ, Timothy, R 402-280-2770 297 H
tlannon@creighton.edu
LANOUE, David 706-568-2056 127 D
lanoue_david@columbusstate.edu
LANOUETTE, Ruth, M 920-832-6528 547 J
ruth.m.lanouette@lawrence.edu
LANPHEAR, Shawna 406-994-3211 295 E
slanphear@montana.edu
LANPHER, Jim 803-754-4100 457 D
LANSER, Michael 920-693-1123 554 A
michael.lanser@gotoltc.edu
LANSWERK, Marcy 507-284-9387 262 G
landswerk.marcy@mayo.edu
LANTAGNE, Douglas, O 802-656-2990 514 F
doug.lantagne@uvm.edu
LANTING, Mark 815-802-8709 154 J
mlanting@kcc.edu
LANTINGA, Sherri 712-722-6212 183 H
lantinga@dordt.edu
LANTIS, Jeffrey, S 517-437-7341 252 E
jeff.lantis@hillsdale.edu
LANTZ, Dona 215-568-4012 436 H
dlantz@moore.edu
LANTZ, Glen 563-588-6784 183 B
glen.lantz@clarke.edu
LANTZ, James, D 989-328-1220 256 A
jlantz@montcalm.edu
LANTZ, Mary Jan 409-944-1281 486 H
mlantz@gc.edu
LANTZ, Susan 570-577-1601 423 D
susan.lantz@bucknell.edu
LANTZ, Tracey, J 660-626-2391 278 F
tlantz@atsu.edu
LANTZY, Robert 303-722-5724 85 L
rlantzy@lincolntech.com
LANUZZA, Jerry 980-598-1434 365 G
jerry.lanuzza@jwu.edu
LANZA, Anna Marie 212-757-1190 323 B
amlanza@funeraleducation.org
LANZA-KADUCE, Linda 352-395-5493 117 E
linda.lanza-kaduce@sfcollege.edu
LANZALACO, Joseph, M 585-385-8367 348 F
jlanzalaco@sjfc.edu
LANZI, Lesley 518-762-4651 334 D
lesley.lanzi@fmcc.suny.edu
LANZILLO, Lee-Ann 617-349-8875 236 G
llanzill@lesley.edu
LANZILLO, Susan 508-626-4534 238 D
slanzillo@framingham.edu
LANZILOTTI, Salvatore 808-734-9520 141 E
ssl@hawaii.edu
LANZONE, Peggie 602-371-1188 17 C
LAOS, Joel 303-762-6903 83 I
joel.laos@denverseminary.edu
LAP, James 718-260-5565 328 E
jlap@citytech.cuny.edu
LAPAGLIA, Karen 814-838-7673 429 B
LAPAILLE, Christine, M 703-993-8860 519 A
clapaille@gmu.edu
LAPALOMBARA, Catherine 301-322-0414 225 F
lapalocx@pgcc.edu
LAPENNA, Alan, G 860-444-8322 558 E
Alan.G.Lapenna@uscg.mil
LAPERUTA, Domenick 718-960-8593 327 C
domenick.laperuta@lehman.cuny.edu
LAPHAM, Steve 301-891-4161 229 B
security@wau.edu
LAPHAM, Steve 301-891-4161 229 B
slapham@wau.edu
LAPIDUS, Chaim, D 410-484-7200 225 C
LAPIDUS, Richard, S 909-869-2400 33 G
rslapidus@csupomona.edu

LASSLEY, Joan, K ... 559-323-2100 ... 66 C
jlassley@sjcl.edu

LASSNER, David, K ... 808-956-3501 ... 140 J
david@hawaii.edu

LASTER, Jill, L ... 817-257-7790 ... 498 F
j.laster@tcu.edu

LASTIMADO, Benedict ... 626-585-7503 ... 61 E
bxlastimado@pasadena.edu

LASTINGER, Michael ... 304-293-6955 ... 544 E
michael.lastinger@mail.wvu.edu

LASTORIA, Michael, D ... 585-567-9622 ... 336 B
michael.lastoria@houghton.edu

LASTRA, Sarai ... 787-743-7979 ... 565 F
ut_slastra@suagm.edu

LASURE, Keith ... 864-941-8687 ... 460 D
lasure.k@ptc.edu

LATAIF, Louis ... 617-353-2668 ... 232 G
lelataif@bu.edu

LATANE, Jane ... 520-383-8401 ... 18 L

LATCHAW HIRSH, Sharon 610-527-0200 ... 445 I
shirsh@rosemont.edu

LATCHUM, Lucy, L ... 757-594-7702 ... 517 I
llatchum@cnu.edu

LATCOVICH, Mark, A ... 440-943-7600 ... 401 G
mal@dioceseofcleveland.org

LATERRA, Frank ... 631-687-1247 ... 349 B
flaterra@sjcny.edu

LATERRA, Frank ... 718-940-5852 ... 349 A
flaterra@sjcny.edu

LATHAM, Adrienne ... 615-329-8632 ... 468 G
alatham@fisk.edu

LATHAM, Amy ... 662-562-3201 ... 276 E
a_latham@northwestms.edu

LATHAM, Angela ... 708-456-0300 ... 166 C
alatham@triton.edu

LATHAM, Brenda ... 209-381-6410 ... 57 C
latham.b@mccd.edu

LATHAM, Clara ... 940-397-4757 ... 491 A
clara.latham@mwsu.edu

LATHAM, Karen, K ... 701-323-6734 ... 381 B
klatham@mohs.org

LATHAM, Marcus ... 912-449-7525 ... 138 G
mlatham@waycross.edu

LATHAM, Marilae ... 618-664-7110 ... 151 D
marilae.latham@greenville.edu

LATHAM, Mark ... 802-831-1226 ... 515 A
mlatham@vermontlaw.edu

LATHAM, Michael ... 718-817-4700 ... 334 C
latham@fordham.edu

LATHAM, Sarah, C ... 205-726-4502 ... 6 G
sclatham@samford.edu

LATHAM, Sarah, V ... 256-782-5276 ... 4 L
slatham@jsu.edu

LATHAM, Tricia ... 580-477-7725 ... 414 C
tricia.latham@wosc.edu

LATHY, Ed ... 614-222-3255 ... 388 F
elathy@ccad.edu

LATIF, Niaz ... 219-989-3251 ... 178 G
nlatif@purduecal.edu

LATIF, Niaz ... 219-989-8320 ... 178 G
nlatif@purduecal.edu

LATIMER, Dewana ... 731-425-2624 ... 475 B
dlatimer@jscc.edu

LATIMER, Tanisha ... 864-941-8363 ... 460 D
latimer.t@ptc.edu

LATIMORE, Leatrice, D ... 504-286-5033 ... 214 I
llatimor@suno.edu

LATIMORE, Nancy, J ... 717-361-1407 ... 428 E
latimonj@etown.edu

LATIMORE, Robbie ... 229-931-2004 ... 136 G
rlatimore@southgatech.edu

LATIN, Quintin ... 256-761-6221 ... 7 H
qlatin@talladega.edu

LATINO, Jennifer, A ... 910-814-5577 ... 362 F
latinoj@campbell.edu

LATINVILLE, Darlene ... 213-624-1200 ... 46 L
dlatinville@fidm.edu

LATIOLAIS, Perry ... 281-487-1170 ... 498 E
platiolais@txchiro.edu

LATIOLAIS, Scott ... 212-749-2802 ... 339 I
slatiolais@msmnyc.edu

LATO, Tracy ... 314-792-6480 ... 283 K
lato@kenrick.edu

LATORELLA, Jacqueline ... 813-253-6219 ... 122 H
jlatorella@ut.edu

LATORTUE, Paul ... 787-751-7410 ... 567 F
prlatortue@aol.com

LATOUF, Christina ... 646-660-6114 ... 326 D
christina_latouf@baruch.cuny.edu

LATOUR, Bill ... 217-641-4290 ... 154 G
blatour@jwcc.edu

LATOUR, Terry, S ... 814-393-2343 ... 442 A
tlatour@clarion.edu

LATOURETTE, Cathy ... 503-725-4930 ... 418 G
latourettec@pdx.edu

LATSHAW, Todd, M ... 717-867-6330 ... 434 C
latshaw@lvc.edu

LATTA, Bruce, J ... 410-293-1801 ... 558 H
latta@usna.edu

LATTA, Judi, M ... 202-238-2338 ... 98 B
jlatta@howard.edu

LATTA, Marcia, S ... 765-658-4212 ... 170 I

LATTA, Mark, A ... 402-280-2860 ... 297 H
marklatta@creighton.edu

LATTA, Stanley ... 814-865-5423 ... 438 F
sxl1@psu.edu

LATTER, George ... 619-849-2317 ... 62 L
georgelatter@pointloma.edu

LATTER, Gerald ... 212-327-8925 ... 347 H
latter@rockefeller.edu

LATTIMER, Sean ... 603-577-6481 ... 304 J
lattimer@dwc.edu

LATTIMORE, Dan, L ... 901-678-2991 ... 474 C
dlattimr@memphis.edu

LATTIMORE, John ... 704-484-4020 ... 369 B
lattimorej@clevelandcommunitycollege.edu

LATTIMORE, Mark ... 478-825-6296 ... 129 C
lattimorem@fvsu.edu

LATTIMORE, Michael, P ... 973-353-1670 ... 314 E
mikelatt@andromeda.rutgers.edu

LATUSZEK, Doty, A ... 260-422-5561 ... 172 L
dalatuszek@indianatech.edu

LATUSZEK, Mark ... 773-907-4000 ... 147 A
mlatuszek@ccc.edu

LATZ, Gil ... 503-725-5350 ... 418 G
latzg@pdx.edu

LAU, Bradley, A ... 503-554-2312 ... 415 I
blau@georgefox.edu

LAU, Danny ... 678-717-3779 ... 129 D
dlau@gsc.edu

LAU, David ... 248-370-2466 ... 257 C
lau@oakland.edu

LAU, John ... 760-355-6235 ... 50 K
john.lau@imperial.edu

LAU, Kimberly ... 831-459-2418 ... 75 A
lau@ucsc.edu

LAU, Lawrence ... 310-577-3000 ... 79 K
lau@yosan.edu

LAU, Ron ... 323-563-5820 ... 39 D
ronlau@cdrewu.edu

LAU, Stuart ... 808-956-8010 ... 141 B
stuartl@hawaii.edu

LAUB, James, A ... 561-803-2302 ... 114 C
james_laub@pba.edu

LAUB, Jeffrey, W ... 434-832-7707 ... 526 A
laubj@cvcc.vccs.edu

LAUB, Richard ... 970-223-2669 ... 85 A
rlaub@ibmc.edu

LAUBAUCH, Harold ... 954-262-1303 ... 114 B
harold@nsu.nova.edu

LAUBE, Irene, H ... 919-536-7211 ... 369 G
laubei@durhamtech.edu

LAUBE, Philip ... 740-826-8101 ... 396 I
plaube@muskingum.edu

LAUBERSHEIMER,
David, E ... 217-786-2240 ... 156 I
david.laubersheimer@llcc.edu

LAUDER, Frank ... 617-873-0137 ... 233 B
finaid@cambridgecollege.edu

LAUDER, Sue, M ... 978-665-3314 ... 238 C
slauder@fitchburgstate.edu

LAUDERBACK, Cindy ... 360-417-6233 ... 536 B
clauderback@pencol.edu

LAUDISIO, Janine ... 305-628-6796 ... 116 G
jlaudisio@stu.edu

LAUER, Andrew, J ... 212-790-0310 ... 361 I
andrewlauer@yu.edu

LAUER, Bonnie ... 570-740-0734 ... 435 C
blauer@luzerne.edu

LAUER, Brenda ... 970-521-6713 ... 86 E
brenda.lauer@njc.edu

LAUER, James ... 828-298-3325 ... 380 C
jlauer@warren-wilson.edu

LAUER, John ... 719-389-6618 ... 81 L
jlauer@coloradocollege.edu

LAUER, Jonathan, D ... 717-766-2511 ... 436 D
jlauer@messiah.edu

LAUER, Larry, D ... 817-257-7808 ... 498 F
l.lauer@tcu.edu

LAUER, Michael ... 314-977-3873 ... 289 F
mlauer9@slu.edu

LAUERMAN, Meg ... 402-472-0088 ... 300 H
mlauerman1@unl.edu

LAUFENBERG, Helen ... 608-822-2308 ... 555 B

LAUFENBERG, Linda, J ... 563-588-6385 ... 183 B
linda.laufenberg@clarke.edu

LAUFER, Marilyn ... 334-844-1486 ... 1 G
laufema@auburn.edu

LAUFFENBURGER,
Linda, M ... 937-327-7811 ... 406 B
llauffenburger@wittenberg.edu

LAUGEL, JoAnn, E ... 812-488-2364 ... 180 B
jl25@evansville.edu

LAUGHLIN, Edward ... 978-478-3400 ... 247 C
elaughlin@zbc.edu

LAUGHLIN, Fredrick, L ... 231-995-1197 ... 256 G
flaughlin@nmc.edu

LAUGHLIN, Janet ... 434-791-5630 ... 516 D
jlaughlin@averett.edu

LAUGHLIN, Jill, N ... 715-394-8350 ... 552 D
jlaughli@uwsuper.edu

LAUGHLIN, Judith ... 724-938-4430 ... 441 G
laughlin@calu.edu

LAUGHLIN, Karen, L ... 850-644-2740 ... 119 C
klaughlin@admin.fsu.edu

LAUGHLIN, Larry, W ... 301-295-3016 ... 558 A
llaughlin@usuhs.mil

LAUGHLIN, Lynn ... 217-732-3168 ... 156 F
llaughli@lincolnchristian.edu

LAUGHLIN, Patricia ... 312-567-3827 ... 153 B
plaughli@iit.edu

LAUGHLIN, Ronda ... 360-752-8334 ... 531 C
rlaughlin@btc.ctc.edu

LAUGHLIN, Sally ... 802-635-1251 ... 515 E
sally.laughlin@jsc.edu

LAUGHLIN, Sherry ... 601-318-6170 ... 278 E
slaughlin@wmcarey.edu

LAUGHRAN, Patrick ... 508-626-4357 ... 238 D
plaughran@framingham.edu

LAUGHTER, Ray ... 832-813-6621 ... 490 C
ray.laughter@lonestar.edu

LAUGHTER, Terry ... 910-277-5223 ... 376 A
laughterth@sapc.edu

LAUGHTON, John ... 609-771-2278 ... 308 G
jlaughto@tcnj.edu

LAUINGER, Curt ... 605-394-4034 ... 466 E
curt.lauinger@wdt.edu

LAUN, Mary Ann ... 626-585-7221 ... 61 E
malaun@pasadena.edu

LAUNDRY, William ... 518-564-2280 ... 354 B
laundrwd@plattsburgh.edu

LAUNIUS, Michael ... 509-963-3610 ... 531 G
launiusm@cwu.edu

LAURANZON, Anne Marie 804-752-7317 ... 522 F
alauranz@rmc.edu

LAURENCE, David ... 928-776-7666 ... 19 E
david.laurence@yc.edu

LAURENT, Joyce ... 574-257-3365 ... 169 F
laurenj@bethelcollege.edu

LAURENT, Robert ... 574-257-3353 ... 169 F
laurenb@bethelcollege.edu

LAURENZ, Jamie ... 575-562-2312 ... 318 A
jamie.laurenz@enmu.edu

LAURENZI, Kellie, L ... 412-397-5201 ... 445 G
laurenzi@rmu.edu

LAURETANO, Angela ... 914-632-5400 ... 341 G
alauretano@monroecollege.edu

LAURIA, Dorothy, M ... 203-582-8258 ... 93 E
dorothy.lauria@quinnipiac.edu

LAURIA, Maryann ... 718-982-2365 ... 327 A

LAURIN, Janet ... 714-533-3946 ... 37 C
jlaurin@calums.edu

LAURITZEN, Rhonda ... 801-627-8388 ... 510 D
lauritzr@owatc.edu

LAURSEN, Gary ... 907-474-6295 ... 10 J
galaursen@alaska.edu

LAUSCH, Mark, C ... 608-243-4508 ... 554 B
mlausch@matcmadison.edu

LAUSELL, Ana, C ... 787-891-0925 ... 562 G
amelon@aguadilla.inter.edu

LAUTERBACH, Lisa ... 734-487-1118 ... 250 H
lisa.lauterbach@emich.edu

LAUTH, Thomas, P ... 706-542-2059 ... 138 C
tplauth@uga.edu

LAUX, Dan ... 402-461-7301 ... 298 C
dlaux@hastings.edu

LAVALLA, Daniel, N ... 215-368-5000 ... 422 H
dlavalla@biblical.edu

LAVALLEE, David ... 518-320-1251 ... 351 D
david.lavallee@suny.edu

LAVANIA, Ambrish ... 803-793-5263 ... 457 F
lavaniaa@denmarktech.edu

LAVASTIDA, Jose, I ... 504-866-7426 ... 213 I
rector@nds.edu

LAVELLE, Helen ... 312-942-2030 ... 163 B
helen_lavelle@rush.edu

LAVELLI, Lucinda ... 352-392-0207 ... 120 B
llavelli@arts.ufl.edu

LAVENDER, Earl ... 615-966-5834 ... 470 D
earl.lavender@lipscomb.edu

LAVENDER, Martha ... 256-927-1801 ... 3 J
mlavender@gadsdenstate.edu

LAVENDER, Melissa ... 850-747-3211 ... 110 E
mlavender@gulfcoast.edu

LAVENDER, Michael, K ... 828-652-0681 ... 371 G
michaell@mcdowelltech.edu

LAVERNIA, Enrique, J ... 530-752-0554 ... 73 F
lavernia@ucdavis.edu

LAVERRIERE, Robert, J ... 937-255-6234 ... 556 H
robert.laverriere@afit.edu

LAVERY, Jim ... 740-389-4636 ... 395 G
laveryj@mtc.edu

LAVERY, Roger ... 765-285-6000 ... 169 D
rlavery@bsu.edu

LAVES, Beth ... 270-745-1900 ... 207 C
beth.laves@wku.edu

LAVIAL, Pierre ... 772-672-8222 ... 101 D

LAVIGNA, Robert ... 608-890-3888 ... 550 G
rlavigna@ohr.wisc.edu

LAVIGNE, JR., F. Travis ... 985-857-3737 ... 210 H
tlavigne@ftcc.edu

LAVIGNE, Robert, W ... 508-213-2217 ... 243 J
robert.lavigne@nichols.edu

LAVIN, Aisha ... 706-667-4170 ... 125 C
alavin@aug.edu

LAVIN, Marjorie, W ... 518-587-2100 ... 355 F
marjorie.lavin@esc.edu

LAVIN, Thomas, J ... 401-456-8094 ... 454 A
tlavin@ric.edu

LAVINDER, Katherine, W ... 540-831-5376 ... 522 D
kawhitfie@radford.edu

LAVINE, Danielle, R ... 207-942-6781 ... 217 B
dlavine@bts.edu

LAVINE, John ... 847-491-2045 ... 160 D
j-lavine@northwestern.edu

LAVINE, Steven, D ... 661-255-1050 ... 32 C
slavine@calarts.edu

LAVIOLETTE, Marc ... 239-590-7891 ... 119 A
mlaviole@fgcu.edu

LAVISTA, Daniel, J ... 213-891-2201 ... 54 F
preid@email.laccd.edu

LAVIT, Daniel, A ... 270-809-2160 ... 204 F
dan.lavit@murraystate.edu

LAVITT, Melissa ... 208-426-3776 ... 142 F
melissalavitt@boisestate.edu

LAVOIE, Chuck ... 802-468-1250 ... 515 C
chuck.lavoie@castleton.edu

LAVOIE, Debra ... 207-216-4312 ... 219 C
dlavoie@yccc.edu

LAVOIE, Kathleen, H ... 518-564-3150 ... 354 B
lavoiekh@plattsburgh.edu

LAVOIE, Lisa ... 860-255-3805 ... 91 C

LAVORATA, Christina, M ... 304-367-4101 ... 543 E

LAVORATA, Christina, M ... 304-367-4101 ... 543 E
chris.lavorata@fairmontstate.edu

LAVOY, Angel ... 787-761-0640 ... 561 B

LAVU, Maritza ... 916-484-8401 ... 56 A
lavum@arc.losrios.edu

LAW, Christina ... 631-632-6280 ... 352 C
christina.law@stonybrook.edu

LAW, Frederick, W ... 440-525-7096 ... 394 F
flaw@lakelandcc.edu

LAW, John, W ... 630-844-5438 ... 145 C
jlaw@aurora.edu

LAW, Kenneth, C ... 740-377-2520 ... 402 F
klawtsbc@zoominternet.net

LAW, Mary Conley ... 360-438-4356 ... 536 F
marylaw@stmartin.edu

LAW, Melinda ... 980-598-1004 ... 365 G
melinda.law@jwu.edu

LAW, Peter ... 740-695-9500 ... 384 J
plaw@btc.edu

LAW, William, D ... 727-341-3241 ... 116 F
law.bill@spcollege.edu

LAWERENCE, Gail ... 325-235-7333 ... 499 I
gail.lawerence@sweetwater.tstc.edu

LAWERENCE, JR.,
Kenneth ... 215-204-4455 ... 447 G
kenneth.lawrence@temple.edu

LAWHON, Cathy ... 949-824-1151 ... 73 H
clawhon@uci.edu

LAWHON, John ... 940-898-3250 ... 502 B
jlawhon@twu.edu

LAWHON, Kevin, A ... 304-442-3058 ... 545 C
kevin.lawhon@mail.wvu.edu

LAWHON, R. Lynn ... 864-488-4608 ... 459 A
llawhon@limestone.edu

LAWHON, William ... 941-487-4323 ... 119 D
wlawhon@ncf.edu

LAWHORN, Janice ... 928-428-8509 ... 14 C
janice.lawhorn@eac.edu

LAWHORNE, Sara ... 205-329-7900 ... 3 B
sara.lawhorne@ecacolleges.com

LAWING, Kim ... 910-362-7003 ... 368 E
klawing@cfcc.edu

LAWING, Martha, A ... 603-862-2053 ... 306 E
anne.lawing@unh.edu

LAWLER, Gary, M ... 570-450-3032 ... 439 J
gml13@psu.edu

LAWLER, Greg ... 805-966-3888 ... 31 A
glawler@brooks.edu

LAWLER, Karen ... 704-378-1418 ... 365 H
klawler@jcsu.edu

LAWLER, Marie ... 925-631-4013 ... 64 F
mrl2@stmarys-ca.edu

LAWLER, Nicola ... 256-761-6207 ... 7 H
Nllawler@talladega.edu

LAWLER, Shirley ... 417-447-8152 ... 287 G
lawlers@otc.edu

LAWLESS, Daniel, M ... 843-349-2021 ... 456 G
dan@coastal.edu

LAWLESS, J. Alan ... 918-343-7715 ... 411 H
alawless@rsu.edu

LAWLESS, Richard ... 516-572-7317 ... 342 C
richard.lawless@ncc.edu

LAWLEY, Thomas, J ... 404-727-5631 ... 129 A
tlawley@emory.edu

LAWLIS, Philip, J ... 717-796-5357 ... 436 D
plawlis@messiah.edu

LAWLOR, Andrew, C ... 814-732-1040 ... 442 D
lawlor@edinboro.edu

LAWLOR, David, D ... 202-994-9487 ... 97 F
ddlawlor@gwu.edu

LAWLOR, Edward, F ... 314-935-6693 ... 292 J
elawlor@wustl.edu

LAWLOR, Jill ... 508-286-8207 ... 246 E
jlawlor@wheatonma.edu

LAWN, Jeanine, M ... 814-269-7037 ... 449 D
lawn@pitt.edu

LAWRENCE, Alfred, C ... 915-831-4463 ... 486 E
alawren4@epcc.edu

LAWRENCE, Barbara ... 718-270-2187 ... 352 D
barbara.lawrence@downstate.edu

LAWRENCE, Barbara ... 646-660-6500 ... 326 D
barbara_lawrence@baruch.cuny.edu

LAWRENCE, Charles ... 206-296-6384 ... 537 F
lawrence@seattleu.edu

LEAVITT, Rose ... 402-354-7137 .... 299 E
rose.leavitt@methodistcollege.edu
LEAVITT, Stephen, C ... 518-388-6116 .... 358 E
leavitts@union.edu
LEBAR, Peter, M ... 814-332-5369 .... 421 E
pete.lebar@allegheny.edu
LEBBE, Duane ... 504-568-4832 .... 213 A
dlebbe@lsuhsc.edu
LEBEAU, Bryan ... 913-758-6115 .... 197 B
lebeau87@stmary.edu
LEBEAU, Michael ... 205-226-4719 .... 2 C
mlebeau@bsc.edu
LEBEL, Paul ... 701-777-2011 .... 381 D
paul.lebel@email.und.edu
LEBER, Frank, W ... 312-329-4388 .... 158 H
fleber@moody.edu
LEBESCH, Anna, M ... 386-312-4061 .... 116 D
annalebesch@sjrstate.edu
LEBESCO, Kathleen ... 212-774-4861 .... 340 D
klebesco@mmm.edu
LEBHERZ, Joe ... 301-682-8315 .... 225 A
lebherz@msmary.edu
LEBICA, John ... 508-362-2131 .... 240 A
jlebica@capecod.edu
LEBIODA, Ed ... 805-437-8547 ..... 33 I
ed.lebioda@csuci.edu
LEBLANC, Ann ... 757-352-4222 .... 523 B
aleblanc@regent.edu
LEBLANC, Bruce ... 309-796-5431 .... 145 E
leblancb@bhc.edu
LEBLANC, Debbie ... 207-947-4591 .... 217 D
dleblanc@bealcollege.edu
LEBLANC, Elva, C ... 817-515-7750 .... 496 A
elva.leblanc@tccd.edu
LEBLANC, Erica ... 310-434-4227 ..... 68 D
leblanc_erica@smc.edu
LEBLANC, Jacqueline ... 212-752-1530 .... 338 C
jacqueline.leblanc@limcollege.edu
LEBLANC, Jerry, L ... 337-482-6235 .... 216 D
jerrylukeleblanc@louisiana.edu
LEBLANC, Nina ... 337-439-5765 .... 208 H
nina@deltatech.edu
LEBLANC, Paul ... 603-645-9631 .... 306 B
p.leblanc@snhu.edu
LEBLANC, Robert ... 713-525-3540 .... 504 D
leblancr@stthom.edu
LEBLANC, Thomas, J ... 305-284-3356 .... 122 F
leblanc@miami.edu
LEBLANC, William ... 401-825-2225 .... 453 B
leblanc@ccri.edu
LEBLEU BURNS, Michele .. 408-864-8218 ..... 47 G
lebleuburnsmichele@deanza.edu
LEBO, Cathy, J ... 410-516-4107 .... 223 F
lebo@jhu.edu
LEBO, Nikki ... 765-269-5483 .... 176 B
nlebo@ivytech.edu
LEBO, Russ ... 559-734-9000 ..... 66 E
russl@sjvc.edu
LEBRON, Maria ... 312-226-6294 .... 156 E
finaid@lexingtoncollege.edu
LEBRON, Nestor, A ... 787-864-2222 .... 563 D
nalebron@inter.edu
LEBSOCK, Gale ... 760-384-6215 ..... 52 N
glebsock@cerrocoso.edu
LECHEHEB, Kamel ... 718-488-1082 .... 338 H
kamel.lecheheb@liu.edu
LECHER, Mark ... 317-738-8178 .... 171 C
mlecher@franklincollege.edu
LECHKO, Amy ... 440-646-8336 .... 405 B
alechko@ursuline.edu
LECHLER, Terry ... 254-299-8652 .... 490 E
tlechler@mclennan.edu
LECHNER, David ... 402-472-2191 .... 300 F
dlechner@nebraska.edu
LECHOWSKI, Piotr ... 312-372-4900 .... 149 D
plechowski@devry.edu
LECHTENBERG, Melanie .... 217-641-4310 .... 154 G
mlechtenberg@jwcc.edu
LECHTENBERG, Victor, L ... 765-494-9095 .... 178 F
vll@purdue.edu
LECK, Kathleen, M ... 847-574-5196 .... 155 G
kleck@lfgsm.edu
LECK, Marie ... 575-538-6109 .... 321 I
leckm@wnmu.edu
LECKERMAN, Natalie ... 215-780-1315 .... 446 G
nleckerman@salus.edu
LECKONBY, Larry, W ... 843-953-5030 .... 456 C
larry.leckonby@citadel.edu
LECKRONE, Michael, J ... 260-982-5004 .... 177 F
mjleckrone@manchester.edu
LECLAIR, Jane ... 518-608-8256 .... 333 F
jleclair@excelsior.edu
LECLERC, Robin ... 248-204-2203 .... 254 E
rleclerc@ltu.edu
LECONTE, Pier ... 787-844-8181 .... 567 E
pier.leconte@upr.edu
LECOUNT, Heidi ... 919-760-8633 .... 366 G
lecounth@meredith.edu
LECOURT, Nancy ... 707-965-6234 ..... 60 J
LECRONE, Jeffrey, L ... 570-321-4112 .... 435 D
lecrone@lycoming.edu
LEDBETTER, Beverly, E ... 401-863-9900 .... 452 J
beverly_ledbetter@brown.edu

LEDBETTER, Kim, M ... 828-652-0602 .... 371 G
kims@mcdowelltech.edu
LEDBETTER, Lisa ... 704-216-3620 .... 373 C
lisa.ledbetter@rccc.edu
LEDBETTER, Neal ... 251-442-2429 .... 9 B
neall@mail.umobile.edu
LEDBETTER, Sam ... 256-549-8690 .... 3 J
sledbetter@gadsdenstate.edu
LEDBETTER, Sherry ... 312-553-5766 .... 146 H
sledbetter@ccc.edu
LEDBETTER, William, B ... 828-652-0674 .... 371 G
bradl@mcdowelltech.edu
LEDDY, Michael ... 401-341-2195 .... 454 D
mike.leddy@salve.edu
LEDDY, Patrick ... 671-735-2442 .... 559 D
greyleddy@uguam.uog.edu
LEDERBERG, Amy, R ... 404-413-3505 .... 131 C
alederberg@gsu.edu
LEDERER, Benjamin ... 718-851-0183 .... 347 C
LEDERMAN, Linda, C ... 480-965-0668 ..... 12 B
linda.lederman@asu.edu
LEDERMANN, Stacy, A ... 585-385-8142 .... 348 F
sledermann@sjfc.edu
LEDESMA, Amadeo ... 575-527-7530 .... 319 G
amadeol@nmsu.edu
LEDESMA, John ... 916-649-2400 ..... 31 C
LEDESMA, Mark ... 206-726-5028 .... 532 G
mledesma@cornish.edu
LEDFORD, Christine ... 757-594-8459 .... 517 I
christine.ledford@cnu.edu
LEDFORD, Howard ... 706-335-9337 .... 132 J
hledford@laniertech.edu
LEDFORD, Julia ... 270-686-4627 .... 202 E
julia.ledford@kctcs.edu
LEDFORD, Kristin ... 304-766-3206 .... 542 F
kledford@kvctc.edu
LEDFORD, Laura ... 217-362-6499 .... 158 F
lledford@millikin.edu
LEDFORD, Randy ... 336-249-8186 .... 369 F
rledford@davidsonccc.edu
LEDFORD, Robert ... 407-708-2126 .... 117 G
ledfordr@seminolestate.edu
LEDFORD, Terry ... 864-941-8559 .... 460 D
ledford.t@ptc.edu
LEDFORD, Tommy, R ... 828-765-7351 .... 371 F
tledford@mayland.edu
LEDMAN, Robert ... 520-383-8401 ..... 18 L
rledman@tocc.cc.az.us
LEDOUX, Michael, W ... 610-499-4345 .... 451 F
mwledoux@widener.edu
LEDUC, Don ... 517-371-5140 .... 259 B
leducd@cooley.edu
LEDUC, Paul, D ... 518-564-2090 .... 354 B
leducpd@plattsburgh.edu
LEDVINA, Anne ... 205-226-7722 .... 2 C
aledvina@bsc.edu
LEDWIN, Richard ... 323-259-2613 ..... 59 H
ledwin@oxy.edu
LEDY, Ann ... 651-757-4007 .... 263 A
aledy@cva.edu
LEDYARD, Christopher, L .. 740-283-6437 .... 390 M
cledyard@franciscan.edu
LEE, Alberta, G ... 585-292-2106 .... 341 H
alee@monroecc.edu
LEE, Allisha ... 270-707-3950 .... 202 A
allisha.lee@kctcs.edu
LEE, Amanda ... 910-362-7475 .... 368 E
alee@cfcc.edu
LEE, IHM, Andrea, J ... 651-690-6525 .... 271 E
ajlee@stkate.edu
LEE, Ann, B ... 812-941-2356 .... 174 D
alee@ius.edu
LEE, Barbara ... 831-646-4014 ..... 57 G
blee@mpc.edu
LEE, Barton ... 813-974-7380 .... 120 D
blee@usf.edu
LEE, Ben ... 212-229-8947 .... 342 E
leeb@newschool.edu
LEE, Benjamin, G ... 605-336-6588 .... 465 B
benlee@sfseminary.edu
LEE, Bert ... 410-276-0306 .... 226 D
blee@host.sdc.edu
LEE, Beth, I ... 714-879-3901 ..... 50 G
bilee@hiu.edu
LEE, Bo Min ... 714-527-0691 ..... 45 J
LEE, Brenda ... 419-530-7730 .... 404 F
brenda.lee@utoledo.edu
LEE, Brian ... 601-877-4063 .... 273 C
brain.lee@sodexo.com
LEE, Brian ... 617-627-3143 .... 245 F
brian.lee@tufts.edu
LEE, Carla ... 314-340-3307 .... 282 I
leec@hssu.edu
LEE, Catherine ... 910-362-7033 .... 368 E
clee@cfcc.edu
LEE, Catherine ... 334-844-1350 .... 1 G
leecath@auburn.edu
LEE, Charley ... 714-527-0691 ..... 45 J
LEE, Chenetta ... 334-876-9303 .... 4 B
chenetta.lee@wccs.edu
LEE, Cheuk ... 212-237-8881 .... 328 A
clee@jjay.cuny.edu
LEE, Chow ... 510-574-1281 ..... 44 D
clee@devry.edu

LEE, Chris ... 602-978-7591 ..... 18 K
chris.lee@thunderbird.edu
LEE, Chris ... 270-706-8622 .... 201 F
chris.lee@kctcs.edu
LEE, Chris ... 800-955-2527 .... 282 G
clee@grantham.edu
LEE, Chris ... 615-794-4254 .... 472 D
clee@omorecollege.edu
LEE, Christopher ... 804-819-4685 .... 525 F
clee@vccs.edu
LEE, Chui-Chun ... 845-257-3719 .... 352 B
leec@newpaltz.edu
LEE, Chul ... 302-736-2371 ..... 96 G
leechul@wesley.edu
LEE, Cindy ... 352-588-8869 .... 116 E
cindy.lee@saintleo.edu
LEE, Crystal ... 225-675-8270 .... 211 J
clee@rpcc.edu
LEE, Curtis ... 253-964-6595 .... 536 C
clee@pierce.ctc.edu
LEE, D. Lynn ... 443-412-2258 .... 223 B
llee@harford.edu
LEE, Dana ... 914-594-4567 .... 343 F
dana_lee@nymc.edu
LEE, Darin, N ... 208-496-2311 .... 142 G
leed@byui.edu
LEE, David, C ... 706-542-5969 .... 138 C
dclee@uga.edu
LEE, David, D ... 270-745-5204 .... 207 C
david.lee@wku.edu
LEE, Dean ... 870-972-3880 ..... 20 C
deanlee@astate.edu
LEE, Delores ... 310-243-3691 ..... 34 B
dslee@csudh.edu
LEE, Dennis ... 229-225-5087 .... 137 D
dlee@southwestgatech.edu
LEE, Dewain ... 907-786-1214 ..... 10 I
aydos@uaa.alaska.edu
LEE, Diana ... 405-491-6310 .... 412 D
dlee@snu.edu
LEE, Diane, M ... 410-455-2859 .... 227 D
dlee@umbc.edu
LEE, Donald, E ... 252-493-7262 .... 372 E
dlee@email.pittcc.edu
LEE, Donna, A ... 404-471-6391 .... 123 G
dlee@agnesscott.edu
LEE, Donzell ... 601-877-6122 .... 273 C
dlee@alcorn.edu
LEE, Doug ... 724-852-3630 .... 451 B
dlee@waynesburg.edu
LEE, Douglas, J ... 319-335-0444 .... 182 C
douglas-lee@uiowa.edu
LEE, E. Joseph ... 207-893-7711 .... 219 F
jlee@sjcme.edu
LEE, Elaine ... 808-454-4793 .... 141 C
elainel@hawaii.edu
LEE, Elwyn, C ... 832-842-5932 .... 503 B
eclee@uh.edu
LEE, Eric ... 617-973-1101 .... 245 E
elee@suffolk.edu
LEE, Frieda ... 415-338-2356 ..... 36 F
friedale@sfsu.edu
LEE, Giljae ... 218-726-7179 .... 272 B
glee@umn.edu
LEE, Grayce ... 504-468-2900 .... 215 B
drlee@southwest.edu
LEE, Greg ... 217-641-4351 .... 154 G
lee@jwcc.edu
LEE, Harlan ... 425-564-2212 .... 531 B
harlan.lee@bellevuecollege.edu
LEE, Herbert ... 831-459-2351 ..... 75 A
vpaa@ucsc.edu
LEE, Herman, C ... 760-744-1150 ..... 61 C
hlee@palomar.edu
LEE, Hesseung ... 215-965-4015 .... 436 H
hlee@moore.edu
LEE, Humphrey ... 256-331-5214 .... 6 B
hlee@nwscc.edu
LEE, Il Soo ... 714-533-3946 ..... 37 C
islee@calums.edu
LEE, Ingrid ... 928-226-4315 ..... 13 H
ingrid.lee@coconino.edu
LEE, Irene ... 907-277-1000 ..... 10 F
contact@chartercollege.edu
LEE, J. Steve ... 251-442-2390 .... 9 B
stevel@mail.umobile.edu
LEE, Jae ... 510-580-3507 ..... 79 G
jlee@cci.edu
LEE, Jay ... 208-769-3302 .... 143 H
jalee@nic.edu
LEE, Joe ... 617-873-0615 .... 233 B
Joe.Lee@cambridgecollege.edu
LEE, John ... 707-826-3961 ..... 36 D
john.lee@humboldt.edu
LEE, Jonathan ... 310-233-4471 ..... 54 I
leej@lahc.edu
LEE, Jonathan ... 860-509-9556 ..... 92 D
jlee@hartsem.edu
LEE, Jonathan, E ... 540-375-2237 .... 523 D
lee@roanoke.edu
LEE, Joni, C ... 501-569-3186 ..... 24 E
jclee@ualr.edu
LEE, Julie ... 707-965-6303 ..... 60 J
jzlee@puc.edu

LEE, Julie ... 229-333-5925 .... 138 F
julielee@valdosta.edu
LEE, Katherine ... 317-921-4921 175
klee@ivytech.edu
LEE, Katrina, K ... 919-658-2502 .... 367 D
klee@moc.edu
LEE, Keum Hee ... 213-385-2322 ..... 79 E
LEE, Kevin ... 620-862-5252 .... 190 D
kevin.lee@barclaycollege.edu
LEE, Kim ... 601-923-1681 .... 277 B
klee@rts.edu
LEE, Kyu, H ... 253-752-2020 .... 533 J
revkhlee@faithseminary.edu
LEE, Kyu Jong ... 770-279-0507 .... 129 E
hmanklee@hotmail.com
LEE, Larry ... 361-698-1700 .... 485 F
llee@delmar.edu
LEE, Larry, K ... 814-332-2324 .... 421 E
larry.lee@allegheny.edu
LEE, Laura ... 205-726-2898 .... 6 G
lhlee@samford.edu
LEE, Leon ... 212-226-7300 .... 346 E
llee@pbcny.edu
LEE, Linda, J ... 414-288-7206 .... 548 D
linda.j.lee@marquette.edu
LEE, Linda, S ... 657-725-7789 ..... 71 F
lslee@stanford.edu
LEE, Lisa ... 714-533-3946 ..... 37 C
lisa@calums.edu
LEE, Lisa ... 212-410-8032 .... 343 B
llee@nycpm.edu
LEE, Lisa ... 610-328-8402 .... 447 E
llee2@swarthmore.edu
LEE, Marc, D ... 202-806-6131 ..... 98 B
mdlee2@howard.edu
LEE, Margaret, B ... 847-635-1801 .... 160 E
plee@oakton.edu
LEE, Marsha ... 662-246-6314 .... 275 F
mlee@msdelta.edu
LEE, Marty ... 707-527-4689 ..... 68 E
mlee@santarosa.edu
LEE, Mary ... 623-572-3416 ..... 16 F
mleexx@midwestern.edu
LEE, Mary, Y ... 617-627-4733 .... 245 F
mary.lee@tufts.edu
LEE, SSJ, Mary Esther ... 215-248-7062 .... 425 C
leem@chc.edu
LEE, Mary W, L ... 630-515-7311 .... 158 E
mleexx@midwestern.edu
LEE, Maurice ... 704-357-8020 .... 361 N
mlee@aii.edu
LEE, Maurice, A ... 501-450-3167 ..... 25 H
mauricel@uca.edu
LEE, Mei-Lin ... 210-436-3414 .... 493 C
mlee@stmarytx.edu
LEE, Michael ... 510-490-6900 ..... 79 G
mlee@cci.edu
LEE, Michael, D ... 229-226-1621 .... 137 F
mlee@thomasu.edu
LEE, Michael, E ... 814-860-5141 .... 433 C
elee@lecom.edu
LEE, Michele, S ... 864-429-8728 .... 462 G
michele@mailbox.sc.edu
LEE, Mike ... 386-752-1822 .... 108 C
mike.lee@fgc.edu
LEE, Ming-Tung "Mike" ... 916-278-6312 ..... 35 E
mikelee@csus.edu
LEE, Mona ... 808-734-9522 .... 141 E
monal@hawaii.edu
LEE, Moses ... 616-395-7190 .... 252 F
lee@hope.edu
LEE, Norma ... 423-697-2478 .... 474 D
LEE, Otto ... 619-388-6965 ..... 65 E
olee@sdccd.edu
LEE, Pamela ... 512-313-3000 .... 483 G
pamela.lee@concordia.edu
LEE, Penny ... 765-455-9415 .... 173 E
pennlee@iuk.edu
LEE, Peter ... 415-354-9155 ..... 32 B
plee@baychef.com
LEE, Peter ... 212-243-5150 .... 334 E
lee@gts.edu
LEE, Raeann ... 614-416-6239 .... 385 E
rlee@bradfordschoolcolumbus.edu
LEE, Randall ... 601-635-6375 .... 274 C
rlee@eccc.edu
LEE, Randolph ... 860-297-2413 ..... 94 C
randolph.lee@trincoll.edu
LEE, Rebecca ... 909-621-8277 ..... 69 A
rebecca.lee@scrippscollege.edu
LEE, Rebecca, R ... 478-757-3551 .... 126 G
blee@centralgatech.edu
LEE, Rickey, C ... 205-929-1641 .... 5 H
rlee@miles.edu
LEE, Robert, E ... 563-884-5123 ..... 60 L
robert.lee@palmer.edu
LEE, Robert, E ... 563-884-5123 .... 188 C
robert.lee@palmer.edu
LEE, Robert, E ... 563-884-5123 .... 114 E
robert.lee@palmer.edu
LEE, Robert, L ... 575-835-5143 .... 319 A
lee@prrc.nmt.edu
LEE, Roger, R ... 770-720-5537 .... 135 F
rrl@reinhardt.edu

LELE, Pradeep 281-618-7123 490 C
pradeep.m.lele@lonestar.edu

LELIAERT, Deborah, S 940-565-2108 504 B
leliaert@unt.edu

LELII, Linda 215-884-8942 452 C
academicdean@woninstitute.edu

LELIK, Mary 312-996-3254 166 F
lelik@uic.edu

LELNER, Larry 315-279-5235 337 K
Lehner@mail.keuka.edu

LELONG, Kristine, D 504-865-3858 213 F
klelong@loyno.edu

LELOUDIS, James, L 919-843-7754 378 D
leloudis@email.unc.edu

LEMA, Barbara 508-286-8206 246 E
blema@wheatoncollege.edu

LEMAHIEU, Dan 847-735-5083 155 F
lemahieu@lakeforest.edu

LEMAHIEU, Keith 219-864-2400 178 B
klemahieu@midamerica.edu

LEMAIRE, Renée 334-222-6591 5 F
rlemaire@lbwcc.edu

LEMANN, Nicholas 212-854-6056 330 F
nl2124@columbia.edu

LEMANSKI, Kenneth 413-572-5210 239 C
klamanski@wsc.ma.edu

LEMANSKI, Larry 903-886-5018 497 E
larry_lemanski@tamu-commerce.edu

LEMASTER, Charles 254-647-3214 492 E
clemaster@rangercollege.edu

LEMASTER, Courtney 270-852-3107 203 E

LEMASTER, J. Michael 937-258-8251 392 C

LEMASTERS, Michael 724-357-2696 442 E
michael.lemasters@iup.edu

LEMASTERS, Phil 325-793-3898 490 F
plemasters@mcm.edu

LEMASTERS, Rosanna 740-695-1720 400 A
stclair@ohio.edu

LEMAY, Eileen 563-589-0300 189 G
elemay@wartburgseminary.edu

LEMAY, Elaine 510-869-6739 64 J
elemay@samuelmerritt.edu

LEMAY, Jerret 315-312-2237 354 A
jerret.lemay@oswego.edu

LEMAY, Mitch 415-485-9467 41 I
mitchell.lemay@marin.edu

LEMBKE, Roberta 507-786-3097 271 H
lembke@stolaf.edu

LEMBKE, Roberta 507-786-2222 271 H
lembke@stolaf.edu

LEMBO, Vincent, J 617-373-2157 244 A

LEMBURG, Mary 713-718-8505 487 G
mary.lemburg@hccs.edu

LEMCKE, Jim, R 406-243-6131 295 A
jim.lemcke@umontana.edu

LEMCOE, Diane 908-526-1200 313 E
dlemcoe@raritanval.edu

LEMERY, Cynthia 518-327-6399 345 H
clemery@paulsmiths.edu

LEMIESZ, Linda 212-353-4115 331 B
lemiesz@cooper.edu

LEMIEUX, Carlene, P 207-893-7754 219 F
clemieux@sjcme.edu

LEMIEUX, Louis, N 202-994-9610 97 F
llemleux@gwu.edu

LEMKE, Angela 276-376-4517 525 C
aml7u@uvawise.edu

LEMKE, Chris 616-222-1360 250 C
chris.lemke@cornerstone.edu

LEMKE, Gregory, J 218-477-5869 268 A
greg.lemke@mnstate.edu

LEMKE, Steve, W 504-282-4455 213 H
slemke@nobts.edu

LEMLER, Bradley, K 574-372-5100 171 E
lemlerbk@grace.edu

LEMLEY, David 310-506-4275 61 G
david.lemley@pepperdine.edu

LEMMA, Paulette 860-832-2364 91 G
lemma@ccsu.edu

LEMOI, Tina 978-762-4000 241 A
tlemoi@northshore.edu

LEMOINE, Holly, D 516-759-2040 360 A
hlemoine@webb-institute.edu

LEMOINE, Sandra, M 318-342-1235 216 E
slemoine@ulm.edu

LEMON, Jason 619-260-4585 76 A
jasonlemon@sandiego.edu

LEMON, Jason 402-474-5315 298 E
jlemon@kaplanuniversity.edu

LEMON, Ronald, E 304-896-7425 542 J
ronl@southern.wvnet.edu

LEMON, William, J 314-824-2002 291 F
lemonj@umsl.edu

LEMOND, Charles 901-843-3890 472 I
lemond@rhodes.edu

LEMONIS, Samuel 601-857-3204 274 E
splemonis@hindscc.edu

LEMONNIER, Janet 973-642-8724 315 C
janet.wagman-lemonnier@shu.edu

LEMONS, James 434-832-7680 526 A
lemonsj@cvcc.vccs.edu

LEMONS, L. Jay 570-372-4130 447 D
supres@susqu.edu

LEMONS, Mike 803-641-3345 462 B
mikel@usca.edu

LEMUEL, Robert, L 989-964-4393 258 A
lemuel@svsu.edu

LEMURA, Linda, M 315-445-4312 338 B
lemuralm@lemoyne.edu

LEMUS, Maria De Jesus 773-371-5453 146 B
mlemus@ctu.edu

LEMUS, Tony 303-762-6925 83 I
tony.lemus@denverseminary.edu

LENA, Hugh, F 401-865-2155 453 F
hlena@providence.edu

LENAHAN, Robert 631-632-6350 352 C
robert.lenahan@stonybrook.edu

LENARD, Mary 262-595-2644 551 E
mary.lenard@uwp.edu

LENARZ, Josh 708-239-4824 165 I
joshua.lenarz@trnty.edu

LENCHAK, Timothy, A 563-876-3353 183 G
tlenchak@dwci.edu

LENCZOWSKI, John 202-462-2101 98 C
lenczowski@iwp.edu

LENDIO, Darolyn 808-956-9901 140 J
lendio@hawaii.edu

LENFEST, Richard 413-572-5405 239 C
rlenfest@wsc.ma.edu

LENGERICH, Shannon 847-925-6889 151 E
slengeri@harpercollege.edu

LENHARDT, Rachel 712-325-3282 186 B
rlenhardt@iwcc.edu

LENHARDT, Steven 617-994-6928 237 A
slenhardt@bhe.mass.edu

LENHART, Steven 212-343-1234 341 B
slenhart@mcny.edu

LENIG, Joni, L 931-540-2752 474 F
jlenig@columbiastate.edu

LENIHAN, Bernard 908-709-7605 316 B
lenihan@ucc.edu

LENIHAN, Gerald 973-642-8252 315 C
gerald.lenihan@shu.edu

LENINGER, Edward, F 630-466-7900 167 G
eleninger@waubonsee.edu

LENKER, Michael 509-533-8280 532 E
mlenker@scc.spokane.edu

LENN, Jeffrey 202-994-4950 97 F
djlenn@gwu.edu

LENNEMAN, Marc 406-447-4336 294 A
mlenneman@carroll.edu

LENNERTZ, Reid 239-590-7960 119 A
rlennert@fgcu.edu

LENNEY, Raina 202-885-5936 97 B
lenney@american.edu

LENNIE, Peter 585-273-5000 358 I
lennie@rochester.edu

LENNIHAN, Louise 212-817-7280 327 B
llennihan@gc.cuny.edu

LENNON, Gerald, P 610-758-3165 434 E
gpl0@lehigh.edu

LENNON, John 845-848-4061 332 C
john.lennon@dc.edu

LENNOX, Marybeth 802-287-8238 513 D
lennoxmb@greenmtn.edu

LENO, Leah 218-879-0813 266 F
leah@fdltcc.edu

LENO, Mclissa 218-733-5903 267 B
m.leno@lsc.edu

LENO, Tom 701-224-5497 382 B
thomas.leno@bismarckstate.edu

LENOIR, Lawrence 202-541-5256 99 G
llenoir@wtu.edu

LENON, Mary Jane 401-865-2566 453 F
mjlenon@providence.edu

LENORE-JENKINS, Shani 314-529-9350 284 F
slenore@maryville.edu

LENROW, Jon 215-670-9359 438 D
jlenrow@peirce.edu

LENSING, Peggy 563-387-1015 187 A
lensinpe@luther.edu

LENSINK, Scott 217-234-5222 155 H
slensink@lakeland.cc.il.us

LENSMEYER, Kris 573-592-5319 293 C
Kris.Lensmeyer@westminster-mo.edu

LENT, Scott 903-223-3087 498 C
scott.lent@tamut.edu

LENTING, Amy 312-225-6288 167 E
alenting@vandercook.edu

LENTINI, James, P 513-529-6010 396 D
james.lentini@muohio.edu

LENTINO, Nicholas 860-727-6765 92 C
nlentino@goodwin.edu

LENTNER, Nikolaus 914-251-6070 354 D
nikolaus.lentner@purchase.edu

LENTO, Joseph 718-260-5430 328 E
jlento@citytech.cuny.edu

LENTSCH, Michael 515-964-6216 183 E
mjlentsch@dmacc.edu

LENTZ, Alice 828-726-2234 368 D
alentz@cccti.edu

LENTZ, Bernard, F 215-895-4971 427 G
bfl25@drexel.edu

LENTZ, Heather 605-995-7227 464 E
heather.lentz@mitchelltech.edu

LENTZ, Lynette 402-375-7241 299 I
lylentz1@wsc.edu

LENWAY, Stefanie, A 517-355-8377 255 D
lenway@msu.edu

LENZ, Christopher 323-343-3237 35 B
clenz@cslanet.calstatela.edu

LENZ, Elizabeth, R 614-292-8900 398 H
lenz.23@osu.edu

LENZ, Joe 515-271-3939 184 A
joe.lenz@drake.edu

LENZ, Mary 320-762-4648 265 I
maryl@alextech.edu

LENZ, Patrick, J 510-987-9101 73 D
patrick.lenz@ucop.edu

LENZ, Suzanne 603-623-0313 305 F
suzannelenz@nhia.edu

LENZI, John 413-545-2313 237 C
jlenzi@registrar.umass.edu

LENZI, Patrick 610-436-1048 443 F
plenzi@wcupa.edu

LENZY, Cherjanet 814-332-3332 421 E
cherjanet.lenzy@allegheny.edu

LEO, Vince 612-874-3665 265 E
vince_leo@mcad.edu

LEOGRANDE, William, M 202-885-6234 97 B
wleogra@american.edu

LEON, Dante, J 425-235-5831 536 E
dleon@rtc.edu

LEON, Georgina 787-257-7373 565 E
ue_gleon@suagm.edu

LEON, Gloria 914-606-6744 360 D
gloria.leon@sunywcc.edu

LEON, Juan, C 787-844-8812 567 E
jleon@uprp.edu

LEON, Julio, S 719-549-2306 83 B
julio.leon@colostsate-pueblo.edu

LEON GUERRERO,
Barbara, B 671-735-5519 559 B
csi@guamcc.edu

LEON GUERRERO,
Deborah, D 671-735-2585 559 D
deborah@uguam.uog.edu

LEONARD, Billy 713-975-7527 499 F

LEONARD, Brenda 704-330-6626 369 A
brenda.leonard@cpcc.edu

LEONARD, David, M 540-458-8752 530 A
dleonard@wlu.edu

LEONARD, Debbie 305-809-3203 108 F
debbie.leonard@fkcc.edu

LEONARD, III, Edward, F 785-227-3380 190 G
president@bethanylb.edu

LEONARD, Gloria, J 314-516-5362 291 F
gloria_leonard@umsl.edu

LEONARD, Joseph, G 202-296-5254 97 F
gleonard@gwu.edu

LEONARD, Katie 570-702-8925 431 K
kleonard@johnson.edu

LEONARD, Katy 205-226-4647 2 C
kleonard@bsc.edu

LEONARD, Kevin, M 585-292-5627 325 D
kmleonard@bryantstratton.edu

LEONARD, Nora 757-388-2900 523 J

LEONARD, Patricia, L 910-962-3117 379 C
leonard@uncw.edu

LEONARD, Patricia, Y 810-989-5523 258 B
pleonard@sc4.edu

LEONARD, OSFS, Peter 610-282-1100 426 I
peter.leonard@desales.edu

LEONARD, Robert 256-824-2233 9 A
robert.leonard@uah.edu

LEONARD, Steve 317-738-8316 171 C
sleonard@franklincollege.edu

LEONARD, Susan 435-613-5230 511 E
susan.leonard@ceu.edu

LEONARD, Thomas, C 510-642-3773 73 F
toml@berkeley.edu

LEONARD, Vee 239-590-1101 119 A
vleonard@fgcu.edu

LEONARD, William 617-735-9883 234 E
leonard@emmanuel.edu

LEONARD-RAY, Pamela 843-574-6411 461 G
Pamela.Leonard-Ray@tridenttech.edu

LEONARD-ROCK, Pearl 608-663-2256 547 C
prock@edgewood.edu

LEONE, Kavita 860-727-6788 92 C
kleone@goodwin.edu

LEONE, Therese, M 510-430-2228 57 D
tmleone@mills.edu

LEONHARDT, Chuck 970-351-1890 88 F
charles.leonhardt@unco.edu

LEONHARDT, Joe 303-753-6046 87 F

LEONOR, JR., Samuel, E 951-785-2090 53 D
sleonor@lasierra.edu

LEONOWICH, Donna 860-343-5778 90 D
dleonowich@mxcc.commnet.edu

LEOPARD, David 912-525-6157 136 B
dleopard@scad.edu

LEOPARD, David 706-379-3111 139 F

LEOPARD, Tim 205-348-8157 8 F
tleopard@fa.ua.edu

LEOPARDI, Dino 607-844-8222 357 H
leopard@tc3.edu

LEOUSIS, Kim 251-442-2290 9 B
kiml@mail.umobile.edu

LEPAGE, Francoise 415-485-3284 45 B
flepage@dominican.edu

LEPAGE, G. Peter 607-255-4146 331
gpl3@cornell.edu

LEPAGE, Greg 425-739-8108 535
greg.lepage@lwtc.edu

LEPAGE, Joe 512-863-1915 495
lepagej@southwestern.edu

LEPAGE, Sharon 808-440-4263 140
slepage@chaminade.edu

LEPKE, Allen 605-995-2958 464
allepke@dwu.edu

LEPLEY, Pamela, D 804-828-6057 525
pdlepley@vcu.edu

LEPORE, Gina 212-982-3456 60
glepore@pacificcollege.edu

LEPORE, Gina 212-982-3456 345 C

LEPORE, Lynne 302-225-6256 96 E
leporel@gbc.edu

LEPOWSKY, Steven 860-679-4885 94
lepowsky@nso2.uchc.edu

LEPPANEN, Hannu 906-487-7285 251 C
hannu.leppanen@finlandia.edu

LEPPERT, Glenn, W 620-862-5252 190 D
registrar@barclaycollege.edu

LEPPO, Robin, L 559-323-2100 66 C
rleppo@sjcl.edu

LEPUS, Jennifer 410-455-3751 227 D
jlepus@umbc.edu

LERBINGER, Jan 617-585-1284 243 E
jan.lerbinger@necmusic.edu

LERCH, Carol 508-929-8119 239 D
clerch@worcester.edu

LERCH, Derek 530-283-0202 47 B
dlerch@frc.edu

LERCH, Maureen, T 330-684-8951 403 C
mlerch@uakron.edu

LERER, Nava 516-877-3236 322 A
lerer@adelphi.edu

LERER, Seth 858-534-6270 74 D
slerer@ucsd.edu

LERMAN, Linda 203-857-7211 90 G
llerman@ncc.commnet.edu

LERMAN, Steven 202-994-6510 97 F
Lerman@gwu.edu

LERNER, Bart 602-216-3114 11 F
blerner@argosy.edu

LERNER, Bart 602-216-3114 144 G
blerner@argosy.edu

LERNER, Dan 802-828-8740 402 I
dan.lerner@myunion.edu

LERNER, Darryl 305-892-7064 111 K
darryl.lerner@jwu.edu

LERNER, Sandra 718-960-6959 327 C
sandra.lerner@lehman.cuny.edu

LERNER, Sharon 212-817-7413 327 B
slerner@gc.cuny.edu

LEROSEN, Genene 804-523-5550 526 F
glerosen@reynolds.edu

LEROUX, Kerri 269-927-8601 254 B
leroux@lakemichigancollege.edu

LEROY, Glen, S 248-204-2803 254 E
gleroy@ltu.edu

LEROY, JoNan 503-838-8483 419 C
leroyj@wou.edu

LERUD, Theodore 630-617-3661 150 F
tedl@elmhurst.edu

LERUD-HECK, Joanne, V 303-273-3690 82 F
jvlerud@mines.edu

LESAGE, Jasper 712-707-7102 188 B
lesage@nwciowa.edu

LESAN, Thomas, L 641-782-7081 189 A
lesan@swcciowa.edu

LESAVOY, Barbara 585-395-5700 352 F
blesavoy@brockport.edu

LESCAULT, JR.,
Maurice, A 434-971-3291 557 D
moe.lescault@us.army.mil

LESCHES, Elchonon 718-363-2034 357 E

LESCINSKI, CSJ, Joan 563-333-6213 188 D
officeofthepresident@sau.edu

LESEANE, Reginald 912-358-3389 136 C
leseaner@savannahstate.edu

LESEN, Beth 212-650-5913 326 H
blesen@ccny.cuny.edu

LESEN, Beth 212-650-5426 326 H

LESESNE, David, L 804-752-7305 522 F
davidlesesne@rmc.edu

LESGOLD, Alan, M 412-648-1738 449 A
al@pitt.edu

LESH, Aja 626-815-6000 30 E
alesh@apu.edu

LESHAN, Tim, E 617-373-8528 244 A

LESHIN, Laurie 518-276-6305 347 D
leshl@rpi.edu

LESHKEVICH, Pete 734-973-3729 260 B
pleshkev@wccnet.edu

LESHOK, Paul 414-443-3658 549 A
leshokp@mtmary.edu

LESICK, Lawrence, T 610-499-1225 451 F
ltlesick@widener.edu

LESKO, Wayne 703-284-1620 521 A
wayne.lesko@marymount.edu

LESLIE, Benjamin, C 704-406-4239 364 B
bleslie@gardner-webb.edu

LEWIS, Carol, E ... 907-474-7083 ... 10 J
celewis@alaska.edu
LEWIS, Carolyn ... 256-372-5690 ... 1 A
carolyn.lewis@aamu.edu
LEWIS, Carolyn ... 201-559-3560 ... 310 C
lewisc@felician.edu
LEWIS, Cassandra, B ... 601-877-3905 ... 273 C
cblewis@alcorn.edu
LEWIS, Charles ... 601-974-1023 ... 275 D
lewiscr@millsaps.edu
LEWIS, Christopher ... 517-371-5140 ... 259 B
lewisch@cooley.edu
LEWIS, Cindy ... 805-493-3199 ... 32 H
clewis@clunet.edu
LEWIS, Craig ... 425-388-9031 ... 533 H
clewis@everettcc.edu
LEWIS, Crissy ... 864-578-8770 ... 460 F
clewis@sherman.edu
LEWIS, Daniel, G ... 925-631-4616 ... 64 F
dlewis@stmarys-ca.edu
LEWIS, Daphne ... 704-216-3463 ... 373 C
daphne.lewis@rccc.edu
LEWIS, David ... 801-281-7630 ... 510 I
david.lewis@stevenshenager.edu
LEWIS, David, E ... 585-275-5240 ... 358 I
david.lewis@rochester.edu
LEWIS, David, R ... 802-356-6824 ... 97 A
david.r.lewis@wilmu.edu
LEWIS, David, W ... 317-274-0462 ... 174 B
dlewis@iupui.edu
LEWIS, Dawanna ... 713-221-8974 ... 503 D
lewisd@uhd.edu
LEWIS, Debra ... 415-485-9326 ... 41 I
debra.lewis@marin.edu
LEWIS, Dewey, H ... 910-938-6225 ... 369 C
lewisd@coastalcarolina.edu
LEWIS, Donald ... 651-641-3262 ... 264 J
dlewis@luthersem.edu
LEWIS, Donald, E ... 205-916-2800 ... 4 D
donl@bhm.herzing.edu
LEWIS, Donald, M ... 651-523-2941 ... 264 C
dlewis02@gw.hamline.edu
LEWIS, Donna ... 601-925-3967 ... 275 E
dlewis@mc.edu
LEWIS, Donna, M ... 304-647-6566 ... 542 H
dlewis@newriver.edu
LEWIS, Doris ... 269-965-3931 ... 253 H
lewisd@kellogg.edu
LEWIS, E. Charles ... 817-202-6720 ... 495 C
lewis@swau.edu
LEWIS, Earl ... 404-727-6055 ... 129 A
earl.lewis@emory.edu
LEWIS, Earnestine ... 434-949-1064 ... 527 H
earnestine.lewis@southside.edu
LEWIS, Eleanor ... 717-867-6302 ... 434 C
lewis@lvc.edu
LEWIS, Eva ... 423-697-2659 ... 474 D
LEWIS, Felicia ... 502-597-6286 ... 203 D
felicia.lewis@kysu.edu
LEWIS, Fred ... 423-279-7665 ... 475 E
fdlewis@northeaststate.edu
LEWIS, Gary ... 970-945-8691 ... 82 C
LEWIS, Georj, L ... 912-478-3326 ... 131 A
glewis@georgiasouthern.edu
LEWIS, Gillian, O ... 206-546-4700 ... 537 G
glewis@shoreline.edu
LEWIS, Goldene ... 718-270-6121 ... 328 D
goldene@mec.cuny.edu
LEWIS, Gregory, V ... 616-824-2977 ... 58 H
LEWIS, Gretchen ... 650-321-5655 ... 64 G
info@stpatricksseminary.org
LEWIS, Hal, M ... 312-322-1715 ... 165 C
LEWIS, III, Henry ... 305-626-3600 ... 108 H
LEWIS, Jack, M ... 540-674-3601 ... 527 B
jlewis@nr.edu
LEWIS, Jacyn ... 415-955-2038 ... 27 A
jlewis@alliant.edu
LEWIS, James, E ... 206-934-5157 ... 537 B
james.lewis@seattlecolleges.edu
LEWIS, Jan ... 541-737-4605 ... 418 B
jan_lewis@ous.edu
LEWIS, Jan, P ... 253-535-7283 ... 535 K
lewisjp@plu.edu
LEWIS, Jane, L ... 209-946-2125 ... 75 D
jlewis@pacific.edu
LEWIS, Jeanne ... 609-652-4201 ... 313 F
jeanne.lewis@stockton.edu
LEWIS, Jeannie, M ... 559-323-2100 ... 66 C
jlewis@sjcl.edu
LEWIS, Jeff ... 909-607-7283 ... 62 H
jeff_lewis@pitzer.edu
LEWIS, Jerry ... 817-272-0979 ... 505 A
jerrylewis@uta.edu
LEWIS, Jim ... 817-272-2584 ... 505 A
jimlewis@uta.edu
LEWIS, Jim ... 806-743-2530 ... 501 E
jim.lewis@ttuhsc.edu
LEWIS, Jim, D ... 704-637-4720 ... 363 C
jdlewis@catawba.edu
LEWIS, Joan, B ... 610-796-8264 ... 421 F
joan.lewis@alvernia.edu
LEWIS, John, C ... 801-422-2533 ... 509 D
john_lewis@byu.edu
LEWIS, John, H ... 901-448-2745 ... 477 C
jlewis51@uthsc.edu
LEWIS, John, L ... 815-753-0936 ... 160 A
jlewis@niu.edu
LEWIS, Joi ... 510-430-2130 ... 57 D
jlewis@mills.edu
LEWIS, Joseph, S ... 949-824-8792 ... 73 H
jslewis@uci.edu
LEWIS, Judith ... 716-829-7776 ... 332 F
lewisj@dyc.edu
LEWIS, Judith, H ... 914-323-5279 ... 340 A
lewisj@mville.edu
LEWIS, Karen ... 925-609-6650 ... 38 B
klewis@cc.edu
LEWIS, Karen ... 615-327-6262 ... 471 A
klewis@mmc.edu
LEWIS, Katherine, P ... 570-340-6094 ... 435 F
kplewis@marywood.edu
LEWIS, Kathie ... 559-730-3826 ... 42 B
kathiel@cos.edu
LEWIS, Kayli ... 407-277-0311 ... 106 G
kalewis@evergladesuniversity.edu
LEWIS, JR., Kenneth, A ... 252-492-2061 ... 374 D
lewis@vgcc.edu
LEWIS, Kenneth, D ... 803-536-7132 ... 460 G
kdlewis@scsu.edu
LEWIS, Kent ... 270-852-3289 ... 203 E
klewis@kwc.edu
LEWIS, Leontye ... 910-672-1265 ... 377 E
llewis8@uncfsu.edu
LEWIS, Leslie ... 607-274-3533 ... 336 G
llewis@ithaca.edu
LEWIS, Linda, E ... 870-543-5906 ... 23 H
llewis@seark.edu
LEWIS, Lindsey, C ... 781-891-2551 ... 231 F
llewis@bentley.edu
LEWIS, Lisa ... 860-486-2240 ... 94 E
lisa.lewis@uconn.edu
LEWIS, Lisa ... 805-898-4010 ... 47 C
llewis@fielding.edu
LEWIS, Lori ... 336-917-5577 ... 376 C
lori.lewis@salem.edu
LEWIS, Lori, A ... 740-376-4704 ... 395 F
lori.lewis@marietta.edu
LEWIS, Lynn ... 864-646-1437 ... 461 F
llewis@tctc.edu
LEWIS, Lynn ... 434-381-6106 ... 524 E
llewis@sbc.edu
LEWIS, Mark ... 781-768-8355 ... 244 D
mark.lewis@regiscollege.edu
LEWIS, Mark ... 325-674-2867 ... 478 H
mark.lewis@acu.edu
LEWIS, Mary ... 651-641-8892 ... 263 C
lewis@csp.edu
LEWIS, Mary ... 772-462-7444 ... 110 L
mlewis@irsc.edu
LEWIS, Michael ... 785-749-8451 ... 193 B
michael.lewis@bie.edu
LEWIS, Michael ... 614-251-4589 ... 398 F
lewism2@ohiodominican.edu
LEWIS, Michael, D ... 315-267-2146 ... 354 C
lewismd@potsdam.edu
LEWIS, Mike ... 419-448-3186 ... 402 E
lewismr@tiffin.edu
LEWIS, Nichole, R ... 919-516-4242 ... 376 B
nrlewis@st-aug.edu
LEWIS, Nora, E ... 215-898-6419 ... 448 I
nlewis@sas.upenn.edu
LEWIS, Pamela ... 765-459-0561 ... 176 A
plewis@ivytech.edu
LEWIS, Penny ... 412-566-2433 ... 434 B
plewis@paculinary.com
LEWIS, Phil ... 405-425-5560 ... 409 E
phil.lewis@oc.edu
LEWIS, Preston ... 325-942-2248 ... 480 E
preston.lewis@angelo.edu
LEWIS, Raphael ... 501-370-5222 ... 23 B
rlewis@philander.edu
LEWIS, Rebecca ... 585-245-5546 ... 353 C
lewis@geneseo.edu
LEWIS, Rebecca, B ... 423-439-6155 ... 473 E
bakerr@etsu.edu
LEWIS, Richard ... 928-350-1307 ... 18 C
rlewis@prescott.edu
LEWIS, Richard ... 330-325-2511 ... 397 C
rwl@neoucom.edu
LEWIS, Rita, F ... 704-461-6726 ... 362 B
ritalewis@bac.edu
LEWIS, Rob ... 859-985-3323 ... 198 F
lewisro@berea.edu
LEWIS, Robin ... 606-326-2423 ... 201 B
Robin.Lewis@kctcs.edu
LEWIS, Rosalyn ... 318-247-0430 ... 215 E
lewisros@gram.edu
LEWIS, S. Kay ... 206-543-6107 ... 538 F
sklewis@uw.edu
LEWIS, Sandra, A ... 716-673-3358 ... 352 A
sandra.lewis@fredonia.edu
LEWIS, Scott ... 801-506-4030 ... 19 C
scott.lewis@phoenix.edu
LEWIS, Shelia ... 714-816-0366 ... 72 I
slewis@tuiu.edu
LEWIS, Shelia ... 619-477-6310 ... 73 A
slewis@usuniversity.edu
LEWIS, Shirley ... 707-864-7000 ... 70 A
shirley.lewis@solano.edu
LEWIS, Steven ... 207-942-6781 ... 217 B
slewis@bts.edu
LEWIS, Susan, A ... 617-262-5000 ... 232 B
susan.lewis@the-bac.edu
LEWIS, Teresa ... 626-584-5416 ... 48 A
tlewis@fuller.edu
LEWIS, Thomas ... 443-287-9900 ... 223 F
tomlewis@jhu.edu
LEWIS, Thomas, C ... 404-413-1404 ... 131 C
tomlewis@gsu.edu
LEWIS, Thomas, L ... 215-780-1280 ... 446 G
president@salus.edu
LEWIS, Tim, D ... 402-363-5638 ... 301 F
tim.lewis@york.edu
LEWIS, Trevor ... 305-626-3750 ... 108 H
trevor.lewis@fmuniv.edu
LEWIS, Urick ... 610-526-6032 ... 430 D
ulewis@harcum.edu
LEWIS, Victoria ... 831-479-6406 ... 31 F
vilewis@cabrillo.edu
LEWIS, Vivian ... 585-273-2760 ... 358 I
vivian.lewis@rochester.edu
LEWIS, Walter ... 518-587-2100 ... 355 F
walter.lewis@esc.edu
LEWIS, William, A ... 601-403-1201 ... 277 A
wlewis@prcc.edu
LEWIS, SR., William, T ... 540-231-3811 ... 529 B
wtlewiss@vt.edu
LEWIS, Zach ... 314-529-9434 ... 284 F
zlewis@maryville.edu
LEWIS-BOYD, Janice ... 313-593-5200 ... 259 E
jckboyd@umd.umich.edu
LEWIS-BRIM, Cathy ... 863-638-7241 ... 123 B
cathy.lewis-brim@warner.edu
LEWIS-JASPER, Vera ... 409-944-1496 ... 486 H
vlewis@gc.edu
LEWIS LOGUE, Judith ... 619-260-4720 ... 76 A
jllogue@sandiego.edu
LEWIS-MOTTS, Irene ... 330-494-6170 ... 402 A
imotts@starkstate.edu
LEWIS SAULO, Mileva ... 650-292-5579 ... 64 J
msaulo@samuelmerritt.edu
LEWIS-THOMAS, Janice ... 256-726-7840 ... 6 C
jthomas@oakwood.edu
LEWIT, Jonathan, D ... 845-257-3130 ... 352 B
lewit@newpaltz.edu
LEWKIEWICZ, Debra ... 845-434-5750 ... 356 H
dlewkiew@sullivan.suny.edu
LEWTER, Andy ... 865-981-8215 ... 470 F
andy.lewter@maryvillecollege.edu
LEWTHWAITE,
Barbara-Jayne ... 908-852-1400 ... 308 F
lewthwaiteb@centenarycollege.edu
LEWTON, John, C ... 260-480-4212 ... 176 D
clewton@ivytech.edu
LEWY, MariLynn, J ... 941-752-5384 ... 118 E
lewym@scf.edu
LEX, Andrea, A ... 301-322-0723 ... 225 F
lexaa@pgcc.edu
LEX, Fredric ... 414-256-1202 ... 549 A
lexf@mtmary.edu
LEXOW, Les ... 636-227-2100 ... 284 E
les.lexow@logan.edu
LEY, Jessica ... 802-287-4318 ... 513 D
LEYBA, Cindy ... 505-661-4686 ... 321 E
cleyba@unm.edu
LEYBA, Marylou ... 415-239-3291 ... 39 H
mleyba@ccsf.edu
LEYBOLD-TAYLOR, Karla ... 276-944-6117 ... 518 I
kleybold@ehc.edu
LEYDEN, John, J ... 401-865-2390 ... 453 F
jleyden@providence.edu
LEYDON, Betty ... 609-258-5601 ... 313 A
betty@princeton.edu
LEYDON, John ... 919-962-4908 ... 377 A
jleydon@northcarolina.edu
LEYDON, Pamela, F ... 904-819-6423 ... 107 A
pleydon@flagler.edu
LEYSER, Becky ... 510-845-6232 ... 71 H
bleyser@sksm.edu
LEYSON, Rebecca ... 302-225-6256 ... 96 E
leysonr@gbc.edu
LEYSTER, Susan ... 360-438-4381 ... 536 F
leysters@stmartin.edu
LEYVA, Alberto ... 770-962-7580 ... 132 A
aleyva@gwinnetttech.edu
LEYVA-PUEBLA, Ricardo ... 206-934-6455 ... 537 B
ricardo.leyva-puebla@seattlecolleges.edu
LEZAK JANOW, Roseann ... 860-509-9501 ... 92 D
rlezak@hartsem.edu
LE'I, Emilia ... 684-699-9155 ... 558 I
e.lei@amsamoa.edu
LI, Al ... 314-434-4044 ... 281 A
al.li@covenantseminary.edu
LI, Benn ... 212-924-5900 ... 357 A
benn@swedishinstitute.edu
LI, Frank ... 530-898-4767 ... 34 A
fli@csuchico.edu
LI, Jenny ... 415-485-3271 ... 45 B
jli@dominican.edu
LI, Kevin ... 773-481-8250 ... 147 F
kli@ccc.edu
LI, Rui ... 610-430-4959 ... 443
rli@wcupa.edu
LI, Shao ... 512-444-8082 ... 499
LI, Sheng ... 714-533-1495 ... 70 E
sli@southbaylo.edu
LI, Yan ... 415-355-1601 ... 28 E
yanli@actcm.edu
LI, Yi ... 937-775-2611 ... 406 C
yi.li@wright.edu
LI, Zhan ... 925-631-4604 ... 64 F
zgl1@stmarys-ca.edu
LI-BUGG, Cherry ... 707-527-4392 ... 68 E
wli-bugg@santarosa.edu
LIANG, Bruce, T ... 860-679-2413 ... 94 E
bliang@uchc.edu
LIANG, Bryan, A ... 619-239-0391 ... 37 D
bliang@cwsl.edu
LIANG, John Paul ... 713-780-9777 ... 480 A
info@acaom.edu
LIANG, Mark ... 714-564-6040 ... 63 F
liang_mark@sac.edu
LIANG, Sherry ... 510-628-8027 ... 54 B
controller@lincolnuca.edu
LIAO-TROTH, Matthew, A ... 478-445-5497 ... 129 F
matthew.liao-troth@gcsu.edu
LIBBERTON, Larry ... 563-242-4023 ... 181 G
larry.libberton@ashford.edu
LIBBY, Betsy ... 207-755-5334 ... 218 G
blibby@cmcc.edu
LIBBY, Elizabeth ... 847-735-6011 ... 155 F
libby@lakeforest.edu
LIBBY, John ... 210-486-3135 ... 479 D
jlibby@alamo.edu
LIBBY, Laura, E ... 207-741-5501 ... 219 A
llibby@smccme.edu
LIBBY, Wendy, B ... 386-822-7250 ... 121 E
wlibby@stetson.edu
LIBEN, Lucy ... 212-924-5900 ... 357 A
lucy@swedishinstitute.edu
LIBERATORE, Anthony, F ... 217-424-6338 ... 158 F
aliberatore@millikin.edu
LIBERATORE, Debra ... 518-454-5145 ... 330 C
liberatd@strose.edu
LIBERATOS, James, D ... 318-257-4287 ... 215 F
schisto@latech.edu
LIBERATOSCIOLI, Daniel ... 215-222-4200 ... 445 F
president@walnuthillcollege.edu
LIBERATOSCIOLI, Peggy ... 215-222-4200 ... 445 F
pl@walnuthillcollege.edu
LIBERMAN, Ira ... 718-438-1002 ... 340 H
yliberman@yeshivanet.com
LIBERTELLI, Joseph ... 202-274-7338 ... 99 F
jlibertelli@udc.edu
LIBERTY, Bob ... 254-526-1310 ... 482 F
bob.liberty@ctcd.edu
LIBET, Alice, Q ... 843-792-4930 ... 459 C
libeta@musc.edu
LIBMAN, Peter ... 516-463-6913 ... 335 H
peter.libman@hofstra.edu
LIBUTTI, Dean ... 401-874-4405 ... 454 E
dean@uri.edu
LICALSI, Pam ... 760-773-2508 ... 41 H
plicalsi@collegeofthedesert.edu
LICARI, Michael, J ... 319-273-2518 ... 182 D
michael.licari@uni.edu
LICATA, Betty Jo ... 330-941-3064 ... 406 F
bjlicata@ysu.edu
LICATA, Christine, M ... 585-475-2953 ... 347 G
cmlnbt@rit.edu
LICATE, Susan ... 440-376-7253 ... 394 E
slicate@lec.edu
LICCIARDI, Anne ... 916-558-2201 ... 56 D
licciaa@scc.losrios.edu
LICHMAN, Jordan ... 703-821-8570 ... 524 D
jlichman@stratford.edu
LICHT, Daniel ... 914-395-2301 ... 350 C
dlicht@sarahlawrence.edu
LICHT, Jodi ... 212-752-1530 ... 338 C
jodi.licht@limcollege.edu
LICHTBLAU, Jobey, L ... 701-231-9581 ... 381 H
jobey.lichtblau@ndsu.edu
LICHTENBERG, John, W ... 248-689-8282 ... 260 A
jlichtenberg@walshcollege.edu
LICHTENBERG, Tami ... 218-625-4921 ... 262 I
tlichten@css.edu
LICHTENFELD, Randy ... 505-821-4800 ... 19 C
randy.lichtenfeld@phoenix.edu
LICHTENSTEIN, Art ... 501-450-5202 ... 25 H
artl@uca.edu
LICHTENSTEIN, Gregg ... 619-594-5281 ... 36 E
lichtens@mail.sdsu.edu
LICHTLE, Richard ... 419-358-3314 ... 385 B
lichtler@bluffton.edu
LICKISS, Steve ... 619-388-7455 ... 65 H
slickiss@sdccd.edu
LIDDELL, Alan, C ... 908-526-1200 ... 313 E
aliddell@raritanval.edu
LIDDELL, Marilynn ... 970-339-6210 ... 80 G
marsi.liddell@aims.edu
LIDDELL, Peter, E ... 315-255-1743 ... 325 H
pliddell@twcny.rr.com
LIDDICOAT, Al ... 805-756-2844 ... 33 F
aliddico@calpoly.edu

LINDSAY, Doug 907-564-8287 10 D
dlindsay@alaskapacific.edu
LINDSAY, Elise 216-368-2517 386 E
exl4@case.edu
LINDSAY, Gloria, A 540-857-7583 528 E
glindsay@virginiawestern.edu
LINDSAY, John 401-232-6154 453 A
jlindsay@bryant.edu
LINDSAY, Jonathan 614-222-3234 388 F
jlindsay@ccad.edu
LINDSAY, Kristen 419-448-2058 391 G
klindsay@heidelberg.edu
LINDSAY, Larry 765-677-2103 174 E
larry.lindsay@indwes.edu
LINDSAY, Laura, F 225-578-1248 212 F
aclind@lsu.edu
LINDSAY, Max, P 989-358-7200 247 G
lindsaym@alpenacc.edu
LINDSAY, Terry 773-244-4588 159 G
tlindsay@northpark.edu
LINDSAY, Twila 410-923-4585 99 D
twila.lindsay@strayer.edu
LINDSAY-BRISBIN, Melanie 719-502-4689 86 G
melanie.lindsay-brisbin@ppcc.edu
LINDSETH, Becky 218-683-8630 268 E
becky.lindseth@northlandcollege.edu
LINDSETH, Paul, G 218-755-4143 266 B
plindseth@bemidjistate.edu
LINDSEY, April 336-887-3000 365 J
alindsey@laureluniversity.edu
LINDSEY, Beverly 662-846-4648 274 B
blindsey@deltastate.edu
LINDSEY, Bruce, M 314-935-6200 292 J
blindsey@wustl.edu
LINDSEY, Candice 903-566-7221 506 C
clindsey@uttyler.edu
LINDSEY, DeLois 860-768-5122 95 A
lindsey@hartford.edu
LINDSEY, Earlene 205-652-3528 10 A
elindsey@uwa.edu
LINDSEY, Greg 612-625-9505 272 D
linds301@umn.edu
LINDSEY, John 336-887-3000 365 J
jlindsey@laureluniversity.edu
LINDSEY, Larry, J 989-837-4376 257 A
larryl@northwood.edu
LINDSEY, Lee 707-476-4100 42 A
lee-lindsey@redwoods.edu
LINDSEY, Stephen 626-914-8806 39 G
slindsey@citruscollege.edu
LINDSEY-LLOYD, Karen 601-925-3901 275 E
lloyd@mc.edu
LINDSLEY, Bonnie, G 419-372-0677 385 D
blindsl@bgsu.edu
LINDSTAEDT, William 415-502-2422 74 E
bill.lindstaedt@ucsf.edu
LINDSTROM, Richard 559-442-8277 72 A
richard.lindstrom@fresnocitycollege.edu
LINDSTROM, Ryan 801-863-8303 511 C
lindstry@uvu.edu
LINDTORTH, Scott, A 919-684-0539 363 I
scott.lindroth@duke.edu
LINDUSKA, Kim 515-964-6628 183 E
kjlinduska@dmacc.edu
LINDVALL, Sherie, J 651-638-6233 261 I
s-lindvall@bethel.edu
LINEAR, Felicia 636-227-2100 284 E
felicia.linear@logan.edu
LINEBACH, Pamela 513-745-5671 403 F
pamela.linebach@uc.edu
LINEBACK, Pamela 513-745-5720 403 F
pamela.lineback@uc.edu
LINEBAUGH, Craig, W 703-726-8220 97 F
cline@gwu.edu
LINEBERGER, Marilyn 404-880-8049 126 I
mlineberger@cau.edu
LINEBERGER, Susanne, B 386-312-4050 116 D
susannelineberger@sjrstate.edu
LINEBURG, Robert 540-831-5228 522 D
rlineburg@radford.edu
LINEHAN, Rob 765-998-4905 179 F
rblinehan@taylor.edu
LINEHAN, Sarah, J 518-743-2263 322 B
linehans@sunyacc.edu
LINER, Andrea, H 903-510-2405 502 E
alin2@tjc.edu
LINFANTE, Felix 973-877-2538 310 A
linfante@essex.edu
LING, Jack, T 937-229-2541 404 A
jack.ling@notes.udayton.edu
LINGEN, BVM, Joan 563-588-6406 183 B
joan.lingen@clarke.edu
LINGENFELTER, Michelle 330-382-7415 393 F
mweekley@kent.edu
LINGENFELTER, Shelly 330-337-4267 393 H
mweekley@kent.edu
LINGER, Frederick, S 740-427-5250 394 C
lingerf@kenyon.edu
LINGER, JR., Jerry 859-371-9393 198 D
jlinger@beckfield.edu
LINGERFELT, Harley 912-525-4001 136 B
harley@scad.edu
LINGLE, Ronald, K 910-938-6211 369 C
lingler@coastalcarolina.edu
LINGO, Melissa, L 386-763-2783 114 E
melissa.lingo@palmer.edu
LINGRELL, Scott 678-839-6423 138 D
slingrel@westga.edu
LINGUA, Jane 310-954-4132 57 H
jlingua@msmc.la.edu
LINHART, Lisa 303-762-6980 83 I
lisa.linhart@denverseminary.edu
LINIO, Rick 304-442-3104 545 C
rick.linio@mail.wvu.edu
LINK, Harvey 701-671-2112 382 E
harvey.link@ndscs.edu
LINK, Johnson 864-656-7389 456 E
jwl@clemson.edu
LINK, Laura 612-874-3700 265 E
laura_link@mcad.edu
LINK, Lisa 616-222-1426 250 C
lisa.link@cornerstone.edu
LINK, Matthew, C 660-543-8538 291 B
link@ucmo.edu
LINK, Rebecca, C 717-815-1336 452 F
rlink@ycp.edu
LINK, Robert 419-434-4528 404 B
link@findlay.edu
LINK, Rosemary, J 515-961-1615 188 F
rosemary.link@simpson.edu
LINKINS, Arthur 903-334-6650 498 C
arthur.linkins@tamut.edu
LINKOFF, Debbie 440-449-1700 384 F
debbie.linkoff@atsinstitute.edu
LINN, Brent 901-375-4400 471 E
brentlinn@midsouthcc.org
LINN, Cindy 740-453-0762 400 D
linnc@ohio.edu
LINN, Gary 970-247-7294 84 G
linn_g@fortlewis.edu
LINN, Joseph, G 785-628-4222 192 F
jlinn@fhsu.edu
LINN, Reid, J 540-568-6131 520 C
linnrj@jmu.edu
LINN, Richard, T 716-827-4351 358 B
linnr@trocaire.edu
LINN, Timon 410-263-2371 225 G
timon.linn@sjca.edu
LINNANE, SJ, Brian, F 410-617-2201 224 A
president@loyola.edu
LINNE, Gil 860-628-4751 92 F
glinne@lincolncollegene.edu
LINNEBUR, Michael 316-942-4291 195 C
linneburm@newmanu.edu
LINNEHAN, Frank 215-895-2000 427 G
Linnehf@drexel.edu
LINNEHAN, JR., James, F 978-656-3151 240 F
linnehanj@middlesex.mass.edu
LINNELL, Jim 505-277-2111 321 C
jlinnell@unm.edu
LINNENBURGER, Jane, C 309-677-2515 145 H
jane@bradley.edu
LINNEVERS, David 831-582-3094 35 C
dlinnevers@csumb.edu
LINNEY, Jean, A 610-519-4606 450 G
jean.linney@villanova.edu
LINO, Paulette 510-723-2665 38 L
plino@chabotcollege.edu
LINRUD, JoAnn 701-858-3110 381 G
joann.linrud@minotstateu.edu
LINSCHEID, David 316-284-5251 190 H
dlin@bethelks.edu
LINSENBIGLER, John 865-573-4517 469 J
jlinsen@johnsonU.edu
LINSKY, Faith 603-283-2163 303 F
flinsky@antiochne.edu
LINSON, Marci 417-690-2636 280 C
linson@cofo.edu
LINSON, Phil 323-856-7792 28 D
plinson@afi.com
LINSTROM, Richard 702-895-5185 302 K
richard.linstrom@unlv.edu
LINTHICUM, Glen 615-248-1243 476 E
glinthicum@trevecca.edu
LINTON, Leon, E 847-229-9595 164 E
LINTON, Meg 310-665-6907 60 B
mlinton@otis.edu
LINTON, Pamela 212-752-1530 338 C
pamela.linton@limcollege.edu
LINTON, Peggy 334-493-3573 5 F
plinton@lbwcc.edu
LINVILLE, Raymond, N 540-831-7600 522 D
rlinvill@radford.edu
LINZER, Daniel, I 847-491-5117 160 D
dlinzer@northwestern.edu
LINZMEYER, Kathryn 510-723-6751 38 L
klinzmeyer@chabotcollege.edu
LINZY, Chad 812-535-5101 179 C
clinzy@smwc.edu
LINZY, Nancy 314-513-4433 289 B
nlinzy@stlcc.edu
LIPAN, Petruta 314-977-3571 289 F
lipanp@slu.edu
LIPE, Leslie 503-338-2450 415 B
llipe@clatsopcc.edu
LIPHART, Jodi 904-826-0084 122 G
jliphart@usa.edu
LIPHART, Kristy 715-682-1496 549 C
kliphart@northland.edu
LIPIEC, Susan 216-373-5211 397 E
slipiec@ndc.edu
LIPINSKI, Ann Marie 773-702-3627 166 D
annmarie@uchicago.edu
LIPINSKI, Barbara 805-962-8179 28 L
LIPINSKI, Marion, A 410-706-0025 227 C
mlipinski@umaryland.edu
LIPINSKI, Tomas, A 317-278-2376 174 B
tlipinsk@iupui.edu
LIPJANKIC, Kanita 916-649-8168 52 F
klipjankic@kaplan.edu
LIPKEY, Debra 202-651-5000 97 E
debra.lipkey@gallaudet.edu
LIPKIN, Michael 845-574-4466 347 I
LIPMAN, Sheryl, H 901-678-2155 474 C
slipman@memphis.edu
LIPMAN, Steven 617-266-1400 231 G
LIPOLD, Tony 949-582-4547 70 F
tlipold@saddleback.edu
LIPP, Dawn 317-554-8326 169 H
dlipp@brownmackie.edu
LIPP, Evan, E 508-767-7285 230 E
elipp@assumption.edu
LIPPARD, Rodney 704-216-3686 373 C
rodney.lippard@rccc.edu
LIPPARD, Rodney, U 252-399-6501 362 A
relippard@barton.edu
LIPPE, Karen, M 561-868-3735 114 D
lippek@palmbeachstate.edu
LIPPERT, Wendy, S 717-766-2511 436 D
wlippert@messiah.edu
LIPPIELLO, Stephen 304-214-8809 543 A
slippiello@wvncc.edu
LIPPIG, Mari 919-508-2502 375 D
mlippig@peace.edu
LIPPIN, Carol, A 732-987-2360 310 D
lippin@georgian.edu
LIPPINCOTT, Andi 315-279-5313 337 K
alippinc@keuka.edu
LIPPINCOTT, Doug 315-279-5641 337 K
dlippinc@mail.keuka.edu
LIPPINCOTT, Margaret 617-928-4596 243 A
mmlippincott@mountida.edu
LIPPMAN, Fred 954-262-1508 114 B
flippman@nsu.nova.edu
LIPPMAN, Stuart 212-463-0400 357 J
stuartl@touro.edu
LIPSCOMB, Donnie 423-869-6353 470 C
donnie.lipscomb@lmunet.edu
LIPSCOMB, Natasha 704-216-3622 373 C
natasha.lipscomb@rccc.edu
LIPSCOMB, Sharyon 225-578-8833 212 E
slipsc1@lsu.edu
LIPSETT, Teresa 787-743-7979 565 F
LIPSHITZ, Rita 773-973-0241 151 H
lipshitz@htc.edu
LIPSKIER, Hershel 973-267-9404 313 C
LIPTON, Jeffrey 631-656-2122 334 B
jlipton@ftc.edu
LIPTON, Mitchell 212-353-4121 331 B
lipton@cooper.edu
LIRA, Juan 956-326-2680 497 B
jlira@tamiu.edu
LIRA, Ken 760-776-7428 41 H
klira@collegeofthedesert.edu
LIRLEY, Sean 719-336-1543 85 K
sean.lirley@lamarcc.edu
LISBOA, Sandra 787-738-2161 567 A
sandra.lisboa@upr.edu
LISCHKA, Rosemary, L 913-288-7246 193 J
rlischka@kckcc.edu
LISENBY, Sadie 901-321-3527 467 G
slisenby@cbu.edu
LISI, Peter 860-768-2446 95 A
lisi@hartford.edu
LISK, III, Earl, B 419-372-0644 385 D
elisk@bgsu.edu
LISKA, Ida 321-253-2929 106 A
iliska@cci.edu
LISKO, Adele 816-941-0430 281 E
alisko@devry.edu
LISKOV, Barbara 617-253-5886 242 A
liskov@csail.mit.edu
LISLE, Kristy 352-323-3630 112 M
lislek@lscc.edu
LISNIK, John 207-621-3317 219 I
lisnik@maine.edu
LISNITZER, Ivan, M 718-270-1234 352 D
ilisnitzer@downstate.edu
LISS, Ron 505-428-1301 320 E
ron.liss@sfcc.edu
LIST, Kathleen, L 941-359-7587 115 K
klist@ringling.edu
LISTER, Basil, M 816-604-6748 285 E
basil.lister@mcckc.edu
LISTER, Carole, B 864-597-4230 463 F
listercb@wofford.edu
LISTER, Charlotte, T 302-857-1290 96 D
clister@dtcc.edu
LISTON, Brenda 614-947-6532 391 A
listonb@franklin.edu
LISTON, Jed 406-243-2361 295 A
jed.liston@umontana.edu
LISTON, Robert, E 703-432-4682 557 E
robert.liston@usmc.mil
LISTOPAD, Darlene 559-438-4222 49 G
darlene_listopad@heald.edu
LISTWAK, Jeffrey, A 412-397-5277 445 G
listwak@rmu.edu
LISZKA, James 518-564-5402 354 B
jlisz001@plattsburgh.edu
LITCHFIELD, Greg 802-862-9616 512 H
glitchfield@burlington.edu
LITCHFIELD, Randy, I 740-362-3125 396 A
rlitchfield@mtso.edu
LITCHKE, Gwen 218-322-2329 267 A
gwen.litchke@itascacc.edu
LITCHMAN, Jennifer, B 410-706-3477 227 C
jlitchman@umaryland.edu
LITKE, Russell 505-566-3262 320 D
litker@sanjuancollege.edu
LITOLFF, Edwin 225-342-6950 215 D
elitolff@uls.state.la.us
LITSCHEL, David 805-966-3888 31 A
dlitschel@brooks.edu
LITT, Jacquelyn 732-932-9721 314 D
dcdean@rci.rutgers.edu
LITT, Jacquelyn, S 573-882-0647 291 D
littj@missouri.edu
LITT, Matt 913-360-7580 190 F
mlitt@benedictine.edu
LITTERAL, Dan 602-387-7000 19 C
dan.litteral@phoenix.edu
LITTERAL, Samuel 304-896-7426 542 J
saml@southern.wvnet.edu
LITTLE, Albert, P 386-312-4116 116 D
allittle@sjrstate.edu
LITTLE, Andrew, P 410-777-2227 221 B
aplittle1@aacc.edu
LITTLE, Bert 254-968-9463 496 F
little@tarleton.edu
LITTLE, Beth, E 304-788-6815 545 A
belittle@mail.wvu.edu
LITTLE, Brittany 919-508-2340 375 D
blittle@peace.edu
LITTLE, Colleen 802-447-6319 514 D
clittle@svc.edu
LITTLE, Daniel 313-593-5500 259 E
delittle@umd.umich.edu
LITTLE, Donald 843-863-7102 456 B
dlittle@csuniv.edu
LITTLE, Ellen, B 325-674-2625 478 H
ellen.little@acu.edu
LITTLE, Glenn, W 863-784-7218 117 I
glenn.little@southflorida.edu
LITTLE, Greg 314-968-7129 293 A
littlegr@webster.edu
LITTLE, Greg 248-340-0600 248 E
greg.little@baker.edu
LITTLE, Jill, M 586-445-7576 254 F
littlej@macomb.edu
LITTLE, Joanna 281-487-1170 498 E
jlittle@txchiro.edu
LITTLE, Judith, W 510-642-3726 73 E
jwlittle@berkeley.edu
LITTLE, Karen 513-244-8437 387 D
karen.little@ccuniversity.edu
LITTLE, Karen, A 419-289-5032 384 D
klittle@ashland.edu
LITTLE, Kevin, K 831-656-2508 557 H
kllittle@nps.edu
LITTLE, Leigh Ann 302-736-2315 96 G
littlele@wesley.edu
LITTLE, Linda 910-521-6494 379 B
linda.little@uncp.edu
LITTLE, Lynn 325-646-2502 488 A
llittle@hputx.edu
LITTLE, Michael, S 757-683-3189 521 L
mlittle@odu.edu
LITTLE, Pamela, M 919-866-5805 374 E
pmlittle@waketech.edu
LITTLE, Patricia, L 330-471-8359 395 E
plittle@malone.edu
LITTLE, Paul 254-710-2161 481 I
baylor@bkstr.com
LITTLE, Philip 312-752-2110 155 B
philip.little@kendall.edu
LITTLE, Scott 601-968-5956 273 F
slittle@belhaven.edu
LITTLE, Shanon 415-257-1302 45 B
shanon.little@dominican.edu
LITTLE, Steve, G 718-951-5116 326 G
slittle@brooklyn.cuny.edu
LITTLE, Ted, A 336-334-7555 377 F
talittle@ncat.edu
LITTLE, Theresa 610-917-1429 450 D
tdlittle@vfcc.edu
LITTLE, Thurlis, J 252-335-3396 377 D
tjlittle@mail.ecsu.edu
LITTLE-BERRY, Teri 352-854-2322 103 D
berryt@cf.edu
LITTLE OWL, Barbara 701-255-3285 383 D
blittleowl@uttc.edu
LITTLE WHITEMAN, Iona 701-627-4738 380 F
llittl@fbcc.bia.edu

LOF, Gregory .... 617-724-6313 .... 242 E glof@mghihp.edu
LOFFLER, Alicia .... 847-491-4647 .... 160 D a-loffler@kellogg.northwestern.edu
LOFFREDO, Joe .... 585-475-2829 .... 347 G jjlrgr@rit.edu
LOFFREDO, Rosemarie ...... 212-998-2910 .... 344 B rl2330@nyu.edu
LOFGREN, Richard .... 859-323-5220 .... 206 H lofgren@uky.edu
LOFLAND, Jessica .... 580-349-1362 .... 410 B jlofland@opsu.edu
LOFLIN, Gene .... 704-290-5853 .... 373 F gloflin@spcc.edu
LOFQUIST, Vicki .... 651-795-1810 .... 267 D vicki.lofquist@metrostate.edu
LOFSTEAD, Rebecca, B ...... 304-293-9358 .... 544 E becky.lofstead@mail.wvu.edu
LOFT, Jan .... 507-537-6218 .... 269 G Jan.Loft@smsu.edu
LOFTHOUSE, David, R ...... 951-785-2938 ...... 53 D dlofthou@lasierra.edu
LOFTIN, Lynn .... 580-559-5252 .... 407 J lloftin@ecok.edu
LOFTIN, R. Bowen .... 979-845-2217 .... 497 C president@tamu.edu
LOFTON, Antwan .... 202-806-6077 ...... 98 B antwan.lofton@howard.edu
LOFTON, Fiona .... 803-786-3862 .... 457 C flofton@columbiasc.edu
LOFTON, Lucky .... 510-659-6105 ...... 59 I llofton@ohlone.edu
LOFTUS, Edna, A .... 910-277-5256 .... 376 A eaol@sapc.edu
LOFTUS, Edward, J .... 570-577-1458 .... 423 D edward.loftus@bucknell.edu
LOFTUS, James, P .... 414-410-4001 .... 546 D jploftus@stritch.edu
LOFTUS, Kate .... 262-472-1392 .... 552 E loftusk@uww.edu
LOFTUS, Lindsey, H .... 330-325-6674 .... 397 C lloftus@neoucom.edu
LOFTUS, Marie .... 718-933-6700 .... 341 G mloftus@monroecollege.edu
LOFTUS, Robert .... 508-929-8017 .... 239 D FrRob@worcester.edu
LOFTUS, Roger .... 507-786-3068 .... 271 H loftus@stolaf.edu
LOFTUS-BERLIN, Eileen .... 973-278-5400 .... 323 J eml@BerkeleyCollege.edu
LOGAN, David, A .... 401-254-4509 .... 454 C dlogan@law.rwu.edu
LOGAN, Erin .... 405-682-7821 .... 409 F elogan@occc.edu
LOGAN, Ethan .... 806-742-1480 .... 501 D ethan.logan@ttu.edu
LOGAN, Gary, L .... 512-863-1442 .... 495 G glogan@southwestern.edu
LOGAN, Irene, F .... 804-524-5902 .... 529 C ilogan@vsu.edu
LOGAN, Linda .... 269-749-6669 .... 257 D llogan@olivetcollege.edu
LOGAN, Lori .... 817-531-6571 .... 502 A llogan@txwes.edu
LOGAN, Mark .... 909-652-6702 ...... 39 B mark.logan@chaffey.edu
LOGAN, Mike .... 712-274-6400 .... 189 H mike.logan@witcc.edu
LOGAN, Renita, G .... 910-938-6145 .... 369 C loganr@coastalcarolina.edu
LOGAN, Robin .... 210-829-3933 .... 503 F rlogan@uiwtx.edu
LOGAN, Ruth .... 585-594-6260 .... 347 F loganr@roberts.edu
LOGAN, Sarah .... 325-942-2259 .... 480 E sarah.logan@angelo.edu
LOGAN, Shannon .... 212-229-5687 .... 342 E logans@newschool.edu
LOGAN, Steve .... 214-768-2422 .... 494 F loganse@smu.edu
LOGAN, Timothy, M .... 254-710-6665 .... 481 I tim_logan@baylor.edu
LOGAN, Tonya .... 740-264-5591 .... 390 F tlogan@egcc.edu
LOGAN, Traci, A .... 781-891-3472 .... 231 F tlogan@bentley.edu
LOGAN, Vanessa .... 602-243-8046 ...... 16 E vanessa.logan@smcmail.maricopa.edu
LOGAN-BENNETT, Lorie .... 410-704-2386 .... 228 E lloganbennett@towson.edu
LOGAR, Antonette, M .... 605-394-2471 .... 466 A toni.logar@sdsmt.edu
LOGEL, Mark, J .... 812-488-2941 .... 180 B ml44@evansville.edu
LOGGAN, Todd .... 503-251-2836 .... 420 H tloggan@uws.edu
LOGIE, Bryan .... 912-201-6021 .... 136 H blogie@southuniversity.edu
LOGSDON, Michael .... 301-387-3333 .... 222 H michael.logsdon@garrettcollege.edu
LOGSDON, Paul .... 417-865-2811 .... 282 A logsdonp@evangel.edu
LOGSDON, Paul, M .... 419-772-2180 .... 398 G p-logsdon@onu.edu
LOGSDON-CONRADSEN, Susan .... 706-236-5494 .... 125 G sconradsen@berry.edu
LOGSTON, Susan, E .... 203-285-2187 ...... 90 A slogston@gwcc.commnet.edu
LOGUE, Alexandra .... 212-794-5414 .... 326 C academicaffairs@mail.cuny.edu
LOGUE, Christin .... 423-614-8415 .... 470 A clogue@leeuniversity.edu
LOGUE, Holly .... 908-737-4376 .... 311 B hologue@kean.edu
LOGUE, Mary .... 805-565-6251 ...... 78 F mlogue@westmont.edu
LOGUE, Rose, M .... 814-393-2223 .... 442 A rlogue@clarion.edu
LOGUE, Susan .... 618-536-5535 .... 164 I slogue@siu.edu
LOH, Wallace, D .... 301-405-1000 .... 227 B wdloh@umd.edu
LOHDEN, Bethany, L .... 636-584-6503 .... 281 I lohdenb@eastcentral.edu
LOHIDE, Kurt .... 507-457-5061 .... 270 B klohide@winona.edu
LOHMANN, Jack .... 404-894-2966 .... 130 D jack.lohmann@carnegie.gatech.edu
LOHMANN, Steven, L .... 580-327-8406 .... 409 C sllohmann@nwosu.edu
LOHRENZ, Steven .... 508-910-6353 .... 237 E slohrenz@umassd.edu
LOHRI-POSEY, Brenda ...... 740-695-9500 .... 384 J bposey@btc.edu
LOHRMEYER, Robert .... 208-792-2225 .... 143 F rlohrmey@lcsc.edu
LOHSANDT, Marie, A .... 605-256-5122 .... 465 G marie.lohsandt@dsu.edu
LOHSE, MaryPat .... 617-349-8669 .... 236 G mlohse@lesley.edu
LOILAND, Cheri .... 253-680-7206 .... 531 A cloiland@bates.ctc.edu
LOILAND, Sharon .... 701-777-3178 .... 381 D sharon.loiland@email.und.edu
LOISEAU, Marvin .... 617-423-4630 .... 231 E mloiseau@bfit.edu
LOISELLE, Helene .... 407-582-1701 .... 122 I hloiselle@valenciacollege.edu
LOIVOS, Scott .... 801-840-4800 .... 509 I sloivos@cci.edu
LOIZZO, Joseph, A .... 740-284-7217 .... 390 M jloizzo@franciscan.edu
LOJKO, Frank .... 435-652-7511 .... 512 A lojko@dixie.edu
LOJKO, Frank .... 435-652-7595 .... 512 A lojko@dixie.edu
LOKEY, Cheryl, P .... 318-323-2889 .... 208 E cheryl.lokey@careertc.edu
LOKEY, Pat .... 480-423-6653 ...... 16 D pat.lokey@sccmail.maricopa.edu
LOKKEN, Jay, M .... 608-785-8017 .... 551 B lokken.jay@uwlax.edu
LOKKEN, Pamela, S .... 314-935-5752 .... 292 J lokken@wustl.edu
LOKMAN, Lawrence, H ...... 310-825-9045 ...... 74 A llokman@support.ucla.edu
LOKUTA, Sharon .... 260-422-5561 .... 172 L slokuta@indianatech.edu
LOLATTE, Richard, J .... 203-773-8501 ...... 89 H rjlolatte@albertus.edu
LOLLAR, Cay .... 662-862-8032 .... 274 G cllollar@iccms.edu
LOMAN, Sharon Kerrigan .. 610-902-1070 .... 423 H sharon.kerrigan.loman@cabrini.edu
LOMANTO, Susan, M .... 973-972-5332 .... 316 E lomanto@umdnj.edu
LOMAS, Mark .... 704-499-9200 ...... 99 D
LOMAX, Terri, L .... 919-515-2117 .... 378 B terri_lomax@ncsu.edu
LOMBARD, Amy .... 724-938-4418 .... 441 G lombard@calu.edu
LOMBARD, Anne, E .... 315-470-6658 .... 355 A
LOMBARD, Gary, A .... 405-682-7810 .... 409 F glombard@occc.edu
LOMBARD, J. Anthony ...... 423-478-7716 .... 472 F alombard@ptseminary.edu
LOMBARD, Karen, L .... 515-574-1140 .... 185 F lombard@iowacentral.edu
LOMBARDI, Eugenia, A ..... 410-617-5055 .... 224 A jlombardi@loyola.edu
LOMBARDI, George, J .... 203-371-7989 ...... 93 G lombardig@sacredheart.edu
LOMBARDI, John .... 773-777-4220 .... 160 C jlombardi@nc.edu
LOMBARDI, John, V .... 225-578-2111 .... 212 E lombardi@lsu.edu
LOMBARDI, Mark .... 314-529-9330 .... 284 F president@maryville.edu
LOMBARDI, Phillip .... 401-232-6374 .... 453 A plombard@bryant.edu
LOMBARDI, Ryan, T .... 740-593-1800 .... 399 G lombardi@ohio.edu
LOMBARDO, Frank .... 386-506-3200 .... 103 J lombarf@DaytonaState.edu
LOMBARDO, Joann .... 860-486-5519 ...... 94 E joann.lombardo@uconn.edu
LOMBARDO, John .... 631-851-6225 .... 356 D lombarj@sunysuffolk.edu
LOMBARDO, Michael .... 503-777-7542 .... 420 A lombardm@reed.edu
LOMBARDO, Pam .... 805-893-2040 ...... 74 F pam.lombardo@ehs.ucsb.edu
LOMBARDO, Roberto .... 386-506-3159 .... 103 J lombarr@DaytonaState.edu
LOMBARDO, Tony .... 225-578-5603 .... 212 F lombardo@lsu.edu
LOMBELLA, Jim .... 860-253-3128 ...... 89 K jlombella@acc.commnet.edu
LOMENA, Sandra .... 305-821-3333 .... 109 A slomena@mm.fnc.edu
LOMETTI, Guy .... 718-405-3343 .... 330 A guy.lometti@mountsaintvincent.edu
LONABOCKER, Louise, M . 617-552-3300 .... 232 D louise.lonabocker.1@bc.edu
LONDA, Ivan .... 212-962-0002 .... 342 G
LONDON, Howard .... 508-531-1295 .... 238 B hlondon@bridgew.edu
LONDON, Howard .... 508-531-1218 .... 238 B hlondon@bridgew.edu
LONDON, Manuel .... 631-632-8304 .... 352 C manuel.london@stonybrook.edu
LONDON, Marjorie .... 860-244-7624 ...... 89 J mlondon@commnet.edu
LONDON, Michael .... 415-422-4400 ...... 76 B melondon@usfca.edu
LONDON-JONES, Emily .... 504-280-6687 .... 213 E elondon@uno.edu
LONE HILL, Karen .... 605-455-6100 .... 464 H klonehill@olc.edu
LONEKER, Ronald .... 973-290-4235 .... 309 A rloneker@cse.edu
LONERGAN, Dennis .... 718-862-7349 .... 339 H dennis.lonergan@manhattan.edu
LONERGAN, Joel, C .... 256-824-6414 .... 9 A joel.lonergan@uah.edu
LONERGAN, Penny .... 913-758-6111 .... 197 B longergan@stmary.edu
LONERGAN, Peter, E .... 716-880-2177 .... 340 E peter.e.lonergan@medaille.edu
LONEY, Carl, E .... 937-327-7307 .... 406 B cloney@wittenberg.edu
LONEY, Teresa, A .... 816-604-1517 .... 285 D teresa.loney@mcckc.edu
LONG, Andrew .... 970-521-6652 ...... 86 E andrew.long@njc.edu
LONG, Andrew .... 360-992-2505 .... 532 A along@clark.edu
LONG, Antonio .... 404-756-4477 .... 124 I along@atlm.edu
LONG, Aubrey, E .... 386-481-2800 .... 101 I longa@cookman.edu
LONG, Bobbie .... 972-548-6866 .... 483 D blong@collin.edu
LONG, Brenda, J .... 252-222-6151 .... 368 F bjl@carteret.edu
LONG, C. Adam .... 864-488-4583 .... 459 A along@limestone.edu
LONG, Carol, S .... 585-245-5531 .... 353 C long@geneseo.edu
LONG, Carrilyn .... 330-494-6170 .... 402 A clong@starkstate.edu
LONG, Catherine, E .... 607-255-2946 .... 331 C cel3@cornell.edu
LONG, Charla .... 615-966-2500 .... 470 D charla.long@lipscomb.edu
LONG, Christina .... 620-665-3521 .... 193 F longc@hutchcc.edu
LONG, Curt .... 563-588-6657 .... 183 B curt.long@clarke.edu
LONG, Daniel .... 313-664-7675 .... 250 A dlong@collegeforcreativestudies.edu
LONG, Dennis .... 425-739-8313 .... 535 B dennis.long@lwtc.edu
LONG, Donald .... 651-748-2626 .... 266 D donald.long@century.edu
LONG, II, Gardner, J .... 478-757-3498 .... 126 G gardner@centralgatech.edu
LONG, Gerard, E .... 210-562-6285 .... 506 E longg@uthscsa.edu
LONG, Hosea .... 501-686-5650 ...... 24 F longhoseaw@uams.edu
LONG, J, D .... 304-457-6266 .... 540 B longjd@ab.edu
LONG, Jack, L .... 214-828-8232 .... 497 A jlong@bcd.tamhsc.edu
LONG, Jeanine .... 229-227-2668 .... 137 D jlong@southwestgatech.edu
LONG, Jeff, C .... 570-389-4198 .... 441 F jlong@bloomu.edu
LONG, Jennifer .... 405-224-3140 .... 413 E jlong@usao.edu
LONG, Jesse .... 806-720-7657 .... 490 D jesse.long@lcu.edu
LONG, Jewel, B .... 757-727-5486 .... 519 C jewel.long@hamptonu.edu
LONG, Jim .... 573-592-4225 .... 293 E jim.long@williamwoods.edu
LONG, Joanne .... 845-437-5255 .... 359 D long@vassar.edu
LONG, Joe .... 210-690-9000 .... 487 C jlong@hallmarkcollege.edu
LONG, K, O .... 325-793-3850 .... 490 F longk@mcm.edu
LONG, Kathleen, A .... 352-273-6324 .... 120 B longka@nursing.ufl.edu
LONG, Kathleen, A .... 352-392-6004 .... 120 B longka@ufl.edu
LONG, Kathleen, M .... 304-147-3823 .... 545 F long@wvwc.edu
LONG, Kenneth .... 610-683-4188 .... 442 F klong@kutztown.edu
LONG, Larry .... 501-279-4335 ...... 21 H llong@harding.edu
LONG, Larry .... 913-588-6587 .... 197 A llong@kumc.edu
LONG, Laurel .... 256-824-2259 .... 9 A laurel.long@uah.edu
LONG, Lauren .... 703-993-2909 .... 519 A llong3@gmu.edu
LONG, Lisa .... 256-761-6466 .... 7 H lelong@talladega.edu
LONG, Marcus .... 314-367-8700 .... 288 I mlong@stlcop.edu
LONG, Mary, C .... 773-995-5343 .... 146 D mlong20@csu.edu
LONG, Melissa .... 802-862-9616 .... 512 H mhowanitz@burlington.edu
LONG, Nathan .... 513-585-2051 .... 387 C
LONG, Patricia, N .... 785-594-8311 .... 190 C president@bakeru.edu
LONG, Paul, D .... 816-604-1080 .... 285 D paul.long@mcckc.edu
LONG, Richard .... 802-860-2755 .... 513 A rlong@champlain.edu
LONG, Robert, F .... 270-809-3537 .... 204 F bob.long@murraystate.edu
LONG, Ronald, B .... 770-484-1204 .... 133 D lru@lru.edu
LONG, Sally .... 410-386-8110 .... 221 G slong@carrollcc.edu
LONG, Shane .... 207-741-5544 .... 219 A slong@smccme.edu
LONG, Sherry .... 606-368-6133 .... 197 H sherrylong@alc.edu
LONG, Steven .... 573-288-6533 .... 281 D slong@culver.edu
LONG, Susan .... 909-594-5611 ...... 58 A slong@mtsac.edu
LONG, Suzette .... 630-466-7900 .... 167 G slong@waubonsee.edu
LONG, Terri .... 909-594-5611 ...... 58 A tlong@mtsac.edu
LONG, Tim .... 312-369-7282 .... 148 B tlong@colum.edu
LONG, Vicki .... 316-322-3152 .... 191 D vlong@butlercc.edu
LONG, III, William .... 518-743-2273 .... 322 B longw@sunyacc.edu
LONG, William, J .... 404-413-5100 .... 131 C long@gsu.edu
LONG-COFFEE, Michelle ... 310-287-4597 ...... 55 F longcofm@wlac.edu
LONGABAUGH, Richard ...... 262-646-6518 .... 549 B rlongabaugh@nashotah.edu
LONGACRE, Jeffrey .... 301-295-1917 .... 558 A jlongacre@usuhs.mil
LONGAKER, Frank .... 540-986-1800 .... 205 D frank@ncbt.edu
LONGAKER, Frank .... 540-986-1800 .... 205 A frank@national-college.edu
LONGAKER, Frank .... 540-986-1800 .... 541 E frank@national-college.edu
LONGAKER, Frank .... 540-986-1800 .... 521 E frank@ncbt.edu
LONGAKER, Frank, E .... 540-986-1800 .... 521 J frank@national-college.edu
LONGATAN, Nancy .... 503-760-3131 .... 414 F nancy@birthingway.edu
LONGENBACH, David .... 609-894-9311 .... 308 C dlongenb@bcc.edu
LONGENECKER, Jack, R .... 717-361-1263 .... 428 E longenjr@etown.edu
LONGENECKER, Lyn .... 717-544-5711 .... 433 E
LONGENECKER, Margot ..... 503-552-1696 .... 417 D mlongenecker@ncnm.edu
LONGENECKER, Penni .... 717-544-4912 .... 433 E
LONGFIELD, Bradley, J .... 563-599-3122 .... 189 B blongfie@dbq.edu
LONGHTA, Karie, L .... 217-786-2263 .... 156 I karie.longhta@llcc.edu
LONGJOHN, Gerald .... 616-222-1423 .... 250 C gerald.longjohn@cornerstone.edu
LONGLEY, S. Catherine ..... 207-725-3242 .... 217 E clongley@bowdoin.edu
LONGMAN, Mikel .... 970-351-2245 ...... 88 F mikel.longman@unco.edu
LONGNION, Lloyd .... 423-472-7141 .... 474 E llongnion@clevelandstatecc.edu
LONGO, Laura .... 732-224-2259 .... 308 B llongo@brookdalecc.edu
LONGO, Rick .... 978-921-4242 .... 242 F rlongo@montserrat.edu

LOUCHE, Suzee, S .... 321-674-8099.... 108 E
slouche@fit.edu
LOUCHOUARN, Patrick ..... 409-740-4710.... 497 D
louchoup@tamug.edu
LOUCKS, Brenda, C .... 781-280-3511.... 240 F
loucksb@middlesex.mass.edu
LOUCKS, C. Melvin .... 626-448-0023.... 51 H
LOUCY, Brian, M .... 315-445-4181.... 338 B
loucyb@lemoyne.edu
LOUD, Tammy .... 616-698-7111.... 250 E
tloud@davenport.edu
LOUDEN, Sandy .... 731-352-4095.... 467 C
loudens@bethelu.edu
LOUDEN, William, F .... 812-488-2376.... 180 B
bl9@evansville.edu
LOUDEN-HANES,
Marie, A .... 419-434-4504.... 404 B
louden-hanes@findlay.edu
LOUDENSLAGER, Anne ...... 570-662-4809.... 443 B
aloudens@mansfield.edu
LOUDER, Corey .... 660-626-2203.... 278 F
clouder@atsu.edu
LOUDERBACK, Joseph ...... 732-729-3822.... 309 D
jlouderback@devry.edu
LOUDIN, Rose Ellen .... 304-473-8600.... 545 F
loudin_r@wvwc.edu
LOUDON, Tina .... 360-650-3240.... 539 C
tina.loudon@wwu.edu
LOUGEE, Barbara .... 802-635-1485.... 515 E
barbara.lougee@jsc.edu
LOUGEE, Wendy, P .... 612-624-1807.... 272 D
wlougee@umn.edu
LOUGHERY, James, F .... 215-968-8041.... 423 E
loughery@bucks.edu
LOUGHLEY, Heather .... 614-433-0095...... 19 C
heather.loughley@phoenix.edu
LOUGHMAN, Ann .... 518-262-5435.... 322 E
loughma@mail.amc.edu
LOUGHRAN, Sean .... 203-837-9330...... 92 A
loughrans@wcsu.edu
LOUIE, Irwin, K .... 818-779-8423...... 53 B
ilouie@kingsuniversity.edu
LOUIS, Charles .... 951-827-5535...... 74 C
charles.louis@ucr.edu
LOUIS, Michael, A .... 314-505-7301.... 280 H
louism@csl.edu
LOUKUS, Kitti .... 906-487-7208.... 251 C
kitty.loukus@finlandia.edu
LOUNSBERRY, Gary .... 336-887-3000.... 365 J
glounsberry@laureluniversity.edu
LOUNSBERY, Michelle ...... 605-367-7464.... 466 C
michelle.lounsbery@southeasttech.edu
LOUREIRO, Rita, D .... 561-237-7035.... 113 D
rloureiro@lynn.edu
LOUSTAUNAU, Jeffrey .... 207-326-2251.... 219 D
j.loustaunau@mma.edu
LOUTH, Richard .... 212-998-2118.... 344 B
richard.louth@nyu.edu
LOUTHERBACK, George ..... 254-295-4698.... 504 A
gloutherback@umhb.edu
LOUTTIT, Julianne, E .... 724-287-8711.... 423 F
julianne.louttit@bc3.edu
LOUWAGIE, Vincent .... 210-349-9928.... 491 E
vlouwagie@ost.edu
LOVALLO, Charles, G .... 973-877-3400.... 310 A
lovallo@essex.edu
LOVATO, Barbara .... 505-925-8991.... 321 G
bgassman@unm.edu
LOVATO, Mildred, P .... 575-461-4413.... 318 F
mildredl@mesalands.edu
LOVE, Anne .... 718-420-4212.... 359 G
alove@wagner.edu
LOVE, Charles .... 864-503-5577.... 463 A
clove@uscupstate.edu
LOVE, David .... 814-393-2334.... 442 A
dlove@clarion.edu
LOVE, Deborah, E .... 504-862-8083.... 215 C
dlove1@tulane.edu
LOVE, Jan .... 404-727-6324.... 129 A
jlove3@emory.edu
LOVE, Jane .... 864-294-2248.... 458 D
jane.love@furman.edu
LOVE, Jeffrey, M .... 248-340-0600.... 248 E
love@baker.edu
LOVE, Julie, N .... 970-247-7503...... 84 G
studenthousing@fortlewis.edu
LOVE, Kathy, S .... 912-443-3024.... 136 D
klove@savannahtech.edu
LOVE, Lisa, L .... 480-965-9743...... 12 B
athletics.director@asu.edu
LOVE, Louise .... 312-369-7495.... 148 B
llove@colum.edu
LOVE, Nyassa .... 510-885-2743...... 34 C
nyassa.love@csueastbay.edu
LOVE, Peter .... 860-701-5071...... 93 B
love_p@mitchell.edu
LOVE, Robert .... 417-862-9533.... 282 D
rlove@globaluniversity.edu
LOVE, Ronald .... 662-254-3624.... 276 C
rlove@mvsu.edu
LOVE, Tommy .... 503-838-8281.... 419 C
lovet@wou.edu
LOVE, Tony .... 432-552-2633.... 507 C
love_t@utpb.edu

LOVEDAY, Joyce .... 253-589-4333.... 532 B
joyce.loveday@cptc.edu
LOVELACE, Betty, M .... 614-236-6611.... 386 C
blovelac@capital.edu
LOVELACE, Diane .... 215-641-6584.... 436 G
dlovelac@mc3.edu
LOVELACE, Everett .... 209-384-6192...... 57 C
everett.lovelace@mccd.edu
LOVELACE, Rhonda .... 501-370-5297...... 23 B
rlovelace@philander.edu
LOVELADY, III, Artis .... 832-252-4617.... 483 A
artis@cbshouston.edu
LOVELAND, David, A .... 607-746-4013.... 355 E
lovelada@delhi.edu
LOVELAND, George .... 540-365-4428.... 518 J
gloveland@ferrum.edu
LOVELESS, Cecelia .... 360-596-5204.... 538 B
cloveless@spscc.ctc.edu
LOVELESS, Cindy .... 940-397-4241.... 491 A
cindy.loveless@mwsu.edu
LOVELESS, Elizabeth, B ...... 563-333-6271.... 188 D
LovelessElizabethB@sau.edu
LOVELESS, Shelly .... 406-247-3000.... 296 A
sloveless@msubillings.edu
LOVELIDGE, Robert .... 979-830-4194.... 482 A
rlovelidge@blinn.edu
LOVELIS, Buffy .... 580-559-5651.... 407 J
blovelis@ecok.edu
LOVELL, Ava .... 505-272-2885.... 321 C
alovell@salud.unm.edu
LOVELL, Ellen .... 719-336-1541...... 85 K
library@lamarcc.edu
LOVELL, Ellen, M .... 802-258-9245.... 513 F
emlovell@marlboro.edu
LOVELL, JR., Ernest, L .... 601-403-1183.... 277 A
elovell@prcc.edu
LOVELL, Michael, R .... 414-229-4331.... 551 C
mlovell@uwm.edu
LOVELL, Sharon .... 540-568-2705.... 520 C
lovellse@jmu.edu
LOVELL, Susan .... 212-472-1500.... 343 G
slovell@nysid.edu
LOVELL, Susan .... 706-562-1681.... 127 D
lovell_susan@columbusstate.edu
LOVELY, Christine .... 916-278-6940...... 35 E
clovely@csus.edu
LOVERIDGE, Robert .... 801-863-8161.... 511 C
loveriro@uvu.edu
LOVERIDGE, Thomas, J .... 801-581-5469.... 510 L
tom.loveridge@utah.edu
LOVERIN, Michelle .... 616-538-2330.... 251 F
mloverin@gbcol.edu
LOVERING, James .... 802-387-6795.... 513 E
jlovering@landmark.edu
LOVETT, Christopher, M ...... 814-886-6400.... 437 A
clovett@mtaloy.edu
LOVETT, David, L .... 717-477-1164.... 443 D
dllove@ship.edu
LOVETT, Eric .... 423-493-4100.... 476 C
lovette@tntemple.edu
LOVETT, Kenyatta .... 615-230-3530.... 476 A
ken.lovett@volstate.edu
LOVETT, Leslie .... 304-367-4602.... 542 I
Leslie.Lovett@pierpont.edu
LOVETT, Michael .... 256-215-4247....... 2 F
mlovett@cacc.edu
LOVETT, Rod, M .... 217-351-2409.... 161 B
rlovett@parkland.edu
LOVETT, Susan, B .... 423-493-4260.... 476 C
lovetts@tntemple.edu
LOVICK, Reed .... 252-527-6223.... 371 D
rlovick@lenoircc.edu
LOVIG, Kristin .... 641-269-4974.... 185 A
lovigkk@grinnell.edu
LOVIK, Eric .... 252-335-0821.... 369 D
eric_lovik@albemarle.edu
LOVINCE, Thomas .... 504-671-5627.... 210 G
tlovin@dcc.edu
LOVING, Julie .... 434-832-7630.... 526 A
lovingj@cvcc.vccs.edu
LOVINGOOD, Deborah, F ...... 630-466-7900.... 167 G
dlovingood@waubonsee.edu
LOVINGOOD, Linda .... 828-835-4242.... 374 C
llovingood@tricountycc.edu
LOVINS, Darrell .... 601-318-6610.... 278 E
dlovins@wmcarey.edu
LOVINS, Greg, M .... 828-262-2030.... 377 B
lovinsgm@appstate.edu
LOVINS, Sandy .... 813-974-8063.... 120 D
slovins@usf.edu
LOVITT, Carl, R .... 860-832-2228...... 91 G
lovittcar@ccsu.edu
LOVSTUEN, Brenda, C .... 319-895-4292.... 183 D
blovstuen@cornellcollege.edu
LOVVORN, Judi .... 229-217-4163.... 134 C
jlovvorn@moultrietech.edu
LOW, Beverly .... 315-228-7368.... 329 H
balow@colgate.edu
LOW, Catherine Yu-Ling .... 808-371-5443.... 140 E
cfo@orientalmedicine.edu
LOW, Don .... 209-575-6060...... 80 B
lowd@mjc.edu
LOW, Douglas .... 812-749-1298.... 178 D
dlow@oak.edu

LOW, Joanne .... 415-561-1850...... 39 H
jlow@ccsf.edu
LOW, Ryan .... 207-778-7271.... 220 C
ryan.lowr@maine.edu
LOW, Wai Hoa .... 808-521-2288.... 140 E
whlow@orientalmedicine.edu
LOWBRIDGE, John .... 270-824-1835.... 202 C
john.lowbridge@kctcs.edu
LOWDEN, Paul .... 616-732-1194.... 250 E
plowden@davenport.edu
LOWDENBACK, Roy .... 502-863-8044.... 200 G
roy_lowdenback@georgetowncollege.edu
LOWDER, Diane, M .... 804-752-7218.... 522 F
dianelowder@rmc.edu
LOWDERMILK, Robert, S .. 336-342-4261.... 373 B
lowdermilkr@rockinghamcc.edu
LOWE, Brenda .... 806-720-7307.... 490 D
brenda.lowe@lcu.edu
LOWE, Byrce .... 662-254-3590.... 276 C
blowe@mvsu.edu
LOWE, Carmen .... 617-627-4239.... 245 F
carmen.lowe@tufts.edu
LOWE, Carrie, B .... 865-573-4517.... 469 J
cblowe@johnsonU.edu
LOWE, Charles .... 561-297-3500.... 118 H
clowe@fau.edu
LOWE, Charles .... 860-486-3619...... 94 E
charles.lowe@uconn.edu
LOWE, Chris .... 616-222-1420.... 250 C
chris.lowe@cornerstone.edu
LOWE, Ellen .... 760-591-3012.... 122 G
elowe@usa.edu
LOWE, JR., Eugene, Y .... 847-491-5255.... 160 D
eyljr@northwestern.edu
LOWE, Flora .... 563-242-4023.... 181 G
flora.lowe@ashford.edu
LOWE, JR., James .... 251-405-7130....... 2 D
jlowe@bishop.edu
LOWE, Janet, S .... 307-766-3307.... 556 E
jlowe@uwyo.edu
LOWE, John .... 912-525-4895.... 136 B
jlowe@scad.edu
LOWE, Judy .... 423-697-2686.... 474 D
LOWE, Kathy .... 707-638-5806...... 72 H
kathy.lowe@tu.edu
LOWE, Kayarda .... 334-872-2533........ 6 H
LOWE, Mark, S .... 701-483-2328.... 381 E
mark.lowe@dickinsonstate.edu
LOWE, Mary Margaret .... 502-863-8403.... 200 G
marymargaret_lowe@georgetowncollege.edu
LOWE, Melissa .... 502-585-9911.... 205 I
mlowe@spalding.edu
LOWE, Rick, D .... 910-630-7027.... 366 H
rlowe@methodist.edu
LOWE, Robt, S .... 630-844-5290.... 145 C
slowe@aurora.edu
LOWE, Ryan .... 816-322-0110.... 279 H
ryan.lowe@calvary.edu
LOWE, Scott .... 573-592-5289.... 293 C
Scott.Lowe@westminster-mo.edu
LOWE, Sharon .... 772-462-7476.... 110 L
slowe@irsc.edu
LOWE, Sharon, B .... 757-823-8141.... 521 K
sblowe@nsu.edu
LOWE, Stephen, H .... 864-427-3681.... 462 G
lowesh@mailbox.sc.edu
LOWE, Steve, D .... 864-379-8779.... 457 G
LOWE, Susan, G .... 620-229-6334.... 196 C
susan.lowe@sckans.edu
LOWE, Tamara, A .... 330-684-8931.... 403 C
lowe@uakron.edu
LOWE, William .... 563-242-4023.... 181 G
william.lowe@ashford.edu
LOWE, William, J .... 219-980-6701.... 173 F
wjlowe@iun.edu
LOWE-CARPENTER,
Dianne .... 307-778-5222.... 556 B
dlowe-ca@lccc.wy.edu
LOWE-SCHNEIDER,
Kathryn .... 812-866-7081.... 171 F
lowe@hanover.edu
LOWENBERG, Jaime .... 915-351-8100.... 480 C
LOWENBERG, Ron .... 714-895-8369...... 41 A
rlowenberg@gwc.cccd.edu
LOWENGRUB, Morton .... 212-960-5217.... 361 I
lowengru@yu.edu
LOWENSTEIN, Marc .... 609-652-4514.... 313 F
marc.lowenstein@stockton.edu
LOWENTHAL, Benjamin .... 410-455-1720.... 227 D
blowenth@umbc.edu
LOWENTHAL, Cynthia, J .... 843-953-0760.... 457 B
lowenthalc@cofc.edu
LOWENTHAL, Tina .... 626-395-2758...... 32 E
tina.lowenthal@caltech.edu
LOWERY, Anne, B .... 251-442-2270........ 9 B
alowery@umobile.edu
LOWERY, Anne, B .... 251-422-2270........ 9 B
alowery@umobile.edu
LOWERY, Anne, B .... 251-442-2270........ 9 B
alowery@umobile.edu
LOWERY, Carla .... 662-329-8543.... 276 B
clowery@ir.muw.edu
LOWERY, Daniel .... 219-473-4333.... 170 D
dlowery@ccsj.edu

LOWERY, Juliet, J .... 540-375-2099.... 523 D
lowery@roanoke.edu
LOWERY, Kathryn .... 601-266-6775.... 278 A
kathryn.lowery@usm.edu
LOWERY, Peg .... 941-752-5390.... 118 E
loweryp@scf.edu
LOWERY-HART, Russell .... 806-371-5226.... 479 H
rdloweryhart@actx.edu
LOWERY-MOORE, Hollis .... 409-880-8661.... 500 F
hollis.moore@lamar.edu
LOWES, JR., Guy .... 304-236-7633.... 542 J
guyl@southern.wvnet.edu
LOWINSKI, Diann .... 218-879-0727.... 266 F
dlowinski@fdltcc.edu
LOWN, Maris .... 908-709-7006.... 316 B
maris.lown@ucc.edu
LOWNDES, Robert, P .... 617-373-2170.... 244 A
LOWRANCE, Gwendolyn ...... 828-898-3360.... 366 A
lowranceg@lmc.edu
LOWRANCE, Jeffrey .... 704-330-6666.... 369 A
jeff.lowrance@cpcc.edu
LOWRANCE, Vicki .... 254-647-3234.... 492 E
vlow@rangercollege.edu
LOWREY, Lang .... 212-243-5150.... 334 E
lowrey@gts.edu
LOWREY, Monte, C .... 618-537-6911.... 157 G
mlowrey@mckendree.edu
LOWRIE, Kalie .... 325-649-8046.... 488 A
klowrie@hputx.edu
LOWRY, Charles .... 304-253-7351.... 541 D
clowry@mountainstate.edu
LOWRY, David .... 405-425-1941.... 409 E
david.lowry@oc.edu
LOWRY, Douglas .... 585-274-1010.... 358 I
dlowry@esm.rochester.edu
LOWRY, Elisabeth .... 415-503-6258...... 66 A
elowry@sfcm.edu
LOWRY, Jenny .... 410-617-2451.... 224 A
jlowry@loyola.edu
LOWRY, John .... 615-966-5951.... 470 D
john.lowry@lipscomb.edu
LOWRY, Kevin .... 847-543-2264.... 147 H
klowry@clcillinois.edu
LOWRY, III, L. Randolph .. 615-966-1787.... 470 D
randy.lowry@lipscomb.edu
LOWRY, Sharon .... 661-722-6300...... 28 J
salowry@avc.edu
LOWY, Esther .... 323-822-9700...... 72 G
tourola@touro.edu
LOWY, Laurence .... 212-410-8007.... 343 B
llowy@nycpm.edu
LOWY, Vivien .... 213-624-1200...... 46 L
vlowy@fidm.edu
LOY, Barry, J .... 978-867-4263.... 235 E
barry.loy@gordon.edu
LOY, Marty .... 715-346-3169.... 552 B
LOY, Terry .... 740-695-9500.... 384 J
teloy@btc.edu
LOYD, Ann .... 478-471-2714.... 133 E
ann.loyd@maconstate.edu
LOYD, James .... 706-649-1449.... 127 E
jloyd@columbustech.edu
LOYD, Jo Lynn .... 972-279-6511.... 479 I
jloyd@amberton.edu
LOYD, Marta .... 479-788-7021...... 24 D
mloyd@uafortsmith.edu
LOYD, Nicole .... 610-861-1503.... 436 I
loyd@moravian.edu
LOYD-PAIGE, Michelle .... 616-526-8703.... 249 E
lopa@calvin.edu
LOYNAZ, Oscar .... 305-348-6796.... 119 B
oscar.loynaz@fiu.edu
LOYOLA, David .... 956-380-8196.... 493 A
dloyola@riogrande.edu
LOZA, Frank .... 325-670-1461.... 487 D
floza@hsutx.edu
LOZADA, Jose .... 787-727-7020.... 568 B
jlozada@sagrado.edu
LOZADA, Mary .... 610-796-8256.... 421 F
mary.lozada@alvernia.edu
LOZADA, Sally .... 740-753-7047.... 392 A
lozada_s@hocking.edu
LOZANO, Fran .... 408-848-4702...... 48 B
flozano@gavilan.edu
LOZANO, Wilson .... 787-857-3600.... 563 A
wlozano@br.inter.edu
LOZEN, Stephen .... 617-423-4630.... 231 E
slozen@bfit.edu
LOZOYA, Lynnette .... 909-599-5433...... 54 A
llozoya@lifepacific.edu
LTAIF, Nicholas, G .... 518-381-1274.... 350 E
ltaifng@sunysccc.edu
LU, Gail .... 415-451-2824...... 66 B
glu@sfts.edu
LU, James .... 951-343-4590...... 31 G
jlu@calbaptist.edu
LU, Shou-En .... 732-235-9764.... 317 A
lus2@umdnj.edu
LU, Wei .... 305-595-9500.... 100 D
LU, Yubin .... 651-631-0204.... 261 D
yubinlu39@yahoo.com
LU, Yue .... 626-289-7719...... 26 J
LUACES, Lourdes .... 787-780-0070.... 560 F
rhumanos@caribbean.edu

LUNDBERG, Shon, R .... 515-964-0601.... 184 G
lundbergs@faith.edu
LUNDBERG-SPRAGUE,
Sheryl .... 808-974-7663.... 141 F
lundberg@hawaii.edu
LUNDBLAD, Larry, A .... 218-855-8053.... 266 C
llundblad@clcmn.edu
LUNDBLAD, Tracey .... 302-736-2372...... 96 G
luncbltr@wesley.edu
LUNDBURG, Wes .... 907-834-1666...... 11 B
plundburg@pwscc.edu
LUNDEEN, Bruce .... 810-766-4017.... 248 C
bruce.lundeen@baker.edu
LUNDEEN, Sally .... 414-229-4189.... 551 C
slundeen@uwm.edu
LUNDELL, Milo, F .... 847-317-8039.... 166 B
mlundell@tiu.edu
LUNDEN, Steve, M .... 509-313-5624.... 534 A
slunden@plant.gonzaga.edu
LUNDERMAN, Dedria .... 850-729-5361.... 114 A
lundermand@nwfsc.edu
LUNDQUIST, Daniel .... 518-244-2018.... 348 A
1lundqd@sage.edu
LUNDQUIST, Sara .... 714-564-6085...... 63 F
lundquist_sara@sac.edu
LUNDRIGAN, Kathleen .... 513-244-4330.... 388 D
kathleen_lundrigan@mail.msj.edu
LUNDSTREM, Karen .... 718-260-5140.... 328 E
klundstrem@citytech.cuny.edu
LUNDSTROM, Linda .... 781-595-6768.... 236 I
llundstrom@mariancourt.edu
LUNDY, Constance, L .... 484-365-7785.... 434 H
lundy@lincoln.edu
LUNDY, Elizabeth .... 503-594-3020.... 415 A
elizabethl@clackamas.edu
LUNDY, Jennifer .... 412-365-1145.... 425 B
jlundy@chatham.edu
LUNDY, Noah .... 207-974-4633.... 218 H
nlundy@emcc.edu
LUNGSTRUM, Anthony .... 573-592-1638.... 293 E
anthony.lungstrum@williamwoods.edu
LUNIN, Jeanne .... 212-353-4107.... 331 B
lunin@cooper.edu
LUNNERMON, JR.,
James, G .... 410-651-6434.... 227 E
jglunnermonii@umes.edu
LUNSFORD, Dale, A .... 903-233-3100.... 489 K
dalelunsford@letu.edu
LUNSFORD, Dan, G .... 828-689-1141.... 366 F
dlunsford@mhc.edu
LUNSFORD, Frances, M .... 336-599-1181.... 372 D
lunsfof@piedmontcc.edu
LUO, Candace .... 408-260-0208...... 47 D
doctoral@fivebranches.edu
LUOMA, Kari .... 906-932-4231.... 251 E
karil@gogebic.edu
LUONG, Carmen .... 718-482-5511.... 328 C
carmenl@lagcc.cuny.edu
LUONG, Huan .... 972-860-8102.... 484 G
hluong@dcccd.edu
LUOTTO, John .... 304-326-1234.... 541 G
jluotto@salemu.edu
LUPIEN, Alfred .... 605-322-8090.... 464 F
alfred.lupien@mtmc.edu
LUPIN, Daniel .... 928-777-3762...... 14 D
lupind@erau.edu
LUPINETTI, Jude .... 985-867-2225.... 214 F
acdean@sjasc.edu
LUPO, Bernadette .... 413-662-5203.... 238 F
bernadette.lupo@mcla.edu
LUPO, Susan .... 734-462-4400.... 258 C
slupo@schoolcraft.edu
LUPTAK, Andrew, J .... 262-243-5700.... 546 I
andrew.luptak@cuw.edu
LUPTON, Deborah .... 410-337-6135.... 222 I
dlupton@goucher.edu
LUPTON, Mark .... 704-272-5406.... 373 F
mlupton@spcc.edu
LURIA, J .... 845-731-3700.... 361 K
yv@ksrnet.com
LUSBY, Mary Lee .... 402-354-7058.... 299 E
marylee.lusby@methodistcollege.edu
LUSH, Mary Jean .... 662-246-6304.... 275 F
mjlush@msdelta.edu
LUSH, Susan .... 617-369-3870.... 244 G
slush@mfa.org
LUSHBAUGH, Jeffery .... 609-777-3083.... 316 A
jlushbaugh@tesc.edu
LUSHBAUGH, Terry .... 304-263-0979.... 541 J
LUSIGNAN, Susan, C .... 585-389-2147.... 342 D
slusign6@naz.edu
LUSK, D. Claude .... 806-291-3436.... 508 B
luskc@wbu.edu
LUSK, David .... 252-493-7319.... 372 E
dlusk@email.pittcc.edu
LUSK, Ju-Hsin .... 423-697-3338.... 474 D
LUSK, Kent, R .... 919-516-4420.... 376 B
krlusk@st-aug.edu
LUSK, Susan .... 310-954-4037...... 57 H
slusk@msmc.la.edu
LUSSIER, Dan .... 731-989-6672.... 468 K
dlussier@fhu.edu
LUSSIER, Michel .... 207-741-5519.... 219 A
mlussier@smccme.edu

LUST, Kevin .... 217-789-1017.... 156 I
kevin.lust@llcc.edu
LUSTIG, Alice .... 732-235-5378.... 316 G
lustigac@umdnj.edu
LUSTIG, Kevin .... 928-541-7777...... 16 I
klustig@ncu.edu
LUSTIG, Lowell .... 617-559-8600.... 235 I
llustig@hebrewcollege.edu
LUTCHEN, Kenneth, R .... 617-353-2800.... 232 G
klutch@bu.edu
LUTER, Gary, S .... 813-253-3333.... 122 H
gluter@ut.edu
LUTES, Jean .... 610-519-6518.... 450 G
jean.lutes@villanova.edu
LUTES, Natalie .... 303-556-5025...... 85 N
lutesn@mscd.edu
LUTGEN, Roxanne .... 715-365-4413.... 554 F
rlutgen@nicoletcollege.edu
LUTGEN, Roxanne, M .... 715-365-4413.... 554 F
rlutgen@nicoletcollege.edu
LUTHER, Judith .... 502-585-9911.... 205 I
jluther@spalding.edu
LUTHER, Nikol .... 208-792-5272.... 143 F
ncluther@lcsc.edu
LUTHER, Patricia .... 760-245-4271...... 77 E
Pat.Luther@vvc.edu
LUTOMSKI, Robert .... 212-229-5459.... 342 E
lutomskr@newschool.edu
LUTRICK, Candee .... 972-825-4612.... 495 D
clutrick@sagu.edu
LUTRICK, Donny .... 972-825-4824.... 495 D
dlutrick@sagu.edu
LUTTMAN, Paul .... 765-966-2656.... 176 F
pluttman@ivytech.edu
LUTTRELL, Curt .... 503-768-6036.... 416 F
luttrell@lclark.edu
LUTY, Carl .... 410-617-2697.... 224 A
cluty@loyola.edu
LUTY, Paul, J .... 503-943-7308.... 420 G
luty@up.edu
LUTZ, Cathleen, A .... 570-321-4069.... 435 D
lutz@lycoming.edu
LUTZ, Charles .... 419-448-3351.... 402 E
clutz@tiffin.edu
LUTZ, Dan .... 765-285-8984.... 169 D
dlutz@bsu.edu
LUTZ, Debra, K .... 989-686-9386.... 250 F
dklutz@delta.edu
LUTZ, Heather .... 434-961-5275.... 527 F
hlutz@pvcc.edu
LUTZ, J. Gary .... 610-758-3708.... 434 E
jgl3@lehigh.edu
LUTZ, Kim, L .... 810-766-4271.... 248 C
kim.lutz@baker.edu
LUTZ, Missy .... 803-321-5120.... 459 G
missy.lutz@newberry.edu
LUTZ, Natalie .... 816-654-7032.... 283 J
nlutz@kcumb.edu
LUTZ, Nate, K .... 612-874-3780.... 265 E
nate_lutz@mcad.edu
LUTZ, Paula .... 406-994-4288.... 295 E
plutz@montana.edu
LUTZ, Susan .... 303-871-2118...... 88 E
susan.lutz@du.edu
LUTZ-DAVIDSON, Stacy .... 719-389-6953...... 81 L
sdavidson@coloradocollege.edu
LUTZKA, David, R .... 218-722-4000.... 263 H
davidl@dbumn.edu
LUU, Khien .... 563-876-3353.... 183 G
kluu@dwci.com
LUUKKONEN, John .... 212-594-4000.... 357 G
jluukkonen@tcicollege.edu
LUVERA, Michael .... 509-963-2959.... 531 G
luveram@cwu.edu
LUX, David .... 401-232-6433.... 453 A
dlux@bryant.edu
LUX, Kate .... 312-662-4033.... 144 C
klux@adler.edu
LUXNER, Catherine .... 570-961-4703.... 435 F
luxner@marywood.edu
LUXTON, Andrea, T .... 269-471-3404.... 247 H
aluxton@andrews.edu
LUXTRUM, Janet .... 253-680-7125.... 531 A
jluxtrum@bates.ctc.edu
LUY, Peggy, S .... 217-424-6330.... 158 F
pluy@millikin.edu
LUYMES, Robyn .... 616-732-1157.... 250 E
rluymes3@davenport.edu
LUZADER, Timothy, B .... 765-494-3981.... 178 F
tluzader@purdue.edu
LUZAR, E. Jane .... 317-278-5082.... 174 B
ejluzar@iupui.edu
LUZURIAGA, Katherine .... 508-856-6282.... 238 A
Katherine.Luzuriaga@umassmed.edu
LUZZI, David, E .... 617-373-2152.... 244 A
LY, Geisce .... 707-962-2661...... 42 A
geisce-ly@redwoods.edu
LY, Vi .... 323-265-8723...... 54 G
lyv@elac.edu
LYBYER, Debra .... 208-792-2313.... 143 F
dlybyer@lcsc.edu
LYDDON, Jan .... 614-947-6536.... 391 A
lyddonj@franklin.edu

LYDDON, Jerri, L .... 620-417-1151.... 196 B
jerrilynn.lyddon@sccc.edu
LYDDON, Susan .... 718-482-5169.... 328 C
slyddon@lagcc.cuny.edu
LYDEN, Michael, P .... 814-824-3652.... 436 C
mlyden@mercyhurst.edu
LYDER, Courtney .... 310-825-9621...... 74 A
clyder@sonnet.ucla.edu
LYDIC, R. Jeffrey .... 724-847-6581.... 429 G
jlydic@geneva.edu
LYDON, Carol Ann .... 828-694-1882.... 368 B
ca_lydon@blueridge.edu
LYDON, Christopher, P .... 401-865-2535.... 453 F
clydon@providence.edu
LYDY, Kenneth, A .... 937-382-6661.... 405 H
kenneth_lydy@wilmington.edu
LYGHT, Bill .... 912-201-6104.... 136 H
blyght@southuniversity.edu
LYGRISSE, Glenn .... 316-322-3231.... 191 D
glygrisse@butlercc.edu
LYKE, Alan, D .... 719-884-5000...... 86 D
LYKINS, Elyce, M .... 570-385-6125.... 440 C
eml10@psu.edu
LYKINS, Jason .... 660-263-3900.... 279 J
jlykins@cccb.edu
LYKINS, Karen .... 931-372-3214.... 474 B
klykins@tntech.edu
LYKOUDIS, Michael, N .... 574-631-7473.... 180 D
lykoudis.1@nd.edu
LYLE, Aaron .... 310-314-6103...... 29 J
LYLE, Charles .... 863-297-5282.... 115 A
clyle@polk.edu
LYLE, Dennis, J .... 847-566-6401.... 167 D
rectorusml@usml.edu
LYLE, Donald, L .... 724-458-2122.... 430 B
dllyle@gcc.edu
LYLE, J. Gary .... 410-777-2836.... 221 B
jglyle@aacc.edu
LYLE, Lisa .... 732-729-3868.... 309 D
llyle@devry.edu
LYLE, William .... 215-489-4987.... 426 H
William.Lyle@delval.edu
LYLES, Carol, S .... 256-765-4201........ 9 D
cslyles@una.edu
LYMAN, Barbara, G .... 717-477-1371.... 443 D
bglyman@ship.edu
LYMAN, Bob .... 601-266-5002.... 278 A
bob.lyman@usm.edu
LYMPANY, John .... 859-985-3990.... 198 F
john_lympany@berea.edu
LYN, Janice .... 504-280-5413.... 213 E
lgallese@uno.edu
LYNCH, Bruce, G .... 336-334-4556.... 379 A
bglynch@uncg.edu
LYNCH, Christine .... 561-297-2536.... 118 H
clynch13@fau.edu
LYNCH, Christopher .... 251-460-7725........ 9 E
clynch@usouthal.edu
LYNCH, Craig .... 312-553-2500.... 146 G
clynch@ccc.edu
LYNCH, Cynthia .... 414-847-3340.... 548 G
cynthialynch@miad.edu
LYNCH, Cynthia, D .... 414-847-3340.... 548 G
cynthialynch@miad.edu
LYNCH, Darlene .... 219-980-6614.... 173 F
darlynch@iun.edu
LYNCH, Dianne .... 828-227-7100.... 379 E
dlynch@wcu.edu
LYNCH, Dianne .... 573-876-7210.... 290 G
dlynch@stephens.edu
LYNCH, Gerald, J .... 765-494-4388.... 178 F
lynch@purdue.edu
LYNCH, James .... 315-792-5316.... 341 E
jlynch@mvcc.edu
LYNCH, Janet, D .... 815-288-5511.... 163 I
lynchj@svcc.edu
LYNCH, Jennifer .... 718-982-2293.... 327 A
Jennifer.Lynch@csi.cuny.edu
LYNCH, Jim Hughes .... 912-279-5713.... 127 B
jlynch@ccga.edu
LYNCH, Joe .... 717-337-6518.... 429 H
jlynch@gettysburg.edu
LYNCH, Julie .... 219-769-3321.... 169 I
jlynch@brownmackie.edu
LYNCH, Julie .... 512-499-4309.... 504 E
jlynch@utsystem.edu
LYNCH, Kathryn .... 781-283-3583.... 246 B
klynch@wellesley.edu
LYNCH, Kevin, P .... 315-268-6728.... 329 C
klynch@clarkson.edu
LYNCH, Kim .... 763-433-1865.... 265 J
kim.lynch@anokaramsey.edu
LYNCH, Kris .... 252-399-6329.... 362 A
klynch@barton.edu
LYNCH, Lisa .... 781-736-3883.... 233 A
lisalynch@brandeis.edu
LYNCH, Lisa, A .... 989-729-3422.... 249 A
lisa.lynch@baker.edu
LYNCH, Maggie .... 707-476-4100...... 42 A
maggie-lynch@redwoods.edu
LYNCH, Michael .... 508-999-8845.... 237 E
mlynch4@umassd.edu
LYNCH, Michael .... 315-568-3052.... 342 H
mlynch@nycc.edu

LYNCH, Michael, F .... 703-993-3840.... 519 A
mlynch@gmu.edu
LYNCH, Paul .... 703-284-1608.... 521 A
paul.lynch@marymount.edu
LYNCH, Richard, E .... 972-708-7340.... 486 I
dick_lynch@gial.edu
LYNCH, Robert .... 240-567-7306.... 224 E
bob.lynch@montgomerycollege.edu
LYNCH, Robert, P .... 407-888-8689.... 107 J
blynch@fcim.edu
LYNCH, Rose .... 908-835-2306.... 317 C
lynchr@warren.edu
LYNCH, Stephen, J .... 401-865-2233.... 453 F
sjlynch@providence.edu
LYNCH, Susan, M .... 570-286-3058.... 436 B
smh@mccannschool.com
LYNCH, William, F .... 215-895-2167.... 427 G
wfl27@drexel.edu
LYNCH MAESTAS,
Michael .... 785-864-2277.... 196 F
mvlm@ku.edu
LYNDGAARD, David .... 320-363-3350.... 271 F
dlyndgaard@csbsju.edu
LYNEMA, Dawn, A .... 616-988-3624.... 254 A
dlynema@kuyper.edu
LYNG, Heather .... 802-287-8231.... 513 D
gmc@bkstr.com
LYNG-GLIDDI, Diana, L .... 518-327-6314.... 345 H
dlyngglíddi@paulsmiths.edu
LYNK, Angel .... 334-347-2623........ 3 G
alynk@escc.edu
LYNN, Angela .... 309-298-1891.... 168 A
an-lynn@wiu.edu
LYNN, Candace .... 253-854-4960.... 535 D
candace@nacstaff.com
LYNN, Crystal .... 540-828-5356.... 516 K
clynn@bridgewater.edu
LYNN, Dahlia .... 207-780-4524.... 220 G
dlynn@usm.maine.edu
LYNN, Kathy .... 802-865-6485.... 513 A
lynn@champlain.edu
LYNN, Ken .... 281-998-6306.... 493 D
ken.lynn@sjcd.edu
LYNN, Laura .... 410-662-2797.... 272 F
laura.lynn@waldenu.edu
LYNN, Mary Evelyn .... 423-473-2368.... 474 E
melynn@clevelandstatecc.edu
LYNN, Michael .... 219-785-5380.... 178 H
mlynn@pnc.edu
LYNN, Richard .... 251-809-1556........ 5 B
richard.lynn@jdcc.edu
LYNN, Richardson, R .... 404-872-3593.... 125 B
rlynn@johnmrshall.edu
LYNN, Robert .... 407-708-2044.... 117 G
lynnr@seminolestate.edu
LYNN, Terence .... 413-775-1440.... 240 B
terencel@gcc.mass.edu
LYNN, Vicki .... 501-450-1494...... 22 A
lynn@hendrix.edu
LYNN, William .... 570-208-5946.... 432 E
williamlynn@kings.edu
LYNNE, Christopher .... 928-541-7777...... 16 I
clynne@ncu.edu
LYNOTT, Patricia .... 603-645-9596.... 306 B
p.lynott@snhu.edu
LYON, Bob .... 423-425-4717.... 477 D
bob-lyon@utc.edu
LYON, Chris .... 913-588-5080.... 197 A
clyon2@kumc.edu
LYON, Douglas, W .... 603-526-3750.... 304 A
dlyon@colby-sawyer.edu
LYON, JR., James, C .... 773-442-4100.... 159 H
j-lyonjr@neiu.edu
LYON, K, B .... 317-931-2306.... 170 E
blyon@cts.edu
LYON, Larry .... 254-710-3588.... 481 I
larry_lyon@baylor.edu
LYON, Lisa .... 808-974-7636.... 141 A
llyon@hawaii.edu
LYON, Mary Eilleen .... 616-331-2221.... 252 A
lyonme@gvsu.edu
LYON, Misty .... 309-341-5422.... 146 A
mlyon@sandburg.edu
LYON, Tammy .... 910-938-6247.... 369 C
lyont@coastalcarolina.edu
LYON, Wade .... 620-417-1064.... 196 B
wade.lyon@sccc.edu
LYONS, Anthony .... 620-227-9203.... 192 B
alyons@dc3.edu
LYONS, Becky .... 406-657-2240.... 295 F
blyons@msubillings.edu
LYONS, Charles, M .... 207-216-4311.... 219 C
clyons@yccc.edu
LYONS, Cheryl, C .... 501-450-3140...... 25 H
clyons@uca.edu
LYONS, Cindy .... 239-590-7904.... 119 A
clyons@fgcu.edu
LYONS, Darrin .... 518-255-5227.... 354 E
lyonsd@cobleskill.edu
LYONS, Dennis .... 508-373-5777.... 241 F
dennis.lyons@mcphs.edu
LYONS, Eilene .... 314-513-4401.... 289 B
elyons@stlcc.edu
LYONS, Gary .... 405-425-1932.... 409 E
gary.lyons@oc.edu

MACKIN, OFM, Kevin .... 845-569-3202.... 342 A
kevin.mackin@msmc.edu
MACKIN, Mary Beth .... 262-472-1533.... 552 E
mackinm@uww.edu
MACKINNEY, Eleanor .... 847-214-7374.... 150 D
epmackinney@aol.com
MACKINNON, George .... 847-619-7290.... 162 I
gmackinnon@roosevelt.edu
MACKINTOSH, Carol .... 315-792-3228.... 359 C
cmackintosh@utica.edu
MACKLIN, James, F .... 518-629-7353.... 336 C
j.macklin@hvcc.edu
MACKNIK, Heather .... 315-652-6500.... 325 A
hmmacknik@bryantstratton.edu
MACKSEY-ETHIER,
Jennifer .... 413-662-5210.... 238 F
j.ethier@mcla.edu
MACLACHLAN, Scott .... 561-207-5325.... 114 D
maclachs@palmbeachstate.edu
MACLAREN, James .... 504-865-5225.... 215 C
maclaren@tulane.edu
MACLAUGHLIN, Cordy ...... 808-984-3471.... 142 B
cordym@hawaii.edu
MACLEAN, Richard .... 907-277-1000...... 10 F
richard.maclean@chartercollege.edu
MACLEISH, Padraic .... 760-872-2000...... 43 H
padraicm@deepsprings.edu
MACLELLAN, Shannon .... 734-995-4892.... 250 B
macles@cuaa.edu
MACLENNAN, Kevin, L ...... 303-492-6694...... 88 B
kevin.maclennan@colorado.edu
MACLENNAN, Marcia, M .. 785-827-5541.... 194 D
maclenn@kwu.edu
MACLENNAN, Richard .... 301-387-3056.... 222 H
rick.maclennan@garrettcollege.edu
MACLEOD, Ann-Mary .... 505-925-8550.... 321 G
annmary@unm.edu
MACLEOD, Catherine .... 212-431-2830.... 343 E
cmacleod@nyls.edu
MACLEOD, David, J .... 563-588-8000.... 184 F
dmacleod@emmaus.edu
MACLEOD, Kelly .... 727-726-1153.... 103 B
kellymacleod@clearwater.edu
MACLEOD, Melissa, A .... 724-458-2050.... 430 B
mamacleod@gcc.edu
MACLEOD, Peter .... 510-883-2056...... 45 A
pmacleod@dspt.edu
MACLEOD, Robert .... 813-974-6015.... 120 D
rmacleod@usf.edu
MACLEOD, Stephen, C .... 978-867-4068.... 235 E
steve.macleod@gordon.edu
MACMAHON, James .... 435-797-2478.... 511 B
jim.macmahon@usu.edu
MACMASTER, Donald .... 989-358-7344.... 247 G
macmastd@alpenacc.edu
MACMILLAN, Cynthia .... 609-984-1130.... 316 A
cmacmillan@tesc.edu
MACMILLAN, David, F ...... 415-422-2047...... 76 B
macmillan@usfca.edu
MACMUNN, Craig .... 207-221-8702.... 218 C
cmacmunn@kaplan.edu
MACNAMARA, Timothy .... 307-778-1256.... 556 B
tmacnama@lccc.wy.edu
MACNAUGHTON,
Christopher, J .... 317-738-8109.... 171 C
cmacnaughton@franklincollege.edu
MACNAUGHTON, Kevin, J 919-515-2732.... 378 B
kevin_macnaughton@ncsu.edu
MACNEIL, M. A. J. Lex ...... 630-515-7275.... 158 E
lmacne@midwestern.edu
MACNEIL, Monty, R .... 860-679-2808...... 94 F
macneil@nso.uchc.edu
MACNEIL, Roderick, L .... 860-679-2808...... 94 E
MacNeil@nso.uchc.edu
MACNEW, James .... 215-637-7700.... 430 H
jmacnew@holyfamily.edu
MACON, Rebecca, D .... 706-542-6020.... 138 C
rmacon@uga.edu
MACONACHY, William ...... 301-369-2800.... 221 F
wvmaconachy@capitol-college.edu
MACOPSON, Elmer, R .... 828-652-0603.... 371 G
elmerm@mcdowelltech.edu
MACOSKO, Ron .... 830-792-7421.... 494 A
rpmacosko@schreiner.edu
MACPHERSON, Corey .... 617-745-3525.... 234 C
corey.s.macpherson@enc.edu
MACREADY, Neil, A .... 909-748-8049...... 75 F
neil_macready@redlands.edu
MACREADY, Valda .... 214-637-3530.... 508 A
vmacready@wadecollege.edu
MACRINA, Francis, L .... 804-827-2262.... 525 E
macrina@vcu.edu
MACRITCHIE, Andrea .... 508-854-4461.... 241 C
MACRO, Venessa .... 515-271-3133.... 184 A
venessa.macro@drake.edu
MACTAGGART, Julie .... 563-589-3619.... 189 B
jmactaggart@dbq.edu
MACUILA, Terry .... 606-242-0974.... 203 A
terry.macuila@kctcs.edu
MACUMBER, Linda, K .... 563-333-6336.... 188 D
MacumberLindaK@sau.edu
MACUR, Kenneth .... 608-663-2200.... 547 C
kmacur@edgewood.edu
MACWILLIAMS, Erika .... 305-809-3277.... 108 F
erika.macwilliams@fkcc.edu

MADACSI, Nancy .... 908-852-1400.... 308 F
library@centenarycollege.edu
MADAIO-O'BRIEN,
Melanie .... 617-353-2256.... 232 G
asmelmad@bu.edu
MADAMA, Patrick .... 732-906-2551.... 311 E
PMadama@middlesexcc.edu
MADANIPOUR, Manouche 617-928-7376.... 243 A
mmadanipour@mountida.edu
MADDALI, Ramesh .... 601-877-6146.... 273 C
rmaddali@alcorn.edu
MADDEN, Beverly .... 650-574-6538...... 67 F
maddenb@smccd.edu
MADDEN, Charles, E .... 478-387-4804.... 130 E
MADDEN, Deanna .... 808-983-4152.... 140 C
dmadden@tokai.edu
MADDEN, Fred, H .... 856-415-2272.... 310 E
fmadden@gccnj.edu
MADDEN, Joe .... 936-639-1301.... 480 D
jmadden@angelina.edu
MADDEN, John .... 575-624-7111.... 318 B
john.madden@roswell.enmu.edu
MADDEN, Margaret, E .... 315-267-2108.... 354 C
maddenme@potsdam.edu
MADDEN, Mike .... 417-447-8170.... 287 G
maddenm@otc.edu
MADDEN, Paul .... 740-351-3421.... 401 I
pmadden@shawnee.edu
MADDEN, Richard .... 931-363-9844.... 470 E
rmadden@martinmethodist.edu
MADDEN, Sarah .... 732-729-3752.... 309 D
smadden@devry.edu
MADDEN, Susan .... 240-567-5274.... 224 E
susan.madden@montgomerycollege.edu
MADDEN, Warren, R .... 515-294-6162.... 182 B
wmadden@iastate.edu
MADDEN-BRENHOLTS,
Linda, R .... 412-578-6654.... 424 G
maddenbrenholtslr@carlow.edu
MADDIGAN, Susan .... 508-362-2131.... 240 A
smaddigan@capecod.edu
MADDIRALA, James .... 601-979-2244.... 275 A
james.maddirala@jsums.edu
MADDISON, Justin .... 701-774-4240.... 382 F
justin.maddison@willistonstate.edu
MADDOCKS, Peter .... 617-989-4328.... 246 C
maddocksp@wit.edu
MADDOX, Cheryl, Y .... 704-847-5600.... 376 H
cmaddox@ses.edu
MADDOX, Cole .... 404-364-8535.... 135 A
cmaddox@oglethorpe.edu
MADDOX, Dusty .... 407-226-6465.... 104 D
dmaddox@devry.edu
MADDOX, Gregory, H .... 713-313-7889.... 499 G
maddox_gh@tsu.edu
MADDOX, Janet, H .... 404-364-8462.... 135 A
jmaddox@oglethorpe.edu
MADDOX, Julie, A .... 219-464-5333.... 181 A
julie.maddox@valpo.edu
MADDOX, Kelley, L .... 770-534-6270.... 126 B
kmaddox@brenau.edu
MADDOX, Kenneth .... 256-372-5616........ 1 A
kenneth.maddox@aamu.edu
MADDOX, Lori, B .... 615-353-3305.... 475 D
lori.maddox@nscc.edu
MADDOX, Nedra .... 704-484-4103.... 369 B
maddox@clevelandcommunitycollege.edu
MADDOX, Rebecca .... 706-295-6321.... 130 C
rmaddox@highlands.edu
MADDOX, Ronald, W .... 910-893-1686.... 362 F
maddox@campbell.edu
MADDOX, Tangella .... 312-341-3584.... 162 I
tmaddox@roosevelt.edu
MADDUX, Gary .... 256-824-2679...... 9 A
gary.maddux@us.army.mil
MADDY, Angela, M .... 620-792-9322.... 190 E
maddya@bartonccc.edu
MADDY, Faith, D .... 314-968-7457.... 293 A
faithmaddy41@webster.edu
MADELONE, Laura .... 607-436-2526.... 353 E
madelolm@oneonta.edu
MADER, James .... 412-346-2100.... 444 D
jmader@pia.edu
MADER, Louis .... 212-772-4521.... 327 E
lmader@hunter.cuny.edu
MADER, Sharon, B .... 504-280-6556.... 213 E
smader@uno.edu
MADGES, William .... 610-660-1282.... 446 C
wmadges@sju.edu
MADHAVARAU, Leela .... 909-748-8285...... 75 F
leela_madhavarau@redlands.edu
MADIGAN, Kay .... 330-652-9919.... 390 H
kaymadigan@eticollege.edu
MADIN, Laurence, P .... 508-289-2515.... 247 A
lmadin@whoi.edu
MADISON, Anna .... 617-287-7232.... 237 D
anna.madison@umb.edu
MADISON, Jennifer .... 940-898-3103.... 502 B
jmadison@twu.edu
MADISON, Jennifer, L .... 716-372-7978.... 345 C
jmadison@obi.edu
MADISON, Katheryn .... 541-684-4644.... 419 F
kmadison@pioneerpacific.edu
MADISON, Olivia, M .... 515-294-1442.... 182 B
omadison@iastate.edu

MADISON, Ryan, D .... 817-923-8459.... 483 C
Madison@kenrick.edu
MADISON, Sandra .... 305-899-4933.... 101 F
smadison@mail.barry.edu
MADLOCK, Calvin .... 661-722-6300...... 28 J
cmadlock@avc.edu
MADONNA, JR.,
Richard, A .... 212-280-7100.... 358 G
rmadonna@uts.columbia.edu
MADOO, Ceres .... 310-665-6895...... 60 B
cmadoo@otis.edu
MADORE, Keith, L .... 207-768-9568.... 220 F
keith.madore@umpi.edu
MADORMA, James .... 708-342-3250.... 149 L
jmadorma@devry.edu
MADOSKI, Larry, D .... 714-542-8086...... 52 K
lmadoski@kensington.edu
MADRAY, Van .... 252-493-7750.... 372 E
vmadray@email.pittcc.edu
MADRIAGA, Rogelio, L ...... 670-234-5498.... 559 F
rogerm@nmcnet.edu
MADRID, Maria, E .... 787-728-1515.... 568 B
mmadrid@sagrado.edu
MADRID, Regina .... 505-454-2534.... 318 E
rmadrid@luna.edu
MADRIGAL, Joseph .... 650-738-4333...... 67 G
madrigalj@smccd.edu
MADSEN, Alice .... 206-878-3710.... 534 E
amadsen@highline.edu
MADSEN, Gary, L .... 512-223-7087.... 481 B
gmadsen@austincc.edu
MADSEN, Jan, D .... 402-280-3386.... 297 H
janmadsen@creighton.edu
MADSEN, Kirsten .... 541-684-7250.... 417 F
kmadsen@northwestchristian.edu
MADSEN, Sandra, K .... 509-527-4571.... 538 G
sandra.madsen@wwcc.edu
MADSEN, Stephanie, D ...... 410-382-4674.... 224 D
smadsen@mcdaniel.edu
MADSON, Greg .... 406-791-5359.... 296 H
gmadson01@ugf.edu
MADULI, Ed .... 408-741-2082...... 77 K
ed_maduli@wvm.edu
MAEA, Cheri .... 703-414-4056.... 518 B
cmaea@devry.edu
MAEDA, John .... 401-454-6764.... 454 B
president@risd.edu
MAELSON, Diane, C .... 215-204-3745.... 447 G
diane.maleson@temple.edu
MAENE, Sara .... 304-876-5112.... 544 A
smaene@shepherd.edu
MAES, Sue, C .... 785-532-5644.... 194 B
scmaes@ksu.edu
MAESTAS, Belen .... 719-587-7321...... 80 F
bmaestas@adams.edu
MAESTAS, Joseph .... 970-945-8691...... 82 C
MAESTAS, Ricardo .... 432-837-8032.... 501 B
rmaestas@sulross.edu
MAESTAS, Richard .... 303-360-4751...... 83 E
richard.maestas@ccaurora.edu
MAESTAS, Stacy .... 307-778-1240.... 556 B
smaestas@lccc.wy.edu
MAESTRI, Madalena .... 480-860-2700...... 14 G
mmaestri@taliesin.edu
MAFAHER, Zlaeddln .... 202-319-5373...... 97 C
mafaher@cua.edu
MAFFEI, Melody .... 209-667-3623...... 36 C
mmafei@csustan.edu
MAFICO, Temba, L .... 404-527-7704.... 132 D
tmafico@itc.edu
MAFREDI, Juan, J .... 412-624-0790.... 449 A
manfredi@pitt.edu
MAGAI, Carol .... 718-488-1177.... 338 H
carol.magai@liu.edu
MAGALONG, Mariles .... 510-235-7800...... 43 B
mmagalong@contracosta.edu
MAGARA, Melanie, S .... 815-753-1681.... 160 A
mmagara@niu.edu
MAGAZU, Daniel .... 508-626-1220.... 238 D
dmagazu@framingham.edu
MAGDALENO, Jose .... 718-960-8241.... 327 C
joseph.magdaleno@lehman.cuny.edu
MAGDZIARZ, Wayne .... 312-915-6403.... 157 A
wmagdzi@luc.edu
MAGEE, JR., David, E .... 423-439-4441.... 473 E
magee@etsu.edu
MAGEE, Dolores, B .... 870-759-4184...... 26 B
dmagee@wbcoll.edu
MAGEE, Jim .... 610-341-1720.... 428 D
jmagee@eastern.edu
MAGEE, Kenneth, W .... 734-763-3434.... 259 D
kmagee@umich.edu
MAGEE, Maggie .... 207-947-4591.... 217 D
mmagee@bealcollege.edu
MAGEE, Patricia .... 504-568-4800.... 213 A
pmagee@lsuhsu.edu
MAGEE, Rosemary .... 404-727-6020.... 129 A
rosemary.magee@emory.edu
MAGEE, Rosie .... 717-262-2006.... 452 B
rmagee@wilson.edu
MAGEE, Tiffany .... 225-768-1701.... 214 B
tiffany.magee@ololcollege.edu
MAGEE, Vicki .... 815-802-8258.... 154 J
vmagee@kcc.edu

MAGEEAN, Deirdre .... 252-328-9471.... 377 C
mageeand@ecu.edu
MAGER, Donald, N .... 704-378-1295.... 365 H
dmager@jcsu.edu
MAGERS, Dwight, E .... 423-236-2992.... 473 A
magers@southern.edu
MAGET, Douglas .... 212-854-6991.... 323 G
dmaget@barnard.edu
MAGGARD, Bradley .... 517-265-5161.... 247 D
MAGGART, Wanda, S .... 919-536-7250.... 369 G
maggartw@durhamtech.edu
MAGGELAKIS, Sophia .... 585-475-2483.... 347 G
sxmsma@rit.edu
MAGGIO, Chris .... 318-357-5286.... 216 B
maggioc@nsula.edu
MAGGIO, Cindy .... 318-676-7811.... 211 H
cindy.maggio@nwltc.edu
MAGGIO, Evelyn .... 718-270-5103.... 328 D
emaggio@mec.cuny.edu
MAGGIOTTO, Michael, A .. 765-285-1042.... 169 D
mmaggiotto@bsu.edu
MAGGITTI, Sara .... 610-902-8566.... 423 H
sara.maggitti@cabrini.edu
MAGGS, Gregory, E .... 202-994-1000...... 97 F
MAGGS, Mark .... 814-234-7755.... 447 C
mmaggs@southhills.edu
MAGHROORI, Ray .... 951-222-8043...... 63 I
ray.maghroori@rcc.edu
MAGHSOUD, Amanda, F ... 803-323-4891.... 463 D
maghsouda@winthrop.edu
MAGID, Bruce, R .... 781-736-2256.... 233 A
bmagid@brandeis.edu
MAGIDA, David .... 802-485-2145.... 514 A
davem@norwich.edu
MAGIE, CM, Sandra, C ...... 713-686-4345.... 504 D
smagie@stthom.edu
MAGIERA, Steve, L .... 239-590-1119.... 119 A
smagiera@fgcu.edu
MAGIERA, Steve, L .... 239-590-1067.... 119 A
smagiera@fgcu.edu
MAGILL, Jim .... 828-298-3325.... 380 C
jmagill@warren-wilson.edu
MAGINN, Julie .... 908-526-1200.... 313 E
jmaginn@raritanval.edu
MAGLION, Joyce .... 973-408-3631.... 309 F
jmaglion@drew.edu
MAGNAN, Carolyn .... 860-832-3715...... 91 G
magnanc@ccsu.edu
MAGNAN, Chris .... 305-892-7007.... 111 K
chris.magnan@jwu.edu
MAGNER, Brent .... 402-363-5636.... 301 F
brent.magner@york.edu
MAGNER, Kevin .... 714-867-5009...... 70 C
MAGNO, Jan .... 760-355-6265...... 50 K
janis.magno@imperial.edu
MAGNO, Janis .... 760-355-6245...... 50 K
janis.magno@imperial.edu
MAGNUS, Keith, B .... 317-940-9385.... 170 C
kmagnus@butler.edu
MAGNUSON, Audrey .... 210-458-6846.... 506 B
audrey.magnuson@utsa.edu
MAGNUSON, Janae .... 414-443-3644.... 549 A
magnusoj@mtmary.edu
MAGNUSON, Kolly, J .... 320-222-6094.... 268 I
kelly.magnuson@ridgewater.edu
MAGNUSON, Kendyl .... 530-741-6989...... 80 E
kmagnuso@yccd.edu
MAGNUSON, Mark .... 218-733-7628.... 267 B
m.magnuson@lsc.edu
MAGNUSON, Nancy .... 410-337-6364.... 222 I
nmagnuso@goucher.edu
MAGNUSON, Nancy, M .... 314-516-5671.... 291 F
magnuson@umsl.edu
MAGNUSSON, Selena .... 706-295-6866.... 130 F
smagnussen@gntc.edu
MAGNUSSON DURHAM,
Nancy .... 615-966-5275.... 470 D
nancy.durham@lipscomb.edu
MAGOLIS, David .... 570-389-4921.... 441 F
dmagolis@bloomu.edu
MAGOON, Martha, W .... 330-438-7430.... 397 C
mwm@neoucom.edu
MAGOWAN, Mike .... 941-379-0404.... 100 G
mmagowan@argosy.edu
MAGRATH, C. Peter .... 607-777-2131.... 351 F
president@binghamton.edu
MAGRATH, Lynda, L .... 914-654-5566.... 330 B
lmagrath@cnr.edu
MAGRIBY, Steve .... 813-253-6265.... 122 H
smagriby@ut.edu
MAGRUDER, Jack .... 660-626-2391.... 278 F
wjmagruder@atsu.edu
MAGUET, Kathryn, L .... 570-577-3700.... 423 D
kathryn.maguet@bucknell.edu
MAGUIRE, Adam .... 617-262-5000.... 232 B
adam.maguire@the-bac.edu
MAGUIRE, Chris .... 715-422-5322.... 554 C
chris.maguire@mstc.edu
MAGUIRE, Eric .... 607-274-1555.... 336 G
emaguire@ithaca.edu
MAGUIRE, Karen .... 212-355-1501.... 326 B
MAGUIRE, Roberta, S .... 920-424-7364.... 551 D
maguire@uwosh.edu

MALEY, David, C 607-274-3480 336 G maley@ithaca.edu
MALEY, Leasa, A 814-362-7539 449 B maley@pitt.edu
MALEY, Robert 215-968-8116 423 E maleyr@bucks.edu
MALEY, Sandra, J 609-497-7720 312 F human.resources@ptsem.edu
MALFITANO, Gregory, J 561-237-7277 113 D gmalfitano@lynn.edu
MALHAS, Faris, A 419-372-7581 385 C fmalhas@bgsu.edu
MALHAS, Faris, A 304-442-3161 545 C faris.malhas@mail.wvu.edu
MALHOTRA, Devinder 320-308-4909 269 C dmmalhotra@stcloudstate.edu
MALIANDI, Paula 973-655-7900 311 G maliandip@mail.montclair.edu
MALIEKAL, Jose 585-395-2394 352 F jmalieka@brockport.edu
MALIG, Jannet 562-860-2451 38 J jmalig@cerritos.edu
MALIK, Christopher, P 716-839-8332 331 G cmalik@daemen.edu
MALIK, David, J 219-980-6966 173 F dmalik@iun.edu
MALIK, Rick 312-225-6288 167 E rmalik@vandercook.edu
MALIK, Tarun 980-598-1020 365 G tarun.malik@jwu.edu
MALIK, Zafar, A 312-939-0111 150 B zafar@eastwest.edu
MALIN, John 217-854-3231 145 F jmali@blackburn.edu
MALINOWSKI, Sarah 201-761-6239 314 F
MALISCH, Susan, M 773-508-7750 157 A smalisc@luc.edu
MALISOS, Gary 561-273-6500 117 J gmalisos@southuniversity.edu
MALIWESKY, Martin 614-287-3669 388 G mmaliwes@cscc.edu
MALIZIA, Michael 727-816-3190 114 F malizim@phcc.edu
MALKEMES, Janet 704-330-4806 369 A janet.malkemes@cpcc.edu
MALKEWICZ, Lisa 574-257-3206 169 F malkew@bethelcollege.edu
MALKOWSKI, Brenda 417-255-7966 286 G brendamalkowski@missouristate.edu
MALKOWSKI, Keith 989-686-9449 250 F
MALL, Scot 502-423-0149 19 C scot.mall@phoenix.edu
MALLACH, Sachi 610-526-6005 430 D smallach@harcum.edu
MALLAMACE, Debra, L 732-750-1800 307 G dlm@berkeleycollege.edu
MALLARD, Kina, S 865-471-3219 467 E kmallard@cn.edu
MALLERY, Mike 503-352-2258 419 E mallerym@pacificu.edu
MALLET, Chris 801-274-3280 512 E cmallet@wgu.edu
MALLET, Colleen 845-437-5276 359 D
MALLETT, Kristi 918-343-7796 411 H kmallett@rsu.edu
MALLETTE, Julia, R 919-515-2334 378 B julie_mallette@ncsu.edu
MALLETTE, Richard 847-735-5277 155 F mallette@lakeforest.edu
MALLIA, Maria 201-559-6072 310 C malliam@felician.edu
MALLINSON, Jeff 425-249-4766 538 D jeff.mallinson@tlc.edu
MALLINSON, Stacie 425-249-4758 538 D stacie.mallinson@tlc.edu
MALLO, Ted, A 330-972-6021 403 B tamallo@uakron.edu
MALLORY, Carolyn, R 361-570-4130 503 E malloryc@uhv.edu
MALLORY, Dale, E 585-292-3040 341 H dmallory@monroecc.edu
MALLORY, David, G 716-270-5348 333 D mallory@ecc.edu
MALLORY, Kristen 909-621-8267 40 D kristen.mallory@cmc.edu
MALLORY, Kristin 304-734-6605 542 D kmallory@bridgemont.edu
MALLORY, Tim 714-459-1114 78 C tmallory@wsulaw.edu
MALLOW, Richard 909-484-4311 46 F
MALLOY, Dorothy, A 610-519-7857 450 G dorothy.malloy@villanova.edu
MALLOY, Jeffrey 812-535-5219 179 C jmalloy@smwc.edu
MALLOY, Kathleen, A 724-925-4028 451 E malloyka@wccc.edu
MALLOY, Leanne 317-955-6150 177 G lmalloy@marian.edu
MALLOY, Michael, J 508-373-5611 241 F michael.malloy@mcphs.edu
MALLOY, SJ, Richard 570-941-6153 450 B malloyr2@scranton.edu
MALLOY, Thomas, K 610-499-4174 451 F tkmalloy@widener.edu
MALLOZZI, Catherine 321-253-2929 106 A cmallozz@cci.edu
MALM, James 719-549-2940 83 B james.malm@colostate-pueblo.edu
MALMBERG, Margaret, A 954-262-6936 114 B mm2439@nsu.nova.edu
MALMBERG, Meg 692-625-5379 559 E mmalmberg@cmi.edu
MALMBERG, Steve 692-625-2502 559 E smalmberg@cmi.edu
MALMGREN, Betty, M 707-253-3372 58 F bmalmgren@napavalley.edu
MALMGREN, Carol, E 217-333-2034 167 B cemalm@illinois.edu
MALMGREN, Irene 626-914-8881 39 G imalmgren@citruscollege.edu
MALMQUIST, Laine 847-628-2011 154 I lmalmquist@judsonu.edu
MALMROSE, John 843-792-2721 459 C malmrose@musc.edu
MALONE, Allison 870-574-4544 24 A amalone@sautech.edu
MALONE, Anne, B 412-362-5610 444 G amalone@pts.edu
MALONE, Brenda, R 919-962-1554 378 D brenda_malone@unc.edu
MALONE, Brian 505-277-8900 321 C bmalone@unm.edu
MALONE, Dan 214-333-6883 484 C dan@dbu.edu
MALONE, Dean 630-515-7145 16 F dmalon@midwestern.edu
MALONE, Dean, P 630-515-7145 158 E dmalon@midwestern.edu
MALONE, Deborah 610-282-1100 426 I deborah.malone@desales.edu
MALONE, Elbert, R 803-536-8213 460 G malone@scsu.edu
MALONE, Jill 727-725-2688 105 J mmalone@cci.edu
MALONE, John 651-962-6925 272 E j9malone@stthomas.edu
MALONE, Judith, A 781-891-2016 231 F jmalone@bentley.edu
MALONE, Kathy 219-980-6701 173 F kalmalon@iun.edu
MALONE, Lora 817-272-2594 505 A lmalone@uta.edu
MALONE, Marisa 317-554-8327 169 H mamalone@brownmackie.edu
MALONE, Mary Frances 203-254-4000 92 B malone@fairfield.edu
MALONE, Michael, F 413-545-5270 237 C mmalone@umass.edu
MALONE, Michael, P 815-753-6065 160 A mmalone@niu.edu
MALONE, Nina, R 310-233-4651 54 I malonenr@lahc.edu
MALONE, Pamela 528-587-2100 355 F pamela.malone@esc.edu
MALONE, Ted 907-786-1520 10 I antem2@uaa.alaska.edu
MALONE, Virginia, J 314-340-3339 282 I malonev@hssu.edu
MALONE-FENNER, Shirley 617-879-2248 246 F smalone-fenner@wheelock.edu
MALONEY, Barry, M 508-929-8020 239 D bmaloney@worcester.edu
MALONEY, Cordelia 312-996-8586 166 F cordelia@uic.edu
MALONEY, Dena 661-362-3305 41 G dena.maloney@canyons.edu
MALONEY, Gerald, J 404-894-0881 130 D jerry.maloney@bks.gatech.edu
MALONEY, Jay 719-389-6785 81 L jmaloney@coloradocollege.edu
MALONEY, Kathryn, A 530-752-2396 73 F kamaloney@ucdavis.edu
MALONEY, Krisellen 210-458-4889 506 B krisellen.maloney@utsa.edu
MALONEY, Marge 925-424-1103 39 A mmaloney@laspositascollege.edu
MALONEY, Maureen 203-358-0700 94 D mmaureen@bridgeport.edu
MALONEY, Maureen, A 510-649-2464 48 H maloney@gtu.edu
MALONEY, Michael 212-280-1530 358 G mmaloney@uts.columbia.edu
MALONEY, Michelle 610-917-1406 450 D mmmaloney@vfcc.edu
MALONEY, Patrick, T 508-831-6710 247 B ptmaloney@wpi.edu
MALONEY, Rebecca, S 504-866-7426 213 I rmaloney@nds.edu
MALONEY, Shari 320-762-4466 265 I sharim@alextech.edu
MALONEY, Vicky, G 803-778-6612 455 G maloneyvg@cctech.edu
MALOOF, Lisa 770-868-4069 132 J lmaloof@laniertech.edu
MALOSH, Ann 541-917-4923 416 H malosha@linnbenton.edu
MALOTT, F. Stephen 573-341-4122 292 A malott@mst.edu
MALOTT, Michelle, L 218-477-2574 268 A michelle.malott@mnstate.edu
MALOVEY, Troy 412-200-3002 19 C troy.malovey@phoenix.edu
MALOY, Michael, T 610-436-3309 443 F mmaloy@wcupa.edu
MALOY, Stanley 619-594-5142 36 E smaloy@sciences.sdsu.edu
MALOY, Vicky 319-368-6465 187 E vmaloy@mtmercy.edu
MALPASS, Scott, C 574-631-8877 180 D malpass.1@nd.edu
MALSBURY, Sara 402-481-8375 297 B sara.malsbury@bryanlgh.org
MALSHEIMER, Cheryl 305-809-3201 108 F cheryl.malsheimer@fkcc.edu
MALSON, Don, G 573-875-7421 280 E dgmalson@ccis.edu
MALTA, Anthony 318-342-3547 216 E malta@ulm.edu
MALTBIE, Randy 256-840-4112 7 B rmaltbie@snead.edu
MALTBY, Lee 773-878-3728 163 D lmaltby@staugustine.edu
MALTBY, Marc 270-686-4544 202 E marc.maltby@kctcs.edu
MALTESE, Vincent 734-384-4128 255 G vmaltese@monroeccc.edu
MALTESE, Vincent 734-384-4152 255 G vmaltese@monroeccc.edu
MALTINO, Frank 973-408-3955 309 F fmaltino@drew.edu
MALUTICH, Steve 832-201-3626 480 B smalutich@houston.aiuniv.edu
MALVEAUX, Brent 251-343-8200 6 F brent.malveaux@remingtoncollege.edu
MALVEAUX, Julianne 336-517-2225 362 C jmalveaux@bennett.edu
MALVERS, Dennis 978-656-3116 240 F malversd@middlesex.mass.edu
MALY, Lonn, D 651-641-8203 263 C maly@csp.edu
MALYJ, Marianne 219-980-6627 173 F mmalyj@iun.edu
MALZACHER, Valerie, I 715-425-3224 552 A valerie.i.malzacher@uwrf.edu
MAMA, Robin 732-571-3586 311 F rmama@monmouth.edu
MAMARCHEV, Helen 239-590-1022 119 A hmamarchev@fgcu.edu
MAMARIL, Liz 858-653-6740 52 C
MAMONIS, JR., Peter 619-275-4700 46 K peter@fashioncareerscollege.com
MAN, Gordon 808-734-9124 141 E goman@hawaii.edu
MANAHAN, Jamie 773-298-3329 163 G manahan@sxu.edu
MANAHAN, Richard, A 423-439-5381 473 E manahanr@etsu.edu
MANAHAN, Ronald, E 574-372-5100 171 E manahare@grace.edu
MANALO, John, F 670-234-5498 559 F johnm@nmcnet.edu
MANARO, James, V 410-778-7204 229 D jmanaro2@washcoll.edu
MANASERI, Christopher 808-455-0260 142 A cmanaser@hawaii.edu
MANAUTOU, Teresa 787-864-2222 563 D tmantou@inter.edu
MANAZIR, Theodore 802-728-1275 515 G tmanazir@vtc.vsc.edu
MANCE, Charles 724-938-1535 441 G mance@calu.edu
MANCE, Jerry 757-455-3349 529 F jmance@vwc.edu
MANCHESTER, Betsy 323-953-4000 54 H manchepb@lacitycollege.edu
MANCHESTER-MOLAK, Ann 401-865-2406 453 F ammolak@providence.edu
MANCHUR, Fred, M 937-395-8775 394 D fred.manchur@khnetwork.org
MANCINI, Donna 610-896-1230 430 G dmancini@haverford.edu
MANCINI, Fabrizio 972-438-6932 492 C fmancini@parkercc.edu
MANCINI, Lisa 636-696-2300 290 A lmancini@sbc-stpeters.com
MANCINI, Nicholas 610-785-6263 446 A nmancini@adphila.org
MANCINI-BROWN, Darlene 860-512-3660 90 C dmancini_brown@mcc.commnet.edu
MANCOSH, Bridget 412-392-3992 444 H bmancosh@pointpark.edu
MANCUSO, Tracy 928-532-6170 17 B
MANDAKOVIC, Tomislav 305-899-3532 101 F tmandakovic@mail.barry.edu
MANDALA, Jim 973-408-3395 309 F jmandala@drew.edu
MANDARINO, James 505-454-3199 318 I jfmandarino@nmhu.edu
MANDAYAM, Shreekanth 856-256-5150 314 A shreek@rowan.edu
MANDEL, Christine 315-655-7887 325 I cmandel@cazenovia.edu
MANDEL, Jeffrey 570-389-4311 441 F jmandel@bloomu.edu
MANDEL, Rhonda 315-312-2285 354 A rhonda.mandel@oswego.edu
MANDEL, Robert 323-856-7741 28 D rmandel@afi.com
MANDELKERN, Michael 714-432-5786 41 B mmandelkern@occ.cccd.edu
MANDERBACH, Kim, K 206-934-6763 537 B kim.manderbach@seattlecolleges.edu
MANDEREN, Michael, C 440-775-8413 397 F michael.manderen@oberlin.edu
MANDERSCHEID, David, C 402-472-6262 300 H dmanderschied2@unl.edu
MANDEVILLE, Dick, G 509-777-4536 539 F rmandeville@whitworth.edu
MANDEVILLE, Kenneth 304-327-4067 543 C kmandeville@bluefieldstate.edu
MANDL, Michael, J 404-727-6018 129 A michael.mandl@emory.edu
MANDOLESE, Jennifer 617-670-4468 235 B jmandolese@fisher.edu
MANDRACHIA, Florence 718-409-7342 356 C 0858mgr@fheg.follett.com
MANDRACHIA, Michael 215-641-6528 436 G mmandrac@mc3.edu
MANDRAFINA, Diane 201-447-7887 307 F dmandrafina@bergen.edu
MANDYAM, Raja 512-454-1188 480 F info@aoma.edu
MANDZIK, Carol, I 607-436-3369 353 E mandzicl@oneonta.edu
MANER, Edward 863-667-5777 118 A elmaner@seu.edu
MANERI, Wendy, L 315-568-3262 342 H wmaneri@nycc.edu
MANESS, Terry, S 254-710-1211 481 I terry_maness@baylor.edu
MANETAS, Magda 609-771-2201 308 G mmanetas@tcnj.edu
MANETAS, Peter 609-771-2323 308 G manetas@tcnj.edu
MANETH, Amber 785-227-3380 190 G manetha@bethanylb.edu
MANEV, Ivan 207-581-1968 220 A imanev@maine.edu
MANEY, Jon 803-641-3293 462 B jonm@usca.edu
MANEY, Robert, L 814-863-6188 438 F rlm1@psu.edu
MANFREDO, Francis, A 315-859-4144 335 A fmanfred@hamilton.edu
MANGAN, DeWayne 512-313-3000 483 G dewayne.mangan@concordia.edu
MANGAN, John 215-893-5252 426 E john.mangan@curtis.edu
MANGAN, Kathryn 510-567-6174 68 G kmangan@sum.edu
MANGAN, William 712-279-5402 182 E william.mangan@briarcliff.edu
MANGAN-FLOOD, Mary 920-923-7166 548 C mmanganflood@marianuniversity.edu
MANGANARO, Marc, J 509-313-5522 534 A manganaro@gonzaga.edu
MANGANELLO, Janice 973-642-8595 315 C janice.manganello@shu.edu
MANGELS, Andrew, P 413-545-2141 237 C amangels@admin.umass.edu
MANGELS, Kathy, M 573-651-2570 290 D kmangels@semo.edu
MANGELSDORF, Sarah, C 847-491-3448 160 D dean@wcas.northwestern.edu
MANGHAM, Neal 505-863-7679 321 D nmangham@gallup.unm.edu
MANGIACAPRA, Vincent, P 203-932-7058 95 B vmangiacapra@newhaven.edu
MANGINE, John, J 814-332-4356 421 E johnmangine@allegheny.edu
MANGINI, William 860-913-2005 92 C bmangini@goodwin.edu
MANGINO, Christine 718-518-6753 327 D smangino@hostos.cuny.edu
MANGIONE, Robert 718-990-6411 348 G mangionr@stjohns.edu
MANGIONE, Terri, L 716-888-2130 325 G mangiont@canisius.edu
MANGLES, Lenore 715-365-4637 554 F lmangles@nicoletcollege.edu
MANGLITZ, Elaine 678-466-5448 127 A elainemanglitz@clayton.edu
MANGLITZ, Marci 706-213-2116 124 H mmanglitz@athenstech.edu
MANGLONA, Gregorio, T 671-777-5591 559 B safety@guamcc.edu
MANGOLD, Melissa 636-651-1600 289 I mmangold@sbc-fenton.com
MANGRO, Nelly 408-934-4900 49 I nelly_mangro@heald.edu
MANGUM, Audrey 954-492-5353 102 J amangum@citycollege.edu

MARCHANT, T. Eston 919-718-7246 368 H bmarchant@cccc.edu

MARCHASE, Richard, B 205-934-1294 8 G marchase@uab.edu

MARCHBANKS, Pete 979-845-8423 497 C pete-marchbanks@tamu.edu

MARCHELLETTA, Barbara 207-947-4591 217 D bmarchelletta@bealcollege.edu

MARCHELLO, Sara, L 757-221-2801 517 J sallie.marchello@wm.edu

MARCHESE, Cynthia, C 212-687-4303 307 G ccm@berkeleycollege.edu

MARCHESE, Cynthia, C 212-687-3730 323 J ccm@berkeleycollege.edu

MARCHESE, Paul 718-631-6690 329 A pmarchese@qcc.cuny.edu

MARCHETTI, Joseph 609-652-4688 313 F joseph.marchetti@stockton.edu

MARCHEWKA, Tony 814-871-7421 429 F marchewk001@gannon.edu

MARCHILDON, Scott 207-221-4230 220 H smarchildon@une.edu

MARCHIONE, Susan, M 716-839-8447 331 G smarchio@daemen.edu

MARCHIONINI, Gary 919-962-8363 378 D gary@ils.unc.edu

MARCHIORI, Dennis, M 563-884-5500 60 L dennis.marchiori@palmer.edu

MARCHIORI, Dennis, M 563-884-5500 188 C dennis.marchiori@palmer.edu

MARCHIORI, Dennis, M 563-884-5500 114 E dennis.marchiori@palmer.edu

MARCHU, Gene 760-773-2567 41 H gmarchu@collegeofthedesert.edu

MARCI, Mark 412-281-2600 446 H mmarci@western-school.com

MARCIAL, Myriam 787-891-0925 562 G mmarcial@aguadilla.inter.edu

MARCIL, Alvina, O 680-488-2471 560 A alvinam@palau.edu

MARCIL, B.J 870-743-3000 22 G bjmarcil@northark.edu

MARCILLE, Andrea, M 868-701-6393 558 E Andrea.M.Marcille@uscg.mil

MARCIN, Heidi, C 585-785-1609 334 A marcinhc@flcc.edu

MARCINEK, Myron 570-961-4786 435 F mmarcinek@marywood.edu

MARCOCCIA, Louis, G 315-443-3037 357 B lmarcocc@syr.edu

MARCOE, Timothy 570-784-3123 441 F frtim@bloomu.edu

MARCOLINE, Beverly, J 315-792-3041 359 C bmarcoline@utica.edu

MARCONE, Luigi 203-837-9314 92 A marconel@wcsu.edu

MARCOTTE, Sharon 218-335-4253 264 I sharon.marcotte@lltc.edu

MARCUM, Jada 513-244-4955 388 D jada_marcum@mail.msj.edu

MARCUM, Judith, W 859-846-5834 204 D jmarcum@midway.edu

MARCUM, Marie 603-542-7744 304 H mmarcum@ccsnh.edu

MARCUM, Roger, L 859-336-5082 205 F rmarcum@sccky.edu

MARCUS, Dave 212-261-1651 343 D dmarcu02@nyit.edu

MARCUS, Debra 503-467-5196 414 H dmarcus@cc.edu

MARCUS, Jamie, E 207-778-7000 220 C

MARCUS, John 508-541-1508 234 B jmarcus@dean.edu

MARCUS, Lynn 978-762-4000 241 A lmarcus@northshore.edu

MARCUS, Nancy 850-644-3500 119 C nmarcus@fsu.edu

MARCUS, Robert, J 317-940-9910 170 C rmarcus@butler.edu

MARCUS, William 406-243-4154 295 A william.marcus@umontana.edu

MARCUS BURGER, Sally 304-766-3131 544 D marcussc@wvstateu.edu

MARCUS-NEWHALL, Amy 909-607-2822 69 A amy.marcus-newhall@scrippscollege.edu

MARCUSE, Adrian, G 212-752-1530 338 C adrian.marcuse@limcollege.edu

MARCUSE, Elizabeth, S 212-752-1530 338 C elizabeth.marcuse@limcollege.edu

MARCY, Mary, B 415-485-3200 45 B president@dominican.edu

MARCZYNSKI, Jerry 775-784-4898 303 A marczyns@unr.edu

MARDEN, Rose 210-341-1366 491 E rmarden@ost.edu

MARDIROSIAN, Haig 813-253-6100 122 H hmardirosian@ut.edu

MARDIS, Michael 502-852-5787 207 A mike.mardis@louisville.edu

MAREK, Cynthia 507-457-1443 271 G cmarek@smumn.edu

MAREK, Diane 847-318-8550 160 C dmarek@nc.edu

MAREK, Robin 401-232-6804 453 A rmarek@bryant.edu

MAREK, Sandra 660-263-4110 287 B sandram@macc.edu

MARES, Manuel 305-821-3333 109 A mmares@mm.fnc.edu

MARES, Manuel 305-821-3333 109 C mmares@mm.fnc.edu

MARES, Maria 787-864-2222 563 D mmares@inter.edu

MAREZ, Alice 510-436-2407 62 D amarez@peralta.edu

MARFELL, Julie 859-253-3637 200 E julie.marfell@frontier.edu

MARFISE, Larry, J 813-253-6240 122 H lmarfise@ut.edu

MARGERUM, Eric, W 812-888-5127 181 B emargerum@vinu.edu

MARGHEIM, Jeffrey 386-822-7020 121 E jmarghei@stetson.edu

MARGIOTTA, Nina 412-397-5866 445 G margiotta@rmu.edu

MARGISON, Richard, L 205-934-5493 8 G margison@uab.edu

MARGLIOTTI, Garrett, D 412-578-6010 424 G gdmargliotti@carlow.edu

MARGON, Bruce 831-459-2425 75 A margon@ucsc.edu

MARGULES, Gary, S 954-262-7507 114 B margules@nsu.nova.edu

MARGULIES, Anne 617-495-9092 235 H anne_margulies@harvard.edu

MARGULIES, L 718-853-8500 357 I

MARGULIES, Mordechai 718-854-2290 324 A

MARHAVER, Brian 315-866-1550 335 E marhavebt@herkimer.edu

MARI-MUTT, Jose, A 787-265-3810 567 C jmari@uprm.edu

MARIANI, Cynthia 860-231-5387 93 H cmariani@sjc.edu

MARIANI, Elsa 787-257-7373 565 E emariani@suagm.edu

MARIANI, Michael, A 716-625-6300 324 K mamariani@bryantstratton.edu

MARIANI, William 716-829-8194 332 F marianiw@dyc.edu

MARIANO, Anthony, A 802-485-2230 514 A tmariano@norwich.edu

MARIANS, Kenneth, J 646-888-6639 339 E kmarians@sloankettering.edu

MARICHAL-LUGO, Carlos 787-993-8866 566 G carlos.marichal@upr.edu

MARICK, Gregory, J 714-830-0250 29 K gmarick@aii.edu

MARICS, Joseph, F 417-268-1000 279 B jmarics@agts.edu

MARIGLIANO, Tom 312-752-2262 155 B thomas.marigliano@kendall.edu

MARIN, Gerardo 415-422-2199 76 B marin@usfca.edu

MARIN CRESPO, Reinaldo 787-896-2252 561 K rmarin@edpcollege.edu

MARINACCIO, Jessica 212-854-1222 330 F jm996@columbia.edu

MARINACE, Betsy 973-684-6861 312 E bmarinace@pccc.edu

MARINELLI, Bryan, D 401-865-1822 453 F bmarinel@providence.edu

MARINETTI, Mike 920-465-2454 551 A marinetm@uwgb.edu

MARINI, Jacob 212-237-8449 328 A jmarini@jjay.cuny.edu

MARINI, Janice, K 215-955-2244 448 B janice.marini@jefferson.edu

MARINI, Mario 724-589-2022 448 A mmarini@thiel.edu

MARINIS, Jeremy 419-448-3301 402 E marinisjj@tiffin.edu

MARINO, Chris 864-646-1836 461 F cmarino@tctc.edu

MARINO, Dana 616-222-1533 250 C dana.marino@cornerstone.edu

MARINO, James 856-225-6046 314 C jmarino@camden.rutgers.edu

MARINO, Lucille 785-864-7431 196 F lmarino@ku.edu

MARINO, Mary Ellen 505-438-8884 320 H maryellen@acupuncturecollege.edu

MARINO, Michael 717-295-1100 452 I michael.marino@yti.edu

MARINO, Patricia 518-262-9550 322 E marinop@mail.amc.edu

MARINO, Robert 585-389-2604 342 D rmarino9@naz.edu

MARINO, Robert 209-667-3153 36 C rmarino@csustan.edu

MARINO, Steve 831-647-6408 57 F steve.marino@miis.edu

MARINUCCI, Dorothy 718-817-3000 334 C marinucci@fordham.edu

MARION, Anne 407-628-6264 121 H amarion@teu.edu

MARION, D. Keith 803-754-4100 457 D

MARION, Joseph 504-286-5389 214 I jmarion@suno.edu

MARION, Lucy, N 706-721-3771 130 B lumarion@georgiahealth.edu

MARION, Michael 916-691-7738 56 B marionm@crc.losrios.edu

MARION, Paul 978-934-3107 237 F paul_marion@uml.edu

MARION, Paul 419-448-3413 402 E marionp@tiffin.edu

MARION, Phyllis, C 619-239-0391 37 D pmarion@cwsl.edu

MARIS, Charles 309-677-3777 145 H cmaris@bradley.edu

MARIUCCI, Robert 805-546-3210 43 F rmariucc@cuesta.edu

MARIUS, Philippe 718-982-2604 327 A philippe.marius@csi.cuny.edu

MARIX, Amy 225-578-3103 212 F

MARIZ, George 360-650-3446 539 C george.mariz@wwu.edu

MARK, Bobbi 212-854-5262 323 G bmark@barnard.edu

MARK, ASC, JoAnn 316-942-4291 195 C markj@newmanu.edu

MARK, Joseph, T 802-468-1203 515 C joe.mark@castleton.edu

MARK, Joy 620-947-3121 196 E joym@tabor.edu

MARK, Robbins 260-399-7700 180 E mrobbins@sf.edu

MARK JONES, John 903-468-8144 497 E john_markjones@tamu-commerce.edu

MARKELL, Dawn 517-338-3048 249 H dmarkell@cleary.edu

MARKER, John 831-582-4796 35 C jmarker@csumb.edu

MARKERT, Stephen 713-221-8946 503 D markerts@uhd.edu

MARKEY, John 210-341-1366 491 E eowens@ost.edu

MARKEY, Mindy 937-393-3431 401 K mmarkey@sscc.edu

MARKEY, Nanette 301-696-3620 223 C markey@hood.edu

MARKGRAF, Karl, F 715-836-4411 550 H markgraf@uwec.edu

MARKHAM, Ian, S 703-461-1701 522 C imarkham@vts.edu

MARKHAM, Joseph 770-962-7580 132 A jmarkham@gwinnetttech.edu

MARKIEWICZ, Renee, J 508-849-3333 230 C rmarkiewicz@annamaria.edu

MARKIN, Rodney 402-559-7687 301 A rmarkin@unmc.edu

MARKLE, Chris, A 570-372-4425 447 D marklec@susqu.edu

MARKLE, Elizabeth 775-831-1314 303 E emarkle@sierranevada.edu

MARKLE, Sue 412-346-2100 444 D smarkle@pia.edu

MARKLE, William, J 610-359-5113 426 G wmarkle@dccc.edu

MARKLEY, Bradley, A 717-766-2511 436 D bmarkley@messiah.edu

MARKLEY, Neil 707-664-4068 37 B neil.markley@sonoma.edu

MARKLEY, Rebecca 800-962-7682 293 B bmarkley@wma.ed

MARKMAN, Rebecca 949-851-6200 46 M rmarkman@fidm.edu

MARKOVICH, Alan 740-753-7075 392 A markovich_a@hocking.edu

MARKOVICH, Matt 415-485-9591 41 I matt.markovich@marin.edu

MARKOVICH, Sue 330-499-9600 393 I smarkov@kent.edu

MARKOW, David 207-454-1003 219 B dmarkow@wccc.me.edu

MARKOWITZ, Marianne 315-448-5040 349 C

MARKOWITZ, Michael 215-637-7700 430 H

MARKOWSKI, Vincent 201-684-7432 313 D vmarkows@ramapo.edu

MARKS, Andrea, M 210-567-7020 506 E marksa@uthscsa.edu

MARKS, Bruce 406-444-0351 294 J bmarks@mgslp.state.mt.us

MARKS, Debra, J 714-449-7463 70 G dmarks@scco.edu

MARKS, Ellen 906-487-2500 255 E ebmarks@mtu.edu

MARKS, Erica 718-260-3298 346 C emarks@poly.edu

MARKS, Ian, R 440-510-1112 386 A irmarks@bryantstratton.edu

MARKS, Janice, L 443-518-4617 223 D jmarks@howardcc.edu

MARKS, Leota 913-288-7200 193 J lmarks@kckcc.edu

MARKS, Lily 303-724-5369 88 D lily.marks@ucdenver.edu

MARKS, Mary 603-668-6706 304 E mmarks@ccsnh.edu

MARKS, Michelle 703-993-8773 519 A mmarks@gmu.edu

MARKS, Ronald 504-865-5314 215 C rmarks@tulane.edu

MARKS, RuthAnn 952-888-4777 270 F rmarks@nwhealth.edu

MARKS, William 410-293-1521 558 H pao@usna.edu

MARKSBURY, Nancy 516-299-2281 339 A nancy.marksbury@liu.edu

MARKSBURY, Rick 504-865-5555 215 C rmarksby@tulane.edu

MARKSON, Alison, W 617-333-2120 234 A amarkson1109@curry.edu

MARKULY, Mark 206-296-5330 537 F markulym@seattleu.edu

MARKWELL, Cheryl 541-245-7641 420 B cmarkwell@roguecc.edu

MARKWOOD, Christopher, L 361-825-5700 497 F chris.markwood@tamucc.edu

MARLAIRE, Natalyn, M 715-852-1399 553 F nmarlaire@cvtc.edu

MARLAND, Jaime 401-427-6954 454 B jmarland@risd.edu

MARLATT, Julie, R 815-740-2270 167 C jmarlatt@stfrancis.edu

MARLER, Dan 970-542-3157 86 A dan.marler@morgancc.edu

MARLER, Joan, H 678-717-3760 129 D jmarler@gsc.edu

MARLEY, Bernard 812-749-1404 178 D bmarley@oak.edu

MARLEY, Chad 307-778-1346 556 B cmarley@lccc.wy.edu

MARLEY, Phillip 660-263-3900 279 J pmarley@cccb.edu

MARLEY, Robert 406-994-2272 295 E rmarley@coe.montana.edu

MARLEY-FREDERICK, Christine 606-546-1364 206 F cmarley@unionky.edu

MARLIN, Nancy, A 619-594-6881 36 E nmarlin@mail.sdsu.edu

MARLINK, Terry, A 916-830-6320 29 L

MARLIS, Beth 323-860-1138 58 E bethm@mi.edu

MARLOWE, Bethany 803-323-4503 463 D marloweb@winthrop.edu

MARLOWE, June 314-991-6220 280 A jmarlowe@chamberlain.edu

MARLOWE, Mike 770-531-6332 132 J mike@laniertech.edu

MARMOLEJO, William 323-953-4000 54 H marmolwa@lacitycollege.edu

MARMON, Richard 623-935-8075 15 H rich.marmon@estrellamountain.edu

MARMUR, Michael 212-824-2215 391 E mmarmur@huc.edu

MARNICH, Darlene 412-392-3474 444 H dmarnich@pointpark.edu

MAROLDO, Brian 516-686-7449 343 D bmaroldo@nyit.edu

MARONE, Phillip, J 215-955-7750 448 B phillip.marone@jefferson.edu

MARONI, Paul, L 860-439-2044 91 E plmar@conncoll.edu

MAROTTA, Marsha 413-572-5374 239 C mmarotta@wsc.ma.edu

MAROVICH, Diana 219-785-5373 178 H dmarovich@pnc.edu

MARQUARDT, Clifford, L 740-377-2520 402 F cmark@zoominternet.net

MARQUARDT, Larry 515-271-1430 183 F larry.marquardt@dmu.edu

MARQUARDT, Scott, E 608-342-1584 551 F marquars@uwplatt.edu

MARQUART, James, W 972-883-2935 505 D marquart@utdallas.edu

MARQUES, Javier 305-348-2111 119 B javier.marques@fiu.edu

MARQUES, Jeffrey 413-775-1700 240 B marquesj@gcc.mass.edu

MARQUEZ, A. Laura 575-492-2560 319 B lmarquez@nmjc.edu

MARQUEZ, Edward 913-621-8713 192 C emarquez@donnelly.edu

MARQUEZ, Ivan 914-337-9300 331 A ivan.marquez@concordia-ny.edu

MARQUEZ, Kenneth, L 719-587-7227 80 F klmarque@adams.edu

MARQUEZ, Krishna 787-746-1400 562 C kmarquez@huertas.edu

MARQUEZ, Lonnie, G 575-835-5606 319 A lmarquez@admin.nmt.edu

MARQUEZ, Moses 505-454-2500 318 E mmarquez@luna.edu

MARQUEZ, Nora 650-843-3450 61 A nmarquez@paloaltou.edu

MARQUEZ, Norma 770-916-3712 128 E nmarquez@devry.edu

MARQUEZ, Silvia 415-703-9573 31 J smarquez@cca.edu

MARQUEZ BELL, Mary 516-876-3073 353 D bellm@oldwestbury.edu

MARTIN, Dave .... 724-852-3463 .... 451 B
dmartin@waynesburg.edu
MARTIN, David .... 570-674-6294 .... 436 F
dmartin@misericordia.edu
MARTIN, David .... 212-787-5300 .... 322 G
MARTIN, David .... 910-893-1610 .... 362 F
dmartin@campbell.edu
MARTIN, David .... 718-420-4341 .... 359 G
dmartin@wagner.edu
MARTIN, David .... 323-469-3300 .... 27 H
MARTIN, David .... 502-852-4653 .... 207 A
dcmart02@louisville.edu
MARTIN, David .... 502-852-8220 .... 207 A
dcmart02@louisville.edu
MARTIN, David .... 414-847-3213 .... 548 G
davidmartin@miad.edu
MARTIN, David, G .... 585-385-8079 .... 348 F
dmartin@sjfc.edu
MARTIN, David, W .... 605-394-2400 .... 466 A
david.martin@sdsmt.edu
MARTIN, Debbie .... 973-290-4208 .... 309 A
dmartin@cse.edu
MARTIN, Deborah .... 312-629-6800 .... 164 A
dmartin@saic.edu
MARTIN, Deborah .... 717-477-1121 .... 443 D
dkmart@ship.edu
MARTIN, Deborah, M .... 210-486-0881 .... 479 F
dmartin82@alamo.edu
MARTIN, Deidre .... 803-641-3448 .... 462 B
deidrem@usca.edu
MARTIN, Diana .... 859-246-6353 .... 201 D
diana.martin@kctcs.edu
MARTIN, Diane .... 704-463-3052 .... 375 E
diane.martin@fsmail.pfeiffer.edu
MARTIN, Diane, C .... 202-994-0511 .... 97 F
dmartin@gwu.edu
MARTIN, Donald .... 843-863-7504 .... 456 B
dmartin@csuniv.edu
MARTIN, Donald, L .... 262-554-2010 .... 158 D
dlcdcphd@comcast.net
MARTIN, Donald, L .... 262-554-2010 .... 548 F
dlcdcphd@comcast.net
MARTIN, Donna, P .... 270-901-1116 .... 201 E
donna.martin@kctcs.edu
MARTIN, Dorothy .... 718-429-6600 .... 359 E
dorothy.martin@vaughn.edu
MARTIN, Dorothy, J .... 205-348-4894 .... 8 F
dot@ua.edu
MARTIN, Earl, F .... 509-313-6289 .... 534 A
martine@gonzaga.edu
MARTIN, III, Earl Joe .... 225-752-4230 .... 208 L
jmartin@iticollege.edu
MARTIN, Edd .... 254-295-4524 .... 504 A
emartin@umhb.edu
MARTIN, Edward .... 775-445-4272 .... 303 B
marti691@wnc.edu
MARTIN, Edward .... 931-363-9832 .... 470 E
emartin@martinmethodist.edu
MARTIN, Elaine, R .... 508-856-2399 .... 238 A
elaine.martin@umassmed.edu
MARTIN, Elizabeth .... 906-487-7253 .... 251 C
beth.martin@finlandia.edu
MARTIN, Emily .... 251-580-2101 .... 5 A
emartin@faulknerstate.edu
MARTIN, Eric .... 212-752-1530 .... 338 C
eric.martin@limcollege.edu
MARTIN, Etienne .... 614-287-2491 .... 388 G
emarti10@cscc.edu
MARTIN, G. Steven .... 510-642-1508 .... 73 E
gsm@berkeley.edu
MARTIN, Gale .... 610-796-8376 .... 421 F
gale.martin@alvernia.edu
MARTIN, Geoffrey .... 419-530-1242 .... 404 F
geoffrey.martin@utoledo.edu
MARTIN, George, E .... 512-448-8411 .... 493 B
georgem@stedwards.edu
MARTIN, George, M .... 716-888-8208 .... 325 G
martin@canisius.edu
MARTIN, Gina .... 212-924-5900 .... 357 A
gina@swedishinstitute.edu
MARTIN, Greg .... 515-964-6368 .... 183 E
gcmartin@dmacc.edu
MARTIN, Gregg, F .... 717-245-4400 .... 558 D
MARTIN, Harold, L .... 336-334-7940 .... 377 F
hmartin@ncat.edu
MARTIN, Irene .... 860-343-5740 .... 90 D
imartin@mxcc.commnet.edu
MARTIN, Jack .... 815-967-7302 .... 162 G
jmartin@rockfordcareercollege.edu
MARTIN, James .... 409-747-9055 .... 507 B
j5martin@utmb.edu
MARTIN, James, J .... 501-882-8851 .... 20 D
jjmartin@asub.edu
MARTIN, Jan .... 323-469-3300 .... 27 H
MARTIN, Jan .... 212-787-5300 .... 322 G
MARTIN, Jana .... 918-293-5339 .... 410 E
jana.s.martin@okstate.edu
MARTIN, Jaye .... 502-897-4085 .... 205 H
jmartin@sbts.edu
MARTIN, Jennifer .... 940-898-3415 .... 502 B
jmartin@twu.edu
MARTIN, Jessica .... 323-241-5270 .... 55 C
martinjm@lasc.edu
MARTIN, Jill .... 800-567-2344 .... 546 G
jmartin@menominee.edu
MARTIN, Jim .... 248-340-0600 .... 248 E
james.martin@baker.edu
MARTIN, Jim David .... 415-575-6165 .... 32 D
jmartin@ciis.edu
MARTIN, Jimmy .... 832-813-6680 .... 490 C
james.d.martin@lonestar.edu
MARTIN, Joel, W .... 413-545-6330 .... 237 C
jmartin@provost.umass.edu
MARTIN, John .... 860-486-2709 .... 94 E
jmartin@foundation.uconn.edu
MARTIN, John .... 502-597-6242 .... 203 D
john.martin@kysu.edu
MARTIN, John .... 916-631-8108 .... 33 C
MARTIN, John .... 208-769-3316 .... 143 H
jfmartin@nic.edu
MARTIN, John, A .... 585-594-6100 .... 347 F
presidentsoffice@roberts.edu
MARTIN, John, A .... 585-594-6100 .... 344 F
presidentsoffice@roberts.edu
MARTIN, John, O .... 413-545-0361 .... 237 C
jomartin@admin.umass.edu
MARTIN, John, R .... 318-487-5443 .... 210 C
jmartin@ltc.edu
MARTIN, JR., John, R .... 817-515-7765 .... 496 A
john.martin@tccd.edu
MARTIN, John, U .... 941-487-4444 .... 119 D
jmartin@ncf.edu
MARTIN, Joshua .... 508-854-7513 .... 241 C
jmartin@qcc.mass.edu
MARTIN, Joshua .... 417-833-2551 .... 279 I
jmartin@cbcag.edu
MARTIN, Juanita, K .... 330-972-7082 .... 403 B
juanita@uakron.edu
MARTIN, Jules .... 212-998-1300 .... 344 B
jules.martin@nyu.edu
MARTIN, Julie .... 802-322-1622 .... 513 C
julie.martin@goddard.edu
MARTIN, Karen, O .... 912-279-5750 .... 127 B
kmartin@ccga.edu
MARTIN, Katherine .... 336-841-9000 .... 365 A
kmartin@highpoint.edu
MARTIN, Kathy .... 704-406-4636 .... 364 B
kmartin@gardner-webb.edu
MARTIN, Kathy .... 208-792-2282 .... 143 F
kmartin@lcsc.edu
MARTIN, Kathy .... 712-274-5148 .... 187 D
martink@morningside.edu
MARTIN, Kathy .... 615-963-5254 .... 474 A
kmartin@tnstate.edu
MARTIN, Keith .... 918-343-7631 .... 411 H
kmartin@rsu.edu
MARTIN, Kelley .... 906-487-7230 .... 251 C
kelley.martin@finlandia.edu
MARTIN, Ken, E .... 252-222-6243 .... 368 F
kem@carteret.edu
MARTIN, Kenneth .... 903-875-7307 .... 491 B
kenneth.martin@navarrocollege.edu
MARTIN, Kenneth, M .... 717-815-1211 .... 452 F
kmartin@ycp.edu
MARTIN, Kevin .... 302-225-6241 .... 96 E
martink@gbc.edu
MARTIN, Kevin .... 618-650-2345 .... 165 A
kemartin@siue.edu
MARTIN, Krystal, N .... 501-882-8906 .... 20 D
knmartin@asub.edu
MARTIN, Kyle, R .... 208-496-1010 .... 142 G
martink@byui.edu
MARTIN, Lance, E .... 706-886-6831 .... 137 G
lmartin@tfc.edu
MARTIN, Laura .... 404-471-6000 .... 123 G
MARTIN, Lawrence .... 631-632-7035 .... 352 C
lawrence.martin@stonybrook.edu
MARTIN, Leandra .... 408-288-3716 .... 67 C
leandra.martin@sjcc.edu
MARTIN, Lee .... 419-448-2169 .... 391 G
lmartin@heidelberg.edu
MARTIN, Leigh, S .... 770-720-5634 .... 135 F
lsm@reinhardt.edu
MARTIN, Linda .... 609-586-4800 .... 311 C
martinl@mccc.edu
MARTIN, Lisa .... 504-865-3428 .... 213 F
lmartin@loyno.edu
MARTIN, Lisa .... 918-343-7614 .... 411 H
lmartin@rsu.edu
MARTIN, Lizbeth, J .... 510-436-1040 .... 50 F
martin@hnu.edu
MARTIN, Lois .... 612-977-5307 .... 262 A
lois.martin@capella.edu
MARTIN, Louisa .... 603-668-2211 .... 306 B
l.martin@snhu.edu
MARTIN, Louisa, A .... 210-431-5005 .... 493 C
lmartin@stmarytx.edu
MARTIN, Lynn .... 734-973-3507 .... 260 B
lgmartin@wccnet.edu
MARTIN, Lynn .... 515-271-1681 .... 183 F
lynn.martin@dmu.edu
MARTIN, Maggie .... 229-391-5135 .... 123 F
mmartin@abac.edu
MARTIN, Malissa .... 513-244-4542 .... 388 D
malissa_martin@mail.msj.edu
MARTIN, Marcus, L .... 434-243-2079 .... 525 B
mlm8n@Virginia.EDU
MARTIN, Marie .... 651-604-4131 .... 265 D
MARTIN, Marie .... 803-780-1229 .... 463 B
martin@voorhees.edu
MARTIN, Mariel, L .... 518-580-8212 .... 351 B
mariel@skidmore.edu
MARTIN, Mark, A .... 248-204-2126 .... 254 E
mmartin@ltu.edu
MARTIN, Mark, A .... 989-837-4497 .... 257 A
martinm@northwood.edu
MARTIN, Michael .... 212-636-6875 .... 334 C
mimartin@law.fordham.edu
MARTIN, Michael .... 408-541-0100 .... 41 C
mmartin@cogswell.edu
MARTIN, Michael .... 918-647-1361 .... 407 E
mmartin@carlalbert.edu
MARTIN, Michael, V .... 225-578-6977 .... 212 F
chancellor@lsu.edu
MARTIN, Michele .... 802-586-7711 .... 514 E
mmartin@sterlingcollege.edu
MARTIN, Michelle .... 609-894-9311 .... 308 C
mmartin@bcc.edu
MARTIN, Michelle, D .... 757-823-8275 .... 521 K
mdmartin@nsu.edu
MARTIN, Mirta, M .... 804-524-5166 .... 529 C
mmartin@vsu.edu
MARTIN, Mona .... 310-434-4692 .... 68 D
martin_mona@smc.edu
MARTIN, Norman, D .... 708-709-7834 .... 161 C
nomartin@prairiestate.edu
MARTIN, Pamela .... 641-673-1182 .... 189 I
martinp@wmpenn.edu
MARTIN, Pamela, S .... 217-245-3046 .... 152 C
psmartin@ic.edu
MARTIN, Patricia .... 507-786-3009 .... 271 H
martinp@stolaf.edu
MARTIN, Patricia, A .... 937-775-3133 .... 406 C
patricia.martin@wright.edu
MARTIN, Paul .... 518-276-8711 .... 347 D
martip@rpi.edu
MARTIN, Paul .... 617-730-7155 .... 243 I
paul.martin@newbury.edu
MARTIN, Paul .... 510-841-1905 .... 27 J
pmartin@absw.edu
MARTIN, Peggy Murray .... 305-626-3749 .... 108 H
pmartin@fmuniv.edu
MARTIN, Peter, A .... 386-763-2651 .... 114 E
peter.martin@palmer.edu
MARTIN, Quincy .... 708-456-0300 .... 166 C
qmartin@triton.edu
MARTIN, Rafael .... 972-883-4824 .... 505 D
rafael.martin@utdallas.edu
MARTIN, Randy .... 870-972-2093 .... 20 C
rmartin@astate.edu
MARTIN, Ray .... 254-295-4590 .... 504 A
rmartin@umhb.edu
MARTIN, Richard, D .... 706-776-0105 .... 135 D
dmartin@piedmont.edu
MARTIN, Robert .... 810-766-8756 .... 248 H
robert.martin@baker.edu
MARTIN, Robert .... 845-758-7419 .... 323 F
martin@bard.edu
MARTIN, Robert .... 505-424-2302 .... 318 C
rmartin@iaia.edu
MARTIN, Robert, C .... 989-774-3368 .... 249 G
martin1rc@cmich.edu
MARTIN, Robert, E .... 303-233-4697 .... 82 G
robt@schooloftrades.com
MARTIN, Robert, K .... 217-581-5983 .... 150 C
rmartin@eiu.edu
MARTIN, Ron .... 618-262-8641 .... 152 I
martinr@iecc.edu
MARTIN, Ron .... 417-690-3248 .... 280 C
martin@cofo.edu
MARTIN, Ronald, C .... 814-732-2743 .... 442 D
martinr@edinboro.edu
MARTIN, Rosalynn .... 256-782-5007 .... 4 L
martin@jsu.edu
MARTIN, Roy, J .... 225-578-2284 .... 212 F
rjmartin@lsu.edu
MARTIN, Ruth .... 619-201-8685 .... 65 D
Ruth.Martin@sdcc.edu
MARTIN, Ryan .... 201-360-4024 .... 310 F
rmartin@hccc.edu
MARTIN, Sally, L .... 920-498-6866 .... 555 A
sally.martin@nwtc.edu
MARTIN, Scott .... 706-355-5037 .... 124 H
smartin@athenstech.edu
MARTIN, Shane .... 310-338-7457 .... 56 E
smartin@lmu.edu
MARTIN, Sherry, J .... 251-809-1532 .... 5 B
sherry.martin@jdcc.edu
MARTIN, Staci .... 903-983-8200 .... 489 F
smartin@kilgore.edu
MARTIN, Stephen, A .... 334-727-8531 .... 8 C
smartin@mytu.tuskegee.edu
MARTIN, Susan .... 734-487-2211 .... 250 H
sue.martin@emich.edu
MARTIN, Susan, D .... 865-974-2445 .... 477 B
sdmartin@utk.edu
MARTIN, RN, Susan, E .... 828-884-8244 .... 362 D
martinse@brevard.edu
MARTIN, Susan, M .... 630-942-3324 .... 147 G
martinsu@cod.edu
MARTIN, Susan, M .... 540-868-7087 .... 526 H
smartin@lfcc.edu
MARTIN, Susie .... 310-377-5501 .... 56 F
smartin@marymountpv.edu
MARTIN, Suzanne .... 985-858-5744 .... 210 H
smartin@ftcc.edu
MARTIN, Suzanne, B .... 513-529-3831 .... 396 D
sue.martin@muohio.edu
MARTIN, Terry .... 318-487-7201 .... 209 B
martin@lacollege.edu
MARTIN, Terry .... 321-433-7000 .... 101 J
martint@brevardcc.edu
MARTIN, Theodore, D .... 845-938-3103 .... 558 G
8uscc@usma.edu
MARTIN, Theresa, M .... 201-559-6022 .... 310 C
martint@felician.edu
MARTIN, Thomas, K .... 972-758-3817 .... 483 D
tmartin@collin.edu
MARTIN, Timothy, J .... 515-574-1097 .... 185 F
martin@iowacentral.edu
MARTIN, Timothy, R .... 508-767-7373 .... 230 E
timartin@assumption.edu
MARTIN, Tod, J .... 402-363-5678 .... 301 F
tjmartin@york.edu
MARTIN, Todd .... 561-803-2127 .... 114 C
todd_martin@pba.edu
MARTIN, Tom .... 361-593-3419 .... 498 A
katdm00@tamuk.edu
MARTIN, Tony, L .... 336-386-3222 .... 374 B
martint@surry.edu
MARTIN, Traci .... 410-337-6191 .... 222 I
tmartin@goucher.edu
MARTIN, Troy, R .... 585-567-9328 .... 336 B
troy.martin@houghton.edu
MARTIN, Valerie, G .... 570-372-4288 .... 447 D
vmartin@susqu.edu
MARTIN, Vicki, J .... 414-297-7269 .... 554 D
martinv@matc.edu
MARTIN, Wayne .... 540-453-2347 .... 525 G
martinw@brcc.edu
MARTIN, Wendy .... 207-859-1101 .... 219 G
martinw@thomas.edu
MARTIN, Wendy .... 909-607-0723 .... 40 C
wendy.martin@cgu.edu
MARTIN, William .... 225-675-8270 .... 211 J
bmartin@rpcc.edu
MARTIN, William, E .... 724-836-9927 .... 449 C
wem1@pitt.edu
MARTIN, William, J .... 570-326-3761 .... 440 K
bmartin@pct.edu
MARTIN-HALL, Margaret .... 870-575-8702 .... 25 B
hallm@uapb.edu
MARTIN II, Ralph, C .... 617-373-2101 .... 244 A
MARTIN-OSORIO,
Carol, J .... 615-353-3268 .... 475 D
carol.martin-osorio@nscc.edu
MARTIN PALMER,
Barbara .... 301-447-5371 .... 225 A
palmer@msmary.edu
MARTIN-REND, Jill .... 814-653-8265 .... 423 F
jill.martin-rend@bc3.edu
MARTIN-SCHRAMM,
Karen, B .... 563-387-1527 .... 187 A
marschka@luther.edu
MARTIN TSE, Jennifer .... 315-464-4604 .... 352 E
martinj@upstate.edu
MARTIN-VEGA, Louis, A .... 919-515-2311 .... 378 B
louis_martin-vega@ncsu.edu
MARTINDALE, Ginger .... 480-517-8175 .... 16 C
ginger.martindale@riosalado.edu
MARTINDELL, Donald, K .... 312-329-4451 .... 158 H
dmartindell@moody.edu
MARTINE, Brian, J .... 256-824-2337 .... 9 A
brian.martine@uah.edu
MARTINEAU, Jim .... 503-594-3271 .... 415 A
jmartineau@clackamas.edu
MARTINELLI, Joseph, L .... 301-322-0417 .... 225 F
martinjl@pgcc.edu
MARTINELLI, Robert, J .... 916-558-2120 .... 56 D
martinr@scc.losrios.edu
MARTINELLI-FERNANDEZ,
Susan .... 309-298-1828 .... 168 A
martinelli-fernandez@wiu.edu
MARTINELLO, Peter .... 859-282-9999 .... 203 G
pmartinello@lincolntech.com
MARTINESI, Anthony .... 718-390-3165 .... 359 G
tmartine@wagner.edu
MARTINETTI, Roseann .... 570-702-8919 .... 431 K
rmartinetti@johnson.edu
MARTINEZ, Abelardo .... 787-276-8240 .... 566 H
abelardo.martinez@upr.edu
MARTINEZ, Ailin .... 787-480-2439 .... 561 D
aimartinez@sanjuancapital.com
MARTINEZ, Betty .... 863-686-1444 .... 105 I
bmartine@cci.edu
MARTINEZ, Carlos .... 817-531-4959 .... 502 A
cmartinez@txwes.edu
MARTINEZ, Carmella .... 505-747-2118 .... 320 A
carmella@nnmc.edu
MARTINEZ, Carriann .... 719-549-3056 .... 87 B
carriann.martinez@pueblocc.edu
MARTINEZ, Charles .... 541-346-3175 .... 419 B
vpdivers@uoregon.edu
MARTINEZ, Cristina .... 830-792-7281 .... 494 A
cimartinez@schreiner.edu

MASON, Mary Ellen .... 410-777-2707.... 221 B
memason@aacc.edu
MASON, Mary Jo .... 203-371-7955.... 93 G
masonm@sacredheart.edu
MASON, Matthew .... 717-560-8254.... 433 D
mmason@lbc.edu
MASON, Michael .... 636-949-4978.... 284 C
mmason@lindenwood.edu
MASON, Natasha .... 912-583-3291.... 126 C
nmason@bpc.edu
MASON, Phil .... 912-279-5710.... 127 B
pmason@ccga.edu
MASON, Phyllis .... 740-245-7228.... 404 E
pmason@rio.edu
MASON, Rachel .... 562-860-2451...... 38 J
rmason@cerritos.edu
MASON, Rick .... 606-242-0138.... 203 A
rick.mason@kctcs.edu
MASON, Rochelle .... 719-389-6800...... 81 L
rmason@coloradocollege.edu
MASON, Ron .... 203-837-8736...... 92 A
masonr@wcsu.edu
MASON, Ronald .... 203-582-3950...... 93 E
ronaldv.p.mason@quinnipiac.edu
MASON, JR., Ronald, F .... 225-771-4680.... 214 G
ronald_mason@sus.edu
MASON, JR., Russell, D ... 701-627-4738.... 380 F
rmason@fbcc.bia.edu
MASON, Sally .... 319-335-3549.... 182 C
sally-mason@uiowa.edu
MASON, Stephen .... 502-597-6260.... 203 D
stephen.mason@kysu.edu
MASON, Steven, D .... 903-233-3230.... 489 K
stevenmason@letu.edu
MASON, Terry, W .... 515-294-5056.... 182 B
oriole@iastate.edu
MASON, Thelma .... 212-650-5816.... 326 H
tmason@ccny.cuny.edu
MASON, Tisa .... 785-628-4277.... 192 F
tmason@fhsu.edu
MASON, Trisha .... 207-602-2451.... 220 H
tmason@une.edu
MASON, William, F .... 315-386-7777.... 355 D
masonw@canton.edu
MASON JENNINGS,
Martha .... 269-749-7644.... 257 D
mjennings@olivetcollege.edu
MASON-JOHNSON,
Angela .... 312-942-7100.... 163 B
angela_mason-johnson@rush.edu
MASON-KINSEY,
Natalie, L .... 718-951-4128.... 326 G
nmasonkinsey@brooklyn.cuny.edu
MASOUM, Nazi .... 949-794-9090...... 71 E
nazim@stanbridge.edu
MASS, Gregory .... 973-596-5745.... 312 C
mass@njit.edu
MASSA, Gary, R .... 513-745-3335.... 406 E
massag@xavier.edu
MASSA, Kenneth .... 901-321-3307.... 467 G
kmassa@cbu.edu
MASSA, Laurie .... 216-397-4661.... 392 M
lmassa@jcu.edu
MASSA, Margot .... 808-974-7348.... 141 A
margota@hawaii.edu
MASSA, Robert, J .... 610-330-5120.... 433 B
massar@lafayette.edu
MASSA, Tina .... 518-587-2100.... 355 F
tina.massa@esc.edu
MASSANO, Donna, R .... 508-999-8043.... 237 E
dmassano@umassd.edu
MASSARI, Lydia, I .... 787-751-0178.... 565 D
ac_lmassari@suagm.edu
MASSARI, Mark .... 805-893-3400...... 74 F
mark.massari@athletics.ucsb.edu
MASSARO, Chris John .... 615-898-2450.... 473 F
cmassaro@mtsu.edu
MASSARO, Patrick, W ...... 724-287-8711.... 423 F
patrick.massaro@bc3.edu
MASSARO, Vincent .... 212-343-1234.... 341 B
vmassaro@mcny.edu
MASSARONI, Larry .... 914-606-7895.... 360 D
larry.massaroni@sunywcc.edu
MASSE, Carol .... 414-847-3270.... 548 G
carolmasse@miad.edu
MASSE, Joni .... 303-530-2100...... 81 E
jmasse@bcmt.org
MASSE, Michelle .... 225-578-4807.... 212 F
mmasse@lsu.edu
MASSE, Raymond .... 207-755-5258.... 218 G
rmasse@cmcc.edu
MASSE, Wendy .... 860-434-5232...... 93 A
wmasse@lymeacademy.edu
MASSELL, Krista .... 706-379-3111.... 139 F
klmassell@yhc.edu
MASSENA, James, R .... 269-471-3307.... 247 H
massenaj@andrews.edu
MASSENBURG, Gerald .... 973-353-5541.... 314 E
geraldm@andromeda.rutgers.edu
MASSENGALE, Kathy .... 505-662-5919.... 321 E
kmasseng@unm.edu
MASSEY, Anne .... 812-855-2809.... 173 C
amassey@indiana.edu
MASSEY, April .... 202-274-5591...... 99 F
amassey@udc.edu
MASSEY, Bethany .... 615-966-6302.... 470 D
bethany.massey@lipscomb.edu
MASSEY, David .... 503-883-2259.... 416 G
dmassey@linfield.edu
MASSEY, Dennis .... 252-493-7220.... 372 E
dmassey@email.pittcc.edu
MASSEY, Diane .... 610-647-4400.... 431 B
dmassey@immaculata.edu
MASSEY, Edwin, R .... 772-462-4701.... 110 L
emassey@irsc.edu
MASSEY, Gary .... 573-875-7756.... 280 E
gamassey@ccis.edu
MASSEY, Janet .... 610-358-4260.... 437 C
jmassey@neumann.edu
MASSEY, Laura .... 503-614-7700.... 419 G
laura.massey@pcc.edu
MASSEY, Marge .... 972-279-6511.... 479 I
mmassey@amberton.edu
MASSEY, Michael .... 919-209-2087.... 371 C
mtmassey@johnstoncc.edu
MASSEY, Pamela, L .... 501-450-3237...... 25 H
pamm@uca.edu
MASSEY, Perry, A .... 910-672-1475.... 377 E
pmassey@uncfsu.edu
MASSEY, Rufus .... 706-368-6945.... 125 G
wmassey@berry.edu
MASSEY, Sandra .... 870-512-7841...... 20 F
sandra_massey@asun.edu
MASSEY, Therisa .... 281-873-0262.... 483 E
library@commonwealth.edu
MASSEY, Thomas, P .... 508-793-7408.... 233 C
tmassey@clarku.edu
MASSEY, Walter .... 312-899-5136.... 164 A
wmassey@saic.edu
MASSEY, Walter, T .... 404-413-3407.... 131 C
wmassey@gsu.edu
MASSI, Christopher, A ...... 301-846-2479.... 222 G
cmassi@frederick.edu
MASSIE, Chase .... 580-581-2245.... 407 D
cmassie@cameron.edu
MASSIE, Maribeth .... 207-221-4519.... 220 H
bmassie@une.edu
MASSIE, Matt .... 937-512-2772.... 401 J
matt.massie@sinclair.edu
MASSIE, Patricia .... 606-759-7141.... 202 D
patee.massie@kctcs.edu
MASSIE, Timmian .... 845-575-3000.... 340 C
timmian.massie@marist.edu
MASSING, Lisa .... 850-201-6065.... 121 F
massingl@tcc.fl.edu
MASSIS, Bruce .... 614-287-2461.... 388 G
bmassis@cscc.edu
MASSMAN, Joseph .... 816-654-7105.... 283 J
jmassman@kcumb.edu
MASSOELS, William .... 219-866-6184.... 179 B
billm@saintjoe.edu
MASSON, Mary .... 802-654-2234.... 514 B
mmasson@smcvt.edu
MASSUCCO, Julie .... 802-241-3378.... 515 B
julie.massucco@vsc.edu
MAST, Amy, H .... 330-684-8982.... 403 C
amast1@uakron.edu
MAST, Gregg, A .... 732-247-5241.... 312 A
gmast@nbts.edu
MAST, Maura .... 617-287-6330.... 237 D
maura.mast@umb.edu
MAST, Russell, F .... 229-333-5941.... 138 F
rmast@valdosta.edu
MAST HEWITT, Marilyn ..... 630-620-2136.... 160 B
registrar@seminary.edu
MAST HEWITT, Marilyn, R 630-620-2196.... 160 B
registrar@seminary.edu
MASTANDUNO, Michael ... 603-646-3999.... 305 A
michael.mastanduno@dartmouth.edu
MASTELLER, John, Q .... 805-525-4417...... 72 E
jmasteller@thomasaquinas.edu
MASTERNAK, Donald .... 517-629-0350.... 247 E
dmasternak@albion.edu
MASTERS, Bradley .... 318-345-9239.... 210 I
misit@ladelta.edu
MASTERS, Carolyn, B .... 814-871-7605.... 429 F
masters004@gannon.edu
MASTERS, Deborah, C .... 415-338-1681...... 36 F
dmasters@sfsu.edu
MASTERS, Debra, G .... 405-466-2952.... 408 G
dgmasters@lunet.edu
MASTERS, Janelle .... 701-224-5525.... 382 B
janelle.masters@bismarckstate.edu
MASTERS, Karen .... 617-296-8300.... 236 E
karen_masters@laboure.edu
MASTERS, Rebecca .... 803-323-2225.... 463 D
mastersr@winthrop.edu
MASTERSON, Ana .... 928-757-0860...... 16 G
amasterson@mohave.edu
MASTERSON, Christine ..... 425-602-3015.... 530 K
cmasters@bastyr.edu
MASTERSON, John, A .... 620-365-5116.... 190 A
masterson@allencc.edu
MASTERSON, Lisanne .... 828-694-1806.... 368 B
lisannem@blueridge.edu
MASTERSON, Regina .... 212-650-7908.... 326 H
rmasterson@ccny.cuny.edu
MASTERSON, Robert .... 559-730-3862...... 42 B
bobm@cos.edu
MASTERSON, Thomas, J ... 989-774-1850.... 249 G
maste1tj@cmich.edu
MASTRANGELO, Joseph ..... 212-799-5000.... 337 H
MASTRE, Tom, M .... 831-656-1095.... 557 H
tmastre@nps.edu
MASTRINE, Bettye Jo .... 330-263-2139.... 388 E
bmastrine@wooster.edu
MASTRO, Steve .... 707-654-1074...... 32 I
smastro@csum.edu
MASTROIANNI, Michael ..... 815-921-2195.... 162 F
m.mastroianni@rockvalleycollege.edu
MASTROMARINO, Daniel .. 718-409-7381.... 356 C
dmastromarino@sunymaritime.edu
MASTROMONICO, Jeff ...... 803-641-2837.... 462 B
jeffm@usca.edu
MASUDA, Walter .... 530-741-6761...... 80 E
wmasuda@yccd.edu
MASULLO, Sharon .... 215-567-7080.... 422 C
smasullo@edmc.edu
MASUTANI, Carol .... 808-734-9528.... 141 E
masutani@hawaii.edu
MATA, Armando .... 773-907-4360.... 147 A
amata@ccc.edu
MATA, Cindy .... 956-364-4647.... 499 J
cindy.mata@harlingen.tstc.edu
MATA, Margaret .... 325-942-2012.... 480 E
margaret.mata@angelo.edu
MATA, Sherri .... 817-531-6552.... 502 A
smata@txwes.edu
MATACHEK, John .... 651-523-2252.... 264 C
jmatachek@hamline.edu
MATANYI, Eric, J .... 708-534-4044.... 151 C
ematanyi@govst.edu
MATE, Robert, L .... 765-494-5860.... 178 F
rmate@purdue.edu
MATECHEN, John .... 724-653-2218.... 427 F
jmatechen@dec.edu
MATEI, Eugen .... 626-584-5298...... 48 A
MATEJKOVIC, Edward, M .. 610-436-3555.... 443 F
ematejkovic@wcupa.edu
MATERN, Cindy, L .... 509-527-5172.... 539 E
matern@whitman.edu
MATHENA, Cindy .... 904-826-0084.... 122 G
cmathena@usa.edu
MATHENEY, H. Scott .... 630-617-3025.... 150 F
hscottm@elmhurst.edu
MATHENY, Christopher ..... 920-735-2401.... 553 G
matheny@fvtc.edu
MATHENY, Jacqueline, S .. 716-932-2541.... 340 E
jacqueline.s.matheny@medaille.edu
MATHENY, Kevin .... 503-493-6521.... 415 E
kmatheny@cu-portland.edu
MATHENY, Stephen .... 828-286-3636.... 371 A
smatheny@isothermal.edu
MATHER, Bruce, J .... 630-617-3178.... 150 F
brucem@elmhurst.edu
MATHER, Jannah, H .... 801-581-6194.... 510 L
jmather@socwk.utah.edu
MATHER, Kim .... 978-867-4246.... 235 E
kim.mather@gordon.edu
MATHER, William .... 407-888-4000.... 113 A
wmather@orlando.chefs.edu
MATHERLY, Cathy .... 276-326-4348.... 516 I
cmatherly@bluefield.edu
MATHERLY, Cheryl .... 918-631-3225.... 413 F
cheryl-matherly@utulsa.edu
MATHERS, Jill .... 402-474-5315.... 298 E
jmathers@kaplanuniversity.edu
MATHERSON, Akua, J .... 336-334-7631.... 377 F
amathers@ncat.edu
MATHES, James .... 850-644-1841.... 119 C
jmathes@admin.fsu.edu
MATHES, Jennifer .... 314-991-6430.... 281 G
jmathes@devry.edu
MATHES, Leon .... 504-865-3148.... 213 F
mathes@loyno.edu
MATHESON, Marian, F ...... 413-542-5187.... 230 A
mfmatheson@amherst.edu
MATHESON, Regina, M ...... 563-333-5838.... 188 D
MATHEU, Federico, M ...... 787-766-1717.... 565 G
um_fmatheu@suagm.edu
MATHEW, Bruce, E .... 608-785-9214.... 555 D
mathewb@westerntc.edu
MATHEW, Prakash, C .... 701-231-7701.... 381 H
prakash.mathew@ndsu.edu
MATHEW, Roy .... 915-747-5117.... 505 E
rmathew@utep.edu
MATHEW, Thomson .... 918-495-7016.... 411 C
tmathew@oru.edu
MATHEWS, Beth .... 912-688-6016.... 134 H
bmathews@ogeecheetech.edu
MATHEWS, Bill .... 334-683-5156........ 5 D
bmathews@judson.edu
MATHEWS, Carla, R .... 248-341-2188.... 257 B
crmathew@oaklandcc.edu
MATHEWS, Darren .... 970-247-7428...... 84 G
mathews_d@fortlewis.edu
MATHEWS, David, M .... 269-782-1270.... 258 E
president@swmich.edu
MATHEWS, Jeanne .... 706-236-2226.... 125 G
jmathews@berry.edu
MATHEWS, Jennifer .... 508-565-1915.... 245 D
jmathews@stonehill.edu
MATHEWS, Karen .... 937-376-6076.... 386 H
kmathews@centralstate.edu
MATHEWS, Marc .... 859-233-8100.... 206 E
mmathews@transy.edu
MATHEWS, Paul .... 410-234-4622.... 225 E
MATHEWS, Rebecca, B .... 618-537-6940.... 157 G
rbmathews@mckendree.edu
MATHEWS, Stacy .... 601-984-1117.... 277 H
smathews@umc.edu
MATHIAS, Carol, A .... 985-448-4646.... 216 A
carol.mathias@nicholls.edu
MATHIAS, Paul .... 610-917-2007.... 450 D
pmathias@vfcc.edu
MATHIASEN, Rebecca .... 402-354-7034.... 299 E
rebecca.mathiasen@methodistcollege.edu
MATHIE, Craig .... 435-283-7100.... 512 B
craig.mathie@snow.edu
MATHIES, Bonnie .... 419-586-0341.... 406 C
bonnie.mathies@wright.edu
MATHIES, Bonnie .... 419-586-0321.... 406 D
bonnie.mathies@wright.edu
MATHIES, Richard .... 510-642-4192...... 73 E
rich@zinc.cchem.berkeley.edu
MATHIESEN, Gaylan .... 218-739-3375.... 264 K
gmathiesen@lbs.edu
MATHIEU, David, J .... 612-312-1269.... 272 F
david.mathieu@waldenu.edu
MATHIEU, Dickens .... 617-627-3336.... 245 F
dickens.mathieu@tufts.edu
MATHIOS, Alan, D .... 607-255-2589.... 331 C
adm5@cornell.edu
MATHIS, Bob, D .... 512-863-1425.... 495 G
bmathis@southwestern.edu
MATHIS, Carolyn .... 626-529-8437...... 60 G
cmathis@pacificoaks.edu
MATHIS, Claude .... 915-831-2857.... 486 E
cmathis1@epcc.edu
MATHIS, Clay, P .... 361-593-5401.... 498 A
clay.mathis@tamuk.edu
MATHIS, Jennifer, M .... 864-388-8307.... 458 J
jmathis@lander.edu
MATHIS, Jon .... 503-255-0332.... 417 C
jmathis@multnomah.edu
MATHIS, Kala .... 931-553-0071.... 471 G
kala.mathis@miller-motte.com
MATHIS, Martha .... 802-485-2640.... 514 A
martham@norwich.edu
MATHIS, Maureen .... 610-660-1306.... 446 C
mmathis@sju.edu
MATHIS, Richard .... 601-403-1175.... 277 A
rmathis@prcc.edu
MATHIS, Sabrina, K .... 270-809-3279.... 204 F
sabrina.mathis@murraystate.edu
MATHIS, Shawn .... 501-450-1333...... 22 A
mathis@hendrix.edu
MATHIS, Teri .... 229-391-5045.... 123 F
tmathis@abac.edu
MATHIS, Tina .... 559-438-4222...... 49 G
tina_mathis@heald.edu
MATHIS-STUMP, Becky, D 304-865-6021.... 541 F
becky.mathis-stump@ovu.edu
MATHISON HANCE,
Marjorie .... 651-690-6516.... 271 E
mmhance@stkate.edu
MATHO, Diego, L .... 617-262-5000.... 232 B
diego.matho@the-bac.edu
MATHWEG, Cathy, M .... 920-923-8138.... 548 C
cmathweg@marianuniversity.edu
MATIENZO-CARRERO,
Ivonne .... 787-764-0000.... 567 F
ivonne.matienzo@upr.edu
MATIJEVIC, Patricia .... 970-339-6374...... 80 G
pat.matijevic@aims.edu
MATILDA, Mecca .... 831-476-9424...... 47 E
finaid@fivebranches.edu
MATIS, Michael .... 207-255-1237.... 220 E
mmatis@maine.edu
MATISON, Kim .... 253-566-5194.... 538 C
kmatison@tacomacc.edu
MATISTA, Theresa .... 916-568-3164...... 55 J
matistt@losrios.edu
MATITIA, Abraham .... 440-943-5300.... 401 D
MATKIN, Gary, W .... 949-824-5525...... 73 H
gmatkin@uci.edu
MATKIN, Neil .... 281-476-1501.... 493 E
neil.matkin@sjcd.edu
MATKOWSKI, Bette .... 303-256-9462...... 85 H
bmatkowski@jwu.edu
MATLAK, Richard, E .... 508-793-2497.... 233 D
rmatlak@holycross.edu
MATLOCK, David, N .... 276-739-2473.... 528 D
dmatlock@vhcc.edu
MATLOCK, Jack .... 501-975-8522...... 23 B
jmatlock@philander.edu
MATLOCK, John .... 405-425-5500.... 409 E
john.matlock@oc.edu
MATLOCK, John, H .... 734-936-1055.... 259 D
matlock@umich.edu
MATLOCK, Kathy .... 910-642-7141.... 373 G
kmatlock@sccnc.edu
MATNEY, Bob .... 419-755-4705.... 397 B
bmatney@ncstatecollege.edu
MATNEY, Paul .... 806-371-5123.... 479 H
jpmatney@actx.edu

MAXSON, Robert 785-243-1435 191 H
rmaxson@cloud.edu
MAXWELL, Alice 850-201-6049 121 F
maxwella@tcc.fl.edu
MAXWELL, Barbara 480-219-6009 278 F
bmaxwell@atsu.edu
MAXWELL, Bruce 606-783-9575 204 E
b.maxwell@moreheadstate.edu
MAXWELL, Bruce 509-682-6835 539 B
bmaxwell@wvc.edu
MAXWELL, Cathy 770-962-7580 132 A
cmaxwell@gwinnetttech.edu
MAXWELL, Chris 706-245-7226 128 K
cmaxwell@ec.edu
MAXWELL, David, E 515-271-2191 184 A
david.maxwell@drake.edu
MAXWELL, Gloria 816-604-4290 285 I
gloria.maxwell@mcckc.edu
MAXWELL, Jack 785-242-5200 195 F
jack.maxwell@ottawa.edu
MAXWELL, James 972-524-3341 495 F
MAXWELL, III, James, D 515-964-0601 184 G
maxwellj@faith.edu
MAXWELL, James, R 218-755-3732 266 B
jmaxwell@bemidjistate.edu
MAXWELL, JR., John, B 205-348-1202 8 F
jmaxwell@cchs.ua.edu
MAXWELL, Kim 970-542-3169 86 A
kim.maxwell@morgancc.edu
MAXWELL, Lafayette 919-572-1625 361 M
lmaxwell@apexsot.edu
MAXWELL, Melvin 601-877-3000 273 C
mmaxwell@alcorn.edu
MAXWELL, Richard 662-254-3412 276 C
rmax@mvsu.edu
MAXWELL, Rick 972-860-4722 484 F
rmaxwell@dcccd.edu
MAXWELL, Simon 785-594-8341 190 C
simon.maxwell@bakeru.edu
MAXWELL, Toni 405-422-1203 411 G
maxwellt@redlandscc.edu
MAXWELL, Valarie 940-397-4346 491 A
valarie.maxwell@mwsu.edu
MAXWELL, Veda 501-370-5284 23 B
vmaxwell@philander.edu
MAXWELL-DOHERTY,
Melissa 805-493-3330 32 H
revmmmd@clunet.edu
MAXWELL-DOHERTY,
Scott 805-493-3230 32 H
revsjmd@clunet.edu
MAY, Bobbie Jo, C 919-496-1567 374 D
may@vgcc.edu
MAY, Brian 325-942-2169 480 E
brian.may@angelo.edu
MAY, Brian, J 325-942-2165 480 E
brian.may@angelo.edu
MAY, Bryan 803-778-7841 455 G
maybw@cctech.edu
MAY, Carol 920-735-2542 553 G
mayc@fvtc.edu
MAY, Cecil 334-386-7154 3 H
cmay@faulkner.edu
MAY, Chad, L 215-637-7700 430 H
cmay@holyfamily.edu
MAY, Christopher, V 314-977-3185 289 F
cmay8@slu.edu
MAY, Daniel, J 419-434-4553 404 B
may@findlay.edu
MAY, David, J 603-862-2727 306 E
david.may@unh.edu
MAY, Gary, S 404-894-6825 130 D
gary.may@coe.gatech.edu
MAY, Gordon, F 248-942-3300 257 B
gfmay@oaklandcc.edu
MAY, Grace 973-761-9025 315 B
grace.may@shu.edu
MAY, Janet 520-206-4740 17 I
MAY, Janet 712-279-5227 182 E
janet.may@briarcliff.edu
MAY, Janet, B 205-934-8132 8 G
jmay@uab.edu
MAY, Jay 931-393-1630 475 C
jmay@mscc.edu
MAY, Jefferson, J 864-388-8314 458 J
jmay@lander.edu
MAY, Jerry, A 734-647-6000 259 D
jamay@umich.edu
MAY, Joe 225-922-1643 209 C
jmay@lctcs.edu
MAY, Katharyn, A 608-263-9725 550 G
kamay@wisc.edu
MAY, Kevin, J 570-348-6293 435 F
kmay@marywood.edu
MAY, Lori, K 901-345-1000 472 G
lori.may@remingtoncollege.edu
MAY, Mariani 310-577-3000 79 K
slmay@yosan.edu
MAY, Mary 817-810-0226 483 G
mary.may@concordia.edu
MAY, Mel, A 216-987-2204 389 A
mel.may@tri-c.edu
MAY, Mona Leiann 404-237-7573 125 F
mlmay@bauder.edu
MAY, Nancy, S 617-373-2700 244 A
MAY, Nina 609-586-4800 311 C
mayn@mccc.edu
MAY, Paul, A 508-213-2377 243 J
paul.may@nichols.edu
MAY, Rebecca, L 269-471-3315 247 H
rmay@andrews.edu
MAY, Robert, E 276-739-2432 528 D
rmay@vhcc.edu
MAY, Ron 574-936-8898 168 I
ron.may@ancilla.edu
MAY, Ronald 253-964-6736 536 C
rmay@pierce.ctc.edu
MAY, Sarah, E 478-301-2413 133 F
may_se@mercer.edu
MAY, Susan, A 920-735-5731 553 G
may@fvtc.edu
MAY, Tobi 518-562-4170 329 D
tobi.may@clinton.edu
MAY, Vicki, L 602-749-4615 13 M
vmay@devry.edu
MAY, Walter, P 770-720-5540 135 F
wpm@reinhardt.edu
MAY, William, V 254-710-1221 481 I
william_may@baylor.edu
MAY-RICCIUTI, Heather 304-829-7335 540 E
hricciuti@bethanywv.edu
MAYABB, Patricia 214-841-3634 485 E
pmayabb@dts.edu
MAYATT, Darlene 601-484-8724 275 C
dmayatt@mcc.cc.ms.us
MAYBANK, Denise, B 517-355-7535 255 D
maybank@msu.edu
MAYBELL, Steven, A 206-281-2824 537 D
maybes@spu.edu
MAYBRAY, Hugh 516-364-0808 343 A
hmaybray@nycollege.edu
MAYBURY, Greg 616-395-7671 252 F
maybury@hope.edu
MAYDEN, Kimberly, A 618-537-6825 157 G
kamayden@mckendree.edu
MAYDEN, Sharrie 702-895-0970 302 K
sharrie.mayden@unlv.edu
MAYEDA, Rachel 415-955-2153 27 F
rmayeda@alliant.edu
MAYER, Betty 651-779-5837 266 D
betty.mayer@century.edu
MAYER, Brenna, S 914-654-5289 330 B
bmayer@cnr.edu
MAYER, Charles 336-249-8186 369 F
cmayer@davidsonccc.edu
MAYER, Connie, M 518-445-2321 322 D
cmaye@albanylaw.edu
MAYER, Donna 410-704-4679 228 E
dmayer@towson.edu
MAYER, Lorri, A 617-984-1768 244 C
lmayer@quincycollege.edu
MAYER, Louis, J 610-660-1321 446 C
lmayer@sju.edu
MAYER, Marni Saling 360-752-8325 531 C
msmayer@btc.ctc.edu
MAYER, Stephan 323-660-6166 40 G
stephan.mayer@cleveland.edu
MAYER, William, A 202-885-3200 97 B
bill.mayer@american.edu
MAYER, Zelig 718-854-2290 324 A
MAYERS, Darryl 617-287-5458 237 D
darryl.mayers@umb.edu
MAYES, David, M 501-882-4420 20 D
dmmayes@asub.edu
MAYES, Florence 803-738-7512 459 D
maysf@midlandstech.edu
MAYES, John, A 203-432-3503 95 D
john.mayes@yale.edu
MAYES, Linda, F 651-631-5145 270 E
lfmayes@nwc.edu
MAYES, Michara, N 713-313-6815 499 G
mayesmn@tsu.edu
MAYES, Randy, L 814-362-5027 449 B
rlm50@pitt.edu
MAYES, Rick 479-936-5162 22 H
rmayes@nwacc.edu
MAYES, JR., Robert, G 251-981-3771 2 H
robert@columbiasouthern.edu
MAYEWSKI, Raymond 585-275-4786 358 I
Raymond_Mayewski@URMC.Rochester.edu
MAYFIELD, Amanda, B 860-439-2088 91 E
amanda.mayfield@conncoll.edu
MAYFIELD, Andrea 662-476-5025 274 D
amayfield@eastms.edu
MAYFIELD, Andrea 662-476-5025 274 D
MAYFIELD, Blayne 405-744-3471 410 C
blayne.mayfield@okstate.edu
MAYFIELD, Buddy 660-831-4176 286 I
mayfieldb@moval.edu
MAYFIELD, Connie 562-860-2451 38 J
cmayfield@cerritos.edu
MAYFIELD, Donny 423-746-5253 476 D
dmayfield@twcnet.edu
MAYFIELD, Gary 601-925-3849 275 E
mayfield@mc.edu
MAYFIELD, Joyce 704-523-5279 99 D
jam@strayer.edu
MAYFIELD, Mike, W 828-262-2070 377 B
mayfldmw@appstate.edu
MAYFIELD, Panny 662-621-4157 273 I
pmayfield@coahomacc.edu
MAYFIELD, Rachel 660-831-4139 286 I
mayfieldr@moval.edu
MAYFIELD, William 662-329-7152 276 B
wmayfield@bu.muw.edu
MAYHALL, Randall 918-781-7246 407 B
mayhallr@bacone.edu
MAYHER, Michael, E 440-525-7255 394 F
mmayher@lakelandcc.edu
MAYHEW, Glen 540-985-8539 520 D
Grmayhew@jchs.edu
MAYHEW, Kelly 619-388-3136 65 F
kmayhew@sdccd.edu
MAYHEW, Marty 520-206-6661 17 I
mmayhew@pima.edu
MAYHEW, Sally, A 618-537-6838 157 G
samayhew@mckendree.edu
MAYHEW, Steven 620-231-7000 195 I
MAYHEW, Susan, L 276-498-4190 515 J
MAYHORNE, John, F 443-412-2382 223 B
jmayhorne@harford.edu
MAYHUE, Richard, L 818-909-5517 56 G
rmayhue@tms.edu
MAYKUS, Janet 512-404-4862 481 D
jmaykus@austinseminary.edu
MAYLE, David, K 804-745-2444 516 L
dkmayle@bryantstratton.edu
MAYLE, Glenn 928-344-7500 12 C
glenn.mayle@azwestern.edu
MAYLER, Teresa 252-536-7207 370 F
maylert@halifaxcc.edu
MAYLONE, Theresa, M 718-990-2517 348 G
maylonet@stjohns.edu
MAYNARD, Barbara 314-256-8858 279 A
maynard@ai.edu
MAYNARD, C. Jack 812-237-2309 173 A
provost@indstate.edu
MAYNARD, David 909-537-5300 36 A
dmaynard@csusb.edu
MAYNARD, Francyenne 972-273-3109 485 B
fmaynard@dcccd.edu
MAYNARD, Kimberly, L 304-896-7345 542 J
kimm@southern.wvnet.edu
MAYNARD, Nelly 773-821-2453 146 D
nmaynard@csu.edu
MAYNARD, Pamela 973-877-3115 310 A
maynard@essex.edu
MAYNARD, Rebecca, A 207-768-2715 218 J
bmaynard@nmcc.edu
MAYNARD, Scott 662-325-3344 276 A
smaynard@career.msstate.edu
MAYNARD NELSON,
Jeanette 612-861-7554 261 C
jeanette@alfredadler.edu
MAYNARD-REID, Pedrito 509-527-2028 538 H
pedrito.maynard-reid@wallawalla.edu
MAYNE, Florence, P 512-499-4517 504 E
fmayne@utsystem.edu
MAYNE, Kevin 860-701-5002 93 B
mayne_k@mitchell.edu
MAYO, Bob 518-276-8300 347 D
mayor@rpi.edu
MAYO, Cindy 870-743-3000 22 G
cmayo@northark.edu
MAYO, Dan 252-493-7304 372 E
dmayo@email.pittcc.edu
MAYO, Donna 706-272-4507 127 G
dmayo@daltonstate.edu
MAYO, Douglas 507-389-2021 267 H
douglas.mayo@mnsu.edu
MAYO, Karen 859-246-6525 201 D
karen.mayo@kctcs.edu
MAYO, Sandra 512-245-2361 501 C
sm37@txstate.edu
MAYO, Sandra, L 818-947-2617 55 E
mayosl@lavc.edu
MAYO, Stephen, L 626-395-4951 32 E
steve@mayo.caltech.edu
MAYO, William, E 337-491-2684 212 C
william.mayo@sowela.edu
MAYOL, Myrna 787-250-0000 566 D
myrna.mayol@upr.edu
MAYORGA, Oscar, J 518-783-2330 350 I
MAYRAND, Leslie 325-486-6247 480 E
leslie.mayrand@angelo.edu
MAYROSE, Julie 920-686-6125 550 E
Julie.Mayrose@sl.edu
MAYROSE, William 413-775-1212 240 B
mayroseb@gcc.mass.edu
MAYS, JR., Allen, R 217-245-3162 152 C
amays@ic.edu
MAYS, Anna 972-860-8261 484 G
amays@dcccd.edu
MAYS, Beth, A 410-777-2480 221 B
bamays@aacc.edu
MAYS, Jon 513-861-6400 402 I
jon.mays@myunion.edu
MAYS, Kelli, L 304-253-7351 541 D
kmays@mountainstate.edu
MAYS, Louis, E 937-393-3431 401 K
lmays@sscc.edu
MAYS, Marilyn 972-273-3501 485 B
mmays@dccd.edu
MAYS, Nathaniel 617-349-8539 230 D
nmays@lesley.edu
MAYS, Nathaniel 617-349-8539 236 G
nmays@lesley.edu
MAYS, Robert 706-737-1471 125 C
rmays@aug.edu
MAYS, Shirley, L 602-682-6800 17 G
smays@phoenixlaw.edu
MAYSILLES, Michael, E 973-618-3236 308 D
mmaysilles@caldwell.edu
MAYSON, Adrianna 845-434-5750 356 H
amayson@sullivan.suny.edu
MAZACHEK, Juliann 785-670-4483 197 D
jmazachek@wufoundation.org
MAZE, Louis 254-867-4810 500 B
louis.maze@tstc.edu
MAZEL, David 719-587-7771 80 F
dbmazel@adams.edu
MAZER, Vicki 301-687-7053 228 C
vmmazer@frostburg.edu
MAZEY, Mary Ellen 419-372-2211 385 C
mmazey@bgsu.edu
MAZGULSKI, Judy 860-343-5868 90 D
jmazgulski@mxcc.commnet.edu
MAZIAR, Christine, M 574-631-2749 180 D
maziar.1@nd.edu
MAZINGO, Pam 252-527-6223 371 D
pmazingo@lenoircc.edu
MAZOR, Lori 212-998-2134 344 B
lori.mazor@nyu.edu
MAZOROL, Patrick 651-635-8050 261 I
p-mazorol@bethel.edu
MAZUK, Melody 484-384-2955 428 D
mazuk@eastern.edu
MAZUK, Melody 484-384-2947 438 C
semlibr@eastern.edu
MAZUR, Joe 772-462-7340 110 L
fmazur@irsc.edu
MAZUR, Paul 973-300-2100 315 F
pmazur@sussex.edu
MAZURAK, Kristina 208-459-5170 143 A
kmazurak@collegeofidaho.edu
MAZURKIEWICZ,
Claudia, J 540-868-7182 526 H
cmazurkiewicz@lfcc.edu
MAZZA, Diane 203-392-5405 91 I
boutaughd1@southernct.edu
MAZZA, Jennifer 845-398-4034 349 H
jmazza@stac.edu
MAZZA, Joseph 760-757-2121 57 E
jmazza@miracosta.edu
MAZZA, Lorraine, R 814-362-7520 449 B
mazza@pitt.edu
MAZZA, Nicholas 850-644-9702 119 C
nfmazza@fsu.edu
MAZZA, Rachelle, E 617-730-7111 243 I
rachelle.mazza@newbury.edu
MAZZA, S. Paul 814-234-7755 447 C
pmazza@southhills.edu
MAZZA, Stephen, W 785-864-4550 196 F
smazza@ku.edu
MAZZARELLI, Carla 845-431-8953 332 E
Mazzarel@sunydutchess.edu
MAZZARELLI, Juli 419-995-8479 392 L
mazzarelli.j@rhodesstate.edu
MAZZARESE, John, A 412-359-1000 448 D
MAZZARESE, John, A 412-359-1000 448 E
jmazzarese@triangle-tech.edu
MAZZARO, Rocky 734-995-7308 250 B
mazzar@cuaa.edu
MAZZEI, Robert, W 607-746-4559 355 E
mazzeirw@delhi.edu
MAZZOCCO, Lisa 213-740-6426 76 C
lisa.mazzocco@usc.edu
MAZZOLA, Frank 603-358-2242 307 A
fmazzola@keene.edu
MAZZOLA, Gregory 603-645-9635 306 B
g.mazzola@snhu.edu
MAZZUTO, Rick 818-677-3208 35 D
rick.mazzuto@csun.edu
MAÑJON, Sonia, B 860-685-3927 95 C
smanjon@wesleyan.edu
MBEWE, Luka 909-731-7599 78 H
lmbewe@westwood.edu
MBOMEH, Gabriel, A 240-895-4305 226 A
gambomeh@smcm.edu
MBUWAYESANGO,
Dora, R 704-636-6077 365 B
dmbuwayesango@hoodseminary.edu
MBYIRUKIRA, James 256-726-7157 6 C
mbyirukira@oakwood.edu
MC CAIG, Robert 732-571-3413 311 F
rmccaig@monmouth.edu
MC DONALD, Molly 408-554-6993 68 C
mmcdonald@scu.edu
MC GINTY, Sabrina 518-244-6891 348 A
mcgins@sage.edu
MC GOVERN, Michael 516-678-5000 341 F
mmcgovern@molloy.edu
MC NULTY, Margaret, B 814-949-5035 438 H
mbm7@psu.edu
MCABEE, Linda, R 336-334-7862 377 F
lrmcabee@ncat.edu

MCCARTHY, Ashley 607-431-4990 335 B mccarthya3@hartwick.edu
MCCARTHY, Barbara 914-773-3741 345 F bmccarthy@pace.edu
MCCARTHY, Barbara 860-253-3102 89 K bmccarthy@acc.commnet.edu
MCCARTHY, Belinda, R 417-836-5000 286 F belindamccarthy@missouristate.edu
MCCARTHY, Beth, W 336-841-9148 365 A bmccarth@highpoint.edu
MCCARTHY, Brittny 818-677-2123 35 D brittny.mccarthy@csun.edu
MCCARTHY, Carla, M 401-841-2220 557 I
MCCARTHY, Casey, J 218-755-3888 266 B cmccarthy@bemidjistate.edu
MCCARTHY, Christian 508-767-7424 230 E cmccarthy@assumption.edu
MCCARTHY, Claire, H 212-353-4266 331 B mccart3@cooper.edu
MCCARTHY, Colby 610-861-1330 436 I mectm01@moravian.edu
MCCARTHY, Daniel 985-549-2055 216 C dmccarthy@selu.edu
MCCARTHY, David, B 402-461-7397 298 C dmccarthy@hastings.edu
MCCARTHY, David, W 706-886-6831 137 G dmccarthy@tfc.edu
MCCARTHY, Douglas 602-285-7245 16 B douglas.mccarthy@pcmail.maricopa.edu
MCCARTHY, Elizabeth, K 508-678-2811 239 F elizabeth.mccarthy@bristolcc.edu
MCCARTHY, Faith 530-221-4275 69 C registrar@shasta.edu
MCCARTHY, Faith 530-221-4275 69 C shastaonline@clearwire.net
MCCARTHY, Gregory, J 701-231-7193 381 H greg.mccarthy@ndsu.edu
MCCARTHY, Hannah, M 617-730-7035 243 I hannah.mccarthy@newbury.edu
MCCARTHY, Helen 802-831-1225 515 A hmccarthy@vermontlaw.edu
MCCARTHY, James 646-660-6500 326 D james_mccarthy@baruch.cuny.edu
MCCARTHY, James 609-652-4335 313 F james.mccarthy@stockton.edu
MCCARTHY, James 610-861-5506 437 G jmccarthy@northampton.edu
MCCARTHY, Joan 402-461-7700 298 C jmccarthy@hastings.edu
MCCARTHY, Joel 315-364-3311 360 C jmccarthy@wells.edu
MCCARTHY, John, H 617-373-2240 244 A
MCCARTHY, Katherine 815-753-5600 160 A kmccarthy1@niu.edu
MCCARTHY, Kelly 708-235-3966 151 C kmccarthy@govst.edu
MCCARTHY, Kevin 704-355-2000 363 B kevin.mccarthy@carolinashealthcare.org
MCCARTHY, Kevin 315-568-3267 342 H kmccarthy@nycc.edu
MCCARTHY, Kevin 704-330-6907 369 A kevin.mccarthy@cpcc.edu
MCCARTHY, Kevin 518-255-5217 354 E mccartk@cobleskill.edu
MCCARTHY, Kevin 425-564-2191 531 B kevin.mccarthy@bellevuecollege.edu
MCCARTHY, Kevin, E 630-637-5134 159 F kemccarthy@nactrl.edu
MCCARTHY, Kristen 410-837-6151 229 A jschwartz@ubalt.edu
MCCARTHY, Lisa 609-771-2082 308 G mccarthy@tcnj.edu
MCCARTHY, Margo, M 203-576-5556 94 A mmccarthy@stvincentscollege.edu
MCCARTHY, Mark, D 216-397-4213 392 M mmccarthy@jcu.edu
MCCARTHY, Mary 607-778-5210 324 G mccarthy_m@sunybroome.edu
MCCARTHY, Merrill, N 828-669-8012 367 C mnmccarthy@montreat.edu
MCCARTHY, SJ, Michael 408-554-4715 68 C mcmccarthy@scu.edu
MCCARTHY, Michael, E 585-385-8025 348 F mmccarthy@sjfc.edu
MCCARTHY, Mike 210-924-4338 481 G mike.mccarthy@bua.edu
MCCARTHY, Monique 239-687-5423 101 B mmccarthy@avemarialaw.edu
MCCARTHY, Pamela 413-585-2840 245 B pmccarth@smith.edu
MCCARTHY, Patricia 724-357-2218 442 E mccarthy@iup.edu
MCCARTHY, Paul, J 214-860-2010 484 I pmccarthy@dcccd.edu
MCCARTHY, Peter, X 386-506-3107 103 J mccartp@DaytonaState.edu
MCCARTHY, Regina, K 603-641-4142 306 F regina.mccarthy@unh.edu
MCCARTHY, Robert, L 860-486-2128 94 E r.mccarthy@uconn.edu
MCCARTHY, Rosemary 412-536-1173 432 F rosemary.mccarthy@laroche.edu
MCCARTHY, Sherry 573-592-4368 293 E smccarth@williamwoods.edu
MCCARTHY, William 207-893-7721 219 F wmccarth@sjcme.edu
MCCARTIN, Sean 541-485-1780 417 E seanmccartin@newhop.edu
MCCARTNEY, Kathleen 617-495-3401 235 H hgsedean@gse.harvard.edu
MCCARTNEY, Mary 614-221-7770 396 B
MCCARTNEY, William, G 765-496-2270 178 F mccart@purdue.edu
MCCARTNEY, JR., William, L 252-328-6050 377 C mccartneyw@ecu.edu
MCCARTY, Alison 617-964-1100 230 B amccarty@ants.edu
MCCARTY, II, Gerald 810-766-4206 248 H gerald.mccartyii@baker.edu
MCCARTY, Josh 870-759-4143 26 B jmccarty@wbcoll.edu
MCCARTY, Kyla 417-690-3292 280 C mccarty@cofo.edu
MCCARTY, Richard, C 615-322-4219 477 F richard.mccarty@vanderbilt.edu
MCCARTY, Susan 212-772-4850 327 E susan.mccarty@hunter.cuny.edu
MCCARTY, Therese, A 518-388-6102 358 E mccartyt@union.edu
MCCARTY-HARRIS, Yulanda 330-941-3370 406 F ymccartyharris@ysu.edu
MCCARVEL, Thomas, J 406-447-4409 294 A tmccarve@carroll.edu
MCCASKEY, Michael, J 518-255-5427 354 E mccaskmj@cobleskill.edu
MCCASKILL, Angela 202-651-5000 97 E angela.mccaskill@gallaudet.edu
MCCASKILL, Rock 864-644-5538 461 B rmccaskill@swu.edu
MCCASKILL, Sharrell 202-651-5642 97 E sharrell.mccaskill@gallaudet.edu
MCCASKILL, Susan 828-339-4251 373 H susanm@southwesterncc.edu
MCCASLIN, Blake 423-746-5332 476 D mccaslin@twcnet.edu
MCCASLIN, John 931-553-0071 471 G john.mccaslin@miller-motte.com
MCCASLIN, Joy 818-710-2910 55 B mccaslin@piercecollege.edu
MCCASLIN, Julie 423-746-5214 476 D jmccaslin@twcnet.edu
MCCASLIN, Randall 814-732-1346 442 D rmccaslin@edinboro.edu
MCCASLIN, Sharon 314-889-4567 282 C smccaslin@fontbonne.edu
MCCAUGHTRY, Samuel, L 814-456-7504 428 F mccaughtrys@eriebc.edu
MCCAUL, Kevin, D 701-231-7411 381 H kevin.mccaul@ndsu.edu
MCCAULEY, Brian 618-374-5180 161 D brian.mccauley@principia.edu
MCCAULEY, Dennis 215-968-8394 423 E mccauley@bucks.edu
MCCAULEY, Howard 816-271-4266 287 A admissn@missouriwestern.edu
MCCAULEY, Kevin, R 805-893-8182 74 F kevin.mccauley@chancellor.ucsb.edu
MCCAULEY, Linda 404-727-7976 129 A linda.mccauley@emory.edu
MCCAULEY, Lisa, M 570-208-5832 432 E lisamccauley@kings.edu
MCCAULEY, Pat 402-461-7419 298 C pmccauley@hastings.edu
MCCAULEY, Terry, L 248-232-4550 257 B tlmccaul@oaklandcc.edu
MCCAUSLAND, Randy 850-644-2591 119 C rmccausland@admin.fsu.edu
MCCAUSLIN, Lauren 617-243-2139 236 F lmccauslin@lasell.edu
MCCAW, Ian, J 254-710-1222 481 I ian_mccaw@baylor.edu
MCCAW, Matt, S 312-939-0111 150 B matt@eastwest.edu
MCCAWLEY, Loree, L 831-479-6234 31 F lomccawl@cabrillo.edu
MCCAY, Bill 509-865-8520 534 D mccay_b@heritage.edu
MCCAY, Patrick 603-623-0313 305 F pmccay@nhia.edu
MCCAY, T. Dwayne 321-674-8889 108 E tdmccay@fit.edu
MCCLAFFERTY, Joe 406-496-4301 296 C jmcclafferty@mtech.edu
MCCLAIN, Beth 309-694-5323 152 B bmcclain@icc.edu
MCCLAIN, Davina 318-357-4592 216 B mcclaind@nsula.edu
MCCLAIN, Elman 425-235-7836 536 E emcclain@rtc.edu
MCCLAIN, Erika 731-394-7497 469 M emcclain@lanecollege.edu
MCCLAIN, James 626-914-8794 39 G jmcclain@citruscollege.edu
MCCLAIN, James, W 870-838-2910 20 A jmcclain@smail.anc.edu
MCCLAIN, Jeremy 662-846-4300 274 B jmcclain@deltastate.edu
MCCLAIN, June 912-427-5847 124 A jmcclain@altamahatech.edu
MCCLAIN, Lisa, L 504-520-7593 217 A lmcclain@xula.edu
MCCLAIN, Mark 937-766-7933 386 F mcclain@cedarville.edu
MCCLAIN, Samantha, E 515-574-1080 185 F mcclain@iowacentral.edu
MCCLAIN, Tim 360-486-8875 536 F tmc@stmartin.edu
MCCLANAHAN, Ana, M 919-513-2311 374 E ammcclanahan@waketech.edu
MCCLANAHAN, Keith 501-882-8811 20 D mkmcclanahan@asub.edu
MCCLANAHAN, Thomas, H 559-278-0840 34 D thomas_mcclanahan@csufresno.edu
MCCLANE, Curren 202-639-1835 97 D cmclane@corcoran.org
MCCLAY, Diana, D 423-439-5890 473 E mcclayd@etsu.edu
MCCLAY, Kelly 609-343-4939 307 D mcclay@atlantic.edu
MCCLEAN, Freda 212-220-8316 326 E fmcclean@bmcc.edu
MCCLEAN, Jerry 209-954-5033 66 D jmcclean@deltacollege.edu
MCCLEANON, Charles 312-850-7154 147 C cmccleanon@ccc.edu
MCCLEARY, Keith 517-264-3981 247 D
MCCLEARY, Louise 413-265-2395 233 E mcclearyl@elms.edu
MCCLEARY, Tim 406-638-3121 294 G mcclearyt@lbhc.cc.mt.us
MCCLEERY, Steve 575-392-5004 319 B smccleery@nmjc.edu
MCCLEISH, Joan, M 515-643-6625 187 C jmccleish@mercydesmoines.org
MCCLELLAN, Cissy 802-860-2711 513 A mcclella@champlain.edu
MCCLELLAN, Craig 304-326-1465 541 G cmcclellan@salemu.edu
MCCLELLAN, Debralee 301-846-2477 222 G dmcclellan@frederick.edu
MCCLELLAN, Edie 414-847-3233 548 G ediemcclellan@miad.edu
MCCLELLAN, Fletcher 717-361-1555 428 E mcclelef@etown.edu
MCCLELLAN, George, S 260-481-6844 174 A mcclellg@ipfw.edu
MCCLELLAN, Jane 201-200-3196 312 B
MCCLELLAN, Jeffrey, C 618-536-3331 164 H jmclell@siue.edu
MCCLELLAN, Mack 405-878-2229 409 D mark.mcclellan@okbu.edu
MCCLELLAN, Melanie 678-839-6423 138 D melmcc@westga.edu
MCCLELLAN, Mia, C 619-482-6369 71 C mmcclellan@swccd.edu
MCCLELLAN, Patricia 828-251-6001 378 C pmcclell@unca.edu
MCCLELLAN, Steven, J 501-569-3202 24 E sjmcclellan@ualr.edu
MCCLELLAND, Charles, F 713-313-7216 499 G mcclellandcf@tsu.edu
MCCLELLAND, Dareen 260-665-4102 180 A mcclellandd@trine.edu
MCCLELLAND, Lou 303-492-8631 88 B lou.mcclelland@colorado.edu
MCCLELLAND, Scott 954-382-6575 122 C smcclelland@tiu.edu
MCCLELLAND, II, Thomas, H 337-475-5908 215 G tmcclelland@mcneese.edu
MCCLELLON, Leslie 303-352-3786 83 F leslie.mcclellon@ccd.edu
MCCLENAGAN, Cindy, M 806-291-1106 508 B cindym@wbu.edu
MCCLENDON, Bev 479-788-7082 24 D bmcclendon@uafortsmith.edu
MCCLENDON, Mark 817-515-5100 496 A mark.mcclendon@tccd.edu
MCCLENDON, Mark, B 406-466-6012 408 G mbmcclendon@lunet.edu
MCCLENDON, Rodney, P 979-862-1065 497 C rpm@tamu.edu
MCCLEON, Mitch 601-635-2111 274 C mmcleon@eccc.edu
MCCLESKEY, Tom 770-426-2660 133 B thomas.mccleskey@life.edu
MCCLINTOCK, Charles 805-898-2930 47 C cmcclintock@fielding.edu
MCCLINTOCK, Kate 707-527-4797 68 E kmcclintock@santarosa.edu
MCCLINTOCK, Marta 724-938-4251 441 G mcclintock@calu.edu
MCCLINTOCK, Melvin, A 240-895-4309 226 A mamcclintock@smcm.edu
MCCLINTOCK, Patty 812-237-2305 173 A patty.mcclintock@indstate.edu
MCCLINTOCK, Richard, C 434-223-6261 519 B rmcclintock@email.hsc.edu
MCCLINTON, JR., Flandus 225-771-5021 214 H flandus_mcclinton@subr.edu
MCCLINTON, Marguerite 214-379-5518 492 D mmcclinton@pqc.edu
MCCLISTER, Lisa 813-988-5131 107 I mcclisterl@floridacollege.edu
MCCLONEY, Maurice 512-505-3084 488 B mmccloney@htu.edu
MCCLOSKEY, Denise 814-827-4423 449 E denisem1@pitt.edu
MCCLOSKEY, Erin, E 814-472-3100 446 B emccloskey@francis.edu
MCCLOSKEY, James 412-396-5286 428 C mccloskey@duq.edu
MCCLOSKEY, James, M 302-356-6880 97 A james.m.mccloskey@wilmu.edu
MCCLOSKEY, JR., John, R 610-796-3005 421 F john.mccloskey@alvernia.edu
MCCLOUD, Alyssa 973-408-3250 309 F amccloud@drew.edu
MCCLOUD, Alyssa 973-313-6146 315 B alyssa.mccloud@shu.edu
MCCLOUD, Donald 269-387-3956 260 F donald.mccloud@wmich.edu
MCCLOUD, Elizabeth, K 717-361-1404 428 E mcclouek@etown.edu
MCCLOY, Eric 215-572-8521 422 B mccloy@arcadia.edu
MCCLUNEY, Alice 828-286-3636 371 A amccluney@isothermal.edu
MCCLUNG, Alan 423-614-8410 470 A amcclung@leeuniversity.edu
MCCLUNG, Denise 304-424-8230 545 B denise.mcclung@mail.wvu.edu
MCCLUNG, Hugh 281-649-3308 487 F hmcclung@hbu.edu
MCCLUNG, Mary 770-537-6065 139 B mary.mcclung@westgatech.edu
MCCLUNG, Philip, L 336-734-7212 370 C pmcclung@forsythtech.edu
MCCLURE, Alyssa 903-223-3060 498 C amcclure@tamut.edu
MCCLURE, Amy 740-368-3562 400 F aamcclur@owu.edu
MCCLURE, Carter, B 843-686-6503 469 M cmcclure@lanecollege.edu
MCCLURE, Dan 503-821-8970 419 D dan@pnca.edu
MCCLURE, David 254-526-1166 482 F david.mcclure@ctcd.edu
MCCLURE, Guy 256-233-8296 1 F guy.mcclure@athens.edu
MCCLURE, H. Lawrence 215-780-1331 446 G larry@salus.edu
MCCLURE, Jennifer 847-214-7319 150 D jmcclure@elgin.edu
MCCLURE, Joy 770-394-8300 124 F jmcclure@aii.edu
MCCLURE, Kelly 215-991-3573 432 G mcclure@lasalle.edu
MCCLURE, Ken 417-836-5233 286 F kmcclure@missuristate.edu
MCCLURE, Kitara 509-533-7378 532 E kmcclure@scc.spokane.edu
MCCLURE, Larry 215-780-1400 446 G larry@salus.edu
MCCLURE, Melissa 503-821-8960 419 D melissa@pnca.edu
MCCLURE, Mike 541-956-7237 420 B mmclure@roguecc.edu
MCCLURE, RET., Robert 845-446-1522 558 G Robert.McClure@wpaog.org
MCCLURE, Ryan 727-726-1153 103 B ryanmcclure@clearwater.edu
MCCLURE, Wesley, C 731-426-7595 469 M mcclure@lanecollege.edu
MCCLURE, William 972-929-9324 486 B wmcclure@devry.edu
MCCLURE, William, S 413-545-2111 237 C billmcclure@contined.umass.edu
MCCLUSKEY, Denise 419-824-3509 395 D dmccluskey@lourdes.edu
MCCLUSKEY, Eugene 207-768-2786 218 J emccluskey@nmcc.edu
MCCLUSKEY, Jennifer 314-529-9561 284 F jmccluskey@maryville.edu
MCCLUSKEY, Peter 860-255-3510 91 C pmccluskey@txcc.commnet.edu
MCCLUSKEY-FAWCETT, Kathleen, A 785-864-2768 196 F kamf@ku.edu
MCCLUSKY, John 830-372-8002 499 C jmcclusky@tlu.edu
MCCLYMONT, Jay 717-766-2511 436 D jmcclymont@messiah.edu
MCCOEY, Margaret 215-951-1222 432 G mccoey@lasalle.edu
MCCOLGIN, Cathleen, C 315-498-7271 345 D mccolgic@sunyocc.edu
MCCOLLETT, Sherry 207-621-3141 220 B umafa@maine.edu
MCCOLLOCH, Mark 443-840-1021 222 D mmocolloch@ccbcmd.edu
MCCOLLOUGH, Laura, L 907-474-1886 10 J lcmccollough@alaska.edu

MCCULLOUGH, Jonathan, W 903-434-8115 491 D jmccullough@ntcc.edu

MCCULLOUGH, Kenneth, C 540-654-1057 524 H kmccullo@umw.edu

MCCULLOUGH, Larry, D 336-887-3000 365 J lmccullough@laureluniversity.edu

MCCULLOUGH, Laura, L 304-414-4445 542 F lmccullough@kvctc.edu

MCCULLOUGH, Leah 828-298-3325 380 C lmccullough@warren-wilson.edu

MCCULLOUGH, Lindsey 617-353-9717 232 G lmccullo@bu.edu

MCCULLOUGH, Lois, N 419-783-2317 389 G lmccullough@defiance.edu

MCCULLOUGH, Markisha 912-427-1969 124 A mmccullough@altamahatech.edu

MCCULLOUGH, Randy 419-559-2353 402 D rmccullough01@terra.edu

MCCULLOUGH, Richard, D 412-268-1180 424 H rm5g@andrew.cmu.edu

MCCULLOUGH, Robert, R 216-368-5445 386 E robert.mccullough@case.edu

MCCULLOUGH, Sherri 719-502-2061 86 G sherri.mccullough@ppcc.edu

MCCULLOUGH, Willie, G 606-326-2068 201 B willie.mccullough@kctcs.edu

MCCULLUM, B. J 309-854-1723 145 E mccullumb@bhc.edu

MCCULLY, Clare 617-730-7089 243 I clare.mccully@newbury.edu

MCCUNE, John 716-673-3373 352 A thomas.mccune@fredonia.edu

MCCURDY, Clantha 617-727-9420 237 A cmccurdy@osfa.mass.edu

MCCURDY, Debra, L 419-995-8200 392 L mccurdy.d@rhodesstate.edu

MCCURDY, Eugene, M 608-796-3921 553 A emmccurdy@viterbo.edu

MCCURDY, John, D 931-431-9700 472 B jmccurdy@nci.edu

MCCURDY, Lauren 205-226-4625 2 C lmccurdy@bsc.edu

MCCURDY, Lyndon, C 937-327-7325 406 B lmccurdy@wittenberg.edu

MCCURLEY, Steve 918-540-6196 408 J smccurley@neo.edu

MCCURREN, Cynthia 616-331-3558 252 A mccurrec@gvsu.edu

MCCURRY, Faith 803-535-1424 460 C mccurryf@octech.edu

MCCURRY, Mel, K 828-286-3636 371 A mmccurry@isothermal.edu

MCCURRY, Rickey, N 812-877-8211 179 A rickey.mccurry@rose-hulman.edu

MCCURRY, Rickey, N 618-453-7174 164 I rmccurry@siu.edu

MCCUSKEY, Beth, M 765-494-1022 178 F bmccuske@purdue.edu

MCCUTCHAN, Molly, M 734-384-4245 255 G mmccutchan@monroeccc.edu

MCCUTCHEN, Michael, F 731-989-6901 468 K mmccutchen@fhu.edu

MCCUTCHEN, Sam 325-649-8052 488 A smccutchen@hputx.edu

MCCUTCHEON, Bruce, E 610-330-5530 433 B mccutchb@lafayette.edu

MCCUTCHEON, Fran 508-588-9100 240 E

MCCUTCHEON, John, F 413-545-9682 237 C jmccutch@admin.umass.edu

MCCUTCHEON, Kathleen 614-292-4164 398 H

MCCUTCHEON, Robert, R 304-637-1216 540 F mccutcheonr@dewv.edu

MCCUTCHEON, Ron 541-885-1120 418 E ron.mccutcheon@oit.edu

MCDADE, Linda 570-348-6249 435 F lmcdade@marywood.edu

MCDADE, Lucinda 909-625-8767 40 C lucinda.mcdade@cgu.edu

MCDADE, William 773-834-3861 166 D wmcdade@bsd.uchicago.edu

MCDADE-CLAY, W. Thomas 585-340-9648 329 G tmcdadeclay@crcds.edu

MCDAID, James 617-879-7960 238 E jmcdaid@massart.edu

MCDANIEL, Brenda 540-362-7439 519 E bmcdaniel@hollins.edu

MCDANIEL, C. Joan 846-846-5781 204 D jmcdaniel@midway.edu

MCDANIEL, Carla 573-897-5000 284 D

MCDANIEL, Cindy 810-762-5620 256 C cindy.mcdanie@mcc.edu

MCDANIEL, Cliff 817-461-8741 480 H

MCDANIEL, Craig 706-295-6928 130 F cmcdaniel@gntc.edu

MCDANIEL, Donna, N 402-557-7184 297 A donna.mcdaniel@bellevue.edu

MCDANIEL, Garry 614-947-6126 391 A mcdanieg@franklin.edu

MCDANIEL, Gary, R 949-214-3055 42 K gary.mcdaniel@cui.edu

MCDANIEL, Jervaise 618-842-3711 152 F mcdanielj@iecc.edu

MCDANIEL, John 615-322-1741 477 F john.mcdaniel@vanderbilt.edu

MCDANIEL, Joy 580-371-2371 408 I jmcdaniel@mscok.edu

MCDANIEL, Juley 620-223-2700 192 G juleym@fortscott.edu

MCDANIEL, Julie 937-484-1337 405 A jmcdaniel@urbana.edu

MCDANIEL, Kay 225-359-9207 209 K kmcdaniel@catc.edu

MCDANIEL, Kristina, D 573-840-9695 290 J mcdank@trcc.edu

MCDANIEL, Lance 304-384-5258 543 D mcdaniell26@mycu.concord.edu

MCDANIEL, Laura 701-231-8330 381 H laura.mcdaniel@ndsu.edu

MCDANIEL, Lucinda 870-933-7900 20 B lmcdaniel@asusystem.edu

MCDANIEL, Mary, W 864-388-8242 458 J mmcdaniel@lander.edu

MCDANIEL, Mary Lee 601-857-3395 274 E mlmcdaniel@hindscc.edu

MCDANIEL, Mick, R 607-844-8222 357 H mcdanim@tc3.edu

MCDANIEL, Peter 864-250-7000 99 D

MCDANIEL, Sonya 706-355-5114 124 H smcdaniel@athenstech.edu

MCDANIEL, Stephen, L 601-877-6693 273 C mcdaniel@alcorn.edu

MCDANIEL, Stephen, L 601-877-6296 273 C mcdaniel@alcorn.edu

MCDANIEL, Thomas 610-921-7672 421 D tmcdaniel@alb.edu

MCDANNELL, Carol 419-448-3441 402 E cmcdannell@tiffin.edu

MCDAVID, Courtney 860-832-3003 91 G mcdavidc@ccsu.edu

MCDAVIS, Roderick, J 740-593-1804 399 G mcdavis@ohio.edu

MCDAVIS, Roderick, J 740-593-1804 400 C mcdavis@ohio.edu

MCDERMOTT, A. Keith 617-541-2454 241 D kmcderm@rcc.mass.edu

MCDERMOTT, Ann, B 508-793-2443 233 D amcdermo@holycross.edu

MCDERMOTT, Betsy 585-385-8143 348 F emcdermott@sjfc.edu

MCDERMOTT, Brian 308-398-7387 297 C bmcdermott@cccneb.edu

MCDERMOTT, Christine 315-568-3105 342 H cmcdermott@nycc.edu

MCDERMOTT, Christine 302-736-2491 96 G mcdermch@wesley.edu

MCDERMOTT, Colleen 515-727-2100 186 D

MCDERMOTT, Dennis 718-489-5362 348 E dmcdermott@stfranciscollege.edu

MCDERMOTT, Diane 312-226-6294 156 E busofc@lexingtoncolleg.edu

MCDERMOTT, Emily 617-287-6500 237 D emily.mcdermott@umb.edu

MCDERMOTT, Harry 520-621-7428 19 B mcdermott@health.arizona.edu

MCDERMOTT, Joan 303-556-8300 85 N mcdermoj@mscd.edu

MCDERMOTT, John, R 563-588-7132 186 I john.mcdermott@loras.edu

MCDERMOTT, Marty 231-777-0462 256 D marty.mcdermott@muskegoncc.edu

MCDERMOTT, Patrice 410-455-3150 227 D mcdermot@umbc.edu

MCDERMOTT, Richard, L 713-500-4963 506 D richard.l.mcdermott@uth.tmc.edu

MCDERMOTT, Robert, B 610-785-6268 446 A deanofmencdscs@adphila.org

MCDERMOTT, Robin 440-375-7000 394 E rmcdermott@lec.edu

MCDERMOTT, Thomas 410-234-4900 225 E

MCDEVITT, Brigid 206-587-6314 537 A bmcdevitt@sccd.ctc.edu

MCDEVITT, Matthew 718-405-3400 330 A matthew.mcdevitt@mountsaintvincent.edu

MCDIARMID, Bill 919-966-7000 378 D bmcd@email.unc.edu

MCDILL, M. Augustus 843-661-1128 458 C mmcdill@fmarion.edu

MCDILL, Sandy 602-787-7352 16 A sandy.mcdill@pvmail.maricopa.edu

MCDOLE, Rob 803-754-4100 457 D

MCDONAGH, David 212-749-2802 339 I dmcdonagh@msmnyc.edu

MCDONALD, Anita, D 814-375-4705 439 D adm10@psu.edu

MCDONALD, Ann, M 978-632-6600 240 G a_mcdonald@mwcc.mass.edu

MCDONALD, Anna 805-898-4018 47 C amcdonald@fielding.edu

MCDONALD, Barbara 218-322-2402 267 A barbara.mcdonald@itascacc.edu

MCDONALD, Barbara, E 575-439-3721 319 E bobi@nmsua.nmsu.edu

MCDONALD, Becky 937-298-3399 394 D becky.mcdonald@kcma.edu

MCDONALD, Carl 912-260-4203 136 F carl.mcdonald@sgc.edu

MCDONALD, Cathy 701-328-4111 381 C cathy.mcdonald@ndus.edu

MCDONALD, Chanchai 901-448-4930 477 C cmcdon12@uthsc.edu

MCDONALD, Clay 281-487-1170 498 E cmcdonald@txchiro.edu

MCDONALD, David 503-838-8211 419 C mcdonald@wou.edu

MCDONALD, Debbie 626-966-4576 28 E info@agu.edu

MCDONALD, Deborah 845-938-5706 558 G addimssion@usma.edu

MCDONALD, Denise 434-544-8665 520 H mcdonald@lynchburg.edu

MCDONALD, Dennis 518-454-5170 330 C mcdonald@strose.edu

MCDONALD, Dotty 337-550-1313 212 H

MCDONALD, Eric 864-587-4200 461 D mcdonalde@smcsc.edu

MCDONALD, Evelyn 901-321-3530 467 G emcdonal@cbu.edu

MCDONALD, Frank 212-346-1800 345 F fmcdonald@pace.edu

MCDONALD, Fritz 319-368-6473 187 E fmcdonald@mtmercy.edu

MCDONALD, Gary 415-422-2699 76 B mcdonald@usfca.edu

MCDONALD, Ginger 978-478-3400 247 C gmcdonald@zbc.edu

MCDONALD, J. David 316-978-3285 197 F david.mcdonald@wichita.edu

MCDONALD, Jack, J 203-582-8621 93 E jack.mcdonald@quinnipiac.edu

MCDONALD, James 435-586-7898 511 A mcdonaldj@suu.edu

MCDONALD, CSC, James, E 574-631-9800 180 D mcdonald.46@nd.edu

MCDONALD, James, L 415-451-2810 66 B jmcdonald@sfts.edu

MCDONALD, Jan 864-977-7151 460 A jan.mcdonald@ngu.edu

MCDONALD, Jason 503-943-7147 420 G mcdonaja@up.edu

MCDONALD, Jennifer 714-241-6163 40 J jmcdonald@coastline.edu

MCDONALD, Jessyna 202-274-5533 99 F jmcdonald@udc.edu

MCDONALD, Joan, T 215-895-2902 427 G mcdonajt@drexel.edu

MCDONALD, Joseph 518-631-9869 358 F mcdonalj@uniongraduatecollege.edu

MCDONALD, Joseph, A 330-471-8318 395 E jmcdonald@malone.edu

MCDONALD, Julia, J 270-745-5394 207 C julia.mcdonald@wku.edu

MCDONALD, Katie 603-228-1541 306 G kmcdonald@piercelaw.edu

MCDONALD, Kevin 585-475-6795 347 G kgmpro@rit.edu

MCDONALD, Krista 513-785-3100 396 E mcdonak@muohio.edu

MCDONALD, Kurt 417-690-3200 280 C purch@cofo.edu

MCDONALD, Latrice 601-928-6206 275 G latrice.mcdonald@mgccc.edu

MCDONALD, Leander 701-766-1133 380 E leander.mcdonald@littlehoop.edu

MCDONALD, Lori 949-214-3074 42 K lori.mcdonald@cui.edu

MCDONALD, Lucy 408-541-0100 41 C lmcdonald@cogswell.edu

MCDONALD, Martha 626-914-8602 39 G mmcdonald@citruscollege.edu

MCDONALD, Mary 910-277-5047 376 A MHM@sapc.edu

MCDONALD, Mary, E 706-542-9167 138 C marymcd@uga.edu

MCDONALD, Matt, C 507-786-3255 271 H mcdonamc@stolaf.edu

MCDONALD, Michael 567-661-7203 400 H michael_mcdonald6@owens.edu

MCDONALD, Michael, A 269-337-7162 253 F Michael.McDonald@kzoo.edu

MCDONALD, Patrick, S 716-880-2345 340 E patrick.s.mcdonald@medaille.edu

MCDONALD, Paul, R 626-966-4576 28 E paulmcdonald@agu.edu

MCDONALD, Pete 706-295-6960 130 F pmcdonald@gntc.edu

MCDONALD, Peter 559-278-2403 34 D pmcdonald@csufresno.edu

MCDONALD, Sallie 671-735-2233 559 D salliemcd@uguam.uog.edu

MCDONALD, Scott 979-458-0996 497 C smcdonald@tamu.edu

MCDONALD, Shireen, E 505-925-8530 321 G semcdonald@salud.unm.edu

MCDONALD, Steve 760-744-1150 61 C smcdonald@palomar.edu

MCDONALD, Steven 401-277-4955 454 B smcdonal@risd.edu

MCDONALD, Sue 818-932-3026 44 N smcdonald@devry.edu

MCDONALD, Susan, K 785-827-5541 194 D smcdonald@kwu.edu

MCDONALD, Terrence, J 734-764-0322 259 D tmcd@umich.edu

MCDONALD, Tim 706-265-7515 132 J tmcdonal@laniertech.edu

MCDONALD, Timothy 816-501-4077 288 D timothy.mcdonald@rockhurst.edu

MCDONALD, Todd 231-348-6603 256 E tmcdonald@ncmich.edu

MCDONALD, Todd, M 602-942-4141 14 E tmcdonal@cci.edu

MCDONALD, Tom 212-229-5900 342 E mcdonalt@newschool.edu

MCDONALD, William 315-866-0300 335 E mcdonaldwh@herkimer.edu

MCDONALD, William 617-951-2350 243 C bill.mcdonald@necb.edu

MCDONALD, William, A 973-748-9000 308 A bill_mcdonald@bloomfield.edu

MCDONALD, William, H 203-596-8590 93 D wmcdonald@post.edu

MCDONALD, William, M 706-542-7774 138 C bmcdonal@uga.edu

MCDONALD-RASH, Jean 848-932-7057 314 B jrash@rci.rutgers.edu

MCDONNEL, Wendy 605-221-3100 464 C wmcdonnel@kilian.edu

MCDONNELL, Betty 217-641-4549 154 G mcdonnell@jwcc.edu

MCDONNELL, Brian, A 401-341-2185 454 D mcdonneb@salve.edu

MCDONNELL, Constance, F 570-941-7640 450 B mcdonnellc1@scranton.edu

MCDONNELL, Heidi 908-852-1400 308 F 0553txt@fheg.follett.com

MCDONNELL, John 716-270-5612 333 B mcdonnellj@ecc.edu

MCDONNELL, John 773-481-8253 147 F jmcdonnell@ccc.edu

MCDONNELL, John 215-991-3778 432 G mcdonnell72@lasalle.edu

MCDONNELL, Joseph 207-780-4020 220 G jmcdonnell@usm.maine.edu

MCDONNELL, Teresa, H 603-513-1308 306 H tessa.mcdonnell@granite.edu

MCDONOUGH, Ann 702-774-4619 302 K ann.mcdonough@unlv.edu

MCDONOUGH, David 508-793-7258 233 C dmcdonough@clarku.edu

MCDONOUGH, Eileen 305-899-3085 101 F emcdonough@mail.barry.edu

MCDONOUGH, Kathleen 413-552-2261 240 C kmcdonough@hcc.edu

MCDONOUGH, Michael, J 585-292-2170 341 H mmcdonough@monroecc.edu

MCDONOUGH, Patrick 610-807-9221 431 C

MCDONOUGH, Peter, G 609-258-2511 313 A pmcd@princeton.edu

MCDONOUGH, JR., Peter, J 848-932-7741 314 B mcdonough@oldqueens.rutgers.edu

MCDONOUGH, Shawna 630-889-6701 159 E smcdonough@nuhs.edu

MCDORMAN, Heather 636-922-8277 288 E hmcdorman@stchas.edu

MCDOUGAL, Jacob, N 209-667-3836 36 C jmcdougal@csustan.edu

MCDOUGAL, Tammy 731-426-7526 469 M tmcdougal@lanecollege.edu

MCDOUGALL, Gerald, S 573-651-2112 290 D gmcdougall@semo.edu

MCDOUGALL, Gordon, A 804-828-8192 525 E gamcdougall@vcu.edu

MCDOUGLE, James, L 304-260-4380 542 C jmcdougl@blueridgectc.edu

MCDOUGLE, Larry 567-661-7210 400 H larry_mcdougle@owens.edu

MCDOWELL, Amy 802-763-7170 515 A amcdowell@vermontlaw.edu

MCDOWELL, Charles, E 608-243-4137 554 B cemcdowell@matcmadison.edu

MCDOWELL, Denise 913-288-7299 193 J dmcdowell@kckcc.edu

MCDOWELL, Denise 717-262-2010 452 B dmcdowell@wilson.edu

MCDOWELL, Jackie 706-236-2202 125 G jmcdowell@berry.edu

MCDOWELL, James 860-512-3603 90 C jmcdowell@mcc.commnet.edu

MCDOWELL, N. Renee 724-653-2212 427 F rmcdowell@dec.edu

MCDOWELL, Pamela 507-786-3011 271 H mcdowell@stolaf.edu

MCDOWELL, Paul 860-486-2434 94 E Paul.McDowell@uconn.edu

MCDOWELL, Richard 406-791-5302 296 H rmcdowell01@ugf.edu

MCDOWELL, Scott 615-966-5690 470 D scott.mcdowell@lipscomb.edu

MCDOWELL, Stephanie 785-227-3380 190 G mcdowells@bethanylb.edu

MCGLOTHIN, Kris 302-735-7696 96 G bkwesley@bncollege.edu
MCGLOTHIN-ELLER, Vince 847-866-3907 151 B vince.mcglothin-eller@garrett.edu
MCGLOTHLAN, Mary 503-255-0332 417 C mmcglothlan@multnomah.edu
MCGLOTHLIN, Michael, G 276-498-4190 515 J
MCGLOUGHLIN, Stephen 916-691-7589 56 B mcglous@crc.losrios.edu
MCGLYNN, J. Douglas 262-646-6522 549 B dmcglynn@nashotah.edu
MCGLYNN, Ken 443-518-4802 223 D kmcglynn@howardcc.edu
MCGLYNN, Maureen 503-399-4784 414 J maureen.mcglynn@chemeketa.edu
MCGOFF, Michael, F 607-777-2143 351 F mmcgoff@binghamton.edu
MCGOLDRICK, Deirdre, E 253-535-7444 535 K mcgoldde@plu.edu
MCGOLDRICK, John 215-951-1015 432 G mcgoldri@lasalle.edu
MCGONAGLE, W. Brad 409-740-4502 497 D mcgonagw@tamug.edu
MCGONAGLE CRIDER, Theresa 251-380-3871 7 F tcrider@shc.edu
MCGONIGAL, Terry, P 509-777-4345 539 F tmcgonigal@whitworth.edu
MCGONIGLE, Gregory 440-775-5191 397 F greg.mcgonigle@oberlin.edu
MCGONIGLE, Mary 610-519-4070 450 G mary.mcgonigle@villanova.edu
MCGONIGLE, Robert, B 570-208-5875 432 E rbmcgoni@kings.edu
MCGONIGLE, Steve 215-951-1075 432 G mcgonigle@lasalle.edu
MCGOUGH, Cris 870-230-5083 21 I mcgougc@hsu.edu
MCGOUGH, David 802-635-1323 515 E david.mcgough@jsc.edu
MCGOUGH, Marsha 425-602-3036 530 K mmcgough@bastyr.edu
MCGOVERN, Bruce 713-646-2920 494 E bmcgovern@stcl.edu
MCGOVERN, Daniel 516-686-7533 343 D dmcgover@nyit.edu
MCGOVERN, Eileen 610-892-1554 441 C emcgovern@pit.edu
MCGOVERN, Lorrie 352-588-7390 116 E lorrie.mcgovern@saintleo.edu
MCGOVERN, Margie 612-861-7554 261 C margie@alfredadler.edu
MCGOVERN, Mark, S 401-865-2702 453 F mmcgovrn@providence.edu
MCGOVERN, Martin, P 508-565-1321 245 D mmcgovern@stonehill.edu
MCGOVERN, Terry 615-230-3352 476 A terry.mcgovern@volstate.edu
MCGOVERN, Thomas 617-236-8800 235 B tmcgovern@fisher.edu
MCGOWAN, Bruce, W 918-877-8101 408 G bwmcgowan@lunet.edu
MCGOWAN, Carl 904-398-4141 121 D
MCGOWAN, Charlotte 269-782-1347 258 E cmcgowan@swmich.edu
MCGOWAN, Chris 573-651-2163 290 D cwmcgowan@semo.edu
MCGOWAN, Debra, P 252-321-4289 372 E dmcgowan@email.pittcc.edu
MCGOWAN, James 516-877-3162 322 A mcgowan2@adelphi.edu
MCGOWAN, Jeanne 215-641-5571 430 C mcgowan.j@gmc.edu
MCGOWAN, Jennifer 909-447-2506 40 E jmcgowan@cst.edu
MCGOWAN, Joanna 610-892-1401 439 B jxm1019@psu.edu
MCGOWAN, John 205-348-5610 8 F john.mcgowan@ua.edu
MCGOWAN, John, P 256-824-2623 9 A john.mcgowan@uah.edu
MCGOWAN, Joseph, J 502-272-8234 198 E jmcgowan@bellarmine.edu
MCGOWAN, Joumana 909-594-5611 58 A jmcgowan@mtsac.edu
MCGOWAN, Kent, M 716-878-4901 353 A mcgowakm@buffalostate.edu
MCGOWAN, Kevin 239-687-5335 101 B kmcgowan@avemarialaw.edu
MCGOWAN, Lisa 717-846-5000 452 G
MCGOWAN, Paul 617-552-3055 232 D paul.mcgowan.2@bc.edu
MCGOWAN, Sindi 770-537-5746 139 B sindi.mcgowan@westgatech.edu
MCGOY, Jeff 618-634-3236 164 C
MCGRADY, Patricia 973-543-6528 307 C acstreasurer@acs350.org
MCGRAIL, Annmarie 914-773-3741 345 F amcgrail@pace.edu
MCGRAIL, Frederick, J 610-758-4487 434 E fjm208@lehigh.edu
MCGRAIL, III, James, J 740-264-5591 390 F jmcgrail@egcc.edu
MCGRAIL, Margaret 914-674-3031 340 G mmcgrail@mercy.edu
MCGRANAHAN, Mary, S 617-552-3300 232 D mary.mcgranahan.1@bc.edu
MCGRANE, Jack, V 973-748-9000 308 A jack_mcgrane@bloomfield.edu
MCGRANE, Wendy 417-625-9386 286 E mcgrane-w@mssu.edu
MCGRANN, Loretta, A 718-940-5980 349 A lmcgrann@sjcny.edu
MCGRANN, Loretta, A 631-687-5142 349 B lmcgrann@sjcny.edu
MCGRATH, Abigail 312-567-3497 153 B amcgrat1@iit.edu
MCGRATH, Andrew, S 608-757-7764 553 E amcgrath@blackhawk.edu
MCGRATH, Charlene 859-441-4500 201 G
MCGRATH, Deborah, F 603-526-3609 304 A dmcgrath@colby-sawyer.edu
MCGRATH, Debra 312-369-7151 148 B dmcgrath@colum.edu
MCGRATH, Elizabeth, Z 660-944-2914 280 F emcgrath@conception.edu
MCGRATH, Jamie 260-399-7700 180 E jmcgrath@sf.edu
MCGRATH, Janet 716-827-2428 358 B mcgrath@trocaire.edu
MCGRATH, Jim 802-831-1233 515 A jmcgrath@vermontlaw.edu
MCGRATH, John 212-594-4000 357 G jmcgrath@tcicollege.edu
MCGRATH, Karen 802-485-2015 514 A karenm@norwich.edu
MCGRATH, Laurie 503-552-1694 417 D lmcgrath@ncnm.edu
MCGRATH, Mark 215-242-1501 425 C mcgrathm@chc.edu
MCGRATH, Robert 404-407-7401 130 D robert.mcgrath@gtri.gatech.edu
MCGRATH, Tim 619-388-2600 65 G tmcgrath@sdccd.edu
MCGRATH, William 212-346-1200 345 F wmcgrath@pace.edu
MCGRATH FLORANCE, Darlene 201-447-7873 307 F dflorance@bergen.edu
MCGRAW, Annette 716-375-2234 348 C amcgraw@sbu.edu
MCGRAW, Darryl, D 919-866-5108 374 E ddmcgraw@waketech.edu
MCGRAW, Jason 610-896-1228 430 G jmcgraw@haverford.edu
MCGRAW, Linda, J 315-445-4185 338 B mcgrawl@lemoyne.edu
MCGRAW, Matt 540-863-2866 526 B mmcgraw@dslcc.edu
MCGRAW, Packy 518-694-7257 322 C packy.mcgraw@acphs.edu
MCGRAW, Paul 660-562-1181 287 E pmcgraw@nwmissouri.edu
MCGREAL, Paul, E 937-229-3795 404 A pmcgreal1@notes.udayton.edu
MCGREEVEY, Michael 315-364-3275 360 C mmcgreevey@wells.edu
MCGREEVY, John, T 574-631-6642 180 D mcgreevy.5@nd.edu
MCGREGOR, Patricia 860-297-2120 94 C patricia.mcgregor@trincoll.edu
MCGREGOR, Wilson, E 254-710-2663 481 I bud_mcgregor@baylor.edu
MCGREGORY, Richard 262-472-4985 552 E mcgregor@uww.edu
MCGREW, Kevin 218-723-6198 262 I kmcgrew@css.edu
MCGREW, Paula, L 304-473-8461 545 F mcgrew_p@wwc.edu
MCGREW, Shea 906-487-3443 255 E smcgrew@mtu.edu
MCGRIFF, Ilona 336-517-2201 362 C imcgriff@bennett.edu
MCGRIFF, Sheryl 313-993-1017 259 C mcgrifsj@udmercy.edu
MCGRIFF-POWERS, Kathleen 716-851-1017 333 B mcgrifpowers@ecc.edu
MCGRISKEN, June 718-489-5352 348 E jmcgrisken@stfranciscollege.edu
MCGUCKIN, Corrie, A 812-374-5173 175 J cmcguckin@ivytech.edu
MCGUCKIN, Denis 516-686-7791 343 D dmcgucki@nyit.edu
MCGUCKIN, Tammy, L 850-474-2382 121 C tmcguckin@uwf.edu
MCGUFFEY, Michael, J 304-696-3648 543 G mcguffey@marshall.edu
MCGUFFIN, Steven 740-699-2484 400 A mcguffin@ohiou.edu
MCGUIGAN, Richard 937-769-1809 383 K rmcguigan@antioch.edu
MCGUIGAN, Richard 937-769-1809 383 K
MCGUINESS, Ilona 410-617-5547 224 A imcguiness@loyola.edu
MCGUINNESS, Maureen 940-565-2648 504 B moe@unt.edu
MCGUINNESS, Paul, M 219-785-5730 178 H mcguinpm@pnc.edu
MCGUINNESS, Thomas, P 617-552-3310 232 D thomas.mcguinness.1@bc.edu
MCGUIRE, Ann 216-421-8019 387 H amcguire@cia.edu
MCGUIRE, Christine 617-353-4176 232 G chmcguir@bu.edu
MCGUIRE, David 561-273-6500 117 J ddmcguire@southuniversity.edu
MCGUIRE, David 561-697-9200 136 H dmcguire@southuniversity.edu
MCGUIRE, David, T 435-586-7755 511 A mcguire@suu.edu
MCGUIRE, Deborah, M 336-838-6524 375 A debi.mcguire@wilkescc.edu
MCGUIRE, Ellen 570-504-7000 425 F
MCGUIRE, Jane 615-230-3204 476 A jane.mcguire@volstate.edu
MCGUIRE, Janelle 810-989-2356 249 B janelle.mcguire@baker.edu
MCGUIRE, Jim 206-239-2302 530 H jmcguire@aii.edu
MCGUIRE, John, M 636-922-8380 288 E jmcguire@stchas.edu
MCGUIRE, Katherine 404-471-6176 123 G kmcguire@agnesscott.edu
MCGUIRE, Kathleen 508-541-1615 234 B kmcguire@dean.edu
MCGUIRE, Mark, T 740-284-5249 390 M mmcguire@franciscan.edu
MCGUIRE, Michael, D 202-687-3439 98 A mcguirmd@georgetown.edu
MCGUIRE, Michael, J 785-670-1763 197 D michael.mcguire@washburn.edu
MCGUIRE, Nancy 712-279-5455 182 E nancy.mcguire@briarcliff.edu
MCGUIRE, Nona, S 614-236-6908 386 C nmcguire@capital.edu
MCGUIRE, Patricia, A 202-884-9050 99 E mcguirep@trinitydc.edu
MCGUIRE, Patrick 315-781-3304 335 G
MCGUIRE, Phyllis 415-239-3014 39 H pmcguire@ccsf.edu
MCGUIRE, Rachel, L 641-422-4104 187 F mcguirac@niacc.edu
MCGUIRE, Ruth, A 651-631-5343 270 E ramcguire@nwc.edu
MCGUIRE, Scott 847-851-5468 83 D smcguire@coloradotech.edu
MCGUIRE, Shaun 718-488-3378 338 H Shaun.McGuire@liu.edu
MCGUIRE, Tara 402-280-3973 297 H taramcguire@creighton.edu
MCGUIRE, William, G 812-941-2243 174 D wgmcguir@ius.edu
MCGUIRE-CLOSSON, Margaret 610-861-4558 437 G mclosson@northampton.edu
MCGUIRK, Dewey 813-880-8017 111 A deweymcguirk@academy.edu
MCGUIRL-HADLEY, Joy 508-999-8148 237 E jhadley@umassd.edu
MCGUKIN, Wanda, R 678-839-6431 138 D wmcgukin@westga.edu
MCGURGAN, Susan 513-231-2223 384 E smcgurgan@athenaeum.edu
MCGURIK, Paul 972-660-5701 490 A
MCGURIMAN, Timothy 312-915-7802 157 A tmcguri@luc.edu
MCGURL, George 802-468-1241 515 C george.mcgurl@castleton.edu
MCGURN, Joseph, P 740-283-6278 390 M jmcgurn@franciscan.edu
MCGURREN, Cynthia 978-542-7591 239 B cmcgurren@salemstate.edu
MCGURTY, Thomas, S 617-627-3264 245 F thomas.mcgurty@tufts.edu
MCGUTHRY, John, W 909-869-6322 33 G sndoda@csupomona.edu
MCHALE, Barbara 215-641-5521 430 C mchale.b@gmc.edu
MCHARGUE, Jackie 828-250-2370 378 C jmchargu@unca.edu
MCHARRIS, Michael 315-792-5489 341 E mmcharris@mvcc.edu
MCHENRY, Bart 949-582-4907 70 F bmchenry@saddleback.edu
MCHENRY, Stephanie 216-687-3673 388 C s.y.mchenry@csuohio.edu
MCHONE, Michael, L 276-223-4798 528 F wcmchom@wcc.vccs.edu
MCHUGH, Carol, G 203-285-2061 90 A cmchugh@gwcc.commnet.edu
MCHUGH, Elizabeth 360-867-6808 533 I mchughe@evergreen.edu
MCHUGH, Eveline 330-337-6403 383 H college@awc.edu
MCHUGH, Kevin 207-786-6341 217 C kmchugh@bates.edu
MCHUGH, Larry 215-567-7080 422 C lmchugh@aii.edu
MCHUGH, Mary 865-251-1800 472 K library@southcollegetn.edu
MCHUGH, Tina 203-285-2092 90 A tmchugh@gwcc.commnet.edu
MCHUGH, Tracy 630-889-6607 159 E tmchugh@nuhs.edu
MCILLECE, Michelle 319-399-8844 183 C mmcillec@coe.edu
MCILNAY, Sandy 816-604-4616 285 [illegible] sandy.mcilnay@mcckc.edu
MCILVANE, Amy 770-426-2648 133 B mcilvane@life.edu
MCILWAINE, Tammy 704-991-0311 374 A tmcilwaine7455@stanly.edu
MCINALLY, David, W 814-332-3782 421 E dave.mcinally@allegheny.edu
MCINERNEY, Tammy 203-837-8290 92 A hammershoyt@wcsu.edu
MCINNES, Allen 806-742-3171 501 D allen.mcinnes@ttu.edu
MCINNIS, Dion 281-283-2021 503 C mcinnis@uhcl.edu
MCINNIS, Robert, L 704-216-6400 366 D rmcinnis@livingstone.edu
MCINNIS, W. Dale 910-410-1806 372 G mcinnisd@richmondcc.edu
MCINTIRE, Dennis, K 770-720-9221 135 F dkm@reinhardt.edu
MCINTIRE, Mary 713-348-2599 492 J maryb@rice.edu
MCINTOSH, Becky, R 864-941-8358 460 D mcintosh.b@ptc.edu
MCINTOSH, Carl, R 803-938-3733 462 F mcintocr@uscsumter.edu
MCINTOSH, Cecilia, A 423-439-4221 473 E mcintosc@etsu.edu
MCINTOSH, Craig 518-276-3992 347 D mcintc@rpi.edu
MCINTOSH, Gary 425-889-7790 535 I gary.mcintosh@northwestu.edu
MCINTOSH, Gayle 253-879-3905 538 E gmcintosh@pugetsound.edu
MCINTOSH, Glenn 248-370-3352 257 C mcintosh@oakland.edu
MCINTOSH, Jennifer 304-293-5496 542 D jennifer.mcintosh@mail.wvu.edu
MCINTOSH, Jennifer, A 304-293-5496 544 E jennifer.mcintosh@mail.wvu.edu
MCINTOSH, Joe 817-515-5377 496 A joe.mcintosh@tccd.edu
MCINTOSH, Joe, E 336-734-7297 370 C jmcintosh@forsythtech.edu
MCINTOSH, John 256-331-5323 6 B jmcintosh@nwscc.edu
MCINTOSH, John, L 574-520-4338 174 C jmcintos@iusb.edu
MCINTOSH, Jonathan 208-882-1566 143 G jmcintosh@nsa.edu
MCINTOSH, Julie 419-434-4062 404 B mcintosh@findlay.edu
MCINTOSH, Keith 520-206-4809 17 I kwmcintosh@pima.edu
MCINTOSH, Tanisha 734-432-5755 254 G tmcintosh@madonna.edu
MCINTOSH, Tim 541-683-5141 415 J tmcintoch@gutcnberg.edu
MCINTOSH-DOTY, Mikail 512-313-3000 483 G mikail.doty@concordia.edu
MCINTURF, Rob 910-962-2682 379 C mcinturfr@uncw.edu
MCINTYRE, Deborah 918-293-5234 410 E deborah.mcintyre@okstate.edu
MCINTYRE, Faye, S 678-839-6467 138 D fmcintyr@westga.edu
MCINTYRE, Jacqueline 516-364-0808 343 A jMcIntyre@nycollege.edu
MCINTYRE, James 513-244-8616 387 D james.mcintyre@ccuniversity.edu
MCINTYRE, James, P 617-552-3246 232 D james.mcintyre.1@bc.edu
MCINTYRE, John 641-844-5668 185 J john.mcintyre@iavalley.edu
MCINTYRE, Julie 518-244-2255 348 A mcinitj@sage.edu
MCINTYRE, Karen 412-392-3976 444 H kmcintyre@pointpark.edu
MCINTYRE, Kevin 806-743-7717 501 E kevin.mcintyre@ttuhsc.edu
MCINTYRE, Kevin, M 610-527-0200 445 I kmcintyre@rosemont.edu
MCINTYRE, Leonard, A 803-536-7173 460 G lamcintyre@scsu.edu
MCINTYRE, Mary, F 412-396-6668 428 C mcintyre@duq.edu
MCINTYRE, Michael 601-643-8404 274 A mike.mcintyre@colin.edu
MCINTYRE, Pam 636-422-2240 289 E pmcintyre@stlcc.edu
MCINTYRE, Richard 401-874-4126 454 E mcintyre@uri.edu
MCINTYRE, Susan, H 252-222-6230 368 F shm@carteret.edu
MCINTYRE, William, A 603-882-6923 304 F bmcintyre@ccsnh.edu
MCINTYRE, Willie 910-672-1157 377 E wmcintyre@uncfsu.edu

MCLAUGHLIN, Joyce .... 978-934-4237.... 237 F Joyce_McLaughlin@uml.edu

MCLAUGHLIN, Katharine, M .... 716-851-1685.... 333 B mclaughlink@ecc.edu

MCLAUGHLIN, Kevin .... 415-503-6253..... 66 A kmclaughlin@sfcm.edu

MCLAUGHLIN, Kevin .... 401-863-9525.... 452 J kevin_mclaughlin@brown.edu

MCLAUGHLIN, Laura .... 636-227-2100.... 284 E Laura.McLaughlin@logan.edu

MCLAUGHLIN, Laurie .... 951-487-6410..... 58 B lmclaugh@msjc.edu

MCLAUGHLIN, Laurie, L ... 612-626-1499.... 272 D mclau001@umn.edu

MCLAUGHLIN, LaVerne ..... 229-430-4799.... 123 H laverne.mclaughlin@asurams.edu

MCLAUGHLIN, Leah .... 918-647-1370.... 407 E lmclaughlin@carlalbert.edu

MCLAUGHLIN, Margaret .... 386-752-1822.... 108 C maggie.mclaughlin@fgc.edu

MCLAUGHLIN, Margaret, K .... 412-578-6071.... 424 G mclaughlinmk@carlow.edu

MCLAUGHLIN, Marianne .... 718-892-3090.... 327 A marianne.mclaughlin@csi.cuny.edu

MCLAUGHLIN, Mark .... 513-745-3409.... 406 E mclaughlin@xavier.edu

MCLAUGHLIN, Mark, W .... 860-832-0065..... 91 G mclaughlinm@ccsu.edu

MCLAUGHLIN, Mary .... 603-526-3755.... 304 A mmclaughlin@colby-sawyer.edu

MCLAUGHLIN, Mary, R ..... 518-454-5170.... 330 C mclaughr@strose.edu

MCLAUGHLIN, Mike .... 319-398-4947.... 186 H mclaug@kirkwood.edu

MCLAUGHLIN, Neil .... 203-837-9308..... 92 A mclaughlinn@wcsu.edu

MCLAUGHLIN, Nora .... 503-777-7774.... 420 A nora.mclaughlin@reed.edu

MCLAUGHLIN, Patricia, A . 401-598-1010.... 453 C pmclaughlin@jwu.edu

MCLAUGHLIN, Patrick, A .. 260-481-6128.... 174 A mclaughp@ipfw.edu

MCLAUGHLIN, Sabrina ...... 850-474-2433.... 121 C smclaughlin2@uwf.edu

MCLAUGHLIN, Sally, J ...... 309-655-7100.... 163 E sally.j.mclaughlin@osfhealthcare.org

MCLAUGHLIN, Sandee ...... 805-591-6220..... 43 F smclaugh@cuesta.edu

MCLAUGHLIN, Stephen, P 262-595-2571.... 551 E stephen.mclaughlin@uwp.edu

MCLAUGHLIN, Steven ...... 404-385-3383.... 130 D steven.mclaughlin@provost.gatech.edu

MCLAUGHLIN, Suzanne .... 816-483-9600.... 289 H sue.mclaughlin@spst.edu

MCLAUGHLIN, Virginia, L . 757-221-2315.... 517 J vamcla@wm.edu

MCLAURIN, Lisa, H .... 919-209-2178.... 371 C lhmclaurin@johnstoncc.edu

MCLAWHORN, David .... 252-940-6201.... 367 I davidmcl@beaufortccc.edu

MCLAWHORN, Toni, D ..... 540-375-2303.... 523 D mclawhorn@roanoke.edu

MCLEAN, Amber .... 906-635-2382.... 254 C amclean@lssu.edu

MCLEAN, Anita .... 609-258-3285.... 313 A amclean@princeton.edu

MCLEAN, Brandon .... 402-844-7102.... 300 A brandon@northeast.edu

MCLEAN, Edward .... 910-672-1315.... 377 E emclean@uncfsu.edu

MCLEAN, H. Elizabeth .... 843-661-1175.... 458 C hmclean@fmarion.edu

MCLEAN, Jack .... 773-508-3912.... 157 A jmclean@luc.edu

MCLEAN, James, E .... 205-348-6052........ 8 F jmclean@bamaed.ua.edu

MCLEAN, Janna .... 815-939-5231.... 160 F jmclean@olivet.edu

MCLEAN, Jennifer .... 570-326-3761.... 440 K jmclean@pct.edu

MCLEAN, Karen, P .... 515-271-1463.... 183 F karen.mclean@dmu.edu

MCLEAN, Matthew .... 731-425-8835.... 475 B mmclean@jscc.edu

MCLEAN, Michael, F .... 805-525-4417..... 72 E mmclean@thomasaquinas.edu

MCLEAN, Mit .... 252-638-7232.... 369 E mcleanm@cravencc.edu

MCLEAN, Natalie .... 336-273-4431.... 362 C nmclean@bennett.edu

MCLEAN, Pat .... 417-690-3441.... 280 C mclean@cofu.edu

MCLEAN, Sandra .... 972-438-6932.... 492 C smclean@parkercc.edu

MCLEAN, Steven .... 661-362-5933..... 41 G steven.mclean@canyons.edu

MCLEAN, Treasa .... 863-638-2984.... 123 C mcleantj@webber.edu

MCLEAN, Valis .... 620-365-5116.... 190 A mclean@allencc.edu

MCLEAN, William, H .... 847-491-7050.... 160 D wmclean@northwestern.edu

MCLEAN-NELSON, Deborah .... 907-842-5109...... 10 J dlmclean@alaska.edu

MCLEANE, David .... 870-574-4458..... 24 A dmcleane@sautech.edu

MCLELLAN, Carolyn .... 757-822-7124.... 528 C cmclellan@tcc.edu

MCLELLAN, Holly, H .... 251-626-3303........ 8 D hmclellan@ussa.edu

MCLELLAN, Keith, C .... 805-965-0581..... 68 B mclellan@sbcc.edu

MCLELLAN, Mark, R .... 352-392-1784.... 120 B mrm1@ufl.edu

MCLELLAN, Mark, R .... 435-797-1180.... 511 B mark.mclellan@usu.edu

MCLELLAND, Brandy .... 310-243-3569..... 34 B bmclelland@csudh.edu

MCLEMORE, Lelan, E .... 262-524-7177.... 546 E lmclemor@carrollu.edu

MCLEMORE, Maria, R .... 651-201-1745.... 265 H maria.mclemore@so.mnscu.edu

MCLENDON, Brenda .... 325-649-8055.... 488 A bmclendon@hputx.edu

MCLENDON, George, L ..... 713-348-4026.... 492 J mclendon@rice.edu

MCLENDON, Ginny .... 252-823-5166.... 370 A mclendong@edgecombe.edu

MCLENDON, Joan, S .... 919-209-2079.... 371 C jsmclendon@johnstoncc.edu

MCLENDON, Valerie .... 636-227-2100.... 284 E valerie.mclendon@logan.edu

MCLENNAN, Dale .... 978-232-2101.... 234 F dmclenna@endicott.edu

MCLENNAN, William, L ..... 650-723-1762..... 71 F mclennan@stanford.edu

MCLEOD, Allan .... 215-871-6652.... 444 B allanm@pcom.edu

MCLEOD, Carol .... 504-278-6418.... 211 I cmcleod@nunez.edu

MCLEOD, Gregory, K .... 904-808-7400.... 116 D gregmcleod@sjrstate.edu

MCLEOD, James, E .... 314-935-7747.... 292 J jemcleod@wustl.edu

MCLEOD, Joetta .... 701-255-3285.... 383 D jmcleod@uttc.edu

MCLEOD, Lorena .... 843-661-8341.... 458 A lorena.mcleod@fdtc.edu

MCLEOD, Margo .... 912-525-6133.... 136 B mmcleod@scad.edu

MCLEOD, Mark .... 404-727-7457.... 129 A rmcleod@emory.edu

MCLEOD, Martha .... 860-253-3001...... 89 K mmcleod@acc.commnet.edu

MCLEOD, Michael .... 863-784-7441.... 117 I michael.mcleod@southflorida.edu

MCLEOD, Michael, J .... 516-877-3177.... 322 A mcleod@adelphi.edu

MCLEOD, Pat .... 419-448-3353.... 402 E mcleodp@tiffin.edu

MCLEOD, Philip, D .... 610-917-1401.... 450 D pdmcleod@vfcc.edu

MCLEOD, Steve .... 901-761-1353.... 469 A smcleod@hst.edu

MCLEOD, Susan .... 910-576-6222.... 372 A

MCLEOD, Terry .... 706-867-3230.... 134 D tmcleod@northgeorgia.edu

MCLEOD, Toni .... 954-262-4932.... 114 B toni@nsu.nova.edu

MCLESKEY, Stephanie .... 828-689-1128.... 366 F smcleskey@mhc.edu

MCLIN, SR., Kevin, J .... 334-727-4553........ 8 C kjones2056@mytu.tuskegee.edu

MCLLWAIN, Daryl .... 207-780-5510.... 220 G darylmc@usm.maine.edu

MCLOGAN, Matthew, E ...... 616-331-2190.... 252 A mcloganm@gvsu.edu

MCLOUD, Debbie .... 479-575-2159..... 24 C dmcloud@uark.edu

MCLOUGHLIN, John .... 516-299-3848.... 339 A john.mcloughlin@liu.edu

MCLOUGHLIN, John .... 516-299-2824.... 339 A john.mclouglin@liu.edu

MCLOUGHLIN, Suzanne .... 516-876-3109.... 353 D mcloughlins@oldwestbury.edu

MCLURE, Amanda .... 954-783-7339.... 106 D amclure@cci.edu

MCMAHAN, Carla .... 864-977-7090.... 460 A carla.mcmahan@ngu.edu

MCMAHAN, David .... 423-636-7315.... 476 F dmcmahan@tusculum.edu

MCMAHAN, Kerrin .... 323-265-8723..... 54 G mcmahakm@elac.edu

MCMAHAN, Mendi, M .... 214-333-5119.... 484 C mendi@dbu.edu

MCMAHAN, Michael .... 661-362-3320..... 41 G michael.mcmahan@canyons.edu

MCMAHAN, Oliver, L .... 423-478-7037.... 472 F omcmahan@ptseminary.edu

MCMAHAN, Robert .... 828-227-2159.... 379 E rmcmahan@wcu.edu

MCMAHAN, Robert, K .... 810-762-9864.... 253 I mcmahan@kettering.edu

MCMAHAN, Shari .... 657-278-7000..... 34 E smcmahan@fullerton.edu

MCMAHAN, Terry .... 239-513-1122.... 110 K tmcmahan@hodges.edu

MCMAHILL, Janet, M .... 515-271-3726.... 184 A janet.mcmahill@drake.edu

MCMAHON, Bernadette, B . 312-369-7436.... 148 B bmcmahon@colum.edu

MCMAHON, Christopher ... 516-773-5535.... 558 F mcmahon@usmma.edu

MCMAHON, Cindy .... 212-962-0002.... 342 G cmcmahon@nyci.edu

MCMAHON, Cyndi .... 978-867-4236.... 235 E cyndi.mcmahon@gordon.edu

MCMAHON, David .... 413-748-3210.... 245 C dmcmahon@spfldcol.edu

MCMAHON, Doug .... 727-864-8587.... 104 K mcmahodh@eckerd.edu

MCMAHON, James, P .... 414-288-7208.... 548 D james.mcmahon@marquette.edu

MCMAHON, Jessica .... 252-527-6223.... 371 D jmcmahon@lenoircc.edu

MCMAHON, Kathleen, N ... 401-254-3161.... 454 C kmcmahon@rwu.edu

MCMAHON, Kevin .... 213-613-2200..... 70 H kevin_mcmahon@sciarc.edu

MCMAHON, M.J .... 928-523-6515..... 17 A mj.mcmahon@nau.edu

MCMAHON, Margaret, J .... 814-827-4418.... 449 E mcmahon@pitt.edu

MCMAHON, Marie .... 619-388-7497..... 65 H mmcmahon@sdccd.edu

MCMAHON, Mary Pat .... 207-725-3225.... 217 E mmcmahon@bowdoin.edu

MCMAHON, Melody, L ...... 773-371-5460.... 146 B mmcmahon@ctu.edu

MCMAHON, Natalie .... 601-276-2000.... 277 E nmcmahon@smcc.edu

MCMAHON, Patricia .... 513-862-2743.... 391 D

MCMAHON, Rebecca .... 216-987-4865.... 389 A rebecca.mcmahon@tri-c.edu

MCMAHON, Renee, M .... 406-447-5501.... 294 A rmcmahon@carroll.edu

MCMAHON, Roberta .... 708-524-6790.... 150 A rmcmahon@dom.edu

MCMAHON, Shelly, A .... 740-368-3201.... 400 F samcmaho@owu.edu

MCMAHON, Stephen .... 802-654-2516.... 514 B smcmahon@smcvt.edu

MCMAHON, Timothy, J ..... 412-359-1000.... 448 F tmcmahon@triangle-tech.edu

MCMAHON, Timothy, J ..... 412-359-1000.... 448 E tmcmahon@triangle-tech.edu

MCMAINS, Robert, E .... 765-494-8000.... 178 F remcmains@purdue.edu

MCMAKIN, Sandy .... 210-805-3005.... 503 F mcmakin@uiwtx.edu

MCMANIGLE, John .... 301-295-3016.... 558 A jmcmanigle@usuhs.mil

MCMANNESS, Matthew ...... 215-951-1050.... 432 G mcmanness@lasalle.edu

MCMANUS, Amy .... 919-497-3330.... 366 E amcmanus@louisburg.edu

MCMANUS, Bill .... 864-977-2094.... 460 A bill.mcmanus@ngu.edu

MCMANUS, Cecil .... 919-546-8417.... 376 D cmcmanus@shawu.edu

MCMANUS, D. Kim .... 804-758-6705.... 527 G kmcmanus@rappahannock.edu

MCMANUS, Janet .... 816-501-3618.... 279 C janet.mcmanus@avila.edu

MCMANUS, Jeffrey .... 239-348-4715.... 101 C jeff.mcmanus@avemaria.edu

MCMANUS, Michael .... 303-797-5654..... 80 J michael.mcmanus@arapahoe.edu

MCMANUS, Michael, L ...... 619-702-9400..... 32 G mcmismism@aol.com

MCMANUS, Robert .... 631-244-3000.... 332 D ir@dowling.edu

MCMANUS, Teresa .... 718-289-5439.... 326 F teresa.mcmanus@bcc.cuny.edu

MCMASTER, Dennis .... 724-503-1001.... 451 A dmcmaster@washjeff.edu

MCMASTER, Jeff .... 617-217-9036.... 231 C jmcmaster@baystate.edu

MCMASTER, Robert .... 612-625-9883.... 272 D mcmaster@umn.edu

MCMASTER, Susan .... 803-774-3311.... 455 G mcmastersm@cctech.edu

MCMASTERS, Mark .... 405-325-2252.... 413 C mark.mcmasters-1@ou.edu

MCMATH, Robert .... 479-575-7678..... 24 C rmcmath@uark.edu

MCMEANS, Orlando, F ...... 304-766-4291.... 544 D mcmeanso@wvstateu.edu

MCMEEKIN, Bill .... 253-840-8419.... 536 C bmcmeekin@pierce.ctc.edu

MCMELLON-WELLS, Pamela, Y .... 856-225-6140.... 314 C pmcwells@camden.rutgers.edu

MCMENAMIN, Margaret, M .... 908-709-7100.... 316 B mcmenamin@ucc.edu

MCMICHAEL, Cyndi .... 248-204-4109.... 254 E cmcmichael@ltu.edu

MCMICHAEL, Joe .... 919-735-5151.... 374 F mcm@waynecc.edu

MCMICHAEL, Robert .... 717-560-8240.... 433 bmcmichael@lbc.edu

MCMICKLE, Marvin, A .... 585-340-9680.... 329 mmcmickle@crcds.edu

MCMILLAN, Bryan .... 910-221-2224.... 364 C

MCMILLAN, Caroline .... 912-486-7056.... 128 cmcmillan@ega.edu

MCMILLAN, Cindy .... 251-343-8200........ 6 cindy.mcmillan@remingtoncollege.edu

MCMILLAN, Douglas .... 580-745-2200.... 412 C dmcmillan@se.edu

MCMILLAN, Douglas .... 580-745-2206.... 412 C dmcmillan@se.edu

MCMILLAN, Forrest .... 325-670-1250.... 487 D fmcmill@hsutx.edu

MCMILLAN, Howard .... 601-974-1250.... 275 D mcmilhl1@millsaps.edu

MCMILLAN, Jacqueline ...... 937-775-4271.... 406 C jacqueline.mcmillan@wright.edu

MCMILLAN, Jane .... 580-745-2604.... 412 C jmcmillan@se.edu

MCMILLAN, Joseph .... 512-444-8082.... 499 E jtmcmillan@texastcm.edu

MCMILLAN, Judy .... 757-822-5121.... 528 C jmcmillan@tcc.edu

MCMILLAN, Karon .... 601-925-3212.... 275 E kmcmilla@mc.edu

MCMILLAN, III, Lex, O ..... 610-921-7600.... 421 D lmcmillan@alb.edu

MCMILLAN, Marilyn .... 212-998-2001.... 344 B marilyn.mcmillan@nyu.edu

MCMILLAN, Mark, A .... 817-515-5331.... 496 A mark.mcmillan@tccd.edu

MCMILLAN, Mary .... 310-303-7302...... 56 F mmcmillan@marymountpv.edu

MCMILLAN, Minnie .... 334-874-5700........ 3 A mmcmillan@concordiaselma.edu

MCMILLEN, Bonnie, K .... 814-362-0968.... 449 B mcmillen@pitt.edu

MCMILLEN, Jeremy .... 903-675-6371.... 502 D jmcmillen@tvcc.edu

MCMILLEN, Mike .... 859-246-6770.... 201 D mike.mcmillen@kctcs.edu

MCMILLEN, William, E ...... 419-530-2739.... 404 F william.mcmillen@utoledo.edu

MCMILLIAN, Carey .... 816-271-4582.... 287 A mcmilli@missouriwestern.edu

MCMILLIN, Barbara .... 731-668-5314.... 476 G bmcmilli@uu.edu

MCMILLIN, David .... 417-626-1234.... 287 F dmcmillin@occ.edu

MCMILLIN, Jennifer .... 417-626-1234.... 287 F jmcmillin@occ.edu

MCMILLIN, Larry, M .... 208-467-8493.... 143 I lmmcmillin@nnu.edu

MCMILLIN, Lisa .... 601-635-2111.... 274 C lmcmillan@eccc.edu

MCMILLIN, Nicole .... 605-367-4821.... 466 C nicole.mcmillin@southeasttech.edu

MCMILLION, Annie .... 304-647-6213.... 544 C amcmillion@osteo.wvsom.edu

MCMILLION, David .... 706-776-0114.... 135 D dmcmillion@piedmont.edu

MCMILLION, Eric, C .... 859-858-3511.... 198 B eric.mcmillion@asbury.edu

MCMILLON, Avis .... 732-224-2967.... 308 B amcmillon@brookdalecc.edu

MCMINIMY, Gisele .... 316-295-5377.... 192 H mcminimy@friends.edu

MCMOORE-GRAY, Vicki .... 704-216-6222.... 366 D vmcmoore@livingstone.edu

MCMOY, Johnny .... 478-374-6402.... 133 G jmcmoy@mgc.edu

MCMULLAN, James .... 601-679-3570.... 274 D jmcmullan@eastms.edu

MCMULLEN, Eileen .... 215-567-7080.... 422 C emcmullen@aii.edu

MCMULLEN, Judith .... 216-987-4836.... 389 A judith.mcmullen@tri-c.edu

MCMULLEN, Justine .... 816-279-7000.... 278 H faid@acot.edu

MCMULLEN, Kenneth, J .... 704-366-5066.... 375 H kmcmullen@rts.edu

MCMULLEN, Linda, H .... 706-880-8021.... 132 I lmcmullen@lagrange.edu

MCMULLEN, Michael .... 315-498-2566.... 345 D mcmullem@sunyocc.edu

MCMULLEN, Patricia .... 202-319-5403...... 97 C mcmullep@cua.edu

MCMULLEN, Ruth .... 707-524-1721...... 68 E rmcmullen@santarosa.edu

MCMULLEN, William, T ..... 409-740-4478.... 497 D mcmullew@tamug.edu

MCMULLIN, Sallie, D .... 434-395-2060.... 520 G mcmullinsd@longwood.edu

MCMURDOCK, Linda .... 310-338-3756...... 56 E lmcmurdock@lmu.edu

MCMURRAY, Aaron, P ...... 509-777-3730.... 539 F amcmurray@whitworth.edu

MCMURRAY, Brock .... 661-763-7811...... 72 C bmcmurray@taftcollege.edu

MCMURRAY, Jeffrey .... 903-886-5852.... 497 E jeffrey_mcmurray@tamu-commerce.edu

MCMURRAY, Kelly 678-359-5339 131 D
kelly1m@gdn.edu
MCMURRY, Marna, R 910-256-0255 367 D
mdavenport@moc.edu
MCMURTRY, Kim 828-669-8012 367 C
kmcmurtry@montreat.edu
MCMURTRY, Tom, O 828-669-8012 367 C
tmcmurtry@montreat.edu
MCNAB, Pat 513-727-3300 396 F
MCNABB, David 970-521-6655 86 E
david.mcnabb@njc.edu
MCNABB, Deana, M 406-338-5421 293 F
deana_mcnabb@bfcc.org
MCNABB, Jane 206-546-6224 537 G
jmcnabb@shoreline.edu
MCNABB, Terry 319-399-8870 183 C
tmcnabb@coe.edu
MCNAIR, Betty-Ann, W 832-252-4691 483 A
bettyann.mcnair@cbshouston.edu
MCNAIR, Christopher, L 325-670-1401 487 D
cmcnair@hsutx.edu
MCNAIR, Don 541-463-5306 416 D
mcnaird@lanecc.edu
MCNAIR, Lily, D 718-390-3211 359 G
lily.mcnair@wagner.edu
MCNAIR, Michael 202-885-2527 97 B
mmcnair@american.edu
MCNAIR, Mike 409-882-3933 500 G
mike.mcnair@lsco.edu
MCNAIR, Phil 304-724-3700 540 C
pmcnair@apus.edu
MCNAIR, Sheila 804-524-6948 529 C
smcnair@vsu.edu
MCNAIRY, Francine, G 717-872-3591 443 C
mupresident@millersville.edu
MCNALL, Mike 309-457-2122 158 G
mike@monm.edu
MCNALLY, Beth 712-749-2052 182 G
mcnallyb@bvu.edu
MCNALLY, Elizabeth, B 740-376-4683 395 F
beth.mcnally@marietta.edu
MCNALLY, Minta, A 336-758-4237 380 B
mcnallma@wfu.edu
MCNALLY, Neal, P 330-941-2489 406 F
npmcnally@ysu.edu
MCNALLY, Pamela 913-758-4389 197 B
mcnally37@stmary.edu
MCNALLY, Patrick 313-496-2689 260 C
pmcnall1@wcccd.edu
MCNALLY, Robin 508-793-7467 233 C
rmcnally@clarku.edu
MCNALLY, Steven, L 303-492-5489 88 B
steve.mcnally@colorado.edu
MCNALLY, Susanne 315-781-3467 335 G
banks@hws.edu
MCNALLY, Tom 803-777-3142 462 A
tom@gwm.sc.edu
MCNAMARA, Anne 602-639-7500 14 I
MCNAMARA, Bob 800-686-7022 92 F
bmcnamara@lincolncollegene.edu
MCNAMARA, John 862-906-5102 89 L
jmcnamara@ccc.commnet.edu
MCNAMARA, John 815-394-5152 162 H
jmcnamara@rockford.edu
MCNAMARA, John, M 312-987-2393 154 F
6mcnamar@jmls.edu
MCNAMARA, Joyce 773-777-4220 160 C
jmcnamara@nc.edu
MCNAMARA, Judith 215-572-2124 422 B
severin@arcadia.edu
MCNAMARA, Julia, M 203-773-8529 89 H
mcnamara@albertus.edu
MCNAMARA, Kimberly 360-475-7230 535 J
kmcnamara@olympic.edu
MCNAMARA, Kristine, E 401-598-1565 453 C
kmcnamara@jwu.edu
MCNAMARA, Mary, E 651-255-6106 271 I
memcnamara@unitedseminary.edu
MCNAMARA, Ryan 727-726-1153 103 B
MCNAMARA, Thomas 508-929-8097 239 D
tmcnamara@worcester.edu
MCNAMARA, Thomas 610-282-1100 426 I
tom.mcnamara@desales.edu
MCNAMEE, Barbara 734-384-4244 255 G
bmcnamee@monroeccc.edu
MCNAMEE, Jane 314-587-2433 284 A
MCNAMEE, Kathleen 870-612-2081 25 E
kathleen.mcnamee@uaccb.edu
MCNAMEE, Mark, G 540-231-6123 529 B
mmcnamee@vt.edu
MCNANEY, Duane 903-983-8107 489 F
dmcnaney@kilgore.edu
MCNANNAY, Dawn 541-259-5800 416 H
mcnannd@linnbenton.edu
MCNEAL, Deborah 662-621-4124 273 I
dmcneal@coahomacc.edu
MCNEAL, Nadine, G 731-989-6644 468 K
nmcneal@fhu.edu
MCNEALEY, Ernest 205-366-8800 7 G
emcnealey@stillman.edu
MCNEALY, Tara, F 843-953-5336 456 C
tara.mcnealy@citadel.edu
MCNEAR, Jack 502-597-5853 203 D
jack.mcnear@kysu.edu
MCNEAR, Kristy 970-225-4860 81 I
krmcnear@collegeamerica.edu
MCNEEL, Jon, T 402-449-2858 298 B
deanofmen@graceu.edu
MCNEELY, Bonnie 405-974-2884 413 B
bmcneely@ucok.edu
MCNEELY, Malone, C 828-448-6020 374 G
mmcneely@wpcc.edu
MCNEELY, Shelley 608-785-9880 555 D
mcneelys@westerntc.edu
MCNEELY, Stanton 985-858-5704 210 H
smcneely@ftcc.edu
MCNEER, James, B 804-862-6220 523 C
jmcneer@rbc.edu
MCNEESE, Beverly 402-363-5690 301 F
bdmcneese@york.edu
MCNEESE, Margaret 713-500-5116 506 D
margaret.c.mcneese@uth.tmc.edu
MCNEESE, Tim, D 402-363-5683 301 F
tdmcnesse@york.edu
MCNEICE-STALLARD,
Barbara 909-594-5611 58 A
bmcneice-stallard@mtsac.edu
MCNEIL, Denise, M 810-989-5571 258 B
dmcneil@sc4.edu
MCNEIL, J. Derek 206-876-6105 537 E
dmcneil@theseattleschool.edu
MCNEIL, Jacquelyn 941-752-5231 118 E
mcneilj@scf.edu
MCNEIL, Marilyn 732-571-3415 311 F
mmcneil@monmouth.edu
MCNEIL, Roger 606-783-2158 204 E
r.mcneil@moreheadstate.edu
MCNEIL, Ronald, D 217-206-6533 167 A
mcneil.ron@uis.edu
MCNEIL, Sybil 478-757-5200 139 A
smcneil@wesleyancollege.edu
MCNEIL, Vickie, J 336-334-5099 379 A
vlmcnei2@uncg.edu
MCNEIL, Wanda 314-340-3511 282 I
mcneilj@hssu.edu
MCNEILL, Denise 806-720-7527 490 D
denise.mcneill@lcu.edu
MCNEILL, Janette, N 336-454-1126 370 E
jnmcneill@gtcc.edu
MCNEILL, Kathy 210-999-7472 502 C
kathy.mcneill@trinity.edu
MCNEILL, Kevin 910-576-6222 372 A
mcneillk@montgomery.edu
MCNEILL, Patricia 707-664-2133 37 B
patricia.mcneill@sonoma.edu
MCNEILL, JR., Robert, J 215-489-2375 426 H
Robert.McNeill@delval.edu
MCNEILL, Savonne 704-922-6420 370 D
mcneill.savonne@gaston.edu
MCNEILL, William, T 336-506-4157 367 G
mcneillt@alamancecc.edu
MCNERNEY, David 515-271-1408 183 F
david.mcnerney@dmu.edu
MCNERNEY, Norma, L 203-857-7020 90 G
nmcnerney@ncc.commnet.edu
MCNESBY, Gerard, M 302-739-4057 96 A
gmcnesby@dtcc.edu
MCNEW, G. Lonnie 410-704-3256 228 E
lmcnew@towson.edu
MCNEW, Janet, M 813-258-7360 122 H
provost@ut.edu
MCNICOL, Greg, L 915-747-7116 505 E
gmcnicol@utep.edu
MCNIECE, Elaine, M 501-450-3124 25 H
elainem@uca.edu
MCNIEL, Donna 209-946-2325 75 D
dmcniel@pacific.edu
MCNIVEN, Spencer 860-628-4751 92 F
smcniven@lincolncollegene.edu
MCNULTY, Alison 307-268-3123 555 F
amcnulty@caspercollege.edu
MCNULTY, Edward, J 312-629-9159 164 A
emcnulty@saic.edu
MCNULTY, Frederick, C 219-785-5241 178 H
fmcnulty@pnc.edu
MCNULTY, Mary Kate 215-572-2877 422 B
mcnultym@arcadia.edu
MCNULTY, Priscilla 612-977-5901 262 A
priscilla.mcnulty@capella.edu
MCNULTY, Sean, J 602-386-4117 11 H
sean.mcnulty@arizonachristian.edu
MCNULTY, Sharon 973-290-4134 309 A
mcnulty@cse.edu
MCNUTT, Anne 205-387-0511 2 B
amcnutt@bscc.edu
MCNUTT, Paula 406-447-4404 294 A
pmcnutt@carroll.edu
MCPARTLAN, Edward, J 914-337-9300 331 A
ed.mcpartlan@concordia-ny.edu
MCPARTLON, Shannon 313-664-7460 250 A
smcpartlon@collegeforcreativestudies.edu
MCPEAK, Charlene 586-286-2097 254 F
mcpeakc@macomb.edu
MCPEAK, Geniece 850-747-6918 101 G
gmcpeak@baymedical.org
MCPEAK, Patrick 315-255-1743 325 H
patrick.mcpeak@cayuga-cc.edu
MCPEAK, Ronie 615-444-2462 467 I
rmcpeak@cumberland.edu
MCPHAIL, Brenda, M 314-516-6503 291 F
bmcphail@umsl.edu
MCPHAIL, Craig 828-898-5241 366 A
mcphail@lmc.edu
MCPHAIL, Mark 262-472-1221 552 E
mcphailm@uww.edu
MCPHAIL NAPLES,
Fabienne 714-895-8319 41 A
fmcphailnaples@gwc.cccd.edu
MCPHATTER, Anna 443-885-4325 224 F
anna.mcphatter@morgan.edu
MCPHEE, Gary 781-280-3230 240 F
mcpheeg@middlesex.mass.edu
MCPHEE, Gary, R 781-280-3530 240 F
mcpheeg@middlesex.mass.edu
MCPHEE, Sidney, A 615-898-2623 473 F
sidney.mcphee@mtsu.edu
MCPHEETERS, Andrew 503-768-7936 416 F
mcpheete@lclark.edu
MCPHERON, Bruce, A 814-865-2541 438 F
bam10@psu.edu
MCPHERREN, Ann, C 260-359-4225 172 K
amcpherren@huntington.edu
MCPHERSON, Evelyn 806-743-2860 501 D
evelyn.mcpherson@ttuhsc.edu
MCPHERSON, John 765-285-5600 169 D
jmcphers@bsu.edu
MCPHERSON, Lindsey 713-525-3639 504 D
guthmanl@stthom.edu
MCPHERSON, Mary, L 972-860-5097 484 I
mmcpherson@dcccd.edu
MCPHERSON, Melissa 231-876-3112 248 F
melissa.mcpherson@baker.edu
MCPHERSON, Michael 305-809-3280 108 F
michael.mcpherson@fkcc.edu
MCPHERSON, Robert 713-743-5003 503 B
rmcpherson@uh.edu
MCPHERSON, Sean 570-586-2400 422 F
smacpherson@bbc.edu
MCPHERSON, Terry 704-378-1237 365 H
tmcpherson@jcsu.edu
MCPHERSON, Tremayne 708-342-3711 149 L
tmcpherson@devry.edu
MCPHERSON, Winnifred 954-486-7728 122 E
MCPHERSON-BARNES,
Penny 856-256-4086 314 A
barnesp@rowan.edu
MCPHIE-OLIVEIRA,
Laura, E 401-341-2103 454 D
mcphiel@salve.edu
MCPHILIMY, Betty, L 847-491-2622 160 D
b-mcphilimy@northwestern.edu
MCPIKE, Julie 618-468-3600 156 C
jmcpike@lc.edu
MCQUADE, Robert, K 574-631-7727 180 D
mcquade.10@nd.edu
MCQUADE, Shauna, N 301-784-5000 221 A
smcquade@allegany.edu
MCQUARIE, Audra 602-557-6151 19 C
audra.mcquarie@phoenix.edu
MCQUARRIE, Laurie 207-942-6781 217 B
lmcquarrie@bts.edu
MCQUATE, Craig 617-369-3252 244 G
cmcquate@mfa.org
MCQUAY-PENINGER,
Laurel 310-434-3718 68 D
mcquay-peninger_laurel@smc.edu
MCQUEEN, Angus 540-887-7012 520 I
amcqueen@mbc.edu
MCQUEEN, Candice 615-966-5708 470 D
candice.mcqueen@lipscomb.edu
MCQUEEN, Elaine 803-754-3950 463 E
MCQUEEN, Lee 308-865-1700 300 G
mcqueenlv@unk.edu
MCQUEEN, Mary 361-698-1317 485 F
mmcqueen2@delmar.edu
MCQUEEN, Rebecca 704-463-3404 375 E
rebecca.mcqueen@fsmail.pfeiffer.edu
MCQUERE, Gordon 785-670-1561 197 D
gordon.mcquere@washburn.edu
MCQUERRY, Marcia 405-878-2025 409 D
marcia.mcquerry@okbu.edu
MCQUESTEN, Pamela 323-259-1451 59 H
pmcquesten@oxy.edu
MCQUILKIN, Scott, A 509-777-4386 539 F
smcquilkin@whitworth.edu
MCQUINN, Robert 847-467-2469 160 D
r.mcquinn@northwestern.edu
MCQUISTION, Chris 615-383-4848 478 E
cmcquistion@watkins.edu
MCQUOWN, Daniel 517-629-0492 247 E
dmcquown@albion.edu
MCRAE, Alphonzo 910-272-3500 373 A
mcrae@robeson.edu
MCRAE, Georgia, D 414-288-7596 548 D
georgia.mcrae@marquette.edu
MCRAE, Jim 206-780-6214 530 I
jim.mcrae@bgi.edu
MCRAE, John 865-974-5267 477 B
jmcrae1@utk.edu
MCRAE, Kevin 406-444-0328 294 J
kmcrae@montana.edu
MCRAE, Marcia, A 229-248-2596 125 E
mmcrae@bainbridge.edu
MCRAE, Mary 972-881-5797 483 D
mmcrae@collin.edu
MCRAE, Maureen 323-259-2548 59 H
mmclevy@oxy.edu
MCRAE, Richard 502-897-4720 205 H
rjmcrae@sbts.edu
MCRANEY, Laura 706-233-7409 136 E
lmcraney@shorter.edu
MCRELL, Michael 620-341-5214 192 D
mcrellmi@emporia.edu
MCREYNOLDS, Betsy, A 417-667-8181 280 I
bmcreynolds@cottey.edu
MCREYNOLDS, Irene 386-226-6151 105 B
mcreynoi@erau.edu
MCREYNOLDS, Jeffrey 573-288-6343 281 D
kcapps@culver.edu
MCREYNOLDS, Karla 573-288-6544 281 D
kmcreynolds@culver.edu
MCREYNOLDS, Kevin 801-524-8138 510 A
kmcreynolds@ldsbc.edu
MCREYNOLDS, Shawn 276-223-4810 528 F
wcmcres@wcc.vccs.edu
MCROBBIE, Michael 812-855-4613 173 C
iupres@indiana.edu
MCROBBIE, Michael, A 812-855-4613 173 B
iupres@indiana.edu
MCROBERTS, Karen 207-786-6232 217 C
kmcrober@bates.edu
MCROBIE, Karen 415-442-6599 48 E
kmcrobie@ggu.edu
MCRORIE, Sally, E 850-644-5244 119 C
smcrorie@fsu.edu
MCSHAN, Jim, C 713-313-1382 499 G
mcshanjc@tsu.edu
MCSHANE, Bridget 860-439-2314 91 E
bamcs@conncoll.edu
MCSHANE, SJ, Joseph, M 718-817-3000 334 C
MCSHANE, Kathi 510-849-8247 60 H
kmcshane@psr.edu
MCSHANE, Kevin 414-302-7000 546 C
kemcshane@bryantstratton.edu
MCSHEA, Anitra, M 570-941-7680 450 B
mcsheaa2@scranton.edu
MCSHEEHY, Diane, M 303-458-4223 87 E
dmcsheehy@regis.edu
MCSHERRY, Brenda 573-442-2211 290 G
MCSHURLEY, Mark, C 540-636-2900 517 H
markm@christendom.edu
MCSPADDEN, Galen, W 620-417-1550 196 B
galen.mcspadden@sccc.edu
MCSPADDEN, Jean 903-675-6304 502 D
jmcspadden@tvcc.edu
MCSPADDEN, Nancy 870-307-7474 22 D
nmcspadden@lyon.edu
MCSWAIN, Michael 704-484-4115 369 B
mcswain@clevelandcommunitycollege.edu
MCSWAIN, Roderick 251-665-4139 2 D
rmcswain@bishop.edu
MCSWEENEY, Frances 509-335-5581 539 A
fkmcs@wsu.edu
MCSWEENEY, Kevin, D 608-262-2748 550 G
kmcsweeney@wisc.edu
MCTAGGART, Rob 906-487-7346 251 C
rob.mctaggart@finlandia.edu
MCTEAGUE, Michael 740-699-2354 400 A
mcteague@ohio.edu
MCTERNAN, Edmund 518-464-8500 333 F
mmcternan@excelsior.edu
MCTIERNAN, Kerri-Ann 212-217-4210 333 G
kerriann_mctiernan@fitnyc.edu
MCTYSON, Pascha 914-323-5490 340 A
pascha.mctyson@mville.edu
MCVAUGH, William, B 540-985-9935 520 D
wbmcvaugh@jchs.edu
MCVAY, Danny 318-487-7137 209 B
mcvay@lacollege.edu
MCVAY, Janine 413-565-1000 231 B
jmcvay@baypath.edu
MCVAY, John 509-527-2066 538 H
john.mcvay@wallawalla.edu
MCVAY, John, R 575-624-8150 319 C
mcvay@nmmi.edu
MCVAY-DYCHE, Jennifer 541-552-7672 419 A
mcvaydycj@sou.edu
MCVEAN, Aaron 530-541-4660 53 F
mcvean@ltcc.edu
MCVEARRY, Kenneth 301-447-5274 225 A
mcvearry@msmary.edu
MCVEETY, Cassie 503-491-7213 417 B
cassie.mcveety@mhcc.edu
MCVEIGH, Paul, J 703-323-4224 527 C
pmcveigh@nvcc.edu
MCVETY, Paul, J 401-598-1775 453 C
pmcvety@jwu.edu
MCVEY, Greg 573-288-6424 281 D
gmcvey@culver.edu
MCWADE, Patricia, A 202-687-4547 98 A
mcwadep@georgetown.edu
MCWAINE, Lamar 281-998-6150 493 F
lamar.mcwaine@sjcd.edu
MCWEENY, Charles, A 740-593-1808 399 G
mcweeny@ohio.edu
MCWHA, Jena, P 315-443-9626 357 B
jpmcwha@syr.edu

MCWHERTER, Karen .... 731-661-5337.... 476 G
kmcwhert@uu.edu
MCWHORTER, Lois, A .... 606-878-4801.... 202 F
lois.mcwhorter@kctcs.edu
MCWHORTER, Shirlyon, J . 305-348-2785.... 119 B
shirlyon.mcwhorter@fiu.edu
MCWILLIAM, Jan .... 310-314-6102.... 29 J
MCWILLIAMS, Stephen, T . 610-519-4095.... 450 G
stephen.mcwilliams@villanova.edu
MCWILLIAMS, Thomas ...... 480-219-6111.... 278 F
tmcwilliams@atsu.edu
MCWILLIE, Betty, E .... 901-321-3330.... 467 G
mcwillie@cbu.edu
MEA, William .... 718-390-3315.... 359 G
william.mea@wagner.edu
MEACHEN, Ed .... 608-263-2571.... 550 F
emeachen@uwsa.edu
MEAD, Amanda (Ame) .... 314-889-4514.... 282 C
amead@fontbonne.edu
MEAD, Dana, G .... 717-361-1359.... 428 E
meaddg@etown.edu
MEAD, David, B .... 817-515-6604.... 496 A
david.mead@tccd.edu
MEAD, JR., George, F .... 337-475-5785.... 215 G
mead@mcneese.edu
MEAD, JR., George, F .... 334-475-5785.... 215 G
mead@mcneese.edu
MEAD, K. Ann .... 270-745-2434.... 207 C
ann.mead@wku.edu
MEAD, Stephen, W .... 630-752-5113.... 168 F
stephen.mead@wheaton.edu
MEAD, Steven .... 860-255-3473.... 91 C
smead@txcc.commnet.edu
MEAD, Susan .... 845-431-8036.... 332 E
mead@sunydutchess.edu
MEADE, Elizabeth .... 610-606-4637.... 424 I
MEADE, Haley .... 212-431-2164.... 343 E
hmeade@nyls.edu
MEADE, Linda, B .... 724-946-7339.... 451 C
meadelb@westminster.edu
MEADE, Marianne .... 610-989-1240.... 450 E
mmeade@vfmac.edu
MEADERS, Kennedy .... 662-329-7436.... 276 B
kmeaders@pd.muw.edu
MEADERS-BOOTH,
Jacqueline, D .... 314-984-7611.... 289 D
jmeadersbooth@stlcc.edu
MEADOR, Diane .... 907-796-6457..... 11 A
diane.meador@uas.alaska.edu
MEADOR, JR., John, M ..... 607-777-2346.... 351 F
jmeador@binghamton.edu
MEADOR, Mark .... 615-966-6223.... 470 D
mark.meador@lipscomb.edu
MEADOR, Michele .... 775-673-7249.... 302 J
mmeador@tmcc.edu
MEADOR, Roy .... 517-750-1200.... 258 F
rmeador@arbor.edu
MEADOR, Ruby .... 870-762-3125..... 20 A
rmeador@smail.anc.edu
MEADOR, Ryan .... 816-943-7316.... 281 E
rmeador@devry.edu
MEADORS, Emily, J .... 606-539-4217.... 206 G
emily.meadors@ucumberlands.edu
MEADORS, Mark .... 918-343-7860.... 411 H
mmeadors@rsu.edu
MEADOWS, David, J .... 804-524-5995.... 529 C
pbullock@vsu.edu
MEADOWS, Dean .... 863-638-7255.... 123 B
dean.meadows@warner.edu
MEADOWS, Dennis .... 304-696-2599.... 543 G
meadowsd@marshall.edu
MEADOWS, Ed .... 850-484-1700.... 114 G
emeadows@pensacolastate.edu
MEADOWS, Evelyn .... 928-724-6950..... 14 A
emeadows@dinecollege.edu
MEADOWS, Margery .... 650-738-4201.... 67 G
meadows@smccd.edu
MEADOWS, Mark .... 619-482-6494.... 71 C
mmeadows@swccd.edu
MEADOWS, Richard, G ...... 414-229-5895.... 551 C
meadows@uwm.edu
MEADOWS, Robyn, L .... 717-541-3920..... 96 H
rlmeadows@widener.edu
MEADOWS, Steve .... 304-384-5180.... 543 D
meadows@concord.edu
MEADOWS, Wanda .... 334-244-3260...... 2 A
wmeadow2@aum.edu
MEAGHER, Paula, G .... 915-831-4530.... 486 E
pmeagher@epcc.edu
MEAGHER, Peter .... 503-517-7712.... 420 A
meagherp@reed.edu
MEALER, Donna .... 731-286-3312.... 475 A
mealer@dscc.edu
MEALY, Betty .... 864-644-5213.... 461 B
bmealy@swu.edu
MEANA, Marta .... 702-895-0184.... 302 K
marta.meana@unlv.edu
MEANER, Christopher, M .. 412-578-6069.... 424 G
meanercm@carlow.edu
MEANEY, Hank .... 516-561-0050.... 325 F
MEANEY, Heather, L .... 518-381-1250.... 350 E
meaneyhl@sunysccc.edu
MEANS, Bill .... 704-337-2374.... 375 G
meansb@queens.edu
MEANS, Gary, A .... 724-925-4061.... 451 E
meansg@wccc.edu
MEANS, Jay, C .... 618-536-6666.... 164 I
jmeans@cos.siu.edu
MEANS, John .... 918-335-6892.... 411 B
jmeans@okwu.edu
MEANS, Margie .... 706-776-0123.... 135 D
mmeans@piedmont.edu
MEANS, Steve .... 800-686-7022.... 92 F
smeans@lincolncollegene.edu
MEANY, David .... 509-359-6335.... 533 D
dmeany@ewu.edu
MEANY, Mary, T .... 920-832-6561.... 547 J
mary.t.meany@lawrence.edu
MEARA, Mark .... 609-894-9311.... 308 C
mmeara@bcc.edu
MEARNS, Geoffrey, s .... 216-687-3588.... 388 C
g.mearns@csuohio.edu
MEARS, Bobby .... 757-789-1747.... 526 D
bmears@es.vccs.edu
MEARS, Laura .... 301-846-2429.... 222 G
lmears@frederick.edu
MEARS, Michael, J .... 941-752-5267.... 118 E
mearsm@scf.edu
MEARS, Philip, N .... 325-942-2191.... 480 E
nolen.mears@angelo.edu
MEARS, Ted .... 320-252-1489.... 269 C
husky@bkstr.com
MEASAMER, Ronnie .... 919-718-7409.... 368 H
rmeasamer@cccc.edu
MEASE, Ervin, J .... 610-799-1112.... 434 D
emease@lccc.edu
MEASE, Stephen .... 802-865-6432.... 513 A
smease@champlain.edu
MEASELS, D. Clark .... 865-471-3328.... 467 E
cmeasels@cn.edu
MECCA, Kim .... 570-504-0920.... 433 A
meccak@lackawanna.edu
MECH, Terrence, F .... 570-208-5943.... 432 E
tfmech@kings.edu
MECHAM, Melissa, E .... 425-637-1010.... 531 I
mmecham@cityu.edu
MECHAM, Steven, J .... 435-797-1967.... 511 B
steve.mecham@usu.edu
MECHE, Eddie, P .... 337-475-5501.... 215 G
emeche@mcneese.edu
MECHE, Lance .... 972-825-4747.... 495 D
LMeche@sagu.edu
MECHNIG, Virginia .... 630-353-7049.... 149 A
vmechnig@devry.edu
MECK, Bill .... 319-208-5069.... 188 G
bmeck@scciowa.edu
MECK, Heather, J .... 814-472-3264.... 446 B
hmeck@francis.edu
MECKEL, David .... 415-703-9561..... 31 J
dmeckel@cca.edu
MECKERT, Bill .... 802-225-3225.... 513 H
bill.meckert@neci.edu
MECONI, Honey .... 585-275-8318.... 358 I
honey.meconi@rochester.edu
MEDA, Pat .... 626-529-8261.... 60 G
pmeda@pacificoaks.edu
MEDAGLIA, Frank .... 804-594-1414.... 526 G
fmedaglia@jtcc.edu
MEDALEN, Brenda, L .... 605-336-6588.... 465 B
bmedalen@sfseminary.edu
MEDBURY, Doug .... 425-235-2352.... 536 E
dmedbury@rtc.edu
MEDCALF, Elizabeth .... 301-687-4161.... 228 C
emedcalf@frostburg.edu
MEDDERS, Alan, G .... 256-765-4100....... 9 D
agmedders@una.edu
MEDDERS, Mike, W .... 903-566-7393.... 506 C
mmedders@uttyler.edu
MEDDINGS, Nancy .... 805-922-6966..... 26 K
nmeddings@hancockcollege.edu
MEDEARIS, Ellen .... 919-667-2500.... 363 I
ellen.medearis@duke.edu
MEDEIROS, Brad .... 508-626-4911.... 238 D
bmedeiros@framingham.edu
MEDEIROS, Christopher, J 617-682-1507.... 234 G
cmedeiros@eds.edu
MEDEIROS, Dave .... 803-786-3007.... 457 C
dave@columbiasc.edu
MEDEIROS, Denis, M .... 816-235-1301.... 291 E
medeirosd@umkc.edu
MEDEMA, Pam .... 815-288-5511.... 163 I
medemap@svcc.edu
MEDENBLIK, Jackie .... 708-239-4821.... 165 I
jackie.medenblik@trnty.edu
MEDENBLIK, Julius, T .... 616-957-6024.... 249 F
jmedenblik@calvinseminary.edu
MEDFORD, Mike .... 404-687-4576.... 127 C
medfordm@ctsnet.edu
MEDINA, JR., Alfredo .... 518-782-6558.... 350 I
amedina@siena.edu
MEDINA, Amber .... 402-461-7757.... 298 C
amedina@hastings.edu
MEDINA, Angel .... 407-447-7300.... 109 H
amedina@flatech.edu
MEDINA, Cynthia .... 303-751-8700.... 81 D
medina@bel-rea.com
MEDINA, Deborah, M .... 716-851-1828.... 333 B
medina@ecc.edu
MEDINA, Kim .... 303-256-9785.... 85 H
kmedina@jwu.edu
MEDINA, Lilia .... 626-914-8591..... 39 G
lmedina@citruscollege.edu
MEDINA, Mara .... 787-780-0070.... 560 F
mmedina@caribbean.edu
MEDINA, Maria .... 973-684-5651.... 312 E
mmedina@pccc.edu
MEDINA, Nancy .... 773-442-5240.... 159 H
n-medina4@neiu.edu
MEDINA, Reinalda .... 718-997-4455.... 328 F
reinalda.medina@qc.cuny.edu
MEDINA, Virginia .... 787-780-0070.... 560 F
vcucurella@caribbean.edu
MEDINA, Widylia .... 787-890-2681.... 566 E
widylia.medina@upr.edu
MEDINA KEISER, Isabel .... 719-587-7011.... 80 F
isabelmedinakeiser@adams.edu
MEDINAC, Slawko, F .... 716-878-4521.... 353 A
medinasf@buffalostate.edu
MEDLEY, Absolom .... 404-237-7573.... 125 F
amedley@bauder.edu
MEDLEY, Brenda .... 504-520-7392.... 217 A
bdmedley@xula.edu
MEDLEY, Dawn .... 417-823-3477.... 290 B
dmedley@forest.edu
MEDLEY, Lara .... 303-273-3200.... 82 F
lara.medley@is.mines.edu
MEDLEY, Mike .... 435-896-9714.... 512 B
michael.medley@snow.edu
MEDLEY-WEEKS, Clarice ... 214-379-5565.... 492 D
cweeks@pqc.edu
MEDLIN, Mary Ann .... 360-736-9391.... 531 H
mmedlin@centralia.edu
MEDLIN, Melissa, T .... 256-765-4276....... 9 D
mtmedlin@una.edu
MEDLOCK, Vicky .... 540-665-4936.... 523 K
vmedlock@su.edu
MEDRANO, Jennifer .... 801-832-2126.... 512 F
jmedrano@westminstercollege.edu
MEDRO, Alfred .... 619-265-0107..... 62 K
amedro@platt.edu
MEDWICK, Peter .... 215-972-2017.... 440 I
pmedwick@pafa.edu
MEE, Christine, L .... 843-349-2091.... 456 G
christin@coastal.edu
MEE, David .... 615-460-6785.... 467 B
david.mee@belmont.edu
MEE, Gail, C .... 313-845-9650.... 252 D
gmee@hfcc.edu
MEECE, Jill, N .... 606-679-8501.... 202 F
jill.meece@kctcs.edu
MEEHAN, Betty, H .... 706-721-7720.... 130 B
emeehan@georgiahealth.edu
MEEHAN, Gabriel, M .... 916-484-8354..... 56 A
meehang@arc.losrios.edu
MEEHAN, Kenneth .... 714-992-7064.... 59 D
kmeehan@fullcoll.edu
MEEHAN, Martin, T .... 978-934-2201.... 237 F
martin_meehan@uml.edu
MEEHAN, Mary, J .... 414-382-6064.... 545 H
mary.meehan@alverno.edu
MEEHAN, Nicole .... 312-915-7666.... 157 A
nleduc@luc.edu
MEEHAN, Patricia .... 856-227-7200.... 308 E
pmeehan@camdencc.edu
MEEHAN, Paula, T .... 616-632-2852.... 248 A
meehapau@aquinas.edu
MEEHAN, William, A .... 256-782-5881........ 4 L
pres@jsu.edu
MEEHL, John .... 440-375-7000.... 394 E
jmeehl@lec.edu
MEEK, Laura .... 614-251-4642.... 398 F
meekl@ohiodominican.edu
MEEK, Leslie .... 320-589-6200.... 272 C
meekles@morris.umn.edu
MEEK, Scott .... 602-787-7902..... 16 A
scott.meek@pvmail.maricopa.edu
MEEK, Tequecie .... 662-252-8000.... 277 C
tmeek@rustcollege.edu
MEEKER, April, M .... 605-642-6092.... 465 F
april.meeker@bhsu.edu
MEEKER, Lorelei .... 812-855-5646.... 173 C
lmeeker@indiana.edu
MEEKER, Ralph .... 630-829-6187.... 145 D
rmeeker@ben.edu
MEEKER, Steve, L .... 605-642-6385.... 465 F
steve.meeker@bhsu.edu
MEEKER, William, C .... 408-944-6004..... 60 L
bill.meeker@palmer.edu
MEEKMA, Glenn, A .... 269-471-3484.... 247 H
meekma@andrews.edu
MEEKS, Andy .... 859-572-5575.... 205 E
meeksa@nku.edu
MEEKS, Debbie .... 912-449-7524.... 138 G
dmeeks@waycross.edu
MEEKS, Glenn .... 773-995-2042.... 146 D
gmeeks@csu.edu
MEEKS, Gregory .... 870-972-3057..... 20 C
gmeeks@astate.edu
MEEKS, Harry, L .... 812-888-4511.... 181 B
hmeeks@vinu.edu
MEEKS, J. Duane .... 561-803-2610.... 114 C
duane_meeks@pba.edu
MEEKS, Joseph, D .... 770-423-6742.... 132
jmeeks@kennesaw.edu
MEEKS, Laura, M .... 740-264-5591.... 390
lmeeks@egcc.edu
MEEKS, Mark .... 478-445-5851.... 129
mark.meeks@gcsu.edu
MEEKS, Matthew .... 972-241-3371.... 484
mmeeks@dallas.edu
MEEKS, Susan .... 478-387-4801.... 130
MEEKS, Tom .... 216-373-5206.... 397
tmeeks@ndc.edu
MEEKS, Toni .... 505-888-8898.... 320
toni@acupuncturecollege.edu
MEEKS-SJOSTROM, Diana 404-237-7573.... 125
dsjostrom@bauder.edu
MEENAN, Robert, F .... 617-638-4640.... 232
rmeenan@bu.edu
MEER, Jonathan, D .... 609-896-5167.... 313
jmeer@rider.edu
MEERNIK, James .... 940-565-3946.... 504
james.meernik@unt.edu
MEERTS, John .... 860-685-3800..... 95 C
jmeerts@wesleyan.edu
MEES, Robert, L .... 618-985-2637.... 154
robertmees@jalc.edu
MEESE, JoAnna .... 724-439-4900.... 433 H
jmeese@laurel.edu
MEESKE, Susan .... 303-870-3601.... 298 C
smeeske@hastings.edu
MEFFORD, David .... 650-508-3502..... 59 G
dmmefford@ndnu.edu
MEGAHED, Nivine .... 312-261-3200.... 159 D
nivine.megahed@nl.edu
MEGALE, Nicole .... 517-264-3850.... 247 D
MEGGINSON, Vicki .... 217-206-6058.... 167 A
megginson.vicki@uis.edu
MEGHREBLIAN, Caren ...... 415-865-0198..... 30 B
meghrebc@aii.edu
MEGORDEN, Timothy, M .. 218-299-4161.... 263 B
megorden@cord.edu
MEGREDY, Jill .... 785-227-3380.... 190 G
megredyj@bethanylb.edu
MEHA, Arapata .... 808-675-3739.... 139 I
mehaa@byuh.edu
MEHAFFEY, Bryan .... 239-280-2507.... 101 C
bryan.mehaffey@avemaria.edu
MEHALIK, Susan .... 724-503-1001.... 451 A
smehalik@washjeff.edu
MEHDIZADEH, Mojden ..... 925-229-1000..... 43 A
mmehdizadeh@4cd.edu
MEHL, Sandra .... 309-341-7793.... 155 E
smehl@knox.edu
MEHL, Shelley .... 501-450-3127..... 25 H
shelleym@uca.edu
MEHLENBACHER, Robert .. 407-569-1169.... 107 G
bob.mehlenbacher@fcc.edu
MEHLER, Mark .... 609-771-2495.... 308 G
mehler@tcnj.edu
MEHLHOFF, Monte .... 605-626-7781.... 465 H
mehlhofm@northern.edu
MEHLIG, Lisa .... 815-921-4070.... 162 F
l.mehlig@rockvalleycollege.edu
MEHNERT-MELAND,
Karen, B .... 218-477-2447.... 268 A
meland@mnstate.edu
MEHOLIC, Christine .... 732-987-2327.... 310 D
meholicc@georgian.edu
MEHRING, Teresa, A .... 620-341-5171.... 192 D
tmehring@emporia.edu
MEHTA, Usha .... 775-850-0700.... 302 E
umehta@morrison.neumont.edu
MEI, Jeffrey .... 617-731-7170.... 244 B
meijeffery@pmc.edu
MEIDINGER, Joddy .... 605-229-8454.... 464 I
joddy.meidinger@presentation.edu
MEIER, Barry .... 951-222-8420..... 64 B
barry.meier@rcc.edu
MEIER, Beth, A .... 919-760-8427.... 366 G
meierb@meredith.edu
MEIER, Gayle .... 770-394-8300.... 124 F
gmeier@aii.edu
MEIER, Harvey .... 402-486-2502.... 300 D
hameier@ucollege.edu
MEIER, Jared .... 970-248-1698..... 82 B
jmeier@mesastate.edu
MEIER, Jay .... 701-224-5666.... 382 B
jay.meier@bismarckstate.edu
MEIER, Karen .... 757-683-5026.... 521 L
kmeier@odu.edu
MEIER, Kenneth .... 530-895-2547..... 31 E
meierke@butte.edu
MEIER, Neal .... 513-487-1174.... 402 I
neal.meier@myunion.edu
MEIER, Richard .... 360-752-8440.... 531 C
dmeier@btc.ctc.edu
MEIER, Susan .... 812-535-5299.... 179 C
smeier@smwc.edu
MEIER, Thomas, K .... 607-735-1790.... 333 A
tmeier@elmira.edu
MEIER WELTZIEN, Lynn ... 406-683-7180.... 295 B
l_weltzien1@umwestern.edu
MEIERS, Chris .... 913-588-0146.... 197 A
cmeiers@kumc.edu

MENINGALL, Jennifer, D ... 813-974-9084 ... 120 D
jmeningall@usf.edu
MENJARES, Pete ... 562-777-4048 ... 30 H
pete.menjares@biola.edu
MENK, David, A ... 507-933-6539 ... 264 B
dmenk@gustavus.edu
MENKE, Laura ... 319-208-5193 ... 188 G
lmenke@scciowa.edu
MENKE, Pamela ... 305-237-3715 ... 113 H
pmenke@mdc.edu
MENKE, Scott ... 262-595-2155 ... 551 E
scott.menke@uwp.edu
MENLOVE, Ronda, R ... 435-797-3728 ... 511 B
ronda.menlove@usu.edu
MENN, Esther ... 773-256-0762 ... 157 B
emenn@lstc.edu
MENNE, Renee, A ... 563-588-7130 ... 186 I
renee.menne@loras.edu
MENNEKE, Beth, R ... 314-505-7761 ... 280 H
mennekeb@csl.edu
MENNICKE, Susan ... 512-863-1857 ... 495 G
mennicks@southwestern.edu
MENNINGER, Gaynia ... 785-242-5200 ... 195 F
gaynia.menninger@ottawa.edu
MENNINGER, Jay, E ... 802-656-3290 ... 514 F
jay.menninger@uvm.edu
MENNS, Melvin ... 202-722-8111 ... 99 D
melvin.menns@strayer.edu
MENOGAN, Kelle ... 601-977-7828 ... 277 F
kem2galoo@aol.com
MENON, Ajay ... 970-491-2398 ... 83 A
ajay.menon@colostate.edu
MENON, Vanaja ... 262-595-2167 ... 551 E
vanaja.menon@uwp.edu
MENSAH, Michael, O ... 570-941-7569 ... 450 B
mensahm2@scranton.edu
MENSAH, Vincent ... 304-424-8223 ... 545 B
vincent.mensah@mail.wvu.edu
MENSAH-DARTEY, Virgil ... 678-422-4100 ... 99 D
MENSCHING, Ron ... 630-889-6606 ... 159 E
rmensching@nuhs.edu
MENSES, Jilma ... 503-725-4432 ... 418 G
ljmeneses@pdx.edu
MENSHOUSE, Nancy, L ... 606-326-2199 ... 201 B
nancy.menshouse@kctcs.edu
MENTE, Patrick, J ... 607-436-2596 ... 353 E
mentepj@oneonta.edu
MENTGES, Jack ... 978-368-2224 ... 230 F
jack.mentges@auc.edu
MENTZER, Cathy ... 717-264-4141 ... 452 B
cmentzer@wilson.edu
MENY, Eileen, M ... 617-912-9128 ... 232 E
emeny@bostonconservatory.edu
MENZ, Leslie, E ... 309-655-2180 ... 163 E
leslie.menz@osfhealthcare.org
MENZANO, Silvestro ... 703-284-6861 ... 521 A
silvestro.menzano@marymount.edu
MENZEL, Carol, A ... 410-334-2946 ... 229 E
cmenzel@worwic.edu
MENZEL, JR., Stephen, W 909-652-6180 ... 39 B
steve.menzel@chaffey.edu
MENZER, Paul ... 540-887-7058 ... 520 I
pmenzer@mbc.edu
MENZIES, Andre' ... 504-816-4570 ... 208 I
amenzies@dillard.edu
MENZIES, John, K ... 973-275-2516 ... 315 B
john.menzies@shu.edu
MEOLA, Christine ... 212-346-1095 ... 345 F
cmeola@pace.edu
MERANTE, Monica, M ... 315-445-4561 ... 338 B
merantmm@lemoyne.edu
MERCADE, Leticia ... 787-815-0000 ... 566 F
MERCADO, Caroline ... 570-372-4753 ... 447 D
mercado@susqu.edu
MERCADO, Carolyn ... 787-894-2828 ... 568 A
carolyn.mercado@upr.edu
MERCADO, Christopher ... 386-734-3303 ... 117 F
cmercado@ftccollege.edu
MERCADO, Eric ... 718-289-5338 ... 326 F
eric.mercado@bcc.cuny.edu
MERCADO, Frank ... 201-360-4043 ... 310 F
fmercado@hccc.edu
MERCADO, Harry ... 787-740-3555 ... 566 A
hmercado@uccaribe.edu
MERCADO, Juan Carlos ... 212-925-6625 ... 326 H
jmercado@ccny.cuny.edu
MERCADO, Leo, A ... 843-953-3020 ... 456 C
leo.mercado@citadel.edu
MERCADO, Luis ... 305-418-4220 ... 115 B
lmercado@pupr.edu
MERCADO, Maritza E, M ... 212-247-3434 ... 339 G
mmercado@mandl.edu
MERCADO-OCASIO,
Iris, M ... 787-894-2828 ... 566 D
iris.mercado@upr.edu
MERCED, Randolph ... 215-717-6827 ... 448 H
rmerced@uarts.edu
MERCER, Brenda, D ... 919-735-5151 ... 374 F
bdmercer@waynecc.edu
MERCER, David, M ... 585-567-9322 ... 336 B
david.mercer@houghton.edu
MERCER, Ellen ... 920-923-8112 ... 548 C
emercer@marianuniversity.edu
MERCER, Frank ... 386-506-4461 ... 103 J
mercerf@DaytonaState.edu
MERCER, JR., John ... 704-463-3352 ... 375 E
john.mercer@fsmail.pfeiffer.edu
MERCER, John, D ... 850-872-3807 ... 110 E
jmercer@gulfcoast.edu
MERCER, Karen ... 319-895-4342 ... 183 D
kmercer@cornellcollege.edu
MERCER, Larry ... 301-552-1400 ... 229 C
lmercer@bible.edu
MERCER, Laura ... 937-512-4571 ... 401 J
laura.mercer@sinclair.edu
MERCER, Leneil ... 313-487-7420 ... 209 B
mercer@lacollege.edu
MERCER, Leslie, K ... 651-201-1862 ... 265 H
leslie.mercer@so.mnscu.edu
MERCER, Paul ... 207-326-2337 ... 219 D
paul.mercer@mma.edu
MERCER, Peter, P ... 201-684-7607 ... 313 D
pmercer@ramapo.edu
MERCER, Sally, A ... 240-895-4309 ... 226 A
samercer@smcm.edu
MERCER, Tracy ... 605-773-3455 ... 465 D
tracym@sdbor.edu
MERCHANT, Betty ... 210-458-4370 ... 506 B
betty.merchant@utsa.edu
MERCHANT, Janie ... 575-646-6014 ... 319 D
jpence@nmsu.edu
MERCHANT, Joshua ... 517-629-0242 ... 247 E
jmerchant@albion.edu
MERCHANT, Walter, G ... 540-563-8000 ... 524 A
wmerchant@skyline.edu
MERCHLEWITZ, Ann, E ... 507-457-1587 ... 271 G
amerchle@smumn.edu
MERCIER, Casey ... 601-477-4223 ... 275 B
casey.mercier@jcjc.edu
MERCIER, Collette, R ... 801-627-8304 ... 510 D
mercierc@owatc.edu
MERCIER, William, C ... 812-237-7829 ... 173 A
william.mercier@indstate.edu
MERCINCAVAGE, Janet, E . 570-208-5878 ... 432 E
jemercin@kings.edu
MERCK, II, William, F ... 407-823-2351 ... 120 A
william.merck@ucf.edu
MERCOGLIANO, Amy ... 609-771-2495 ... 308 G
mercogli@tcnj.edu
MERCOMES, Brenda, W ... 617-541-5383 ... 241 D
brendam@rcc.mass.edu
MERCURIO, Gloria ... 201-761-6125 ... 314 F
gmercurio@spc.edu
MERCURIO, Joseph, P ... 617-353-6500 ... 232 G
mercurio@bu.edu
MERCURIO, Michelle ... 703-414-4069 ... 518 B
mmercurio@devry.edu
MERCURIO, Sherry ... 614-947-6581 ... 391 A
mercuris@franklin.edu
MERDINGER, Joan ... 408-924-2450 ... 37 A
joan.merdinger@sjsu.edu
MERDINGER, Sandy ... 406-444-0056 ... 294 J
smerdinger@montana.edu
MEREAU, Amanda ... 617-349-8540 ... 230 D
amereau@lesley.edu
MEREDITH, Brian ... 270-745-6169 ... 207 C
MEREDITH, Brian ... 901-678-2843 ... 474 C
bmeredith@memphis.edu
MEREDITH, Daniel ... 864-941-8442 ... 460 D
meredith.d@ptc.edu
MEREDITH, Don, L ... 901-761-1354 ... 469 A
hstlib@hst.edu
MEREDITH, Gloria ... 847-578-3270 ... 163 A
gloria.meredith@rosalindfranklin.edu
MEREDITH, Jennifer ... 850-718-2258 ... 102 H
meredithj@chipola.edu
MEREDITH, John, R ... 517-750-1200 ... 258 F
randym@arbo.edu
MEREDITH, Joyce ... 740-587-6515 ... 389 H
meredithj@denison.edu
MEREDITH, Marc ... 310-665-6815 ... 60 B
marcm@otis.edu
MEREDITH, Patricia ... 813-463-7194 ... 100 H
pmeredith@argosy.edu
MEREDITH, Patricia ... 813-463-7163 ... 144 G
pmeredith@argosy.edu
MEREDITH, Polly ... 661-362-2203 ... 56 G
pmeredith@masters.edu
MEREDITH, Steven ... 573-681-5109 ... 284 B
meredith@lincolnu.edu
MERELLA, Bartholomew, J . 202-541-5264 ... 99 G
merella@wtu.edu
MERES, Cynthia, L ... 607-436-3388 ... 353 E
merescl@oneonta.edu
MERFALEN, Barbara, K ... 670-234-5498 ... 559 F
barbaram@nmcnet.edu
MERFELD, Kendra, S ... 319-352-8512 ... 189 F
kendra.merfeld@wartburg.edu
MERGEN, Amy ... 419-824-3677 ... 395 D
amergen@lourdes.edu
MERGENTHAL, James ... 215-895-0476 ... 427 G
jem38@drexel.edu
MERGET, Kathleen ... 845-451-1776 ... 331 F
k_merget@culinary.edu
MERGIOTTI, James, J ... 215-670-9494 ... 438 D
president@peirce.edu
MERGL, Francine, R ... 716-888-8211 ... 325 G
merglf@canisius.edu
MERGLER, Nancy, L ... 405-325-3221 ... 413 C
nmergler@ou.edu
MERICKEL, Mark ... 707-664-2394 ... 37 B
mark.merickel@sonoma.edu
MERICLE, Margaret, E ... 559-442-8210 ... 72 A
margaret.mericle@fresnocitycollege.edu
MERIDITH, Pamela ... 870-759-4139 ... 26 B
pmeridith@wbcoll.edu
MERIGOLD, Mary ... 716-896-0700 ... 359 F
merigoldm@villa.edu
MERILAT, Meliinda ... 832-252-0745 ... 483 A
melinda.merilat@cbshouston.edu
MERILLAT, Jason, C ... 610-566-1776 ... 452 A
jmerillat@williamson.edu
MERIMEE, Nancy, S ... 913-971-3427 ... 195 A
nsmerimee@mnu.edu
MERINGOLO,
Salvatore, M ... 540-654-1372 ... 524 H
tmeringo@umw.edu
MERINO, Robert ... 281-998-6150 ... 493 D
robert.merino@sjcd.edu
MERIWETHER, Jan ... 434-947-8127 ... 522 E
jmeriwether@randolphcollege.edu
MERIWETHER, Jason ... 615-329-8854 ... 468 G
jmeriwether@fisk.edu
MERJIL, Mark ... 909-384-8990 ... 65 C
mmerjil@sbccd.cc.ca.us
MERK, James, T ... 334-285-5177 ... 4 K
jmerk@ingram.cc.al.us
MERKEL, Cynthia, F ... 906-635-2674 ... 254 C
cmerkel@lssu.edu
MERKEL, Denise ... 520-417-4148 ... 13 G
merkeld@cochise.edu
MERKEL, Diane ... 518-564-2195 ... 354 B
diane.merkel@plattsburgh.edu
MERKEL, Luz, I ... 509-777-4225 ... 539 F
lmerkel@whitworth.edu
MERKEL-VEER, Chelly ... 701-766-1302 ... 380 E
chelly.merkel@littlehoop.edu
MERKIN, Yitzchok ... 301-962-5111 ... 229 F
ymerkin@yeshiva.edu
MERKLE, Barbara ... 940-397-4334 ... 491 A
barbara.merkle@mwsu.edu
MERKLE, Ben ... 208-882-1566 ... 143 G
bmerkle@nsa.edu
MERKLE, H. Bart ... 616-331-3585 ... 252 A
merkleb@gvsu.edu
MERKLE, Jean ... 563-425-5765 ... 189 C
merklej@uiu.edu
MERKLE, Joseph, F ... 717-815-1460 ... 452 F
jmerkle@ycp.edu
MERKLE, Karen, L ... 410-386-8107 ... 221 G
kmerkle@carrollcc.edu
MERKLE, Patricia ... 315-568-3277 ... 342 H
pmerkle@nycc.edu
MERKLEY, Brett ... 801-524-8132 ... 510 A
bmerkley@idsbc.edu
MERKT, Mary Lou ... 864-294-2140 ... 458 D
marylou.merkt@furman.edu
MERKX, Gilbert ... 919-684-5830 ... 363 I
gilbert.merkx@duke.edu
MERL, Jill ... 808-544-9364 ... 140 B
jmerl@hpu.edu
MERLI, Janet ... 201-559-6040 ... 310 C
merlij@felician.edu
MERLIN, Howard, E ... 484-365-7404 ... 434 H
hmerlin@lincoln.edu
MERLINO, Deborah ... 617-521-3805 ... 245 A
deborah.merlino@simmons.edu
MERLINO, Keith ... 412-809-5100 ... 444 F
merlino@pti.edu
MERLO, Barbara ... 254-526-1223 ... 482 F
barbara.merlo@ctcd.edu
MEROLLI, Roy, H ... 845-575-3000 ... 340 C
roy.merolli@marist.edu
MERRELL, Donna ... 660-248-6214 ... 279 K
dmerrell@centralmethodist.edu
MERRELL, Linda ... 859-525-6510 ... 204 H
lkmerrell@national-college.edu
MERRELL, Melinda, M ... 425-235-5846 ... 536 E
mmerrell@rtc.edu
MERRELL, Sue ... 937-512-2917 ... 401 J
sue.merrell@sinclair.edu
MERRICK, Bernard, D ... 412-365-1231 ... 425 B
merrick@chatham.edu
MERRICK, Donna ... 432-264-5105 ... 487 I
dmerrick@howardcollege.edu
MERRICK, Jocelyn ... 413-662-5193 ... 238 F
j.merrick@mcla.edu
MERRICK, Robyn ... 225-771-4680 ... 214 G
robyn_merrick@sus.edu
MERRICK, Robyn ... 225-771-4200 ... 214 H
robyn_merrick@sus.edu
MERRIFIELD, Mary ... 314-529-9510 ... 284 F
mmerrifield@maryville.edu
MERRIGAN, John ... 660-543-4233 ... 291 B
merrigan@ucmo.edu
MERRIHEW, Mark, W ... 620-417-1202 ... 196 B
mark.merrihew@sccc.edu
MERRILL, Andy ... 440-375-7000 ... 394 E
amerrill@lec.edu
MERRILL, Ben ... 802-728-1329 ... 515 G
bmerrill@vtc.edu
MERRILL, Chad ... 828-694-1901 ... 368 E
chadm@blueridge.edu
MERRILL, Dale ... 714-997-6849 ... 39 C
merrill@chapman.edu
MERRILL, H. Donald ... 704-233-8284 ... 380 D
dmerrill@wingate.edu
MERRILL, Joanne ... 603-897-8257 ... 305 G
jmerrill@rivier.edu
MERRILL, Kristin ... 513-244-8151 ... 387 D
kristin.merrill@ccuniversity.edu
MERRILL, Martha, C ... 860-439-2200 ... 91 E
mcmer@conncoll.edu
MERRILL, Melvin ... 229-391-4894 ... 123 F
mmerrill@abac.edu
MERRILL, Michael ... 212-647-7801 ... 355 F
michael.merrill@esc.edu
MERRILL, Paul ... 256-331-5223 ... 6 B
merrill@nwscc.edu
MERRILL, Scott, M ... 508-793-2438 ... 233 D
smerrill@holycross.edu
MERRILL, Steve ... 801-601-4917 ... 509 B
ssmerrill@argosy.edu
MERRILL, Timothy, W ... 804-752-7212 ... 522 F
timothymerrill@rmc.edu
MERRILL-DOSS, Jean ... 573-518-2262 ... 286 B
jeanmer@mineralarea.edu
MERRIMAN, William, J ... 718-862-7374 ... 339 H
william.merriman@manhattan.edu
MERRIMAN, JR.,
William, R ... 620-229-6223 ... 196 C
dick.merriman@sckans.edu
MERRION, Margaret, M ... 269-387-5810 ... 260 F
margaret.merrion@wmich.edu
MERRITT, Adam ... 910-392-4660 ... 367 B
adam.merritt@miller-motte.com
MERRITT, Christine, C ... 315-859-4111 ... 335 A
cmerritt@hamilton.edu
MERRITT, Deborah, J ... 804-745-2444 ... 516 L
djmerritt@bryantstratton.edu
MERRITT, Fred, E ... 937-766-4969 ... 386 F
merritf@cedarville.edu
MERRITT, Jaci, M ... 903-434-8103 ... 491 D
jmerritt@ntcc.edu
MERRITT, James, A ... 608-246-6330 ... 554 B
jamerritt1@matcmadison.edu
MERRITT, John, D ... 502-231-5221 ... 204 A
jdmerritt@louisvillebiblecollege.org
MERRITT, Judy, M ... 205-853-1200 ... 5 C
jmerritt@jeffstateonline.com
MERRITT, Nancy ... 812-237-2000 ... 173 A
nancy.merritt@indstate.edu
MERRITT, Scott ... 318-869-5708 ... 208 F
smerritt@centenary.edu
MERRITT, Stephen, R ... 610-519-7499 ... 450 G
stephen.merritt@villanova.edu
MERRITT, Susan, M ... 212-346-1810 ... 345 F
smerritt@pace.edu
MERRITT, Wayne ... 704-406-3939 ... 364 B
wmerritt@gardner-webb.edu
MERRITT MILLER, Beth ... 916-278-6231 ... 35 E
merrittmillerb@csus.edu
MERRYMAN, Ed ... 408-554-5076 ... 68 C
emerryman@scu.edu
MERRYMAN, Jason ... 423-236-2893 ... 473 A
jasonmerryman@southern.edu
MERRYMAN, Marjorie ... 212-749-2802 ... 339 I
mmerryman@msmnyc.edu
MERSETH, Juel, O ... 507-344-7854 ... 261 H
juel.merseth@blc.edu
MERSON, Michael, H ... 919-681-7760 ... 363 I
michael.merson@duke.edu
MERTEN, Alan, G ... 703-993-8700 ... 519 A
amerten@gmu.edu
MERTEN, Elizabeth ... 712-749-2062 ... 182 G
mertenl@bvu.edu
MERTES, Scott ... 989-773-6622 ... 255 F
smertes@midmich.edu
MERTH, LeAnn ... 402-486-2535 ... 300 D
lemerth@ucollege.edu
MERTH, Paula, B ... 651-290-6376 ... 273 B
paula.merth@wmitchell.edu
MERTHA, George, V ... 601-877-6154 ... 273 C
mgeorge@alcorn.edu
MERVINE, Ed ... 310-577-3000 ... 79 K
financialaid@yosan.edu
MERVYN, Frances ... 617-327-6777 ... 242 C
frances_mervyn@mspp.edu
MERYHEW, Barb ... 307-268-2249 ... 555 F
bmeryhew@caspercollege.edu
MERZ, Nancy ... 816-235-1154 ... 291 E
merzn@umkc.edu
MERZ, Soon, O ... 512-223-7035 ... 481 B
smerz@austincc.edu
MESA, Tina ... 210-486-3901 ... 479 D
tmesa@alamo.edu
MESAROS, Cyndi ... 805-922-6966 ... 26 K
cmesaros@hancockcollege.edu
MESCH, Barry ... 617-559-8613 ... 235 I
bmesch@hebrewcollege.edu
MESCHIEVITZ, Catherine ... 561-297-3282 ... 118 H
cmeschie@fau.edu
MESCON, Timothy, S ... 706-507-8950 ... 127 D
mescon_timothy@columbusstate.edu
MESEROLE, Brooke ... 910-362-7062 ... 368 E
bmeserole@cfcc.edu

MEYERS, Rosalind, R .... 404-894-1822.... 130 D
rosalind.meyers@gatech.edu
MEYERS, Shelly, A .... 864-488-8207.... 459 A
smeyers@limestone.edu
MEYERS, Tom, J .... 574-535-7346.... 171 D
tomjm@goshen.edu
MEYINSSE, Joseph .... 225-771-5390.... 214 H
joseph_meyinsse@subr.edu
MEZA, Juan .... 209-228-4400.... 74 B
jmeza@ucmerced.edu
MEZIERE, Kevin .... 858-653-6740..... 52 C
MEZNEK, James .... 805-652-5502..... 77 A
jmeznek@vcccd.edu
MEZYNSKI, David .... 914-961-8313.... 349 I
dmezynski@svots.edu
MEZZANINI, Frank .... 352-588-8215.... 116 E
frank.mezzanini@saintleo.edu
MHLABA, S. Leonard .... 617-228-2032.... 239 G
smhlaba@bhcc.mass.edu
MIAH, Abdul, J .... 804-523-5330.... 526 F
amiah@reynolds.edu
MIARA, Lee, S .... 973-278-5400.... 323 J
lsm@berkeleycollege.edu
MIARA, Lee, S .... 973-278-5400.... 307 G
lsm@berkeleycollege.edu
MIAZGA, John .... 325-942-2212.... 480 E
john.miazga@angelo.edu
MICA, Christine .... 202-319-5304..... 97 C
mica@cua.edu
MICALIZIO, Beatrice .... 562-427-0861...... 44 G
bmicalizio@devry.edu
MICALIZIO, Karen .... 530-895-2555...... 31 E
micalizioka@butte.edu
MICARE, Dennis .... 386-506-3920.... 103 J
micared@DaytonaState.edu
MICCO, Melissa, A .... 412-397-5264.... 445 G
micco@rmu.edu
MICHAEL, Bernardo, A .... 717-766-2511.... 436 D
bmichael@messiah.edu
MICHAEL, Bob .... 706-864-1998.... 134 D
bmichael@northgeorgia.edu
MICHAEL, Cheryl .... 410-334-2884.... 229 E
cmichael@worwic.edu
MICHAEL, Debra .... 615-329-8604.... 468 G
dmichael@fisk.edu
MICHAEL, Gage .... 719-549-3006..... 87 B
Michael.Gage@pueblocc.edu
MICHAEL, Gregory, C .... 413-782-1343.... 246 D
gmichael@wne.edu
MICHAEL, Jennifer .... 617-732-2871.... 241 F
jennifer.michael@bos.mcphs.edu
MICHAEL, Jody .... 810-762-0048.... 256 C
jody.michael@mcc.edu
MICHAEL, Joshua, B .... 570-586-2400.... 422 F
jmichael@bbc.edu
MICHAEL, Larry, L .... 570-326-3761.... 440 K
lmichael@pct.edu
MICHAEL, Lloyd, H .... 713-798-4842.... 481 H
lmichael@bcm.edu
MICHAEL, Marge, M .... 701-252-3467.... 381 A
mmichael@jc.edu
MICHAEL, III, Max .... 205-934-7730....... 8 G
maxm@uab.edu
MICHAEL, Noreen, M .... 340-693-1003.... 568 C
nmichae@uvi.edu
MICHAEL, Pamela .... 315-312-2102.... 354 A
pamela.michael@oswego.edu
MICHAEL, Sandra .... 215-637-7700.... 430 H
smichael@holyfamily.edu
MICHAEL, Steve, O .... 215-572-2924.... 422 B
michaels@arcadia.edu
MICHAEL-PICKETT,
Stephanie .... 704-922-6215.... 370 D
michael.stephanie@gaston.edu
MICHAELIDES, Anthony ...... 661-362-3253...... 41 G
anthony.michaelides@canyons.edu
MICHAELIDES, Barbara ..... 318-342-5550.... 216 E
michaelides@ulm.edu
MICHAELIS, Jim .... 801-863-8996.... 511 C
michaeji@uvu.edu
MICHAELIS, Margaret .... 408-864-8857...... 47 G
michaelismargaret@deanza.edu
MICHAELIS, Randall, B ...... 509-777-4303.... 539 F
rmichaelis@whitworth.edu
MICHAELS, Alan, C .... 614-292-2631.... 398 H
michaels.23@osu.edu
MICHAELS, Andrea, P .... 508-793-7773.... 233 C
amichaels@clarku.edu
MICHAELS, Brent .... 910-678-8209.... 370 B
michaelb@faytechcc.edu
MICHAELS, Cathy .... 718-262-2238.... 329 B
ctsia@york.cuny.edu
MICHAELS, Daniel .... 217-228-5432.... 161 E
dmichaels@quincy.edu
MICHAELS, George, H .... 805-893-2378.... 74 F
george@id.ucsb.edu
MICHAELS, Jeff, A .... 717-477-1171.... 443 D
jamich@ship.edu
MICHAELS, Lynda .... 570-389-4061.... 441 F
lmichael@bloomu.edu
MICHAELS, Meredith .... 949-824-4923.... 73 H
m.michaels@uci.edu
MICHAELS, Sheri .... 319-385-6229.... 186 A
sheri.michaels@iwc.edu
MICHAELS, Sue .... 916-660-7272..... 69 F
smichaels@sierracollege.edu
MICHAELSEN, Kevin .... 919-760-8565.... 366 G
michaelsen@meredith.edu
MICHAELSON, Dorcas, M . 651-523-2210.... 264 C
dmichaelson01@hamline.edu
MICHAELSON, John .... 425-640-1559.... 533 E
john.michaelson@edcc.edu
MICHAELSON FISHER,
Bonnie .... 410-778-7261.... 229 D
bfisher2@washcoll.edu
MICHAJLA, Patty .... 425-640-1516.... 533 E
pmichajl@edcc.edu
MICHAL, Barbara, M .... 706-419-1275.... 127 F
michal@covenant.edu
MICHALAK, Sarah .... 919-962-1301.... 378 D
smichala@email.unc.edu
MICHALENKO, John .... 412-397-4399.... 445 G
michalenko@rmu.edu
MICHALERYA, William, D . 610-758-5802.... 434 E
wdm1@lehigh.edu
MICHALOWSKI, Sam .... 718-982-2007.... 327 A
sam.michalowski@csi.cuny.edu
MICHALSKI, Greg .... 904-632-3017.... 109 E
gmichals@fscj.edu
MICHALSKI, Monica .... 718-489-5274.... 348 E
mmichalski@stfranciscollege.edu
MICHALSON, JR.,
Gordon, E .... 941-487-4100.... 119 D
michalson@ncf.edu
MICHAUD, Marco, J .... 860-439-5477.... 91 E
marco.michaud@conncoll.edu
MICHAUD, Paul .... 912-478-7765.... 131 A
pmichaud@georgiasouthern.edu
MICHAUD, Paul .... 908-526-1200.... 313 E
pmichaud@raritanval.edu
MICHEALS, Deborah .... 724-480-3515.... 426 A
deb.micheals@ccbc.edu
MICHELINI, Debra .... 847-543-2383.... 147 H
dmichelini@clcillinois.edu
MICHELINI, Rick, H .... 724-287-8711.... 423 F
rick.michelini@bc3.edu
MICHELL, Peter .... 925-631-4571..... 64 F
pmichell@stmarys-ca.edu
MICHELS, Fredrick, A .... 906-635-2404.... 254 C
fmichels@lssu.edu
MICHELS, Therese .... 402-557-7115.... 297 A
therese.michels@bellevue.edu
MICHELSON, Stuart .... 386-822-7405.... 121 E
smichels@stetson.edu
MICIAK, Alan, R .... 412-396-1372.... 428 C
miciaka@duq.edu
MICKANIS, Judith, L .... 570-577-3171.... 423 D
mickanis@bucknell.edu
MICKELSEN, Scott .... 308-367-5253.... 301 C
MICKELSON, Doug .... 414-256-1252.... 549 A
mickelsd@mtmary.edu
MICKENS, Charles .... 517-371-5140.... 259 B
mickensc@cooley.edu
MICKENS, George .... 623-245-4600.... 18 M
gmickens@uticorp.com
MICKENS, Helen .... 517-371-5140.... 259 B
mickensh@cooley.edu
MICKENS, Kendrick .... 610-359-5340.... 426 G
kmickens@dccc.edu
MICKENSON, Melanie .... 570-408-4100.... 451 G
melanie.mickelson@wilkes.edu
MICKEY, James, C .... 210-458-4133.... 506 B
jim.mickey@utsa.edu
MICKEY-BOGGS, Shari ...... 513-745-3657.... 406 E
mickeyboggss@xavier.edu
MICKLES, Muriel, B .... 434-832-7656.... 526 A
micklesm@cvcc.vccs.edu
MICKOOL, Richard .... 937-525-3815.... 406 B
rmickool@wittenberg.edu
MICUCCI, Nicholas .... 201-360-4243.... 310 F
nmicucci@hccc.edu
MIDANIK, Lorraine, T .... 510-642-5039..... 73 E
swdean@berkeley.edu
MIDCAP, Richard, D .... 410-827-5858.... 222 B
rmidcap@chesapeake.edu
MIDDEKER, Vicki .... 303-464-2322..... 87 D
vmiddeker@westwood.edu
MIDDENDORF, Sandra .... 651-641-3599.... 264 J
smiddendorf001@luthersem.edu
MIDDENDORF, Terry .... 651-523-2302.... 264 C
tmiddendorf@hamline.edu
MIDDLEBROOK, Sharon ..... 254-659-7502.... 487 E
smiddlebrook@hillcollege.edu
MIDDLESWARTH, Jean, E . 336-575-3901.... 370 C
jmiddles@forsythtech.edu
MIDDLETON, Antoinette ..... 212-220-1267.... 326 E
amiddleton@bmcc.cuny.edu
MIDDLETON, Charles, R ... 312-341-3800.... 162 I
cmiddleton@roosevelt.edu
MIDDLETON, David .... 973-761-9080.... 315 B
david.middleton@shu.edu
MIDDLETON, Dawcett .... 405-733-7450.... 411 I
wzjones@rose.edu
MIDDLETON, Jacqueline .... 330-263-2580.... 388 E
jkmiddleton@wooster.edu
MIDDLETON, James, E ...... 541-383-7201.... 414 I
jmiddleton@cocc.edu
MIDDLETON, Jeffrey .... 520-494-5287..... 13 F
jeff.middleton@centralaz.edu
MIDDLETON, Joan .... 301-934-7853.... 222 C
joanm@csmd.edu
MIDDLETON, Joan .... 301-934-7568.... 222 C
joanm@csmd.edu
MIDDLETON, Joseph .... 718-960-8421.... 327 C
joseph.middleton@lehman.cuny.edu
MIDDLETON, Kenna .... 859-622-1515.... 200 D
kenna.middleton@eku.edu
MIDDLETON, Lowell .... 757-727-5640.... 519 C
lowell.middleton@hamptonu.edu
MIDDLETON, Lyle .... 501-329-6872...... 21 C
lmiddleton@cbc.edu
MIDDLETON, Melinda, L ... 812-877-8259.... 179 A
melinda.l.middleton@rose-hulman.edu
MIDDLETON, Michael, A ... 573-882-3394.... 291 D
middletonm@missouri.edu
MIDDLETON, Nigel, T .... 303-273-3327..... 82 F
nmiddlet@mines.edu
MIDDLETON, Norma, L ..... 336-316-2151.... 364 E
nmiddlet@guilford.edu
MIDDLETON, Pam .... 843-574-6303.... 461 G
pamela.middleton@tridenttech.edu
MIDDLETON, Renee, A ...... 740-593-4400.... 399 G
middletr@ohio.edu
MIDDLETON, Rich .... 859-622-2966.... 200 D
rich.middleton@eku.edu
MIDDLETON, Rodney, C ... 989-328-1202.... 256 A
rodm@montcalm.edu
MIDDLETON, Whittaker, V . 803-535-5347.... 456 D
wmiddleton@claflin.edu
MIDGETT, Pam .... 940-397-4182.... 491 A
pam.midgett@mwsu.edu
MIDGETTE, Juanita .... 252-335-3586.... 377 D
jmidgette@mail.ecsu.edu
MIDGLEY, Michael, T .... 512-223-7579.... 481 B
midgley@austincc.edu
MIDHA, Chand .... 330-972-7857.... 403 B
cmidha@uakron.edu
MIDKIFF, Lindsay .... 870-633-4480...... 21 F
lindsay.midkiff@eacc.edu
MIDKIFF, Lori, A .... 304-929-5472.... 542 H
lmidkiff@newriver.edu
MIDKIFF, Mike .... 903-923-2136.... 486 D
mmidkiff@etbu.edu
MIDKIFF, JR., Robert, M .. 570-577-1561.... 423 D
robert.midkiff@bucknell.edu
MIDKIFF, Sabrina .... 713-500-3015.... 506 D
sabrina.midkiff@uth.tmc.edu
MIDONECK, Shari, R .... 212-746-2088.... 360 B
srmidone@med.cornell.edu
MIDTHUN, Steve .... 414-277-7224.... 548 H
midthun@msoe.edu
MIEDEMA, Linda .... 321-433-5014.... 101 J
miedemal@brevardcc.edu
MIEKLE, Tom .... 909-594-5611...... 58 A
tmiekle@mtsac.edu
MIELE, Carol .... 201-493-3617.... 307 F
cmiele@bergen.edu
MIELKE, David, E .... 734-487-4140.... 250 H
david.mielke@emich.edu
MIERS, Michael .... 508-849-3326.... 230 C
mmiers@annamaria.edu
MIES, Jay .... 620-672-5641.... 196 A
jaym@prattcc.edu
MIGLAW, Kari, L .... 831-656-2077.... 557 H
klmiglaw@nps.edu
MIGLER, Jerry .... 218-299-6506.... 267 G
jerry.migler@minnesota.edu
MIGLORIE, JR., Frank, G . 802-773-5900.... 513 B
fmiglorie@csj.edu
MIGLORIE, Patricia .... 802-773-5900.... 513 B
pmiglorie@csj.edu
MIGNAULT, Richard .... 845-451-1369.... 331 F
r_mignau@culinary.edu
MIGNOGNA, Janice .... 215-780-1235.... 446 G
janice@salus.edu
MIGNOGNA, Janice .... 215-780-1400.... 446 G
janice@salus.edu
MIGUEL, George .... 520-383-8401..... 18 L
gmiguel@tocc.cc.az.us
MIGYANKO, Stephanie, M 724-439-4900.... 433 H
smigyanko@laurel.edu
MIHAL, Roxanne, E .... 617-228-2027.... 239 G
rmihal@bhcc.mass.edu
MIHALAKIS, Marina .... 401-454-6764.... 454 B
mmihalak@risd.edu
MIHALCIN, Patricia .... 724-287-8711.... 423 F
patricia.mihalcin@bc3.edu
MIHALEVICH, Rick .... 573-897-5000.... 284 D
MIHALIC, Angela .... 214-648-2168.... 507 D
angela.mihalic@utsouthwestern.edu
MIHALIK, Brian .... 803-777-1611.... 462 A
MIHALY, Christine .... 734-973-3477.... 260 B
cmihaly@wccnet.edu
MIHALY, Marc .... 802-831-1214.... 515 A
mmihaly@vermontlaw.edu
MIHALYOV, David .... 585-395-2577.... 352 F
dmihalyo@brockport.edu
MIHARA, Darrell .... 425-388-9581.... 533 H
dmihara@everettcc.edu
MIHEL, George, J .... 815-288-5511.... 163 I
mihelg@svcc.edu
MIHELICH, Lucinda .... 719-549-3080..... 87 B
Cindy.Mihelich@pueblocc.edu
MIHLBACHLER, Dennis ..... 217-532-6961.... 155
dennis.mihlbachler@doc.illinois.gov
MIHM-HEROLD,
Wendy, A .... 563-562-3263.... 187
mihm-heroldw@portal.nicc.edu
MIHOPULOS, Sheryl, L ..... 516-877-3365.... 322 A
mihopulos@adelphi.edu
MIKE, James .... 717-477-1151.... 443 D
jhmike@ship.edu
MIKE, Joe .... 651-846-3335.... 261 E
jmike@argosy.edu
MIKEL, Ed .... 206-268-4617.... 530 F
emikel@antioch.edu
MIKELL, Ashley .... 802-865-6428.... 513 A
mikell@champlain.edu
MIKESELL, Brian .... 413-528-7274.... 231 A
bmikesell@simons-rock.edu
MIKESELL, Leslie .... 530-283-0202...... 47 E
lmikesell@frc.edu
MIKESIC, Patrick .... 785-594-8447.... 190 C
patrick.mikesic@bakeru.edu
MIKEWORTH, Becky, L ..... 618-544-8657.... 152 G
mikeworthb@iecc.edu
MIKHAIL, Osama, I .... 713-500-3047.... 506 D
osama.i.mikhail@uth.tmc.edu
MIKKELSEN, Andrea .... 507-457-5024.... 270 B
amikkelsen@winona.edu
MIKKELSEN, Carmelita ...... 251-580-2213........ 5 A
cmikkelsen@faulknerstate.edu
MIKKELSEN, Morris, E ...... 319-273-2611.... 182 D
morris.mikkelsen@uni.edu
MIKLUSAK, Courtney .... 619-239-0391...... 37 D
cmiklusak@cwsl.edu
MIKNAVICH, Marie .... 315-866-0300.... 335 E
miknavimt@herkimer.edu
MIKOWSKI, Thomas .... 616-632-2853.... 248 A
mikowtho@aquinas.edu
MIKSA, Anthony .... 815-455-8673.... 157 F
tmiksa@mchenry.edu
MIKUS, Robert .... 443-352-4012.... 226 E
rmikus@stevenson.edu
MIKUSZEWSKI, Barbara .... 216-987-4497.... 389 A
barbara.mikuszewski@tri-c.edu
MILACCI, Fred .... 434-592-4043.... 520 F
fmilacci@liberty.edu
MILADIN, Judith, G .... 315-255-1743.... 325 H
miladin@cayuga-cc.edu
MILAM, B. Hofler .... 336-758-7415.... 380 B
MILAM, John, H .... 540-868-7249.... 526 H
jmilam@lfcc.edu
MILAM, Kathy, L .... 937-382-6661.... 405 H
kathy_milam@wilmington.edu
MILAM, Linda .... 918-781-7247.... 407 B
milaml@bacone.edu
MILANO, Joy .... 616-222-3000.... 254 A
jmilano@kuyper.edu
MILANO, Todd, A .... 717-728-2200.... 425 A
toddmilano@centralpenn.edu
MILARDOVICH, Julia .... 916-278-6322...... 35 E
juliam@csus.edu
MILASINOVIC, Milan .... 212-752-1530.... 338 C
milan.milasinovic@limcollege.edu
MILAVETZ, Barry .... 701-777-4278.... 381 D
barry.milavetz@email.und.edu
MILBOURNE, John, M ...... 321-674-7160.... 108 E
jmilbour@fit.edu
MILBURN, Milo, C .... 740-283-3771.... 390 M
mmilburn@franciscan.edu
MILBURN, Tim, R .... 208-467-8644.... 143 I
trmilburn@nnu.edu
MILBURY, Roy, S .... 774-455-7573.... 237 B
rmilbury@umassp.edu
MILBY, Kevin, S .... 859-238-5534.... 199 D
kevin.milby@centre.edu
MILDON, Todd, B .... 206-616-6811.... 538 F
tmildon@uw.edu
MILEHAM, Mardi .... 503-883-2217.... 416 G
mmileham@linfield.edu
MILENTIS, John .... 260-480-4156.... 176 D
jmilentis@ivytech.edu
MILES, Arletha .... 914-773-3856.... 345 F
lmiles@pace.edu
MILES, Belinda .... 216-987-2004.... 389 A
belinda.miles@tri-c.edu
MILES, Billie .... 802-654-2930.... 514 B
bmiles@smcvt.edu
MILES, Candice .... 202-274-5000...... 99 F
cmiles@udc.edu
MILES, Cindy .... 619-644-7569...... 48 I
cindy.miles@gcccd.edu
MILES, David, A .... 201-692-2227.... 310 B
dmiles@fdu.edu
MILES, Donald .... 814-472-3360.... 446 B
dmiles@francis.edu
MILES, Donald .... 803-593-9231.... 455 A
milesd@atc.edu
MILES, Frank .... 334-244-3467........ 2 A
fmiles1@aum.edu
MILES, Herb, E .... 979-230-3474.... 482 B
herb.miles@brazosport.edu
MILES, Jason .... 425-889-7800.... 535 I
jason.miles@northwestu.edu
MILES, Jennifer .... 662-329-7129.... 276 B
jmiles@vpss.muw.edu

MILES, Kevin, J 610-799-1169 434 D kmiles@lccc.edu
MILES, Kim 626-585-7401 61 E kxmiles@pasadena.edu
MILES, Linda 252-398-6505 363 E milesl@chowan.edu
MILES, Lora 618-650-2020 165 A
MILES, Martin 757-727-5635 519 C martin.miles@hamptonu.edu
MILES, Mary, E 502-852-6688 207 A maryelizabeth.miles@louisville.edu
MILES, Ray 337-475-5192 215 G rmiles@mcneese.edu
MILES, Richard 513-721-7944 391 C rmiles@gbs.edu
MILES, Stephannie 704-461-6873 362 B stephanniemiles@bac.edu
MILES, Stephen 941-487-4200 119 D miles@ncf.edu
MILES, Suzanne 520-206-4999 17 I smiles@pima.edu
MILES, Suzanne 520-206-6577 17 I smiles@pima.edu
MILES, Tom 478-445-4027 129 F tom.miles@gcsu.edu
MILES, Vernon 870-230-5134 21 I vmiles@hsu.edu
MILES, Veryl, V 202-319-5139 97 C miles@cua.edu
MILES, Vickie 334-670-5628 8 B vmiles@troy.edu
MILES, Wendy 508-373-9705 231 D wendy.miles@becker.edu
MILESKI, Annette 269-782-1463 258 E ascheid@swmich.edu
MILETTI, Linnette 787-841-2000 564 I lmiletti@email.pucpr.edu
MILEUR, Jean-Pierre 607-777-2141 351 F jpmileur@binghamton.edu
MILEWSKI, Douglas, J 973-275-2473 311 A douglas.milewski@shu.edu
MILEY, Abigail 812-488-2272 180 B am275@evansville.edu
MILFORD, David 518-244-2207 348 A milford@sage.edu
MILFORD, Michael 909-514-1808 44 B mmilford@devry.edu
MILFORD, William 516-299-2045 309 A william.milford@liu.edu
MILHAM, Donna 616-451-3511 250 E dmilham@davenport.edu
MILHAUSEN, Michael 503-399-6527 414 J michael.milhausen@chemeketa.edu
MILHIZER, Eugene, R 239-687-5301 101 B ermilhizer@avemarialaw.edu
MILHOLLAND, Tom, A 325-674-2918 478 H milholland@acu.edu
MILHOUSE, Songie 708-596-2000 164 F smilhouse@ssc.edu
MILICH, Marianne 219-980-6618 173 F mmilich@iun.edu
MILICI, Roger 212-636-6545 334 C milici@fordham.edu
MILIONIS, Daren 503-375-7012 415 F dmilionis@corban.edu
MILIOTTO, Mark 847-328-9300 164 B mark.miliotto@seabury.edu
MILJEVICH, Greg 715-365-4486 554 F gmiljevidh@nicoletcollege.edu
MILKOWSKI, Rose 312-629-6182 164 A rmilkowski@saic.edu
MILLA, Rosalinda 619-477-6310 73 A rmilla@usuniversity.edu
MILLAGE, Mark 605-221-3114 464 C mmillage@kilian.edu
MILLAN, Brett 956-872-7263 494 D bmillan@southtexascollege.edu
MILLANE, Maureen 716-839-8334 331 G mmillane@daemen.edu
MILLAR, Kenneth 562-985-4691 35 A kmillar@csulb.edu
MILLAR, Norman 818-767-0888 79 D norman.millar@woodbury.edu
MILLARD, Bill 765-677-2520 174 E bill.millard@indwes.edu
MILLARD, Chris 801-626-6055 511 D cmillard@weber.edu
MILLARD, Cristi 801-957-4145 512 C cristi.millard@slcc.edu
MILLARD, Jill 704-272-5397 373 F jmillard@spcc.edu
MILLARD, Timothy 606-783-9555 204 E t.millard@moreheadstate.edu
MILLAY, David 501-569-3390 24 E dlmillay@ualr.edu
MILLAY, David, L 501-569-3390 24 E dlmillay@ualr.edu
MILLEN, Elaine 603-447-3970 306 H elaine.millen@granite.edu
MILLEN, Mark 717-767-3400 452 I mark.millen@yti.edu
MILLEN, Mark 717-757-1100 452 I mark.millen@yti.edu
MILLEN, Tom 404-727-6052 129 A tom.millen@emory.edu
MILLENBACH, Judy 503-699-6266 416 I jmillenbach@marylhurst.edu
MILLENDER, Angelia 954-201-7486 102 A amillender@broward.edu
MILLER, Alan 504-988-7566 215 C amiller@tulane.edu
MILLER, Alex 864-977-7010 460 A alex.miller@ngu.edu
MILLER, Amanda, L 419-995-8260 399 B miller.1491@osu.edu
MILLER, Amy 215-568-9215 436 E amiller@mccworks.org
MILLER, Andrea Lewis 337-491-2678 212 C andrea.miller@sowela.edu
MILLER, Andrew 863-667-5703 118 A aemiller@seu.edu
MILLER, Andrew, T 607-255-2000 331 C atm65@cornell.edu
MILLER, Anita, L 814-871-5847 429 F miller064@gannon.edu
MILLER, Ann, M 336-841-9021 365 A amiller@highpoint.edu
MILLER, Anne 212-217-4190 333 G anne_miller@fitnyc.edu
MILLER, Annie 513-785-3280 396 E mille152@muohio.edu
MILLER, Anthony, A 540-545-7257 523 K amiller@su.edu
MILLER, Anthony, G 301-369-2800 221 F agmiller@capitol-college.edu
MILLER, Antoinette 216-791-5000 388 B axm120@case.edu
MILLER, Arnold, R 304-696-2677 543 G miller@marshall.edu
MILLER, Ashley 270-384-8065 203 H
MILLER, Ave 770-962-7580 132 A amiller@gwinnetttech.edu
MILLER, Avery 312-942-7091 163 B avery_miller@rush.edu
MILLER, Barbara 443-352-4369 226 E blmiller@stevenson.edu
MILLER, Barbara, A 215-968-8414 423 E millerb@bucks.edu
MILLER, Barbara, H 214-828-8268 497 A bmiller@bcd.tamhsc.edu
MILLER, Barbara, R 301-447-5072 225 A brmiller@msmary.edu
MILLER, Barbara Kaye 602-682-6800 17 G bmiller@phoenixlaw.edu
MILLER, Becky 913-360-7410 190 F beckymiller@benedictine.edu
MILLER, Becky 812-298-2361 177 A rmiller@ivytech.edu
MILLER, Beth 409-880-2292 500 E bbmiller@lit.edu
MILLER, Beth 505-925-8687 321 C schlbeth@unm.edu
MILLER, Bethany 859-622-6682 200 D bethany.miller@eku.edu
MILLER, Betsy 575-538-6118 321 I millerb@wnmu.edu
MILLER, Bettina 340-693-1421 568 C bmiller@uvi.edu
MILLER, Beverly 858-598-1200 30 A bmiller@aii.edu
MILLER, Bill 830-372-8120 499 C bmiller@tlu.edu
MILLER, BJ 540-432-4304 518 E bj.miller@emu.edu
MILLER, Bo 601-968-8797 273 F bmiller@belhaven.edu
MILLER, Bonnie 575-769-4014 317 K bonnie.miller@clovis.edu
MILLER, Brandon 254-710-3771 481 I brandon_miller@baylor.edu
MILLER, Brian 252-493-7241 372 E bmiller@email.pittcc.edu
MILLER, Brian 616-451-3511 250 E bmiller@davenport.edu
MILLER, Brian 501-244-5129 19 F brian.miller@arkansasbaptist.edu
MILLER, Bridget 315-655-7225 325 I bmmiller@cazenovia.edu
MILLER, Butch 970-248-1503 82 B rmiller@mesastate.edu
MILLER, Cantrell 304-442-3185 542 D cantrell.miller@mail.wvu.edu
MILLER, Cantrell, L 304-442-3185 545 C cantrell.miller@mail.wvu.edu
MILLER, Cantrell, L 304-442-3185 542 D cantrell.miller@mail.wvu.edu
MILLER, Carla 231-591-3825 251 B millerc@ferris.edu
MILLER, Carlyle, H 212-746-1058 360 B chm2031@med.cornell.edu
MILLER, Carol, A 262-472-1130 552 E millerc@uww.edu
MILLER, Carol, J 701-231-7761 381 H carol.miller@ndsu.edu
MILLER, Caroline, B 513-556-3379 403 D caroline.miller@uc.edu
MILLER, Carolyn 740-284-5822 390 M cmiller@franciscan.edu
MILLER, Cary Beth 615-383-4848 478 E cmiller@watkins.edu
MILLER, Catherine 203-857-3342 90 G cmiller@ncc.commnet.edu
MILLER, Cecile 478-274-7643 134 G cmiller@oftc.edu
MILLER, Chandra 918-293-5266 410 E chandra.miller@okstate.edu
MILLER, Chani 908-354-6057 317 G
MILLER, Charles 337-521-8990 212 B charles.miller@southlouisiana.edu
MILLER, Charles 281-649-3300 487 F cmiller@hbu.edu
MILLER, Cheryl 503-552-1510 417 D cmiller@ncnm.edu
MILLER, Cheryl 540-857-7201 528 E ccmiller@virginiawestern.edu
MILLER, Cheryl, L 860-439-2085 91 E cheryl.miller@conncoll.edu
MILLER, Cheryl, W 773-752-5757 146 E cmiller@ctschicago.edu
MILLER, Chris 312-752-2428 155 B chris.miller@kendall.edu
MILLER, Chris 847-317-7036 166 B cmiller@tiu.edu
MILLER, Chris, E 570-326-3761 440 K cmiller@pct.edu
MILLER, Christine 507-292-5130 269 B christinem.miller@roch.edu
MILLER, Christine, A 724-946-7148 451 C millerca@westminster.edu
MILLER, Clarence (Hank) 845-687-5065 358 C millerh@sunyulster.edu
MILLER, Colleen 320-589-6006 272 C mille593@morris.umn.edu
MILLER, Colleen 419-383-6805 404 F colleen.miller@utoledo.edu
MILLER, Craig 484-384-2953 438 C semregis@eastern.edu
MILLER, Dale 870-972-3053 20 C dmiller@astate.edu
MILLER, Dale, J 518-381-1280 350 E millerdj@sunysccc.edu
MILLER, Dan 662-329-7114 276 B dmiller@finaid.muw.edu
MILLER, Daniel 505-473-6708 320 F daniel.miller@santafeuniversity.edu
MILLER, Daniel, D 317-955-6058 177 G dmiller@marian.edu
MILLER, Daniel, P 570-321-4139 435 D millerda@lycoming.edu
MILLER, Darlene 973-877-3101 310 A dmiller@essex.edu
MILLER, Darrel 704-337-2574 375 G millerd@queens.edu
MILLER, David 507-389-7444 269 F david.miller@southcentral.edu
MILLER, David 606-546-1291 206 F dkmiller@unionky.edu
MILLER, David 501-686-7609 24 F dlmiller2@uams.edu
MILLER, David 312-362-8720 148 F miller@cdm.depaul.edu
MILLER, David 563-425-5293 189 C millerd@uiu.edu
MILLER, David 330-263-2317 388 E dmiller@wooster.edu
MILLER, David, E 304-293-8676 544 E dave.miller@mail.wvu.edu
MILLER, David, J 208-282-2517 143 D milldave@isu.edu
MILLER, David, J 515-294-8079 182 B djmille@iastate.edu
MILLER, David, P 617-333-2101 234 A dmiller@curry.edu
MILLER, Debbie 262-564-3220 553 H millerd@gtc.edu
MILLER, Deborah 714-997-6603 39 C dmiller@chapman.edu
MILLER, Deborah 419-772-2464 398 G d-miller@onu.edu
MILLER, Debra 217-357-3129 146 A dmiller@sandburg.edu
MILLER, Debra, M 570-326-3761 440 K dmiller2@pct.edu
MILLER, Dennis 201-447-7104 307 F dmiller@bergen.edu
MILLER, Dennis, L 414-443-8853 553 B dennis.miller@wlc.edu
MILLER, Dennis, R 570-662-4293 443 B dmiller@mansfield.edu
MILLER, Dianna, L 956-721-5820 489 G vpi@laredo.edu
MILLER, Dolores, M 563-562-3263 187 G millerd@nicc.edu
MILLER, Donna 502-213-5333 202 B donna.miller@kctcs.edu
MILLER, Donna 603-513-5118 306 G donna.miller@law.unh.edu
MILLER, Dorothy, A 816-604-1258 285 D dorothy.miller@mcckc.edu
MILLER, Doug 417-626-1234 287 F miller.doug@occ.edu
MILLER, Drew 936-294-1720 501 A adm007@shsu.edu
MILLER, Drucilla, W 423-798-7942 476 B drucilla.miller@ws.edu
MILLER, Dyan 925-424-1275 39 A dmiller@laspositascollege.edu
MILLER, E. John 701-231-7933 381 H ej.miller@ndsu.edu
MILLER, Earl 845-675-4790 344 G earl.miller@nyack.edu
MILLER, Edgar 803-777-8134 462 A ewmiller@gwm.sc.edu
MILLER, JR., Edward, D 410-955-3180 223 F emiller@jhmi.edu
MILLER, Eileen 503-399-5016 414 J eileen.miller@chemeketa.edu
MILLER, Elinor 303-964-5758 87 E emiller@regis.edu
MILLER, Elizabeth 805-922-6966 26 K emiller@hancockcollege.edu
MILLER, Elizabeth, K 651-638-6215 261 I e-miller@bethel.edu
MILLER, Ellen, B 540-828-5755 516 K emiller@bridgewater.edu
MILLER, Elvert 718-270-6002 328 D miller@mec.cuny.edu
MILLER, Enola 225-359-9231 209 K emiller@catc.edu
MILLER, Enrico, A 315-267-2484 354 C millerea@potsdam.edu
MILLER, Evan 201-967-9667 307 G
MILLER, Faith 706-272-4462 127 G fmiller@daltonstate.edu
MILLER, Fayneese, S 802-656-3424 514 F fayneese.miller@uvm.edu
MILLER, JR., Frank, P 717-771-4057 440 G fpm1@psu.edu
MILLER, Fred 907-852-3333 10 G fred.miller@ilisagvik.edu
MILLER, Fred 864-294-3800 458 D fred.miller@furman.edu
MILLER, Frederick 805-493-3960 32 H fdmiller@clunet.edu
MILLER, Galen, P 989-386-6644 255 F gpmiller@midmich.edu
MILLER, Gary 407-366-9493 115 I gmiller@rts.edu
MILLER, Gary 415-451-2806 66 B maintenance@sfts.edu
MILLER, George 901-722-3311 473 B
MILLER, Gerry 212-650-8687 326 H gmiller@ccny.cuny.edu
MILLER, Gina 412-536-1085 432 F gina.miller@laroche.edu
MILLER, Gina, L 678-547-6169 133 F miller_gl@mercer.edu
MILLER, Glen 503-399-5210 414 J glen.miller@chemeketa.edu
MILLER, Glenn 609-652-4378 313 F glenn.miller@stockton.edu
MILLER, Glenn 800-962-7682 293 B gmiller@wma.edu
MILLER, Glynis, K 972-860-7010 484 H GlynisMiller@dcccd.edu
MILLER, Harry, E 484-664-3464 437 B hmiller@muhlenberg.edu
MILLER, Henry 580-559-5760 407 J bmiller@ecok.edu
MILLER, Jack 619-574-6909 60 E jmiller@pacificcollege.edu
MILLER, Jacqueline 781-899-5500 232 A srmiller@blessedjohnxxiii.edu
MILLER, Jacquelyn 206-296-5446 537 F jcmiller@seattleu.edu
MILLER, Jaime, M 708-709-3513 161 C jmmiller@prairiestate.edu
MILLER, James 630-637-5500 159 F jlmiller@noctrl.edu
MILLER, James 201-447-7124 307 F jmiller@bergen.edu
MILLER, James 518-327-6215 345 H jmiller@paulsmiths.edu
MILLER, James 814-732-2826 442 D jbmiller@edinboro.edu
MILLER, James, C 701-231-6834 381 H james.c.miller@ndsu.edu
MILLER, James, D 804-289-8694 525 A jmiller@richmond.edu
MILLER, James, G 585-475-6637 347 G jgm6527@rit.edu
MILLER, James, M 419-995-8460 399 B miller.154@osu.edu
MILLER, James, P 573-629-2003 282 H jmiller@hlg.edu
MILLER, James, S 401-863-7940 452 J james_s_miller@brown.edu
MILLER, Jeanne, C 607-436-2513 353 E millerjc@oneonta.edu
MILLER, Jeanne, M 904-632-3232 109 E jmmiller@fscj.edu
MILLER, Jeanne, Y 570-669-7010 434 D jmiller@lccc.edu

MILLER, Jeff ... 541-956-7270 ... 420 B jmiller@roguec.edu

MILLER, Jeff ... 574-296-6206 ... 169 C jmiller@ambs.edu

MILLER, Jeff ... 803-754-4100 ... 457 D

MILLER, Jeffrey ... 314-529-9350 ... 284 F jeffmiller@maryville.edu

MILLER, Jess ... 541-440-4600 ... 420 F jess.miller@umpqua.edu

MILLER, Jessica, K ... 608-796-3013 ... 553 A jkmiller@viterbo.edu

MILLER, Jim ... 603-513-1338 ... 306 H jim.miller@granite.edu

MILLER, Jim ... 828-227-7124 ... 379 E jimmiller@wcu.edu

MILLER, Joan ... 386-226-4833 ... 105 C joan.dove@erau.edu

MILLER, Joanne ... 508-793-7320 ... 233 C jmiller@clarku.edu

MILLER, Joel, C ... 319-895-4107 ... 183 D jmiller@cornellcollege.edu

MILLER, John ... 404-527-4520 ... 126 F jmiller@carver.edu

MILLER, John ... 256-840-4195 ... 7 B jmiller@snead.edu

MILLER, John ... 503-352-2215 ... 419 E jmiller@pacificu.edu

MILLER, John, H ... 936-468-4008 ... 495 H jhmiller@sfasu.edu

MILLER, John, S ... 208-732-6280 ... 143 B jmiller@csi.edu

MILLER, John, W ... 860-832-3000 ... 91 G millerjw@ccsu.edu

MILLER, II, John, W ... 434-971-3301 ... 557 D john.millerII@conus.army.mil

MILLER, Jolene ... 765-269-5720 ... 176 B jomiller@ivytech.edu

MILLER, Jonathan ... 407-646-2306 ... 116 B jxmiller@rollins.edu

MILLER, Jonathan ... 508-854-4334 ... 241 C jmiller@qcc.mass.edu

MILLER, Jonathan, L ... 413-755-4230 ... 241 E jmiller@stcc.edu

MILLER, Joseph, C ... 334-833-4398 ... 4 E joseph.miller@huntingdon.edu

MILLER, Judith ... 740-264-5591 ... 390 F jmiller@egcc.edu

MILLER, Judith, E ... 904-620-2720 ... 120 C j.miller@unf.edu

MILLER, Judith, G ... 334-347-2623 ... 3 G jmiller@escc.edu

MILLER, Judy ... 989-686-9472 ... 250 F jamiller@delta.edu

MILLER, Judy ... 814-536-5168 ... 424 C jmiller@crbc.net

MILLER, Julie ... 716-839-8245 ... 331 G 0134mgr@fheg.follett.com

MILLER, Julie, H ... 313-577-2034 ... 260 D aa6560@wayne.edu

MILLER, K, C ... 480-994-9244 ... 18 I kc@swiha.org

MILLER, Kara ... 248-218-2029 ... 257 F kmiller@rc.edu

MILLER, Karen ... 507-223-7252 ... 268 B karen.miller@mnwest.edu

MILLER, Karen ... 216-987-4240 ... 389 A karen.miller@tri-c.edu

MILLER, Karen ... 419-448-2202 ... 391 G kmiller@heidelberg.edu

MILLER, Karen, L ... 913-588-1665 ... 197 A kmiller@kumc.edu

MILLER, Kate ... 605-995-2901 ... 464 B kamiller1@dwu.edu

MILLER, Kate, C ... 979-845-3651 ... 497 C kcmiller@tamu.edu

MILLER, Kathleen ... 239-590-7600 ... 119 A kmiller@fgcu.edu

MILLER, Kathleen, M ... 573-882-2011 ... 291 C millerkm@umsystem.edu

MILLER, SSJ, Kathryn ... 215-248-7167 ... 425 C kmiller@chc.edu

MILLER, Kay ... 707-654-1135 ... 32 I kmiller@csum.edu

MILLER, Keith ... 864-250-8175 ... 458 F keith.miller@gvltec.edu

MILLER, Keith, T ... 804-524-5070 ... 529 C ktmiller@vsu.edu

MILLER, Kelly ... 317-788-3437 ... 180 C kmiller@uindy.edu

MILLER, Ken ... 407-646-2999 ... 116 B kmiller@rollins.edu

MILLER, Ken ... 502-456-6506 ... 206 C kmiller@sullivan.edu

MILLER, Kenneth ... 909-599-5433 ... 54 A kmiller@lifepacific.edu

MILLER, Kenneth ... 740-857-1311 ... 401 F kmiller@rosedale.edu

MILLER, Kenneth, C ... 330-369-3200 ... 402 H tbcmail@tbc-trumbullbusiness.com

MILLER, Kenneth, P ... 814-898-6111 ... 439 E kqm3@psu.edu

MILLER, Kent ... 573-288-6373 ... 281 D kmiller@culver.edu

MILLER, Kevin ... 800-686-7022 ... 92 F kmiller@lincolncollegene.edu

MILLER, Kevin ... 920-403-3045 ... 550 C kevin.miller@snc.edu

MILLER, Kevin, D ... 973-408-3109 ... 309 F theoadm@drew.edu

MILLER, Kieron ... 562-907-4236 ... 79 B kmiller@whittier.edu

MILLER, Kimberly, A ... 410-822-5400 ... 222 B kmiller@chesapeake.edu

MILLER, Kimberly, D ... 812-877-8176 ... 179 A kimberly.miller@rose-hulman.edu

MILLER, Kimberly, M ... 814-269-2074 ... 449 D kimiller@pitt.edu

MILLER, Kimela ... 575-835-5888 ... 319 A kmiller@admin.nmt.edu

MILLER, Kolby ... 270-247-8521 ... 204 C kmiller@midcontinent.edu

MILLER, Kris ... 775-753-2135 ... 302 H krism@gwmail.gbcnv.edu

MILLER, L. Christopher ... 414-288-7206 ... 548 D l.christopher.miller@marquette.edu

MILLER, Larry ... 228-896-2506 ... 275 G larry.miller@mgccc.edu

MILLER, Larry ... 256-840-4111 ... 7 B lmiller@snead.edu

MILLER, Larry, S ... 270-686-4502 ... 202 E larry.miller@kctcs.edu

MILLER, Laura ... 717-766-2511 ... 436 D lmiller@messiah.edu

MILLER, Lavonna ... 618-842-3711 ... 152 F millerl@iecc.edu

MILLER, Lawrence, H ... 302-454-3917 ... 96 C miller@dtcc.edu

MILLER, Lawrence, W ... 540-432-4133 ... 518 E millerlw@emu.edu

MILLER, Leangela ... 559-737-6214 ... 42 B leangelam@cos.edu

MILLER, Lee ... 740-826-8171 ... 396 I leem@muskingum.edu

MILLER, Lester ... 908-526-1200 ... 313 E lmiller@raritanval.edu

MILLER, Lewis, R ... 317-940-9714 ... 170 C lmiller@butler.edu

MILLER, Linda ... 618-395-1169 ... 152 H millerli@iecc.edu

MILLER, Linda, G ... 270-809-2154 ... 204 F linda.miller@murraystate.edu

MILLER, Linda, J ... 262-691-5526 ... 555 C lmiller@wctc.edu

MILLER, Lisa ... 708-210-5767 ... 164 F lmiller@ssc.edu

MILLER, Lisa ... 563-244-7002 ... 184 C lmiller@eicc.edu

MILLER, Lisa ... 620-672-5641 ... 196 A lisam@prattcc.edu

MILLER, Lisa ... 805-378-1572 ... 77 B lisamiller@vcccd.edu

MILLER, Lisa ... 516-678-5000 ... 341 F lmiller@molloy.edu

MILLER, Lisa, R ... 318-342-5431 ... 216 E lmiller@ulm.edu

MILLER, Lori ... 412-261-2647 ... 432 B lmiller@kaplan.edu

MILLER, Lucy, T ... 727-816-3448 ... 114 F millerl@phcc.edu

MILLER, Lyn ... 765-983-1214 ... 171 B millely@earlham.edu

MILLER, M. Brad ... 407-851-2525 ... 106 E brmiller@cci.edu

MILLER, Marc, D ... 706-737-1418 ... 125 C mmiller@aug.edu

MILLER, Marcia ... 202-685-2650 ... 557 F millerm@ndu.edu

MILLER, Marcus, J ... 803-786-5150 ... 459 B mmiller@ltss.edu

MILLER, Margaret, C ... 847-543-2101 ... 147 H ecd185@clcillinois.edu

MILLER, Margaret, L ... 423-439-4300 ... 473 E millerml@etsu.edu

MILLER, Margaret, M ... 609-258-5813 ... 313 A mmmiller@princeton.edu

MILLER, Marilynn ... 406-657-2244 ... 295 F mmiller@msubillings.edu

MILLER, Mark ... 318-869-5117 ... 208 F mmiller@centenary.edu

MILLER, Mark ... 304-253-7351 ... 541 D mmiller@mountainstate.edu

MILLER, Mark, A ... 303-245-4775 ... 86 B markm@naropa.edu

MILLER, Mark, A ... 740-376-4741 ... 395 F mark.miller@marietta.edu

MILLER, Marlene, R ... 702-968-2023 ... 303 D mmiller@roseman.edu

MILLER, Marsha ... 912-279-5728 ... 127 B mmiller@ccga.edu

MILLER, Martha ... 704-357-8020 ... 361 N mmiller@aii.edu

MILLER, Marty, L ... 757-823-9539 ... 521 K mlmiller@nsu.edu

MILLER, Martyn, J ... 215-204-7708 ... 447 G martyn.miller@temple.edu

MILLER, Mary ... 203-432-2900 ... 95 D mary.miller@yale.edu

MILLER, Mary, E ... 209-228-4430 ... 74 B MMiller7@UCMerced.edu

MILLER, Mary, K ... 828-327-7000 ... 368 G mkmiller@cvcc.edu

MILLER, MaryAnne ... 617-228-2102 ... 239 G mmiller@bhcc.mass.edu

MILLER, Matt ... 989-386-6600 ... 255 F mmiller@midmich.edu

MILLER, Matthew ... 973-300-2338 ... 315 F mmiller@sussex.edu

MILLER, Matthew ... 678-839-5500 ... 138 D mmiller@westga.edu

MILLER, Matthew, A ... 574-372-5100 ... 171 E millerma@grace.edu

MILLER, Megan ... 410-225-2420 ... 224 C memiller@mica.edu

MILLER, Melinda, A ... 315-386-7085 ... 355 D millerm@canton.edu

MILLER, Melissa ... 843-661-8104 ... 458 A melissa.miller@fdtc.edu

MILLER, Melissa, A ... 585-785-1639 ... 334 A millerma@flcc.edu

MILLER, Melissa, C ... 386-312-4106 ... 116 D melissamiller@sjrstate.edu

MILLER, Melody ... 806-743-7826 ... 501 E melody.miller@ttuhsc.edu

MILLER, Melvin ... 802-485-2134 ... 514 A miller@norwich.edu

MILLER, Merianne ... 828-251-6676 ... 378 C mmiller@unca.edu

MILLER, Merrill ... 315-228-1000 ... 329 H mmiller@colgate.edu

MILLER, Michael ... 805-893-2118 ... 74 F Mike.Miller@sa.ucsb.edu

MILLER, Michael ... 715-682-1202 ... 549 C mmiller@northland.edu

MILLER, Michael ... 406-683-7636 ... 295 B m_miller@umwestern.edu

MILLER, Michael ... 715-425-0629 ... 552 A michael.miller@uwrf.edu

MILLER, Michael, A ... 512-471-4110 ... 505 B mike.miller@austin.utexas.edu

MILLER, Michael, C ... 704-463-3030 ... 375 E mike.miller@fsmail.pfeiffer.edu

MILLER, Michael, D ... 805-756-2344 ... 33 F mdmiller@calpoly.edu

MILLER, Michael, H ... 410-293-1500 ... 558 H millerm@usna.edu

MILLER, Michael, R ... 330-471-8205 ... 395 E mimiller@malone.edu

MILLER, Michael, S ... 510-436-1360 ... 50 F mmiller@hnu.edu

MILLER, Michael Patrick ... 708-524-5921 ... 150 A mmiller@dom.edu

MILLER, Michelle ... 802-860-2729 ... 513 A miller@champlain.edu

MILLER, Michelle, R ... 757-727-5447 ... 519 C

MILLER, Mike ... 530-895-2298 ... 31 E millermi@butte.edu

MILLER, Mike ... 336-386-8121 ... 374 B millerm@surry.edu

MILLER, Miryom, R ... 845-434-5240 ... 361 L lehu5@aol.com

MILLER, Morris ... 253-589-5565 ... 532 B morris.miller@cptc.edu

MILLER, Nancy ... 517-787-0800 ... 253 E millernancya@jccmi.edu

MILLER, Nancy ... 530-938-5404 ... 42 C millern@siskiyous.edu

MILLER, Nancy, B ... 205-726-2915 ... 6 G ndmiller@samford.edu

MILLER, Nancy, W ... 323-226-6301 ... 55 G

MILLER, Nelson ... 616-301-6800 ... 259 B millern@cooley.edu

MILLER, Nora, R ... 662-329-7145 ... 276 B nmiller@vpfa.muw.edu

MILLER, Pam ... 985-380-2436 ... 211 K

MILLER, Pamela ... 505-566-3217 ... 320 D millerp@sanjuancollege.edu

MILLER, Pamela ... 402-241-6405 ... 300 A pamm@northeast.edu

MILLER, Parks ... 706-776-0102 ... 135 D parksmiller@piedmont.edu

MILLER, Patricia, A ... 816-322-0110 ... 279 H pat.miller@calvary.edu

MILLER, Patrick ... 817-257-7825 ... 498 F p.miller@tcu.edu

MILLER, Paul ... 662-243-1902 ... 274 D pmiller@eastms.edu

MILLER, Paul ... 310-476-9777 ... 28 F pmiller@ajula.edu

MILLER, Pearce ... 412-566-2433 ... 434 B pmiller@paculinary.com

MILLER, Peggy ... 806-742-2781 ... 501 D peggy.miller@ttu.edu

MILLER, Peter ... 215-596-8542 ... 450 A p.miller@usciences.edu

MILLER, Peter, J ... 413-205-3201 ... 229 G peter.miller@aic.edu

MILLER, Peter, R ... 207-795-2842 ... 217 F millerpe@cmhc.org

MILLER, Phillip, E ... 212-824-2261 ... 335 C pmiller@huc.edu

MILLER, Rachel, S ... 620-327-8213 ... 193 rachelsm@hesston.edu

MILLER, Randall, C ... 304-260-4380 ... 542 rmiller@blueridgectc.edu

MILLER, Randi ... 201-360-4073 ... 310 rmiller@hccc.edu

MILLER, Ray ... 402-363-5656 ... 301 lrmiller@york.edu

MILLER, Ray ... 402-449-2920 ... 298 rmiller6053@graceu.edu

MILLER, Richard ... 504-362-6364 ... 68 rmiller@sum.edu

MILLER, Richard ... 219-947-8400 ... 177 rkmiller@kaplan.edu

MILLER, Richard, A ... 970-247-7426 ... 84 miller_r@fortlewis.edu

MILLER, Richard, B ... 417-625-9565 ... 286 miller-r@mssu.edu

MILLER, Richard, C ... 270-745-5468 ... 207 C richard.c.miller@wku.edu

MILLER, Richard, K ... 781-292-2301 ... 235 C richard.miller@olin.edu

MILLER, Richard, L ... 713-500-3603 ... 506 D richard.l.miller@uth.tmc.edu

MILLER, Rick ... 262-691-5323 ... 555 C rmiller@wctc.edu

MILLER, Rob ... 913-758-6160 ... 197 B millerr@stmary.edu

MILLER, Rob ... 908-852-1400 ... 308 F millerr@centenarycollege.edu

MILLER, Robbins ... 501-882-8876 ... 20 D ermiller@asub.edu

MILLER, Robert ... 352-392-1336 ... 120 B rmiller@admin.ufl.edu

MILLER, Robert, B ... 626-585-7123 ... 61 E rbmiller@pasadena.edu

MILLER, Robert, B ... 626-585-7665 ... 61 E rbmiller@pasadena.edu

MILLER, Robert, G ... 901-333-4368 ... 475 H rgmiller1@southwest.tn.edu

MILLER, Robert, H ... 225-771-5170 ... 214 H rhmillerjr@aol.com

MILLER, Robert, L ... 217-581-7249 ... 150 C rlmiller@eiu.edu

MILLER, Robert, M ... 864-294-2111 ... 458 D bob.miller@furman.edu

MILLER, Robert, R ... 540-828-5383 ... 516 K rmiller@bridgewater.edu

MILLER, Rodney, E ... 316-978-3389 ... 197 F rodney.miller@wichita.edu

MILLER, Rodney, E ... 706-419-1134 ... 127 F miller@covenant.edu

MILLER, Roger ... 269-488-4257 ... 253 G rmiller@kvcc.edu

MILLER, Roger, M ... 205-329-7909 ... 3 B roger.miller@ecacolleges.com

MILLER, Roland, G ... 847-543-2551 ... 147 H com624@clcillinois.edu

MILLER, Ross ... 973-642-3888 ... 307 G rem@berkeleycollege.edu

MILLER, Ross ... 973-642-3888 ... 323 J rem@berkeleycollege.edu

MILLER, Ruby ... 480-517-8152 ... 16 C ruby.miller@riosalado.edu

MILLER, Rush, G ... 412-648-7747 ... 449 A rgmiller@pitt.edu

MILLER, Ruth ... 785-594-4530 ... 190 C ruth.miller@bakeru.edu

MILLER, Ruth ... 650-306-3125 ... 67 E miller@smccd.edu

MILLER, Ruth, H ... 812-464-1824 ... 180 F rhmiller@usi.edu

MILLER, Ryan ... 918-561-1109 ... 410 D ryan.miller@okstate.edu

MILLER, Sally ... 707-664-4444 ... 37 B sally.miller@sonoma.edu

MILLER, Samira ... 323-822-9700 ... 72 G samira.miller@touro.edu

MILLER, Samuel ... 828-227-7147 ... 379 E sammiller@wcu.edu

MILLER, Samuel, T ... 229-928-1387 ... 131 B

MILLER, Sandra ... 973-720-2659 ... 317 D millers@wpunj.edu

MILLER, Sandra ... 716-827-4348 ... 358 B millers@trocaire.edu

MILLER, Sarah ... 763-424-0848 ... 268 D smiller2@nhcc.edu

MILLER, Scott, D ... 304-829-7111 ... 540 E smiller@bethanywv.edu

MILLER, Shari, K ... 716-673-3438 ... 352 A shari.miller@fredonia.edu

MILLER, Sharon ... 973-267-9404 ... 313 C rca079@aol.com

MILLER, Sharon ... 248-232-4175 ... 257 B semiller@oaklandcc.edu

MILLER, Sharon ... 863-297-1093 ... 115 A smiller@polk.edu

MILLER, Stacey ... 954-783-7339 ... 106 D smiller@cci.edu

MILLER, Stacey, A ... 802-656-3434 ... 514 F stacey.miller@uvm.edu

MILLER, Stan, W ... 574-535-7515 ... 171 D stanreg@goshen.edu

MINDERMAN, James, W ... 812-888-4227.... 181 B
jwminderman@vinu.edu

MINDINGALL, Marilyn, P .. 478-301-2680.... 133 F
mindingall_m@mercer.edu

MINE, Jodi .... 808-933-0803.... 141 F
mine@hawaii.edu

MINEAR, Dorothy, J .... 850-245-0466.... 118 F
dorothy.minear@flbog.edu

MINEO, Michael .... 718-817-4931.... 334 C
mineo@fordham.edu

MINER, Donald, L .... 608-262-0063.... 550 G
dminer@bussvc.wisc.edu

MINER, Judy, C .... 650-949-7200...... 47 H
minerjudy@fhda.edu

MINER, Kathleen .... 907-564-8265...... 10 D
kminer@alaskapacific.edu

MINER, Madonne .... 801-626-6424.... 511 D
madonneminer@weber.edu

MINER, Marlene, R .... 513-745-5660.... 403 F
marlene.miner@uc.edu

MINERVINI, Ron .... 617-730-7222.... 243 I
ron.minervini@newbury.edu

MINFORD, Joell .... 412-392-3422.... 444 H
jminford@pointpark.edu

MING, Amanda .... 248-476-1122.... 255 C
aming@mispp.edu

MINGEE, Sheila .... 217-477-2747.... 156 A
smingee@lakeviewcol.edu

MINGENBACK, Mary .... 620-341-5413.... 192 D
mmingenb@emporia.edu

MINGER, David .... 503-491-7316.... 417 B
david.minger@mhcc.edu

MINGLE, James, J .... 607-255-3903.... 331 C
jjm19@cornell.edu

MINGO, Rhonda .... 864-596-9016.... 457 E
rhonda.mingo@converse.edu

MINGO, Susan .... 207-454-1032.... 219 B
smingo@wccc.me.edu

MINGO, Susan .... 207-454-1046.... 219 B
smingo@wccc.me.edu

MINGUILLON, Janie .... 925-631-4572...... 64 F
mmingui@stmarys-ca.edu

MINHAS, Omer .... 419-772-2529.... 398 G
o-minhas@onu.edu

MINICK, Evelyn .... 610-660-1905.... 446 C
minick@sju.edu

MINICK, Thomas, R .... 239-280-2525.... 101 C
thomas.minick@avemaria.edu

MINIEA, D. Scott .... 573-592-1633.... 293 E
scott.miniea@williamwoods.edu

MINIFIE, Elizabeth .... 401-341-2266.... 454 D
minifiee@salve.edu

MINIS, Elizabeth .... 816-604-4114.... 285 I
lisa.minis@mcckc.edu

MINIX, Dean .... 254-968-9141.... 496 F
minix@tarleton.edu

MINK, Randy, L .... 412-397-4307.... 445 G
mink@rmu.edu

MINK-SALAS, Kandy .... 657-278-3211...... 34 E
kmink@fullerton.edu

MINKIEWICZ, Jennifer, V .. 216-221-8584.... 405 D
jennifermink@vmcad.edu

MINKLER, James .... 509-533-3538.... 532 F
jamesm@spokanefalls.edu

MINKLER, Jim .... 509-533-3764.... 532 D
jimm@spokanefalls.edu

MINKS, Larry .... 580-745-2500.... 412 C
lminks@se.edu

MINNE, Erin .... 309-438-7681.... 153 C
eminne@ilstu.edu

MINNER, Sam, H .... 540-831-5404.... 522 D
sminner@radford.edu

MINNICH, Bryan .... 785-827-5541.... 194 D
bryan.minnich@kwu.edu

MINNICH, Donna .... 973-596-3603.... 312 C
donna.minnich@njit.edu

MINNICH, Peggy .... 513-244-4531.... 388 D
peggy_minnich@mail.msj.edu

MINNICH, Thomas .... 304-734-6699.... 542 D
tminnich@bridgemont.edu

MINNICH, William .... 650-991-3525...... 44 C
wminnich@devry.edu

MINNICK, Ann, M .... 651-696-6036.... 265 A
aminnick@macalester.edu

MINNICK, Charlie .... 563-242-4023.... 181 G
charlie.minnick@ashford.edu

MINNICK, Susan .... 262-691-5392.... 555 C
sminnick@wctc.edu

MINNICK, William, C .... 712-707-7226.... 188 B
bminnick@nwciowa.edu

MINNIHAN, Jacki .... 815-921-4482.... 162 F
j.minnihan@rockvalleycollege.edu

MINNIS, Phil .... 618-985-3741.... 154 E
philminnis@jalc.edu

MINNIS, Sarah, L .... 919-536-7200.... 369 G
minniss@durhamtech.edu

MINNIS, Stephen, D .... 913-360-7400.... 190 F
sminnis@benedictine.edu

MINNITI, Lea .... 513-745-2872.... 406 E
minnitil@xavier.edu

MINNOCK, Ed .... 508-531-6189.... 238 B
eminnock@bridgew.edu

MINOR, Dan .... 970-675-3272...... 82 D
dan.minor@cncc.edu

MINOR, Diana, Y .... 909-869-3704...... 33 G
dyminor@csupomona.edu

MINOR, Diane .... 312-553-2636.... 146 G
dminor1@ccc.edu

MINOR, DoVeanna, F .... 205-348-8462.......... 8 F
dfulton@as.ua.edu

MINOR, Frankie, D .... 573-882-7275.... 291 D
minorf@missouri.edu

MINOR, JR., Hassan .... 202-806-2530...... 98 B
svp@howard.edu

MINOR, Leslie .... 541-383-7238.... 414 I
lminor@cocc.edu

MINOR, Lloyd, B .... 410-516-3355.... 223 F
lminor@jhu.edu

MINOR, Lottie .... 901-369-0835...... 99 D
lottie.minor@strayer.edu

MINOR, Scott .... 916-631-8108...... 33 C

MINOR, Tamra .... 518-956-8110.... 351 E
tminor@uamail.albany.edu

MINOW, Martha .... 617-495-4601.... 235 H
minow@law.harvard.edu

MINTER, Dee .... 478-471-2031.... 133 E
dee.minter@maconstate.edu

MINTER, Doug .... 309-268-8385.... 151 G
doug.minter@heartland.edu

MINTER, Doug .... 507-933-7527.... 264 B
dminter@gustavus.edu

MINTER, Michael .... 972-825-4818.... 495 D
mminter@sagu.edu

MINTER, Terry .... 972-825-4628.... 495 D
tminter@sagu.edu

MINTERN, Janet .... 252-493-7286.... 372 E
jmintern@email.pittcc.edu

MINTON, Joyce .... 336-838-6251.... 375 A
joyce.minton@wilkescc.edu

MINTON, Randy, F .... 912-583-3109.... 126 C
rminton@bpc.edu

MINTZ, Alan, E .... 718-933-6700.... 341 G
amintz@monroecollege.edu

MINTZ, Elizabeth .... 732-356-1595.... 315 D
bmintz@somerset.edu

MINTZ, Marcia, B .... 202-687-6400...... 98 A
mbm23@georgetown.edu

MINUS, Bertha .... 904-470-8051.... 105 A
bertha.minus@ewc.edu

MINUS, Daryl .... 252-638-1088.... 369 E
minusd@cravencc.edu

MINUS, Molly, E .... 512-448-8581.... 493 B
mollym@stedwards.edu

MIRABAL, Elizabeth .... 602-216-3163...... 11 F
emirabal@argosy.edu

MIRABAL, Gloria .... 787-480-2355.... 561 D
gmirabal@sanjuancapital.com

MIRABELL, Julie, L .... 440-964-4316.... 393 E
jmirabell@kent.edu

MIRABELLA, Mike .... 949-851-6200...... 46 M
mmirabella@fidm.edu

MIRABILE, Kathleen .... 602-212-0501...... 17 D
kmirabile@theparalegalinstitute.edu

MIRABILE, Kathleen .... 800-231-3803...... 12 G

MIRABITO, Donna .... 248-689-8282.... 260 A
dmirabit@walshcollege.edu

MIRABITO, Michael .... 570-348-6209.... 435 F
mirabito@marywood.edu

MIRACKY, SJ, James, F .... 410-617-2327.... 224 A
jjmiracky@loyola.edu

MIRACLE, William, D .... 540-828-5380.... 516 K
wmiracle@bridgewater.edu

MIRANDA, Albert .... 714-484-7394...... 59 C
amiranda@cypresscollege.edu

MIRANDA, Alex .... 805-969-3626...... 60 K
amiranda@pacifica.edu

MIRANDA, Candida .... 312-567-3134.... 153 B
miranda@iit.edu

MIRANDA, Deana .... 312-935-6657.... 162 E
dmiranda@robertmorris.edu

MIRANDA, Elizabeth .... 787-250-1912.... 563 E
emiranda@metro.inter.edu

MIRANDA, Gloria .... 310-660-3735...... 45 D
gmiranda@elcamino.edu

MIRANDA, Jakelin .... 305-273-4499.... 103 C
jakelin@cbt.edu

MIRANDA, Jose .... 954-923-4440.... 112 K
registrar@keycollege.edu

MIRANDA, Mark .... 732-571-3593.... 311 F
mmiranda@monmouth.edu

MIRANDA, Mirta .... 305-593-1223.... 102 D
mmiranda@albizu.edu

MIRANDA, Paul .... 718-429-6600.... 359 E
paul.miranda@vaughn.edu

MIRANDA, Rick .... 970-491-6614...... 83 A
rick.miranda@colostate.edu

MIRANDA, Robert .... 714-992-7090...... 59 D
bmiranda@fullcoll.edu

MIRANDA, Rowan, A .... 734-764-7270.... 259 D
rowanm@umich.edu

MIRANDA-RODRÍGUEZ,
Edna .... 787-993-8860.... 566 G
edna.miranda1@upr.edu

MIRANTE, Aida .... 401-341-2140.... 454 D
mirantea@salve.edu

MIRCH, Mary .... 818-240-1000...... 48 C
mmirch@glendale.edu

MIRECKI, Julie .... 920-693-1193.... 554 A
julie.mirecki@gotoltc.edu

MIRELES, Rod .... 936-261-1905.... 496 E
rmireles@pvamu.edu

MIRENDA, Rosalie, M .... 610-558-5501.... 437 C
rmirenda@neumann.edu

MIRES, Mike .... 208-769-7783.... 143 H

MIRIZZI, Ray .... 513-569-1561.... 387 F
raymond.mirizzi@cincinnatistate.edu

MIRMIRAN, Amir .... 305-348-2522.... 119 B
amir.mirmiran@fiu.edu

MIROCHA, Ken .... 563-441-4116.... 184 E
kmirocha@eicc.edu

MIRON, Luis .... 504-865-3530.... 213 F
lmiron@loyno.edu

MIRON, Nancy .... 323-343-3050...... 35 B
nmiron@cslanet.calstatela.edu

MIROTZNIK, Jerrold .... 718-951-5024.... 326 G
jerrym@brooklyn.cuny.edu

MIRR, Jim .... 415-354-9167...... 32 B
jmirr@baychef.com

MIRRO, Roberta .... 631-249-3048.... 356 A
sm711/bncollege@bncollege.com

MIRSHAB, Bahman .... 713-525-2100.... 504 D
mirshab@stthom.edu

MIRVIS, Diane, C .... 203-576-4740...... 94 D
dmirvis@bridgeport.edu

MIRZA, Zoaib .... 312-662-4233.... 144 C

MISAK, M. David .... 580-774-3275.... 412 F
david.misak@swosu.edu

MISANTONE, Louis .... 781-762-1211.... 235 A
drlou@fine-ne.com

MISCAVAGE, Denise .... 570-674-6248.... 436 F
dmiscava@misericordia.edu

MISCH, Donald .... 303-492-0025...... 88 B
donald.misch@colorado.edu

MISCHE, Terri .... 320-308-6675.... 269 C
tamische@stcloudstate.edu

MISCHKE, Joel, P .... 414-443-8812.... 553 B
joel.mischke@wlc.edu

MISERENDINO, Peter .... 203-287-3026...... 93 C
paier.admin@snet.net

MISGEN, Sherry .... 312-899-5216.... 164 A
smisgen@saic.edu

MISHEK, Mark .... 651-213-4006.... 264 D
mmishek@hazelden.org

MISHLER, Jeremy .... 231-591-2345.... 251 B
mishlerj@ferris.edu

MISHOE, Shelley .... 757-683-4960.... 521 L
smishoe@odu.edu

MISHRA, Banamber .... 337-475-5010.... 215 G
bmishra@mcneese.edu

MISHRA, Sharda, D .... 615-327-6156.... 471 A
smishra@mmc.edu

MISIANO, Chris .... 434-592-3144.... 520 F
cjmisiano@liberty.edu

MISICK, Jennifer .... 718-289-5906.... 326 F
jennifer.misick@bcc.cuny.edu

MISKO, Elaine, J .... 412-578-6137.... 424 G
miskoej@carlow.edu

MISKOVIC, Linda .... 714-628-4901...... 63 G
miskovic_linda@sccollege.edu

MISKY, Allison .... 860-231-5505...... 93 H
amisky@sjc.edu

MISLA, Abel .... 787-841-2000.... 564 I
abel_misla@email.pucpr.edu

MISNER, John .... 706-776-0115.... 135 D
jmisner@piedmont.edu

MISRA, Hara, P .... 540-231-4000.... 518 H

MISRA, Ravi, P .... 414-955-8778.... 548 E
rmisra@mcw.edu

MISSAKIAN, Anais .... 401-454-6184.... 454 B
amissaki@risd.edu

MISSEL, Chris .... 912-588-2580.... 124 A
cmissel@altamahatech.edu

MISSELL, Katherine .... 619-260-4551...... 76 A
kmissell@sandiego.edu

MISSURELLI, David .... 262-551-6200.... 546 F
dmissurelli@carthage.edu

MISTICK, Barbara, K .... 717-262-2000.... 452 B
barbara.mistick@wilson.edu

MISTO, RSM, Leona .... 401-341-2229.... 454 D
mistol@salve.edu

MITCHAM, Aaron .... 412-396-5098.... 428 C
mitchama@duq.edu

MITCHAM, Larry, G .... 678-359-5059.... 131 D
larrym@gdn.edu

MITCHELL, Alan .... 256-331-5362.......... 6 B
mitchell@nwscc.edu

MITCHELL, Amanda .... 706-754-7724.... 134 E
amitchell@northgatech.edu

MITCHELL, Andrea .... 954-783-7339.... 106 D
amitchell@cci.edu

MITCHELL, Antoinette .... 202-884-9504...... 99 E
mitchellan@trinitydc.edu

MITCHELL, Audrey .... 256-765-4124.......... 9 D
admitchell@una.edu

MITCHELL, Bede .... 912-478-5116.... 131 A
wbmitch@georgiasouthern.edu

MITCHELL, Ben, L .... 601-984-6300.... 277 H
blmitchell@umc.edu

MITCHELL, Beth .... 828-765-7351.... 371 F
bmitchell@mayland.edu

MITCHELL, Betsy .... 626-395-6148...... 32 E
betsy.mitchell@caltech.edu

MITCHELL, Bonnie .... 508-626-4651.... 238 D
bonniem@framingham.edu

MITCHELL, Bradley, J .... 937-382-6661.... 405 H
brad_mitchell@wilmington.edu

MITCHELL, Brenda .... 479-788-7519...... 24 D
bmitchel@uafortsmith.edu

MITCHELL, Brenda, S .... 301-322-0858.... 225 F
bmitchell@pgcc.edu

MITCHELL, Brian .... 504-865-5261.... 215 C
brian@tulane.edu

MITCHELL, Brian, S .... 504-314-2818.... 215 C
brian@tulane.edu

MITCHELL, Carl .... 910-678-8373.... 370 B
mitchelc@faytechcc.edu

MITCHELL, Cathryn .... 912-538-3101.... 137 A
cmitchell@southeasterntech.edu

MITCHELL, Cathy .... 806-894-9611.... 494 C
cmitchell@southplainscollege.edu

MITCHELL, Cecile .... 907-786-1558...... 10 I
ancom@uaa.alaska.edu

MITCHELL, Charles .... 607-735-1937.... 333 A
cmitchell@elmira.edu

MITCHELL, Chase .... 435-283-7340.... 512 B
chase.mitchell@snow.edu

MITCHELL, Chrisie .... 845-431-8976.... 332 E
chrisie.mitchell@sunydutchess.edu

MITCHELL, Cindy .... 765-269-5380.... 176 B
cmitchell@ivytech.edu

MITCHELL, Craig .... 206-517-4541.... 537 C
cmitchell@siom.edu

MITCHELL, Daisy .... 773-481-8830.... 147 F
dmitchell@ccc.edu

MITCHELL, Dan .... 434-592-4152.... 520 F
dmitchell@liberty.edu

MITCHELL, David .... 415-503-6218...... 66 A
dlmitchell@sfcm.edu

MITCHELL, David .... 401-598-1249.... 453 C
dmitchell@jwu.edu

MITCHELL, David, B .... 301-405-5726.... 227 B
chief@umpd.umd.edu

MITCHELL, David, C .... 360-475-7100.... 535 J
dmitchell@olympic.edu

MITCHELL, Debbie .... 760-921-5408...... 61 B
dmitchell@paloverde.edu

MITCHELL, Debbie .... 734-432-4076.... 254 G
doffman@madonna.edu

MITCHELL, Debra .... 562-947-8755...... 71 A
debramitchell@scuhs.edu

MITCHELL, Dennis .... 601-484-0221.... 276 A
dmitchell@meridian.msstate.edu

MITCHELL, Don .... 602-386-4183...... 11 H
don.mitchell@arizonachristian.edu

MITCHELL, Donald .... 217-206-6690.... 167 A
mitchell.donald@uis.edu

MITCHELL, III, Earnest, L . 731-426-7604.... 469 M
ernest@lanecollege.edu

MITCHELL, Elizabeth, T ...... 210-458-4105.... 506 B
liz.mitchell@utsa.edu

MITCHELL, IV, Enzley .... 312-567-7124.... 153 B
emitche2@iit.edu

MITCHELL, Eugene, S .... 610-796-8413.... 421 F
gene.mitchell@alvernia.edu

MITCHELL, Franklin, L .... 864-488-8239.... 459 A
fmitchell@limestone.edu

MITCHELL, Gary .... 575-763-0535.... 508 B
mitchellg@wbu.edu

MITCHELL, Geoffrey .... 601-984-1115.... 277 H
gmitchell@umc.edu

MITCHELL, Gerald, A .... 919-866-5143.... 374 E
gamitchell@waketech.edu

MITCHELL, Gregory .... 843-477-2032.... 458 G
greg.mitchell@hgtc.edu

MITCHELL, Gregory .... 903-886-5719.... 497 E
gregory_mitchell@tamu-commerce.edu

MITCHELL, Horace .... 661-654-2241...... 33 H
hmitchell@csub.edu

MITCHELL, James .... 212-678-4084.... 357 F
jm331@tc.columbia.edu

MITCHELL, James, M .... 334-876-9231.......... 4 B
jmitchell@wccs.edu

MITCHELL, James, W .... 202-806-6565...... 98 B
jwmitchell@howard.edu

MITCHELL, Jaynie .... 281-476-1501.... 493 E
jaynie.mitchell@sjcd.edu

MITCHELL, Jeff .... 319-398-4983.... 186 H
jmitche@kirkwood.edu

MITCHELL, Jennie .... 812-535-5279.... 179 C
jmitchel@smwc.edu

MITCHELL, Jennifer, E .... 757-455-8785.... 529 F
jemitchell@vwc.edu

MITCHELL, Joan .... 978-367-2345.... 230 F
joan.mitchell@auc.edu

MITCHELL, Joan .... 801-274-3280.... 512 E
jmitchell@wgu.edu

MITCHELL, Joann .... 215-898-6630.... 448 I
joannm@pobox.upenn.edu

MITCHELL, John .... 912-344-2529.... 124 E
john.mitchell@armstrong.edu

MITCHELL, Judy .... 815-280-6640.... 154 H
jmitchel@jjc.edu

MITCHELL, Karen .... 615-230-3505.... 476 A
karen.mitchell@volstate.edu

MOHR, Thomas ... 303-373-2008 ... 87 G
MOHR, Wayne, C ... 570-389-4303 ... 441 F
wmohr@bloomu.edu
MOHRBACHER, Bob ... 509-793-2055 ... 531 D
Bobm@bigbend.edu
MOHRE, Trudy ... 325-649-8022 ... 488 A
tmohre@hputx.edu
MOHS, Marlene ... 651-690-6932 ... 271 E
mmohn@stkate.edu
MOHSEN, Bashir ... 201-216-9901 ... 309 G
MOHSINI, Virga ... 617-824-7858 ... 234 D
virga_mohsini@emerson.edu
MOHUN, Susan ... 205-391-2223 ... 7 A
smohun@sheltonstate.edu
MOIANI, Thomas ... 215-596-7532 ... 450 A
t.moiani@usciences.edu
MOINESTER, Eli ... 610-526-6197 ... 430 D
emoinester@harcum.edu
MOIOLA, Tena ... 858-566-1200 ... 43 J
tmoiola@disd.edu
MOIR, Chris ... 216-987-3492 ... 389 A
chris.moir@tri-c.edu
MOIR, Margaret (Peg), A ... 419-755-4704 ... 397 B
pmoir@ncstatecollege.edu
MOIST, Kirk, L ... 715-833-6224 ... 553 F
kmoist@cvtc.edu
MOJICA, Agnes ... 787-892-4320 ... 563 G
amojica@sg.inter.edu
MOJICA, Francis, J ... 787-723-4481 ... 560 H
francismojica@yahoo.com
MOJICA, Jorge, E ... 787-852-1430 ... 562 D
jmojica@microjuris.com
MOJICA, Luis ... 787-780-0070 ... 560 F
lmojica@caribbean.edu
MOJOCK, Charles, R ... 352-365-3523 ... 112 M
mojockc@lscc.edu
MOK, Jacqueline ... 520-621-5288 ... 19 B
jlmok@email.arizona.edu
MOKEL, Haroon ... 202-408-2400 ... 99 D
haroon.mokel@strayer.edu
MOKOSSO, Henry, E ... 504-286-5250 ... 214 I
hmokosso@suno.edu
MOKRZECKI, Elizabeth ... 413-572-8019 ... 239 C
emokrzecki@wsc.ma.edu
MOKUAU, Noreen, K ... 808-956-6300 ... 141 B
noreen@hawaii.edu
MOLALENGE, Teshome, H 540-828-5751 ... 516 K
tmolalen@bridgewater.edu
MOLAND, Millie ... 970-248-1304 ... 82 B
mmoland@mesastate.edu
MOLASSO, Billy ... 619-947-6787 ... 391 A
molassob@franklin.edu
MOLD, Jean ... 435-722-6900 ... 510 J
MOLDAVAN, Carla ... 706-295-6306 ... 130 C
cmoldava@highlands.edu
MOLDE, Alan, I ... 507-933-7622 ... 264 B
amolde@gustavus.edu
MOLDENHAUER, Susan ... 307-766-6620 ... 556 E
amsm@uwyo.edu
MOLDER, Kandi ... 918-335-6237 ... 411 B
kmolder@okwu.edu
MOLDSTAD, Donald, L ... 507-344-7312 ... 261 H
donm@blc.edu
MOLDSTAD, Jonathan, L ... 507-344-7889 ... 261 H
jmoldstad@blc.edu
MOLEN, Brent ... 801-426-8234 ... 509 F
president@ucdh.edu
MOLEN, Kenneth ... 801-226-1081 ... 509 F
director@ucdh.edu
MOLENAAR, James, H ... 320-222-5211 ... 268 I
jim.molenaar@ridgewater.edu
MOLENKAMP, Kathy, L ... 616-538-2330 ... 251 F
kmolenkamp@gbcol.edu
MOLER, Misty ... 704-216-3623 ... 373 C
misty.moler@rccc.edu
MOLESWORTH, Mark, D ... 608-342-1567 ... 551 F
moleswom@uwplatt.edu
MOLEY, Linda ... 620-252-7115 ... 191 I
lmoley@coffeyville.edu
MOLIDOR, Christian ... 225-578-1351 ... 212 F
molidor@lsu.edu
MOLIFE, Brenda ... 508-531-1201 ... 238 B
bmolife@bridgew.edu
MOLIKEN, Laura ... 610-409-3606 ... 450 C
lmoliken@ursinus.edu
MOLINA, Carlos ... 718-518-6658 ... 327 D
cmolina@hostos.cuny.edu
MOLINA, Carlos ... 202-495-3876 ... 98 D
cmolina@dhs.edu
MOLINA, Jose, A ... 787-738-2161 ... 567 A
jose.molina3@upr.edu
MOLINA, Michael ... 806-742-2116 ... 501 D
michael.molina@ttu.edu
MOLINARO, Brian ... 315-792-5545 ... 341 E
bmolinaro@mvcc.edu
MOLITIERNO, Jason, J ... 203-396-8324 ... 93 G
molitiernoj@sacredheart.edu
MOLIVER, Donald ... 732-571-3422 ... 311 F
dmoliver@monmouth.edu
MOLL, Amy ... 208-426-5719 ... 142 F
amoll@boisestate.edu
MOLL, Jonathan ... 781-239-4022 ... 230 G
jmoll@babson.edu
MOLL, Monica, M ... 419-372-2346 ... 385 C
mmoll@bgsu.edu
MOLL, Stephen ... 305-919-5700 ... 119 B
molls@fiu.edu
MOLLA, Mike ... 410-225-2215 ... 224 C
mmolla@mica.edu
MOLLAHAN, David, J ... 334-683-2301 ... 5 G
dmollahan@marionmilitary.edu
MOLLBERG, Barbara, J ... 507-285-7111 ... 269 B
barb.mollberg@roch.edu
MOLLENKAMP, Brian, L ... 734-207-9581 ... 256 B
bmollenkamp@mts.edu
MOLLENKOPF, Robert ... 724-480-3387 ... 426 A
robert.mollenkopf@ccbc.edu
MOLLER, Edward ... 617-928-4515 ... 243 A
enmoller@mountida.edu
MOLLER, Jerry, E ... 806-371-5297 ... 479 H
jemoller@actx.edu
MOLLER, Steffen ... 503-594-3390 ... 415 A
steffenm@clackamas.edu
MOLLEUR, Sherri ... 802-322-1626 ... 513 C
sherri.molleur@goddard.edu
MOLLICONI, Mary ... 402-461-7320 ... 298 C
mmolliconi@hastings.edu
MOLLIS, Kristi, L ... 561-912-1211 ... 106 G
kmollis@evergladesuniversity.edu
MOLLOY, Christopher, J ... 732-445-2675 ... 314 D
cmolloy1@pharmacy.rutgers.edu
MOLLOY, Elizabeth ... 678-891-2450 ... 130 G
Elizabeth.Molloy@gpc.edu
MOLLOY, Marcie, A ... 410-822-5400 ... 222 B
mamolloy@chesapeake.edu
MOLNAR, Imre ... 313-664-7890 ... 250 A
imolnar@collegeforcreativestudies.edu
MOLNAR, Susan ... 617-254-2610 ... 244 E
MOLONEY, Jacqueline ... 978-934-2943 ... 237 F
jacqueline_moloney@uml.edu
MOLS, Frank ... 717-867-6118 ... 434 C
mols@lvc.edu
MOLYNEUX, Annette ... 215-895-1415 ... 427 G
ajm26@drexel.edu
MOLZ, Chris ... 215-222-4200 ... 445 F
cmolz@walnuthillcollege.edu
MOMAN, Orthella, P ... 601-977-7778 ... 277 F
omoman@tougaloo.edu
MOMAN, Tim ... 602-432-8414 ... 11 C
MOMANY, Christopher, P . 517-265-5161 ... 247 D
cmomany@adrian.edu
MOMAYEZI, Betty ... 678-466-4143 ... 127 A
bettymomayezi@clayton.edu
MOMAYEZI, Nasser ... 678-466-4700 ... 127 A
nassermomayezi@clayton.edu
MOMBERG, Joel ... 813-974-1899 ... 120 D
jmomberg@usf.edu
MOMINEY, Michael ... 954-262-8252 ... 114 B
mominey@nsu.nova.edu
MONACO, A, G ... 225-578-8200 ... 212 F
amonaco@lsu.edu
MONACO, Anthony, P ... 617-627-3300 ... 245 F
anthony.monaco@tufts.edu
MONACO, Dennis ... 978-232-2357 ... 234 F
dmonaco@endicott.edu
MONACO, Frank, J ... 914-923-2658 ... 345 F
fmonaco@pace.edu
MONACO, Salvatore ... 415-738-8107 ... 1 E
smonaco@aju.edu
MONAGAN, Paul, R ... 903-510-2130 ... 502 E
pmon@tjc.edu
MONAGHAN, Thomas, S .. 239-280-2522 ... 101 C
tmonaghan@avemaria.edu
MONAHAN, JR.,
Charles, F ... 617-732-2880 ... 241 F
charles.monahan@mcphs.edu
MONAHAN, Daniel ... 508-565-1373 ... 245 D
dmonahan@stonehill.edu
MONAHAN, Helena ... 210-805-5880 ... 503 F
helena@uiwtx.edu
MONAHAN, Joseph ... 732-987-2662 ... 310 D
monahanj@georgian.edu
MONAHAN, Quin ... 704-461-6802 ... 362 B
quinmonahan@bac.edu
MONAN, SJ, J. Donald ... 617-552-2128 ... 232 D
j.donald.monan@bc.edu
MONASCH, Chris, P ... 718-990-6223 ... 348 G
monaschc@stjohns.edu
MONCHEK, Lana ... 305-595-9500 ... 100 D
MONCHER, Gary, R ... 510-261-8500 ... 61 F
gmoncher@patten.edu
MONCHUSIE, David ... 816-584-6434 ... 287 H
david.monchusie@park.edu
MONCK-MARCELLINO,
Caitlin ... 718-780-0322 ... 324 F
caitlin.monck-marcellino@brooklaw.edu
MONCRIFFE, Pritchard ... 405-466-3215 ... 408 G
pmoncriffe@lunet.edu
MONCURE, Betty ... 601-979-2227 ... 275 A
betty.j.moncure@jsums.edu
MONCURE, Thomas, M ... 703-993-2619 ... 519 A
tmoncure@gmu.edu
MONDAY, JR., Elden, R ... 206-239-2315 ... 530 H
emonday@aii.edu
MONDAY, Eric, N ... 225-578-4342 ... 212 F
emonday@lsu.edu
MONDAY, Kathryn, J ... 804-289-8771 ... 525 A
kmonday@richmond.edu
MONDEH, Sama ... 205-247-8151 ... 7 G
smondeh@stillman.edu
MONDEIK, Shelly ... 715-675-3331 ... 554 G
mondeik@ntc.edu
MONDELLI, Robert ... 973-684-6626 ... 312 E
rmondelli@pccc.edu
MONDOU, Sherry, B ... 253-879-3204 ... 538 E
smondou@pugetsound.edu
MONDROS, Jacqueline ... 212-452-7085 ... 327 E
jmondros@hunter.cuny.edu
MONDZIEL, Marlene ... 804-819-4902 ... 525 F
mmondziel@vccs.edu
MONE, Jennifer ... 516-463-7310 ... 335 H
jennifer.mone@hofstra.edu
MONETA, Larry ... 919-684-3737 ... 363 I
larry.moneta@duke.edu
MONEY, Barbara ... 972-599-3151 ... 483 D
bmoney@collin.edu
MONEY, Royce ... 325-674-4974 ... 478 H
moneyr@acu.edu
MONEYHAM, Valerie, Z ... 850-474-2041 ... 121 C
vmoneyha@uwf.edu
MONFETTE, Francine ... 401-341-2231 ... 454 D
monfettf@salve.edu
MONFORTON, Jeffrey, M .. 313-883-8501 ... 257 G
monforton.jeffrey@shms.edu
MONGE, Eduardo ... 714-997-6847 ... 39 C
monge@chapman.edu
MONGE, John, A ... 734-462-4400 ... 258 C
jmonge@schoolcraft.edu
MONGELLI, Antoinette ... 310-983-3525 ... 74 A
mongelli@volunteer.ucla.edu
MONGEON, Mike ... 508-373-9458 ... 231 D
MONGER, Leah ... 231-591-3727 ... 251 B
mongerl@ferris.edu
MONGER, Malika, S ... 608-243-4449 ... 554 B
mmonger@matcmadison.edu
MONGILLO, Anne, M ... 516-463-6776 ... 335 H
anne.mongillo@hofstra.edu
MONHEIT, Alan, C ... 732-235-2865 ... 317 A
monheiac@umdnj.edu
MONHEIT, Yidel ... 718-853-2442 ... 361 C
MONHOLLEN, Steve ... 859-280-1218 ... 203 F
smonhollen@lextheo.edu
MONHOLLON, Michael ... 325-670-5870 ... 487 D
mmonholl@hsutx.edu
MONIACI, Steve, C ... 281-649-3096 ... 487 F
smoniaci@hbu.edu
MONIODIS, Paul ... 410-837-5244 ... 229 A
pmoniodis@ubalt.edu
MONIZ, Karyn ... 980-598-1108 ... 365 G
karyn.moniz@jwu.edu
MONIZ, Richard ... 980-598-1603 ... 365 G
richard.moniz@jwu.edu
MONK, David, H ... 814-865-2526 ... 438 F
dhm6@psu.edu
MONK, Suzanne ... 662-476-5014 ... 274 D
smonk@eastms.edu
MONK, Tammy ... 304-384-5325 ... 543 D
careerservices@concord.edu
MONKS, Birgit ... 909-652-6876 ... 39 B
birgit.monks@chaffey.edu
MONKS, Laura ... 931-430-0028 ... 475 C
lmonks@mscc.edu
MONN, Linda, S ... 717-749-6191 ... 440 A
lsm4@psu.edu
MONNAT, Angela, B ... 585-385-8042 ... 348 F
amonnat@sjfc.edu
MONNES, Mark, J ... 419-755-4824 ... 397 B
mmonnes@ncstatecollege.edu
MONNIN, Nancy ... 907-852-3333 ... 10 G
humanresources@ilisagvik.edu
MONNOT, Charles ... 405-208-5295 ... 410 A
cmonnot@okcu.edu
MONOD, Kelly ... 941-752-5491 ... 118 E
monodk@scf.edu
MONREAL, Ismare ... 305-892-7567 ... 111 K
ismare.monreal@jwu.edu
MONREAL, Raul ... 602-243-8040 ... 16 E
raul.monreal@smcmail.maricopa.edu
MONROE, Dennis ... 334-420-4266 ... 7 I
dmonroe@trenholmstate.edu
MONROE, Joseph, W ... 859-257-5770 ... 206 H
joe.monroe@uky.edu
MONROE, JP ... 541-346-2085 ... 419 B
jpmonroe@uoregon.edu
MONROE, Judith ... 407-823-2351 ... 120 A
judith.monroe@ucf.edu
MONROE, Larry, D ... 606-474-3282 ... 200 J
lmonroe@kcu.edu
MONROE, Michele, A ... 310-866-4050 ... 29 C
mmonroe@argosy.edu
MONROE, Murphy ... 312-369-7133 ... 148 B
mmonroe@colum.edu
MONROE, Randall, L ... 570-326-3761 ... 440 K
rmonroe@pct.edu
MONROE, Thomas ... 618-468-5700 ... 156 C
twmonroe@lc.edu
MONROE, W. Sam ... 409-984-6100 ... 500 H
sam.monroe@lamarpa.edu
MONROE, Walter ... 386-481-2497 ... 101 I
monroew@cookman.edu
MONROE, William ... 713-743-9007 ... 503
wmonroe@uh.edu
MONS, Marie ... 404-894-4582 ... 130
marie.mons@finaid.gatech.edu
MONSON, Amy ... 859-442-1149 ... 201
amy.monson@kctcs.edu
MONSON, Terry ... 906-487-7338 ... 251
terry.monson@finlandia.edu
MONTAG, Jerry ... 616-331-3327 ... 252 A
montagj@gvsu.edu
MONTAG, John, J ... 402-465-2401 ... 299
jmontag@nebrwesleyan.edu
MONTAGNINO, Chris ... 513-551-5151 ... 19 C
chris.montagnino@phoenix.edu
MONTAGUE, Evan ... 517-483-1046 ... 254 D
montage@lcc.edu
MONTAGUE, Marlena, O ... 671-735-5641 ... 559 B
marlena.montague@guamcc.edu
MONTAGUE, Orinthia ... 952-487-8283 ... 268 C
orinthia.montague@normandale.edu
MONTALBAN, Silvia ... 646-557-4409 ... 328 A
smontalban@jjay.cuny.edu
MONTALBANO, Ivonne ... 713-221-8060 ... 503 D
montalbanoi@uhd.edu
MONTALVO, Alfredo ... 787-725-8120 ... 562 A
amontalvo0035@eap.edu
MONTALVO, Carmen ... 787-878-5475 ... 562 H
cmontalv@arecibo.inter.edu
MONTALVO, Francisco, N . 787-279-1912 ... 563 B
fmontalvo@bayamon.inter.edu
MONTALVO, Luis ... 617-262-5000 ... 232 B
luis.montalvo@the-bac.edu
MONTALVO, Provi ... 787-878-5475 ... 562 H
pmontalvo@arecibo.inter.edu
MONTANEZ, John ... 212-220-8011 ... 326 E
jmontanez@bmcc.cuny.edu
MONTANEZ, Robert ... 916-691-7204 ... 56 B
montanr@crc.losrios.edu
MONTANEZ-LOPEZ, Nilda 787-740-3001 ... 566 A
nmontanez@uccaribe.edu
MONTANO, Marrybell ... 801-818-8900 ... 510 E
marrybell.montano@provocollege.edu
MONTANO-CORDOVA,
Ruby, S ... 909-593-3511 ... 75 C
rmontano-cordova@laverne.edu
MONTAVON, Victoria, A ... 513-556-1515 ... 403 D
victoria.montavon@uc.edu
MONTAZAR, Ali, J ... 203-932-7167 ... 95 B
amontazar@newhaven.edu
MONTECALVO, Frank ... 814-472-3002 ... 446 B
fmontecalvo@francis.edu
MONTEFUSCO, Anthony ... 401-254-3023 ... 454 C
amontefusco@rwu.edu
MONTEIRO, F. Marconi ... 210-924-4338 ... 481 G
marconi.monteiro@bua.edu
MONTEIRO, Kenneth, P ... 415-338-1693 ... 36 F
monteiro@sfsu.edu
MONTEIRO, Manuel, P ... 617-353-4477 ... 232 G
mmonteir@bu.edu
MONTEITH, Delos, D ... 828-339-4236 ... 373 H
delos@southwesterncc.edu
MONTEITH, Monte ... 505-346-2340 ... 321 B
mmonteith@sipi.bia.edu
MONTEL, Gary, E ... 260-982-5223 ... 177 F
gemontel@manchester.edu
MONTELEONE, Paul ... 318-473-6477 ... 212 G
pmonteleone@lsua.edu
MONTELONGO, Angie ... 713-525-3572 ... 504 D
montela@stthom.edu
MONTEMAGNO, Carlo, D . 513-556-2933 ... 403 D
carlo.montemagno@uc.edu
MONTEMAYOR, Brenda ... 254-867-3061 ... 500 B
brenda.montemayor@tstc.edu
MONTEMAYOR, Roland ... 415-452-5703 ... 39 H
rmontema@ccsf.edu
MONTERECY, Monty ... 206-934-3628 ... 536 H
orestes.monterecy@seattlecolleges.edu
MONTERO, Janina ... 310-825-1404 ... 74 A
jmontero@saonet.ucla.edu
MONTES, Bruce, A ... 773-508-7601 ... 157 A
bmontes@luc.edu
MONTES, Darlene ... 818-364-7792 ... 55 A
montesd@lamission.edu
MONTES, Porfirio ... 787-863-2390 ... 563 C
porfirio.montes@fajardo.inter.edu
MONTES, Susan, R ... 305-284-6021 ... 122 F
smontes@miami.edu
MONTES-BURGOS,
Carmen ... 787-993-8952 ... 566 G
carmen.montes1@upr.edu
MONTES-MORALES,
Maria ... 718-782-2200 ... 324 C
mmontes@boricuacollege.edu
MONTESI, Christy ... 662-846-4646 ... 274 B
cmontesi@deltastate.edu
MONTESINO, María del C . 787-720-1022 ... 560 D
recaudaciones@atlanticcollege.edu
MONTEVIRGEN, Alexis, S . 510-748-2288 ... 62 B
amontevirgen@peralta.edu
MONTGOMERY, Carol ... 312-362-5361 ... 148 F
cmontgo1@depaul.edu
MONTGOMERY, Cathy ... 912-427-6265 ... 124 A
cmontgomery@altamahatech.edu
MONTGOMERY, Clyde ... 405-466-3423 ... 408 G
cmontgomery@lunet.edu

MONTGOMERY, Dale ... 479-619-4234 ... 22 H
dmontgom@nwacc.edu
MONTGOMERY, Darrell ... 330-337-6403 ... 383 H
business@awc.edu
MONTGOMERY, Doug, B ... 336-272-7102 ... 364 D
montgomeryd@greensborocollege.edu
MONTGOMERY, E. Dean ... 386-481-2030 ... 101 I
montgomd@cookman.edu
MONTGOMERY, Jacque ... 303-724-1528 ... 88 D
Jacque.Montgomery@UCDenver.edu
MONTGOMERY, Joe ... 509-544-4935 ... 532 C
jmontgomery@columbiabasin.edu
MONTGOMERY, John ... 951-343-4963 ... 31 G
jmontgomery@calbaptist.edu
MONTGOMERY, John ... 575-562-4002 ... 318 A
john.montgomery@enmu.edu
MONTGOMERY, Joseph ... 803-780-1039 ... 463 B
jmontgomery@voorhees.edu
MONTGOMERY, Keith ... 715-261-6223 ... 552 F
keith.montgomery@uwc.edu
MONTGOMERY, Kit, P ... 214-333-5242 ... 484 C
kit@dbu.edu
MONTGOMERY, Laura, M ... 630-752-5227 ... 168 F
Laura.Montgomery@wheaton.edu
MONTGOMERY, Lea, A ... 904-264-2172 ... 116 A
lea.montgomery@iwsfla.org
MONTGOMERY, Lisa ... 312-567-3777 ... 153 B
montgomeryl@iit.edu
MONTGOMERY, Lisa, P ... 843-792-5050 ... 459 C
montgoml@musc.edu
MONTGOMERY, Lyman ... 937-708-5798 ... 405 G
lmontgomery@wilberforce.edu
MONTGOMERY, Martha ... 254-442-5114 ... 482 G
martha.montgomery@cisco.edu
MONTGOMERY, Nancy ... 562-860-2451 ... 38 J
nmontgomery@cerritos.edu
MONTGOMERY, Nancy ... 575-439-3798 ... 319 E
nancy@nmsua.nmsu.edu
MONTGOMERY, Roark ... 903-875-7487 ... 491 B
roark.montgomery@navarrocollege.edu
MONTGOMERY, Robert, J ... 248-232-4806 ... 257 B
rjmontgo@oaklandcc.edu
MONTGOMERY,
Soncerey, L ... 336-750-2314 ... 380 A
montgomerysl@wssu.edu
MONTGOMERY, Susan ... 740-453-0762 ... 400 D
montgomer@ohio.edu
MONTGOMERY, Tammy ... 916-484-8101 ... 56 A
montgot2@arc.losrios.edu
MONTGOMERY,
Toni-Marie ... 847-491-7552 ... 160 D
t-montgomery@northwestern.edu
MONTGOMERY, Tonya ... 502-597-6434 ... 203 D
tonya.montgomery@kysu.edu
MONTGOMERY, Trent ... 256-372-5725 ... 1 A
trent.montgomery@aamu.edu
MONTGOMERY-BORONICO,
Christie ... 203-932-7236 ... 95 B
cmontgomery-boronico@newhaven.edu
MONTI, Joseph ... 407-644-1408 ... 116 B
jmonti@rollins.edu
MONTICINO, Michael ... 940-565-2497 ... 504 B
MONTIEL, Richard ... 805-437-3384 ... 33 I
richard.montiel@csuci.edu
MONTIJO, Minerva ... 716-896-0700 ... 359 F
montijom@villa.edu
MONTINI, Christine ... 330-494-1214 ... 385 I
cmontini@edmc.edu
MONTOGMERY, Nash, D ... 757-823-8462 ... 521 K
ndmontgomery@nsu.edu
MONTONE, Richard ... 413-644-4776 ... 231 A
rmontone@simons-rock.edu
MONTOYA, Alex ... 360-992-2080 ... 532 A
amontoya@clark.edu
MONTOYA, Alfredo ... 505-747-2122 ... 320 A
alfredo@nnmc.edu
MONTOYA, Bernadette ... 575-646-2447 ... 319 D
bermonto@nmsu.edu
MONTOYA, Mitzi, M ... 480-727-1955 ... 12 B
mitzi.montoya@asu.edu
MONTOYA, Natalie, R ... 405-878-5416 ... 412 A
nrmontoya@stgregorys.edu
MONTOYA, Rolando ... 305-237-3635 ... 113 H
rmontoya@mdc.edu
MONTOYA, Sharon ... 928-428-8286 ... 14 C
sharon.montoya@eac.edu
MONTOYA, Valerie ... 505-346-2330 ... 321 B
vmontoya@sipi.bia.edu
MONTPLAISIR, Daniel ... 386-226-4928 ... 105 B
montplad@erau.edu
MONTRALLO, Pamela ... 435-652-7522 ... 512 A
montrall@dixie.edu
MONTREAL, Steven ... 262-243-5700 ... 546 I
steve.montreal@cuw.edu
MONTS, Lester, P ... 734-764-3982 ... 259 D
lmonts@umich.edu
MOO-YOUNG, Keith ... 302-343-4500 ... 35 B
kmooyou@exchange.calstate.edu
MOODY, B ... 207-941-7000 ... 218 A
moodyb@husson.edu
MOODY, Bill ... 678-717-3630 ... 129 D
bmoody@gsc.edu
MOODY, Brad ... 501-760-4213 ... 22 F
bmoody@npcc.edu
MOODY, Charles ... 602-850-8000 ... 17 H
cmoody@phoenixseminary.edu
MOODY, Christopher, M ... 302-855-5927 ... 96 B
cmoody@dtcc.edu
MOODY, D. L ... 817-461-8741 ... 480 H
dlmoody@abconline.org
MOODY, Donna ... 618-235-2700 ... 165 B
donna.moody@swic.edu
MOODY, Jan ... 601-928-6207 ... 275 G
janet.moody@mgccc.edu
MOODY, Jeff, T ... 219-942-1459 ... 170 F
jmoody@ccredu.com
MOODY, Linda ... 213-477-2560 ... 57 H
lmoody@msmc.la.edu
MOODY, Marilyn ... 208-426-1234 ... 142 F
marilynmoody@boisestate.edu
MOODY, Marla ... 417-447-4842 ... 287 G
moodym@otc.edu
MOODY, Michelle, L ... 757-594-8819 ... 517 I
mlmoody@cnu.edu
MOODY, Monica ... 478-757-5224 ... 139 A
mmoody@wesleyancollege.edu
MOODY, Nancy, B ... 423-636-7301 ... 476 F
nmoody@tusculum.edu
MOODY-SHEPHERD,
Eleanor ... 212-870-1222 ... 344 A
emoody.shepherd@nyts.edu
MOOLENAR-WIRSY,
Pamela ... 678-891-2433 ... 130 G
Pamela.Moolenar-Wirsy@gpc.edu
MOON, Agnes ... 410-225-2347 ... 224 C
amoon@mica.edu
MOON, Beverly ... 662-846-4834 ... 274 B
bmoon@deltastate.edu
MOON, David ... 719-255-3566 ... 88 C
cmoon@uccs.edu
MOON, Deborah, J ... 412-268-6011 ... 424 H
deborahm@andrew.cmu.edu
MOON, Deok Joo ... 678-735-5471 ... 129 E
admin@gcuniv.edu
MOON, Don ... 434-592-3237 ... 520 F
donmoon@liberty.edu
MOON, Freddie, P ... 256-766-6610 ... 4 C
pmoon@hcu.edu
MOON, Gary, W ... 404-233-3949 ... 135 G
gmoon@richmont.edu
MOON, Greg ... 503-517-1880 ... 421 B
gmoon@westernseminary.edu
MOON, Greta ... 760-245-4271 ... 77 E
Greta.Moon@vvc.edu
MOON, Hyon ... 949-480-4139 ... 69 I
hmoon@soka.edu
MOON, Lee, L ... 904-620-2833 ... 120 C
l.moon@unf.edu
MOON, Mary ... 212-757-1190 ... 323 B
mmoon@funeraleducation.org
MOON, Michael, J ... 503-370-6017 ... 421 C
mmoon@willamette.edu
MOON, Pamela ... 270-926-4040 ... 199 K
pmoon@daymarcollege.edu
MOON, Richard ... 321-433-7202 ... 101 J
moonr@brevardcc.edu
MOON, Susan ... 573-288-6441 ... 281 D
smoon@culver.edu
MOONEY, Carol Ann ... 574-284-4602 ... 179 D
mooney@saintmarys.edu
MOONEY, Catherine ... 209-954-5642 ... 66 D
cmooney@deltacollege.edu
MOONEY, Debra ... 513-745-3204 ... 406 E
mooney@xavier.edu
MOONEY, Dee ... 575-492-2115 ... 321 H
dmooney@usw.edu
MOONEY, Hank ... 918-465-1804 ... 408 A
hmooney@eosc.edu
MOONEY, Kim ... 603-899-4284 ... 305 B
mooneyk@franklinpierce.edu
MOONEY, Mary, K ... 806-371-5311 ... 479 H
mkmooney@actx.edu
MOONEY, Sandra, N ... 281-649-3256 ... 487 F
smooney@hbu.edu
MOONEYHAN, Allen ... 870-512-7864 ... 20 F
allen_mooneyhan@asun.edu
MOONO, Steady ... 215-641-6547 ... 436 G
smoono@mc3.edu
MOORADIAN, Ronald, G ... 562-903-4757 ... 30 H
ron.mooradian@biola.edu
MOORE, Albert ... 408-741-2146 ... 77 K
albert_moore@wvm.edu
MOORE, Alicia ... 541-383-7262 ... 414 I
amoore@cocc.edu
MOORE, Allison, O ... 816-654-7204 ... 283 J
aomoore@kcumb.edu
MOORE, Allyson, L ... 203-432-0800 ... 95 D
allyson.moore@yale.edu
MOORE, Alvin, L ... 512-505-3151 ... 488 B
almoore@htu.edu
MOORE, Amanda ... 501-450-1303 ... 22 A
moore@hendrix.edu
MOORE, Anita, W ... 662-252-8000 ... 277 C
amoore@rustcollege.edu
MOORE, Ann ... 601-403-1250 ... 277 A
amoore@prcc.edu
MOORE, Anne ... 413-236-1641 ... 239 E
amoore@berkshirecc.edu
MOORE, Anne, C ... 605-677-5371 ... 465 E
anne.moore@usd.edu
MOORE, Anthony ... 270-384-8108 ... 203 H
moorea@lindsey.edu
MOORE, Arthur, L ... 859-238-5575 ... 199 D
art.moore@centre.edu
MOORE, Barbara ... 662-329-7288 ... 276 B
bmoore@edhs.muw.edu
MOORE, Barbara ... 585-340-9593 ... 329 G
bmoore@crcds.edu
MOORE, Barbara ... 914-251-6018 ... 354 D
barbara.moore@purchase.edu
MOORE, Barbara, C ... 803-705-4604 ... 455 D
mooreb@benedict.edu
MOORE, Barbe ... 724-357-4077 ... 442 E
bmoore@iup.edu
MOORE, Barry, L ... 561-993-1134 ... 114 D
mooreb@palmbeachstate.edu
MOORE, Becky ... 706-865-2134 ... 138 A
bmoore@truett.edu
MOORE, III, Berrien ... 405-325-3095 ... 413 C
berrien@ou.edu
MOORE, Bert, S ... 972-883-2355 ... 505 D
bmoore@utdallas.edu
MOORE, Beverly ... 845-434-5750 ... 356 H
bmoore@sullivan.suny.edu
MOORE, Billy ... 662-846-4200 ... 274 B
bmoore@deltastate.edu
MOORE, Brad ... 505-224-4423 ... 317 J
bmoore28@cnm.edu
MOORE, Brett, C ... 607-735-1724 ... 333 A
bmoore@elmira.edu
MOORE, Brian ... 845-561-0800 ... 342 A
MOORE, Bridget ... 325-670-1482 ... 487 D
bmoore@jsutx.edu
MOORE, Carl, C ... 251-460-6419 ... 9 E
ccmoore@usouthal.edu
MOORE, Charles ... 657-278-4343 ... 34 E
cmoore@fullerton.edu
MOORE, Christina ... 229-245-2460 ... 139 E
christina.moore@wiregrass.edu
MOORE, Christine ... 619-961-4323 ... 72 F
cmoore@tjsl.edu
MOORE, Claire, E ... 443-352-4306 ... 226 E
cmoore@stevenson.edu
MOORE, Cynthia ... 310-434-4305 ... 68 D
moore_cynthia@smc.edu
MOORE, Dan ... 580-745-2006 ... 412 C
dmoore@se.edu
MOORE, Daniel ... 603-535-2525 ... 307 B
dmoore@plymouth.edu
MOORE, Daniel, J ... 812-877-8110 ... 179 A
daniel.j.moore@rose-hulman.edu
MOORE, Danny, B ... 252-398-6448 ... 363 E
moored@chowan.edu
MOORE, Daryl, J ... 209-667-3959 ... 36 C
dmoore@csustan.edu
MOORE, David ... 563-589-3351 ... 189 B
dmoore@dbq.edu
MOORE, Davis ... 314-644-9196 ... 289 C
dfmoore@stlcc.edu
MOORE, Debbie ... 706-886-6831 ... 137 G
dmoore@tfc.edu
MOORE, Deborah, D ... 785-670-1538 ... 197 D
deborah.moore@washburn.edu
MOORE, Debra, J ... 601-362-9991 ... 273 E
debra.moore@antonellicollege.edu
MOORE, Denise ... 913-469-8500 ... 193 I
dmoore56@jccc.edu
MOORE, Denise ... 404-215-3486 ... 134 A
dmoore@morehouse.edu
MOORE, Dennis, T ... 585-785-1294 ... 334 A
mooredt@flcc.edu
MOORE, Dirk, S ... 276-944-6810 ... 518 I
dsmoore@ehc.edu
MOORE, Donald ... 609-652-4633 ... 313 F
donald.moore@stockton.edu
MOORE, Edward ... 504-456-3141 ... 208 A
MOORE, Edwin ... 707-965-7103 ... 60 J
emoore@puc.edu
MOORE, Elinore ... 773-838-7528 ... 147 E
emoore20@ccc.edu
MOORE, Elma, L ... 937-327-7012 ... 406 B
emoore@wittenberg.edu
MOORE, Erin, K ... 985-549-5861 ... 216 C
erin.moore@selu.edu
MOORE, Ernest ... 404-880-6423 ... 126 I
emoore@cau.edu
MOORE, Evelyn, J ... 319-399-8526 ... 183 C
emoore@coe.edu
MOORE, Francis, X ... 434-395-2034 ... 520 G
moorefx@longwood.edu
MOORE, Frederick, V ... 712-749-2103 ... 182 G
mooref@bvu.edu
MOORE, Garret ... 740-587-6482 ... 389 H
moore@denison.edu
MOORE, Gary ... 802-828-8556 ... 514 G
MOORE, George, E ... 215-204-6542 ... 447 G
george.moore@temple.edu
MOORE, Gillian ... 312-369-7963 ... 148 B
gmoore@colum.edu
MOORE, Ginger ... 903-233-4382 ... 489 K
gingermoore@letu.edu
MOORE, Ginnie ... 740-351-3281 ... 401 I
gmoore@shawnee.edu
MOORE, Glen ... 601-928-6297 ... 275 G
glen.moore@mgccc.edu
MOORE, Gordon ... 404-894-3959 ... 130 D
gordon.moore@omed.gatech.edu
MOORE, Gregory, R ... 859-323-5823 ... 206 H
grmoor2@uky.edu
MOORE, Gwendolyn ... 912-443-5711 ... 136 D
gmoore@savannahtech.edu
MOORE, Gwendolyn ... 334-874-5700 ... 3 A
gmoore@concordiaselma.edu
MOORE, Hallie ... 216-791-5000 ... 388 B
hallie.moore@case.edu
MOORE, Harry ... 215-751-8800 ... 426 B
hmoore@ccp.edu
MOORE, Holly ... 206-934-6867 ... 537 B
holly.moore@seattlecolleges.edu
MOORE, Honour ... 215-827-0567 ... 430 H
hmoore@holyfamily.edu
MOORE, Hsiao-Ping, H ... 248-204-3500 ... 254 E
hmoore@ltu.edu
MOORE, Jacques ... 207-859-4732 ... 217 G
jrmoore@colby.edu
MOORE, James ... 520-494-5345 ... 13 F
james.moore7@centralaz.edu
MOORE, James, E ... 215-951-1017 ... 432 G
mooreje@lasalle.edu
MOORE, James, R ... 847-317-8036 ... 166 B
jmoore@tiu.edu
MOORE, Jamillah, K ... 323-953-4000 ... 54 H
moorejk@lacitycollege.edu
MOORE, Jana ... 928-317-6052 ... 12 C
jana.moore@azwestern.edu
MOORE, Janice ... 717-728-2219 ... 425 A
janicemoore@centralpenn.edu
MOORE, Jason ... 205-391-5809 ... 7 A
jmoore@sheltonstate.edu
MOORE, Jeanie ... 704-216-3500 ... 373 C
jeanie.moore@rccc.edu
MOORE, Jeff ... 703-365-9286 ... 515 H
MOORE, Jennie ... 617-670-4427 ... 235 B
jmoore@fisher.edu
MOORE, Jennifer ... 626-815-6000 ... 30 E
jmoore@apu.edu
MOORE, Joe ... 812-265-2580 ... 176 G
ljmoore@ivytech.edu
MOORE, John, F ... 540-231-8991 ... 529 B
jmoore1@vt.edu
MOORE, III, John, V ... 215-204-5005 ... 447 G
john.mooreiii@temple.edu
MOORE, Johnnie ... 434-582-2250 ... 520 F
jrmoore@liberty.edu
MOORE, Johnny ... 870-762-3180 ... 20 A
jmoore@smail.anc.edu
MOORE, Johnny, M ... 903-510-2261 ... 502 E
jmoo@tjc.edu
MOORE, Joseph ... 630-942-2371 ... 147 G
moorej7718@cod.edu
MOORE, Joseph, B ... 617-349-8500 ... 230 D
jbmoore@lesley.edu
MOORE, Joseph, B ... 617-349-8500 ... 236 G
jbmoore@lesley.edu
MOORE, Joy, A ... 740-389-4636 ... 395 G
moorej@mtc.edu
MOORE, Juanna, S ... 214-828-8907 ... 497 A
jmoore@bcd.tamhsc.edu
MOORE, Judy ... 815-599-3457 ... 152 A
judy.moore@highland.edu
MOORE, Judy, S ... 574-535-7522 ... 171 D
judysm@goshen.edu
MOORE, Karen ... 816-604-5229 ... 285 F
karen.moore@mcckc.edu
MOORE, Kathy, J ... 740-826-8114 ... 396 I
moore@muskingum.edu
MOORE, Keirsten ... 614-236-6679 ... 386 C
kmoore@capital.edu
MOORE, Keith, E ... 757-455-3354 ... 529 F
kmoore@vwc.edu
MOORE, Kelly, T ... 630-743-0682 ... 168 C
kmoore@westwood.edu
MOORE, Kenneth ... 937-512-3107 ... 401 J
kenneth.moore@sinclair.edu
MOORE, Kimberly ... 434-295-0136 ... 521 E
kmoore@ncbt.edu
MOORE, Kristen ... 913-451-1431 ... 195 F
kristen.moore@ottawa.edu
MOORE, Kristen ... 913-451-1431 ... 195 G
MOORE, Lara ... 541-962-3368 ... 418 C
lmoore@eou.edu
MOORE, Laura ... 567-661-7410 ... 400 H
laura_moore@owens.edu
MOORE, Lesa ... 251-442-2207 ... 9 B
lesam@mail.umobile.edu
MOORE, Leslie ... 253-833-9111 ... 534 C
lmoore@greenriver.edu
MOORE, Lew ... 501-279-4347 ... 21 H
lmoore@harding.edu
MOORE, Lew Rita ... 513-861-6400 ... 402 I
lewrita.moore@munion.edu
MOORE, Linda ... 617-824-8570 ... 234 D
linda_moore@emerson.edu
MOORE, Linda ... 309-671-2734 ... 158 B

MOORE, Linda ... 641-844-5690 ... 185 J
linda.moore@iavalley.edu

MOORE, Linda, H ... 217-351-2551 ... 161 B
lmoore@parkland.edu

MOORE, Lisa ... 925-631-4328 ... 64 F
lmoore@stmarys-ca.edu

MOORE, Lisia ... 916-649-8168 ... 52 F
lmoore@kaplan.edu

MOORE, Lorna, G ... 336-758-5301 ... 380 B
moore@wfu.edu

MOORE, Lynn ... 541-440-4600 ... 420 F
lynn.moore@umpqua.edu

MOORE, Lynn ... 603-752-1113 ... 304 I
lmoore@ccsnh.edu

MOORE, Mal, M ... 205-348-3600 ... 8 F
mmoore@ia.ua.edu

MOORE, Marcia, K ... 843-953-8200 ... 457 B
moorem@cofc.edu

MOORE, Margie ... 405-262-2552 ... 411 G
moorem@redlandscc.edu

MOORE, Marilyn, A ... 814-871-7614 ... 429 F
moore037@gannon.edu

MOORE, Mark ... 402-363-5600 ... 301 F
dmark.moore@gmail.com

MOORE, Mark ... 405-974-2754 ... 413 B
mmoore@ucok.edu

MOORE, Mark ... 740-351-3207 ... 401 I
mmoore@shawnee.edu

MOORE, Marlene ... 503-370-6285 ... 421 C
moorem@willamette.edu

MOORE, Martha ... 734-372-4900 ... 259 B
moorem@cooley.edu

MOORE, Mary ... 410-287-1053 ... 222 A
mmoore@cecil.edu

MOORE, Mary, C ... 317-788-6150 ... 180 C
moore@uindy.edu

MOORE, Mary, E ... 617-353-3050 ... 232 G
mmoore@bu.edu

MOORE, Mary Pat ... 319-296-4255 ... 185 C
mary.moore@hawkeyecollege.edu

MOORE, Mary Rita ... 708-456-0300 ... 166 C
mpatrice@triton.edu

MOORE, Matt ... 605-995-2187 ... 464 B
mamoore@dwu.edu

MOORE, Maureen ... 352-588-8121 ... 116 E
maureen.moore@saintleo.edu

MOORE, Mazie ... 314-889-1421 ... 282 C
mmoore@fontbonne.edu

MOORE, Melody, L ... 804-706-5122 ... 526 G
mmoore@jtcc.edu

MOORE, Michael ... 989-729-3437 ... 249 A
michael.moore@baker.edu

MOORE, Michael ... 701-777-6772 ... 381 D
michael.moore@research.und.edu

MOORE, Michael, A ... 231-843-5900 ... 260 E
mamoore@westshore.edu

MOORE, Michael, P ... 509-865-8585 ... 534 D
moore_m@heritage.edu

MOORE, Michael, R ... 317-274-0622 ... 174 B
mmoore1@iupui.edu

MOORE, Mickey ... 423-614-8430 ... 470 A
mmoore@leeuniversity.edu

MOORE, Mike ... 949-480-4155 ... 69 I
mmoore@soka.edu

MOORE, Mike, K ... 701-788-4706 ... 381 F
Mike.Moore@mayvillestate.edu

MOORE, Mitchell, L ... 540-665-1298 ... 523 K
mmoore7@su.edu

MOORE, Monika ... 909-607-9226 ... 40 C
monika.moore@cgu.edu

MOORE, Nancy ... 908-526-1200 ... 313 E
nmoore@raritanval.edu

MOORE, Nicole ... 314-889-1496 ... 282 C
nmoore@fontbonne.edu

MOORE, Paige ... 803-758-2700 ... 455 B
pmoore@allenuniversity.edu

MOORE, Pamela ... 541-684-4644 ... 419 F
pmoore@pioneerpacific.edu

MOORE, Patrice ... 504-671-6535 ... 210 G
pmoore@dcc.edu

MOORE, Paul ... 229-732-5910 ... 124 C
paulmoore@andrewcollege.edu

MOORE, Paul, A ... 419-372-8556 ... 385 C
pmoore@bgsu.edu

MOORE, Penny ... 918-456-5511 ... 409 A
moorepl@nsuok.edu

MOORE, Philip, S ... 803-777-2814 ... 462 A
philmoore@sc.edu

MOORE, R. Bartley ... 202-687-0454 ... 98 A
rbm9@georgetown.edu

MOORE, Ray ... 334-876-9248 ... 4 B
rmoore@wccs.edu

MOORE, Renee ... 210-805-5864 ... 503 F
reneem@uiwtx.edu

MOORE, Renee, R ... 865-639-6604 ... 475 F
rmoore@pstcc.edu

MOORE, Robert, G ... 719-389-6693 ... 81 L
robert.moore@coloradocollege.edu

MOORE, Robert, M ... 207-859-1104 ... 219 G
iavp@thomas.edu

MOORE, Robin ... 402-761-8270 ... 300 C
rmoore@southeast.edu

MOORE, Robin ... 757-822-1724 ... 528 C
rmoore@tcc.edu

MOORE, Rochelle, I ... 240-567-5036 ... 224 E
rochelle.hopkins@montgomerycollege.edu

MOORE, Roderick, B ... 276-964-7286 ... 528 A
rod.moore@sw.edu

MOORE, Roy ... 615-898-2813 ... 473 F
roy.moore@mtsu.edu

MOORE, Rudi ... 317-543-3617 ... 177 H
rmoore@martin.edu

MOORE, Russell ... 303-492-2890 ... 88 B
rmoore@colorado.edu

MOORE, Russell, D ... 502-897-4897 ... 205 H
rmoore@sbts.edu

MOORE, Russell, D ... 502-897-4112 ... 205 H
rmoore@sbts.edu

MOORE, Sandra ... 859-622-6587 ... 200 D
sandra.moore@eku.edu

MOORE, Sarah ... 253-879-3207 ... 538 E
smoore@pugetsound.edu

MOORE, Scott ... 713-718-2870 ... 487 G
scott.moore@hccs.edu

MOORE, Sean ... 603-862-3827 ... 306 E
sean.moore@unh.edu

MOORE, Sharamie, T ... 337-475-5493 ... 215 G
strahan@mcneese.edu

MOORE, Sharon ... 860-412-7273 ... 91 A
smoore@qvcc.commnet.edu

MOORE, Sharyn ... 650-543-3798 ... 57 B
smoore@menlo.edu

MOORE, Shirley ... 937-778-7861 ... 390 G
smoore@edisonohio.edu

MOORE, Stephan ... 770-394-8300 ... 124 F
smoore@aii.edu

MOORE, Stephanie ... 773-947-6281 ... 157 E
smoore@mccormick.edu

MOORE, Steven, C ... 239-590-1919 ... 119 A
cmoore@fgcu.edu

MOORE, Stuart ... 251-380-2240 ... 7 F
smoore@shc.edu

MOORE, Sue ... 417-447-8856 ... 287 G
moores@otc.edu

MOORE, Susan ... 845-431-8686 ... 332 E
moore@sunydutchess.edu

MOORE, Sylvia ... 406-444-0314 ... 294 J
smoore@montana.edu

MOORE, Tamara ... 719-255-4322 ... 88 C
tamara.moore@uccs.edu

MOORE, Teresa ... 806-291-3752 ... 508 B
teresam@wbu.edu

MOORE, Teri, D ... 540-674-3600 ... 527 B
tmoore@nr.edu

MOORE, Terry, R ... 740-588-1383 ... 407 A
tmoore@zanestate.edu

MOORE, Theresa ... 608-796-3172 ... 553 A
trmoore@viterbo.edu

MOORE, Thomas ... 870-972-3030 ... 20 C
tmoore@astate.edu

MOORE, Thomas, J ... 989-774-3500 ... 249 G
thomas.j.moore@cmich.edu

MOORE, Tim ... 706-379-5166 ... 139 F
tsmoore@yhc.edu

MOORE, Timothy ... 847-214-7651 ... 150 D
tmoore@elgin.edu

MOORE, Timothy ... 518-255-5323 ... 354 E
mooretw@cobleskill.edu

MOORE, Tina ... 217-234-5346 ... 155 H
tmoore@lakeland.cc.il.us

MOORE, Todd, B ... 620-792-9241 ... 190 E
mooret@bartonccc.edu

MOORE, Todd, H ... 316-284-5230 ... 190 H
tmoore@bethelks.edu

MOORE, JR., Tom, A ... 205-329-7871 ... 3 B
tom.moore@ecacolleges.com

MOORE, Tonja ... 305-348-2168 ... 119 B
tonja.moore@fiu.edu

MOORE, Tony ... 225-771-3201 ... 214 G
tony_moore@sus.edu

MOORE, Torin, Y ... 413-542-2161 ... 230 A
tmoore@amherst.edu

MOORE, Tyler, J ... 972-860-7696 ... 484 H
TMoore@dcccd.edu

MOORE, Wayne ... 956-882-6567 ... 505 C
wayne.moore@utb.edu

MOORE, William ... 201-692-7200 ... 310 B
wmoore@fdu.edu

MOORE, William, T ... 912-478-5258 ... 131 A
tmoore@georgiasouthern.edu

MOORE, Winifred, B ... 843-953-7477 ... 456 C
bo.moore@citadel.edu

MOORE, Yvonne ... 323-660-6166 ... 40 G
yvonne.moore@cleveland.edu

MOORE-ASSEM,
Carolyn, D ... 919-530-5294 ... 378 A
cassem@nccu.edu

MOORE-JONES,
Yolanda, V ... 919-536-7201 ... 369 G
jonesym@durhamtech.edu

MOORE-LINN, Cathleen ... 671-735-2944 ... 559 D
cmoore@uguam.uog.edu

MOORE-PIZON, Thomas ... 813-621-0041 ... 105 G
tmoore@cci.edu

MOORE-RAMSEY, Donna ... 216-987-5339 ... 389 A
donna.moore-ramsey@tri-c.edu

MOOREHEAD, Shaylon ... 225-928-3005 ... 208 C

MOORER, Glynda, M ... 517-355-2488 ... 255 D
moorerg@msu.edu

MOORES, Lisa ... 301-295-3764 ... 558 A
lmoores@usuhs.mil

MOORHEAD, Tracey, A ... 219-299-3654 ... 263 B
moorhead@cord.edu

MOORHOUSE, Dian ... 954-262-5393 ... 114 B
dian@nsu.nova.edu

MOORING, Linda ... 252-246-1343 ... 375 B
lmooring@wilsoncc.edu

MOORMAN, Annorrah ... 309-556-3052 ... 153 E
amoorman@iwu.edu

MOORMAN, Cathy ... 765-998-5123 ... 179 F
ctmoorman@taylor.edu

MOORMAN, Jeanne, M ... 419-995-8481 ... 399 B
moorman.35@osu.edu

MOORMAN, Jo Ann ... 386-267-0565 ... 103 I
director@daytonacollege.edu

MOORMAN, Thomas, D ... 817-735-2505 ... 504 C
tmoorman@hsc.unt.edu

MOORS, Dean ... 402-462-4000 ... 297 C
dmoors@cccneb.edu

MOORWOOD, Woody ... 626-815-3855 ... 30 E
wmoorwood@apu.edu

MOOS, Floyd ... 661-362-3386 ... 41 G
floyd.moos@canyons.edu

MOOS, Holly ... 509-793-2010 ... 531 D
hollym@bigbend.edu

MOOS, Michael ... 317-917-3623 ... 177 H
mmoos@martin.edu

MOOS, William, H ... 509-335-0200 ... 539 A
bill.moos@wsu.edu

MOOSBRUGGER,
Daniel, P ... 706-865-2134 ... 138 A
dmoosbrugger@truett.edu

MOOSE, Richard, E ... 315-267-2377 ... 354 C
moosere@potsdam.edu

MOOSMANN, Gloria ... 216-987-4788 ... 389 A
gloria.moosmann@tri-c.edu

MOOT, Bradley ... 212-678-8035 ... 337 G
brmoot@jtsa.edu

MORA, Aracely ... 714-628-4880 ... 63 G
mora_aracely@sccollege.edu

MORA, Isabelle ... 206-876-6100 ... 537 E
imora@theseattleschool.edu

MORA, Michelle ... 818-240-1000 ... 48 C
mmora@glendale.edu

MORA, Peter, L ... 609-343-4901 ... 307 D
mora@atlantic.edu

MORAGA, Gloria ... 916-278-6156 ... 35 E
gmoraga@csus.edu

MORAH, Emeka, O ... 937-708-5705 ... 405 G
emorah@wilberforce.edu

MORAIN, Claudia ... 530-752-9841 ... 73 F
cmmorain@ucdavis.edu

MORAIN, Tom ... 641-784-5053 ... 184 H
tmorain@gracelend.edu

MORALE, Joseph, L ... 903-927-3232 ... 509 A
jmorale@wileyc.edu

MORALE, Sonja ... 903-566-7059 ... 506 C
smorale@uttyler.edu

MORALES, Ada ... 787-882-2065 ... 565 I
colocaiones@unitecpr.net

MORALES, Adelina, C ... 325-942-2073 ... 480 E
adelina.morales@angelo.edu

MORALES, Angel ... 787-852-1430 ... 562 D

MORALES, Aurea ... 718-963-4112 ... 324 C
amorales@boricuacollege.edu

MORALES, Cheryl ... 909-607-2650 ... 62 H
cheryl_morales@pitzer.edu

MORALES, David ... 713-221-8513 ... 503 D
MoralesD@uhd.edu

MORALES, Edwin ... 787-786-3030 ... 560 E
emorales@ucb.edu.pr

MORALES, George ... 806-743-2952 ... 501 F
george.morales@ttuhsc.edu

MORALES, Ileana ... 787-878-5475 ... 562 H
imorales@arecibo.inter.edu

MORALES, Irma ... 787-863-2390 ... 563 C
irma.morales@fajardo.inter.edu

MORALES, James ... 435-797-1712 ... 511 B
james.morales@usu.edu

MORALES, Jossue ... 787-891-0925 ... 562 G
jomorales@aguadilla.inter.edu

MORALES, Karen, G ... 787-841-2000 ... 564 I

MORALES, Lidia ... 305-821-3333 ... 109 A
lmorales@mm.fnc.edu

MORALES, Lidia ... 305-821-3333 ... 109 B
lmorales@mm.fnc.edu

MORALES, Lidia ... 305-821-3333 ... 109 C
lmorales@mm.fnc.edu

MORALES, Milagros ... 787-850-9312 ... 567 B
milagros.morales@upr.edu

MORALES, Milga ... 718-951-5352 ... 326 G
milga@brooklyn.cuny.edu

MORALES, Nora ... 361-354-2239 ... 482 I
moralesn@coastlbend.edu

MORALES, Ramona ... 305-593-1223 ... 102 D
rmorales@albizu.edu

MORALES, Robert ... 805-965-0581 ... 68 B
moralesr@sbcc.edu

MORALES, Rosalia ... 787-864-2222 ... 563 D
rmorales@inter.edu

MORALES, Sandra ... 787-857-3600 ... 563 A
smorales@br.inter.edu

MORALES, Tomás, D ... 718-982-2400 ... 327
president@csi.cuny.edu

MORALES-MARTINEZ,
Maria ... 787-264-1912 ... 563
marimo@sg.inter.edu

MORAMARCO, Jacques ... 310-453-8300 ... 45
jacques@emperors.edu

MORAN, Alan ... 216-987-3484 ... 389
alan.moran@tri-c.edu

MORAN, Carmella ... 630-844-5132 ... 145
cmoran@aurora.edu

MORAN, Christyn ... 610-527-0200 ... 445
christyn@rosemont.edu

MORAN, Elizabeth ... 715-422-5326 ... 554 C
elizabeth.moran@mstc.edu

MORAN, Francis, J ... 540-234-9261 ... 525 G
moranf@brcc.edu

MORAN, James ... 303-871-2591 ... 88 E
jmoran@du.edu

MORAN, James, J ... 615-353-3249 ... 475 D
josh.moran@nscc.edu

MORAN, James, M ... 203-576-4735 ... 94 D
jmoran@bridgeport.edu

MORAN, Jim ... 814-732-2711 ... 442 D

MORAN, Kathryn, A ... 317-788-3367 ... 180 C
kmoran@uindy.edu

MORAN, Ken ... 502-456-6504 ... 206 C
kmoran@sullivan.edu

MORAN, Maggie ... 662-562-3277 ... 276 E
mmoran@northwestms.edu

MORAN, Michael ... 413-565-1000 ... 231 B
mmoran@baypath.edu

MORAN, Patricia ... 610-606-4609 ... 424 I
pmoran@cedarcrest.edu

MORAN, Patrick ... 307-766-4175 ... 556 E
therock@uwyo.edu

MORAN, Paul, J ... 570-208-5948 ... 432 E
pjmoran@kings.edu

MORAN, S. Bradley ... 401-874-6530 ... 454 E
moran@uri.edu

MORAN, Sam, E ... 540-365-4250 ... 518 J
semoran@ferrum.edu

MORAN, Stephanie ... 303-404-5157 ... 84 H
steph.moran@frontrange.edu

MORAN, Terry ... 412-566-2433 ... 434 B
tmoran@paculinary.com

MORAN, Tracy ... 585-389-2030 ... 342 D
tmoran8@naz.edu

MORAN, Virginia ... 760-245-4271 ... 77 E
Virginia.Moran@vvc.edu

MORAN, Wes ... 706-378-2903 ... 125 G
wmoran@berry.edu

MORAN-BROWN, Carol ... 802-865-6426 ... 513 A
moran@champlain.edu

MORANO, Lori ... 518-464-8648 ... 333 F
lmorano@excelsior.edu

MORANSKI, Karen ... 217-206-7413 ... 167 A
moranski.karen@uis.edu

MORANT, Blake ... 336-758-5430 ... 380 B
morantbd@wfu.edu

MORAVEC, Todd ... 518-564-2072 ... 354 B
moraveta@plattsburgh.edu

MORAZ, Kristen, L ... 561-237-7602 ... 113 D
kmoraz@lynn.edu

MORBER, Timothy, T ... 330-471-8279 ... 395 E
tmorber@malone.edu

MORCIGLIO, Jean ... 517-483-1862 ... 254 D
morcigj@lcc.edu

MORDACH, Christine, A ... 978-837-5196 ... 242 D
christine.mordach@merrimack.edu

MORDACH, John ... 312-942-5600 ... 163 B
john_morcach@rush.edu

MORDI, John ... 787-765-1915 ... 564 B
jmordi@inter.edu

MORDICA, Joy ... 731-427-2554 ... 469 M
jmordica@lanecollege.edu

MORDOSKY, Anthony, A ... 856-256-4402 ... 314 A
mordosky@rowan.edu

MOREA, Marilisa ... 312-467-8606 ... 146 C
mmorea@thechicagoschool.edu

MOREAU, Donald ... 603-641-7350 ... 305 H
dmoreau@anselm.edu

MOREAU, Joseph ... 315-312-5500 ... 354 A
jmoreau@oswego.edu

MOREAU, Matt ... 740-389-6786 ... 399 D
moreau.1@osu.edu

MOREAU, Steve ... 904-620-2665 ... 120 C
smoreau@unf.edu

MOREDOCK, Gerald, M ... 615-248-7773 ... 476 E
gmoredock@trevecca.edu

MOREE, Chris ... 318-676-7811 ... 211 H
chris.moree@nwltc.edu

MOREFIELD, Bill, R ... 423-318-2735 ... 476 B
bill.morefield@ws.edu

MOREHEAD, Jere, W ... 706-583-0690 ... 138 C
morehead@uga.edu

MOREHEAD, Kaleybra ... 870-543-5963 ... 23 H
kmorehead@seark.edu

MOREHEAD, Kaleybra, M ... 870-543-5963 ... 23 H
kmorehead@seark.edu

MOREHEAD, Michael, A ... 575-646-5858 ... 319 D
mmorehea@nmsu.edu

MOREHOUSE, JR.,
Percy, A ... 303-556-2939 ... 85 N
morehoup@mscd.edu

MORRIS, Carlton, E 334-727-8565 8 C clae@tuskegee.edu

MORRIS, Charles 860-297-2222 94 C charles.morris@trincoll.edu

MORRIS, Cheryl 405-631-3399 84 I cherylm@heritage-education.com

MORRIS, Cheryl 405-631-3399 408 C

MORRIS, Clark, W 816-781-7700 293 D morrisc@william.jewell.edu

MORRIS, Craig 541-552-6319 419 A cmorris@sou.edu

MORRIS, Dan 702-651-5500 302 G dan.morris@csn.edu

MORRIS, Daryl 334-244-3295 2 A dmorris@aum.edu

MORRIS, David 602-243-8127 16 E david.morris@smcmail.maricopa.edu

MORRIS, Delesa 561-803-2022 114 C delesa_morris@pba.edu

MORRIS, Diana 800-567-2344 546 G dmorris@menominee.edu

MORRIS, Diane 202-639-1816 97 D dmorris@corcoran.org

MORRIS, Don 314-968-7450 293 A morrisdo@webster.edu

MORRIS, Dottie 603-358-2206 307 A dmorris@keene.edu

MORRIS, Doug, D 740-374-8716 405 F ddmorris@wscc.edu

MORRIS, Duncan, D 860-253-3052 89 K dmorris@acc.commnet.edu

MORRIS, Emma, W 404-669-2058 135 E emma.morris@point.edu

MORRIS, Gary 315-312-2255 354 A gary.morris@oswego.edu

MORRIS, Genevieve 251-380-3020 7 F gmorris@shc.edu

MORRIS, Geri 419-227-3141 404 D geri@unoh.edu

MORRIS, Glenn 352-335-2332 100 B

MORRIS, Henry 507-389-6125 267 H henry.morris@mnsu.edu

MORRIS, Jacqueline 205-366-8950 7 G jmorris@stillman.edu

MORRIS, Jake 615-966-2000 470 D jake.morris@lipscomb.edu

MORRIS, Jay 740-699-2489 400 A morrisj@ohiou.edu

MORRIS, Jeffery, B 785-532-6415 194 B jbmorris@ksu.edu

MORRIS, Jennifer, M 650-325-5621 64 G jennifer.morris@stpatricksseminary.org

MORRIS, Jerry, R 606-474-3121 200 J jmorris@kcu.edu

MORRIS, Jim 386-752-1822 108 C jim.morris@fgc.edu

MORRIS, Joe 601-923-1700 277 B jmorris@rts.edu

MORRIS, Joe, E 205-853-1200 5 C jmorris@jeffstateonline.com

MORRIS, John 808-739-8555 140 A jmorris@chaminade.edu

MORRIS, John, F 215-204-1492 447 G john.morris@temple.edu

MORRIS, John, K 801-581-4466 510 L john.morris@legal.utah.edu

MORRIS, John, S 208-885-6478 144 B jmorris@uidaho.edu

MORRIS, Julia, M 304-457-6205 540 B auviljm@ab.edu

MORRIS, Karen 803-641-3489 462 B karenm@usca.edu

MORRIS, Karen 703-709-5875 522 B kmorris@potomac.edu

MORRIS, Katherine, W 937-775-2809 406 C kathy.morris@wright.edu

MORRIS, Kathleen 912-279-5743 127 B kmorris@ccga.edu

MORRIS, Kenneth, W 319-895-4484 183 D kmorris@cornellcollege.edu

MORRIS, Kevin 936-294-1794 501 A upd_khm@shsu.edu

MORRIS, Kizzy 570-422-2820 442 C kmorris@po-box.esu.edu

MORRIS, Kyle 307-755-2160 556 G kmorris@wyotech.edu

MORRIS, LaSonia 318-670-9319 215 A lmorris@susla.edu

MORRIS, Laura 832-813-6793 490 C laura.k.morris@lonestar.edu

MORRIS, Lela 817-598-6488 508 C morris@wc.edu

MORRIS, Linda, M 570-327-4770 440 K lmorris@pct.edu

MORRIS, Lonnie 301-860-3427 228 A lmorris@bowiestate.edu

MORRIS, Loren, L 620-665-3523 193 F morrisl@hutchcc.edu

MORRIS, M. Scott 404-894-2499 130 D scott.morris@ohr.gatech.edu

MORRIS, Marie, S 765-641-4020 169 A msmorris@anderson.edu

MORRIS, Mark 360-438-4394 536 F mmorris@stmartin.edu

MORRIS, Matt 417-255-7260 286 G mattmorris@missouristate.edu

MORRIS, Mellasenah 410-234-4655 225 E

MORRIS, Michele, M 561-237-7788 113 D mmorris@lynn.edu

MORRIS, Mitzi 214-637-3530 508 A mmorris@wadecollege.edu

MORRIS, Nancy 615-230-3272 476 A nancy.morris@volstate.edu

MORRIS, Nerissa, E 305-284-4476 122 F nmorris@miami.edu

MORRIS, Nora 763-433-1632 265 J nora.morris@anokaramsey.edu

MORRIS, Pamela 941-752-5201 118 E morrisp@scf.edu

MORRIS, Pearl, A 505-863-7576 321 D pmorris@gallup.unm.edu

MORRIS, Phil 803-822-3559 459 D morrisp@midlandstech.edu

MORRIS, Princilla, E 615-329-8888 468 G psmart@fisk.edu

MORRIS, Rachel 216-373-5320 397 E rmorris@ndc.edu

MORRIS, Reggie 323-241-5200 55 C morrisr@lasc.du

MORRIS, Renea 740-593-2563 399 G morrisr@ohio.edu

MORRIS, Rick 864-977-7777 460 A publicsafety@ngu.edu

MORRIS, Rita, R 740-351-3208 401 I rmorris@shawnee.edu

MORRIS, III, Robert 520-459-1610 508 B morrisb@wbu.edu

MORRIS, Robert, D 404-413-2502 131 C robinmorris@gsu.edu

MORRIS, Robert, J 765-285-1300 169 D rmorris@bsu.edu

MORRIS, Sandra, L 843-792-8720 459 C morriss@musc.edu

MORRIS, Sarah, L 816-235-1023 291 E morrissl@umkc.edu

MORRIS, Sheila, D 423-585-6942 476 B sheila.morris@ws.edu

MORRIS, Steve 270-789-5017 199 C srmorris@campbellsville.edu

MORRIS, Steve 606-539-4209 206 G steve.morris@ucumberlands.edu

MORRIS, Tammy, H 336-599-1181 372 D morrist@piedmontcc.edu

MORRIS, Tina 731-286-3346 475 A morris@dscc.edu

MORRIS, Tina 731-286-3345 475 A morris@dscc.edu

MORRIS, Tina 731-286-3265 475 A morris@dscc.edu

MORRIS, Tom 570-586-2400 422 F tmorris@bbc.edu

MORRIS, Tracy, L 815-224-0393 153 D tracy_morris@ivcc.edu

MORRIS, Trevor 817-531-7587 502 A tmorris@txwes.edu

MORRIS, Trisha, A 814-362-7624 449 B tmorris@pitt.edu

MORRIS, Valerie, B 843-953-8222 457 B morrisv@cofc.edu

MORRIS, Vincent, E 630-752-5013 168 F vincent.morris@wheaton.edu

MORRIS, Wanda 310-900-1600 45 E morris_w@compton.edu

MORRIS, Wayne 618-262-8641 152 I morrisw@iecc.edu

MORRIS, Wendi 478-296-6179 134 G wmorris@oftc.edu

MORRIS, Will 432-685-4641 490 G wmorris@midland.edu

MORRIS, William, F 317-921-4887 175 G bmorris@ivytech.edu

MORRIS, William, G 315-267-2579 354 C morriswg@potsdam.edu

MORRIS, William, R 512-492-3060 480 F wmorris@aoma.edu

MORRIS, Willie 630-753-9091 160 C wmorris@nc.edu

MORRIS-POWELL, Donna 336-334-7593 377 F demorris@ncat.edu

MORRIS-SMITH, Carrie 402-530-1918 19 C carrie.morris@phoenix.edu

MORRISETTE, Joanna 919-735-5151 374 F jmmorrisette@waynecc.edu

MORRISON, Barry, F 401-232-6017 453 A bmorriso@bryant.edu

MORRISON, Bart 304-357-4372 541 H Bartmorrison@ucwv.edu

MORRISON, Bennett 440-834-3726 393 G bmorri11@kent.edu

MORRISON, Brenda, M 443-412-2409 223 B bmorrison@harford.edu

MORRISON, Carol 239-513-1122 110 K cmorrison@hodges.edu

MORRISON, Darrell, R 870-235-4013 23 I drmorrison@saumag.edu

MORRISON, David 770-534-6167 126 B dmorrison@brenau.edu

MORRISON, David, J 717-221-1300 430 E djmorris@hacc.edu

MORRISON, Don 641-628-5280 183 A morrisond@central.edu

MORRISON, Edwina 406-444-6570 294 J emorrison@montana.edu

MORRISON, Gail, A 217-443-8764 148 E morrison@dacc.edu

MORRISON, Gale, M 805-893-4175 74 F gale.morrison@graddiv.ucsb.edu

MORRISON, George, H 304-236-7640 542 J georgem@southern.wvnet.edu

MORRISON, Holly 478-757-2647 133 E holly.morrison@maconstate.edu

MORRISON, James 617-746-1990 236 B James.Morrison@hult.edu

MORRISON, Jason 580-477-7767 414 C jason.morrison@wosc.edu

MORRISON, Jean 617-353-2000 232 G jmorrison@bu.edu

MORRISON, Jenni 419-783-2380 389 G jmorrison@defiance.edu

MORRISON, Jennifer 800-523-1578 121 H jmorrison@teu.edu

MORRISON, Jennifer, K 508-767-7007 230 E jemorrison@assumption.edu

MORRISON, Julie 734-973-5010 260 B jmorriso@wccnet.edu

MORRISON, Kelly, S 434-381-6337 524 E morrison@sbc.edu

MORRISON, Kirk 858-513-9240 181 G kirk.morrison@ashford.edu

MORRISON, Leonard 781-891-2575 231 F lmorrison@bentley.edu

MORRISON, Marty, G 540-654-2287 524 H mmorris3@umw.edu

MORRISON, Maureen, V 203-773-8542 89 H morrison@albertus.edu

MORRISON, Nancy 212-998-4924 344 B nancy.morrison@nyu.edu

MORRISON, Rebecca, L 414-955-4949 548 E rmorriso@mcw.edu

MORRISON, Rob 503-682-3903 419 F rmorrison@pioneerpacific.edu

MORRISON, Rodney 856-225-6510 314 C rodneymo@camden.rutgers.edu

MORRISON, Rodney 419-448-2391 391 G rmorriso@heidelberg.edu

MORRISON, Scott, D 540-828-5376 516 K smorriso@bridgewater.edu

MORRISON, Sharon 580-745-2702 412 C smorrison@se.edu

MORRISON, Thomas 812-855-6992 173 B morrison@indiana.edu

MORRISON, Tim 909-607-1113 40 B tim_morrison@cuc.claremont.edu

MORRISON, Tom 812-855-6992 173 C morrisot@indiana.edu

MORRISON-BEEDY, Dianne 813-974-2191 120 D dmbeedy@health.usf.edu

MORRISON-SHETLAR, Alison 336-278-6490 364 A amorrison4@elon.edu

MORRISS-OLSON, Melissa 413-565-1000 231 B mmolson@baypath.edu

MORRISSETTE, Gina 617-296-8300 236 E gina_morrissette@laboure.edu

MORRISSEY, Aileen 386-506-3475 103 J morrisa@DaytonaState.edu

MORRISSEY, Ann, M 401-874-4846 454 E morrissey@uri.edu

MORRISSEY, Bob 641-683-5259 185 D bmorriss@indianhills.edu

MORRISSEY, Deb 715-682-1269 549 C dmorrissey@northland.edu

MORRISSEY, Jeff, P 417-836-5770 286 F jeffmorrissey@missouristate.edu

MORRISSEY, Marietta 973-655-4314 311 G morrisseym@mail.montclair.edu

MORRISSEY, Morgan 518-445-3207 322 D mmorr@albanylaw.edu

MORRISSEY, Sharron 919-807-7100 367 F morrissey@nccommunitycolleges.edu

MORRO, Robert 610-519-4589 450 G robert.morro@villanova.edu

MORROBEL-SOSA, Anny 915-747-5536 505 E amorrobel@utep.edu

MORROS, Lucy, S 636-949-2000 284 C lmorros@lindenwood.edu

MORROW, Andrew, B 717-221-1300 430 E abmorrow@hacc.edu

MORROW, Barbara 802-586-7111 514 E bmorrow@sterlingcollege.edu

MORROW, Barbara, A 314-340-5763 282 I morrowb@hssu.edu

MORROW, David 215-222-4200 445 F dmorrow@walnuthillcollege.edu

MORROW, David, M 518-762-4651 334 D dmorrow@fmcc.suny.edu

MORROW, Dorothy 402-557-7296 297 A dorothy.morrow@bellevue.edu

MORROW, Jacqueline, R 717-720-4045 442 E

MORROW, Jean 575-769-4915 317 K jean.morrow@clovis.edu

MORROW, Jean 617-585-1250 243 E jean.morrow@necmusic.edu

MORROW, Jeffrey, S 330-665-1084 398 D jeff@ocm.edu

MORROW, Joyce 319-273-2700 182 D joyce.morrow@uni.edu

MORROW, Laurie 318-357-3162 211 G lmorrow@ltc.edu

MORROW, Liz 573-681-5011 284 B morrowl@lincolnu.edu

MORROW, Marjann 325-574-7608 508 F mmorrow@wtc.edu

MORROW, S. Rex 219-785-5550 178 H smorrow@pnc.edu

MORROW, Wanda 713-646-1825 494 E wmorrow@stcl.edu

MORSBERGER, Michael, J 202-994-6419 97 F mjm@gwu.edu

MORSE, Charles, C 508-831-5540 247 B cmorse@wpi.edu

MORSE, Danielle 781-595-6768 236 I dmorse@mariancourt.edu

MORSE, Marc 702-651-3008 302 G marc.morse@csn.edu

MORSE, Mark 212-349-4330 334 G mmorse@globe.edu

MORSE, MaryKate 503-554-6158 415 I mkmorse@georgefox.edu

MORSE, Robert 603-526-3698 304 A rmorse@colby-sawyer.edu

MORSE, William 253-879-2808 538 E wmorse@pugetsound.edu

MORSETTE, Clarice 406-395-4313 296 G camorsette@yahoo.com

MORSMAN, Elaine 607-587-4061 355 C morsmaem@alfredstate.edu

MORSOVILLO, Michael 708-524-6793 150 A morsomike@dom.edu

MORT, Dale 717-569-7071 433 D dmort@lbc.edu

MORTALI, Jill, M 603-646-3007 305 A jill.m.mortali@dartmouth.edu

MORTEN, George 805-437-8516 33 I george.morten@csuci.edu

MORTENSEN, Alan 815-584-2806 155 H alan.mortensen@doc.illinois.gov

MORTENSEN, Brad 801-626-6002 511 D bmortensen@weber.edu

MORTENSEN, Daniel, W 610-917-1409 450 D dwmortensen@vfcc.edu

MORTENSEN, John, D 435-797-0792 511 B john.mortensen@usu.edu

MORTENSEN, Larry 719-587-7402 80 F lsmorten@adams.edu

MORTENSON, Donald, W 206-281-2522 537 D dmort@spu.edu

MORTHLAND, Betsey 309-796-5285 145 E morthlandb@bhc.edu

MORTIMER, Ian 802-651-5911 513 A mortimer@champlain.edu

MORTIMER, Lee, E 513-556-0364 403 D lee.mortimer@uc.edu

MORTIMER, Theresa 617-287-6800 237 D theresa.mortimer@umb.edu

MORTLAND, Stephen 765-998-5206 179 F stmortlan@taylor.edu

MORTON, Allen 203-837-9600 92 A mortona@wcsu.edu

MORTON, Amy, M 508-831-5874 247 B ammorton@wpi.edu

MORTON, Brad 973-290-4477 309 A bmorton@cse.edu

MORTON, Clarresa 540-665-4500 523 K cmorton@su.edu

MORTON, Cornel, N 805-756-1521 33 F cmorton@calpoly.edu

MORTON, Danny 704-484-4032 369 B morton@clevelandcommunitycollege.edu

MORTON, Darren, M 718-990-6707 348 G mortond@stjohns.edu

MORTON, Diane 301-846-2442 222 G dmorton@frederick.edu

MORTON, Evelyn 713-348-4052 492 J evelyn.morton@rice.edu

MORTON, John 808-956-7038 140 J jmorton@hawaii.edu

MORTON, John, F 808-956-7038 141 D jmorton@hawaii.edu

MORTON, Lea-Ann 573-341-4254 292 A mortonl@mst.edu

MORTON, Leo, E 816-235-1101 291 E mortonle@umkc.edu

MORTON, Lisa 414-276-5200 170 F lmorton@ccredu.com

MORTON, Lynn 704-337-2506 375 G mortonl@queens.edu

MORTON, Marcia 417-667-8181 280 I mmorton@cottey.edu

MORTON, Margaret 212-353-4208 331 B mortonnyc@cooper.edu

MORTON, Mary 518-587-2100 355 F mary.morton@esc.edu

MUCH, Kari .... 507-389-1455 .... 267 H
karen.much@mnsu.edu

MUCHAL, Stacey .... 570-961-7868 .... 433 A
muchals@lackawanna.edu

MUCHANE, Mary, W .... 704-894-2644 .... 363 F
mamuchane@davidson.edu

MUCHANE, Mur, K .... 704-894-2402 .... 363 F
mumuchane@davidson.edu

MUCHLINSKI, Alan .... 323-343-3820 ...... 35 B
amuchli@exchange.calstatela.edu

MUCK, Dan .... 605-995-3065 .... 464 E
dan.muck@mitchelltech.edu

MUCK, Terry .... 859-858-2261 .... 198 A

MUDD, Sara .... 864-231-6062 .... 455 C
smudd@andersonuniversity.edu

MUDD, Stephen, B .... 314-505-7313 .... 280 H
mudds@csl.edu

MUDRAK, Jeff .... 859-233-8701 .... 206 E
jmudrak@transy.edu

MUECKE, Mary .... 718-409-7444 .... 356 C
mmuecke@sunymaritime.edu

MUECKE, Nancy .... 641-648-4611 .... 185 I
nancy.muecke@iavalley.edu

MUECKE, Nancy .... 641-648-8502 .... 185 H
Nancy.Muecke@iavalley.edu

MUEHE, Roger .... 615-383-3230 .... 466 H
mueher@dominicancampus.org

MUEHSAM, Mitchell .... 936-294-1254 .... 501 A
mmuehsam@shsu.edu

MUELLENBACH, Joanne .... 570-504-9627 .... 425 F

MUELLER, Al .... 815-753-6104 .... 160 A
amueller@niu.edu

MUELLER, Alan, C .... 336-316-2313 .... 364 E
muelleracc@guilford.edu

MUELLER, Andrew .... 212-966-0300 .... 342 F
andrew@nyaa.edu

MUELLER, Beverley, D .... 757-594-7002 .... 517 I
bmueller@cnu.edu

MUELLER, Brian .... 602-639-7500 ...... 14 I

MUELLER, Bruce .... 312-567-6480 .... 153 B
muellerb@itt.edu

MUELLER, Carla .... 636-949-4731 .... 284 C
cmueller@lindenwood.edu

MUELLER, Cheryl .... 419-227-3141 .... 404 D
camuell@unoh.edu

MUELLER, Chris .... 715-425-3505 .... 552 A
chris.mueller@uwrf.edu

MUELLER, Dennis .... 510-574-1131 ...... 44 D
dmueller@devry.edu

MUELLER, Donna, G .... 585-292-2527 .... 341 H
dmueller@monroecc.edu

MUELLER, Edward .... 561-868-3032 .... 114 D
muellere@palmbeachstate.edu

MUELLER, Harry .... 765-289-2291 .... 175 K
hmueller@ivytech.edu

MUELLER, John, P .... 414-410-4059 .... 546 D
jpmueller@stritch.edu

MUELLER, Joseph .... 307-382-1647 .... 556 F
jmueller@wwcc.wy.edu

MUELLER, Julie .... 636-949-4901 .... 284 C
jmueller@lindenwood.edu

MUELLER, Kathyrn .... 714-432-5646 ...... 41 B
kmueller@occ.cccd.edu

MUELLER, Marifaith .... 217-228-5432 .... 161 E
muellma@quincy.edu

MUELLER, Martin .... 212-229-5896 .... 342 E
muellerm@newschool.edu

MUELLER, Michael .... 817-735-5475 .... 504 C
mmueller@hsc.unt.edu

MUELLER, Michelle, K .... 810-989-5607 .... 258 B
mmueller@sc4.edu

MUELLER, OSU, Pam .... 270-686-4319 .... 198 G
pam.mueller@brescia.edu

MUELLER, Ralph .... 860-768-4648 ...... 95 A
rmueller@hartford.edu

MUELLER, Steven, D .... 937-229-3141 .... 404 A
Steven.Mueller@notes.udayton.edu

MUELLER, Steven, P .... 949-214-3386 ...... 42 K
steve.mueller@cui.edu

MUELLER, Tim .... 701-224-2437 .... 381 C

MUELLER, Vilma .... 973-618-3384 .... 308 D
vmueller@caldwell.edu

MUELLER, William, J .... 423-266-4574 .... 135 G
bmueller@richmont.edu

MUELLER-ROEBKE, Jenny 402-643-7374 .... 297 F
jenny.roebke@cune.edu

MUENSTER, Bettina .... 212-237-8506 .... 328 A
bmuenster@jjay.cuny.edu

MUERTZ, Julie, A .... 618-235-2700 .... 165 B
julie.muertz@swic.edu

MUESELER, Christine .... 724-838-4232 .... 447 B
mueseler@setonhill.edu

MUETHER, John .... 407-366-9493 .... 277 B
jmuether@rts.edu

MUETHER, John, R .... 407-366-9493 .... 115 I
jmuether@rts.edu

MUFFETT, Andrew .... 765-269-5900 .... 176 B
amuffett@ivytech.edu

MUGDH, Mrinal .... 281-283-3020 .... 503 C
mugdh@uhcl.edu

MUGG, Heather .... 404-727-9326 .... 129 A
hmugg@emory.edu

MUGGEP, Louis .... 845-398-4174 .... 349 H
lmuggeo@stac.edu

MUGGLETON, Mary .... 585-271-3657 .... 348 B
mmuggleton@stbernards.edu

MUGLER, Dale, H .... 330-972-5365 .... 403 B
dmugler@uakron.edu

MUGRIDGE, Philip .... 610-341-1721 .... 428 D
pmugridg@eastern.edu

MUGWANYA, Edmond, M . 818-779-8448 ...... 53 B
emugwanya@kingsuniversity.edu

MUHA, Beth .... 202-885-2591 ...... 97 B
beth@american.edu

MUHA, David .... 973-408-3206 .... 309 F
dmuha@drew.edu

MUHA, Priscilla .... 925-631-4522 ...... 64 F
pdm2@stmarys-ca.edu

MUHA, Susan .... 216-987-3110 .... 389 A
susan.muha@tri-c.edu

MUHAMMED, Robert .... 336-750-3299 .... 380 A
muhammedr@wssu.edu

MUHL, V. Jane .... 920-433-6666 .... 546 A
jane.muhl@bellincollege.edu

MUHLFELDER, Leslie, F .... 610-330-5060 .... 433 B
muhlfell@lafayette.edu

MUILENBURG, Gene .... 651-855-6302 .... 464 G
gmuilenburg@national.edu

MUIR, Bernard .... 302-831-4006 ...... 96 F
bmm@udel.edu

MUIR, JR., Harry, P .... 262-521-5435 .... 552 F
harry.muir@uwc.edu

MUIR, Julie .... 916-649-8168 ...... 52 F

MUIR, Karen .... 614-287-2512 .... 388 G
kmuir@cscc.edu

MUIR, Thorton .... 770-426-2624 .... 133 B
tmuir@life.edu

MUIR, Troy .... 330-337-6403 .... 383 H
business@awc.edu

MUKASA, Samuel .... 603-862-1781 .... 306 E
sam.mukasa@unh.edu

MUKERJEA, Rabindra, N ... 765-494-9708 .... 178 F
rnmukerjea@purdue.edu

MUKHARJI, Indrani .... 847-491-3005 .... 160 D
indrani@northwestern.edu

MULADORE, James, G ...... 989-964-4045 .... 258 A
jgm@svsu.edu

MULARCZYK, Linda .... 508-767-7157 .... 230 E
lmularczyk@assumption.edu

MULCAHEY, William .... 319-363-8213 .... 187 E
mulcahey@mtmercy.edu

MULCAHY, OP, Bernard ... 202-495-3821 ...... 98 D
bmulcahy@dhs.edu

MULCAHY, Kevin, F .... 716-878-4698 .... 353 A
mulcahkf@buffalostate.edu

MULCAHY, Mary .... 814-362-0259 .... 449 B
mnp1@pitt.edu

MULCAHY, R. Timothy ...... 612-624-5054 .... 272 D
mulcahy@umn.edu

MULCAHY, Sean .... 913-360-7500 .... 190 F
smulcahy@benedictine.edu

MULDER, Craig, A .... 231-995-1061 .... 256 G
cmulder@nmc.edu

MULDER, Lori .... 616-395-7811 .... 252 F
mulderl@hope.edu

MULDERICK, Thomas, J .... 610-799-1941 .... 434 D
tmulderick@lccc.edu

MULERO, Daritza .... 787-258-1501 .... 561 E
dmulero@columbiaco.edu

MULFORD, David, H .... 540-375-2290 .... 523 D
mulford@roanoke.edu

MULGREW, Frank .... 203-591-5040 ...... 93 D
fmulgrew@post.edu

MULHALL, Lawrence, P ..... 864-833-8301 .... 460 E
lmulhall@presby.edu

MULHERIN, April, C .... 207-778-7081 .... 220 C
april.mulherin@maine.edu

MULHERN, Jean, K .... 937-382-6661 .... 405 H
jean_mulhern@wilmington.edu

MULHOLLAND, William ...... 413-236-2122 .... 239 E
wmulholl@berkshirecc.edu

MULIK, James .... 692-625-3994 .... 559 E
jmulik@cmi.edu

MULKERN, Denise .... 973-972-4339 .... 316 C
mulkernde@umdnj.edu

MULKEY, Amelia .... 850-973-1604 .... 113 J
mulkeya@nfcc.edu

MULKEY, Betty .... 859-572-5763 .... 205 E
mulkey@nku.edu

MULKEY, Stephen .... 207-948-3131 .... 219 H
smulkey@unity.edu

MULKEY, Tom .... 575-492-2144 .... 321 H
tmulkey@usw.edu

MULL, Ray .... 304-327-4062 .... 543 C
rmull@bluefieldstate.edu

MULLALY, Lisa .... 703-396-6608 .... 518 D
lmullaly@devry.edu

MULLANE, Michael .... 207-992-1970 .... 218 A
mullanem@husson.edu

MULLANE, Patrick, D .... 717-245-1740 .... 427 E
mullanep@dickinson.edu

MULLANE, William, S .... 512-223-1024 .... 481 B
wmullane@austincc.edu

MULLANEY, Kathryn, L ...... 315-229-5896 .... 349 E
kmullaney@stlawu.edu

MULLARKEY, Patrick .... 570-208-5928 .... 432 E
patrickmullarkey@kings.edu

MULLEN, Adrienne, A .... 323-265-8613 ...... 54 G
mullenaa@elac.edu

MULLEN, Deborah, F .... 404-687-4520 .... 127 C
mullend@ctsnet.edu

MULLEN, Denise .... 503-297-5544 .... 417 G
dmullen@ocac.edu

MULLEN, Eric .... 616-234-4164 .... 251 G
emullen@grcc.edu

MULLEN, OSB, Godfrey ..... 812-357-6981 .... 179 E
gmullen@saintmeinrad.edu

MULLEN, James, H .... 814-332-5380 .... 421 E
james.mullen@allegheny.edu

MULLEN, Jennifer .... 757-683-3580 .... 521 L
jmullen@odu.edu

MULLEN, Kate .... 518-327-6480 .... 345 H
kmullen@paulsmiths.edu

MULLEN, Kathi .... 603-822-5440 .... 306 H
kathi.mullen@granite.edu

MULLEN, Kelly .... 847-317-7121 .... 166 B
kmullen@tiu.edu

MULLEN, OFM, Kevin ...... 518-783-2302 .... 350 I
kmullen@siena.edu

MULLEN, Kimberly .... 703-562-1691 .... 127 D
mullen_kimberly@columbusstate.edu

MULLEN, Michael .... 610-361-5222 .... 437 C
mullenm@neumann.edu

MULLEN, Micheal, D .... 859-257-3027 .... 206 H
mike.mullen@uky.edu

MULLEN, Patty .... 415-955-2041 ...... 27 A
pmullen@alliant.edu

MULLEN, Shirley, A .... 585-567-9310 .... 336 B
shirley.mullen@houghton.edu

MULLEN, Steve, L .... 716-851-1294 .... 333 C
mullens@ecc.edu

MULLEN, Steven, K .... 214-333-5170 .... 484 C
stevem@dbu.edu

MULLEN, William .... 612-874-3762 .... 265 E
william_mullen@mcad.edu

MULLENDORE, Heather ...... 304-829-7905 .... 540 E
hmullendore@bethanywv.edu

MULLENS, Rob, A .... 541-346-1228 .... 419 B
mullens@uoregon.edu

MULLER, Christopher .... 617-353-3261 .... 232 G
cmuller@bu.edu

MULLER, David .... 212-241-8716 .... 342 B

MULLER, Eugene, W .... 973-748-9000 .... 308 A
eugene_muller@bloomfield.edu

MULLER, Janet .... 502-213-2179 .... 202 B
janet.muller@kctcs.edu

MULLER, Janice, J .... 301-295-3356 .... 558 A
jmuller@usuhs.mil

MULLER, Joe .... 405-974-2502 .... 413 B
jmuller@ucok.edu

MULLER, John, B .... 402-557-7001 .... 297 A
john.muller@bellevue.edu

MULLER, Joseph .... 860-253-3055 ...... 89 K
jmuller@acc.commnet.edu

MULLER, Joyce, D .... 410-857-2292 .... 224 D
jmuller@mcdaniel.edu

MULLER, Katharine .... 310-434-3701 ...... 68 D
muller_katharine@smc.edu

MULLER, Kathy .... 304-865-6127 .... 541 F
kathy.muller@ovu.edu

MULLER, Ralph, W .... 215-662-2203 .... 448 I
ralph.muller@uphs.upenn.edu

MULLER, Robin .... 803-321-5155 .... 459 G
robin.muller@newberry.edu

MULLER, Steve .... 802-387-1632 .... 513 E
smuller@landmark.edu

MULLER, Susan, M .... 270-809-3590 .... 204 F
smuller1@murraystate.edu

MULLERY, Colleen .... 707-826-5086 ...... 36 D
cbm1@humboldt.edu

MULLHOLLAND, Krista ..... 262-595-2301 .... 551 E
bookstore@uwp.edu

MULLIGAN, Brendan .... 617-369-3458 .... 244 G
bmulligan@mfa.org

MULLIGAN, Diane .... 503-977-4532 .... 419 G
dmulliga@pcc.edu

MULLIGAN, Maura .... 617-989-4232 .... 246 C
mulliganm@wit.edu

MULLIGAN, Rob .... 916-608-6500 ...... 56 C

MULLIGAN, Susan, C .... 973-877-3071 .... 310 A
mulligan@essex.edu

MULLIGAN, Thomas, E ..... 330-569-5940 .... 391 H
mulligante@hiram.edu

MULLIKEN, Taffy .... 719-502-3019 ...... 86 G
taffy.mulliken@ppcc.edu

MULLIKIN, Demeri, C .... 651-757-4004 .... 263 A
dmullikin@cva.edu

MULLIKIN, Jane .... 419-473-2700 .... 389 B
jmullikin@daviscollege.edu

MULLIN, Carol .... 610-359-5318 .... 426 G
cmullin@dccc.edu

MULLIN, OSB, Douglas .... 320-363-2737 .... 271 F
dmullin@csbsju.edu

MULLIN, John .... 972-377-1575 .... 483 D
jmullin@collin.edu

MULLIN, John, R .... 413-545-5271 .... 237 C
jmullin@provost.umass.edu

MULLIN, Mark, E .... 573-341-4175 .... 292 A
memullin@mst.edu

MULLIN, Virginia .... 617-735-9756 .... 234 E
mullin@emmanuel.edu

MULLINAX, Carl, F .... 814-866-8120 .... 433 [illegible]
cmullinax@lecom.edu

MULLINAX, Kenneth .... 334-229-4104 .... 1 [illegible]
kmullinax@alasu.edu

MULLINAX, Melissa .... 828-328-7244 .... 366 E
melissa.mullinax@lr.edu

MULLINS, Andrew, P .... 662-915-7111 .... 277 G
amullins@olemiss.edu

MULLINS, Ann, M .... 662-846-4670 .... 274 E
amullins@deltastate.edu

MULLINS, Brian .... 859-622-2821 .... 200 D
brian.mullins@eku.edu

MULLINS, JR., C. David ... 423-439-4343 .... 473 E
mullinsc@etsu.edu

MULLINS, Catherine .... 802-387-6736 .... 513 E
cmullins@landmark.edu

MULLINS, Dixie .... 409-772-5302 .... 507 B
dimullin@utmb.edu

MULLINS, James, L .... 765-494-2900 .... 178 F
jmullins@purdue.edu

MULLINS, Judy .... 660-785-4150 .... 291 A
jmullins@truman.edu

MULLINS, Liza .... 904-256-7082 .... 111 J
lmullin1@ju.edu

MULLINS, Rhonda .... 606-218-5200 .... 207 B
rhondamullins@pc.edu

MULLINS, Sharon .... 281-425-6388 .... 489 J
smullins@lee.edu

MULLINS, Steve .... 714-879-3901 ...... 50 G
smullins@hiu.edu

MULLINS, William .... 740-826-8120 .... 396 I
wmullins@muskingum.edu

MULLIS, Joe, W .... 910-678-8217 .... 370 B
mullisj@faytechcc.edu

MULLIS, Terri .... 913-758-6114 .... 197 B
mullis15@stmary.edu

MULLIS, Tres .... 540-458-8165 .... 530 A
tmullis@wlu.edu

MULLOWNEY, Glenda, K ... 425-235-7873 .... 536 E
gmullowney@rtc.edu

MULLOWNEY, William, J .. 407-582-3411 .... 122 I
bmullowney@valenciacollege.edu

MULLOY, Josetta .... 251-380-3470 .... 7 F
mulloy@shc.edu

MULQUEEN, Joann .... 914-831-0418 .... 330 D
jmulqueen@cw.edu

MULRENAN, Holly .... 203-576-5518 ...... 94 A
hmulrenan@stvincentscollege.edu

MULROE, Michael .... 312-942-6214 .... 163 B
mike_mulroe@rush.edu

MULROONEY, Bill .... 310-660-3418 ...... 45 D
bmulroon@elcamino.edu

MULROONEY, Debra .... 503-253-3443 .... 417 H
dmulrooney@ocom.edu

MULROY, William, T .... 610-526-1407 .... 421 G
william.mulroy@theamericancollege.edu

MULROY-DEGENHART,
Carmella .... 814-865-7611 .... 438 F
qum11@psu.edu

MULRYAN, Michael .... 714-879-3901 ...... 50 G
mdmulryan@hiu.edu

MULSHINE, James, L .... 312-942-3589 .... 163 B
james_l_mulshine@rush.edu

MULSO, Sara, K .... 651-641-8857 .... 263 C
smulso@csp.edu

MULSO, William .... 507-537-6267 .... 269 G
William.Mulso@smsu.edu

MULTARI, James .... 516-678-5000 .... 341 F
jmultari@molloy.edu

MULTHAUF, Christopher .... 847-574-5270 .... 155 G
cmulthauf@lfgsm.edu

MULTOP, Kevin .... 541-383-7578 .... 414 I
kmultop@cocc.edu

MULUMBA, Syokwaa .... 201-360-4183 .... 310 F
smulumba@hccc.edu

MULVEY, Julie .... 508-588-9100 .... 240 E

MULVEY, Kristin .... 815-280-2201 .... 154 H
kmulvey@jjc.edu

MULVEY, Lisa .... 516-299-2263 .... 339 A
lisa.mulvey@liu.edu

MULVIHILL, Kelleyrobin .... 617-989-4127 .... 246 C
mulvihillk@wit.edu

MULVIHILL, Rosemary ...... 781-768-7029 .... 244 D
rosemary.mulvihill@regiscollege.edu

MULVILLE, Matthew, H ..... 716-888-2220 .... 325 G
mulville@canisius.edu

MUMA, Richard, D .... 316-978-5761 .... 197 F
richard.muma@wichita.edu

MUMFORD, John .... 814-827-4409 .... 449 E
mumford@pitt.edu

MUMFORD, John, W .... 814-641-3452 .... 431 L
mumford@juniata.edu

MUMFORD, Thomas .... 801-524-8123 .... 510 A
tmumford@ldsbc.edu

MUMMERT, John .... 650-949-7070 ...... 47 H
mummertjohn@foothill.edu

MUMMERT, Kelly .... 304-243-2226 .... 545 G
kmummert@wju.edu

MUMMERT, Vernon .... 718-982-3149 .... 327 A
vernon.mummert@csi.cuny.edu

MUMPER, Michael .... 719-587-7436 ...... 80 F
mmumper@adams.edu

MUNA, Esther, A .... 671-735-5700 .... 559 B
gccpresident@guamcc.edu

MURPHY, Robert ... 508-767-7225 ... 230 E
rtmurphy@assumption.edu
MURPHY, Robert, P ... 716-829-8199 ... 332 F
murphyrp@dyc.edu
MURPHY, Sean ... 407-888-4000 ... 113 A
smurphy1@careered.com
MURPHY, Stephen, C ... 203-432-8090 ... 95 D
stephen.murphy@yale.edu
MURPHY, Steven, J ... 773-298-3310 ... 163 G
murphy@sxu.edu
MURPHY, Susan, H ... 607-255-7595 ... 331 C
shm1@cornell.edu
MURPHY, Susan, L ... 415-422-2620 ... 76 B
murphy@usfca.edu
MURPHY, Suzanne ... 212-678-3755 ... 357 F
smurphy@tc.columbia.edu
MURPHY, Suzanne, K ... 215-596-8888 ... 450 A
s.murphy@usciences.edu
MURPHY, Thomas ... 516-876-3215 ... 353 D
murphyt@oldwestbury.edu
MURPHY, Todd ... 323-343-2500 ... 35 B
tmurphy@cslanet.calstatela.edu
MURPHY, Wayne ... 718-289-5245 ... 326 F
wayne.murphy@bcc.cuny.edu
MURPHY CHURCH, Linda 401-709-8408 ... 454 B
lchurch@risd.edu
MURPHY-FREEBOLIN,
Lorie ... 563-588-6571 ... 183 B
lorie.murphy-freebolin@clarke.edu
MURPHY-STETZ,
Katherine ... 312-567-3080 ... 153 B
murphy@iit.edu
MURR, Christopher ... 512-245-3975 ... 501 C
cm18@txstate.edu
MURRAH, Matt ... 214-333-6887 ... 484 C
matt@dbu.edu
MURRAY, Adam, L ... 270-809-5604 ... 204 F
adam.murray@murraystate.edu
MURRAY, Adrienne, M ... 704-894-2915 ... 363 F
admurray@davidson.edu
MURRAY, Ann ... 307-778-1113 ... 556 B
amurray@lccc.wy.edu
MURRAY, Ann Marie ... 315-866-0300 ... 335 E
murrayam@herkimer.edu
MURRAY, Barbara, M ... 909-748-8544 ... 75 F
barbara_murray@redlands.edu
MURRAY, Betty ... 254-968-9070 ... 496 F
murray@tarleton.edu
MURRAY, Brooke ... 814-393-2572 ... 442 A
bmurray@clarion.edu
MURRAY, Charles ... 205-387-0511 ... 2 B
cmurray@bscc.edu
MURRAY, Cherry, A ... 617-495-5829 ... 235 H
camurray@seas.harvard.edu
MURRAY, Christopher, D .. 208-885-6154 ... 144 B
chrismurray@uidaho.edu
MURRAY, David ... 732-224-2449 ... 308 B
dmurray@brookdalecc.edu
MURRAY, Deborah ... 423-614-8175 ... 470 A
debmurray@leeuniversity.edu
MURRAY, Debra, H ... 717-361-1164 ... 428 E
murraydh@etown.edu
MURRAY, Dennis, J ... 845-575-3000 ... 340 C
dennis.murray@marist.edu
MURRAY, Don ... 402-486-2536 ... 300 D
domurray@ucollege.edu
MURRAY, Douglas, J ... 575-624-8020 ... 319 C
dmurray@nmmi.edu
MURRAY, Eric ... 425-352-8810 ... 531 F
emurray@cascadia.edu
MURRAY, Eric, H ... 404-816-4533 ... 132 B
ericm@atl.herzing.edu
MURRAY, Frank ... 509-542-4835 ... 532 C
fmurray@columbiabasin.edu
MURRAY, George, W ... 803-754-4100 ... 457 D
MURRAY, Gloria, J ... 812-941-2385 ... 174 D
glomurra@ius.edu
MURRAY, Harris ... 803-535-1255 ... 460 C
murrayh@octech.edu
MURRAY, Harris ... 803-535-1257 ... 460 C
murrayh@octech.edu
MURRAY, Helen ... 260-399-7700 ... 180 E
hmurray@sf.edu
MURRAY, Hope, W ... 302-739-4050 ... 96 A
hmurray@dtcc.edu
MURRAY, Jay, E ... 203-596-4630 ... 93 D
jmurray@post.edu
MURRAY, Jill ... 570-504-8111 ... 433 A
murrayj@lackawanna.edu
MURRAY, Joanne, S ... 781-283-2492 ... 246 B
jmurray@wellesley.edu
MURRAY, John ... 812-237-2785 ... 173 A
john.murray@indstate.edu
MURRAY, Karen ... 254-968-9103 ... 496 F
kmurray@tarleton.edu
MURRAY, Kathleen, M ... 651-696-6160 ... 265 A
kmurray@macalester.edu
MURRAY, Louise ... 973-290-4430 ... 309 A
lmurray@cse.edu
MURRAY, Lynne ... 202-651-5006 ... 97 E
lynne.murray@gallaudet.edu
MURRAY, Mark ... 904-264-2172 ... 116 A
mark.murray@iws.edu
MURRAY, Meghan ... 858-635-4290 ... 27 E
mmurray@alliant.edu
MURRAY, Michael ... 626-584-2040 ... 48 A
mdmurray@fuller.edu
MURRAY, Michele ... 206-296-6066 ... 537 F
mmurray@seattleu.edu
MURRAY, Nancy, K ... 219-464-5989 ... 181 A
nancy.murray@valpo.edu
MURRAY, Percy ... 903-923-2421 ... 509 A
pmurray@wileyc.edu
MURRAY, Peter ... 650-949-7259 ... 47 H
murraypeter@foothill.edu
MURRAY, Peter, J ... 410-706-2461 ... 227 C
pmurray@umaryland.edu
MURRAY, Renae ... 561-803-2155 ... 114 C
renae_murray@pba.edu
MURRAY, Robert ... 208-769-3474 ... 143 H
robert_murray@nic.edu
MURRAY, Robert ... 309-556-3031 ... 153 E
bmurray@iwu.edu
MURRAY, Robert ... 845-398-4125 ... 349 H
rmurray@stac.edu
MURRAY, Robert ... 860-444-8520 ... 558 E
robert.murray@uscga.edu
MURRAY, Robert, C ... 434-223-6020 ... 519 B
rcmurray@email.hsc.edu
MURRAY, Rose-Marie ... 305-949-9500 ... 105 F
rmurray@cci.edu
MURRAY, Sharon ... 518-292-1753 ... 348 A
murras2@sage.edu
MURRAY, Shelba, M ... 828-652-0657 ... 371 G
shelbam@mcdowelltech.edu
MURRAY, Steven ... 870-338-6474 ... 25 D
MURRAY, Steven ... 657-278-2614 ... 34 E
smurray@fullerton.edu
MURRAY, Susan ... 509-682-6435 ... 539 B
smurray@wvc.edu
MURRAY, Tamsen ... 714-879-3901 ... 50 G
tmurray@hiu.edu
MURRAY, Thomas ... 336-770-3277 ... 379 D
murrayt@uncsa.edu
MURRAY, Thomas, K ... 563-387-1862 ... 187 A
murrayto@luther.edu
MURRAY, Thomas, M ... 703-784-2105 ... 557 E
thomas.murray@usmc.mil
MURRAY, Trish ... 704-894-2099 ... 363 F
trmurray@davidson.edu
MURRAY, William, G ... 516-671-2213 ... 360 A
bmurray@webb-institute.edu
MURRAY-JENSEN, Julie ... 541-880-2221 ... 416 C
jensen@klamathcc.edu
MURRAY-LAURY, Janice ... 908-737-7080 ... 311 B
jmurray@kean.edu
MURRAY-RUST, Catherine 404-894-8914 ... 130 D
catherine.rust@library.gatech.edu
MURRELL, James, T ... 931-363-9823 ... 470 E
jmurrell@martinmethodist.edu
MURRELL, Terry ... 712-274-6400 ... 189 H
terry.murrell@witcc.edu
MURRIL, Antoinette ... 312-567-3012 ... 153 B
amurril@iit.edu
MURRIN, Michael ... 716-926-8900 ... 335 F
mmurrin@hilbert.edu
MURRY, Eric ... 623-245-4600 ... 18 M
emurry@uticorp.com
MURRY, LaKeisha ... 901-381-3939 ... 478 D
keisha@visible.edu
MURRY, Tracy ... 941-487-4504 ... 119 D
tmurry@ncf.edu
MURTAGH, Michael ... 309-467-6315 ... 150 H
mmurtagh@eureka.edu
MURTAGH GITTO, Ann ... 413-528-7297 ... 231 A
agitto@simons-rock.edu
MURTAUGH, Kelly ... 651-423-8319 ... 266 E
kelly.murtaugh@dctc.edu
MURTAUGH, Peter, T ... 314-286-4813 ... 288 B
ptmurtaugh@ranken.edu
MURTHA, Brenda ... 605-274-5217 ... 463 H
brenda.murtha@augie.edu
MURTHA, Paul ... 718-982-2113 ... 327 A
Paul.Murtha@csi.cuny.edu
MURUAKO, Dominic ... 205-366-8854 ... 7 G
dmuruako@stillman.edu
MURVIN, David ... 561-391-1148 ... 104 H
dmurvin@dmac.edu
MURY, Hal ... 919-209-2000 ... 371 C
hemury@johnstoncc.edu
MUSAL, Edward ... 914-251-6923 ... 354 D
edward.musal@purchase.edu
MUSCARELLA, Joseph ... 516-572-0605 ... 342 C
joseph.muscarella@ncc.edu
MUSCARI, Kathy, L ... 740-283-6267 ... 390 M
kmuscari@franciscan.edu
MUSCENTE, Catherine ... 516-678-5000 ... 341 F
cmuscente@molloy.edu
MUSCIO, Fugen ... 270-809-3538 ... 204 F
fugen.muscio@murraystate.edu
MUSCOPLAT, Charles, C ... 612-624-6252 ... 272 D
cmuscop@umn.edu
MUSE, Clyde ... 601-857-3240 ... 274 E
vcmuse@hindscc.edu
MUSE, Douglas ... 870-612-2167 ... 25 E
douglas.muse@uaccb.edu
MUSE, Justin ... 540-365-4441 ... 518 J
jmuse@ferrum.edu
MUSE, William ... 406-243-5661 ... 295 A
bill.muse@umontana.edu
MUSEWICZ, Suellen ... 570-961-7824 ... 433 A
musewiczs@lackawanna.edu
MUSGRAVE, Dan ... 575-624-8214 ... 319 C
musgrave@nmmi.edu
MUSGROVE, Karen ... 318-678-6031 ... 209 J
kmusgrove@bpcc.edu
MUSGROVE, Robert ... 320-629-5120 ... 268 G
musgrover@pinetech.edu
MUSHRUSH, Tiffany ... 440-646-8370 ... 405 B
tmushrush@ursuline.edu
MUSICK, Chris ... 614-823-1370 ... 400 G
cmusick@otterbein.edu
MUSICK, Kelly ... 409-933-8496 ... 483 B
kmusick@com.edu
MUSIL, Erin ... 415-865-0198 ... 30 B
emusil@aii.edu
MUSKAVITCH, John, W ... 909-389-3269 ... 65 B
jmuskavitch@craftonhills.edu
MUSKIN, Michael ... 970-351-1408 ... 88 F
michael.muskin@unco.edu
MUSKOPF, James ... 314-719-3635 ... 282 C
jmuskopf@fontbonne.edu
MUSOLF, David, E ... 608-262-3956 ... 550 G
musolf@secfac.wisc.edu
MUSOLF, Shelly, R ... 260-422-5561 ... 172 L
srmusolf@indianatech.edu
MUSSA-MULDOON,
Carla, R ... 310-233-4450 ... 54 I
muldoonc@lahc.edu
MUSSANO, Frank, P ... 717-815-1365 ... 452 F
fmussano@ycp.edu
MUSSELMAN, Don ... 606-546-1209 ... 206 F
dmusselman@unionky.edu
MUSSELMAN, Kathy, I ... 615-898-2929 ... 473 F
kathy.musselm@mtsu.edu
MUSSELWHITE, Laura ... 706-204-2368 ... 130 C
lmusselw@highlands.edu
MUSSER, Jeff ... 616-331-2207 ... 252 A
musserj@gvsu.edu
MUSSER, Steve ... 717-560-8248 ... 433 D
MUSSO, Daniele ... 913-360-7975 ... 190 F
dmusso@benedictine.edu
MUSTAF, Mustafa ... 201-216-9901 ... 309 G
MUSTER, Robert ... 612-659-6104 ... 267 E
robert.muster@minneapolis.edu
MUSTERMAN, Cynthia, A .. 314-421-0949 ... 290 H
musterman@siba.edu
MUTONE, Paul ... 860-297-4224 ... 94 C
paul.mutone@trincoll.edu
MUTUA, Makau, W ... 716-645-2052 ... 351 G
mutua@buffalo.edu
MUYSKENS, James, L ... 718-997-5550 ... 328 F
james.muyskens@qc.cuny.edu
MUYSKENS, Judy, A ... 402-465-2110 ... 299 J
provost@nebrwesleyan.edu
MUZIA, Raymond ... 757-825-2900 ... 528 B
muziar@tncc.edu
MUÑIZ, Maria ... 787-841-2000 ... 564 I
mmuniz@email.pucpr.edu
MUÑOZ, Ivette ... 787-725-8120 ... 562 A
imunoz@eap.edu
MUÑOZ-MUÑOZ,
Miguel, A ... 787-250-0000 ... 566 D
miguel.munoz3@upr.edu
MWAURA, John ... 973-748-9000 ... 308 A
john_mwaura@bloomfield.edu
MWENJA, Dominic ... 858-653-3000 ... 33 A
dmwenja@calmu.edu
MYAZOE, Diane, C ... 692-528-5033 ... 559 E
dcmyazoe@yahoo.com
MYDLOWEC, Sally, P ... 215-885-2360 ... 435 E
smydlowec@manor.edu
MYER, Bonnie ... 360-736-9391 ... 531 H
bmyer@centralia.edu
MYER, Marci ... 206-934-3669 ... 536 H
marci.myer@seattlecolleges.edu
MYEROWITZ, Rachel ... 240-895-4373 ... 226 A
rmyerowitz@smcm.edu
MYERS, Alvin, B ... 434-395-2300 ... 520 G
myersab@longwood.edu
MYERS, Amy, A ... 717-291-4082 ... 429 E
amy.myers@fandm.edu
MYERS, Barbara ... 912-358-3051 ... 136 C
myersb@savannahstate.edu
MYERS, Bradley, A ... 614-292-1556 ... 398 H
myers.7@osu.edu
MYERS, Bradley, A ... 614-292-1556 ... 399 C
myers.7@osu.edu
MYERS, Camille ... 843-525-8359 ... 461 E
cmyers@tcl.edu
MYERS, Charles ... 219-473-4367 ... 170 D
cmyers@ccsj.edu
MYERS, Charles ... 215-596-8791 ... 450 A
c.myers@usciences.edu
MYERS, Cheryl ... 706-649-1290 ... 127 E
cmyers@columbustech.edu
MYERS, Cheryl ... 504-571-1290 ... 210 G
cmyers@dcc.edu
MYERS, Chris ... 707-864-7000 ... 70 A
chris.myers@solano.edu
MYERS, Dale ... 830-792-7235 ... 494 A
dtmyers@schreiner.edu
MYERS, Daniel, J ... 574-631-2799 ... 180
dmyers@nd.edu
MYERS, Deborah, L ... 828-298-3325 ... 380
dmyers@warren-wilson.edu
MYERS, Donald ... 202-885-2700 ... 97
don@american.edu
MYERS, Donald, C ... 901-333-5259 ... 475
dmyers@southwest.tn.edu
MYERS, Eveadean ... 701-231-7703 ... 381
evie.myers@ndsu.edu
MYERS, Gary, D ... 504-282-4455 ... 213
gmeyers@nobts.edu
MYERS, Gary, L ... 417-864-7220 ... 282
gmyers@cci.edu
MYERS, Gary, L ... 662-325-2646 ... 276
gmyers@deanas.msstate.edu
MYERS, Greeley ... 325-793-4603 ... 490
myers.greeley@mcm.edu
MYERS, James ... 650-325-9122 ... 64 G
vat2ins@aol.com
MYERS, James ... 618-537-6828 ... 157 G
jamyers@mckendree.edu
MYERS, James, L ... 803-536-8480 ... 460 G
myers@scsu.edu
MYERS, Jeannette ... 843-661-1291 ... 458 C
jmyers@fmarion.edu
MYERS, Jimmy ... 239-590-7406 ... 119 A
jimyers@fgcu.edu
MYERS, Joe ... 931-393-1553 ... 475 C
jmyers@mscc.edu
MYERS, John ... 413-528-7293 ... 231 A
johnm@simons-rock.edu
MYERS, Jolene ... 406-377-9410 ... 294 C
myers@dawson.edu
MYERS, Julie, K ... 845-758-7518 ... 323 F
myers@bard.edu
MYERS, Karen, S ... 330-287-1275 ... 399 A
myers.444@osu.edu
MYERS, Kelly ... 815-802-8260 ... 154 J
kmyers@kcc.edu
MYERS, Keri ... 316-320-7312 ... 191 D
kmyers7@butlercc.edu
MYERS, Kevin ... 361-570-4840 ... 503 E
myersk@uhv.edu
MYERS, Kim ... 916-660-7100 ... 69 F
MYERS, Laura ... 740-593-2620 ... 399 G
myersl@ohio.edu
MYERS, Lynne, M ... 508-793-2265 ... 233 D
lmyers@holycross.edu
MYERS, Marci ... 620-223-2700 ... 192 G
marcim@fortscott.edu
MYERS, Margaret ... 701-777-2015 ... 381 D
margaret.myers@email.und.edu
MYERS, Mark ... 907-474-5837 ... 10 J
mdmyers@alaska.edu
MYERS, Mark ... 432-264-3752 ... 487 I
mmyers@howardcollege.edu
MYERS, Mary, L ... 320-222-7534 ... 268 I
mary.myers@ridgewater.edu
MYERS, Mary Beth ... 317-274-1505 ... 174 B
mbmyers@iupui.edu
MYERS, Michael ... 847-982-2500 ... 151 H
myers@htc.edu
MYERS, Michelle ... 816-584-6727 ... 287 H
michelle.meyers@park.edu
MYERS, Nathan, D ... 419-289-5970 ... 384 D
nmyers@ashland.edu
MYERS, Patricia ... 518-587-2100 ... 355 F
patricia.myers@esc.edu
MYERS, Patricia, A ... 330-672-7890 ... 393 D
pmyers@kent.edu
MYERS, Patricia, T ... 865-539-7242 ... 475 F
pmyers@pstcc.edu
MYERS, Paul ... 503-943-7134 ... 420 G
myers@up.edu
MYERS, Perry ... 903-983-8258 ... 489 F
pmyers@kilgore.edu
MYERS, Randy, E ... 620-665-3579 ... 193 F
myersr@hutchcc.edu
MYERS, Regan ... 847-925-6826 ... 151 E
rmyers@harpercollege.edu
MYERS, Robert ... 574-257-3524 ... 169 F
myersr@bethelcollege.edu
MYERS, Robert ... 310-434-4200 ... 68 D
myers_robert@smc.edu
MYERS, Robert ... 301-790-2800 ... 223 A
myersr@hagerstowncc.edu
MYERS, Robert ... 870-762-3191 ... 20 A
rmyers@smail.anc.edu
MYERS, Robert ... 918-335-6226 ... 411 B
rmyers@okwu.edu
MYERS, Robert, V ... 312-821-6300 ... 144 E
MYERS, Sara ... 404-687-4547 ... 127 C
myerss@ctsnet.edu
MYERS, Sara, J ... 386-312-4037 ... 116 D
sallymyers@sjrstate.edu
MYERS, Talbert ... 919-209-2071 ... 371 C
t_myers@johnstoncc.edu
MYERS, Thomas ... 314-505-7329 ... 280 H
myerst@csl.edu
MYERS, Tim ... 972-825-4723 ... 495 D
tmyers@sagu.edu
MYHRE, Terry ... 801-304-4224 ... 509 E
tmyhre@globeuniversity.edu

NAVA, Robert ... 415-338-2506 ... 36 F
rjnava@sfsu.edu

NAVA, Robert ... 415-338-2517 ... 36 F
rjnava@sfsu.edu

NAVARDAUSKAS, Amy ... 219-785-5307 ... 178 H
adavis@pnc.edu

NAVARI, Shelley ... 802-860-6405 ... 513 A
navari@champlain.edu

NAVARRETE, Nancy ... 602-285-7392 ... 16 B
nancy.navarrete@pcmail.maricopa.edu

NAVARRETTE, Lupe ... 325-235-7368 ... 500 C
jose.navarrette@tstc.edu

NAVARRETTE, Ricardo, D ... 707-524-1651 ... 68 E
rnavarrette@santarosa.edu

NAVARRO, Carlos ... 408-273-2693 ... 58 G
cnavarro@nhu.edu

NAVARRO, David ... 619-388-7560 ... 65 H
dnavarro@sdccd.edu

NAVARRO, JoAnn ... 607-777-3060 ... 351 F
navarro@binghamton.edu

NAVARRO, Lesia ... 951-487-3245 ... 58 B
lnavarro@msjc.edu

NAVARRO, Leslie, A ... 708-656-8000 ... 159 C
leslie.navarro@morton.edu

NAVARRO, Renee ... 415-476-7700 ... 74 E
renee.navarro@ucsf.edu

NAVARRO, Victor ... 480-732-7020 ... 15 G
victor.navarro@cgcmail.maricopa.edu

NAVE, Felicia, M ... 926-261-2175 ... 496 E
fmnave@pvamu.edu

NAVE, Jeffery, W ... 504-282-4455 ... 213 H
jnave@nobts.edu

NAVIN, Thomas, P ... 413-545-9474 ... 237 C
tnavin@admin.umass.edu

NAVIN, Tom ... 802-258-3173 ... 514 C
tom.navin@worldlearning.org

NAVLAKHA, Jainendra ... 305-348-2026 ... 119 B
navlakha@cis.fiu.edu

NAVRAN, Darius ... 216-432-8971 ... 387 A
Navran@ChancellorU.edu

NAVRATIL, Gerald ... 212-854-6574 ... 330 F
gan2@columbia.edu

NAWN, Ruth ... 603-513-1320 ... 306 H
ruth.nawn@granite.edu

NAYLER, Ronald ... 847-467-5810 ... 160 D
r-nayler@northwestern.edu

NAYLOR, Bob ... 435-722-6900 ... 510 J

NAYLOR, David ... 843-863-7154 ... 456 B
dnaylor@csuniv.edu

NAYLOR, Patricia ... 973-408-3103 ... 309 F
pnaylor@drew.edu

NAYLOR, Richard ... 508-373-9453 ... 231 D
richard.naylor@becker.edu

NAYLOR, Suzette ... 816-802-3519 ... 283 I
snaylor@kcai.edu

NAYLOR, Tere, E ... 816-932-1620 ... 289 G
tnaylor@saint-lukes.org

NAYLOR, Tracy ... 270-686-9550 ... 198 G
tracy.naylor@brescia.edu

NAYLOR-JOHNSON, Darrell ... 912-525-8031 ... 136 B
dnaylorj@scad.edu

NAYLOR MOORE, Barbara ... 662-252-8000 ... 277 C
bmoore@rustcollege.edu

NAZARENKO, Tatiana ... 805-565-6070 ... 78 F
tnazarenko@westmont.edu

NAZARIAN, Nick ... 909-652-6541 ... 39 B
nick.nazarian@chaffey.edu

NAZARIO, Lisa ... 201-200-2335 ... 312 B
lnazario@njcu.edu

NAZARIO-COLON, Ricardo ... 270-745-5066 ... 207 C
ricardo.nazariocolon@wku.edu

NAZARIO-TORRES, Juan, C ... 787-620-2040 ... 560 B
jcnazario@aupr.edu

NAZEMETZ, Alex, P ... 814-362-7555 ... 449 B
nazemetz@pitt.edu

NDIAYE, Momar ... 309-438-5365 ... 153 C
mndiaye@ilstu.edu

NEACE, Thomas ... 606-487-3204 ... 201 H
thomas.neace@kctcs.edu

NEAD, Margaret, A ... 585-271-3778 ... 329 G
mnead@crcds.edu

NEAL, Bill ... 704-484-4097 ... 369 B
nealb@clevelandcommunitycollege.edu

NEAL, Bill ... 985-549-2217 ... 216 C
wneal@selu.edu

NEAL, Brenda ... 304-260-4380 ... 542 C
bneal@blueridgectc.edu

NEAL, Brigette ... 313-664-7470 ... 250 A
bneal@collegeforcreativestudies.edu

NEAL, Charles ... 870-307-7398 ... 22 D
cneal@lyon.edu

NEAL, Charles, V ... 607-587-4019 ... 355 C
nealcv@alfredstate.edu

NEAL, Diane, H ... 318-670-9230 ... 215 A
dneal@susla.edu

NEAL, Donna, V ... 252-493-7309 ... 372 E
dneal@email.pittcc.edu

NEAL, Elizabeth ... 513-562-8766 ... 384 A
eneal@artacademy.edu

NEAL, Ernest ... 803-778-7814 ... 455 G
nealej@cctech.edu

NEAL, Gary, W ... 210-999-7411 ... 502 C
gneal@trinity.edu

NEAL, James ... 212-854-2247 ... 330 F
jneal@columbia.edu

NEAL, Joan ... 610-902-8234 ... 423 H
joan.neal@cabrini.edu

NEAL, Kathleen, E ... 860-701-5380 ... 93 B
neal_k@mitchell.edu

NEAL, Kurtis, R ... 325-942-2168 ... 480 E
kurtis.neal@angelo.edu

NEAL, JR., L. Cameron ... 972-881-5891 ... 483 D
cneal@collin.edu

NEAL, Lyle ... 402-761-8224 ... 300 C
lneal@southeast.edu

NEAL, Mary, Y ... 804-752-7259 ... 522 F
mneal@rmc.edu

NEAL, Michael, A ... 661-654-2287 ... 33 H
mneal@csub.edu

NEAL, Nicole ... 740-351-3245 ... 401 I
nneal@shawnee.edu

NEAL, Phillip ... 270-901-1114 ... 201 E
phil.neal@kctcs.edu

NEAL, Robin ... 916-484-8172 ... 56 A
nealr@arc.losrios.edu

NEAL, Rodney ... 909-558-4543 ... 54 D
rneal@llu.edu

NEAL, Shandon ... 225-771-3590 ... 214 H

NEAL, Shannon ... 504-816-4228 ... 208 I
sneal@dillard.edu

NEAL, Stephanie, A ... 304-696-4325 ... 542 G
neal@mctc.edu

NEAL, Steven, M ... 330-287-1211 ... 399 A
neal.2@osu.edu

NEAL, Thomas, G ... 409-984-6156 ... 500 H
tom.neal@lamarpa.edu

NEAL, Thomas, M ... 714-547-9625 ... 31 I
tneal@calcoast.edu

NEAL, Tom ... 503-838-8043 ... 419 C
nealt@wou.edu

NEAL, W. Anthony ... 336-517-2392 ... 362 C
tneal@bennett.edu

NEAL, William, G ... 808-675-3457 ... 139 I
nealw@byuh.edu

NEAL, Willie ... 214-860-8784 ... 485 A
wneal@dcccd.edu

NEAL, Willie, H ... 434-381-6144 ... 524 E
wneal@sbc.edu

NEAL, Zeal ... 501-279-4331 ... 21 H
zneal@harding.edu

NEALEIGH, Michael ... 405-224-3140 ... 413 E
mnealeigh@usao.edu

NEALEN, Mary Kaye ... 406-791-5378 ... 296 H
mnealen@ugf.edu

NEALON, Ann ... 570-702-8913 ... 431 K
anealon@johnson.edu

NEALON, Bonnie ... 765-658-4294 ... 170 I
bnealon@depauw.edu

NEALON, Jacquelyn ... 516-686-7925 ... 343 D
jnealon@nyit.edu

NEALON, Marisol ... 415-575-6120 ... 32 D
mmendoza@ciis.edu

NEALON, Michael ... 517-483-1016 ... 254 D
nealonm@lcc.edu

NEALON-WOODS, Michele ... 312-379-1683 ... 146 C
mnealon-woods@thechicagoschool.edu

NEAR, Hollis ... 206-726-5040 ... 532 G
hnear@cornish.edu

NEARY, Dan ... 425-889-5204 ... 535 I
dan.neary@northwestu.edu

NEARY, Michele, A ... 847-491-8466 ... 160 D
m-neary@northwestern.edu

NEARY, Robert ... 315-866-0300 ... 335 E
nearyrd@herkimer.edu

NEAS, Bonita ... 701-231-8640 ... 381 H
bonnie.neas@ndsu.edu

NEASE, Owen ... 504-282-4455 ... 213 H
financialaid@nobts.edu

NEATH-FOSTER, Jacqueline ... 978-368-2459 ... 230 F
jacqueline.neathfoster@auc.edu

NEAU, George ... 510-567-6174 ... 68 G
chancellor@sum.edu

NEAULT, Lynn ... 619-388-7800 ... 65 H
lneault@sdccd.edu

NEAULT, Lynn, C ... 619-388-6922 ... 65 E
lneault@sdccd.edu

NEAVE, Jessica ... 617-217-9204 ... 231 C
jneave@baystate.edu

NEAVES, Mitchell ... 340-693-1046 ... 568 C
mneaves@uvi.edu

NEAVILL, Michael ... 513-244-8436 ... 387 D
michael.neavill@ccuniversity.edu

NEBEKER-CHRISTENSEN, Annie ... 801-581-7066 ... 510 L
anebeker@sa.utah.edu

NEBEL, Andreia ... 402-552-6178 ... 297 D
nebel@clarksoncollege.edu

NEBESKY, Michael ... 864-656-2390 ... 456 E
mnebeske@clemson.edu

NECESSARY, David ... 276-739-2448 ... 528 D
dnecessary@vhcc.edu

NECESSARY, Russell, D ... 276-328-0322 ... 525 C
rdn2f@uvawise.edu

NECHIPURENKO, Erin ... 508-626-4951 ... 238 D
enechipurenko@framingham.edu

NECOCHEA, Juan ... 408-273-2677 ... 58 G
jnecochea@nhu.edu

NECULA, Cristina ... 718-960-2416 ... 327 C
cristina.necula@lehman.cuny.edu

NEDDERMAN, Robert, M ... 402-461-7410 ... 298 C
bnedderman@hastings.edu

NEDEAU, Patricia ... 312-893-7160 ... 150 G
pnedeau@erikson.edu

NEDELL, Thomas ... 617-373-2240 ... 244 A

NEDERHOFF, Arlan ... 712-722-6010 ... 183 H
anederho@dordt.edu

NEDERHOOD, Al ... 323-319-9500 ... 72 J

NEE, Michael ... 310-578-1080 ... 28 K
mnee@antioch.edu

NEEB, Jennifer, K ... 610-799-1120 ... 434 D
jneeb@lccc.edu

NEEDHAM, Frankie ... 828-898-8763 ... 366 A
needham@lmc.edu

NEEDHAM, James ... 361-825-2778 ... 497 F
james.needham@tamucc.edu

NEEDHAM, Jodie ... 312-427-2737 ... 154 F
6needham@jmls.edu

NEEDHAM, Michele ... 630-466-7900 ... 167 G
mneedham@waubonsee.edu

NEEFE, Diane ... 608-785-9539 ... 555 D
neefed@westerntc.edu

NEEL, Ellen ... 623-845-3371 ... 15 J
e.neel@gcmail.maricopa.edu

NEEL, Tom, H ... 617-348-6558 ... 246 A
neel@urbancollege.edu

NEELEY, Megan ... 423-323-0201 ... 475 E
mneeley@northeaststate.edu

NEELY, Dail ... 940-397-6273 ... 491 A
dail.neely@mwsu.edu

NEELY, Erin ... 740-695-9500 ... 384 J
eneely@btc.edu

NEELY, Jennifer ... 615-248-1237 ... 476 E
jneely@trevecca.edu

NEELY, Kate ... 662-476-5043 ... 274 D
kneely@eastms.edu

NEELY, Monty, K ... 503-838-8271 ... 419 C
neelyk@wou.edu

NEELY, Nicole ... 814-827-4430 ... 449 E
mailliar@pitt.edu

NEELY, Patricia ... 415-494-8240 ... 1 E
pneely@aju.edu

NEELY, Renee ... 575-562-2314 ... 318 A
renee.neely@enmu.edu

NEELY, Robert ... 940-898-3301 ... 502 B
rneely@twu.edu

NEENAN, Benedict, T ... 660-944-2859 ... 280 F
benedict@conception.edu

NEENAN, SJ, William, B ... 617-552-1650 ... 232 D
william.neenan.1@bc.edu

NEESAM, Jaci, E ... 415-422-6762 ... 76 B
neesam@usfca.edu

NEESE, John, M ... 325-670-1273 ... 487 D
jneese@hsutx.edu

NEESE, Susan ... 253-680-7025 ... 531 A
sneese@bates.ctc.edu

NEESMITH, Debra ... 704-216-3640 ... 373 C
debra.neesmith@rccc.edu

NEEVE, Tasia, S ... 415-442-7833 ... 48 E
tneeve@ggu.edu

NEEVEL, Ken ... 616-392-8555 ... 260 G
ken@westernsem.edu

NEF, Dennis, L ... 559-278-4468 ... 34 D
dennisn@csufresno.edu

NEFF, Ann, M ... 620-431-2820 ... 195 B
aneff@neosho.edu

NEFF, Jon ... 319-398-7195 ... 186 H
jneff@kirkwood.edu

NEFF, Kathryn ... 573-518-2378 ... 286 B
kneff@mineralarea.edu

NEFF, Laura, A ... 740-587-6271 ... 389 H
neffl@denison.edu

NEFF, Scott ... 740-774-6300 ... 389 C
sneff@daymarcollege.edu

NEFF, Sherri, A ... 913-288-7201 ... 193 J
sneff@kckcc.edu

NEGASH, Worku ... 408-855-5232 ... 78 A
worku.negash@edu.com

NEGBENEBOR, Anthony, I ... 704-406-4622 ... 364 B
anegbenebor@gardner-webb.edu

NEGIP, Marilyn ... 617-243-2242 ... 236 F
mnegip@lasell.edu

NEGLIA, Frank, A ... 973-290-4344 ... 309 A
fneglia@cse.edu

NEGLIA, Michael, S ... 904-620-2923 ... 120 C
mneglia@unf.edu

NEGRETE, Rena ... 714-992-7077 ... 59 D
rnegrete@fullcoll.edu

NEGRON, Elizabeth ... 787-757-1520 ... 566 H

NEGRON, Gisela ... 787-257-7373 ... 565 E
gnegron@suagm.edu

NEGRON, Lillian ... 787-786-3030 ... 560 E
lnegron@ucb.edu.pr

NEGRON, Luz ... 787-743-4041 ... 561 E
lznegron@columbiaco.edu

NEGRON, Olga ... 787-832-6000 ... 562 E
mortiz@icprjc.edu

NEGRON, Pablo, E ... 518-629-7154 ... 336 C
p.negron@hvcc.edu

NEGRON, Rebecca, M ... 517-750-1200 ... 258 F
rnegron@arbor.edu

NEGRON-PORTILLO, Luis, M ... 787-751-1912 ... 564 A
lmnegron@inter.edu

NEHER, Kenneth, R ... 618-650-2536 ... 165 A
kneher@siue.edu

NEHER, William ... 317-940-9815 ... 170 C
neher@butler.edu

NEHLS, Wally ... 574-807-7632 ... 169 F
nehlsw@bethelcollege.edu

NEHRBAS, Mark, H ... 740-284-5870 ... 390 M
mnehrbas@franciscan.edu

NEHRING, Matthew, S ... 719-587-7504 ... 80 F
msnehrin@adams.edu

NEHRING, Wendy, M ... 423-439-7051 ... 473 E
nehringw@etsu.edu

NEICE, Joan ... 602-978-7254 ... 18 K
joan.neice@thunderbird.edu

NEIDECK, Robert ... 765-998-5222 ... 179 F
rbneideck@taylor.edu

NEIDERBACH, Michael, A ... 607-871-2329 ... 322 F
neiderbach@alfred.edu

NEIDORF, David ... 760-872-2000 ... 43 H
dneidorf@deepsprings.edu

NEIDY, Jon ... 309-677-2374 ... 145 H
neidy@bradley.edu

NEIFERT, Roger ... 316-322-3144 ... 191 D
rneifert@butlercc.edu

NEIGHBOR, Edward ... 407-823-5269 ... 120 A
james.neighbor@ucf.edu

NEIGHBORS, Ira ... 504-284-5484 ... 214 I
ineighbo@suno.edu

NEIGHBORS, Janie ... 940-668-7333 ... 491 C
jneighbors@nctc.edu

NEIGLER, Peter ... 904-731-4949 ... 105 H
pneigler@cci.edu

NEIHEISEL, Steve ... 208-885-5690 ... 144 B
steven@uidaho.edu

NEIHOF, JR., John, E ... 606-693-5000 ... 203 C
jneihof@kmbc.edu

NEIKIRK, Mark ... 859-572-1449 ... 205 E
neikirkm1@nku.edu

NEIL, Amy ... 631-244-3207 ... 332 D
neila@dowling.edu

NEIL, Jon ... 518-580-5490 ... 351 B
jneil@skidmore.edu

NEIL, Linda ... 773-481-8408 ... 147 F
lneil@ccc.edu

NEIL, Stephanie ... 206-876-6100 ... 537 E
sneil@theseattleschool.edu

NEILL, Christine ... 602-243-8185 ... 16 E
christine.neill@smcmail.maricopa.edu

NEILL, Sarah ... 617-521-2124 ... 245 A
sarah.neill@simmons.edu

NEILSEN, Ardis ... 805-922-6966 ... 26 K
aneilsen@hancockcollege.edu

NEILSON, Leanne ... 805-493-3145 ... 32 H
neilson@clunet.edu

NEILSON, Richard, P ... 516-671-2215 ... 360 A
rneilson@webb-institute.edu

NEIMAN, Gershon ... 845-731-3700 ... 361 K

NEIMEYER, Nicole ... 419-227-3141 ... 404 D
nniemeye@unoh.edu

NEIN, Daniel, F ... 207-786-6207 ... 217 C
dnein@bates.edu

NEINER, Catherine ... 404-471-6425 ... 123 G
cneiner@agnesscott.edu

NEISEL, Bridgette ... 330-490-7337 ... 405 E
bneisel@walsh.edu

NEISES, Marlene ... 414-382-6017 ... 545 H
marlene.neises@alverno.edu

NEITZ, Stephen ... 717-815-1924 ... 452 F
sneitz@ycp.edu

NEITZEL, Alan ... 405-736-0315 ... 411 I
aneitzel@rose.edu

NEJAD, Hassan ... 201-684-7406 ... 313 D
hnejad@ramapo.edu

NEJMAN, Michael ... 847-925-6175 ... 151 E
mnejman@harpercollege.edu

NELANT, Dan ... 304-326-1522 ... 541 G
dnelant@salemu.edu

NELKENBAUM, Avrohom Yaakov ... 718-645-0536 ... 341 D

NELLENBACK, Marie, A ... 315-255-1743 ... 325 H
marie.nellenback@cayuga-cc.edu

NELLER, Irene ... 562-903-4727 ... 30 H
irene.neller@biola.edu

NELLESEN, Gary ... 909-594-5611 ... 58 A
gnellese@mtsac.edu

NELLIGAN, Julie ... 630-829-6077 ... 145 D
jnelligan@ben.edu

NELLIS, M. Duane ... 208-885-6365 ... 144 B
dnellis@uidaho.edu

NELLIS, Virginia ... 802-258-9233 ... 513 F
gnellis@marlboro.edu

NELMS, Chad ... 864-231-2025 ... 455 C
cnelms@andersonuniversity.edu

NELMS, Charlie ... 919-530-6104 ... 378 A
cnelms@nccu.edu

NELMS, Jim, A ... 936-261-1932 ... 496 E
janelms@pvamu.edu

NESTOR, Sally 970-542-3151 86 A
sally.nestor@morgancc.edu
NETHERTON, James, S 478-301-2710 133 F
netherton_js@mercer.edu
NETTELL, Katie 701-662-1517 382 D
katie.nettell@lrsc.edu
NETTLES, Evelyn 615-963-7004 474 A
enettles1@tnstate.edu
NETTLES, Ronald, E 601-643-8300 274 A
ronnie.nettles@colin.edu
NETTLETON, Patricia, A 859-371-9393 198 D
panettleton@beckfield.edu
NETTLETON, Peter 859-371-9393 198 D
pnettleton@beckfield.edu
NETZHAMMER, Emile 603-358-2105 307 A
mnetzhammer@keene.edu
NEU, Frances 727-341-3319 116 F
neu.frances@spcollege.edu
NEUBAUER, Kirk 563-387-1434 187 A
neubauki@luther.edu
NEUBAUER, Lane, B 215-951-5157 432 G
neubauer@lasalle.edu
NEUBAUER, Sarah Jo 925-609-6650 38 B
sneubauer@carrington.edu
NEUBAUER, Trish 563-387-1567 187 A
neubautr@luther.edu
NEUBERGER, Boruch 410-484-7200 225 C
NEUBERGER, Paul, M 920-923-7613 548 C
NEUBERGER, Sheftel, M 410-484-7200 225 C
NEUDIGATE, Marcia 859-341-5627 199 B
mneudigate@brownmackie.edu
NEUENDORF, Karen 734-995-7439 250 B
neuenke@cuaa.edu
NEUERBURG, Kent 985-549-2135 216 C
kent.neuerburg@selu.edu
NEUFELD, Amy 913-621-8772 192 C
aneufeld@donnelly.edu
NEUFELD, Don 626-812-3020 30 E
dneufeld@apu.edu
NEUFELD, Iris 419-358-3322 385 B
neufeldi@bluffton.edu
NEUFELD, Jane, F 773-508-3852 157 A
jneufe@luc.edu
NEUFELD, Kenley 805-965-0581 68 B
neufeld@sbcc.edu
NEUFELDT, Ellen 757-683-3442 521 L
eneufeld@odu.edu
NEUFVILLE, Janette 301-576-0123 229 B
jneufvil@wau.edu
NEUFVILLE, Mortimer, H 410-651-6101 227 E
mhneufville@umes.edu
NEUHARD, Ian 772-462-7898 110 L
ineuhard@irsc.edu
NEUHARDT, Erin 978-232-2109 234 F
eneuhard@endicott.edu
NEUHAUSER, John, J 802-654-2212 514 B
jneuhauser@smcvt.edu
NEUHOF, Jennifer 718-817-3727 334 C
neuhof@fordham.edu
NEUHOFF, Martin, C 260-422-5561 172 L
mcneuhoff@indianatech.edu
NEULS, Daniel 281-476-1501 493 E
daniel.neuls@sjcd.edu
NEUMAN, Dawn 805-437-8441 33 I
dawn.neuman@csuci.edu
NEUMAN, Paul 928-317-7659 12 C
paul.neuman@azwestern.edu
NEUMAN, Yisroel 732-367-1060 307 H
NEUMANN, Edith, F 619-477-6310 73 A
eneumann@usuniveristy.edu
NEUMANN, Gregory 716-645-3131 351 G
buffalo@bkstr.com
NEUMANN, Jessica 785-670-1727 197 D
jessica.neumann1@washburn.edu
NEUMANN, Kathleen 309-298-1066 168 A
k-neumann@wiu.edu
NEUMANN, Pamela, R 716-839-8325 331 G
pneumann@daemen.edu
NEUMANN, Yoram 619-477-6310 73 A
yneumann@usuniversity.edu
NEUMAYR, Mark 928-523-6517 17 A
mark.neumayr@nau.edu
NEUN, Stephen 603-283-2150 303 F
sneun@antiochne.edu
NEUNER, Jerome, L 716-888-2120 325 G
neuner@canisius.edu
NEUPAUER, Nicholas, C 724-287-8711 423 F
nicholas.neupauer@bc3.edu
NEUTENS, James, J 865-305-9290 477 C
jneutens@mc.utmck.edu
NEVAREZ, Anel 714-300-0300 70 I
anevarez@scitech.edu
NEVAREZ, Gerard 575-646-3635 319 D
gerardn@nmsu.edu
NEVE, Nancy 906-635-2080 254 C
nneve@lssu.edu
NEVEAU, Judy 310-434-4303 68 D
neveau_judy@smc.edu
NEVELS, Andrea 773-244-5565 159 G
anevels@northpark.edu
NEVELS, JR., Harry, V 434-848-1825 523 G
hnevels@saintpauls.edu
NEVEU, Debra 504-816-4546 208 I
dneveu@dillard.edu
NEVILLE, David 858-642-8163 58 I
dneville@nu.edu
NEVILLE, Nancy 216-421-7427 387 H
nneville@cia.edu
NEVILLS, Landee 417-328-1826 290 E
lnevills@sbuniv.edu
NEVIN, Amy 518-631-9844 358 F
nevina@uniongraduatecollege.edu
NEVINS, Daniel 212-678-8067 337 G
danevins@jtsa.edu
NEVINS, Jeff 918-595-7895 412 H
jnevins@tulsacc.edu
NEVINS, Katherine, J 651-638-6292 261 I
nevkat@bethel.edu
NEVOIS, Dana, A 636-797-3000 283 H
dnevois@jeffco.edu
NEW, Dustin 864-379-8725 457 G
new@erskine.edu
NEW, Lynn 903-923-2093 486 D
lnew@etbu.edu
NEW, Michael, J 802-654-2635 514 B
mnew@smcvt.edu
NEW, William, G 409-772-6015 507 B
wgnew@utmb.edu
NEWBANKS, Rex 740-826-8155 396 I
rexn@muskingum.edu
NEWBERG, Bella 760-750-4444 36 B
newberg@csusm.edu
NEWBERN, Judson 615-322-2715 477 F
judson.newbern@vanderbilt.edu
NEWBERRY, Anthony 502-213-2121 202 B
tony.newberry@kctcs.edu
NEWBERRY, Beth 502-585-9911 205 I
bnewberry@spalding.edu
NEWBERRY, Elesha 901-272-5139 471 B
registrar@mca.edu
NEWBERRY, Elizabeth 651-450-3654 266 I
enewber@inverhills.edu
NEWBERRY, Leanna, J 620-421-6700 194 E
leannan@labette.edu
NEWBERRY, Robert 575-624-7180 318 B
robert.newberry@roswell.enmu.edu
NEWBOLD, Pamela 330-823-6572 404 C
newbolph@mountunion.edu
NEWBORN, Janis 256-726-7460 6 C
jnewborn@oakwood.edu
NEWBURN, Rita 501-244-5125 19 F
rita.newburn@arkansasbaptist.edu
NEWBY, Belita 256-726-8245 6 C
bfleming@oakwood.edu
NEWBY, Greg 907-450-8663 10 J
gbnewby@alaska.edu
NEWBY, Gretchen 314-275-3548 161 D
gretchen.newby@principia.edu
NEWBY, Matt 952-446-4312 263 E
newbym@crown.edu
NEWBY, Stephen, M 206-281-2938 537 D
newbys@spu.edu
NEWBY, Teresa 952-446-4484 263 E
newbyt@crown.edu
NEWBY, Vanessa 708-534-4551 151 C
vnewby@govst.edu
NEWCOMB, Ron 770-975-4000 126 H
NEWCOMB, Sherri 718-631-6381 329 A
snewcomb@qcc.cuny.edu
NEWCOMB, Terry 315-364-3370 360 C
tnewcomb@wells.edu
NEWCOMBE, David, A 540-365-4463 518 J
dnewcombe@ferrum.edu
NEWCOMBE, Rodd 321-674-7110 108 E
newcombe@fit.edu
NEWCOME, Beth 304-367-4298 542 I
Beth.Newcome@pierpont.edu
NEWCOMER, Jan, A 501-450-3130 25 H
jann@uca.edu
NEWELL, Alton, E 724-503-1001 451 A
anewell@washjeff.edu
NEWELL, Bridget 801-832-2822 512 F
bnewell@westminstercollege.edu
NEWELL, Cindy 785-826-2638 194 C
cnewell@salina.k-state.edu
NEWELL, Diane 251-380-9090 3 H
dnewell@faulkner.edu
NEWELL, Glen, C 336-334-7731 377 F
gcnewell@ncat.edu
NEWELL, James 856-256-4012 314 A
newell@rowan.edu
NEWELL, James 718-270-2488 352 D
james.newell@downstate.edu
NEWELL, Jennifer, M 585-343-0055 334 F
jmnewell@genesee.du
NEWELL, JR., John, H 843-953-7154 457 B
newellj@cofc.edu
NEWELL, Keith 912-260-4377 136 F
keith.newell@sgc.edu
NEWELL, Patricia 239-489-9027 104 L
NEWELL, Peggy 617-636-3536 245 F
peggy.newell@tufts.edu
NEWELL, Peggy 617-627-6550 245 F
peggy.newell@tufts.edu
NEWELL, Rand, E 207-948-3131 219 H
rnewell@unity.edu
NEWELL, Tamara, J 405-425-5475 409 E
tammy.newell@oc.edu
NEWGARD, Debra 651-905-3400 261 J
NEWGARD, Debra 612-977-5414 262 A
debra.newgard@capella.edu
NEWGENT, Matt 405-262-2552 411 G
newgentm@redlandscc.edu
NEWHALL, JR., Edward 401-454-6307 454 B
enewhall@risd.edu
NEWHOFF, Marilyn 619-594-6516 36 E
mnewhoff@mail.sdsu.edu
NEWHOUSE, Dollie, J 843-661-1677 458 C
dnewhouse@fmarion.edu
NEWHOUSE, Gary 847-635-1640 160 E
garyn@oakton.edu
NEWHOUSE, Greg 619-388-7673 65 H
gnewhous@sdccd.edu
NEWHOUSE, Greg 619-388-7673 65 H
gnewhouse@sdccd.edu
NEWHOUSE, Roger 419-995-8139 392 L
newhouse.r@rhodesstate.edu
NEWHOUSE, Valerie, K 712-362-0434 185 G
vnewhouse@iowalakes.edu
NEWINS, Anne 209-384-6185 57 C
newins.a@mccd.edu
NEWITZ, Laurie, H 718-780-7503 324 F
laurie.newitz@brooklaw.edu
NEWKIRK, Charlene 412-469-6300 425 H
cnewkirk@ccac.edu
NEWKIRK, Vann 478-827-7594 129 C
newkirkv@fvsu.edu
NEWKIRK, Vann 256-372-5104 1 A
vann.newkirk@aamu.edu
NEWKIRK, William 401-454-6283 454 B
bnewkirk@risd.edu
NEWKOFSKY, Stephen 315-268-6467 329 C
steve.newkofsky@clarkson.edu
NEWKOME, George, R 330-972-6458 403 B
newkome@uakron.edu
NEWLAND, Jamesetta 212-346-1600 345 F
jnewland@pace.edu
NEWLIN, Toni 765-998-5211 179 F
tnnewlin@taylor.edu
NEWMAN, Allison 518-276-6359 347 D
newmaa3@rpi.edu
NEWMAN, Andy 308-635-6026 301 E
newmana@wncc.edu
NEWMAN, Barry 212-242-2255 358 A
barry.newman@tsca.edu
NEWMAN, Beth 513-732-5218 403 E
jenny.newman@uc.edu
NEWMAN, Bryan 714-378-1878 19 C
bryan.newman@phoenix.edu
NEWMAN, Carolyn 631-656-3191 334 B
cnewman@ftc.edu
NEWMAN, Carrie 814-824-3311 436 C
cnewman@mercyhurst.edu
NEWMAN, David, E 607-274-3177 336 G
dnewman@ithaca.edu
NEWMAN, Denise 269-965-3931 253 H
newmand@kellogg.edu
NEWMAN, Denise 989-328-1245 256 A
denisen@montcalm.edu
NEWMAN, Elizabeth 781-239-4538 230 G
enewman1@babson.edu
NEWMAN, Ethel 321-433-7060 101 J
newmane@brevardcc.edu
NEWMAN, Gail 925-439-2181 43 D
gnewman@losmedanos.edu
NEWMAN, Geoffrey, W 973-655-5104 311 G
newmang@mail.montclair.edu
NEWMAN, J. Bonnie 603-271-2739 304 B
jbnewman@ccsnh.edu
NEWMAN, James 201-216-8722 315 E
jnewman@stevens.edu
NEWMAN, Janet 715-422-5476 554 C
janet.newman@mstc.edu
NEWMAN, Janis, J 713-313-1183 499 G
newmanjj@tsu.edu
NEWMAN, Jeanine 337-491-2030 212 C
jeanine.newman@sowela.edu
NEWMAN, Kathleen 410-516-4065 223 F
knewman@jhu.edu
NEWMAN, Kay, S 334-387-3877 1 D
kaynewman@amridgeuniversity.edu
NEWMAN, Keith 765-677-2105 174 E
keith.newman@indwes.edu
NEWMAN, Kevin 907-822-3201 10 C
knewman@akbible.edu
NEWMAN, Larry, M 609-896-5152 313 G
newman@rider.edu
NEWMAN, Linda, L 734-764-7401 259 D
newmanll@umich.edu
NEWMAN, Lori, L 563-884-5408 188 C
lori.newman@palmer.edu
NEWMAN, Marc, A 919-516-4092 376 B
manewman@st-aug.edu
NEWMAN, Melissa 606-546-1226 206 F
melissa.newman@unionky.edu
NEWMAN, Michael 212-463-0400 357 J
michael.newman@touro.edu
NEWMAN, Michelle 901-333-4217 475 H
mnewman@southwest.tn.edu
NEWMAN, Nancy, J 402-465-2375 299 J
njn@nebrwesleyan.edu
NEWMAN, Norm 260-480-4202 176 D
nnewman@ivytech.edu
NEWMAN, Rebecca 303-753-6046 87 F
rnewman@rmcad.edu
NEWMAN, Richard 321-674-7999 108 E
jrnewman@fit.edu
NEWMAN, Robert, D 801-581-8816 510 L
robert.newman@hum.utah.edu
NEWMAN, Russ 858-635-4535 27 A
rnewman@alliant.edu
NEWMAN, Russ 858-635-4535 27 E
rnewman@alliant.edu
NEWMAN, Sandra 713-973-3028 486 A
snewman@devry.edu
NEWMAN, Scott 918-293-4666 410 E
scott.newman@okstate.edu
NEWMAN, Vaughn 405-273-5331 408 B
vnewman@familyoffaithcollege.edu
NEWMEN, Patricia, N 207-859-4460 217 G
pnnewmen@colby.edu
NEWNHAM, David 916-484-8433 56 A
newnhad@arc.losrios.edu
NEWSCHWANDER, Gregg 334-844-5662 1 G
gen0002@auburn.edu
NEWSCHWANDER, Gregg 334-244-3658 2 A
gnewschw@aum.edu
NEWSOM, Debbie 859-622-5012 200 D
debbie.newsom@eku.edu
NEWSOM, M. Nadine 765-459-0561 176 A
mnewson@ivytech.edu
NEWSOM, Stephanie, R 319-352-8539 189 F
stephanie.newsom@wartburg.edu
NEWSOM, Thomas, W 214-692-8080 480 I
tnewsom@aii.edu
NEWSOME, Chevelle 916-278-6470 35 E
cnewsome@csus.edu
NEWSOME, Gary 815-939-5120 160 F
gnewsome@olivet.edu
NEWSOME, John, T 601-984-1738 277 H
jtnewsome@umc.edu
NEWSOME, Mark 336-506-4121 367 G
mark.newsome@alamancecc.edu
NEWSOME, Moses 718-270-5024 328 D
mnewsome@mec.cuny.edu
NEWSOME, Pam 612-874-3798 265 E
pam_newsome-prochniak@mcad.edu
NEWSOME, Sarah 850-973-9675 113 J
newsomes@nfcc.edu
NEWSON-HORST, Adele 443-885-3509 224 F
adele.newsonhorst@morgan.edu
NEWTON, Andrea 541-463-5315 416 D
newtona@lanecc.edu
NEWTON, Andrew 706-721-4018 130 B
anewton@georgiahealth.edu
NEWTON, Ann 808-544-0265 140 B
anewton@hpu.edu
NEWTON, Billy 505-566-3775 320 D
newtonb@sanjuancollege.edu
NEWTON, Carolyn 330-263-2004 388 E
cnewton@wooster.edu
NEWTON, Diane, D 501-450-3184 25 H
dnewton@uca.edu
NEWTON, Dorian 510-430-2262 57 D
newton@mills.edu
NEWTON, Dusty 308-865-8702 300 G
newtond@unk.edu
NEWTON, Eric, D 864-242-5100 455 E
NEWTON, Fred 602-387-7000 19 C
fred.newton@apollogrp.edu
NEWTON, H. Joseph 979-845-7361 497 C
jnewton@tamu.edu
NEWTON, Jeff 419-530-4484 404 F
jeff.newton2@utoledo.edu
NEWTON, Jeffrey, L 617-253-3952 242 A
jeffreynewton@mit.edu
NEWTON, John 630-617-3020 150 F
newtonj@elmhurst.edu
NEWTON, Joseph, A 229-333-5974 138 F
jnewton@valdosta.edu
NEWTON, Kristi, L 626-395-6215 32 E
knewton@caltech.edu
NEWTON, LaCresha 501-370-4001 19 F
lacresha.newton@arkansasbaptist.edu
NEWTON, Lynette 402-826-8688 298 A
lynette.newton@doane.edu
NEWTON, Mallory 580-477-7701 414 C
mallory.newton@wosc.edu
NEWTON, Martin 205-726-2131 6 G
cnewton@samford.edu
NEWTON, Michael 559-438-4222 49 G
michael_newton@heald.edu
NEWTON, Michael, L 270-384-8099 203 H
newtonm@lindsey.edu
NEWTON, Nell, J 574-631-6789 180 D
nell.newton@nd.edu
NEWTON, Sandra 252-492-2061 374 D
newton@vgcc.edu
NEWTON, Steven, D 517-750-1200 258 F
snewton@arbor.edu
NEWTON, Traci 910-892-3178 364 F
tnewton@heritagebiblecollege.edu
NEWTON, Verne 845-575-3000 340 C
verne.newton@marist.edu

NIELSON, Brittany .... 719-235-4026...... 19 C
Brittany.Nielson@phoenix.edu
NIELSON, Jay .... 307-855-2105.... 555 G
jnielson@cwc.edu
NIELSON, Joel .... 330-672-3120.... 393 D
jnielson@kent.edu
NIELSON, Marian, J .... 315-733-2300.... 359 A
mnielson@uscny.edu
NIELSON, Niel, B .... 706-419-1117.... 127 F
nielson@covenant.edu
NIELSON, P. Douglas .... 808-675-3510.... 139 I
nielsond@byuh.edu
NIELSON, Robert .... 218-726-8168.... 272 B
rnielson@d.umn.edu
NIELSON, Robert .... 435-283-7037.... 512 B
rob.nielson@snow.edu
NIEMAN, Charles, L .... 412-624-7123.... 449 A
cnieman@pitt.edu
NIEMAN, Donald .... 607-777-2144.... 351 F
dnieman@binghamton.edu
NIEMAN, James .... 860-509-9516...... 92 D
NIEMAN, James .... 860-509-9516...... 92 D
jnieman@hartsem.edu
NIEMAN, Kenneth, F .... 765-641-4182.... 169 A
kfnieman@anderson.edu
NIEMAN, Larry .... 312-935-6231.... 162 E
lnieman@robertmorris.edu
NIEMAN, Paul .... 818-710-4121...... 55 B
niemanp@piercecollege.edu
NIEMANN, Trish .... 480-732-7030...... 15 G
trish.niemann@cgcmail.maricopa.edu
NIEMEYER, Donna, A .... 402-844-7351.... 300 A
donna@northeast.edu
NIEMI, JR., Albert, W .... 214-768-3012.... 494 F
aniemi@cox.smu.edu
NIEMI, Becky .... 970-675-3219...... 82 D
rebecca.niemi@cncc.edu
NIEMI, Jayne, L .... 651-696-6200.... 265 A
niemi@macalester.edu
NIEMIEC, Catherine .... 602-274-1885...... 17 F
cniemiec@pihma.edu
NIEMIEC, Mary, P .... 312-355-0423.... 166 F
mniemiec@uic.edu
NIENABER, Mary Kay .... 218-733-7626.... 267 B
m.nienaber@lsc.edu
NIENABER, Steve .... 859-572-1366.... 205 E
nienabers1@nku.edu
NIENART, Marilyn .... 607-431-4104.... 335 B
nienartm@hartwick.edu
NIENHUIS, Nancy, E .... 617-964-1100.... 230 B
nnienhuis@ants.edu
NIENSTEDT, Barbara .... 856-415-2173.... 310 E
bnienstedt@gccnj.edu
NIERENBERG, Susan .... 716-829-8777.... 332 F
nierenbs@dyc.edu
NIES, Charles .... 209-228-7620...... 74 B
CNies@UCMerced.edu
NIESE, Vicki, J .... 419-772-2057.... 398 G
v-niese@onu.edu
NIESKES, Ed .... 715-232-1285.... 552 C
nieskese@uwstout.edu
NIESKES, Edward .... 715-232-1683.... 552 C
nieskese@uwstout.edu
NIETO, Erma, M .... 940-898-3270.... 502 B
enieto@twu.edu
NIETO, Hollis, B .... 323-259-2598...... 59 H
hnieto@oxy.edu
NIETO, Linda, A .... 402-552-3039.... 297 D
nieto@clarksoncollege.edu
NIEUWEBOER, Mariyn .... 603-577-6511.... 304 J
nieuweboer@dwc.edu
NIEUWSMA, Randal, G .... 616-526-6334.... 249 E
nieuwr@calvin.edu
NIEVES, Alfredo .... 787-766-1717.... 565 G
alnieves@suagm.edu
NIEVES, Beatriz .... 787-766-1717.... 565 G
um_bnieves@suagm.edu
NIEVES, Danily .... 787-882-2065.... 565 I
NIEVES, Drusila, F .... 845-675-4564.... 344 G
drusila.nieves@nyack.edu
NIEVES, Gladys, T .... 787-765-3560.... 561 J
gnieves@edpcollege.edu
NIEVES, Ivette .... 787-279-1912.... 563 B
inieves@bayamon.inter.edu
NIEVES, Lamberto, C .... 201-761-6085.... 314 F
lnieves@spc.edu
NIEVES, Lourdes .... 305-821-3333.... 109 A
lourdes@mm.fnc.edu
NIEVES, Lourdes .... 305-821-3333.... 109 B
lourdes@mm.fnc.edu
NIEVES, Lourdes .... 305-821-3333.... 109 C
lourdes@mm.fnc.edu
NIEVES, Lourdes, M .... 787-765-1915.... 564 B
lmnieves@inter.edu
NIEVES, Mayra .... 212-237-8624.... 328 A
mnieves@jjay.cuny.edu
NIEVES, Nancy .... 787-265-3858.... 567 C
nnieves@uprm.edu
NIEVES, Ricardo .... 787-780-0070.... 560 F
rnieves@caribbean.edu
NIEVES, Wilfredo .... 860-906-5101...... 89 L
wnieves@ccc.commnet.edu
NIEVES VAZQUEZ, Gladys 787-765-3560.... 561 K
nievglad@edpcollege.edu

NIEWENHOUS, Susan .... 208-792-2395.... 143 F
sniewenh@lcsc.edu
NIEWOONDER, Patricia .... 269-488-4434.... 253 G
pniewoonder@kvcc.edu
NIGGLI, Susan .... 585-275-7761.... 358 I
sniggli@admin.rochester.edu
NIGH, Theresa .... 317-738-8090.... 171 C
tnigh@franklincollege.edu
NIGHTINGALE, Charles .... 443-518-4615.... 223 D
cnightingale@howardcc.edu
NIGHTINGALE, Lisa .... 972-860-8051.... 484 G
lnightingale@dcccd.edu
NIGRO, Georgia, N .... 207-786-6202.... 217 C
gnigro@bates.edu
NIGRO, Mary .... 516-299-3605.... 339 A
mary.nigro@liu.edu
NIGRO, Nick .... 419-473-2700.... 389 B
nnigro@daviscollege.edu
NIGRO, Richard, A .... 215-951-1360.... 432 G
nigro@lasalle.edu
NIGRO, Stephen, M .... 413-542-2101.... 230 A
smnigro@amherst.edu
NIGUIDULA, Amanda .... 305-348-3532.... 119 B
amanda.niguidula@fiu.edu
NIKIAS, C.L, M .... 213-740-2111...... 76 C
uscpresident@usc.edu
NIKOLAKIS, Michael .... 251-580-2121...... 5 A
mnikolakis@faulknerstate.edu
NILA, Ed .... 818-386-5605...... 62 F
enila@pgi.edu
NILAND, Eileen, A .... 716-888-2620.... 325 G
nilande@canisius.edu
NILAND, Joe .... 251-442-2288...... 9 B
jnmobile@hotmail.com
NILE, Lauren, N .... 818-677-2077...... 35 D
lauren.nile@csun.edu
NILES, Mark .... 206-296-4000.... 537 F
nilesm@seattleu.edu
NILES, Maryann .... 781-280-3703.... 240 F
nilesm@middlesex.mass.edu
NILES, Stephanie .... 267-502-2798.... 423 B
stephanie.niles@brynathyn.edu
NILGES, John .... 573-897-5000.... 284 D
NILL, Jack .... 417-862-9533.... 282 D
info@globaluniversity.edu
NILSEN, Kenneth .... 201-216-5206.... 315 E
knilsen@stevens.edu
NILSEN, Spencer .... 510-654-2934...... 46 J
snilsen@expression.edu
NILSON, Brent .... 303-530-2100...... 81 E
bnilson@bcmt.org
NILSSON, Martin .... 603-577-6505.... 304 J
nilsson@dwc.edu
NIMMER, Carole, E .... 660-543-4580.... 291 B
cnimmer@ucmo.edu
NIMMER, Raymond .... 713-743-2100.... 503 B
rnimmer@uh.edu
NIMMER-WILLIAMS,
Yolanda, E .... 713-313-6823.... 499 G
nimmerye@tsu.edu
NIMMO, Steven .... 706-776-0113.... 135 D
snimmo@piedmont.edu
NIMOCKS, Mittie .... 608-342-1491.... 551 F
nimocksm@uwplatt.edu
NIMON, Opie .... 312-949-7610.... 152 D
onimon@ico.edu
NIMPS, Roger, L .... 419-995-8369.... 399 B
nimps.1@osu.edu
NIMS, Vince .... 510-848-5232...... 47 I
vnims@fst.edu
NING, Bin .... 734-487-4924.... 250 H
bin.ning@emich.edu
NINOS, Katherine .... 505-471-5756.... 321 A
NIP, Kit .... 319-385-6250.... 186 A
knip@iwc.edu
NIPP, Tim, J .... 731-881-7601.... 477 E
timnipp@utm.edu
NIPPER, G. Edward .... 870-235-4031...... 23 I
genipper@saumag.edu
NIPPER, Susan, H .... 252-451-8221.... 372 B
snipper@nash.cc.nc.us
NIPPERT, Karen, F .... 901-333-4283.... 475 H
knippert@southwest.tn.edu
NIROOMAND, Farhang .... 361-570-4230.... 503 E
niroomandf@uhv.edu
NIROUMAND, Madjid .... 714-432-5940...... 41 B
mniroumand@occ.cccd.edu
NISBET, Jane, A .... 603-862-1948.... 306 E
jan.nisbet@unh.edu
NISBETT, Nancy .... 713-348-6200.... 492 J
nnisbett@rice.edu
NISENBOYM, Svetlana .... 718-261-5800.... 324 D
snisenboym@bramsonort.edu
NISH, Melinda .... 714-432-5015...... 41 B
mnish@occ.cccd.edu
NISH, Nancy .... 573-288-6536.... 281 D
nnish@culver.edu
NISHIDA, Susan .... 808-454-4700.... 141 C
susan@uhwo.hawaii.edu
NISHIDA, Susan, S .... 808-454-4750.... 141 C
susan@uhwo.hawaii.edu
NISHIGUCHI, Earl, K .... 808-245-8274.... 141 H
earln@hawaii.edu

NISHIME, Jeanie .... 310-660-3472...... 45 D
jnishime@elcamino.edu
NISHIMOTO, Ann .... 808-454-4742.... 141 C
ann@uhwo.hawaii.edu
NISHIMOTO, John, H .... 714-449-7409...... 70 G
jnishimoto@scco.edu
NISSEL, Chaim .... 646-685-0115.... 361 I
drnissel@yu.edu
NISSEN, Jill .... 314-367-8700.... 288 I
jnissen@stlcop.edu
NISSEN, John .... 802-387-7145.... 513 E
johnnissen@landmark.edu
NISSLEY, Nick .... 513-569-1601.... 387 F
nick.nissley@cincinnatistate.edu
NISWANDER, Frederick .... 252-328-6975.... 377 C
niswanderf@ecu.edu
NISWONGER, Joseph, R .... 414-410-4504.... 546 D
jrniswonger@stritch.edu
NITECKI, Danuta .... 215-895-2750.... 427 G
dan44@drexel.edu
NITSCH, Wanda .... 760-591-3012.... 122 G
wnitsch@usa.edu
NITTA, Gary .... 808-245-8230.... 141 H
gnitta@hawaii.edu
NIVELE, Joanne .... 303-581-9955.... 320 H
Joanne@acupuncturecollege.edu
NIX, Julie .... 256-782-5815...... 4 L
jnix@jsu.edu
NIX, Preston, L .... 504-282-4455.... 213 H
pnix@nobts.edu
NIX, Rachel .... 870-574-1521...... 24 A
rnix@sautech.edu
NIX, Sheila .... 210-431-2178.... 493 C
snix@stmarytx.edu
NIX, Stephan .... 361-593-2000.... 498 A
stephan.nix@tamuk.edu
NIXON, Andrea .... 507-222-4043.... 262 B
anixon@carleton.edu
NIXON, David .... 414-256-1203.... 549 A
nixond@mtmary.edu
NIXON, David, E .... 734-384-4166.... 255 G
dnixon@monroeccc.edu
NIXON, Gwen .... 314-513-4290.... 289 B
gnixon@stlcc.edu
NIXON, Jude .... 978-542-7267.... 239 B
jnixon@salemstate.edu
NIXON, LeAnne .... 601-477-4008.... 275 B
leanne.nixon@jcjc.edu
NIXON, Monica .... 206-296-6070.... 537 F
mnixon@seattleu.edu
NIXON, Philip .... 256-726-7398...... 6 C
pnixon@oakwood.edu
NIXON, Stanley .... 252-335-0821.... 369 D
snixon@albemarle.edu
NIXON, Susan .... 318-487-7401.... 209 B
nixon@lacollege.edu
NIXON, Terry .... 325-793-4721.... 490 F
tnixon@mcm.edu
NIXON, Timothy, P .... 269-471-3211.... 247 H
tnixon@andrews.edu
NIXON, Tina, S .... 334-833-4410...... 4 E
tnixon@huntingdon.edu
NIXON, Valerie, B .... 607-587-3985.... 355 C
nixonvb@alfredstate.edu
NIXON HUDSON, Linda ... 410-951-3010.... 228 B
lhudson@coppin.edu
NJIE, Valerie .... 412-402-9779.... 422 I
vnjie@mcg-btc.org
NJOGU, Wamucii, E .... 773-442-5700.... 159 H
w-njogu@neiu.edu
NNADI, Eucharia, E .... 702-968-2038.... 303 D
ennadi@roseman.edu
NNAZOR, Reginald .... 937-376-6007.... 386 H
rnnazor@centralstate.edu
NNOROMELE, Patrick, C ... 859-622-2973.... 200 D
patrick.nnoromele@eku.edu
NOACK, Kelly .... 309-794-7477.... 145 B
kellynoack@augustana.edu
NOAH, Tara .... 660-359-3948.... 287 D
tnoah@mail.ncmissouri.edu
NOBILE, Bryan .... 601-643-8468.... 274 A
bryan.nobile@colin.edu
NOBLE, Ann .... 281-649-3304.... 487 F
aanoble@hbu.edu
NOBLE, Barbara .... 314-340-3621.... 282 I
nobleb@hssu.edu
NOBLE, Deborah .... 215-968-8408.... 423 E
nobled@bucks.edu
NOBLE, Doug .... 540-654-1235.... 524 H
dnoble@umw.edu
NOBLE, Eric .... 415-565-4784...... 73 G
noblee@uchastings.edu
NOBLE, Janice .... 925-424-1324...... 39 A
jnoble@laspositascollege.edu
NOBLE, John, H .... 413-597-2311.... 246 G
john.h.noble@williams.edu
NOBLE, Kathleen .... 402-474-5315.... 298 E
knoble@kaplanuniversity.edu
NOBLE, Kathleen, A .... 817-515-5034.... 496 A
kathleen.noble@tccd.edu
NOBLE, Melanie .... 859-858-3511.... 198 B
melanie.noble@asbury.edu
NOBLE, Ronald, J .... 209-667-3177...... 36 C
rnoble@csustan.edu

NOBLE, Seth .... 970-542-3248...... 86 A
seth.noble@morgancc.edu
NOBLE, Shlomo .... 585-473-2810.... 357 C
NOBLE-GOODMAN, Stuart 909-748-8142...... 75 F
stuart_noblegoodman@redlands.edu
NOBLES, Joann .... 478-825-6278.... 129 C
noblesj@fvsu.edu
NOBLES, Rodney .... 262-691-5362.... 555 C
rnobles@wctc.edu
NOBLES, Susan, Q .... 252-493-7287.... 372 E
snobles@email.pittcc.edu
NOBLES, Tammy .... 573-681-5271.... 284 B
noblest@lincolnu.edu
NOBLETT, Jeffrey .... 719-389-6681...... 81 L
jnoblett@coloradocollege.edu
NOBLIN, Patricia .... 973-300-2754.... 315 F
pnoblin@sussex.edu
NOBLITT, Jeff .... 630-466-7900.... 167 G
jnoblitt@waubonsee.edu
NOBLITT, Mariea .... 610-740-3780.... 424 I
kowens@cedarcrest.edu
NOBLITT, William .... 620-341-5454.... 192 D
wnoblitt@emporia.edu
NOBUO, Adora .... 680-488-2471.... 560 A
adoraa@palau.edu
NOCE, Joe .... 215-780-1294.... 446 G
pcobookstore@mattmccoy.com
NOCELLA, Frank .... 973-300-2115.... 315 F
fnocella@sussex.edu
NOCKUNAS, Michael .... 413-572-5468.... 239 C
mnockunas@wsc.ma.edu
NODA, Keisuke .... 845-752-3000.... 358 D
dpknoda@aol.com
NODGE, Andrea .... 734-432-5737.... 254 G
anodge@madonna.edu
NODINE, Chad .... 276-328-0196.... 525 C
jcn5g@uvawise.edu
NODLAND, Rita .... 701-224-5692.... 382 B
rita.nodland@bismarckstate.edu
NODZENSKI, Peter .... 309-796-5374.... 145 E
nodzenskip@bhc.edu
NOE, Bryan, D .... 205-934-8227...... 8 G
bnoe@uab.edu
NOE, Godfrey, F .... 678-891-2568.... 130 G
gnoe@gpc.edu
NOEHRE, Edwin .... 608-258-2401.... 554 B
enoehre@matcmadison.edu
NOEL, Amy .... 910-592-8084.... 373 D
anoel@sampsoncc.edu
NOEL, Bill .... 502-451-0815.... 206 B
bnoel@sullivan.edu
NOEL, Bill .... 502-451-0815.... 206 C
bnoel@sullivan.edu
NOEL, Cheryl, A .... 724-925-4058.... 451 E
noelc@wccc.edu
NOEL, Erin .... 559-453-2000...... 47 K
erin.noel@fresno.edu
NOEL, Henry .... 413-205-3510.... 229 G
henry.noel@aic.edu
NOEL, JR., J. Andrew .... 607-255-7266.... 331 C
athletic_dir@cornell.edu
NOEL, Joanne .... 732-356-1595.... 315 D
jnoel@somerset.edu
NOEL, John, D .... 563-562-3263.... 187 G
noelj@portal.nicc.edu
NOEL, Michael .... 714-620-3712...... 29 D
mnoel@argosy.edu
NOEL, Michelle .... 775-673-7000.... 302 J
mnoel@tmcc.edu
NOEL, Norma .... 575-646-4986.... 319 D
nnoel@nmsu.edu
NOEL, Shawn .... 301-387-3052.... 222 H
shawn.noel@garrettcollege.edu
NOEL, Terry .... 724-532-5095.... 446 E
terry.noel@email.stvincent.edu
NOEL-ELKINS, Amelia .... 309-438-3217.... 153 C
anoelel@ilstu.edu
NOELL, Sarah .... 860-768-4408...... 95 A
snoell@hartford.edu
NOFFSINGER, Lynda, D .... 336-888-6352.... 365 A
lnoffsin@highpoint.edu
NOFRI, Julia, E .... 203-365-4837...... 93 G
nofrij@sacredheart.edu
NOFTSINGER, Mark, P .... 540-375-2283.... 523 D
noftsinger@roanoke.edu
NOFTZGER, Richard, L .... 724-852-3271.... 451 B
noftzger@waynesburg.edu
NOGUCHI, Motohisa .... 773-834-2500.... 165 G
NOHLGREN, Bethany .... 845-758-7099.... 323 F
nohlgren@bard.edu
NOHRE, Kathy .... 320-762-4591.... 265 I
kathyn@alextech.edu
NOHRIA, Nitin .... 617-495-6653.... 235 H
nnohria@hbs.harvard.edu
NOJAN, Mehran .... 315-312-2345.... 354 A
mehran.nojan@oswego.edu
NOLAN, Beth .... 202-994-6503...... 97 F
bnolan@gwu.edu
NOLAN, Brian .... 301-447-5223.... 225 A
nolan@msmary.edu
NOLAN, Cathy, M .... 301-784-5000.... 221 A
cnolan@allegany.edu
NOLAN, Charles, S .... 781-292-2201.... 235 C
charles.nolan@olin.edu

NOTA, Michele .... 401-874-2242 .... 454 E
mnota@advance.uri.edu
NOTARESCHI, Rey, T .... 330-325-6796 .... 397 C
rtn@neoucom.edu
NOTCHICK, Thomas, K ...... 570-348-6241 .... 435 F
notchick@marywood.edu
NOTO, Lisa .... 707-664-3019 ...... 37 B
lisa.noto@sonoma.edu
NOTO, Robert, A .... 517-353-3530 .... 255 D
notor@msu.edu
NOTT, Graham .... 760-630-1555 ...... 52 J
grahamn@kaplan.edu
NOTTKE, Janine .... 906-487-7267 .... 251 C
janine.nottke@finlandia.edu
NOVACK, Van .... 562-985-5462 ...... 35 A
vnovack@csulb.edu
NOVAK, JR., Albert, J .... 412-624-6800 .... 449 A
albert.novak@ia.pitt.edu
NOVAK, Amy .... 605-995-2661 .... 464 B
amnovak@dwu.edu
NOVAK, Brian .... 425-352-8545 .... 531 F
bnovak@cascadia.edu
NOVAK, Bunny .... 507-453-2700 .... 267 F
bnovak@southeastmn.edu
NOVAK, Diane .... 832-813-6544 .... 490 C
diane.novak@lonestar.edu
NOVAK, Elaine .... 815-224-0483 .... 153 D
elaine_novak@ivcc.edu
NOVAK, J. Michael .... 563-884-5626 .... 188 C
michael.novak@palmer.edu
NOVAK, J. Michael .... 563-884-5626 .... 114 E
michael.novak@palmer.edu
NOVAK, J. Michael .... 563-884-5626 ...... 60 L
michael.novak@palmer.edu
NOVAK, James .... 248-683-0504 .... 254 G
jnovak@madonna.edu
NOVAK, Jeffrey .... 570-702-8920 .... 431 K
jnovak@johnson.edu
NOVAK, Jerry .... 734-995-7340 .... 250 B
novakj@cuaa.edu
NOVAK, John .... 219-980-6905 .... 173 F
jmnovak@iun.edu
NOVAK, Mark .... 408-924-2655 ...... 37 A
mnovak@cemail.sjsu.edu
NOVAK, Mike .... 479-248-7236 ...... 21 G
mnovak@ecollege.edu
NOVAK, Peter, J .... 415-422-6251 ...... 76 B
novakp@usfca.edu
NOVAK, Thomas .... 207-893-6636 .... 219 F
tnovak@sjcme.edu
NOVAK, Thomas .... 617-585-1308 .... 243 E
tom.novak@necmusic.edu
NOVAK, Wendy .... 907-277-1000 ...... 10 F
contact@chartercollege.edu
NOVELLO, Ruth .... 979-275-2104 .... 315 B
ruth.novello@shu.edu
NOVISKY, Ronnell .... 330-869-3600 .... 385 F
NOVKOVIC, Meredith .... 973-290-4130 .... 309 A
mbeebe@cse.edu
NOVO, Frank .... 617-964-1111 .... 230 B
fnovo@ants.edu
NOVOBILSKI, Andy .... 870-972-3079 ...... 20 C
anovobilski@astate.edu
NOVOTNY, April .... 614-236-6565 .... 386 C
anovotny@capital.edu
NOVOTNY, Doreen .... 650-949-6210 ...... 47 H
NOVOTNY, Dorene .... 650-949-6210 ...... 47 F
novotnydorene@fhda.edu
NOVOTNY, Frank, J .... 719-587-7622 ...... 80 F
fjnovotn@adams.edu
NOVOTNY, Jodi .... 425-235-2464 .... 536 E
jnovotny@rtc.edu
NOVOTNY, Matthew .... 330-941-3552 .... 406 F
Mmnovotny@ysu.edu
NOVOTNY, Richard, J .... 440-525-7358 .... 394 F
rnovotny@lakelandcc.edu
NOWACZYK, Ronald .... 203-932-7257 ...... 95 B
rnowaczyk@newhaven.edu
NOWACZYK, Ronald .... 814-393-2223 .... 442 A
rnowaczyk@clarion.edu
NOWAK, Bill .... 502-213-2104 .... 202 B
bill.nowak@kctcs.edu
NOWAK, Jack .... 541-880-2224 .... 416 C
nowak@klamathcc.edu
NOWAK, Janice .... 904-470-8192 .... 105 A
janice.nowak@ewc.edu
NOWAK, Karen .... 213-251-3636 ...... 29 H
knowak@aii.edu
NOWAK, Linda, I .... 209-667-3288 ...... 36 C
lnowak@csustan.edu
NOWAK, Meg .... 607-431-4501 .... 335 B
nowakm@hartwick.edu
NOWAK, Susan .... 585-389-2731 .... 342 D
snowak8@naz.edu
NOWAK, Thomas, S .... 845-848-4000 .... 332 C
thomas.nowak@dc.edu
NOWAK, Tom .... 574-936-8898 .... 168 I
tom.nowak@ancilla.edu
NOWAK, Tony, J .... 414-847-3240 .... 548 G
tonynowak@miad.edu
NOWAKOWSKI, Rodney .... 205-934-3036 .... 8 G
rnowakow@uab.edu
NOWEL, OP, Mark, D .... 401-865-2649 .... 453 F
mnowel@providence.edu
NOWELL, Cheryl .... 305-348-2434 .... 119 B
nowell@fiu.edu
NOWELL, Sharon .... 386-481-2073 .... 101 I
pietys@cookman.edu
NOWICKI, Carol .... 510-885-3763 ...... 34 C
carol.nowicki@csueastbay.edu
NOWICKI, Ewa .... 415-869-2900 .... 236 B
ewa.nowicki@hult.edu
NOWICKI, Laura .... 740-593-1969 .... 399 G
nowicki@ohio.edu
NOWICKI, Maria .... 419-251-1583 .... 395 H
maria.nowicki@mercycollege.edu
NOWICKI, Stephen .... 919-668-2728 .... 363 I
snowicki@duke.edu
NOWLAN, Marilyn, L .... 860-727-6782 ...... 92 C
mnowlan@goodwin.edu
NOWLIN, Bill .... 918-456-5511 .... 409 A
nowlin@nsuok.edu
NOWLIN, Brian .... 562-985-5537 ...... 35 A
bnowlin@csulb.edu
NOWLIN, Jane, R .... 405-946-7799 .... 411 E
janen@plattcollege.org
NOWLIN, Steve .... 626-396-2397 ...... 29 G
stephen.nowlin@artcenter.edu
NOWOGORSKI, Barbara .... 570-961-7835 .... 433 A
nowogorskib@lackawanna.edu
NOYA, Christine, A .... 443-352-4477 .... 226 E
cnoya@stevenson.edu
NOYA, Roberto .... 207-778-7050 .... 220 C
roberto.noya@maine.edu
NOYER, Rich .... 206-878-3710 .... 534 E
rnoyer@highline.edu
NOYES, Charlie .... 617-989-4407 .... 246 C
noyesc1@wit.edu
NOYES, Daniel .... 585-567-6260 .... 336 B
daniel.noyes@houghton.edu
NOYES, Doug .... 605-455-6076 .... 464 H
NOYES, Linda .... 516-299-3281 .... 338 F
Linda.Noyes@liu.edu
NOZICA, Thomas .... 304-357-4823 .... 541 H
thomasnozica@ucwv.edu
NRI, Monique, N .... 212-229-5592 .... 342 E
nrim@newschool.edu
NTOKO, Alfred .... 718-262-2804 .... 329 B
NTUEN, Celestine .... 336-334-7995 .... 377 F
ntuen@ncat.edu
NUARA, Frank .... 212-875-4619 .... 323 E
fnuara@bankstreet.edu
NUBEL, Anna .... 402-280-2222 .... 297 H
annanubel@creighton.edu
NUCCI, John, A .... 617-573-8000 .... 245 E
jnucci@suffolk.edu
NUCCI, Lisa .... 813-342-3726 ...... 19 C
lisa.nucci@phoenix.edu
NUCCIO, Beth .... 248-340-0600 .... 248 E
beth.nuccio@baker.edu
NUCKOLS, Jack .... 304-734-6623 .... 542 D
jnuckols@bridgemont.edu
NUCKOLS, Melanie .... 336-734-7332 .... 370 C
mnuckols@forsythtech.edu
NUESELL, Jerry, J .... 919-508-2314 .... 375 D
jnuesell@peace.edu
NUESELL, Lisa .... 919-381-6912 .... 367 D
lnuesell@moc.edu
NUEST, Arlen .... 620-278-4240 .... 196 D
anuest@sterling.edu
NUFER, Ken .... 719-549-2187 ...... 83 B
ken.nufer@colostate-pueblo.edu
NUGEN, Deb .... 402-399-2442 .... 297 E
dnugen@csm.edu
NUGENT, Barli .... 212-799-5000 .... 337 H
NUGENT, Christine, R .... 828-298-3325 .... 380 C
cnugent@warren-wilson.edu
NUGENT, Joe .... 831-479-6140 ...... 31 F
jonugent@cabrillo.edu
NUGENT, John, D .... 860-439-5266 ...... 91 E
john.nugent@connccoll.edu
NUGENT, Kim .... 713-777-4433 .... 508 I
knugent@westwood.edu
NUGENT, Kim .... 713-973-3100 .... 486 A
knugent@devry.edu
NUGENT, S. Georgia .... 740-427-5111 .... 394 C
nugent@kenyon.edu
NULL, David .... 608-265-1988 .... 550 G
dnull@library.wisc.edu
NULL, Greg .... 800-444-1440 .... 444 D
gnull@pia.edu
NULPH, Wendy .... 972-438-6932 .... 492 C
wnulph@parkercc.edu
NUMRICH, Camille .... 401-825-2237 .... 453 B
cnumrich@ccri.edu
NUNAMAKER, Gail .... 989-386-6692 .... 255 F
gnunamaker@midmich.edu
NUNAN, David .... 714-772-3330 ...... 28 I
davidnunan@gmail.com
NUNES, Grafton, J .... 216-421-7410 .... 387 H
gnunes@cia.edu
NUNES, Victoria .... 650-306-3274 ...... 67 E
nunes@smccd.edu
NUNEZ, Antonio .... 505-471-5756 .... 321 A
dean@swc.edu
NUNEZ, Awilda .... 787-257-0000 .... 566 H
awilda.nunez@upr.edu
NUNEZ, Cheryl, L .... 513-745-3539 .... 406 E
nunezc@xavier.edu
NUNEZ, Elaine .... 787-786-3030 .... 560 E
enunez@ucb.edu.pr
NUNEZ, Elsa, M .... 860-465-5221 ...... 91 H
nunez@easternct.edu
NUNEZ, Francisco .... 787-780-5134 .... 564 E
fnunez@nationalcollegepr.edu
NUNEZ, Gabriel .... 305-593-1223 .... 102 D
gnunez@albizu.edu
NUNEZ, Ivon .... 973-596-3478 .... 312 C
nunez@njit.edu
NUNEZ, Jessica .... 830-591-7226 .... 495 B
jnunez@swtjc.cc.tx.us
NUNEZ, Jose .... 650-358-6836 ...... 67 D
nunezj@smccd.edu
NUNEZ, Jose Ramon .... 562-938-4695 ...... 54 E
jnunez@lbcc.edu
NUNEZ, Juan .... 617-287-4818 .... 237 D
juan.nunez@umb.edu
NUNEZ, Lois .... 617-928-4500 .... 243 A
lanunez@mountida.edu
NUNEZ, Michael, W .... 909-593-3511 ...... 75 C
mnunez@laverne.edu
NUNEZ, Rigo .... 503-552-1664 .... 417 D
rnunez@ncnm.edu
NUNEZ, William .... 402-472-2116 .... 300 H
wnunez2@unl.edu
NUNEZ, William, J .... 402-472-2097 .... 300 H
wnunez2@unl.edu
NUNEZ, III, William, J .... 337-550-1201 .... 212 H
NUNEZ, Yancy .... 806-894-9611 .... 494 C
ynunez@southplainscollege.edu
NUNLEY, Beth .... 815-802-8142 .... 154 J
bnunley@kcc.edu
NUNLEY, Ernest, L .... 276-739-2510 .... 528 D
enunley@vhcc.edu
NUNLEY, Gayle, R .... 802-656-8513 .... 514 F
gayle.nunley@uvm.edu
NUNLEY, Jeff .... 813-988-5131 .... 107 I
bookstore@floridacollege.edu
NUNN, Dana .... 970-248-1868 ...... 82 B
dnunn@mesastate.edu
NUNN, Diane, L .... 203-773-4474 ...... 89 H
dlnunn@albertus.edu
NUNN, Helen, S .... 570-372-4450 .... 447 D
nunn@susqu.edu
NUNN, Lori .... 540-674-3615 .... 527 B
lnunn@nr.edu
NUNN, Rod .... 314-539-5302 .... 289 A
rodnunn@stlcc.edu
NUNN GORMAN,
Yolanda, J .... 818-386-5650 ...... 62 F
ynunn@pgi.edu
NUNNA, Ramakrishna .... 559-278-2500 ...... 34 D
rnunna@csufresno.edu
NUNNALLY, Gladys .... 804-524-6714 .... 529 C
nunnally@vsu.edu
NUNNELLEY, William, A ... 205-726-2800 .... 6 G
wanunnel@samford.edu
NUNNELLY, Laura .... 505-473-6270 .... 320 F
laura.nunnelly@santafeuniversity.edu
NUNZIATA, Ray .... 813-620-1446 .... 110 A
NUNZIATA, Raymond .... 813-205-4442 .... 100 F
NURNBERGER, Charles .... 757-825-2717 .... 528 B
nurnbergerc@tncc.edu
NURU-HOLM, Njeri .... 216-687-9335 .... 388 C
n.nuru-holm@csuohio.edu
NUSBAUM, Nancy .... 512-245-2244 .... 501 C
nn01@txstate.edu
NUSENBAUM, Tatiana .... 212-349-4330 .... 334 G
tnusenbaum@globe.edu
NUSSBAUM, Daniel .... 860-231-5770 ...... 93 H
dnussbaum@sjc.edu
NUSSBAUM, Irwin .... 860-768-7904 ...... 95 A
nussbaum@hartford.edu
NUSSBAUM, Renee .... 419-755-4772 .... 397 B
rnussbau@ncstatecollege.edu
NUSSBAUMER, John .... 248-751-7800 .... 259 B
nussbauj@cooley.edu
NUSSEL, Jay .... 260-399-7700 .... 180 E
jnussel@sf.edu
NUTI, Larry .... 925-631-4901 ...... 64 F
lnuti@stmarys-ca.edu
NUTT, Jill, M .... 616-234-4031 .... 251 G
jnutt@grcc.edu
NUTTALL, Neil .... 660-359-3948 .... 287 D
nnuttall@mail.ncmissouri.edu
NUTTER, Cheryl .... 419-251-1519 .... 395 H
cheryl.nutter@mercycollege.edu
NUTTER, Doug .... 301-860-3402 .... 228 A
dnutter@bowiestate.edu
NUTTER, Mark, E .... 740-374-8716 .... 405 F
mnutter@wscc.edu
NUTTER, Susan .... 207-973-1036 .... 218 A
nutters@husson.edu
NUTTER, Susan, K .... 919-515-7188 .... 378 B
susan_nutter@ncsu.edu
NUTTLE, Louise, C .... 423-439-6000 .... 473 E
nuttle@etsu.edu
NUTTY, David .... 207-780-4276 .... 220 G
dnutty@usm.maine.edu
NWAGBARAOCHA,
Joel, O .... 202-419-0400 ...... 99 D
president@strayer.edu
NWAKEZE, Peter .... 718-933-6700 .... 341 G
pnwakeze@monroecollege.edu
NWANKWO, Charles .... 337-491-2442 .... 212 C
charles.nwankwo@sowela.edu
NWANNE, Andrew, I .... 260-422-5561 .... 172 L
ainwanne@indianatech.edu
NWAOHA, Ugo .... 909-941-9410 ...... 62 J
unwaoha@plattcollege.edu
NWARIAKU, Fiemu, E .... 214-648-9968 .... 507 D
fiemu.nwariku@utsouthwestern.edu
NWOKEAFOR, Cosmos .... 301-860-3232 .... 228 A
cnwokeafor@bowiestate.edu
NWOSU, Peter .... 615-963-2515 .... 474 A
pnwosu@tnstate.edu
NYAMAPFENE, Kingston ... 713-313-4275 .... 499 G
nyamapfenek@tsu.edu
NYBERG, Christopher, L .... 315-684-6083 .... 354 F
nybergcl@morrisville.edu
NYBERG, Christopher, L .... 315-684-6056 .... 354 F
nybergcl@morrisville.edu
NYBERG, Connie .... 307-855-2207 .... 555 G
cnyberg@cwc.edu
NYCE, Douglas, J .... 540-432-4206 .... 518 E
douglas.nyce@emu.edu
NYCZ, Mandy .... 920-403-3181 .... 550 C
mandy.nycz@snc.edu
NYE, David, J .... 303-963-3197 ...... 81 K
dnye@ccu.edu
NYE, Fumiko .... 954-783-7339 .... 106 D
fnye@cci.edu
NYE, Jamey .... 916-691-7344 ...... 56 B
nyej@crc.losrios.edu
NYE, Linda, R .... 276-223-4869 .... 528 F
wcnyexl@wcc.vccs.edu
NYE, Valerie .... 505-473-6575 .... 320 F
valerie.nye@santafeuniversity.edu
NYGAARD, Steve .... 415-422-6824 ...... 76 B
ssnygaard@usfca.edu
NYGARD, Gordon, A .... 206-281-2308 .... 537 D
gnygard@spu.edu
NYGREEN, Ted .... 914-606-6789 .... 360 D
ted.nygreen@sunywcc.edu
NYHAMMER, Diane, L .... 815-921-4007 .... 162 F
d.nyhammer@rockvalleycollege.edu
NYHART, Brant .... 602-386-4178 ...... 11 H
brant.nyhart@arizonachristian.edu
NYHUS, Orrin .... 763-433-1346 .... 265 J
orrin.nyhus@anokaramsey.edu
NYIRENDA, Stanley, M .... 410-651-7531 .... 227 E
snyirenda@umes.edu
NYKIEL, Ronald .... 207-941-7111 .... 218 A
nykielr@husson.edu
NYLANDER, Albert .... 662-846-4700 .... 274 B
nylander@deltastate.edu
NYLEN, Judith .... 718-636-3506 .... 346 D
jnylen@pratt.edu
NYMAN, Walter, D .... 570-326-3761 .... 440 K
wnyman@pct.edu
NYPAVER, David .... 330-972-6876 .... 403 B
nypaver@uakron.edu
NYQUIST, J. Paul .... 312-329-4112 .... 158 H
paul.nyquist@moody.edu
NYQUIST, Paul .... 734-207-9581 .... 256 B
pnyquist@mts.edu
NYRE, Joseph, E .... 914-633-2203 .... 336 E
JNyre@iona.edu
NYSSE, Sheila .... 920-686-6275 .... 550 E
Sheila.Nysse@sl.edu
NYSTROM, David .... 562-903-4703 ...... 30 H
david.nystrom@biola.edu
NYUL, Renata .... 617-373-7666 .... 244 A
NZAMUTUMA, Issumael .... 978-368-2399 .... 230 F
issumael.nzamatuma@auc.edu
NZEOGWU, Okeleke .... 702-968-1659 .... 303 D
onzeogwu@roseman.edu
NZINGA-JOHNSON,
Sekile .... 585-389-2747 .... 342 D
snzinga3@na.edu

O

O BRIEN, John, P .... 315-445-4444 .... 338 B
obrienjp@lemoyne.edu
OAKAR, Margaret .... 216-373-5375 .... 397 E
moakar@ndc.edu
OAKES, Brian .... 410-617-2475 .... 224 A
boakes@loyola.edu
OAKES, Edward .... 540-831-7515 .... 522 D
eoakes@radford.edu
OAKES, Janna .... 303-797-5930 ...... 80 J
janna.oakes@arapahoe.edu
OAKES, Mary .... 312-369-6802 .... 148 B
moakes@colum.edu
OAKES, Ronald, L .... 660-263-3900 .... 279 J
president@cccb.edu
OAKLEY, Christina .... 561-912-1211 .... 106 G
coakley@evergladesuniversity.edu
OAKLEY, Danielle .... 608-262-8350 .... 550 G
droakley@uhs.wisc.edu
OAKLEY, Eloy .... 562-938-4122 ...... 54 E
eoakley@lbcc.edu

OKANDA, Fred 731-426-7599 469 M
fokanda@lanecollege.edu
OKAY, Kathleen 973-300-2153 315 F
kokay@sussex.edu
OKEKE, Charles 702-651-7425 302 G
charles.okeke@csn.edu
OKEREKE, Augustine 718-270-4953 328 D
augokereke@mec.cuny.edu
OKOJIE, Felix, A 601-979-2931 275 A
felix.a.okojie@jsums.edu
OKOLI, Chuks 617-541-5363 241 D
cokoli@rcc.mass.edu
OKORONKWO, Josephine 504-286-5361 214 I
jokoronkwo@suno.edu
OKREPKIE, Phyllis 605-394-4959 464 G
pokrepkie@national.edu
OKUDA, Alex, H 949-480-4159 69 I
aokuda@soka.edu
OKUN, Gail 973-278-5400 323 J
gso@BerkeleyCollege.edu
OKUN, Gail 973-278-5400 307 G
gso@berkeleycollege.edu
OLAFSON, Donna 913-288-7179 193 J
dolafson@kckcc.edu
OLALDE, Patricia 312-369-7248 148 B
polalde@colum.edu
OLASKY, Marvin 212-659-7200 338 A
OLAVARRIA RODRIGUEZ,
Zenaida 787-896-2252 561 K
zolavarria@edpcollege.edu
OLAVE, Ricardo 312-777-8680 153 A
rolave@aii.edu
OLBERDING, Kristina 513-562-8773 384 A
financialaid@artacademy.edu
OLBERT, Doug 602-850-8000 17 H
dolbert@phoenixseminary.edu
OLCESE, Charles, A 620-235-4680 195 I
colcese@pittstate.edu
OLCHEFSKE, Mark, C 641-422-4191 187 F
olchemar@niacc.edu
OLCZAK, Joe, A 724-836-9898 449 C
gaujo6@pitt.edu
OLD BEAR, Te-Atta 406-638-3106 294 G
oldbeart@lbhc.cc.mt.us
OLDANI, John 636-949-4993 284 C
joldani@lindenwood.edu
OLDEHOFF, Allison 212-217-4114 333 G
allison_oldehoff@fitnyc.edu
OLDENKAMP, Mike 712-324-5061 188 A
mikeo@nwicc.edu
OLDFIELD, Curt, E 563-556-5110 187 G
oldfieldc@portal.nicc.edu
OLDFIELD, Melody, K 541-737-3871 418 F
university.marketing@oregonstate.edu
OLDHAM, Betty, A 208-496-1112 142 G
oldhamb@byui.edu
OLDHAM, Bruce, E 913-971-3656 195 A
beoldham@mnu.edu
OLDHAM, Larry, R 731-989-6649 468 K
loldham@fhu.edu
OLDHAM, Phillip 423-425-4633 477 D
phil-oldham@utc.edu
OLDHAM, Steve 254-295-4505 504 A
soldham@umhb.edu
OLDHAM, Todd, M 585-292-3057 341 H
toldham@monroecc.edu
OLDHAM, Vickie 478-825-6319 129 C
oldhamv@fvsu.edu
OLDHOUSER DAVIS, Kay 803-938-3746 462 F
kayo@uscsumter.edu
OLDS, Carole 719-502-3249 86 G
carole.olds@ppcc.edu
OLDS, G. Richard 951-827-4564 74 C
richard.olds@ucr.edu
OLDS, Kim 617-217-9040 231 C
kolds@baystate.edu
OLEGERIIL, Jay 680-488-2471 560 A
jayo@palau.edu
OLEJNICZAK, Kraig, J 219-464-5085 181 A
kraig.olejniczak@valpo.edu
OLEKA, Sam 502-597-6411 203 D
sam.oleka@kysu.edu
OLEKS, Judith 301-790-2800 223 A
oleksj@hagerstowncc.edu
OLEKSIW, Steven 718-780-7982 324 F
steven.oleksiw@brooklaw.edu
OLEN, Lynda 251-380-4195 7 F
lolen@shc.edu
OLENICK, Erin 510-666-8248 26 G
eolinick@aimc.edu
OLENIK, Joseph 914-251-6915 354 D
joe.olenik@purchase.edu
OLER, Elizabeth 312-935-4232 153 F
eoler@icsw.edu
OLER, Gregory, S 410-516-8000 223 F
goler@jhu.edu
OLESIUK, Sue 828-254-1921 367 H
solesiuk@abtcch.edu
OLESON-BRIGGS, Susan 704-330-6022 369 A
susan.oleson@cpcc.edu
OLESZEWSKI, Susan 215-276-6070 446 G
sueo@salus.edu
OLGUIN, Albert 310-900-1600 45 E
olguin_a@compton.edu
OLGUIN, Javier, E 972-860-5306 484 H
JavierEOlguin@dcccd.edu
OLGUIN-RYAN, Elizabeth 915-831-6325 486 E
eolguin@epcc.edu
OLIAN, Judy, D 310-825-7982 74 A
judy.olian@anderson.ucla.edu
OLIARO, Paul, M 559-278-2541 34 D
poliaro@csufresno.edu
OLIN, Jen 207-948-3131 219 H
jolin@unity.edu
OLIN, Robert, F 205-348-5972 8 F
olin@as.ua.edu
OLINER, Alex 212-349-4330 334 G
aoliner@globe.edu
OLINER, Martin 212-349-4330 334 G
moliner@globe.edu
OLING-SISAY, Mary 740-351-3251 401 I
moling-sisay@shawnee.edu
OLINGER, CSC, Gerard, J 503-943-8532 420 G
OLINGER, Richard, P 814-868-7767 433 C
rpolinger@mch1.org
OLINGER, Ronald, J 913-360-7413 190 F
rolinger@benedictine.edu
OLINGY, Jeff 423-697-3204 474 D
OLION, LaDelle 910-672-1074 377 E
lolion@uncfsu.edu
OLIPHANT, Uretz, S 217-333-5465 167 B
uretz.oliphant@carle.com
OLIVA, Giacomo 212-217-4040 333 G
giacomo_oliva@fitnyc.edu
OLIVA, Giacomo, M 402-472-9339 300 H
goliva2@unl.edu
OLIVA, Joseph, E 718-990-6421 348 G
olivaj@stjohns.edu
OLIVA, Robert 718-951-5696 326 G
boliva@brooklyn.cuny.edu
OLIVARES, Carlos 787-279-1912 563 B
colivares@bayamon.inter.edu
OLIVARES, Cecilia 309-268-8061 151 G
cecilia.olivares@heartland.edu
OLIVARES, Dora 956-364-4119 499 J
dora.olivares@harlingen.tstc.edu
OLIVAREZ, Juan 616-632-2880 248 A
jro002@aquinas.edu
OLIVE, David, W 276-326-4466 516 I
dolive@bluefield.edu
OLIVE, Nancy 605-331-6770 466 D
nancy.olive@usiouxfalls.edu
OLIVE-TAYLOR, Becky 336-278-6500 364 A
oliveb@elon.edu
OLIVEIRA, Sandra, J 401-865-2602 453 F
solivei6@providence.edu
OLIVER, Alice 954-446-6172 100 E
aoliver@aiufl.edu
OLIVER, Bob 435-283-7221 512 B
bob.oliver@snow.edu
OLIVER, Carolyne, B 713-313-7097 499 G
olivercb@tsu.edu
OLIVER, Cary 615-226-3990 471 I
coliver@nadcedu.com
OLIVER, Daniel, T 831-656-2511 557 H
dtoliver@nps.edu
OLIVER, David 805-654-6339 77 D
doliver@vcccd.edu
OLIVER, David, J 515-294-3220 182 B
doliver@iastate.edu
OLIVER, Denita 256-215-4290 2 F
doliver@cacc.edu
OLIVER, Diana 301-846-2435 222 G
doliver@frederick.edu
OLIVER, Donna, H 662-254-3425 276 C
doliver@mvsu.edu
OLIVER, James 229-430-4702 123 H
james.oliver@asurams.edu
OLIVER, Janet, W 231-995-1076 256 G
joliver@nmc.edu
OLIVER, Jeanette, J 713-313-7104 499 G
oliver_jj@tsu.edu
OLIVER, Jeanne 503-352-2740 419 E
jeanne1@pacificu.edu
OLIVER, Jeannie 901-369-0835 99 D
OLIVER, Jenea 816-235-6011 291 E
oliverj@umkc.edu
OLIVER, Kenneth 361-593-2411 498 A
kenneth.oliver@tamuk.edu
OLIVER, Lillian, M 787-723-4481 560 H
loliver@ceaprc.org
OLIVER, OSF, M. Marilyn 260-399-7700 180 E
moliver@sf.edu
OLIVER, Melvin, L 805-893-8354 74 F
moliver@ltsc.ucsb.edu
OLIVER, Patricia Belton 713-743-2400 503 B
pboliver@uh.edu
OLIVER, Richard, E 573-884-6705 291 D
oliverr@missouri.edu
OLIVER, Rick 303-991-1575 80 H
rick.oliver@americansentinel.edu
OLIVER, Robert, C 605-274-4111 463 H
rob.oliver@augie.edu
OLIVER, Ruben, D 405-466-2996 408 G
rdoliver@lunet.edu
OLIVER, Samuel W. "Dub" 903-923-2222 486 D
doliver@etbu.edu
OLIVER, Sandi 803-738-7699 459 D
olivers@midlandstech.edu
OLIVER, Sharon 207-581-1561 220 A
smoliver@maine.edu
OLIVER, Sharon, J 919-530-6335 378 A
soliver@nccu.edu
OLIVER, Shawn 609-497-7818 312 F
shawn.oliver@ptsem.edu
OLIVER, Sylvester, W 662-252-8000 277 C
syoliver@rustcollege.edu
OLIVER, Thomas 830-372-8050 499 C
toliver@tlu.edu
OLIVER PUTNAM,
Patricia, T 619-260-7430 76 A
poliver@sandiego.edu
OLIVER TORRES,
Marie, A 787-480-2351 561 D
mtorres@sanjuancapital.com
OLIVERA, Robert 510-261-8500 61 F
robert.olivera@patten.edu
OLIVERAS, Esteban 202-274-5248 99 F
eoliveras@udc.edu
OLIVERAS, Ivette 787-848-1589 564 G
registraduria@popac.edu
OLIVERI, Carl 570-340-6016 435 F
coliveri@marywood.edu
OLIVERIA, Steve 707-468-3081 57 A
OLIVERO, Paula 724-738-2683 443 E
paula.olivero@sru.edu
OLIVERSON, Richard 316-942-4291 195 C
oliversonr@newmanu.edu
OLIVETTE, Michael 914-606-6912 360 D
michael.olivette@sunywcc.edu
OLIVIER, Deborah 215-568-9215 436 E
dolivier@mccworks.org
OLIVIERI, Janies 787-250-1912 563 E
jolivieri@metro.inter.edu
OLIVIERI-LENAHAN,
Elizabeth 914-633-2547 336 E
eolivieri@iona.edu
OLIVO, Claudia 973-300-2306 315 F
colivo@sussex.edu
OLIVO, Cynthia, D 626-585-7074 61 E
cdolivo@pasadena.edu
OLKHOVSKAYA, Elena 510-436-1037 50 F
olkhovskaya@hnu.edu
OLLEY, Lorraine 847-566-6401 167 D
lolley@usml.edu
OLLILA, Les 715-324-6900 549 D
les.ollila@ni.edu
OLLIVER, James 727-394-6111 116 F
olliver.james@spcollege.edu
OLLSEN, Annette 713-973-3201 486 A
aollsen@keller.edu
OLMSTEAD, Audrey 248-689-8282 260 A
aolmstea@walshcollege.edu
OLMSTEAD, Karen, L 410-543-6489 228 D
klolmstead@salisbury.edu
OLMSTEAD, Steve 918-293-4744 410 E
steve.olmstead@okstate.edu
OLMSTEAD, Thomas 505-473-6027 320 F
thomas.olmstead@santafeuniversity.edu
OLMSTEAD, Wayne 775-753-2274 302 H
wayneo@gwmail.gbcnv.edu
OLMSTED, Jane 270-745-5787 207 C
jane.olmsted@wku.edu
OLNEY, Douglas, P 218-755-2764 266 B
dolney@bemidjistate.edu
OLNEY, Richard 941-487-4242 119 D
olney@ncf.edu
OLSEN, Ann, E 502-272-8133 198 E
aolsen@bellarmine.edu
OLSEN, Burke 540-261-8416 524 C
burke.olsen@svu.edu
OLSEN, Danny, R 801-422-5648 509 D
danny_olsen@byu.edu
OLSEN, Gary, R 610-519-4580 450 G
gary.olsen@villanova.edu
OLSEN, Jim 651-255-6164 271 I
jolsen@unitedseminary.edu
OLSEN, Jo 218-723-7040 262 I
jolsen@css.edu
OLSEN, John, S 901-843-3795 472 I
olsen@rhodes.edu
OLSEN, Julene 435-722-6900 510 J
OLSEN, Julie, A 765-361-6206 181 C
olsenj@wabash.edu
OLSEN, Kenneth, E 732-255-0400 312 D
kolsen@ocean.edu
OLSEN, Kris 714-628-7303 39 C
kolsen@chapman.edu
OLSEN, Matthew 918-495-7707 411 C
maolsen@oru.edu
OLSEN, Michelle 701-224-2540 381 C
michelle.olsen@ndus.edu
OLSEN, Morgan, R 480-727-9920 12 B
morgan.r.olsen@asu.edu
OLSEN, Randy, J 801-422-2905 509 D
randy_olsen@byu.edu
OLSEN, Renee 208-792-2151 143 F
rmolsen@lcsc.edu
OLSEN, JR., Robert, C 516-671-2277 360 A
rolsen@webb-institute.edu
OLSEN, Steve 515-244-4221 181 D
olsens@aib.edu
OLSEN, Steven, A 310-825-3444 74 A
solsen@conet.ucla.edu
OLSEN, Ted 425-602-3101 530 K
tolsen@bastyr.edu
OLSEN, Todd 435-613-5217 511 E
todd.olsen@ceu.edu
OLSHINSKY, Martin 304-214-8800 543 A
molshinsky@wvncc.edu
OLSON, Bette 402-465-2237 299 J
bolson@nebrwesleyan.edu
OLSON, Brian 847-317-6400 166 B
briano@tiu.edu
OLSON, Cari 701-858-3323 381 G
cari.olson@minotstateu.edu
OLSON, Chris 916-608-6500 56 C
OLSON, Craige, J 801-581-8951 510 L
dentaled@hsc.utah.edu
OLSON, David 785-227-3380 190 G
olsond@bethanylb.edu
OLSON, Diane 701-349-3621 383 B
dianeolson@trinitybiblecollege.edu
OLSON, Don 218-723-6471 262 I
dolson@css.edu
OLSON, Doug, A 715-833-6237 553 F
dolson@cvtc.edu
OLSON, Douglas 708-456-0300 166 C
dolson@triton.edu
OLSON, Dustin 805-893-4151 74 F
dustin.olson@police.ucsb.edu
OLSON, Eric 215-895-2079 427 G
eric.j.olson@drexel.edu
OLSON, Gail, M 651-201-1750 265 H
gail.olson@so.mnscu.edu
OLSON, Gretchen, S 515-271-2084 184 A
gretchen.olson@drake.edu
OLSON, Heidi, L 320-222-5209 268 I
heidi.olson@ridgewater.edu
OLSON, Ian 907-474-5317 10 J
inolson@alaska.edu
OLSON, Jeffery, D 651-638-6241 261 I
jeff-olson@bethel.edu
OLSON, Jeffrey 605-455-6055 464 H
jolson@olc.edu
OLSON, Jerry 580-349-1344 410 B
jolson@opsu.edu
OLSON, Joan, G 612-874-3745 265 E
joan_olson@mcad.edu
OLSON, Joe 541-440-4600 420 F
Joe.Olson@umpqua.edu
OLSON, John 425-388-9407 533 H
jolson@everettcc.edu
OLSON, Judith 760-591-3012 122 G
jolson@usa.edu
OLSON, Kerry, J 409-882-3362 500 G
kerry.olson@lsco.edu
OLSON, Ketlyn 802-225-3306 513 H
katelyn.olson@neci.edu
OLSON, Ksenia 218-723-6139 262 I
kolson@nebook.com
OLSON, Laura, A 605-331-6627 466 D
laura.olson@usiouxfalls.edu
OLSON, Linda 610-341-5930 428 D
lolson@eastern.edu
OLSON, Lois, A 612-330-1162 261 G
olson3@augsburg.edu
OLSON, Louise 401-454-6323 454 B
lolson@risd.edu
OLSON, Lynette 320-308-5382 269 D
lolson@sctcc.edu
OLSON, Lynette 620-235-4113 195 I
lolson@pittstate.edu
OLSON, Lynn 207-893-7801 219 F
lolson@sjcme.edu
OLSON, Lynn, F 508-793-7294 233 C
lolson@clarku.edu
OLSON, Mark 773-244-5728 159 G
molson@northpark.edu
OLSON, Mark, J 703-812-4757 520 E
molson@leland.edu
OLSON, Marlene 860-343-5869 90 D
molson@mxcc.commnet.edu
OLSON, MaryEllen 325-674-2000 478 H
meo10b@acu.edu
OLSON, Matthew 781-280-3802 240 F
olsonm@middlesex.mass.edu
OLSON, Matthew 715-324-6900 549 D
matt.olson@ni.edu
OLSON, Maureen 404-894-1420 130 D
maureen.olson@health.gatech.edu
OLSON, Megan 907-786-1764 10 I
anmo@uaa.alaska.edu
OLSON, Nancy 641-585-8147 189 E
olsonn@waldorf.edu
OLSON, Nancy 217-732-3168 156 F
nolson@lincolnchristian.edu
OLSON, Neil 573-882-3768 291 D
olsonne@missouri.edu
OLSON, Phillip 413-545-1378 237 C
polson@aux.umass.edu
OLSON, Ray, A 614-235-4136 402 G
rolson@TLSohio.edu
OLSON, Robert 605-626-3336 465 H
olsonr@northern.edu

ORTA, Jose 305-223-4561 116 C
ORTALE, Lynn 215-248-7030 425 C
ortalel@chc.edu
ORTBERG, Jennifer, L 714-895-8965 41 A
jortberg@gwc.cccd.edu
ORTEGA, Ana, M 787-743-7979 565 F
ut_aortega@suagm.edu
ORTEGA, Bertha, P 509-865-8529 534 D
ortega_b@heritage.edu
ORTEGA, Carmen 787-257-7373 565 E
ue_cortega@suagm.edu
ORTEGA, Carolyn, M 973-655-7327 311 G
ortegac@mail.montclair.edu
ORTEGA, David 210-486-1227 479 F
dortega@alamo.edu
ORTEGA, David, F 541-485-1780 417 E
davidortega@newhope.edu
ORTEGA, Janet 602-243-8287 16 E
ORTEGA, Jeff 916-722-8200 37 H
jortega@cc.edu
ORTEGA, John 951-639-5185 58 B
jortega@msjc.edu
ORTEGA, Luz, D 787-480-2407 561 D
lortega@sanjuancapital.com
ORTEGA, Suzanne 919-962-4614 377 A
stortega@northcarolina.edu
ORTEGO, Sheila 505-428-1201 320 E
sheila.ortego@sfcc.edu
ORTEGON, Ricardo 212-986-4343 323 J
ricardo@berkeleycollege.edu
ORTEGON, Ricardo 212-986-4343 307 G
ricardo@berkeleycollege.edu
ORTELLI, Tracy, A 502-410-6200 200 F
tortelli@galencollege.edu
ORTEN, Mark 740-587-8504 389 H
ortenm@denison.edu
ORTH, Linda 423-425-4669 477 D
linda-orth@utc.edu
ORTIZ, Ann 910-893-1669 362 F
ortiz@campbell.edu
ORTIZ, Ariel 787-766-1717 565 G
um_aortiz@suagm.edu
ORTIZ, Carmen 562-997-5584 44 G
cortiz@devry.com
ORTIZ, Christine 617-253-4860 242 A
cortiz@mit.edu
ORTIZ, Daniel 617-287-5910 237 D
daniel.ortiz@umb.edu
ORTIZ, Edna 787-786-3030 560 E
eortiz@ucb.edu.pr
ORTIZ, Eduardo 787-250-1912 563 E
ehortiz@metro.inter.edu
ORTIZ, Elizabeth 818-947-2361 55 E
ortizme@lavc.edu
ORTIZ, Elizabeth, F 312-362-8588 148 F
eortiz4@depaul.edu
ORTIZ, Emma, L 773-838-7530 147 E
eortiz@ccc.edu
ORTIZ, Eugene 505-661-4682 321 E
eortiz3@unm.edu
ORTIZ, Francisco 787-761-0640 561 B
francisco_1152@hotmail.com
ORTIZ, Hilda, L 787-863-2390 563 C
hilda.ortiz@fajardo.inter.edu
ORTIZ, Holly 661-835-1111 67 J
ORTIZ, Holly 805-967-9677 67 K
ORTIZ, Holly 661-835-1111 67 I
ORTIZ, Holly 805-922-8256 67 L
ORTIZ, Holly 805-339-2999 68 A
ORTIZ, J. Michael 909-869-2290 33 G
jmo@csupomona.edu
ORTIZ, James, O 207-741-5501 219 A
jortiz@smccme.edu
ORTIZ, Jamie, S 956-326-3068 497 B
jortiz@tamiu.edu
ORTIZ, Jeanne 562-907-4233 79 B
jortiz@whittier.edu
ORTIZ, Jessy 718-405-3204 330 A
jessy.ortiz@mountsaintvincent.edu
ORTIZ, Johnathan 505-454-2548 318 E
jortiz@luna.edu
ORTIZ, Jose, E 787-857-3600 563 A
jeortiz@br.inter.edu
ORTIZ, Jose, M 805-922-6966 26 K
jortiz@hancockcollege.edu
ORTIZ, Juan Carlos 213-481-1313 69 E
ORTIZ, Judy 503-352-7309 419 E
ortiz@pacificu.edu
ORTIZ, Kendra 787-780-0070 560 F
kortiz@caribbean.edu
ORTIZ, Kristina 212-752-1530 338 C
kristina.ortiz@limcollege.edu
ORTIZ, Larry 310-243-2107 34 B
lortiz@csudh.edu
ORTIZ, Laura 630-942-2971 147 G
ortizl@cod.edu
ORTIZ, Lillian 203-575-8034 90 E
lortiz@nvcc.commnet.edu
ORTIZ, Lourdes 787-279-1912 563 B
lortiz@bayamon.inter.edu
ORTIZ, Lourdes, Z 787-257-0000 566 H
lourdes.ortiz2@upr.edu
ORTIZ, Luz 787-864-2222 563 D
luzortiz@inter.edu
ORTIZ, Luz, M 787-832-6000 562 E
mortiz@icprjc.edu
ORTIZ, Luz, M 215-503-4094 448 B
luz.ortiz@jefferson.edu
ORTIZ, Mario 219-785-5476 178 H
mortiz@pnc.edu
ORTIZ, Migdalia 787-279-1912 563 B
morti@bayamon.inter.edu
ORTIZ, Myrta 787-815-0000 566 F
ORTIZ, Noe 210-486-4600 479 C
nortiz@alamo.edu
ORTIZ, Noel 787-753-6335 562 E
nortiz@icprjc.edu
ORTIZ, Norma 787-620-2040 560 B
nortiz@aupr.edu
ORTIZ, Nuria 650-289-3336 64 G
nuria.ortiz@stpatrickseminary.org
ORTIZ, Rafael 787-725-6500 560 G
rortiz@albizu.edu
ORTIZ, Ralph 559-734-9000 66 E
ralpho@sjvc.edu
ORTIZ, Rosa 787-738-2161 567 A
rosa.ortiz1@upr.edu
ORTIZ, Samantha 303-556-3519 88 D
Samantha.Ortiz@ucdenver.edu
ORTIZ, Vivian 781-239-3101 240 D
vortiz@massbay.edu
ORTIZ, Zoraida 787-743-7979 565 F
zortiz@suagm.edu
ORTIZ-ALVAREZ, Jorge 787-993-8916 566 G
jorge.ortiz@upr.edu
ORTIZ ALVAREZ, Lelis Antonio 954-322-4460 112 B
ORTIZ-CINTRÓN, Jesús 787-993-8878 566 G
jesus.ortiz3@upr.edu
ORTIZ-CINTRÓN, Jesús 787-993-8869 566 G
jesus.ortiz3@upr.edu
ORTIZ COLÓN, Yadira 787-725-8120 562 A
yortiz@eap.edu
ORTIZ FLORES, Ileana 787-896-2252 561 K
iortiz@edpcollege.edu
ORTIZ PARRA, Erika Jose 954-322-4460 112 B
ORTIZ PARRA, Lelis 954-322-4460 112 B
ORTIZ-PRINCE, Yvonne 512-505-3035 488 B
yoprince@htu.edu
ORTIZ-ZAYAS, Jose, E 787-857-3600 563 A
jeortiz@br.inter.edu
ORTMAN, William, B 973-618-3259 308 D
wortman@caldwell.edu
ORTMEIER, Shane 605-882-5284 464 D
ortmeies@lakeareatech.edu
ORTMEYER, Rose Ann 573-681-5044 284 B
ortmeyr@lincolnu.edu
ORTNER, Richard 617-912-9134 232 E
rortner@bostonconservatory.edu
ORTOLANI, Brent 918-343-7771 411 H
bortolani@rsu.edu
ORTON, Mozelle 801-957-4561 512 C
mozelle.orton@slcc.edu
ORTON, Susan 207-786-6337 217 C
sorton@bates.edu
ORTSTADT, Andrew, D 314-935-8604 292 J
aortstadt@wustl.edu
ORUM-ALEXANDER, Gail 323-563-5851 39 D
gailorum@cdrewu.edu
ORVIS, Arleen 563-387-1005 187 A
orvisarl@luther.edu
ORWIG, Greg 509-777-4580 539 F
gorwig@whitworth.edu
ORWIGHO, Godfrey 419-530-3955 404 F
godfrey.ovwigho@utoledo.edu
ORZA, Deanna 770-781-6770 132 J
dorza@laniertech.edu
ORZECHOWSKI, Laurie 419-824-3959 395 D
lorzechowski@lourdes.edu
ORZECHOWSKI, Michael 212-280-1301 358 G
morzechowski@uts.columbia.edu
ORZOFF, Jordan 909-706-3811 78 D
jorzoff@westernu.edu
ORZOLEK, Jeffrey, P 540-831-5376 522 D
jorzolek@radford.edu
ORZOLEK, Mariah 419-783-2358 389 G
morzolek@defiance.edu
OSACHY, Lisa, A 412-578-6306 424 G
osachyla@carlow.edu
OSAGIE, Linda 214-860-8604 485 A
losagie@dcccd.edu
OSANTOWSKI, Kimberly 248-204-3940 254 E
kosantows@ltu.edu
OSAWA, Steve 510-659-6111 59 I
sosawa@ohlone.edu
OSBAHR, Diane 712-325-3235 186 B
dosbahr@iwcc.edu
OSBON, Cindy 301-846-2593 222 G
cosbon@frederick.edu
OSBORN, Bennie, I 530-752-1361 73 F
biosburn@ucdavis.edu
OSBORN, Bill 928-757-0817 16 G
bosborn@mohave.edu
OSBORN, Carolyn, S 830-792-7282 494 A
cosborn@schreiner.edu
OSBORN, Dan 586-791-6610 248 G
daniel.osborn@baker.edu
OSBORN, David, R 303-762-6918 83 I
david.osborn@denverseminary.edu
OSBORN, Edward, H 860-465-5303 91 H
osborne@easternct.edu
OSBORN, Elizabeth, A 240-895-4385 226 A
eaosborn@smcm.edu
OSBORN, Jeffrey 609-771-2724 308 G
josborn@tcnj.edu
OSBORN, Lou 714-704-2727 78 G
losborn@westwood.edu
OSBORN, Matthew 419-267-1381 397 D
mosborn@northweststate.edu
OSBORN, Micahel, A 614-885-5585 401 B
mosborn@pcj.edu
OSBORN, Richard, E 423-439-8300 473 E
osbornr@etsu.edu
OSBORNE, Becky 217-353-2005 161 B
bosborne@parkland.edu
OSBORNE, Curtis 510-649-2477 48 H
cosborne@gtu.edu
OSBORNE, David, L 610-785-6530 446 A
developmentscs@adphila.org
OSBORNE, Jackie 619-482-6330 71 C
josborne@swccd.edu
OSBORNE, John 305-428-5700 113 I
josborne@aii.edu
OSBORNE, John 405-425-5463 409 E
john.osborne@oc.edu
OSBORNE, John, N 270-745-5747 207 C
john.osborne@wku.edu
OSBORNE, Kenneth, T 401-254-3166 454 C
kosborne@rwu.edu
OSBORNE, Larry 808-735-4825 140 A
losborne@chaminade.edu
OSBORNE, Margaret, H 315-255-1743 325 H
osbornem@cayuga-cc.edu
OSBORNE, Mark 610-989-1301 450 E
mosborne@vfmac.edu
OSBORNE, Matthew, S 517-750-1200 258 F
mosborne@arbor.edu
OSBORNE, Michael 207-974-4685 218 H
mosborne@emcc.edu
OSBORNE, Michelle 518-454-5141 330 C
osbornem@strose.edu
OSBORNE, Nancy 805-898-2905 47 C
nosborne@fielding.edu
OSBORNE, Shelley 704-991-0203 374 A
sosborne7501@stanly.edu
OSBORNE, Steven, C 843-953-5574 457 B
osbornes@cofc.edu
OSBORNE, Tom 402-472-3011 300 H
tosborne2@unl.edu
OSBORNE, Travis, G 530-226-4978 69 H
tosborne@simpsonu.edu
OSBORNE-ADAMS, Dawn 607-777-2388 351 F
ombudsman@binghamton.edu
OSBORNE-ELLIOTT, Miriam 340-692-4187 568 C
mosborn@uvi.edu
OSBORNE-LONG, Faith 518-564-2090 354 B
faith.long@plattsburgh.edu
OSBOURNE, John 304-829-7395 540 E
josbourne@bethanywv.edu
OSBURN, Jan 254-867-3014 500 B
jan.osburn@tstc.edu
OSBURN, Monica, Z 910-521-6202 379 B
monica.osburn@uncp.edu
OSBURN, Toby, W 337-475-5607 215 G
tosburn@mcneese.edu
OSEBY, Todd 651-779-3276 266 D
todd.oseby@century.edu
OSEEKEY, Leonard 716-829-7677 332 F
oseekey@dyc.edu
OSEGUEDA, Roberto 915-747-5680 505 E
osegueda@utep.edu
OSENGA, Annette 510-780-4500 53 I
aosenga@lifewest.edu
OSGOOD, Dorothy 803-705-4623 455 D
osgoodd@benedict.edu
OSGOOD, Ken 303-273-3596 82 F
kosgood@mines.edu
OSHERSON, Julie 802-387-6732 513 E
josherson@landmark.edu
OSHIRO, Cathie, R 620-792-9234 190 E
oshiroc@bartonccc.edu
OSHIRO, Robyn 808-454-4700 141 C
OSINGA, Mark, L 864-596-9041 457 E
mark.osinga@converse.edu
OSIRIM, Mary 610-526-5074 423 C
OSIRIS, Charles 805-922-6966 26 K
cosiris@hancockcollege.edu
OSKAMP, Shirley 802-287-8388 513 D
oskamps@greenmtn.edu
OSMANSON, Deb 402-449-2844 298 B
dosmanson@graceu.edu
OSMER, Kelly 978-659-1212 241 B
kosmer@necc.mass.edu
OSMER, Patrick, S 614-292-6031 398 H
osmer.1@osu.edu
OSMUN, Molly, M 641-844-5706 185 J
molly.osmun@iavalley.edu
OSSORIO, Devon 573-288-6571 281 D
dossorio@culver.edu
OST, Sue 406-265-3525 295 G
osts@msun.edu
OSTASH, Heather 760-384-6249 52 N
hostash@cerrocoso.edu
OSTDIEK, Donald 713-348-4786 492 J
dho@rice.edu
OSTEEN-COCHRANE, Kieta 321-433-7515 101 J
osteen-cochranek@brevardcc.edu
OSTENDORF, Carole 414-372-4345 547 I
carole@lakeside.edu
OSTENDORF, Ellen 410-337-6431 222 I
OSTENDORFF, Stephen 516-678-5000 341 F
sostendorff@molloy.edu
OSTER, Ashley 704-687-5827 378 E
aoster@uncc.edu
OSTER, Ben Zion 323-937-3763 79 J
OSTER, Joseph 410-704-2364 228 E
joster@towson.edu
OSTER, Sharon, M 203-432-6035 95 D
sharon.oster@yale.edu
OSTERBIND, Kelly 256-782-5400 4 L
kosterbi@jsu.edu
OSTERHAGE, Keith 414-288-5327 548 D
keith.osterhage@marquette.edu
OSTERHOLT, James 505-984-6109 320 C
josterholt@sjcsf.edu
OSTERHOUDT, Lori, B 607-746-4692 355 E
osterhlb@delhi.edu
OSTERTHUN, Stu 402-323-3401 300 C
sosterthun@southeast.edu
OSTIN, Daniel 732-235-4565 316 G
ostindj@umdnj.edu
OSTLER, Jon 435-283-7361 512 B
jon.ostler@snow.edu
OSTOJIC, Diane 708-596-2000 164 F
dostojic@ssc.edu
OSTOLAZA, Magda, A 787-257-7373 565 E
ue_mostolaza@suagm.edu
OSTRANDER, David 352-588-8250 116 E
david.ostrander@saintleo.edu
OSTRANDER, Doris 202-298-2551 97 D
dostrander@corcoran.org
OSTRANDER, Gary, K 808-956-7837 141 B
gko@hawaii.edu
OSTRANDER, Jean, M 641-422-4177 187 F
ostrajea@niacc.edu
OSTRANDER, Richard 616-222-1589 250 C
rick.ostrander@cornerstone.edu
OSTRANDER, Tammy 218-723-6173 262 I
tostrand@css.edu
OSTROSKE, Georgette 516-918-3607 324 E
gostroske@bcl.edu
OSTROSKI, Erin, B 570-348-6248 435 F
ostroski@marywood.edu
OSTROTH, David 508-531-1276 238 B
dostroth@bridgew.edu
OSTROW, James 617-243-2111 236 F
jostrow@lasell.edu
OSTROWSKI, Ally 303-753-6046 87 F
aostrowski@rmcad.edu
OSTRYE, Mary, E 317-921-4313 175 G
mostrye@ivytech.edu
OSTWINKLE, Christopher, M 563-556-5110 187 G
ostwinkc@nicc.edu
OSUNDE, Samuel 662-254-9041 276 C
sosunde@mvsu.edu
OSWALD, Gloria 305-626-3641 108 H
goswald@fmuniv.edu
OSWALD, Mike, R 208-356-1320 142 G
oswaldrm@byui.edu
OSWALD, P.J 503-517-1800 421 B
pjoswald@westernseminary.edu
OSWALD, Pete 217-854-3231 145 F
pete.oswald@blackburn.edu
OSWALD, Phil 920-403-3016 550 C
phil.oswald@snc.edu
OSWALD, Sharon 662-325-2580 276 A
soswald@cobilan.msstate.edu
OSWALT, Natalie 936-591-9075 492 A
jshannon@panola.edu
OTAIGBE, Michael, I 703-878-2810 99 D
mio@strayer.edu
OTERO, Emeterio, M 585-262-1610 341 H
eotero@monroecc.edu
OTERO, Juan 787-766-1717 565 G
juotero@suagm.edu
OTERO, Rafael 956-882-7304 505 C
rafael.otero@utb.edu
OTHMAN, Saib 630-844-4229 145 C
sothman@aurora.edu
OTIS, Averl, R 716-673-3398 352 A
averl.otis@fredonia.edu
OTO, Rod, M 507-222-4190 262 B
roto@carleton.edu
OTOUPAL, Vince 831-582-3534 35 C
votoupal@csumb.edu
OTSUKA, Tami 714-532-6067 39 C
otsuka@chapman.edu
OTT, Deanna 501-329-6872 21 C
dott@cbc.edu
OTT, Jay, W 719-884-5000 86 D
jwott@nbc.edu

O'BRIEN, David, J 850-474-2626 121 C
dobrien@uwf.edu
O'BRIEN, David, J 937-229-2105 404 A
David.OBrien@notes.udayton.edu
O'BRIEN, David, M 671-735-2905 559 D
dobrien@uguam.uog.edu
O'BRIEN, Diane, E 570-408-4734 451 G
diane.obrien@wilkes.edu
O'BRIEN, Eddie 706-865-2134 138 A
eobrien@truett.edu
O'BRIEN, Eileen 978-542-7529 239 B
eobrien@salemstate.edu
O'BRIEN, Elizabeth 415-749-4581 65 I
eobrien@sfai.edu
O'BRIEN, Frances, L 304-293-5040 544 E
frances.o'brien@mail.wvu.edu
O'BRIEN, Gwen 574-284-4595 179 D
gobrien@saintmarys.edu
O'BRIEN, Irene 973-353-5541 314 E
jobrien@andromeda.rutgers.edu
O'BRIEN, J. Patrick 806-651-2100 498 D
pobrien@mail.wtamu.edu
O'BRIEN, J. Randall 865-471-3200 467 E
robrien@cn.edu
O'BRIEN, Jack 409-740-4830 497 D
obrienj@tamug.edu
O'BRIEN, Janet, L 912-478-5371 131 A
jlobrien@georgiasouthern.edu
O'BRIEN, Jennifer 815-394-4376 162 H
jobrien@rockford.edu
O'BRIEN, Jim 480-965-9118 12 B
james.obrien@asu.edu
O'BRIEN, Jim 254-526-1365 482 F
jim.obrien@ctcd.edu
O'BRIEN, John 763-424-0820 268 D
jobrien@nhcc.edu
O'BRIEN, John, F 617-422-7221 243 G
O'BRIEN, Kathleen 414-382-6084 545 H
kathleen.obrien@alverno.edu
O'BRIEN, Kathleen, A 612-624-3557 272 D
kobrien@umn.edu
O'BRIEN, Kelly 860-297-2046 94 C
kelly.obrien@trincoll.edu
O'BRIEN, Kevin 865-573-4517 469 J
kobrien@johnsonU.edu
O'BRIEN, Margaret, A 605-256-5049 465 G
peg.o'brien@dsu.edu
O'BRIEN, Mary 707-546-4000 45 G
mobrien@empirecollege.com
O'BRIEN, Mary Eileen 845-848-7801 332 C
mary.eileen.obrien@dc.edu
O'BRIEN, Maureen 310-287-4379 55 F
obrienma@wlac.edu
O'BRIEN, Maureen 724-830-1075 447 B
obrien@setonhill.edu
O'BRIEN, Michael, E 419-530-4987 404 F
michael.obrien6@utoledo.edu
O'BRIEN, Michael, J 217-442-7232 148 E
mobrien@dacc.edu
O'BRIEN, Michael, J 610-841-3333 441 D
mobrien@psb.edu
O'BRIEN, Michael, J 573-882-4421 291 D
obrienm@missouri.edu
O'BRIEN, Mike 412-237-3168 425 H
mobrien@ccac.edu
O'BRIEN, Paul, R 772-462-7376 110 L
pobrien@irsc.edu
O'BRIEN, Stacey 217-641-4241 154 G
obrien@jwcc.edu
O'BRIEN, Susan 256-824-6133 9 A
susan.obrien@uah.edu
O'BRIEN, Susan, M 609-633-6460 316 A
sobrien@tesc.edu
O'BRIEN, Suzanne 810-989-5747 258 B
sobrien@sc4.edu
O'BRIEN, Wayne, R 434-395-2409 520 G
obrienwr@longwood.edu
O'BRIEN, William, A 304-255-0793 543 D
obrien@concord.edu
O'BRIEN, William, T 724-287-8711 423 F
william.obrien@bc3.edu
O'BRIEN FRIEDERICHS,
Jane 781-239-2461 240 D
jobrienfriederichs@massbay.edu
O'BRYANT, Theresa, M 413-662-5231 238 F
theresa.obryant@mcla.edu
O'BRYON, Laura 541-552-8106 419 A
obryon@sou.edu
O'CALLAGHAN, Cecelia 608-771-2161 308 G
ocallagh@tcnj.edu
O'CALLAGHAN, Cindy 617-735-9779 234 E
ocallac@emmanuel.edu
O'CALLAGHAN, Karen 516-463-6605 335 H
karen.ocallaghan@hofstra.edu
O'CALLAGHAN, Scott 802-447-6359 514 D
socall@svc.edu
O'CARROLL, Theresa 708-974-5248 159 A
ocarroll@morainevalley.edu
O'CINNSEALAIGH,
Benedict 513-231-2223 384 E
bocinnsealaigh@athenaeum.edu
O'CONNELL, Catharine 540-887-7030 520 I
coconnell@mbc.edu
O'CONNELL, Colleen 215-884-8942 452 C
planning@woninstitute.edu
O'CONNELL, Daniel 978-867-4246 235 E
daniel.oconnell@gordon.edu
O'CONNELL, Danny, J 330-941-3549 406 F
djoconnell@ysu.edu
O'CONNELL, David, J 563-333-6092 188 D
OConnellDavidJ@sau.edu
O'CONNELL, Dorothy, J 978-656-3236 240 F
oconnelld@middlesex.mass.edu
O'CONNELL, Erin, E 206-281-2175 537 D
ocone@spu.edu
O'CONNELL, Heather, A 302-356-6814 97 A
heather.a.oconnell@wilmu.edu
O'CONNELL, Janet 360-473-1120 533 F
O'CONNELL, Mark 269-965-3931 253 H
oconnellm@kellogg.edu
O'CONNELL, Maurice, J 757-594-7160 517 I
maury@cnu.edu
O'CONNELL, Ralph, A 914-594-4900 343 F
ralph_oconnell@nymc.edu
O'CONNELL, Robert, G 617-333-2050 234 A
boconnel@curry.edu
O'CONNELL, Sean, P 203-773-8539 89 H
oconnell@albertus.edu
O'CONNER, Terrence 305-628-6516 116 G
toconner@stu.edu
O'CONNER, William, J 585-385-8424 348 F
boconnor@sjfc.edu
O'CONNOR, Barbara, R 217-333-1216 167 B
boconnr@illinois.edu
O'CONNOR, OSFS,
Bernard, F 610-282-1100 426 I
boconnor@desales.edu
O'CONNOR, Bill 425-564-5454 531 B
bill.oconnor@bellevuecollege.edu
O'CONNOR, Bob 315-781-3535 335 G
oconnor@hws.edu
O'CONNOR, Carol 870-972-3973 20 C
coconnor@astate.edu
O'CONNOR, Charles, D 260-481-6977 174 A
oconnorc@ipfw.edu
O'CONNOR, Christi 323-953-4000 54 H
oconnoca@lacitycollege.edu
O'CONNOR,
Christopher, K 617-254-2610 244 E
O'CONNOR, Claudia 703-284-6901 521 A
claudia.oconnor@marymount.edu
O'CONNOR, Colleen, M 973-720-2125 317 D
oconnorc1@wpunj.edu
O'CONNOR, Daniel 661-395-4231 52 M
doconnor@bakersfieldcollege.edu
O'CONNOR, Deirdre, M 570-577-3141 423 D
deirdre.oconnor@bucknell.edu
O'CONNOR, Diane 215-641-6416 436 G
doconnor@mc3.edu
O'CONNOR, Edward, R 203-582-5202 93 E
edward.oconnor@quinnipiac.edu
O'CONNOR, Ellen 617-287-5100 237 D
ellen.oconnor@umb.edu
O'CONNOR, Ellen, M 215-955-6835 448 B
ellen.oconnor@jefferson.edu
O'CONNOR, Erin 617-521-2420 245 A
erin.oconnor3@simmons.edu
O'CONNOR, James 212-229-5300 342 E
oconnorj@newschool.edu
O'CONNOR, James 319-273-2761 182 D
james.oconnor@uni.edu
O'CONNOR, James 404-894-9044 130 D
james.oconnor@oit.gatech.edu
O'CONNOR, Jeremiah 508-793-2564 233 D
joconnor@holycross.edu
O'CONNOR, Jim 707-638-5997 72 H
jim.oconnor@tu.edu
O'CONNOR, Jody 415-575-6153 32 D
joconnor@ciis.edu
O'CONNOR, John 214-768-2011 494 F
joconnor@smu.edu
O'CONNOR, John 860-444-8280 558 E
John.C.OConnor@uscg.mil
O'CONNOR, Joseph 607-778-5379 324 G
oconnor_j@sunybroome.edu
O'CONNOR, Joyce, E 773-371-5408 146 B
joyceoco@ctu.edu
O'CONNOR, Kathleen 617-243-2199 236 F
koconner@lasell.edu
O'CONNOR, Kathleen 608-663-6715 547 C
koconnor@edgewood.edu
O'CONNOR, Kevin 949-582-4788 70 F
koconnor@saddleback.edu
O'CONNOR, Kevin, J 559-456-2777 27 B
koconnor@alliant.edu
O'CONNOR, Margaret 314-454-7557 282 E
maoconnor@bjc.org
O'CONNOR, Margaret, J 770-720-5921 135 F
poc@reinhardt.edu
O'CONNOR, Mark, F 617-552-3315 232 D
mark.oconnor.1@bc.edu
O'CONNOR, Martin 570-348-6211 435 F
oconnor@marywood.edu
O'CONNOR, Mary 480-731-8403 15 F
mary.oconnor@domail.maricopa.edu
O'CONNOR, Matthew, L 203-582-8297 93 E
matthew.oconnor@quinnipiac.edu
O'CONNOR, Michael 815-802-8908 154 J
moconnor@kcc.edu
O'CONNOR, Michael, J 828-262-3190 377 B
oconnormj@appstate.edu
O'CONNOR, Patricia 714-459-1175 78 C
poconnor@wsulaw.edu
O'CONNOR, Patricia, G 619-275-4700 46 K
patoatfcc@aol.com
O'CONNOR, Patrick 708-974-5555 159 A
oconnorp@morainevalley.edu
O'CONNOR, Sheila 402-457-2733 298 H
soconnor7@mccneb.edu
O'CONNOR, Thomas, J 703-993-3256 519 A
toconno2@gmu.edu
O'CONNOR, William, R 386-822-7500 121 E
woconnor@stetson.edu
O'CONNOR-BENSON, Pat 239-597-7101 119 A
poconnor@fgcu.edu
O'CONNOR-GOMEZ,
Doreen 562-907-4352 79 B
doconnor@whittier.edu
O'CONNOR-JOHNSTON,
Elizabeth 508-362-2131 240 A
eoconnorjohnston@capecod.edu
O'DANIEL, Carolyn 502-213-5333 202 B
O'DANIEL, Dale 850-718-2299 102 H
odanield@chipola.edu
O'DANIEL, Rosemary 309-341-5456 146 A
O'DAY, Gail, R 336-758-4315 380 B
odaygr@wfu.edu
O'DAY, Jim 406-243-5331 295 A
jim.oday@umontana.edu
O'DAY, Rey 951-222-8485 64 B
rey.oday@rcc.edu
O'DAY, Steven, P 717-291-3989 429 E
steven.oday@fandm.edu
O'DELL, Carol, S 912-583-3125 126 C
codell@bpc.edu
O'DELL, Cynthia 219-980-6509 173 F
codell@iun.edu
O'DELL, Greg 734-487-1222 250 H
godell@emich.edu
O'DELL, Jacqueline 417-781-5633 292 C
jacqueline.odell@vatterott.edu
O'DELL, James 617-912-9166 232 E
jodell@bostonconservatory.edu
O'DELL, Tim 843-661-8300 458 A
tim.odell@fdtc.edu
O'DESKY, Ryan 608-249-6611 547 D
O'DONLEY, Rudy 918-465-1802 408 A
rodonley@eosc.edu
O'DONNELL, Anne 215-893-5272 426 E
anne.odonnell@curtis.edu
O'DONNELL, Bill 217-228-5432 161 E
odonnbi@quincy.edu
O'DONNELL, Bill, J 574-520-4218 174 C
odonnell@iusb.edu
O'DONNELL, Brennan 718-862-7301 339 H
brennan.odonnell@manhattan.edu
O'DONNELL, Cynthia 941-355-9080 104 J
c.odonnell@ewcollege.org
O'DONNELL, David 303-292-0015 83 H
d.odonnell@denverschoolofnursing.org
O'DONNELL, Eileen 617-327-6777 242 C
eileen_healy@mspp.edu
O'DONNELL, Eileen 215-635-7300 430 A
busoffice@gratz.edu
O'DONNELL, OP, Gabriel 202-495-3832 98 D
dean@dhs.edu
O'DONNELL, James 402-375-7394 299 I
jaodonn1@wsc.edu
O'DONNELL, James, J 202-687-6400 98 A
provost@georgetown.edu
O'DONNELL, John 781-239-3101 240 D
jodonnell@massbay.edu
O'DONNELL, Karen 813-880-8011 111 A
kodonnell@academy.edu
O'DONNELL, Kevin 802-225-3356 513 H
kevin.odonnell@neci.edu
O'DONNELL, Matthew 206-543-1829 538 F
odonnel@uw.edu
O'DONNELL, Michael 520-319-3300 12 L
miodonnell@brownmackie.edu
O'DONNELL, Michael 512-499-4601 504 E
modonnell@utsystem.edu
O'DONNELL, Michael 262-741-8538 553 H
odonnellm@gtc.edu
O'DONNELL, SSJ, Patricia 215-248-7125 425 C
podonnel@chc.edu
O'DONNELL, Patrick 562-860-2451 38 J
podonnell@cerritos.edu
O'DONNELL, Ralph 660-944-2920 280 F
rodonnell@conception.edu
O'DONNELL, Timothy, T 540-636-2900 517 H
president@christendom.edu
O'DONOGHUE, Patricia 312-362-8666 148 F
podonog1@depaul.edu
O'DONOVAN, Stephen 254-526-1934 482 F
stephen.o'donovan@ctcd.edu
O'DOWD, Kathleen 734-432-5300 254 G
kodowd@madonna.edu
O'DRISCOLL, Brian 503-352-2917 419 E
odriscob@pacificu.edu
O'DRISCOLL, Dean 435-865-8054 511 A
odriscoll@suu.edu
O'DUOR, Charles 850-412-5480 118 G
charles.oduor@famu.edu
O'DWYER, Anne 413-528-7240 231 A
aodwyer@simons-rock.edu
O'DWYER, Timothy 503-768-7860 416 F
odwyer@lclark.edu
O'FARRELL, Kevin, D 727-376-6911 122 B
kofarrell@trinitycollege.edu
O'FARRELL, Mark, T 727-376-6911 122 B
mofarrell@trinitycollege.edu
O'FLAHERTY, Kevin 215-646-7300 430 C
oflaherty.k@gmc.edu
O'GORMAN, Deb 775-829-9000 302 J
dogorman@tmcc.edu
O'GORMAN, Jane 706-864-1918 134 D
jogorman@northgeorgia.edu
O'GORMAN, Kathryn 513-569-1695 387 F
kathy.ogorman@cincinnatistate.edu
O'GORMAN, Ryan 845-848-7600 332 C
ryan.ogorman@dc.edu
O'GRADY, Elaine 845-561-0800 342 A
elaine.ogrady@msmc.edu
O'GRADY EISENMANN,
Sharon 610-660-1290 446 C
seisenma@sju.edu
O'GUYNN, Valerie 310-900-1600 45 E
o'guynn_v@compton.edu
O'GWYNN, Martin 405-585-5411 409 D
marty.o'gwynn@okbu.edu
O'HAGAN, Jill 860-412-7311 91 A
johagan@qvcc.commnet.edu
O'HAGAN, Patricia 808-734-9569 141 E
ohaganp@hawaii.edu
O'HAIR, Dan 859-257-7805 206 H
O'HAIR, Mary, J 859-257-2813 206 H
O'HALLA, Kevin 616-234-3638 251 G
kohalla@grcc.edu
O'HALLORAN, Teresa 715-836-2387 550 H
ohallote@uwec.edu
O'HANIAN, Hunter 617-879-7045 238 E
hohanian@massart.edu
O'HARA, Bradley 225-342-6950 215 D
bohara@uls.state.la.us
O'HARA, Christine, S 716-286-8776 344 D
cso@niagara.edu
O'HARA, Colleen 773-298-3780 163 G
ohara@sxu.edu
O'HARA, Edward 203-837-9109 92 A
oharae@wcsu.edu
O'HARA, James, P 609-896-5367 313 G
johara@rider.edu
O'HARA, Marcy 805-565-6114 78 F
mohara@westmont.edu
O'HARA, Noreen 914-323-5165 340 A
oharan@mville.edu
O'HARA, Patrick 715-732-3888 555 A
patrick.ohara@nwtc.edu
O'HARA, William, T 401-232-6477 453 A
wohara@bryant.edu
O'HARE, Katie 617-323-6662 242 C
katie_ohare@mspp.edu
O'HARE, Lyn 828-296-9990 380 C
lohare@warren-wilson.edu
O'HARE, Susan 610-861-1588 436 I
mesio01@moravian.edu
O'HEA, Barbara, J 563-556-5110 187 G
o'heab@nicc.edu
O'HEARN, Christopher 760-245-4271 77 E
Christopher.O'Hearn@vvc.edu
O'HERN, Susan 518-465-8500 333 F
sohern@excelsior.edu
O'HERRON, Virginia 757-683-4141 521 L
voherron@odu.edu
O'KANE, Gail 612-659-6299 267 E
gail.okane@minneapolis.edu
O'KARMA, Theodore 818-345-8414 42 D
tokarma@columbiacollege.edu
O'KEEFE, Barbara, J 847-491-7023 160 D
b-okeefe@northwestern.edu
O'KEEFE, Louise 256-824-2445 9 A
Louise.OKeefe@uah.edu
O'KEEFE, Martha 540-891-3094 526 E
mokeefe@germanna.edu
O'KEEFE, Mildred 516-876-3247 353 D
okeefem@oldwestbury.edu
O'KEEFE, Paterick 716-829-7753 332 F
O'KEEFE, Paul 508-830-5063 239 A
pokeefe@maritime.edu
O'KEEFE, Paul 781-736-2120 233 A
pokeefe@brandeis.edu
O'KEEFE, Steve 618-985-3741 154 E
steveokeefe@jalc.edu
O'KEEFE, Susan 732-571-3521 311 F
okeefe@monmouth.edu
O'KEEFE, Tim 701-777-2611 381 D
timo@undalumni.org
O'KEEFFE, Mary Ellen 206-934-3701 536 H
maryellen.okeeffe@seattlecolleges.edu
O'KEEFFE, Michael 727-341-3352 116 F
okeeffe.mike@spcollege.edu
O'KELLY, Keiren 773-371-5442 146 B
kokelly@ctu.edu
O'KIEF, Kristy 605-995-2656 464 B
krokief@dwu.edu

P

PADRON, Joshua ... 954-499-9700 ... 104 C
jpadron@devry.edu
PADULA, Fernando ... 915-747-5594 ... 505 E
lfpadula@utep.edu
PAEPLOW, Randall, K ... 863-784-7083 ... 117 I
randall.paeplow@southflorida.edu
PAESE, Paul ... 765-455-9441 ... 173 E
jpcpaese@iuk.edu
PAESLER, Dennis ... 218-683-8577 ... 268 E
dennis.paesler@northlandcollege.edu
PAFF, John, W ... 260-359-4051 ... 172 K
jpaff@huntington.edu
PAGÁN, José, V ... 787-728-1515 ... 568 B
jvpagan@sagrado.edu
PAGÁN, María ... 787-848-1520 ... 564 G
mpagan@popac.edu
PAGAN, Alba ... 617-850-1261 ... 236 A
apagan@hchc.edu
PAGAN, Andres ... 787-765-1915 ... 564 B
apagan@inter.edu
PAGAN, Damaris ... 787-765-1915 ... 564 B
dpagan@inter.edu
PAGAN, Deomedes ... 787-815-0000 ... 566 F
PAGAN, Hector ... 787-878-5475 ... 562 H
hpagan@arecibo.inter.edu
PAGAN, Nellie ... 787-766-1717 ... 565 G
npaganm@suagm.edu
PAGAN, Nydia ... 787-780-0070 ... 560 F
mpagan@caribbean.edu
PAGAN, Virgen ... 787-480-2406 ... 561 D
vpagan01@sanjuancapital.com
PAGAN, Vivian ... 212-349-4330 ... 334 G
vivian@globe.edu
PAGAN, Yolanda ... 787-891-0925 ... 562 G
ypagan@ns.inter.edu
PAGANELLI, John ... 508-531-1328 ... 238 B
jpaganelli@bridgew.edu
PAGANI-SOTO, Juan, C ... 787-765-4210 ... 561 A
jcpagani@cempr.edu
PAGANO, Amy, E ... 724-458-3850 ... 430 B
aepagano@gcc.edu
PAGANO, Jan ... 772-462-7635 ... 110 L
jpagano@irsc.edu
PAGANO, Jeffrey, M ... 716-839-8254 ... 331 G
jpagano@daemen.edu
PAGANO, Michael, A ... 312-996-2671 ... 166 F
mapagano@uic.edu
PAGANO, Michael, A ... 312-413-3375 ... 166 F
mapagano@uic.edu
PAGE, Beth, M ... 276-739-2506 ... 528 D
bpage@vhcc.edu
PAGE, Beverly ... 206-726-5004 ... 532 G
bpage@cornish.edu
PAGE, Bob ... 913-588-7332 ... 197 A
bpage@kumc.edu
PAGE, Cedric, D ... 505-662-0330 ... 321 E
cpage11@unm.edu
PAGE, Cheryl ... 417-268-6412 ... 279 D
cpage@gobbc.edu
PAGE, Daniel, R ... 870-235-4171 ... 23 I
drpage@saumag.edu
PAGE, David ... 501-370-5270 ... 23 B
dpage@philander.edu
PAGE, Dorian ... 435-586-7721 ... 511 A
page@suu.edu
PAGE, Hugh, R ... 574-631-7242 ... 180 D
page.6@nd.edu
PAGE, Jamie ... 502-585-9911 ... 205 I
jpage@spalding.edu
PAGE, Kim ... 207-255-1220 ... 220 E
kpage@maine.edu
PAGE, Mark ... 813-880-8005 ... 111 B
mpage@academy.edu
PAGE, Michael, J ... 781-891-2921 ... 231 F
mpage@bentley.edu
PAGE, Pamela ... 254-442-5121 ... 482 G
pam.page@cisco.edu
PAGE, Paula ... 918-456-5511 ... 409 A
page@nsuok.edu
PAGE, Reginald ... 609-586-4800 ... 311 C
pager@mccc.edu
PAGE, Richard, K ... 208-496-1121 ... 142 G
pager@byui.edu
PAGE, Robert ... 706-295-6300 ... 130 C
rpage@highlands.edu
PAGE, Robert ... 706-842-0341 ... 472 E
bobpage860@charter.net
PAGE, Robert, E ... 480-965-1288 ... 12 B
robert.page@asu.edu
PAGE, Sally, J ... 701-777-4171 ... 381 D
sally.page@email.und.edu
PAGE, Scott ... 828-565-4167 ... 370 G
spage@haywood.edu
PAGE, Scott ... 503-494-8050 ... 418 D
PAGE, Susan ... 708-456-0300 ... 166 C
spage@triton.edu
PAGE, Yolanda ... 870-575-8051 ... 25 B
pagey@uapb.edu
PAGE-SMITH, Julie ... 231-843-5949 ... 260 E
jsmith@westshore.edu
PAGE-STADLER, Jaime ... 920-424-2027 ... 551 D
pagestad@uwosh.edu
PAGEL, Bruce ... 352-371-2833 ... 104 I
director@dragonrises.edu

PAGEL, Richard ... 714-432-5024 ... 41 B
rpagel@occ.cccd.edu
PAGLIARO, Phil ... 610-399-2299 ... 441 H
ppagliaro@cheyney.edu
PAGLIARULO, John ... 617-573-8115 ... 245 E
jpagliar@suffolk.edu
PAGNAM, Charles, J ... 508-856-4340 ... 238 A
charles.pagnam@umassmed.edu
PAGNOTTA, Cindy ... 914-831-2700 ... 339 D
lisa.dorado@liu.edu
PAGOLU, John ... 692-625-8092 ... 559 E
cmilib@ntamar.net
PAGOTTO, Louise ... 808-734-9519 ... 141 E
pagotto@hawaii.edu
PAGUIA, Cheryl, L ... 510-580-6740 ... 79 G
cpaguia@cci.edu
PAGURA, Annie ... 443-412-2418 ... 223 B
apagura@harford.edu
PAHCODDY, JR., Lee ... 785-749-8467 ... 193 B
lpahcoddy@haskell.edu
PAHL, Jennifer ... 989-964-4011 ... 258 A
jkpahl@svsu.edu
PAHL, Kim ... 920-693-1136 ... 554 A
kim.pahl@gotoltc.edu
PAHUT, Amberly ... 406-683-7306 ... 295 B
a_pahut@umwestern.edu
PAI, Bipin ... 219-989-2694 ... 178 G
bipinpai@purduecal.edu
PAI, Edward ... 323-953-4000 ... 54 H
epai@lacitycollege.edu
PAIER, Daniel, L ... 203-287-3022 ... 93 C
PAIER, Jonathan, E ... 203-287-3180 ... 93 C
paier.jep@snet.net
PAIER, Maureen, E ... 203-287-3035 ... 93 C
paier.fin@snet.net
PAIGE, Ellen, M ... 904-256-7024 ... 111 J
epaige@ju.edu
PAIGE, CSC, John, R ... 574-239-8375 ... 172 J
jpaige@hcc-nd.edu
PAIGE, Joseph, P ... 860-832-2225 ... 91 G
paigejop@ccsu.edu
PAIGE, Joy ... 704-378-1024 ... 365 H
jpaige@jcsu.edu
PAIKOWSKI, Gary ... 903-463-8707 ... 487 A
paikowski@grayson.edu
PAINE, Clarke, C ... 717-291-3991 ... 429 E
clarke.paine@fandm.edu
PAINE, Gage, E ... 210-458-4136 ... 506 B
gage.paine@utsa.edu
PAINE, James ... 636-227-2100 ... 284 E
james.paine@logan.edu
PAINE, Paula ... 785-242-5200 ... 195 G
PAINE, Paula ... 785-242-5200 ... 195 F
paula.paine@ottawa.edu
PAINE, Paula ... 785-242-5200 ... 178 E
PAINE, Paula ... 785-242-5200 ... 17 C
PAINE, Paula ... 785-242-5200 ... 549 E
PAINO, Tracy ... 612-343-4768 ... 270 C
trpaino@northcentral.edu
PAINO, Troy, D ... 660-785-4100 ... 291 A
tpaino@truman.edu
PAIR-CUNNINGHAM, Stephanie, S ... 301-322-0649 ... 225 F
pairss@pgcc.edu
PAIZ, Larry, P ... 214-350-9722 ... 483 H
larry.paiz@crid.com
PAJAK, Daniel, T ... 304-829-7217 ... 540 E
dpajak@bethanywv.edu
PAJE-MANALO, Leila, L ... 603-862-3491 ... 306 E
leila.paje-manalo@unh.edu
PAJIC, Natasa ... 859-233-8213 ... 206 E
npajic@transy.edu
PAKALA, James, C ... 314-434-4044 ... 281 A
jim.pakala@covenantseminary.edu
PAKOWSKI, Lawrence ... 910-755-7324 ... 368 C
pakowskil@brunswickcc.edu
PAKSTIS, John ... 978-934-4331 ... 237 F
john_pakstis@uml.edu
PALACIO, Michelle ... 305-348-1757 ... 119 B
michelle.palacio@fiu.edu
PALAGONIA, Michael ... 802-635-1205 ... 515 E
michael.palagonia@jsc.edu
PALAMIOTIS, Nikki ... 678-915-4276 ... 137 C
npalamio@spsu.edu
PALAMOUNTAIN, Valerie ... 434-961-5333 ... 527 F
vpalamountain@pvcc.edu
PALAN, Kay ... 269-387-5050 ... 260 F
kay.palan@wmich.edu
PALANGI, Anthony ... 518-743-2246 ... 322 B
palangia@sunyacc.edu
PALANISWAMY, Usha ... 407-277-0311 ... 106 G
upalaniswamy@evergladesuniversity.edu
PALANTZAS, Nicholas ... 781-821-2222 ... 240 E
PALARDY, William, B ... 781-899-5500 ... 232 A
rev.palardy@blessedjohnxxiii.edu
PALASOTA, Joanna, E ... 713-525-3151 ... 504 D
palasota@stthom.edu
PALASOTA, John ... 713-525-6918 ... 504 D
japalaso@stthom.edu
PALATELLA, Anna Marie ... 724-925-4091 ... 451 E
palatellaa@wccc.edu
PALAZOLA, Cecelia ... 901-272-5142 ... 471 B
cpalazola@mca.edu

PALAZZO, Robert ... 518-276-8031 ... 347 D
palazr@rpi.edu
PALCZEWSKI, Christine ... 716-896-0700 ... 359 F
cepalcz@villa.edu
PALCZEWSKI, Christine, E ... 716-896-0700 ... 359 F
cepalcz@villa.edu
PALEFSKY, Lou ... 212-875-4679 ... 323 E
finaid@bankstreet.edu
PALEN, Lisa ... 203-575-8100 ... 90 E
lpalen@nvcc.commnet.edu
PALERMO, Heather ... 406-771-4305 ... 296 B
hpalermo@msugf.edu
PALERMO, Lisa ... 651-730-5100 ... 264 A
lpalermo@globeuniversity.edu
PALERMO, Pam ... 231-995-1533 ... 256 G
ppalermo@nmc.edu
PALERMO, Pamela, J ... 440-964-4274 ... 393 E
ppalermo@kent.edu
PALESE, Rick ... 312-225-6288 ... 167 E
rpalese@vandercook.edu
PALEY, Noelle ... 607-753-2336 ... 353 B
noelle.paley@cortland.edu
PALIK, Pelma ... 691-320-2480 ... 559 A
pelmap@comfsm.fm
PALINKAS, Robert, D ... 217-333-2711 ... 167 B
palinkas@illinois.edu
PALINSKY, David, W ... 661-336-5147 ... 52 L
dpalinsk@kccd.edu
PALIWAL, Rupendra ... 203-396-8084 ... 93 G
paliwalr@sacredheart.edu
PALLA, Joe ... 707-527-1000 ... 68 E
jpalla@santarosa.edu
PALLADINO, Mark ... 215-951-2700 ... 444 C
palladinom@philau.edu
PALLADINO, Michael ... 732-571-3421 ... 311 F
mpalladi@monmouth.edu
PALLADINO, Michael ... 212-752-1530 ... 338 C
michael.palladino@limcollege.edu
PALLADINO, Michael, A ... 215-898-9386 ... 448 I
mikep@isc.upenn.edu
PALLADINO, Richard ... 914-633-2351 ... 336 E
rpalladino@iona.edu
PALLADINO, Robert ... 740-283-6405 ... 390 M
rpalladino@franciscan.edu
PALLAVICINI, Maria, G ... 209-946-2551 ... 75 D
mpallavicini@pacific.edu
PALLEJA, Sandra ... 212-237-8873 ... 328 A
spalleja@jjay.cuny.edu
PALLONE, Donna, L ... 724-287-8711 ... 423 F
donna.pallone@bc3.edu
PALM, Don ... 530-747-5220 ... 56 D
palmd@scc.losrios.edu
PALM, Elizabeth, A ... 847-735-5107 ... 155 F
palm@lakeforest.edu
PALM, Matt ... 419-448-2020 ... 391 G
mpalm@heidelberg.edu
PALM, Risa, I ... 404-413-2574 ... 131 C
risapalm@gsu.edu
PALM, Ryan ... 814-824-3320 ... 436 C
rpalm@mercyhurst.edu
PALMA, Eugene ... 516-877-3505 ... 322 A
palma@adelphi.edu
PALMA, Yazmin ... 305-273-4499 ... 103 C
yazmin@cbt.edu
PALMATIER, Bob ... 205-940-7806 ... 8 A
bpalmatier@edaff.com
PALMER, April, A ... 843-383-8214 ... 457 A
apalmer@coker.edu
PALMER, Betty, G ... 404-627-2681 ... 126 A
betty.palmer@beulah.org
PALMER, Brian ... 904-256-7374 ... 111 J
bpalmer@ju.edu
PALMER, Bruce ... 281-283-3300 ... 503 C
palmer@uhcl.edu
PALMER, Bruce, H ... 508-999-8634 ... 237 E
bpalmer@umassd.edu
PALMER, C. Eddie ... 337-482-6965 ... 216 D
palmer@louisiana.edu
PALMER, C. Patrick ... 517-264-7606 ... 258 D
ppalmer@sienaheights.edu
PALMER, Charles ... 813-545-4527 ... 458 B
charlespalmer@forrrestcollege.edu
PALMER, Colleen ... 617-585-1295 ... 243 E
colleen.palmer@necmusic.edu
PALMER, Daniel, E ... 330-675-8823 ... 394 A
dpalmer1@kent.edu
PALMER, Doreen, E ... 603-641-4164 ... 306 F
doreen.palmer@unh.edu
PALMER, Douglas, J ... 979-862-6649 ... 497 C
dpalmer@tamu.edu
PALMER, Eric ... 810-766-4237 ... 248 C
ericpalmer@baker.edu
PALMER, Eric ... 810-766-4238 ... 248 H
eric.palmer@baker.edu
PALMER, Eric, F ... 804-287-6591 ... 525 A
epalmer@richmond.edu
PALMER, Gail ... 785-670-1151 ... 197 D
gail.palmer@washburn.edu
PALMER, Gary ... 620-223-2700 ... 192 G
garyp@fortscott.edu
PALMER, Gregory ... 914-323-5194 ... 340 A
palmerg@mville.edu
PALMER, Harvey, J ... 585-475-2146 ... 347 G
hjpeen@rit.edu

PALMER, Jacqueline ... 202-408-2400 ... 99 D
PALMER, Jan, E ... 304-293-6978 ... 544 E
jpalmer@hsc.wvu.edu
PALMER, Janice ... 860-832-1791 ... 91 G
palmerj@ccsu.edu
PALMER, Jeffrey, L ... 302-831-3007 ... 96 F
jpalmer@udel.edu
PALMER, John ... 320-308-3143 ... 269 C
jwpalmer@stcloudstate.edu
PALMER, John ... 651-846-1482 ... 269 E
john.palmer@saintpaul.edu
PALMER, Jonathan ... 618-374-5148 ... 161 D
president@principia.edu
PALMER, Joseph ... 315-792-5318 ... 341 E
jpalmer@mvcc.edu
PALMER, Joyce ... 315-792-5477 ... 341 E
jpalmer@mvcc.edu
PALMER, Julio ... 787-841-2000 ... 564 I
jpalmer@email.pucpr.edu
PALMER, Kevin ... 573-875-7329 ... 280 E
kpalmer@ccis.edu
PALMER, Linda ... 801-422-3605 ... 509 D
linda_palmer@byu.edu
PALMER, Lisa ... 706-771-4089 ... 125 D
lpalmer@augustatech.edu
PALMER, Magali ... 787-279-1912 ... 563 B
mpalmer@bayamon.inter.edu
PALMER, Magaly ... 787-279-1912 ... 563 B
mpalmer@bayamon.inter.edu
PALMER, Maria, T ... 336-334-7800 ... 377 F
mtpalmer@ncat.edu
PALMER, Marila, D ... 903-233-3130 ... 489 K
marilapalmer@letu.edu
PALMER, Mel ... 706-548-8505 ... 135 D
mpalmer@piedmont.edu
PALMER, Michael, D ... 757-352-4406 ... 523 B
mpalmer@regent.edu
PALMER, Nikki ... 907-822-3201 ... 10 C
info@akbible.edu
PALMER, Patricia ... 501-812-2210 ... 23 C
ppalmer@pulaskitech.edu
PALMER, Ron ... 304-637-1252 ... 540 F
palmerr@dewv.edu
PALMER, Roxanne ... 772-672-8222 ... 101 D
PALMER, Russell, A ... 516-877-3249 ... 322 A
palmer@adelphi.edu
PALMER, Sallie ... 702-369-9944 ... 301 G
spalmer@aii.edu
PALMER, Sandra ... 203-575-8046 ... 90 E
spalmer@nvcc.commnet.edu
PALMER, Scott ... 952-888-4777 ... 270 F
spalmer@nwhealth.edu
PALMER, Susan, M ... 320-363-5298 ... 262 H
spalmer@csbsju.edu
PALMER, Tom ... 706-864-1786 ... 134 D
tpalmer@northgeorgia.edu
PALMER, Vanessa ... 931-372-3888 ... 474 B
vpalmer@tntech.edu
PALMER PRANGE, Raphaella, M ... 217-362-6410 ... 158 F
rpalmer@millikin.edu
PALMERI, Marian, K ... 570-208-5900 ... 432 E
mkpalmer@kings.edu
PALMERTREE, Bill ... 940-898-3972 ... 502 B
bpalmertree@twu.edu
PALMIERI, Becky ... 518-587-2100 ... 355 F
becky.palmieri@esc.edu
PALMIERI, Ernie ... 914-251-6530 ... 354 D
ernie.palmieri@purchase.edu
PALMIERI, Mark ... 315-279-5418 ... 337 K
mpalmier@mail.keuka.edu
PALMIERI, Robert ... 315-866-0300 ... 335 E
palmierrh@herkimer.edu
PALMIERI-MOUDED, Kimberly, J ... 718-390-4345 ... 348 G
palmierk@stjohns.edu
PALMINI, Bill ... 415-565-4611 ... 73 G
palminib@uchastings.edu
PALMITER, Lia Richards ... 570-961-4799 ... 435 F
lpalmiter@marywood.edu
PALMORE, Marcus ... 703-709-5875 ... 522 B
mpalmore@potomac.edu
PALMOUR, Mack ... 678-717-3861 ... 129 D
mpalmour@gsc.edu
PALO, Eric, E ... 425-235-2331 ... 536 E
epalo@rtc.edu
PALOK, Debra ... 623-845-3536 ... 15 J
debra.palok@gcmail.maricopa.edu
PALOMBI, Barbara ... 616-331-3266 ... 252 A
palombib@gvsu.edu
PALOMBO, Tom, J ... 336-316-2290 ... 364 E
tpalombo@guilford.edu
PALOMO, Giovanni ... 212-226-5500 ... 323 C
gpalomo@aii.edu
PALOMO, William ... 671-735-2364 ... 559 D
safety@uguam.uog.edu
PALONE, James, E ... 330-471-8255 ... 395 E
jpalone@malone.edu
PALONSKY, Stuart, B ... 573-882-3893 ... 291 D
palonskys@missouri.edu
PALOS, Jim ... 773-481-8175 ... 147 F
jpalos4@ccc.edu
PALOV, Susan, K ... 814-269-2090 ... 449 D
palov@pitt.edu

PARK, Kathryn 409-933-8201 483 B
kpark@com.edu

PARK, Linda 315-279-5208 337 K
lpark@mail.keuka.edu

PARK, Matthew 940-397-4501 491 A
matthew.park@mwsu.edu

PARK, Mi 562-926-1023 63 B
mhpark@ptsa.edu

PARK, Michelle 714-533-1495 70 B
isa@southbaylo.edu

PARK, Mimi 714-533-1495 70 B
mimi@southbaylo.edu

PARK, Myung 425-739-8287 535 B
myung.park@lwtc.edu

PARK, No Hee 310-206-6063 74 A
npark@dent.ucla.edu

PARK, Shelley, S 859-622-2361 200 D
shelley.park@eku.edu

PARK, Sunny 806-720-7507 490 D
sunny.park@lcu.edu

PARKE, Lydia 215-780-1417 446 G
lparke@salus.edu

PARKER, Aaron, L 601-426-6346 277 D
aparker@southeasternbaptist.edu

PARKER, Anthony, O 229-430-3502 123 I
aparker@albanytech.edu

PARKER, Barbara 315-268-6445 329 C
bparker@clarkson.edu

PARKER, Beverly 318-670-9571 215 A
bparker@susla.edu

PARKER, Brian 212-659-3610 338 A

PARKER, Bruce 212-243-5150 334 E
bparker@gts.edu

PARKER, Cassandra 202-274-5323 99 F
cparker@udc.edu

PARKER, Cathy 601-484-8799 275 C
cparker@mcc.cc.ms.us

PARKER, Charles, R 850-263-3261 101 E
crparker@baptistcollege.edu

PARKER, Collier, B 570-340-6000 435 F
cbparker@marywood.edu

PARKER, Craig 502-897-4885 205 H
cparker@sbts.edu

PARKER, Cynthia 706-295-6346 130 C
cparker@highlands.edu

PARKER, Cynthia, L 401-598-1345 453 C
cparker@jwu.edu

PARKER, Dana, C 610-436-2627 443 F
dparker@wcupa.edu

PARKER, Danny, M 864-231-2145 455 C
dparker@andersonuniversity.edu

PARKER, Darnell 410-778-7457 229 D
dparker2@washcoll.edu

PARKER, Darrell, F 864-503-5566 463 A
dparker@uscupstate.edu

PARKER, David 336-506-4301 367 G
parkerdw@alamancecc.edu

PARKER, Deborah 870-762-3151 20 A
dparker@smail.anc.edu

PARKER, Deborah 423-425-4467 477 D
debbie-parker@utc.edu

PARKER, Diane 617-243-2137 236 F
dparker@lasell.edu

PARKER, Donna 610-526-6004 430 D
dparker@harcum.edu

PARKER, Dorothy 214-333-5106 484 C
dorothy@dbu.edu

PARKER, Frank 936-294-1781 501 A
fparker@shsu.edu

PARKER, G. Randy 336-334-4822 370 E

PARKER, Gail, C 318-342-1961 216 E
gparker@ulm.edu

PARKER, George 530-741-6700 80 C

PARKER, Gilbert, A 607-729-1581 332 A
gparker@davisny.edu

PARKER, Heather 530-251-3331 53 G
hparker@lassencollege.edu

PARKER, Heidi 641-673-1031 189 I
parkerh@wmpenn.edu

PARKER, Jack 617-353-4639 232 G
jjparker@bu.edu

PARKER, James 605-677-5331 465 E
james.parker@usd.edu

PARKER, James, T 801-581-6857 510 L
jparker@purchasing.utah.edu

PARKER, Janet 210-458-4211 506 B
janet.parker@utsa.edu

PARKER, Janet 910-892-3178 364 F
jparker@heritagebiblecollege.edu

PARKER, Janice, C 312-658-5100 165 E
janice.parker@tbiil.edu

PARKER, Jeffrey 303-315-2750 88 D
jeff.parker@ucdenver.edu

PARKER, Jerome, S 610-359-5100 426 G
jparker@dccc.edu

PARKER, Jill 530-752-2599 73 F
jblack@ucdavis.edu

PARKER, Jim, O 504-816-8592 213 H
jparker@nobts.edu

PARKER, Jo Ellen 434-381-6210 524 E
jparker@sbc.edu

PARKER, John 231-995-1019 256 G
jparker@nmc.edu

PARKER, Johnny, F 205-391-2379 7 A
jparker@sheltonstate.edu

PARKER, Jonathan, K 951-343-4213 31 G
jparker@calbaptist.edu

PARKER, Joyce, E 310-233-4551 54 I
parkerje@lahc.edu

PARKER, Karen, L 434-582-2445 520 F
kparker@liberty.edu

PARKER, Kathleen 320-363-5195 262 H
kparker@csbsju.edu

PARKER, Kathleen 320-363-2121 271 F
kparker@csbsju.edu

PARKER, Kathy, P 585-275-8902 358 I
kathy_parker@urmc.rochester.edu

PARKER, Keith 561-732-4424 117 A
kparker@svdp.edu

PARKER, Keith, S 310-794-6811 74 A
kparker@support.ucla.edu

PARKER, Kelly 419-473-2700 389 B
kparker@daviscollege.edu

PARKER, Kevin 845-758-7511 323 F
parker@bard.edu

PARKER, Kim 713-646-1803 494 E
kparker@stcl.edu

PARKER, Kim 214-637-3530 508 A
kparker@wadecollege.edu

PARKER, Kim 423-478-6235 474 E
kparker01@clevelandstatecc.edu

PARKER, Kyle 479-788-7008 24 D
kparker@uafortsmith.edu

PARKER, Lee 715-394-8217 552 D
lparker@uwsuper.edu

PARKER, Linda 843-863-8054 456 B
lparker@csuniv.edu

PARKER, Linda, M 518-388-6123 358 E
parkerl@union.edu

PARKER, Maria 870-584-4471 25 C
mparker@cccua.edu

PARKER, Maria, D 205-665-6050 9 C
parkermd@montevallo.edu

PARKER, Mark 901-761-1356 469 A
mparker@hst.edu

PARKER, Mark 405-208-5315 410 A
mparker@okcu.edu

PARKER, Mary 310-393-0411 61 D
mfparker@rand.org

PARKER, Mary Jo 713-221-8471 503 D
parkerm@uhd.edu

PARKER, Melanie, L 617-253-4733 242 A
mlparker@mit.edu

PARKER, Micah 951-343-4318 31 G
miparker@calbaptist.edu

PARKER, Mike 731-352-4239 467 C
parkerm@bethelu.edu

PARKER, Pamela, H 205-348-8256 8 F
pparker@advance.ua.edu

PARKER, Peggy 910-892-3178 364 F
pparker@heritagebiblecollege.edu

PARKER, Pennie 407-646-2636 116 B
pparker@rollins.edu

PARKER, Philip 812-464-1865 180 F
plparker@usi.edu

PARKER, Pippin 212-229-5859 342 E
parkerp@newschool.edu

PARKER, Randy 252-492-2061 374 D
rparker@vgcc.edu

PARKER, Rebecca 510-845-6232 71 H
rparker@sksm.edu

PARKER, Richard, L 989-328-1291 256 A
rickp@montcalm.edu

PARKER, Robert 404-471-6236 123 G
rparker@agnesscott.edu

PARKER, Robert 304-766-3061 544 D
parkerf@wvstateu.edu

PARKER, Robin, L 513-529-6734 396 D
parkerrl@muohio.edu

PARKER, Rodney 410-617-2310 224 A
rparker1@loyola.edu

PARKER, Roger, C 510-885-3692 34 C
roger.parker@csueastbay.edu

PARKER, Ron 979-230-3480 482 B
ron.parker@brazosport.edu

PARKER, Sandra 513-745-5736 403 F
sandra.parker@uc.edu

PARKER, Savander 408-274-7900 67 B
savander.parker@evc.edu

PARKER, Scotty 770-537-5750 139 B
scotty.parker@westgatech.edu

PARKER, Sherry 407-277-0311 106 G
sparker@evergladesuniversity.edu

PARKER, Sirena 662-329-7127 276 B
sparker@ss.muw.edu

PARKER, Sonia 801-957-4446 512 C
sonia.parker@slcc.edu

PARKER, Teresa 740-389-4636 395 G
parkert@mtc.edu

PARKER, Terri 803-765-6023 455 B
tparker@allenuniversity.edu

PARKER, Terry 303-273-3399 82 F
tparker@mines.edu

PARKER, Thomas, H 413-542-2328 230 A
admissions@amherst.edu

PARKER, Tim 205-879-5588 3 H
tparker@faulkner.edu

PARKER, Wayne, M 267-502-2565 423 B
wayne.parker@anc-gc.org

PARKER, Willis 202-274-5060 99 F
wparker@udc.edu

PARKER, Zoann 302-328-7508 96 G
parker@wesle.edu

PARKER AMES, Gwen 845-675-4446 344 G
gwen.ames@nyack.edu

PARKER-JEFFRIES, Terry 704-463-3057 375 E
terry.jeffries@fsmail.pfeiffer.edu

PARKER-KELLY, Darlene 323-563-9340 39 D
darleneparkerkelly@cdrewu.edu

PARKES, Marty 314-529-9340 284 F
mparkes@maryville.edu

PARKHURST, Abbie 540-828-5782 516 K
aparkhur@bridgewater.edu

PARKIN, Richard, C 413-755-4489 241 E
rparkin@stcc.edu

PARKINSON, Alan, R 801-422-4327 509 D
alan_parkinson@byu.edu

PARKINSON, Ann 252-335-0821 369 D
aparkinson@albemarle.edu

PARKINSON, David 435-797-1645 511 B
david.parkinson@usu.edu

PARKINSON, III,
Henry, C 978-665-3160 238 C
hparkinson@fitchburgstate.edu

PARKINSON, Michael 314-529-9553 284 F
mparkinson@maryville.edu

PARKISON, Kathy 765-455-9205 173 E
kparkiso@iuk.edu

PARKS, Ann 660-263-4110 287 B
annp@macc.edu

PARKS, Barbara, E 803-786-3962 457 C
beparks@columbiasc.edu

PARKS, Brenda 309-298-1944 168 A
bs-parks@wiu.edu

PARKS, Carlton 626-284-2777 27 D
cparks@alliant.edu

PARKS, Cherri, S 303-963-3357 81 K
cparks@ccu.edu

PARKS, Colin 202-462-2101 98 C
parks@iwp.edu

PARKS, Cynthia 706-737-1431 125 C
cparks@aug.edu

PARKS, Dave 908-737-4840 311 B
dparks@kean.edu

PARKS, Earl 202-651-5494 97 E
earl.parks@gallaudet.edu

PARKS, Erik, I 312-939-4975 151 F
eparks@interiordesign.edu

PARKS, Joseph 573-875-4842 291 F
parksj@umsl.edu

PARKS, Julie 616-234-3714 251 G
jparks@grcc.edu

PARKS, Marshall 970-351-1814 88 F
marshall.parks@unco.edu

PARKS, Maureen 217-333-2590 166 E
mparks@uillinois.edu

PARKS, Michael 210-567-2791 506 E
parksm@uthscsa.edu

PARKS, Sherrie 325-235-7402 500 C
sherrie.parks@tstc.edu

PARKS, Susie 619-201-8670 65 D
Susie.Parks@sdcc.edu

PARKS, Susie, M 619-201-8670 65 D
Susie.Parks@sdcc.edu

PARKS, Thomas, N 801-581-7236 510 L
tom.parks@utah.edu

PARKS, Tom 617-262-5000 232 B
thomas.parks@the-bac.edu

PARKS, Valerie 915-779-8031 483 F
vparks@computercareercenter.com

PARKS, Vanasia Conley 423-425-4536 477 D
vanasia-parks@utc.edu

PARKS POOLEY,
Barbara, D 319-368-6470 187 E
bpooley@mtmercy.edu

PARKYN, David, L 773-244-5710 159 G
dparkyn@northpark.edu

PARLE, Joseph, D 713-785-5995 483 A
joe.parle@cbshouston.edu

PARLETT, Lynda, W 910-272-3235 373 A
lparlett@robeson.edu

PARLETT, Ray, M 585-567-9333 336 B
ray.parlett@houghton.edu

PARMANN, Maureen 810-767-4000 248 H
maureen.parmann@baker.edu

PARMER, Harry 949-582-4585 70 F
hparmer@saddleback.edu

PARMER, Marsha 503-223-2245 416 E
mparmer@westernculinary.com

PARMETER, John 515-271-1465 183 F
john.parmeter@dmu.edu

PARMLEY, Kelli, A 804-828-6683 525 E
kparmley@vcu.edu

PARNELL, Lauren 912-583-3211 126 C
lparnell@bpc.edu

PARNELL, Paul 562-908-3402 63 H
pparnell@riohondo.edu

PARNELL, Rob Roy 512-463-1808 500 D
robroy.parnell@tsus.edu

PARNELL, Todd 417-873-7201 281 H
tparnell@drury.edu

PARNES, Marvin, G 734-936-3933 259 D
mgparnes@umich.edu

PARNHAM, Gary 617-236-8800 235 B
gparnham@fisher.edu

PARNUM CADBURY,
Sarah 218-951-5144 432 G
cadbury@lasalle.edu

PAROLINI, Roger, K 630-844-5489 145 C
rparolin@aurora.edu

PARPART, Amanda, L 605-256-5244 465 G
amanda.parpart@dsu.edu

PARR, Ronald, G 901-333-4737 475 H
rgparr@southwest.tn.edu

PARR-BARRETT, Cindy, A 217-443-8759 148 E
cparrett@dacc.edu

PARRA, Carlos, P 423-236-2746 473 A
cpaarra@southern.edu

PARRA DE ORTIZ,
Alicia, F 954-322-4460 112 B

PARRAVICINI, Marcelo, S 203-591-5042 93 D
mparravicini@post.edu

PARRECO, Callie 303-477-7240 84 I
calliep@heritage-education.com

PARRENT, Jonathan, V 270-824-8571 202 C
jay.parrent@kctcs.edu

PARRENT, Rick 615-230-3321 476 A
rick.parrent@volstate.edu

PARRENT, Robert, W 501-450-5074 25 H
rparrent@uca.edu

PARRETT, Brenda, J 601-643-8301 274 A
brenda.parrett@colin.edu

PARRIERA, Keri 360-383-3330 539 D
kparrier@whatcom.ctc.edu

PARRILL, Jacqueline 740-366-9407 386 G
parrill.9@osu.edu

PARRIOTT, Karen 307-532-8264 555 H
karen.parriott@ewc.wy.edu

PARRIS, Elliott 301-860-4705 228 A
eparris@bowiestate.edu

PARRIS, Gina 864-294-2322 458 D
gina.parris@furman.edu

PARRISH, Austen 213-738-5728 71 D
academicaffairs@swlaw.edu

PARRISH, Cheney 800-962-7682 293 B
cparrish@wma.edu

PARRISH, Dave 770-531-6420 132 J
dparrish@laniertech.edu

PARRISH, Debra, J 906-353-4600 253 J
dparrish@kbocc.org

PARRISH, Gretchan 336-342-4261 373 B
parrishg@rockinghamcc.edu

PARRISH, Holly, A 717-240-5247 439 C
hap15@psu.edu

PARRISH, J. Michael 408-924-4800 37 A
mparrish@science.sjsu.edu

PARRISH, Jenni 415-565-4881 73 G
parrishj@uchastings.edu

PARRISH, John 336-342-4261 373 B
parrishj@rockinghamcc.edu

PARRISH, Paula 858-566-1200 43 J
pparrish@disd.edu

PARROTT, Mike 843-208-8040 462 C
rparrot@uscb.edu

PARROTT, Roger 601-968-5919 273 F
president@belhaven.edu

PARROTT-ROBBINS,
Rebecca 606-242-0256 203 A
rebecca.robbins@kctcs.edu

PARRY, John 970-491-3939 83 A
john.parry@colostate.edu

PARRY, John 216-687-4808 388 C
john.parry@csuohio.edu

PARRY, Laura, S 518-783-8282 350 I
lparry@siena.edu

PARRY, Rodney, R 605-357-1300 465 E
rodney.parry@usd.edu

PARRY, Susan 845-341-4251 345 E
susan.parry@sunyorange.edu

PARSCAL, Tina 866-621-0124 88 G
tina.parscal@rockies.edu

PARSHALL, William 267-468-8022 447 G
william.parshall@temple.edu

PARSLEY, Nancy, L 847-578-8401 163 A
nancy.parsley@rosalindfranklin.edu

PARSNIK, Pamela 570-674-6310 436 F
pparsnik@misericordia.edu

PARSON, Alayne 303-871-2693 88 E
alayne.parson@du.edu

PARSON, Lisa 620-278-4264 196 D
lparson@sterling.edu

PARSON, Willie 803-376-5708 455 B
wparson@allenuniversity.edu

PARSON, Willie, L 803-376-5700 455 B
wparson@allenuniversity.edu

PARSONS, Amy 970-491-5257 83 A
amy.parsons@colostate.edu

PARSONS, Brigitte 715-365-4406 554 F
bparsons@nicoletcollege.edu

PARSONS, Carole, H 603-526-3674 304 A
cparsons@colby-sawyer.edu

PARSONS, Duncan, A 423-323-3191 475 E
daparsons@northeaststate.edu

PARSONS, Edy 319-363-8213 187 E
eparsons@mtmercy.edu

PARSONS, JR., Frank, R 334-833-4294 4 E fparsons@huntingdon.edu
PARSONS, Geoffrey, J 843-349-2054 456 G parsons@coastal.edu
PARSONS, James 951-222-8856 64 B jim.parsons@rcc.edu
PARSONS, James 207-859-1250 219 G maintenance@thomas.edu
PARSONS, Larry, R 304-473-8042 545 F parsons@wvwc.edu
PARSONS, Mark 417-625-9396 286 E parons-m@mssu.edu
PARSONS, Marty 479-619-4217 22 H mparsone1@nwacc.edu
PARSONS, Pamela 406-771-4314 296 B pparsons@msugf.edu
PARSONS, Patrick 309-694-5593 152 B patrick.parsons@icc.edu
PARSONS, Paul, F 336-278-5724 364 A pparsons@elon.edu
PARSONS, Priscilla 409-880-7691 500 F priscilla.parsons@lamar.edu
PARSONS, Timothy, I 765-447-9550 172 G timothy.parsons@harrison.edu
PART, Howard 937-775-2933 406 C howard.part@wright.edu
PARTAIN, Julie 229-931-2249 136 G jpartain@southgatech.edu
PARTAIN, Pam 706-272-2985 127 G ppartain@daltonstate.edu
PARTAIN, Suzanne 303-333-4224 81 C spartain@aspen.edu
PARTARRIEU, Roberto 703-416-1441 519 F rpartarrieu@ipsciences.edu
PARTCH, Nancy 815-825-2086 155 C nancy.partch@kishwaukeecollege.edu
PARTEE, Ben 805-965-0581 68 B partee@sbcc.edu
PARTEN, Janice 559-278-2364 34 D jparten@csufresno.edu
PARTIN, Vicki 859-246-6414 201 D vicki.partin@kctcs.edu
PARTLETT, David 404-712-8815 129 A david.partlett@emory.edu
PARTON, Becky 217-786-2351 156 I becky.parton@llcc.edu
PARTON, Dwayne 918-781-3680 407 B partond@bacone.edu
PARTON, Sabrena 706-233-7465 136 E sparton@shorter.edu
PARTON, William 479-968-0417 20 G wparton@atu.edu
PARTRIDGE, Kristen 405-325-3163 413 C kpartridge@ou.edu
PARTRIDGE, Patrick 801-274-3280 512 E ppartridge@wgu.edu
PARVIZI, Nasrin 607-753-5582 353 B nasrin.parvizi@cortland.edu
PARZIALE, Anthony 561-868-3239 114 D parziala@palmbeachstate.edu
PARZY, Robert 847-925-6649 151 E rparzy@harpercollege.edu
PASBRIG, Chris, A 262-524-7343 546 E cpasbrig@carrollu.edu
PASCAL, Kenneth, C 713-623-2040 480 J kpascal@aii.edu
PASCAL, Sandra, E 617-989-4478 246 C pascals@wit.edu
PASCALE, Lynn 203-287-3031 93 C paier.admission@snet.net
PASCARIELLO, Jacqueline 631-632-6840 352 C jacqueline.pascariello@stonybrook.edu
PASCHAL, Jerry, L 205-348-5848 8 F jpaschal@sa.ua.edu
PASCHAL, Linda, L 414-955-8208 548 E lpaschal@mcw.edu
PASCHALL, Bill 303-477-7240 84 I billp@heritage-education.com
PASCHALL, Danny 562-903-4874 30 H danny.paschall@biola.edu
PASCO, Myra 303-404-5473 84 H myra.pasco@frontrange.edu
PASCOE, Frank, H 815-740-3216 167 C fpascoe@stfrancis.edu
PASCOE, Tammie 903-983-8105 489 F tpascoe@kilgore.edu
PASCUA, Arnel 818-240-1000 48 C apascua@glendale.edu
PASCUA, Vance 916-577-2200 79 C vpascua@jessup.edu
PASCUAL, Candice 727-725-2688 105 J cpascual@cci.edu
PASCUAL, Mytha 310-900-1600 45 E pascual_m@compton.edu
PASCUCCI, Richard, A 215-871-6690 444 B richardp@pcom.edu
PASEK, Heidi 406-771-4397 296 B hpasek@msugf.edu
PASHA, Stephanie 508-831-6655 247 B spasha@wpi.edu
PASIAK, David 315-498-2492 345 D
PASKETT, Lindy 307-855-2120 555 G lpaskett@cwc.edu
PASKOFF, Beth, M 225-578-1480 212 F bpaskoff@lsu.edu
PASKUS, John 413-236-2109 239 E jpaskus@berkshirecc.edu
PASKVAN, Brian 567-661-7742 400 H brian_paskvan@owens.edu
PASOUR, Katherine 828-328-7126 366 B katherine.pasour@lr.edu
PASQUERELLA, Lynn 413-538-2500 242 G commish@mtholyoke.edu
PASQUINI, Angela 212-749-2802 339 I finaid@msmnyc.edu
PASS-STERN, Bernice 212-614-6176 346 A bstern@chpnet.org
PASSALACQUA, Dominic 315-792-3393 359 C dpassalacqua@utica.edu
PASSARO, Joanne 262-524-7364 546 E jpassaro@carrollu.edu
PASSESER, Scott 212-312-4440 332 B spasseser@devry.edu
PASSET, Joanne 765-973-8521 173 D jpasset@iue.edu
PASSIN, Cathey 610-647-4400 431 B cpassin@immaculata.edu
PASSMORE, Joe 423-746-5333 476 D jpassmore@twcnet.edu
PASTERIS, Marc 309-467-6305 150 H mpasteris@eureka.edu
PASTIDES, Harris 803-777-2001 462 A pastides@sc.edu
PASTIN, John, R 856-256-4550 314 A pastin@rowan.edu
PASTOOR, Robert, A 740-376-4736 395 F bob.pastoor@marietta.edu
PASTOR, Richard 386-506-4414 103 J pastorr@DaytonaState.edu
PASTORE, Michael, A 315-255-1743 325 H michael.pastore@cayuga-cc.edu
PASTORELLA, Mark, J 585-262-1509 341 H mpastorella@monroecc.edu
PASTORIZA, Nelida 718-518-4412 327 D npastoriza@hostos.cuny.edu
PASTORRES-PALFFY, Elizabeth 916-485-3276 402 I beth.pastorres-palffy@myunion.edu
PASTRANA, Livia, D 787-728-1515 568 B lpastrana@sagrado.edu
PASTRANA, Marie Luz 787-765-3560 561 J lpastrana@edpcollege.edu
PASTRANA, Marilyn 787-765-3560 561 J mpastrana@edpcollege.edu
PASTRANA MURIEL, Marilyn 787-765-3560 561 K mpastrana@edpcollege.edu
PASTULA, Matthew 670-234-5498 559 F matthewp@nmcnet.edu
PASTULA, Robert, G 256-765-4357 9 D rpastula@una.edu
PASZKIEWICZ, Wendy 312-662-4211 144 C paszk@adler.edu
PATACCA, Pam 330-339-3391 394 B ppatacca@kent.edu
PATANICZEK, Dennis, A 410-543-6335 228 D dapataniczek@salisbury.edu
PATANKAR, Manoj 314-977-3078 289 F patankar@slu.edu
PATANO, Alexander 215-591-5700 427 A apatano@devry.edu
PATAWARAN, Arrileen 773-995-2063 146 D apatawar@csu.edu
PATCH, Sara 802-447-4013 514 D spatch@svc.edu
PATCHETT, Heather 423-636-7303 476 F
PATCHETT, Margaret, B 704-403-3077 362 E margaret.patchett@carolinashealthcare.org
PATCHETT, Sandra 765-269-5105 176 B spatchet@ivytech.edu
PATCHNER, Michael 317-274-8362 174 B patchner@iupui.edu
PATE, David, S 585-385-8034 348 F dpate@sjfc.edu
PATE, Doug 919-209-2007 371 C mdpate@johnstoncc.edu
PATE, Jane 731-286-3347 475 A pate@dscc.edu
PATE, Juston 606-759-7141 202 D juston.pate@kctcs.edu
PATE, Nino 671-734-1812 559 C npate@piu.edu
PATE, Susan 386-506-3769 103 J pates@DaytonaState.edu
PATEE, Carla 602-227-9378 192 B cpatee@dc3.edu
PATEE, Greg 620-227-9355 192 B gpatee@dc3.edu
PATEGAS, Dianna 203-582-8797 93 E dianna.pategas@quinnipiac.edu
PATEL, Dipak 312-935-6681 162 E dipakpatel@robertmorris.edu
PATEL, Jagdish 718-518-4409 327 D jpatel@hostos.cuny.edu
PATEL, Maqbool 410-951-3780 228 B mpatel@coppin.edu
PATEL, Narendra, H 404-880-8064 126 I npatel@cau.edu
PATEL, Sonia 979-209-7336 482 A sonia.patel@blinn.edu
PATELLA, Cathleen 315-364-3289 360 C cpatella@wells.edu
PATENAUDE, Craig 301-934-7643 222 C cpatenaude@csmd.edu
PATERSON, Brent 309-438-5451 153 C bgpater@ilstu.edu
PATERSON, Robert 516-678-5000 341 F rpaterson@molloy.edu
PATERSON, Valeria 617-682-1593 234 G vpaterson@eds.edu
PATERSON, Wendy, A 585-385-7316 348 F wpaterson@sjfc.edu
PATH, Bill, R 402-844-7054 300 A billp@northeast.edu
PATI, Niranjan 856-256-4025 314 A pati@rowan.edu
PATNAUDE, Valerie 603-897-8533 305 G vpatnaude@rivier.edu
PATO, Rosevonne 684-699-7834 558 I r.pato@amsamoa.edu
PATON, John 203-582-8574 93 E john.paton@quinnipiac.edu
PATON, Valerie 806-742-2184 501 D valerie.paton@ttu.edu
PATOTA, Nancy 914-633-2413 336 E NPatota@iona.edu
PATOUT, Gerald 337-550-1380 212 H
PATRIA, Patty 508-373-1981 231 D patty.patria@becker.edu
PATRIARCA, Linda 252-328-1000 377 C patriarcal@ecu.edu
PATRIAS, Marla, H 218-755-2876 266 B mpatrias@bemidjistate.edu
PATRICK, Beth 606-783-2447 204 E b.patrick@moreheadstate.edu
PATRICK, Carmel 518-381-1442 350 E patricc@sunysccc.edu
PATRICK, Craig 718-933-6700 341 G cpatrick@monroecollege.edu
PATRICK, Diane 616-234-4105 251 G dpatrick@grcc.edu
PATRICK, Diane, D 616-234-4101 251 G dpatrick@grcc.edu
PATRICK, Dolores 618-468-6300 156 C dpatrick@lc.edu
PATRICK, Edward 404-880-8067 126 I epatrick@cau.edu
PATRICK, Gary 707-476-4385 42 A garry-patrick@redwoods.edu
PATRICK, James, A 817-923-8459 483 C jpatrick@cstm.edu
PATRICK, Jamie 919-497-3245 366 E jpatrick@louisburg.edu
PATRICK, Julietta 815-455-8613 157 F jpatrick@mchenry.edu
PATRICK, Kevin 662-241-6405 276 B kpatrick@ss.muw.edu
PATRICK, Kim 616-331-2280 252 A patricki@gvsu.edu
PATRICK, Laura 949-376-6000 53 E lpatrick@lagunacollege.edu
PATRICK, Michelle 859-846-5391 204 D mpatrick@midway.edu
PATRICK, Paul, G 864-379-6675 457 G ppatrick@erskine.edu
PATRICK, Randy 863-667-5029 118 A rpatrick@seu.edu
PATRICK, Vernell 973-877-3023 310 A patrick@essex.edu
PATRICK-TURNER, Ronne 617-373-5416 244 A
PATRIQUIN, Charlotte 413-538-2225 242 G cpatriqu@mtholyoke.edu
PATRO, Rick 410-843-8490 272 F rick.patro@laureate.net
PATSCHECK, Valerie 805-437-8878 33 I valerie.patscheck@csuci.edu
PATTANAYAK, Arjendu 507-222-4300 262 B apattana@carleton.edu
PATTARINI, Stephen, M 315-792-3032 359 C spattarini@utica.edu
PATTEE, Bob 254-295-4524 504 A rpattee@umhb.edu
PATTEE, TOR, Daniel, J 740-283-6245 390 M dpattee@franciscan.edu
PATTEN, Don 570-586-2400 422 F dpatten@bbc.edu
PATTEN, Lori 802-468-1211 515 C lori.patten@castleton.edu
PATTEN, Patricia, C 757-455-3201 529 F ppatten@vwc.edu
PATTEN-LEMONS, Rebecca 317-921-4667 175 I rpatten@ivytech.edu
PATTEN WALLACE, Kaye 419-530-7963 404 F kaye.pattenwallace@utoledo.edu
PATTENAUDE, Richard, L 207-973-3205 219 I pattenaude@maine.edu
PATTENGALE, Jerry 765-677-2170 174 E jerry.pattengale@indwes.edu
PATTERSON, Abbie, L 310-233-4031 54 I patteral@lahc.edu
PATTERSON, Anne 940-552-6291 507 E apatterson@vernoncollege.edu
PATTERSON, Barbara, A 580-774-3261 412 F barbara.patterson@swosu.edu
PATTERSON, Becky 502-852-3385 207 A becky.patterson@louisville.edu
PATTERSON, Ben 805-565-6210 78 F bpatters@westmont.edu
PATTERSON, Bernie 715-346-2123 552 B
PATTERSON, Brian 262-879-0200 549 E
PATTERSON, Charles 912-478-5465 131 A cpatterson@georgiasouthern.edu
PATTERSON, Charles 912-478-2647 131 A cpatterson@georgiasouthern.edu
PATTERSON, Corey 325-674-2950 478 H pattersonc@acu.edu
PATTERSON, Cynthia 252-638-7304 369 E pattersc@cravencc.edu
PATTERSON, Cynthia, M 561-237-7172 113 D cpatterson@lynn.edu
PATTERSON, Dale 918-540-6319 408 J dale.patterson@neo.edu
PATTERSON, Darrin 330-337-6403 383 H college@awc.edu
PATTERSON, Deborah 276-466-7907 528 G deborahpatteson@vic.edu
PATTERSON, Diana, L 724-773-3558 438 I dlp25@psu.edu
PATTERSON, Donald, W 570-484-2255 443 A dpatters@lhup.edu
PATTERSON, Dorothy 803-780-1192 463 B pattersn@voorhees.edu
PATTERSON, Eddie 803-780-1249 463 B epatterson@voorhees.edu
PATTERSON, Felicia, L 410-777-2718 221 B flpatterson@aacc.edu
PATTERSON, Frank 850-644-0453 119 C fpatterson@fsu.edu
PATTERSON, Franklin 386-481-2020 101 I pattersonf@cookman.edu
PATTERSON, Hope 575-439-3729 319 E hope@nmsua.nmsu.edu
PATTERSON, Howard 903-566-7316 506 C hpatterson@uttyler.edu
PATTERSON, James 908-852-1400 308 F pattersonj@centenarycollege.edu
PATTERSON, James 860-738-6482 90 F jpatterson@nwcc.commnet.edu
PATTERSON, Jana Lynn, F 336-278-7200 364 A patters@elon.edu
PATTERSON, Jeff 405-789-7661 412 E jeff.patterson@swcu.edu
PATTERSON, Joanna 414-382-6009 545 H
PATTERSON, John, A 478-301-5544 133 F patterson_ja@mercer.edu
PATTERSON, John, D 620-235-4108 195 I jpatters@pittstate.edu
PATTERSON, Johnny 318-274-6568 215 E pattersonj@gram.edu
PATTERSON, Joi 219-473-4305 170 D jpatterson@ccsj.edu
PATTERSON, Joyce, D 337-475-5232 215 G alumni@mcneese.edu
PATTERSON, Kathy 740-374-8716 405 F
PATTERSON, Kay 731-286-3207 475 A kpatterson@dscc.edu
PATTERSON, Laura 815-838-0500 156 D patterla@lewisu.edu
PATTERSON, Laura, M 734-763-7109 259 D lmpatter@umich.edu
PATTERSON, Lisa 614-823-1589 400 G lphillips@otterbein.edu
PATTERSON, Liz 313-993-1254 259 C patterew@udmercy.edu
PATTERSON, Loretta 316-322-3294 191 D lpatterson@butlercc.edu
PATTERSON, Lorna 360-596-5292 538 B lpatterson@spscc.ctc.edu
PATTERSON, Meg, A 540-857-6500 528 E mpatterson@virginiawestern.edu
PATTERSON, Michael 410-225-2422 224 C mpatters@mica.edu
PATTERSON, Michael 415-503-6237 66 A mpatterson@sfcm.edu
PATTERSON, Norma, J 602-216-2600 11 F npatterson@argosy.edu
PATTERSON, Paige 817-923-1921 495 E presidentsoffice@swbts.edu
PATTERSON, Patrick 615-333-3344 472 A ppatterson@national-college.edu
PATTERSON, Ralph 864-388-8350 458 J rpatterson@lander.edu
PATTERSON, Robert, K 650-723-2300 71 F bob.patterson@stanford.edu
PATTERSON, Roger, D 509-335-5524 539 A roger.patterson@wsu.edu
PATTERSON, Ron, K 901-448-2747 477 C rpatte10@uthsc.edu
PATTERSON, Sarah 254-867-3842 500 B sarah.patterson@tstc.edu
PATTERSON, Sharon 414-443-8556 553 B sharon.patterson@wlc.edu
PATTERSON, Stanley 334-387-3877 1 D stanleypatterson@amridgeuniversity.edu

PATTERSON, Steve ... 217-228-5432 ... 161 E
pattest@quincy.edu
PATTERSON, Susan ... 518-458-5358 ... 330 C
patterss@strose.edu
PATTERSON, Teresa ... 559-244-2637 ... 71 I
teresa.patterson@scccd.edu
PATTERSON, Thomas ... 334-387-3877 ... 1 D
thomaspatterson@amridgeuniversity.edu
PATTERSON, Thomas ... 509-533-7033 ... 532 E
tomp@spokanefalls.edu
PATTERSON, Tim ... 802-586-7711 ... 514 E
tpatterson@sterlingcollege.edu
PATTERSON, Tom ... 509-533-3844 ... 532 F
tomp@spokanefalls.edu
PATTERSON, III, U, L ... 704-484-4025 ... 369 B
patterson@clevelandcommunitycollege.edu
PATTERSON, Van ... 903-693-2044 ... 492 A
vpatterson@panola.edu
PATTERSON, Vanessa ... 805-965-0581 ... 68 B
patterson@sbcc.edu
PATTERSON, Vicki ... 832-252-4624 ... 483 A
vicki@cbhouston.edu
PATTERSON-DIAZ, Alyce .. 304-896-7355 ... 542 J
alycep@southern.wvnet.edu
PATTERSON-RANDLES,
Sandra, R ... 812-941-2200 ... 174 D
srpr@ius.edu
PATTI, Christopher, M ... 510-642-7122 ... 73 E
cpatti@berkeley.edu
PATTI, Eden ... 641-423-2530 ... 186 F
peden@kaplan.edu
PATTILLO, Andre ... 404-215-2752 ... 134 A
apattill@morehouse.edu
PATTILLO, Baker ... 936-468-2201 ... 495 H
bpattillo@sfasu.edu
PATTON, Amy ... 570-408-4400 ... 451 G
amy.patton@wilkes.edu
PATTON, Bess, L ... 252-789-0284 ... 371 E
bpatton@martincc.edu
PATTON, Chad ... 434-949-1045 ... 527 H
chad.patton@southside.edu
PATTON, Jeanette ... 405-974-2658 ... 413 B
jpatton@ucok.edu
PATTON, Jeremy ... 575-439-3737 ... 319 E
jpatton@nmsua.nmsu.edu
PATTON, Jerry, R ... 760-773-2500 ... 41 H
jpatton@collegeofthedesert.edu
PATTON, Kathlyn ... 361-354-2221 ... 482 I
jfkpat@coastalbend.edu
PATTON, Laurie ... 919-684-4510 ... 363 I
laurie.patton@duke.edu
PATTON, Mary ... 817-257-7660 ... 498 F
m.patton@tcu.edu
PATTON, Molly ... 704-403-1755 ... 362 E
molly.patton@carolinashealthcare.org
PATTON, Paul, E ... 606-218-5261 ... 207 B
pep@pc.edu
PATTON, Philip, L ... 319-273-2283 ... 182 D
philip.patton@uni.edu
PATTON, Seth, H ... 740-587-6262 ... 389 H
patton@denison.edu
PATTON, Simonee ... 229-317-6925 ... 128 A
simonee.patton@darton.edu
PATTON, Temple ... 419-995-8132 ... 399 B
patton.112@osu.edu
PATTY, Jeff ... 706-295-6775 ... 130 C
jpatty@highlands.edu
PATTY, Stacy ... 806-720-7652 ... 490 D
stacy.patty@lcu.edu
PATWARY, Mohsin ... 718-270-6218 ... 328 D
mohsin@mec.cuny.edu
PATZ, Cecilia ... 310-243-3866 ... 34 B
cptaz@csudh.edu
PATZ, Thomas ... 317-738-8025 ... 171 C
tpatz@franklincollege.edu
PAUGH, Jennifer ... 262-641-9944 ... 545 I
PAUGH, Jerry ... 714-449-7487 ... 70 G
jpaugh@scco.edu
PAUGH, Mark ... 352-854-2322 ... 103 D
paughm@cf.edu
PAUKEN, Patrick ... 419-372-2226 ... 385 C
paukenp@bgsu.edu
PAUL, Alyson ... 706-864-1902 ... 134 D
arpaul@northgeorgia.edu
PAUL, Beth ... 386-822-7010 ... 121 E
bpaul@stetson.edu
PAUL, Dana ... 706-880-8253 ... 132 I
dpaul@lagrange.edu
PAUL, David ... 360-416-7738 ... 538 A
dave.paul@skagit.edu
PAUL, Emilia ... 303-556-3559 ... 85 N
epaul@mscd.edu
PAUL, Ivan ... 217-641-4553 ... 154 G
ipaul@jwcc.edu
PAUL, Jeremy ... 860-570-5127 ... 94 E
jeremy.paul@uconn.edu
PAUL, Jina ... 402-552-3100 ... 297 D
PAUL, John ... 503-534-4018 ... 416 I
jpaul@marylhurst.edu
PAUL, Joseph, S ... 601-266-5020 ... 278 A
joe.paul@usm.edu
PAUL, Mary ... 619-849-2215 ... 62 L
marypaul@pointloma.edu

PAUL, Michelle ... 417-455-5566 ... 281 C
mpaul@crowder.edu
PAUL, Nancy, A ... 607-777-2400 ... 351 F
npaul@binghamton.edu
PAUL, Neha ... 202-541-5249 ... 99 G
npaul@wtu.edu
PAUL, Prem, S ... 402-472-3123 ... 300 H
ppaul2@unl.edu
PAUL, Rob ... 630-515-4526 ... 149 A
rpaul@devry.edu
PAUL, Roberta ... 217-228-5432 ... 161 E
paulro@quincy.edu
PAUL, Shelly ... 561-912-1211 ... 106 G
spaul@evergladesuniversity.edu
PAUL, Sonia ... 256-726-7134 ... 6 C
spaul@oakwood.edu
PAUL, Tina ... 870-612-2017 ... 25 E
tina.paul@uaccb.edu
PAUL, Tina ... 870-612-2016 ... 25 E
tina.paul@uaccb.edu
PAUL, Tonya ... 419-772-3106 ... 398 G
t-paul@onu.edu
PAUL, William ... 225-248-1015 ... 213 G
PAULAUSKAS, Ted ... 508-767-7279 ... 230 E
tpaulaus@assumption.edu
PAULDINE, David, J ... 630-515-4566 ... 149 A
dpauldine@devry.edu
PAULE, Romeo ... 415-949-7308 ... 47 H
pauleromeo@fhda.edu
PAULETTI, Daniel ... 610-436-2552 ... 443 F
dpauletti@wcupa.edu
PAULEY, Amy, I ... 585-785-1541 ... 334 A
pauleyai@flcc.edu
PAULEY, Ann ... 202-884-9725 ... 99 E
pauleya@trinitydc.edu
PAULEY, Edward ... 817-923-1921 ... 495 E
epauley@swbts.edu
PAULEY-HEARD, LeAnn ... 847-628-1565 ... 154 I
lpauleyheard@judsonu.edu
PAULI, Mary Louise ... 781-891-2660 ... 231 F
mpauli@bentley.edu
PAULI, Wayne, E ... 605-256-5800 ... 465 G
wayne.pauli@dsu.edu
PAULIEN, Jon ... 909-558-4536 ... 54 D
jpaulien@llu.edu
PAULIN, Christopher ... 860-512-2753 ... 90 C
cpaulin@mcc.commnet.edu
PAULINE, Rose Lee ... 215-951-1014 ... 432 G
pauline@lasalle.edu
PAULISON, Wayne ... 918-631-2616 ... 413 F
wayne-paulison@utulsa.edu
PAULK, Carol ... 912-443-3025 ... 136 D
cpaulk@savannahtech.edu
PAULK, Mona ... 229-468-2102 ... 139 E
mona.paulk@wiregrass.edu
PAULK, Taylor ... 405-912-9018 ... 408 D
books@hc.edu
PAULLI, OFM, Kenneth, P 518-783-4290 ... 350 I
kpaulli@siena.edu
PAULNACK, Karl ... 617-912-9124 ... 232 E
kpaulnack@bostonconservatory.edu
PAULO, Joseph ... 803-754-4100 ... 457 D
PAULOS, Christine ... 651-748-2619 ... 266 D
christine.paulos@century.edu
PAULOSKI, SP, Pam ... 773-371-5420 ... 146 B
presoffice@ctu.edu
PAULS, Kenton ... 712-707-7111 ... 188 B
kenton.pauls@nwciowa.edu
PAULS, Robin, H ... 618-985-3741 ... 154 E
robinpauls@jalc.edu
PAULS, Toni ... 503-517-1324 ... 421 A
tpauls@warnerpacific.edu
PAULSEN, A. William ... 912-201-8000 ... 136 H
bpaulsen@southuniversity.edu
PAULSEN, John, E ... 937-327-7317 ... 406 B
jpaulsen@wittenberg.edu
PAULSON, Cheri ... 781-239-3845 ... 230 G
cpaulson@babson.edu
PAULSON, Chuck ... 612-659-6102 ... 267 E
chuck.paulson@minneapolis.edu
PAULSON, Dennis ... 623-572-3415 ... 16 F
dpauls@midwestern.edu
PAULSON, Dennis, J ... 630-515-7352 ... 158 E
dpauls@midwestern.edu
PAULSON, Diane ... 763-488-2518 ... 266 G
diane.paulson@hennepintech.edu
PAULSON, Janet ... 503-594-3162 ... 415 A
jpaulson@clackamas.edu
PAULSON, Lawrie ... 701-252-3467 ... 381 A
paulson@jc.edu
PAULSON, Nancy ... 218-855-8054 ... 266 C
npaulson@clcmn.edu
PAULSON, Nicole ... 612-798-3718 ... 265 G
npaulson@msbcollege.edu
PAULSON, Robert ... 361-593-3106 ... 498 A
robert.paulson@tamuk.edu
PAULSON, Stephen, M ... 423-775-7333 ... 467 D
steve@bryan.edu
PAULSON, Veronica ... 605-626-2518 ... 465 H
paulsonv@northern.edu
PAULUS, Jim ... 620-947-3121 ... 196 E
jimp@tabor.edu
PAULUS, Michael ... 206-281-2414 ... 537 D

PAULUS, Michael, L ... 419-372-2891 ... 385 C
mpaulus@bgsu.edu
PAULY, John, J ... 414-288-7511 ... 548 D
john.pauly@marquette.edu
PAULY, Susan, E ... 336-721-2603 ... 376 C
susan.pauly@salem.edu
PAUR, Dave ... 435-613-5357 ... 511 E
dave.paur@ceu.edu
PAUSTIAN, Kevin, W ... 563-884-5721 ... 188 C
kevin.paustian@palmer.edu
PAUSTIAN, Tony ... 515-633-2439 ... 183 E
adpaustian@dmacc.edu
PAVE, Adam ... 909-607-0109 ... 40 F
adam_pave@kgi.edu
PAVEGLIO, Kevin ... 757-671-7171 ... 518 G
kpaveglio@ecpi.edu
PAVEK, Annette ... 320-762-4411 ... 265 I
annettep@alextech.edu
PAVELCHAK, Mark ... 323-343-2730 ... 35 B
PAVELOI, Chris ... 330-499-9600 ... 393 I
cpaveloi@kent.edu
PAVER, Bob, C ... 512-863-1676 ... 495 G
paver@southwestern.edu
PAVER, Jonathan ... 706-456-0300 ... 166 C
jpaver@triton.edu
PAVEY, Carl, E ... 517-750-1200 ... 258 F
cpavey@arbor.edu
PAVEZA, Gregory ... 203-392-7036 ... 91 I
pavezag1@southernct.edu
PAVIN, Anna ... 805-437-8425 ... 33 I
anna.pavin@csuci.edu
PAVLIK, Donna ... 773-298-3258 ... 163 G
pavlik@sxu.edu
PAVLIK, Joni, P ... 919-718-7222 ... 368 H
jpavlik@cccc.edu
PAVLOVICH, Mark, G ... 610-436-3303 ... 443 F
mpavlovich@wcupa.edu
PAVON, Tracie ... 515-961-1630 ... 188 F
tracie.pavon@simpson.edu
PAVONE, Cassandra ... 828-689-1196 ... 366 F
cpavone@mhc.edu
PAVONE, Gerri Lynn ... 586-445-7242 ... 254 F
pavoneg@macomb.edu
PAVONE, Joseph ... 401-825-2114 ... 453 B
jpavone@ccri.edu
PAVONE, Peter, J ... 414-276-5200 ... 546 C
pjpavone@bryantstratton.edu
PAVY, Edwin, C ... 270-789-5227 ... 199 C
ecpavy@campbellsville.edu
PAWLAK, Katherine ... 863-680-3964 ... 109 D
kpawlak@flsouthern.edu
PAWLAK, Therese ... 906-932-4231 ... 251 E
theresep@gogebic.edu
PAWLAWSKI, Eddie ... 615-547-1225 ... 467 I
epawlawski@cumberland.edu
PAWLEY, JR., John ... 360-779-9993 ... 535 E
jpawley@nca.edu
PAWLICKI, Frederick, W ... 785-864-4790 ... 196 F
fpawlick@ku.edu
PAWLOSKI, Chris, J ... 989-964-7122 ... 258 A
cjpawlos@svsu.edu
PAWLOW, Thomas, A ... 618-744-0426 ... 157 G
tapawlow@mckendree.edu
PAWLOWSKI, Ceceile ... 716 896-0700 ... 359 F
pawlowskic@villa.edu
PAWLOWSKI, Eugene ... 212-998-2775 ... 344 B
gene.pawlowski@nyu.edu
PAWLOWSKI, Randy ... 407-708-2320 ... 117 G
pawlowsr@seminolestate.edu
PAWLUK, Steve ... 951-785-2320 ... 53 D
spawluk@lasierra.edu
PAXSON, Christina, H ... 609-258-4800 ... 313 A
cpaxson@princeton.edu
PAXTON, Helen, S ... 973-353-5262 ... 314 E
paxton@andromeda.rutgers.edu
PAXTON, Mike ... 303-546-3543 ... 86 B
mikep@naropa.edu
PAXTON, Patricia, A ... 330-287-1254 ... 399 A
bxsosuati@bncollege.com
PAYBA, Shane ... 808-984-3496 ... 142 B
payba@hawaii.edu
PAYDAR, Nasser, H ... 765-973-8201 ... 173 D
paydar@iue.edu
PAYDEN, Bryant ... 703-335-0752 ... 99 D
bp@strayer.edu
PAYLO, Keith ... 412-392-3862 ... 444 H
kpaylo@pointpark.edu
PAYNE, Angela ... 601-481-1357 ... 275 C
apayne@mcc.cc.ms.us
PAYNE, Anna Beth ... 570-372-4238 ... 447 D
paynea@susqu.edu
PAYNE, Annaliese ... 812-535-5183 ... 179 C
apayne@smwc.edu
PAYNE, Betsy ... 828-262-6432 ... 377 B
paynebp@appstate.edu
PAYNE, Brandi ... 406-994-2845 ... 295 E
bpayne@montana.edu
PAYNE, Bryson ... 706-864-1915 ... 134 D
bpayne@northgeorgia.edu
PAYNE, C. Michael ... 740-264-5591 ... 390 F
mpayne@egcc.edu
PAYNE, Carol ... 404-894-5596 ... 130 D
carol.payne@business.gatech.edu

PAYNE, Cathy ... 276-326-4233 ... 516 I
cpayne@bluefield.edu
PAYNE, Charles, R ... 765-285-5466 ... 169 D
cpayne@bsu.edu
PAYNE, Dan ... 406-683-7142 ... 295 B
d_payne@umwestern.edu
PAYNE, Darrell ... 318-487-7559 ... 209 B
payne@lacollege.edu
PAYNE, Deborah ... 618-985-3741 ... 154 E
deborahpayne@jalc.edu
PAYNE, Don ... 303-762-6943 ... 83 I
don.payne@denverseminary.edu
PAYNE, Donna, G ... 252-328-6940 ... 377 C
payned@ecu.edu
PAYNE, Gail, D ... 434-381-6324 ... 524 E
payne@sbc.edu
PAYNE, George, M ... 240-567-2582 ... 224 E
george.payne@montgomerycollege.edu
PAYNE, Hal, D ... 716-878-5550 ... 353 A
paynehd@buffalostate.edu
PAYNE, JR., Harry, E ... 813-988-5131 ... 107 I
president@floridacollege.edu
PAYNE, Harvey ... 803-754-4100 ... 457 D
PAYNE, Jack, M ... 352-392-1971 ... 120 B
jackpayne@ifas.ufl.edu
PAYNE, James ... 309-438-5669 ... 153 C
jepayne@ilstu.edu
PAYNE, James, R ... 803-535-5301 ... 456 D
japayne@claflin.edu
PAYNE, Jennifer ... 802-586-7711 ... 514 E
jpayne@sterlingcollege.edu
PAYNE, John, F ... 671-735-5558 ... 559 B
john.payne2@guamcc.edu
PAYNE, John, K ... 802-654-2629 ... 514 B
jpayne@smcvt.edu
PAYNE, Judith ... 605-256-5693 ... 465 G
judy.payne@dsu.edu
PAYNE, June, P ... 765-285-1264 ... 169 D
jpayne@bsu.edu
PAYNE, Karen, W ... 570-326-3761 ... 440 K
kpayne@pct.edu
PAYNE, Kathryn, E ... 215-951-1941 ... 432 G
paynek@lasalle.edu
PAYNE, Kent ... 847-214-7552 ... 150 D
kpayne@elgin.edu
PAYNE, Lisa ... 618-437-5321 ... 162 B
payne@rlc.edu
PAYNE, Lynn ... 303-784-8045 ... 85 I
lpayne@international.edu
PAYNE, Maggie ... 530-898-4570 ... 34 A
mpayne@csuchico.edu
PAYNE, Mary ... 515-271-1452 ... 183 F
mary.payne@dmu.edu
PAYNE, Michael, J ... 215-951-1841 ... 432 G
payne@lasalle.edu
PAYNE, Molly ... 617-732-2218 ... 241 F
molly.payne@mcphs.edu
PAYNE, Natalie ... 215-965-4039 ... 436 H
npayne@moore.edu
PAYNE, O, J ... 641-648-6101 ... 185 I
orintheo.payne@iavalley.edu
PAYNE, Pat ... 617-349-8850 ... 234 G
ppayne@lesley.edu
PAYNE, Patricia ... 617-349-8841 ... 230 D
ppayne@lesley.edu
PAYNE, Patricia ... 617-349-8841 ... 236 G
ppayne@lesley.edu
PAYNE, Paula ... 478-387-4901 ... 130 E
PAYNE, Ralph, C ... 304-256-0279 ... 542 H
rpayne@newriver.edu
PAYNE, Shari, L ... 412-397-6235 ... 445 G
payne@rmu.edu
PAYNE, Sherri ... 702-651-2678 ... 302 G
sherri.payne@csn.edu
PAYNE, Stephen, D ... 269-471-6534 ... 247 H
stephen@andrews.edu
PAYNE, Stephen, D ... 269-405-2837 ... 252 C
stephen@andrews.edu
PAYNE, Steven, W ... 772-462-7805 ... 110 L
spayne@irsc.edu
PAYNE, Susan, B ... 919-334-1520 ... 374 E
sbpayne@waketech.edu
PAYNE, Suzie ... 562-860-2451 ... 38 J
rpayne@cerritos.edu
PAYNE, Sylvia, M ... 317-274-4417 ... 174 B
payne@iupui.edu
PAYNE, Tena ... 270-534-3342 ... 203 B
tena.payne@kctcs.edu
PAYNE, Terry ... 828-298-3325 ... 380 C
tpayne@warren-wilson.edu
PAYNE, Thomas, L ... 573-882-3846 ... 291 D
paynet@missouri.edu
PAYNE, Valley, C ... 318-670-9324 ... 215 A
vpayne@susla.edu
PAYNE, Wesley, A ... 573-840-9689 ... 290 J
wpayne@trcc.edu
PAYNE, William ... 218-726-7033 ... 272 B
PAYNTER, Ronald ... 212-817-7609 ... 327 B
rpaynter@gc.cuny.edu
PAYSEUR, Victoria, F ... 515-271-3116 ... 184 A
victoria.payseur@drake.edu
PAYTON, Alvin ... 229-333-2123 ... 139 E
alvin.payton@wiregrass.edu

PELCHAT, Kate .... 262-347-2911.... 547 B
kpelchat@devry.edu
PELESKY, Tim .... 301-784-5000.... 221 A
tpelesky@allegany.edu
PELIO, JR., Joseph .... 516-299-4213.... 338 F
joe.pelio@liu.edu
PELISSERO, John, P .... 312-915-7585.... 157 A
jpeliss@luc.edu
PELKEY, Bob, O .... 671-735-2862.... 559 D
bpelkey@uguam.uog.edu
PELKEY, Dave .... 253-566-6007.... 538 C
dpelkey@tacomacc.edu
PELL, Alice, N .... 607-255-7993.... 331 C
ap19@cornell.edu
PELLEGRIN, Amy, E .... 304-367-4135.... 543 E
Amy.Pellegrin@fairmontstate.edu
PELLEGRINI, Larry .... 570-674-6307.... 436 F
lpellegr@misericordia.edu
PELLEGRINO, Anthony ...... 413-565-1000.... 231 B
apellegrino@baypath.edu
PELLEGRINO, Debra, A ..... 570-941-6305.... 450 B
pellegrinod2@scranton.edu
PELLEGRINO, Karen, A ...... 203-254-4100.... 92 B
kpellegrino@fairfield.edu
PELLEGRINO, Thomas, C .. 203-254-4000...... 92 B
tpellegrino@fairfield.edu
PELLEGRINO, Thomas, R .. 757-446-8488.... 518 F
pellegtr@evms.edu
PELLERITO, Chris .... 989-386-6660.... 255 F
cpellerito@midmich.edu
PELLETIER, David, J .... 573-629-3092.... 282 H
dpelletier@hlg.edu
PELLETIER, Jo-Ann, M ...... 508-678-2811.... 239 F
jo-ann.pelletier@bristolcc.edu
PELLETIER, Kathe .... 612-977-5701.... 262 A
kathe.pelletier@capella.edu
PELLETIER, Kristan, M .... 518-629-7328.... 336 C
k.pelletier@hvcc.edu
PELLETIER, Vincent .... 847-214-7363.... 150 D
vpelletier@eglin.edu
PELLETT, Tracy .... 509-963-1404.... 531 G
tracy.pellett@cwu.edu
PELLEY, Sue .... 304-214-8825.... 543 A
spelley@wvncc.edu
PELLICANE, Patrick, J .... 501-569-8661...... 24 E
pjpellicane@ualr.edu
PELLICCIA, Michael, C ...... 516-572-7538.... 342 C
michael.pelliccia@ncc.edu
PELLICCIOTTI, Joseph .... 219-980-6841.... 173 F
jpelli@iun.edu
PELLICCIOTTI, M. Beth ...... 219-989-2239.... 178 G
pellicmb@purduecal.edu
PELLICO, Gary .... 317-921-4882.... 175 I
gpellico@ivytech.edu
PELLINEN, Brian .... 603-882-6923.... 304 F
bpellinen@ccsnh.edu
PELLISH, Catherine .... 303-404-5022...... 84 H
catherine.pellish@frontrange.edu
PELLY, Micheal .... 714-997-6982...... 39 C
pelly@chapman.edu
PELPHREY, Barry .... 304-766-4189.... 544 D
bpelphrey@wvstateu.edu
PELRINE, JR., John, P ...... 773-298-3121.... 163 G
pelrine@sxu.edu
PELT, Micheal .... 812-749-1542.... 178 D
mpelt@oak.edu
PELTIER, Beverly .... 706-771-4023.... 125 D
bpeltier@augustatech.edu
PELTIER, Linda, M .... 937-778-7802.... 390 G
lpeltier@edisonohio.edu
PELTIER, Matthew, S .... 423-652-4740.... 469 L
mspeltie@king.edu
PELTO, Bill, L .... 828-262-3020.... 377 B
peltowl@appstate.edu
PELTON, Jack .... 208-426-4203.... 142 F
jpelton@boisestate.edu
PELTON, Mark .... 478-445-2753.... 129 F
mark.pelton@gcsu.edu
PELTON, Woody .... 336-278-6700.... 364 A
wpelton@elon.edu
PELTSVERGER, Boris .... 229-931-2100.... 131 B
PELUSI, Mario, J .... 309-556-3061.... 153 E
mpelusi@iwu.edu
PELUSO, Constance .... 718-631-6297.... 329 A
cpeluso@qcc.cuny.edu
PELUSO, Kerry .... 404-727-0551.... 129 A
kerry.peluso@emory.edu
PELUSO-VERDEND, Gary .. 918-610-8303.... 411 D
gary.peluso@ptstulsa.edu
PELY, Laszlo .... 410-617-2421.... 224 A
lpely@loyola.edu
PELZ, Beth .... 713-221-8575.... 503 D
pelzb@uhd.edu
PELZEL, Carolyn, A .... 603-646-3095.... 305 A
carolyn.a.pelzel@dartmouth.edu
PELZEL, Morris .... 812-749-1202.... 178 D
mpelzel@oak.edu
PEMBERTON, Barbara .... 870-245-5541...... 22 I
pembertonb@obu.edu
PEMBERTON, Cynthia, L ... 816-235-1868.... 291 E
pembertonc@umkc.edu
PEMBERTON, Dana, L .... 406-338-5441.... 293 F
danalou@bfcc.org
PEMBERTON, Laurie .... 805-922-6966...... 26 K
laurie.pemberton@hancockcollege.edu
PEMBERTON, Loren .... 509-533-3503.... 532 F
lorenp@spokanefalls.edu
PEMBERTON, Richard .... 573-897-5000.... 284 D
PEMBERTON, Rochelle .... 218-335-4202.... 264 I
shelly.pemberton@lltc.edu
PEMBROOK, Randall, G .... 785-670-1649.... 197 D
randy.pembrook@washburn.edu
PEMSTEIN, Debra .... 845-758-7405.... 323 F
pemstein@bard.edu
PENA, Andrew .... 915-747-5202.... 505 E
ampena@utep.edu
PENA, Augusto, E .... 828-262-6252.... 377 B
penaae@appstate.edu
PENA, Daniel .... 210-458-4245.... 506 B
daniel.pena@utsa.edu
PENA, Diana, A .... 956-872-3558.... 494 D
dpena@southtexascollege.edu
PENA, Fred .... 254-298-8321.... 496 B
fred.pena@templejc.edu
PENA, Jesus .... 610-683-4700.... 442 F
pena@kutztown.edu
PENA, JR., Jose, A .... 956-721-5312.... 489 G
jpena@laredo.edu
PENA, Juanita .... 719-846-5537...... 87 J
juanita.pena@trinidadstate.edu
PENA, Laura .... 915-532-3737.... 508 E
lpena@westerntech.edu
PENA, Maria .... 360-417-6340.... 536 B
mpena@pencol.edu
PENA, Maria, E .... 787-850-9376.... 567 B
maria.pena1@upr.edu
PENA, Nova .... 915-595-1935.... 489 B
PENA, Philip .... 708-656-8000.... 159 C
philip.pena@morton.edu
PENA, Robert .... 361-593-4783.... 498 A
robert.pena@tamuk.edu
PENA, Sandra, V .... 956-326-2361.... 497 B
sandra@tamiu.edu
PENA, Stan .... 325-649-8608.... 488 A
spena@hputx.edu
PENA-WARFIELD,
Roseanna .... 508-362-2131.... 240 A
rpenawar@capecod.edu
PENCE, Bill .... 540-868-7061.... 526 H
bpence@lfcc.edu
PENCE, Heather .... 404-297-9522.... 128 B
penceh@dekalbtech.edu
PENCE, Lorence, L .... 304-647-6295.... 544 C
lpence@osteo.wvsom.edu
PENCE, Nadine, S .... 765-361-6434.... 181 C
pencen@wabash.edu
PENCE, Susan .... 505-473-6175.... 320 F
susan.pence@santafeuniversity.edu
PENCIU, Christian .... 972-929-9315.... 486 B
cpenciu@devry.edu
PENDER, Consuela .... 912-478-5409.... 131 A
cpender@georgiasouthern.edu
PENDERGAST,
Katherine, N .... 617-373-2230.... 244 A
PENDERGAST, Linda .... 309-672-5534.... 158 B
lpendergast@mcon.edu
PENDERGRAFT, Susan .... 336-386-3380.... 374 B
pendergrafts@surry.edu
PENDERGRASS, Margaret .. 919-843-5048.... 378 D
mjpender@email.unc.edu
PENDERGRASS, Toni .... 281-922-3403.... 493 G
toni.pendergrass@sjcd.edu
PENDERGRAST, Runan .... 859-246-6305.... 201 D
runan.pendergrast@kctcs.edu
PENDHARKAR, Hemant ..... 781-239-2225.... 240 D
hpendharkar@massbay.edu
PENDLETON, Brandon .... 312-553-5654.... 146 H
bpendleton2@ccc.edu
PENDLETON, Dennis, F ...... 530-757-8663...... 73 F
dfpendleton@ucdavis.edu
PENDLETON, Edith .... 239-489-9213.... 104 L
ependleton@edison.edu
PENDLETON, Janis, S .... 803-327-7402.... 456 F
jpendleton@clintonjuniorcollege.edu
PENDLETON, Kathy, J .... 502-852-6585.... 207 A
kathy.pendleton@louisville.edu
PENDLETON, Laura .... 509-574-4937.... 540 A
lpendleton@yvcc.edu
PENDLETON, Laurence .... 615-963-7923.... 474 A
laurence.pendleton@tnstate.edu
PENDLETON, Penny .... 479-788-7121...... 24 D
ppendlet@uafortsmith.edu
PENDSE, Ravi .... 316-978-5053.... 197 F
ravi.pendse@wichita.edu
PENFIELD, Gary, M .... 401-456-8123.... 454 A
gpenfield@ric.edu
PENISTEN, Douglas .... 918-456-5511.... 409 A
penisten@nsuok.edu
PENKALA, Robert .... 586-445-7636.... 254 F
penkalar@macomb.edu
PENKE, Ann, K .... 920-565-1242.... 547 H
penkea@lakeland.edu
PENKOVA, Snejanka .... 787-764-0270.... 567 F
snejanka.penkova@upr.edu
PENLAND, Joni, M .... 502-410-6200.... 200 F
jpenland@galencollege.edu
PENLAND, Lynn, R .... 812-488-2360.... 180 B
lp22@evansville.edu
PENLAND, Nathan .... 417-328-1828.... 290 E
npenland@sbuniv.edu
PENLER, Karen .... 216-373-6364.... 397 E
kpenler@ndc.edu
PENN, Ann, E .... 919-966-3576.... 378 D
ann_penn@unc.edu
PENN, Cris .... 614-688-4940.... 398 H
penn.4@osu.edu
PENN, Deborah .... 620-947-3121.... 196 E
deborahp@tabor.edu
PENN, Mark, A .... 330-325-6262.... 397 C
mpenn@neoucom.edu
PENN, Ray .... 423-869-6312.... 470 C
rpenn@lmunet.edu
PENNA, Anthony .... 617-552-3475.... 232 D
anthony.penna.1@bc.edu
PENNA, Nancy .... 612-977-5522.... 262 A
nancy.penna@capella.edu
PENNA, Nancy .... 218-299-3250.... 263 B
penna@cord.edu
PENNARTZ, Kathy .... 940-397-4214.... 491 A
kathy.pennartz@mwsu.edu
PENNETTI, Dianna .... 212-854-3362.... 323 G
dpennetti@barnard.edu
PENNEY, R. William .... 386-822-7045.... 121 E
bpenney@stetson.edu
PENNIECOOK, Tricia, Y ...... 909-558-4578...... 54 D
tpenniecook@llu.edu
PENNINGS, Rhonda, R .... 712-324-5061.... 188 A
rpennings@nwicc.edu
PENNINGTON, Amy .... 479-964-0832...... 20 G
apennington@atu.edu
PENNINGTON, Karen, L ...... 973-655-4311.... 311 G
penningtonk@mail.montclair.edu
PENNINGTON, Laurie .... 928-428-8231...... 14 C
laurie.pennington@eac.edu
PENNINGTON, Paul .... 513-244-8181.... 387 D
paul.pennington@ccuniversity.edu
PENNINGTON, Rebecca, A 814-375-4766.... 439 D
rxs163@psu.edu
PENNINGTON, Ronald .... 636-922-8271.... 288 E
rpennington@stchas.edu
PENNINGTON, Sabrina ...... 765-966-2656.... 176 F
spenning@ivytech.edu
PENNINGTON, Sandra .... 801-375-5125.... 510 F
spennington@rmuohp.edu
PENNINGTON, Sherry, R .... 417-667-8181.... 280 I
spennington@cottey.edu
PENNINI, Susan, W .... 617-333-2165.... 234 A
spennini@curry.edu
PENNIPEDE, Barbara, S ..... 914-923-2699.... 345 F
bpennipede@pace.edu
PENNISON, Bret .... 504-865-2290.... 213 F
bmpennis@loyno.edu
PENNIX, James .... 540-831-5371.... 522 D
jpennix@radford.edu
PENNO, Tina .... 412-566-2433.... 434 B
tmcclaren@paculinary.com
PENNOCK, Denise .... 714-628-4844...... 63 G
pennock_denise@sccollege.edu
PENNOCK, Margaret .... 605-367-7667.... 466 C
margaret.pennock@southeasttech.edu
PENNOYER, Douglas .... 562-903-4844...... 30 H
doug.pennoyer@biola.edu
PENNY, Helen .... 229-333-5366.... 139 E
helen.penny@wiregrass.edu
PENNY, Rick .... 440-525-7320.... 394 F
rpenny@lakelandcc.edu
PENNY, Robert .... 601-923-1600.... 277 B
bpenny@rts.edu
PENNYWEIT, Shalana .... 209-473-5200...... 50 C
shalana_pennyweit@heald.edu
PENNYWELL, Judith .... 219-989-1104.... 178 G
Judith.Pennywell@purduecal.edu
PENROD, Donald .... 562-985-5091...... 35 A
dpenrod@csulb.edu
PENROSE, Betsy, S .... 315-786-2249.... 337 F
bpenrose@sunyjefferson.edu
PENRY, Jason, C .... 325-942-2116.... 480 E
jason.penry@angelo.edu
PENSE, Christine .... 610-861-5312.... 437 G
cpense@northampton.edu
PENSIS, Claude .... 602-639-7500...... 14 I
PENSKAR, Donald .... 269-387-8804.... 260 F
donald.penskar@wmich.edu
PENSON, Amy, M .... 828-286-3636.... 371 A
apenson@isothermal.edu
PENTACOST, Pat .... 417-624-7070.... 284 G
ppentacost@messengercollege.edu
PENTICUFF, Joy .... 512-313-3000.... 483 G
joy.penticuff@concordia.edu
PENYACK, Megan .... 781-595-6768.... 236 I
mpenyack@mariancourt.edu
PENZENSTADLER, SSND,
Joan .... 414-256-1226.... 549 A
penzenj@mtmary.edu
PENZIUL, Carl .... 607-844-8222.... 357 H
penziuc@tc3.edu
PEOPLE, Yasha .... 732-247-5241.... 312 A
ypeople@nbts.edu
PEOPLES, Gerald, C .... 601-877-6380.... 273 C
gpeoples@alcorn.edu
PEOPLES, Gregory, A .... 734-487-0074.... 250 H
gregory.peoples@emich.edu
PEOPLES, Verjanis .... 225-771-2290.... 214 H
verjanis_peoples@subr.edu
PEPALL, Lynne .... 617-627-3106.... 245 F
lynne.pepall@tufts.edu
PEPE, Alicia .... 518-292-1915.... 348 A
pepea@sage.edu
PEPE, Gerald, J .... 757-446-5800.... 518 F
pepegj@evms.edu
PEPE, James .... 718-982-3209.... 327 A
James.Pepe@csi.cuny.edu
PEPICELLO, William .... 602-387-7000...... 19 C
bill.pepicello@phoenix.edu
PEPIN, James .... 334-649-5000.... 557 B
PEPIN, Phyllis, A .... 409-944-1222.... 486 H
ppepin@gc.edu
PEPION, Kenneth .... 970-247-7334...... 84 G
pepion_k@fortlewis.edu
PEPITO, Bobby .... 714-542-8086...... 52 K
bpepito@kensington.edu
PEPITONE, Christine .... 518-828-4181.... 330 E
christine.pepitone@sunycgcc.edu
PEPITONE, Dianne .... 914-831-0367.... 330 D
dpepitone@cw.edu
PEPLINSKI, Michael .... 724-938-4950.... 441 G
peplinski@calu.edu
PEPLOW, Nena .... 309-677-3223.... 145 H
nena@bradley.edu
PEPOY, Joseph .... 586-791-6610.... 248 G
joe.pepoy@baker.edu
PEPPARD, Paul .... 407-569-1366.... 107 G
paul.peppard@fcc.edu
PEPPARD, Sandra .... 407-569-1331.... 107 G
sandi.peppard@fcc.edu
PEPPARD, Timothy .... 216-397-4444.... 392 M
tpeppard@jcu.edu
PEPPERS, Larry, C .... 540-458-8602.... 530 A
pepperst@wlu.edu
PEPPIN, Patricia .... 480-461-7456...... 15 K
pat.peppin@mcmail.maricopa.edu
PERAGALLO, Nilda, P .... 305-284-2107.... 122 F
nperagallo@miami.edu
PERALES, Jose .... 585-385-8067.... 348 F
jperales@sjfc.edu
PERALES, Kris .... 515-244-4221.... 181 D
peralesk@aib.edu
PERALEZ, Esther .... 816-271-5609.... 287 A
eperalez@missouriwestern.edu
PERALTA, Tracy .... 505-925-8800.... 321 G
tlperalt@unm.edu
PERANANAMGAM, Reetha 419-448-2193.... 391 G
rperanan@heidelberg.edu
PERANTONI, Janet, L .... 908-526-1200.... 313 E
jperanto@raritanval.edu
PERCHINSKY, Tessa, A .... 715-833-6256.... 553 F
tperchinsky@cvtc.edu
PERCIANTE, Linda, K .... 303-963-3237...... 81 K
lperciante@ccu.edu
PERCIANTE, Terence, H ...... 630-752-5873.... 168 F
terry.perciante@wheaton.edu
PERCUOCO, Robert, E .... 563-884-5460.... 188 C
robert.percuoco@palmer.edu
PERCUOCO, Robert, E .... 563-884-5460.... 114 E
robert.percuoco@palmer.edu
PERCUOCO, Robert, E .... 563-884-5460...... 60 L
robert.percuoco@palmer.edu
PERCY, Paul, M .... 423-652-4811.... 469 L
PERCY, Steve .... 410-837-5353.... 229 A
spercy@ubalt.edu
PERDIKIS, Galen .... 904-953-7035.... 262 G
perdikis.galen@mayo.edu
PERDOMO, Jose, A .... 425-235-2352.... 536 E
jperdomo@rtc.edu
PERDOMO, Lisa .... 513-487-1261.... 402 I
lisa.perdomo@myunion.edu
PERDUE, Jean .... 405-789-7661.... 412 E
jean.perdue@swcu.edu
PERDUE, K. Alan .... 304-876-5009.... 544 A
aperdue@shepherd.edu
PERDUE, Robin, A .... 843-383-8025.... 457 A
rperdue@coker.edu
PERDUE, Tina, K .... 740-376-4730.... 395 F
tina.perdue@marietta.edu
PERDUE, Wendy, C .... 804-289-8740.... 525 A
PEREA, Jake, E .... 415-338-2687...... 36 F
pjoost@sfsu.edu
PEREBOOM, Maarten, L ...... 410-543-6450.... 228 D
mlpereboom@salisbury.edu
PERECHI, Reuben .... 904-470-8078.... 105 A
rperechi@ewc.edu
PERECMAN, Dov .... 845-434-5240.... 361 L
dperecman@fallsburgyeshiva.com
PEREGOY, Robert .... 406-275-4976.... 296 F
bob_peregoy@skc.edu
PEREIRA, Augie .... 718-357-0500.... 349 F
apereira@edaff.com
PEREIRA, Freyja .... 707-527-4512...... 68 E
fpereira@santarosa.edu
PEREIRA, Kim .... 309-438-2559.... 153 C
kpereira@ilstu.edu
PEREIRA, Sandra .... 508-849-3363.... 230 C
spereira@annamaria.edu

PERRY, George 210-458-4450 506 B
george.perry@utsa.edu
PERRY, George 304-260-4380 542 C
PERRY, Gretchen 845-758-7276 323 F
gperry@bard.edu
PERRY, James 903-813-2277 481 A
jperry@austincollege.edu
PERRY, Janet 405-682-1611 409 F
jcperry@occc.edu
PERRY, Jason 801-581-8514 510 L
jason.perry@utah.edu
PERRY, Jerry 303-724-2152 88 D
jerry.perry@ucdenver.edu
PERRY, Jessica, M 787-743-7979 565 F
ut_jperry@suagm.edu
PERRY, Johanna, L 914-337-9300 331 A
johanna.perry@concordia-ny.edu
PERRY, John 815-802-8552 154 J
jperry@kcc.edu
PERRY, John, F 864-503-5242 463 A
jperry@uscupstate.edu
PERRY, Jonathan, C 479-575-5276 24 C
jperry@uark.edu
PERRY, Judy, A 432-837-8058 501 B
jperry@sulross.edu
PERRY, Katherine 315-498-2602 345 D
perryka@sunyocc.edu
PERRY, Kimberly 530-895-2484 31 E
perryki@butte.edu
PERRY, Kristine 973-300-2772 315 F
kperry@sussex.edu
PERRY, Mansco 651-696-6735 265 A
mperry@macalester.edu
PERRY, Margaret 202-495-3828 98 D
advance@dhs.edu
PERRY, Maria 215-884-8942 452 C
cfo@woninstitute.edu
PERRY, Marilynn 732-571-3489 311 F
mperry@monmouth.edu
PERRY, Mark 417-862-9533 282 D
mperry@globaluniversity.edu
PERRY, Mark 559-734-9000 66 L
president@sjvc.edu
PERRY, Mark 559-734-9000 66 E
president@sjvc.edu
PERRY, Mark 559-734-9000 66 K
president@sjvc.edu
PERRY, Mark 559-734-9000 66 H
markp@sjvc.edu
PERRY, Mark, A 559-734-9000 66 G
president@sjvc.edu
PERRY, Marva 781-239-3151 240 D
mperry@massbay.edu
PERRY, Mary Elaine 610-660-1045 446 C
mperry01@sju.edu
PERRY, Maryann, B 508-565-1105 245 D
mperry@stonehill.edu
PERRY, Melissa 386-312-4058 116 D
melissaperry@sjrstate.edu
PERRY, Meredith 423-425-4431 477 D
meredith-perry@utc.edu
PERRY, Michael 559-734-9000 66 E
mikep@sjvc.edu
PERRY, Michael 321-674-7127 108 E
perrymj@fit.edu
PERRY, Michael, J 315-386-7315 355 D
perrymj@canton.edu
PERRY, Nancy 410-386-8231 221 G
nperry@carrollcc.edu
PERRY, Nauleen, A 302-857-1080 96 D
nperry@dtcc.edu
PERRY, Pat, B 252-246-1327 375 B
pperry@wilsoncc.edu
PERRY, Paul 231-995-1114 256 G
pperry@nmc.edu
PERRY, Renee 602-285-7433 16 B
renee.perry@pcmail.maricopa.edu
PERRY, Robert, K 423-746-5209 476 D
rkperry@twcnet.edu
PERRY, Roberta 610-526-2967 445 I
rperry@rosemont.edu
PERRY, Robin 704-637-4384 363 C
raperry@catawba.edu
PERRY, Roslyn 606-783-2571 204 E
ro.perry@moreheadstate.edu
PERRY, Sam, J 773-508-3598 157 A
sperry@luc.edu
PERRY, Scott 312-777-8664 153 A
smperry@aii.edu
PERRY, Stephanie, D 276-328-0240 525 C
sdh9y@uvawise.edu
PERRY, Steve 864-294-2458 458 D
steve.perry@furman.edu
PERRY, Steven 201-684-7363 313 D
sperry@ramapo.edu
PERRY, Steven 325-738-3341 500 C
steven.perry@tstc.edu
PERRY, Steven, R 607-436-2513 353 E
perrysr@oneonta.edu
PERRY, Stuart 320-363-2189 271 F
sperry@csbsju.edu
PERRY, Sue, A 856-691-8600 309 C
sperry@cccnj.edu
PERRY, Thomas, D 740-376-4408 395 F
tom.perry@marietta.edu
PERRY, Tom 479-524-7122 22 C
tperry@jbu.edu
PERRY, Traci 740-376-4720 395 F
traci.perry@marietta.edu
PERRY, Walter 215-596-8890 450 A
w.perry@usciences.edu
PERRY, Wayne 334-387-3877 1 D
wayneperry@amridgeuniversity.edu
PERRY, William, L 217-581-2011 150 C
wlperry@eiu.edu
PERRY-JOHNSON, Arlethia 770-423-6350 132 H
aperryjo@kennesaw.edu
PERRY-NAUSE, Sharon 419-448-3504 402 E
perrynauses@tiffin.edu
PERRY-THOMPSON, Laura 814-269-7070 449 D
lpt@pitt.edu
PERRYMAN, Lance 970-491-7051 83 A
lance.perryman@colostate.edu
PERRYMAN, Larry 707-468-3069 57 A
lperryman@mendocino.edu
PERRYMAN, Nancy, S 309-655-4119 163 E
nancy.s.perryman@osfhealthcare.org
PERSAUD, Damindra 718-261-5800 324 D
dpersaud@bramsonort.edu
PERSAUD, June 973-877-3407 310 A
persaud@essex.edu
PERSAUD, Roxanne 718-489-5379 348 E
rpersaud@stfranciscollege.edu
PERSEK, Carol 828-884-8251 362 D
persekca@brevard.edu
PERSHING, David, W 801-581-5057 510 L
david.pershing@utah.edu
PERSICHITTE, Kay, A 307-766-3145 556 E
kpersi@uwyo.edu
PERSICO, Frank, G 202-319-5100 97 C
persico@cua.edu
PERSICO, Sebastian, T 212-817-7600 327 B
spersico@gc.cuny.edu
PERSINGER, Bill 931-221-6309 473 D
persingerb@apsu.edu
PERSKY, David 352-588-8291 116 E
david.persky@saintleo.edu
PERSKY, Ira 718-982-3035 327 A
ira.persky@csi.cuny.edu
PERSKY, Ira 718-982-2240 327 A
ira.persky@csi.cuny.edu
PERSON, Andy 914-330-1450 340 G
aperson@mercy.edu
PERSON, Mark 601-979-2021 275 A
mark.s.person@jsums.edu
PERSON, Ruth, J 810-762-5725 259 F
rjperson@umflint.edu
PERSON, Walter 202-686-0876 99 A
walter.person@potomac.edu
PERSONS, William 334-229-4276 1 C
wpersons@alasu.edu
PERSSON, Carol 413-572-5365 239 C
cpersson@wsc.ma.edu
PERSSON, Katherine 218-312-1640 490 C
katherine.persson@lonestar.edu
PERTL, Brian, G 920-832-6614 547 J
brian.g.pertl@lawrence.edu
PERUGGI, Regina, S 718-368-5109 328 B
president@kbcc.cuny.edu
PERUSO, Dominick, F 814-472-3005 446 B
dperuso@francis.edu
PERUSSE, Charles, E 919-962-1000 377 A
ceperusse@northcarolina.edu
PERVI, Susan, D 202-319-5714 97 C
pervi@cua.edu
PERVIER, Curt 432-685-4677 490 G
cpervier@midland.edu
PERZESKI, Donna, M 216-916-7506 398 E
dmp@ocpm.edu
PESARCHICK, Robert, A 610-785-6204 446 A
academicdtdscs@adphila.org
PESCADOR, Susan 516-918-3717 324 E
spescador@bcl.edu
PESCINSKI, Robert 973-618-3552 308 D
rpescinski@caldwell.edu
PESCOVITZ, Ora, H 734-647-9351 259 D
opescovi@umich.edu
PESEK, James, G 814-393-2600 442 A
jpesek@clarion.edu
PESHEK, Mary 712-274-5274 187 D
peshek@morningside.edu
PESIGAN, Jason 213-252-5100 26 C
PESKA, Don 817-735-2149 504 C
dpeska@hsc.unt.edu
PESOLD, Dan 314-968-7130 293 A
pesoldd@webster.edu
PESOTSKI, Chris 215-717-6170 448 H
cpesotski@uarts.edu
PESSINK, Martin 903-983-8650 489 F
mpessink@kilgore.edu
PESTA, Donna 518-255-5624 354 E
Pestadh@cobleskill.edu
PESTA, John 570-408-4641 451 G
john.pesta@wilkes.edu
PESTANA, John 508-565-1315 245 D
jpestana@stonehill.edu
PESTELLO, Fred, P 315-445-4120 338 B
president@lemoyne.edu
PETA, Jamie 303-546-5283 86 B
jamiep@naropa.edu
PETAK, Katty 402-399-2411 297 E
vpetak@csm.edu
PETCHER, Douglas 312-362-7595 148 F
dpetcher@depaul.edu
PETCHIK, Carl, A 202-319-5515 97 C
petchik@cua.edu
PETE, Mary, C 907-543-4502 10 J
mpete@alaska.edu
PETER, Beth, C 651-641-8795 263 C
peter@csp.edu
PETER, David 812-888-4166 181 B
dpeter@vinu.edu
PETER, Florence, L 692-625-3394 559 E
flpeter@cmi.edu
PETER, Joakim 691-330-2620 559 A
jojo@comfsm.fm
PETER, Lori 660-263-3900 279 J
lbp@cccb.edu
PETERKA, Cynthia, J 443-518-4809 223 D
cpeterka@howardcc.edu
PETERMAN, Francine 718-997-5220 328 F
francine.peterman@qc.cuny.edu
PETERS, Anna 212-659-3610 338 A
PETERS, Bob 360-736-9391 531 H
bpeters@centralia.edu
PETERS, Brian, S 847-491-8420 160 D
b-peters2@northwestern.edu
PETERS, Christopher 214-234-4850 486 F
cpeters@cci.edu
PETERS, Clark 814-732-2921 442 D
cpeters@edinboro.edu
PETERS, Craig 605-367-5462 466 C
craig.peters@southeasttech.edu
PETERS, Daniel, J 402-461-7303 298 C
dpeters@hastings.edu
PETERS, David 407-569-1320 107 G
david.peters@fcc.edu
PETERS, David, R 304-473-8540 545 F
PETERS, Deborah 406-896-5832 295 F
deborah.peters@msubillings.edu
PETERS, Doug, D 218-477-2306 268 A
petersd@mnstate.edu
PETERS, Earic 323-953-4000 54 H
peterseb@lacitycollege.edu
PETERS, Ellen 207-786-8211 217 C
cpeters@bates.edu
PETERS, Ellen 253-879-3104 538 E
epeters@pugetsound.edu
PETERS, Fred, M 903-510-2627 502 E
fpet@tjc.edu
PETERS, Gordon, C 801-818-8900 510 E
gordonp@provocollege.edu
PETERS, Heather 815-825-2086 155 C
heather.peters@kishwaukeecollege.edu
PETERS, Hermina, P 202-274-6256 99 F
hpeters@udc.edu
PETERS, J. Lee 860-768-4165 95 A
lpeters@hartford.edu
PETERS, James 616-538-2330 251 F
jpeters@gbcol.edu
PETERS, Jana 661-763-7809 72 C
jpeters@taftcollege.edu
PETERS, Jerry 760-252-2411 30 F
jpeters@barstow.edu
PETERS, Jesse 910-521-6635 379 B
peters@uncp.edu
PETERS, John, E 270-824-8593 202 C
john.peters@kctcs.edu
PETERS, John, G 815-753-9500 160 A
jpeters@niu.edu
PETERS, Joyce 662-685-4771 273 H
jpeters@bmc.edu
PETERS, Kathleen 321-433-7730 101 J
petersk@brevardcc.edu
PETERS, Kirk 860-255-3561 91 C
kpeters@txcc.commnet.edu
PETERS, Larry 580-349-1560 410 B
lpeters@opsu.edu
PETERS, Laurie 765-459-0561 176 A
lpeters@ivytech.edu
PETERS, Lee 617-262-5000 232 B
lee.peters@the-bac.edu
PETERS, Leonard 203-432-3262 95 D
leonard.peters@yale.edu
PETERS, Libby 606-436-5721 201 H
libby.peters@kctcs.edu
PETERS, RET., MaryAnn 401-841-7004 557 I
PETERS, MaryAnne 610-341-5834 428 D
mpeters@eastern.edu
PETERS, Matthew 570-702-8914 431 K
mpeters@johnson.edu
PETERS, Melissa 386-481-2580 101 I
petersm@cookman.edu
PETERS, Michael, P 505-984-6098 320 C
president@sjcsf.edu
PETERS, Michele 716-827-4333 358 B
petersm@trocaire.edu
PETERS, Monica 936-633-5250 480 D
mpeters@angelina.edu
PETERS, Pamela, J 607-746-4635 355 E
peterspj@delhi.edu
PETERS, Randall 770-228-7366 137 B
rpeters@sctech.edu
PETERS, Ronald, E 404-527-7702 132 D
rpeters@itc.edu
PETERS, Sarah 503-961-6200 418 A
speters@pioneerpacific.edu
PETERS, Sheila 615-329-8575 468 G
speters@fisk.edu
PETERS, Steve 316-295-5567 192 H
steve_peters@friends.edu
PETERS, Sue 925-631-4842 64 F
speters@stmarys-ca.edu
PETERS, Suzanne 413-545-0356 237 C
sepeters@finaid.umass.edu
PETERS, Timothy, C 949-214-3363 42 K
tim.peters@cui.edu
PETERS, Tom, D 308-398-7365 297 C
tpeters@cccneb.edu
PETERS-NGUYEN, Diane 808-735-4772 140 A
dpeters@chaminade.edu
PETERSDORFF, Joe 478-988-6800 133 H
jpetersdorff@middlegatech.edu
PETERSEN, Aaron 517-437-7341 252 E
aaron.petersen@hillsdale.edu
PETERSEN, Barbara 814-255-8321 425 G
bpetersen@state.pa.us
PETERSEN, Calvin 402-280-2796 297 H
creighton@bkstr.com
PETERSEN, Dana 207-216-4454 219 C
dpetersen@yccc.edu
PETERSEN, Debra 260-459-4545 175 A
dpetersen@ibcfortwayne.edu
PETERSEN, Donna 813-974-6603 120 D
dpeters@hsc.usf.edu
PETERSEN, Dorene 503-244-0726 414 D
dorenepetersen@achs.edu
PETERSEN, George 805-493-3419 32 H
gjpeters@clunet.edu
PETERSEN, Glenn 507-457-5031 270 B
gpetersen@winona.edu
PETERSEN, Karl 314-768-7800 286 D
kpetersen@missouricollege.com
PETERSEN, Kristin 402-471-2505 299 F
kpetersen@nscs.edu
PETERSEN, Linda 785-243-1435 191 H
lpetersen@cloud.edu
PETERSEN, Mark, A 336-758-6053 380 B
map@wfu.edu
PETERSEN, Mark, T 540-378-5125 523 D
petersen@roanoke.edu
PETERSEN, Marty 425-602-3027 530 K
mpetersen@bastyr.edu
PETERSEN, Mary, S 206-296-2043 537 F
marypete@seattleu.edu
PETERSEN, Melinda 503-725-8212 418 G
melinda.petersen@pdx.edu
PETERSEN, Owe, G 414-277-7114 548 H
petersen@msoe.edu
PETERSEN, Page 507-433-0650 269 A
ppeterse@riverland.edu
PETERSEN, Rita, A 201-559-6022 310 C
petersenr@felician.edu
PETERSEN, Stephen 847-925-6255 151 E
speterse@harpercollege.edu
PETERSEN, Stephen, H 901-678-5426 474 C
shptrsen@memphis.edu
PETERSEN, Ted 815-802-8602 154 J
tpetersen@kcc.edu
PETERSEN, Tina 916-577-2200 79 C
tpetersen@jessup.edu
PETERSON, Andrew 215-596-8877 450 A
a.peterson@usciences.edu
PETERSON, Andrew, J 704-366-4853 277 B
apeterson@rts.edu
PETERSON, Ann 713-348-4679 492 J
annp@rice.edu
PETERSON, Arthur 626-571-8811 76 D
arthurp@uwest.edu
PETERSON, Barbara 732-224-2643 308 B
bpeterson@brookdalecc.edu
PETERSON, Bill 706-233-7469 136 E
bpeterson@shorter.edu
PETERSON, Brent 212-472-1500 343 G
bpeterson@nysid.edu
PETERSON, Brittany 952-446-4160 263 E
petersonb@crown.edu
PETERSON, Bruce, A 320-308-6639 269 D
bpeterson@sctcc.edu
PETERSON, Bruce, E 740-376-4736 395 F
bruce.peterson@marietta.edu
PETERSON, Carolyn 919-546-3750 376 D
cpeterson@shawu.edu
PETERSON, Cathie 651-846-1490 269 E
cathie.peterson@saintpaul.edu
PETERSON, Chad 612-436-7520 265 G
cpeterson@msbcollege.edu
PETERSON, JR., Charles 804-523-5821 526 F
cpeterson@reynolds.edu
PETERSON, Charles, D 701-231-7456 381 H
charles.peterson@ndsu.edu
PETERSON, Charles, I 773-244-5615 159 G
cpeterson@northpark.edu

ETERSON, Chris .... 501-569-3167...... 24 E
tlcampbell@ualr.edu
ETERSON, Chris .... 405-717-6226.... 412 D
cpeterson@snu.edu
ETERSON, Christine .... 202-319-5590...... 97 C
petersoc@cua.edu
ETERSON, Christine .... 202-319-5050...... 97 C
petersoc@cua.edu
ETERSON, Christine .... 443-423-1467.... 224 C
cpetersn@mica.edu
ETERSON, Cindy .... 706-776-0103.... 135 D
cpeterson@piedmont.edu
PETERSON, Cindy .... 913-971-3533.... 195 A
cpeterso@mnu.edu
PETERSON, Curt, M .... 304-293-3449.... 544 E
Curt.Peterson@mail.wvu.edu
PETERSON, Cynthia .... 903-923-2257.... 486 D
cpeterson@etbu.edu
PETERSON, David .... 309-672-5916.... 158 B
dpeterson@mcon.edu
PETERSON, David .... 651-675-4700.... 264 H
dpeterson@twincitiesculinary.com
PETERSON, David, C .... 208-467-8527.... 143 I
dpeterson@nnu.edu
PETERSON, Deborah, A ...... 952-885-5412.... 270 F
dpeterson@nwhealth.edu
PETERSON, Dennis, R .... 563-884-5442.... 188 C
dennis.peterson@palmer.edu
PETERSON, Derek .... 605-688-4163.... 466 B
derek.peterson@sdstate.edu
PETERSON, Dolores .... 610-372-4721.... 445 B
dpeterson@racc.edu
PETERSON, Don .... 209-384-6182...... 57 C
peterson.d@mccd.edu
PETERSON, Donna, C .... 612-626-9234.... 272 D
peter011@umn.edu
PETERSON, Elaine .... 641-844-5763.... 185 J
elaine.peterson@iavalley.edu
PETERSON, Frances .... 606-759-7141.... 202 D
frances.peterson@kctcs.edu
PETERSON, Freddie .... 318-274-2222.... 215 E
petersonf@gram.edu
PETERSON, G. P. (Bud) .... 404-894-5051.... 130 D
bud.peterson@gatech.edu
PETERSON, Greg .... 562-938-4140...... 54 E
gpeterson@lbcc.edu
PETERSON, Greg .... 507-457-2800.... 270 B
gpeterson@winona.edu
PETERSON, Heather .... 609-343-5008.... 307 D
hpeterso@atlantic.edu
PETERSON, Jacqueline, D . 508-793-2414.... 233 D
jpeterso@holycross.edu
PETERSON, James .... 510-540-7747...... 54 B
jamespeterson@lincolnuca.edu
PETERSON, James .... 616-234-4017.... 251 G
jpeter@grcc.edu
PETERSON, James, R .... 509-527-4686.... 538 G
PETERSON, JoAnn .... 712-279-1633.... 182 E
joann.peterson@briarcliff.edu
PETERSON, Joe .... 435-613-5220.... 511 E
joe.peterson@ceu.edu
PETERSON, John, A .... 671-735-2153.... 559 D
jpeterson@uguam.uog.edu
PETERSON, Joyce, C .... 218-722-4000.... 263 H
joycep@dbumn.edu
PETERSON, Julie .... 773-702-0689.... 166 D
juliep@uchicago.edu
PETERSON, Kate, M .... 541-737-0759.... 418 F
kate.peterson@oregonstate.edu
PETERSON, Kathy .... 269-782-1492.... 258 E
kpeterson@swmich.edu
PETERSON, Kenneth .... 505-786-4186.... 318 H
kpeterson@navajotech.edu
PETERSON, Kent, A .... 414-277-7176.... 548 H
peterson@msoe.edu
PETERSON, Kim .... 907-786-1706...... 10 I
afkmp@uaa.alaska.edu
PETERSON, Kirk .... 937-484-1242.... 405 A
kpeterson@urbana.edu
PETERSON, Klay .... 864-503-5254.... 463 A
kpeterson@uscupstate.edu
PETERSON, Kurtis, M .... 860-882-1690...... 94 B
PETERSON, Larry, E .... 618-634-3221.... 164 C
larryp@shawneecc.edu
PETERSON, Laura .... 940-397-4919.... 491 A
laura.peterson@mwsu.edu
PETERSON, Laura, K .... 614-235-4136.... 402 G
lpeterson@TLSohio.edu
PETERSON, Leland .... 802-586-7711.... 514 E
lpeterson@sterlingcollege.edu
PETERSON, Linda .... 305-899-3020.... 101 F
lpeterson@mail.barry.edu
PETERSON, Linda .... 813-974-6061.... 120 D
lpeterso@admin.usf.edu
PETERSON, Linda .... 215-885-2360.... 435 E
PETERSON, Linda, C .... 865-694-6404.... 475 F
lcpeterson@pstcc.edu
PETERSON, Linda, K .... 810-762-9940.... 253 I
lpeterso@kettering.edu
PETERSON, Linda, M .... 563-556-5110.... 187 G
petersol@nicc.edu
PETERSON, Lori .... 612-330-1637.... 261 G
petersol@augsburg.edu
PETERSON, Lori .... 406-447-5432.... 294 A
lpeterson@carroll.edu
PETERSON, Maggie .... 406-496-4316.... 296 C
mpeterson@mtech.edu
PETERSON, Marc .... 214-768-3417.... 494 F
mpeterso@smu.edu
PETERSON, Margaret .... 406-496-4316.... 296 D
mpeterson@mtech.edu
PETERSON, Margrette .... 510-869-6512...... 64 J
mpeterson@samuelmerritt.edu
PETERSON, Mark .... 651-450-3373.... 266 I
mpeters@inverhills.edu
PETERSON, Melissa, E ...... 716-851-1775.... 333 D
petersonm@ecc.edu
PETERSON, Michael, E .... 260-422-5561.... 172 L
mepterson@indianatech.edu
PETERSON, Michael, W ...... 512-448-8788.... 493 B
michaelp@stedwards.edu
PETERSON, Michele .... 970-247-7435...... 84 G
peterson_m@fortlewis.edu
PETERSON, Michele .... 505-566-3363.... 320 D
petersonm@sanjuancollege.edu
PETERSON, Michelle .... 507-285-7180.... 269 B
michelle.peterson@roch.edu
PETERSON, Mike .... 707-476-4100...... 42 A
PETERSON, Nedra .... 818-767-0888...... 79 D
nedra.peterson@woodbury.edu
PETERSON, Nicole .... 931-221-7979.... 473 D
petersonn@apsu.edu
PETERSON, Norman .... 406-994-7150.... 295 E
normp@montana.edu
PETERSON, Norris, A .... 253-535-7645.... 535 K
petersna@plu.edu
PETERSON, Pamela .... 831-459-5380...... 75 A
pgpeters@ucsc.edu
PETERSON, Pamela .... 561-912-2166.... 106 G
ppeterson@evergladesuniversity.edu
PETERSON, Paul .... 218-683-8800.... 268 E
PETERSON, Penelope, L ..... 847-491-3828.... 160 D
p-peterson@northwestern.edu
PETERSON, Phyllis .... 815-740-3399.... 167 C
ppeterson@stfrancis.edu
PETERSON, Polly, J .... 701-252-3467.... 381 A
ppeterso@jc.edu
PETERSON, Randolph, L .... 479-979-1431...... 26 A
rpeterson@ozarks.edu
PETERSON, Rebecca .... 802-865-6425.... 513 A
peterson@champlain.edu
PETERSON, Robert .... 801-840-4800.... 509 I
rpeterson@cci.edu
PETERSON, Robert, P .... 508-856-4296.... 238 A
robert.peterson@umassmed.edu
PETERSON, Ross .... 435-797-1158.... 511 B
ross.peterson@usu.edu
PETERSON, Roy .... 262-243-5700.... 546 I
roy.peterson@cuw.edu
PETERSON, Scott .... 740-392-6868.... 396 H
scott.peterson@mvnu.edu
PETERSON, Stella .... 770-426-2930.... 133 B
peterson@life.edu
PETERSON, Steven .... 313-425-3700.... 248 D
steven.peterson@baker.edu
PETERSON, Susan, K .... 785-532-6221.... 194 B
skp@ksu.edu
PETERSON, Thomas .... 732-906-2512.... 311 E
TPeterson@middlesexcc.edu
PETERSON, Timothy .... 763-279-2475.... 261 J
tpeterson@browncollege.edu
PETERSON, Trayce .... 765-983-1501.... 171 B
petertr@earlham.edu
PETERSON, Tyler .... 334-244-3615........ 2 A
PETERSON, Val, L .... 801-863-8424.... 511 C
petersva@uvu.edu
PETERSON, Vance, T .... 818-677-4400...... 35 D
vance.peterson@csun.edu
PETERSON, Wendy .... 509-335-5586.... 539 A
wendyp@wsu.edu
PETERSON, Wes .... 360-538-4243.... 534 B
wpeterso@ghc.edu
PETERSON, Wilbur (Pete) .. 615-547-1275.... 467 I
ppeterson@cumberland.edu
PETERSON-SENIUK,
Peggy .... 419-473-2700.... 389 B
pseniuk@daviscollege.edu
PETERSON-VEATCH, Ross . 574-535-7508.... 171 D
rosspv@goshen.edu
PETH, Rita .... 510-885-3938...... 34 C
rita.peth@csueastbay.edu
PETHE-COOK, Marlyn .... 813-253-6231.... 122 H
mpethe@ut.edu
PETHICK, Michael .... 231-591-3900.... 251 B
pethicj@ferris.edu
PETILLO, John, J .... 203-371-7900...... 93 G
petilloj@sacredheart.edu
PETINAK, Craig .... 909-384-8978...... 65 C
cpetinak@sbccd.cc.ca.us
PETIPRIN, Gary .... 502-272-8480.... 198 E
gpetiprin@bellarmine.edu
PETISCE, Virginia, C .... 508-457-1313.... 243 B
vpetisce@ngs.edu
PETIT, Charles, P .... 617-912-9113.... 232 E
cpetit@bostonconservatory.edu
PETIT WILSON, Valerie ...... 401-863-2216.... 452 J
valerie_wilson@brown.edu
PETITT, Charles, W .... 336-725-8344.... 375 F
petittc@pbc.edu
PETITT, Pamela .... 206-268-4022.... 530 F
ppetitt@antioch.edu
PETITTI, Mario .... 440-525-7328.... 394 F
mpetitti@lakelandcc.edu
PETKASH, John .... 607-778-5011.... 324 G
petkash_j@sunybroome.edu
PETKE, Debra .... 860-434-5232...... 93 A
dpetke@lymeacademy.edu
PETKO, Karen .... 330-823-7288.... 404 C
petkokl@mountunion.edu
PETLEY, Kathleen .... 518-629-4574.... 336 C
k.petley@hvcc.edu
PETR, Carrie .... 402-826-8271.... 298 A
carrie.petr@doane.edu
PETRAGNANI, Joseph, F ... 610-660-1528.... 446 C
petragna@sju.edu
PETRANOVICH, Ron .... 505-863-7596.... 321 D
ronp@gallup.unm.edu
PETRAS, Donna .... 586-263-6266.... 254 F
petrasd@macomb.edu
PETREE, Daniel .... 585-395-2623.... 352 F
dpetree@brockport.edu
PETRELLA, Yvonne .... 315-312-2270.... 354 A
yvonne.petrella@oswego.edu
PETRI, Basia .... 503-682-1862.... 419 F
bpetri@pioneerpacific.edu
PETRI, Elizabeth .... 413-662-5219.... 238 F
e.petri@mcla.edu
PETRICCA, Joe .... 323-856-7721...... 28 D
jpetricca@afi.com
PETRICHENKO,
Kathleen, J .... 410-822-5400.... 222 B
kpetrichenko@chesapeake.edu
PETRICK, Joseph .... 802-287-8377.... 513 D
petrickj@greenmtn.edu
PETRICK, Laurie .... 920-832-6525.... 547 J
laurie.a.petrick@lawrence.edu
PETRIDIS, Heather .... 626-815-4570...... 30 E
hpetridis@apu.edu
PETRIE, Bruce, F .... 575-234-9214.... 319 F
bpetrie@cavern.nmsu.edu
PETRIE, Mark, J .... 716-878-3641.... 353 A
petriemj@buffalostate.edu
PETRIE, Nancy .... 914-337-9300.... 331 A
nancy.petrie@concordia-ny.edu
PETRIKAT, Douglas .... 714-547-9625...... 31 I
dpetrikat@calcoast.edu
PETRILLO, Emilia .... 410-328-8404.... 227 C
epetr001@umaryland.edu
PETRILLO, Tracee .... 781-239-5695.... 230 G
tpetrillo@babson.edu
PETRITUS, Paul .... 585-720-0660.... 325 C
ppetritus@bryantstratton.edu
PETRIZZO, Louis, S .... 631-451-4235.... 356 D
petrizl@sunysuffolk.edu
PETRO, John, G .... 412-321-7550.... 423 G
PETRO, Patrice, S .... 414-229-4523.... 551 C
ppetro@uwm.edu
PETRO, Tony .... 239-687-5443.... 101 B
tpetro@avemarialaw.edu
PETROCCIA, Anthony, M .... 315-568-3256.... 342 H
apetrocc@nycc.edu
PETROCCO-NAPULI,
Kristina, L .... 315-568-3886.... 342 H
kpetrocco@nycc.edu
PETROFF, Les .... 317-738-8108.... 171 C
lpetroff@franklincollege.edu
PETROKA, Louise, A .... 203-285-2393...... 90 A
lpetroka@gwcc.commnet.edu
PETRONE, Jill .... 253-943-2800.... 533 B
jpetrone@devry.edu
PETROSIAN, Anahid .... 956-872-6790.... 494 D
anahid@southtexascollege.edu
PETROSINO, James, A ...... 585-292-3672.... 341 H
jpetrosino@monroecc.edu
PETROSINO, Linda .... 419-372-8243.... 385 C
lpetros@bgsu.edu
PETROSINO, Susan .... 860-832-1786...... 91 G
petrosinos@ccsu.edu
PETROSKI, Paul, S .... 410-706-8338.... 227 C
ppetrosk@umaryland.edu
PETROSKY, Elaine .... 330-675-8864.... 394 A
epetrosk@kent.edu
PETROSKY, Joseph .... 586-498-4181.... 254 F
petroskyj@macomb.edu
PETROSKY, Snezena .... 641-472-7000.... 187 B
spetrosky@mum.edu
PETROVIC, Louis .... 508-910-9842.... 237 E
lpetrovic@umassd.edu
PETROVICH, Jason, G .... 765-658-4218.... 170 I
jpetrovich@depauw.edu
PETROVICH, Tamberly .... 831-582-4137...... 35 C
tpetrovich@csumb.edu
PETRUCCI, Michele .... 724-357-2295.... 442 E
michelep@iup.edu
PETRUCCIO, Diane .... 440-646-8390.... 405 B
dpetruc@ursuline.edu
PETRUS, John .... 412-536-1033.... 432 F
john.petrus@laroche.edu
PETRUS, Robin .... 607-778-5045.... 324 G
petrus_r@sunybroome.edu
PETRUSCH, Suzanne, M .... 210-436-3995.... 493 C
spetrusch@stmarytx.edu
PETRUSO, Karl .... 817-272-7215.... 505 A
petruso@uta.edu
PETRUZZELLI, Barbara, W . 845-561-0800.... 342 A
barbara.petruzzelli@msmc.edu
PETRUZZELLI, Dominic, A 973-655-6500.... 311 G
petruzzellid@mail.montclair.edu
PETRY, Laura .... 312-332-0707.... 165 H
PETRY, Ric .... 614-222-3227.... 388 F
rpetry@ccad.edu
PETRYSHAK, Bruce .... 615-898-5570.... 473 F
bruce.petryshak@mtsu.edu
PETRYSHYN, Laryssa .... 716-829-8119.... 332 F
petryshl@dyc.edu
PETSCH, Verl, E .... 307-532-8248.... 555 H
verl.petsch@ewc.wy.edu
PETSCHE, Daniel .... 660-944-2875.... 280 F
daniel@conception.edu
PETT-CONKLIN, Linda .... 713-525-3535.... 504 D
lmpc@stthom.edu
PETTAY, Robert .... 949-812-7462...... 27 C
rpettay@alliant.edu
PETTEGREW, Larry .... 800-672-3060.... 376 E
PETTEWAY, Venetia, S .... 810-762-7899.... 253 I
vpettewa@kettering.edu
PETTIBONE, Dennis .... 423-236-2741.... 473 A
dlpettib@southern.edu
PETTIBONE, John, C .... 770-720-5939.... 135 F
jcp@reinhardt.edu
PETTIFORD, Anthony .... 937-376-6223.... 386 H
apettiford@centralstate.edu
PETTIFORD, Jacqueline, L . 336-334-4822.... 370 E
jlpettiford@gtcc.edu
PETTIGREW, Frank, E .... 419-289-5051.... 384 D
fpettigr@ashland.edu
PETTIGREW, Jason .... 605-229-8350.... 464 I
jason.pettigrew@presentation.edu
PETTINARI, Gayle .... 719-549-3329...... 87 B
gayle.pettinari@pueblocc.edu
PETTINGER, Connie .... 708-209-3045.... 148 C
constance.pettinger@cuchicago.edu
PETTINICO, JR., Nicholas . 860-832-1766...... 91 G
pettinico@ccsu.edu
PETTIS, Curtis .... 937-376-6349.... 386 H
cpettis@centralstate.edu
PETTIS, Stephanie .... 251-575-3156........ 1 B
spettis@ascc.edu
PETTIS-WALDEN,
Karen, M .... 804-523-5029.... 526 F
kpettis-walden@reynolds.edu
PETTIT, Charlene, M .... 920-924-3112.... 554 E
cpettit@morainepark.edu
PETTIT, Cyndi .... 214-333-5235.... 484 C
cyndi@dbu.edu
PETTIT, Gretchen, A .... 636-584-6535.... 281 I
PETTIT, Jillian, P .... 336-841-9283.... 365 A
jpettit@highpoint.edu
PETTIT, Patricia, A .... 217-424-6488.... 158 F
ppettit@millikin.edu
PETTITT, Maureen .... 360-416-7919.... 538 A
maureen.pettitt@skagit.edu
PETTUS, Algray, L .... 936-261-1387.... 496 E
alpettus@pvamu.edu
PETTY, Daniel, W .... 813-988-5131.... 107 I
pettyd@floridacollege.edu
PETTY, Jamie .... 706-295-7733.... 130 C
jpetty@highlands.edu
PETTY, JoBeth .... 601-968-8901.... 273 F
JBpetty@belhaven.edu
PETTY, Leslie .... 734-462-4400.... 258 C
lpetty@schoolcraft.edu
PETTY, Leslie .... 708-802-6213.... 163 G
petty@sxu.edu
PETTY, Marcia, L .... 504-865-3030.... 213 F
mlpetty@loyno.edu
PETTY, Mark .... 319-385-6231.... 186 A
mpetty@iwc.edu
PETTY, Michael, E .... 812-429-1411.... 176 I
mpetty@ivytech.edu
PETTY, Mikel, D .... 256-824-4368........ 9 A
mikel.petty@uah.edu
PETTY, Rachel .... 202-274-5194...... 99 F
rpetty@udc.edu
PETTY, Tricia, L .... 304-293-8500.... 544 E
tricia.petty@mail.wvu.edu
PETTY, Yolanda .... 478-471-5364.... 133 E
yolanda.petty@maconstate.edu
PETTY-WARD, Paula, J ...... 931-540-2572.... 474 F
ppettyward@columbiastate.edu
PETTYJOHN, Susan, H .... 828-262-2340.... 377 B
pettyjohnsh@appstate.edu
PETULA, Eileen, E .... 610-328-8399.... 447 E
epetula1@swarthmore.edu
PETZ, Dan .... 620-672-5641.... 196 A
danp@prattcc.edu
PETZNICK, Michelle, L .... 641-422-4205.... 187 F
petznmic@niacc.edu
PEUGH-WADE, Martha, A . 415-422-2444...... 76 B
peugh@usfca.edu
PEULER, Todd .... 616-647-5100...... 19 C
Todd.Peuler@phoenix.edu
PEWE, Richard, P .... 517-607-2518.... 252 E
rich.pewe@hillsdale.edu
PEYTON, James .... 206-878-3710.... 534 E
jpeyton@highline.edu

PEYTON, Janice 936-273-7392 490 C
janice.peyton@lonestar.edu
PEYTON, Marcia 706-754-7789 134 E
mpeyton@northgatech.edu
PEYTON, Virginia 501-812-2206 23 C
vpeyton@pulaskitech.edu
PEZOLD, Frank 361-825-2349 497 F
frank.pezold@tamucc.edu
PEZZAROSSI, Alba 773-481-8872 147 F
apezzarossi@ccc.edu
PEZZELLE, Patrick 406-293-2721 294 D
ppezzell@fvcc.edu
PEZZI, Eileen 315-464-7853 352 E
pezzie@upstate.edu
PEZZOLI, Jean 808-984-3290 142 B
pezzoli@hawaii.edu
PEZZULLO, Christopher 207-772-5437 220 H
cpezzullo@une.edu
PEZZUTO, John 808-933-2909 141 A
pezzuto@hawaii.edu
PEÑA, Rosa 787-797-1166 564 D
rpena@mechtech.edu
PFAFF, Jason 402-530-1902 19 C
Jason.Pfaff@phoenix.edu
PFANNENSTIEHL, Craig 617-217-9050 231 C
cfp@baystate.edu
PFAUTZ, Chris 804-594-1556 526 G
cpfautz@jtcc.edu
PFEFER, Mark, T 913-234-0796 191 G
mark.pfefer@cleveland.edu
PFEFFER, Carole 502-272-8184 198 E
cpfeffer@bellarmine.edu
PFEFFER, Miriam 718-782-2200 324 C
mpfeffer@boricuacollege.edu
PFEFFER, Richard 732-224-2262 308 B
rpfeffer@brookdalecc.edu
PFEFFER, Richard, J 732-224-2262 308 B
rpfeffer@brookdalecc.edu
PFEIFER, Alan, D 815-288-5511 163 I
pfeifer@svcc.edu
PFEIFER, Brette 785-460-5509 191 J
brette.pfeifer@colbycc.edu
PFEIFER, Donald 413-236-2131 239 E
dpfeifer@berkshirecc.edu
PFEIFER, Joseph 503-251-5775 420 H
jpfeifer@uws.edu
PFEIFER, Justin 785-587-2800 194 F
justinpfeifer@matc.net
PFEIFER, Tad 308-535-3684 298 I
pfeifert@mpcc.edu
PFEIFFER, Charlotte, D 574-520-5536 174 C
cpfeifer@iusb.edu
PFEIFFER, Francine 202-220-1336 314 B
francine@rutgers.edu
PFEIFFER, Jay 717-262-2006 452 B
jay.pfeiffer@wilson.edu
PFEIFFER, Kelley 636-922-8544 288 F
kpfeiffer@stchas.edu
PFEIFFER, Marcia, F 314-513-4208 289 B
mpfeiffer@stlcc.edu
PFEIFFER, Mary 716-829-7808 332 F
pfeiffer@dyc.edu
PFEIFFER, Patricia, D 772-462-7301 110 L
ppfeiffe@irsc.edu
PFEIFFER, Pattie 919-735-5151 374 F
ppfeiffer@waynecc.edu
PFEIFFER, William, S 828-298-3325 380 C
president@warren-wilson.edu
PFEIFLE, Barbara 859-280-1224 203 F
bpfeifle@lextheo.edu
PFEIL, Robert 716-286-8689 344 D
fpfeil@niagara.edu
PFEILSTICKER, Carole 561-297-2738 118 H
pfeilsti@fau.edu
PFENDER, Alison 724-653-2197 427 F
apfender@dec.edu
PFISTER, Kathrine 815-479-7529 157 F
kpfister@mchenry.edu
PFLEIGER, Kelly 215-368-5000 422 H
kpfleiger@biblical.edu
PFLUKE, Deanna 585-266-0430 333 E
dpfluke@cci.edu
PFURSICH, Fred 562-907-4236 79 B
fpfursich@whittier.edu
PFUTZENREUTER,
Richard, H 612-625-4517 272 D
pfutz001@umn.edu
PHAIAH, Peter 218-281-8505 272 A
phaiah@umn.edu
PHAIRE-WASHINGTON,
Linda 334-229-8343 1 C
lphaire@alasu.edu
PHAKITTHONG, Rachelle 715-675-3331 554 G
phakitth@ntc.edu
PHALEN, Kathleen 617-975-9014 234 E
phalenka@emmanuel.edu
PHAM, Hue 714-432-5764 41 B
hpham@occ.cccd.edu
PHAM, Michael 206-587-4193 537 A
mpham@sccd.ctc.edu
PHAM, Tom, C 617-984-1699 244 C
tpham@quincycollege.edu
PHAN, Minh 504-866-7426 213 I
frphan@nds.edu

PHAN, Nga 619-684-8800 59 A
nphan@newschoolarch.edu
PHAN, Phil 410-234-9402 223 F
pphan@jhu.edu
PHARO, SCN, Diane 812-357-6598 179 E
dpharo@saintmeinrad.edu
PHARR, Christine 402-399-2419 297 E
msellers@csm.edu
PHARR, Dianne 254-442-5151 482 G
dianne.pharr@cisco.edu
PHARR, Maria 252-638-7284 369 E
pharr@cravencc.edu
PHEASANT, Clayton, N 570-348-6285 435 F
pheasant@marywood.edu
PHEASANT, Joel, C 814-641-5334 431 L
pheasaj@juniata.edu
PHELAN, Carol 617-585-1139 243 E
carol.phelan@necmusic.edu
PHELAN, Carol 516-877-3154 322 A
phelan@adelphi.edu
PHELAN, Daniel, J 517-787-0800 253 E
phelandanielj@jccmi.edu
PHELAN JOHNSON,
Marcia 860-297-2041 94 C
marcia.johnson@trincoll.edu
PHELAN-NINH, Jennifer 315-792-7500 356 B
jennifer.phelan@sunyit.edu
PHELON, Elmer 212-237-8541 328 A
ephelon@jjay.cuny.edu
PHELPS, Bill 870-245-5567 22 I
phelpswr@obu.edu
PHELPS, Brian 360-383-3365 539 D
bphelps@whatcom.ctc.edu
PHELPS, Camille 580-745-2080 412 C
cphelps@se.edu
PHELPS, Craig 480-219-6012 278 F
cphelps@atsu.edu
PHELPS, Cynthia 212-960-5836 361 I
cphelps@yu.edu
PHELPS, Dani, J 610-841-3333 441 D
dphelps@psb.edu
PHELPS, Debbie 620-331-4100 193 G
dphelps@indycc.edu
PHELPS, Dennis, L 504-282-4455 213 H
dphelps@nobts.edu
PHELPS, Devon, N 419-995-8389 399 B
phelps.2@osu.edu
PHELPS, Esther 330-337-6403 383 H
depemp@raex.com
PHELPS, Gary, L 330-471-8127 395 E
gphelps@malone.edu
PHELPS, Gina, S 601-977-0960 278 C
gina.phelps@vc.edu
PHELPS, Hilary 860-343-5856 90 D
hphelps@mxcc.commnet.edu
PHELPS, Janet 603-668-6706 304 E
jphelps@ccsnh.edu
PHELPS, Jean 718-262-2285 329 B
phelps@york.cuny.edu
PHELPS, Joel 802-447-6306 514 D
jphelps@svc.edu
PHELPS, Jon 407-679-0100 110 C
jphelps@fullsail.com
PHELPS, Martha 270-824-8591 202 C
martha.phelps@kctcs.edu
PHELPS, Sarah, M 202-319-5142 97 C
phelpss@cua.edu
PHELPS, Sherri 870-245-5410 22 I
phelpss@obu.edu
PHELPS-ELLERKER, Lena 863-784-7303 117 I
lena.phelps@southflorida.edu
PHENICIE, Christopher, N 864-488-4549 459 A
cphenicie@limestone.edu
PHENIX, Amy 612-626-1616 272 D
PHENIX, Morgan, S 540-868-7111 526 H
mphenix@lfcc.edu
PHIFER, James, R 319-399-8686 183 C
jphifer@coe.edu
PHILBECK, Daniel, L 864-587-4223 461 D
philbed@smcsc.edu
PHILBERT, Martin, A 734-763-4523 259 D
philbert@umich.edu
PHILBIN, Kathleen 585-389-2451 342 D
kphilbi8@naz.edu
PHILIP, Chuck 574-289-7001 176 C
cphilip@ivytech.edu
PHILIP, George, M 518-956-8010 351 E
presmail@uamail.albany.edu
PHILIPKOSKY, Thomas, G 843-953-6907 456 C
tom.philipkosky@citadel.edu
PHILIPP, Diane 517-437-7341 252 E
diane.philipp@hillsdale.edu
PHILIPP, Shirin 617-349-9600 236 G
PHILIPPA, Laine, M 414-410-4187 546 D
lmphilippa@stritch.edu
PHILIPPON, Roger 207-755-5357 218 G
rphilippon@cmcc.edu
PHILIPS, JR., Billy, U 806-743-1388 501 E
billy.philips@ttuhsc.edu
PHILLEY, Tim 918-495-6970 411 C
tphilley@oru.edu
PHILLIP, Thomas, G 262-243-5700 546 I
thomas.phillip@cuw.edu

PHILLIPS, Adrian 313-496-2820 260 C
aphilli1@wcccd.edu
PHILLIPS, Adrienne 662-252-8000 277 C
aphillips@rustcollege.edu
PHILLIPS, Alice 502-447-1000 206 A
aphillips@spencerian.edu
PHILLIPS, Allison 336-838-6491 375 A
allison.phillips@wilkescc.edu
PHILLIPS, Amy 719-590-6708 83 D
aphillips@coloradotech.edu
PHILLIPS, Andrew, T 410-293-1583 558 H
atphillip@usna.edu
PHILLIPS, Brad, C 607-733-7177 332 I
bphillips@ebi-college.com
PHILLIPS, Brian 562-903-4897 30 H
brian.phillips@biola.edu
PHILLIPS, Bridget 217-479-7031 157 D
bridget.phillips@mac.edu
PHILLIPS, Calvin 956-665-2262 506 A
phillipscd@utpa.edu
PHILLIPS, Carol 910-938-6343 369 C
phillipsc@coastalcarolina.edu
PHILLIPS, Carolyn 850-484-1140 114 G
cphillips@pensacolastate.edu
PHILLIPS, Christopher, G 410-706-2261 227 C
cphillip@umaryland.edu
PHILLIPS, Cinda, K 812-749-1271 178 D
cphillip@oak.edu
PHILLIPS, Cindy 417-477-8212 287 G
phillipc@otc.edu
PHILLIPS, Cliff 407-831-9816 102 I
cphillips@citycollege.edu
PHILLIPS, Cynthia 610-841-3333 441 D
cphillips@psb.edu
PHILLIPS, Dave 870-777-5722 25 F
dave.phillips@uacch.edu
PHILLIPS, Dave 615-248-1683 476 E
dphillips@trevecca.edu
PHILLIPS, Denese 805-966-3888 31 A
Denese.Phillips@brooks.edu
PHILLIPS, Denise 972-721-5168 502 F
dphilli@udallas.edu
PHILLIPS, Dianna 732-224-2265 308 B
PHILLIPS, Dianne 225-768-1736 214 B
marilyn.phillips@ololcollege.edu
PHILLIPS, Dorothy, E 606-679-8501 202 F
dorothy.phillips@kctcs.edu
PHILLIPS, Douglas 585-275-3311 358 I
dphillips@admin.rochester.edu
PHILLIPS, E. Clorisa 276-466-7910 528 G
PHILLIPS, Earnest 702-895-2388 302 K
earnest.phillips@unlv.edu
PHILLIPS, Eddie 312-850-7125 147 C
ephillips@ccc.edu
PHILLIPS, Edward 504-520-6787 217 A
ephillips@xula.edu
PHILLIPS, Elaine, W 405-273-5331 408 B
ephillips@familyoffaithcollege.edu
PHILLIPS, Faith 740-366-9492 399 E
phillips.495@osu.edu
PHILLIPS, Faith 740-366-9492 386 G
phillips.495@osu.edu
PHILLIPS, Gail, G 615-353-3703 475 D
gail.phillips@nscc.edu
PHILLIPS, Gary, A 765-361-6224 181 C
phillipg@wabash.edu
PHILLIPS, Gina 817-531-6548 502 A
gphillips@txwes.edu
PHILLIPS, Glen 478-387-4731 130 E
PHILLIPS, Heather 218-477-4363 268 A
phillipshe@mnstate.edu
PHILLIPS, Hugh, H 334-833-4581 4 E
bphillips@huntingdon.edu
PHILLIPS, Idelia, P 941-752-5218 118 E
phillii@scf.edu
PHILLIPS, J. Lynn 757-569-6701 527 E
ledwards@pdc.edu
PHILLIPS, James, J 847-491-8880 160 D
j-phillips@northwestern.edu
PHILLIPS, James, K 910-630-7149 366 H
jphillips@methodist.edu
PHILLIPS, James, L 713-798-6598 481 H
phillips@bcm.edu
PHILLIPS, Janet 540-224-6973 520 D
jephillips@jchs.edu
PHILLIPS, Jeffrey, J 404-880-8480 126 I
jphillips@cau.edu
PHILLIPS, Jennifer 212-592-2000 350 F
jphillips2@sva.edu
PHILLIPS, Jennifer 315-859-4243 335 A
jlphillips@hamilton.edu
PHILLIPS, Joanne 423-775-6596 472 E
jphillips@ogs.edu
PHILLIPS, John, A 619-260-4523 76 A
jphillips@sandiego.edu
PHILLIPS, John, C 216-373-5308 397 E
jphillips@ndc.edu
PHILLIPS, Joseph, M 206-296-5700 537 F
phillipsj@seattleu.edu
PHILLIPS, June 318-670-6365 215 A
jphillips@susla.edu
PHILLIPS, Karen 413-775-1305 240 B
phillips@gcc.mass.edu

PHILLIPS, Kevin, J 203-932-7318 95 E
kphillips@newhaven.edu
PHILLIPS, Kimberley, L 718-951-3136 326 G
KPhillips@brooklyn.cuny.edu
PHILLIPS, Larry, M 936-639-1301 480 D
phillips@angelina.edu
PHILLIPS, Laurel, E 814-362-7531 449 B
leb2@pitt.edu
PHILLIPS, Linda 601-968-5934 273 F
lphillips@belhaven.edu
PHILLIPS, Linda 580-581-2238 407 D
lindap@cameron.edu
PHILLIPS, Lynette 516-299-2461 338 F
Lynette.Phillips@liu.edu
PHILLIPS, Margaret, R 304-293-2545 544 E
margaret.phillips@mail.wvu.edu
PHILLIPS, Mari Anne 417-667-8181 280 I
mphillips@cottey.edu
PHILLIPS, Marie 413-265-2365 233 E
phillipsmarie@elms.edu
PHILLIPS, Mary, T 678-915-7230 137 C
phillips@spsu.edu
PHILLIPS, Matthew 815-394-5003 162 H
mphillips@rockford.edu
PHILLIPS, Melissa, C 828-733-5883 371 F
mphillips@mayland.edu
PHILLIPS, Michael, C 843-953-4942 457 B
phillipsm@cofc.edu
PHILLIPS, Mike 309-796-5012 145 E
phillipsm@bhc.edu
PHILLIPS, Monika 870-512-7703 20 F
monika_phillips@asun.edu
PHILLIPS, Morgan 910-642-7141 373 G
mphillips@sccnc.edu
PHILLIPS, Myra 804-524-5352 529 C
mhphilli@vsu.edu
PHILLIPS, Nyambura, M 609-894-9311 308 C
nphillip@bcc.edu
PHILLIPS, Pamela 920-498-5418 555 A
pamela.phillips@nwtc.edu
PHILLIPS, Patricia 401-454-6563 454 B
pphillip02@risd.edu
PHILLIPS, Patricia, L 757-789-1723 526 D
phillips@es.vccs.edu
PHILLIPS, Phil, E 310-506-7227 61 G
phil.phillips@pepperdine.edu
PHILLIPS, Rachel 215-965-4025 436 H
rphillips@moore.edu
PHILLIPS, Ralph 480-860-2700 14 G
rphillips@taliesin.edu
PHILLIPS, Ralph, N 724-847-6766 429 G
rphillip@geneva.edu
PHILLIPS, Raymond, B 207-859-4209 217 G
Ray.Phillips@colby.ed
PHILLIPS, Rebecca, J 724-847-6843 429 G
PHILLIPS, Richard 276-523-7467 527 A
rphillips@me.vccs.edu
PHILLIPS, Richard, W 901-722-0220 473 B
rphillips@sco.edu
PHILLIPS, Rita, M 515-294-0548 182 B
rphillip@iastate.edu
PHILLIPS, Robyn 509-452-5100 536 A
PHILLIPS, Sandra 828-297-3811 368 D
sphillips@cccti.edu
PHILLIPS, Sandy 724-222-5330 438 E
sphillips@penncommercial.edu
PHILLIPS, Shannon 843-863-7035 456 B
sphillip@csuniv.edu
PHILLIPS, Sheri 417-865-2811 282 A
phillipss@evangel.edu
PHILLIPS, Stephen, S 443-412-2286 223 B
sphillips@harford.edu
PHILLIPS, Steve 845-675-4741 344 G
steve.phillips@nyack.edu
PHILLIPS, Sue 570-702-8916 431 K
sphillips@johnson.edu
PHILLIPS, Susan, D 518-956-8030 351 E
sdphil@uamail.albany.edu
PHILLIPS, Susan, M 850-436-8444 123 A
susan.phillips@vc.edu
PHILLIPS, Susanne, D 610-399-2217 441 H
sphillips@cheyney.edu
PHILLIPS, Teri, P 253-535-7187 535 K
phillitp@plu.edu
PHILLIPS, Terry Don 864-656-1935 456 E
pterry@clemson.edu
PHILLIPS, Timothy 563-333-6259 188 D
PhillipsTimothy@sau.edu
PHILLIPS, Tina, A 610-499-1161 451 F
taphillips@widener.edu
PHILLIPS, Tom 570-389-4775 441 F
tphilli2@bloomu.edu
PHILLIPS, Valerie 619-596-2766 26 I
valerie@advancedtraining.edu
PHILLIPS, Wendy, S 724-838-7399 424 G
phillipsws@carlow.edu
PHILLIPS, William 859-622-3515 200 D
william.phillips@eku.edu
PHILLIPS, William 401-232-6045 453 A
wphillip@bryant.edu
PHILLIPS, Wilma, D 334-386-7274 3 H
wphillips@faulkner.edu
PHILLIPS, Winfred, M 352-392-9271 120 B
wphil@ufl.edu

PILLING, Georgene ... 215-572-2946 ... 422 B
pilling@arcadia.edu
PILLON, Greg, S ... 615-460-6645 ... 467 B
greg.pillon@belmont.edu
PILLOTE, Lauren ... 303-753-6046 ... 87 F
PILLOW, Kirk, E ... 215-717-6388 ... 448 H
kpillow@uarts.edu
PILLOW-PRICE, Kathy ... 870-307-7373 ... 22 D
kprice@lyon.edu
PILON, Simone ... 317-738-8256 ... 171 C
spilon@franklincollege.edu
PILSNER, Joseph ... 713-942-5049 ... 504 D
pilsnerj@stthom.edu
PILTZ, Anthony ... 406-657-1020 ... 296 E
plitza@rocky.edu
PIMENTEL, German ... 787-840-8894 ... 567 E
german.pimentel@upr.edu
PIMENTEL, Robert ... 559-934-2793 ... 77 H
robertpimentel@whccd.edu
PIMENTEL, Rosa ... 787-250-1912 ... 563 E
rmpimentel@metro.inter.edu
PIMMENTEL, Myshel ... 209-386-6777 ... 57 C
pimmentel.m@mccd.edu
PIMOMO, Rose ... 509-865-8512 ... 534 D
pimomo_r@heritage.edu
PINA, Bernard ... 575-527-7610 ... 319 G
bepina@nmsu.edu
PINA, Elsa ... 915-351-8100 ... 480 C
PINA, Jason ... 401-254-5306 ... 454 C
jpina@rwu.edu
PINA, Jason, B ... 401-874-2101 ... 454 E
jbpina@uri.edu
PINA HOUDE, Ana Maria . 915-351-8100 ... 480 C
PINCHBACK, Keith ... 501-882-8855 ... 20 D
gkpinchback@asub.edu
PINCHOT, III, Gifford ... 206-780-6203 ... 530 I
gifford.pinchot@bgi.edu
PINCKNEY, Al ... 414-297-6279 ... 554 D
pincknea@matc.edu
PINCKNEY, Jloundia ... 843-574-6120 ... 461 G
jloundia.pinckney@tridenttech.edu
PINDAR, Kassy ... 702-579-3556 ... 302 C
kpindar@kaplan.edu
PINDAR, Marianne ... 570-459-1573 ... 433 A
pindarm@lackawanna.edu
PINDER, Walt ... 912-427-5778 ... 124 A
wpinder@altamahatech.edu
PINE, Gary ... 626-815-5081 ... 30 E
PINE, John ... 412-392-4750 ... 444 H
jpine@pointpark.edu
PINE, Karey ... 585-475-6230 ... 347 G
ktprla@rit.edu
PINEDA, Gladys ... 212-423-2768 ... 335 D
gladys.pineda@helenefuld.edu
PINEDA, Marika ... 541-463-5824 ... 416 D
pinedam@lanecc.edu
PINEDO, Ciriaco ... 909-652-6160 ... 39 B
cid.pinedo@chaffey.edu
PINEIRO, Mildred ... 787-728-1515 ... 568 B
mpineiro@sagrado.edu
PINEIRO, Pedro ... 718-997-4446 ... 328 F
pedro.pineiro@qc.cuny.edu
PINER, Brandy ... 803-981-7391 ... 463 G
bpiner@yorktech.edu
PINERO, Luis, A ... 608-263-2378 ... 550 G
lapinero@vc.wisc.edu
PINES, Darryll, J ... 301-405-3869 ... 227 B
pines@umd.edu
PINESCHI, David ... 916-348-4689 ... 45 H
dpineschi@epic.edu
PINESETT, JoDell ... 714-300-0300 ... 70 I
jpinesett@scitech.edu
PINET, Celine ... 408-741-2140 ... 78 B
celine.pinet@westvalley.edu
PINI, John ... 781-891-2228 ... 231 F
jpini@bentley.edu
PINI, John, A ... 781-891-2228 ... 231 F
jpini@bentley.edu
PINION, Tyson ... 419-448-3438 ... 402 E
piniont@tiffin.edu
PINIZZOTTO, Russell ... 617-989-4485 ... 246 C
pinizzottor@wit.edu
PINK, Kathy ... 641-844-5739 ... 185 H
Kathy.Pink@iavalley.edu
PINK, Kevin ... 641-683-5128 ... 185 D
kpink@indianhills.edu
PINK, Rodney ... 718-488-6012 ... 338 H
rodney.pink@liu.edu
PINK, Thomas, A ... 906-635-2315 ... 254 C
tpink@lssu.edu
PINKALL, Rita ... 620-672-5641 ... 196 A
ritap@prattcc.edu
PINKARD, Elfred, A ... 704-378-1000 ... 365 H
epinkard@jcsu.edu
PINKE, Taylor, A ... 813-258-7401 ... 122 H
tpinke@ut.edu
PINKERMAN, Loren, L ... 706-880-8234 ... 132 I
lpinkerman@lagrange.edu
PINKERTON, Frank ... 909-652-6290 ... 39 B
frank.pinkerton@chaffey.edu
PINKERTON, Mary ... 262-472-1712 ... 552 E
pinkertm@uww.edu
PINKERTON, Susan ... 602-274-4300 ... 13 A
spinkerton@brymanschool.edu
PINKHAM, JoEllen ... 585-389-2060 ... 342 D
jpinkha0@naz.edu
PINKHAM, Wesley, M ... 818-779-8413 ... 53 B
wpinkham@kingsuniversity.edu
PINKNEY, Adrell, L ... 504-286-5229 ... 214 I
apinkney@suno.edu
PINKNEY, Dwayne ... 919-962-1091 ... 378 D
dpinkney@email.unc.edu
PINKOWSKI, JR.,
Richard, J ... 716-926-8820 ... 335 F
rickp@hilbert.edu
PINKSTON, Cody ... 920-748-8365 ... 549 I
pinkstonc@ripon.edu
PINKSTON, Glen, P ... 580-581-2225 ... 407 D
glenp@cameron.edu
PINKSTON, Paul ... 920-465-2373 ... 551 A
pinkstop@uwgb.edu
PINKSTON, Scott ... 870-368-7371 ... 23 A
spinkston@ozarka.edu
PINKSTON, Terri, B ... 405-325-3021 ... 413 C
terri@ou.edu
PINKSTON-MCKEE, Ria ... 773-291-6251 ... 147 D
rmckee@ccc.edu
PINN, Carolyn ... 518-381-1331 ... 350 E
taylorc@sunysccc.edu
PINNELL, Yalonda ... 417-829-1421 ... 19 C
Yalonda.Pinnell@phoenix.edu
PINNER, Ray ... 256-824-6350 ... 9 A
ray.pinner@uah.edu
PINNEY, Denise, M ... 973-642-8871 ... 315 C
denise.pinney@shu.edu
PINNICK, Denise ... 812-749-1267 ... 178 D
dpinnick@oak.edu
PINNICK, Maureen ... 317-738-8028 ... 171 C
mpinnick@franklincollege.edu
PINO, Alejandro, J ... 563-588-7205 ... 186 I
alejandro.pino@loras.edu
PINO, Diana ... 713-718-5115 ... 487 G
diana.pino@hccs.edu
PINO, Lori ... 510-780-4500 ... 53 I
lpino@lifewest.edu
PINOCCI, Tina, M ... 856-256-4604 ... 314 A
pinocci@rowan.edu
PINOTTI, Gerald ... 708-209-3032 ... 148 C
jerry.pinotti@cuchicago.edu
PINS, Jacqueline, J ... 608-757-7772 ... 553 E
jpins@blackhawk.edu
PINSKY, Linda ... 212-986-4343 ... 323 J
lsp@berkeleycollege.edu
PINSKY, Linda ... 973-278-5400 ... 307 G
lsp@BerkeleyCollege.edu
PINSON, J. Matthew ... 615-383-1340 ... 468 J
president@fwbbc.edu
PINTAK, Lawrence, E ... 509-335-8535 ... 539 A
lpintak@wsu.edu
PINTER-LUCKE, Claudia, L 909-869-3328 ... 33 G
clpinterluck@csupomona.edu
PINTO, Brian ... 610-921-6728 ... 421 D
bpinto@alb.edu
PINTO, David ... 609-652-4555 ... 313 F
david.pinto@stockton.edu
PINTO, John ... 712-274-5158 ... 187 D
pinto@morningside.edu
PINTO, Neville ... 502-852-6281 ... 207 A
ngpint01@louisville.edu
PINTO, Savlo ... 773-291-6501 ... 147 D
spinto3@ccc.edu
PIONG, Chee ... 561-912-1211 ... 106 G
cpiong@evergladesuniversity.edu
PIOTRKOWSKI, Joann ... 440-646-8327 ... 405 B
jpiotrkowski@ursuline.edu
PIOTROWSKI, Kevin ... 603-513-1326 ... 306 H
kevin.piotrowski@granite.edu
PIPER, Dianne ... 340-693-1141 ... 568 C
dpiper@uvi.edu
PIPER, Everett, G ... 918-335-6234 ... 411 B
epiper@okwu.edu
PIPER, Renee ... 985-446-8111 ... 216 A
renee.piper@nicholls.edu
PIPER, Richard ... 913-627-4126 ... 193 J
rpiper@kckcc.edu
PIPER, Terry ... 305-899-3649 ... 101 F
tpiper@mail.barry.edu
PIPER, Wendy, L ... 740-368-3177 ... 400 F
wlpiper@owu.edu
PIPERATA, Diana ... 215-637-7700 ... 430 H
dpiperata@holyfamily.edu
PIPES, Dianne, L ... 210-431-4373 ... 493 C
dpipes@stmarytx.edu
PIPES, III, J. Kelly ... 336-838-6424 ... 375 A
kelly.pipes@wilkescc.edu
PIPINSKI, Ann, L ... 570-702-8901 ... 431 K
apipinski@johnson.edu
PIPITONE, Linda ... 314-889-1493 ... 282 C
lpipitone@fontbonne.edu
PIPKIN, Lisa, W ... 252-334-2020 ... 367 A
lisa.pipkin@macuniversity.edu
PIPPIN, Jeff ... 310-506-7500 ... 61 G
jeff.pippin@pepperdine.edu
PIRIUS, Landon ... 763-424-0712 ... 268 D
lpirius@nhcc.edu
PIRKLE, Bill ... 803-641-3395 ... 462 B
billp@usca.edu
PIRKLE, Martha ... 706-880-8245 ... 132 I
mpirkle@lagrange.edu
PIRKUL, Hasan ... 972-883-6813 ... 505 D
hpirkul@utdallas.edu
PIRRELLO, Joe ... 212-226-5500 ... 323 C
jpirrello@aii.edu
PIRRMAN, Martin, E ... 706-880-8232 ... 132 I
mpirrman@lagrange.edu
PIRSCHEL, C. Sue ... 419-434-5333 ... 404 B
pirschel@findlay.edu
PIRTLE, Gina ... 219-473-4379 ... 170 D
gpirtle@ccsj.edu
PIRTLE, Pamela ... 847-491-7458 ... 160 D
p-pirtle@northwestern.edu
PIRTLE, Ron ... 601-968-8990 ... 273 F
rpirtle@belhaven.edu
PISA, Michael, C ... 315-312-3572 ... 354 A
mike.pisa@oswego.edu
PISANI, Carol ... 973-290-4364 ... 309 A
cpisani@cse.edu
PISANI, Carol ... 973-290-4491 ... 309 A
cpisani@cse.edu
PISANI, Roger ... 973-290-4209 ... 309 A
rpisani@cse.edu
PISANO, Douglas, J ... 617-732-2874 ... 241 F
douglas.pisano@mcphs.edu
PISANO, Etta, D ... 843-792-2842 ... 459 C
pisanoe@musc.edu
PISANO, Rebecca, L ... 410-704-2451 ... 228 E
rpisano@towson.edu
PISCHKE, Kevin ... 916-577-2200 ... 79 C
kpischke@jessup.edu
PISCITIELLO, Anthony, M .. 507-457-1700 ... 271 G
tpisciti@smumn.edu
PISCOPO, Carmine, R ... 401-865-2727 ... 453 F
cpiscopo@providence.edu
PISHKIN, Richard, J ... 617-228-2427 ... 239 G
rpishkin@bhcc.mass.edu
PISORS, Jesse ... 918-495-6610 ... 411 C
jpisors@oru.edu
PISTILLI, Fran ... 860-738-6325 ... 90 F
fpistilli@nwcc.commnet.edu
PISTILLO, Jason ... 602-383-8228 ... 19 A
jay@uat.edu
PISTORINO, Thomas, G ... 781-768-7075 ... 244 D
t.pistorino@regiscollege.edu
PISZKER, James ... 814-824-2429 ... 436 C
jpiszker@mercyhurst.edu
PITARO, Teresa ... 781-239-4452 ... 230 G
tpitaro@babson.edu
PITCHER, Brian, L ... 509-358-7551 ... 539 A
bpitcher@wsu.edu
PITCHER, Carole, D ... 302-295-1133 ... 97 A
carole.d.pitcher@wilmu.edu
PITCHER, Christopher, G ... 302-295-1152 ... 97 A
christopher.g.pitcher@wilmu.edu
PITCHER, Darren ... 406-874-6165 ... 294 H
pitcherd@milescc.edu
PITCHER, John, K ... 856-691-8600 ... 309 C
jpitcher@cccnj.edu
PITCHER, Mark ... 276-944-6242 ... 518 I
mpitcher@ehc.edu
PITCHER, Paula ... 609-343-5015 ... 307 D
ppitcher@atlantic.edu
PITCHFORD, Jeffery, L ... 501-450-3185 ... 25 H
jeffp@uca.edu
PITCHFORD, Nicola ... 415-480-1880 ... 45 B
nicola.pitchford@dominican.edu
PITEGOFF, Peter ... 207-780-4344 ... 220 G
pitegoff@usm.maine.edu
PITHIS, Nancy ... 617-236-8800 ... 235 B
npithis@fisher.edu
PITMAN, Bruce ... 716-645-2711 ... 351 G
cas-dean@buffalo.edu
PITMAN, Bruce, M ... 208-885-6757 ... 144 B
bpitman@uidaho.edu
PITNEY, Pat ... 907-474-7907 ... 10 J
kppitney@alaska.edu
PITONAK, Audrey ... 304-357-4745 ... 541 H
audreypitonak@ucwv.edu
PITONZO, Beth ... 505-224-4427 ... 317 J
bpitonzo@cnm.edu
PITRE, Donna ... 985-632-5177 ... 211 L
PITRE, Jude ... 318-276-2401 ... 210 D
PITSCHMANN, Louis, A ... 205-348-7561 ... 8 F
lpitschm@bama.ua.edu
PITSIRI, Lisa ... 405-736-0315 ... 411 I
lpitsiri@rose.edu
PITT, Ronald, E ... 401-456-8003 ... 454 A
rpitt@ric.edu
PITT, Tina ... 408-453-9900 ... 50 E
tpitt@henley-putnam.edu
PITTARELLI, Edward ... 201-689-7037 ... 307 F
epittarrelli@bergen.edu
PITTENGER, David ... 304-696-2350 ... 543 G
pittengerd@marshall.edu
PITTENGER, Mike ... 858-635-4475 ... 27 E
mpittenger@alliant.edu
PITTENGER, Susan, D ... 315-568-3069 ... 342 H
spittenger@nycc.edu
PITTER, Keiko ... 503-768-7227 ... 416 F
PITTER, Yeruchem ... 516-225-4700 ... 346 K
PITTMAN, Alexander ... 419-586-0360 ... 406 D
alex.pittman@wright.edu
PITTMAN, Crystal ... 864-941-8328 ... 460 D
pittman.cg@ptc.edu
PITTMAN, Dale ... 626-585-7136 ... 61 [illegible]
depittman@pasadena.edu
PITTMAN, Don, A ... 918-610-8303 ... 411 D
don.pittman@ptstulsa.edu
PITTMAN, Edward, L ... 845-437-5426 ... 359 D
edpittman@vassar.edu
PITTMAN, Jane, D ... 540-665-3489 ... 523 K
jpittman@su.edu
PITTMAN, Julia ... 410-462-8380 ... 221 D
jpitman@bccc.edu
PITTMAN, Karan ... 229-732-5944 ... 124 C
karanpittman@andrewcollege.edu
PITTMAN, Kathy, L ... 985-549-2150 ... 216 C
kpittman@selu.edu
PITTMAN, L. Monique ... 269-471-3297 ... 247 H
pittman@andrews.edu
PITTMAN, Laurie, S ... 815-224-0417 ... 153 D
laurie_pittman@ivcc.edu
PITTMAN, Marty ... 251-442-2236 ... 9 B
mpittman@mail.umobile.edu
PITTMAN, Michelle ... 912-478-0880 ... 131 A
mepittman@georgiasouthern.edu
PITTMAN, Nancy ... 918-610-8303 ... 411 D
nancy.pittman@ptstulsa.edu
PITTMAN, Patrick ... 910-362-7043 ... 368 E
ppittman@cfcc.edu
PITTMAN, Stanley, G ... 260-982-5270 ... 177 F
sgpittman@manchester.edu
PITTMAN, Stephanie, M ... 262-554-2010 ... 548 F
eph08@aol.com
PITTMAN, Sue ... 715-232-1151 ... 552 C
pittmans@uwstout.edu
PITTMAN, Suzanne ... 478-445-6283 ... 129 F
suzanne.pittman@gcsu.edu
PITTMAN, W. Randall ... 205-726-2331 ... 6 G
rpittman@samford.edu
PITTMAN-SCHULZ,
Kimberley ... 707-826-3132 ... 36 D
KimberleyPS@humboldt.edu
PITTMON, Alex ... 805-965-0581 ... 68 B
pittmona@sbcc.edu
PITTS, Beverly, J ... 317-788-3211 ... 180 C
bpitts@uindy.edu
PITTS, Carl ... 770-531-6305 ... 132 J
cpitts@laniertech.edu
PITTS, Chuck ... 713-942-9505 ... 487 H
capitts@hgst.edu
PITTS, Debi ... 303-837-0825 ... 81 B
pittsd@aii.edu
PITTS, Eleanor ... 205-929-6389 ... 5 E
epitts@lawsonstate.edu
PITTS, Gail, S ... 248-341-2151 ... 257 B
gspitts@oaklandcc.edu
PITTS, Gary ... 229-227-2414 ... 137 D
gpitts@southwestgatech.edu
PITTS, James, E ... 850-644-0538 ... 119 C
jpitts@admin.fsu.edu
PITTS, Karen, H ... 315-684-6068 ... 354 F
pittskh@morrisville.edu
PITTS, Lawrence, H ... 510-987-9020 ... 73 D
lawrence.pitts@ucop.edu
PITTS, Mark ... 619-849-2548 ... 62 L
markpitts@pointloma.edu
PITTS, Mike ... 417-328-1412 ... 290 E
mpitts@sbuniv.edu
PITTS, Otis ... 828-328-7179 ... 366 B
otis.pitts@lr.edu
PITTS, Paul ... 618-650-2333 ... 165 A
ppitts@siue.edu
PITTS, T. Michael ... 423-439-4213 ... 473 E
pittsm@etsu.edu
PITTS-TAYLOR, Victoria ... 212-817-8895 ... 327 B
womstu@gc.cuny.edu
PITZER, Timothy, G ... 330-471-8434 ... 395 E
tpitzer@malone.edu
PITZNER, Alex ... 717-901-5124 ... 430 F
apitzner@harrisburgu.edu
PIUMETTI FARLAND, Lisa 310-338-7896 ... 56 E
lpiumett@lmu.edu
PIUROWSKI, Robert, C ... 914-337-9300 ... 331 A
robert.piurowski@concordia-ny.edu
PIVERAL, Joyce ... 660-562-1671 ... 287 E
piveral@nwmissouri.edu
PIVEROTTO, Angela ... 724-738-2051 ... 443 E
angela.piverotto@sru.edu
PIWETZ, Eileen ... 432-685-4519 ... 490 G
epiwetz@midland.edu
PIXLEY, Alan ... 479-788-7093 ... 24 D
apixley@uafortsmith.edu
PIXLEY, Sue ... 641-683-5106 ... 185 D
spixley@indianhills.edu
PIXLEY, Susan ... 320-629-5161 ... 268 G
pixleys@pinetech.edu
PIXLEY, Susan ... 651-846-1471 ... 269 E
susan.pixley@saintpaul.edu
PIXLEY, Zaide, E ... 269-337-5755 ... 253 F
Zaide.Pixley@kzoo.edu
PIZAM, Abraham ... 407-903-8010 ... 120 A
abraham.pizam@ucf.edu
PIZER, Lori ... 518-292-7785 ... 348 A
inst_res@sage.edu
PIZIO, Jennifer ... 419-251-1710 ... 395 H
jennifer.pizio@mercycollege.edu
PIZZANO, Patti ... 704-461-6573 ... 362 B
pattipizzano@bac.edu

ZZO, Lauren 610-341-5843 428 D
lpizzo@eastern.edu
ZZO, Philip, A 650-724-5688 71 F
philip.pizzo@stanford.edu
ZZUTI, Linda, J 309-677-3153 145 H
lindap@bradley.edu
ZZUTO, William, J 203-236-9818 94 E
william.j.pizzuto@uconn.edu
JATAK, Jennifer 203-932-7082 95 B
jpjatak@newhaven.edu
LACCO, Christopher 401-598-2900 453 C
cplacco@jwu.edu
LACE, Linna, F 816-235-6230 291 E
placel@umkc.edu
LACE, Ted, P 816-654-7286 283 J
tplace@kcumb.edu
LACEK, Robert, L 574-289-7001 176 C
rplacek@ivytech.edu
LACEY, David 800-556-3656 57 B
dplacey@menlo.edu
LACIDI, Kathleen 434-381-6596 524 E
kplacidi@sbc.edu
LAEHN, Kristin, H 253-535-7615 535 K
plaehnkh@plu.edu
LAGENS, Leslie, F 325-649-8705 488 A
lplagens@hputx.edu
LAGGEMEYER, Ted 775-674-7552 302 J
tplaggemeyer@tmcc.edu
LAISTOW, Vicki 651-426-8241 266 E
vicki.plaistow@dctc.edu
LAKE, John 417-865-2811 282 A
plakej@evangel.edu
PLANCHOCK, Norann 318-677-3100 216 B
planchockn@nsula.edu
PLANELL, Lilia 787-728-1515 568 B
lplanell@sagrado.edu
PLANETA, Michael 815-740-3496 167 C
mplaneta@stfrancis.edu
PLANK, Donna 254-295-4591 504 A
dplank@umhb.edu
PLANK, Kirke, E 608-743-4472 553 E
kplank@blackhawk.edu
PLANK, Kirke, E 608-757-7727 553 E
kplank@blackhawk.edu
PLANK, Mary Beth 407-679-0100 110 C
mbplank@fullsail.com
PLANO, Gwendolyn 949-451-5214 70 E
gplano@ivc.edu
PLANT, David 419-783-2306 389 G
dplant@defiance.edu
PLANT, Fred, W 219-464-5436 181 A
fred.plant@valpo.edu
PLANT, Ken 801-375-5455 510 H
stevenprovo@aol.com
PLANT, Maureen, C 301-443-5362 225 A
mplant@msmary.edu
PLANTE, Dawn, M 440-525-7327 394 F
dplante@lakelandcc.edu
PLANTE, John, J 412-396-4937 428 C
plantej@duq.edu
PLANTE, Kathleen, G 504-280-6218 213 E
kplante@uno.edu
PLANTEFABER, Lisa 413-572-5733 239 C
lplantefaber@wsc.ma.edu
PLANTES, Peter, J 214-648-9796 507 D
peter.plantes@utsouthwestern.edu
PLAPLER, Dina 860-679-4593 94 F
dplapler@foundation.uconn.edu
PLASS, Susan 541-278-5838 414 G
splass@bluecc.edu
PLASSE, Robert 413-572-8131 239 C
rplasse@wsc.ma.edu
PLATA, Ernest, J 903-923-2476 509 A
eplata@wileyc.edu
PLATER-ZYBERK, Elizabeth, M 305-284-5000 122 F
epz@miami.edu
PLATI, Heather 207-893-7898 219 F
hplati@sjcme.edu
PLATSOUCAS, Christopher 757-683-3274 521 L
cplatsoucas@odu.edu
PLATT, Jamie 805-966-3888 31 A
jplatt@brooks.edu
PLATT, Jeffrey 716-829-7766 332 F
plattjh@dyc.edu
PLATT, Mary 714-997-6607 39 C
platt@chapman.edu
PLATT, Rich 240-895-4922 226 A
rdplatt@smcm.edu
PLATT, Sharon 412-536-1120 432 F
sharon.platt@laroche.edu
PLATT, Steve 541-278-5904 414 G
splatt@bluecc.edu
PLATTER, Michael 202-408-2400 99 D
PLATUKUS, Graceann 570-740-0355 435 C
gplatukus@luzerne.edu
PLAYER, Kathy 602-639-7500 14 I
PLAZA, Gloria 312-935-6625 162 E
gplaza@robertmorris.edu
PLEAS, Dorothy, J 630-637-5156 159 F
djpleas@noctrl.edu
PLEAS-BAILEY, Dawn, E 620-229-6336 196 C
dawn.pleas-bailey@sckans.edu

PLEASANT, Klint 248-218-2058 257 F
kpleasant@rc.edu
PLEASANT, Robert 740-533-4600 400 C
pleasanr@ohio.edu
PLEASANTS, David, J 608-796-3913 553 A
djpleasants@viterbo.edu
PLECENIK, Jeanne 914-455-2650 340 G
jplecenik@mercy.edu
PLEGER, Kimberly 253-680-7102 531 A
kpleger@bates.ctc.edu
PLEGER, Tom 608-356-8351 552 F
thomas.pleger@uwc.edu
PLEMMONS, Donna 501-450-1351 22 A
plemmons@hendrix.edu
PLEMONS, Debbie 312-578-3884 168 B
dplemons@westwood.edu
PLENN, Lee 610-527-0200 445 I
lplenn@rosemont.edu
PLESEK, Joseph 219-981-4951 176 E
jplesek@ivytech.edu
PLESS, Beth 812-330-6049 175 H
bpless@ivytech.edu
PLESSNER, Von, R 419-267-1350 397 D
vplessner@northweststate.edu
PLETCHER, Ann, M 864-596-9086 457 E
ann.pletcher@converse.edu
PLETCHER, Barbara 561-297-2145 118 H
pletcher@fau.edu
PLETCHER, Jill, M 316-978-3435 197 F
jill.pletcher@wichita.edu
PLETCHER, Kathy 920-465-2383 551 A
pletchek@uwgb.edu
PLETSCHER, Anthony, W 215-368-5000 422 H
tpletscher@biblical.edu
PLEUSS, Carol, J 330-684-8928 403 C
cjpleus@uakron.edu
PLEWE, Stanley, J 435-652-7504 512 A
splewe@dixie.edu
PLINSKE, Kathleen, A 407-582-4100 122 I
kplinske@valenciacollege.edu
PLINSKI, Christie 503-491-7197 417 B
christie.plinski@mhcc.edu
PLISKA, John 415-338-2037 36 F
jpliska@sfsu.edu
PLOEGER, SM, Bernard 808-735-4741 140 A
bploeger@chaminade.edu
PLONSKY, Christine, A 512-471-4780 505 B
chris.plonsky@athletics.utexas.edu
PLOTKIN, David 503-699-6316 416 I
dplotkin@marylhurst.edu
PLOTKIN, Helen, S 501-450-1225 22 A
plotkin@hendrix.edu
PLOTKOWSKI, Paul 616-331-6260 252 A
plotkowp@gvsu.edu
PLOTNICK, Tamra 212-346-1244 345 F
tplotnick@pace.edu
PLOTT, Richard, K 956-364-4050 499 J
richard.plott@harlingen.tstc.edu
PLOTTS, Debra 334-214-4866 2 G
debra.plotts@cv.edu
PLOTTS, Donald, L 419-755-4811 397 B
dplotts@ncstatecollege.edu
PLOTTS, Douglas, J 610-861-1560 436 I
plottsd@moravian.edu
PLOTTS, John 972-721-5266 502 F
jplotts@udallas.edu
PLOTTS, John, E 415-476-4148 74 E
John.Plotts@ucsf.edu
PLOWMAN, Donde 402-472-9500 300 H
dplowman2@unl.edu
PLOWMAN, Ernest 617-369-3619 244 G
eplowman@mfa.org
PLOWUCHA, Beverly 607-778-5187 324 G
plowucha_b@sunybroome.edu
PLUCHUTA, Alexander 610-359-5057 426 G
apluchut@dccc.edu
PLUG, Dawn 330-339-3391 394 B
dplug@kent.edu
PLUHTA, Elizabeth, A 206-934-5141 537 B
elizabeth.pluhta@seattlecolleges.edu
PLUMB, Anne, M 901-572-2842 467 A
anne.plumb@bchs.edu
PLUMB, Richard 310-338-2834 56 E
rplumb@lmu.edu
PLUMLY, Wayne, L 229-245-3825 138 F
lwplumly@valdosta.edu
PLUMMER, Dale, H 610-566-1776 452 A
dplummer@williamson.edu
PLUMMER, David 575-461-4413 318 F
davidp@mesalands.edu
PLUMMER, Deborah, L 508-856-2179 238 A
deborah.plummer@umassmed.edu
PLUMMER, Dianne 617-989-4036 246 C
plummerd@wit.edu
PLUMMER, James, D 650-723-3938 71 F
plummer@ee.stanford.edu
PLUMMER, James, D 513-556-1299 403 D
james.plummer@uc.edu
PLUMMER, Lisa 610-902-8549 423 H
lisa.m.plummer@cabrini.edu
PLUMMER, Meredith 760-366-5284 43 E
mplummer@cmccd.edu
PLUMMER, Robert, M 423-439-4218 473 E
plummerb@etsu.edu

PLUMMER, Troy, A 515-263-6050 184 I
tplummer@grandview.edu
PLUMMER, Vince 701-671-2319 382 E
vince.plummer@ndscs.edu
PLUNKETT, Christine 802-862-9616 512 H
cplunkett@burlington.edu
PLUNKETT, Jackie 314-529-9398 284 F
jplunkett@maryville.edu
PLUNKETT, James, C 215-951-1500 432 G
plunkett@lasalle.edu
PLUNKETT, Nancy 916-638-1616 49 K
nancy_plunkett@heald.edu
PLUTCHAK, Scott 205-934-5460 8 G
tscott@uab.edu
PLUTCHOK, Yisroel 718-438-5476 360 F
PLUTE, David 307-754-6025 556 D
David.Plute@northwestcollege.edu
PLUTINO-CALABRESE, Stella 585-389-2465 342 D
splutin2@naz.edu
PLYLER, Chris, P 803-777-7695 462 A
plyler.chris@sc.edu
PLYMALE, Chad, E 304-457-6247 540 B
plymalece@ab.edu
PLYMPTON, Margaret, F 610-758-3178 434 E
mfp3@lehigh.edu
PNACEK, Kevin, M 517-780-4579 248 I
kevin.pnacek@baker.edu
PNIOWER, Arianne 617-277-3915 232 F
POARCH, Mark 828-726-2737 368 D
mpoarch@cccti.edu
POATS, Lillian, B 713-313-7978 499 G
poats_lb@tsu.edu
POBAT, Peter 718-368-5109 328 B
ppobat@kbcc.cuny.edu
POBLENZ, Scott, B 978-468-7111 235 F
spoblenz@gcts.edu
POBLETE, Juan 831-459-4792 75 A
jpoblete@ucsc.edu
POBYWAJLO, Margaret, F 603-641-4156 306 F
margaret.pobywajlo@unh.edu
POCHARD, Brad 864-294-3406 458 D
brad.pochard@furman.edu
POCHE, Paulette, M 985-549-5638 216 C
ppoche@selu.edu
POCOCK, Beth 828-884-8287 362 D
pocockba@brevard.edu
PODELL, David 212-517-0520 340 D
dpodell@mmm.edu
PODEMSKI, Richard, S 850-474-7713 121 C
rpodemski@uwf.edu
PODESTA, David 601-977-0960 3 B
david.podesta@vecacolleges.com
PODGORAK, Anne, E 715-394-8203 552 D
apodgora@uwsuper.edu
PODIS, JoAnne 440-646-8107 405 B
jpodis@ursuline.edu
PODOLEFSKY, Aaron, M 716-878-4101 353 A
podoleam@buffalostate.edu
PODOLSKY, Daniel, K 214-648-2508 507 D
priscilla.alderman@utsouthwestern.edu
POE, JR., Donald 704-463-3041 375 E
don.poe@fsmail.pfeiffer.edu
POE, Elmer 252-328-9066 377 C
poee@ecu.edu
POE, Greg 704-406-4630 364 B
gpoe@gardner-webb.edu
POEHLER, M, J 816-802-3393 283 I
mpoehler@kcai.edu
POEHLERT, Edward 760-757-2121 57 E
epoehlert@miracosta.edu
POELKER, Scott 843-574-6198 461 G
scott.poelker@tridenttech.edu
POELKING, Karen, L 216-373-5234 397 E
kpoelking@ndc.edu
POELMAN, Keith, A 801-524-8135 510 A
kpoelman@idsbc.edu
POELVOORDE, Tracy, L 309-779-7708 166 A
poelvoordet@trinityqc.com
POERTNER, Gary 949-582-4840 70 D
gpoertner@socccd.org
POETZL, Steven 541-485-1780 417 E
stevepoetzl@newhope.edu
POFF, Elaine, G 954-262-7261 114 B
poff@nsu.nova.edu
POFF, Robert, C 812-246-3301 176 H
rpoff@ivytech.edu
POGGENDORF, Brenda, P 540-375-2270 523 D
poggendorf@roanoke.edu
POGLIANO, Mark 734-462-4400 258 C
mpogliano@schoolcraft.edu
POGUE, Brian, W 603-646-2106 305 A
brian.w.pogue@dartmouth.edu
POGUE, Frank, G 318-247-3811 215 E
POGUE, Gregory 609-771-3078 308 G
pogueg@tcnj.edu
POHAS, Joanie 310-338-3068 56 E
jpohas@lmu.edu
POHL, Charles, A 215-503-6988 448 B
charles.pohl@jefferson.edu
POHL, Don 314-286-3653 288 B
dpohl@ranken.edu
POHL, Henry, S 518-262-5919 322 E
pohlh@mail.amc.edu

POHL, Laurie 617-353-9814 232 G
lpohl@bu.edu
POHL, Sara 815-825-2086 155 C
sarapohl@kishwaukeecollege.edu
POHLIG, Holly 407-646-2161 116 B
hpohlig@rollins.edu
POHLMAN, Chuck, M 402-844-7181 300 A
chuckp@northeast.edu
POHLMAN, Nancy, A 815-740-3496 167 C
npohlman@stfrancis.edu
POHLSON, Scott 605-677-5434 465 E
scott.pohlson@usd.edu
POINDEXTER, Freddy, D 816-654-7910 283 J
fpoindexter@kcumb.edu
POINDEXTER, Jeanne 757-382-9900 99 D
POINDEXTER, Mark 989-774-4308 249 G
poind1m@cmich.edu
POINTDEXTER, Michael, C 916-558-2142 56 D
poindem@scc.losrios.edu
POINTER, Shandretta 813-621-0041 105 G
spointer@cci.edu
POINTER, Steven 847-317-7180 166 B
spointer@tiu.edu
POINTS, Dan 405-733-7359 411 I
dpoints@rose.edu
POINTS, Emily 309-694-5353 152 B
epeterson@icc.edu
POIRIER, Clare 508-999-8002 237 E
cpoirier@umassd.edu
POIRIER, Janet, L 603-641-7010 305 H
jpoirier@anselm.edu
POIRIER, Jean-Nicholas 315-568-3074 342 H
npoirier@nycc.edu
POIRRIER, Gail, P 337-482-6808 216 D
poirrier@louisiana.edu
POISEL, Mark Allen 212-346-1200 345 F
mpoisel@pace.edu
POITER, Emilia 410-532-5184 225 D
epoiter@ndm.edu
POITIER, Thomas 803-376-5700 455 B
tpoitier@allenuniversity.edu
POKORA, Thomas 810-766-4103 248 H
tom.pokora@baker.edu
POKORNY, Anita, R 330-325-6476 397 C
app@neoucom.edu
POKOT, Elena 262-472-1001 552 E
pokote@uww.edu
POKRAS, Martha 617-627-3389 245 F
martha.pokras@tufts.edu
POL, Lou 402-554-2303 301 B
lpol@unomaha.edu
POLACK, Joseph 330-499-9600 393 I
jpolack@kent.edu
POLAND, Jennifer 724-222-5330 438 E
jpoland@penncommercial.edu
POLAND, Russell 615-327-6171 471 A
rpoland@mmc.edu
POLANIECKI, Andrew 574-239-8315 172 J
apolaniecki@hcc-nd.edu
POLATAJKO, Mark 216-987-4727 389 A
mark.polatajko@tri-c.edu
POLAZZI, Eileen, M 973-748-9000 308 A
eileen_polazzi@bloomfield.edu
POLCYN, Laura, J 253-535-8225 535 K
polcyn@plu.edu
POLCZYNSKI, Mimi 618-545-3363 155 A
mpolczynski@kaskaskia.edu
POLD, Rein, A 814-393-2166 442 A
rpold@clarion.edu
POLDEN, Donald, J 408-554-4362 68 C
dpolden@scu.edu
POLDING, John 973-720-2887 317 D
poldingj@wpunj.edu
POLE, Rhonda 605-995-2902 464 B
rhpole@dwu.edu
POLEMENI, Anthony 212-463-0400 357 J
apolemeni@touro.edu
POLESHEK, Jeffrey, A 941-359-7635 115 K
jpoleshe@ringling.edu
POLETTI, Ed 215-972-2053 440 I
epoletti@pafa.edu
POLGAR, Rebecca 410-234-4673 225 E
POLHEMUS, Clyta, L 209-664-6507 36 C
cpolhemus@csustan.edu
POLICANO, Andrew, J 949-824-8470 73 H
policano@uci.edu
POLIGALA, Kimberly 325-793-4991 490 F
poligala.kimberly@mcm.edu
POLIN, Mark 360-676-2772 535 F
mpolin@nwic.edu
POLIN, Michael 941-782-5927 433 C
mpolin@lecom.edu
POLINAK, Peter 315-781-3337 335 G
polinak@hws.edu
POLING, Jana 503-255-0332 417 C
jpoling@multnomah.edu
POLING-BOLLAS, Betty 513-241-4338 383 L
betty.bollas@antonellicollege.edu
POLIRSTOK, Susan 908-737-3750 311 B
polirsts@kean.edu
POLIS, Kathi 704-330-6976 369 A
kathy.polis@cpcc.edu
POLISI, Joseph, W 212-799-5000 337 H

POLIZZI, Dianne 617-243-2133 236 F
dpolizzi@lasell.edu

POLK, Ali 831-476-9424 47 E
marketing@fivebranches.edu

POLK, Alisa, L 540-636-2900 517 H
finaid@christendom.edu

POLK, Anjanetta 765-459-0561 176 A
apolk5@ivytech.edu

POLK, Charles, H 304-253-7351 541 D
drpolk@mountainstate.edu

POLK, Christopher, S 313-577-2300 260 D
cpolk@wayne.edu

POLK, Laura 301-934-7506 222 C
laurap@csmd.edu

POLK-BRIDGES, Dawn 214-692-8080 480 I
dpolkbridges@aii.edu

POLKOWSKI, James, R 734-462-4400 258 C
jpolkows@schoolcraft.edu

POLL, Michael 704-945-7314 375 E
michael.poll@fsmail.pfeiffer.edu

POLLACK, Ann, M 310-794-0387 74 A
apollack@resadmin.ucla.edu

POLLACK, Dianne 802-241-4620 515 B
dianne.pollak@vsc.edu

POLLACK, Gary 509-335-4750 539 A
gary.pollack@wsu.edu

POLLACK, Glenn 914-251-5976 354 D
glenn.pollack@purchase.edu

POLLACK, Martha, E 734-763-1282 259 D
pollackm@umich.edu

POLLACK, Meyer 323-731-2383 60 I
pollack@psuca.edu

POLLACK, Naomi 847-982-2500 151 H

POLLACK, Pamela 718-951-3118 326 G
pamela@brooklyn.cuny.edu

POLLACK, Tessa, M 210-434-6711 491 G
tmpollack@lake.ollusa.edu

POLLAK, Georgia, B 212-960-5285 361 I
gpollak@yu.edu

POLLARD, Al 254-299-8669 490 E
apollard@mclennan.edu

POLLARD, III, Alton, B 202-806-0500 98 B
abpollard@howard.edu

POLLARD, Charles 479-524-7200 22 C
cpollard@jbu.edu

POLLARD, Cindy 573-882-9724 291 C
pollardcg@umsystem.edu

POLLARD, Cindy 503-517-1026 421 A
cpollard@warnerpacific.edu

POLLARD, DeRionne, P 240-567-5264 224 E
president@montgomerycollege.edu

POLLARD, Jamie, B 515-294-0123 182 B
jbp@iastate.edu

POLLARD, Janet, L 361-593-2439 498 A
janet.pollard@tamuk.edu

POLLARD, Jeffrey, W 703-993-2380 519 A
pollard2@gmu.edu

POLLARD, Jennie 972-860-8201 484 G
jpollard@dcccd.edu

POLLARD, Jennifer, A 716-645-2450 351 G
pollardj@buffalo.edu

POLLARD, Kristi 970-248-1182 82 B
kpollard@mesastate.edu

POLLARD, Leslie 256-726-7000 6 C
lpollard@oakwood.edu

POLLARD, Mary Lee 518-464-8500 333 F
mpollard@excelsior.edu

POLLARD, Natalie, M 609-896-5340 313 G
pollardn@rider.edu

POLLARD, Pamela 914-606-6851 360 D
pamela.pollard@sunywcc.edu

POLLARD, Richard 657-278-2714 34 E
rpollard@fullerton.edu

POLLARD, Sherry 573-882-8420 291 D
pollards@missouri.edu

POLLARD, Thomas, D 203-432-3565 95 D
thomas.pollard@yale.edu

POLLARD, William, F 859-233-8121 206 E
wpollard@transy.edu

POLLARD, William, L 718-270-5000 328 D
wlpollard@mec.cuny.edu

POLLCHIK, Allan 740-774-7200 399 H
pollchic@ohio.edu

POLLE, Sarah 213-613-2200 70 H
directors_office@sciarc.edu

POLLENZ, Hal 212-678-8000 337 G
hapollenz@jtsa.edu

POLLERT, Tim 708-596-2000 164 F
tpollert@ssc.edu

POLLEY, Debra Lee 518-454-2066 330 C
polleyd@strose.edu

POLLION, Sean 231-348-6621 256 E
spollion@ncmich.edu

POLLITZ, John, H 715-836-3715 550 H
pollitjh@uwec.edu

POLLMAN, Janeen 701-228-5458 382 C
bookcell@dakotacollege.edu

POLLOCK, Charles, R 413-782-1233 246 D
cpollock@wne.edu

POLLOCK, Jill 303-860-5600 88 A
jill.pollock@cu.edu

POLLOCK, Kevin, A 810-989-5545 258 B
kapollock@sc4.edu

POLLOCK, Matthew 570-586-2400 422 F
mpollock@bbc.edu

POLLOCK, Shannon 770-975-4000 126 H

POLLOM, Andrew 708-209-3248 148 C
andrew.pollom@cuchicago.edu

POLO, Jose, R 787-738-2161 567 A
rechumanos@upr.edu

POLOAI, Sal 684-699-9155 558 I
s.poloai@amsamoa.edu

POLONSKY, Kenneth 773-702-9306 166 D
polonsky@bsd.uchicago.edu

POLSBY, Daniel, D 703-993-8087 519 A
polsby@gmu.edu

POLSDOFER, Duane 641-585-8121 189 E
polsdofed@waldorf.edu

POLSELLI, Larry 616-554-5827 250 E
lpolselli@davenport.edu

POLSKY, John 212-686-9244 323 A

POLSON, Mary, E 717-245-1835 427 E
polsonm@dickinson.edu

POLSON, William Jerry 580-745-2212 412 C
jpolson@se.edu

POLTERSDORF, Todd 973-300-2253 315 F
tpoltersdorf@sussex.edu

POLVERINI, Peter, J 734-763-3311 259 D
neovas@umich.edu

POLVINALE, Lorraine, K 410-778-7812 229 D
lpolvinale2@washcoll.edu

POLYCHRONIS, Paul, D 660-543-4060 291 B
ppolychr@ucmo.edu

POLYOT, Susan 207-947-4591 217 D
spolyot@bealcollege.edu

POLZ, Sue 708-226-3870 162 E
spolz@robertmorris.edu

POMAJZL, Jacque 402-826-8294 298 A
jacque.pomajzl@doane.edu

POMALES, Eleuterio 787-758-2525 567 D
eleuterio.pomales@upr.edu

POMALES, Reinaldo 787-758-2525 567 D
reinaldo.pomales@upr.edu

POMERENK, Julia 509-335-5511 539 A
pomerenk@wsu.edu

POMEROY, Claire 916-734-3578 73 F
claire.pomeroy@ucdmc.ucdavis.edu

POMEROY, Donald, G 304-442-3313 545 C
donald.pomeroy@mail.wvu.edu

POMFRET, Margaret 419-289-5102 384 D
mpomfret@ashland.edu

POMMERER, Ron 701-845-7700 382 A
ron.pommerer@vcsu.edu

POMPEI, Eric 310-314-6160 29 J

POMPER, Gwen, E 303-492-8223 88 B
gwen.pomper@colorado.edu

POMPEY, JR., Robert 336-334-7587 377 F
rpompey@ncat.edu

POMPLUN, Joann 605-626-2283 465 H
jpomplun@northern.edu

POMYKALSKI, James 570-372-4529 447 D
pomykalski@susqu.edu

PONCE, Chris, B 909-621-8192 63 A
chris.ponce@pomona.edu

PONCE, Christy 915-831-6614 486 E
cponce29@epcc.edu

PONCE, Omar 787-766-1717 565 G
um_oponce@suagm.edu

PONCELET, Jolene 507-453-2662 267 F
jponcelet@southeastmn.edu

POND, Eugene, W 214-841-3725 485 E
epond@dts.edu

POND, Justin 972-929-9750 486 B
jpond@devry.edu

PONDER, Anne 828-251-6500 378 C
chanoffi@unca.edu

PONDER, Betty, J 828-251-6100 378 C
bponder@unca.edu

PONDER, Denis 928-314-9515 12 C
denis.ponder@azwesteren.edu

PONDER, Leslee 940-397-4350 491 A
leslee.ponder@mwsu.edu

PONDER, Nathan 318-473-6591 212 G
nponder@lsua.edu

PONESSE, Matthew 614-253-2741 398 F
ponessem@ohiodominican.edu

PONOROFF, Lawrence 520-621-1498 19 B
lponoroff@law.arizona.edu

PONREMY, Sue 708-524-6965 150 A
sponremy@dom.edu

PONS, Jose, L 787-844-8181 567 E
jpons@uprp.edu

PONSETTO, Jean 773-325-7504 148 F
jlentipo@depaul.edu

PONTEP, Tanya 818-654-1721 62 F
tpontep@pgi.edu

PONTI, Marilyn, K 509-527-5986 539 E
pontimk@whitman.edu

PONTICELLI, Jan 530-741-6795 80 E
jpontice@yccd.edu

PONTINEN, Jodi 218-749-7753 267 C
j.pontinen@mr.mnscu.edu

PONTIOUS, Sharon 304-348-7741 119 B
Sharon.Pontious@fiu.edu

PONTIUS, JR., John, M 518-608-8384 333 F
jpontius@excelsior.edu

PONTO, Patricia, A 269-337-7191 253 F
Pat.Ponto@kzoo.edu

PONTON, Cynthia, L 434-381-6136 524 E
cponton@sbc.edu

PONTON, Dennis, K 716-878-5903 353 A
pontondk@buffalostate.edu

PONTURO, Joseph 973-328-5500 309 B
jponturo@ccm.edu

POOL, Deborah, A 845-938-6947 558 G
8drm@usma.edu

POOL, Jeff, B 859-985-3235 198 F
jeff_pool@berea.edu

POOL, Madonna 301-387-3743 222 H
madonna.pool@garrettcollege.edu

POOLE, Bill 817-272-3571 505 A
bpoole@uta.edu

POOLE, Cary 817-531-4872 502 A
cpoole@txwes.edu

POOLE, David 951-343-4409 31 G
dpoole@calbaptist.edu

POOLE, Dennis, L 803-777-5291 462 A
dennis.poole@sc.edu

POOLE, John, K 434-832-7615 526 A
poolej@cvcc.vccs.edu

POOLE, John (Jake) 907-474-6560 10 J
jcpoole@alaska.edu

POOLE, Lana 573-875-7237 280 E
llpoole@ccis.ede

POOLE, Mary Ellen 415-503-6251 66 A
abeckett@sfcm.edu

POOLE, Paula 717-560-8257 433 D
ppoole@lbc.edu

POOLE, Penny 806-291-3406 508 B
poolep@wbu.edu

POOLE, Robert, S 615-327-6273 471 A
rpoole@mmc.edu

POOLE, Russell 303-724-0425 88 D
russell.poole@ucdenver.edu

POOLE, Sherilyn 708-235-7594 151 C
spoole@govst.edu

POOLE, Stan 870-245-5196 22 I
pooles@obu.edu

POOLE, Thomas, G 814-865-2507 438 F
tgp1@psu.edu

POOLE, Warren, E 252-335-3670 377 D
wepoole@mail.ecsu.edu

POOLER, Anne 207-581-2441 220 A
pooler@maine.edu

POOLER, Suzanne 207-859-1102 219 G
poolers@thomas.edu

POOLER, Traci, M 270-384-8100 203 H
poolert@lindsey.edu

POOLER, III, Willis 270-384-8070 203 H
poolerw@lindsey.edu

POOLEY, Allison 602-429-1198 19 D
allison.pooley@wintu.edu

POOLMAN, Leslie, J 717-245-1320 427 E
poolman@dickinson.edu

POON, Christine, A 614-292-2666 398 H
poon.36@osu.edu

POON, Gordon 408-864-8945 47 G
gordonpoon@deanza.edu

POOR, H. Vincent 609-258-1816 313 A
poor@princeton.edu

POOR, P, J 218-755-2988 266 B
ppoor@bemidjistate.edu

POORANDI, Masood 386-481-2340 101 I
poorandm@cookman.edu

POORE, Sharon 859-442-1175 201 G
sharon.poore@kctcs.edu

POORMAN, Brad 325-793-4910 490 F
bpoorman@mcm.edu

POORMAN, Julie 617-266-1400 231 G

POORMAN, Julie 252-328-6373 377 C
poormanj@ecu.edu

POORMAN, CSC, Mark, L 503-943-7207 420 G

POOS, Lawrence, R 202-319-5115 97 C
poos@cua.edu

POOVEY, Gena, E 864-488-4509 459 A
gpoovey@limestone.edu

POOVEY, Sara 256-439-6833 3 J
sbrenizer@gadsdenstate.edu

POPA, Hope 312-662-4011 144 C

POPE, Angel 804-257-5726 529 D
vuu@bkstr.com

POPE, Bonnie, G 334-734-7428 370 C
bpope@forsythtech.edu

POPE, Christina 315-464-4582 352 E
popec@upstate.edu

POPE, Eric 248-204-2210 254 E
epope@ltu.edu

POPE, Iris 760-872-2000 43 H
buck@deepsprings.edu

POPE, John 770-412-4034 137 B
jpope@sctech.edu

POPE, Joseph 337-392-3102 216 B
popej@nsula.edu

POPE, Karen, K 308-432-6366 299 G
kpope@csc.edu

POPE, Kiesha, L 804-523-5137 526 F
kpope@reynolds.edu

POPE, Myron 405-974-5370 413 B
mpope5@ucok.edu

POPE, Sharon 570-372-4439 447
popes@susqu.edu

POPE, Tom 606-589-3023 203
tom.pope@kctcs.edu

POPE-DAVIS, Donald, B 574-631-8052 180
pope-davis.1@nd.edu

POPENFOOSE, G. Stephen 574-372-5100 171
popenfgs@grace.edu

POPHAM, Heidi 706-295-6598 130
hpopham@gntc.edu

POPIELSKI, Kathy 716-827-4343 358 E
popielskik@trocaire.edu

POPIELSKI, Michael 574-289-7001 176 C
mpopielski@ivytech.edu

POPIOLEK, Marcus 313-664-7665 250 A
mpopiolek@collegeforcreativestudies.edu

POPKIN, Eric 719-389-6657 81 L
epopkin@coloradocollege.edu

POPKO, John, P 206-296-6222 537 F
jpopko@seattleu.edu

POPLAWSKI, Lisa 509-359-4555 533 D
lpoplawski@ewu.edu

POPLOWSKI, Kira 909-621-8219 62 H
kira_poplowski@pitzer.edu

POPOLI, John, N 847-574-5210 155 G
jpopoli@lfgsm.edu

POPOLOSKI, Tanya 603-623-0313 305 F
tpopoloski@nhia.edu

POPOOLA, Joseph, K 803-934-3290 459 F
jpopoola@morris.edu

POPOVICH, Donna, B 813-253-6237 122 H
dpopovich@ut.edu

POPOVICH, Joseph 443-885-3372 224 F
joseph.popovich@morgan.edu

POPOVICH, Paulette, M 330-684-8940 403 C
popovic@uakron.edu

POPOVICS, Alexander, J 518-629-7307 336 C
a.popovics@hvcc.edu

POPP, Connie 414-382-6352 545 H
connie.popp@alverno.edu

POPP, Randall 918-594-8031 410 D
randall.popp@okstate.edu

POPP, William, C 770-720-5568 135 F
wcp@reinhardt.edu

POPPE, Jan, R 989-964-2058 258 A
jrpoppe@svsu.edu

POPPE, Kenneth 860-832-1633 91 G
poppe@ccsu.edu

POPPELL, John, E 352-392-1336 120 B
poppell@ufl.edu

POPPER, Deborah 718-982-2222 327 A
deborah.popper@csi.cuny.edu

POPPO, Kristin 617-873-0232 233 B
Kristin.Poppo@cambridgecollege.edu

PORADA, Kenneth 740-245-7214 404 E
kporada@rio.edu

PORAT, Moshe 215-204-1836 447 G
moshe.porat@temple.edu

PORCARELLO, Irene 713-718-7071 487 G
irene.porcarello@hccs.edu

PORCH, Linda 215-965-4037 436 H
lporch@moore.edu

PORCHE, Demetrius 504-568-4106 213 A
dporch@lsuhsc.edu

PORCHE, JR., Francis 337-491-2445 212 C
francis.porche@sowela.edu

PORCHIA, Christine 910-678-8583 370 B
porchiac@faytechcc.edu

PORETTE, Joanne 845-848-7813 332 C
joanne.porette@dc.edu

PORFIDO, Nancy 609-343-5095 307 D
porfido@atlantic.edu

PORNKITTICHOTCHAROEN, Gib 617-541-5352 241 D
gibp@rcc.mass.edu

PORPIGLIA, Karen, R 716-673-3109 352 A
karen.porpiglia@fredonia.edu

PORRAS, Francisco 928-692-3076 16 G
fporras@mohave.edu

PORRECA, Richard, F 303-492-3224 88 B
richard.porreca@colorado.edu

PORRETT, Susan 810-989-2112 249 B
susan.porrett@baker.edu

PORT, Jeffrey, L 651-638-6439 261 I
jport@bethel.edu

PORTELA, Stanley 787-752-4540 566 H
stanley.portela@upr.edu

PORTELA IRIGOYEN, Celso, E 787-725-8120 562 A
cportela@centro.eap.edu

PORTER, Aaron, K 423-775-7574 467 D
aaron.porter@bryan.edu

PORTER, Andrea 215-646-7300 430 C
porter.a@gmc.edu

PORTER, Andrew, C 215-898-7014 448 I
andyp@gse.upenn.edu

PORTER, Ava 540-985-8531 520 D
agporter@jchs.edu

PORTER, Barbara, A 540-831-5408 522 D
bporter@radford.edu

PORTER, Barbara, A 202-994-3121 97 F
porter@gwu.edu

PORTER, Betsy, A 412-624-7164 449 A
bporter@pitt.edu

PORTER, Brandi, K ... 814-886-6445 ... 437 A bporter@mtaloy.edu
PORTER, Brenda, I ... 607-871-2186 ... 322 F porterbi@alfred.edu
PORTER, Brian ... 818-932-3036 ... 44 N bporter@devry.edu
PORTER, Charles ... 251-405-7118 ... 2 D cporter@bishop.edu
PORTER, Christine, M ... 540-654-1058 ... 524 H cjporter@umw.edu
PORTER, Clifford ... 229-430-4660 ... 123 H clifford.porter@asurams.edu
PORTER, Clyde ... 972-860-7760 ... 484 E cporter@dcccd.edu
PORTER, Curtis, R ... 505-277-6465 ... 321 C cporter@unm.edu
PORTER, Curtiss, E ... 412-675-9080 ... 439 H cep6@psu.edu
PORTER, Cyndi ... 916-631-8108 ... 33 C
PORTER, David ... 731-661-5343 ... 476 G dporter@uu.edu
PORTER, David, S ... 401-874-2370 ... 454 E david.porter@uri.edu
PORTER, DeeDee ... 619-388-3976 ... 65 F dporter@sdccd.edu
PORTER, Diane ... 719-549-3303 ... 87 B diane.porter@pueblocc.edu
PORTER, Fonda ... 919-497-3205 ... 366 E fporter@louisburg.edu
PORTER, Frank ... 937-376-6649 ... 386 H fporter@centralstate.edu
PORTER, Hallie ... 202-885-3810 ... 97 B porter@american.edu
PORTER, Hugh ... 503-777-7573 ... 420 A hugh.porter@reed.edu
PORTER, J. Davidson (Dusty) ... 410-225-2422 ... 224 C dporter@mica.edu
PORTER, James, L ... 601-366-8880 ... 278 D jporter@wbs.edu
PORTER, Jeff ... 276-656-0309 ... 527 D jporter@ph.vccs.edu
PORTER, Jefferson ... 734-647-6073 ... 259 D jkporter@umich.edu
PORTER, Jennifer ... 718-405-3337 ... 330 A jennifer.porter@mountsaintvincent.edu
PORTER, Jennifer ... 813-882-0100 ... 99 D
PORTER, Jennifer, C ... 617-735-9772 ... 234 E porterj@emmanuel.edu
PORTER, John ... 518-320-1530 ... 351 D john.porter@suny.edu
PORTER, John, B ... 570-961-4772 ... 435 F porter@marywood.edu
PORTER, Jon, K ... 802-656-0123 ... 514 F jon.porter@uvm.edu
PORTER, Jonathan ... 501-312-0007 ... 23 D jonathan.porter@remingtoncollege.edu
PORTER, Joseph, B ... 518-608-8370 ... 333 F jporter@excelsior.edu
PORTER, Kary ... 252-638-7266 ... 369 E porterk@cravencc.edu
PORTER, Katherine ... 360-438-4312 ... 536 F kporter@stmartin.edu
PORTER, Kevin ... 404-761-8861 ... 135 E kevin.porter@point.edu
PORTER, Kim ... 314-763-6013 ... 289 C kporter54@stlcc.edu
PORTER, Lawrence, B ... 973-761-9584 ... 311 A lawrence.porter@shu.edu
PORTER, Lisa, M ... 607-587-3938 ... 355 C porterlm@alfredstate.edu
PORTER, Mark, J ... 401-863-3870 ... 452 J mark_porter@brown.edu
PORTER, Mary ... 914-395-2303 ... 350 C mporter@slc.edu
PORTER, Mary Kay ... 301-652-8477 ... 222 E mporter@devry.edu
PORTER, Michael ... 651-962-4376 ... 272 E mporter@stthomas.edu
PORTER, Nadine ... 240-684-5566 ... 227 F human-resources@umuc.edu
PORTER, Narda ... 276-328-0116 ... 525 C nnb3h@uvawise.edu
PORTER, Natalie ... 415-955-2149 ... 27 F nporter@alliant.edu
PORTER, Randey ... 559-438-4222 ... 49 G randey_porter@heald.edu
PORTER, Rebecca ... 701-858-3126 ... 381 G rebecca.porter@minotstateu.edu
PORTER, Rebecca, E ... 317-274-0401 ... 174 B rporter@iupui.edu
PORTER, Rod ... 619-388-7442 ... 65 H rporter@sdccd.edu
PORTER, Ruth Ellen ... 912-583-3101 ... 126 C rporter@bpc.edu
PORTER, Sharon ... 864-587-4272 ... 461 D portersd@smcsc.edu
PORTER, Steve ... 620-665-3552 ... 193 F porters@hutchcc.edu
PORTER, Susie ... 801-581-8094 ... 510 L s.porter@utah.edu
PORTER, Timothy ... 702-895-2058 ... 302 K tim.porter@unlv.edu
PORTER, Tina ... 773-256-3000 ... 158 A tporter@meadville.edu
PORTER, Tracy ... 863-297-3743 ... 115 A tporter@polk.edu
PORTER, Vincent ... 210-829-2770 ... 503 F porterv@uiwtx.edu
PORTER, Wilma, B ... 248-341-2182 ... 257 B wbporter@oaklandcc.edu
PORTERA, Malcolm ... 205-348-5861 ... 8 E mportera@uasystem.ua.edu
PORTERFIELD, Daniel, R ... 717-291-3911 ... 429 E daniel.porterfield@fandm.edu
PORTERFIELD, Deana, L ... 626-812-3015 ... 30 E dporterfield@apu.edu
PORTERFIELD, Kent ... 314-977-2226 ... 289 F kporter6@slu.edu
PORTERFIELD, Kim ... 512-245-9645 ... 501 C kp10@txstate.edu
PORTERFIELD, Robyn, J ... 540-831-5407 ... 522 D rjporterf@radford.edu
PORTERVINT, Bernice ... 360-676-2772 ... 535 F bportervint@nwic.edu
PORTIER, Bonnie ... 301-447-5288 ... 225 A bportier@msmary.edu
PORTILLO, Cesar ... 425-564-2445 ... 531 B cesar.portillo@bellevuecollege.edu
PORTILLO MAZAL, Diego ... 508-270-4115 ... 240 D dportillomazal@massbay.edu
PORTLOCK, Jeremy ... 785-594-8415 ... 190 C jeremy.portlock@bakerU.edu
PORTNER, Matthew, D ... 419-289-5251 ... 384 D mportner@ashland.edu
PORTNEY, Leslie ... 617-726-8009 ... 242 E lportney@mghihp.edu
PORTNOY, Robert, N ... 402-472-7450 ... 300 H rportnoy1@unl.edu
PORTO, Enrico, A ... 304-367-4111 ... 543 E rick.porto@fairmontstate.edu
PORTWINE, Ronald, E ... 989-964-2064 ... 258 A report@svsu.edu
PORTWOOD, Sharon, G ... 704-687-7913 ... 378 E sgportwo@uncc.edu
PORTZ, Margaret, A ... 610-758-5794 ... 434 E mak5@lehigh.edu
POSADAS, Jorge ... 210-486-0130 ... 479 F jposadas@alamo.edu
POSAMENTIER, Alfred ... 914-674-7350 ... 340 G aposamentier@mercy.edu
POSEJPAL, Gigi ... 312-369-7458 ... 148 B gposejpal@colum.edu
POSENDEK, Jeff ... 260-665-4143 ... 180 A posendekj@trine.edu
POSER, Susan ... 402-472-2161 ... 300 H sposer1@unl.edu
POSEY, Della ... 601-979-2244 ... 275 A della.r.posey@jsums.edu
POSEY, Denise ... 276-466-7872 ... 528 G doliver@vic.edu
POSEY, Jeff ... 601-643-8411 ... 274 A jeff.posey@colin.edu
POSEY, Josephine, M ... 601-877-6386 ... 273 C posey@alcorn.edu
POSEY, Monica ... 513-569-1511 ... 387 F monica.posey@cincinnatistate.edu
POSHARD, Glenn ... 618-536-3471 ... 164 H poshard@siu.edu
POSHEK, Joe ... 714-432-5536 ... 41 B jposhek@occ.cccd.edu
POSILLICO, Joseph, J ... 973-618-3500 ... 308 D jposillico@caldwell.edu
POSING, Mary ... 815-802-8202 ... 154 J mposing@kcc.edu
POSIVAK, Donna ... 610-861-4137 ... 437 G dposivak@northampton.edu
POSKANZER, JR., Steven, G ... 507-222-4305 ... 262 B president@carleton.edu
POSKEY, Cynthia ... 985-536-4418 ... 212 A
POSLER, Brian ... 812-465-7020 ... 180 F bposler@usi.edu
POSLUSNY, Matthew ... 610-499-4377 ... 451 F mposlusny@widener.edu
POSMAN, Jerold ... 212-650-7401 ... 326 H jposman@ccny.cuny.edu
POSNER, Kenneth ... 352-588-8992 ... 116 E kenneth.posner@saintleo.edu
POSNER, Sylvia ... 212-824-2211 ... 391 E sposner@huc.edu
POSS, Regena, B ... 615-547-1227 ... 467 I rposs@cumberland.edu
POSSEHL, DeAnn, L ... 262-595-2320 ... 551 E deann.possehl@uwp.edu
POST, Jack ... 215-717-6080 ... 448 H jpost@uarts.edu
POST, Julie ... 770-962-7580 ... 132 A jpost@gwinnetttech.edu
POST, Michael ... 301-447-5214 ... 225 A post@msmary.edu
POST, Nichole ... 607-729-1581 ... 332 A npost@davisny.edu
POST, Regina ... 937-327-6404 ... 406 B rpost@wittenberg.edu
POST, Robert ... 610-361-5233 ... 437 C postr@neumann.edu
POST, Robert, C ... 203-432-1660 ... 95 D robert.post@yale.edu
POST, Scott ... 870-612-2139 ... 25 E scott.post@uaccb.edu
POST, William ... 530-898-6212 ... 34 A bpost@csuchico.edu
POST-LUNDQUIST, Beth ... 518-580-5750 ... 351 B bpostlun@skidmore.edu
POSTEL, Doug ... 318-251-4145 ... 211 B doug.postel@ltc.edu
POSTEL, Doug ... 318-368-3179 ... 210 L dpostel@ltc.edu
POSTEMA, Miles, J ... 231-591-3894 ... 251 B postemam@ferris.edu
POSTER, Elizabeth, C ... 817-272-2776 ... 505 A poster@uta.edu
POSTER, Michael, C ... 563-333-6032 ... 188 D PosterMichaelC@sau.edu
POSTLETHWAITE, Martha ... 651-255-6156 ... 271 I mpostlethwaite@unitedseminary.edu
POSTLEWAIT, Cheryl ... 913-288-7230 ... 193 J cpostlewait@kckcc.edu
POSTLEWATE, Rusty ... 410-455-3260 ... 227 D rpost@umbc.edu
POSTMA, Kurt ... 616-538-2330 ... 251 F kpostma@gbcol.edu
POSTMA, Laura ... 906-248-8420 ... 249 C lpostma@bmcc.edu
POSTON, Fred, L ... 517-355-5014 ... 255 D poston@msu.edu
POSTON, Fulton ... 386-481-2970 ... 101 I postonf@cookman.edu
POSTON, Kyle ... 619-574-6909 ... 60 E kposton@pacificcollege.edu
POSTON, Linda, K ... 845-675-4434 ... 344 G linda.poston@nyack.edu
POSTON, Michael ... 949-824-4521 ... 73 H mposton@uci.edu
POSTON, Michael, J ... 336-316-2178 ... 364 E mposton@guilford.edu
POSTON, Muriel ... 518-580-5705 ... 351 B mposton@skidmore.edu
POSTON, R. Stephen ... 704-233-8194 ... 380 D poston@wingate.edu
POSTON, Tammy, A ... 757-446-8447 ... 518 F postonta@evms.edu
POSTUPACK, Mary Frances ... 570-422-7966 ... 442 C mpostupack@po-box.esu.edu
POTASH, David ... 617-333-2233 ... 234 A dpotash@curry.edu
POTEET, Tanya, J ... 614-236-6408 ... 386 C tpoteet@capital.edu
POTEMPA, John, S ... 708-656-8000 ... 159 C john.potempa@morton.edu
POTEMPA, Kathleen, M ... 734-764-7185 ... 259 D potempa@umich.edu
POTESTIO, Dena Sue ... 719-549-2380 ... 83 B denasue.potestio@colostate-pueblo.edu
POTH, Jean, C ... 978-556-3624 ... 241 B jpoth@necc.mass.edu
POTO, Waliah ... 330-339-3391 ... 394 B wpoto@kent.edu
POTOKA, Lisa ... 843-383-8173 ... 457 A lpotoka@coker.edu
POTRAFKA, Mark ... 573-341-4209 ... 292 A markp@mst.edu
POTTEIGER, Jeffrey ... 616-331-2675 ... 252 A potteigj@gvsu.edu
POTTENGER, John, R ... 256-824-2313 ... 9 A john.pottenger@uah.edu
POTTER, Adam ... 315-786-2364 ... 337 F apotter@sunyjefferson.edu
POTTER, Aletha, E ... 603-899-4130 ... 305 B potterl@franklinpierce.edu
POTTER, Barbara ... 618-252-5400 ... 164 G barb.potter@sic.edu
POTTER, Cheryl, J ... 704-406-4269 ... 364 B cpotter@gardner-webb.edu
POTTER, Cindy ... 817-531-4821 ... 502 A cpotter@txwes.edu
POTTER, Danny ... 903-589-4072 ... 490 B dpotter@lonmorris.edu
POTTER, Douglas, E ... 704-847-5600 ... 376 H dpotter@ses.edu
POTTER, III, Earl, H ... 320-308-2122 ... 269 C president@stcloudstate.edu
POTTER, Gia ... 606-218-5211 ... 207 B gpotter@pc.edu
POTTER, James ... 406-265-3727 ... 295 G potterj@msun.edu
POTTER, Janet, L ... 410-827-5834 ... 222 B jpotter@chesapeake.edu
POTTER, Jay ... 704-330-4409 ... 369 A jay.potter@cpcc.edu
POTTER, John ... 617-827-5962 ... 237 D john.potter@umb.edu
POTTER, John, M ... 937-766-7855 ... 386 F potterj@cedarville.edu
POTTER, Kay, C ... 205-853-1200 ... 5 C kpotter@jeffstateonline.com
POTTER, Laura, L ... 615-353-3217 ... 475 D laura.potter@nscc.edu
POTTER, Lawrence, T ... 814-332-2777 ... 421 E lawrence.potter@allegheny.edu
POTTER, Linda ... 937-294-0592 ... 401 H linda@saa.edu
POTTER, Mary ... 716-829-7756 ... 332 F potterm@dyc.edu
POTTER, Mike ... 425-739-8387 ... 535 B mike.potter@lwtc.edu
POTTER, Patricia, E ... 858-642-8801 ... 58 I ppotter@nu.edu
POTTER, Robert, A ... 401-254-3498 ... 454 C bobpotter@rwu.edu
POTTER, Rollin, R ... 501-450-3293 ... 25 H rpotter@uca.edu
POTTER, Rosemary ... 608-263-7678 ... 552 F rosemary.potter@uwex.uwc.edu
POTTER, Sarah ... 207-786-6120 ... 217 C spotter@bates.edu
POTTER, Sarah ... 802-865-5445 ... 513 A spotter@champlain.edu
POTTER, Scott ... 740-389-4636 ... 395 G potters@mtc.edu
POTTER, Stephen, L ... 336-841-9125 ... 365 A spotter@highpoint.edu
POTTER, Tammy ... 270-534-3278 ... 203 B tammy.potter@kctcs.edu
POTTER, Teri, L ... 603-535-2376 ... 307 B tpotter@plymouth.edu
POTTER, Theresa ... 909-607-2760 ... 49 D theresa_potter@hmc.edu
POTTER, Theresa, M ... 540-365-4201 ... 518 J tpotter@ferrum.edu
POTTER, Thomas, L ... 207-255-1221 ... 220 E potter@maine.edu
POTTER, Tim ... 937-294-0592 ... 401 H tim@saa.edu
POTTER, William ... 985-732-6640 ... 211 C
POTTER, William ... 231-591-2428 ... 251 B william_potter@ferris.edu
POTTER, William, G ... 706-542-0621 ... 138 C wpotter@uga.edu
POTTERVELD, Riess ... 510-849-8223 ... 60 H rpotterveld@psr.edu
POTTORFF, Carol ... 916-484-8428 ... 56 A pottorc@arc.losrios.edu
POTTORFF, JR., James, P ... 785-864-3276 ... 196 F jpottorff@ku.edu
POTTORFF, Linda ... 605-721-5228 ... 464 G lpottorff@national.edu
POTTS, Charles ... 310-434-4180 ... 68 D potts_charles@smc.edu
POTTS, Claudia, J ... 314-984-7204 ... 289 D cpotts10@stlcc.edu
POTTS, David, E ... 334-683-5102 ... 5 D dpotts@judson.edu
POTTS, Flo, E ... 918-595-7224 ... 412 H fpotts@tulsacc.edu
POTTS, Glenn, T ... 715-425-3335 ... 552 A glenn.t.potts@uwrf.edu
POTTS, Joe ... 785-864-3617 ... 196 F jpotts@ku.edu
POTTS, Jonathan ... 412-397-5291 ... 445 G potts@rmu.edu
POTTS, Marilyn, S ... 304-293-2121 ... 544 E marilyn.potts@mail.wvu.edu
POTTS, Steven ... 310-506-4000 ... 61 G steve.potts@pepperdine.edu
POTTS-BELL, Martha ... 319-385-6488 ... 186 A martha.potts-bell@iwc.edu
POTTS-RUSK, Lorethea, H ... 812-888-5848 ... 181 B lpotts-rusk@vinu.edu
POTVIN, David ... 601-968-5904 ... 273 F dpotvin@belhaven.edu
POTVIN, Martha ... 406-994-2452 ... 295 E
POTVIN-GIORDANO, Claudine ... 518-629-7451 ... 336 C c.potvingiordano@hvcc.edu
POU, Patricia ... 618-931-0600 ... 165 B patricia.pou@swic.edu
POUDRIER-AARONSON, Lucinda ... 508-999-8145 ... 237 E laaronson@umassd.edu
POULIN, Eric ... 413-775-1834 ... 240 B pouline@gcc.mass.edu
POULIOS, Nanette ... 248-689-8282 ... 260 A npoulios@walshcollege.edu
POULLARD, Jonathan ... 510-642-6770 ... 73 E poullard@berkeley.edu
POULLARD-BURTON, Lisa ... 646-660-6097 ... 326 D lpburton@baruch.cuny.edu
POULOS, Ted, P ... 847-543-2221 ... 147 H tpoulos@clcillinois.edu
POUND, Lee Eliff ... 417-625-9355 ... 286 E pound-l@mssu.edu
POUNDER, Diana, G ... 501-450-3175 ... 25 H dianap@uca.edu
POUNDERS, Kenneth ... 662-720-7207 ... 276 D kwpounders@nemcc.edu
POUNDS, Dennis, J ... 304-462-4125 ... 543 F dennis.pounds@glenville.edu
POURE, Charles ... 602-286-8241 ... 15 I charles.poure@gwmail.maricopa.edu
POUREETEZADI, Sasan ... 480-461-7000 ... 15 K
POURHAMIDI, Jaleh ... 702-968-1652 ... 303 D jpourhamidi@roseman.edu

POURIER, Marilyn .... 605-455-6045.... 464 H
mpourier@olc.edu
POURIET, Zacarias .... 787-480-2470.... 561 D
zpoueriet@sanjuancapital.com
POURZANJANI, Omid .... 714-895-8156...... 41 A
opourzanjani@gwc.cccd.edu
POVENTUD, Irem .... 787-841-2000.... 564 I
ipoventud@email.pucpr.edu
POVLACK, Maria .... 716-827-2418.... 358 B
povlackm@trocaire.edu
POWAZEK, Jack .... 310-825-7286...... 74 A
powazek@facnet.ucla.edu
POWAZEK, Jack, J .... 310-825-2411...... 74 A
powazek@ucla.edu
POWE, David, L .... 601-984-1018.... 277 H
dpowe@umc.edu
POWEL, Wayne .... 814-472-3004.... 446 B
wpowel@francis.edu
POWELL, Aaron .... 360-867-6238.... 533 I
powella@evergreen.edu
POWELL, Alex .... 617-876-0956.... 236 H
alex.powell@longy.edu
POWELL, April .... 559-453-2027...... 47 K
agp@fresno.edu
POWELL, Betty .... 713-221-8072.... 503 D
powellb@uhd.edu
POWELL, Betty .... 610-606-4637.... 424 I
bpowell@cedarcrest.edu
POWELL, Brett .... 870-245-5410...... 22 I
powellb@obu.edu
POWELL, Carl .... 734-487-4591.... 250 H
crpowell@emich.edu
POWELL, Charles .... 203-432-7458...... 95 D
charles.powell@yale.edu
POWELL, Curtis, N .... 518-276-6359.... 347 D
powelc2@rpi.edu
POWELL, Darrin .... 859-336-1746.... 201 F
darrin.powell@kctcs.edu
POWELL, Dave .... 269-964-4744.... 260 F
dave.powell@wmich.edu
POWELL, DeAnna .... 254-968-9431.... 496 F
powell@tarleton.edu
POWELL, Deborah, L .... 434-381-6179.... 524 E
dpowell@sbc.edu
POWELL, Debra .... 303-937-4200...... 82 A
dpowell@chu.edu
POWELL, Denise .... 912-538-3162.... 137 A
dpowell@southeasterntech.edu
POWELL, Edna .... 310-506-6464...... 61 G
edna.powell@pepperdine.edu
POWELL, Glenn .... 706-721-1896.... 130 B
gpowell@georgiahealth.edu
POWELL, Gregory, S .... 903-693-2022.... 492 A
gpowell@panola.edu
POWELL, Hiram .... 386-481-2957.... 101 I
powellh@cookman.edu
POWELL, Jack, P .... 317-955-6312.... 177 G
jpowell@marian.edu
POWELL, James .... 318-798-6868.... 208 B
POWELL, Jami, D .... 859-238-5573.... 199 D
jami.powell@centre.edu
POWELL, Jane .... 213-738-6836...... 71 D
jpowell@swlaw.edu
POWELL, Jason, B .... 860-832-2398...... 91 G
powell@ccsu.edu
POWELL, Jay .... 205-970-9215........ 7 D
jpowell@sebc.edu
POWELL, Jennifer .... 601-477-5454.... 275 B
jennifer.powell@jcjc.edu
POWELL, Jill .... 704-355-8894.... 363 B
jill.powell@carolinashealthcare.org
POWELL, John .... 304-734-6689.... 542 D
jpowell@bridgemont.edu
POWELL, John .... 304-766-5727.... 542 F
jpowell@kvctc.edu
POWELL, JR., John, W .... 843-953-5200.... 456 C
john.powell@citadel.edu
POWELL, John Michael .... 610-558-5542.... 437 C
powellj@neumann.edu
POWELL, Karan, H .... 304-724-3700.... 540 C
kpowell@apus.edu
POWELL, Karen .... 650-378-7359...... 67 F
powellk@smccd.edu
POWELL, Katherine .... 706-236-1707.... 125 G
kpowell@berry.edu
POWELL, Kathleen, I .... 740-587-6521.... 389 H
powellk@denison.edu
POWELL, Kellie .... 432-837-8614.... 501 B
kpowell@sulross.edu
POWELL, Kevin .... 804-524-5691.... 529 C
manager525@nebook.com
POWELL, Larry .... 318-678-6000.... 209 J
lpowell@bpcc.edu
POWELL, Larry .... 575-769-4919.... 317 K
larry.powell@clovis.edu
POWELL, Linda .... 503-883-2627.... 416 G
lpowell@linfield.edu
POWELL, Lyn .... 352-854-2322.... 103 D
powelll@cf.edu
POWELL, Marjorie, L .... 410-706-3950.... 227 C
mlpowell@af.umaryland.edu
POWELL, Nancy, L .... 606-679-8501.... 202 F
nancy.powell@kctcs.edu
POWELL, Necole .... 314-367-8700.... 288 I
npowell@stlcop.edu
POWELL, Patsy .... 912-871-1603.... 134 H
ppowell@ogeecheetech.edu
POWELL, Patty .... 615-230-3440.... 476 A
patty.powell@volstate.edu
POWELL, Patty, T .... 615-230-3441.... 476 A
patty.powell@volstate.edu
POWELL, Paula, R .... 270-384-8001.... 203 H
powellp@lindsey.edu
POWELL, Peter .... 615-445-3456.... 468 E
ppowell@devry.edu
POWELL, R. Tony, A .... 270-809-2664.... 204 F
tony.powell@murraystate.edu
POWELL, Randall .... 936-294-3981.... 501 A
rrp014@shsu.edu
POWELL, Richard, S .... 904-620-2015.... 120 C
rsp@unf.edu
POWELL, Rick .... 573-875-7325.... 280 E
rpowell@ccis.edu
POWELL, Rick .... 405-491-6333.... 412 D
rpowell@snu.edu
POWELL, Scott .... 231-439-6349.... 256 E
spowell@ncmich.edu
POWELL, Shalisa .... 219-769-3321.... 169 I
sdpowell@brownmackie.edu
POWELL, Skeet .... 254-298-8692.... 496 B
skeetpowell@templejc.edu
POWELL, Sue .... 601-936-5555.... 274 E
cspowell@hindscc.edu
POWELL, Theresa, A .... 215-204-6556.... 447 G
theresa.powell@temple.edu
POWELL, Thomas .... 252-789-0293.... 371 E
tpowell@martincc.edu
POWELL, Thomas, H .... 301-447-5600.... 225 A
powell@msmary.edu
POWELL, Todd .... 785-628-4233.... 192 F
tpowell@fhsu.edu
POWELL, Todd .... 803-799-9082.... 461 A
jtpowell@southuniversity.edu
POWELL, III, Tommie .... 504-278-6423.... 211 I
tpowell@nunez.edu
POWELL, Wayne .... 828-328-7334.... 366 B
powellw@lr.edu
POWELL, William, W .... 601-266-4964.... 278 A
william.powell@usm.edu
POWELL-COHEN, Sheila .... 305-626-3657.... 108 H
shelia.powellcohen@fmuniv.edu
POWER, Christopher .... 513-745-5700.... 403 F
christopher.power@uc.edu
POWER, Colleen .... 510-883-7153...... 45 A
cpower@dspt.edu
POWER, Suzanne .... 858-635-4682...... 27 E
spower@alliant.edu
POWER-BARNES,
Marie, R .... 609-984-4839.... 316 A
mpowerbarnes@tesc.edu
POWER ROBISON,
Elizabeth .... 562-907-4219...... 79 B
eprobison@whittier.edu
POWERS, Amber .... 215-576-0800.... 445 C
apowers@rrc.edu
POWERS, Andrew .... 740-593-1911.... 399 G
powersa@ohio.edu
POWERS, Barbara .... 989-686-9032.... 250 F
bjpowers@delta.edu
POWERS, Cindy .... 304-896-7382.... 542 J
cindyw@southern.wvnet.edu
POWERS, Colleen .... 203-576-4487...... 94 D
cpowers@bridgeport.edu
POWERS, Danielle .... 856-227-7200.... 308 E
dpowers@camdencc.edu
POWERS, David .... 206-296-5300.... 537 F
powersda@seattleu.edu
POWERS, Elizabeth, A .... 401-232-6085.... 453 A
bpowers@bryant.edu
POWERS, Frank .... 509-533-3429.... 532 F
frankp@spokanefalls.edu
POWERS, John .... 650-926-0250...... 71 F
jfpowers@stanford.edu
POWERS, Jon, R .... 740-368-3082.... 400 F
jrpowers@owu.edu
POWERS, Keri .... 508-531-1324.... 238 B
keri.powers@bridgew.edu
POWERS, Lisa, M .... 814-865-7517.... 438 F
lmr8@psu.edu
POWERS, Lynn .... 407-708-2138.... 117 G
powers@seminolestate.edu
POWERS, Mark, R .... 508-626-4545.... 238 D
mpowers@framingham.edu
POWERS, Patrick .... 407-646-2115.... 116 B
ppowers@rollins.edu
POWERS, Peter, K .... 717-766-2511.... 436 D
ppowers@messiah.edu
POWERS, Richard .... 512-313-3000.... 483 G
richard.powers@concordia.edu
POWERS, Shirley, A .... 402-844-7141.... 300 A
shirleyp@northeast.edu
POWERS, Suzanne .... 417-328-1689.... 290 E
spowers@sbuniv.edu
POWERS, Terri .... 510-666-8248...... 26 G
POWERS, Tim .... 949-794-9090...... 71 E
tpowers@stanbridge.edu
POWERS, Tyrone .... 410-777-7496.... 221 B
tpowers@aacc.edu
POWERS, William, B .... 312-987-1435.... 154 F
6powers@jmls.edu
POWERS, JR., William, C .... 512-471-1232.... 505 B
president@po.utexas.edu
POWERS-LEE, Susan, G .... 617-373-2842.... 244 A
POWERS-SCHAUB, Gail .... 231-777-5331.... 248 J
gail.powersschaub@baker.edu
POWLESS, David .... 205-970-9225........ 7 D
dpowless@sebc.edu
POWLESS, Donna .... 800-567-2344.... 546 G
dpowless@menominee.edu
POWLEY, Mary, R .... 585-385-8057.... 348 F
mpowley@sjfc.edu
POWLISON, Lisa, B .... 802-654-2212.... 514 B
lpowlison@smcvt.edu
POYTHRESS, James, W .... 540-857-6004.... 528 E
jpoythress@virginiawestern.edu
POZEGA, Jon, A .... 425-235-2463.... 536 E
jpozega@rtc.edu
POZNANSKI, Brad, F .... 603-656-6023.... 305 H
bfpoznanski@anselm.edu
PRABHU, Vilas, A .... 717-872-3596.... 443 C
vilas.prabhu@millersville.edu
PRACHER, Mark .... 310-287-4467...... 55 F
prachem@wlac.edu
PRADO, Lenore .... 305-628-6514.... 116 G
lprado@stu.edu
PRADO, Marivi .... 305-474-6880.... 116 G
mprado@stu.edu
PRAEGER, Pam .... 509-533-3535.... 532 D
pamp@spokanefalls.edu
PRAET, Diane, M .... 313-993-3313.... 259 C
praetdm@udmercy.edu
PRAETORIUS, Elizabeth .... 718-409-7204.... 356 C
lpraetorius@sunymaritime.edu
PRAETZEL, Gary, D .... 716-286-8270.... 344 D
gdp@niagara.edu
PRALL, J Andrew .... 260-399-7700.... 180 E
jprall@sf.edu
PRANGER, Henriette, M .... 860-727-6740...... 92 C
hpranger@goodwin.edu
PRANGLIN, Roxie .... 806-651-2037.... 498 D
rpranglin@wtamu.edu
PRASAD, Lorraine .... 718-997-5760.... 328 F
lorraine.prasad@qc.cuny.edu
PRASAD, Vishwanath .... 940-369-7487.... 504 B
vprasad@unt.edu
PRASIFKA, Matthew .... 713-525-3512.... 504 D
prasifm@stthom.edu
PRASKI, Pat .... 989-729-3457.... 249 A
pat.praski@baker.edu
PRASLOVA, Ludmilla .... 714-556-3610...... 76 E
lpraslova@vanguard.edu
PRASSE, David, P .... 312-915-6992.... 157 A
dprasse@luc.edu
PRASTER, Donald, O .... 570-326-3761.... 440 K
dpraster@pct.edu
PRATER, Bob .... 913-469-8500.... 193 I
bprater@jccc.edu
PRATER, Loretta .... 573-651-2178.... 290 D
lprater@semo.edu
PRATER, Margaret .... 731-286-3585.... 475 A
prater@nwtnworks.org
PRATER, Michael .... 574-520-4319.... 174 C
maprater@lusb.edu
PRATER, Susan .... 405-974-2303.... 413 B
sprater@ucok.edu
PRATHER, Alphonse .... 931-552-7600.... 468 A
aprather@daymarinstitute.edu
PRATHER, Kerry, N .... 317-738-8121.... 171 C
kprather@franklincollege.edu
PRATHER, Ruth, L .... 407-582-2822.... 122 I
rprather@valenciacollege.edu
PRATHER, Tammy .... 662-329-7131.... 276 B
tprather@registrar.muw.edu
PRATT, Andrew, L .... 816-781-7700.... 293 D
pratta@william.jewell.edu
PRATT, Anne .... 802-251-7607.... 513 F
apratt@marlboro.edu
PRATT, Barbara .... 908-835-2355.... 317 C
pratt@warren.edu
PRATT, Bernard .... 207-778-7009.... 220 C
ben.pratt@maine.edu
PRATT, Charles .... 201-200-2141.... 312 B
cpratt@njcu.edu
PRATT, Dan .... 913-288-7150.... 193 J
dpratt1@kckcc.edu
PRATT, Edward .... 337-482-6266.... 216 D
pratt@louisiana.edu
PRATT, Edward .... 225-771-4545.... 214 H
edward_pratt@subr.edu
PRATT, Edward, E .... 561-297-0567.... 118 H
epratt2@fau.edu
PRATT, Eric .... 601-925-7652.... 275 E
epratt@mc.edu
PRATT, G. Michael .... 513-529-1809.... 396 D
prattgm@muohio.edu
PRATT, G. Michael .... 513-785-3200.... 396 E
pratt@muohio.edu
PRATT, Harold .... 417-836-4252.... 286 F
PRATT, James .... 812-749-1215.... 178 D
jpratt@oak.edu
PRATT, Jonathan, R .... 763-417-8250.... 262 C
PRATT, Kris .... 812-749-1408.... 178 D
kpratt@oak.edu
PRATT, Linda .... 760-921-5410...... 61 B
lpratt@paloverde.edu
PRATT, Linda .... 402-472-5242.... 300 F
lpratt@nebraska.edu
PRATT, Marcy .... 703-414-4115.... 149 A
mpratt@devry.edu
PRATT, Michael .... 205-652-3565...... 10 A
mpratt@uwa.edu
PRATT, Patricia .... 205-652-3547...... 10 A
ppratt@uwa.edu
PRATT, Patricia .... 205-652-3550...... 10 A
ppratt@uwa.edu
PRATT, Robert, C .... 517-750-1200.... 258 F
bpratt@arbor.edu
PRATT, Sarah .... 213-740-8867...... 76 C
pratt@usc.edu
PRATT, Shawn .... 253-854-4960.... 535 D
spratt@nacstaff.com
PRATT, JR., Theodore, W .... 360-650-3450.... 539 C
ted.pratt@cc.wwu.edu
PRATT, JR., Walter, F .... 803-777-6857.... 462 A
wpratt@law.sc.edu
PRATT-CLARKE, Menah .... 217-333-0885.... 167 B
menahpc@illinois.edu
PRAY, G. Jon .... 414-288-7532.... 548 D
jon.pray@marquette.edu
PRAYOR, Sharon .... 773-291-6210.... 147 D
sprayor@ccc.edu
PREAS, Derek .... 903-468-3148.... 497 E
derek_preas@tamu-commerce.edu
PREATHER, Gary .... 817-515-6742.... 496 A
gary.preather@tccd.edu
PREBLE, Edwin, G .... 575-624-8070.... 319 C
preble@nmmi.edu
PRECHTER, Patricia .... 504-394-7744.... 214 A
pprechter@olhcc.edu
PRECHTL, Gregory, D .... 716-673-3101.... 352 A
gregory.prechtl@fredonia.edu
PRECIADO, Danielle .... 510-723-6608...... 38 L
dpreciado@chabotcollege.edu
PRECISE, Leigh .... 816-483-9600.... 289 H
leighp@spst.edu
PRECZEWSKI, Stanley .... 478-445-4444.... 129 F
president@gcsu.edu
PRECZEWSKI, Stanley .... 678-407-5231.... 130 A
spreczewski@ggc.edu
PREDIC, Beba .... 303-937-4202...... 82 A
bpredic@chu.edu
PREECE, Barbara .... 760-750-4350...... 36 B
bpreece@csusm.edu
PREECE, Jennifer, J .... 301-405-2033.... 227 B
preece@umd.edu
PREGEANT, Gene, E .... 985-549-5888.... 216 C
gpregeant@selu.edu
PREGITZER, Kurt .... 208-885-6442.... 144 B
kpregitzer@uidaho.edu
PREHN, Kevin .... 858-279-4500...... 52 H
kprehn@kaplan.edu
PREISINGER, George, T .... 248-370-2127.... 257 C
preising@oakland.edu
PREISLER, Karen .... 979-532-6381.... 508 J
karenp@wcjc.edu
PREISSER, Grant .... 912-525-5000.... 136 B
gpreisse@scad.edu
PRELLWITZ, Andrew .... 920-748-8175.... 549 I
prellwitz@ripon.edu
PRELOCK, Patricia, A .... 802-656-2216.... 514 F
patricia.prelock@uvm.edu
PREMNATH, Devadasan, N .... 585-271-3657.... 348 B
dnprem@stbernards.edu
PREMO, Brenda .... 909-469-5385...... 78 D
bpremo@westernu.edu
PREMO, Greg, V .... 253-535-8787.... 535 K
premogv@plu.edu
PRENATT, Ann, B .... 314-935-7746.... 292 J
aprenatt@wustl.edu
PRENDERGAST, Debra, L .... 708-709-3689.... 161 C
dprendergast@prairiestate.edu
PRENDERGAST, Jocelyn .... 781-762-1211.... 235 A
drlyn@fine-ne.com
PRENDERGAST, Nancy .... 847-635-1661.... 160 E
nprender@oakton.edu
PRENDERGAST,
Thomas, M .... 419-755-4712.... 397 B
tprendergast@ncstatecollege.edu
PRENGAMAN, Diane .... 410-225-2285.... 224 C
dprengam@mica.edu
PRENOVOST, Jason .... 206-878-3710.... 534 E
jprenovo@highline.edu
PRENTICE, Ernest, D .... 402-559-6045.... 301 A
edprenti@unmc.edu
PRENTICE, Marilyn .... 847-214-7992.... 150 D
mprentice@elgin.edu
PRENTISS, Kay .... 508-849-3228.... 230 C
kprentiss@annamaria.edu
PREOCANIN, Shelley .... 812-866-7097.... 171 F
preocanins@hanover.edu
PREPEJCHAL, Mary .... 956-364-4041.... 499 J
mary.prepejchal@harlingen.tstc.edu
PRESCOD-CAESAR,
Pamela .... 315-228-7411.... 329 H
pprescodcaesar@colgate.edu

PRIOLEAU-TAYLOR, Erica . 803-536-7061.... 460 G
esprioleau@scsu.edu

PRIOR, David, B .... 512-499-4233.... 504 E
dprior@utsystem.edu

PRIOR, David, J .... 276-328-0122.... 525 C
djp4s@uvawise.edu

PRIOR, Roberta .... 203-285-2209..... 90 A
rprior@gwcc.commnet.edu

PRISCO, Anne .... 310-338-2700..... 56 E
aprisco@lmu.edu

PRISELAC, Thomas .... 310-423-6252..... 38 I

PRISLIN, Radmila .... 619-594-4163..... 36 E
rprislin@sunstroke.sdsu.edu

PRISLOVSKY, Andrew .... 901-321-3278.... 467 G
aprislov@cbu.edu

PRITCHARD, Brett .... 256-215-4254....... 2 F
bpritchard@cacc.edu

PRITCHARD, Lamar .... 713-743-1253.... 503 B
flpritchard@uh.edu

PRITCHARD, Mandie .... 541-440-4600.... 420 F
mandie.pritchard@umpqua.edu

PRITCHARD, Michael, H .... 301-846-2417.... 222 G
mpritchard@frederick.edu

PRITCHARD, Rod .... 319-399-8605.... 183 C
rpritcha@coe.edu

PRITCHARD, Sarah, M ...... 847-491-7640.... 160 D
spritchard@northwestern.edu

PRITCHARD, Tom .... 425-564-2206.... 531 B
thomas.pritchard@bellevuecollege.edu

PRITCHETT, Alondrea, J ..... 334-229-4737....... 1 C
apritchett@alasu.edu

PRITCHETT, Beth .... 304-327-4139.... 543 C
bpritchett@bluefieldstate.edu

PRITCHETT, David, R .... 205-665-6131....... 9 C
pritchettdr@montevallo.edu

PRITCHETT, H. Franklin ..... 678-839-6582.... 138 D
fpritche@westga.edu

PRITCHETT, Merrill, R .... 410-837-6207.... 229 A
mpritchett@ubalt.edu

PRITCHETT, Nikki .... 850-644-2003.... 119 C
npritchett@admin.fsu.edu

PRITCHETT, Wendell .... 856-225-6095.... 314 C
chancellor@camden.rutgers.edu

PRITTS, Barry, R .... 304-473-8040.... 545 F
pritts@wvwc.edu

PRITZ, Stephen, J .... 352-392-1374.... 120 B
spritz@ufl.edu

PRITZKER, Barry .... 518-580-5654.... 351 B
bpritzke@skidmore.edu

PRITZL, Kurt, J .... 202-319-5259..... 97 C
pritzl@cua.edu

PRIVETT, James, E .... 803-938-3758.... 462 F
jamesp@uscsumter.edu

PRIVETT, SJ, Stephen, A ... 415-422-6762..... 76 B
privett@usfca.edu

PROBST, A. J .... 573-897-5000.... 284 D

PROBST, Laura .... 305-348-3133.... 119 B
laura.probst@fiu.edu

PROBST, Mark .... 804-523-5790.... 526 F
mprobst@reynolds.edu

PROBST, Robert .... 513-556-9808.... 403 D
Robert.probst@uc.edu

PROBSTFELD, Carol, F ...... 941-752-5326.... 118 E
probstc@scf.edu

PROBY, James .... 719-638-6580..... 84 E
jproby@cci.edu

PROCARIO-FOLEY, Carl .... 914-633-2632.... 336 E
cprocariofoley@iona.edu

PROCHNOW, Allen, J .... 262-243-5700.... 546 I
allen.prochnow@cuw.edu

PROCK, Jim .... 870-972-2656..... 20 C
jprock@astate.edu

PROCTER, Ken .... 478-445-4441.... 129 F
ken.procter@gcsu.edu

PROCTER, Sharon .... 313-664-7889.... 250 A
sprocter@collegeforcreativestudies.edu

PROCTOR, Catherine .... 732-247-5241.... 312 A
cproctor@nbts.edu

PROCTOR, Christina .... 530-541-4660..... 53 F
proctor@ltcc.edu

PROCTOR, David, B .... 570-484-2018.... 443 A
dproctor@lhup.edu

PROCTOR, Ed .... 870-743-3000..... 22 G
eproctor@northark.edu

PROCTOR, Matt .... 417-626-1234.... 287 F
pres@occ.edu

PROCTOR, Michael, A .... 520-626-5531..... 19 B
mproctor@arizona.edu

PROCTOR, Patricia .... 501-374-0804..... 19 F
patricia.proctor@arkansasbaptist.edu

PROCTOR, R. Leland .... 336-599-1181.... 372 D
proctol@piedmontcc.edu

PROCTOR, William, L .... 904-819-6210.... 107 A
proctorw@flagler.edu

PROCTOR-ROGERS,
Cheryl .... 312-362-8937.... 148 F
cprogers@depaul.edu

PROEFROCK, Steve .... 269-467-9945.... 251 D
sproefrock@glenoaks.edu

PROENZA, Luis, M .... 330-972-7074.... 403 B
proenza@uakron.edu

PROFETA, Glen .... 714-432-5861..... 41 B
gprofeta@occ.cccd.edu

PROFETA, Patricia, C .... 772-462-7590.... 110 L
pprofeta@irsc.edu

PROFETA, Philip, S .... 585-275-5811.... 358 I
philip_profeta@urmc.rochester.edu

PROFFITT, David .... 757-352-4876.... 523 B
jdowney@regent.edu

PROFFITT, Randall, K .... 813-374-5122.... 175 J
rproffit@ivytech.edu

PROFFITT, Roger .... 620-227-9422.... 192 B
rproffitt@dc3.edu

PROFFITT, Ron .... 276-739-2421.... 528 D
rproffitt@vhcc.edu

PROFIT, Loretta .... 225-634-2636.... 210 A
lprofit@catc.edu

PROFITT, Adam .... 513-721-7944.... 391 C
adamprofitt@gbs.edu

PROGAR, Patrick, R .... 973-618-3212.... 308 D
progar@caldwell.edu

PROHASKA, Jonathan .... 603-577-6414.... 304 J
prohaska_jonathan@dwc.edu

PROITE, Rosanne .... 512-245-2931.... 501 C
rp45@txstate.edu

PROKOVICH, Jeffrey, D ..... 724-458-3846.... 430 B
jdprokovich@gcc.edu

PROMADES, Frederick, C .. 401-341-2117.... 454 D
promadef@salve.edu

PROMBO, James, R .... 815-772-7218.... 159 B
jprombo@morrison.tec.il.us

PRONCHICK, Stephen .... 707-654-1106..... 32 I
spronchick@csum.edu

PRONKO, Nick, G .... 814-871-7471.... 429 F
pronko001@gannon.edu

PROPER, Amy .... 703-329-9100..... 99 D

PROPER, Sheryle, A .... 814-332-2701.... 421 E
sheryle.proper@allegheny.edu

PROPHET, Mary Webb .... 740-587-6215.... 389 H
prophet@denison.edu

PROPP, Timothy .... 602-978-7593..... 18 K
tim.propp@thunderbird.edu

PROPST, Daisy, M .... 670-243-5498.... 559 F
daisym@nmcnet.edu

PROPST, Jennifer .... 828-448-6051.... 374 G
jpropst@wpcc.edu

PROPST, Joan, L .... 304-457-6251.... 540 B
propstjl@ab.edu

PROPST, Kent .... 660-248-6238.... 279 K
kpropst@centralmethodist.edu

PROPST, Marlene .... 541-917-4784.... 416 H
propstm@linnbenton.edu

PROPST, William, S .... 310-794-6027..... 74 A
wpropst@finance.ucla.edu

PROSPER, Yamilette .... 787-891-0925.... 562 G
yprosper@aguadilla.inter.edu

PROSSER, Deborah .... 678-717-3587.... 129 D
dprosser@gsc.edu

PROSSER, Robert, D .... 731-352-4240.... 467 C
prosserb@bethelu.edu

PROSSER, Sally .... 620-672-5641.... 196 A
sallyp@prattcc.edu

PROSSER, Steve .... 731-352-4000.... 467 C
prossers@bethelu.edu

PROTAS, Elizabeth, J .... 409-772-3001.... 507 B
eprotas@utmb.edu

PROTHERO, Charles, L ...... 570-945-8015.... 432 C
charlie.prothero@keystone.edu

PROTO, Angelo, B .... 516-877-3680.... 322 A
proto@adelphi.edu

PROTSKY, Julia .... 440-449-1700.... 384 F
julia.protsky@atsinstitute.edu

PROUDFIT, Ann .... 216-987-5892.... 389 A
ann.proudfit@tri-c.edu

PROUDFOOT, Donald, W .. 903-510-2975.... 502 E
dpro@tjc.edu

PROUDFOOT, Tony .... 765-285-1560.... 169 D
tproudfoot@bsu.edu

PROUGH, Gene .... 850-718-2288.... 102 H
proughg@chipola.edu

PROULX, David, R .... 603-862-2421.... 306 E
david.proulx@unh.edu

PROULX, Dennis .... 802-468-1249.... 515 C
dennis.proulx@castleton.edu

PROULX, Diane .... 402-399-2456.... 297 E
dproulx@csm.edu

PROULX, Gena .... 815-280-2207.... 154 H
gproulx@jjc.edu

PROULX-CURRY, Pamela .. 207-974-4603.... 218 H
pproulx-curry@emcc.edu

PROUSE, Margaret, R .... 302-857-1065..... 96 D
mprouse@dtcc.edu

PROUT, Deborah .... 775-831-1314.... 303 E
dprout@sierranevada.edu

PROUT, Tont .... 692-625-8424.... 559 E
tprout@cmi.edu

PROUT, Wilson .... 716-926-8910.... 335 F
wprout@hilbert.edu

PROUTY, Steve .... 941-752-5204.... 118 E
proutys@scf.edu

PROVAN, Amy .... 410-532-5379.... 225 D
aprovan@ndm.edu

PROVENCHER, Susan .... 603-668-6660.... 305 C

PROVENCIO-VASQUEZ,
Elias .... 915-747-8217.... 505 E
eprovenciovasquez@utep.edu

PROVENZA, Joseph, S ...... 904-819-6359.... 107 A
jprovenza@flagler.edu

PROVINCE, Anne .... 512-492-3051.... 480 F
aprovince@aoma.edu

PROVINE, Rick, E .... 765-658-4435.... 170 I
provine@depauw.edu

PROVOST, David, J .... 802-865-6400.... 513 A
djprovost@champlain.edu

PROVOST, Norman .... 212-757-1190.... 323 B
nprovost@funeraleducation.org

PRUCE, Dora .... 216-397-4565.... 392 M
dpruce@jcu.edu

PRUCHNICKI, Jennifer .... 580-581-2209.... 407 D
jpruchni@cameron.edu

PRUCNAL, James, R .... 256-549-8242....... 3 J
jprucnal@gadsdenstate.edu

PRUDDEN, Laura .... 978-934-4774.... 237 F
laura_prudden@uml.edu

PRUDEN, Elizabeth .... 513-487-1232.... 402 I
elizabeth.pruden@myunion.edu

PRUDHOMME, Harvey, J .. 503-370-6348.... 421 C
hprudhom@willamette.edu

PRUE, Stephen .... 785-832-6644.... 193 B
stephen.prue@bie.edu

PRUETT, James, P .... 860-444-8255.... 558 E
James.P.Pruett@uscg.mil

PRUETT, Karol .... 903-983-8178.... 489 F
kpruett@kilgore.edu

PRUETT, Kristine .... 570-408-4676.... 451 G
kristine.pruett@wilkes.edu

PRUETT, Robert, R .... 919-658-7760.... 367 D
rpruett@moc.edu

PRUIT, John .... 214-860-8613.... 485 A
jpruit@dcccd.edu

PRUITT, Aaron .... 541-684-7217.... 417 F
aaronp@northwestchristian.edu

PRUITT, Chris .... 402-449-2917.... 298 B
cpruitt@graceu.edu

PRUITT, Dennis, A .... 803-777-4172.... 462 A
dpruitt@sc.edu

PRUITT, George, A .... 609-984-1105.... 316 A
gpruitt@tesc.edu

PRUITT, John .... 408-848-4732..... 48 B
jpruitt@gavilan.edu

PRUITT, Karl .... 205-929-6348....... 5 E
kpruitt@lawsonstate.edu

PRUITT, Kylie .... 615-297-7545.... 466 H
pruittk@aquinascollege.edu

PRUITT, Leah, L .... 864-587-4225.... 461 D
pruittl@smcsc.edu

PRUITT, Nancy, J .... 276-935-4349.... 516 A
npruitt@asl.edu

PRUITT, Samory, T .... 205-348-8376....... 8 F
samory.pruitt@ua.edu

PRULL, Richard, W .... 401-456-8437.... 454 A
rprull@ric.edu

PRUNENCA, Mary Ellen ..... 602-978-7200..... 18 K
maryellen.prunenca@thunderbird.edu

PRUNTY, Bonnie, S .... 607-274-3141.... 336 G
bprunty@ithaca.edu

PRUNTY, Kathleen, A .... 909-869-3380..... 33 G
kaprunty@csupomona.edu

PRUNTY, Patricia .... 845-431-8402.... 332 E
prunty@sunydutchess.edu

PRUNTY, Rose .... 715-365-4401.... 554 I
rprunty@nicoletcollege.edu

PRUNTY, Rose .... 715-365-4525.... 554 F
rprunty@nicoletcollege.edu

PRUS, Mark .... 607-753-2207.... 353 B
mark.prus@cortland.edu

PRUSHA, Todd .... 319-398-5565.... 186 H
tprusha@kirkwood.edu

PRUSKOWSKI, Nancy .... 215-968-8514.... 423 E
pruskows@bucks.edu

PRUSS, Linda .... 513-244-4408.... 388 D
linda_pruss@mail.msj.edu

PRUSSIN, Shari .... 212-217-4000.... 333 G
shari_prussin@fitnyc.edu

PRUTOW, Dennis, J .... 412-731-8690.... 445 E
dprutow@rpts.edu

PRY, George .... 412-809-5100.... 444 F
pry.georgel@pti.edu

PRYCE-SHEEHAN, Linda ... 559-453-2038..... 47 K
linda.pryce-sheehan@fresno.edu

PRYLES, Kathryn .... 508-588-9100.... 240 E

PRYOR, Benjamin .... 419-530-2075.... 404 F
benjamin.pryor@utoledo.edu

PRYOR, Charles .... 212-752-1530.... 338 C
charles.pryor@limcollege.edu

PRYOR, Douglas .... 305-809-3184.... 108 F
douglas.pryor@fkcc.edu

PRYOR, Glen, E .... 435-586-7737.... 511 A
pryor@suu.edu

PRYOR, Jaime .... 661-726-1911..... 73 C

PRYOR, Kelly, L .... 304-367-4131.... 543 E
kelly.pryor@fairmontstate.edu

PRYOR, Kim .... 336-342-4261.... 373 B
pryork@rockinghamcc.edu

PRYOR, Raymond, G .... 570-208-5828.... 432 E
rgpryor@kings.edu

PRYSTOWSKY, Richard .... 740-366-9151.... 386 G
rprystow@cotc.edu

PRZYBLYSKI, Jeannene ..... 415-749-4534..... 65 I
jprzyblyski@sfai.edu

PRZYGOCKI, Ginny .... 989-686-9276.... 250 F
vlprzygo@delta.edu

PRZYGODA, Melitha, R ..... 203-576-4588..... 94 D
mprzygod@bridgeport.edu

PRZYWARA, Richard, T ..... 610-430-4156.... 443 F
rprzywara@wcufoundation.org

PSAILA, Marisa .... 585-475-4932.... 347 G
mxpdar@rit.edu

PSARRIS, Kleanthis .... 718-951-3170.... 326 G
LPsarris@brooklyn.cuny.edu

PTAK, David, H .... 402-844-7046.... 300 A
davep@northeast.edu

PUCCI, Tom .... 724-938-4351.... 441 G
pucci@calu.edu

PUCCIARELLI, Matthew, G . 718-990-7614.... 348 G
pucciarm@stjohns.edu

PUCINE, Richard .... 315-792-5309.... 341 E
rpucine@mvcc.edu

PUCK, Steve .... 800-962-7682.... 293 B
spuck@wma.edu

PUCKETT, Benjamin .... 727-726-1153.... 103 B
benpuckett@clearwater.edu

PUCKETT, Christopher .... 303-315-6619..... 88 D
chris.puckett@ucdenver.edu

PUCKETT, Jack .... 252-492-2061.... 374 D
puckett@vgcc.edu

PUCKETT, Jackie, A .... 864-488-4585.... 459 A
jpuckett@limestone.edu

PUCKETT, Jeff .... 608-363-2651.... 546 B
puckettj@beloit.edu

PUCKETT-BOLER, Laura .... 864-503-5194.... 463 A
lpuckett-boler@uscupstate.edu

PUDDESTER, Frederick, W 413-597-4421.... 246 G
frederick.w.puddester@williams.edu

PUDNEY, JR., Terry .... 315-652-6500.... 325 A
tmpudneyjr@bryantstratton.edu

PUENTE, Miguel .... 509-865-8508.... 534 D
puente_m@heritage.edu

PUENTE, Miguel .... 509-865-8697.... 534 D
puente_m@heritage.edu

PUEPPKE, Steven, G .... 517-355-0123.... 255 D
pueppke@msu.edu

PUETT, Debbie .... 828-286-3636.... 371 A
dpuett@isothermal.edu

PUFFER, Anna, L .... 606-436-5721.... 201 H
lois.puffer@kctcs.edu

PUGESEK, Peggy .... 847-543-2210.... 147 H
pugjesekpj@clcillinois.edu

PUGH, Benjamin, W .... 318-670-9302.... 215 A
bpugh@susla.edu

PUGH, Chad .... 405-789-7661.... 412 E
chad.pugh@swcu.edu

PUGH, Daniel .... 479-575-5004..... 24 C
djpugh@uark.edu

PUGH, David .... 912-525-6980.... 136 B
dpugh@scad.edu

PUGH, Jason .... 601-928-6233.... 275 G
jason.pugh@mgccc.edu

PUGH, John .... 907-796-6568..... 11 A
john.pugh@uas.alaska.edu

PUGH, LaSandra .... 225-771-3170.... 214 H
sandy_pugh@subr.edu

PUGH, Maureen, N .... 570-372-4157.... 447 D
pugh@susqu.edu

PUGH, Nathaniel .... 631-451-4129.... 356 D
pughn@sunysuffolk.edu

PUGH, Paul, F .... 610-519-4200.... 450 G
paul.pugh@villanova.edu

PUGH, W. Russ .... 330-684-8916.... 403 C
wrp@uakron.edu

PUGH-SEEMSTER, Nora ..... 405-682-7831.... 409 F
npseemster@occc.edu

PUGLIESE, Gloria .... 215-951-1882.... 432 G
pugliese@lasalle.edu

PUGLIESE, Mike, A .... 918-663-9000.... 411 F
mikep@plattcollege.org

PUGLIESE, Stephen .... 610-647-4400.... 431 B
spugliese@immaculata.edu

PUGLIESI, Karen, L .... 928-523-1580..... 17 A
karen.pugliesi@nau.edu

PUGLISI, Michael, J .... 276-944-6662.... 518 I
mpuglisi@ehc.edu

PUGNAIRE, Michele, P ...... 508-856-4250.... 238 A
michele.pugnaire@umassmed.edu

PUHALA, Kimberly .... 617-984-1727.... 244 C
kpuhala@quincycollege.edu

PUHL, Diane .... 313-927-1443.... 255 A
dpuhl@marygrove.edu

PUICH, Sam .... 801-302-2800.... 510 C
sam.puich@neumont.edu

PUIG, Ivan, O .... 787-257-7373.... 565 E
ivpuig@suagm.edu

PUKYS, Gail .... 330-499-9600.... 393 I
gpukys@kent.edu

PUKYS, Suzanna .... 512-863-1987.... 495 G
pukyss@southwestern.edu

PULAKOS, Joan .... 208-885-6716.... 144 B
pulakos@uidaho.edu

PULASKI, Edward .... 315-792-3087.... 359 C

PULAVARTI, Srinivas .... 804-289-6010.... 525 A
spulavar@richmond.edu

PULEIO, Samuel, T .... 814-393-2280.... 442 A
spuleio@clarion.edu

Q

QUIGLEY, William, R .... 304-293-6600.... 544 E
william.quigley@mail.wvu.edu
QUILES, Elisa .... 787-257-7373.... 565 E
equiles@suagm.edu
QUILES, Ismael .... 787-738-2161.... 567 A
ismael.quiles@upr.edu
QUILL, Robin .... 508-929-8013.... 239 D
rquill@worcester.edu
QUILLEN, Carol .... 713-348-4033.... 492 J
quillen@rice.edu
QUILLEN, Carol, E .... 704-894-2201.... 363 F
caquillen@davidson.edu
QUILLEN, David .... 630-466-7900.... 167 G
dquillen@waubonsee.edu
QUILLIAN, Benjamin, F ..... 562-951-4600...... 33 E
bquillian@calstate.edu
QUILLIN, Paul .... 718-862-7249.... 339 H
q515mgr@sheg.fullett.com
QUIMBY, Kristyn .... 574-520-4154.... 174 C
krirhawk@iusb.edu
QUIMBY, Linda .... 603-899-4059.... 305 B
quimbyl@franklinpierce.edu
QUINCY, Barbara, I .... 724-946-7928.... 451 C
quincybi@westminster.edu
QUINDT, Willie .... 308-635-6083.... 301 E
wquindt@wncc.edu
QUINE, Jay, A .... 832-252-4604.... 483 A
jay.quine@cbshouston.edu
QUINLAN, Carolyn .... 517-265-5161.... 247 D
QUINLAN, Catherine .... 213-821-2344...... 76 C
cquinlan@usc.edu
QUINLAN, Mickey .... 318-869-5701.... 208 F
mquinlan@centenary.edu
QUINLAN BRAME, Julie ... 414-382-6371.... 545 H
julie.quinlan@alverno.edu
QUINLEY, Melissa .... 828-254-1921.... 367 H
mquinley@abtech.edu
QUINLIVAN, Gary .... 724-537-4597.... 446 E
gary.quinlivan@email.stvincent.edu
QUINN, Aaron .... 740-245-7234.... 404 E
aquinn@rio.edu
QUINN, Anita .... 906-487-2281.... 255 E
aquin@mtu.edu
QUINN, Anthony .... 734-384-4279.... 255 G
aquinn@monroeccc.edu
QUINN, Arthur .... 561-732-4424.... 117 A
aquinn@svdp.edu
QUINN, Bill .... 281-487-1170.... 498 E
bquinn@txchiro.edu
QUINN, Brian .... 657-278-3058...... 34 E
bquinn@fullerton.edu
QUINN, Brigid .... 402-878-2380.... 298 G
bquinn@littlepriest.edu
QUINN, Catherine .... 215-248-7137.... 425 C
quinnc@chc.edu
QUINN, Charles, C .... 512-223-8119.... 481 B
cquinn@austincc.edu
QUINN, Christine, J .... 312-261-3200.... 159 D
christine.quinn@nl.edu
QUINN, Christopher .... 207-221-8761.... 218 C
cquinn@kaplan.edu
QUINN, Edward, M .... 202-687-4134...... 98 A
quinne@georgetown.edu
QUINN, Edwin .... 601-979-2329.... 275 A
edwin.h.quinn@jsums.edu
QUINN, Erin .... 802-443-5253.... 513 G
quinn@middlebury.edu
QUINN, Evelyn .... 732-987-2314.... 310 D
quinne@georgian.edu
QUINN, Frank .... 619-849-2338...... 62 L
frankquinn@pointloma.edu
QUINN, Gina .... 952-838-1870.... 263 F
vquinn@devry.edu
QUINN, Jack, F .... 716-851-1200.... 333 C
jquinn@ecc.edu
QUINN, Jack, F .... 716-851-1200.... 333 B
jquinn@ecc.edu
QUINN, Jack, F .... 716-851-1200.... 333 D
jquinn@ecc.edu
QUINN, John .... 605-394-4800.... 464 G
jquinn@national.edu
QUINN, JR., John, F .... 401-341-2206.... 454 D
quinnj@salve.edu
QUINN, Joseph, G .... 718-817-3013.... 334 C
jgquinn@fordham.edu
QUINN, Kathryn, L .... 518-388-6103.... 358 E
quinnk@union.edu
QUINN, Kathy .... 314-529-9476.... 284 F
kquinn@maryville.edu
QUINN, Kevin .... 920-403-3051.... 550 C
kevin.quinn@snc.edu
QUINN, Kevin, C .... 315-443-8338.... 357 B
kcquinn@syr.edu
QUINN, SJ, Kevin, P .... 570-941-7500.... 450 B
presidentquinn@scranton.edu
QUINN, Kim .... 630-743-0669.... 168 C
kquinn@westwood.edu
QUINN, Kimbra .... 806-894-9611.... 494 C
kquinn@southplainscollege.edu
QUINN, Laurie .... 603-332-8335.... 306 H
laurie.quinn@granite.edu
QUINN, Leslie .... 913-469-8500.... 193 I
lquinn2@jccc.edu
QUINN, Linda .... 402-941-6280.... 299 A
quinzti@midlandu.edu
QUINN, Marisa, A .... 401-863-2453.... 452 J
marisa_quinn@brown.edu
QUINN, Michael .... 206-296-5500.... 537 F
quinnm@seattleu.edu
QUINN, Michael, G .... 585-292-2151.... 341 H
mquinn@monroecc.edu
QUINN, Michael, P .... 401-598-2945.... 453 C
MQuinn@jwu.edu
QUINN, Michelle .... 970-351-1120...... 88 F
michelle.quinn@unco.edu
QUINN, Patrick .... 714-997-6947...... 39 C
pjquinn@chapman.edu
QUINN, Patrick, A .... 315-792-3006.... 359 C
pquinn@utica.edu
QUINN, Penny .... 620-792-9303.... 190 E
quinnp@bartonccc.edu
QUINN, Regina .... 601-979-3950.... 275 A
regina.quinn@jsums.edu
QUINN, Robert, E .... 563-588-7736.... 186 I
bob.quinn@loras.edu
QUINN, Sarah, F .... 610-660-1230.... 446 C
squinn@sju.edu
QUINN, Shaman .... 603-668-6660.... 305 C
QUINN, Shaman .... 307-754-6232.... 556 D
Shaman.Quinn@northwestcollege.edu
QUINN, Sharon .... 410-455-2540.... 227 D
squinn@umbc.edu
QUINN, Sherry .... 313-927-1509.... 255 A
squinn@marygrove.edu
QUINN, Stephanie .... 815-226-4065.... 162 H
squinn@rockford.edu
QUINN, Stephen .... 973-618-3320.... 308 D
squinn@caldwell.edu
QUINN, Susan .... 707-524-1598...... 68 E
squinn@santarosa.edu
QUINN, Tania .... 914-654-5257.... 330 B
tquinn@cnr.edu
QUINN, Teresa .... 845-437-5370.... 359 D
QUINN, Thomas .... 989-275-5000.... 253 K
tom.quinn@kirtland.edu
QUINN, Wade .... 252-493-7271.... 372 E
wquinn@email.pittcc.edu
QUINN, William, P .... 302-356-6775...... 97 A
william.p.quinn@wilmu.edu
QUINNETT, Jim .... 325-793-4611.... 490 F
jquinnett@mcm.edu
QUINNINE, Michael .... 510-580-6742...... 79 G
mquinnine@cci.edu
QUINONES, Angel .... 787-848-1589.... 564 G
ppcadmin@popac.edu
QUINONES, Carlos, A .... 787-753-0039.... 564 C
QUINONES, Denise .... 310-377-5501...... 56 F
dquinones@marymountpv.edu
QUINONES, Eva, Z .... 787-265-3800.... 567 C
quinones_e@rigel.uprm.edu
QUINONES, Irma .... 787-758-2525.... 567 D
irma.quinones1@upr.edu
QUINONES, Jose .... 787-257-0000.... 566 H
jose.quinones@upr.edu
QUINONES, Rosa .... 787-257-0000.... 566 H
rosa.quinones1@upr.edu
QUINONES VELEZ,
Mildred .... 787-896-2252.... 561 K
mquinones@edpcollege.edu
QUINONEZ, Virginia .... 312-329-6623.... 146 C
vquinonez@thechicagoschool.edu
QUINT, Doug .... 620-242-0586.... 194 H
quintd@mcpherson.edu
QUINT, Julie .... 314-256-8808.... 279 A
QUINTA, Ron .... 510-659-6191...... 59 I
rquinta@ohlone.edu
QUINTAL, Jorge .... 336-334-5536.... 379 A
j_quinta@uncg.edu
QUINTAL, Rollande .... 508-849-3340.... 230 C
rquintal@annamaria.edu
QUINTANA, Elena .... 312-662-4021.... 144 C
lkunard@adler.edu
QUINTANA, Javier .... 787-279-1912.... 563 B
jquintana@bayamon.inter.edu
QUINTANA, Karla .... 505-428-1203.... 320 E
karla.quintana@sfcc.edu
QUINTANA, Lawrence .... 505-454-2502.... 318 E
lquintana@luna.edu
QUINTANA, Rosaura .... 787-815-0000.... 566 F
rquintana@upra.edu
QUINTANA HERNANDEZ,
Carmen .... 787-896-2252.... 561 K
cquintana@edpcollege.edu
QUINTANILLA, Hector .... 817-531-4840.... 502 A
hquintanilla@txwes.edu
QUINTANILLA, Kelly .... 361-825-2659.... 497 F
kelly.quintanilla@tamucc.edu
QUINTERO-DEVLAEMINCK,
Monica .... 503-682-1862.... 419 F
monicaqd@pioneerpacific.edu
QUINTERO-JIMENEZ,
Noel .... 787-725-6500.... 560 G
nquintero@albizu.edu
QUINTONG, Joel, R .... 203-416-3417...... 93 G
quintongj@sacredheart.edu
QUINTYNE, Renee .... 845-398-4207.... 349 H
rquintyn@stac.edu
QUINZE, Tiffany .... 217-228-5432.... 161 E
dar@quincy.edu
QUIRAY, Maria .... 508-626-4559.... 238 D
mquiray@framingham.edu
QUIREY, Debbie .... 405-744-2212.... 409 B
dquirey@okstate.edu
QUIRK, Donna .... 312-915-8723.... 157 A
dquirk@luc.edu
QUIRK, Joe .... 360-442-2207.... 535 C
jquirk@lowercolumbia.edu
QUIRK, Patrick .... 239-687-5501.... 101 B
pquirk@avemarialaw.edu
QUIRK, Wayne .... 509-963-3101.... 531 G
quirkw@cwu.edu
QUIRK-BAILEY, Sheila ...... 847-925-6668.... 151 E
squirk@harpercollege.edu
QUIROS, Kristi .... 830-372-8060.... 499 C
kquiros@tlu.edu
QUIROZ, Gloria .... 773-878-3256.... 163 D
gquiroz@staugustine.edu
QUISENBERRY, JR.,
Henry, L .... 334-347-2623........ 3 G
cquisenberry@escc.edu
QUISENBERRY, Sharon ..... 515-294-6344.... 182 B
sharronq@iastate.edu
QUIST, Arlene .... 605-455-6011.... 464 H
aquist@olc.edu
QUISTGARD, Fred .... 207-216-4406.... 219 C
fquistgard@yccc.edu
QUITUGUA, Jose, C .... 671-735-5522.... 559 B
facility@guamcc.edu
QURESHI, Aamir .... 202-872-4700...... 99 C
aamir@sanz.edu

R

R-HENRY, Karen .... 248-414-6900.... 255 B
krhenry@mji.edu
RAAB, Amy .... 614-257-5015.... 390 B
araab@devry.edu
RAAB, Jennifer, J .... 212-772-4242.... 327 E
jennifer.raab@hunter.cuny.edu
RAAB, Keith .... 541-881-5828.... 420 E
kraab@tvcc.cc
RAAB, Lettie, M .... 936-261-5900.... 496 E
lmraab@pvamu.edu
RAAB, Maryrose .... 315-792-7215.... 356 B
maryrose.raab@sunyit.edu
RAADA, Hank .... 602-639-7500...... 14 I
RAAK, Daniel .... 605-361-0200.... 464 A
draak@sf.coloradotech.edu
RABALAIS, Nicole .... 615-248-1237.... 476 E
nrabalais@trevecca.edu
RABB, Harriet .... 212-327-8070.... 347 H
harriet.rabb@rockefeller.edu
RABBITT, Kara, M .... 973-720-2180.... 317 D
rabbittk@wpunj.edu
RABBITT, Rhonda, M .... 608-796-3384.... 553 A
rmrabbitt@viterbo.edu
RABENDA-BAJKOWSKA,
Lucy .... 202-408-2400...... 99 D
RABENOLD, Scott .... 865-974-1000.... 477 A
RABENSTEIN, Dallas .... 951-827-5034...... 74 C
dallas.rabenstein@ucr.edu
RABIDEAU, Melissa .... 314-837-6777.... 288 F
mrabideau@slcconline.edu
RABIDEAU, Shelly, S .... 317-940-8423.... 170 C
srabidea@butler.edu
RABIL, Alison .... 919-684-3501.... 363 I
alison.rabil@duke.edu
RABIN, Adele .... 858-635-4801...... 27 E
arabin@alliant.edu
RABINEAU, Kevin .... 269-965-3931.... 253 H
rabineauk@kellogg.edu
RABINOVICH, Oleg .... 718-818-6470.... 349 G
RABINOVICH, Sheryl .... 213-624-1200...... 46 L
srabinovich@fidm.edu
RABINOWITCH, Janet .... 812-855-4773.... 173 C
jrabinow@indiana.edu
RABINOWITZ, Celia, E .... 240-895-4267.... 226 A
cerabinowitz@smcm.edu
RABINOWITZ, Eli .... 718-377-0777.... 346 G
RABINOWITZ, Stuart .... 516-463-6800.... 335 H
president@hofstra.edu
RABINOWITZ, Vita .... 212-772-4150.... 327 E
vita.rabinowitz@hunter.cuny.edu
RABITOY, Eric .... 626-914-8788...... 39 G
erabitoy@citruscollege.edu
RABLE, Michelle, A .... 419-824-3816.... 395 D
mrable@lourdes.edu
RABY, Susan .... 315-312-2260.... 354 A
susan.raby@oswego.edu
RACCANELLO, Paul .... 415-485-3223...... 45 B
raccanello@dominican.edu
RACE, Debbie .... 828-251-6417.... 378 C
drace@unca.edu
RACE, John .... 614-251-4303.... 398 F
racej@ohiodominican.edu
RACE, Mary Jo .... 412-624-4200.... 449 A
mar6@pitt.edu
RACER, Jennifer .... 419-755-4040.... 397 B
racer.5@osu.edu
RACHAL, Michael .... 504-865-2486.... 213 F
rachal@loyno.edu
RACHAVONG, Darrelene .... 972-883-6236.... 505
dar@utdallas.edu
RACHFORD, Jennifer .... 909-607-2201...... 63
jennifer.rachford@pomona.edu
RACHITA, David, A .... 281-283-2568.... 503
rachita@uhcl.edu
RACINA, Kris .... 907-474-7700...... 10
khracina@alaska.edu
RACINE, Anne .... 406-338-5411.... 293
anne_racine@bfcc.org
RACINE, Gail, M .... 508-767-7283.... 230
gracine@assumption.edu
RACINE, Leo .... 508-678-2811.... 239
leo.racine@bristolcc.edu
RACINE, Rudy .... 603-668-6660.... 305 C
RACKETT, Peter .... 516-773-5564.... 558 F
rackettp@usmma.edu
RACKLEY, Denise, Q .... 910-592-8084.... 373 D
drackley@sampsoncc.edu
RACKLEY, J. Mike .... 662-325-9311.... 276 A
mike.rackley@msstate.edu
RACKLEY, Richard, W .... 865-688-9422.... 468
info@fountainheadcollege.com
RACKLEY, Steven, P .... 419-434-4651.... 404 B
rackley@findlay.edu
RACKLIFFE, Jerry, J .... 404-413-3000.... 131 C
jracklif@gsu.edu
RACKOFF, Jerome, S .... 570-577-3623.... 423 D
jerry.rackoff@bucknell.edu
RACYNSKI, Patricia, A .... 205-934-5121........ 8 G
trish@uab.edu
RADAKOVICH, Dan .... 404-894-5411.... 130 D
drad@athletics.gatech.edu
RADANT, Tia .... 651-450-3397.... 266 I
tradant@inverhills.edu
RADCLIFFE, Denise .... 651-730-5100.... 264 A
dradcliffe@globeuniversity.edu
RADCLIFFE, Shelby, K .... 570-577-3200.... 423 D
shelby.radcliffe@bucknell.edu
RADCLIFFE, Steve .... 513-244-4381.... 388 D
steve_radcliffe@mail.msj.edu
RADDATZ, Susan .... 651-423-8205.... 266 E
susan.raddatz@dctc.edu
RADECKE, Mark Wm .... 570-372-4220.... 447 D
radecke@susqu.edu
RADECKI, Pete .... 417-873-7899.... 281 H
pradecki@drury.edu
RADEL, Marie .... 765-455-9468.... 173 E
meradel@iuk.edu
RADEL, Nicholas, F .... 864-294-2795.... 458 D
nick.radel@furman.edu
RADEMACHER, Eric .... 513-556-3304.... 403 D
eric.rademacher@uc.edu
RADER, Claude, K .... 410-951-3858.... 228 B
drader@coppin.edu
RADER, Rachel .... 931-372-3016.... 474 B
rrader@tntech.edu
RADERSTORF, D. Michael . 404-413-0776.... 131 C
mraderstorf@gsu.edu
RADFORD, Amy, J .... 901-843-3870.... 472 I
radford@rhodes.edu
RADFORD, Laurie .... 503-552-1617.... 417 D
lradford@ncnm.edu
RADFORD, Marilyn .... 270-384-8022.... 203 H
radfordm@lindsey.edu
RADFORD, Ron .... 256-395-2211........ 7 E
rradford@suscc.edu
RADFORD-HILL, Sheila ..... 563-387-1486.... 187 A
radfsh01@luther.edu
RADFORD-WEDEMEYER,
Margaret-Ann .... 410-337-6183.... 222 I
margaret-ann.radford-wedemeyer@goucher.edu
RADIONOFF, Kathleen, A .. 608-258-2309.... 554 B
kradionoff@matcmadison.edu
RADKE, Cheryl .... 623-245-4600...... 18 M
cradke@uticorp.com
RADKE, Laurie .... 920-498-6995.... 555 A
laurie.radke@nwtc.edu
RADKE, William .... 405-974-3371.... 413 B
wradke@ucok.edu
RADLIFF, Mary .... 518-255-5211.... 354 E
radliffmd@cobleskill.edu
RADLO, Dolores .... 508-373-9705.... 231 D
dolores.radlo@becker.edu
RADLOWSKI, Mark, E .... 315-792-5467.... 341 E
mradlowski@mvcc.edu
RADNEY, Ron .... 661-654-3271...... 33 H
rradney@csub.edu
RADOVANIC, Joyce, A .... 814-269-7114.... 449 D
joyceara@pitt.edu
RADSON, Darrell .... 906-487-3555.... 255 E
dradson@mtu.edu
RADT, Jennifer .... 513-732-5327.... 403 E
jennifer.radt@uc.edu
RADTKE, Elizabeth, L .... 651-523-2201.... 264 C
bradtke@hamline.edu
RADTKE, Eric, C .... 708-709-3638.... 161 C
eradtke@prairiestate.edu
RADULESCU, Eugen .... 713-348-6725.... 492 J
eugen@rice.edu
RADVANSKY, Sandy, M .... 740-284-5357.... 390 M
sradvansky@franciscan.edu
RADWAN, Ann, B .... 320-308-4287.... 269 C
abradwan@stcloudstate.edu

RAMIREZ, Juan .... 909-469-5622 .... 78 D
jramirez@westernu.edu
RAMIREZ, Kathy .... 406-447-5185 .... 294 A
kramirez@carroll.edu
RAMIREZ, Laura, M .... 323-265-8973 .... 54 G
ramirelm@elac.edu
RAMIREZ, Lisa .... 317-554-8300 .... 169 H
earamirez@brownmackie.edu
RAMIREZ, Loida, R .... 787-744-8519 .... 561 I
lramirez@ediccollege.com
RAMIREZ, Maria Luisa .... 956-721-5394 .... 489 G
mlramirez@laredo.edu
RAMIREZ, Maribel .... 305-628-6704 .... 116 G
mramirez2@stu.edu
RAMIREZ, Mayra, I .... 787-723-4481 .... 560 H
mramirez@ceaprc.org
RAMIREZ, Minita .... 956-326-2278 .... 497 B
minita@tamiu.edu
RAMIREZ, Richard, M .... 805-756-2091 .... 33 F
rramirez@calpoly.edu
RAMIREZ, Sam .... 361-825-5826 .... 497 F
samuel.ramirez@tamucc.edu
RAMIREZ, Sam .... 440-826-2908 .... 384 H
sramirez@bw.edu
RAMIREZ, Sara .... 617-824-8454 .... 234 D
sara_ramirez@emerson.edu
RAMIREZ, Yvonne .... 718-430-2541 .... 361 I
yramire1@aecom.yu.edu
RAMIREZ HERNANDEZ,
Edith .... 787-896-2252 .... 561 K
eramirez@edpcollege.edu
RAMIREZ-MENDEZ,
Pablo, A .... 787-890-2681 .... 566 E
pablo.ramirez@upr.edu
RAMIREZ-RIVERA, Rafael .. 787-878-5475 .... 562 H
rramirez@arecibo.inter.edu
RAMIREZ SILVA, Juan .... 787-815-0000 .... 566 F
upra_rect@upr.clu.edu
RAMIREZ-SOTO, Ismael .... 508-999-8006 .... 237 E
IRamirezsoto@umassd.edu
RAMM, Jennifer .... 254-295-5527 .... 504 A
jramm@umhb.edu
RAMMING, Ron .... 918-463-2931 .... 407 H
rronald@connorsstate.edu
RAMON, Luciano .... 956-794-4002 .... 489 G
lramon@laredo.edu
RAMON, Ralph .... 325-574-7625 .... 508 F
rramon@wtc.edu
RAMON, Scott .... 312-629-6100 .... 164 A
sramon@saic.edu
RAMOS, Anthony .... 210-805-1201 .... 503 F
aramos@uiwtx.edu
RAMOS, Antonio .... 787-284-1912 .... 563 F
aramos@ponce.inter.edu
RAMOS, Charlene .... 248-204-2334 .... 254 E
cramos@ltu.edu
RAMOS, Daisy .... 787-738-2161 .... 567 A
daisy.ramos@upr.edu
RAMOS, Daniel .... 909-941-9410 .... 62 J
dramos@plattcollege.edu
RAMOS, Edith .... 787-878-6000 .... 562 E
eramos@icprjc.edu
RAMOS, Edwin .... 787-746-1400 .... 562 C
eramos@huertas.edu
RAMOS, Gladys .... 787-738-2161 .... 567 A
gladys.ramos@upr.edu
RAMOS, Harry .... 714-830-0203 .... 29 K
hramos@aii.edu
RAMOS, Irma .... 951-487-3156 .... 58 B
iramos@msjc.edu
RAMOS, Jorge .... 787-765-3560 .... 561 J
RAMOS, Josue .... 787-878-5475 .... 562 H
jramos@arecibo.inter.edu
RAMOS, Julio .... 787-720-4476 .... 566 B
biblioteca@colmizpa.edu
RAMOS, Kianna .... 651-675-4700 .... 264 H
kramos@twincitiesculinary.com
RAMOS, Maria .... 903-886-5091 .... 497 E
maria_ramos@tamu-commerce.edu
RAMOS, Maria, A .... 787-863-2390 .... 563 C
maria.ramos@fajardo.inter.edu
RAMOS, Nancy, L .... 401-254-3455 .... 454 C
nramos@rwu.edu
RAMOS, Patricia .... 310-434-3311 .... 68 D
ramos_patricia@smc.edu
RAMOS, Paula .... 978-368-2294 .... 230 F
paula.ramos@auc.edu
RAMOS, Rebecca .... 401-865-2345 .... 453 F
rramos@providence.edu
RAMOS, Richard, O .... 515-961-1536 .... 188 F
rich.ramos@simpson.edu
RAMOS, Rudy .... 310-900-1600 .... 45 E
ramos_r@compton.edu
RAMOS, Theresa .... 505-277-5251 .... 321 C
tramos@unm.edu
RAMOS, Wilberto .... 256-761-8757 .... 7 H
wramos@talladega.edu
RAMOS-ESCOBAR,
Jorge, L .... 787-767-4300 .... 567 F
jose.ramos29@upr.edu
RAMOS-ROMAN,
Constancia .... 787-725-6500 .... 560 G
cramos@albizu.edu
RAMPENTHAL, Janet .... 619-849-2209 .... 62 L
janetrampenthal@pointloma.edu
RAMPERSAD, Dave .... 334-386-7105 .... 3 H
drampersad@faulkner.edu
RAMPEY, Julie .... 918-343-7545 .... 411 H
jrampey@rsu.edu
RAMPINO, Tatiana .... 203-576-5990 .... 94 A
trampino@stvincentscollege.edu
RAMPP, Carrie, E .... 570-577-1557 .... 423 D
carrie.rampp@bucknell.edu
RAMPY, Bill .... 512-245-6761 .... 501 C
wr15@txstate.edu
RAMS, Richard .... 714-484-7374 .... 59 C
rrams@cypresscollege.edu
RAMSAMMY, Jillian .... 352-854-2322 .... 103 D
jillian.ramsammy@cf.edu
RAMSAY, John .... 434-223-7154 .... 519 B
jramsay@hsc.edu
RAMSAY, John, G .... 484-664-3134 .... 437 B
ramsay@muhlenberg.edu
RAMSBOTTOM, Mary, M .. 317-940-9516 .... 170 C
mramsbot@butler.edu
RAMSDELL, Twyla .... 651-213-4180 .... 264 D
tramsdell@hazelden.org
RAMSDEN-MEIER, Joanna 319-226-2004 .... 181 E
ramsdejl@ihs.org
RAMSETH, Mark, R .... 614-235-4136 .... 402 G
mramseth@TLSohio.edu
RAMSEY, Berkley, C .... 434-797-8400 .... 526 C
bramsey@dcc.vccs.edu
RAMSEY, Betty Jo .... 910-642-7141 .... 373 G
bjramsey@sccnc.edu
RAMSEY, David .... 813-253-6227 .... 122 H
dramsey@ut.edu
RAMSEY, Dawn .... 678-915-4287 .... 137 C
dramsey@spsu.edu
RAMSEY, Derrick .... 410-951-3748 .... 228 B
dramsey@coppin.edu
RAMSEY, Donna, M .... 440-834-3728 .... 393 G
dramsey@kent.edu
RAMSEY, Ebony .... 336-750-3350 .... 380 A
ramseye@wssu.edu
RAMSEY, Gerald .... 619-388-3246 .... 65 F
gramsey@sdccd.edu
RAMSEY, Heather .... 215-567-7080 .... 422 C
hramsey@edmc.edu
RAMSEY, James, R .... 502-852-5417 .... 207 A
jrrams02@louisville.edu
RAMSEY, Jason .... 719-590-6766 .... 83 D
jramsey@coloradotech.edu
RAMSEY, Joel .... 620-223-2700 .... 192 G
joelr@fortscott.edu
RAMSEY, John .... 253-833-9111 .... 534 C
jramsey@greenriver.edu
RAMSEY, Julie, L .... 717-337-6921 .... 429 H
ramsey@gettysburg.edu
RAMSEY, Marleen .... 509-527-4289 .... 538 G
marleen.ramsey@wwcc.edu
RAMSEY, Marty .... 828-227-7335 .... 379 E
mramsey@wcu.edu
RAMSEY, Nancy .... 931-540-2553 .... 474 F
nramsey@columbiastate.edu
RAMSEY, Natasha .... 217-228-5432 .... 161 E
ramsera@quincy.edu
RAMSEY, Paul, G .... 206-543-7718 .... 538 F
pramsey@uw.edu
RAMSEY, Renee .... 928-541-7777 .... 16 I
rramsey@ncu.edu
RAMSEY, Sandy, M .... 828-898-8748 .... 366 A
ramsey@lmc.edu
RAMSEY, Tom .... 425-249-4748 .... 538 D
tom.ramsey@tlc.edu
RAMSEY, Vickie .... 530-257-6181 .... 53 G
vramsey@lassencollege.edu
RAMSEY-BARNES,
Robinette .... 215-951-1050 .... 432 G
barnes@lasalle.edu
RAMSEY-HAMACHER,
Paige .... 352-588-8489 .... 116 E
paige.ramsey.hamacher@saintleo.edu
RAMSEYER, Larry, E .... 989-686-9234 .... 250 F
leramsey@delta.edu
RAMSOWER, Reagan .... 254-710-3554 .... 481 I
reagan_ramsower@baylor.edu
RAMTHUN, Sarah, J .... 515-574-1021 .... 185 F
ramthun_s@iowacentral.edu
RAMÍREZ-SILVA, Juan .... 787-815-0000 .... 566 D
rectoria@upra.edu
RANABARGAR, Kerry, D ... 620-431-2820 .... 195 B
kranabargar@neosho.edu
RANALDI, Diane .... 413-565-1000 .... 231 B
dranaldi@baypath.edu
RANALLI, Carlee, K .... 814-641-3103 .... 431 L
ranallc@juniata.edu
RANALLI, George .... 212-650-7118 .... 326 H
gr1@ccny.cuny.edu
RANCE, DeLonn, L .... 417-268-1000 .... 279 B
drance@agts.edu
RANCOURT, Ann .... 603-358-2118 .... 307 A
arancour@keene.edu
RAND, Amy .... 417-455-5740 .... 281 C
arand@crowder.edu
RAND, Kathryn .... 701-777-2104 .... 381 D
rand@law.und.edu
RAND, Steven .... 207-780-5107 .... 220 G
srand@usm.maine.edu
RAND, Valarie .... 312-280-3500 .... 153 A
vrand@aii.edu
RANDALL, Archie .... 307-433-8363 .... 556 A
RANDALL, Charles .... 650-493-4430 .... 51 C
crandall@itp.edu
RANDALL, Christina, E .... 517-750-1200 .... 258 F
crandall@arbor.edu
RANDALL, Comer, H .... 864-833-2820 .... 460 E
chrandal@presby.edu
RANDALL, Donna, M .... 517-629-0210 .... 247 E
drandall@albion.edu
RANDALL, Greg .... 256-840-4166 .... 7 B
grandall@snead.edu
RANDALL, Greg .... 509-682-6465 .... 539 B
grandall@wvc.edu
RANDALL, John .... 949-214-3358 .... 42 K
john.randall@cui.edu
RANDALL, Karen, M .... 630-942-2592 .... 147 G
randall@cod.edu
RANDALL, Kathleen .... 315-792-3164 .... 359 C
krandall@utica.edu
RANDALL, Kenneth, C .... 205-348-5117 .... 8 F
kcrandal@law.ua.edu
RANDALL, Meridith .... 707-468-3010 .... 57 A
mrandall@mendocino.edu
RANDALL, Monica .... 410-951-3845 .... 228 B
mrandall@coppin.edu
RANDALL, Robin .... 508-286-8232 .... 246 E
rrandall@wheatonma.edu
RANDALL, Ruth .... 913-469-8500 .... 193 I
ruthrandall@jccc.edu
RANDALL, Taylor .... 801-587-3869 .... 510 L
taylor.randall@utah.edu
RANDAZZA, Paula .... 603-897-8303 .... 305 G
prandazza@rivier.edu
RANDAZZO, Jennifer, L .... 563-884-5888 .... 188 C
jennifer.randazzo@palmer.edu
RANDAZZO, Mary .... 248-204-2309 .... 254 E
mrandazzo@ltu.edu
RANDAZZO, Nick .... 504-366-5409 .... 208 J
nick70053@aol.com
RANDAZZO, Nino .... 312-935-4000 .... 162 E
nrandazzo@robertmorris.edu
RANDEL, Jess .... 785-460-5481 .... 191 J
jess.randel@colbycc.edu
RANDELS, George .... 209-946-2011 .... 75 D
RANDERS, Mary .... 650-543-3925 .... 57 B
mary.randers@menlo.edu
RANDERSON, Mike .... 573-875-7661 .... 280 E
dmranderson@ccis.edu
RANDHAWA, Sabah, U .... 541-737-2111 .... 418 F
osu.provost@oregonstate.edu
RANDLE, Benjamin .... 716-829-7836 .... 332 F
randleb@dyc.edu
RANDLE, John .... 231-591-2892 .... 251 B
randlej@ferris.edu
RANDLE, William, M .... 336-334-7979 .... 377 F
RANDLES, Christopher, M . 217-351-2513 .... 161 B
crandles@parkland.edu
RANDLES, Jill, A .... 559-323-2100 .... 66 C
jrandles@sjcl.edu
RANDO, Robert, A .... 937-775-3409 .... 406 C
robert.rando@wright.edu
RANDOLPH, Amanda .... 828-689-1103 .... 366 F
arandolph@mhc.edu
RANDOLPH, Robert, M .... 617-258-5484 .... 242 A
randolph@mit.edu
RANDOLPH, Susan .... 816-501-2450 .... 279 C
susan.randolph@avila.edu
RANDOLPH, Tamela .... 573-651-2408 .... 290 D
trandolph@semo.edu
RANDORF, Lori .... 330-672-5368 .... 393 D
lrandorf@kent.edu
RANDY GREEN, Jonathan . 937-327-6406 .... 406 B
jgreen@wittenberg.edu
RANE-SZOSTAK, Donna .... 949-582-4324 .... 70 F
draneszostak@saddleback.edu
RANELLI, F. Edward .... 850-474-2348 .... 121 C
eranelli@uwf.edu
RANES, Rodney .... 618-395-7777 .... 152 H
ranesr@iecc.edu
RANES, Zachary, T .... 727-376-6911 .... 122 B
zranes@trinitycollege.edu
RANEY, Jonna, G .... 405-878-2178 .... 409 D
jonna.raney@okbu.edu
RANEY, Kristen, A .... 715-833-6491 .... 553 F
kraney@cvtc.edu
RANGE, Ronald .... 205-391-2644 .... 7 A
rrange@sheltonstate.edu
RANGE, Shirley .... 615-329-8768 .... 468 G
srange@fisk.edu
RANGEL, Andrea .... 806-894-9611 .... 494 C
arangel@southplainscollege.edu
RANGEL, Juan, M .... 816-604-1503 .... 285 D
juan.rangel@mcckc.edu
RANGUETTE, Renea, L .... 608-757-7700 .... 553 E
rranguette@blackhawk.edu
RANHEIM, John .... 314-434-4044 .... 281 A
john.ranheim@covenantseminary.edu
RANIERI, Ann, E .... 610-526-6084 .... 430 D
aranieri@harcum.edu
RANIERI, Tracey, M .... 607-436-2446 .... 353 E
ranieritm@oneonta.edu
RANJEL, Mary .... 210-924-4338 .... 481 G
mary.ranjel@bua.edu
RANK, Carin .... 413-559-5385 .... 235 G
RANK, Mark .... 717-815-1218 .... 452 F
mrank@ycp.edu
RANKIN, Arthur .... 318-473-6581 .... 212 G
arankin@lsua.edu
RANKIN, David, F .... 870-235-4001 .... 23 [illegible]
dfrankin@saumag.edu
RANKIN, Emily .... 909-621-8054 .... 69 A
emily.rankin@scrippscollege.edu
RANKIN, James, M .... 479-575-5900 .... 24 C
rankinj@uark.edu
RANKIN, Jason, A .... 501-450-5015 .... 25 H
jrankin@uca.edu
RANKIN, Jeffrey, D .... 309-457-2314 .... 158 G
jeffr@monm.edu
RANKIN, Joni .... 316-684-5335 .... 196 C
joni.rankin@sckans.edu
RANKIN, Mary Ann .... 512-471-3285 .... 505 B
rankin@mail.utexas.edu
RANKIN, Mona, G .... 516-876-3160 .... 353 D
rankinm@oldwestbury.edu
RANKIN, Stephanie, A .... 717-361-1569 .... 428 E
rankins@etown.edu
RANKIN, Stephen .... 214-768-4502 .... 494 F
rankins@smu.edu
RANSDELL, Gary, A .... 270-745-4346 .... 207 C
gary.ransdell@wku.edu
RANSDELL, Junell, A .... 217-786-4506 .... 156 I
junell.ransdell@llcc.edu
RANSOM, Scott, B .... 817-735-2509 .... 504 C
Scott.Ransom@unthsc.edu
RANSOME, Sheri .... 205-726-2487 .... 6 G
shransom@samford.edu
RANTA, Richard, R .... 901-678-2350 .... 474 C
rranta@memphis.edu
RANTZ, Kristen .... 406-791-5291 .... 296 H
krantz01@ugf.edu
RANTZ, Ricky .... 805-735-3366 .... 26 K
rrantz@hancockcollege.edu
RAO, Ashok .... 585-475-7181 .... 347 G
arao@saunders.rit.edu
RAO, B. Madhu .... 419-372-3411 .... 385 C
rao@bgsu.edu
RAO, Julie, M .... 585-245-5553 .... 353 C
rao@geneseo.edu
RAO, Michael .... 804-828-1200 .... 525 E
president@vcu.edu
RAO, MrinaLini, C .... 217-333-3077 .... 166 E
meenarao@uillinois.edu
RAPACCIOLI, Donna .... 718-817-4100 .... 334 C
rapaccioli@fordham.edu
RAPANOS, John .... 212-986-4343 .... 307 G
jmr@berkeleycollege.edu
RAPANOS, John .... 212-986-4343 .... 323 J
jmr@berkeleycollege.edu
RAPAPORT, Ross, J .... 989-774-3381 .... 249 G
rapap1rj@cmich.edu
RAPE, Bruce, M .... 217-443-8786 .... 148 E
brape@dacc.edu
RAPELYE, Janet, L .... 609-258-6150 .... 313 A
jrapelye@princeton.edu
RAPER, Lorraine .... 252-246-1339 .... 375 B
lraper@wilsoncc.edu
RAPESS, Paul .... 516-299-2214 .... 339 A
paul.rapess@liu.edu
RAPIER, Brenda .... 706-419-1126 .... 127 F
rapier@covenant.edu
RAPIER, Debbie, A .... 859-344-3513 .... 206 D
debbie.rapier@thomasmore.edu
RAPOSA, Donna .... 781-239-2500 .... 240 D
draposa@massbay.edu
RAPOSA, Kristina .... 781-292-2300 .... 235 C
RAPOZA, Mark, F .... 401-865-2064 .... 453 F
mrapoza@providence.edu
RAPP, Cynthia, K .... 620-417-1012 .... 196 B
cynthia.rapp@sccc.edu
RAPP, Gary .... 316-295-5838 .... 192 H
rappg@friends.edu
RAPP, John .... 713-798-4517 .... 481 H
jrapp@bcm.edu
RAPP, Karen .... 323-260-8108 .... 54 G
rappk@elac.edu
RAPP, Norman .... 615-329-8848 .... 468 G
nrapp@fisk.edu
RAPP, Peter .... 503-494-8744 .... 418 D
RAPP, Timothy .... 301-295-4231 .... 558 A
trapp@usuhs.mil
RAPP, Virginia .... 310-660-3773 .... 45 D
vrapp@elcamino.edu
RAPPAPORT, Anne .... 618-468-3420 .... 156 C
arappaport@lc.edu
RAPPLEY, Marsha, D .... 517-353-1730 .... 255 D
rappley@msu.edu
RAPPLEYE, Warren .... 254-647-3234 .... 492 E
wrappleye@rangercollege.edu
RAPTOSH, Joseph .... 412-321-8383 .... 423 G
RARIG, Jenny, M .... 610-359-5148 .... 426 G
jrarig@dccc.edu
RASBAND, James, R .... 801-422-6383 .... 509 D
james_rasband@byu.edu
RASBERRY, Charles, J .... 914-395-2522 .... 350 C

ASBERRY, Sandra .... 601-968-8703.... 273 F
srasberry@belhaven.edu
ASCATI, Ralph, J .... 770-499-3550.... 132 H
rrascati@kennesaw.edu
ASCH, Carla .... 785-670-1074.... 197 D
carla.rasch@washburn.edu
ASCH, J. Lee .... 608-785-9210.... 555 D
raschl@westerntc.edu
ASCO, Glenn .... 770-975-4000.... 126 H
ASCOE, Monica .... 716-851-1102.... 333 D
rascoe@ecc.edi
ASHED, D. Omar .... 864-622-6031.... 455 C
orashed@andersonuniversity.edu
ASHED, Jamal, A .... 906-227-2947.... 256 F
jrashed@nmu.edu
ASHID, Jerry, T .... 570-321-4137.... 435 D
rashid@lycoming.edu
ASK, Brenda .... 970-330-8008...... 80 G
brenda.rask@aims.edu
ASK, Brenda .... 970-339-6332...... 80 G
brenda.rask@aims.edu
ASKA, Sandra .... 214-902-8191.... 480 K
sraska@atienterprises.edu
ASKIN, David .... 718-434-0784.... 325 J
ASKOB, Gary, E .... 405-271-2232.... 413 D
gary-raskob@ouhsc.edu
RASMUSSEN, Bob .... 417-626-1234.... 287 F
rasmussen.bob@occ.edu
RASMUSSEN, Bob .... 801-863-8491.... 511 C
bob.rasmussen@uvu.edu
RASMUSSEN, Brock .... 612-874-3749.... 265 E
brock_rasmussen@mcad.edu
RASMUSSEN, Bruce, D ...... 402-280-2720.... 297 H
bdrass@creighton.edu
RASMUSSEN, Cheryl .... 785-442-6021.... 193 D
crasmussen@highlandcc.edu
RASMUSSEN, Clyde .... 509-793-2053.... 531 D
clyder@bigbend.edu
RASMUSSEN, Connie, A .... 308-432-6366.... 299 G
crasmussen@csc.edu
RASMUSSEN, David, W ..... 850-644-5488.... 119 C
dwrasmussen@admin.fsu.edu
RASMUSSEN, Dillon .... 312-578-3897.... 168 B
drasmussen@westwood.edu
RASMUSSEN, Don .... 303-546-5284.... 86 B
donald@naropa.edu
RASMUSSEN, George, A .... 361-593-3712.... 498 A
allen.rasmussen@tamuk.edu
RASMUSSEN, Jack, L .... 801-626-6273.... 511 D
jrasmussen@weber.edu
RASMUSSEN, Karla, R .... 757-455-3290.... 529 F
krasmussen@vwc.edu
RASMUSSEN, Lowell, C ..... 320-589-6100.... 272 C
rasmuslc@morris.umn.edu
RASMUSSEN, Mabel .... 407-277-0311.... 106 G
mrasmussen@evergladesuniversity.edu
RASMUSSEN, Michele, A .. 610-526-5375.... 423 C
mrasmuss@brynmawr.edu
RASMUSSEN, Phil .... 425-889-5271.... 535 I
phil.rasmussen@northwestu.edu
RASMUSSEN, Rob .... 815-479-7599.... 157 F
rrasmuss@mchenry.edu
RASMUSSEN, Robert, H .... 225-578-2154.... 212 E
rrasmus@lsu.edu
RASMUSSEN, Robert, K ..... 213-740-6473...... 76 C
rrasmussen@law.usc.edu
RASMUSSON, Beth .... 605-626-2655.... 465 H
rasmussb@northern.edu
RASNAKE, Martha, L .... 276-964-7389.... 528 A
martha.rasnake@sw.edu
RASNICK, JR., William, B . 423-439-7900.... 473 E
rasnick@etsu.edu
RASOR, Mark .... 918-540-6213.... 408 J
mrasor@neo.edu
RASPILLER, Ted .... 979-209-7210.... 482 A
ted.raspiller@blinn.edu
RASSOUL, Hamid .... 321-674-8778.... 108 E
rassoul@fit.edu
RAST, Lawrence, R .... 260-452-2101.... 170 G
lawrence.rast@ctsfw.edu
RASUL, David .... 916-558-2376...... 56 D
rasuld@scc.losrios.edu
RASZEWSKI, Thomas .... 410-864-3621.... 226 B
traszewski@stmarys.edu
RATANASIRIPONG, Paul ... 562-985-4001...... 35 A
pratanas@csulb.edu
RATCHFORD, Jerome .... 770-423-6310.... 132 H
jratchfo@kennesaw.edu
RATCLIFF, Christine, L ...... 662-252-8000.... 277 C
cratcliff@rustcollege.edu
RATCLIFF, Terry, D .... 509-777-3499.... 539 F
tratcliff@whitworth.edu
RATCLIFFE, Jackson .... 415-485-3225...... 45 B
jratcliffe@dominican.edu
RATCLIFFE, R. Samuel ...... 540-464-7560.... 529 A
ratcliffers@vmi.edu
RATERS, Michael, P .... 765-361-6289.... 181 C
ratersm@wabash.edu
RATH, Phillip, S .... 812-888-5101.... 181 B
prath@vinu.edu
RATHBONE, Thomas, M .... 607-436-3224.... 353 E
rathbotm@oneonta.edu
RATHBUN, Robert, D .... 570-577-3200.... 423 D
bob.rathbun@bucknell.edu

RATHBURN, III,
Carlisle, B .... 903-223-3001.... 498 C
carlisle.rathburn@tamut.edu
RATHE, Dean .... 303-914-6303...... 87 C
dean.rathe@rrcc.edu
RATHEL, Angela, W .... 850-263-3261.... 101 E
awrathel@baptistcollege.edu
RATHJE, James, A .... 507-354-8221.... 265 B
rathjeja@mlc-wels.edu
RATHJEN, Arthur, H .... 920-424-1020.... 551 D
rathjena@uwosh.edu
RATHKE, Debra .... 567-661-7247.... 400 H
debra_rathke@owens.edu
RATHKE, Sheila, W .... 412-624-4248.... 449 A
rathke@pitt.edu
RATHMELL, Daniel .... 607-729-1581.... 332 A
danrathmell@davisny.edu
RATIGAN, Jim .... 702-895-2380.... 302 K
james.ratigan@unlv.edu
RATLIFF, Brian, L .... 276-935-4349.... 516 A
bratliff@asl.edu
RATLIFF, Ceci .... 509-542-4811.... 532 C
cratliff@columbiabasin.edu
RATLIFF, Gerald, L .... 315-267-2108.... 354 C
ratlifgl@potsdam.edu
RATLIFF, Jill .... 606-783-9555.... 204 E
ji.ratliff@moreheadstate.edu
RATLIFF, John .... 704-272-5375.... 373 F
jratliff@spcc.edu
RATLIFF, Kelly, M .... 530-754-6170...... 73 F
kmratliff@ucdavis.edu
RATLIFF, Kerry .... 606-368-6064.... 197 H
kerryratliff@alc.edu
RATLIFF, Kevin .... 540-453-2264.... 525 G
ratliffk@brcc.edu
RATLIFF, Thomas .... 765-677-2116.... 174 E
thomas.ratliff@indwes.edu
RATLIFF, Vickie .... 276-523-7462.... 527 A
vratliff@me.vccs.edu
RATLIFFE, Celina .... 503-699-6315.... 416 I
cratliffe@marylhurst.edu
RATNER, Hilary, H .... 313-577-5600.... 260 D
aa3411@wayne.edu
RATNER, Neil .... 845-352-3431.... 361 G
shaareitorah@optonline.net
RATTIGAN, Paulette .... 401-232-6320.... 453 A
prattiga@bryant.edu
RATTO, Lisa .... 510-783-2100...... 49 H
lica_ratto@hoald.odu
RATTY, Michael .... 617-732-2130.... 241 F
michael.ratty@mcphs.edu
RATZLAFF, Kalen .... 617-876-0956.... 236 H
kalen.ratzlaff@longy.edu
RAU, Don, A .... 913-588-1405.... 197 A
drau@kumc.edu
RAUB, Tammara .... 607-871-2128.... 322 F
raubt@alfred.edu
RAUCH, Dena .... 319-398-5476.... 186 H
dena.rauch@kirkwood.edu
RAUCH, Kenneth, E .... 260-422-5561.... 172 L
kerauch@indianatech.edu
RAUCKHORST, Ashlee .... 740-774-7200.... 399 H
rauckhor@ohio.edu
RAUDENBUSH, Joan, M ..... 215-881-7386.... 438 G
jmr28@psu.edu
RAUDENBUSH, Reid, C ...... 410-778-7855.... 229 D
rraudenbush2@washcoll.edu
RAUH, Mitchell, J .... 801-375-5125.... 510 F
mrauh@rmuohp.edu
RAULT, Pamela, V .... 504-280-7083.... 213 E
pkvrana@uno.edu
RAULUK, Ruth .... 412-392-3996.... 444 H
rrauluk@pointpark.edu
RAUP, Kristin, A .... 412-578-6534.... 424 G
raupka@carlow.edu
RAUSCH, Diane .... 805-986-5826...... 77 C
drausch@vcccd.edu
RAUSCHER, Victor, E .... 518-445-2302.... 322 D
vraus@albanylaw.edu
RAUSCHKOLB, Arlen .... 212-875-4645.... 323 E
arauschkolb@bankstreet.edu
RAUTZHAN, Peter .... 610-282-1100.... 426 I
peter.rautzhan@desales.edu
RAVALIN, Tamara .... 559-737-3879...... 42 B
tamarar@cos.edu
RAVE, Carole .... 360-676-2772.... 535 F
crave@nwic.edu
RAVELLI, James, B .... 503-943-7540.... 420 G
ravelli@up.edu
RAVENELL, Alma .... 903-927-3275.... 509 A
arravenell@wileyc.edu
RAVENELL, Johnnie .... 704-337-2330.... 375 G
ravenellj@queens.edu
RAVENELLE, Robert, G ...... 508-767-7325.... 230 E
rravenel@assumption.edu
RAVERTA, Paul, E .... 413-236-1003.... 239 E
praverta@berkshirecc.edu
RAVINDRA, Krishnaswamy 314-977-8843.... 289 F
ravindrak@slu.edu
RAVISHANKER, Ganesan .... 781-283-2095.... 246 B
gravisha@wellesley.edu
RAWDING, Bridget .... 978-837-5211.... 242 D
bridget.rawding@merrimack.edu
RAWICZ, Diane .... 707-654-1039...... 32 I
drawicz@csum.edu

RAWITCH, Allen, B .... 913-588-1258.... 197 A
arawitch@kumc.edu
RAWITCH, Cynthia, Z .... 818-677-2957...... 35 D
cynthia.rawitch@csun.edu
RAWITSCH, Mark .... 707-468-3082...... 57 A
mrawitsc@mendocino.edu
RAWL, Carolyn, D .... 334-244-3934........ 2 A
crawl@aum.edu
RAWLEIGH, Camilla, B ...... 717-815-6521.... 452 F
crawleig@ycp.edu
RAWLES, Scott .... 318-869-5011.... 208 F
srawles@centenary.edu
RAWLEY, Albert .... 434-791-5654.... 516 D
brawley@averett.edu
RAWLING, Brenda .... 580-559-5350.... 407 J
brawling@ecok.edu
RAWLINGS, Ava .... 618-545-3030.... 155 A
arawlings@kaskaskia.edu
RAWLINGS, Becky .... 360-383-3404.... 539 D
brawling@whatcom.ctc.edu
RAWLINGS, Douglas, H .... 207-778-7292.... 220 C
rawling@maine.edu
RAWLINGS, Gilbert .... 410-276-0306.... 226 D
grawlings@host.sdc.edu
RAWLINGS, Kristiaan .... 505-473-6678.... 320 F
kristiaan.rawlings@santafeuniversity.edu
RAWLINGS, Lynnette .... 330-385-7463.... 393 F
lrawling@kent.edu
RAWLINS, Benjamin .... 615-327-6141.... 471 A
brawlins@mmc.edu
RAWLINS, V. Lane .... 940-565-2026.... 504 B
president@unt.edu
RAWLINSON, Eddy .... 214-860-2392.... 484 I
erawlinson@dcccd.edu
RAWLINSON, Ina, R .... 919-735-5151.... 374 F
irrawlinson@waynecc.edu
RAWLINSON, Rachel .... 812-429-1432.... 176 I
rrawlinson@ivytech.edu
RAWLS, Terry .... 415-808-1430...... 49 E
terry_rawls@heald.edu
RAWN, Mary, K .... 973-275-2891.... 315 B
mary.rawn@shu.edu
RAWSON, Shawn .... 269-782-1474.... 258 E
srawson01@swmich.edu
RAY, Aisha .... 312-893-7137.... 150 G
aray@erikson.edu
RAY, Anita .... 706-245-7226.... 128 K
aray@ec.edu
RAY, Barry, D .... 864-231-2015.... 455 C
bray@andersonuniversity.edu
RAY, Bernard .... 615-327-6294.... 471 A
bray@mmc.edu
RAY, Brandon .... 360-442-2254.... 535 C
bray@lowercolumbia.edu
RAY, Cara .... 678-717-3622.... 129 D
cray@gsc.edu
RAY, Chad .... 704-330-6909.... 369 A
chad.ray@cpcc.edu
RAY, JR., Charles, A .... 504-816-8010.... 213 H
cray@nobts.edu
RAY, David .... 870-460-1033...... 25 A
ray@uamont.edu
RAY, David, H .... 405-325-6426.... 413 C
dray@ou.edu
RAY, Donald, W .... 828-298-3325.... 380 C
dray@warren-wilson.edu
RAY, Douglas .... 305-623-2445.... 116 G
dray@stu.edu
RAY, Edward, J .... 541-737-4133.... 418 F
pres.office@oregonstate.edu
RAY, Gary .... 940-898-3010.... 502 B
gray@twu.edu
RAY, Janell .... 713-942-9505.... 487 H
jray@hgst.edu
RAY, Jeff .... 678-915-7234.... 137 C
jray@spsu.edu
RAY, Jerry .... 912-583-3115.... 126 C
jray@bpc.edu
RAY, Jess, D .... 309-438-2264.... 153 C
jdray@ilstu.edu
RAY, Joe, F .... 662-246-6308.... 275 F
jray@msdelta.edu
RAY, John, C .... 979-230-3202.... 482 B
john.ray@brazosport.edu
RAY, Johnnie, D .... 480-965-7393...... 12 B
johnnie.ray@asu.edu
RAY, Judy, K .... 336-841-9201.... 365 A
jray@highpoint.edu
RAY, Kate .... 904-953-2919.... 262 G
kray@mayo.edu
RAY, Katerina, R .... 419-372-8575.... 385 C
krray@bgsu.edu
RAY, Kathlin, D .... 775-784-6500.... 303 A
RAY, Keith, H .... 217-732-3168.... 156 F
pres@lincolnchristian.edu
RAY, Ken .... 813-253-7054.... 110 I
kray6@hccfl.edu
RAY, Lee Ann .... 979-458-7236.... 496 G
Ray@tamhsc.edu
RAY, Marsha, M .... 215-751-8000.... 426 B
mray@ccp.edu
RAY, Monica .... 256-372-5555...... 1 A
monica.ray@aamu.edu

RAY, Nicholas, T .... 812-941-2411.... 174 D
nicray@ius.edu
RAY, JR., R. Richard .... 616-395-7785.... 252 F
ray@hope.edu
RAY, Rhonda .... 503-760-3131.... 414 F
rhonda@birthingway.edu
RAY, Roxie, L .... 203-576-4290...... 94 D
roxieray@bridgeport.edu
RAY, S. Alan .... 630-617-3100.... 150 F
president@elmhurst.edu
RAY, Sally .... 270-745-2283.... 207 C
sally.ray@wku.edu
RAY, Sarah .... 802-443-5000.... 513 G
ray@middlebury.edu
RAY, Scott .... 903-923-2148.... 486 D
sray@etbu.edu
RAY, Shawn .... 305-892-7015.... 111 K
shawn.ray@jwu.edu
RAY, Valerie .... 765-966-2656.... 176 F
vray@ivytech.edu
RAY, William .... 503-352-2786.... 419 E
raywb@pacificu.edu
RAYBUCK, Diane, R .... 330-972-6427.... 403 B
drr9@uakron.edu
RAYBURN, Bentley .... 719-590-6797...... 83 D
brayburn@coloradotech.edu
RAYBURN, John .... 713-500-3079.... 506 D
john.rayburn@uth.tmc.edu
RAYBURN, Judy, M .... 731-881-7020.... 477 E
jrayburn@utm.edu
RAYBURN, T. Monroe .... 202-319-5765...... 97 C
rayburn@cua.edu
RAYCHOUDHURY,
Samir, S .... 803-705-4648.... 455 D
raychoudhurys@benedict.edu
RAYE, Brenda .... 330-494-1214.... 385 I
braye@brownmackie.edu
RAYER, Susan, S .... 859-233-8193.... 206 E
careerdevelopment@transy.edu
RAYMAN, Jack, R .... 814-865-2377.... 438 F
jxr1@psu.edu
RAYMOND, Annette .... 973-748-9000.... 308 A
annette_raymond@bloomfield.edu
RAYMOND, Chris .... 413-572-5243.... 239 C
craymond@wsc.ma.edu
RAYMOND, Diane .... 603-428-2223.... 305 E
draymond@nec.edu
RAYMOND, Donald, M ...... 207-834-7521.... 220 D
raymond@maine.edu
RAYMOND, SR., John, R .. 414-955-8225.... 548 E
jraymond@mcw.edu
RAYMOND, Margaret .... 608-262-1234.... 550 G
mraymond2@wisc.edu
RAYMOND, Mary, P .... 845-437-5285.... 359 D
maraymond@vassar.edu
RAYMOND, Monica .... 805-339-6370...... 67 I
RAYMOND, Monica .... 805-339-6370...... 67 J
RAYMOND, Monica .... 805-339-6370...... 67 L
RAYMOND, Monica .... 805-339-6370...... 68 A
RAYMOND, Richard .... 419-448-2227.... 391 G
rraymond@heidelberg.edu
RAYMOND, Sarah .... 406-496-4384.... 296 C
sraymond@mtech.edu
RAYMOND, Thomas .... 605-455-6012.... 464 H
traymond@olc.edu
RAYMOND, Tom .... 605-455-6044.... 464 H
traymond@olc.edu
RAYMUNDO, Laurie .... 671-735-2184.... 559 D
lraymundo@gmail.com
RAYNER, Jill .... 706-864-1688.... 134 D
jprayner@northgeorgia.edu
RAYNOR, Bill .... 781-239-2665.... 240 D
braynor@massbay.edu
RAYNOR, Jamie .... 803-641-3480.... 462 B
jamier@usca.edu
RAYNOR, Nathan .... 706-865-2134.... 138 A
nraynor@truett.edu
RAZIANO, Deborah, A .... 985-448-4110.... 216 A
deborah.raziano@nicholls.edu
RAZO, Bridget .... 661-722-6300...... 28 J
brazo@avc.edu
RAZO, Gabriel .... 312-553-5901.... 146 H
grazo@ccc.edu
RAZZAGHI, Farzaneh .... 956-665-2755.... 506 A
farzaneh@utpa.edu
RAZZANO, Joe .... 270-831-9644.... 201 I
joe.razzano@kctcs.edu
RE, Doug .... 415-239-3759...... 39 H
dre@ccsf.edu
RE, John .... 864-225-7653.... 458 B
johnre@forrestcollege.edu
RE, Robin .... 740-774-6300.... 389 C
rre@daymarcollege.edu
RE, Robin .... 740-687-6126.... 389 E
rre@daymarcollege.edu
REA, Ann, W .... 207-947-4591.... 217 D
librarian@bealcollege.edu
REA, Dennis .... 406-657-1746.... 295 F
drea@msubillings.edu
REA, Gail .... 314-454-8848.... 282 E
grea@bjc.org
REA, Kenneth, W .... 318-257-4262.... 215 F
rea@latech.edu

REA, Laura, C .... 956-326-2355 .... 497 B
lrea@tamiu.edu
READ, Allison .... 860-297-2013 .... 94 C
allison.read@trincoll.edu
READ, Deborah, A .... 937-229-2973 .... 404 A
deborah.read@notes.udayton.edu
READ, Marsha .... 775-327-2363 .... 303 A
read@unr.edu
READ, Melissa, P .... 508-541-1652 .... 234 B
mread@dean.edu
READ, Simon .... 240-895-4442 .... 226 A
sread@smcm.edu
READEY, Mary, L .... 614-292-0257 .... 398 H
readey.3@osu.edu
READING, Sarah .... 781-239-2782 .... 240 D
sreading@massbay.edu
READY, Catherine .... 407-843-3984 .... 110 B
careers@fortiscollege.edu
READY, Deana .... 573-592-4236 .... 293 E
deana.ready@williamwoods.edu
REAGAN, Cheryl .... 518-562-4110 .... 329 D
cheryl.reagan@clinton.edu
REAGAN, Daniel, W .... 603-641-4131 .... 306 F
dan.reagan@unh.edu
REAGAN, Judith, E .... 913-588-1480 .... 197 A
jreagan@kumc.edu
REAGAN, Kate, M .... 423-869-6389 .... 470 C
kate.reagan@lmunet.edu
REAGAN, Margy .... 202-884-9707 .... 99 E
reaganm@trinitydc.edu
REAGAN, Melinda .... 972-279-6511 .... 479 I
mreagan@amberton.edu
REAGINS-LILLY,
Soncia, R .... 512-471-5017 .... 505 B
soncia.r.lilly@austin.utexas.edu
REAGLE, Mike .... 859-622-3855 .... 200 D
mike.reagle@eku.edu
REAGLES, Patricia, J .... 507-344-7306 .... 261 H
patti.reagles@blc.edu
REALE, SJ, Frank .... 314-977-2500 .... 289 F
realef@slu.edu
REALE, SJ, Frank .... 314-977-7065 .... 289 F
reale@slu.edu
REALE, Todd, D .... 502-272-8242 .... 198 E
treale@bellarmine.edu
REALIVASQUEZ, Yvonne .... 432-837-8032 .... 501 B
yrealivasquez@sulross.edu
REAM, Debbie .... 213-477-2505 .... 57 H
dream@msmc.la.edu
REAP, Mary .... 413-265-2293 .... 233 E
reapm@elms.edu
REARDON, Colleen .... 708-524-6643 .... 150 A
creardon@dom.edu
REARDON, Maureen .... 508-457-1313 .... 243 B
mreardon@ngs.edu
REARDON, Pat .... 256-824-2561 .... 9 A
reardonp@uah.edu
REARDON, Penny .... 304-434-8000 .... 542 E
reardon@eastern.wvnet.edu
REARDON, Richard .... 208-667-2588 .... 144 B
rreardon@uidaho.edu
REARDON, Thomas, J .... 662-915-5056 .... 277 G
sparky@olemiss.edu
REARDON, Timothy .... 440-646-8312 .... 405 B
treardon@ursuline.edu
REARIC, Sue .... 619-644-7576 .... 48 I
sue.rearic@gcccd.edu
REAS, Rae-Ellen .... 425-640-1401 .... 533 E
raeellen.reas@edcc.edu
REASH, Brenda .... 252-222-6000 .... 368 F
REASONER, Carroll .... 319-335-2841 .... 182 C
carroll-reasoner@uiowa.edu
REASONER, Elliott .... 630-743-0689 .... 168 C
sreasoner@westwood.edu
REASSO, Robert .... 207-973-1069 .... 218 A
reassor@husson.edu
REAUME, Vicki .... 734-487-0250 .... 250 H
vicky.reaume@emich.edu
REAVES, Donald, J .... 336-750-2041 .... 380 A
chancellorsoffice@wssu.edu
REAVES, Kenneth, M .... 863-680-3007 .... 109 D
kreaves@flsouthern.edu
REAVES, Leonard .... 419-448-3271 .... 402 E
reavesl@tiffin.edu
REAVES, Mary, B .... 708-709-3501 .... 161 C
mreaves@prairiestate.edu
REAVES, Nicole .... 724-925-6952 .... 451 E
reavesn@wccc.edu
REAVIS, Bob .... 785-654-2416 .... 190 A
breavis@allencc.edu
REAVIS, Ralph .... 434-528-5276 .... 529 E
reavis@vul.edu
REBER, Christopher, M .... 814-676-6591 .... 442 A
creber@clarion.edu
REBER, Christopher, M .... 814-676-6591 .... 442 B
creber@clarion.edu
REBHOLZ, Catherine, R .... 414-276-5200 .... 546 C
krrebholz@bryantstratton.edu
REBIMBUS, Michael .... 803-705-4357 .... 455 D
rebimbus@benedict.edu
REBORATTI, Ed .... 610-282-1100 .... 426 I
ed.reboratti@desales.edu
REBORI, Christine .... 636-949-4477 .... 284 C
crebori@lindenwood.edu
REBRO, Jan .... 425-637-1010 .... 531 I
jrebro@cityu.eu
REBULL, Patrick .... 305-237-0564 .... 113 H
prebull@mdc.edu
RECA, Michael, F .... 609-896-5080 .... 313 G
reca@rider.edu
RECCHIA, Karen .... 318-678-6000 .... 209 J
krecchia@bpcc.edu
RECH, Tara .... 510-594-3670 .... 31 J
trech@cca.edu
RECHEIUNGEL, Winfred .... 680-488-3036 .... 560 A
winfredr@palau.edu
RECHLIN, Mike .... 304-358-2000 .... 540 H
mike@future.edu
RECHTSCHAFFEN,
Joyce, A .... 202-220-1364 .... 313 A
jrechtsc@princeton.edu
RECINOS, Diane .... 973-278-5400 .... 307 G
dr@berkeleycollege.edu
RECINOS, Diane .... 973-278-5000 .... 323 J
dr@berkeleycollege.edu
RECK, Gwen .... 409-984-6115 .... 500 H
gwen.reck@lamarpa.edu
RECK, Ronald .... 732-987-2416 .... 310 D
reckr@georgian.edu
RECK, Una Mae .... 574-520-4220 .... 174 C
maereck@iusb.edu
RECKER, OSB, Ralph .... 503-845-3320 .... 417 A
ralph.recker@mtangel.edu
RECKER, Sandy, M .... 563-588-7362 .... 186 I
sandy.recker@loras.edu
RECKNER, Angela, T .... 215-489-2203 .... 426 H
Angela.Reckner@delval.edu
RECKTENWALD, Kay .... 561-297-0026 .... 118 H
kreckten@fau.edu
RECNY, Beverly .... 540-535-3592 .... 523 K
brecny@su.edu
RECOD, Pamela .... 910-323-5614 .... 362 G
RECORD, Ann .... 731-668-7240 .... 478 F
ann.record@wtbc.edu
RECORD, Kim .... 336-334-5952 .... 379 A
ksrecord@uncg.edu
RECTOR, Billy, C .... 713-313-6898 .... 499 G
rectorbc@tsu.edu
RECTOR, Brenda .... 865-882-4526 .... 475 G
rectorbw@roanestate.edu
RECTOR, Dave .... 360-596-5305 .... 538 B
drector@spscc.stc.edu
RECTOR, David .... 660-785-7607 .... 291 A
daverec@truman.edu
RECTOR, Jeff .... 423-493-4224 .... 476 C
rectorj@tntemple.edu
RECTOR, Jeff .... 423-493-4220 .... 476 C
rectorj@tntemple.edu
RECTOR, Lallene, J .... 847-866-3904 .... 151 B
ljr@garrett.edu
RECTOR, Larry .... 865-573-4517 .... 469 J
lrector@johnsonU.edu
RECTOR, Patricia .... 918-465-1769 .... 408 A
prector@eosc.edu
RECTOR, Rob .... 417-447-4852 .... 287 G
rectorr@otc.edu
RECZNIK, Joel, S .... 740-284-5236 .... 390 M
jrecznik@franciscan.edu
RECZNIK, John .... 740-283-6497 .... 390 M
jlrecznik@franciscan.edu
RECZNIK, Mark, E .... 740-284-5845 .... 390 M
mrecznik@franciscan.edu
REDD, Annie .... 386-481-2520 .... 101 I
redda@cookman.edu
REDD, Randy .... 901-751-8453 .... 471 D
rredd@mabts.edu
REDD, Rea .... 724-852-3254 .... 451 B
rredd@waynesburg.edu
REDD, Scott .... 407-366-9493 .... 115 I
sredd@rts.edu
REDD, Theresa, M .... 202-806-0870 .... 98 B
tredd@howard.edu
REDDA, Kinfe, K .... 850-412-5102 .... 118 G
kinfe.redda@famu.edu
REDDAY, Darlene .... 605-698-3966 .... 465 C
dredday@swc.tc
REDDER, Kelly .... 585-475-7412 .... 347 G
karrar@rit.edu
REDDER, Vince .... 605-995-2631 .... 464 B
viredder@dwu.edu
REDDERSON, Jeff, P .... 864-294-3262 .... 458 D
jeff.redderson@furman.edu
REDDICK, Amanda .... 678-891-2782 .... 130 G
Amanda.Reddick@gpc.edu
REDDICK, Michael .... 317-788-3372 .... 180 C
mreddick@uindy.edu
REDDICK, Niles .... 229-391-4782 .... 123 F
nreddick@abac.edu
REDDING, Melanie .... 865-471-3229 .... 467 E
mredding@cn.edu
REDDING, Michael, W .... 541-346-5022 .... 419 B
mredding@uoregon.edu
REDDING, Russell .... 215-345-1500 .... 426 H
russell.redding@delval.edu
REDDINGTON, Kathleen .... 575-527-7604 .... 319 G
kredding@nmsu.edu
REDDY, Chandra .... 615-963-7561 .... 474 A
creddy@tnstate.edu
REDDY, Indra, K .... 361-593-4271 .... 496 G
ireddy@pharmacy.tamhsc.edu
REDDY, John, M .... 724-337-1000 .... 424 E
jreddy@careerta.edu
REDDY, Michael, S .... 205-934-4720 .... 8 G
mreddy@uab.edu
REDDY, N. Mohan .... 216-368-1156 .... 386 E
mohan.reddy@case.edu
REDDY, Narem .... 678-466-4100 .... 127 A
naremreddy@clayton.edu
REDDY, JR., Robert, A .... 440-775-8142 .... 397 F
rob.reddy@oberlin.edu
REDDY, Venkateshwar .... 719-255-3408 .... 88 C
vreddy@uccs.edu
REDEKER, Michael .... 314-505-7000 .... 280 H
redekerm@csl.edu
REDES, Cliff .... 231-876-3105 .... 248 F
cliff.redes@baker.edu
REDFERN, Mylan .... 432-552-2220 .... 507 C
redfern_m@utpb.edu
REDFERN, Paul, W .... 717-337-6829 .... 429 H
predfern@gettysburg.edu
REDFERN, Vance .... 575-538-6310 .... 321 I
redfernw@wnmu.edu
REDFIELD, David .... 916-484-8408 .... 56 A
redfied@arc.losrios.edu
REDHEAD, Catherine .... 406-683-7450 .... 295 B
c_redhead@umwestern.edu
REDHORN-CHAMBERLAIN,
Sharon .... 402-878-2380 .... 298 G
sredhorn@littlepriest.edu
REDIKER, Nicole .... 207-941-7176 .... 219 E
redikern@nescom.edu
REDING, Terrence .... 585-345-6850 .... 334 F
tareding@genesee.edu
REDINGER, Larry, L .... 909-594-5611 .... 58 A
lredinge@mtsac.edu
REDINGTON, Joseph .... 570-674-6756 .... 436 F
jredingt@misericordia.edu
REDLEAF-COLLETT, Betty .. 989-775-4123 .... 257 H
collett.betty@sagchip.edu
REDLER, Susan .... 212-431-2121 .... 343 E
sredler@nyls.edu
REDLICH, Philip, N .... 414-805-5726 .... 548 E
predlich@mcw.edu
REDLIN, Greg .... 662-846-4004 .... 274 B
gredlin@deltastate.edu
REDLINGER, Lawrence, J .. 972-883-6188 .... 505 D
redling@utdallas.edu
REDMAN, Barbara, K .... 313-577-4070 .... 260 D
ae9080@wayne.edu
REDMAN, Carol .... 618-395-7777 .... 152 E
redmanc@iecc.edu
REDMAN, Chris .... 785-749-8497 .... 193 B
president@haskell.edu
REDMAN, Donald, L .... 717-334-6286 .... 435 A
dredman@ltsg.edu
REDMAN, Robert, R .... 503-255-0332 .... 417 C
rredman@multnomah.edu
REDMAN, Thomas, J .... 978-232-2005 .... 234 F
tredman@endicott.edu
REDMAN, Wendy .... 907-450-8007 .... 10 H
wendy.redman@alaska.edu
REDMOND, Carmen .... 650-949-6166 .... 47 G
redmondcarmen@fhda.edu
REDMOND, Carmen .... 650-949-6166 .... 47 H
redmondcarmen@foothill.edu
REDMOND, Michael, J .... 303-458-4944 .... 87 E
mredmond@regis.edu
REDMOND, Minor (Will) .... 717-871-5344 .... 443 C
minor.redmond@millersville.edu
REDMOND, Thomas, E .... 202-274-5935 .... 99 F
tredmond@udc.edu
REDONNETT, Rosa .... 207-973-3231 .... 219 I
rosar@maine.edu
REDTOMAHAWK, James .... 701-255-3285 .... 383 D
jredtomahawk@uttc.edu
REDWINE, Elaine, S .... 970-247-7142 .... 84 G
redwine_e@fortlewis.edu
REDWINE, Marian .... 405-491-6336 .... 412 D
maredwin@snu.edu
REDWINE, Mike .... 405-491-6638 .... 412 D
mredwine@snu.edu
REDWINE, William .... 606-783-2081 .... 204 E
b.redwine@moreheadstate.edu
REECE, Albert .... 410-706-7410 .... 227 C
deanmed@som.umaryland.edu
REECE, Bryan .... 562-860-2451 .... 38 J
breece@cerritos.edu
REECE, Bryan, A .... 214-860-2306 .... 484 I
breece@dcccd.edu
REECE, David .... 910-695-3831 .... 373 E
reeced@sandhills.edu
REECE, E. Albert .... 410-706-7410 .... 227 C
deanmed@som.umaryland.edu
REECE, Jeremy .... 870-733-6786 .... 22 E
jreece@midsouthcc.edu
REECE, Marilyn .... 256-228-6001 .... 6 A
reecem@nacc.edu
REECE, Ronda .... 405-945-8631 .... 410 F
REECE, Sheila .... 903-785-7661 .... 492 B
sreece@parisjc.edu
REECE, Terry .... 805-546-3283 .... 43 F
treece@cuesta.edu
REECK-IRBY, Joanne .... 612-330-1111 .... 261 G
reeck@augsburg.edu
REED, Albert .... 505-428-1314 .... 320 E
al.reed@sfcc.edu
REED, Alexis .... 304-876-5157 .... 544 A
apalladi@shepherd.edu
REED, Ann .... 304-462-4117 .... 543 F
ann.reed@glenville.edu
REED, Anne, E .... 207-941-7176 .... 219 E
reeda@nescom.edu
REED, Annie, G .... 818-947-2320 .... 55 F
reedag@lavc.edu
REED, Beverly .... 630-942-4218 .... 147 G
reedbe@cod.edu
REED, Beverly, S .... 301-322-0495 .... 225 F
reedbs@pgcc.edu
REED, Brian, V .... 802-656-0903 .... 514 F
brian.reed@uvm.edu
REED, Bruce .... 956-665-2292 .... 506 A
bjreed@utpa.edu
REED, Burton, J .... 402-554-2262 .... 301 B
breed@unomaha.edu
REED, Charlene, K .... 330-672-2121 .... 393 D
creed2@kent.edu
REED, Charles, B .... 562-951-4700 .... 33 E
creed@calstate.edu
REED, Chelsea, S .... 317-738-8119 .... 171 C
creed@franklincollege.edu
REED, Christine .... 805-922-6966 .... 26 K
creed@hancockcollege.edu
REED, Christopher, S .... 603-526-3797 .... 304 A
chreed@colby-sawyer.edu
REED, Claudia .... 310-954-4371 .... 57 H
creed@msmc.la.edu
REED, Dale, K .... 620-417-1014 .... 196 B
dale.reed@sccc.edu
REED, Dallas .... 662-254-3636 .... 276 C
dfreed@mvsu.edu
REED, Dan .... 530-898-6451 .... 34 A
dmreed@csuchico.edu
REED, David, D .... 906-487-3043 .... 255 E
ddreed@mtu.edu
REED, Dee .... 812-535-5212 .... 179 C
dreed@smwc.edu
REED, Dennis, J .... 818-947-2625 .... 55 E
reeddj@lavc.edu
REED, Diane .... 757-594-7202 .... 517 I
dreed@cnu.edu
REED, Don .... 620-278-4247 .... 196 D
dreed@sterling.edu
REED, Donna .... 503-977-4497 .... 419 G
donna.reed@pcc.edu
REED, Doug .... 870-245-5167 .... 22 I
reedd@obu.edu
REED, Edward, J .... 260-480-4250 .... 176 D
ereed@ivytech.edu
REED, Elizabeth .... 305-899-4013 .... 101 F
ereed@mail.barry.edu
REED, Eloise .... 903-923-3222 .... 500 A
eloise.reed@marshall.tstc.edu
REED, Francesca .... 703-284-5901 .... 521 A
francesca.reed@marymount.edu
REED, Gary .... 214-645-0137 .... 507 D
gary.reed@utsouthwestern.edu
REED, Gary, D .... 217-581-6260 .... 150 C
gdreed@eiu.edu
REED, Harry .... 713-646-1852 .... 494 E
hreed@stcl.edu
REED, Helen .... 970-351-2601 .... 88 F
helen.reed@unco.edu
REED, James, D .... 806-651-2055 .... 498 D
jreed@mail.wtamu.edu
REED, Jeff .... 515-292-9694 .... 181 F
REED, Jeffrey, G .... 920-923-8760 .... 548 C
jreed@marianuniversity.edu
REED, Jerry .... 570-389-4040 .... 441 F
jreed@bloomu.edu
REED, John .... 425-249-4800 .... 538 D
john.reed@tlc.edu
REED, John .... 617-253-6700 .... 242 A
reedjs@mit.edu
REED, Jon .... 304-253-7351 .... 541 D
jreed@mountainstate.edu
REED, Jonathan .... 909-593-3511 .... 75 C
jreed@laverne.edu
REED, Karen, A .... 419-755-4538 .... 397 B
kreed@ncstatecollege.edu
REED, Kathleen, O .... 717-334-6286 .... 435 A
kreed@ltsg.edu
REED, Kathy, S .... 217-581-3227 .... 150 C
ksreed@eiu.edu
REED, Kendall .... 515-271-1515 .... 183 F
kendall.reed@dmu.edu
REED, Kenneth .... 575-492-2132 .... 321 H
kreed@usw.edu
REED, Kevin .... 310-206-1355 .... 74 A
kreed@conet.ucla.edu
REED, Kimberly .... 270-745-2434 .... 207 C
kim.reed@wku.edu
REED, Knyja .... 312-935-4119 .... 162 E
kreed@robertmorris.edu
REED, Lee .... 202-687-2435 .... 98 A
athletics@georgetown.edu

REID, John .... 805-437-8444 ..... 33 I
john.reid@csuci.edu
REID, Julia .... 503-760-3131 .... 414 F
julia@birthingway.edu
REID, Kandace .... 585-266-0430 .... 333 E
kreid@cci.edu
REID, JR., Karl, N .... 405-744-5140 .... 410 C
karl.reid@okstate.edu
REID, Kathleen, A .... 413-782-1211 .... 246 D
kreid@wne.edu
REID, Kevin .... 478-757-2511 .... 133 E
kevin.reid@maconstate.edu
REID, Lenzy .... 706-355-5008 .... 124 H
lreid@athenstech.edu
REID, Marda .... 845-257-3171 .... 352 B
reidm@newpaltz.edu
REID, Mark .... 206-281-2624 .... 537 D
mreid@spu.edu
REID, Melissa .... 606-546-1610 .... 206 F
REID, Michael .... 325-942-2017 .... 480 E
michael.reid@angelo.edu
REID, Michelle .... 330-499-9600 .... 393 I
mreid6@kent.edu
REID, Michelle .... 701-231-8887 .... 381 H
michelle.reid@ndsu.edu
REID, Pamela, T .... 860-231-5221 ..... 93 H
preid@sjc.edu
REID, Paula .... 505-747-2153 .... 320 A
preid@nnmc.edu
REID, Richard, H .... 337-475-5588 .... 215 G
rreid@mcneese.edu
REID, Robert, D .... 540-568-3254 .... 520 C
reidrd@jmu.edu
REID, Shannon .... 603-271-2722 .... 304 B
REID, Stanley, G .... 512-476-2772 .... 481 C
president@austingrad.edu
REID, JR., Thomas, G .... 412-731-8690 .... 445 E
treid@rpts.edu
REID, Tina, S .... 864-592-4683 .... 461 C
reidt@sccsc.edu
REID, Victoria .... 410-528-7602 .... 272 F
victoria.reid@waldenu.edu
REID-CHASSIAKOS, Linda 818-677-3689 .... 35 D
linda.reid.chassiakos@csun.edu
REID-HART, De Reese .... 773-602-5118 .... 147 B
REID-MARTINEZ,
Kathaleen .... 405-691-3800 .... 408 H
kreidmartinez@macu.edu
REIDELL, Mary Frances .... 412-578-6174 .... 424 G
reidellmf@carlow.edu
REIDENBERG, Marcus, M . 212-746-6227 .... 360 B
mmreid@med.cornell.edu
REIDHEAD, Van, A .... 570-422-3539 .... 442 C
vreidhead@po-box.esu.edu
REIDOUT, Valerie .... 610-683-4060 .... 442 F
reidout@kutztown.edu
REIDY, Connie .... 319-277-0220 .... 186 D
REIDY, Fran .... 352-588-8246 .... 116 E
fran.reidy@saintleo.edu
REIDY, Joseph, P .... 202-806-2550 ..... 98 B
jreidy@howard.edu
REIDY, Robert, C .... 650-723-6324 ..... 71 F
rcr@stanford.edu
REIDY, Stephanie .... 410-462-8245 .... 221 D
sreidy@bccc.edu
REIF, Karyn .... 312-942-3691 .... 163 B
karyn_reif@rush.edu
REIF, L. Rafael .... 617-253-4500 .... 242 A
reif@mit.edu
REIF, Steven, J .... 248-246-2511 .... 257 B
sjreif@oaklandcc.edu
REIFENHEISER, Paul .... 845-434-5750 .... 356 H
preifenh@sullivan.suny.edu
REIFF, Henry, B .... 410-857-2512 .... 224 D
hreiff@mcdaniel.edu
REIFF, Marianne .... 802-322-1719 .... 513 C
marianne.reiff@goddard.edu
REIFLER, Sylvia .... 617-217-9237 .... 231 C
sreifler@baystate.edu
REIGELMAN, Milton, M .... 859-238-5287 .... 199 D
milton.reigelman@centre.edu
REIGH, Darryel .... 405-224-3140 .... 413 E
dreigh@usao.edu
REIGHARD, Erica .... 814-262-6440 .... 441 A
ereighard@pennhighlands.edu
REIGHLEY, Twila .... 319-335-2110 .... 182 C
twila-reighley@uiowa.edu
REIGOSA, Teresa .... 305-237-3536 .... 113 H
treigosa@mdc.edu
REILENDER, Catherine, L .. 859-846-5315 .... 204 D
creilender@midway.edu
REILLY, Anne, H .... 773-508-7478 .... 157 A
areilly@luc.edu
REILLY, James .... 312-553-2540 .... 146 G
jreilly1@ccc.edu
REILLY, James .... 304-724-3700 .... 540 C
jreilly@apus.edu
REILLY, Karen .... 301-624-2862 .... 222 G
kreilly@frederick.edu
REILLY, Karen .... 701-671-2189 .... 382 E
karen.reilly@ndscs.edu
REILLY, Kevin, P .... 608-262-2321 .... 550 F
kreilly@uwsa.edu

REILLY, Kristie .... 908-737-3460 .... 311 B
kreilly@kean.edu
REILLY, Madelyn .... 412-396-4895 .... 428 C
reillym@duq.edu
REILLY, Marie, T .... 814-863-7033 .... 439 C
mtr12@psu.edu
REILLY, MaryBeth .... 718-982-2426 .... 327 A
MaryBeth.Reilly@csi.cuny.edu
REILLY, Maureen .... 518-743-2306 .... 322 B
reillym@sunyacc.edu
REILLY, P, J .... 201-360-4361 .... 310 F
preilly@hccc.edu
REILLY, Patricia .... 617-627-2000 .... 245 F
patricia.reilly@tufts.edu
REILLY, Paul, J .... 215-951-1100 .... 432 G
reilly@lasalle.edu
REILLY, Seamus .... 217-353-2170 .... 161 B
sereilly@parkland.edu
REILLY, Susan .... 561-297-3850 .... 118 H
sreilly@fau.edu
REILLY-KELLY, Tracy .... 360-992-2163 .... 532 A
tkelly@clark.edu
REILLY-MYKLEBUST,
Alice .... 715-425-9884 .... 552 A
alice.m.reilly-myklebust@uwrf.edu
REIMAN, Dennis, M .... 904-997-2940 .... 109 E
dennis.reiman@fscj.edu
REIMANN, Jan .... 573-334-9181 .... 285 A
jan@metrobusinesscollege.edu
REIMANN, Rick .... 518-587-2100 .... 355 F
rick.reimann@esc.edu
REIMER, Carol .... 907-822-3201 ..... 10 C
registrar@akbible.edu
REIMER, Dawn .... 763-424-0817 .... 268 D
dreimer@nhcc.edu
REIMER, Kevin .... 559-453-5556 ..... 47 K
kevin.reimer@fresno.edu
REIMER, Linda .... 212-229-5350 .... 342 E
reimerl@newschool.edu
REIMER, Martin .... 712-274-6400 .... 189 H
martin.reimer@witcc.edu
REIMER, Michael .... 201-360-4156 .... 310 F
mreimer@hccc.edu
REIMONDO, Sue .... 859-985-3212 .... 198 F
sue_reimondo@berea.edu
REIN, Kim .... 303-914-6260 ..... 87 C
kim.rein@rrcc.edu
REINA, Juana .... 914-606-6710 .... 360 D
juana.reina@sunywcc.edu
REINBOLD, Sue .... 607-729-8915 .... 332 I
sreinbold@ebi-college.com
REINCKE, Nancy .... 515-271-2161 .... 184 A
nancy.reincke@drake.edu
REINDL, Kay .... 209-478-0800 ..... 50 I
kreindl@humphreys.edu
REINEMUND, Steven .... 336-758-5110 .... 380 B
steve@wfu.edu
REINER, Rachel .... 732-414-2834 .... 317 F
REINERT, Duane .... 660-944-2852 .... 280 F
dreinert@conception.edu
REINERT, Stephen, L .... 732-932-7787 .... 314 D
sreinert@rci.rutgers.edu
REING, Linda .... 212-875-4605 .... 323 E
alumrel@bankstreet.edu
REINHARDT, Alan, J .... 508-213-2201 .... 243 J
alan.reinhardt@nichols.edu
REINHARDT, Brian .... 510-885-3690 ..... 34 C
brian.reinhardt@csueastbay.edu
REINHARDT, Douglas, E ... 207-859-4760 .... 217 G
dereinha@colby.edu
REINHARDT, John, W .... 402-472-1344 .... 301 A
jreinhardt@unmc.edu
REINHARDT, Rosemary ..... 208-426-1422 .... 142 F
rosemaryreinhardt@boisestate.edu
REINHARDT, Sharon .... 209-384-6188 ..... 57 C
reinhardt.s@mccd.edu
REINHART, Charles, W ...... 812-888-4480 .... 181 B
creinhart@vinu.edu
REINHART, Kellee, C .... 205-348-5938 ...... 8 E
kreinhar@uasystem.ua.edu
REINHART, Loretta, M .... 330-471-8168 .... 395 E
loreinhart@malone.edu
REINHART, Rachel .... 419-372-0451 .... 385 C
rvanna@bgsu.edu
REINHART, Rose .... 315-568-3329 .... 342 H
rreinhart@nycc.edu
REINHARTSEN, Steven, C . 336-506-4146 .... 367 G
reinhart@alamancecc.edu
REINKE, Brenda .... 405-682-7510 .... 409 F
breinke@occc.edu
REINKE, Jane .... 763-424-0819 .... 268 D
jreinke@nhcc.edu
REINLAND, Jeffrey, E .... 509-527-4312 .... 538 G
jeffrey.reinland@wwcc.edu
REINSCH FRIESE, Ellen ..... 937-775-2709 .... 406 C
ellen.friese@wright.edu
REINSCHMIDT, Cheryl .... 323-856-7698 ..... 28 D
creinschmidt@afi.com
REINTS, Cindi, P .... 319-895-4216 .... 183 D
creints@cornellcollege.edu
REIS, Elizabeth .... 708-974-5283 .... 159 A
reis@morainevalley.edu
REIS, Paul .... 203-837-9805 ..... 92 A
reisp@wcsu.edu

REISBERG, Jeff .... 727-873-4552 .... 121 B
reisberg@mail.usf.edu
REISECK, Carol, J .... 708-209-3262 .... 148 C
carol.reiseck@cuchicago.edu
REISER, Robert .... 650-843-3515 ..... 61 A
rreiser@paloaltou.edu
REISETTER, Mary .... 641-585-8681 .... 189 E
reisettem@waldorf.edu
REISETTER-HART, Judith ... 414-382-6431 .... 545 H
judith.reisetter@alverno.edu
REISH, Brenda, J .... 800-287-8822 .... 169 E
reishbr@bethanyseminary.edu
REISH, Joseph, G .... 269-387-5202 .... 260 F
joe.reish@wmich.edu
REISIG, Jerry .... 212-870-1213 .... 344 A
jreisig@nyts.edu
REISINGER, Amanda, B ..... 740-588-1275 .... 407 A
amreisinger@zanestate.edu
REISINGER, Scot, H .... 319-368-6472 .... 187 E
sreisinger@mtmercy.edu
REISINGER, Tracy .... 503-699-6253 .... 416 I
treisinger@marylhurst.edu
REISKE, Matthew .... 573-882-6574 .... 291 D
reiskem@missouri.edu
REISMAN, Lonn .... 254-968-9178 .... 496 F
reisman@tarleton.edu
REISS, Michael, A .... 718-377-0777 .... 346 G
REISS, Mitchell, B .... 410-778-7201 .... 229 D
mreiss2@washcoll.edu
REISS, Richard .... 201-692-7003 .... 310 B
reissr@fdu.edu
REISS, Yona .... 212-960-5347 .... 361 I
yreiss@yu.edu
REISS, Yona .... 212-960-5344 .... 361 I
yreiss@yu.edu
REISSENWEBER, Beth, W .. 630-844-5490 .... 145 C
breissen@aurora.edu
REISSER, Linda .... 503-978-5292 .... 419 G
lreisser@pcc.edu
REIST, David .... 785-442-6010 .... 193 D
dreist@highlandcc.edu
REITCHEL, Meghan .... 207-859-1105 .... 219 G
registrar@thomas.edu
REITER, Emily .... 213-613-2200 ..... 70 H
emily_reiter@sciarc.edu
REITER, Laurie .... 800-567-2344 .... 546 G
lreiter@menominee.edu
REITER, Sharon, L .... 909-869-3016 ..... 33 G
slreiter@csupomona.edu
REITER, Susan, M .... 727-341-3267 .... 116 F
reiter.susan@spcollege.edu
REITMAN, Bruce .... 617-627-3158 .... 245 F
bruce.reitman@tufts.edu
REITMAN, Zipora .... 845-574-4000 .... 347 I
REITNOUR, Brian .... 585-567-9622 .... 336 B
brian.reitnour@houghton.edu
REITNOUR, Matthew .... 585-567-9561 .... 336 B
matthew.reitnour@houghton.edu
REITTER, Kim .... 314-977-2828 .... 289 F
reitterk@slu.edu
REITZ, Nancy .... 916-484-8215 ..... 56 A
reitzn@arc.losrios.edu
REJONIS, Michele .... 304-829-7411 .... 540 E
mrejonis@bethanywv.edu
REKE, Daniel, R .... 937-778-7878 .... 390 G
dreke@edisonohio.edu
REKOW, Dianne .... 212-998-2414 .... 344 B
edr1@nyu.edu
REKOW, Dianne .... 718-260-3761 .... 346 C
drekow@poly.edu
REKOWSKI, Lois, T .... 740-264-5591 .... 390 F
lrekowski@egcc.edu
REL, Ricardo .... 575-646-5909 .... 319 D
rrel@nmsu.edu
RELAY, Lyn .... 718-368-5034 .... 328 B
lrelay@kbcc.cuny.edu
RELEFORD, Michele .... 336-750-2171 .... 380 A
relefordmi@wssu.edu
RELIHAN, Constance, C .... 334-844-4900 ...... 1 G
relihco@auburn.edu
RELL, Amy .... 303-556-3850 ..... 83 F
amy.rell@ccd.edu
RELLINGER, Brian, A .... 740-368-3131 .... 400 F
barellin@owu.edu
RELYEA, Michelle .... 718-488-1039 .... 338 H
michelle.relyea@liu.edu
RELYEA, Steven, W .... 858-534-3390 ..... 74 D
srelyea@ucsd.edu
REMBACZ, Mark .... 307-382-1646 .... 556 F
mrembacz@wwcc.wy.edu
REMBAUGH, Fredi .... 213-749-4208 ..... 50 D
frembaugh@huc.edu
REMBERT, Johnny .... 904-470-8277 .... 105 A
jlrembert@ewc.edu
REMELIUS, Terisa, C .... 361-593-3612 .... 498 A
terisa.remelius@tamuk.edu
REMELTS, Glenn, A .... 616-526-6299 .... 249 E
remelt@calvin.edu
REMENDER, Kathleen, A ... 810-762-9794 .... 253 I
kremende@kettering.edu
REMIAS, Roberta .... 586-498-4170 .... 254 F
remiasr@macomb.edu

REMIERES-MORIN,
Pamela 207-755-5224 218
premieres@cmcc.edu
REMINGTON, Debra 440-375-7040 394
dremington@lec.edu
REMINGTON, Joan 305-919-4500 119
joan.remington@fiu.edu
REMINGTON, Judith, V 847-491-8413 160
j-remington@northwestern.edu
REMINGTON, William, B ... 301-405-4683 227
bremingt@umd.edu
REMLEY, Daniel, C .... 570-577-1195 .... 423 D
dan.remley@bucknell.edu
REMMENGA, Kurt .... 641-784-5190 .... 184 H
remmenga@graceland.edu
REMMERS, Dawn .... 817-272-0777 .... 505 A
dremmers@uta.edu
REMO, Tom .... 845-938-4262 .... 558 G
Tom.Remo@usma.edu
REMSBURG, Barbara .... 801-587-0851 .... 510 L
bremsburg@housing.utah.edu
REMSBURG, Katherine, M . 317-738-8135 .... 171 C
kremsburg@franklincollege.edu
REMULLA, Regan .... 323-259-2970 ..... 59 H
rremulla@oxy.edu
REMY, Douglas .... 602-386-4143 ..... 11 H
douglas.remy@arizonachristian.edu
REN, Linda .... 510-592-9688 ..... 59 F
linda@npu.edu
REN, Wei .... 714-816-0366 ..... 72 I
registration@tuiu.edu
RENACIA, Victorina M, Y .. 671-735-2978 .... 559 D
vrenacia@uguam.uog.edu
RENAGHAN, Dorothy .... 617-287-5450 .... 237 D
dorothy.renaghan@umb.edu
RENAGHAN, Maureen .... 626-857-4147 ..... 39 G
mestrada@citruscollege.edu
RENARD, Jessica .... 561-273-6500 .... 117 J
jrenard@southuniversity.edu
RENAUD, Angela .... 401-598-1400 .... 453 C
arenaud@jwu.edu
RENAUD, Robert, E .... 717-245-1072 .... 427 E
renaudr@dickinson.edu
RENAUD, Steve .... 512-444-8082 .... 499 B
info@texastcm.edu
RENAULT, Heather, M .... 518-783-2423 .... 350 I
hrenault@siena.edu
RENBARGER, Bridgette .... 402-399-2646 .... 297 E
brenbarger@csm.edu
RENCIS, Joseph .... 931-372-3172 .... 474 B
jrencis@tntech.edu
RENDEL, Barbara .... 513-244-8124 .... 387 D
barbara.rendel@ccuniversity.edu
RENDER, Philip .... 843-477-2171 .... 458 G
philip.render@hgtc.edu
RENDON, James .... 860-444-8286 .... 558 E
James.E.Rendon@uscg.mil
RENDON, Michael .... 361-825-2414 .... 497 F
michael.rendon@tamucc.edu
RENDON, Mindy, P .... 785-670-1065 .... 197 D
mindy.rendon@washburn.edu
RENDON, Rudolph, L .... 512-448-8445 .... 493 B
rudolphr@stedwards.edu
RENEAU, Daniel, D .... 318-257-3785 .... 215 F
reneau@latech.edu
RENER, Christine .... 616-331-3498 .... 252 A
renerc@gvsu.edu
RENEW, Steve .... 760-773-2551 ..... 41 H
srenew@collegeofthedesert.edu
RENEY, Richard .... 978-762-4000 .... 241 A
rreney@northshore.edu
RENFRO, Chrissy .... 307-778-5222 .... 556 B
crenfro@lccc.wy.edu
RENFRO, Glen, G .... 423-652-6368 .... 469 L
gerenfro@king.edu
RENFRO, Linda .... 541-245-7517 .... 420 B
lrenfro@roguecc.edu
RENFRO, Roy, E .... 903-463-8717 .... 487 A
renfror@grayson.edu
RENFROW, Michael .... 574-520-4839 .... 174 C
crenfrow@iusb.edu
RENGIIL, Yoichi, K .... 671-735-2249 .... 559 D
yoichi@uguam.uog.edu
RENICH FRASER, Elouise . 484-384-2941 .... 438 C
semdean@eastern.edu
RENICK, James .... 601-979-2323 .... 275 A
james.c.renick@jsums.edu
RENICK, Timothy, M .... 404-413-2580 .... 131 C
trenick@gsu.edu
RENIFF, William, M .... 440-826-2212 .... 384 H
breniff@bw.edu
RENK, Mike .... 701-671-2217 .... 382 E
mike.renk@ndscs.edu
RENKEN, Tracy .... 202-884-9095 ..... 99 E
renkent@trinitydc.edu
RENN, Joanne, M .... 757-455-3303 .... 529 F
jrenn@vwc.edu
RENNA, Matt .... 914-773-3813 .... 345 F
mrenna@pace.edu
RENNELL, Valerie, D .... 814-641-3141 .... 431 L
rennelv@juniata.edu
RENNER, Cathy .... 812-488-2519 .... 180 B
cr4@evansville.edu
RENNER, Daniel .... 303-446-4854 ..... 86 C
renner@dcpa.org

ENNER, Tami .... 312-662-4142.... 144 C
ENNER, Tom, L .... 616-395-7860.... 252 F
trenner@hope.edu
ENNERT, Mordechai .... 718-438-5476.... 360 F
ENNIE, Christopher .... 810-989-5642.... 258 B
ccrennie@sc4.edu
ENNIE, Robert, J .... 904-997-2901.... 109 E
rrennie@fscj.edu
ENNIER, James, A .... 806-651-2777.... 498 D
jrennier@mail.wtamu.edu
ENNIGER, Phyllis, R .... 904-632-3327.... 109 E
prenning@fscj.edu
ENNINGER, Laura .... 304-876-5461.... 544 A
lrenning@shepherd.edu
ENNIX, Louise .... 843-525-8318.... 461 E
lrennix@tcl.edu
ENO, Adam .... 301-846-2560.... 222 G
areno@frederick.edu
ENO, Eric .... 210-486-5484.... 479 B
ereno@alamo.edu
ENO-MUNRO, Jane .... 843-953-6378.... 457 B
munroj@cofc.edu
ENOLA, Elaine .... 409-944-1387.... 486 H
erenola@gc.edu
ENSBERGER, Jeffrey, L ... 713-646-1853.... 494 E
jrensberger@stcl.edu
ENTENBACH, Amy .... 404-364-8303.... 135 A
arentenbach@oglethorpe.edu
ENTMEESTER, Matt, G ..... 920-433-6657.... 546 A
matt.rentmeester@bellincollege.edu
RENTNER, Terry .... 419-372-2079.... 385 C
trentne@bgsu.edu
RENTON, Steve .... 559-730-3902...... 42 B
stever@cos.edu
RENTON, Steve .... 559-737-6216...... 42 B
stever@cos.edu
RENTSCH, Janet, D .... 989-964-7120.... 258 A
jrentsch@svsu.edu
RENTSCHLER, Gina .... 417-865-2811.... 282 A
rentschlerg@evangel.edu
RENTTO, Jessica .... 619-594-6018...... 36 E
jrentto@mail.sdsu.edu
RENTZ, Bruce .... 616-451-3511.... 250 E
brentz@davenport.edu
RENTZ, Linda, T .... 517-586-3010.... 249 H
lrentz@cleary.edu
RENTZ, Shirley, A .... 618-537-6533.... 157 G
sarentz@mckendree.edu
RENVILLE, Allen .... 530-895-2239...... 31 E
renvilleal@butte.edu
RENWICK, Michael, D .... 860-297-2055...... 94 C
michael.renwick@trincoll.edu
RENY, Denise .... 207-741-5568.... 219 A
dreny@smccme.edu
RENY, James .... 207-741-5888.... 219 A
jreny@smccme.edu
RENZ, Amy Button .... 785-532-5050.... 194 B
arenz@ksu.edu
RENZ, Christopher, M .... 510-883-2084...... 45 A
crenz@dspt.edu
RENZEMA, Rich .... 616-538-2330.... 251 F
rrenzema@gbcol.edu
RENZI, Edward .... 401-454-6468.... 454 B
erenzi@risd.edu
RENZI, Michael John .... 408-741-2056...... 78 B
michael.renzi@westvalley.edu
RENZI, Paul, F .... 540-458-8596.... 530 A
RENZULLI, Virgil, N .... 480-965-4980...... 12 B
renzulli@asu.edu
REOHR, Janet .... 716-896-0700.... 359 F
reohrj@villa.edu
REPAC, Richard, A .... 301-687-4331.... 228 C
rrepac@frostburg.edu
REPAIRE, Anne, K .... 304-442-3143.... 545 C
anne.repaire@mail.wvu.edu
REPAIRE, Anne, K .... 304-442-3151.... 545 C
anne.repaire@mail.wvutech.edu
REPENNING, Thomas .... 301-934-7630.... 222 C
tomr@csmd.edu
REPETSKI, Michael .... 330-941-1457.... 406 F
michael.repetski@cis.ysu.edu
REPHANN, Lola .... 212-752-1530.... 338 C
lola.rephann@limcollege.edu
REPMAN, Denise .... 504-671-5330.... 210 G
drepma@dcc.edu
REPP, A. Drew .... 260-399-7700.... 180 E
arepp@sf.edu
REPP, Philip, C .... 765-285-1034.... 169 D
prepp@bsu.edu
REPPERT, Angela .... 610-398-5300.... 434 F
areppert@lincolntech.com
REPPERT, David .... 610-796-8463.... 421 F
david.reppert@alvernia.edu
REPPMANN, Aron .... 708-239-4750.... 165 I
aron.reppmann@trnty.edu
REQUA, Cynthia .... 253-589-5535.... 532 B
cynthia.requa@cptc.edu
RERKO, Renee, L .... 651-603-6318.... 263 C
rerko@csp.edu
RESEBURG, Rhoda .... 503-493-6509.... 415 E
rreseburg@cu-portland.edu
RESETAR, Patrick .... 216-475-7520.... 401 E
RESH-KAMP, Jamie .... 301-387-3742.... 222 H
jamie.reshkamp@garrettcollege.edu
RESIDES, Diane, L .... 443-412-2142.... 223 B
dresides@harford.edu
RESNICK, Coleen .... 508-541-1655.... 234 B
cresnick@dean.edu
RESNIK, Kim .... 770-394-8300.... 124 F
kresnik@aii.edu
RESSLER, Koreen .... 701-854-8001.... 383 A
koreenr@sbci.edu
RESTINE, Nan .... 940-898-2202.... 502 B
lrestine@twu.edu
RESTO-OLIVO, Josephine .. 787-620-2040.... 560 B
jolivo@aupr.edu
RESTO TORRES, Juan .... 787-765-4210.... 561 A
jresto@cempr.edu
RESTUM, John .... 734-207-9581.... 256 B
jrestum@mts.edu
RETALLIC, Whitney .... 617-731-7620.... 244 B
RETCHIN, Sheldon, M .... 804-828-9771.... 525 E
retchin@mcvh-vcu.edu
RETCHLESS, Lindsay .... 814-362-5273.... 449 B
lhr2@pitt.edu
RETELLE, Mary Louise .... 508-849-3333.... 230 C
mretelle@annamaria.edu
RETHANS, Arno .... 530-898-6101...... 34 A
arethans@csuchico.edu
RETIF, Earl .... 504-865-5731.... 215 C
eretif@tulane.edu
RETKA, James .... 218-683-8643.... 268 E
james.retka@northlandcollege.edu
RETTERER, Oscar .... 717-291-4169.... 429 E
oscar.retterer@fandm.edu
RETTIG, Glenn .... 567-429-3563.... 400 H
glenn_rettig@owens.edu
RETTIG, James .... 410-293-6900.... 558 H
RETTIG, Perry, R .... 920-424-1410.... 551 D
rettig@uwosh.edu
RETTLER, Peter, J .... 262-335-5706.... 554 E
prettler@morainepark.edu
RETZAK, Lynn .... 920-693-1282.... 554 A
lynn.retzak@gotoltc.edu
REUSCH, Rita, T .... 801-581-3386.... 510 L
reuschr@law.utah.edu
REUSS, Patricia, B .... 406-657-2168.... 295 F
preuss@msubillings.edu
REUTER, Meg .... 212-431-2345.... 343 E
mreuter@nyls.edu
REUTER, Rocky, J .... 614-236-6226.... 386 C
rreuter@capital.edu
REUTER, Sara .... 541-885-1628.... 418 E
sara.reuter@oit.edu
REUTER, Sarah .... 860-768-5101...... 95 A
reuter@hartford.edu
REUTER, William, D .... 716-851-1700.... 333 B
reuter@ecc.edu
REUTTER, John .... 256-551-3119........ 4 J
john.reutter@drakestate.edu
REVELEY, III, W. Taylor .... 757-221-1693.... 517 J
taylor@wm.edu
REVELL, Leana .... 863-784-7120.... 117 I
leana.revell@southflorida.edu
REVELS, Judith, A .... 910-272-3347.... 373 A
jrevels@robeson.edu
REVELS, Tim, D .... 864-578-8770.... 460 F
trevels@sherman.edu
REVELT, Joseph, E .... 717-871-2390.... 443 C
joseph.revelt@millersville.edu
REVENAUGH, Ken .... 314-392-2356.... 286 C
revenaug@mobap.edu
REVENIS, Anthony .... 301-295-3068.... 558 A
arevenis@usuhs.mil
REVERE, Paul .... 503-493-6512.... 415 E
prevere@cu-portland.edu
REVIERE, Rebecca, L .... 202-806-5326...... 98 B
rreviere@howard.edu
REX, Barbara .... 805-493-3175...... 32 H
rex@clunet.edu
REX, Lisa Youngkin .... 610-330-5060.... 433 B
rexl@lafayette.edu
REX, Michael, G .... 419-995-8301.... 392 L
rex.m@rhodesstate.edu
REXILIUS-TUTHILL, Reiko . 518-327-6319.... 345 H
rtuthill@paulsmiths.edu
REXROAT, Dee, A .... 319-895-4241.... 183 D
drexroat@cornellcollege.edu
REXRODE, Richard, R .... 660-263-3900.... 279 J
rrr@cccb.edu
REY, Michael .... 970-225-4860...... 81 I
michael.rey@collegeamerica.edu
REYER, Otto .... 909-469-5350...... 78 D
oreyer@westernu.edu
REYES, Alicia .... 773-702-8666.... 166 D
areyes1@uchicago.edu
REYES, Angel .... 718-782-2200.... 324 C
areyes@boricuacollege.edu
REYES, Arnaldo .... 787-850-9349.... 567 B
arnaldo.reyes@upr.edu
REYES, Arturo .... 707-864-7000...... 70 A
arturo.reyes@solano.edu
REYES, Elvira .... 617-876-0956.... 236 H
elvira.reyes@longy.edu
REYES, George, R .... 512-223-8007.... 481 B
rey@austincc.edu
REYES, Ginger .... 805-437-8521...... 33 I
ginger.reyes@csuci.edu
REYES, Hector .... 787-894-2828.... 568 A
hector.reyes4@upr.edu
REYES, Jennifer .... 201-447-7456.... 307 F
jreyes@bergen.edu
REYES, Livette .... 787-894-2828.... 568 A
livette.reyes@upr.edu
REYES, Lolita, C .... 671-735-5611.... 559 B
lolita.reyes@guamcc.edu
REYES, Monica, B .... 989-964-7489.... 258 A
mbreyes@svsu.edu
REYES, Ray .... 619-660-4206...... 48 J
ray.reyes@gcccd.edu
REYES, Raymond .... 509-313-3667.... 534 A
reyes@gu.gonzaga.edu
REYES, Robert, G .... 214-860-2090.... 484 I
rreyes@dcccd.edu
REYES-ROSELLO, Rosana .. 845-341-4537.... 345 E
rosana.reyesrosello@sunyorange.edu
REYMANN, Linda .... 443-352-4203.... 226 E
lreymann@stevenson.edu
REYNA, Cynthia .... 870-862-8131...... 23 G
creyna@southark.edu
REYNA, Deirdre .... 956-721-5140.... 489 G
dreyna@laredo.edu
REYNA, Dorotea .... 415-575-6135...... 32 D
dreyna@ciis.edu
REYNA, Farrah .... 318-869-5073.... 208 F
freyna@centenary.edu
REYNA, Janan .... 847-290-7400.... 145 A
jreyna@argosy.edu
REYNA, Marilu, A .... 210-932-6269.... 498 B
mreyna@tamusa.tamus.edu
REYNA, Mario .... 956-872-6116.... 494 D
reyna@southtexascollege.edu
REYNA, Oscar, E .... 956-326-2468.... 497 B
oreyna@tamiu.edu
REYNA, Roberto .... 978-368-2371.... 230 F
roberto.reyna@auc.edu
REYNA, Tony .... 713-942-5920.... 504 D
reynat@stthom.edu
REYNA, Yolanda .... 210-486-3333.... 479 D
yreyna@alamo.edu
REYNARD, Betty .... 409-839-2048.... 500 E
bjreynard@lit.edu
REYNDERS, John, C .... 712-274-5100.... 187 D
reynders@morningside.edu
REYNOLDS, Angela .... 479-968-0396...... 20 G
areynolds@atu.edu
REYNOLDS, Angela .... 330-337-6403.... 383 H
areynolds@awc.edu
REYNOLDS, Anne .... 478-445-5331.... 129 F
anne.reynolds@gcsu.edu
REYNOLDS, Brad .... 706-865-2134.... 138 A
breynolds@truett.edu
REYNOLDS, Brent .... 573-288-6420.... 281 D
breynolds@culver.edu
REYNOLDS, Carolyn, H ...... 276-523-2400.... 527 A
creynolds@me.vccs.edu
REYNOLDS, Colleen .... 309-268-8188.... 151 G
colleen.reynolds@heartland.edu
REYNOLDS, Curtis, A .... 352-392-1141.... 120 B
curtrey@ufl.edu
REYNOLDS, Cynthia .... 847-318-8550.... 160 C
careynolds@nc.edu
REYNOLDS, Dean, S .... 317-931-4226.... 170 E
dreynolds@cts.edu
REYNOLDS, Debra .... 860-738-6309...... 90 F
dreynolds@nwcc.commnet.edu
REYNOLDS, Diane, L .... 804-828-3430.... 525 E
dlreynol@vcu.edu
REYNOLDS, Don .... 334-386-7240........ 3 H
dreynolds2@faulkner.edu
REYNOLDS, Eleanor, L .... 248-370-3364.... 257 C
reynolds@oakland.edu
REYNOLDS, Elizabeth, P ..... 304-293-4245.... 544 E
liz.reynolds@mail.wvu.edu
REYNOLDS, Ellen .... 914-395-2329.... 350 C
REYNOLDS, Gail .... 740-374-8716.... 405 F
greynolds@wscc.edu
REYNOLDS, Gary .... 719-255-3505...... 88 C
greynold@uccs.edu
REYNOLDS, Glenn .... 757-826-1883.... 516 H
REYNOLDS, Holly .... 770-718-5314.... 126 B
hreynolds@brenau.edu
REYNOLDS, Jack .... 706-272-4456.... 127 G
jreynolds@daltonstate.edu
REYNOLDS, James .... 708-456-0300.... 166 C
jreyno11@triton.edu
REYNOLDS, James, M .... 937-383-8503.... 405 H
jim_reynolds@wilmington.edu
REYNOLDS, Jeff .... 970-339-6484...... 80 G
jeff.reynolds@aims.edu
REYNOLDS, John, C .... 626-815-3887...... 30 E
jreynolds@apu.edu
REYNOLDS, Judith .... 719-389-6384...... 81 L
jreynolds@coloradocollege.edu
REYNOLDS, Judith, L .... 617-573-8302.... 245 E
jreynolds@suffolk.edu
REYNOLDS, Karen .... 802-773-5900.... 513 B
kreynolds@csj.edu
REYNOLDS, Kay .... 978-665-3140.... 238 C
kay.reynolds@fitchburgstate.edu
REYNOLDS, Kevin .... 503-725-3886.... 418 G
reynoldsk@pdx.edu
REYNOLDS, Kevin, W .... 330-941-2742.... 406 F
kwreynolds@ysu.edu
REYNOLDS, Kimberly .... 785-243-1435.... 191 H
kreynolds@cloud.edu
REYNOLDS, Lana .... 405-382-9218.... 412 B
l.reynolds@sscok.edu
REYNOLDS, Larry .... 920-923-8132.... 548 C
lreynolds@marianuniversity.edu
REYNOLDS, Linda .... 859-572-5208.... 205 E
reynoldsl@nku.edu
REYNOLDS, Liz .... 914-594-4229.... 343 F
nymc@bkstr.com
REYNOLDS, Lois .... 865-694-6693.... 475 F
lreynolds@pstcc.edu
REYNOLDS, Lois, G .... 865-694-6523.... 475 F
lreynolds@pstcc.edu
REYNOLDS, Mary .... 630-753-9087.... 160 C
mreynolds@nc.edu
REYNOLDS, Michael, C ...... 334-844-4367........ 1 G
reynom2@auburn.edu
REYNOLDS, Nancy, W .... 270-686-4244.... 198 G
nancy.reynolds@brescia.edu
REYNOLDS, Norman .... 812-749-1272.... 178 D
nreynolds@oak.edu
REYNOLDS, Patrick, D .... 315-859-4607.... 335 A
preynold@hamilton.edu
REYNOLDS, Patsy .... 618-536-4405.... 164 I
pradmit@siu.edu
REYNOLDS, Randall .... 615-460-6443.... 467 B
randall.reynolds@belmont.edu
REYNOLDS, Richard .... 617-627-3334.... 245 F
dick.reynolds@tufts.edu
REYNOLDS, Richard, E .... 614-823-3529.... 400 G
rreynolds@otterbein.edu
REYNOLDS, Roger .... 910-576-6222.... 372 A
reynoldsr@montgomery.edu
REYNOLDS, Ross .... 651-905-3469.... 261 J
rreynolds@browncollege.edu
REYNOLDS, Scott .... 615-226-3990.... 471 I
sreynolds@nadcedu.com
REYNOLDS, Sean, B .... 847-491-3741.... 160 D
sean.reynolds@northwestern.edu
REYNOLDS, Sharon, P .... 336-633-0234.... 372 F
spreynolds@randolph.edu
REYNOLDS, Stephanie, C .. 315-792-5456.... 341 E
sreynolds@mvcc.edu
REYNOLDS, Steve .... 480-245-7960...... 14 K
steve.reynolds@lbconline.edu
REYNOLDS, Thomas, E .... 303-458-4087...... 87 E
treynold@regis.edu
REYNOLDS, Thomas, L .... 704-687-7248.... 378 E
tlreynol@uncc.edu
REYNOLDS, Todd, A .... 618-537-6857.... 157 G
treynold@mckendree.edu
REYNOLDS, Virginia .... 916-691-7359...... 56 B
mcreyng@crc.losrios.edu
REYNOLDS, Wally .... 815-455-8547.... 157 F
wreynold@mchenry.edu
REYNOLDS, Wanda, L .... 509-313-3583.... 534 A
reynolds@gu.gonzaga.edu
REYNOLDS, William, D .... 616-395-7748.... 252 F
reynold@hope.edu
REYNOLDS, William, F .... 973-596-3004.... 312 C
william.reynolds@njit.edu
REYNOLDS, William, G .... 202-687-2461...... 98 A
wgr2@georgetown.edu
REYNOLDS, JR.,
William, H .... 860-297-2355...... 94 C
william.reynolds@trincoll.edu
REYNOLDS, Yoke San, L .... 434-924-0716.... 525 B
ysr4n@virginia.edu
REYNVAAN, Debbie .... 360-538-4101.... 534 B
dreynvaa@ghc.edu
REZAC, Ken .... 402-461-2503.... 297 C
krezac@cccneb.edu
REZAI, Saeed .... 801-832-2527.... 512 F
srezai@westminstercollege.edu
REZNIK, Inna .... 516-572-7637.... 342 C
inna.reznik@ncc.edu
RHAME, Pamela .... 912-525-5100.... 136 B
prhame@scad.edu
RHAMES, Ronald .... 803-822-3261.... 459 D
rhamesr@midlandstech.edu
RHEA, Jessica .... 239-590-7016.... 119 A
jrhea@fgcu.edu
RHEA, Mitchell .... 423-478-6231.... 474 E
MRhea01@clevelandstatecc.edu
RHEA, Teresa, R .... 256-549-8230........ 3 J
trhea@gadsdenstate.edu
RHEAD, Lori .... 608-363-2630.... 546 B
rheadl@beloit.edu
RHEAULT, Wendy .... 847-578-8805.... 163 A
wendy.rheault@rosalindfranklin.edu
RHEAUME, Steve .... 603-535-2266.... 307 B
srheaume@plymouth.edu
RHEE, Anthony .... 334-241-9703........ 8 B
arhee@troy.edu
RHEIN, John .... 610-430-4163.... 443 F
jrhein@wcupa.edu
RHEINSCHMIDT,
Richard, E .... 319-399-8643.... 183 C
rrheinsc@coe.edu
RHEW, Steven, W .... 336-334-5806.... 379 A
steve_rhew@uncg.edu

RHI-KLEINERT, Susan 818-364-7778 55 A
Rhiks@lamission.edu
RHIM, Choonhee, L 323-265-8625 54 G
rhimcl@elac.edu
RHIMES, Ilee 213-740-7197 76 C
irhimes@usc.edu
RHINE, Lisa 859-572-6447 205 E
rhinel1@nku.edu
RHINE, Marjorie 262-472-1268 552 E
rhinem@uww.edu
RHINE, Randy 308-432-6231 299 G
rrhine@csc.edu
RHINEHARDT, Kimrey 919-843-0381 377 A
kwr@northcarolina.edu
RHINEHART, Erna 208-769-3315 143 H
erna_rhinehart@nic.edu
RHINEHART, Leslie, L 814-362-7658 449 B
llr5@pitt.edu
RHINEHART, Marilyn 913-469-8500 193 I
marilynr@jccc.edu
RHOADES, Andy 512-245-3459 501 C
sr20@txstate.edu
RHOADES, IV, Mack, B 713-743-9370 503 B
mrhoades@uh.edu
RHOADES, Margot 301-447-5215 225 A
margot_rhoades@msmary.edu
RHOADES, Richard, G 256-824-6343 9 A
richard.rhoades@uah.edu
RHOADES, Samuel, T 804-257-5811 529 D
strhoades@aol.com
RHOADES, Valerie 719-346-9300 86 A
valerie.rhoades@morgancc.edu
RHOADES WILLIAMS,
Castine 706-821-8311 135 C
crhoades@paine.edu
RHOADS, Bill 620-768-2909 192 G
billr@fortscott.edu
RHOADS, George 732-235-9700 317 A
rhoads@umdnj.edu
RHOADS, Jeff 928-717-7679 19 E
jeff.rhoads@yc.edu
RHOADS, Judith, L 270-824-8562 202 C
judithl.rhoads@kctcs.edu
RHOADS, Kay, M 803-934-3255 459 F
krhoads@morris.edu
RHOADS, Linden 206-543-0905 538 F
lrhoads@uw.edu
RHOADS, Michael 802-839-8317 513 H
michael.rhoads@neci.edu
RHOADS, Sandy 618-536-7751 164 I
srhoads@siu.edu
RHODA, Christopher 207-859-1124 219 G
chris@thomas.edu
RHODA, Karen 248-689-8282 260 A
krhoda@walshcollege.edu
RHODARMER, Melanie 828-251-6700 378 C
mrhodarm@unca.edu
RHODE, Carolyn 336-506-4128 367 G
carolyn.rhode@alamancecc.edu
RHODE, Charles, G 404-894-4114 130 D
chuck.rhode@facilities.gatech.edu
RHODEN, Brenda 256-761-6204 7 H
brhoden@talladega.edu
RHODEN, Deborah 256-840-4137 7 B
drhoden@snead.edu
RHODEN, Joyce 334-727-8011 8 C
jrhoden@tuskegee.edu
RHODEN, Laura 336-744-0900 362 H
laura@carolina.edu
RHODEN, Richard, R 337-475-5887 215 G
rrhoden@mcneese.edu
RHODES, Anthony, P 212-592-2000 350 F
arhodes@sva.edu
RHODES, Ashley 713-777-4433 508 I
arhodes@westwood.edu
RHODES, Benjamin, J 309-556-3710 153 E
brhodes@iwu.edu
RHODES, Carla 706-880-8240 132 I
crhodes@lagrange.edu
RHODES, Carol, C 302-739-4060 96 A
crhodes1@dtcc.edu
RHODES, Chuck 707-664-4033 37 B
chuck.rhodes@sonoma.edu
RHODES, David 318-371-3035 211 F
drhodes@ltc.edu
RHODES, David, J 251-578-1313 6 E
jrhodes@rstc.edu
RHODES, David, J 212-592-2000 350 F
drhodes@sva.edu
RHODES, David, J 740-376-4503 395 F
david.rhodes@marietta.edu
RHODES, Dawn, M 317-274-4511 174 B
dawnrhod@iupui.edu
RHODES, Edward 703-993-4180 519 A
edrhodes@gmu.edu
RHODES, Fred, W 502-272-8150 198 E
frhodes@bellarmine.edu
RHODES, Gale 502-852-5727 207 A
gale.rhodes@louisville.edu
RHODES, Gary, L 804-523-5200 526 F
grhodes@reynolds.edu
RHODES, Jack, W 843-953-3708 456 C
jack.rhodes@citadel.edu
RHODES, Jim 828-694-1839 368 B
jimr@blueridge.edu
RHODES, John 410-225-2201 224 C
jrhodes@mica.edu
RHODES, Kaia 916-789-8600 49 L
kaia_rhodes@heald.edu
RHODES, Kathy 360-596-5240 538 B
krhodes@spscc.ctc.edu
RHODES, Kay 806-742-5170 501 D
kay.rhodes@ttu.edu
RHODES, Lawrence 212-799-5000 337 H
RHODES, Lisa, D 404-270-5728 137 E
lrhodes@spelman.edu
RHODES, Marlene 314-644-9245 289 C
mrhodes@stlcc.edu
RHODES, Michelle 616-331-3234 252 A
rhodesmi@gvsu.edu
RHODES, Phil 281-649-3417 487 F
prhodes@hbu.edu
RHODES, Robert 575-492-2640 319 B
rrhodes@nmjc.edu
RHODES, Ruth 312-225-6288 167 E
rrhodes@vandercook.edu
RHODES, Scott 352-588-8283 116 E
scott.rhodes02@saintleo.edu
RHODES, Simon 317-274-7211 174 B
srhodes@iupui.edu
RHODES, Tammy 479-968-0272 20 G
trhodes@atu.edu
RHODES, Tiffany 510-276-3888 38 E
trhodes@cc.edu
RHODES, Vincent, A 757-446-7070 518 F
rhodesva@evms.edu
RHOLES, Julia 662-915-7092 277 G
jrholes1@olemiss.edu
RHONE, Henry, G 804-828-1244 525 E
hgrhone@vcu.edu
RHOR, William 603-887-7438 303 G
physical_plant@chestercollege.edu
RHOTEN, Darrell 305-386-9900 105 E
drhoten@cci.edu
RHOTON, James, M 843-863-7050 456 B
jrhoton@csuniv.edu
RHOTON, Patrick, L 740-392-6868 396 H
prhoton@mvnu.edu
RHUE, Monika 704-371-6741 365 H
mrhue@jcsu.edu
RHUEMS, Ken 417-455-5596 281 C
krhuems@crowder.edu
RHYNE, Sandra 803-754-4100 457 D
RHYNE, Teresa, L 757-455-3345 529 F
trhyne@vwc.edu
RHYNEER, Madeleine 503-370-6021 421 C
mrhyneer@willamette.edu
RHYNER, Jennifer 262-554-2010 158 D
midwestcollegefa@aol.com
RHYNER, Jennifer, L 262-554-2010 548 F
mwcfinancialaid@aol.com
RHYNS, Ukeyco 773-602-5016 147 B
urhyns@ccc.edu
RIAL, Scott 847-543-2652 147 H
srial@clcillinois.edu
RIAS, Curtis 212-650-7073 326 H
curtis@ccny.cuny.edu
RIAT, Douglas, A 785-864-4036 196 F
driat@ku.edu
RIBAKOW, Larry 410-484-7200 225 C
RIBAR, Tom 724-852-3302 451 B
tribar@waynesburg.edu
RIBARICH, Marie 914-654-5320 330 B
mribarich@cnr.edu
RIBEAU, Sidney 202-806-2500 98 B
sidney.ribeau@howard.edu
RIBERDY, Michelle 413-552-2547 240 C
mriberdy@hcc.edu
RIBICH, Fred, D 319-352-8320 189 F
fred.ribich@wartburg.edu
RIBICH, Fred, D 319-352-8284 189 F
fred.ribich@wartburg.edu
RIBNIK, Emily 330-499-9600 393 I
eribnik@kent.edu
RIBORDY, J. Clark 785-242-5200 195 F
clark.ribordy@ottawa.edu
RIBORDY, J. Clark 785-242-5200 195 G
RIBORDY, J. Clark 785-242-5200 178 E
RIBORDY, J. Clark 785-242-5200 17 C
RIBORDY, J. Clark 785-242-5200 549 E
RICATTO, Pascal, J 201-493-3572 307 F
pjricatto@bergen.edu
RICCA, Beth 201-684-7455 313 D
bricca@ramapo.edu
RICCARDI, Andy 215-204-7939 447 G
ariccard@temple.edu
RICCARDI, JR., Louis, D 415-442-7224 48 E
lriccardi@ggu.edu
RICCARDI, Richard 203-392-5232 91 I
riccardir1@southernct.edu
RICCARDI, Valerie 610-892-1511 441 C
vriccardi@pit.edu
RICCI, Jose, L 787-728-1515 568 B
jricci@sagrado.edu
RICCI, Jose, L 787-727-7727 568 B
jricci@sagrado.edu
RICCIARDI, Julie, E 919-508-2362 375 D
jricciardi@peace.edu
RICCIO, JudyAnn 203-365-4899 93 G
riccioj@sacredheart.edu
RICCIO, Richard, A 201-692-7050 310 B
riccio@fdu.edu
RICE, Adrian 212-824-2220 391 E
arice@huc.edu
RICE, Ann 803-584-3446 462 E
annerice@mailbox.sc.edu
RICE, Ann, M 916-734-0751 73 F
ann.rice@ucdmc.ucdavis.edu
RICE, Carnellia, N 910-362-7065 368 E
crice@cfcc.edu
RICE, Charles, L 301-295-3013 558 A
crice@usuhs.edu
RICE, Cheryl 330-494-6170 402 A
crice@starkstate.edu
RICE, Cheryl, A 678-836-6280 138 D
crice@westga.edu
RICE, Clementine 810-766-4192 248 H
clementine.rice@baker.edu
RICE, Cynthia, E 410-706-3171 227 C
crice@umaryland.edu
RICE, Dan 701-777-2674 381 D
dan.rice@email.und.edu
RICE, Daniel, B 785-628-4260 192 F
drice@fhsu.edu
RICE, Debi 253-752-2020 533 J
financialaid@faithseminary.edu
RICE, Denise 434-848-6447 523 G
drice@saintpauls.edu
RICE, Dennis 925-631-4794 64 F
drice@stmarys-ca.edu
RICE, Donald 202-885-8694 100 A
drice@wesleyseminary.edu
RICE, Donna 918-465-1814 408 A
drice@eosc.edu
RICE, Donnie 256-352-8041 10 B
donnie.rice@wallacestate.edu
RICE, Edward 662-246-6442 275 F
erice@msdelta.edu
RICE, Elaine, K 610-785-6216 446 A
financeopsscs@adphila.org
RICE, Eric, L 253-752-2020 533 J
deanofstudents@faithseminary.edu
RICE, Gary 907-786-1544 10 I
angar@uaa.alaska.edu
RICE, Heather 256-228-6001 6 A
riceh@nacc.edu
RICE, Howard, T 270-809-2535 204 F
hal.rice@murraystate.edu
RICE, James, P 570-577-3655 423 D
rice@bucknell.edu
RICE, James, W 320-222-7474 268 I
jim.rice@ridgewater.edu
RICE, Jodie 213-381-3333 53 C
jrice@lac.edu
RICE, John 775-753-2260 302 H
johnr@gwmail.gbcnv.edu
RICE, Jonah 618-252-5400 164 G
jonah.rice@sic.edu
RICE, Larry 305-892-5366 111 K
larry.rice@jwu.edu
RICE, Larry, D 918-343-7612 411 H
lrice@rsu.edu
RICE, Leo 617-349-8598 236 G
lrice@lesley.edu
RICE, Linda 757-822-5201 528 C
lrice@tcc.edu
RICE, Malcolm 256-824-6347 9 A
malcom.rice@uah.edu
RICE, Margaret 718-960-4992 327 C
margaret.rice@lehman.cuny.edu
RICE, Margaret, H 361-570-4145 503 E
ricem@uhv.edu
RICE, Mark, P 218-477-2062 268 A
ricem@mnstate.edu
RICE, Michele 814-262-6447 441 A
mrice@pennhighlands.edu
RICE, Nathan 806-743-3238 501 E
nathan.rice@ttuhsc.edu
RICE, Patrick 305-809-3228 108 F
patrick.rice@fkcc.edu
RICE, Peggy 815-836-5350 156 D
ricepe@lewisu.edu
RICE, Peter 201-684-7601 313 D
price@ramapo.edu
RICE, Priscilla 215-968-8450 423 E
ricep@bucks.edu
RICE, Prudence, M 618-453-4540 164 I
price@siu.edu
RICE, Rachel 207-768-9447 220 F
rachel.rice@umpi.edu
RICE, Sabra, L 336-249-8186 369 F
slrice@davidsonccc.edu
RICE, Sammie 313-496-2771 260 C
srice1@wcccd.edu
RICE, Scott 217-333-0560 167 B
serice@uillinois.edu
RICE, Sharyn 978-632-6600 240 G
s_rice@mwcc.mass.edu
RICE, Sherwin 910-879-5646 368 A
srice@bladencc.edu
RICE, Stephen, C 301-295-3896 558 A
srice@usuhs.mil
RICE, Stuart, A 773-834-2493 165 G
sarice@ttic.edu
RICE, Susan, I 336-633-0282 372 F
sirice@randolph.edu
RICE, Tammy 949-582-4701 70 F
trice@saddleback.edu
RICE, Teresa 337-269-0620 207 F
teresar@bluecliffcollege.com
RICE, Thomas 310-206-9345 74 A
trice@conet.ucla.edu
RICE, Thomas, M 712-274-5222 187 D
rice@morningside.edu
RICE, Thomas, W 319-335-0256 182 C
tom-rice@uiowa.edu
RICE-CLAYBORN, Kathy 501-450-3134 25 H
kathyc@uca.edu
RICE-EVANS, Marla, D 910-962-7055 379 C
riceevansm@uncw.edu
RICE MCADAMS, Beverly 864-231-2075 455 C
bmcadams@andersonuniversity.edu
RICH, Arthur 402-457-2681 298 H
aarich@mccneb.edu
RICH, Jack, W 325-674-2013 478 H
richj@acu.edu
RICH, Jeffrey 218-723-6112 262 I
jrich4@css.edu
RICH, Jim 309-341-5296 146 A
jrich@sandburg.edu
RICH, John 860-885-2326 91 B
jrich@trcc.commnet.edu
RICH, Kathy 781-280-3501 240 F
richk@middlesex.mass.edu
RICH, Laura 910-893-4364 362 F
richl@campbell.edu
RICH, Martha 315-279-5368 337 K
mrich@mail.keuka.edu
RICH, Mary, L 203-576-5756 94 A
mrich@stvincentscollege.edu
RICH, Melanie, M 315-464-6548 352 E
richm@upstate.edu
RICH, Scott 620-278-4294 196 D
srich@sterling.edu
RICH, Steven 617-236-8800 235 B
srich@fisher.edu
RICH, Steven, W 217-581-6616 150 C
swrich@eiu.edu
RICH, Tammy 570-484-2128 443 A
trich@lhup.edu
RICH, Timothy, A 651-631-5489 270 E
tarich@nwc.edu
RICH-COATES, Robin 757-789-1748 526 D
rrich-coates@es.vccs.edu
RICHARD, Christine, G 201-291-1111 307 G
cgr@berkeleycollege.edu
RICHARD, Christine, G 201-291-1111 323 J
cgr@berkeleycollege.edu
RICHARD, Delores 662-621-4205 273 I
drichard@coahomacc.edu
RICHARD, M.S.,
Edward, J 314-792-6107 283 K
richard@kenrick.edu
RICHARD, Ellen 415-439-2309 28 C
erichard@act-sf.org
RICHARD, Francis, D 904-620-2700 120 C
drichard@unf.edu
RICHARD, George 440-826-2325 384 H
grichard@bw.edu
RICHARD, J. Randall 330-745-5008 397 C
jrr1@neoucom.edu
RICHARD, Mark 256-840-4110 7 B
mrichard@snead.edu
RICHARD, Mark 814-871-7763 429 F
richard004@gannon.edu
RICHARD, Matasar, A 212-431-2840 343 E
rmatasar@nyls.edu
RICHARD, Robert 337-482-6923 216 D
bookstore@louisiana.edu
RICHARD, Roseann 707-654-1175 32 I
rrichard@csum.edu
RICHARD, Ryan 318-255-7950 215 F
ryan@latechalumni.org
RICHARD, Thomas 603-358-2326 307 A
trichard@keene.edu
RICHARD, Thomas, J 207-768-2795 218 J
trichard@nmcc.edu
RICHARD, Valerie 704-403-3507 362 E
valerie.richard@carolinashealthcare.org
RICHARDELLO, Denise 413-662-5201 238 F
denise.richardello@mcla.edu
RICHARDI, Rocco 508-588-9100 240 E
RICHARDS, Calvin, R 214-860-2232 484 I
crichards@dcccd.edu
RICHARDS, Char 262-524-6891 546 E
crichard@carrollu.edu
RICHARDS, Charlie 262-646-6528 549 B
crichards@nashotah.edu
RICHARDS, Connie, L 229-333-5699 138 F
clrichards@valdosta.edu
RICHARDS, David 626-584-5458 48 A
finaid-assocdir@dept.fuller.edu
RICHARDS, David, G 208-496-3524 142 G
richardsd@byui.edu
RICHARDS, David, J 517-321-0242 252 B
drichards@glcc.edu

RIDGE, Sean ... 865-573-4517 .... 469 J
sridge@johnsonU.edu

RIDGEDELL, Ken, W ... 985-549-2121 .... 216 C
kridgedell@selu.edu

RIDGELL, Reilly, A ... 671-735-5530 .... 559 B
deansoffice@guamcc.edu

RIDGELY, Barbara, S ... 302-739-4622 .... 96 A
bridgely@dtcc.edu

RIDGELY, Glenda ... 864-388-8305 .... 458 J
gridgely@lander.edu

RIDGEWAY, Larry ... 662-915-5050 .... 277 G
lridgewa@olemiss.edu

RIDGLE, Saadia ... 601-928-6225 .... 275 G
saadia.ridgle@mgccc.edu

RIDGWAY, Dan ... 216-649-8900 .... 398 E
dridgway@ocpm.edu

RIDGWAY, Susan, M ... 989-837-4219 .... 257 A
ridgway@northwood.edu

RIDINGS, Maureen ... 508-541-1656 .... 234 B
mridings@dean.edu

RIDINGTON, M. Thomas ... 610-341-4377 .... 428 D
tridingt@eastern.edu

RIDLEY, Carolyn, L ... 859-858-3511 .... 198 B
carolyn.ridley@asbury.edu

RIDLEY, Emmett, L ... 804-524-5068 .... 529 C
eridley@vsu.edu

RIDLEY, Scott ... 806-742-1988 .... 501 D
scott.ridley@ttu.edu

RIDLEY, JR., Wadell ... 610-660-1223 .... 446 C
wridley@sju.edu

RIDLON, Walter ... 207-755-5409 .... 218 G
wridlon@cmcc.edu

RIDOUT, Thomas, M ... 563-562-3263 .... 187 G
ridoutt@nicc.edu

RIDPATH, Amy ... 540-374-4300 .... 99 D

RIEBENACK, Kristen, R ... 260-399-7700 .... 180 E
kriebenack@sf.edu

RIECK, Ray ... 217-234-5224 .... 155 H
rrieck@lakeland.cc.il.us

RIEDEL, Eric ... 612-312-2393 .... 272 F
eric.riedel@waldenu.edu

RIEDEL, Eric, R ... 330-569-5240 .... 391 H
riedeler@hiram.edu

RIEDEL, Herbert, H ... 334-222-6591 .... 5 F
hriedel@lbwcc.edu

RIEDER, Richard ... 217-420-6029 .... 158 F
rrieder@millikin.edu

RIEDER, JR., Robert, W ... 256-824-6633 .... 9 A
riederr@uah.edu

RIEDINGER, Jeffrey, M ... 517-355-2352 .... 255 D
ispdean@msu.edu

RIEDINGER, Kirk ... 303-691-5700 .... 89 D

RIEDY, Joshua ... 701-777-2661 .... 381 D
joshua.riedy@email.und.edu

RIEDY, Joshua ... 701-777-4237 .... 381 D
joshua.riedy@email.und.edu

RIEFKOHL, Jorge ... 787-780-0070 .... 560 F
jriefkohl@caribbean.edu

RIEGELNEGG, F. Dennis ... 219-866-6157 .... 179 B
fdr@saintjoe.edu

RIEGLE, Nancy ... 202-639-1763 .... 97 D

RIEHL, Gretchen, K ... 972-860-7140 .... 484 H
GRiehl@dcccd.edu

RIEHL, Shelle ... 360-438-4463 .... 536 F
rshahanriehl@stmartin.edu

RIEHS, Steven ... 630-515-7702 .... 149 A
sriehs@devry.edu

RIEKEMAN, Guy, F ... 770-426-2601 .... 133 B
riekeman@life.edu

RIEL, Paul ... 904-620-4663 .... 120 C
priel@unf.edu

RIELLY, Kevin, B ... 518-743-2335 .... 322 B
riellyk@sunyacc.edu

RIEMAN, Barbara, M ... 716-851-1421 .... 333 C
rieman@ecc.edu

RIENDEAU, Russ ... 312-261-3200 .... 159 D

RIENZI, Beth ... 661-654-6324 .... 33 H
brienzi@csub.edu

RIEPMA, Edward ... 949-794-9090 .... 71 E
eriepma@stanbridge.edu

RIES, Barry ... 507-389-2321 .... 267 H
barry.ries@mnsu.edu

RIES, Cheryl ... 906-487-7317 .... 251 C
cheryl.ries@finlandia.edu

RIES, Heidi, R ... 937-255-3633 .... 556 H
heidi.ries@afit.edu

RIES, Karen ... 641-423-2530 .... 186 F
revans@kaplan.edu

RIES, Kenneth ... 320-629-5195 .... 268 G
riesk@pinetech.edu

RIES, Suzanne ... 662-241-7494 .... 276 B
sries@ss.muw.edu

RIES, Thomas Karl ... 651-641-8211 .... 263 C
ries@csp.edu

RIESENBERG, Carol ... 509-533-7075 .... 532 D
criesenberg@spokanefalls.edu

RIESENBERG, Carol ... 509-533-7075 .... 532 E
criesenberg@scc.spokane.edu

RIESGO, Andrea ... 760-366-5285 .... 43 E
ariesgo@cmccd.edu

RIESSLAND, Larry ... 308-865-8524 .... 300 G
riesslandl@unk.edu

RIESTER, Jon ... 812-866-7021 .... 171 F
riester@hanover.edu

RIESTER, Leslie ... 503-977-8288 .... 419 G
lriester@pcc.edu

RIESTRA, Miguel ... 787-622-8000 .... 115 B
mriestra@pupr.edu

RIESTRA, Miguel, A ... 787-622-8000 .... 566 C
mriestra@pupr.edu

RIETKERK, Kristen ... 910-221-2224 .... 364 C

RIFFE, Angie ... 304-253-7351 .... 541 D
ariffe@mountainstate.edu

RIFFE, Cindy ... 918-335-6842 .... 411 B
criffe@okwu.edu

RIFFE, Denver ... 304-487-3845 .... 541 E
driffe@educorp.edu

RIFFE, Mike ... 229-209-5270 .... 124 C
mikeriffe@andrewcollege.edu

RIFFE, Tony ... 304-425-2323 .... 541 K

RIFFEE, William, H ... 352-273-6309 .... 120 B
riffee@cop.ufl.edu

RIFFEL, Beth ... 620-947-3121 .... 196 E
bethr@tabor.edu

RIFFEY, Candy ... 701-323-8623 .... 381 B
criffey@mohs.org

RIFFLE, Robert ... 562-860-2451 .... 38 J
rriffle@cerritos.edu

RIFKIN, Benjamin ... 609-771-2277 .... 308 G
rifkin@tcnj.edu

RIGBY, Heather ... 248-476-1122 .... 255 C
hrigby@mispp.edu

RIGEL, Bill ... 863-638-7243 .... 123 B
bill.rigel@warner.edu

RIGG, Jenny ... 307-778-4326 .... 556 B
jrigg@lccc.wy.edu

RIGGERT, Mark ... 402-557-7070 .... 297 A
bubookstore@fheg.follett.com

RIGGINS, David, W ... 828-689-1219 .... 366 F
driggins@mhc.edu

RIGGINS, Lana ... 919-546-8598 .... 376 D
lriggins@shawu.edu

RIGGINS, Shawn ... 816-364-5399 .... 292 G
shawn.riggins@vatterott-college.edu

RIGGLE, Elise ... 419-755-4313 .... 397 B
riggle.17@osu.edu

RIGGLE, Priscilla ... 660-785-7777 .... 291 A
priggle@truman.edu

RIGGLEMAN, John, S ... 517-750-1200 .... 258 F
srigglem@arbor.edu

RIGGLEMAN, Tim ... 304-434-8000 .... 542 E
torigglem@eastern.wvnet.edu

RIGGS, Allen ... 435-283-7125 .... 512 B
allen.riggs@snow.edu

RIGGS, Becky ... 870-862-8131 .... 23 G
briggs@southark.edu

RIGGS, Channing ... 612-624-6868 .... 272 D
riggs035@umn.edu

RIGGS, David ... 765-677-2808 .... 174 E
david.riggs@indwes.edu

RIGGS, Jim ... 417-455-5466 .... 281 C
jriggs@crowder.edu

RIGGS, John ... 405-208-7909 .... 410 A
jriggs@okcu.edu

RIGGS, Joyce ... 270-824-8581 .... 202 C
joyce.riggs@kctcs.edu

RIGGS, M. Peggy ... 516-299-4206 .... 338 F
peggy.riggs@liu.edu

RIGGS, Maria ... 718-482-5040 .... 328 C
mariarig@lagcc.cuny.edu

RIGGS, Robert, F ... 214-841-3617 .... 485 E
rriggs@dts.edu

RIGNEY, Doug ... 205-934-5493 .... 8 G
drigney@uab.edu

RIGNEY, Jack ... 330-941-1909 .... 406 F
jprigney@ysu.edu

RIGNEY, Margaret ... 918-463-2931 .... 407 H
mrigney@connorsstate.edu

RIGSBEE, Craig ... 530-895-2521 .... 31 E
rigsbeecr@butte.edu

RIGSBEE, David ... 217-641-4533 .... 154 G
drigsbee@jwcc.edu

RIGSBY, Dave ... 503-370-6217 .... 421 C
drigsby@willamette.edu

RIGSBY, Ellen, M ... 309-467-6311 .... 150 H
eraid@eureka.edu

RIHACEK, Robin ... 708-210-5754 .... 164 F
rrihacek@ssc.edu

RIHL-LEWINSKY, Elizabeth ... 215-572-2956 .... 422 B
rihll@arcadia.edu

RIIS, Janet ... 406-447-5423 .... 294 A
jriis@carroll.edu

RIKEL, Randy ... 903-223-3005 .... 498 C
randy.rikel@tamut.edu

RIKER, Dave ... 210-458-4263 .... 506 B
dave.riker@utsa.edu

RILES, Warren ... 912-478-5197 .... 131 A
rileswl@georgiasouthern.edu

RILEY, Anthony, G ... 806-894-9611 .... 494 C
triley@southplainscollege.edu

RILEY, Bruce ... 608-785-8218 .... 551 B
riley.bruc@uwlax.edu

RILEY, Carla ... 320-589-6066 .... 272 C
rileycj@morris.umn.edu

RILEY, Christine ... 828-251-6500 .... 378 C
criley@unca.edu

RILEY, Doreen, K ... 216-397-4345 .... 392 M
driley@jcu.edu

RILEY, Edward ... 617-254-2610 .... 244 E

RILEY, Eileen ... 412-809-5100 .... 444 F
riley@pti.edu

RILEY, Elaine ... 254-526-1106 .... 482 F
elaine.riley@ctcd.edu

RILEY, Francis, D ... 617-495-1780 .... 235 H
francis_riley@harvard.edu

RILEY, George, F ... 610-519-7715 .... 450 G
george.riley@villanova.edu

RILEY, Jamie, R ... 434-395-2394 .... 520 G
rileyjr@longwood.edu

RILEY, Jeannette, E ... 508-999-8279 .... 237 E
j1riley@umassd.edu

RILEY, Jill ... 732-987-2228 .... 310 D
riley@georgian.edu

RILEY, Ken ... 432-685-4569 .... 490 G
kriley@midland.edu

RILEY, Kimberly ... 816-604-4523 .... 285 I
kim.riley@mcckc.edu

RILEY, Mark ... 870-584-4471 .... 25 C
mriley@cccua.edu

RILEY, P. Thomas ... 703-654-1040 .... 524 H
priley@umw.edu

RILEY, Patrick ... 440-684-6022 .... 405 B
priley@ursuline.edu

RILEY, Robert, A ... 717-867-6202 .... 434 C
riley@lvc.edu

RILEY, Robert, K ... 253-535-7119 .... 535 K
rileyrk@plu.edu

RILEY, Ryan, T ... 717-901-5140 .... 430 F
rriley@harrisburgu.edu

RILEY, Sabrina ... 402-486-2514 .... 300 D
sariley@ucollege.edu

RILEY, Sarah ... 900-652-6176 .... 39 B
sarah.riley@chaffey.edu

RILEY, Scott, T ... 218-285-2205 .... 268 H
sriley@rrcc.mnscu.edu

RILEY, Susan ... 513-732-5324 .... 403 E
rileysu@email.uc.edu

RILEY, Tammy ... 606-478-7200 .... 205 C
tmriley@national-college.edu

RILEY, Tisa, R ... 717-221-1300 .... 430 E
trriley@hacc.edu

RILEY, Toni ... 301-431-5410 .... 225 B
triley@nlc.edu

RILEY, Vicki ... 304-214-8857 .... 543 A
vriley@wvncc.edu

RILEY, Wayne, J ... 615-327-6904 .... 471 A
wjriley@mmc.edu

RILEY HAUSER, Ellen ... 715-682-4591 .... 555 E
ellen.hauser@witc.edu

RILING, Dean ... 918-836-6886 .... 412 G
driling@mail.spartan.edu

RILLING, David, S ... 864-488-4573 .... 459 A
drilling@limestone.edu

RILLORTA, Rhoda ... 704-355-3243 .... 363 B
rhoda.rillorta@carolinashealthcare.org

RIMA, Kyle ... 801-832-2008 .... 512 F
krima@westminstercollege.edu

RIMAI, Monica ... 503-725-4444 .... 418 G
monica.rimai@pdx.edu

RIMER, Barbara, K ... 919-966-3215 .... 378 D
brimer@unc.edu

RIMER, Michelle ... 828-328-7473 .... 366 B
michelle.rimer@lr.edu

RIMIRCH, Bruce ... 680-488-2471 .... 560 A
brucer@palau.edu

RIMMER, Jessica ... 405-691-3800 .... 408 H
jrimmer@macu.edu

RIMMER, Kelly, R ... 717-240-5217 .... 439 C
kog2@psu.edu

RIMPAU, Jim ... 406-994-4390 .... 295 E
rimpau@montana.edu

RINARD, Pat ... 727-341-3064 .... 116 F
rinard.pat@spcollege.edu

RINAS, Craig ... 972-825-4612 .... 495 D
crinas@sagu.edu

RINCHICH, Jack, L ... 304-357-4857 .... 541 H
jackrinchich@ucwv.edu

RINCK, Jared ... 816-604-6740 .... 285 E
jared.rinck@mcckc.edu

RINCON, Frank, L ... 909-537-5185 .... 36 A
frincon@csusb.edu

RINCON, Mary Beth ... 219-989-2251 .... 178 G
mbrincon@purduecal.edu

RINDE, Carla, M ... 610-409-3599 .... 450 C
crinde@ursinus.edu

RINDE, Pat, J ... 701-252-3467 .... 381 A
rinde@jc.edu

RINDERKNECHT, Bethany ... 319-368-6467 .... 187 E
brinderknecht@mtmercy.edu

RINDERKNECHT, Deborah ... 814-269-2989 .... 449 D
drinderk@pitt.edu

RINDO, Michael, J ... 715-836-4742 .... 550 H
rindomj@uwec.edu

RINDO, Michael, J ... 715-836-2327 .... 550 H
rindomj@uwec.edu

RINDO, Michael, J ... 715-836-4741 .... 550 H
rindomj@uwec.edu

RINDSKOPF PARKER, Elizabeth ... 916-739-7151 .... 75 D
elizabeth@pacific.edu

RINEHART, Dorothy, C ... 859-238-5459 .... 199 [illegible]
dotti.rinehart@centre.edu

RINEHART, Gerald, D ... 612-624-3560 .... 272 D
g-rine@umn.edu

RINEHART, Kenton, W ... 845-575-3000 .... 340 C
kent.rinehart@marist.edu

RINEHART, Richard, J ... 570-577-3213 .... 423 D
r.rinehart@bucknell.edu

RINEHART, Shelley ... 281-998-6150 .... 493 G
shelley.rinehart@sjcd.edu

RINER, William, F ... 803-313-7104 .... 462 D
wriner@mailbox.sc.edu

RINEY, Don ... 928-317-6470 .... 12 C
don.riney@azwestern.edu

RINEY, OSU, Judith, N ... 270-686-4288 .... 198 G
judith.riney@brescia.edu

RING, David ... 631-244-3054 .... 332 D
ringd@dowling.edu

RING, Joshua ... 828-328-7927 .... 366 B
joshua.ring@lr.edu

RING, Patricia ... 702-992-2110 .... 302 I
patricia.ring@nsc.nevada.edu

RING, Ray ... 212-817-7390 .... 327 B
rring@gc.cuny.edu

RING, Timothy ... 513-585-2402 .... 387 C

RINGA, Melanie ... 914-961-8313 .... 349 I
finance@svots.edu

RINGELBERG, Kirstin ... 336-278-5249 .... 364 A
kringelberg@elon.edu

RINGENBERG, Ron ... 574-296-6212 .... 169 C
rringenb@ambs.edu

RINGER-FISHER, Denise ... 412-261-2647 .... 432 B
dringer-fisher@kaplan.edu

RINGGER, Nick ... 907-822-3201 .... 10 C
nringger@akbible.edu

RINGGOLD, Briar ... 580-477-7700 .... 414 C
briar.ringgold@wosc.edu

RINGLAND, Inez ... 708-524-6873 .... 150 A
iringland@dom.edu

RINGLE, John ... 217-206-6190 .... 167 A
ringle.john@uis.edu

RINGLE, Martin, D ... 503-777-7254 .... 420 A
martin.ringle@reed.edu

RINGLE, Suzanne ... 602-286-8110 .... 15 I
suzanne.ringle@gwmail.maricopa.edu

RINGLEN, Ringlen, P ... 691-320-2480 .... 559 A
rringlen@comfsm.fm

RINGLER, Neil, H ... 315-470-6606 .... 355 A
neilringler@esf.edu

RINGO, Teresa, T ... 936-294-1060 .... 501 A
reg_tat@shsu.edu

RINGOLD, Debra ... 503-370-6440 .... 421 C
dringold@willamette.edu

RINGOLD, Gordon ... 831-459-4229 .... 75 A
ringold@ucsc.edu

RINGSTAD, Ann ... 907-474-5922 .... 10 J
atringstad@alaska.edu

RINGWOOD, Karen ... 203-597-9036 .... 94 D
klozada@bridgeport.edu

RINI, Anthony ... 617-373-4774 .... 244 A

RINI, Lisa ... 212-686-9040 .... 360 E
lrini@woodtobecoburn.edu

RINK, Darrel, C ... 479-788-7390 .... 24 D
drink@uafortsmith.edu

RINKE, Patricia, A ... 515-263-2912 .... 184 I
prinke@grandview.edu

RINKENBAUGH, Bill ... 316-322-3297 .... 191 D
brinkenb@butlercc.edu

RINKER, Jonathan, A ... 304-877-6428 .... 540 D
jon.rinker@abc.edu

RINKER, Linda ... 616-554-5183 .... 250 E
lrinker@davenport.edu

RINKINEN, Ross ... 906-487-7314 .... 251 C
ross.rinkinen@finlandia.edu

RINN, Martha ... 830-372-8110 .... 499 C
mrinn@tlu.edu

RINNE, Henry ... 479-788-7431 .... 24 D
hrinne@uafortsmith.edu

RINNE, Jason ... 660-831-4088 .... 286 I
rinnej@moval.edu

RIO, Deborah ... 661-362-3298 .... 41 G
debbie.rio@canyons.edu

RIONI, Dominic ... 860-628-4751 .... 92 F
drioni@lincolncollegene.edu

RIORDAN, Catherine, A ... 360-650-3480 .... 539 C
catherine.riordan@wwu.edu

RIORDAN, Charles ... 302-831-1073 .... 96 F
riordan@udel.edu

RIORDAN, Charles ... 410-617-2195 .... 224 A
criordan@loyola.edu

RIORDAN, Christine ... 303-871-4324 .... 88 E
christine.riordan@du.edu

RIORDAN, Jennifer ... 717-564-4112 .... 432 A
jriordan@kaplan.edu

RIORDAN, Kevin ... 708-596-2000 .... 164 F
kriordan@ssc.edu

RIORDAN, Marsha ... 641-673-1045 .... 189 I
riordanm@wmpenn.edu

RIORDAN, Phil ... 561-237-7749 .... 113 D
priordan@lynn.edu

RIOS, Adlin ... 787-728-1545 .... 568 B
adlinrios@sagrado.edu

RIOS, Alfonso ... 323-357-6209 .... 54 G
riosa@elac.edu

RIVEROS-SCHAFER, Enrique ..... 415-338-1511 ..... 36 F
eriveros@sfsu.edu
RIVERS, Andrew ..... 202-806-2500 ..... 98 B
andrew.rivers@howard.edu
RIVERS, Christina ..... 707-967-2911 ..... 58 F
crivers@napavalley.edu
RIVERS, Denise, Z ..... 716-286-8761 ..... 344 D
dzr@niagara.edu
RIVERS, John, D ..... 330-471-8133 ..... 395 E
jrivers@malone.edu
RIVERS, Larry, E ..... 478-825-6315 ..... 129 C
riversl@fvsu.edu
RIVERS, Nancy, A ..... 434-982-2662 ..... 525 B
nan9k@virginia.edu
RIVERS, Verna ..... 340-693-1087 ..... 568 C
vrivers@uvi.edu
RIVES, Dan ..... 812-855-3027 ..... 173 B
drives@indiana.edu
RIVES, Dan ..... 812-855-2239 ..... 173 C
drives@indiana.edu
RIVES, Joseph ..... 309-762-8090 ..... 168 A
j-rives@wiu.edu
RIVET, Elizabeth ..... 413-565-1000 ..... 231 B
erivete@baypath.edu
RIVETT, Donna ..... 772-462-7656 ..... 110 L
drivett@irsc.edu
RIVINIUS, DeeLynn ..... 727-873-4264 ..... 121 B
rivinius@mail.usf.edu
RIX, Mary Sue ..... 318-869-5137 ..... 208 F
msrix@centenary.edu
RIXEN, Mary ..... 580-371-2371 ..... 408 I
mrixen@mscok.edu
RIZA, Robert ..... 254-659-7791 ..... 487 E
rriza@hillcollege.edu
RIZK, Michelle ..... 907-450-8191 ..... 10 H
michelle.rizk@alaska.edu
RIZVI, S. Abu ..... 802-656-9102 ..... 514 F
abu.rizvi@uvm.edu
RIZVI, Syed ..... 714-628-4967 ..... 63 G
rizvi_syed@sccollege.edu
RIZVI, Teresa, J ..... 937-229-3241 ..... 404 A
teri.rizvi@notes.udayton.edu
RIZZA, James ..... 508-767-7419 ..... 230 E
j.rizza@assumption.edu
RIZZA, Robert, A ..... 507-538-5027 ..... 262 D
rizza.robert@mayo.edu
RIZZI, Gino ..... 518-828-4181 ..... 330 E
rizzi@sunycgcc.edu
RIZZO, Barbara ..... 847-635-2604 ..... 160 E
rizzo@oakton.edu
RIZZO, Bryan ..... 734-432-5604 ..... 254 G
brizzo@madonna.edu
RIZZO, Christina ..... 315-786-2291 ..... 337 F
crizzo@sunyjefferson.edu
RIZZO, Christopher ..... 724-773-3957 ..... 438 I
clr4@psu.edu
RIZZO, Frank ..... 703-284-1650 ..... 521 A
frank.rizzo@marymount.edu
RIZZO, Matt ..... 802-831-1206 ..... 515 A
mrizzo@vermontlaw.edu
RIZZO, Pete ..... 402-844-7151 ..... 300 A
pete@northeast.edu
RIZZUTO, James, T ..... 719-384-6821 ..... 86 F
jim.rizzuto@ojc.edu
ROA, Irma ..... 323-464-2777 ..... 27 I
iroa@ca.aada.org
ROACH, Bill ..... 864-587-4396 ..... 461 D
roachb@smcsc.edu
ROACH, Colleen ..... 617-228-2177 ..... 239 G
croach@bhcc.mass.edu
ROACH, David ..... 315-228-7611 ..... 329 H
droach@colgate.edu
ROACH, J. Terrance ..... 301-405-4942 ..... 227 B
troach@umd.edu
ROACH, Jack ..... 843-661-8121 ..... 458 A
jack.roach@fdtc.edu
ROACH, Ron ..... 709-379-3111 ..... 139 F
rroach@yhc.edu
ROACH, Tracy ..... 660-263-3900 ..... 279 J
troach@cccb.edu
ROACH, Virginia ..... 212-875-4668 ..... 323 E
vroach@bankstreet.edu
ROACHE, Marjorie ..... 708-596-2000 ..... 164 F
mroache@ssc.edu
ROADCUP, David ..... 513-244-8184 ..... 387 D
david.roadcup@ccuniversity.edu
ROADES, Nicole ..... 937-393-3431 ..... 401 K
nroades@sscc.edu
ROADRUCK, Nancy, L ..... 330-972-7425 ..... 403 B
nancy5@uakron.edu
ROAF, Sterling, A ..... 404-756-1650 ..... 134 B
aroaf@msm.edu
ROAMES, Jeff ..... 626-529-8079 ..... 60 G
jroames@pacificoaks.edu
ROAN, Colt ..... 870-460-1028 ..... 25 A
roan@uamont.edu
ROAN, John, A ..... 214-648-3572 ..... 507 D
john.roan@utsouthwestern.edu
ROAN, Kimberly ..... 763-576-4813 ..... 266 A
kroan@anokatech.edu
ROAN, Lisa, A ..... 607-733-7177 ..... 332 I
lroan@ebi-college.com
ROAN, Tina ..... 440-684-6085 ..... 405 B
troan@ursuline.edu
ROANE, Kevin ..... 732-571-3561 ..... 311 F
kroane@monmouth.edu
ROARK, Bob ..... 479-899-6644 ..... 21 B
rroark@bryancollege.com
ROARK, Deborah ..... 817-531-4498 ..... 502 A
droark@txwes.edu
ROARK, Donna ..... 606-487-3128 ..... 201 H
donna.roark@kctcs.edu
ROARK, Harold ..... 503-352-3060 ..... 419 E
roark@pacificu.edu
ROARK, Ian ..... 432-335-6685 ..... 491 F
iroark@odessa.edu
ROARK, Jack ..... 406-756-3872 ..... 294 D
jroark@fvcc.edu
ROARK, Tony ..... 208-426-2030 ..... 142 F
troark@boisestate.edu
ROATCH, Gay ..... 910-576-6222 ..... 372 A
roatchg@montgomery.edu
ROATH, Cindy ..... 303-937-4255 ..... 82 A
croath@chu.edu
ROBACK, Joseph ..... 570-941-7540 ..... 450 B
robackj2@scranton.edu
ROBAIN LACAILLE, Jemma ..... 718-482-5077 ..... 328 C
jlacaille@lagcc.cuny.edu
ROBAR, Stephen ..... 814-362-7586 ..... 449 B
robar@pitt.edu
ROBARDS, Darren ..... 708-456-0300 ..... 166 C
drobards@triton.edu
ROBARDS, Paul ..... 478-934-3149 ..... 133 G
probards@mgc.edu
ROBB, Annette, D ..... 937-255-6800 ..... 556 H
annette.robb@afit.edu
ROBB, Cameraon ..... 602-216-3171 ..... 11 F
crobb@argosy.edu
ROBB, James ..... 517-371-5140 ..... 259 B
robbj@cooley.edu
ROBB, Jim ..... 870-743-3000 ..... 22 G
jrobb@northark.edu
ROBB, Mercy ..... 630-829-6095 ..... 145 D
mrobb@ben.edu
ROBB, Sarah ..... 620-431-2820 ..... 195 B
srobb@neosho.edu
ROBB, Susan, E ..... 804-828-6772 ..... 525 E
sarobb@vcu.edu
ROBB SHIMKO, Molly ..... 724-830-4620 ..... 447 B
shimko@setonhill.edu
ROBBEN, Richard, W ..... 734-764-3400 ..... 259 D
rrobben@umich.edu
ROBBERT, Sharon ..... 708-239-4771 ..... 165 I
sharon.robbert@trnty.edu
ROBBIE, Kimberly ..... 510-659-6165 ..... 59 I
krobbie@ohlone.edu
ROBBINS, Canty ..... 901-678-3855 ..... 474 C
crobbns1@memphis.edu
ROBBINS, Charles ..... 707-527-4498 ..... 68 E
crobbins@santarosa.edu
ROBBINS, David, O ..... 740-368-3101 ..... 400 F
dorobbin@owu.edu
ROBBINS, Dennis ..... 626-815-3004 ..... 30 E
drobbins@apu.edu
ROBBINS, Dorothy ..... 417-864-7220 ..... 282 B
drobbins@cci.edu
ROBBINS, Gayle, M ..... 706-542-2273 ..... 138 C
grobbins@uga.edu
ROBBINS, George ..... 518-276-6216 ..... 347 D
robbig@rpi.edu
ROBBINS, Ginger ..... 601-925-3210 ..... 275 E
grobbins@mc.edu
ROBBINS, Kelly ..... 509-574-4775 ..... 540 A
krobbins@yvcc.edu
ROBBINS, Mark ..... 315-443-2255 ..... 357 B
robbinsm@syr.edu
ROBBINS, Marty ..... 512-472-2471 ..... 494 B
mrobbins@ssw.edu
ROBBINS, Mary, A ..... 817-515-6528 ..... 496 A
mary.robbins@tccd.edu
ROBBINS, Nickey, L ..... 870-508-6108 ..... 20 E
nrobbins@asumh.edu
ROBBINS, Patricia, A ..... 903-923-3262 ..... 500 A
pat.robbins@marshall.tstc.edu
ROBBINS, Richard ..... 260-399-7700 ..... 180 E
rrobbins@sf.edu
ROBBINS, Robert ..... 954-201-7554 ..... 102 A
rrobbins@broward.edu
ROBBINS, Ruth ..... 215-965-4038 ..... 436 H
rrobbins@moore.edu
ROBBINS, Sandra ..... 617-735-9715 ..... 234 E
robbins@emmanuel.edu
ROBBINS, Scott, D ..... 731-881-7775 ..... 477 E
sdrobbins@utm.edu
ROBBINS, Shawna, L ..... 760-252-2411 ..... 30 F
srobbins@barstow.edu
ROBBINS, Stacey ..... 773-291-6413 ..... 147 D
ssrobbins@ccc.edu
ROBBINS, Thomas ..... 802-241-2531 ..... 515 B
thomas.robbins@vsc.edu
ROBBINS, Thomas, G ..... 617-353-5533 ..... 232 G
tqresq@bu.edu
ROBBINS SMITH, Patricia ..... 562-860-2451 ..... 38 J
probbinssmith@cerritos.edu
ROBECK, Judy ..... 507-433-0511 ..... 269 A
jrobeck@riverland.edu
ROBEL, Lauren ..... 812-855-8886 ..... 173 C
lrobel@indiana.edu
ROBELOTTO, Vince ..... 706-379-3111 ..... 139 F
vrobelotto@yhc.edu
ROBERDS, Lauren ..... 314-644-9673 ..... 289 A
lroberds@stlcc.edu
ROBERS, Pam ..... 262-551-5778 ..... 546 F
probers@carthage.edu
ROBERSON, Angela, M ..... 309-677-1000 ..... 145 H
nickie@bradley.edu
ROBERSON, Glen ..... 765-269-5156 ..... 176 B
groberso@ivytech.edu
ROBERSON, James, A ..... 919-335-1020 ..... 374 E
jaroberson@waketech.edu
ROBERSON, James, L ..... 904-620-1360 ..... 120 C
len.roberson@unf.edu
ROBERSON, Janet ..... 434-791-5891 ..... 516 D
roberson@averett.edu
ROBERSON, John ..... 910-893-1224 ..... 362 F
robersonj@campbell.edu
ROBERSON, Julie, A ..... 423-652-6301 ..... 469 L
jarobers@king.edu
ROBERSON, Larry ..... 912-443-5828 ..... 136 D
lroberson@savannahtech.edu
ROBERSON, Marla ..... 864-646-1753 ..... 461 F
mrobers1@tctc.edu
ROBERSON, Miriam, C ..... 904-819-6204 ..... 107 A
robersonm@flagler.edu
ROBERSON, Richard, E ..... 717-766-2511 ..... 436 D
rroberso@messiah.edu
ROBERSON, Rita, G ..... 304-236-7648 ..... 542 J
ritar@southern.wvnet.edu
ROBERSON, Rose ..... 415-452-5257 ..... 39 H
rroberso@ccsf.edu
ROBERSON, Steve ..... 336-334-5393 ..... 379 A
shrobers@uncg.edu
ROBERSON, Terry, G ..... 205-665-6015 ..... 9 C
roberson@montevallo.edu
ROBERSON, Valerie ..... 815-280-2238 ..... 154 H
vroberso@jjc.edu
ROBERSTSON, Sandra, L ..... 501-569-3204 ..... 24 E
slrobertson@ualr.edu
ROBERT, Bernadette ..... 310-954-4099 ..... 57 H
brobert@msmc.la.edu
ROBERT, Charlyn, A ..... 508-213-2368 ..... 243 J
charlie.robert@nichols.edu
ROBERT, Jean ..... 908-852-1400 ..... 308 F
robertj@centenarycollege.edu
ROBERT, Kleinschmidt ..... 732-255-0400 ..... 312 D
rkleinschmidt@ocean.edu
ROBERTON, Margaret, R ..... 919-866-5838 ..... 374 E
mrroberton@waketech.edu
ROBERTS, Aaron ..... 402-643-7233 ..... 297 F
aaron.roberts@cune.edu
ROBERTS, Al ..... 434-736-2005 ..... 527 H
al.roberts@southside.edu
ROBERTS, Alan, L ..... 772-462-7235 ..... 110 L
aroberts@irsc.edu
ROBERTS, Alex ..... 509-533-3514 ..... 532 D
AlexR@spokanefalls.edu
ROBERTS, Alex ..... 509-533-3514 ..... 532 F
alexr@spokanefalls.edu
ROBERTS, Amanda ..... 573-876-7101 ..... 290 G
aroberts@stephens.edu
ROBERTS, Amy ..... 412-281-2600 ..... 446 H
aroberts@western-school.com
ROBERTS, Amy, L ..... 315-684-6041 ..... 354 F
robertal@morrisville.edu
ROBERTS, Antonia ..... 803-793-5197 ..... 457 F
robertsa@denmarktech.edu
ROBERTS, Barbara ..... 360-676-2772 ..... 535 F
broberts@nwic.edu
ROBERTS, Betsy ..... 707-527-4811 ..... 68 E
eroberts@santarosa.edu
ROBERTS, Betty ..... 334-556-2418 ..... 4 A
broberts@wallace.edu
ROBERTS, Bianca ..... 661-255-1050 ..... 32 C
broberts@calarts.edu
ROBERTS, Bob, E ..... 304-293-3136 ..... 544 E
bob.roberts@mail.wvu.edu
ROBERTS, Brent ..... 406-657-2320 ..... 295 F
broberts@msubillings.edu
ROBERTS, Carolyn ..... 313-927-1474 ..... 255 A
croberts@marygrove.edu
ROBERTS, Catherine, C ..... 480-342-4850 ..... 262 G
roberts.catherine@mayo.edu
ROBERTS, Charles ..... 360-676-2772 ..... 535 F
chroberts@nwic.edu
ROBERTS, Charlie, W ..... 225-578-3814 ..... 212 F
croberts@lsualumni.org
ROBERTS, Cheryl ..... 503-399-6591 ..... 414 J
cheryl.roberts@chemeketa.edu
ROBERTS, Cheryl, A ..... 340-692-4192 ..... 568 C
crobert@uvi.edu
ROBERTS, Christine, B ..... 919-209-2116 ..... 371 C
cbroberts@johnstoncc.edu
ROBERTS, Clancy ..... 615-329-8663 ..... 468 G
croberts@fisk.edu
ROBERTS, Colleen, T ..... 540-831-5500 ..... 522 D
ctroberts@radford.edu
ROBERTS, Craig, W ..... 573-651-2513 ..... 290 D
croberts@semo.edu
ROBERTS, Creighton ..... 912-358-3004 ..... 136 C
robertsc@savannahstate.edu
ROBERTS, Curt ..... 801-626-8940 ..... 511 D
curtroberts@weber.edu
ROBERTS, Cynthia, A 412-624-8076 449
croberts@bc.pitt.edu
ROBERTS, Daniel, A 800-469-0236 211
daniel.roberts@ltc.edu
ROBERTS, Dave 775-674-7616 302
droberts@tmcc.edu
ROBERTS, David 203-932-7435 95
droberts@newhaven.edu
ROBERTS, David 860-465-5395 91
robertsda@easternct.edu
ROBERTS, Dennis ..... 408-554-5406 ..... 68 C
droberts@scu.edu
ROBERTS, Dennis ..... 530-938-5313 ..... 42 C
robertsd@siskiyous.edu
ROBERTS, Doug ..... 707-527-1709 ..... 68 E
droberts@santarosa.edu
ROBERTS, Ed 432-264-5055 487
eroberts@howardcollege.edu
ROBERTS, Ellen ..... 706-507-8503 ..... 127 D
roberts_ellen@columbusstate.edu
ROBERTS, II, Ernst, E ..... 915-831-2000 ..... 486 E
ROBERTS, Eugene ..... 860-486-3114 ..... 94 E
eugene.roberts@uconn.edu
ROBERTS, III, Francis (Tri), A ..... 859-246-6556 ..... 201 D
tri.roberts@kctcs.edu
ROBERTS, Franklin, D ..... 207-778-7215 ..... 220 C
froberts@maine.edu
ROBERTS, Gail ..... 229-225-5206 ..... 137 D
groberts@southwestgatech.edu
ROBERTS, Gail ..... 419-448-2013 ..... 391 G
groberts@heidelberg.edu
ROBERTS, Gary ..... 617-627-3313 ..... 245 F
gary.roberts@tufts.edu
ROBERTS, Gary, A ..... 501-450-3416 ..... 25 H
garyr@uca.edu
ROBERTS, Gary, O ..... 607-871-2715 ..... 322 F
roberts@alfred.edu
ROBERTS, Gary, R ..... 317-274-2581 ..... 174 B
robertsg@iupui.edu
ROBERTS, Gayla ..... 903-675-6212 ..... 502 D
groberts@tvcc.edu
ROBERTS, George ..... 870-862-8131 ..... 23 G
groberts@southark.edu
ROBERTS, Glenda, V ..... 607-746-4545 ..... 355 E
robertgv@delhi.edu
ROBERTS, Glenn ..... 978-632-6600 ..... 240 G
g_roberts@mwcc.mass.edu
ROBERTS, Gregory ..... 509-533-3556 ..... 532 F
gregoryr@spokanefalls.edu
ROBERTS, Gregory, W ..... 434-982-3200 ..... 525 B
groberts@Virginia.EDU
ROBERTS, Gregory, W ..... 425-739-8251 ..... 535 B
greg.roberts@lwtc.edu
ROBERTS, Heather ..... 916-660-7900 ..... 69 F
ROBERTS, Ian ..... 402-461-7455 ..... 298 C
iroberts@hastings.edu
ROBERTS, James ..... 843-863-8083 ..... 456 B
jroberts@csuniv.edu
ROBERTS, James ..... 410-951-3800 ..... 228 B
jroberts@coppin.edu
ROBERTS, James ..... 570-674-6758 ..... 436 F
jroberts@misericordia.edu
ROBERTS, James, S ..... 919-684-3501 ..... 303 I
james.roberts@duke.edu
ROBERTS, Jayne ..... 850-718-2209 ..... 102 H
robertsj@chipola.edu
ROBERTS, Jean ..... 231-777-0519 ..... 256 D
jean.roberts@muskegoncc.edu
ROBERTS, Jean ..... 231-777-0261 ..... 256 D
jean.roberts@muskegoncc.edu
ROBERTS, Jean, L ..... 425-637-1010 ..... 531 I
jroberts@cityu.edu
ROBERTS, Jeanette, C ..... 608-262-1414 ..... 550 G
jroberts@pharmacy.wisc.edu
ROBERTS, Jeanne ..... 813-253-6203 ..... 122 H
jroberts@ut.edu
ROBERTS, Jeffrey, T ..... 765-494-1730 ..... 178 F
jtrob@purdue.edu
ROBERTS, Jennifer ..... 740-364-9644 ..... 399 E
roberts.862@osu.edu
ROBERTS, Jennifer ..... 617-730-7103 ..... 243 I
jennifer.roberts@newbury.edu
ROBERTS, Jennifer ..... 740-364-9644 ..... 386 G
jroberts@cotc.edu
ROBERTS, Jeri ..... 207-948-3131 ..... 219 H
jroberts@unity.edu
ROBERTS, Jessie, R ..... 985-549-2001 ..... 216 C
jroberts@selu.edu
ROBERTS, Jill, J ..... 903-813-2335 ..... 481 A
jjroberts@austincollege.edu
ROBERTS, Jim, O ..... 910-893-1240 ..... 362 F
roberts@campbell.edu
ROBERTS, Jimmy ..... 254-298-8340 ..... 496 B
jdr@templejc.edu
ROBERTS, John ..... 903-593-8311 ..... 499 A
jroberts@texascollege.edu
ROBERTS, John ..... 713-743-3000 ..... 503 B
jwroberts@uh.edu
ROBERTS, Jon ..... 501-279-4257 ..... 21 H
jroberts@harding.edu
ROBERTS, Juanita ..... 334-727-8894 ..... 8 C
jroberts@tuskegee.edu

ROBERTS, Karen 954-201-7423 102 A jiroff@broward.edu
ROBERTS, Karen 559-737-6257 42 B karenr@cos.edu
ROBERTS, Kay Lynn 580-745-2977 412 C kroberts@se.edu
ROBERTS, Kelley 706-867-3280 134 D karoberts@northgeorgia.edu
ROBERTS, Kevin 518-564-5022 354 B robertkw@plattsburgh.edu
ROBERTS, Kevin, J 325-674-2675 478 H robertsk@acu.edu
ROBERTS, Larry 641-844-5766 185 J larry.roberts@iavalley.edu
ROBERTS, II, Laurence, W 315-792-3340 359 C lroberts@utica.edu
ROBERTS, Leonard 973-748-9000 308 A leonard_roberts@bloomfield.edu
ROBERTS, Lila 678-466-4357 127 A lilaroberts@clayton.edu
ROBERTS, Lisa 618-374-5068 161 D
ROBERTS, Lonnie, V 912-427-5816 124 A lroberts@altamahatech.edu
ROBERTS, Malcolm 808-942-1000 140 H careers.hnl.ed@remingtoncollege.edu
ROBERTS, Mark 740-284-5345 390 M mroberts@franciscan.edu
ROBERTS, Mark, A 407-823-2771 120 A roberts@ucf.edu
ROBERTS, Mary 478-445-5384 129 F mary.roberts@gcsu.edu
ROBERTS, Mary Margaret 662-329-7295 276 B mmroberts@alumni.muw.edu
ROBERTS, Matthew, J 805-756-6000 33 F mjroberts@calpoly.edu
ROBERTS, Melvin 856-227-7200 308 E mroberts@camdencc.edu
ROBERTS, Michael, H 843-349-2282 456 G mroberts@coastal.edu
ROBERTS, Michelle, A 662-846-4000 274 B mroberts@deltastate.edu
ROBERTS, Mike 319-398-5411 186 H mrobert@kirkwood.edu
ROBERTS, Nancy 610-606-4640 424 I nroberts@cedarcrest.edu
ROBERTS, Patrick, S 330-569-5278 391 H robertsps@hiram.edu
ROBERTS, Patty, J 318-869-5747 208 F pjrobert@centenary.edu
ROBERTS, Paul 229-225-4098 137 D proberts@southwestgatech.edu
ROBERTS, Paul 205-970-9233 7 D proberts@sebc.edu
ROBERTS, Paul 715-232-1184 552 C robertsp@uwstout.edu
ROBERTS, Paul, G 773-508-8901 157 A prober2@luc.edu
ROBERTS, Pauline 225-923-2524 207 E
ROBERTS, Phyllis, A 276-964-7588 528 A phyllis.roberts@sw.edu
ROBERTS, R. Philip 816-414-3700 286 A president@mbts.edu
ROBERTS, Randal, R 503-517-1860 421 B rroberts@westernseminary.edu
ROBERTS, Randall 606-886-3863 201 C randall.roberts@kctcs.edu
ROBERTS, Richard 201-684-7616 313 D rroberts@ramapo.edu
ROBERTS, Richard 423-775-6596 472 E rroberts@ogs.edu
ROBERTS, Rick 904-620-2955 120 C rtrobert@unf.edu
ROBERTS, Robin 479-575-4804 24 C
ROBERTS, Robin 317-738-8759 171 C rroberts@franklincollege.edu
ROBERTS, Robin 302-857-6120 95 F rroberts@desu.edu
ROBERTS, Ruth 972-825-4656 495 D rroberts@sagu.edu
ROBERTS, Sallyann 815-226-4083 162 H sroberts@rockford.edu
ROBERTS, Scott 702-895-2816 302 K scott.roberts@unlv.edu
ROBERTS, Sean 616-824-2977 58 H
ROBERTS, Shandel 415-433-9200 68 F sroberts@saybrook.edu
ROBERTS, Shannon 215-248-7111 425 C roberts@chc.edu
ROBERTS, Sharon, A 727-577-1497 200 F
ROBERTS, Stephen, W 248-370-2445 257 C swrobert@oakland.edu
ROBERTS, Steve 817-531-4403 502 A sroberts@txwes.edu
ROBERTS, Susan 262-564-3224 553 H robertss@gtc.edu
ROBERTS, Thomas, J 239-590-7021 119 A troberts@fgcu.edu
ROBERTS, Tom 562-951-4583 33 E troberts@calstate.edu
ROBERTS, Vanessa 325-793-4681 490 F vroberts@mcm.edu
ROBERTS, Vanice, W 706-233-7464 136 E vroberts@shorter.edu
ROBERTS, Vonnie, W 405-466-2999 408 G vwroberts@lunet.edu
ROBERTS, Wayne 601-643-8351 274 A wayne.roberts@colin.edu
ROBERTS, William 201-692-2629 310 B william_roberts@fdu.edu
ROBERTS, William, P 630-874-4702 159 D broberts@nl.edu
ROBERTS, William, R 906-487-2622 255 E wrrobert@mtu.edu
ROBERTS-CORB, Carol 562-985-4187 35 A crcorb@csulb.edu
ROBERTSON, Alan, D 708-709-3568 161 C arobertson@prairiestate.edu
ROBERTSON, Alice 269-956-3931 253 H robertsona@kellogg.edu
ROBERTSON, Beverly 828-689-1244 366 F brobertson@mhc.edu
ROBERTSON, Blake 501-337-5000 21 D brobertson@otcweb.edu
ROBERTSON, Carole 312-488-6006 146 C crobertson@thechicagoschool.edu
ROBERTSON, Charlotta 619-388-2801 65 G crobertson@sdccd.edu
ROBERTSON, Christopher 205-929-1655 5 H admissions@miles.edu
ROBERTSON, Courtney 941-907-2262 106 G crobertson@evergladesuniversity.edu
ROBERTSON, Craig, L 618-537-6856 157 G clrobertson@mckendree.edu
ROBERTSON, Darlene 937-769-1820 383 K drobertson@antioch.edu
ROBERTSON, Debbie 405-382-9248 412 B d.robertson@sscok.edu
ROBERTSON, Debora 712-279-1771 182 E debora.robertson@briarcliff.edu
ROBERTSON, Dennis 903-923-2320 486 D drobertson@etbu.edu
ROBERTSON, Diana 785-864-7224 196 F drobertson@ku.edu
ROBERTSON, Don 507-537-6018 269 G Don.Robertson@smsu.edu
ROBERTSON, Don, E 270-809-6831 204 F don.robertson@murraystate.edu
ROBERTSON, Donna, V 312-567-3230 153 B robertson@iit.edu
ROBERTSON, Doug 504-456-3141 208 A
ROBERTSON, Douglas 305-348-3681 119 B douglas.robertson@fiu.edu
ROBERTSON, Gloria 269-660-8021 257 E robertsong@millercollege.edu
ROBERTSON, Ian 828-298-3325 380 C irobert@warren-wilson.edu
ROBERTSON, J. D 435-652-7576 512 A jrobertson@dixie.edu
ROBERTSON, Jennifer 903-675-6215 502 D jrobertson@tvcc.edu
ROBERTSON, Jill 303-273-3207 82 F jill.robertson@is.mines.edu
ROBERTSON, John 402-844-7011 300 A johnr@northeast.edu
ROBERTSON, Jon, H 561-237-7701 113 D jrobertson@lynn.edu
ROBERTSON, Joseph, E 503-494-8252 418 D
ROBERTSON, Leonard, A 972-721-5236 502 F lrobertson@udallas.edu
ROBERTSON, Mary 870-512-7812 20 F mary_robertson@asun.edu
ROBERTSON, Michael 901-722-3226 473 B mike.robertson@sco.edu
ROBERTSON, Patricia 843-574-6057 461 G patricia.robertson@tridenttech.edu
ROBERTSON, Paul 402-878-2380 298 G probertson@littlepriest.edu
ROBERTSON, Randall, A 336-734-7334 370 C rrobertson@forsythtech.edu
ROBERTSON, Richard, J 760-757-2121 57 E drobertson@miracosta.edu
ROBERTSON, Roby, D 501-569-8572 24 E rdrobertson@ualr.edu
ROBERTSON, Russell 847-578-3000 163 A russell.robertson@rosalindfranklin.edu
ROBERTSON, Sandra, L 501-569-8736 24 E slrobertson@ualr.edu
ROBERTSON, Sharon, N 703-323-3198 527 C srobertson@nvcc.edu
ROBERTSON, Stacey, M 309-677-3538 145 H smr@bradley.edu
ROBERTSON, Summer 704-406-3271 364 B srobertson@gardner-webb.edu
ROBERTSON, Thomas, S 215-898-4715 448 I robertson@wharton.upenn.edu
ROBERTSON, William, J 717-866-5775 428 I wrobertson@evangelical.edu
ROBESON, Dan 518-292-8657 348 A robesd@sage.edu
ROBICHAUD, Betin 508-213-2292 243 J betin.robichaud@nichols.edu
ROBICHAUD, Karen 615-966-5602 470 D karen.robichaud@lipscomb.edu
ROBICHAUD, Rob 208-321-8800 142 H rrobichaud@brownmackie.edu
ROBICHAUX, Renee 337-550-1233 212 H
ROBIE, Curt, D 413-572-5280 239 C crobie@wsc.ma.edu
ROBILLARD, Jean, E 319-335-8064 182 C jean-robillard@uiowa.edu
ROBILLARD, Marc 617-353-3502 232 G robillrd@bu.edu
ROBIN, Brandon 318-487-7498 209 B brandonrobin@lacollege.edu
ROBIN, Florence, K 818-719-6409 55 B robinfk@piercecollege.edu
ROBIN, Tracy 212-229-1671 342 E robint@newschool.edu
ROBINETTE, Stephen, H 417-836-4127 286 F steverobinette@missouristate.edu
ROBINS, Linda 580-371-2371 408 I lrobins@mscok.edu
ROBINS, Luke 318-397-6100 210 J lrobins@ladelta.edu
ROBINS, Luke 318-345-9262 210 I lrobins@ladelta.edu
ROBINS, Mary 650-543-3735 57 B mrobins@menlo.edu
ROBINSON, Albert 410-951-3803 228 B arobinson@coppin.edu
ROBINSON, Alfred, L 573-681-6156 284 B robinsona@lincolnu.edu
ROBINSON, Andrew 603-358-2108 307 A arobinso@keene.edu
ROBINSON, Beatriz, G 305-474-6846 116 G brobinson@stu.edu
ROBINSON, Bev 208-459-5680 143 A brobinson@collegeofidaho.edu
ROBINSON, Beverly 615-329-8657 468 G brobinson@fisk.edu
ROBINSON, Beverly 972-825-4798 495 D brobinson@sagu.edu
ROBINSON, Bonnell 617-585-6676 230 D robinson@lesley.edu
ROBINSON, Carrie 318-670-9663 215 A crobinson@susla.edu
ROBINSON, Cassandra, M 301-860-4000 228 A crobinson@bowiestate.edu
ROBINSON, Chad 970-943-3123 89 B crobinson@western.edu
ROBINSON, Charles 479-575-7955 24 C cfrobins@uark.edu
ROBINSON, Charles, D 318-795-4107 213 D drobinso@lsus.edu
ROBINSON, Charles, F 510-987-9800 73 D charles.robinson@ucop.edu
ROBINSON, Chase, F 212-817-7200 327 B crobinson@gc.cuny.edu
ROBINSON, Cheryl 407-582-6883 122 I crobinson@valenciacollege.edu
ROBINSON, Christine 407-708-2566 117 G robinsoc@seminolestate.edu
ROBINSON, Christine, M 414-410-4183 546 D cmrobinson@stritch.edu
ROBINSON, Christopher, D 336-246-3900 375 A chris.robinson@wilkescc.edu
ROBINSON, Connie 813-935-5700 115 J connierobinson@remingtoncollege.edu
ROBINSON, Constance, V 315-267-2573 354 C harpercv@potsdam.edu
ROBINSON, Cynthia, R 910-277-5738 376 A robinscr@sapc.edu
ROBINSON, Daniel 909-469-5561 78 D drobinson@westernu.edu
ROBINSON, David 405-945-3241 410 F
ROBINSON, David 503-494-4460 418 D
ROBINSON, Dawnelle 334-285-5177 4 K drobinson@ingram.cc.al.us
ROBINSON, Deborah 732-255-0400 312 D drobinson@ocean.edu
ROBINSON, Deborah, M 330-588-2586 395 E drobinson@malone.edu
ROBINSON, Deborah, P 850-201-6109 121 F robinsd@tcc.fl.edu
ROBINSON, Debra A, G 573-341-6154 292 A debrar@mst.edu
ROBINSON, OSB, Denis 812-357-6522 179 E drobinson@saintmeinrad.edu
ROBINSON, Denise 859-572-5688 205 E robinson@nku.edu
ROBINSON, Dindy 817-257-5019 498 F d.robinson@tcu.edu
ROBINSON, Dollye M, E 601-979-7036 275 A dollye.robinson@jsums.edu
ROBINSON, Dorothy, K 203-432-4949 95 D dorothy.robinson@yale.edu
ROBINSON, Douglas, W 562-985-5587 35 A drobinso@csulb.edu
ROBINSON, Duan 731-426-7525 469 M drobinson@lanecollege.edu
ROBINSON, D'Wayne 404-880-8798 126 I erobinson@cau.edu
ROBINSON, Edna 281-476-1501 493 E edna.robinson@sjcd.edu
ROBINSON, Edward 202-686-0876 99 A library@potomac.edu
ROBINSON, Edward, G 608-757-7713 553 E erobinson@blackhawk.edu
ROBINSON, Elaine 816-483-9600 289 H elaine.robinson@spst.edu
ROBINSON, Evangeline, W 601-979-2282 275 A evangeline.w.robinson@jsums.edu
ROBINSON, Francine 937-376-6142 386 H frobinson@centralstate.edu
ROBINSON, Gail, D 901-334-5826 471 C grobinson@memphisseminary.edu
ROBINSON, Gary 607-431-4420 335 B robinsong@hartwick.edu
ROBINSON, Gary 859-336-5082 205 F grobinson@sccky.edu
ROBINSON, Genevieve 314-889-4760 282 C grobinson@fontbonne.edu
ROBINSON, Gina 910-755-7343 368 C robinsong@brunswickcc.edu
ROBINSON, Gregory 773-291-6211 147 D grobinson@ccc.edu
ROBINSON, Irene, M 281-756-3501 479 G irobinson@alvincollege.edu
ROBINSON, J. Edward 718-960-8245 327 C je.robinson@lehman.cuny.edu
ROBINSON, Jane, L 614-947-6001 391 A robinsoj@franklin.edu
ROBINSON, Janet 419-824-3676 395 D jrobinson@lourdes.edu
ROBINSON, Janice, S 212-678-3732 357 F jsr167@tc.columbia.edu
ROBINSON, Jeannette 973-877-3084 310 A robinson@essex.edu
ROBINSON, Jerrell, W 212-237-8717 328 A jrobinson@jjay.cuny.edu
ROBINSON, JoAnne 706-771-5730 125 D jrobinso@augustatech.edu
ROBINSON, Joel, L 859-572-5825 205 E robinsonjoe@nku.edu
ROBINSON, Judith, G 757-446-5841 518 F robinsjg@evms.edu
ROBINSON, Karen 415-380-1616 48 D karenrobinson@ggbts.edu
ROBINSON, Kasi 404-681-6500 134 A krobinso@morehouse.edu
ROBINSON, Katheryn 787-257-0000 566 H katheryn.robinson@upr.edu
ROBINSON, Kelley 518-244-2201 348 A robink3@sage.edu
ROBINSON, Kenneth, I 714-808-4830 59 B krobinson@nocccd.edu
ROBINSON, Kent 502-213-2118 202 B kent.robinson@kctcs.edu
ROBINSON, Kevin 559-734-9000 66 E kevinr@sjvc.edu
ROBINSON, Kevin 435-586-1966 511 A robinson_kl@suu.edu
ROBINSON, Kevin, W 610-660-1357 446 C krobinso@sju.edu
ROBINSON, Kristin 602-331-7500 12 D klrobinson@aii.edu
ROBINSON, LaNita 218-733-7616 267 B l.robinson@lsc.edu
ROBINSON, Larry 973-761-9655 315 B larry.robinson@shu.edu
ROBINSON, Larry, J 701-845-7217 382 A larry.robinson@vcsu.edu
ROBINSON, Liz 646-660-6590 326 D liz_robinson@baruch.cuny.edu
ROBINSON, Lorene, K 302-857-6050 95 F lrobinso@desu.edu
ROBINSON, Lorne, T 651-696-6358 265 A robinson@macalester.edu
ROBINSON, Louester 843-722-5556 461 G lou.robinson@tridenttech.edu
ROBINSON, Lynne, P 301-447-5296 225 A lrobinso@msmary.edu
ROBINSON, Marcia 610-399-2033 441 H marciarobinson@cheyney.edu
ROBINSON, Margaret, A 620-229-6232 196 C margaret.robinson@sckans.edu
ROBINSON, Mark 323-343-2730 35 B mrobinson@cslanet.calstatela.edu
ROBINSON, Mary 410-276-0306 226 D mrobinson@host.sdc.edu
ROBINSON, Mary 510-869-6131 64 J mrobinson@samuelmerritt.edu
ROBINSON, Mary 716-896-0700 359 F robinsonm@villa.edu
ROBINSON, Mary Kate 713-623-2040 480 J mkrobinson@aii.edu
ROBINSON, Meri 706-507-8433 127 D robinson_meri@columbusstate.edu
ROBINSON, Michael 405-744-6528 410 C michael.robinson@okstate.edu
ROBINSON, Michele' 847-925-6221 151 E mrobinso@harpercollege.edu
ROBINSON, Mick 406-444-6570 294 J mirobinson@montana.edu
ROBINSON, Mike 205-226-4935 2 C mrobinso@bsc.edu
ROBINSON, Mitch 931-221-7883 473 D robinsonm@apsu.edu
ROBINSON, Morris 318-678-6005 209 J mrobinson@bpcc.edu
ROBINSON, Myra 703-729-8800 99 D

ROBINSON, Neal 802-654-2512 514 B
nrobinson@smcvt.edu
ROBINSON, Nechelle 800-533-3378 138 B
nrobinson@uofa.edu
ROBINSON, Nell 334-244-3424 2 A
nrobins3@aum.edu
ROBINSON, Norm 615-248-1296 476 E
nrobinson@trevecca.edu
ROBINSON, Oscar 937-769-1823 383 K
orobinson@antioch.edu
ROBINSON, Pam 405-878-2243 409 D
pam.robinson@okbu.edu
ROBINSON, Patricia 920-993-5133 553 G
robinson@fvtc.edu
ROBINSON, Patty 661-362-3992 41 G
patty.robinson@canyons.edu
ROBINSON, Paul, A 734-647-3502 259 D
probins@umich.edu
ROBINSON, Perry, H 740-587-6624 389 H
robinson@denison.edu
ROBINSON, Peter, J 585-275-4036 358 I
Peter_Robinson@URMC.Rochester.edu
ROBINSON, Ralph 302-857-7381 95 F
rrobinson@desu.edu
ROBINSON, Regina 318-670-9617 215 A
rrobinson@susla.edu
ROBINSON, Richard 770-836-4713 139 B
richard.robinson@westgatech.edu
ROBINSON, Richard, A 401-825-2109 453 B
rrobinson@ccri.edu
ROBINSON, Robbie 225-342-6950 215 D
rrobinson@uls.state.la.us
ROBINSON, Robert 909-621-8136 63 A
robert.robinson@pomona.edu
ROBINSON, Robert 210-458-5868 506 B
rob.robison@utsa.edu
ROBINSON, Robert 802-654-2524 514 B
rrobinson@smcvt.edu
ROBINSON, Robert, L 717-815-1553 452 F
rrobinso@ycp.edu
ROBINSON, Robin 508-626-4688 238 D
rrobinson@framingham.edu
ROBINSON, Ronald, R 864-597-4051 463 F
robinsonrr1@wofford.edu
ROBINSON, Rosemary 256-824-6203 9 A
rosemary.robinson@uah.edu
ROBINSON, Roy 253-879-3653 538 E
rrobinson@pugetsound.edu
ROBINSON, Rufus 843-746-5100 99 D
ROBINSON, Sandra, L 407-823-5529 120 A
sandra.robinson@ucf.edu
ROBINSON, Sandra, T 313-922-3311 260 C
srobins1@wcccd.edu
ROBINSON, Sandy 216-987-4867 389 A
sandy.robinson@tri-c.edu
ROBINSON, Scott 901-320-9740 478 B
srobinson@victory.edu
ROBINSON, Sharon 518-244-2466 348 A
robins@sage.edu
ROBINSON, Sharon 704-233-8249 380 D
s.robinson@wingate.edu
ROBINSON, Sharon 970-204-8239 84 H
sharon.robinson@frontrange.edu
ROBINSON, Sharon 580-745-2362 412 C
srobinson@se.edu
ROBINSON, Shawn 813-253-7755 110 I
srobinson37@hccfl.edu
ROBINSON, Sid 909-537-5007 36 A
sidr@csusb.edu
ROBINSON, Stephanie, R 559-442-4600 72 A
stephanie.robinson@fresnocitycollege.edu
ROBINSON, Steve 304-293-2641 544 E
steve.robinsonr@mail.wvu.edu
ROBINSON, Sunnie 860-444-8508 558 E
Sunnie.Robinson@uscg.mil
ROBINSON, T. Joan 443-885-3350 224 F
joan.robinson@morgan.edu
ROBINSON, Terry 217-875-7200 162 D
terryr@richland.edu
ROBINSON, Theotis 865-974-0518 477 A
trobins4@tennessee.edu
ROBINSON, Timothy 904-620-2657 120 C
trobinso@unf.edu
ROBINSON, Tom 308-635-6182 301 E
robinson@wncc.edu
ROBINSON, Tracey 954-499-9849 104 C
trobinson2@devry.edu
ROBINSON, Tray 530-898-4764 34 A
trobinson@csuchico.edu
ROBINSON, Vickie, S 919-658-7757 367 D
vrobinson@moc.edu
ROBINSON, Wade, A 316-978-3021 197 F
wade.robinson@wichita.edu
ROBINSON, Walter, A 510-642-2316 73 E
wrobinson@berkeley.edu
ROBINSON, Warren 803-705-4662 455 D
robinson@benedict.edu
ROBINSON, Wayne 718-473-8960 328 E
wrobinson@citytech.cuny.edu
ROBINSON, Wayne 718-260-4900 328 E
wrobinson@citytech.cuny.edu
ROBINSON, Wayne 307-855-2104 555 G
wrobinson@cwc.edu
ROBINSON, Wayne, G 919-718-7214 368 H
wrobinson@cccc.edu
ROBINSON, Wendi 614-947-6768 391 A
robinsow@franklin.edu
ROBINSON, Wendy 212-616-7299 335 D
wendy.robinson@helenefuld.edu
ROBINSON, Wendy 515-964-6222 183 E
wsrobinson@dmacc.edu
ROBINSON, William 410-621-2355 227 E
wrobinson3@umes.edu
ROBINSON-ARMSTRONG,
Abbie 310-338-7598 56 E
arobinso@lmu.edu
ROBINSON-GARDNER,
Dorris, R 601-979-2455 275 A
dorris.r.gardner@jsums.edu
ROBINSON KLOOS,
Jennifer 651-690-8831 271 E
jrkloos@stkate.edu
ROBINSON-LEWIS,
Denise 973-720-2885 317 D
lewisd@wpunj.edu
ROBINSON-LONG, James 303-546-3566 86 B
james@naropa.edu
ROBINSON-WRIGHT,
Monique 615-230-3447 476 A
monique.wright@volstate.edu
ROBISON, Dan 312-280-3500 153 A
drobison@aii.edu
ROBISON, Jeff 540-261-8410 524 C
jeff.robison@svu.edu
ROBISON, Linda, K 504-280-6207 213 E
lrobison@uno.edu
ROBISON, Lori 419-267-1342 397 D
lrobison@northweststate.edu
ROBISON, Margaret 910-362-7101 368 E
mrobison@cfcc.edu
ROBISON, Mike 662-562-3438 276 E
jmrobison@northwestms.edu
ROBISON, Mike 559-438-4222 49 G
mike_robison@heald.edu
ROBISON, Richard 707-654-1093 32 I
rrobison@csum.edu
ROBISON, Ruth, E 808-974-7313 141 A
rrobison@hawaii.edu
ROBISON, Sue 304-326-1415 541 G
srobison@salemu.edu
ROBISON, Timothy 928-350-2103 18 C
trobison@prescott.edu
ROBITAILLE, Marilyn 254-968-9632 496 F
robitaille@tarleton.edu
ROBITZ, Krista 229-317-6929 128 A
krista.robitz@darton.edu
ROBLES, Doris 787-620-2040 560 B
drobles@aupr.edu
ROBLES, Elizabeth 213-477-2769 57 H
erobles@msmc.la.edu
ROBLES, Laura 310-243-2547 34 B
lrobles@csudh.edu
ROBLES, Ray 787-864-2222 563 D
rayroble@inter.edu
ROBLES, Ruben 909-748-8289 75 F
ruben_robles@redlands.edu
ROBNETT, Regi 207-221-4102 220 H
rrobnett@une.edu
ROBOLE, Donna 715-425-3502 552 A
donna.robole@uwrf.edu
ROBOMAN, Lourdes 691-350-2296 559 A
comfsmyap@comfsm.fm
ROBOTHAM, Donald 212-817-8013 327 B
drobotham@gc.cuny.edu
ROBUCK, Chris 503-594-3090 415 A
chrisr@clackamas.edu
ROBY, Mary 704-406-4293 364 B
ROBY, Peter, P 617-373-2672 244 A
ROCA, Carmen 305-592-1223 560 G
croca@albizu.edu
ROCA, Carmen 305-593-1223 102 D
croca@albizu.edu
ROCA, Joan 507-389-5953 267 H
joan.roca@mnsu.edu
ROCAP, Donna 845-431-8066 332 E
rocap@sunydutchess.edu
ROCCHETTI, Lisa 310-453-8300 45 F
lisa@emperors.edu
ROCCO, Denine, M 330-972-2672 403 B
drocco@uakron.edu
ROCCO, Frederick 508-678-2811 239 F
frederick.rocco@bristolcc.edu
ROCCO, Karen, S 412-362-8500 444 E
pims5808@aol.com
ROCHA, Amy 714-338-1303 29 K
arocha@aii.edu
ROCHA, Collette, G 323-343-3075 35 B
crocha@cslanet.calstate.edu
ROCHA, Daniel 210-486-3200 479 D
drocha@alamo.edu
ROCHA, Mark, W 626-585-7201 61 E
mwrocha@pasadena.edu
ROCHA, Roger 205-747-1001 19 C
roger.rocha@phoenix.edu
ROCHAT, Angela 970-247-7695 84 G
rochat_a@fortlewis.edu
ROCHE, Amarilis 787-848-1589 564 G
aeconomica@popac.edu
ROCHE, Daniel 973-655-4158 311 G
roched@mail.montclair.edu
ROCHE, Denise, A 716-829-7673 332 F
roche@dyc.edu
ROCHE, Isabel 802-440-4406 512 G
iroche@bennington.edu
ROCHE, James 413-545-6330 237 C
jroche@provost.umass.edu
ROCHE, Jason 313-993-1092 259 C
rochejj@udmercy.edu
ROCHE, Mary Beth 570-504-1589 433 A
rochem@lackawanna.edu
ROCHE, Scott 407-708-2174 117 G
roches@seminolestate.edu
ROCHE, Sibyl 651-757-4051 263 A
sjroche@cva.edu
ROCHE, Stephen, H 407-303-8016 108 D
stephen.roche@fhchs.edu
ROCHEFORT, Mary 218-723-6505 262 I
mrochefo@css.edu
ROCHELEAU, James 916-485-3276 402 I
james.rocheleau@myunion.edu
ROCHELEAU, Richard 310-338-6534 56 E
rrochele@lmu.edu
ROCHLITZ, Mendel 718-853-8500 357 I
ROCHON, Gilbert, L 334-727-8501 8 C
ROCHON, Ronald, S 812-465-1617 180 F
rochon@usi.edu
ROCHON, Sandra 978-762-4000 241 A
srochon@northshore.edu
ROCHON, Thomas, R 607-274-3111 336 G
president@ithaca.edu
ROCK, Arlene, M 413-782-1538 246 D
arock@wne.edu
ROCK, David 662-915-7063 277 G
rock@olemiss.edu
ROCK, David 727-786-4707 102 F
drock@cfi.edu
ROCK, Harry 413-748-3914 245 C
hrock@spfldcol.edu
ROCK, Jennifer 215-489-2917 426 H
Jennifer.Rock@delval.edu
ROCK, John 305-348-0570 119 B
John.Rock@fiu.edu
ROCK, John 504-568-8448 213 A
jrock@lsuhsc.edu
ROCK, Susan 516-299-3057 339 A
susan.rock@liu.edu
ROCK, Thomas 212-678-3083 357 F
tpr4@tc.columbia.edu
ROCKE, Mike 562-947-8755 71 A
mikerocke@scuhs.edu
ROCKECHARLIE, Barbara 704-372-0266 365 I
brockecharlie@kingscollegecharlotte.edu
ROCKENBACH,
Freddi-beth 215-567-7080 422 C
frockenbach@aii.edu
ROCKETT, Jeri, M 651-962-6780 272 E
gmrockett@stthomas.edu
ROCKETT, Kathryn, S 516-299-2523 338 F
kathryn.rockett@liu.edu
ROCKETT, Sandra 731-286-3238 475 A
rockett@dscc.edu
ROCKEY, Marci 217-786-2320 156 I
marci.rockey@llcc.edu
ROCKEY, Nancy, M 717-221-1774 430 E
nmrockey@hacc.edu
ROCKEY, Tim 210-486-0926 479 F
trockey@alamo.edu
ROCKHILL, Linda 718-779-1430 346 B
info@plazacollege.edu
ROCKHILL, Wendy 206-587-6921 537 A
wrockhill@sccd.ctc.edu
ROCKHOLD, Robin 601-984-2810 277 H
rrockhold@umc.edu
ROCKLAND-MILLER,
Harry, S 413-545-2337 237 C
rockmill@uhs.umass.edu
ROCKLIN, Thomas, R 319-335-3557 182 C
thomas-rocklin@uiowa.edu
ROCKS, JR., Thomas, E 412-261-2647 432 B
trocks@kaplan.edu
ROCQUE, Marc 215-527-2961 422 B
rocquem@arcadia.edu
ROCQUEMORE, Ronda 773-481-8103 147 F
rrocquemore@ccc.edu
RODARTE, Isabel 505-747-2241 320 A
irodarte@nnmc.edu
RODARTE, Kathleen 626-585-7439 61 E
kmrodarte@pasadena.edu
RODARTE, Susana 915-831-2018 486 E
srodart7@epcc.edu
RODAS, Daniel, J 516-299-2049 338 F
daniel.rodas@liu.edu
RODAS, Mary 516-364-0808 343 A
mrodas@nycollege.edu
RODDA, Robert 330-263-2062 388 E
rrodda@wooster.edu
RODDEN, Greg, A 863-638-7215 123 B
greg.rodden@warner.edu
RODDINI, Martin 516-572-7331 342 C
martin.roddini@ncc.edu
RODDY, Chris 269-927-8620 254 B
croddy@lakemichigancollege.edu
RODDY, Jackie 615-217-9347 468 B
jroddy@daymarinstitute.edu
RODDY, Lowell 931-221-7213 473 D
roddyl@apsu.edu
RODDY, Shirley 405-691-3800 408 H
sroddy@macu.edu
RODE, Joe 817-515-7741 496 A
joe.rode@tccd.edu
RODECKER, Daniel 518-580-5860 351 B
drodecke@skidmore.edu
RODENFELS, Clint, R 512-223-4721 481 B
crodenfe@austincc.edu
RODERICK, Gerald, K 410-778-7810 229 D
jroderick2@washcoll.edu
RODERICK, Michellle 508-999-8081 237 E
mroderick1@umassd.edu
RODES, Virginia 219-473-4372 170 D
vrodes@ccsj.edu
RODGER, Doug 712-324-5061 188 A
drodger@nwicc.edu
RODGERS, Anthony 904-470-8167 105 A
arrodgers@ewc.edu
RODGERS, Ardie 405-733-7434 411 I
arodgers@rose.edu
RODGERS, Beverly 218-335-4262 264 I
beverly.rodgers@lltc.edu
RODGERS, JR., Bob 404-233-3949 135 G
brodgers@richmont.edu
RODGERS, Christie 636-949-4697 284 C
crodgers@lindenwood.edu
RODGERS, Christopher 718-817-4755 334 C
chrodgers@fordham.edu
RODGERS, Denise, V 973-972-3645 316 C
rodgerdv@umdnj.edu
RODGERS, Forrest 509-963-2160 531 G
rodgers@cwu.edu
RODGERS, Fredrick 716-896-0700 359 F
rodgersf@villa.edu
RODGERS, Harold 574-257-3320 169 F
rodgerh@bethelcollege.edu
RODGERS, Janie 706-357-5281 124 H
jrodgers@athenstech.edu
RODGERS, Kenneth, G 919-530-5079 378 A
krodgers@nccu.edu
RODGERS, Laurie, A 314-719-3661 282 C
lrodgers@fontbonne.edu
RODGERS, Mark 708-366-3316 150 A
mrodgers@dom.edu
RODGERS, Mary, P 662-246-6263 275 F
mrodgers@msdelta.edu
RODGERS, Mike 214-818-1369 484 A
mrodgers@criswell.edu
RODGERS, Norma, L 918-595-7868 412 H
nrodgers@tulsacc.edu
RODGERS, Phillip 503-725-5442 418 G
prodgers@pdx.edu
RODGERS, Ronald, F 603-862-0960 306 D
ron.rodgers@usnh.edu
RODGERS, Ronald, F 603-862-0960 306 E
ron.rogers@unh.edu
RODGERS, Ruby 270-534-3184 203 B
ruby.rodgers@kctcs.edu
RODGERS, Ruth 317-955-6321 177 G
rrodgers@marian.edu
RODGERS, Teresa, P 334-670-3219 8 B
trodgers@troy.edu
RODGERS, Terreta 404-225-4604 125 A
trodgers@atlantatech.edu
RODGERS, Thomas, C 585-385-8184 348 F
trodgers@sjfc.edu
RODGERS, Victor 671-735-5640 559 B
victor.rodgers@guamcc.edu
RODIN, Merrill 213-477-2861 57 H
mrodin@msmc.la.edu
RODKIN, Carolyn 510-848-5232 47 I
crodkin@fst.edu
RODKIN, Dan 352-395-4171 117 E
dan.rodkin@sfcollege.edu
RODLER, Trina 323-856-7699 28 D
trodler@afi.com
RODNE, Anne 561-912-1211 106 G
arodne@evergladesuniversity.edu
RODNER, Richard 909-621-8099 40 D
richard.rodner@cmc.edu
RODNEY, Joel, M 717-771-4120 440 G
jmr45@psu.edu
RODNEY, Mae, L 336-750-2440 380 A
rodneyml@wssu.edu
RODNING, Janet, M 770-720-5954 135 F
jmr@reinhardt.edu
RODOCKER, Jason, L 540-458-8753 530 A
jrodocker@wlu.edu
RODOLF, Mark 405-974-3611 413 B
mrodolf@ucok.edu
RODOLFA, Emil, R 530-752-0871 73 F
errodolfa@ucdavis.edu
RODRICK SCHNAATH,
Heidi 215-967-1112 435 B
hrodrick-schnaath@ltsp.edu
RODRIGUE, Kelly, J 985-448-4154 216 A
kelly.rodrigue@nicholls.edu
RODRIGUE, Morris 530-242-7760 69 D
mrodrigue@shastacollege.edu
RODRIGUES, Leon 651-638-6810 261 I
l-rodrigues@bethel.edu

ROGERS, Bryan, L 734-763-4093 259 D
blrogers@umich.edu
ROGERS, Cheryl, L 903-510-3217 502 E
crog@tjc.edu
ROGERS, Chris 610-647-4400 431 B
crogers@immaculata.edu
ROGERS, Cindy, A 972-860-8186 484 G
car3810@dcccd.edu
ROGERS, Craig, L 270-789-5057 199 C
crogers@campbellsville.edu
ROGERS, Dana 409-882-3372 500 G
dana.rogers@lsco.edu
ROGERS, Dana, N 409-882-3397 500 G
dana.rogers@lsco.edu
ROGERS, David, E 315-684-6054 354 F
rogersde@morrisville.edu
ROGERS, Donna 252-789-0290 371 E
drogers@martincc.edu
ROGERS, Dwayne 318-487-7216 209 B
rogers@lacollege.edu
ROGERS, Elizabeth 410-752-4710 221 E
lrogers@bic.edu
ROGERS, Elizabeth 931-372-3317 474 B
erogers@tntech.edu
ROGERS, Elizabeth, A 336-278-6350 364 A
rogers@elon.edu
ROGERS, Frederick, A 507-222-4173 262 B
frogers@carleton.edu
ROGERS, Gail 423-746-5202 476 D
grogers@twcnet.edu
ROGERS, Gannon 707-668-5663 43 I
ROGERS, George 440-826-8094 384 H
gerogers@bw.edu
ROGERS, Glen 414-382-6269 545 H
glen.rogers@alverno.edu
ROGERS, Greg 623-845-4526 15 J
greg.rogers@gcmail.maricopa.edu
ROGERS, Greg 412-392-3924 444 H
grogers@pointpark.edu
ROGERS, Gregory 401-254-3116 454 C
grogers@rwu.edu
ROGERS, Harry, C 215-898-7091 448 I
library@pobox.upenn.edu
ROGERS, Hudson 239-590-7329 119 A
hrogers@fgcu.edu
ROGERS, J. Orion 540-831-5958 522 D
jorogers@radford.edu
ROGERS, Jack, T 541-737-3010 418 F
jack.rogers@oregonstate.edu
ROGERS, James 212-327-8506 347 H
jrogers@mail.rockefeller.edu
ROGERS, James 212-517-0435 340 D
jrogers@mmm.edu
ROGERS, Janet 614-287-2727 388 G
jrogers@cscc.edu
ROGERS, Jason 615-460-6441 467 B
jason.rogers@belmont.edu
ROGERS, Jeanette 205-853-1200 5 C
jrogers@jeffstateonline.com
ROGERS, Jenica, P 315-267-2482 354 C
rogersjp@potsdam.edu
ROGERS, Jesse 858-598-1200 30 A
jrogers@aii.edu
ROGERS, Jesse, W 940-397-4211 491 A
jesse.rogers@mwsu.edu
ROGERS, Jessica 941-487-4900 119 D
ncalum@ncf.edu
ROGERS, Jevita 703-993-2349 519 A
jdefreit@gmu.edu
ROGERS, John, W 413-205-3378 229 G
john.rogers@aic.edu
ROGERS, Johnell 803-934-3256 459 F
jrogers@morris.edu
ROGERS, Jolayne 816-322-0110 279 H
jolayne.rogers@calvary.edu
ROGERS, Jolene, R 712-362-0491 185 G
jrogers@iowalakes.edu
ROGERS, Jolynn 509-359-2383 533 D
jrogers@ewu.edu
ROGERS, Joseph 320-363-2082 271 F
jrogers@csbsju.edu
ROGERS, Joseph, T 610-527-0200 445 I
jtrogers@rosemont.edu
ROGERS, Joyce 317-916-7850 175 G
jrogers@ivytech.edu
ROGERS, Joyce 602-978-7332 18 K
joyce.rogers@thunderbird.edu
ROGERS, Judith 340-692-4132 568 C
jrogers@uvi.edu
ROGERS, Judy, R 417-667-8181 280 I
jrogers@cottey.edu
ROGERS, Kathleen, R 617-521-2276 245 A
kathleen.rogers@simmons.edu
ROGERS, Ken 509-527-2511 538 H
ken.rogers@wallawalla.edu
ROGERS, Leslie, D 252-493-7322 372 E
lrogers@email.pittcc.edu
ROGERS, Lisa, C 615-898-5345 473 F
lisa.rogers@mtsu.edu
ROGERS, Mary 619-388-6591 65 E
mrogers@sdccd.edu
ROGERS, Meryl 631-851-6296 356 G
rogersm@sunysuffolk.edu
ROGERS, Michael, B 607-735-1891 333 A
mrogers@elmira.edu
ROGERS, Michael, F 843-953-7696 456 C
mike.rogers@citadel.edu
ROGERS, Michael, Q 904-470-8151 105 A
michael.rogers0904@ewc.edu
ROGERS, Mike 209-946-2569 75 D
mrogers@pacific.edu
ROGERS, Nancy, B 812-237-7900 173 A
nancy.rogers@indstate.edu
ROGERS, Patricia, A 781-891-2622 231 F
progers@bentley.edu
ROGERS, Patricia, L 218-755-2965 266 B
progers@bemidjistate.edu
ROGERS, Pete 303-964-5207 87 E
progers@regis.edu
ROGERS, Phil 208-459-5282 143 A
progers@collegeofidaho.edu
ROGERS, Philip 252-328-6105 377 C
rogersp@ecu.edu
ROGERS, Phyllis 864-592-4816 461 C
rogersp@sccsc.edu
ROGERS, Phyllis 254-295-4501 504 A
progers@umhb.edu
ROGERS, Ralph 510-780-4500 53 I
rrogers@lifewest.edu
ROGERS, Ralph, V 219-989-2446 178 G
rvrogers@purduecal.edu
ROGERS, Randy 317-921-4737 175 I
rrogers@ivytech.edu
ROGERS, Randy 336-386-3466 374 B
rogersr@surry.edu
ROGERS, Ray 407-646-2195 116 B
rrogers@rollins.edu
ROGERS, Richard, L 313-664-7474 250 A
rrogers@collegeforcreativestudies.edu
ROGERS, Richard, R 909-593-3511 75 C
rrogers2@laverne.edu
ROGERS, Rodney, K 419-372-2915 385 C
rrogers@bgsu.edu
ROGERS, Russell 201-216-5078 315 E
rrogers@stevens.edu
ROGERS, Ruth, D 253-535-7186 535 K
rogersrd@plu.edu
ROGERS, Sandra 801-422-4916 509 D
sandra_rogers@byu.edu
ROGERS, Scott 828-726-2488 368 D
srogers@cccti.edu
ROGERS, Scott 509-542-4834 532 C
srogers@columbiabasin.edu
ROGERS, Scott, S 330-385-1070 400 E
srogers@ovct.edu
ROGERS, Sharon 609-894-9311 308 C
srogers@bcc.edu
ROGERS, Sheree, O 920-832-6587 547 J
sheree.o.rogers@lawrence.edu
ROGERS, Stacy 859-344-3309 206 D
stacy.rogers@thomasmore.edu
ROGERS, Stephen, K 405-744-8052 410 C
steve.rogers@okstate.edu
ROGERS, Susan 706-379-3111 139 F
srogers@yhc.edu
ROGERS, Susan 972-883-4325 505 D
susan.rogers@utdallas.edu
ROGERS, Tamara, E 617-496-3069 235 H
tamara_rogers@harvard.edu
ROGERS, Tammy 706-880-8344 132 I
trogers@lagrange.edu
ROGERS, Tammy 202-319-5232 97 C
rogerst@cua.edu
ROGERS, Tamy 214-333-5158 484 C
tamy@dbu.edu
ROGERS, Theresa 925-969-3449 52 B
trogers@jfku.edu
ROGERS, Thomas 502-213-7310 202 B
thomas.rogers@kctcs.edu
ROGERS, Tracy 719-587-7990 80 F
tracy_rogers@adams.edu
ROGERS, Vivian, D 757-499-7900 517 A
vdrogers@bryantstratton.edu
ROGERS, W. Timothy 865-974-6593 477 B
timrogers@utk.edu
ROGERS, Warren, W 913-971-3380 195 A
wwrogers@mnu.edu
ROGERSON, Andrew 707-664-2028 37 B
ROGERSON, Joanie 360-736-9391 531 H
jrogerson@centralia.edu
ROGG, Cathie 616-698-7111 250 E
crogg@davenport.edu
ROGGE, Ann 302-736-2445 96 G
roggean@wesley.edu
ROGNSTAD, Lynn, B 605-677-6497 465 E
lynn.rognstad@usd.edu
ROGOFF, Mai-Lan, A 508-856-5652 238 A
mai-lan.rogoff@umassmed.edu
ROGOW, Robert 859-622-1409 200 D
robert.rogow@eku.edu
ROGSTAD, Mark 509-574-4671 540 A
mrogstad@yvcc.edu
ROHALY, Julie 615-217-9347 468 B
jrohaly@daymarinstitute.edu
ROHAN, James, P 920-465-2075 551 A
rohanj@uwgb.edu
ROHDE, Scott, W 608-785-8711 551 B
rohde.scot@uwlax.edu
ROHLEDER, Ann 812-357-6610 179 E
arohleder@saintmeinrad.edu
ROHLEDER, John 651-779-3496 266 D
john.rohleder@century.edu
ROHLENA, Robbie 712-274-5426 187 D
rohlena@morningside.edu
ROHLER, James 740-363-1146 396 A
jrohler@mtso.edu
ROHLFS, Steven 301-447-5295 225 A
rohlfs@msmary.edu
ROHM, Robert, K 937-766-7603 386 F
rohmr@cedarville.edu
ROHNER, Tom 630-889-6638 159 E
trohner@nuhs.edu
ROHR, Ann 970-207-4550 85 M
ROHR, Ann 970-207-4500 89 A
ROHRBACH, Anne, L 814-865-5471 438 F
alr3@psu.edu
ROHRBACH, Daniel, W 937-255-6565 556 H
daniel.rohrbach@afit.edu
ROHRBACK, Jane, T 248-204-3160 254 E
jrohrback@ltu.edu
ROHRBAUGH, Suzanne 252-335-0821 369 D
suzanne_rohrbaugh@albemarle.edu
ROHRER, Douglas 270-901-3490 207 C
douglas.rohrer@wku.edu
ROHRER, Katherine 609-258-7800 313 A
krohrer@princeton.edu
ROHRER, Mary 507-457-2602 270 B
mrohrer@winona.edu
ROHRS, Dawn, M 816-654-7012 283 J
drohrs@kcumb.edu
ROHWER, Keith 402-941-6332 299 A
rohwer@midlandu.edu
ROID, Gale 503-517-1053 421 A
groid@warnerpacific.edu
ROIDT, Joseph, M 304-637-1277 540 F
roidtj@dewv.edu
ROIG, Lizzette, A 787-844-9231 567 E
lizzette.roig@upr.edu
ROISELAND, Kevin, N 319-352-8220 189 F
kevin.roiseland@wartburg.edu
ROJAS, Carmen, I 787-743-4041 561 E
crojas@columbiaco.edu
ROJAS, Jason 860-297-4166 94 C
jason.rojas@trincoll.edu
ROJAS, Rene, L 716-851-1259 333 D
rojas@ecc.edu
ROJAS, Rodney 213-613-2200 70 H
rodney_rojas@sciarc.edu
ROJCEWICZ, Peter, M 206-268-4108 530 F
projcewicz@antioch.edu
ROJO, Richard 209-946-2311 75 D
rrojo@pacific.edu
ROKOS, Jean 231-995-1248 256 G
jrokos@nmc.edu
ROKOS, Nicole 561-297-3880 118 H
nrokos@fau.edu
ROKOWSKY, Israel 845-425-1370 345 B
ROKSANDIC, Stevo 614-234-1644 396 G
sroksandic@mchs.com
ROKUSEK, Jim 605-367-6109 466 C
jim.rokusek@southeasttech.edu
ROLAN, Chris 408-855-5438 78 A
chris.rolan@wvm.edu
ROLAND, Cheryl 269-387-8400 260 F
cheryl.roland@wmich.edu
ROLAND, Christy 515-244-4221 181 D
rolandc@aib.edu
ROLAND, David, E 706-233-7329 136 E
droland@shorter.edu
ROLAND, Desiree 954-322-4460 112 B
ROLAND, Harriet, A 803-533-3790 460 G
rolandha@scsu.edu
ROLAND, Kirc, J 360-442-2471 535 C
kroland@lowercolumbia.edu
ROLAND, Mark 515-244-4221 181 D
rolandm@aib.edu
ROLAND, Meg 503-699-3336 416 I
mroland@marylhurst.edu
ROLD, Gary, F 630-617-3078 150 F
garyr@elmhurst.edu
ROLDAN, Marggi 864-578-8770 460 F
mroldan@sherman.edu
ROLEN, Chris 408-741-2092 77 K
chris_rolen@wvm.edu
ROLEN, Scott 541-917-4420 416 H
rolens@linnbenton.edu
ROLEY, V. Vance 808-956-8377 141 B
vroley@hawaii.edu
ROLFE, Cynthia 405-974-2688 413 B
crolfe@ucok.edu
ROLFE, Rial, D 806-743-2905 501 E
rial.rolfe@ttuhsc.edu
ROLFES, Katherine 337-521-8906 212 B
kroltes@southlouisiana.edu
ROLFSON, Eric, F 207-581-1198 220 A
eric.rolfson@maine.edu
ROLHEISER, Ronald 210-341-1366 491 E
rrolheiser@ost.edu
ROLL, Debbie 907-564-8220 10 D
droll@alaskapacific.edu
ROLLANS, Mary Ann 479-968-0234 20 G
mrollans@atu.edu
ROLLE, Jo Ann 212-752-1530 338 C
joann.rolle@limcollege.edu
ROLLE, Kevin 256-372-5279 1 A
kevin.rolle@aamu.edu
ROLLENE, Jerry 479-524-7212 22 C
jrollene@jbu.edu
ROLLER, Laura 612-330-1720 261 G
roller@augsburg.edu
ROLLER, Steven, A 617-228-2023 239 G
sroller@bhcc.mass.edu
ROLLESTON, George 440-826-2081 384 H
grollest@bw.edu
ROLLEY, LuAnn, K 802-656-7892 514 F
luann.rolley@uvm.edu
ROLLING, OSB, Brendan 913-360-7655 190 F
brolling@benedictine.edu
ROLLINGS, Dave 775-445-4223 303 B
dcr@wnc.edu
ROLLINS, Andrea 619-594-6416 36 E
ROLLINS, Benita 740-362-3374 396 A
brollins@mtso.edu
ROLLINS, Cheryl 443-885-4429 224 F
cheryl.rollins@morgan.edu
ROLLINS, John 562-997-5340 44 G
jrollins@devry.edu
ROLLINS, Karen 860-509-9511 92 D
krollins@hartsem.edu
ROLLINS, Pam 334-420-4253 7 I
prollins@trenholmstate.edu
ROLLINS, Stephen, J 907-786-1825 10 I
srollins@uaa.alaska.edu
ROLLISON, Jeffrey, D 610-647-4400 431 B
jrollison@immaculata.edu
ROLLMAN, Catherine, A 804-752-7270 522 F
crollman@rmc.edu
ROLLO, Ann 315-364-3416 360 C
arollo@wells.edu
ROLLO, J. Michael 239-590-7910 119 A
jmrollo@fgcu.edu
ROLLOCK, Alysa, C 765-494-5830 178 F
acrollock@purdue.edu
ROLLS, Dickie 620-252-7575 191 I
dickier@coffeyville.edu
ROLON, Maricruz 787-743-7979 565 F
mrolon@suagm.edu
ROLON, Reynaldo 787-279-1912 563 B
rrolon@bayamon.inter.edu
ROLPH, Chris 865-573-4517 469 J
crolph@johnsonU.edu
ROM, Cristine 216-421-7440 387 H
crom@cia.edu
ROM, Kjetil 541-881-5746 420 E
krom@tvcc.cc
ROMA, Lawrence, J 607-777-2224 351 F
lroma@binghamton.edu
ROMACK, Thomas 740-264-5591 390 F
tromack@egcc.edu
ROMAGNOLI, Janice 615-655-7274 325 I
jaromagnoli@cazenovia.edu
ROMAIN, Pete 212-517-0414 340 D
promain@mmm.edu
ROMALI, Reagan, F 773-907-4451 147 A
rromali@ccc.edu
ROMAN, Brunilda 787-480-2410 561 D
broman@sanjuancapital.com
ROMAN, Cathy 717-291-4197 429 E
cathy.roman@fandm.edu
ROMAN, Cynthia 734-384-4101 255 G
croman@monroeccc.edu
ROMAN, Elba, I 787-890-2681 566 E
elba.roman@upr.edu
ROMAN, Ivan, F 787-882-2065 565 I
director_ejecutivo@unitecpr.net
ROMAN, Jose Luis 787-480-2461 561 D
jroman@sanjuancapital.com
ROMAN, Juan, E 787-841-2000 564 I
ROMAN, Kristen 312-850-7186 147 C
1118mgr@fheg.follett.com
ROMAN, Marcia 407-404-6014 117 G
romanm@seminolestate.edu
ROMAN, Marcia 407-708-4722 117 G
romanm@seminolestate.edu
ROMAN, Maria 559-791-2364 53 A
mroman@portervillecollege.edu
ROMAN, Nilsa, M 787-891-0925 562 G
nroman@aguadilla.inter.edu
ROMAN, Paul 724-838-4215 447 B
roman@setonhill.edu
ROMAN, Susan 708-524-6986 150 A
sroman@dom.edu
ROMAN, Vladimir 787-763-6425 562 F
vroman@inter.edu
ROMAN-VARGAS,
Madeline 773-489-8910 147 F
mroman-vargas@ccc.edu
ROMANELLO, Mary 202-884-9000 99 E
ROMANO, C. Renee 217-333-1300 167 B
romano3@illinois.edu
ROMANO, Carol, A 301-295-1180 558 A
carol.romano@usuhs.mil
ROMANO, Christopher 201-684-7309 313 D
cromano@ramapo.edu

ROSE, Linda 562-860-2451 38 J lrose@cerritos.edu
ROSE, Linda 714-564-6082 63 F rose_linda@sac.edu
ROSE, Linwood, H 540-568-6868 520 C roselh@jmu.edu
ROSE, Lisa 310-434-4402 68 D rose_lisa@smc.edu
ROSE, Louise 978-681-0800 242 B lrose@mslaw.edu
ROSE, Margie 303-369-5151 86 I fa@plattcolorado.edu
ROSE, Maria, C 304-367-4151 543 E
ROSE, Marie 818-401-1034 42 D mrose@columbiacollege.edu
ROSE, Mary 781-239-5075 230 G rose@babson.edu
ROSE, Melissa 315-859-4413 335 A marose@hamilton.edu
ROSE, Melody 503-725-3137 418 G rosem@pdx.edu
ROSE, Michael, J 215-898-5828 448 I mjrose@pobox.upenn.edu
ROSE, Patricia, L 215-898-3208 448 I prose@pobox.upenn.edu
ROSE, Rachel 276-376-4035 525 C rlb7q@uvawise.edu
ROSE, Rebecca 304-829-7221 540 E rrose@bethanywv.edu
ROSE, Sarah 423-585-6752 476 B sarah.rose@ws.edu
ROSE, Sharon 252-398-1229 363 E rosesh@chowan.edu
ROSE, Steve 509-527-2402 538 H steve.rose@wallawalla.edu
ROSE, Steven 973-684-5900 312 E srose@pccc.edu
ROSE, Susan 713-525-6957 504 D roses@stthom.edu
ROSE, Ted 615-547-1383 467 I trose@cumberland.edu
ROSE, Todd, S 703-993-5012 519 A trose2@gmu.edu
ROSE, Vanessa, R 202-994-0816 97 F vrose@gwu.edu
ROSE, Wanda, F 701-323-6271 381 B wrose@mohs.org
ROSE-STEPHENS, Sodia 954-492-5353 102 J srose-stephens@citycollege.edu
ROSEBERRY, Fred 606-585-8647 201 B Froseberry0001@kctcs.edu
ROSEBLADE, Bob 530-541-4660 53 F roseblade@ltcc.edu
ROSEBOOM, Julie 607-436-2503 353 E roseboj@oneonta.edu
ROSEBORO, Clevell, S 919-516-4145 376 B csroseboro@st-aug.edu
ROSEBORO-BARNES, Edwina 803-981-7162 463 G eroseboro@yorktech.edu
ROSEBROUGH, Tom 731-661-5373 476 G trosebro@uu.edu
ROSELLI, Claudia 708-974-5357 159 A roselli@morainevalley.edu
ROSEMEYER, Abbie 561-803-2180 114 C abbie_rosemeyer@pba.edu
ROSEN, Abbey, E 920-923-7645 548 C aerosen95@marianuniversity.edu
ROSEN, Barry 212-220-1238 326 E brosen@bmcc.cuny.edu
ROSEN, C. Martin 812-941-2262 174 D crosen@ius.edu
ROSEN, David 617-824-8540 234 D david_rosen@emerson.edu
ROSEN, David, M 818-767-0888 79 D david.rosen@woodbury.edu
ROSEN, Janet, S 218-723-6072 262 I jrosen@css.edu
ROSEN, Jeffrey, H 312-915-6562 157 A jrosen9@luc.edu
ROSEN, Jonathan, M 518-262-5686 322 E rosenj@mail.amc.edu
ROSEN, Robert, J 262-551-5702 546 F rrosen@carthage.edu
ROSEN, Sara 785-864-4904 196 F rosen@ku.edu
ROSEN, Sara Thomas 785-864-8040 196 F rosen@ku.edu
ROSEN, Seth 212-431-2169 343 E srosen@nyls.edu
ROSEN, Sharon 407-215-9706 110 H sharon@orl.herzing.edu
ROSEN-BRAND, Amy 716-878-4500 353 A rosenba@buffalostate.edu
ROSEN SINGLETON, Suzanne 202-448-7213 97 E suzanne.singleton@gallaudet.edu
ROSENBALM, Whitney 972-238-6023 485 C wrosenbalm@dcccd.edu
ROSENBAUM, Carol 212-463-0400 357 J carolr@touro.edu
ROSENBAUM, David, R 864-941-8377 460 D rosenbaum.d@ptc.edu
ROSENBAUM, Irving 954-262-1507 114 B irv@nsu.nova.edu
ROSENBAUM, Thomas, F 773-702-8810 166 D provost@uchicago.edu
ROSENBERG, Alannah 949-582-4854 70 F aorrison@saddleback.edu
ROSENBERG, Brian, C 651-696-6207 265 A rosenbergb@macalester.edu
ROSENBERG, Chaim 718-854-2290 324 A
ROSENBERG, Eric 201-216-5488 315 E erosenbe@stevens.edu
ROSENBERG, Harry 702-968-2020 303 D jseip@roseman.edu
ROSENBERG, John 801-422-2779 509 D john_rosenberg@byu.edu
ROSENBERG, Kris 503-251-2821 420 H krosenberg@uws.edu
ROSENBERG, Mark 305-348-2111 119 B mark.rosenberg@fiu.edu
ROSENBERG, Naomi 617-636-2143 245 F naomi.rosenberg@tufts.edu
ROSENBERG, Samuel 201-684-7624 313 D sjrosenb@ramapo.edu
ROSENBERG, Samuel 312-341-3697 162 I srosenbe@roosevelt.edu
ROSENBERG, Sherry 717-564-4112 432 A srosenberg@kaplan.edu
ROSENBERGER, Benjamin 610-372-4721 445 B brosenberger@racc.edu
ROSENBERGER, Jeanne 408-554-4583 68 C jrosenberger@scu.edu
ROSENBERGER, Steven, H 614-823-1150 400 G srosenberger@otterbein.edu
ROSENBLATT, Jim 601-925-7104 275 E jim.rosenblatt@mc.edu
ROSENBLOOM, Stuart 312-461-0600 144 D srosenbloom@aaart.edu
ROSENBLUM, Donald 954-262-8402 114 B donr@nsu.nova.edu
ROSENBLUM, Ken 219-392-3600 176 E krosenbl@ivytech.edu
ROSENBLUM, Yosef 718-854-2290 324 A
ROSENBOOM, David 661-255-1050 32 C drosenbo@calarts.edu
ROSENDAHL, Matthew 715-246-6561 555 E matt.rosendahl@witc.edu
ROSENFELD, Lynn, R 661-255-1050 32 C lynn@calarts.edu
ROSENFELD, Renee 215-637-7700 430 H rlrosenfeld@holyfamily.edu
ROSENFELD, Sholom 718-774-5050 357 E
ROSENFELDT, Mary 513-745-3022 406 E rosenfeldt@xavier.edu
ROSENGART, Sharon 973-720-3019 317 D rosengarts@wpunj.edu
ROSENGARTEN, Jayne 212-650-3733 327 E jayne.rosengarten@hunter.cuny.edu
ROSENGARTEN, Jeffrey 212-960-5239 361 I rosengar@yu.edu
ROSENGARTEN, Lewis 607-753-4808 353 B lewis.rosengarten@cortland.edu
ROSENHECK, Sari 845-434-5750 356 H sarir@sullivan.suny.edu
ROSENHEIN, Jon 212-799-5000 337 H
ROSENKRANS, Jane 949-582-4340 70 F jrosenkrans@saddleback.edu
ROSENRAUCH, Yair 718-259-5300 324 D yrosen@bramsonort.edu
ROSENSAFT, Jean, B 212-824-2209 391 E jrosensaft@huc.edu
ROSENSTEIN, Arthur 858-566-1200 43 J arthur@disd.edu
ROSENSTEIN, Gloria 858-566-1200 43 J gloria@disd.edu
ROSENSTEIN, Ilena 860-768-4418 95 A rosenstei@hartford.edu
ROSENSTEIN, Ilene 213-740-7711 76 C irosenst@usc.edu
ROSENSTOCK, Esther 443-334-2653 226 E erosenstock@stevenson.edu
ROSENSTOCK, Linda 310-825-6381 74 A lindarosenstock@ph.ucla.edu
ROSENSTONE, Steven, J 651-201-1696 265 H
ROSENTHAL, Cheryl 671-824-8595 234 D cheryl_rosenthal@emerson.edu
ROSENTHAL, David, S 617-495-2010 235 H drose@uhs.harvard.edu
ROSENTHAL, Eric 847-925-6677 151 E erosenth@harpercollege.edu
ROSENTHAL, Jeffrey, E 315-255-1743 325 H rosenthal@cayuga-cc.edu
ROSENTHAL, Jonathan, M 309-438-2920 153 C jmrosen@ilstu.edu
ROSENTHAL, Rachel 916-660-7502 69 F rrosenthal@sierracollege.edu
ROSENTHAL, Rich 704-330-6316 369 A rich.rosenthal@cpcc.edu
ROSENTHAL, Robert 860-685-2010 95 C rrosenthal@wesleyan.edu
ROSETH, Lisa 218-723-6016 262 I lroseth@css.edu
ROSEVEAR, Scott, G 570-577-3200 423 D scott.rosevear@bucknell.edu
ROSEVEARE, Mark 864-592-4763 461 C rosevearem@sccsc.edu
ROSHON, William 239-489-9292 104 L wroshon@edison.edu
ROSICKY, John, A 301-322-0524 225 F jrosicky@pgcc.edu
ROSIER, Tamara 616-222-3000 254 A trosier@kuyper.edu
ROSIER, Therese 706-737-1400 125 C trosier@aug.edu
ROSINE, Greg, J 269-387-2072 260 F greg.rosine@wmich.edu
ROSINSKI, Shonda 337-521-8934 212 B srosinski@southlouisiana.edu
ROSKOWSKI, Ed 520-515-3688 13 G roskoe@cochise.edu
ROSKOWSKI, Pamela 415-476-5455 74 E proskowski@police.ucsf.edu
ROSKY, Bruce 818-610-6543 55 B roskybrucer@piercecollege.edu
ROSMUS, Julie 802-773-5900 513 B jrosmus@csj.edu
ROSNER, Christine 215-637-7700 430 H crosner@holyfamily.edu
ROSNER, Julie, A 215-572-2815 422 B rosner@arcadia.edu
ROSNER-SALAZAR, Ari Senghor 303-556-4724 83 F ari.rosner@ccd.edu
ROSNIK, Peter 413-775-1441 240 B rosnick@gcc.mass.edu
ROSOFF, Nancy, G 856-225-6486 314 C nrosoff@camden.rutgers.edu
ROSONET, Kay 228-497-7649 275 G kay.rosonet@mgccc.edu
ROSOWSKY, David 518-276-6298 347 D rosowd@rpi.edu
ROSPOND, Raylene 515-271-1814 184 A raylene.rospond@drake.edu
ROSPOND, Raylene 515-271-2982 184 A
ROSS, Amy 978-232-2161 234 F aross@endicott.edu
ROSS, Anthony, J 651-641-8815 263 C ross@csp.edu
ROSS, Anthony, R 323-343-3100 35 B tross@cslanet.calstatela.edu
ROSS, Arthur, J 304-293-6607 544 E ajross@hsc.wvu.edu
ROSS, Beverly 334-420-4332 7 I bross@trenholmstate.edu
ROSS, Bob 386-226-6198 14 D robert.ross@erau.edu
ROSS, Calvin 850-599-3256 118 G calvin.ross@famu.edu
ROSS, Carla 510-869-6618 64 J cross@samuelmerritt.edu
ROSS, Carmin, E 217-875-7200 162 D cross@richland.edu
ROSS, Christine, C 434-223-6056 519 B cross@email.hsc.edu
ROSS, Christopher 425-637-1010 531 I c.ross@cityu.edu
ROSS, Chrystle, M 229-391-4853 123 F cross@abac.edu
ROSS, Clark, G 704-894-2204 363 F clross@davidson.edu
ROSS, Corey 903-233-4460 489 K CoreyRoss@letu.edu
ROSS, Cynthia, S 580-581-2201 407 D cross@cameron.edu
ROSS, David 501-279-4930 21 H dross@harding.edu
ROSS, David 270-247-8521 204 C dross@midcontinent.edu
ROSS, David, A 972-708-7340 486 I david_ross@gial.edu
ROSS, David, B 573-651-2297 290 D dross@semo.edu
ROSS, David, L 804-828-6610 525 E dlross@vcu.edu
ROSS, Deanna 208-459-5222 143 A dross@collegeofidaho.edu
ROSS, Denise 704-991-0264 374 A dross7926@stanly.edu
ROSS, Donald, E 561-237-7782 113 D dross@lynn.edu
ROSS, Donnah 352-854-2322 103 D rossd@cf.edu
ROSS, Elizabeth 617-735-9701 234 E ross@emmanuel.edu
ROSS, Elizabeth 212-229-8947 342 E rosse@newschool.edu
ROSS, Eric 660-263-4110 287 B ericr@macc.edu
ROSS, JR., Ervin 386-481-2561 101 I rosse@cookman.edu
ROSS, Frank, E 773-442-4600 159 H
ROSS, Gary 706-233-7326 136 E gross@shorter.edu
ROSS, Gary, L 315-228-7401 329 H gross@colgate.edu
ROSS, George, E 989-774-3131 249 G president@cmich.edu
ROSS, Gerald 410-225-2399 224 C gross@mica.edu
ROSS, James 321-433-7095 101 J rossj@brevardcc.edu
ROSS, James, A 734-384-4259 255 G jross@monroeccc.edu
ROSS, James, H 573-884-8738 291 C rossjh@health.missouri.edu
ROSS, Jason 864-977-7026 460 A jason.ross@ngu.edu
ROSS, Jennifer, A 260-422-5561 172 L jaross@indianatech.edu
ROSS, Jerrold 718-990-1305 348 G rossj@stjohns.edu
ROSS, Joann 304-253-7351 541 D jross@mountainstate.edu
ROSS, John 903-589-4014 490 B jross@lonmorris.edu
ROSS, John, A 785-628-4431 192 F jross@fhsu.edu
ROSS, Julie, S 617-627-3360 245 F j.ross@tufts.edu
ROSS, Karen 734-432-5529 254 G kross@madonna.edu
ROSS, Kathleen 650-574-6532 67 F rossk@smccd.edu
ROSS, Keith 314-392-2301 286 C rossk@mobap.edu
ROSS, Ken 863-297-1096 115 A kross@polk.edu
ROSS, Kevin, M 561-237-7823 113 D kross@lynn.edu
ROSS, Larry, W 610-799-1128 434 D lross@lccc.edu
ROSS, Laura 407-708-2058 117 G rossl@seminolestate.edu
ROSS, Lauren 937-512-2625 401 J lauren.ross@sinclair.edu
ROSS, Luana 406-275-4959 296 F luana_ross@skc.edu
ROSS, Lucy 763-576-4797 266 A lross@anokatech.edu
ROSS, Meg 662-562-3204 276 E mross@northwestms.edu
ROSS, Mettha, M 312-939-0111 150 B mettha@eastwest.edu
ROSS, Michael 773-291-6348 147 D mross17@ccc.edu
ROSS, Michael, D 614-885-5585 401 B mross@pcj.edu
ROSS, Mindy 845-341-4541 345 E mindy.ross@sunyorange.edu
ROSS, Nancy, J 207-795-7596 217 F rossnj@cmhc.org
ROSS, Pam 404-669-2487 135 E pam.ross@point.edu
ROSS, Pam 864-231-2032 455 C pbryant@andersonuniversity.edu
ROSS, Patricia, A 937-778-7887 390 G pross@edisonohio.edu
ROSS, Pete 216-987-3471 389 A peter.ross@tri-c.edu
ROSS, Peter, G 989-774-4456 249 G ross1pg@cmich.edu
ROSS, III, Phillip 410-704-4053 228 E pross@towson.edu
ROSS, Rebecca 610-436-2501 443 F rross2@wcupa.edu
ROSS, Reginald 410-951-3596 228 B rross@coppin.edu
ROSS, Richard, S 860-297-2258 94 C richard.ross@trincoll.edu
ROSS, Rick 360-417-6533 536 B rross@pencol.edu
ROSS, Ronald 973-877-3078 310 A ross@essex.edu
ROSS, Roshaunda 309-556-3412 153 E mcaffairs@iwu.edu
ROSS, Ruth, M 360-475-7250 535 J rross@olympic.edu
ROSS, Ryan 303-556-3926 83 F ryan.ross@ccd.edu
ROSS, Sadie 518-587-2100 355 F sadie.ross@esc.edu
ROSS, Scott, T 304-877-6428 540 D admissions@abc.edu
ROSS, Sonia 210-690-9000 487 B sross@hallmarkcollege.edu
ROSS, Sonia 210-690-9000 487 C sross@hallmarkcollege.edu
ROSS, Stephen 541-552-6258 419 A rossS@sou.edu
ROSS, Stephen, C 724-847-6541 429 G scross@geneva.edu
ROSS, Terryl, J 541-737-4381 418 F terryl.ross@oregonstate.edu
ROSS, Thelma 484-365-7583 434 H tross@lincoln.edu
ROSS, Thelma, L 800-561-2606 434 H tross@lincoln.edu
ROSS, Thomas, W 919-962-4622 377 A tomross@northcarolina.edu
ROSS, Todd 626-815-6000 30 E tross@apu.edu
ROSS, Tricia 212-799-5000 337 H

ROWE, Theresa, M 248-370-4326 257 C rowe@oakland.edu
ROWE, Tom 641-472-1144 187 B trowe@mum.edu
ROWE, Wayne 740-389-6786 399 D rowe.31@osu.edu
ROWELL, Amanda 409-882-3345 500 G amanda.rowell@lsco.edu
ROWELL, Amy 251-275-3156 1 B arowell@ascc.edu
ROWELL, Barbara 304-766-3156 544 D browell@wvstateu.edu
ROWELL, Eric 309-794-7578 145 B ericrowell@augustana.edu
ROWELL, Gid 678-466-4477 127 A gidrowell@clayton.edu
ROWELL, Patricia 216-987-5131 389 A patricia.rowell@tri-c.edu
ROWELL, Reda 678-466-4474 127 A redarowell@clayton.edu
ROWEN, Cate 413-585-3022 245 B crowen@smith.edu
ROWETT-JAMES, Kelly, A 336-334-5946 379 A karowett@uncg.edu
ROWH, Mark, C 540-674-3617 527 B mrowh@nr.edu
ROWLAND, Alma, Z 276-739-2436 528 D arowland@vhcc.edu
ROWLAND, Bryan, K 434-395-2030 520 G rowlandbk@longwood.edu
ROWLAND, David, L 219-464-5313 181 A david.rowland@valpo.edu
ROWLAND, Gloria, T 919-516-4200 376 B growland@st-aug.edu
ROWLAND, Linda 706-864-1358 134 D lcgooden@northgeorgia.edu
ROWLAND, Nettie 336-256-0863 377 F rowlandn@ncat.edu
ROWLAND, Randy 913-360-7372 190 F rrowland@benedictine.edu
ROWLAND, Rita, K 626-584-5484 48 A rrowland@fuller.edu
ROWLAND, IV, Roy 863-667-5081 118 A rrowland@seu.edu
ROWLAND, Sheri 850-201-6097 121 F rowlands@tcc.fl.edu
ROWLAND, Wayne 812-749-1288 178 D wrowland@oak.edu
ROWLANDS, Steve 325-674-2626 478 H rowlandss@acu.edu
ROWLES, Brian 863-638-7667 123 B brian.rowles@warner.edu
ROWLETT, Carol 540-857-7277 528 E
ROWLETT, Sharron 603-888-1311 305 G srowlett@rivier.edu
ROWLEY, Becky 575-769-4001 317 K becky.rowley@clovis.edu
ROWLEY, Becky, K 575-769-4921 317 K becky.rowley@clovis.edu
ROWLEY, Bob 630-617-3403 150 F srowley@elmhurst.edu
ROWLEY, Bob 405-425-5109 409 E bob.rowley@oc.edu
ROWLEY, Jason 410-843-6096 272 F jason.rowley@laureate.net
ROWLEY, Jill 409-880-8450 500 F jill.rowley@lamar.edu
ROWLEY, Lisa 503-352-7252 419 E lisajrowley@pacificu.edu
ROWLEY, Richard 951-639-5420 58 B rrowley@msjc.edu
ROWLEY, Susan 802-865-6414 513 A rowley@champlain.edu
ROWLINGS, Julie, M 617-327-6777 242 C julie_rowlings@mspp.edu
ROWSER, F. Diannah 251-578-1313 6 E drowser@rstc.edu
ROWTON, Dustin 405-691-3800 408 H drowton@macu.edu
ROY, Alisa 704-922-6202 370 D roy.alisa@gaston.edu
ROY, Ashok, K 770-423-6021 132 H aroy3@kennesaw.edu
ROY, James 540-868-7050 526 H jroy@lfcc.edu
ROY, James, C 904-276-6783 116 D jimroy@sjrstate.edu
ROY, II, Joe, E 303-492-7311 88 B joe.roy@colorado.edu
ROY, Judy, K 260-422-5561 172 L jkroy@indianatech.edu
ROY, Justin, P 318-342-1043 216 E roy@ulm.edu
ROY, Lara 612-874-3778 265 E lara_roy@mcad.edu
ROY, Leonard 860-628-4751 92 F lroy@lincolncollegene.edu
ROY, Marc 410-337-6044 222 I marc.roy@goucher.edu
ROY, MaryEllen 850-484-1428 114 G mroy@pensacolastate.edu
ROY, Melissa 845-574-4758 347 I mroy@sunyrockland.edu
ROY, Michael, D 802-443-5595 513 G mdroy@middlebury.edu
ROY, Omaira 617-928-4074 243 A Oroy@mountida.edu
ROY, Pallabi 410-337-6062 222 I pallabi.roy@goucher.edu
ROY, Paul 650-493-4430 51 C proy@itp.edu
ROY, Rina 916-484-8108 56 A royr@arc.losrios.edu
ROY, Tracey 218-322-2409 267 C troy@itascacc.edu
ROY, Tracey 218-322-2409 266 H troy@itascacc.edu
ROY, Tracey 218-322-2409 270 A t.roy@itascacc.edu
ROYAL, SR., Bobby, L 609-343-4828 307 D broyal@atlantic.edu
ROYAL, Bryan, K 804-257-5630 529 D bkroyal@vuu.edu
ROYAL, Carmen 609-343-5087 307 D croyal@atlantic.edu
ROYAL, Christina 216-987-4577 389 A tina.royal@tri-c.edu
ROYAL, Robert 540-338-2700 517 D rroyal@cdu.edu
ROYALL, Ann 617-262-5000 232 B ann.royall@the-bac.edu
ROYBAL, Katy 405-425-1876 409 E katy.watson@oc.edu
ROYBAL, Walter 719-587-8281 80 F wsroybal@adams.edu
ROYCE, Lee, G 601-925-3200 275 E lroyce@mc.edu
ROYE, Shauna 202-495-3837 98 D sroye@dhs.edu
ROYEEN, Charlotte 314-977-8501 289 F royeencb@slu.edu
ROYER, Anna 405-945-8611 410 F
ROYER, Drew 603-623-0313 305 F droyer@nhia.edu
ROYER, Joseph, M 765-641-4000 169 A jmroyer@anderson.edu
ROYER, Roma 602-850-8000 17 H rroyer@phoenixseminary.edu
ROYER, Stacie 512-279-2842 507 H stacie.royer@vc.edu
ROYER, Tina 218-749-7730 267 C t.royer@mr.mnscu.edu
ROYOS, Andre 915-779-8031 483 F aroyos@computercareercenter.com
ROYS, Cindy 516-918-3723 324 E croys@bcl.edu
ROYSTER, Jacqueline, J 404-894-1728 130 D jacqueline.royster@iac.gatech.edu
ROYSTER, Robynne 415-703-9532 31 J rroyster@cca.edu
ROYSTON, Rosemary, R 706-379-3111 139 F rosemary@yhc.edu
ROYUK, Brent 402-643-7304 297 F
ROZ, Mugur 617-850-1545 236 A mroz@hchc.edu
ROZADA, Mayra 787-891-0925 562 G mrozada@aguadilla.inter.edu
ROZAK, Edward 508-830-5030 239 A erozak@maritime.edu
ROZANSKA, M. Paul 215-637-7700 430 H smprozanska@holyfamily.edu
ROZANSKI, Kathy 856-256-5400 314 A rozanski@rowan.edu
ROZANSKI, Mordechai 609-896-5001 313 G mrozanski@rider.edu
ROZANSKY, Kristen, B 717-531-1315 439 L kbr2@psu.edu
ROZAR, Alva 636-227-2100 284 E alva.rozar@logan.edu
ROZEBOOM, Dave 512-428-8515 493 B daver@stedwards.edu
ROZEK, Charles, E 216-368-4390 386 E cer2@case.edu
ROZELL, Laura 518-327-6291 345 H lrozell@paulsmiths.edu
ROZEMA, Burton, J 708-239-4760 165 I burt.rozema@trnty.edu
ROZEMBAJGIER, John 614-885-5585 401 B jrozembajgier@pcj.edu
ROZEWSKI, Mark 812-464-1849 180 F mrozewski@usi.edu
ROZIN, Miriam 503-399-8486 414 J miriam.rozin@chemeketa.edu
ROZIN, Vladmir 212-463-0400 357 J vladmirr@touro.edu
ROZNOWSKI, James 847-925-6732 151 E jroznows@harpercollege.edu
RUANE, Julia 216-987-5027 389 A julia.ruane@tri-c.edu
RUANO, Norman 773-878-3894 163 D nruano@iwe.staugustine.edu
RUBACK, Ginger 954-492-5353 102 J gruback@citycollege.edu
RUBACK, Sally, A 920-929-2126 554 E sruback@morainepark.edu
RUBBELKE, Thomas, J 651-641-8700 263 C rubbelke@csp.edu
RUBECK, Dustin, D 972-241-3371 484 D drubeck@dallas.edu
RUBEK, Cindy 719-590-6851 83 D crubek@coloradotech.edu
RUBEL, Carol 617-587-5650 243 D rubelc@neco.edu
RUBEL, Katherine 909-607-2609 40 C katherine_rubel@cuc.edu
RUBEL, Robert, J 401-841-3339 557 I
RUBEL, Tom 641-683-5111 185 D trubel@indianhills.edu
RUBEL, Tom 641-683-5252 185 D trubel@indianhills.edu
RUBEMEYER, Susan 636-922-8360 288 E srubemeyer@stchas.edu
RUBEN, Bruce 212-824-2225 335 C bruben@huc.edu
RUBENSTEIN, David 856-256-4222 314 A rubenstein@rowan.edu
RUBENSTEIN, Nancy 419-448-2106 391 G nrubenst@heidelberg.edu
RUBENZAHL, Ira, H 413-755-4906 241 E irubenzahl@stcc.edu
RUBERO, Maria, D 787-250-1912 563 E mdrubero@metro.inter.edu
RUBERTONE, Joseph, D 203-582-8775 93 E joseph.rubertone@quinnipiac.edu
RUBES, Larry 804-706-5041 526 G lrubes@jtcc.edu
RUBEY, Charles 812-298-2329 177 A crubey@ivytech.edu
RUBEY, Daniel, R 516-463-5940 335 H daniel.rubey@hofstra.edu
RUBIN, Andrea 607-962-9231 331 D rubin@corning-cc.edu
RUBIN, Connie 419-530-1464 404 F connie.rubin@utoledo.edu
RUBIN, David 503-788-6644 420 A david.rubin@reed.edu
RUBIN, Gary, N 410-704-2358 228 E grubin@towson.edu
RUBIN, Henry 507-457-5570 270 B hrubin@winona.edu
RUBIN, James 602-787-6546 16 A james.rubin@pvmail.maricopa.edu
RUBIN, Joshua 718-436-2122 357 D
RUBIN, Lisa 770-426-2725 133 B lrubin@life.edu
RUBIN, Marge 920-720-6811 553 G rubin@fvtc.edu
RUBIN, Mark, E 804-827-1313 525 E merubin@vcu.edu
RUBIN, Meyer 908-354-6057 317 G
RUBIN, Moshe 516-239-9002 350 H
RUBIN, Rachel 860-486-2337 94 E rachel.rubin@uconn.edu
RUBIN, Rachel 860-486-2337 94 E Rachel.Rubin@uconn.edu
RUBIN, Steve 719-219-9636 81 J
RUBINO, Cynthia 914-694-1122 323 J cnr@berkeleycollege.edu
RUBINO, John 207-941-7109 218 A rubinoj@husson.edu
RUBINO, Karen, M 401-456-8849 454 A krubino@ric.edu
RUBINO, Linda 718-780-1998 338 E lrubino@chpnet.org
RUBINO, Michael, H 508-767-7156 230 E rubino@assumption.edu
RUBINSTEIN, Mark 603-862-2053 306 E mark.rubinstein@unh.edu
RUBIO, Christian 318-342-1539 216 E rubio@ulm.edu
RUBIO, Christopher 310-689-3200 42 F crubio@kaplan.edu
RUBIO, Olga, D 956-721-5296 489 G drubio@laredo.edu
RUBIO, Paty 518-580-5705 351 B prubio@skidmore.edu
RUBIO, Peter 305-593-1223 102 D prubio@albizu.edu
RUBIO, Sucette 787-780-5134 564 F srubio@nationalcollegepr.edu
RUBLE, Celeste 507-433-0666 269 A celeste.ruble@riverland.edu
RUBLE, Jim 785-227-3380 190 G rublej@bethanylb.edu
RUBLE, Joel 559-925-3127 77 J joelruble@whccd.edu
RUBLE, Michelle 301-934-4711 222 C micheller@csmd.edu
RUBLE, Robert, W 607-735-1802 333 A rruble@elmira.edu
RUBLE, Robert, W 419-772-2020 398 G r-ruble@onu.edu
RUBRITZ, Gerald 814-886-6460 437 A grubritz@mtaloy.edu
RUBSAMEN, Richard 775-831-1314 303 E rrubsamen@sierranevada.edu
RUBY, Carl, A 937-766-7871 386 F rubyc@cedarville.edu
RUBY, Katharine 507-786-3019 271 H ruby@stolaf.edu
RUCCIUS, Frederick, E 215-955-8733 448 B frederick.ruccius@jefferson.edu
RUCH, Doug 678-891-3269 130 G druch@gpc.edu
RUCH, J. Chuck 309-677-3100 145 H cruch@bradley.edu
RUCH, Lisa 815-965-7314 162 G lruch@rockfordcareercollege.edu
RUCH, Nate, P 612-343-4747 270 C npruch@northcentral.edu
RUCHALA, Patsy, L 775-784-6841 303 A pruchala@unr.edu
RUCKENSTEIN, Andrei, E 617-353-4791 232 G andreir@bu.edu
RUCKER, Alena Jewel 304-981-6247 542 D
RUCKER, Cedric, B 540-654-1655 524 H crucker@umw.edu
RUCKER, Marty, K 423-585-6983 476 B marty.rucker@ws.edu
RUCKER, Patricia, A 215-670-9282 438 D parucker@peirce.edu
RUCKER, Paul 206-685-9223 538 F uwalumni@uw.edu
RUCKER, Richard 937-433-3410 390 I rrucker@edaff.com
RUCKER, Robert, E 662-685-4771 273 H erucker@bmc.edu
RUCKER, Robin 937-376-6692 386 H rrucker@centralstate.edu
RUCKER, Sherri, B 615-329-8555 468 G srucker@fisk.edu
RUCKER-FRANKLIN, Yvonne 870-633-4480 21 F yrucker@eacc.edu
RUCKER-SHAMU, Marian 301-860-3849 228 A mshamu@bowiestate.edu
RUD, A.G 509-335-4853 539 A ag.rud@wsu.edu
RUDA, Ryan 620-276-9597 193 A ryan.ruda@gcccks.edu
RUDASILL, Lisa 419-423-2211 385 H lrudasill@brownmackie.edu
RUDASILL, Susann 850-644-1571 119 C srudasill@fsu.edu
RUDAY, Robert, M 813-253-6204 122 H bruday@ut.edu
RUDD, M. David 801-581-8620 510 L david.rudd@csbs.utah.edu
RUDD WEITZEL, Jann 636-949-4846 284 C jweitzel@lindenwood.edu
RUDDELL, Larry 509-682-6795 539 B lruddell@wvc.edu
RUDDEN, David 847-214-7925 150 D drudden@elgin.edu
RUDDICK, Steve, L 913-588-7281 197 A sruddick@kumc.edu
RUDDY, Margaret, E 561-237-7822 113 D mruddy@lynn.edu
RUDE, John 323-267-3724 54 G rudejc@elac.edu
RUDE, Linda, R 417-268-6048 279 D lrude@gobbc.edu
RUDEAU, William 609-771-2187 308 G rudeau@tcnj.edu
RUDECOFF, Christine, A 315-684-6055 354 F rudecoc@morrisville.edu
RUDEEN, P. Kevin 405-271-2288 413 D kevin-rudeen@ouhsc.edu
RUDENGA, Elizabeth 708-239-4739 165 I liz.rudenga@trnty.edu
RUDGERS, Lisa, M 734-763-5800 259 D rudgers@umich.edu
RUDIG, Lynn 608-785-9892 555 D rudigl@westerntc.edu
RUDIGER, Brenda 906-487-2400 255 E brudiger@mtu.edu
RUDIGER, Jennifer 715-232-1151 552 C rudigerj@uwstout.edu
RUDIN, Brent 765-998-5113 179 F brent_rudin@tayloru.edu
RUDLEY, John, M 713-313-7044 499 G rudleyjm@tsu.edu
RUDLOFF, Lynn 512-428-1317 493 B lynnr@stedwards.edu
RUDLOFF, William, J 724-738-2465 443 E william.rudloff@sru.edu
RUDNEY, Gwen 320-589-6411 272 C rudneygl@morris.umn.edu
RUDNICK, Joseph 310-825-1042 74 A jrudnick@college.ucla.edu
RUDNICK, Mark, V 410-334-2911 229 E mrudnick@worwic.edu
RUDNIK, Jeffrey, A 270-686-4324 198 G jeffrey.rudnik@brescia.edu
RUDOLPH, Jacquelyn, T 541-737-3103 418 F human.resources@oregonstate.edu
RUDOLPH, Marva 865-974-2498 477 B mrudolp1@utk.edu
RUDOLPH, Mary Kay 707-524-1516 68 E mrudolph@santarosa.edu
RUDOLPH, Roy 617-876-0956 236 H roy.rudolph@longy.edu
RUDY, Donna 301-790-2800 223 A rudyd@hagerstowncc.edu

RUSSELL, Jessica 910-695-3789 373 E
russellj@sandhills.edu

RUSSELL, Jill, F 413-748-3241 245 C
jrussell@spfldcol.edu

RUSSELL, Jill, T 717-867-6076 434 C
russell@lvc.edu

RUSSELL, Jimmie 253-943-2800 533 B
jrussell@devry.edu

RUSSELL, JoAnne 757-569-6712 527 E
jrussell@pdc.edu

RUSSELL, Joanne 860-512-2603 90 C
jrussell@mcc.commnet.edu

RUSSELL, John, H 325-793-3801 490 F
jrussell@mcm.edu

RUSSELL, John, P 402-559-5343 301 A
jrussel@unmc.edu

RUSSELL, Juanita 601-877-6191 273 C
juanita@alcorn.edu

RUSSELL, Judith 352-273-2505 120 B
jcrussell@ufl.edu

RUSSELL, Kevin 601-968-8746 273 F
krussell@belhaven.edu

RUSSELL, Kim 617-912-9165 232 E
krussell@bostonconservatory.edu

RUSSELL, Kimberly 307-532-8251 555 H
kimberly.russell@ewc.wy.edu

RUSSELL, Kimberly, A 903-510-2382 502 E
krus@tjc.edu

RUSSELL, Leah, R 540-375-2210 523 D
russell@roanoke.edu

RUSSELL, Lisa 541-684-4644 419 F
lrussell@pioneerpacific.edu

RUSSELL, Malcolm 402-486-2501 300 D
marussel@ucollege.edu

RUSSELL, Marilyn 785-749-8470 193 B
mrussell@haskell.edu

RUSSELL, Mark 419-995-8411 392 L
russell.m@rhodesstate.edu

RUSSELL, Mary Jane 802-654-2494 514 B
mrussell@smcvt.edu

RUSSELL, Michael 912-478-5234 131 A
mjrussel@georgiasouthern.edu

RUSSELL, Mike 240-567-3136 224 E
mike.russell@montgomerycollege.edu

RUSSELL, Nell 307-766-3459 556 E
nell@uwyo.edu

RUSSELL, Robert 650-843-3503 61 A
r.russell@paloaltou.edu

RUSSELL, Robert 605-626-7770 465 H
Robert.Russell@northern.edu

RUSSELL, Ronda 406-994-5541 295 E
rrussell@montana.edu

RUSSELL, Ruby 205-853-1200 5 C
rrussell@jeffstateonline.com

RUSSELL, Samuel, J 660-944-2810 280 F
samuel@conception.edu

RUSSELL, Scott 978-232-2113 234 F
srussell@endicott.edu

RUSSELL, Starla 605-394-4034 466 E
starla.russell@wdt.edu

RUSSELL, Stephanie, J 414-288-1881 548 D
stephanie.russell@marquette.edu

RUSSELL, Steve, R 817-735-2525 504 C
srussell@hsc.unt.edu

RUSSELL, Susan 254-659-7631 487 E
srussell@hillcollege.edu

RUSSELL, Terry 636-949-4980 284 C
trussell@lindenwood.edu

RUSSELL, Thad 620-227-9325 192 B
trussell@dc3.edu

RUSSELL, Thomas 312-369-7940 148 B
trussell@colum.edu

RUSSELL, William 860-632-3050 92 E
busoffice@holyapostles.edu

RUSSELL HOLZ,
Stephanie, A 813-253-6233 122 H
srholz@ut.edu

RUSSELL O'GRADY,
Marijo 212-346-1306 345 F
mogrady@pace.edu

RUSSI, Gary, D 248-370-3500 257 C
russi@oakland.edu

RUSSI KIRSHNER, Judith 312-996-5611 166 F
kirshner@uic.edu

RUSSO, Cecilia, M 718-990-6667 348 G
russoc@stjohns.edu

RUSSO, Joseph 215-895-6436 427 G
jr385@drexel.edu

RUSSO, Joseph, A 574-631-6436 180 D
russo.4@nd.edu

RUSSO, Lisa 213-613-2200 70 H
lisarusso@sciarc.edu

RUSSO, Marian 631-687-4590 349 B
mrusso@sjcny.edu

RUSSO, Melissa 412-281-2600 446 H
mrusso@western-school.com

RUSSO, Richard 510-642-2700 73 E
russo@berkeley.edu

RUSSO, Robert 215-699-5700 433 G
rrusso@LSB.edu

RUSSO, Robert, C 203-254-4288 92 B
rcrusso@fairfield.edu

RUSSOM, Kenneth, S 904-819-6230 107 A
krussom@flagler.edu

RUSSOM, Vaughn, N 715-394-8327 552 D
vrussom@uwsuper.edu

RUSSOMANNO, David, J 317-274-0802 174 B
drussoma@iupui.edu

RUSSONIELLO, Maria, J 570-963-2536 440 F
mjr1@psu.edu

RUSSOS, Milton, A 904-632-3123 109 E
mrussos@fscj.edu

RUSSOW, Craig 414-443-8544 553 B
craig.russow@wlc.edu

RUST, Kathleen 630-617-3419 150 F
kathyrst@elmhurst.edu

RUST, Mark, M 410-857-2503 224 D
mrust@mcdaniel.edu

RUST, Melissa 501-686-2532 24 B
mrust@uasys.edu

RUST, Tammy 815-280-2346 154 H
trust@jjc.edu

RUSTON, Lauren 407-478-0500 110 H
laurenr@orl.herzing.edu

RUSTOWICZ, Mary Louis 716-896-0700 359 F
rustowim@villa.edu

RUSZKOWSKI, Betty 727-736-5082 117 F
betty_ruszkowski@schiller.edu

RUTBERG, Barbara 617-824-8275 234 D
barbara_rutberg@emerson.edu

RUTE, Warren 908-526-1200 313 E
wrute@raritanval.edu

RUTENBECK, Jeffrey 802-651-5924 513 A
jrutenbeck@champlain.edu

RUTH, David, A 215-895-2501 427 G
ruthda@drexel.edu

RUTH, Rick 717-477-1835 443 D
reruth@ship.edu

RUTHENBECK, Julie, J 325-942-2255 480 E
julie.ruthenbeck@angelo.edu

RUTHERFORD, Ann, O 406-874-6196 294 H
rutherforda@milescc.edu

RUTHERFORD, Cynthia 215-572-4091 422 B
rutherfc@arcadia.edu

RUTHERFORD, Gina 850-973-9414 113 J
rutherfordg@nfcc.edu

RUTHERFORD, Greg, F 803-327-8050 463 G
grutherford@yorktech.edu

RUTHERFORD, Jeff 916-638-7582 66 K

RUTHERFORD, Joan, M 419-251-1301 395 H
joan.rutherford@mercycollege.edu

RUTHERFORD, John, D 214-648-0400 507 D
john.rutherford@utsouthwestern.edu

RUTHERFORD, Karen, W 803-705-4671 455 D
rutherk@benedict.edu

RUTHERFORD, Laurie, G 713-500-2101 506 D
laurie.g.rutherford@uth.tmc.edu

RUTHERFORD, Lisa, H 608-263-7400 550 G
lrutherford@vc.wisc.edu

RUTHERFORD, Mary 907-450-8034 10 H
mary.rutherford@alaska.edu

RUTHERFORD, Marylyn 973-877-3408 310 A
rutherford@essex.edu

RUTHERFORD, Paul 304-327-4403 543 C
prutherford@bluefieldstate.edu

RUTHERFORD, Van 937-327-7891 406 B
vrutherford@wittenberg.edu

RUTHERMAN, Kathy 270-852-3142 203 E
krutherman@kwc.edu

RUTHRAUFF, Dirk 559-278-6715 34 D
druthrauff@csufresno.edu

RUTKOWSKI, Edmund 718-636-3784 346 D
ekow@pratt.edu

RUTKOWSKI, Sandra 419-824-3762 395 D
srutkowski@lourdes.edu

RUTLAND, Mark 918-495-6888 411 C
mrutland@oru.edu

RUTLEDGE, Catherine 484-365-8087 434 H
crutledge@lincoln.edu

RUTLEDGE, James 662-846-4021 274 B
jrutledge@deltastate.edu

RUTLEDGE, Janet 410-455-1781 227 D
jrutledge@umbc.edu

RUTLEDGE, John, E 803-313-7156 462 D
rutledj@mailbox.sc.edu

RUTLEDGE, Karen 731-286-3242 475 A
rutledge@dscc.edu

RUTLEDGE, Susan 314-392-2355 286 C
rutledges@mobap.edu

RUTLEDGE, Todd 417-269-3873 281 B
trutle@coxcollege.edu

RUTT, Charles, D 660-543-4370 291 B
rutt@ucmo.edu

RUTT, Jack, H 540-432-4478 518 E
ruttj@emu.edu

RUTT, Richard 503-352-7377 419 E
ruttra@pacificu.edu

RUTTEN, Erich 651-962-6561 272 E
erutten@stthomas.edu

RUTTER, Robert 920-403-3964 550 C
bob.rutter@snc.edu

RUUD, William, N 717-477-1301 443 D
wnruud@ship.edu

RUX, Shirley, K 701-788-4754 381 F
Shirley.Rux@mayvillestate.edu

RUYLE, Dianna 217-854-3231 145 F
druyl@blackburn.edu

RUYS, Jasmine 661-362-3466 41 G
jasmine.ruys@canyons.edu

RUYS, John 925-424-1382 39 A
jruys@laspositascollege.edu

RUZICH, Steve 708-596-2000 164 F
sruzich@ssc.edu

RUZICKA, James 402-461-7337 298 C
jruzicka@hastings.edu

RYALL, Patrick 503-768-7294 416 F
ryall@lclark.edu

RYALLS, Kenneth, R 402-354-7258 299 E
ken.ryalls@methodistcollege.edu

RYALS, Reginald 540-423-9055 526 E
rryals@germanna.edu

RYAN, Adam 660-944-2827 280 F
adam@conception.edu

RYAN, Angela 312-341-2007 162 I
aryan@roosevelt.edu

RYAN, Anne 207-221-8723 218 C
aryan@kaplan.edu

RYAN, Barry, T 714-415-6500 77 G
bryan@westcoastuniversity.edu

RYAN, Bruce 607-844-8222 357 H
ryanb@tc3.edu

RYAN, Bryan, K 919-866-5146 374 E
bkryan@waketech.edu

RYAN, Carroll 714-882-7800 33 D

RYAN, Catherine 413-572-5218 239 C
cryan@wsc.ma.edu

RYAN, Chenise 205-934-4076 8 G
cryan@uab.edu

RYAN, Christopher 508-830-5003 239 A
cryan@maritime.edu

RYAN, Curtis, W 801-832-2148 512 F
cryan@westminstercollege.edu

RYAN, Dan 800-962-7682 293 B
dryan@wma.edu

RYAN, David 402-643-7350 297 F
david.ryan@cune.edu

RYAN, Don 570-702-8944 431 K
dryan@johnson.edu

RYAN, Duane 575-562-2112 318 A
duane.ryan@enmu.edu

RYAN, G. Jeremiah 201-447-7237 307 F
gjryan@bergen.edu

RYAN, Gail, L 313-577-6595 260 D
gailryan@wayne.edu

RYAN, Greg 714-992-7092 59 D
gryan@fullcoll.edu

RYAN, Heather 574-237-0774 170 B
hryan@brownmackie.edu

RYAN, Helen, G 502-272-8426 198 E
hryan@bellarmine.edu

RYAN, James 617-262-5000 232 B
James.Ryan@the-bac.edu

RYAN, James 734-462-4400 258 C
jryan@schoolcraft.edu

RYAN, James 570-504-9639 425 F

RYAN, James, G 336-217-5128 377 F
jgryan@ncat.edu

RYAN, Joan 712-325-3200 186 B
jeryan@iwcc.edu

RYAN, CSC, John 570-208-5899 432 E
jjryan@kings.edu

RYAN, John, F 802-656-0693 514 F
john.f.ryan@uvm.edu

RYAN, Joseph 702-579-3519 302 C
jryan2@kaplan.edu

RYAN, Judith 207-228-8304 220 G
judyryan@maine.edu

RYAN, Kathleen 508-541-1515 234 B
kryan@dean.edu

RYAN, Kathleen 617-732-5042 241 F
Kathleen.Ryan@mcphs.edu

RYAN, Kent 386-246-4801 103 J
ryank@DaytonaState.edu

RYAN, Kevin 305-428-5700 113 I
kryan@aii.edu

RYAN, Kyle 781-899-5500 232 A
kryan@blessedjohnxxiii.edu

RYAN, Larry 505-277-2847 321 C
larry@unm.edu

RYAN, Lawrence 310-577-3000 79 K
lryan@yosan.edu

RYAN, Leslie 619-684-8811 59 A
lryan@newschoolarch.edu

RYAN, Linda, S 515-271-2147 184 A
linda.ryan@drake.edu

RYAN, Lori 602-331-7500 12 D
lryan@aii.edu

RYAN, Loyd 501-450-1348 22 A
ryan@hendrix.edu

RYAN, Mark, R 573-882-0314 291 D
ryanmr@missouri.edu

RYAN, Martin 503-222-3225 415 H
mryan@cci.edu

RYAN, Martin, B 973-353-5713 314 E
mbryan@andromeda.rutgers.edu

RYAN, Mary 501-686-6730 24 F
ryanmaryl@uams.edu

RYAN, Mary 419-473-2700 389 B
mryan@daviscollege.edu

RYAN, Mary, A 651-962-6133 272 E
maryan@stthomas.edu

RYAN, Mary, M 859-572-6371 205 E
ryanm@nku.edu

RYAN, Melissa 904-725-0525 103 E
mryan@concorde.edu

RYAN, Michael 617-585-1187 243 E
michael.ryan@necmusic.edu

RYAN, Mike, E 206-934-6790 537 B
michael.ryan@seattlecolleges.edu

RYAN, Molly 661-255-1050 32 C
mryan@calarts.edu

RYAN, Patricia 540-674-3613 527 B
pryan@nr.edu

RYAN, Patricia, C 573-651-2249 290 D
pryan@semo.edu

RYAN, Peter 662-325-3742 276 A
ryan@cvm.msstate.edu

RYAN, Philip 508-362-2131 240 A
pryan@capecod.edu

RYAN, Robert 800-782-2422 33 B
rryan851@earthlink.net

RYAN, Ron 954-262-8856 114 B
ronr@nsu.nova.edu

RYAN, Rosaleen 831-646-4035 57 G
rryan@mpc.edu

RYAN, Scott 817-272-3181 505 A
sdryan@uta.edu

RYAN, Sean 334-683-2333 5 G
sryan@marionmilitary.edu

RYAN, Sean, J 502-272-8376 198 E
sryan@bellarmine.edu

RYAN, Sharon 213-624-1200 46 L
sryan@fidm.edu

RYAN, Spencer 405-878-5177 412 A
shryan@stgregorys.edu

RYAN, Suzanne 812-856-5572 173 C
sryan@indiana.edu

RYAN, Thomas, E 508-767-7205 230 E
tryan@assumption.edu

RYAN, Thomas, J 718-862-7356 339 H
thomas.ryan@manhattan.edu

RYAN, Tiffiney 618-634-3242 164 C
tiffineyr@shawneecc.edu

RYAN, Tim 574-520-4261 174 C
timryan@iusb.edu

RYAN, Tim 845-451-1352 43 G
t_ryan@culinary.edu

RYAN, Tim 845-452-9600 331 F
t_ryan@culinary.edu

RYAN, Valerie 858-642-8513 58 I
vryan@nu.edu

RYAN, Vicky 419-473-2700 389 B
vryan@daviscollege.edu

RYAN, Victoria 239-687-5351 101 B
vryan@avemarialaw.edu

RYAN, Walter, F 812-941-2210 174 D
wryan@ius.edu

RYAN-HOFFMAN,
Maureen 732-987-2218 310 D
ryan-hoffman@georgian.edu

RYBA, Carla 412-367-4000 424 F
director3@careerta.edu

RYCHLEWSKI, Judith, A 816-781-9700 293 D
rychlewskij@william.jewell.edu

RYCHLY, Carol, J 706-737-1400 125 C
crychly@aug.edu

RYCZKOWSKI, Sandy 920-498-6829 555 A
sandra.ryczkowski@nwtc.edu

RYDEN, Tod 325-235-7366 500 C
tod.ryden@tstc.edu

RYDER, Ellen 508-793-2419 233 D
eryder@holycross.edu

RYDER, Laura 717-755-2300 422 E
lryder@aii.edu

RYDER-FOX, Jennifer 530-898-5844 34 A
jrfox@csuchico.edu

RYDL, Chareny, L 979-845-3158 497 C
chareny@tamu.edu

RYE, Colleen 906-635-2626 254 C
crye@lssu.edu

RYEA, Alan, E 802-656-2010 514 F
alan.ryea@uvm.edu

RYERSON, James 703-284-5926 521 A
james.ryerson@marymount.edu

RYERSON, Lisa Marsh 315-364-3265 360 C
president@wells.edu

RYKEN, Barbara 510-869-8692 64 J
bryken@samuelmerritt.edu

RYKEN, Philip, G 630-752-5002 168 F
philip.ryken@wheaton.edu

RYLE, Jerry 203-365-7651 93 G
rylef@sacredheart.edu

RYLES, Ruby 718-368-5000 328 B
rryles@kbcc.cuny.edu

RYMAN, Denny, G 318-342-1622 216 E
ryman@ulm.edu

RYMER, Angie 318-676-7811 211 H
arymer@nwltc.edu

RYON, Diane 704-372-0266 365 I
dryon@kingscollegecharlotte.edu

RYS, Stanley, C 847-566-6401 167 D
srys@usml.edu

RYSLINGE, Birgitte 503-614-7555 419 G
birgitte.ryslinge@pcc.edu

RYSTROM, Andrea 651-779-3953 266 D
andrea.rystrom@century.edu

S

SALAMY, James ... 315-866-0300 ... 335 E
salamyjr@herkimer.edu
SALANE, Linda, B ... 803-786-3748 ... 457 C
lsalane@columbiasc.edu
SALANI, Chris ... 906-487-7378 ... 251 C
chris.salani@finlandia.edu
SALARI, Gholamereza ... 717-394-6211 ... 426 C
rsalari@csb.edu
SALAS, Charles, G ... 860-685-2002 ... 95 C
csalas@wesleyan.edu
SALAS, Ezra ... 209-416-3700 ... 49 J
SALAS-BELTRAN, Rocio ... 714-533-1495 ... 70 B
rsbeltran@southbaylo.edu
SALATINO, Kevin, M ... 207-725-3673 ... 217 E
ksalatin@bowdoin.edu
SALATINO, Michael ... 630-829-6667 ... 145 D
msalatino@ben.edu
SALAVITABAR, Hadi ... 845-257-2930 ... 352 B
salavith@newpaltz.edu
SALAWAY, Kevin, J ... 570-450-3015 ... 439 J
kjs27@psu.edu
SALAY, Lawrence ... 203-285-2046 ... 90 A
lsalay@gwcc.commnet.edu
SALAZ, Eduardo ... 925-631-4212 ... 64 F
els3@stmarys-ca.edu
SALAZ, Mark ... 520-494-5250 ... 13 F
mark.salaz@centralaz.edu
SALAZAR, Alma ... 909-931-7599 ... 78 H
asalazar@westwood.edu
SALAZAR, David ... 562-985-4131 ... 35 A
salazar@csulb.edu
SALAZAR, Ed ... 928-541-7777 ... 16 I
esalazar@ncu.edu
SALAZAR, Michael ... 562-860-2451 ... 38 J
msalazar@cerritos.edu
SALAZAR-VALENTINE, Marcia ... 419-372-8183 ... 385 C
marcias@bgsu.edu
SALBU, Steven, C ... 404-894-2600 ... 130 D
steven.salbu@mgt.gatech.edu
SALCHENBERGER, Linda, M ... 414-288-7141 ... 548 D
linda.salchenberger@marquette.edu
SALCIDO, Kevin, J ... 480-965-6608 ... 12 B
kevin.j.salcido@asu.edu
SALDANA, Irma ... 773-291-6775 ... 147 D
isaldana@ccc.edu
SALDANA, Noe, V ... 210-458-4376 ... 506 B
noe.saldana@utsa.edu
SALDANA-TALLEY, Jane ... 707-778-3931 ... 68 E
lsaldana-talley@santarosa.edu
SALE, Gene ... 561-803-2286 ... 114 C
gene_sale@pba.edu
SALEH, Bahaa ... 407-882-3326 ... 120 A
besaleh@creol.ucf.edu
SALEH, Donald, A ... 315-443-5559 ... 357 B
dasaleh@syr.edu
SALEM, Susan ... 310-954-4112 ... 57 H
ssalem@msmc.la.edu
SALEM, Susan ... 801-957-4447 ... 512 C
susan.salem@slcc.edu
SALEMME, Brenda ... 716-488-3023 ... 337 D
brendasalemme@jamestownbusinesscollege.edu
SALEMME, Kevin ... 978-837-5377 ... 242 D
kevin.salemme@merrimack.edu
SALERNO, Dena ... 570-372-4302 ... 447 D
salerno@susqu.edu
SALESTROM, Charles ... 308-535-3681 ... 298 I
salestromc@mpcc.edu
SALFI, Maureen ... 716-286-8686 ... 344 D
mes@niagara.edu
SALGADO, Javier ... 787-761-0640 ... 561 B
SALGUERO, Jossie ... 787-766-1912 ... 562 F
jsalguer@inter.edu
SALIBA, Elizabeth ... 602-285-7748 ... 16 B
e.saliba@pcmail.maricopa.edu
SALIBA, Joseph, E ... 937-229-2245 ... 404 A
joseph.saliba@notes.udayton.edu
SALIBA, Tony, E ... 937-229-2306 ... 404 A
Tony.Saliba@notes.udayton.edu
SALIBA, Yvette, C ... 407-303-6413 ... 108 D
yvette.saliba@fhchs.edu
SALICHS, Eduardo ... 787-765-1915 ... 564 B
esalichs@inter.edu
SALIM, Ellis, P ... 810-766-4276 ... 248 C
ellis.salim@baker.edu
SALIMAN, Merna, S ... 816-604-3044 ... 285 H
merna.saliman@mcckc.edu
SALIMBENE, Franklyn, P ... 781-891-2462 ... 231 F
fsalimbene@bentley.edu
SALINAS, Antonio ... 575-439-3601 ... 319 E
antsalin@nmsua.nmsu.edu
SALINAS, Gilberto ... 956-326-2760 ... 497 B
gsalinas@tamiu.edu
SALINAS, Jessica ... 956-665-3361 ... 506 A
lopezj@utpa.edu
SALINAS, Lelia ... 956-872-7209 ... 494 D
lelias1@southtexascollege.edu
SALINAS, Sallie ... 714-241-4901 ... 40 J
ssalinas@coastline.edu
SALINAS, Stacy ... 973-748-9000 ... 308 A
stacy_salinas@bloomfield.edu
SALINE, Terrie ... 309-341-7436 ... 155 E
tsaline@knox.edu
SALINGER, Sharon, V ... 949-824-7761 ... 73 H
sharon.salinger@uci.edu
SALISBURY, Kathleen ... 603-862-0938 ... 306 D
kathleen.salisbury@usnh.edu
SALIVA, Sara ... 787-264-1912 ... 563 G
smsaliva@sg.inter.edu
SALKIN, Patricia, E ... 518-445-2351 ... 322 D
psalk@albanylaw.edu
SALLADA, Paul ... 513-244-4819 ... 388 D
paul_sallada@mail.msj.edu
SALLAN, Veena ... 270-686-4639 ... 202 E
veena.sallan@kctcs.edu
SALLEE, David, L ... 816-781-7700 ... 293 D
salleed@william.jewell.edu
SALLEE, L. James ... 219-785-5667 ... 178 H
jsallee@pnc.edu
SALLEH-BARONE, Normah 708-974-5209 ... 159 A
salleh-barone@morainevalley.edu
SALLER, Richard, P ... 650-723-9784 ... 71 F
rsaller@stanford.edu
SALLEY, Dug ... 610-282-1100 ... 426 I
SALLIN, Dennis ... 573-897-5000 ... 284 D
SALLUSTIO, Joe ... 303-477-7240 ... 84 I
joes@heritage-education.com
SALLY, Dana ... 828-227-7307 ... 379 E
dsally@wcu.edu
SALMEIER, Michael ... 909-599-5433 ... 54 A
SALMERI, Patrice ... 612-330-1166 ... 261 G
salmeri@augsburg.edu
SALMI, SJ, Richard, P ... 251-380-3866 ... 7 F
raslmi@shc.edu
SALMO, James, G ... 401-456-8105 ... 454 A
jsalmo@ric.edu
SALMON, Donald, L ... 563-589-3618 ... 189 B
dsalmon@dbq.edu
SALMON, Edward, L ... 262-646-6508 ... 549 B
elsalmon@dioceseofsc.org
SALMON, Mark ... 334-670-3342 ... 8 B
msalmon@troy.edu
SALMON, Mark ... 816-802-3473 ... 283 I
msalmon@kcai.edu
SALMON, Marla ... 206-543-8736 ... 538 F
msalmon@uw.edu
SALMON, Sheri ... 205-226-4692 ... 2 C
ssalmon@bsc.edu
SALMONA, Riccardo ... 212-799-5000 ... 337 H
SALMOND, Susan, W ... 973-972-4322 ... 316 H
salmonsu@umdnj.edu
SALMONSON, Jason ... 702-579-3513 ... 302 C
jsalmonson@kaplan.edu
SALNAITIS, John ... 719-255-3375 ... 88 C
john.salnaitis@uccs.edu
SALOCKS, Stephen, E ... 617-254-2610 ... 244 E
SALOMANSON, Kristen ... 231-591-3801 ... 251 B
kristen_salomonson@ferris.edu
SALOME, Joann ... 575-835-5206 ... 319 A
jsalome@admin.nmt.edu
SALOMON, Mattisyahu ... 732-367-1060 ... 307 H
SALOMON, Rachel ... 692-625-3394 ... 559 E
rsalomon@cmi.edu
SALOMON-FERNÁNDEZ, Yves ... 781-239-3159 ... 240 D
ysalomonfernandez@massbay.edu
SALOMONE, Joseph, J ... 215-895-4948 ... 427 G
salomojj@drexel.edu
SALOMONSON, Kristen ... 231-591-3801 ... 251 B
kristen_salomonson@ferris.edu
SALOMONSON, Kristen ... 231-591-3801 ... 251 B
Kristen_Salomonson@ferris.edu
SALONE, Chris ... 410-225-2499 ... 224 C
csalone@mica.edu
SALONEN, Neil Albert ... 203-576-4665 ... 94 D
nas@bridgeport.edu
SALONER, Garth ... 650-723-1940 ... 71 F
saloner@stanford.edu
SALOVEY, Peter ... 203-432-4444 ... 95 D
peter.salovey@yale.edu
SALOWITZ, Stewart, I ... 309-556-3206 ... 153 E
salowitz@iwu.edu
SALOWITZ, Susan ... 860-343-5724 ... 90 D
ssalowitz@mxcc.commnet.edu
SALTER, Anne ... 404-364-8514 ... 135 A
asalter@oglethorpe.edu
SALTER, Brooke ... 912-538-3129 ... 137 A
bsalter@southeasterntech.edu
SALTER, M. Lee ... 919-515-2423 ... 378 B
lee_salter@ncsu.edu
SALTER, Ruth ... 229-430-3986 ... 123 H
ruth.salter@asurams.edu
SALTER-SMITH, Cassandra, L ... 716-839-8237 ... 331 G
csalters@daemen.edu
SALTIEL, Henry ... 718-482-6120 ... 328 C
hsaltiel@lagcc.cuny.edu
SALTONSTALL, Thomas, L 617-228-3311 ... 239 G
tlsaltonstall@bhcc.mass.edu
SALTSMAN, George ... 325-674-2996 ... 478 H
saltsman@acu.edu
SALTZ, Ira, S ... 724-983-2825 ... 440 D
SALTZMAN, Robert ... 516-463-4134 ... 335 H
robert.saltzman@hofstra.edu
SALVA, William, M ... 914-337-9300 ... 331 A
william.salva@concordia-ny.edu
SALVADOR, Cinnamon, A ... 337-475-5711 ... 215 G
csalvador@mcneese.edu
SALVADOR, Susan, M ... 585-292-2121 ... 341 H
ssalvador@monroecc.edu
SALVAGE, Lynn ... 718-357-0500 ... 349 F
lsalvage@edaff.com
SALVAGGIO, Brian ... 508-531-1276 ... 238 B
SALVAIL, Leslie, H ... 410-777-2709 ... 221 B
lhsalvail@aacc.edu
SALVANO, Claudia ... 407-328-2096 ... 117 G
salvanoc@seminolestate.edu
SALVATO, Alfred, C ... 215-503-7570 ... 448 B
alfred.salvato@jefferson.edu
SALVATO, Scott ... 516-678-5000 ... 341 F
ssalvato@molloy.edu
SALVESEN, Guy ... 858-646-3114 ... 67 H
gsalvesen@sandfordburnham.org
SALVIDIO, Nanci ... 413-572-8123 ... 239 C
nsalvidio@wsc.ma.edu
SALVUCCI, James ... 443-334-2215 ... 226 E
jsalvucci@stevenson.edu
SALWASSER, Hal, J ... 541-737-1585 ... 418 F
hal.salwasser@oregonstate.edu
SALYER, Breanne ... 276-328-0126 ... 525 C
wbd9q@uvawise.edu
SALYERS, Catherine, A ... 219-866-6187 ... 179 B
cathys@saintjoe.edu
SALYERS-STONER, Connie 740-351-3267 ... 401 I
cstoner@shawnee.edu
SALZMAN, Christine ... 201-714-2198 ... 310 F
csalzman@hccc.edu
SAM, David ... 847-214-7374 ... 150 D
dsam@elgin.edu
SAM, David, A ... 540-423-9039 ... 526 E
dsam@germanna.edu
SAM, Mary ... 218-855-8159 ... 266 C
msam@clcmn.edu
SAMA, Eduardo ... 305-553-6065 ... 107 E
esama@careercollege.edu
SAMAHA, Ahmed ... 803-641-3411 ... 462 B
ahmeds@usca.edu
SAMALOT-RIVERA, OP, Yamil, A ... 787-786-0018 ... 561 H
ysamalot@cedoc.edu
SAMANGO, Melissa ... 610-526-6196 ... 430 D
msamango@harcum.edu
SAMANI, Tresia ... 540-857-7313 ... 528 E
tsamani@virginiawestern.edu
SAMANI, Tresia, B ... 804-758-6704 ... 527 G
tsamani@rappahannock.edu
SAMANT, Ajay ... 904-620-2590 ... 120 C
ajay.samant@unf.edu
SAMANTA, Shivajl ... 434-961-5229 ... 527 F
ssamanta@pvcc.edu
SAMARA, Michael, D ... 802-654-2566 ... 514 B
msamara@smcvt.edu
SAMATAR, Ahmed, I ... 651-696-6564 ... 265 A
samatar@macalester.edu
SAMBERG, Carol ... 212-875-4680 ... 323 E
csamberg@bankstreet.edu
SAMBERG, Wendy ... 203-285-2108 ... 90 A
wsamberg@gwcc.commnet.edu
SAMDAHL, JR., Donald, H ... 540-464-7228 ... 529 A
samdahldh@vmi.edu
SAMDPERIL, Debra ... 617-369-3116 ... 244 G
dsamdperil@smfa.edu
SAMEK, Linda ... 503-554-2871 ... 415 I
lsamek@georgefox.edu
SAMEK, Tom ... 503-375-7031 ... 415 F
tsamek@corban.edu
SAMENFINK, William, H ... 978-232-2402 ... 234 F
bsamenfi@endicott.edu
SAMET, Jan ... 301-696-3934 ... 223 C
jsamet@hood.edu
SAMHAT, Nayef ... 740-427-5114 ... 394 C
samhatn@kenyon.edu
SAMIA, Cris ... 425-564-2973 ... 531 B
cris.samia@bellevuecollege.edu
SAMIIAN, Vida ... 559-278-3056 ... 34 D
vida_samiian@csufresno.edu
SAMITORE, Wendy, C ... 509-527-4262 ... 538 G
wendy.samitore@wwcc.edu
SAMMAKIA, Bahgat ... 607-777-4818 ... 351 F
bahgat@binghamton.edu
SAMMARCO, Ed ... 800-955-2527 ... 282 G
SAMMARCO, Erica, C ... 716-888-2100 ... 325 G
sammarce@canisius.edu
SAMMIS, Robert ... 626-914-8550 ... 39 G
rsammis@citruscollege.edu
SAMMONS, Dallas ... 606-783-2060 ... 204 E
d.sammons@moreheadstate.edu
SAMMONS, Gregory, S ... 607-587-3992 ... 355 C
sammongs@alfredstate.edu
SAMMONS, Kenneth, R ... 509-313-6951 ... 534 A
ksammons@plant.gonzaga.edu
SAMMONS, Morgan ... 415-955-2066 ... 27 A
msammons@alliant.edu
SAMOLEWICZ, Mark ... 201-216-5218 ... 315 E
msamolew@stevens.edu
SAMOLEWSKI, Patrick, C ... 989-964-4221 ... 258 A
pcs@svsu.edu
SAMONS, Jenni ... 517-780-4553 ... 248 I
jenni.samons@baker.edu
SAMORA, Tracy ... 719-549-2850 ... 83 E
tracy.samora@colostate-pueblo.edu
SAMPH, Thomas ... 203-591-5050 ... 93 D
tsamph@post.edu
SAMPITE, Chris ... 318-869-5018 ... 208 F
csampite@centenary.edu
SAMPLE, Bradford, W ... 423-775-7232 ... 467 D
bradford.sample@bryan.edu
SAMPLE, Jay ... 806-291-1725 ... 508 B
samplej@wbu.edu
SAMPLE, Mark ... 704-991-0247 ... 374 A
jsample7479@stanly.edu
SAMPLE, Michael ... 812-855-0850 ... 173 B
mmsample@indiana.edu
SAMPLE, Mike ... 812-855-0850 ... 173 C
mmsample@indiana.edu
SAMPLE, Rick, A ... 301-369-2800 ... 221 F
rsample@capitol-college.edu
SAMPLE-PURTLEBAUGH, Charlene ... 765-288-8681 ... 172 H
charlene.purtlebaugh@harrison.edu
SAMPLER, Georgianna, W ... 818-947-2770 ... 55 E
samplegw@lavc.edu
SAMPLES, Janet ... 859-442-4121 ... 201 G
janet.samples@kctcs.edu
SAMPLES, Jennifer ... 541-684-7210 ... 417 F
jsamples@northwestchristian.edu
SAMPLES, Jim ... 562-903-4751 ... 30 H
jim.samples@biola.edu
SAMPLES, Robert, D ... 314-516-5665 ... 291 F
bob@umsl.edu
SAMPLEY, Curtis ... 334-387-3877 ... 1 D
curtissampley@amridgeuniversity.edu
SAMPSON, Ann ... 660-359-3948 ... 287 D
asampson@mail.ncmissouri.edu
SAMPSON, Betty, J ... 509-865-8600 ... 534 D
sampson_b@heritage.edu
SAMPSON, Christina ... 304-829-7401 ... 540 E
csampson@bethanywv.edu
SAMPSON, Christopher ... 920-465-2527 ... 551 A
sampsonc@uwgb.edu
SAMPSON, Connie, B ... 404-413-3230 ... 131 C
csampson@gsu.edu
SAMPSON, David, G ... 518-381-1370 ... 350 E
sampsodg@sunysccc.edu
SAMPSON, Laura ... 845-434-5750 ... 356 H
lsampson@sullivan.suny.edu
SAMPSON, Marsha ... 406-657-2085 ... 295 F
msampson@msubillings.edu
SAMPSON, Michael ... 203-392-5900 ... 91 I
sampsonm1@southernct.edu
SAMPSON, Robert ... 401-841-1323 ... 557 I
SAMPSON, Sharon ... 412-731-8690 ... 445 E
bookstore@rpts.edu
SAMPSON, Thaddeus ... 717-780-2425 ... 430 E
tsampson@hacc.edu
SAMPSON, Therese ... 609-343-5116 ... 307 D
sampson@atlantic.edu
SAMPSON, Zora, J ... 608-342-1688 ... 551 F
sampsonz@uwplatt.edu
SAMRA, Rajinder ... 925-424-1027 ... 39 A
rsamra@laspositascollege.edu
SAMS, Catherine, T ... 864-656-4233 ... 456 E
willsam@clemson.edu
SAMS, Susan ... 714-997-6829 ... 39 C
sams@chapman.edu
SAMS, Timothy, E ... 518-276-6201 ... 347 D
samst@rpi.edu
SAMSON, Agniel ... 256-726-7357 ... 6 C
samson@oakwood.edu
SAMSON, Kim, M ... 218-477-2133 ... 268 A
samson@mnstate.edu
SAMSON, Linda ... 708-534-4389 ... 151 C
lsamson@govst.edu
SAMSON, Mark ... 406-265-3761 ... 295 G
msamson@msun.edu
SAMUEL, Bryan ... 423-425-5670 ... 477 D
bryan-samuel@utc.edu
SAMUEL, Jacinta ... 692-625-6724 ... 559 E
jsamuel@cmi.edu
SAMUEL, Vincent ... 340-693-1400 ... 568 C
vsamuel@uvi.edu
SAMUEL LOFTUS, Barbara 570-674-6195 ... 436 F
mhinton@misericordia.edu
SAMUELS, A. Dexter ... 615-963-5646 ... 474 A
asamuels@tnstate.edu
SAMUELS, Darlette, C ... 731-426-7595 ... 469 M
dsamuels@lanecollege.edu
SAMUELS, Deby, K ... 615-966-7133 ... 470 D
deby.samuels@lipscomb.edu
SAMUELS, Diana ... 410-276-0306 ... 226 D
dsamuels@host.sdc.edu
SAMUELS, Elena ... 212-220-8061 ... 326 E
esamuels@bmcc.cuny.edu
SAMUELS, Milton ... 617-427-0060 ... 241 D
msamuels@rcc.mass.edu
SAMUELS, Robert ... 401-874-2288 ... 454 E
rsamuels@mail.uri.edu
SAMUELS, Sandra ... 973-353-5231 ... 314 E
szsamuls@newark.rutgers.edu
SAMUELS, Scott ... 248-218-2057 ... 257 F
ssamuels@rc.edu
SAMUELS-JONES, Michelle ... 240-684-2290 ... 227 F
student-services@umuc.edu

SAMUELSON, Cecil, O ...... 801-422-2521.... 509 D
cecil_samuelson@byu.edu
SAMUELSON, Pamela .... 570-372-4272.... 447 D
samuelson@susqu.edu
SAMUELSON, Terri .... 630-466-7900.... 167 G
tsamuelson@waubonsee.edu
SAN JOSE, Rodney .... 309-677-3131.... 145 H
rodney@bradley.edu
SAN NICOLAS, Heidi, E .... 671-735-2481.... 559 D
heidisan@ite.net
SAN NICOLAS, Jennifer .... 760-384-6367...... 52 N
jsannico@cerrocoso.edu
SANABRIA, Roberto, A ...... 773-442-5416.... 159 H
r-sanabria1@neiu.edu
SANAGUSTIN, Mary .... 760-744-1150...... 61 C
msanagustin@palomar.edu
SANAI, Fardin .... 518-956-8062.... 351 E
fsanai@uamail.albany.edu
SANANES, Amram .... 718-339-1090.... 361 D
amramsananes@verizon.net
SANANES, Josh .... 718-339-1090.... 361 D
rjsananes@mikdashmelech.org
SANBORN, Brett .... 303-220-1200...... 81 F
brett.sanborn@cffp.edu
SANBORN, Esther .... 773-298-3419.... 163 G
sanborn@sxu.edu
SANBORN, Jennifer .... 413-538-2500.... 242 G
jsanborn@mtholyoke.edu
SANBORN, Karen .... 734-432-5843.... 254 G
ksanborn@madonna.edu
SANBORN, Merlene .... 207-974-4871.... 218 H
msanborn@emcc.edu
SANCES, Susan .... 312-777-7731.... 144 G
ssances@argosy.edu
SANCHEZ, Alberto .... 623-845-3015...... 15 J
alberto.sanchez@gcmail.maricopa.edu
SANCHEZ, Andrew, E .... 505-925-8508.... 321 G
aesanchz@unm.edu
SANCHEZ, Angel, A .... 209-667-3646...... 36 C
aasanchez@csustan.edu
SANCHEZ, Ann .... 914-961-8313.... 349 I
aks@svots.edu
SANCHEZ, Anna .... 505-224-4687.... 317 J
asanchez420@cnm.edu
SANCHEZ, Anna .... 787-780-0070.... 560 F
asanchez@caribbean.edu
SANCHEZ, Caridad .... 305-821-3333.... 109 A
csanchez@mm.fnc.edu
SANCHEZ, Caridad .... 305-821-3333.... 109 B
csanchez@mm.fnc.edu
SANCHEZ, Caridad .... 305-821-3333.... 109 C
csanchez@mm.fnc.edu
SANCHEZ, Cheryl .... 719-336-1516...... 85 K
cheryl.sanchez@lamarcc.edu
SANCHEZ, Diane .... 210-829-5866.... 503 F
castaned@uiwtx.edu
SANCHEZ, Dwight .... 704-378-3500.... 365 H
dsanchez@jcsu.edu
SANCHEZ, Frank .... 212-794-5775.... 326 C
frank.sanchez@mail.cuny.edu
SANCHEZ, Gregory .... 619-388-3354...... 65 F
gsanchez@sdccd.edu
SANCHEZ, Hector Ruben ... 787-751-1912.... 564 A
rsanchez@inter.edu
SANCHEZ, Henry .... 575-538-6470.... 321 I
sanchezh@wnmu.edu
SANCHEZ, Ines .... 787-850-9348.... 567 B
ines.sanchez@upr.edu
SANCHEZ, Johanna .... 718-780-1898.... 338 E
jsanchez@chpnet.org
SANCHEZ, John .... 210-434-6711.... 491 G
jdsanchez@lake.ollusa.edu
SANCHEZ, Jorge, R .... 714-241-6338...... 40 J
jsanchez@coastline.edu
SANCHEZ, Jose .... 787-878-5475.... 562 H
jsanchez@arecibo.inter.edu
SANCHEZ, Josefina .... 787-850-9361.... 567 B
josefina.sanchez@upr.edu
SANCHEZ, Juan, M .... 512-471-2877.... 505 B
jsanchez@mail.utexas.edu
SANCHEZ, Judy .... 623-845-3481...... 15 J
judy.sanchez@gcmail.maricopa.edu
SANCHEZ, Julian .... 919-684-6756.... 363 I
julian.sanchez@duke.edu
SANCHEZ, Leopoldo, A ...... 314-863-2772.... 280 H
sanchezl@csl.edu
SANCHEZ, Librada .... 973-720-2586.... 317 D
sanchezl@wpunj.edu
SANCHEZ, Lisa .... 323-343-3694...... 35 B
lsanchez@cslanet.calstate.edu
SANCHEZ, Luis .... 520-494-5266...... 13 F
luis.sanchez@centralaz.edu
SANCHEZ, Luiz, P .... 805-922-6966...... 26 K
lsanchez@hancockcollege.edu
SANCHEZ, Mark .... 559-442-8226...... 72 A
mark.sanchez@fresnocitycollege.edu
SANCHEZ, Nancy .... 801-957-4041.... 512 C
nancy.sanchez@slcc.edu
SANCHEZ, Nicolas .... 928-855-7812...... 16 G
nsanchez@mohave.edu
SANCHEZ, Omar .... 305-821-3333.... 109 C
omarsnc@mm.fnc.edu
SANCHEZ, Omar .... 305-821-3333.... 109 B
omarsnc@mm.fnc.edu
SANCHEZ, Omar .... 305-821-3333.... 109 A
omarsnc@mm.fnc.edu
SANCHEZ, Ramiro .... 805-654-6464...... 77 D
rsanchez@vcccd.edu
SANCHEZ, Rebecca .... 951-343-4236...... 31 G
rsanchez@calbaptist.edu
SANCHEZ, Richard, M .... 903-875-7308.... 491 B
richard.sanchez@navarrocollege.edu
SANCHEZ, Roxanne .... 210-434-6711.... 491 G
rlsanchez@lake.ollusa.edu
SANCHEZ, Samuel .... 787-751-1912.... 564 A
ssamuel@inter.edu
SANCHEZ, Steven .... 314-977-2611.... 289 F
ssanche6@slu.edu
SANCHEZ, Victor .... 708-656-8000.... 159 C
victor.sanchez@morton.edu
SANCHEZ, William .... 605-575-2038.... 466 D
william.sanchez@usiouxfalls.edu
SANCHEZ, Willie .... 402-363-5620.... 301 F
willie.sanchez@york.edu
SANCHEZ, Xiomara .... 787-743-4041.... 561 E
xsanchez@columbiaco.edu
SANCILIO, Leonard .... 585-245-5706.... 353 C
sancilio@geneseo.edu
SANCOMB, Danny .... 304-243-2365.... 545 G
athletics@wju.edu
SAND, Scott .... 909-622-8866...... 44 J
ssand@devry.edu
SAND, Sharon .... 845-434-5750.... 356 H
ssand@sullivan.suny.edu
SANDBERG, Curtis .... 859-985-3208.... 198 F
curtis_sandberg@berea.edu
SANDBERG, Gary, A .... 614-235-4136.... 402 G
gsandberg@TLSohio.edu
SANDBERG, Peter .... 507-786-3611.... 271 H
sandberg@stolaf.edu
SANDBERG, Ruth .... 215-635-7300.... 430 A
rsandberg@gratz.edu
SANDBOTHE, Robin .... 913-667-5700.... 191 E
rsandbothe@cbts.edu
SANDBULTE, Deb .... 712-707-7224.... 188 B
debfs@nwciowa.edu
SANDE, Jeff, A .... 218-755-3988.... 266 B
jsande@bemidjistate.edu
SANDE, Nora .... 503-552-1531.... 417 D
nsande@ncnm.edu
SANDEEN, Beverly, A .... 530-752-2616...... 73 F
basandeen@ucdavis.edu
SANDEEN, Cathy .... 310-825-5551...... 74 A
csandeen@unex.ucla.edu
SANDEFUR, Gary .... 608-263-2303.... 550 G
gsandefur@ls.wisc.edu
SANDEL, Robert, H .... 540-857-7311.... 528 E
rsandel@virginiawestern.edu
SANDELL, Stanley, C .... 310-233-4181...... 54 I
sandelsc@lahc.edu
SANDER, Dennis, M .... 620-417-1018.... 196 B
dennis.sander@sccc.edu
SANDER, Eugene .... 520-621-7621...... 19 B
egsander@ag.arizona.edu
SANDER, Phyllis .... 618-634-3334.... 164 C
phylliss@shawneecc.edu
SANDERLIN,
September, C .... 757-683-4324.... 521 L
ssanderl@odu.edu
SANDERS, Allison .... 703-526-5800.... 516 B
asanders@argosy.edu
SANDERS, Alphonso .... 662-254-3484.... 276 C
asanders@mvsu.edu
SANDERS, Angela .... 501-370-5259...... 23 B
asanders@philander.edu
SANDERS, Art .... 515-271-3172.... 184 A
SANDERS, Barbara .... 775-673-7123.... 302 J
bsanders@tmcc.edu
SANDERS, Beth .... 808-322-4850.... 141 F
sanders@hawaii.edu
SANDERS, Betty Jo .... 910-642-7141.... 373 G
bsanders@sccnc.edu
SANDERS, Blanche .... 601-877-6350.... 273 C
blanche@alcorn.edu
SANDERS, Brian .... 209-575-6701...... 80 B
sandersb@mjc.edu
SANDERS, Chris .... 563-425-5832.... 189 C
sandersc@uiu.edu
SANDERS, Chris .... 314-744-5345.... 286 C
sanders@mobap.edu
SANDERS, Clifton .... 801-957-5180.... 512 C
clifton.sanders@slcc.edu
SANDERS, Craig, R .... 970-225-4860...... 81 I
craig.sanders@collegeamerica.edu
SANDERS, Deborah, L .... 903-923-3239.... 500 A
deborah.sanders@marshall.tstc.edu
SANDERS, Donna Sue .... 386-506-3137.... 103 J
sanderds@DaytonaState.edu
SANDERS, Frances .... 913-621-8716.... 192 C
sanders@donnelly.edu
SANDERS, George, E .... 904-646-2205.... 109 E
gsanders@fscj.edu
SANDERS, Gwendolyn .... 252-335-3226.... 377 D
gsanders@mail.ecsu.edu
SANDERS, H. Michael .... 513-745-5717.... 403 F
h.michael.sanders@uc.edu
SANDERS, J. Michael .... 806-742-2120.... 501 D
mike.sanders@ttu.edu
SANDERS, Jack, A .... 423-439-4236.... 473 E
sanders@etsu.edu
SANDERS, Jerry, R .... 651-696-6700.... 265 A
sanders@macalester.edu
SANDERS, Jessica .... 412-566-2433.... 434 B
jsanders@paculinary.com
SANDERS, Jill .... 503-552-1994.... 417 D
jsanders@ncnm.edu
SANDERS, Jo-Ann .... 419-448-2288.... 391 G
jsanders@heidelberg.edu
SANDERS, Jocelyn .... 423-425-4515.... 477 D
jocelyn-sanders@utc.edu
SANDERS, Joe .... 432-552-2620.... 507 C
sanders_j@utpb.edu
SANDERS, JoEllen .... 330-339-3391.... 394 B
jsanders@kent.edu
SANDERS, John .... 740-753-6449.... 392 A
sanders_j@hocking.edu
SANDERS, John, J .... 843-792-3811.... 459 C
sanderjj@musc.edu
SANDERS, Karen .... 386-506-3050.... 103 J
sanderk@DaytonaState.edu
SANDERS, Karen, A .... 217-786-2784.... 156 I
karen.sanders@llcc.edu
SANDERS, Ken .... 908-737-7030.... 311 B
kesander@kean.edu
SANDERS, Kerry .... 248-414-6900.... 255 B
ksanders@mji.edu
SANDERS, Kimberly .... 713-525-3889.... 504 D
sanderk1@stthom.edu
SANDERS, Laurie .... 515-244-4221.... 181 D
lauries@aib.edu
SANDERS, JR.,
Lawrence, L .... 404-756-1321.... 134 B
lsanders@msm.edu
SANDERS, Lee .... 870-574-4455...... 24 A
lsanders@sautech.edu
SANDERS, Leon .... 318-274-6401.... 215 E
sandersl@gram.edu
SANDERS, Liz .... 312-362-5289.... 148 F
lsander3@depaul.edu
SANDERS, Marcy .... 817-272-2101.... 505 A
sanders@uta.edu
SANDERS, Melvin .... 620-241-0723.... 191 F
melvin.sanders@centralchristian.edu
SANDERS, Michael .... 863-638-7239.... 123 B
michael.sanders@warner.edu
SANDERS, Nancy, A .... 815-395-5100.... 163 C
nancysanders@sacn.edu
SANDERS, Nena, F .... 205-726-2861........ 6 G
nfsander@samford.edu
SANDERS, Paul .... 740-366-9416.... 399 E
sanders.102@osu.edu
SANDERS, Paula .... 713-348-2598.... 492 J
sanders@rice.edu
SANDERS, Philip .... 609-984-4099.... 316 A
psanders@tesc.edu
SANDERS, Rich, F .... 208-467-8825.... 143 I
rfsanders@nnu.edu
SANDERS, Richard .... 860-444-8646.... 558 E
Richard.W.Sanders@uscga.edu
SANDERS, Robert .... 662-254-3478.... 276 C
rlsanders@mvsu.edu
SANDERS, Ron .... 254-867-4834.... 500 B
ron.sanders@tstc.edu
SANDERS, Sabrina .... 562-938-5082...... 54 E
ssanders@lbcc.edu
SANDERS, Sally .... 816-271-4287.... 287 A
sanders@missouriwestern.edu
SANDERS, Sandra .... 816-584-6816.... 287 H
sandra.sanders@park.edu
SANDERS, Sue, E .... 817-515-4573.... 496 A
sue.sanders@tccd.edu
SANDERS, RSM,
Susan, M .... 773-298-3981.... 163 G
sanders@sxu.edu
SANDERS, Tiffany .... 256-395-2211........ 7 E
tsanders@suscc.edu
SANDERS, Timothy, J .... 765-494-6838.... 178 F
sanderstj@purdue.edu
SANDERS, Tom .... 330-337-6403.... 383 H
college@awc.edu
SANDERS, Tricia .... 218-281-8326.... 272 A
sand0803@umn.edu
SANDERS, Victoria .... 570-422-2862.... 442 C
vsanders@po-box.esu.edu
SANDERS, W, C .... 507-389-7299.... 269 F
wc.sanders@southcentral.edu
SANDERS-HAWKINS,
Linda .... 202-806-2755...... 98 B
lsanders-hawkins@howard.edu
SANDERS-KELLEY, Kelly ... 731-352-4000.... 467 C
kelleyk@bethelu.edu
SANDERS-MARKS, Tanya .. 412-237-4657.... 425 H
tsander-marks@ccac.edu
SANDERS-MCMURTRY,
Kijua .... 404-471-6064.... 123 G
ksandersmcmurtry@agnesscott.edu
SANDERSON, Carla, D .... 731-661-5355.... 476 G
csanders@uu.edu
SANDERSON, Francie, W .. 919-866-5944.... 374 E
fwsanderson@waketech.edu
SANDERSON, Kevin, L .... 651-675-4701.... 264 H
ksanderson@msp.chefs.edu
SANDERSON, Larry .... 575-492-2787.... 319 B
lsanderson@nmjc.edu
SANDERSON, Laurie .... 757-221-2467.... 517 J
slsand@wm.edu
SANDERSON, Sharon .... 706-886-6831.... 137 G
ssanderson@tfc.edu
SANDFORD, Art .... 805-654-6587...... 77 D
asandford@vcccd.edu
SANDGREN, Eric .... 501-569-3333...... 24 E
exsandgren@ualr.edu
SANDGREN, Peggy .... 303-765-3113...... 84 K
SANDIDGE, Steven .... 817-598-6421.... 508 C
ssandidge@wc.edu
SANDIFER, Betty .... 843-792-0552.... 459 C
sandifbw@musc.edu
SANDIFER, Joyce .... 504-520-5230.... 217 A
jsandife@xula.edu
SANDIFER, William, A .... 803-584-3446.... 462 E
sandifea@mailbox.sc.edu
SANDLOOP, Len .... 757-388-2900.... 523 J
SANDMANN, Warren .... 507-389-1333.... 267 H
warren.sandmann@mnsu.edu
SANDMEYER, Louise, E ...... 814-863-8721.... 438 F
les1@psu.edu
SANDO, Terry .... 701-777-3511.... 381 D
terry.sando@email.und.edu
SANDOVAL, Ann .... 563-344-1500.... 182 F
asandoval@brownmackie.edu
SANDOVAL, Eddie .... 817-515-6532.... 496 A
eddie.sandoval@tccd.edu
SANDOVAL, Greg .... 951-571-6120...... 63 J
greg.sandoval@mvc.edu
SANDOVAL, James, W .... 951-827-4641...... 74 C
james.sandoval@ucr.edu
SANDOVAL, Jessie .... 320-363-5800.... 262 H
jsandoval@csbsju.edu
SANDOVAL, Juan .... 940-397-4117.... 491 A
juan.sandoval@mwsu.edu
SANDOVAL, Victor, A .... 801-878-1401.... 303 D
vsandoval@roseman.edu
SANDQUIST, Rick, A .... 515-574-1347.... 185 F
sandquist@iowacentral.edu
SANDRETTO, Maxine, L ...... 217-333-9634.... 167 B
msandret@uillinois.edu
SANDS, Amy .... 831-647-4116...... 57 F
asands@miis.edu
SANDS, Charles .... 951-343-4619...... 31 G
csands@calbaptist.edu
SANDS, Charlie .... 205-726-2820........ 6 G
ccsands@samford.edu
SANDS, Harlan, M .... 205-975-9934........ 8 G
hsands@uab.edu
SANDS, Timothy, D .... 765-494-9709.... 178 F
tsands@purdue.edu
SANDS HINES, Brenda .... 804-745-2444.... 516 L
bshines@bryantstratton.edu
SANDS-VANKERK, Linda .. 630-942-2621.... 147 G
sands-vankerkl@cod.edu
SANDSTROM, Kent .... 701-231-9588.... 381 H
kent.sandstrom@ndsu.edu
SANDSTROM, Lynne .... 707-826-4031...... 36 D
les37@humboldt.edu
SANDT, Jennifer, A .... 410-334-2920.... 229 E
jsandt@worwic.edu
SANDUM TUNE, Rachel .... 937-327-7411.... 406 B
rtune@wittenberg.edu
SANDUSKY, Brian .... 913-451-1431...... 17 C
SANDUSKY, Brian .... 913-451-1431.... 178 E
SANDUSKY, Brian .... 913-451-1431.... 195 F
brian.sandusky@ottawa.edu
SANDUSKY, Brian .... 913-451-1431.... 195 G
SANDUSKY, Brian .... 913-451-1431.... 549 E
SANDUSKY, Curt .... 301-846-2411.... 222 G
csandusky@frederick.edu
SANDWEISS, Daniel, H .... 207-581-3217.... 220 A
dan.sandweiss@umit.maine.edu
SANDY, Bud .... 309-672-4946.... 158 B
SANDY, Michael, B .... 717-780-3277.... 430 E
mbsandy@hacc.edu
SANER, Eileen .... 574-296-6233.... 169 C
esaner@ambs.edu
SANFILIPPO, Sarah .... 802-447-6311.... 514 D
ssanfilippo@svc.edu
SANFORD, Clarke .... 661-654-2391...... 33 H
csanford@csub.edu
SANFORD, Debra, A .... 330-385-1070.... 400 E
dsanford@ovct.edu
SANFORD, Delacy .... 904-470-8290.... 105 A
dsanford@ewc.edu
SANFORD, Delores, A .... 775-673-7013.... 302 J
dsanford@tmcc.edu
SANFORD, James .... 615-687-6901.... 466 G
jsanford@abcnash.edu
SANFORD, Janell .... 757-826-1883.... 516 H
SANFORD, Marilyn .... 334-844-7771........ 1 G
sanfoma@auburn.edu
SANFORD, Matthew .... 607-431-4460.... 335 B
sanfordm@hartwick.edu
SANFORD, Susan, H .... 315-470-6604.... 355 A
shsanfor@esf.edu
SANFORD, Teresa .... 336-316-2115.... 364 E
tsanford@guilford.edu
SANGER, Bryna .... 212-229-8947.... 342 E
sanger@newschool.edu

SANGER, Kathy 507-625-6556 271 C Kathy.Sanger@Rasmussen.edu

SANGER, Laurel, T 585-292-3398 341 H lsanger@monroecc.edu

SANGER, Patrick 281-756-3663 479 G psanger@alvincollege.edu

SANGHVI, Kamlesh 847-543-2974 147 H ksanghvi@clcillinois.edu

SANGREY-BILLY, Cory 406-395-4313 296 G csangrey@stonechild.edu

SANGUINET, Bonnie, K 314-984-7624 289 D bsanguinet@stlcc.edu

SANIDAD, Daniel 408-855-5139 78 A daniel.sanidad@wvmccd.cc.ca.us

SANJANA, Espi 415-351-3550 65 I esanjana@sfai.edu

SANKEY, Dean, A 715-232-2258 552 C sankeyd@uwstout.edu

SANKEY, Stephen, D 610-785-6510 446 A ssankey@adphila.org

SANKEY, Steve 425-822-8266 535 I steve.sankey@northwestu.edu

SANKO, Jerry 620-672-5641 196 A jerrys@prattcc.edu

SANKS GUIDRY, Beverly 909-469-5341 78 D bguidry@westernu.edu

SANNS, Aaron, D 208-496-1610 142 G sannsa@byui.edu

SANOIR, Carla 561-912-1211 106 G csanoir@evergladesuniversity.edu

SANSBURY, James, E 301-445-1966 227 A sansbury@usmd.edu

SANSEVERE, Susanne 201-360-4284 310 F ssansevere@hccc.edu

SANSEVIRO, Michael, L 770-423-6310 132 H msansevi@kennesaw.edu

SANSING, Joyce 706-355-5018 124 H jsansing@athenstech.edu

SANSING, Lucille 510-215-0277 144 G lsansing@argosy.edu

SANSING, Perry 662-329-7104 276 B psansing@pres.muw.edu

SANSOLA, Steve 845-575-3000 340 C steve.sansola@marist.edu

SANSOM, Mel 501-279-4485 21 H msansom@harding.edu

SANSON, Calvin 352-638-9729 101 H csanson@beaconcollege.edu

SANSON, Jerry 318-473-6470 212 G jsanson@lsua.edu

SANSONE, Joseph 201-360-4006 310 F jsansone@hccc.edu

SANSONE, Linda 716-827-2496 358 B sansonel@trocaire.edu

SANT, Anne, M 508-565-1343 245 D asant@stonehill.edu

SANTANA, Melanie 787-751-0160 561 G msantana@cmpr.gobierno.pr

SANTANA, Pedro 609-652-4601 313 F pedro.santana@stockton.edu

SANTANA, Yara 312-427-2737 154 F 6santanay@jmls.edu

SANTANA-BRAVO, Maydel 305-348-1555 119 B santanam@fiu.edu

SANTANA-SOTO, Yvette 530-749-5002 80 E vsantana@yccd.edu

SANTEE, Wendi 863-638-7246 123 B wendi.santee@warner.edu

SANTELL, Candice 937-769-1343 383 J csantell@antioch.edu

SANTELL, Ross 216-987-2340 389 A ross.santell@tri-c.edu

SANTIAGO, Alfonso 787-841-2000 564 I alfonso.santiago@email.pucpr.edu

SANTIAGO, Carmen, E 787-890-2681 566 E carmen.santiago7@hotmail.com

SANTIAGO, Carol 787-620-2040 560 B csantiago@aupr.edu

SANTIAGO, Dalia 787-882-2065 565 I orientacion@unitecpr.net

SANTIAGO, Delma 787-744-1060 564 D dsantiago@mechtech.edu

SANTIAGO, Edny 787-864-2222 563 D edsantiago@inter.edu

SANTIAGO, Elias 787-765-1915 564 B esantiago@inter.edu

SANTIAGO, George 516-918-3601 324 E gsantiago@bcl.edu

SANTIAGO, Hilda 856-415-2276 310 E hsantiago@gccnj.edu

SANTIAGO, Ivette 787-250-0000 566 D ivette.santiago5@upr.edu

SANTIAGO, Jaime 787-250-1912 563 E jaimesantiago@metro.inter.edu

SANTIAGO, Judith 212-343-1234 341 B jsantiago@mcny.edu

SANTIAGO, Lori 918-622-4877 19 C lori.santiago@phoenix.edu

SANTIAGO, Marilia 787-894-2828 568 A marilia.santiago1@upr.edu

SANTIAGO, Marta 315-312-3702 354 A marta.santiago@oswego.edu

SANTIAGO, Rafael 787-780-0070 560 F rsantiago@caribbean.edu

SANTIAGO, Soriel 787-815-0000 566 F

SANTIAGO, Victor 787-857-3600 563 A vsantiago@br.inter.edu

SANTIAGO, Yinaira 787-260-5665 563 F yinsant@ponce.inter.edu

SANTIAGO-BORRERO, Pedro, J 787-758-2525 567 D pedro.santiago9@upr.edu

SANTIAGO-CANET, Jaime, L 787-841-2000 564 I jstgocan@email.pucpr.edu

SANTIAGO MENDEZ, Rosa 787-881-1212 565 A rsmendez@email.pucpr.edu

SANTIAGO ROSADO, Lydia, E 787-863-2390 563 C lydia.santiago@fajardo.inter.edu

SANTIAGO-TORO, Clarissa 787-723-4481 560 H centroaldia@yahoo.com

SANTICOLA, Jeff 412-566-2433 434 B jsanticola@paculinary.com

SANTILLI, Nicholas, R 216-397-4425 392 M santilli@jcu.edu

SANTILLI, Patricia 508-286-3857 246 E psantill@wheatonma.edu

SANTINI, Cathy 925-969-3584 52 B csantini@jfku.edu

SANTIVASCI, Joeseph 610-436-3085 443 F jsantivasci@wcupa.edu

SANTIZO, Roberto 847-628-2532 154 I rsantizo@judsonu.edu

SANTOMAURO, Kristine, M 302-225-6233 96 E santomk@gbc.edu

SANTORA, Anthony 908-737-6000 311 B afs@kean.edu

SANTORA, Cynthia, S 607-587-4230 355 C santorcs@alfredstate.edu

SANTORE, JR., Chuck 724-439-4900 433 H csantore@laurel.edu

SANTORI, Margarita 787-265-3879 567 C msantori@uprm.edu

SANTORO, Daniella 212-924-5900 357 A ce@swedishinstitute.edu

SANTOS, Adele, N 617-253-4402 242 A ansantos@mit.edu

SANTOS, Allison 312-280-3500 153 A asantos@aii.edu

SANTOS, Ana, B 670-234-5498 559 F anas@nmcnet.edu

SANTOS, Ana, L 973-642-8392 315 C ana.santos@shu.edu

SANTOS, Carlo 408-288-3761 67 A

SANTOS, Carmen, K 671-735-5548 559 B carmen.kweksantos@guamcc.edu

SANTOS, Carol 508-999-8388 237 E csantos1@umassd.edu

SANTOS, Catherine 315-312-2500 354 A santos@oswego.edu

SANTOS, Cynthia 713-221-8136 503 D santosc@uhd.edu

SANTOS, Helena 617-243-2127 236 F hsantos@lasell.edu

SANTOS, Kennia 787-480-2453 561 D ksantos@sanjuancapital.com

SANTOS, Leslie 209-228-2977 74 B LSantos@UCMerced.edu

SANTOS, Mae 323-343-3555 35 B msantos@cslanet.calstatela.edu

SANTOS, Maria 561-273-6500 117 J msantos@southuniversity.edu

SANTOS, Maria del, C 787-743-7979 565 F ut_masantos@suagm.edu

SANTOS, Maricarmen 787-743-7979 565 F m_santos@suagm.edu

SANTOS, Maritza 787-878-5475 562 H msantos@arecibo.inter.edu

SANTOS, Matthew 610-683-4113 442 F santos@kutztown.edu

SANTOS, Michelle, M 671-735-5590 559 B deansoffice@guamcc.edu

SANTOS, Paul 704-330-6689 369 A paul.santos@cpcc.edu

SANTOS, Ramon 305-223-4561 116 C santos@sjvcs.edu

SANTOS, Robert 212-650-8830 326 H rdsantos@ccny.cuny.edu

SANTOS, Sandra 787-758-2525 567 D sandra.santos@upr.edu

SANTOS DE BARONA, Maryann 765-494-2336 178 F msdb@purdue.edu

SANTOSTEFANO, Donald 717-867-6341 434 C facilities-services@lvc.edu

SANTUCCI, George 412-281-2600 446 H gsantucci@western-school.com

SANTUCCI, Wayne 212-517-0544 340 D wsantucci@mmm.edu

SANTULLI, II, John, J 954-262-8832 114 B santulli@nsu.nova.edu

SANYAL, Rajib, N 765-285-8192 169 D rnsanyal@bsu.edu

SAO, Ry-Yon 425-637-1010 531 I rgsao@cityu.edu

SAPARILAS, John, W 919-866-5450 374 E jwsaparilas@waketech.edu

SAPATA, Tony 708-237-5050 160 C tsapata@nc.edu

SAPERSTEIN, Shari 954-262-7202 114 B ssaperst@nsu.nova.edu

SAPERSTONE, Barbara, L 703-323-3222 527 C bsaperstone@nvcc.edu

SAPHIRE, Diane, G 210-999-8483 502 C dsaphire@trinity.edu

SAPIENZA, Matthew 646-746-4275 326 C matthew.sapienza@mail.cuny.edu

SAPIENZA, Michael, C 423-775-7224 467 D misapienza@bryan.edu

SAPIRO, Virginia 617-353-2401 232 G vsapiro@bu.edu

SAPLAD, Thalia 206-546-4512 537 G tsaplad@shoreline.edu

SAPONARA, Manuel 787-878-9218 566 F

SAPONARO, James 315-792-3046 359 C jsaponaro@utica.edu

SAPP, Aimee 573-592-4391 293 E asapp@williamwoods.edu

SAPP, Buddy 912-871-1634 134 H bsapp@ogeecheetech.edu

SAPP, Fred 910-672-1204 377 E fsapp@uncfsu.edu

SAPP, Geneva 509-865-8631 534 D sapp_g@heritage.edu

SAPP, Jeremy, B 512-279-2850 507 H jeremy.sapp@vc.edu

SAPP, Judy 606-877-1421 202 F judy.sapp@kctcs.edu

SAPP, Lauren 850-599-3370 118 G lauren.sapp@famu.edu

SAPP, Marge 843-525-8276 461 E msapp@tcl.edu

SAPP, Mary, M 305-284-3856 122 F msapp@miami.edu

SAPP, Sarah 662-562-3274 276 E ssapp@northwestms.edu

SAPPENFIELD, Elizabeth 317-738-8075 171 C esappenfield@franklincollege.edu

SAPPENFIELD, George, O 336-386-3280 374 B sappeng@surry.edu

SAPPINGTON, Eric 660-831-4168 286 I sappingtone@moval.edu

SAPPINGTON, Lee Ann 970-339-6223 80 G leeann.sappington@aims.edu

SAPYTA, Lynn 630-942-2219 147 G sapytal@cod.edu

SARA, Ligaya 680-488-2471 560 A ligayas@palau.edu

SARA, Tejnder 334-727-8704 8 C tsara@tuskegee.edu

SARAC, Isa 703-591-7042 528 H

SARACCO, Melanie 714-867-5009 70 C

SARACENO, William 509-542-4408 532 C bsaraceno@columbiabasin.edu

SARAJIAN, Charles 973-655-7480 311 G sarajianc@mail.montclair.edu

SARAKA, Mike 570-422-3691 442 C msaraka@esufoundation.org

SARANTAKOS, Paul 217-351-2385 161 B psarantakos@parkland.edu

SARBER, Sarah 765-455-9204 173 E shawkins@iuk.edu

SARGE, Billy 859-344-3402 206 D billy.sarge@thomasmore.edu

SARGEANT, Kari 815-802-8256 154 J ksargeant@kcc.edu

SARGENT, Anneila, I 626-395-6100 32 E afs@caltech.edu

SARGENT, Carol, L 910-576-6222 372 A sargentc@montgomery.edu

SARGENT, Ed 425-739-8100 535 B ed.sargent@lwtc.edu

SARGENT, Frank 401-598-1033 453 C FSargent@jwu.edu

SARGENT, Gary 254-295-4242 504 A gsargent@umhb.edu

SARGENT, Jeffrey 708-456-0300 166 C jsargent@triton.edu

SARGENT, Jenell 404-270-5447 137 E jsargent@spelman.edu

SARGENT, Joey, E 423-585-6836 476 B joe.sargent@ws.edu

SARGENT, Joseph 415-503-6211 66 A jsargent@sfcm.edu

SARGENT, Judy, L 701-777-4251 381 D judy.sargent@email.und.edu

SARGENT, Lori 270-384-8030 203 H sargentl@lindsey.edu

SARGENT, Madeline 215-568-9215 436 E msargent@mccworks.org

SARGENT, Marilyn 707-664-2790 37 B sargenma@sonoma.edu

SARGENT, Mark, L 978-867-4206 235 E mark.sargent@gordon.edu

SARGENT, Peter, E 314-968-7006 293 A sargenpe@webster.edu

SARGENT, Tom, M 910-576-6222 372 A sargentt@montgomery.edu

SARHAN, Mostafa 912-358-4190 136 C vpaa@savannahstate.edu

SARIAN, Richard 216-421-7432 387 H rsarian@cia.edu

SARIDAKIS, Dianne 215-965-4048 436 H dsaridakis@moore.edu

SARIKAS, Bridget 202-806-2411 98 B bridget.sarikas@howard.edu

SARIN, Sanjiv 336-334-7920 377 F sarin@ncat.edu

SARKAR, Amin 256-372-5092 1 A amin.sarkar@aamu.edu

SARKIS, Joseph 508-793-7670 233 C jsarkis@clarku.edu

SARLES, Harry 913-684-3097 558 C harry.sarles@us.army.mil

SARMIENTO, Reine 718-482-5414 328 C rsarmiento@lagcc.cuny.edu

SARNA, Ruth 785-594-8409 190 C ruth.sarna@bakeru.edu

SARNESO, Bernard, J 814-269-7073 449 D sarneso@pitt.edu

SARNOVSKY, Joseph 407-708-2430 117 G sarnovsj@seminolestate.edu

SARRA, Amanda 561-912-1211 106 G asarra@evergladesuniversity.edu

SARRATORE, Steve, T 260-481-6536 174 A sarrator@ipfw.edu

SARRATORI, Peter 315-781-3647 335 G sarratori@hws.edu

SARRAZIN, Catherine 504-671-5410 210 G csarra@dcc.edu

SARRETT, David, C 804-828-7235 525 E dcsarrett@vcu.edu

SARRETT, Michele 304-253-7351 541 D msarrett@mountainstate.edu

SARRIS, Emmanuel 312-850-7090 147 C esarris@ccc.edu

SARSAR, Saliba 732-571-4474 311 F sarsar@monmouth.edu

SARTAIN, S, L 816-559-5612 287 H sartain@park.edu

SARTARELLI, Jose, V 304-293-7800 544 E jose.sartarelli@mail.wvu.edu

SARTIN, Mici 405-691-3800 408 H msartin@macu.edu

SARVELA, Paul 618-536-3465 164 H psarvela@siu.edu

SARVER, Angel, M 417-268-6010 279 D asarver@gobbc.edu

SARVEY, Sharon 252-399-6401 362 A sisarvey@barton.edu

SARVIS, Randall, F 937-382-6661 405 H randy_sarvis@wilmington.edu

SASAKI, Charles 808-734-9517 141 E sasakich@hawaii.edu

SASAKI, Edwin 661-654-2554 33 H esasaki@csub.edu

SASS, Michael 518-694-7367 322 C michael.sass@acphs.edu

SASS, Sharon, A 561-868-3147 114 D sasss@palmbeachstate.edu

SASS, Terricita, E 757-823-8679 521 K tesass@nsu.edu

SASS, Thomas, A 615-383-1340 468 J tom-s@fwbbc.edu

SASSAMAN, Margo, J 717-872-3312 443 C margo.sassaman@millersville.edu

SASSE, Benjamin 402-941-6000 299 A president@midlandu.edu

SASSER, Dell 606-436-5721 201 H dell.sasser@kctcs.edu

SASSER, Jackson 757-822-1080 528 C jsasser@tcc.edu

SASSER, Jackson, N 352-395-5164 117 E j.sasser@sfcollege.edu

SASSER, Jennifer 503-675-3964 416 I jsasser@marylhurst.edu

SASSER, Rachelle 310-900-1600 45 E sasser_r@compton.edu

SASSER, Susan, M 919-735-5151 374 F msm@waynecc.edu

SASSMAN, Jen, L 319-352-8262 189 F jennifer.sassman@wartburg.edu

SASSO, Gary, M 610-758-3221 434 E gms208@lehigh.edu

SASTRY, Shankar 510-642-5771 73 E sastry@coe.berkeley.edu

SATCHER, SR., Robert, L 434-848-6401 523 G rsatcher@saintpauls.edu

SATCHWELL, Carol 315-655-7144 325 I csatchwell@cazenovia.edu

SATELE, Arleen 619-660-4654 48 J arleen.satele@gcccd.edu

SATEY, Linda, S 828-448-3531 374 G lsatey@wpcc.edu

SATHER, Steven, M 609-258-6479 313 A sather@princeton.edu

SATHRUM, Malia 503-399-6566 414 J malia.sathrum@chemeketa.edu

SATKOWIAK, Ann, E 865-539-7153 475 F asatkowiak@pstcc.edu

SATKOWSKI, John 567-661-7204 400 H john_satkowski@owens.edu

ATO, Kay 516-299-2584 339 A kay.sato@liu.edu
ATO, Sara 808-544-0238 140 B ssato@hpu.edu
ATO, Tami, A 714-449-7449 70 G tsato@scco.edu
SATRIANA, Dan 970-351-2399 88 F dan.satriana@unco.edu
SATTAR, Mo 413-565-1000 231 B msattar@baypath.edu
SATTERFIELD, Billy 281-283-2480 503 C satterfield@uhcl.edu
SATTERFIELD, Jay 731-989-6381 468 K jsatterfield@fhu.edu
SATTERLEE, Kevin 208-426-1203 142 F ksatterl@boisestate.edu
SATTERLEE, Richard 718-862-7352 339 H richard.satterlee@manhattan.edu
SATTERLY, Amy 812-749-1392 178 D asatterly@oak.edu
SATTERTHWAITE, Ann 215-596-8948 450 A a.satter@usciences.edu
SATTERTHWAITE, Shad 405-325-3546 413 D shad@ou.edu
SATTERTHWAITE, Shad, B 405-325-3546 413 C shad@ou.edu
SATTLER, Brian 409-880-8396 500 F brian.sattler@lamar.edu
SATTLER, Joan, L 309-677-3180 145 H jls@bradley.edu
SATTLER, Michael 315-472-6603 325 E msattler@bryantstratton.edu
SATTLER, Nancy, J 419-559-2179 402 D nsattler@terra.edu
SAUBERT, IV, Carl, W 636-227-2100 284 E carl.saubert@logan.edu
SAUCEDA, Marshall 310-338-5808 56 E msauceda@lmu.edu
SAUCEMAN, Fred, W 423-439-4317 473 E sauceman@etsu.edu
SAUCIER, Bonnie 503-413-8080 416 G bsaucie@linfield.edu
SAUCIER, Claudia 504-671-5602 210 G csauci@dcc.edu
SAUCIER, Todd 207-581-1138 220 A todd.saucier@umit.maine.edu
SAUDER, Ron 404-727-4499 129 A ron.sauder@emory.edu
SAUDER, Vinita, R 423-236-2580 473 A sauder@southern.edu
SAUDERS, Charlette, R 574-372-5100 171 E saudercr@grace.edu
SAUER, Alan, R 860-297-2043 94 C alan.sauer@trincoll.edu
SAUER, James, L 610-341-5957 428 D jsauer@eastern.edu
SAUER, Jenni 610-647-4400 431 B jsauer@immaculata.edu
SAUER, Marty, R 630-637-5801 159 F mrsauer@noctrl.edu
SAUER, Mike 702-895-1073 302 K sauer@unlv.edu
SAUER, Peter 340-693-1102 568 C psauer@uvi.edu
SAUERESSIG, Sarah 785-587-2800 194 F sarahsaueressig@matc.net
SAUERS, Darlene 724-838-4210 447 B sauers@setonhill.edu
SAUERWEIN, David, A 603-526-3758 304 A dsauerwein@colby-sawyer.edu
SAUERWEIN, Rachel 802-831-1237 515 A cwiegand@vermontlaw.edu
SAUK, John, J 502-852-5295 207 A john.sauk@louisville.edu
SAUL, Amy 610-861-1509 436 I awsaul@moravian.edu
SAUL, J. Beau 607-844-8222 357 H saulj@TC3.edu
SAULE, Mara, R 802-656-2020 514 F mara.saule@uvm.edu
SAULMON, Sharon 405-733-7322 411 I ssaulmon@rose.edu
SAULNIER, Richard 212-237-8118 328 A rsaulnier@jjay.cuny.edu
SAULS, Con 276-466-7935 528 G consauls@vic.edu
SAULS, Jina, M 276-935-4349 516 A jsauls@asl.edu
SAULS, Steve 305-348-3505 119 B steve.sauls@fiu.edu
SAULSBERRY, Keith 334-556-2470 4 A ksaulsberry@wallace.edu
SAUM, Rob 386-506-3484 103 J saumr@DaytonaState.edu
SAUNDERS, Amber 318-676-7811 211 H asaunders@nwltc.edu
SAUNDERS, Benjie 540-831-7109 522 D bookstor@radford.edu
SAUNDERS, Brian 310-544-6487 64 H brian.saunders@usw.salvationarmy.org
SAUNDERS, C. Tom 912-279-5757 127 B tsaunders@ccga.edu
SAUNDERS, Cheryl 612-659-6762 267 E cheryl.saunders@minneapolis.edu
SAUNDERS, Gary 910-576-6222 372 A saundersg@montgomery.edu
SAUNDERS, Gayle, M 217-875-7200 162 D gsaunder@richland.edu
SAUNDERS, Joseph 304-766-3353 544 D saundejs@wvstateu.edu
SAUNDERS, Julie 713-646-1815 494 E jsaunders@stcl.edu
SAUNDERS, Kari 314-744-5301 286 C saundersk@mobap.edu
SAUNDERS, Kathy 716-614-6201 344 C saundersk@niagaracc.suny.edu
SAUNDERS, Keith 319-335-0553 182 C keith-saunders@uiowa.edu
SAUNDERS, Kenneth, K 516-572-7664 342 C kenneth.saunders@ncc.edu
SAUNDERS, Kevin 831-582-3397 35 C kesaunders@csumb.edu
SAUNDERS, Laura 912-871-1600 134 H lsaunders@ogeecheetech.edu
SAUNDERS, Laura 425-564-2301 531 B laura.saunders@bellevuecollege.edu
SAUNDERS, Laverna, M 412-396-6136 428 C lsaunders@duq.edu
SAUNDERS, Lenore 323-953-4000 54 H saundele@lacitycollege.edu
SAUNDERS, Mark 405-878-5402 412 A msaunders@stgregorys.edu
SAUNDERS, Martha 601-266-5001 278 A martha.saunders@usm.edu
SAUNDERS, Mary, M 434-395-2063 520 G saundersmm@longwood.edu
SAUNDERS, Mary Jane 561-297-3450 118 H president@fau.edu
SAUNDERS, Melinda, D 304-896-7364 542 J mindys@southern.wvnet.edu
SAUNDERS, Paris 816-235-1141 291 E saundersp@umkc.edu
SAUNDERS, Robert 334-983-6556 8 B rsaunders@troy.edu
SAUNDERS, Scott 310-314-6063 29 J
SAUNDERS, Scott, D 716-673-3171 352 A scott.saunders@fredonia.edu
SAUNDERS, Shantell 410-752-4710 221 E ssaunders@bic.edu
SAUNDERS, Sharon 850-599-3860 118 G sharon.saunders@famu.edu
SAUNDERS, Sharon 850-599-3410 110 G sharon.saunders@famu.edu
SAUNDERS, Sharon 434-947-8114 522 E ssaunders@randolphcollege.edu
SAUNDERS, Sharon, E 281-649-3206 487 F ssaunders@hbu.edu
SAUNDERS, Tanya, R 607-274-3063 336 G tsaunders@ithaca.edu
SAUNDERS, William, T 713-313-7846 499 G saunders_wt@tsu.edu
SAUNDERS-FIELDS, Christine, V 718-270-7657 352 D christine.saunders-fields@downstate.edu
SAUNDERS-KEURJIAN, J.C 310-434-4144 68 D keurjian_jc@smc.edu
SAUNDERS-WHITE, Debra 910-962-3888 379 C whiteds@uncw.edu
SAURENNANN, Denise 215-951-2985 432 G saurennann@lasalle.edu
SAUTER, David, M 513-529-8781 396 D sauterdm@muohio.edu
SAUTER, Marcia, K 260-399-7700 180 E msauter@sf.edu
SAUTNER, Elisabeth 407-659-0900 104 E bsautner@devry.edu
SAUTTER, Fred, C 256-824-6147 9 A chris.sautter@uah.edu
SAUVE, Stephanie, L 585-340-9588 329 G ssauve@crcds.edu
SAVAGE, Ann 567-661-7184 400 H elizabeth_savage@owens.edu
SAVAGE, Carin 718-289-5184 326 F carin.savage@bcc.cuny.edu
SAVAGE, Deana, M 432-685-4514 490 G docsavage@midland.edu
SAVAGE, Donna 254-968-9246 496 F dsavage@tarleton.edu
SAVAGE, Jeffery 575-624-8050 319 C savage@nmmi.edu
SAVAGE, Jennie, R 207-768-9551 220 F jennie.savage@umpi.edu
SAVAGE, Mike 510-567-6174 68 G msavage@sum.edu
SAVAGE, Monique, J 517-265-5161 247 D msavage@adrian.edu
SAVAGE, Robert, S 318-473-6492 212 G rsavage@lsua.edu
SAVAGE, Sheryl 508-588-9100 240 E
SAVAGE, Susan 309-457-2337 158 G savage@monm.edu
SAVAGE, Suzanne 757-233-8736 529 F ssavage@vwc.edu
SAVALA, Peggy 714-459-1124 78 C psavala@wsulaw.edu
SAVAS, Steven 781-768-7201 244 D steven.savas@regiscollege.edu
SAVELL, Medrick, H 601-426-6346 277 D msavell@southeasternbaptist.edu
SAVERANCE, R. Kyle 843-383-8017 457 A ksaverance@coker.edu
SAVIANESO, Michael 201-684-7402 313 D msaviane@ramapo.edu
SAVICH, Kim 858-576-1287 19 C kim.savich@phoenix.edu
SAVIDGE, Lawrence 843-574-6051 461 G
SAVILLE, Roy, E 540-831-7812 522 D rsaville@radford.edu
SAVIN, Dorothy 910-695-3724 373 E savind@sandhills.edu
SAVIN, Laura 651-846-1469 269 E laura.savin@saintpaul.edu
SAVINO, Jeffrey, L 814-641-3301 431 L savinoj@juniata.edu
SAVINO, Melissa 212-517-0540 340 D msavino@mmm.edu
SAVINO, Vickie 707-546-4000 45 G vasavino@empirecollege.com
SAVIOR, Valerie 323-259-2623 59 H vsavior@oxy.edu
SAVITSKI, Erin, A 570-208-5923 432 E easavits@kings.edu
SAVOCA, Marianna 631-632-6810 352 C marianna.savoca@stonybrook.edu
SAVOIAN, Roy 509-963-1955 531 G savoianr@cwu.edu
SAVOIE, E. Joseph 337-482-6203 216 D president@louisiana.edu
SAVOIE, Elmy 985-858-2984 210 H esavoie@ftcc.edu
SAVOIE, James 215-717-6394 448 H jsavoie@uarts.edu
SAVOIE, Leslie, L 321-674-7362 108 E lsavoie@fit.edu
SAVOIT, Taina, J 337-475-5065 215 G tsavoit@mcneese.edu
SAVORD, Lauren 951-343-4726 31 G lsavord@calbaptist.edu
SAVORY, Paul, A 402-472-3567 300 H psavory2@unl.edu
SAVRDA, Charles 334-844-5737 1 G savrdce@auburn.edu
SAWYER, Cary, A 757-455-3310 529 F casawyer@vwc.edu
SAWYER, Charles, E 952-888-4777 270 F csawyer@nwhealth.edu
SAWYER, Darrell, R 605-394-2667 466 A darrell.sawyer@sdsmt.edu
SAWYER, David 502-895-3411 204 B dsawyer@lpts.edu
SAWYER, Diane 410-263-2371 225 G diane.sawyer@sjca.edu
SAWYER, Donald, T 510-885-2513 34 C don.sawyer@csueastbay.edu
SAWYER, Gerald, O 315-386-7222 355 D sawyerj@canton.edu
SAWYER, James 586-445-7196 254 F sawyerj@macomb.edu
SAWYER, Janis 501-760-4215 22 F jsawyer@npcc.edu
SAWYER, JD 303-256-9388 85 H jsawyer@jwu.edu
SAWYER, Jeffrey 410-837-5244 229 A jsawyer@ubalt.edu
SAWYER, Jenny, L 502-852-4957 207 A jsawyer@louisville.edu
SAWYER, Joan, U 252-334-2012 367 A joan.sawyer@macuniversity.edu
SAWYER, John 208-882-1566 143 G johnsawyer@nsa.edu
SAWYER, John, E 302-831-1787 96 F sawyerj@udel.edu
SAWYER, Jonathan, C 202-319-5619 97 C sawyerj@cua.edu
SAWYER, Joseph 617-364-3510 232 C jsawyer@boston.edu
SAWYER, Julie 918-444-3083 409 A sawjerjk@nsuok.edu
SAWYER, Katherine 847-925-6319 151 E ksawyer@harpercollege.edu
SAWYER, Lee 860-727-6941 92 C lsawyer@goodwin.edu
SAWYER, Lyn 802-468-1208 515 C lyn.sawyer@castleton.edu
SAWYER, Michael 307-268-2492 555 F msawyer@caspercollege.edu
SAWYER, Penelope 215-641-6573 436 G psawyer@mc3.edu
SAWYER, Penny 404-270-2768 128 G psawyer@devry.edu
SAWYER, Rick 781-736-3600 233 A sawyer@brandeis.edu
SAWYER, Sara 603-271-2722 304 B
SAWYER, Stephen 207-786-6223 217 C ssawyer@bates.edu
SAWYER, Terrence, M 410-617-5161 224 A tsawyer@loyola.edu
SAWYER, Thomas 207-326-2426 219 D tom.sawyer@mma.edu
SAWYER, Thomas 812-941-2287 174 D sawyer@ius.edu
SAWYER, Trisha 252-862-1246 372 H sawyert@roanokechowan.edu
SAWYER, Wm. Gregory 805-437-8546 33 I greg.sawyer@csuci.edu
SAWZAK, Vicki 805-546-3171 43 F vsawzak@cuesta.edu
SAX, Christine 717-477-1348 443 D csax@ship.edu
SAX, Lisa 518-587-2100 355 F lisa.sax@esc.edu
SAXBY, William, R 303-963-3124 81 K wsaxby@ccu.edu
SAXENA, Ashok 479-575-3054 24 C asaxena@uark.edu
SAXENA, Pradeep 585-594-6430 347 F saxenap@roberts.edu
SAXENIAN, AnnaLee 510-642-9980 73 E anno@ischool.berkeley.edu
SAXON, Gerald, D 817-272-5403 505 A saxon@uta.edu
SAXON, Jackie 512-404-4869 481 D jsaxon@austinseminary.edu
SAXON, Joey 940-565-3200 504 B saxon@unt.edu
SAXTON, Brad 203-582-3642 93 E brad.saxton@quinnipiac.edu
SAXTON, Jane 425-602-3024 530 K jsaxton@bastyr.edu
SAXTON, Tresa, M 336-334-3134 379 A tmsaxton@uncg.edu
SAY, Elizabeth, A 818-677-3301 35 D elizabeth.say@csun.edu
SAYEGH, Andre 201-447-9218 307 F asayegh@bergen.edu
SAYEGH, Jean, J 716-376-7509 337 E johnsayegh@mail.sunyjcc.edu
SAYERS, Kevin, W 614-236-6943 386 C ksayers@capital.edu
SAYERS, Kimberly, J 330-287-0100 399 A sayers.1@osu.edu
SAYERS, Sean 787-725-6500 560 G ssayers@sju.albizu.edu
SAYES, Patty 979-230-3241 482 B patty.sayes@brazosport.edu
SAYLER, David 605-677-5309 465 E david.sayler@usd.edu
SAYLES, Bridget, M 540-674-3606 527 B bsayles@nr.edu
SAYLES, Thomas 213-740-5371 76 C sayles@usc.edu
SAYRE, Patrice, M 515-281-6421 182 A psayre@iastate.edu
SAYRE, Richard 309-457-2190 158 G rsayre@monm.edu
SAYRES, Byron, A 304-457-6225 540 B sayresba@ab.edu
SBALBI, Anthony 413-552-2550 240 C asbalbi@hcc.edu
SBERNA, Robert, A 843-953-5111 456 C bob.sberna@citadel.edu
SBRAGIA, Alberta, M 412-624-2137 449 A sbragia@pitt.edu
SBREGA, John, J 508-678-2811 239 F john.sbrega@bristolcc.edu
SCACCIA, Jeff 479-979-1310 26 A jscaccia@ozarks.edu
SCADUTO, Dana, E 717-245-1013 427 E scadutod@dickinson.edu
SCADUTO, George, C 904-256-7024 111 J gscadut@ju.edu
SCAGGS, Susan 228-896-2519 275 G susan.scaggs@mgccc.edu
SCAGLIONE, Kathy, L 515-271-1460 183 F kathleen.scaglione@dmu.edu
SCALA, Kristen 413-236-3065 239 E kscale@berkshirecc.edu
SCALES, Keyana 336-334-7946 377 F kscales@ncat.edu
SCALES, Linda, M 619-260-4654 76 A scales@sandiego.edu
SCALES, Michael 215-204-7184 447 G michael.scales@temple.edu
SCALES, Michael, G 845-675-4777 344 G president@nyack.edu
SCALES, Shari 503-554-2112 415 I sscales@georgefox.edu
SCALES, Suzanne 928-213-6060 13 I
SCALES, Virginia 408-288-3719 67 C virginia.scales@sjcc.edu
SCALESSI, Lisa 708-456-0300 166 C lscaless@triton.edu
SCALF, CPPS, Kevin 219-866-6352 179 B kscalf@saintjoe.edu
SCALI, Justin 706-776-0104 135 D jscali@piedmont.edu
SCALICE, Michael 212-349-4330 334 G mscalice@globe.edu
SCALISE-SMITH, Dale 315-792-3376 359 C dscalis@utica.edu
SCALLEY, Elizabeth 787-766-1912 562 F escalley@inter.edu
SCALZO, Denise 631-244-3159 332 D scalzod@dowling.edu

SCALZO, Jackie ... 413-585-2108 ... 245 B
jscalzo@smith.edu
SCALZO-MCNEIL, Anne ... 508-588-9100 ... 240 E
SCAMMELL, Richard, E ... 518-276-6281 ... 347 D
scammr@rpi.edu
SCANDALIS, Thomas ... 516-686-3722 ... 343 D
tscandal@nyit.edu
SCANDURA, Teresa, A ... 305-284-4154 ... 122 F
scandura@miami.edu
SCANES, Colin, G ... 414-229-2591 ... 551 C
scanes@uwm.edu
SCANLAN, Brian ... 239-280-2483 ... 101 C
brian.scanlan@avemaria.edu
SCANLAN, Patrick ... 440-826-2455 ... 384 H
pscanlan@bw.edu
SCANLAN, Therese, A ... 708-763-6443 ... 162 C
therese.scanlan@resu.edu
SCANLON, Stephen ... 913-588-1100 ... 197 A
sscanlon@kumc.edu
SCANLON, Tom ... 617-732-2775 ... 241 F
tom.scanlon@mcphs.edu
SCANTLING, Edgar (Ed), L 308-865-8502 ... 300 G
scantlinge@unk.edu
SCARAMUZZO, Gail ... 570-961-7848 ... 433 A
scramuzzog@lackawanna.edu
SCARANO, John ... 216-397-4717 ... 392 M
jscarano@jcu.edu
SCARANO, Martin ... 603-862-2013 ... 306 E
marty.scarano@unh.edu
SCARANO, Michael ... 641-585-8163 ... 189 E
michael.scarano@waldorf.edu
SCARBAROUGH, Celeste ... 512-476-2772 ... 481 C
admissions@austingrad.edu
SCARBERRY, Randy ... 606-218-5208 ... 207 B
randy@pc.edu
SCARBORO, Donna ... 202-994-6360 ... 97 F
scarboro@gwu.edu
SCARBORO, Kim ... 850-973-1613 ... 113 J
scarborok@nfcc.edu
SCARBORO, Lynne, B ... 310-338-5236 ... 56 E
lscarbor@lmu.edu
SCARBOROUGH,
Donald, A ... 336-841-9135 ... 365 A
dscarbor@highpoint.edu
SCARBOROUGH, Scott, L . 419-383-3407 ... 404 F
scott.scarborough@utoledo.edu
SCARBROUGH, Frances ... 804-862-6214 ... 523 C
fscarbrough@rbc.edu
SCARCELLE, Ed ... 212-229-5300 ... 342 E
scarcele@newschool.edu
SCARDELLA, Anthony, T ... 732-235-6305 ... 316 G
scardean@umdnj.edu
SCARDINO, Janell ... 402-375-7553 ... 299 I
jascard1@wsc.edu
SCARDINO, Wendy ... 563-588-6513 ... 183 B
wendy.scardino@clarke.edu
SCARINGE, John ... 562-902-3330 ... 71 A
johnscaringe@scuhs.edu
SCARLATOS, Pete ... 561-297-0466 ... 118 H
scarlatos@fau.edu
SCARNECCHIA, Suellyn ... 734-764-0305 ... 259 D
suellyns@umich.edu
SCARPA, Harry, C ... 973-408-3312 ... 309 F
hscarpa@drew.edu
SCARPINO, John ... 407-708-2148 ... 117 G
scarpinj@seminolestate.edu
SCARTELLI, Joseph, P ... 540-831-5265 ... 522 D
jscartel@radford.edu
SCATES, LouAnn, P ... 704-406-4263 ... 364 B
lscates@gardner-webb.edu
SCATLIFFE-WALLACE,
Kathleen ... 847-543-2998 ... 147 H
per286@clcillinois.edu
SCAVONE, Victoria, R ... 248-689-8282 ... 260 A
vscavone@walshcollege.edu
SCAVUZZO, Connie, M ... 312-949-7079 ... 152 D
cscavuzzo@ico.edu
SCAZZOLA, April, K ... 808-974-7664 ... 141 A
komenaka@hawaii.edu
SCERE, Rubie, J ... 318-670-9473 ... 215 A
rscere@susla.edu
SCERRA, Mary ... 603-668-6706 ... 304 E
mscerra@ccsnh.edu
SCHAAD, Dean ... 419-755-4855 ... 397 B
dschaad@ncstatecollege.edu
SCHAAF, Linda, L ... 608-342-1221 ... 551 F
schaafl@uwplatt.edu
SCHAAFSMA, Carol ... 541-917-4201 ... 416 H
schaafc@linnbenton.edu
SCHAAKE, Vicki ... 518-587-2100 ... 355 F
vicki.schaake@esc.edu
SCHAAL, Mary ... 928-344-7772 ... 12 C
mary.schaal@azwestern.edu
SCHAAL, Mary ... 215-503-8390 ... 448 B
mary.schaal@jefferson.edu
SCHAAL, Michael, L ... 810-762-9733 ... 253 I
mschaal@kettering.edu
SCHAB, Diana ... 541-888-2525 ... 420 C
dschab@socc.edu
SCHABERT, Daniel ... 215-646-7300 ... 430 C
schabert.d@gmc.edu
SCHACHT, Linda ... 615-966-6155 ... 470 D
linda.schacht@lipscomb.edu
SCHACHT, Otto, B ... 806-291-1022 ... 508 B
schachto@wbu.edu
SCHACHTER, Crystal ... 845-341-4070 ... 345 E
crystal.schachter@sunyorange.edu
SCHACHTER, Ruth ... 215-567-7080 ... 422 C
rschachter@edmc.edu
SCHACHTER, Shmuel ... 410-484-7200 ... 225 C
SCHACK, Amy ... 914-594-4832 ... 343 F
amy_schack@nymc.edu
SCHACKMUTH, Kurt ... 815-836-5810 ... 156 D
schackku@lewisu.edu
SCHACTLER, Linda ... 509-963-1384 ... 531 G
schactler@cwu.edu
SCHADE, Carrie ... 773-298-3123 ... 163 G
schade@sxu.edu
SCHADE, Herb ... 417-455-5740 ... 281 C
hschade@crowder.edu
SCHADEL, Arlene ... 575-538-6675 ... 321 I
schadela@wnmu.edu
SCHADEMAN, Emily ... 215-248-3648 ... 425 C
schademane@chc.edu
SCHADING, Douglas ... 212-938-5880 ... 355 B
dschading@sunyopt.edu
SCHAECHTER, Alexander ... 718-854-8791 ... 339 F
mh@thejnet.com
SCHAEFER, Carol ... 217-854-3231 ... 145 F
cscha@blackburn.edu
SCHAEFER, Joseph ... 914-674-7473 ... 340 G
jschaefer@mercy.edu
SCHAEFER, Karen, D ... 575-646-2731 ... 319 D
kschaefe@nmsu.edu
SCHAEFER, Karla ... 641-585-8159 ... 189 E
schaeferk@waldorf.edu
SCHAEFER, Kristina, G ... 617-521-2339 ... 245 A
kristina.schaefer@simmons.edu
SCHAEFER, Lynne ... 410-455-2939 ... 227 D
lschaefer@umbc.edu
SCHAEFER, Maryann ... 312-629-6118 ... 164 A
mschaefer@saic.edu
SCHAEFER, Ronald, P ... 618-650-3785 ... 165 A
rschaef@siue.edu
SCHAEFER, Sharon, P ... 813-253-6250 ... 122 H
sschaefer@ut.edu
SCHAEFER, Thomas, G ... 412-536-1198 ... 432 F
thomas.schaefer@laroche.edu
SCHAEFER, Verdell ... 909-558-4509 ... 54 D
vschaefer@llu.edu
SCHAEFER HORVATH,
Virginia ... 716-673-3335 ... 352 A
virginia.horvath@fredonia.edu
SCHAEFFER, Kathi ... 617-984-1676 ... 244 C
kschaeffer@quincycollege.edu
SCHAEFFER, Lisa ... 910-521-6851 ... 379 B
lisa.schaeffer@uncp.edu
SCHAEFFER, Scot ... 563-387-1287 ... 187 A
schasc01@luther.edu
SCHAEFFER, William ... 310-665-6940 ... 60 B
wschaeffer@otis.edu
SCHAEFFER, William, G ... 718-990-6802 ... 348 G
schaeffw@stjohns.edu
SCHAEFFLER, Jan ... 203-332-5220 ... 90 B
jschaeffler@hcc.commnet.edu
SCHAEL, John, M ... 314-935-5288 ... 292 J
schael@wustl.edu
SCHAFER, Christine, L ... 319-352-8500 ... 189 F
christine.schafer@wartburg.edu
SCHAFER, Curtis, P ... 512-245-2645 ... 501 C
cs21@txstate.edu
SCHAFER, Jay ... 413-545-0284 ... 237 C
jschafer@library.umass.edu
SCHAFER, Larry ... 212-746-4070 ... 360 B
lwschafe@med.cornell.edu
SCHAFER, Michael ... 419-772-2190 ... 398 G
m-schafer@onu.edu
SCHAFER, Penny ... 559-456-2777 ... 27 B
pschafer@alliant.edu
SCHAFER, William ... 404-385-8772 ... 130 D
william.schafer@vpss.gatech.edu
SCHAFFER, Andy ... 812-206-8382 ... 174 D
schaffer@purdue.edu
SCHAFFER, Cheryl ... 309-268-8046 ... 151 G
cheryl.schaffer@heartland.edu
SCHAFFER, Connie ... 567-661-7737 ... 400 H
connie_schaffer@owens.edu
SCHAFFER, Edward, J ... 708-709-7836 ... 161 C
eschaffer@prairiestate.edu
SCHAFFER, Frederick, P ... 212-794-5506 ... 326 C
frederick.schaffer@mail.cuny.edu
SCHAFFER, James, P ... 610-330-5000 ... 433 B
schaffej@lafayette.edu
SCHAFFER, Joseph ... 406-771-4305 ... 296 B
jschaffer@msugf.edu
SCHAFFER, Lonnie ... 757-822-1180 ... 528 C
ljschaffer@tcc.edu
SCHAFFER, Lonnie, J ... 757-822-1065 ... 528 C
ljshaffer@tcc.edu
SCHAFFER, Mindy, M ... 410-822-5400 ... 222 B
mschaffer@chesapeake.edu
SCHAFFER, Sandy ... 931-393-1536 ... 475 C
sschaffer@mscc.edu
SCHAFFHAUSER, Anthony . 218-736-1528 ... 267 G
anthony.schaffhauserl@minnesota.edu
SCHAFRICK, James, A ... 203-773-8507 ... 89 H
jschafrick@albertus.edu
SCHAICH, Monte ... 816-331-5700 ... 288 A
mschaich@pcitraining.edu
SCHAKE, Kurt ... 510-267-1340 ... 44 H
kschake@devry.edu
SCHALHAMER, Randall ... 303-975-5024 ... 89 E
rschalhamer@westwood.edu
SCHALK, Lawrence, E ... 269-471-3484 ... 247 H
schalk@andrews.edu
SCHALL, Jeffrey ... 603-752-1113 ... 304 I
jschall@ccsnh.edu
SCHALL, Lawrence, M ... 404-364-8320 ... 135 A
lschall@oglethorpe.edu
SCHALLENKAMP, Kay ... 605-642-6111 ... 465 F
kay.schallenkamp@bhsu.edu
SCHALO, Pamela, A ... 530-226-4702 ... 69 H
pschalo@simpsonu.edu
SCHAMANN, Matthew ... 716-926-8925 ... 335 F
mschamann@hilbert.edu
SCHAMP, Rosemary ... 856-374-4941 ... 308 E
rschamp@camdencc.edu
SCHANCK, Donald, S ... 401-863-9570 ... 452 J
donald_schanck@brown.edu
SCHANDORFF, M. Gene ... 208-467-8665 ... 143 I
meschandorff@nnu.edu
SCHANIEL, William ... 678-839-4780 ... 138 D
wschanie@westga.edu
SCHANTZ, Janet, D ... 317-738-8009 ... 171 C
jschantz@franklincollege.edu
SCHANTZ, Mark ... 205-226-4650 ... 2 C
mschantz@bsc.edu
SCHANZ, Jeff ... 518-276-6205 ... 347 D
schanj@rpi.edu
SCHAPER, Nikki ... 760-757-2121 ... 57 E
nschaper@miracosta.edu
SCHAPER, Sue ... 208-459-5837 ... 143 A
sschaper@collegeofidaho.edu
SCHAPERKOTTER, Nancy .. 715-422-5526 ... 554 C
nancy.schaperkotter@mstc.edu
SCHAPIRA, Ruth ... 215-635-7300 ... 430 A
rschapira@gratz.edu
SCHAPIRO, Chaim ... 973-455-9031 ... 313 C
chaimschap@aol.com
SCHAPIRO, Mendel ... 323-937-3763 ... 79 J
SCHAPIRO, Morton, O ... 847-491-7456 ... 160 D
nu-president@northwestern.edu
SCHAPP, Rebecca, M ... 408-554-4528 ... 68 C
rschapp@scu.edu
SCHAPPERT, Catherine, H . 570-348-6260 ... 435 F
cschappert@marywood.edu
SCHAPPERT, David ... 610-861-1540 ... 436 I
dschappert@moravian.edu
SCHARBACH, Bruce ... 480-857-5560 ... 15 G
bruce.scharbach@cgcmail.maricopa.edu
SCHARER, Lloyd, S ... 517-321-0242 ... 252 B
lscharer@glcc.edu
SCHARFENBERGER,
James ... 315-312-3214 ... 354 A
scharfen@oswego.edu
SCHARLE, Joyce ... 215-646-7300 ... 430 C
scharle.j@gmc.edu
SCHARMAN, Janet, S ... 801-422-2387 ... 509 D
jan_scharman@byu.edu
SCHARPER, Alice ... 805-965-0581 ... 68 B
scharper@sbcc.edu
SCHARRON, Edna ... 787-250-0000 ... 566 D
edna.scharron@upr.edu
SCHARTMAN, Laura, A ... 248-370-2387 ... 257 C
schartma@oakland.edu
SCHATTEN, Steve, A ... 610-758-3375 ... 434 E
sas308@lehigh.edu
SCHATTMAN, Lisa ... 858-566-1200 ... 43 J
lschattman@disd.edu
SCHATZ, Julianne ... 336-272-7102 ... 364 D
julies@greensborocollege.edu
SCHATZBERG, Kathleen ... 508-362-2131 ... 240 A
kschatzb@capecod.edu
SCHATZEL, Kim ... 313-593-5248 ... 259 E
schatzel@umd.umich.edu
SCHAUB, Dawn ... 904-264-9122 ... 106 C
dschaub@cci.edu
SCHAUB, J. Michael ... 202-687-3493 ... 98 A
jms46@georgetown.edu
SCHAUB, Linda ... 517-750-1200 ... 258 F
lindas@arbor.edu
SCHAUB, Mark ... 616-331-3898 ... 252 A
schaubm@gvsu.edu
SCHAUBACH, Bryan ... 540-857-7273 ... 528 E
bschaubach@virginiawestern.edu
SCHAUER, Ariane ... 310-377-5501 ... 56 F
aschauer@marymountpv.edu
SCHAUER, Rhonda ... 701-224-2497 ... 381 C
rhonda.schauer@ndus.edu
SCHAULAND, Vicky, M ... 920-433-6635 ... 546 A
vicky.schauland@bellincollege.edu
SCHAUMANN, Niels, B ... 651-290-6313 ... 273 B
niels.schaumann@wmitchell.edu
SCHAUS, Deborah ... 256-233-8136 ... 1 F
deborah.schaus@athens.edu
SCHAUS, Jim ... 740-593-0982 ... 399 G
schaus@ohio.edu
SCHEARS, Ben ... 620-441-5245 ... 192 A
schears@cowley.edu
SCHEBLER, Meg ... 563-242-4023 ... 181 G
meg.schebler@ashford.edu
SCHEBLO, David ... 765-459-0561 ... 176 A
dscheblo@ivytech.edu
SCHECHTER, Aaron, M ... 718-377-0777 ... 346 G
SCHECHTER, Mendel ... 718-377-0777 ... 346 G
SCHECK, Stephen ... 503-838-8226 ... 419 C
schecks@wou.edu
SCHEDIN, Karen ... 508-373-9410 ... 231 D
karen.schedin@becker.edu
SCHEER, Brenda, C ... 801-581-8254 ... 510 L
scheer@arch.utah.edu
SCHEER, Steve, M ... 260-480-4221 ... 176 D
sscheer@ivytech.edu
SCHEERER, Jerry ... 214-860-8735 ... 485 A
jscheerer@dcccd.edu
SCHEERER, Teresa ... 215-785-0111 ... 440 H
SCHEESSELE, Jennifer ... 314-977-3838 ... 289 F
jscheess@slu.edu
SCHEETT, Rod ... 701-355-8181 ... 383 E
scheett@umary.edu
SCHEETZ, Anita, A ... 406-768-6341 ... 294 F
ascheetz@fpcc.edu
SCHEFF, Deborah, M ... 314-977-2802 ... 289 F
scheff@slu.edu
SCHEFFEL, Debora ... 303-784-8045 ... 85 I
dscheffel@international.edu
SCHEFFEL, Kent ... 618-468-5000 ... 156 C
kscheffe@lc.edu
SCHEFFKE, Joan ... 435-797-7191 ... 511 B
joan.scheffke@usu.edu
SCHEFFLER, Keith ... 281-425-6489 ... 489 J
kscheffl@lee.edu
SCHEHR, Terra ... 410-617-2271 ... 224 A
tschehr@loyola.edu
SCHEIB, Keith ... 606-212-0501 ... 17 D
kscheib@theparalegalinstitute.edu
SCHEIB, Roger ... 620-417-1240 ... 196 B
roger.scheib@sccc.edu
SCHEIBMEIR, Alan ... 903-463-8600 ... 487 A
scheibmeir@grayson.edu
SCHEIBMEIR, Monica, S ... 785-670-1526 ... 197 D
monica.scheibmeir@washburn.edu
SCHEID, Cheryl, R ... 901-448-4930 ... 477 C
cscheid@uthsc.edu
SCHEIDENHELM, Carol ... 773-508-7489 ... 157 A
cschei1@luc.edu
SCHEIDT, Douglas ... 585-395-2510 ... 352 F
dscheidt@brockport.edu
SCHEINBERG, Mark, E ... 860-727-6757 ... 92 C
mscheinberg@goodwin.edu
SCHEINMAN, Steven, J ... 315-464-9720 ... 352 E
scheinms@upstate.edu
SCHEIRING, Michael, J ... 609-984-1110 ... 316 A
mscheiring@tesc.edu
SCHEIZERER, Carrie ... 614-221-7770 ... 396 B
SCHELCHER, Cindy ... 408-741-2165 ... 78 B
cindy.schelcher@westvalley.edu
SCHELCHER, Cindy ... 408-741-2165 ... 78 B
cindy.schelcher@wvm.edu
SCHELCHER, Cynthia ... 408-741-2165 ... 77 K
cindy_schelcher@wvm.edu
SCHELDT, Suzanne ... 206-934-4700 ... 536 H
suzanne.scheldt@seattlecolleges.edu
SCHELL, Courtney ... 307-755-2122 ... 556 G
cschell@wyotechstaff.edu
SCHELL, John ... 407-823-5711 ... 120 A
rick.schell@ucf.edu
SCHELL, Karen ... 518-292-1719 ... 340 A
schelk@sage.edu
SCHELL, Michael, J ... 541-885-1452 ... 418 E
michael.schell@oit.edu
SCHELLACK, Emil, F ... 913-971-3299 ... 195 A
cpolice@mnu.edu
SCHELLENBERGER,
Lauren ... 573-288-6429 ... 281 D
SCHELLHARDT,
Thomas, G ... 319-273-2382 ... 182 D
tom.schellhardt@uni.edu
SCHELLHAUSE, Vaughn, R 419-586-0329 ... 406 D
vaughn.schellhause@wright.edu
SCHEMENT, Jorge, R ... 732-932-7500 ... 314 D
comminfo.dean@rutgers.edu
SCHEMMEL, Evelyn, A ... 808-955-1500 ... 140 D
evelyn_schemmel@heald.edu
SCHEMPER, Lugene, L ... 616-526-6121 ... 249 F
lschempe@calvin.edu
SCHENCK, Ken ... 765-677-2258 ... 174 E
ken.schenck@indwes.edu
SCHENCK, Robert, B ... 252-335-0821 ... 369 D
rschenck@albemarle.edu
SCHENEWERK, Randal ... 573-875-7256 ... 280 E
raschenewerk@ccis.edu
SCHENK, Christy ... 623-572-3325 ... 16 F
cschen@midwestern.edu
SCHENK, Daniel, L ... 812-429-1389 ... 176 I
dschenk@ivytech.edu
SCHENK, Dina ... 312-467-2114 ... 146 C
dschenk@tcsedsystem.edu
SCHENK, Evelyn ... 989-275-5000 ... 253 K
evelyn.schenk@kirtland.edu
SCHENK, Glenn ... 310-287-4275 ... 55 F
schenkga@wlac.edu
SCHENK, Kim ... 925-685-1230 ... 43 C
kschenk@dvc.edu
SCHENK, Margie ... 812-429-1423 ... 176 I
mschenk@ivytech.edu

SCHMIDT, Chuck .... 509-542-4747 .... 532 C
cschmidt@columbiabasin.edu

SCHMIDT, Clayton, F .... 334-387-3877 .... 1 D
claytonschmidt@amridgeuniversity.edu

SCHMIDT, Constance, R .... 615-898-5191 .... 473 F
cschmidt@mtsu.edu

SCHMIDT, Curt .... 612-659-6902 .... 267 E
curt.schmidt@minneapolis.edu

SCHMIDT, Dan .... 701-224-5735 .... 382 B
daniel.j.schmidt@bismarckstate.edu

SCHMIDT, David, E .... 785-628-4487 .... 192 F
dschmidt@fhsu.edu

SCHMIDT, David, O .... 701-777-4151 .... 381 D
david.schmidt@research.und.edu

SCHMIDT, Denise .... 973-328-5245 .... 309 B
dschmidt@ccm.edu

SCHMIDT, Don .... 615-771-7821 .... 478 G
dschmidt@williamsoncc.edu

SCHMIDT, Emily .... 802-862-9616 .... 512 H
eschmidt@burlington.edu

SCHMIDT, Eric, R .... 608-796-3017 .... 553 A
erschmidt@viterbo.edu

SCHMIDT, Ernest .... 515-964-0601 .... 184 G
schmidte@faith.edu

SCHMIDT, Gene .... 989-386-6604 .... 255 F
gschmidt@midmich.edu

SCHMIDT, Harry, R .... 847-259-1840 .... 146 F
hschmidt@christianlifecollege.edu

SCHMIDT, James .... 507-457-5020 .... 270 B
jschmidt@winona.edu

SCHMIDT, James, W .... 312-996-2695 .... 166 F
jschmidt@uic.edu

SCHMIDT, Jaqueline, L ...... 620-341-5221 .... 192 D
jschmidt@emporia.edu

SCHMIDT, Jaqueline, L ...... 620-341-5223 .... 192 D
jschmidt@emporia.edu

SCHMIDT, Jeffrey .... 410-704-3414 .... 228 E
jschmidt@towson.edu

SCHMIDT, John .... 334-670-3201 .... 8 B
jschmidt@troy.edu

SCHMIDT, Jolene .... 515-271-3957 .... 184 A
jolene.schmidt@drake.edu

SCHMIDT, Jona, M .... 605-256-5857 .... 465 G
jona.schmidt@dsu.edu

SCHMIDT, Julie .... 402-826-8200 .... 298 A
julie.schmidt@doane.edu

SCHMIDT, Karen .... 309-556-3172 .... 153 E
karens@iwu.edu

SCHMIDT, Keith, E .... 712-749-2230 .... 182 G
schmidt@bvu.edu

SCHMIDT, Ken .... 512-313-3000 .... 483 G
ken.schmidt@concordia.edu

SCHMIDT, Kristopher .... 563-242-4023 .... 181 G
kris.schmidt@ashford.edu

SCHMIDT, Mark .... 312-595-1006 .... 166 D
pdas@uchicago.edu

SCHMIDT, Martin, A .... 617-253-7817 .... 242 A
schmidt@mtl.mit.edu

SCHMIDT, Mellis .... 505-747-2213 .... 320 A
mschmidt@nnmc.edu

SCHMIDT, Michael, E .... 402-554-2336 .... 301 B
mschmidt@unomaha.edu

SCHMIDT, Michele .... 920-498-5658 .... 555 A
michele.schmidt@nwtc.edu

SCHMIDT, Michelle .... 575-769-4110 .... 317 K
michelle.schmidt@clovis.edu

SCHMIDT, Patricia .... 631-656-2176 .... 334 B
pschmidt@ftc.edu

SCHMIDT, Patty .... 309-649-6272 .... 165 D
patty.schmidt@src.edu

SCHMIDT, Phil .... 801-274-3280 .... 512 E
pschmidt@wgu.edu

SCHMIDT, Rachel .... 216-687-5594 .... 388 C
r.m.schmidt@csuohio.edu

SCHMIDT, Rachelle, M .... 651-846-1348 .... 269 E
rachelle.schmidt@saintpaul.edu

SCHMIDT, Soren .... 906-487-7239 .... 251 C
soren.schmidt@finlandia.edu

SCHMIDT, Steven, P .... 208-426-1614 .... 142 F
sschmid2@boisestate.edu

SCHMIDT, Susan .... 712-324-5061 .... 188 A
sschmidt@nwicc.edu

SCHMIDT, Tabitha .... 816-802-3445 .... 283 I
tschmidt@kcai.edu

SCHMIDT, Wayne .... 765-677-2245 .... 174 E
wayne.schmidt@indwes.edu

SCHMIDT-NORRIS, Jenae .... 607-778-5001 .... 324 G
schmidt_j@sunybroome.edu

SCHMIEDEL, Mary, E .... 202-687-3911 .... 98 A
schmiedm@georgetown.edu

SCHMIEDL, Joe .... 808-544-1105 .... 140 B
jschmiedl@hpu.edu

SCHMIEG, Rose, A .... 540-665-5534 .... 523 K
rschmieg@su.edu

SCHMIESING, David, A ..... 740-284-6513 .... 390 M
dschmiesing@franciscan.edu

SCHMILL, Stuart .... 617-258-5514 .... 242 A
stucrew@mit.edu

SCHMINKE, Elyse .... 303-477-7240 .... 84 I
elyses@heritage-education.com

SCHMISEK, Brian .... 972-721-4068 .... 502 F
schmisek@udallas.edu

SCHMIT, Joan .... 608-262-4240 .... 550 G
jschmit@bus.wisc.edu

SCHMIT, Matt .... 563-441-4125 .... 184 E

SCHMIT, Shelly, M .... 641-422-4211 .... 187 F
schmishe@niacc.edu

SCHMITH, Sue, C .... 404-876-1227 .... 126 D
sue.schmith@bccr.edu

SCHMITT, Barbara .... 570-662-4854 .... 443 B
bschmitt@mansfield.edu

SCHMITT, Deborah, F .... 716-851-1270 .... 333 C
schmitt@ecc.edu

SCHMITT, Karen, R .... 907-786-6494 ...... 10 I
apkrs@uaa.alaska.edu

SCHMITT, Linda .... 732-356-1595 .... 315 D
lschmitt@somerset.edu

SCHMITT, Patrick .... 253-840-8421 .... 536 C
pschmitt@pierce.ctc.edu

SCHMITT, Sue, A .... 206-296-5760 .... 537 F
sschmitt@seattleu.edu

SCHMITTLEIN, David, C .... 617-253-2804 .... 242 A
dschmitt@mit.edu

SCHMITZ, Cody .... 612-343-4410 .... 270 C
cschmitz@northcentral.edu

SCHMITZ, Diane .... 503-399-6031 .... 414 J
diane.schmitz@chemeketa.edu

SCHMITZ, Donna .... 701-252-3467 .... 381 A
dschmitz@jc.edu

SCHMITZ, Homer .... 314-977-8188 .... 289 F
schmitzh@slu.edu

SCHMITZ, Nisa .... 314-340-3391 .... 282 I
schmitzn@hssu.edu

SCHMITZ, Polly, C .... 509-527-5168 .... 539 E
schmitpc@whitman.edu

SCHMITZ, Stevie .... 406-657-1134 .... 296 E
schmitzs@rocky.edu

SCHMOKE, Kurt, L .... 202-806-8000 ...... 98 B
kschmoke@law.howard.edu

SCHMOLL, Beverly, J .... 419-530-5451 .... 404 F
beverly.schmoll@utoledo.edu

SCHMOLL, Bob .... 788-227-3380 .... 190 G
schmollb@bethanylb.edu

SCHMONSKY, Judy .... 518-694-7222 .... 322 C
judith.schmonsky@acphs.edu

SCHMOOCK, Allen .... 208-792-2215 .... 143 F
atschmoock@lcsc.edu

SCHMOTTER, James, W .... 203-837-8300 ...... 92 A
schmotterj@wcsu.edu

SCHMOTZER, Mark .... 516-299-3547 .... 338 F
mark.schmotzer@liu.edu

SCHMOYER, Andrea .... 312-379-1617 .... 146 C
aschmoyer@thechicagoschool.edu

SCHMUTTE, Gregory, T ...... 413-205-3449 .... 229 G
gregory.schmutte@aic.edu

SCHMUTTE, Jerry .... 712-274-5313 .... 187 D
schmutte@morningside.edu

SCHMUTZ, Betsy .... 314-968-6960 .... 293 A
schmutz@webster.edu

SCHNABEL, Bobby .... 812-856-1079 .... 173 C
schnabel@indiana.edu

SCHNACKENBERG, Scott .. 212-678-3706 .... 357 F
sps19@tc.columbia.edu

SCHNAIDMAN, Yaakov .... 570-346-1747 .... 452 E

SCHNAITTER, Roger .... 309-556-3111 .... 153 E
dstudent@iwu.edu

SCHNALL, David .... 212-340-7705 .... 361 I
dschnall@yu.edu

SCHNAPP, Derek .... 217-206-6716 .... 167 A
schnapp.derek@uis.edu

SCHNARR, Carmin, A .... 812-888-4332 .... 181 B
cschnarr@vinu.edu

SCHNEBERGER, Scott .... 618-374-5155 .... 161 D
scott.schneberger@principia.edu

SCHNECK, Ken .... 802-258-9238 .... 513 F
kschneck@marlboro.edu

SCHNEIDER, Ali .... 814-871-7490 .... 429 F
schneider@gannon.edu

SCHNEIDER, Alvin .... 281-425-6489 .... 489 J
aschneider@lee.edu

SCHNEIDER, Amy, J .... 620-792-9302 .... 190 E
schneidera@bartonccc.edu

SCHNEIDER, Audrey .... 215-204-4607 .... 447 G
audrey.schneider@temple.edu

SCHNEIDER, Carolyn .... 866-621-0124 .... 88 G
carolyn.schneider@rockies.edu

SCHNEIDER, Carrie .... 651-423-8244 .... 266 E
carrie.schneider@dctc.edu

SCHNEIDER, Chad .... 740-389-4636 .... 395 G
schneiderc@mtc.edu

SCHNEIDER, Debbie .... 314-531-7925 .... 289 F
bksustlouis@bncollege.com

SCHNEIDER, Edward, D ..... 530-226-4156 .... 69 H
eschneider@simpsonu.edu

SCHNEIDER, JR.,
Elmer, E .... 979-845-8058 .... 497 C
eschneider@tamu.edu

SCHNEIDER, Greg .... 913-288-7155 .... 193 J
gschneid@kckcc.edu

SCHNEIDER, Helen .... 410-617-2995 .... 224 A
hschneider@loyola.edu

SCHNEIDER, Howard .... 631-632-6265 .... 352 C
howard.schneider@stonybrook.edu

SCHNEIDER, Jed, S .... 315-445-4500 .... 338 B
schneij@lemoyne.edu

SCHNEIDER, Jeffrey, A ...... 814-332-3355 .... 421 E
jschneider@allegheny.edu

SCHNEIDER, Joan .... 660-562-1250 .... 287 E
jschneider@nwmissouri.edu

SCHNEIDER, Joanne .... 315-228-7362 .... 329 H
jschneider@colgate.edu

SCHNEIDER, Judith .... 732-987-2255 .... 310 D
schneiderj@georgian.edu

SCHNEIDER, Julia .... 816-271-4369 .... 287 A
schneide@missouriwestern.edu

SCHNEIDER, Karen .... 510-436-1160 ...... 50 F
schneider@hnu.edu

SCHNEIDER, Kenneth, J .... 507-266-7095 .... 262 D
schneider.kenneth@mayo.edu

SCHNEIDER, Marc .... 770-426-2700 .... 133 B
marcs@life.edu

SCHNEIDER, Marcia .... 214-648-7518 .... 507 D
marcia.schneider@utsouthwestern.edu

SCHNEIDER, Mark .... 641-269-3018 .... 185 A

SCHNEIDER, Matthew .... 608-249-6611 .... 547 D
mschneider@msn.herzing.edu

SCHNEIDER, Michael, P .... 620-242-0405 .... 194 H
schneidm@mcpherson.edu

SCHNEIDER, Pamela .... 732-987-2234 .... 310 D
schneiderp@georgian.edu

SCHNEIDER, Richard, W ... 802-485-2065 .... 514 A
pres@norwich.edu

SCHNEIDER, Scott .... 563-588-6354 .... 183 B
scott.schneider@clarke.edu

SCHNEIDER, Sharyn .... 510-594-3706 ...... 31 J
sschneider@cca.edu

SCHNEIDER, Steve .... 402-872-2393 .... 299 H
sschneider@peru.edu

SCHNEIDER, Suzanne .... 718-357-0500 .... 349 F
sschneider@edaff.com

SCHNEIDER, Tammi .... 909-607-3217 ...... 40 C
tammi.schneider@cgu.edu

SCHNEIDER, Tina .... 419-995-8326 .... 392 L
tschneider@lima.ohio-state.edu

SCHNEIDER, Tina .... 419-995-8326 .... 399 B
schneider.290@osu.edu

SCHNEIDER, Tom .... 727-864-8409 .... 104 K
schneite@eckerd.edu

SCHNEIDER, Valetta, L ..... 308-635-6040 .... 301 E
vschneid@wncc.edu

SCHNEIDER, Wayne, R ..... 785-827-5541 .... 194 D
kwaynes@kwu.edu

SCHNEIDERMAN,
Edward, S .... 718-933-6700 .... 341 G
eschneid@monroecollege.edu

SCHNEIKART-LUEBBE,
Christine .... 316-978-3149 .... 197 F
christine.luebbe@wichita.edu

SCHNEITER, Ellen .... 207-621-3300 .... 220 B
ellen.schneiter@maine.edu

SCHNEITER, R. Wane .... 540-464-7212 .... 529 A
schneiterrw@vmi.edu

SCHNELL, Ann, B .... 585-785-1532 .... 334 A
schnelab@flcc.edu

SCHNELL, Bill .... 610-353-7630 .... 425 E
wschnell@kaplan.edu

SCHNELL, Carolyn, A .... 701-231-7189 .... 381 H
carolyn.schnell@ndsu.edu

SCHNELL, Judy .... 308-635-6106 .... 301 E
jschnell@wncc.edu

SCHNELLER, Barbara .... 610-436-2513 .... 443 F
bschneller@wcupa.edu

SCHNEPF, Chester, H .... 203-285-2151 ...... 90 A
cschnepf@gwcc.commnet.edu

SCHNICK, Robert, M .... 814-866-8165 .... 433 C
rschnick@lecom.edu

SCHNITZ, James, E .... 801-274-3280 .... 512 E
jschnitz@wgu.edu

SCHNITZ, Janet, W .... 801-274-3280 .... 512 E
jazbell@wgu.edu

SCHNITZER, Carol, N .... 518-580-5849 .... 351 B
cschnitz@skidmore.edu

SCHNOOR, Chuck .... 520-494-5303 ...... 13 F
chuck.schnoor@centralaz.edu

SCHNOOR, Neal .... 402-375-7389 .... 299 I
neschno1@wsc.edu

SCHNORBUS, Richard .... 228-392-2994 .... 278 B
richard.schnorbus@vc.edu

SCHNUPP, Chris .... 718-357-0500 .... 349 F
cschnupp@edaff.com

SCHNUR, Fred .... 212-678-8008 .... 337 G
frschnur@jtsa.edu

SCHNURBUSCH, James .... 314-918-2567 .... 281 J
jschnurbusch@eden.edu

SCHNURR, Dean, D .... 419-372-0613 .... 385 D
dschnur@bgsu.edu

SCHNYDMAN, Jerome, D .. 410-516-4351 .... 223 F
jds1@jhu.edu

SCHOBER, Kelly Lyons ...... 717-290-8719 .... 433 F
kschober@lancasterseminary.edu

SCHOBER, Michael .... 212-229-5777 .... 342 E
schober@newschool.edu

SCHOCHET, Ezra, B .... 323-937-3763 ...... 79 J
eschochet@yoec.edu

SCHODOWSKI, Francis .... 717-872-3820 .... 443 C
francis.schodowski@millersville.edu

SCHODZINSKI, E.J .... 740-699-2356 .... 400 A
schodzin@ohio.edu

SCHODZINSKI, E.J .... 740-699-2503 .... 400 A
schodzin@ohio.edu

SCHOEFFLER, Susan .... 775-445-3249 .... 303 B
schoeffs@wnc.edu

SCHOELER, Mary .... 715-394-8266 .... 552 [illegible]
mschoele@uwsuper.edu

SCHOELLES, SSJ,
Patricia, A .... 585-271-3657 .... 348 [illegible]
pschoelles@stbernards.edu

SCHOEN, David .... 716-286-8001 .... 344 [illegible]
schoen@niagara.edu

SCHOEN, Linda .... 614-251-4715 .... 398 [illegible]
schoenl@ohiodominican.edu

SCHOEN, Linda, M .... 503-223-2245 .... 416 [illegible]
lschoen@westernculinary.com

SCHOENBACHLER, Denise 815-753-1755 .... 160 A
denises@niu.edu

SCHOENECKE, Marvin .... 417-690-2204 .... 280 C
schoenecke@cofo.edu

SCHOENECKER, Craig, V ... 651-201-1864 .... 265 H
craig.schoenecker@so.mnscu.edu

SCHOENECKER, Mark .... 719-587-7696 ...... 80 F

SCHOENEFELD, Dale, A .... 918-631-2881 .... 413 F
schoend@utulsa.edu

SCHOENER, Lois .... 607-735-1890 .... 333 A
lschoener@elmira.edu

SCHOENFELD, Diane .... 617-573-8454 .... 245 E
dschoenf@suffolk.edu

SCHOENFELD, Michael .... 802-443-3177 .... 513 G
schoenfe@middlebury.edu

SCHOENFELD, Michael, J . 919-681-3788 .... 363 I
michael.schoenfeld@duke.edu

SCHOENFELDER, Louis ..... 605-995-2191 .... 464 B
loschoen@dwu.edu

SCHOENGOOD,
Matthew, G .... 212-817-7400 .... 327 B
mschoengood@gc.cuny.edu

SCHOENHOFF, Tiffany .... 404-669-4019 .... 135 E
tiffany.schoenhoff@point.edu

SCHOENLE, JR.,
Gerald, W .... 716-645-2230 .... 351 G
gws3@buffalo.edu

SCHOENWALD, Ira, S .... 309-438-8311 .... 153 C
ischoen@ilstu.edu

SCHOENWETTER, Beth ...... 414-256-0169 .... 549 A
schoenwb@mtmary.edu

SCHOEPHOERSTER,
Richard, T .... 915-747-5460 .... 505 E
schoephoerster@utep.edu

SCHOER, Jill, R .... 715-394-8598 .... 552 D
jschoer@uwsuper.edu

SCHOETTLE, William .... 517-371-5140 .... 259 B
schoettw@cooley.edu

SCHOFE, Kathy, D .... 706-737-1444 .... 125 C
kschofe@aug.edu

SCHOFFMAN, Garth, D ...... 330-684-8938 .... 403 C
gds@uakron.edu

SCHOFIELD, Anna, M .... 614-222-3274 .... 388 F
aschofield@ccad.edu

SCHOFIELD, Audrey .... 561-803-2075 .... 114 C
audrey_schofield@pba.edu

SCHOFIELD, Krystal .... 813-253-6239 .... 122 H
kschofield@ut.edu

SCHOFIELD, Ronald .... 312-553-3384 .... 146 G
rschofield@ccc.edu

SCHOFIELD, Sherri .... 906-248-8424 .... 249 C
sschofield@bmcc.edu

SCHOH, Eric .... 402-375-7520 .... 299 I
erschoh1@wsc.edu

SCHOKNECHT, Pat .... 407-646-2700 .... 116 B
pschoknecht@rollins.edu

SCHOLBE, Karen .... 314-529-9392 .... 284 F
kscholbe@maryville.edu

SCHOLES, J. Scott .... 208-732-6250 .... 143 B
sscholes@csi.edu

SCHOLL, Heather .... 847-214-7177 .... 150 D
hscholl@elgin.edu

SCHOLL, Timothy .... 402-474-5315 .... 298 E
tscholl@kaplanuniversity.edu

SCHOLL-FIEDLER, Anne .... 410-455-2216 .... 227 D
afielder@umbc.edu

SCHOLLA, James .... 320-308-5028 .... 269 D
jscholla@sctcc.edu

SCHOLLE, Peter, A .... 575-835-5302 .... 319 A
bureau@gis.nmt.edu

SCHOLLES, Holly .... 503-760-3131 .... 414 F
holly@birthingway.edu

SCHOLLMEIER, John .... 507-457-1436 .... 271 G
jschollm@smumn.edu

SCHOLTE, Hugh .... 509-793-2291 .... 531 D

SCHOLTEN, Brian .... 607-274-3075 .... 336 G
bscholten@ithaca.edu

SCHOLZ, Ben .... 201-761-7109 .... 314 F
bscholz@spc.edu

SCHOLZ, Daniel, J .... 414-410-4010 .... 546 D
djscholz@stritch.edu

SCHOLZ, Greg .... 603-428-2470 .... 305 E
gscholz@nec.edu

SCHOLZ, Joan, M .... 262-243-5700 .... 546 I
joan.scholz@cuw.edu

SCHOLZ, Stephen, G .... 919-516-4384 .... 376 B
sgscholz@st-aug.edu

SCHOLZE, Roberta .... 217-351-2383 .... 161 B
rscholze@parkland.edu

SCHON, Al .... 314-918-2523 .... 281 J
aschon@eden.edu

SCHONBERGER, Barry, K .. 812-464-1862 .... 180 F
bkschonb@usi.edu

SCHULZ, Leslie .... 928-523-4331...... 17 A
leslie.schulz@nau.edu
SCHULZ, Michael .... 406-683-7492.... 295 B
m_schulz@umwestern.edu
SCHULZ, Paul, A .... 914-337-9300.... 331 A
paul.schulz@concordia-ny.edu
SCHULZ, Robert .... 619-594-5901....... 36 E
rschulz@mail.sdsu.edu
SCHULZ, Steve .... 712-792-8308.... 183 E
sdschulz@dmacc.edu
SCHULZ, Timothy, J .... 906-487-2005.... 255 E
schulz@mtu.edu
SCHULZE, Christine, L .... 218-299-4544.... 263 B
schulze@cord.edu
SCHULZE, Edee .... 651-638-6300.... 261 I
e-schulze@bethel.edu
SCHULZE, Lori, A .... 920-748-8310.... 549 I
schulzel@ripon.edu
SCHUMACHER, Betty, A .... 701-845-7412.... 382 A
betty.schumacher@vcsu.edu
SCHUMACHER, Bryan, J .... 605-394-2215.... 466 A
bryan.schumacher@sdsmt.edu
SCHUMACHER, Casey .... 217-544-6464.... 163 F
SCHUMACHER, Charlotte .. 806-291-3549.... 508 B
schumacherc@wbu.edu
SCHUMACHER, Daniel .... 815-836-5247.... 156 D
schumada@lewisu.edu
SCHUMACHER, Gail .... 847-318-8550.... 160 C
gschumacher@nc.edu
SCHUMACHER, Jane .... 803-641-3328.... 462 B
janes@usca.edu
SCHUMACHER, Janette ...... 484-664-3180.... 437 B
schumach@muhlenberg.edu
SCHUMACHER, Lawrence .. 847-318-8550.... 160 C
lschumacher@nc.edu
SCHUMACHER, Lillian .... 419-448-3053.... 402 E
schumacherlb@tiffin.edu
SCHUMACHER, Marie .... 505-566-3212.... 320 D
schumacherm@sanjuancollege.edu
SCHUMACHER,
Mary Jeanne .... 812-357-6501.... 179 E
mschumacher@saintmeinrad.edu
SCHUMACHER, Ron .... 419-448-3584.... 402 E
schumacherrm@tiffin.edu
SCHUMACHER, Scott .... 701-671-2446.... 382 E
scott.schumacher.1@ndscs.edu
SCHUMACHER, Tom .... 928-649-6513...... 19 E
tom.schumacher@yc.edu
SCHUMACHER-BRIGHT,
Erin .... 503-943-7125.... 420 G
bright@up.edu
SCHUMAKER, Ashley, L .... 304-558-0699.... 543 B
schumaker@hepc.wvnet.edu
SCHUMAKER, Terry, W ..... 641-422-4222.... 187 F
schumter@niacc.edu
SCHUMAN, Alan, M .... 410-386-8495.... 221 G
aschuman@carrollcc.edu
SCHUMAN, Shmuel .... 847-982-2500.... 151 H
schuman@htc.edu
SCHUMANN, Brian .... 816-861-1000.... 292 D
brian.schumann@vatterott-college.edu
SCHUMANN, James, E .... 320-363-5211.... 262 H
jschumann@csbsju.edu
SCHUMANN, Kenneth .... 503-352-2180.... 419 E
schumank@pacificu.edu
SCHUMANN, Patricia, J .... 304-637-1340.... 540 F
schumannp@dewv.edu
SCHUMANN, Sherry .... 972-548-6803.... 483 D
sschumann@collin.edu
SCHUMM, Gregory, F .... 419-586-0325.... 406 D
gregory.schumm@wright.edu
SCHURE, Matthew .... 215-871-6800.... 444 B
mschure@pcom.edu
SCHURIG, Gerhardt .... 540-231-7910.... 529 B
gschurig@vt.edu
SCHURMAN, Jane .... 610-869-5113.... 426 G
jschurman@dccc.edu
SCHURMANN, Linda .... 605-886-6777.... 464 F
lschurmann@mtmc.edu
SCHUSTAL, S .... 203-325-4351...... 89 I
SCHUSTER, Alice, M .... 570-326-3761.... 440 K
aschuste@pct.edu
SCHUSTER, Alice-Ann .... 845-451-1262.... 331 F
a_schust@culinary.edu
SCHUSTER, Julian, Z .... 314-968-8242.... 293 A
julianschuster31@webster.edu
SCHUSTER, Kathryn, A .... 712-325-3204.... 186 B
schuster@iwcc.edu
SCHUSTER, Leslie .... 401-456-9723.... 454 A
lschuster@ric.edu
SCHUSTER, Marilyn, R .... 413-585-3000.... 245 B
mschuste@smith.edu
SCHUSTER, Sheldon, M ..... 909-607-0108...... 40 F
sheldon_schuster@kgi.edu
SCHUSTER, Stacy .... 609-771-3214.... 308 G
schuster@tcnj.edu
SCHUSTER-MATLOCK,
Tracy .... 563-333 6049.... 188 D
SchusterTracy@sau.edu
SCHUSTEREIT, Roger .... 254-659-7821.... 487 E
SCHUTT, Stephen, D .... 847-735-5100.... 155 F
presiden@lakeforest.edu
SCHUTTA, Katharine .... 312-629-6821.... 164 A
kschutta@saic.edu
SCHUTTE, Janet, L .... 260-422-5561.... 172 L
jlschutte@indianatech.edu
SCHUTTE, Jessica .... 657-278-3125...... 34 E
jschutte@fullerton.edu
SCHUTTE, Thomas, F .... 718-636-3647.... 346 D
tschutte@pratt.edu
SCHUTTINGA, Bethany ...... 712-722-6076.... 183 H
bethanys@dordt.edu
SCHUTZ, Christine .... 208-459-5524.... 143 A
cschutz@collegeofidaho.edu
SCHUTZ, David .... 505-747-5432.... 320 A
dschutz@nnmc.edu
SCHUTZ, Greg .... 615-366-3933.... 473 C
greg.schutz@tbr.edu
SCHUTZLER, Lyndon .... 831-646-4221...... 57 G
lschutzler@mpc.edu
SCHUYLER, Lori, G .... 804-289-8781.... 525 A
lschuyle@richmond.edu
SCHUYLER, Peter .... 508-678-2811.... 239 F
peter.schuyler@bristolcc.edu
SCHWAB, Daniel, J .... 734-384-4202.... 255 G
dschwab@monroeccc.edu
SCHWAB, Duane .... 701-662-1534.... 382 D
duane.schwab@lrsc.edu
SCHWAB, Etta .... 503-654-8000.... 419 F
eschwab@pioneerpacific.edu
SCHWAB, Gregory .... 432-837-8432.... 501 B
gschwab@sulross.edu
SCHWAB, Gregory .... 432-837-8203.... 501 B
gschwab@sulross.edu
SCHWAB, Kenneth, L .... 615-868-6503.... 471 F
kschwab@mtsa.edu
SCHWAB, Linda .... 615-383-4848.... 478 E
lschwab@watkins.edu
SCHWAB, Mary, S .... 540-828-5487.... 516 K
mschwab@bridgewater.edu
SCHWAB, Missie .... 812-535-5220.... 179 C
mschwab@smwc.edu
SCHWAB, Pat .... 573-334-9181.... 285 A
pat@metrobusinesscollege.edu
SCHWAB, Steve .... 352-335-4000.... 102 K
sschwab@citycollege.edu
SCHWAB, Steve, J .... 901-448-4796.... 477 C
sschwab@uthsc.edu
SCHWAB, Stewart, J .... 607-255-3527.... 331 C
sjs15@cornell.edu
SCHWABACH, Katie .... 315-866-0300.... 335 E
schwabaka@herkimer.edu
SCHWABE, Denise .... 800-727-6713...... 92 C
dschwabe@goodwin.edu
SCHWABENBAUER, Lori .... 215-637-7700.... 430 H
lschwaben@holyfamily.edu
SCHWAGER, Kathleen .... 860-255-3571...... 91 C
kschwager@txcc.commnet.edu
SCHWAIG, Kathy, S .... 770-423-6425.... 132 H
kschwaig@kennesaw.edu
SCHWAIGER, Patsy .... 513-244-4371.... 388 D
patsy_schwaiger@mail.msj.edu
SCHWALBACH, Eileen .... 414-256-1207.... 549 A
schwale@mtmary.edu
SCHWALLER, John, F .... 315-267-2100.... 354 C
schwaljf@potsdam.edu
SCHWAM, Michael .... 561-547-6130.... 107 E
mschwam@careercollege.edu
SCHWAN-HONDROS,
Linda .... 614-508-7203.... 392 B
SCHWANER, Terry .... 419-434-4377.... 404 B
schwaner@findlay.edu
SCHWANHOLT, Anne .... 215-635-7300.... 430 A
aschwanholt@gratz.edu
SCHWANKE, Deborah .... 785-460-5411.... 191 J
debbie.schwanke@colbycc.edu
SCHWANKE, Shellie .... 309-467-6316.... 150 H
sschwanke@eureka.edu
SCHWANTES, Kathy, M ...... 320-222-5206.... 268 I
kathy.schwantes@ridgewater.edu
SCHWARCK, Susanne .... 567-661-7341.... 400 H
susanne_schwarck@owens.edu
SCHWARTZ, Celeste, M ..... 215-641-6492.... 436 G
cschwartz@mc3.edu
SCHWARTZ, Cory .... 909-384-8514...... 65 C
cschwartz@sbccd.cc.ca.us
SCHWARTZ, David .... 845-783-9901.... 359 B
vtamds@gmail.com
SCHWARTZ, David, J .... 248-370-3465.... 257 C
schwart3@oakland.edu
SCHWARTZ, Deborah .... 419-824-3760.... 395 D
dschwartz@lourdes.edu
SCHWARTZ, Doreen .... 847-635-1632.... 160 E
doreen@oakton.edu
SCHWARTZ, Ernest .... 718-384-5460.... 361 E
SCHWARTZ, Frank, J .... 973-655-4213.... 311 G
schwartzf@mail.montclair.edu
SCHWARTZ, Gary .... 718-960-6093.... 327 C
gary.schwartz@lehman.cuny.edu
SCHWARTZ, Gary .... 760-252-2411...... 30 F
gschwartz@barstow.edu
SCHWARTZ, Hayim .... 718-268-4700.... 347 B
SCHWARTZ, Janis .... 973-720-2175.... 317 D
schwartzj@wpunj.edu
SCHWARTZ, Joel, D .... 757-221-2460.... 517 J
jxschw@wm.edu
SCHWARTZ, John, R .... 607-777-2275.... 351 F
jschwart@binghamton.edu
SCHWARTZ, Judy, A .... 972-860-7184.... 484 H
JudySchwartz@dcccd.edu
SCHWARTZ, Kenneth .... 504-865-5389.... 215 C
kschwartz@tulane.edu
SCHWARTZ, Lance, W .... 507-344-7427.... 261 H
schwartz@blc.edu
SCHWARTZ, Leonard .... 718-261-5800.... 324 D
lschwrtz@ortopsusa.org
SCHWARTZ, Liz .... 701-252-3467.... 381 A
lschwart@jc.edu
SCHWARTZ, Mary, L .... 301-295-3013.... 558 A
mary.schwartz@usuhs.mil
SCHWARTZ, Mary Beth .... 803-327-8042.... 463 G
mbschwartz@yorktech.edu
SCHWARTZ, Pam .... 618-393-2982.... 152 E
schwartzp@iecc.edu
SCHWARTZ, Patti .... 412-392-3959.... 444 H
pschwartz@pointpark.edu
SCHWARTZ, Regina, L .... 330-684-8786.... 403 C
reginas@uakron.edu
SCHWARTZ, Robert .... 206-296-5831.... 537 F
schwartr@seattleu.edu
SCHWARTZ, Robert, W .... 573-341-7887.... 292 A
rwschwar@mst.edu
SCHWARTZ, Sandor .... 718-963-1212.... 337 I
kyrs@thejnet.com
SCHWARTZ, Shuly .... 212-678-8826.... 337 G
shschwartz@jtsa.edu
SCHWARTZ, Stephen .... 413-265-2367.... 233 E
schwartzs@elms.edu
SCHWARTZ, Steven .... 212-938-5712.... 355 B
sschwartz@sunyopt.edu
SCHWARTZ, Steven, J .... 970-247-7196...... 84 G
schwartz_s@fortlewis.edu
SCHWARTZ, Teri .... 310-825-7891...... 74 A
tschwartz@tft.ucla.edu
SCHWARTZ, Terry .... 719-255-4047...... 88 C
tschwart@uccs.edu
SCHWARTZ, Victor .... 212-960-5330.... 361 I
vschwar1@yu.edu
SCHWARTZBAUER,
Jon, C .... 864-578-8770.... 460 F
jschwartzbauer@sherman.edu
SCHWARTZMILLER, Paul .. 412-237-3034.... 425 H
pschwartzmiller@ccac.edu
SCHWARTZSTEIN,
Linda, A .... 703-993-8789.... 519 A
lschwar1@gmu.edu
SCHWARZ, John .... 409-740-4528.... 497 D
schwarzj@tamug.edu
SCHWARZ, Jurgen, G .... 410-651-6072.... 227 E
jgschwarz@umes.edu
SCHWARZ, Kristine .... 805-962-8179...... 28 L
kschwarz@antioch.edu
SCHWARZ, May, L .... 614-235-4136.... 402 G
mschwarz@TLSohio.edu
SCHWARZ, Steven .... 718-997-5903.... 328 F
steven.schwarz@qc.cuny.edu
SCHWARZ, Thomas, J .... 914-251-6010.... 354 D
thomas.schwarz@purchase.edu
SCHWARZ, Todd, K .... 208-732-6325.... 143 B
tschwarz@csi.edu
SCHWARZCHILD, Michael . 203-837-8691...... 92 A
schwarzchildm@wcsu.edu
SCHWARZENBACH,
Arlene, K .... 319-352-8227.... 189 F
arlene.schwarzenbach@wartburg.edu
SCHWARZER, Chris .... 770-394-8300.... 124 F
cschwarzer@aii.edu
SCHWEBEL, Lisa .... 718-951-4114.... 326 G
lisas@brooklyn.cuny.edu
SCHWEER, Harlan, M .... 630-942-3821.... 147 G
schweer@cod.edu
SCHWEHN, Mark, R .... 219-464-5310.... 181 A
mark.schwehn@valpo.edu
SCHWEIGER, Theresa .... 941-756-0690.... 433 C
tschweiger@lecom.edu
SCHWEIGERT, Rich .... 303-534-6290...... 82 I
rich.schweigert@colostate.edu
SCHWEITZER, Aileen, E ..... 757-825-2871.... 528 B
schweitzera@tncc.edu
SCHWEITZER, Carrie .... 972-860-4848.... 484 F
cschweitzer@dcccd.edu
SCHWEITZER, Cathie .... 413-748-3333.... 245 C
cschweitzer@spfldcol.edu
SCHWEITZER, Connie, J .... 989-964-4160.... 258 A
schw@svsu.edu
SCHWEITZER, Glenna, L .... 734-763-9954.... 259 D
glenna@umich.edu
SCHWEITZER, Laura .... 518-631-9841.... 358 F
schweitzerl@uniongraduatecollege.edu
SCHWEITZER, Mike .... 210-999-8409.... 502 C
mschweit@trinity.edu
SCHWEITZER, Steven, J .... 800-287-8822.... 169 E
schwest@bethanyseminary.edu
SCHWENK, Terry .... 978-232-2066.... 234 F
terrys@endicott.edu
SCHWENN, John, O .... 706-272-4438.... 127 G
jschwenn@daltonstate.edu
SCHWERDT, Mark .... 603-880-8308.... 306 C
tmc@thomasmorecollege.edu
SCHWERTNER, Melanie ...... 325-574-6503.... 508 F
mschwertner@wtc.edu
SCHWIEBERT, Ryan .... 828-339-4600.... 373 H
ryans@southwesterncc.edu
SCHWIEGER, Susan .... 603-887-7413.... 303 G
susan.schwieger@chestercollege.edu
SCHWIETERMAN, Jerry ..... 219-473-4239.... 170 D
jschwieterman@ccsj.edu
SCHWIETZ, Michele .... 970-351-2161...... 88 F
michele.schwietz@unco.edu
SCHWINGENDORF,
Keith, E .... 219-785-5449.... 178 H
kschwingendorf@pnc.edu
SCHWINKE, Victoria .... 573-897-5000.... 284 D
SCIAME, Joseph, A .... 718-990-1941.... 348 G
sciamej@stjohns.edu
SCIAME-GIESECKE, Sue .... 765-455-9227.... 173 E
sgieseck@iuk.edu
SCIANNA, Dominic .... 718-990-6185.... 348 G
sciannad@stjohns.edu
SCIANNAMEO, Louise, C .. 412-578-2090.... 424 G
sciannameolc@carlow.edu
SCIBILIA, Joanne .... 617-552-3344.... 232 D
joanne.scibilia.1@bc.edu
SCIGLITANO, JR.,
Anthony, C .... 973-275-5847.... 315 B
anthony.sciglitano@shu.edu
SCIMECA, Joel .... 970-225-4860...... 81 I
joel.scimeca@collegeamerica.edu
SCIMONE, Bill .... 603-623-0313.... 305 F
bscimone@nhia.edu
SCIOLA, Michael, A .... 860-685-3377...... 95 C
msciola@wesleyan.edu
SCIPIO, Julius .... 478-825-6330.... 129 C
scipioj@fvsu.edu
SCIPLE, Melinda .... 662-476-5040.... 274 D
msciple@eastms.edu
SCISM, Bruce .... 615-230-3555.... 476 A
bruce.scism@volstate.edu
SCISM, Darby .... 773-508-2876.... 157 A
dscism@luc.edu
SCIUTO, Jim .... 925-631-8043...... 64 F
jsciuto@stmarys-ca.edu
SCLAFANI, Joseph .... 813-253-6130.... 122 H
jsclafani@ut.edu
SCLAFANI, Sandra .... 212-875-4675.... 323 E
ssclafani@bankstreet.edu
SCOBEE, Georgia .... 225-216-8608.... 209 I
scobeeg@mybrcc.edu
SCOBEY, David .... 212-229-5613.... 342 E
scobeyd@newschool.edu
SCOBY, Jerry, L .... 231-591-2164.... 251 B
scobyj@ferris.edu
SCOFIELD, Elizabeth, A ...... 215-951-1040.... 432 G
scofield@lasalle.edu
SCOFIELD, Jeff .... 808-974-7324.... 141 A
jscofiel@hawaii.edu
SCOGGINS, Amy .... 229-227-2687.... 137 D
ascoggins@southwestgatech.edu
SCOGGINS, M, W .... 303-273-3280...... 82 F
presoffice@mines.edu
SCOGIN, James .... 903-223-3110.... 498 C
james.scogin@tamut.edu
SCOLERI, Marc .... 212-226-5500.... 323 C
mscoleri@aii.edu
SCOLLARD, Connie .... 602-337-3044...... 12 K
cscollard@brownmackie.edu
SCOMA, Sam .... 309-796-5650.... 145 E
scomas@bhc.edu
SCOPA, Pat .... 606-589-3042.... 203 A
pat.scopa@kctcs.edu
SCOPAS, Constantine .... 212-686-9244.... 323 A
SCOPELLITI, Theresa .... 570-961-7840.... 433 A
scopellitit@lackawanna.edu
SCORDINO, Anthony .... 914-606-6521.... 360 D
anthony.scordino@sunywcc.edu
SCORSE, Bill .... 417-873-7200.... 281 H
bscorse@drury.edu
SCORZELLO, Joseph .... 617-254-2610.... 244 E
SCOT, Stacey .... 717-728-2214.... 425 A
staceyscott@centralpenn.edu
SCOTKA, Mary, F .... 210-434-6711.... 491 G
mscotka@lake.ollusa.edu
SCOTT, A. Nicole .... 260-422-5561.... 172 L
anscott@indianatech.edu
SCOTT, Adrienne .... 610-353-7630.... 425 E
ascott@kaplan.edu
SCOTT, Alexander .... 201-559-6187.... 310 C
scotta@felician.edu
SCOTT, Alicia .... 404-756-4054.... 124 I
ascott@atlm.edu
SCOTT, Angela .... 305-899-3666.... 101 F
ascott@mail.barry.edu
SCOTT, Anne .... 940-898-2586.... 502 B
ascott2@twu.edu
SCOTT, Annie .... 860-343-5767...... 90 D
ascott@mxcc.commnet.edu
SCOTT, Arthur, L .... 610-861-5458.... 437 G
ascott@northampton.edu
SCOTT, Bette, J .... 405-325-1974.... 413 C
bscott@ou.edu
SCOTT, Bill .... 260-399-7700.... 180 E
bscott@sf.edu
SCOTT, Billy .... 662-254-3319.... 276 C
bscott@mvsu.edu
SCOTT, Bob .... 580-349-1597.... 410 B
bobs@opsu.edu

SEAMAN, Sally .... 860-434-5232 .... 93 A
sseaman@lymeacademy.edu

SEAMAN, Sara .... 501-760-4101 .... 22 F
sseaman@npcc.edu

SEAMAN, Scott, H .... 740-593-2705 .... 399 G
seaman@ohio.edu

SEAMANS, Nancy, H .... 404-413-2700 .... 131 C
nseamans@gsu.edu

SEAMS, Jennifer .... 304-645-6383 .... 544 C
jseams@osteo.wvsom.edu

SEANE, Oupa .... 904-620-2475 .... 120 C
oseane@unf.edu

SEARCH, Sally .... 850-201-8505 .... 121 F
searchs@tcc.fl.edu

SEARCY, Douglas, N .... 540-654-1062 .... 524 H
dsearcy@umw.edu

SEARCY, Scott .... 641-585-8227 .... 189 E
searcys@waldorf.edu

SEARCY, Tim .... 318-487-7601 .... 209 B
searcy@lacollege.edu

SEARCY, Tony, V .... 336-386-3246 .... 374 B
searcyt@surry.edu

SEARING, Linda .... 585-389-2870 .... 342 D
lsearin9@naz.edu

SEARLE, Diana .... 510-567-6174 .... 68 G
dsearle@sum.edu

SEARLE, Kenneth .... 510-567-6174 .... 68 G
ksearles@sum.edu

SEARLE, Mark, S .... 480-965-7405 .... 12 B
mark.searle@asu.edu

SEARS, Andrew, L .... 585-475-4786 .... 347 G

SEARS, Connie .... 562-938-4053 .... 54 E
csears@lbcc.edu

SEARS, David .... 240-567-7492 .... 224 E
david.sears@montgomerycollege.edu

SEARS, Gary, W .... 603-641-4101 .... 306 F
gsw@unh.edu

SEARS, James, R .... 313-577-4301 .... 260 D
aa0830@wayne.edu

SEARS, John .... 303-220-1200 .... 81 F
john.sears@cffp.edu

SEARS, Judith .... 575-234-9225 .... 319 F
jsears@cavern.nmsu.edu

SEARS, Laura .... 402-826-6773 .... 298 A
laura.sears@doane.edu

SEARS, Paul .... 419-434-4439 .... 404 B
sears@findlay.edu

SEARS, Richard .... 678-839-5353 .... 138 D
rsears@westga.edu

SEARS, Robert, E .... 864-644-5064 .... 461 B
rsears@swu.edu

SEARS, Stephen, R .... 956-326-2480 .... 497 B
steve.sears@tamiu.edu

SEARS, Steven, A .... 401-865-2425 .... 453 F
ssears@providence.edu

SEARS, Tad .... 218-723-6017 .... 262 I
tsears@css.edu

SEARSON, Robert .... 216-987-3943 .... 389 A
robert.searson@tri-c.edu

SEASTEDT, R. Erik .... 518-255-5514 .... 354 E
seastere@cobleskill.edu

SEATON, Ann .... 845-758-6822 .... 323 F
aseaton@bard.edu

SEATON, William, J .... 609-984-1120 .... 316 A
bseaton@tesc.edu

SEAVER, Catherine .... 860-512-2623 .... 90 C
cseaver@mcc.commnet.edu

SEAVER, Earl, J .... 815-753-0494 .... 160 A
eseaver@niu.edu

SEAVER, Kent .... 972-273-3430 .... 485 B
kseaver@dcccd.edu

SEAVERS, Norm .... 954-201-7813 .... 102 A
nseavers@broward.edu

SEAWORTH, H, P .... 701-224-2583 .... 381 C
pat.seaworth@ndus.edu

SEAWORTH, Timothy .... 701-355-8150 .... 383 E
seaworth@umary.edu

SEAY, Jeanie .... 540-831-6667 .... 522 D
jseay@radford.edu

SEBASTAIN, Juliann, G .... 314-516-6066 .... 291 F
sebastainj@umsl.edu

SEBASTIAN, Christina .... 518-445-3361 .... 322 D
cseba@albanylaw.edu

SEBASTIAN, David, L .... 765-641-4032 .... 169 A
dlsebastian@anderson.edu

SEBASTIAN, Denise .... 573-518-2249 .... 286 B
denise@mineralarea.edu

SEBASTIAN, Donald, H .... 973-596-2963 .... 312 C
sebastian@njit.edu

SEBASTIAN, Jayakiran .... 215-248-7378 .... 435 B
jsebastian@ltsp.edu

SEBASTIAN, Pam .... 660-831-4142 .... 286 I
sebastianp@moval.edu

SEBASTIAN-FRUEHAUF,
Tracie .... 724-503-1001 .... 451 A
tfruehauf@washjeff.edu

SEBASTIANI, Richard .... 713-221-8225 .... 503 D
sebastianir@uhd.edu

SEBOLT, George, W .... 412-291-6210 .... 422 D
gsebolt@aii.edu

SEBOLT, Kevin, G .... 740-284-5192 .... 390 M
ksebolt@franciscan.edu

SEBOLT, Lara .... 412-291-6315 .... 422 D
lsebolt@aii.edu

SECHLER, Elizabeth, J .... 570-348-6236 .... 435 F
ejsechler@marywood.edu

SECHLER, Elizabeth, S .... 540-464-7345 .... 529 A
sechleres@vmi.edu

SECHRIST, Ann .... 770-972-7580 .... 132 A
asechrist@gwinnetttech.edu

SECHRIST, Paul, W .... 405-682-7503 .... 409 F
psechrist@occc.edu

SECKAR, Donna, J .... 336-334-5454 .... 379 A
djseckar@uncg.edu

SECKMAN, Colleen .... 740-695-9500 .... 384 J
cseckman@btc.edu

SECOLSKY, Charles .... 973-328-5056 .... 309 B
csecolsky@ccm.edu

SECORD, Anne-Marie .... 858-541-7913 .... 58 I
asecord@nu.edu

SECRIST, Tammi .... 304-336-8281 .... 544 B
tsecrist@westliberty.edu

SECTTOR, Stuart, A .... 937-328-3857 .... 387 G
secttors@clarkstate.edu

SEDA, Eduardo .... 787-878-6000 .... 562 E
eseda@icprjc.edu

SEDA, Eric .... 718-357-0500 .... 349 F
eseda@edaff.com

SEDANO, George .... 510-594-5033 .... 31 J
gsedano@cca.edu

SEDBERRY, Angela .... 910-576-6222 .... 372 A
sedberrya@montgomery.edu

SEDDIKI, Mohamed .... 973-877-3080 .... 310 A
seddiki@essex.edu

SEDER, Diana .... 909-607-7785 .... 40 D
diana.seder@cmc.edu

SEDERBURG, William, A .... 801-321-7103 .... 510 K
wsederburg@utahsbr.edu

SEDGWICK, Timothy, F .... 703-461-1721 .... 522 C
tsedgwick@vts.edu

SEDILLO, Eileen .... 505-454-3430 .... 318 I
sedillo_e@nmhu.edu

SEDILLO, Robert .... 928-226-4283 .... 13 H
bobby.sedillo@coconino.edu

SEDLACEK, Bernard .... 402-457-2529 .... 298 H
bsedlacek@mccneb.edu

SEDLACEK, Beverly .... 402-354-7249 .... 299 E
bev.sedlacek@methodistcollege.edu

SEDLAK, John .... 570-740-0234 .... 435 C
jsedlak@luzerne.edu

SEDORE, Ann .... 315-470-7481 .... 331 E

SEDORE, Christopher, M .... 315-443-1984 .... 357 B
cmsedore@syr.edu

SEDWICK, Nils .... 408-571-3766 .... 44 M
nsedwick@devry.edu

SEDWICK, Susan, W .... 512-471-6424 .... 505 B
sedwick@austin.utexas.edu

SEE, David .... 501-337-5000 .... 21 D
dsee@otcweb.edu

SEE, Leslie .... 304-260-4380 .... 542 C
lsee@blueridgectc.edu

SEEBECK, Bob .... 918-293-5412 .... 410 E
bob.seebeck@okstate.edu

SEEBER, Ronald .... 607-255-1256 .... 331 C
rs60@cornell.edu

SEEBERGER, Debra .... 410-704-2360 .... 228 E
dseeberger@towson.edu

SEEBO, Elane .... 806-291-3417 .... 508 B
seeboe@wbu.edu

SEED, Anne .... 510-869-6610 .... 64 J
aseed@samuelmerritt.edu

SEEDHOUSE, Julie .... 406-247-5781 .... 295 F
jseedhouse@msubillings.edu

SEEGER, Mat .... 313-577-5342 .... 260 D
aa4331@wayne.edu

SEEGERS, Heidi .... 319-385-6375 .... 186 A
hseegers@iwc.edu

SEEGMILLER, Jesse .... 540-261-2746 .... 524 C
jesse.seegmiller@svu.edu

SEEHERMAN, Elisa .... 215-717-6075 .... 448 H
careerservices@uarts.edu

SEEKINS, Travis, P .... 325-670-1589 .... 487 D
seekins@hsutx.edu

SEEKLANDER, Marlene .... 605-882-5284 .... 464 D
seeklanm@lakeareatech.edu

SEEL, Max .... 906-487-2440 .... 255 E
seel@mtu.edu

SEELIG, Dayna, S .... 606-783-5282 .... 204 E
d.seelig@moreheadstate.edu

SEELY, Bruce, E .... 906-487-2156 .... 255 E
bseely@mtu.edu

SEEM, Mark, D .... 212-242-2255 .... 358 A
mark.seem@tsca.edu

SEEM, Susan .... 585-395-2525 .... 352 F
sseem@brockport.edu

SEEMAN, Steve, C .... 563-588-8000 .... 184 F
financialaid@emmaus.edu

SEEMANN, Jeffrey, R .... 979-845-8585 .... 497 C
jseemann@tamu.edu

SEEMANN, Jeffrey, R .... 979-845-8585 .... 496 D
jseemann@tamu.edu

SEESE, Christine .... 410-225-2222 .... 224 C
cseese@mica.edu

SEESE, Robert, M .... 512-245-7966 .... 501 C
rs20@txstate.edu

SEESTEDT-STANFORD,
Linda .... 828-227-7495 .... 379 E
lstanford@wcu.edu

SEETHOFF, Terrance, L .... 906-227-2300 .... 256 F
tseethof@nmu.edu

SEETHOFF, Terrance, L .... 906-227-2920 .... 256 F
tseethof@nmu.edu

SEEVERS, JR., Gary .... 417-862-9533 .... 282 D
president@globaluniversity.edu

SEEVERS, Scott .... 402-643-7233 .... 297 F
scott.seevers@cune.edu

SEFCIK, Jeff .... 325-942-2333 .... 480 E
jeff.sefcik@angelo.edu

SEFFERS, Tracy .... 304-876-5463 .... 544 A
tseffers@shepherd.edu

SEFTON, Ellen .... 904-680-7728 .... 107 H
esefton@fcsl.edu

SEGAL, Gordon .... 691-320-2480 .... 559 A
gsegal@comfsm.fm

SEGAR, Robert, B .... 530-752-2172 .... 73 F
rbsegar@ucdavis.edu

SEGAR, Thomas .... 304-876-5214 .... 544 A
tsegar@shepherd.edu

SEGARRA, Carlos .... 787-264-1912 .... 563 G
carlos-segarra@sg.inter.edu

SEGARRA, Jose .... 787-878-5475 .... 562 H
jsegarra@arecibo.inter.edu

SEGARS, Glenda .... 662-862-8383 .... 274 G
grsegars@iccms.edu

SEGAWA, Mike .... 253-879-2837 .... 538 E
msegawa@pugetsound.edu

SEGAY, Gary .... 928-724-6738 .... 14 A
gsegay@dinecollege.edu

SEGER, Christine .... 765-966-2656 .... 176 F
crethlake@ivytech.edu

SEGGELKE, Linda .... 217-732-3168 .... 156 F
lseggelke@lincolnchristian.edu

SEGGERMAN, Richard, W .... 319-352-8276 .... 189 F
richard.seggerman@wartburg.edu

SEGOVIA, Ric .... 708-456-0300 .... 166 C
rsegovia@triton.edu

SEGOVIS, James .... 401-232-6206 .... 453 A
jsegovis@bryant.edu

SEGRAN, Sam .... 806-742-5151 .... 501 D
sam.segran@ttu.edu

SEGRAVE, Jeffrey, O .... 518-580-5590 .... 351 B
jsegrave@skidmore.edu

SEGRAVES, Daniel, L .... 314-921-9290 .... 292 B
dsegraves@ugst.edu

SEGREE, E. Ramone .... 718-482-5006 .... 328 C
rsegree@lagcc.cuny.edu

SEGURA, Bill .... 254-867-4891 .... 500 B
bill.segura@systems.tstc.edu

SEGURA, Oneida .... 305-821-3333 .... 109 B
osegura@mm.fnc.edu

SEGURA, Oneida .... 305-821-3333 .... 109 A
osegura@mm.fnc.edu

SEHEULT, Erin .... 909-558-4508 .... 54 D
eseheult@llu.edu

SEHGAL, Varun .... 718-518-6641 .... 327 D
vsehgal@hostos.cuny.edu

SEHL, JR., Patrick .... 316-295-5488 .... 192 H
sehl@friends.edu

SEHLOFF, John, M .... 507-344-7342 .... 261 H
john@blc.edu

SEIBEL, Kathleen .... 619-239-0391 .... 37 D
kseibel@cwsl.edu

SEIBENHAR, Neil .... 315-279-5428 .... 337 K
nseiben@mail.keuka.edu

SEIBERT, Susan .... 618-650-3708 .... 165 A
sseiber@siue.edu

SEIBLE, Frieder .... 858-534-6237 .... 74 D
fseible@ucsd.edu

SEIBOLD, Kathy .... 208-459-5882 .... 143 A
kseibold@collegeofidaho.edu

SEIBOLD, Kathy .... 716-896-0700 .... 359 F
seiboldke@villa.edu

SEIBRING, Scott .... 309-556-3096 .... 153 E
iwufaid@iwu.edu

SEIBRING, Steve, D .... 309-556-3135 .... 153 E
sseibrin@iwu.edu

SEICHRIST, Pipa .... 305-538-3193 .... 113 G

SEIDEL, Andrew, B .... 214-841-3514 .... 485 E
aseidel@dts.edu

SEIDEL, Angela .... 814-536-5168 .... 424 C
aseidel@crbc.net

SEIDEL, Angela .... 814-536-5168 .... 424 B
aseidel@crbc.net

SEIDEL, Ethan, A .... 410-857-2200 .... 224 D
eseidel@mcdaniel.edu

SEIDEL, Tina .... 618-344-5600 .... 289 I
tseidel@sbc-collinsville.com

SEIDELMAN, James, E .... 801-832-2581 .... 512 F
cseidelman@westminstercollege.edu

SEIDEMANN, Jonathan .... 410-484-7200 .... 225 C

SEIDEN, David .... 732-235-4690 .... 316 G
seiden@umdnj.edu

SEIDEN, Dena .... 813-879-6000 .... 106 F
dseiden@cci.edu

SEIDEN, Peggy .... 610-328-8489 .... 447 E
pseiden1@swarthmore.edu

SEIDENSTICKER,
Duane, P .... 414-847-3274 .... 548 G
duaneseidensticker@miad.edu

SEIDL, Daniel, J .... 920-498-5712 .... 555 A
daniel.seidl@nwtc.edu

SEIDLER, Nick 414-277-6922 548
seidler@msoe.edu

SEIDMAN, Stephen, B 512-245-2119 501
ss76@txstate.edu

SEIF, Gershon 874-982-2500 151
seif@htc.edu

SEIFERT, Alice 914-923-2616 345
aseifert@pace.edu

SEIFERT, Sheila 406-874-6163 294
seiferts@milescc.edu

SEIFFERT, Ronald, J 614-251-4741 398
seifferr@ohiodominican.edu

SEIFRIED, Brent .... 970-267-3202 .... 19 C
brent.seifried@phoenix.edu

SEIGART, Denise .... 443-334-2821 .... 226 E
dseigart@stevenson.edu

SEIGEL, Denise .... 516-299-3392 .... 339 A
denise.seigel@liu.edu

SEIGLE, Mark .... 310-243-3771 .... 34 B
mseigle@csudh.edu

SEIJO, Haydee .... 787-764-2960 .... 567 F
hseijo@degi.uprrp.edu

SEILER, Gary .... 651-793-1920 .... 267 D
gary.seiler@metrostate.edu

SEILER, Susan .... 414-256-1230 .... 549 A
mktg@mtmary.edu

SEIMITS, Kristin .... 414-297-6641 .... 554 D
seimitsk@matc.edu

SEIN, Laurie .... 303-280-7653 .... 84 C
lsein@devry.edu

SEINFELD, Lynn .... 847-635-2186 .... 160 E
lynns@oakton.edu

SEIPEL, Joseph, H .... 804-828-2787 .... 525 E
jseipel@vcu.edu

SEIPP, JR., Dale, E .... 503-554-2252 .... 415 I
dseipp@georgefox.edu

SEITHEL, William, W .... 312-362-7552 .... 148 F
wseithel@depaul.edu

SEITZ, Gina .... 801-281-7630 .... 510 I
gina.seitz@stevenshenager.edu

SEITZ, Kathy .... 828-726-2269 .... 368 D
kseitz@cccti.edu

SEITZ, Rebecca .... 573-592-4222 .... 293 E
rebecca.seitz@williamwoods.edu

SEITZ, William .... 409-740-4748 .... 497 D
seitzw@tamug.edu

SEITZ, William, A .... 409-740-4409 .... 497 D
seitzw@tamug.edu

SEITZER, Joan, M .... 410-827-5808 .... 222 B
jseitzer@chesapeake.edu

SEIVERS, Lana .... 615-898-2874 .... 473 F
lseivers@mtsu.edu

SEIVWRIGHT, Hazel .... 718-488-1223 .... 338 H
hazel.seivwright@liu.edu

SEIXAS, Karyn .... 626-395-6161 .... 32 E
karyn@caltech.edu

SEJDINAJ, John, A .... 574-631-4130 .... 180 D
sejdinaj.1@nd.edu

SEK, Mary, S .... 610-861-1567 .... 436 I
memss01@moravian.edu

SEKELSKY, Mary Jo, S .... 810-762-3434 .... 259 F
maryjoss@umflint.edu

SEKHRI, Kiran .... 313-496-2811 .... 260 C
ksekhri1@wcccd.edu

SEKUL, Michelle .... 601-928-6267 .... 275 G
michelle.sekul@mgccc.edu

SEKULICH, Brad .... 704-687-7747 .... 378 E
sekulich@uncc.edu

SEKWAT, Alex .... 615-963-5139 .... 474 A
asekwat@tnstate.edu

SELANDER, Ralph .... 843-349-5296 .... 458 G
ralph.selander@hgtc.edu

SELBE, James, E .... 270-707-3705 .... 202 A
james.selbe@kctcs.edu

SELBE, James, H .... 240-684-2303 .... 227 F
jselbe@umuc.edu

SELBY, Rosemary .... 478-553-2055 .... 134 F
rselby@oftc.edu

SELBY, Sara .... 912-449-7580 .... 138 G
sselby@waycross.edu

SELBY, Sara, E .... 912-449-7580 .... 138 G
sselby@waycross.edu

SELBY, Steve .... 714-992-7081 .... 59 D
sselby@fullcoll.edu

SELBY, Terri, P .... 802-654-2462 .... 514 B
tselby@smcvt.edu

SELBY, Zachary .... 614-508-7228 .... 392 B
zselby@hondros.edu

SELDEN, Richard .... 410-234-4525 .... 225 E

SELDERS, Ronald, J .... 304-637-1268 .... 540 F
seldersr@dewv.edu

SELF, George .... 520-515-5385 .... 13 G
selfg@cochise.edu

SELF, Michael .... 615-329-8697 .... 468 G
mself@fisk.edu

SELF, Phyllis .... 309-298-2762 .... 168 A
p-self@wiu.edu

SELF, Sheila .... 918-456-5511 .... 409 A
selfsj@nsuok.edu

SELF-DAVIS, LeAnn .... 731-989-6931 .... 468 K
ldavis@fhu.edu

SELGO, Tim .... 616-331-8800 .... 252 A
selgot@gvsu.edu

SEWARD, Karen .... 518-629-7356.... 336 C
k.seward@hvcc.edu
SEWARD, Stephen .... 860-231-5503..... 93 H
sseward@sjc.edu
SEWART, John, J .... 650-574-6196...... 67 F
sewart@smccd.edu
SEWELL, Ann, C .... 817-257-5070.... 498 F
a.sewell@tcu.edu
SEWELL, Arleen .... 684-699-9155.... 558 I
a.sewell@amsamoa.edu
SEWELL, Daniel, R .... 415-433-9200...... 68 F
SEWELL, Daniel, R .... 805-898-2916...... 47 C
dsewell@fielding.edu
SEWELL, Devona .... 352-854-2322.... 103 D
sewelld@cf.edu
SEWELL, Jason .... 423-472-7141.... 474 E
jsewell@clevelandstatecc.edu
SEWELL, Keli .... 864-977-7733.... 460 A
keli.sewell@ngu.edu
SEWELL, Lisa .... 610-519-4646.... 450 G
lisa.sewell@villanova.edu
SEWELL, Robert .... 760-245-4271...... 77 E
Robert.Sewell@vvc.edu
SEWELL, Said .... 478-825-1070.... 129 C
sewell@fvsu.edu
SEWELL, Stacy .... 845-398-4137.... 349 H
ssewell@stac.edu
SEWELL, Tanisha .... 585-266-0430.... 333 E
tsewell@cci.edu
SEWELL, Thomas, R .... 423-585-2644.... 476 B
thomas.sewell@ws.edu
SEWELL, Zennabelle .... 212-261-1682.... 343 D
zsewell@nyit.edu
SEWNUNDUN,
Kalyani (Sandhya) .... 972-929-6777.... 486 B
kpatel@devry.edu
SEXSON, Marla .... 620-229-6364.... 196 C
marla.sexson@sckans.edu
SEXTER, Jay .... 646-981-4500.... 357 J
jsexter@touro.edu
SEXTON, Eric, L .... 316-978-3250.... 197 F
eric.sexton@goshockers.com
SEXTON, Gary .... 330-941-1778.... 406 F
sexton@wysu.org
SEXTON, Glenna, W .... 970-247-7331...... 84 G
sexton_g@fortlewis.edu
SEXTON, John .... 212-998-2345.... 344 B
john.sexton@nyu.edu
SEXTON, Michele, D .... 620-235-4187.... 195 I
msexton@pittstate.edu
SEXTON, Mike .... 408-554-4700...... 68 C
mbsexton@scu.edu
SEXTON, Robert, M .... 215-572-3816.... 451 D
bsexton@wts.edu
SEXTON, Steve .... 615-248-7792.... 476 E
ssexton@trevecca.edu
SEXTON, Susan .... 651-690-6565.... 271 E
swsexton@stkate.edu
SEXTON, Susan, K .... 937-229-4333.... 404 A
susan.sexton@notes.udayton.edu
SEXTON-JOHNSON, Sara . 509-359-2442.... 533 D
ssextonjohns@ewu.edu
SEYBERT, David, W .... 412-396-4877.... 428 C
seybert@duq.edu
SEYBOLD, Marc, P .... 516-876-3379.... 353 D
seyboldm@oldwestbury.edu
SEYDEL, Tim .... 541-962-3740.... 418 C
tseydel@eou.edu
SEYLE, David, C .... 229-732-5928.... 124 C
davidseyle@andrewcollege.edu
SEYMAN, Elaine .... 503-222-3225.... 415 H
eseyman@cci.edu
SEYMOUR, Charlena .... 617-521-2077.... 245 A
charlena.seymour@simmons.edu
SEYMOUR, Cheryl .... 518-562-4125.... 329 D
cheryl.stein@clinton.edu
SEYMOUR, Daniel .... 713-718-5016.... 487 G
daniel.seymour@hccs.edu
SEYMOUR, Dennis .... 815-939-5302.... 160 F
dseymour@olivet.edu
SEYMOUR, G. Kim .... 580-928-5533.... 412 F
kim.seymour@swosu.edu
SEYMOUR, Jodi, L .... 641-784-5112.... 184 H
seymour@graceland.edu
SEYMOUR, Michael .... 763-433-1335.... 265 J
michael.seymour@anokaramsey.edu
SEYMOUR, Richard, R .... 252-335-0821.... 369 D
rseymour@albemarle.edu
SEYMOUR, Teresa .... 318-473-6424.... 212 G
tseymour@lsua.edu
SEYMOUR-ROUTE,
Paulette .... 508-856-5758.... 238 A
Paulette.SeymourRoute@umassmed.edu
SFEIR, Raymond .... 714-997-6551...... 39 C
SFRAGA, Mike .... 907-474-6533...... 10 J
msfraga@alaska.edu
SGANGA, Fred .... 631-444-8606.... 352 C
fred.sganga@stonybrook.edu
SGRECCI, Carl, E .... 607-274-3118.... 336 G
csgrecci@ithaca.edu
SHAAK, Melissa, J .... 781-239-4398.... 230 G
shaak@babson.edu
SHABAHANG, Homa .... 909-593-3511...... 75 C
hshabahang@laverne.edu

SHABAKA, Macheo .... 310-900-1600...... 45 E
shabaka_m@compton.edu
SHABAN, Hisham .... 954-446-6107.... 100 E
hshaban@aiufl.edu
SHABAZZ, David .... 928-692-3016...... 16 G
dshabazz@mohave.edu
SHABAZZ, Mensimah .... 860-343-5897...... 90 D
mshabazz@mxcc.commnet.edu
SHABAZZ, Ricky .... 310-900-1600...... 45 E
shabazz_r@compton.edu
SHABAZZ, Roxie .... 910-672-1784.... 377 E
rshabazz@uncfsu.edu
SHABLIN, Steven, J .... 248-370-3470.... 257 C
shablin@oakland.edu
SHACHTER, Amy, M .... 408-554-7041...... 68 C
ashachter@scu.edu
SHACKELFORD, Barbara .... 662-720-4089.... 276 D
bshack@nemcc.edu
SHACKELFORD, Carol .... 601-635-2111.... 274 C
cshackelford@eccc.edu
SHACKELFORD,
Cynthia, K .... 205-665-6230...... 9 C
shackelc@montevallo.edu
SHACKELFORD, Harper ..... 910-678-8413.... 370 B
shackelh@faytechcc.edu
SHACKELFORD, Judy .... 217-544-6464.... 163 F
SHACKELFORD, Michelle .. 918-540-6188.... 408 J
mshackelford@neo.edu
SHACKLEFORD, Keith .... 949-451-5407...... 70 E
kshackleford@ivc.edu
SHACKLEFORD, Michael ... 804-524-5350.... 529 C
mshackle@vsu.edu
SHACKLEFORD, JR.,
Robert, S .... 336-633-0287.... 372 F
rsshackleford@randolph.edu
SHACKLETON, Larry .... 434-592-3007.... 520 F
lshackleton@liberty.edu
SHADAIR, Maureen, M .... 206-934-5378.... 537 B
maureen.shadair@seattlecolleges.edu
SHADDY, Deborah .... 913-758-6143.... 197 B
shaddy15@stmary.edu
SHADDY, Robert .... 718-997-3760.... 328 F
robert.shaddy@qc.cuny.edu
SHADE, Christina .... 206-393-3545...... 29 D
cshade@argosy.edu
SHADE-DAVISON,
Stephanie .... 580-745-2267.... 412 C
sdavison@se.edu
SHADFAR, Cyrus .... 913-621-8720.... 192 C
cshadfar@donnelly.edu
SHADICK, Richard .... 212-346-1526.... 345 F
rshadick@pace.edu
SHADIX, Brian .... 404-270-2788.... 128 G
bshadix@devry.edu
SHADKO, Jacqueline .... 248-942-3300.... 257 B
jashadko@oaklandcc.edu
SHADLE, Joseph .... 513-745-3567.... 406 E
shadle@xavier.edu
SHADOIAN, Holly, L .... 401-456-8884.... 454 A
hshadoian@ric.edu
SHADOW, Cyndie .... 913-217-4600.... 190 B
SHADWICK, Monte .... 785-827-5541.... 194 D
monte.shadwick@kwu.edu
SHAFER, Angela .... 812-669-0728.... 171 H
angela.shafers@harrison.edu
SHAFER, Carol .... 570-286-3058.... 436 B
cshafer@mccannschool.com
SHAFER, Glenn .... 973-353-1604.... 314 E
gshafer@business.rutgers.edu
SHAFER, Glenn, R .... 973-353-1604.... 314 D
gshafer@business.rutgers.edu
SHAFER, Jack, L .... 610-499-4454.... 451 F
jlshafer@widener.edu
SHAFER, Jesse .... 215-951-2850.... 444 C
shaferj@philau.edu
SHAFER, John, R .... 317-738-8080.... 171 C
jshafer@franklincollege.edu
SHAFER, Kathrynne, G .... 717-691-6003.... 436 D
kshafer@messiah.edu
SHAFER, Pamela .... 832-559-4217.... 490 C
pamela.n.shafer@lonestar.edu
SHAFER, Patricia .... 215-951-2930.... 444 C
shafert@philau.edu
SHAFER, Ron .... 912-588-2501.... 124 A
rshafer@altamahatech.edu
SHAFER, Stephanie, C .... 540-432-4118.... 518 E
stephanie.shafer@emu.edu
SHAFFER, Alan, D .... 740-392-6868.... 396 H
alan.shaffer@mvnu.edu
SHAFFER, Brian, W .... 901-843-3976.... 472 I
shaffer@rhodes.edu
SHAFFER, Chris .... 334-983-6556...... 8 B
shafferc@troy.edu
SHAFFER, Chris .... 503-494-6057.... 418 D
SHAFFER, Christopher .... 740-351-3207.... 401 I
cshaffer@shawnee.edu
SHAFFER, Germaine .... 606-436-5721.... 201 H
germaine.shaffer@kctcs.edu
SHAFFER, Janet .... 765-998-5330.... 179 F
jnshaffer@taylor.edu
SHAFFER, Jessica .... 207-216-4401.... 219 C
jshaffer@yccc.edu
SHAFFER, Jon .... 231-591-3755.... 251 B
John_Shaffer@ferris.edu

SHAFFER, Linda .... 816-501-2422.... 279 C
linda.shaffer@avila.edu
SHAFFER, Myra .... 864-388-8351.... 458 J
mshaffer@lander.edu
SHAFFER, Patti .... 724-357-2621.... 442 E
Patty.Shaffer@iup.edu
SHAFFER, Tamera, L .... 812-877-8003.... 179 A
tamera.shaffer@rose-hulman.edu
SHAFFER, Teresa .... 574-830-0375.... 176 C
tshaffer@ivytech.edu
SHAFFER, Wendy .... 978-556-3858.... 241 B
wshaffer@necc.mass.edu
SHAFFER FRYLING,
Michelle .... 724-357-2302.... 442 E
mfryling@iup.edu
SHAFFER LILIENTHAL,
Robin .... 641-844-5730.... 185 H
robin.lilienthal@iavalley.edu
SHAFFNER, Donna, L .... 716-888-2500.... 325 G
shaffned@canisius.edu
SHAFKOWITZ, Marshall, J 312-944-0882.... 156 B
SHAFQAT, Sahar .... 240-895-4910.... 226 A
sshafqat@smcm.edu
SHAH, Kashif .... 708-974-5348.... 159 A
shah@morainevalley.edu
SHAH, Monal .... 954-499-9703.... 149 A
mshah@devry.edu
SHAH, Sadiq .... 805-437-8898...... 33 I
sadiq.shah@csuci.edu
SHAH-GORDON, Ruta .... 718-390-3423.... 359 G
rshahgor@wagner.edu
SHAHAN, J. Michael .... 409-882-3314.... 500 G
mike.shahan@lsco.edu
SHAHEED, Kate .... 510-885-2839...... 34 C
kate.shaheed@csueastbay.edu
SHAHIN, Hamdi .... 201-559-6076.... 310 C
shahinh@felician.edu
SHAHRABI, Kamal .... 631-420-2115.... 356 A
kamal.shahrabi@farmingdale.edu
SHAHROKHI, Hossein .... 713-221-8542.... 503 D
shahrokhi@uhd.edu
SHAIKH, Usama .... 516-876-3323.... 353 D
shaikhu@oldwestbury.edu
SHAILOR, Barbara .... 203-432-8187...... 95 D
barbara.shailor@yale.edu
SHAIN, Yeruchim .... 732-431-1600.... 315 G
SHAINDLIN, Andrew .... 412-268-6286.... 424 H
shaindlin@andrew.cmu.edu
SHAINK, Dick .... 810-762-0453.... 256 C
dick.shaink@mcc.edu
SHAKE, Miranda .... 217-554-6846.... 156 A
mshake@lakeviewcol.edu
SHAKER, Lucy, G .... 773-244-5526.... 159 G
lshaker@northpark.edu
SHAKLEE, Ronald .... 330-941-4740.... 406 F
rshaklee@ysu.edu
SHALALA, Donna, E .... 305-284-5155.... 122 F
dshalala@miami.edu
SHALAMOV, Marina .... 718-261-5800.... 324 D
mshalamov@bramsonort.edu
SHALITA, Mindi .... 609-984-1114.... 316 A
mshalita@tesc.edu
SHALLA, Annie .... 970-521-6702...... 86 E
annie.shalla@njc.edu
SHALLBERG, Mary Ann, H 281-283-2004.... 503 C
shallberg@uhcl.edu
SHALLCROSS, Dorothy .... 303-797-5647...... 80 J
dorothy.shallcross@arapahoe.edu
SHALLENBERGER,
Grant, W .... 409-740-4943.... 497 D
shalleng@tamug.edu
SHALLO, Michael, J .... 914-594-4574.... 343 F
michael_shallo@nymc.edu
SHALVA, Sara .... 617-559-8610.... 235 I
sshalva@hebrewcollege.edu
SHAMASH, Yacov .... 631-632-8380.... 352 C
yacov.shamash@stonybrook.edu
SHAMBACH, Teresa .... 330-369-3200.... 402 H
tbcmail@tbc-trumbullbusiness.com
SHAMBAUGH, Jeannine .... 330-363-5420.... 384 G
jshambaugh@aultman.com
SHAMGOCHIAN, Maureen 508-929-8938.... 239 D
mshamgochian@worcester.edu
SHAMIM, Jina .... 415-476-8850...... 74 E
jinashamim@ucsf.edu
SHAMPENY, Renelle .... 518-587-2100.... 355 F
renelle.shampeny@esc.edu
SHAMS, Arian .... 714-300-0300...... 70 I
ashams@scitech.edu
SHAMS, Nazila .... 714-300-0300...... 70 I
nshams@scitech.edu
SHAMS, Parviz .... 714-300-0300...... 70 I
pshams@scitech.edu
SHANAFELT, Rebecca, S ... 727-816-3288.... 114 F
shanafr@phcc.edu
SHANAHAN, James .... 440-365-5222.... 395 C
SHANAHAN, Judy .... 636-949-4900.... 284 C
jshanahan@lindenwood.edu
SHANAHAN, Megan .... 906-353-4600.... 253 J
megan@kbocc.org
SHANBLATT, Stephanie .... 517-483-1156.... 254 D
shanbls@lcc.edu
SHANDLEY, Thomas, C ..... 704-894-2225.... 363 F
toshandley@davidson.edu

SHANE, J. Michael .... 716-372-2155.... 348
jmshane@eznet.net
SHANEBERGER, Roy .... 314-539-5207.... 289
rshaneberger@stlcc.edu
SHANER, Carl, L .... 570-326-3761.... 440
c.shaner@pct.edu
SHANGRAW, R, F .... 480-965-1225...... 12
rick.shangraw@asu.edu
SHANK, Barbara, W .... 651-962-5801.... 272
bwshank@stthomas.edu
SHANK, Harold .... 304-865-6003.... 541
harold.shank@ovu.edu
SHANK, Larry .... 740-826-6109.... 396
lshank@muskingum.edu
SHANK, Leanne, M .... 540-458-8940.... 530
lshank@wlu.edu
SHANK, Matthew, D .... 703-284-1598.... 521
matthew.shank@marymount.edu
SHANK, Scott .... 434-381-6100.... 524
sshank@sbc.edu
SHANK, Theresa .... 301-790-2800.... 223
tmshank@hagerstowncc.edu
SHANKAR, Jai .... 831-647-3537...... 57
jshankar@miis.edu
SHANKAR, Jille .... 509-533-4152.... 532 F
jilles@spokanefalls.edu
SHANKEL, James, V .... 724-741-1028.... 424 G
shankeljv@carlow.edu
SHANKLIN, Bart .... 309-298-1544.... 168 A
b-shanklin@wiu.edu
SHANKLIN, Carol .... 785-532-7927.... 194 B
shanklin@ksu.edu
SHANKLIN, Iris .... 404-756-4916.... 124
ishanklin@atlm.edu
SHANKMAN, Kimberly, C . 913-360-7413.... 190 F
kshankman@benedictine.edu
SHANKS, Alane, K .... 617-541-5343.... 241 D
ashanks@rcc.mass.edu
SHANKS, Alane, K .... 617-731-7101.... 244 B
ashanks@pmc.edu
SHANKS, Carol .... 314-918-2501.... 281 J
cshanks@eden.edu
SHANKS, Martha .... 828-254-1921.... 367 H
mshanks@abtech.edu
SHANKWEILER, Jean .... 310-660-3350...... 45 D
jshankweiler@elcamino.edu
SHANLEY, OP, Brian, J ..... 401-865-2153.... 453 F
bshanley@providence.edu
SHANLEY, Deborah, A .... 718-951-5214.... 326 G
dshanley@brooklyn.cuny.edu
SHANLEY, James, E .... 406-768-6310.... 294 F
jshanley@fpcc.edu
SHANLEY, Mark, G .... 540-831-5433.... 522 D
mshanley@radford.edu
SHANLEY, Michael, V .... 978-665-3421.... 238 C
mshanley@fitchburgstate.edu
SHANMUGARATNAM,
Carol .... 781-283-2308.... 246 B
cshanmug@wellesley.edu
SHANNON, Beth .... 301-431-6400.... 225 B
SHANNON, Carol .... 989-386-6622.... 255 F
cshannon@midmich.edu
SHANNON, Cheryl .... 203-285-2321...... 90 A
cshannon@gwcc.commnet.edu
SHANNON, David .... 405-878-2381.... 409 D
david.shannon@okbu.edu
SHANNON, Henry, D .... 909-652-6100...... 39 B
henry.shannon@chaffey.edu
SHANNON, Jeff .... 479-575-2702...... 24 C
jshannon@uark.edu
SHANNON, Jim .... 901-321-3305.... 467 G
jshannon@cbu.edu
SHANNON, Joe .... 903-693-2028.... 492 A
jshannon@panola.edu
SHANNON, John, T .... 973-655-4214.... 311 G
shannonj@mail.montclair.edu
SHANNON, Kathi, R .... 509-682-6420.... 539 B
krshannon@wvc.edu
SHANNON, Kelly .... 312-915-6159.... 157 A
kshann2@luc.edu
SHANNON, Linda, A .... 718-990-6578.... 348 G
shannonl@stjohns.edu
SHANNON, Mike .... 956-872-3535.... 494 D
mshannon@southtexascollege.edu
SHANNON, Pat .... 208-426-1125.... 142 F
pshannon@boisestate.edu
SHANNON, Randy .... 757-822-2181.... 528 C
rshannon@tcc.edu
SHANNON, Scott, S .... 315-470-6537.... 355 A
sshannon@esf.edu
SHANNON, Tim .... 312-467-2166.... 146 C
tshannon@tcsfound.org
SHANTZ, Dale .... 989-275-5000.... 253 K
dale.shantz@kirkland.edu
SHAO, Alan, T .... 843-953-6651.... 457 B
shaoa@cofc.edu
SHAO, Dawei .... 505-888-8898.... 320 H
drshao@acupuncturecollege.edu
SHAPE, Ronald .... 605-721-5220.... 464 G
rshape@national.edu
SHAPIRO, Adam .... 760-750-4195...... 36 B
ashapiro@csusm.edu
SHAPIRO, Adrian .... 713-973-3123.... 486 A
ashapiro@devry.edu

SHEEHAN, Timothy .... 651-213-4166.... 264 D
tsheehan@hazelden.org
SHEEHAN MASSARO, Maureen .... 937-327-7517.... 406 B
mmassaro@wittenberg.edu
SHEEHEY, John, D .... 802-654-2571.... 514 B
jsheehey@smcvt.edu
SHEEHY, Colette .... 434-924-3349.... 525 B
cc@virginia.edu
SHEEHY, Harry .... 603-646-2465.... 305 A
harry.sheehy@dartmouth.edu
SHEEHY, Molly, H .... 978-656-3105.... 240 F
sheehym@middlesex.mass.edu
SHEEKS, Gina .... 706-507-8730.... 127 D
sheeks_gina@columbusstate.edu
SHEELEY, Brian .... 859-344-3572.... 206 D
brian.sheeley@thomasmore.edu
SHEELEY, Robert, G .... 203-392-6050...... 91 I
sheeleyr1@southernct.edu
SHEERAN, Janet, W .... 405-878-5363.... 412 A
jwsheeran@stgregorys.edu
SHEERAN, Michael, J .... 303-458-4190...... 87 E
president@regis.edu
SHEERAN, Robert, M .... 513-745-3151.... 406 E
sheeran@xavier.edu
SHEERAN, Thomas .... 240-567-4119.... 224 E
thomas.sheeran@montgomerycollege.edu
SHEERER, Marilyn .... 252-328-5419.... 377 C
sheererm@ecu.edu
SHEETS, Christine .... 740-593-4094.... 399 G
sheetsch@ohio.edu
SHEETS, Heather .... 312-467-2381.... 146 C
heathersheets@thechicagoschool.edu
SHEETS, Helene .... 419-824-3965.... 395 D
hsheets@lourdes.edu
SHEETS, Julie .... 573-518-2206.... 286 B
jsheets@mineralarea.edu
SHEFFER, Ilene .... 574-520-4344.... 174 C
isheffer@iusb.edu
SHEFFER, Mary .... 603-513-5175.... 306 G
mary.sheffer@law.unh.edu
SHEFFIELD, Ann, D .... 814-332-2357.... 421 E
ann.sheffield@allegheny.edu
SHEFFIELD, Betty .... 251-580-2134........ 5 A
bsheffield@faulknerstate.edu
SHEFFIELD, Jared .... 319-296-4223.... 185 C
jared.sheffield@hawkeyecollege.edu
SHEFFIELD, Jared .... 541-440-4600.... 420 F
jared.sheffield@umpqua.edu
SHEFFIELD, Linda .... 434-736-2002.... 527 H
linda.sheffield@southside.edu
SHEFFIELD, Ric, S .... 740-427-5117.... 394 C
sheffier@kenyon.edu
SHEFFLETTE, Nancy, A ...... 501-882-4581...... 20 D
nasheffletle@asub.edu
SHEFTIC, Alissa .... 269-467-9945.... 251 D
asheftic@glenoaks.edu
SHEGAN, Christine .... 570-662-4900.... 443 B
cshegan@mansfield.edu
SHEHEANE, Dene .... 404-894-1238.... 130 D
dene.sheheane@dev.gatech.edu
SHEHEE, Amy .... 859-985-3002.... 198 F
sheheea@berea.edu
SHEHU, Aida .... 904-363-6221.... 117 C
ashehu@sbjacksonville.com
SHEIBLEY, Thomas, J .... 610-660-1030.... 446 C
tsheible@sju.edu
SHEIDLER, Ann .... 419-473-2700.... 389 B
asheidler@daviscollege.edu
SHEIN, David .... 845-758-7454.... 323 F
shein@bard.edu
SHEKLETON, James, F .... 605-773-3455.... 465 D
jims@sdbor.edu
SHELANGOSKI, Bryan .... 502-456-6506.... 206 C
bshelangoski@sullivan.edu
SHELB, Jane .... 937-775-5515.... 406 C
jane.schelb@wright.edu
SHELBY, Barbara .... 740-588-1315.... 407 A
bshelby@zanestate.edu
SHELBY, R. Dennis .... 312-935-4232.... 153 F
rdshelby@icsw.edu
SHELBY, Valerie, J .... 601-979-1240.... 275 A
valerie.j.shelby@jsums.edu
SHELDON, Clayton, D .... 610-499-4239.... 451 F
cdsheldon@widener.edu
SHELDON, Frederick, H ...... 225-578-2887.... 212 F
fsheld@lsu.edu
SHELDON, Jane .... 308-865-8525.... 300 G
sheldonj@unk.edu
SHELDON, Jeannette .... 954-783-7339.... 106 D
jsheldon@cci.edu
SHELDON, Marianne .... 510-430-3221...... 57 D
mshel@mills.edu
SHELDON, Michael .... 207-221-4591.... 220 H
msheldon@une.edu
SHELDON, Scott .... 415-451-2822...... 66 B
ssheldon@sfts.edu
SHELDON, Tim .... 212-229-5456.... 342 E
sheldont@newschool.edu
SHELDON, Todd .... 402-363-5601.... 301 F
tlsheldon@york.edu
SHELENBERGER, Donald, E .... 724-946-7143.... 451 C
shelende@westminster.edu

SHELEY, Joseph, F .... 916-278-6331...... 35 E
sheleyj@csus.edu
SHELL, Cathy .... 828-898-8740.... 366 A
shell@lmc.edu
SHELL, Cathy .... 828-898-8723.... 366 A
shell@lmc.edu
SHELL, Chris .... 734-487-2382.... 250 H
chris.shell@emich.edu
SHELL, Larry .... 405-744-5370.... 410 C
larry.shell@okstate.edu
SHELL, Martin .... 650-723-4186...... 71 F
mshell@stanford.edu
SHELLBERG, David .... 303-797-5703...... 80 J
david.shellberg@arapahoe.edu
SHELLEDY, David .... 312-942-7120.... 163 B
david_shelledy@rush.edu
SHELLENBARGER, Lauren . 623-935-8808...... 15 H
lauren.shellenbarger@estrellamountain.edu
SHELLENBARGER, Lauren . 602-243-8084...... 16 E
SHELLEY, Chris .... 815-288-5511.... 163 I
shellec@svcc.edu
SHELLEY, Daniel .... 585-475-6736.... 347 G
drsadm@rit.edu
SHELLEY, Ena, M .... 317-940-9752.... 170 C
eshelley@butler.edu
SHELLEY, Jeff .... 205-929-3416........ 5 E
jshelley@lawsonstate.edu
SHELLEY, MargE .... 913-469-8500.... 193 I
mshelley@jccc.edu
SHELLEY, Michael .... 773-256-0721.... 157 B
mshelley@lstc.edu
SHELLEY, Stephen .... 940-397-4110.... 491 A
stephen.shelley@mwsu.edu
SHELLY, Peggy .... 215-780-1284.... 446 G
pshelly@salus.edu
SHELLY, Thomas, R .... 248-218-2011.... 257 F
rshelly@rc.edu
SHELMAN, Gary .... 210-486-3920.... 479 D
jshelman@alamo.edu
SHELOW, Stephen, G .... 814-865-1864.... 438 F
sps8@psu.edu
SHELPMAN, David .... 740-286-1554.... 389 D
dshelpman@daymarcollege.edu
SHELTON, Alice .... 317-955-6022.... 177 G
ashelton@marian.edu
SHELTON, Amy .... 615-794-4254.... 472 D
ashelton@omorecollege.edu
SHELTON, Charlita .... 877-442-0505...... 88 G
charlita.shelton@rockies.edu
SHELTON, Diane, E .... 641-784-5302.... 184 H
shelton@graceland.edu
SHELTON, Garry, M .... 540-857-7282.... 528 E
mshelton@virginiawestern.edu
SHELTON, Joyce, A .... 847-317-7172.... 166 B
SHELTON, M. Dwight .... 540-231-8775.... 529 B
mdsjr@vt.edu
SHELTON, Maria, T .... 817-515-5389.... 496 A
maria.shelton@tccd.edu
SHELTON, Myles .... 409-944-1200.... 486 H
mshelton@gc.edu
SHELTON, Nancy, B .... 434-395-2129.... 520 G
sheltonnb@longwood.edu
SHELTON, Paige .... 713-623-2040.... 480 J
pashelton@aii.edu
SHELTON, Randall .... 918-456-5511.... 409 A
sheltonr@nsuok.edu
SHELTON, Robby, C .... 931-363-9890.... 470 E
rshelton@martinmethodist.edu
SHELTON, Roosevelt .... 502-597-6415.... 203 D
roosevelt.shelton@kysu.edu
SHELTON, Scott .... 252-328-6964.... 377 C
sheltonj@ecu.edu
SHELTON, Sharron .... 940-552-6291.... 507 E
sshelton@vernoncollege.edu
SHELTON, Tanya, L .... 304-457-6310.... 540 B
sheltontl@ab.edu
SHELTON, Terri, L .... 336-256-0426.... 379 A
shelton@uncg.edu
SHELTON, Treva .... 812-866-7056.... 171 F
shelton@hanover.edu
SHELTON, Vickie .... 806-371-5017.... 479 H
vlshelton@actx.edu
SHELTON, W. Brian .... 706-886-6831.... 137 G
bshelton@tfc.edu
SHELTON-CLARK, Anne ..... 662-621-4220.... 273 I
ashelton-clark@coahomacc.edu
SHEMMER, Rosalie .... 914-323-5484.... 340 A
shemmerr@mville.edu
SHEMTOV, Kasriel .... 248-414-6900.... 255 B
rabbi@theshul.net
SHEMWELL, James .... 870-762-3134...... 20 A
jshemwell@smail.anc.edu
SHEMWELL, Latasha .... 270-926-4040.... 199 K
lshemwell@daymarcollege.edu
SHEN, Shiji .... 908-737-3470.... 311 B
sshen@kean.edu
SHEN, Sunny .... 516-739-1545.... 343 C
academic_dean@nyctcm.edu
SHENDY, Jo Ellen .... 858-642-8024...... 58 I
jshendy@nu.edu
SHENETTE, John .... 413-585-2400.... 245 B
jshenett@smith.edu
SHENK, Sara, W .... 574-295-3726.... 169 C
swshenk@ambs.edu

SHENNAN, Andrew .... 781-283-3583.... 246 B
ashennan@wellesley.edu
SHENODA, Matthew .... 661-255-1050...... 32 C
shenoda@calarts.edu
SHENOY, Kallya .... 661-654-3425...... 33 H
SHENTON, Helen .... 617-495-3650.... 235 H
helen_shenton@harvard.edu
SHEPARD, Bruce .... 360-650-3480.... 539 C
president@wwu.edu
SHEPARD, II, Charles .... 419-434-4628.... 404 B
shepard@findlay.edu
SHEPARD, Dave .... 757-221-2255.... 517 J
dbshep@wm.edu
SHEPARD, James, P .... 334-844-1007........ 1 G
jshepard@auburn.edu
SHEPARD, Julie .... 412-396-5894.... 428 C
shepardj@duq.edu
SHEPARD, Kathy, J .... 717-728-2261.... 425 A
kathyshepard@centralpenn.edu
SHEPARD, Ken .... 570-586-2400.... 422 F
kshepard@bbc.edu
SHEPARD, Loretta .... 303-492-6937...... 88 B
lorrie.shepard@colorado.edu
SHEPARD, Nancy .... 530-938-5331...... 42 C
shepard@siskiyous.edu
SHEPARD, Richard, K .... 303-477-7240...... 84 I
rshepard@heritage-education.com
SHEPARD, Robert, S .... 919-684-3363.... 363 I
robert.shepard@duke.edu
SHEPARD, Robin .... 209-381-6470...... 57 C
shepard.r@mccd.edu
SHEPARD, Thom .... 704-337-2464.... 375 G
shepardt@queens.edu
SHEPARD-SMITH, Andrew 931-221-7881.... 473 D
shepardsmitha@apsu.edu
SHEPARDSON, Andrew, J . 781-891-2161.... 231 F
ashepardson@bentley.edu
SHEPARDSON, J. Andrew . 781-891-2161.... 231 F
ashepardson@bentley.edu
SHEPARDSON, Timothy, M .... 715-738-3852.... 553 F
tshepardson@cvtc.edu
SHEPAS, Rick .... 724-852-3245.... 451 B
SHEPELSKY, Ernie .... 718-429-6600.... 359 E
ernie.shepelsky@vaughn.edu
SHEPERD, Marilyn .... 314-889-4701.... 282 C
msheperd@fontbonne.edu
SHEPHARD, Debra .... 605-882-5284.... 464 D
shephard@lakeareatech.edu
SHEPHERD, Candace, H .... 334-271-1670........ 6 D
cshepherd@princeinstitute.edu
SHEPHERD, Chad .... 314-367-8700.... 288 I
cshepherd@stlcop.edu
SHEPHERD, Gay .... 931-372-3234.... 474 B
gshepherd@tntech.edu
SHEPHERD, Gregory, J ...... 305-284-3420.... 122 F
shepherd@miami.edu
SHEPHERD, Janet .... 563-589-3775.... 189 B
jshepher@dbq.edu
SHEPHERD, Janet .... 563-425-5788.... 189 C
shepherdj@uiu.edu
SHEPHERD, Joseph, E .... 626-395-5802...... 32 E
joseph.e.shepherd@caltech.edu
SHEPHERD, Judy .... 434-949-1049.... 527 H
judy.shepherd@southside.edu
SHEPHERD, Karla, M .... 410-837-5744.... 229 A
kshepherd@ubalt.edu
SHEPHERD, Kila .... 406-444-0845.... 295 C
kila.shepherd@umhelena.edu
SHEPHERD, Margaret, A .... 206-543-7604.... 538 F
mshep@uw.edu
SHEPHERD, Nancy .... 505-566-3264.... 320 D
shepherdn@sanjuancollege.edu
SHEPHERD, Paul .... 715-425-4444.... 552 A
paul.shepherd@uwrf.edu
SHEPHERD, Susan, B .... 330-363-4349.... 384 G
sshepherd@aultman.com
SHEPHERD, Tamara, A .... 703-461-1723.... 522 C
tshepherd@vts.edu
SHEPHERD, Teanca .... 724-503-1001.... 451 A
tshepherd@washjeff.edu
SHEPHERD-GREGG, Debbie .... 740-392-6868.... 396 H
dshepher@mvnu.edu
SHEPPARD, Beth .... 847-328-9300.... 164 B
beth.sheppard@seabury.edu
SHEPPARD, Beth, M .... 847-866-3877.... 151 B
beth.sheppard@garrett.edu
SHEPPARD, Blair, H .... 919-660-7725.... 363 I
blair.sheppard@dukece.edu
SHEPPARD, Charles .... 714-459-1152...... 78 C
csheppard@wsulaw.edu
SHEPPARD, Elizabeth .... 478-387-4882.... 130 E
SHEPPARD, Ellen .... 704-355-5316.... 363 B
ellen.sheppard@carolinascollege.edu
SHEPPARD, Ellen .... 704-355-5316.... 363 B
ellen.sheppard@carolinashealthcare.org
SHEPPARD, Eric, J .... 757-727-6970.... 519 C
eric.sheppard@hamptonu.edu
SHEPPARD, James, A .... 620-229-6227.... 196 C
james.sheppard@sckans.edu
SHEPPARD, Matt .... 218-299-6519.... 267 G
matt.sheppard@minnesota.edu

SHEPPARD, Nancy .... 412-809-5100.... 444 F
sheppard@pti.edu
SHEPPARD, Phillip .... 508-588-9100.... 240 E
SHEPPARD, Tina, F .... 573-341-4218.... 292 A
tinas@mst.edu
SHEPPARD, Vicki .... 336-917-5090.... 376 C
vicki.sheppard@salem.edu
SHEPPERD, Rhonda .... 304-253-7351.... 541 D
shepperd@mountainstate.edu
SHEPPERSON, Dale .... 317-632-5553.... 177 E
dshepperson@lincolntech.com
SHEPROW, Lauren .... 631-632-4896.... 352 C
lauren.sheprow@stonybrook.edu
SHER, Daniel, P .... 303-492-7505...... 88 B
daniel.sher@colorado.edu
SHER, Ephraim, Y .... 845-434-5240.... 361 L
esher@fallsburgyeshiva.com
SHERADIN, Pamela .... 315-364-3221.... 360 C
psheridan@wells.edu
SHEREMAN, Sandra .... 562-985-5537...... 35 A
ssherem@csulb.edu
SHEREN, Deborah .... 216-373-5347.... 397 E
dsheren@ndc.edu
SHERER, Michael .... 574-535-7406.... 171 D
msherer@goshen.edu
SHERER, Tyler .... 619-594-2522...... 36 E
tsherer@mail.sdsu.edu
SHERIDAN, Chris .... 216-368-2774.... 386 E
cxs131@case.edu
SHERIDAN, David .... 908-709-7516.... 316 B
sheridan@ucc.edu
SHERIDAN, Debra .... 305-348-6457.... 119 B
debra.sheridan@fiu.edu
SHERIDAN, Eileen .... 617-730-7010.... 243 I
eileen.sheridan@newbury.edu
SHERIDAN, John .... 620-341-5208.... 192 D
jsherida@emporia.edu
SHERIDAN, Maureen, E ..... 570-208-5865.... 432 E
mesherid@kings.edu
SHERIDAN, Neil, G .... 810-762-9728.... 253 I
nsherida@kettering.edu
SHERIDAN, Nora .... 978-556-3616.... 241 B
nsheridan@necc.mass.edu
SHERIDAN, Pamela .... 610-436-3383.... 443 F
psheridan@wcupa.edu
SHERIDON, Paul .... 541-485-1780.... 417 E
paulsheridon@newhope.edu
SHERIFF, Robyn .... 435-613-5233.... 511 E
robyn.sheriff@ceu.edu
SHERIFF-TAYLOR, Patricia 601-979-2127.... 275 A
patricia.sherriff-taylor@jsums.edu
SHERLIN, Joe, H .... 423-439-4210.... 473 E
sherlin@etsu.edu
SHERLOCK, Jean .... 818-733-2600...... 58 J
SHERLOCK, Julia, B .... 989-774-3068.... 249 G
julia.b.sherlock@cmich.edu
SHERMAN, Ann .... 617-243-2162.... 236 F
asherman@lasell.edu
SHERMAN, Ann, M .... 906-227-2330.... 256 F
asherman@nmu.edu
SHERMAN, Cassie .... 312-235-3505.... 164 D
cassie@shimer.edu
SHERMAN, Catherine .... 724-503-1001.... 451 A
csherman@washjeff.edu
SHERMAN, Curt .... 402-643-7369.... 297 F
curt.sherman@cune.edu
SHERMAN, Dawn, C .... 508-213-2440.... 243 J
dawn.sherman@nichols.edu
SHERMAN, Debra .... 985-732-6640.... 211 C
SHERMAN, JR., Douglas .. 401-739-5000.... 453 E
dsherman@neit.edu
SHERMAN, Fred .... 650-949-6119...... 47 F
shermanfred@fhda.edu
SHERMAN, Gary .... 860-231-5360...... 93 H
gsherman@sjc.edu
SHERMAN, George .... 718-631-6273.... 329 A
gsherman@qcc.cuny.edu
SHERMAN, George .... 434-832-7606.... 526 A
shermang@cvcc.vccs.edu
SHERMAN, George, M .... 978-232-2009.... 234 F
gsherman@endicott.edu
SHERMAN, Glen .... 973-720-2761.... 317 D
shermang@wpunj.edu
SHERMAN, Helen .... 803-780-1266.... 463 B
hsherman@voorhees.edu
SHERMAN, Hugh .... 740-593-2000.... 399 G
shermanh@ohio.edu
SHERMAN, III, James .... 605-856-5880.... 465 A
james.sherman@sintegleska.edu
SHERMAN, Jo Lynne .... 509-533-7411.... 532 E
jsherman@scc.spokane.edu
SHERMAN, Julee .... 660-248-6203.... 279 K
jsherman@centralmethodist.edu
SHERMAN, Kristen .... 617-670-4419.... 235 B
ksherman01@fisher.edu
SHERMAN, Linda .... 301-447-5366.... 225 A
lsherman@msmary.edu
SHERMAN, Malcolm .... 781-736-2000.... 233 A
msherman@brandeis.edu
SHERMAN, Mary .... 303-797-5092...... 80 J
mary.sherman@arapahoe.edu
SHERMAN, Mike .... 330-972-7593.... 403 B
provost@uakron.edu

SHERMAN, Robert, A ... 631-656-2117 ... 334 B
rsherman@ftc.edu
SHERMAN, Roger, H ... 631-656-2189 ... 334 B
rhsherman@ftc.edu
SHERMAN, Ruth, D ... 617-333-2364 ... 234 A
rsherman@curry.edu
SHERMAN, Sharon ... 609-896-5120 ... 313 G
sherman@rider.edu
SHERMIS, Mark, D ... 330-972-7680 ... 403 B
shermis@uakron.edu
SHERRARD, Catherine, E ... 812-246-3301 ... 176 H
csherrard@ivytech.edu
SHERRELL, J. Michael ... 865-974-2178 ... 477 B
jsherrel@utk.edu
SHERRELL, Jeff ... 205-226-4939 ... 2 C
jsherrel@bsc.edu
SHERRICK, Rebecca, L ... 630-844-5476 ... 145 C
sherrick@aurora.edu
SHERRILL, Audrey ... 704-922-6223 ... 370 D
sherrill.audrey@gaston.edu
SHERRILL, Christy ... 501-812-2214 ... 23 C
csherrill@pulaskitech.edu
SHERRILL, Jan-Mitchell ... 412-392-8026 ... 444 H
jsherrill@pointpark.edu
SHERRILL, Linda, G ... 517-750-1200 ... 258 F
lsherrill@arbor.edu
SHERROD, Vicki ... 478-289-2105 ... 128 J
vsherrod@ega.edu
SHERRON, Catherine ... 859-344-3387 ... 206 D
catherine.sherron@thomasmore.edu
SHERRY, Jan, P ... 916-568-3042 ... 55 J
sherryj@losrios.edu
SHERRY, Michael ... 716-652-8900 ... 326 A
msherry@cks.edu
SHERRY, Richard, J ... 651-638-6287 ... 261 I
r-sherry@bethel.edu
SHERSTAD, Brian, P ... 616-538-2330 ... 251 F
bsherstad@gbcol.edu
SHERWEN, Laurie ... 215-596-8501 ... 450 A
l.sherwen@usciences.edu
SHERWIN, Paul ... 415-338-1541 ... 36 F
psherwin@sfsu.edu
SHERWOOD, David, G ... 262-646-6535 ... 549 B
dsherwood@nashotah.edu
SHERWOOD, James ... 631-451-4330 ... 356 E
sherwoj@sunysuffolk.edu
SHERWOOD, Marian, D ... 814-332-2983 ... 421 E
marian.sherwood@allegheny.edu
SHERWOOD, Mary ... 361-825-2621 ... 497 F
mary.sherwood@tamucc.edu
SHERWOOD,
Mary Frances ... 337-491-2657 ... 212 C
mary.sherwood@sowela.edu
SHERWOOD, Peter, M ... 405-744-5663 ... 410 C
peter.sherwood@okstate.edu
SHERWOOD, Robbie ... 510-780-4500 ... 53 I
rsherwood@lifewest.edu
SHERWOOD, Susan ... 410-290-7100 ... 223 H
SHESKI, Harry ... 505-287-6641 ... 319 H
hsheski@nmsu.edu
SHESTON, Andy, W ... 757-594-7509 ... 517 I
asheston@cnu.edu
SHETLER, Clay, E ... 574-535-7351 ... 171 D
clayes@goshen.edu
SHEUCRAFT, Derrek, G ... 615-353-3272 ... 475 D
derrek.sheucraft@nscc.edu
SHEVACH, Shirley ... 718-518-6650 ... 327 D
sshevach@hostos.cuny.edu
SHEVRIN, Amy ... 614-222-4000 ... 388 F
ashevrin@ccad.edu
SHEW, Amy, E ... 856-351-2682 ... 315 A
ashew@salemcc.edu
SHEWMAKER, Stephen, M ... 706-542-0006 ... 138 C
sshew@uga.edu
SHI, J. Steve ... 706-542-7912 ... 138 C
sshi@uga.edu
SHI, Yuwei ... 831-647-4155 ... 57 F
yuwei.shi@miis.edu
SHIAO, Jerry ... 408-435-8989 ... 69 G
jshiao@svuca.edu
SHIBA, Margaret ... 808-933-0829 ... 141 A
mshiba@hawaii.edu
SHIBATA, Martin, C ... 805-756-2501 ... 33 F
mshibata@calpoly.edu
SHIBAZAKI, Kozue ... 210-567-2648 ... 506 E
shibazaki@uthscsa.edu
SHIBLEY, Deborah ... 254-526-1347 ... 482 F
deborah.shibley@ctcd.edu
SHIBLEY, Lisa, R ... 717-871-2390 ... 443 C
lisa.shibley@millersville.edu
SHIBLEY, Robert ... 716-829-3981 ... 351 G
rshibley@buffalo.edu
SHIBUYA, Hisatake ... 323-462-1384 ... 58 E
SHICKLE, Richard, C ... 540-665-4533 ... 523 K
rshickle@su.edu
SHIDELER, Lorri, P ... 814-641-3605 ... 431 L
shidell@juniata.edu
SHIDEMANTLE, Ronald, C ... 412-397-3408 ... 445 G
shidemantle@rmu.edu
SHIEH, Charles ... 863-638-2975 ... 123 C
shiehc@webber.edu
SHIELDS, Brenda ... 610-399-2080 ... 441 H
bshields@cheyney.edu
SHIELDS, Brian ... 301-552-1400 ... 229 C
bshields@bible.edu
SHIELDS, Carolyn, C ... 313-577-1620 ... 260 D
SHIELDS, Daniel ... 845-848-7818 ... 332 C
daniel.shields@dc.edu
SHIELDS, JR., David, P ... 256-765-4223 ... 9 D
dpshields@una.edu
SHIELDS, Deanna, J ... 304-367-4775 ... 543 E
deanna.shields@fairmontstate.edu
SHIELDS, Dennis, J ... 608-342-1234 ... 551 F
shieldsd@uwplatt.edu
SHIELDS, Francis ... 860-439-2570 ... 91 E
fjshi@conncoll.edu
SHIELDS, Geoffrey, B ... 802-831-1237 ... 515 A
jshields@vermontlaw.edu
SHIELDS, George, C ... 570-577-3292 ... 423 D
george.shields@bucknell.edu
SHIELDS, Gregory, J ... 803-799-9082 ... 461 A
gshields@southuniversity.edu
SHIELDS, Jerri ... 575-392-5018 ... 319 B
jshields@nmjc.edu
SHIELDS, Joan ... 201-761-6475 ... 314 F
jshields@spc.edu
SHIELDS, Jonathan ... 402-486-2897 ... 300 D
joshield@ucollege.edu
SHIELDS, Joseph ... 740-593-0371 ... 399 G
SHIELDS, Katie ... 610-660-1231 ... 446 C
kshields@sju.edu
SHIELDS, Lauren ... 410-386-8442 ... 221 G
lshields@carrollcc.edu
SHIELDS, Michelle ... 517-787-0800 ... 253 E
shieldsmichellm@jccmi.edu
SHIELDS, Michelle ... 517-780-4550 ... 248 I
michelle.shields@baker.edu
SHIELDS, Pete ... 478-445-5651 ... 129 F
pete.shields@gcsu.edu
SHIELDS, Peter, C ... 781-736-4520 ... 233 A
pshields@brandeis.edu
SHIELDS, Portia, H ... 615-963-7401 ... 474 A
president@tnstate.edu
SHIELDS, Ronald ... 402-363-5661 ... 301 F
ron.shields@york.edu
SHIELDS, Sally ... 309-649-6250 ... 165 D
sally.shields@src.edu
SHIELDS, Theodosia, T ... 919-530-5233 ... 378 A
tshields@nccu.edu
SHIELDS, Todd ... 479-575-5900 ... 24 C
tshild@uark.edu
SHIELDS, Vickie ... 509-359-6081 ... 533 D
vshields@ewu.edu
SHIELDS, William, A ... 814-827-4420 ... 449 E
was14@pitt.edu
SHIELL, Steve ... 907-834-1622 ... 11 B
sshiell@pwscc.edu
SHIFFERT, John ... 678-466-4460 ... 127 A
johnshiffert@clayton.edu
SHIFFLER, Ronald ... 912-478-7412 ... 131 A
shiffler@georgiasouthern.edu
SHIFFLER, Ronald ... 912-478-2622 ... 131 A
shiffler@georgiasouthern.edu
SHIFFLETT, Lee, A ... 540-568-7926 ... 520 C
shiffla@jmu.edu
SHIFFLETT, Pamela, D ... 540-423-9039 ... 526 E
pshifflett@germanna.edu
SHIFFMAN, Paul ... 518-464-8803 ... 333 F
pshiffman@excelsior.edu
SHIFLETT, Matt ... 304-457-6256 ... 540 B
shiflettmk@ab.edu
SHIGEHARA, Deborah ... 808-974-7531 ... 141 F
deborahs@hawaii.edu
SHIKOSKI, Richard, L ... 608-757-7759 ... 553 E
dshikoski@blackhawk.edu
SHILL, Deb ... 641-269-3230 ... 185 A
shilldeb@grinnell.edu
SHILLET, Gary ... 212-592-2000 ... 350 F
gshillet@sva.edu
SHILS, Nancy ... 215-895-1106 ... 450 A
n.shils@usciences.edu
SHIMABUKURO, Julie ... 314-935-4893 ... 292 J
jshimabukuro@wustl.edu
SHIMALA, Deanne ... 219-473-4310 ... 170 D
dshimala@ccsj.edu
SHIMEK, Dennis, W ... 209-667-3351 ... 36 C
dshimek@csustan.edu
SHIMEK, Gary, S ... 414-277-7181 ... 548 H
shimek@msoe.edu
SHIMIZU, Jeffery ... 310-434-4317 ... 68 D
shimizu_jeffery@smc.edu
SHIMIZU, Stacey ... 309-556-3190 ... 153 E
abroad@iwu.edu
SHIMMEL, Debra, L ... 717-815-1232 ... 452 F
dshimmel@ycp.edu
SHIMMEL, Kurt ... 724-738-2008 ... 443 E
kurt.shimmel@sru.edu
SHIMROCK, Dana ... 301-387-3003 ... 222 H
dana.shimrock@garrettcollege.edu
SHIMSHAK, Susan ... 414-256-1210 ... 549 A
shimshas@mtmary.edu
SHIN, David, H ... 714-527-0691 ... 45 J
info@evangelia.edu
SHIN, Jason ... 714-533-3946 ... 37 C
jshin@calums.edu
SHIN, Jason ... 714-533-1495 ... 70 B
jshin@southbaylo.edu
SHINAGEL, Michael ... 617-495-2930 ... 235 H
michael_shinagel@harvard.edu
SHINBERGER, Darcie, R ... 309-298-1993 ... 168 A
dr-shinberger@wiu.edu
SHINDELL, J. Robert ... 512-505-3030 ... 488 B
rshindell@htu.edu
SHINDLER, Kenda E, G ... 573-592-4216 ... 293 E
kshindle@williamwoods.edu
SHINE, Kenneth, I ... 512-499-4224 ... 504 E
kshine@utsystem.edu
SHINER, Mark ... 315-228-7680 ... 329 H
mshiner@colgate.edu
SHINER WILSON, Carol ... 484-664-3130 ... 437 B
cwilson@muhlenberg.edu
SHINGLE, Betty ... 724-222-5330 ... 438 E
bshingle@penncommercial.edu
SHINGLES, Samuel, D ... 662-254-3435 ... 276 C
SHINGLES, Stan, L ... 989-774-3686 ... 249 G
shing1sl@cmich.edu
SHINN, Clinton, W ... 276-935-4349 ... 516 A
wshinn@asl.edu
SHINN, David ... 217-641-4514 ... 154 G
dshinn@jwcc.edu
SHINN, Larry, D ... 859-985-3520 ... 198 F
larry_shinn@berea.edu
SHINVILLE, Padriac ... 309-268-8000 ... 151 G
padriac.shinville@heartland.edu
SHIPES, Bertie ... 912-427-5800 ... 124 A
bshipes@altamahatech.edu
SHIPLEY, Aletha ... 614-287-2640 ... 388 G
ashipley@cscc.edu
SHIPLEY, David ... 205-726-2064 ... 6 G
dsshiple@samford.edu
SHIPLEY, Donna, M ... 724-653-2202 ... 427 F
dshipley@dec.edu
SHIPLEY, John, R ... 305-284-6297 ... 122 F
jshipley@miami.edu
SHIPLEY, Robert ... 918-631-3092 ... 413 F
robert-shipley@utulsa.edu
SHIPLEY, Suzanne ... 304-876-5107 ... 544 A
sshipley@shepherd.edu
SHIPMAN, Doug ... 618-395-7777 ... 152 H
shipmand@iecc.edu
SHIPMAN, Jean, P ... 801-581-8771 ... 510 L
jean.shipman@utah.edu
SHIPMAN, Richard ... 517-353-5940 ... 255 D
shipmanr@msu.edu
SHIPP, Ben ... 254-295-4618 ... 504 A
bshipp@umhb.edu
SHIPP, Judith ... 217-206-7122 ... 167 A
shipp.judy@uis.edu
SHIPP, Kevin ... 325-235-7337 ... 500 C
kevin.shipp@tstc.edu
SHIPP, Melvin, D ... 614-292-3246 ... 398 H
shipp.25@osu.edu
SHIPP, Tina ... 251-981-3771 ... 2 H
tina.shipp@columbiasouthern.edu
SHIPPEE, Ellen ... 603-535-2255 ... 307 B
eshippee@plymouth.edu
SHIPPEN, Tyler ... 312-777-7600 ... 144 H
tshippen@argosy.edu
SHIPPEY, JR., Robert, C ... 276-326-4202 ... 516 I
rshippey@bluefield.edu
SHIPPS, Mark, H ... 740-368-3310 ... 400 F
mhshipps@owu.edu
SHIPSHOCK, Amy ... 651-675-4700 ... 264 H
ashipshock@twincitiesculainary.com
SHIPULA, Anthony, J ... 570-675-9107 ... 440 E
ajs39@psu.edu
SHIPWAY, Ann, M ... 304-260-4380 ... 542 C
ashipway@blueridgectc.edu
SHIRACHI, Susan ... 808-933-0816 ... 141 A
shirachi@hawaii.edu
SHIRAH, Hank ... 850-484-2500 ... 114 G
hshirah@pensacolastate.edu
SHIRAI, Calvin ... 808-245-8333 ... 141 H
shiraic@hawaii.edu
SHIRAS, Susan ... 805-966-3888 ... 31 A
sshiras@brooks.edu
SHIRAZI, Rhonda ... 251-380-2255 ... 7 F
rshirazi@shc.edu
SHIREMAN, Kimberly ... 336-342-4261 ... 373 B
shiremank@rockinghamcc.edu
SHIRES, William ... 304-647-6273 ... 544 C
wshires@osteo.wvsom.edu
SHIREY, Benton ... 859-622-3311 ... 200 D
benton.shirey@eku.edu
SHIREY, Bo ... 740-446-4367 ... 391 B
bshirey@gallipoliscareercollege.edu
SHIREY, Brian, D ... 302-739-4064 ... 96 A
bshirey@dtcc.edu
SHIREY, Jeanette ... 740-446-4367 ... 391 B
finaid@gallipoliscareercollege.edu
SHIREY, Robert, L ... 740-446-4367 ... 391 B
gcc@gallipoliscareercollege.edu
SHIRK, Wendy ... 918-495-7742 ... 411 C
wshirk@oru.edu
SHIRLEY, Amy ... 617-730-7158 ... 243 I
amy.shirley@newbury.edu
SHIRLEY, Curtis, D ... 217-424-3965 ... 158 F
cshirley@millikin.edu
SHIRLEY, Dana, R ... 816-501-2410 ... 279 C
dana.shirley@avila.edu
SHIRLEY, Dustin ... 425-889-5206 ... 535 I
dustin.shirley@northwestu.edu
SHIRLEY, John ... 607-753-7668 ... 353 B
john.shirley@cortland.edu
SHIRLEY, Kelly ... 704-355-4275 ... 363 B
kelly.shirley@carolinashealthcare.org
SHIRLEY, Natalie ... 405-947-3230 ... 410 F
SHIRLEY, Phil, E ... 806-874-4800 ... 482 H
phil.shirley@clarendoncollege.edu
SHIRLEY, Robert ... 334-387-3877 ... 1 D
robertshirley@amridgeuniversity.edu
SHIRLEY, Steven, W ... 701-845-7102 ... 382 A
steven.shirley@vcsu.edu
SHIRLEY, JR., Thomas, R ... 215-951-2720 ... 444 C
shirleyt@philau.edu
SHIRLEY, Vikki ... 850-245-0466 ... 118 F
vikki.shirley@flbog.edu
SHIRVANI, Hamid ... 209-667-3201 ... 36 C
president@csustan.edu
SHISIDO, Jack, L ... 831-656-2192 ... 557 H
jlshishi@nps.edu
SHISLER, Kirk, L ... 540-432-4203 ... 518 E
kirk.shisler@emu.edu
SHISLER-RAPP, Susan, M ... 610-359-5040 ... 426 G
srapp@dccc.edu
SHIVELY, Bruce, L ... 775-784-6516 ... 303 A
shively@unr.edu
SHIVELY, C. Randall ... 618-437-5321 ... 162 B
shively@rlc.edu
SHIVELY, Marnie ... 209-588-5105 ... 80 A
shively@yosemite.edu
SHIVERS, Sandra ... 914-594-3723 ... 343 F
sandra_shivers@nymc.edu
SHIVOKEVICH, Heather ... 631-244-3318 ... 332 D
shivokeh@dowling.edu
SHKOP, Esther ... 773-973-0241 ... 151 H
shkop@htc.edu
SHLAFER, David ... 352-395-5486 ... 117 E
david.shlafer@sfcollege.edu
SHMIDMAN, Michael, A ... 212-463-0400 ... 357 J
michaels@touro.edu
SHNIDMAN, Avrohom ... 410-484-7200 ... 225 C
SHOAF, Victoria, L ... 718-990-6800 ... 348 G
shoafv@stjohns.edu
SHOCK, Stephanie ... 701-662-1655 ... 382 D
stephanie.shock@lrsc.edu
SHOCKEY, James, W ... 520-626-2422 ... 10 B
jshockey@email.arizona.edu
SHOCKEY, Sherri, L ... 260-982-5237 ... 177 F
slshockey@manchester.edu
SHOCKLEY, Darlas ... 641-683-5174 ... 185 D
dshockle@indianhills.edu
SHOCKLEY, David, R ... 828-726-2214 ... 368 D
dshockley@cccti.edu
SHOCKLEY, Robin, L ... 614-234-5213 ... 396 G
rshockley@mccn.edu
SHOCKLEY-ZALABAK,
Pam ... 719-255-3436 ... 88 C
exec1@uccs.edu
SHOE, Maurice (Buddy) ... 405-691-3800 ... 408 H
bshoe@macu.edu
SHOEMAKE, James, M ... 214-388-5466 ... 485 D
difs@dallasinstitute.edu
SHOEMAKE, Kellie ... 910-695-3714 ... 373 E
shoemakek@sandhills.edu
SHOEMAKE, Monte ... 417-626-1234 ... 287 F
shoemake.monte@occ.edu
SHOEMAKER, Chris ... 229-732-5912 ... 124 C
chaplain@andrewcollege.edu
SHOEMAKER, Chris ... 276-326-4212 ... 516 I
cshoemaker@bluefield.edu
SHOEMAKER, Cindy ... 717-262-2006 ... 452 B
cshoemaker@wilson.edu
SHOEMAKER, Lorna ... 317-931-2365 ... 170 E
lshoemaker@cts.edu
SHOEMAKER, Norm ... 619-849-2784 ... 62 L
normshoemaker@pointloma.edu
SHOEMAKER, Patricia, B ... 540-831-5439 ... 522 D
pshoemak@radford.edu
SHOEMAKER, Peter ... 202-319-5220 ... 97 C
shoemaker@cua.edu
SHOEMAKER, Polly ... 803-754-4100 ... 457 D
SHOEMAKER, Scott ... 619-849-2565 ... 62 L
scottshoemaker@pointloma.edu
SHOENBERGER, George ... 301-985-7124 ... 227 F
cfo@umuc.edu
SHOENER, Gary ... 570-504-7949 ... 433 A
shoenerg@lackawanna.edu
SHOENER, Pattie ... 504-282-4455 ... 213 H
pshoener@nobts.edu
SHOESMITH, Meighan ... 425-558-0299 ... 533 C
smeighan@digipen.edu
SHOFIELD, Joanna ... 513-785-3024 ... 396 E
shofiej@muohio.edu
SHOFIELD, Joanna ... 513-785-3024 ... 396 F
SHOGE, Ruth, C ... 410-778-7292 ... 229 D
rshoge2@washcoll.edu
SHOGER, Diane, L ... 585-262-1504 ... 341 H
dshoger@monroecc.edu
SHOJAI, Siamack ... 860-832-3228 ... 91 G
shojaisia@ccsu.edu
SHOLOCK, Adale ... 610-436-2122 ... 443 F
asholock@wcupa.edu

SHOLTEN, Bryan .... 303-963-3398 .... 81 K bsholten@ccu.edu

SHOMAKER, Darrell .... 540-985-8362 .... 520 D dkshomaker@jchs.edu

SHOMAKER, T, S .... 512-324-7377 .... 507 B tsshomak@utmb.edu

SHOMAKER, Thomas, S .... 979-436-0201 .... 496 G Shomaker@medicine.tamhsc.edu

SHOMAN, Marta .... 719-589-7023 .... 87 J marta.shoman@trinidadstate.edu

SHOMO, Thomas, H .... 434-223-6262 .... 519 B tshomo@hsc.edu

SHOMOUR, Carlisa .... 505-346-2346 .... 321 B cshomour@sipi.bia.edu

SHONBRUN, Anne .... 718-270-4551 .... 352 D anne.shonbrun@downstate.edu

SHONESY, Linda .... 256-216-3366 .... 1 F linda.shonesy@athens.edu

SHONKWILER, David, L ..... 608-246-6801 .... 554 B dshonkwiler@matcmadison.edu

SHONTZ, Gary, B .... 319-273-3576 .... 182 D gary.shontz@uni.edu

SHONTZ, Susan, F .... 814-641-3304 .... 431 L shontzs@juniata.edu

SHOOP, David .... 803-799-9082 .... 461 A dshoop@southuniversity.edu

SHOOT, Madge .... 217-234-5375 .... 155 H mbailey1292@lakeland.cc.il.us

SHOPE, Mark .... 334-556-2295 .... 4 A mshope@wallace.edu

SHOPE, Mary Ann .... 501-907-6670 .... 23 C mashope@pulaskitech.edu

SHOPE, Ronald, J .... 402-449-2872 .... 298 B rshope@graceu.edu

SHOPSHIRE, Sandra .... 208-282-2997 .... 143 D shopsand@isu.edu

SHOPTAW, Merrell, E .... 479-968-0218 .... 20 G mshoptaw@atu.edu

SHOQUIST, Carmen .... 763-424-0902 .... 268 D cshoquist@nhcc.edu

SHOR, Mark .... 212-463-0400 .... 357 J mshor@touro.edu

SHOR, Stuart, B .... 212-817-7604 .... 327 B sshor@gc.cuny.edu

SHORB, Deanna .... 641-269-4981 .... 185 A shorb@grinnell.edu

SHORB, Stephen .... 402-554-2640 .... 301 B sshorb@unomaha.edu

SHORE, Cecilia, M .... 513-529-9266 .... 396 D shorec@muohio.edu

SHORE, Daniel .... 617-496-2650 .... 235 H dan_shore@harvard.edu

SHORE, Elliott .... 610-526-5270 .... 423 C eshore@brynmawr.edu

SHORE, Jim .... 412-521-6200 .... 445 H jim.shore@rosedaletech.org

SHORE, Michael, J .... 815-599-3491 .... 152 A mike.shore@highland.edu

SHORE, Muriel .... 201-559-6030 .... 310 C shorem@felician.edu

SHORE, Sara .... 612-798-3757 .... 265 G sshore@msbcollege.edu

SHORES, Dennis .... 610-647-4400 .... 431 B dshores@immaculata.edu

SHORES, Jonathan .... 828-669-8012 .... 367 C jeshores@montreat.edu

SHORES, Robin, H .... 610-690-6879 .... 447 E rshores1@swarthmore.edu

SHOREY, David .... 978-468-7111 .... 235 F shorey@gcts.edu

SHORT, Al .... 303-861-1151 .... 83 G ashort@concorde.edu

SHORT, Andrea .... 217-732-3168 .... 156 F ashort@lincolnchristian.edu

SHORT, Anthony, E .... 419-372-7019 .... 385 C ashort@bgsu.edu

SHORT, Brent .... 352-588-8258 .... 116 E brent.short@saintleo.edu

SHORT, Donna .... 828-652-0631 .... 371 G donnasho@mcdowelltech.edu

SHORT, Donna .... 828-652-0631 .... 371 G donnas@mcdowelltech.edu

SHORT, Emily .... 615-230-3477 .... 476 A emily.short@volstate.edu

SHORT, Emily .... 615-230-3447 .... 476 A emily.short@volstate.edu

SHORT, Evelyn .... 360-417-6381 .... 536 B eshort@pencol.edu

SHORT, Frank .... 585-395-2350 .... 352 F fshort@brockport.edu

SHORT, John .... 920-929-3602 .... 552 F john.short@uwc.edu

SHORT, Kyla .... 918-343-7865 .... 411 H kshort@rsu.edu

SHORT, Myriah .... 740-753-7020 .... 392 A short_m@hocking.edu

SHORT, Rosanna .... 623-935-8941 .... 15 H rosanna.short@estrellamountain.edu

SHORT, Royce, B .... 864-242-5100 .... 455 E

SHORT, Susan .... 651-757-4003 .... 263 A sshort@cva.edu

SHORT, Trey .... 309-556-3017 .... 153 E tshort@iwu.edu

SHORT, William .... 407-646-2619 .... 116 B wshort@rollins.edu

SHORT, SM, William .... 510-848-5232 .... 47 I wshort@fst.edu

SHORT-THOMPSON, Cady 513-745-5660 .... 403 F shortcw@ucmail.uc.edu

SHORTBULL, Thomas, H ... 605-455-6022 .... 464 H tshortb@olc.edu

SHORTELL, Stephen, M ..... 510-642-2082 .... 73 E shortell@berkeley.edu

SHORTER, William, H .... 540-831-5794 .... 522 D wshorter@radford.edu

SHORTER-GOODEN, Kumea .... 626-284-2777 .... 27 D kshorter-gooden@alliant.edu

SHORTY, Ursula .... 225-771-2790 .... 214 H ursula_shorty@subr.edu

SHOSTACK, Pauline .... 315-498-2708 .... 345 D

SHOTICK, Joyce .... 309-677-2422 .... 145 H jas@bradley.edu

SHOTSBERGER, Paul .... 864-644-5354 .... 461 B pshotsberger@swu.edu

SHOTT, Brandy .... 704-233-8028 .... 380 D b.shott@wingate.edu

SHOTT, Diane, T .... 276-326-4201 .... 516 I dshott@bluefield.edu

SHOTWELL SMITH, Mary . 706-233-7278 .... 136 E msmith@shorter.edu

SHOUDY, Peter, D .... 610-499-1036 .... 96 H ppshoudy@widener.edu

SHOUDY, Peter, D .... 610-499-1036 .... 451 F pdshoudy@widener.edu

SHOULDIS, Martha, K .... 203-576-5277 .... 94 A mshouldis@stvincentscollege.edu

SHOUN, Stan .... 314-286-4801 .... 288 B sshoun@ranken.edu

SHOUP, John .... 951-343-4205 .... 31 G jshoup@calbaptist.edu

SHOUP, Terry .... 408-554-6940 .... 68 C tshoup@scu.edu

SHOURDS, Rita, H .... 812-246-3301 .... 176 H rshourds@ivytech.edu

SHOURESHI, Rahmat .... 516-686-7630 .... 343 D

SHOVLAIN, Raymond, J .... 563-333-6233 .... 188 D ShovlainRaymondJ@sau.edu

SHOWALTER, Marc, K .... 662-915-3784 .... 277 G mshowalt@olemiss.edu

SHOWALTER, Martha .... 734-973-3722 .... 260 B showalter@wccnet.edu

SHOWALTER, Rodney, J .... 540-338-1776 .... 522 A

SHOWALTER, Stephanie .... 215-836-2222 .... 422 A finaid@antonelli.edu

SHOWELL, JR., Charles .... 937-376-6441 .... 386 H cshowell@centralstate.edu

SHOWELL, Jeffrey, A .... 419-372-8603 .... 385 C jashowe@bgsu.edu

SHOWERS, Anita .... 434-961-6574 .... 527 F ashowers@pvcc.edu

SHOWERS, Jerel .... 713-973-3034 .... 486 A jshowers@devry.edu

SHOWERS, Shane .... 315-568-3125 .... 342 H sshowers@nycc.edu

SHOWS, Alicia .... 601-276-2000 .... 277 E showsa@smcc.edu

SHOWS, Deidre .... 601-318-6583 .... 278 E dede.shows@wmcarey.edu

SHOWS, John .... 601-928-6397 .... 275 G john.shows1@mgcc.edu

SHOWS-PEREZ, Cindy .... 337-482-6497 .... 216 D cperez@louisiana.edu

SHPER, Paul .... 802-322-1656 .... 513 C paul.shper@goddard.edu

SHRAGG, Diane .... 619-239-0391 .... 37 D dshragg@cwsl.edu

SHRAUNER, Bob, L .... 816-604-6538 .... 285 E bob.shrauner@mcckc.edu

SHREFFLER, Christine .... 314-344-4440 .... 285 K cshreff@aol.com

SHREVE, Harlan, N .... 304-788-6922 .... 545 A hnshreve@mail.wvu.edu

SHREVE, Teresa .... 205-348-7625 .... 8 F tshreve@bama.ua.edu

SHREVES, Phillip .... 660-543-4040 .... 291 B pshreves@ucmo.edu

SHRIDHAR, Malayppan ..... 313-593-5030 .... 259 E mals@umd.umich.edu

SHRIER, Douglas, M .... 540-868-7199 .... 526 H dshrier@lfcc.edu

SHRIMPTON, Nikki .... 315-472-5730 .... 355 F nikki.shrimpton@esc.edu

SHRINER, Michael, B .... 409-772-3501 .... 507 B mshriner@utmb.edu

SHRIVER, Michael .... 970-542-3174 .... 86 A michael.shriver@morgancc.edu

SHRIVER, Michaele .... 804-862-6212 .... 523 C mshriver@rbc.edu

SHRODE, Scott .... 828-328-7108 .... 366 B scott.shrode@lr.edu

SHROKA, Julie .... 847-543-2847 .... 147 H julieshroka@clcillinois.edu

SHROPSHIRE, Kevin .... 276-656-0288 .... 527 D

SHROPSHIRE, Martin, W ... 336-386-3453 .... 374 B shropsm@surry.edu

SHROYER, Margaret (Peg) . 320-308-5030 .... 269 D pshroyer@sctcc.edu

SHRUBB, Richard .... 507-372-3491 .... 268 B richard.shrubb@mnwest.edu

SHRUM, Kayse .... 918-561-8201 .... 410 D kayse.shrum@okstate.edu

SHU, Wen Li .... 913-621-8767 .... 192 C wshu@donnelly.edu

SHUBERT, Bruce .... 785-532-6226 .... 194 B bshubert@ksu.edu

SHUBERT, David .... 316-942-4291 .... 195 C shubertd@newmanu.edu

SHUBERT, Lisa, A .... 507-344-7324 .... 261 H lshubert@blc.edu

SHUCK, Richard .... 765-658-4020 .... 170 I dickshuck@depauw.edu

SHUFORD, Bettina .... 919-966-4045 .... 378 D bcshufor@email.unc.edu

SHUFORD, Eddie .... 828-652-0652 .... 371 G eddieshuford@mcdowelltech.edu

SHUFORD, Frank, S .... 336-838-6420 .... 375 A frank.shuford@wilkescc.edu

SHUFORD, Susan .... 828-898-8841 .... 366 A shufords@lmc.edu

SHUGART, Carol .... 912-287-5809 .... 135 B cshugart@okefenokeetech.edu

SHUGART, Sanford, C .... 407-582-3250 .... 122 I sshugart@valenciacollege.edu

SHUJAA, Mwalimu .... 225-771-4582 .... 214 H mwalimu_shujaa@subr.edu

SHULAMITH, Mellman .... 815-836-5455 .... 156 D mellmash@lewisu.edu

SHULL, A. Hope .... 731-989-6067 .... 468 K hshull@fhu.edu

SHULL, Craig, L .... 706-233-7203 .... 136 E cshull@shorter.edu

SHULL, Roger .... 806-894-9611 .... 494 C rshull@southplainscollege.edu

SHULL, Roxanna .... 260-459-4600 .... 175 A rshull@ibcfortwayne.edu

SHULMAN, Brian .... 973-275-2168 .... 315 B brian.shulman@shu.edu

SHULMAN, Jacob .... 732-367-1060 .... 307 H yshulman@bmg.edu

SHULNAK, Jody .... 360-992-2447 .... 532 A jshulnak@clark.edu

SHULTES, Kenneth, E .... 717-245-1272 .... 427 E shultes@dickinson.edu

SHULTIS, Terri .... 415-442-7079 .... 48 E tshultis@ggu.edu

SHULTS, Charlene .... 432-552-2370 .... 507 C shults_c@utpb.edu

SHULTS, Joel .... 719-587-7901 .... 80 F jshults@adams.edu

SHULTZ, Cathleen, M .... 501-279-4475 .... 21 H shultz@harding.edu

SHULTZ, Christopher .... 949-824-5337 .... 73 H chris.shultz@uci.edu

SHULTZ, Edward .... 808-956-8922 .... 141 B shultz@hawaii.edu

SHULTZ, John, C .... 419-289-5160 .... 384 D jshultz@ashland.edu

SHULTZ, Kari .... 423-236-2484 .... 473 A kshultz@southern.edu

SHULTZ, Richard, D .... 608-342-1561 .... 551 F shultz@uwplatt.edu

SHULTZ, Walter, J .... 570-326-3761 .... 440 K wshultz@pct.edu

SHULUK, William .... 239-489-9356 .... 104 L wshuluk@edison.edu

SHUMAKE, Connie, C .... 502-852-3551 .... 207 A ccshum01@louisville.edu

SHUMAKER, Anne .... 276-466-7869 .... 528 G anneshumaker@vic.edu

SHUMAKER, Anne, W .... 276-466-7868 .... 528 G anneshumaker@vic.edu

SHUMAKER, Deb .... 989-275-5000 .... 253 K deb.shumaker@kirtland.edu

SHUMAKER, Elizabeth .... 512-404-4803 .... 481 D eshumaker@austinseminary.edu

SHUMAKER, Jeffrey .... 304-384-5266 .... 543 D jshumaker@concord.edu

SHUMAKER, Lisa .... 412-372-3900 .... 424 D director2@careerta.edu

SHUMAKER, Nancy .... 507-285-7461 .... 269 B nancy.shumaker@roch.edu

SHUMAKER, Steve .... 570-586-2400 .... 422 F sshumaker@bbc.edu

SHUMAN, Jenny .... 478-296-6117 .... 134 G jshuman@oftc.edu

SHUMAN, Michaeline, M .. 814-332-2381 .... 421 E michaeline.shuman@allegheny.edu

SHUMAN, Ruth .... 617-243-2140 .... 236 F rshuman@lasell.edu

SHUMAN, Shari, A .... 904-620-2002 .... 120 C sshuman@unf.edu

SHUMATE, Donna, L .... 919-209-2125 .... 371 C dlshumate@johnstoncc.edu

SHUMPERT, Glenn .... 803-641-3444 .... 462 B glenns@usca.edu

SHUMWAY, Nicolas .... 713-348-4810 .... 492 J shumway@rice.edu

SHUPALA, Christine .... 361-825-2643 .... 497 F christine.shupala@tamucc.edu

SHUPE, Della .... 952-885-5417 .... 270 dshupe@nwhealth.edu

SHUPE, Gary .... 217-641-4505 .... 154 C gshupe@jwcc.edu

SHUPE, John .... 845-257-3335 .... 352 E shupej@newpaltz.edu

SHUPP, Edward, K .... 610-758-4200 .... 434 E eks0@lehigh.edu

SHUPP, Matthew, R .... 610-892-1289 .... 439 E mrs32@psu.edu

SHUPP, Michael, D .... 515-263-6136 .... 184 mshupp@grandview.edu

SHUPPY, Brian, L .... 801-626-6114 .... 511 D bshuppy@weber.edu

SHUR, Barry .... 303-724-2911 .... 88 D Barry.Shur@ucdenver.edu

SHURAN, Melanie .... 847-578-3403 .... 163 A melanie.shuran@rosalindfranklin.edu

SHURES, Aaron, G .... 217-206-6003 .... 167 A shures.aaron@uis.edu

SHURMAN, Susan, J .... 732-445-4181 .... 314 D sschurman@smlr.rutgers.edu

SHURTZ, Mary Ann .... 703-734-5325 .... 524 D mshurtz@stratford.edu

SHURTZ, II, Richard, R ..... 703-821-8570 .... 524 D rshurtz@stratford.edu

SHUSTER, Arthur .... 828-298-3325 .... 380 C ashuster@warren-wilson.edu

SHUSTER, Patricia .... 603-641-7150 .... 305 H pshuster@anselm.edu

SHUTE, Marcus, W .... 404-880-6990 .... 126 I mwshute@cau.edu

SHUTE, William .... 202-955-9091 .... 504 E wshute@utsystem.edu

SHUTLER, Troy .... 419-755-4896 .... 397 B tshutler@ncstatecollege.edu

SHUTT, Allison .... 501-450-3897 .... 22 A shutt@hendrix.edu

SHUTT, Barbara, C .... 207-859-5415 .... 217 G bcshutt@colby.edu

SHUTT, Gary .... 405-744-4800 .... 410 C gary.shutt@okstate.edu

SHUTTER, Susan, S .... 412-578-6351 .... 424 G shutterss@carlow.edu

SHYDIAN, Joanne .... 706-750-4954 .... 36 B jshydian@csusm.edu

SHYTLE, Louise .... 606-326-2077 .... 201 B louise.shytle@kctcs.edu

SIAMUNDELE, Andre .... 315-364-3215 .... 360 C asiamundele@wells.edu

SIAS, Mary, E .... 502-597-6260 .... 203 D mary.sias@kysu.edu

SIBAL, Thomas .... 574-936-8898 .... 168 I tom.sibal@ancilla.edu

SIBENALLER-WOODALL, Beth .... 712-324-5061 .... 188 A beths@nwicc.edu

SIBERIO, Victor .... 787-265-3862 .... 567 C vsiberio@uprm.edu

SIBERIO TORRES, Victor .. 787-265-3862 .... 567 C v_siberio@rumac.uprm.edu

SIBERT, Alan .... 706-864-1940 .... 134 D aksibert@northgeorgia.edu

SIBERT, Pamela .... 816-802-3421 .... 283 I psibert@kcai.edu

SIBERT, Sonja .... 775-753-2181 .... 302 H sonjas@gwmail.gbcnv.edu

SIBLEY, Debra .... 504-568-6107 .... 213 A dsible@lsuhsc.edu

SICARD, OP, Kenneth, R ... 401-865-2055 .... 453 F ksicard@providence.edu

SICARD, Rex, E .... 785-243-1435 .... 191 H rsicard@cloud.edu

SICHTERMAN, David .... 313-927-1391 .... 255 A dsichterman@marygrove.edu

SICIENSKY, Emily .... 931-540-2704 .... 474 F esiciensky@columbiastate.edu

SICILIANO, Julie .... 413-782-1553 .... 246 D jsicilia@wne.edu

SICILIANO, Stephen, N ...... 231-995-1373 .... 256 G ssiciliano@nmc.edu

SICKBERT, Alan, A .... 651-523-2421 .... 264 C asickbert01@hamline.edu

SIDBURY, Carmen .... 404-270-5705 .... 137 E csidbury@spelman.edu

SIDDARAJU, Raj .... 309-649-6387 .... 165 D raj.siddaraju@src.edu

SIDDENS, Nancy .... 217-732-3168 .... 156 F nsiddens@lincolnchristian.edu

SIDDIQI, Melanie .... 909-652-6780 .... 39 B melanie.siddiqi@chaffey.edu

SIDDIQI, Muhammad .... 708-656-8000 .... 159 C muhammad.siddiqi@morton.edu

SIDDIQUI, Martuza .... 651-793-1910 .... 267 D

SIDEBOTTOM, Daniel .... 607-753-2501 .... 353 B daniel.sidebottom@cortland.edu

SIDEBOTTOM, Sara, L .... 859-572-5588 .... 205 E sidebottoms@nku.edu

SIDERAS, John, F .... 216-368-4340 .... 386 E john.sideras@case.edu

SIDERS, Janet .... 229-931-2000 .... 131 B

SIDES, Diane, O .... 573-651-2256 .... 290 D dosides@semo.edu

SIMMONS, Bette, M .... 973-328-5171.... 309 B
bsimmons@ccm.edu
SIMMONS, Blair .... 510-869-1592..... 64 J
bsimmons@samuelmerritt.edu
SIMMONS, Charles, W ...... 410-276-0306.... 226 D
csimmons@host.sdc.edu
SIMMONS, Chuck .... 845-758-7878.... 323 F
simmons@bard.edu
SIMMONS, D. Glenn .... 602-279-1011.... 508 B
simmonsg@wbu.edu
SIMMONS, Dale .... 847-628-1001.... 154 I
dsimmons@judsonu.edu
SIMMONS, Donald .... 605-995-2937.... 464 B
dosimmon@dwu.edu
SIMMONS, Eddie .... 843-574-6268.... 461 G
eddie.simmons@tridenttech.edu
SIMMONS, Edna .... 410-951-3069.... 228 B
esimmons@coppin.edu
SIMMONS, Edna .... 410-951-3384.... 228 B
esimmons@coppin.edu
SIMMONS, Elaine, R .... 620-792-9214.... 190 E
simmonse@bartonccc.edu
SIMMONS, Elizabeth, H ..... 517-353-6486.... 255 D
esimmons@msu.edu
SIMMONS, Gail .... 914-323-5262.... 340 A
simmonsg@mville.edu
SIMMONS, Georgia .... 812-265-2580.... 176 G
gsimmons@ivytech.edu
SIMMONS, Gregory .... 410-455-1452.... 227 D
gsimmons@umbc.edu
SIMMONS, Hezekiah, N ..... 585-292-3320.... 341 H
hsimmons@monroecc.edu
SIMMONS, Howard, L ...... 410-276-0306.... 226 D
hsimmons@host.sdc.edu
SIMMONS, James, M .... 409-880-8405.... 500 F
james.simmons@lamar.edu
SIMMONS, Jay, K .... 319-385-6204.... 186 A
jay.simmons@iwc.edu
SIMMONS, Kathy .... 405-466-3228.... 408 G
ksimmons@lunet.edu
SIMMONS, Kenith .... 808-974-7707.... 141 A
simmons@hawaii.edu
SIMMONS, Kirsten .... 910-277-3943.... 376 A
simmonskm@sapc.edu
SIMMONS, Kistie .... 928-776-3219..... 18 C
ksimmons@prescott.edu
SIMMONS, Kitty .... 951-785-2397..... 53 D
ksimmons@lasierra.edu
SIMMONS, Laura, L .... 309-655-3450.... 163 E
laura.l.simmons@osfhealthcare.org
SIMMONS, Leroy .... 704-216-6195.... 366 D
lsimmons@livingstone.edu
SIMMONS, Linda .... 541-881-5756.... 420 E
lsimmons@tvcc.cc
SIMMONS, Lysa .... 315-498-2228.... 345 D
simmonsl@sunyocc.edu
SIMMONS, Michael .... 724-738-3333.... 443 E
michael.simmons@sru.edu
SIMMONS, Michelle .... 765-459-0561.... 176 A
msimmons@ivytech.edu
SIMMONS, Michelle .... 419-372-2723.... 385 C
msimmon@bgsu.edu
SIMMONS, Pat .... 478-471-2717.... 133 E
pat.simmons@maconstate.edu
SIMMONS, Patricia .... 270-824-1795.... 202 C
patricia.simmons@kctcs.edu
SIMMONS, Paul, M .... 651-962-6706.... 272 E
pmsimmons@stthomas.edu
SIMMONS, Regina Ray ...... 404-756-4047.... 124 I
rsimmons@atlm.edu
SIMMONS, Richard, E .... 864-488-8344.... 459 A
rsimmons@limestone.edu
SIMMONS, Rick .... 318-257-2912.... 215 F
simmons@latech.edu
SIMMONS, Robert, A .... 816-235-1368.... 291 E
simmonsr@umkc.edu
SIMMONS, Rosemary, E .... 618-453-5371.... 164 I
rsimmons@siu.edu
SIMMONS, Ruth, J .... 401-863-2234.... 452 J
president@brown.edu
SIMMONS, Sara .... 910-521-6271.... 379 B
sara.simmons@uncp.edu
SIMMONS, Sarah, J .... 304-442-3178.... 545 C
bkswvuit@bncollege.com
SIMMONS, Sheila .... 912-583-3184.... 126 C
ssimmons@bpc.edu
SIMMONS, Tacuma .... 410-276-0306.... 226 D
tsimmons@host.sdc.edu
SIMMONS, Terry .... 262-564-3108.... 553 H
simmonst@gtc.edu
SIMMONS, Thomas .... 419-772-2450.... 398 G
t-simmons@onu.edu
SIMMONS, Timothy, J .... 414-288-5048.... 548 D
tim.simmons@marquette.edu
SIMMONS, Todd .... 480-517-8137..... 16 C
todd.simmons@riosalado.edu
SIMMONS, Todd, H .... 541-737-4611.... 418 F
todd.simmons@oregonstate.edu
SIMMONS-JOHNSON,
Deborah .... 713-718-7332.... 487 G
deborah.johnson@hccs.edu
SIMMONS-WALSTON,
Valerie .... 770-531-3110.... 126 B
vsimmons-walston@brenau.edu

SIMMS, Carl .... 559-442-8255..... 71 I
carl.simms@scccd.edu
SIMMS, Jamie .... 503-491-7620.... 417 B
jamie.simms@mhcc.edu
SIMMS, Rebecca .... 859-246-6761.... 201 D
rebecca.simms@kctcs.edu
SIMMS, Tracy .... 541-463-5889.... 416 D
simmst@lanecc.edu
SIMON, SR., Aaron .... 225-928-3005.... 208 C
aaronsimon@camelotcollege.com
SIMON, Bashe .... 212-463-0400.... 357 J
simonb@touro.edu
SIMON, Carol .... 616-395-7903.... 252 F
simon@hope.edu
SIMON, Carol .... 916-348-4689..... 45 H
csimon@epic.edu
SIMON, D. Fred .... 541-346-5851.... 419 B
denis@uoregon.edu
SIMON, Dale .... 319-887-3614.... 186 H
dale.simon@kirkwood.edu
SIMON, Donald, E .... 718-933-6700.... 341 G
dsimon@monroecollege.edu
SIMON, Ellis .... 212-650-5310.... 326 H
esimon@ccny.cuny.edu
SIMON, George, A .... 419-866-0261.... 402 B
gasimon@stautzenberger.com
SIMON, Jan .... 217-351-3818.... 161 B
jsimon@parkland.edu
SIMON, Janet .... 406-657-2278.... 295 F
jsimon@msubillings.edu
SIMON, Jill, K .... 651-641-8211.... 263 C
simon@csp.edu
SIMON, John .... 919-660-0330.... 363 I
john.simon@duke.edu
SIMON, Kathryn, C .... 859-233-8124.... 206 E
ksimon@transy.edu
SIMON, Lou Anna, K .... 517-355-6560.... 255 D
laksimon@msu.edu
SIMON, Marche .... 510-261-8500..... 61 F
marche.simon@patten.edu
SIMON, Marlene .... 310-954-4135..... 57 H
msimon@msmc.la.edu
SIMON, Michelle, S .... 914-422-4407.... 345 F
msimon@pace.edu
SIMON, Patric, D .... 405-466-3262.... 408 G
pdsimon@lunet.edu
SIMON, Paul, M .... 203-837-8494..... 92 A
simonp@wcsu.edu
SIMON, Robert .... 724-357-2217.... 442 E
rjsimon@iup.edu
SIMON, Rose, A .... 336-917-5421.... 376 C
rose.simon@salem.edu
SIMON, Scott .... 419-824-3743.... 395 D
ssimon@lourdes.edu
SIMON, Tina, L .... 419-372-2700.... 385 C
tsimon@bgsu.edu
SIMON, Toby .... 401-232-6855.... 453 A
tsimon@bryant.edu
SIMON, William .... 314-615-6908.... 291 F
bsimon@emergingtech.org
SIMON, Yvonne .... 603-314-1420.... 306 B
ysimon@snhu.edu
SIMONDS, Linda, A .... 413-565-1000.... 231 B
lsimonds@baypath.edu
SIMONE, Beverly .... 319-208-5050.... 188 G
bsimone@scciowa.edu
SIMONE, Carmen .... 307-268-2540.... 555 F
csimone@caspercollege.edu
SIMONE, John .... 609-586-4800.... 311 C
simonej@mccc.edu
SIMONE, Lucian .... 203-285-2223..... 90 A
lsimone@gwcc.commnet.edu
SIMONE, Michael .... 323-265-8789..... 54 G
simonems@elac.edu
SIMONE, Tony .... 360-538-4154.... 534 B
tsimone@ghc.edu
SIMONEAUX, Catherine ..... 504-865-3231.... 213 F
cmsimone@loyno.edu
SIMONEAUX, Michel .... 706-865-2134.... 138 A
msimoneaux@truett.edu
SIMONEAUX, Mike .... 912-583-2241.... 126 C
msimoneaux@bpc.edu
SIMONEAUX, Wendy .... 225-578-8878.... 212 E
wendys@lsu.edu
SIMONELLI, Ray .... 937-769-1845.... 383 K
rsimonelli@antioch.edu
SIMONETTI, Salvatore, J ... 585-245-5651.... 353 C
simonetti@geneseo.edu
SIMONI, Mary .... 518-276-3315.... 347 D
simonm@rpi.edu
SIMONIAN, Yasmen .... 801-626-7117.... 511 D
ysimonian@weber.edu
SIMONS, Earl, G .... 718-262-3795.... 329 B
esimons@york.cuny.edu
SIMONS, Ernest .... 704-290-5828.... 373 F
esimons@spcc.edu
SIMONS, Kathleen .... 513-745-3202.... 406 E
simonsk@xavier.edu
SIMONS, Kenneth, B .... 414-955-4577.... 548 E
ksimons@mcw.edu
SIMONS, Michael, A .... 718-990-6601.... 348 G
simonsm@stjohns.edu
SIMONS, Richard, J .... 717-531-3876.... 439 L
rxs14@psu.edu

SIMONS, Robert, E .... 336-599-1181.... 372 D
simonsr@piedmontcc.edu
SIMONS, Sherri, J .... 308-432-6355.... 299 G
ssimons@csc.edu
SIMONS, Shino .... 626-812-3053..... 30 E
ssimons@apu.edu
SIMONTON, Mary .... 334-291-4963........ 2 G
mary.simonton@cv.edu
SIMOTAS, Monica .... 718-405-3290.... 330 A
monica.simotas@mountsaintvincent.edu
SIMPER, Craig, J .... 435-797-1156.... 511 B
craig.simper@usu.edu
SIMPKINS, Alice, M .... 706-396-8111.... 135 C
asimpkins@paine.edu
SIMPKINS, Pamela, P .... 540-831-5419.... 522 D
ppsimpkin@radford.edu
SIMPSON, Amanda .... 940-898-3456.... 502 B
asimpson1@twu.edu
SIMPSON, Andrea .... 336-386-3263.... 374 B
simpsoaj@surry.edu
SIMPSON, Andrea, M .... 414-906-4663.... 551 C
amsimp@uwm.edu
SIMPSON, Andrew, L .... 651-631-5239.... 270 E
alsimpson@nwc.edu
SIMPSON, Angela .... 606-589-3025.... 203 A
angela.simpson@kctcs.edu
SIMPSON, Anita .... 580-628-6237.... 409 B
anita.simpson@north-ok.edu
SIMPSON, Atticus .... 843-921-6916.... 460 B
asimpson@netc.edu
SIMPSON, Benjamin, I .... 214-841-3627.... 485 E
bsimpson@dts.edu
SIMPSON, Brandy .... 701-228-5613.... 382 C
brandy.simpson@dakotacollege.edu
SIMPSON, Brendt .... 315-228-6208.... 329 H
bsimpson@colgate.edu
SIMPSON, Carol .... 757-683-3079.... 521 L
csimpson@odu.edu
SIMPSON, Cindy .... 708-209-3156.... 148 C
cindy.simpson@cuchicago.edu
SIMPSON, Connie .... 303-797-5601..... 80 J
connie.simpson@arapahoe.edu
SIMPSON, Cynthia, F .... 718-990-6333.... 348 G
simpsoc1@stjohns.edu
SIMPSON, Daniel, L .... 302-857-1126..... 96 D
dsimpson@dtcc.edu
SIMPSON, Deborah, E .... 414-955-4332.... 548 E
dsimpson@mcw.edu
SIMPSON, Dennis .... 303-986-2320..... 82 E
dennis@csha.net
SIMPSON, Devon .... 503-297-5544.... 417 G
dsimpson@ocac.edu
SIMPSON, Donald, E .... 417-836-5514.... 286 F
donsimpson@missouristate.edu
SIMPSON, Gina .... 303-986-2320..... 82 E
gina@csha.net
SIMPSON, JR., Grant, W .. 512-448-8651.... 493 B
grants@stedwards.edu
SIMPSON, Jack .... 423-461-8955.... 471 H
jasimpson@milligan.edu
SIMPSON, Jacklyn, A .... 704-687-7501.... 378 E
jasimpso@uncc.edu
SIMPSON, III, James, D ... 904-632-5049.... 109 E
jsimpson@fscj.edu
SIMPSON, James, E .... 434-395-2093.... 520 G
simpsonje@longwood.edu
SIMPSON, Jane .... 678-839-5306.... 138 D
jsimpson@westga.edu
SIMPSON, Johnnie .... 910-410-1855.... 372 G
johnnies@richmondcc.edu
SIMPSON, Juliene .... 973-290-4207.... 309 A
jsimpson@cse.edu
SIMPSON, Kurt .... 815-599-3501.... 152 A
kurt.simpson@highland.edu
SIMPSON, Larry .... 662-562-3219.... 276 E
jlsimpson@northwestms.edu
SIMPSON, Lawrence, J ...... 617-266-1400.... 231 G
SIMPSON, Mallory, M .... 815-753-9506.... 160 A
mmsimpson@niu.edu
SIMPSON, Mark .... 801-626-6047.... 511 D
marksimpson1@weber.edu
SIMPSON, Matthew .... 252-335-3532.... 377 D
mdsimpson@mail.escu.edu
SIMPSON, Micah .... 205-970-9243........ 7 D
msimpson@sebc.edu
SIMPSON, Michael .... 518-564-2155.... 354 B
simpsome@plattsburgh.edu
SIMPSON, Michael, A .... 304-788-6886.... 545 A
masimpson@mail.wvu.edu
SIMPSON, Michael, J .... 415-338-2218..... 36 F
msimpson@sfsu.edu
SIMPSON, Nancy, P .... 864-231-2029.... 455 C
nsimpson@andersonuniversity.edu
SIMPSON, Patricia .... 605-642-6132.... 465 F
SIMPSON, Peggy, A .... 810-762-9527.... 253 I
psimpson@kettering.edu
SIMPSON, Philip .... 321-433-7780.... 101 J
simpsonp@brevardcc.edu
SIMPSON, Phyllis .... 225-768-1713.... 214 B
psimpson@ololcollege.edu
SIMPSON, Ralph .... 484-365-7528.... 434 H
rsimpson@lincoln.edu
SIMPSON, Rebecca .... 502-852-6397.... 207 A
becky.simpson@louisville.edu

SIMPSON, Renee, K .... 407-582-1506.... 122
rsimpson@valenciacollege.edu
SIMPSON, Richard .... 614-236-6383.... 386
rsimpson@law.capital.edu
SIMPSON, Robert .... 248-222-1503.... 250
robert.simpson@cornerstone.edu
SIMPSON, Robert .... 714-484-7331..... 59
rsimpson@cypresscollege.edu
SIMPSON, Robert .... 731-661-5219.... 476
rsimpson@uu.edu
SIMPSON, Robert, L .... 810-762-7949.... 253
rsimpson@kettering.edu
SIMPSON, Sarah .... 803-780-1263.... 463
simpson@voorhees.edu
SIMPSON, Scott .... 909-607-8135..... 40
scott.simpson@cgu.edu
SIMPSON, Stephen, J .... 301-687-4211.... 228
ssimpson@frostburg.edu
SIMPSON, Suzanne .... 662-846-4050.... 274
ssimpson@deltastate.edu
SIMPSON, Ted .... 410-225-2531.... 224
tsimpson@mica.edu
SIMPSON, Teresa .... 409-880-8879.... 500 F
teresa.simpson@lamar.edu
SIMPSON, Todd .... 402-872-2304.... 299 H
tsimpson@peru.edu
SIMPSON, Tony .... 909-537-5166..... 36 A
tsimpson@csusb.edu
SIMPSON, Traci .... 305-899-3150.... 101 F
tsimpson@mail.barry.edu
SIMPSON, Vornadette .... 301-552-1400.... 229 C
vsimpson@bible.edu
SIMS, Alan .... 215-596-8813.... 450 A
a.sims@usciences.edu
SIMS, Bradford (Brad) .... 812-237-3166.... 173 A
bradford.sims@indstate.edu
SIMS, Charles, E .... 206-934-4136.... 536 G
charles.sims@seattlecolleges.edu
SIMS, Dale .... 615-366-3921.... 473 C
dale.sims@tbr.edu
SIMS, Damon .... 814-865-0909.... 438 F
drs37@psu.edu
SIMS, David .... 478-471-2780.... 133 E
david.sims@maconstate.edu
SIMS, Donald, R .... 662-254-3551.... 276 C
d-ray@mvsu.edu
SIMS, Dora .... 281-756-3524.... 479 G
dsims@alvincollege.edu
SIMS, Frank .... 641-673-1703.... 189 I
simsf@wmpenn.edu
SIMS, Gayle .... 919-536-7250.... 369 G
simso@durhamtech.edu
SIMS, Gayle .... 704-687-7208.... 378 E
ogsims@uncc.edu
SIMS, George, E .... 251-380-2262........ 7 F
gsims@shc.edu
SIMS, Glenn .... 910-410-1684.... 372 G
glenns@richmondcc.edu
SIMS, Jack .... 814-871-7464.... 429 F
sims003@gannon.edu
SIMS, Jane .... 402-354-7073.... 299 E
jane.sims@methodistcollege.edu
SIMS, John .... 973-720-2397.... 317 D
simsj@wpunj.edu
SIMS, Kathy, L .... 310-206-7774..... 74 A
ksims@career.ucla.edu
SIMS, Lesley .... 510-436-1405..... 50 F
sims@hnu.edu
SIMS, Leslie .... 304-424-8221.... 545 B
leslie.sims@mail.wvu.edu
SIMS, Marcella .... 251-405-7133........ 2 D
msims@bishop.edu
SIMS, Mary, J .... 831-656-3658.... 557 H
mjsims@nps.edu
SIMS, Mary, L .... 803-536-8198.... 460 G
msims@scsu.edu
SIMS, Michelle .... 229-317-6729.... 128 A
michelle.sims@darton.edu
SIMS, Michelle .... 850-436-8444.... 123 A
michelle.sims@vc.edu
SIMS, Patricia .... 256-551-1717........ 4 J
patricia.sims@drakestate.edu
SIMS, Phil, W .... 903-875-7543.... 491 B
phil.sims@navarrocollege.edu
SIMS, Roberta, L .... 570-577-3310.... 423 D
roberta.sims@bucknell.edu
SIMS, Sue, A .... 803-938-3729.... 462 F
sues@uscsumter.edu
SIMS, Suzanne .... 256-216-3314........ 1 F
suzanne.sims@athens.edu
SIMS-TUCKER, Bernita, M . 410-651-3553.... 227 E
bsimstucker@umes.edu
SIMSHEUSER, Carrie, L ..... 816-654-7072.... 283 J
csimsheuser@kcumb.edu
SIMSON, Earl, L .... 401-456-8106.... 454 A
esimson@ric.edu
SIMSON, Gary, J .... 478-301-2602.... 133 F
simson_g@mercer.edu
SINATRA, Ann .... 610-989-1327.... 450 E
asinatra@vfmac.edu
SINCAVAGE, Joseph .... 610-436-3535.... 443 F
jsincavage@wcupa.edu
SINCLAIR, Joyce .... 512-313-3000.... 483 G
joyce.sinclair@concordia.edu

SKINNER, Katherine .... 615-460-6407.... 467 B
kathryn.skinner@belmont.edu

SKINNER, Margaret .... 307-766-4847.... 556 E
mjf@uwyo.edu

SKINNER, Patricia, A .... 704-922-6475.... 370 D
skinner.pat@gaston.edu

SKINNER, Randall .... 928-428-8252...... 14 C
randy.skinner@eac.edu

SKINNER, Regina .... 609-343-5086.... 307 D
rskinner@atlantic.edu

SKINNER, Rick .... 580-774-3788.... 412 F
rick.skinner@swosu.edu

SKINNER, Robert, E .... 504-520-7304.... 217 A
rskinner@xula.edu

SKINNER, II, Robert, N ..... 304-473-8557.... 545 F
skinner_b@wvwc.edu

SKINNER, Timothy .... 954-545-4500.... 117 H
library@sfbc.edu

SKINNER, William, F .... 920-993-6025.... 547 J
william.f.skinner@lawrence.edu

SKIPP, Steven, I .... 904-819-6258.... 107 A
sskipp@flagler.edu

SKIPPER, Bob .... 270-745-4295.... 207 C
bob.skipper@wku.edu

SKIPPER, Curt .... 601-635-2111.... 274 C
cskipper@eccc.edu

SKIPPER, Eric .... 678-717-3698.... 129 D
eskipper@gsc.edu

SKIPPER, Mark .... 612-374-5800.... 263 I
mskipper@dunwoody.edu

SKIPPER, Wray .... 229-931-2354.... 136 G
wskipper@southgatech.edu

SKIVIAT, David, M .... 740-283-6223.... 390 M
dskiviat@franciscan.edu

SKLEDER, Anne .... 610-902-8300.... 423 H
as3436@cabrini.edu

SKLYAR, Mila .... 703-821-8570.... 524 D
msklyar@stratford.edu

SKOGEN, Larry, C .... 701-224-5431.... 382 B
larry.skogen@bismarckstate.edu

SKOLNIK, Richard, J .... 315-312-3168.... 354 A
richard.skolnik@oswego.edu

SKONER, Peter, R .... 814-742-3085.... 446 B
pskoner@francis.edu

SKOPITZ, Ronald, J .... 678-915-4962.... 137 C
rskopitz@spsu.edu

SKORACZEWSKI, Paul .... 715-682-1841.... 549 C
pskoraczewski@northland.edu

SKORLINSKI, James, E ..... 414-229-4304.... 551 C
jimsk@uwm.edu

SKORTON, David, J .... 607-255-5201.... 331 C
president@cornell.edu

SKOUGSTAD, Becky .... 303-753-6046...... 87 F
bskougstad@rmcad.edu

SKRADE, Mark .... 417-823-3477.... 290 B
mskrade@forest.edu

SKRAMSTAD, Sam .... 970-945-8691...... 82 C

SKRANKA, Jay .... 507-457-5480.... 270 B
skranka@winona.edu

SKRESLET, Stanley .... 804-355-0671.... 524 F
sskreslet@upsem.edu

SKRHA, Pattie .... 440-826-8011.... 384 H
pskrha@bw.edu

SKROCKI, Martin, P .... 516-773-5374.... 558 F
skrockim@usmma.edu

SKRUTSKI, Stanley, F .... 570-348-6225.... 435 F
skrutski@marywood.edu

SKRZYPEK, Larry, A .... 304-243-2241.... 545 G
larrys@wju.edu

SKUCE, Anne .... 812-941-2212.... 174 D
askuce@ius.edu

SKUL, Jeanne .... 864-503-5960.... 463 A
jskul@uscupstate.edu

SKURJA, JR., Michael .... 801-375-5125.... 510 F
mskurja@rmuohp.edu

SLAATS, Jacqueline .... 847-735-5285.... 155 F
slaats@lakeforest.edu

SLABACH, Frederick, G ...... 817-531-4401.... 502 A
fslabach@txwes.edu

SLABAUGH, Dawn .... 530-938-5373...... 42 C
slabaugh@siskiyous.edu

SLABAUGH, Katie .... 765-285-1545.... 169 D
kslabaugh@bsu.edu

SLABAUGH, Scott .... 330-829-8207.... 404 C
slabausa@mountunion.edu

SLABIK, Sandra .... 610-558-5291.... 437 C
slabiks@neumann.edu

SLACK, Craig .... 301-314-7164.... 227 B
cslack@umd.edu

SLACK, David .... 785-227-3380.... 190 G
slackd@bethanylb.edu

SLACK, Gregory, C .... 315-268-6475.... 329 C
gslack@clarkson.edu

SLACK, Karen .... 320-762-4463.... 265 I
karens@alextech.edu

SLACK, Robert .... 626-914-8581...... 39 G
rslack@citruscollege.edu

SLACUM, Scott .... 302-736-2493...... 96 G
slacumsc@wesley.edu

SLADE, Brenda .... 212-854-2091.... 323 G
bslade@barnard.edu

SLADE, Patricia .... 973-877-3209.... 310 A
slade@essex.edu

SLADKI, Joseph .... 304-724-3700.... 540 C
jsladki@apus.edu

SLAFF, Sara .... 410-576-7847.... 226 A

SLAGELL, Jeff .... 662-846-4440.... 274 B
jslagell@deltastate.edu

SLAGLE, Jeff .... 727-576-6500.... 112 G
jslagle@keisercareer.edu

SLAGTER, Eelco, A .... 212-746-5784.... 360 B
eas2008@med.cornell.edu

SLAICH, Lucy .... 410-704-2050.... 228 E
lslaich@towson.edu

SLAMA, John .... 763-231-3151.... 264 E
slama@mpls.herzing.edu

SLANGER, William, D .... 701-231-7418.... 381 H
william.slanger@ndsu.edu

SLANGER, Zvi Dov .... 410-486-0006.... 221 C

SLANN, Martin .... 903-566-7368.... 506 C
mslann@uttyler.edu

SLATER, Amanda .... 480-994-9244...... 18 I
amandas@swiha.net

SLATER, Glenn .... 215-785-0111.... 440 H

SLATER, Jamie .... 704-337-2516.... 375 G
slaterj@queens.edu

SLATER, Janet .... 217-333-2350.... 167 B
slaterj@illinois.edu

SLATER, Lois .... 406-275-4820.... 296 F
lois_slater@skc.edu

SLATER, Peter .... 212-594-4000.... 357 G
pslater@tcicollege.edu

SLATER, Sarah .... 541-485-1780.... 417 E
registrar@newhope.edu

SLATER, Wayne, A .... 941-377-4880.... 113 F

SLATON, Christa, D .... 575-646-3500.... 319 D
cslaton@nmsu.edu

SLATON, Gwendolyn .... 973-877-3233.... 310 A
slaton@essex.edu

SLATON, William .... 404-816-4533.... 132 B
wslaton@atl.herzing.edu

SLATTERY, Kathryn .... 815-836-5275.... 156 D
slatteka@lewisu.edu

SLAUGHTER, Beverly, J ..... 321-433-5150.... 101 J
slaughterb@brevardcc.edu

SLAUGHTER, Clinton .... 530-895-2366...... 31 E
slaughtercl@butte.edu

SLAUGHTER, Craig, A .... 765-658-4030.... 170 I
craigslaughter@depauw.edu

SLAUGHTER, Gayle, R .... 713-798-6644.... 481 H
gayles@bcm.edu

SLAUGHTER, Jacqueline ..... 512-245-2273.... 501 C
js47@txstate.edu

SLAUGHTER, John .... 254-647-3234.... 492 E
jslaughter@rangercollege.edu

SLAUGHTER, Katie .... 954-545-4500.... 117 H
registrar@sfbc.edu

SLAUGHTER, Millicent .... 956-721-5746.... 489 G
mslaughter@laredo.edu

SLAUGHTER, Sabra, C .... 843-792-2228.... 459 C
slaughsc@musc.edu

SLAUGHTER, Shirley .... 510-981-2840...... 62 A
sslaughter@peralta.edu

SLAUTA, Katherine .... 619-235-2049...... 46 N
kslauta@fidm.edu

SLAVENS, Joseph, C .... 530-226-4108...... 69 H
jslavens@simpsonu.edu

SLAVIN, Dennis .... 646-660-6504.... 326 D
dennis_slavin@baruch.cuny.edu

SLAVIN, Joan, L .... 714-850-4800...... 72 D
slavin@taftu.edu

SLAVIN, Kevin, B .... 914-606-6733.... 360 D
kevin.slavin@sunywcc.edu

SLAVIN, Pat .... 775-673-7812.... 302 J
pslavin@tmcc.edu

SLAVITT, Lesley .... 312-341-2351.... 162 I
lslavitt@roosevelt.edu

SLAWSKI, Richard .... 212-650-7061.... 326 H
rslawski@ccny.cuny.edu

SLAWSON, Linda .... 903-785-7661.... 492 B
lslawson@parisjc.edu

SLAWSON, Mark .... 617-873-0106.... 233 B
Mark.Slawson@cambridgecollege.edu

SLAWTER, Laura .... 336-917-5312.... 376 C
laura.slawter@salem.edu

SLAY, Jack, C .... 706-880-8256.... 132 I
jslay@lagrange.edu

SLAYDEN, Jon, N .... 417-268-6351.... 279 D
jslayden@gobbc.edu

SLAYMAKER, Valerie .... 651-213-4746.... 264 D
vslaymaker@hazelden.org

SLAYTER, Don .... 904-724-2229.... 118 B

SLAYTON, Deborah, L .... 217-424-6348.... 158 F
dslayton@millikin.edu

SLAYTON, Deborah, L .... 217-420-6774.... 158 F
dslayton@millikin.edu

SLAYTON, William .... 260-399-7700.... 180 E
wslayton@sf.edu

SLEBODA, Cheryl .... 508-849-3420.... 230 C
csleboda@annamaria.edu

SLEBODNIK, Robert .... 585-292-5627.... 325 D
rslebodnik@bryantstratton.edu

SLED, Jill .... 503-682-1862.... 419 F
jsled@pioneerpacific.edu

SLEDGE, Danny .... 269-927-8120.... 254 B
selmon@lakemichigancollege.edu

SLEDGE, Donald .... 205-929-6442........ 5 E
dsledge@lawsonstate.edu

SLEDGE, Janet .... 386-506-3899.... 103 J
sledgej@DaytonaState.edu

SLEEMAN, Geoffrey .... 313-664-7480.... 250 A
gsleeman@collegeforcreativestudies.edu

SLEEVI, Timothy .... 269-948-9500.... 253 H
sleevit@kellogg.edu

SLEIGH-LAYMAN, Staci ..... 509-963-2205.... 531 G
staci@cwu.edu

SLEIGHT, Garth .... 406-874-6212.... 294 H
sleightg@milescc.edu

SLEIGHT, Weldon .... 308-367-5200.... 301 C
wsleight2@unl.edu

SLEJKO, Christa .... 972-273-3010.... 485 B
cslejko@dcccd.edu

SLEMMER, Duane, L .... 208-467-8360.... 143 I
dlslemmer@nnu.edu

SLENSKI, Brian .... 517-321-0242.... 252 B
bslenski@glcc.edu

SLEPITZA, Ron .... 816-501-3750.... 279 C
ron.slepitza@avila.edu

SLESH, Jenny .... 724-222-5330.... 438 E
jslesh@penncommercial.edu

SLESNICK, Daniel, A .... 512-471-4363.... 505 B
slesnick@austin.utexas.edu

SLETTEDAHL, Gene, A .... 507-354-8221.... 265 B
slettega@mlc-wels.edu

SLETTEN, Michael, L .... 206-296-5990.... 537 F
sletten@seattleu.edu

SLEVA, Michael .... 616-451-3511.... 250 E
msleva@davenport.edu

SLEVIN, Kathleen, F .... 757-221-2601.... 517 J
keslev@wm.edu

SLIFE, Joye .... 706-245-7226.... 128 K
jslife@ec.edu

SLIFE, Madonna .... 618-634-3375.... 164 C
madonnas@shawneecc.edu

SLIGH, Gary .... 352-323-3670.... 112 M
slighg@lscc.edu

SLIKE, Robert .... 808-543-8019.... 140 B
rslike@hpu.edu

SLIMAN, George, S .... 412-578-8826.... 424 G
slimangs@carlow.edu

SLINEY, Dee .... 425-352-8269.... 531 F
dsliney@cascadia.edu

SLINGER, Michael, J .... 302-477-2111...... 96 H
mjslinger@widener.edu

SLINKER, Bryan, K .... 509-335-9515.... 539 A
slinker@vetmed.wsu.edu

SLISZ, John, P .... 716-851-1851.... 333 B
slisz@ecc.edu

SLISZ, Judith .... 718-862-7579.... 339 H
judith.slisz@manhattan.edu

SLIZ, Mark .... 708-237-5000.... 160 C
msliz@nc.edu

SLIZEWSKI, Tom .... 803-593-9231.... 455 A
slizewst@atc.edu

SLOAN, Barbara .... 850-201-8680.... 121 F
sloanb@tcc.fl.edu

SLOAN, Barry .... 310-287-4278...... 55 F
sloanba@wlac.edu

SLOAN, Candice, Y .... 864-587-4282.... 461 D
sloanc@smcsc.edu

SLOAN, Charles, B .... 919-497-3320.... 366 E
csloan@louisburg.edu

SLOAN, Damon, N .... 815-740-3399.... 167 C
dsloan@stfrancis.edu

SLOAN, Jeff .... 405-912-9455.... 408 D
jsloan@hc.edu

SLOAN, Lee .... 361-698-1259.... 485 F
lsloan@delmar.edu

SLOAN, Michael .... 309-694-5512.... 152 B
msloan@icc.edu

SLOAN, Robert, B .... 281-649-3153.... 487 F
rsloan@hbu.edu

SLOAN, Roberta .... 936-294-2771.... 501 A

SLOAN, Ron .... 765-289-2291.... 175 K
rsloan9@ivytech.edu

SLOAN, Susan .... 310-243-3639...... 34 B
ssloan@csudh.edu

SLOAN, Susan .... 315-364-3264.... 360 C
ssloan@wells.edu

SLOAN, Susan .... 503-253-3443.... 417 H
ssloan@ocom.edu

SLOANE, Tomecca .... 919-760-8633.... 366 G
sloaneto@meredith.edu

SLOAS, Ike .... 901-843-3880.... 472 I

SLOAT, Deborah, L .... 605-394-1201.... 466 A
deborah.sloat@sdsmt.edu

SLOAT, James .... 724-503-1001.... 451 A
jsloat@washjeff.edu

SLOBERT, Yantee .... 585-385-8423.... 348 F
yslobert@sjfc.edu

SLOCUM, Cameron, W .... 409-772-3448.... 507 B
cwslocum@utmb.edu

SLOCUM, Jeff .... 315-655-7290.... 325 I
jslocum@cazenovia.edu

SLOCUM, Stacy, S .... 585-385-8388.... 348 F
sslocum@sjfc.edu

SLOCUMB, Douglas .... 423-478-7036.... 472 F
dslocumb@ptseminary.edu

SLOKA, Sandra, L .... 815-740-5026.... 167 C
ssloka@stfrancis.edu

SLOMBIA, Sonia .... 937-376-6574.... 386 H
sslombia@centralstate.edu

SLOMOVITS, Mendel .... 732-414-2834.... 317 F

SLOMOVITS, Yosef .... 732-367-1060.... 307 H

SLON, Dennis .... 310-338-5127...... 56 E
dslon@lmu.edu

SLONAC, Kevin .... 262-551-5727.... 546 F
kslonac@carthage.edu

SLONE, Jason .... 866-944-4228.... 402 E
slonej@tiffin.edu

SLOSS, Robert, E .... 401-232-6046.... 453 A
rsloss@bryant.edu

SLOTE, Ben, L .... 814-332-3391.... 421 E
ben.slote@allegheny.edu

SLOTKIN, Jacquelyn, H ...... 619-239-0391...... 37 D
jslotkin@cwsl.edu

SLOTTOW, Timothy, P .... 734-764-7272.... 259 D
tslottow@umich.edu

SLOUGH, Rebecca .... 574-296-6228.... 169 C
rslough@ambs.edu

SLOVAK, Jeffrey .... 708-534-4981.... 151 C
jslovak@govst.edu

SLOVER, Kimberly, S .... 603-526-3647.... 304 A
kslover@colby-sawyer.edu

SLOWENSKY, Joseph .... 714-744-7882...... 39 C
jslowens@chapman.edu

SLUDER, Richard, D .... 660-543-4811.... 291 B
sluder@ucmo.edu

SLUDER, Robin .... 423-478-7727.... 472 F
rsluder@ptseminary.edu

SLUIS, Kimberly .... 630-637-5152.... 159 F
kasluis@noctrl.edu

SLUSARCZYK, Richard .... 212-226-7300.... 346 E
rslusar@pbcny.edu

SLUSHER, Cindy .... 503-222-3225.... 415 H
cslusher@cci.edu

SLUSHER, Jennifer .... 540-985-8502.... 520 D
jjslusher@jchs.edu

SLUSHER, Max .... 609-894-9311.... 308 C
gslusher@bcc.edu

SLUSSER, Brenda .... 208-377-8080.... 142 I
bslusser@cc.edu

SLUSSER, Karen, L .... 570-389-4055.... 441 F
kslusse2@bloomu.edu

SLUTSKY, Madeleine .... 317-613-4800.... 169 B

SLY, Douglas, P .... 509-793-2004.... 531 D
dougs@bigbend.edu

SMAIL, John .... 704-687-3679.... 378 E
jsmail@uncc.edu

SMALES, Sandra .... 617-984-1723.... 244 C
ssmales@quincycollege.edu

SMALL, Angus .... 901-435-1627.... 470 B
angus_small@loc.edu

SMALL, Barbara .... 847-925-6682.... 151 E
bsmall@harpercollege.edu

SMALL, Brenda, L .... 423-585-6772.... 476 B
brenda.small@ws.edu

SMALL, Brent .... 575-562-2194.... 318 A
brent.small@enmu.edu

SMALL, Cindy .... 406-265-3787.... 295 G
csmall@msun.edu

SMALL, Dan .... 253-566-5030.... 538 C
dsmall@tacomacc.edu

SMALL, Daniel, F .... 202-994-6620...... 97 F
dsmall@gwu.edu

SMALL, Daphne .... 650-949-7046...... 47 H
smalldaphne@foothill.edu

SMALL, Darlene .... 843-383-8039.... 457 A
dsmall@coker.edu

SMALL, David .... 406-638-3110.... 294 G
smalld@lbhc.cc.mt.us

SMALL, David, B .... 713-743-5100.... 503 B
dsmall@uh.edu

SMALL, Elizabeth .... 610-527-0200.... 445 I
esmall@rosemont.edu

SMALL, Gillian .... 212-794-5417.... 326 C
gillian.small@mail.cuny.edu

SMALL, Hank .... 843-863-7080.... 456 B
hsmall@csuniv.edu

SMALL, Jacquelyn .... 863-667-5157.... 118 A
jrsmall@seu.edu

SMALL, Joe, A .... 509-526-6432.... 538 G
joe.small@wwcc.edu

SMALL, John, J .... 630-637-5701.... 159 F
jjsmall@noctrl.edu

SMALL, Jonathan .... 617-951-2350.... 243 C
jonathan.small@necb.edu

SMALL, Jonathan, A .... 317-940-9249.... 170 C
jasmall@butler.edu

SMALL, Latrenda .... 954-783-7339.... 106 D
lsmall@cci.edu

SMALL, Linda .... 313-993-1540.... 259 C
smalll@udmercy.edu

SMALL, Melissa .... 434-592-5280.... 520 F
mjeenigenburg@liberty.edu

SMALL, Natissia .... 314-516-5128.... 291 F
smalln@umsl.edu

SMALL, Virginia .... 718-246-6456.... 338 H
virginia.small@liu.edu

SMALLEN, David, L .... 315-859-4169.... 335 A
dsmallen@hamilton.edu

SMALLEN, David, L .... 315-859-4169.... 335 A

SMALLEY, David .... 217-732-3155.... 156 G
dsmalley@lincolncollege.edu

SMITH, Delois ... 256-824-4600 ... 9 A
delois.smith@uah.edu
SMITH, Denise, M ... 603-862-3396 ... 306 E
denise.smith@unh.edu
SMITH, Denise Dwight ... 704-687-2231 ... 378 E
ddsmith@uncc.edu
SMITH, Dennis ... 216-987-5556 ... 389 A
dennis.smith@tri-c.edu
SMITH, Derek ... 215-489-2476 ... 426 H
Derek.Smith@delval.edu
SMITH, Devin ... 402-643-7328 ... 297 F
devin.smith@cune.edu
SMITH, Diane ... 309-677-3229 ... 145 H
dms@bradley.edu
SMITH, Diane ... 210-999-8201 ... 502 C
dsmith@trinity.edu
SMITH, Diane, K ... 513-562-6260 ... 384 A
dksmith@artacademy.edu
SMITH, Dianne ... 510-204-0718 ... 39 F
dsmith@cdsp.edu
SMITH, Don ... 229-931-2731 ... 136 G
dsmith@southgatech.edu
SMITH, Donald ... 270-745-6256 ... 207 C
donald.smith@wku.edu
SMITH, Donald, A ... 336-316-2162 ... 364 E
dsmith4@guilford.edu
SMITH, Donald, E ... 716-286-8348 ... 344 D
des@niagara.edu
SMITH, Donald, E ... 732-445-1750 ... 314 B
don.smith@rutgers.edu
SMITH, Donald, K ... 412-397-4484 ... 445 G
smithd@rmu.edu
SMITH, Donald, R ... 318-342-1050 ... 216 E
dosmith@ulm.edu
SMITH, Donald, S ... 608-757-7723 ... 553 E
dsmith@blackhawk.edu
SMITH, Donna ... 601-925-3313 ... 275 E
dsmith@mc.edu
SMITH, Donna ... 815-802-8402 ... 154 J
dsmith@kcc.edu
SMITH, Donna ... 610-861-1384 ... 436 I
medgs01@moravian.edu
SMITH, Dorothy ... 504-816-4527 ... 208 I
dsmith@dillard.edu
SMITH, Dorothy ... 213-763-5507 ... 55 D
smithd@lattc.edu
SMITH, Dorsey ... 334-244-3232 ... 2 A
dsmith@aum.edu
SMITH, Douglas ... 570-422-3534 ... 442 C
dsmith@po-box.esu.edu
SMITH, Douglas, F ... 610-796-8393 ... 421 F
doug.smith@alvernia.edu
SMITH, Douglas, J ... 508-565-1341 ... 245 D
dsmith@stonehill.edu
SMITH, Drew ... 870-230-5265 ... 21 I
smithc@hsu.edu
SMITH, Dustin ... 479-788-7591 ... 24 D
dusmith@uafortsmith.edu
SMITH, Dwayne ... 813-974-2267 ... 120 D
mdsmith8@usf.edu
SMITH, Dwayne ... 314-340-3511 ... 282 I
smithd@hssu.edu
SMITH, Dwight, L ... 973-328-5090 ... 309 B
dsmith@ccm.edu
SMITH, III, Earl ... 713-743-1899 ... 503 B
esmith@uh.edu
SMITH, Ed ... 334-387-3877 ... 1 D
edsmith@amridgeuniversity.edu
SMITH, Ed ... 601-477-4029 ... 275 B
edd.smith@jcjc.edu
SMITH, Ed ... 615-771-7821 ... 478 G
ed@williamsoncc.edu
SMITH, Eddie, C ... 662-621-4144 ... 273 I
esmith@coahomacc.edu
SMITH, Edmond, C ... 276-964-7338 ... 528 A
ed.smith@sw.edu
SMITH, Edward ... 601-984-1350 ... 277 H
ejsmith@umc.edu
SMITH, Eileen ... 740-389-6786 ... 399 D
smith.1394@osu.edu
SMITH, Elizabeth ... 925-631-4278 ... 64 F
jes5@stmarys-ca.edu
SMITH, Elizabeth ... 802-225-3262 ... 513 H
elizabeth.smith@neci.edu
SMITH, Ellie ... 760-366-3791 ... 43 E
esmith@cmccd.edu
SMITH, Elmer, R ... 770-216-2960 ... 132 C
ers@ict-ils.edu
SMITH, Emily ... 252-527-6223 ... 371 D
esmith@lenoircc.edu
SMITH, Emily ... 972-929-9316 ... 486 B
esmith7@devry.edu
SMITH, Emory ... 229-243-5309 ... 125 E
emory.smith@bainbridge.edu
SMITH, Ephraim, P ... 562-951-4710 ... 33 E
esmith@calstate.edu
SMITH, Eric ... 210-690-9000 ... 487 C
esmith@hallmarkcollege.edu
SMITH, Eric ... 315-464-5763 ... 352 E
smither@upstate.edu
SMITH, Eric, L ... 906-227-1314 ... 256 F
esmith@nmu.edu
SMITH, Erik ... 207-255-1327 ... 220 E
erik.smith@maine.edu

SMITH, Erin ... 970-204-8121 ... 84 H
erin.smith@frontrange.edu
SMITH, Erling, A ... 805-756-2246 ... 33 F
esmith21@calpoly.edu
SMITH, Eva ... 425-640-1171 ... 533 E
esmith@edcc.edu
SMITH, Farnum ... 916-577-2200 ... 79 C
fsmith@jessup.edu
SMITH, Felicia ... 770-593-2257 ... 131 E
gjcfs@mindspring.com
SMITH, Frank ... 760-245-4271 ... 77 E
Frank.Smith@vvc.edu
SMITH, Frank, E ... 423-869-7088 ... 470 C
frank.smith@lmunet.edu
SMITH, Fred, R ... 740-376-4791 ... 395 F
fred.smith@marietta.edu
SMITH, Frederick, M ... 517-264-7876 ... 258 D
fsmith@sienaheights.edu
SMITH, Fritz ... 562-907-4951 ... 79 B
fritz@whittier.edu
SMITH, G, T ... 304-637-1243 ... 540 F
buck@dewv.edu
SMITH, G. Ben ... 704-637-4111 ... 363 C
gbsmith@catawba.edu
SMITH, Gary ... 315-279-5352 ... 337 K
gsmith@mail.keuka.edu
SMITH, Gary ... 435-283-7300 ... 512 B
gary.smith@snow.edu
SMITH, Gary, R ... 701-231-7494 ... 381 H
gary.smith@ndsu.edu
SMITH, Geary ... 815-455-8788 ... 157 F
gsmith@mchenry.edu
SMITH, Gene ... 919-735-5151 ... 374 F
gsmith@waynecc.edu
SMITH, Gene ... 614-292-7572 ... 398 H
smith.5407@osu.edu
SMITH, George ... 207-879-8757 ... 218 B
SMITH, George ... 617-349-8886 ... 236 G
ggsmith@lesley.edu
SMITH, George ... 425-640-1668 ... 533 E
gsmith@edcc.edu
SMITH, George, L ... 229-931-2302 ... 131 B
SMITH, George, S ... 508-999-8008 ... 237 E
g1smith@umassd.edu
SMITH, Gerald ... 817-461-8741 ... 480 H
gsmith@abconline.org
SMITH, Gladys ... 313-927-1259 ... 255 A
gsmith8938@marygrove.edu
SMITH, Glenn, C ... 503-280-8512 ... 415 E
glenns@cu-portland.edu
SMITH, Glenn, R ... 610-526-7935 ... 423 C
gsmith@brynmawr.edu
SMITH, Gloria ... 337-521-8922 ... 212 B
gsmith@southlouisiana.edu
SMITH, Grady ... 601-276-2000 ... 277 E
gsmith@smcc.edu
SMITH, Greg ... 503-554-2570 ... 415 I
gsmith@georgefox.edu
SMITH, Greg ... 563-344-1500 ... 182 F
grsmith@brownmackie.edu
SMITH, Greg ... 757-363-2121 ... 516 E
directoramn@tidetech.com
SMITH, Greg, P ... 308-398-7300 ... 297 C
gpsmith@cccneb.edu
SMITH, Gregory ... 662-720-7449 ... 276 D
gsmith@nemcc.edu
SMITH, Gregory ... 510-885-3249 ... 34 C
gregory.smith@csueastbay.edu
SMITH, Gregory ... 714-449-7456 ... 70 G
gsmith@scco.edu
SMITH, Gregory ... 610-399-2240 ... 441 H
psimon@cheyney.edu
SMITH, Gregory, L ... 920-465-2343 ... 551 A
smithg@uwgb.edu
SMITH, Gretna ... 757-822-1708 ... 528 C
gsmith@tcc.edu
SMITH, Harold ... 252-940-6219 ... 367 I
harolds@beaufortccc.edu
SMITH, Heather ... 508-531-1295 ... 238 B
h2smith@bridgew.edu
SMITH, Helen ... 602-243-8032 ... 16 E
helen.smith@smcmail.maricopa.edu
SMITH, Henry ... 617-824-8123 ... 234 D
henry_smith@emerson.edu
SMITH, Henry, H ... 340-693-1062 ... 568 C
hsmith@uvi.edu
SMITH, Henry, L ... 765-677-2100 ... 174 E
henry.smith@indwes.edu
SMITH, Howard, W ... 620-235-4518 ... 195 I
smith@pittstate.edu
SMITH, I. Darchele ... 704-357-8020 ... 361 N
idsmith@aii.edu
SMITH, Idelia ... 413-552-2228 ... 240 C
ismith@hcc.edu
SMITH, Ileana, M ... 302-855-1674 ... 96 B
ismith@dtcc.edu
SMITH, J, R ... 630-752-5061 ... 168 F
jr.smith@wheaton.edu
SMITH, J. Fitz ... 937-327-7076 ... 406 B
jfsmith@wittenberg.edu
SMITH, Jace ... 541-463-5561 ... 416 D
smithj@lanecc.edu
SMITH, Jack, W ... 713-500-3909 ... 506 D
jack.w.smith@uth.tmc.edu

SMITH, Jackie ... 623-572-3601 ... 16 F
jsmith@midwestern.edu
SMITH, Jacquelyn, M ... 630-515-6388 ... 158 E
jsmith@midwestern.edu
SMITH, Jake ... 612-343-4179 ... 270 C
jesmith@northcentral.edu
SMITH, James ... 718-429-6600 ... 359 E
james.smith@vaughn.edu
SMITH, James ... 718-489-5306 ... 348 E
jsmith@stfranciscollege.edu
SMITH, James ... 575-492-2159 ... 321 H
jsmith@usw.edu
SMITH, James ... 909-384-8600 ... 65 C
jsmith@sbccd.cc.ca.us
SMITH, James ... 740-654-6711 ... 399 G
SMITH, James ... 740-654-6711 ... 400 B
SMITH, James, E ... 317-788-3360 ... 180 C
jesmith@uindy.edu
SMITH, James, M ... 605-626-2521 ... 465 H
James.Smith@northern.edu
SMITH, Jane, L ... 630-942-2481 ... 147 G
smithja@cod.edu
SMITH, Janet ... 423-869-6287 ... 470 C
janet.smith@lmunet.edu
SMITH, Janet ... 601-643-8383 ... 274 A
janet.smith@colin.edu
SMITH, Janet, F ... 931-540-2510 ... 474 F
janet.smith@columbiastate.edu
SMITH, Jarret, L ... 540-828-5469 ... 516 K
jlsmith@bridgewater.edu
SMITH, Jason ... 312-567-7112 ... 153 B
jsmith31@iit.edu
SMITH, Jason ... 415-503-6281 ... 66 A
SMITH, Jean ... 718-780-0638 ... 324 F
jean.smith@brooklaw.edu
SMITH, Jean, L ... 610-989-1438 ... 450 E
jsmith@vfmac.edu
SMITH, Jeanne ... 304-734-6617 ... 542 D
jsmith@bridgemont.edu
SMITH, Jeannean ... 903-813-2431 ... 481 A
jsmith@austincollege.edu
SMITH, Jeannie ... 901-678-4530 ... 474 C
jesmith@memphis.edu
SMITH, Jeff ... 912-525-4500 ... 136 B
jesmith@scad.edu
SMITH, Jeff ... 912-681-5667 ... 134 H
tjsmith@ogeecheetech.edu
SMITH, Jeff ... 941-487-4353 ... 119 D
jsmith@ncf.edu
SMITH, Jeff ... 806-720-7482 ... 490 D
jeff.smith@lcu.edu
SMITH, Jeffrey ... 919-546-8238 ... 376 D
jeffrey.smith@shawu.edu
SMITH, Jennifer, B ... 270-745-4586 ... 207 C
Jennifer.breiwa.smith@wku.edu
SMITH, Jenny ... 828-328-7252 ... 366 B
jenny.smith@lr.edu
SMITH, Jeremy ... 601-276-2000 ... 277 E
jsmith@smcc.edu
SMITH, Jerome ... 803-934-3217 ... 459 F
jsmith@morris.edu
SMITH, Jerry ... 229-217-4210 ... 134 C
jsmith@moultrietech.edu
SMITH, Jerry ... 928-344-7535 ... 12 C
jerry.smith@azwestern.edu
SMITH, Jesse ... 661-255-1050 ... 32 C
jsmith@calarts.edu
SMITH, Jesse, R ... 601-477-4100 ... 275 B
jesse.smith@jcjc.edu
SMITH, Jessie, C ... 615-329-8731 ... 468 G
jcsmith@fisk.edu
SMITH, Jill ... 765-998-5384 ... 179 F
jlgodorhazy@taylor.edu
SMITH, Jill, A ... 818-677-2118 ... 35 D
jill.smith@csun.edu
SMITH, Jim ... 806-291-3440 ... 508 B
smithj@wbu.edu
SMITH, Jim, O ... 812-330-6062 ... 175 H
josmith@ivytech.edu
SMITH, Jimmy, L ... 601-877-6170 ... 273 C
jsmith@alcorn.edu
SMITH, Jo ... 615-353-3303 ... 475 D
jo.smith@nscc.edu
SMITH, Joan ... 303-914-6276 ... 87 C
joan.smith@rrcc.edu
SMITH, Joan ... 303-914-6410 ... 87 C
joan.smith@rrcc.edu
SMITH, Joan, E ... 209-575-6508 ... 79 L
smithj@yosemite.edu
SMITH, Joanne, H ... 512-245-2152 ... 501 C
js14@txstate.edu
SMITH, Jody, D ... 818-779-8043 ... 53 B
jsmith@kingsuniversity.edu
SMITH, Joe Lee ... 321-433-5502 ... 101 J
smithj@brevardcc.edu
SMITH, Joel, M ... 607-746-4600 ... 355 E
smithjm@delhi.edu
SMITH, Joel, M ... 607-746-4520 ... 355 E
smithjm@delhi.edu
SMITH, Joel, M ... 412-268-2649 ... 424 H
joelms@andrew.cmu.edu
SMITH, John ... 412-536-1088 ... 432 F
john.smith@laroche.edu

SMITH, John ... 251-460-6171 ... 9
johnsmith@usouthal.edu
SMITH, John ... 515-271-2969 ... 184 A
john.smith@drake.edu
SMITH, John ... 847-925-6416 ... 151 B
jsmith@harpercollege.edu
SMITH, John ... 919-530-5133 ... 378 A
jsmith@nccu.edu
SMITH, John, W ... 401-454-6501 ... 454 E
SMITH, John David ... 304-384-5241 ... 543 D
jdsmith@concord.edu
SMITH, Johnny ... 828-286-3636 ... 371 A
jsmith@isothermal.edu
SMITH, Joianne ... 847-635-1739 ... 160 E
joismith@oakton.edu
SMITH, Jonathan, E ... 216-397-4605 ... 392 M
jsmith@jcu.edu
SMITH, Joseph, T ... 410-706-7302 ... 227 C
jtsmith@af.umaryland.edu
SMITH, Joy, S ... 864-656-0471 ... 456 E
joy@clemson.edu
SMITH, Joyce ... 256-726-7356 ... 6 C
jsmith@oakwood.edu
SMITH, Joyya ... 912-478-8746 ... 131 A
jsmith@georgiasouthern.edu
SMITH, Judith, L ... 310-206-3961 ... 74 A
judis@college.ucla.edu
SMITH, Judy ... 814-824-3650 ... 436 C
jsmith@mercyhurst.edu
SMITH, Juli ... 661-654-2066 ... 33 H
jsmith101@csub.edu
SMITH, Julia ... 870-574-4498 ... 24 A
jsmith@sautech.edu
SMITH, June ... 402-481-8705 ... 297 B
june.smith@bryanlgh.org
SMITH, Kara ... 337-475-5148 ... 215 G
ksmith2@mcneese.edu
SMITH, Karen ... 432-552-2530 ... 507 C
smith_k@utpb.edu
SMITH, Karen, J ... 251-981-3771 ... 2 H
karen.smith@columbiasouthern.edu
SMITH, Karen, J ... 914-831-0343 ... 330 D
ksmith@cw.edu
SMITH, Karina ... 541-888-7316 ... 420 C
ksmith@socc.edu
SMITH, Katherine ... 702-968-2010 ... 303 D
ksmith@roseman.edu
SMITH, Kathleen, E ... 562-902-3367 ... 71 A
kathleensmith@scuhs.edu
SMITH, Kathleen, M ... 502-852-5419 ... 207 A
kathleen@louisville.edu
SMITH, Kathryn ... 503-517-7462 ... 420 A
smithk@reed.edu
SMITH, Kathy ... 760-630-1555 ... 52 J
ksmith@kaplan.edu
SMITH, Kathy ... 614-292-2991 ... 398 H
SMITH, Kathy ... 614-234-2230 ... 396 G
ksmith@mccn.edu
SMITH, Kathy, S ... 336-888-6391 ... 365 A
ksmith@highpoint.edu
SMITH, Katie, J ... 651-631-5222 ... 270 E
kjsmith@nwc.edu
SMITH, Katrina ... 806-291-3540 ... 508 B
smithk@wbu.edu
SMITH, Kay ... 515-244-4221 ... 181 D
smithk@aib.edu
SMITH, Keisha ... 954-499-9661 ... 104 C
ksmith@devry.edu
SMITH, Keith ... 252-451-8264 ... 372 B
ksmith@nash.cc.nc.us
SMITH, Keith ... 973-328-5400 ... 309 B
ksmith@ccm.edu
SMITH, Keith ... 731-989-6053 ... 468 K
ksmith@fhu.edu
SMITH, Kelly ... 231-876-3107 ... 248 F
kelly.smith@baker.edu
SMITH, Kelly ... 907-564-8289 ... 10 D
kelsmith@alaskapacific.edu
SMITH, Kenneth ... 508-929-8121 ... 239 D
kenneth.smith@worcester.edu
SMITH, Kenneth, A ... 724-847-6610 ... 429 G
kasmith@geneva.edu
SMITH, Kent ... 740-593-2561 ... 399 G
smithk1@ohio.edu
SMITH, Kevin ... 419-995-8294 ... 399 B
smith.178@osu.edu
SMITH, Kevin ... 773-291-6455 ... 147 D
ksmith@ccc.edu
SMITH, Kevin, B ... 409-880-8400 ... 500 F
kevin.smith@lamar.edu
SMITH, Kevin, H ... 901-678-2421 ... 474 C
ksmith@memphis.edu
SMITH, Khrystal ... 864-503-5125 ... 463 A
ksmith@uscupstate.edu
SMITH, Kimberly ... 860-701-6540 ... 558 E
Kimberly.R.Smith@uscg.mil
SMITH, Kris ... 808-544-0840 ... 140 B
ksmith@hpu.edu
SMITH, Kris, M ... 703-993-8841 ... 519 A
ksmitr@gmu.edu
SMITH, Krista ... 229-928-1331 ... 131 B
SMITH, Kristen ... 510-430-3131 ... 57 D
krsmith@mills.edu

SMITH, Scott .... 314-977-2501.... 289 F
ssmit134@slu.edu
SMITH, Scott .... 845-938-3833.... 558 G
Scott.Smith@usma.edu
SMITH, Scott, A .... 803-786-3672.... 457 C
scsmith@columbiasc.edu
SMITH, Scott, R .... 251-460-7093....... 9 E
srsmith@usouthal.edu
SMITH, Sean .... 805-565-6061...... 78 F
sesmith@westmont.edu
SMITH, Sharina .... 417-328-1803.... 290 E
ssmith@sbuniv.edu
SMITH, Sharon .... 609-984-1180.... 316 A
registrar@tesc.edu
SMITH, Sharon .... 616-632-2902.... 248 A
smithsha@aquinas.edu
SMITH, Sharon, P .... 828-652-0697.... 371 G
sharons@mcdowelltech.edu
SMITH, Sharon, P .... 724-836-9911.... 449 C
upgpres@pitt.edu
SMITH, Sharon Ann .... 618-374-5199.... 161 D
SMITH, Shawn .... 217-732-3168.... 156 F
ssmith@lincolnchristian.edu
SMITH, Shawn .... 541-881-5835.... 420 E
ssmith@tvcc.cc
SMITH, Sheila .... 585-271-3657.... 348 B
ssmith@stbernards.edu
SMITH, Shelley .... 256-840-4128........ 7 B
ssmith@snead.edu
SMITH, Sheryl, E .... 330-672-2480.... 393 D
sesmith@kent.edu
SMITH, Shirley .... 714-484-7455...... 59 C
ssmith@cypresscollege.edu
SMITH, Smret .... 815-836-5332.... 156 D
smithsm@lewisu.edu
SMITH, Solomon, S .... 405-466-3275.... 408 G
sssmith@lunet.edu
SMITH, Sonya .... 901-448-5568.... 477 C
sonya@uthsc.edu
SMITH, Stacie .... 904-680-7724.... 107 H
ssmith@fcsl.edu
SMITH, Stacy, A .... 989-837-4140.... 257 A
smithsta@northwood.edu
SMITH, Stan .... 702-895-3197.... 302 K
stan.smith@unlv.edu
SMITH, Stanley, B .... 864-656-2171.... 456 E
sbsmith@clemson.edu
SMITH, Stephanie .... 800-782-2422...... 33 B
smsmith@mail.cnuas.edu
SMITH, Stephanie, S .... 302-739-6819...... 96 A
ssmith@dtcc.edu
SMITH, Stephen .... 706-864-1890.... 134 D
ssmith@northgeorgia.edu
SMITH, Stephen .... 206-546-4694.... 537 G
spsmith@shoreline.edu
SMITH, Stephen, C .... 415-338-3879...... 36 F
scsmith@sfsu.edu
SMITH, Stephen, E .... 918-465-1723.... 408 A
ssmith@eosc.edu
SMITH, Stephen, M .... 985-549-2282.... 216 C
ssmith@selu.edu
SMITH, Stephen, P .... 215-951-1153.... 432 G
smiths@lasalle.edu
SMITH, Steve .... 865-974-4127.... 477 B
SMITH, Steve .... 951-343-4360...... 31 G
ssmith@calbaptist.edu
SMITH, Steve .... 910-410-1850.... 372 G
ssmith@richmondcc.edu
SMITH, Steve .... 512-837-2665.... 489 H
jbrooks@tca.edu
SMITH, Steve .... 907-450-8389...... 10 H
steve.smith@alaska.edu
SMITH, Steve .... 256-765-4233........ 9 D
wssmith@una.edu
SMITH, Steve .... 970-521-6657...... 86 E
steve.smith@njc.edu
SMITH, Steve .... 716-829-7600.... 332 F
smith@dyc.edu
SMITH, Steve .... 802-586-7711.... 514 E
ssmith@sterlingcollege.edu
SMITH, Steven .... 707-826-3256...... 36 D
ss7006@humboldt.edu
SMITH, Steven .... 601-977-4462.... 277 F
ssmith@tougaloo.edu
SMITH, Steven .... 817-923-1921.... 495 E
swsmith@swbts.edu
SMITH, Steven .... 410-455-1511.... 227 D
smithst@umbc.edu
SMITH, Steven .... 715-344-3063.... 554 C
steve.smith@mstc.edu
SMITH, Steven, F .... 989-774-7328.... 249 G
smith1sf@cmich.edu
SMITH, Steven, J .... 413-565-1000.... 231 B
ssmith@baypath.edu
SMITH, Steven, N .... 262-243-5700.... 546 I
steve.smith@cuw.edu
SMITH, Steven, R .... 619-239-0391...... 37 D
ssmith@cwsl.edu
SMITH, Stuart .... 501-812-2256...... 23 C
ssmith@pulaskitech.edu
SMITH, Stuart, A .... 859-858-3511.... 198 B
stuart.smith@asbury.edu
SMITH, Sue .... 916-361-1660...... 38 C
ssmith@cc.edu

SMITH, Susan .... 858-534-3583...... 74 D
susmith@ucsd.edu
SMITH, Susan .... 414-382-6042.... 545 H
sue.smith@alverno.edu
SMITH, Susan, A .... 678-717-3730.... 129 D
ssmith@gsc.edu
SMITH, Susan, C .... 607-436-2770.... 353 E
smithsc@oneonta.edu
SMITH, Susan, K .... 937-775-2620.... 406 C
susan.smith@wright.edu
SMITH, Susan, L .... 305-628-6661.... 116 G
ssmith@stu.edu
SMITH, Susan, M .... 563-589-3400.... 189 B
ssmith@dbq.edu
SMITH, Susanne .... 937-512-3009.... 401 J
susanne.smith@sinclair.edu
SMITH, Susanne .... 614-947-6160.... 391 A
smiths@franklin.edu
SMITH, Suzan .... 901-320-9769.... 478 B
srsmith@victory.edu
SMITH, Sybil .... 781-736-3443.... 233 A
sysmith@brandeis.edu
SMITH, Sybil .... 425-352-8133.... 531 F
ssmith@cascadia.edu
SMITH, Sylvia, A .... 706-880-8229.... 132 I
ssmith@lagrange.edu
SMITH, Tamalea .... 908-709-7093.... 316 B
tsmith@ucc.edu
SMITH, Tara .... 501-812-2314...... 23 C
tsmith@pulaskitech.edu
SMITH, Teresa .... 850-201-8590.... 121 F
smitht@tcc.fl.edu
SMITH, Teresa, C .... 217-245-3002.... 152 C
tcsmith@ic.edu
SMITH, Teresa, H .... 318-342-5320.... 216 E
tsmith@ulm.edu
SMITH, Teresa, L .... 504-278-6491.... 211 I
tsmith@nunez.edu
SMITH, Teresea, I .... 714-879-3901...... 50 G
tlsmith@hiu.edu
SMITH, Terrance .... 478-825-6473.... 129 C
smitht0@fvsu.edu
SMITH, Terry .... 713-646-1708.... 494 E
tsmith@stcl.edu
SMITH, Terry, B .... 573-875-7500.... 280 E
tsmith@ccis.edu
SMITH, Terry, L .... 814-732-2477.... 442 D
tlsmith@edinboro.edu
SMITH, Terry, S .... 512-505-3004.... 488 B
tssmith@htu.edu
SMITH, Theresa .... 515-643-6732.... 187 C
tsmith@mercydesmoines.org
SMITH, Therese, A .... 989-328-1284.... 256 A
terrys@montcalm.edu
SMITH, Thomas .... 314-392-2264.... 286 C
smitht@mobap.edu
SMITH, Thomas .... 970-351-2838...... 88 F
thomas.smith@unco.edu
SMITH, Thomas .... 918-456-5511.... 409 A
smith199@nsuok.edu
SMITH, Thomas, J .... 616-234-3951.... 251 G
tsmith@grcc.edu
SMITH, Thomas, P .... 570-941-7620.... 450 B
smitht3@scranton.edu
SMITH, Thomas, W .... 610-519-4651.... 450 G
thomas.w.smith@villanova.edu
SMITH, Tiffany .... 770-426-2780.... 133 B
tiffany.smith@life.edu
SMITH, Tim .... 773-838-7526.... 147 E
tsmith2@ccc.edu
SMITH, Timothy .... 731-661-5201.... 476 G
tsmith@uu.edu
SMITH, Tom .... 479-575-3208...... 24 C
tecsmith@uark.edu
SMITH, Tom, G .... 920-403-3866.... 550 C
tom.smith@snc.edu
SMITH, Tomesa .... 256-352-8233...... 10 B
tomesa.smith@wallacestate.edu
SMITH, Tommy .... 504-671-5608.... 210 G
tsmith@dcc.edu
SMITH, Tonia .... 305-949-9500.... 105 F
tsmith@cci.edu
SMITH, Tracy .... 617-912-9193.... 232 E
tsmith@bostonconservatory.edu
SMITH, Tracy .... 980-598-1006.... 365 G
tracy.smith@jwu.edu
SMITH, Tracy, D .... 501-882-8806...... 20 D
tdsmith@asub.edu
SMITH, Travis, G .... 315-386-7417.... 355 D
smitht@canton.edu
SMITH, Trent .... 620-276-9510.... 193 A
trent.smith@gcccks.edu
SMITH, Tricia, G .... 410-334-2892.... 229 E
tgsmith@worwic.edu
SMITH, Valerie .... 609-258-3040.... 313 A
SMITH, Vanessa .... 713-779-1110.... 493 H
vsmith@sbhouston.com
SMITH, Verne, R .... 302-477-2248...... 96 H
vrsmith@widener.edu
SMITH, Vernon .... 480-517-8270...... 16 C
vernon.smith@riosalado.edu
SMITH, Vicki .... 301-784-5000.... 221 A
vsmith@allegany.edu

SMITH, Vicki .... 315-536-5666.... 337 K
vlsmith@mail.keuka.edu
SMITH, Vicky .... 319-368-6464.... 187 E
vsmith@mtmercy.edu
SMITH, Vicky .... 815-455-8725.... 157 F
vsmith@mchenry.edu
SMITH, Victoria .... 315-279-5255.... 337 K
vsmith@mail.keuka.edu
SMITH, W. Andrew (Andy) . 512-475-6608.... 505 B
andy.smith@universityunions.utexas.edu
SMITH, W. Gaines .... 334-844-5546........ 1 G
smithwg@aces.edu
SMITH, W. Stuart .... 843-792-4000.... 459 C
smithstu@musc.edu
SMITH, Wade .... 864-592-4670.... 461 C
smithwa@sccsc.edu
SMITH, Wallace Charles .... 484-384-2950.... 438 C
sempres@eastern.edu
SMITH, Walter .... 301-846-2674.... 222 G
wsmith@frederick.edu
SMITH, Walter, L .... 765-641-4156.... 169 A
wlsmith@anderson.edu
SMITH, Wendall .... 610-896-1000.... 430 G
w1smith@haverford.edu
SMITH, Wendy, B .... 724-847-6104.... 429 G
wbsmith@geneva.edu
SMITH, Wendy, D .... 209-667-3351...... 36 C
wsmith@csustan.edu
SMITH, Wendy, M .... 307-674-6446.... 556 C
wsmith@sheridan.edu
SMITH, Whitman .... 662-915-7226.... 277 G
whitman@olemiss.edu
SMITH, Will .... 740-389-6786.... 399 D
smith.4818@osu.edu
SMITH, William .... 760-921-5442...... 61 B
wsmith@paloverde.edu
SMITH, William, G .... 252-335-3225.... 377 D
wgsmith@mail.ecsu.edu
SMITH, William, H .... 617-824-3450.... 234 D
william_smith@emerson.edu
SMITH, Willie .... 337-948-0239.... 209 D
wsmith@acadiana.edu
SMITH, Willie .... 337-363-2197.... 209 E
wsmith@acadiana.edu
SMITH, Willie .... 337-948-0384.... 209 G
wsmith@ltc.edu
SMITH, Wilma Quarker ...... 251-578-1313........ 6 E
wsmith@rstc.edu
SMITH, Zana .... 513-875-3344.... 387 B
zana.smith@chatfield.edu
SMITH-BATES, Jacqui, S ... 206-281-2488.... 537 D
jacquisb@spu.edu
SMITH-BROWN,
Stephanie .... 870-543-5996...... 23 H
sbrown@seark.edu
SMITH-BRUSH, Lynn .... 972-273-3464.... 485 B
lsmith@dcccd.edu
SMITH-BUTLER, Lisa .... 843-377-2144.... 456 A
lsbutler@charlestonlaw.edu
SMITH-CAMPBELL, Vesta .. 517-338-3042.... 249 H
vscampbell@cleary.edu
SMITH-COPPES, John .... 320-251-5600.... 271 D
john.smith-coppes@Rasmussen.edu
SMITH GLASPER, Marcia .. 203-392-5491...... 91 I
smithglaspm1@southernct.edu
SMITH-HOWELL, Deb .... 402-554-3378.... 301 B
dsmith-howell@unomaha.edu
SMITH-HUPP, Karen .... 301-934-7701.... 222 C
karens@csmd.edu
SMITH-KELLER, Keley .... 563-387-1025.... 187 A
SMITH-KIAWU, Rena .... 718-997-5100.... 328 F
rena.smithkiawu@qc.cuny.edu
SMITH MORGAN, Terry ...... 334-683-5100........ 5 D
tmorgan1@judson.edu
SMITH-PATTERSON, Trina 817-515-7711.... 496 A
trina.patterson@tccd.edu
SMITH QUIST, Bonnie ...... 614-947-6068.... 391 A
quistb@frankli.edu
SMITH-ROBINSON,
Marilyn .... 404-225-4612.... 125 A
msmithro@atlantatech.edu
SMITH-SEBASTO,
Nicholas .... 908-737-3613.... 311 B
nsmithse@kean.edu
SMITH-WILLIAMS,
Michelle .... 708-534-4503.... 151 C
msmith-williams@govst.edu
SMITH-WORTHINGTON,
Darlene .... 252-493-7429.... 372 E
dsmith@email.pittcc.edu
SMITHER, Sheila .... 620-331-4100.... 193 G
ssmither@indycc.edu
SMITHERS, John, A .... 401-598-1509.... 453 C
jsmithers@jwu.edu
SMITHEY, Van .... 386-752-1822.... 108 C
van.smithey@fgc.edu
SMITHSOM, Ryan .... 517-780-4568.... 248 I
ryan.smithson@baker.edu
SMITHSON, Bud .... 620-417-1651.... 196 B
bud.smithson@sccc.edu
SMITHSON, John, W .... 610-660-1216.... 446 C
smithson@sju.edu
SMITLEY, Debra, K .... 309-438-3320.... 153 C
dsmitle@ilstu.edu

SMITS, Karen, J .... 920-498-5615.... 555
karen.smits@nwtc.edu
SMITS, Peter, N .... 559-278-6050...... 34
peter_smits@csufresno.edu
SMITS, Sally, A .... 414-425-8300.... 550
ssmits@shst.edu
SMITTER, Roger .... 410-827-5847.... 222
rsmitter@chesapeake.edu
SMOCK, Cathy .... 979-458-7177.... 496
cathy-smock@tamus.edu
SMOKOWSKI, Peter .... 617-358-7000.... 232 C
psmokows@bu.edu
SMOLINSKI, James, A .... 937-224-0061.... 395 A
jsmolinski@swcollege.net
SMOLKER, David .... 813-223-3888.... 119 D
davids@bsbfirm.com
SMOLKO, Rita, M .... 330-287-1296.... 399 A
smolko.3@osu.edu
SMOLLA, Rodney, A .... 864-294-2100.... 458 D
rod.smolla@furman.edu
SMOLSKI, Lisa .... 401-456-2809.... 454 A
lsmolski@ric.edu
SMOOT, Kathy .... 606-487-3088.... 201 H
Kathy.Smoot@kctcs.edu
SMOOT, Lori .... 410-334-2898.... 229 E
lsmoot@worwic.edu
SMOROL, Bobbie, H .... 315-792-3128.... 359 C
bsmorol@utica.edu
SMOTHERA, Roderick, L .... 512-505-3070.... 488 B
rlsmothers@htu.edu
SMOTHERS, Traci .... 504-762-3004.... 210 G
tsmoth@dcc.edu
SMRHA, Judith .... 785-594-8337.... 190 C
judy.smrha@bakeru.edu
SMULSON, Erik .... 202-687-0100...... 98 A
ems62@georgetown.edu
SMUNT, Timothy, L .... 414-229-6256.... 551 C
tsmunt@uwm.edu
SMURDON, Melissa, J .... 317-940-8200.... 170 C
msmurdon@butler.edu
SMUTZ, Wayne, D .... 814-863-6726.... 438 F
wds4@psu.edu
SMYER, Michael, A .... 570-577-1561.... 423 D
smyer@bucknell.edu
SMYKIL, Paula .... 603-899-4341.... 305 B
smykilp@franklinpierce.edu
SMYLE, Faye .... 707-253-3106...... 58 F
fsmyle@napavalley.edu
SMYRE HINES, Beverly ...... 706-771-4156.... 125 D
bsmyre@augustatech.edu
SMYTH, Nancy, J .... 716-645-1267.... 351 G
sw-dean@buffalo.edu
SMYTH, Vince .... 904-620-2875.... 120 C
vsmyth@unf.edu
SMYTH-MCGAHA, Bonnie . 501-882-8826...... 20 D
bmsmyth@asub.edu
SMYTHE, Jennifer .... 503-352-2770.... 419 E
smythej@pacificu.edu
SNAPE, Kevin .... 216-987-3208.... 389 A
kevin.snape@tri-c.edu
SNAPP, Diana .... 207-326-2243.... 219 D
diana.snapp@mma.edu
SNAPP, John .... 325-670-1507.... 487 D
John.Snapp@hsutx.edu
SNARE, Charles .... 308-432-6246.... 299 G
csnare@csc.edu
SNAVELY, Deanne .... 724-357-2609.... 442 E
Deanne.Snavely@iup.edu
SNAVELY, Grace, N .... 617-364-3510.... 232 C
gsnavely@boston.edu
SNEAD, L. Rucker .... 434-223-6106.... 519 B
rsnead@hsc.edu
SNEDDEN, Kelly .... 316-942-4291.... 195 C
sneddenk@newmanu.edu
SNEDDON, Jay, N .... 208-732-6247.... 143 B
jsneddon@csi.edu
SNEED, Bronwyn, C .... 870-235-4023...... 23 I
bcsneed@saumag.edu
SNEED, Carlos .... 651-523-2423.... 264 C
csneed@hamline.edu
SNEED, Donna .... 314-984-7513.... 289 D
dsneed20@stlcc.edu
SNEED, Janice .... 318-670-9471.... 215 A
jsneed@susla.edu
SNEED, Mike .... 501-812-2238...... 23 C
msneed@pulaskitech.edu
SNEERINGER, Tim .... 814-827-4440.... 449 E
sneering@pitt.edu
SNELL, Carolyn, R .... 803-535-5338.... 456 D
csnell@claflin.edu
SNELL, Cudore, L .... 202-806-7300...... 98 B
csnell@howard.edu
SNELL, Kim .... 937-298-3399.... 394 D
kim.snell@kcma.edu
SNELL, Laurence, I .... 904-632-3294.... 109 E
lsnell@fscj.edu
SNELL, Sara .... 803-786-3029.... 457 C
ssnell@columbiasc.edu
SNELLGROVE, Michael, R . 256-824-2560........ 9 A
michael.snellgrove@uah.edu
SNELLING, John .... 602-787-6840...... 16 A
john.snelling@pvmail.maricopa.edu
SNELSON, Pamela .... 717-291-3843.... 429 E
pam.snelson@fandm.edu

SNIDER, Ann ..... 614-253-3537 .... 398 F snidera@ohiodominican.edu
SNIDER, Darlene ..... 509-527-3689 .... 538 G darlene.snider@wwcc.edu
SNIDER, Dean, C ..... 509-527-5288 .... 539 E sniderdc@whitman.edu
SNIDER, Dwayne ..... 254-968-9103 .... 496 F snider@tarleton.edu
SNIDER, Glen ..... 928-428-8217 ..... 14 C glen.snider@eac.edu
SNIDER, James, M ..... 301-784-5000 .... 221 A jsnider@allegany.edu
SNIDER, Katharine, J ..... 717-291-3989 .... 429 E kate.snider@fandm.edu
SNIDER, Kevin, J ..... 724-334-6051 .... 440 B kjs33@psu.edu
SNIDER, Lisa ..... 318-371-3035 .... 211 F lsnider@ltc.edu
SNIDER, Lora ..... 859-622-2246 .... 200 D lora.snider@eku.edu
SNIDER, Neil ..... 205-652-3614 ..... 10 A nsnider@uwa.edu
SNIP, Bob ..... 502-897-4703 .... 205 H besnip@sbts.edu
SNIPES, Lloyd ..... 803-327-7402 .... 456 F
SNITKER, Connie ..... 319-363-8213 .... 187 E csnitker@mtmercy.edu
SNODDY, Catherine, E ..... 304-697-7550 .... 540 I csnoddy@huntingtonjuniorcollege.edu
SNODDY, Rebeckah ..... 765-973-8585 .... 173 D rrieder@iue.edu
SNODGRASS, Burnie, L ..... 417-836-4040 .... 286 F bsnodgrass@missouristate.edu
SNODGRASS, Gregory ..... 512-245-2208 .... 501 C gs03@txstate.edu
SNODGRASS, Madelyn ..... 512-472-4133 .... 494 B msnodgrass@ssw.edu
SNODGRASS, Mark, T ..... 815-740-3432 .... 167 C msnodgrass@stfrancis.edu
SNODGRASS, Steven ..... 217-732-3155 .... 156 G ssnodgrass@lincolncollege.edu
SNODGRASS, Wendell ..... 563-425-5202 .... 189 C snodgrassw@uiu.edu
SNOE, Terri ..... 412-392-4207 .... 444 H tsnoe@pointpark.edu
SNOOK, Dawn ..... 704-637-4402 .... 363 C dsnook@catawba.edu
SNOREK, Karen ..... 507-332-5890 .... 269 F karen.snorek@southcentral.edu
SNOVER, Lydia, S ..... 617-253-5838 .... 242 A lsnover@mit.edu
SNOW, Barbara ..... 607-962-9223 .... 331 D snow@corning-cc.edu
SNOW, Brent ..... 210-932-6217 .... 498 B brent.snow@tamusa.tamus.edu
SNOW, Bruce, M ..... 801-422-5054 .... 509 D bruce_snow@byu.edu
SNOW, Cathy, C ..... 478-757-5173 .... 139 A csnow@wesleyancollege.edu
SNOW, Fredrick ..... 800-955-2527 .... 282 G
SNOW, Gregory, J ..... 408-944-6008 .... 60 L greg.snow@palmer.edu
SNOW, Joe ..... 918-781-7245 .... 407 B snowj@bacone.edu
SNOW, Kathryn ..... 815-288-5511 .... 163 I snowk@svcc.edu
SNOW, Laura ..... 816-483-9600 .... 289 H laura.snow@spst.edu
SNOW, Laura ..... 801-581-5113 .... 510 L laura.snow@utah.edu
SNOW, LeAnn ..... 510-841-1905 ..... 27 J lflesher@absw.edu
SNOW, Marie ..... 904-470-8124 .... 105 A marie.snow@ewc.edu
SNOW, Natalie ..... 610-683-4153 .... 442 F snow@kutztown.edu
SNOW, Nicholas ..... 973-761-9018 .... 315 B nicholas.snow@shu.edu
SNOW-FLAMER, Keith ..... 707-476-4177 ..... 42 A keith-snowflamer@redwoods.edu
SNOWDEN, Bradley, C ..... 540-665-5455 .... 523 K bsnowden@su.edu
SNOWDEN, Kent ..... 334-241-9576 ..... 8 B kesnowden@troy.edu
SNOWDEN, Michael ..... 912-344-2567 .... 124 E michael.snowden@armstrong.edu
SNOWDEN, Michael, T ..... 337-475-5426 .... 215 G msnowden@mcneese.edu
SNOWDEN, Monique, L ..... 805-898-4154 .... 47 C msnowden@fielding.edu
SNOWHILL, Lucia ..... 805-893-5383 .... 74 F snowhill@library.ucsb.edu
SNUFFIN, Gary ..... 901-722-3260 .... 473 B gsnuffin@sco.edu
SNUGGS, Jean ..... 916-484-8201 .... 56 A snuggsj@arc.losrios.edu
SNUGGS, Kristi, L ..... 252-823-5166 .... 370 A snuggsk@edgecombe.edu
SNYDER, Alan, J ..... 610-758-6964 .... 434 E ajs410@lehigh.edu
SNYDER, Alan, R ..... 301-687-4242 .... 228 C arsnyder@frostburg.edu
SNYDER, Andrea ..... 717-545-4747 .... 432 D
SNYDER, Angie, P ..... 479-248-7236 ..... 21 G angie@ecollege.edu
SNYDER, Arthur, E ..... 260-422-5561 .... 172 L aesnyder@indianatech.edu
SNYDER, Barbara, H ..... 801-581-7793 .... 510 L bsnyder@sa.utah.edu
SNYDER, Barbara, R ..... 216-368-4344 .... 386 E barbara.snyder@case.edu
SNYDER, Brandy ..... 432-837-8189 .... 501 B bsnyder@sulross.edu
SNYDER, C. Vernon ..... 419-530-4249 .... 404 F vernon.snyder@utoledo.edu
SNYDER, Carla ..... 903-223-3013 .... 498 C carla.snyder@tamut.edu
SNYDER, Chris ..... 724-830-1895 .... 447 B csnyder@setonhill.edu
SNYDER, Clint, W ..... 330-325-6755 .... 397 C cwsnyder@neoucom.edu
SNYDER, Connie ..... 229-248-2504 .... 125 E csnyder@bainbridge.edu
SNYDER, Cynthia, L ..... 540-654-1011 .... 524 H csnyder@umw.edu
SNYDER, Daniel, C ..... 303-975-5010 .... 89 E dsnyder@westwood.edu
SNYDER, David ..... 415-485-9506 .... 41 I david.snyder@marin.edu
SNYDER, David, W ..... 717-545-4747 .... 432 D
SNYDER, Dee Dee ..... 330-287-1223 .... 399 A snyder.426@osu.edu
SNYDER, Denis ..... 360-475-7421 .... 535 J dsnyder@olympic.edu
SNYDER, Diane, E ..... 210-485-0010 .... 479 B dsnyder12@alamo.edu
SNYDER, Dianne, O ..... 704-403-1521 .... 362 E dianne.snyder@carolinashealthcare.org
SNYDER, Donald ..... 702-895-3308 .... 302 K donald.snyder@unlv.edu
SNYDER, Donald, W ..... 610-799-1121 .... 434 D dsnyder@lccc.edu
SNYDER, Gerry ..... 505-473-6292 .... 320 F gerry.snyder@santafeuniversity.edu
SNYDER, Grant, S ..... 610-359-5060 .... 426 G gsnyder@dccc.edu
SNYDER, Gregory, J ..... 810-762-3488 .... 259 F gsnyders@umflint.edu
SNYDER, Jackie ..... 315-866-0300 .... 335 E snyderje@herkimer.edu
SNYDER, Jan, E ..... 712-324-5061 .... 188 A jsnyder@nwicc.edu
SNYDER, Jane ..... 617-232-8026 .... 232 F snyderj@bgsp.edu
SNYDER, Jane ..... 314-719-3627 .... 282 C jsnyder@fontbonne.edu
SNYDER, Jason ..... 205-970-9235 ..... 7 D jsnyder@sebc.edu
SNYDER, Jeff, B ..... 651-631-5142 .... 270 E jbsnyder@nwc.edu
SNYDER, Jim ..... 859-336-5082 .... 205 F jsnyder@sccky.edu
SNYDER, John, F ..... 724-738-2028 .... 443 E john.snyder@sru.edu
SNYDER, John, R ..... 419-995-8300 .... 399 B snyder.4@osu.edu
SNYDER, Jon, D ..... 212-875-4466 .... 323 E jsnyder@bankstreet.edu
SNYDER, Julie, A ..... 419-372-9623 .... 385 C jmaiuri@bgsu.edu
SNYDER, Katherine ..... 301-687-4105 .... 228 C ksnyder@frostburg.edu
SNYDER, Keith ..... 423-236-2929 .... 473 A kasnyder@southern.edu
SNYDER, Kenneth ..... 517-629-0213 .... 247 E ksnyder@albion.edu
SNYDER, Kevin, C ..... 336-841-9107 .... 365 A ksnyder@highpoint.edu
SNYDER, Ky, L ..... 619-260-2930 .... 76 A kysnyder@sandiego.edu
SNYDER, Lisa ..... 864-977-7669 .... 460 A lisa.snyder@ngu.edu
SNYDER, Lisa, M ..... 260-356-4070 .... 172 K lsnyder@huntington.edu
SNYDER, Lorraine, G ..... 312-915-6411 .... 157 A lsnyde2@luc.edu
SNYDER, Marcella ..... 304-336-8345 .... 544 B msnyder@westliberty.edu
SNYDER, Marian, L ..... 610-799-1734 .... 434 D msnyder@lccc.edu
SNYDER, Mary ..... 719-255-4119 .... 88 C mary.snyder@uccs.edu
SNYDER, Mary Beth ..... 248-370-4200 .... 257 C mbsnyder@oakland.edu
SNYDER, Matthew ..... 315-792-5331 .... 341 E msnyder2@mvcc.edu
SNYDER, Paul ..... 239-590-7050 .... 119 A psnyder@fgcu.edu
SNYDER, Peggy, J ..... 620-235-4176 .... 195 I psnyder@pittstate.edu
SNYDER, Reonna ..... 515-244-4221 .... 181 D snyderr@aib.edu
SNYDER, Rob, A ..... 724-287-8711 .... 423 F rob.snyder@bc3.edu
SNYDER, Robert, A ..... 707-826-3722 .... 36 D ras1@humboldt.edu
SNYDER, Robert, J ..... 610-282-1100 .... 426 I robert.snyder@desales.edu
SNYDER, Ryan ..... 716-270-5119 .... 333 D ascsnyderr@ecc.edu
SNYDER, Sandra ..... 503-552-1514 .... 417 D ssnyder@ncnm.edu
SNYDER, Sheri ..... 580-628-6208 .... 409 B sheri.snyder@north-ok.edu
SNYDER, Stephen, D ..... 513-529-6225 .... 396 D snydersd@muohio.edu
SNYDER, Stephen, E ..... 229-931-2037 .... 131 B
SNYDER, Steven, C ..... 540-636-2900 .... 517 H ssnyder@christendom.edu
SNYDER, Susan, M ..... 716-829-3316 .... 351 G student-health@buffalo.edu
SNYDER, Terry ..... 610-896-1272 .... 430 G tsnyder@haverford.edu
SNYDER, Thomas, J ..... 317-921-4265 .... 175 G tsnyder@ivytech.edu
SNYDER, Timothy, L ..... 410-617-2495 .... 224 A tlsnyder@loyola.edu
SNYDER, Vicki ..... 740-392-6868 .... 396 H vsnyder@mvnu.edu
SNYDER, Victoria ..... 706-321-8167 .... 135 C vsnyder@paine.edu
SNYDER, Walter, W ..... 816-654-7122 .... 283 J wsnyder@kcumb.edu
SOARDS, Kathy ..... 419-267-1314 .... 397 D ksoards@northweststate.edu
SOARES, Danene ..... 619-660-4674 ..... 48 J danene.soares@gcccd.edu
SOBA, Steven ..... 603-645-9611 .... 306 B s.soba@snhu.edu
SOBANET, Jennifer ..... 303-404-5560 .... 84 H jennifer.sobanet@frontrange.edu
SOBANIA, Neal, W ..... 253-531-7203 .... 535 K sobania@plu.edu
SOBASKI, Kenneth, J ..... 714-816-0366 ..... 72 I ksobaski@tuiu.edu
SOBCZYK, Jim ..... 415-502-5256 ..... 74 E jsobczyk@ucsf.edu
SOBEK, Christine, J ..... 630-466-7900 .... 167 G csobek@waubonsee.edu
SOBH, Tarek, M ..... 203-576-4111 .... 94 D sobh@bridgeport.edu
SOBIESUO, Andrew ..... 843-953-5537 .... 457 B sobiesuoa@cofc.edu
SOBINA, Debra ..... 814-676-6591 .... 442 B dsobina@clarion.edu
SOBISCH, Andreas ..... 216-397-4183 .... 392 M sobisch@jcu.edu
SOBKY-SHAFFER, Yvette ..... 310-665-6819 ..... 60 B ysobky@otis.edu
SOBOLESKE, Mark ..... 303-986-2320 ..... 82 E marks@csha.net
SOBOTOR, William, J ..... 901-572-2772 .... 467 A bill.sobotor@bchs.edu
SOBOTTA, Sharon ..... 925-631-4193 ..... 64 F ssobotta@stmarys-ca.edu
SOCCI, Patrick, J ..... 516-463-5676 .... 335 H patrick.socci@hofstra.edu
SOCHOCKY, Anna ..... 505-984-6102 .... 320 C
SOCORRO, Julio ..... 954-965-7272 .... 107 B
SODANO, Carol Rae ..... 305-899-3310 .... 101 F csodano@mail.barry.edu
SODEN, Richard ..... 212-938-4030 .... 355 B rsoden@sunyopt.edu
SODERQUIST, Rich ..... 815-802-8173 .... 154 J rsoderquist@kcc.edu
SOEFFING, William ..... 605-331-6759 .... 466 D william.soeffing@usiouxfalls.edu
SOEFFKER-CULICERTO, Heike, I ..... 304-929-6731 .... 542 H hsoeffker@newriver.edu
SOFFA, Kari ..... 661-362-5417 ..... 41 G Kari.soffa@canyons.edu
SOFISH, Marion ..... 408-283-7500 ..... 37 A marion.sofish@sjsu.edu
SOFO, Dianna ..... 973-290-4478 .... 309 A dsofo@cse.edu
SOFRANKO, Greg ..... 724-938-4274 .... 441 G sofranko@calu.edu
SOGLIUZZO, SJ, Louis, P ..... 315-445-4113 .... 338 B sogliulp@lemoyne.edu
SOHAN, Donna ..... 860-412-7261 ..... 91 A dsohan@qvcc.commnet.edu
SOHM, Michael ..... 952-446-4161 .... 263 E sohmm@crown.edu
SOHN, Eugene ..... 718-518-4284 .... 327 D esohn@hostos.cuny.edu
SOHN-ROBENSON, Sunhee ..... 315-268-6633 .... 329 C ssohnrob@clarkson.edu
SOHOLT, Pam, B ..... 701-788-4823 .... 381 F Pam.Soholt@mayvillestate.edu
SOIFER, Aviam ..... 808-956-6363 .... 141 B soifer@hawaii.edu
SOIFER, B, T ..... 626-395-4241 ..... 32 E pmachair@caltech.edu
SOIFER, Yitzchok ..... 845-362-3053 .... 323 H
SOIFFER, Stephen ..... 718-260-5400 .... 328 E ssoiffer@citytech.cuny.edu
SOILEAU, M, J ..... 407-823-5538 .... 120 A mj@ucf.edu
SOJKA, Gregory, S ..... 513-732-5209 .... 403 E sojkagy@email.uc.edu
SOKANY, Stephen, G ..... 330-672-2222 .... 393 D ssokany@kent.edu
SOKENU, Julius ..... 805-378-1448 ..... 77 B jsokenu@vcccd.edu
SOKOL, Karen, A ..... 973-642-8738 .... 315 C karen.sokol@shu.edu
SOKOL, Moshe, Z ..... 718-820-4800 .... 357 J sokolm@touro.edu
SOKOLS, Patricia, L ..... 864-488-8255 .... 459 A psokols@limestone.edu
SOKOLSKY, Pierre, V ..... 801-581-6958 .... 510 L ps@physics.utah.edu
SOLA, Peter, L ..... 651-631-5349 .... 270 E plsola@nwc.edu
SOLAN, George ..... 252-399-6399 .... 362 A gsolan@barton.edu
SOLAND, Nathan ..... 507-786-3310 .... 271 H solandn@stolaf.edu
SOLANDER, Sondra, K ..... 620-431-2820 .... 195 B ssolander@neosho.edu
SOLANO, Hugo ..... 787-725-6500 .... 560 G nsolano@sju.albizu.edu
SOLANO, Laura ..... 719-549-3221 ..... 87 B Laura.Solano@pueblocc.edu
SOLARI, Joe, P ..... 317-788-3425 .... 180 C jsolari@uindy.edu
SOLAZZO, Liz ..... 336-506-4172 .... 367 G solazzol@alamancecc.edu
SOLBACH, Robin ..... 732-987-2681 .... 310 D solbach@georgian.edu
SOLBERG, Bennett ..... 703-821-8570 .... 524 D bsolberg@stratford.edu
SOLBERG, Eric, J ..... 563-588-7969 .... 186 I eric.solberg@loras.edu
SOLBERG, Larry ..... 715-425-3774 .... 552 A larry.c.solberg@uwrf.edu
SOLBERG, Lori ..... 605-995-2805 .... 464 B losolber@dwu.edu
SOLBERG, Susan, R ..... 708-709-3758 .... 161 C ssolberg@prairiestate.edu
SOLBRIG, Ronald ..... 208-282-2330 .... 143 D solbrona@isu.edu
SOLDAVIN, Raymond, C ..... 212-817-7130 .... 327 B rsoldavin@gc.cuny.edu
SOLDWISCH, Sandie ..... 708-763-1598 .... 162 C sandie.soldwisch@resu.edu
SOLEM, Jan ..... 701-774-4214 .... 382 F jan.solem@willistonstate.edu
SOLEMSAAS, Rachel ..... 425-564-2446 .... 531 B rachel.solemsaas@bellevuecollege.edu
SOLES, David ..... 212-998-8259 .... 344 B david.soles@nyu.edu
SOLES, Jason ..... 903-923-2011 .... 486 D jsoles@etbu.edu
SOLHAUG, Michael, J ..... 757-446-5804 .... 518 F solhaumj@evms.edu
SOLHEIM, Derek, N ..... 319-352-8330 .... 189 F derek.solheim@wartburg.edu
SOLHEIM, Joan, C ..... 704-847-5600 .... 376 H jsolheim@ses.edu
SOLINGA, Elaine, F ..... 860-439-2058 ..... 91 E efsol@conncoll.edu
SOLINGER, Diane, P ..... 218-477-2322 .... 268 A solinger@mnstate.edu
SOLIS, JR., Federico ..... 956-764-5866 .... 489 G fsolis@laredo.edu
SOLIS, Robert ..... 774-455-7711 .... 237 B rsolis@umassp.edu
SOLIS, Vincent, R ..... 956-764-5950 .... 489 G vincent.solis@laredo.edu
SOLITRO, Patricia, A ..... 508-854-4203 .... 241 C pats@qcc.mass.edu
SOLIZ, Sandra ..... 713-525-3103 .... 504 D solizs@stthom.edu
SOLL, Andy ..... 978-542-6120 .... 239 B asoll@salemstate.edu
SOLLARS, David ..... 785-670-2045 .... 197 D david.sollars@washburn.edu
SOLLENBERGER, Donna, K ..... 409-772-6116 .... 507 B dksoll@utmb.edu
SOLLER, Dan ..... 301-447-7407 .... 225 A soller@msmary.edu
SOLLEY, Anna ..... 602-285-7433 ..... 16 B anna.solley@pcmail.maricopa.edu
SOLLINS, Amy ..... 415-565-4832 ..... 73 G sollinsa@uchastings.edu
SOLLOSI, Nancy, B ..... 336-334-4822 .... 370 E nbsollosi@gtcc.edu
SOLMS, Daniel ..... 765-677-2138 .... 174 E daniel.solms@indwes.edu
SOLODUCHA, Kathy, J ..... 816-501-4250 .... 288 D kathy.soloducha@rockhurst.edu
SOLOFF, Laura ..... 310-314-6021 ..... 29 J
SOLOMEN, Joy ..... 856-256-4686 .... 314 A solomen@rowan.edu
SOLOMITA, Lynn ..... 310-660-3670 ..... 45 D lsolomita@elcamino.edu
SOLOMON, Daniel, L ..... 919-515-7277 .... 378 B d_solomon@ncsu.edu
SOLOMON, Debbie ..... 425-235-2352 .... 536 E dsolomon@rtc.edu

SOLOMON, Eric, S .... 214-828-8408.... 497 A
esolomon@bcd.tamhsc.edu
SOLOMON, Jeffrey, S .... 508-831-5288.... 247 B
solomon@wpi.edu
SOLOMON, Jeremy .... 781-239-3122.... 240 D
jsolomon@massbay.edu
SOLOMON, Laura .... 212-217-3650.... 333 G
laura_solomon@fitnyc.edu
SOLOMON, Mark, R .... 248-689-8282.... 260 A
msolomon@walshcollege.edu
SOLOMON, Mary Ellen ...... 412-392-6190.... 444 H
mesolomon@pointpark.edu
SOLOMON, Mendel .... 973-267-9404.... 313 C
rabbisolo@aol.com
SOLOMON, Michelle .... 256-726-7508........ 6 C
msolomon@oakwood.edu
SOLOMON, Rayman, L .... 856-225-6191.... 314 C
raysol@camlaw.rutgers.edu
SOLOMON, Robert .... 912-754-2879.... 136 D
rsolomon@savannahtech.edu
SOLOMON, Samuel, B .... 617-373-2597.... 244 A
SOLOMON, Shoshana .... 973-267-9404.... 313 C
rca226@aol.com
SOLOMON, Sigrid, B .... 937-382-6661.... 405 H
sigrid_solomon@wilmington.edu
SOLOMON, William, G ...... 478-301-2771.... 133 F
solomon_wg@mercer.edu
SOLOMONS, Len, P .... 731-881-7626.... 477 E
lsolomon@utm.edu
SOLOMONS, Mary, L .... 518-580-5619.... 351 B
msolomon@skidmore.edu
SOLOMONSON, Heidi ...... 651-213-4126.... 264 D
SOLORZANO, Fernando .... 562-985-4101...... 35 A
fsolorza@csulb.edu
SOLT, Karen .... 630-942-2292.... 147 G
soltka@cod.edu
SOLT, Michael .... 562-985-5306...... 35 A
msolt@csulb.edu
SOLTAN, Joanna .... 617-369-3655.... 244 G
jsoltan@smfa.edu
SOLTIS, Corinne .... 907-796-6255...... 11 A
corinne.soltic@uas.alaska.edu
SOLTIS, Karen .... 412-291-6322.... 422 D
ksoltis@aii.edu
SOLTIS, Kay, W .... 253-535-8725.... 535 K
soltiskw@plu.edu
SOLTMAN, Jackie .... 231-876-3104.... 248 F
jackie.soltman@baker.edu
SOLTMAN, Mary .... 360-596-5210.... 538 B
msoltman@spscc.ctc.edu
SOLTOW, Allen, R .... 918-631-2766.... 413 F
allen-soltow@utulsa.edu
SOLTYS, Jonathan .... 630-889-6620.... 159 E
jsoltys@nuhs.edu
SOLTZ, David, L .... 570-389-4526.... 441 F
dsoltz@bloomu.edu
SOM, Andrew .... 415-338-3145...... 36 F
asom@sfsu.edu
SOMERA, R. Ray, D .... 671-735-5528.... 559 B
reneray.somera@guamcc.edu
SOMERO, Marty .... 970-351-2502...... 88 F
marty.somero@unco.edu
SOMERS, Christine .... 570-674-6314.... 436 F
csomers@misericordia.edu
SOMERS, Cindy .... 303-797-5972...... 80 J
cindy.somers@arapahoe.edu
SOMERS, Jeanne .... 216-397-3053.... 392 M
jsomers@jcu.edu
SOMERS, Kevin .... 870-743-3000...... 22 G
ksomers@northark.edu
SOMERS, Michael .... 508-531-1256.... 238 B
msomers@bridgew.edu
SOMERS, Micki .... 870-743-3000...... 22 G
msomers@northark.edu
SOMERS, Robert, J .... 410-455-2695.... 227 D
somers@umbc.edu
SOMERS, Vickie, L .... 336-278-5584.... 364 A
somersv@elon.edu
SOMERSON, Rosanne .... 401-454-6134.... 454 B
rsomerso@risd.edu
SOMERVELL, Ronald .... 703-284-6941.... 521 A
ronald.somervell@marymount.edu
SOMERVILLE, Charles ...... 304-696-2424.... 543 G
somervil@marshall.edu
SOMERVILLE, Dionne, D ... 570-389-4062.... 441 F
dsomervi@bloomu.edu
SOMERVILLE, Mary .... 303-556-2805...... 88 D
Mary.Somerville@ucdenver.edu
SOMERVILLE, Tim .... 951-719-2994...... 63 C
doc@golfcollege.edu
SOMERVILLE, Tom .... 216-987-4883.... 389 A
tom.somerville@tri-c.edu
SOMICH, Michael, L .... 919-613-7611.... 363 I
msomich@duke.edu
SOMMA, Ann Marie .... 518-743-2232.... 322 B
sommaa@sunyacc.edu
SOMMA, Lauren .... 951-781-2727...... 64 C
SOMMA, Victor .... 508-425-1216.... 241 C
vsomma@qcc.mass.edu
SOMMER, Brooks .... 202-462-2101...... 98 C
sommer@iwp.edu
SOMMER, John .... 201-360-4042.... 310 F
jsommer@hccc.edu

SOMMER, Maralyn, T .... 870-230-5320...... 21 I
sommerm@hsu.edu
SOMMER, Sally, W .... 419-358-3317.... 385 B
sommers@bluffton.edu
SOMMER, Toni .... 805-546-3120...... 43 F
tsommer@cuesta.edu
SOMMER-KRESSE, Sue ..... 843-953-6684.... 457 B
sommerkresses@cofc.edu
SOMMERFELD, Curtis ...... 541-956-7238.... 420 B
curt@roguecc.edu
SOMMERFELDT, Scott, D .. 801-422-2674.... 509 D
scott_sommerfeldt@byu.edu
SOMMERS, Bill .... 970-945-8691...... 82 C
SOMMERS, Janet, B .... 651-631-5201.... 270 E
jbsommers@nwc.edu
SOMMERS, Mary .... 308-865-8520.... 300 G
sommersm@unk.edu
SOMMERS, Mary, C .... 713-942-5048.... 504 D
sommers@stthom.edu
SOMMERS, Rhoda, C .... 330-471-8538.... 395 E
rsommers@malone.edu
SOMMERVILLE, Jan .... 616-632-2881.... 248 A
sommejan@aquinas.edu
SOMMERVILLE, Sandi ...... 407-905-2200.... 115 C
SOMMERVILLE, Tim .... 407-905-2200.... 115 C
SOMPOLSKI, Robert .... 847-635-1690.... 160 E
somplski@oakton.edu
SOMVICHIAN, Kamol .... 323-731-2383...... 60 I
ksomvichian@psuca.edu
SONDER, Henk, E .... 401-456-9577.... 454 A
hsonder@ric.edu
SONDEY, Joann .... 914-831-0288.... 330 D
jsondey@cw.edu
SONDEY, Stephen .... 201-684-7496.... 313 D
ssondey@ramapo.edu
SONENBERG, Dave .... 402-437-2619.... 300 C
dsonenbe@southeast.edu
SONES, Rodney .... 740-477-7786.... 398 C
SONES, Ronald .... 434-592-3377.... 520 F
rsones@liberty.edu
SONEY, Ralph, G .... 252-862-1308.... 372 H
soneyr@roanokechowan.edu
SONG, A. Li .... 516-364-0808.... 343 A
asong@nycollege.edu
SONG, Hee Sook .... 770-279-0507.... 129 E
financial.aid@gcuniv.edu
SONG, Hee Sook .... 770-279-0507.... 129 E
academic@gcuniv.edu
SONG, Moon Ho .... 770-279-0507.... 129 E
mhsong2001@hotmail.com
SONGER, Dan .... 814-362-7506.... 449 B
songer@pitt.edu
SONGSTER, Nora .... 707-546-4000...... 45 G
nsongster@empirecollege.com
SONGSTER, Roger .... 402-941-6128.... 299 A
songster@midlandu.edu
SONI, P. Sarita .... 812-855-3931.... 173 C
sonip@indiana.edu
SONI, P. Sarita, E .... 812-855-4440.... 174 B
sonip@indiana.edu
SONI, Varun .... 213-740-6110...... 76 C
vasoni@usc.edu
SONIDO, Eleanor .... 310-900-1600...... 45 E
sonido_e@compton.edu
SONJA, Daniels .... 310-243-3784...... 34 B
sdaniels@csudh.edu
SONKA, Steven, T .... 217-333-9525.... 167 B
ssonka@illinois.edu
SONNEMA, Roy .... 719-549-2865...... 83 B
roy.sonnema@colostate-pueblo.edu
SONNENBERG, Jeff .... 602-557-1740...... 19 C
jeff.sonnenberg@phoenix.edu
SONNENBERG, Judith ...... 512-863-1252.... 495 G
sonnenbj@southwestern.edu
SONNENBERGER, David .... 630-829-6538.... 145 D
dsonnenberger@ben.edu
SONNENBLICK, Carol .... 718-552-1170.... 328 E
csonnenblick@citytech.cuny.edu
SONNENFELD, Gerald ...... 864-656-7701.... 456 E
sonneng@clemson.edu
SONNENSTEIN, Mark .... 718-933-6700.... 341 G
ssonnenstein@monroecollege.edu
SONNENSTRAHL, Samuel . 202-651-5060...... 97 E
samuel.sonnenstrahl@gallaudet.edu
SONNER, Mary .... 423-636-7345.... 476 F
msonner@tusculum.edu
SONNLEITNER,
Thomas, G .... 920-424-3030.... 551 D
sonnleit@uwosh.edu
SONNTAG, Dave .... 509-313-6192.... 534 A
sonntagd@gonzaga.edu
SONNTAG, Gabriela .... 909-748-8096...... 75 F
gabriela_sonntag@redlands.edu
SONNTAG, Michael, E ...... 207-768-9520.... 220 F
michael.sonntag@umpi.edu
SONOBE, Blake, I .... 580-774-3771.... 412 F
blake.sonobe@swosu.edu
SONODA, Kazuhiro .... 509-865-8581.... 534 D
sonoda_k@heritage.edu
SONQUIST, Eric, J .... 805-893-8585...... 74 F
eric.sonquist@ia.ucsb.edu
SONSTEBY, Jill .... 651-638-6254.... 261 I
jks44888@bethel.edu

SOOHOO, Liane .... 206-239-2222.... 530 H
lsoohoo@aii.edu
SOONS, Peter, D .... 802-654-2374.... 514 B
psoons@smcvt.edu
SOOS, Lori .... 716-286-8390.... 344 D
lsoos@niagara.edu
SOOY, Lindsay .... 419-448-2340.... 391 G
lsooy@heidelberg.edu
SOPCICH, Joseph, M .... 913-469-8500.... 193 I
jsopcich@jccc.edu
SOPCZYK, Debbie .... 518-464-8728.... 333 F
dsopczyk@excelsior.edu
SOPER, Elaine .... 304-647-6260.... 544 C
esoper@osteo.wvsom.edu
SOPER, Sarah .... 765-973-8231.... 173 D
saeaton@iue.edu
SOPKO, Bryn .... 503-943-7331.... 420 G
sopko@up.edu
SOPP, Linda .... 413-577-4016.... 237 C
lsopp@admin.umass.edu
SOPRANO, Kenneth .... 215-248-7022.... 425 C
sopranok@chc.edu
SORA, Gail .... 603-623-0313.... 305 F
gsora@nhia.edu
SORACI, Ross .... 617-739-1700.... 243 F
rsoraci@aii.edu
SORANNO, James .... 212-998-2815.... 344 B
james.soranno@nyu.edu
SORBER, Ken .... 801-274-3280.... 512 E
ksorber@wgu.edu
SORBER, Todd .... 973-684-5656.... 312 E
tsorber@pccc.edu
SORCE, Tanya .... 973-290-4465.... 309 A
tsorce@cse.edu
SORDELET, Teresa .... 260-399-7700.... 180 E
tsordelet@sf.edu
SORELLE, Patrick .... 920-465-2323.... 551 A
sorellep@uwgb.edu
SORENSEN, Carl, K .... 804-289-8166.... 525 A
csorense@richmond.edu
SORENSEN, Charles, W ..... 715-232-2441.... 552 C
sorensenc@uwstout.edu
SORENSEN, Cheri .... 602-387-5814...... 19 C
cheri.sorensen@phoenix.edu
SORENSEN, Christine, K ... 808-956-7703.... 141 B
sorens@hawaii.edu
SORENSEN, Dennis .... 815-802-8360.... 154 J
dsorensen@kcc.edu
SORENSEN, Gary .... 928-428-8247...... 14 C
gary.sorensen@eac.edu
SORENSEN, Niles, F .... 704-687-7201.... 378 E
nfsorens@uncc.edu
SORENSEN, Rachel .... 515-244-4221.... 181 D
sorensenr@aib.edu
SORENSEN, Richard, E ...... 540-231-6601.... 529 B
sorensen@vt.edu
SORENSEN, Robin .... 704-378-1048.... 365 H
rsorensen@jcsu.edu
SORENSEN, Roseann, T .... 718-390-4536.... 348 G
sorenser@stjohns.edu
SORENSEN, Zak .... 616-538-2330.... 251 F
zsorensen@gbcol.edu
SORENSON, Andrew, J ...... 860-701-6194.... 558 E
Andrew.J.Sorenson@uscg.mil
SORENSON, Shad .... 801-863-7072.... 511 C
shad.sorenson@uvu.edu
SOREY, Kellie .... 757-822-1122.... 528 C
ksorey@tcc.edu
SORG, Charlotte .... 419-267-1317.... 397 D
csorg@northweststate.edu
SORIA, Deborah, B .... 831-479-5007...... 31 F
desoria@cabrillo.edu
SORIA, Laura .... 773-777-4220.... 160 C
lsoria@nc.edu
SORIANO, Esteban .... 831-755-6822...... 49 C
esoriano@hartnell.edu
SORIERO, Julie .... 617-253-4499.... 242 A
jsoriero@mit.edu
SORK, Victoria .... 310-825-7755...... 74 A
vlsork@ucla.edu
SORLEY, Julie .... 740-477-7801.... 398 C
SOROCHTY, Roger, W ...... 918-631-2895.... 413 F
roger-sorochty@utulsa.edu
SOROKA, Leonard, G .... 215-637-7700.... 430 H
lsoroka@holyfamily.edu
SOROKES, Lawrence .... 716-375-2304.... 348 C
lsorokes@sbu.edu
SORRELL, Carson .... 315-792-7456.... 356 B
sorrelc@sunyit.edu
SORRELL, Clyde, H .... 240-567-5271.... 224 E
rocky.sorrell@montgomerycollege.edu
SORRELL, Garry .... 660-596-7301.... 290 F
gsorrell@sfccmo.edu
SORRELL, Michael, J .... 214-379-5550.... 492 D
president@pqc.edu
SORRELLS, Glenn .... 972-279-6511.... 479 I
gsorrells@amberton.edu
SORRELS, Paul .... 830-279-3013.... 501 B
psorrels@sulross.edu
SORRENTINO,
Donna Marie .... 603-862-2930.... 306 E
dms@unh.edu
SORRENTINO, Sebastian ... 860-768-4034...... 95 A
sorrentin@hartford.edu

SORRENTO, Anthony .... 973-300-2769.... 315 F
asorrento@sussex.edu
SORROW, Russ, L .... 770-484-1204.... 133 D
rsorrow@lru.edu
SORTOR, Janet, M .... 207-741-5504.... 219 A
jsortor@smccme.edu
SORTOR, Marci, J .... 507-786-3004.... 271 H
sortor@stolaf.edu
SORUM, Alan .... 907-834-1667...... 11 B
asorum@pwscc.edu
SOSA, Dona .... 212-343-1234.... 341 B
dsosa@mcny.edu
SOSA, Horacio .... 856-256-4129.... 314 A
sosa@rowan.edu
SOSA, Ismael .... 830-591-7281.... 495 B
ismael.sosa@swtjc.cc.tx.us
SOSA, Leticia .... 787-761-0640.... 561 B
biblioteca@cbp.edu
SOSA, Victor .... 603-862-2001.... 306 E
victor.sosa@unh.edu
SOSA-HEGARTY, Dina, M . 972-860-7205.... 484 H
DinaSosa-Hegarty@dcccd.edu
SOSSEN, Nina .... 413-545-4741.... 237 C
nsossen@admin.umass.edu
SOSTER, Jennifer, C .... 765-658-4198.... 170 I
jsoster@depauw.edu
SOTHERDEN, James, J ...... 717-691-6012.... 436 D
jsotherd@messiah.edu
SOTHERLAND, Paul, R ...... 269-337-7012.... 253 F
Paul.Sotherland@kzoo.edu
SOTHMANN, Mark, S .... 843-792-3031.... 459 C
sothmann@musc.edu
SOTIROS, James .... 707-638-5460...... 72 H
james.sotiros@tu.edu
SOTO, Amilcar .... 787-878-5475.... 562 H
asoto@arecibo.inter.edu
SOTO, Arlene .... 541-756-6445.... 420 C
asoto@socc.edu
SOTO, Bobby .... 214-333-5360.... 484 C
bobby@dbu.edu
SOTO, Carlos .... 813-253-7860.... 110 I
csoto@hccfl.edu
SOTO, Edgar .... 520-206-3260...... 17 I
esoto@pima.edu
SOTO, Emilia .... 787-269-4510.... 566 A
esoto@uccaribe.edu
SOTO, Emilia .... 787-740-6631.... 566 A
emsoto@uccaribe.edu
SOTO, Grisselle .... 787-725-8120.... 562 A
gsoto0056@eap.edu
SOTO, Heriberto .... 787-751-1912.... 564 A
herisoto@inter.edu
SOTO, Jose .... 402-323-3412.... 300 C
jsoto@southeast.edu
SOTO, Limaris .... 787-725-8120.... 562 A
lisotoa@eap.edu
SOTO, Luis, A .... 787-864-2222.... 563 D
luissoto@inter.edu
SOTO, Monica .... 305-899-3057.... 101 F
msoto@mail.barry.edu
SOTO-CRUZ, Nilsa .... 787-834-5151.... 565 B
nsoto@email.pucpr.edu
SOTO-GREENE, Maria, L .... 973-972-9151.... 316 F
sotogrml@umdnj.edu
SOTO MENDEZ, Aracelia .. 787-896-2252.... 561 K
asoto@edpcollege.edu
SOTO TRUJILLO,
Benjamin .... 787-878-4146.... 566 F
SOTONA, Shirley .... 404-876-1227.... 126 D
shirley.sotona@bccr.edu
SOTTER, Trudy .... 724-964-8811.... 437 D
tsotterfa@aol.com
SOUBA, JR., Wiley, W ...... 603-650-1200.... 305 A
wiley.w.souba.jr@dartmouth.edu
SOUBA, JR., Wiley, W ...... 614-292-1200.... 398 H
souba.1@osu.edu
SOUCIE, James .... 207-326-2241.... 219 D
jim.soucie@mma.edu
SOUCY, Erin .... 207-834-7830.... 220 D
esoucy@maine.edu
SOUCY, Ken, R .... 937-229-2641.... 404 A
ken.soucy@notes.udayton.edu
SOUCY, Matthew, R .... 906-786-5802.... 249 D
soucym@baycollege.edu
SOUHRADA, Rick .... 209-384-6135...... 57 C
souhrada.r@mccd.edu
SOULES, Robert, C .... 518-388-6176.... 358 E
soulesr@union.edu
SOULLIERE, Robert .... 260-399-7700.... 180 E
rsoulliere@sf.edu
SOULSBY, Eric .... 928-344-7609...... 12 C
eric.soulsby@azwestern.edu
SOURBEER, Dan .... 760-744-1150...... 61 C
dsourbeer@palomar.edu
SOUSA, Jorge, E .... 919-516-4016.... 376 B
jsousa@st-aug.edu
SOUSA, Marsha .... 907-796-6531...... 11 A
mcsousa@uas.alaska.edu
SOUSA, Marsha .... 907-796-6518...... 11 A
marsha.sousa@uas.alaska.edu
SOUSA, Sheryl, A .... 781-736-3630.... 233 A
sousa@brandeis.edu
SOUSA-PEOPLES, Kim ...... 336-334-5231.... 379 A
ksp@uncg.edu

SPELOCK, Angela 304-253-7351 541 D
aspelock@mountainstate.edu

SPENCE, Bob, C 254-710-3731 481 I
bob_spence@baylor.edu

SPENCE, Colleen 617-427-0060 241 D
cspenc@rcc.mass.edu

SPENCE, Joe 918-456-5511 409 A
spence001@nsuok.edu

SPENCE, Mary 716-829-7736 332 F
spencem@dyc.edu

SPENCE, Robert, H 417-865-2811 282 A
spencer@evangel.edu

SPENCE, Sasha 718-982-2699 327 A
Sasha.Spence@csi.cuny.edu

SPENCE, Weymouth 301-891-4128 229 B
wspence@wau.edu

SPENCER, A. Clayton 617-495-9093 235 H
clayton_spencer@harvard.edu

SPENCER, Amanda 254-867-3820 500 B
amanda.spencer@tstc.edu

SPENCER, Andrea, M 914-773-3870 345 F
aspencer@pace.edu

SPENCER, Catherine 212-636-6522 334 C
caspencer@fordham.edu

SPENCER, Dan 254-298-8619 496 B
dan.spencer@templejc.edu

SPENCER, Deborah 860-231-5390 93 H
dspencer@sjc.edu

SPENCER, Denise 802-447-4631 514 D
dspencer@svc.edu

SPENCER, Dorothy, A 252-744-2212 377 C
spencerdo@ecu.edu

SPENCER, Edward 540-231-6272 529 B
espencer@vt.edu

SPENCER, Elizabeth, A 530-226-4602 69 H
bspencer@simpsonu.edu

SPENCER, Erin 254-298-8590 496 B
erin.spencer@templejc.edu

SPENCER, Estelle, H 413-205-3461 229 G
estelle.spencer@aic.edu

SPENCER, Florence 803-750-2500 99 D

SPENCER, James, D 570-321-4316 435 D
spencer@lycoming.edu

SPENCER, Janie, M 608-785-8495 551 B
spencer.jane@uwlax.edu

SPENCER, Jed 801-626-6586 511 D
jedspencer@weber.edu

SPENCER, Jeremy 508-626-4500 238 D
jspencer1@framingham.edu

SPENCER, John 617-735-9780 234 E
spencerj@emmanuel.edu

SPENCER, John 304-384-5334 543 D
spencer@concord.edu

SPENCER, John, D 817-515-4591 496 A
john.spencer@tccd.edu

SPENCER, Joseph 419-559-2347 402 D

SPENCER, Judith 662-325-3713 276 A
jspencer@hrm.msstate.edu

SPENCER, Keith, J 417-667-8181 280 I
kspencer@cottey.edu

SPENCER, Kellie 407-569-1175 107 G
admissions@fcc.edu

SPENCER, Krystal, F 812-888-4587 181 B
kspencer@vinu.edu

SPENCER, Lisa 575-769-4115 317 K
lisa.spencer@clovis.edu

SPENCER, Mark 781-736-3508 233 A
mspencer@brandeis.edu

SPENCER, Mark 918-335-6865 411 B
mspencer@okwu.edu

SPENCER, Mary 414-277-4517 548 H
spencer@msoe.edu

SPENCER, Megan, T 757-455-3115 529 F
mspencer@vwc.edu

SPENCER, Meleah 417-873-7444 281 H
mspencer02@drury.edu

SPENCER, Melinda 404-657-1334 138 E
melinda.spencer@usg.edu

SPENCER, Ray 217-351-2376 161 B
rcspencer@parkland.edu

SPENCER, Rick, E 630-637-5209 159 F
respencer@noctrl.edu

SPENCER, Robin 510-261-8500 61 F
Robin.spencer@patten.edu

SPENCER, Roger, W 276-739-2407 528 D
rspencer@vhcc.edu

SPENCER, Ruth 845-437-6820 359 D
ruspencer@vassar.edu

SPENCER, Sandra, L 217-353-2637 161 B
sspencer@parkland.edu

SPENCER, Scott 703-284-1520 521 A
scott.spencer@marymount.edu

SPENCER, Shannon 419-372-6389 385 C
spensha@bgsu.edu

SPENCER, Sonya 972-860-8142 484 G
sspencer@dcccd.edu

SPENCER, Stephanie 575-769-4956 317 K
stephanie.spencer@clovis.edu

SPENCER, Theodore, L 734-647-0102 259 D
tsz@umich.edu

SPENCER, Tiffany 618-453-4188 164 I
spencer@siu.edu

SPENCER, Yvette 205-226-7720 2 C
yspencer@bsc.edu

SPENGLER, Gregory, C 410-706-1264 227 C
gspengle@umaryland.edu

SPENNY, Nancy 219-877-3100 170 A
nspenny@brownmackie.edu

SPERBER, Greg 619-574-6909 60 E
gsperber@pacificcollege.edu

SPERLING, Linda 256-352-8128 10 B
linda.sperling@wallacestate.edu

SPERLING, Michael 914-674-7500 340 G
msperling@mercy.edu

SPERLING, William 206-546-4788 537 G
wsperling@shoreline.edu

SPERO, Filomena 630-617-3788 150 F
Filomenas@elmhurst.edu

SPEROS, Michael 916-278-4239 35 E
msperos@csus.edu

SPEROS, Michael 916-278-6655 35 E
msperos@saclink.csus.edu

SPERRY, Richard, J 801-585-9602 510 L
richard.sperry@hsc.utah.edu

SPESSARD, James, H 336-841-9226 365 A
jspess@highpoint.edu

SPETKA, Rosemary, V 315-792-5495 341 E
rspetka@mvcc.edu

SPETMAN, Randy 850-644-1079 119 C
rspetman@admin.fsu.edu

SPETTER, Bryan 317-738-8026 171 C
bspetter@franklincollege.edu

SPEWOCK, Kelly J, K 412-291-6244 422 D
kspewock@aii.edu

SPEZIA, Robert 313-883-8576 257 G
spezia.robert@shms.edu

SPEZIALE, Michael 570-408-4679 451 G
michael.speziale@wilkes.edu

SPEZIANI, Humberto, M 305-284-5450 122 F
hmspez@miami.edu

SPEZZA, Nicholas 505-224-4111 317 J
nspezza@cnm.edu

SPEZZACATENA, Maricel 305-273-4499 103 C
maricel@cbt.edu

SPICE, Jim 719-255-3111 88 C
jspice@uccs.edu

SPICER, Donald, Z 301-445-2729 227 A
dspicer@usmd.edu

SPICER, Erin 850-484-1706 114 G
espicer@pensacolastate.edu

SPICER, Julie 515-244-4221 181 D
spicerj@aib.edu

SPICER, Kim, A 479-979-1320 26 A
kaspicer@ozarks.edu

SPICER, Mistie 740-351-3635 401 I
mspicer@shawnee.edu

SPICER, Thomas 303-273-3368 82 F
tspicer@mines.edu

SPICKLER, Angela 717-396-7833 440 J
aspickler@pcad.edu

SPIEGEL, Allen, M 212-430-2801 361 I
spiegel@aecom.yu.edu

SPIEGEL, Allen, M 212-960-3179 361 I
aspiegel@aecom.yu.edu

SPIEGEL, Benjamin 732-367-1060 307 H

SPIEGEL, John 516-572-7118 342 C
john.spiegel@ncc.edu

SPIEGEL, Mary, K 205-348-8185 8 F
mary.spiegel@ua.edu

SPIEGEL, Sara 773-697-2419 149 C
sspiegel@devry.edu

SPIELER, Emily, A 617-373-3307 244 A

SPIELMANN, Dan 920-465-2067 551 A
spielmad@uwgb.edu

SPIELVOGEL, Jennifer 216-987-4767 389 A
jennifer.spielvogel@tri-c.edu

SPIERS, Cynthia, E 419-995-8331 392 L
spiers.c@rhodesstate.edu

SPIERS, Jessica 419-227-3141 404 D
jspiers@unoh.edu

SPIERS, William 850-201-8399 121 F
spiersw@tcc.fl.edu

SPIES, Brent 314-889-4564 282 C
bspies@fontbonne.edu

SPIES, Carolyn, I 973-748-9000 308 A
carolyn_spies@bloomfield.edu

SPIES, Gail 563-288-6004 184 D
gspies@eicc.edu

SPIES, Richard, R 401-863-9995 452 J
richard_spies@brown.edu

SPIGELMYER, Francie, P 724-287-8711 423 F
frances.spigelmyer@bc3.edu

SPIGELMYER, Kathleen 215-248-7025 425 C
spigelmyerk@chc.edu

SPIKER, Robert 304-876-5395 544 A
rspiker@shepherd.edu

SPIKER, William, J 440-826-3623 384 H
wspiker@bw.edu

SPILDE, Mary 541-463-5200 416 D
spildem@lanecc.edu

SPILKER, Christopher 313-883-8651 257 G
spilker.christopher@shms.edu

SPILLER, JoAnn 760-384-6221 52 N
jspiller@cerrocoso.edu

SPILLER, Judith 603-862-2165 306 E
judy.spiller@unh.edu

SPILLETT, Margaret 315-255-1743 325 H
margaret.spillett@cayuga-cc.edu

SPILLMAN, Tom 951-487-3945 58 B
tspillma@msjc.edu

SPILLUM, Carol 605-274-4090 463 H
carol.spillum@augie.edu

SPILMAN, Todd 505-473-6295 320 F
todd.spilman@laureate.net

SPINA, Anthony 716-829-7648 332 F
spinaaw@dyc.edu

SPINA, Eric, F 315-443-2494 357 B
efspina@syr.edu

SPINA, Matthew, R 609-497-7870 312 F
admissions@ptsem.edu

SPINA, Nicolas, A 812-888-4588 181 B
nspina@vinu.edu

SPINATO, Donna 903-886-5860 497 E
donna_spinato@tamu-commerce.edu

SPINAZZA, Terri 208-426-2168 142 F
tspinazz@boisestate.edu

SPINDEL, Donna 304-696-2818 543 G
spindel@marshall.edu

SPINDLE, William 907-786-4620 10 I
anwhs@uaa.alaska.edu

SPINDLER, Deborah 858-635-4700 27 E
dspindler@alliant.edu

SPINELLI, Paul 727-341-3070 116 F
spinelli.paul@spcollege.edu

SPINELLI, JR., Stephen 215-951-2727 444 C
spinellis@philau.edu

SPINELLI-SEXTER, Eva 212-463-0400 357 J
espinelli@touro.edu

SPINHIRNE, Raymond, J 512-448-8662 493 B
rays@stedwards.edu

SPINILLO, Anthony 570-340-6057 435 F
spinillo@marywood.edu

SPINNER, Cornelia, V 202-274-6649 99 F
cspinner@udc.edu

SPINNER, Michael, S 203-773-8578 89 H
mspinner@albertus.edu

SPINNEY, Molly, P 724-946-7330 451 C
mspinney@westminster.edu

SPINNEY, Robert, G 540-338-1776 522 A

SPINOSA, Tony 202-685-3946 557 F
spinosat@ndu.edu

SPINRAD, Rick 541-737-3467 418 F
rick.spinrad@oregonstate.edu

SPIREA, Roxana 561-912-2166 106 G
rspirea@evergladesuniversity.edu

SPIRES, Carol 770-531-6396 132 J
cspires@laniertech.edu

SPIRES, Chris 803-641-3463 462 B
chriss@usca.edu

SPIRES, Tracy, M 864-379-8805 457 G
tspires@erskine.edu

SPIRIDON, Charles, P 203-837-8663 92 A
spiridonc@wcsu.edu

SPIRO, Elaine 215-489-2346 426 H
Elaine.Spiro@delval.edu

SPIRO, Louis, M 585-395-2129 352 F
lspiro@brockport.edu

SPIRO, Mark 413-559-5528 235 G
mkstr@hampshire.edu

SPISAK, Art, L 319-335-1685 182 C

SPISAK, Arthur, L 417-836-6370 286 F
artspisak@missouristate.edu

SPITTAL, Ryan 815-939-5452 160 F
rspittal@olivet.edu

SPITTLER, Holly, J 814-362-7657 449 B
spittler@pitt.edu

SPITZ, Catherine 309-556-3120 153 E
cspitz@iwu.edu

SPITZ, Cody 575-562-2178 318 A
cody.spitz@enmu.edu

SPITZER, Michael 516-876-4062 355 F
michael.spitzer@esc.edu

SPITZER, Michael, H 610-785-6520 446 A
dirapopasformscs@adphila.org

SPIVACK, James 410-704-2512 228 E
jspivack@towson.edu

SPIVAK, Howard 718-951-5342 326 G
howards@brooklyn.cuny.edu

SPIVAK, Michael 641-472-7000 187 B
mspivak@mum.edu

SPIVEY, Margaret, C 301-790-2800 223 A
spiveym@hagerstowncc.edu

SPIVEY, Sheila, D 904-620-2528 120 C
sspivey@unf.edu

SPIVEY, Susan, M 319-363-0481 186 D

SPIWAK, Doug 847-925-6969 151 E
dspiwak@harpercollege.edu

SPIZUOCO, Dennis 610-989-1322 450 E
dspizuoco@vfmac.edu

SPIZZIRRRI, Erica 609-984-1588 316 A
espizzirri@tesc.edu

SPLINTER, Ann 507-389-7289 269 F
ann.splinter@southcentral.edu

SPOALES, Gary 304-724-3700 540 C
gspoales@apus.edu

SPOERRI, Tamara, D 207-725-3837 217 E
tspoerri@bowdoin.edu

SPOHN, Andy 517-265-5161 247 D
aspohn@adrian.edu

SPOHN, Debborah 661-395-4211 52 M
dspohn@bakersfieldcollege.edu

SPOHR, Robert 989-328-1251 256 A
robs@montcalm.edu

SPOLTORE, Janet, D 860-439-2692 91 E
janet.spoltore@conncoll.edu

SPONG, Mark, W 972-883-2974 505 D
mspong@utdallas.edu

SPONG, Melinda 859-572-1464 205 E
spongm1@nku.edu

SPONG, Robert 301-790-2800 223 A
spongr@hagerstowncc.edu

SPONSELLER, Eric 814-871-7238 429 F
sponsell001@gannon.edu

SPOONER, David 518-276-6890 347 D
spoond@rpi.edu

SPOONER, John 616-538-2330 251 F
jspooner@gbcol.edu

SPOONER, Judith 330-869-3600 385 F
jspooner@brownmackie.edu

SPOONER, Matt 310-476-9777 28 F
mspooner@ajula.edu

SPOONER, Natalie, M 315-786-2268 337 F
nspooner@sunyjefferson.edu

SPOOR, Darlene 619-660-4670 48 J
darlene.spoor@gcccd.edu

SPOOR, Suzanne, J 410-777-2448 221 B
sjspoor@aacc.edu

SPOR, Arvid 310-660-3483 45 D
aspor@elcamino.edu

SPORE, MaryBeth 724-537-4567 446 E
marybeth.spore@email.stvincent.edu

SPORE, Robert, B 540-464-7322 529 A
sporerb@vmi.edu

SPORES, Jon 360-383-3440 539 D
jspores@whatcom.ctc.edu

SPORLEDER, Brian, R 414-276-5200 546 C
brsporleder@bryantstratton.edu

SPORS, Jonathon, L 217-443-8577 148 E
jspors@dacc.edu

SPORTSMAN, Joseph, S 513-244-4389 388 D
scott_sportsman@mail.msj.edu

SPORTSMAN, Susan 940-397-4594 491 A
susan.sportsman@mwsu.edu

SPOSILI, Michael 518-580-5610 351 B
msposili@skidmore.edu

SPOTO, Mary 352-588-8463 116 E
mary.spoto@saintleo.edu

SPOTZ, Jason 440-375-7000 394 E
jspotz@lec.edu

SPRADLEY, Minou 619-388-3520 65 F
mspradl@sdccd.edu

SPRADLIN, Michael, R 901-751-8453 471 D
mspradlin@mabts.edu

SPRADLING, Jane 337-550-1216 212 H

SPRADLING, John 903-785-7661 492 B
jspradling@parisjc.edu

SPRADLING, Steve 330-494-6170 402 A
sspradling@starkstate.edu

SPRAGG, Anna 203-582-5257 93 E
anna.spragg@quinnipiac.edu

SPRAGG, Elizabeth 989-358-7247 247 G
spragge@alpenacc.edu

SPRAGGE, Phyllis 650-940-7730 47 H
spraggephyllis@foothill.edu

SPRAGGINS, Lynn 256-378-2022 2 F
lspraggins@cacc.edu

SPRAGGINS, Timothy 334-244-3220 2 A
tspraggins@aum.edu

SPRAGUE, Brinton 425-739-8127 535 B
brinton.sprague@lwtc.edu

SPRAGUE, Carol 413-545-0698 237 C
sprague@research.umass.edu

SPRAGUE, Jennifer 505-984-6041 320 C
jsprague@sjcsf.edu

SPRAGUE, Jennifer 303-477-7240 84 I
jennifers@heritage-education.com

SPRAGUE, Jon, E 419-772-2276 398 G
j-sprague@onu.edu

SPRAGUE, Karen, U 541-346-1246 419 B
kus@uoregon.edu

SPRAGUE, Robert, L 310-287-4398 55 F
spragurl@wlac.edu

SPRAGUE, Todd 360-867-6042 533 I
spraguet@evergreen.edu

SPRAGUE, Viola, M 810-762-9668 253 I
vsprague@kettering.edu

SPRAKE, Timothy 425-637-1010 531 I
tsprake@cityu.edu

SPRAKER, Matt 615-248-1245 476 E
mspraker@trevecca.edu

SPRANZA, John 706-295-6363 130 C
jspranza@highlands.edu

SPRATLIN, Jim 334-386-7265 3 H
jspratlin@faulkner.edu

SPRATLIN, Steve 256-395-2211 7 E
sspratlin@suscc.edu

SPRATT, Bruce, R 404-413-3071 131 C
bspratt@gsu.edu

SPRATT, Sharon 270-706-8478 201 F
sharon.spratt@kctcs.edu

SPRATT, Wanda 530-339-3610 69 D
wspratt@shastacollege.edu

SPRAW, Deanna 419-434-4589 404 B
spraw@findlay.edu

STANAITIS, Judith 610-558-5544 437 C stanaitj@neumann.edu
STANBACK STROUD, Regina 650-738-4110 67 G stroudr@smccd.edu
STANCEL, George, M 713-500-9880 506 D george.m.stancel@uth.tmc.edu
STANCIL, Daphne 910-410-1732 372 G daphnes@richmondcc.edu
STANCIL, Jay 606-546-1292 206 F jstancil@unionky.edu
STANCIU, Hope 330-490-7142 405 E hstanciu@walsh.edu
STANDAERT, Kristin 312-567-8829 153 B standaert@iit.edu
STANDAHL, Jerry, J 757-569-6719 527 E jstandahl@pdc.edu
STANDERFER, Mary 479-394-7622 23 E mstanderfer@rmcc.edu
STANDERFER, Steve 661-722-6300 28 J sstanderfer@avc.edu
STANDEVEN, Valerie 402-474-5315 298 E vstandeven@kaplanuniversity.edu
STANDFUSS, Chuck 651-696-6280 265 A standfuss@macalester.edu
STANDIFIRD, Stephen 812-488-2856 180 B ss500@evansville.edu
STANDISH, David 361-593-3312 498 A kamrf00@tamuk.edu
STANDISH, Leanna 425-602-3000 530 K ljs@bastyr.edu
STANDLEA, Donna 909-607-3305 40 C donna.standlea@cgu.edu
STANDLEY, James, D 936-468-2807 495 H jstandley@sfasu.edu
STANDLEY, Susan 309-794-7207 145 B suestandley@augustana.edu
STANDRIDGE, Joe 254-968-9065 496 F jstandr@tarleton.edu
STANEK, Karla, E 608-785-8515 551 B stanek.karl@uwlax.edu
STANESKI, Richard, A 570-422-3201 442 C richard.staneski@po-box.esu.edu
STANFIELD, B. Jane 205-348-5256 8 F jstanfie@bama.ua.edu
STANFIELD, Lori, J 785-539-3571 194 G ljstanfield@mccks.edu
STANFIELD, Margot, J 509-313-5995 534 A stanfield@gu.gonzaga.edu
STANFIELD, Vincent (Shelby) 512-475-7510 505 B s.stanfield@mail.utexas.edu
STANFILL, Sandy 731-968-5722 475 B sstanfill@jscc.edu
STANFORD, Forrest 704-971-8500 363 D
STANFORD, Jeanne 805-893-4411 74 F stanford-j@sa.ucsb.edu
STANFORD, Linda, O 517-355-5767 255 D stanford@msu.edu
STANFORD, Roger, J 715-858-1857 553 F rstanford@cvtc.edu
STANFORD, Steve 601-925-3205 275 E stanford@mc.edu
STANFORD, Virgil 760-252-2411 30 F vstanford@barstow.edu
STANFORD, Yvonne 662-621-4287 273 I ystanford@coahomacc.edu
STANGE, Carl 507-457-5100 270 B cstange@winona.edu
STANGE, Pat 402-460-2152 297 C pstange@cccneb.edu
STANGE, Randy 620-665-3594 193 F stanger@hutchcc.edu
STANGE, Von 319-335-3000 182 C von-stange@uiowa.edu
STANGER, Winn 801-626-6876 511 D wstanger@weber.edu
STANGLEIN, Neil 573-592-1658 293 E neil.stanglein@williamwoods.edu
STANGLIN, Gerald, M 903-983-8104 489 F gstanglin@kilgore.edu
STANGO, Linda 203-575-8016 90 E lstango@nvcc.commnet.edu
STANICIC, Rob 281-998-6150 493 D rob.stanicic@sjcd.edu
STANIEWICZ, Theodore 215-489-2228 426 H Theodore.Staniewicz@delval.edu
STANKEY, Lindy, J 651-631-5344 270 E ljstankey@nwc.edu
STANKEY, Michael 940-898-3350 502 B mstankey1@twu.edu
STANKIEWICZ, Donna 973-684-5218 312 E dstankiewicz@pccc.edu
STANKOVICH, Joseph 518-580-5719 351 B jstankov@skidmore.edu
STANKOWSKI, Lisa 231-843-5802 260 E lmstankowski@westshore.edu
STANLEY, Allen, D 501-569-8474 24 E adstanley@ualr.edu
STANLEY, Brian 478-471-2864 133 E brian.stanley@maconstate.edu
STANLEY, Carol 706-355-5019 124 H cstanley@athenstech.edu
STANLEY, Carol A, J 434-924-4122 525 B cas4b@virginia.edu
STANLEY, Cheryl 413-572-5713 239 C cstanley@westfield.ma.edu
STANLEY, Chris 252-334-2043 367 A chris.stanley@macuniversity.edu
STANLEY, Christine 979-458-2905 497 C cstanley@tamu.edu
STANLEY, Christine, A 979-845-3210 497 C cstanley@tamu.edu
STANLEY, Cole 405-974-2361 413 B cstanley2@ucok.edu
STANLEY, David 724-838-4270 447 B stanley@setonhill.edu
STANLEY, Deborah 301-860-3543 228 A dstanley@bowiestate.edu
STANLEY, Deborah, F 315-312-2211 354 A deborah.stanley@oswego.edu
STANLEY, Donna, G 276-523-7493 527 A dstanley@me.vccs.edu
STANLEY, Graydon, A 208-732-6221 143 B gstanley@csi.edu
STANLEY, Harold, W 214-768-3454 494 F hstanley@smu.edu
STANLEY, Jack 806-457-4200 486 G jstanley@fpctx.edu
STANLEY, Jay 910-879-5503 368 A jstanley@bladencc.edu
STANLEY, Jennifer 401-254-3123 454 C jstanley@rwu.edu
STANLEY, Jeremiah 904-596-2333 122 A jstanley@tbc.edu
STANLEY, John 812-488-2238 180 B js405@evansville.edu
STANLEY, Karen 317-917-5707 175 G kstanley@ivytech.edu
STANLEY, Lori 563-387-1005 187 A stanleyl@luther.edu
STANLEY, Mark 712-325-3375 186 B mstanley@iwcc.edu
STANLEY, N, J 570-321-4131 435 D stanley@lycoming.edu
STANLEY, Patricia 319-296-4230 185 C patricia.stanley@hawkeyecollege.edu
STANLEY, Rene 731-286-3205 475 A stanley@dscc.edu
STANLEY, Richard, H 480-727-8307 12 B richard.h.stanley@asu.edu
STANLEY, Robert 773-244-4585 159 G rstanley@northpark.edu
STANLEY, OP, Ronald 845-848-4042 332 C ron.stanley@dc.edu
STANLEY, Samuel, L 631-632-6265 352 C samuel.stanley@stonybrook.edu
STANLEY, Tuesday, L 816-604-1253 285 D tuesday.stanley@mcckc.edu
STANLEY, Valarie, J 203-432-0849 95 D valarie.stanley@yale.edu
STANLEY-MCAULAY, Deborah 203-436-4072 95 D deborah.stanley-mcaulay@yale.edu
STANO, Diana 440-646-8101 405 B dstano@ursuline.edu
STANSBURY, Calvin 252-536-4330 370 F stans@halifaxcc.edu
STANSBURY, Donald, M 757-683-3446 521 L dstansbe@odu.edu
STANSLOSKI, Donald 419-434-5327 404 B stansloski@findlay.edu
STANTON, Amanda 806-291-3414 508 B stanton@wbu.edu
STANTON, Cecilia 651-793-1508 267 D cecilia.stanton@metrostate.edu
STANTON, Karen 251-380-2777 7 F kstanton@shc.edu
STANTON, Kate 405-271-2416 413 D kate-stanton@ouhsc.edu
STANTON, Lisa 541-956-7024 420 B lstanton@roguecc.edu
STANTON, Marian 410-276-0306 226 D mstanton@host.sdc.edu
STANTON, Mark 626-812-3087 30 E mstanton@apu.edu
STANTON, Maureen, L 530-752-2072 73 F mlstanton@ucdavis.edu
STANTON, Michael, J 508-213-2285 243 J michael.stanton@nichols.edu
STANTON, Paul 617-627-4239 245 F paul.stanton@tufts.edu
STANTON, Paul, E 413-565-1000 231 B pstanton@baypath.edu
STANTON, JR., Paul, E 423-439-4211 473 E stantonp@etsu.edu
STANTON, Susan, S 914-606-6931 360 D susan.stanton@sunywcc.edu
STANWOOD, Julie 617-585-6722 230 D stanwood@lesley.edu
STANZA, Tami, D 313-496-2616 260 C tstanza1@wcccd.edu
STANZESKI, Marialice 215-885-2360 435 E mstanzeski@manor.edu
STANZIANI, Anthony 212-312-4301 332 B astanziani@devry.edu
STAPEL, Joe 231-777-5300 248 J joe.stapel@baker.edu
STAPLES, Lynn 610-285-5082 439 K lmf20@psu.edu
STAPLES, William, A 281-283-2004 503 C president@uhcl.edu
STAPLETON, Gregg 864-646-1796 461 F gstaplet@tctc.edu
STAPLETON, Marilyn 518-243-4471 332 G
STAPLETON, Michael, F 706-867-2781 134 D mfstapleton@northgeorgia.edu
STAPLETON, Sarah 931-598-3349 472 J sstaplet@sewanee.edu
STAPLETON, Scot 205-552-1217 3 B scot.stapleton@ecacolleges.com
STAPLETON-SMITH, Jeannie 914-968-6200 349 D jeannie.stapleton-smith@archny.org
STAPP, Robert 310-578-1080 28 K rstapp@antiochla.edu
STARACE, Melissa 610-861-4589 437 G mstarace@northampton.edu
STARASTA, Mike 217-732-3155 156 G mstarasta@lincolncollege.edu
STARBIRD, S. Andrew 408-554-4523 68 C sstarbird@scu.edu
STARCEVICH, Joe 641-856-2224 185 D jstarcev@indianhills.edu
STARCEVICH, Mick 319-398-5501 186 H mstarce@kirkwood.edu
STARCK, Brenda 602-286-8060 15 I brenda.starck@gwmail.maricopa.edu
STARCK, Patricia, L 713-500-2001 506 D patricia.l.starck@uth.tmc.edu
STARCZEWSKI, Kirk 518-587-2100 355 F kirk.starczewski@esc.edu
STARER, Paul 650-949-7534 47 H starerpaul@foothill.edu
STARGARDTER, Steven, A 925-969-3302 52 B stargardter@jfku.edu
STARGEL, Denton, L 201-761-7425 314 F
STARICH, Gale, H 770-718-5304 126 B gstarich@brenau.edu
STARK, Anne, M 906-227-1052 256 F astark@nmu.edu
STARK, Carl 870-230-5324 21 I starkc@hsu.edu
STARK, Debra 201-684-7221 313 D dstark@ramapo.edu
STARK, Deidra 818-947-2508 55 E starkdk@lavc.edu
STARK, JR., Gary 480-657-3223 13 L gstark@devry.edu
STARK, Inger 510-464-3224 62 C istark@peralta.edu
STARK, Jared, A 402-363-5635 301 F jastark@york.edu
STARK, John, D 307-766-6242 556 E jdstark@uwyo.edu
STARK, Linda 407-569-1380 107 G library@fcc.edu
STARK, Lou, W 319-399-8843 183 C lstark@coe.edu
STARK, Michael, M 608-246-6737 554 B mmstark@matcmadison.edu
STARK, Nicole 661-255-1050 32 C nstark@calarts.edu
STARK, Paul 419-448-2066 391 G pstark@heidelberg.edu
STARK, Ruth 212-650-6849 326 H stark@sci.ccny.cuny.edu
STARK, Wayne, F 434-381-6151 524 E wstark@sbc.edu
STARKE, Christhina 800-962-7682 293 B cstarke@wma.edu
STARKE, Sandra 607-777-6226 351 F sstarke@binghamton.edu
STARKE, Sandra 607-777-2728 351 F sstarke@binghamton.edu
STARKE, William 724-266-3838 448 G wstarke@tsm.edu
STARKEL, Henry, A 203-932-7033 95 B hstarkel@newhaven.edu
STARKEY, Alysia 785-826-2637 194 C astarkey@sal.ksu.edu
STARKEY, Amanda, M 618-235-2700 165 B amanda.starkey@swic.edu
STARKEY, Jeremy 304-424-8379 545 B jeremy.starkey@mail.wvu.edu
STARKEY, Shawn, M 810-989-5540 258 B sstarkey@sc4.edu
STARKEY, Stan, R 865-882-4565 475 G starkeys@roanestate.edu
STARKEY, Terry 870-574-4421 24 A tstarkey@sautech.edu
STARKMAN, Eve 212-824-2285 335 C estarkman@huc.edu
STARKMAN, Kenneth, J 608-243-4440 554 B kstarkman@matcmadison.edu
STARKOFF, Kathleen 614-292-6553 398 H starkoff.3@osu.edu
STARKOVICH, Steven 253-535-7126 535 K starkosp@plu.edu
STARKS, Jacqueline, M 610-660-1081 446 C jstarks@sju.edu
STARKS, Marilyn 662-621-4154 273 I mstarks@coahomacc.edu
STARKS, Sam, B 215-898-6993 448 oaaeop@pobox.upenn.edu
STARKSON, Mary Jo, H 507-344-7310 261 maryjo.starkson@blc.edu
STARKWEATHER, Cathy 989-386-6688 255 cstarkweather@midmich.edu
STARKWEATHER, Peter 702-895-2263 302 peter.starkweather@unlv.edu
STARLEY, Monica 478-445-4444 129 F monica.starley@gcsu.edu
STARLING, Buddy 334-670-3175 8 B bstar@troy.edu
STARLING, Cordia 706-272-2457 127 G cstarling@daltonstate.edu
STARLING, Sharron 206-726-5018 532 G sstarling@cornish.edu
STARLING, William, J 910-592-8081 373 D bstarlin@sampsoncc.edu
STARMER, Jamie 530-898-5253 34 A jstarmer@csuchico.edu
STARNER, Wendy, S 717-766-2511 436 D wstarner@messiah.edu
STARNES, Gina 318-795-4239 213 D gina.starnes@lsus.edu
STARNES, Scott 434-592-4191 520 F sastarnes@liberty.edu
STARNES, Shane 704-461-6200 362 B shanestarnes@bac.edu
STAROS, James, V 413-545-6223 237 C jstaros@provost.umass.edu
STAROTOLI, Jeremiah 610-789-6700 445 A jstarotoli@prismcareerinstitute.edu
STARR, Bettie, C 270-384-8030 203 H starrb@lindsey.edu
STARR, Brian 806-720-7405 490 D brian.starr@lcu.edu
STARR, Clara, H 415-241-2249 39 H cstarr@ccsf.edu
STARR, Dolores 904-256-7016 111 J dstarr@ju.edu
STARR, J. Barton 561-803-2250 114 C barton_starr@pba.edu
STARR, Kenneth, W 254-710-3555 481 I ken_starr@baylor.edu
STARR, Margaret, J 309-692-4092 158 C mstarr@midstate.edu
STARR, Peter 202-885-2446 97 B pstarr@american.edu
STARR, Sharon 704-922-6366 370 D starr.sharon@gaston.edu
STARR, Terry 913-621-8718 192 C tstarr@donnelly.edu
STARR, Valorie 620-278-4463 196 D vstarr@sterling.edu
STARR-COHEN, Debra 305-597-9599 108 A miami@fanh.com
STARR FIEDLER, Heather 412-392-3409 444 H hstarr@pointpark.edu
STARR JOHNSON, Joyce 314-862-3456 282 C jjohnson@fontbonne.edu
STARRATT, Christopher 305-899-4571 101 F cstarratt@mail.barry.edu
STARRATT, Joseph 509-335-4558 539 A jstarratt@wsu.edu
STARRETT, David 573-986-7477 290 D dstarrett@semo.edu
STARTUP, Allison 770-720-5542 135 F afs@reinhardt.edu
STARTUP, Kenneth, M 870-759-4128 26 B kstartup@wbcoll.edu
STASA, Joan 419-530-2814 404 F joan.stasa@utoledo.edu
STASCHAK, John, J 716-250-7500 324 H jjstaschak@bryantstratton.edu
STASHER, Jesse 702-968-2004 303 D jstasher@roseman.edu
STASOLLA, Debbie 609-896-5228 313 G dstasolla@rider.edu
STASSEN, Anne, K 215-972-2039 440 I astassen@pafa.edu
STASSIS, Bassel 973-684-6500 312 E bstassis@pccc.edu
STATE, Timothy 847-735-6022 155 F state@lakeforest.edu
STATEN, Shannon, D 502-852-6636 207 A sdstat01@louisville.edu
STATES, Hollyce 508-588-9100 240 E
STATMORE, Kelly 215-906-4139 93 D kstatmore@post.edu
STATMORE, Michael 203-591-5056 93 D mstatmore@post.edu
STATON, Ann 940-898-3326 502 B astaton@twu.edu
STATON, JR., Robert, E 864-833-8578 460 E restaton@presby.edu
STATON, Wendell 478-445-6341 129 F wendell.staton@gcsu.edu
STATTON, Thomas, M 301-766-3653 223 G tstatton@kaplan.edu
STAUB, Robert, H 318-342-5360 216 E staub@ulm.edu
STAUDER, Ellen Keck 503-777-7258 420 A estauder@reed.edu

STEINER, Frederick, R 512-471-1922 505 B
fsteiner@austin.utexas.edu
STEINER, Glen, D 708-209-3328 148 C
glen.steiner@cuchicago.edu
STEINER, James, D 563-589-3210 189 B
jsteiner@dbq.edu
STEINER, Joseph, F 307-766-6556 556 E
jspharmd@uwyo.edu
STEINER, Rita, L 410-617-2504 224 A
rsteiner@loyola.edu
STEINER, Rochelle 213-740-6264 76 C
rochelle.steiner@usc.edu
STEINER, Terry 406-657-1078 296 E
steinert@rocky.edu
STEINER, William, W 808-974-7393 141 A
steiner@hawaii.edu
STEINER-LANG, Kathy 314-935-5910 292 J
ksteiner@wustl.edu
STEINFELD, Peter, K 712-749-2205 182 G
steinfeld@bvu.edu
STEINFELD, Trudy 212-998-4735 344 B
trudy.steinfeld@nyu.edu
STEINHAGEN, Robert 206-316-2458 530 J
roberts@bgu.edu
STEINHOFF, Cynthia, K 410-777-2483 221 B
cksteinhoff@aacc.edu
STEINKAMP, Janet 320-308-5933 269 D
jsteinkamp@sctcc.edu
STEINKE, Robin, J 717-334-6286 435 A
rsteinke@ltsg.edu
STEINKEOWAY, Louise, A 407-851-2525 106 B
lsteinke@cci.edu
STEINKIRCHNER,
Linda, M 585-385-5242 348 F
lsteinkirchner@sjfc.edu
STEINMAN, Alan 616-331-3749 252 A
steinmaa@gvsu.edu
STEINMETZ, Amanda 307-674-6446 556 C
asteinmetz@sheridan.edu
STEINMETZ, Edward, J 570-941-4289 450 B
steinmetze1@scranton.edu
STEINMETZ, Joseph, E 614-292-1677 398 H
steinmetz.53@osu.edu
STEINMETZ, Michael 859-253-3637 200 E
michael.steinmetz@frontier.edu
STEINMETZ, Paul 203-837-8771 92 A
steinmetzp@wcsu.edu
STEINMETZ, Paul, M 203-837-9805 92 A
steinmetzp@wcsu.edu
STEINMETZ, Rob, R 717-221-1798 430 E
rrsteinm@hacc.edu
STEINNERD, Sarah 573-651-2588 290 D
ssteinnerd@semo.edu
STEINOUR, David 703-726-3602 97 F
steinour@gwu.edu
STEINROCK, Timothy, J 610-921-7654 421 D
tsteinrock@alb.edu
STEINRUCK, Jessica, M 202-231-3344 557 G
jessica.steinruck@dia.mil
STEINWAY, Harry, R 845-561-0800 342 A
harry.steinway@msmc.edu
STEINWEDEL, Cheryl 419-227-3141 404 D
csteinwedel@unoh.edu
STEITZ, John, A 740-284-5177 390 M
jsteitz@franciscan.edu
STEJSKAL, Pat 815-479-7530 157 F
pstejakal@mchenry.edu
STEJSKAL, Patricia 815-479-7530 157 F
pstejskal@mchenry.edu
STEKETEE, Gail 617-353-3760 232 G
steketee@bu.edu
STELK, Cheryl 478-988-6800 133 H
cstelk@middlegatech.edu
STELLA, Mark 304-384-5356 543 D
markstella@hotmail.com
STELLA, Steven 518-454-5139 330 C
stellas@strose.edu
STELLAR, James 718-997-5900 328 F
james.stellar@qc.cuny.edu
STELMACH, Kim 508-373-9432 231 D
kim.stelmach@becker.edu
STELTER, Caroline, W 804-758-6728 527 G
cstelter@rappahannock.edu
STELZER, Stuart, P 479-979-1381 26 A
sstelzer@ozarks.edu
STEM, Elaine 252-492-2061 374 D
stem@vgcc.edu
STEMBRIDGE, Allen, F 269-471-3622 247 H
stem@andrews.edu
STEMBRIDGE,
Catherine, L 847-491-8056 160 D
c-stembridge@northwestern.edu
STEMKOSKI, Stephen 315-859-4301 335 A
sstemkos@hamilton.edu
STEMLEY, Gemma 610-399-2275 441 H
gstemley@cheyney.edu
STEMM, Wallis 480-610-3961 13 K
wstemm@devry.edu
STEMMER, John, K 502-272-8140 198 E
jstemmer@bellarmine.edu
STEMMONS, Sylvia, M 217-786-2260 156 I
sylvia.stemmons@llcc.edu
STEMP, Andy 907-852-3333 10 G
businessoffice@ilisagvik.edu

STEMPER, Diane, L 614-292-3600 398 H
stemper.1@osu.edu
STEN, Andrea 503-493-6529 415 E
asten@cu-portland.edu
STENBECK, Amber, L 919-508-2037 375 D
astenbeck@peace.edu
STENBERG, Richard, W 937-327-7460 406 B
rstenberg@wittenberg.edu
STENBERG, Steve 503-517-1238 421 A
sstenberg@warnerpacific.edu
STENDARDI, Deborah, M 585-475-5040 347 G
dmsgrl@rit.edu
STENDER, Julie 435-652-7703 512 A
stender@dixie.edu
STENEHJEM, Keith, A 701-788-4755 381 F
Keith.Stenehjem@mayvillestate.edu
STENGEL, Mark 805-546-3159 43 F
mark_stengel@cuesta.edu
STENGER, JR., Harvey, G 716-645-2992 351 G
provost@buffalo.edu
STENGER, Karen 440-826-2726 384 H
kstenger@bw.edu
STENKO, Michael 860-465-4509 91 H
stenkom@easternct.edu
STENNES-SPIDAHL,
Naomi, R 608-796-3481 553 A
nrstennesspidahl@viterbo.edu
STENNETT, Debbie 806-291-3500 508 B
stennettd@wbu.edu
STENNETTE, Jan 434-544-8381 520 H
stennette@lynchburg.edu
STENNIS, Jackie 662-476-5065 274 D
jstennis@eastms.edu
STENSON, Charlene 701-845-7105 382 A
c.stenson@vcsu.edu
STENSON, Charlene 701-845-7105 382 A
charlene.stenson@vcsu.edu
STENSON, Christopher 773-602-5078 147 B
cstenson@ccc.edu
STENSON, Linnea 612-659-6103 267 E
linnea.stenson@minneapolis.edu
STENSRUD, Scott 808-544-0278 140 B
sstensrud@hpu.edu
STEORTS, Ken 901-381-3939 478 D
ken@visible.edu
STEPANOVICH, Michael 661-395-4840 52 M
mstepano@bakersfieldcollge.edu
STEPHAN, Larry 928-777-3770 14 D
larry.stephan@erau.edu
STEPHAN, Lisa, M 920-565-1255 547 H
stephanlm@lakeland.edu
STEPHAN, Scott 517-629-0960 247 E
sstephan@alpha.albion.edu
STEPHAN, Sharon, R 402-472-7554 300 F
sstephan@nebraska.edu
STEPHAN, W. Karl 989-837-4211 257 A
stephan@northwood.edu
STEPHAN, William, B 317-231-2114 173 C
wstephan@indiana.edu
STEPHAN, William, B 812-855-0850 173 B
wstephan@clarian.org
STEPHAN HAINS,
Theresa, R 716-878-6711 353 A
stephatr@buffalostate.edu
STEPHEN, Carolyn 530-895-2311 31 E
stephenca@butte.edu
STEPHEN, Cathleen 610-607-6205 445 B
cstephen@racc.edu
STEPHEN BURT,
M. Rachel 317-940-9867 170 C
rstephen@butler.edu
STEPHEN-SELBY,
Heather, M 425-235-2352 536 E
heatherstephen-selby@rtc.edu
STEPHENOFF, Gail, C 614-292-5648 398 H
stephenoff.1@osu.edu
STEPHENS, Amy, M 503-255-0332 417 C
astephens@multnomah.edu
STEPHENS, Arthur 828-227-7203 379 E
stephena@wcu.edu
STEPHENS, Barbara 229-248-2530 125 E
bstephen@bainbridge.edu
STEPHENS, Barry 270-686-4516 202 E
barry.stephens@kctcs.edu
STEPHENS, Charlene 302-736-2505 96 G
stephech@wesley.edu
STEPHENS, Crystal 661-726-1911 73 C
STEPHENS, David 877-442-0505 88 G
david.stephens@rockies.edu
STEPHENS, David, J 931-363-9865 470 E
dstephens@martinmethodist.edu
STEPHENS, Diane, S 818-677-5929 35 D
diane.stephens@csun.edu
STEPHENS, Elisa 415-274-2200 26 E
STEPHENS, Fred, W 407-303-5752 108 D
fred.stephens@fhchs.edu
STEPHENS, Gail, M 870-230-5081 21 I
stepheg@hsu.edu
STEPHENS, Janice 256-378-2003 2 F
jstephens@cacc.edu
STEPHENS, Jay 435-613-5240 511 E
jay.stephens@ceu.edu
STEPHENS, Jerry, W 205-934-6360 8 G
jerryws@uab.edu

STEPHENS, Josh 806-720-7502 490 D
josh.stephens@lcu.edu
STEPHENS, Joyanne, G 954-236-1282 118 H
jsteph@fau.edu
STEPHENS, June 626-914-8825 39 G
jstephens@citruscollege.edu
STEPHENS, Kevin, N 309-655-2291 163 E
kevin.n.stephens@osfhealthcare.org
STEPHENS, Mackie 334-222-6591 5 F
mstephens@lbwcc.edu
STEPHENS, Mark 931-372-3224 474 B
mstephens@tntech.edu
STEPHENS, Mary 213-624-1200 46 L
mstephens@fidm.edu
STEPHENS, Mary, E 562-985-1658 35 A
mestephe@csulb.edu
STEPHENS, Mary Ann 330-672-2121 393 D
STEPHENS, Michael 323-259-2651 59 H
mstephens@oxy.edu
STEPHENS, JR.,
Norman, L 863-784-7110 117 I
norman.stephens@southflorida.edu
STEPHENS, Patricia 915-779-8031 483 F
pstephens@computercareercenter.com
STEPHENS, Ralph 361-593-3814 498 A
ralph.stephens@tamuk.edu
STEPHENS, Richard 704-637-4466 363 C
rstephens@catawba.edu
STEPHENS, Robert, E 816-654-7533 283 J
rstephens@kcumb.edu
STEPHENS, Ronald 270-769-1614 207 C
ron.stephens@wku.edu
STEPHENS, Rusty 252-246-1223 375 B
rstephens@wilsoncc.edu
STEPHENS, Sandra, S 901-722-3220 473 B
sandra@sco.edu
STEPHENS, Sharon 215-968-8468 423 E
stephens@bucks.edu
STEPHENS, Sonya 812-855-8783 173 C
sonsteph@indiana.edu
STEPHENS, Steve 678-466-4300 127 A
stevestephens@clayton.edu
STEPHENS, Tom 916-577-2200 79 C
tstephens@jessup.edu
STEPHENS, Virginia, L 203-396-8302 93 G
stephensv@sacredheart.edu
STEPHENS-HELM, Jennifer 304-724-3700 540 C
jstephens@apus.edu
STEPHENSON, Alan, H 828-694-1821 368 B
ah_stephenson@blueridge.edu
STEPHENSON, Cathy 828-694-1807 368 B
ck_stephenson@blueridge.edu
STEPHENSON, Devin 573-840-9698 290 J
dstephenson@trcc.edu
STEPHENSON, Diane 217-732-3155 156 G
dstephenson@lincolncollege.edu
STEPHENSON, E. Frank 252-398-6278 363 E
stephf@chowan.edu
STEPHENSON, Errol 954-973-4760 100 J
estephenson@atienterprises.edu
STEPHENSON, Melissa, K 603-924-2481 305 E
mstephenson@nec.edu
STEPHENSON, Norman, J 308-635-6121 301 E
stephens@wncc.edu
STEPHENSON, Rod 206-878-3710 534 E
rstephen@highline.edu
STEPHENSON, Sally 716-851-1698 333 D
stephenson@ecc.edu
STEPHENSON, Susan, E 850-474-2487 121 C
sstephenson@uwf.edu
STEPHENSON, Thomas 610-328-8319 447 E
tstephe1@swarthmore.edu
STEPHERSON, Kenneth 814-824-2273 436 C
kstepherson@mercyhurst.edu
STEPHNEY, Jessie 601-877-6471 273 C
jstephney@alcorn.edu
STEPIEN, E. Rick 808-544-0205 140 B
rstepien@hpu.edu
STEPIEN, Michael 614-947-6045 391 A
stepienm@franklin.edu
STEPLETON, Jon 719-502-2017 86 G
jon.stepleton@ppcc.edu
STEPNER, Michael 619-684-8789 59 A
mstepner@newschoolarch.edu
STEPNIAK, Michael, J 540-665-4600 523 K
mstepnia@su.edu
STEPP, James, D 207-768-9560 220 F
james.stepp@umpi.edu
STEPP, Jim 606-368-6454 197 H
jamesstepp@alc.edu
STEPP, Joe, A 606-368-6027 197 H
joestepp@alc.edu
STEPP, Perry, L 606-474-3253 200 J
plstepp@kcu.edu
STEPP, Thomas, L 803-777-3106 462 A
tstepp@sc.edu
STEPPE-JONES, Cecelia 919-530-6466 378 A
csteppej@nccu.edu
STERK, Claire, E 404-727-0785 129 A
claire.sterk@emory.edu
STERK, Jim 619-594-6357 36 E
adsdsu@mail.sdsu.edu
STERKOWITZ, Robert 708-974-5250 159 A
sterkowitz@morainevalley.edu

STERLING, Alan 972-721-5347 502 F
asterling@udallas.edu
STERLING, Althea 718-951-5916 326 G
asterling@brooklyn.cuny.edu
STERLING, Greg, E 574-631-8052 180 D
sterling.1@nd.edu
STERLING, Julie, L 740-588-1209 407 A
jsterling@zanestate.edu
STERLING, Marcia 505-566-3588 320 D
sterlingm@sanjuancollege.edu
STERLING, Michael 740-695-9500 384 J
msterling@btc.edu
STERLING, Monique 610-992-1700 99 D
STERLING, Rita, M 501-569-3302 24 E
rmsterling@ualr.edu
STERLING, Sean 949-812-7446 27 C
ssterling@alliant.edu
STERLING, Walter, J 505-984-6070 320 C
dean@sjcsf.edu
STERMAN, Laura, F 314-513-4258 289 B
lsterman@stlcc.edu
STERN, Dana 419-473-2700 389 B
dstern@daviscolleg.edu
STERN, David 651-523-2088 264 C
dstern02@hamline.edu
STERN, David 901-448-5529 477 C
dstern@uthsc.edu
STERN, David 901-448-5293 477 C
dstern@uthsc.edu
STERN, Deborah 215-576-0800 445 C
dstern@rrc.edu
STERN, Dennis 802-831-1155 515 A
dstern@vermontlaw.edu
STERN, Donna 203-371-7929 93 G
sternd@sacredheart.edu
STERN, Hal, S 949-824-7405 73 H
icsdean@uci.edu
STERN, Joshua 215-572-2932 422 B
sternj@arcadia.edu
STERN, Joyce 641-269-3702 185 A
sternjm@grinnell.edu
STERN, Kevin, D 214-841-3426 485 E
kstern@dts.edu
STERN, Lorna 215-572-2145 422 B
sternl@arcadia.edu
STERN, Robert A, M 203-432-2279 95 D
robert.stern@yale.edu
STERN, Sam 541-737-4661 418 F
sam.stern@oregonstate.edu
STERN, Shannyn 928-541-7777 16 I
sstern@ncu.edu
STERN, Sharon 254-710-1010 481 I
sharon_stern@baylor.edu
STERN, Steve 608-263-1841 550 G
sjstern@wisc.edu
STERN, Susan 262-695-3451 555 C
sstern1@wctc.edu
STERNBERG, Les 803-777-3828 462 A
lstern@gwm.sc.edu
STERNBURG, Robert 405-744-5627 410 C
provost@okstate.edu
STERNER, Dennis, W 509-777-4411 539 F
dsterner@whitworth.edu
STERNER, Sheri 714-432-5081 41 B
ssterner@occ.cccd.edu
STERNS, Teresa, G 304-462-4110 543 F
teresa.sterns@glenville.edu
STEROS, Bryan 973-642-8088 315 C
bryan.steros@shu.edu
STERRETT, Joseph, D 610-758-4320 434 E
jds7@lehigh.edu
STERRETT, Myra 352-395-5150 117 E
myra.sterrett@sfcollege.edu
STERRITT, Patricia 252-335-0821 369 D
psterritt@albemarle.edu
STERRY, Barbara 954-262-5365 114 B
sterry@nsu.nova.edu
STETLER, P. Daniel 772-546-5534 110 J
danstetler@hsbc.edu
STETS, OSF, Rosemary 610-796-5509 421 F
rosemary.stets@alvernia.edu
STEUER, Axel, D 217-245-3001 152 C
asteuer@ic.edu
STEUERWALD, Brian 317-917-3260 177 H
bsteu@martin.edu
STEVANUS, Linda 301-387-3011 222 H
linda.stevanus@garrettcollege.edu
STEVEN, Donald, A 609-896-5010 313 G
dsteven@rider.edu
STEVENS, Adrian 909-607-8684 62 H
adrian_stevens@pitzer.edu
STEVENS, Alison 206-587-5492 537 A
astevens@sccd.ctc.edu
STEVENS, Andrea, N 662-329-7431 276 B
astevens@dev.muw.edu
STEVENS, Andrew 303-914-6201 87 C
andrew.stevens@rrcc.edu
STEVENS, Anne, A 704-461-6718 362 B
annestevens@bac.edu
STEVENS, Audrey 937-484-1319 405 A
astevens@urbana.edu
STEVENS, Blaine, K 413-205-3264 229 G
blaine.stevens@aic.edu

STICHNOTE, Lynn, K .... 573-341-4198.... 292 A
lks@mst.edu
STICK, Jim .... 515-964-6429.... 183 E
jwstick@dmacc.edu
STICKANS, Dana .... 812-374-5332.... 175 J
dstickans@ivytech.edu
STICKEL, Marianne .... 415-458-3722.... 45 B
mstickel@dominican.edu
STICKELMAIER, Laurie, W . 330-263-2581.... 388 E
lstickelmaier@wooster.edu
STICKLEY, Ronald, G .... 540-665-4530.... 523 K
rstickle3@su.edu
STICKNEY, Carey .... 318-345-9130.... 210 I
cstickney@ladelta.edu
STIEFEL, Debra .... 815-288-5511.... 163 I
stiefed@svcc.edu
STIEFEL, Ethan .... 336-770-3207.... 379 D
stiefele@uncsa.edu
STIEFEL, Joseph .... 727-394-6058.... 159 E
jstiefel@nuhs.edu
STIEFEL, Karen, A .... 210-297-9630.... 481 E
STIEFEL, Sheryl .... 425-602-3008.... 530 K
sstiefel@bastyr.edu
STIEFFEL, Deborah .... 570-372-4396.... 447 D
stieffel@susqu.edu
STIELOW, Fred .... 304-724-3700.... 540 C
fstielow@apus.edu
STIENBARGER, Mary Ann . 765-983-1346.... 171 B
stienma@earlham.edu
STIFEL, David .... 860-412-7363.... 91 A
dstifel@qvcc.commnet.edu
STIFF, Cindra, K .... 270-852-3113.... 203 E
cindrast@kwc.edu
STIFFIN, Rose Mary .... 305-626-3697.... 108 H
rstiffin@fmuniv.edu
STIFFLER, Daniel, J .... 314-367-8700.... 288 I
daniel.stiffler@stlcop.edu
STIFTER, Michael, J .... 715-425-3827.... 552 A
michael.j.stifter@uwrf.edu
STIGER, Barry, R .... 570-326-3761.... 440 K
bstiger@pct.edu
STIGER, Bob .... 870-512-7801.... 20 F
bob_stiger@asun.edu
STIGER, Kathleen .... 323-241-5338.... 55 C
stigerk@lasc.edu
STIGER, Tim, A .... 405-224-3140.... 413 E
tstiger@usao.edu
STIGLITZ, Eloise .... 760-750-4056.... 36 B
estiglitz@csusm.edu
STILES, Andrea .... 513-244-4844.... 388 D
andrea_stiles@mail.msj.edu
STILES, Betsy .... 610-902-8202.... 423 H
egs34@cabrini.edu
STILES, Chip .... 978-837-5357.... 242 D
stilesc@merrimack.edu
STILES, Diane .... 785-890-3641.... 195 E
diane.stiles@nwktc.edu
STILES, Gary, L .... 919-668-6330.... 363 I
stile003@mc.duke.edu
STILES, J. Bruce .... 901-448-5106.... 477 C
jstiles@uthsc.edu
STILES, Marsha .... 610-861-1369.... 436 I
mlstiles@moravian.edu
STILES, Michael, D .... 712-279-3149.... 188 E
stilesmd@stlukescollege.edu
STILL, Guy, M .... 856-225-2900.... 314 C
guystill@camden.rutgers.edu
STILL, Kathy .... 276-376-0130.... 525 C
kls72d@uvawise.edu
STILLE, Brand, R .... 864-597-4130.... 463 F
stillebr@wofford.edu
STILLERMAN, Harry .... 704-878-4321.... 371 H
hstillerman@mitchellcc.edu
STILLEY, Dana .... 845-574-4224.... 347 I
dstilley@sunyrockland.edu
STILLMAN, Bruce .... 516-367-8497.... 329 F
stillman@cshl.edu
STILLMAN, John, P .... 801-581-3655.... 510 L
john.stillman@hsc.utah.edu
STILWELL, Martha .... 269-965-3931.... 253 H
stilwellm@kellogg.edu
STIMAC, John .... 217-581-2017.... 150 C
jpstimac@eiu.edu
STIMAC, Robin .... 816-604-3071.... 285 H
robin.stimac@mcckc.edu
STIMELING, Kurt, W .... 315-268-6620.... 329 C
kstimeli@clarkson.edu
STIMPERT, Cathy .... 419-755-4047.... 399 C
stimpert.9@osu.edu
STIMPLE, Janet .... 216-687-3831.... 388 C
j.stimple@csuohio.edu
STINCHCOMB, Jan .... 410-225-2289.... 224 C
jstinchc@mica.edu
STINE, June .... 312-341-2407.... 162 I
jstine@roosevelt.edu
STINE, Karen .... 334-244-3678.... 2 A
kstine@aum.edu
STINE, Maxine .... 804-288-1000.... 523 F
mstine@rsht.edu
STINE, Terry, E .... 208-376-7731.... 142 E
terrys@boisebible.edu
STINEMETZ, Charles, L .... 740-368-3112.... 400 F
clstinem@owu.edu

STINER, Carol .... 202-685-2514.... 557 F
stinerc@ndu.edu
STINER, Margaret .... 440-826-8061.... 384 H
mstiner@bw.edu
STINES, Marsha .... 828-627-4529.... 370 G
mstines@haywood.edu
STINESPRING, James, M .. 304-457-6243.... 540 B
stinespringjm@ab.edu
STINGLE, Janice .... 920-686-6231.... 550 E
Janice.Stingle@sl.edu
STINNER, Erin .... 308-635-6081.... 301 E
stinnere@wncc.edu
STINNER, Jerry .... 818-677-2004.... 35 D
jerry.stinner@csun.edu
STINNETT, Gary, W .... 704-687-4269.... 378 E
gwstinne@uncc.edu
STINSON, Barbara, J .... 715-425-3141.... 552 A
barbara.stinson@uwrf.edu
STINSON, Becky .... 573-592-4237.... 293 E
bstinson@williamwoods.edu
STINSON, Charlie .... 256-761-6301.... 7 H
cstinson@talladega.edu
STINSON, Christine, H .... 540-365-4311.... 518 J
cstinson@ferrum.edu
STINSON, Christopher .... 312-850-7010.... 147 C
cstinson@ccc.edu
STINSON, Claire .... 931-372-3311.... 474 B
cstinson@tntech.edu
STINSON, Greg .... 219-464-5212.... 181 A
greg.stinson@valpo.edu
STINSON, Kandi, M .... 513-745-4236.... 406 E
stinson@xavier.edu
STINSON, Mark .... 636-573-9300.... 286 H
mstinson@motech.edu
STINSON, Matt .... 330-823-7803.... 404 C
stinsomp@mountunion.edu
STINSON, Monica .... 510-574-1103.... 44 D
mstinson@devry.edu
STINSON, Pamela .... 580-628-6210.... 409 B
pamela.stinson@north-ok.edu
STINSON, Randy .... 502-897-4205.... 205 H
rstinson@sbts.edu
STINSON, Randy .... 502-897-4813.... 205 H
rstinson@sbts.edu
STINSON, Shakitha .... 512-505-3029.... 488 B
slstinson@htu.edu
STINSON, Willette .... 937-708-5629.... 405 G
wstinson@wilberforce.edu
STINTON, Martha .... 808-853-1040.... 140 G
marthas@pacrim.edu
STIPCAK, Sondra, L .... 570-321-4322.... 435 D
stipcak@lycoming.edu
STIREWALT, Jesse .... 218-879-0708.... 266 F
housing@fdltcc.edu
STIRLING, Diane, S .... 704-894-2462.... 363 F
distirling@davidson.edu
STIRLING, James, S .... 301-405-3372.... 227 B
jstirlin@umd.edu
STIRLING, Joan, R .... 870-368-2007.... 23 A
jstirling@ozarka.edu
STIRLING, Wynn, C .... 801-422-4465.... 509 D
wynn_stirling@byu.edu
STIRTON, Rob .... 734-462-4400.... 258 C
rstirton@schoolcraft.edu
STIRTZ, Michele, D .... 402-552-2543.... 297 D
stirtz@clarksoncollege.edu
STISO, Joseph .... 978-632-6600.... 240 G
j_stiso@mwcc.mass.edu
STITH, Kay, K .... 405-878-5434.... 412 A
kkstith@stgregorys.edu
STITH, Kevin, U .... 740-368-3398.... 400 F
kustith@owu.edu
STITH, Melvin, T .... 315-443-9494.... 357 B
mtstith@syr.edu
STITHEM, Diana .... 928-757-0881.... 16 G
dstithem@mohave.edu
STITSWORTH, Michael .... 507-786-3002.... 271 H
stitswor@stolaf.edu
STITT, Sarah .... 734-973-8576.... 260 B
stitt@wccnet.edu
STITT, Teresa .... 989-686-9422.... 250 F
tfstitt@delta.edu
STITTS, Doria, K .... 336-750-2345.... 380 A
stittsd@wssu.edu
STIVER, Keith .... 510-723-6923.... 38 L
kstiver@chabotcollege.edu
STIVERS, Mary Elizabeth .... 515-263-2805.... 184 I
mestivers@grandview.edu
STOB, Jeffrey, A .... 616-526-6280.... 249 E
stobje@calvin.edu
STOB, Michael .... 616-526-7114.... 249 E
stob@calvin.edu
STOBER, Dan .... 650-723-7162.... 71 F
dan.stober@stanford.edu
STOBNICKE, Michelle .... 505-428-1659.... 320 E
michelle.stobnicke@sfcc.edu
STOBO, John, D .... 510-987-9071.... 73 D
john.stobo@ucop.edu
STOCCO, Douglas, M .... 806-743-2556.... 501 E
doug.stocco@ttuhsc.edu
STOCCO, Douglas, M .... 806-743-3600.... 501 E
doug.stocco@ttuhsc.edu
STOCK, Carolmarie .... 513-569-1236.... 387 F
carolmarie.stock@cincinnatistate.edu

STOCK, Jack, P .... 810-762-7873.... 253 I
jstock@kettering.edu
STOCK, Kenneth .... 708-656-8000.... 159 C
kenneth.stock@morton.edu
STOCK, Laura, D .... 573-651-2021.... 290 D
lstock@semo.edu
STOCK, Lawrence, E .... 724-287-8711.... 423 F
larry.stock@bc3.edu
STOCK, Lisa, A .... 630-942-2351.... 147 G
stockl@cod.edu
STOCK, Renee .... 304-829-7572.... 540 E
rstock@bethanywv.edu
STOCK, Susan .... 312-341-3548.... 162 I
sstock@roosevelt.edu
STOCK, Tom .... 320-363-2969.... 271 F
tstock@csbsju.edu
STOCK, Tom .... 315-866-0300.... 335 E
stockte@herkimer.edu
STOCK KUPPERMAN,
Gretel, L .... 608-796-3272.... 553 A
glstock@viterbo.edu
STOCKE, Mike .... 253-964-6534.... 536 C
mstocke@pierce.ctc.edu
STOCKER, Jane Ellen .... 708-596-2000.... 164 F
jstocker@ssc.edu
STOCKER, Susan, J .... 440-964-4211.... 393 E
sjstocke@kent.edu
STOCKER, Todd .... 651-641-8213.... 263 C
stocker@csp.edu
STOCKERT, Brian .... 619-388-2600.... 65 G
bstockert@sdccd.edu
STOCKERT, Patricia, A .... 309-655-4124.... 163 E
patricia.a.stockert@osfhealthcare.org
STOCKING, Lynn .... 406-243-7801.... 295 D
lynn.stocking@umontana.edu
STOCKS, Morris, H .... 662-915-5315.... 277 G
mhstocks@olemiss.edu
STOCKS, Sherri .... 757-352-4843.... 523 B
sstocks@regent.edu
STOCKSLADER, Jon Jay .... 716-286-8189.... 344 D
js@niagara.edu
STOCKSTILL, Stephanie .... 281-756-3531.... 479 G
sstockstill@alvincollege.edu
STOCKTON, Carl, A .... 281-283-3000.... 503 C
stockton@uhcl.edu
STOCKTON, Jim .... 870-743-3000.... 22 G
stockton@northark.edu
STOCKTON, Nancy .... 812-855-5711.... 173 C
stocktnj@indiana.edu
STOCKTON, Thomas, B .... 336-841-4592.... 365 A
tstockto@highpoint.edu
STOCKWELL, John, C .... 864-503-5200.... 463 A
jstockwell@uscupstate.edu
STODDARD, Eric .... 928-541-7777.... 16 I
estoddard@ncu.edu
STODDARD, Reed, J .... 208-496-9370.... 142 G
stoddardr@byui.edu
STODDARD, Richard, S .... 614-292-1279.... 398 H
stoddard.1@osu.edu
STODDART, Scott, F .... 212-217-4320.... 333 G
scott_stoddart@fitnyc.edu
STODDART, Sue, A .... 920-923-7177.... 548 C
sstoddart@marianuniversity.edu
STOECKLIN, Dennis, J .... 503-280-8503.... 415 E
dstoecklin@cu-portland.edu
STOEFFEL, Virginia .... 845-431-8906.... 332 E
Virginia.stoeffel@sunydutchess.edu
STOEHR, Gary .... 716-829-7796.... 332 F
stoehrg@dyc.edu
STOFAN, John .... 510-217-4701.... 29 F
jstofan@argosy.edu
STOFFER, Dale, R .... 419-289-5985.... 384 D
dstoffer@ashland.edu
STOFFERS, Jill .... 831-647-6571.... 57 F
jill.stoffers@miis.edu
STOFFLE, Carla .... 520-621-6432.... 19 B
stofflec@library.arizona.edu
STOFFREGEN-DEYOUNG,
Margaret .... 260-399-7700.... 180 E
mstoffregendeyoung@sf.edu
STOFFT, Lori .... 928-314-9595.... 12 C
lorraine.stofft@azwestern.edu
STOGNER, Becky .... 806-651-2311.... 498 D
bstogner@mail.wtamu.edu
STOHLER, Christian, S .... 410-706-7461.... 227 C
cstohler@dental.umaryland.edu
STOICESCU, Dan .... 410-287-6060.... 222 A
dstoicescu@cecil.edu
STOIK, Julene .... 712-274-6400.... 189 H
julie.stoik@witcc.edu
STOJEVICH, Jean .... 218-733-5908.... 267 B
j.stojevich@lsc.edu
STOJKOVIC, Stan .... 414-229-4400.... 551 C
stojkovi@uwm.edu
STOKAN, Matthew .... 724-852-3227.... 451 B
mstokan@waynesburg.edu
STOKELY, Madlyn .... 212-772-4847.... 327 E
madlyn.stokely@hunter.cuny.edu
STOKER, Susan .... 765-269-5609.... 176 B
sstoker1@ivytech.edu
STOKES, Allison .... 585-275-4321.... 358 I
allison.stokes@rochester.edu
STOKES, Butch .... 662-325-2663.... 276 A
butch@registrar.msstate.edu

STOKES, Douglas .... 803-535-1393.... 460 C
stokesd@octech.edu
STOKES, Ellen, E .... 410-704-3255.... 228 E
estokes@towson.edu
STOKES, Garnett, S .... 706-542-1538.... 138 C
gstokes@franklin.uga.edu
STOKES, Garnett, S .... 850-644-1816.... 119 C
STOKES, H. Bruce .... 951-343-4487.... 31 G
hbstokes@calbaptist.edu
STOKES, Judi .... 845-431-8405.... 332 E
judi.stokes@sunydutchess.edu
STOKES, Larry .... 912-358-4190.... 136 C
stokesl@savannahstate.edu
STOKES, Leroy .... 336-334-4822.... 370 E
lstokes@gtcc.edu
STOKES, Madeline .... 251-405-4457.... 2 D
mstokes@bishop.edu
STOKES, Mark .... 423-636-7319.... 476 F
mstokes@tusculum.edu
STOKES, Mark .... 423-636-7316.... 476 F
STOKES, Maureen, O .... 760-252-2411.... 30 F
mstokes@barstow.edu
STOKES, Michael .... 423-478-6218.... 474 E
mstokes@clevelandstatecc.edu
STOKES, Mickey, E .... 662-476-5068.... 274 D
mstokes@eastms.edu
STOKES, Robert, D .... 610-519-4311.... 450 G
robert.stokes@villanova.edu
STOKES, Timothy .... 253-566-5022.... 538 C
tstokes@tacomacc.edu
STOKES-WILSON, Lynette . 312-850-7301.... 147 C
lstokes@ccc.edu
STOKKE, Renae .... 303-632-2300.... 83 C
rstokke@coloradotech.edu
STOLAR, Larry .... 972-438-6932.... 492 C
lstolar@parkercc.edu
STOLAR, Steven, M .... 856-691-8600.... 309 C
sstolar@cccnj.edu
STOLL, August .... 732-255-0400.... 312 D
astoll@ocean.edu
STOLL, James, G .... 978-542-6401.... 239 B
jstoll@salemstate.edu
STOLL, Laura, K .... 573-341-4081.... 292 A
lstoll@mst.edu
STOLL, Nancy, C .... 617-573-8239.... 245 E
nstoll@suffolk.edu
STOLL, Sherideen, S .... 419-372-8262.... 385 C
sstoll@bgsu.edu
STOLL, William, S .... 314-935-7574.... 292 J
stoll@wustl.edu
STOLLER, Brett .... 309-649-6211.... 165 D
brett.stoller@src.edu
STOLLERY, Chris .... 206-726-5052.... 532 G
cstollery@cornish.edu
STOLLSTEIMER, Terry .... 248-370-2160.... 257 C
stollste@oakland.edu
STOLPER, Edward, M .... 626-395-6336.... 32 E
ems@caltech.edu
STOLPER, Lauren, B .... 626-395-6361.... 32 E
lstolper@caltech.edu
STOLT, Wilbur .... 701-777-2617.... 381 D
wilbur.stolt@email.und.edu
STOLTZ, Jacqueline, C .... 860-701-5040.... 93 B
stoltz_j@mitchell.edu
STOLTZ, Marlene .... 406-756-3846.... 294 D
mstoltz@fvcc.edu
STOLTZ-LOIKE, Marion .... 212-287-3510.... 357 J
mstoltz-loike@touro.edu
STOLWORTHY, Charity .... 970-675-3203.... 82 D
charity.stolworthy@cncc.edu
STOLZ, Rebecca .... 323-259-2691.... 59 H
rstolz@oxy.edu
STOMBER, Richard .... 973-720-2277.... 317 D
stomberr@wpunj.edu
STOMPER, Jeffrey, A .... 847-543-2531.... 147 H
stomper@clcillinois.edu
STONE, Adam .... 815-753-1747.... 160 A
ajstone@niu.edu
STONE, Barbara .... 312-235-3507.... 164 D
b.stone@shimer.edu
STONE, Brad .... 310-338-5807.... 56 E
bstone@lmu.edu
STONE, David .... 815-753-9282.... 160 A
dastone@niu.edu
STONE, David .... 314-968-6968.... 293 A
stoneda@webster.edu
STONE, David, M .... 212-854-9962.... 330 F
dms2148@columbia.edu
STONE, Denise .... 503-255-0332.... 417 C
dstone@multnomah.edu
STONE, Dennis .... 704-971-8500.... 363 D
STONE, Dennis, K .... 214-648-1908.... 507 D
dennis.stone@utsouthwestern.edu
STONE, Doreen .... 218-935-0417.... 273 A
dstone@wetcc.org
STONE, Eddie .... 931-393-1593.... 475 C
estone@mscc.edu
STONE, Emily .... 925-685-1230.... 43 C
estone@dvc.edu
STONE, Gaylund, K .... 262-243-5700.... 546 I
gaylund.stone@cuw.edu
STONE, Glenice .... 662-720-7237.... 276 D
gstone@nemcc.edu

STRAUTZ-SPRINGBORN, Shelly ... 989-328-1243 ... 256 A
shellys@montcalm.edu
STRAVERS, Meredith ... 269-965-3931 ... 253 H
straversm@kellogg.edu
STRAWBRIDGE, Richard ... 603-623-0313 ... 305 F
rickstrawbridge@nhia.edu
STRAWLEY, George ... 252-473-2264 ... 369 D
gstrawley@albemarle.edu
STRAWN, Brad ... 405-491-6608 ... 412 D
bstrawn@snu.edu
STRAWN, Roxanna ... 920-686-6150 ... 550 E
Roxanna.Strawn@sl.edu
STRAWN, Scott ... 405-491-6335 ... 412 D
sstrawn@snu.edu
STRAWSER, Jerry ... 979-845-4711 ... 497 C
jstrawser@tamu.edu
STRAWSER, Joyce, A ... 973-761-9225 ... 315 B
joyce.strawser@shu.edu
STRAYER, Colleen ... 419-530-2516 ... 404 F
colleen.strayer@utoledo.edu
STRAYER, James, E ... 308-398-7355 ... 297 C
jstrayer@cccneb.edu
STRAYER, John, C ... 610-892-1504 ... 441 C
jstrayer@pit.edu
STRAZDAS, Peter, J ... 269-387-8584 ... 260 F
peter.strazdas@wmich.edu
STREAR, Jay ... 310-476-9777 ... 28 F
jstrear@ajula.edu
STREBE, Chet, A ... 715-675-3331 ... 554 G
strebe@ntc.edu
STRECKENBEIN, Mark ... 609-343-5127 ... 307 D
strecken@atlantic.edu
STRECKER, Bill ... 636-922-8607 ... 288 E
STRECKER, Deborah ... 610-896-1129 ... 430 G
dstrecke@haverford.edu
STREET, Aaron, J ... 870-235-5011 ... 23 I
ajstreet@saumag.edu
STREET, Helen ... 662-252-8000 ... 277 C
hstreet@rustcollege.edu
STREET, Kathleen, A ... 909-869-2572 ... 33 G
kastreet@csupomona.edu
STREET, Kenneth ... 936-639-1301 ... 480 D
kstreet@angelina.edu
STREET, Margaret, F ... 573-629-3006 ... 282 H
mstreet@hlg.edu
STREET, Scott, V ... 617-266-1400 ... 231 G
STREET, Sheila ... 336-506-4186 ... 367 G
streets@alamancecc.edu
STREETER, Holly ... 319-425-5340 ... 189 C
streeterh@uiu.edu
STREETER, Kelley ... 860-231-5228 ... 93 H
kstreeter@sjc.edu
STREETER, Lucy ... 808-739-4686 ... 140 A
lstreete@chaminade.edu
STREETER, Montrose ... 315-781-3900 ... 335 G
streeter@hws.edu
STREETER, William, W ... 262-595-2141 ... 551 E
william.streeter@uwp.edu
STREFF, Frederick, M ... 540-674-3637 ... 527 B
fstreff@nr.edu
STREFF, Kevin, F ... 605-256-5077 ... 465 G
kevin.streff@dsu.edu
STREGE, Ron ... 715-346-3574 ... 552 B
rstrege@uwsp.edu
STREHLOW, Betty, J ... 320-222-5203 ... 268 I
betty.strehlow@ridgewater.edu
STREID, David ... 641-472-1130 ... 187 B
dstreid@mum.edu
STREIM, Nancy ... 212-678-7407 ... 357 F
streim@tc.edu
STREIN, Nancy ... 718-951-5163 ... 326 G
nstrein@brooklyn.cuny.edu
STREIT, Gary, W ... 719-884-5000 ... 86 D
gwstreit@nbc.edu
STREIT, Linda, A ... 678-547-6799 ... 133 F
streit_la@mercer.edu
STRENGTH, Carli ... 817-591-1081 ... 100 J
STRETCHER, Gary, D ... 409-984-6209 ... 500 H
gary.stretcher@lamarpa.edu
STREUBERT, Helen, J ... 210-434-6711 ... 491 G
hjstreubert@lake.ollusa.edu
STREUFERT, Billie ... 605-331-6602 ... 466 D
billie.streufert@usiouxfalls.edu
STREY, Mary, M ... 641-628-5188 ... 183 A
streym@central.edu
STRICHERZ, Shanda, L ... 605-336-6588 ... 465 B
shandas@sfseminary.edu
STRICKER, Edward, M ... 412-624-4569 ... 449 A
edstrick@pitt.edu
STRICKLAND, Angelique ... 770-938-4711 ... 133 A
STRICKLAND, Brian ... 251-580-2214 ... 5 A
bstrickland@faulknerstate.edu
STRICKLAND, Carolyn, R ... 570-326-3761 ... 440 K
cstrickl@pct.edu
STRICKLAND, Claire ... 207-581-1593 ... 220 A
claire.strickland@umit.maine.edu
STRICKLAND, Earnestine, J ... 512-505-3082 ... 488 B
eestrickland@htu.edu
STRICKLAND, Fatisha ... 215-591-5729 ... 427 A
fstrickland@devry.edu
STRICKLAND, Gary ... 912-279-5831 ... 127 B
gstrickland@ccga.edu
STRICKLAND, Gary, E ... 605-336-6588 ... 465 B
gstrickland@sfseminary.edu
STRICKLAND, Haywood, L ... 903-927-3200 ... 509 A
hstrickland@wileyc.edu
STRICKLAND, Joy ... 303-963-3012 ... 81 K
jstrickland@ccu.edu
STRICKLAND, Katherine, F ... 540-857-6020 ... 528 E
kstrickland@virginiawestern.edu
STRICKLAND, Kathleen, M ... 724-738-2007 ... 443 E
kathleen.strickland@sru.edu
STRICKLAND, Ken ... 229-217-4188 ... 134 C
kstrickland@moultrietech.edu
STRICKLAND, Ken ... 901-272-5107 ... 471 B
kstrickland@mca.edu
STRICKLAND, Kristine ... 225-216-8068 ... 209 I
kristinestrickland@lctcs.edu
STRICKLAND, LeAnne ... 910-892-3178 ... 364 F
lstrickland@heritagebiblecollege.edu
STRICKLAND, Les ... 480-423-6510 ... 16 D
les.strickland@sccmail.maricopa.edu
STRICKLAND, Liz, F ... 870-575-8471 ... 25 B
stricklandl@uapb.edu
STRICKLAND, Mark ... 727-341-3408 ... 116 F
strickland.mark@spcollege.edu
STRICKLAND, Michael, D ... 615-460-6420 ... 467 B
mike.strickland@belmont.edu
STRICKLAND, Michele ... 478-553-2097 ... 134 F
mstrickland@oftc.edu
STRICKLAND, Pamela ... 732-235-9721 ... 317 A
ohmanpa@umdnj.edu
STRICKLAND, Randy ... 502-585-7101 ... 205 I
rstrickland@spalding.edu
STRICKLAND, Samuel ... 919-866-5826 ... 374 E
sstrickland@waketech.edu
STRICKLAND, Sandra, W ... 252-335-0821 ... 369 D
sstrickland@albemarle.edu
STRICKLAND, Sherry ... 254-559-7707 ... 500 C
sherry.strickland@tstc.edu
STRICKLAND, Sidney ... 215-327-8084 ... 347 H
strickland@rockefeller.edu
STRICKLAND, Tim, H ... 252-246-1375 ... 375 B
tstrickland@wilsoncc.edu
STRICKLAND, Tina ... 229-217-4141 ... 134 C
tstrickland@moultrietech.edu
STRICKLAND, Tonya ... 229-248-2569 ... 125 E
tstrickland@bainbridge.edu
STRICKLAND, Valerie ... 770-962-7580 ... 132 A
vstrickland@gwinnetttech.edu
STRICKLAND, Wayne, G ... 503-255-0332 ... 417 C
udub@multnomah.edu
STRICKLER, Michael, M ... 540-464-7102 ... 529 A
stricklermm@vmi.edu
STRICKLER, Tammy ... 505-224-3067 ... 317 J
STRICKLER, Tammy ... 505-224-4325 ... 317 J
tammys@cnm.edu
STRICKLIN, Jan ... 503-352-2890 ... 419 E
jstricklin@pacificu.edu
STRICKLIN, Linda ... 208-792-2439 ... 143 F
lsstricklin@lcsc.edu
STRICKLIN, Scott ... 662-325-8082 ... 276 A
sas24@msstate.edu
STRIEGEL, Nicole ... 417-455-5636 ... 281 C
nstriege@crowder.edu
STRIKWERDA, Carl, J ... 717-361-1193 ... 428 E
strikwerda@etown.edu
STRIMKOVSKY, Lauri ... 215-248-7168 ... 425 C
strimkovsky@chc.edu
STRIMPLE, Karen ... 620-252-7555 ... 191 I
karens@coffeyville.edu
STRINE, Michael ... 434-924-3252 ... 525 B
ms6vu@virginia.edu
STRINGER, Christopher ... 609-292-2108 ... 316 A
cstringer@tesc.edu
STRINGER, Cindy ... 254-647-3120 ... 492 E
STRINGER, Janet ... 650-306-3291 ... 67 E
stringerj@smccd.net
STRINGER, Martin ... 714-628-4816 ... 63 G
stringer_martin@sccollege.edu
STRINGER, Sarah ... 334-727-8254 ... 8 C
ssstringer@tuskegee.edu
STRINGER, Scott ... 601-984-5167 ... 277 H
sstringer@umc.edu
STRINGER, Story ... 970-225-4860 ... 81 I
story.stringer@collegeamerica.edu
STRINGER, Tommy ... 903-875-7380 ... 491 B
tommy.stringer@navarrocollege.edu
STRINGFELLOW, Alan ... 405-682-7522 ... 409 F
astringfellow@occc.edu
STRINGFELLOW, Catherine ... 256-395-2211 ... 7 E
cstringfellow@suscc.edu
STRIPE-PORTILLO, Jennifer ... 213-615-7264 ... 146 C
jstripe@thechicagoschool.edu
STRIPLING, Rosanne ... 903-223-3003 ... 498 C
rosanne.stripling@tamut.edu
STRIPLING, William, R ... 870-972-2048 ... 20 C
ricks@astate.edu
STRITIKUS, Tom ... 206-543-2100 ... 538 F
tstrit@uw.edu
STRMISKA, Kenneth, D ... 920-565-1478 ... 547 H
strmiskakd@lakeland.edu
STROBECK, Carol ... 973-290-4418 ... 309 A
cstrobeck@cse.edu
STROBEL, Corbin ... 620-665-3537 ... 193 F
strobelc@hutchcc.edu
STROBEL, Judy ... 406-874-6207 ... 294 H
strobelj@milescc.edu
STROBEL, Nathan ... 414-443-8825 ... 553 B
nathan.strobel@wlc.edu
STROBLE, Elizabeth, J ... 314-968-6996 ... 293 A
stroble@webster.edu
STROCKBINE, Richard ... 972-721-5207 ... 502 F
dick@udallas.edu
STRODE, Rhoda ... 918-687-6747 ... 407 H
rhoda.strode@connorsstate.edu
STRODEMIER, Tammy ... 360-736-9391 ... 531 H
tstrodmeier@centralia.edu
STROEH, Mark ... 713-692-0077 ... 484 B
STROH, Melinda ... 617-353-3635 ... 232 G
strohm@bu.edu
STROHM, Bobbie, A ... 858-499-0202 ... 41 E
bstrohm@coleman.edu
STROHM, Leslie, C ... 919-962-1219 ... 378 D
leslie_strohm@unc.edu
STROHM, Shelly ... 203-332-5179 ... 90 B
sstrohm@hcc.commnet.edu
STROHMETZ, David ... 732-263-5121 ... 311 F
dstrohme@monmouth.edu
STROHMEYER, George ... 814-871-5873 ... 429 F
strohmey002@gannon.edu
STROHMEYER, George ... 814-871-7436 ... 429 F
strohmeyer@gannon.edu
STROJNY, Duane ... 517-371-5140 ... 259 B
strojnyd@cooley.edu
STROKER, Robert ... 215-204-8301 ... 447 G
robert.stroker@temple.edu
STROKER, Robert ... 215-782-2715 ... 447 G
robert.stroker@temple.edu
STROLLO, Ronald, A ... 330-941-2385 ... 406 F
rastrollo@ysu.edu
STROLLO HOLBROOK, Toni ... 407-646-2280 ... 116 B
tsholbrook@rollins.edu
STROM, Donald ... 314-935-5514 ... 292 J
don_strom@wustl.edu
STROM, G. L. (Jack) ... 701-349-3621 ... 383 B
jackstrom@trinitybiblecollege.edu
STROM, Laura, A ... 618-650-3330 ... 165 A
lstrom@siue.edu
STROM, Siri, J ... 509-865-8613 ... 534 D
strom_s@heritage.edu
STROM, Steven ... 845-451-1552 ... 331 F
s_strom@culinary.edu
STROMAN, Gerry, G ... 765-455-9316 ... 173 E
gstroman@iuk.edu
STROMAN, Jay ... 706-379-3111 ... 139 F
jtstroman@yhc.edu
STROMAN, Kozman ... 305-430-1168 ... 108 H
kozman.stroman@fmuniv.edu
STROMAN, Lauren ... 713-718-8091 ... 487 G
lauren.stroman@hccs.edu
STROMBERG, Lori, S ... 308-635-6703 ... 301 E
stromber@wncc.edu
STROMMEN, Kim ... 215-204-7000 ... 447 G
strommen@temple.edu
STROMQUIST, Eric ... 503-961-6200 ... 418 A
estromquist@pioneerpacific.edu
STROMQUIST, Eric ... 888-624-2433 ... 419 F
estromquist@pioneerpacific.edu
STRONACH, Bruce ... 215-204-7000 ... 447 G
bruce.stronach@temple.edu
STRONG, Charles ... 318-371-3035 ... 211 H
cstrong@nwltc.edu
STRONG, Charles, T ... 318-371-3035 ... 211 F
cstrong@ltc.edu
STRONG, Charmaine, R ... 724-838-4242 ... 447 B
strong@setonhill.edu
STRONG, Chuck ... 662-562-3494 ... 276 E
cwstrong@northwestms.edu
STRONG, Douglas, M ... 206-281-2473 ... 537 D
dstrong@spu.edu
STRONG, Gary, E ... 310-825-1201 ... 74 A
gstrong@library.ucla.edu
STRONG, Harry ... 619-688-0800 ... 42 J
hstrong@concorde.edu
STRONG, James, T ... 209-667-3203 ... 36 C
jtstrong@csustan.edu
STRONG, Karen ... 702-895-4074 ... 302 K
karen.strong@unlv.edu
STRONG, Kira ... 641-673-1014 ... 189 I
strongk@wmpenn.edu
STRONG, Kirk ... 801-422-2507 ... 509 D
kirk_strong@byu.edu
STRONG, III, L. Thomas ... 504-282-4455 ... 213 H
tstrong@nobts.edu
STRONG, Mike ... 909-389-3210 ... 65 B
mstrong@craftonhills.edu
STRONG, Pennie ... 478-757-3463 ... 126 G
pms@centralgatech.edu
STRONG, Robert, A ... 540-458-8418 ... 530 A
strongr@wlu.edu
STRONG, Shirley ... 415-575-6171 ... 32 D
sstrong@ciis.edu
STRONG, Walter, L ... 504-816-4359 ... 208 I
wstrong@dillard.edu
STRONG, Zebedee, D ... 817-515-4206 ... 496 A
zeb.strong@tccd.edu
STRONGWATER, Steven ... 631-444-2701 ... 352 [illegible]
steven.strongwater@stonybrook.edu
STROTHER, Jennielle ... 512-472-4133 ... 494 [illegible]
jstrother@ssw.edu
STROTHER, Jennifer ... 425-564-4250 ... 531 [illegible]
jennifer.strother@bellevuecollege.edu
STROTHER, William ... 318-670-6472 ... 215 A
wstrother@susla.edu
STROTHMAN, Gary ... 815-825-2086 ... 155 C
gstrothmn@kishwaukeecollege.edu
STROUD, Annie ... 608-663-3317 ... 547 C
astroud@edgewood.edu
STROUD, Clarke ... 405-271-4000 ... 413 D
clarke-stroud@ouhsc.edu
STROUD, Clarke ... 405-325-3161 ... 413 C
cstroud@ou.edu
STROUD, George ... 610-902-8417 ... 423 H
george.stroud@cabrini.edu
STROUD, Jonathan, M ... 319-895-4215 ... 183 D
jstroud@cornellcollege.edu
STROUD, Lewis ... 910-277-5149 ... 376 A
stroudl@sapc.edu
STROUD, Nancy ... 478-471-2728 ... 133 E
nancy.stroud@maconstate.edu
STROUD, Ron ... 915-831-2614 ... 486 E
jstroud2@epcc.edu
STROUGAL, Susan ... 630-829-6018 ... 145 D
sstrougal@ben.edu
STROUP-BENHAM, Christine ... 303-315-2835 ... 88 D
christine.stroup-benham@ucdenver.edu
STROUSE, Nancy ... 702-895-2811 ... 302 K
nancy.strouse@unlv.edu
STROUSE, Robert, K ... 714-850-4800 ... 89 F
Strouse@TaftU.edu
STROUSE, Robert, K ... 714-850-4800 ... 72 D
strouse@taftu.edu
STROUTH, Crystal ... 507-372-3451 ... 268 B
crystal.strouth@mnwest.edu
STROUTS, Paul, A ... 850-644-4444 ... 119 C
pstrouts@admin.fsu.edu
STRUBE, Chris ... 908-852-1400 ... 308 F
strubec@centenarycollege.edu
STRUBEL, John ... 843-863-8044 ... 456 B
jstrubel@csuniv.edu
STRUBLE, Dan ... 828-669-8012 ... 367 C
dstruble@montreat.edu
STRUBLE, Lee, E ... 585-292-2902 ... 341 H
lstruble@monroecc.edu
STRUBLE, Robert ... 716-896-0700 ... 359 F
restruble@villa.edu
STRUBY, Shannon ... 402-354-7104 ... 299 E
shannon.struby@methodistcollege.edu
STRUCHTEMEYER, Derek, L ... 770-720-5549 ... 135 F
dls@reinhardt.edu
STRUCK, Kathy ... 605-367-4625 ... 466 C
kathy.struck@southeasttech.edu
STRUCKMEYER, Jacqueline ... 931-221-7466 ... 473 D
struckmeyerj@apsu.edu
STRUDWICK, Daniel ... 217-228-5432 ... 161 E
strudda@quincy.edu
STRUEBEL, Phil, J ... 716-884-9120 ... 324 J
pjstruebel@bryantstratton.edu
STRUGAR-FRITSCH, Chris ... 517-483-1813 ... 254 D
strugarj@lcc.edu
STRULOEFF, Mark ... 503-699-6252 ... 416 I
mstruloeff@marylhurst.edu
STRUNK, Jeffrey ... 859-572-6448 ... 205 E
strunk@nku.edu
STRUNK, Mary, C ... 518-783-2314 ... 350 I
strunk@siena.edu
STRUNK, Paul, J ... 570-961-4760 ... 435 F
pjstrunk@marywood.edu
STRUNK, Vicki ... 502-447-7634 ... 205 B
STRUPP, Kerry ... 920-923-7666 ... 548 C
kstrupp@marianuniversity.edu
STRUPPA, Daniele, C ... 714-997-6826 ... 39 C
struppa@chapman.edu
STRYBOS, John ... 210-485-0701 ... 479 B
jstrybos@alamo.edu
STRYDOM, Peet ... 901-381-3939 ... 478 D
peet@visible.edu
STRYDOM, Sue ... 901-381-3939 ... 478 D
sue@visible.edu
STRYKER, H. Ford ... 814-865-4402 ... 438 F
hfs2@psu.edu
STRYKER, Joanne ... 401-454-6177 ... 454 B
jstryker@risd.edu
STRYKER, Marcy ... 518-464-8527 ... 333 F
mstryker@excelsior.edu
STRYSICK, Michael, P ... 859-238-5710 ... 199 D
michael.strysick@centre.edu
STUARD, Avis ... 504-520-7583 ... 217 A
astuard@xula.edu
STUART, Alesia, K ... 251-578-1313 ... 6 E
akstuart@rstc.edu
STUART, Ann ... 940-898-3201 ... 502 B
astuart@twu.edu
STUART, Beverly ... 206-268-4507 ... 530 F
bstuart@antioch.edu
STUART, Carol, M ... 252-334-2010 ... 367 A
carol.stuart@macuniversity.edu

SULLIVAN, Bryce .... 615-460-6437.... 467 B
bryce.sullivan@belmont.edu
SULLIVAN, Charles .... 973-642-8766.... 315 C
charles.sullivan@shu.edu
SULLIVAN, Cheryl .... 231-995-1147.... 256 G
csullivan@nmc.edu
SULLIVAN, Cheryl .... 559-638-3641...... 72 B
cheyrl.sullivan@reedleycollege.edu
SULLIVAN, Chris .... 619-388-2797...... 65 G
csullivan@sdccd.edu
SULLIVAN, Christopher, B . 585-385-8001.... 348 F
csullivan@sjfc.edu
SULLIVAN, Claudia .... 541-956-7176.... 420 B
csullivan@roguecc.edu
SULLIVAN, Cliff .... 252-985-5123.... 375 C
csullivan@ncwc.edu
SULLIVAN, Colin .... 401-341-2268.... 454 D
colin.sullivan@salve.edu
SULLIVAN, Crystal, C .... 937-229-3369.... 404 A
crystal.sulllivan@notes.udayton.edu
SULLIVAN, Dan .... 919-658-7748.... 367 D
dsullivan@moc.edu
SULLIVAN, David .... 772-462-2505.... 110 L
dsulliva@irsc.edu
SULLIVAN, Debra .... 704-357-8020.... 361 N
dtsullivan@aii.edu
SULLIVAN, Durrelle .... 360-736-9391.... 531 H
dsullivan@centralia.edu
SULLIVAN, E. Thomas .... 612-625-0051.... 272 D
sulli059@umn.edu
SULLIVAN, Edward .... 212-220-8014.... 326 E
esullivan@bmcc.cuny.edu
SULLIVAN, Edward .... 657-278-8325...... 34 E
esullivan@fullerton.edu
SULLIVAN, Eileen, G .... 630-617-3050.... 150 F
esullivan@elmhurst.edu
SULLIVAN, Ellen, R .... 512-448-8664.... 493 B
ellenrs@stedwards.edu
SULLIVAN, Erin .... 540-831-5226.... 522 D
esullivan12@radford.edu
SULLIVAN, SSJ,
Florence, E .... 215-248-7122.... 425 C
fsulliva@chc.edu
SULLIVAN, George, J .... 610-359-4151.... 426 G
gsulliva@dccc.edu
SULLIVAN, Geraldine, M ... 440-646-8322.... 405 B
gsullivan@ursuline.edu
SULLIVAN, Glenda, F .... 423-425-4553.... 477 D
glenda-sullivan@utc.edu
SULLIVAN, Glenn, D .... 502-451-0815.... 206 B
gds@sullivan.edu
SULLIVAN, Glenn, D .... 502-451-0815.... 206 C
gds@sullivan.edu
SULLIVAN, Helen .... 817-461-8741.... 480 H
hsullivan@abconline.org
SULLIVAN, Hillary .... 914-632-5400.... 341 G
hsullivan@monroecollege.edu
SULLIVAN, Holly .... 865-273-8884.... 470 F
holly.sullivan@maryvillecollege.edu
SULLIVAN, Jack .... 973-328-5252.... 309 B
jsullivan@ccm.edu
SULLIVAN, Jem .... 202-495-3820...... 98 D
jrsullivan@dhs.edu
SULLIVAN, Joan, D .... 781-768-7212.... 244 D
joan.sullivan@regiscollege.edu
SULLIVAN, John .... 727-864-8331.... 104 K
sullivjf@eckerd.edu
SULLIVAN, John .... 615-383-4848.... 478 E
jsullivan@watkins.edu
SULLIVAN, John, L .... 508-586-1572.... 238 A
john.sullivan@umassmed.edu
SULLIVAN, John, M .... 508-286-3484.... 246 E
jsulliva@wheatonma.edu
SULLIVAN, Jolene .... 417-455-5618.... 281 C
jsullivan@crowder.edu
SULLIVAN, Joseph .... 805-965-0581...... 68 B
sullivanj@sbcc.edu
SULLIVAN, Julie, H .... 619-260-4553...... 76 A
jsullivan@sandiego.edu
SULLIVAN, Kathleen .... 207-892-6766.... 219 F
ksullivan@sjcme.edu
SULLIVAN, Kathleen .... 845-848-7804.... 332 C
kathleen.sullivan@dc.edu
SULLIVAN, Kathleen, A ...... 412-536-1819.... 432 F
kathleen.sullivan@laroche.edu
SULLIVAN, Kenneth, A .... 775-445-4246.... 303 B
ken@wnc.edu
SULLIVAN, Kristie .... 910-695-3907.... 373 E
sullivank@sandhills.edu
SULLIVAN, Kristin .... 817-272-2761.... 505 A
knsull@uta.edu
SULLIVAN, Kristopher, T .... 401-232-6707.... 453 A
ktsulliv@bryant.edu
SULLIVAN, Laura .... 715-682-4591.... 555 E
laura.sullivan@witc.edu
SULLIVAN, Lawrence .... 212-237-8364.... 328 A
lsullivan@jjay.cuny.edu
SULLIVAN, Leah .... 440-646-8126.... 405 B
lsullivan@ursuline.edu
SULLIVAN, Leo, V .... 617-552-3335.... 232 D
leo.sullivan.1@bc.edu
SULLIVAN, Leslie .... 269-749-7638.... 257 D
lsullivan@olivetcollege.edu
SULLIVAN, Liam .... 603-623-0313.... 305 F
lsullivan@nhia.edu
SULLIVAN, Linda .... 310-434-3427...... 68 D
sullivan_linda@smc.edu
SULLIVAN, Lynette, D .... 419-559-2391.... 402 D
lsullivan@terra.edu
SULLIVAN, Lynn .... 352-395-5514.... 117 E
lynn.sullivan@sfcollege.edu
SULLIVAN, Margaret .... 727-873-4151.... 121 B
msullivan@mail.usf.edu
SULLIVAN, Margaret .... 727-873-4264.... 120 D
msullivan@mail.usf.edu
SULLIVAN, Marie .... 603-888-1311.... 305 G
mariesullivan@rivier.edu
SULLIVAN, Mark .... 937-327-6181.... 406 B
msullivan@wittenberg.edu
SULLIVAN, Martha .... 508-793-2276.... 233 D
sullivan@holycross.edu
SULLIVAN, Mary .... 908-526-1200.... 313 E
msullivan@raritanval.edu
SULLIVAN, Mary .... 617-879-2257.... 246 F
msullivan@wheelock.edu
SULLIVAN, Mary .... 570-740-0429.... 435 C
msullivan@luzerne.edu
SULLIVAN, Mary, A .... 570-326-3761.... 440 K
msulliva@pct.edu
SULLIVAN, Melanie, P .... 502-272-8477.... 198 E
msullivan@bellarmine.edu
SULLIVAN, Melanie, R .... 860-629-6122...... 93 B
sullivan_m@mitchell.edu
SULLIVAN, Melissa .... 603-623-0313.... 305 F
msullivan@nhia.edu
SULLIVAN, Michael .... 413-265-2494.... 233 E
sullivanm@elms.edu
SULLIVAN, Monty .... 225-922-2373.... 209 C
msullivan@lctcs.edu
SULLIVAN, Myron .... 605-642-6297.... 465 F
myron.sullivan@bhsu.edu
SULLIVAN, Nancy .... 508-541-1641.... 234 B
nsullivan@dean.edu
SULLIVAN, Nancy .... 419-448-3188.... 402 E
sullivann@tiffin.edu
SULLIVAN, Oliver .... 212-686-9244.... 323 A
SULLIVAN, Pat .... 513-618-1922.... 387 E
psullivan@ccms.edu
SULLIVAN, Patricia .... 402-354-7024.... 299 E
pat.sullivan@methodistcollege.edu
SULLIVAN, Patrick .... 610-499-4202.... 451 F
ptsullivan@widener.edu
SULLIVAN, Paul .... 231-591-2614.... 251 B
sullivanp@ferris.edu
SULLIVAN, Peter .... 715-324-6900.... 549 D
peter.sullivan@ni.edu
SULLIVAN, R. Mark .... 518-454-5120.... 330 C
sullivam@strose.edu
SULLIVAN, JR.,
Richard, F .... 617-333-2302.... 234 A
rsulliva@curry.edu
SULLIVAN, Richard, J .... 574-239-8401.... 172 J
rsullivan@hcc-nd.edu
SULLIVAN, Robert .... 352-588-8432.... 116 E
robert.sullivan02@saintleo.edu
SULLIVAN, Robert, S .... 858-822-0830...... 74 D
rssullivan@ucsd.edu
SULLIVAN, Roger, B .... 607-436-2513.... 353 F
sullivrb@oneonta.edu
SULLIVAN, Ruth, D .... 401-825-2488.... 453 B
rsullivan@ccri.edu
SULLIVAN, Samuel .... 706-737-1422.... 125 C
ssullivan@aug.edu
SULLIVAN, Scott .... 817-257-7601.... 498 F
s.sullivan@tcu.edu
SULLIVAN, Sean .... 708-456-0300.... 166 C
ssulliva@triton.edu
SULLIVAN, Sean .... 508-793-7160.... 233 C
ssullivan@clarku.edu
SULLIVAN, Sean, P .... 716-645-2287.... 351 G
sps@buffalo.edu
SULLIVAN, Shawn, P .... 715-675-3331.... 554 G
sullivan@ntc.edu
SULLIVAN, Skip .... 770-537-7940.... 139 B
skip.sullivan@westgatech.edu
SULLIVAN, Slade .... 325-674-2485.... 478 H
sullivans@acu.edu
SULLIVAN, Stephanie .... 770-426-2632.... 133 B
stephanie.sullivan@life.edu
SULLIVAN, Stephen, B .... 508-854-4375.... 241 C
sbsullivan@qcc.mass.edu
SULLIVAN, Susan .... 812-749-1223.... 178 D
ssullivan@oak.edu
SULLIVAN, Suzanne .... 601-968-8746.... 273 F
ssullivan@belhaven.edu
SULLIVAN, Teresa, A .... 434-924-3337.... 525 B
SULLIVAN, Thomas .... 660-944-2860.... 280 F
thomas@conception.edu
SULLIVAN, Thomas .... 617-243-2059.... 236 F
tpsullivan@lasell.edu
SULLIVAN, Thomas, B .... 512-448-8727.... 493 B
toms@stedwards.edu
SULLIVAN, Thomas, P .... 517-586-3012.... 249 H
tsullivan@cleary.edu
SULLIVAN, Timothy, J .... 508-929-8073.... 239 D
tsullivan@worcester.edu
SULLIVAN, Toyette .... 410-386-8429.... 221 G
tsullivan@carrollcc.edu
SULLIVAN, Tracy .... 708-235-2179.... 151 C
tsullivan@govst.edu
SULLIVAN, Wayne .... 662-862-8101.... 274 G
jwsullivan@iccms.edu
SULLIVAN ALIOTO,
Kathleen .... 415-239-3816...... 39 H
ksalioto@ccsf.edu
SULLIVAN-CROWLEY,
Lianne, C .... 609-258-2430.... 313 A
lsulliva@princeton.edu
SULLIVAN-TRAINOR,
Deborah .... 651-638-6804.... 261 I
suldeb@bethel.edu
SULLIVAN-WILLIAMS,
Lizziel .... 856-256-4226.... 314 A
sullivan@rowan.edu
SULLO, Fred .... 914-654-5555.... 330 B
fsullo@cnr.edu
SULTON, James .... 732-224-2020.... 308 B
jsulton@brookdalecc.edu
SULZBACH, J. Bonnie .... 443-412-2119.... 223 B
bsulzbach@harford.edu
SUMADI, Mohammad .... 813-882-0100...... 99 D
SUMAJIT, Rosemary .... 808-845-9143.... 141 G
rosea@hawaii.edu
SUMAYA, Isabel .... 661-654-6489...... 33 H
isumaya@csub.edu
SUMEREL, Marie, B .... 919-760-8341.... 366 G
sumerelm@meredith.edu
SUMICHRAST, Robert, T ..... 706-542-8100.... 138 C
busdean@terry.uga.edu
SUMMA, Louise, J .... 860-892-5734...... 91 B
lsumma@trcc.commnet.edu
SUMMA-WOLFE, Cathy .... 415-485-9528...... 41 I
cathy.summawolfe@marin.edu
SUMMARY, Sherry .... 618-985-3741.... 154 E
sherrysummary@jalc.edu
SUMMER, Gail .... 540-365-4208.... 518 J
gsummer@ferrum.edu
SUMMER-LAMBRECHT,
Jennifer .... 763-424-0946.... 268 D
jsummer@nhcc.edu
SUMMERER, Mike .... 860-679-3030...... 94 F
summerer@uchc.edu
SUMMERFIELD, Julie .... 610-896-1177.... 430 G
jsummerf@haverford.edu
SUMMERFIELD, Liane .... 703-284-6478.... 521 A
liane.summerfield@marymount.edu
SUMMERLIN, Chris .... 478-471-2317.... 133 E
chris.summerlin@maconstate.edu
SUMMERLIN, Timothy .... 830-792-7345.... 494 A
tsummerlin@schreiner.edu
SUMMERS, Amanda .... 281-425-6875.... 489 J
asummers@lee.edu
SUMMERS, Carol .... 206-934-7791.... 536 H
carol.summers@seattlecolleges.edu
SUMMERS, Cynthia .... 312-362-7294.... 148 F
csummers@depaul.edu
SUMMERS, David .... 614-236-6467.... 386 C
dsummers@capital.edu
SUMMERS, Eric, J .... 985-549-3850.... 216 C
esummers@selu.edu
SUMMERS, Geoffrey, P .... 410-455-5827.... 227 D
gsummers@umbc.edu
SUMMERS, Greg .... 715-346-4446.... 552 B
gsummers@uwsp.edu
SUMMERS, James .... 214-379-5430.... 492 D
jsummers@pqc.edu
SUMMERS, Janie, K .... 314-286-3665.... 288 B
jksummers@ranken.edu
SUMMERS, Jean .... 816-932-2073.... 289 G
gsummers@saint-lukes.org
SUMMERS, Jerry .... 903-923-2084.... 486 D
jsummers@etbu.edu
SUMMERS, Karen, L .... 434-381-6230.... 524 E
ksummers@sbc.edu
SUMMERS, LeRoy .... 706-821-8232.... 135 C
lsummers@paine.edu
SUMMERS, Lori .... 201-200-3489.... 312 B
lsummers@njcu.edu
SUMMERS, Matthew, A .... 304-637-1373.... 540 F
summersm@dewv.edu
SUMMERS, Michael .... 757-822-7122.... 528 C
msummers@tcc.edu
SUMMERS, Micheal .... 806-291-1165.... 508 B
summersm@wbu.edu
SUMMERS, Nathan .... 937-294-0592.... 401 H
nathan@saa.edu
SUMMERS, Richard, G .... 931-598-1917.... 472 J
rsummers@sewanee.edu
SUMMERS, Robert .... 870-512-7716...... 20 F
robert_summers@asun.edu
SUMMERS, Tony, E .... 972-238-6202.... 485 C
tesummers@dcccd.edu
SUMMERS, Tony, E .... 972-238-6203.... 485 C
tesummers@dcccd.edu
SUMMERS, Wally .... 229-931-2040.... 136 G
wsummers@southgatech.edu
SUMMERS, Wally .... 229-931-2044.... 136 G
wsummers@southgatech.edu
SUMMERS, Zaneta .... 704-878-3351.... 371 H
zsummers@mitchellcc.edu
SUMMERSELL, Charley .... 518-587-2100.... 355 F
charley.summersell@esc.edu
SUMMERVILLE, Jamie .... 270-247-8521.... 204 C
jsummerville@midcontinent.edu
SUMMERVILLE, Rachele ...... 541-888-7259.... 420 C
rsummerville@socc.edu
SUMMINS, Lisa .... 908-835-2322.... 317 C
lsummins@warren.edu
SUMNER, Amanda .... 918-561-8459.... 410 D
amanda.sumner@okstate.edu
SUMNER, Don .... 405-878-5283.... 412 A
dbsumner@stgregorys.edu
SUMNER, Henry, A .... 610-558-5513.... 437 C
hsumner@neumann.edu
SUMNER, Janice .... 704-357-8020.... 361 N
jsumner@aii.edu
SUMNER, Karen .... 605-575-2030.... 466 D
karen.sumner@usiouxfalls.edu
SUMNER, Sarah, C .... 530-226-4144...... 69 H
ssumner@simpsonu.edu
SUMNER, Wesley .... 321-674-6218.... 108 E
wsumner@fit.edu
SUMPLE, Coreen .... 860-244-7630...... 89 J
csumple@commnet.edu
SUMPTER, Warner, I .... 410-651-6590.... 227 E
wisumpter@umes.edu
SUMRALL, Glenn .... 601-974-6455.... 273 F
gsumrall@belhaven.edu
SUN, Yanling .... 973-655-4091.... 311 G
suny@mail.montclair.edu
SUN, Zafer .... 707-864-7124...... 70 A
zafer.sun@solano.edu
SUNATA, Cem .... 805-756-6016...... 33 F
csunata@calpoly.edu
SUNBURY, Mary Ann .... 704-463-3203.... 375 E
maryann.sunbury@fsmail.pfeiffer.edu
SUND, Andrew, C .... 773-878-7502.... 163 D
asund@staugustine.edu
SUNDBERG, Lori, H .... 847-735-5030.... 155 F
lsundberg@lakeforest.edu
SUNDBERG, Lori, L .... 309-341-5214.... 146 A
lsundberg@sandburg.edu
SUNDBORG, SJ,
Stephen, V .... 206-296-1891.... 537 F
sundborg@seattleu.edu
SUNDBY, Oliver .... 307-532-8304.... 555 H
oliver.sundby@ewc.wy.edu
SUNDEEN, Joseph, T .... 626-529-8234...... 60 G
tsundeen@pacificoaks.edu
SUNDERLAND, Jon, D .... 509-313-6115.... 534 A
sunderland@gonzaga.edu
SUNDERMAN, Rick .... 614-947-6605.... 391 A
sundermr@franklin.edu
SUNDERMANN, Brigitte .... 970-255-2600...... 82 B
bsunderm@mesastate.edu
SUNDET, Rosemary .... 979-830-4075.... 482 A
rosemary.sundet@blinn.edu
SUNDGREN, Donald, E .... 434-982-5834.... 525 B
des5j@virginia.edu
SUNDQUIST, Mike .... 209-575-6081...... 80 B
sundquistm@yosemite.cc.ca.us
SUNDSMO, Alecia, D .... 717-245-1485.... 427 E
sundsmoa@dickinson.edu
SUNDSTEDT, Bernard .... 815-226-3371.... 162 H
bsunstedt@rockford.edu
SUNDSTROM, Sandra .... 507-786-3357.... 271 H
sundstro@stolaf.edu
SUNDSTROM, William .... 408-551-7045...... 68 C
wsundstrom@scu.edu
SUNDY, Carolyn .... 606-589-3052.... 203 A
carolyn.sundy@kctcs.edu
SUNI, Ellen, Y .... 816-235-1007.... 291 E
sunie@umkc.edu
SUNLEAF, Arthur, W .... 563-588-7137.... 186 I
arthur.sunleaf@loras.edu
SUNSER, James .... 585-345-6812.... 334 F
jmsunser@genesee.edu
SUNSHINE, Eugene, S .... 847-491-5534.... 160 D
e-sunshine@northwestern.edu
SUNSHINE, Lisbet .... 415-338-1120...... 36 F
lisbet@sfsu.edu
SUNSHINE, Phyllis .... 410-337-6046.... 222 I
psunshine@goucher.edu
SUOREZ, Paula .... 760-384-6298...... 52 N
pasouroez@cerrocoso.edu
SUPALLA, Don, D .... 507-285-7215.... 269 B
donald.supalla@roch.edu
SUPERNAW, Robert, B .... 704-233-8015.... 380 D
supernaw@wingate.edu
SUPERVILLE, Claude, R .... 713-313-4244.... 499 G
superville_cr@tsu.edu
SUPOWITZ, Paul, A .... 412-624-2901.... 449 A
psupowit@pitt.edu
SUPPLEE, Edwin .... 845-938-3327.... 558 G
8uscc@usma.edu
SUPPLEE, JR., Jack .... 859-257-8288.... 206 H
supplee@uky.edu
SUPPLEE, Janice .... 937-766-8319.... 386 F
suppleej@cedarville.edu
SUPURGECI, Jonna .... 605-668-1515.... 464 F
jsupurgeci@mtmc.edu
SURAMEK, Mae .... 859-985-3110.... 198 F
mae_suramek@berea.edu
SURATY-CLARKE,
Mercedes .... 713-743-1185.... 503 B
msclarke@uh.edu

SWARTZ, Mark 212-410-8457 343 B mswartz@nycpm.edu
SWARTZ, Mary, K 757-683-3623 521 L mswartz@odu.edu
SWARTZ, Terri 510-885-3291 34 C terri.swartz@csueastbay.edu
SWARTZBECK, Susan 724-589-2150 448 A swartzbeck@thiel.edu
SWARTZENDRUBER, Loren, E 540-432-4100 518 E lorens@emu.edu
SWARTZENTRUBER, Dale, E 740-368-3811 400 F deswartz@owu.edu
SWARTZLANDER, Barbara 207-602-2363 220 H bswartzlander@une.edu
SWARTZWELDER, Roger, L 205-329-7903 3 B roger.swartzwelder@ecacolleges.com
SWATCHICK, Abby 610-568-1474 421 F abby.swatchick@alvernia.edu
SWATCHICK, Matthew, J 570-385-6000 440 C mjs48@psu.edu
SWATFAGER-HANEY, Patricia 410-532-5308 225 D pswatfagerhaney@ndm.edu
SWAYZE, Faye 951-785-2006 53 D fswayze@lasierra.edu
SWEANEY, Anne, L 706-542-4879 138 C aseaney@fcs.uga.edu
SWEANY, Lisa 912-344-2730 124 E lisa.sweany@armstrong.edu
SWEARENGIN, Paul 412-237-3050 425 H pswearengin@ccac.edu
SWEARER, Randy 215-951-2705 444 C swearerr@philau.edu
SWEARINGEN, Jodie 651-423-8216 266 E jodie.swearingen@dctc.edu
SWEARINGER, Lee 808-942-1000 140 H careers.hnl.ea@remingtoncollege.edu
SWEARINGIN, Bubba 940-325-2591 508 C bswearingin@wc.edu
SWEAT, Mary Lee 504-864-7047 213 F sweat@loyno.edu
SWEATMAN, Robert, A 217-245-3289 152 C rsweatma@ic.edu
SWEDE, Marci 860-343-5779 90 D mswede@mxcc.commnet.edu
SWEEDEN, Debi 270-926-4040 199 K dsweeden@daymarcollege.edu
SWEEDLER, Alan, R 619-594-1354 36 E asweedler@sciences.sdsu.edu
SWEEK, Cristina 541-278-5753 414 G csweek@bluecc.edu
SWEELEY, Rebecca 209-228-4667 74 B RSweeley@UCMerced.edu
SWEEN, Barbara 859-572-6695 205 E sweenb@nku.edu
SWEENER, Kathleen 518-629-7320 336 C k.sweener@hvcc.edu
SWEENEY, Daniel, J 315-386-7120 355 D sweenedj@canton.edu
SWEENEY, Gladys, A 703-416-1441 519 F gsweeney@ipsciences.edu
SWEENEY, Jeff 503-699-6269 416 I jsweeney@marylhurst.edu
SWEENEY, John, M 401-865-2281 453 F john.sweeney@providence.edu
SWEENEY, Katherine 706-737-1405 125 C ksweeney@aug.edu
SWEENEY, Kathleen, J 978-656-3046 240 F sweeneyk@middlesex.mass.edu
SWEENEY, Laurie Beth 614-222-3268 388 F lsweeney@ccad.edu
SWEENEY, Marc 937-766-7480 386 F msweeney@cedarville.edu
SWEENEY, Michael 510-883-2083 45 A msweeney@dspt.edu
SWEENEY, Michael, E 513-231-2223 384 E msweeney@athenaeum.edu
SWEENEY, Michael, L 423-461-1511 468 F msweeney@ecs.edu
SWEENEY, Richard, T 973-596-3208 312 C richard.sweeney@njit.edu
SWEENEY, Robert, D 434-924-1008 525 B rds2j@virginia.edu
SWEENEY, Robert, J 937-775-3346 406 C robert.sweeney@wright.edu
SWEENEY, Susan, Y 518-327-6400 345 H ssweeney@paulsmiths.edu
SWEENEY, Timothy 252-335-0821 369 D timothy_sweeney@albemarle.edu
SWEENEY, Trina, D 304-204-4340 544 D sweeneyt@wvstateu.edu
SWEENEY, Victoria 630-889-6572 159 E vsweeney@nuhs.edu
SWEENEY, Vince 608-265-2822 550 G vsweeney@wisc.edu
SWEENEY, Yvette, M 636-922-8238 288 E ysweeney@stchas.edu
SWEET, Brett 615-343-6735 477 F brett.sweet@vanderbilt.edu
SWEET, Chris 503-821-8926 419 D csweet@pnca.edu
SWEET, Chris 503-699-6268 416 I csweet@marylhurst.edu
SWEET, Darryl 415-565-4604 73 G sweetd@uchastings.edu
SWEET, David 972-721-5288 502 F dsweet@udallas.edu
SWEET, David, M 315-279-5249 337 K dsweet@mail.keuka.edu
SWEET, Doris Ann 508-767-7272 230 E dasweet@assumption.edu
SWEET, Fred 616-222-1329 250 C fred.sweet@cornerstone.edu
SWEET, Lu 307-382-1639 556 F lsweet@wwcc.wy.edu
SWEET, Nathan 206-876-6100 537 E facilities@theseattleschool.edu
SWEET, Paul, R 616-538-2330 251 F psweet@gbcol.edu
SWEET, Stephanie 631-244-3047 332 D sweets@dowling.edu
SWEET, Stephen, A 919-658-7493 367 D ssweet@moc.edu
SWEET, Susan, W 570-662-4849 443 B ssweet@mansfield.edu
SWEET, Tracy 802-241-1188 515 B tracy.sweet@vsc.edu
SWEET-MCGREGOR, Denise 928-344-1723 12 C denise.sweet-mcgregor@azwestern.edu
SWEET-PRZYBYSZ, Jodie, L 574-239-8374 172 J jsweet@hcc-nd.edu
SWEETANA, Michael 610-282-1100 426 I michael.sweetana@desales.edu
SWEETEN, Katie 918-540-6211 408 J katiebs@neo.edu
SWEETENBURG-LEE, Penni 804-257-5656 529 D pbsweetenburg@vuu.edu
SWEETING, Bonnie 828-327-7000 368 G bsweetin@cvcc.edu
SWEETING, Don 407-366-9943 277 B dsweeting@rts.edu
SWEETING, Donald, W 407-366-9493 115 I dsweeting@rts.edu
SWEETLAND, Dennis 603-641-7052 305 H dsweetla@anselm.edu
SWEETLAND, Jane 805-437-8918 33 I jane.sweetland@csuci.edu
SWEEZEY, Gail, M 717-337-6100 429 H gsweezey@gettysburg.edu
SWEGAN, Gary, D 419-372-7799 385 C gswegan@bgsu.edu
SWEITZER, JR., Frank, X 716-839-8222 331 G fsweitze@daemen.edu
SWEITZER, Frederick 860-768-4504 95 A sweitzer@hartford.edu
SWEITZER-RILEY, Beth, E 260-982-5052 177 F besweitzer-riley@manchester.edu
SWEIZER, Jim 703-330-5398 540 C jsweizer@apus.edu
SWENDER, Herbert 620-276-9602 193 A herbert.swender@gcccks.edu
SWENGLER, Eleni 410-386-8157 221 G eswengler@carrollcc.edu
SWENSON, Andrew 402-643-7220 297 F andrew.swenson@cune.edu
SWENSON, Beth, I 701-788-4750 381 F Beth.Swenson@mayvillestate.edu
SWENSON, Craig, D 312-899-9900 144 G cswenson@argosy.edu
SWENSON, Jeffrey, F 612-330-1241 261 G swensonj@augsburg.edu
SWENSON, Michael 507-457-2773 270 B mswenson@winona.edu
SWENSON, III, Ralph, M 802-656-2699 514 F ralph.swenson@uvm.edu
SWENSON, Randy, L 630-889-6545 159 E rswenson@nuhs.edu
SWENSON, Tammy 423-697-4418 474 D
SWENSON, Terry 909-558-8348 54 D tswenson@llu.edu
SWENTON, Gina, D 860-628-4751 92 F gswenton@lincolncollegene.edu
SWERBINSKY, Megan 216-791-5000 388 B megan.swerbinsky@case.edu
SWERDLOW, Nadia 818-364-7842 55 A swerdln@lamission.edu
SWETICH, Mary 775-289-3589 302 H marys@gwmail.gbcnv.edu
SWETS, Paul 325-942-2024 480 E paul.swets@angelo.edu
SWETT, Denise 650-949-7524 47 H swettdenise@foothill.edu
SWETT, Denise 650-949-6952 47 H swettdenise@fhda.edu
SWICK, Dean 901-722-3202 473 B dswick@sco.edu
SWICK, Pat 229-732-5930 124 C patswick@andrewcollege.edu
SWICKARD, Allison 719-502-2666 86 G allison.swickard@ppcc.edu
SWIECH, Carol, A 603-641-4148 306 F carol.swiech@unh.edu
SWIECINSKI, Deborah, L 757-683-3127 521 L dswiecin@odu.edu
SWIFT, Carole 563-441-2467 186 E cswift@kucampus.edu
SWIFT, Catherine 406-444-0328 294 J cswift@montana.edu
SWIFT, Rick 803-754-4100 457 D
SWIFT, Sheila 318-670-9646 215 A sswift@susla.edu
SWIFT, Vikki 208-792-2269 143 F vswift@lcsc.edu
SWIFT, William 978-632-6600 240 G w_swift@mwcc.mass.edu
SWIGART, Scott, A 585-385-8430 348 F sswigart@sjfc.edu
SWIGER, John 559-448-8282 66 G johns@sjvc.edu
SWIHART, Karin 620-278-4276 196 D kswihart@sterling.edu
SWINDALL, Linda 727-864-8217 104 K swindal@eckerd.edu
SWINDELL, George 843-349-5238 458 G george.swindell@hgtc.edu
SWINDELL, Hal 252-940-6444 367 I HalGS@beaufortccc.edu
SWINDELL, Jim 256-306-2539 2 E jes@calhoun.edu
SWINDLE, Jackquline 713-718-5206 487 G jackquline.swindle@hccs.edu
SWINDLE, Richard, V 678-547-6456 133 F swindle_rv@mercer.edu
SWINDOLL, George 843-349-5238 458 G george.swindoll@hgtc.edu
SWINEY, John 509-963-3031 531 G swineyj@cwu.edu
SWINEY, Karen 910-521-6222 379 B karen.swiney@uncp.edu
SWINEY, R. Preston 910-521-6228 379 B preston.swiney@uncp.edu
SWINK, Doug 816-235-1213 291 E swinkd@umkc.edu
SWINK, Esther 615-248-1201 476 E eswink@trevecca.edu
SWINKLER, Mary 724-357-2555 442 E Mary.Swinkler@iup.edu
SWINNEY, Victoria 405-208-5071 410 A vswinney@okcu.edu
SWINSON, Kathy 618-392-7777 152 E swinsonk@iecc.edu
SWINSON, Phyllis 570-422-2820 442 C pswinson@po-box.esu.edu
SWINT, JR., Otis, J 252-638-7323 369 E swinto@cravencc.edu
SWINTON, Brent, E 202-238-2444 98 B bswinton@howard.edu
SWINTON, David, H 803-705-4681 455 D swintond@benedict.edu
SWINTON, Kelly 515-244-4221 181 D swintonk@aib.edu
SWIRSKI, Thomas 219-981-4213 173 F tswirski@iun.edu
SWIRSKY, David, M 203-285-2305 90 A dswirsky@gwcc.commnet.edu
SWISHER, Gary 614-251-4734 398 F swisherg@ohiodominican.edu
SWISHER, Susan 773-298-3070 163 G swisher@sxu.edu
SWISHER, Wayne 701-777-2786 381 D wayne.swisher@email.und.edu
SWISHER, William, K 859-344-3600 206 D bill.swisher@thomasmore.edu
SWISS, Jane, M 260-399-7700 180 E jswiss@sf.edu
SWITANOWSKI, Lori 562-860-2451 38 J lswitanowski@cerritos.edu
SWITZER, Aimee 304-776-6290 540 G aswitzer@cci.edu
SWITZER, Devon 718-409-7260 356 C dswitzer@sunymaritime.edu
SWITZER, Gloria 714-459-1107 78 C gswitzer@wsulaw.edu
SWITZER, Jacki, S 260-422-5561 172 L jsswitzer@indianatech.edu
SWITZER, Ron 864-592-4770 461 C switzerr@sccsc.edu
SWITZER, Teri 719-255-3115 88 C tswitzer@uccs.edu
SWOMLEY, Brian 610-917-3939 450 D blswomley@vfcc.edu
SWORD, Joey, C 540-831-5421 522 D jcsword@radford.edu
SWORDER, David, D 858-534-5556 74 D dsworder@ucsd.edu
SWORDS, Jason 229-317-6449 128 A jason.swords@darton.edu
SYBEL, Lauri 802-728-1320 515 G lsybel@vtc.vsc.edu
SYDOW, Debbie, L 315-498-2211 345 D president@sunyocc.edu
SYED, Naim 603-668-6706 304 E nsyed@ccsnh.edu
SYGIELSKI, John, J 717-221-1300 430 E rryoung@hacc.edu
SYKES, Andrew 651-846-3388 261 E asykes@argosy.edu
SYKES, Arthur 972-860-7688 484 H ArtSykes@dcccd.edu
SYKES, David 860-343-5704 90 D dsykes@mxcc.commnet.edu
SYKES, Elaine 410-951-4154 228 B esykes@coppin.edu
SYKES, Eric 617-824-8268 234 D eric_sykes@emerson.edu
SYKES, Gwendolyn 404-215-2675 134 A gsykes@morehouse.edu
SYKES, JR., John, D 434-949-1019 527 H john.sykes@southside.edu
SYKES, Margaret, D 937-778-7855 390 G mmyers@edisonohio.edu
SYKES, Reginald 251-575-3156 1 B rlsykes@ascc.edu
SYKES, Sheila 978-665-3102 238 C ssykes@fitchburgstate.edu
SYKORA, Terrance 563-876-3353 183 G
SYKTICH, Jackie, D 814-371-6920 427 H mainc@dbcollege.com
SYLER-JONES, Tracy 817-257-7811 498 F t.syler-jones@tcu.edu
SYLVAIN, Anne 617-236-8800 235 B asylvain@fisher.edu
SYLVESTER, Barbara 732-750-1800 307 G bms@Berkeleycollege.edu
SYLVESTER, Barbara, N 903-813-2457 481 A bsylvester@austincollege.edu
SYLVESTER, Douglas 480-965-9066 12 B douglas.sylvester@asu.edu
SYLVESTER, James 860-444-2683 558 E jsylvester@cgaalumni.org
SYLVESTER, Lori 918-495-7708 411 C lsylvester@oru.edu
SYLVESTER, Sue 510-869-8628 64 J ssylvester@samuelmerritt.edu
SYLVIA, Bane 740-351-3398 401 I bsylvia@shawnee.edu
SYLVIA, Lorraine 814-262-3822 441 A lsylvia@pennhighlands.edu
SYLWESTER, Donald 402-643-7446 297 F don.sylwester@cune.edu
SYMANCYK, Daniel, F 410-777-2587 221 B dfsymancyk@aacc.edu
SYMANK, Kathryn, B 979-862-4572 497 C k-symank@tamu.edu
SYMANOSKIE, Chris 304-724-3700 540 C csymanoskie@apus.edu
SYMINGTON, Susan, K 508-362-2131 240 A sklinesy@capecod.edu
SYMONDS, Andrea 802-831-1209 515 A asymonds@vermontlaw.edu
SYMONDS, Brian 818-345-8508 42 D bsymonds@columbiacollege.edu
SYMONS, Gretchen, A 814-332-2159 421 E gretchen.symons@allegheny.edu
SYNDER, Brittany 305-809-3233 108 F brittany.snyder@fkcc.edu
SYNDER, Jane 617-277-3915 232 F synderj@bgsp.edu
SYNDER, Ned 937-461-5174 396 C ned.synder@staffmiamijacobs.edu
SYNODI, George, S 203-832-7273 95 B gsynodi@newhaven.edu
SYPHER, Beverly, D 765-494-9709 178 F bdsypher@purdue.edu
SYREK, Richard 845-574-4465 347 I rsyrek@sunyrockland.edu
SYRONEY, Mark 216-916-8074 398 E msyroney@ocpm.edu
SYTSMA, Richard 616-957-6016 249 F rsytsma@calvinseminary.edu
SYVERTSON, Debra 701-228-5454 382 C deb.syvertson@dakotacollege.edu
SYVERUD, Kent, D 314-935-6420 292 J kdsyverud@wustl.edu
SZABADOS, Anna 801-957-3334 512 C anna.szabados@slcc.edu
SZABO, Julia 419-358-3245 385 B szaboj@bluffton.edu
SZABO, Mihaela, A 304-336-8270 544 B mszabo@westliberty.edu
SZAFRAN, Zvi 678-915-7238 137 C zszafran@spsu.edu
SZAJ, Christine, M 612-330-1023 261 G szaj@augsburg.edu
SZAKAS, Joe, S 207-621-3198 220 B szakas@maine.edu
SZALANKIEWICZ, Linda 413-552-2155 240 C lszalankiewicz@hcc.edu
SZALKIEWICZ, Joe 858-653-6740 52 C
SZANI, Phyllis 201-200-3350 312 B pszani@njcu.edu
SZANTO, Edit 208-732-6863 143 B eszanto@csi.edu
SZASZ-PALMER, Suzy 434-395-2431 520 G palmerss@longwood.edu
SZATMARY, David, P 206-685-6306 538 F dszatmar@uw.edu
SZCZERBACKI, David 518-454-5160 330 C szczerbd@strose.edu

TANNER, William, P 785-827-5541 194 D
buck.tanner@kwu.edu
TANNER-HAROLD, Donna 217-351-2429 161 B
dtanner@parkland.edu
TANNIRU, Mohan, R 248-370-3286 257 C
tanniru@oakland.edu
TANON, Alma 408-270-6432 67 B
alma.tanon@evc.edu
TANOUYE, Allyson, M 808-956-7927 141 B
atanouye@hawaii.edu
TANSEY, Barbara 910-678-8307 370 B
tanseyb@faytechcc.edu
TANSLEY, Robert 203-596-4502 93 D
btansley@post.edu
TANTILLO, Richard, C 315-859-4412 335 A
rtantill@hamilton.edu
TANTSITS, SCC, Gerardine 973-543-6528 307 C
deanregistrar@acs350.org
TANZER, Ken 415-703-9592 31 J
ktanzer@cca.edu
TANZER, Kim 434-924-7019 525 B
kmt8t@Virginia.EDU
TAPHORN, Rick, J 423-775-7207 467 D
rick.taphorn@bryan.edu
TAPIA, Damaris 773-442-4205 159 H
d-tapia1@neiu.edu
TAPIA, Erren 219-473-4257 170 D
etapia@ccsj.edu
TAPIA, Ismael 787-763-1010 562 E
mvelez@icprjc.edu
TAPIA, Ivette 323-660-6166 40 G
ivette.tapia@cleveland.edu
TAPIA, Luis 787-894-2828 568 A
luis.tapia@upr.edu
TAPIA URZUA, Andres 412-291-6423 422 D
atapia-urzua@aii.edu
TAPLEY, Robyn 321-674-8050 108 E
rtapley@fit.edu
TAPP, Paul 903-923-2042 486 D
ptapp@etbu.edu
TAPP, Rita 903-785-7661 492 B
rtapp@parisjc.edu
TAPPAN, Charlene 860-512-2912 90 C
ctappan@mcc.commnet.edu
TAPPER, Janet 503-251-5757 420 H
jtapper@uws.edu
TAPSCOTT, Michael, R 202-994-1463 97 F
tapscott@gwu.edu
TARANTELLI, Thomas, L 518-276-6234 347 D
tarant@rpi.edu
TARANTO, John, A 816-501-3630 279 C
john.taranto@avila.edu
TARAS, Marilyn 636-422-2240 289 E
mtaras@stlcc.edu
TARBELL, Levi 641-673-1024 189 I
tarbelll@wmpenn.edu
TARBELL, Mary 413-755-4855 241 E
Tarbell@stcc.edu
TARBETT, Matthew 740-695-9500 384 J
mtarbett@btc.edu
TARBOX, James 619-594-4379 36 E
jtarbox@mail.sdsu.edu
TARBOX, Norm 801-626-6003 511 D
ntarbox@weber.edu
TARBOX, Sandra 717-477-1131 443 D
sltarbox@ship.edu
TARBY, Jay 216-397-1703 392 M
tarby@jcu.edu
TARDIF, Mark 207-948-3131 219 H
mtardif@unity.edu
TARENCE, Elaine, P 334-387-3877 1 D
elainetarence@amridgeuniversity.edu
TARGETT, Nancy, M 302-831-2841 96 F
ntargett@udel.edu
TARGONSKI, Conrad, A 608-796-3804 553 A
catargonski@viterbo.edu
TARGONSKI, David 704-461-6248 362 B
davidtargonski@bac.edu
TARGOWNIK, George 718-982-2080 327 A
George.Targownik@csi.cuny.edu
TARMAN, Christopher 949-451-5766 70 E
ctarman@ivc.edu
TARNOWSKI, Jeffrey 678-891-2520 130 G
Jeffrey.Tarnows@gpc.edu
TARNOWSKI, Susan 612-332-3361 261 F
starnowski@aii.edu
TARO, Thomas 680-488-2746 560 A
tarothomas@yahoo.com
TAROLA, Robert 202-806-2411 98 B
robert.tarola@howard.edu
TARPEY, Andrea 413-755-4847 241 E
tarpey@stcc.edu
TARPEY, Gerard 914-923-2804 345 F
gtarpey@pace.edu
TARPLEE, Marc 803-327-8017 463 G
mtarplee@yorktech.edu
TARPLEY, Billy 870-230-5518 21 I
tarpleyb@hsu.edu
TARPLEY, Sue 706-236-2292 125 G
starpley@berry.edu
TARQUINO, Beth, A 716-250-7500 324 H
batarquino@bryantstratton.edu
TARR, Barbara, L 818-779-8240 53 B
btarr@kingsuniversity.edu
TARR, Steven 610-526-1425 421 G
steven.tarr@theamericancollege.edu
TARRANT, David 952-446-4120 263 E
tarrantd@crown.edu
TARRANT, Kaneesha 562-938-4268 54 E
ktarrant@lbcc.edu
TARRANT, Melissa 706-233-7205 136 E
mtarrant@shorter.edu
TARSA, Michael 845-938-2022 558 G
8gc@usma.edu
TARSIA, Robert 805-893-4080 74 F
robert.tarsia@audit.ucsb.edu
TART, Judy 202-884-9704 99 E
tartj@trinitydc.edu
TART, Judye 910-592-8081 373 D
jtart@sampsoncc.edu
TART, Kathryn 361-570-4376 503 E
tartk@uhv.edu
TART, Marla, L 919-866-5901 374 E
mltart@waketech.edu
TART, Sylvia 910-642-7141 373 G
start@sccnc.edu
TARTAGLIA, Joseph, F 973-596-5279 312 C
tartaglia@njit.edu
TARVER, Beverly 706-721-2821 130 B
btarver@georgiahealth.edu
TARVER, Jerome, S 301-736-3631 224 B
jerome.tarver@msbbcs.edu
TARVER, Micheal 479-968-0274 20 G
mtarver@atu.edu
TARVER, Stephanie, B 337-562-4249 215 G
starver@mcneese.edu
TARVER, III, Walter, L 609-652-4804 313 F
walter.tarver@stockton.edu
TARVER-ROSS, Cassandra 334-244-3610 2 A
ctarverr@aum.edu
TARVIN, Patricia 412-809-5100 444 F
tarvin@pti.edu
TASA, Ken 979-230-3320 482 B
ken.tasa@brazosport.edu
TASHIMA, Jaye 760-245-4271 77 E
Jaye.Tashima@vvc.edu
TASHMAN, Jodi, L 215-699-5700 433 G
jtashman@LSB.edu
TASKAR, Yana 425-455-2242 533 A
ytaskar@keller.edu
TASSIN, Shannon 318-487-7151 209 B
tassin@lacollege.edu
TASSON, Dana 503-725-2800 418 G
tassond@pdx.edu
TASSONI, John, P 513-529-7135 396 D
tassonjp@muohio.edu
TASTAD, Renee 303-404-5332 84 H
renee.tastad@frontrange.edu
TATARKA, Donna 973-290-4700 309 A
dtatarka@cse.edu
TATE, Allen 717-391-7285 447 H
tate@stevenscollege.edu
TATE, Charlotte 312-996-6695 166 F
tate@uic.edu
TATE, David 307-382-1882 556 F
dtate@wwcc.wy.edu
TATE, Don 864-587-4227 461 D
tated@smcsc.edu
TATE, Horace 973-408-3246 309 F
htate@drew.edu
TATE, Kippy 334-229-6994 1 C
ktate@alasu.edu
TATE, Louella, H 512-223-0045 481 B
ltate@austincc.edu
TATE, Mike 254-968-9107 496 F
tate@tarleton.edu
TATE, Nancy, A 785-670-1648 197 D
nancy.tate@washburn.edu
TATE, Pam 417-255-7230 286 G
pamtate@missouristate.edu
TATE, Randall 870-972-2056 20 C
rtate@astate.edu
TATE, Robert, H 863-680-4347 109 D
rtate@flsouthern.edu
TATE, Susan, E 614-236-6813 386 C
state@capital.edu
TATE, Thomas, L 334-683-2321 5 G
ttate@marionmilitary.edu
TATE, Verlanda 205-929-1440 5 H
vtate@miles.edu
TATE, William, A 417-833-2551 279 I
wtate@cbcag.edu
TATGE, Kellie 320-762-4489 265 I
kelliet@alextech.edu
TATLOCK, Mark 661-362-2222 56 G
mtatlock@masters.edu
TATMAN, Sandi 925-969-3456 52 B
statman@jfku.edu
TATNALL, Amber 207-216-4392 219 C
atatnall@yccc.edu
TATOM, Lisa 936-294-1750 501 A
ljt002@shsu.edu
TATRO, Clayton 620-223-2700 192 G
claytont@fortscott.edu
TATRO, Donna, E 609-258-2845 313 A
tatro@princeton.edu
TATRO, Fred 617-364-3510 232 C
ftatro@boston.edu
TATSUI, Kiyoko 310-689-3200 42 F
ktatsui@kaplan.edu
TATUM, Ashley 940-668-7323 491 C
atatum@nctc.edu
TATUM, Beverly Daniel 404-270-5001 137 E
presidentsoffice@spelman.edu
TATUM, Judy, B 313-577-3291 260 D
jtatum@wayne.edu
TATUM, Lance 334-670-3365 8 B
ltatum@troy.edu
TATUM, Leila 770-426-2917 133 B
leila.tatum@life.edu
TATUM, Tanya 850-599-3777 118 G
tanya.tatum@famu.edu
TATUM, Terry 361-825-2693 497 F
terry.tatum@tamucc.edu
TATUM, Veronda 870-862-8131 23 G
vtatum@southark.edu
TAUB, Carol 503-253-3443 417 H
ctaub@ocom.edu
TAUBER, Hendy 323-937-3763 79 J
htauber@yoec.edu
TAUBMAN, Mark, B 585-275-0017 358 I
Mark_Taubman@URMC.Rochester.edu
TAUER, Ritamarie 281-649-3702 487 F
rtauer@hbu.edu
TAUPIER, Andrea, S 413-748-3609 245 C
ataupier@spfldcol.edu
TAUSZ, Jerrad 816-204-2109 19 C
jerrad.tausz@phoenix.edu
TAUZIN, Kristie, R 985-448-4509 216 A
kristie.tauzin@nicholls.edu
TAVADA, Dwight, L 810-762-9825 253 I
dtavada@kettering.edu
TAVAKOLI, Assad 910-672-1527 377 E
atavakoli@uncfsu.edu
TAVAKOLI, Sue 623-935-8020 15 H
sue.tavakoli@estrellamountain.edu
TAVARES, Shirley, A 787-725-8120 562 A
investigacion@eap.edu
TAVAREZ, Luis, A 856-256-4276 314 A
tavarez@rowan.edu
TAVELLI, Nancy, J 509-527-5297 539 E
tavelln@whitman.edu
TAVES, Bennett, C 206-934-6629 537 B
ben.taves@seattlecolleges.edu
TAVES, Michael, E 607-274-3061 336 G
taves@ithaca.edu
TAVES, Michael, E 607-274-3867 336 G
taves@ithaca.edu
TAWYEA, Edward, W 215-503-8848 448 B
edward.tawyea@jefferson.edu
TAYEBI, Kandi 936-294-1971 501 A
kanditayebi@shsu.edu
TAYEH, Raja 402-826-6776 298 A
raja.tayeh@doane.edu
TAYLOE, John 252-398-1232 363 E
tayloj@chowan.edu
TAYLOR, Alicia 256-306-2621 2 E
ataylor@calhoun.edu
TAYLOR, Amanda 404-297-9522 128 B
taylora@dekalbtech.edu
TAYLOR, Andrea 562-985-5197 35 A
ataylor@csulb.edu
TAYLOR, Angie 859-441-4500 201 G
TAYLOR, Anna 770-233-5560 137 B
ataylor@sctech.edu
TAYLOR, Anne Marie 925-969-3491 52 B
amtaylor@jfku.edu
TAYLOR, Barbara 540-423-9032 526 E
btaylor@germanna.edu
TAYLOR, Barry 305-348-3662 119 B
barry.taylor@fiu.edu
TAYLOR, Beck, A 509-777-3200 539 F
btaylor@whitworth.edu
TAYLOR, Bill 641-782-7081 189 A
taylor@swcciowa.edu
TAYLOR, Bill 408-741-2642 78 B
bill.taylor@westvalley.edu
TAYLOR, Bill 713-348-6000 492 J
wtaylor@rice.edu
TAYLOR, Blair 276-326-4282 516 I
btaylor@bluefield.edu
TAYLOR, Brandon 334-683-2378 5 G
btaylor@marionmilitary.edu
TAYLOR, Brandy 912-871-1616 134 H
btaylor@ogeecheetech.edu
TAYLOR, Brenda 251-405-7008 2 D
btaylor@bishop.edu
TAYLOR, Brian 808-956-6182 141 B
taylorb@hawaii.edu
TAYLOR, Brian 402-935-9400 299 C
btaylor@nechristian.edu
TAYLOR, Carmen 406-275-4972 296 F
carmen_taylor@skc.edu
TAYLOR, Carol, A 714-556-3610 76 E
officeofthepresident@vanguard.edu
TAYLOR, Cecil, R 251-442-2406 9 B
ctaylor@mail.umobile.edu
TAYLOR, Celeste 706-355-5081 124 H
ctaylor@athenstech.edu
TAYLOR, Charles 404-237-7573 125 F
ctaylor@bauder.edu
TAYLOR, Charles 256-331-5462 6 B
taylor@nwscc.edu
TAYLOR, Charles 417-873-7391 281 H
ctaylor@drury.edu
TAYLOR, JR., Charles, E 704-233-8218 380 D
taylor@wingate.edu
TAYLOR, Charles, S 937-775-2225 406 C
charles.taylor@wright.edu
TAYLOR, Chelsa 276-739-2423 528 D
ctaylor@vhcc.edu
TAYLOR, Cherilyn, Y 803-536-7245 460 G
ctaylor@scsu.edu
TAYLOR, Cheryl, A 417-268-1000 279 B
ctaylor@agts.edu
TAYLOR, Chris 801-863-8484 511 C
taylorch@uvu.edu
TAYLOR, Christopher 575-562-2343 318 A
chris.taylor@enmu.edu
TAYLOR, Craig 541-463-5364 416 D
taylorc@lanecc.edu
TAYLOR, Craig, B 503-554-2911 415 I
ctaylor@georgefox.edu
TAYLOR, Curtis, J 712-722-6006 183 H
curtis@dordt.edu
TAYLOR, Cynthia, S 972-860-7191 484 H
CynthiaSTaylor@dcccd.edu
TAYLOR, Cyrus, C 216-368-4437 386 E
casdean@case.edu
TAYLOR, Dale 740-351-3758 401 I
dtaylor@shawnee.edu
TAYLOR, Daniel 216-432-8945 387 A
dataylor@chancelloru.edu
TAYLOR, Danny 615-966-7650 470 D
danny.taylor@lipscomb.edu
TAYLOR, David 713-500-4535 506 D
david.taylor@uth.tmc.edu
TAYLOR, David 276-326-4257 516 I
dtaylor@bluefield.edu
TAYLOR, David 276-326-4206 516 I
dtaylor@bluefield.edu
TAYLOR, David, E 202-885-2121 97 B
taylor@american.edu
TAYLOR, David, M 205-652-3531 10 A
dmt@uwa.edu
TAYLOR, David, M 205-652-3531 10 A
dmt@uwa.edi
TAYLOR, Deb, A 864-622-6063 455 C
dtaylor@andersonuniversity.edu
TAYLOR, Debora, W 512-448-8450 493 B
deboraw@stedwards.edu
TAYLOR, Deborah 562-777-4069 30 H
deborah.taylor@biola.edu
TAYLOR, Deborah, A 603-526-3760 304 A
dtaylor@colby-sawyer.edu
TAYLOR, Deborah, D 336-734-7178 370 C
ddtaylor@forsythtech.edu
TAYLOR, Delores, T 804-827-8730 525 E
dttaylor@vcu.edu
TAYLOR, Denise 760-921-5429 61 B
dtaylor@paloverde.edu
TAYLOR, Dennis 318-869-5360 208 F
dtaylor@centenary.edu
TAYLOR, Donnis, D 740-392-6868 396 H
denny.taylor@mvnu.edu
TAYLOR, Dickerson, E 706-233-7240 136 E
dtaylor@shorter.edu
TAYLOR, Dinny, S 413-597-3072 246 G
dinny.s.taylor@williams.edu
TAYLOR, Don 949-582-4541 70 F
dtaylor@saddleback.edu
TAYLOR, Don 415-338-3326 36 F
dtaylor@sfsu.edu
TAYLOR, Donald 630-829-6240 145 D
dtaylor@ben.edu
TAYLOR, Donald, R 870-307-7203 22 D
dtaylor@lyon.edu
TAYLOR, Doug 404-687-4568 127 C
taylord@ctsnet.edu
TAYLOR, Dustin 910-678-8236 370 B
taylord@faytechcc.edu
TAYLOR, Ed 206-616-7175 538 F
edtaylor@uw.edu
TAYLOR, Edward 608-663-2333 547 C
etaylor@edgewood.edu
TAYLOR, Eileen 317-578-7353 178 C
TAYLOR, Ella 503-838-8757 419 C
taylore@wou.edu
TAYLOR, Ellen 540-831-5771 522 D
eltaylor@radford.edu
TAYLOR, Erica 901-320-9730 478 B
etaylor@victory.edu
TAYLOR, G. Christine 765-494-6969 178 F
taylorgc@purdue.edu
TAYLOR, Gary 865-251-1800 472 K
gtaylor@southcollegetn.edu
TAYLOR, Gene, F 701-231-5614 381 H
gene.taylor@ndsu.edu
TAYLOR, George, R 410-951-3551 228 B
gtaylor@coppin.edu
TAYLOR, Geraldine, S 781-891-2222 231 F
gtaylor@bentley.edu
TAYLOR, Gia 480-423-6300 16 D
gia.taylor@sccmail.maricopa.edu

TEIG, Trisha .... 801-832-2235 .... 512 F
tteig@westminstercollege.edu
TEIPEL, Julie .... 312-280-3500 .... 153 A
jteipel@aii.edu
TEIS, Lawrence, B .... 512-245-2114 .... 501 C
lt10@txstate.edu
TEITELBAUM, Aharon .... 845-783-0994 .... 359 B
TEITELBAUM, Jeremy .... 860-486-2713 .... 94 E
Jeremy.Teitelbaum@uconn.edu
TEITELBAUM, Kenneth .... 618-453-2415 .... 164 I
kteitelb@siu.edu
TEITLBAUM, Zalman .... 718-963-9770 .... 358 H
yab@utsb.org
TEJADA, Carlos .... 716-286-8769 .... 344 D
ctejada@niagara.edu
TEKIELE, Todd .... 517-629-0318 .... 247 E
ttekiele@albion.edu
TEKIPPE, Stephanie, S .... 319-352-8628 .... 189 F
stephanie.tekippe@wartburg.edu
TELFER, Richard, J .... 262-472-1918 .... 552 E
telferr@uww.edu
TELFORD, Rebecca, P .... 937-778-7809 .... 390 G
btelford@edisonohio.edu
TELL, Barbara .... 310-954-4348 .... 57 H
btell@msmc.la.edu
TELLEEN, Jane, A .... 651-523-2202 .... 264 C
jtelleen@hamline.edu
TELLEI, Patrick, U .... 680-488-1669 .... 560 A
tellei@palau.edu
TELLER, Ryan .... 402-486-2538 .... 300 D
ryteller@ucollege.edu
TELLES, Cathy .... 602-749-4660 .... 13 M
ctelles@devry.edu
TELLEZ, Kenneth .... 575-528-7070 .... 319 G
ktellez@nmsu.edu
TELLI, Suzette .... 615-297-7545 .... 466 H
tellis@aquinascollege.edu
TELLO, Al .... 949-451-5472 .... 70 E
atello@ivc.edu
TEMAAT, Beverly .... 620-227-9119 .... 192 B
bgtemaat@dc3.edu
TEMPEL, Eugene, R .... 812-855-6679 .... 173 C
etempel@indiana.edu
TEMPERA, Jeffrey, L .... 631-451-4506 .... 356 D
temperj@sunysuffolk.edu
TEMPKIN, Aron .... 802-485-2624 .... 514 A
TEMPLE, Austin .... 318-357-6699 .... 216 B
temple@nsula.edu
TEMPLE, David, W .... 315-464-5476 .... 352 E
templed@upstate.edu
TEMPLE, Gary, M .... 817-202-6755 .... 495 C
gtemple@swau.edu
TEMPLE, Glena, G .... 608-796-3392 .... 553 A
ggtemple@viterbo.edu
TEMPLE, Jack .... 334-387-3877 .... 1 D
jacktemple@amridgeuniversity.edu
TEMPLE, Jim .... 661-362-3535 .... 41 G
james.temple@canyons.edu
TEMPLE, Lori .... 702-895-3628 .... 302 K
lorit@unlv.edu
TEMPLE, Michael, P .... 252-398-6226 .... 363 E
templm@chowan.edu
TEMPLE, Robert .... 619-482-6309 .... 71 C
rtemple@swccd.edu
TEMPLE, Susan .... 281-998-6150 .... 493 D
susan.temple@sjcd.edu
TEMPLE, Vickie .... 318-678-6025 .... 209 J
vtemple@bpcc.edu
TEMPLEMAN, John, N .... 440-826-2071 .... 384 H
jtemplem@bw.edu
TEMPLER, Lisa .... 409-933-8262 .... 483 B
ltempler@com.edu
TEMPLETON, Debra, R .... 540-831-6030 .... 522 D
drtemplet@radford.edu
TEMPLETON, Etheldra .... 215-871-6486 .... 444 B
etheldrat@pcom.edu
TEMPLETON, Heidi .... 660-785-4016 .... 291 A
heidi@truman.edu
TEMPLETON, Linda, B .... 219-980-6767 .... 173 F
litemple@iun.edu
TEMPLETON, Rosalyn .... 406-265-3726 .... 295 G
rosalyn.templeton@msun.edu
TEMPLETON, William .... 907-786-4005 .... 10 I
anwgt@uaa.alaska.edu
TEMPLETON-CORNELL,
Vicki, L .... 315-267-2190 .... 354 C
templevl@postdam.edu
TEMPLIN, Carl, R .... 435-586-5401 .... 511 A
templin@suu.edu
TEMPLIN, JR., Robert, G .. 703-323-3101 .... 527 C
rtemplin@nvcc.edu
TEMTE, Anne, T .... 218-683-8610 .... 268 E
anne.temte@northlandcollege.edu
TENA, Lydia .... 915-831-8818 .... 486 E
lpere121@epcc.edu
TENBOSCH, Courtney .... 513-771-2424 .... 385 G
ctenbosch@brownmackie.edu
TENCHER, Donald, E .... 401-456-8007 .... 454 A
dtencher@ric.edu
TENCZAR, JR., Robert, C .. 773-298-3326 .... 163 G
tenczar@sxu.edu
TENDALL, Michael, W .... 309-794-7357 .... 145 B
adsmt@augustana.edu
TENDALL, Stephen .... 563-333-6423 .... 188 D
TendallStephen@sau.edu
TENENBAUM, Elchonon .... 707-638-5507 .... 72 H
rabbi@tu.edu
TENEROWICZ, Nathan .... 814-269-7077 .... 449 D
ntenerow@pitt.edu
TENGERES, Laura, N .... 954-308-2224 .... 100 I
tengeresl@aii.edu
TENGLIN, Ingrid, K .... 773-244-5601 .... 159 G
itenglin@northpark.edu
TENIENTE-MATSON,
Cynthia .... 559-278-2083 .... 34 D
cmatson@csufresno.edu
TENNANT, Linda, A .... 706-236-2282 .... 125 G
ltennant@berry.edu
TENNANT, Otto .... 270-789-5034 .... 199 C
otennant@campbellsville.edu
TENNASSEE, Paul, N .... 202-274-6277 .... 99 F
ptennassee@udc.edu
TENNEN, Elaine .... 805-654-6346 .... 77 D
elainetennen@vcccd.edu
TENNENT, Lee .... 864-646-1777 .... 461 F
ltennent@tctc.edu
TENNENT, Timothy, C .... 859-858-2202 .... 198 A
TENNER, Jack, D .... 409-880-1783 .... 500 F
jack.tenner@lamar.edu
TENNESON, Richard, J .... 563-387-1010 .... 187 A
tennesri@luther.edu
TENNEY, David .... 713-348-8036 .... 492 J
dtenney@rice.edu
TENNEY, Peter .... 509-462-3722 .... 531 E
ptenney@cc.edu
TENNYSON, Pat .... 423-869-6286 .... 470 C
ptennyson@lmunet.edu
TENNYSON, Tenis .... 406-791-5305 .... 296 H
ttennyson@ugf.edu
TENUTA, Robert, M .... 815-740-3372 .... 167 C
rtenuta@stfrancis.edu
TEODORESCU, Daniel .... 404-727-5278 .... 129 A
dteodor@emory.edu
TEPATTI, Eileen, G .... 217-786-2885 .... 156 I
eileen.tepatti@llcc.edu
TEPE, Chabha .... 636-227-2100 .... 284 E
chabha.tepe@logan.edu
TEPE, Rodger, E .... 636-227-2100 .... 284 E
rodger.tepe@logan.edu
TEPROVICH, Amy .... 239-489-9316 .... 104 L
ateprovich@edison.edu
TEPSA, Kristin .... 906-353-4602 .... 253 J
ktepsa@kbocc.org
TERAQAWACHI, Lori .... 808-984-3406 .... 142 B
loritera@hawaii.edu
TERAVEST, Daniel, J .... 707-253-3341 .... 58 F
dteravest@napavalley.edu
TERCERO, Lily, F .... 817-515-5171 .... 496 A
lily.tercero@tccd.edu
TERCHEK, Daniel .... 212-472-1500 .... 343 G
dterchek@nysid.edu
TEREBESSY, Hilarie .... 312-942-7100 .... 163 B
hilarie_terebessy@rush.edu
TERENZIO, Marion .... 973-748-9000 .... 308 A
marion_terenzio@bloomfield.edu
TERESA, Daniel .... 831-755-6840 .... 49 C
dteresa@hartnell.edu
TERESHINSKI, Robert .... 605-668-1584 .... 464 F
rtereshinski@mtmc.edu
TERESI, Mark .... 847-566-6401 .... 167 D
mteresi@usml.edu
TERHAAR, Jody, L .... 320-363-5580 .... 262 H
jterhaar@csbsju.edu
TERHORST, Dan .... 760-480-8474 .... 78 E
dterhorst@wscal.edu
TERHUNE, James, S .... 207-859-4780 .... 217 G
jterhune@colby.edu
TERKLA, Dawn, G .... 617-627-3274 .... 245 F
dawn.terkla@tufts.edu
TERMOTT, Kenneth .... 732-247-5241 .... 312 A
ktermott@nbts.edu
TERNES, Roger .... 715-425-3246 .... 552 A
roger.ternes@uwrf.edu
TERP, Douglas, C .... 207-859-4770 .... 217 G
dcterp@colby.edu
TERP, Jeff .... 317-921-4225 .... 175 G
jterp@ivytech.edu
TERPACK, Sallie, A .... 814-732-1024 .... 442 D
terpack@edinboro.edu
TERPENNING, Marlene, K . 740-284-5179 .... 390 M
mterpenning@franciscan.edu
TERPSTRA, Duane .... 616-451-3511 .... 250 E
dterpstra@davenport.edu
TERPSTRA, Joylita .... 423-478-7707 .... 472 F
jterpstra@ptseminary.edu
TERRACINA, Lorraine .... 718-270-2187 .... 352 D
lterracina@downstate.edu
TERRANOVA, Paul .... 913-588-7068 .... 197 A
pterranova@kumc.edu
TERRASS, Richard .... 617-726-0781 .... 242 E
rterrass@mghihp.edu
TERREGINO, Carol, A .... 732-235-4576 .... 316 G
terregca@umdnj.edu
TERRELL, Bill .... 915-532-3737 .... 508 E
bterrell@westerntech.edu
TERRELL, Billie, P .... 815-740-3399 .... 167 C
bterrell@stfrancis.edu
TERRELL, C. Jeffrey .... 404-233-3949 .... 135 G
jterrell@richmont.edu
TERRELL, Charles .... 304-434-8001 .... 542 E
cterrell@eastern.wvnet.edu
TERRELL, Gaither, M .... 336-316-2143 .... 364 E
gterrell@guilford.edu
TERRELL, Jan (Denny) .... 717-477-1375 .... 443 D
dterrell@ship.edu
TERRELL, Janice .... 704-355-4305 .... 363 B
janice.terrell@carolinascollege.edu
TERRELL, Mark .... 814-860-5121 .... 433 C
hbell@lecom.edu
TERRELL, Patricia .... 208-282-2315 .... 143 D
terrpatr@isu.edu
TERRELL, Peg, J .... 765-966-2656 .... 176 F
pterrell@ivytech.edu
TERRELL, Sherri, I .... 915-747-5302 .... 505 E
siterrell@utep.edu
TERRELL, Tracy .... 509-963-3076 .... 531 G
terrell@cwu.edu
TERRELL-BAMIRO, Caryl ... 480-732-7134 .... 15 G
caryl.terrell-bamiro@cgcmail.maricopa.edu
TERRELL-POWELL,
Yvonne, L .... 206-546-4509 .... 537 G
yterrell@shoreline.edu
TERRIO, Dan, M .... 509-527-4981 .... 539 E
terrio@whitman.edu
TERRIO, Paul, L .... 612-330-1049 .... 261 G
terriop@augsburg.edu
TERRONE, Maria .... 718-997-5590 .... 328 F
maria.terrone@qc.cuny.edu
TERRONEZ, Randy .... 515-244-4221 .... 181 D
terronezr@aib.edu
TERRY, Alicia .... 760-757-2121 .... 57 E
aterry@miracosta.edu
TERRY, Andy .... 205-853-1200 .... 5 C
atterry@jeffstateonline.com
TERRY, Bill .... 845-758-7495 .... 323 F
wterry@bard.edu
TERRY, Brooks .... 904-680-7700 .... 107 H
bterry@fcsl.edu
TERRY, Bryan, J .... 973-655-4153 .... 311 G
terryb@mail.montclair.edu
TERRY, Carol .... 707-826-5728 .... 36 D
ct7002@humboldt.edu
TERRY, Carol, S .... 401-454-6278 .... 454 B
cterry@risd.edu
TERRY, Denise .... 574-372-5100 .... 171 E
Denise.Terry@grace.edu
TERRY, Ditamichelle .... 804-745-2444 .... 516 L
ddterry@bryantstratton.edu
TERRY, Esther .... 336-517-2154 .... 362 C
eterry@bennett.edu
TERRY, George .... 618-468-6000 .... 156 C
gterry@lc.edu
TERRY, Heidi .... 816-654-7152 .... 283 J
hterry@kcumb.edu
TERRY, Homer .... 606-436-5721 .... 201 H
homer.terry@kctcs.edu
TERRY, James, E .... 304-696-2486 .... 543 G
terry@marshall.edu
TERRY, James, H .... 401-354-2335 .... 454 D
terryj@salve.edu
TERRY, Jan, M .... 217-245-1097 .... 156 I
jan.terry@llcc.edu
TERRY, John .... 605-718-6551 .... 464 G
jterry@national.edu
TERRY, Justyn .... 724-266-3838 .... 448 G
jterry@tsm.edu
TERRY, Karen .... 212-237-8040 .... 328 A
kterry@jjay.cuny.edu
TERRY, Laura, C .... 423-439-4210 .... 473 E
terryl@etsu.edu
TERRY, Martin, L .... 419-434-4521 .... 404 B
terry@findlay.edu
TERRY, Missy, D .... 503-554-2101 .... 415 I
terrym@georgefox.edu
TERRY, Neil, W .... 806-651-2530 .... 498 D
nterry@mail.wtamu.edu
TERRY, Penelope .... 718-951-5924 .... 326 G
pterry@brooklyn.cuny.edu
TERRY, Sabrina, D .... 276-223-4702 .... 528 F
wcterrs@wcc.vccs.edu
TERRY, Sara Beth .... 334-833-4062 .... 4 E
sbterry@huntingdon.edu
TERRY, Stephen, B .... 843-383-8035 .... 457 A
sterry@coker.edu
TERRY, Susan .... 206-543-0535 .... 538 F
nahe@uw.edu
TERRY, Terri .... 205-348-0609 .... 8 F
teri.terry@ua.edu
TERRY, Tina .... 606-886-3863 .... 201 C
tina.terry@kctcs.edu
TERRY, Troy, M .... 864-294-2213 .... 458 D
troy.terry@furman.edu
TERVALA, Debra .... 301-934-7846 .... 222 C
dtervala@csmd.edu
TERWILLIGER, Jason .... 502-863-8437 .... 200 G
jason_terwilliger@georgetowncollege.edu
TESAR, Dan .... 714-992-7048 .... 59 D
dtesar@fullcoll.edu
TESFAGIORGIS, Gebre, H .. 515-294-1181 .... 182 B
gebretes@iastate.edu
TESFAMARIAM, Biniam .... 575-234-9249 .... 319 F
bini2005@cavern.nmsu.edu
TESH, J. Michael .... 210-567-2590 .... 506 E
tesh@uthscsa.edu
TESH, Mike .... 336-758-5160 .... 380 B
teshjm@wfu.edu
TESKE, Paul .... 303-315-2805 .... 88 D
Paul.Teske@ucdenver.edu
TESKEY, Michael .... 503-777-7593 .... 420 A
michael.teskey@reed.edu
TESORIERE, Joseph .... 518-564-4601 .... 354 B
tesorijp@plattsburgh.edu
TESS, Dan, E .... 570-484-2238 .... 443 A
dtess@lhup.edu
TESS, Paul, A .... 507-354-8221 .... 265 B
tesspa@mlc-wels.edu
TESSIER, Michael, A .... 812-488-2956 .... 180 B
mt28@evansville.edu
TESSIER, Nanci .... 804-287-6425 .... 525 A
ntessier@richmond.edu
TESSIER-LAVIGNE, Marc ... 212-327-8080 .... 347 H
marctl@rockefeller.edu
TESSLER, Mark, A .... 734-764-9200 .... 259 D
tessler@umich.edu
TESSMANN, Cary, A .... 262-691-5214 .... 555 C
ctessmann@wctc.edu
TESTINI, Ann .... 906-487-7361 .... 251 C
ann.testini@finlandia.edu
TESTY, Kellye, Y .... 206-543-2586 .... 538 F
lawdean@uw.edu
TETEN, Dixie .... 402-872-2226 .... 299 H
dteten@peru.edu
TETER, Steve .... 620-862-5252 .... 190 D
steve.teter@barclaycollege.edu
TETLOW, Wendolyn, E .... 906-786-5802 .... 249 D
tetloww@baycollege.edu
TETRAULT, Martha, R .... 413-597-2681 .... 246 G
martha.r.tetrault@williams.edu
TETREAU, Jerry, C .... 480-245-7969 .... 14 K
jerry.tetreau@ibconline.edu
TETREAULT, Jules .... 603-899-4178 .... 305 B
tetreaj@franklinpierce.edu
TETREAULT, Robert, G .... 401-456-8216 .... 454 A
rtetreault@ric.edu
TETRICK, Angel .... 225-922-1643 .... 209 C
atetrick@lctcs.edu
TETSTILL, John .... 636-422-2040 .... 289 E
JHTetstill@stlcc.edu
TETTER, Stephanie .... 831-646-4082 .... 57 G
stetter@mpc.edu
TETZLAFF-BELHASEN,
Chris, M .... 361-698-1308 .... 485 F
chris@delmar.edu
TETZLOFF, Jason .... 320-308-5377 .... 269 D
jtetzloff@sctcc.edu
TETZLOFF, Lisa .... 920-465-2200 .... 551 A
tetzlofl@uwgb.edu
TEVIS, Glenna, J .... 712-274-5269 .... 187 D
tevis@morningside.edu
TEW, Glade .... 808-675-3590 .... 139 I
glade.tew@byuh.edu
TEW, JR., John .... 816-584-6410 .... 287 H
john.tew@park.edu
TEW, Mark .... 325-649-8002 .... 488 A
mtew@hputx.edu
TEW, Rebecca .... 706-560-2039 .... 127 D
tew_rebecca@columbusstate.edu
TEWS, Anne .... 269-927-8117 .... 254 B
tews@lakemichigancollege.edu
TEXIDOR, Migdalia .... 787-250-1912 .... 563 E
mtexidor@metro.inter.edu
TEYMOURTASH, Janet, L .. 415-422-6636 .... 76 B
janet@usfca.edu
TEZENO, Albert .... 318-274-6190 .... 215 E
tezenoa@gram.edu
THACKER, Judy .... 619-275-4700 .... 46 K
judy@fashioncareerscollege.com
THACKER, Karen, S .... 610-796-8306 .... 421 F
karen.thacker@alvernia.edu
THACKER, Linda .... 314-529-6573 .... 284 F
lthacker@maryville.edu
THACKER, Terry .... 615-383-4848 .... 478 E
tthacker@watkins.edu
THACKER, Victor, L .... 304-637-1292 .... 540 F
thackert@dewev.edu
THAI, Khi .... 954-762-5650 .... 118 H
thai@fau.edu
THAMES, Brenda .... 916-484-8375 .... 56 A
thamesb@arc.losrios.edu
THAMES, James, H .... 214-841-3678 .... 485 E
jthames@dts.edu
THAMES, Jamie .... 478-757-4024 .... 139 A
jthames@wesleyancollege.edu
THAMES, Kathleen .... 337-482-6397 .... 216 D
kat@louisiana.edu
THAMES, Kathleen, A .... 337-482-6397 .... 216 D
kat@louisiana.edu
THANNICKAL, Steve .... 918-495-6620 .... 411 C
sthannical@oru.edu
THAO-FEHUK, May .... 651-905-3420 .... 261 J
mthaofehuk@browncollege.edu
THARAKAN, Ana .... 312-499-1813 .... 149 D
atharakan@devry.edu
THARP, Brent .... 912-478-5444 .... 131 A
btharp@georgiasouthern.edu
THARP, Carla .... 201-761-7364 .... 314 F

THOMAS, Mary, E ... 248-204-2406 ... 254 E
mthomas@ltu.edu
THOMAS, Mary Beth ... 617-735-9766 ... 234 E
thomasmb@emmanuel.edu
THOMAS, Matthew, D ... 507-933-7510 ... 264 B
news@gustavus.edu
THOMAS, Maurice ... 856-351-2697 ... 315 A
mthomas@salemcc.edu
THOMAS, Maxcie ... 870-575-8101 ... 25 B
thomasm@uapb.edu
THOMAS, May ... 540-362-6519 ... 519 E
mthomas@hollins.edu
THOMAS, Melissa ... 503-554-2214 ... 415 I
mthomas@georgefox.edu
THOMAS, Michael ... 618-985-3741 ... 152 E
thomasm@iecc.edu
THOMAS, Michael ... 601-979-3060 ... 275 A
michael.thomas@jsums.edu
THOMAS, Michael ... 513-556-4603 ... 403 D
thommi@uc.edu
THOMAS, Mike, R ... 618-235-2700 ... 165 B
michael.thomas@swic.edu
THOMAS, Miriam ... 765-459-0561 ... 176 A
mthomas@ivytech.edu
THOMAS, Nancy ... 248-204-3203 ... 254 E
nthomas@ltu.edu
THOMAS, Natalie ... 903-233-4171 ... 489 K
nataliethomas@letu.edu
THOMAS, Nathan ... 309-677-3221 ... 145 H
nthomas@bradley.edu
THOMAS, Nichole, E ... 315-268-3854 ... 329 C
nthomas@clarkson.edu
THOMAS, Otis ... 443-885-3160 ... 224 F
otis.thomas@morgan.edu
THOMAS, Pam ... 630-889-6661 ... 159 E
pthomas@nuhs.edu
THOMAS, Patricia, A ... 202-274-6314 ... 99 F
pthomas@udc.edu
THOMAS, Paul ... 443-627-7322 ... 272 F
paul.thomas@waldenu.edu
THOMAS, Paul ... 901-333-5760 ... 475 H
pthomas@southwest.tn.edu
THOMAS, Pauline ... 870-575-8970 ... 25 B
thomas@uapb.edu
THOMAS, Peter, A ... 508-831-6074 ... 247 B
pthomas@wpi.edu
THOMAS, Peter, I ... 419-530-4229 ... 404 F
peter.thomas@utoledo.edu
THOMAS, Phil ... 319-208-5053 ... 188 G
pthomas@scciowa.edu
THOMAS, Randi Malcolm ... 513-529-4151 ... 396 D
randi.thomas@muohio.edu
THOMAS, Reggie ... 714-256-1311 ... 48 D
reggiethomas@ggbts.edu
THOMAS, Renard ... 661-362-3327 ... 41 G
renard.thomas@canyons.edu
THOMAS, Rhonda ... 662-329-7138 ... 276 B
rthomas@acadsupp.muw.edu
THOMAS, Richard ... 253-943-3158 ... 533 B
rthomas@devry.edu
THOMAS, Richard, R ... 847-491-2325 ... 160 D
r-thomas2@northwestern.edu
THOMAS, Rikki ... 757-727-5250 ... 519 C
rikki.thomas@hamptonu.edu
THOMAS, Robert, J ... 570-941-6486 ... 450 B
thomasm5@scranton.edu
THOMAS, Robert, L ... 313-577-2515 ... 260 D
aa0817@wayne.edu
THOMAS, Ron ... 651-423-8213 ... 266 E
ron.thomas@dctc.edu
THOMAS, Ronald, C ... 718-262-2332 ... 329 B
rthomas@york.cuny.edu
THOMAS, Ronald, R ... 253-879-3201 ... 538 E
president@pugetsound.edu
THOMAS, Rosemary, M ... 410-546-6939 ... 228 D
rmthomas@salisbury.edu
THOMAS, Ryan ... 801-626-7931 ... 511 D
ryanthomas2@weber.edu
THOMAS, Sam ... 662-915-7690 ... 277 G
sethomas@olemiss.edu
THOMAS, Sandra ... 760-252-2411 ... 30 F
sthomas@barstow.edu
THOMAS, Sandra ... 217-641-4344 ... 154 G
thomas@jwcc.edu
THOMAS, Sandra ... 405-974-2690 ... 413 B
sthomas@ucok.edu
THOMAS, Shawn ... 229-391-4910 ... 123 F
sthomas@abac.edu
THOMAS, Shawn, O ... 806-651-2006 ... 498 D
sthomas@mail.wtamu.edu
THOMAS, Stacey ... 765-455-9391 ... 173 E
stathoma@iuk.edu
THOMAS, Stephen, J ... 212-746-2999 ... 360 B
sjthoma@med.cornell.edu
THOMAS, Stephen, W ... 252-328-4400 ... 377 C
thomass@ecu.edu
THOMAS, Steve ... 432-685-4521 ... 490 G
steve@midland.edu
THOMAS, Stuart ... 970-339-6232 ... 80 G
stuart.thomas@aims.edu
THOMAS, Susan, L ... 618-650-3674 ... 165 A
suthoma@siue.edu
THOMAS, Suzanne, W ... 330-471-8239 ... 395 E
sthomas@malone.edu
THOMAS, Sylvia ... 951-222-8620 ... 64 B
sylvia.thomas@rcc.edu
THOMAS, Teresa ... 615-898-2600 ... 473 F
tthomas@mtsu.edu
THOMAS, Teresa ... 412-268-3580 ... 424 H
ts2h@andrew.cmu.edu
THOMAS, Terri ... 502-456-6505 ... 206 C
tthomas@sullivan.edu
THOMAS, Terry ... 919-572-1625 ... 361 M
THOMAS, Todd ... 423-652-6045 ... 469 L
tthomas@king.edu
THOMAS, Todd, S ... 518-464-8526 ... 333 F
tthomas@excelsior.edu
THOMAS, Tracy ... 205-226-4902 ... 2 C
tthomas@bsc.edu
THOMAS, Troy ... 405-842-8007 ... 19 C
troy.thomas@phoenix.edu
THOMAS, Tyrone ... 843-355-4152 ... 463 C
thomast@wiltech.edu
THOMAS, Valerie, A ... 410-455-3142 ... 227 D
valerie.thomas@umbc.edu
THOMAS, Vanrea ... 718-270-4885 ... 328 D
vanrea@mec.cuny.edu
THOMAS, Verian ... 850-599-3505 ... 118 G
verian.thomas@famu.edu
THOMAS, W, E ... 252-335-3292 ... 377 D
wethomas@mail.ecsu.edu
THOMAS, Wade, L ... 607-436-3458 ... 353 E
thomaswl@oneonta.edu
THOMAS, Wanda ... 330-675-8821 ... 393 D
wthomas4@kent.edu
THOMAS, Wilbert, L ... 757-727-5356 ... 519 C
bill.thomas@hamptonu.edu
THOMAS, William, A ... 713-313-6816 ... 499 G
thomaswa@tsu.edu
THOMAS, Willie, G ... 302-855-1689 ... 96 B
wthomas6@dtcc.edu
THOMAS-GLOVER, Linda ... 757-789-1775 ... 526 D
lglover@es.vccs.edu
THOMAS-GOLDEN,
Tammalyn, M ... 919-516-4533 ... 376 B
THOMAS-MADDOX,
Candice ... 740-654-6711 ... 400 B
thomas@ohio.edu
THOMAS-MOBLEY, Linda ... 619-684-8843 ... 59 A
lthomas@newschoolarch.edu
THOMAS-PARROTT,
Sharon ... 630-515-4577 ... 149 A
stparrott@devry.edu
THOMAS-SMITH,
E. Joahanne ... 936-261-2175 ... 496 E
ejthomas-smith@pvamu.edu
THOMAS TROUPE,
Jennifer ... 978-921-4242 ... 242 F
jtroupe@montserrat.edu
THOMAS-WILLIAMS,
Regina ... 912-443-5708 ... 136 D
rthomas@savannahtech.edu
THOMASI, SR., Edward, J ... 203-773-8506 ... 89 H
ethomasi@albertus.edu
THOMASON, Chris ... 870-777-5722 ... 25 F
Chris.Thomason@uaccb.edu
THOMASON, Don, A ... 513-244-8162 ... 387 D
don.thomason@ccuniversity.edu
THOMASON, Jerry ... 870-743-3000 ... 22 G
jthomaso@northark.edu
THOMASON, Mary ... 870-574-4719 ... 24 A
mthomaso@sautech.edu
THOMASON, Tommy, N ... 713-221-8100 ... 503 D
thomasont@uhd.edu
THOMASSON, James ... 617-364-3510 ... 232 C
jthomasson@boston.edu
THOMASSON, Janice ... 574-284-4610 ... 179 D
janicet@saintmarys.edu
THOMASSON, Kim ... 859-253-0621 ... 205 A
kthomasson@national-college.edu
THOMASSON, Susan ... 704-355-3921 ... 363 B
susan.thomasson@carolinas.org
THOMES, Christopher, P ... 850-747-3250 ... 110 E
cthomes@gulfcoast.edu
THOMFORDE,
Christopher, M ... 610-861-1364 ... 436 I
thomforde@moravian.edu
THOMLINSON, Gene ... 417-865-2811 ... 282 A
thomlinsong@evangel.edu
THOMMPSON, Troy, J ... 336-841-9404 ... 365 A
tthompso@highpoint.edu
THOMPSOM, Cathy ... 423-614-8200 ... 470 A
cthompson@leeuniversity.edu
THOMPSON, Adelia, P ... 757-594-8759 ... 517 I
adelia.thompson@cnu.edu
THOMPSON, Al ... 509-359-2466 ... 533 D
athompson@ewu.edu
THOMPSON, Al ... 715-346-2481 ... 552 B
THOMPSON, Alan ... 406-444-0835 ... 295 C
thompsona@umhelena.edu
THOMPSON, Allan ... 903-923-2175 ... 486 D
athompson@etbu.edu
THOMPSON, Allison, L ... 318-342-6917 ... 216 E
althompson@ulm.edu
THOMPSON, Alton ... 302-857-6100 ... 95 F
athompson@desu.edu
THOMPSON, Amber ... 719-336-1592 ... 85 K
amber.thompson@lamarcc.edu
THOMPSON, Amber ... 828-286-3636 ... 371 A
athompson@isothermal.edu
THOMPSON, Amy ... 631-687-5713 ... 349 B
althompson@sjcny.edu
THOMPSON, Amy ... 718-940-5713 ... 349 A
althompson@sjcny.edu
THOMPSON, Amy ... 229-732-5938 ... 124 C
amythompson@andrewcollege.edu
THOMPSON, Amy, S ... 440-964-4224 ... 393 E
asthomps@kent.edu
THOMPSON, Andrew ... 605-455-6049 ... 464 H
athompson@olc.edu
THOMPSON, Ann ... 270-706-8444 ... 201 F
ann.thompson@kctcs.edu
THOMPSON, Ann, E ... 508-849-3342 ... 230 C
athompson@annamaria.edu
THOMPSON, Anne ... 912-344-2589 ... 124 E
anne.thompson@armstrong.edu
THOMPSON, Annette ... 210-283-5091 ... 503 F
athompson@uiwtx.edu
THOMPSON, Anthony ... 804-257-5837 ... 529 D
athompson@vuu.edu
THOMPSON, Barbara, A ... 260-359-4049 ... 172 K
bthompson@huntington.edu
THOMPSON, Berte ... 717-766-2511 ... 436 D
bthompso@messiah.edu
THOMPSON, Beth ... 423-614-8357 ... 470 A
bthompson@leeuniversity.edu
THOMPSON, Beth ... 903-434-8106 ... 491 D
bthompson@ntcc.edu
THOMPSON, Bianca ... 973-972-8514 ... 316 H
thompsbm@umdnj.edu
THOMPSON, Bianca ... 973-972-8551 ... 317 B
thompsbm@umdnj.edu
THOMPSON, Bill ... 919-735-5151 ... 374 F
billt@waynecc.edu
THOMPSON, Bill, T ... 919-735-5151 ... 374 F
billt@waynecc.edu
THOMPSON, Bob ... 405-912-9453 ... 408 D
bthompson@hc.edu
THOMPSON, Bobby, W ... 540-365-4233 ... 518 J
bthompson@ferrum.edu
THOMPSON, Bradley ... 901-751-8453 ... 471 D
bthompson@mabts.edu
THOMPSON, Brenda ... 512-863-1290 ... 495 G
THOMPSON, Brenda, L ... 812-888-4125 ... 181 B
bthompson@vinu.edu
THOMPSON, Brenda, S ... 304-293-3837 ... 544 E
brenda.thompson@mail.wvu.edu
THOMPSON, Brian, L ... 904-819-6249 ... 107 A
bthompson@flagler.edu
THOMPSON, C. Marty ... 405-271-2673 ... 413 D
marty-thompson@ouhsc.edu
THOMPSON, Carey ... 901-843-3000 ... 472 I
THOMPSON, Carly ... 863-686-1444 ... 105 I
cthompso@cci.edu
THOMPSON, Carlyle ... 718-270-4987 ... 328 D
carlyle@mec.cuny.edu
THOMPSON, Carmela ... 716-878-4017 ... 353 A
thompsc@buffalostate.edu
THOMPSON, Caro ... 802-322-1644 ... 513 C
caro.thompson@goddard.edu
THOMPSON, Carolyn, J ... 505-277-2123 ... 321 C
cjtc@unm.edu
THOMPSON, Charles ... 404-270-2918 ... 128 G
cthompson1@devry.edu
THOMPSON, Charles, G ... 413-542-2221 ... 230 A
cgthompson@amherst.edu
THOMPSON, Charles, S ... 423-652-4742 ... 469 L
csthomps@king.edu
THOMPSON, Cheryl ... 402-559-2792 ... 301 A
cbthompson@unmc.edu
THOMPSON,
Christopher, J ... 651-962-5771 ... 272 E
cjthompson@stthomas.edu
THOMPSON, Cindy ... 651-675-4700 ... 264 H
cthompson@msp.chefs.edu
THOMPSON, Clare, A ... 563-333-6293 ... 188 D
ThompsonClareA@sau.edu
THOMPSON, Claudette ... 305-386-9900 ... 105 E
cthompson@cci.edu
THOMPSON, Cole, P ... 970-207-4500 ... 89 A
THOMPSON, Corinne, B ... 802-656-7898 ... 514 F
corinne.thompson@uvm.edu
THOMPSON, Cory ... 404-297-9522 ... 128 B
thompsonc@dekalbtech.edu
THOMPSON, Craig ... 646-888-6639 ... 339 E
cthompson@mskcc.org
THOMPSON, Cynthia ... 217-206-7715 ... 167 A
thompson.cynthia@uis.edu
THOMPSON, Daniel, J ... 651-290-6362 ... 273 B
dan.thompson@wmitchell.edu
THOMPSON, Darci ... 405-425-5065 ... 409 E
darci.thompson@oc.edu
THOMPSON, Darlene ... 334-214-4807 ... 2 G
darlene.thompson@cv.edu
THOMPSON, Dave ... 714-546-7600 ... 40 J
dthompson@coastline.edu
THOMPSON, Dave ... 417-777-5062 ... 279 E
dthompson@texascountytech.edu
THOMPSON, David ... 304-424-8303 ... 545 B
dave.thompson@mail.wvu.edu
THOMPSON, David ... 434-961-5447 ... 527 F
dthompson@pvcc.edu
THOMPSON, Dawn ... 503-777-7500 ... 420 A
dthomp@reed.edu
THOMPSON, Dawn, M ... 302-831-8939 ... 96 F
dawnt@udel.edu
THOMPSON, Debbi, N ... 864-597-4208 ... 463 F
thompsondn@wofford.edu
THOMPSON, Deborah ... 864-833-8278 ... 460 E
dthompson@presby.edu
THOMPSON, Deborah, L ... 269-337-7318 ... 253 F
Debbie.Roberts@kzoo.edu
THOMPSON, Debra ... 480-731-8510 ... 15 F
debra.thompson@domail.maricopa.edu
THOMPSON, Delores ... 575-492-2519 ... 319 B
dthompson@nmjc.edu
THOMPSON, Dennis, F ... 580-774-3764 ... 412 F
dennis.thompson@swosu.edu
THOMPSON, Desiree ... 207-454-1020 ... 219 B
dthompson@wccc.me.edu
THOMPSON, Destiny, S ... 512-505-3037 ... 488 B
dsthompson@htu.edu
THOMPSON, Devon, N ... 903-593-8311 ... 499 A
dthompson@texascollege.edu
THOMPSON, Diane ... 518-587-2100 ... 355 F
diane.thompson@esc.edu
THOMPSON, Dick ... 207-973-3224 ... 219 I
dick.thompson@maine.edu
THOMPSON, Donovan ... 718-289-5796 ... 326 F
donovan.thompson@bcc.cuny.edu
THOMPSON, Dwayne, E ... 714-895-8727 ... 41 A
dthompson@gwc.cccd.edu
THOMPSON, E. Maria ... 607-436-2517 ... 353 E
thompsem@oneonta.edu
THOMPSON, Edward, J ... 516-678-5000 ... 341 F
ethompson@molloy.edu
THOMPSON, Eichelle ... 414-256-1210 ... 549 A
thompsoe@mtmary.edu
THOMPSON, Eileen ... 617-879-2413 ... 246 F
ethompson@wheelock.edu
THOMPSON, Emily ... 816-604-3022 ... 285 H
emily.thompson@mcckc.edu
THOMPSON, Eric ... 617-369-3486 ... 244 G
ethompson@smfa.edu
THOMPSON, Fannie, G ... 301-736-3631 ... 224 B
fannie.thompson@msbbcs.edu
THOMPSON, Fred ... 615-460-6670 ... 467 B
fred.thompson@belmont.edu
THOMPSON, Gary ... 701-845-7197 ... 382 A
gary.thompson@vcsu.edu
THOMPSON, Gary ... 330-263-2165 ... 388 E
gthompson@wooster.edu
THOMPSON, Gary, B ... 518-783-2550 ... 350 I
thompson@siena.edu
THOMPSON, III,
George, R ... 803-938-3839 ... 462 F
bobt@uscsumter.edu
THOMPSON, Greg ... 843-349-5247 ... 458 G
greg.thompson@hgtc.edu
THOMPSON, Greg ... 407-366-9493 ... 115 I
gthompson@rts.edu
THOMPSON, Greg ... 513-861-6400 ... 402 I
greg.thompson@myunion.edu
THOMPSON, Gregory ... 850-644-5260 ... 119 C
gwthompson@fsu.edu
THOMPSON, Gregory ... 843-349-5247 ... 458 G
gregory.thompson@hgtc.edu
THOMPSON, III,
H. Lawrence ... 724-266-3838 ... 448 G
lthompson@tsm.edu
THOMPSON, Helen ... 330-287-1231 ... 399 A
thompson.959@osu.edu
THOMPSON, Herbert ... 386-481-2672 ... 101 I
thompsoh@cookman.edu
THOMPSON, Howard ... 563-425-5307 ... 189 C
thompsonh@uiu.edu
THOMPSON, Jack ... 479-619-4140 ... 22 H
jthompson19@nwacc.edu
THOMPSON, James ... 301-736-3631 ... 224 B
james.thompson@msbbcs.edu
THOMPSON, James, E ... 573-882-4378 ... 291 D
thompsonje@missouri.edu
THOMPSON, James, P ... 865-974-7262 ... 477 B
jthompson@utk.edu
THOMPSON, James, V ... 916-563-3276 ... 56 A
thompsj@arc.losrios.edu
THOMPSON, Jane, W ... 412-624-6576 ... 449 A
jthompson@bc.pitt.edu
THOMPSON, Janet ... 908-526-1200 ... 313 E
jthompso@raritanval.edu
THOMPSON, Janet, K ... 507-786-8254 ... 271 H
thompsjk@stolaf.edu
THOMPSON, Jean-Noel ... 325-674-6802 ... 478 H
jnthompson@acu.edu
THOMPSON, Jeff, S ... 256-824-2605 ... 9 A
jeff.thompson@uah.edu
THOMPSON, Jeffrey, M ... 909-537-5315 ... 36 A
jthompso@csusb.edu
THOMPSON, Jeffrey, S ... 775-784-4591 ... 303 A
thompson@physics.unr.edu
THOMPSON, Jennifer ... 212-280-1317 ... 358 G
jthompson@uts.columbia.edu
THOMPSON, Jennifer ... 815-921-4272 ... 162 F
j.thompson@rockvalleycollege.edu
THOMPSON, Jeremy ... 718-951-5882 ... 326 G
JeremyThompson@brooklyn.cuny.edu

THRANE, Linda .... 713-348-6281.... 492 J
thrane@rice.edu
THRASHER, Barbara, S ...... 434-947-8143.... 522 E
bthrasher@randolphcollege.edu
THRASHER, James, T .... 724-458-2200.... 430 B
jtthrasher@gcc.edu
THRASHER, Stephanie .... 405-945-7799.... 411 F
stephaniet@plattcollege.org
THRIFT, Jerry, L .... 910-755-7381.... 368 C
thriftj@brunswickcc.edu
THRO, William, E .... 757-594-7571.... 517 I
wthro@cnu.edu
THROCKMORTON, Julie .... 724-503-1001.... 451 A
jthrockmorton@washjeff.edu
THROENER, Mary, E .... 660-562-1127.... 287 E
mthroen@nwmissouri.edu
THROGMORTON, Daniel ... 916-563-3206..... 55 J
throgd@losrios.edu
THRONE, James .... 954-492-5353.... 102 J
jthrone@citycollege.edu
THRONEBERRY, Angela .... 575-646-2431.... 319 D
athroneb@nmsu.edu
THRONEBURG, Dennis ...... 217-234-5296.... 155 H
dthroneb@lakeland.cc.il.us
THROOP, Elizabeth .... 712-749-2422.... 182 G
throope@bvu.edu
THROOP, William, M .... 802-287-8214.... 513 D
throopw@greenmtn.edu
THROWER, Linda .... 619-482-6325...... 71 C
lthrower@swccd.edu
THROWER, Minda .... 816-501-4057.... 288 D
minda.thrower@rockhurst.edu
THROWER, Raymond, H ..... 507-933-8809.... 264 B
rthrower@gustavus.edu
THRUMAN, Michelle .... 815-588-3575.... 152 A
michelle.thruman@highland.edu
THRUSH, Claudia .... 570-389-4012.... 441 F
cthrush@bloomu.edu
THUHA, Permy, K .... 601-877-6118.... 273 C
pthuha@alcorn.edu
THULIN, Frederick .... 847-679-3135.... 155 D
fthulin@ksi.edu
THUM, Dennis, L .... 605-331-6777.... 466 D
dennis.thum@usiouxfalls.edu
THURBER, John, P .... 609-984-1155.... 316 A
jthurber@tesc.edu
THURBER, Mike .... 918-587-6789.... 413 A
mthurber@twsweld.com
THURLER, Kimberly, M ...... 617-627-3175.... 245 F
kim.thurler@tufts.edu
THURLOW, III, George ..... 805-893-4799...... 74 F
george.thurlow@ia.ucsb.edu
THURLOW, Hugh .... 303-753-6046...... 87 F
hthurlow@rmcad.edu
THURLOW, Kim .... 765-966-2656.... 176 F
kthurlow@ivytech.edu
THURMAN, Blake .... 716-839-8228.... 331 G
bthurman@daemen.edu
THURMAN, Constance .... 309-341-5251.... 146 A
cthurman@sandburg.edu
THURMAN, Kerri, L .... 217-443-8850.... 148 E
kthurman@dacc.edu
THURMAN, Laurence .... 951-372-7000...... 64 A
THURMAN, Lynne, F .... 580-774-3267.... 412 F
lynne.thurman@swosu.edu
THURMAN, Mike .... 270-831-9790.... 201 I
mike.thurman@kctcs.edu
THURMAN, Todd, A .... 580-774-3068.... 412 F
todd.thurman@swosu.edu
THURMER, Karen .... 276-326-4461.... 516 I
kthurmer@bluefield.edu
THURMOND, Bradley .... 765-459-0561.... 176 A
bthurmond@ivytech.edu
THURMOND, Wade .... 636-651-1600.... 289 I
wthurmond@sbc-fenton.com
THURSBY, Randall .... 701-231-7922.... 381 C
randall.thursby@ndus.edu
THURSTON, Cathryn, Q ..... 202-231-4011.... 557 G
cathryn.thurston@dia.mil
THURSTON, Maureen .... 720-279-8992...... 84 J
mthurston@religiousscience.org
THURSTON, William .... 919-546-8457.... 376 D
wthursto@shawu.edu
THURY, Spencer .... 641-673-1088.... 189 I
thurys@wmpenn.edu
THWEATT, Herbert .... 684-699-4834.... 558 I
h.thweatt@amsamoa.edu
THYEN, Gary, L .... 651-962-6107.... 272 E
glthyen@stthomas.edu
THYGESON, William .... 215-503-8189.... 448 B
william.thygeson@jefferson.edu
THYREEN, Timothy, R .... 724-627-8191.... 451 B
thyreen@waynesburg.edu
TIAGA, Sally .... 760-776-7441...... 41 H
stiaga@collegeofthedesert.edu
TIBBETTS, John .... 518-629-4552.... 336 C
j.tibbetts@hvcc.edu
TICE, Elizabeth .... 858-513-9240.... 181 G
elizabeth.tice@ashford.edu
TICE, Gene, E .... 270-684-9797.... 207 C
gene.tice@wku.edu
TICE, Jared .... 252-399-6372.... 362 A
jtice@barton.edu
TICE, William .... 312-942-6584.... 163 B
bill_h_tice@rush.edu
TICHENOR, Kristin, R .... 508-831-5286.... 247 B
tichenor@wpi.edu
TICK, Michael .... 859-257-1701.... 206 H
TICKEL, Kirby .... 580-628-6789.... 409 B
kirby.tickel@north-ok.edu
TIDEMANN, Gail .... 605-688-4154.... 466 B
gail.tidemann@sdstate.edu
TIDWELL, Jerry .... 731-661-5496.... 476 G
tidwell@uu.edu
TIDWELL, Michael .... 570-389-4745.... 441 F
mtidwell@bloomu.edu
TIEDE, Lori .... 775-445-3259.... 303 B
tiedel@wnc.edu
TIEDEMAN, Angie .... 303-340-7524...... 83 E
TIEDEMANN, Andrew .... 617-824-8540.... 234 D
andrew_tiedemann@emerson.edu
TIEDEMANN, Elizabeth ...... 724-836-7182.... 449 C
tiedeman@pitt.edu
TIEDT, Penny .... 608-785-6501.... 551 B
tiedt.penn@uwlax.edu
TIEFENTHALER, Jill .... 719-389-6748...... 81 L
president@coloradocollege.edu
TIELL, Bonnie .... 419-448-3261.... 402 E
btiell@tiffin.edu
TIEMANN, Kathleen .... 701-777-2011.... 381 D
kathleen.tiemann@as.und.edu
TIEMEIER, Thomas, L .... 563-884-5653.... 188 C
tom.tiemeier@palmer.edu
TIEMEIER, Thomas, L .... 563-884-5653...... 60 L
tom.tiemeier@palmer.edu
TIEMEIER, Thomas, L .... 563-884-5653.... 114 E
tom.tiemeier@palmer.edu
TIEN, Anita .... 617-552-0753.... 232 D
anita.tien.1@bc.edu
TIEN, James, M .... 305-284-6035.... 122 F
jmtien@miami.edu
TIEN, Norman, C .... 216-368-3227.... 386 E
norman.tien@case.edu
TIENOU, Tite .... 847-317-8086.... 166 B
tedsdean@tiu.edu
TIERCE, Joan .... 662-472-2312.... 274 F
jtierce@holmescc.edu
TIERNAN, Bernadette .... 973-720-2463.... 317 D
tiernanb@wpunj.edu
TIERNEY, Deborah, J .... 515-961-1699.... 188 F
deb.tierney@simpson.edu
TIERNEY, JoAnn .... 413-662-5421.... 238 F
j.tierney@mcla.edu
TIERNEY, Kathleen .... 610-526-5364.... 423 C
ktierney01@brynmawr.edu
TIERNEY, Kevin .... 315-279-5228.... 337 K
ktierney@mail.keuka.edu
TIERNEY, RN, Margaret, A 718-390-4447.... 348 G
tierneym@stjohns.edu
TIERNO, Mark, J .... 315-655-7116.... 325 I
mtierno@cazenovia.edu
TIERNO, Scott .... 603-668-2211.... 306 B
s.tierno@snhu.edu
TIETJE, Brian .... 805-756-7434...... 33 F
btietje@calpoly.edu
TIETJEN, David .... 801-440-0886.... 509 B
dtietjenr@argosy.edu
TIETZ, Leah Jo .... 406-444-6570.... 294 J
ltietz@montana.edu
TIFFANY, David, M .... 716-673-3321.... 352 A
david.tiffany@fredonia.edu
TIFFANY, Janice .... 641-784-5120.... 184 H
tiffany@graceland.edu
TIFFIN, Doug .... 972-708-7338.... 486 I
gial_dean-academic@gial.edu
TIFFIN, Douglas, R .... 972-708-7338.... 486 I
doug.tiffin@gial.edu
TIFFNEY, Bruce, H .... 805-893-3827...... 74 F
bruce.tiffney@ccs.ucsb.edu
TIFFT, Thomas, W .... 440-943-7600.... 401 G
twt@dioceseofcleveland.org
TIGHE, Kevin .... 434-239-5222.... 521 D
TIGHE, Peter .... 718-262-2351.... 329 B
ptighe@york.cuny.edu
TIGNOR, Buddy .... 828-627-4576.... 370 G
mtignor@haywood.edu
TIGNOR, Marlene .... 307-778-1104.... 556 B
mtignor@lccc.wy.edu
TIGUE, Patrick .... 413-755-4482.... 241 E
tigue@stcc.edu
TIKHON, Bishop .... 570-561-1818.... 446 D
bptikhon@stots.edu
TILDEN, Kevin .... 949-214-3127...... 42 K
kevin.tilden@cui.edu
TILDEN, Marsha, A .... 740-368-3163.... 400 F
matilden@owu.edu
TILFORD, Joseph .... 336-770-3214.... 379 D
tilford@uncsa.edu
TILGHMAN, Norman, G .... 410-651-6458.... 227 E
ngtilghman@umes.edu
TILGHMAN, Patricia, E ...... 410-651-6449.... 227 E
petilghman@umes.edu
TILGHMAN, Rochelle .... 314-340-3335.... 282 I
tilghman@hssu.edu
TILGHMAN, Shirley, M .... 609-258-6100.... 313 A
smt@princeton.edu
TILL, Ellen, P .... 850-474-2080.... 121 C
etill@uwf.edu
TILL, Kimberly, B .... 214-841-3459.... 485 E
ktill@dts.edu
TILL, Stacey .... 602-331-7500...... 12 D
TILLAR, JR., Thomas, C ..... 540-231-6285.... 529 B
ttillar@vt.edu
TILLARD, Bill .... 386-506-4433.... 103 J
tillarw@DaytonaState.edu
TILLBERG, Rebecca .... 310-287-4361...... 55 F
tillberw@wlac.edu
TILLER, Donzelle .... 610-399-2427.... 441 H
dtiller@cheyney.edu
TILLER, Matt .... 615-966-6190.... 470 D
matt.tiller@lipscomb.edu
TILLERY, Carmen .... 812-237-3888.... 173 A
carmen.tillery@indstate.edu
TILLERY, Frank .... 972-438-6932.... 492 C
ftillery@parkercc.edu
TILLERY, Marcus, D .... 706-821-8255.... 135 C
mtillery@paine.edu
TILLERY, Mariann, W .... 336-841-9286.... 365 A
mtillery@highpoint.edu
TILLETT, Guy .... 605-394-4976.... 464 G
gtillett@national.edu
TILLETT, Kerry .... 609-771-3139.... 308 G
thompsok@tcnj.edu
TILLETT, Marcie .... 270-686-4216.... 198 G
marcie.tillett@brescia.edu
TILLEY, Amy .... 479-394-7622...... 23 E
atilley@rmcc.edu
TILLEY, Jeff .... 979-830-4129.... 482 A
jeff.tilley@blinn.edu
TILLEY, Neil .... 828-689-1306.... 366 F
ntilley@mhc.edu
TILLINGHAST, David, H .... 508-531-1380.... 238 B
dtillinghast@bridgew.edu
TILLMAN, Henry .... 225-771-5497.... 214 G
henry_tillman@sus.edu
TILLMAN, Ivy .... 706-721-1379.... 130 B
itillman@georgiahealth.edu
TILLMAN, Joseph, L .... 910-296-2506.... 371 B
jtillman@jamessprunt.edu
TILLMAN, Keith .... 815-280-2385.... 154 H
ktillman@jjc.edu
TILLMAN, Krista .... 704-337-2273.... 375 G
tillmank@queens.edu
TILLMAN, Rosalyn, P .... 865-329-3101.... 475 F
rtillman@pstcc.edu
TILLMAN, JR., Walter, T ... 225-771-4680.... 214 G
walter_tillman@subr.edu
TILLOTSON, O.CARM.,
Frederick, J .... 202-541-5228...... 99 G
ftillotson@wtu.edu
TILLOTSON, Jeanette .... 607-778-5195.... 324 G
tillotson_j@sunybroome.edu
TILLQUIST, John .... 951-571-6471...... 64 B
john.tillquist@rcc.edu
TILMA, Lisa .... 316-295-5525.... 192 H
lisa_tilma@friends.edu
TILOT, Nicole .... 262-243-5700.... 546 I
nicole.tilot@cuw.edu
TILSON, E. Vincent .... 704-233-8115.... 380 D
tilson@wingate.edu
TILTON, Brent .... 715-232-2346.... 552 C
tiltonb@uwstout.edu
TILTON, James .... 401-863-2721.... 452 J
james_tilton@brown.edu
TILTON, Roger, L .... 803-754-4100.... 457 D
TIMBERLAKE, Dan .... 208-426-1603.... 142 F
dantimberlake@boisestate.edu
TIMBERLAKE, Gregory .... 419-755-4740.... 397 B
gtimberlake@ncstatecollege.edu
TIMKO, Michael, A .... 724-503-1001.... 451 A
mtimko@washjeff.edu
TIMLIN, Laynee, H .... 757-455-3366.... 529 F
etimlin@vwc.edu
TIMMANN, Claudia .... 928-757-0802...... 16 G
ctimmann@mohave.edu
TIMMANN, David .... 610-436-2984.... 443 F
dtimmann@wcupa.edu
TIMMER, Amy .... 517-371-5140.... 259 B
timmera@cooley.edu
TIMMER, JR., James .... 616-526-6037.... 249 E
jrt3@calvin.edu
TIMMERMAN, Annemarie .. 828-627-4608.... 370 G
atimmerman@haywood.edu
TIMMERMAN, David, M ...... 309-457-2325.... 158 G
dtimmerman@monm.edu
TIMMERMANS, Steven .... 708-239-4791.... 165 I
steven.timmermans@trnty.edu
TIMMONS, George .... 518-464-8830.... 333 F
gtimmons@excelsior.edu
TIMMONS, Joseph, F .... 918-631-2710.... 413 F
joseph-timmons@utulsa.edu
TIMMONS, Keona .... 843-746-5100...... 99 D
TIMMONS, Ray .... 803-593-9231.... 455 A
timmons@atc.edu
TIMMONS, Susan .... 864-941-8307.... 460 D
timmons.s@ptc.edu
TIMMONS, Tim .... 708-239-4787.... 165 I
tim.timmons@trnty.edu
TIMMONS, Tom .... 847-969-2820.... 154 A
TIMMS, Lindsay .... 478-757-5233.... 139 A
ltimms@wesleyancollege.edu
TIMMS, Luis .... 415-869-2900.... 236 B
lius.timms@hult.edu
TIMPANO, Anne .... 540-654-1013.... 524 H
atimpano@umw.edu
TIMPSON, Brigham, J .... 312-341-2322.... 162 I
btimpson@roosevelt.edu
TIMS, Deana .... 870-512-7811...... 20 F
deana_tims@asun.edu
TIMS, Ray, L .... 919-532-5523.... 374 E
rltims@waketech.edu
TINAJERO, Josefina, V .... 915-747-5572.... 505 E
tinajero@utep.edu
TINANT, Jason .... 605-455-6001.... 464 H
jtinant@olc.edu
TINCHER, Steve .... 765-966-2656.... 176 F
stincher@ivytech.edu
TINCHER-LADNER, Lynn ...... 601-928-6383.... 275 G
lynn.tincher-ladner@mgccc.edu
TINDALL, Amanda .... 502-212-2255.... 202 B
amanda.tindall@kctcs.edu
TINDALL, David, W .... 206-281-2982.... 537 D
dtindall@spu.edu
TINDALL, Michelle .... 804-706-5228.... 526 G
mtindall@jtcc.edu
TINDELL, Tyrone .... 703-729-8800...... 99 D
TINEBRA, Karen .... 973-877-3053.... 310 A
tinebra@essex.edu
TINEBRA, Vincent .... 502-447-7634.... 205 B
TINES, Charles .... 361-698-1561.... 485 F
ctines@delmar.edu
TING, John .... 978-934-2576.... 237 F
john_ting@uml.edu
TINGEY, Jeff .... 208-282-4064.... 143 D
tingjeff@isu.edu
TINGEY, Kent, M .... 208-282-3198.... 143 D
tingkent@isu.edu
TINGLE, Caroline, D .... 386-312-4270.... 116 D
carolinetingle@sjrstate.edu
TINGLEFF, Brian, P .... 515-643-6663.... 187 C
btingleff@mercydesmoines.org
TINGSON-GATUZ, Connie .. 734-432-5883.... 254 G
ctingson-gatuz@madonna.edu
TINK, Fletcher, L .... 816-960-2008.... 280 B
ftink@cityvision.edu
TINKER, Nancy .... 860-465-5348...... 91 H
tinkern@easternct.edu
TINKEY, Jim .... 412-536-1011.... 432 F
jim.tinkey@laroche.edu
TINKHAM, Brenda, S .... 252-398-6304.... 363 E
tinkhb@chowan.edu
TINSLEY, Cheryl, K .... 828-884-8264.... 362 D
tinsleck@brevard.edu
TINSLEY, Harold .... 410-337-6170.... 222 I
htinsley@goucher.edu
TINSLEY, Joseph .... 706-821-8320.... 135 C
jtinsley@paine.edu
TINSLEY, Marie .... 718-473-8700.... 328 E
mtinsley@citytech.cuny.edu
TINTERA, Judi, E .... 321-674-6303.... 108 E
jtintera@fit.edu
TIO, Adrian .... 508-999-9295.... 237 E
atio@umassd.edu
TIONGSON, Lenie .... 703-821-8570.... 524 D
ltiongson@stratford.edu
TIPMORE, Barbara .... 270-686-4530.... 202 E
barbara.tipmore@kctcs.edu
TIPPENS, Darryl .... 310-506-4261...... 61 G
darryl.tippens@pepperdine.edu
TIPPETT, Bryan .... 623-935-8030...... 15 H
bryan.tippett@estrellamountain.edu
TIPPEY, Dawn .... 859-858-2325.... 198 A
TIPPIN, Peggy .... 270-444-9676.... 200 A
ptippin@daymarcolleg.edu
TIPPIN, Rick .... 270-534-3216.... 203 B
rick.tippin@kctcs.edu
TIPPS, David .... 910-392-4660.... 367 B
dtipps@miller-motte.com
TIPPS, Donna, F .... 256-765-4231........ 9 D
dftipps@una.edu
TIPPS, Jane .... 615-898-2670.... 473 F
jtipps@mtsu.edu
TIPS, Jean .... 817-735-5031.... 504 C
jtips@hsc.unt.edu
TIPTON, Alan .... 361-593-2244.... 498 A
a-tipton@tamuk.edu
TIPTON, Alzada .... 630-617-3063.... 150 F
tiptona@elmhurst.edu
TIPTON, Carol .... 361-593-3528.... 498 A
c-tipton@tamuk.edu
TIPTON, Joellen, N .... 936-294-1808.... 501 A
joellen@shsu.edu
TIPTON, Melanie, K .... 918-610-8303.... 411 D
melanie.tipton@ptstulsa.edu
TIPTON-ROGERS, Donna ...... 828-835-4204.... 374 C
dtipton@tricounty.edu
TIRADO, Betty, M .... 607-436-2081.... 353 E
tiradoem@oneonta.edu
TIRONE, Shannon .... 330-941-3732.... 406 F
stirone@ysu.edu
TIRPAK, Anne, M .... 773-371-5417.... 146 B
atirpak@ctu.edu

TONEY, Rosie ... 501-372-6883 ... 19 F
rosie.toney@arkansasbaptist.edu

TONG, Diep ... 704-330-6859 ... 369 A
diep.tong@cpcc.edu

TONG, Vincent, P ... 203-285-2415 ... 90 A
vtong@gwcc.commnet.edu

TONI, Keith ... 508-678-2811 ... 239 F
keith.toni@bristolcc.edu

TONIONI, Renee ... 630-466-7900 ... 167 G
rtonioni@waubonsee.edu

TONJES, Janet ... 402-643-7290 ... 297 F
janet.tonjes@cune.edu

TONKINSON, John, P ... 212-924-5900 ... 357 A
cfo@swedishinstitute.edu

TONN, Mike ... 620-665-3382 ... 193 F
tonnm@hutchcc.edu

TONN, Sheri, J ... 253-535-7121 ... 535 K
tonnsj@plu.edu

TONN BOOKER, Paulette, L ... 507-344-7840 ... 261 H
ptbooker@blc.edu

TONNER, Shawn ... 706-864-1514 ... 134 D
sctonner@northgeorgia.edu

TONNESON, Jennifer ... 704-219-7165 ... 373 C
jennifer.tonneson@rccc.edu

TONNESON, Julie, A ... 612-625-4517 ... 272 D
tonne001@umn.edu

TONREY, Donna, A ... 215-991-3726 ... 432 G
tonrey@lasalle.edu

TOOEY, Mary, J ... 410-706-2693 ... 227 C
mjtooey@hshsl.umaryland.edu

TOOHEY, Katherine, M ... 413-205-3352 ... 229 G
tina.toohey@aic.edu

TOOKE-RAWLINS, Dixie ... 540-231-4000 ... 518 H

TOOLE, Genesis ... 602-285-7230 ... 16 B

TOOLE, Lisa ... 570-702-8903 ... 431 K
ltoole@johnson.edu

TOOLE, Raymond, L ... 610-359-5330 ... 426 G
rtoole@dccc.edu

TOOLEY, Elaine ... 585-567-9211 ... 336 B
elaine.tooley@houghton.edu

TOOLEY, Liz ... 406-657-1680 ... 295 F
ltooley@msubillings.edu

TOOLIN, Cynthia ... 860-632-3033 ... 92 E
registrar@holyapostles.edu

TOOMAJIAN, JR., Charles, R ... 413-597-4286 ... 246 G
charles.r.toomajian@williams.edu

TOOMBS, Jean ... 216-791-5000 ... 388 B
jst4@case.edu

TOOMEY, Elaine ... 617-323-6662 ... 242 C
elaine_toomey@mspp.edu

TOOMEY, Kimberly ... 732-224-2268 ... 308 B
ktoomey@brookdalecc.edu

TOOMEY, Marcia, D ... 978-232-2060 ... 234 F
mtoomey@endicott.edu

TOOMEY, Richard ... 408-554-4966 ... 68 C
rtoomey@scu.edu

TOOMEY, Richard, J ... 812-237-2510 ... 173 A
richard.toomey@indstate.edu

TOON, Rhonda ... 678-359-5124 ... 131 D
rhondat@gdn.edu

TOONE, Danette ... 785-243-1435 ... 191 H
dtoone@cloud.edu

TOOREDMAN, Kathryn ... 312-899-9900 ... 144 G
ktooredman@argosy.edu

TOOTE, Christopher ... 903-769-5712 ... 488 M
christopher_toote@jarvis.edu

TOOTE, Christopher ... 903-769-5775 ... 488 M
christopher_toote@jarvis.edu

TOOTHMAN, Kristin ... 330-337-4226 ... 393 H
ktoothman@kent.edu

TOOTOONCHI, Ahmad ... 301-687-4019 ... 228 C
tootoonchi@frostburg.edu

TOOZE, John ... 212-327-8000 ... 347 H
john.tooze@rockefeller.edu

TOPHAM, Susan ... 619-660-4302 ... 48 J
susan.topham@gcccd.edu

TOPLIFF, Michael, L ... 575-835-5735 ... 319 A
mtopliff@nmt.edu

TOPP, Joelle ... 517-371-5140 ... 259 B
toppj@cooley.edu

TOPPE, Michele ... 503-725-4422 ... 418 G
toppem@pdx.edu

TOPPER, David ... 717-477-1124 ... 443 D
datopp@ship.edu

TOPPER, Janet ... 610-341-5955 ... 428 D
jtopper@eastern.edu

TOPPER, Maria, L ... 301-447-5211 ... 225 A
mtopper@msmary.edu

TOPPING, Ann, V ... 585-262-1676 ... 341 H
atopping@monroecc.edu

TOPPING, Scott ... 269-782-1249 ... 258 E
stopping@swmich.edu

TOPPING, Thomas, E ... 585-785-1209 ... 334 A
toppinte@flcc.edu

TOPPING, W. Frank ... 205-929-1448 ... 5 H
wftopping@miles.edu

TOPPLE, Dianne ... 518-828-4181 ... 330 E
dianne.topple@sunycgcc.edu

TOPSHE, Joyce ... 860-685-3757 ... 95 C
jtopshe@wesleyan.edu

TORABI, Mo ... 812-855-4808 ... 173 C
torabi@indiana.edu

TORAN, Peter ... 410-837-5582 ... 229 A
ptoran@ubalt.edu

TORBERT, Edgar, C ... 404-413-2574 ... 131 C
etorbert@gsu.edu

TORBORG-VERMILYEA, Kate ... 843-208-8115 ... 462 C
ktorgorg@uscb.edu

TORCHIA, Richard ... 215-572-2131 ... 422 B
torchia@arcadia.edu

TORDENTI, Laura ... 860-832-1605 ... 91 G
tordentilau@ccsu.edu

TORELL, Kurt, C ... 412-675-9052 ... 439 H
kct10@psu.edu

TORELLO, Tom ... 212-346-1200 ... 345 F
ttorello@pace.edu

TORES, Evelyn ... 787-264-1912 ... 563 G
evetores@sg.inter.edu

TORGERSEN, Arlene ... 360-538-4066 ... 534 B
atorgers@ghc.edu

TORGERSON, Jane ... 817-257-7940 ... 498 F
j.torgerson@tcu.edu

TORGERSON, Richard, L ... 563-387-1001 ... 187 A
rtorgers@luther.edu

TORGERSON, Roberta ... 218-879-0803 ... 266 F
roberta@fdltcc.edu

TORGERSON, Tad, H ... 406-874-6181 ... 294 H
torgerson@milescc.edu

TORICK, Marc ... 717-396-7833 ... 440 J
mtorick@pcad.edu

TORIGOE, Eileen ... 808-734-9575 ... 141 E
eileent@hawaii.edu

TORIMIRO, Frederic, B ... 540-365-4404 ... 518 J
ftorimiro@ferrum.edu

TORLINE, Donald, R ... 586-791-6610 ... 248 G
don.torline@baker.edu

TORMEY, Robert ... 714-816-0366 ... 72 I
rtormey@tuiu.edu

TORNAMBE, Matthew, J ... 716-375-7673 ... 348 C
mtornamb@sbu.edu

TORNO, Keith ... 616-222-3000 ... 254 A
ITDirector@kuyper.edu

TORNQUIST, Kristi ... 320-308-2022 ... 269 C

TORNQUIST, Kristi ... 605-688-5106 ... 466 B
kristi.tornquist@sdstate.edu

TORO, Elba ... 787-878-5475 ... 562 H
etoro@arecibo.inter.edu

TORO, Francisco ... 787-844-2318 ... 567 E
francisco.toro@upr.edu

TORO-RAMOS, Zulma ... 316-978-3400 ... 197 F
zulma.toro-ramos@wichita.edu

TORO-ZAPATA, Rogelio ... 787-264-1912 ... 563 G
rtoro@sg.inter.edu

TOROK, Cathy ... 301-387-3035 ... 222 H
cathy.torok@garrettcollege.edu

TOROK, Michael ... 209-588-5143 ... 80 A
torokm@yosemite.edu

TORPEY GARGANTA, Kathleen ... 508-678-2811 ... 239 F
kathy.garganta@bristolcc.edu

TORPEY GARGANTA, Kathy ... 508-678-2811 ... 239 F
kathy.garganta@bristolcc.edu

TORRANCE, Iain, R ... 609-497-7800 ... 312 F
president@ptsem.edu

TORRANCE, Peggy, L ... 218-299-3339 ... 263 B
torrance@cord.edu

TORRE, Patrick ... 203-932-7224 ... 95 B
ptorre@newhaven.edu

TORRE, Timothy ... 908-737-7140 ... 311 B
ttore@kean.edu

TORRENCE, Gary, G ... 314-367-8700 ... 288 I
gtorrence@stlcop.edu

TORRENCE, Michael, L ... 610-799-1089 ... 434 D
mtorrence@lccc.edu

TORRENS, Michael ... 435-797-0220 ... 511 B
michael.torrens@usu.edu

TORRENS-BURTON, Jonathan ... 507-284-3627 ... 262 F

TORRES, Ana, D ... 787-834-9595 ... 565 J
atorres@uaa.edu

TORRES, Angela ... 787-751-1912 ... 564 A
antorres@inter.edu

TORRES, Antoinette ... 215-895-0253 ... 427 G
at59@drexel.edu

TORRES, Aurelio ... 956-364-4222 ... 499 J
aurelio.torres@harlingen.tstc.edu

TORRES, Betania ... 863-667-5463 ... 118 A
btorres@seu.edu

TORRES, Briget ... 210-486-4177 ... 479 C
btorres@alamo.edu

TORRES, Carmen ... 787-864-2222 ... 563 D
cjtorres@inter.edu

TORRES, Carmen ... 787-892-4300 ... 563 G
cdtorres@sg.inter.edu

TORRES, Carmen ... 702-579-3531 ... 302 C
ctorres2@kaplan.edu

TORRES, Carolyn ... 510-574-1271 ... 44 D
ctorres@devry.edu

TORRES, Cathy ... 305-809-3250 ... 108 F
cathy.torres@fkcc.edu

TORRES, Christine ... 281-998-6150 ... 493 F
christine.torres@sjcd.edu

TORRES, Dario ... 787-265-3867 ... 567 C
d_torres@rumad.uprm.edu

TORRES, David ... 951-222-8000 ... 63 I
david.torres@rcc.edu

TORRES, David ... 951-222-8075 ... 64 B
david.torres@rcc.edu

TORRES, Eliseo, S ... 505-277-0952 ... 321 C
cheo@unm.edu

TORRES, Elsie, M ... 787-258-1501 ... 561 E
etorres@columbiaco.edu

TORRES, Ernie, M ... 803-536-7011 ... 460 G
etorres@scsu.edu

TORRES, Evelyn ... 787-882-2065 ... 565 I
directora_planificacion@unitecpr.net

TORRES, Frank ... 623-845-3904 ... 15 J
frank.torres@gcmail.maricopa.edu

TORRES, Gaile ... 406-395-4313 ... 296 G
gtorres@stonechild.edu

TORRES, Gema, C ... 787-279-1912 ... 563 B
gtorres@bayamon.inter.edu

TORRES, Helen ... 210-486-0393 ... 479 F
htorres@alamo.edu

TORRES, Jannett ... 787-780-0070 ... 560 F
jtorres@caribbean.edu

TORRES, Jocely ... 787-480-2464 ... 561 D
jtorres@sanjuancapital.com

TORRES, Jorge ... 787-894-2828 ... 568 A
jtorres@uprm.edu

TORRES, Jorge, A ... 787-257-7373 ... 565 E
jotorres@suagm.edu

TORRES, Jose, A ... 787-840-2575 ... 564 H

TORRES, Jose Arnaldo ... 787-881-1212 ... 565 A
joseatorres@email.pucpr.edu

TORRES, Juan, C ... 817-515-3055 ... 496 A
juan.torres@tccd.edu

TORRES, Julio ... 954-499-9815 ... 149 A
jtorres@devry.edu

TORRES, Kristen ... 480-644-0267 ... 18 A
ktorres@pmi.edu

TORRES, Lisabelle ... 954-446-6386 ... 100 E
ltorres@aiufl.edu

TORRES, Lourdes ... 718-518-4151 ... 327 D
ltorres@hostos.cuny.edu

TORRES, Luz ... 718-862-7313 ... 339 H
luz.torres@manhattan.edu

TORRES, Maribel ... 787-884-6000 ... 562 E
mtorres@icprjc.edu

TORRES, Mariela ... 212-752-1530 ... 338 C
mariela.torres@limcollege.edu

TORRES, Marlon ... 718-262-2916 ... 329 B
mtorres@york.cuny.edu

TORRES, Michael ... 516-678-5000 ... 341 F
mtorres@molly.edu

TORRES, Migdalia ... 787-257-7373 ... 565 E
ue_mtorres@suagm.edu

TORRES, Miguel ... 787-894-2828 ... 568 A

TORRES, Myrna ... 787-743-4041 ... 561 E
mtorres@columbiaco.edu

TORRES, Nitza, J ... 787-864-2222 ... 563 D
njtorres@inter.edu

TORRES, Norma ... 787-265-3811 ... 567 C
norma_t@dediego.uprm.edu

TORRES, Omar ... 661-362-3135 ... 41 G
omar.torres@canyons.edu

TORRES, Orlando ... 787-257-0000 ... 566 H
orlando.torres5@yahoo.com

TORRES, Rhonda ... 817-598-6212 ... 508 C
rtorres@wc.edu

TORRES, Roberto ... 787-832-4040 ... 567 C
torresr@uprm.edu

TORRES, Rosie ... 787-832-4040 ... 567 C
servmed@uprm.edu

TORRES, Wilmarie ... 787-743-4041 ... 561 E
wtorres@columbiaco.edu

TORRES-CLEMENTE, Sandra, M ... 787-250-0000 ... 566 D
sandra.torres6@upr.edu

TORRES DUGGAN, Nancy ... 626-396-2210 ... 29 G
nancy.torresduggan@artcenter.edu

TORRES-LUGO, Irmannette ... 787-738-2161 ... 567 A
irmannette.torres@upr.edu

TORRES-PETRILLI, Diana ... 212-678-8011 ... 337 G
dipetrilli@jtsa.edu

TORRES-SÁNCHEZ, Jorge, L ... 787-993-8965 ... 566 G
jorge.torres17@upr.edu

TORRES-SANTOS, Raymond ... 562-985-4376 ... 35 A
rtsantos@csulb.edu

TORRES SEGARRA, Aurea ... 787-896-2252 ... 561 K
atorres@edpcollege.edu

TORRES-VARGAS, Jorge ... 787-620-2040 ... 560 B
jtorres@aupr.edu

TORRESCANO, Moises ... 210-829-3928 ... 503 F
moisest@uiwtx.edu

TORRESDAL, Pamela, C ... 563-387-1375 ... 187 A
torrespa@luther.ed

TORRIJAS, Christopher ... 574-239-8390 ... 172 J
ctorrijas@hcc-nd.edu

TORRY, Phyllis ... 901-435-1555 ... 470 B
phyllis_torry@loc.edu

TORTAROLO, John ... 760-744-1150 ... 61 C
jtortarolo@palomar.edu

TORTORELLI, Aldo ... 212-752-1530 ... 338 C
aldo.tortorelli@limcollege.edu

TORTORICI, Marianne ... 209-384-6105 ... 57 C
marianne.tortorici@mccd.edu

TORTURELLI, Joseph ... 201-360-4693 ... 310 F
jtorturelli@hccc.edu

TORULAGHA, Priye ... 305-430-1185 ... 108 H
Priye.Torulagha@fmuniv.edu

TORVESTAD, Pat ... 501-686-8999 ... 24 F
ptorvestad@uams.edu

TORVIK, Stan ... 307-778-1174 ... 556 B
storvik@lccc.wy.edu

TOSCANO, James, P ... 757-822-1015 ... 528 C
jtoscano@tcc.edu

TOSCHKOFF, Marisa, L ... 989-837-4337 ... 257 A
toschkof@northwood.edu

TOSCHLOG, Ingrid ... 317-274-5944 ... 174 B
itoschlo@iupui.edu

TOSH, Carol ... 901-333-5025 ... 475 H
catosh@southwest.tn.edu

TOSO, Mary ... 605-274-5530 ... 463 H
mary.toso@augie.edu

TOSSAS, Ezer ... 954-322-4460 ... 112 B

TOSTE, Mary, I ... 619-388-2795 ... 65 G
mtoste@sdccd.edu

TOSTEN, Lori ... 717-262-2017 ... 452 B
ltosten@wilson.edu

TOSTEN, Rod ... 717-337-6601 ... 429 H
rtosten@gettysburg.edu

TOSTENSON, Wendi ... 229-217-4142 ... 134 C
wtostenson@moultrietech.edu

TOSTI-LANE, Dave ... 206-726-5136 ... 532 G
dtostilane@cornish.edu

TOSTON, Margaret, Y ... 731-881-7710 ... 477 E
mtoston@utm.edu

TOTH, Jessica, L ... 314-768-1234 ... 283 C

TOTH, Joseph ... 732-255-0400 ... 312 D
jtoth@ocean.edu

TOTINO, Robert ... 617-989-4325 ... 246 C
totinor@wit.edu

TOTTEN, Herman, L ... 940-565-2445 ... 504 B
totten@unt.edu

TOTTEN, Julie ... 402-554-2322 ... 301 B
jtotten@unomaha.edu

TOTTEN, Rita ... 714-952-9066 ... 28 A

TOTTEN, Willette ... 870-575-4713 ... 25 B
tottenw@uapb.edu

TOTTERMAN, Henrik ... 617-746-1990 ... 236 B
henrik.totterman@hult.edu

TOTTY, Angie, D ... 501-882-4432 ... 20 D
adtotty@asub.edu

TOU, Phillip ... 510-763-7787 ... 26 F
ktou@acchs.edu

TOUCHETTE, Lindsey ... 239-590-1016 ... 119 A
ltouchet@fgcu.edu

TOUGAS, Tim ... 320-762-4402 ... 265 I
timt@alextech.edu

TOULIATOS-MILES, Diane, H ... 314-516-5904 ... 291 F
touliatosd@umsl.edu

TOUMA, Elizabeth ... 415-503-6261 ... 66 A
eat@sfcm.edu

TOUSSAINT, Jess ... 630-466-7900 ... 167 G
jtoussaint@waubonsee.edu

TOUTAIN, Henry, P ... 740-427-5137 ... 394 C
toutainh@kenyon.edu

TOUTGES, Greg, A ... 218-477-2131 ... 268 A
toutges@mnstate.edu

TOUZEAU, Karen, E ... 573-882-4256 ... 291 D
touzeauk@missouri.edu

TOUZEAU, Leigh, A ... 865-539-7013 ... 475 F
latouzeau@pstcc.edu

TOVAR, Cindy ... 312-225-6288 ... 167 E
ctovar@vandercook.edu

TOVAR, Rina ... 386-822-7200 ... 121 E
rtovar@stetson.edu

TOVARES, Carlos ... 951-571-6162 ... 63 J
carlos.tovares@mvc.edu

TOVES, Louise, M ... 671-735-2995 ... 559 D
lmtoves@uguam.uog.edu

TOVEY, David ... 419-755-4222 ... 399 C
tovey.2@osu.edu

TOWAI, Gibson ... 680-488-2471 ... 560 A
gibs2y@yahoo.com

TOWERS, George ... 304-384-6303 ... 543 D
towrers@concord.edu

TOWERS, Joel ... 212-229-8950 ... 342 E
towersj@newschool.edu

TOWLE, David, C ... 319-273-2676 ... 182 D
david.towle@uni.edu

TOWLE, Roger, K ... 724-458-3355 ... 430 B
rktowle@gcc.edu

TOWLE, Thomas ... 603-271-7755 ... 304 G
ttowle@ccsnh.edu

TOWLES, Warren ... 515-643-7316 ... 187 C
wtowles@mercydesmoines.org

TOWNE, Becky, L ... 713-942-9505 ... 487 H
btowne@hgst.edu

TOWNER, Daniel ... 802-634-1401 ... 515 E
daniel.towner@jsc.edu

TOWNER, Mark ... 978-232-2255 ... 234 F
mtowner@endicott.edu

TOWNLEY, Rod ... 704-216-3850 ... 373 C
rod.townley@rccc.edu

TOWNS, Elmer, L ... 434-582-2169 ... 520 F
eltowns@liberty.edu

TOWNS, Gail ... 732-987-2266 ... 310 D
townsg@georgian.edu

TOWNSEND, Bill .... 601-925-3257 .... 275 E btownsen@mc.edu
TOWNSEND, Candace, V .... 337-475-5635 .... 215 G ctownsend@mcneese.edu
TOWNSEND, Debra .... 315-228-7417 .... 329 H dtownsend@colgate.edu
TOWNSEND, Elizabeth, R .. 336-599-1181 .... 372 D townsee@piedmontcc.edu
TOWNSEND, George .... 913-667-5700 .... 191 E gtownsend@cbts.edu
TOWNSEND, Heidi .... 360-779-9993 .... 535 E htownsend@nca.edu
TOWNSEND, James, R ...... 903-233-4341 .... 489 K jamestownsend@letu.edu
TOWNSEND, Janis .... 972-721-4142 .... 502 F jtownsend@udallas.edu
TOWNSEND, Joshua, W .... 410-334-2958 .... 229 E jtownsend@worwic.edu
TOWNSEND, Joyce .... 636-949-4971 .... 284 C jtownsend@lindenwood.edu
TOWNSEND, Karen .... 617-879-7065 .... 238 E ktownsend@massart.edu
TOWNSEND, Lani .... 818-774-0550 .... 46 G
TOWNSEND, Lori .... 757-388-2900 .... 523 J
TOWNSEND, SR., Michael, M ..... 803-793-5100 .... 457 F townsendm@denmarktech.edu
TOWNSEND, Pam .... 256-331-5233 ...... 6 B townsend@nwscc.edu
TOWNSEND, Ralph .... 507-457-5017 .... 270 B rtownsend@winona.edu
TOWNSEND, Sonia .... 281-998-6150 .... 493 G sonia.townsend@sjcd.edu
TOWNSEND-GAMBLE, Jennifer .... 803-533-3750 .... 460 G jgamble2@scsu.edu
TOWNSHEND, John, R ...... 301-405-1691 .... 227 B jtownshe@umd.edu
TOWNSLEY, Debra, M .... 919-508-2220 .... 375 D dmtownsley@peace.edu
TOWNSLEY, Michael .... 801-565-5110 .... 509 G mtownsley@devry.edu
TOWNSLEY, R. Mike .... 260-422-5561 .... 172 L rmtownsley@indianatech.edu
TOWNSLEY, Stacy .... 620-229-6208 .... 196 C stacy.townsley@sckans.edu
TOWSLEY, Scott .... 507-574-4929 .... 540 A stowsley@yvcc.edu
TOY, Charles .... 517-371-5140 .... 259 B toyc@cooley.edu
TOY, Sharon, S .... 405-744-5984 .... 410 C sharon.toy@okstate.edu
TOY-HALE, Bernadette .... 270-686-4506 .... 202 E bernie.hale@kctcs.edu
TOYAMA, Gordon, K .... 503-370-6265 .... 421 C gtoyama@willamette.edu
TOZER, Thomas, J .... 615-898-2919 .... 473 F ttozer@mtsu.edu
TRACEY, SC, Kathleen .... 718-405-3775 .... 330 A kathleen.tracey@mountsaintvincent.edu
TRACEY, Kevin, J .... 516-562-3467 .... 332 H
TRACEY, Patrick .... 401-739-5000 .... 453 E ptracey@neit.edu
TRACHTA, Yvonne .... 361-593-4338 .... 498 A yvonne.trachta@tamuk.edu
TRACHTE, Kent, C .... 717-291-4000 .... 429 E kent.trachte@fandm.edu
TRACIA, Michele .... 617-739-1700 .... 243 F mtracia@aii.edu
TRACY, Anne, M .... 419-372-2211 .... 385 C atracy@bgsu.edu
TRACY, Carla, B .... 309-794-7266 .... 145 B carlatracy@augustana.edu
TRACY, David .... 508-588-9100 .... 240 E
TRACY, II, Edward .... 313-993-1554 .... 259 C tracyeg@udmercy.edu
TRACY, Gene .... 757-221-2470 .... 517 J ertrac@wm.edu
TRACY, Geofrey, L .... 419-372-8262 .... 385 C gtracy@bgsu.edu
TRACY, Gloria .... 941-752-5323 .... 118 E tracyg@scf.edu
TRACY, Heidi, L .... 614-823-1400 .... 400 G htracy@otterbein.edu
TRACY, James, W .... 859-257-5294 .... 206 H tracy@uky.edu
TRACY, Jerry, W .... 818-767-0888 .... 79 D jerry.tracy@woodbury.edu
TRACY, Kim .... 773-442-4190 .... 159 H k-tracy@neiu.edu
TRACY, Lindsay .... 303-256-9452 .... 85 H lindsay.morgantracy@jwu.edu
TRACY, Morgan, A .... 859-858-3511 .... 198 B morgan.tracy@asbury.edu
TRACY, Rhonda .... 304-424-8242 .... 545 B rhonda.tracy@mail.wvu.edu
TRACY, Roy .... 505-786-4111 .... 318 H rtracy@navajotech.edu
TRACY, Sandra, G .... 901-843-3800 .... 472 I tracy@rhodes.edu
TRACY, Scott .... 951-343-4218 ..... 31 G stracy@calbaptist.edu
TRACY, Tim .... 859-323-7601 .... 206 H
TRACY, William, F .... 608-262-4930 .... 550 G wftracy@wisc.edu
TRACZYK, Joyce .... 763-433-1243 .... 265 J joyce.traczyk@anokaramsey.edu
TRADO, Donna .... 828-327-7000 .... 368 G dtrado@cvcc.edu
TRAFFIE, Tim .... 651-523-2015 .... 264 C ttraffie@hamline.edu
TRAFFORD, Beth .... 501-812-2232 ..... 23 C btrafford@pulaskitech.edu
TRAFLET, Dianne, M .... 973-761-9353 .... 311 A dianne.traflet@shu.edu
TRAGNI, Carolyn .... 914-674-7582 .... 340 G ctragni@mercy.edu
TRAHAN, Michael .... 409-984-6378 .... 500 H michael.trahan@lamarpa.edu
TRAHAN, Tonya .... 337-269-0620 .... 207 F tonyat@bluecliffcollege.com
TRAIGER, Jeff .... 816-235-5660 .... 291 E traigerj@umkc.edu
TRAINA, Louis .... 239-513-1122 .... 110 K ltraina@hodges.edu
TRAINA, Samuel .... 209-228-2857 ..... 74 B STraina@UCMerced.edu
TRAINER, Diane, M .... 610-799-1737 .... 434 D dtrainer@lccc.edu
TRAINER, James, F .... 610-519-7578 .... 450 G james.trainer@villanova.edu
TRAINER, Jason .... 218-793-2437 .... 268 E jason.trainer@northlandcollege.edu
TRAINER, Jill .... 916-278-4655 ..... 35 E jill.trainer@csus.edu
TRAINER, Karin .... 609-258-3170 .... 313 A ktrainer@princeton.edu
TRAINO, Joe .... 928-226-4285 ..... 13 H joe.traino@coconino.edu
TRAINOR, David .... 860-493-0032 ..... 91 F trainord@ct.edu
TRAINOR, Joseph, G .... 215-596-8862 .... 450 A j.traino@usciences.edu
TRAINOR, Judith, L .... 508-831-5423 .... 247 B jtrainor@wpi.edu
TRAINOR, Timothy .... 845-938-2000 .... 558 G 8dean@usma.edu
TRAKINAT, Mary Beth .... 309-268-8172 .... 151 G marybeth.trakinat@heartland.edu
TRAMDACK, Philip, J .... 724-738-2630 .... 443 E philip.tramdack@sru.edu
TRAMEL, Caitlin .... 212-636-6520 .... 334 C ctramel@fordham.edu
TRAMEL, Terry .... 405-789-7661 .... 412 E terry.tramel@swcu.edu
TRAMELLI, Marianne .... 212-678-3148 .... 357 F mt772@tc.columbia.edu
TRAMMEL, Sheila .... 318-257-2235 .... 215 F strammel@latech.edu
TRAMMELL, C. David .... 859-858-3511 .... 198 B david.trammell@asbury.edu
TRAMMELL, Genie .... 918-293-5210 .... 410 E genie.trammell@okstate.edu
TRAMMELL, Janice .... 409-880-8419 .... 500 F janice.trammell@lamar.edu
TRAMMELL, NaTonia .... 508-831-5796 .... 247 B ntrammell@wpi.edu
TRAMMELL, Webster, B .... 732-224-2282 .... 308 B wtrammell@brookdalecc.edu
TRAMONTANO, William, A .... 718-951-5864 .... 326 G tramontano@brooklyn.cuny.edu
TRAMONTE, Michael .... 713-500-3158 .... 506 D michael.tramonte@uth.tmc.edu
TRAMPF, Judith, M .... 262-472-4672 .... 552 E trampfj@uww.edu
TRAMUTA, Daniel, M .... 716-673-3253 .... 352 A daniel.tramuta@fredonia.edu
TRAMUTA, Daniel, M .... 716-673-3181 .... 352 A daniel.tramuta@fredonia.edu
TRAN, Deborah .... 415-565-4740 .... 73 G trand@uchastings.edu
TRAN, Dzung .... 602-243-8128 ..... 16 E dzung.tran@smcmail.maricopa.edu
TRAN, Hanh .... 818-364-7608 ..... 55 A tranh@lamission.edu
TRAN, Hieu .... 502-456-6504 .... 206 C htran@sullivan.edu
TRAN, My Linh .... 773-907-6814 .... 147 A mtran@ccc.edu
TRAN, Tuy .... 919-530-7244 .... 378 A ttran@nccu.edu
TRAN, Vu .... 310-825-3101 .... 74 A vtran@saonet.ucla.edu
TRANCHINA, Anthony .... 985-447-0924 .... 211 L anthony.tranchina@ltc.edu
TRANDAHL, Pamela .... 651-675-4700 .... 264 H ptrandahl@msp.chefs.edu
TRANEL, Mark .... 314-516-5273 .... 291 F mtranel@umsl.edu
TRANQUADA, Jim .... 323-259-2990 ..... 59 H jtranqua@oxy.edu
TRANQUILLI, Andrew, A ... 203-582-8774 .... 93 E andy.tranquilli@quinnipiac.edu
TRANSUE, Mary .... 678-717-3410 .... 129 D mtransue@gsc.edu
TRANSUE, Pamela .... 253-566-5100 .... 538 C ptransue@tacomacc.edu
TRANT, John, M .... 956-665-2404 .... 506 A
TRANT, Meg .... 617-217-9018 .... 231 C mtrant@baystate.edu
TRAPANICK, Benjamin, J .. 508-626-4505 .... 238 D btrapanick@framingham.edu
TRAPP, Chris .... 740-389-6786 .... 399 D trapp.22@osu.edu
TRAPP, Daniel .... 313-883-8540 .... 257 G trapp.daniel@shms.edu
TRAPP, Harry .... 301-369-2800 .... 221 F htrapp@capitol-college.edu
TRAPP, Lori .... 734-973-3529 .... 260 B lori@wccnet.edu
TRAPP, Rachel .... 256-331-5237 ...... 6 B rachel.trapp@nwscc.edu
TRASK, Mark .... 239-489-9099 .... 104 L mark.trask@edison.edu
TRASK, III, Tallman .... 919-684-6600 .... 363 I t3@duke.edu
TRATHEN, Edwin .... 518-891-2915 .... 344 E etrathen@nccc.edu
TRAUB, Gilbert .... 718-409-7385 .... 356 C gtraub@sunymaritime.edu
TRAUBE, Eve .... 212-410-8006 .... 343 B etraube@nycpm.edu
TRAUGH, Cecelia .... 718-488-1088 .... 338 H cecelia.traugh@liu.edu
TRAUPMAN-CARR, Carol .. 610-861-1348 .... 436 I caroltcarr@moravian.edu
TRAUTH, Denise, M .... 512-245-2121 .... 501 C president@txstate.edu
TRAUTMAN, Stewart .... 352-854-2322 .... 103 D trautmas@cf.edu
TRAUTMANN, Roger .... 503-255-0332 .... 417 C rtrautmann@multnomah.edu
TRAVENICK, Ron .... 510-659-6107 ..... 59 I rtravenick@ohlone.edu
TRAVER, Cherrice, A .... 518-388-6530 .... 358 E traverc@union.edu
TRAVER, Virginia .... 239-687-5409 .... 101 B vtraver@avemarialaw.edu
TRAVER, William .... 518-458-5337 .... 330 C traverw@strose.edu
TRAVERS, Nan .... 518-587-2100 .... 355 F nan.travers@esc.edu
TRAVERSI, Diane .... 707-527-4508 ..... 68 E dtraversi@santarosa.edu
TRAVERSO, Celeste .... 787-620-2040 .... 560 B ctraverso@aupr.edu
TRAVERSO, Susan .... 717-361-1416 .... 428 E traversos@etown.edu
TRAVIESO, Charlotte .... 504-865-5901 .... 215 C ctraviel@tulane.edu
TRAVIS, Annie .... 662-252-8094 .... 277 C
TRAVIS, Antonio, W .... 404-756-4023 .... 124 I atravis@atlm.edu
TRAVIS, Artie, L .... 301-860-3391 .... 228 A atravis@bowiestate.edu
TRAVIS, Brantly, D .... 270-809-2155 .... 204 F brantly.travis@murraystate.edu
TRAVIS, Deborah, J .... 916-691-7321 ..... 56 B travisd@crc.losrios.edu
TRAVIS, Douglas, B .... 512-472-4133 .... 494 B dtravis@ssw.edu
TRAVIS, Frederick .... 641-472-7000 .... 187 B ftravis@mum.edu
TRAVIS, Heather .... 515-961-1579 .... 188 F heather.travis@simpson.edu
TRAVIS, Jeremy .... 212-237-8600 .... 328 A jtravis@jjay.cuny.edu
TRAVIS, Joseph, A .... 850-644-4404 .... 119 C jtravis@fsu.edu
TRAVIS, Kay .... 270-554-9200 .... 203 B
TRAVIS, Larry .... 513-244-8191 .... 387 D larry.travis@ccuniversity.edu
TRAVIS, Patricia, J .... 914-594-4575 .... 343 F pat_travis@nymc.edu
TRAVIS, Scott .... 616-395-7251 .... 252 F remenschneider@hope.edu
TRAVIS, Shawn .... 985-858-5713 .... 210 H stravis@ftcc.edu
TRAVIS, Shirley .... 703-993-1918 .... 519 A stravis1@gmu.edu
TRAVIS, Terry, K .... 215-951-1540 .... 432 G travis@lasalle.edu
TRAVIS, Thomas .... 631-687-1275 .... 349 B ttravis@sjcny.edu
TRAVIS, Thomas, G .... 718-940-5723 .... 349 A ttravis@sjcny.edu
TRAVIS, Tom .... 770-962-7580 .... 132 A ttravis@gwinnetttech.edu
TRAVISANO, Jacqueline .... 718-990-8328 .... 348 G travisaj@stjohns.edu
TRAWEEK, Vicki .... 817-598-6218 .... 508 C vtraweek@wc.edu
TRAWICK, Rebecca .... 909-652-6493 ..... 39 B rebecca.trawick@chaffey.edu
TRAWICK, Thomas .... 404-880-8812 .... 126 I ttrawick@cau.edu
TRAXLER, Matt .... 651-450-3885 .... 266 I mtraxle@inverhills.edu
TRAXLER, Sue .... 507-222-5608 .... 262 B straxler@carleton.edu
TRAYLOR, Delores .... 256-761-6246 ...... 7 H ddtraylor@talladega.edu
TRAYLOR, Judy, G .... 903-434-8242 .... 491 D jtraylor@ntcc.edu
TRAYLOR, Lauren .... 732-987-2478 .... 310 D traylorl@georgian.edu
TRAYNOR, Kathy .... 603-623-0313 .... 305 F ktraynor@nhia.edu
TRAYNOR, Kathy .... 715-682-1296 .... 549 C ktraynor@northland.edu
TRAYNUM, Elise .... 415-565-4715 ..... 73 G traynume@uchastings.edu
TRAYSTMAN, Richard .... 303-724-8155 ..... 88 D richard.traystman@ucdenver.edu
TREACY, SJ, Jack, R .... 408-554-4372 ..... 68 C jtreacy@scu.edu
TREADAWAY, Glenda .... 828-262-6311 .... 377 B treadaway@appstate.edu
TREADWAY, Jay .... 828-898-8730 .... 366 A treadway@lmc.edu
TREADWELL, Andrew .... 772-462-4804 .... 110 L atreadwe@irsc.edu
TREADWELL, Jane, B .... 217-206-6597 .... 167 A treadwell.jane@uis.edu
TREADWELL, Larry .... 305-474-6860 .... 116 G ltreadwell@stu.edu
TREADWELL, Melinda, D ... 603-358-2220 .... 307 A mtreadwe@keene.edu
TREAKLE-MOORE, Evelyn . 202-806-7540 ..... 98 B etreakle-moore@howard.edu
TREANOR, Laura .... 810-989-2374 .... 249 B laura.treanor@baker.edu
TREANOR, Shirley .... 650-949-7364 ..... 47 H barkershirley@foothill.edu
TREANOR, William, M .... 202-662-9031 ..... 98 A wtreanor@georgetown.edu
TREASE, Tracy .... 303-632-2300 ..... 83 C ttrease@coloradotech.edu
TREAT, Bruce, J .... 585-785-1216 .... 334 A treatbo@flcc.edu
TREAT, Tod .... 217-875-7200 .... 162 D ttreat@richland.edu
TREBAR, Robert .... 440-375-7000 .... 394 E rtrebar@lec.edu
TREBER, Karen, A .... 301-687-4102 .... 228 C ktreber@frostburg.edu
TREBON, Thomas, J .... 406-447-4401 .... 294 A ttrebon@carroll.edu
TREBOW, Elizabeth .... 818-654-1707 ..... 62 F etrebow@pgi.edu
TRECARTIN, Ralph, R .... 585-395-2119 .... 352 F rtrecart@brockport.edu
TRECKER, Stan .... 617-585-6651 .... 236 G strecker@lesley.edu
TRECKER, Stan .... 617-585-6651 .... 230 D strecker@aiboston.edu
TREDUP, Fred .... 702-895-3201 .... 302 K fred.tredup@unlv.edu
TREDWAY, Walter .... 417-328-1531 .... 290 E wtredway@sbuniv.edu
TREECE, T. Gerald .... 713-646-1776 .... 494 E gtreece@stcl.edu
TREESE WILSON, Jennifer 415-955-2000 ...... 27 A jtreese@alliant.edu
TREFFILETTI, Elaine .... 914-674-7540 .... 340 G eegliskis@mercy.edu
TREFT, Paul .... 712-274-5221 .... 187 D treft@morningside.edu
TREGRE, Calvin, S .... 504-520-7539 .... 217 A ctregre@xula.edu
TRELA, D, J .... 810-762-3234 .... 259 F djtrela@umflint.edu
TRELISKY, Nina .... 973-720-2305 .... 317 D treliskyn@wpunj.edu
TRELLA, Joseph .... 610-282-1100 .... 426 I joseph.trella@desales.edu
TRELOW, Cheryl, D .... 660-543-4255 .... 291 B trelow@ucmo.edu
TREMBLAY, Christopher, W .... 313-593-5300 .... 259 E cwtrem@umd.umich.edu
TREMBLAY, Pamela .... 706-880-8313 .... 132 I ptremblay@lagrange.edu
TREMBLE, Gayle .... 912-443-5724 .... 136 D gtremble@savannahtech.edu
TREML, Colleen .... 216-368-4286 .... 386 E colleen.treml@case.edu
TREMPE, James, P .... 419-530-2844 .... 404 F James.Trempe@utoledo.edu
TRENDE, Richard .... 715-425-3133 .... 552 A richard.trende@uwrf.edu
TRENDT, Diana, J .... 608-342-1183 .... 551 F trendtd@uwplatt.edu
TRENKELBACH, Henry .... 330-382-7420 .... 393 F htrenkel@kent.edu
TRENKELBACH, Henry .... 330-337-4206 .... 393 H htrenkel@kent.edu
TRENSCH, Kit .... 678-915-7307 .... 137 C ktrensch@spsu.edu
TRENT, Coe Ann .... 336-342-4261 .... 373 B trentc@rockinghamcc.edu
TRENTACOSTE, Peter .... 859-572-5448 .... 205 E trentacosp1@nku.edu
TREPAL, Michael, J .... 212-410-8067 .... 343 B mtrepal@nycpm.edu

TREPKOWSKI, Patti .... 616-234-4226.... 251 G ptrepkow@grcc.edu
TREPKOWSKI, Ronald, E ... 989-964-4285.... 258 A ret@svsu.edu
TRESER-OSGOOD, Nancy, J .... 909-621-8110...... 63 A nancy.treser-osgood@pomona.edu
TRESOLINI, Carol .... 919-962-3907.... 378 D carol_tresolini@med.unc.edu
TRESS, Samuel, D .... 410-837-5520.... 229 A stress@ubalt.edu
TRESSEL, Ryan .... 336-841-4519.... 365 A rtressel@highpoint.edu
TRESSLER, Dan .... 575-538-6000.... 321 I tresslerd@wumu.edu
TRETHEWAY, Catherine ..... 518-828-4181.... 330 E tretheway_c@sunycgcc.edu
TRETHEWAY, Earl .... 518-828-4181.... 330 E tretheway@sunycgcc.edu
TREUTHART, Jean, M .... 717-718-0328.... 430 E jmtreuth@hacc.edu
TREVAN, Timothy, J .... 818-677-2160...... 35 D timothy.j.trevan@csun.edu
TREVATHAN, Michael, R ... 318-342-5242.... 216 E trevathan@ulm.edu
TREVINO, Jorge .... 210-486-2886.... 479 E jtrevino@alamo.edu
TREVINO, Martha, S .... 956-764-5946.... 489 G martha.trevino@laredo.edu
TREVINO, Mary .... 956-326-2275.... 497 B maryt@tamiu.edu
TREVINO, Melba .... 956-872-3113.... 494 D melbat@southtexascollege.edu
TREVINO, Michael .... 415-565-4892...... 73 G trevinom@uchastings.edu
TREVINO, Miguel, A .... 956-326-2283.... 497 B mtrevino@tamiu.edu
TREVINO, Monica .... 405-224-3140.... 413 E mtrevino@usao.edu
TREVINO, Rick .... 805-654-6400...... 77 D rtrevino@vcccd.edu
TREVINO BAUER, Blanca .. 956-882-7081.... 505 C blanca.bauer@utb.edu
TREVIS, Michael .... 310-660-3101...... 45 D mtrevis@elcamino.edu
TREVISAN, Maurizio .... 212-650-5275.... 326 H mtrevisan@ccny.cuny.edu
TREVISAN, Sandi .... 619-388-7752...... 65 H strevisa@sdccd.edu
TREVOR, Mary .... 928-350-1101...... 18 C mtrevor@prescott.edu
TREVOR, Tyler .... 406-444-0311.... 294 J ttrevor@montana.edu
TREW, Marcy .... 330-494-1214.... 385 I mtrew@brownmackie.edu
TREWERN, Jay .... 972-825-4606.... 495 D jtrewern@sagu.edu
TREWYN, Ronald, W .... 785-532-6195.... 194 B trewyn@ksu.edu
TREXLER, William, H .... 814-886-6421.... 437 A wtrexler@mtaloy.edu
TREZ, Joseph, W .... 843-953-5092.... 456 C joe.trez@citadel.edu
TREZEVANT, Bill .... 608-342-1234.... 551 F trezevantb@uwplatt.edu
TREZISE, Rene, M .... 304-788-6872.... 545 A rmtrezise@mail.wvu.edu
TRIANTAFILOU, Nicholas, C .... 617-850-1280.... 236 A pres_office@hchc.edu
TRIBBLE, Judy .... 812-535-5255.... 179 C jtribble@smwc.edu
TRIBBLE, Keith .... 407-823-2261.... 120 A ktribble@athletics.ucf.edu
TRIBBLE, Sherman .... 919-572-1625.... 361 M
TRIBLE, Paul, S .... 757-594-7001.... 517 I ptrible@cnu.edu
TRIBLEY, Walt .... 509-682-6665.... 539 B wtribley@wvc.edu
TRIBLEY, Walt .... 509-682-6605.... 539 B wtribley@wvc.edu
TRIBUS, Brian .... 845-938-3808.... 558 G Brian.Tribus@usma.edu
TRICARICO, Kerri .... 212-998-2913.... 344 B kerri.tricarico@nyu.edu
TRICARICO, Mary Ann .... 617-739-1700.... 243 F mtricarico@aii.edu
TRICE, Gwinetta, L .... 229-430-4739.... 123 H gwinetta.trice@asurams.edu
TRICE, Matt .... 229-430-6618.... 123 I mtrice@albanytech.edu
TRICE, Sarah .... 803-822-3321.... 459 D trices@midlandstech.edu
TRICHE, Casie .... 985-448-4077.... 216 A casie.triche@nicholls.edu
TRICHE, III, Charles, W .... 337-482-6396.... 216 D ctriche@louisiana.edu
TRICKETT, David G, H .... 303-765-3102...... 84 K dgtrickett@iliff.edu
TRICOLI, Anthony, S .... 678-891-2700.... 130 G Anthony.Tricoli@gpc.edu
TRICOLI, Robin, J .... 423-442-2001.... 469 B president@hiwassee.edu
TRICOMI, Terri .... 510-981-2955...... 62 A ttricomi@peralta.edu

TRIDENTE, Teresa .... 201-216-5176.... 315 E ttrident@stevens.edu
TRIERWEILER, Charles, S . 205-329-7907...... 3 B chuck.trierweiler@ecacolleges.com
TRIETLEY, JR., Richard, C 716-375-2513.... 348 C rtrietley@sbu.edu
TRIEZENBERG, Glenn, E ... 616-526-6485.... 249 E gtriezen@calvin.edu
TRIGALO, Ophir .... 312-567-3290.... 153 B trigalo@iit.edu
TRIGG, Debra .... 510-659-7376...... 59 I dtrigg@ohlone.edu
TRIGGS, Patricia .... 360-475-7480.... 535 J ptriggs@olympic.edu
TRILLER, Mark, V .... 608-757-7701.... 553 E mtriller@blackhawk.edu
TRILLI, Victor .... 316-942-4291.... 195 C trilliv@newmanu.edu
TRIMARCHI, Valarie .... 703-302-1380.... 530 D vtrimarchi@westwood.edu
TRIMBLE, Ferris, E .... 323-241-5467...... 55 C trimblfe@lasc.edu
TRIMBLE, Joe .... 615-966-5672.... 470 D joe.trimble@lipscomb.edu
TRIMBLE, Karen .... 530-741-6700...... 80 C
TRIMBLE, LaDonna .... 661-722-6300...... 28 J ltrimble@avc.edu
TRIMBLE, Marshall .... 480-423-6314...... 16 D marshall.trimble@sccmail.maricopa.edu
TRIMBLE, Michael, D .... 203-365-7557...... 93 G trimblem@sacredheart.edu
TRIMBOLI, James .... 716-614-6202.... 344 C trimboli@niagaracc.suny.edu
TRIMBOLI, Thomas, A .... 843-953-5528.... 457 B trimbolit@cofc.edu
TRIMIEW, Darryl .... 718-270-4947.... 328 D dtrimiew@mec.cuny.edu
TRIMMER, Susan .... 570-389-5138.... 441 F strimmer@bloomufdn.org
TRINIDAD, Vanessa .... 787-884-6000.... 562 E vtrinidad@icprjc.edu
TRINKLEIN, Andrea .... 404-727-4144.... 129 A ajtrink@emory.edu
TRINKO, Lynn, A .... 419-995-8412.... 399 B trinko.1@osu.edu
TRIONFI, Thomas, P .... 989-774-3166.... 249 G trion1tp@cmich.edu
TRIPATHI, Satish, K .... 716-645-2901.... 351 G president@buffalo.edu
TRIPEPI, Matt .... 513-745-3081.... 406 E tripepi@xavier.edu
TRIPLET, Jeff .... 503-977-4406.... 419 G jtriplet@pcc.edu
TRIPLETT, Beth .... 563-588-6468.... 183 B beth.triplett@clarke.edu
TRIPLETT, Clark .... 314-392-2221.... 286 C triplett@mobap.edu
TRIPLETT, Jill .... 404-270-5677.... 137 E jtriple1@spelman.ed
TRIPLETT, Karen .... 612-624-1347.... 272 D ktrip@groupwise.umn.edu
TRIPLETT, Lynn .... 781-768-7315.... 244 D lynn.triplett@regiscollege.edu
TRIPLETT, Melinda, S .... 810-762-9517.... 253 I mtriplett@kettering.edu
TRIPLETT, Neal .... 919-668-9995.... 363 I neal.triplett@duke.edu
TRIPLETT, R. Gilbert .... 214-828-8101.... 497 A gtriplett@bcd.tamhsc.edu
TRIPLITT, Tom, A .... 864-294-3464.... 458 D tom.triplitt@furman.edu
TRIPODI, Michael .... 908-737-7020.... 311 B mtripodi@kean.edu
TRIPP, Harry, E .... 814-393-2351.... 442 A htripp@clarion.edu
TRIPP, Susan .... 315-866-0300.... 335 E trippsk@herkimer.edu
TRIPPETT, William .... 608-263-7727.... 552 F william.trippett@uwc.edu
TRIPURANENI, Vinaya, L .. 909-593-3511...... 75 C vtripuraneni@laverne.edu
TRISCIUZZI, Andrea .... 410-234-4670.... 225 E
TRITAK, Ann .... 201-761-6272.... 314 F atritak@spc.edu
TRITLE, Madonna .... 219-785-5244.... 178 H mtritle@pnc.edu
TRIVEDI, Tushar .... 201-761-6264.... 314 F ttrivedi@spc.edu
TRIVUNOVICH, Nick .... 813-974-4903.... 120 D ntrivuno@usf.edu
TRIZZINO-PECOR, June .... 212-965-8340.... 322 A trizzino@adelphi.edu
TRNCAK, Stephen .... 281-998-6348.... 493 D stephen.trncak@sjcd.edu
TROASTLE, Greta, J .... 304-637-1331.... 540 F troastleg@dewv.edu
TROCHIM, Shawn .... 254-299-8811.... 490 E strochim@mclennan.edu
TROCHUCK, Mike .... 708-239-4836.... 165 I mike.trochuck@trnty.edu
TROCINO, Sherry, M .... 607-735-1770.... 333 A strocino@elmira.edu
TROHA, James .... 419-448-2383.... 391 G jtroha@heidelberg.edu

TROIANO, Peter, F .... 203-392-5556...... 91 I troianop2@southernct.edu
TROILO, David .... 212-938-5658.... 355 B dtroilo@sunyopt.edu
TROJAN, John .... 908-526-1200.... 313 E jtrojan@raritanval.edu
TROLLINGER, Richard, W .. 859-238-5209.... 199 D richard.trollinger@centre.edu
TROMANHAUSER, David, C .... 423-775-7308.... 467 D david.tromanhauser@bryan.edu
TROMBELLA, Jerry .... 201-559-6185.... 310 C trombellaj@felician.edu
TROMPETTER, Linda .... 570-674-6482.... 436 F ltrompet@misericordia.edu
TRON, Dionn, M .... 513-529-3637.... 396 D trondm@muohio.edu
TRONGALE, Nicholas .... 630-889-6673.... 159 E ntrongale@nuhs.edu
TRONSEN, William .... 802-440-4868.... 512 G tronsen@bennington.edu
TRONTO, Stacie .... 252-328-9025.... 377 C trontos@ecu.edu
TROPP, Judybeth .... 619-961-4319...... 72 F jtropp@tjsl.edu
TROSSET, Carol .... 413-559-5890.... 235 G
TROST, Patricia, G .... 708-709-3637.... 161 C ptrost@prairiestate.edu
TROSVIG, Kelli .... 206-616-0114.... 538 F kelli@uw.edu
TROTMAN, Joylyn .... 256-726-8436...... 6 C jtrotman@oakwood.edu
TROTTA, Neil .... 617-236-8867.... 235 B ntrotta@fisher.edu
TROTTER, Dennis, C .... 402-461-7326.... 298 C dennis_trotter@hastings.edu
TROTTER, Johnny .... 706-295-6974.... 130 F jtrotter@gntc.edu
TROTTER, Steve .... 360-867-6185.... 533 I trotters@evergreen.edu
TROTTIER, Sheila .... 701-477-7862.... 383 C strottier@tm.edu
TROTTY, Willie, F .... 936-261-1550.... 496 E wftrotty@pvamu.edu
TROTTY, Willie, F .... 936-261-3500.... 496 E wftrotty@pvamu.edu
TROUP, James .... 203-575-8220...... 90 E jtroup@nvcc.commnet.edu
TROUP, Pat .... 251-981-3771...... 2 H pat.troup@columbiasouthern.edu
TROUPE, Bonnie, L .... 508-565-1069.... 245 D btroupe@stonehill.edu
TROUT, Curtis, C .... 309-556-3195.... 153 E ctrout@iwu.edu
TROUT, Darice .... 847-925-6070.... 151 E dtrout@harpercollege.edu
TROUT, Margaret .... 503-370-6971.... 421 C mtrout@willamette.edu
TROUTEN, Stefanie, K .... 304-336-8900.... 544 B strouten@westliberty.edu
TROUTMAN, Dara, L .... 402-472-7143.... 300 F dtroutman@nebraska.edu
TROUTMAN, Donald .... 570-321-4064.... 435 D troutman@lycoming.edu
TROUTT, Amy .... 618-545-3048.... 155 A atroutt@kaskaskia.edu
TROUTT, William, E .... 901-843-3730.... 472 I trouttw@rhodes.edu
TROWBRIDGE, Christian, A .... 302-295-1151...... 97 A christian.a.trowbridge@wilmu.edu
TROWBRIDGE, Cory, D ..... 816-322-0110.... 279 H security@calvary.edu
TROWBRIDGE, Cory, D ..... 816-322-0110.... 279 H cory.trowbridge@Calvary.edu
TROWBRIDGE, Larry .... 217-479-7079.... 157 D larry.trowbridge@mac.edu
TROWBRIDGE, Raymond .... 518-828-4181.... 330 E trowbridge@sunycgcc.edu
TROXEL, Steve .... 620-365-5116.... 190 A troxel@allencc.edu
TROXLER, Debra, J .... 302-571-5380...... 96 C dtroxler@dtcc.edu
TROY, Randy .... 260-399-7700.... 180 E rtroy@sf.edu
TROY, Robert, C .... 718-960-7825.... 327 C robert.troy@lehman.cuny.edu
TROY, Shawn .... 989-386-6616.... 255 F stroy@midmich.edu
TROYER, Carol, A .... 717-334-6286.... 435 A ctroyer@ltsg.edu
TROYER, Cindy .... 903-566-7461.... 506 C ctroyer@uttyler.edu
TROYER, Lisa .... 217-333-3070.... 166 E troyer@uillinois.edu
TROYER, Marilyn .... 419-289-5350.... 384 D mtroyer2@ashland.edu
TROYER, Mark, J .... 859-858-3511.... 198 B mark.troyer@asbury.edu
TROYER, Stephen .... 330-337-6403.... 383 H college@awc.edu
TRUBACZ, Joe .... 907-450-8022...... 10 H joe.trubacz@alaska.edu
TRUCKENMILLER, Greg ..... 518-762-4651.... 334 D gtrucken@fmcc.suny.edu

TRUDEAU, Dave .... 252-492-2061.... 374 D trudeau@vgcc.edu
TRUDEAU, Sara, L .... 202-526-3799...... 98 E
TRUDEAU, Scott .... 248-204-3850.... 254 E strudeau@ltu.edu
TRUDEAU, Skip .... 765-998-5368.... 179 F sktrudeau@taylor.edu
TRUDELL, Kyle .... 573-288-6450.... 281 D ktrudell@culver.edu
TRUE, Don .... 803-593-9231.... 455 A true@atc.edu
TRUE, Douglas, K .... 319-335-3552.... 182 C douglas-true@uiowa.edu
TRUE, Elizabeth .... 617-928-4042.... 243 A eatrue@mountida.edu
TRUE, Jeanette .... 605-882-5284.... 464 D truej@lakeareatech.edu
TRUE, Reiko .... 415-955-2100...... 27 F rtrue@alliant.edu
TRUELOVE, Elaine, M .... 478-757-3414.... 126 G truelove@centralgatech.edu
TRUEMAN, Amy .... 607-844-8222.... 357 H truemaa@TC3.edu
TRUEMAN, Carl .... 215-887-5511.... 451 D ctrueman@wts.edu
TRUESDALE, Karen .... 678-891-2542.... 130 G ktruesda@gpc.edu
TRUESDELL, Cheryl, B .... 260-481-6506.... 174 A truesdel@ipfw.edu
TRUESDELL, Joanne .... 503-594-3000.... 415 A joannet@clackamas.edu
TRUESDELL, Nancy, D .... 920-832-6596.... 547 J nancy.d.truesdell@lawrence.edu
TRUETT, William, M .... 704-272-5363.... 373 F wtruett@spcc.edu
TRUFANT, Nicole .... 207-602-2157.... 220 H ntrufant@une.edu
TRUILLO, Lawrence, T .... 607-778-5207.... 324 G truillo_l@sunybroome.edu
TRUITT, Bettie .... 309-796-5373.... 145 E truittb@bhc.edu
TRUITT, Jennifer .... 217-228-5432.... 161 E truitje@quincy.edu
TRUITT, Terry, C .... 765-641-4354.... 169 A tctruitt@anderson.edu
TRUJILLO, Claudia .... 530-895-2400...... 31 E trujillocl@butte.edu
TRUJILLO, Fidel, J .... 505-454-3020.... 318 I fidel@nmhu.edu
TRUJILLO, George .... 301-985-7283.... 227 F gtrujillo@umuc.edu
TRUJILLO, Tamara .... 707-638-5317...... 72 H tamara.trujillo@tu.edu
TRULLINGER, Robert .... 914-948-6206.... 355 F robert.trullinger@esc.edu
TRULOVE, Milyon .... 651-523-2207.... 264 C mtrulove01@hamline.edu
TRUMAN, Grace, H .... 561-868-3122.... 114 D trumang@palmbeachstate.edu
TRUMAN, Kevin, Z .... 816-235-2399.... 291 E trumank@umkc.edu
TRUMBALL, Bill .... 207-948-3131.... 219 H btrumball@unity.edu
TRUMBOWER, Jeffrey, A ... 802-654-2492.... 514 B jtrumbower@smcvt.edu
TRUMPICK, Susan, A .... 518-743-2248.... 322 B trumpics@sunyacc.edu
TRUMPOWER, Peter .... 330-494-6170.... 402 A ptrumpower@starkstate.edu
TRUMPS, Thomas, H .... 540-464-7313.... 529 A trumpsth@vmi.edu
TRUONG, Chris .... 714-564-6043...... 63 F truong_chris@sac.edu
TRUONG, Tina .... 575-439-3703.... 319 E ttruong@nmsua.nmsu.edu
TRUONG, Tina .... 575-439-3703.... 319 E ttruong@nmsu.edu
TRUPP, Kim, L .... 334-844-4580...... 1 G truppki@auburn.edu
TRUSCHKE, Michael, E .... 310-506-4392...... 61 G michael.truschke@pepperdine.edu
TRUSHEIM, Dale, W .... 410-778-7709.... 229 D dtrusheim2@washcoll.edu
TRUSKOWSKI, Marilyn, C . 413-662-5598.... 238 F marilyn.truskowski@mcla.edu
TRUSTY, Denise .... 606-886-3863.... 201 C denise.trusty@kctcs.edu
TRUSZ, Robert, J .... 740-351-3610.... 401 I btrusz@shawnee.edu
TRUTNA, Kevin .... 530-741-6766...... 80 E ktrutna@yccd.edu
TRUXILLO, Betty, D .... 225-923-2524.... 207 E director@brsc.edu
TRYON, Sandy .... 515-964-6408.... 183 E sbtryon@dmacc.edu
TRZASKA, Ken, J .... 906-932-4231.... 251 E kent@gogebic.edu
TRZEBIATOWSKI, Brian .... 773-481-8287.... 147 F btrzebiatowski@ccc.edu
TRZOP, Chasity .... 502-968-7191.... 199 A ctrzop@brownmackie.edu
TSACOUMIS, Stephanie .... 202-687-6843...... 98 A st73@georgetown.edu

TURNER, Donna, S ... 803-786-3178 ... 457 C
dturner@columbiasc.edu
TURNER, Eddie, C ... 806-291-3615 ... 508 B
turnere@wbu.edu
TURNER, Ellen ... 941-907-2262 ... 106 G
eturner@evergladesuniversity.edu
TURNER, Emily ... 212-312-4414 ... 332 B
eturner@devry.edu
TURNER, Eric, A ... 870-759-4110 ... 26 B
eturner@wbcoll.edu
TURNER, Fran ... 205-391-2663 ... 7 A
fturner@sheltonstate.edu
TURNER, Franklin, R ... 714-539-6561 ... 71 G
TURNER, Gary ... 615-844-5276 ... 468 J
gturner@fwbbc.edu
TURNER, Helen ... 601-984-5009 ... 277 H
hturner@umc.edu
TURNER, J. Leigh ... 979-845-7725 ... 497 C
jl-turner@tamu.edu
TURNER, James ... 607-844-8222 ... 357 H
turnerj@TC3.edu
TURNER, James ... 303-691-5700 ... 89 D
TURNER, James, C ... 434-924-2670 ... 525 B
jct4w@virginia.edu
TURNER, Jana, D ... 901-572-2455 ... 467 A
jana.turner@bchs.edu
TURNER, Janet ... 503-943-7311 ... 420 G
Turnerj@up.edu
TURNER, Jermaine ... 256-539-0834 ... 4 F
reg@hbc1.edu
TURNER, Joe ... 239-513-1122 ... 110 K
jturner@hodges.edu
TURNER, John, H ... 541-278-5950 ... 414 G
jturner@bluecc.edu
TURNER, John, T ... 910-695-3704 ... 373 E
turnerj@sandhills.edu
TURNER, Joseph, T ... 252-473-5936 ... 369 D
joseph_turner@albemarle.edu
TURNER, June ... 760-921-5558 ... 61 B
june.turner@paloverde.edu
TURNER, Kara ... 443-885-3350 ... 224 F
kara.turner@morgan.edu
TURNER, Kerry ... 202-541-5235 ... 99 G
kturner@wtu.edu
TURNER, Larry ... 704-355-7577 ... 363 B
larry.turner@carolinashealthcare.org
TURNER, Lathan, E ... 252-328-6495 ... 377 C
turnerla@ecu.edu
TURNER, Laurie, L ... 253-535-7361 ... 535 K
turnerll@plu.edu
TURNER, Leslie ... 561-803-2473 ... 114 C
leslie_turner@pba.edu
TURNER, Linda ... 309-796-5345 ... 145 E
turnerl@bhc.edu
TURNER, Lois "Casey" ... 215-895-6711 ... 427 G
lat59@drexel.edu
TURNER, Louise ... 406-586-3585 ... 294 I
louise.turner@montanabiblecollege.edu
TURNER, Margaret ... 410-951-3700 ... 228 B
mturner@coppin.edu
TURNER, Marietta ... 217-351-2505 ... 161 B
mturner@parkland.edu
TURNER, Mary ... 916-558-2226 ... 56 D
turnerm@scc.losrios.edu
TURNER, Matt ... 304-696-6713 ... 543 G
turner6@marshall.edu
TURNER, Michael ... 858-279-4500 ... 52 H
mturner@kaplan.edu
TURNER, Michael ... 661-722-6300 ... 28 J
sturner29@avc.edu
TURNER, Michael ... 218-723-6387 ... 262 I
mturner@css.edu
TURNER, Michael, C ... 334-387-3877 ... 1 D
mcturner@amridgeuniversity.edu
TURNER, Mitzi ... 270-247-8521 ... 204 C
mturner@midcontinent.edu
TURNER, Nancy, L ... 608-342-1789 ... 551 F
turnern@uwplatt.edu
TURNER, Pat, A ... 530-752-6068 ... 73 F
paturner@ucdavis.edu
TURNER, Patrick ... 318-397-6166 ... 210 J
patrick.turner@myneltc.edu
TURNER, Paul ... 859-246-6717 ... 201 D
paul.turner@kctcs.edu
TURNER, Paul, S ... 561-237-7245 ... 113 D
pturner@lynn.edu
TURNER, Peter ... 315-268-6544 ... 329 C
pturner@clarkson.edu
TURNER, R. Gerald ... 214-768-3300 ... 494 F
mjj@smu.edu
TURNER, Rachel ... 305-626-3605 ... 108 H
rachel.turner@fmuniv.edu
TURNER, Ralph ... 850-599-3430 ... 118 G
ralph.turner@famu.edu
TURNER, Raymond ... 256-372-5721 ... 1 A
raymond.turner@aamu.edu
TURNER, Rebecca, E ... 256-782-5485 ... 4 L
bturner@jsu.edu
TURNER, Rebecca, O ... 256-782-5540 ... 4 L
rturner@jsu.edu
TURNER, Robert ... 910-296-2416 ... 371 B
rturner@jamessprunt.edu
TURNER, JR., Robert, L ... 804-524-5569 ... 529 C
rturner@vsu.edu
TURNER, Ron ... 740-389-6786 ... 399 D
turner.27@osu.edu
TURNER, Sally, J ... 716-673-3424 ... 352 A
sally.turner@fredonia.edu
TURNER, Sandra ... 212-242-2255 ... 358 A
TURNER, Sarah ... 319-296-4432 ... 185 C
sarah.turner@hawkeyecollege.edu
TURNER, Sarah ... 304-384-5348 ... 543 D
slrner@concord.edu
TURNER, Sharon, P ... 859-323-5786 ... 206 H
spturn2@uky.edu
TURNER, Stephen, R ... 219-785-5401 ... 178 H
sturner@pnc.edu
TURNER, Steven ... 580-559-5539 ... 407 J
sturner@ecok.edu
TURNER, Sue, Z ... 912-443-5485 ... 136 D
sturner@savannahtech.edu
TURNER, Sylvia, C ... 714-564-5600 ... 63 F
turner_sylvia@sac.edu
TURNER, Tara ... 410-951-3812 ... 228 B
tturner@coppin.edu
TURNER, Terrance, A ... 903-233-4441 ... 489 K
terryturner@letu.edu
TURNER, Terry ... 913-588-4871 ... 197 A
tturner@kumc.edu
TURNER, Thomas, H ... 540-375-2311 ... 523 D
turner@roanoke.edu
TURNER, Tony ... 478-757-3432 ... 126 G
tturner@centralgatech.edu
TURNER, Vickie ... 662-243-1940 ... 274 D
vturner@eastms.edu
TURNER, Walter ... 404-627-2681 ... 126 A
walter.turner@beulah.org
TURNER, Wilson ... 812-298-2320 ... 177 A
wturner15@ivytech.edu
TURNER, Zoa Ann ... 972-524-3341 ... 495 F
TURNER-MURRAY,
Sonya, M ... 740-587-6647 ... 389 H
turner@denison.edu
TURNER-SAMPLE,
Margaret ... 480-517-4556 ... 16 C
margaret.turner-sample@riosalado.edu
TURNER-WATTS, Sheryl ... 864-503-5490 ... 463 A
sturner-watts@uscupstate.edu
TURNER-WILLIAMS,
Melva, K ... 318-670-9331 ... 215 A
mturner@susla.edu
TURNEY, Keith ... 303-273-3333 ... 82 F
keith.turney@is.mines.edu
TURNIS, Jane ... 719-389-6138 ... 81 L
jturnis@coloradocollege.edu
TURNOCK, Madeline ... 503-493-8550 ... 415 E
mturnock@cu-portland.edu
TURNQUIST, David, C ... 303-724-1100 ... 88 D
david.turnquist@ucdenver.edu
TURNQUIST, James ... 906-487-2313 ... 255 E
jaturnqu@mtu.edu
TURNQUIST, Sandra ... 906-487-7240 ... 251 C
sandra.turnquist@finlandia.edu
TURPEN, James ... 402-559-4388 ... 301 A
jterpen@unmc.edu
TURPIN, Craig ... 502-213-2110 ... 202 B
craig.turpin@kctcs.edu
TURPIN, Jennifer, E ... 415-422-6136 ... 76 B
turpinj@usfca.edu
TURPIN, John, C ... 336-841-9000 ... 365 A
jturpin@highpoint.edu
TURTELTAUB, Rhea ... 310-794-5567 ... 74 A
rheat@support.ucla.edu
TURZAI, Eric, C ... 717-361-1157 ... 428 E
turzaiec@etown.edu
TURZANSKI, Edward, A ... 215-951-1391 ... 432 G
turzansk@lasalle.edu
TUSACK, Donna ... 619-594-7500 ... 36 E
donna.tusack@sdsu.edu
TUSCHAK, Mark ... 830-792-7215 ... 494 A
mctuschak@schreiner.edu
TUSKI, Donald ... 207-775-5098 ... 218 E
dtuski@meca.edu
TUTEN, Jane ... 803-641-3460 ... 462 B
janet@usca.edu
TUTHILL, George, F ... 603-535-2286 ... 307 B
gftuthilli@plymouth.edu
TUTHILL, John ... 775-673-7090 ... 302 J
jtuthill@tmcc.edu
TUTHILL-RANGER, Nina ... 503-961-6200 ... 418 A
ntuthill@pioneerpacific.edu
TUTSOCK, Robert, J ... 989-964-4082 ... 258 A
tutsock@svsu.edu
TUTT, Betty, R ... 573-592-4354 ... 293 E
btutt@williamwoods.edu
TUTT, Larry ... 270-831-9783 ... 201 I
larry.tutt@kctcs.edu
TUTTER, Catherine ... 617-369-3602 ... 244 G
ctutter@smfa.edu
TUTTLE, David, M ... 210-999-8843 ... 502 C
dtuttle@trinity.edu
TUTTLE, Gail ... 315-792-3016 ... 359 C
gtuttle@utica.edu
TUTTLE, Gail, C ... 336-841-9120 ... 365 A
gtuttle@highpoint.edu
TUTTLE, James ... 253-589-5533 ... 532 B
jim.tuttle@cptc.edu
TUTTLE, Jeffrey, P ... 215-368-7538 ... 424 A
jtuttle@cbs.edu
TUTTLE, Tina ... 760-384-6208 ... 52 N
ttuttle@cerrocoso.edu
TUYTSCHAEVERS, Mary ... 575-492-2873 ... 319 B
mtuytschaevers@nmjc.edu
TVARKUNAS, Michael ... 662-476-5059 ... 274 D
mtvar@eastms.edu
TVRDY, Peggy ... 402-826-8260 ... 298 A
peggy.tvrdy@doane.edu
TWADDELL, Gerald, E ... 859-344-3307 ... 206 D
gerald.twaddell@thomasmore.edu
TWEED, Emily ... 952-888-4777 ... 270 F
etweed@nwhealth.edu
TWEED, James ... 617-243-2225 ... 236 F
jtweed@lasell.edu
TWEEDIE, Frank ... 401-598-2503 ... 453 C
ftweedie@jwu.edu
TWIGGS, Sarah ... 706-764-3523 ... 130 F
stwiggs@gntc.edu
TWILLEY, Robert ... 337-482-6541 ... 216 D
rtwilley@louisiana.edu
TWISS, Camilie ... 603-594-2567 ... 306 A
TWISS, Jenn ... 435-797-0077 ... 511 B
jenn.twiss@usu.edu
TWIST, Tony ... 317-299-0333 ... 179 G
TWITCHELL, Barbara ... 775-829-9041 ... 302 J
btwitchell@tmcc.edu
TWOHIG, James ... 936-639-1301 ... 480 D
jtwohig@angelina.edu
TWOMBLY, Kelly ... 785-442-6022 ... 193 D
ktwombly@highlandcc.edu
TWOREK, Amy ... 312-935-6031 ... 162 E
atworek@robertmorris.edu
TWYMAN, Edward ... 262-595-2345 ... 551 E
twyman@uwp.edu
TYBURSKI, Marcelle ... 315-228-7431 ... 329 H
mtyburski@colgate.edu
TYBURSKI, Mike ... 415-514-2036 ... 74 E
mtyburski@hr.ucsf.edu
TYBURSKI, Robert, L ... 315-228-7445 ... 329 H
rtyburski@colgate.edu
TYDINGS, Flora, W ... 706-355-5110 ... 124 H
ftydings@athenstech.edu
TYE, Ann ... 559-451-0334 ... 19 C
ann.tye@phoenix.edu
TYISKA, Felecia ... 903-769-5730 ... 488 M
felecia_tyiska@jarvis.edu
TYKOCINSKI, Mark, L ... 215-955-1628 ... 448 B
mark.tykocinski@jefferson.edu
TYKSINSKI, Deborah ... 315-792-7151 ... 356 B
deborah.tyksinski@sunyit.edu
TYKWINSKI, Joseph ... 701-845-7332 ... 382 A
joe.tykwinski@vcsu.edu
TYLER, Alan ... 360-438-4495 ... 536 F
atyler@stmartin.edu
TYLER, Arthur, Q ... 713-718-8464 ... 487 G
art.tyler@hccs.edu
TYLER, Carol ... 304-829-7567 ... 540 E
ctyler@bethanywv.edu
TYLER, Greg ... 251-626-3303 ... 8 D
gtyler@ussa.edu
TYLER, Gwendolyn, J ... 609-896-5058 ... 313 G
tyler@rider.edu
TYLER, Harold ... 310-660-3504 ... 45 D
htyler@elcamino.edu
TYLER, Jaimee ... 517-578-7178 ... 235 D
jtyler@gibbsboston.edu
TYLER, Jeanie ... 619-388-3924 ... 65 F
jtyler@sdccd.edu
TYLER, Julie ... 901-320-9700 ... 478 B
juliet@victory.edu
TYLER, Karlene, M ... 620-242-0441 ... 194 H
tylerk@mcpherson.edu
TYLER, Ken ... 304-473-8099 ... 545 F
tyler@wvwc.edu
TYLER, Maurice ... 336-334-7856 ... 377 F
tylerm@ncat.edu
TYLER, Melvin, C ... 816-235-1141 ... 291 E
tylerm@umkc.edu
TYLER, Ralph ... 203-332-5081 ... 90 B
rtyler@hcc.commnet.edu
TYLER, Rico ... 773-325-4680 ... 148 F
rtyler@depaul.edu
TYLER, Victoria ... 914-455-3515 ... 340 G
vtyler@mercy.edu
TYLER, Wanda ... 203-932-7427 ... 95 B
wtyler@newhaven.edu
TYMANN, Daniel ... 978-867-4260 ... 235 E
dan.tymann@gordon.edu
TYMAS-JONES, Raymond ... 801-581-3887 ... 510 L
r.tymasjones@finearts.utah.edu
TYMKOW, Tony, A ... 708-534-4108 ... 151 C
ttymkow@govst.edu
TYMOCZKO, Michelle ... 303-477-7240 ... 84 I
michellet@heritage-education.com
TYMUS, Peter ... 516-299-3370 ... 338 F
peter.tymus@liu.edu
TYNAN, George ... 858-534-5556 ... 74 D
gtynan@ucsd.edu
TYNDALL, Brad ... 970-945-8691 ... 82 C
TYNER, Dennis, J ... 785-242-5200 ... 195 F
dennis.tyner@ottawa.edu
TYNER, Kathy ... 619-482-6344 ... 71 C
ktyner@swccd.edu
TYNER, Kathy ... 214-638-0484 ... 489 E
ktyner@kdstudio.com
TYNER, Lee ... 662-915-7792 ... 277 G
ltyner@olemiss.edu
TYNES, Craig ... 601-403-1155 ... 277 A
ctynes@prcc.edu
TYNES, James ... 212-220-1377 ... 326 E
jtynes@bmcc.cuny.edu
TYNES, Sheryl, R ... 210-999-8201 ... 502 C
stynes@trinity.edu
TYNON, Kathy ... 402-872-2365 ... 299 H
ktynon@peru.edu
TYNSKY, Troy ... 507-284-3293 ... 262 G
tynsky.troy@mayo.edu
TYO, Keith, D ... 518-564-3930 ... 354 B
tyokd@plattsburgh.edu
TYPOLT, Jeanie ... 406-586-3585 ... 294 I
jeanie.typolt@montanabiblecollege.edu
TYPOLT, Ty ... 406-586-3585 ... 294 I
typoltj@hotmail.com
TYRE, Yulanda ... 334-244-3553 ... 2 A
ytyre@aum.edu
TYREE, Jonathan ... 434-947-8112 ... 522 E
jtyree@randolphcollege.edu
TYREE, Lawrence ... 305-809-3204 ... 108 F
larry.tyree@fkcc.edu
TYREE, Shelley, M ... 205-665-6155 ... 9 C
tyreelm@montevallo.edu
TYRELL, Steven, J ... 607-587-3911 ... 355 C
tyrellsj@alfredstate.edu
TYRRELL, Elizabeth ... 408-270-6453 ... 67 B
elizabeth.tyrrell@evc.edu
TYRRELL, Wil ... 914-323-5341 ... 340 A
wil.tyrrell@mville.edu
TYSON, AJ ... 252-862-1307 ... 372 H
tysona@roanokechowan.edu
TYSON, Claire ... 209-667-3866 ... 36 C
ctyson@csustan.edu
TYSON, James, E ... 512-505-3149 ... 488 B
jetyson@htu.edu
TYSON, Linda ... 252-399-6330 ... 362 A
ltyson@barton.edu
TYSON, Molly ... 440-775-8472 ... 397 F
molly.tyson@oberlin.edu
TYSON, Thomas, N ... 410-334-2913 ... 229 E
ttyson@worwic.edu
TYSON, William, R ... 919-893-9101 ... 368 H
btyson@cccc.edu
TYSON-LOFQUIST, Beth ... 828-227-7495 ... 379 E
btyson@wcu.edu
TYSZLER, Ira ... 212-463-0400 ... 357 J
tysz@touro.edu
TYUS, Bing ... 863-297-1004 ... 115 A
btyus@polk.edu
TZENG, Julia ... 415-371-0002 ... 60 A
TZENG, Walker ... 415-371-0002 ... 60 A

U

UBARRI-DE LEÓN, Lydia ... 787-993-8858 ... 566 G
lydia.ubarri@upr.edu
UBELL, Robert, N ... 718-260-3407 ... 346 C
rubell@poly.edu
UBER, Rhonda ... 719-549-2890 ... 83 B
rhonda.uber@colostate-pueblo.edu
UCCI, Martha ... 508-565-1033 ... 245 D
mucci@stonehill.edu
UCHIN, Robert, A ... 954-262-7311 ... 114 B
ruchin@nsu.nova.edu
UDA, Jon ... 208-426-1304 ... 142 F
jonuda@boisestate.edu
UDALL, David ... 928-428-8295 ... 14 C
david.udall@eac.edu
UDAS, Ken ... 774-455-7601 ... 237 B
kudas@umassonline.net
UDD, Kris, J ... 402-449-2811 ... 298 B
registrar@graceu.edu
UDDIN, Rita ... 718-260-5610 ... 328 E
ruddin@citytech.cuny.edu
UDE, Georgia ... 931-363-9863 ... 470 E
gude@martinmethodist.edu
UDE, Wayne ... 360-331-0307 ... 535 G
UDEH, Igwe, E ... 504-286-5331 ... 214 I
iudeh@suno.edu
UDELHOFEN, Angela, M ... 608-342-1125 ... 551 F
rulea@uwplatt.edu
UDEN, Michael ... 262-243-5700 ... 546 I
michael.uden@cuw.edu
UDEOGALANYA, Anthony ... 718-270-6200 ... 328 D
anthonyu@mec.cuny.edu
UDIS-KESSLER, Amanda ... 719-227-8177 ... 81 L
audiskessler@coloradocollege.edu
UDKOW, David ... 516-686-7902 ... 343 D
dudkow@nyit.edu
UDLER, Sonya, G ... 703-247-2500 ... 99 D
sonya.udler@strayer.edu
UDOM, Udoh ... 615-871-2260 ... 99 D
UDOVIC, Edward, R ... 312-362-8042 ... 148 F
eudovic@depaul.edu
UDOVIC, CM, Edward, R ... 312-362-8042 ... 148 F
eudovic@depaul.edu
UDPA, Satish, S ... 517-355-5113 ... 255 D
udpa@msu.edu

V

VACHON DANHO, Renee 508-541-1712 234 B rdanho@dean.edu
VACHON DANHO, Renee 401-456-8091 454 A rdanho@ric.edu
VACIK, Stephen, M 785-460-5400 191 J steve.vacik@colbycc.edu
VACLAVIK, Sharon 361-572-6480 507 G sharon.vaclavik@victoriacollege.edu
VADALA, Mark 978-837-5134 242 D mark.vadala@merrimack.edu
VADEN, David 716-250-7500 324 H dvaden@bryantstratton.edu
VADEN, Sandra, D 856-691-8600 309 C svaden@cccnj.edu
VADEN-GOAD, Linda 508-626-4582 238 D lvadengoad@framingham.edu
VADER, Patricia 909-469-5318 78 D pvader@westernu.edu
VAGLIENTI, Kendra 972-860-4555 484 F kvaglienti@dcccd.edu
VAGNER, Bryan 618-453-4913 164 I bvagner@siu.edu
VAHEY, Karen, A 718-990-2160 348 G vaheyk@stjohns.edu
VAHLBUSCH, Jefford, B 715-836-3621 550 H vahlbujb@uwec.edu
VAHLE, Kirby, L 214-648-2400 507 D kirby.vahle@utsouthwestern.edu
VAHSEN, Steven, S 410-293-1568 558 H vahsen@usna.edu
VAIDYA, Ashish 323-343-3800 35 B avaidya@calstatela.edu
VAIL, Mita, K 757-455-3217 529 F mvail@vwc.edu
VAILAS, Arthur, C 208-282-3440 143 D vailarth@isu.edu
VAILLANCOURT, Allison 520-621-1684 19 B vaillana@email.arizona.edu
VAINNER, Thomas 517-787-0800 253 E vainnerthomasl@jccmi.edu
VAIRO, Carl, A 610-565-1095 452 A cvairo@williamson.edu
VAITHYLINGAM, Mugunth 702-651-5900 302 G mugunth.vaithylingam@csn.edu
VAKALIS, Marianne 973-278-5400 307 G mpv@berkeleycollege.edu
VAKALIS, Marianne 212-986-4343 323 J mpv@berkeleycollege.edu
VAKAMUDI, Ramesh 404-413-0721 131 C fmdrkv@gsu.edu
VALADEZ, James 909-748-8791 75 F james_valadez@redlands.edu
VALADEZ, Martin 509-542-4430 532 C mvaladez@columbiabasin.edu
VALAND, Steven, B 864-250-8185 458 F steve.valand@gvltec.edu
VALASEK, Thomas 908-526-1200 313 E tvalasek@raritanval.edu
VALBUENA, Al 301-860-3957 228 A avalbuena@bowiestate.edu
VALCKE, Catherine 765-455-9411 173 E chightow@iuk.edu
VALCOURT, George 813-491-6125 159 D george.valcourt@nl.edu
VALDES, Jose, L 305-821-3333 109 B jvaldes@mm.fnc.edu
VALDES, Jose, L 305-821-3333 109 C jvaldes@mm.fnc.edu
VALDES, Jose, L 305-821-3333 109 A jvaldes@mm.fnc.edu
VALDES, Mario 262-243-5700 546 I mario.valdes@cuw.edu
VALDESPINO, Maria 954-499-9832 104 C mvaldespino@devry.edu
VALDEZ, Al 951-785-2115 53 D avaldez@lasierra.edu
VALDEZ, Cristobal, O 937-778-7801 390 G cvaldez@edisonohio.edu
VALDEZ, Jose, L 305-231-3326 109 C jvaldes@mm.Fnc.edu
VALDEZ, Jude 210-458-2401 506 B jude.valdez@utsa.edu
VALDEZ, Julian 305-273-4499 103 C julian@cbt.edu
VALDEZ-FAULI, Mariana 202-408-2400 99 D
VALDIVIA, Monica 818-767-0888 79 D monica.valdivia@woodbury.edu
VALDIVIA, Nicolas 562-985-8391 35 A nvaldiv2@csulb.edu
VALE, SSJ, Carol Jean 215-248-7021 425 C cvale@chc.edu
VALE, Darla 513-244-4295 388 D darla_vale@mail.msj.edu
VALEK, Alan 216-791-5000 388 B ajv2@case.edu
VALEK, Millicent, M 979-230-3200 482 B millicent.valek@brazosport.edu
VALENCIA, Jhon 253-833-9111 534 C jvalencia@greenriver.edu
VALENCIA, Marilyn, F 216-397-4268 392 M mvalencia@jcu.edu
VALENCIA, Steven, J 580-327-8478 409 C sjvalencia@nwosu.edu
VALENCUELE, Arthur 808-955-1500 140 D arthur_valencuele@heald.edu
VALENTE, Bianca 610-359-5292 426 G bvalente@dccc.edu
VALENTE, Elizabeth 510-869-6243 64 J evalente@samuelmerritt.edu
VALENTE, Jason 517-787-0800 253 E valentejasonh@jccmi.edu
VALENTE, Mario 760-757-2121 57 E mvalente@miracosta.edu
VALENTE, Paula, R 716-880-2879 340 E paula.r.valente@medaille.edu
VALENTI, Anthony 973-300-2350 315 F tvalenti@sussex.edu
VALENTI, Antony 239-732-3776 104 L avalenti@edison.edu
VALENTI, Joseph 845-561-0800 342 A jospeh.valenti@msmc.edu
VALENTIN, Annette 787-786-3030 560 E anvalentin@ucb.edu.pr
VALENTIN, Cruz Belinda 787-763-6888 567 F cruz.valentin1@upr.edu
VALENTIN, Joe 727-726-1153 103 B joevalentin@clearwater.edu
VALENTIN, Julio 407-708-2281 117 G valentij@seminolestate.edu
VALENTIN, Luz, C 787-786-3030 560 E lvalentin@ucb.edu.pr
VALENTINE, Ann, M 812-298-2201 177 A valentine@ivytech.edu
VALENTINE, Bryan 505-984-6096 320 C bvalentine@sjcsf.edu
VALENTINE, Bryan 814-269-7064 449 D bvalen@pitt.edu
VALENTINE, Carey, G 248-204-3800 254 E campfac@ltu.edu
VALENTINE, Christy 870-972-3780 20 C cvalentine@astate.edu
VALENTINE, Jared 503-517-1008 421 A jvalentine@warnerpacific.edu
VALENTINE, Leanne 712-749-2164 182 G valentinel@bvu.edu
VALENTINE, Maureen 724-503-1001 451 A mvalentine@washjeff.edu
VALENTINE, Peggy 336-750-2570 380 A valentinepe@wssu.edu
VALENTINE, Richard, D 573-288-6323 281 D rvalentine@culver.edu
VALENTINE, Robert 212-463-0400 357 J robert.valentine@touro.edu
VALENTINE, Robert 415-749-4515 65 I rvalentine@sfai.edu
VALENTINE, Sidney 803-327-8017 463 G
VALENTINE, Tony 305-626-3619 108 H tvalentine@fmuniv.edu
VALENTINI, Ron 828-327-7000 368 G rvalenti@cvcc.edu
VALENTINO, Christina, L 831-459-3778 75 A basonline@ucsc.edu
VALENTINO, Lisa 407-971-5010 117 G valentil@seminolestate.edu
VALENTO, Bernard 585-395-2751 352 F bvalento@brockport.edu
VALENZA, John, A 713-500-4021 506 D john.a.valenza@uth.tmc.edu
VALENZIANO, Patricia 708-709-2947 161 C pvalenziano@prairiestate.edu
VALENZUELA, Cesario, E 432-837-8076 501 B cesariov@sulross.edu
VALENZUELA, Eileen 925-439-2181 43 D evalenzuela@losmedanos.edu
VALENZUELA, Ernesto 520-494-5459 13 F ernesto.valenzuela@centralaz.edu
VALERA, Luis 702-895-2389 302 K luis.valera@unlv.edu
VALERA, Marc 718-817-3842 334 C valera@fordham.edu
VALERIANO, Oscar 323-265-8777 54 G valerio@elac.edu
VALERIANO, Zaira 432-685-4534 490 G zaira@midland.edu
VALERIO, Brett 414-443-8785 553 B brett.valerio@wlc.edu
VALERIO, Marilyn 402-354-7027 299 E marilyn.valerio@methodistcollege.edu
VALERIO, Sandra 361-698-1277 485 F svalerio@delmar.edu
VALERIO, Vance, R 325-942-2193 480 E vance.valerio@angelo.edu
VALERY, Suzanne 805-922-6966 26 K svalery@hancockcollege.edu
VALEZENO, Dennis 907-786-4708 10 I afdvp@uaa.alaska.edu
VALIENTE, Barbara 323-259-2660 59 H bgillett@oxy.edu
VALINE, Debra, K 608-785-8006 551 B valine.debr@uwlax.edu
VALINE, Janet, E 814-269-7081 449 D valine@pitt.edu
VALINES, Francisco 305-348-2347 119 B valinesf@fiu.edu
VALINTIS, Michelle 503-253-3443 417 H mvalintis@ocom.edu
VALK, Dana 323-259-2602 59 H dvalk@oxy.edu
VALKINBURG, David 740-753-6591 392 A valkinburg_d@hocking.edu
VALKO, Christi 814-536-5168 424 C cvalko@crbc.net
VALLANCE, Brenda, J 512-448-8550 493 B brendav@stedwards.edu
VALLANDINGHAM, Richard 309-796-5047 145 E vallandinghamd@bhc.edu
VALLAR, Larry 304-243-2359 545 G
VALLE, Sondra, E 518-629-7622 336 C s.valle@hvcc.edu
VALLEJO, Isabel 408-273-2695 58 G ivallejo@nhu.edu
VALLEJO, Maria, M 561-868-3400 114 D vallejom@palmbeachstate.edu
VALLES, Arleen 575-835-5162 319 A avalles@admin.nmt.edu
VALLEY, Clinton 951-785-2266 53 D cvalley@lasierra.edu
VALLEY, Cynthia, K 412-268-2922 424 H cvza@andrew.cmu.edu
VALLEY, Timothy 414-277-7150 548 H valley@msoe.edu
VALLOZZI, Jason 412-359-1000 448 F jvallozzi@triangle-tech.edu
VALOSKY, Kenneth, G 610-519-4530 450 G ken.valosky@villanova.edu
VALTIERRA, J. Guadalupe 219-981-4404 176 E jvaltier@ivytech.edu
VALTOS, Jennifer 770-426-2762 133 B jvaltos@life.edu
VALUCKAS, Christine, A 410-287-1027 222 A cvaluckas@cecil.edu
VAMVAKIDES, Judite 203-396-2872 93 G vamvakidesj@sacredheart.edu
VAN AKEN, Troy, D 724-589-2100 448 A tvanaken@thiel.edu
VAN ALFEN, Neal, K 530-752-1605 73 F nkvanalfen@ucdavis.edu
VAN ALLEN, George, H 615-353-3236 475 D george.vanallen@nscc.edu
VAN ALLEN, Terry 810-766-6842 259 F terryva@umflint.edu
VAN ALSTINE, Tim 309-298-1106 168 A t-vanalstine@wiu.edu
VAN ARNAM, Sherrie 718-940-5754 349 A svanarnam@sjcny.edu
VAN AUKEN, James 757-457-7121 516 C james.vanauken@atlanticuniv.edu
VAN BAAREN, Valerie, L 973-655-5225 311 G vanbaarenv@mail.montclair.edu
VAN BERGEIJK, Ernst 631-348-3117 343 D evanberg@nyit.edu
VAN BERGEN, Mildred 516-876-4076 355 F mildred.vanbergen@esc.edu
VAN BERKOM, Debbie 701-224-5431 382 B debbie.vanberkom@bismarckstate.edu
VAN BIBBER, Karl 831-656-3241 557 H kavanbibb@nps.edu
VAN BLARCOM, Ronald 949-214-3135 42 K ron.vanblarcom@cui.edu
VAN BRUNT, Brian 270-745-2701 207 C brian.vanbrunt@wku.edu
VAN BRUNT, Troy, G 956-721-5326 489 G troyvb@laredo.edu
VAN BUREN, David, P 608-342-1262 551 F vanburen@uwplatt.edu
VAN BUREN, Mary 386-226-6525 105 B vanburem@erau.edu
VAN BUSKIRK, Christina, P 717-245-1640 427 E vanbuski@dickinson.edu
VAN CANNEYT, Donna, S 901-678-2810 474 C dvncnnyt@memphis.edu
VAN CLEAVE, Martha 503-883-2308 416 G mvcleave@linfield.edu
VAN CLEAVE, Robb 541-506-6150 415 C rvancleave@cgcc.cc.or.us
VAN CLEAVE, Samuel, J 480-423-6003 16 D samuel.vancleave@sccmail.maricopa.edu
VAN CLEAVE, William 504-865-5767 215 C wvanclea@tulane.edu
VAN CLEEF, Sarah, E 903-510-2033 502 E svan@tjc.edu
VAN DAM, Dale 530-642-5644 56 C
VAN DE BOOGAARD, Eric 719-587-7951 80 F evdb@adams.edu
VAN DE CAR, Katharyn 702-651-4516 302 G kathy.vandecar@csn.edu
VAN DE LOO, John 715-365-4553 554 F vandeloo@nicoletcollege.edu
VAN DE MOORTELL, Raymond 617-254-2610 244 E
VAN DE PUTTE, Andre 312-629-6100 164 A avande2@saic.edu
VAN DEKKER, Angela 718-817-3800 334 C avandekker@fordham.edu
VAN DEN ABBEELE, Georges 617-373-5173 244 A
VAN DEN BERG, Rex 805-922-6966 26 K rvandenberg@hancockcollege.edu
VAN DEN BERGHE, Bruce 651-962-6060 272 b9vandenberg@stthomas.edu
VAN DEN HUL, Richard, D 360-650-3182 539 rich.vandenhul@wwu.edu
VAN DENEND, Michael, J 616-526-6142 249 vanden@calvin.edu
VAN DER BURG, Anna 860-685-2810 95 C avanderburg@wesleyan.edu
VAN DER GIESSEN, Hans 203-576-4668 94 D hvdg@bridgeport.edu
VAN DER KARR, Carol 607-753-2206 353 E carol.vanderkarr@cortland.edu
VAN DER KLEY, Jan 269-387-2365 260 F jan.vanderkley@wmich.edu
VAN DER LEEUW, Sander 480-965-6214 12 B vanderle@asu.edu
VAN DER MEID, J. Scott 781-736-3483 233 A svanderm@brandeis.edu
VAN DER POL, Willem 657-278-2065 34 E wvanderpol@fullerton.edu
VAN DER VEER, Mary Caroline 518-587-2100 355 F marycaroline.powers@esc.edu
VAN DER WEELE, Eileen 662-329-8549 276 B evanderweele@audit.muw.edu
VAN DERVEER, Rachael 724-847-6596 429 G 0643mgr@fheg.follett.com
VAN DEVEN, Randy 903-468-8181 497 E randy_vandeven@tamu-commerce.edu
VAN DINE, Kathryn, L 563-588-8000 184 F registrar@emmaus.edu
VAN DONSELAAR, Brian 712-722-6299 183 H brianvd@dordt.edu
VAN DOREN, Greg 218-935-0417 273 A greg.vandoren@wctcc.org
VAN DUSER, Kathy 773-371-5450 146 B admissions@ctu.edu
VAN DUYNE, Patrick 815-280-6696 154 H pvanduyn@jjc.edu
VAN DUZER, Jeffrey, B 206-281-2087 537 D vandj@spu.edu
VAN DYCK, Judy 503-725-4878 418 G vandyckj@pdx.edu
VAN DYK, Leanne 616-392-8555 260 G leanne.vandyk@westernsem.edu
VAN DYKE, James 920-923-8083 548 C jvandyke@marianuniversity.edu
VAN DYKE, Jon 217-234-5378 155 H jvandyke@lakeland.cc.il.us
VAN DYKE, Michael, J 802-728-1213 515 G mvandyke@vtc.vsc.edu
VAN DYKE, Patricia 716-829-7802 332 F vandykep@dyc.edu
VAN DYKEN, Douglas 616-395-7810 252 F vandyken@hope.edu
VAN ECK, Thomas, A 616-526-8553 249 E tveck@calvin.edu
VAN ELLIS, Wayne 562-907-4241 79 B wvanellis@law.whittier.edu
VAN ESS, Jami 928-226-4209 13 H jami.vaness@coconino.edu
VAN ESSEN, Quentin 712-722-6080 183 H quentin@dordt.edu
VAN FOSSEN, Brian, F 570-340-6024 435 F bvanfossen@marywood.edu
VAN FOSSEN, Dell Jean 951-785-2088 53 D dvanfoss@lasierra.edu
VAN FOSSEN, Drew 920-403-4427 550 C drew.vanfossen@snc.edu
VAN GALEN, Dean, A 715-425-3201 552 A dean.vangalen@uwrf.edu
VAN GIESON, Christine, N 805-893-3641 74 F christine.vangieson@sa.ucsb.edu
VAN GIESON, Cindy 517-780-4554 248 I cindy.vangieson@baker.edu
VAN GILDER, Holly 330-490-7144 405 E hvangilder@walsh.edu
VAN GINHOVEN, Lee, H 269-927-8611 254 B vanginhoven@lakemichigancollege.edu
VAN GOOR, Nelia, A 980-598-1007 365 G nelia.vangoor@jwu.edu
VAN GORDON, Beth 219-980-7202 173 F vgordon@iun.edu
VAN GORDON, Elizabeth 574-520-4463 174 C vgordon@iusb.edu
VAN GRONINGEN, Willis 708-239-4880 165 I bill.vangroningen@trnty.edu
VAN GRUENSVEN, Sheryl 920-465-2326 551 A vangrues@uwgb.edu
VAN GUNDY, Doug 304-473-8243 545 F vangundy@wvwc.edu
VAN HAMERSVELD, Pete 310-243-3825 34 B pvanhamersveld@csudh.edu
VAN HARPEN, Robin 414-229-2629 551 C rvanharp@uwm.edu
VAN HEMERT, Ann 641-628-7645 183 A
VAN HEMERT, John, L 540-674-3660 527 B jvanhemert@nr.edu
VAN HOLLAND, Phyllis, L 360-417-6291 536 B pvanholland@pencol.edu
VAN HOOK, Dianne, G 661-362-3400 41 G dianne.vanhook@canyons.edu

AN HOOK, Jayson .... 423-614-8695.... 470 A
jvanhook@leeuniversity.edu
AN HORN, Brian, W .... 270-809-4159.... 204 F
brian.vanhorn@murraystate.edu
AN HORN, Donald, L ...... 304-696-6433.... 543 G
vanhorn@marshall.edu
AN HORN, Fred .... 478-387-4778.... 130 E
VAN HORN, Keith, F .... 419-267-1303.... 397 D
kvanhorn@northweststate.edu
VAN HORN, Stu .... 916-608-6500...... 56 C
VAN HORN, Wayne .... 601-925-3297.... 275 E
wvanhorn@mc.edu
VAN HOUT, Vicky .... 920-735-5731.... 553 G
VAN HOUTEN, Michael ...... 517-629-0567.... 247 E
mvanhouten@albion.edu
VAN KEUREN, Karen, A .... 585-785-1206.... 334 A
vankeuka@flcc.edu
VAN KIRK, Shannon .... 541-278-5916.... 414 G
svankirk@bluecc.edu
VAN KLEY, Sandy .... 712-707-7145.... 188 B
svankley@nwciowa.edu
VAN LANINGHAM,
Kathy, M .... 479-575-5910...... 24 C
kvl@uark.edu
VAN LEAR, Michael, C ...... 808-955-1500.... 140 D
michael_vanlear@heald.edu
VAN LEIDEN, Melissa .... 785-594-8306.... 190 C
melissa.vanleiden@bakeru.edu
VAN LOO, Scott, D .... 419-289-5088.... 384 D
svanloo@ashland.edu
VAN MARTER, Dianne .... 313-831-5200.... 251 A
dvanmarter@etseminary.edu
VAN MEETEREN, Lisa .... 909-748-8047...... 75 F
lisa_vanmeeteren@redlands.edu
VAN METER, Gary .... 805-645-6471...... 77 D
gvanmeter@vcccd.edu
VAN NAME, Carol .... 805-922-6966...... 26 K
cvanname@hancockcollege.edu
VAN NATTA, Gretchen .... 312-341-2479.... 162 I
gvannatta@roosevelt.edu
VAN NESS, Forrest, L .... 314-516-6680.... 291 F
vannessf@umsl.edu
VAN NIEKERK, Andre .... 818-767-0888...... 79 D
andre.vanniekerk@woodbury.edu
VAN NORMAN, Karen .... 973-761-9076.... 315 B
karen.vannorman@shu.edu
VAN OMMEREN, Ryan .... 805-493-3211...... 32 H
rvommere@clunet.edu
VAN OORT, Harlan .... 712-707-7190.... 188 B
hvanoort@nwciowa.edu
VAN ORMAN, Kit .... 315-364-3317.... 360 C
kit@wells.edu
VAN ORMAN, Sarah, A ..... 608-262-1885.... 550 G
svanorman@uhs.wisc.edu
VAN ORNAM, Donald, C .. 423-236-2750.... 473 A
dvanorn@southern.edu
VAN ORSDEL, Lee .... 616-331-2621.... 252 A
vanorsdl@gvsu.edu
VAN PELT, Cynthia .... 734-487-0455.... 250 H
cynthia.vanpelt@emich.edu
VAN PELT, Richard .... 626-585-7201...... 61 E
rpvanpelt@pasadena.edu
VAN PELT, Richard .... 626-585-7277...... 61 E
rpvanpelt@pasadena.edu
VAN RIPER, Lisa .... 804-289-8778.... 525 A
lvanripe@richmond.edu
VAN SCHARREL, Mark, H . 773-256-0676.... 157 B
mvanscha@lstc.edu
VAN SCHYNDEL,
C. Richard .... 208-467-8445.... 143 I
crvanschyndel@nnu.edu
VAN SHERRILL, Martin ..... 256-372-4735........ 1 A
martin.sherrill@aamu.edu
VAN SICKLE, Frederick, M 212-854-1754.... 330 F
VAN SICKLE, Lee .... 773-298-3410.... 163 G
vansickle@sxu.edu
VAN SLYCK, Abigail, A ..... 860-439-2731...... 91 E
abigail.van-slyck@conncoll.edu
VAN SOELEN, Timothy ...... 712-722-6228.... 183 H
timothyv@dcrdt.edu
VAN SOMEREN, Charles ... 202-462-2101...... 98 C
vansomeren@iwp.edu
VAN STEENHUYSE,
Kathleen .... 319-398-4911.... 186 H
kvanste@kirkwood.edu
VAN STRATEN, Amy .... 920-831-4355.... 553 G
vanstrat@fvtc.edu
VAN TASSEL, Kristin .... 785-227-3380.... 190 G
vantasselk@bethanylb.edu
VAN THUYNE, Michael, E . 215-637-7700.... 430 H
mvanthuyne@holyfamily.edu
VAN TIL, Seth, J .... 724-458-3887.... 430 B
sjvantil@gcc.edu
VAN TRAN, Lac .... 312-942-3400.... 163 B
lac_tran@rush.edu
VAN UUM, Elizabeth .... 314-516-5774.... 291 F
vanuum@umsl.edu
VAN VACTOR, Myra .... 425-564-2255.... 531 B
myra.vanvactor@bellevuecollege.edu
VAN VALEN, Gretchen .... 607-274-3846.... 336 G
gvanvalen@ithaca.edu
VAN VECHTEN, Daniel ...... 513-244-4466.... 388 D
daniel_van_vechten@mail.msj.edu
VAN VLECK, Thomas .... 660-626-2138.... 278 F
tvanvleck@atsu.edu
VAN VOLKENBURGH,
Linda, C .... 513-861-6400.... 402 I
linda.van@myunion.edu
VAN VOORHIS, Sue, N ..... 612-625-8098.... 272 D
vanvo002@umn.edu
VAN WAGNER, Molly .... 715-425-3195.... 552 A
molly.van-wagner@uwrf.edu
VAN WAGONER,
Randall, J .... 315-792-5333.... 341 E
rvanwagoner@mvcc.edu
VAN WEELDEN, Kathy ...... 603-428-2235.... 305 E
kvanweelden@nec.edu
VAN WICKLIN, Bob .... 585-567-9340.... 336 B
bob.vanwicklin@houghton.edu
VAN WIE, Lisa .... 518-629-8143.... 336 C
l.vanwie@hvcc.edu
VAN WINGERDEN,
Thomas, J .... 616-526-6378.... 249 E
tjv6@calvin.edu
VAN WINKLE, Julian .... 847-543-2641.... 147 H
jvanwinkle@clcillinois.edu
VAN WINKLE, Robynne ..... 541-440-4600.... 420 F
robynne.vanwinkle@umpqua.edu
VAN WYK, Christopher ..... 973-408-3502.... 309 F
cvanwyk@drew.edu
VAN WYK, Sharon .... 304-724-3700.... 540 C
svanwyk@apus.edu
VAN ZANDT, David .... 212-229-5600.... 342 E
VAN ZINDEREN, Gary .... 701-252-3467.... 381 A
gvanzind@jc.edu
VAN ZWOL, R. William ..... 520-318-2700...... 12 E
rvanzwol@aii.edu
VAN ZYL, Henry .... 609-292-4000.... 316 A
phvanzyl@tesc.edu
VANARSDALL, Cathy .... 765-361-6421.... 181 C
vanarsdc@wabash.edu
VANASSE, Dennis .... 508-849-3372.... 230 C
dvanasse@annamaria.edu
VANAUSDLE, Steven, L ..... 509-527-4274.... 538 G
steven.vanausdle@wwcc.edu
VANCAMP, Grayson .... 773-947-6283.... 157 E
gvancamp@mccormick.edu
VANCE, Carl .... 503-768-7801.... 416 F
cvance@lclark.edu
VANCE, Debra .... 812-330-6111.... 175 H
dvance@ivytech.edu
VANCE, Elaine .... 202-651-5288...... 97 E
janet.vance@gallaudet.edu
VANCE, Linda, B .... 407-582-2586.... 122 I
lvance@valenciacollege.edu
VANCE, Mary Lee .... 715-394-8580.... 552 D
mvance@uwsuper.edu
VANCE, Mickey .... 601-635-6208.... 274 C
mvance@eccc.edu
VANCE, Richard, N .... 765-658-4233.... 170 I
VANCE, Robert .... 414-577-2658.... 159 D
rvance@nl.edu
VANCE, W, C .... 816-235-1208.... 291 E
vancewc@umkc.edu
VANCKO, Candace .... 518-255-5111.... 354 E
vanckocs@cobleskill.edu
VANCKO, Candace, S .... 607-746-4090.... 355 E
vanckocs@delhi.edu
VANCLEAVE, Donna .... 804-819-4695.... 525 F
dvancleave@vccs.edu
VANCO, Peggy .... 414-229-4853.... 551 C
pvanco@uwm.edu
VANDE VOORT, Lee .... 641-628-5152.... 183 A
vandevoortl@central.edu
VANDE YACHT, Dan .... 715-425-3342.... 552 A
daniel.vandeyacht@uwrf.edu
VANDE ZANDE, Carleen ..... 920-424-3190.... 551 D
vandezac@uwosh.edu
VANDEGRIFT, OP,
Raymond .... 202-495-3856...... 98 D
rvandegrift@dhs.edu
VANDEGRIFT, Vaughn .... 618-650-2481.... 165 A
vandegr@siue.edu
VANDELINDER, David .... 313-993-1639.... 259 C
vandelda@udmercy.edu
VANDELL, Deborah, L .... 949-824-8026...... 73 H
dvandell@uci.edu
VANDEN BERGE, Philip .... 616-957-6042.... 249 F
pvberge@calvinseminary.edu
VANDEN BOOM,
Leonard, A .... 414-277-7154.... 548 H
vandenbo@msoe.edu
VANDENAVOND, Steve .... 920-465-2641.... 551 A
vandenas@uwgb.edu
VANDENBERG, Ed .... 281-476-1501.... 493 E
ed.vandenberg@sjcd.edu
VANDENBERG, Patricia ...... 413-538-2899.... 242 G
pvandenb@mtholyoke.edu
VANDENBERGHE, Claire ... 585-395-5415.... 352 F
cvandenb@brockport.edu
VANDER HOEK, Nancy .... 605-229-8545.... 464 I
nancy.vanderhoek@presentation.edu
VANDER HOOVEN, James 603-524-3207.... 304 D
jvanderhooven@ccsnh.edu
VANDER HORN, Alexis, A 563-884-5102...... 60 L
alexis.vanderhorn@palmer.edu
VANDER HORN, Alexis, A 563-884-5102.... 188 C
alexis.vanderhorn@palmer.edu
VANDER PLOEG, Scott ..... 270-824-8684.... 202 C
scott.vanderploeg@kctcs.edu
VANDER VELDE, George ... 708-239-4792.... 165 I
george.vandervelde@trnty.edu
VANDER WERF, Dave .... 712-722-6020.... 183 H
davevw@dordt.edu
VANDER ZWAAG, Lora ..... 712-274-6400.... 189 H
lora.vanderzwaag@witcc.edu
VANDERBILT, Michelle ...... 253-943-2800.... 533 B
mvanderbilt@devry.edu
VANDERBILT, William .... 616-395-7850.... 252 F
vanderbilt@hope.edu
VANDERBOUT, Jenne .... 660-543-8000.... 291 B
vanderbout@ucmo.edu
VANDERBURG, Judy, J ...... 503-838-8490.... 419 C
vanderj@wou.edu
VANDERBURGH, Paul, M . 937-229-2390.... 404 A
Paul.Vanderburgh@udayton.edu
VANDERFORD, Brenda ...... 304-766-5107.... 544 D
bvanderf@wvstateu.edu
VANDERGRIFT, Peggy, L .. 205-853-1200........ 5 C
pvandy@jeffstateonline.com
VANDERHART, Mark .... 219-864-2400.... 178 B
mvanderhart@midamerica.edu
VANDERHILL, Dan .... 517-750-1200.... 258 F
danv@arbor.edu
VANDERHILL, Steven, T .... 214-528-8600.... 492 F
VANDERHOFF, Jessica ...... 860-906-5021...... 89 L
jvanderhoff@ccc.commnet.edu
VANDERHOOF, Karen .... 973-328-5012.... 309 B
kvanderhoof@ccm.edu
VANDERHORN, Alexis, A .. 563-884-5102.... 114 E
alexis.vanderhorn@palmer.edu
VANDERLAND, Helen .... 804-819-4951.... 525 F
hvanderland@vccs.edu
VANDERLICK, T. Kyle .... 203-432-4220...... 95 D
kyle.vanderlick@yale.edu
VANDERMAAS-PEELER,
Maureen .... 336-278-6453.... 364 A
vanderma@elon.edu
VANDERPOL, Diane .... 801-832-2013.... 512 F
dvanderpol@westminstercollege.edu
VANDERPOOL, Janet .... 660-359-3948.... 287 D
jvanderpool@mail.ncmissouri.edu
VANDERPOOL, Molly .... 765-973-8415.... 173 D
moberry@iue.edu
VANDERSLICE, Ronna, J .... 580-581-2339.... 407 D
rvanderslice@cameron.edu
VANDERSPOEL, James ...... 906-932-4231.... 251 E
jimv@gogebic.edu
VANDERSTAAY, Steven, L . 360-650-3004.... 539 C
steven.vanderstaay@wwu.edu
VANDERSTEL, David .... 317-917-3388.... 177 H
dvanderstel@martin.edu
VANDERVEEN, R Pete, L .. 323-442-1369...... 76 C
phardean@usc.edu
VANDERVELDEN, Michael . 208-459-5851.... 143 A
mvandervelden@collegeofidaho.edu
VANDERVOORT,
Patricia, A .... 361-582-2587.... 507 G
patricia.vandervoort@victoriacollege.edu
VANDERVORT,
Michael, W .... 512-471-7117.... 505 B
mike.vandervort@austin.utexas.edu
VANDERWEL, David .... 616-395-7777.... 252 F
vanderwel@hope.edu
VANDERWOUDE, Chris ..... 703-658-4304.... 517 H
coachvw@christendom.edu
VANDERWOUDE, Katrina .. 248-218-2109.... 257 F
kvanderwoude@rc.edu
VANDERWYST, Roxann, S . 715-233-5358.... 553 F
rvanderwyst@cvtc.edu
VANDERZWAAG, George .. 585-275-4301.... 358 I
george.vanderzwaag@rochester.edu
VANDEVANDER, David, R . 540-828-5316.... 516 K
devandeva@bridgewater.edu
VANDEVER, Jennifer .... 618-650-5234.... 165 A
jvandev@siue.edu
VANDEVILLE, Denise .... 906-487-7379.... 251 C
denise.vandeville@finlandia.edu
VANDEVOORDE, Eric .... 765-269-5458.... 176 B
evandevoorde@ivytech.edu
VANDEWALKER, Sara, L ... 217-443-8777.... 148 E
slong@dacc.edu
VANDIJK, Carol .... 623-572-3323...... 16 F
cvandi@midwestern.edu
VANDIVER, Russell .... 770-531-6304.... 132 J
vandiver@laniertech.edu
VANDYKE, Jacki .... 262-691-5266.... 555 C
jvandyke@wctc.edu
VANDYKE, Rhonda, L .... 276-964-7388.... 528 A
rhonda.vandyke@sw.edu
VANDYKE COLBY,
Rhonda .... 540-665-4500.... 523 K
rcolby@su.edu
VANECEK, Frank .... 802-485-2725.... 514 A
vanecek@norwich.edu
VANEERDEN, Kathy, S .... 262-335-5757.... 554 E
kvaneerden@morainepark.edu
VANEGAS, Jorge .... 979-845-1221.... 497 C
jvanegas@tamu.edu
VANEK, Susan .... 574-284-4594.... 179 D
svanek@saintmarys.edu
VANFLEET, Rita .... 402-552-3516.... 297 D
vanfleetrita@clarksoncollege.edu
VANG, Mai .... 715-346-2002.... 552 B
mavang@uwsp.edu
VANG, Pakou .... 651-773-1741.... 266 D
pakou.vang@century.edu
VANGALDER, Jeanette .... 970-351-2341...... 88 F
jeanette.vangalder@unco.edu
VANGARELLI, Kim .... 570-226-4625.... 433 A
vangarellik@lackawanna.edu
VANGSGARD, Mark, D .... 651-962-6095.... 272 E
mdvangsgard@stthomas.edu
VANGSNESS, Jane .... 701-231-8012.... 381 C
jane.vangsness@ndus.edu
VANHECKE, JoNes .... 507-933-7526.... 264 B
jvanheck@gustavus.edu
VANHEE, Tonya .... 970-943-2493...... 89 B
tvanhee@western.edu
VANHIMBERGEN,
Thomas, W .... 414-410-4002.... 546 D
twvanhimbergen@stritch.edu
VANHOORELBEKE, Jack ...... 989-964-4109.... 258 A
jvh@svsu.edu
VANIS, Mary .... 602-371-1188...... 17 C
VANIS, Mary .... 602-371-1188.... 195 F
mary.vanis@ottawa.edu
VANKERCKHOVE, Iris .... 718-409-5514.... 356 C
ivankerckhove@sunymaritime.edu
VANKEUREN, James, P ...... 419-289-5377.... 384 D
jvankeu1@ashland.edu
VANKO, David .... 410-704-2121.... 228 E
dvanko@towson.edu
VANLANDINGHAM,
Brenda .... 662-246-6301.... 275 F
bvanlandingham@msdelta.edu
VANLANDINGHAM, Liz .... 303-360-4769...... 83 E
liz.vanlandingham@ccaurora.edu
VANLONDEN, April .... 800-287-8822.... 169 E
vanloap@earlham.edu
VANLONDON, April .... 765-983-1816.... 171 B
vonloap@earlham.edu
VANLONE, Jeffrey .... 315-781-3000.... 335 G
vanlone@hws.edu
VANMETER, Terry .... 270-789-5031.... 199 C
twvanmeter@campbellsville.edu
VANN, Allen .... 305-348-2465.... 119 B
Allen.Vann@fiu.edu
VANN, Andre, D .... 919-530-7453.... 378 A
avann@nccu.edu
VANN, Wendy .... 252-862-1234.... 372 H
vannw@roanokechowan.edu
VANNESS, Kathryn, A .... 540-375-2257.... 523 D
vanness@roanoke.edu
VANNEY, Greg, T .... 563-387-1350.... 187 A
vanneygr@luther.edu
VANNEY, Pete .... 715-365-4419.... 554 F
pvanney@nicoletcollege.edu
VANNIMAN, Dawn .... 810-762-0045.... 256 C
dawn.vanniman@mcc.edu
VANNOY, Judy .... 276-326-4260.... 516 I
jvannoy@bluefield.edu
VANNOY, Roger .... 423-869-6285.... 470 C
athletics@lmunet.edu
VANOVER, Chance .... 405-425-5086.... 409 E
chance.vanover@oc.edu
VANOVERSCHELDE, Jim ... 512-223-7246.... 481 B
jvanover@austincc.edu
VANRHEENEN, Mark .... 248-218-2049.... 257 F
mvanrheenen@rc.edu
VANSAGHI, Tom, M .... 816-604-1090.... 285 D
tom.vansaghi@mcckc.edu
VANSELL, Kimberly .... 660-543-4123.... 291 B
VANSICKLE, Cissy .... 301-387-3083.... 222 H
cissy.vansickle@garrettcollege.edu
VANSTEEN, John .... 631-656-3187.... 334 B
jvansteen@ftc.edu
VANSTRYDONCK,
Gerald, E .... 585-340-9640.... 329 G
gvanstrydonck@crcds.edu
VANSWEDEN, James, A ..... 269-337-7291.... 253 F
James.VanSweden@kzoo.edu
VANTILBURG, Mark, W ...... 330-941-3518.... 406 F
mwvantilburg@ysu.edu
VANTOORN, Kay .... 817-531-4414.... 502 A
kvantoorn@txwes.edu
VANTYLE, Peter, R .... 315-568-3146.... 342 H
pvantyle@nycc.edu
VANVOORST, James, R ...... 607-777-2157.... 351 F
vanvoors@binghamton.edu
VANWAART, Ellen .... 712-325-3244.... 186 B
evanwaart@iwcc.edu
VANWINKLE, David, B .... 847-969-4922.... 145 A
dvanwinkle@argosy.edu
VANZANT, Michael .... 740-392-6868.... 396 H
mvanzant@mvnu.edu
VARAHRAMYAN, Kody .... 317-274-1020.... 174 B
kvarahra@iupui.edu
VARANO, Babette .... 201-684-7028.... 313 D
blanni@ramapo.edu
VARAS, Elaine, P .... 973-972-7030.... 316 C
varas@umdnj.edu
VARBLE, Susan .... 504-762-3031.... 210 G
svarbl@dcc.edu
VARDAMAN, Lee .... 334-808-6319........ 8 B
vardaman@troy.edu
VARDANEGA, Dave .... 415-749-4570...... 65 I
dvardanega@sfai.edu

VARDEMAN, Vicki 575-492-2725 319 B
vvardeman@nmjc.edu

VARELA, Julio 956-380-8104 493 A
jvarela@riogrande.edu

VARELA, Lorell 787-834-9595 565 J

VARGA, Alane, P 315-792-3100 359 C
avarga@utica.edu

VARGA, Ann Marie 407-646-2159 116 B
avarga@rollins.edu

VARGA, Shane 269-782-1321 258 E
svarga@swmich.edu

VARGAS, Elizabeth 787-728-1515 568 B
evargas@sagrado.edu

VARGAS, Erin 909-931-7599 78 H
evargas@westwood.edu

VARGAS, Ileana 787-765-1915 564 B
ivargas@inter.edu

VARGAS, Jose 714-628-5941 63 G
vargas_jose@sccollege.edu

VARGAS, Jose 760-744-1150 61 C
jvargas@palomar.edu

VARGAS, Lizzette 787-753-6335 562 E
lvargas@icpruc.edu

VARGAS, Magda 787-841-2000 564 I
mivargas@email.pucpr.edu

VARGAS, Manuel 336-750-2370 380 A
vargasma@wssu.edu

VARGAS, Mark, A 773-298-3350 163 G
vargas@sxu.edu

VARGAS, Phillip 210-434-6711 491 G
pvargas@lake.ollusa.edu

VARGAS, Wanda 787-891-0925 562 G
wvargas@aguadilla.inter.edu

VARGAS, Yanina 413-552-2231 240 C
yvargas@hcc.edu

VARGAS-ABURTO, Carlos 610-683-4212 442 F
cvargas@kutztown.edu

VARGO, Karen 574-520-4878 174 C
kvargo@iusb.edu

VARHUS, Sara 585-389-2011 342 D
svarhus0@naz.edu

VARI, April, L 717-245-1639 427 E
varia@dickinson.edu

VARKONYI, Istvan, L 215-204-3177 447 G
istvan.varkonyi@temple.edu

VARLAND, Roger, M 517-750-1200 258 F
rvarland@arbor.edu

VARLOTTA, Lori 916-278-6060 35 E
varlotta@csus.edu

VARN, James, S 603-862-3290 306 E
jim.varn@unh.edu

VARNAU, Chris 317-931-2316 170 E
cvarnau@cts.edu

VARNELL, Jonathan, P 336-316-2153 364 E
jvarnell@guilford.edu

VARNER, Donna, A 757-594-8816 517 I
dvarner@cnu.edu

VARNER, Jeanine, B 325-674-2024 478 H
jeanine.varner@acu.edu

VARNER, Jenny, M 336-249-8186 369 F
jmvarner@davidsonccc.edu

VARNER, Katy 502-213-7303 202 B
katy.varner@kctcs.edu

VARNER, Mary, C 610-526-1302 421 G
mary.varner@theamericancollege.edu

VARNER, Stu 501-279-4331 21 H
svarner@harding.edu

VARNET, Harvey 843-208-8025 462 C
varnet@uscb.edu

VARNET, Harvey 843-208-8203 462 C
varnet@uscb.edu

VARNEY, Donna 304-645-6373 544 C
dvarney@osteo.wvsom.edu

VARNEY, Janice 269-639-8442 254 B
varney@lakemichigancollege.edu

VARNEY, Ruth 804-594-1559 526 G
rvarney@jtcc.edu

VARNSON, Stacie 701-483-2999 381 E
stacie.varnson@dickinsonstate.edu

VARNUM, Linda, J 603-526-3738 304 A
lindav@colby-sawyer.edu

VARONA, Juan, N 787-738-4660 567 A
juan.varona@upr.edu

VARONA-ECHEANDÍA, Juan, N 787-738-2161 566 D
juan.varona@upr.edu

VARSA, Barbara 301-314-7735 227 B
bvarsa@umd.edu

VARSALONA, Jack, P 302-356-6818 97 A
donna.m.quinn@wilmu.edu

VARSALONA, Jacque, R 302-295-1168 97 A
jacqueline.r.varsalona@wilmu.edu

VARSHNEY, Sanjay 916-278-6011 35 E
varshney@csus.edu

VARTEBEDIAN, Robert, A 816-271-4237 287 A
president@missouriwestern.edu

VARVILLE, Paul 956-872-2330 494 D
pbvarvil@southtexascollege.edu

VARVIS, Stephen 559-453-2031 47 K
slvarvis@fresno.edu

VARWIG, Jana 410-704-2270 228 E
jvarwig@towson.edu

VASARHELYI, Marina 914-323-5139 340 A
marina.vasarhelyi@mville.edu

VASBINDER, Linda, M 609-984-1105 316 A
lvasbinder@tesc.edu

VASCONCELLOS, Tina 510-986-6992 62 C
tvasconcellos@peralta.edu

VASCURA, Jacquelyn, L 740-826-8084 396 I
jkent@muskingum.edu

VASILOPOULOS, Helena 312-752-2104 155 B
helena.vasilopoulos@kendall.edu

VASKELIS, Frank, M 650-358-6720 67 D
vaskelis@smccd.edu

VASQUEZ, Albert 310-434-4302 68 D
vasquez_albert@smc.edu

VASQUEZ, Andrew 830-372-8017 499 C
avasquez@tlu.edu

VASQUEZ, Graciela 562-860-2451 38 J
gvasquez@cerritos.edu

VASQUEZ, James 718-260-5244 328 E
jvazquez@citytech.cuny.edu

VASQUEZ, Jeffrey 206-934-3643 536 H
jeffrey.vasquez@seattlecolleges.edu

VASQUEZ, Lisa, R 972-758-3894 483 D
lvasquez@collin.edu

VASQUEZ, Patricia 617-745-3851 234 C
patty.vasquez@enc.edu

VASQUEZ, Rafeal 305-593-1223 102 D
rvasquez@albuzu.edu

VASQUEZ, Sandy 915-747-7873 505 E
svasquez@utep.edu

VASQUEZ, Sharon 860-768-4505 95 A
svasquez@hartford.edu

VASQUEZ DE VELASCO, Guillermo, P 765-285-5863 169 D
guillermo@bsu.edu

VASQUEZ ESPINOSA, Ramon, E 787-265-3822 567 C
reve@ece.uprm.edu

VASQUEZ-HUERTA, Jessika 310-665-6898 60 B
otisaid@otis.edu

VASQUEZ-MARTINEZ, Ernesto 787-622-8000 115 B
evazquez@pupr.edu

VASQUEZ-OSBORN, Wendy 909-915-3800 29 B
wvasquez-osborn@argosy.edu

VASS, Robert 203-576-4228 94 D
rvass@bridgeport.edu

VASSALLO, Barbara 207-221-8713 218 C
bvassallo@kaplan.edu

VASSAR, David, K 713-348-4043 492 J
dvassar@rice.edu

VASSAR, Pam 913-469-8500 193 I
pvassar@jccc.edu

VASTINE-NORMAN, Paula 817-515-6456 496 A
paula.vastinenorman@tccd.edu

VATANDOOST, Nossi 615-514-2787 472 C
nossi@nossi.edu

VATER, Ruth 608-363-2218 546 B
vaterr@beloit.edu

VATISTAS, Vatistas 262-551-6001 546 F
vvatistas@carthage.edu

VAUBEL, Thomas, M 920-748-8117 549 I
vaubelt@ripon.edu

VAUGHAN, Bruce, F 757-455-3309 529 F
bvaughan@vwc.edu

VAUGHAN, Cheryl 804-763-6300 99 D
cheryl.vaughan@strayer.edu

VAUGHAN, Chris 309-794-7292 145 B
chrisvaughan@augustana.edu

VAUGHAN, Dixie, L 740-374-8716 405 F
dvaughan@wscc.edu

VAUGHAN, Greg 562-903-4752 30 H
greg.vaughan@biola.edu

VAUGHAN, Jennie 812-330-6007 175 H
jvaughan@ivytech.edu

VAUGHAN, Jesse 804-524-5877 529 C
jvaughan@vsu.edu

VAUGHAN, Jim 208-376-7731 142 E
jvaughan@boisebible.edu

VAUGHAN, Joan, T 708-534-4105 151 C
jvaughan@govst.edu

VAUGHAN, Joseph 909-621-8613 49 D
joseph_vaughan@hmc.edu

VAUGHAN, II, Juan, E 252-862-1375 372 H
vaughanje@roanokechowan.edu

VAUGHAN, Karen 208-526-1200 313 E
kvaughan@raritanval.edu

VAUGHAN, Larry, F 615-547-1222 467 I
lvaughan@cumberland.edu

VAUGHAN, Leslie 617-989-4510 246 C
vaughanl@wit.edu

VAUGHAN, Michael, B 801-626-6006 511 D
mvaughan@weber.edu

VAUGHAN, Peter 212-636-6616 334 C
pvaughan@fordham.edu

VAUGHAN, JR., Robert, A 678-466-4100 127 A
robertvaughan@clayton.edu

VAUGHAN, Sally, J 585-385-8196 348 F
svaughan@sjfc.edu

VAUGHAN-COOKE, Melanie 502-213-2183 202 B
melanie.vaughan-cooke@kctcs.edu

VAUGHN, Arthur 678-915-3282 137 C
avaughn@spsu.edu

VAUGHN, Bobby 650-508-3500 59 G
bvaughn@ndnu.edu

VAUGHN, Cathy 541-440-4600 420 F
cathy.vaughn@umpqua.edu

VAUGHN, Deborah, S 662-915-1687 277 G
dvaughn@olemiss.edu

VAUGHN, Denise 919-278-2673 376 D
dvaughn@shawu.edu

VAUGHN, Edward, L 601-877-6227 273 C
elvaughn@alcorn.edu

VAUGHN, Jason 417-328-1714 290 E
jvaughn@sbuniv.edu

VAUGHN, Jennifer 270-852-3118 203 E
jvaughn@kwc.edu

VAUGHN, Joseph 660-543-4621 291 B
vaughn@ucmo.edu

VAUGHN, Joyce 870-575-8969 25 B
vaughnj@uapb.edu

VAUGHN, Karen, A 910-642-7141 373 G
kvaughn@sccnc.edu

VAUGHN, Katherine 870-743-3000 22 G
kvaughn@northark.edu

VAUGHN, Kellie 270-789-5001 199 C
kpvaughn@campbellsville.edu

VAUGHN, La'Mont 847-578-3204 163 A
lamont.vaughn@rosalindfranklin.edu

VAUGHN, Linda 904-743-1122 112 A
lvaughn@jones.edu

VAUGHN, Lori 413-565-1000 231 B
lvaughn@baypath.edu

VAUGHN, Michele 847-543-2153 147 H
mvaughn@clcillinois.edu

VAUGHN, Nancy 256-372-5835 1 A
nancy.vaughn@aamu.edu

VAUGHN, Patrick 636-422-2240 289 E
pvaughn20@stlcc.edu

VAUGHN, Patti 617-262-5000 232 B
Patti.Vaughn@the-bac.edu

VAUGHN, Renata 870-972-2054 20 C
rvaughn@astate.edu

VAUGHN, Robert 323-856-7661 28 D
rvaughn@afi.com

VAUGHN, Robert 610-372-4721 445 B
rvaughn@racc.edu

VAUGHN, Ronald, L 813-253-6201 122 H
president@ut.edu

VAUGHN, Suzanne, A 661-395-4301 52 M
svaughn@bakersfieldcollege.edu

VAUGHN, Tarva 256-549-8671 3 J
tvaughn@gadsdenstate.edu

VAUGHT, Wayne 816-235-2815 291 E
vaughtw@umkc.edu

VAUPEL, Chris 516-877-3258 322 A
cpvaupel@adelphi.edu

VAUPEL, Richard, D 423-493-4215 476 C
vaupelr@tntemple.edu

VAUX, Alan, C 618-453-2466 164 I
alanvaux@siu.edu

VAVASOUR, JoEllen, L 914-654-5541 330 B
jvavasour@cnr.edu

VAVOLIZZA, Ann 845-848-4001 332 C
ann.vavolizza@dc.edu

VAWTER, Cheryl, D 509-777-4518 539 F
cvawter@whitworth.edu

VAYDA, Melissa, M 717-728-2248 425 A
melissavayda@centralpenn.edu

VAYDA, Michael, E 479-575-2034 24 C
mvayda@uark.edu

VAZ, Maria, J 248-204-2400 254 E
provost@ltu.edu

VAZQUEZ, Airlyn 787-882-2065 565 I
biblioteca@unitecpr.net

VAZQUEZ, Carmen 718-289-5151 326 F
carmen.vazquez@bcc.cuny.edu

VAZQUEZ, Carmen 305-593-1223 102 D
cvazquez@albizu.edu

VAZQUEZ, Carmen, M 619-260-4588 76 A
carmenvazquez@sandiego.edu

VAZQUEZ, David 239-590-1123 119 A
dvazquez@fgcu.edu

VAZQUEZ, Frank 888-384-0849 27 G
frankv@allied.edu

VAZQUEZ, Jaime 787-780-0070 560 F
jvazquez@caribbean.edu

VAZQUEZ, Juan, A 714-628-4930 63 G
vazquez_juan@sccollege.edu

VAZQUEZ, Magda 787-878-5475 562 H
mava@arecibo.inter.edu

VAZQUEZ, Maria 787-864-2222 563 D
mavazrom@inter.edu

VAZQUEZ, Marie 402-457-2430 298 H
mvazquez@mccneb.edu

VAZQUEZ, Silvio 805-565-6200 78 F

VAZQUEZ, Trina 828-277-5521 376 F
tvazquez@southcollegenc.edu

VAZQUEZ, Vilmaris 787-878-5475 562 H
vvazquez@arecibo.inter.edu

VAZQUEZ-BARQUET, Ernesto 787-754-8000 566 C
evazquez@pupr.edu

VAZQUEZ-BARQUET, Ernesto 787-622-8000 115 B
evazquez@pupr.edu

VAZQUEZ-SKILLINGS, Rebecca, D 614-823-1354 400
rvazquez-skillings@otterbein.edu

VAZQUEZTELL, Hernán 787-250-0000 566
hernan.vazqueztell@upr.edu

VEACH, Grace 863-667-5061 118
gveach@seu.edu

VEACH, Leslie 252-985-5369 375
lveach@ncwc.edu

VEAL, Sharon 478-553-2056 134
sveal@oftc.edu

VEATH, Lois 308-432-6203 299 G
lveath@csc.edu

VEAZEY, Barbara 270-534-3082 203
barbara.veazey@kctcs.edu

VECCHIO, John 716-827-4344 358
vecchioj@trocaire.edu

VECCHIO, Maria 201-559-6017 310 C
vecchiom@felician.edu

VECCHIONE, Tom 336-278-6538 364 A
tvecchione@elon.edu

VECHINI, Jose, A 787-864-2222 563 D
javechi@inter.edu

VEDDER, Lori 810-762-3444 259 F
lvedder@umflint.edu

VEDIA, Roxanne 956-721-5437 489 G
rvedia@laredo.edu

VEDVICK, Kathryn, A 206-934-6415 537 B
kathy.vedvick@seattlecolleges.edu

VEECH, Guthrie 314-837-6777 288 F
gveech@slcconline.edu

VEEDER, Samantha 585-389-2310 342 D
sveeder0@naz.edu

VEEN, Leslie 415-451-2834 66 B
lveen@sfts.edu

VEENA, Sneh, B 509-865-8530 534 D
veena_s@heritage.edu

VEENSTRA, Derick, A 301-369-2800 221 F
rveenstra@capitol-college.edu

VEENSTRA, Dianne, M 301-369-2800 221 F
dveenstra@capitol-college.edu

VEENSTRA, Myron 701-777-2127 381 D
myron.veenstra@email.und.edu

VEENSTRA, Tim 517-586-3014 249 H
tveenstra@cleary.edu

VEGA, Aixa 787-834-9595 565 J
avega@uaa.edu

VEGA, Barbara 432-837-8810 501 B
bvega@sulross.edu

VEGA, Daisy 787-882-2065 565 I
recursoshumanos@unitecpr.net

VEGA, Elsa 305-593-1223 102 D
evega@albizu.edu

VEGA, Erlinda 787-264-1912 563 G
yaremi@sg.inter.edu

VEGA, Eva 787-746-1400 562 C
evega@huertas.edu

VEGA, Frances, T 219-981-4957 176 E
fvega@ivytech.edu

VEGA, Fredrick 787-250-1912 563 E
fredrickvega@metro.inter.edu

VEGA, Javier 212-592-2000 350 F
jvega@sva.edu

VEGA, Juan 787-844-8181 567 E
juan.vega@upr.edu

VEGA, Manfredo 787-620-2040 560 B
mvega@aupr.edu

VEGA, Zaida 787-766-1717 565 G
zvega@suagm.edu

VEGA-LA SERNA, Jennifer 559-730-3700 42 B
jenniferl@cos.edu

VEHR, Gregory, J 513-556-3028 403 D
greg.vehr@uc.edu

VEHRKENS, Kenneth, T 201-692-2671 310 B
vehrkens@fdu.edu

VEIT, Kenneth, J 215-871-6770 444 B
kenv@pcom.edu

VEITCH, Bradley 913-385-7700 197 G

VEITCH, Jonathan 323-259-2691 59 H

VEITH, Gene, E 540-338-1776 522 A

VEJSICKY, Janet 740-826-8139 396 I
janv@muskingum.edu

VELA, JR., Cesar, E 956-721-5370 489 G
cvela@laredo.edu

VELA, Rene 219-981-4421 176 E
rvela5@ivytech.edu

VELA, Robert, H 210-486-0930 479 F
rvela63@alamo.edu

VELA, SM, Rudy 210-431-8094 493 C
rvela3@stmarytx.edu

VELARDE, Jose 847-543-2602 147 H
jvelarde@clcillinois.edu

VELARDE, Katie 719-549-2199 83 B
katie.velarde@colostate-pueblo.edu

VELARDE, Mary 915-779-8031 483 F
mvelarde@computercareercenter.com

VELARDI, Lisa Marie 866-967-8822 109 G
lvelardi@flatech.edu

VELASCO, Jessica 425-889-5212 535 I
jessica.velasco@northwestu.edu

VELASCO, Steven, C 805-893-2434 74 F
steve.velasco@bap.ucsb.edu

VELASQUEZ, Kimberly 503-223-2245 416 E
kvelasquez@westernculinary.com

VIDINHA, Phyllis 808-245-8213 141 H
pvidinha@hawaii.edu

VIDLER, Anthony 212-353-4220 331 B
vidler@cooper.edu

VIDMAR, Melissa 540-831-5248 522 D
mvidmar@radford.edu

VIDOVIC, Lou 314-652-0300 288 H

VIDRINE, Christopher 504-568-5976 213 A
cvidri@lsuhsc.edu

VIEBROCK, Stan 816-654-7216 283 J
sviebrock@kcumb.edu

VIECK, Jana, L 812-888-5090 181 B
jvieck@vinu.edu

VIEIRA, Elvira 973-877-1912 310 A
vieira@essex.edu

VIEIRA, Margarida 508-531-1207 238 B
mvieira@bridgew.edu

VIEIRA, Michael 508-678-2811 239 F
michael.vieira@bristolcc.edu

VIEIRA, Nelson 201-360-4131 310 F
nvieira@hccc.edu

VIEIRA, Patricia, S 401-865-1962 453 F
pvieira@providence.edu

VIEIRA, Robert 503-494-7878 418 D

VIEIRA, Stanley 617-349-8498 236 G
svieira@lesley.edu

VIEIRA, Stephen, A 401-825-2004 453 B
savieira@ccri.edu

VIEL, Thomas 815-921-4304 162 F
t.viel@rockvalleycollege.edu

VIELE, Dan 314-968-6905 293 A
vieleda@webster.edu

VIEN, Michele 518-694-7216 322 C
michele.vien@acphs.edu

VIENCEK, Jenifer 708-237-5050 160 C
jviencek@nc.edu

VIENNA, Michael, P 410-548-3503 228 D
mpvienna@salisbury.edu

VIENNE, Charlie 936-294-1840 501 A
cvienne@shsu.edu

VIERA, Lisandra 787-740-1611 566 A
lisandra.viera@uccaribe.edu

VIERA, Michelle 615-963-5880 474 A
mviera@tnstate.edu

VIERS, Christopher 812-855-4418 173 C
cviers@indiana.edu

VIERSEN, Alan 619-388-7693 65 H
aviersen@sdccd.edu

VIERTEL, Cynthia, S 920-748-8312 549 I
viertelc@ripon.edu

VIERUS, Glen 979-830-4181 482 A
gvierus@blinn.edu

VIERZBA, Shawn 320-363-2144 271 F
svierzba@csbsjhu.edu

VIESELMEYER, Dian 949-214-3035 42 K
dian.vieselmeyer@cui.edu

VIETMEIER, Barbara 847-617-6698 166 B
bvietmei@tiu.edu

VIETOR, Sandi 605-274-4127 463 H
sandi.vietor@augie.edu

VIETS, Hermann 414-277-7101 548 H
viets@msoe.edu

VIETTI, Jacqueline 316-322-3100 191 D
jvietti@butlercc.edu

VIEW, John, E 315-470-6670 355 A
jeview@esf.edu

VIEW, Sean 801-832-2502 512 F
sview@westminstercollege.edu

VIEWEG, Bruce, W 218-299-4737 263 B
bvieweg@cord.edu

VIGEANT, Paul 508-999-9143 237 E
pvigeant@umassd.edu

VIGGIANO, Thomas, R 507-284-3268 262 F
viggiano.thomas@mayo.edu

VIGIL, Damian 505-566-3084 320 D
vigild@sanjuancollege.edu

VIGIL, James 505-473-6349 320 F
james.vigil@laureate.net

VIGIL, James 304-876-5219 544 A
jvigil@shepherd.edu

VIGIL, Jim 417-833-2551 279 I
jvigil@cbcag.edu

VIGIL, Kathryn 505-661-4688 321 E
kaguilar@unm.edu

VIGIL, Renee 719-587-7526 80 F
reneevigil@adams.edu

VIGIL-GARCIA, Nickie 575-624-8035 319 C
vigil-garcia@nmmi.edu

VIGLIETTA, Eileen, P 304-243-2346 545 G
eileen@wju.edu

VIGNA, Natan 951-785-2100 53 D
nvigna@lasierra.edu

VIGNATO, Linda 631-687-2671 349 B
lvignato@sjcny.edu

VIGNERON, David 978-232-2376 234 F
dvignero@endicott.edu

VIGNES, Mark 225-359-9209 209 K
mvignes@catc.edu

VIGNOCCHI, Carmela 805-922-6966 26 K
cvignocchi@hancockcollege.edu

VIGO, Luisa 787-763-6199 567 F
egcti.upr@upr.edu

VIHOS, Lisa, B 920-565-1295 547 H
vihosl@lakeland.edu

VIJITHA-KUMARA, Kanaka 309-467-6434 150 H
kumara@eureka.edu

VIKANDER, David 507-537-6281 269 G
David.Vikander@smsu.edu

VILA CRUZ, Geraldo 608-246-6442 554 B
gvilacruz@matcmadison.edu

VILABOY, Teresa 619-388-7485 65 H
tvilaboy@sdccd.edu

VILARDI, Theresa, J 845-758-7432 323 F
vilardi@webjogger.net

VILARINO, Ivonne 787-844-8181 567 E
ivonne.vilarino@upr.edu

VILE, John, R 615-898-2152 473 F
john.vile@mtsu.edu

VILENSKI, Daniel, P 401-254-3159 454 C
dvilenski@rwu.edu

VILES, Vickery 541-383-7258 414 I
vviles@cocc.edu

VILIC, Boris 609-896-5033 313 G
bvilic@rider.edu

VILLA, Christopher, M 559-442-4600 72 A
chris.villa@fresnocitycollege.edu

VILLA, Cindy 915-747-5113 505 E
cvilla@utep.edu

VILLA, Humberto 787-758-2525 567 D
humberto.villa@upr.edu

VILLA, William 808-739-4695 140 A
william.villa@chaminade.edu

VILLAIZAN, Sonia 787-878-5475 562 H
svillaiz@arecibo.inter.edu

VILLALOBOS, Bobbi 562-938-4113 54 E
bvillalobos@lbcc.edu

VILLALPANDO, Octavio 801-581-7569 510 L
octavio.villalpando@utah.edu

VILLAMIL, Juanita 787-758-2525 567 D
juanita.villamil1@upr.edu

VILLAMIL, Margarita 787-844-8181 567 E
margarita.villamil@upr.edu

VILLAMIL, Olga 787-250-1912 563 E
ovillamil@metro.inter.edu

VILLANI, Christine 718-260-3360 346 C
cvillani@poly.edu

VILLANTI, Athony 315-792-3053 359 C
avillanti@utica.edu

VILLANUEVA, Christina 210-431-6789 493 C
cvillanueva@stmarytx.edu

VILLANUEVA, Daniel 310-900-1600 45 E
dvillanueva@elcamino.edu

VILLANUEVA, Donna Mae 818-719-6444 55 B
villandm@piercecollege.edu

VILLANUEVA, Gil 804-289-8640 525 A
gvillanu@richmond.edu

VILLANUEVA, Rebecca 432-264-5608 487 I
rvillanueva@howardcollege.edu

VILLANUEVA, Sumaya 212-484-1346 328 A
svillanueva@jjay.cuny.edu

VILLANUEVA, Teresa 575-562-2991 318 A
teresa.villanueva@enmu.edu

VILLANUEVA, Teresa 830-569-4222 482 I
terry@coastalbend.edu

VILLANUEVE, Lauren 215-717-6000 448 H
lvillanueve@uarts.edu

VILLAR, Abby 843-661-8351 458 A
abby.villar@fdtc.edu

VILLAR, Jeremy 323-953-4000 54 H
villarjv@lacitycollege.edu

VILLAREAL, Henry 650-574-6590 67 F
henry.villareal@smccd.edu

VILLARREAL, Abe 575-538-6336 321 I
news@wnmu.edu

VILLARREAL, Elisabeth 210-829-2736 503 F
villaret@uiwtx.edu

VILLARREAL, Ernesto 423-461-8492 471 H
ebvillarreal@milligan.edu

VILLARREAL, Graciela, B 832-822-3441 481 H
gbv@bcm.edu

VILLARREAL, James 210-436-3472 493 C
jvillarreal64@stmarytx.edu

VILLARREAL, Oscar 956-665-2770 506 A
oscar@utpa.edu

VILLARREAL, Patricia 414-229-5923 551 C
pavillar@uwm.edu

VILLARREAL, Rene 956-882-8213 505 C
rene.villarreal@utb.edu

VILLARREAL, Rene 956-882-8295 505 C
rene.villarreal@utb.edu

VILLARREAL, Rick 940-565-2662 504 B
rickv@unt.edu

VILLARS, James 651-290-6475 273 B
jim.villars@wmitchell.edu

VILLARUAL, Elizabeth 210-486-3713 479 D
eaguilar-villarr@alamo.edu

VILLEGAS, Veronica 305-273-4499 103 C
veronica@cbt.edu

VILLEGAS-VIDAL, Ludi 818-364-7643 55 A
villegl@lamission.edu

VILLENEUVE, Martha 603-897-8260 305 G
mvilleneuve@rivier.edu

VILLERS, Koreen 304-457-1700 540 B
villerskr@ab.edu

VILLOLDO, Sergio 305-418-4220 115 B
svilloldo@pupr.edu

VILLOLDO, Sergio 787-754-8000 566 C
svilloldo@pupr.edu

VINARSKI, Cynthia, A 412-396-6596 428 C
vinarski@duq.edu

VINCENT, Andrew 502-897-4785 205 H
avincent@sbts.edu

VINCENT, Endas 225-771-3670 214 G
endas_vincent@sus.edu

VINCENT, Endas 225-771-3670 214 H
endas_vincent@subr.edu

VINCENT, Eugenia 951-222-8711 64 B
eugenia.vincent@rcc.edu

VINCENT, Gregory, J 512-471-3212 505 B
gvincent@mail.utexas.edu

VINCENT, Herb 225-578-3861 212 F
vincent@lsu.edu

VINCENT, Michael 928-523-5011 17 A
michael.vincent@nau.edu

VINCENT, Pat 270-399-1578 199 J
pvincent@daymarcollege.edu

VINCENT, Sara 860-512-2909 90 C
svincent@mcc.commnet.edu

VINCENT, Stephanie 617-739-1700 243 F
svincent@aii.edu

VINCENT, William, B 215-572-3802 451 D
bvincent@wts.edu

VINCENT, William, K 951-639-5201 58 B
bvincent@msjc.edu

VINCIGUERRA, Michael, J 815-740-3369 167 C
mvinciguerra@stfrancis.edu

VINCZE, John 203-285-2310 90 A
jvincze@gwcc.commnet.edu

VINES, Dennis, R 770-484-1204 133 D
lru@lru.edu

VINES, Donny 205-802-1200 3 C
donny.vines@vc.edu

VINES, Erin 707-864-7256 70 A
erin.vines@solano.edu

VINES, Robert 239-590-7044 119 A
rvines@fgcu.edu

VINEY, Rhonda, L 601-342-1845 551 F
vineyr@uwplatt.edu

VINEYARD, Ed 580-548-2207 409 B
edwin.vineyar@north-ok.edu

VINEYARD, John, P 931-598-1890 472 J
jpvineya@sewanee.edu

VINEYARD, Judy 618-985-3741 154 E
judyvineyard@jalc.edu

VINGER, Christopher, J 973-642-3888 307 G
cjv@berkeleycollege.edu

VINGER, Christopher, J 973-642-3888 323 J
cjv@berkeleycollege.edu

VINIAR, Barbara, A 410-827-5802 222 B
bviniar@chesapeake.edu

VINING, Isaac 404-225-4750 125 A
ivining@atlantatech.edu

VINK, Cher 715-468-2815 555 E
cher.vink@witc.edu

VINOVRSKI, Bernie 559-278-2061 34 D
bernard_vinovrski@csufresno.edu

VINSKI, Jerome 908-526-1200 313 E
jvinski@raritanval.edu

VINSON, Bonita 214-932-1111 489 K
bonitavinson@letu.edu

VINSON, Larry, J 402-552-6108 297 D
vinson@clarksoncollege.edu

VINSON, Valerie 404-880-8773 126 I
vvinson@cau.edu

VINSON, Wendy 706-245-7226 128 K
wvinson@ec.edu

VINT, Patricia 734-432-5595 254 G
pvint@madonna.edu

VINZANT, Doug 307-766-5768 556 E
dvinzant@uwyo.edu

VINZANT, Jeffrey, P 334-244-3576 2 A
jvinzant@aum.edu

VIOLA, Jennifer 615-217-9347 468 B
jviola@daymarinstitute.edu

VIOLA, Joe 541-383-7776 414 I
jviola@cocc.edu

VIOLANTE, Marc, N 847-543-2580 147 H
mviolante@clcillinois.edu

VIOLANTE, Thomas 203-575-8132 90 E
tviolante@nvcc.commnet.edu

VIOLETTE, Glenn 650-949-7394 47 H
violettglenn@foothill.edu

VIOLLT, Kathleen 312-935-4155 162 E
kviollt@robertmorris.edu

VIOLLT, Michael, P 312-935-6600 162 E
mviollt@robertmorris.edu

VIOTTI, Karen 901-321-3254 467 G
kviotti@cbu.edu

VIRASAWMI, Errol 516-364-0808 343 A
egv@nycollege.edu

VIRELLA, Francisco 702-369-9944 301 G
fvirella@aii.edu

VIRELLA, Grisobelle 787-844-8181 567 E
griso@uprp.edu

VIRELLO, Mark 617-296-8300 236 E
mark_virello@laboure.edu

VIRES, Charles 731-989-6171 468 K
cvires@fhu.edu

VIRGINT, Jacqueline 505-428-1409 320 E
jacqueline.virgint@sfcc.edu

VIRIJEVICH, Diana 219-989-2056 178 G
dvirijev@purduecal.edu

VIRK, Sunny 718-960-8261 327
sunny.virk@lehman.cuny.edu

VIRTS, Paul, H 651-631-5096 270
phvirts@nwc.edu

VIRTUCCI, Tom 954-262-7304 114
tomv@nsu.nova.edu

VISCI, Chip 805-756-7008 33
vcisci@calpoly.edu

VISCOMI, Susan 716-926-8800 335 F
sviscomi@hilbert.edu

VISCONAGE, Elizabeth, L 410-864-4261 226 E
bvisconage@stmarys.edu

VISCUSI, Raymond 610-359-5070 426 G
rviscusi@dccc.edu

VISENTIN, Peter 203-837-8680 92 A
narduccid@wcsu.edu

VISHWANATHA, J, K 817-735-2560 504 C
jvishwan@hsc.unt.edu

VISKER, Thomas 574-257-3417 169 F
viskert@bethelcollege.edu

VISOT, Cynthia, S 813-974-1678 120 D
cvisot@usf.edu

VISSCHER, Caitlin 508-373-9527 231 D

VISSCHER, Petra 410-225-4255 224 C
pvisscher@mica.edu

VISUANO, Denise 503-838-8349 419 C
visuanod@wou.edu

VITA, Claudine 610-526-6012 430 D
cvita@harcum.edu

VITAGLIANO, James, V 617-726-3136 242 E
jvitagliano@mghihp.edu

VITAL, Allen 256-372-4170 1 A
allen.vital@aamu.edu

VITALE, Bob 319-385-6270 186 A
bob.vitale@iwc.edu

VITALE, Frank 410-888-9048 226 F
fvitale@tai.edu

VITALE, James, M 215-670-9306 438 D
jmvitale@peirce.edu

VITALE, Jean 718-261-5800 324 D
jvitale@bramsonort.edu

VITALE, Joseph 973-328-5060 309 B
jvitale@ccm.edu

VITALE, Lori 816-995-2806 288 C
lori.vitale@researchcollege.edu

VITALE, Michael 386-506-3079 103 J
vitalem@daytonastate.edu

VITALOS, Mark 610-606-4642 424 I
mavitalo@cedarcrest.edu

VITANGELI, Kory, M 317-788-3485 180 C
kvitangeli@uindy.edu

VITATOE, David, A 216-397-1984 392 M
dvitatoe@jcu.edu

VITATOE, Steven, P 216-397-4277 392 M
svitatoe@jcu.edu

VITELLI, Chris 209-588-5142 80 A
vitellic@yosemite.edu

VITELLI, Mary 407-628-6303 116 B
mvitelli@rollins.edu

VITI, Elizabeth 717-337-6823 429 H
eviti@gettysburg.edu

VITO, Melissa 520-621-0963 19 B
mmvito@email.arizona.edu

VITO, Raymond 404-894-2792 130 D
raymond.vito@provost.gatech.edu

VITO, Ron 951-222-8490 64 B
ron.vito@rcc.edu

VITOLA, Anthony 203-332-5034 90 B
avitola@hcc.commnet.edu

VITOLINS, Constance, M 570-326-3761 440 K
cvitolin@pct.edu

VITTER, Jeffrey, S 785-864-4904 196 F
jsv@ku.edu

VITTES, Elliot 407-823-2373 120 A
elliot@ucf.edu

VITTETOE, Stanley 727-791-2475 116 F
vittetoe.stan@spcollege.edu

VITUCCI, Alanna 602-557-3901 19 C
alanna.vitucci@apollogrp.edu

VIVEIROS, Derek 508-678-2811 239 F
derek.viveiros@bristolcc.edu

VIVEIROS, Nelia 215-204-3745 447 G
nelia.viveiros@temple.edu

VIVERETTE, Maggie, J 229-333-5463 138 F
mviveret@valdosta.edu

VIVERITO, Diane 708-974-5334 159 A
viverito@morainevalley.edu

VIVIAN, Daniel 716-645-4540 351 G
dtvivian@buffalo.edu

VIVILECCHIA, Joe 603-623-0313 305 F
jvivilecchia@nhia.edu

VIVONA, Joseph, F 301-445-1923 227 A
jvivona@usmd.edu

VIZCARRONDO, Maria, J 787-279-1912 563 B
mvizcarrondo@bayamon.inter.edu

VIZZINI, Anthony, J 269-276-3253 260 F
anthony.vizzini@wmich.edu

VLAHAKIS, Stacy 312-752-2232 155 B
stacy.vlahakis@kendall.edu

VLAHAKIS, Valerie 217-641-4561 154 G

VLAHOS, Christopher, J 216-368-6280 386 E
christopher.vlahos@case.edu

VLAHOV, David 415-476-1805 74 E
david.vlahov@nursing.ucsf.edu

WADE, John, M .... 423-461-1540 .... 468 F jwade@ecs.edu
WADE, Julian, P .... 404-297-9522 .... 128 B wadej@dekalbtech.edu
WADE, Keith .... 706-865-2134 .... 138 A kwade@truett.edu
WADE, Lara .... 813-974-9060 .... 120 D larawade@usf.edu
WADE, Marcia .... 310-434-4010 .... 68 D wade_marcia@smc.edu
WADE, Margaret .... 432-685-4615 .... 490 G mwade@midland.edu
WADE, Mark .... 215-572-2986 .... 422 B wade@arcadia.edu
WADE, Melissa .... 954-969-9771 .... 108 B melissaw@steinerleisure.com
WADE, Michael .... 812-855-9973 .... 173 C mjwade@indiana.edu
WADE, Noreen .... 516-572-3559 .... 342 C noreen.wade@ncc.edu
WADE, Patti, P .... 601-974-1019 .... 275 D wadepp@millsaps.edu
WADE, Susan .... 785-594-8382 .... 190 C susan.wade@bakeru.edu
WADE, Tina .... 952-487-8428 .... 268 C tina.wade@normandale.edu
WADE, Trisha .... 803-799-9082 .... 461 A twade@southuniversity.edu
WADE, Virginia .... 310-377-5501 .... 56 F vwade@marymountpv.edu
WADE, William .... 218-726-8831 .... 272 B wwade@d.umn.edu
WADE, William, C .... 334-844-3500 .... 1 G wadewil@auburn.edu
WADE ATTEBERRY, Mary . 317-788-3310 .... 180 C matteberry@uindy.edu
WADELL, John .... 219-866-6176 .... 179 B jwadell@saintjoe.edu
WADHVANI, Rashmi .... 212-472-1500 .... 343 G rwadhvani@nysid.edu
WADIAN, Becky .... 563-425-5270 .... 189 C wadianb@uiu.edu
WADKINS, Jesse, E .... 479-248-7236 .... 21 G jwadkins@ecollege.edu
WADLINGTON, Laura .... 865-471-3270 .... 467 E lwadlington@cn.edu
WADSWORTH, Frank .... 765-455-9446 .... 173 E fwadswo@iuk.edu
WADSWORTH, Michael ..... 517-629-0224 .... 247 E mwadsworth@albion.edu
WAECHTER, Julie .... 719-587-7165 .... 80 F jmwaecht@adams.edu
WAFA, Marwan, A .... 812-372-8266 .... 174 B
WAGEMESTER, Doug .... 319-398-4909 .... 186 H dwageme@kirkwood.edu
WAGENER, Pam .... 815-825-2086 .... 155 C pam.wagener@kishwaukeecollege.edu
WAGENER, William, C .... 304-336-8177 .... 544 B wagenerw@westliberty.edu
WAGER, Carrie, A .... 972-860-7040 .... 484 H CWager@dcccd.edu
WAGER, Lisa .... 212-217-4700 .... 333 G lisa_wager@fitnyc.edu
WAGES, Charlene .... 843-661-1146 .... 458 C cwages@fmarion.edu
WAGES, Sam .... 210-805-5836 .... 503 F wages@uiwtx.edu
WAGGENER, Shelton .... 510-642-4096 .... 73 E shelw@berkeley.edu
WAGGONER, Bill .... 970-339-6290 .... 80 G bill.waggoner@aims.edu
WAGGONER, George, W ... 240-895-3115 .... 226 A gwwaggoner@smcm.edu
WAGGONER, Janet .... 303-404-5408 .... 84 H janet.waggoner@frontrange.edu
WAGGONER, Julia .... 715-682-1302 .... 549 C jwaggoner@northland.edu
WAGGONER, R. Greg .... 970-943-2079 .... 89 B gwaggoner@western.edu
WAGGONER, Reneau .... 502-213-2620 .... 202 B reneau.waggoner@kctcs.edu
WAGGONER, Todd .... 417-862-9533 .... 282 D twaggoner@globaluniversity.edu
WAGGONER, Wes .... 817-257-7490 .... 498 F w.waggoner@tcu.edu
WAGNER, Anne Marie .... 513-244-4810 .... 388 D anne_marie_wagner@mail.msj.edu
WAGNER, Anthony, E .... 215-204-6545 .... 447 G anthony.wagner@temple.edu
WAGNER, Betty, J .... 989-774-3968 .... 249 G betty.j.wagner@cmich.edu
WAGNER, Claire, M .... 513-529-7592 .... 396 D wagnercm@muohio.edu
WAGNER, Colette .... 718-951-5637 .... 326 G cwagner@brooklyn.cuny.edu
WAGNER, Cori .... 217-479-7141 .... 157 D cori.wagner@mac.edu
WAGNER, Danielle .... 610-558-5502 .... 437 C wagnerd@neumann.edu
WAGNER, Dave .... 615-966-5683 .... 470 D dave.wagner@lipscomb.edu
WAGNER, David, L .... 916-278-6078 .... 35 E wagnerdl@csus.edu
WAGNER, Donald, I .... 901-678-4265 .... 474 C diwagner@memphis.edu
WAGNER, Donald, R .... 678-839-6636 .... 138 D dwagner@westga.edu
WAGNER, Hudlin .... 507-222-4248 .... 262 B hwagner@carleton.edu
WAGNER, James, M .... 214-648-2168 .... 507 D james.wagner@utsouthwestern.edu
WAGNER, James, W .... 404-727-6013 .... 129 A james.wagner@emory.edu
WAGNER, Jane .... 617-682-1511 .... 234 G jwagner@eds.edu
WAGNER, Janel .... 605-229-8427 .... 464 I janel.wagner@presentation.edu
WAGNER, Janet, M .... 609-652-4534 .... 313 F janet.wagner@stockton.edu
WAGNER, Jean .... 503-491-6113 .... 417 B jean.wagner@mhcc.edu
WAGNER, Jeanne .... 717-901-5117 .... 430 F JWagner@HarrisburgU.edu
WAGNER, Jeff .... 515-961-1626 .... 188 F jeff.wagner@simpson.edu
WAGNER, JoAnn .... 937-529-2201 .... 403 A jwagner@united.edu
WAGNER, Jodi .... 509-527-2772 .... 538 H jodi.wagner@wallawalla.edu
WAGNER, Joseph .... 413-592-3189 .... 233 E wagnerj@elms.edu
WAGNER, Karen .... 212-799-5000 .... 337 H
WAGNER, Ken .... 808-675-3760 .... 139 I wagnerk@byuh.edu
WAGNER, Kevin, J .... 740-826-6129 .... 396 I kevinw@muskingum.edu
WAGNER, Kimberly, M .... 260-481-6174 .... 174 A wagnerk@ipfw.edu
WAGNER, Lana .... 325-649-8011 .... 488 A lwagner@hputx.edu
WAGNER, Laura .... 219-866-6116 .... 179 B lwagner@saintjoe.edu
WAGNER, Linda .... 863-686-1444 .... 105 I lwagner@cci.edu
WAGNER, Linda, L .... 814-871-7401 .... 429 F wagner001@gannon.edu
WAGNER, Lynn .... 252-246-1293 .... 375 B lwagner@wilsoncc.edu
WAGNER, Mara .... 617-277-3915 .... 232 F wagnerm@bgsp.edu
WAGNER, Marci, K .... 724-450-4089 .... 430 B mkwagner@gcc.edu
WAGNER, Marilyn, D .... 940-565-3487 .... 504 B mwagner@unt.edu
WAGNER, Mary .... 803-777-7700 .... 462 A mary.wagner@sc.edu
WAGNER, Michael, F .... 603-646-2349 .... 305 A michael.f.wagner@dartmouth.edu
WAGNER, Nancy, B .... 860-832-2050 .... 91 G wagnernab@ccsu.edu
WAGNER, Owen, W .... 724-946-7335 .... 451 C owagner@westminster.edu
WAGNER, Patrick .... 920-403-3017 .... 550 C pat.wagner@snc.edu
WAGNER, Rich .... 612-374-5800 .... 263 I rwagner@dunwoody.edu
WAGNER, Richard, A .... 413-796-2306 .... 246 D rwagner@wne.edu
WAGNER, Richard, T .... 240-895-3421 .... 226 A rtwagner@smcm.edu
WAGNER, Robin .... 717-337-7000 .... 429 H rowagner@gettysburg.edu
WAGNER, Roger .... 760-366-5289 .... 43 E rwagner@cmccd.edu
WAGNER, Shirley .... 978-665-3167 .... 238 C swagner@fitchburgstate.edu
WAGNER, Steve .... 218-733-5934 .... 267 B s.wagner@lsc.edu
WAGNER, Susan .... 603-577-6559 .... 304 J wagner@dwc.edu
WAGNER, Susan .... 520-795-0787 .... 12 A financialaid@asaom.edu
WAGNER, Teresa, J .... 315-464-4252 .... 352 E wagnert@upstate.edu
WAGNER, Timothy .... 614-287-2408 .... 388 G twagner@cscc.edu
WAGNER, Tracy, A .... 941-359-7511 .... 115 K twagner@ringling.edu
WAGNER, Tricia .... 417-269-8316 .... 281 B twagner@coxcollege.edu
WAGNER, Virginia .... 414-382-6115 .... 545 H virginia.wagner@alverno.edu
WAGNER, William .... 415-371-0002 .... 60 A
WAGNER-FOSSEN, Dena ... 406-771-4312 .... 296 B dfossen@msugf.edu
WAGNER-LIND, Wendy ..... 954-308-2620 .... 100 I wwagner@aii.edu
WAGNER WEICK, Cynthia 209-946-2650 .... 75 D cweick@pacific.edu
WAGNITZ, Jeff .... 206-878-3710 .... 534 E jwagnitz@highline.edu
WAGNON, Bill .... 205-226-4901 .... 2 C bwagnon@bsc.edu
WAGONER, Dale .... 510-723-7202 .... 38 L dwagoner@chabotcollege.edu
WAGONSELLER, Rick .... 814-732-1094 .... 442 D rwagonseller@edinboro.edu
WAGOR, Walter .... 330-499-9600 .... 393 I
WAGSTAFF, Grayson .... 202-319-5417 .... 97 C wagstaff@cua.edu
WAGSTAFF, John .... 310-660-3262 .... 45 D jwagstaff@elcamino.edu
WAGSTAFF, Robert .... 617-951-2350 .... 243 C robert.wagstaff@necb.edu
WAGUESPACK, Cathy .... 504-394-7744 .... 214 A cwaguespack@olhcc.edu
WAGUESPACK, F. Poche ... 251-981-3771 .... 2 H poche@columbiasouthern.edu
WAHEED, Mohammed, A .. 307-855-2186 .... 555 G mwaheed@cwc.edu
WAHL, Christopher .... 201-360-4178 .... 310 F cwahl@hccc.edu
WAHL, Doug, J .... 715-232-2501 .... 552 C wahld@uwstout.edu
WAHL, John .... 435-722-6900 .... 510 J
WAHL, Lynette .... 651-523-3000 .... 264 C lwahl@hamline.edu
WAHL, Robert .... 860-255-3472 .... 91 C rwahl@txcc.commnet.edu
WAHL, Terry .... 812-357-6442 .... 179 E twahl@saintmeinrad.edu
WAHLBECK, Mary .... 630-428-9548 .... 149 J mwahlbeck@devry.edu
WAHLBERG, David .... 715-682-1307 .... 549 C dwahlberg@northland.edu
WAHLER, Rick .... 661-362-2267 .... 56 G rwahler@masters.edu
WAHLERS, Mark, E .... 503-280-8578 .... 415 E mwahlers@cu-portland.edu
WAHLERT, Christine, A ..... 816-654-7285 .... 283 J cwahlert@kcumb.edu
WAHLFELDT, Tracy, D .... 217-443-8772 .... 148 E twahlfeldt@dacc.edu
WAHLSTROM, David, A ..... 617-989-4552 .... 246 C wahlstromd@wit.edu
WAHLSTROM, Tomi .... 813-463-7187 .... 100 H twahlstrom@argosy.edu
WAHR, David .... 567-661-7401 .... 400 H david_wahr@owens.edu
WAHR, Linda .... 312-329-2213 .... 158 H lwahr@moody.edu
WAIALEALE, Mary .... 541-485-1780 .... 417 E mary@enewhope.org
WAID, Monica, K .... 941-359-7511 .... 115 K mwaid@ringling.edu
WAID, Patti, W .... 209-228-4483 .... 74 B pwaid@UCMerced.edu
WAIDE, Linda .... 256-331-5321 .... 6 B lwaide@nwscc.edu
WAINDLE, Kaylene .... 207-741-5571 .... 219 A kwaindle@smccme.edu
WAINES, Bridgette .... 904-680-7780 .... 107 H bwaines@fcsl.edu
WAINSCOTT, Denise .... 606-546-1218 .... 206 F wainscot@unionky.edu
WAINWRIGHT, Lisa .... 312-899-1236 .... 164 A lwainwright@saic.edu
WAINWRIGHT, William, S 985-732-6640 .... 211 C
WAIS, Marc .... 212-998-4410 .... 344 B marc.wais@nyu.edu
WAIT, Mark .... 615-322-7660 .... 477 F mark.wait@vanderbilt.edu
WAITE, Boyd, A .... 410-293-1582 .... 558 H waite@usna.edu
WAITE, Burton, L .... 208-524-3000 .... 143 C burton.waite@my.eitc.edu
WAITE, Dan .... 949-214-3472 .... 42 K dan.waite@cui.edu
WAITE, George .... 616-234-3818 .... 251 G gwaite@grcc.edu
WAITE, Greg .... 714-953-6500 .... 46 A
WAITE, Joann .... 509-313-5870 .... 534 A waite@gonzaga.edu
WAITE, Lori .... 909-652-6020 .... 39 B lori.waite@chaffey.edu
WAITE, Michelle .... 402-472-2116 .... 300 H mwaite1@unl.edu
WAITE, Ruth, M .... 414-410-4390 .... 546 D rmwaite@stritch.edu
WAITE, William .... 973-300-2100 .... 315 F wwaite@sussex.edu
WAITE, Zauyah .... 412-365-2794 .... 425 B zwaite@chatham.edu
WAITE-FRANZEN, Ellen, J 603-646-2643 .... 305 A ellen.waite-franzen@dartmouth.edu
WAITERS, Ernest .... 301-860-4040 .... 228 A ewaiters@bowiestate.edu
WAITES, Alan .... 785-460-5402 .... 191 J alan.waites@colbycc.edu
WAITZ, Ian, A .... 617-253-0218 .... 242 A iaw@mit.edu
WAJERT, Susan, C .... 309-779-7710 .... 166 A wajertsc@ihs.org
WAJLER, Nancy .... 847-925-6910 .... 151 E nwajler@harpercollege.edu
WAKE, Sue .... 606-539-4201 .... 206 G sue.wake@ucumberlands.edu
WAKE, Warren, K .... 412-291-6358 .... 422 D wwake@aii.edu
WAKEFIELD, Jill .... 206-934-3872 .... 536 G jill.wakefield@seattlecolleges.edu
WAKEFIELD, Larry .... 229-430-4609 .... 123 [illegible] larry.wakefield@asurams.edu
WAKELING, William, M ..... 617-373-5001 .... 244 A
WAKEMAN, Wendy .... 626-584-5423 .... 48 A wwakeman@fuller.edu
WALBERT, Janet, E .... 215-572-2088 .... 422 B walbertj@arcadia.edu
WALBERT, Mark .... 309-438-2430 .... 153 C mswalber@ilstu.edu
WALBERT, Tim .... 501-812-2366 .... 23 C twalbert@pulaskitech.edu
WALBORN, Ronald .... 845-770-5716 .... 344 G ronald.walborn@nyack.edu
WALBORN, Wanda, F .... 845-675-4457 .... 344 G wanda.walborn@nyack.edu
WALBURN, Carson, S .... 740-826-8468 .... 396 I cwalburn@muskingum.edu
WALCH, Darlene, M .... 906-227-2117 .... 256 F dwalch@umu.edu
WALCHESKI, Michael .... 651-603-6184 .... 263 C walcheski@csp.edu
WALCHONSKY, OSBM, Marie Francis .... 215-885-2360 .... 435 E sfrancis@manor.edu
WALCK, Brad .... 405-382-9231 .... 412 B b.walck@sscok.edu
WALCROFT, Marie, B .... 215-699-5700 .... 433 G mwalcroft@LSB.edu
WALCZAK, David .... 954-463-3000 .... 100 I dwalczak@aii.edu
WALD, Jonathan, D .... 941-355-9080 .... 104 J
WALDECK, Steve .... 661-362-2767 .... 56 G swaldeck@masters.edu
WALDEN, Barbara, A .... 906-786-5802 .... 249 D waldenb@baycollege.edu
WALDEN, Daniel .... 323-242-5511 .... 55 C waldendw@lasc.edu
WALDEN, Valerie .... 361-570-4815 .... 503 E waldenv@uhv.edu
WALDERT, Wolfgang .... 847-328-9300 .... 164 B wolf.waldert@seabury.edu
WALDMANN, Robert, G ... 718-429-6600 .... 359 E robert.waldmann@vaughn.edu
WALDNER, George, W .... 717-815-1221 .... 452 F gwaldner@ycp.edu
WALDNER, Joanne, L .... 978-232-2013 .... 234 F jwaldner@endicott.edu
WALDNER, Louann .... 559-737-4838 .... 42 B louannw@cos.edu
WALDO, Susan .... 575-646-1722 .... 319 D swaldo@nmsu.edu
WALDO, Susan .... 575-646-1631 .... 319 D swaldo@nmsu.edu
WALDON, James, G .... 814-871-5814 .... 429 F waldon001@gannon.edu
WALDREN, Henry "Tre", M .... 419-995-8081 .... 392 L waldren.t@rhodesstate.edu
WALDREP, Dwain .... 205-970-9231 .... 7 D dwaldrep@sebc.edu
WALDRIP, Brenda .... 601-318-6188 .... 278 E brenda.waldrip@wmcarey.edu
WALDRON, David, E .... 512-448-8453 .... 493 B dwaldron@stedwards.edu
WALDRON, Gregory, T .... 860-439-2408 .... 91 E gregory.waldron@conncoll.edu
WALDRON, Janet .... 207-581-1541 .... 220 A janet.waldron@umit.maine.edu
WALDRON, Jerome, F .... 410-546-6933 .... 228 D jfwaldron@salisbury.edu
WALDRON, Kathleen .... 973-720-2222 .... 317 D waldronk@wpunj.edu
WALDRON, Sara .... 973-408-3390 .... 309 F swaldron@drew.edu
WALDROP, Heath .... 870-862-8131 .... 23 G hwaldrop@southark.edu
WALDROP, Tony, G .... 407-823-2303 .... 120 A twaldrop@ucf.edu
WALDROUP, Linda, L .... 812-888-4333 .... 181 B lwaldroup@vinu.edu
WALDRUP, Bobby, E .... 904-620-2700 .... 120 C bwaldrup@unf.edu
WALDRUP, J. Charles .... 336-334-7592 .... 377 F cwaldrup@ncat.edu
WALDSTEIN, Edith, J .... 319-352-8272 .... 189 F edith.waldstein@wartburg.edu
WALDVOGEL, Craig .... 708-342-3233 .... 149 L cwaldvogel@devry.edu
WALDVOGEL, Marlene .... 517-264-7190 .... 258 D mwaldvogel@sienaheights.edu
WALEK, Chuck .... 972-708-7574 .... 486 I chuck_walek@gial.edu
WALENGA, Gail, A .... 513-529-7506 .... 396 D walengga@muohio.edu
WALENTA, Michael .... 616-331-6737 .... 252 A walentam@gvsu.edu
WALERIUS, Kenneth .... 419-434-4601 .... 404 B walerius@findlay.edu
WALESBY, Anthony, J .... 734-763-0325 .... 259 D walesby@umich.edu
WALETZKO, Chuck .... 952-487-8146 .... 268 C chuck.waletzko@normandale.edu
WALFORD, Ron .... 502-213-5101 .... 202 B ronald.walford@kctcs.edu

WALLACE, John ... 203-596-4512 ... 93 D
jwallace@post.edu
WALLACE, Jon, R ... 626-812-3075 ... 30 E
jwallace@apu.edu
WALLACE, Joyce ... 214-333-5229 ... 484 C
joycew@dbu.edu
WALLACE, Juanita ... 210-567-8800 ... 506 E
wallacej@uthscsa.edu
WALLACE, Julia, E ... 920-465-2334 ... 551 A
wallacej@uwgb.edu
WALLACE, Kim ... 303-404-5671 ... 84 H
kim.wallace@frontrange.edu
WALLACE, Larry ... 423-746-5329 ... 476 D
lwallace@twcnet.edu
WALLACE, Laura, J ... 434-592-7330 ... 520 F
jwallac@liberty.edu
WALLACE, Leigh ... 229-217-4143 ... 134 C
lwallace@moultrietech.edu
WALLACE, Linda ... 765-455-9288 ... 173 E
lwallace@iuk.edu
WALLACE, Linda ... 240-895-4289 ... 226 A
llwallace@smcm.edu
WALLACE, Lula ... 773-481-8752 ... 147 F
lwallace@ccc.edu
WALLACE, Lynn, H ... 215-702-4337 ... 444 A
lwallace@pbu.edu
WALLACE, Marcus, L ... 580-327-8418 ... 409 C
mlwallace@nwosu.edu
WALLACE, Mark ... 562-860-2451 ... 38 J
mwallace@cerritos.edu
WALLACE, Maureen ... 303-975-5027 ... 89 E
mwallace2@westwood.edu
WALLACE, Michael ... 804-524-5598 ... 529 C
mwallace@vsu.edu
WALLACE, Paul, N ... 724-946-7306 ... 451 C
wallace@westminster.edu
WALLACE, Paula, J ... 434-947-8126 ... 522 E
pwallace@randolphcollege.edu
WALLACE, Paula, S ... 912-525-5200 ... 136 B
pwallace@scad.edu
WALLACE, Randy ... 512-499-4527 ... 504 E
rwallace@utsystem.edu
WALLACE, Ray ... 479-788-7030 ... 24 D
rwallace@uafortsmith.edu
WALLACE, Renee, L ... 512-232-3320 ... 505 B
rlwallace@austin.utexas.edu
WALLACE, Richard ... 650-738-4124 ... 67 G
wallacer@smccd.edu
WALLACE, Rosemary, K ... 325-793-4655 ... 490 F
kwallace@mcm.edu
WALLACE, Selina ... 620-431-2820 ... 195 B
swallace@neosho.edu
WALLACE, Shelby ... 802-485-2658 ... 514 A
swallace@norwich.edu
WALLACE, Steve ... 601-923-1600 ... 277 B
swallace@rts.edu
WALLACE, Steven, R ... 904-632-3224 ... 109 E
steven.wallace@fscj.edu
WALLACE, Susan ... 312-893-7120 ... 150 G
jpromer@erikson.edu
WALLACE, Tami ... 615-230-3573 ... 476 A
tami.wallace@volstate.edu
WALLACE, Terry ... 501-370-5359 ... 23 B
twallace@philander.edu
WALLACE, Thomas ... 402-554-2482 ... 301 B
tdwallace@unomaha.edu
WALLACE, Tiffany ... 662-254-3440 ... 276 C
trwallace@mvsu.edu
WALLACE, Tim ... 864-587-4237 ... 461 D
wallacet@smcsc.edu
WALLACE, Tom ... 615-898-2271 ... 473 F
tom.wallace@mtsu.edu
WALLACE, Tony ... 937-433-3410 ... 390 I
twallace@edaff.com
WALLACE, Valeri, E ... 860-628-4751 ... 92 F
vwallace@lincolncollegene.edu
WALLACE, Wayne, E ... 352-392-1601 ... 120 B
waynewallace@crc.ufl.edu
WALLACE, Wilbur ... 803-793-5170 ... 457 F
wallacew@denmarktech.edu
WALLACH, Paul, M ... 914-594-4500 ... 343 F
paul_wallach@nymc.edu
WALLACK, Lawrence ... 503-725-4043 ... 418 G
wallackl@pdx.edu
WALLENDAL, Deborah ... 262-691-5240 ... 555 C
dwallendal@wctc.edu
WALLER, Christal ... 501-370-5333 ... 23 B
cwaller@philander.edu
WALLER, Cynthia, G ... 615-353-3645 ... 475 D
cynthia.waller@nscc.edu
WALLER, Frank ... 301-860-3813 ... 228 A
fwaller@bowiestate.edu
WALLER, Jan ... 507-433-0627 ... 269 A
jwaller@riverland.edu
WALLER, Janet ... 256-824-6282 ... 9 A
janet.waller@uah.edu
WALLER, Jennifer ... 662-645-3555 ... 274 B
jwaller@deltastate.edu
WALLER, Lorie ... 919-735-5151 ... 374 F
loriew@waynecc.edu
WALLER, Steve ... 218-855-8137 ... 266 C
swaller@clcmn.edu
WALLER, Steven, S ... 402-472-2201 ... 300 H
swaller1@unl.edu

WALLERSTEIN, Michael, B 646-312-3310 ... 326 D
president@baruch.cuny.edu
WALLESER, Diane, K ... 608-246-6550 ... 554 B
dwalleser@matcmadison.edu
WALLEY, Anna-Jean ... 559-455-5566 ... 31 H
cccbusiness@hotmail.com
WALLEY, Jim ... 601-477-4173 ... 275 B
jim.walley@jcjc.edu
WALLEY, Wendell, L ... 559-455-5560 ... 31 H
cccpresww@aol.com
WALLIEN, Dayle, L ... 308-635-6551 ... 301 E
walliend@wncc.edu
WALLIN, Celeste ... 212-616-7273 ... 335 D
celeste.wallin@helenefuld.edu
WALLING, Stella ... 603-899-4147 ... 305 B
stella@franklinpierce.edu
WALLIS, Madeline ... 978-762-4000 ... 241 A
mwallis@northshore.edu
WALLIS, Matthew ... 817-257-5808 ... 498 F
matthew.wallis@tcu.edu
WALLIS, Sherry ... 660-263-3900 ... 279 J
publicrelations@cccb.edu
WALLIS, Trevor ... 502-897-4106 ... 205 H
twallis@sbts.edu
WALLIS, W. Jeff ... 718-933-6760 ... 341 G
jwallis@monroecollege.edu
WALLISCHECK, Eric York .. 516-773-5000 ... 558 F
ewallischeck@usmma.edu
WALLNER, Steve ... 262-595-2451 ... 551 E
steve.wallner@uwp.edu
WALLRAPP, Gary, G ... 617-984-1662 ... 244 C
gwallrapp@quincycollege.edu
WALLS, Cindy ... 618-262-8641 ... 152 I
wallsc@iecc.edu
WALLS, George ... 301-369-2800 ... 221 F
ghwalls@capitol-college.edu
WALLS, Kelly ... 276-326-4232 ... 516 I
kwalls@bluefield.edu
WALLS, Lesley ... 617-732-2800 ... 241 F
lesley.walls@mcphs.edu
WALLS, Randy, C ... 417-268-1000 ... 279 B
rwalls@agts.edu
WALLS, Shannon ... 573-876-7156 ... 290 G
swalls@stephens.edu
WALLS, Skip ... 972-686-7878 ... 492 H
WALLS-UPCHURCH,
L. Ida ... 901-448-4444 ... 477 C
iupchurch@uthsc.edu
WALLSTEIN, Shawna ... 713-525-2160 ... 504 D
wallsts@stthom.edu
WALLY, William ... 680-488-6223 ... 560 A
willyw@palau.edu
WALMSLEY, Robert ... 508-626-4012 ... 238 D
mquiray@framingham.edu
WALN, Ursula ... 402-872-2341 ... 299 H
uwaln@peru.edu
WALNOHA, Melinda ... 760-921-5404 ... 61 B
mwalnoha@paloverde.edu
WALPOLE, Arch ... 757-499-7900 ... 517 A
afwalpole@bryantstratton.edu
WALPOLE, Tommy, A ... 318-342-5419 ... 216 E
walpole@ulm.edu
WALRATH, Ron ... 803-786-5150 ... 459 B
rwalrath@ltss.edu
WALSETH, Teri, L ... 218-477-2095 ... 268 A
walseth@mnstate.edu
WALSH, Ann ... 516-299-3874 ... 339 A
ann.walsh@liu.edu
WALSH, Beth ... 541-684-7224 ... 417 F
bethw@northwestchristian.edu
WALSH, Clifton ... 915-747-5611 ... 505 E
cwalsh@utep.edu
WALSH, Cynthia ... 817-257-7855 ... 498 F
c.walsh@tcu.edu
WALSH, Denise ... 559-438-4222 ... 49 G
denise_walsh@heald.edu
WALSH, Donnell ... 636-949-4853 ... 284 C
dwalsh@lindenwood.edu
WALSH, Erin ... 718-405-3345 ... 330 A
erin.walsh@mountsaintvincent.edu
WALSH, Gerald, T ... 914-968-6200 ... 349 D
sjsr@archny.org
WALSH, James ... 312-410-8996 ... 146 C
jwalsh@thechicagoschool.edu
WALSH, James, A ... 904-276-6839 ... 116 D
tonywalsh@sjrstate.edu
WALSH, Jeff ... 352-588-7337 ... 116 E
jeffrey.walsh@saintleo.edu
WALSH, Jessica ... 765-269-5600 ... 176 B
jwalsh27@ivytech.edu
WALSH, John ... 775-682-7190 ... 303 A
WALSH, John ... 978-632-6600 ... 240 G
j_walsh@mwcc.mass.edu
WALSH, John, T ... 909-748-8368 ... 75 F
john_walsh@redlands.edu
WALSH, Joseph, T ... 847-491-3485 ... 160 D
vp-research@northwestern.edu
WALSH, Julianne ... 617-879-7073 ... 238 E
jwalsh@massart.edu
WALSH, Kathleen ... 224-233-2235 ... 159 D
kathleen.walsh@nl.edu
WALSH, Kimberly, A ... 563-588-7417 ... 186 I
kimberly.walsh@loras.edu

WALSH, Lawrence ... 610-436-3564 ... 443 F
lwalsh@wcupa.edu
WALSH, Lindy ... 802-862-9616 ... 512 H
lwalsh@burlington.edu
WALSH, Margaret ... 614-251-4605 ... 398 F
walshm@ohiodominican.edu
WALSH, Margurete ... 215-951-1013 ... 432 G
walshm@lasalle.edu
WALSH, Mark ... 813-974-2660 ... 120 D
mwalsh@usf.edu
WALSH, Mark, C ... 630-844-5111 ... 145 C
mwalsh@aurora.edu
WALSH, Mary, T ... 504-988-8537 ... 215 C
mary@tulane.edu
WALSH, Mary Beth ... 914-597-2163 ... 360 B
mwalsh@burke.org
WALSH, Mary Lee ... 434-961-6540 ... 527 F
mwalsh@pvcc.edu
WALSH, Melissa ... 215-965-4042 ... 436 H
mwalsh@moore.edu
WALSH, Michael ... 570-504-7000 ... 425 F
WALSH, Michael ... 503-943-7205 ... 420 G
walsh@up.edu
WALSH, Michael ... 414-297-6246 ... 554 D
walshm@matc.edu
WALSH, Michael, D ... 540-568-5681 ... 520 C
walshmd@jmu.edu
WALSH, Michael, J ... 518-564-2100 ... 354 B
walshmj@plattsburgh.edu
WALSH, Michela ... 314-513-4218 ... 289 B
mwalsh@stlcc.edu
WALSH, Michele, M ... 781-891-2070 ... 231 F
mwalsh1@bentley.edu
WALSH, Patricia, J ... 417-255-7904 ... 286 G
pwalsh@missouristate.edu
WALSH, Richard ... 541-552-6258 ... 419 A
walshr@sou.edu
WALSH, Rosalie, K ... 406-447-5440 ... 294 A
rwalsh@carroll.edu
WALSH, Susan ... 541-552-6669 ... 419 A
walsh@sou.edu
WALSH, Susan ... 209-384-6082 ... 57 C
walsh.s@mccd.edu
WALSH, Tammy ... 941-359-7505 ... 115 K
twalsh@ringling.edu
WALSH, Thomas, J ... 315-443-2881 ... 357 B
twalsh@syr.edu
WALSH, Timothy ... 919-684-5055 ... 363 I
tim.walsh@duke.edu
WALSH, Timothy, J ... 716-878-4201 ... 353 A
walshtj@buffalostate.edu
WALSH, Timothy, L ... 662-915-7375 ... 277 G
tim@olemiss.edu
WALSHOK, Mary, L ... 858-534-3411 ... 74 D
mwalshok@ucsd.edu
WALSKI, Don ... 507-457-5555 ... 270 B
dwalski@winona.edu
WALSTRUM, John, W ... 253-589-5500 ... 532 B
john.walstrum@cptc.edu
WALT, J, D ... 859-858-2198 ... 198 A
WALT, John, D ... 859-858-2183 ... 198 A
WALTER, Almar ... 419-434-6967 ... 404 B
waltera@findlay.edu
WALTER, B. Kaye ... 317-921-4882 ... 175 I
WALTER, B. Oliver ... 307-766-4106 ... 556 E
owalter@uwyo.edu
WALTER, Blake ... 630-620-2105 ... 160 B
bwalter@seminary.edu
WALTER, Constance ... 701-483-2787 ... 381 E
constance.walter@dickinsonstate.edu
WALTER, George, J ... 610-519-6456 ... 450 G
george.walter@villanova.edu
WALTER, James ... 623-572-3340 ... 16 F
jwalte@midwestern.edu
WALTER, James ... 860-486-3530 ... 94 E
Jim.Walter@uconn.edu
WALTER, Jim ... 706-355-5120 ... 124 H
jwalter@athenstech.edu
WALTER, John, M ... 661-362-2239 ... 56 G
jwalter@masters.edu
WALTER, Kelly ... 617-353-2300 ... 232 G
kwalter@bu.edu
WALTER, Kelly, D ... 972-708-7415 ... 486 I
admissions@gial.edu
WALTER, Kristy ... 617-243-2147 ... 236 F
kwalter@lasell.edu
WALTER, Lisa, A ... 715-232-2266 ... 552 C
walterl@uwstout.edu
WALTER, Robyn, C ... 636-584-6617 ... 281 I
walterr@eastcentral.edu
WALTER, Ruth ... 412-809-5100 ... 444 F
walter@pti.edu
WALTER, Shulem ... 718-855-4092 ... 347 A
WALTER, Susan ... 530-541-4660 ... 53 F
walter@ltcc.edu
WALTER, Tom, G ... 678-717-3553 ... 129 D
twalter@gsc.edu
WALTER, Willis ... 386-481-2087 ... 101 I
walterw@cookman.edu
WALTER-BURKE,
Judith, P ... 707-253-3371 ... 58 F
jwburke@napavalley.edu
WALTER-MACK, Kathy ... 816-604-1587 ... 285 D
kathy.walter-mack@mcckc.edu

WALTER-SCHUMACHER,
Joan ... 414-382-6064 ... 545 F
joan.walter@alverno.edu
WALTERREIT, Jay ... 989-358-7215 ... 247 G
walterrj@alpenacc.edu
WALTERS, Alice ... 845-561-0800 ... 342 A
WALTERS, Carmen ... 504-762-3015 ... 210 G
cwalte@dcc.edu
WALTERS, Dale ... 423-236-2860 ... 473 A
dwalters@southern.edu
WALTERS, Dave ... 270-789-5007 ... 199 C
dlwalters@campbellsville.edu
WALTERS, Evon, W ... 631-548-2565 ... 356 F
waltere@sunysuffolk.edu
WALTERS, Gary, D ... 609-258-3535 ... 313 A
walters@princeton.edu
WALTERS, George ... 760-921-5507 ... 61 B
gwalters@paloverde.edu
WALTERS, Irene, A ... 260-481-6104 ... 174 A
walters@ipfw.edu
WALTERS, Isaac ... 267-256-0200 ... 99 D
WALTERS, Jennifer, L ... 413-585-2797 ... 245 B
jwalters@smith.edu
WALTERS, Jim ... 951-343-4323 ... 31 G
jmwalters@calbaptist.edu
WALTERS, Joanna ... 785-242-5200 ... 178 E
WALTERS, Joanna ... 785-242-5200 ... 195 G
WALTERS, Joanna ... 785-242-5200 ... 17 C
WALTERS, Joanna ... 785-242-5200 ... 549 E
WALTERS, Joanna, L ... 785-242-5200 ... 195 F
joanna.walters@ottawa.edu
WALTERS, Joe ... 303-963-3376 ... 81 K
jwalters@ccu.edu
WALTERS, Jonathan ... 802-485-2420 ... 514 A
jwalters@norwich.edu
WALTERS, June ... 870-762-3102 ... 20 A
jwalters@smail.anc.edu
WALTERS, Kathie ... 319-226-2003 ... 181 E
waltersks@ihs.org
WALTERS, Kelly ... 661-834-0126 ... 66 F
kelly.walters@sjvc.edu
WALTERS, Kent, L ... 904-264-2172 ... 116 A
kwalters@iws.edu
WALTERS, Leigh Anne ... 973-290-4219 ... 309 A
lwalters@cse.edu
WALTERS, Linda ... 212-686-9040 ... 360 E
lwalters@woodtobecoburn.edu
WALTERS, Maria ... 623-245-4600 ... 18 M
mwalters@uticorp.com
WALTERS, Mark ... 608-262-3666 ... 550 G
mwalters@ohr.wisc.edu
WALTERS, Meridee ... 505-428-1232 ... 320 E
meridee.walters@sfcc.edu
WALTERS, Michael ... 309-341-5290 ... 146 A
mwalters@sandburg.edu
WALTERS, Michael, R ... 606-783-2053 ... 204 E
m.walters@moreheadstate.edu
WALTERS, Ray ... 910-678-8244 ... 370 B
waltersr@faytechcc.edu
WALTERS, Richard ... 314-918-2561 ... 281 J
rwalters@eden.edu
WALTERS, Rick ... 803-313-7464 ... 462 D
WALTERS, Ricki ... 507-433-0534 ... 269 A
rwalters@riverland.edu
WALTERS, Robby ... 828-286-3636 ... 371 A
rwalters@isothermal.edu
WALTERS, Robert ... 310-665-6916 ... 60 B
rwalters@otis.edu
WALTERS, Robert ... 540-231-6077 ... 529 B
rwalters@vt.edu
WALTERS, Roland ... 540-365-4267 ... 518 J
rwalters@ferrum.edu
WALTERS, Sherry, L ... 724-653-2181 ... 427 F
swalters@dec.edu
WALTERS, Tamyra ... 269-749-7197 ... 257 D
twalters@olivetcollege.edu
WALTERS, Tanaya ... 980-598-1835 ... 365 G
tanaya.walters@jwu.edu
WALTERS, Timothy, L ... 509-359-2777 ... 533 D
twalters@ewu.edu
WALTERS, Tyler ... 540-231-5595 ... 529 B
tyler.walters@vt.edu
WALTERS, William ... 650-543-3827 ... 57 B
wwalters@menlo.edu
WALTERS DUNLAP, Karen 209-575-6058 ... 80 B
waltersdunlapk@mjc.edu
WALTERS DUNLAP, Karen 209-575-6067 ... 80 B
waltersdunlapk@mjc.edu
WALTHER, Barb ... 734-995-7499 ... 250 B
walthb@cuaa.edu
WALTHERS, Bruce ... 303-914-6388 ... 87 C
bruce.walthers@rrcc.edu
WALTHERS, Kevin, G ... 925-424-1001 ... 39 A
kwalthers@laspositascollege.edu
WALTHOUR, Scott ... 419-434-4657 ... 404 B
walthour@findlay.edu
WALTON, Ali ... 303-871-2287 ... 88 E
Alison.Walton@du.edu
WALTON, Anita ... 919-530-7099 ... 378 A
awalton@nccu.edu
WALTON, Connie ... 318-247-3811 ... 215 E
WALTON, David, G ... 865-539-7096 ... 475 F
dgwalton@pstcc.edu

WARNER, Steve ..... 863-638-2926 .... 123 C
warnerss@webber.edu
WARNER, Susan ..... 516-686-7647 .... 343 D
swarner@nyit.edu
WARNER, Thomas, R ..... 504-278-6468 .... 211 I
twarner@nunez.edu
WARNER, Timothy, R ..... 650-723-4567 .... 71 F
trw@stanford.edu
WARNER, Tony ..... 410-426-8490 .... 221 D
twarner@bccc.edu
WARNICK, Mark ..... 870-236-6901 .... 21 E
mwarnick@crc.edu
WARNKEN, Mindy ..... 914-337-9300 .... 331 A
melinda.warnken@concordia-ny.edu
WARNOCK, Michael ..... 573-882-4329 .... 291 D
warnockm@missouri.edu
WARPNESS, Wm. Guy ..... 307-755-2120 .... 556 G
gwarpness@wyotechstaff.edu
WARREN, Beverly, J ..... 804-828-1345 .... 525 E
bjwarren@vcu.edu
WARREN, Bronson ..... 580-559-5210 .... 407 J
bwarren@ecok.edu
WARREN, Charlotte, J ..... 217-786-2273 .... 156 I
charlotte.warren@llcc.edu
WARREN, Cheryl ..... 925-424-1156 .... 39 A
cwarren@laspositascollege.edu
WARREN, Chris ..... 601-643-8306 .... 274 A
chris.warren@colin.edu
WARREN, David ..... 617-739-1700 .... 243 F
dwarren@aii.edu
WARREN, Debbie ..... 703-284-1619 .... 521 A
debbie.warren@marymount.edu
WARREN, Denise ..... 218-935-0417 .... 273 A
dwarren@wetcc.org
WARREN, Diana ..... 812-535-5284 .... 179 C
dwarren@smwc.edu
WARREN, Doris, C ..... 281-649-3013 .... 487 F
dcwarren@hbu.edu
WARREN, Earl ..... 256-782-5306 .... 4 L
ewarren@jsu.edu
WARREN, Elisabeth, B ..... 940-565-2892 .... 504 B
warren@unt.edu
WARREN, Ernest ..... 513-851-3800 .... 402 C
ernest.warren@templebaptist.edu
WARREN, Glenna ..... 908-852-1400 .... 308 F
warreng@centenarycollege.edu
WARREN, Huldah ..... 828-884-8337 .... 362 D
warrenh@brevard.edu
WARREN, James ..... 212-410-8063 .... 343 B
jwarren@nycpm.edu
WARREN, Jason, D ..... 270-707-3801 .... 202 A
jason.warren@kctcs.edu
WARREN, Joan, D ..... 212-779-5000 .... 337 H
WARREN, John ..... 616-222-1433 .... 250 C
john.warren@cornerstone.edu
WARREN, John, S ..... 850-474-2022 .... 121 C
jwarren@uwf.edu
WARREN, Katonia ..... 407-628-5870 .... 106 B
kwarren@cci.edu
WARREN, Larry ..... 202-865-6660 .... 98 B
lwarren@huhosp.org
WARREN, Lynda ..... 541-956-7016 .... 420 B
lwarren@roguecc.edu
WARREN, Melissa ..... 254-867-3794 .... 500 B
melissa.warren@tstc.edu
WARREN, Nicholas ..... 781-736-4414 .... 233 A
nwarren@brandeis.edu
WARREN, Pamela ..... 920-923-7614 .... 548 C
pwarren@marianuniversity.edu
WARREN, Patricia ..... 503-338-2306 .... 415 B
pwarren@clatsopcc.edu
WARREN, Robert, D ..... 408-554-4300 .... 68 C
rwarren@scu.edu
WARREN, Roscoe ..... 305-626-3741 .... 108 H
rwarren@fmuniv.edu
WARREN, Ruth ..... 252-335-0821 .... 369 D
rwarren@albemarle.edu
WARREN, Sara ..... 410-225-2264 .... 224 C
swarren@mica.edu
WARREN, Scott ..... 254-659-7781 .... 487 E
swarren@hillcollege.edu
WARREN, Shannon ..... 304-645-6382 .... 544 C
swarren@osteo.wvsom.edu
WARREN, Steven, F ..... 785-864-7298 .... 196 F
sfwarren@ku.edu
WARREN, Tim ..... 505-566-4321 .... 320 D
warrent@sanjuancollege.edu
WARREN, V'Ella ..... 206-543-8765 .... 538 F
vwarren@uw.edu
WARREN, Wade ..... 318-487-7436 .... 209 B
warren@lacollege.edu
WARREN, William, J ..... 801-581-6773 .... 510 L
william.warren@utah.edu
WARREN-MARLATT,
Rebeccah ..... 909-389-3355 .... 65 B
rmarla@craftonhills.edu
WARRENER, Mary ..... 845-341-4007 .... 345 E
mary.warrener@sunyorange.edu
WARRICK, JR.,
Douglas, R ..... 803-641-3406 .... 462 B
randyw@usca.edu
WARRICK-JOHNSON,
Deshawn ..... 248-204-2151 .... 254 E
djohnson@ltu.edu

WARRINGTON, Adam ..... 802-654-0505 .... 515 D
adam.warrington@ccv.edu
WARRINGTON, Richard ..... 800-567-2344 .... 546 G
richwarrington@menominee.edu
WARRINGTON, Scott, C ..... 909-869-6989 .... 33 G
scwarrington@csupomona.edu
WARRINGTON, Traci ..... 401-341-2477 .... 454 D
traci.warrington@salve.edu
WARSHAWER, Elizabeth ..... 215-893-5252 .... 426 E
elizabeth.warshawer@curtis.edu
WARTELL, Michael, A ..... 260-481-6103 .... 174 A
wartell@ipfw.edu
WARTGROW, Jerry ..... 303-315-7682 .... 88 D
chancellor@ucdenver.edu
WARTHAN, Nathan ..... 503-375-7006 .... 415 F
nwarthan@corban.edu
WARTHEN, Douglas ..... 740-366-9560 .... 399 E
warthen.5@osu.edu
WARTMAN, Bruce ..... 215-574-9600 .... 431 A
bwartman@hussianart.edu
WARTMAN, Jed, W ..... 207-859-4280 .... 217 G
jwartman@colby.edu
WARTMAN, Lynne ..... 215-574-9600 .... 431 A
lwartman@hussianart.edu
WARTZOK, Douglas ..... 305-348-2151 .... 119 B
wartzok@fiu.edu
WARWICK, Ann ..... 212-938-5600 .... 355 B
awarwick@sunyopt.edu
WARYAS, Diane ..... 702-651-4485 .... 302 G
diane.waryas@csn.edu
WARZYNSKI, Chet ..... 404-894-1099 .... 130 D
chet.warzynski@orgdev.gatech.edu
WASAN, Darsh, T ..... 312-567-3001 .... 153 B
wasan@iit.edu
WASBAUER, Kevin ..... 831-647-3595 .... 57 F
kwasbauer@miis.edu
WASEM, John, E ..... 423-722-1086 .... 468 F
jwasem@ecs.edu
WASESCHA, Anna ..... 860-343-5703 .... 90 D
awasescha@mxcc.commnet.edu
WASHAM, Ronnie ..... 606-337-1722 .... 199 E
rwasham@ccbbc.edu
WASHBURN, Curtis ..... 808-739-4627 .... 140 A
cwashbur@chaminade.edu
WASHBURN, Floyd ..... 843-525-8257 .... 461 E
fwashburn@tcl.edu
WASHBURN, James, B ..... 662-254-3300 .... 276 C
james.washburn@mvsu.edu
WASHBURN, Joseph ..... 252-672-7502 .... 369 E
washburnj@cravencc.edu
WASHBURN, Joyce ..... 785-460-5403 .... 191 J
joyce.washburn@colbycc.edu
WASHBURN, Keith, E ..... 440-365-5222 .... 395 C
WASHBURN, Kevin ..... 505-277-4700 .... 321 C
washburn@law.unm.edu
WASHBURN, Lois, M ..... 904-470-8266 .... 105 A
lois.washburn@ewc.edu
WASHBURN, Robert, B ..... 618-650-2560 .... 165 A
rwashbu@siue.edu
WASHBURN, Terri ..... 248-689-8282 .... 260 A
twashburn@walshcollege.edu
WASHBURNE, Cynthia ..... 860-512-3353 .... 90 C
cwashburne@mcc.commnet.edu
WASHCO, Chris ..... 907-834-1631 .... 11 B
cwashco@pwscc.edu
WASHINGTON, A. Eugene 310-825-5687 .... 74 A
ewashington@mednet.ucla.edu
WASHINGTON, Al ..... 314-264-1000 .... 292 E
alfred.washington@vatterott.edu
WASHINGTON, Andre ..... 859-442-4176 .... 201 G
andre.washington@kctcs.edu
WASHINGTON, Cheryl ..... 334-874-5700 .... 3 A
cwashington@concordiaselma.edu
WASHINGTON,
Christopher, L ..... 614-947-6129 .... 391 A
washingc@franklin.edu
WASHINGTON, Crystal ..... 773-838-7535 .... 147 E
cwashington59@ccc.edu
WASHINGTON, Dana ..... 815-802-8962 .... 154 J
dwashington@kcc.edu
WASHINGTON, Dennis, C . 616-732-1198 .... 250 E
dwashington@davenport.edu
WASHINGTON, DeSandra . 910-678-0037 .... 370 B
washingd@faytechcc.edu
WASHINGTON, Earlie ..... 269-387-2638 .... 260 F
earlie.washington@wmich.edu
WASHINGTON, Eric ..... 718-960-8181 .... 327 C
eric.washington@lehman.cuny.edu
WASHINGTON, Fred, E ..... 936-261-9100 .... 496 E
fewashington@pvamu.edu
WASHINGTON, Fred, E ..... 936-261-2140 .... 496 E
fewashington@pvamu.edu
WASHINGTON, Gregory ..... 847-851-5309 .... 144 F
WASHINGTON, Ingrid ..... 859-442-1148 .... 201 G
ingrid.washington@kctcs.edu
WASHINGTON, J. Leon ..... 610-758-3100 .... 434 E
jnw207@lehigh.edu
WASHINGTON,
James Bernard ..... 252-536-7220 .... 370 F
washingtonj@halifaxcc.edu
WASHINGTON, Jennifer ..... 860-832-3820 .... 91 D
jwashington@charteroak.edu
WASHINGTON, Kaye ..... 318-670-9450 .... 215 A
kwashington@susla.edu

WASHINGTON, Kelvin ..... 803-533-3736 .... 460 G
kwashington@scsu.edu
WASHINGTON,
Kheysia, H ..... 318-670-9417 .... 215 A
kwashington@susla.edu
WASHINGTON,
L. Marshall ..... 717-358-2975 .... 430 E
lmwashin@hacc.edu
WASHINGTON, Leila ..... 410-951-3660 .... 228 B
lwashington@coppin.edu
WASHINGTON, Mary ..... 229-317-6761 .... 128 A
mary.washington@darton.edu
WASHINGTON, Maurice ..... 404-653-7857 .... 134 A
mwashington@morehouse.edu
WASHINGTON, Michael ..... 813-227-4161 .... 111 B
mwashington@online.academy.edu
WASHINGTON, Michael ..... 901-435-1601 .... 470 B
michael_washington@loc.edu
WASHINGTON, Pamela ..... 405-974-5537 .... 413 B
pwashington@ucok.edu
WASHINGTON, Sammie ..... 256-331-5200 .... 6 B
sammiew@nwscc.edu
WASHINGTON, Ted, M ..... 615-353-3228 .... 475 D
ted.washington@nscc.edu
WASHINGTON, William, O 847-317-7091 .... 166 B
coffeew@tiu.edu
WASHINGTON, Willie ..... 803-705-4734 .... 455 D
washingtonw@benedict.edu
WASHINGTON, Winifred ..... 903-769-5723 .... 488 M
winifred_washington@jarvis.edu
WASHINGTON-LACEY,
Bonita ..... 765-983-1515 .... 171 B
washibo@earlham.edu
WASHINGTON-WOODS,
Paula ..... 870-235-4145 .... 23 I
pwwoods@saumag.edu
WASHKEVICH, Stephen ..... 978-632-6600 .... 240 G
s_washkevich@mwcc.mass.edu
WASHKO, Mary Jo ..... 804-523-5345 .... 526 F
mwashko@reynolds.edu
WASHOUSKY, Richard, C . 716-851-1500 .... 333 C
washousky@ecc.edu
WASICSKO, Mark ..... 859-572-5229 .... 205 E
wasicskom1@nku.edu
WASIELEWSKI, Laura ..... 603-656-6051 .... 305 H
lwasielewski@anselm.edu
WASIK, David, G ..... 330-972-7926 .... 403 B
wasik@uakron.edu
WASILENKO, William, J ..... 757-446-8480 .... 518 F
wasilewj@evms.edu
WASILOWSKI, Stuart ..... 704-290-5240 .... 373 F
swasilowski@spcc.edu
WASIOLEK, Sue ..... 919-684-6313 .... 363 I
dean.sue@duke.edu
WASKIE, Kenneth, G ..... 607-777-2184 .... 351 F
kwaskie@binghamton.edu
WASKOSKY, Julia ..... 815-802-8510 .... 154 J
jwaskosky@kcc.edu
WASKOW, Iris ..... 310-476-9777 .... 28 F
iwaskow@ajula.edu
WASLEY, Patrick ..... 415-338-3068 .... 36 F
pwasley@sfsu.edu
WASSBERG, Catherine ..... 651-523-2616 .... 264 C
cwassberg01@hamline.edu
WASSEL, Robert ..... 314-977-2041 .... 289 F
rwassel@slu.edu
WASSENAAR, Dave ..... 714-484-7345 .... 59 C
dwassenaar@cypresscollege.edu
WASSENAAR, JR.,
James, R ..... 305-348-4190 .... 119 B
wassenaa@fiu.edu
WASSENBERG, Pinky, S ..... 217-206-6523 .... 167 A
wassenberg.pinky@uis.edu
WASSERMAN, Harriet ..... 206-344-4344 .... 537 A
hwasse@sccd.ctc.edu
WASSERMAN, Joy ..... 847-328-1124 .... 391 E
jwasserman@huc.edu
WASSERMAN, Scott ..... 775-784-4901 .... 302 F
scott_wasserman@nshe.nevada.edu
WASSON, Dale ..... 817-272-5401 .... 505 A
wasson@uta.edu
WASSON, George ..... 314-984-7763 .... 289 D
gwasson@stlcc.edu
WASSON, Leslie, A ..... 561-237-7773 .... 113 D
lwasson@lynn.edu
WASSON, Michael ..... 303-280-7485 .... 84 C
mwasson@devry.edu
WASSON, Tanlee, T ..... 812-941-2293 .... 174 D
tawasson@ius.edu
WASSON, Thomas ..... 601-857-3367 .... 274 E
thwasson@hindscc.edu
WASTLER, Cyndi, L ..... 703-339-2516 .... 99 D
clw@strayer.edu
WASUKANIS, John, T ..... 561-868-3480 .... 114 D
wasukanj@palmbeachstate.edu
WATANABE, Mie ..... 808-956-6423 .... 140 J
mie@hawaii.edu
WATERFIELD, James, R ..... 757-683-4631 .... 521 L
rwater@odu.edu
WATERFIELD, Lisa ..... 757-388-2900 .... 523 J
WATERHOUSE, Lynda ..... 239-513-1135 .... 123 D
lwaterhouse@wolford.edu
WATERMAN, Ann-Marie ..... 202-274-6110 .... 99 F
awaterman@udc.edu

WATERMAN, Christopher .. 310-206-6469 .... 74 A
cwater@arts.ucla.edu
WATERS, Barry, D ..... 989-774-7493 .... 249 G
water1b@cmich.edu
WATERS, Christine ..... 810-424-5294 .... 259 F
cwaters@umflint.edu
WATERS, Christopher, C ..... 336-278-5055 .... 364 A
cwaters@elon.edu
WATERS, Gary ..... 706-236-2251 .... 125 G
gwaters@berry.edu
WATERS, Gloria, S ..... 617-353-2704 .... 232 G
gwaters@bu.edu
WATERS, Gloriana ..... 212-794-5353 .... 326 C
gloriana.waters@mail.cuny.edu
WATERS, Gregory, L ..... 973-655-7374 .... 311 G
watersg@mail.montclair.edu
WATERS, Jeff ..... 417-328-1632 .... 290 E
jwaters@sbuniv.edu
WATERS, Jennifer ..... 312-369-7831 .... 148 B
jwaters@colum.edu
WATERS, Joan ..... 334-291-4951 .... 2 G
joan.waters@cv.edu
WATERS, John, B ..... 512-472-4133 .... 494 B
jwaters@ssw.edu
WATERS, Karita ..... 615-966-1791 .... 470 D
karita.waters@lipscomb.edu
WATERS, Kerry ..... 480-994-9244 .... 18 I
kwaters@swiha.net
WATERS, Lynne, T ..... 808-956-8109 .... 140 J
lynnew@hawaii.edu
WATERS, Marlo ..... 707-965-6676 .... 60 J
mwaters@puc.edu
WATERS, Melissa ..... 770-426-2901 .... 133 B
melissa.waters@life.edu
WATERS, Michelle ..... 252-335-0821 .... 369 D
michelle_waters@albemarle.edu
WATERS, Myra ..... 410-837-5159 .... 229 A
mwaters@ubalt.edu
WATERS, Ron ..... 707-476-4331 .... 42 A
ron-waters@redwoods.edu
WATERS, Roy, S ..... 318-257-2893 .... 215 F
roy@latech.edu
WATERS, Sarah ..... 419-372-2011 .... 385 C
waterss@bgsu.edu
WATERS, Shari ..... 714-997-6726 .... 39 C
swaters@chapman.edu
WATERS, Sharon ..... 570-326-3761 .... 440 K
swaters@pct.edu
WATERS, Taylor ..... 410-263-2371 .... 225 G
taylor.waters@sjca.edu
WATFORD, John ..... 229-271-4049 .... 136 G
jwatford@southgatech.edu
WATFORD, Lettie ..... 229-931-2145 .... 131 B
WATHEN, Cory ..... 916-691-7418 .... 56 B
wathenc@crc.losrios.edu
WATHEN, James ..... 270-686-4465 .... 202 E
jim.wathen@kctcs.edu
WATKIN, Anna Maria, S ..... 217-351-2596 .... 161 B
amwatkin@parkland.edu
WATKIN, Steve ..... 661-654-3277 .... 33 H
swatkin@csub.edu
WATKINS, Alison, L ..... 941-359-6111 .... 115 K
awatkins@ringling.edu
WATKINS, Anita ..... 919-962-7096 .... 377 A
awatkins@northcarolina.edu
WATKINS, Brenda, F ..... 864-488-4544 .... 459 A
bwatkins@limestone.edu
WATKINS, Bryan ..... 773-244-5770 .... 159 G
bjwatkins@northpark.edu
WATKINS, Caryl ..... 718-982-2300 .... 327 A
Caryl.Watkins@csi.cuny.edu
WATKINS, II, Curtis, E ..... 850-201-8291 .... 121 F
watkinsc@tcc.fl.edu
WATKINS, Dan ..... 215-612-6600 .... 425 D
dwatkins@chicareers.com
WATKINS, Daniel ..... 601-979-2433 .... 275 A
daniel.watkins@jsums.edu
WATKINS, Dorla ..... 816-584-6231 .... 287 H
dorla.watkins@park.edu
WATKINS, Faye ..... 757-727-5371 .... 519 C
faye.watkins@hamptonu.edu
WATKINS, Fran ..... 480-423-6133 .... 16 D
fran.watkins@sccmail.maricopa.edu
WATKINS, Frank ..... 772-462-7475 .... 110 L
fwatkins@irsc.edu
WATKINS, Jameson ..... 913-588-7387 .... 197 A
jwatkins@kumc.edu
WATKINS, Jennifer ..... 918-463-2931 .... 407 H
jennifer.watkins@connorsstate.edu
WATKINS, Joe ..... 619-849-2650 .... 62 L
jwatkins@pointloma.edu
WATKINS, John ..... 724-938-1569 .... 441 G
watkins@calu.edu
WATKINS, Kristin ..... 503-977-4696 .... 419 G
kwatkins@pcc.edu
WATKINS, Laurie ..... 307-382-1647 .... 556 F
lwatkins@wwcc.wy.edu
WATKINS, Lee ..... 610-896-1023 .... 430 G
lwatkins@haverford.edu
WATKINS, Lori ..... 334-556-2361 .... 4 A
lwatkins@wallace.edu
WATKINS, Marie ..... 585-389-2304 .... 342 D
mwatkin2@naz.edu

WEAVER, Don ... 620-327-8219 ... 193 C
donw@hesston.edu
WEAVER, Donna Jo ... 812-888-4220 ... 181 B
dweaver@vinu.edu
WEAVER, Gina ... 585-345-6808 ... 334 F
gmweaver@genesee.edu
WEAVER, H. Danny ... 816-654-7102 ... 283 J
hweaver@kcumb.edu
WEAVER, Harrison ... 415-380-1376 ... 48 D
harryweaver@ggbts.edu
WEAVER, James ... 540-231-3977 ... 529 B
weaverj@vt.edu
WEAVER, Jennifer, L ... 717-337-3855 ... 430 E
jlweaver@hacc.edu
WEAVER, John ... 325-674-2387 ... 478 H
WEAVER, JR., Joseph, B ... 405-744-5982 ... 410 C
WEAVER, JR., Joseph, B ... 405-744-2690 ... 410 C
joe.weaver@okstate.edu
WEAVER, Julie ... 231-439-6306 ... 256 E
jweaver@ncmich.edu
WEAVER, Larry ... 903-875-7380 ... 491 B
larry.weaver@navarrocollege.edu
WEAVER, Laura ... 925-485-5215 ... 38 L
lweaver@clpccd.org
WEAVER, Laura ... 925-485-5215 ... 38 K
lgweaver@clpccd.org
WEAVER, Laura ... 925-485-5215 ... 39 A
lgweaver@clpccd.org
WEAVER, Laura ... 219-785-5742 ... 178 H
lweaver@pnc.edu
WEAVER, Linza, M ... 757-569-6735 ... 527 E
lweaver@pdc.edu
WEAVER, Lloyd, J ... 205-329-7922 ... 3 B
lloyd.weaver@ecacolleges.com
WEAVER, Mary, O ... 570-326-2869 ... 437 F
director_nbi@comcast.net
WEAVER, Melanie ... 419-772-2272 ... 398 G
m-weaver@onu.edu
WEAVER, Neal ... 806-651-2070 ... 498 D
nweaver@mail.wtamu.edu
WEAVER, Priscilla ... 928-724-6610 ... 14 A
pweaver@dinecollege.edu
WEAVER, Sandie ... 562-903-4760 ... 30 H
sandie.weaver@biola.edu
WEAVER, Sean ... 505-545-3380 ... 318 I
slweaver@nmhu.edu
WEAVER, Shannon ... 972-273-3390 ... 485 B
sweaver@dcccd.edu
WEAVER, Susan, F ... 724-653-2211 ... 427 F
sweaver@dec.edu
WEAVER, Susan, M ... 330-382-7432 ... 393 F
sweaver@kent.edu
WEAVER, Terri, E ... 312-996-7808 ... 166 F
teweaver@uic.edu
WEAVER, Theresa ... 906-635-2733 ... 254 C
tweaver@lssu.edu
WEAVER, Tim ... 304-829-7242 ... 540 E
tweaver@bethanywv.edu
WEAVER, Vicki ... 660-359-3948 ... 287 D
vweaver@mail.ncmissouri.edu
WEAVER, Vickie, L ... 609-896-5029 ... 313 G
weaver@rider.edu
WEAVER, William, H ... 478-757-2549 ... 133 E
bill.weaver@maconstate.edu
WEAVER-GRIGGS, Linda ... 803-327-8024 ... 463 G
lwgriggs@yorktech.edu
WEAVER HART, Ann ... 215-204-7405 ... 447 G
president@temple.edu
WEAVERLING, Kenneth, J ... 302-454-3978 ... 96 C
weave@dtcc.edu
WEAVIL, Vicki ... 336-770-3266 ... 379 D
weavilv@uncsa.edu
WEBB, Andrew ... 505-880-2877 ... 317 H
WEBB, Arla, J ... 443-518-4690 ... 223 D
awebb@howardcc.edu
WEBB, Barbara ... 989-686-9228 ... 250 F
brwebb@delta.edu
WEBB, Bill ... 918-495-7163 ... 411 C
bwebb@oru.edu
WEBB, Brandon ... 979-209-7285 ... 482 A
brandon.webb@blinn.edu
WEBB, Brandon, R ... 918-647-1210 ... 407 E
bwebb@carlalbert.edu
WEBB, Brent, W ... 801-422-6201 ... 509 D
WEBB, Brian ... 802-828-8740 ... 402 I
brian.webb@myunion.edu
WEBB, Brian ... 336-386-3530 ... 374 B
webbb@surry.edu
WEBB, Burton, J ... 208-467-8539 ... 143 I
bwebb@nnu.edu
WEBB, Carol ... 281-487-1170 ... 498 E
cwebb@txchiro.edu
WEBB, Carolyn, S ... 318-670-9314 ... 215 A
cwebb@susla.edu
WEBB, Charles, H ... 517-750-1200 ... 258 F
cwebb@arbor.edu
WEBB, Charlie ... 806 720-7156 ... 490 D
charlie.webb@lcu.edu
WEBB, Cheryl, A ... 803-327-7402 ... 456 F
cwebb@clintonjuniorcollege.edu
WEBB, Chloe ... 641-844-5708 ... 185 J
chloe.webb@iavalley.edu
WEBB, Dan ... 423-425-4729 ... 477 D
dan-webb@utc.edu
WEBB, Dann ... 478-988-6800 ... 133 H
dwebb@middlegatech.edu
WEBB, David ... 775-831-1314 ... 303 E
dwebb@sierranevada.edu
WEBB, Dixie ... 931-221-6346 ... 473 D
webbd@apsu.edu
WEBB, Donna ... 229-391-5001 ... 123 F
dwebb@abac.edu
WEBB, Donnetta ... 916-558-2408 ... 56 D
webbd@scc.losrios.edu
WEBB, Duncan ... 312-461-0600 ... 144 D
dwebb@aaart.edu
WEBB, Eddie ... 916-484-8569 ... 56 A
webbe@losrios.edu
WEBB, Elnora, T ... 510-464-3236 ... 62 C
ewebb@peralta.edu
WEBB, Greg ... 270-444-9676 ... 200 A
gwebb@daymarcollege.edu
WEBB, Heather ... 630-652-8373 ... 149 B
hwebb@devry.edu
WEBB, Jacqueline, F ... 603-526-3621 ... 304 A
jwebb@colby-sawyer.edu
WEBB, James, D ... 806-651-1240 ... 498 D
jwebb@mail.wtamu.edu
WEBB, Jay, K ... 434-544-8218 ... 520 H
webb@lynchburg.edu
WEBB, Jeanie ... 405-733-7374 ... 411 I
jwebb@rose.edu
WEBB, Joe, B ... 626-584-5491 ... 48 A
jwebb@fuller.edu
WEBB, Joshua, M ... 989-964-4359 ... 258 A
jmwebb@svsu.edu
WEBB, Karen ... 805-756-2171 ... 33 F
kwebb@calpoly.edu
WEBB, Karen Schuster ... 415-955-2050 ... 27 A
kwebb@alliant.edu
WEBB, Kathleen, M ... 937-229-4263 ... 404 A
kathleen.webb@notes.udayton.edu
WEBB, Kathy ... 606-546-1616 ... 206 F
kwebb@unionky.edu
WEBB, Katonja ... 773-602-5000 ... 147 B
kwebb@ccc.edu
WEBB, Keith ... 404-270-5279 ... 137 E
kwebb5@spelman.edu
WEBB, Ken ... 619-680-4430 ... 32 A
ken.webb@cc-sd.edu
WEBB, Kenneth ... 903-785-7661 ... 492 B
kwebb@parisjc.edu
WEBB, Kristine, W ... 904-620-2769 ... 120 C
kwebb@unf.edu
WEBB, Kyla ... 615-230-3343 ... 476 A
kyla.webb@volstate.edu
WEBB, Kyle ... 901-843-3760 ... 472 I
webb@rhodes.edu
WEBB, Lee ... 870-512-7849 ... 20 F
lee_webb@asun.edu
WEBB, Lindsie, B ... 330-684-8941 ... 403 C
llamb@uakron.edu
WEBB, Lisa ... 214-768-4564 ... 494 F
lisawebb@smu.edu
WEBB, Maria ... 973-443-8533 ... 310 B
mwebb@fdu.edu
WEBB, Mark, F ... 931-598-1284 ... 472 J
mwebb@sewanee.edu
WEBB, Michael ... 815-921-2151 ... 162 F
m.webb@rockvalleycollege.edu
WEBB, Michelle ... 207-453-5120 ... 218 I
mwebb@kvcc.me.edu
WEBB, Randall, J ... 318-357-6441 ... 216 B
webb@nsula.edu
WEBB, Randy ... 870-733-6750 ... 22 E
rwebb@midsouthcc.edu
WEBB, Raymond, J ... 847-566-6401 ... 167 D
rwebb@usml.edu
WEBB, Reggie ... 863-669-2305 ... 115 A
rwebb@polk.edu
WEBB, Reggie ... 540-828-8014 ... 516 K
rwebb@bridgewater.edu
WEBB, Reginald ... 863-669-2305 ... 115 A
rwebb@polk.edu
WEBB, Richard, E ... 610-896-1290 ... 430 G
rwebb@haverford.edu
WEBB, Robert, L ... 781-891-2283 ... 231 F
rwebb@bentley.edu
WEBB, Steffani ... 913-588-1400 ... 197 A
swebb@kumc.edu
WEBB, Susan ... 785-242-5200 ... 195 F
susan.webb@ottawa.edu
WEBB, Terrance ... 608-246-6270 ... 554 B
tswebb@matcmadison.edu
WEBB, Terry ... 607-777-4787 ... 351 F
twebb@binghamton.edu
WEBB, Truly ... 651-793-1272 ... 267 D
truly.webb@metrostate.edu
WEBB, Vicki ... 870-307-7227 ... 22 D
vwebb@lyon.edu
WEBB, Vincent ... 936-294-1632 ... 501 A
vjw002@shsu.edu
WEBB, Virginia, E ... 610-526-1308 ... 421 G
virginia.webb@theamericancollege.edu
WEBB, W. Roger ... 405-974-2311 ... 413 B
webb@ucok.edu
WEBB, Walter, W ... 815-939-5333 ... 160 F
wwebb@olivet.edu
WEBB, JR., William, C ... 810-762-3324 ... 259 F
bwebb@umflint.edu
WEBB SHARPE, Lisa ... 517-483-1106 ... 254 D
sharpel@lcc.edu
WEBBER, Chris ... 618-395-7777 ... 152 H
webberc@iecc.edu
WEBBER, Eleanor ... 802-635-1309 ... 515 E
eleanor.webber@jsc.edu
WEBBER, Henry, S ... 314-935-7877 ... 292 J
HWEBBER@wustl.edu
WEBBER, Karen, B ... 303-458-3561 ... 87 E
kwebber@regis.edu
WEBBER, Ken, P ... 641-422-4275 ... 187 F
webbeken@niacc.edu
WEBBER, Leah ... 617-928-4513 ... 243 A
lwebber@mountida.edu
WEBBER, Louise ... 909-621-8265 ... 40 C
louise.webber@cgu.edu
WEBBER, Mike ... 415-422-2508 ... 76 B
webberm@usfca.edu
WEBBER, Tracy, E ... 828-765-7351 ... 371 F
twebber@mayland.edu
WEBBER-COLBERT,
Wilma, F ... 662-915-7735 ... 277 G
wcolbert@olemiss.edu
WEBER, Allison ... 920-693-1631 ... 554 A
allison.weber@gotoltc.edu
WEBER, Brad ... 620-252-7076 ... 191 I
bradw@coffeyville.edu
WEBER, Bruce, W ... 302-831-1211 ... 96 F
WEBER, Cate ... 651-846-3330 ... 261 E
cweber@argosy.edu
WEBER, Charlotte ... 304-696-4812 ... 543 G
cweber@rcbi.org
WEBER, Cheryl ... 617-585-1157 ... 243 E
cheryl.weber@necmusic.edu
WEBER, Chris ... 231-995-1039 ... 256 G
cweber@nmc.edu
WEBER, Dave ... 507-285-7217 ... 269 B
dave.weber@roch.edu
WEBER, Dave, N ... 507-285-7217 ... 269 B
dave.weber@roch.edu
WEBER, Dawn ... 419-289-4142 ... 384 D
dweber1@ashland.edu
WEBER, Donna, J ... 715-836-3871 ... 550 H
weberdj@uwec.edu
WEBER, Donna, M ... 715-232-2314 ... 552 C
weberd@uwstout.edu
WEBER, Eric ... 801-957-4136 ... 512 C
eric.weber@slcc.edu
WEBER, Ernest ... 718-270-2431 ... 352 D
ernest.weber@downstate.edu
WEBER, Girard, W ... 847-543-2201 ... 147 H
jweber@clcillinois.edu
WEBER, J. Christopher ... 570-577-1795 ... 423 D
weber@bucknell.edu
WEBER, Jacqueline, J ... 573-592-5307 ... 293 C
Jackie.Weber@westminster-mo.edu
WEBER, Jeff ... 414-443-8819 ... 553 B
jeff.weber@wlc.edu
WEBER, Joan ... 509-574-4984 ... 540 A
jweber@yvcc.edu
WEBER, Jodi ... 903-434-8114 ... 491 D
jweber@ntcc.edu
WEBER, Joe ... 931-221-7618 ... 473 D
weberj@apsu.edu
WEBER, John ... 219-785-5273 ... 178 H
jweber@pnc.edu
WEBER, Jolanta, A ... 509-313-6504 ... 534 A
weberj@gonzaga.edu
WEBER, Joseph, F ... 979-845-4728 ... 497 C
vpsa@tamu.edu
WEBER, Julie ... 575-646-3202 ... 319 D
jeweber@nmsu.edu
WEBER, Karen ... 415-749-4504 ... 65 I
kweber@sfai.edu
WEBER, Keith, A ... 513-244-4350 ... 388 D
keith.weber@mail.msj.edu
WEBER, Kevin ... 502-585-9911 ... 205 I
kweber@spalding.edu
WEBER, Leann ... 701-228-5426 ... 382 C
leann.weber@dakotacollege.edu
WEBER, Lou Anne ... 864-503-5197 ... 463 A
lweber@uscupstate.edu
WEBER, Margaret ... 740-284-5244 ... 390 M
mweber@franciscan.edu
WEBER, Margaret, J ... 310-568-5615 ... 61 G
margaret.weber@pepperdine.edu
WEBER, Mark ... 920-498-5663 ... 555 A
mark.weber@nwtc.edu
WEBER, Mark ... 330-672-2962 ... 393 D
mweber@kent.edu
WEBER, Marsha, L ... 218-477-2076 ... 268 A
marsha.weber@mnstate.edu
WEBER, MaryEllen ... 214-648-3684 ... 507 D
maryellen.weber@utsouthwestern.edu
WEBER, Melissa, A ... 570-577-1201 ... 423 D
melissa.weber@bucknell.edu
WEBER, Merlin, D ... 530-226-4501 ... 69 H
mweber@simpsonu.edu
WEBER, Nancy ... 843-525-8226 ... 461 E
nweber@tcl.edu
WEBER, Peter, M ... 401-863-7799 ... 452 J
peter_weber@brown.edu
WEBER, Phil ... 740-857-1311 ... 401 [illegible]
pweber@rosedale.edu
WEBER, Randy ... 620-365-5116 ... 190 A
weber@allencc.edu
WEBER, Scott ... 716-645-6029 ... 351 [illegible]
sweber@buffalo.edu
WEBER, OP, Sharon, R ... 517-264-7102 ... 258 D
srweber@sienaheights.edu
WEBER, Susan ... 212-501-3050 ... 323 [illegible]
weber@bgc.bard.edu
WEBER, Teresa ... 914-323-6304 ... 340 A
teresa.weber@mville.edu
WEBER, William, V ... 217-581-2921 ... 150 C
wvweber@eiu.edu
WEBLEY, Radha ... 707-826-4502 ... 36 D
rw76@humboldt.edu
WEBSTER, Alex ... 425-637-1010 ... 531 [illegible]
alexwebster@cityu.edu
WEBSTER, Carita ... 281-476-1501 ... 493 E
carita.webster@sjcd.edu
WEBSTER, Frank, R ... 404-816-4533 ... 132 B
fwebster@atl.herzing.edu
WEBSTER, Fred ... 406-275-4800 ... 296 F
WEBSTER, James, N ... 660-248-6223 ... 279 K
jwebster@centralmethodist.edu
WEBSTER, Jeremy ... 740-593-2723 ... 399 G
webstej1@ohio.edu
WEBSTER, Jerry ... 419-559-2395 ... 402 D
jwebster@terra.edu
WEBSTER, John, W ... 951-785-2041 ... 53 D
jwebster@lasierra.edu
WEBSTER, Kacy ... 515-727-2100 ... 186 G
kwebster@hamiltonia.edu
WEBSTER, LaTika ... 317-738-8080 ... 171 C
lwebster@franklincollege.edu
WEBSTER, Leatha, E ... 909-593-3511 ... 75 C
lwebster@laverne.edu
WEBSTER, Linda ... 573-592-5288 ... 293 C
Linda.Webster@westminster-mo.edu
WEBSTER, Lynn ... 208-459-5325 ... 143 A
lwebster@collegeofidaho.edu
WEBSTER, Margo ... 510-204-0753 ... 39 F
mwebster@cdsp.edu
WEBSTER, Mary, L ... 626-395-6304 ... 32 E
mwebster@caltech.edu
WEBSTER, Matthew, H ... 859-344-3306 ... 206 D
matthew.webster@thomasmore.edu
WEBSTER, Michael ... 610-361-2222 ... 437 C
websterm@neumann.edu
WEBSTER, Michael, N ... 410-857-2202 ... 224 D
mwebster@mcdaniel.edu
WEBSTER, Ondes ... 865-471-3352 ... 467 E
owebster@cn.edu
WEBSTER, Reede, O ... 612-659-6312 ... 267 E
reede.webster@minneapolis.edu
WEBSTER, Richard, C ... 410-334-2896 ... 229 E
rwebster@worwic.edu
WEBSTER, Robert, O ... 518-437-4550 ... 351 E
rwebster@uamail.albany.edu
WEBSTER, Scott ... 508-999-8202 ... 237 E
swebster@umassd.edu
WEBSTER, Tom ... 903-923-2157 ... 486 D
twebster@etbu.edu
WEBSTER, Valerie ... 229-293-6135 ... 136 F
valerie.webster@sgc.edu
WEBSTER, Wayne, P ... 920-748-8351 ... 549 I
websterw@ripon.edu
WEBSTER, William, C ... 212-243-5150 ... 334 E
webster@gts.edu
WECHNER, Richard ... 615-232-7384 ... 469 D
rwechner@iadtnashville.com
WECHSLER, Barton, J ... 573-882-3304 ... 291 D
wechslerb@missouri.edu
WECKMAN, Judith ... 859-985-3791 ... 198 F
judith_weckman@berea.edu
WECKMUELLER, Beth, L ... 414-229-6164 ... 551 C
bethw@uwm.edu
WEDDERBURN, Anette ... 301-860-3939 ... 228 A
awedderburn@bowiestate.edu
WEDDINGTON, Brenda ... 773-907-4755 ... 147 A
bweddington@ccc.edu
WEDDINGTON, Hank ... 828-328-7035 ... 366 B
hank.weddington@lr.edu
WEDDLE-WEST, Karen, D ... 901-678-2531 ... 474 C
kweddle@memphis.edu
WEDEL, Allen ... 316-284-5242 ... 190 H
awedel@bethelks.edu
WEDES, Lloyd ... 713-973-3137 ... 486 A
lwedes@devry.edu
WEDGE, Luann ... 616-234-4170 ... 251 G
lwedge@grcc.edu
WEDIG, Tyler ... 319-895-4378 ... 183 D
twedig@cornellcollege.edu
WEDLER, Andrea ... 518-445-2388 ... 322 D
awedl@albanylaw.edu
WEDLER-JOHNSON,
Darlene ... 941-752-5247 ... 118 E
wedlerd@scf.edu
WEDLOCK, Monica ... 404-687-4516 ... 127 C
wedlockm@ctsnet.edu
WEDMAN, John ... 573-882-4546 ... 291 D
wedmanj@missouri.edu
WEE, Liang, C ... 563-562-3263 ... 187 G
weel@portal.nicc.edu

WEISS, Daniel, H .... 610-330-5200.... 433 B
weissd@lafayette.edu
WEISS, David .... 210-567-3709.... 506 E
weissd@uthscsa.edu
WEISS, Dennis .... 609-652-4548.... 313 F
dennis.weiss@stockton.edu
WEISS, Don .... 816-941-0430.... 281 E
dweiss@devry.edu
WEISS, Ira, R .... 919-515-5560.... 378 B
ira_weiss@ncsu.edu
WEISS, Jack, M .... 225-578-8491.... 213 C
WEISS, Janet, A .... 734-764-4401.... 259 D
janetw@umich.edu
WEISS, Jeffery, I .... 718-990-6357.... 348 G
weissj@stjohns.edu
WEISS, Joseph, H .... 267-502-2632.... 423 B
joe.weiss@anc-gc.org
WEISS, Karen .... 618-252-5400.... 164 G
karen.weiss@sic.edu
WEISS, Kay .... 909-384-8535...... 65 C
kweiss@sbccd.cc.ca.us
WEISS, Mark .... 541-917-4780.... 416 H
weissm@linnbenton.edu
WEISS, Mark .... 503-838-8990.... 419 C
weissm@wou.edu
WEISS, Michelle .... 860-412-7353...... 91 A
mweiss@qvcc.commnet.edu
WEISS, Roy .... 773-702-0344.... 166 D
rweiss@medicine.bsd.uchicago.edu
WEISSINGER, Ellen .... 402-472-3751.... 300 H
eweissinger1@unl.edu
WEISSKOPF, Vera .... 229-931-2259.... 131 B
WEISSMAN, Julie .... 314-246-4256.... 293 A
julieweissman22@webster.edu
WEISSMAN, Neil, B .... 717-245-1321.... 427 E
weissmne@dickinson.edu
WEISWEAVER, Tom .... 253-833-9111.... 534 C
tweisweaver@greenriver.edu
WEITER, Stephen .... 315-470-6715.... 355 A
spweiter@esf.edu
WEITZ, Anna, D .... 610-607-6210.... 445 B
aweitz@racc.edu
WEITZ, Sue, D .... 509-313-4107.... 534 A
weitz@gu.gonzaga.edu
WEITZER, Joseph .... 262-695-7824.... 555 C
jweitzer@wctc.edu
WEITZER, William .... 203-254-4000...... 92 B
wweitzer@fairfield.edu
WEITZMAN, Lauren .... 801-581-6826.... 510 L
lweitzman@sa.utah.edu
WELBORN, Ruth, B .... 512-245-3300.... 501 C
rw01@txstate.edu
WELBOURNE, Claudia .... 315-279-6868.... 337 K
cwelbour@mail.keuka.edu
WELBURN, Janice .... 414-288-7214.... 548 D
janice.welburn@marquette.edu
WELBURN, Marsha .... 617-928-4599.... 243 A
mwelburn@mountida.edu
WELBURN, William .... 414-288-8028.... 548 D
william.welburn@marquette.edu
WELCH, Alexis .... 252-527-6223.... 371 D
awelch@lenoircc.edu
WELCH, Bashen .... 205-929-1445........ 5 H
bwelch@miles.edu
WELCH, C. Brigid .... 209-946-2949...... 75 D
bwelch@pacific.edu
WELCH, Charles, L .... 501-660-1000...... 20 B
president@asusystem.edu
WELCH, Charles, L .... 870-230-5091...... 21 I
cwelch@hsu.edu
WELCH, Denise .... 903-693-1121.... 492 A
dwelch@panola.edu
WELCH, Dirk .... 940-397-4972.... 491 A
dirk.welch@mwsu.edu
WELCH, Dotty .... 740-588-1220.... 407 A
dwelch@zanestate.edu
WELCH, Doug .... 417-626-1234.... 287 F
welch.doug@occ.edu
WELCH, Edwin, H .... 304-357-4713.... 541 H
edwinwelch@ucwv.edu
WELCH, Eric .... 901-321-3419.... 467 G
ewelch@cbu.edu
WELCH, Felicia .... 602-978-7412...... 18 K
felicia.welch@thunderbird.edu
WELCH, Frances, C .... 843-953-5613.... 457 B
welchf@cofc.edu
WELCH, James (Emory) ..... 863-667-5805.... 118 A
jewelch@seu.edu
WELCH, Jennifer, C .... 315-464-4570.... 352 E
welchj@upstate.edu
WELCH, Joe Ben .... 225-675-8270.... 211 J
jbwelch@rpcc.edu
WELCH, John .... 412-362-5610.... 444 G
jwelch@pts.edu
WELCH, Kathy .... 407-691-1098.... 116 B
kjwelch@rollins.edu
WELCH, Lena .... 615-248-1393.... 476 E
lwelch@trevecca.edu
WELCH, Lynne .... 908-709-7167.... 316 B
welch@ucc.edu
WELCH, Mark .... 202-885-3287...... 97 B
mark@american.edu
WELCH, Mary Ellen .... 540-665-5436.... 523 K
shenandoah@bkstr.com
WELCH, Matthew, D .... 337-562-4220.... 215 G
WELCH, Michael .... 847-578-3238.... 163 A
michael.welch@rosalindfranklin.edu
WELCH, Olga, M .... 412-396-1360.... 428 C
welcho@duq.edu
WELCH, Patricia .... 443-885-3385.... 224 F
pwelch@morgan.edu
WELCH, Paul .... 858-635-4709...... 27 E
pwelch@alliant.edu
WELCH, Paul .... 508-626-4640.... 238 D
pwelch@framingham.edu
WELCH, Raymond .... 201-447-7184.... 307 F
rwelch@bergen.edu
WELCH, Regina .... 804-627-5300.... 516 J
WELCH, Renee .... 970-351-2127...... 88 F
renee.welch@unco.edu
WELCH, Ronald, W .... 843-953-6588.... 456 C
rwelch1@citadel.edu
WELCH, Sandra, T .... 210-458-4706.... 506 B
sandra.welch@utsa.edu
WELCH, Shari, L .... 814-863-9938.... 439 C
slg1@psu.edu
WELCH, Sharon .... 773-256-3000.... 158 A
swelch@meadville.edu
WELCH, Sherri, L .... 856-691-8600.... 309 C
swelch@cccnj.edu
WELCH, Susan .... 518-564-5062.... 354 B
welchst@plattsburgh.edu
WELCH, Susan .... 814-865-7691.... 438 F
sxw11@psu.edu
WELCH, Sylvia .... 503-978-5841.... 419 G
swelch@pcc.edu
WELCH, Tammy .... 575-528-7069.... 319 G
welchta@nmsu.edu
WELCH, Terry .... 828-227-7100.... 379 E
welcht@wcu.edu
WELCH, Vince .... 706-245-7226.... 128 K
vwelch@ec.edu
WELCH, Walter .... 859-572-6421.... 205 E
welchw1@nku.edu
WELDEN, David .... 770-962-7580.... 132 A
dwelden@gwinnetttech.edu
WELDEN, Soraya .... 601-484-8628.... 275 C
swelden@mcc.cc.ms.us
WELDON, Ann-Marie .... 980-598-1528.... 365 G
ann-marie.weldon@jwu.edu
WELDON, James .... 803-780-1119.... 463 B
jweldon@voorhees.edu
WELDON, Leslie .... 618-634-3337.... 164 C
lesliew@shawneecc.edu
WELDON, Rich .... 803-593-9231.... 455 A
weldon@atc.edu
WELDON, Stephanie, J ...... 603-668-6706.... 304 E
sjweldon@ccsnh.edu
WELGE, Vicky, L .... 217-443-8702.... 148 E
voliver@dacc.edu
WELKER, Dan .... 928-428-8300...... 14 C
dan.welker@eac.edu
WELKER, Joan, C .... 570-484-2181.... 443 A
jwelker@lhup.edu
WELKER, Josh .... 217-641-4110.... 154 G
jwelker@jwcc.edu
WELKER, Mark .... 336-758-3898.... 380 B
welker@wfu.edu
WELKEY, Sharon .... 210-832-2115.... 503 F
welkey@uiwtx.edu
WELLBAUM, Robert, W ..... 334-844-1139........ 1 G
wellbrw@auburn.edu
WELLBORN, Linda .... 417-865-2811.... 282 A
wellbornl@evangel.edu
WELLE, David .... 760-872-2000...... 43 H
dwelle@deepsprings.edu
WELLER, John, F .... 513-745-5600.... 403 F
john.weller@uc.edu
WELLER, Steve .... 972-438-6932.... 492 C
sweller@parkercc.edu
WELLER, Vicki .... 410-617-2201.... 224 A
vweller@loyola.edu
WELLER-DENGEL, Pamela . 507-389-6061.... 267 H
pamela.weller-dengel@mnsu.edu
WELLHAM, Ann .... 301-387-3045.... 222 H
ann.wellham@garrettcollege.edu
WELLHAUSEN, Chad .... 712-542-5117.... 186 B
cwellhausen@iwcc.edu
WELLINGTON, Eric, R .... 610-359-5127.... 426 G
ewellington@dccc.edu
WELLIVER, Suzy, L .... 610-799-1946.... 434 D
swelliver@lccc.edu
WELLMAN, Barbara .... 217-228-5432.... 161 E
wellmba@quincy.edu
WELLMAN, Christopher ..... 660-543-4331.... 291 B
cwellman@ucmo.edu
WELLMAN, Ronald, D .... 336-758-5616.... 380 B
wellmanr@wfu.edu
WELLNER, Justin .... 831-582-3044...... 35 C
jwellner@csumb.edu
WELLS, Ann .... 229-248-2516.... 125 E
ann.wells@bainbridge.edu
WELLS, Barbara .... 239-433-6951.... 104 L
bwells@edison.edu
WELLS, Barbara .... 865-981-8278.... 470 F
barbara.wells@maryvillecollege.edu
WELLS, Barbara .... 901-333-4259.... 475 H
bwells@southwest.tn.edu
WELLS, Barbara, G .... 662-915-7265.... 277 G
wells@olemiss.edu
WELLS, Beth .... 503-845-3243.... 417 A
beth.wells@mtangel.edu
WELLS, Betty, E .... 419-755-4756.... 397 B
bwells@ncstatecollege.edu
WELLS, Billy .... 706-864-1630.... 134 D
bewells@northgeorgia.edu
WELLS, Bonnie .... 860-439-5001...... 91 E
bonnie.wells@conncoll.edu
WELLS, Brent .... 281-283-2180.... 503 C
wellsb@uhcl.edu
WELLS, Brian, J .... 502-776-1443.... 205 G
WELLS, C. Gene .... 812-488-2664.... 180 B
gw5@evansville.edu
WELLS, Carole .... 610-683-4212.... 442 F
wells@kutztown.edu
WELLS, Cathy .... 253-833-9111.... 534 C
cwells@greenriver.edu
WELLS, Christina .... 217-479-7030.... 157 D
christina.wells@mac.edu
WELLS, Christopher, J .... 765-658-4226.... 170 I
christopherwells@depauw.edu
WELLS, Christopher, J .... 765-658-4060.... 170 I
christopherwells@depauw.edu
WELLS, Dan .... 812-877-8205.... 179 A
dan.wells@rose-hulman.edu
WELLS, David, A .... 817-515-5250.... 496 A
david.wells@tccd.edu
WELLS, David, J .... 315-386-7411.... 355 D
wellsd@canton.edu
WELLS, Debra .... 724-335-5336.... 437 H
dwells@oaa.edu
WELLS, Elaine .... 212-938-5690.... 355 B
ewells@sunyopt.edu
WELLS, Gail, V .... 716-878-4631.... 353 A
wellsgv@buffalostate.edu
WELLS, Gail, W .... 859-572-5788.... 205 E
wells@nku.edu
WELLS, Henry, D .... 919-572-1625.... 361 M
registrar@apexsot.edu
WELLS, Jayne, E .... 608-785-9141.... 555 D
wellsj@westerntc.edu
WELLS, Jeremy .... 612-330-1177.... 261 G
wells@augsburg.edu
WELLS, Jeremy .... 515-727-2100.... 186 G
jeremywells@hamiltonia.edu
WELLS, Johann .... 478-825-6200.... 129 C
wellsj@fvsu.edu
WELLS, Johann .... 334-291-4954........ 2 G
johann.wells@cv.edu
WELLS, John, M .... 252-335-0821.... 369 D
jmwells@albemarle.edu
WELLS, John, T .... 804-684-7103.... 517 J
wells@vims.edu
WELLS, John, W .... 828-689-1250.... 366 F
jwells@mhc.edu
WELLS, Jovita .... 202-274-6260...... 99 F
jwells@udc.edu
WELLS, Keith, P .... 303-762-6963...... 83 I
keith.wells@denverseminary.edu
WELLS, La Shawn .... 925-609-6650...... 38 B
lbwells@cc.edu
WELLS, Linda, S .... 617-353-2852.... 232 G
lwells@bu.edu
WELLS, Lisa .... 540-887-7330.... 520 I
lwells@mbc.edu
WELLS, Marilyn .... 570-422-3536.... 442 C
mwells@po-box.esu.edu
WELLS, Mary .... 603-668-6660.... 305 C
WELLS, Nick .... 785-460-4684.... 191 J
nick.wells@colbycc.edu
WELLS, Paul, S .... 740-374-8716.... 405 F
pwells1@wscc.edu
WELLS, R. Hal .... 612-874-3634.... 265 E
hal_wells@mcad.edu
WELLS, Rebecca .... 270-831-9682.... 201 I
rebecca.wells@kctcs.edu
WELLS, Regina, A .... 302-454-3941...... 96 C
rwells@dtcc.edu
WELLS, Richard .... 731-661-6595.... 476 G
rwells@uu.edu
WELLS, Richard, H .... 920-424-0200.... 551 D
wellsr@uwosh.edu
WELLS, JR., Robert, J .... 864-656-0244.... 456 E
rjwells@clemson.edu
WELLS, Sarah .... 813-463-7153.... 100 H
swells@argosy.edu
WELLS, Sherry .... 913-758-6123.... 197 B
wellss@stmary.edu
WELLS, Sherry .... 409-880-8968.... 500 F
sherry.wells@lamar.edu
WELLS, Teri .... 304-896-7443.... 542 J
teriw@southern.wvnet.edu
WELLS, Twyla, C .... 919-209-2119.... 371 C
tcwells@johnstoncc.edu
WELLS, Virginia, D .... 757-221-4386.... 517 J
vdwell@wm.edu
WELLS, Warren .... 660-785-4121.... 291 A
wwells@truman.edu
WELLS, Will .... 419-995-8213.... 392 L
wells.w@rhodesstate.edu
WELLS, William .... 207-780-4995.... 220 G
wells@maine.edu
WELLS, William, C .... 419-995-8213.... 392 L
wells.w@rhodesstate.edu
WELLS, William, T .... 336-758-5154.... 380 B
wellswt@wfu.edu
WELLS-BOOTH, Shawna .... 352-787-7660.... 101 F
swells@beaconcollege.edu
WELP, Cindy .... 712-274-5114.... 187 D
welp@morningside.edu
WELSCH, Cheryl .... 845-434-5750.... 356 H
cwelsch@sullivan.suny.edu
WELSCH, Colleen .... 269-782-1204.... 258 E
cwelsch@swmich.edu
WELSCH, Gabriel .... 814-641-3131.... 431 L
welschg@juniata.edu
WELSH, Connie .... 406-444-0614.... 294 J
cwelsh@montana.edu
WELSH, David .... 860-255-3513...... 91 C
dwelsh@txcc.commnet.edu
WELSH, John .... 213-740-6977...... 76 C
john@fms.usc.edu
WELSH, Johnelle .... 254-526-1298.... 482 F
johnelle.welsh@ctcd.edu
WELSH, Judith .... 540-338-2700.... 517 D
jwelsh@cdu.edu
WELSH, Marcia, G .... 410-704-2125.... 228 E
mwelsh@towson.edu
WELSH, Marcia, G .... 410-704-2356.... 228 E
mwelsh@towson.edu
WELSH, Patrick, J .... 610-785-6265.... 446 A
deanofmentdscs@adphila.org
WELSH, Sarah .... 617-264-7756.... 234 E
swelsh@emmanuel.edu
WELSH, Steven .... 985-448-4325.... 216 A
steve.welsh@nicholls.edu
WELSH, Susan .... 478-757-5137.... 139 A
swelsh@wesleyancollege.edu
WELSH, Susan, T .... 478-757-5155.... 139 A
swelsh@wesleyancollege.edu
WELSH, Suzanne, P .... 610-328-8316.... 447 E
swelsh1@swarthmore.edu
WELSH, Tasha, D .... 636-797-3000.... 283 H
twelsh@jeffco.edu
WELSH, Tracy .... 605-688-4121.... 466 B
tracy.welsh@sdstate.edu
WELSH, William, J .... 570-941-7600.... 450 B
welshw2@scranton.edu
WELTER, Linda .... 617-879-2233.... 246 F
lwelter@wheelock.edu
WELTER, Stephen .... 619-594-2978...... 36 E
WELTJEN, Scott .... 716-270-5239.... 333 D
weltjen@ecc.edu
WELTON, Ronald, J .... 516-876-3135.... 353 D
weltonr@oldwestbury.edu
WELTY, Ann .... 843-574-6100.... 461 G
ann.welty@tridenttech.edu
WELTY, Jessica .... 918-335-6268.... 411 B
jwelty@okwu.edu
WELTY, John, D .... 559-278-2324...... 34 D
john_welty@csufresno.edu
WELZ, Linda .... 626-914-8811...... 39 G
lwelz@citruscollege.edu
WEN, Hui-Men .... 941-487-4601.... 119 D
hwen@ncf.edu
WEN, Joseph .... 620-341-5274.... 192 D
hwen@emporia.edu
WENBERG, Carrie .... 314-889-1403.... 282 C
cwenberg@fontbonne.edu
WENCK, Lisa, M .... 607-436-2518.... 353 E
wenckim@oneonta.edu
WENDALL, Alan, B .... 215-951-1916.... 432 G
wendall@lasalle.edu
WENDEL, Shirley, A .... 913-288-7626.... 193 J
swendel@kckcc.edu
WENDELN, Sheila .... 803-321-5140.... 459 G
sheila.wendeln@newberry.edu
WENDEROFF, Karen .... 212-220-8021.... 326 E
kwenderoff@bmcc.cuny.edu
WENDEROTH, Christine .... 773-753-0735.... 157 E
cwendero@lstc.edu
WENDEROTH, Christine .... 773-256-0735.... 157 B
cwenderoth@jkmlibrary.org
WENDLE, William, D .... 276-328-0139.... 525 C
wdw8m@uvawise.edu
WENDLER, David, O .... 507-354-8221.... 265 B
wendledo@mlc-wels.edu
WENDLER, Dee .... 503-725-3752.... 418 G
wendler@pdx.edu
WENDOVER, Wendy .... 303-963-3268...... 81 K
wwendover@ccu.edu
WENDT, Bill .... 478-445-5589.... 129 F
bill.wendt@gcsu.edu
WENDT, Bob .... 907-822-3201...... 10 C
bwendt@akbible.edu
WENDT, Donna .... 706-771-4150.... 125 D
dwendt@augustatech.edu
WENDT, Hunter .... 586-498-4090.... 254 F
wendth@macomb.edu
WENDT, Ted .... 559-278-3027...... 34 D
twendt@csufresno.edu
WENDT, Tim .... 217-353-3673.... 161 B
twendt@parkland.edu
WENDTH, Norman .... 978-368-2200.... 230 F
norman.wendth@auc.edu

WESTPHAL, Stephen, A ..... 231-995-1130.... 256 G
swestphal@nmc.edu

WESTRA, Jeff .... 608-249-6611.... 547 D
careers@msn.herzing.edu

WESTRA, Kayla .... 507-372-3435.... 268 B
kayla.westra@mnwest.edu

WESTRA, Robert, C .... 704-847-5600.... 376 H
cwoodside@ses.edu

WESTRICK, Karyn, J .... 419-434-4758.... 404 B
westrick@findlay.edu

WESTWATER, Julia .... 508-289-3379.... 247 A
jwestwater@whoi.edu

WETENDORF, Trey .... 432-335-6708.... 491 F
twetendorf@odessa.edu

WETHERBEE-METCALF,
Pamela .... 410-617-2330.... 224 A
pwetherbeemetcalf@loyola.edu

WETHERELL, Bill .... 386-506-3813.... 103 J
wetherb@DaytonaState.edu

WETHERILL, G. Richard ..... 580-559-5455.... 407 J
rwethrll@ecok.edu

WETHERILL, Karen .... 910-962-3354.... 379 C
wetherillk@uncw.edu

WETHERINGTON, Lee .... 252-527-6223.... 371 D
lwetherington@lenoircc.edu

WETHERS, Gaynelle .... 585-389-2008.... 342 D
gwether9@naz.edu

WETMORE, Angela .... 615-248-1739.... 476 E
awetmore@trevecca.edu

WETMORE, Dawn .... 567-661-7338.... 400 H
dawn_wetmore@owens.edu

WETMORE, Jill .... 989-964-4064.... 258 A
jwetmore@svsu.edu

WETSELL, Linda, S .... 814-332-4790.... 421 E
linda.wetsell@allegheny.edu

WETSIT, Larry .... 406-768-6311.... 294 F
lwetsit@fpcc.edu

WETSTEIN, Kenneth, A ...... 419-783-2587.... 389 G
kwetstein@defiance.edu

WETSTEIN, Matthew .... 209-954-5472...... 66 D
mwetstein@deltacollege.edu

WETTAN, Richard .... 718-997-2795.... 328 F
richard.wettan@qc.cuny.edu

WETTER, Kevin .... 808-356-5261.... 140 B
kvetter@hpu.edu

WETTICK, Elizabeth .... 412-383-1805.... 449 A
wettickes@upmc.edu

WETZEL, Barbara .... 716-896-0700.... 359 F
wetzel@villa.edu

WETZEL, Derrick .... 610-282-1100.... 426 I
derrick.wetzel@desales.edu

WETZEL, Kim .... 415-675-5200...... 47 A
kwetzel@fidm.edu

WETZEL, Mary, E .... 717-728-2260.... 425 A
marywetzel@centralpenn.edu

WETZEL, Shelby .... 307-754-6110.... 556 D
Shelby.Wetzel@northwestcollege.edu

WETZEL, Stephanie .... 707-668-5663...... 43 I

WETZEL, Suzanne, M .... 734-384-4206.... 255 G
swetzel@monroeccc.edu

WETZEL HARDER, Wendy 949-480-4081...... 69 I
wwharder@soka.edu

WETZSTEIN, James .... 219-464-5096.... 181 A
james.wetzstein@valpo.edu

WEXLER, Arthur .... 609-343-4905.... 307 D
wexler@atlantic.edu

WEXLER, Joan, G .... 718-780-7900.... 324 F
joan.wexler@brooklaw.edu

WEXLER, Jon .... 201-692-7304.... 310 B
jwexler@fdu.edu

WEXLER, Judie .... 415-575-6104...... 32 D
jwexler@ciis.edu

WEXLER, Robert .... 310-476-9777...... 28 F
rwexler@ajula.edu

WEYAND, Joel .... 402-826-8242.... 298 A
joel.weyand@doane.edu

WEYERS, Lori, A .... 715-675-3331.... 554 G
weyers@ntc.edu

WEYGAND, Robert, A .... 401-874-2433.... 454 E
bobw@uri.edu

WEYGANT, Susan .... 914-923-2397.... 345 F
sweygant@pace.edu

WEYHENMEYER,
James, A .... 404-413-3516.... 131 C
jweyhenmeyer@gsu.edu

WEYMAN, Crystal .... 216-687-3595.... 388 C
c.weyman@csuohio.edu

WHALEN, David .... 517-607-2321.... 252 E
david.whalen@hillsdale.edu

WHALEN, David .... 845-451-1406.... 331 F
d_whalen@culinary.edu

WHALEN, Eileen .... 206-744-3036.... 538 F
whalene@uw.edu

WHALEN, F. Richard .... 757-683-3018.... 521 L
dwhalen@odu.edu

WHALEN, Jeff .... 209-588-5126...... 80 A
whalenj@yosemite.edu

WHALEN, Lynn .... 217-786-2219.... 156 I
lynn.whalen@llcc.edu

WHALEN, Michael .... 419-251-1824.... 395 H
michael.whalen@mercycollege.edu

WHALEN, Patricia .... 814-824-3070.... 436 C
pwhalen@mercyhurst.edu

WHALEN, Paul .... 818-719-6444...... 55 B
whalenpl@piercecollege.edu

WHALEN, Peggy .... 507-453-2401.... 267 F
wwhalen@southeastmn.edu

WHALEN, Philip, E .... 843-348-2350.... 456 G
pwhalen@coastal.edu

WHALEN, Scott .... 315-255-1743.... 325 H
scott.whalen@cayuga-cc.edu

WHALEN, Tricia .... 507-433-0374.... 269 A
twhalen@riverland.edu

WHALEY, Chris .... 865-882-4513.... 475 G
whaleycl@roanestate.edu

WHALEY, David, J .... 802-485-2300.... 514 A
davew@norwich.edu

WHALEY, Michael .... 636-949-4561.... 284 C

WHALEY, Michael .... 636-949-4561.... 284 C
mwhaley@lindenwood.edu

WHALEY, Michael, J .... 860-685-3160...... 95 C
mwhaley@wesleyan.edu

WHALEY, Mitchell, H .... 765-285-5818.... 169 D
mwhaley@bsu.edu

WHALEY, Sheree .... 530-242-7667...... 69 D
swhaley@shastacollege.edu

WHALEY, Stephanie .... 912-344-2658.... 124 E
stephanie.whaley@armstrong.edu

WHALEY, Tammey, E .... 864-503-5210.... 463 A
twhaley@uscupstate.edu

WHANG, John, E .... 213-381-0081...... 51 F
johnewhang@hotmail.com

WHANG, Kyu-Jung .... 607-255-4394.... 331 C
kw253@cornell.edu

WHARTON, Barbara, I .... 614-823-1576.... 400 G
bwharton@otterbein.edu

WHARTON, Beverly, A .... 712-279-5400.... 182 E
beverly.wharton@briarcliff.edu

WHARTON, Bill .... 636-227-2100.... 284 E
bill.wharton@logan.edu

WHARTON, Bob .... 903-233-3610.... 489 K
bobwharton@letu.edu

WHARTON, George .... 513-556-5503.... 403 D
george.wharton@uc.edu

WHARTON, Kristin .... 704-233-8366.... 380 D
kwharton@wingate.edu

WHARTON, Martha, L .... 410-617-2988.... 224 A
mwharton1@loyola.edu

WHARTON, Randy .... 567-661-7457.... 400 H
william_wharton@owens.edu

WHARTON, Robert, A .... 605-394-2411.... 466 A
robert.wharton@sdsmt.edu

WHATELY, Lorrie .... 253-752-2020.... 533 J
admissions@faithseminary.edu

WHATLEY, Katherine, M ..... 706-236-2216.... 125 G
kwhatley@berry.edu

WHATLEY, Melissa .... 657-278-2380...... 34 E
mkwhatley@fullerton.edu

WHATLEY, Sherri .... 903-566-7247.... 506 C
swhatley@uttyler.edu

WHATLEY, Thomas, S .... 318-342-5015.... 216 E
whatley@ulm.edu

WHEAT, Gary .... 417-626-1234.... 287 F
gwheat@occ.edu

WHEAT, Zach .... 434-243-2096.... 525 B
zjw6b@virginia.edu

WHEATLEY, Diane .... 757-789-1754.... 526 D
dwheatley@es.vccs.edu

WHEATLEY, Jennifer .... 541-956-7291.... 420 B
jwheatley@roguecc.edu

WHEATLEY, Joyce .... 757-382-5687.... 518 C
jwheatley@devry.edu

WHEATLEY, Vesta, M .... 817-515-7795.... 496 A
vesta.wheatley@tccd.edu

WHEATLY, Michele, G .... 304-293-5701.... 544 E
michele.wheatly@mail.wvu.edu

WHEATLY, Stephen .... 805-493-3828...... 32 H
wheatly@clunet.edu

WHEATON, David, M .... 651-696-6211.... 265 A
wheaton@macalester.edu

WHEATON, Janilee, B .... 216-687-2277.... 388 C
j.wheaton@csuohio.edu

WHEATON, Jeremy .... 224-293-5961...... 83 D
jwheaton@coloradotech.edu

WHEATON, Tom .... 605-642-6446.... 465 F
tom.wheaton@bhsu.edu

WHEATON-COX, Ruth, L ... 608-757-7678.... 553 E
rwheaton-cox@blackhawk.edu

WHEELAN, Elliot .... 804-524-5090.... 529 C
ewheelan@vsu.edu

WHEELAND, Craig .... 610-519-4520.... 450 G
craig.wheeland@villanova.edu

WHEELDON, Tim, T .... 515-263-6152.... 184 I
twheeldon@grandview.edu

WHEELER, Amber .... 603-882-6923.... 304 F
awheeler@ccsnh.edu

WHEELER, Brad .... 812-855-4717.... 173 C
bwheeler@indiana.edu

WHEELER, Brad, C .... 812-855-3478.... 173 B
bwheeler@indiana.edu

WHEELER, Cassandra, L .... 956-326-2260.... 497 B
cwheeler@tamiu.edu

WHEELER, Cecilia, B .... 919-528-4737.... 374 D
wheelerc@vgcc.edu

WHEELER, Darrell, P .... 312-915-7024.... 157 A
dwheeler@luc.edu

WHEELER, Ed, R .... 678-359-5017.... 131 D
edw@gdn.edu

WHEELER, Erin .... 518-631-9850.... 358 F
wheelere@uniongraduatecollege.edu

WHEELER, Frank, E .... 402-363-5646.... 301 F
fwheeler@york.edu

WHEELER, Gary .... 269-467-9945.... 251 D
gwheeler@glenoaks.edu

WHEELER, H. William .... 434-592-3003.... 520 F
hwwheeler@liberty.edu

WHEELER, Ike .... 870-512-7865...... 20 F
ike_wheeler@asun.edu

WHEELER, John, D .... 216-368-5555.... 386 E
john.wheeler@case.edu

WHEELER, John, J .... 269-387-2966.... 260 F
john.j.wheeler@wmich.edu

WHEELER, Jolene .... 928-724-6694...... 14 A
jwheeler@dinecollege.edu

WHEELER, Karen, J .... 501-569-3204...... 24 E
kjwheeler@ualr.edu

WHEELER, Kathleen, B .... 402-363-5696.... 301 F
kbwheeler@york.edu

WHEELER, Laurie .... 707-965-7200...... 60 J
lwheeler@puc.edu

WHEELER, Lawrence .... 503-725-4928.... 418 G
wheelerl@pdx.edu

WHEELER, Linda .... 706-272-4547.... 127 G
lwheeler@daltonstate.edu

WHEELER, Lisa .... 318-678-6000.... 209 J
lwheeler@bpcc.edu

WHEELER, Lisa .... 952-487-8286.... 268 C
lisa.wheeler@normandale.edu

WHEELER, Margaret .... 314-991-6200.... 280 A
mwheeler@devry.com

WHEELER, Mark .... 208-426-1140.... 142 F
mwheeler@boisestate.edu

WHEELER, Mary .... 254-526-1200.... 482 F
mary.wheeler@ctcd.edu

WHEELER, Mary Anne .... 850-973-1605.... 113 J
wheelerm@nfcc.edu

WHEELER, Michelle .... 248-476-1122.... 255 C
mwheeler@mispp.edu

WHEELER, Michelle .... 919-718-7239.... 368 H
mwheeler@cccc.edu

WHEELER, Nolan .... 360-442-2121.... 535 C
nwheeler@lowercolumbia.edu

WHEELER, Nolan .... 360-442-2201.... 535 C
nwheeler@lowercolumbia.edu

WHEELER, Quentin, D .... 480-965-3391...... 12 B
quentin.wheeler@asu.edu

WHEELER, Richard .... 217-244-4545.... 167 B
rpw@illinois.edu

WHEELER, Susan .... 309-694-8855.... 152 B
swheeler@icc.edu

WHEELER, Susan, L .... 540-568-3727.... 520 C
wheel2sl@jmu.edu

WHEELER, Terry .... 561-803-2501.... 114 C
terry_wheeler@pba.edu

WHEELER, Thomas .... 816-604-5240.... 285 F
thomas.wheeler@mcckc.edu

WHEELER, Tim .... 425-739-8252.... 535 B
tim.wheeler@lwtc.edu

WHEELER-DUNNER,
Aundrea .... 251-405-7168...... 2 D
awheeler@bishop.edu

WHEELESS, Jim .... 912-443-5858.... 136 D
jwheeless@savannahtech.edu

WHEELESS, Kent .... 252-399-6338.... 362 A
kwheeles@barton.edu

WHEELIS, Tina .... 870-368-2008...... 23 A
twheelis@ozarka.edu

WHEELOCK, William .... 330-941-3165.... 406 F
wwheelock@ysu.edu

WHEELWRIGHT,
Steven, C .... 808-675-3700.... 139 I
wheelwrights@byuh.edu

WHEETLEY, John .... 209-473-5200...... 50 C

WHELAN, JR., Donald, J .. 817-257-7785.... 498 F
d.whelan@tcu.edu

WHELAN, Janet .... 410-837-4779.... 229 A
jwhelan@ubalt.edu

WHELAN, John .... 254-710-8562.... 481 I
John_Whelan@baylor.edu

WHELAN, Matthew .... 631-632-6857.... 352 C
matthew.whelan@stonybrook.edu

WHELAN, Michaele .... 781-736-2106.... 233 A
mwhelan@brandeis.edu

WHELAN, Robert .... 718-289-5162.... 326 F
robert.whelan@bcc.cuny.edu

WHELCHEL, Hugh .... 703-448-3393.... 277 B
hwehelchel@rts.edu

WHELCHEL, Hugh .... 703-222-7871.... 523 A
hwhelchel@rts.edu

WHELIHAN, Tom .... 218-846-3778.... 267 G
tom.whelihan@minnesota.edu

WHERRY, Cassandra, J ...... 641-269-3424.... 185 A
wherry@grinnell.edu

WHETTEN, Judd .... 808-675-3400.... 139 I
whettenj@byuh.edu

WHICKER, Paul, R .... 603-283-2391.... 303 F
pwhicker@antioch.edu

WHIDDEN, Frank .... 205-665-6512...... 9 C
fwhidden@montevallo.edu

WHIDDON, Tifini .... 936-633-4555.... 480 D
twhiddon@angelina.edu

WHIFFEN, Sarah, E .... 585-785-1263.... 334 A
whiffes@flcc.edu

WHIGHAM, Steve .... 715-324-6900.... 549 [illegible]
steve.whigham@ni.edu

WHIKEHART, John, R .... 812-330-6001.... 175 F
jwhikeha@ivytech.edu

WHILLOCK, David .... 817-257-5918.... 498 F
d.whillock@tcu.edu

WHIPPLE, P. Michael .... 504-861-5543.... 213 F
pmwhipple@loyno.edu

WHIPPY, Helen J, D .... 671-735-2994.... 559 D
hwhippy@uguam.uog.edu

WHISENAND, Gary, D .... 509-777-4313.... 539 F
gwhisenand@whitworth.edu

WHISENANT, Mary Alice ... 540-365-4235.... 518 J
mwhisenant@ferrum.edu

WHISENHUNT, Denise ...... 619-388-3498...... 65 F
dwhisenh@sdccd.edu

WHISENNAND, Jack .... 405-382-9950.... 412 B
j.whisennand@sscok.edu

WHISETON-COMER, Freda 708-534-4518.... 151 C
fcomer@govst.edu

WHISLER, Janice .... 219-785-5283.... 178 H
jwhisler@pnc.edu

WHISLER, Ruth .... 928-344-7505...... 12 C
ruth.whisler@azwestern.edu

WHISMAN, Linda, A .... 213-738-6729...... 71 D
library@swlaw.edu

WHISNANT, David, M .... 864-597-4294.... 463 F
whistnantdm@wofford.edu

WHISNANT, Rebecca, S .... 937-229-3421.... 404 A
Rebecca.Whisnant@notes.udayton.edu

WHITACKER, Keila .... 405-945-3252.... 410 F

WHITACRE, Aaron .... 540-868-7073.... 526 H
lwhitacre@lfcc.edu

WHITACRE, Caroline .... 614-292-1582.... 398 H
whitacre.3@osu.edu

WHITACRE, Norma .... 360-475-7360.... 535 J
nwhitacre@olympic.edu

WHITAKER, A. Dale .... 765-494-6970.... 178 F
dwhittake@purdue.edu

WHITAKER, Bret .... 740-366-9410.... 399 E
whitaker.77@osu.edu

WHITAKER, Cindy .... 505-254-7575...... 18 J
cwhitaker@theartcenter.edu

WHITAKER, Debbie .... 951-222-8434...... 64 B
debbie.whitaker@rcc.edu

WHITAKER, Deborah .... 276-466-7912.... 528 G
deborahwhitaker@vic.edu

WHITAKER, Evans, P .... 864-231-2100.... 455 C
ewhitaker@andersonuniversity.edu

WHITAKER, Gary .... 903-769-5751.... 488 M
gary_whitaker@jarvis.edu

WHITAKER, Gwen .... 336-734-7471.... 370 C
gwhitaker@forsythtech.edu

WHITAKER, Helene, M .... 610-861-5460.... 437 G
hwhitaker@northampton.edu

WHITAKER, James .... 727-726-1153.... 103 B
jameswhitaker@clearwater.edu

WHITAKER, Janice .... 972-825-4759.... 495 D
jwhitaker@sagu.edu

WHITAKER, Jason .... 859-233-8289.... 206 E
jwhitaker@transy.edu

WHITAKER, Lon .... 406-275-4969.... 296 F
lon_whitaker@skc.edu

WHITAKER, Lon .... 541-962-3773.... 418 C
lwhitake@eou.edu

WHITAKER, Michelle .... 910-672-1958.... 377 E
mwhitaker@uncfsu.edu

WHITAKER, Nashanta .... 336-315-7800...... 99 D

WHITAKER, Rob .... 706-802-5105.... 130 C
rwhitake@highlands.edu

WHITAKER, JR.,
Russell, E .... 804-862-6200.... 523 C
rwhitaker@rbc.edu

WHITAKER, Scott .... 505-428-1268.... 320 E
scott.whitaker@sfcc.edu

WHITAKER, Shari .... 315-655-7332.... 325 I
sswhitaker@cazenovia.edu

WHITAKER, Whit .... 706-236-2227.... 125 G
awhitaker@berry.edu

WHITAKER-HECK,
Rosalynne .... 757-727-5405.... 519 C
rosalynne.whitaker-heck@hamptonu.edu

WHITAKER-LEA, Laura .... 706-864-1900.... 134 D
lwhitaker-lea@northgeorgia.edu

WHITBY, Holly .... 615-248-1320.... 476 E
hwhitby@trevecca.edu

WHITCOMB, Connie, F .... 716-375-2351.... 348 C
cwhitcomb@sbu.edu

WHITCOMB, Michael, E ..... 860-685-5340...... 95 C
mwhitcomb@wesleyan.edu

WHITCUP, Cary .... 703-414-4032.... 518 B
cwhitcup@devry.edu

WHITE, A. Jay .... 812-941-2362.... 174 D
jwhite04@ius.edu

WHITE, Aaron .... 901-272-5136.... 471 B
finaid@mca.edu

WHITE, Adam, J .... 434-381-6113.... 524 E
ajwhite@sbc.edu

WHITE, Alan, R .... 252-328-6249.... 377 C
whiteal@ecu.edu

WHITE, Alison Boord .... 302-225-6343...... 96 E
whitea@gbc.edu

WHITE, Andrew .... 631-632-7100.... 352 C
andrew.white@stonybrook.edu

WHITE, Andrew, W 207-786-6491 217 C awhite@bates.edu
WHITE, Anne 253-964-6623 536 C awhite@pierce.ctc.edu
WHITE, Barbara, A 706-425-3136 138 C barbwhit@uga.edu
WHITE, Barbara, L 972-860-8348 484 H BWhite@dcccd.edu
WHITE, Barbara, W 512-471-1937 505 B bww@austin.utexas.edu
WHITE, Belva 404-727-2584 129 A belva.white@ctrl.emory.edu
WHITE, Betsy 810-989-2117 249 B betsy.white@baker.edu
WHITE, Beverly, E 906-635-2697 254 C bwhite@lssu.edu
WHITE, Bevley, D 251-460-6188 9 E bdwhite@usouthal.edu
WHITE, Bradley 615-963-5817 474 A bwhite2@tnstate.edu
WHITE, Brian 503-768-7307 416 F bdwhite@lclark.edu
WHITE, Brian 419-755-4227 399 C white.808@osu.edu
WHITE, Caleb 608-822-2446 555 B
WHITE, Carol 718-289-5151 326 F carol.white@bcc.cuny.edu
WHITE, Carol, C 919-866-5925 374 E ccwhite@waketech.edu
WHITE, Carolee 315-228-7488 329 H cwhite@colgate.edu
WHITE, Charles, B 210-999-7345 502 C cwhite@trinity.edu
WHITE, Charlie 276-223-4848 528 F wcwhitc@wcc.vccs.edu
WHITE, Chet 202-686-0876 99 A chet.white@potomac.edu
WHITE, Christina, C 770-534-6299 126 B cwhite@brenau.edu
WHITE, Courtney 864-646-1484 461 F cwhite12@tctc.edu
WHITE, Curtis 706-821-8239 135 C cwhite@paine.edu
WHITE, Curtis 419-289-5777 384 D cwhite@ashland.edu
WHITE, Cynthia, L 972-758-3871 483 D clwhite@collin.edu
WHITE, Daniel 907-474-6222 10 J dmwhite@alaska.edu
WHITE, David 252-328-1552 377 C whited@ecu.edu
WHITE, David 336-887-3000 365 J dwhite@laureluniversity.edu
WHITE, David 334-448-5112 8 B whited@troy.edu
WHITE, David 304-424-8225 545 B dave.white@mail.wvu.edu
WHITE, David 570-484-2136 443 A dwhite@lhup.edu
WHITE, David, B 828-254-1921 367 H dwhite@abtech.edu
WHITE, Dawn, H 937-327-7800 406 B dwhite@wittenberg.edu
WHITE, Deborah 330-972-8259 403 B dwhite1@uakron.edu
WHITE, Deborah 810-762-3200 259 F debwhite@umflint.edu
WHITE, Dewayne 212-678-3315 357 F white@exchange.tc.columbia.edu
WHITE, Diane 703-284-1610 521 A diane.white@marymount.edu
WHITE, Donald, T 540-464-7251 529 A whitedt@vmi.edu
WHITE, Donna 304-829-7622 540 E dwhite@bethanywv.edu
WHITE, Douglas 856-691-8600 309 C dwhite@cccnj.edu
WHITE, Eddie 615-248-1242 476 E ewhite@trevecca.edu
WHITE, Edna, M 972-860-8152 484 G ewhite@dcccd.edu
WHITE, Eileen 510-464-3213 62 C ewhite@peralta.edu
WHITE, Elaine, T 718-862-7246 339 H elaine.white@manhattan.edu
WHITE, Elizabeth, J 773-371-5415 146 B ewhite@ctu.edu
WHITE, Ernie 919-735-5151 374 F ewhite@waynecc.edu
WHITE, Evelyn, M 256-761-6216 7 H ewhite@talladega.edu
WHITE, Fred 817-212-4100 502 A fwhite@law.txwes.edu
WHITE, Gary 215-953-5999 99 D gary.white@strayer.edu
WHITE, Gary 615-226-3990 471 I gwhite@nadcedu.com
WHITE, Gary 615-322-2457 477 F religiouslife@vanderbilt.edu
WHITE, Gary, R 805-893-2182 74 F gary.white@sa.ucsb.edu
WHITE, Georgia 520-494-6602 13 F georgia.white1@centralaz.edu
WHITE, Gwen 907-450-8191 10 H gwen.white@alaska.edu
WHITE, Hayne 704-272-5343 373 F hwhite@spcc.edu
WHITE, J, H 334-387-3877 1 D johnwhite@amridgeuniversity.edu
WHITE, Jackie 478-757-3400 126 G jwhite@centralgatech.edu
WHITE, Jacqueline, M 401-865-2811 453 F jwhite@providence.edu
WHITE, James 509-313-4049 534 A whitej@gonzaga.edu
WHITE, James 419-448-3272 402 E jjwhite@tiffin.edu
WHITE, II, James, C 724-503-1001 451 A jwhite@washjeff.edu
WHITE, James, M 410-651-8440 227 E jmwhite@umes.edu
WHITE, Janet, C 608-757-7705 553 E jwhite@blackhawk.edu
WHITE, Jennifer 909-777-3300 46 H
WHITE, Jerre 714-556-3610 76 E jwhite@vanguard.edu
WHITE, Jerry, L 517-750-1200 258 F jwhite@arbor.edu
WHITE, Jessie 254-659-7841 487 E jwhite@hillcollege.edu
WHITE, Jim 231-995-1193 256 G jwhite@nmc.edu
WHITE, Joan 928-226-4217 13 H joan.white@coconino.edu
WHITE, Joel 541-917-4840 416 H whitej@linnbenton.edu
WHITE, John 503-352-7355 419 E whiteja@pacificu.edu
WHITE, John 404-687-4522 127 C whitej@ctsnet.edu
WHITE, John 239-513-1122 110 K jwhite@hodges.edu
WHITE, John, A 413-748-3408 245 C jawhite@spfldcol.edu
WHITE, John, V 702-895-1876 302 K john.white@unlv.edu
WHITE, John, W 434-947-8100 522 E jwwhite@randolphcollege.edu
WHITE, Jonathan 718-409-7220 356 C jwhite@sunymaritime.edu
WHITE, Joshua 617-262-5000 232 B Joshua.White@the-bac.edu
WHITE, Judi 479-394-7622 23 E jwhite@rmcc.edu
WHITE, Judi 918-647-1474 407 E jpwhite@carlalbert.edu
WHITE, Julie 773-481-8920 147 F jwhite@ccc.edu
WHITE, Julie, R 315-464-4816 352 E whitejul@upstate.edu
WHITE, Karen 207-453-5117 218 I kwhite@kvcc.me.edu
WHITE, Karen, K 727-341-4656 116 F white.karenkaufman@spcollege.edu
WHITE, Karen, L 574-520-4477 174 C kwhite@iusb.edu
WHITE, Kelly, L 361-698-1641 485 F kwhite@delmar.edu
WHITE, Kevin 919-684-2431 363 I kwhite@duaa.duke.edu
WHITE, Kristie, L 804-342-5219 529 D klwhite@vuu.edu
WHITE, Kyle 918-335-6289 411 B kwhite@okwu.edu
WHITE, Ladylease 973-877-3494 310 A white@essex.edu
WHITE, Laura, M 863-784-7154 117 I laura.white@southflorida.edu
WHITE, Laurie 617-759-1700 243 F lawhite@aii.edu
WHITE, Laurie 757-822-1085 528 C lwhite@tcc.edu
WHITE, Lawrence 302-831-7361 96 F lawwhite@udel.edu
WHITE, Linda 901-435-1601 470 B linda_white@loc.edu
WHITE, Lisa 417-626-1234 287 F white.lisa@occ.edu
WHITE, Lisa, C 319-895-4361 183 D lwhite@cornellcollege.edu
WHITE, Lori, S 214-768-2821 494 F lswhite@smu.edu
WHITE, Lucinda 859-246-6335 201 D lucinda.white@kctcs.edu
WHITE, Lynn 812-888-4241 181 B lwhite@vinu.edu
WHITE, M. Chrisopher 252-398-6221 363 E whitec@chowan.edu
WHITE, Margie 573-592-1194 293 E margie.white@williamwoods.edu
WHITE, Mark 402-552-6067 297 D whitemark@clarksoncollege.edu
WHITE, Marsha, S 770-720-5512 135 F msw@reinhardt.edu
WHITE, Marshall Sonny 803-738-7600 459 D whites@midlandstech.edu
WHITE, Mary 570-484-2253 443 A mwhite4@lhup.edu
WHITE, Mary Jean 334-745-6437 7 E mjwhite@suscc.edu
WHITE, Mary Jo 303-492-8908 88 B joey.white@colorado.edu
WHITE, Mary Jo 206-934-5378 537 B maryjo.white@seattlecolleges.edu
WHITE, Maureen 860-701-5047 93 B white_m@mitchell.edu
WHITE, Michael 415-896-2123 19 C michael.white@apollogrp.edu
WHITE, Michael 229-317-6726 128 A michael.white@darton.edu
WHITE, Michael 559-638-3641 72 B michael.white@reedleycollege.edu
WHITE, Michael, L 319-399-8643 183 C mwhite@coe.edu
WHITE, Michele, M 540-568-6281 520 C whitemm@jmu.edu
WHITE, Michelle 515-244-4221 181 D whitem@aib.edu
WHITE, Michelle 918-647-1399 407 E mwhite@carlalbert.edu
WHITE, Monica, J 716-673-3271 352 A monica.white@fredonia.edu
WHITE, Norman 863-638-7264 123 B norman.white@warner.edu
WHITE, O. Ivan 903-927-3384 509 A oiwhite@wileyc.edu
WHITE, Olivia, G 301-696-3573 223 C owhite@hood.edu
WHITE, P. Phillip 518-629-7149 336 C p.white@hvcc.edu
WHITE, Pamela 413-755-4452 241 E pjwhite@stcc.edu
WHITE, Pamela 515-294-7800 182 B pjwhite@iastate.edu
WHITE, Patricia 305-284-2394 122 F pwhite@miami.edu
WHITE, Patrick, E 765-361-6221 181 C whitep@wabash.edu
WHITE, Perry, D 316-284-5241 190 H pwhite@bethelks.edu
WHITE, Peter 619-388-3464 65 F pwhite@sdccd.edu
WHITE, R. Barry 315-792-3011 359 C rwhite@utica.edu
WHITE, Randy 260-665-4171 180 A whiter@trine.edu
WHITE, Randy 407-774-6200 541 D rwhite@mountainstate.edu
WHITE, Ray 360-383-3350 539 D rwhite@whatcom.ctc.edu
WHITE, Ray 334-241-9538 8 B grwhite@troy.edu
WHITE, Rebecca 229-209-5145 124 C rebeccawhite@andrewcollege.edu
WHITE, Rebecca, H 706-542-7140 138 C rhwhite@uga.edu
WHITE, Rex 713-221-8505 503 D whiter@uhd.edu
WHITE, Rhonda 336-517-2183 362 C rjwhite@bennett.edu
WHITE, Richard, L 732-932-7353 314 B riwhite@rci.rutgers.edu
WHITE, Richard E, T 206-726-5127 532 G retwhite@cornish.edu
WHITE, Robert 561-803-2528 114 C bob_white@pba.edu
WHITE, Robert 870-574-4463 24 A rwhite@sautech.edu
WHITE, Robert, L 937-327-7411 406 B rwhite@wittenberg.edu
WHITE, Robert, W 931-598-1210 472 J police@sewanee.edu
WHITE, Ronald, G 803-786-3091 457 C rwhite@columbiasc.edu
WHITE, Ronald, J 605-394-2493 466 A ronald.white@sdsmt.edu
WHITE, Roslyn 248-457-2734 252 G
WHITE, Sabrina 706-771-4037 125 D swhite@augustatech.edu
WHITE, Samantha 573-875-7352 280 E sjwhite@ccis.edu
WHITE, Samuel, L 601-877-6142 273 C slwhite@alcorn.edu
WHITE, Samuel, L 601-877-6388 273 C slwhite@alcorn.edu
WHITE, Sharon 203-251-8406 94 E sharon.white@uconn.edu
WHITE, Shawn, A 304-788-6879 545 A sawhite@mail.wvu.edu
WHITE, Shelley 828-254-1921 367 H swhite@abtech.edu
WHITE, Stephanie, M 804-257-5745 529 D swhite@vuu.edu
WHITE, Stephen 718-862-7548 339 H stephen.white@manhattan.edu
WHITE, Stephen 615-898-5454 473 F swhite@mtsu.edu
WHITE, Stephen, E 401-254-3681 454 C swhite@rwu.edu
WHITE, Steven 316-978-3782 197 F steven.white@wichita.edu
WHITE, Susan, E 912-583-3169 126 C swhite@bpc.edu
WHITE, Susan, K 913-627-4125 193 J swhite@kckcc.edu
WHITE, Tamisia 212-870-1226 344 A finaid@nyts.edu
WHITE, Tammy, S 205-652-3651 10 A thw@uwa.edu
WHITE, Terry, A 615-460-6617 467 B terry.white@belmont.edu
WHITE, Thelma 270-706-8814 201 F thelma.white@kctcs.edu
WHITE, Thomas 207-602-2939 220 H twhite5@une.edu
WHITE, Thomas 817-923-1921 495 E twhite@swbts.edu
WHITE, Timothy, L 352-846-0850 120 B tlwhite@ufl.edu
WHITE, Timothy, P 951-827-5201 74 C tim.white@ucr.edu
WHITE, Todd, D 319-895-4167 183 D twhite@cornellcollege.edu
WHITE, Tonya 863-638-2936 123 C whitet@webber.edu
WHITE, W. Scott 704-406-4259 364 B swhite@gardner-webb.edu
WHITE, Wayman 252-335-0821 369 D waywhite@albemarle.edu
WHITE, Wendy, S 215-746-5200 448 I generalcounsel@ogc.upenn.edu
WHITE, William 304-253-7351 541 D wwhite@mountainstate.edu
WHITE, William, H 508-929-8811 239 D wwhite@worcester.edu
WHITE, Woodie 504-286-5117 214 I wwhite@suno.edu
WHITE CASTENADA, April 626-395-8167 32 E april@caltech.edu
WHITED, David 847-317-4194 166 B dwhited@tiu.edu
WHITED, Frances, P 330-287-1216 399 A whited.16@osu.edu
WHITEFORD, Aaron 503-768-7944 416 F ahw@lclark.edu
WHITEHAIR, Bruce 814-332-2451 421 E bwhitehair@allegheny.edu
WHITEHEAD, Carolyn 303-492-5366 88 B carolyn.whitehead@cufund.org
WHITEHEAD, Charles, L 618-931-0600 165 B chuck.whitehead@swic.edu
WHITEHEAD, Doug 435-652-7500 512 A whitehead@dixie.edu
WHITEHEAD, Jayne, E 513-529-4029 396 D whitehje@muohio.edu
WHITEHEAD, Jeff 740-654-6711 400 B whitehej@ohio.edu
WHITEHEAD, Joe 601-266-4884 278 A joe.whitehead@usm.edu
WHITEHEAD, Johnny, C 413-545-2125 237 C jcw@admin.umass.edu
WHITEHEAD, Joyce, E 630-889-6610 159 E jwhitehead@nuhs.edu
WHITEHEAD, Pam 606-589-3155 203 A pamela.whitehead@kctcs.edu
WHITEHEAD, Richard 540-261-4347 524 C richard.whitehead@svu.edu
WHITEHEAD, Ronald, H 269-471-8380 247 H pastorron@andrews.edu
WHITEHEAD, Sharon, F 606-679-8501 202 F sharon.whitehead@kctcs.edu
WHITEHEAD, Teresa 575-769-4066 317 K teresa.whitehead@clovis.edu
WHITEHORN, Michael, A 325-670-1250 487 D mwhite@hsutx.edu
WHITEHOUSE, Eric 239-477-2100 115 E Eric.Whitehouse@rasmussen.edu
WHITELEY, Herbert, E 217-333-2760 167 B hwhiteley@illinois.edu
WHITELEY, Janell 360-475-7504 535 J jwhiteley@olympic.edu
WHITELY, Geoffrey, G 516-918-2787 360 A gwhitely@webb-institute.edu
WHITELY, Patricia, A 305-284-4922 122 F pwhitely@miami.edu
WHITEMAN, Betty 386-822-8869 121 E bwhiteman@stetson.edu
WHITEMAN, Lee 412-536-1169 432 F leona.whiteman@laroche.edu
WHITEMAN, Ray 574-807-7139 169 F ray.whiteman@bethelcollege.edu
WHITEMORE, Alan, T 617-989-4307 246 C whitemorea@wit.edu
WHITENECK, Peter 715-634-4790 547 G pwhiteneck@lco-college.edu
WHITENER, Susan 907-455-2824 10 J mswhitener@alaska.edu
WHITESIDE, Harold 615-898-2900 473 F harold.whiteside@mtsu.edu
WHITESIDE, Niki 281-998-6150 493 D niki.whiteside@sjcd.edu
WHITEY, Jeff 541-888-7634 420 C jwhitey@socc.edu

Name	Phone	Code	Email
WHITFIELD, Gary	209-588-5112	80 A	whitfieldg@yosemite.edu
WHITFIELD, Walter, V	252-789-0232	371 E	wwhitfield@martincc.edu
WHITFILL, Jill	731-352-4083	467 C	whitfillj@bethelu.edu
WHITFORD, Betty Lou	334-844-4448	1 G	blw0017@auburn.edu
WHITFORD, Jewel, L	406-395-4313	296 G	jewelwhitford@hotmail.com
WHITHAM, Bruce	856-256-4981	314 A	whitham@rowan.edu
WHITHAUS, Becky	573-897-5000	284 D	
WHITING, Ernestine	410-843-8506	272 F	ernestine.whiting@laureate.net
WHITING, Mary	870-460-1026	25 A	whitingm@uamont.edu
WHITING, Melinda	215-893-5275	426 E	melinda.whiting@curtis.edu
WHITING, Raymond, A	706-729-2040	125 C	rwhiting@aug.edu
WHITING, Sarah, M	713-348-4044	492 J	sarah.whiting@rice.edu
WHITING, Scott	334-874-5700	3 A	swhiting@concordiaselma.edu
WHITING, Shari, K	315-859-4313	335 A	swhiting@hamilton.edu
WHITING, Svea	970-943-7057	89 B	swhiting@western.edu
WHITING, Todd	704-366-4853	375 H	twhiting@rts.edu
WHITIS, Andrew	419-783-2490	389 G	awhitis@defiance.edu
WHITIS, Matt	815-939-5350	160 F	mwhitis@olivet.edu
WHITIS, Sarah	530-842-1245	42 C	swhitis@siskiyous.edu
WHITLATCH, Frank	707-826-5101	36 D	frank@humboldt.edu
WHITLATCH, Michael, D	712-749-2172	182 G	whitlatch@bvu.edu
WHITLEDGE, Terry	907-474-7229	10 J	terry@ims.uaf.edu
WHITLEY, Darrell, S	252-985-5105	375 C	dwhitley@ncwc.edu
WHITLEY, Kay, E	432-837-8226	501 B	kwhitley@sulross.edu
WHITLEY, Peggy	281-312-1493	490 C	peggy.whitley@lonestar.edu
WHITLING, Jacqueline	570-484-3045	443 A	jwhitlin@lhup.edu
WHITLOCK, Bill	864-646-1583	461 F	wwhitloc@tctc.edu
WHITLOCK, David, W	405-878-2002	409 D	david.whitlock@okbu.edu
WHITLOCK, Doug	859-622-2977	200 D	doug.whitlock@eku.edu
WHITLOCK, Mary	661-836-6300	52 D	mwhitlock@kaplan.edu
WHITLOCK, Pamela, B	910-962-3167	379 C	whitlock@uncw.edu
WHITLOCK, Roger	601-635-2111	274 C	rwhitlock@eccc.edu
WHITLOCK, Sharon, K	765-494-9708	178 F	whitlock@purdue.edu
WHITLOCK, Stephen	678-839-6426	138 D	swhitlock@westga.edu
WHITLOCK, Tonya	674-423-2000	139 B	tonya.whitlock@westgatech.edu
WHITLOCK, Veronica	212-472-1500	343 G	vwhitlock@nysid.edu
WHITMAN, Carl, E	209-667-3343	36 C	cwhitman@csustan.edu
WHITMAN, Chris	734-764-0747	259 D	cwhitman@umich.edu
WHITMAN, David	651-604-4118	265 D	
WHITMAN, Deirdre	914-674-7316	340 G	dwhitman@mercy.edu
WHITMAN, John	510-885-3674	34 C	john.whitman@csueastbay.edu
WHITMAN, Joshua	608-785-8616	551 B	whitman.josh@uwlax.edu
WHITMAN, Rebecca, R	616-234-4010	251 G	rwhitman@grcc.edu
WHITMAN, William, D	989-386-6696	255 F	wwhitman@midmich.edu
WHITMER, Ann	517-629-0440	247 E	awhitmer@albion.edu
WHITMER, Daniel, J	812-888-4204	181 B	dwhitmer@vinu.edu
WHITMIRE, Teresa	479-619-4175	22 H	twhitmire@nwacc.edu
WHITMORE, Joe	256-782-5777	4 L	whitmore@jsu.edu
WHITMORE, Karen	973-328-5671	309 B	kwhitmore@ccm.edu
WHITMORE, Kimberly, N	515-574-1138	185 F	whitmore@iowacentral.edu
WHITMORE, Michele	802-635-1452	515 E	michele.whitmore@jsc.edu
WHITMORE-HANSEN, Anne	518-564-2090	354 B	anne.hansen@plattsburgh.edu
WHITNABLE, Michael, D	740-374-8716	405 F	mwhitnable@wscc.edu
WHITNEY, Candice	408-848-4754	48 B	cwhitney@gavilan.edu
WHITNEY, Cynthia	732-987-2244	310 D	whitneyc@georgian.edu
WHITNEY, Gleaves	616-331-3298	252 A	whitneyg@gvsu.edu
WHITNEY, Glenda	573-897-5000	284 D	
WHITNEY, Heidi	802-468-6072	515 C	heidi.whitney@castleton.edu
WHITNEY, Jarrid	626-395-6341	32 E	
WHITNEY, Joan, G	610-519-4050	450 G	joan.whitney@villanova.edu
WHITNEY, Karen, M	814-393-2220	442 A	president@clarion.edu
WHITNEY, Marian, D	315-684-6066	354 F	whitnemd@morisville.edu
WHITNEY, Patricia, C	207-859-5002	217 G	pcwhitne@colby.edu
WHITNEY, Patrick, F	312-595-4900	153 B	whitney@id.iit.edu
WHITNEY, Paul	401-874-5224	454 E	pwhitney@uri.edu
WHITNEY, Phyllis	319-385-6206	186 A	phyllis.whitney@iwc.edu
WHITNEY, Richard	805-962-8179	28 L	rwhitney@antioch.edu
WHITNEY, Richard, A	907-786-4754	10 I	rich.whitney@uaa.alaska.edu
WHITSON, Brian	757-221-7876	517 J	bwwhit@wm.edu
WHITSON, Caroline, B	803-786-3178	457 C	cwhitson@columbiasc.edu
WHITSON, Robert, E	405-744-2474	410 C	bob.whitson@okstate.edu
WHITSON, Tony	901-435-1733	470 B	tony_whitson@loc.edu
WHITT, Alton	205-934-0850	8 G	awhitt@uab.edu
WHITT, Cynthia, L	423-869-6394	470 C	cindy.whitt@lmunet.edu
WHITT, David, T	205-726-2386	6 G	dtwhitt@samford.edu
WHITT, Edith, L	828-689-1151	366 F	ewhitt@mhc.edu
WHITT, Marc	859-622-2301	200 D	marc.whitt@eku.edu
WHITT, Paul	715-324-6900	549 D	paul.whitt@ni.edu
WHITTAKER, Debra, B	727-816-3405	114 F	whittad@phcc.edu
WHITTAKER, Denise	619-482-6301	71 C	dwhittaker@swccd.edu
WHITTAKER, Mark	904-819-6290	107 A	mark@flagler.edu
WHITTAKER, Robert, E	802-626-6427	515 F	robert.whittaker@lyndonstate.edu
WHITTAKER-DAVIS, Sharon	205-366-8838	7 G	swhittaker@stillman.edu
WHITTELSEY, Lucia, W	207-859-4832	217 G	lwwhitte@colby.edu
WHITTEMORE, Nancy	661-255-1050	32 C	nwhittem@calarts.edu
WHITTEN, Deborah	864-656-8128	456 E	dbw@clemson.edu
WHITTEN, Pamela	517-355-3410	255 D	pwhitten@msu.edu
WHITTEN, Patrice	850-484-1561	114 G	pwhitten@pensacolastate.edu
WHITTENBURG, Scott, L	504-280-6321	213 E	swhitten@uno.edu
WHITTEY, Chris	216-421-7455	387 H	cwhittey@cia.edu
WHITTEY, Christopher	207-775-3052	218 E	cwhittey@meca.edu
WHITTINGHAM, Michelle	831-459-1453	75 A	michelle@ucsc.edu
WHITTINGHAM, Rachel	501-329-6872	21 C	
WHITTINGTON, Christine, A	336-272-7102	364 D	cwhittington@greensborocollege.edu
WHITTINGTON, Connie	318-869-5101	208 F	cwhitt@centenary.edu
WHITTINGTON, Donna	225-675-8270	211 J	dwhittington@rpcc.edu
WHITTINGTON, Gerald, O	336-278-5434	364 A	whitting@elon.edu
WHITTINGTON, Jennifer	304-776-6290	540 G	jbennett@cci.edu
WHITTINGTON, Lee	828-765-7351	371 F	lwhittington@mayland.edu
WHITTINGTON, Ray	312-362-6781	148 F	rwhittin@depaul.edu
WHITTLER, Kim	410-752-4710	221 E	kwhittler@bic.edu
WHITTLESEY, Valerie, D	770-423-6023	132 H	vwhittle@kennesaw.edu
WHITTON, Mary Lou	913-768-1900	191 A	mwhitton@brownmackie.edu
WHITTUM, Terry, E	904-256-7099	111 J	twhittu@ju.edu
WHITTY, Jennifer	707-654-1720	32 I	jwhitty@csum.edu
WHITWELL, Jeff	615-898-2700	473 F	jwhitwel@mtsu.edu
WHITWORTH, Bruce	559-278-2795	34 D	bwhitwor@csufresno.edu
WHITWORTH, Ling, Y	434-395-2319	520 G	whitworthly@longwood.edu
WHORLEY, Frank	410-951-2600	228 B	fwhorley@coppin.edu
WHTE, Alisa	940-397-4226	491 A	alisa.white@mwsu.edu
WHYNOTT, Anne	262-564-2758	553 H	whynotta@gtc.edu
WHYTE, Cassandra	304-766-3249	544 D	whytec@wvstateu.edu
WHYTE, Novia, P	516-463-6928	335 H	novia.p.whyte@hofstra.edu
WHYTE, William	262-564-3228	553 H	whytew@gtc.edu
WIAFE, Ronald	216-373-5274	397 E	rwiafe@ndc.edu
WIATER, Patrick	518-255-5423	354 E	wiaterpa@cobleskill.edu
WIBBELL, Lee	217-641-4314	154 G	lwibbel@jwcc.edu
WIBBENMEYER, Kana	773-508-3489	157 A	kwibben@luc.edu
WICHERN, Adam	718-405-3776	330 A	adam.wichern@mountsaintvincent.edu
WICHERT, Jerome, L	580-774-3786	412 F	jerome.wichert@swosu.edu
WICHMAN, Beth	210-458-4142	506 B	beth.wichman@utsa.edu
WICHROSKI, Pamela, J	207-786-6207	217 C	pwichros@bates.edu
WICHRYK, Adam, T	215-489-2220	426 H	Adam.Wichryk@delval.edu
WICK, Michael, R	715-836-2033	550 H	wickmr@uwec.edu
WICKEHAM, Daniel	414-955-8826	548 E	dwickeha@mcw.edu
WICKER, Wesley, K	770-423-6976	132 H	wwicker@kennesaw.edu
WICKER-MCCREE, Ingrid	919-530-7057	378 A	iwicker@nccu.edu
WICKERT, Jonathan, A	515-294-5933	182 B	wickert@iastate.edu
WICKES, David	503-251-2810	420 H	dwickes@uws.edu
WICKIZER, Della, H	434-395-2074	520 G	wickizerdh@longwood.edu
WICKLESS, Megan	402-552-6119	297 D	wicklessmegan@clarksoncollege.edu
WICKLIFFE, Cari, S	314-977-2350	289 F	wicklics@slu.edu
WICKLUND, Greg, A	817-202-6743	495 C	wicklund@swau.edu
WICKLUND, Joe	218-723-6479	262 I	jwicklun@css.edu
WICKMAN, Larry	575-461-4413	318 F	larryw@mesalands.edu
WICKS, Michelle, D	304-204-4093	542 F	mwicks@kvctc.edu
WICKS, Natalie	313-993-1000	259 C	wicksnk@udmercy.edu
WIDDERS, Pat	479-788-7390	24 D	pwidders@uafortsmith.edu
WIDDIG, Bernd	617-552-3827	232 D	bernd.widdig.1@bc.edu
WIDENHOFER, Stephen, B	217-424-6300	158 F	swidenhofer@millikin.edu
WIDGER, Deborah	575-646-4034	319 D	dwidger@nmsu.edu
WIDGER, Mari Jo	308-535-3773	298 I	widgerm@mpcc.edu
WIDMER, Robert, D	309-268-8100	151 G	rob.widmer@heartland.edu
WIDMER, Roger, H	312-669-5141	150 E	rwidmer@ellis.edu
WIDNER, Bobby	229-430-2837	123 I	bwidner@albanytech.edu
WIDNER, Zachary	540-985-9701	520 D	rrwidner@jchs.edu
WIDNEY, Kaye, C	304-293-2831	544 E	kaye.widney@mail.wvu.edu
WIEBE, Harold, D	740-368-3656	400 F	hdwiebe@owu.edu
WIEBE, Henry, A	573-341-4579	292 A	wiebe@mst.edu
WIECHMANN, Lauri	309-341-5461	146 A	lwiechmann@sandburg.edu
WIECHOWSKI, Linda	248-689-8282	260 A	lwiechow@walshcollege.edu
WIECKOWSKI, Ellen, G	412-397-6901	445 G	wieckowski@rmu.edu
WIED, Christine	979-830-4224	482 A	cwied@blinn.edu
WIEDA, Karen, S	636-584-6551	281 I	wiedaks@eastcentral.edu
WIEDEN, Ted	925-685-1230	43 C	twieden@dvc.edu
WIEDOWER, Judith	913-758-6314	197 B	wiedowerj@stmary.edu
WIEDOWER, CSC, Veronique	574-284-4886	179 D	vwiedowe@saintmarys.edu
WIEGAND, Stephanie	425-640-1423	533 E	stephanie.wiegand@edcc.edu
WIEGANDT, Scott, P	502-272-8496	198 E	swiegandt@bellarmine.edu
WIEGEL, Lisa	563-288-6003	184 D	lwiegel@eicc.edu
WIEGENSTEIN, Steve, C	573-875-8700	280 E	scwiegenstein@ccis.edu
WIEGERS, Lynn	818-677-2325	35 D	lynn.wiegers@csun.edu
WIEGERT, Tim	517-750-1200	258 F	twiegert@arbor.edu
WIEGMANN, Dawn, R	319-352-8437	189 F	dawn.wiegmann@wartburg.edu
WIEHE, Wallace	678-891-3016	130 G	Wallace.Wiehe@gpc.edu
WIELAND, John	502-213-3653	202 B	john.wieland@kctcs.edu
WIELECHOWSKI, Robert, A	734-462-4400	258 C	rwielech@schoolcraft.edu
WIELENGA, Jay	712-707-7111	188 B	jayw@nwciowa.edu
WIELHORSKI, Karen	281-283-3930	503 C	wielhorski@uhcl.edu
WIELINSKI, Peter	218-631-7810	267 G	peter.wielinski@minnesota.edu
WIELK, Lawrence, J	203-371-7916	93 G	wielkl@sacredheart.edu
WIEMERS, Eugene, L	207-786-6261	217 C	ewiemers@bates.edu
WIEMEYER, Steve, R	402-449-2820	298 B	swiemeyer@graceu.edu
WIENCEK, John, M	813-974-3780	120 D	jwiencek@eng.usf.edu
WIENER, Evelyn	215-662-2869	448 I	wiener@pobox.upenn.edu
WIENER, Howard	516-773-5754	558 F	wienerh@usmma.edu
WIENER, Madeleine	858-635-4428	27 E	mwiener@alliant.edu
WIENER, Stuart, A	702-968-2008	303 D	swiener@roseman.edu
WIENER, William, R	336-334-5375	379 A	wrwiener@uncg.edu
WIENS, Ann	312-499-4214	164 A	awiens@saic.edu
WIENS, Chris	620-242-0436	194 H	wiensc@mcpherson.edu
WIER, Karry	219-877-3100	170 A	kwier@brownmackie.edu
WIERDA, Bruce	231-777-0657	256 D	bruce.wierda@muskegoncc.edu
WIERGACZ, Nora	219-464-5335	181 A	nora.wiergacz@valpo.edu
WIERS, Alison	336-334-4822	370 E	ajwiers@gtcc.edu
WIERTEL, Anthony	716-926-8818	335 F	twiertel@hilbert.edu
WIERZBICKI, Andrzej	251-460-6280	9 E	awierzbi@jaguar1.usouthal.edu
WIESCHOWSKI, Marilyn	269-467-9945	251 D	mwieschowski@glenoaks.edu
WIESE, Barry	281-487-1170	498 E	bwiese@txchiro.edu
WIESE, Karen	641-269-4939	185 A	wiese@grinnell.edu
WIESE, Vicki	605-995-3023	464 E	vicki.wiese@mitchelltech.edu
WIESE, Warren, K	218-477-2171	268 A	wiese@mnstate.edu
WIESEHAN, Terry	765-973-8221	173 D	twieseha@iue.edu
WIESEMANN, Lois	801-957-4255	512 C	lois.wiesemann@slcc.edu
WIESEN, Elizabeth	207-893-6630	219 F	lwiesen@sjcme.edu
WIESENBURG, Denis	601-266-5116	278 A	denis.wiesenburg@usm.edu
WIESENTHAL, Steve	773-834-3529	166 D	swiesenthal@uchicago.edu
WIESNER, Bob	803-641-3522	462 B	bobw@usca.edu
WIESNER, Don	316-942-4291	195 C	wiesnerd@newmanu.edu
WIETZ, Ophelia	305-220-4120	115 D	libdir@ptcmatt.com
WIEWEL, Wim	503-725-4419	418 G	president@pdx.edu
WIEZBICKI-STEVENS, Kathy	413-565-1000	231 B	kwiezbic@baypath.edu
WIG, Jeff	218-894-5172	266 C	jwig@clcmn.edu
WIGAND, Debra	920-686-6121	550 E	Debra.Wigand@sl.edu
WIGENT, Rodney	215-596-7545	450 A	r.wigent@usciences.edu
WIGFALL, Arthur	212-463-0400	357 J	arthur.wigfall@touro.edu
WIGGAM, Marilyn	614-257-5034	390 B	mwiggam@devry.edu

WILKINS, Wendy, K .... 575-646-1727.... 319 D
provost@nmsu.edu
WILKINSON, Cathryn .... 630-942-2425.... 147 G
wilkin@cod.edu
WILKINSON, Christine, K .. 480-965-7782...... 12 B
c.wilkinson@asu.edu
WILKINSON, J. Brian .... 205-853-1200......... 5 C
jwilkinson@jeffstateonline.com
WILKINSON, James .... 662-254-3554.... 276 C
jgwilkinson@mvsu.edu
WILKINSON, Jay .... 515-961-1288.... 188 F
jay.wilkinson@simpson.edu
WILKINSON, Julie .... 941-782-5678.... 433 C
jwilkinson@lecom.edu
WILKINSON, Karen .... 304-776-6290.... 540 G
kwilkinson@cci.edu
WILKINSON, Kevin .... 305-949-9500.... 105 F
kwilkinson@cci.edu
WILKINSON, Lonnie .... 225-771-3015.... 214 H
lonnie_wilkinson@subr.edu
WILKINSON, Michelle .... 206-268-4114.... 530 F
mwilkinson@antioch.edu
WILKINSON, Missy, A ...... 309-649-6329.... 165 D
missy.wilkinson@src.edu
WILKINSON, Patrick, J ...... 920-424-2147.... 551 D
wilkinso@uwosh.edum
WILKINSON, Richard, S .... 512-448-8441.... 493 B
richw@stedwards.edu
WILKINSON, Robert, B ...... 620-235-4132.... 195 I
wilkinsn@pittstate.edu
WILKINSON, Shirley, S ..... 205-329-7915........ 3 B
shirley.wilkinson@ecacolleges.com
WILKINSON, Tim .... 406-657-2326.... 295 F
timothy.wilkinson@msubillings.edu
WILKINSON, W. David ...... 601-974-1172.... 275 D
wilkiwd@millsaps.edu
WILKINSON, William, J .... 215-204-4775.... 447 G
william.wilkinson@temple.edu
WILKISON, Debra .... 972-881-5761.... 483 D
dwilkison@collin.edu
WILKOSKI, Donna, M .... 215-698-8203.... 423 E
wilkoski@bucks.edu
WILKS, Barbara .... 704-378-1042.... 365 H
bwilks@jcsu.edu
WILKS, David .... 302-736-2508...... 96 G
WILKS, Preston .... 509-793-2194.... 531 D
prestonw@bigbend.edu
WILKS, Ronald, W .... 317-788-3517.... 180 C
wilks@uindy.edu
WILL, Kris .... 303-986-2320...... 82 E
kris@csha.net
WILL, Matthew, W .... 317-788-3370.... 180 C
mwill@uindy.edu
WILLAMON, Nancy, R .... 217-351-2533.... 161 B
nwillamon@parkland.edu
WILLAMS, Mike .... 501-279-4312...... 21 H
mwilliams@harding.edu
WILLAN, William .... 740-533-4600.... 400 C
willanw@ohio.edu
WILLAN, William .... 740-533-4610.... 399 G
willanw@ohio.edu
WILLARD, Joseph .... 215-991-3586.... 432 G
willard@lasalle.edu
WILLARD, Judith, A .... 716-286-8418.... 344 D
jaw@niagara.edu
WILLARD, Paul .... 205-970-9206........ 7 D
pwillard@sebc.edu
WILLARD, Timothy, J .... 314-286-4871.... 288 B
tjwillard@ranken.edu
WILLBORG, Erik .... 406-657-1110.... 296 E
erik.willborg@rocky.edu
WILLCOX, Jan, M .... 540-231-4000.... 518 H
WILLCOX, Wayne .... 912-344-2689.... 124 E
wayne.willcox@armstrong.edu
WILLEKENS, Rene, G .... 623-935-8069...... 15 H
rene.willekens@estrellamountain.edu
WILLEMSEN, David, W ...... 417-268-1000.... 279 B
dwillemsen@agts.edu
WILLENBORG, Andy, B ..... 563-589-0217.... 189 G
awillenborg@wartburgseminary.edu
WILLENS, Babette .... 805-962-8179...... 28 L
bwillens@antioch.edu
WILLENSKY, Violet, J .... 908-526-1200.... 313 E
vwillens@raritanval.edu
WILLERTH, Dale .... 630-466-7900.... 167 G
dwillerth@waubonsee.edu
WILLETT, Brian .... 205-726-2902........ 6 G
bewillet@samford.edu
WILLETT, Dana .... 931-221-7779.... 473 D
willettd@apsu.edu
WILLETT, Edward, M .... 618-537-6959.... 157 G
ewillett@mckendree.edu
WILLETT, Heather .... 910-695-3726.... 373 E
willetth@sandhills.edu
WILLETTS, Jeffrey, G .... 703-812-4757.... 520 E
jwilletts@leland.edu
WILLEY, Jim .... 765-643-7133.... 175 K
jwilley@ivytech.edu
WILLEY, John, H .... 231-591-3825.... 251 B
willeyj1@ferris.edu
WILLEY, Sue, J .... 317-788-3246.... 180 C
swilley@uindy.edu
WILLFAHRT, Connie .... 715-422-5525.... 554 C
connie.willfahrt@mstc.edu

WILLGING, Gregory, A ...... 563-556-5110.... 187 G
willging@nicc.edu
WILLGING, Pete .... 815-599-3421.... 152 A
pete.willging@highland.edu
WILLIAM, Perez .... 212-431-2888.... 343 E
wperez@nyls.edu
WILLIAMS, Alfred .... 860-412-7212...... 91 A
awilliams@qvcc.commnet.edu
WILLIAMS, Amanda .... 913-288-7218.... 193 J
awilliams@kckcc.edu
WILLIAMS, Amanda .... 813-880-8042.... 111 A
adiaz@academy.edu
WILLIAMS, Angela .... 803-738-7691.... 459 D
williamsa@midlandstech.edu
WILLIAMS, Ann .... 662-254-3347.... 276 C
admsn@mvsu.edu
WILLIAMS, Ann, M .... 610-285-5000.... 439 K
auw2@psu.edu
WILLIAMS, Annette .... 540-453-2332.... 525 G
williamsa@brcc.edu
WILLIAMS, Annette, M .... 212-746-6005.... 360 B
dean@med.cornell.edu
WILLIAMS, Annie .... 719-549-2116...... 83 B
annie.williams@colostate-pueblo.edu
WILLIAMS, Anthony, T ...... 325-674-5288.... 478 H
williamsa@acu.edu
WILLIAMS, Antonio .... 410-706-7032.... 227 C
awilliams@police.umaryland.edu
WILLIAMS, Arley .... 307-766-4839.... 556 E
awilli44@uwyo.edu
WILLIAMS, Audrey .... 352-365-3510.... 112 M
williama@lscc.edu
WILLIAMS, Audrey .... 865-694-6545.... 475 F
ajwilliams@pstcc.edu
WILLIAMS, Barry .... 570-208-5932.... 432 E
barrywilliams@kings.edu
WILLIAMS, Benecia .... 573-681-5271.... 284 B
williamb@lincolnu.edu
WILLIAMS, Benecia, R ...... 573-681-5096.... 284 B
williamb@lincolnu.edu
WILLIAMS, Bert .... 478-387-4782.... 130 E
WILLIAMS, Betty, B .... 843-383-8055.... 457 A
bwilliams@coker.edu
WILLIAMS, Bob .... 386-506-3697.... 103 J
williab@DaytonaState.edu
WILLIAMS, Bobby .... 936-294-1735.... 501 A
ath_brw@shsu.edu
WILLIAMS, Brad .... 954-262-7282.... 114 B
bradwill@nsu.nova.edu
WILLIAMS, Bradley, E .... 530-226-4172...... 69 H
bwilliams@simpsonu.edu
WILLIAMS, Brian, G .... 216-397-4296.... 392 M
bwilliams@jcu.edu
WILLIAMS, Bridgett .... 678-891-3400.... 130 G
bridgett.williams@gpc.edu
WILLIAMS, Brockton .... 615-343-4411.... 477 F
brock.williams@vanderbilt.edu
WILLIAMS, Byron, C .... 225-771-4680.... 214 G
byronc_williams@sus.edu
WILLIAMS, Calvin .... 607-962-9233.... 331 D
williams@corning-cc.edu
WILLIAMS, Calvin, H .... 717-815-1226.... 452 F
cwilliam@ycp.edu
WILLIAMS, Cameron .... 906-487-7368.... 251 C
cam.williams@finlandia.edu
WILLIAMS, Carl, M .... 610-399-2297.... 441 H
cwilliams@cheyney.edu
WILLIAMS, Carla .... 601-877-6188.... 273 C
cwilliams@alcorn.edu
WILLIAMS, Carmen .... 701-777-4358.... 381 D
carmen.williams@email.und.edu
WILLIAMS, Carol .... 804-763-6711...... 99 D
ctw@strayer.edu
WILLIAMS, Carol .... 336-272-7102.... 364 D
carolw@greensborocollege.edu
WILLIAMS, Carol .... 325-674-2940.... 478 H
carol.williams@acu.edu
WILLIAMS, Carol, K .... 478-301-2670.... 133 F
williams_ck@mercer.edu
WILLIAMS, Carolane .... 410-462-7799.... 221 D
cwilliams@bccc.edu
WILLIAMS, Carolyn .... 903-983-8277.... 489 F
cwilliams@kilgore.edu
WILLIAMS, Carrie, R .... 334-683-2350........ 5 G
cwilliams@marionmilitary.edu
WILLIAMS, Catherine, M .... 541-737-2494.... 418 F
catherine.williams@oregonstate.edu
WILLIAMS, Cathy .... 315-781-3696.... 335 G
cwilliams@hws.edu
WILLIAMS, Cathy .... 417-865-2811.... 282 A
williamsc@evangel.edu
WILLIAMS, Celeastia .... 818-767-0888...... 79 D
celeastia.williams@woodbury.edu
WILLIAMS, Chad .... 336-633-0183.... 372 F
gcwilliams@randolph.edu
WILLIAMS, Charles .... 410-651-6508.... 227 E
cwilliams@umes.edu
WILLIAMS, Charles .... 630-829-6025.... 145 D
WILLIAMS, Charles, F .... 704-637-4550.... 363 C
cwilliam@catawba.edu
WILLIAMS, Charlie .... 908-737-3330.... 311 B
chwillia@kean.edu
WILLIAMS, Charlotte .... 828-328-7214.... 366 B
charlotte.williams@lr.edu

WILLIAMS,
Charlotte Treby .... 609-258-7097.... 313 A
trebyw@princeton.edu
WILLIAMS, Cheryl .... 949-214-3310...... 42 K
cheryl.williams@cui.edu
WILLIAMS, Chris .... 502-456-6504.... 206 C
cwilliams@sullivan.edu
WILLIAMS, Chris .... 864-644-5303.... 461 B
cwilliams@swu.edu
WILLIAMS, Chris, J .... 765-641-4235.... 169 A
cjwilliams@anderson.edu
WILLIAMS, Christal, D ...... 816-802-3558.... 283 I
cdwilliams@kcai.edu
WILLIAMS, Christine .... 906-786-5802.... 249 D
williamc@baycollege.edu
WILLIAMS, Christopher ...... 516-299-3834.... 338 F
christopher.williams@liu.edu
WILLIAMS, Christopher ..... 507-288-4563.... 263 D
cwilliams@crossroadscollege.edu
WILLIAMS, Chuck, R .... 317-940-8491.... 170 C
crwillia@butler.edu
WILLIAMS, Clara .... 770-671-1200.... 124 D
crwilliams@argosy.edu
WILLIAMS, Clara, A .... 615-687-6895.... 466 G
cawilliams@abcnash.edu
WILLIAMS, Clark .... 541-278-5796.... 414 G
clwilliams@bluecc.edu
WILLIAMS, Clifford, S .... 860-832-3898...... 91 D
cwilliams@charteroak.edu
WILLIAMS, Coameca .... 662-846-4640.... 274 B
0089mgr@fheg.follett.com
WILLIAMS, Connie .... 803-793-5129.... 457 F
williamsco@denmarktech.edu
WILLIAMS, Connie .... 225-928-3005.... 208 C
WILLIAMS, Connie .... 513-556-6998.... 403 D
connie.williams@uc.edu
WILLIAMS, Corey .... 773-907-4667.... 147 A
cwilliams369@ccc.edu
WILLIAMS, Crystal .... 503-771-1112.... 420 A
williamsc@reed.edu
WILLIAMS, Crystal, G .... 919-516-4197.... 376 B
cgwilliams@st-aug.edu
WILLIAMS, Cynthia .... 662-621-4126.... 273 I
cwilliams@coahomacc.edu
WILLIAMS, D. Newell .... 817-257-7231.... 482 C
n.williams@tcu.edu
WILLIAMS, Damon .... 608-265-5228.... 550 G
damon.williams@provost.wisc.edu
WILLIAMS, Dan .... 940-397-4239.... 491 A
dan.williams@mwsu.edu
WILLIAMS, III, Daniel, A .. 202-806-6763...... 98 B
dwilliams@howard.edu
WILLIAMS, Darlene .... 318-357-6100.... 216 B
darlene@nsula.edu
WILLIAMS, Darlene .... 510-261-8500...... 61 F
Darlene.Williams@patten.edu
WILLIAMS, Darrell, W .... 479-979-1208...... 26 A
dwwillia@ozarks.edu
WILLIAMS, David .... 916-608-6500...... 56 C
WILLIAMS, David .... 325-793-4694.... 490 F
dwilliams@mcm.edu
WILLIAMS, David .... 615-322-8333.... 477 F
david.williams@vanderbilt.edu
WILLIAMS, David, B .... 614-292-6446.... 398 H
WILLIAMS, David, L .... 313-577-4501.... 260 D
ad4287@wayne.edu
WILLIAMS, David, S .... 706-542-3240.... 138 C
dwilliam@uga.edu
WILLIAMS, Dawn .... 504-816-4914.... 208 I
dwilliams@dillard.edu
WILLIAMS, Deborah, H ...... 864-941-8367.... 460 D
williams.d@ptc.edu
WILLIAMS, Debra, J .... 724-925-4200.... 451 E
williamsd@wccc.edu
WILLIAMS, Denise .... 217-641-4231.... 154 G
williams@jwcc.edu
WILLIAMS, Dennis .... 405-789-6400.... 412 D
dwilliam@snu.edu
WILLIAMS, Diann, W .... 870-543-5929...... 23 H
dwilliams@seark.edu
WILLIAMS, Donald .... 330-672-2312.... 393 D
dwilliams@kent.edu
WILLIAMS, Donald .... 570-674-6315.... 436 F
frdon@misericordia.edu
WILLIAMS, Donald, E .... 407-303-5671.... 108 D
don.williams@fhchs.edu
WILLIAMS, Donald, J .... 540-231-5991.... 529 B
dowilli3@vt.edu
WILLIAMS, Donald, S .... 906-487-2538.... 255 E
dswillia@mtu.edu
WILLIAMS, Donna, M .... 610-799-1107.... 434 D
dwilliams@lccc.edu
WILLIAMS, Donyel .... 312-553-3164.... 146 H
dwilliams@ccc.edu
WILLIAMS, Doug .... 515-965-7024.... 183 E
dcwilliams@dmacc.edu
WILLIAMS, Drew, H .... 214-841-3636.... 485 E
dwilliams@dtc.edu
WILLIAMS, E. Keith .... 404-756-4003.... 124 I
kwilliams@atlm.edu
WILLIAMS, Earl .... 941-554-3781.... 100 G
eawilliams@argosy.edu
WILLIAMS, Eddie, R .... 815-753-6009.... 160 A
ewilliam@niu.edu

WILLIAMS, Edward .... 336-506-4178.... 367 G
edward.williams@alamancecc.edu
WILLIAMS, Elizabeth .... 803-778-7873.... 455 G
williamsel@cctech.edu
WILLIAMS, Elizabeth, N ..... 240-895-4467.... 226 A
enwilliams@smcm.edu
WILLIAMS, Emmit .... 310-243-3799...... 34 E
ewilliams@csudh.edu
WILLIAMS, Eric .... 616-234-3720.... 251 G
ewilliam@grcc.edu
WILLIAMS, Erik, W .... 540-857-8914.... 528 E
ewilliams@virginiawestern.edu
WILLIAMS, Erika, T .... 817-515-3049.... 496 A
erika.williams@tccd.edu
WILLIAMS, Eunice .... 315-498-2565.... 345 D
williame@sunyocc.edu
WILLIAMS, F. Clark .... 615-343-2100.... 477 F
f.clark.williams@vanderbilt.edu
WILLIAMS, Falecia, D .... 407-582-1235.... 122 I
fawilliams@valenciacollege.edu
WILLIAMS, Fathia .... 985-858-5728.... 210 H
fwilliams@ftcc.edu
WILLIAMS, Felica .... 304-327-4212.... 543 C
fblanks@bluefieldstate.edu
WILLIAMS, Frank .... 716-839-8225.... 331 G
fwilliam@daemen.edu
WILLIAMS, Frank .... 580-559-5256.... 407 J
fwilliams@ecok.edu
WILLIAMS, Frank, G .... 217-245-3003.... 152 C
fwilliam@ic.edu
WILLIAMS, Fred .... 714-808-4746...... 59 B
fwilliams@nocccd.edu
WILLIAMS, G. Keith .... 404-880-6389.... 126 I
gkwilliams@cau.edu
WILLIAMS, Gail, C .... 757-446-5869.... 518 F
williamsgc@evms.edu
WILLIAMS, Gary .... 956-384-2866.... 493 A
gwilliams@riogrande.edu
WILLIAMS, George .... 615-327-6815.... 471 A
gwilliams@mmc.edu
WILLIAMS, George, D .... 919-516-4236.... 376 B
gewilliams@st-aug.edu
WILLIAMS, Georgia, E .... 252-398-6439.... 363 E
willig@chowan.edu
WILLIAMS, Gerald .... 256-761-6128........ 7 H
gwilliams@talladega.edu
WILLIAMS, Gerhild, S .... 314-935-5106.... 292 J
gerhildwilliams@wustl.edu
WILLIAMS, Gerry .... 303-333-4224...... 81 C
WILLIAMS, Glorya, E .... 229-430-4654.... 123 H
glorya.williams@asurams.edu
WILLIAMS, Gregory, D .... 432-335-6410.... 491 F
gwilliams@odessa.edu
WILLIAMS, Gregory, G .... 713-313-1962.... 499 G
williamsg@tsu.edu
WILLIAMS, Gregory, H .... 513-556-2201.... 403 D
president@uc.edu
WILLIAMS, H. James .... 616-331-7100.... 252 A
williahj@gvsu.edu
WILLIAMS, Harry, L .... 302-857-6001...... 95 F
hwilliams@desu.edu
WILLIAMS, Heidi .... 724-938-5700.... 441 G
williams_h@calu.edu
WILLIAMS, Helen .... 626-815-5348...... 30 E
hwilliams@apu.edu
WILLIAMS, Hila .... 937-708-5252.... 405 G
hwilliams@wilberforce.edu
WILLIAMS, Hillary, A .... 512-505-3075.... 488 B
hawilliams@htu.edu
WILLIAMS, Irma .... 201-761-6052.... 314 F
ssmith@spc.edu
WILLIAMS, Jack .... 615-383-1340.... 468 J
jack@fwbbc.edu
WILLIAMS, Jacqueline .... 718-951-5352.... 326 G
williams@brooklyn.cuny.edu
WILLIAMS, Jacqueline, H .. 410-951-6481.... 228 B
jwilliams@coppin.edu
WILLIAMS, James .... 303-871-2203...... 88 E
james.herbert@du.edu
WILLIAMS, James .... 408-298-2181...... 67 C
james.williams@sjcc.edu
WILLIAMS, James .... 417-865-2811.... 282 A
williamsj@evangel.edu
WILLIAMS, James .... 414-297-6492.... 554 D
williaje@matc.edu
WILLIAMS, James, C .... 317-738-8213.... 171 C
jwilliams@franklincollege.edu
WILLIAMS, James, E .... 620-341-5267.... 192 D
jwilliam@emporia.edu
WILLIAMS, James, F .... 303-492-7511...... 88 B
james.williams@colorado.edu
WILLIAMS, James, L .... 800-553-3378.... 138 B
jwilliams@uofa.edu
WILLIAMS, JR., James, L . 540-464-7119.... 529 A
williamsjl@vmi.edu
WILLIAMS, James, V .... 904-256-7025.... 111 J
jwillia3@ju.edu
WILLIAMS, Jan .... 410-617-2928.... 224 A
jwilliams@loyola.edu
WILLIAMS, Jan, R .... 865-974-5061.... 477 B
jwilli3@utk.edu
WILLIAMS, Jane .... 401-456-8013.... 454 A
jwilliams@ric.edu

WILLIAMS, Teresa, G .... 704-233-8210.... 380 D
tgwilliams@wingate.edu
WILLIAMS, Terri .... 404-364-8320.... 135 A
twilliams1@oglethorpe.edu
WILLIAMS, Terri, B .... 724-847-6892.... 429 G
twilliam@geneva.edu
WILLIAMS, Terria, C .... 803-535-5720.... 456 D
twilliams@claflin.edu
WILLIAMS, Terry .... 601-484-8615.... 275 C
twilliam@mcc.cc.ms.us
WILLIAMS, Theodore, D .... 304-829-7465.... 540 E
twilliams@bethanywv.edu
WILLIAMS, Thomas .... 218-281-8583.... 272 A
will3140@umn.edu
WILLIAMS, Tiffaney .... 706-821-8282.... 135 C
tiwilliams@paine.edu
WILLIAMS, Tiffany, S .... 816-235-5599.... 291 E
williamsti@umkc.edu
WILLIAMS, Tim .... 502-895-3411.... 204 B
twilliams@lpts.edu
WILLIAMS, Timothy .... 765-973-8320.... 173 D
timwill@iue.edu
WILLIAMS, Todd .... 901-320-9700.... 478 B
twilliams@victory.edu
WILLIAMS, Todd, J .... 215-702-4861.... 444 A
president@pbu.edu
WILLIAMS, Todd Allyn ...... 888-316-9377.... 387 A
WILLIAMS, Tom .... 318-678-6000.... 209 J
twilliams@bpcc.edu
WILLIAMS, Tonjua, L .... 727-341-3344.... 116 F
williams.tonjua@spcollege.edu
WILLIAMS, Tracey, Y .... 270-707-3825.... 202 A
twilliams0139@kctcs.edu
WILLIAMS, Traci, N .... 423-746-5213.... 476 D
twilliams@twcnet.edu
WILLIAMS, Trudy .... 412-392-8085.... 444 H
twilliams@pointpark.edu
WILLIAMS, Trysta .... 785-587-2800.... 194 F
trystawilliams@matc.net
WILLIAMS, Tyler, R .... 208-496-1331.... 142 G
williamst@byui.edu
WILLIAMS, Valerie .... 405-271-2688.... 413 D
valerie-williams@ouhsc.edu
WILLIAMS, Valerie, A .... 305-626-3622.... 108 H
vwilliam@fmuniv.edu
WILLIAMS, Vaughn, A .... 770-423-6210.... 132 H
vwilliam@kennesaw.edu
WILLIAMS, Velma, J .... 804-828-1347.... 525 E
vjwillia@vcu.edu
WILLIAMS, Vera, A .... 985-549-2241.... 216 C
vera.williams@selu.edu
WILLIAMS, Vicki .... 662-846-4011.... 274 B
vwilliams@deltastate.edu
WILLIAMS, Vickie .... 334-214-4803........ 2 G
vickie.williams@cv.edu
WILLIAMS, Victoria .... 610-796-5511.... 421 F
victoria.williams@alvernia.edu
WILLIAMS, Walter .... 205-929-6317........ 5 E
wwilliams@lawsonstate.edu
WILLIAMS, Wanda, K .... 713-500-3864.... 506 D
wanda.k.williams@uth.tmc.edu
WILLIAMS, Wendy, E .... 843-953-5506.... 457 B
williamsw@cofc.edu
WILLIAMS, William, F .... 724-738-2001.... 443 F
william.williams@sru.edu
WILLIAMS, William, T .... 303-458-4122...... 87 E
wwilliam@regis.edu
WILLIAMS, Willie .... 713-718-8570.... 487 G
willie.williams@hccs.edu
WILLIAMS, Wilma, L .... 870-235-4097...... 23 I
wlwilliams@saumag.edu
WILLIAMS, Yolanda .... 813-879-6000.... 106 F
ywilliams@cci.edu
WILLIAMS, Yolanda .... 407-708-2069.... 117 G
williamy@seminolestate.edu
WILLIAMS, Zena .... 773-380-6850.... 168 D
zwilliams@westwood.edu
WILLIAMS-BETHEA,
Melanie .... 212-678-3702.... 357 F
mwilliams@tc.edu
WILLIAMS-COTE, Anna .... 617-984-1626.... 244 C
awilliams@quincycollege.edu
WILLIAMS-GAUDIOSO,
Amy .... 610-359-5341.... 426 G
awilliam@dccc.edu
WILLIAMS-GOLDSTEIN,
Brittany .... 201-684-7609.... 313 D
bwillia1@ramapo.edu
WILLIAMS-KIRKSEY,
Shirley .... 404-880-6774.... 126 I
skirksey@cau.edu
WILLIAMS LOSTON,
Adena .... 210-486-2900.... 479 B
aloston@alamo.edu
WILLIAMS LOSTON,
Adena .... 210-486-2900.... 479 E
aloston@alamo.edu
WILLIAMS MALLETT,
Denise .... 313-993-1496.... 259 C
williamd@udmercy.edu
WILLIAMS-PEREZ, Kendra 319-226-2040.... 181 E
williakb@ihs.org
WILLIAMS-ROBERTS,
Deborah .... 810-762-9650.... 253 I
droberts@kettering.edu

WILLIAMS RUSHIN,
Palisa .... 859-246-6522.... 201 D
palisa.rushin@kctcs.edu
WILLIAMSON, Angela .... 417-690-2208.... 280 C
awilliamson@cofo.edu
WILLIAMSON, Bob .... 360-992-2123.... 532 A
bwilliamson@clark.edu
WILLIAMSON, Carla .... 919-658-7749.... 367 D
cwilliamson@moc.edu
WILLIAMSON, Carol .... 641-628-7667.... 183 A
williamsonc@central.edu
WILLIAMSON, Celia .... 940-565-4961.... 504 B
celia@unt.edu
WILLIAMSON, Colin, W ..... 570-326-3761.... 440 K
cwilliam@pct.edu
WILLIAMSON, Dale, E .... 308-432-6221.... 299 G
dwilliamson@csc.edu
WILLIAMSON, Dean .... 936-261-2188.... 496 E
cdwilliamson@pvamu.edu
WILLIAMSON, Debbie .... 843-863-7050.... 456 B
dwilliam@csuniv.edu
WILLIAMSON, Debra .... 906-353-4600.... 253 J
dwilliamson@kbocc.org
WILLIAMSON, Donna .... 717-544-4912.... 433 E
WILLIAMSON, Donna, S .... 540-365-4216.... 518 J
dswilliamson@ferrum.edu
WILLIAMSON, Douglas ..... 910-893-1258.... 362 F
dwilliamson@campbell.edu
WILLIAMSON, Emily, L ...... 828-448-3120.... 374 G
ewilliamson@wpcc.edu
WILLIAMSON, George .... 619-849-2610...... 62 L
georgewilliamson@pointloma.edu
WILLIAMSON, Gerald .... 706-886-6831.... 137 G
jerryw@tfc.edu
WILLIAMSON, Handy .... 573-882-9061.... 291 D
williamsonha@missouri.edu
WILLIAMSON, Harold, A .... 573-882-5606.... 291 C
williamsonh@health.missouri.edu
WILLIAMSON, JR.,
Harold, A .... 573-882-5606.... 291 D
williamsonh@health.missouri.edu
WILLIAMSON, Heather ...... 254-442-5001.... 482 G
heather.williamson@cisco.edu
WILLIAMSON, James, D .... 410-704-4862.... 228 E
jwilliamson@towson.edu
WILLIAMSON, James, E .... 706-542-5813.... 138 C
administration@police.uga.edu
WILLIAMSON, James, R .... 858-784-8469...... 69 B
WILLIAMSON, Jay, C .... 330-325-6588.... 397 C
jcw@neoucom.edu
WILLIAMSON, Jeff .... 507-372-3408.... 268 B
jeff.williamson@mnwest.edu
WILLIAMSON, Joann .... 803-641-3668.... 462 B
joannw@usca.edu
WILLIAMSON, Katherine .... 252-492-2061.... 374 D
williamsonk@vgcc.edu
WILLIAMSON, Kimberly .... 252-493-7217.... 372 E
kwilliamson@email.pittcc.edu
WILLIAMSON, Kimberly .... 773-481-8186.... 147 F
kwilliamson13@ccc.edu
WILLIAMSON, Laurel .... 281-998-6184.... 493 D
laurel.williamson@sjcd.edu
WILLIAMSON, Marty .... 661-654-2111...... 33 H
mwilliamson@csub.edu
WILLIAMSON, Marvel .... 405-208-5900.... 410 A
mwilliamson@okcu.edu
WILLIAMSON, Michael ...... 650-738-4331...... 67 G
willliamsonm@smccd.edu
WILLIAMSON, Michael ...... 650-738-4221...... 67 G
williamsonm@smccd.edu
WILLIAMSON, Nancy .... 301-985-7080.... 227 F
legal-affairs@umuc.edu
WILLIAMSON, Nancy .... 516-572-7406.... 342 C
nancy.williamson@ncc.edu
WILLIAMSON, Pamela .... 757-823-2037.... 521 K
pwilliamson@nsu.edu
WILLIAMSON, Patricia, A .. 815-224-0440.... 153 D
patty_williamson@ivcc.edu
WILLIAMSON, Pauline .... 410-532-3164.... 225 D
pwilliamson@ndm.edu
WILLIAMSON, Randall, H . 202-231-3351.... 557 G
randall.williamson@dia.mil
WILLIAMSON, Rhea .... 707-826-4189...... 36 D
Rhea.Williamson@humboldt.edu
WILLIAMSON, Sean .... 706-245-7226.... 128 K
swilliamson@ec.edu
WILLIAMSON, Sharon .... 603-526-3756.... 304 A
sewillia@colby-sawyer.edu
WILLIAMSON, Sharon .... 806-742-4250.... 501 D
sharon.williamson@ttu.edu
WILLIAMSON, Sheila, D .... 336-599-1181.... 372 D
willias1@piedmontcc.edu
WILLIAMSON, Stephanie ... 801-281-7630.... 510 I
stephanie.williamson@stevenshenager.edu
WILLIAMSON, Sue .... 306-416-7679.... 538 A
sue.williamson@skagit.edu
WILLIAMSON, Tari .... 704-366-5066.... 375 H
twilliamson@rts.edu
WILLIAMSON, Tom .... 651-450-3680.... 266 I
twillia@inverhills.edu
WILLIAMSON, Tommy .... 336-721-2824.... 376 C
tommy.williamson@salem.edu
WILLIAR, Marc, G .... 904-819-6220.... 107 A
mwilliar@flagler.edu

WILLIARD, Stacey .... 724-266-3838.... 448 G
swilliard@tsm.edu
WILLIFORD, A. Michael .... 740-593-1059.... 399 G
willifor@ohio.edu
WILLIFORD, Craig .... 847-317-8084.... 166 B
cwilliford@tiu.edu
WILLIFORD, Darryl .... 301-860-4186.... 228 A
dwilliford@bowiestate.edu
WILLIFORD, David .... 615-383-1340.... 468 J
dwilliford@fwbbc.edu
WILLIFORD, Don .... 325-670-1491.... 487 D
willifrd@hsutx.edu
WILLIFORD, G. Craig .... 954-382-6400.... 122 C
WILLIFORD, Joey .... 662-720-7564.... 276 D
jewilliford@nemcc.edu
WILLIFORD, Lynn, E .... 919-962-1339.... 378 D
lynn_williford@unc.edu
WILLIFORD, Pamela, K ..... 325-670-1347.... 487 D
pwillifo@hsutx.edu
WILLIHNGANZ, Shirley, C 502-852-6153.... 207 A
scwill01@louisville.edu
WILLILAMS, Glenn .... 314-275-3524.... 161 D
WILLINGER, Katie .... 920-693-1247.... 554 A
katie.willinger@gotoltc.edu
WILLINGHAM, Becky .... 615-771-7821.... 478 G
bwillingham@williamsoncc.edu
WILLINGHAM, Brian .... 213-637-1360...... 78 I
bwillingham@westwood.edu
WILLINGHAM, Gloria .... 805-898-2914...... 47 C
gwillingham@fielding.edu
WILLINGHAM, Paul .... 281-283-2222.... 503 C
willingham@uhcl.edu
WILLINGHAM, Ralph .... 817-598-6248.... 508 C
rwillingham@wc.edu
WILLINGHAM, Ricky .... 256-551-5219........ 4 J
ricky.willingham@drakestate.edu
WILLINGHAM, Sonnie .... 904-332-0910...... 84 I
sonniew@heritage-education.com
WILLINGHAM, Sonnie .... 904-332-0910.... 110 G
WILLINGHAM-HINTON,
Shelley, M .... 919-516-4190.... 376 B
swhinton@st-aug.edu
WILLIS, Adrienne .... 601-877-6325.... 273 C
awillis@alcorn.edu
WILLIS, Bob .... 334-983-6556........ 8 B
rwillis@troy.edu
WILLIS, Brandon .... 904-596-2476.... 122 A
bwillis@tbc.edu
WILLIS, Brenda, G .... 404-756-5791.... 134 B
bwillis@msm.edu
WILLIS, Brian .... 828-254-1921.... 367 H
bwillis@abtech.edu
WILLIS, Chris .... 251-460-6121........ 9 E
cmwillis@usouthal.edu
WILLIS, Christopher .... 412-536-1194.... 432 F
christopher.willis@laroche.edu
WILLIS, Cliff, K .... 814-332-2860.... 421 E
cliff.willis@allegheny.edu
WILLIS, Connie .... 510-748-2211...... 62 B
cwillis@peralta.edu
WILLIS, Darley .... 716-851-1118.... 333 B
willis@ecc.edu
WILLIS, Dave .... 541-463-5566.... 416 D
willisd@lanecc.edu
WILLIS, Doug .... 318-257-3267.... 215 F
doug@latech.edu
WILLIS, Eric, R .... 319-352-8470.... 189 F
rick.willis@wartburg.edu
WILLIS, Gary .... 800-962-7682.... 293 B
gwillis@wma.edu
WILLIS, Georgia .... 410-752-4710.... 221 E
gwillis@bic.edu
WILLIS, Harvey .... 973-328-5232.... 309 B
hwillis@ccm.edu
WILLIS, Jason .... 859-572-5746.... 205 E
willisj2@nku.edu
WILLIS, Jeff .... 270-384-8097.... 203 H
willisj@lindsey.edu
WILLIS, Kent .... 903-589-4072.... 490 B
kwillis@lonmorris.edu
WILLIS, Kim .... 309-677-4118.... 145 H
goblue@bradley.edu
WILLIS, Kimberley, D .... 585-292-2197.... 341 H
kwillis@monroecc.edu
WILLIS, Lisa .... 312-850-7066.... 147 C
lwillis04@ccc.edu
WILLIS, Lori, A .... 541-383-7572.... 414 I
lwillis@cocc.edu
WILLIS, Mark, D .... 804-828-0138.... 525 E
mdwillis@vcu.edu
WILLIS, Michaela .... 402-872-2221.... 299 H
mwillis@peru.edu
WILLIS, Paul .... 229-386-3202.... 123 F
pwillis@abac.edu
WILLIS, Russ .... 601-266-4050.... 278 A
russ.willis@usm.edu
WILLIS, Russ .... 601-266-5005.... 278 A
russ.willis@usm.edu
WILLIS, Tamie, L .... 405-425-5320.... 409 E
tamie.willis@oc.edu
WILLIS, Wanda, J .... 904-470-8251.... 105 A
wanda.willi098@ewc.edu
WILLIS-CAMPBELL, Lesia . 718-522-9073.... 323 D
lwillis-campbell@asa.edu

WILLIS-HASLIP, Shirlee .... 907-786-6190...... 10
sawillishaslip@uaa.alaska.edu
WILLIS-RIVERA, Jennifer ... 715-425-3531.... 552 A
jennifer.willis-rivera@uwrf.edu
WILLISON, Brian .... 608-249-6611.... 547 D
bwillison@msn.herzing.edu
WILLITS, Lynn .... 314-529-9333.... 284 F
lwillits@maryville.edu
WILLITS, Mary Lou .... 802-287-8316.... 513 D
willitsml@greenmtn.edu
WILLKIE, Dan .... 619-388-7527...... 65 H
dwillkie@sdccd.edu
WILLLIAMS, Sarah .... 386-481-2060.... 101 I
williams@cookman.edu
WILLMAN, Katharine .... 248-645-3360.... 250 D
kwillman@cranbrook.edu
WILLMANN, Ellie .... 207-326-2232.... 219 D
ellie.willmann@mma.edu
WILLMON, John .... 314-421-0949.... 290 H
jwillmon@siba.edu
WILLMON, Nixon .... 256-228-6001........ 6 A
willmonn@nacc.edu
WILLMORE, Sharman .... 513-732-5296.... 403 E
sharman.willmore@uc.edu
WILLNER, Donald .... 315-792-5469.... 341 E
dwillner@mvcc.edu
WILLOME, Donna .... 585-389-2501.... 342 D
dwillom0@naz.edu
WILLOUGHBY, Case .... 212-772-4882.... 327 E
case.willoughby@hunter.cuny.edu
WILLOUGHBY, Dan .... 714-992-7037...... 59 D
dwilloughby@fullcoll.edu
WILLOUGHBY, J. Michael 512-245-2581.... 501 C
jw02@txstate.edu
WILLOUGHBY, Karen, P ... 412-536-1201.... 432 F
karen.willoughby@laroche.edu
WILLOUGHBY, Thomas ..... 303-871-3383...... 88 E
twilloug@du.edu
WILLRICH, Penny, L .... 602-682-6800...... 17 G
pwillrich@phoenixlaw.edu
WILLS, Deleen .... 503-375-7003.... 415 F
dwills@corban.edu
WILLS, Deri .... 803-641-3787.... 462 B
deriw@usca.edu
WILLS, G. Benjamin .... 702-968-1611.... 303 D
bwills@roseman.edu
WILLS, Joe .... 530-898-4143...... 34 A
jwills@csuchico.edu
WILLS, Mark .... 714-620-3751...... 29 D
mwills@argosy.edu
WILLS, Mike .... 417-836-7635.... 286 F
mikewills@missouristate.edu
WILLS, Mike .... 573-592-1191.... 293 E
mike.wills@williamwoods.edu
WILLS, Penelope .... 928-776-2022...... 19 E
penny.wills@yc.edu
WILLS, Russell .... 870-575-7187...... 25 B
willsr@uapb.edu
WILLS, Yvonne .... 636-922-8315.... 288 E
ywills@stchas.edu
WILLSON, Robert, W .... 692-625-3031.... 559 E
rwwillson@cmi.edu
WILLSON, Steve .... 479-394-7622...... 23 E
swillson@rmcc.edu
WILLY, Randy .... 312-669-5258.... 150 E
rwilly@ellis.edu
WILMER, Elizabeth .... 540-857-7385.... 528 E
ewilmer@virginiawestern.edu
WILMER, Susan .... 215-895-1970.... 427 G
wilmers@drexel.edu
WILMER, Wesley .... 402-449-2945.... 298 B
wwilmer232@graceu.edu
WILMES, Douglas, R .... 304-788-6865.... 545 A
drwilmes@mail.wvu.edu
WILMES, Gerald .... 660-562-1350.... 287 E
gwilmes@nwmissouri.edu
WILMES, Regina .... 856-566-6726.... 316 I
wilmesrr@umdnj.edu
WILMESHERR, Jon .... 828-765-7351.... 371 F
jwilmesherr@mayland.edu
WILMOTH, Dirk, E .... 276-944-6814.... 518 I
dwilmoth@ehc.edu
WILMOTH, Jamie .... 865-882-4270.... 475 G
wilmoth@roanestate.edu
WILMOTH, Joe, J .... 304-462-4112.... 543 F
joe.wilmoth@glenville.edu
WILMOTH, Karen, L .... 304-637-1374.... 540 F
wilmothk@dewv.edu
WILMOTH, Nikki .... 254-659-7771.... 487 E
nwilmoth@hillcollege.edu
WILMOWSKY, Joseph .... 718-774-3430.... 325 J
WILSEY, Mary, M .... 585-785-1360.... 334 A
wilseym@flcc.edu
WILSFORD, Elda .... 765-289-2291.... 175 K
ewilsfor@ivytech.edu
WILSON, Alan, G .... 660-263-3900.... 279 J
awilson@cccb.edu
WILSON, Alla .... 570-422-3589.... 442 C
awilson@po-box.esu.edu
WILSON, Amy .... 202-319-6916...... 97 C
wilsonae@cua.edu
WILSON, Amy .... 206-876-6100.... 537 E
awilson@theseattleschool.edu

WILSON, Tracy 859-282-8989 132 C
twilson@ict-ils.edu
WILSON, Tressey, D 936-361-1700 496 E
tdwilson@pvamu.edu
WILSON, Valerie 870-574-4514 24 A
vwilson@sautech.edu
WILSON, Valvia 601-977-7844 277 F
vwilson@tougaloo.edu
WILSON, Vicki 859-246-6316 201 D
vicki.wilson@kctcs.edu
WILSON, Vicki 724-852-3375 451 B
vwilson@waynesburg.edu
WILSON, Victor, K 843-953-5522 457 B
wilsonw@cofc.edu
WILSON, Wade 979-230-3215 482 B
wade.wilson@brazosport.edu
WILSON, Warren 605-642-6930 465 F
warren.wilson@bhsu.edu
WILSON, Wendy 229-430-2766 123 H
wendy.wilson@asurams.edu
WILSON, William 423-323-3191 475 E
wrwilson@northeaststate.edu
WILSON, William, P 207-859-4692 217 G
wpwilson@colby.edu
WILSON, Yolanda 336-734-7251 370 C
ywilson@forsythtech.edu
WILSON, Yvette 212-280-1396 358 G
ywilson@uts.columbia.edu
WILSON-ANSTEY, Elizabeth, A 212-746-1057 360 B
eaanstey@med.cornell.edu
WILSON-BARKER, Sharon 207-992-1934 218 A
wilsonbarkers@husson.edu
WILSON-FENNELL, Nicole 734-462-4400 258 C
nwilson@schoolcraft.edu
WILSON-HALE, Brenda 518-276-6247 347 D
wilsob6@rpi.edu
WILSON-OYELARAN, Eileen, B 269-337-7220 253 F
wilsonoy@kzoo.edu
WILSON-PARKER, Sharnita, L 252-335-3747 377 D
slwilson@mail.ecsu.edu
WILSON-PORTER, Cyndi 210-829-2706 503 F
porter@uiwtx.edu
WILSON-STALLINGS, Samaria 617-682-1508 234 G
swilson@eds.edu
WILSON-TAYLOR, Sharon 312-369-7221 148 B
swilson-taylor@colum.edu
WILT, Jason 269-782-2702 258 E
jwilt@swmich.edu
WILT, Jeff 816-604-6704 285 E
jeff.wilt@mcckc.edu
WILT, Larry, M 410-455-2356 227 D
wilt@umbc.edu
WILTBANK, J. Kelley 207-973-3229 219 I
university.counsel@maine.edu
WILTENBURG, Robert, E 314-935-4806 292 J
rewilten@wustl.edu
WILTENMUTH, III, John, P 540-654-1047 524 H
jwiltenm@umw.edu
WILTGEN, JR., James, N 501-450-1223 22 A
wiltgen@hendrix.edu
WILTON, Courtney 503-594-3010 415 A
courtneyw@clackamas.edu
WILTON, John 510-642-3100 73 E
vcaf@berkeley.edu
WILTRAKIS, Frank 734-462-4400 258 C
fpw@schoolcraft.edu
WILTSCHEK, Walt 260-982-5243 177 F
wjwiltschek@manchester.edu
WILTSE, Mary Alane 518-828-4181 330 E
wiltse@sunycgcc.edu
WILTSE, Mike 989-686-9110 250 F
michaelwiltse@delta.edu
WILTZIUS, Pierre 805-893-5024 74 F
mlpsdean@ltsc.ucsb.edu
WIMBERLEY, Bernadette, H 302-225-6312 96 E
wimberlb@gbc.edu
WIMBERLY, Frances 706-396-8171 135 C
fwimberly@paine.edu
WIMBERLY, Theresa 318-676-7811 211 H
twimberly@nwltc.edu
WIMBISH, Gary 301-891-4112 229 B
chaplain@wau.edu
WIMBISH, Jennifer, L 972-860-8251 484 G
jwimbish@dcccd.edu
WIMBUSH, James 812-855-2739 173 C
jwimbush@indiana.edu
WIMER, Valinda 386-822-8850 121 E
vwimer@stetson.edu
WIMES, Edward, D 402-472-7161 300 F
ewimes@nebraska.edu
WIMMER, Edward, E 419-372-0709 385 D
ewimmer@bgsu.edu
WIMS, Daniel, K 256-372-5275 1 A
daniel.wims@aamu.edu
WIMS, Lois 914-674-7438 340 G
lwims@mercy.edu
WIN, Judith 413-528-7350 231 A
jwin@simons-rock.edu
WIN, U. Ba 413-528-7392 231 A
bawin@simons-rock.edu
WINANT, Richard, M 718-270-7411 352 D
rwinant@downstate.edu
WINCH, Eric, D 973-642-8289 315 C
eric.winch@shu.edu
WINCHELL, Barbra 845-561-0800 342 A
WINCHESTER, Andrea 731-425-2644 475 B
awinchester@jscc.edu
WINCHESTER, Elizabeth, A 314-977-2354 289 F
wincheea@slu.edu
WINCHESTER, Gina, S 270-809-5086 204 F
gina.winchester@murraystate.edu
WINCHESTER, Paul 316-295-5836 192 H
winchp@friends.edu
WINCHESTER, Samuel 800-672-3060 376 E
WINCHESTER, Sara 732-255-0400 312 D
swinchester@ocean.edu
WIND, Heidi 314-595-3400 278 G
hwind@anthemcollege.edu
WIND, Joseph, E 859-572-5916 205 E
wind@nku.edu
WINDERL, James 845-434-5750 356 H
jwinderl@sullivan.suny.edu
WINDERS, Tim 806-894-9611 494 C
twinders@southplainscollege.edu
WINDHAM, Ana, M 210-999-7306 502 C
awindham@trinity.edu
WINDHAM, Don 772-462-7357 110 L
dwindham@irsc.edu
WINDHAM, Greg 662-720-7210 276 D
gwindham@nemcc.edu
WINDHAM, Jameka 216-373-5287 397 E
jwindham@ndc.edu
WINDHAM, James, R 662-915-7448 277 G
jwindham@olemiss.edu
WINDLE, Frank, H 215-871-6750 444 B
frankwi@pcom.edu
WINDLE, Lawrence, B 956-380-8100 493 A
rgbipresident@riogrande.edu
WINDROW, Vincent 615-898-5812 473 F
vwindrow@mtsu.edu
WINDSOR, Lang 281-756-3639 479 G
lwindsor@alvincollege.edu
WINDY BOY, Helen 406-395-4313 296 G
hwindyboy@stonechild.edu
WINE, Stony 252-527-6223 371 D
swine@lenoircc.edu
WINEBARGER, Conley, F 336-734-7182 370 C
cwinebarger@forsythtech.edu
WINEBRAKE, James, J 585-475-2447 347 G
jjwgpt@rit.edu
WINEGAR, Lucien, T 570-372-4422 447 D
winegar@susqu.edu
WINEGARD, Kathryn 660-248-6208 279 K
kwinegar@centralmethodist.edu
WINEGARD, Tanya 402-280-2718 297 H
wingard@creighton.edu
WINEGARDEN, Alan, D 651-641-8258 263 C
winegarden@csp.edu
WINER, Toby, R 212-346-1200 345 F
twiner@pace.edu
WINES, Ed 952-487-8159 268 C
ed.wines@normandale.edu
WINES, Margaret 212-616-7250 335 D
margaret.wines@helenefuld.edu
WINFIELD, Robert, A 734-763-6880 259 D
rwinf@umich.edu
WINFIELD, Ted 802-656-3244 514 F
ted.winfield@uvm.edu
WINFREE, Kemp, W 304-746-1991 543 G
kwinfree@marshall.edu
WINFREE, Terri, L 708-709-3953 161 C
twinfree@prairiestate.edu
WINFREY, Steve 606-759-7141 202 D
steve.winfrey@kctcs.edu
WINFREY GRIFFIN, Polly 609-258-6191 313 A
polly@princeton.edu
WING, Barbara, R 928-776-2311 19 E
barbara.wing@yc.edu
WING, Derek 425-602-3107 530 K
media@bastyr.edu
WING, Edward 401-863-3330 452 J
edward_wing_md@brown.edu
WING, Kattie 479-575-3806 24 C
kattie@uark.edu
WINGARD, Alan, B 706-233-7248 136 E
awingard@shorter.edu
WINGARD, Larry, R 724-847-6733 429 G
lwingard@geneva.edu
WINGATE, C. Keith 415-565-4682 73 G
wingatek@uchastings.edu
WINGATE, Margaret 850-201-8366 121 F
wingatem@tcc.fl.edu
WINGATE, Susan, F 903-923-3231 500 A
susan.wingate@marshall.tstc.edu
WINGE, Jennifer, D 814-332-4351 421 E
jdwinge@allegheny.edu
WINGER, Heather 260-459-4590 175 A
hwinger@ibcfortwayne.edu
WINGER, Philip, E 570-372-4135 447 D
winger@susqu.edu
WINGER, Philip, G 716-375-2622 348 C
pwinger@sbu.edu
WINGET, Paul 515-244-4221 181 D
wingetp@aib.edu
WINGETT, Max, F 276-656-0201 527 D
mwingett@ph.vccs.edu
WINGFIELD, Albert, B 260-452-2106 170 G
al.wingfield@ctsfw.edu
WINGFIELD, Rob 912-449-7598 138 G
rwing@waycross.edu
WINGFIELD, Tim 865-573-4517 469 J
twingfield@johnsonU.edu
WINGLER, Barbara 661-763-7881 72 C
bwingler@taftcollege.edu
WINGLER, Mike 336-838-6178 375 A
michael.wingler@wilkescc.edu
WINGO, Charles, M 404-364-8364 135 A
cwingo@oglethorpe.edu
WINGO, Nancie 505-984-6103 320 C
alumni@sjcsf.edu
WINGROVE, Betty 765-289-2291 175 K
bwingrov@ivytech.edu
WINGS, Aaron 319-398-5403 186 H
aaron.wings@kirkwood.edu
WINIGER, Brent 701-355-8303 383 E
bwiniger@umary.edu
WININGS, Kathy 845-752-3000 358 D
academics@uts.edu
WINISTORFER, Paul, M 540-231-5481 529 B
pwinisto@vt.edu
WINK, Edward, F 612-624-1648 272 D
ewink@umn.edu
WINKELBAUER, Brian 303-273-3140 82 F
bwinkelb@mines.edu
WINKELMAN, Bryce 360-596-5333 538 B
bwinkelman@spscc.ctc.edu
WINKELMANN, John, F 608-363-2350 546 B
winkelj@beloit.edu
WINKLER, Carol, J 314-286-3651 288 B
cjwinkler@ranken.edu
WINKLER, Chris 512-313-3000 483 G
chris.winkler@concordia.edu
WINKLER, David 502-456-6509 206 B
dwinkler@sctd.edu
WINKLER, Janet 678-466-5050 127 A
janetwinkler@clayton.edu
WINKLER, Linda 570-408-4600 451 G
WINKLER, Roy 765-289-2291 175 K
rwinkler@ivytech.edu
WINKLER, Sandy 864-592-3765 461 C
winklers@sccsc.edu
WINKLEY, Robert 617-585-1280 243 E
robert.winkley@necmusic.edu
WINN, Emmett 334-844-5771 1 G
winne@auburn.edu
WINN, Jewel 615-963-7401 474 A
jwinn@tnstate.edu
WINN, Regina 318-670-9411 215 A
rwinn@susla.edu
WINNEY, Maureen 518-587-2100 355 F
maureen.winney@esc.edu
WINNIFORD, Janet 801-626-6008 511 D
jwinniford@weber.edu
WINNINGHAM, Laura 909-389-3323 65 B
lwinningham@craftonhills.edu
WINOGRAD, Katharine, W 505-224-4412 317 J
winograd@cnm.edu
WINQUIST, Melissa 480-858-9100 18 H
m.winquist@scnm.edu
WINRICH, J. Steven 859-238-5317 199 D
steve.winrich@centre.edu
WINSHIP, Nancy, K 781-736-4002 233 A
winship@brandeis.edu
WINSLOW, Bridgette 517-265-5161 247 D
WINSLOW, Chris 775-674-7500 302 J
cwinslow@tmcc.edu
WINSLOW, Christopher, J 508-289-2325 247 A
cwinslow@whoi.edu
WINSLOW, Kathy 252-985-5134 375 C
kwinslow@ncwc.edu
WINSLOW, Kellen 937-376-6289 386 H
kwinslow@centralstate.edu
WINSLOW, Richard, P 816-781-7700 293 D
winslowr@william.jewell.edu
WINSLOW, Valerie 908-737-7100 311 B
vwinslow@kean.edu
WINSLOW-SCHABER, Deborah, J 716-888-2240 325 G
winslowd@canisius.edu
WINSOME, Thais 408-855-5217 78 A
thais.winsome@wvm.edu
WINSON, Mark 218-733-7613 267 B
m.winson@lsc.edu
WINSOR, Susan, A 803-593-5611 455 A
winsor@atc.edu
WINSTEL, Susan, M 412-578-6330 424 G
winstelsm@carlow.edu
WINSTON, Bruce, E 757-352-4306 523 B
brucwin@regent.edu
WINSTON, David 870-512-7829 20 F
david_winston@asun.edu
WINSTON, Eric 312-369-7418 148 B
ewinston@colum.edu
WINSTON, Jeannie 501-569-3345 24 E
eewinston@ualr.edu
WINSTON, Kathleen 951-639-5560 58 E
kwinston@msjc.edu
WINSTON, Mark, D 973-353-5222 314 E
winstonm@andromeda.rutgers.edu
WINSTON, JR., Matthew, M 706-542-0054 138 C
mwinston@uga.edu
WINSTON, Robert, P 717-245-1363 427 E
winston@dickinson.edu
WINSTON, Van Buren 212-217-3400 333 G
vanburen_winston@fitnyc.edu
WINSTON-MUIR, Jeanni 301-846-2489 222 G
jwinston-muir@frederick.edu
WINTER, Adam 602-749-4622 13 M
awinter@devry.edu
WINTER, Barbara, J 620-235-4152 195 I
bwinter@pittstate.edu
WINTER, Karla, R 563-562-3263 187 G
winterk@nicc.edu
WINTER, Melanie 540-665-3499 523 K
mwinter@su.edu
WINTER, Roy 213-252-5100 26 C
WINTER, Stacey, O 701-231-8954 381 H
stacey.winter@ndsu.edu
WINTER, Tara 518-255-5418 354 E
wintert@cobleskill.edu
WINTER, Valerie 609-894-9311 308 C
vwinter@bcc.edu
WINTER, Walt 850-484-1903 114 G
wwinter@pensacolastate.edu
WINTER, William 775-784-6656 303 A
WINTER, JR., William, F 618-650-5380 165 A
wwinter@siue.edu
WINTERBAUER, Nancy, S 848-932-7832 314 B
winterbauer@oldqueens.rutgers.edu
WINTEREGG, Steven 937-766-3235 386 F
winteregg@cedarville.edu
WINTERER, James, C 651-962-6404 272 E
jcwinterer@stthomas.edu
WINTERFIELD, Catherine 973-300-2119 315 F
cwinterfield@sussex.edu
WINTERHALTER, Teresa 912-344-3135 124 E
teresa.winterhalter@armstrong.edu
WINTERMEYER, Stephen, F 317-274-8214 174 B
swinter@iupui.edu
WINTERS, Amy 308-635-6195 301 E
winters4@wncc.edu
WINTERS, Amy 845-687-5124 358 C
wintersa@sunyulster.edu
WINTERS, Chet 610-372-4721 445 B
cwinters@racc.edu
WINTERS, Curt, D 215-702-4206 444 A
cwinters@pbu.edu
WINTERS, Genevieve 480-517-8418 16 C
genevieve.winters@riosalado.edu
WINTERS, Hyla 702-651-4554 302 G
hyla.winters@csn.edu
WINTERS, James, W 630-617-6447 150 F
jwinters@elmhurst.edu
WINTERS, Jill 414-961-3897 549 A
jwinters@ccon.edu
WINTERS, Jill, M 414-326-2301 546 H
jwinters@ccon.edu
WINTERS, Rick 540-261-8492 524 C
rick.winters@svu.edu
WINTERS, Todd 618-453-2469 164 I
tw3a@siu.edu
WINTERS-DUNN, Teresa 413-265-2210 233 E
wintersdunnt@elms.edu
WINTERS-PALACIO, C.M 312-850-3527 147 C
cwinterspalacio@ccc.edu
WINTERSTEEN, Wendy 515-294-2518 182 B
wwinters@iastate.edu
WINTERSTEIN, James, F 630-889-6604 159 E
jwinterstein@nuhs.edu
WINWARD, Cindy 866-680-2756 510 B
office@midwifery.edu
WIORA, Margaret, A 630-637-5454 159 F
mawiora@noctrl.edu
WIORKOWSKI, John 972-883-2274 505 D
wiorkow@utdallas.edu
WIPF, Peggy 701-328-4114 381 C
peggy.wipf@ndus.edu
WIPPERMAN, Gary, L 319-352-8353 189 F
gary.wipperman@wartburg.edu
WIPPMAN, David 612-625-4841 272 D
dwippman@umn.edu
WIRAG, J. Robert 407-823-2094 120 A
j.wirag@ucf.edu
WIRT, Gary, L 302-225-6260 96 E
wirtgl@gbc.edu
WIRT, Susan 706-507-8463 127 D
wirt_susan@columbusstate.edu
WIRTH, Diane 209-575-6507 79 L
wirthd@yosemite.edu
WIRTH, Michael 865-974-3031 477 B
mwirth@utk.edu
WIRTH, Ross 614-947-6128 391 A
wirthr@franklin.edu
WIRTH, Sandy 860-913-2063 92 C
swirth@goodwin.edu
WIRTZ, James, J 831-656-3781 557 H
jwirtz@nps.edu

WOLF JOHNSON, Cynthia 704-687-7226 378 E cwolfjo@uncc.edu
WOLFE, Agata 201-216-8162 315 E awolfe@stevens.edu
WOLFE, Andrew 315-792-7234 356 B andrew.wolfe@sunyit.edu
WOLFE, Connie 336-386-8121 374 B wolfec@surry.edu
WOLFE, David 732-255-0400 312 D dwolfe@ocean.edu
WOLFE, Debbie 336-386-3401 374 B wolfed@surry.edu
WOLFE, Elizabeth 304-696-6007 543 G mccormi8@marshall.edu
WOLFE, Gregory 508-565-1357 245 D gwolfe@stonehill.edu
WOLFE, JR., James 812-941-2330 174 D
WOLFE, James, F 540-231-4000 518 H
WOLFE, Joel 205-970-9208 7 D jwolfe@sebc.edu
WOLFE, Johanna 713-221-8909 503 D wolfej@uhd.edu
WOLFE, John, R 419-586-0326 406 D john.wolfe@wright.edu
WOLFE, John, S 812-877-8590 179 A john.s.wolfe@rose-hulman.edu
WOLFE, Jonathan 409-880-7633 500 E jcwolfe@lit.edu
WOLFE, Karl 507-288-2886 261 G wolfek@augsburg.edu
WOLFE, Katherine, J 402-465-2312 299 J kjw@nebrwesleyan.edu
WOLFE, Katrin, A 814-269-7011 449 D kawolfe@pitt.edu
WOLFE, Lisa, C 636-797-3000 283 H lwolfe@jeffco.edu
WOLFE, Madelaine 619-660-4452 48 J madelaine.wolfe@gcccd.edu
WOLFE, Martha 270-706-8554 201 F martha.wolfe@kctcs.edu
WOLFE, N, J 212-217-4370 333 G nj_wolfe@fitnyc.edu
WOLFE, Peggy, L 337-475-5820 215 G pwolfe@mcneese.edu
WOLFE, Shea 312-329-6633 146 C swolfe@thechicagoschool.edu
WOLFE, Thomas, V 315-443-4263 357 B tvwolfe@syr.edu
WOLFE, Vicki, L 205-970-9245 7 D vwolfe@sebc.edu
WOLFE-LEE, Chyerl 360-650-3774 539 C chyerl.wolfe-lee@wwu.edu
WOLFE-STEPRO, Charlene 603-668-6706 304 E cwolfe@ccsnh.edu
WOLFENDEN, Robert, W 610-758-3430 434 E rww3@lehigh.edu
WOLFER, Diane 513-671-1920 384 I
WOLFER, Diane, G 859-371-9393 198 D dwolfer@beckfield.edu
WOLFERSBERGER, Mary, J 815-280-2476 154 H mwolfers@jjc.edu
WOLFERT, Kelly 920-693-1171 554 A ltc.bookstore@gotoltc.edu
WOLFERTZ, Joanne, R 203-576-5238 94 A jwolfertz@stvincentscollege.edu
WOLFF, Susan 815-939-5203 160 F swolff@olivet.edu
WOLFF, Susan 541-506-6030 415 C swolff@cgcc.cc.or.us
WOLFF, Timothy 775-784-4666 303 A tawolff@unr.edu
WOLFGANG, Frank, F 215-489-2268 426 H Frank.Wolfgang@delval.edu
WOLFGRAM SALZ, Kim 507-284-3163 262 E wolfgramsalz.kim@mayo.edu
WOLFINGER, Elizabeth 919-760-8514 366 G wolfingere@meredith.edu
WOLFORD, Gail 859-985-3150 198 F gail_wolford@berea.edu
WOLFORD, Norman, R 239-513-1135 123 D
WOLFRAM, Dietmar 414-229-4709 551 C dwolfram@uwm.edu
WOLFSON, Amy 508-793-2541 233 D awolfson@holycross.edu
WOLFSON, Bob, E 619-594-6304 36 E bwolfson@foundation.sdsu.edu
WOLFSON, Elizabeth 805-962-8179 28 L
WOLFSON, Moshe 718-941-8000 341 A
WOLFSON, Warren 312-362-8088 148 F wwolfson@depaul.edu
WOLGAMOTT, Gary, D 580-774-3249 412 F gary.wolgamott@swosu.edu
WOLIN, Richard, R 231-995-2003 256 G rwolin@nmc.edu
WOLINSKY, Lawrence, E 214-828-8300 497 A wolinsky@bcd.tamhsc.edu
WOLINSKY, Lawrence, E 214-828-8300 496 G lwatkins@bcd.tamhsc.edu
WOLK, David, S 802-468-1201 515 C dave.wolk@castleton.edu
WOLKEN, James 401-454-6420 454 B jwolken@risd.edu
WOLKING, Daryl 540-338-1776 522 A
WOLLAS, Robyn 615-771-7821 478 G rwollas@williamsoncc.edu
WOLLENS, Jack 360-383-3016 539 D jwollens@whatcom.ctc.edu
WOLLER, Eric, K 507-344-7790 261 H ewoller@blc.edu
WOLLMAN, Julie 617-879-2448 246 F jwollman@wheelock.edu
WOLLMAN, Rick 712-274-5320 187 D wollman@morningside.edu
WOLLMERING, Jerry 660-785-4235 291 A jerryw@truman.edu
WOLMAN, Tara 413-552-2495 240 C twolman@hcc.edu
WOLMARK, Mordechai 845-352-3431 361 G mwolmark@optonline.net
WOLOSCHUK, Peter 617-731-7089 244 B woloschp@pmc.edu
WOLPERN, Kevin 952-888-4777 270 F kwolpern@nwhealth.edu
WOLPERT, Ann, J 617-253-5297 242 A awolpert@mit.edu
WOLPERT, David 330-823-2286 404 C wolperds@mountunion.edu
WOLPIN, Aryeh 718-232-7800 360 K
WOLPIN, Chaim 718-232-7800 360 K
WOLPIN, Ken 908-737-3290 311 B wolpin@kean.edu
WOLSZCZAK, Jennifer 219-785-5299 178 H jwolszczak@pnc.edu
WOLSZON, Linda 817-257-7863 498 F l.wolszon@tcu.edu
WOLTMANN, Tanya, L 312-341-2006 162 I twoltman@roosevelt.edu
WOLTZ, Rita 804-819-4906 525 F rwoltz@vccs.edu
WOMACK, Donna 318-678-6000 209 J dwomack@bpcc.edu
WOMACK, Joe 541-684-7241 417 F jwomack@northwestchristian.edu
WOMACK, Kenneth, A 814-949-5000 438 H kaw16@psu.edu
WOMACK, Steve 615-383-4848 478 E swomack@watkins.edu
WOMACK, Wayne 479-788-7407 24 D wwomack@uafortsmith.edu
WOMACK, William 918-495-7088 411 C wwomack@oru.edu
WOMBLE, Jeff 910-672-1474 377 E jwomble@uncfsu.edu
WOMBLE, Lynn, Z 903-813-2891 481 A lwomble@austincollege.edu
WOMBLE, Ron 620-235-4124 195 I kwomble@pittstate.edu
WOMELSDUFF, Gary, E 206-281-2678 537 D womelg@spu.edu
WOMER, N. Keith 314-516-6109 291 F womerk@umsl.edu
WON, Cha Hi 714-527-0691 45 J
WON, Chul 213-487-0150 45 C aromc@dula.edu
WONCH, Stephen 616-632-2885 248 A sjw001@aquinas.edu
WONDERLIN, Julie 812-298-2296 177 A jwonderl@ivytech.edu
WONDERS, Christopher 717-477-1251 443 D cawonders@ship.edu
WONDRA, Ellen 847-328-9300 164 B ellen.wondra@seabury.edu
WONG, Erwin 212-220-8322 326 E ewong@bmcc.cuny.edu
WONG, Julie 727-873-4882 121 B juliewong@mail.usf.edu
WONG, Kathy 828-227-7218 379 E wong@wcu.edu
WONG, Krista 217-732-3168 156 F kwong@lincolnchristian.edu
WONG, Leslie, E 906-227-2242 256 F lwong@nmu.edu
WONG, Michael 808-455-0491 142 A mckwong@hawaii.edu
WONG, Nancy, C 323-265-8820 54 G wongnc@elac.edu
WONG, Paul 619-594-5456 36 E pwong@sdsu.edu
WONG, Raymond 909-868-4108 44 J rwong@devry.edu
WONG, Richard 804-355-0671 524 F rwong@upsem.edu
WONG, Tony 562-809-5100 47 J
WONG, Waiyan 512-444-8082 499 B faid@texastcm.edu
WONG, Walter 510-643-1640 73 E oua2wong@berkeley.edu
WONG-NICKERSON, Agnes 415-338-2582 36 F agnesw@sfsu.edu
WONGSAROJ, Ben 305-623-4100 108 H ben.wongsaroj@fmuniv.edu
WOO, Carolyn, Y 574-631-7992 180 D woo.5@nd.edu
WOO, Debra 201-200-3003 312 B dwoo@njcu.edu
WOO, Don 708-239-4861 165 I don.woo@trnty.edu
WOO, Ho, K 714-517-1945 30 G
WOO, Meredith, J 434-924-4611 525 B mjw8q@virginia.edu
WOO, Michael 909-869-2661 33 G
WOO, Tommy Lee 650-723-2300 71 F
WOOD, Amy 828-328-7728 366 B amy.wood@lr.edu
WOOD, Amy, B 615-963-5772 474 A awood@tnstate.edu
WOOD, Andy 662-472-2312 274 F awood@holmescc.edu
WOOD, Barbara 702-968-2055 303 D bwood@roseman.edu
WOOD, Bob, G 410-677-4819 228 D bgwood@salisbury.edu
WOOD, Bonnie 985-867-2237 214 F rouquette@sjasc.edu
WOOD, Brent 330-499-9600 393 I bwood11@kent.edu
WOOD, Bret 405-733-7413 411 I bwood@rose.edu
WOOD, Carol, S 434-924-1400 525 B cwood@virginia.edu
WOOD, Cathy, R 202-319-5606 97 C woodcr@cua.edu
WOOD, Charlene 828-479-9256 374 C cwaldroup@tricountycc.edu
WOOD, Charles 850-201-6428 121 F woodc@tcc.fl.edu
WOOD, II, Charles 304-896-7386 542 J charlesw@southern.wvnet.edu
WOOD, Chris 302-736-2316 96 G chriswood@wesley.edu
WOOD, Chris 903-923-2062 486 D cwood@etbu.edu
WOOD, Cliff, L 845-574-4214 347 I cwood@sunyrockland.edu
WOOD, Cristel 671-734-1812 559 C cwood@piu.edu
WOOD, Cynthia, L 256-765-4328 9 D clwood@una.edu
WOOD, Dan 828-884-8366 362 D dan.wood@brevard.edu
WOOD, Darrow 718-260-5497 328 E dwood@citytech.cuny.edu
WOOD, David 206-665-4600 180 A woodd@trine.edu
WOOD, David 713-973-3000 149 A dwood4@devry.edu
WOOD, David 713-973-3010 486 A dbwood@devry.edu
WOOD, David, H 906-227-2112 256 F dwood@nmu.edu
WOOD, David, S 864-597-4020 463 F woodds@wofford.edu
WOOD, Debra 704-216-6079 366 D dwood@livingstone.edu
WOOD, Donna, G 918-595-7841 412 H dwood@tulsacc.edu
WOOD, Doug 480-219-6111 278 F dwood@atsu.edu
WOOD, Douglas, M 717-766-2511 436 D dwood@messiah.edu
WOOD, Elizabeth, A 607-778-5319 324 G wood_e@sunybroome.edu
WOOD, Elizabeth, B 609-258-3354 313 A lizwood@princeton.edu
WOOD, Erin 701-662-1598 382 D erin.wood@lrsc.edu
WOOD, Evelyn 606-487-3141 201 H evelyn.wood@kctcs.edu
WOOD, Fred 423-478-6229 474 E fwood@clevelandstatecc.edu
WOOD, Fred, E 530-752-6866 73 F fewood@ucdavis.edu
WOOD, Gail 607-753-2221 353 B gail.wood@cortland.edu
WOOD, Gary, M 262-595-2430 551 E gary.wood@uwp.edu
WOOD, Gaye 704-991-0221 374 A gwood7693@stanly.edu
WOOD, Gayle, E 865-539-7160 475 F gwood@pstcc.edu
WOOD, Jack 989-686-9822 250 F jackwood@delta.edu
WOOD, Jan 510-204-0716 39 F jwood@cdsp.edu
WOOD, Jane 816-584-6483 287 H jane.wood@park.edu
WOOD, Janice, R 707-965-6315 60 J jwood@puc.edu
WOOD, Jason 307-855-2111 555 G jswood@cwc.edu
WOOD, Jeff 509-574-4691 540 A jwood@yvcc.edu
WOOD, Jeffrey, A 309-438-7602 153 C jwood@ilstu.edu
WOOD, Jerry 402-826-8258 298 A jerry.wood@doane.edu
WOOD, Jocelyn 215-222-4200 445 F jmwood@walnuthillcollege.edu
WOOD, John 314-286-4855 288 E jewood@ranken.edu
WOOD, John 307-855-2162 555 G jwood@cwc.edu
WOOD, Joseph, S 410-837-5244 229 A jwood@ubalt.edu
WOOD, Joyce 765-998-5117 179 F jywood@taylor.edu
WOOD, Joyce 205-929-1810 5 H jduganwood@aol.com
WOOD, Julia, H 865-694-6530 475 F jwood@pstcc.edu
WOOD, Kathryn 909-748-8069 75 F kathryn_wood@redlands.edu
WOOD, Kathryn 671-735-2658 559 D kwood@uguam.uog.edu
WOOD, Kelley 325-670-1251 487 D kwood@hsutx.edu
WOOD, Kim 865-251-1800 472 K kwood@southcollegetn.edu
WOOD, Kris 270-706-8412 201 F kris.wood@kctcs.edu
WOOD, Kurt, W 563-884-5127 60 L kurt.wood@palmer.edu
WOOD, Kurt, W 563-884-5127 188 C kurt.wood@palmer.edu
WOOD, Kurt, W 563-884-5127 114 E kurt.wood@palmer.edu
WOOD, Larry, E 931-598-1374 472 J lwood@sewanee.edu
WOOD, Laura 617-627-3345 245 F laura.wood@tufts.edu
WOOD, Laura 903-923-8207 492 A lwood@panola.edu
WOOD, Leslie, A 989-328-1214 256 A lesliew@montcalm.edu
WOOD, Lynn 617-873-0154 233 B Lynn.Wood@cambridgecollege.edu
WOOD, Lynsey 207-221-8752 218 C
WOOD, M. Ann 517-371-5140 259 B woodann@cooley.edu
WOOD, Mark 909-621-8146 63 A mark.wood@pomona.edu
WOOD, Mark, D 310-233-4426 54 I woodmd@lahc.edu
WOOD, Mark, U 530-226-4603 69 H mwood@simpsonu.edu
WOOD, Martin 719-255-3438 88 C mwood@uccs.edu
WOOD, Marty 715-836-2542 550 H mwood@uwec.edu
WOOD, Michael 952-446-4100 263 E woodm@crown.edu
WOOD, Michael 609-652-4294 313 F michael.wood@stockton.edu
WOOD, Michael 570-408-4300 451 G michael.wood@wilkes.edu
WOOD, Michael, A 316-978-3575 197 F mike.wood@wichita.edu
WOOD, Michael, T 301-369-2800 221 F president@capitol-college.edu
WOOD, SC, Monica 914-968-6200 349 D mwood@corriganlibrary.org
WOOD, Murray 661-362-3433 41 G murray.wood@canyons.edu
WOOD, Pamela, R 919-658-7753 367 D pwood@moc.edu
WOOD, Richard, C 806-743-2200 501 E richard.wood@ttuhsc.ttu.edu
WOOD, Richard, J 251-460-7021 9 E rwood@usouthal.edu
WOOD, Robert 904-620-4200 120 C robert.wood@unf.edu
WOOD, Robert 610-989-1257 450 E rwood@vfmac.edu
WOOD, Robert, A 740-368-3945 400 F rawood@owu.edu
WOOD, Robert, D 919-515-6121 378 B bob_wood@ncsu.edu
WOOD, Robert, H 315-268-6474 329 C rwood@clarkson.edu
WOOD, Robert, S 901-334-5830 471 C rswood@memphisseminary.edu
WOOD, Ronald, A 507-537-6272 269 G Ron.Wood@smsu.edu
WOOD, Scott, A 208-885-6195 144 B swood@uidaho.edu
WOOD, Shelia 504-286-5368 214 I swood@suno.edu
WOOD, Sherri, L 573-882-0683 291 D woods@missouri.edu
WOOD, Steve 828-835-4254 374 C swood@tricountycc.edu
WOOD, Susan 804-819-4972 525 F swood@vccs.edu
WOOD, Therese 269-749-7623 257 D twood@olivetcollege.edu
WOOD, Tim 616-331-2240 252 A woodt@gvsu.edu
WOOD, Tom 615-966-6174 470 D tom.wood@lipscombs.edu
WOOD, Vicky 740-389-4636 395 G woodv@mtc.edu

WORDEN, Sylvia 714-432-5026 41 B sworden@occ.cccd.edu
WORK, Christine 845-341-4763 345 E christine.work@sunyorange.edu
WORK, Denise 402-552-2796 297 D workdenise@clarksoncollege.edu
WORKMAN, Andrew 510-430-2347 57 D aworkman@mills.edu
WORKMAN, Christine 410-857-2267 224 D cworkman@mcdaniel.edu
WORKMAN, Greg 336-887-3000 365 J gworkman@laureluniversity.edu
WORKMAN, Mark, E 904-620-2700 120 C mworkman@unf.edu
WORKMAN, Nikki 740-389-4636 395 G workman@mtc.edu
WORKU, Adu 707-965-6242 60 J aworku@puc.edu
WORLAND, Brooke, A 317-738-8159 171 C bworland@franklincollege.edu
WORLAND, Marcia 765-459-0561 176 A mworland@ivytech.edu
WORLEY, Brian 909-621-8112 40 D brian.worley@cmc.edu
WORLEY, David 303-765-3107 84 K dworley@iliff.edu
WORLEY, Glenn 601-925-3370 275 E gworley@mc.edu
WORLEY, Jewell, B 276-376-1004 525 C ljw4k@uvawise.edu
WORLEY, Louise 717-815-1446 452 F lworley@ycp.edu
WORLEY, Mark 972-241-3371 484 D mworley@dallas.edu
WORLEY, Paul 828-835-9564 374 C pworley@tricountycc.edu
WORLEY, Phil, W 956-721-5416 489 G pworley@laredo.edu
WORM, Lori, M 920-424-3033 551 D worm@uwosh.edu
WORM, Roberta 402-891-9411 301 D roberta.worm@vatterott-college.edu
WORMACK, Janet 240-567-5292 224 E janet.wormack@montgomerycollege.edu
WORMAN, Ernie 803-947-2052 459 G ernie.worman@newberry.edu
WORMLEY, David, N 814-865-7537 438 F dnw2@psu.edu
WORMLEY, Nicholas George 203-582-3719 93 E nicholas.wormley@quinnipiac.edu
WORMSER, Jennifer 949-376-6000 53 E jwormser@lagunacollege.edu
WORNALL, Robyn 707-253-3373 58 F rwornall@napavalley.edu
WORRELL, Cortney 718-409-7477 356 C cworrell@sunymaritime.edu
WORRELL, Dan, L 479-575-5949 24 C dworrell@uark.edu
WORSHAM, Earl 610-361-5323 437 C worshame@neumann.edu
WORSLEY, Christina 925-685-1230 43 C cworsley@dvc.edu
WORSTER, Kathy, A 434-395-2016 520 G worsterks@longwood.edu
WORTH, Ben 859-246-6353 201 D ben.worth@kctcs.edu
WORTH, Bill 702-933-9700 301 I bworth@devry.edu
WORTH, Donald 575-492-2741 319 B dworth@nmjc.edu
WORTH, Joe 314-513-4161 289 B jworth@stlcc.edu
WORTH, John 207-326-2276 219 D john.worth@mma.edu
WORTHAM, Dan 901-321-3256 467 G dwortham@cbu.edu
WORTHAM, Donald 651-403-8638 262 I dwortham@css.edu
WORTHAM, Trudy 361-570-4110 503 E worthamt@uhv.edu
WORTHEN, Cynthia 703-526-5800 516 B cworthen@argosy.edu
WORTHEN, Kevin 585-389-2880 342 D kworthe6@naz.edu
WORTHEN, Kevin, J 801-422-2640 509 D kevin_worthen@byu.edu
WORTHEN, Shannon 479-248-7236 21 G sworthen@ecollege.edu
WORTHERLY, Churchill, B 443-885-4022 224 F churchill.wortherly@morgan.edu
WORTHINGTON, Evelyn 956-380-8183 493 A eworthington@riogrande.edu
WORTHINGTON, Jacki 800-962-7682 293 B jworthington@wma.edu
WORTHINGTON, Joni 919-962-4929 377 A worthj@northcarolina.edu
WORTHINGTON, Roger, L 573-882-5838 291 D worthingtonr@missouri.edu
WORTHY, Mark 225-752-4233 208 L mworthy@iticollege.edu
WORTHY, Vernon 404-215-2666 134 A vworthy@morehouse.edu
WORTLEY, Gary 706-507-8043 127 D wortley_gary@columbusstate.edu
WORTMANN, Barbara 973-300-2124 315 F bwortmann@sussex.edu
WOSSUM, Doris, F 931-363-9895 470 E dwossum@martinmethodist.edu
WOTEN, Elizabeth 708-209-3528 148 C lizz.woten@cuchicago.edu
WOUGHTER, Kathy 607-871-2132 322 F woughter@alfred.edu
WOY, Robert 702-365-7690 302 D
WOZNEY, Nancee 507-453-2722 267 F nwozney@southeastmn.edu
WOZNIAK, Andrew 630-889-6878 159 E awozniak@nuhs.edu
WOZNIAK, Linda 570-945-8202 432 C linda.wozniak@keystone.edu
WOZNIAK, Thomas, P 413-782-1317 246 D twozniak@wne.edu
WOZNICK, Aimee 716-896-0700 359 F woznicka@villa.edu
WRASMAN, PHJC, Carleen 574-936-8898 168 I carleen.wrasman@ancilla.edu
WRAY, Chuck 704-922-6432 370 D wray.chuck@gaston.edu
WRAY, JR., James, M 859-280-1245 203 F swray@lextheo.edu
WRAY, Kyle 405-744-9082 410 C kyle.wray@okstate.edu
WRAY, Lois 804-862-6206 523 C lwray@rbc.edu
WRAY, Roger 434-949-1040 527 H roger.wray@southside.edu
WRAY, Theresa 818-386-5679 62 F twray@pgi.edu
WRAY, Virginia, F 870-307-7202 22 D vwray@lyon.edu
WRAY, Warren, K 573-341-4138 292 A wkwray@mst.edu
WREFORD, Paul, W 618-235-2700 165 B paul.wreford@swic.edu
WREN, Brent, M 256-824-6681 9 A brent.wren@uah.edu
WREN, Emily, C 317-274-4553 174 B ewren@iupui.edu
WREN, Jan 606-539-4328 206 G jan.wren@ucumberlands.edu
WREN, Lanell, E 530-221-4275 69 C lwren@shasta.edu
WREN, Richard 312-553-5641 146 H rwren@ccc.edu
WRENN, Christy 318-869-5059 208 F cwrenn@centenary.edu
WRENN, Donna, C 508-793-3391 233 D dwrenn@holycross.edu
WRENN, Will 910-296-1974 371 B wwrenn@jamessprunt.edu
WRIGHT, Adam 314-387-7000 19 C adam.wright@phoenix.edu
WRIGHT, Adam 214-333-5597 484 C adam@dbu.edu
WRIGHT, Adriene 305-626-1443 108 H adriene.wright@fmuniv.edu
WRIGHT, Alexis 843-355-4165 463 C wrighta@wiltech.edu
WRIGHT, Alexis, S 212-875-4422 323 E awright@bankstreet.edu
WRIGHT, Allison 212-247-3434 339 G awright@mandl.edu
WRIGHT, Andrew 417-836-5518 286 F
WRIGHT, Angie 478-757-5192 139 A awright@wesleyancollege.edu
WRIGHT, Anita 559-934-2144 77 H anitawright@whccd.edu
WRIGHT, Ann 515-244-4221 181 D wrighta@aib.edu
WRIGHT, Ardene, T 225-771-2680 214 H trisha_wright@subr.edu
WRIGHT, Arthuree, R 202-806-7234 98 B arwright@howard.edu
WRIGHT, Barbara 803-778-6695 455 G wrightb@cctech.edu
WRIGHT, Barbara 918-293-4952 410 E barbara.wright@okstate.edu
WRIGHT, Barbara 304-357-4813 541 H barbarawright@ucwv.edu
WRIGHT, Beth 817-272-3291 505 A b.wright@uta.edu
WRIGHT, Bob 425-388-9913 533 H rwright@everettcc.edu
WRIGHT, Bonnie, M 864-488-8318 459 A bwright@limestone.edu
WRIGHT, Brandon 801-622-1573 510 G brandon.wright@stevenshenager.edu
WRIGHT, Brant 248-689-8282 260 A bwright@walshcollege.edu
WRIGHT, Bruce, A 520-247-4645 19 B wrightb@email.arizona.edu
WRIGHT, Carl 318-274-2275 215 E wrightc@gram.edu
WRIGHT, Carol 918-781-7263 407 B wrightc@bacone.edu
WRIGHT, Cathleen 830-372-8078 499 C cwright@tlu.edu
WRIGHT, Cathy 770-254-7280 138 D cwright@westga.edu
WRIGHT, Cathy 502-213-7273 202 B catherine.wright@kctcs.edu
WRIGHT, Charles, W 803-938-3867 462 F wrightcw@uscsumter.edu
WRIGHT, Chatt, G 808-544-0202 140 B cwright@hpu.edu
WRIGHT, Claudia 830-758-5006 501 B crwright@sulross.edu
WRIGHT, Cory 718-270-4842 328 D cwright@mec.cuny.edu
WRIGHT, Craig, J 516-572-7121 342 C craig.wright@ncc.edu
WRIGHT, Dale, F 585-567-9321 336 B dale.wright@houghton.edu
WRIGHT, Daniel, W 386-763-2671 114 E daniel.wright@palmer.edu
WRIGHT, David 505-566-3837 320 D wrightd@sanjuancollege.edu
WRIGHT, David 336-386-8121 374 B wrightd@surry.edu
WRIGHT, David, A 610-738-0536 443 F dwright@wcupa.edu
WRIGHT, David, W 765-677-3060 174 E david.wright@indwes.edu
WRIGHT, David, W 717-337-6400 429 H dwright@gettysburg.edu
WRIGHT, Deborah, G 757-825-3527 528 B wrightd@tncc.edu
WRIGHT, Dee 515-271-4526 184 A dee.wright@drake.edu
WRIGHT, Denis, G 904-646-2005 109 E dwright@fscj.edu
WRIGHT, Don 559-651-2500 66 E donw@sjvc.edu
WRIGHT, Donna 270-789-5010 199 C dwright@campbellsville.edu
WRIGHT, Doris, N 870-230-5089 21 I wrightd@hsu.edu
WRIGHT, Earl 731-881-7733 477 E ewright@utm.edu
WRIGHT, Edwin, R 610-499-4281 451 F erwright@widener.edu
WRIGHT, Elizabeth, A 215-893-5279 426 E elizabeth.wright@curtis.edu
WRIGHT, Elizabeth, J 570-450-3503 439 J ejw12@psu.edu
WRIGHT, Fran 617-745-3723 234 C fran.c.wright@enc.edu
WRIGHT, Gary 404-215-2636 134 A gwright@morehouse.edu
WRIGHT, Gayla 509-359-6824 533 D gwright@ewu.edu
WRIGHT, George, C 936-261-2111 496 E gcwright@pvamu.edu
WRIGHT, Gregory, R 610-292-9852 445 D greg.wright@reseminary.edu
WRIGHT, III, Hervey 316-295-5803 192 H wright@friends.edu
WRIGHT, Irvin 570-389-4492 441 F iwright@bloomu.edu
WRIGHT, James 949-582-4820 70 F jwright@saddleback.edu
WRIGHT, James 510-659-6220 59 I jwright@ohlone.edu
WRIGHT, Jason 315-568-3268 342 H jwright@nycc.edu
WRIGHT, Jeffrey 207-326-2215 219 D jeff.wright@mma.edu
WRIGHT, Jeffrey 802-287-8395 513 D jwright@greenmtn.edu
WRIGHT, Jeffrey, E 765-641-4544 169 A jewright@anderson.edu
WRIGHT, Jill 309-694-5361 152 B jwright@icc.edu
WRIGHT, Jimmy 606-886-3863 201 C jimmy.wright@kctcs.edu
WRIGHT, Jo Rae 919-681-3257 363 I jrwright@duke.edu
WRIGHT, Joann 708-974-5358 159 A wright@morainevalley.edu
WRIGHT, John 207-780-4485 220 G jwright@usm.maine.edu
WRIGHT, John 845-561-0800 342 A john.wright@msmc.edu
WRIGHT, John, E 304-336-8180 544 B jewright@westliberty.edu
WRIGHT, John, W 352-392-0466 120 B jwright@jou.ufl.edu
WRIGHT, Julie 573-288-6640 281 D jwright@culver.edu
WRIGHT, Karen, F 270-384-7313 203 H wrightk@lindsey.edu
WRIGHT, Karen, M 606-679-8501 202 F karen.wright@kctcs.edu
WRIGHT, Karl 340-692-4021 568 C kwright@uvi.edu
WRIGHT, Kay 979-230-3377 482 B kay.wright@brazosport.edu
WRIGHT, Keith 770-619-3647 128 G kwright@devry.edu
WRIGHT, Keith 703-414-4129 518 B kwright@devry.edu
WRIGHT, Kristine, A 612-626-0302 272 D wrigh084@umn.edu
WRIGHT, Larisa 513-244-4414 388 D larisa_wright@mail.msj.edu
WRIGHT, LeAnne 903-223-3078 498 C leanne.wright@tamut.edu
WRIGHT, Leroy 231-591-2686 251 B wrightl@ferris.edu
WRIGHT, Linda 717-901-5112 430 F LWright@HarrisburgU.net
WRIGHT, Logan, S 816-483-9600 289 H lswright@spst.edu
WRIGHT, Lori 216-791-5000 388 B lxw21@case.edu
WRIGHT, Lynn, C 304-724-3700 540 C lwright@apus.edu
WRIGHT, Matt 706-419-1556 127 F
WRIGHT, Matthew 615-322-2451 477 F matthew.wright@vanderbilt.edu
WRIGHT, May, F 270-824-8649 202 C may.wright@kctcs.edu
WRIGHT, Meghan 828-898-8729 366 A wrightm@lmc.edu
WRIGHT, Michael 660-543-4272 291 B mwright@ucmo.edu
WRIGHT, Michael 229-931-2351 136 G mwright@southgatech.edu
WRIGHT, Michael, G 313-577-8155 260 D dx2558@wayne.edu
WRIGHT, Mike 717-757-1100 452 I mike.wright@yti.edu
WRIGHT, Milton 773-838-7606 147 E mwright@ccc.edu
WRIGHT, Nathan 218-322-2323 267 A nathan.wright@itascacc.edu
WRIGHT, III, Neil, W 859-622-1478 200 D neil.wright@eku.edu
WRIGHT, Norman 801-863-8239 511 C norman.wright@uvu.edu
WRIGHT, Nova 540-863-2868 526 B nwright@dslcc.edu
WRIGHT, Paul 610-902-8562 423 H paul.r.wright@cabrini.edu
WRIGHT, Paul, G 727-816-3466 114 F wrightp@phcc.edu
WRIGHT, Peter 603-228-1541 306 G peter.wright@law.unh.edu
WRIGHT, Phil 503-584-7261 414 J phil.wright@chemeketa.edu
WRIGHT, Randy 314-968-6918 293 A wrightra@webster.edu
WRIGHT, Raymond, M 401-874-2186 454 E wrightr@egr.uri.edu
WRIGHT, Renee 814-838-7673 429 B
WRIGHT, Rick 863-638-2918 123 C wrightrm@webber.edu
WRIGHT, Rick, L 785-539-3571 194 G rwright@mcck.edu
WRIGHT, Robert 602-383-8228 19 A rwright@uat.edu
WRIGHT, Robert 304-624-7695 541 L rwright@wvbc.edu
WRIGHT, Robert, E 936-468-2605 495 H wrightre@sfasu.edu
WRIGHT, Robin 859-441-4500 201 G robin.wright@kctcs.edu
WRIGHT, Rodner, B 850-599-3244 118 G rodner.wright@famu.edu
WRIGHT, Ron 337-550-1307 212 H
WRIGHT, Ron 504-762-3000 210 G rwrigh@dcc.edu
WRIGHT, Russell 206-393-3557 530 G rwwright@argosy.edu
WRIGHT, Sean 205-726-4591 6 G swright@samford.edu
WRIGHT, Shelly, A 845-257-3291 352 B wrights@newpaltz.edu
WRIGHT, Sheri 760-757-2121 57 E swright@miracosta.edu
WRIGHT, Sherry 870-230-5352 21 I wrights@hsu.edu
WRIGHT, Sonia 707-253-3378 58 F swright@napavalley.edu
WRIGHT, Stan 318-357-5716 216 B ralphw@nsula.edu
WRIGHT, Stephanie 336-334-4822 370 E swweeks@gtcc.edu
WRIGHT, Susan 515-271-3623 184 A susan.wright@drake.edu
WRIGHT, Susan, F 716-878-4301 353 A orrsf@buffalostate.edu
WRIGHT, Theo 504-394-7744 214 A twright@olhcc.edu
WRIGHT, Thomas 518-828-4181 330 E wright@sunycgcc.edu
WRIGHT, Thomas 423-473-2750 474 E twright@clevelandstatecc.edu
WRIGHT, Tim 910-592-8081 373 D twright@sampsoncc.edu
WRIGHT, Timothy, S 863-680-4297 109 D twright@flsouthern.edu
WRIGHT, Travis, E 919-761-2278 376 G twright@sebts.edu

YAMAMOTO, Louise 808-734-9513 141 E
yamamotl@hawaii.edu
YAMAMOTO, Roy 808-675-3406 139 I
roy.yamamoto@byuh.edu
YAMAMURA, Whitney 916-691-7326 56 B
yamamuw@crc.losrios.edu
YAMANE, Noreen 808-974-7659 141 F
noreeny@hawaii.edu
YAMAUCHI, Kent 626-585-7273 61 E
ktyamauchi@pasadena.edu
YAMAWAKI, Hideki 909-607-8494 40 C
hideki.yamawaki@cgu.edu
YAMBA, Mohamed 724-938-4240 441 G
yamba@calu.edu
YAMEEN, Deanna 508-588-9100 240 E
YAMILKOSKI, Vince, J 770-534-6134 126 B
vyamilkoski@brenau.edu
YAMÍN, Isabel 787-728-1515 568 B
iyamin@sagrado.edu
YAN, Raymond 425-558-0299 533 C
ryan@digipen.edu
YAN, Ruth 319-226-2080 181 E
yanl2@ihs.org
YANCEY, Gary 850-729-5364 114 A
yanceyg@nwfsc.edu
YANCEY, Jennifer, L 361-582-2519 507 G
jennifer.yancey@victoriacollege.edu
YANCEY, John 904-620-2638 120 C
jyancey@unf.edu
YANCEY, Laurica 252-398-6454 363 E
yancel@chowan.edu
YANCHAK, Frank 614-947-6723 391 A
yanchakf@franklin.edu
YANCHICK, Victor, A 804-828-3006 525 E
vyanchick@vcu.edu
YANCKELLO, Robert 407-823-2711 120 A
bob.yanckello@ucf.edu
YANDA, Alan 503-228-6528 414 E
ayanda@aii.edu
YANG, Alan, I 808-956-7408 141 B
alany@hawaii.edu
YANG, Alice 831-459-2328 75 A
ayang@ucsc.edu
YANG, Henry, T 805-893-2231 74 F
henry.yang@chancellor.ucsb.edu
YANG, Hong 401-232-6885 453 A
hyang@bryant.edu
YANG, Honggang 954-262-3048 114 B
yang@nsu.nova.edu
YANG, Kuan 281-487-1170 498 E
kyang@txchiro.edu
YANG, Neng 503-838-8590 419 C
yangn@wou.edu
YANG, Nicole 920-693-1120 554 A
nicole.yang@gotoltc.edu
YANG, Olivia 509-335-5571 539 A
olivia.yang@wsu.edu
YANG, Steve 651-450-3330 266 I
syang@inverhills.edu
YANG, Xuemei 541-684-7318 417 F
yxm@northwestchristian.edu
YANG, Zhahui 626-448-0023 51 H
zyang@itsla.edu
YANISH, Paula 970-339-6537 80 G
paula.yanish@aims.edu
YANKE, Gaylyn 505-287-6633 319 H
gyanke@nmsu.edu
YANKELEWITZ, Yoel 718-846-1940 361 F
yyankelewitz@gmail.com
YANKELITIS, Wendy 570-348-6201 435 F
yankelitis@marywood.edu
YANKEY, Terry, L 606-474-3222 200 J
tly@kcu.edu
YANNA, Dan 304-876-5236 544 A
dyanna@shepherd.edu
YANNICK, Lisa 610-436-3075 443 F
lyannick@wcupa.edu
YANNIELLO, Michael, C 516-876-3146 353 D
yanniellom@oldwestbury.edu
YANNUZZI, Raymond 856-227-7200 308 E
ryannuzzi@camdencc.edu
YAO, Min 858-534-3396 74 D
myao@ucsd.edu
YAQUB, Samia 530-895-2203 31 E
yaqubsa@butte.edu
YAQUINTA, Donald 304-243-2044 545 G
dony@wju.edu
YARBERRY, Cindy 406-444-6897 295 C
yarberryc@umhelena.edu
YARBERRY, Megan, J 808-885-9226 140 I
YARBOROUGH, Josh 615-525-2800 466 I
jyarbrough@argosy.edu
YARBROUGH, Boyd 864-294-2216 458 D
boyd.yarbrough@furman.edu
YARBROUGH, David 707-546-4000 45 G
dyarbrough@empirecollege.com
YARBROUGH, David 337-482-1015 216 D
yarbrough@louisiana.edu
YARBROUGH, Howard 423-697-4785 474 D
YARBROUGH, J. Keith 432-552-2415 507 C
yarbrough_k@utpb.edu
YARBROUGH, Keva 770-650-3000 99 D
YARBROUGH, Laura 870-762-3105 20 A
lyarbrough@smail.anc.edu
YARBROUGH, Laura, L 336-249-8186 369 F
llyarbro@davidsoncc.edu
YARBROUGH, Mark, M 214-841-3460 485 E
myarbrough@dts.edu
YARBROUGH, Nancy, J 731-881-7800 477 E
nyarbrough@utm.edu
YARBROUGH, Nancy, J 731-881-7805 477 E
nyarbrough@utm.edu
YARBROUGH, Sharon, L 865-694-6526 475 F
slyarbrough@pstcc.edu
YARDE, Winston 718-281-5212 329 A
wyarde@qcc.cuny.edu
YARDLEY, Katherine, W 207-778-7153 220 C
kyardley@maine.edu
YARDLEY, Owen 402-472-3555 300 H
oyardley2@unl.edu
YARKIN, Cherisa 206-587-6903 537 A
cyarkin@sccd.ctc.edu
YARLOTT, JR., David 406-638-3107 294 G
davidyarlott@lbhc.cc.mt.us
YARNELL, Allen, L 406-994-2826 295 E
ayarnell@montana.edu
YARNELL, Thomas, V 614-823-1502 400 G
tyarnell@otterbein.edu
YARRISH, Julie 310-434-3762 68 D
yarrish_julie@smc.edu
YASBIN, Ronald 314-516-5504 291 F
yasbinr@umsl.edu
YASECKO, Susan 847-543-2218 147 H
syasecko@clcillinois.edu
YASINSAC, Alec 251-460-6390 9 E
yasinsac@usouthal.edu
YASINSKI, W. Arnold 503-370-6728 421 C
ayasinski@willamette.edu
YASMAN, Shannon 805-493-3838 32 H
yasman@clunet.edu
YASSIN, Raef 954-499-9777 104 C
ryassin@devry.edu
YASUDA, Cathy 541-881-5585 420 E
cyasuda@tvcc.cc
YASUHARA, Eri, F 909-537-5800 36 A
eyasuha@csusb.edu
YASUHARA, June 808-739-4603 140 A
jyasuhar@chaminade.edu
YATES, Bill 228-497-9602 275 G
george.yates@mgccc.edu
YATES, Brian 434-592-4108 520 F
bcyates@liberty.edu
YATES, Dorothy, C 307-766-5320 556 E
dyates4@uwyo.edu
YATES, Emma 310-423-6252 38 I
YATES, Frances 765-973-8470 173 D
fyates@iue.edu
YATES, James 918-647-1230 407 E
jyates@carlalbert.edu
YATES, Kristin 402-472-5242 300 F
kyates@nebraska.edu
YATES, Lucian 936-261-3600 496 E
lyates@pvamu.edu
YATES, Mark 903-923-2339 486 D
myates@etbu.edu
YATES, Marvin, L 985-549-5250 216 C
myates@selu.edu
YATES, Melodie 216-687-0389 388 C
m.yates@csuohio.edu
YATES, Patricia, A 978-934-2355 237 F
patricia_yates@uml.edu
YATES, Susan 559-442-4600 72 A
susan.yates@fresnocitycollege.edu
YATES, Todd 210-431-4217 493 C
tyates@stmarytx.edu
YATES, Yvonne 270-247-8521 204 C
yyates@midcontinent.edu
YATES-MATTINGLY, Shelia 516-745-5769 403 F
shelia.yates@uc.edu
YATIM, Fouad 617-570-4855 245 E
fyatim@suffolk.edu
YATS, Kirk, M 989-774-3674 249 G
yats1km@cmich.edu
YAU, Lishan 864-294-3609 458 D
lishan.yau@furman.edu
YAU, Yeeka 919-658-7708 367 D
yyau@moc.edu
YAUGHN, Valerie, E 912-201-8000 136 H
vyaughn@southuniversity.edu
YAUN, John 304-696-3152 543 G
yaun@marshall.edu
YAUNEY, Alan, J 518-381-1256 350 E
yauneyaj@sunysccc.edu
YAW, Brian 503-255-0332 417 C
byaw@multnomah.edu
YAW, Edward, J 973-328-5031 309 B
eyaw@ccm.edu
YAW, Steve 574-257-3346 169 F
yaws@bethelcollege.edu
YAZDANI, Linda 303-914-6536 87 C
linda.yazdani@rrcc.edu
YAZDI, Aliakbar, R 205-853-1200 5 C
ayazdi@jeffstateonline.com
YBANEZ, Elsa 210-436-3725 493 C
eybanez@stmarytx.edu
YBARRA, Tomas 509-574-4640 540 A
tybarra@yvcc.edu
YBARRONDO, Brent 719-587-7481 80 F
baybarro@adams.edu
YDOYAGA, Shannon 972-238-6376 485 C
shannony@dcccd.edu
YE, Michael, H 240-895-4696 226 A
mhye@smcm.edu
YEAGER, Brad 303-937-4290 82 A
byeager@chu.edu
YEAGER, Brad 303-937-4200 82 A
byeager@chu.edu
YEAGER, Carolyn, G 717-245-1686 427 E
yeager@dickinson.edu
YEAGER, Clark 503-768-7548 416 F
yeager@lclark.edu
YEAGER, David 812-866-7076 171 F
yeagerd@hanover.edu
YEAGER, Eric 972-599-3121 483 D
eyeager@collin.edu
YEAGER, Michelle 314-652-0300 288 H
myeager@slchcmail.com
YEAGER, Phyllis 859-442-1150 201 G
phyllis.yeager@kctcs.edu
YEAGER, Robert, E 812-749-1210 178 D
ryeager@oak.edu
YEAGLE, Philip, L 973-353-5213 314 E
pyeagle@andromeda.rutgers.edu
YEAGLEY, William 989-774-3081 249 G
yeagl1b@cmich.edu
YEAKEL, Lois, M 610-799-1961 434 D
lyeakel@lccc.edu
YEAKLEY, Randall 903-233-3808 489 K
randyyeakley@letu.edu
YEARWOOD, George, A 919-508-2035 375 D
ryearwood@peace.edu
YEATTS, Beth, A 330-941-3142 406 F
bayeatts@ysu.edu
YEATTS, Debra 910-630-7385 366 H
dyeatts@methodist.edu
YEATTS, George, D 843-953-5304 456 C
dewey.yeatts@citadel.edu
YEAZEL, Bill 913-288-7690 193 J
yeazel@kckcc.edu
YEAZELL, Stephen, C 310-825-8404 74 A
yeazell@law.ucla.edu
YECK, Laura 254-647-3237 492 E
lyeck@rangercollege.edu
YEE, Atom 408-554-4455 68 C
ayee@scu.edu
YEE, Carole 818-947-2326 55 E
yeec@lavc.edu
YEE, David 415-239-3669 39 H
dyee@ccsf.edu
YEE, Elena 805-565-6132 78 F
eyee@westmont.edu
YEE, Robert 617-989-4590 246 C
yeer@wit.edu
YEE, Sandra, G 313-577-4020 260 D
aj0533@wayne.edu
YEE, Shirley, W 412-291-6246 422 D
syee@aii.edu
YEH, Elizabeth 612-659-6306 267 E
elizabeth.yeh@minneapolis.edu
YEH, Frank 662-252-8000 277 C
fyeh@rustcollege.edu
YEH, Li-An 919-530-7001 378 A
lyeh@nccu.edu
YEHL, Robert, F 870-230-5014 21 I
yehlb@hsu.edu
YEHUDAH, Shoshana 212-463-0400 357 J
shulys@touro.edu
YEIGH, Bjong, W 315-792-7400 354 F
wolf.yeigh@sunyit.edu
YEIGH, Bjong, W 315-792-7400 356 B
wolf.yeigh@sunyit.edu
YEKEL, Herb 219-473-4227 170 D
hyekel@ccsj.edu
YEKOVICH, Robert 713-348-4837 492 J
yekovr@rice.edu
YELIN, Louise 914-251-6550 354 D
louise.yelin@purchase.edu
YELLE, Dave 413-565-1000 231 B
dyelle@baypath.edu
YELLE, Richard, W 203-576-4222 94 D
ryelle@bridgeport.edu
YELLEN, David, N 312-915-7120 157 A
dyellen@luc.edu
YELNOSKY, Robert, E 814-641-3707 431 L
yelnosr@juniata.edu
YELTON, Shauna, N 205-726-2835 6 G
snyelton@samford.edu
YELVINGTON, Philip, R 901-321-3396 467 G
pyelving@cbu.edu
YELVINGTON, Sherry 901-272-5125 471 B
syelvington@mca.edu
YEN, Charlie 310-434-3002 68 D
yen_charlie@smc.edu
YEN, Flora, B 916-568-3132 55 J
yenf@losrios.edu
YEN, Johanna, C 954-763-9840 101 A
atom@atom.edu
YEN, S.C. Max 260-481-6839 174 A
yens@ipfw.edu
YENA, John, A 401-598-1100 453 C
jyena@jwu.edu
YENCHA, Tom 304-424-8309 545 B
tom.yencha@mail.wvu.edu
YENSAN, Lester, K 401-874-5371 454 E
yensan@mail.uri.edu
YENSON, Evelyn 206-934-3227 536 G
evelyn.yenson@seattlecolleges.edu
YENTES, Matt 863-638-2963 123 C
yentesms@webber.edu
YEO, Frederick, L 920-424-3322 551 D
yeof@uwosh.edu
YEOMAN, Matlynn, B 910-642-7141 373 G
myeoman@sccnc.edu
YEOMANS, Jennifer 603-888-1311 305 G
jyeomans@rivier.edu
YEONOPOLUS, Jim 254-526-1781 482 F
jim.yeonopolus@ctcd.edu
YEP, Katie 651-846-1372 269 E
katie.yep@saintpaul.edu
YEPES, Maria, E 323-265-8957 54 G
yepesme@elac.edu
YEPES, Maria Elena 323-265-8957 54 G
yepesme@elac.edu
YERGER, Linda 360-475-7300 535 J
lyerger@olympic.edu
YERGER, Mark 570-577-1795 423 D
mark.yerger@bucknell.edu
YERGER, Stacy 610-796-8317 421 F
stacy.yerger@alvernia.edu
YERK, Melanie 239-939-4766 118 D
myerk@swfc.edu
YESKEVICZ, Bevin 334-277-3390 3 F
bevin.yeskevicz@vc.edu
YESSO, John, M 440-964-4343 393 E
jyesso@kent.edu
YESTRAMSKI, Joanne 978-934-3450 237 F
Joanne_Yestramski@uml.edu
YETMAN, Barbara, H 215-968-8045 423 E
yetmanb@bucks.edu
YETMAR, Theresa 785-594-8316 190 C
theresa.yetmar@bakeru.edu
YEVIN, G. Bernard 336-734-7224 370 C
byevin@forsythtech.edu
YEW, Phillip 213-487-0110 45 C
chinese@dula.edu
YIANOUKOS, Steven, J 315-268-6622 329 C
stevey@clarkson.edu
YIGZAW, Erika 503-244-0726 414 D
erikayigzaw@achs.edu
YIH, T, C 562-985-5314 35 A
yih@csulb.edu
YIN, Kong 713-221-8975 503 D
YinK@uhd.edu
YINGLING, Julie, R 419-434-4550 404 B
yinglingj@findlay.edu
YINGLING, Kevin, W 304-696-3170 543 G
YIP, Yunny 415-749-4524 65 I
yyip@sfai.edu
YIRKA, Carl, A 802-831-1443 515 A
cyirka@vermontlaw.edu
YLINEN, Jeff 612-374-5800 263 I
jylinen@dunwoody.edu
YOACHIM, Maureen 610-740-3725 424 I
bookstore@cedarcrest.edu
YOAKUM, Katrina, M 785-864-3261 196 F
kyoakum@ku.edu
YOANNONE, Carol 412-237-4421 425 H
cyoannone@ccac.edu
YOCHUM, Denise 253-964-6776 536 C
dyochum@pierce.ctc.edu
YOCHUM, Gilbert, R 757-683-3521 521 L
gyochum@odu.edu
YOCKEY, Glenn 830-372-8040 499 C
gyockey@tlu.edu
YOCOM, Jim 574-520-4806 174 C
jyocom@iusb.edu
YOCUM, Stephanie 559-730-3988 42 B
stephaniey@cos.edu
YODER, Alfred 740-857-1311 401 F
ayoder@rosedale.edu
YODER, Anita, R 574-535-7114 171 D
anitay@goshen.edu
YODER, Brad, L 260-422-5561 172 L
blyoder@indianatech.edu
YODER, Brent 620-327-8231 193 C
brenty@hesston.edu
YODER, Chris, K 610-341-5840 428 D
ckuhl@eastern.edu
YODER, Dan 541-440-4600 420 F
dan.yoder@umpqua.edu
YODER, Donna, K 814-886-6368 437 A
dyoder@mtaloy.edu
YODER, Ernest 989-774-7570 249 G
yoder1el@cmich.edu
YODER, James, A 508-289-2252 247 A
jyoder@whoi.edu
YODER, Janette, K 574-535-7545 171 D
janetteky@goshen.edu
YODER, Julie 301-387-3101 222 H
julie.yoder@garrettcollege.edu
YODER, Kathleen 937-484-1353 405 A
registrar@urbana.edu
YODER, Ken 619-201-8692 65 D
Ken.Yoder@sdcc.edu

YODER, Mari 419-267-1268 397 D myoder@northweststate.edu
YODER, Norris 828-328-7145 366 B norris.yoder@lr.edu
YODER, Robert, E 574-535-7244 171 D robertey@goshen.edu
YODER, Twila, K 540-432-4100 518 E yodertk@emu.edu
YOHE, Roger 480-461-7151 15 K roger.yohe@mcmail.maricopa.edu
YOHNK, Dean 262-595-2188 551 E yohnk@uwp.edu
YOHO, Robert 515-271-1464 183 F robert.yoho@dmu.edu
YOHO, Steven, K 912-201-8105 136 H syoho@southuniversity.edu
YOIA, Dominic 203-582-5224 93 E dominic.yoia@quinnipiac.edu
YOK, Larry 206-878-3710 534 E lyok@highline.edu
YOKLIC, Deborah 520-206-4650 17 I dyoklic@pima.edu
YOKOTOBI, Fusako 760-245-4271 77 E Fusako.Yokotobi@vvc.edu
YOKOYAMA, Janis, K 213-738-6714 71 D deansoffice@swlaw.edu
YOLITZ, Brian, D 651-201-1777 265 H brian.yolitz@so.mnscu.edu
YON, Larry 704-216-3541 373 C larry.yon@rccc.edu
YONAN, Jonathan 610-225-5704 428 D jyonan@eastern.edu
YONEMITSU, Lori 206-546-4552 537 G lyonemitsu@shoreline.edu
YONG, Henry, C 408-270-6471 67 B henry.yong@evc.edu
YONG, Yan Yan 540-834-1048 526 E yyong@germanna.edu
YONGUE, Marelle 337-482-6826 216 D darlene@louisiana.edu
YONKERS, Molly 507-933-7588 264 B
YONUTAS, Dave 352-395-5379 117 E dave.yonutas@sfcollege.edu
YOON, Michelle 562-926-1023 63 B
YOON, Victor 770-279-0507 129 E dryoon@gcuniv.edu
YOON, Youngjune 213-381-2221 64 I koreandean@samra.edu
YOPP, Jan 919-962-8266 378 D jan_yopp@unc.edu
YOPP, John 859-257-2756 206 H jyopp@uky.edu
YORDAN, Carlos 973-408-3365 309 F cyordan@drew.edu
YORK, A. Jerome 210-567-7050 506 E york@uthscsa.edu
YORK, Aaron 903-875-7328 491 B aaron.york@navarrocollege.edu
YORK, Allison 319-398-4998 186 H ayork@kirkwood.edu
YORK, Brenda 406-994-2824 295 E byork@montana.edu
YORK, Corey 914-251-6080 354 D corey.york@purchase.edu
YORK, David 512-492-3032 480 F dyork@aoma.edu
YORK, Guy, L 352-395-5164 117 E guy.york@sfcollege.edu
YORK-LEMELIN, Lisa 207-453-5128 218 I lyork@kvcc.me.edu
YORKER, Beatrice 323-343-4600 35 B byorker@calstatela.edu
YORTSOS, Yannis, C 213-740-0617 76 C yortsos@usc.edu
YOSHIDA, James 808-974-7658 141 F jamesyos@hawaii.edu
YOSHIKAWA, Naoto 808-983-4105 140 C yoshinao@tokai.edu
YOSHIMURA, Nancy 949-480-4045 69 I nyoshimura@soka.edu
YOSHINA, Eileen 360-596-5383 538 B eyoshina@spscc.ctc.edu
YOSHINO, Lori 909-621-8856 62 H lori_yoshino@pitzer.edu
YOST, Edward 703-339-3041 99 D edward.yost@strayer.edu
YOST, Kathy 253-589-5602 532 B kathy.yost@cptc.edu
YOST, Robert, A 704-334-6882 367 E ryost@nlts.edu
YOU, Nancy 714-816-0366 72 I nyou@tuiu.edu
YOUATT, June, P 517-432-1075 255 D youatt@msu.edu
YOUHOUSE, John 610-558-5518 437 C youhousej@neumann.edu
YOUMANS, Art 201-761-7403 314 F ayoumans@spc.edu
YOUNCE, Thomas, C 919-515-3000 378 B tom_younce@ncsu.edu
YOUNESSI, Houman 860-548-7880 93 F youneh@rpi.edu
YOUNG, Al 205-929-3424 5 E ayoung@lawsonstate.edu
YOUNG, Alan, E 802-773-5900 513 B
YOUNG, Alissa 270-707-3717 202 A alissa.young@kctcs.edu
YOUNG, Amanda 864-644-5558 461 B ayoung@swu.edu
YOUNG, Amber 954-923-4440 112 K financial@keycollege.edu
YOUNG, Amy 973-278-5400 307 G amy@berkeleycollege.edu
YOUNG, Andrew 812-888-4323 181 B ayoung@vinu.edu
YOUNG, Ann, S 859-238-5480 199 D ann.young@centre.edu
YOUNG, Barbara 662-562-3202 276 E ba_young@northwestms.edu
YOUNG, Benjamin 317-916-7918 175 G byoung@ivytech.edu
YOUNG, Beth 815-825-2086 155 C beth.young@kishwaukeecollege.edu
YOUNG, Betty 478-553-2090 134 F byoung@oftc.edu
YOUNG, Betty, K 713-718-7628 487 G betty.young@hccs.edu
YOUNG, Bradley, J 310-233-4066 54 I youngbj@lahc.edu
YOUNG, Brandon 815-288-5561 155 H brandon.young@doc.illinois.gov
YOUNG, Brenda 626-815-4527 30 E byoung@apu.edu
YOUNG, Brian, A 402-280-2121 297 H bay@creighton.edu
YOUNG, Carol 724-852-3332 451 B cyoung@waynesburg.edu
YOUNG, Cathy 617-912-9139 232 E cyoung@bostonconservatory.edu
YOUNG, Charles 910-879-5561 368 A cyoung@bladencc.edu
YOUNG, Charlotte 321-674-7400 108 E cyoung@fit.edu
YOUNG, Cheryl, D 513-529-8600 396 D youngcd@muohio.edu
YOUNG, Clifford 909-537-5717 36 A cyoung@csusb.edu
YOUNG, Connie 217-554-6899 156 A cyoung@lakeviewcol.edu
YOUNG, Dallin 435-652-7571 512 A youngdal@dixie.edu
YOUNG, Dan 336-316-2898 364 E youngfd@guilford.edu
YOUNG, Dana 541-881-5580 420 E dyoung@tvcc.cc
YOUNG, Danielle 440-775-8692 397 F danielle.young@oberlin.edu
YOUNG, Darlene, P 812-941-2306 174 D dyoung01@ius.edu
YOUNG, David 270-237-3577 200 B dayoung@daymarcollege.edu
YOUNG, David, A 602-496-1446 12 B david.young@asu.edu
YOUNG, David, L 434-582-2071 520 F dlyoung@liberty.edu
YOUNG, Deborah 606-589-3323 203 A deborah.young@kctcs.edu
YOUNG, Deborah 718-270-6059 328 D young@mec.cuny.edu
YOUNG, Denise 706-867-3281 134 D dyoung@northgeorgia.edu
YOUNG, Dennis 513-244-4727 388 D dennis_young@mail.msj.edu
YOUNG, Djuana 713-743-9570 503 B ddyoung@uh.edu
YOUNG, Donald, R 336-744-0900 362 H don@carolina.edu
YOUNG, Donna 480-423-6300 16 D donna.young@sccmail.maricopa.edu
YOUNG, Doug 937-484-1308 405 A dyoung@urbana.edu
YOUNG, Eldon 714-484-7177 59 C eyoung@cypresscollege.edu
YOUNG, Evelyn 661-654-2241 33 H eyoung3@csub.edu
YOUNG, F. Rick 662-476-8442 274 D ryoung@eastms.edu
YOUNG, F. Russell 601-928-6205 275 G russell.young@mgccc.edu
YOUNG, Gary 406-247-3009 295 F gyoung@msubillings.edu
YOUNG, Gary 406-657-2367 295 F gyoung@msubillings.edu
YOUNG, Gary, R 318-869-5746 208 F gryoung@centenary.edu
YOUNG, Gene 936-294-1510 501 A young@shsu.edu
YOUNG, Gerald 507-222-4056 262 B gyoung@carleton.edu
YOUNG, Gwyn 601-643-8318 274 A gwyn.young@colin.edu
YOUNG, Harry, A 215-204-3317 447 G harry.young@temple.edu
YOUNG, Hester 843-863-8020 456 B hyoung@csuniv.edu
YOUNG, J, A 540-828-5706 516 K jyoung@bridgewater.edu
YOUNG, J.R 412-536-1100 432 F JR.young@laroche.edu
YOUNG, Jackie 502-585-7130 205 I jyoung04@spalding.edu
YOUNG, James 708-656-8000 159 C james.young@morton.edu
YOUNG, James, B 847-491-8542 160 D jbyoung@northwestern.edu
YOUNG, Jan 435-613-5205 511 E jan.young@ceu.edu
YOUNG, Janet 209-228-4419 74 B JYoung@UCMerced.edu
YOUNG, Jay 614-251-4715 398 F youngj@ohiodominican.edu
YOUNG, Jeff 931-372-3311 474 B jyoung@tntech.edu
YOUNG, Jessica 970-943-3045 89 B jyoung@western.edu
YOUNG, Joanna, C 603-862-3530 306 E joanna.young@unh.edu
YOUNG, John 973-328-5026 309 B jyoung@ccm.edu
YOUNG, John 315-781-3748 335 G jyoung@hws.edu
YOUNG, John 303-360-4707 83 E john.young@ccaurora.edu
YOUNG, John 937-327-7800 406 B jyoung@wittenberg.edu
YOUNG, John, O 203-392-6275 91 I youngj1@southernct.edu
YOUNG, John, O 989-837-4423 257 A young@northwood.edu
YOUNG, John, W 770-720-5522 135 F jyw@reinhardt.edu
YOUNG, Johnny 810-762-3456 259 F jyung@umflint.edu
YOUNG, Jon 910-672-1460 377 E jyoung@uncfsu.edu
YOUNG, Jonathan 804-524-5987 529 C jyoung@vsu.edu
YOUNG, Jordan, M 802-862-9616 512 H jyoung@burlington.edu
YOUNG, Joseph 619-388-7672 65 H jyoung@sdccd.edu
YOUNG, Julian, M 843-661-1228 458 C jyoung@fmarion.edu
YOUNG, K. Richard 801-422-3094 509 D richard_young@byu.edu
YOUNG, JR., Karl, J 985-380-2436 211 K kyoung@ltc.edu
YOUNG, Kay 817-598-6303 508 C kyoung@wc.edu
YOUNG, Kay, F 508-213-2114 243 J kay.young@nichols.edu
YOUNG, Kelly 325-674-2795 478 H kelly.young@acu.edu
YOUNG, Kenneth 516-678-8000 341 F kyoung@molloy.edu
YOUNG, Kerry, A 315-786-2279 337 F kyoung@sunyjefferson.edu
YOUNG, Kimberly 760-252-2411 30 F kyoung@barstow.edu
YOUNG, Kristen 702-895-0143 302 K kristen.young@unlv.edu
YOUNG, Kristine 775-881-7509 303 E kyoung@sierranevada.edu
YOUNG, Kristine, M 217-351-2542 161 B kyoung@parkland.edu
YOUNG, Laura, R 336-334-4374 379 A lryoung2@uncg.edu
YOUNG, Lavern 312-949-7430 152 D lyoung@ico.edu
YOUNG, Lester, C 909-869-2204 33 G lcyoung@csupomona.edu
YOUNG, Linda, C 334-556-2234 4 A lyoung@wallace.edu
YOUNG, Linda, K 512-223-7889 481 B lyoung@austincc.edu
YOUNG, Linda, L 440-826-2127 384 H lyoung@bw.edu
YOUNG, Lisa 718-270-5000 328 D lisa@mec.cuny.edu
YOUNG, Llewellyn 928-344-7517 12 C llewellyn.young@azwestern.edu
YOUNG, Lloyd, Y 313-577-1574 260 D eg1264@wayne.edu
YOUNG, Margaret 505-454-3522 318 I young_m@nmhu.edu
YOUNG, Margaret 337-550-1203 212 H myoung@lsue.edu
YOUNG, Marie 814-472-3022 446 B myoung@francis.edu
YOUNG, Marilyn 803-376-5737 455 B myoung@allenuniversity.edu
YOUNG, Marilyn, C 803-376-5827 455 B myoung@allenuniversity.edu
YOUNG, Mark, S 303-762-6902 83 I president@denverseminary.edu
YOUNG, Mary 603-513-1307 306 H mary.young@granite.edu
YOUNG, Melanie 610-328-8397 447 E myoung1@swarthmore.edu
YOUNG, Michael 508-531-1704 238 B myoung@bridgew.edu
YOUNG, Michael 212-674-2600 58 J
YOUNG, Michael, D 805-893-3651 74 F michael.young@sa.ucsb.edu
YOUNG, Michael, E 270-809-6831 204 F mike.young@murraystate.edu
YOUNG, Michael, K 206-543-5010 538 F president@uw.edu
YOUNG, Michael, W 212-327-8000 347 H michael.young@rockefeller.edu
YOUNG, Michelle, L 315-268-4268 329 C myoung@clarkson.edu
YOUNG, Mike 719-502-2403 86 G michael.young@ppcc.edu
YOUNG, Miles 903-434-8146 491 D mgyoung@ntcc.edu
YOUNG, Misty 573-681-5580 284 B youngm@lincolnu.edu
YOUNG, Monty 215-646-7300 430 C young.monty@gmc.edu
YOUNG, Nancy 620-242-0427 194 H youngn@mcpherson.edu
YOUNG, Nancy 410-455-2393 227 D nyoung@umbc.edu
YOUNG, Nancy, N 336-750-8764 380 A youngnn@wssu.edu
YOUNG, Nicole 731-989-6768 468 K nyoung@fhu.edu
YOUNG, Norman 860-768-7819 95 A young@hartford.edu
YOUNG, Paul, J 740-588-1225 407 A pyoung@zanestate.edu
YOUNG, Paul, R 307-674-6446 556 C pyoung@sheridan.edu
YOUNG, Peter, C 240-684-5268 227 F cio@umuc.edu
YOUNG, Randy 660-359-3948 287 D ryoung@mail.ncmissouri.edu
YOUNG, Raymond 609-984-1141 316 A ryoung@tesc.edu
YOUNG, Rena 270-707-3732 202 A rena.young@kctcs.edu
YOUNG, Richard 207-581-1700 220 A ryoung@maine.edu
YOUNG, Robert 423-236-2805 473 A ryoung@southern.edu
YOUNG, Robert, B 440-365-5222 395 C
YOUNG, Robert, F 843-349-2277 456 G ryoung@coastal.edu
YOUNG, Robert, J 214-378-1703 484 E ryoung@dcccd.edu
YOUNG, Robin 509-533-7067 532 E ryoung@scc.spokane.edu
YOUNG, Roddy, O 603-646-9249 305 A roddy.o.young@dartmouth.edu
YOUNG, Roger 512-863-1346 495 G youngr@southwestern.edu
YOUNG, Ronald 269-782-1272 258 E hyoung@swmich.edu
YOUNG, Ronald, R 717-221-1300 430 E rryoung@hacc.edu
YOUNG, Rosemary 513-732-5232 403 E rosemary.young@uc.edu
YOUNG, Sam 301-846-2495 222 G syoung@frederick.edu
YOUNG, Sam 619-849-2562 62 L samyoung@pointloma.edu
YOUNG, Sean, B 262-243-5700 546 I sean.young@cuw.edu
YOUNG, Shauna 216-361-2786 387 A syoung@chancelloru.edu
YOUNG, Sheridan 580-581-2408 407 D
YOUNG, Sheryl 828-765-7351 371 F syoung@mayland.edu
YOUNG, Stephen, K 405-271-5444 413 D stephen-young@ouhsc.edu
YOUNG, Stephen, W 513-732-5318 403 E steve.young@uc.edu
YOUNG, Steve 828-694-1891 368 B sd_young@blueridge.edu
YOUNG, Steve 850-718-2203 102 H youngs@chipola.edu
YOUNG, Tammy 479-394-7622 23 E tyoung@rmcc.edu
YOUNG, Tammy 404-756-4016 124 I tyoung@atlm.edu
YOUNG, Tasheka 718-368-5597 328 B tyoung@kbcc.cuny.edu
YOUNG, Tellis 260-399-7700 180 E tyoung@sf.edu
YOUNG, Teresa 806-291-3585 508 B youngt@wbu.edu
YOUNG, Terry 325-793-4683 490 F tyoung@mcm.edu
YOUNG, Terry, E 864-429-8728 462 G tyoung@mailbox.sc.edu
YOUNG, Thomas, C 315-268-4430 329 C young@clarkson.edu
YOUNG, Tim 714-556-3610 76 E tyoung@vanguard.edu
YOUNG, Tom 507-933-7551 264 B tyoung3@gustavus.edu
YOUNG, Tommy 903-923-2137 486 D tyoung@etbu.edu

YOUNG, Tyrone .... 410-651-6411.... 227 E
tyoung@umes.edu
YOUNG, Virginia, E .... 804-752-7256.... 522 F
vyoung@rmc.edu
YOUNG, Von .... 217-351-2884.... 161 B
vyoung@parkland.edu
YOUNG, W. Dale .... 304-724-3700.... 540 C
dyoung@apus.edu
YOUNG, William .... 757-727-5000.... 519 C
william.young@hamptonu.edu
YOUNG, William, R .... 512-223-7069.... 481 B
pyoung@austincc.edu
YOUNG CHOI, Mun .... 860-486-2221...... 94 E
mun.choi@uconn.edu
YOUNG SWITZER, Jo .... 260-982-5050.... 177 F
jyswitzer@manchester.edu
YOUNG-YASSINE,
Debra, L .... 610-526-6118.... 430 D
elaharcum@harcum.edu
YOUNGBEAR-TIBBETS,
Holly .... 800-567-2344.... 546 G
hyoungbear@menominee.edu
YOUNGBLOOD, Betty .... 586-263-6242.... 257 C
youngblo@oakland.edu
YOUNGBLOOD, Cecil .... 608-363-2237.... 546 B
youngblc@beloit.edu
YOUNGBLOOD, Joseph ..... 607-777-4351.... 316 A
jyoungblood@tesc.edu
YOUNGBLOOD, Kent .... 270-247-8521.... 204 C
kyoungblood@midcontinent.edu
YOUNGBLOOD, Kerry, L .... 252-222-6140.... 368 F
youngbloodk@carteret.edu
YOUNGBLOOD, Merna ...... 618-842-3711.... 152 F
youngbloodm@iecc.edu
YOUNGBLOOD, Pamela .... 979-532-6542.... 508 J
pamy@wcjc.edu
YOUNGBLOOD, Randy ...... 205-226-4700........ 2 C
ryoungbl@bsc.edu
YOUNGBLOOD, Rick .... 601-477-4014.... 275 B
rick.youngblood@jcjc.edu
YOUNGBLUT, William .... 305-348-7835.... 119 B
william.youngblut@fiu.edu
YOUNGE, Jeffrey, W .... 507-344-7328.... 261 H
jyounge@blc.edu
YOUNGER, Donna .... 847-635-1656.... 160 E
dyounger@oakton.edu
YOUNGER, Larry, J .... 270-686-9572.... 198 G
larry.younger@brescia.edu
YOUNGER, Phyllis .... 205-929-6441........ 5 E
pyounger@lawsonstate.edu
YOUNGERS, Jane, A .... 210-567-2333.... 506 E
youngers@uthscsa.edu
YOUNGLOVE, Ted .... 661-722-6300...... 28 J
tyounglove@avc.edu
YOUNGQUIST, Jim, L .... 501-569-8476...... 24 E
jlyoungquist@ualr.edu
YOUNGQUIST, Joan .... 360-416-7675.... 538 A
joan.youngquist@skagit.edu
YOUNGS, Joel .... 309-764-2213.... 145 E
youngsj@bhc.edu
YOUNGS, JR., Thomas, E . 412-624-8785.... 449 A
tyoungs@bc.pitt.edu
YOUNKIN, Michelle .... 402-486-2529.... 300 D
miyounki@ucollege.edu
YOUNT, Diana .... 617-964-1100.... 230 B
dyount@ants.edu
YOUNT, Rebecca, H .... 401-333-7159.... 453 B
ryount@ccri.edu
YOUNT, Richard, L .... 808-544-0272.... 140 B
ryount@hpu.edu
YOUNT, Sara .... 502-272-8401.... 198 E
syount@bellarmine.edu
YOUNT, Tim, M .... 248-276-8229.... 248 E
YOURDAN, Marilyn, R .... 316-978-3620.... 197 F
marilyn.yourdan@wichita.edu
YOURMAN, Mitchell .... 215-335-0800.... 434 G
myourman@lincolntech.com
YOUSE, Lauren .... 573-629-3122.... 282 H
Lauren.Youse@hlg.edu
YOVANOVICH, Michele ...... 239-590-7900.... 119 A
myovanov@fgcu.edu
YOW, Deborah .... 919-515-2109.... 378 B
d_yow@ncsu.edu
YOWELL, Lee, P .... 706-886-6831.... 137 G
lyowell@tfc.edu
YOWELL, Susan, K .... 308-635-6104.... 301 E
yowells@wncc.edu
YOXALL, Andrea, G .... 620-417-1125.... 196 B
andrea.yoxall@sccc.edu
YOXALL, Daniel .... 210-434-6711.... 491 G
dyoxall@lake.ollusa.edu
YSAIS, David .... 213-763-7063...... 55 D
dpysais@lattc.edu
YSEBAERT, Emily .... 920-498-5612.... 555 A
emily.ysebaert@nwtc.edu
YSURSA, Bernie, J .... 618-235-2700.... 165 B
bernard.ysursa@swic.edu
YU, Alexander .... 330-471-8303.... 395 E
ayu@malone.edu
YU, Bin .... 401-456-8160.... 454 A
byu@ric.edu
YU, Dennis .... 510-592-9688...... 59 F
wub@npu.edu
YU, Diane .... 212-998-2340.... 344 B
diane.yu@nyu.edu
YU, James .... 626-571-5110...... 54 C
YU, Lei .... 713-313-7282.... 499 G
yu_lx@tsu.edu
YU, Maya .... 505-438-8884.... 320 H
maya@acupuncturecollege.edu
YU, Roger .... 516-686-7700.... 343 D
ryu@nyit.edu
YUAN, Qing .... 301-387-3043.... 222 H
qing.yuan@garrettcollege.edu
YUASA, Miyoko .... 808-946-3773.... 139 H
YUCHA, Carolyn .... 702-895-4070.... 302 K
carolyn.yucha@unlv.edu
YUDIN, Lee, S .... 671-735-2002.... 559 D
lyudin@uguam.uog.edu
YUDOF, Mark, G .... 510-987-9074...... 73 D
president@ucop.edu
YUDT, Angela, L .... 312-355-2412.... 166 F
ayudt@uic.edu
YUEN, Dan .... 212-924-5900.... 357 A
YUEN, Jeffrey .... 212-924-5900.... 357 A
jyuen@swedishinstitute.edu
YUEN, Sylvia .... 808-956-8234.... 141 B
syuen@hawaii.edu
YUHAS, Rosemary .... 717-867-6234.... 434 C
yuhas@lvc.edu
YUILLE, Thomasina, A .... 570-577-1592.... 423 D
thomasina.yuille@bucknell.edu
YULFO, Monserrate .... 787-891-0925.... 562 G
myulfo@aguadilla.inter.edu
YUN, Erin .... 443-518-3825.... 223 D
eyun@howardcc.edu
YUNDEM, Mustafa .... 414-229-3262.... 551 C
yundem@uwm.edu
YUNEK, Brent, W .... 949-824-6362...... 73 H
bwyunek@uci.edu
YUNG, Josephine .... 360-438-4375.... 536 F
jyung@stmartin.edu
YUNGBLUT, Michelle .... 972-438-6932.... 492 C
myungblut@parkercc.edu
YUNKAI, Chen .... 910-672-1957.... 377 E
ychen@uncfsu.edu
YUNKER, Kristin, L .... 585-343-0055.... 334 F
klyunker@genesee.edu
YURA, Catherine, A .... 304-293-2547.... 544 E
cathy.yura@mail.wvu.edu
YURACHEK, Hunter, R .... 843-349-2813.... 456 G
hunter@coastal.edu
YURACKO, Kimberly, A ..... 312-503-3466.... 160 D
k-yuracko@law.northwestern.edu
YURKO WALL, Suzanne ...... 203-773-6989...... 89 H
yurkowall@albertus.edu
YURKUS, Betina, D .... 228-392-2994.... 278 B
betina.yurkus@vc.edu
YUST, Rob .... 417-625-9395.... 286 E
yust-r@mssu.edu
YUSUFOV, Daniil .... 303-937-4572...... 82 A
dyusufov@chu.edu
YUTUC, Lloyd .... 301-891-4477.... 229 B
ylloyd@wau.edu
YZZI, Nicholas, Y .... 215-368-7538.... 424 A

Z

ZABALA, Juan .... 409-880-8921.... 500 F
juan.zabala@lamar.edu
ZABALETA, Lynn Marie ..... 978-368-2218.... 230 F
lynn.zabaleta@auc.edu
ZABEL, Darcy .... 316-295-5436.... 192 H
dzabel@friends.edu
ZABOJNIK, Linda, S .... 972-860-7370.... 484 H
LindaZabojnik@dcccd.edu
ZABORA, James, R .... 202-319-5454...... 97 C
zabora@cua.edu
ZABORAC, Tom .... 309-647-7030.... 155 H
tom.zaborac@doc.illinois.gov
ZABOROWSKI, Joseph, J .. 402-280-2100.... 297 H
josephzaborowski@creighton.edu
ZABOSKI, Gerald .... 570-941-7669.... 450 B
zaboskig1@scranton.edu
ZABRISKI, Michele .... 570-340-6058.... 435 F
mzabriski@marywood.edu
ZABRISKIE, Mark .... 541-737-5774.... 418 F
mark.zabriskie@oregonstate.edu
ZACHARIAH, Sajit .... 216-687-4625.... 388 C
sajit.zachariah@csuohio.edu
ZACHARIAH, Sujith .... 708-456-0300.... 166 C
szachari@triton.edu
ZACHARIAS, Holly .... 252-399-6366.... 362 A
hzacharias@barton.edu
ZACHARIAS, Larry .... 972-883-2232.... 505 D
larry.zacharias@utdallas.edu
ZACHARY, Jane, E .... 413-538-2302.... 242 G
jzachary@mtholyoke.edu
ZACHARY, Samuel .... 859-572-5495.... 205 E
zachary@nku.edu
ZACHMEYER, Dru .... 805-756-6473...... 33 F
dzachmey@calpoly.edu
ZACHOCKI, Peter .... 312-567-5983.... 153 B
pzachock@iit.edu
ZACK, Gary, L .... 314-719-8017.... 282 C
gzack@fontbonne.edu
ZACKER, John .... 301-314-7775.... 227 B
jzacker@umd.edu
ZACKIN, Freda .... 973-972-4380.... 316 C
zackinfr@umdnj.edu
ZACOVIC, Anne .... 206-934-5661.... 536 H
anne.zacovic@seattlecolleges.edu
ZACOVIC, Mark, J .... 619-660-4221...... 48 J
mark.zacovic@gcccd.edu
ZADOYEN, Larisa .... 310-476-9777...... 28 F
lzadoyen@ajula.edu
ZAEHRING, Craig .... 617-541-5399.... 241 D
czaehr@rcc.mass.edu
ZAFFUTO, George, T .... 412-536-1115.... 432 F
george.zaffuto@laroche.edu
ZAGER, Stacy .... 516-918-3675.... 324 E
szager@bcl.edu
ZAGORA, Marilyn, A .... 716-338-1020.... 337 E
marilynzagora@mail.sunyjcc.edu
ZAGORSKI, Joe .... 530-938-5216...... 42 C
jzagorski@siskiyous.edu
ZAHED, Fereshtah .... 803-705-4771.... 455 D
zahedf@benedict.edu
ZAHN, Jeffrey, A .... 920-403-3071.... 550 C
jeffrey.zahn@snc.edu
ZAHN, JoAnn .... 503-491-7273.... 417 B
joann.zahn@mhcc.edu
ZAHN, Karla .... 920-693-1172.... 554 A
karla.zahn@gotoltc.edu
ZAHN, Patricia .... 314-516-5267.... 291 F
zahnp@umsl.edu
ZAHN, Paul .... 305-892-7050.... 111 K
paul.zahn@jwu.edu
ZAHNER, Kathryn, L .... 631-423-0483.... 350 G
kzahner@icseminary.edu
ZAHZAM, Nancy, L .... 718-780-7915.... 324 F
nancy.zahzam@brooklaw.edu
ZAIDI, Syed, S .... 570-422-3077.... 442 C
zaidi@po-box.esu.edu
ZAIDMAN, Ron .... 831-476-9424...... 47 E
president@fivebranches.edu
ZAIDMAN, Ron .... 408-260-0208...... 47 D
president@fivebranches.edu
ZAIMES, Leon .... 617-559-8783.... 235 I
lzaimes@hebrewcollege.edu
ZAIS, Diana, P .... 781-239-4382.... 230 G
prescottzais@babson.edu
ZAJAC, SND, Brendon .... 440-943-7600.... 401 G
brendonzajac@gmail.com
ZAJACESKOWSKI, John .... 518-244-2253.... 348 A
zajacj@sage.edu
ZAJCHOWSKI, Ann .... 860-727-6757...... 92 C
azajchowski@goodwin.edu
ZAK, Diane, S .... 605-677-5671.... 465 E
diane.zak@usd.edu
ZAKAHI, Walter .... 507-389-1712.... 267 H
walter.zakahi@mnsu.edu
ZAKARIA, Roland .... 619-574-6909...... 60 E
rzakaria@pacificcollege.edu
ZAKARIN, Joann .... 619-596-2766...... 26 I
jo@advancedtraining.edu
ZAKEL, Lori .... 937-512-2881.... 401 J
lori.zakel@sinclair.edu
ZAKERY, Fatemeh .... 314-256-8163.... 282 I
zakeryf@hssu.edu
ZAKOWSKI, Paul .... 630-942-2895.... 147 G
zakows@cod.edu
ZAKRI, Kathleen, M .... 315-652-6500.... 325 A
kzakri@bryantstratton.edu
ZAKRZEWSKI, Bruce .... 269-927-8162.... 254 B
zakrzewski@lakemichigancollege.edu
ZAKRZEWSKI, Mary .... 215-885-2360.... 435 E
mzak@manor.edu
ZALACCA, James, A .... 315-267-2314.... 354 C
zalaccja@potsdam.edu
ZALAPI, Diane .... 248-476-1122.... 255 C
dzalapi@mispp.edu
ZALETEL, Cora .... 719-549-2576...... 83 B
cora.zaletel@colostate-pueblo.edu
ZALOOM, Victor .... 409-880-8229.... 500 F
victor.zaloom@lamar.edu
ZALOT, Marcella, K .... 207-859-4904.... 217 G
mkzalot@colby.edu
ZAMBARDI, Victor, A .... 248-370-3112.... 257 C
zambardi@oakland.edu
ZAMBELLA, BethAnn .... 717-361-1428.... 428 E
zambell@etown.edu
ZAMBELLI, William, W .... 914-337-9300.... 331 A
william.zambelli@concordia-ny.edu
ZAMBITO, Angela, R .... 304-336-8490.... 544 B
azambito@westliberty.edu
ZAMBLE, Anthony .... 773-244-5568.... 159 G
azamble@northpark.edu
ZAMBONI, Garnett .... 785-825-5422.... 191 B
kzamboni@brownmackie.edu
ZAMBONINO, Maria .... 773-878-3813.... 163 D
mzambonino@staugustine.edu
ZAMBRANA, Maritza .... 787-279-1912.... 563 B
mzambrana@bayamon.inter.edu
ZAMBRANO, Thomas .... 732-987-2613.... 310 D
zambrano@georgian.edu
ZAMBRUN, Christina .... 260-665-4242.... 180 A
zambrunc@trine.edu
ZAMKOFF, Arthur .... 215-895-0502.... 427 G
az36@drexel.edu
ZAMMETT, Louis .... 804-257-5750.... 529 D
lzammett@vuu.edu
ZAMOJSKI, David .... 617-353-4380.... 232 G
zamojski@bu.edu
ZAMORA, Felix, A .... 214-860-8700.... 485 A
fzamora@dcccd.edu
ZAMORA, Juan .... 305-628-6593.... 116 G
jzamora@stu.edu
ZAMORA, Teri .... 956-364-4400.... 499 J
teri.zamora@harlingen.tstc.edu
ZAMORA-AGUILAR,
Beatrice .... 619-482-6379...... 71 C
bzamora@swccd.edu
ZAMPANO, Gary .... 570-941-4273.... 450 B
zampanog1@scranton.edu
ZAMZOW, Wes .... 706-737-1400.... 125 C
wzamzow@aug.edu
ZANDBERGEN, Dianne, V . 616-222-3000.... 254 A
diannez@kuyper.edu
ZANDER, Douglas .... 717-872-3371.... 443 C
doug.zander@millersville.edu
ZANDER, Kirk .... 406-756-3806.... 294 D
kzander@fvcc.edu
ZANDERS, Ann .... 225-216-8723.... 209 I
zandersa@mybrcc.edu
ZANDERS, Joan, A .... 703-323-3014.... 527 C
jzanders@nvcc.edu
ZANE, Cynthia, A .... 716-926-8923.... 335 F
czane@hilbert.edu
ZANE, Gary .... 207-948-3131.... 219 H
gzane@unity.edu
ZANE, Ken .... 860-628-4751...... 92 F
kzane@lincolncollegene.edu
ZANELLA-LITKE, Joanne ... 508-999-8942.... 237 E
jzanella@umassd.edu
ZANETTI, Mary, L .... 508-856-6009.... 238 A
Mary.Zanetti@umassmed.edu
ZANFINI-PARKER,
Christine .... 508-767-7329.... 230 E
chparker@assumption.edu
ZANG, Connie .... 740-366-9246.... 386 G
czang@cotc.edu
ZANG, Frank .... 208-426-5391.... 142 F
frankzang@boisestate.edu
ZANG, Paul .... 810-766-4112.... 248 H
paul.zang@baker.edu
ZANGER, Kate .... 563-588-6313.... 183 B
kate.zanger@clarke.edu
ZANGHI, Palma .... 716-896-0700.... 359 F
zanghi@villa.edu
ZANGHI, Palma, M .... 716-896-0700.... 359 F
zanghi@villa.edu
ZANIOS, Jamie, T .... 641-422-4162.... 187 F
zaniojam@niacc.edu
ZANJANI, Mellissia .... 609-586-4800.... 311 C
zanjanim@mccc.edu
ZANK, Gary .... 256-824-6575........ 9 A
gary.zank@uah.edu
ZANKICH, Mark, A .... 310-233-4171...... 54 I
zankicma@lahc.edu
ZANKO, Michael .... 973-655-5457.... 311 G
zankom@mail.montclair.edu
ZANON, Lewis .... 847-855-2649.... 149 H
lzanon@keller.edu
ZANSITIS, Richard, A .... 713-348-5237.... 492 J
zansitis@rice.edu
ZANT, Don .... 662-325-2231.... 276 A
dzant@budgetplan.msstate.edu
ZAPALSKA, Alina, M .... 860-444-8334.... 558 E
alina.m.zapalska@uscg.mil
ZAPATA, B. Cecilia .... 607-436-2830.... 353 E
zapatabc@oneonta.edu
ZAPATA, Fred .... 210-999-7401.... 502 C
fred.zapata@trinity.edu
ZAPATA, Jesse, T .... 210-458-2700.... 506 B
jesse.zapata@utsa.edu
ZAPATA, Sergio .... 915-351-8100.... 480 C
ZAPOLSKI, Mike .... 309-794-7223.... 145 B
mikezapolski@augustana.edu
ZAPPALA, Henry, W .... 617-824-8281.... 234 D
hank_zappala@emerson.edu
ZAPPALORTI, Robert, E .... 203-287-3028...... 93 C
paier.admin@snet.net
ZAPPE, Christopher .... 717-337-6820.... 429 H
czappe@gettysburg.edu
ZAPPI, Mark, E .... 337-482-6685.... 216 D
zappi@louisiana.edu
ZAPPIA, Gerard .... 585-389-2570.... 342 D
gzappia4@naz.edu
ZAPPONE, Michael .... 412-291-6248.... 422 D
mzappone@aii.edu
ZAPROROZHETZ,
Laurene, E .... 937-255-5894.... 556 H
laurene.zaprorozhetz@afit.edu
ZARAGOZA, Federico .... 210-485-0015.... 479 B
fzaragoza@alamo.edu
ZARCONI, Joseph .... 330-375-3107.... 397 C
zarconij@summa-health.org
ZAREMBA, Terah .... 269-965-3931.... 253 H
zarembat@kellogg.edu
ZARET, David .... 812-855-5021.... 173 C
zaret@indiana.edu
ZARING, Gayle .... 618-544-8657.... 152 G
zaringg@iecc.edu
ZARKOWSKI, Pamela .... 313-993-1585.... 259 C
zarkowp1@udmercy.edu

ZILLMER, Eric, A .... 215-895-1977.... 427 G
zillmer@drexel.edu
ZIMA, Bonita .... 920-498-5753.... 555 A
bonita.zima@nwtc.edu
ZIMBELMAN, Joel .... 530-898-5351...... 34 A
jzimbelman@csuchico.edu
ZIMIC, Deborah, L .... 410-843-6995.... 272 F
deborah.zimic@laureate.net
ZIMLICH, Robert .... 251-626-3303........ 8 D
rzimlich@ussa.edu
ZIMLICH, Robert, L .... 502-272-8263.... 198 E
bzimlich@bellarmine.edu
ZIMMER, Brandi .... 785-738-9056.... 195 D
bzimmer@ncktc.edu
ZIMMER, Robert, J .... 773-702-8001.... 166 D
president@uchicago.edu
ZIMMER, Scott .... 858-635-4553...... 27 E
szimmer@alliant.edu
ZIMMER, Tim .... 618-262-8641.... 152 I
zimmert@iecc.edu
ZIMMERLEE, Karla, J .... 530-898-5201...... 34 A
kzimmerlee@csuchico.edu
ZIMMERMAN, Barri .... 410-543-6165.... 228 D
ebzimmerman@salisbury.edu
ZIMMERMAN, Christine .... 315-229-5394.... 349 E
christinezimmerman@stlawu.edu
ZIMMERMAN, David .... 540-432-0943.... 521 G
ZIMMERMAN, Debbie .... 706-776-0100.... 135 D
dzimmerman@piedmont.edu
ZIMMERMAN, Deborah, B 512-448-8540.... 493 B
debbiez@stedwards.edu
ZIMMERMAN, Doug, R .... 814-871-7663.... 429 F
zimmerman001@gannon.edu
ZIMMERMAN, Eileen, P .... 207-753-6970.... 217 C
ezimmerm@bates.edu
ZIMMERMAN, Ellen .... 508-626-4582.... 238 D
ezimmerman@framingham.edu
ZIMMERMAN, Gail .... 603-358-2842.... 307 A
gzimmerman@keene.edu
ZIMMERMAN, Heidi .... 615-898-2025.... 473 F
heidi.zimmer@mtsu.edu
ZIMMERMAN, Jean .... 269-467-9945.... 251 D
jzimmerman@glenoaks.edu
ZIMMERMAN, Jeffrey, A .... 260-422-5561.... 172 L
jazimmerman@indianatech.edu
ZIMMERMAN, Jeremy .... 951-343-5023...... 31 G
jzimmerman@calbaptist.edu
ZIMMERMAN, Jerry .... 301-387-3074.... 222 H
jerry.zimmerman@garrettcollege.edu
ZIMMERMAN, Jill .... 661-722-6300...... 28 J
jzimmerman@avc.edu
ZIMMERMAN, Joe .... 316-295-5700.... 192 H
zimmerj@friends.edu
ZIMMERMAN, John, A .... 916-339-1500...... 58 D
jzimmerman@mticollege.edu
ZIMMERMAN, Judith, D .... 860-727-6714...... 92 C
jzimmerman@goodwin.edu
ZIMMERMAN, Julia .... 850-644-5211.... 119 C
jazimmerman@fsu.edu
ZIMMERMAN, Lynn .... 404-712-1238.... 129 A
ZIMMERMAN, Michael .... 586-445-7159.... 254 F
zimmermanm@macomb.edu
ZIMMERMAN, Michael .... 575-646-3411.... 319 D
mzimmerm@nmsu.edu
ZIMMERMAN, Michael .... 360-867-6400.... 533 I
mz@evergreen.edu
ZIMMERMAN, Midge .... 757-455-3230.... 529 F
mlzimmerman@vwc.edu
ZIMMERMAN, Nancy .... 704-637-4307.... 363 C
nzimmera@catawba.edu
ZIMMERMAN, Niel .... 509-828-1224.... 533 D
nzimmerman@cwu.edu
ZIMMERMAN, Paul, H .... 610-330-5136.... 433 B
zimmermp@lafayette.edu
ZIMMERMAN, Robert, E .... 479-575-3301...... 24 C
bobz@uark.edu
ZIMMERMAN, Sarah, E .... 419-866-0261.... 402 B
sezimmerman@stautzenberger.com
ZIMMERMAN, Sari .... 415-565-4619...... 73 G
zimmerma@uchastings.edu
ZIMMERMAN, Stephanie .... 217-875-7200.... 162 D
szimmerman@richland.edu
ZIMMERMAN, Susan .... 518-255-5413.... 354 E
zimmersj@cobleskill.edu
ZIMMERMAN, Thomas, P .... 260-452-2152.... 170 G
thomas.zimmerman@ctsfw.edu
ZIMMERMAN, Timothy .... 606-679-8501.... 202 F
timothy.zimmerman@kctcs.edu
ZIMMERMAN, Zvi .... 847-982-2500.... 151 H
zimmerman@htc.edu
ZIMMERMANN, Christian .... 301-934-7513.... 222 C
czimmermann@csmd.edu
ZIMMERMANN, Griz .... 440-375-7000.... 394 E
griz@lec.edu
ZIMMERMANN, Joanna .... 281-998-6150.... 493 G
joanna.zimmermann@sjcd.edu
ZIMMERS, Jennifer, J .... 208-732-6277.... 143 B
jzimmers@csi.edu
ZIMPHER, Nancy, L .... 518-320-1355.... 351 D
chancellor@suny.edu
ZIMPRICH, Janet .... 651-846-3329.... 261 E
jzimprich@argosy.edu
ZINDT, Gina .... 309-341-7200.... 155 E
gzindt@knox.edu

ZINGA, Patricia .... 708-456-0300.... 166 C
pzinga@triton.edu
ZINGARO, Louise, S .... 434-381-6316.... 524 E
lzingaro@sbc.edu
ZINGG, Paul, J .... 530-898-5201...... 34 A
pzingg@csuchico.edu
ZINGRONE, Nancy, L .... 757-457-7174.... 516 C
nancy.zingrone@atlanticuniv.edu
ZINGSHEIM, Shairon .... 510-659-6201...... 59 I
szingsheim@ohlone.edu
ZINK, Abbey .... 203-837-8839...... 92 A
zinka@wcsu.edu
ZINK, Bill .... 812-535-5213.... 179 C
bzink@smwc.edu
ZINK, Diane .... 315-568-3065.... 342 H
dzink@nycc.edu
ZINK, Ellen, L .... 615-353-3224.... 475 D
ellen.zink@nscc.edu
ZINK, Glenda .... 330-494-6170.... 402 A
gzink@starkstate.edu
ZINK, Janis, I .... 918-631-2565.... 413 F
janis-zink@utulsa.edu
ZINK, Larry, W .... 502-852-7072.... 207 A
lwzink01@louisville.edu
ZINK, Paul .... 618-537-6981.... 157 G
pwzink@mckendree.edu
ZINK, Rosemary .... 231-777-0314.... 256 D
ZINKAN, Rob .... 765-973-8444.... 173 D
rzinkan@iue.edu
ZINKUS, Michael .... 508-626-4357.... 238 D
mzinkus@framingham.edu
ZINN, Annalisa, J .... 208-582-3395...... 93 E
annalisa.zinn@quinnipiac.edu
ZINN, David .... 540-362-6435.... 519 E
coachzinn@gmail.com
ZINNANTI, Len .... 212-772-4460.... 327 E
lzinnant@hunter.cuny.edu
ZINNERMAN-BETHEA,
Darlene .... 803-705-4733.... 455 D
bethead@benedict.edu
ZINNI, Amanda .... 440-375-7150.... 394 E
azinni@lec.edu
ZINS, Rosemary, S .... 718-281-5144.... 329 A
rzins@qcc.cuny.edu
ZINSMEISTER, Robin, O .... 252-335-0821.... 369 D
rogriffin@albemarle.edu
ZINTAK, Jane .... 570-385-6260.... 440 C
jqz1@psu.edu
ZIONTS, Paul .... 773-325-7740.... 148 F
pzionts@depaul.edu
ZIPF, Marianne, C .... 718-779-1430.... 346 B
mzipf@plazacollege.edu
ZIPPERLEN, Marlene .... 254-295-4573.... 504 A
mzipperlen@umhb.edu
ZIRBLIS, Ellalou .... 802-485-2631.... 514 A
ellalou@norwich.edu
ZIRIAX, Danny .... 918-495-7018.... 411 C
dziriax@oru.edu
ZIRKIN, Barbara .... 443-352-4039.... 226 E
bzirkin@stevenson.edu
ZISOOK, Joshua .... 847-982-2500.... 151 H
jzissok@htc.edu
ZITTEL, Kimberly .... 716-829-7816.... 332 F
zittelk@dyc.edu
ZITZELSBERGER, Robert .... 304-829-7591.... 540 E
rzitzelsberger@bethanywv.edu
ZITZNER, Linda .... 510-430-2024...... 57 D
lzitzner@mills.edu
ZITZOW, Larry, L .... 701-777-4137.... 381 D
larry.zitzow@email.und.edu
ZIVIN, Joselyn .... 312-261-3200.... 159 D
joselyn.zivin@nl.edu
ZIX, Theresa .... 626-396-2477...... 29 G
theresa.zix@artcenter.edu
ZIZOS, Anthony .... 603-862-0209.... 306 E
anthony.zizos@unh.edu
ZLATA, William .... 212-772-4482.... 327 E
bill.zlata@hunter.cuny.edu
ZLATANOV, Milla .... 408-541-0100...... 41 C
mzlatanov@cogswell.edu
ZLEVOR, Mark .... 262-564-3096.... 553 H
zlevorm@gtc.edu
ZMUDA, Rebecca .... 239-280-2563.... 101 C
rebecca.zmuda@avemaria.edu
ZNAMENSKIS, Nik .... 802-225-3235.... 513 H
nik.znamenskis@neci.edu
ZOBRIST, Vicki .... 402-399-2391.... 297 E
vzobrist@csm.edu
ZOCH, Brandon .... 252-398-6464.... 363 E
zochbr@chowan.edu
ZODY, John .... 812-330-6067.... 175 H
jzody1@ivytech.edu
ZOELLER, Marisa .... 502-272-8335.... 198 E
mzoeller@bellarmine.edu
ZOELLNER, Mark .... 605-229-8585.... 464 I
mark.zoellner@presentation.edu
ZOLA, Carol .... 724-838-4212.... 447 B
zola@setonhill.edu
ZOLA, Gary .... 513-221-7444.... 391 E
GZola@cn.huc.edu
ZOLA, Stuart, M .... 404-727-7707.... 129 A
szola@rmy.emory.edu
ZOLFO, Elana .... 631-244-3395.... 332 D
zolfoe@dowling.edu

ZOLFO, Elana .... 631-244-3420.... 332 D
zolfoe@dowling.edu
ZOLLARS, Scott, M .... 620-421-6700.... 194 E
scottz@labette.edu
ZOLLER, Karen .... 216-373-5267.... 397 E
kzoller@ndc.edu
ZOLLI, Frank, A .... 203-576-4279...... 94 D
zolli@bridgeport.edu
ZOLLINGER, Richard .... 704-330-6730.... 369 A
richard.zollinger@cpcc.edu
ZOLLNER, Michele .... 412-304-0727.... 429 A
mzollner@cci.edu
ZOLNOWSKY, W. David .... 605-256-5675.... 465 G
david.zolnowsky@dsu.edu
ZOLOTH, Stephen, R .... 617-373-3323.... 244 A
ZOLTOWSKY, Jordan .... 718-818-6470.... 349 G
ZONA, Jean .... 508-531-1211.... 238 B
jzona@bridgew.edu
ZONDLO, Tim .... 763-433-1427.... 265 J
tim.zondlo@anokaramsey.edu
ZONER, Kathy, R .... 607-255-0412.... 331 C
krz1@cornell.edu
ZONN, Sidney .... 412-397-5345.... 445 G
zonns@rmu.edu
ZOOK, Letha .... 304-357-4875.... 541 H
lethazook@ucwv.edu
ZOOK, Rosemarie, E .... 248-689-8282.... 260 A
rzook@walshcollege.edu
ZOPPOLI, David .... 860-727-6768...... 92 C
dzoppoli@goodwin.edu
ZORDAN, Anthony, J .... 815-740-3395.... 167 C
azordan@stfrancis.edu
ZORIC, Joseph .... 740-284-5801.... 390 M
jzoric@franciscan.edu
ZORIC, Virginia, L .... 740-284-5254.... 390 M
gzoric@franciscan.edu
ZORN, David, C .... 303-837-0825...... 81 B
zornd@aii.edu
ZORN, Diane .... 941-955-8862.... 115 K
ZORN, Jenny .... 909-537-5024...... 36 A
jzorn@csusb.edu
ZORN, Karen .... 617-876-0956.... 236 H
karen.zorn@longy.edu
ZOZAYA, Pat .... 702-651-5078.... 302 G
pat.zozaya@csn.edu
ZRIMSEK, Becky .... 507-222-4205.... 262 B
rzrimsek@carleton.edu
ZUBERBUELER, OP,
Mary Anne .... 615-297-7545.... 466 H
srmanne@aquinascollege.edu
ZUBIZARRETA, John .... 803-786-3014.... 457 C
jzubizarreta@columbiasc.edu
ZUCALLA, Fred, P .... 315-733-2300.... 359 A
fzucalla@uscny.edu
ZUCCARELLI, Anthony, J .... 909-558-4528...... 54 D
azuccarelli@llu.edu
ZUCCHETTO, Vincent .... 718-960-8242.... 327 C
vincent.zucchetto@lehman.cuny.edu
ZUCCONI, Michael, J .... 540-432-4211.... 518 E
michael.zucconi@emu.edu
ZUCH, Michel .... 979-830-4163.... 482 A
michel.zuch@binn.edu
ZUCKER, Avraham .... 718-382-8702.... 360 J
ZUCKER, Lauren .... 610-543-2500...... 99 D
ZUCKERMAN, Derek .... 914-633-2336.... 336 E
dzuckerman@iona.edu
ZUCKERMAN-AVILES,
Stephanie, B .... 716-878-5811.... 353 A
zuckersb@buffalostate.edu
ZUDEKOFF, Rosanne .... 203-773-8502...... 89 H
zudekoff@albertus.edu
ZUEHLKE, Karen, A .... 920-924-6320.... 554 E
zkuehlke@morainepark.edu
ZUELKE, Bill .... 503-534-4073.... 416 I
bzuelke@marylhurst.edu
ZUFELT, Jeffrey, A .... 717-262-2010.... 452 B
jzufelt@wilson.edu
ZUG, Mary Ann .... 515-271-1440.... 183 F
maryann.zug@dmu.edu
ZUHLKE, James .... 610-436-3316.... 443 F
jzuhlke@wcupa.edu
ZUICHES, Carol .... 773-702-8604.... 166 D
czuiches@uchicago.edu
ZUKER, Fred .... 281-487-1170.... 498 E
fzuker@txchiro.edu
ZUKOR, Tevya, M .... 540-654-1053.... 524 H
tzukor@umw.edu
ZUKOWSKI, Joanne .... 803-325-2873.... 463 G
jzukowski@yorktech.edu
ZUKOWSKI, Kimberly, J .... 716-286-8568.... 344 D
kjz@niagara.edu
ZUMBACH, Deborah, J .... 319-335-3815.... 182 C
deborah-zumbach@uiowa.edu
ZUMWALT, Debra, L .... 650-723-6397...... 71 F
zumwalt@stanford.edu
ZUMWINKEL, Donna .... 314-984-7590.... 289 D
dzumwinkel@stlcc.edu
ZUNGOLO, Eileen, H .... 412-396-6554.... 428 C
zungolo@duq.edu
ZUNIGA, Donna, P .... 936-291-0452.... 489 J
dzuniga@lee.edu
ZUNIGA, Kelly .... 713-718-8596.... 487 G
kelly.zuniga@hccs.edu

ZUNIGA, Leo .... 210-485-0035.... 479 B
lzuniga@alamo.edu
ZUPAN, Mark .... 585-275-3316.... 358 I
mark.zupan@simon.rochester.edu
ZUPANCICH, Patti .... 218-235-2166.... 270 A
p.zupancich@vcc.edu
ZURAW, Peter .... 781-283-2474.... 246 B
pzuraw@wellesley.edu
ZURAWSKY, Walter .... 718-260-3725.... 346 C
zurawsky@poly.edu
ZUREK, Ronald, M .... 775-784-4031.... 303 A
zurek@unr.edu
ZUROW, Rick .... 503-977-4450.... 419 G
rick.zurow@pcc.edu
ZUSCHIN, Andrea, P .... 540-365-4456.... 518 J
azuschin@ferrum.edu
ZUTES, Spring .... 661-726-1911...... 73 C
ZUVERS, Larry .... 419-267-1308.... 397 D
lzuvers@northweststate.edu
ZUZACK, Judith, A .... 724-287-8711.... 423 F
judith.zuzack@bc3.edu
ZUZEVICH, Theresa .... 661-362-3644...... 41 G
theresa.zuzevich@canyons.edu
ZUZOLO, Renee .... 330-652-9919.... 390 H
reneezuzolo@eticollege.edu
ZVACEK, Susan, M .... 785-864-2600.... 196 F
szvacek@ku.edu
ZVARITCH, Jeanne .... 330-337-6403.... 383 H
college@awc.edu
ZVOSEC, Almut .... 216-421-7447.... 387 H
azvosec@cia.edu
ZWEIG, Yitzchak .... 305-534-7050.... 121 G
yzweig@talmudicu.edu
ZWEIG, Yochanan .... 305-534-7050.... 121 G
rosh@talmudicu.edu
ZWICK, Ann, O .... 606-679-8501.... 202 F
ann.zwick@kctcs.edu
ZWICKEY, Heather .... 503-552-1742.... 417 D
hzwickey@ncnm.edu
ZWIER, Robert .... 585-594-6659.... 347 F
zwier_robert@roberts.edu
ZWIREN, Martin .... 718-960-1117.... 327 C
martin.zwiren@lehman.cuny.edu
ZWISLER, Stasia .... 847-574-5222.... 155 G
szwisler@lfgsm.edu
ZWYGART-STAUFFACHER,
Mary, C .... 715-836-5287.... 550 H
zwygarmc@uwec.edu
ZYLAK, David, D .... 240-895-4911.... 226 A
ddzylak@smcm.edu
ZYLSTRA, Art .... 206-264-9100.... 530 J
artz@bgu.edu
ZYLSTRA, Brian .... 641-628-5641.... 183 A
zylstrab@central.edu
ZYLSTRA, Carl, E .... 712-722-6002.... 183 H
czylstra@dordt.edu
ZYLSTRA, Jim .... 608-266-1739.... 553 D
jim.zylstra@wtcsystem.edu
ZYMARIS, Joyce .... 508-588-9100.... 240 E

Accreditation Index of Institutions by Regional, National, Professional and Specialized Agencies

Degree levels are shown by the following symbols: (C) diploma/certificate; (A) associate; (B) baccalaureate; (M) master's; (S) beyond master's but less than doctorate; (FP) first professional; (D) doctorate.

AA: Commission on Accreditation of Allied Health Education Programs: anesthesiologist assistant (M)

AAB: Aviation Accreditation Board International: aviation (A,B)

AAFCS: American Association of Family and Consumer Sciences: family and consumer science (B)

ABHES: Accrediting Bureau of Health Education Schools: allied health (C,A,B)

ACBSP: Accreditation Council for Business Schools and Programs: business administration, management, accounting and related business fields (A,B,M)

ACCSC: Accrediting Commission of Career Schools and Colleges: occupational, trade, and technical education (A,B,M)

ACFEI: American Culinary Federation, Inc.: culinary arts and culinary management (C,A,B)

ACICS: Accrediting Council for Independent Colleges and Schools: business and business related programs (C,A,B,M)

Art Institute of Las Vegas, The ... NV ... 301
Everest College ... NV ... 302
ITT Technical Institute ... NV ... 302
Morrison University ... NV ... 302
Lebanon College ... NH ... 305
Eastwick College ... NJ ... 309
Brookline College ... NM ... 317
Carrington College - Albuquerque ... NM ... 317
ITT Technical Institute ... NM ... 318
Art Institute of New York City, The ... NY ... 323
ASA Institute of Business & Computer Technology ... NY ... 323
Elmira Business Institute ... NY ... 332
Everest Institute ... NY ... 333
ITT Technical Institute ... NY ... 337
Long Island Business Institute ... NY ... 338
Mildred Elley ... NY ... 341
Olean Business Institute ... NY ... 345
Professional Business College ... NY ... 346
SBI Campus-An Affiliate of Sanford-Brown ... NY ... 350
Art Institute of Charlotte, The ... NC ... 361
ITT Technical Institute ... NC ... 365
King's College ... NC ... 365
Living Arts College @ School of Communication Arts ... NC ... 366
Miller-Motte Technical College ... NC ... 367
South College ... NC ... 376
Academy of Court Reporting ... OH ... 383
ATS Institute of Technology ... OH ... 384
Beckfield College ... OH ... 384
Bradford School ... OH ... 385
Brown Mackie College-Akron ... OH ... 385
Brown Mackie College-Cincinnati ... OH ... 385
Brown Mackie College-Findlay ... OH ... 385
Brown Mackie College-North Canton ... OH ... 385
Daymar College-Chillicothe ... OH ... 389
Daymar College-Jackson ... OH ... 389
Daymar College-Lancaster ... OH ... 389
Daymar College-New Boston ... OH ... 389
Fortis College ... OH ... 390
Gallipolis Career College ... OH ... 391
Hondros College ... OH ... 392
ITT Technical Institute ... OH ... 392
Lincoln College ... OH ... 394
Lincoln College of Technology ... OH ... 394
Lincoln College of Technology ... OH ... 395
Miami-Jacobs Career College ... OH ... 396
Ohio Business College ... OH ... 397
Ohio Business College ... OH ... 398
Ohio Business College, Lorain Branch ... OH ... 398
Ohio Valley College of Technology ... OH ... 400
Stautzenberger College ... OH ... 402
Trumbull Business College ... OH ... 402
Brown Mackie College-Tulsa ... OK ... 407
Clary Sage College ... OK ... 407
Community Care College ... OK ... 407
ITT Technical Institute ... OK ... 408
Oklahoma Technical College ... OK ... 411
Carrington College - Portland ... OR ... 414
Everest College ... OR ... 415
ITT Technical Institute ... OR ... 416
Le Cordon Bleu College of Culinary Arts in Portland ... OR ... 416
Oregon Culinary Institute ... OR ... 418
Pioneer Pacific College ... OR ... 419
Art Institute of Philadelphia ... PA ... 422
Art Institute of York - Pennsylvania, The ... PA ... 422
Bradford School ... PA ... 423
Cambria-Rowe Business College ... PA ... 424
Consolidated School of Business ... PA ... 426
Douglas Education Center ... PA ... 427
DuBois Business College ... PA ... 427
DuBois Business College ... PA ... 428
Erie Business Center South ... PA ... 428
Erie Business Center, Main ... PA ... 428
Everest Institute ... PA ... 429
Fortis Institute ... PA ... 429
ITT Technical Institute ... PA ... 431
Kaplan Career Institute ... PA ... 432
Kaplan Career Institute - ICM Campus ... PA ... 432
Lansdale School of Business ... PA ... 433
Laurel Business Institute ... PA ... 433
Laurel Technical Institute ... PA ... 434
McCann School of Business & Technology .. PA ... 435
McCann School of Business & Technology .. PA ... 436
Newport Business Institute ... PA ... 437
Pace Institute ... PA ... 438
Penn Commercial Business/Technical School ... PA ... 438
Pennsylvania Institute of Health and Technology ... PA ... 441
South Hills School of Business and Technology ... PA ... 447
Yorktowne Business Institute ... PA ... 452
Atlantic College ... PR ... 560
EDIC College ... PR ... 561
Humacao Community College ... PR ... 562
John Dewey College ... PR ... 564
National College of Business and Technology ... PR ... 564
Brown Mackie College-Greenville ... SC ... 455
Forrest Junior College ... SC ... 458
Golf Academy of America ... SC ... 458
ITT Technical Institute ... SC ... 458
Miller-Motte Technical College ... SC ... 459
Daymar Institute ... TN ... 468
International Academy of Design and Technology ... TN ... 469
ITT Technical Institute ... TN ... 469
Miller-Motte Technical College ... TN ... 471
National College of Business and Technology ... TN ... 471
National College of Business and Technology ... TN ... 472
Virginia College School of Business and Health ... TN ... 478
West Tennessee Business College ... TN ... 478
Anamarc College ... TX ... 480
Career Point College ... TX ... 482
Court Reporting Institute of Dallas ... TX ... 483
Court Reporting Institute of Houston ... TX ... 483
Everest College ... TX ... 486
International Academy of Design and Technology ... TX ... 488
International Business College ... TX ... 488
ITT Technical Institute ... TX ... 488
Le Cordon Bleu College of Culinary Arts in Austin ... TX ... 489
Le Cordon Bleu College of Culinary Arts in Dallas ... TX ... 489
Sanford-Brown College-Houston ... TX ... 493
Texas School of Business ... TX ... 499
Texas School of Business-Friendswood ... TX ... 499
Texas School of Business-Southwest ... TX ... 499
Vet Tech Institute of Houston ... TX ... 507
Virginia College at Austin ... TX ... 507
Westwood College-Dallas ... TX ... 508
Westwood College-Fort Worth ... TX ... 508
Westwood College-Houston South ... TX ... 508
Art Institute of Salt Lake City, The ... UT ... 509
Broadview University ... UT ... 509
Eagle Gate College ... UT ... 509
Everest College ... UT ... 509
ITT Technical Institute ... UT ... 509
Neumont University ... UT ... 510
Bon Secours Memorial College of Nursing ... VA ... 516
California University of Management and Sciences Virginia ... VA ... 517
ITT Technical Institute ... VA ... 519
ITT Technical Institute ... VA ... 520
Miller-Motte Technical College ... VA ... 521
National College ... VA ... 521
Sanford-Brown College ... VA ... 523
Sentara College of Health Sciences ... VA ... 523
Stratford University ... VA ... 524
Virginia International University ... VA ... 528
Westwood College-Annandale ... VA ... 530
Westwood College-Arlington Ballston ... VA ... 530
Bainbridge Graduate Institute ... WA ... 530
Carrington College - Spokane ... WA ... 531
Everest College ... WA ... 533
International Academy of Design and Technology ... WA ... 534
ITT Technical Institute ... WA ... 534
ITT Technical Institute ... WA ... 535
ITT Technical Institute ... WV ... 541
Mountain State College ... WV ... 541
National College ... WV ... 541
Valley College - Martinsburg Campus ... WV ... 541
West Virginia Business College ... WV ... 541
West Virginia Business College ... WV ... 542
West Virginia Junior College ... WV ... 545
ITT Technical Institute ... WI ... 547
Sanford-Brown College-Milwaukee ... WI ... 550
Institute of Business and Medical Careers ... WY ... 556

ACUP: Accreditation Commission for Acupuncture and Oriental Medicine: acupuncture (C,FP,M,D)

Arizona School of Acupuncture and Oriental Medicine ... AZ ... 12
Asian Institute of Medical Studies ... AZ ... 12
Phoenix Institute of Herbal Medicine and Acupuncture ... AZ ... 17
Academy of Chinese Culture and Health Sciences ... CA ... 26
Acupuncture and Integrative Medicine College-Berkeley ... CA ... 26
@Alhambra Medical University ... CA ... 26
American College of Traditional Chinese Medicine ... CA ... 28
Dongguk University ... CA ... 45
Emperor's College of Traditional Oriental Medicine ... CA ... 45
Five Branches University: Graduate School of Traditional Chinese Medicine ... CA ... 47
Pacific College of Oriental Medicine ... CA ... 60
Samra University of Oriental Medicine ... CA ... 64
South Baylo University ... CA ... 70
Southern California University of Health Sciences ... CA ... 71
Southern California University School of Oriental Medicine and Acupuncture ... CA ... 71
@Stanton University ... CA ... 71
University of East-West Medicine ... CA ... 75
Yo San University of Traditional Chinese Medicine ... CA ... 79
Colorado School of Traditional Chinese Medicine ... CO ... 82
Institute of Taoist Education and Acupuncture ... CO ... 85
Southwest Acupuncture College ... CO ... 87
University of Bridgeport ... CT ... 94
Academy for Five Element Acupuncture ... FL ... 100
Acupuncture & Massage College ... FL ... 100
Atlantic Institute of Oriental Medicine ... FL ... 101
Dragon Rises College of Oriental Medicine .. FL ... 104
East West College of Natural Medicine ... FL ... 104
Florida College of Integrative Medicine ... FL ... 107
Institute of Clinical Acupuncture and Oriental Medicine ... HI ... 140
Traditional Chinese Medical College of Hawaii ... HI ... 140
World Medicine Institute ... HI ... 142
Midwest College of Oriental Medicine ... IL ... 158
National University of Health Sciences ... IL ... 159
Pacific College of Oriental Medicine ... IL ... 161
@Kansas College of Chinese Medicine ... KS ... 194
Tai Sophia Institute ... MD ... 226
New England School of Acupuncture ... MA ... 243
American Academy of Acupuncture and Oriental Medicine ... MN ... 261
Northwestern Health Sciences University ... MN ... 270
Southwest Acupuncture College ... NM ... 320
Southwest Acupuncture College-Albuquerque ... NM ... 320
New York Chiropractic College ... NY ... 342
New York College of Health Professions ... NY ... 343
New York College of Traditional Chinese Medicine ... NY ... 343
Pacific College of Oriental Medicine ... NY ... 345
Swedish Institute College of Health Sciences NY ... 357
Tri-State College of Acupuncture ... NY ... 358
American Institute of Alternative Medicine ... OH ... 383
National College of Natural Medicine ... OR ... 417
Oregon College of Oriental Medicine ... OR ... 417
Won Institute of Graduate Studies ... PA ... 452
American College of Acupuncture and Oriental Medicine ... TX ... 480
AOMA Graduate School of Integrative Medicine ... TX ... 480
Texas College of Traditional Chinese Medicine ... TX ... 499
Bastyr University ... WA ... 530
Seattle Institute of Oriental Medicine ... WA ... 537
Midwest College of Oriental Medicine ... WI ... 548

ADNUR: National League for Nursing: nursing (A)

Alabama Southern Community College ... AL ... 1
Bevill State Community College ... AL ... 2
Bishop State Community College ... AL ... 2
Calhoun Community College ... AL ... 2
Central Alabama Community College ... AL ... 2
Gadsden State Community College ... AL ... 3
George C. Wallace Community College - Dothan ... AL ... 4
George Corley Wallace State Community College - Selma ... AL ... 4
James H. Faulkner State Community College ... AL ... 5
Jefferson Davis Community College ... AL ... 5
Jefferson State Community College ... AL ... 5
Lawson State Community College ... AL ... 5
Lurleen B. Wallace Community College ... AL ... 5
Northeast Alabama Community College ... AL ... 6
Northwest - Shoals Community College ... AL ... 6
Shelton State Community College ... AL ... 7
Snead State Community College ... AL ... 7
Southern Union State Community College ... AL ... 7
Troy University ... AL ... 8
University of Mobile ... AL ... 9
University of West Alabama, The ... AL ... 10
Wallace State Community College - Hanceville ... AL ... 10
University of Alaska Anchorage ... AK ... 10
Arizona Western College ... AZ ... 12
Central Arizona College ... AZ ... 13
Chandler-Gilbert Community College ... AZ ... 15
Cochise College ... AZ ... 13
Estrella Mountain Community College ... AZ ... 15
Gateway Community College ... AZ ... 15
Glendale Community College ... AZ ... 15
Mesa Community College ... AZ ... 15
Mohave Community College ... AZ ... 16
Northland Pioneer College ... AZ ... 17
Paradise Valley Community College ... AZ ... 16
Phoenix College ... AZ ... 16
Pima County Community College District ... AZ ... 17
Scottsdale Community College ... AZ ... 16
Yavapai College ... AZ ... 19
Arkansas Northeastern College ... AR ... 20
Arkansas State University ... AR ... 20
East Arkansas Community College ... AR ... 21
National Park Community College ... AR ... 22
North Arkansas College ... AR ... 22
Phillips Community College of the University of Arkansas ... AR ... 25
Southeast Arkansas College ... AR ... 23
Southern Arkansas University ... AR ... 23
University of Arkansas at Fort Smith ... AR ... 24
University of Arkansas at Little Rock ... AR ... 24
University of Arkansas Community College at Batesville ... AR ... 25
Cerritos College ... CA ... 38
Chaffey College ... CA ... 39
College of Marin ... CA ... 41
College of the Canyons ... CA ... 41
College of the Desert ... CA ... 41
Cypress College ... CA ... 59
El Camino College ... CA ... 45
Evergreen Valley College ... CA ... 67
Golden West College ... CA ... 41
Grossmont College ... CA ... 49
Long Beach City College ... CA ... 54
Los Angeles Harbor College ... CA ... 54
Los Angeles Pierce College ... CA ... 55
Los Angeles Valley College ... CA ... 55
Monterey Peninsula College ... CA ... 57
Moorpark College ... CA ... 77
Ohlone College ... CA ... 59
Pacific Union College ... CA ... 60
Palomar College ... CA ... 61
Riverside City College ... CA ... 64
Saddleback College ... CA ... 70
San Bernardino Valley College ... CA ... 65
San Diego City College ... CA ... 65
San Joaquin Delta College ... CA ... 66
Santa Ana College ... CA ... 63
Santa Barbara City College ... CA ... 68
Santa Monica College ... CA ... 68
Southwestern College ... CA ... 71
Aims Community College ... CO ... 80
Arapahoe Community College ... CO ... 80
Colorado Mountain College ... CO ... 82
Front Range Community College ... CO ... 84
Morgan Community College ... CO ... 86
Otero Junior College ... CO ... 86
Pueblo Community College ... CO ... 87
Capital Community College ... CT ... 89
Gateway Community College ... CT ... 90
Goodwin College ... CT ... 92
Naugatuck Valley Community College ... CT ... 90
Norwalk Community College ... CT ... 90
St. Vincent's College ... CT ... 94
Three Rivers Community College ... CT ... 91
Delaware Technical and Community College Owens Campus ... DE ... 96
Delaware Technical and Community College Stanton-Wilmington Campus ... DE ... 96
Delaware Technical and Community College Terry Campus ... DE ... 96
University System of the District of Columbia DC ... 99
Broward College ... FL ... 102
College of Central Florida ... FL ... 103
Daytona State College ... FL ... 103
Edison State College ... FL ... 104
Florida Gateway College ... FL ... 108
Florida Hospital College of Health Sciences . FL ... 108
Florida State College at Jacksonville ... FL ... 109
Gulf Coast State College ... FL ... 110
Hillsborough Community College ... FL ... 110
Indian River State College ... FL ... 110
Lake-Sumter Community College ... FL ... 112
Miami Dade College ... FL ... 113
Palm Beach State College ... FL ... 114
Pasco-Hernando Community College ... FL ... 114
Pensacola State College ... FL ... 114
Polk State College ... FL ... 115
St. Petersburg College ... FL ... 116
Santa Fe College ... FL ... 117
Seminole State College of Florida ... FL ... 117
State College of Florida, Manatee-Sarasota . FL ... 118
Valencia College ... FL ... 122
Abraham Baldwin Agricultural College ... GA ... 123
Athens Technical College ... GA ... 124
Bainbridge College ... GA ... 125
College of Coastal Georgia ... GA ... 127
Columbus Technical College ... GA ... 127
Dalton State College ... GA ... 127
Darton College ... GA ... 128
Georgia Highlands College ... GA ... 130
Georgia Northwestern Technical College ... GA ... 130
Georgia Perimeter College ... GA ... 130
Gordon College ... GA ... 131
Gwinnett Technical College ... GA ... 132
Macon State College ... GA ... 133
Middle Georgia College ... GA ... 133
North Georgia College & State University ... GA ... 134
South Georgia College ... GA ... 136
Southwest Georgia Technical College ... GA ... 137
West Georgia Technical College ... GA ... 139
Kapiolani Community College ... HI ... 141
University of Hawaii Hawaii Community College ... HI ... 141
University of Hawaii Kauai Community College ... HI ... 141
University of Hawaii Maui College ... HI ... 142
Brigham Young University-Idaho ... ID ... 142
College of Southern Idaho ... ID ... 143
Idaho State University ... ID ... 143
North Idaho College ... ID ... 143
Black Hawk College ... IL ... 145
Carl Sandburg College ... IL ... 146
City Colleges of Chicago Harry S Truman College ... IL ... 147
City Colleges of Chicago Richard J. Daley College ... IL ... 147
College of DuPage ... IL ... 147
College of Lake County ... IL ... 147
Elgin Community College ... IL ... 150
Harper College ... IL ... 151
Heartland Community College ... IL ... 151
Illinois Central College ... IL ... 152
Illinois Eastern Community Colleges Frontier Community College ... IL ... 152
Illinois Eastern Community Colleges Lincoln Trail College ... IL ... 152
Illinois Eastern Community Colleges Olney Central College ... IL ... 152

Universidad Metropolitana ... PR ... 565
University of Puerto Rico at Arecibo ... PR ... 566
University of Puerto Rico-Humacao ... PR ... 567
Community College of Rhode Island ... RI ... 453
New England Institute of Technology ... RI ... 453
Aiken Technical College ... SC ... 455
Central Carolina Technical College ... SC ... 455
Florence - Darlington Technical College ... SC ... 458
Greenville Technical College ... SC ... 458
Horry-Georgetown Technical College ... SC ... 458
Midlands Technical College ... SC ... 459
Orangeburg-Calhoun Technical College ... SC ... 460
Piedmont Technical College ... SC ... 460
Spartanburg Community College ... SC ... 461
Technical College of the Lowcountry ... SC ... 461
Tri-County Technical College ... SC ... 461
Trident Technical College ... SC ... 461
University of South Carolina Lancaster ... SC ... 462
York Technical College ... SC ... 463
Dakota Wesleyan University ... SD ... 464
Presentation College ... SD ... 464
University of South Dakota, The ... SD ... 465
Aquinas College ... TN ... 466
Chattanooga State Community College ... TN ... 474
Cleveland State Community College ... TN ... 474
Columbia State Community College ... TN ... 474
Dyersburg State Community College ... TN ... 475
Jackson State Community College ... TN ... 475
Lincoln Memorial University ... TN ... 470
Motlow State Community College ... TN ... 475
Northeast State Technical Community College ... TN ... 475
Roane State Community College ... TN ... 475
Southern Adventist University ... TN ... 473
Southwest Tennessee Community College ... TN ... 475
Tennessee State University ... TN ... 474
Walters State Community College ... TN ... 476
Alvin Community College ... TX ... 479
Amarillo College ... TX ... 479
Angelo State University ... TX ... 480
Austin Community College District ... TX ... 481
Baptist Health System School of Health Professions ... TX ... 481
Blinn College ... TX ... 482
Brookhaven College ... TX ... 484
Central Texas College ... TX ... 482
College of the Mainland ... TX ... 483
Collin County Community College District ... TX ... 483
Del Mar College ... TX ... 485
El Centro College ... TX ... 484
El Paso Community College ... TX ... 486
Galveston College ... TX ... 486
Grayson County College ... TX ... 487
Houston Baptist University ... TX ... 487
Howard College ... TX ... 487
Kilgore College ... TX ... 489
Lamar University ... TX ... 500
Laredo Community College ... TX ... 489
Lee College ... TX ... 489
Lone Star College System ... TX ... 490
McLennan Community College ... TX ... 490
Midland College ... TX ... 490
Navarro College ... TX ... 491
North Central Texas College ... TX ... 491
Odessa College ... TX ... 491
Panola College ... TX ... 492
Paris Junior College ... TX ... 492
San Antonio College ... TX ... 479
San Jacinto College Central ... TX ... 493
San Jacinto College South ... TX ... 493
South Plains College ... TX ... 494
Tarrant County College District ... TX ... 496
Temple College ... TX ... 496
Texarkana College ... TX ... 496
Texas Southmost College ... TX ... 499
Trinity Valley Community College ... TX ... 502
University of Texas at Brownsville, The ... TX ... 505
Victoria College ... TX ... 507
Weatherford College ... TX ... 508
Broadview University ... UT ... 509
Dixie State College of Utah ... UT ... 512
Provo College ... UT ... 510
Salt Lake Community College ... UT ... 512
Stevens-Henager College ... UT ... 510
Utah State University-College of Eastern Utah ... UT ... 511
Utah Valley University ... UT ... 511
Weber State University ... UT ... 511
Castleton State College ... VT ... 515
Southern Vermont College ... VT ... 514
Vermont Technical College ... VT ... 515
University of the Virgin Islands ... VI ... 568
Blue Ridge Community College ... VA ... 525
Dabney S. Lancaster Community College ... VA ... 526
Germanna Community College ... VA ... 526
J. Sargeant Reynolds Community College ... VA ... 526
John Tyler Community College ... VA ... 526
Mountain Empire Community College ... VA ... 527
Norfolk State University ... VA ... 527
Northern Virginia Community College ... VA ... 527
Patrick Henry Community College ... VA ... 527
Piedmont Virginia Community College ... VA ... 527
Southwest Virginia Community College ... VA ... 528
Thomas Nelson Community College ... VA ... 528
Tidewater Community College ... VA ... 528
Virginia Highlands Community College ... VA ... 528
Wytheville Community College ... VA ... 528
Bellevue College ... WA ... 531
Big Bend Community College ... WA ... 531
Clark College ... WA ... 532
Columbia Basin College ... WA ... 532
Everett Community College ... WA ... 533
Grays Harbor College ... WA ... 534
Highline Community College ... WA ... 534
Lower Columbia College ... WA ... 535
North Seattle Community College ... WA ... 536
Olympic College ... WA ... 535
Peninsula College ... WA ... 536
Pierce College District ... WA ... 536
Seattle Central Community College ... WA ... 537
Shoreline Community College ... WA ... 537
Skagit Valley College ... WA ... 538
South Puget Sound Community College ... WA ... 538
Tacoma Community College ... WA ... 538
Walla Walla Community College ... WA ... 538
Wenatchee Valley College ... WA ... 539
Whatcom Community College ... WA ... 539
Yakima Valley Community College ... WA ... 540
Blue Ridge Community and Technical College ... WV ... 542
Bluefield State College ... WV ... 543
Davis & Elkins College ... WV ... 540
Fairmont State University ... WV ... 543
Kanawha Valley Community & Technical College ... WV ... 542
Marshall University ... WV ... 543
Southern West Virginia Community and Technical College ... WV ... 542
University of Charleston ... WV ... 541
West Virginia Northern Community College ... WV ... 543
West Virginia University at Parkersburg ... WV ... 545
Blackhawk Technical College ... WI ... 553
Cardinal Stritch University ... WI ... 546
Chippewa Valley Technical College ... WI ... 553
College of Menominee Nation ... WI ... 546
Fox Valley Technical College ... WI ... 553
Gateway Technical College ... WI ... 553
Herzing University ... WI ... 547
Lakeshore Technical College ... WI ... 554
Madison Area Technical College ... WI ... 554
Mid-State Technical College ... WI ... 554
Milwaukee Area Technical College ... WI ... 554
Moraine Park Technical College ... WI ... 554
Nicolet Area Technical College ... WI ... 554
Northcentral Technical College ... WI ... 554
Northeast Wisconsin Technical College ... WI ... 555
Southwest Wisconsin Technical College ... WI ... 555
Waukesha County Technical College ... WI ... 555
Western Technical College ... WI ... 555
Wisconsin Indianhead Technical College ... WI ... 555
Casper College ... WY ... 555
Central Wyoming College ... WY ... 555
Laramie County Community College ... WY ... 556
Northern Wyoming Community College District ... WY ... 556
Northwest College ... WY ... 556
Western Wyoming Community College ... WY ... 556

ANEST: Council on Accreditation of Nurse Anesthesia Educational Programs: nurse anesthesia (C,M,D)

Samford University ... AL ... 6
University of Alabama at Birmingham ... AL ... 8
Midwestern University ... AZ ... 16
Arkansas State University ... AR ... 20
California State University-Fullerton ... CA ... 34
Loma Linda University ... CA ... 54
Samuel Merritt University ... CA ... 64
University of Southern California ... CA ... 76
Central Connecticut State University ... CT ... 91
Fairfield University ... CT ... 92
Georgetown University ... DC ... 98
Barry University ... FL ... 101
Bay Medical Center ... FL ... 101
Florida Gulf Coast University ... FL ... 119
Florida Hospital College of Health Sciences ... FL ... 108
Florida International University ... FL ... 119
University of Miami ... FL ... 122
University of North Florida ... FL ... 120
University of South Florida ... FL ... 120
Wolford College ... FL ... 123
Georgia Health Sciences University ... GA ... 130
Mercer University ... GA ... 133
DePaul University ... IL ... 148
Millikin University ... IL ... 158
Rosalind Franklin University of Medicine & Science ... IL ... 163
Rush University ... IL ... 163
Southern Illinois University Edwardsville ... IL ... 165
University of Iowa ... IA ... 182
Newman University ... KS ... 195
University of Kansas Medical Center ... KS ... 197
Murray State University ... KY ... 204
Louisiana State University Health Sciences Center-New Orleans ... LA ... 213
Our Lady of the Lake College ... LA ... 214
University of New England ... ME ... 220
Uniformed Services University of the Health Sciences ... MD ... 558
University of Maryland Baltimore ... MD ... 227
Boston College ... MA ... 232
Northeastern University ... MA ... 244
Michigan State University ... MI ... 255
Oakland University ... MI ... 257
University of Detroit Mercy ... MI ... 259
University of Michigan-Flint ... MI ... 259
Wayne State University ... MI ... 260
Mayo School of Health Sciences ... MN ... 262
Saint Mary's University of Minnesota ... MN ... 271
University of Minnesota-Twin Cities ... MN ... 272
Goldfarb School of Nursing at Barnes-Jewish College ... MO ... 282
Missouri State University ... MO ... 286
University of Missouri - Kansas City ... MO ... 291
Webster University ... MO ... 293
Bryan LGH College of Health Sciences ... NE ... 297
Clarkson College ... NE ... 297
UMDNJ-School of Nursing ... NJ ... 316
Albany Medical College ... NY ... 322
Columbia University in the City of New York ... NY ... 330
State University of New York at Buffalo ... NY ... 351
State University of New York Health Science Center at Brooklyn ... NY ... 352
Carolinas College of Health Sciences ... NC ... 363
Duke University ... NC ... 363
East Carolina University ... NC ... 377
University of North Carolina at Greensboro ... NC ... 379
Wake Forest University ... NC ... 380
Western Carolina University ... NC ... 379
University of North Dakota Main Campus ... ND ... 381
Case Western Reserve University ... OH ... 386
Lourdes University ... OH ... 395
Otterbein University ... OH ... 400
University of Akron, Main Campus, The ... OH ... 403
University of Cincinnati Main Campus ... OH ... 403
Youngstown State University ... OH ... 406
Oregon Health & Science University ... OR ... 418
Bloomsburg University of Pennsylvania ... PA ... 441
Drexel University ... PA ... 427
Gannon University ... PA ... 429
La Roche College ... PA ... 432
La Salle University ... PA ... 432
Saint Joseph's University ... PA ... 446
Saint Vincent College ... PA ... 446
Thomas Jefferson University ... PA ... 448
University of Pennsylvania ... PA ... 448
University of Pittsburgh ... PA ... 449
University of Scranton, The ... PA ... 450
Villanova University ... PA ... 450
York College of Pennsylvania ... PA ... 452
Inter American University of Puerto Rico Arecibo Campus ... PR ... 562
Medical University of South Carolina ... SC ... 459
University of South Carolina Columbia ... SC ... 462
Mount Marty College ... SD ... 464
Lincoln Memorial University ... TN ... 470
Middle Tennessee School of Anesthesia ... TN ... 471
Union University ... TN ... 476
University of Tennessee at Chattanooga ... TN ... 477
University of Tennessee Health Science Center ... TN ... 477
University of Tennessee, Knoxville ... TN ... 477
Baylor College of Medicine ... TX ... 481
Texas Christian University ... TX ... 498
Texas Wesleyan University ... TX ... 502
University of Texas Health Science Center at Houston (UTHealth), The ... TX ... 506
Westminster College ... UT ... 512
Old Dominion University ... VA ... 521
Virginia Commonwealth University ... VA ... 525
Gonzaga University ... WA ... 534
Marshall University ... WV ... 543
Mountain State University ... WV ... 541
University of Wisconsin-La Crosse ... WI ... 551

ARCPA: Accreditation Review Commission on Education for the Physician Assistant: physician assisting programs (C,A,B,M)

Birmingham-Southern College ... AL ... 2
University of Alabama at Birmingham ... AL ... 8
University of South Alabama ... AL ... 9
Midwestern University ... AZ ... 16
Harding University Main Campus ... AR ... 21
Loma Linda University ... CA ... 54
Riverside City College ... CA ... 64
Samuel Merritt University ... CA ... 64
San Joaquin Valley College, Inc. ... CA ... 66
Stanford University ... CA ... 71
Touro University-California ... CA ... 72
University of California-Davis ... CA ... 73
University of Southern California ... CA ... 76
Western University of Health Sciences ... CA ... 78
Red Rocks Community College ... CO ... 87
University of Colorado Denver|Anschutz Medical Campus ... CO ... 88
Quinnipiac University ... CT ... 93
Yale University ... CT ... 95
George Washington University ... DC ... 97
Howard University ... DC ... 98
Barry University ... FL ... 101
#Keiser University ... FL ... 112
Miami Dade College ... FL ... 113
Nova Southeastern University ... FL ... 114
University of Florida ... FL ... 120
Emory University ... GA ... 129
Georgia Health Sciences University ... GA ... 130
Mercer University ... GA ... 133
South University ... GA ... 136
Idaho State University ... ID ... 143
#City Colleges of Chicago Malcolm X College ... IL ... 147
Midwestern University ... IL ... 158
#Northwestern University ... IL ... 160
Rosalind Franklin University of Medicine & Science ... IL ... 163
#Rush University ... IL ... 163
Southern Illinois University Carbondale ... IL ... 164
Butler University ... IN ... 170
#Indiana State University ... IN ... 173
University of Saint Francis ... IN ... 180
Des Moines University ... IA ... 183
University of Iowa ... IA ... 182
Wichita State University ... KS ... 197
University of Kentucky ... KY ... 206
#University of the Cumberlands ... KY ... 206
Louisiana State University in Shreveport ... LA ... 213
#Our Lady of the Lake College ... LA ... 214
University of New England ... ME ... 220
Anne Arundel Community College ... MD ... 221
Towson University ... MD ... 228
University of Maryland Eastern Shore ... MD ... 227
Massachusetts College of Pharmacy and Health Sciences ... MA ... 241
Northeastern University ... MA ... 244
Springfield College ... MA ... 245
Central Michigan University ... MI ... 249
Grand Valley State University ... MI ... 252
University of Detroit Mercy ... MI ... 259
Wayne State University ... MI ... 260
Western Michigan University ... MI ... 260
Augsburg College ... MN ... 261
#Mississippi College ... MS ... 275
Missouri State University ... MO ... 286
Saint Louis University ... MO ... 289
Rocky Mountain College ... MT ... 296
Union College ... NE ... 300
University of Nebraska Medical Center ... NE ... 301
#Franklin Pierce University ... NH ... 305
Seton Hall University ... NJ ... 315
UMDNJ-School of Health Related Professions ... NJ ... 317
University of New Mexico Main Campus ... NM ... 321
Albany Medical College ... NY ... 322
City University of New York The City College ... NY ... 326
City University of New York York College ... NY ... 329
Daemen College ... NY ... 331
D'Youville College ... NY ... 332
Hofstra University ... NY ... 335
Le Moyne College ... NY ... 338
Long Island University Brooklyn Campus ... NY ... 338
Mercy College ... NY ... 340
New York Institute of Technology ... NY ... 343
Pace University ... NY ... 345
Rochester Institute of Technology ... NY ... 347
St. John's University ... NY ... 348
State University of New York at Stony Brook ... NY ... 352
State University of New York Health Science Center at Brooklyn ... NY ... 352
#State University of New York Upstate Medical University ... NY ... 352
Touro College ... NY ... 357
Wagner College ... NY ... 359
Weill Cornell Medical College ... NY ... 360
#Campbell University ... NC ... 362
Duke University ... NC ... 363
East Carolina University ... NC ... 377
Methodist University ... NC ... 366
Wake Forest University ... NC ... 380
Wingate University ... NC ... 380
University of North Dakota Main Campus ... ND ... 381
Cleveland State University ... OH ... 388
Cuyahoga Community College ... OH ... 389
Kettering College of Medical Arts ... OH ... 394
Marietta College ... OH ... 395
#University of Findlay, The ... OH ... 404
#University of Mount Union ... OH ... 404
University of Toledo ... OH ... 404
University of Oklahoma Health Sciences Center ... OK ... 413
Oregon Health & Science University ... OR ... 418
Pacific University ... OR ... 419
Arcadia University ... PA ... 422
Chatham University ... PA ... 425
DeSales University ... PA ... 426
Drexel University ... PA ... 427
Duquesne University ... PA ... 428
Gannon University ... PA ... 429
King's College ... PA ... 432
Lock Haven University of Pennsylvania ... PA ... 443
Marywood University ... PA ... 435
Pennsylvania College of Technology ... PA ... 440
Philadelphia College of Osteopathic Medicine ... PA ... 444
Philadelphia University ... PA ... 444
Saint Francis University ... PA ... 446
Salus University ... PA ... 446
Seton Hill University ... PA ... 447
#University of Pittsburgh ... PA ... 449
Medical University of South Carolina ... SC ... 459
University of South Dakota, The ... SD ... 465
#Bethel University ... TN ... 467
#Lincoln Memorial University ... TN ... 470
South College ... TN ... 472
Trevecca Nazarene University ... TN ... 476
Baylor College of Medicine ... TX ... 481
Texas Tech University ... TX ... 501
University of North Texas Health Science Center at Fort Worth ... TX ... 504

ART: National Association of Schools of Art and Design: art and design (C,A,B,M,D)

AUD: American Speech-Language-Hearing Association: audiology (M,D)

BBT: Commission on Accreditation of Allied Health Education Programs: blood bank technology (C,M)

Rush University ... IL ... 163
Johns Hopkins University ... MD ... 223
University of Cincinnati Main Campus ... OH ... 403
University of Texas Health Science Center at San Antonio ... TX ... 506
University of Texas Medical Branch, The ... TX ... 507
University of Texas Southwestern Medical Center at Dallas ... TX ... 507

BI: Association for Biblical Higher Education: bible college education (C,A,B,M,D)

Heritage Christian University ... AL ... 4
Huntsville Bible College ... AL ... 4
Selma University ... AL ... 6
Southeastern Bible College ... AL ... 7
Alaska Bible College ... AK ... 10
Ecclesia College ... AR ... 21
Bethesda Christian University ... CA ... 30
@Eternity Bible College ... CA ... 45
@Grace Mission University ... CA ... 48
Hope International University ... CA ... 50
@Horizon College of San Diego ... CA ... 50
@International Reformed University and Seminary ... CA ... 51
King's University, The ... CA ... 53
Life Pacific College ... CA ... 54
Olivet University ... CA ... 60
Presbyterian Theological Seminary in America ... CA ... 63
School of Urban Missions ... CA ... 68
William Jessup University ... CA ... 79
World Mission University ... CA ... 79
Nazarene Bible College ... CO ... 86
Florida Christian College ... FL ... 107
Hobe Sound Bible College ... FL ... 110
Robert E. Webber Institute for Worship Studies, The ... FL ... 116
@South Florida Bible College ... FL ... 117
Trinity College of Florida ... FL ... 122
Beulah Heights University ... GA ... 126
#Carver College ... GA ... 126
Toccoa Falls College ... GA ... 137
@New Hope Christian College-Hawaii ... HI ... 140
Boise Bible College ... ID ... 142
Lincoln Christian University ... IL ... 156
Moody Bible Institute ... IL ... 158
Crossroads Bible College ... IN ... 170
Emmaus Bible College ... IA ... 184
Faith Baptist Bible College and Seminary ... IA ... 184
Barclay College ... KS ... 190
Manhattan Christian College ... KS ... 194
Clear Creek Baptist Bible College ... KY ... 199
Kentucky Mountain Bible College ... KY ... 203
@Louisville Bible College ... KY ... 204
@Simmons College of Kentucky ... KY ... 205
Washington Bible College/Capital Bible Seminary ... MD ... 229
Zion Bible College ... MA ... 247
Grace Bible College ... MI ... 251
Great Lakes Christian College ... MI ... 252
Kuyper College ... MI ... 254
#Crossroads College ... MN ... 263
Oak Hills Christian College ... MN ... 270
Southeastern Baptist College ... MS ... 277
Baptist Bible College ... MO ... 279
Calvary Bible College and Theological Seminary ... MO ... 279
Central Bible College ... MO ... 279
Central Christian College of the Bible ... MO ... 279
Ozark Christian College ... MO ... 287
Saint Louis Christian College ... MO ... 288
@Montana Bible College ... MT ... 294
Grace University ... NE ... 298
Nebraska Christian College ... NE ... 299
Somerset Christian College ... NJ ... 315
Davis College ... NY ... 332
@Carolina Bible College ... NC ... 362
Carolina Christian College ... NC ... 362
@Grace College of Divinity ... NC ... 364
Laurel University ... NC ... 365
Mid-Atlantic Christian University ... NC ... 367
Trinity Bible College ... ND ... 383
Allegheny Wesleyan College ... OH ... 383
Cincinnati Christian University ... OH ... 387
God's Bible School and College ... OH ... 391
Ohio Christian University ... OH ... 398
Rosedale Bible College ... OH ... 401
Tri-State Bible College ... OH ... 402
Family of Faith College ... OK ... 408
Multnomah University ... OR ... 417
New Hope Christian College ... OR ... 417
Baptist Bible College and Seminary ... PA ... 422
Lancaster Bible College ... PA ... 433
Philadelphia Biblical University ... PA ... 444
Colegio Biblico Pentecostal De Puerto Rico ... PR ... 561
Universidad Pentecostal Mizpa ... PR ... 566
Columbia International University ... SC ... 457
W.L. Bonner College ... SC ... 463
@All Saints Bible College ... TN ... 466
American Baptist College ... TN ... 466
Free Will Baptist Bible College ... TN ... 468
Johnson University ... TN ... 469
@Mid-South Christian College ... TN ... 471
Williamson Christian College ... TN ... 478
Arlington Baptist College ... TX ... 480
Baptist University of the Americas ... TX ... 481
College of Biblical Studies-Houston ... TX ... 483
Dallas Christian College ... TX ... 484
Rio Grande Bible Institute ... TX ... 493
@Bethel College ... VA ... 516
@Washington Baptist University ... VA ... 530
Appalachian Bible College ... WV ... 540

BUS: AACSB-The Association to Advance Collegiate Schools of Business: business and management (B,M,D)

Auburn University ... AL ... 1
Auburn University at Montgomery ... AL ... 2
Birmingham-Southern College ... AL ... 2
Jacksonville State University ... AL ... 4
Samford University ... AL ... 6
Tuskegee University ... AL ... 8
University of Alabama at Birmingham ... AL ... 8
University of Alabama in Huntsville ... AL ... 9
University of Alabama, The ... AL ... 8
University of Montevallo ... AL ... 9
University of South Alabama ... AL ... 9
University of Alaska Anchorage ... AK ... 10
University of Alaska Fairbanks ... AK ... 10
Arizona State University ... AZ ... 12
Northern Arizona University ... AZ ... 17
Thunderbird School of Global Management ... AZ ... 18
University of Arizona ... AZ ... 19
Arkansas State University ... AR ... 20
Arkansas Tech University ... AR ... 20
Henderson State University ... AR ... 21
Ouachita Baptist University ... AR ... 22
Southern Arkansas University ... AR ... 23
University of Arkansas at Little Rock ... AR ... 24
University of Arkansas Main Campus ... AR ... 24
University of Central Arkansas ... AR ... 25
California Polytechnic State University-San Luis Obispo ... CA ... 33
California State Polytechnic University-Pomona ... CA ... 33
California State University-Bakersfield ... CA ... 33
California State University-Chico ... CA ... 34
California State University-East Bay ... CA ... 34
California State University-Fresno ... CA ... 34
California State University-Fullerton ... CA ... 34
California State University-Long Beach ... CA ... 35
California State University-Los Angeles ... CA ... 35
California State University-Northridge ... CA ... 35
California State University-Sacramento ... CA ... 35
California State University-San Bernardino ... CA ... 36
California State University-Stanislaus ... CA ... 36
Chapman University ... CA ... 39
Claremont Graduate University ... CA ... 40
Loyola Marymount University ... CA ... 56
Monterey Institute of International Studies ... CA ... 57
Naval Postgraduate School ... CA ... 557
Pepperdine University ... CA ... 61
San Diego State University ... CA ... 36
San Francisco State University ... CA ... 36
San Jose State University ... CA ... 37
Santa Clara University ... CA ... 68
Sonoma State University ... CA ... 37
Stanford University ... CA ... 71
University of California-Berkeley ... CA ... 73
University of California-Davis ... CA ... 73
University of California-Irvine ... CA ... 73
University of California-Los Angeles ... CA ... 74
University of California-Riverside ... CA ... 74
University of California-San Diego ... CA ... 74
University of San Diego ... CA ... 76
University of San Francisco ... CA ... 76
University of Southern California ... CA ... 76
University of the Pacific ... CA ... 75
Colorado State University ... CO ... 83
Colorado State University-Pueblo ... CO ... 83
Fort Lewis College ... CO ... 84
United States Air Force Academy ... CO ... 558
University of Colorado at Colorado Springs ... CO ... 88
University of Colorado Boulder ... CO ... 88
University of Colorado Denver|Anschutz Medical Campus ... CO ... 88
University of Denver ... CO ... 88
University of Northern Colorado ... CO ... 88
Fairfield University ... CT ... 92
Quinnipiac University ... CT ... 93
Sacred Heart University ... CT ... 93
United States Coast Guard Academy ... CT ... 558
University of Connecticut ... CT ... 94
University of Hartford ... CT ... 95
Yale University ... CT ... 95
Delaware State University ... DE ... 95
University of Delaware ... DE ... 96
American University ... DC ... 97
George Washington University ... DC ... 97
Georgetown University ... DC ... 98
Howard University ... DC ... 98
Barry University ... FL ... 101
Florida Atlantic University ... FL ... 118
Florida Gulf Coast University ... FL ... 119
Florida International University ... FL ... 119
Florida State University ... FL ... 119
Jacksonville University ... FL ... 111
Rollins College ... FL ... 116
Stetson University ... FL ... 121
University of Central Florida ... FL ... 120
University of Florida ... FL ... 120
University of Miami ... FL ... 122
University of North Florida ... FL ... 120
University of South Florida ... FL ... 120
University of South Florida St. Petersburg ... FL ... 121
University of Tampa ... FL ... 122
University of West Florida ... FL ... 121
Augusta State University ... GA ... 125
Berry College ... GA ... 125
Clark Atlanta University ... GA ... 126
Clayton State University ... GA ... 127
Columbus State University ... GA ... 127
Dalton State College ... GA ... 127
Emory University ... GA ... 129
Georgia College & State University ... GA ... 129
Georgia Institute of Technology ... GA ... 130
Georgia Southern University ... GA ... 131
Georgia Southwestern State University ... GA ... 131
Georgia State University ... GA ... 131
Kennesaw State University ... GA ... 132
Mercer University ... GA ... 133
Morehouse College ... GA ... 134
North Georgia College & State University ... GA ... 134
Savannah State University ... GA ... 136
University of Georgia ... GA ... 138
University of West Georgia ... GA ... 138
Valdosta State University ... GA ... 138
University of Hawaii at Hilo ... HI ... 141
University of Hawaii at Manoa ... HI ... 141
Boise State University ... ID ... 142
Idaho State University ... ID ... 143
University of Idaho ... ID ... 144
Bradley University ... IL ... 145
DePaul University ... IL ... 148
Eastern Illinois University ... IL ... 150
Illinois Institute of Technology ... IL ... 153
Illinois State University ... IL ... 153
Loyola University Chicago ... IL ... 157
Northern Illinois University ... IL ... 160
Northwestern University ... IL ... 160
Southern Illinois University Carbondale ... IL ... 164
Southern Illinois University Edwardsville ... IL ... 165
University of Chicago ... IL ... 166
University of Illinois at Chicago ... IL ... 166
University of Illinois at Springfield ... IL ... 167
University of Illinois at Urbana-Champaign ... IL ... 167
Western Illinois University ... IL ... 168
Ball State University ... IN ... 169
Butler University ... IN ... 170
Indiana State University ... IN ... 173
Indiana University Bloomington ... IN ... 173
Indiana University Kokomo ... IN ... 173
Indiana University Northwest ... IN ... 173
Indiana University-Purdue University Fort Wayne ... IN ... 174
Indiana University South Bend ... IN ... 174
Indiana University Southeast ... IN ... 174
Purdue University Main Campus ... IN ... 178
University of Evansville ... IN ... 180
University of Notre Dame ... IN ... 180
University of Southern Indiana ... IN ... 180
Valparaiso University ... IN ... 181
Drake University ... IA ... 184
Iowa State University ... IA ... 182
University of Iowa ... IA ... 182
University of Northern Iowa ... IA ... 182
Emporia State University ... KS ... 192
Kansas State University ... KS ... 194
Pittsburg State University ... KS ... 195
University of Kansas Main Campus ... KS ... 196
Washburn University ... KS ... 197
Wichita State University ... KS ... 197
Bellarmine University ... KY ... 198
Eastern Kentucky University ... KY ... 200
Morehead State University ... KY ... 204
Murray State University ... KY ... 204
Northern Kentucky University ... KY ... 205
University of Kentucky ... KY ... 206
University of Louisville ... KY ... 207
Western Kentucky University ... KY ... 207
Grambling State University ... LA ... 215
Louisiana State University and Agricultural and Mechanical College ... LA ... 212
Louisiana State University in Shreveport ... LA ... 213
Louisiana Tech University ... LA ... 215
Loyola University New Orleans ... LA ... 213
McNeese State University ... LA ... 215
Nicholls State University ... LA ... 216
Northwestern State University ... LA ... 216
Southeastern Louisiana University ... LA ... 216
Southern University and A&M College ... LA ... 214
Tulane University ... LA ... 215
University of Louisiana at Lafayette ... LA ... 216
University of Louisiana at Monroe ... LA ... 216
University of New Orleans ... LA ... 213
University of Maine ... ME ... 220
University of Southern Maine ... ME ... 220
Frostburg State University ... MD ... 228
Loyola University Maryland ... MD ... 224
Morgan State University ... MD ... 224
Salisbury University ... MD ... 228
Towson University ... MD ... 228
University of Baltimore ... MD ... 229
University of Maryland College Park ... MD ... 227
University of Maryland Eastern Shore ... MD ... 227
Babson College ... MA ... 230
Bentley University ... MA ... 231
Boston College ... MA ... 232
Boston University ... MA ... 232
Brandeis University ... MA ... 233
Clark University ... MA ... 233
Harvard University ... MA ... 235
Massachusetts Institute of Technology ... MA ... 242
Northeastern University ... MA ... 244
Simmons College ... MA ... 245
Suffolk University ... MA ... 245
University of Massachusetts ... MA ... 237
University of Massachusetts Boston ... MA ... 237
University of Massachusetts Dartmouth ... MA ... 237
University of Massachusetts Lowell ... MA ... 237
Western New England University ... MA ... 246
Worcester Polytechnic Institute ... MA ... 247
Central Michigan University ... MI ... 249
Eastern Michigan University ... MI ... 250
Grand Valley State University ... MI ... 252
Michigan State University ... MI ... 255
Michigan Technological University ... MI ... 255
Northern Michigan University ... MI ... 256
Oakland University ... MI ... 257
Saginaw Valley State University ... MI ... 258
University of Detroit Mercy ... MI ... 259
University of Michigan-Ann Arbor ... MI ... 259
University of Michigan-Dearborn ... MI ... 259
University of Michigan-Flint ... MI ... 259
Wayne State University ... MI ... 260
Western Michigan University ... MI ... 260
Minnesota State University Duluth ... MN ... 268
Minnesota State University, Mankato ... MN ... 267
St. Cloud State University ... MN ... 269
University of Minnesota Duluth ... MN ... 272
University of Minnesota-Twin Cities ... MN ... 272
Winona State University ... MN ... 270
Jackson State University ... MS ... 275
Millsaps College ... MS ... 275
Mississippi State University ... MS ... 276
University of Mississippi ... MS ... 277
University of Southern Mississippi ... MS ... 278
Drury University ... MO ... 281
Missouri State University ... MO ... 286
Missouri Western State University ... MO ... 287
Rockhurst University ... MO ... 288
Saint Louis University ... MO ... 289
Southeast Missouri State University ... MO ... 290
Truman State University ... MO ... 291
University of Central Missouri ... MO ... 291
University of Missouri - Columbia ... MO ... 291
University of Missouri - Kansas City ... MO ... 291
University of Missouri - Saint Louis ... MO ... 291
Washington University in St. Louis ... MO ... 292
Montana State University ... MT ... 295
Montana State University - Billings ... MT ... 295
University of Montana - Missoula, The ... MT ... 295
Creighton University ... NE ... 297
University of Nebraska at Kearney ... NE ... 300
University of Nebraska at Omaha ... NE ... 301
University of Nebraska - Lincoln ... NE ... 300
University of Nevada, Las Vegas ... NV ... 302
University of Nevada, Reno ... NV ... 303
Dartmouth College ... NH ... 305
University of New Hampshire ... NH ... 306
College of New Jersey, The ... NJ ... 308
Fairleigh Dickinson University ... NJ ... 310
Monmouth University ... NJ ... 311
Montclair State University ... NJ ... 311
New Jersey Institute of Technology ... NJ ... 312
Ramapo College of New Jersey ... NJ ... 313
Rider University ... NJ ... 313
Rowan University ... NJ ... 314
Rutgers the State University of New Jersey Camden Campus ... NJ ... 314
Rutgers the State University of New Jersey Newark Campus ... NJ ... 314
Seton Hall University ... NJ ... 315
William Paterson University of New Jersey ... NJ ... 317
New Mexico State University Main Campus ... NM ... 319
University of New Mexico Main Campus ... NM ... 321
Adelphi University ... NY ... 322
Alfred University ... NY ... 322
Baruch College/City University of New York ... NY ... 326
Canisius College ... NY ... 325
Clarkson University ... NY ... 329
Columbia University in the City of New York ... NY ... 330
Cornell University ... NY ... 331
Fordham University ... NY ... 334
Hofstra University ... NY ... 335
Iona College ... NY ... 336
Ithaca College ... NY ... 336
Le Moyne College ... NY ... 338
Long Island University C.W. Post Campus ... NY ... 339
Manhattan College ... NY ... 339
Marist College ... NY ... 340
New York University ... NY ... 344
Niagara University ... NY ... 344
Pace University ... NY ... 345
Rensselaer Polytechnic Institute ... NY ... 347
Rochester Institute of Technology ... NY ... 347
St. Bonaventure University ... NY ... 348
St. John Fisher College ... NY ... 348
St. John's University ... NY ... 348
Siena College ... NY ... 350
State University of New York at Albany ... NY ... 351
State University of New York at Binghamton ... NY ... 351
State University of New York at Buffalo ... NY ... 351

BUSA: AACSB-The Association to Advance Collegiate Schools of Business: accounting (B,M,D)

CACREP: Council for Accreditation of Counseling & Related Educational Programs: addiction counseling, career counseling, marriage, couple and family counseling, mental health counseling, school counseling, student affairs and college counseling and counselor education and supervision (M,D)

Augusta State University ... GA ... 125
Clark Atlanta University ... GA ... 126
Columbus State University ... GA ... 127
Georgia Southern University ... GA ... 131
Georgia State University ... GA ... 131
Mercer University ... GA ... 133
North Georgia College & State University ... GA ... 134
University of Georgia ... GA ... 138
University of West Georgia ... GA ... 138
Valdosta State University ... GA ... 138
Boise State University ... ID ... 142
Idaho State University ... ID ... 143
Northwest Nazarene University ... ID ... 143
Argosy University, Chicago ... IL ... 144
Argosy University, Schaumburg ... IL ... 145
Bradley University ... IL ... 145
Chicago State University ... IL ... 146
Concordia University Chicago ... IL ... 148
Eastern Illinois University ... IL ... 150
Governors State University ... IL ... 151
Northeastern Illinois University ... IL ... 159
Northern Illinois University ... IL ... 160
Roosevelt University ... IL ... 162
Southern Illinois University Carbondale ... IL ... 164
Triton College ... IL ... 166
University of Illinois at Springfield ... IL ... 167
Western Illinois University ... IL ... 168
Ball State University ... IN ... 169
Butler University ... IN ... 170
Grace College and Seminary ... IN ... 171
Indiana State University ... IN ... 173
Indiana University Bloomington ... IN ... 173
Indiana University South Bend ... IN ... 174
Indiana Wesleyan University ... IN ... 174
Purdue University Main Campus ... IN ... 178
Valparaiso University ... IN ... 181
University of Iowa ... IA ... 182
University of Northern Iowa ... IA ... 182
Emporia State University ... KS ... 192
Kansas State University ... KS ... 194
MidAmerica Nazarene University ... KS ... 195
Pittsburg State University ... KS ... 195
Eastern Kentucky University ... KY ... 200
Lindsey Wilson College ... KY ... 203
Western Kentucky University ... KY ... 207
Louisiana State University and Agricultural and Mechanical College ... LA ... 212
Loyola University New Orleans ... LA ... 213
Northwestern State University ... LA ... 216
Our Lady of Holy Cross College ... LA ... 214
Southeastern Louisiana University ... LA ... 216
Southern University and A&M College ... LA ... 214
University of Louisiana at Monroe ... LA ... 216
University of New Orleans ... LA ... 213
University of Southern Maine ... ME ... 220
Loyola University Maryland ... MD ... 224
University of Maryland College Park ... MD ... 227
Bridgewater State University ... MA ... 238
Andrews University ... MI ... 247
Eastern Michigan University ... MI ... 250
Michigan State University ... MI ... 255
Oakland University ... MI ... 257
University of Detroit Mercy ... MI ... 259
Wayne State University ... MI ... 260
Western Michigan University ... MI ... 260
Capella University ... MN ... 262
Minnesota State University Moorhead ... MN ... 268
Minnesota State University, Mankato ... MN ... 267
St. Cloud State University ... MN ... 269
Walden University ... MN ... 272
Winona State University ... MN ... 270
Delta State University ... MS ... 274
Jackson State University ... MS ... 275
Mississippi College ... MS ... 275
Mississippi State University ... MS ... 276
University of Mississippi ... MS ... 277
Southeast Missouri State University ... MO ... 290
University of Central Missouri ... MO ... 291
University of Missouri - Saint Louis ... MO ... 291
Montana State University ... MT ... 295
University of Montana - Missoula, The ... MT ... 295
University of Nebraska at Kearney ... NE ... 300
University of Nebraska at Omaha ... NE ... 301
University of Nevada, Las Vegas ... NV ... 302
University of Nevada, Reno ... NV ... 303
Antioch University New England ... NH ... 303
Plymouth State University ... NH ... 307
College of New Jersey, The ... NJ ... 308
Kean University ... NJ ... 311
Monmouth University ... NJ ... 311
Montclair State University ... NJ ... 311
Rider University ... NJ ... 313
Rutgers the State University of New Jersey New Brunswick Campus ... NJ ... 314
UMDNJ-School of Health Related Professions ... NJ ... 317
William Paterson University of New Jersey ... NJ ... 317
New Mexico State University Main Campus ... NM ... 319
University of New Mexico Main Campus ... NM ... 321
Canisius College ... NY ... 325
City University of New York Brooklyn College ... NY ... 326
City University of New York Herbert H. Lehman College ... NY ... 327
City University of New York Hunter College ... NY ... 327
Long Island University C.W. Post Campus ... NY ... 339
St. Bonaventure University ... NY ... 348
St. John Fisher College ... NY ... 348
St. John's University ... NY ... 348
State University of New York College at Plattsburgh ... NY ... 354
State University of New York, The College at Brockport ... NY ... 352
Syracuse University Main Campus ... NY ... 357
University of Rochester ... NY ... 358
Appalachian State University ... NC ... 377
Gardner-Webb University ... NC ... 364
North Carolina Agricultural and Technical State University ... NC ... 377
North Carolina Central University ... NC ... 378
North Carolina State University ... NC ... 378
University of North Carolina at Chapel Hill ... NC ... 378
University of North Carolina at Charlotte ... NC ... 378
University of North Carolina at Greensboro ... NC ... 379
Wake Forest University ... NC ... 380
Western Carolina University ... NC ... 379
North Dakota State University Main Campus. ND ... 381
Bowling Green State University ... OH ... 385
Cleveland State University ... OH ... 388
Heidelberg University ... OH ... 391
John Carroll University ... OH ... 392
Kent State University Main Campus ... OH ... 393
Ohio University Main Campus ... OH ... 399
University of Akron, Main Campus, The ... OH ... 403
University of Cincinnati Main Campus ... OH ... 403
University of Dayton ... OH ... 404
University of Toledo ... OH ... 404
Walsh University ... OH ... 405
Wright State University Main Campus ... OH ... 406
Xavier University ... OH ... 406
Youngstown State University ... OH ... 406
Oklahoma State University ... OK ... 410
Lewis and Clark College ... OR ... 416
Oregon State University ... OR ... 418
Portland State University ... OR ... 418
Southern Oregon University ... OR ... 419
California University of Pennsylvania ... PA ... 441
Duquesne University ... PA ... 428
Edinboro University of Pennsylvania ... PA ... 442
Gannon University ... PA ... 429
Geneva College ... PA ... 429
Indiana University of Pennsylvania ... PA ... 442
Marywood University ... PA ... 435
Neumann University ... PA ... 437
Penn State University Park ... PA ... 438
Shippensburg University of Pennsylvania ... PA ... 443
Slippery Rock University of Pennsylvania ... PA ... 443
University of Scranton, The ... PA ... 450
West Chester University of Pennsylvania ... PA ... 443
Citadel, The Military College of South Carolina, The ... SC ... 456
Clemson University ... SC ... 456
South Carolina State University ... SC ... 460
University of South Carolina Columbia ... SC ... 462
Winthrop University ... SC ... 463
South Dakota State University ... SD ... 466
University of South Dakota, The ... SD ... 465
East Tennessee State University ... TN ... 473
Middle Tennessee State University ... TN ... 473
University of Memphis, The ... TN ... 474
University of Tennessee at Chattanooga ... TN ... 477
University of Tennessee, Knoxville ... TN ... 477
Vanderbilt University ... TN ... 477
St. Mary's University ... TX ... 493
Sam Houston State University ... TX ... 501
Stephen F. Austin State University ... TX ... 495
Texas A & M University - Commerce ... TX ... 497
Texas A & M University - Corpus Christi ... TX ... 497
Texas State University-San Marcos ... TX ... 501
Texas Tech University ... TX ... 501
Texas Woman's University ... TX ... 502
University of Houston - Victoria ... TX ... 503
University of Mary Hardin-Baylor ... TX ... 504
University of North Texas ... TX ... 504
University of Texas at Brownsville, The ... TX ... 505
University of Texas at San Antonio ... TX ... 506
University of Vermont ... VT ... 514
Argosy University, Washington DC ... VA ... 516
College of William & Mary ... VA ... 517
Eastern Mennonite University ... VA ... 518
James Madison University ... VA ... 520
Lynchburg College ... VA ... 520
Marymount University ... VA ... 521
Old Dominion University ... VA ... 521
Radford University ... VA ... 522
Regent University ... VA ... 523
University of Virginia ... VA ... 525
Virginia Commonwealth University ... VA ... 525
Virginia Polytechnic Institute and State University ... VA ... 529
Central Washington University ... WA ... 531
Eastern Washington University ... WA ... 533
Gonzaga University ... WA ... 534
Seattle University ... WA ... 537
Western Washington University ... WA ... 539
West Virginia University ... WV ... 544
University of Wisconsin-Oshkosh ... WI ... 551
University of Wisconsin-Whitewater ... WI ... 552
University of Wyoming ... WY ... 556

CEA: Commission on English Language Program Accreditation: english language (C)

University of Alabama, The ... AL ... 8
University of North Alabama ... AL ... 9
University of Arizona ... AZ ... 19
University of Arkansas Main Campus ... AR ... 24
California State University-Long Beach ... CA ... 35
San Jose State University ... CA ... 37
University of California-Irvine ... CA ... 73
University of California-San Diego ... CA ... 74
University of Southern California ... CA ... 76
Arapahoe Community College ... CO ... 80
Colorado State University ... CO ... 83
University of Colorado Boulder ... CO ... 88
University of Denver ... CO ... 88
University of Connecticut ... CT ... 94
University of Delaware ... DE ... 96
Georgetown University ... DC ... 98
University of Central Florida ... FL ... 120
University of Florida ... FL ... 120
University of Miami ... FL ... 122
University of South Florida ... FL ... 120
Valencia College ... FL ... 122
Georgia State University ... GA ... 131
University of Hawaii at Hilo ... HI ... 141
University of Hawaii at Manoa ... HI ... 141
University of Hawaii Hawaii Community College ... HI ... 141
Harper College ... IL ... 151
Southern Illinois University Carbondale ... IL ... 164
University of Illinois at Chicago ... IL ... 166
Western Illinois University ... IL ... 168
Indiana State University ... IN ... 173
University of Iowa ... IA ... 182
University of Northern Iowa ... IA ... 182
Kansas State University ... KS ... 194
University of Kansas Main Campus ... KS ... 196
University of Maryland College Park ... MD ... 227
Boston University ... MA ... 232
Michigan State University ... MI ... 255
Western Michigan University ... MI ... 260
Missouri State University ... MO ... 286
University of Central Missouri ... MO ... 291
College of Southern Nevada ... NV ... 302
State University of New York at Buffalo ... NY ... 351
University of North Carolina at Greensboro ... NC ... 379
Ohio State University Main Campus, The ... OH ... 398
Xavier University ... OH ... 406
University of Oregon ... OR ... 419
Drexel University ... PA ... 427
Duquesne University ... PA ... 428
Penn State University Park ... PA ... 438
University of Pennsylvania ... PA ... 448
University of Pittsburgh ... PA ... 449
Wilkes University ... PA ... 451
University of South Carolina Columbia ... SC ... 462
Lone Star College System ... TX ... 490
Texas A & M University ... TX ... 497
University of Houston ... TX ... 503
University of North Texas ... TX ... 504
University of Utah, The ... UT ... 510
Utah State University ... UT ... 511
Saint Michael's College ... VT ... 514
George Mason University ... VA ... 519
Virginia Polytechnic Institute and State University ... VA ... 529
Eastern Washington University ... WA ... 533
Gonzaga University ... WA ... 534
University of Washington ... WA ... 538
Washington State University ... WA ... 539

CHIRO: Council on Chiropractic Education: chiropractic education (FP)

Cleveland Chiropractic College ... CA ... 40
Life Chiropractic College West ... CA ... 53
Palmer College of Chiropractic, West Campus ... CA ... 60
Southern California University of Health Sciences ... CA ... 71
University of Bridgeport ... CT ... 94
Palmer College of Chiropractic, Florida Campus ... FL ... 114
Life University ... GA ... 133
National University of Health Sciences ... IL ... 159
Palmer College of Chiropractic ... IA ... 188
Cleveland Chiropractic College - Kansas City ... KS ... 191
Northwestern Health Sciences University ... MN ... 270
Logan College of Chiropractic ... MO ... 284
D'Youville College ... NY ... 332
New York Chiropractic College ... NY ... 342
University of Western States ... OR ... 420
Sherman College of Chiropractic ... SC ... 460
Parker University ... TX ... 492
Texas Chiropractic College ... TX ... 498

CIDA: Council for Interior Design Accreditation: interior design (B,M)

Auburn University ... AL ... 1
Samford University ... AL ... 6
University of Alabama, The ... AL ... 8
Virginia College ... AL ... 3
Arizona State University ... AZ ... 12
Art Institute of Phoenix, The ... AZ ... 12
Southwest University of Visual Arts ... AZ ... 18
Harding University Main Campus ... AR ... 21
University of Arkansas Main Campus ... AR ... 24
University of Central Arkansas ... AR ... 25
Academy of Art University ... CA ... 26
Art Institute of California-Los Angeles, The ... CA ... 29
Art Institute of California-Orange County, The ... CA ... 29
California College of the Arts ... CA ... 31
California State Polytechnic University-Pomona ... CA ... 33
California State University-Fresno ... CA ... 34
California State University-Northridge ... CA ... 35
California State University-Sacramento ... CA ... 35
Design Institute of San Diego ... CA ... 43
Interior Designers Institute ... CA ... 51
San Diego State University ... CA ... 36
Woodbury University ... CA ... 79
Art Institute of Colorado, The ... CO ... 81
Colorado State University ... CO ... 83
Rocky Mountain College of Art & Design ... CO ... 87
George Washington University ... DC ... 97
Art Institute of Fort Lauderdale, The ... FL ... 100
Florida International University ... FL ... 119
Florida State University ... FL ... 119
International Academy of Design and Technology ... FL ... 111
Miami International University of Art & Design ... FL ... 113
Ringling College of Art and Design ... FL ... 115
University of Florida ... FL ... 120
American InterContinental University ... GA ... 124
Art Institute of Atlanta, The ... GA ... 124
Brenau University ... GA ... 126
Georgia Southern University ... GA ... 131
Savannah College of Art and Design ... GA ... 136
University of Georgia ... GA ... 138
Brigham Young University-Idaho ... ID ... 142
University of Idaho ... ID ... 144
Columbia College Chicago ... IL ... 148
Harrington College of Design ... IL ... 151
Illinois Institute of Art, The ... IL ... 153
Illinois State University ... IL ... 153
International Academy of Design and Technology ... IL ... 153
Southern Illinois University Carbondale ... IL ... 164
Ball State University ... IN ... 169
Indiana State University ... IN ... 173
Indiana University Bloomington ... IN ... 173
Indiana University-Purdue University Indianapolis ... IN ... 174
Purdue University Main Campus ... IN ... 178
Iowa State University ... IA ... 182
Kansas State University ... KS ... 194
University of Kentucky ... KY ... 206
University of Louisville ... KY ... 207
Louisiana State University and Agricultural and Mechanical College ... LA ... 212
Louisiana Tech University ... LA ... 215
University of Louisiana at Lafayette ... LA ... 216
Boston Architectural College ... MA ... 232
Endicott College ... MA ... 234
Mount Ida College ... MA ... 243
Newbury College ... MA ... 243
Suffolk University ... MA ... 245
Wentworth Institute of Technology ... MA ... 246
Central Michigan University ... MI ... 249
College for Creative Studies ... MI ... 250
Eastern Michigan University ... MI ... 250
Ferris State University ... MI ... 251
International Academy of Design and Technology ... MI ... 252
Lawrence Technological University ... MI ... 254
Michigan State University ... MI ... 255
Western Michigan University ... MI ... 260
University of Minnesota-Twin Cities ... MN ... 272
Mississippi State University ... MS ... 276
University of Southern Mississippi ... MS ... 278
Maryville University of Saint Louis ... MO ... 284
University of Missouri - Columbia ... MO ... 291
University of Nebraska at Kearney ... NE ... 300
University of Nebraska - Lincoln ... NE ... 300
Art Institute of Las Vegas, The ... NV ... 301
University of Nevada, Las Vegas ... NV ... 302
Kean University ... NJ ... 311
Southwest University of Visual Arts ... NM ... 320
Cornell University ... NY ... 331
Fashion Institute of Technology ... NY ... 333
New York Institute of Technology ... NY ... 343
New York School of Interior Design ... NY ... 343
Pratt Institute ... NY ... 346
Rochester Institute of Technology ... NY ... 347
School of Visual Arts ... NY ... 350
State University of New York College at Buffalo ... NY ... 353
Syracuse University Main Campus ... NY ... 357
Villa Maria College of Buffalo ... NY ... 359
Appalachian State University ... NC ... 377
East Carolina University ... NC ... 377
High Point University ... NC ... 365
Meredith College ... NC ... 366
University of North Carolina at Greensboro ... NC ... 379
Western Carolina University ... NC ... 379
North Dakota State University Main Campus. ND ... 381
Columbus College of Art & Design ... OH ... 388
Kent State University Main Campus ... OH ... 393
Miami University ... OH ... 396
Ohio State University Main Campus, The ... OH ... 398
Ohio University Main Campus ... OH ... 399
University of Akron, Main Campus, The ... OH ... 403
University of Cincinnati Main Campus ... OH ... 403
Oklahoma Christian University ... OK ... 409
Oklahoma State University ... OK ... 410
University of Central Oklahoma ... OK ... 413

CLPSY: American Psychological Association: clinical psychology (D)

CNCE: Accrediting Council for Continuing Education and Training: continuing education (C,A)

COE: Council on Occupational Education: occupational, trade, and technical education (A)

COMTA: Commission on Massage Therapy Accreditation: massage therapy, bodywork, aesthetics/esthetics and skin care (C,A)

CONST: American Council for Construction Education: construction education (A,B)

Auburn University ... AL ... 1
Jefferson State Community College ... AL ... 5
Arizona State University ... AZ ... 12
Northern Arizona University ... AZ ... 17
John Brown University ... AR ... 22
University of Arkansas at Little Rock ... AR ... 24
California Polytechnic State University-San Luis Obispo ... CA ... 33
California State University-Chico ... CA ... 34
California State University-Fresno ... CA ... 34
California State University-Northridge ... CA ... 35
California State University-Sacramento ... CA ... 35
Colorado State University ... CO ... 83
Central Connecticut State University ... CT ... 91
Florida International University ... FL ... 119
Santa Fe College ... FL ... 117
University of Florida ... FL ... 120
University of North Florida ... FL ... 120
Georgia Institute of Technology ... GA ... 130
Georgia Southern University ... GA ... 131
Southern Polytechnic State University ... GA ... 137
Boise State University ... ID ... 142
Bradley University ... IL ... 145
Illinois State University ... IL ... 153
John A. Logan College ... IL ... 154
Southern Illinois University Edwardsville ... IL ... 165
Indiana State University ... IN ... 173
Purdue University Main Campus ... IN ... 178
Kansas State University ... KS ... 194
Eastern Kentucky University ... KY ... 200
Northern Kentucky University ... KY ... 205
Louisiana State University and Agricultural and Mechanical College ... LA ... 212
University of Louisiana at Monroe ... LA ... 216
University of Maryland Eastern Shore ... MD ... 227
Wentworth Institute of Technology ... MA ... 246
Eastern Michigan University ... MI ... 250
Ferris State University ... MI ... 251
Michigan State University ... MI ... 255
Minnesota State University Moorhead ... MN ... 268
Minnesota State University, Mankato ... MN ... 267
University of Southern Mississippi ... MS ... 278
Missouri State University ... MO ... 286
State Fair Community College ... MO ... 290
University of Central Missouri ... MO ... 291
University of Nebraska - Lincoln ... NE ... 300
University of Nevada, Las Vegas ... NV ... 302
Central New Mexico Community College ... NM ... 317
University of New Mexico Main Campus ... NM ... 321
Alfred State College ... NY ... 355
State University of New York College of Technology at Delhi ... NY ... 355
East Carolina University ... NC ... 377
North Carolina Agricultural and Technical State University ... NC ... 377
Western Carolina University ... NC ... 379
North Dakota State University Main Campus. ND ... 381
Bowling Green State University ... OH ... 385
Cincinnati State Technical and Community College ... OH ... 387
Columbus State Community College ... OH ... 388
University of Cincinnati Main Campus ... OH ... 403
University of Oklahoma Norman Campus ... OK ... 413
Oregon State University ... OR ... 418
Drexel University ... PA ... 427
Pennsylvania College of Technology ... PA ... 440
Roger Williams University ... RI ... 454
Clemson University ... SC ... 456
South Dakota State University ... SD ... 466
North Lake College ... TX ... 485
Texas A & M University ... TX ... 497
University of Houston ... TX ... 503
Brigham Young University ... UT ... 509
Weber State University ... UT ... 511
Virginia Polytechnic Institute and State University ... VA ... 529
Central Washington University ... WA ... 531
Edmonds Community College ... WA ... 533
University of Washington ... WA ... 538
Washington State University ... WA ... 539
Milwaukee School of Engineering ... WI ... 548
University of Wisconsin-Stout ... WI ... 552

COPSY: American Psychological Association: counseling psychology (D)

Auburn University ... AL ... 1
Arizona State University ... AZ ... 12
Colorado State University ... CO ... 83
University of Denver ... CO ... 88
University of Northern Colorado ... CO ... 88
Howard University ... DC ... 98
University of Florida ... FL ... 120
University of Miami ... FL ... 122
Georgia State University ... GA ... 131
University of Georgia ... GA ... 138
Loyola University Chicago ... IL ... 157
Southern Illinois University Carbondale ... IL ... 164
University of Illinois at Urbana-Champaign ... IL ... 167
Ball State University ... IN ... 169
Indiana State University ... IN ... 173
Indiana University Bloomington ... IN ... 173
Purdue University Main Campus ... IN ... 178
University of Notre Dame ... IN ... 180
Iowa State University ... IA ... 182
University of Iowa ... IA ... 182
University of Kansas Main Campus ... KS ... 196
University of Kentucky ... KY ... 206
University of Louisville ... KY ... 207
Louisiana Tech University ... LA ... 215
University of Maryland College Park ... MD ... 227
Boston College ... MA ... 232
Western Michigan University ... MI ... 260
University of Minnesota-Twin Cities ... MN ... 272
University of Saint Thomas ... MN ... 272
University of Southern Mississippi ... MS ... 278
University of Missouri - Columbia ... MO ... 291
University of Missouri - Kansas City ... MO ... 291
University of Nebraska - Lincoln ... NE ... 300
Seton Hall University ... NJ ... 315
New Mexico State University Main Campus . NM ... 319
Fordham University ... NY ... 334
New York University ... NY ... 344
State University of New York at Albany ... NY ... 351
Teachers College, Columbia University ... NY ... 357
University of North Dakota Main Campus ... ND ... 381
Cleveland State University ... OH ... 388
University of Akron, Main Campus, The ... OH ... 403
Oklahoma State University ... OK ... 410
University of Oklahoma Norman Campus ... OK ... 413
University of Oregon ... OR ... 419
Lehigh University ... PA ... 434
Penn State University Park ... PA ... 438
Tennessee State University ... TN ... 474
University of Memphis, The ... TN ... 474
University of Tennessee, Knoxville ... TN ... 477
Our Lady of the Lake University ... TX ... 491
Texas A & M University ... TX ... 497
Texas Tech University ... TX ... 501
Texas Woman's University ... TX ... 502
University of Houston ... TX ... 503
University of North Texas ... TX ... 504
University of Texas at Austin ... TX ... 505
Brigham Young University ... UT ... 509
University of Utah, The ... UT ... 510
Virginia Commonwealth University ... VA ... 525
Washington State University ... WA ... 539
West Virginia University ... WV ... 544
Marquette University ... WI ... 548
University of Wisconsin-Madison ... WI ... 550
University of Wisconsin-Milwaukee ... WI ... 551

CORE: Council of Rehabilitation Education: rehabilitation counseling (M)

Alabama Agricultural and Mechanical University ... AL ... 1
@Alabama State University ... AL ... 1
Auburn University ... AL ... 1
Troy University ... AL ... 8
University of Alabama at Birmingham ... AL ... 8
University of Alabama, The ... AL ... 8
University of Arizona ... AZ ... 19
Arkansas State University ... AR ... 20
University of Arkansas at Little Rock ... AR ... 24
University of Arkansas Main Campus ... AR ... 24
California State University-Fresno ... CA ... 34
California State University-Los Angeles ... CA ... 35
California State University-Sacramento ... CA ... 35
California State University-San Bernardino ... CA ... 36
San Diego State University ... CA ... 36
San Francisco State University ... CA ... 36
University of Northern Colorado ... CO ... 88
Central Connecticut State University ... CT ... 91
George Washington University ... DC ... 97
Florida Atlantic University ... FL ... 118
Florida State University ... FL ... 119
University of South Florida ... FL ... 120
Fort Valley State University ... GA ... 129
Georgia State University ... GA ... 131
Thomas University ... GA ... 137
University of Hawaii at Manoa ... HI ... 141
University of Idaho ... ID ... 144
@Adler School of Professional Psychology ... IL ... 144
Illinois Institute of Technology ... IL ... 153
Northeastern Illinois University ... IL ... 159
Northern Illinois University ... IL ... 160
Southern Illinois University Carbondale ... IL ... 164
University of Illinois at Urbana-Champaign ... IL ... 167
Ball State University ... IN ... 169
Drake University ... IA ... 184
University of Iowa ... IA ... 182
Emporia State University ... KS ... 192
University of Kentucky ... KY ... 206
Louisiana State University Health Sciences Center-New Orleans ... LA ... 213
Southern University and A&M College ... LA ... 214
University of Southern Maine ... ME ... 220
Coppin State University ... MD ... 228
University of Maryland College Park ... MD ... 227
University of Maryland Eastern Shore ... MD ... 227
Assumption College ... MA ... 230
Springfield College ... MA ... 245
University of Massachusetts Boston ... MA ... 237
Michigan State University ... MI ... 255
Wayne State University ... MI ... 260
Western Michigan University ... MI ... 260
Minnesota State University, Mankato ... MN ... 267
St. Cloud State University ... MN ... 269
Jackson State University ... MS ... 275
Mississippi State University ... MS ... 276
Maryville University of Saint Louis ... MO ... 284
Montana State University - Billings ... MT ... 295
UMDNJ-School of Health Related Professions ... NJ ... 317
New Mexico Highlands University ... NM ... 318
City University of New York Hunter College . NY ... 327
Hofstra University ... NY ... 335
State University of New York at Buffalo ... NY ... 351
East Carolina University ... NC ... 377
@North Carolina Agricultural and Technical State University ... NC ... 377
University of North Carolina at Chapel Hill ... NC ... 378
@Winston-Salem State University ... NC ... 380
Bowling Green State University ... OH ... 385
Kent State University Main Campus ... OH ... 393
Ohio University Main Campus ... OH ... 399
@Wilberforce University ... OH ... 405
Wright State University Main Campus ... OH ... 406
East Central University ... OK ... 407
Langston University ... OK ... 408
Portland State University ... OR ... 418
Western Oregon University ... OR ... 419
Edinboro University of Pennsylvania ... PA ... 442
Penn State University Park ... PA ... 438
University of Pittsburgh ... PA ... 449
University of Scranton, The ... PA ... 450
Bayamon Central University ... PR ... 560
Pontifical Catholic University of Puerto Rico, The ... PR ... 564
University of Puerto Rico-Rio Piedras Campus ... PR ... 567
Salve Regina University ... RI ... 454
South Carolina State University ... SC ... 460
University of South Carolina Columbia ... SC ... 462
South Dakota State University ... SD ... 466
University of Memphis, The ... TN ... 474
University of Tennessee, Knoxville ... TN ... 477
Stephen F. Austin State University ... TX ... 495
Texas Tech University Health Sciences Center ... TX ... 501
University of North Texas ... TX ... 504
University of Texas at Austin ... TX ... 505
University of Texas at El Paso ... TX ... 505
University of Texas - Pan American ... TX ... 506
University of Texas Southwestern Medical Center at Dallas ... TX ... 507
Utah State University ... UT ... 511
Virginia Commonwealth University ... VA ... 525
Western Washington University ... WA ... 539
West Virginia University ... WV ... 544
University of Wisconsin-Madison ... WI ... 550
University of Wisconsin-Stout ... WI ... 552

CS: ABET, Inc.: computer science (B)

Alabama Agricultural and Mechanical University ... AL ... 1
Auburn University ... AL ... 1
Jacksonville State University ... AL ... 4
University of Alabama at Birmingham ... AL ... 8
University of Alabama in Huntsville ... AL ... 9
University of Alabama, The ... AL ... 8
University of North Alabama ... AL ... 9
University of South Alabama ... AL ... 9
University of Alaska Fairbanks ... AK ... 10
Arizona State University ... AZ ... 12
Northern Arizona University ... AZ ... 17
Arkansas Tech University ... AR ... 20
University of Arkansas at Little Rock ... AR ... 24
University of Arkansas Main Campus ... AR ... 24
University of Central Arkansas ... AR ... 25
California Polytechnic State University-San Luis Obispo ... CA ... 33
California State Polytechnic University-Pomona ... CA ... 33
California State University-Chico ... CA ... 34
California State University-Dominguez Hills .. CA ... 34
California State University-Fullerton ... CA ... 34
California State University-Long Beach ... CA ... 35
California State University-Los Angeles ... CA ... 35
California State University-Northridge ... CA ... 35
California State University-Sacramento ... CA ... 35
California State University-San Bernardino ... CA ... 36
San Diego State University ... CA ... 36
San Francisco State University ... CA ... 36
San Jose State University ... CA ... 37
University of California-Berkeley ... CA ... 73
University of California-Davis ... CA ... 73
University of California-Los Angeles ... CA ... 74
University of California-Riverside ... CA ... 74
University of California-Santa Barbara ... CA ... 74
University of Southern California ... CA ... 76
University of the Pacific ... CA ... 75
Metropolitan State College of Denver ... CO ... 85
United States Air Force Academy ... CO ... 558
University of Colorado at Colorado Springs .. CO ... 88
University of Colorado Boulder ... CO ... 88
University of Colorado Denver|Anschutz Medical Campus ... CO ... 88
Central Connecticut State University ... CT ... 91
Quinnipiac University ... CT ... 93
Southern Connecticut State University ... CT ... 91
University of Connecticut ... CT ... 94
University of New Haven ... CT ... 95
George Washington University ... DC ... 97
Howard University ... DC ... 98
University System of the District of Columbia DC ... 99
Florida Agricultural and Mechanical University ... FL ... 118
Florida Atlantic University ... FL ... 118
Florida Institute of Technology ... FL ... 108
Florida International University ... FL ... 11
Florida Memorial University ... FL ... 10
Florida State University ... FL ... 11
University of Central Florida ... FL ... 12
University of North Florida ... FL ... 12
University of South Florida ... FL ... 12
Armstrong Atlantic State University ... GA ... 124
Georgia Institute of Technology ... GA ... 13
Georgia Southern University ... GA ... 13
Kennesaw State University ... GA ... 132
Macon State College ... GA ... 133
Mercer University ... GA ... 133
Southern Polytechnic State University ... GA ... 137
University of West Georgia ... GA ... 138
Boise State University ... ID ... 142
Idaho State University ... ID ... 143
University of Idaho ... ID ... 144
Illinois Institute of Technology ... IL ... 153
Illinois State University ... IL ... 153
Southern Illinois University Carbondale ... IL ... 164
Southern Illinois University Edwardsville ... IL ... 165
University of Illinois at Chicago ... IL ... 166
University of Illinois at Urbana-Champaign ... IL ... 167
Indiana University-Purdue University Fort Wayne ... IN ... 174
Indiana University-Purdue University Indianapolis ... IN ... 174
Purdue University Main Campus ... IN ... 178
Rose-Hulman Institute of Technology ... IN ... 179
University of Evansville ... IN ... 180
University of Notre Dame ... IN ... 180
Iowa State University ... IA ... 182
Kansas State University ... KS ... 194
University of Kansas Main Campus ... KS ... 196
Eastern Kentucky University ... KY ... 200
University of Kentucky ... KY ... 206
University of Louisville ... KY ... 207
Grambling State University ... LA ... 215
Louisiana State University and Agricultural and Mechanical College ... LA ... 212
Louisiana State University in Shreveport ... LA ... 213
Louisiana Tech University ... LA ... 215
McNeese State University ... LA ... 215
Nicholls State University ... LA ... 216
Southeastern Louisiana University ... LA ... 216
Southern University and A&M College ... LA ... 214
University of Louisiana at Lafayette ... LA ... 216
University of Louisiana at Monroe ... LA ... 216
University of New Orleans ... LA ... 213
University of Maine ... ME ... 220
University of Southern Maine ... ME ... 220
Bowie State University ... MD ... 228
Johns Hopkins University ... MD ... 223
Loyola University Maryland ... MD ... 224
Towson University ... MD ... 228
United States Naval Academy ... MD ... 558
University of Maryland Baltimore County ... MD ... 227
Fitchburg State University ... MA ... 238
Massachusetts Institute of Technology ... MA ... 242
Northeastern University ... MA ... 244
Salem State University ... MA ... 239
Tufts University ... MA ... 245
University of Massachusetts Boston ... MA ... 237
University of Massachusetts Dartmouth ... MA ... 237
Westfield State University ... MA ... 239
Worcester Polytechnic Institute ... MA ... 247
Calvin College ... MI ... 249
Grand Valley State University ... MI ... 252
Kettering University ... MI ... 253
Oakland University ... MI ... 257
University of Michigan-Ann Arbor ... MI ... 259
University of Michigan-Dearborn ... MI ... 259
Western Michigan University ... MI ... 260
St. Cloud State University ... MN ... 269
University of Minnesota Duluth ... MN ... 272
Jackson State University ... MS ... 275
Mississippi State University ... MS ... 276
Mississippi Valley State University ... MS ... 276
University of Mississippi ... MS ... 277
University of Southern Mississippi ... MS ... 278
Missouri State University ... MO ... 286
Missouri University of Science & Technology MO ... 292
Southeast Missouri State University ... MO ... 290
University of Missouri - Kansas City ... MO ... 291
Montana State University ... MT ... 295
Montana Tech of The University of Montana MT ... 296
University of Montana - Missoula, The ... MT ... 295
University of Nebraska at Omaha ... NE ... 301
University of Nebraska - Lincoln ... NE ... 300
University of Nevada, Las Vegas ... NV ... 302
University of Nevada, Reno ... NV ... 303
University of New Hampshire ... NH ... 306
College of New Jersey, The ... NJ ... 308
Fairleigh Dickinson University ... NJ ... 310
Montclair State University ... NJ ... 311
New Jersey Institute of Technology ... NJ ... 312
Rowan University ... NJ ... 314
Stevens Institute of Technology ... NJ ... 315
William Paterson University of New Jersey .. NJ ... 317
New Mexico Institute of Mining and Technology ... NM ... 319
University of New Mexico Main Campus ... NM ... 321
City University of New York College of Staten Island ... NY ... 327
City University of New York The City College ... NY ... 326
Iona College ... NY ... 336
Pace University ... NY ... 345

CVT: Commission on Accreditation of Allied Health Education Programs: cardiovascular technology (C,A,B)

CYTO: Commission on Accreditation of Allied Health Education Programs: cytotechnology (C,A,B,M)

DA: American Dental Association: dental assisting (C,A)

Bates Technical College ... WA ... 531
Bellingham Technical College ... WA ... 531
Clover Park Technical College ... WA ... 532
Lake Washington Technical College ... WA ... 535
Renton Technical College ... WA ... 536
South Puget Sound Community College ... WA ... 538
Spokane Community College ... WA ... 532
Blackhawk Technical College ... WI ... 553
Fox Valley Technical College ... WI ... 553
Gateway Technical College ... WI ... 553
Northeast Wisconsin Technical College ... WI ... 555
Western Technical College ... WI ... 555

DANCE: National Association of Schools of Dance: dance (C,B,M,D)

University of Alabama, The ... AL ... 8
University of Arizona ... AZ ... 19
California Institute of the Arts ... CA ... 32
California State University-Fullerton ... CA ... 34
California State University-Long Beach ... CA ... 35
Chapman University ... CA ... 39
Loyola Marymount University ... CA ... 56
San Jose State University ... CA ... 37
University of California-Santa Barbara ... CA ... 74
University of Hartford ... CT ... 95
Florida State University ... FL ... 119
Jacksonville University ... FL ... 111
Miami Dade College ... FL ... 113
University of Florida ... FL ... 120
Brenau University ... GA ... 126
University of Georgia ... GA ... 138
University of Illinois at Urbana-Champaign ... IL ... 167
Ball State University ... IN ... 169
Butler University ... IN ... 170
University of Iowa ... IA ... 182
Wichita State University ... KS ... 197
Towson University ... MD ... 228
Hope College ... MI ... 252
Oakland University ... MI ... 257
University of Michigan-Ann Arbor ... MI ... 259
Wayne State University ... MI ... 260
Western Michigan University ... MI ... 260
St. Olaf College ... MN ... 271
University of Minnesota-Twin Cities ... MN ... 272
Belhaven University ... MS ... 273
University of Southern Mississippi ... MS ... 278
University of Missouri - Kansas City ... MO ... 291
Montclair State University ... NJ ... 311
Rutgers the State University of New Jersey New Brunswick Campus ... NJ ... 314
University of New Mexico Main Campus ... NM ... 321
Barnard College ... NY ... 323
Fordham University ... NY ... 334
State University of New York, The College at Brockport ... NY ... 352
University of North Carolina at Greensboro ... NC ... 379
Kent State University Main Campus ... OH ... 393
Ohio State University Main Campus, The ... OH ... 398
Ohio University Main Campus ... OH ... 399
University of Akron, Main Campus, The ... OH ... 403
University of Cincinnati Main Campus ... OH ... 403
Mercyhurst College ... PA ... 436
Point Park University ... PA ... 444
Slippery Rock University of Pennsylvania ... PA ... 443
Temple University ... PA ... 447
Columbia College ... SC ... 457
Winthrop University ... SC ... 463
Southern Methodist University ... TX ... 494
Texas Christian University ... TX ... 498
Texas Woman's University ... TX ... 502
University of Texas at Austin ... TX ... 505
Brigham Young University ... UT ... 509
Southern Utah University ... UT ... 511
University of Utah, The ... UT ... 510
James Madison University ... VA ... 520
Virginia Commonwealth University ... VA ... 525
University of Wisconsin-Stevens Point ... WI ... 552

DENT: American Dental Association: dentistry (FP)

University of Alabama at Birmingham ... AL ... 8
Midwestern University ... AZ ... 16
Loma Linda University ... CA ... 54
University of California-Los Angeles ... CA ... 74
University of California-San Francisco ... CA ... 74
University of Southern California ... CA ... 76
University of the Pacific ... CA ... 75
Western University of Health Sciences ... CA ... 78
United States Air Force Academy ... CO ... 558
University of Colorado DenverlAnschutz Medical Campus ... CO ... 88
University of Connecticut Health Center ... CT ... 94
Howard University ... DC ... 98
Jacksonville University ... FL ... 111
Nova Southeastern University ... FL ... 114
University of Florida ... FL ... 120
University of Miami ... FL ... 122
Emory University ... GA ... 129
Georgia Health Sciences University ... GA ... 130
Idaho State University ... ID ... 143
Loyola University Chicago ... IL ... 157
Midwestern University ... IL ... 158
Southern Illinois University Edwardsville ... IL ... 165
University of Illinois at Chicago ... IL ... 166
Indiana University-Purdue University Indianapolis ... IN ... 174
University of Iowa ... IA ... 182
Wichita State University ... KS ... 197
University of Kentucky ... KY ... 206
University of Louisville ... KY ... 207
Louisiana State University Health Sciences Center at Shreveport ... LA ... 213
Louisiana State University Health Sciences Center-New Orleans ... LA ... 213
Johns Hopkins University ... MD ... 223
University of Maryland Baltimore ... MD ... 227
Boston University ... MA ... 232
Harvard University ... MA ... 235
Tufts University ... MA ... 245
University of Massachusetts at Worcester ... MA ... 238
University of Detroit Mercy ... MI ... 259
University of Michigan-Ann Arbor ... MI ... 259
Mayo School of Health Sciences ... MN ... 262
University of Minnesota-Twin Cities ... MN ... 272
University of Mississippi Medical Center ... MS ... 277
Saint Louis University ... MO ... 289
University of Missouri - Kansas City ... MO ... 291
Creighton University ... NE ... 297
University of Nebraska Medical Center ... NE ... 301
Roseman University of Health Sciences ... NV ... 303
University of Nevada, Las Vegas ... NV ... 302
UMDNJ-New Jersey Dental School ... NJ ... 316
University of New Mexico Main Campus ... NM ... 321
Columbia University in the City of New York ... NY ... 330
Mount Sinai School of Medicine ... NY ... 342
New York Medical College ... NY ... 343
New York University ... NY ... 344
State University of New York at Buffalo ... NY ... 351
State University of New York at Stony Brook ... NY ... 352
State University of New York Upstate Medical University ... NY ... 352
University of Rochester ... NY ... 358
Weill Cornell Medical College ... NY ... 360
Yeshiva University ... NY ... 361
East Carolina University ... NC ... 377
University of North Carolina at Chapel Hill ... NC ... 378
Wake Forest University ... NC ... 380
Case Western Reserve University ... OH ... 386
Ohio State University Main Campus, The ... OH ... 398
University of Cincinnati Main Campus ... OH ... 403
University of Toledo ... OH ... 404
University of Oklahoma Health Sciences Center ... OK ... 413
Oregon Health & Science University ... OR ... 418
Drexel University ... PA ... 427
Lake Erie College of Osteopathic Medicine ... PA ... 433
Seton Hill University ... PA ... 447
Temple University ... PA ... 447
Thomas Jefferson University ... PA ... 448
University of Pennsylvania ... PA ... 448
University of Pittsburgh ... PA ... 449
University of Puerto Rico-Medical Sciences Campus ... PR ... 567
Medical University of South Carolina ... SC ... 459
Meharry Medical College ... TN ... 471
University of Tennessee Health Science Center ... TN ... 477
University of Tennessee, Knoxville ... TN ... 477
Vanderbilt University ... TN ... 477
Texas A & M Health Science Center Baylor College of Dentistry ... TX ... 497
University of Texas Health Science Center at Houston (UTHealth), The ... TX ... 506
University of Texas Health Science Center at San Antonio ... TX ... 506
University of Texas M.D. Anderson Cancer Center, The ... TX ... 507
University of Texas Medical Branch, The ... TX ... 507
University of Utah, The ... UT ... 510
University of Virginia ... VA ... 525
Virginia Commonwealth University ... VA ... 525
University of Washington ... WA ... 538
West Virginia University ... WV ... 544
Marquette University ... WI ... 548
Medical College of Wisconsin ... WI ... 548

DETC: Distance Education and Training Council: home study schools (A,B,M, FP,D)

Andrew Jackson University ... AL ... 1
Columbia Southern University ... AL ... 2
American Graduate School of Education ... AZ ... 11
Brighton College ... AZ ... 12
Dunlap-Stone University ... AZ ... 14
Harrison Middleton University ... AZ ... 14
National Paralegal College ... AZ ... 16
Paralegal Institute, The ... AZ ... 17
Penn Foster College ... AZ ... 17
Sessions College for Professional Design ... AZ ... 18
Sonoran Desert Institute ... AZ ... 18
Abraham Lincoln University ... CA ... 26
Allied American University ... CA ... 27
American Graduate University ... CA ... 28
Anaheim University ... CA ... 28
Applied Professional Training, Inc. ... CA ... 29
California Coast University ... CA ... 31
California Intercontinental University ... CA ... 32
California Miramar University ... CA ... 33
California National University for Advanced Studies ... CA ... 33
California Southern University ... CA ... 33
Concord Law School of Kaplan University ... CA ... 42
Henley-Putnam University ... CA ... 50
Perelandra College ... CA ... 62
Taft Law School ... CA ... 72
University of Philosophical Research ... CA ... 75
American Sentinel University ... CO ... 80
Aspen University ... CO ... 81
Holmes Institute of Consciousness Studies ... CO ... 84
McKinley College ... CO ... 85
U.S. Career Institute ... CO ... 89
William Howard Taft University ... CO ... 89
Yorktown University ... CO ... 89
Teacher Education University ... FL ... 121
University of St. Augustine for Health Sciences ... FL ... 122
Ashworth University ... GA ... 124
University of Atlanta ... GA ... 138
Babel University Professional School of Translation ... HI ... 139
Kona University ... HI ... 140
Ellis University ... IL ... 150
Antioch School of Church Planting and Leadership Development ... IA ... 181
INSTE Bible College ... IA ... 185
Southwest University ... LA ... 215
Griggs University ... MI ... 252
American College of Technology ... MO ... 278
City Vision College ... MO ... 280
Global University ... MO ... 282
Grantham University ... MO ... 282
Cleveland Institute of Electronics ... OH ... 388
Lakewood College ... OH ... 394
American College of Healthcare Sciences ... OR ... 414
Huntington College of Health Sciences ... TN ... 469
Western Governors University ... UT ... 512
Atlantic University ... VA ... 516
Catholic Distance University, The ... VA ... 517
University of Management & Technology ... VA ... 524
World College ... VA ... 530
Northwest Institute of Literary Arts ... WA ... 535
American Public University System ... WV ... 540
Martinsburg Institute ... WV ... 541

DH: American Dental Association: dental hygiene (C,A)

Tri-State Institute ... AL ... 8
Wallace State Community College - Hanceville ... AL ... 10
University of Alaska Anchorage ... AK ... 10
University of Alaska Fairbanks ... AK ... 10
Carrington College - Mesa ... AZ ... 13
Mesa Community College ... AZ ... 15
Mohave Community College ... AZ ... 16
Northern Arizona University ... AZ ... 17
Phoenix College ... AZ ... 16
Pima County Community College District ... AZ ... 17
Rio Salado College ... AZ ... 16
University of Arkansas at Fort Smith ... AR ... 24
University of Arkansas for Medical Sciences ... AR ... 24
Cabrillo College ... CA ... 31
Carrington College California - Sacramento ... CA ... 38
Carrington College California - San Jose ... CA ... 38
Cerritos College ... CA ... 38
Chabot College ... CA ... 38
Concorde Career College ... CA ... 42
Cypress College ... CA ... 59
Diablo Valley College ... CA ... 43
Foothill College ... CA ... 47
Fresno City College ... CA ... 72
Loma Linda University ... CA ... 54
Moreno Valley College ... CA ... 63
Oxnard College ... CA ... 77
Pasadena City College ... CA ... 61
Sacramento City College ... CA ... 56
San Joaquin Valley College, Inc. ... CA ... 66
Santa Rosa Junior College ... CA ... 68
Shasta College ... CA ... 69
Southwestern College ... CA ... 71
Taft College ... CA ... 72
University of Southern California ... CA ... 76
University of the Pacific ... CA ... 75
West Coast University ... CA ... 77
West Los Angeles College ... CA ... 55
Colorado Northwestern Community College ... CO ... 82
Community College of Denver ... CO ... 83
Pueblo Community College ... CO ... 87
Lincoln College of New England ... CT ... 92
Tunxis Community College ... CT ... 91
University of Bridgeport ... CT ... 94
University of New Haven ... CT ... 95
Delaware Technical and Community College Stanton-Wilmington Campus ... DE ... 96
Howard University ... DC ... 98
Brevard Community College ... FL ... 101
Broward College ... FL ... 102
Daytona State College ... FL ... 103
Edison State College ... FL ... 104
Florida State College at Jacksonville ... FL ... 109
Gulf Coast State College ... FL ... 110
Hillsborough Community College ... FL ... 110
Indian River State College ... FL ... 110
Miami Dade College ... FL ... 113
Palm Beach State College ... FL ... 114
Pasco-Hernando Community College ... FL ... 114
Pensacola State College ... FL ... 114
St. Petersburg College ... FL ... 116
Sanford-Brown Institute ... FL ... 117
Santa Fe College ... FL ... 117
South Florida Community College ... FL ... 117
State College of Florida, Manatee-Sarasota ... FL ... 118
Tallahassee Community College ... FL ... 121
Valencia College ... FL ... 12
Athens Technical College ... GA ... 12
Central Georgia Technical College ... GA ... 126
Clayton State University ... GA ... 12
Columbus Technical College ... GA ... 127
Darton College ... GA ... 128
Georgia Health Sciences University ... GA ... 130
Georgia Highlands College ... GA ... 130
Georgia Perimeter College ... GA ... 130
Lanier Technical College ... GA ... 132
Middle Georgia Technical College ... GA ... 133
Savannah Technical College ... GA ... 136
Southeastern Technical College ... GA ... 137
West Georgia Technical College ... GA ... 139
Wiregrass Georgia Technical College ... GA ... 139
University of Hawaii at Manoa ... HI ... 141
University of Hawaii Maui College ... HI ... 142
Carrington College - Boise ... ID ... 142
College of Southern Idaho ... ID ... 143
Idaho State University ... ID ... 143
Carl Sandburg College ... IL ... 146
City Colleges of Chicago Kennedy-King College ... IL ... 147
College of DuPage ... IL ... 147
College of Lake County ... IL ... 147
Harper College ... IL ... 151
Illinois Central College ... IL ... 152
John A. Logan College ... IL ... 154
Lake Land College ... IL ... 155
Lewis and Clark Community College ... IL ... 156
Parkland College ... IL ... 161
Prairie State College ... IL ... 161
Rock Valley College ... IL ... 162
Southern Illinois University Carbondale ... IL ... 164
Indiana University Northwest ... IN ... 173
Indiana University-Purdue University Fort Wayne ... IN ... 174
Indiana University-Purdue University Indianapolis ... IN ... 174
Indiana University South Bend ... IN ... 174
Ivy Tech Community College of Indiana-East Central ... IN ... 175
Ivy Tech Community College of Indiana-North Central ... IN ... 176
University of Southern Indiana ... IN ... 180
Des Moines Area Community College ... IA ... 183
Hawkeye Community College ... IA ... 185
Iowa Central Community College ... IA ... 185
Iowa Western Community College ... IA ... 186
Kirkwood Community College ... IA ... 186
Flint Hills Technical College ... KS ... 192
Johnson County Community College ... KS ... 193
Manhattan Area Technical College ... KS ... 194
Wichita State University ... KS ... 197
Big Sandy Community and Technical College ... KY ... 201
Bluegrass Community and Technical College ... KY ... 201
Henderson Community College ... KY ... 201
University of Louisville ... KY ... 207
Western Kentucky University ... KY ... 207
Louisiana State University Health Sciences Center-New Orleans ... LA ... 213
Southern University at Shreveport-Louisiana ... LA ... 215
University of Louisiana at Monroe ... LA ... 216
University of Maine at Augusta ... ME ... 220
University of New England ... ME ... 220
Allegany College of Maryland ... MD ... 221
Baltimore City Community College ... MD ... 221
Community College of Baltimore County, The ... MD ... 222
University of Maryland Baltimore ... MD ... 227
Bristol Community College ... MA ... 239
Cape Cod Community College ... MA ... 240
Massachusetts College of Pharmacy and Health Sciences ... MA ... 241
Middlesex Community College ... MA ... 240
Mount Ida College ... MA ... 243
Mount Wachusett Community College ... MA ... 240
Quinsigamond Community College ... MA ... 241
Springfield Technical Community College ... MA ... 241
Baker College of Auburn Hills ... MI ... 248
Baker College of Port Huron ... MI ... 249
Delta College ... MI ... 250
Ferris State University ... MI ... 251
Grand Rapids Community College ... MI ... 251
Kalamazoo Valley Community College ... MI ... 253
Kellogg Community College ... MI ... 253
Lansing Community College ... MI ... 254
Mott Community College ... MI ... 256
Oakland Community College ... MI ... 257
University of Detroit Mercy ... MI ... 259
University of Michigan-Ann Arbor ... MI ... 259
Wayne County Community College District ... MI ... 260
Argosy University, Twin Cities ... MN ... 261
Century College ... MN ... 266
Herzing University ... MN ... 264
Lake Superior College ... MN ... 267
Minnesota State University Moorhead ... MN ... 268
Minnesota State University, Mankato ... MN ... 267
Normandale Community College ... MN ... 268
Rochester Community and Technical College ... MN ... 269
Saint Cloud Technical and Community College ... MN ... 269
University of Minnesota-Twin Cities ... MN ... 272
Meridian Community College ... MS ... 275
Mississippi Delta Community College ... MS ... 275
Northeast Mississippi Community College ... MS ... 276

DIETC: American Dietetic Association: coordinated dietetics programs (B,M)

DIETD: American Dietetic Association: didactic dietetics programs

Tennessee Technological University ... TN ... 474
University of Memphis, The ... TN ... 474
University of Tennessee at Chattanooga ... TN ... 477
University of Tennessee at Martin ... TN ... 477
University of Tennessee, Knoxville ... TN ... 477
Abilene Christian University ... TX ... 478
Baylor University ... TX ... 481
Lamar University ... TX ... 500
Prairie View A & M University ... TX ... 496
Sam Houston State University ... TX ... 501
Stephen F. Austin State University ... TX ... 495
Texas A & M University ... TX ... 497
Texas A & M University - Kingsville ... TX ... 498
Texas Christian University ... TX ... 498
Texas Southern University ... TX ... 499
Texas State University-San Marcos ... TX ... 501
Texas Tech University ... TX ... 501
Texas Woman's University ... TX ... 502
University of Houston ... TX ... 503
University of Texas at Austin ... TX ... 505
University of the Incarnate Word ... TX ... 503
Brigham Young University ... UT ... 509
Utah State University ... UT ... 511
University of Vermont ... VT ... 514
James Madison University ... VA ... 520
Norfolk State University ... VA ... 521
Radford University ... VA ... 522
Virginia Polytechnic Institute and State University ... VA ... 529
Virginia State University ... VA ... 529
Bastyr University ... WA ... 530
Central Washington University ... WA ... 531
Seattle Pacific University ... WA ... 537
Washington State University ... WA ... 539
Marshall University ... WV ... 543
West Virginia University ... WV ... 544
University of Wisconsin-Green Bay ... WI ... 551
University of Wisconsin-Madison ... WI ... 550
University of Wisconsin-Stevens Point ... WI ... 552
University of Wisconsin-Stout ... WI ... 552
University of Wyoming ... WY ... 556

DIETI: American Dietetic Association: dietetic post-baccalaureate internships

Oakwood University ... AL ... 6
University of Alabama at Birmingham ... AL ... 8
University of Alaska Anchorage ... AK ... 10
Arizona State University ... AZ ... 12
University of Arkansas for Medical Sciences ... AR ... 24
University of Central Arkansas ... AR ... 25
California Polytechnic State University-San Luis Obispo ... CA ... 33
California State Polytechnic University-Pomona ... CA ... 33
California State University-Chico ... CA ... 34
California State University-Fresno ... CA ... 34
California State University-Long Beach ... CA ... 35
California State University-Northridge ... CA ... 35
California State University-Sacramento ... CA ... 35
San Francisco State University ... CA ... 36
San Jose State University ... CA ... 37
University of California-Davis ... CA ... 73
University of California-Los Angeles ... CA ... 74
@University of California-San Diego ... CA ... 74
University of California-San Francisco ... CA ... 74
University of Southern California ... CA ... 76
University of Northern Colorado ... CO ... 88
Saint Joseph College ... CT ... 93
University of Connecticut ... CT ... 94
University of Delaware ... DE ... 96
Florida State University ... FL ... 119
University of Florida ... FL ... 120
University of North Florida ... FL ... 120
Emory University ... GA ... 129
Life University ... GA ... 133
University of Georgia ... GA ... 138
Idaho State University ... ID ... 143
Benedictine University ... IL ... 145
@Bradley University ... IL ... 145
Eastern Illinois University ... IL ... 150
Illinois State University ... IL ... 153
Loyola University Chicago ... IL ... 157
Northern Illinois University ... IL ... 160
Rush University ... IL ... 163
Southern Illinois University Carbondale ... IL ... 164
University of Illinois at Urbana-Champaign ... IL ... 167
Ball State University ... IN ... 169
Indiana University-Purdue University Indianapolis ... IN ... 174
Iowa State University ... IA ... 182
University of Iowa ... IA ... 182
University of Kansas Medical Center ... KS ... 197
Eastern Kentucky University ... KY ... 200
Murray State University ... KY ... 204
University of Kentucky ... KY ... 206
Louisiana Tech University ... LA ... 215
McNeese State University ... LA ... 215
Southern University and A&M College ... LA ... 214
Tulane University ... LA ... 215
University of Louisiana at Lafayette ... LA ... 216
University of Maine ... ME ... 220
Johns Hopkins University ... MD ... 223
University of Maryland Baltimore ... MD ... 227
University of Maryland College Park ... MD ... 227
University of Maryland Eastern Shore ... MD ... 227
Boston University ... MA ... 232
Simmons College ... MA ... 245
University of Massachusetts ... MA ... 237
Andrews University ... MI ... 247
Central Michigan University ... MI ... 249
Michigan State University ... MI ... 255
University of Michigan-Ann Arbor ... MI ... 259
Western Michigan University ... MI ... 260
Concordia College ... MN ... 263
Mayo School of Health Sciences ... MN ... 262
University of Minnesota-Twin Cities ... MN ... 272
Mississippi State University ... MS ... 276
University of Southern Mississippi ... MS ... 278
Cox College ... MO ... 281
Saint Louis University ... MO ... 289
Southeast Missouri State University ... MO ... 290
@Montana State University ... MT ... 295
University of Nebraska - Lincoln ... NE ... 300
University of Nebraska Medical Center ... NE ... 301
University of Nevada, Las Vegas ... NV ... 302
University of Nevada, Reno ... NV ... 303
Keene State College ... NH ... 307
University of New Hampshire ... NH ... 306
College of Saint Elizabeth ... NJ ... 309
Montclair State University ... NJ ... 311
UMDNJ-School of Health Related Professions ... NJ ... 317
@New Mexico State University Main Campus ... NM ... 319
University of New Mexico Main Campus ... NM ... 321
City University of New York Brooklyn College ... NY ... 326
City University of New York Herbert H. Lehman College ... NY ... 327
City University of New York Hunter College ... NY ... 327
City University of New York Queens College ... NY ... 328
Cornell University ... NY ... 331
Long Island University C.W. Post Campus ... NY ... 339
New York University ... NY ... 344
Sage Colleges, The ... NY ... 348
State University of New York at Buffalo ... NY ... 351
State University of New York at Stony Brook ... NY ... 352
State University of New York College at Oneonta ... NY ... 353
Syracuse University Main Campus ... NY ... 357
Teachers College, Columbia University ... NY ... 357
Appalachian State University ... NC ... 377
East Carolina University ... NC ... 377
@Lenoir-Rhyne University ... NC ... 366
Meredith College ... NC ... 366
North Carolina Central University ... NC ... 378
University of North Carolina at Greensboro ... NC ... 379
Western Carolina University ... NC ... 379
Bowling Green State University ... OH ... 385
Case Western Reserve University ... OH ... 386
Kent State University Main Campus ... OH ... 393
Mount Carmel College of Nursing ... OH ... 396
Ohio State University Main Campus, The ... OH ... 398
Oklahoma State University ... OK ... 410
University of Central Oklahoma ... OK ... 413
University of Oklahoma Health Sciences Center ... OK ... 413
Oregon Health & Science University ... OR ... 418
Oregon State University ... OR ... 418
@Cedar Crest College ... PA ... 424
Immaculata University ... PA ... 431
Indiana University of Pennsylvania ... PA ... 442
Marywood University ... PA ... 435
Penn State University Park ... PA ... 438
University of Puerto Rico-Medical Sciences Campus ... PR ... 567
University of Rhode Island ... RI ... 454
Medical University of South Carolina ... SC ... 459
Winthrop University ... SC ... 463
University of South Dakota, The ... SD ... 465
East Tennessee State University ... TN ... 473
Lipscomb University ... TN ... 470
University of Memphis, The ... TN ... 474
University of Tennessee at Martin ... TN ... 477
University of Tennessee, Knoxville ... TN ... 477
Vanderbilt University ... TN ... 477
Baylor College of Medicine ... TX ... 481
Lamar University ... TX ... 500
Prairie View A & M University ... TX ... 496
Sam Houston State University ... TX ... 501
Stephen F. Austin State University ... TX ... 495
Texas A & M University ... TX ... 497
Texas A & M University - Kingsville ... TX ... 498
Texas State University-San Marcos ... TX ... 501
Texas Tech University ... TX ... 501
Texas Woman's University ... TX ... 502
University of Houston ... TX ... 503
University of Texas Health Science Center at Houston (UTHealth), The ... TX ... 506
University of the Incarnate Word ... TX ... 503
Brigham Young University ... UT ... 509
Utah State University ... UT ... 511
University of Virginia ... VA ... 525
Virginia Commonwealth University ... VA ... 525
Virginia Polytechnic Institute and State University ... VA ... 529
Virginia State University ... VA ... 529
Bastyr University ... WA ... 530
Central Washington University ... WA ... 531
Marshall University ... WV ... 543
West Virginia University ... WV ... 544
Mount Mary College ... WI ... 549
University of Wisconsin-Green Bay ... WI ... 551
University of Wisconsin-Madison ... WI ... 550
University of Wisconsin-Stout ... WI ... 552
Viterbo University ... WI ... 553

DIETT: American Dietetic Association: dietetic technician (A)

Central Arizona College ... AZ ... 13
Chandler-Gilbert Community College ... AZ ... 15
Paradise Valley Community College ... AZ ... 16
Black River Technical College ... AR ... 21
Cosumnes River College ... CA ... 56
Los Angeles City College ... CA ... 54
Merritt College ... CA ... 62
Orange Coast College ... CA ... 41
@Santa Rosa Junior College ... CA ... 68
Gateway Community College ... CT ... 90
Lincoln College of New England ... CT ... 92
Florida State College at Jacksonville ... FL ... 109
@Hillsborough Community College ... FL ... 110
Harper College ... IL ... 151
@Parkland College ... IL ... 161
Delgado Community College ... LA ... 210
Southern Maine Community College ... ME ... 219
Baltimore City Community College ... MD ... 221
Laboure College ... MA ... 236
Wayne County Community College District ... MI ... 260
Normandale Community College ... MN ... 268
Saint Louis Community College at Florissant Valley ... MO ... 289
Southeast Community College ... NE ... 300
Truckee Meadows Community College ... NV ... 302
University of New Hampshire ... NH ... 306
Camden County College ... NJ ... 308
Middlesex County College ... NJ ... 311
Erie Community College North Campus ... NY ... 333
La Guardia Community College/City University of New York ... NY ... 328
State University of New York College of Agriculture and Technology at Morri sville ... NY ... 354
Suffolk County Community College Eastern Campus ... NY ... 356
Trocaire College ... NY ... 358
Westchester Community College ... NY ... 360
Gaston College ... NC ... 370
Cincinnati State Technical and Community College ... OH ... 387
Columbus State Community College ... OH ... 388
Cuyahoga Community College ... OH ... 389
Owens Community College ... OH ... 400
Sinclair Community College ... OH ... 401
Youngstown State University ... OH ... 406
@Oklahoma State University - Oklahoma City ... OK ... 410
Community College of Allegheny County ... PA ... 425
Penn State University Park ... PA ... 438
Southwest Tennessee Community College ... TN ... 475
Tarrant County College District ... TX ... 496
Milwaukee Area Technical College ... WI ... 554

DMOLS: National Accrediting Agency for Clinical Laboratory Sciences: diagnostic molecular scientist (C,B)

University of Connecticut ... CT ... 94
University of Kansas Medical Center ... KS ... 197
Michigan State University ... MI ... 255
Northern Michigan University ... MI ... 256
State University of New York Upstate Medical University ... NY ... 352
University of North Carolina at Chapel Hill ... NC ... 378
Texas Tech University Health Sciences Center ... TX ... 501
University of Texas M.D. Anderson Cancer Center, The ... TX ... 507

DMS: Commission on Accreditation of Allied Health Education Programs: diagnostic medical sonography (C,A,B)

Lurleen B. Wallace Community College ... AL ... 5
Trenholm State Technical College ... AL ... 7
Wallace State Community College - Hanceville ... AL ... 10
Gateway Community College ... AZ ... 15
Arkansas State University ... AR ... 20
University of Arkansas at Fort Smith ... AR ... 24
University of Arkansas for Medical Sciences ... AR ... 24
Charles Drew University of Medicine & Science ... CA ... 39
Cypress College ... CA ... 59
Foothill College ... CA ... 47
Loma Linda University ... CA ... 54
Merced College ... CA ... 57
Orange Coast College ... CA ... 41
Santa Barbara City College ... CA ... 68
University of California-San Diego ... CA ... 74
University of Colorado DenverlAnschutz Medical Campus ... CO ... 88
Delaware Technical and Community College Owens Campus ... DE ... 96
Delaware Technical and Community College Stanton-Wilmington Campus ... DE ... 96
George Washington University ... DC ... 97
Broward College ... FL ... 102
Cambridge Institute of Allied Health & Technology ... FL ... 102
Central Florida Institute ... FL ... 102
Florida Hospital College of Health Sciences ... FL ... 108
Hillsborough Community College ... FL ... 110
Keiser University ... FL ... 112
Miami Dade College ... FL ... 113
Nova Southeastern University ... FL ... 114
Palm Beach State College ... FL ... 11
Sanford-Brown Institute ... FL ... 11
Valencia College ... FL ... 12
Athens Technical College ... GA ... 12
Georgia Health Sciences University ... GA ... 13
Georgia Northwestern Technical College ... GA ... 13
Ogeechee Technical College ... GA ... 134
Sanford-Brown College ... GA ... 136
Boise State University ... ID ... 14
College of DuPage ... IL ... 147
Harper College ... IL ... 151
John A. Logan College ... IL ... 154
Rush University ... IL ... 163
Southern Illinois University Carbondale ... IL ... 164
Triton College ... IL ... 166
University of Southern Indiana ... IN ... 180
Mercy College of Health Sciences ... IA ... 187
University of Iowa ... IA ... 182
University of Kansas Medical Center ... KS ... 197
Washburn University ... KS ... 197
Bowling Green Technical College ... KY ... 201
Jefferson Community and Technical College ... KY ... 202
Morehead State University ... KY ... 204
St. Catharine College ... KY ... 205
West Kentucky Community and Technical College ... KY ... 203
Delgado Community College ... LA ... 210
Louisiana State University at Eunice ... LA ... 212
Kennebec Valley Community College ... ME ... 218
Johns Hopkins University ... MD ... 223
Montgomery College ... MD ... 224
University of Maryland Baltimore County ... MD ... 227
Bunker Hill Community College ... MA ... 239
Middlesex Community College ... MA ... 240
Springfield Technical Community College ... MA ... 241
Baker College of Auburn Hills ... MI ... 248
Baker College of Owosso ... MI ... 249
Delta College ... MI ... 250
Ferris State University ... MI ... 251
Grand Valley State University ... MI ... 252
Jackson Community College ... MI ... 253
Lansing Community College ... MI ... 254
Oakland Community College ... MI ... 257
Argosy University, Twin Cities ... MN ... 261
Mayo School of Health Sciences ... MN ... 262
St. Catherine University ... MN ... 271
Saint Cloud Technical and Community College ... MN ... 269
Hinds Community College ... MS ... 274
Itawamba Community College ... MS ... 274
Saint Louis Community College at Forest Park ... MO ... 289
Sanford-Brown College ... MO ... 289
University of Missouri - Columbia ... MO ... 291
Bryan LGH College of Health Sciences ... NE ... 297
Nebraska Methodist College ... NE ... 299
University of Nebraska Medical Center ... NE ... 301
College of Southern Nevada ... NV ... 302
NHTI-Concord's Community College ... NH ... 304
Bergen Community College ... NJ ... 307
Gloucester County College ... NJ ... 310
UMDNJ-School of Health Related Professions ... NJ ... 317
Central New Mexico Community College ... NM ... 317
New Mexico State University Dona Ana Community College ... NM ... 319
Hudson Valley Community College ... NY ... 336
Long Island University Brooklyn Campus ... NY ... 338
New York University ... NY ... 344
Rochester Institute of Technology ... NY ... 347
State University of New York Health Science Center at Brooklyn ... NY ... 352
Asheville - Buncombe Technical Community College ... NC ... 367
Caldwell Community College and Technical Institute ... NC ... 368
Cape Fear Community College ... NC ... 368
Forsyth Technical Community College ... NC ... 370
Johnston Community College ... NC ... 371
Pitt Community College ... NC ... 372
South Piedmont Community College ... NC ... 373
Southwestern Community College ... NC ... 373
Central Ohio Technical College ... OH ... 386
Cincinnati State Technical and Community College ... OH ... 387
Cuyahoga Community College ... OH ... 389
Kettering College of Medical Arts ... OH ... 394
Lorain County Community College ... OH ... 395
Owens Community College ... OH ... 400
University of Rio Grande ... OH ... 404
Oklahoma State University - Oklahoma City ... OK ... 410
University of Oklahoma Health Sciences Center ... OK ... 413
Community College of Allegheny County ... PA ... 425
Harrisburg Area Community College ... PA ... 430
Lackawanna College ... PA ... 433
Lancaster General College of Nursing and Health Sciences ... PA ... 433
Misericordia University ... PA ... 436
Mount Aloysius College ... PA ... 437
Northampton Community College ... PA ... 437
Sanford-Brown Institute-Pittsburgh ... PA ... 446
South Hills School of Business and Technology ... PA ... 447
Thomas Jefferson University ... PA ... 448
Community College of Rhode Island ... RI ... 453
Greenville Technical College ... SC ... 458
Horry-Georgetown Technical College ... SC ... 458

Southeast Technical Institute ... SD ... 466
Baptist Memorial College of Health Sciences TN ... 467
Chattanooga State Community College ... TN ... 474
Vanderbilt University ... TN ... 477
Volunteer State Community College ... TN ... 476
Alvin Community College ... TX ... 479
Angelina College ... TX ... 480
Austin Community College District ... TX ... 481
Del Mar College ... TX ... 485
El Centro College ... TX ... 484
El Paso Community College ... TX ... 486
Lamar Institute of Technology ... TX ... 500
Lone Star College System ... TX ... 490
Midland College ... TX ... 490
Sanford-Brown College-Houston ... TX ... 493
Temple College ... TX ... 496
Texas Southmost College ... TX ... 499
Tyler Junior College ... TX ... 502
University of Texas at Brownsville, The ... TX ... 505
Tidewater Community College ... VA ... 528
Bellevue College ... WA ... 531
Seattle University ... WA ... 537
Spokane Community College ... WA ... 532
Tacoma Community College ... WA ... 538
Mountain State University ... WV ... 541
West Virginia University ... WV ... 544
Blackhawk Technical College ... WI ... 553
Chippewa Valley Technical College ... WI ... 553
Northeast Wisconsin Technical College ... WI ... 555
University of Wisconsin-Madison ... WI ... 550
Laramie County Community College ... WY ... 556

DNUR: National League for Nursing: nursing (C)

Bon Secours Memorial College of Nursing ... VA ... 516
Sentara College of Health Sciences ... VA ... 523

DT: American Dental Association: dental laboratory technology (C,A)

Pima County Community College District ... AZ ... 17
Los Angeles City College ... CA ... 54
Pasadena City College ... CA ... 61
Indian River State College ... FL ... 110
Atlanta Technical College ... GA ... 125
Idaho State University ... ID ... 143
Indiana University-Purdue University Fort Wayne ... IN ... 174
Kirkwood Community College ... IA ... 186
Bluegrass Community and Technical College KY ... 201
Louisiana State University Health Sciences Center-New Orleans ... LA ... 213
Middlesex Community College ... MA ... 240
Erie Community College-South Campus ... NY ... 333
New York City College of Technology/City University of New York ... NY ... 328
Durham Technical Community College ... NC ... 369
Portland Community College ... OR ... 419
San Antonio College ... TX ... 479
J. Sargeant Reynolds Community College ... VA ... 526
Bates Technical College ... WA ... 531

EEG: Commission on Accreditation of Allied Health Education Programs: electroneurodiagnostic technology (C,A)

Gateway Community College ... AZ ... 15
Orange Coast College ... CA ... 41
Lincoln Land Community College ... IL ... 156
Kirkwood Community College ... IA ... 186
Scott Community College ... IA ... 184
Laboure College ... MA ... 236
Mayo School of Health Sciences ... MN ... 262
Minneapolis Community and Technical College ... MN ... 267
DeVry University - North Brunswick Campus. NJ ... 309
Catawba Valley Community College ... NC ... 368
Pamlico Community College ... NC ... 372
Cuyahoga Community College ... OH ... 389
Harcum College ... PA ... 430
Southeast Technical Institute ... SD ... 466
McLennan Community College ... TX ... 490
Western Technical College ... WI ... 555

EH: New England Association of Schools and Colleges, Commission on Institutions of Higher Education (NEASC-CIHE)

&Monterey Institute of International Studies ... CA ... 57
&Johnson & Wales University - Denver Campus ... CO ... 85
Albertus Magnus College ... CT ... 89
Asnuntuck Community College ... CT ... 89
Capital Community College ... CT ... 89
Central Connecticut State University ... CT ... 91
Charter Oak State College ... CT ... 91
Connecticut College ... CT ... 91
Eastern Connecticut State University ... CT ... 91
Fairfield University ... CT ... 92
Gateway Community College ... CT ... 90
Goodwin College ... CT ... 92
Hartford Seminary ... CT ... 92
Holy Apostles College and Seminary ... CT ... 92
Housatonic Community College ... CT ... 90
Lincoln College of New England ... CT ... 92
Lyme Academy College of Fine Arts ... CT ... 93
Manchester Community College ... CT ... 90
Middlesex Community College ... CT ... 90
Mitchell College ... CT ... 93
Naugatuck Valley Community College ... CT ... 90
Northwestern Connecticut Community-Technical College ... CT ... 90
Norwalk Community College ... CT ... 90
Post University ... CT ... 93
Quinebaug Valley Community College ... CT ... 91
Quinnipiac University ... CT ... 93
Sacred Heart University ... CT ... 93
Saint Joseph College ... CT ... 93
St. Vincent's College ... CT ... 94
Southern Connecticut State University ... CT ... 91
Three Rivers Community College ... CT ... 91
Trinity College ... CT ... 94
Tunxis Community College ... CT ... 91
United States Coast Guard Academy ... CT ... 558
University of Bridgeport ... CT ... 94
University of Connecticut ... CT ... 94
&University of Connecticut Health Center ... CT ... 94
University of Hartford ... CT ... 95
University of New Haven ... CT ... 95
Wesleyan University ... CT ... 95
Western Connecticut State University ... CT ... 92
Yale University ... CT ... 95
&Johnson & Wales University ... FL ... 111
Bangor Theological Seminary ... ME ... 217
Bates College ... ME ... 217
Bowdoin College ... ME ... 217
Central Maine Community College ... ME ... 218
Central Maine Medical Center College of Nursing and Health Professions ... ME ... 217
Colby College ... ME ... 217
College of the Atlantic ... ME ... 217
Eastern Maine Community College ... ME ... 218
Husson University ... ME ... 218
@Institute for Doctoral Studies in the Visual Arts ... ME ... 218
Kennebec Valley Community College ... ME ... 218
Maine College of Art ... ME ... 218
Maine Maritime Academy ... ME ... 219
Northern Maine Community College ... ME ... 218
Saint Joseph's College of Maine ... ME ... 219
Southern Maine Community College ... ME ... 219
Thomas College ... ME ... 219
Unity College ... ME ... 219
University of Maine ... ME ... 220
University of Maine at Augusta ... ME ... 220
University of Maine at Farmington ... ME ... 220
University of Maine at Fort Kent ... ME ... 220
University of Maine at Machias ... ME ... 220
University of Maine at Presque Isle ... ME ... 220
University of New England ... ME ... 220
University of Southern Maine ... ME ... 220
Washington County Community College ... ME ... 219
York County Community College ... ME ... 219
American International College ... MA ... 229
Amherst College ... MA ... 230
Andover Newton Theological School ... MA ... 230
Anna Maria College ... MA ... 230
&Art Institute of Boston at Lesley University, The ... MA ... 230
Assumption College ... MA ... 230
Babson College ... MA ... 230
Bard College at Simon's Rock ... MA ... 231
Bay Path College ... MA ... 231
Bay State College ... MA ... 231
Becker College-Worcester ... MA ... 231
Benjamin Franklin Institute of Technology ... MA ... 231
Bentley University ... MA ... 231
Berklee College of Music ... MA ... 231
Berkshire Community College ... MA ... 239
Boston Architectural College ... MA ... 232
Boston College ... MA ... 232
Boston Conservatory, The ... MA ... 232
Boston Graduate School of Psychoanalysis . MA ... 232
Boston University ... MA ... 232
Brandeis University ... MA ... 233
Bridgewater State University ... MA ... 238
Bristol Community College ... MA ... 239
Bunker Hill Community College ... MA ... 239
Cambridge College ... MA ... 233
Cape Cod Community College ... MA ... 240
Clark University ... MA ... 233
College of Our Lady of the Elms ... MA ... 233
College of the Holy Cross ... MA ... 233
Conway School of Landscape Design ... MA ... 233
Curry College ... MA ... 234
Dean College ... MA ... 234
Eastern Nazarene College ... MA ... 234
Emerson College ... MA ... 234
Emmanuel College ... MA ... 234
Endicott College ... MA ... 234
Fisher College ... MA ... 235
Fitchburg State University ... MA ... 238
Framingham State University ... MA ... 238
Franklin W. Olin College of Engineering ... MA ... 235
Gordon College ... MA ... 235
Gordon-Conwell Theological Seminary ... MA ... 235
Greenfield Community College ... MA ... 240
Hampshire College ... MA ... 235
Harvard University ... MA ... 235
Hebrew College ... MA ... 235
Hellenic College-Holy Cross Greek Orthodox School of Theology ... MA ... 236
Holyoke Community College ... MA ... 240
Hult International Business School ... MA ... 236
Laboure College ... MA ... 236
Lasell College ... MA ... 236
Lesley University ... MA ... 236
Longy School of Music of Bard College ... MA ... 236
Marian Court College ... MA ... 236
Massachusetts Bay Community College ... MA ... 240
Massachusetts College of Art and Design ... MA ... 238
Massachusetts College of Liberal Arts ... MA ... 238
Massachusetts College of Pharmacy and Health Sciences ... MA ... 241
Massachusetts Institute of Technology ... MA ... 242
Massachusetts Maritime Academy ... MA ... 239
Massachusetts School of Law at Andover ... MA ... 242
Massachusetts School of Professional Psychology ... MA ... 242
Massasoit Community College ... MA ... 240
Merrimack College ... MA ... 242
MGH Institute of Health Professions ... MA ... 242
Middlesex Community College ... MA ... 240
Montserrat College of Art ... MA ... 242
Mount Holyoke College ... MA ... 242
Mount Ida College ... MA ... 243
Mount Wachusett Community College ... MA ... 240
National Graduate School of Quality Systems Management, The ... MA ... 243
New England College of Business and Finance ... MA ... 243
New England College of Optometry, The ... MA ... 243
New England Conservatory of Music ... MA ... 243
New England Institute of Art, The ... MA ... 243
Newbury College ... MA ... 243
Nichols College ... MA ... 243
North Shore Community College ... MA ... 241
Northeastern University ... MA ... 244
Northern Essex Community College ... MA ... 241
Pine Manor College ... MA ... 244
Quincy College ... MA ... 244
Quinsigamond Community College ... MA ... 241
Regis College ... MA ... 244
Roxbury Community College ... MA ... 241
Saint John's Seminary ... MA ... 244
Salem State University ... MA ... 239
Simmons College ... MA ... 245
Smith College ... MA ... 245
Springfield College ... MA ... 245
Springfield Technical Community College ... MA ... 241
Stonehill College ... MA ... 245
Suffolk University ... MA ... 245
Tufts University ... MA ... 245
University of Massachusetts ... MA ... 237
University of Massachusetts at Worcester ... MA ... 238
University of Massachusetts Boston ... MA ... 237
University of Massachusetts Dartmouth ... MA ... 237
University of Massachusetts Lowell ... MA ... 237
Urban College of Boston ... MA ... 246
Wellesley College ... MA ... 246
Wentworth Institute of Technology ... MA ... 246
Western New England University ... MA ... 246
Westfield State University ... MA ... 239
Wheaton College ... MA ... 246
Wheelock College ... MA ... 246
Williams College ... MA ... 246
Woods Hole Oceanographic Institution ... MA ... 247
Worcester Polytechnic Institute ... MA ... 247
Worcester State University ... MA ... 239
Chester College of New England ... NH ... 303
Colby-Sawyer College ... NH ... 304
Daniel Webster College ... NH ... 304
Dartmouth College ... NH ... 305
Franklin Pierce University ... NH ... 305
Granite State College ... NH ... 306
Great Bay Community College ... NH ... 304
Hesser College ... NH ... 305
Keene State College ... NH ... 307
Lakes Region Community College ... NH ... 304
Manchester Community College ... NH ... 304
Nashua Community College ... NH ... 304
New England College ... NH ... 305
@New Hampshire Institute of Art ... NH ... 305
NHTI-Concord's Community College ... NH ... 304
Plymouth State University ... NH ... 307
River Valley Community College ... NH ... 304
Rivier College ... NH ... 305
Saint Anselm College ... NH ... 305
Southern New Hampshire University ... NH ... 306
#Thomas More College of Liberal Arts, The ... NH ... 306
University of New Hampshire ... NH ... 306
&University of New Hampshire at Manchester NH ... 306
University of New Hampshire School of Law - formerly Franklin Pierce Law Ce nter ... NH ... 306
White Mountains Community College ... NH ... 304
&Johnson & Wales University-Charlotte ... NC ... 365
Brown University ... RI ... 452
Bryant University ... RI ... 453
Community College of Rhode Island ... RI ... 453
Johnson & Wales University ... RI ... 453
Mater Ecclesiae College ... RI ... 453
Naval War College ... RI ... 557
New England Institute of Technology ... RI ... 453
Providence College ... RI ... 453
Rhode Island College ... RI ... 454
Rhode Island School of Design ... RI ... 454
Roger Williams University ... RI ... 454
Salve Regina University ... RI ... 454
University of Rhode Island ... RI ... 454
Bennington College ... VT ... 512
Burlington College ... VT ... 512
Castleton State College ... VT ... 515
Champlain College ... VT ... 513
College of St. Joseph ... VT ... 513
Community College of Vermont ... VT ... 515
Goddard College ... VT ... 513
Green Mountain College ... VT ... 513
Johnson State College ... VT ... 515
Landmark College ... VT ... 513
Lyndon State College ... VT ... 515
Marlboro College ... VT ... 513
Middlebury College ... VT ... 513
Norwich University ... VT ... 514
Saint Michael's College ... VT ... 514
School for International Training ... VT ... 514
Southern Vermont College ... VT ... 514
Sterling College ... VT ... 514
University of Vermont ... VT ... 514
Vermont College of Fine Arts ... VT ... 514
Vermont Law School ... VT ... 515
Vermont Technical College ... VT ... 515

EMT: Commission on Accreditation of Allied Health Education Programs: emergency medical technician-paramedic (C,A,B)

Bevill State Community College ... AL ... 2
Bishop State Community College ... AL ... 2
Calhoun Community College ... AL ... 2
Gadsden State Community College ... AL ... 3
George C. Wallace Community College - Dothan ... AL ... 4
James H. Faulkner State Community College ... AL ... 5
Jefferson State Community College ... AL ... 5
Lurleen B. Wallace Community College ... AL ... 5
Northeast Alabama Community College ... AL ... 6
Northwest - Shoals Community College ... AL ... 6
Southern Union State Community College ... AL ... 7
Trenholm State Technical College ... AL ... 7
University of South Alabama ... AL ... 9
Wallace State Community College - Hanceville ... AL ... 10
University of Alaska Fairbanks ... AK ... 10
Arkansas Northeastern College ... AR ... 20
Arkansas State University-Beebe ... AR ... 20
Arkansas Tech University ... AR ... 20
Black River Technical College ... AR ... 21
East Arkansas Community College ... AR ... 21
National Park Community College ... AR ... 22
North Arkansas College ... AR ... 22
NorthWest Arkansas Community College ... AR ... 22
South Arkansas Community College ... AR ... 23
Southeast Arkansas College ... AR ... 23
University of Arkansas at Monticello ... AR ... 25
University of Arkansas Community College at Batesville ... AR ... 25
University of Arkansas Community College at Hope ... AR ... 25
University of Arkansas for Medical Sciences AR ... 24
American River College ... CA ... 56
Bakersfield College ... CA ... 52
Butte College ... CA ... 31
California State University-Sacramento ... CA ... 35
City College of San Francisco ... CA ... 39
Crafton Hills College ... CA ... 65
Cuesta College ... CA ... 43
Foothill College ... CA ... 47
Fresno City College ... CA ... 72
Imperial Valley College ... CA ... 50
Mendocino College ... CA ... 57
Mt. San Antonio College ... CA ... 58
Napa Valley College ... CA ... 58
Palomar College ... CA ... 61
Riverside City College ... CA ... 64
Saddleback College ... CA ... 70
Santa Rosa Junior College ... CA ... 68
Southwestern College ... CA ... 71
University of Antelope Valley ... CA ... 73
University of California-Los Angeles ... CA ... 74
Ventura College ... CA ... 77
Victor Valley College ... CA ... 77
Aims Community College ... CO ... 80
Arapahoe Community College ... CO ... 80
Colorado Mesa University ... CO ... 82
Colorado Mountain College ... CO ... 82
Community College of Aurora ... CO ... 83
Pikes Peak Community College ... CO ... 86
Pueblo Community College ... CO ... 87
Capital Community College ... CT ... 89
Delaware Technical and Community College Terry Campus ... DE ... 96
George Washington University ... DC ... 97
Brevard Community College ... FL ... 101
Broward College ... FL ... 102
College of Central Florida ... FL ... 103
Daytona State College ... FL ... 103
Edison State College ... FL ... 104
Florida Gateway College ... FL ... 108
Florida State College at Jacksonville ... FL ... 109
Gulf Coast State College ... FL ... 110
Hillsborough Community College ... FL ... 110
Indian River State College ... FL ... 110
Miami Dade College ... FL ... 113
Palm Beach State College ... FL ... 114
Pasco-Hernando Community College ... FL ... 114
Pensacola State College ... FL ... 114
Polk State College ... FL ... 115

Institution	State	Page
St. Petersburg College	FL	116
Santa Fe College	FL	117
Seminole State College of Florida	FL	117
Tallahassee Community College	FL	121
Valencia College	FL	122
Gwinnett Technical College	GA	132
Brigham Young University-Idaho	ID	142
College of Southern Idaho	ID	143
Idaho State University	ID	143
Loyola University Chicago	IL	157
Indiana University-Purdue University Indianapolis	IN	174
Ivy Tech Community College of Indiana-Bloomington	IN	175
Ivy Tech Community College of Indiana-Columbus	IN	175
Ivy Tech Community College of Indiana-Kokomo	IN	176
Ivy Tech Community College of Indiana-North Central	IN	176
Ivy Tech Community College of Indiana-Northeast	IN	176
Ivy Tech Community College of Indiana-Southwest	IN	176
Ivy Tech Community College of Indiana-Wabash Valley	IN	177
Vincennes University	IN	181
Kirkwood Community College	IA	186
Mercy College of Health Sciences	IA	187
University of Iowa	IA	182
Western Iowa Tech Community College	IA	189
Barton County Community College	KS	190
Coffeyville Community College	KS	191
Cowley County Community College	KS	192
Flint Hills Technical College	KS	192
Garden City Community College	KS	193
Hutchinson Community College and Area Vocational School	KS	193
Johnson County Community College	KS	193
Kansas City Kansas Community College	KS	193
Eastern Kentucky University	KY	200
Bossier Parish Community College	LA	209
Delgado Community College	LA	210
Louisiana State University and Agricultural and Mechanical College	LA	212
South Louisiana Community College	LA	212
Anne Arundel Community College	MD	221
Community College of Baltimore County, The	MD	222
Howard Community College	MD	223
University of Maryland Baltimore County	MD	227
Kalamazoo Valley Community College	MI	253
Lansing Community College	MI	254
Century College	MN	266
Inver Hills Community College	MN	266
Northland Community and Technical College	MN	268
Ridgewater College	MN	268
Rochester Community and Technical College	MN	269
Saint Cloud Technical and Community College	MN	269
South Central College	MN	269
East Central Community College	MS	274
East Mississippi Community College	MS	274
Hinds Community College	MS	274
Holmes Community College	MS	274
Itawamba Community College	MS	274
Jones County Junior College	MS	275
Mississippi Gulf Coast Community College	MS	275
Northwest Mississippi Community College	MS	276
IHM Academy of EMS	MO	283
Montana State University - Billings	MT	295
Creighton University	NE	297
Metropolitan Community College	NE	298
College of Southern Nevada	NV	302
NHTI-Concord's Community College	NH	304
Central New Mexico Community College	NM	317
Eastern New Mexico University-Roswell	NM	318
New Mexico State University Dona Ana Community College	NM	319
Santa Fe Community College	NM	320
University of New Mexico Main Campus	NM	321
City University of New York Borough of Manhattan Community College	NY	326
Dutchess Community College	NY	332
Herkimer County Community College	NY	335
Hudson Valley Community College	NY	336
Monroe Community College	NY	341
St. John's University	NY	348
State University of New York College of Agriculture and Technology at Coble skill	NY	354
Catawba Valley Community College	NC	368
Southwestern Community College	NC	373
Western Carolina University	NC	379
Bismarck State College	ND	382
Columbus State Community College	OH	388
University of Cincinnati Main Campus	OH	403
Youngstown State University	OH	406
Oklahoma City Community College	OK	409
Chemeketa Community College	OR	414
Oregon Health & Science University	OR	418
Harrisburg Area Community College	PA	430
Pennsylvania College of Technology	PA	440
Greenville Technical College	SC	458
Horry-Georgetown Technical College	SC	458
Trident Technical College	SC	461
Chattanooga State Community College	TN	474
Columbia State Community College	TN	474
Jackson State Community College	TN	475
Northeast State Technical Community College	TN	475
Roane State Community College	TN	475
Southwest Tennessee Community College	TN	475
Tennessee Technological University	TN	474
Volunteer State Community College	TN	476
Walters State Community College	TN	476
Austin Community College District	TX	481
Blinn College	TX	482
Brazosport College	TX	482
Brookhaven College	TX	484
Central Texas College	TX	482
College of the Mainland	TX	483
Galveston College	TX	486
Houston Community College	TX	487
Lone Star College System	TX	490
San Jacinto College Central	TX	493
San Jacinto College North	TX	493
South Plains College	TX	494
Tarrant County College District	TX	496
Temple College	TX	496
Texas Southmost College	TX	499
University of Texas at Brownsville, The	TX	505
University of Texas Health Science Center at San Antonio	TX	506
University of Texas Southwestern Medical Center at Dallas	TX	507
Wharton County Junior College	TX	508
Dixie State College of Utah	UT	512
University of Utah, The	UT	510
Utah Valley University	UT	511
Weber State University	UT	511
Central Virginia Community College	VA	526
J. Sargeant Reynolds Community College	VA	526
Jefferson College of Health Sciences (Formerly Community Hospital)	VA	520
National College	VA	521
Northern Virginia Community College	VA	527
Piedmont Virginia Community College	VA	527
Southwest Virginia Community College	VA	528
Tidewater Community College	VA	528
Virginia Commonwealth University	VA	525
Central Washington University	WA	531
Clark College	WA	532
Columbia Basin College	WA	532
Spokane Community College	WA	532
Tacoma Community College	WA	538
University of Washington	WA	538
Waukesha County Technical College	WI	555
Laramie County Community College	WY	556

ENG: ABET, Inc.: engineering (B,M)

Institution	State	Page
Alabama Agricultural and Mechanical University	AL	1
Auburn University	AL	1
Tuskegee University	AL	8
University of Alabama at Birmingham	AL	8
University of Alabama in Huntsville	AL	9
University of Alabama, The	AL	8
University of South Alabama	AL	9
University of Alaska Anchorage	AK	10
University of Alaska Fairbanks	AK	10
Arizona State University	AZ	12
Embry-Riddle Aeronautical University-Prescott Campus	AZ	14
Northern Arizona University	AZ	17
University of Arizona	AZ	19
Arkansas State University	AR	20
Arkansas Tech University	AR	20
Harding University Main Campus	AR	21
John Brown University	AR	22
University of Arkansas at Little Rock	AR	24
University of Arkansas Main Campus	AR	24
California Institute of Technology	CA	32
California Maritime Academy	CA	32
California Polytechnic State University-San Luis Obispo	CA	33
California State Polytechnic University-Pomona	CA	33
California State University-Chico	CA	34
California State University-East Bay	CA	34
California State University-Fresno	CA	34
California State University-Fullerton	CA	34
California State University-Long Beach	CA	35
California State University-Los Angeles	CA	35
California State University-Northridge	CA	35
California State University-Sacramento	CA	35
Harvey Mudd College	CA	49
Humboldt State University	CA	36
Loyola Marymount University	CA	56
National Test Pilot Institute	CA	58
Naval Postgraduate School	CA	557
San Diego State University	CA	36
San Francisco State University	CA	36
San Jose State University	CA	37
Santa Clara University	CA	68
Stanford University	CA	71
University of California-Berkeley	CA	73
University of California-Davis	CA	73
University of California-Irvine	CA	73
University of California-Los Angeles	CA	74
University of California-Riverside	CA	74
University of California-San Diego	CA	74
University of California-Santa Barbara	CA	74
University of California-Santa Cruz	CA	75
University of San Diego	CA	76
University of Southern California	CA	76
University of the Pacific	CA	75
Colorado School of Mines	CO	82
Colorado State University	CO	83
Colorado State University-Pueblo	CO	83
Colorado Technical University	CO	83
Fort Lewis College	CO	84
United States Air Force Academy	CO	558
University of Colorado at Colorado Springs	CO	88
University of Colorado Boulder	CO	88
University of Colorado Denver|Anschutz Medical Campus	CO	88
University of Denver	CO	88
Central Connecticut State University	CT	91
Fairfield University	CT	92
Trinity College	CT	94
United States Coast Guard Academy	CT	558
University of Bridgeport	CT	94
University of Connecticut	CT	94
University of Hartford	CT	95
University of New Haven	CT	95
Yale University	CT	95
University of Delaware	DE	96
Catholic University of America, The	DC	97
George Washington University	DC	97
Howard University	DC	98
University System of the District of Columbia	DC	99
Embry-Riddle Aeronautical University	FL	105
Florida Agricultural and Mechanical University	FL	118
Florida Atlantic University	FL	118
Florida Gulf Coast University	FL	119
Florida Institute of Technology	FL	108
Florida International University	FL	119
Florida State University	FL	119
University of Central Florida	FL	120
University of Florida	FL	120
University of Miami	FL	122
University of North Florida	FL	120
University of South Florida	FL	120
University of West Florida	FL	121
Georgia Institute of Technology	GA	130
Mercer University	GA	133
University of Georgia	GA	138
University of Hawaii at Manoa	HI	141
Boise State University	ID	142
Brigham Young University-Idaho	ID	142
Idaho State University	ID	143
University of Idaho	ID	144
Bradley University	IL	145
Illinois Institute of Technology	IL	153
Northern Illinois University	IL	160
Northwestern University	IL	160
Olivet Nazarene University	IL	160
Southern Illinois University Carbondale	IL	164
Southern Illinois University Edwardsville	IL	165
University of Illinois at Chicago	IL	166
University of Illinois at Urbana-Champaign	IL	167
Indiana Institute of Technology	IN	172
Indiana University-Purdue University Fort Wayne	IN	174
Indiana University-Purdue University Indianapolis	IN	174
Purdue University Calumet	IN	178
Purdue University Main Campus	IN	178
Rose-Hulman Institute of Technology	IN	179
Taylor University	IN	179
Trine University	IN	180
University of Evansville	IN	180
University of Notre Dame	IN	180
University of Southern Indiana	IN	180
Valparaiso University	IN	181
Dordt College	IA	183
Iowa State University	IA	182
St. Ambrose University	IA	188
University of Iowa	IA	182
Kansas State University	KS	194
University of Kansas Main Campus	KS	196
Wichita State University	KS	197
Murray State University	KY	204
University of Kentucky	KY	206
University of Louisville	KY	207
Western Kentucky University	KY	207
Louisiana State University and Agricultural and Mechanical College	LA	212
Louisiana Tech University	LA	215
McNeese State University	LA	215
Southern University and A&M College	LA	214
Tulane University	LA	215
University of Louisiana at Lafayette	LA	216
University of New Orleans	LA	213
Maine Maritime Academy	ME	219
University of Maine	ME	220
University of Southern Maine	ME	220
Capitol College	MD	221
Johns Hopkins University	MD	223
Loyola University Maryland	MD	224
Morgan State University	MD	224
United States Naval Academy	MD	558
University of Maryland Baltimore County	MD	227
University of Maryland College Park	MD	227
Boston University	MA	232
Franklin W. Olin College of Engineering	MA	235
Harvard University	MA	235
Massachusetts Institute of Technology	MA	242
Merrimack College	MA	242
Northeastern University	MA	244
Smith College	MA	245
Suffolk University	MA	245
Tufts University	MA	24
University of Massachusetts	MA	23
University of Massachusetts Dartmouth	MA	23
University of Massachusetts Lowell	MA	23
Wentworth Institute of Technology	MA	24
Western New England University	MA	24
Worcester Polytechnic Institute	MA	24
Andrews University	MI	24
Baker College of Flint	MI	24
Calvin College	MI	24
Central Michigan University	MI	24
Ferris State University	MI	25
Grand Valley State University	MI	25
Hope College	MI	25
Kettering University	MI	25
Lake Superior State University	MI	25
Lawrence Technological University	MI	25
Michigan State University	MI	255
Michigan Technological University	MI	255
Oakland University	MI	257
Saginaw Valley State University	MI	258
University of Detroit Mercy	MI	259
University of Michigan-Ann Arbor	MI	259
University of Michigan-Dearborn	MI	259
Wayne State University	MI	260
Western Michigan University	MI	260
Minnesota State University, Mankato	MN	267
St. Cloud State University	MN	269
University of Minnesota Duluth	MN	272
University of Minnesota-Twin Cities	MN	272
University of Saint Thomas	MN	272
Winona State University	MN	270
Jackson State University	MS	275
Mississippi State University	MS	276
University of Mississippi	MS	277
Missouri University of Science & Technology	MO	292
Saint Louis University	MO	289
Southeast Missouri State University	MO	290
University of Missouri - Columbia	MO	291
University of Missouri - Kansas City	MO	291
University of Missouri - Saint Louis	MO	291
Washington University in St. Louis	MO	292
Carroll College	MT	294
Montana State University	MT	295
Montana Tech of The University of Montana	MT	296
University of Nebraska - Lincoln	NE	300
University of Nevada, Las Vegas	NV	302
University of Nevada, Reno	NV	303
Daniel Webster College	NH	304
Dartmouth College	NH	305
University of New Hampshire	NH	306
College of New Jersey, The	NJ	308
Fairleigh Dickinson University	NJ	310
Monmouth University	NJ	311
New Jersey Institute of Technology	NJ	312
Princeton University	NJ	313
Rowan University	NJ	314
Rutgers the State University of New Jersey New Brunswick Campus	NJ	314
Stevens Institute of Technology	NJ	315
New Mexico Institute of Mining and Technology	NM	319
New Mexico State University Main Campus	NM	319
University of New Mexico Main Campus	NM	321
Alfred University	NY	322
City University of New York College of Staten Island	NY	327
City University of New York The City College	NY	326
Clarkson University	NY	329
Columbia University in the City of New York	NY	330
Cooper Union	NY	331
Cornell University	NY	331
Hofstra University	NY	335
Manhattan College	NY	339
New York Institute of Technology	NY	343
Polytechnic Institute of New York University	NY	346
Rensselaer Polytechnic Institute	NY	347
Rochester Institute of Technology	NY	347
State University of New York at Binghamton	NY	351
State University of New York at Buffalo	NY	351
State University of New York at New Paltz	NY	352
State University of New York at Stony Brook	NY	352
State University of New York College of Environmental Science and Forestry	NY	355
State University of New York Maritime College	NY	356
Syracuse University Main Campus	NY	357
Union College	NY	358
United States Merchant Marine Academy	NY	558
United States Military Academy	NY	558
University of Rochester	NY	358
Webb Institute	NY	360
Duke University	NC	363
East Carolina University	NC	377
North Carolina Agricultural and Technical State University	NC	377
North Carolina State University	NC	378
University of North Carolina at Charlotte	NC	378
North Dakota State University Main Campus	ND	381
University of North Dakota Main Campus	ND	381
Air Force Institute of Technology	OH	556
Case Western Reserve University	OH	386
Cedarville University	OH	386
Central State University	OH	386
Cleveland State University	OH	388
Marietta College	OH	395
Miami University	OH	396

ENGR: ABET, Inc.: applied science (A, B,M)

ENGT: ABET, Inc.: engineering technology (A,B)

Bluefield State College ... WV ... 543
Bridgemont Community and Technical College ... WV ... 542
Fairmont State University ... WV ... 543
West Virginia University Institute of Technology ... WV ... 545
Milwaukee School of Engineering ... WI ... 548
Northeast Wisconsin Technical College ... WI ... 555

EXSC: Commission on Accreditation of Allied Health Education Programs: exercise science (B,M)

Central Connecticut State University ... CT ... 91
Southern Connecticut State University ... CT ... 91
Georgia State University ... GA ... 131
University of Louisiana at Monroe ... LA ... 216
University of Southern Maine ... ME ... 220
Salisbury University ... MD ... 228
Springfield College ... MA ... 245
Westfield State University ... MA ... 239
St. Catherine University ... MN ... 271
Missouri Baptist University ... MO ... 286
University of North Carolina at Charlotte ... NC ... 378
North Dakota State University Main Campus. ND ... 381
University of Mary ... ND ... 383
Kent State University Main Campus ... OH ... 393
Ohio Northern University ... OH ... 398
University of Central Oklahoma ... OK ... 413
Bloomsburg University of Pennsylvania ... PA ... 441
East Stroudsburg University of Pennsylvania PA ... 442
Eastern University ... PA ... 428
Indiana University of Pennsylvania ... PA ... 442
Slippery Rock University of Pennsylvania ... PA ... 443
West Chester University of Pennsylvania ... PA ... 443
Lyndon State College ... VT ... 515
Liberty University ... VA ... 520
Lynchburg College ... VA ... 520
Old Dominion University ... VA ... 521

FOR: Society of American Foresters: forestry (B,M,FP)

Alabama Agricultural and Mechanical University ... AL ... 1
Auburn University ... AL ... 1
University of Alaska Fairbanks ... AK ... 10
Northern Arizona University ... AZ ... 17
University of Arkansas at Monticello ... AR ... 25
California Polytechnic State University-San Luis Obispo ... CA ... 33
Humboldt State University ... CA ... 36
University of California-Berkeley ... CA ... 73
Colorado State University ... CO ... 83
Yale University ... CT ... 95
University of Florida ... FL ... 120
University of Georgia ... GA ... 138
University of Idaho ... ID ... 144
Southern Illinois University Carbondale ... IL ... 164
University of Illinois at Urbana-Champaign ... IL ... 167
Purdue University Main Campus ... IN ... 178
Iowa State University ... IA ... 182
University of Kentucky ... KY ... 206
Louisiana State University and Agricultural and Mechanical College ... LA ... 212
Louisiana Tech University ... LA ... 215
University of Maine ... ME ... 220
University of Massachusetts ... MA ... 237
Michigan State University ... MI ... 255
Michigan Technological University ... MI ... 255
University of Minnesota-Twin Cities ... MN ... 272
Mississippi State University ... MS ... 276
University of Missouri - Columbia ... MO ... 291
University of Montana - Missoula, The ... MT ... 295
University of New Hampshire ... NH ... 306
Paul Smith's College of Arts and Sciences .. NY ... 345
State University of New York College of Environmental Science and Forestry ... NY ... 355
#Duke University ... NC ... 363
North Carolina State University ... NC ... 378
Ohio State University Main Campus, The ... OH ... 398
Oklahoma State University ... OK ... 410
Oregon State University ... OR ... 418
Penn State University Park ... PA ... 438
Clemson University ... SC ... 456
University of Tennessee, Knoxville ... TN ... 477
Stephen F. Austin State University ... TX ... 495
Texas A & M University ... TX ... 497
Utah State University ... UT ... 511
Virginia Polytechnic Institute and State University ... VA ... 529
University of Washington ... WA ... 538
Washington State University ... WA ... 539
West Virginia University ... WV ... 544
University of Wisconsin-Madison ... WI ... 550
University of Wisconsin-Stevens Point ... WI ... 552

FUSER: American Board of Funeral Service Education: funeral service education (C,A,B)

Bishop State Community College ... AL ... 2
Jefferson State Community College ... AL ... 5
Mesa Community College ... AZ ... 15
Arkansas State University-Mountain Home ... AR ... 20
University of Arkansas Community College at Hope ... AR ... 25
American River College ... CA ... 56
Cypress College ... CA ... 59
Arapahoe Community College ... CO ... 80
Lincoln College of New England ... CT ... 92
University System of the District of Columbia DC ... 99
Florida State College at Jacksonville ... FL ... 109
Miami Dade College ... FL ... 113
St. Petersburg College ... FL ... 116
Gupton Jones College of Funeral Service ... GA ... 131
Ogeechee Technical College ... GA ... 134
Carl Sandburg College ... IL ... 146
City Colleges of Chicago Malcolm X College IL ... 147
Southern Illinois University Carbondale ... IL ... 164
Worsham College of Mortuary Science ... IL ... 168
Ivy Tech Community College-Central Indiana IN ... 175
Ivy Tech Community College of Indiana-Northwest ... IN ... 176
Mid-America College of Funeral Service ... IN ... 178
Vincennes University ... IN ... 181
Des Moines Area Community College ... IA ... 183
Kansas City Kansas Community College ... KS ... 193
Delgado Community College ... LA ... 210
Community College of Baltimore County, The ... MD ... 222
FINE Mortuary College ... MA ... 235
Mount Ida College ... MA ... 243
Wayne State University ... MI ... 260
University of Minnesota-Twin Cities ... MN ... 272
East Mississippi Community College ... MS ... 274
Holmes Community College ... MS ... 274
Mississippi Gulf Coast Community College .. MS ... 275
Northwest Mississippi Community College ... MS ... 276
Saint Louis Community College at Forest Park ... MO ... 289
Mercer County Community College ... NJ ... 311
American Academy McAllister Institute of Funeral Service ... NY ... 323
Hudson Valley Community College ... NY ... 336
Nassau Community College ... NY ... 342
Simmons Institute of Funeral Service, Inc. ... NY ... 351
Fayetteville Technical Community College ... NC ... 370
Cincinnati College of Mortuary Science ... OH ... 387
University of Central Oklahoma ... OK ... 413
Mt. Hood Community College ... OR ... 417
Northampton Community College ... PA ... 437
Pittsburgh Institute of Mortuary Science ... PA ... 444
Piedmont Technical College ... SC ... 460
John A. Gupton College ... TN ... 469
Amarillo College ... TX ... 479
Commonwealth Institute of Funeral Service . TX ... 483
Dallas Institute of Funeral Service ... TX ... 485
San Antonio College ... TX ... 479
John Tyler Community College ... VA ... 526
Tidewater Community College ... VA ... 528
Milwaukee Area Technical College ... WI ... 554

HSA: Commission on Accreditation of Healthcare Management Education: healthcare management (M)

University of Alabama at Birmingham ... AL ... 8
Arizona State University ... AZ ... 12
University of Arkansas for Medical Sciences AR ... 24
California State University-Long Beach ... CA ... 35
San Diego State University ... CA ... 36
University of California-Los Angeles ... CA ... 74
University of Southern California ... CA ... 76
University of Colorado DenverlAnschutz Medical Campus ... CO ... 88
Yale University ... CT ... 95
George Washington University ... DC ... 97
Georgetown University ... DC ... 98
University of Central Florida ... FL ... 120
University of Florida ... FL ... 120
University of Miami ... FL ... 122
University of North Florida ... FL ... 120
Armstrong Atlantic State University ... GA ... 124
Georgia State University ... GA ... 131
Governors State University ... IL ... 151
Northwestern University ... IL ... 160
Rush University ... IL ... 163
Indiana University-Purdue University Indianapolis ... IN ... 174
University of Iowa ... IA ... 182
University of Kansas Main Campus ... KS ... 196
University of Kentucky ... KY ... 206
Tulane University ... LA ... 215
University of Southern Maine ... ME ... 220
Johns Hopkins University ... MD ... 223
Boston University ... MA ... 232
Simmons College ... MA ... 245
University of Michigan-Ann Arbor ... MI ... 259
University of Minnesota-Twin Cities ... MN ... 272
University of Saint Thomas ... MN ... 272
Saint Louis University ... MO ... 289
University of Missouri - Columbia ... MO ... 291
Baruch College/City University of New York . NY ... 326
Columbia University in the City of New York NY ... 330
Cornell University ... NY ... 331
New York University ... NY ... 344
Union Graduate College ... NY ... 358
University of North Carolina at Chapel Hill ... NC ... 378
University of North Carolina at Charlotte ... NC ... 378
Ohio State University Main Campus, The ... OH ... 398
Xavier University ... OH ... 406
University of Oklahoma Health Sciences Center ... OK ... 413
Penn State University Park ... PA ... 438
Temple University ... PA ... 447
University of Pennsylvania ... PA ... 448
University of Pittsburgh ... PA ... 449
University of Scranton, The ... PA ... 450
Widener University ... PA ... 451
University of Puerto Rico-Medical Sciences Campus ... PR ... 567
Medical University of South Carolina ... SC ... 459
University of South Carolina Columbia ... SC ... 462
University of Memphis, The ... TN ... 474
Baylor University ... TX ... 481
Texas A & M University ... TX ... 497
Texas State University-San Marcos ... TX ... 501
Texas Tech University ... TX ... 501
Texas Woman's University ... TX ... 502
Trinity University ... TX ... 502
University of Houston - Clear Lake ... TX ... 503
George Mason University ... VA ... 519
Marymount University ... VA ... 521
Virginia Commonwealth University ... VA ... 525
University of Washington ... WA ... 538
Washington State University ... WA ... 539

HT: National Accrediting Agency for Clinical Laboratory Sciences: histologic technology (C,A,B)

Phoenix College ... AZ ... 16
Pima County Community College District ... AZ ... 17
California State University-Sacramento ... CA ... 35
Mt. San Antonio College ... CA ... 58
Goodwin College ... CT ... 92
Delaware Technical and Community College Stanton-Wilmington Campus ... DE ... 96
Barry University ... FL ... 101
Florida State College at Jacksonville ... FL ... 109
Miami Dade College ... FL ... 113
Darton College ... GA ... 128
Elgin Community College ... IL ... 150
Indiana University-Purdue University Indianapolis ... IN ... 174
Harford Community College ... MD ... 223
Lansing Community College ... MI ... 254
Argosy University, Twin Cities ... MN ... 261
Mayo School of Health Sciences ... MN ... 262
North Hennepin Community College ... MN ... 268
State University of New York College of Agriculture and Technology at Coble skill .. NY ... 354
Davidson County Community College ... NC ... 369
University of North Dakota Main Campus ... ND ... 381
Columbus State Community College ... OH ... 388
Lakeland Community College ... OH ... 394
Youngstown State University ... OH ... 406
Drexel University ... PA ... 427
Harcum College ... PA ... 430
University of Pittsburgh ... PA ... 449
Community College of Rhode Island ... RI ... 453
Medical University of South Carolina ... SC ... 459
Houston Community College ... TX ... 487
St. Philip's College ... TX ... 479
Tarleton State University ... TX ... 496
University of Texas Health Science Center at San Antonio ... TX ... 506
University of Texas M.D. Anderson Cancer Center, The ... TX ... 507
Old Dominion University ... VA ... 521
Clover Park Technical College ... WA ... 532

IACBE: International Assembly for Collegiate Business Education: business programs in institutions that grant bachelor/graduate degrees (A,B, M,D)

#Stillman College ... AL ... 7
John Brown University ... AR ... 22
University of the Ozarks ... AR ... 26
Azusa Pacific University ... CA ... 30
California Maritime Academy ... CA ... 32
#National University ... CA ... 58
Pacific Union College ... CA ... 60
Albertus Magnus College ... CT ... 89
Goldey-Beacom College ... DE ... 96
Wilmington University ... DE ... 97
Edward Waters College ... FL ... 105
Hodges University ... FL ... 110
Lynn University ... FL ... 113
Nova Southeastern University ... FL ... 114
Palm Beach Atlantic University ... FL ... 114
Saint Leo University ... FL ... 116
Southeastern University ... FL ... 118
Webber International University ... FL ... 123
Toccoa Falls College ... GA ... 137
University of Guam ... GU ... 559
Lewis-Clark State College ... ID ... 143
Lincoln College ... IL ... 156
McKendree University ... IL ... 157
National-Louis University ... IL ... 159
North Park University ... IL ... 159
Robert Morris University ... IL ... 162
Rockford College ... IL ... 162
Bethel College ... IN ... 169
Grace College and Seminary ... IN ... 171
Marian University ... IN ... 177
Oakland City University ... IN ... 178
Purdue University Calumet ... IN ... 178
Saint Joseph's College ... IN ... 179
Ashford University ... IA ... 181
Maharishi University of Management ... IA ... 18
Northwestern College ... IA ... 18
University of Saint Mary ... KS ... 19
Campbellsville University ... KY ... 19
Kentucky Wesleyan College ... KY ... 20
Lindsey Wilson College ... KY ... 20
Spalding University ... KY ... 20
#Our Lady of Holy Cross College ... LA ... 214
Husson University ... ME ... 218
University of Maine at Fort Kent ... ME ... 220
Capitol College ... MD ... 221
Mount St. Mary's University ... MD ... 225
University of Maryland College Park ... MD ... 227
American International College ... MA ... 229
College of Our Lady of the Elms ... MA ... 233
Fitchburg State University ... MA ... 238
Nichols College ... MA ... 243
Springfield College ... MA ... 245
Wentworth Institute of Technology ... MA ... 246
Andrews University ... MI ... 247
Baker College of Allen Park ... MI ... 248
Baker College of Auburn Hills ... MI ... 248
Baker College of Cadillac ... MI ... 248
Baker College of Clinton Township ... MI ... 248
Baker College of Flint ... MI ... 248
Baker College of Jackson ... MI ... 248
Baker College of Muskegon ... MI ... 248
Baker College of Owosso ... MI ... 249
Baker College of Port Huron ... MI ... 249
Davenport University ... MI ... 250
Lawrence Technological University ... MI ... 254
Walsh College of Accountancy and Business Administration ... MI ... 260
Bemidji State University ... MN ... 266
Saint Mary's University of Minnesota ... MN ... 271
Belhaven University ... MS ... 273
#Avila University ... MO ... 279
Culver-Stockton College ... MO ... 281
#Harris-Stowe State University ... MO ... 282
Stephens College ... MO ... 290
University of Montana Western, The ... MT ... 295
Bellevue University ... NE ... 297
Clarkson College ... NE ... 297
College of Saint Mary ... NE ... 297
Concordia University ... NE ... 297
Grace University ... NE ... 298
Wayne State College ... NE ... 299
Roseman University of Health Sciences ... NV ... 303
Centenary College ... NJ ... 308
Felician College ... NJ ... 310
Cazenovia College ... NY ... 325
Daemen College ... NY ... 331
Dominican College of Blauvelt ... NY ... 332
Dowling College ... NY ... 332
D'Youville College ... NY ... 332
Excelsior College ... NY ... 333
Keuka College ... NY ... 337
Manhattanville College ... NY ... 340
Medaille College ... NY ... 340
Roberts Wesleyan College ... NY ... 347
St. Thomas Aquinas College ... NY ... 349
State University of New York College at Potsdam ... NY ... 354
Vaughn College of Aeronautics and Technology ... NY ... 359
Montreat College ... NC ... 367
Dickinson State University ... ND ... 381
Jamestown College ... ND ... 381
Minot State University ... ND ... 381
University of Mary ... ND ... 383
Chancellor University ... OH ... 387
Defiance College, The ... OH ... 389
Franklin University ... OH ... 391
Lake Erie College ... OH ... 394
Lourdes University ... OH ... 395
Malone University ... OH ... 395
University of Rio Grande ... OH ... 404
Urbana University ... OH ... 405
Ursuline College ... OH ... 405
Bacone College ... OK ... 407
Oklahoma Wesleyan University ... OK ... 411
Southwestern Oklahoma State University ... OK ... 412
Eastern Oregon University ... OR ... 418
Marylhurst University ... OR ... 416
Northwest Christian University ... OR ... 417
Oregon Institute of Technology ... OR ... 418
Gwynedd-Mercy College ... PA ... 430
#Mercyhurst College ... PA ... 436
Misericordia University ... PA ... 436
Pennsylvania College of Technology ... PA ... 440
Philadelphia Biblical University ... PA ... 444
Point Park University ... PA ... 444
Saint Francis University ... PA ... 446
Seton Hill University ... PA ... 447
Universidad Politecnica De Puerto Rico ... PR ... 566
Salve Regina University ... RI ... 454
Charleston Southern University ... SC ... 456
National American University ... SD ... 464
Presentation College ... SD ... 464
University of Sioux Falls ... SD ... 466
Bryan College ... TN ... 467
Southern Adventist University ... TN ... 473
Concordia University Texas ... TX ... 483
Howard Payne University ... TX ... 488
LeTourneau University ... TX ... 489
Southwestern Adventist University ... TX ... 495
Hampton University ... VA ... 519
Davis & Elkins College ... WV ... 540

IFSAC: International Fire Service Accreditation Congress Degree Assembly: fire and emergency related degree (A,B)

IPSY: American Psychological Association: pre-doctoral internships in professional psychology

JOUR: Accrediting Council on Education for Journalism and Mass Communications: journalism and mass communications (B,M)

KIN: Commission on Accreditation of Allied Health Education Programs: kinesiotherapy (B)

LAW: American Bar Association: law (FP)

University of Iowa ... IA ... 182
University of Kansas Main Campus ... KS ... 196
Washburn University ... KS ... 197
Northern Kentucky University ... KY ... 205
University of Kentucky ... KY ... 206
University of Louisville ... KY ... 207
Louisiana State University Paul M. Hebert Law Center ... LA ... 213
Loyola University New Orleans ... LA ... 213
Southern University and A&M College ... LA ... 214
Tulane University ... LA ... 215
University of Southern Maine ... ME ... 220
University of Baltimore ... MD ... 229
University of Maryland Baltimore ... MD ... 227
Boston College ... MA ... 232
Boston University ... MA ... 232
Harvard University ... MA ... 235
New England Law | Boston ... MA ... 243
Northeastern University ... MA ... 244
Suffolk University ... MA ... 245
Western New England University ... MA ... 246
Michigan State University ... MI ... 255
Thomas M. Cooley Law School ... MI ... 259
University of Detroit Mercy ... MI ... 259
University of Michigan-Ann Arbor ... MI ... 259
Wayne State University ... MI ... 260
Hamline University ... MN ... 264
University of Minnesota-Twin Cities ... MN ... 272
University of Saint Thomas ... MN ... 272
William Mitchell College of Law ... MN ... 273
Mississippi College ... MS ... 275
University of Mississippi ... MS ... 277
Saint Louis University ... MO ... 289
University of Missouri - Columbia ... MO ... 291
University of Missouri - Kansas City ... MO ... 291
Washington University in St. Louis ... MO ... 292
University of Montana - Missoula, The ... MT ... 295
Creighton University ... NE ... 297
University of Nebraska - Lincoln ... NE ... 300
University of Nevada, Las Vegas ... NV ... 302
University of New Hampshire School of Law - formerly Franklin Pierce Law Ce nter ... NH ... 306
Rutgers the State University of New Jersey Camden Campus ... NJ ... 314
Rutgers the State University of New Jersey Newark Campus ... NJ ... 314
Seton Hall University School of Law ... NJ ... 315
University of New Mexico Main Campus ... NM ... 321
Albany Law School ... NY ... 322
Brooklyn Law School ... NY ... 324
City University of New York Queens College ... NY ... 328
Columbia University in the City of New York ... NY ... 330
Cornell University ... NY ... 331
Fordham University ... NY ... 334
Hofstra University ... NY ... 335
New York Law School ... NY ... 343
New York University ... NY ... 344
Pace University ... NY ... 345
St. John's University ... NY ... 348
State University of New York at Buffalo ... NY ... 351
Syracuse University Main Campus ... NY ... 357
Touro College ... NY ... 357
Yeshiva University ... NY ... 361
Campbell University ... NC ... 362
Charlotte School of Law ... NC ... 363
Duke University ... NC ... 363
Elon University ... NC ... 364
North Carolina Central University ... NC ... 378
University of North Carolina at Chapel Hill ... NC ... 378
Wake Forest University ... NC ... 380
University of North Dakota Main Campus ... ND ... 381
Capital University ... OH ... 386
Case Western Reserve University ... OH ... 386
Cleveland State University ... OH ... 388
Ohio Northern University ... OH ... 398
Ohio State University Main Campus, The ... OH ... 398
University of Akron, Main Campus, The ... OH ... 403
University of Cincinnati Main Campus ... OH ... 403
University of Dayton ... OH ... 404
University of Toledo ... OH ... 404
Oklahoma City University ... OK ... 410
University of Oklahoma Norman Campus ... OK ... 413
University of Tulsa ... OK ... 413
Lewis and Clark College ... OR ... 416
University of Oregon ... OR ... 419
Willamette University ... OR ... 421
Drexel University ... PA ... 427
Duquesne University ... PA ... 428
Penn State Dickinson School of Law, The ... PA ... 439
Temple University ... PA ... 447
University of Pennsylvania ... PA ... 448
University of Pittsburgh ... PA ... 449
Villanova University ... PA ... 450
Widener University ... PA ... 451
Inter American University of Puerto Rico School of Law ... PR ... 564
Pontifical Catholic University of Puerto Rico, The ... PR ... 564
University of Puerto Rico-Rio Piedras Campus ... PR ... 567
Roger Williams University ... RI ... 454
Charleston School of Law ... SC ... 456
University of South Carolina Columbia ... SC ... 462
University of South Dakota, The ... SD ... 465
University of Memphis, The ... TN ... 474
University of Tennessee, Knoxville ... TN ... 477
Vanderbilt University ... TN ... 477
Baylor University ... TX ... 481
St. Mary's University ... TX ... 493
South Texas College of Law ... TX ... 494
Southern Methodist University ... TX ... 494
Texas Southern University ... TX ... 499
Texas Tech University ... TX ... 501
Texas Wesleyan University ... TX ... 502
University of Houston ... TX ... 503
University of Texas at Austin ... TX ... 505
Brigham Young University ... UT ... 509
University of Utah, The ... UT ... 510
Vermont Law School ... VT ... 515
Appalachian School of Law ... VA ... 516
College of William & Mary ... VA ... 517
George Mason University ... VA ... 519
Judge Advocate General's Legal Center & School, The ... VA ... 557
Liberty University ... VA ... 520
Regent University ... VA ... 523
University of Richmond ... VA ... 525
University of Virginia ... VA ... 525
Washington and Lee University ... VA ... 530
Gonzaga University ... WA ... 534
Seattle University ... WA ... 537
University of Washington ... WA ... 538
West Virginia University ... WV ... 544
Marquette University ... WI ... 548
University of Wisconsin-Madison ... WI ... 550
University of Wyoming ... WY ... 556

LIB: American Library Association: librarianship (FP)

University of Alabama, The ... AL ... 8
University of Arizona ... AZ ... 19
San Jose State University ... CA ... 37
University of California-Los Angeles ... CA ... 74
University of Denver ... CO ... 88
#Southern Connecticut State University ... CT ... 91
Catholic University of America, The ... DC ... 97
Florida State University ... FL ... 119
University of South Florida ... FL ... 120
#Valdosta State University ... GA ... 138
University of Hawaii at Manoa ... HI ... 141
Dominican University ... IL ... 150
University of Illinois at Urbana-Champaign ... IL ... 167
Indiana University Bloomington ... IN ... 173
University of Iowa ... IA ... 182
Emporia State University ... KS ... 192
University of Kentucky ... KY ... 206
Louisiana State University and Agricultural and Mechanical College ... LA ... 212
University of Maryland College Park ... MD ... 227
Simmons College ... MA ... 245
University of Michigan-Ann Arbor ... MI ... 259
Wayne State University ... MI ... 260
St. Catherine University ... MN ... 271
University of Southern Mississippi ... MS ... 278
University of Missouri - Columbia ... MO ... 291
Rutgers the State University of New Jersey New Brunswick Campus ... NJ ... 314
City University of New York Queens College ... NY ... 328
Long Island University C.W. Post Campus ... NY ... 339
Pratt Institute ... NY ... 346
St. John's University ... NY ... 348
State University of New York at Albany ... NY ... 351
#State University of New York at Buffalo ... NY ... 351
Syracuse University Main Campus ... NY ... 357
North Carolina Central University ... NC ... 378
University of North Carolina at Chapel Hill ... NC ... 378
University of North Carolina at Greensboro ... NC ... 379
Kent State University Main Campus ... OH ... 393
University of Oklahoma Norman Campus ... OK ... 413
Clarion University of Pennsylvania ... PA ... 442
Drexel University ... PA ... 427
University of Pittsburgh ... PA ... 449
University of Puerto Rico-Rio Piedras Campus ... PR ... 567
University of Rhode Island ... RI ... 454
University of South Carolina Columbia ... SC ... 462
University of Tennessee, Knoxville ... TN ... 477
Texas Woman's University ... TX ... 502
University of North Texas ... TX ... 504
University of Texas at Austin ... TX ... 505
University of Washington ... WA ... 538
University of Wisconsin-Madison ... WI ... 550
University of Wisconsin-Milwaukee ... WI ... 551

LSAR: American Society of Landscape Architects: landscape architecture (B,M)

Auburn University ... AL ... 1
Arizona State University ... AZ ... 12
University of Arizona ... AZ ... 19
University of Arkansas Main Campus ... AR ... 24
California Polytechnic State University-San Luis Obispo ... CA ... 33
California State Polytechnic University-Pomona ... CA ... 33
University of California-Berkeley ... CA ... 73
University of California-Davis ... CA ... 73
University of Southern California ... CA ... 76
Colorado State University ... CO ... 83
University of Colorado Denver|Anschutz Medical Campus ... CO ... 88
University of Connecticut ... CT ... 94
Florida Agricultural and Mechanical University ... FL ... 118
Florida International University ... FL ... 119
University of Florida ... FL ... 120
University of Georgia ... GA ... 138
University of Idaho ... ID ... 144
Illinois Institute of Technology ... IL ... 153
University of Illinois at Urbana-Champaign ... IL ... 167
Ball State University ... IN ... 169
Purdue University Main Campus ... IN ... 178
Iowa State University ... IA ... 182
Kansas State University ... KS ... 194
University of Kentucky ... KY ... 206
Louisiana State University and Agricultural and Mechanical College ... LA ... 212
Morgan State University ... MD ... 224
University of Maryland College Park ... MD ... 227
Boston Architectural College ... MA ... 232
Harvard University ... MA ... 235
University of Massachusetts ... MA ... 237
Michigan State University ... MI ... 255
University of Michigan-Ann Arbor ... MI ... 259
University of Minnesota-Twin Cities ... MN ... 272
Mississippi State University ... MS ... 276
University of Nevada, Las Vegas ... NV ... 302
Rutgers the State University of New Jersey New Brunswick Campus ... NJ ... 314
University of New Mexico Main Campus ... NM ... 321
City University of New York The City College ... NY ... 326
Cornell University ... NY ... 331
State University of New York College of Environmental Science and Forestry ... NY ... 355
North Carolina Agricultural and Technical State University ... NC ... 377
North Carolina State University ... NC ... 378
North Dakota State University Main Campus. ND ... 381
Ohio State University Main Campus, The ... OH ... 398
Oklahoma State University ... OK ... 410
University of Oklahoma Norman Campus ... OK ... 413
University of Oregon ... OR ... 419
Chatham University ... PA ... 425
Penn State University Park ... PA ... 438
Philadelphia University ... PA ... 444
Temple University ... PA ... 447
University of Pennsylvania ... PA ... 448
Rhode Island School of Design ... RI ... 454
University of Rhode Island ... RI ... 454
Clemson University ... SC ... 456
Texas A & M University ... TX ... 497
Texas Tech University ... TX ... 501
University of Texas at Arlington, The ... TX ... 505
University of Texas at Austin ... TX ... 505
Utah State University ... UT ... 511
University of Virginia ... VA ... 525
Virginia Polytechnic Institute and State University ... VA ... 529
University of Washington ... WA ... 538
Washington State University ... WA ... 539
West Virginia University ... WV ... 544
University of Wisconsin-Madison ... WI ... 550

M: Middle States Association of Colleges and Schools, Commission on Higher Education (MSA/CHE)

&American Academy of Dramatic Arts, Los Angeles Campus ... CA ... 27
&Culinary Institute of America at Greystone, The ... CA ... 43
&Hebrew Union College-Jewish Institute of Religion (California Branch) ... CA ... 50
&Rensselaer at Hartford ... CT ... 93
Delaware College of Art and Design ... DE ... 95
Delaware State University ... DE ... 95
Delaware Technical and Community College Owens Campus ... DE ... 96
Delaware Technical and Community College Stanton-Wilmington Campus ... DE ... 96
Delaware Technical and Community College Terry Campus ... DE ... 96
Goldey-Beacom College ... DE ... 96
University of Delaware ... DE ... 96
Wesley College ... DE ... 96
Wilmington University ... DE ... 97
American University ... DC ... 97
Catholic University of America, The ... DC ... 97
Corcoran College of Art and Design ... DC ... 97
Gallaudet University ... DC ... 97
George Washington University ... DC ... 97
Georgetown University ... DC ... 98
Howard University ... DC ... 98
Institute of World Politics, The ... DC ... 98
National Defense University ... DC ... 557
National Intelligence University ... DC ... 557
Pontifical Faculty of the Immaculate Conception at the Dominican House of S tudies ... DC ... 98
Pontifical John Paul II Institute for Studies on Marriage and Family ... DC ... 98
Potomac College ... DC ... 99
@Radians College ... DC ... 99
Strayer University ... DC ... 99
Trinity Washington University ... DC ... 99
University System of the District of Columbia DC ... 99
Washington Theological Union ... DC ... 99
Wesley Theological Seminary ... DC ... 100
&Carlos Albizu University Miami Campus ... FL ... 102
&Polytechnic University Puerto Rico ... FL ... 115
Allegany College of Maryland ... MD ... 221
Anne Arundel Community College ... MD ... 221
#Baltimore City Community College ... MD ... 221
Bowie State University ... MD ... 22
Capitol College ... MD ... 22
Carroll Community College ... MD ... 22
Cecil College ... MD ... 22
Chesapeake College ... MD ... 22
College of Southern Maryland ... MD ... 22
Community College of Baltimore County, The ... MD ... 22
Coppin State University ... MD ... 22
Frederick Community College ... MD ... 22
Frostburg State University ... MD ... 228
Garrett College ... MD ... 22
Goucher College ... MD ... 22
Hagerstown Community College ... MD ... 223
Harford Community College ... MD ... 223
Hood College ... MD ... 223
Howard Community College ... MD ... 223
Johns Hopkins University ... MD ... 223
Loyola University Maryland ... MD ... 224
Maryland Institute College of Art ... MD ... 224
McDaniel College ... MD ... 224
Montgomery College ... MD ... 224
Morgan State University ... MD ... 224
Mount St. Mary's University ... MD ... 225
National Labor College ... MD ... 225
Notre Dame of Maryland University ... MD ... 225
&Peabody Institute of Johns Hopkins University ... MD ... 225
Prince George's Community College ... MD ... 225
St. John's College ... MD ... 225
St. Mary's College of Maryland ... MD ... 226
Saint Mary's Seminary and University ... MD ... 226
Salisbury University ... MD ... 228
@SANS Technology Institute, The ... MD ... 226
Sojourner-Douglass College ... MD ... 226
Stevenson University ... MD ... 226
Tai Sophia Institute ... MD ... 226
Towson University ... MD ... 228
Uniformed Services University of the Health Sciences ... MD ... 558
United States Naval Academy ... MD ... 558
University of Baltimore ... MD ... 229
University of Maryland Baltimore ... MD ... 227
University of Maryland Baltimore County ... MD ... 227
University of Maryland College Park ... MD ... 227
University of Maryland Eastern Shore ... MD ... 227
University of Maryland University College ... MD ... 227
Washington Adventist University ... MD ... 229
Washington Bible College/Capital Bible Seminary ... MD ... 229
Washington College ... MD ... 229
Wor-Wic Community College ... MD ... 229
Assumption College for Sisters ... NJ ... 307
Atlantic Cape Community College ... NJ ... 307
Bergen Community College ... NJ ... 307
Berkeley College ... NJ ... 307
Bloomfield College ... NJ ... 308
Brookdale Community College ... NJ ... 308
Burlington County College ... NJ ... 308
Caldwell College ... NJ ... 308
Camden County College ... NJ ... 308
Centenary College ... NJ ... 308
College of New Jersey, The ... NJ ... 308
College of Saint Elizabeth ... NJ ... 309
County College of Morris ... NJ ... 309
Cumberland County College ... NJ ... 309
Drew University ... NJ ... 309
Essex County College ... NJ ... 310
Fairleigh Dickinson University ... NJ ... 310
Felician College ... NJ ... 310
Georgian Court University ... NJ ... 310
Gloucester County College ... NJ ... 310
Hudson County Community College ... NJ ... 310
&Immaculate Conception Seminary of Seton Hall University ... NJ ... 311
Kean University ... NJ ... 311
Mercer County Community College ... NJ ... 311
Middlesex County College ... NJ ... 311
Monmouth University ... NJ ... 311
Montclair State University ... NJ ... 311
New Jersey City University ... NJ ... 312
New Jersey Institute of Technology ... NJ ... 312
Ocean County College ... NJ ... 312
Passaic County Community College ... NJ ... 312
Princeton Theological Seminary ... NJ ... 312
Princeton University ... NJ ... 313
Ramapo College of New Jersey ... NJ ... 313
Raritan Valley Community College ... NJ ... 313
Richard Stockton College of New Jersey, The ... NJ ... 313
Rider University ... NJ ... 313
Rowan University ... NJ ... 314
&Rutgers the State University of New Jersey Camden Campus ... NJ ... 314
Rutgers the State University of New Jersey New Brunswick Campus ... NJ ... 314
&Rutgers the State University of New Jersey Newark Campus ... NJ ... 314
Saint Peter's College ... NJ ... 314
Salem Community College ... NJ ... 315
Seton Hall University ... NJ ... 315
&Seton Hall University School of Law ... NJ ... 315
Somerset Christian College ... NJ ... 315
Stevens Institute of Technology ... NJ ... 315
Sussex County Community College ... NJ ... 315
Thomas Edison State College ... NJ ... 316
&UMDNJ-Graduate School of Biomedical Sciences ... NJ ... 316

MAAB: Accrediting Bureau of Health Education Schools: medical assisting (C)

MAC: Commission on Accreditation of Allied Health Education Programs: medical assisting (C,A)

rocaire College ... NY ... 358
Wood Tobé-Coburn School ... NY ... 360
lamance Community College ... NC ... 367
sheville - Buncombe Technical Community College ... NC ... 367
Cabarrus College of Health Sciences ... NC ... 362
Carteret Community College ... NC ... 368
Central Carolina Community College ... NC ... 368
Central Piedmont Community College ... NC ... 369
College of the Albemarle ... NC ... 369
Craven Community College ... NC ... 369
Davidson County Community College ... NC ... 369
Durham Technical Community College ... NC ... 369
Edgecombe Community College ... NC ... 370
Forsyth Technical Community College ... NC ... 370
Gaston College ... NC ... 370
Guilford Technical Community College ... NC ... 370
Haywood Community College ... NC ... 370
James Sprunt Community College ... NC ... 371
Johnston Community College ... NC ... 371
King's College ... NC ... 365
Lenoir Community College ... NC ... 371
Living Arts College @ School of Communication Arts ... NC ... 366
Martin Community College ... NC ... 371
Mayland Community College ... NC ... 371
Miller-Motte Technical College ... NC ... 367
Mitchell Community College ... NC ... 371
Montgomery Community College ... NC ... 372
Nash Community College ... NC ... 372
Pamlico Community College ... NC ... 372
Pitt Community College ... NC ... 372
South College ... NC ... 376
South Piedmont Community College ... NC ... 373
Stanly Community College ... NC ... 374
Surry Community College ... NC ... 374
Tri-County Community College ... NC ... 374
Vance-Granville Community College ... NC ... 374
Wake Technical Community College ... NC ... 374
Wayne Community College ... NC ... 374
Western Piedmont Community College ... NC ... 374
Wilkes Community College ... NC ... 375
Rasmussen College - Fargo/Moorhead ... ND ... 382
Akron Institute of Herzing University ... OH ... 383
Belmont Technical College ... OH ... 384
Bradford School ... OH ... 385
Brown Mackie College-Akron ... OH ... 385
Brown Mackie College-Cincinnati ... OH ... 385
Bryant & Stratton College ... OH ... 386
#Cincinnati State Technical and Community College ... OH ... 387
Clark State Community College ... OH ... 387
Columbus State Community College ... OH ... 388
Cuyahoga Community College ... OH ... 389
Davis College ... OH ... 389
Eastern Gateway Community College - Jefferson County Campus ... OH ... 390
Edison State Community College ... OH ... 390
Fortis College ... OH ... 390
Hocking College ... OH ... 392
James A. Rhodes State College ... OH ... 392
Lakeland Community College ... OH ... 394
Lorain County Community College ... OH ... 395
Marion Technical College ... OH ... 395
Miami-Jacobs Career College ... OH ... 396
Northwest State Community College ... OH ... 397
Ohio Business College ... OH ... 397
Ohio Business College, Lorain Branch ... OH ... 398
Ohio University Lancaster Campus ... OH ... 400
Ohio Valley College of Technology ... OH ... 400
Owens Community College ... OH ... 400
Sinclair Community College ... OH ... 401
Southern State Community College ... OH ... 401
Stark State College ... OH ... 402
Stautzenberger College ... OH ... 402
University of Akron, Main Campus, The ... OH ... 403
University of Cincinnati-Clermont College ... OH ... 403
University of Cincinnati-Raymond Walters College ... OH ... 403
University of Northwestern Ohio ... OH ... 404
Youngstown State University ... OH ... 406
Zane State College ... OH ... 407
Tulsa Community College ... OK ... 412
Central Oregon Community College ... OR ... 414
Clackamas Community College ... OR ... 415
Columbia Gorge Community College ... OR ... 415
Everest College ... OR ... 415
Heald College, Portland ... OR ... 416
Lane Community College ... OR ... 416
Linn-Benton Community College ... OR ... 416
Mt. Hood Community College ... OR ... 417
Portland Community College ... OR ... 419
Berks Technical Institute ... PA ... 422
Bradford School ... PA ... 423
Butler County Community College ... PA ... 423
Career Training Academy ... PA ... 424
Central Pennsylvania College ... PA ... 425
Community College of Allegheny County ... PA ... 425
Community College of Philadelphia ... PA ... 426
Delaware County Community College ... PA ... 426
Everest Institute ... PA ... 429
Fortis Institute ... PA ... 429
Harrisburg Area Community College ... PA ... 430
Kaplan Career Institute ... PA ... 432
Kaplan Career Institute - ICM Campus ... PA ... 432
Lehigh Carbon Community College ... PA ... 434
McCann School of Business & Technology ... PA ... 435
McCann School of Business & Technology ... PA ... 436
Montgomery County Community College ... PA ... 436
Mount Aloysius College ... PA ... 437
Penn Commercial Business/Technical School ... PA ... 438
Pittsburgh Technical Institute ... PA ... 444
Westmoreland County Community College ... PA ... 451
YTI Career Institute ... PA ... 452
Aiken Technical College ... SC ... 455
Central Carolina Technical College ... SC ... 455
Forrest Junior College ... SC ... 458
Greenville Technical College ... SC ... 458
Midlands Technical College ... SC ... 459
Miller-Motte Technical College ... SC ... 459
Orangeburg-Calhoun Technical College ... SC ... 460
Piedmont Technical College ... SC ... 460
South University Columbia Campus ... SC ... 461
Spartanburg Community College ... SC ... 461
Tri-County Technical College ... SC ... 461
Trident Technical College ... SC ... 461
Colorado Technical University ... SD ... 464
Lake Area Technical Institute ... SD ... 464
Mitchell Technical Institute ... SD ... 464
National American University ... SD ... 464
Presentation College ... SD ... 464
Chattanooga State Community College ... TN ... 474
Cleveland State Community College ... TN ... 474
Concorde Career College ... TN ... 467
Miller-Motte Technical College ... TN ... 471
National College of Business and Technology ... TN ... 471
National College of Business and Technology ... TN ... 472
South College ... TN ... 472
Cisco Junior College ... TX ... 482
College of the Mainland ... TX ... 483
Computer Career Center ... TX ... 483
El Centro College ... TX ... 484
El Paso Community College ... TX ... 486
Hallmark College of Technology ... TX ... 487
Houston Community College ... TX ... 487
Kaplan College ... TX ... 489
Lone Star College System ... TX ... 490
Northeast Texas Community College ... TX ... 491
Richland College ... TX ... 485
San Antonio College ... TX ... 479
San Jacinto College North ... TX ... 493
Texas State Technical College Harlingen ... TX ... 499
Westwood College-Dallas ... TX ... 508
Westwood College-Fort Worth ... TX ... 508
Westwood College-Houston South ... TX ... 508
Broadview University ... UT ... 509
Everest College ... UT ... 509
Latter-Day Saints Business College ... UT ... 510
Ogden-Weber Applied Technology College ... UT ... 510
Salt Lake Community College ... UT ... 512
Stevens-Henager College ... UT ... 510
Bryant & Stratton College ... VA ... 516
Bryant & Stratton College ... VA ... 517
National College ... VA ... 521
Tidewater Community College ... VA ... 528
Clark College ... WA ... 532
Clover Park Technical College ... WA ... 532
Everett Community College ... WA ... 533
Highline Community College ... WA ... 534
Lake Washington Technical College ... WA ... 535
Lower Columbia College ... WA ... 535
North Seattle Community College ... WA ... 536
Olympic College ... WA ... 535
Renton Technical College ... WA ... 536
Skagit Valley College ... WA ... 538
South Puget Sound Community College ... WA ... 538
Spokane Community College ... WA ... 532
Wenatchee Valley College ... WA ... 539
Whatcom Community College ... WA ... 539
Yakima Valley Community College ... WA ... 540
Huntington Junior College ... WV ... 540
Marshall University ... WV ... 543
Mountain State University ... WV ... 541
Mountwest Community and Technical College ... WV ... 542
National College ... WV ... 541
West Virginia Northern Community College ... WV ... 543
Blackhawk Technical College ... WI ... 553
Bryant & Stratton College ... WI ... 546
Chippewa Valley Technical College ... WI ... 553
Concordia University Wisconsin ... WI ... 546
Fox Valley Technical College ... WI ... 553
Gateway Technical College ... WI ... 553
Lac Courte Oreilles Ojibwa Community College ... WI ... 547
Madison Area Technical College ... WI ... 554
Mid-State Technical College ... WI ... 554
Milwaukee Area Technical College ... WI ... 554
Moraine Park Technical College ... WI ... 554
Nicolet Area Technical College ... WI ... 554
Northcentral Technical College ... WI ... 554
Northeast Wisconsin Technical College ... WI ... 555
Southwest Wisconsin Technical College ... WI ... 555
Waukesha County Technical College ... WI ... 555
Western Technical College ... WI ... 555
Wisconsin Indianhead Technical College ... WI ... 555

MACTE: Montessori Accreditation Council for Teacher Education: Montessori teacher education

South Mountain Community College ... AZ ... 16
Saint Mary's College of California ... CA ... 64
Barry University ... FL ... 101
Palm Beach State College ... FL ... 114
Kennesaw State University ... GA ... 132
Chaminade University of Honolulu ... HI ... 140
Indiana University South Bend ... IN ... 174
St. Catherine University ... MN ... 271
Xavier University ... OH ... 406
Oklahoma City University ... OK ... 410
Chestnut Hill College ... PA ... 425
Lander University ... SC ... 458
Belmont University ... TN ... 467

MEAC: Midwifery Education Accreditation Council: midwifery education (C,A)

National College of Midwifery ... NM ... 318
Birthingway College of Midwifery ... OR ... 414
Midwives College of Utah ... UT ... 510
Bastyr University ... WA ... 530

MED: Liaison Committee on Medical Education: medicine (FP)

University of Alabama at Birmingham ... AL ... 8
University of South Alabama ... AL ... 9
University of Arizona ... AZ ... 19
University of Arkansas for Medical Sciences ... AR ... 24
Loma Linda University ... CA ... 54
Stanford University ... CA ... 71
University of California-Davis ... CA ... 73
University of California-Irvine ... CA ... 73
University of California-Los Angeles ... CA ... 74
University of California-San Diego ... CA ... 74
University of California-San Francisco ... CA ... 74
University of Southern California ... CA ... 76
University of Colorado Denver/Anschutz Medical Campus ... CO ... 88
University of Connecticut Health Center ... CT ... 94
Yale University ... CT ... 95
George Washington University ... DC ... 97
Georgetown University ... DC ... 98
Howard University ... DC ... 98
#Florida Atlantic University ... FL ... 118
#Florida International University ... FL ... 119
Florida State University ... FL ... 119
#University of Central Florida ... FL ... 120
University of Florida ... FL ... 120
University of Miami ... FL ... 122
University of South Florida ... FL ... 120
Emory University ... GA ... 129
Georgia Health Sciences University ... GA ... 130
Mercer University ... GA ... 133
Morehouse School of Medicine ... GA ... 134
University of Hawaii at Manoa ... HI ... 141
Loyola University Chicago ... IL ... 157
Northwestern University ... IL ... 160
Rosalind Franklin University of Medicine & Science ... IL ... 163
Rush University ... IL ... 163
Southern Illinois University Carbondale ... IL ... 164
University of Chicago ... IL ... 166
University of Illinois at Chicago ... IL ... 166
Indiana University-Purdue University Indianapolis ... IN ... 174
University of Iowa ... IA ... 182
University of Kansas Medical Center ... KS ... 197
University of Kentucky ... KY ... 206
University of Louisville ... KY ... 207
Louisiana State University Health Sciences Center at Shreveport ... LA ... 213
Louisiana State University Health Sciences Center-New Orleans ... LA ... 213
Tulane University ... LA ... 215
Johns Hopkins University ... MD ... 223
Uniformed Services University of the Health Sciences ... MD ... 558
University of Maryland Baltimore ... MD ... 227
Boston University ... MA ... 232
Harvard University ... MA ... 235
Tufts University ... MA ... 245
University of Massachusetts at Worcester ... MA ... 238
Michigan State University ... MI ... 255
#Oakland University ... MI ... 257
University of Michigan-Ann Arbor ... MI ... 259
Wayne State University ... MI ... 260
Mayo Medical School ... MN ... 262
University of Minnesota-Twin Cities ... MN ... 272
University of Mississippi Medical Center ... MS ... 277
Saint Louis University ... MO ... 289
University of Missouri - Columbia ... MO ... 291
University of Missouri - Kansas City ... MO ... 291
Washington University in St. Louis ... MO ... 292
Creighton University ... NE ... 297
University of Nebraska Medical Center ... NE ... 301
University of Nevada, Reno ... NV ... 303
Dartmouth College ... NH ... 305
#Rowan University ... NJ ... 314
UMDNJ-New Jersey Medical School ... NJ ... 316
UMDNJ-Robert Wood Johnson Medical School ... NJ ... 316
University of New Mexico Main Campus ... NM ... 321
Albany Medical College ... NY ... 322
Columbia University in the City of New York ... NY ... 330
#Hofstra University ... NY ... 335
Mount Sinai School of Medicine ... NY ... 342
New York Medical College ... NY ... 343
New York University ... NY ... 344
State University of New York at Buffalo ... NY ... 351
State University of New York at Stony Brook ... NY ... 352
State University of New York Health Science Center at Brooklyn ... NY ... 352
State University of New York Upstate Medical University ... NY ... 352
University of Rochester ... NY ... 358
Weill Cornell Medical College ... NY ... 360
Yeshiva University ... NY ... 361
Duke University ... NC ... 363
East Carolina University ... NC ... 377
University of North Carolina at Chapel Hill ... NC ... 378
Wake Forest University ... NC ... 380
University of North Dakota Main Campus ... ND ... 381
Case Western Reserve University ... OH ... 386
Northeastern Ohio Universities Colleges of Medicine and Pharmacy ... OH ... 397
Ohio State University Main Campus, The ... OH ... 398
University of Cincinnati Main Campus ... OH ... 403
University of Toledo ... OH ... 404
Wright State University Main Campus ... OH ... 406
University of Oklahoma Health Sciences Center ... OK ... 413
Oregon Health & Science University ... OR ... 418
#Commonwealth Medical College, The ... PA ... 425
Drexel University ... PA ... 427
Penn State Milton S. Hershey Medical Center College of Medicine ... PA ... 439
Temple University ... PA ... 447
Thomas Jefferson University ... PA ... 448
University of Pennsylvania ... PA ... 448
University of Pittsburgh ... PA ... 449
#Ponce School of Medicine ... PR ... 564
San Juan Bautista School of Medicine ... PR ... 565
Universidad Central Del Caribe ... PR ... 566
University of Puerto Rico-Medical Sciences Campus ... PR ... 567
Brown University ... RI ... 452
Medical University of South Carolina ... SC ... 459
University of South Carolina Columbia ... SC ... 462
University of South Dakota, The ... SD ... 465
East Tennessee State University ... TN ... 473
Meharry Medical College ... TN ... 471
University of Tennessee Health Science Center ... TN ... 477
Vanderbilt University ... TN ... 477
Baylor College of Medicine ... TX ... 481
Texas A & M University ... TX ... 497
Texas Tech University ... TX ... 501
Texas Tech University Health Sciences Center ... TX ... 501
University of Texas Health Science Center at Houston (UTHealth), The ... TX ... 506
University of Texas Health Science Center at San Antonio ... TX ... 506
University of Texas Medical Branch, The ... TX ... 507
University of Texas Southwestern Medical Center at Dallas ... TX ... 507
University of Utah, The ... UT ... 510
University of Vermont ... VT ... 514
Eastern Virginia Medical School ... VA ... 518
University of Virginia ... VA ... 525
Virginia Commonwealth University ... VA ... 525
#Virginia Polytechnic Institute and State University ... VA ... 529
University of Washington ... WA ... 538
Marshall University ... WV ... 543
West Virginia University ... WV ... 544
Medical College of Wisconsin ... WI ... 548
University of Wisconsin-Madison ... WI ... 550

MFCD: American Association for Marriage and Family Therapy: marriage and family therapy (M,D)

Auburn University ... AL ... 1
Alliant International University-Fresno & Sacramento ... CA ... 27
Alliant International University-Irvine ... CA ... 27
Alliant International University-Los Angeles ... CA ... 27
Alliant International University-San Diego ... CA ... 27
Chapman University ... CA ... 39
Hope International University ... CA ... 50
Loma Linda University ... CA ... 54
San Diego State University ... CA ... 36
University of San Diego ... CA ... 76
Colorado State University ... CO ... 83
Central Connecticut State University ... CT ... 91
Fairfield University ... CT ... 92
Saint Joseph College ... CT ... 93
Southern Connecticut State University ... CT ... 91
University of Connecticut ... CT ... 94
Florida State University ... FL ... 119
Nova Southeastern University ... FL ... 114
Mercer University ... GA ... 133
University of Georgia ... GA ... 138
Valdosta State University ... GA ... 138
Northern Illinois University ... IL ... 160
Northwestern University ... IL ... 160
Christian Theological Seminary ... IN ... 170
Purdue University Calumet ... IN ... 178
Purdue University Main Campus ... IN ... 178
Iowa State University ... IA ... 182
Friends University ... KS ... 192
Kansas State University ... KS ... 194
Louisville Presbyterian Theological Seminary ... KY ... 204
University of Kentucky ... KY ... 206
University of Louisville ... KY ... 207
University of Louisiana at Monroe ... LA ... 216

University of Maryland College Park ... MD ... 227
University of Massachusetts Boston ... MA ... 237
Michigan State University ... MI ... 255
Argosy University, Twin Cities ... MN ... 261
Bethel University ... MN ... 261
St. Cloud State University ... MN ... 269
Saint Mary's University of Minnesota ... MN ... 271
University of Minnesota-Twin Cities ... MN ... 272
Reformed Theological Seminary ... MS ... 277
University of Southern Mississippi ... MS ... 278
Saint Louis University ... MO ... 289
School of Professional Psychology at Forest Institute, The ... MO ... 290
University of Nebraska - Lincoln ... NE ... 300
University of Nevada, Las Vegas ... NV ... 302
Antioch University New England ... NH ... 303
University of New Hampshire ... NH ... 306
Seton Hall University ... NJ ... 315
Iona College ... NY ... 336
Syracuse University Main Campus ... NY ... 357
University of Rochester ... NY ... 358
Appalachian State University ... NC ... 377
East Carolina University ... NC ... 377
Pfeiffer University ... NC ... 375
North Dakota State University Main Campus. ND ... 381
Ohio State University Main Campus, The ... OH ... 398
University of Akron, Main Campus, The ... OH ... 403
Oklahoma State University ... OK ... 410
Lewis and Clark College ... OR ... 416
University of Oregon ... OR ... 419
Drexel University ... PA ... 427
La Salle University ... PA ... 432
Seton Hill University ... PA ... 447
University of Rhode Island ... RI ... 454
Converse College ... SC ... 457
Abilene Christian University ... TX ... 478
St. Mary's University ... TX ... 493
Texas Tech University ... TX ... 501
University of Houston - Clear Lake ... TX ... 503
Brigham Young University ... UT ... 509
Utah State University ... UT ... 511
Virginia Polytechnic Institute and State University ... VA ... 529
Antioch University Seattle ... WA ... 530
Pacific Lutheran University ... WA ... 535
Seattle Pacific University ... WA ... 537
Edgewood College ... WI ... 547
University of Wisconsin-Stout ... WI ... 552

MIDWF: Accreditation Commission for Midwifery Education: nurse midwifery (C,M,D)

California State University-Fullerton ... CA ... 34
San Diego State University ... CA ... 36
University of California-San Francisco ... CA ... 74
University of Colorado Denver|Anschutz Medical Campus ... CO ... 88
Yale University ... CT ... 95
Georgetown University ... DC ... 98
University of Florida ... FL ... 120
University of Miami ... FL ... 122
Emory University ... GA ... 129
University of Illinois at Chicago ... IL ... 166
University of Indianapolis ... IN ... 180
University of Kansas Medical Center ... KS ... 197
Frontier Nursing University ... KY ... 200
University of Michigan-Ann Arbor ... MI ... 259
Wayne State University ... MI ... 260
University of Minnesota-Twin Cities ... MN ... 272
UMDNJ-School of Health Related Professions ... NJ ... 317
UMDNJ-School of Nursing ... NJ ... 316
University of New Mexico Main Campus ... NM ... 321
Columbia University in the City of New York NY ... 330
New York University ... NY ... 344
State University of New York at Stony Brook NY ... 352
State University of New York Health Science Center at Brooklyn ... NY ... 352
East Carolina University ... NC ... 377
Case Western Reserve University ... OH ... 386
Ohio State University Main Campus, The ... OH ... 398
University of Cincinnati Main Campus ... OH ... 403
Oregon Health & Science University ... OR ... 418
Philadelphia University ... PA ... 444
University of Pennsylvania ... PA ... 448
University of Puerto Rico-Medical Sciences Campus ... PR ... 567
Vanderbilt University ... TN ... 477
Baylor University ... TX ... 481
@Texas Tech University ... TX ... 501
University of Utah, The ... UT ... 510
Shenandoah University ... VA ... 523
@Seattle University ... WA ... 537
University of Washington ... WA ... 538
Marquette University ... WI ... 548

MIL: Commission on Accreditation of Allied Health Education Programs: medical illustrator (M)

Georgia Health Sciences University ... GA ... 130
University of Illinois at Chicago ... IL ... 166
Johns Hopkins University ... MD ... 223
University of Texas Southwestern Medical Center at Dallas ... TX ... 507

MLTAB: Accrediting Bureau of Health Education Schools: medical laboratory technician (C)

Herzing University ... FL ... 110
Spencerian College ... KY ... 205
Spencerian College ... KY ... 206
Southwestern Oklahoma State University ... OK ... 412

MLTAD: National Accrediting Agency for Clinical Laboratory Sciences: medical laboratory technician (A)

Calhoun Community College ... AL ... 2
Gadsden State Community College ... AL ... 3
Jefferson State Community College ... AL ... 5
Wallace State Community College - Hanceville ... AL ... 10
University of Alaska Anchorage ... AK ... 10
Phoenix College ... AZ ... 16
Pima County Community College District ... AZ ... 17
Arkansas State University ... AR ... 20
Arkansas State University-Beebe ... AR ... 20
National Park Community College ... AR ... 22
North Arkansas College ... AR ... 22
Phillips Community College of the University of Arkansas ... AR ... 25
De Anza College ... CA ... 47
Southwestern College ... CA ... 71
Arapahoe Community College ... CO ... 80
Delaware Technical and Community College Owens Campus ... DE ... 96
Brevard Community College ... FL ... 101
Florida State College at Jacksonville ... FL ... 109
Indian River State College ... FL ... 110
Keiser University ... FL ... 112
Miami Dade College ... FL ... 113
St. Petersburg College ... FL ... 116
Central Georgia Technical College ... GA ... 126
College of Coastal Georgia ... GA ... 127
Dalton State College ... GA ... 127
Darton College ... GA ... 128
DeKalb Technical College ... GA ... 128
Lanier Technical College ... GA ... 132
North Georgia Technical College ... GA ... 134
Okefenokee Technical College ... GA ... 135
Southeastern Technical College ... GA ... 137
Southwest Georgia Technical College ... GA ... 137
West Georgia Technical College ... GA ... 139
Wiregrass Georgia Technical College ... GA ... 139
Kapiolani Community College ... HI ... 141
Elgin Community College ... IL ... 150
Illinois Central College ... IL ... 152
John A. Logan College ... IL ... 154
John Wood Community College ... IL ... 154
Kankakee Community College ... IL ... 154
Kaskaskia College ... IL ... 155
Oakton Community College ... IL ... 160
Rend Lake College ... IL ... 162
Shawnee Community College ... IL ... 164
Southeastern Illinois College ... IL ... 164
Southern Illinois University Carbondale ... IL ... 164
Southern Illinois University Edwardsville ... IL ... 165
Southwestern Illinois College ... IL ... 165
Harrison College - Indianapolis East Campus ... IN ... 172
Ivy Tech Community College of Indiana-North Central ... IN ... 176
Ivy Tech Community College of Indiana-Southern Indiana ... IN ... 176
Ivy Tech Community College of Indiana-Wabash Valley ... IN ... 177
Des Moines Area Community College ... IA ... 183
Hawkeye Community College ... IA ... 185
Iowa Central Community College ... IA ... 185
Barton County Community College ... KS ... 190
Seward County Community College/Area Technical School ... KS ... 196
Eastern Kentucky University ... KY ... 200
Henderson Community College ... KY ... 201
Madisonville Community College ... KY ... 202
Somerset Community College ... KY ... 202
Southeast Kentucky Community and Technical College ... KY ... 203
Acadiana Technical College Lafayette Campus ... LA ... 209
Delgado Community College ... LA ... 210
Louisiana State University at Alexandria ... LA ... 212
MedVance Institute-Baton Rouge ... LA ... 213
Southern University at Shreveport-Louisiana LA ... 215
University of Maine at Augusta ... ME ... 220
University of Maine at Presque Isle ... ME ... 220
Allegany College of Maryland ... MD ... 221
Anne Arundel Community College ... MD ... 221
Community College of Baltimore County, The ... MD ... 222
Bristol Community College ... MA ... 239
Mount Wachusett Community College ... MA ... 240
Springfield Technical Community College ... MA ... 241
Baker College of Allen Park ... MI ... 248
Baker College of Owosso ... MI ... 249
Baker College of Port Huron ... MI ... 249
Ferris State University ... MI ... 251
Kellogg Community College ... MI ... 253
Macomb Community College ... MI ... 254
Northern Michigan University ... MI ... 256
Alexandria Technical & Community College . MN ... 265
Argosy University, Twin Cities ... MN ... 261
Hibbing Community College, A Technical and Community College ... MN ... 266
Lake Superior College ... MN ... 267
Minnesota State Community and Technical College ... MN ... 267
Minnesota West Community and Technical College ... MN ... 268
North Hennepin Community College ... MN ... 268
Rasmussen College - Mankato ... MN ... 271
Rasmussen College - St. Cloud ... MN ... 271
Saint Paul College-A Community & Technical College ... MN ... 269
South Central College ... MN ... 269
Copiah-Lincoln Community College ... MS ... 274
Hinds Community College ... MS ... 274
Meridian Community College ... MS ... 275
Mississippi Delta Community College ... MS ... 275
Mississippi Gulf Coast Community College .. MS ... 275
Northeast Mississippi Community College ... MS ... 276
Pearl River Community College ... MS ... 277
Moberly Area Community College ... MO ... 287
Ozarks Technical Community College ... MO ... 287
Saint Louis Community College at Forest Park ... MO ... 289
Three Rivers Community College ... MO ... 290
Central Community College ... NE ... 297
Mid-Plains Community College ... NE ... 298
Southeast Community College ... NE ... 300
College of Southern Nevada ... NV ... 302
River Valley Community College ... NH ... 304
Camden County College ... NJ ... 308
Mercer County Community College ... NJ ... 311
Middlesex County College ... NJ ... 311
Central New Mexico Community College ... NM ... 317
San Juan College ... NM ... 320
University of New Mexico-Gallup ... NM ... 321
Broome Community College ... NY ... 324
City University of New York Bronx Community College ... NY ... 326
Dutchess Community College ... NY ... 332
Erie Community College North Campus ... NY ... 333
Farmingdale State College ... NY ... 356
Nassau Community College ... NY ... 342
Orange County Community College ... NY ... 345
Alamance Community College ... NC ... 367
Asheville - Buncombe Technical Community College ... NC ... 367
Beaufort County Community College ... NC ... 367
Central Piedmont Community College ... NC ... 369
Coastal Carolina Community College ... NC ... 369
College of the Albemarle ... NC ... 369
Davidson County Community College ... NC ... 369
Halifax Community College ... NC ... 370
Sandhills Community College ... NC ... 373
Southeastern Community College ... NC ... 373
Southwestern Community College ... NC ... 373
Stanly Community College ... NC ... 374
Wake Technical Community College ... NC ... 374
Western Piedmont Community College ... NC ... 374
Bismarck State College ... ND ... 382
Rasmussen College - Bismarck ... ND ... 382
Cincinnati State Technical and Community College ... OH ... 387
Clark State Community College ... OH ... 387
Columbus State Community College ... OH ... 388
Cuyahoga Community College ... OH ... 389
Eastern Gateway Community College - Jefferson County Campus ... OH ... 390
Edison State Community College ... OH ... 390
Lakeland Community College ... OH ... 394
Lorain County Community College ... OH ... 395
Marion Technical College ... OH ... 395
Shawnee State University ... OH ... 401
Stark State College ... OH ... 402
Washington State Community College ... OH ... 405
Youngstown State University ... OH ... 406
Zane State College ... OH ... 407
Northeastern Oklahoma Agricultural and Mechanical College ... OK ... 408
Rose State College ... OK ... 411
Seminole State College ... OK ... 412
Tulsa Community College ... OK ... 412
Portland Community College ... OR ... 419
Community College of Allegheny County ... PA ... 425
Community College of Philadelphia ... PA ... 426
Fortis Institute ... PA ... 429
Harcum College ... PA ... 430
Harrisburg Area Community College ... PA ... 430
Mercyhurst College ... PA ... 436
Montgomery County Community College ... PA ... 436
Mount Aloysius College ... PA ... 437
Penn State Hazleton ... PA ... 439
Reading Area Community College ... PA ... 445
Community College of Rhode Island ... RI ... 453
Florence - Darlington Technical College ... SC ... 458
Greenville Technical College ... SC ... 458
Midlands Technical College ... SC ... 459
Spartanburg Community College ... SC ... 461
Tri-County Technical College ... SC ... 461
Trident Technical College ... SC ... 461
York Technical College ... SC ... 463
Lake Area Technical Institute ... SD ... 464
Mitchell Technical Institute ... SD ... 464
Fortis Institute ... TN ... 468
Jackson State Community College ... TN ... 475
Northeast State Technical Community College ... TN ... 475
Southwest Tennessee Community College .. TN ... 475
Volunteer State Community College ... TN ... 476
Amarillo College ... TX ... 479
Austin Community College District ... TX ... 481
Central Texas College ... TX ... 482
Del Mar College ... TX ... 485
El Centro College ... TX ... 484
El Paso Community College ... TX ... 486
Grayson County College ... TX ... 487
Houston Community College ... TX ... 487
Lamar State College-Orange ... TX ... 500
Laredo Community College ... TX ... 489
McLennan Community College ... TX ... 490
Navarro College ... TX ... 491
Northeast Texas Community College ... TX ... 491
St. Philip's College ... TX ... 479
San Jacinto College Central ... TX ... 493
Sanford-Brown College-Houston ... TX ... 493
Tarleton State University ... TX ... 496
Texas Southmost College ... TX ... 499
Tyler Junior College ... TX ... 502
University of Texas at Brownsville, The ... TX ... 505
Victoria College ... TX ... 507
Weber State University ... UT ... 511
J. Sargeant Reynolds Community College ... VA ... 526
Northern Virginia Community College ... VA ... 527
Wytheville Community College ... VA ... 528
Clover Park Technical College ... WA ... 532
Shoreline Community College ... WA ... 537
Wenatchee Valley College ... WA ... 539
Marshall University ... WV ... 543
Pierpont Community & Technical College ... WV ... 542
Southern West Virginia Community and Technical College ... WV ... 542
Blackhawk Technical College ... WI ... 553
Chippewa Valley Technical College ... WI ... 553
Madison Area Technical College ... WI ... 554
Milwaukee Area Technical College ... WI ... 554
Moraine Park Technical College ... WI ... 554
Northcentral Technical College ... WI ... 554
Northeast Wisconsin Technical College ... WI ... 555
Western Technical College ... WI ... 555
Casper College ... WY ... 555

MT: National Accrediting Agency for Clinical Laboratory Sciences: medical technology (C,B)

Auburn University at Montgomery ... AL ... 2
Tuskegee University ... AL ... 8
University of Alabama at Birmingham ... AL ... 8
University of Alaska Anchorage ... AK ... 10
DeVry University - Phoenix Campus ... AZ ... 13
Arkansas State University ... AR ... 20
University of Arkansas for Medical Sciences AR ... 24
California State University-Dominguez Hills .. CA ... 34
Loma Linda University ... CA ... 54
San Francisco State University ... CA ... 36
San Jose State University ... CA ... 37
University of California-Davis ... CA ... 73
University of California-Irvine ... CA ... 73
University of Hartford ... CT ... 95
University of Delaware ... DE ... 96
George Washington University ... DC ... 97
Howard University ... DC ... 98
Florida Gulf Coast University ... FL ... 119
Florida Hospital College of Health Sciences . FL ... 108
University of Central Florida ... FL ... 120
University of West Florida ... FL ... 121
Armstrong Atlantic State University ... GA ... 124
Georgia Health Sciences University ... GA ... 130
Thomas University ... GA ... 137
University of Hawaii at Manoa ... HI ... 141
Idaho State University ... ID ... 143
Illinois State University ... IL ... 153
Loyola University Chicago ... IL ... 157
Northern Illinois University ... IL ... 160
Rush University ... IL ... 163
University of Illinois at Springfield ... IL ... 167
Indiana University-Purdue University Indianapolis ... IN ... 174
Allen College ... IA ... 181
Mercy College of Health Sciences ... IA ... 187
St. Luke's College ... IA ... 188
University of Kansas Medical Center ... KS ... 197
Wichita State University ... KS ... 197
Bellarmine University ... KY ... 198
Eastern Kentucky University ... KY ... 200
University of Kentucky ... KY ... 206
Louisiana State University Health Sciences Center at Shreveport ... LA ... 213
Louisiana State University Health Sciences Center-New Orleans ... LA ... 213
McNeese State University ... LA ... 215
Our Lady of the Lake College ... LA ... 214
University of Louisiana at Monroe ... LA ... 216
Morgan State University ... MD ... 224
Salisbury University ... MD ... 228
Stevenson University ... MD ... 226
University of Maryland Baltimore ... MD ... 227
University of Massachusetts Dartmouth ... MA ... 237
University of Massachusetts Lowell ... MA ... 237
Andrews University ... MI ... 247
Eastern Michigan University ... MI ... 250
Ferris State University ... MI ... 251
Grand Valley State University ... MI ... 252
Michigan State University ... MI ... 255
Northern Michigan University ... MI ... 256
Saginaw Valley State University ... MI ... 258

MUS: National Association of Schools of Music: music (B,M,D)

Nebraska Wesleyan University ... NE ... 299
University of Nebraska at Kearney ... NE ... 300
University of Nebraska at Omaha ... NE ... 301
University of Nebraska - Lincoln ... NE ... 300
Wayne State College ... NE ... 299
University of Nevada, Las Vegas ... NV ... 302
University of Nevada, Reno ... NV ... 303
Keene State College ... NH ... 307
University of New Hampshire ... NH ... 306
College of New Jersey, The ... NJ ... 308
Kean University ... NJ ... 311
Montclair State University ... NJ ... 311
New Jersey City University ... NJ ... 312
Rider University ... NJ ... 313
Rowan University ... NJ ... 314
Rutgers the State University of New Jersey New Brunswick Campus ... NJ ... 314
William Paterson University of New Jersey ... NJ ... 317
Eastern New Mexico University Main Campus ... NM ... 318
New Mexico State University Main Campus ... NM ... 319
University of New Mexico Main Campus ... NM ... 321
College of Saint Rose, The ... NY ... 330
Hartwick College ... NY ... 335
Houghton College ... NY ... 336
Ithaca College ... NY ... 336
Nassau Community College ... NY ... 342
Nazareth College of Rochester ... NY ... 342
Nyack College ... NY ... 344
Roberts Wesleyan College ... NY ... 347
Schenectady County Community College ... NY ... 350
State University of New York at Binghamton ... NY ... 351
State University of New York at Fredonia ... NY ... 352
State University of New York at New Paltz ... NY ... 352
State University of New York College at Buffalo ... NY ... 353
State University of New York College at Oneonta ... NY ... 353
State University of New York College at Oswego ... NY ... 354
State University of New York College at Potsdam ... NY ... 354
Syracuse University Main Campus ... NY ... 357
University of Rochester ... NY ... 358
Appalachian State University ... NC ... 377
Brevard College ... NC ... 362
Chowan University ... NC ... 363
East Carolina University ... NC ... 377
Elizabeth City State University ... NC ... 377
Fayetteville State University ... NC ... 377
Gardner-Webb University ... NC ... 364
Greensboro College ... NC ... 364
Mars Hill College ... NC ... 366
Meredith College ... NC ... 366
North Carolina Agricultural and Technical State University ... NC ... 377
Pfeiffer University ... NC ... 375
Queens University of Charlotte ... NC ... 375
Salem College ... NC ... 376
University of North Carolina at Greensboro ... NC ... 379
University of North Carolina at Pembroke ... NC ... 379
University of North Carolina at Wilmington ... NC ... 379
Western Carolina University ... NC ... 379
Wingate University ... NC ... 380
Winston-Salem State University ... NC ... 380
Dickinson State University ... ND ... 381
Minot State University ... ND ... 381
North Dakota State University Main Campus ... ND ... 381
University of North Dakota Main Campus ... ND ... 381
Valley City State University ... ND ... 382
Ashland University ... OH ... 384
Baldwin-Wallace College ... OH ... 384
Bluffton University ... OH ... 385
Bowling Green State University ... OH ... 385
Capital University ... OH ... 386
Case Western Reserve University ... OH ... 386
Cedarville University ... OH ... 386
Central State University ... OH ... 386
Cincinnati Christian University ... OH ... 387
Cleveland Institute of Music ... OH ... 388
Cleveland State University ... OH ... 388
College of Mount St. Joseph ... OH ... 388
College of Wooster, The ... OH ... 388
Heidelberg University ... OH ... 391
Hiram College ... OH ... 391
Kent State University Main Campus ... OH ... 393
Miami University ... OH ... 396
Mount Vernon Nazarene University ... OH ... 396
Muskingum University ... OH ... 396
Oberlin College ... OH ... 397
Ohio Northern University ... OH ... 398
Ohio State University Main Campus, The ... OH ... 398
Ohio University Main Campus ... OH ... 399
Ohio Wesleyan University ... OH ... 400
Otterbein University ... OH ... 400
Sinclair Community College ... OH ... 401
University of Akron, Main Campus, The ... OH ... 403
University of Cincinnati Main Campus ... OH ... 403
University of Dayton ... OH ... 404
University of Mount Union ... OH ... 404
University of Toledo ... OH ... 404
Wittenberg University ... OH ... 406
Wright State University Main Campus ... OH ... 406
Xavier University ... OH ... 406
Youngstown State University ... OH ... 406
Cameron University ... OK ... 407
East Central University ... OK ... 407
Northeastern State University ... OK ... 409
Oklahoma Baptist University ... OK ... 409
Oklahoma Christian University ... OK ... 409
Oklahoma City University ... OK ... 410
Oklahoma State University ... OK ... 410
Oral Roberts University ... OK ... 411
Southeastern Oklahoma State University ... OK ... 412
Southern Nazarene University ... OK ... 412
Southwestern Oklahoma State University ... OK ... 412
University of Central Oklahoma ... OK ... 413
University of Oklahoma Norman Campus ... OK ... 413
University of Science and Arts of Oklahoma ... OK ... 413
University of Tulsa ... OK ... 413
George Fox University ... OR ... 415
Linfield College ... OR ... 416
Marylhurst University ... OR ... 416
Pacific University ... OR ... 419
Portland State University ... OR ... 418
Southern Oregon University ... OR ... 419
University of Oregon ... OR ... 419
University of Portland ... OR ... 420
Western Oregon University ... OR ... 419
Willamette University ... OR ... 421
Bloomsburg University of Pennsylvania ... PA ... 441
Bucknell University ... PA ... 423
Bucks County Community College ... PA ... 423
Carnegie Mellon University ... PA ... 424
Clarion University of Pennsylvania ... PA ... 442
Curtis Institute of Music ... PA ... 426
Duquesne University ... PA ... 428
Edinboro University of Pennsylvania ... PA ... 442
Elizabethtown College ... PA ... 428
Immaculata University ... PA ... 431
Indiana University of Pennsylvania ... PA ... 442
Kutztown University of Pennsylvania ... PA ... 442
Lebanon Valley College ... PA ... 434
Mansfield University of Pennsylvania ... PA ... 443
Marywood University ... PA ... 435
Mercyhurst College ... PA ... 436
Messiah College ... PA ... 436
Millersville University of Pennsylvania ... PA ... 443
Moravian College ... PA ... 436
Penn State University Park ... PA ... 438
Philadelphia Biblical University ... PA ... 444
Seton Hill University ... PA ... 447
Slippery Rock University of Pennsylvania ... PA ... 443
Susquehanna University ... PA ... 447
Temple University ... PA ... 447
University of the Arts, The ... PA ... 448
West Chester University of Pennsylvania ... PA ... 443
Westminster College ... PA ... 451
York College of Pennsylvania ... PA ... 452
Rhode Island College ... RI ... 454
University of Rhode Island ... RI ... 454
Anderson University ... SC ... 455
Charleston Southern University ... SC ... 456
Claflin University ... SC ... 456
Coastal Carolina University ... SC ... 456
Coker College ... SC ... 457
College of Charleston ... SC ... 457
Columbia College ... SC ... 457
Converse College ... SC ... 457
Furman University ... SC ... 458
Lander University ... SC ... 458
Limestone College ... SC ... 459
Newberry College ... SC ... 459
North Greenville University ... SC ... 460
Presbyterian College ... SC ... 460
South Carolina State University ... SC ... 460
Southern Wesleyan University ... SC ... 461
University of South Carolina Aiken ... SC ... 462
University of South Carolina Columbia ... SC ... 462
Winthrop University ... SC ... 463
Augustana College ... SD ... 463
Black Hills State University ... SD ... 465
Northern State University ... SD ... 465
South Dakota State University ... SD ... 466
University of South Dakota, The ... SD ... 465
Austin Peay State University ... TN ... 473
Belmont University ... TN ... 467
Carson-Newman College ... TN ... 467
East Tennessee State University ... TN ... 473
Fisk University ... TN ... 468
Lee University ... TN ... 470
Lipscomb University ... TN ... 470
Maryville College ... TN ... 470
Middle Tennessee State University ... TN ... 473
Southern Adventist University ... TN ... 473
Tennessee State University ... TN ... 474
Tennessee Technological University ... TN ... 474
Trevecca Nazarene University ... TN ... 476
Union University ... TN ... 476
University of Memphis, The ... TN ... 474
University of Tennessee at Chattanooga ... TN ... 477
University of Tennessee at Martin ... TN ... 477
University of Tennessee, Knoxville ... TN ... 477
Vanderbilt University ... TN ... 477
Abilene Christian University ... TX ... 478
Amarillo College ... TX ... 479
Angelo State University ... TX ... 480
Baylor University ... TX ... 481
Dallas Baptist University ... TX ... 484
Del Mar College ... TX ... 485
East Texas Baptist University ... TX ... 486
Hardin-Simmons University ... TX ... 487
Howard Payne University ... TX ... 488
Lamar University ... TX ... 500
Midwestern State University ... TX ... 491
Odessa College ... TX ... 491
Prairie View A & M University ... TX ... 496
St. Mary's University ... TX ... 493
Sam Houston State University ... TX ... 501
Southern Methodist University ... TX ... 494
Southwestern Baptist Theological Seminary ... TX ... 495
Southwestern University ... TX ... 495
Stephen F. Austin State University ... TX ... 495
Tarleton State University ... TX ... 496
Texas A & M University - Commerce ... TX ... 497
Texas A & M University - Corpus Christi ... TX ... 497
Texas A & M University - Kingsville ... TX ... 498
Texas Christian University ... TX ... 498
Texas Southmost College ... TX ... 499
Texas State University-San Marcos ... TX ... 501
Texas Tech University ... TX ... 501
Texas Wesleyan University ... TX ... 502
Texas Woman's University ... TX ... 502
University of Houston ... TX ... 503
University of Mary Hardin-Baylor ... TX ... 504
University of North Texas ... TX ... 504
University of Texas at Arlington, The ... TX ... 505
University of Texas at Austin ... TX ... 505
University of Texas at Brownsville, The ... TX ... 505
University of Texas at El Paso ... TX ... 505
University of Texas at San Antonio ... TX ... 506
University of Texas - Pan American ... TX ... 506
Wayland Baptist University ... TX ... 508
West Texas A & M University ... TX ... 498
Brigham Young University ... UT ... 509
Snow College ... UT ... 512
Southern Utah University ... UT ... 511
University of Utah, The ... UT ... 510
Utah State University ... UT ... 511
Weber State University ... UT ... 511
Christopher Newport University ... VA ... 517
George Mason University ... VA ... 519
Hampton University ... VA ... 519
James Madison University ... VA ... 520
Longwood University ... VA ... 520
Norfolk State University ... VA ... 521
Old Dominion University ... VA ... 521
Radford University ... VA ... 522
Shenandoah University ... VA ... 523
University of Mary Washington ... VA ... 524
Virginia Commonwealth University ... VA ... 525
Virginia Polytechnic Institute and State University ... VA ... 529
Virginia State University ... VA ... 529
Central Washington University ... WA ... 531
Eastern Washington University ... WA ... 533
Pacific Lutheran University ... WA ... 535
Seattle Pacific University ... WA ... 537
University of Puget Sound ... WA ... 538
University of Washington ... WA ... 538
Walla Walla University ... WA ... 538
Washington State University ... WA ... 539
Western Washington University ... WA ... 539
Whitworth University ... WA ... 539
Marshall University ... WV ... 543
Shepherd University ... WV ... 544
West Liberty University ... WV ... 544
West Virginia University ... WV ... 544
West Virginia Wesleyan College ... WV ... 545
Alverno College ... WI ... 545
Carthage College ... WI ... 546
Lawrence University ... WI ... 547
Silver Lake College ... WI ... 550
University of Wisconsin-Eau Claire ... WI ... 550
University of Wisconsin-Green Bay ... WI ... 551
University of Wisconsin-La Crosse ... WI ... 551
University of Wisconsin-Madison ... WI ... 550
University of Wisconsin-Milwaukee ... WI ... 551
University of Wisconsin-Oshkosh ... WI ... 551
University of Wisconsin-Platteville ... WI ... 551
University of Wisconsin-River Falls ... WI ... 552
University of Wisconsin-Stevens Point ... WI ... 552
University of Wisconsin-Superior ... WI ... 552
University of Wisconsin-Whitewater ... WI ... 552
Viterbo University ... WI ... 553
Casper College ... WY ... 555
Northwest College ... WY ... 556
University of Wyoming ... WY ... 556

NAIT: The Association of Technology, Management, and Applied Engineering: technology, applied technology, engineering technology and technology-related programs (A,B,M)

Jacksonville State University ... AL ... 4
Arizona State University ... AZ ... 12
University of Arkansas at Fort Smith ... AR ... 24
University of Arkansas at Pine Bluff ... AR ... 25
California Polytechnic State University-San Luis Obispo ... CA ... 33
California State University-Chico ... CA ... 34
College of the Redwoods Community College District ... CA ... 42
San Jose State University ... CA ... 37
Central Connecticut State University ... CT ... 91
Idaho State University ... ID ... 143
Eastern Illinois University ... IL ... 150
Illinois State University ... IL ... 153
Northern Illinois University ... IL ... 160
Southern Illinois University Carbondale ... IL ... 164
Indiana State University ... IN ... 173
Ivy Tech Community College-Central Indiana ... IN ... 175
Ivy Tech Community College of Indiana-Bloomington ... IN ... 17
Ivy Tech Community College of Indiana-Columbus ... IN ... 17
Ivy Tech Community College of Indiana-East Central ... IN ... 17
Ivy Tech Community College of Indiana-Kokomo ... IN ... 17
Ivy Tech Community College of Indiana-Lafayette ... IN ... 17
Ivy Tech Community College of Indiana-North Central ... IN ... 17
Ivy Tech Community College of Indiana-Northeast ... IN ... 176
Ivy Tech Community College of Indiana-Northwest ... IN ... 17
Ivy Tech Community College of Indiana-Richmond ... IN ... 176
Ivy Tech Community College of Indiana-Southern Indiana ... IN ... 17
Ivy Tech Community College of Indiana-Southwest ... IN ... 176
Ivy Tech Community College of Indiana-Wabash Valley ... IN ... 177
Purdue University Main Campus ... IN ... 178
Iowa State University ... IA ... 182
University of Northern Iowa ... IA ... 182
Eastern Kentucky University ... KY ... 200
Morehead State University ... KY ... 204
Western Kentucky University ... KY ... 207
Acadiana Technical College Lafayette Campus ... LA ... 209
Baton Rouge Community College ... LA ... 209
Capital Area Technical College Baton Rouge Campus ... LA ... 209
Delgado Community College ... LA ... 210
L.E. Fletcher Technical Community College ... LA ... 210
Nicholls State University ... LA ... 216
Northeast Louisiana Technical College Delta-Ouachita Campus ... LA ... 210
Nunez Community College ... LA ... 211
South Central Louisiana Technical College River Parishes Campus ... LA ... 212
South Louisiana Community College ... LA ... 212
Southeastern Louisiana University ... LA ... 216
Southern University at Shreveport-Louisiana ... LA ... 215
University of Louisiana at Lafayette ... LA ... 216
University of Southern Maine ... ME ... 220
Central Michigan University ... MI ... 249
Bemidji State University ... MN ... 266
Minnesota State University Moorhead ... MN ... 268
St. Cloud State University ... MN ... 269
Alcorn State University ... MS ... 273
Holmes Community College ... MS ... 274
Jackson State University ... MS ... 275
Mississippi Gulf Coast Community College ... MS ... 275
Crowder College ... MO ... 281
East Central College ... MO ... 281
Linn State Technical College ... MO ... 284
Missouri State University ... MO ... 286
Southeast Missouri State University ... MO ... 290
State Fair Community College ... MO ... 290
University of Central Missouri ... MO ... 291
University of Nebraska at Kearney ... NE ... 300
Farmingdale State College ... NY ... 356
State University of New York College at Buffalo ... NY ... 353
East Carolina University ... NC ... 377
Elizabeth City State University ... NC ... 377
North Carolina Agricultural and Technical State University ... NC ... 377
University of North Dakota Main Campus ... ND ... 381
Bowling Green State University ... OH ... 385
Kent State University Main Campus ... OH ... 393
Ohio Northern University ... OH ... 398
Ohio University Main Campus ... OH ... 399
Owens Community College ... OH ... 400
Southwestern Oklahoma State University ... OK ... 412
California University of Pennsylvania ... PA ... 441
Clarion University-Venango Campus ... PA ... 442
Millersville University of Pennsylvania ... PA ... 443
Pennsylvania College of Technology ... PA ... 440
Cleveland State Community College ... TN ... 474
Jackson State Community College ... TN ... 475
Middle Tennessee State University ... TN ... 473
Nashville State Community College ... TN ... 475
Northeast State Technical Community College ... TN ... 475
Tennessee State University ... TN ... 474
Tennessee Technological University ... TN ... 474
Walters State Community College ... TN ... 476
Texas A & M University - Kingsville ... TX ... 498
Texas Southern University ... TX ... 499
University of Texas at Tyler ... TX ... 506
Norfolk State University ... VA ... 521
Pierpont Community & Technical College ... WV ... 542
University of Wisconsin-Platteville ... WI ... 551

NATUR: Council on Naturopathic Medical Education: naturopathic medical education (FP)

Southwest College of Naturopathic Medicine & Health Sciences ... AZ ... 18
University of Bridgeport ... CT ... 94
@National University of Health Sciences ... IL ... 159
National College of Natural Medicine ... OR ... 417
Bastyr University ... WA ... 530

NH: North Central Association of Colleges and Schools, The Higher Learning Commission (NCA)

Ohio Valley University ... WV ... 541
Pierpont Community & Technical College ... WV ... 542
&Potomac State College of West Virginia University ... WV ... 545
Salem International University ... WV ... 541
Shepherd University ... WV ... 544
Southern West Virginia Community and Technical College ... WV ... 542
University of Charleston ... WV ... 541
West Liberty University ... WV ... 544
West Virginia Northern Community College ... WV ... 543
West Virginia State University ... WV ... 544
West Virginia University ... WV ... 544
West Virginia University at Parkersburg ... WV ... 545
&West Virginia University Institute of Technology ... WV ... 545
West Virginia Wesleyan College ... WV ... 545
Wheeling Jesuit University ... WV ... 545
Alverno College ... WI ... 545
Bellin College, Inc. ... WI ... 546
Beloit College ... WI ... 546
Blackhawk Technical College ... WI ... 553
Cardinal Stritch University ... WI ... 546
Carroll University ... WI ... 546
Carthage College ... WI ... 546
Chippewa Valley Technical College ... WI ... 553
College of Menominee Nation ... WI ... 546
Columbia College of Nursing ... WI ... 546
Concordia University Wisconsin ... WI ... 546
&DeVry University - Milwaukee Center ... WI ... 547
&DeVry University - Waukesha Center ... WI ... 547
Edgewood College ... WI ... 547
Fox Valley Technical College ... WI ... 553
Gateway Technical College ... WI ... 553
Herzing University ... WI ... 547
Lac Courte Oreilles Ojibwa Community College ... WI ... 547
Lakeland College ... WI ... 547
Lakeshore Technical College ... WI ... 554
Lawrence University ... WI ... 547
Madison Area Technical College ... WI ... 554
Maranatha Baptist Bible College & Seminary ... WI ... 548
Marian University ... WI ... 548
Marquette University ... WI ... 548
Medical College of Wisconsin ... WI ... 548
Mid-State Technical College ... WI ... 554
Milwaukee Area Technical College ... WI ... 554
Milwaukee Institute of Art & Design ... WI ... 548
Milwaukee School of Engineering ... WI ... 548
Moraine Park Technical College ... WI ... 554
Mount Mary College ... WI ... 549
Nicolet Area Technical College ... WI ... 554
Northcentral Technical College ... WI ... 554
Northeast Wisconsin Technical College ... WI ... 555
Northland College ... WI ... 549
&Ottawa University Wisconsin ... WI ... 549
&Rasmussen College - Appleton ... WI ... 549
&Rasmussen College - Green Bay ... WI ... 549
&Rasmussen College - Wausau ... WI ... 549
Ripon College ... WI ... 549
Sacred Heart School of Theology ... WI ... 550
Saint Norbert College ... WI ... 550
Silver Lake College ... WI ... 550
Southwest Wisconsin Technical College ... WI ... 555
University of Wisconsin Colleges ... WI ... 552
University of Wisconsin-Eau Claire ... WI ... 550
University of Wisconsin-Green Bay ... WI ... 551
University of Wisconsin-La Crosse ... WI ... 551
University of Wisconsin-Madison ... WI ... 550
University of Wisconsin-Milwaukee ... WI ... 551
University of Wisconsin-Oshkosh ... WI ... 551
University of Wisconsin-Parkside ... WI ... 551
University of Wisconsin-Platteville ... WI ... 551
University of Wisconsin-River Falls ... WI ... 552
University of Wisconsin-Stevens Point ... WI ... 552
University of Wisconsin-Stout ... WI ... 552
University of Wisconsin-Superior ... WI ... 552
University of Wisconsin-Whitewater ... WI ... 552
Viterbo University ... WI ... 553
Waukesha County Technical College ... WI ... 555
Western Technical College ... WI ... 555
Wisconsin Indianhead Technical College ... WI ... 555
Wisconsin Lutheran College ... WI ... 553
Wisconsin School of Professional Psychology ... WI ... 553
Casper College ... WY ... 555
Central Wyoming College ... WY ... 555
Eastern Wyoming College ... WY ... 555
Laramie County Community College ... WY ... 556
Northern Wyoming Community College District ... WY ... 556
Northwest College ... WY ... 556
University of Wyoming ... WY ... 556
Western Wyoming Community College ... WY ... 556

NMT: Joint Review Committee on Education Programs in Nuclear Medicine Technology: nuclear medicine technology (C,A,B)

University of Alabama at Birmingham ... AL ... 8
Gateway Community College ... AZ ... 15
University of Arkansas for Medical Sciences ... AR ... 24
University of California-Los Angeles ... CA ... 74
Gateway Community College ... CT ... 90
Lincoln College of New England ... CT ... 92
Delaware Technical and Community College Stanton-Wilmington Campus ... DE ... 96
Cambridge Institute of Allied Health & Technology ... FL ... 102
Florida Hospital College of Health Sciences ... FL ... 108
Hillsborough Community College ... FL ... 110
Santa Fe College ... FL ... 117
Armstrong Atlantic State University ... GA ... 124
Georgia Health Sciences University ... GA ... 130
College of DuPage ... IL ... 147
Triton College ... IL ... 166
Indiana University-Purdue University Indianapolis ... IN ... 174
Mercy College of Health Sciences ... IA ... 187
University of Iowa ... IA ... 182
University of Kansas Medical Center ... KS ... 197
Bluegrass Community and Technical College ... KY ... 201
Jefferson Community and Technical College ... KY ... 202
Delgado Community College ... LA ... 210
Central Maine Medical Center College of Nursing and Health Professions ... ME ... 217
Johns Hopkins University ... MD ... 223
Prince George's Community College ... MD ... 225
Massachusetts College of Pharmacy and Health Sciences ... MA ... 241
Regis College ... MA ... 244
Salem State University ... MA ... 239
Springfield Technical Community College ... MA ... 241
University of Massachusetts at Worcester ... MA ... 238
Worcester State University ... MA ... 239
Ferris State University ... MI ... 251
Macomb Community College ... MI ... 254
Mayo School of Health Sciences ... MN ... 262
Saint Mary's University of Minnesota ... MN ... 271
University of Mississippi Medical Center ... MS ... 277
Saint Louis University ... MO ... 289
University of Missouri - Columbia ... MO ... 291
University of Nebraska Medical Center ... NE ... 301
University of Nevada, Las Vegas ... NV ... 302
Gloucester County College ... NJ ... 310
UMDNJ-School of Health Related Professions ... NJ ... 317
City University of New York Bronx Community College ... NY ... 326
Molloy College ... NY ... 341
State University of New York at Buffalo ... NY ... 351
Caldwell Community College and Technical Institute ... NC ... 368
Forsyth Technical Community College ... NC ... 370
University of North Carolina at Chapel Hill ... NC ... 378
Cuyahoga Community College ... OH ... 389
Kent State University Salem Campus ... OH ... 393
Ohio State University Main Campus, The ... OH ... 398
University of Cincinnati Main Campus ... OH ... 403
University of Findlay, The ... OH ... 404
University of Oklahoma Health Sciences Center ... OK ... 413
Cedar Crest College ... PA ... 424
Community College of Allegheny County ... PA ... 425
Lancaster General College of Nursing and Health Sciences ... PA ... 433
Misericordia University ... PA ... 436
Robert Morris University ... PA ... 445
Thomas Jefferson University ... PA ... 448
University of Puerto Rico-Medical Sciences Campus ... PR ... 567
Midlands Technical College ... SC ... 459
Southeast Technical Institute ... SD ... 466
Baptist Memorial College of Health Sciences ... TN ... 467
Chattanooga State Community College ... TN ... 474
South College ... TN ... 472
University of Tennessee, Knoxville ... TN ... 477
Vanderbilt University ... TN ... 477
Amarillo College ... TX ... 479
Baylor University ... TX ... 481
Del Mar College ... TX ... 485
Galveston College ... TX ... 486
Houston Community College ... TX ... 487
University of the Incarnate Word ... TX ... 503
University of Utah, The ... UT ... 510
University of Vermont ... VT ... 514
Old Dominion University ... VA ... 521
Virginia Commonwealth University ... VA ... 525
Bellevue College ... WA ... 531
Kanawha Valley Community & Technical College ... WV ... 542
West Virginia University ... WV ... 544
#Wheeling Jesuit University ... WV ... 545

NRPA: National Recreation and Park Association: recreation, park resources, and leisure studies (B)

Arizona State University ... AZ ... 12
Northern Arizona University ... AZ ... 17
Arkansas Tech University ... AR ... 20
California Polytechnic State University-San Luis Obispo ... CA ... 33
California State University-Chico ... CA ... 34
California State University-Fresno ... CA ... 34
California State University-Long Beach ... CA ... 35
California State University-Sacramento ... CA ... 35
San Francisco State University ... CA ... 36
San Jose State University ... CA ... 37
Metropolitan State College of Denver ... CO ... 85
Georgia Southern University ... GA ... 131
University of Georgia ... GA ... 138
University of Idaho ... ID ... 144
Chicago State University ... IL ... 146
Eastern Illinois University ... IL ... 150
Illinois State University ... IL ... 153
Southern Illinois University Carbondale ... IL ... 164
University of Illinois at Urbana-Champaign ... IL ... 167
University of St. Francis ... IL ... 167
Western Illinois University ... IL ... 168
Indiana State University ... IN ... 173
Indiana University Bloomington ... IN ... 173
University of Northern Iowa ... IA ... 182
Kansas State University ... KS ... 194
Pittsburg State University ... KS ... 195
Eastern Kentucky University ... KY ... 200
Western Kentucky University ... KY ... 207
University of Maine at Machias ... ME ... 220
Frostburg State University ... MD ... 228
Springfield College ... MA ... 245
Central Michigan University ... MI ... 249
Ferris State University ... MI ... 251
Minnesota State University, Mankato ... MN ... 267
University of Mississippi ... MS ... 277
University of Southern Mississippi ... MS ... 278
Missouri State University ... MO ... 286
Southeast Missouri State University ... MO ... 290
University of Missouri - Columbia ... MO ... 291
University of New Hampshire ... NH ... 306
Ithaca College ... NY ... 336
Saint Joseph's College, New York - Suffolk Campus ... NY ... 349
State University of New York College at Cortland ... NY ... 353
State University of New York, The College at Brockport ... NY ... 352
Appalachian State University ... NC ... 377
East Carolina University ... NC ... 377
North Carolina Central University ... NC ... 378
North Carolina State University ... NC ... 378
University of North Carolina at Greensboro ... NC ... 379
University of North Carolina at Wilmington ... NC ... 379
Winston-Salem State University ... NC ... 380
Bowling Green State University ... OH ... 385
Kent State University Main Campus ... OH ... 393
Ohio University Main Campus ... OH ... 399
University of Toledo ... OH ... 404
Oklahoma State University ... OK ... 410
California University of Pennsylvania ... PA ... 441
East Stroudsburg University of Pennsylvania ... PA ... 442
Lock Haven University of Pennsylvania ... PA ... 443
Slippery Rock University of Pennsylvania ... PA ... 443
Temple University ... PA ... 447
York College of Pennsylvania ... PA ... 452
Benedict College ... SC ... 455
Clemson University ... SC ... 456
Middle Tennessee State University ... TN ... 473
University of Tennessee, Knoxville ... TN ... 477
Texas A & M University ... TX ... 497
Texas State University-San Marcos ... TX ... 501
University of North Texas ... TX ... 504
Brigham Young University ... UT ... 509
University of Utah, The ... UT ... 510
Utah State University ... UT ... 511
George Mason University ... VA ... 519
Longwood University ... VA ... 520
Old Dominion University ... VA ... 521
Radford University ... VA ... 522
Virginia Wesleyan College ... VA ... 529
Eastern Washington University ... WA ... 533
Western Washington University ... WA ... 539
University of Wisconsin-La Crosse ... WI ... 551

NUR: National League for Nursing: nursing (B,M)

Oakwood University ... AL ... 6
Troy University ... AL ... 8
Tuskegee University ... AL ... 8
University of Alaska Anchorage ... AK ... 10
Arkansas State University ... AR ... 20
Arkansas Tech University ... AR ... 20
Harding University Main Campus ... AR ... 21
Southern Arkansas University ... AR ... 23
University of Arkansas at Fort Smith ... AR ... 24
University of Arkansas at Little Rock ... AR ... 24
University of Arkansas at Monticello ... AR ... 25
University of Arkansas at Pine Bluff ... AR ... 25
California State University-East Bay ... CA ... 34
Pacific Union College ... CA ... 60
Sonoma State University ... CA ... 37
Colorado State University-Pueblo ... CO ... 83
Metropolitan State College of Denver ... CO ... 85
Platt College ... CO ... 86
Quinnipiac University ... CT ... 93
Delaware State University ... DE ... 95
Wesley College ... DE ... 96
University System of the District of Columbia ... DC ... 99
Bethune Cookman University ... FL ... 101
Florida Agricultural and Mechanical University ... FL ... 118
Florida Hospital College of Health Sciences ... FL ... 108
Indian River State College ... FL ... 110
Miami Dade College ... FL ... 113
State College of Florida, Manatee-Sarasota ... FL ... 118
University of Tampa ... FL ... 122
Albany State University ... GA ... 123
Augusta State University ... GA ... 125
College of Coastal Georgia ... GA ... 127
Georgia College & State University ... GA ... 129
Georgia Southwestern State University ... GA ... 131
Gordon College ... GA ... 131
LaGrange College ... GA ... 132
Macon State College ... GA ... 133
North Georgia College & State University ... GA ... 134
Piedmont College ... GA ... 135
Thomas University ... GA ... 137
University of Guam ... GU ... 559
Hawaii Pacific University ... HI ... 140
University of Hawaii at Hilo ... HI ... 141
Boise State University ... ID ... 142
Brigham Young University-Idaho ... ID ... 142
Bradley University ... IL ... 145
Chicago State University ... IL ... 146
Governors State University ... IL ... 151
Lakeview College of Nursing ... IL ... 156
Methodist College of Nursing ... IL ... 158
Rockford College ... IL ... 162
Saint Francis Medical Center College of Nursing ... IL ... 163
St. John's College ... IL ... 163
Bethel College ... IN ... 169
Indiana State University ... IN ... 173
Indiana University East ... IN ... 173
Indiana University Northwest ... IN ... 173
Indiana University-Purdue University Fort Wayne ... IN ... 174
Indiana University-Purdue University Indianapolis ... IN ... 174
Purdue University Calumet ... IN ... 178
Purdue University North Central Campus ... IN ... 178
Saint Mary's College ... IN ... 179
University of Evansville ... IN ... 180
Vincennes University ... IN ... 181
Allen College ... IA ... 181
Briar Cliff University ... IA ... 182
Iowa Wesleyan College ... IA ... 186
Emporia State University ... KS ... 192
Kansas Wesleyan University ... KS ... 194
Frontier Nursing University ... KY ... 200
Kentucky State University ... KY ... 203
Midway College ... KY ... 204
Northern Kentucky University ... KY ... 205
Thomas More College ... KY ... 206
Dillard University ... LA ... 208
Grambling State University ... LA ... 215
Louisiana State University at Alexandria ... LA ... 212
Loyola University New Orleans ... LA ... 213
McNeese State University ... LA ... 215
Our Lady of Holy Cross College ... LA ... 214
Our Lady of the Lake College ... LA ... 214
University of New England ... ME ... 220
Bowie State University ... MD ... 228
Coppin State University ... MD ... 228
Notre Dame of Maryland University ... MD ... 225
Stevenson University ... MD ... 226
Washington Adventist University ... MD ... 229
Anna Maria College ... MA ... 230
Atlantic Union College ... MA ... 230
Endicott College ... MA ... 234
Regis College ... MA ... 244
University of Massachusetts Dartmouth ... MA ... 237
Andrews University ... MI ... 247
Davenport University ... MI ... 250
Ferris State University ... MI ... 251
Lake Superior State University ... MI ... 254
St. Catherine University ... MN ... 271
Alcorn State University ... MS ... 273
Chamberlain College of Nursing - St. Louis ... MO ... 280
Lincoln University ... MO ... 284
Missouri Southern State University ... MO ... 286
Southwest Baptist University ... MO ... 290
Webster University ... MO ... 293
Montana State University - Northern ... MT ... 295
Salish Kootenai College ... MT ... 296
Bryan LGH College of Health Sciences ... NE ... 297
Clarkson College ... NE ... 297
College of Saint Mary ... NE ... 297
Midland University ... NE ... 299
Nebraska Wesleyan University ... NE ... 299
Great Basin College ... NV ... 302
Roseman University of Health Sciences ... NV ... 303
Franklin Pierce University ... NH ... 305
Rivier College ... NH ... 305
College of Saint Elizabeth ... NJ ... 309
Kean University ... NJ ... 311
New Jersey City University ... NJ ... 312
Ramapo College of New Jersey ... NJ ... 313
Thomas Edison State College ... NJ ... 316
UMDNJ-School of Nursing ... NJ ... 316
Eastern New Mexico University Main Campus ... NM ... 318
City University of New York College of Staten Island ... NY ... 327
City University of New York Medgar Evers College ... NY ... 328
City University of New York York College ... NY ... 329
Daemen College ... NY ... 331
Elmira College ... NY ... 333
Excelsior College ... NY ... 333
Farmingdale State College ... NY ... 356
Keuka College ... NY ... 337
New York City College of Technology/City University of New York ... NY ... 328
Saint Joseph's College, New York ... NY ... 349
State University of New York College of Technology at Delhi ... NY ... 355
Wagner College ... NY ... 359
Barton College ... NC ... 362
Gardner-Webb University ... NC ... 364
North Carolina Agricultural and Technical State University ... NC ... 377

NURSE: Commission on Collegiate Nursing Education: nursing (B,M)

NW: Northwest Association of Schools and Colleges, Commission on Colleges (NASC)

pokane Community College ... WA ... 532
pokane Falls Community College ... WA ... 532
acoma Community College ... WA ... 538
rinity Lutheran College ... WA ... 538
niversity of Puget Sound ... WA ... 538
niversity of Washington ... WA ... 538
Valla Walla Community College ... WA ... 538
Valla Walla University ... WA ... 538
Vashington State University ... WA ... 539
Venatchee Valley College ... WA ... 539
Vestern Washington University ... WA ... 539
Vhatcom Community College ... WA ... 539
Vhitman College ... WA ... 539
Vhitworth University ... WA ... 539
'akima Valley Community College ... WA ... 540

NY: New York State Board of Regents

American Academy of Dramatic Arts ... NY ... 323
Bramson O R T College ... NY ... 324
Christie's Education, Inc. ... NY ... 326
Cold Spring Harbor Laboratory/Watson School of Biological Sciences ... NY ... 329
Elmezzi Graduate School of Molecular Medicine, The ... NY ... 332
Globe Institute of Technology ... NY ... 334
Holy Trinity Orthodox Seminary ... NY ... 336
Institute of Design and Construction ... NY ... 336
Louis V. Gerstner Jr. Graduate School of Biomedical Sciences at Memorial Sl oan-Kettering Cancer Ctr ... NY ... 339
Memorial Hospital School of Nursing ... NY ... 340
New York Academy of Art ... NY ... 342
New York Career Institute ... NY ... 342
New York College of Health Professions ... NY ... 343
Northeastern Seminary ... NY ... 344
Rabbi Isaac Elchanan Theological Seminary NY ... 346
Richard Gilder Graduate School at the American Museum of Natural History ... NY ... 347
Rockefeller University ... NY ... 347
Salvation Army School for Officer Training ... NY ... 350
Samaritan Hospital School of Nursing ... NY ... 350
Technical Career Institutes ... NY ... 357
Union Graduate College ... NY ... 358
USC The Business College ... NY ... 359
Wood Tobé-Coburn School ... NY ... 360

OPD: Commission on Opticianry Accreditation: opticianry (A)

Middlesex Community College ... CT ... 90
Hillsborough Community College ... FL ... 110
Miami Dade College ... FL ... 113
DeKalb Technical College ... GA ... 128
Ogeechee Technical College ... GA ... 134
Indiana University Bloomington ... IN ... 173
Baker College of Jackson ... MI ... 248
College of Southern Nevada ... NV ... 302
Camden County College ... NJ ... 308
Essex County College ... NJ ... 310
Raritan Valley Community College ... NJ ... 313
Southwestern Indian Polytechnic Institute ... NM ... 321
Erie Community College North Campus ... NY ... 333
New York City College of Technology/City University of New York ... NY ... 328
Technical Career Institutes ... NY ... 357
Durham Technical Community College ... NC ... 369
Roane State Community College ... TN ... 475
Tyler Junior College ... TX ... 502
J. Sargeant Reynolds Community College ... VA ... 526
Seattle Central Community College ... WA ... 537

OPE: Commission on Accreditation of Allied Health Education Programs: orthotics and prosthetics (C,B,M)

California State University-Dominguez Hills .. CA ... 34
St. Petersburg College ... FL ... 116
Georgia Institute of Technology ... GA ... 130
Northwestern University ... IL ... 160
Eastern Michigan University ... MI ... 250
Century College ... MN ... 266
University of Pittsburgh ... PA ... 449
University of Texas Southwestern Medical Center at Dallas ... TX ... 507
University of Washington ... WA ... 538

OPLT: Commission on Opticianry Accreditation: opthalmic laboratory technician (C)

Southwestern Indian Polytechnic Institute ... NM ... 321

OPT: American Optometric Association: optometry (FP)

University of Alabama at Birmingham ... AL ... 8
@Midwestern University ... AZ ... 16
Southern California College of Optometry ... CA ... 70
University of California-Berkeley ... CA ... 73
@Western University of Health Sciences ... CA ... 78
Nova Southeastern University ... FL ... 114
Illinois College of Optometry ... IL ... 152
Indiana University Bloomington ... IN ... 173
New England College of Optometry, The ... MA ... 243
Ferris State University ... MI ... 251
University of Missouri - Saint Louis ... MO ... 291
State University of New York College of Optometry ... NY ... 355
Ohio State University Main Campus, The ... OH ... 398
Northeastern State University ... OK ... 409
Pacific University ... OR ... 419
Salus University ... PA ... 446
Inter American University of Puerto Rico School of Optometry ... PR ... 564
Southern College of Optometry ... TN ... 473
University of Houston ... TX ... 503
@University of the Incarnate Word ... TX ... 503

OPTR: American Optometric Association: optometric residency programs

University of Alabama at Birmingham ... AL ... 8
Southern California College of Optometry ... CA ... 70
University of California-Berkeley ... CA ... 73
Nova Southeastern University ... FL ... 114
Illinois College of Optometry ... IL ... 152
Indiana University Bloomington ... IN ... 173
New England College of Optometry, The ... MA ... 243
Ferris State University ... MI ... 251
University of Missouri - Saint Louis ... MO ... 291
State University of New York College of Optometry ... NY ... 355
Ohio State University Main Campus, The ... OH ... 398
Northeastern State University ... OK ... 409
Pacific University ... OR ... 419
Salus University ... PA ... 446
Inter American University of Puerto Rico Bayamon Campus ... PR ... 563
Southern College of Optometry ... TN ... 473
University of Houston ... TX ... 503

OPTT: American Optometric Association: optometric technician (A)

Indiana University Bloomington ... IN ... 173
Madison Area Technical College ... WI ... 554

OSTEO: American Osteopathic Association, Office of Osteopathic Education: osteopathic medicine (FP)

Midwestern University ... AZ ... 16
Touro University-California ... CA ... 72
Western University of Health Sciences ... CA ... 78
@Rocky Vista University ... CO ... 87
Nova Southeastern University ... FL ... 114
Midwestern University ... IL ... 158
Des Moines University ... IA ... 183
University of Pikeville ... KY ... 207
University of New England ... ME ... 220
Michigan State University ... MI ... 255
@William Carey University ... MS ... 278
A. T. Still University of Health Sciences ... MO ... 278
Kansas City University of Medicine & Biosciences ... MO ... 283
UMDNJ-School of Osteopathic Medicine ... NJ ... 316
New York Institute of Technology ... NY ... 343
Touro College ... NY ... 357
Ohio University Main Campus ... OH ... 399
Oklahoma State University Center for Health Sciences College of Osteopathic Medicine OK ... 410
Lake Erie College of Osteopathic Medicine .. PA ... 433
Philadelphia College of Osteopathic Medicine ... PA ... 444
Lincoln Memorial University ... TN ... 470
University of North Texas Health Science Center at Fort Worth ... TX ... 504
Edward Via College of Osteopathic Medicine VA ... 518
@Pacific Northwest University of Health Sciences ... WA ... 536
West Virginia School of Osteopathic Medicine ... WV ... 544

OT: American Occupational Therapy Association: occupational therapy (B, M,D)

Alabama State University ... AL ... 1
#Tuskegee University ... AL ... 8
University of Alabama at Birmingham ... AL ... 8
University of South Alabama ... AL ... 9
Midwestern University ... AZ ... 16
University of Central Arkansas ... AR ... 25
California State University-Dominguez Hills .. CA ... 34
Dominican University of California ... CA ... 45
Loma Linda University ... CA ... 54
Samuel Merritt University ... CA ... 64
San Jose State University ... CA ... 37
University of Southern California ... CA ... 76
Colorado State University ... CO ... 83
Quinnipiac University ... CT ... 93
Sacred Heart University ... CT ... 93
Howard University ... DC ... 98
Barry University ... FL ... 101
#Florida Agricultural and Mechanical University ... FL ... 118
Florida Gulf Coast University ... FL ... 119
Florida International University ... FL ... 119
Nova Southeastern University ... FL ... 114
University of Florida ... FL ... 120
University of St. Augustine for Health Sciences ... FL ... 122
Brenau University ... GA ... 126
Georgia Health Sciences University ... GA ... 130
Idaho State University ... ID ... 143
Chicago State University ... IL ... 146
Governors State University ... IL ... 151
Midwestern University ... IL ... 158
Rush University ... IL ... 163
University of Illinois at Chicago ... IL ... 166
Indiana University-Purdue University Indianapolis ... IN ... 174
University of Indianapolis ... IN ... 180
University of Southern Indiana ... IN ... 180
St. Ambrose University ... IA ... 188
University of Kansas Medical Center ... KS ... 197
Eastern Kentucky University ... KY ... 200
Spalding University ... KY ... 205
Louisiana State University Health Sciences Center at Shreveport ... LA ... 213
Louisiana State University Health Sciences Center-New Orleans ... LA ... 213
Husson University ... ME ... 218
University of New England ... ME ... 220
University of Southern Maine ... ME ... 220
Towson University ... MD ... 228
American International College ... MA ... 229
Bay Path College ... MA ... 231
Boston University ... MA ... 232
Salem State University ... MA ... 239
Springfield College ... MA ... 245
Tufts University ... MA ... 245
Worcester State University ... MA ... 239
Baker College of Flint ... MI ... 248
Eastern Michigan University ... MI ... 250
Grand Valley State University ... MI ... 252
Saginaw Valley State University ... MI ... 258
Wayne State University ... MI ... 260
Western Michigan University ... MI ... 260
College of Saint Scholastica, The ... MN ... 262
St. Catherine University ... MN ... 271
University of Minnesota-Twin Cities ... MN ... 272
University of Mississippi Medical Center ... MS ... 277
A. T. Still University of Health Sciences ... MO ... 278
Maryville University of Saint Louis ... MO ... 284
Rockhurst University ... MO ... 288
Saint Louis University ... MO ... 289
University of Missouri - Columbia ... MO ... 291
Washington University in St. Louis ... MO ... 292
College of Saint Mary ... NE ... 297
Creighton University ... NE ... 297
University of New Hampshire ... NH ... 306
Kean University ... NJ ... 311
Richard Stockton College of New Jersey, The ... NJ ... 313
Seton Hall University ... NJ ... 315
University of New Mexico Main Campus ... NM ... 321
Western New Mexico University ... NM ... 321
#City University of New York York College ... NY ... 329
Columbia University in the City of New York NY ... 330
Dominican College of Blauvelt ... NY ... 332
D'Youville College ... NY ... 332
Ithaca College ... NY ... 336
Keuka College ... NY ... 337
Long Island University Brooklyn Campus ... NY ... 338
Mercy College ... NY ... 340
New York Institute of Technology ... NY ... 343
New York University ... NY ... 344
Sage Colleges, The ... NY ... 348
State University of New York at Buffalo ... NY ... 351
State University of New York at Stony Brook NY ... 352
State University of New York Health Science Center at Brooklyn ... NY ... 352
Touro College ... NY ... 357
Utica College ... NY ... 359
East Carolina University ... NC ... 377
Lenoir-Rhyne University ... NC ... 366
University of North Carolina at Chapel Hill ... NC ... 378
Winston-Salem State University ... NC ... 380
University of Mary ... ND ... 383
University of North Dakota Main Campus ... ND ... 381
Cleveland State University ... OH ... 388
Ohio State University Main Campus, The ... OH ... 398
Shawnee State University ... OH ... 401
University of Findlay, The ... OH ... 404
University of Toledo ... OH ... 404
Xavier University ... OH ... 406
University of Oklahoma Health Sciences Center ... OK ... 413
Pacific University ... OR ... 419
Alvernia University ... PA ... 421
Chatham University ... PA ... 425
Duquesne University ... PA ... 428
Elizabethtown College ... PA ... 428
Gannon University ... PA ... 429
Misericordia University ... PA ... 436
Philadelphia University ... PA ... 444
Saint Francis University ... PA ... 446
Temple University ... PA ... 447
Thomas Jefferson University ... PA ... 448
University of Pittsburgh ... PA ... 449
University of Scranton, The ... PA ... 450
University of the Sciences in Philadelphia ... PA ... 450
University of Puerto Rico-Medical Sciences Campus ... PR ... 567
Medical University of South Carolina ... SC ... 459
University of South Dakota, The ... SD ... 465
Belmont University ... TN ... 467
Milligan College ... TN ... 471
Tennessee State University ... TN ... 474
University of Tennessee at Chattanooga ... TN ... 477
University of Tennessee Health Science Center ... TN ... 477
Texas Tech University Health Sciences Center ... TX ... 501
Texas Woman's University ... TX ... 502
University of Texas at El Paso ... TX ... 505
University of Texas Health Science Center at San Antonio ... TX ... 506
University of Texas Medical Branch, The ... TX ... 507
University of Texas - Pan American ... TX ... 506
University of Utah, The ... UT ... 510
James Madison University ... VA ... 520
Jefferson College of Health Sciences (Formerly Community Hospital) ... VA ... 520
Radford University ... VA ... 522
Shenandoah University ... VA ... 523
Virginia Commonwealth University ... VA ... 525
Eastern Washington University ... WA ... 533
University of Puget Sound ... WA ... 538
University of Washington ... WA ... 538
West Virginia University ... WV ... 544
Concordia University Wisconsin ... WI ... 546
Mount Mary College ... WI ... 549
University of Wisconsin-La Crosse ... WI ... 551
University of Wisconsin-Madison ... WI ... 550
University of Wisconsin-Milwaukee ... WI ... 551

OTA: American Occupational Therapy Association: occupational therapy assistant (C,A)

Wallace State Community College - Hanceville ... AL ... 10
Brown Mackie College-Phoenix ... AZ ... 12
Brown Mackie College-Tucson ... AZ ... 12
Pima Medical Institute-Mesa ... AZ ... 18
Pima Medical Institute-Tucson ... AZ ... 18
Pulaski Technical College ... AR ... 23
South Arkansas Community College ... AR ... 23
Grossmont College ... CA ... 49
Sacramento City College ... CA ... 56
Santa Ana College ... CA ... 63
Pima Medical Institute-Denver ... CO ... 86
Pueblo Community College ... CO ... 87
Housatonic Community College ... CT ... 90
Lincoln College of New England ... CT ... 92
Manchester Community College ... CT ... 90
Delaware Technical and Community College Owens Campus ... DE ... 96
Delaware Technical and Community College Stanton-Wilmington Campus ... DE ... 96
Daytona State College ... FL ... 103
Florida Hospital College of Health Sciences . FL ... 108
Florida State College at Jacksonville ... FL ... 109
Keiser University ... FL ... 112
Polk State College ... FL ... 115
State College of Florida, Manatee-Sarasota . FL ... 118
Augusta Technical College ... GA ... 125
Brown Mackie College-Atlanta ... GA ... 126
Darton College ... GA ... 128
Georgia Northwestern Technical College ... GA ... 130
Middle Georgia College ... GA ... 133
Kapiolani Community College ... HI ... 141
Brown Mackie College-Boise ... ID ... 142
City Colleges of Chicago Wilbur Wright College ... IL ... 147
Illinois Central College ... IL ... 152
John A. Logan College ... IL ... 154
Kaskaskia College ... IL ... 155
Lewis and Clark Community College ... IL ... 156
Lincoln Land Community College ... IL ... 156
Parkland College ... IL ... 161
Rend Lake College ... IL ... 162
Shawnee Community College ... IL ... 164
South Suburban College of Cook County ... IL ... 164
Southeastern Illinois College ... IL ... 164
Brown Mackie College-Fort Wayne ... IN ... 169
Brown Mackie College-Indianapolis ... IN ... 169
Brown Mackie College-Merrillville ... IN ... 169
Brown Mackie College-South Bend ... IN ... 170
University of Southern Indiana ... IN ... 180
Kirkwood Community College ... IA ... 186
Brown Mackie College-Kansas City ... KS ... 191
Brown Mackie College-Salina ... KS ... 191
Newman University ... KS ... 195
Brown Mackie College-Hopkinsville ... KY ... 198
Brown Mackie College-Louisville ... KY ... 199
Brown Mackie College-Northern Kentucky ... KY ... 199
Jefferson Community and Technical College KY ... 202
Madisonville Community College ... KY ... 202
Bossier Parish Community College ... LA ... 209
Delgado Community College ... LA ... 210
University of Louisiana at Monroe ... LA ... 216
Kennebec Valley Community College ... ME ... 218
Allegany College of Maryland ... MD ... 221
Community College of Baltimore County, The ... MD ... 222
Bristol Community College ... MA ... 239
North Shore Community College ... MA ... 241
Quinsigamond Community College ... MA ... 241
Springfield Technical Community College ... MA ... 241
Baker College of Allen Park ... MI ... 248
Baker College of Muskegon ... MI ... 248
Grand Rapids Community College ... MI ... 251
Macomb Community College ... MI ... 254
Mott Community College ... MI ... 256
Wayne County Community College District .. MI ... 260
Anoka Technical College ... MN ... 266
Northland Community and Technical College MN ... 268
St. Catherine University ... MN ... 271

Holmes Community College ... MS ... 274
Itawamba Community College ... MS ... 274
Pearl River Community College ... MS ... 277
East Central College ... MO ... 281
Metropolitan Community College - Penn Valley ... MO ... 285
Moberly Area Community College ... MO ... 287
Ozarks Technical Community College ... MO ... 287
St. Charles Community College ... MO ... 288
Saint Louis Community College at Meramec ... MO ... 289
Sanford-Brown College ... MO ... 289
State Fair Community College ... MO ... 290
University of Missouri - Kansas City ... MO ... 291
Central Community College ... NE ... 297
College of Southern Nevada ... NV ... 302
River Valley Community College ... NH ... 304
Eastern New Mexico University-Roswell ... NM ... 318
Erie Community College North Campus ... NY ... 333
Jamestown Community College ... NY ... 337
La Guardia Community College/City University of New York ... NY ... 328
Maria College of Albany ... NY ... 340
Mercy College ... NY ... 340
Orange County Community College ... NY ... 345
Rockland Community College ... NY ... 347
Suffolk County Community College Grant Campus ... NY ... 356
#Touro College ... NY ... 357
Cabarrus College of Health Sciences ... NC ... 362
Cape Fear Community College ... NC ... 368
Durham Technical Community College ... NC ... 369
Pitt Community College ... NC ... 372
North Dakota State College of Science ... ND ... 382
Brown Mackie College-Akron ... OH ... 385
Brown Mackie College-Findlay ... OH ... 385
Cincinnati State Technical and Community College ... OH ... 387
Cuyahoga Community College ... OH ... 389
James A. Rhodes State College ... OH ... 392
Kent State University Ashtabula Campus ... OH ... 393
Kent State University East Liverpool Campus ... OH ... 393
Owens Community College ... OH ... 400
Shawnee State University ... OH ... 401
Sinclair Community College ... OH ... 401
Stark State College ... OH ... 402
Zane State College ... OH ... 407
Brown Mackie College-Tulsa ... OK ... 407
Murray State College ... OK ... 408
Oklahoma City Community College ... OK ... 409
Southwestern Oklahoma State University ... OK ... 412
Tulsa Community College ... OK ... 412
Community College of Allegheny County ... PA ... 425
Harcum College ... PA ... 430
Kaplan Career Institute - ICM Campus ... PA ... 432
Lehigh Carbon Community College ... PA ... 434
Mercyhurst College ... PA ... 436
Penn State Berks ... PA ... 439
Penn State DuBois ... PA ... 439
Penn State Mont Alto ... PA ... 440
Pennsylvania College of Technology ... PA ... 440
#University of Puerto Rico-Humacao ... PR ... 567
Community College of Rhode Island ... RI ... 453
New England Institute of Technology ... RI ... 453
Greenville Technical College ... SC ... 458
Trident Technical College ... SC ... 461
Lake Area Technical Institute ... SD ... 464
Nashville State Community College ... TN ... 475
Roane State Community College ... TN ... 475
Amarillo College ... TX ... 479
Austin Community College District ... TX ... 481
Del Mar College ... TX ... 485
Houston Community College ... TX ... 487
Laredo Community College ... TX ... 489
Lone Star College System ... TX ... 490
Navarro College ... TX ... 491
Panola College ... TX ... 492
St. Philip's College ... TX ... 479
South Texas College ... TX ... 494
Salt Lake Community College ... UT ... 512
Jefferson College of Health Sciences (Formerly Community Hospital) ... VA ... 520
Southwest Virginia Community College ... VA ... 528
Tidewater Community College ... VA ... 528
Virginia Highlands Community College ... VA ... 528
Green River Community College ... WA ... 534
Lake Washington Technical College ... WA ... 535
Pima Medical Institute-Seattle ... WA ... 536
Mountain State University ... WV ... 541
Fox Valley Technical College ... WI ... 553
Madison Area Technical College ... WI ... 554
Milwaukee Area Technical College ... WI ... 554
Western Technical College ... WI ... 555
Wisconsin Indianhead Technical College ... WI ... 555
Casper College ... WY ... 555

PA: National Accrediting Agency for Clinical Laboratory Sciences: pathologist's assistant (C,A,B,M)

Quinnipiac University ... CT ... 93
Rosalind Franklin University of Medicine & Science ... IL ... 163
Indiana University-Purdue University Indianapolis ... IN ... 174
University of Maryland Baltimore ... MD ... 227
Wayne State University ... MI ... 260
Duke University ... NC ... 363
Drexel University ... PA ... 427
West Virginia University ... WV ... 544

PDPSY: American Psychological Association: post-doctoral residency in professional psychology

University of California-Los Angeles ... CA ... 74
University of Southern California ... CA ... 76
University of Massachusetts at Worcester ... MA ... 238
University of Michigan-Ann Arbor ... MI ... 259
University of Rochester ... NY ... 358
University of Oklahoma Health Sciences Center ... OK ... 413
Brown University ... RI ... 452
Virginia Commonwealth University ... VA ... 525
University of Washington ... WA ... 538
Medical College of Wisconsin ... WI ... 548

PERF: Commission on Accreditation of Allied Health Education Programs: perfusionist (C,B,M)

Midwestern University ... AZ ... 16
University of Arizona ... AZ ... 19
Quinnipiac University ... CT ... 93
Barry University ... FL ... 101
Rush University ... IL ... 163
University of Iowa ... IA ... 182
University of Nebraska Medical Center ... NE ... 301
Long Island University C.W. Post Campus ... NY ... 339
State University of New York Upstate Medical University ... NY ... 352
Ohio State University Main Campus, The ... OH ... 398
University of Pittsburgh ... PA ... 449
Medical University of South Carolina ... SC ... 459
Vanderbilt University ... TN ... 477
Milwaukee School of Engineering ... WI ... 548

PH: Council on Education for Public Health: public health (B,M,D)

University of Alabama at Birmingham ... AL ... 8
University of Alaska Anchorage ... AK ... 10
University of Arizona ... AZ ... 19
University of Arkansas for Medical Sciences ... AR ... 24
California State University-Fresno ... CA ... 34
California State University-Fullerton ... CA ... 34
California State University-Long Beach ... CA ... 35
California State University-Northridge ... CA ... 35
Loma Linda University ... CA ... 54
San Diego State University ... CA ... 36
San Francisco State University ... CA ... 36
San Jose State University ... CA ... 37
Touro University-California ... CA ... 72
University of California-Berkeley ... CA ... 73
University of California-Davis ... CA ... 73
University of California-Los Angeles ... CA ... 74
University of Southern California ... CA ... 76
University of Colorado Denver|Anschutz Medical Campus ... CO ... 88
University of Northern Colorado ... CO ... 88
Southern Connecticut State University ... CT ... 91
University of Connecticut Health Center ... CT ... 94
Yale University ... CT ... 95
George Washington University ... DC ... 97
Florida Agricultural and Mechanical University ... FL ... 118
Florida International University ... FL ... 119
Nova Southeastern University ... FL ... 114
University of Florida ... FL ... 120
University of Miami ... FL ... 122
University of North Florida ... FL ... 120
University of South Florida ... FL ... 120
University of West Florida ... FL ... 121
Armstrong Atlantic State University ... GA ... 124
Emory University ... GA ... 129
Georgia Health Sciences University ... GA ... 130
Georgia Southern University ... GA ... 131
Georgia State University ... GA ... 131
Mercer University ... GA ... 133
Morehouse School of Medicine ... GA ... 134
University of Georgia ... GA ... 138
University of Hawaii at Manoa ... HI ... 141
Idaho State University ... ID ... 143
Northern Illinois University ... IL ... 160
Northwestern University ... IL ... 160
Southern Illinois University Carbondale ... IL ... 164
University of Illinois at Chicago ... IL ... 166
Indiana University Bloomington ... IN ... 173
Indiana University-Purdue University Indianapolis ... IN ... 174
Des Moines University ... IA ... 183
University of Iowa ... IA ... 182
University of Kansas Main Campus ... KS ... 196
Eastern Kentucky University ... KY ... 200
University of Kentucky ... KY ... 206
University of Louisville ... KY ... 207
Western Kentucky University ... KY ... 207
Tulane University ... LA ... 215
Johns Hopkins University ... MD ... 223
Morgan State University ... MD ... 224
Uniformed Services University of the Health Sciences ... MD ... 558
University of Maryland Baltimore ... MD ... 227
University of Maryland College Park ... MD ... 227
Boston University ... MA ... 232
Harvard University ... MA ... 235
Tufts University ... MA ... 245
University of Massachusetts ... MA ... 237
University of Michigan-Ann Arbor ... MI ... 259
Wayne State University ... MI ... 260
University of Minnesota-Twin Cities ... MN ... 272
Jackson State University ... MS ... 275
University of Southern Mississippi ... MS ... 278
Saint Louis University ... MO ... 289
University of Missouri - Columbia ... MO ... 291
University of Nebraska at Omaha ... NE ... 301
University of Nebraska Medical Center ... NE ... 301
University of Nevada, Reno ... NV ... 303
Dartmouth College ... NH ... 305
University of New Hampshire ... NH ... 306
New Jersey Institute of Technology ... NJ ... 312
Rutgers the State University of New Jersey New Brunswick Campus ... NJ ... 314
UMDNJ-School of Public Health ... NJ ... 317
New Mexico State University Main Campus ... NM ... 319
University of New Mexico Main Campus ... NM ... 321
City University of New York Brooklyn College ... NY ... 326
City University of New York Graduate Center ... NY ... 327
City University of New York Herbert H. Lehman College ... NY ... 327
City University of New York Hunter College ... NY ... 327
Columbia University in the City of New York ... NY ... 330
Mount Sinai School of Medicine ... NY ... 342
New York Medical College ... NY ... 343
New York University ... NY ... 344
State University of New York at Albany ... NY ... 351
State University of New York at Buffalo ... NY ... 351
State University of New York at Stony Brook ... NY ... 352
State University of New York Health Science Center at Brooklyn ... NY ... 352
University of Rochester ... NY ... 358
East Carolina University ... NC ... 377
University of North Carolina at Chapel Hill ... NC ... 378
University of North Carolina at Charlotte ... NC ... 378
University of North Carolina at Greensboro ... NC ... 379
Bowling Green State University ... OH ... 385
Case Western Reserve University ... OH ... 386
Cleveland State University ... OH ... 388
Northeastern Ohio Universities Colleges of Medicine and Pharmacy ... OH ... 397
Ohio State University Main Campus, The ... OH ... 398
Ohio University Main Campus ... OH ... 399
University of Akron, Main Campus, The ... OH ... 403
University of Toledo ... OH ... 404
Wright State University Main Campus ... OH ... 406
University of Oklahoma Health Sciences Center ... OK ... 413
Oregon Health & Science University ... OR ... 418
Oregon State University ... OR ... 418
Portland State University ... OR ... 418
Drexel University ... PA ... 427
East Stroudsburg University of Pennsylvania ... PA ... 442
Temple University ... PA ... 447
Thomas Jefferson University ... PA ... 448
University of Pennsylvania ... PA ... 448
University of Pittsburgh ... PA ... 449
West Chester University of Pennsylvania ... PA ... 443
University of Puerto Rico-Medical Sciences Campus ... PR ... 567
Brown University ... RI ... 452
University of South Carolina Columbia ... SC ... 462
East Tennessee State University ... TN ... 473
Meharry Medical College ... TN ... 471
University of Tennessee, Knoxville ... TN ... 477
Vanderbilt University ... TN ... 477
Texas A & M University ... TX ... 497
University of North Texas Health Science Center at Fort Worth ... TX ... 504
University of Texas Health Science Center at Houston (UTHealth), The ... TX ... 506
University of Texas Medical Branch, The ... TX ... 507
Brigham Young University ... UT ... 509
University of Utah, The ... UT ... 510
Eastern Virginia Medical School ... VA ... 518
Old Dominion University ... VA ... 521
University of Virginia ... VA ... 525
Virginia Commonwealth University ... VA ... 525
University of Washington ... WA ... 538
West Virginia University ... WV ... 544
Medical College of Wisconsin ... WI ... 548
University of Wisconsin-La Crosse ... WI ... 551
University of Wisconsin-Madison ... WI ... 550

PHAR: Accreditation Council for Pharmaceutical Education: pharmacy (FP)

Auburn University ... AL ... 1
Samford University ... AL ... 6
Midwestern University ... AZ ... 16
University of Arizona ... AZ ... 19
@Harding University Main Campus ... AR ... 21
University of Arkansas for Medical Sciences ... AR ... 24
@California Northstate College of Pharmacy ... CA ... 33
Loma Linda University ... CA ... 54
Touro University-California ... CA ... 72
University of California-San Diego ... CA ... 74
University of California-San Francisco ... CA ... 74
University of Southern California ... CA ... 76
University of the Pacific ... CA ... 75
Western University of Health Sciences ... CA ... 78
@Regis University ... CO ... 87
University of Colorado Denver|Anschutz Medical Campus ... CO ... 8[illegible]
@Saint Joseph College ... CT ... 9[illegible]
University of Connecticut ... CT ... 94
Howard University ... DC ... 98
Florida Agricultural and Mechanical University ... FL ... 118
Nova Southeastern University ... FL ... 114
Palm Beach Atlantic University ... FL ... 114
University of Florida ... FL ... 120
@University of South Florida ... FL ... 120
Mercer University ... GA ... 133
South University ... GA ... 136
University of Georgia ... GA ... 138
University of Hawaii at Hilo ... HI ... 141
Idaho State University ... ID ... 143
@Chicago State University ... IL ... 146
Midwestern University ... IL ... 158
@Roosevelt University ... IL ... 162
@Rosalind Franklin University of Medicine & Science ... IL ... 163
Southern Illinois University Edwardsville ... IL ... 165
University of Illinois at Chicago ... IL ... 166
Butler University ... IN ... 170
Purdue University Main Campus ... IN ... 178
Drake University ... IA ... 184
University of Iowa ... IA ... 182
University of Kansas Main Campus ... KS ... 196
Sullivan University ... KY ... 206
University of Kentucky ... KY ... 206
University of Louisiana at Monroe ... LA ... 216
Xavier University of Louisiana ... LA ... 217
@Husson University ... ME ... 218
@University of New England ... ME ... 220
@Notre Dame of Maryland University ... MD ... 225
University of Maryland Baltimore ... MD ... 227
@University of Maryland Eastern Shore ... MD ... 227
Massachusetts College of Pharmacy and Health Sciences ... MA ... 241
Northeastern University ... MA ... 244
@Western New England University ... MA ... 246
Ferris State University ... MI ... 251
University of Michigan-Ann Arbor ... MI ... 259
Wayne State University ... MI ... 260
University of Minnesota-Twin Cities ... MN ... 272
University of Mississippi ... MS ... 277
St. Louis College of Pharmacy ... MO ... 288
University of Missouri - Kansas City ... MO ... 291
University of Montana - Missoula, The ... MT ... 295
Creighton University ... NE ... 297
University of Nebraska Medical Center ... NE ... 301
Roseman University of Health Sciences ... NV ... 303
Rutgers the State University of New Jersey New Brunswick Campus ... NJ ... 314
University of New Mexico Main Campus ... NM ... 321
Albany College of Pharmacy and Health Sciences ... NY ... 322
@D'Youville College ... NY ... 332
Long Island University Brooklyn Campus ... NY ... 338
St. John Fisher College ... NY ... 348
St. John's University ... NY ... 348
State University of New York at Buffalo ... NY ... 351
@Touro College ... NY ... 357
Campbell University ... NC ... 362
University of North Carolina at Chapel Hill ... NC ... 378
Wingate University ... NC ... 380
North Dakota State University Main Campus ... ND ... 381
Northeastern Ohio Universities Colleges of Medicine and Pharmacy ... OH ... 397
Ohio Northern University ... OH ... 398
Ohio State University Main Campus, The ... OH ... 398
University of Cincinnati Main Campus ... OH ... 403
University of Findlay, The ... OH ... 404
University of Toledo ... OH ... 404
Southwestern Oklahoma State University ... OK ... 412
University of Oklahoma Health Sciences Center ... OK ... 413
Oregon State University ... OR ... 418
Pacific University ... OR ... 419
Duquesne University ... PA ... 428
Lake Erie College of Osteopathic Medicine ... PA ... 433
@Philadelphia College of Osteopathic Medicine ... PA ... 444
Temple University ... PA ... 447
@Thomas Jefferson University ... PA ... 448
University of Pittsburgh ... PA ... 449
University of the Sciences in Philadelphia ... PA ... 450
Wilkes University ... PA ... 451
University of Puerto Rico-Medical Sciences Campus ... PR ... 567
University of Rhode Island ... RI ... 454
Medical University of South Carolina ... SC ... 459
@Presbyterian College ... SC ... 460
South Dakota State University ... SD ... 466
@Belmont University ... TN ... 467
East Tennessee State University ... TN ... 473
@Lipscomb University ... TN ... 470
@Union University ... TN ... 476
University of Tennessee Health Science Center ... TN ... 477
Texas A & M University - Kingsville ... TX ... 498
Texas Southern University ... TX ... 499
Texas Tech University Health Sciences Center ... TX ... 501
University of Houston ... TX ... 503
University of Texas at Austin ... TX ... 505
University of the Incarnate Word ... TX ... 503
University of Utah, The ... UT ... 510

ppalachian College of Pharmacy ... VA ... 515
ampton University ... VA ... 519
henandoah University ... VA ... 523
irginia Commonwealth University ... VA ... 525
niversity of Washington ... WA ... 538
Vashington State University ... WA ... 539
niversity of Charleston ... WV ... 541
Vest Virginia University ... WV ... 544
oncordia University Wisconsin ... WI ... 546
Jniversity of Wisconsin-Madison ... WI ... 550
niversity of Wyoming ... WY ... 556

PLNG: Planning Accreditation Board: certified planning (B,M)

Alabama Agricultural and Mechanical University ... AL ... 1
Auburn University ... AL ... 1
Arizona State University ... AZ ... 12
University of Arizona ... AZ ... 19
California Polytechnic State University-San Luis Obispo ... CA ... 33
California State Polytechnic University-Pomona ... CA ... 33
San Jose State University ... CA ... 37
University of California-Berkeley ... CA ... 73
University of California-Irvine ... CA ... 73
University of California-Los Angeles ... CA ... 74
University of Southern California ... CA ... 76
University of Colorado Denver|Anschutz Medical Campus ... CO ... 88
Florida Atlantic University ... FL ... 118
Florida State University ... FL ... 119
University of Florida ... FL ... 120
Georgia Institute of Technology ... GA ... 130
University of Hawaii at Manoa ... HI ... 141
University of Illinois at Chicago ... IL ... 166
University of Illinois at Urbana-Champaign ... IL ... 167
Ball State University ... IN ... 169
Iowa State University ... IA ... 182
University of Iowa ... IA ... 182
Kansas State University ... KS ... 194
University of Kansas Main Campus ... KS ... 196
University of Louisville ... KY ... 207
University of New Orleans ... LA ... 213
Morgan State University ... MD ... 224
University of Maryland College Park ... MD ... 227
Harvard University ... MA ... 235
Massachusetts Institute of Technology ... MA ... 242
Tufts University ... MA ... 245
University of Massachusetts ... MA ... 237
Eastern Michigan University ... MI ... 250
Michigan State University ... MI ... 255
University of Michigan-Ann Arbor ... MI ... 259
Wayne State University ... MI ... 260
University of Minnesota-Twin Cities ... MN ... 272
Jackson State University ... MS ... 275
Missouri State University ... MO ... 286
University of Nebraska - Lincoln ... NE ... 300
Rutgers the State University of New Jersey New Brunswick Campus ... NJ ... 314
University of New Mexico Main Campus ... NM ... 321
City University of New York Hunter College ... NY ... 327
Columbia University in the City of New York ... NY ... 330
Cornell University ... NY ... 331
New York University ... NY ... 344
Pratt Institute ... NY ... 346
State University of New York at Albany ... NY ... 351
State University of New York at Buffalo ... NY ... 351
East Carolina University ... NC ... 377
University of North Carolina at Chapel Hill ... NC ... 378
Cleveland State University ... OH ... 388
Ohio State University Main Campus, The ... OH ... 398
University of Cincinnati Main Campus ... OH ... 403
University of Oklahoma Norman Campus ... OK ... 413
Portland State University ... OR ... 418
University of Oregon ... OR ... 419
University of Puerto Rico-Rio Piedras Campus ... PR ... 567
Clemson University ... SC ... 456
University of Memphis, The ... TN ... 474
Texas A & M University ... TX ... 497
Texas Southern University ... TX ... 499
University of Texas at Arlington, The ... TX ... 505
University of Texas at Austin ... TX ... 505
University of Utah, The ... UT ... 510
University of Virginia ... VA ... 525
Virginia Commonwealth University ... VA ... 525
Virginia Polytechnic Institute and State University ... VA ... 529
Eastern Washington University ... WA ... 533
University of Washington ... WA ... 538
University of Wisconsin-Madison ... WI ... 550
University of Wisconsin-Milwaukee ... WI ... 551

PNUR: National League for Nursing: practical nursing (C)

Bevill State Community College ... AL ... 2
Bishop State Community College ... AL ... 2
Calhoun Community College ... AL ... 2
George C. Wallace Community College - Dothan ... AL ... 4
George Corley Wallace State Community College - Selma ... AL ... 4
James H. Faulkner State Community College ... AL ... 5
Jefferson State Community College ... AL ... 5
Lawson State Community College ... AL ... 5
Northeast Alabama Community College ... AL ... 6
Shelton State Community College ... AL ... 7
Snead State Community College ... AL ... 7
Trenholm State Technical College ... AL ... 7
Front Range Community College ... CO ... 84
Pueblo Community College ... CO ... 87
Delaware Technical and Community College Terry Campus ... DE ... 96
College of Central Florida ... FL ... 103
Santa Fe College ... FL ... 117
Augusta Technical College ... GA ... 125
Columbus Technical College ... GA ... 127
Savannah Technical College ... GA ... 136
Carrington College - Boise ... ID ... 142
Carl Sandburg College ... IL ... 146
College of DuPage ... IL ... 147
Lake Land College ... IL ... 155
South Suburban College of Cook County ... IL ... 164
Ivy Tech Community College-Central Indiana ... IN ... 175
Ivy Tech Community College of Indiana-Bloomington ... IN ... 175
Ivy Tech Community College of Indiana-Columbus ... IN ... 175
Ivy Tech Community College of Indiana-East Central ... IN ... 175
Ivy Tech Community College of Indiana-Kokomo ... IN ... 176
Ivy Tech Community College of Indiana-Lafayette ... IN ... 176
Ivy Tech Community College of Indiana-North Central ... IN ... 176
Ivy Tech Community College of Indiana-Northeast ... IN ... 176
Ivy Tech Community College of Indiana-Northwest ... IN ... 176
Ivy Tech Community College of Indiana-Richmond ... IN ... 176
Ivy Tech Community College of Indiana-Southeast ... IN ... 176
Ivy Tech Community College of Indiana-Southern Indiana ... IN ... 176
Ivy Tech Community College of Indiana-Southwest ... IN ... 176
Ivy Tech Community College of Indiana-Wabash Valley ... IN ... 177
Vincennes University ... IN ... 181
Des Moines Area Community College ... IA ... 183
Western Iowa Tech Community College ... IA ... 189
Dodge City Community College ... KS ... 192
Hutchinson Community College and Area Vocational School ... KS ... 193
Wichita Area Technical College ... KS ... 197
Southeast Kentucky Community and Technical College ... KY ... 203
L.E. Fletcher Technical Community College ... LA ... 210
College of Southern Maryland ... MD ... 222
Howard Community College ... MD ... 223
Mount Wachusett Community College ... MA ... 240
Northern Essex Community College ... MA ... 241
Quincy College ... MA ... 244
Quinsigamond Community College ... MA ... 241
Davenport University ... MI ... 250
Grand Rapids Community College ... MI ... 251
Minneapolis Community and Technical College ... MN ... 267
Rochester Community and Technical College ... MN ... 269
Saint Paul College-A Community & Technical College ... MN ... 269
Meridian Community College ... MS ... 275
Mississippi Delta Community College ... MS ... 275
Mississippi Gulf Coast Community College ... MS ... 275
Metropolitan Community College - Penn Valley ... MO ... 285
Southeast Community College ... NE ... 300
Western Nebraska Community College ... NE ... 301
College of Southern Nevada ... NV ... 302
Kaplan College ... NV ... 302
NHTI-Concord's Community College ... NH ... 304
St. Joseph School of Nursing ... NH ... 306
Salem Community College ... NJ ... 315
Union County College ... NJ ... 316
Central New Mexico Community College ... NM ... 317
Farmingdale State College ... NY ... 356
Suffolk County Community College Ammerman Campus ... NY ... 356
Trocaire College ... NY ... 358
Durham Technical Community College ... NC ... 369
Wayne Community College ... NC ... 374
Dickinson State University ... ND ... 381
North Dakota State College of Science ... ND ... 382
United Tribes Technical College ... ND ... 383
Hocking College ... OH ... 392
Lorain County Community College ... OH ... 395
Harrisburg Area Community College ... PA ... 430
Lehigh Carbon Community College ... PA ... 434
Northampton Community College ... PA ... 437
Pennsylvania College of Technology ... PA ... 440
Reading Area Community College ... PA ... 445
Community College of Rhode Island ... RI ... 453
Central Carolina Technical College ... SC ... 455
Greenville Technical College ... SC ... 458
Horry-Georgetown Technical College ... SC ... 458
Midlands Technical College ... SC ... 459
Orangeburg-Calhoun Technical College ... SC ... 460
Technical College of the Lowcountry ... SC ... 461
Tri-County Technical College ... SC ... 461
Trident Technical College ... SC ... 461
University of South Carolina Lancaster ... SC ... 462
York Technical College ... SC ... 463
Lake Area Technical Institute ... SD ... 464
Austin Community College District ... TX ... 481
Cisco Junior College ... TX ... 482
El Centro College ... TX ... 484
Dixie State College of Utah ... UT ... 512
Ogden-Weber Applied Technology College ... UT ... 510
Snow College ... UT ... 512
Uintah Basin Applied Technology College ... UT ... 510
Utah State University-College of Eastern Utah ... UT ... 511
Weber State University ... UT ... 511
Vermont Technical College ... VT ... 515
Chippewa Valley Technical College ... WI ... 553
Milwaukee Area Technical College ... WI ... 554

POD: American Podiatric Medical Association: podiatry (FP)

Midwestern University ... AZ ... 16
Samuel Merritt University ... CA ... 64
@Western University of Health Sciences ... CA ... 78
Barry University ... FL ... 101
Rosalind Franklin University of Medicine & Science ... IL ... 163
Des Moines University ... IA ... 183
New York College of Podiatric Medicine ... NY ... 343
Ohio College of Podiatric Medicine ... OH ... 398
Temple University ... PA ... 447

POLYT: Commission on Accreditation of Allied Health Education Programs: polysomnographic technologist education (C,A)

Wallace State Community College - Hanceville ... AL ... 10
Orange Coast College ... CA ... 41
Central Florida Institute ... FL ... 102
Moraine Valley Community College ... IL ... 159
Mercy College of Health Sciences ... IA ... 187
Johnson County Community College ... KS ... 193
Bluegrass Community and Technical College ... KY ... 201
Bowling Green Technical College ... KY ... 201
West Kentucky Community and Technical College ... KY ... 203
Community College of Baltimore County, The ... MD ... 222
Northern Essex Community College ... MA ... 241
Baker College of Flint ... MI ... 248
Minneapolis Community and Technical College ... MN ... 267
Coahoma Community College ... MS ... 273
Sanford-Brown College ... MO ... 289
Southeast Community College ... NE ... 300
State University of New York at Stony Brook ... NY ... 352
Catawba Valley Community College ... NC ... 368
Central Carolina Community College ... NC ... 368
Lenoir Community College ... NC ... 371
Pitt Community College ... NC ... 372
Sandhills Community College ... NC ... 373
Cuyahoga Community College ... OH ... 389
Mercy College of Ohio ... OH ... 395
Oregon Institute of Technology ... OR ... 418
East Tennessee State University ... TN ... 473
Miller-Motte Technical College ... TN ... 471
Roane State Community College ... TN ... 475
Volunteer State Community College ... TN ... 476
Alvin Community College ... TX ... 479
Texas Southmost College ... TX ... 499
University of Texas at Brownsville, The ... TX ... 505
J. Sargeant Reynolds Community College ... VA ... 526
Highline Community College ... WA ... 534

PSPSY: American Psychological Association: combined professional-scientific psychology (D)

University of California-Santa Barbara ... CA ... 74
Florida State University ... FL ... 119
Northeastern University ... MA ... 244
Pace University ... NY ... 345
State University of New York at Buffalo ... NY ... 351
Yeshiva University ... NY ... 361
Utah State University ... UT ... 511
James Madison University ... VA ... 520

PTA: American Physical Therapy Association: physical therapy (M,D)

Alabama State University ... AL ... 1
University of Alabama at Birmingham ... AL ... 8
University of South Alabama ... AL ... 9
@Midwestern University ... AZ ... 16
Northern Arizona University ... AZ ... 17
Arkansas State University ... AR ... 20
@Harding University Main Campus ... AR ... 21
University of Central Arkansas ... AR ... 25
Azusa Pacific University ... CA ... 30
California State University-Fresno ... CA ... 34
California State University-Long Beach ... CA ... 35
California State University-Northridge ... CA ... 35
California State University-Sacramento ... CA ... 35
Chapman University ... CA ... 39
Loma Linda University ... CA ... 54
Mount St. Mary's College ... CA ... 57
Samuel Merritt University ... CA ... 64
San Francisco State University ... CA ... 36
University of California-San Francisco ... CA ... 74
University of Southern California ... CA ... 76
University of the Pacific ... CA ... 75
Western University of Health Sciences ... CA ... 78
Regis University ... CO ... 87
University of Colorado Denver|Anschutz Medical Campus ... CO ... 88
Quinnipiac University ... CT ... 93
Sacred Heart University ... CT ... 93
University of Connecticut ... CT ... 94
University of Hartford ... CT ... 95
University of Delaware ... DE ... 96
George Washington University ... DC ... 97
Howard University ... DC ... 98
Florida Agricultural and Mechanical University ... FL ... 118
Florida Gulf Coast University ... FL ... 119
Florida International University ... FL ... 119
Nova Southeastern University ... FL ... 114
University of Central Florida ... FL ... 120
University of Florida ... FL ... 120
University of Miami ... FL ... 122
University of North Florida ... FL ... 120
University of St. Augustine for Health Sciences ... FL ... 122
University of South Florida ... FL ... 120
Armstrong Atlantic State University ... GA ... 124
Emory University ... GA ... 129
Georgia Health Sciences University ... GA ... 130
Georgia State University ... GA ... 131
@Mercer University ... GA ... 133
North Georgia College & State University ... GA ... 134
Idaho State University ... ID ... 143
Bradley University ... IL ... 145
Governors State University ... IL ... 151
Midwestern University ... IL ... 158
Northern Illinois University ... IL ... 160
Northwestern University ... IL ... 160
Rosalind Franklin University of Medicine & Science ... IL ... 163
University of Illinois at Chicago ... IL ... 166
Indiana University-Purdue University Indianapolis ... IN ... 174
University of Evansville ... IN ... 180
University of Indianapolis ... IN ... 180
Clarke University ... IA ... 183
Des Moines University ... IA ... 183
St. Ambrose University ... IA ... 188
University of Iowa ... IA ... 182
University of Kansas Medical Center ... KS ... 197
Wichita State University ... KS ... 197
Bellarmine University ... KY ... 198
University of Kentucky ... KY ... 206
Louisiana State University Health Sciences Center at Shreveport ... LA ... 213
Louisiana State University Health Sciences Center-New Orleans ... LA ... 213
Husson University ... ME ... 218
University of New England ... ME ... 220
University of Maryland Baltimore ... MD ... 227
University of Maryland Eastern Shore ... MD ... 227
American International College ... MA ... 229
Boston University ... MA ... 232
@Massachusetts College of Pharmacy and Health Sciences ... MA ... 241
MGH Institute of Health Professions ... MA ... 242
Northeastern University ... MA ... 244
Simmons College ... MA ... 245
Springfield College ... MA ... 245
University of Massachusetts Lowell ... MA ... 237
Andrews University ... MI ... 247
Central Michigan University ... MI ... 249
Grand Valley State University ... MI ... 252
Oakland University ... MI ... 257
University of Michigan-Flint ... MI ... 259
Wayne State University ... MI ... 260
College of Saint Scholastica, The ... MN ... 262
Mayo School of Health Sciences ... MN ... 262
St. Catherine University ... MN ... 271
University of Minnesota-Twin Cities ... MN ... 272
University of Mississippi Medical Center ... MS ... 277
Maryville University of Saint Louis ... MO ... 284
Missouri State University ... MO ... 286
Rockhurst University ... MO ... 288
Saint Louis University ... MO ... 289
Southwest Baptist University ... MO ... 290
University of Missouri - Columbia ... MO ... 291
Washington University in St. Louis ... MO ... 292
University of Montana - Missoula, The ... MT ... 295
Creighton University ... NE ... 297
University of Nebraska Medical Center ... NE ... 301
University of Nevada, Las Vegas ... NV ... 302
Franklin Pierce University ... NH ... 305
Richard Stockton College of New Jersey, The ... NJ ... 313
Rutgers the State University of New Jersey Camden Campus ... NJ ... 314
Seton Hall University ... NJ ... 315
UMDNJ-School of Health Related Professions ... NJ ... 317
University of New Mexico Main Campus ... NM ... 321
City University of New York College of Staten Island ... NY ... 327
City University of New York Hunter College ... NY ... 327
Clarkson University ... NY ... 329
Columbia University in the City of New York ... NY ... 330
Daemen College ... NY ... 331

Dominican College of Blauvelt ... NY ... 332
D'Youville College ... NY ... 332
Ithaca College ... NY ... 336
Long Island University Brooklyn Campus ... NY ... 338
Mercy College ... NY ... 340
Nazareth College of Rochester ... NY ... 342
New York Institute of Technology ... NY ... 343
New York Medical College ... NY ... 343
New York University ... NY ... 344
Sage Colleges, The ... NY ... 348
State University of New York at Buffalo ... NY ... 351
State University of New York at Stony Brook NY ... 352
State University of New York Health Science Center at Brooklyn ... NY ... 352
State University of New York Upstate Medical University ... NY ... 352
Touro College ... NY ... 357
Utica College ... NY ... 359
Duke University ... NC ... 363
East Carolina University ... NC ... 377
Elon University ... NC ... 364
University of North Carolina at Chapel Hill ... NC ... 378
Western Carolina University ... NC ... 379
Winston-Salem State University ... NC ... 380
University of Mary ... ND ... 383
University of North Dakota Main Campus ... ND ... 381
Cleveland State University ... OH ... 388
College of Mount St. Joseph ... OH ... 388
Ohio State University Main Campus, The ... OH ... 398
Ohio University Main Campus ... OH ... 399
University of Cincinnati Main Campus ... OH ... 403
University of Dayton ... OH ... 404
University of Findlay, The ... OH ... 404
University of Toledo ... OH ... 404
Walsh University ... OH ... 405
Youngstown State University ... OH ... 406
Langston University ... OK ... 408
University of Oklahoma Health Sciences Center ... OK ... 413
Pacific University ... OR ... 419
Arcadia University ... PA ... 422
Chatham University ... PA ... 425
Drexel University ... PA ... 427
Duquesne University ... PA ... 428
Gannon University ... PA ... 429
Lebanon Valley College ... PA ... 434
Misericordia University ... PA ... 436
Neumann University ... PA ... 437
Saint Francis University ... PA ... 446
Slippery Rock University of Pennsylvania ... PA ... 443
Temple University ... PA ... 447
Thomas Jefferson University ... PA ... 448
University of Pittsburgh ... PA ... 449
University of Scranton, The ... PA ... 450
University of the Sciences in Philadelphia ... PA ... 450
Widener University ... PA ... 451
University of Puerto Rico-Medical Sciences Campus ... PR ... 567
University of Rhode Island ... RI ... 454
Medical University of South Carolina ... SC ... 459
University of South Carolina Columbia ... SC ... 462
University of South Dakota, The ... SD ... 465
Belmont University ... TN ... 467
East Tennessee State University ... TN ... 473
Tennessee State University ... TN ... 474
University of Tennessee at Chattanooga ... TN ... 477
University of Tennessee Health Science Center ... TN ... 477
Angelo State University ... TX ... 480
Baylor University ... TX ... 481
Hardin-Simmons University ... TX ... 487
Texas State University-San Marcos ... TX ... 501
Texas Tech University Health Sciences Center ... TX ... 501
Texas Woman's University ... TX ... 502
@University of North Texas Health Science Center at Fort Worth ... TX ... 504
University of Texas at El Paso ... TX ... 505
University of Texas Health Science Center at San Antonio ... TX ... 506
University of Texas Medical Branch, The ... TX ... 507
University of Texas Southwestern Medical Center at Dallas ... TX ... 507
@Rocky Mountain University of Health Professions ... UT ... 510
University of Utah, The ... UT ... 510
University of Vermont ... VT ... 514
Hampton University ... VA ... 519
@Lynchburg College ... VA ... 520
Marymount University ... VA ... 521
Old Dominion University ... VA ... 521
@Radford University ... VA ... 522
Shenandoah University ... VA ... 523
Virginia Commonwealth University ... VA ... 525
Eastern Washington University ... WA ... 533
University of Puget Sound ... WA ... 538
University of Washington ... WA ... 538
West Virginia University ... WV ... 544
Wheeling Jesuit University ... WV ... 545
Carroll University ... WI ... 546
Concordia University Wisconsin ... WI ... 546
Marquette University ... WI ... 548
University of Wisconsin-La Crosse ... WI ... 551
University of Wisconsin-Madison ... WI ... 550
University of Wisconsin-Milwaukee ... WI ... 551

PTAA: American Physical Therapy Association: physical therapy assistant (A)

Bishop State Community College ... AL ... 2
Calhoun Community College ... AL ... 2
Community College of the Air Force ... AL ... 557
George C. Wallace Community College - Dothan ... AL ... 4
Jefferson State Community College ... AL ... 5
South University ... AL ... 7
Wallace State Community College - Hanceville ... AL ... 10
@Brookline College ... AZ ... 12
Carrington College - Mesa ... AZ ... 13
Gateway Community College ... AZ ... 15
Mohave Community College ... AZ ... 16
Pima Medical Institute-Mesa ... AZ ... 18
Pima Medical Institute-Tucson ... AZ ... 18
Arkansas State University ... AR ... 20
Arkansas Tech University ... AR ... 20
NorthWest Arkansas Community College ... AR ... 22
South Arkansas Community College ... AR ... 23
@Carrington College California - Pleasant Hill CA ... 38
Cerritos College ... CA ... 38
@College of the Sequoias ... CA ... 42
@Concorde Career College ... CA ... 42
Concorde Career College ... CA ... 42
@Concorde Career College ... CA ... 42
Loma Linda University ... CA ... 54
Ohlone College ... CA ... 59
Sacramento City College ... CA ... 56
#San Diego Mesa College ... CA ... 65
Arapahoe Community College ... CO ... 80
@Concorde Career College ... CO ... 83
Morgan Community College ... CO ... 86
Pima Medical Institute-Denver ... CO ... 86
Pueblo Community College ... CO ... 87
Capital Community College ... CT ... 89
Housatonic Community College ... CT ... 90
Manchester Community College ... CT ... 90
Naugatuck Valley Community College ... CT ... 90
Northwestern Connecticut Community-Technical College ... CT ... 90
Norwalk Community College ... CT ... 90
Tunxis Community College ... CT ... 91
Delaware Technical and Community College Owens Campus ... DE ... 96
Delaware Technical and Community College Stanton-Wilmington Campus ... DE ... 96
Broward College ... FL ... 102
College of Central Florida ... FL ... 103
@Concorde Career Institute ... FL ... 103
Daytona State College ... FL ... 103
Florida Gateway College ... FL ... 108
Florida State College at Jacksonville ... FL ... 109
Gulf Coast State College ... FL ... 110
Herzing University ... FL ... 110
Indian River State College ... FL ... 110
Keiser University ... FL ... 112
Miami Dade College ... FL ... 113
Pensacola State College ... FL ... 114
Polk State College ... FL ... 115
St. Petersburg College ... FL ... 116
Seminole State College of Florida ... FL ... 117
South University ... FL ... 117
State College of Florida, Manatee-Sarasota . FL ... 118
Athens Technical College ... GA ... 124
Chattahoochee Technical College ... GA ... 126
Darton College ... GA ... 128
South University ... GA ... 136
Kapiolani Community College ... HI ... 141
@Carrington College - Boise ... ID ... 142
Idaho State University ... ID ... 143
Black Hawk College ... IL ... 145
College of DuPage ... IL ... 147
Elgin Community College ... IL ... 150
Fox College ... IL ... 151
Illinois Central College ... IL ... 152
Kankakee Community College ... IL ... 154
Kaskaskia College ... IL ... 155
Lake Land College ... IL ... 155
Morton College ... IL ... 159
Oakton Community College ... IL ... 160
Southern Illinois University Carbondale ... IL ... 164
Southwestern Illinois College ... IL ... 165
#Brown Mackie College-Fort Wayne ... IN ... 169
Brown Mackie College-South Bend ... IN ... 170
Ivy Tech Community College of Indiana-East Central ... IN ... 175
Ivy Tech Community College of Indiana-Northwest ... IN ... 176
University of Evansville ... IN ... 180
University of Indianapolis ... IN ... 180
University of Saint Francis ... IN ... 180
Vincennes University ... IN ... 181
@Hawkeye Community College ... IA ... 185
Indian Hills Community College ... IA ... 185
Kirkwood Community College ... IA ... 186
Mercy College of Health Sciences ... IA ... 187
North Iowa Area Community College ... IA ... 187
Western Iowa Tech Community College ... IA ... 189
Colby Community College ... KS ... 191
Hutchinson Community College and Area Vocational School ... KS ... 193
Kansas City Kansas Community College ... KS ... 193
@Labette Community College ... KS ... 194
Washburn University ... KS ... 197
Hazard Community and Technical College ... KY ... 201
Jefferson Community and Technical College KY ... 202
Madisonville Community College ... KY ... 202
Somerset Community College ... KY ... 202
Southeast Kentucky Community and Technical College ... KY ... 203
West Kentucky Community and Technical College ... KY ... 203
Bossier Parish Community College ... LA ... 209
Delgado Community College ... LA ... 210
Louisiana College ... LA ... 209
Our Lady of the Lake College ... LA ... 214
Kennebec Valley Community College ... ME ... 218
Allegany College of Maryland ... MD ... 221
Anne Arundel Community College ... MD ... 221
Baltimore City Community College ... MD ... 221
Carroll Community College ... MD ... 221
Chesapeake College ... MD ... 222
College of Southern Maryland ... MD ... 222
Montgomery College ... MD ... 224
Bay State College ... MA ... 231
Berkshire Community College ... MA ... 239
Mount Wachusett Community College ... MA ... 240
North Shore Community College ... MA ... 241
Springfield Technical Community College ... MA ... 241
Baker College of Allen Park ... MI ... 248
Baker College of Flint ... MI ... 248
Baker College of Muskegon ... MI ... 248
Delta College ... MI ... 250
Finlandia University ... MI ... 251
Henry Ford Community College ... MI ... 252
Kellogg Community College ... MI ... 253
Macomb Community College ... MI ... 254
Mid Michigan Community College ... MI ... 255
Mott Community College ... MI ... 256
Washtenaw Community College ... MI ... 260
Anoka-Ramsey Community College ... MN ... 265
Lake Superior College ... MN ... 267
Northland Community and Technical College MN ... 268
St. Catherine University ... MN ... 271
Hinds Community College ... MS ... 274
Itawamba Community College ... MS ... 274
Meridian Community College ... MS ... 275
Pearl River Community College ... MS ... 277
@Concorde Career College ... MO ... 280
Linn State Technical College ... MO ... 284
Metropolitan Community College - Penn Valley ... MO ... 285
@Mineral Area College ... MO ... 286
Missouri Western State University ... MO ... 287
Ozarks Technical Community College ... MO ... 287
Saint Louis Community College at Meramec MO ... 289
Clarkson College ... NE ... 297
Nebraska Methodist College ... NE ... 299
Northeast Community College ... NE ... 300
Southeast Community College ... NE ... 300
College of Southern Nevada ... NV ... 302
Hesser College ... NH ... 305
River Valley Community College ... NH ... 304
Essex County College ... NJ ... 310
Mercer County Community College ... NJ ... 311
Union County College ... NJ ... 316
@Carrington College - Albuquerque ... NM ... 317
Pima Medical Institute-Albuquerque ... NM ... 320
San Juan College ... NM ... 320
Broome Community College ... NY ... 324
City University of New York Kingsborough Community College ... NY ... 328
Genesee Community College ... NY ... 334
Herkimer County Community College ... NY ... 335
La Guardia Community College/City University of New York ... NY ... 328
Nassau Community College ... NY ... 342
Niagara County Community College ... NY ... 344
Onondaga Community College ... NY ... 345
Orange County Community College ... NY ... 345
Suffolk County Community College Ammerman Campus ... NY ... 356
SUNY Canton-College of Technology ... NY ... 355
Villa Maria College of Buffalo ... NY ... 359
Caldwell Community College and Technical Institute ... NC ... 368
Central Piedmont Community College ... NC ... 369
@Craven Community College ... NC ... 369
Fayetteville Technical Community College ... NC ... 370
Guilford Technical Community College ... NC ... 370
Martin Community College ... NC ... 371
Nash Community College ... NC ... 372
South College ... NC ... 376
Southwestern Community College ... NC ... 373
Surry Community College ... NC ... 374
Clark State Community College ... OH ... 387
Cuyahoga Community College ... OH ... 389
Edison State Community College ... OH ... 390
Hocking College ... OH ... 392
James A. Rhodes State College ... OH ... 392
Kent State University Ashtabula Campus ... OH ... 393
Kent State University East Liverpool Campus ... OH ... 393
Lorain County Community College ... OH ... 395
Marion Technical College ... OH ... 395
North Central State College ... OH ... 397
Owens Community College ... OH ... 400
Professional Skills Institute ... OH ... 401
Shawnee State University ... OH ... 401
Sinclair Community College ... OH ... 401
Stark State College ... OH ... 402
University of Cincinnati Main Campus ... OH ... 403
Washington State Community College ... OH ... 405
Zane State College ... OH ... 407
Carl Albert State College ... OK ... 407
Murray State College ... OK ... 408
Northeastern Oklahoma Agricultural and Mechanical College ... OK ... 408
Oklahoma City Community College ... OK ... 409
Southwestern Oklahoma State University ... OK ... 412
Tulsa Community College ... OK ... 412
@Lane Community College ... OR ... 416
Mt. Hood Community College ... OR ... 417
Butler County Community College ... PA ... 423
California University of Pennsylvania ... PA ... 441
Central Pennsylvania College ... PA ... 425
Community College of Allegheny County ... PA ... 425
Harcum College ... PA ... 430
@Lackawanna College ... PA ... 433
Lehigh Carbon Community College ... PA ... 434
Mercyhurst College ... PA ... 436
Mount Aloysius College ... PA ... 437
#Penn State DuBois ... PA ... 439
@Penn State Fayette, The Eberly Campus ... PA ... 439
Penn State Hazleton ... PA ... 439
Penn State Mont Alto ... PA ... 440
Penn State Shenango ... PA ... 440
University of Pittsburgh at Titusville ... PA ... 449
@Inter American University of Puerto Rico Ponce Campus ... PR ... 563
University of Puerto Rico at Ponce ... PR ... 567
University of Puerto Rico-Humacao ... PR ... 567
Community College of Rhode Island ... RI ... 453
New England Institute of Technology ... RI ... 453
Greenville Technical College ... SC ... 458
Horry-Georgetown Technical College ... SC ... 458
Midlands Technical College ... SC ... 459
Technical College of the Lowcountry ... SC ... 461
Trident Technical College ... SC ... 461
Lake Area Technical Institute ... SD ... 464
Chattanooga State Community College ... TN ... 474
@Concorde Career College ... TN ... 467
@Daymar Institute ... TN ... 468
Jackson State Community College ... TN ... 475
Roane State Community College ... TN ... 475
South College ... TN ... 472
Southwest Tennessee Community College .. TN ... 475
Volunteer State Community College ... TN ... 476
Walters State Community College ... TN ... 476
Amarillo College ... TX ... 479
Austin Community College District ... TX ... 481
Blinn College ... TX ... 482
Del Mar College ... TX ... 485
El Paso Community College ... TX ... 486
Houston Community College ... TX ... 487
Kilgore College ... TX ... 489
Laredo Community College ... TX ... 489
Lone Star College System ... TX ... 490
McLennan Community College ... TX ... 490
Northeast Texas Community College ... TX ... 491
Odessa College ... TX ... 491
St. Philip's College ... TX ... 479
San Jacinto College South ... TX ... 493
@South Plains College ... TX ... 494
South Texas College ... TX ... 494
Tarrant County College District ... TX ... 496
@Victoria College ... TX ... 507
Western Technical College ... TX ... 508
Wharton County Junior College ... TX ... 508
@Dixie State College of Utah ... UT ... 512
Provo College ... UT ... 510
Salt Lake Community College ... UT ... 512
Jefferson College of Health Sciences (Formerly Community Hospital) ... VA ... 520
Medical Careers Institute ... VA ... 521
Northern Virginia Community College ... VA ... 527
Tidewater Community College ... VA ... 528
Wytheville Community College ... VA ... 528
Green River Community College ... WA ... 534
Lake Washington Technical College ... WA ... 535
Olympic College ... WA ... 535
Pima Medical Institute-Seattle ... WA ... 536
Spokane Falls Community College ... WA ... 532
Whatcom Community College ... WA ... 539
Mountain State University ... WV ... 541
Mountwest Community and Technical College ... WV ... 542
Pierpont Community & Technical College ... WV ... 542
Blackhawk Technical College ... WI ... 553
Chippewa Valley Technical College ... WI ... 553
Gateway Technical College ... WI ... 553
@Madison Area Technical College ... WI ... 554
Milwaukee Area Technical College ... WI ... 554
Northeast Wisconsin Technical College ... WI ... 555
@Southwest Wisconsin Technical College ... WI ... 555
Western Technical College ... WI ... 555
Laramie County Community College ... WY ... 556

RABN: Association of Advanced Rabbinical and Talmudic Schools: rabbinical and Talmudic education (B, M,D)

Yeshiva Ohr Elchonon Chabad/West Coast Talmudical Seminary ... CA ... 79
Beth Benjamin Academy of Connecticut ... CT ... 89
Talmudic College of Florida ... FL ... 121
@Yeshiva Gedolah Rabbinical College ... FL ... 123
Telshe Yeshiva-Chicago ... IL ... 165
Bais HaMedrash & Mesivta of Baltimore ... MD ... 221

RAD: Joint Review Committee on Education in Radiologic Technology: radiography (C,A,B)

Shawnee State University ... OH ... 401
Sinclair Community College ... OH ... 401
University of Cincinnati-Raymond Walters College ... OH ... 403
University of Rio Grande ... OH ... 404
Xavier University ... OH ... 406
Zane State College ... OH ... 407
Bacone College ... OK ... 407
Carl Albert State College ... OK ... 407
Rose State College ... OK ... 411
Southwestern Oklahoma State University ... OK ... 412
Tulsa Community College ... OK ... 412
University of Oklahoma Health Sciences Center ... OK ... 413
Western Oklahoma State College ... OK ... 414
Portland Community College ... OR ... 419
Bucks County Community College ... PA ... 423
Community College of Allegheny County ... PA ... 425
Community College of Philadelphia ... PA ... 426
Drexel University ... PA ... 427
Fortis Institute ... PA ... 429
Gannon University ... PA ... 429
Harcum College ... PA ... 430
Harrisburg Area Community College ... PA ... 430
Holy Family University ... PA ... 430
Johnson College ... PA ... 431
Lancaster General College of Nursing and Health Sciences ... PA ... 433
Mansfield University of Pennsylvania ... PA ... 443
Misericordia University ... PA ... 436
Montgomery County Community College ... PA ... 436
Northampton Community College ... PA ... 437
Penn State New Kensington ... PA ... 440
Penn State Schuylkill ... PA ... 440
Pennsylvania College of Technology ... PA ... 440
Sanford-Brown Institute-Pittsburgh ... PA ... 446
Thomas Jefferson University ... PA ... 448
Inter American University of Puerto Rico San German Campus ... PR ... 563
Universidad Central Del Caribe ... PR ... 566
Universidad del Este ... PR ... 565
University of Puerto Rico-Medical Sciences Campus ... PR ... 567
Community College of Rhode Island ... RI ... 453
Aiken Technical College ... SC ... 455
Florence - Darlington Technical College ... SC ... 458
Greenville Technical College ... SC ... 458
Horry-Georgetown Technical College ... SC ... 458
Midlands Technical College ... SC ... 459
Orangeburg-Calhoun Technical College ... SC ... 460
Piedmont Technical College ... SC ... 460
Spartanburg Community College ... SC ... 461
Technical College of the Lowcountry ... SC ... 461
Trident Technical College ... SC ... 461
York Technical College ... SC ... 463
Mitchell Technical Institute ... SD ... 464
Presentation College ... SD ... 464
Austin Peay State University ... TN ... 473
Baptist Memorial College of Health Sciences ... TN ... 467
Chattanooga State Community College ... TN ... 474
Columbia State Community College ... TN ... 474
East Tennessee State University ... TN ... 473
Fortis Institute ... TN ... 468
Jackson State Community College ... TN ... 475
South College ... TN ... 472
Southwest Tennessee Community College ... TN ... 475
University of Tennessee, Knoxville ... TN ... 477
Volunteer State Community College ... TN ... 476
Amarillo College ... TX ... 479
Angelina College ... TX ... 480
Austin Community College District ... TX ... 481
Baptist Health System School of Health Professions ... TX ... 481
Baylor University ... TX ... 481
Blinn College ... TX ... 482
Brookhaven College ... TX ... 484
Coastal Bend College ... TX ... 482
Del Mar College ... TX ... 485
El Centro College ... TX ... 484
El Paso Community College ... TX ... 486
Galveston College ... TX ... 486
Houston Community College ... TX ... 487
Howard College ... TX ... 487
Lamar Institute of Technology ... TX ... 500
Laredo Community College ... TX ... 489
Lone Star College System ... TX ... 490
McLennan Community College ... TX ... 490
Midwestern State University ... TX ... 491
Northeast Texas Community College ... TX ... 491
Odessa College ... TX ... 491
Paris Junior College ... TX ... 492
St. Philip's College ... TX ... 479
San Jacinto College Central ... TX ... 493
Tarrant County College District ... TX ... 496
Texas Southmost College ... TX ... 499
Tyler Junior College ... TX ... 502
University of Texas at Brownsville, The ... TX ... 505
University of Texas M.D. Anderson Cancer Center, The ... TX ... 507
Weatherford College ... TX ... 508
Wharton County Junior College ... TX ... 508
Dixie State College of Utah ... UT ... 512
Salt Lake Community College ... UT ... 512
Champlain College ... VT ... 513
Southern Vermont College ... VT ... 514
Central Virginia Community College ... VA ... 526
Medical Careers Institute ... VA ... 521
Piedmont Virginia Community College ... VA ... 527
RSHT ... VA ... 523
Southwest Virginia Community College ... VA ... 528
Virginia Commonwealth University ... VA ... 525
Virginia Western Community College ... VA ... 528
Carrington College - Spokane ... WA ... 531
Pima Medical Institute-Seattle ... WA ... 536
Spokane Community College ... WA ... 532
Tacoma Community College ... WA ... 538
Bluefield State College ... WV ... 543
Mountain State University ... WV ... 541
Southern West Virginia Community and Technical College ... WV ... 542
University of Charleston ... WV ... 541
West Virginia University ... WV ... 544
Bellin College, Inc. ... WI ... 546
Blackhawk Technical College ... WI ... 553
Chippewa Valley Technical College ... WI ... 553
Lakeshore Technical College ... WI ... 554
Madison Area Technical College ... WI ... 554
Milwaukee Area Technical College ... WI ... 554
Moraine Park Technical College ... WI ... 554
Northcentral Technical College ... WI ... 554
Northeast Wisconsin Technical College ... WI ... 555
Sanford-Brown College-Milwaukee ... WI ... 550
University of Wisconsin-Madison ... WI ... 550
Western Technical College ... WI ... 555
Casper College ... WY ... 555
Laramie County Community College ... WY ... 556

RADDOS: Joint Review Committee on Education in Radiologic Technology: medical dosimetry (C,B)

University of Arkansas at Little Rock ... AR ... 24
Georgia Health Sciences University ... GA ... 130
Southern Illinois University Carbondale ... IL ... 164
Indiana University-Purdue University Indianapolis ... IN ... 174
University of Maryland Baltimore ... MD ... 227
Pitt Community College ... NC ... 372
University of North Carolina at Chapel Hill ... NC ... 378
University of Cincinnati-Raymond Walters College ... OH ... 403
University of Oklahoma Health Sciences Center ... OK ... 413
Thomas Jefferson University ... PA ... 448
University of Texas Health Science Center at San Antonio ... TX ... 506
University of Texas M.D. Anderson Cancer Center, The ... TX ... 507
Bellevue College ... WA ... 531
University of Wisconsin-La Crosse ... WI ... 551

RADMAG: Joint Review Committee on Education in Radiologic Technology: magnetic resonance (C,B)

Thomas Jefferson University ... PA ... 448
West Virginia University ... WV ... 544

RTT: Joint Review Committee on Education in Radiologic Technology: radiation therapist/technologist (C,A,B)

University of Alabama at Birmingham ... AL ... 8
University of South Alabama ... AL ... 9
Gateway Community College ... AZ ... 15
Arkansas State University ... AR ... 20
California State University-Long Beach ... CA ... 35
City College of San Francisco ... CA ... 39
Loma Linda University ... CA ... 54
Gateway Community College ... CT ... 90
Howard University ... DC ... 98
Cambridge Institute of Allied Health & Technology ... FL ... 102
Hillsborough Community College ... FL ... 110
Armstrong Atlantic State University ... GA ... 124
Georgia Health Sciences University ... GA ... 130
Georgia Northwestern Technical College ... GA ... 130
Southern Illinois University Carbondale ... IL ... 164
Indiana University Northwest ... IN ... 173
Indiana University-Purdue University Indianapolis ... IN ... 174
Ivy Tech Community College of Indiana-Bloomington ... IN ... 175
University of Iowa ... IA ... 182
University of Louisville ... KY ... 207
Delgado Community College ... LA ... 210
Southern Maine Community College ... ME ... 219
Laboure College ... MA ... 236
Massachusetts College of Pharmacy and Health Sciences ... MA ... 241
Suffolk University ... MA ... 245
University of Massachusetts at Worcester ... MA ... 238
Baker College of Jackson ... MI ... 248
Grand Valley State University ... MI ... 252
University of Michigan-Flint ... MI ... 259
Wayne State University ... MI ... 260
Argosy University, Twin Cities ... MN ... 261
Mayo School of Health Sciences ... MN ... 262
University of Minnesota-Twin Cities ... MN ... 272
Saint Louis University ... MO ... 289
University of Nebraska Medical Center ... NE ... 301
College of Southern Nevada ... NV ... 302
NHTI-Concord's Community College ... NH ... 304
Bergen Community College ... NJ ... 307
Erie Community College City Campus ... NY ... 333
Nassau Community College ... NY ... 342
State University of New York Upstate Medical University ... NY ... 352
Forsyth Technical Community College ... NC ... 370
Pitt Community College ... NC ... 372
University of North Carolina at Chapel Hill ... NC ... 378
Kent State University Salem Campus ... OH ... 393
Ohio State University Main Campus, The ... OH ... 398
University of Cincinnati-Raymond Walters College ... OH ... 403
University of Oklahoma Health Sciences Center ... OK ... 413
Oregon Health & Science University ... OR ... 418
Community College of Allegheny County ... PA ... 425
Gwynedd-Mercy College ... PA ... 430
Thomas Jefferson University ... PA ... 448
Baptist Memorial College of Health Sciences ... TN ... 467
Chattanooga State Community College ... TN ... 474
Vanderbilt University ... TN ... 477
Amarillo College ... TX ... 479
Galveston College ... TX ... 486
Texas State University-San Marcos ... TX ... 501
University of Texas M.D. Anderson Cancer Center, The ... TX ... 507
University of Texas Southwestern Medical Center at Dallas ... TX ... 507
University of Virginia ... VA ... 525
Virginia Commonwealth University ... VA ... 525
Virginia Western Community College ... VA ... 528
Bellevue College ... WA ... 531
West Virginia University ... WV ... 544
University of Wisconsin-La Crosse ... WI ... 551

SC: Southern Association of Colleges and Schools, Commission on Colleges (SACS)

Air University ... AL ... 557
Alabama Agricultural and Mechanical University ... AL ... 1
Alabama Southern Community College ... AL ... 1
Alabama State University ... AL ... 1
Amridge University ... AL ... 1
Athens State University ... AL ... 1
Auburn University ... AL ... 1
Auburn University at Montgomery ... AL ... 2
Bevill State Community College ... AL ... 2
Birmingham-Southern College ... AL ... 2
Bishop State Community College ... AL ... 2
Calhoun Community College ... AL ... 2
Central Alabama Community College ... AL ... 2
Chattahoochee Valley Community College ... AL ... 2
&Community College of the Air Force ... AL ... 557
Concordia College ... AL ... 3
Enterprise State Community College ... AL ... 3
Faulkner University ... AL ... 3
Gadsden State Community College ... AL ... 3
George C. Wallace Community College - Dothan ... AL ... 4
George Corley Wallace State Community College - Selma ... AL ... 4
Huntingdon College ... AL ... 4
Jacksonville State University ... AL ... 4
James H. Faulkner State Community College ... AL ... 5
Jefferson Davis Community College ... AL ... 5
Jefferson State Community College ... AL ... 5
@J.F. Drake State Technical College ... AL ... 4
Judson College ... AL ... 5
Lawson State Community College ... AL ... 5
Lurleen B. Wallace Community College ... AL ... 5
Marion Military Institute ... AL ... 5
Miles College ... AL ... 5
Northeast Alabama Community College ... AL ... 6
Northwest - Shoals Community College ... AL ... 6
Oakwood University ... AL ... 6
Samford University ... AL ... 6
&School of Advanced Air and Space Studies ... AL ... 557
#Shelton State Community College ... AL ... 7
Snead State Community College ... AL ... 7
&South University ... AL ... 7
Southern Union State Community College ... AL ... 7
Spring Hill College ... AL ... 7
Stillman College ... AL ... 7
Talladega College ... AL ... 7
Troy University ... AL ... 8
Tuskegee University ... AL ... 8
United States Sports Academy ... AL ... 8
University of Alabama at Birmingham ... AL ... 8
University of Alabama in Huntsville ... AL ... 9
University of Alabama, The ... AL ... 8
University of Mobile ... AL ... 9
University of Montevallo ... AL ... 9
University of North Alabama ... AL ... 9
University of South Alabama ... AL ... 9
#University of West Alabama, The ... AL ... 10
Wallace State Community College - Hanceville ... AL ... 10
&Embry-Riddle Aeronautical University-Prescott Campus ... AZ ... 14
Ave Maria University ... FL ... 101
Baptist College of Florida, The ... FL ... 101
Barry University ... FL ... 101
Beacon College ... FL ... 101
Bethune Cookman University ... FL ... 101
Brevard Community College ... FL ... 101
Broward College ... FL ... 102
Chipola College ... FL ... 102
Clearwater Christian College ... FL ... 103
College of Central Florida ... FL ... 103
Daytona State College ... FL ... 103
@Digital Media Arts College ... FL ... 104
Eckerd College ... FL ... 104
Edison State College ... FL ... 104
Edward Waters College ... FL ... 105
Embry-Riddle Aeronautical University ... FL ... 105
&Embry-Riddle Aeronautical University-Worldwide ... FL ... 105
Everglades University ... FL ... 106
Flagler College ... FL ... 107
Florida Agricultural and Mechanical University ... FL ... 118
Florida Atlantic University ... FL ... 118
Florida Christian College ... FL ... 107
Florida College ... FL ... 107
Florida Gateway College ... FL ... 108
Florida Gulf Coast University ... FL ... 119
Florida Hospital College of Health Sciences ... FL ... 108
Florida Institute of Technology ... FL ... 108
Florida International University ... FL ... 119
Florida Keys Community College ... FL ... 108
Florida Memorial University ... FL ... 108
Florida National College Hialeah Campus ... FL ... 109
&Florida National College South Campus ... FL ... 109
&Florida National College Training Center ... FL ... 109
Florida Southern College ... FL ... 109
Florida State College at Jacksonville ... FL ... 109
Florida State University ... FL ... 119
Gulf Coast State College ... FL ... 110
Hillsborough Community College ... FL ... 110
Hodges University ... FL ... 110
Indian River State College ... FL ... 110
Jacksonville University ... FL ... 111
&Keiser University ... FL ... 112
Keiser University ... FL ... 112
&Keiser University ... FL ... 112
Lake-Sumter Community College ... FL ... 112
Lynn University ... FL ... 113
Miami Dade College ... FL ... 113
Miami International University of Art & Design ... FL ... 113
New College of Florida ... FL ... 119
North Florida Community College ... FL ... 113
Northwest Florida State College ... FL ... 114
Nova Southeastern University ... FL ... 114
Palm Beach Atlantic University ... FL ... 114
Palm Beach State College ... FL ... 114
Pasco-Hernando Community College ... FL ... 114
Pensacola State College ... FL ... 114
Polk State College ... FL ... 115
&Reformed Theological Seminary ... FL ... 115
Ringling College of Art and Design ... FL ... 115
Rollins College ... FL ... 116
St. John Vianney College Seminary ... FL ... 116
St. Johns River State College ... FL ... 116
Saint Leo University ... FL ... 116
St. Petersburg College ... FL ... 116
St. Thomas University ... FL ... 116
St. Vincent De Paul Regional Seminary ... FL ... 117
Santa Fe College ... FL ... 117
Seminole State College of Florida ... FL ... 117
South Florida Community College ... FL ... 117
&South University ... FL ... 117
Southeastern University ... FL ... 118
State College of Florida, Manatee-Sarasota ... FL ... 118
Stetson University ... FL ... 121
Tallahassee Community College ... FL ... 121
University of Central Florida ... FL ... 120
University of Florida ... FL ... 120
University of Miami ... FL ... 122
University of North Florida ... FL ... 120
University of South Florida ... FL ... 120
University of South Florida Manatee-Sarasota ... FL ... 121
University of South Florida St. Petersburg ... FL ... 121
University of Tampa ... FL ... 122
University of West Florida ... FL ... 121
Valencia College ... FL ... 122
Warner University ... FL ... 123
Webber International University ... FL ... 123
Abraham Baldwin Agricultural College ... GA ... 123
Agnes Scott College ... GA ... 123
Albany State University ... GA ... 123
Albany Technical College ... GA ... 123
@Altamaha Technical College ... GA ... 124
Andrew College ... GA ... 124
Armstrong Atlantic State University ... GA ... 124
Art Institute of Atlanta, The ... GA ... 124
Athens Technical College ... GA ... 124
Atlanta Metropolitan College ... GA ... 124
Atlanta Technical College ... GA ... 125
Augusta State University ... GA ... 125
Augusta Technical College ... GA ... 125
Bainbridge College ... GA ... 125
Bauder College ... GA ... 125
Berry College ... GA ... 125
Brenau University ... GA ... 126
Brewton-Parker College ... GA ... 126
Central Georgia Technical College ... GA ... 126
Chattahoochee Technical College ... GA ... 126
Clark Atlanta University ... GA ... 126
Clayton State University ... GA ... 127
College of Coastal Georgia ... GA ... 127
Columbia Theological Seminary ... GA ... 127
Columbus State University ... GA ... 127
Columbus Technical College ... GA ... 127
Covenant College ... GA ... 127

Walters State Community College .... TN 476
Watkins College of Art, Design & Film .... TN 478
Abilene Christian University .... TX 478
Alvin Community College .... TX 479
Amarillo College .... TX 479
Amberton University .... TX 479
@American College of Acupuncture and Oriental Medicine .... TX 480
Angelina College .... TX 480
Angelo State University .... TX 480
AOMA Graduate School of Integrative Medicine .... TX 480
Art Institute of Dallas .... TX 480
Art Institute of Houston, The .... TX 480
Austin College .... TX 481
Austin Community College District .... TX 481
Austin Graduate School of Theology .... TX 481
Austin Presbyterian Theological Seminary .... TX 481
Baptist Missionary Association Theological Seminary .... TX 481
Baylor College of Medicine .... TX 481
Baylor University .... TX 481
Blinn College .... TX 482
Brazosport College .... TX 482
Brite Divinity School .... TX 482
Brookhaven College .... TX 484
Cedar Valley College .... TX 484
Central Texas College .... TX 482
Cisco Junior College .... TX 482
Clarendon College .... TX 482
Coastal Bend College .... TX 482
College of Saint Thomas More, The .... TX 483
College of the Mainland .... TX 483
Collin County Community College District .... TX 483
Concordia University Texas .... TX 483
Criswell College .... TX 484
Dallas Baptist University .... TX 484
Dallas Theological Seminary .... TX 485
Del Mar College .... TX 485
East Texas Baptist University .... TX 486
Eastfield College .... TX 484
El Centro College .... TX 484
El Paso Community College .... TX 486
Frank Phillips College .... TX 486
Galveston College .... TX 486
Graduate Institute of Applied Linguistics .... TX 486
Grayson County College .... TX 487
Hardin-Simmons University .... TX 487
Hill College .... TX 487
Houston Baptist University .... TX 487
Houston Community College .... TX 487
Howard College .... TX 487
Howard Payne University .... TX 488
Huston-Tillotson University .... TX 488
Jacksonville College .... TX 488
Jarvis Christian College .... TX 488
Kilgore College .... TX 489
Lamar Institute of Technology .... TX 500
Lamar State College-Orange .... TX 500
Lamar State College-Port Arthur .... TX 500
Lamar University .... TX 500
Laredo Community College .... TX 489
Lee College .... TX 489
LeTourneau University .... TX 489
Lon Morris College .... TX 490
Lone Star College System .... TX 490
Lubbock Christian University .... TX 490
McLennan Community College .... TX 490
McMurry University .... TX 490
Midland College .... TX 490
Midwestern State University .... TX 491
Mountain View College .... TX 485
Navarro College .... TX 491
North Central Texas College .... TX 491
North Lake College .... TX 485
Northeast Texas Community College .... TX 491
Northwest Vista College .... TX 479
Oblate School of Theology .... TX 491
Odessa College .... TX 491
Our Lady of the Lake University .... TX 491
Palo Alto College .... TX 479
Panola College .... TX 492
Paris Junior College .... TX 492
Parker University .... TX 492
#Paul Quinn College .... TX 492
Prairie View A & M University .... TX 496
Ranger College .... TX 492
Rice University .... TX 492
Richland College .... TX 485
St. Edward's University .... TX 493
St. Mary's University .... TX 493
St. Philip's College .... TX 479
Sam Houston State University .... TX 501
San Antonio College .... TX 479
&San Jacinto College Central .... TX 493
&San Jacinto College North .... TX 493
&San Jacinto College South .... TX 493
Schreiner University .... TX 494
Seminary of the Southwest .... TX 494
South Plains College .... TX 494
South Texas College .... TX 494
Southern Methodist University .... TX 494
Southwest Texas Junior College .... TX 495
Southwestern Adventist University .... TX 495
Southwestern Assemblies of God University .... TX 495
Southwestern Baptist Theological Seminary .... TX 495
Southwestern Christian College .... TX 495
Southwestern University .... TX 495
Stephen F. Austin State University .... TX 495
#Sul Ross State University .... TX 501
Tarleton State University .... TX 496
Tarrant County College District .... TX 496
Temple College .... TX 496
Texarkana College .... TX 496
&Texas A & M Health Science Center Baylor College of Dentistry .... TX 497
Texas A & M International University .... TX 497
Texas A & M University .... TX 497
&Texas A & M University at Galveston .... TX 497
Texas A & M University - Commerce .... TX 497
Texas A & M University - Corpus Christi .... TX 497
Texas A & M University - Kingsville .... TX 498
&Texas A & M University-San Antonio .... TX 498
Texas A & M University System Health Science Center .... TX 496
Texas A & M University - Texarkana .... TX 498
Texas Chiropractic College .... TX 498
Texas Christian University .... TX 498
Texas College .... TX 499
Texas Lutheran University .... TX 499
Texas Southern University .... TX 499
Texas Southmost College .... TX 499
Texas State Technical College Harlingen .... TX 499
Texas State Technical College Marshall .... TX 500
Texas State Technical College Waco .... TX 500
Texas State Technical College West Texas .... TX 500
Texas State University-San Marcos .... TX 501
Texas Tech University .... TX 501
Texas Tech University Health Sciences Center .... TX 501
Texas Wesleyan University .... TX 502
Texas Woman's University .... TX 502
Trinity University .... TX 502
Trinity Valley Community College .... TX 502
Tyler Junior College .... TX 502
University of Dallas .... TX 502
University of Houston .... TX 503
University of Houston - Clear Lake .... TX 503
University of Houston - Downtown .... TX 503
University of Houston - Victoria .... TX 503
University of Mary Hardin-Baylor .... TX 504
University of North Texas .... TX 504
University of North Texas Health Science Center at Fort Worth .... TX 504
University of St. Thomas .... TX 504
University of Texas at Arlington, The .... TX 505
University of Texas at Austin .... TX 505
University of Texas at Brownsville, The .... TX 505
University of Texas at Dallas, The .... TX 505
University of Texas at El Paso .... TX 505
University of Texas at San Antonio .... TX 506
University of Texas at Tyler .... TX 506
University of Texas Health Science Center at Houston (UTHealth), The .... TX 506
University of Texas Health Science Center at San Antonio .... TX 506
University of Texas M.D. Anderson Cancer Center, The .... TX 507
University of Texas Medical Branch, The .... TX 507
University of Texas of the Permian Basin .... TX 507
University of Texas - Pan American .... TX 506
University of Texas Southwestern Medical Center at Dallas .... TX 507
University of the Incarnate Word .... TX 503
Vernon College .... TX 507
Victoria College .... TX 507
Wade College Infomart .... TX 508
Wayland Baptist University .... TX 508
Weatherford College .... TX 508
West Texas A & M University .... TX 498
Western Texas College .... TX 508
Wharton County Junior College .... TX 508
Wiley College .... TX 509
@Appalachian College of Pharmacy .... VA 515
Averett University .... VA 516
Blue Ridge Community College .... VA 525
Bluefield College .... VA 516
Bridgewater College .... VA 516
Central Virginia Community College .... VA 526
Christendom College .... VA 517
Christopher Newport University .... VA 517
College of William & Mary .... VA 517
Dabney S. Lancaster Community College .... VA 526
Danville Community College .... VA 526
Eastern Mennonite University .... VA 518
Eastern Shore Community College .... VA 526
Eastern Virginia Medical School .... VA 518
ECPI College of Technology .... VA 518
Emory & Henry College .... VA 518
Ferrum College .... VA 518
George Mason University .... VA 519
Germanna Community College .... VA 526
Hampden-Sydney College .... VA 519
Hampton University .... VA 519
Hollins University .... VA 519
Institute for the Psychological Sciences .... VA 519
J. Sargeant Reynolds Community College .... VA 526
James Madison University .... VA 520
Jefferson College of Health Sciences (Formerly Community Hospital) .... VA 520
John Tyler Community College .... VA 526
Liberty University .... VA 520
Longwood University .... VA 520
Lord Fairfax Community College .... VA 526
Lynchburg College .... VA 520
Marine Corps University .... VA 557
Mary Baldwin College .... VA 520
Marymount University .... VA 521
&Medical Careers Institute .... VA 521
Mountain Empire Community College .... VA 527
New River Community College .... VA 527
Norfolk State University .... VA 521
Northern Virginia Community College .... VA 527
Old Dominion University .... VA 521
Patrick Henry Community College .... VA 527
Paul D. Camp Community College .... VA 527
Piedmont Virginia Community College .... VA 527
Radford University .... VA 522
Randolph College .... VA 522
Randolph-Macon College .... VA 522
Rappahannock Community College .... VA 527
&Reformed Theological Seminary .... VA 523
Regent University .... VA 523
Richard Bland College .... VA 523
Roanoke College .... VA 523
#Saint Paul's College .... VA 523
Shenandoah University .... VA 523
@Southern Virginia University .... VA 524
Southside Virginia Community College .... VA 527
Southwest Virginia Community College .... VA 528
Sweet Briar College .... VA 524
Thomas Nelson Community College .... VA 528
Tidewater Community College .... VA 528
Union Presbyterian Seminary .... VA 524
University of Mary Washington .... VA 524
University of Richmond .... VA 525
University of Virginia .... VA 525
University of Virginia's College at Wise, The .... VA 525
Virginia Commonwealth University .... VA 525
Virginia Highlands Community College .... VA 528
Virginia Intermont College .... VA 528
Virginia Military Institute .... VA 529
Virginia Polytechnic Institute and State University .... VA 529
Virginia State University .... VA 529
Virginia Union University .... VA 529
Virginia Wesleyan College .... VA 529
Virginia Western Community College .... VA 528
Washington and Lee University .... VA 530
Wytheville Community College .... VA 528

SCPSY: American Psychological Association: school psychology (D)

Arizona State University .... AZ 12
University of Arizona .... AZ 19
University of Central Arkansas .... AR 25
University of California-Berkeley .... CA 73
University of California-Riverside .... CA 74
University of Northern Colorado .... CO 88
University of Connecticut .... CT 94
University of Florida .... FL 120
University of South Florida .... FL 120
Georgia State University .... GA 131
University of Georgia .... GA 138
Illinois State University .... IL 153
Northern Illinois University .... IL 160
Ball State University .... IN 169
Indiana State University .... IN 173
Indiana University Bloomington .... IN 173
University of Iowa .... IA 182
University of Kansas Main Campus .... KS 196
University of Kentucky .... KY 206
Louisiana State University and Agricultural and Mechanical College .... LA 212
Tulane University .... LA 215
University of Maryland College Park .... MD 227
University of Massachusetts .... MA 237
Central Michigan University .... MI 249
Michigan State University .... MI 255
University of Minnesota-Twin Cities .... MN 272
Mississippi State University .... MS 276
University of Southern Mississippi .... MS 278
University of Missouri - Columbia .... MO 291
University of Nebraska - Lincoln .... NE 300
Rutgers the State University of New Jersey New Brunswick Campus .... NJ 314
Alfred University .... NY 322
City University of New York Graduate Center .... NY 327
Fordham University .... NY 334
Hofstra University .... NY 335
New York University .... NY 344
St. John's University .... NY 348
State University of New York at Albany .... NY 351
Syracuse University Main Campus .... NY 357
Teachers College, Columbia University .... NY 357
North Carolina State University .... NC 378
University of North Carolina at Chapel Hill .... NC 378
Kent State University Main Campus .... OH 393
Oklahoma State University .... OK 410
University of Oregon .... OR 419
Duquesne University .... PA 428
Lehigh University .... PA 434
Penn State University Park .... PA 438
Temple University .... PA 447
University of Rhode Island .... RI 454
University of South Carolina Columbia .... SC 462
University of Tennessee, Knoxville .... TN 477
Texas A & M University .... TX 497
University of Houston .... TX 503
University of Texas at Austin .... TX 505
University of Utah, The .... UT 510
University of Washington .... WA 538
University of Wisconsin-Madison .... WI 550
University of Wisconsin-Milwaukee .... WI 551

SP: American Speech-Language-Hearing Association: speech-language pathology (M,D)

Alabama Agricultural and Mechanical University .... AL 1
Auburn University .... AL 1
University of Alabama, The .... AL 8
University of Montevallo .... AL 9
University of South Alabama .... AL 9
Arizona State University .... AZ 12
Northern Arizona University .... AZ 17
University of Arizona .... AZ 19
Arkansas State University .... AR 20
@Harding University Main Campus .... AR 21
University of Arkansas at Little Rock .... AR 24
University of Arkansas Main Campus .... AR 24
University of Central Arkansas .... AR 25
California State University-Chico .... CA 34
California State University-East Bay .... CA 34
California State University-Fresno .... CA 34
California State University-Fullerton .... CA 34
California State University-Long Beach .... CA 35
California State University-Los Angeles .... CA 35
California State University-Northridge .... CA 35
California State University-Sacramento .... CA 35
@California State University-San Marcos .... CA 36
@Chapman University .... CA 39
Loma Linda University .... CA 54
San Diego State University .... CA 36
San Francisco State University .... CA 36
San Jose State University .... CA 37
University of Redlands .... CA 75
University of the Pacific .... CA 75
University of Colorado Boulder .... CO 88
University of Northern Colorado .... CO 88
Southern Connecticut State University .... CT 91
University of Connecticut .... CT 94
Gallaudet University .... DC 97
George Washington University .... DC 97
Howard University .... DC 98
University System of the District of Columbia .... DC 99
Florida Atlantic University .... FL 118
Florida International University .... FL 119
Florida State University .... FL 119
Nova Southeastern University .... FL 114
University of Central Florida .... FL 120
University of Florida .... FL 120
University of South Florida .... FL 120
Armstrong Atlantic State University .... GA 124
Georgia State University .... GA 131
University of Georgia .... GA 138
University of West Georgia .... GA 138
Valdosta State University .... GA 138
University of Hawaii at Manoa .... HI 141
Idaho State University .... ID 143
Eastern Illinois University .... IL 150
Governors State University .... IL 151
Illinois State University .... IL 153
Northern Illinois University .... IL 160
Northwestern University .... IL 160
Rush University .... IL 163
Saint Xavier University .... IL 163
Southern Illinois University Carbondale .... IL 164
Southern Illinois University Edwardsville .... IL 165
University of Illinois at Urbana-Champaign .... IL 167
Western Illinois University .... IL 168
Ball State University .... IN 169
Indiana State University .... IN 173
Indiana University Bloomington .... IN 173
Purdue University Main Campus .... IN 178
@St. Ambrose University .... IA 188
University of Iowa .... IA 182
University of Northern Iowa .... IA 182
Fort Hays State University .... KS 192
Kansas State University .... KS 194
University of Kansas Main Campus .... KS 196
Wichita State University .... KS 197
Eastern Kentucky University .... KY 200
Murray State University .... KY 204
University of Kentucky .... KY 206
University of Louisville .... KY 207
Western Kentucky University .... KY 207
Louisiana State University and Agricultural and Mechanical College .... LA 212
Louisiana State University Health Sciences Center at Shreveport .... LA 213
Louisiana State University Health Sciences Center-New Orleans .... LA 213
Louisiana Tech University .... LA 215
Southeastern Louisiana University .... LA 216
#Southern University and A&M College .... LA 214
University of Louisiana at Lafayette .... LA 216
University of Louisiana at Monroe .... LA 216
University of Maine .... ME 220
Loyola University Maryland .... MD 224
Towson University .... MD 228
University of Maryland College Park .... MD 227
Boston University .... MA 232
Emerson College .... MA 234
MGH Institute of Health Professions .... MA 242
Northeastern University .... MA 244
University of Massachusetts .... MA 237
Worcester State University .... MA 239
@Calvin College .... MI 249
Central Michigan University .... MI 249

Eastern Michigan University ..... MI 250
Michigan State University ..... MI 255
Wayne State University ..... MI 260
Western Michigan University ..... MI 260
Minnesota State University Moorhead ..... MN 268
Minnesota State University, Mankato ..... MN 267
St. Cloud State University ..... MN 269
University of Minnesota Duluth ..... MN 272
University of Minnesota-Twin Cities ..... MN 272
Jackson State University ..... MS 275
Mississippi University for Women ..... MS 276
University of Mississippi ..... MS 277
University of Southern Mississippi ..... MS 278
Fontbonne University ..... MO 282
Missouri State University ..... MO 286
Rockhurst University ..... MO 288
Saint Louis University ..... MO 289
Southeast Missouri State University ..... MO 290
Truman State University ..... MO 291
University of Central Missouri ..... MO 291
University of Missouri - Columbia ..... MO 291
University of Montana - Missoula, The ..... MT 295
University of Nebraska at Kearney ..... NE 300
University of Nebraska at Omaha ..... NE 301
University of Nebraska - Lincoln ..... NE 300
University of Nevada, Reno ..... NV 303
University of New Hampshire ..... NH 306
Kean University ..... NJ 311
Montclair State University ..... NJ 311
@Richard Stockton College of New Jersey, The ..... NJ 313
Seton Hall University ..... NJ 315
William Paterson University of New Jersey ..... NJ 317
Eastern New Mexico University Main Campus ..... NM 318
New Mexico State University Main Campus ..... NM 319
University of New Mexico Main Campus ..... NM 321
Adelphi University ..... NY 322
City University of New York Brooklyn College ..... NY 326
City University of New York Herbert H. Lehman College ..... NY 327
City University of New York Hunter College ..... NY 327
City University of New York Queens College ..... NY 328
College of Saint Rose, The ..... NY 330
Hofstra University ..... NY 335
Ithaca College ..... NY 336
Long Island University Brooklyn Campus ..... NY 338
Long Island University C.W. Post Campus ..... NY 339
Mercy College ..... NY 340
@Molloy College ..... NY 341
Nazareth College of Rochester ..... NY 342
New York Medical College ..... NY 343
New York University ..... NY 344
St. John's University ..... NY 348
Saint Joseph's College, New York ..... NY 349
State University of New York at Buffalo ..... NY 351
State University of New York at Fredonia ..... NY 352
State University of New York at New Paltz ..... NY 352
State University of New York College at Buffalo ..... NY 353
State University of New York College at Geneseo ..... NY 353
State University of New York College at Plattsburgh ..... NY 354
Syracuse University Main Campus ..... NY 357
Teachers College, Columbia University ..... NY 357
Touro College ..... NY 357
Appalachian State University ..... NC 377
East Carolina University ..... NC 377
North Carolina Central University ..... NC 378
University of North Carolina at Chapel Hill ..... NC 378
University of North Carolina at Greensboro ..... NC 379
Western Carolina University ..... NC 379
Minot State University ..... ND 381
University of North Dakota Main Campus ..... ND 381
Bowling Green State University ..... OH 385
Case Western Reserve University ..... OH 386
Cleveland State University ..... OH 388
Kent State University Main Campus ..... OH 393
Miami University ..... OH 396
Ohio State University Main Campus, The ..... OH 398
Ohio University Main Campus ..... OH 399
University of Akron, Main Campus, The ..... OH 403
University of Cincinnati Main Campus ..... OH 403
University of Toledo ..... OH 404
Northeastern State University ..... OK 409
Oklahoma State University ..... OK 410
University of Central Oklahoma ..... OK 413
University of Oklahoma Health Sciences Center ..... OK 413
University of Tulsa ..... OK 413
Portland State University ..... OR 418
University of Oregon ..... OR 419
Bloomsburg University of Pennsylvania ..... PA 441
California University of Pennsylvania ..... PA 441
Clarion University of Pennsylvania ..... PA 442
Duquesne University ..... PA 428
East Stroudsburg University of Pennsylvania ..... PA 442
Edinboro University of Pennsylvania ..... PA 442
Indiana University of Pennsylvania ..... PA 442
La Salle University ..... PA 432
Marywood University ..... PA 435
Misericordia University ..... PA 436
Penn State University Park ..... PA 438
Temple University ..... PA 447
University of Pittsburgh ..... PA 449
West Chester University of Pennsylvania ..... PA 443
@Universidad Del Turabo ..... PR 565
University of Puerto Rico-Medical Sciences Campus ..... PR 567
University of Rhode Island ..... RI 454
South Carolina State University ..... SC 460
University of South Carolina Columbia ..... SC 462
University of South Dakota, The ..... SD 465
East Tennessee State University ..... TN 473
Tennessee State University ..... TN 474
University of Memphis, The ..... TN 474
University of Tennessee, Knoxville ..... TN 477
Vanderbilt University ..... TN 477
Abilene Christian University ..... TX 478
Baylor University ..... TX 481
Lamar University ..... TX 500
Our Lady of the Lake University ..... TX 491
Stephen F. Austin State University ..... TX 495
Texas A & M University - Kingsville ..... TX 498
Texas Christian University ..... TX 498
Texas State University-San Marcos ..... TX 501
Texas Tech University Health Sciences Center ..... TX 501
Texas Woman's University ..... TX 502
University of Houston ..... TX 503
University of North Texas ..... TX 504
University of Texas at Austin ..... TX 505
University of Texas at Dallas, The ..... TX 505
University of Texas at El Paso ..... TX 505
University of Texas - Pan American ..... TX 506
West Texas A & M University ..... TX 498
Brigham Young University ..... UT 509
University of Utah, The ..... UT 510
Utah State University ..... UT 511
University of Vermont ..... VT 514
Hampton University ..... VA 519
James Madison University ..... VA 520
Longwood University ..... VA 520
Old Dominion University ..... VA 521
Radford University ..... VA 522
University of Virginia ..... VA 525
Eastern Washington University ..... WA 533
University of Washington ..... WA 538
Washington State University ..... WA 539
Western Washington University ..... WA 539
Marshall University ..... WV 543
West Virginia University ..... WV 544
Marquette University ..... WI 548
University of Wisconsin-Eau Claire ..... WI 550
University of Wisconsin-Madison ..... WI 550
University of Wisconsin-Milwaukee ..... WI 551
University of Wisconsin-River Falls ..... WI 552
University of Wisconsin-Stevens Point ..... WI 552
University of Wisconsin-Whitewater ..... WI 552
University of Wyoming ..... WY 556

SPAA: National Association of Schools of Public Affairs and Administration: public affairs and administration (M)

Auburn University ..... AL 1
Auburn University at Montgomery ..... AL 2
Troy University ..... AL 8
University of Alabama at Birmingham ..... AL 8
Arizona State University ..... AZ 12
University of Arizona ..... AZ 19
Arkansas State University ..... AR 20
University of Arkansas at Little Rock ..... AR 24
California State Polytechnic University-Pomona ..... CA 33
California State University-Bakersfield ..... CA 33
California State University-Chico ..... CA 34
California State University-Dominguez Hills ..... CA 34
California State University-Fresno ..... CA 34
California State University-Fullerton ..... CA 34
California State University-Long Beach ..... CA 35
California State University-Los Angeles ..... CA 35
California State University-San Bernardino ..... CA 36
California State University-Stanislaus ..... CA 36
Naval Postgraduate School ..... CA 557
San Diego State University ..... CA 36
San Francisco State University ..... CA 36
San Jose State University ..... CA 37
University of Southern California ..... CA 76
University of Colorado Denver|Anschutz Medical Campus ..... CO 88
University of Connecticut ..... CT 94
University of Delaware ..... DE 96
American University ..... DC 97
George Washington University ..... DC 97
Howard University ..... DC 98
Florida Atlantic University ..... FL 118
Florida Gulf Coast University ..... FL 119
Florida International University ..... FL 119
Florida State University ..... FL 119
University of Central Florida ..... FL 120
University of North Florida ..... FL 120
University of South Florida ..... FL 120
Albany State University ..... GA 123
Augusta State University ..... GA 125
Clark Atlanta University ..... GA 126
Georgia College & State University ..... GA 129
Georgia Southern University ..... GA 131
Georgia State University ..... GA 131
Kennesaw State University ..... GA 132
Savannah State University ..... GA 136
University of Georgia ..... GA 138
University of West Georgia ..... GA 138
Valdosta State University ..... GA 138
Boise State University ..... ID 142
DePaul University ..... IL 148
Governors State University ..... IL 151
Northern Illinois University ..... IL 160
Southern Illinois University Carbondale ..... IL 164
Southern Illinois University Edwardsville ..... IL 165
University of Illinois at Chicago ..... IL 166
University of Illinois at Springfield ..... IL 167
Indiana University Bloomington ..... IN 173
Indiana University Northwest ..... IN 173
Indiana University-Purdue University Fort Wayne ..... IN 174
Indiana University-Purdue University Indianapolis ..... IN 174
Indiana University South Bend ..... IN 174
Iowa State University ..... IA 182
Kansas State University ..... KS 194
University of Kansas Main Campus ..... KS 196
Wichita State University ..... KS 197
Eastern Kentucky University ..... KY 200
Kentucky State University ..... KY 203
Northern Kentucky University ..... KY 205
University of Kentucky ..... KY 206
University of Louisville ..... KY 207
Western Kentucky University ..... KY 207
Grambling State University ..... LA 215
Louisiana State University and Agricultural and Mechanical College ..... LA 212
Southern University and A&M College ..... LA 214
University of Maine ..... ME 220
University of Baltimore ..... MD 229
University of Maryland Baltimore County ..... MD 227
University of Maryland College Park ..... MD 227
Bridgewater State University ..... MA 238
Harvard University ..... MA 235
Northeastern University ..... MA 244
Suffolk University ..... MA 245
Central Michigan University ..... MI 249
Eastern Michigan University ..... MI 250
Grand Valley State University ..... MI 252
Oakland University ..... MI 257
Wayne State University ..... MI 260
Western Michigan University ..... MI 260
University of Minnesota-Twin Cities ..... MN 272
Jackson State University ..... MS 275
Mississippi State University ..... MS 276
Missouri State University ..... MO 286
Saint Louis University ..... MO 289
University of Missouri - Columbia ..... MO 291
University of Missouri - Kansas City ..... MO 291
University of Missouri - Saint Louis ..... MO 291
University of Nebraska at Omaha ..... NE 301
University of Nevada, Las Vegas ..... NV 302
Kean University ..... NJ 311
Rutgers the State University of New Jersey Camden Campus ..... NJ 314
Rutgers the State University of New Jersey Newark Campus ..... NJ 314
Seton Hall University ..... NJ 315
New Mexico State University Main Campus ..... NM 319
University of New Mexico Main Campus ..... NM 321
Baruch College/City University of New York ..... NY 326
City University of New York John Jay College of Criminal Justice ..... NY 328
Long Island University Brooklyn Campus ..... NY 338
Long Island University C.W. Post Campus ..... NY 339
New School, The ..... NY 342
New York University ..... NY 344
State University of New York at Albany ..... NY 351
State University of New York at Binghamton ..... NY 351
State University of New York, The College at Brockport ..... NY 352
Syracuse University Main Campus ..... NY 357
Appalachian State University ..... NC 377
East Carolina University ..... NC 377
North Carolina State University ..... NC 378
University of North Carolina at Chapel Hill ..... NC 378
University of North Carolina at Charlotte ..... NC 378
University of North Carolina at Greensboro ..... NC 379
University of North Carolina at Wilmington ..... NC 379
University of North Dakota Main Campus ..... ND 381
Cleveland State University ..... OH 388
Kent State University Main Campus ..... OH 393
Ohio State University Main Campus, The ..... OH 398
University of Akron, Main Campus, The ..... OH 403
University of Dayton ..... OH 404
University of Toledo ..... OH 404
Wright State University Main Campus ..... OH 406
Portland State University ..... OR 418
University of Oregon ..... OR 419
Willamette University ..... OR 421
Carnegie Mellon University ..... PA 424
Penn State Harrisburg ..... PA 439
University of Pittsburgh ..... PA 449
Villanova University ..... PA 450
University of Puerto Rico-Rio Piedras Campus ..... PR 567
College of Charleston ..... SC 457
University of South Carolina Columbia ..... SC 462
University of South Dakota, The ..... SD 465
Tennessee State University ..... TN 474
University of Memphis, The ..... TN 474
University of Tennessee at Chattanooga ..... TN 477
Texas A & M University ..... TX 497
Texas State University-San Marcos ..... TX 501
Texas Tech University ..... TX 501
University of North Texas ..... TX 504
University of Texas at Arlington, The ..... TX 505
University of Texas at Austin ..... TX 505
University of Texas at Dallas, The ..... TX 505
University of Texas at El Paso ..... TX 505
University of Texas at San Antonio ..... TX 506
Brigham Young University ..... UT 509
University of Utah, The ..... UT 510
George Mason University ..... VA 519
Old Dominion University ..... VA 521
Virginia Commonwealth University ..... VA 525
Virginia Polytechnic Institute and State University ..... VA 529
Seattle University ..... WA 537
University of Washington ..... WA 538
West Virginia University ..... WV 544

SURGA: Commission on Accreditation of Allied Health Education Programs: surgical assistant (C,A)

College of Southern Idaho ..... ID 143
Vincennes University ..... IN 181
Madisonville Community College ..... KY 202
Macomb Community College ..... MI 254
Wayne County Community College District ..... MI 260
University of Cincinnati Main Campus ..... OH 403
Eastern Virginia Medical School ..... VA 518

SURGT: Commission on Accreditation of Allied Health Education Programs: surgical technology (C,A)

Bevill State Community College ..... AL 2
Calhoun Community College ..... AL 2
James H. Faulkner State Community College ..... AL 5
Lurleen B. Wallace Community College ..... AL 5
Southern Union State Community College ..... AL 7
Virginia College ..... AL 3
Gateway Community College ..... AZ 15
Lamson College ..... AZ 15
Mohave Community College ..... AZ 16
Pima County Community College District ..... AZ 17
North Arkansas College ..... AR 22
South Arkansas Community College ..... AR 23
Southeast Arkansas College ..... AR 23
University of Arkansas at Fort Smith ..... AR 24
University of Arkansas for Medical Sciences ..... AR 24
American Career College-Orange County ..... CA 28
Carrington College California - Citrus Heights ..... CA 37
Carrington College California - San Jose ..... CA 38
Concorde Career College ..... CA 42
Fresno City College ..... CA 72
MiraCosta Community College District ..... CA 57
San Joaquin Valley College-Bakersfield ..... CA 66
San Joaquin Valley College-Fresno ..... CA 66
San Joaquin Valley College-Hesperia ..... CA 66
Skyline College ..... CA 67
Southwestern College ..... CA 71
Aims Community College ..... CO 80
Concorde Career College ..... CO 83
#Everest College ..... CO 84
Manchester Community College ..... CT 90
Brevard Community College ..... FL 101
Central Florida Institute ..... FL 102
Concorde Career Institute ..... FL 103
Daytona State College ..... FL 103
Everest Institute ..... FL 105
Everest University-Brandon Campus ..... FL 105
Florida State College at Jacksonville ..... FL 109
Fortis College ..... FL 109
Gulf Coast State College ..... FL 110
Indian River State College ..... FL 110
Keiser Career College ..... FL 112
Keiser University ..... FL 112
MedVance Institute of Fort Lauderdale ..... FL 113
Palm Beach State College ..... FL 114
Pensacola State College ..... FL 114
Sanford-Brown Institute ..... FL 117
Santa Fe College ..... FL 117
Virginia College ..... FL 123
Albany Technical College ..... GA 123
Athens Technical College ..... GA 124
Augusta Technical College ..... GA 125
Central Georgia Technical College ..... GA 126
Columbus Technical College ..... GA 127
Everest Institute ..... GA 129
Georgia Northwestern Technical College ..... GA 130
Gwinnett Technical College ..... GA 132
Lanier Technical College ..... GA 132
Middle Georgia Technical College ..... GA 133
Moultrie Technical College ..... GA 134
Ogeechee Technical College ..... GA 134
Okefenokee Technical College ..... GA 135
Savannah Technical College ..... GA 136
Southeastern Technical College ..... GA 137
Southern Crescent Technical College ..... GA 137
Southwest Georgia Technical College ..... GA 137
West Georgia Technical College ..... GA 139
Wiregrass Georgia Technical College ..... GA 139
Kapiolani Community College ..... HI 141
College of Southern Idaho ..... ID 143
Eastern Idaho Technical College ..... ID 143
City Colleges of Chicago Malcolm X College ..... IL 147
College of DuPage ..... IL 147
College of Lake County ..... IL 147
Elgin Community College ..... IL 150
Illinois Central College ..... IL 152

SURTEC: Accrediting Bureau of Health Education Schools: surgical technologist (C,A)

SW: Council on Social Work Education: social work (B,M)

Virginia Intermont College VA 528
@Virginia State University VA 529
Virginia Union University VA 529
Eastern Washington University WA 533
Heritage University WA 534
Pacific Lutheran University WA 535
Seattle University WA 537
University of Washington WA 538
Walla Walla University WA 538
Bethany College WV 540
Concord University WV 543
Marshall University WV 543
Mountain State University WV 541
Shepherd University WV 544
West Virginia State University WV 544
West Virginia University WV 544
Carthage College WI 546
Concordia University Wisconsin WI 546
Marian University WI 548
Mount Mary College WI 549
University of Wisconsin-Eau Claire WI 550
University of Wisconsin-Green Bay WI 551
University of Wisconsin-Madison WI 550
University of Wisconsin-Milwaukee WI 551
University of Wisconsin-Oshkosh WI 551
University of Wisconsin-River Falls WI 552
@University of Wisconsin-Stevens Point WI 552
University of Wisconsin-Superior WI 552
University of Wisconsin-Whitewater WI 552
Viterbo University WI 553
University of Wyoming WY 556

TEAC: Teacher Education Accreditation Council: teacher education (B,M,D)

@Northcentral University AZ 16
University of Phoenix AZ 19
Chapman University CA 39
Adams State College CO 80
Colorado State University CO 83
Colorado State University-Pueblo CO 83
Fort Lewis College CO 84
Regis University CO 87
@Flagler College FL 107
@Jose Maria Vargas University FL 112
@University of Miami FL 122
@American InterContinental University IL 144
@Knox College IL 155
@Buena Vista University IA 182
St. Ambrose University IA 188
Tulane University LA 215
University of Southern Maine ME 220
Boston College MA 232
@Cambridge College MA 233
Lesley University MA 236
@University of Massachusetts Boston MA 237
@Adrian College MI 247
@Albion College MI 247
@Alma College MI 247
@Aquinas College MI 248
@Calvin College MI 249
Central Michigan University MI 249
@Cornerstone University MI 250
@Ferris State University MI 251
@Hope College MI 252
@Lake Superior State University MI 254
@Marygrove College MI 255
Michigan State University MI 255
@Michigan Technological University MI 255
Northern Michigan University MI 256
Oakland University MI 257
@Olivet College MI 257
@Robert B. Miller College MI 257
@Siena Heights University MI 258
@Spring Arbor University MI 258
@University of Detroit Mercy MI 259
University of Michigan-Ann Arbor MI 259
@University of Michigan-Dearborn MI 259
@Wayne State University MI 260
Bethel University MN 261
College of Saint Scholastica, The MN 262
@Concordia College MN 263
@Rust College MS 277
@Lindenwood University MO 284
Rockhurst University MO 288
@University of Missouri - Columbia MO 291
William Woods University MO 293
Montana State University MT 295
University of Nebraska - Lincoln NE 300
University of New Hampshire NH 306
Bloomfield College NJ 308
Caldwell College NJ 308
Centenary College NJ 308
College of Saint Elizabeth NJ 309
@Drew University NJ 309
Fairleigh Dickinson University NJ 310
Felician College NJ 310
Georgian Court University NJ 310
@New Jersey City University NJ 312
Princeton University NJ 313
Ramapo College of New Jersey NJ 313
Richard Stockton College of New Jersey, The NJ 313
Rutgers the State University of New Jersey Camden Campus NJ 314
Rutgers the State University of New Jersey New Brunswick Campus NJ 314
Rutgers the State University of New Jersey Newark Campus NJ 314
Saint Peter's College NJ 314
Thomas Edison State College NJ 316
Alfred University NY 322
@Bard College NY 323
@Barnard College NY 323
@Boricua College NY 324
@Cazenovia College NY 325
Colgate University NY 329
College of Mount Saint Vincent NY 330
@College of New Rochelle, The NY 330
@Cornell University NY 331
@Daemen College NY 331
Dominican College of Blauvelt NY 332
@Elmira College NY 333
Hartwick College NY 335
@Hobart and William Smith Colleges NY 335
Hofstra University NY 335
Houghton College NY 336
@Keuka College NY 337
Le Moyne College NY 338
Long Island University Brooklyn Campus NY 338
Long Island University C.W. Post Campus NY 339
Long Island University Hudson Graduate Center at Westchester NY 339
Long Island University Riverhead Campus NY 339
Manhattan College NY 339
Medaille College NY 340
Nazareth College of Rochester NY 342
New York University NY 344
@Pratt Institute NY 346
@Roberts Wesleyan College NY 347
Rochester Institute of Technology NY 347
@St. Francis College NY 348
St. John's University NY 348
@Saint Joseph's College, New York NY 349
St. Lawrence University NY 349
@Sarah Lawrence College NY 350
@Skidmore College NY 351
State University of New York at Albany NY 351
State University of New York at Binghamton NY 351
State University of New York at Buffalo NY 351
State University of New York College at Plattsburgh NY 354
@State University of New York Empire State College NY 355
@Touro College NY 357
Union Graduate College NY 358
Utica College NY 359
@Vassar College NY 359
@Wells College NY 360
@Yeshiva University NY 361
Brevard College NC 362
@Lees-McRae College NC 366
Case Western Reserve University OH 386
Cincinnati Christian University OH 387
College of Mount St. Joseph OH 388
@Lake Erie College OH 394
Lourdes University OH 395
Ohio Christian University OH 398
@University of Findlay, The OH 404
@Wilmington College OH 405
Xavier University OH 406
University of Tulsa OK 413
@Holy Family University PA 430
Robert Morris University PA 445
@Saint Francis University PA 446
Seton Hill University PA 447
Temple University PA 447
@University of Pittsburgh PA 449
@University of Scranton, The PA 450
@Bayamon Central University PR 560
@Caribbean University PR 560
@Inter American University of Puerto Rico Aguadilla Campus PR 562
@Inter American University of Puerto Rico Arecibo Campus PR 562
@Inter American University of Puerto Rico Barranquitas Campus PR 563
@Inter American University of Puerto Rico Fajardo Campus PR 563
@Inter American University of Puerto Rico Guayama Campus PR 563
@Inter American University of Puerto Rico Metropolitan Campus PR 563
@Inter American University of Puerto Rico Ponce Campus PR 563
@Inter American University of Puerto Rico San German Campus PR 563
@National College of Business and Technology PR 564
@Pontifical Catholic University of Puerto Rico-Arecibo Campus PR 565
@Pontifical Catholic University of Puerto Rico-Mayaguez Campus PR 565
@Pontifical Catholic University of Puerto Rico, The PR 564
@Universidad del Este PR 565
@Universidad Del Turabo PR 565
@Universidad Metropolitana PR 565
@Abilene Christian University TX 478
@Rice University TX 492
Texas Lutheran University TX 499
@Texas State University-San Marcos TX 501
@University of Houston - Victoria TX 503
@University of St. Thomas TX 504
University of Texas at Tyler TX 506
Brigham Young University UT 509
Dixie State College of Utah UT 512
Southern Utah University UT 511
@University of Utah, The UT 510
@Utah State University UT 511
Utah Valley University UT 511
@Weber State University UT 511
Westminster College UT 512
Bluefield College VA 516
Emory & Henry College VA 518
Hollins University VA 519
Mary Baldwin College VA 520
Randolph College VA 522
Randolph-Macon College VA 522
Regent University VA 523
Roanoke College VA 523
Shenandoah University VA 523
University of Richmond VA 525
University of Virginia VA 525
University of Virginia's College at Wise, The VA 525
@Washington and Lee University VA 530
Saint Martin's University WA 536
Alderson Broaddus College WV 540
Davis & Elkins College WV 540
@Ohio Valley University WV 541
University of Charleston WV 541
Wheeling Jesuit University WV 545
Lakeland College WI 547

TED: National Council for Accreditation of Teacher Education: teacher education (B,M,S,D)

Alabama Agricultural and Mechanical University AL 1
Alabama State University AL 1
Athens State University AL 1
Auburn University AL 1
Auburn University at Montgomery AL 2
Birmingham-Southern College AL 2
Faulkner University AL 3
Jacksonville State University AL 4
Miles College AL 5
Oakwood University AL 6
Samford University AL 6
Stillman College AL 7
Troy University AL 8
Tuskegee University AL 8
University of Alabama at Birmingham AL 8
University of Alabama in Huntsville AL 9
University of Alabama, The AL 8
University of Montevallo AL 9
University of North Alabama AL 9
University of South Alabama AL 9
University of West Alabama, The AL 10
Alaska Pacific University AK 10
University of Alaska Anchorage AK 10
University of Alaska Fairbanks AK 10
University of Alaska Southeast AK 11
Northern Arizona University AZ 17
Arkansas State University AR 20
Arkansas Tech University AR 20
Harding University Main Campus AR 21
Henderson State University AR 21
Hendrix College AR 22
John Brown University AR 22
Lyon College AR 22
Ouachita Baptist University AR 22
Philander Smith College AR 23
Southern Arkansas University AR 23
University of Arkansas at Fort Smith AR 24
University of Arkansas at Little Rock AR 24
University of Arkansas at Monticello AR 25
University of Arkansas at Pine Bluff AR 25
University of Arkansas Main Campus AR 24
University of Central Arkansas AR 25
University of the Ozarks AR 26
Williams Baptist College AR 26
Azusa Pacific University CA 30
California Lutheran University CA 32
California State University-Bakersfield CA 33
California State University-Chico CA 34
California State University-Dominguez Hills CA 34
California State University-East Bay CA 34
California State University-Fresno CA 34
California State University-Fullerton CA 34
California State University-Long Beach CA 35
California State University-Los Angeles CA 35
California State University-Monterey Bay CA 35
California State University-Northridge CA 35
California State University-San Bernardino CA 36
California State University-San Marcos CA 36
California State University-Stanislaus CA 36
Loyola Marymount University CA 56
San Diego State University CA 36
San Francisco State University CA 36
San Jose State University CA 37
Sonoma State University CA 37
Stanford University CA 71
University of San Diego CA 76
University of the Pacific CA 75
Colorado Mesa University CO 82
Metropolitan State College of Denver CO 85
University of Colorado at Colorado Springs CO 88
University of Colorado Boulder CO 88
University of Colorado Denver/Anschutz Medical Campus CO 88
University of Northern Colorado CO 88
Central Connecticut State University CT 91
Eastern Connecticut State University CT 91
Fairfield University CT 92
Quinnipiac University CT 93
Sacred Heart University CT 93
Southern Connecticut State University CT 91
University of Connecticut CT 94
University of Hartford CT 95
Western Connecticut State University CT 92
Delaware State University DE 95
University of Delaware DE 96
#Wesley College DE 96
Wilmington University DE 97
American University DC 97
Catholic University of America, The DC 97
Gallaudet University DC 97
George Washington University DC 97
Howard University DC 98
Trinity Washington University DC 99
University System of the District of Columbia DC 99
Bethune Cookman University FL 101
Florida Agricultural and Mechanical University FL 118
Florida Atlantic University FL 118
Florida International University FL 119
Florida State University FL 119
Stetson University FL 121
University of Central Florida FL 120
University of Florida FL 120
University of North Florida FL 120
University of South Florida FL 120
University of South Florida St. Petersburg FL 121
University of West Florida FL 121
Albany State University GA 123
Armstrong Atlantic State University GA 124
Augusta State University GA 125
Berry College GA 125
Brenau University GA 126
Brewton-Parker College GA 126
Clark Atlanta University GA 126
Clayton State University GA 127
Columbus State University GA 127
Dalton State College GA 127
Emory University GA 129
Fort Valley State University GA 129
Georgia College & State University GA 129
Georgia Southern University GA 131
Georgia Southwestern State University GA 131
Georgia State University GA 131
Kennesaw State University GA 132
Macon State College GA 133
Mercer University GA 133
North Georgia College & State University GA 134
Paine College GA 135
Point University GA 135
Spelman College GA 137
University of Georgia GA 138
University of West Georgia GA 138
Valdosta State University GA 138
University of Guam GU 559
University of Hawaii at Manoa HI 141
Boise State University ID 142
Idaho State University ID 143
Lewis-Clark State College ID 143
Northwest Nazarene University ID 143
University of Idaho ID 144
Augustana College IL 145
Aurora University IL 145
Bradley University IL 145
Chicago State University IL 146
Concordia University Chicago IL 148
Eastern Illinois University IL 150
Governors State University IL 151
Illinois State University IL 153
Lewis University IL 156
Loyola University Chicago IL 157
McKendree University IL 157
Millikin University IL 158
National-Louis University IL 159
Northeastern Illinois University IL 159
Northern Illinois University IL 160
Olivet Nazarene University IL 160
Roosevelt University IL 162
Saint Xavier University IL 163
Southern Illinois University Carbondale IL 164
Southern Illinois University Edwardsville IL 165
University of St. Francis IL 167
Western Illinois University IL 168
Wheaton College IL 168
Anderson University IN 169
Ball State University IN 169
Bethel College IN 169
Butler University IN 170
DePauw University IN 170
Franklin College of Indiana IN 171
Goshen College IN 171
Grace College and Seminary IN 171
Hanover College IN 171
Huntington University IN 172
Indiana State University IN 173
Indiana University Bloomington IN 173
Indiana University East IN 173
Indiana University Kokomo IN 173
Indiana University Northwest IN 173
Indiana University-Purdue University Fort Wayne IN 174
Indiana University South Bend IN 174
Indiana University Southeast IN 174
Indiana Wesleyan University IN 174
Manchester College IN 177

THEA: National Association of Schools of Theatre: theatre (B,M,D)

THEOL: Association of Theological Schools: theology (M,FP,D)

TRACS: Transnational Association of Christian Colleges and Schools: christian studies education (C,A,B,M,D)

VET: American Veterinary Medical Association: veterinary medicine (FP)

WC: Western Association of Schools and Colleges, Accrediting Commission for Senior Colleges and Universities (WASC-Sr)

WJ: Western Association of Schools and Colleges, Accrediting Commission for Community and Junior Colleges (WASC-ACCJC)

Index of FICE Numbers

Code	Institution	State	Page
002214	Saint John's Seminary	MA	244
002217	Stonehill College	MA	245
002218	Suffolk University	MA	245
002219	Tufts University	MA	245
002221	University of Massachusetts	MA	237
002222	University of Massachusetts Boston	MA	237
002224	Wellesley College	MA	246
002225	Wentworth Institute of Technology	MA	246
002226	Western New England University	MA	246
002227	Wheaton College	MA	246
002228	Wheelock College	MA	246
002229	Williams College	MA	246
002230	Woods Hole Oceanographic Inst	MA	247
002233	Worcester Polytechnic Institute	MA	247
002234	Adrian College	MI	247
002235	Albion College	MI	247
002236	Alma College	MI	247
002237	Alpena Community College	MI	247
002238	Andrews University	MI	247
002239	Aquinas College	MI	248
002240	Bay Noc Community College	MI	249
002241	Calvin College	MI	249
002242	Calvin Theological Seminary	MI	249
002243	Central Michigan University	MI	249
002246	Cleary University	MI	249
002247	Concordia University	MI	250
002248	Cranbrook Academy of Art	MI	250
002249	Davenport University	MI	250
002251	Delta College	MI	250
002259	Eastern Michigan University	MI	250
002260	Ferris State University	MI	251
002261	Mott Community College	MI	256
002262	Kettering University	MI	253
002263	Glen Oaks Community College	MI	251
002264	Gogebic Community College	MI	251
002265	Grace Bible College	MI	251
002266	Cornerstone University	MI	250
002267	Grand Rapids Community College	MI	251
002268	Grand Valley State University	MI	252
002269	Great Lakes Christian College	MI	252
002270	Henry Ford Community College	MI	252
002272	Hillsdale College	MI	252
002273	Hope College	MI	252
002274	Jackson Community College	MI	253
002275	Kalamazoo College	MI	253
002276	Kellogg Community College	MI	253
002277	Lake Michigan College	MI	254
002278	Lansing Community College	MI	254
002279	Lawrence Technological University	MI	254
002282	Madonna University	MI	254
002284	Marygrove College	MI	255
002288	Rochester College	MI	257
002290	Michigan State University	MI	255
002292	Michigan Technological University	MI	255
002293	Lake Superior State University	MI	254
002294	Monroe County Community College	MI	255
002295	Montcalm Community College	MI	256
002296	Baker College of Muskegon	MI	248
002297	Muskegon Community College	MI	256
002299	North Central Michigan College	MI	256
002301	Northern Michigan University	MI	256
002302	Northwestern Michigan College	MI	256
002303	Oakland Community College	MI	257
002307	Oakland University	MI	257
002308	Olivet College	MI	257
002310	St. Clair County Community College	MI	258
002311	Kuyper College	MI	254
002313	Sacred Heart Major Seminary College	MI	257
002314	Saginaw Valley State University	MI	258
002315	Schoolcraft College	MI	258
002316	Siena Heights University	MI	258
002317	Southwestern Michigan College	MI	258
002318	Spring Arbor University	MI	258
002322	Finlandia University	MI	251
002323	University of Detroit Mercy	MI	259
002325	University of Michigan-Ann Arbor	MI	259
002326	University of Michigan-Dearborn	MI	259
002327	University of Michigan-Flint	MI	259
002328	Washtenaw Community College	MI	260
002329	Wayne State University	MI	260
002330	Western Michigan University	MI	260
002331	Western Theological Seminary	MI	260
002332	Anoka-Ramsey Community College	MN	265
002334	Augsburg College	MN	261
002335	Riverland Community College	MN	269
002336	Bemidji State University	MN	266
002337	Bethany Lutheran College	MN	261
002339	Central Lakes College	MN	266
002340	Carleton College	MN	262
002341	College of Saint Benedict	MN	262
002342	St. Catherine University	MN	271
002343	The College of Saint Scholastica	MN	262
002345	University of Saint Thomas	MN	272
002346	Concordia College	MN	263
002347	Concordia University, St. Paul	MN	263
002350	Vermilion Community College	MN	270
002353	Gustavus Adolphus College	MN	264
002354	Hamline University	MN	264
002355	Hibbing Community College	MN	266
002356	Itasca Community College	MN	267
002357	Luther Seminary	MN	264
002358	Macalester College	MN	265
002360	Minnesota State University, Mankato	MN	267
002361	Martin Luther College	MN	265
002362	Minneapolis Cmty & Tech College	MN	267
002365	Minneapolis College of Art Design	MN	265
002366	Crossroads College	MN	263
002367	Minnesota State University Moorhead	MN	268
002369	North Central University	MN	270
002370	North Hennepin Community College	MN	268
002371	Northwestern College	MN	270
002373	Rochester Community & Tech College	MN	269
002375	Southwest Minnesota State Univ	MN	269
002377	St. Cloud State University	MN	269
002379	Saint John's University	MN	271
002380	St Mary's University of Minnesota	MN	271
002382	St. Olaf College	MN	271
002383	Crown College	MN	263
002385	Northland Community & Tech College	MN	268
002386	United Theol Seminary-Twin Cities	MN	271
002388	University of Minnesota Duluth	MN	272
002389	University of Minnesota-Morris	MN	272
002391	William Mitchell College of Law	MN	273
002393	Minnesota State Col-Southeast Tech	MN	267
002394	Winona State University	MN	270
002396	Alcorn State University	MS	273
002397	Belhaven University	MS	273
002398	Blue Mountain College	MS	273
002401	Coahoma Community College	MS	273
002402	Copiah-Lincoln Community College	MS	274
002403	Delta State University	MS	274
002404	East Central Community College	MS	274
002405	East Mississippi Community College	MS	274
002407	Hinds Community College	MS	274
002408	Holmes Community College	MS	274
002409	Itawamba Community College	MS	274
002410	Jackson State University	MS	275
002411	Jones County Junior College	MS	275
002413	Meridian Community College	MS	275
002414	Millsaps College	MS	275
002415	Mississippi College	MS	275
002416	Mississippi Delta Community College	MS	275
002417	Mississippi Gulf Coast Cmty College	MS	275
002422	Mississippi University for Women	MS	276
002423	Mississippi State University	MS	276
002424	Mississippi Valley State University	MS	276
002426	Northeast Mississippi Cmty College	MS	276
002427	Northwest Mississippi Cmty College	MS	276
002430	Pearl River Community College	MS	277
002433	Rust College	MS	277
002435	Southeastern Baptist College	MS	277
002436	Southwest Mississippi Cmty College	MS	277
002439	Tougaloo College	MS	277
002440	University of Mississippi	MS	277
002441	University of Southern Mississippi	MS	278
002447	William Carey University	MS	278
002449	Avila University	MO	279
002450	Calvary Bible Col & Theol Seminary	MO	279
002452	Central Bible College	MO	279
002453	Central Methodist University	MO	279
002454	University of Central Missouri	MO	291
002455	DeVry University-Kansas City Campus	MO	281
002456	Columbia College	MO	280
002457	Concordia Seminary	MO	280
002458	Cottey College	MO	280
002459	Crowder College	MO	281
002460	Culver-Stockton College	MO	281
002461	Drury University	MO	281
002462	Eden Theological Seminary	MO	281
002463	Evangel University	MO	282
002464	Fontbonne University	MO	282
002466	Harris-Stowe State University	MO	282
002467	Conception Seminary College	MO	280
002468	Jefferson College	MO	283
002469	St Louis Cmty Col Center	MO	289
002470	St Louis Cmty Col Florissant Valley	MO	289
002471	St Louis Cmty Col Forest Park	MO	289
002472	St Louis Cmty Col Meramec	MO	289
002473	Kansas City Art Institute	MO	283
002474	Kansas City Univ of Med & BioSci	MO	283
002476	Kenrick-Glennon Seminary	MO	283
002477	A. T. Still Univ of Health Sciences	MO	278
002479	Lincoln University	MO	284
002480	Lindenwood University	MO	284
002482	Maryville University of Saint Louis	MO	284
002484	Metropolitan Cmty Col-Penn Valley	MO	285
002485	Midwestern Baptist Theol Seminary	MO	286
002486	Mineral Area College	MO	286
002488	Missouri Southern State University	MO	286
002489	Missouri Valley College	MO	286
002490	Missouri Western State University	MO	287
002491	Moberly Area Community College	MO	287
002494	Nazarene Theological Seminary	MO	287
002495	Truman State University	MO	291
002496	Northwest Missouri State University	MO	287
002498	Park University	MO	287
002499	Rockhurst University	MO	288
002500	College of the Ozarks	MO	280
002501	Southeast Missouri State University	MO	290
002502	Southwest Baptist University	MO	290
002503	Missouri State University	MO	286
002504	St. Louis College of Pharmacy	MO	288
002506	Saint Louis University	MO	289
002509	Saint Paul School of Theology	MO	289
002512	Stephens College	MO	290
002514	North Central Missouri College	MO	287
002515	Univ of Missouri System Admin	MO	291
002516	University of Missouri - Columbia	MO	291
002517	Missouri Univ of Science Tech	MO	292
002518	Univ of Missouri - Kansas City	MO	291
002519	Univ of Missouri - Saint Louis	MO	291
002520	Washington University in St. Louis	MO	292
002521	Webster University	MO	293
002522	Wentworth Military Academy/Jr Col	MO	293
002523	Westminster College	MO	293
002524	William Jewell College	MO	293
002525	William Woods University	MO	293
002526	Carroll College	MT	294
002527	University of Great Falls	MT	296
002528	Miles Community College	MT	294
002529	Dawson Community College	MT	294
002530	Montana State University - Billings	MT	295
002531	Montana Tech of the Univ of Montana	MT	296
002532	Montana State University	MT	295
002533	Montana State University - Northern	MT	295
002534	Rocky Mountain College	MT	296
002536	The University of Montana-Missoula	MT	295
002537	The University of Montana Western	MT	295
002539	Chadron State College	NE	299
002540	College of Saint Mary	NE	297
002541	Concordia University	NE	297
002542	Creighton University	NE	297
002544	Doane College	NE	298
002547	Grace University	NE	298
002548	Hastings College	NE	298
002551	University of Nebraska at Kearney	NE	300
002553	Midland University	NE	299
002554	University of Nebraska at Omaha	NE	301
002555	Nebraska Wesleyan University	NE	299
002557	Mid-Plains Community College	NE	298
002559	Peru State College	NE	299
002560	Western Nebraska Community College	NE	301
002563	Union College	NE	300
002565	University of Nebraska - Lincoln	NE	300
002566	Wayne State College	NE	299
002567	York College	NE	301
002568	University of Nevada, Reno	NV	303
002569	University of Nevada, Las Vegas	NV	302
002572	Colby-Sawyer College	NH	304
002573	Dartmouth College	NH	305
002575	Franklin Pierce University	NH	305
002579	New England College	NH	305
002580	Southern New Hampshire University	NH	306
002581	NHTI-Concord's Community College	NH	304
002582	Manchester Community College	NH	304
002583	Great Bay Community College	NH	304
002586	Rivier College	NH	305
002587	Saint Anselm College	NH	305
002589	University of New Hampshire	NH	306
002590	Keene State College	NH	307
002591	Plymouth State University	NH	307
002595	Assumption College for Sisters	NJ	307
002596	Atlantic Cape Community College	NJ	307
002597	Bloomfield College	NJ	308
002598	Caldwell College	NJ	308
002599	Centenary College	NJ	308
002600	College of Saint Elizabeth	NJ	309
002601	Cumberland County College	NJ	309
002603	Drew University	NJ	309
002607	Fairleigh Dickinson University	NJ	310
002608	Georgian Court University	NJ	310
002609	Rowan University	NJ	314
002610	Felician College	NJ	310
002611	Immaculate Conception Seminary	NJ	311
002613	New Jersey City University	NJ	312
002615	Middlesex County College	NJ	311
002616	Monmouth University	NJ	311
002617	Montclair State University	NJ	311
002619	New Brunswick Theological Seminary	NJ	312
002620	UMDNJ-New Jersey Medical School	NJ	316
002621	New Jersey Institute of Technology	NJ	312
002622	Kean University	NJ	311
002624	Ocean County College	NJ	312
002625	William Paterson University of NJ	NJ	317
002626	Princeton Theological Seminary	NJ	312
002627	Princeton University	NJ	313
002628	Rider University	NJ	313
002629	Rutgers State Univ Central Office	NJ	314
002631	Rutgers State Univ - Newark	NJ	314
002632	Seton Hall University	NJ	315
002638	Saint Peter's College	NJ	314
002639	Stevens Institute of Technology	NJ	315
002642	The College of New Jersey	NJ	308
002643	Union County College	NJ	316
002649	Santa Fe Univ of Art and Design	NM	320
002650	University of the Southwest	NM	321
002651	Eastern New Mexico University	NM	318
002653	New Mexico Highlands University	NM	318
002654	New Mexico Inst of Mining & Tech	NM	319
002655	New Mexico Junior College	NM	319
002656	New Mexico Military Institute	NM	319
002657	NM State University-Main Campus	NM	319
002658	NM State University-Alamogordo	NM	319

Code	Institution	State	Page
003085	Notre Dame College	OH	397
003086	Oberlin College	OH	397
003088	Ohio College of Podiatric Medicine	OH	398
003089	Ohio Northern University	OH	398
003090	The Ohio State Univ Main Campus	OH	398
003092	The Ohio State University Lima	OH	399
003093	The Ohio State University Mansfield	OH	399
003094	The Ohio State University at Marion	OH	399
003095	The Ohio State University Newark	OH	399
003099	DeVry University - Columbus Campus	OH	390
003100	Ohio University Main Campus	OH	399
003101	Ohio University Eastern Campus	OH	400
003102	Ohio University Chillicothe Campus	OH	399
003104	Ohio University Lancaster Campus	OH	400
003108	Ohio University Zanesville Branch	OH	400
003109	Ohio Wesleyan University	OH	400
003110	Otterbein University	OH	400
003113	Pontifical College Josephinum	OH	401
003115	Rabbinical College of Telshe	OH	401
003116	University of Rio Grande	OH	404
003119	Sinclair Community College	OH	401
003121	Tiffin University	OH	402
003122	United Theological Seminary	OH	403
003123	The Univ of Akron, Main Campus	OH	403
003125	University of Cincinnati Main	OH	403
003127	University of Dayton	OH	404
003131	University of Toledo	OH	404
003133	Urbana University	OH	405
003134	Ursuline College	OH	405
003135	Walsh University	OH	405
003141	Wilberforce University	OH	405
003142	Wilmington College	OH	405
003143	Wittenberg University	OH	406
003144	Xavier University	OH	406
003145	Youngstown State University	OH	406
003146	Western Oklahoma State College	OK	414
003147	Bacone College	OK	407
003149	Southern Nazarene University	OK	412
003150	Cameron University	OK	407
003151	Oklahoma Wesleyan University	OK	411
003152	University of Central Oklahoma	OK	413
003153	Connors State College	OK	407
003154	East Central University	OK	407
003155	Eastern Oklahoma State College	OK	408
003156	Redlands Community College	OK	411
003157	Langston University	OK	408
003158	Murray State College	OK	408
003160	Northeastern Oklahoma A&M College	OK	408
003161	Northeastern State University	OK	409
003162	Northern Oklahoma College	OK	409
003163	Northwestern Oklahoma State Univ	OK	409
003164	Oklahoma Baptist University	OK	409
003165	Oklahoma Christian University	OK	409
003166	Oklahoma City University	OK	410
003167	Univ of Science & Arts of Oklahoma	OK	413
003168	Rogers State University	OK	411
003170	Oklahoma State University	OK	410
003172	Oklahoma State Univ - Okmulgee	OK	410
003174	Oklahoma Panhandle State University	OK	410
003176	Carl Albert State College	OK	407
003178	Seminole State College	OK	412
003179	Southeastern Oklahoma State Univ	OK	412
003180	Southwestern Christian University	OK	412
003181	Southwestern Oklahoma State Univ	OK	412
003183	St. Gregory's University	OK	412
003184	University of Oklahoma Norman	OK	413
003185	University of Tulsa	OK	413
003186	Blue Mountain Community College	OR	414
003188	Central Oregon Community College	OR	414
003189	Clatsop Community College	OR	415
003191	Concordia University	OR	415
003193	Eastern Oregon University	OR	418
003194	George Fox University	OR	415
003196	Lane Community College	OR	416
003197	Lewis and Clark College	OR	416
003198	Linfield College	OR	416
003199	Marylhurst University	OR	416
003203	Mount Angel Seminary	OR	417
003204	Mt. Hood Community College	OR	417
003206	Multnomah University	OR	417
003207	Pacific Northwest College of Art	OR	419
003208	Northwest Christian University	OR	417
003209	Western Oregon University	OR	419
003210	Oregon State University	OR	418
003211	Oregon Institute of Technology	OR	418
003212	Pacific University	OR	419
003213	Portland Community College	OR	419
003216	Portland State University	OR	418
003217	Reed College	OR	420
003218	Chemeketa Community College	OR	414
003219	Southern Oregon University	OR	419
003220	Southwestern Oregon Community Col	OR	420
003221	Treasure Valley Community College	OR	420
003222	Umpqua Community College	OR	420
003223	University of Oregon	OR	419
003224	University of Portland	OR	420
003225	Warner Pacific College	OR	421
003227	Willamette University	OR	421
003228	Bryn Athyn Col of the New Church	PA	423
003229	Albright College	PA	421
003230	Allegheny College	PA	421
003231	Community College of Allegheny Cty	PA	425
003233	Alvernia University	PA	421
003235	Arcadia University	PA	422
003237	Bryn Mawr College	PA	423
003238	Bucknell University	PA	423
003239	Bucks County Community College	PA	423
003240	Butler County Community College	PA	423
003241	Cabrini College	PA	423
003242	Carnegie Mellon University	PA	424
003243	Cedar Crest College	PA	424
003244	Chatham University	PA	425
003245	Chestnut Hill College	PA	425
003247	Misericordia University	PA	436
003249	Community College of Philadelphia	PA	426
003251	Curtis Institute of Music	PA	426
003252	Delaware Valley College	PA	426
003253	Dickinson College	PA	427
003254	The Penn State Dickinson Sch of Law	PA	439
003256	Drexel University	PA	427
003258	Duquesne University	PA	428
003259	Eastern University	PA	428
003260	Palmer Theol Sem of Eastern Univ	PA	438
003262	Elizabethtown College	PA	428
003263	Evangelical Theological Seminary	PA	428
003265	Franklin & Marshall College	PA	429
003266	Gannon University	PA	429
003267	Geneva College	PA	429
003268	Gettysburg College	PA	429
003269	Grove City College	PA	430
003270	Gwynedd-Mercy College	PA	430
003272	Harcum College	PA	430
003273	Harrisburg Area Community College	PA	430
003274	Haverford College	PA	430
003275	Holy Family University	PA	430
003276	Immaculata University	PA	431
003277	Indiana University of Pennsylvania	PA	442
003279	Juniata College	PA	431
003280	Keystone College	PA	432
003282	King's College	PA	432
003283	Lackawanna College	PA	433
003284	Lafayette College	PA	433
003285	Lancaster Bible College	PA	433
003286	Lancaster Theological Seminary	PA	433
003287	La Salle University	PA	432
003288	Lebanon Valley College	PA	434
003289	Lehigh University	PA	434
003290	Lincoln University	PA	434
003291	Lutheran Theol Seminary Gettysburg	PA	435
003292	Lutheran Theol Seminary at Phila	PA	435
003293	Lycoming College	PA	435
003294	Manor College	PA	435
003296	Marywood University	PA	435
003297	Mercyhurst College	PA	436
003298	Messiah College	PA	436
003300	Moore College of Art and Design	PA	436
003301	Moravian College	PA	436
003302	Mount Aloysius College	PA	437
003303	Carlow University	PA	424
003304	Muhlenberg College	PA	437
003305	Erie Business Center South	PA	428
003306	Valley Forge Christian College	PA	450
003309	Peirce College	PA	438
003311	Salus University	PA	446
003313	Widener University	PA	451
003315	Bloomsburg Univ of Pennsylvania	PA	441
003316	California University of PA	PA	441
003317	Cheyney University of Pennsylvania	PA	441
003318	Clarion University of Pennsylvania	PA	442
003319	Clarion University-Venango Campus	PA	442
003320	East Stroudsburg University of PA	PA	442
003321	Edinboro University of Pennsylvania	PA	442
003322	Kutztown University of Pennsylvania	PA	442
003323	Lock Haven University of PA	PA	443
003324	Mansfield University of PA	PA	443
003325	Millersville University of PA	PA	443
003326	Shippensburg University of PA	PA	443
003327	Slippery Rock University of PA	PA	443
003328	West Chester University of PA	PA	443
003329	Penn State University Park	PA	438
003330	Penn State Lehigh Valley	PA	439
003331	Penn State Altoona	PA	438
003332	Penn State Beaver	PA	438
003333	Penn State Erie	PA	439
003334	Penn State Berks	PA	439
003335	Penn State DuBois	PA	439
003336	Penn State Fayette, The Eberly Camp	PA	439
003338	Penn State Hazleton	PA	439
003339	Penn State Greater Allegheny	PA	439
003340	Penn State Mont Alto	PA	440
003341	Penn State New Kensington	PA	440
003342	Penn State Abington	PA	438
003343	Penn State Schuylkill	PA	440
003344	Penn State Worthington-Scranton	PA	440
003345	Penn State Shenango	PA	440
003346	Penn State Wilkes-Barre	PA	440
003347	Penn State York	PA	440
003348	PA St Grt Vlly Sch of Grad Prof Std	PA	439
003350	The University of the Arts	PA	448
003351	Philadelphia Biblical University	PA	444
003352	Philadelphia Col of Osteopathic Med	PA	444
003353	Univ of Sciences in Philadelphia	PA	450
003354	Philadelphia University	PA	444
003356	Pittsburgh Theological Seminary	PA	444
003357	Point Park University	PA	444
003358	Reformed Presbyterian Theo Seminary	PA	445
003359	Robert Morris University	PA	445
003360	Rosemont College	PA	445
003362	Seton Hill University	PA	447
003364	Saint Charles Borromeo Seminary	PA	446
003366	Saint Francis University	PA	446
003367	Saint Joseph's University	PA	446
003368	Saint Vincent College	PA	446
003369	Susquehanna University	PA	447
003370	Swarthmore College	PA	447
003371	Temple University	PA	447
003376	Thiel College	PA	448
003378	University of Pennsylvania	PA	448
003379	University of Pittsburgh	PA	449
003380	Univ of Pittsburgh Bradford	PA	449
003381	Univ of Pittsburgh Greensburg	PA	449
003382	Univ of Pittsburgh at Johnstown	PA	449
003383	Univ of Pittsburgh Titusville	PA	449
003384	The University of Scranton	PA	450
003385	Ursinus College	PA	450
003386	Valley Forge Military College	PA	450
003388	Villanova University	PA	450
003389	Washington & Jefferson College	PA	451
003391	Waynesburg University	PA	451
003392	Westminster College	PA	451
003393	Westminster Theological Seminary	PA	451
003394	Wilkes University	PA	451
003395	Pennsylvania College of Technology	PA	440
003396	Wilson College	PA	452
003399	York College of Pennsylvania	PA	452
003401	Brown University	RI	452
003402	Bryant University	RI	453
003404	Johnson & Wales University	RI	453
003406	Providence College	RI	453
003407	Rhode Island College	RI	454
003408	Community College of Rhode Island	RI	453
003409	Rhode Island School of Design	RI	454
003410	Roger Williams University	RI	454
003411	Salve Regina University	RI	454
003413	Naval War College	RI	557
003414	University of Rhode Island	RI	454
003417	Allen University	SC	455
003418	Anderson University	SC	455
003419	Charleston Southern University	SC	456
003420	Benedict College	SC	455
003421	Bob Jones University	SC	455
003422	Southern Wesleyan University	SC	461
003423	The Citadel Military College of SC	SC	456
003424	Claflin University	SC	456
003425	Clemson University	SC	456
003426	University of South Carolina Sumter	SC	462
003427	Coker College	SC	457
003428	College of Charleston	SC	457
003429	Columbia International University	SC	457
003430	Columbia College	SC	457
003431	Converse College	SC	457
003432	Erskine College	SC	457
003434	Furman University	SC	458
003435	Lander University	SC	458
003436	Limestone College	SC	459
003437	Lutheran Theol Southern Seminary	SC	459
003438	Medical Univ of South Carolina	SC	459
003439	Morris College	SC	459
003440	Newberry College	SC	459
003441	North Greenville University	SC	460
003445	Presbyterian College	SC	460
003446	South Carolina State University	SC	460
003447	Spartanburg Methodist College	SC	461
003448	Univ of South Carolina-Columbia	SC	462
003449	University of South Carolina Aiken	SC	462
003450	Univ of South Carolina Beaufort	SC	462
003451	Coastal Carolina University	SC	456
003453	Univ of South Carolina Lancaster	SC	462
003454	Univ of South Carolina Salkehatchie	SC	462
003455	Voorhees College	SC	463
003456	Winthrop University	SC	463
003457	Wofford College	SC	463
003458	Augustana College	SD	463
003459	Black Hills State University	SD	465
003461	Dakota Wesleyan University	SD	464
003463	Dakota State University	SD	465
003465	Mount Marty College	SD	464
003466	Northern State University	SD	465
003467	Presentation College	SD	464
003469	University of Sioux Falls	SD	466
003470	South Dakota Sch of Mines & Tech	SD	466
003471	South Dakota State University	SD	466
003474	The University of South Dakota	SD	465
003477	Aquinas College	TN	466
003478	Austin Peay State University	TN	473
003479	Belmont University	TN	467
003480	Bethel University	TN	467
003481	Carson-Newman College	TN	467
003482	Christian Brothers University	TN	467
003483	Columbia State Community College	TN	474
003484	Covenant College	GA	127
003485	Cumberland University	TN	467
003486	Lipscomb University	TN	470

Code	Institution	State	Page
666532	DeVry University - Henry County	GA	128
666533	ITT Technical Institute	CA	51
666534	ITT Technical Institute	CA	51
666535	DeVry University - Gurnee	IL	149
666536	ITT Technical Institute	FL	111
666537	ITT Technical Institute	FL	111
666538	ITT Technical Institute	IL	154
666539	ITT Technical Institute	IL	154
666540	ITT Technical Institute	KY	200
666541	ITT Technical Institute	MA	236
666542	ITT Technical Institute	MI	253
666543	ITT Technical Institute	NE	298
666544	ITT Technical Institute	NV	302
666545	ITT Technical Institute	NM	318
666546	ITT Technical Institute	OH	392
666547	ITT Technical Institute	OH	392
666548	ITT Technical Institute	PA	431
666549	ITT Technical Institute	SC	458
666550	ITT Technical Institute	TN	469
666551	ITT Technical Institute	TX	488
666552	ITT Technical Institute	TX	488
666554	ITT Technical Institute	TX	488
666555	ITT Technical Institute	VA	519
666556	DeVry University - Indianapolis	IN	170
666557	DeVry University - Southfield	MI	250
666558	DeVry University - Edina	MN	263
666559	DeVry University - St. Louis Park	MN	263
666560	DeVry University - Henderson	NV	301
666561	DeVry University - Paramus	NJ	309
666562	DeVry University - Raleigh/Durham	NC	363
666563	DeVry University - Cincinnati	OH	390
666564	DeVry University - Dayton	OH	390
666565	DeVry University - Seven Hills	OH	390
666566	DeVry University - Oklahoma City	OK	407
666567	DeVry University - Portland	OR	415
666568	DeVry University - Philadelphia	PA	427
666569	DeVry University - Pittsburgh	PA	427
666570	DeVry University - King of Prussia	PA	427
666571	DeVry University - Memphis	TN	468
666573	DeVry University - Austin	TX	485
666574	DeVry University - Fort Worth	TX	485
666575	DeVry University - Richardson	TX	486
666576	DeVry University - Sandy	UT	509
666577	DeVry University - Chesapeake	VA	518
666582	Santa Barbara Business College	CA	67
666583	Vatterott College - Wichita	KS	197
666584	Vatterott College-O'Fallon	MO	292
666588	DeVry University - Louisville	KY	200
666589	DeVry University - Nashville	TN	468
666590	Everest University-Orange Park	FL	106
666591	Sanz College	DC	99
666595	ITT Technical Institute	GA	132
666596	ITT Technical Institute	IA	186
666597	Westwood College-Atlanta Northlake	GA	139
666599	Westwood College-Annandale	VA	530
666601	Inter Amer Univ of PR Sch Optometry	PR	564
666602	Fortis College	OH	390
666603	Pont Catholic Univ of PR-Arecibo	PR	565
666605	Pont Catholic Univ of PR-Mayaguez	PR	565
666609	ITT Technical Institute	NY	337
666612	Florida Med Trng Inst-Coconut Creek	FL	108
666613	Anthem College-Milwaukee	WI	545
666615	Pacific Col of Oriental Medicine	IL	161
666616	Robert E. Webber Inst Worship Stds	FL	116
666618	Southwest Acupuncture College	CO	87
666619	Art Inst of California-Sacramento	CA	29
666620	Art Inst of California-Sunnyvale	CA	30
666621	Everest Col-Ontario Metro	CA	46
666622	Florida Career College	FL	107
666623	Hallmark College of Aeronautics	TX	487
666624	Florida Career College	FL	107
666628	Reformed Theological Seminary	FL	115
666631	Intl Academy of Design/Tech	FL	111
666632	Intl Academy Design & Tech	MI	252
666636	Academy for Jewish Religion	CA	26
666638	Brandman University	CA	30
666639	Columbia Gorge Community College	OR	415
666640	Evangelia University	CA	45
666641	Georgia Christian University	GA	129
666642	Grace Mission University	CA	48
666643	Gerstner Grad Sch of Biomedical Sci	NY	339
666644	Lutheran Brethren Seminary	MN	264
666647	Tillamook Bay Community College	OR	420
666648	University of Fort Lauderdale	FL	122
666649	NM State Univ Dona Ana Cmty College	NM	319
666650	Kona University	HI	140
666651	Anaheim University	CA	28
666653	Atlantic University	VA	516
666654	Argosy University, Denver	CO	81
666655	Argosy University, Salt Lake City	UT	509
666656	Connecticut State Univ System Ofc	CT	91
666658	Suffolk Cty Cmty Coll Central Admin	NY	356
666659	Prince William Sound Cmty College	AK	11
666660	Westwood College-Arlington Ballston	VA	530
666665	S California Univ Sch Oriental Med	CA	71
666666	SW Acupuncture Col-Albuquerque	NM	320
666668	Argosy University, Nashville	TN	466
666669	ITT Technical Institute	FL	111
666670	California Intercontinental Univ	CA	32
666671	Elmezzi Grad Sch of Molecular Med	NY	332
666673	Beckfield College	OH	384
666675	Charter College-Oxnard	CA	39
666677	MedTech College	IN	177
666678	MedTech College	IN	177
666680	National College	IN	178
666683	Tri-State Institute	AL	8
666687	Global University	MO	282
666688	International Inst Restorative Prac	PA	431
666689	Texas A & M University-San Antonio	TX	498
666690	Florida National Col Training Ctr	FL	109
666691	Floridal National Coll South Campus	FL	109
666692	The Art Institute of Michigan	MI	248
666693	Art Institute of Ohio-Cincinnati	OH	384
666694	Art Institute of Salt Lake City	UT	509
666695	ITT Technical Institute	AL	4
666696	ITT Technical Institute	AZ	14
666697	ITT Technical Institute	CA	51
666700	ITT Technical Institute	IN	175
666701	ITT Technical Institute	MS	274
666702	ITT Technical Institute	MO	283
666703	ITT Technical Institute	NC	365
666704	ITT Technical Institute	NC	365
666705	ITT Technical Institute	NC	365
666706	ITT Technical Institute	OH	392
666707	Yeshiva & Kolel Bais Medrash Elyon	NY	361
666708	ITT Technical Institute	TN	469
666709	ITT Technical Institute	WV	541
666710	Brighton College	AZ	12
666711	California Intrntl Business Univ	CA	32
666712	Heald College, Central Office	CA	49
666713	California Miramar University	CA	33
666714	Future Generations Graduate School	WV	540
666715	Lakewood College	OH	394
666718	Oklahoma Technical College	OK	411
666719	College of Medicine, Mayo Clinic	MN	262
666721	AMDA Col & Conservatory of Perf Art	CA	27
666723	American InterContinental Univ	IL	144
666724	Brookline College	NM	317
666728	Le Cordon Bleu College Dallas	TX	489
666729	Texas School of Business-Southwest	TX	499
666730	Court Reporting Institute Houston	TX	483
666731	Colorado Technical University	SD	464
666732	Colorado Technical University	CO	83
666733	International Academy Design/Tech	TX	488
666734	California Univ Mgmt/Sciences VA	VA	517
666735	Argosy University, Atlanta	GA	124
666736	Argosy University, Chicago	IL	144
666737	Everest College	WA	533
666738	Instit of Business/Medical Careers	WY	556
666739	Sanford-Brown College	AZ	18
666740	Internatl Acad of Design/Tech	CA	51
666741	University of New Mexico-Valencia	NM	321
666742	University of New Mexico-Los Alamos	NM	321
666743	University of New Mexico-Taos	NM	321
666745	Marine Corps University	VA	557
666746	Sch of Avanced Air/Space Studies	AL	557
666747	San Jacinto College North	TX	493
666748	San Jacinto College South	TX	493
666749	Everest College-West LA	CA	46
666751	Carrington College CA-San Leandro	CA	38
666752	Kaplan College	FL	112
666753	Sanford-Brown College	IL	163
666758	Keiser Career College	FL	112
666759	Northwestern Polytechnic University	CA	59
666761	Fortis College, Phoenix	AZ	14
666762	Fortis College	UT	509
666765	Art Institutes International - KC	KS	190
666769	Rasmussen College - Brooklyn Park	MN	271
666770	California Southern University	CA	33
666771	Moreno Valley College	CA	63
666772	Norco College	CA	64
666775	Northwest Institute Literary Arts	WA	535
666776	U.S. Career Institute	CO	89
666777	Hiwassee College	TN	469
666779	Mesivta Keser Torah	NJ	311
666780	Brown Mackie Colllege-Boise	ID	142
666781	Brown Mackie College-Greenville	SC	455
666782	Brown Mackie College-Phoenix	AZ	12
666783	Brown Mackie College-Tulsa	OK	407
666784	Bd of Trustees Cmty-Technical Col	CT	89
666785	Reformed Theological Seminary	NC	375
666786	CA Natl Univ for Advanced Studies	CA	33
666787	Argosy University, Hawaii	HI	139
666788	Argosy University, Washington DC	VA	516
666789	Argosy University, Schaumburg	IL	145
666790	Argosy University, Phoenix	AZ	11
666791	DeVry University - Downers Grove	IL	149
666792	Brown Mackie College-Quad Cities	IA	182
666793	Brown Mackie College-St. Louis	MO	279
666809	College for Financial Planning	CO	81
666811	Antioch University Midwest	OH	383
666812	Antioch University Seattle	WA	530
666813	Inter Amer Univ of PR School of Law	PR	564
666814	Carlos Albizu Univ Miami Campus	FL	102
666828	Bryant & Stratton College Sys Ofc	NY	324
666829	DeVry University - Fremont Campus	CA	44
666830	Florida College of Natural Health	FL	107
666923	Baker College System	MI	248
666925	Chabot-Las Positas CC District	CA	38
666929	International Business College	IN	175
666937	Baker College of Owosso	MI	249
666940	Baker College of Auburn Hills	MI	248
666941	Baker College of Cadillac	MI	24
666942	Baker College of Clinton Township	MI	24
666943	Baker College of Port Huron	MI	24
666970	UMDNJ-School of Nursing	NJ	31
666971	Huntington Col of Health Sciences	TN	46
666974	The JAG Legal Center & School	VA	55
666979	DeVry College of New York	NY	33
666982	American Graduate University	CA	28
666988	DeVry University-Long Beach Campus	CA	44
666989	DeVry Univ - Alpharetta Campus	GA	128
666991	UMDNJ-School of Public Health	NJ	317
666992	Antioch University New England	NH	303
666993	WV Council Cmty/Tech Col Educ	WV	542
666994	Everest Univ-Jacksonville	FL	105
666996	Baker College of Allen Park	MI	248
667002	Rocky Vista University	CO	87
667003	Rich Gilder Grad Sch @ Am Mus Nat H	NY	347
667004	The Commonwealth Medical College	PA	425
667005	Radians College	DC	99
667006	The SANS Technology Institute	MD	226
667007	Sotheby's Institute of Art	NY	351
667008	Five Br Univ: Grad Sch Trad Ch Med	CA	47
667009	National Test Pilot Institute	CA	58
667010	New Hope Christian College-Hawaii	HI	140
667011	Simmons College of Kentucky	KY	205
667012	Carolina Bible College	NC	362
667013	Grace College of Divinity	NC	364
667014	All Saints Bible College	TN	466
667015	Bethel College	VA	516
667016	Faith Theological Seminary	MD	222
667017	American Graduate School of Educ	AZ	11
667018	Sessions College for Prof Design	AZ	18
667019	Appalachian College of Pharmacy	VA	515
667020	CA Northstate College of Pharmacy	CA	33
667021	IHM Academy of EMS	MO	283
667022	Central Florida Institute	FL	102
667023	Saint Francis Seminary	WI	550
667024	Hands-on Medical Massage School	CA	49
667025	Oxman College	CA	60
667026	Antioch Sch Ch Plnt/Ldrship Dev	IA	181
667027	Saint Gregory the Great Seminary	NE	300
667028	LSU Paul M. Hebert Law Center	LA	213
667029	Westwood College	CO	89
667030	NE LA Tech Col Bastrop Camp	LA	210
667031	Sanford-Brown Institute	FL	117
667032	Keiser University	FL	112
667033	Bolivar Technical College	MO	279
667034	Rasmussen College	MN	270
667035	Martinsburg Institute	WV	541
667036	Inst Doctoral Stds in Visual Arrts	ME	218
667037	Keweenaw Bay Ojibwa Cmty Col	MI	253
667038	Medical Careers Institute	VA	521
667039	Riverside Community College Distric	CA	63
667040	San Bernardino Community Col Dist	CA	65
667041	West Hills Community College Dist	CA	77
667042	Carrington Col CA-Citrus Heights	CA	37
667043	Heald College, Modesto	CA	49
667044	San Joaquin Valley College-Hesperia	CA	66
667045	Eternity Bible College	CA	45
667046	Mid-South Christian College	TN	471
667047	Interface College	WA	534
667048	Colorado Academy of Veterinary Tech	CO	81
667049	Abraham Lincoln University	CA	26
667050	Reformed Episcopal Seminary	PA	445
667051	Texas Sch of Business-Friendswood	TX	499
667052	Alhambra Medical University	CA	26
667053	Stanton University	CA	71
667054	Shorter College	AR	23
667055	Redeemer Theological Seminary	TX	492
667056	Shepherd Univ Sch of Theology	CA	69
667057	Sonoran Desert Institute	AZ	18
667058	Univ of So Florida Manatee-Sarasota	FL	121
667059	Rasmussen College - Appleton	WI	549
667060	Rasmussen College - Aurora	IL	161
667061	Rasmussen College-Blaine	MN	270
667062	Rasmussen College - Fort Myers	FL	115
667063	Rasmussen College - Green Bay	WI	549
667064	Rasmussen Col - Mokena/Tinley Park	IL	161
667065	Rasmussen College - Rockford	IL	161
667066	Rasmussen College-Romeoville/Joliet	IL	162
667067	Rasmussen College - Tampa/Brandon	FL	115
667068	Rasmussen College - Wausau	WI	549
667069	Sanford-Burnham Grad Sch Biomed Sci	CA	67
667070	International Technological Univ	CA	51
667071	Cedars-Sinai Med Grad Pgm Biomed Sc	CA	38
667072	John Paul the Great Catholic Univ	CA	52
667073	American Career College-Orange Cnty	CA	28
667074	Midwest Institute-Earth City	MO	285
667075	Bais HaMedrash & Mesivta Baltimore	MD	221
667076	Be'er Yaakov Talmudic Seminary	NY	323
667077	Yeshiva Gedolah Ohr Yisrael	NY	360
667078	Yeshiva Gedolah Zichron Leyma	NJ	317
667079	Daymar College-Madisonville	KY	199
667080	Daymar College-Scottsville	KY	200
667081	Daymar College-Louisville East	KY	199
667082	Daymar College-New Boston	OH	389
667083	Tribeca Flashpoint Media Arts Acad	IL	165
667084	St. Louis Community Coll Wildwood	MO	289

Index of Universities, Colleges and Schools